LONGMAN Language Activator®

LONGMAN

Language Activator®

Helps you write and speak natural English

SECOND EDITION

Longman

longman.com

Pearson Education Limited
Edinburgh Gate, Harlow, Essex CM20 2JE England
and associated companies throughout the world

Visit our website: http://www.longman.com/dictionaries

First published 1993
Second edition 2002
Third impression 2004

Paperback edition
ISBN 0 582 41952 2

Cased edition
ISBN 0 582 41548 9

British Library Cataloguing-in-Publication Data
A catalogue record for this book is available from the British Library.

Library in Congress Cataloging-in-Publication Data
A catalog record for this book is available from the Library of Congress.

Designed by Alex Ingr, Tamandua Design & Typography, London

Set in Monotype Nimrod and Linotype Univers
by Peter Wray, Surrey

Printed in Spain by Cayfosa-Quebecor

▸ Contents

Acknowledgements

Linglex Dictionary and Corpus Advisory Committee
Lord Quirk (Chair)
Professor Geoffrey Leech (Vice-Chair)
Professor Douglas Biber
Professor Gillian Brown
Professor David Crystal
Philip Scholfield
Professor Katie Wales
Professor J C Wells

Director
Della Summers

Editorial Director
Adam Gadsby

Managing Editor
Stephen Bullon

Senior Associate Lexicographer
Chris Fox

Associate Lexicographers
Stella O'Shea
Karen Stern

Senior Editors
Karen Cleveland Marwick
Jo Leigh
Elizabeth Manning
Michael Murphy
Ruth Urbom

Editors
Evadne Adrian-Vallance
Daniel Barron
Elizabeth Beizai
Sheila Dignen
Stephen Handorf
Alex Henderson
Ted Jackson
Martin Stark
Laura Wedgeworth
Deborah Yuill

Pronunciation Adviser
Professor J C Wells

Pronunciation Editor
Dinah Jackson

Editorial Manager
Sheila Dallas

Production Editors
Michael Brooks
Jennifer Sagala

Proofreaders
Judith Aguda
Colin Baldwin
Isabel Griffiths
Nigel Hope
Ruth Noble
Sue Lightfoot

Resources and Systems Manager
Steve Crowdy

Project Manager
Alan Savill

Technical Support Manager
Trevor Satchell

Project & Database Administrator
Denise McKeough

Keyboarder
Pauline Savill

Production
Clive McKeough
Tracy Cassidy

Typesetting
Peter Wray

Text design
Alex Ingr

Photography
Gareth Boden

Preface

When we first published the *Longman Language Activator*® in 1993, it was as a result of research about ELT dictionaries with students and teachers in many different countries. They all said the same thing: 'What we really want is a dictionary that will tell us when it is correct to use a particular word, and how to use it – so that we sound natural and fluent, particularly when we write.' The *Longman Activator* was our solution to this problem – a dictionary with full, in fact very full, definitions, but arranged according to ideas, concepts, and meanings. The student or teacher started with a basic idea, like HAPPY. They looked up that idea in alphabetical order in the *Longman Activator* and were guided, in two or three easy choices, to a more idiomatic word or phrase to express exactly what they meant. So if they meant 'very happy because something good has happened', they found a word like 'delighted'. Then they could read the definition and the corpus-based examples for more understanding of the meaning. In addition, the grammatical constructions and collocations, such as 'delighted about' or 'delighted to hear something', meant they should be able to use the word correctly in their piece of writing.

The editorial team was delighted when Lord Randolph Quirk endorsed the groundbreaking work done by the original lexicographers and publishers. He called the *Longman Activator* 'the dictionary the world has been waiting for'.

For the second edition, there have been major improvements. Based on our now much-larger Longman Corpus Network, 60 per cent of examples have been improved. In response to constructive criticism about the ease of use of the book, the access system has been simplified dramatically. The index, containing all the meanings and phrases in alphabetical order, has been moved to the back in the traditional place. These last two changes are based on the reaction to the *Longman Activator*'s smaller version for intermediate students, the *Longman Essential Activator*, published in 1997.

We hope that the thousands of fans of the *Longman Activator* agree that these improvements make the book even easier and more rewarding to use, and help them expand and refine their use of English vocabulary.

Della Summers
Director – Longman Dictionaries

Introduction

The *Longman Language Activator®* is a dictionary of ideas for teachers and for students at upper intermediate to advanced level. It is different from an ordinary dictionary.

A traditional dictionary is used mainly to ***decode*** the meaning of unknown ***words***. The *Longman Activator*, on the other hand, is specifically designed to be used by students to ***produce*** their ideas in the English language, in other words to ***encode*** their ***ideas***. The *Longman Activator* helps students expand their vocabulary and improve their ability to express themselves by showing them:

- which word has exactly the right meaning for the context
- which subjects and objects go with which particular verbs
- which phrases or collocations the word would normally be used in.

Meaning first

One of the most important innovations of the *Longman Activator* approach is the grouping together of individual word-meanings or phrase-meanings that generally share the same idea, concept, or semantic area. They mean the same thing in a general way, but they entail certain key differences. These differences govern why one word sounds natural or correct in a particular sentence and why another word, apparently very close in meaning to the first word, does not sound right to native or highly proficient speakers of English.

Access

The number of keywords, or concepts, has been reduced from 1052 in the first edition to 866 in the revised *Language Activator*. By reducing the number of keywords, we have simplified the system for finding the word or phrase to express the student's meaning.

Index

One of the new features of this edition is that we have moved the index, containing all the word-meanings and phrase-meanings in the *Longman Activator*, to the back of the book. This makes it easier for teachers and students to check that a word or phrase they are unsure of is correct and means exactly what they think it does.

Keywords or concepts

The 866 keywords chosen as concepts have been tested in classrooms in the UK and checked against the Longman Learner's Corpus in order to validate them. This means that students will already know the meaning of the keywords. The keywords are then divided into smaller sections each with a different heading, such as 'feeling happy' under HAPPY. The student selects the heading that most closely corresponds to the idea that he or she wants to express, and then selects from the menu the words or phrase that fit the meaning or context best. Example sentences taken directly from the spoken and written corpora show how the word or phrase is used in everyday English, along with all the collocations and grammatical patterns they will need to use the word or phrase idiomatically.

Corpus and spoken English

All our work is based on the analysis of millions of words of computerized language known as the 'corpus'. We now have much larger corpora than we did when the original *Longman Activator* was written. Over 300 million words of British and American written and spoken material enable us to reflect English accurately. All Longman ELT/ESL dictionaries cover spoken English – words and expressions such as 'have a great time', 'have fun', 'can't wait', 'hyper'; this is particularly true of the *Longman Activator* which places special emphasis on the spoken language. The Longman Learner's Corpus enables us to predict which words students are most familiar with, and to know which words are problematic and therefore to be avoided in definitions and examples. This information helps us in the formulation of definitions and in the selection of corpus-based examples.

We would like to thank the contributors to the first edition, and the many students and teachers around the world whose invaluable feedback has contributed to the improvements in this, the second edition of the *Longman Language Activator*.

Adam Gadsby
Editorial Director – Longman Dictionaries

Using the *Longman Language Activator*

Here are some examples of how to put your ideas into words using the *Longman Language Activator*.

Look at the picture. What happened here?

She burned the shirt.

Look in the *Longman Language Activator*. Here's how it helps:

The basic word that you know is **burn**. Is there a more exact word?

Read the definitions and examples to find which one matches the picture.

Scorch matches the picture. The surface of the shirt is *burned*, and the iron has left a dark mark on it.

burn

RELATED WORDS

see also **fire, hot, explode**

1 to burn something

- burn
- burn down
- incinerate
- scorch
- singe
- charred

burn /bɜːʳn/ [v T] to damage or destroy something with fire or heat: *She lit a fire and burned his letters one by one.* | **burn a hole in sth** (=make a hole by burning it) *Someone had dropped a cigarette and burned a hole in the carpet.* | **burn sth to a crisp/cinder** (=destroy something completely by burning it) *Most of his possessions had been burnt to a cinder.* —**burnt/burned** /bɜːʳnt, bɜːʳnd/ [adj] *The cake is slightly burnt, I'm afraid.*

burn down /ˌbɜːʳn 'daʊn/ [phr v T] to completely destroy a building by burning it **burn down sth** *Police believe students are responsible for burning down the school.* | **burn sth down** *Her ex-husband threatened to burn the house down with her and the kids inside.*

incinerate /ɪn'sɪnəreɪt/ [v T usually in passive] to destroy unwanted things by burning them in a special machine: *Household waste is usually incinerated after it has been collected.* | *All the clothes that were affected by radiation had to be incinerated.*

scorch /skɔːʳtʃ/ [v T] to burn the surface of something and leave a dark mark on it: *The heater was left on all night and it scorched the wall.* | *Having the iron on a very high heat can scorch the fabric.* —**scorch mark** /'skɔːʳtʃ mɑːʳk/ [n C] *This shirt is ruined – there's a big scorch mark on the back.*

singe /sɪndʒ/ [v T] to damage something such as hair, wool, or paper by burning it slightly so that the ends or edges are burnt: *The flames were hot enough to singe your eyebrows.* | *The rug was singed by a piece of burning coal that had fallen from the fire.*

charred /tʃɑːʳd/ [adj usually before noun] wood, sticks, bones etc that are **charred** are black because they have been damaged by burning: *In the cave they found some charred animal bones.* | *It was nearly impossible to recognize the charred bodies.*

So what happened here?

She *scorched* the shirt.

▸ Look at the picture. What's happening here?

She is not eating very much of her meal because she is thinking about something else. She doesn't look very happy.

eat

1 to eat

- eat
- have
- chew
- swallow
- lick
- consume
- dig in/tuck in
- feed
- chow down

2 to have a meal

- have
- eat
- have something to eat
- grab something/a bite to eat
- have a snack
- snack
- dine

3 to eat a lot or too much

- stuff/gorge yourself
- pig out
- make a pig of yourself
- overeat

4 to eat something very quickly

- wolf down
- bolt down
- gobble up/down
- scoff

5 to eat noisily

- munch
- crunch

6 to eat all of something

- eat up
- finish
- finish off/up
- polish off
- demolish
- devour

7 to eat small amounts of food

- nibble
- pick at
- hardly touch your food/dinner/meal etc

8 to eat less in order to lose weight

- diet
- diet

9 to stop eating or refuse to eat

- fast
- go on (a) hunger strike
- be off your food

10 when you have eaten enough or too much food

- have had enough
- be full
- couldn't eat another thing
- bloated
- on a full stomach

▸ Look in the *Longman Language Activator*. Here's how it helps:

More specific words to describe this picture can be found under the basic word **eat**.

Eat has ten sections. You don't have to read through all of the words and definitions in every section. Read the names of the sections.

Which one fits the picture?

The closest section seems to be number 7 'to eat small amounts of food'. Have a closer look at the words in that section. Do any of them match the picture?

7 to eat small amounts of food

- nibble
- pick at
- hardly touch your food/dinner/meal etc

nibble /ˈnɪbəl/ [v I/T] to eat something by biting very small pieces: *The horse lowered his head and began to nibble the grass.* | **+ on/at** *We stood around drinking wine and nibbling on little snacks.*

pick at /ˈpɪk æt/ [v T] to eat only a small part of a meal, especially because you feel ill or unhappy: *I sat picking at my dinner, wishing I were somewhere else.*

hardly touch your food/dinner/meal etc /ˌhɑːʳdli ˈtʌtʃ jɔːʳ fuːd/ [v phrase] to eat almost none of your dinner, meal etc: *Are you feeling okay? You've hardly touched your dinner.* | *We were so full by the time dessert came that we hardly touched it.*

Pick at is a good choice. She has only eaten a small part of her dinner, and she looks unhappy.

▸ So what is happening in the picture?

She is *picking at* her dinner.

▸ Look at the picture. What's happening here?

She is drawing things while she is on the telephone. She's not really thinking about what she's doing.

▸ Look in the *Longman Language Activator*. Here's how it helps:

The word 'draw' is familiar. Is there a more precise word?

Look at the five words that the *Activator* gives that mean 'to draw a picture, pattern, line etc': **draw, sketch, doodle, scribble** and **trace**. One of them fits the meaning exactly. Reading the examples may make it even clearer which is the best word to choose.

The definition for **doodle** matches what is happening in the picture, and the example sentence 'I always doodle while I'm talking on the phone.' matches too.

▸ So what is she doing?

She's *doodling* on the paper.

draw

RELATED WORDS

▸ *see also* **paint, picture, design, art/culture, pattern**

1 to draw a picture, pattern, line etc

- ▸ draw
- ▸ sketch
- ▸ doodle
- ▸ scribble
- ▸ trace

draw /drɔː/ [v I/T] to make a picture, pattern, line etc using a pen or pencil: *What are you drawing?* | *She can draw really well.* | *I'm good at drawing animals, but I can't draw people.* | **draw a picture of sb/sth** *Mike was sitting outside, drawing a picture of the trees at the bottom of the garden.* | **draw a line/circle/square etc** *Someone had drawn a line under my name.*

sketch /sketʃ/ [v I/T] to make a quick, simple drawing of a person, place etc, without many details: *Maggie grabbed a piece of paper and quickly sketched the bird before it flew away.* | *He sat by the river, sketching.*

doodle /ˈduːdl/ [v I] to draw shapes, lines, or patterns without really thinking about what you are doing, for example when you are thinking about something else or when you feel bored: *I always doodle while I'm talking on the phone.* | **+ on** *Simon was lying on the floor, doodling on a sheet of paper.*

scribble /ˈskrɪbəl/ [v I/T] to quickly draw lines and shapes without making any particular pattern, shape, or picture – use this especially about what small children do before they have learnt to draw or write: *Katie can't draw a real picture yet but she enjoys scribbling with crayons.* | **scribble all over/on sth** *Oh no! One of the kids has scribbled all over my report!*

trace /treɪs/ [v T] to copy a picture by putting transparent paper over it and then drawing along the lines of the picture: *The children traced the map of France and then wrote in the names of the places they had visited.*

listen

2 to secretly listen to someone

- listen in
- eavesdrop
- bug
- tap
- monitor

listen in /ˌlɪsən ˈɪn/ [phr v I] to listen to someone else's conversation when they do not know that you are listening, either on the telephone or when you are near them: *Whenever her boss had one of his 'private meetings', she always used to listen in.* | **+ on** *We tried to listen in on their conversation, but they were talking too quietly.* | *They used to have hours of fun listening in on what people were doing in their hotel rooms.*

eavesdrop /ˈiːvzdrɒp‖-drɑːp/ [v I] to secretly listen to someone else's conversation by standing near them, hiding behind a door etc: *How did you know I was going? You've been eavesdropping, haven't you!* | **+ on** *I caught him eavesdropping on our conversation.* | *Sue was able to eavesdrop on them through the open window.*

bug /bʌg/ [v T] to hide a small piece of electronic recording equipment in someone's room, car, office etc in order to listen secretly to what is said there: *Security agents bugged their offices and managed to get some evidence against them.* | *Wells was convinced the house was bugged and insisted on playing loud music while we talked.*

tap /tæp/ [v T] to connect a piece of electronic recording equipment to a telephone system so that you can listen to people's telephone conversations: *Later we realized our phones had been tapped and the police knew everything.* | *The President had to resign over an illegal phone-tapping operation.*

monitor /ˈmɒnɨtəʳ‖ˈmɑː-/ [v T] to listen to another country's radio or television broadcasts or radio messages in order to get information about that country: *Satellite technology means that enemy airwaves can be monitored more closely than ever before.*

▸ Look at the picture. What's happening here?

The couple on the left are having a private conversation.

The man on the right is secretly listening to their conversation.

▸ Look in the *Longman Language Activator*. Here's how it helps:

Listen is not exact enough. There must be a word that means *'to secretly listen to someone's conversation'*.

Only one of the definitions matches the action in the picture: **eavesdrop**.

The *Activator* shows you that the usual preposition to use with **eavesdrop** is 'on'.

▸ So what is happening in the picture?

He is *eavesdropping*.
or **He is *eavesdropping on* their conversation.**

Look at the picture.

What's the little boy doing?

The little boy is crying. He's very upset.

Look in the *Longman Language Activator*. Here's how it helps:

'Cry' is a basic word. There must be a word that says more clearly what is happening in the picture.

Cry is a main word in the *Longman Language Activator*, and the first section is 'to cry'.

At the word cry you'll find the idiom **cry your eyes out** which means 'to cry a lot because you are very upset'. That fits the picture.

Further down, there is **sob**: 'if you sob, you cry noisily and your body shakes, because you are very sad or because someone has upset you'. This matches too.

After sob is **bawl**: 'to cry loudly – use this especially about young children...' This also seems to match.

▸ So what is he doing?

The little boy is *crying his eyes out.*
or
The little boy is *sobbing.*
or
The little boy is *bawling.*

cry

RELATED WORDS

opposite: —— **laugh**
- to say something loudly *see* **shout**
- *see also* **sad, upset**

1 to cry

- **cry**
- **weep**
- **sob**
- **bawl**
- **snivel/sniffle**
- **whimper**
- **be in tears**
- **your eyes water**
- **tears**

cry /kraɪ/ [v I] if you **cry**, tears come from your eyes, for example because you are sad or upset, or because you have hurt yourself: *I could hear the baby crying in the next room.* | *Kim's eyes were red and she looked as though she'd been crying.* | *Don't cry, I didn't mean to upset you.* | **+ about** *Jenny won't tell me what she's crying about.* | **make sb cry** *The film was so sad, it made me cry.* | **cry and cry** (=cry for a long time) *I sat alone in my room and cried and cried.* | **cry your eyes out** (=cry a lot because you are very upset) *The poor kid's so miserable, he's upstairs crying his eyes out.* | **cry with happiness/joy/relief etc** *She cried with joy when she heard that the children were safe.* | **cry yourself to sleep** (=cry until you fall asleep) *At night I'd cry myself to sleep, thinking about you.* —**cry** [n singular] *You'll feel better when you've had a good cry.*

weep /wiːp/ [v I] especially written to cry quietly and for a long time because you are very sad or you feel a strong emotion: *She sat beside her dying father and wept.* | **weep openly** (=without trying to stop or hide it) *Thousands of French citizens, many weeping openly, bade a silent farewell to Mitterand.* | **weep with emotion/grief/joy etc** *I remember weeping with pride when my first son was born.* | **weep bitterly** (=cry strongly) *His mother wept bitterly and his father sat grim-faced.*

sob /sɒb‖sɑːb/ [v I] if you **sob**, you cry noisily and your body shakes, because you are very sad or because someone has upset you: *The sound of her sobbing kept them awake all night.* | *'Please don't leave me,' he sobbed.* | *The child covered her face with her hands and started to sob uncontrollably.*

bawl /bɔːl/ [v I] to cry loudly – use this especially about young children or people you do not have any sympathy for: *'Stop, bawling,' Dad said crossly, 'and come over here.'* | *The baby was sitting in his high chair, red in the face and bawling.*

snivel/sniffle /ˈsnɪvəl, ˈsnɪfəl/ [v I] to cry in a weak, complaining way and at the same time breathe in air noisily through your nose: *'What are you snivelling about, Jake?'* | *She kept sniffling into her handkerchief and saying how unfair everything was.*

whimper /ˈwɪmpəʳ/ [v I] to make a quiet, continuous, unhappy sound like an animal in pain, or to say something with this sound in your voice: *'I'm sorry,' she whimpered, but Richard wasn't listening.* | **+ with** *Pat whimpered with the pain of the bullet wound in his shoulder.* —**whimper** [n C] *The boy's crying died down to a whimper.*

Look at the picture. What's happening here?

The man is pushing her with his finger in order to wake her up.

Look in the *Longman Language Activator*. Here's how it helps:

By looking up the basic word **push**, you will find other words that would better fit the picture.

The section headings 1 and 2 don't match. Does number 3 'to push someone or something with your finger, elbow, or with something pointed' match? Yes!

The *Activator* gives you a choice of four words in this section. A **nudge** is using the elbow, and the definition for **dig somebody in the ribs** says that it is a push into someone's body not their arm.

So what is happening in the picture?

He is *poking* her to wake her up.
He is *prodding* her.

push

RELATED WORDS

see also **pull, press, squash**

1 to push something or someone

- push
- give sth/sb a push
- shove
- give sth/sb a shove
- hustle
- bundle
- manhandle

2 to push something that has wheels or rolls easily

- push
- wheel
- roll
- trundle

3 to push someone or something with your finger, elbow, or with something pointed

- nudge
- poke
- prod
- dig sb in the ribs

nudge /nʌdʒ/ [v T] to gently push someone with your elbow to get their attention, especially when you do not want anyone else to notice: *Toby nudged my arm. 'That's the guy I told you about,' he whispered.* | *Christine nudged me and giggled.* —**nudge** [n C] *Mark gave me a nudge and indicated two men who had just walked in.*

poke /pəʊk/ [v T] to push someone or something with your finger or with something sharp: *The boys poked the fish with sticks to see if it was still alive* | **poke sb in the eye/side/ribs** *Careful with that stick! You nearly poked me in the eye.* —**poke** [n C] *I gave dad a poke to wake him up.*

prod /prɒd‖prɑːd/ [v T] to gently push someone or something, using your finger or something such as a stick: *Sergeant Thompson raised his stick and prodded the soldier in the chest.* | *They walked around him, prodding and pinching him.* —**prod** [n C] *He gave the dog a quick prod with his foot.*

dig sb in the ribs /ˌdɪg (sb) ɪn ðə ˈrɪbz/ [v phrase] to suddenly push your finger or elbow into someone's body, to get their attention or tell them something: *Jenny dug me sharply in the ribs and told me to be quiet.* | *Edward laughed loudly, digging me in the ribs, wanting me to share the joke.*

▸ **Look at the picture. What is she doing?**

The woman is looking through the gap. She seems to be secretly having a quick look at something.

look

RELATED WORDS

▸ *see also* **see, watch, examine, look for**

3 to look quickly

- ▸ **glance**
- ▸ **take a quick look/ have a quick look**
- ▸ **peek/take a peek**
- ▸ **peep**
- ▸ **take one look**

glance /glɑːns‖glæns/ [v I] to look quickly at someone or something and then look away again **+ at** *Dr Morse kept glancing nervously at his watch.* | *'Some of you may not be happy about what I have to say,' he began, glancing at Janey.* | **+ into/down/ through etc** *Glancing into Neil's room, she noticed that his suitcase was packed.* —**glance** [n C] **+ at** *A quick glance at the map showed that we were on the right road.* | **a backward glance** (=a quick look back at the place you have left) *I walked away without a wave or a backward glance.* | **a sidelong glance** (=a quick look to one side) *Tammy gave her sister a sidelong glance and the two started to giggle.*

take a quick look/have a quick look /ˌteɪk ə kwɪk ˈlʊk, ˌhæv ə kwɪk ˈlʊk/ [v phrase] to look at something quickly in order to check that everything is satisfactory **+ at/around/through etc** *He took a quick look in the mirror, and went out of the house.* | *She had a quick look around the room before letting the guests in.*

peek/take a peek /piːk, ˌteɪk ə ˈpiːk/ [v I/v phrase] to look at something quickly and secretly, especially from a place where you cannot be seen: *When I heard the noise in the next room, I couldn't resist having a peek.* | **+ at** *The little girl peeked at me from behind her grandmother's skirt.* | **+ in/into/ through/over etc** *We tip-toed into the room and peeked in the crib without waking the baby.* | *She opened the door and took a quick peek inside.*

peep /piːp/ [v I] especially British to look at something quickly and secretly, especially from a place where you cannot be seen **+ through/into/round** *Bobby peeped around the corner to see if anyone was coming.* | *We peeped through a crack in the fence and saw Mrs Finley talking to a strange-looking man.*

take one look /teɪk ˌwʌn ˈlʊk/ [v phrase] to look quickly at someone or something that you have not seen before, and immediately decide what your opinion of them is: *They opened the door to the room, took one look, and decided to go to another hotel.* | **+ at** *She took one look at me and said she would not work with me.* | *The teacher took one look at his homework and told him he would have to redo it.*

▸ **Look in the *Longman Language Activator*. Here's how it helps:**

The basic word here is **look**, but there must be a more precise word that means *'to look at something secretly and quickly'*.

Section 3 of **look** has words that mean 'to look quickly'. Read through the entries to see which one fits the meaning exactly.

In this case, there are two entries that fit:
peek/take a peek and **peep**
Use the information included in the entries to use the word correctly.

▸ **So what is the woman in the picture doing?**

She is *peeking through* the gap.
She is *taking a peek* through the gap.
or **She is *peeping* through the gap.**

▸ Look at the pictures. What's happening here?

The woman is holding the little boy, and the little boy is holding a teddy bear.

▸ Look in the *Longman Language Activator*. Here's how it helps:

The pictures are showing emotion.

There must be a better way to describe the pictures that is more specific than 'hold'. Is there a word that will describe both pictures?

▸ **So what is happening in the pictures?**

She's *cuddling* the little boy, and the little boy is *cuddling* the teddy bear.

Look in the *Longman Language Activator* at **hold**. Read the section headings. Section number 6 – 'to put your arms around someone' – is the best match.

Many of the entries in this section have very similar meanings. How can you tell which is the best one? If the definitions do not make it clear, try reading the example sentences.

The definition for **cuddle** explains that it is used especially when you are holding a child, a small animal, or someone you love. The example sentence shows that cuddle is often used with teddy bears, so that also fits.

hold

RELATED WORDS

- have an amount of something inside *see* **contain**
- *see also* **lift, carry, take**

6 to put your arms around someone

- hold
- put your arms around
- hug
- cuddle
- take sb in your arms
- embrace

hold /həʊld/ [v T] to put your arms around someone and **hold** them close to you, especially to show that you love them, or in order to comfort them: *I held her until she went to sleep.* | **hold sb tight** *There was nothing I could say so I just held her tight and let her cry.* | **hold sb in your arms** *She held a baby in her arms.*

put your arms around /ˌpʊt jɔːr ˈɑːʳmz əraʊnd/ [v phrase] to hold someone especially when you want to comfort them or kiss them or show that you love them: *Mama put her arms around me and tried to comfort me.* | *She put her arms around his neck and kissed his cheek.*

hug /hʌg/ [v T] to put your arms around someone and hold them close to you, especially to show that you love them, or to comfort them: *My father hugged me affectionately when I got home.* | *'I'll never forget you,' she said, and we hugged each other for the last time.* | **hug sb close/tight** *Jane threw her arms around him and hugged him tight.* —**hug** [n C] **give sb a hug** *Give me a hug, then it's time for bed.* | **bear hug** (=a very tight hug) *His arms tightened around her in a bear hug.*

cuddle /ˈkʌdl/ [v I/T] to hold someone in your arms for a long time, especially a child, a small animal, or someone you love: *She had fallen asleep in her chair, cuddling a little teddy bear.* | **kiss and cuddle** (=when two people hold each other and kiss each other) *They were kissing and cuddling on the sofa.* —**cuddle** [n C] **give sb a cuddle** *She was giving the baby a cuddle.*

take sb in your arms /ˌteɪk (sb) ɪn jɔːr ˈɑːʳmz/ [v phrase] to gently pull someone towards you and hold them in your arms, especially someone you love: *He took Sophie in his arms and kissed her.* | *Margaret took the little boy in her arms and carried him downstairs.*

embrace /ɪmˈbreɪs/ [v I/T] **formal** put your arms around someone and hold them in a friendly or loving way, especially when you are meeting or leaving someone: *Phoebe ran to embrace her mother.* | *Before my flight was called we stood and embraced.* —**embrace** [n C] *The children rushed into the embrace of their father*

Look at the picture. What's happening here?

She is fastening her seatbelt.

Look in the *Longman Language Activator*. Here's how it helps:

Fasten is a correct word to use here, but there are other ways to say this.

Do any of the entries under section 1 of **fasten/unfasten** match what is shown in the picture?

One of the entries seems to be an exact match.

The definition for **buckle up** and **buckle** says 'to fasten your seatbelt in a car'. These words have a label which means that the words are used in American English not in British English.

So what is the woman in the picture doing?

She's *fastening* her seatbelt.
or
She's *buckling up*.
or
She's *buckling* her seatbelt.

fasten/unfasten

RELATED WORDS

see also **tight, tie/untie, attach, join, stick, clothes**

1 to fasten something

- fasten
- button/button up
- zip up
- do up
- tie
- buckle up

fasten /ˈfɑːsən‖ˈfæ-/ [v T] to join together the two sides of a piece of clothing, bag, belt etc, so that it is closed: *Fasten your coat – it's cold outside.* | *He fastened the bracelet for her.* | *Ella fastened her blouse with shaking fingers.* —**fastened** [adj not before noun] *Please keep your seat belts fastened.*

button/button up /ˈbʌtn, ˌbʌtn ˈʌp/ [v T/phr v T] to fasten the buttons on a piece of clothing: *He began buttoning his shirt and putting on his tie.* | *Stone buttoned up his heavy jacket.* | **button sth up/button up sth** *She buttoned her cardigan up all the way to her neck.* | *I adjusted my tie and buttoned up my coat.* —**buttoned up** [adj] *It was cold and his coat was completely buttoned up.*

zip up [phr v T] ALSO **zip** [v T] especially American /ˌzɪp ˈʌp, zɪp/ to fasten clothes, bags etc with a zip: *I can't zip up these jeans – they're too tight.* | *Can you zip my dress for me?* | **zip sth up** *She took some money out of her purse and quickly zipped it up again.* | **zip up sth** *Roger zipped up the battered black case he carried his guitar in.* —**zipped up** [adj not before noun] *My sleeping bag was fully zipped up.*

do up /ˌduː ˈʌp/ [phr v T] British especially spoken to fasten clothes, or the buttons, zips etc on clothes **do up sth** *Come on then, do up your coat and let's go.* | *When I walked into the room, Allen was doing up his trousers.* | **do sth up** *I can't do this zip up – it's stuck.* | *Are your shoelaces done up properly?* —**done up** /ˌdʌn ˈʌp/ [adj not before noun] *The toggles on his duffel coat were done up wrongly.*

tie /taɪ/ [v T] to fasten something by making a knot: *She tied a scarf around her neck.* | *Do you know how to tie a bow tie?*

buckle up [phr v I] ALSO **buckle** [v T] American /ˌbʌkəl ˈʌp, ˈbʌkəl/ to fasten your seatbelt in a car: *Eighty percent of motorists now buckle up, studies show.* | *Nancy got behind the wheel and buckled up.* | *The new law will require passengers in the rear seats of automobiles to buckle their seatbelts.*

How the *Activator* is organized

The words in the *Longman Language Activator* are organized into groups, based on common words (called *keywords*), that express basic ideas. For example, all the words that are connected with 'happy', such as **glad**, **pleased**, and **delighted**, are grouped together under the keyword HAPPY. Similarly, all the words that are different types of 'taste', such as **sweet**, **sour**, and **spicy**, are grouped together under the keyword TASTE. Showing words together in groups like this makes the *Activator* very useful for building up your vocabulary and for finding a range of different words in the same meaning area.

There are two easy ways to find the words you want using the *Activator*. One way is by looking for keywords in the main dictionary; the other way is by looking for the words in the index.

Go to pages xxii and xxiii, and the colour pages ix-xx, to see how the *Activator* can help you write and speak natural English.

How to use the *Activator* using keywords

When you want, for example, to find a better word to replace 'very happy' in this sentence:

Mary was <u>very happy</u> when she was offered the job.

1 Think of a word or phrase which expresses the basic meaning of what you want to say.

happy

2 Find the keyword 'happy' and choose the most suitable section.

happy

3 very happy because something good has happened

3 Read the definitions and examples of the words in the section, and decide which is the most appropriate one for you to use.

overjoyed /ˌəʊvəʳˈdʒɔɪd/ **[adj] written** very happy about something, especially a piece of good news: *Naturally I was overjoyed when I was offered the part in the play.* | **+ to see/hear/learn/be etc** *My parents were overjoyed to see my brother again.*

4 Use this word to improve your sentence, following the grammatical hints given in the *Activator*.

Mary was <u>overjoyed</u> when she was offered the job.

▸ How to use the *Activator* index

If you know a more precise word and want to find others like it, look it up in the index at the end of the book. Here, you will be directed to the correct keyword. For example, say you want another word that means 'thief'. It does not have its own keyword, but if you look in the index you will find this:

thicken/get thicker ▸ LIQUID 6
thickness ▸ THICK 2
thief ▸ STEAL 5
thin ▸ DETAIL 6; LIQUID 3; THIN 1, 8, 9, 10
be wearing thin ▸ USE 13

This means that you should look at the keyword STEAL, section 5.

steal

5 someone who steals

- ▸ **thief**
- ▸ **robber**
- ▸ **burglar**
- ▸ **shoplifter**
- ▸ **pickpocket**
- ▸ **mugger**
- ▸ **joyrider**
- ▸ **kleptomaniac**

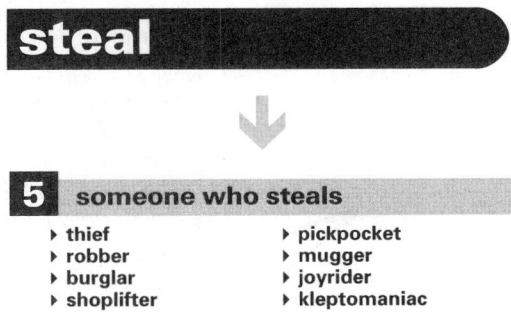

You now have a range of words that you can choose from, all in the same meaning area as 'thief'. The *Activator* will tell you the differences between the words and show you many examples of how they are used in real, everyday English.

Keyword
a basic word or phrase which shows the meaning area

References
useful references to other related keywords in the book

Menu
a list of all the words in the section

Label
tells you whether a word is British or American

Definition
shows you how the word is different from the other words in the section

Pronunciation
shows how each word and phrase is pronounced

party

RELATED WORDS

▸ *see also* **celebrate, invite, drink, dance, meal**

1 a party

▸ **party**
▸ **get-together**
▸ **do**
▸ **shower**
▸ **bash**

party /ˈpɑːʳti/ [n C] a social event, especially in someone's house, when people talk, drink, eat, and dance: *We're having a party at my house. Do you want to come?* | *Did you go to Stella's party?* | **invite sb to a party** *How many people have they invited to the party?* | **surprise party** *We gave her a surprise party at a local bar.* | **a birthday/Halloween/Christmas/engagement etc party** (=to celebrate a birthday, Halloween etc) *Over a hundred children came to the annual Christmas party.* | **dinner party** (=a party at someone's house in the evening, when people have a meal) *I gave my first dinner party last weekend.* | **office party** (=a party for people who work together) *Office parties are fun if you're young, free, and single.* | **fancy dress party** British **/costume party** American (=a party where people wear strange, funny, or historical clothes) *You're invited to a fancy dress party.* | **cocktail party** (=a fairly formal party in the evening, at which alcoholic drinks are served) *I went to a cocktail party in the lobby of the Ritz once.*

get-together /ˈget təˌgeðəʳ/ [n C] an informal party, often to celebrate something: *Shana's picture won first prize, so we had a little get-together to celebrate.* | *a big family get-together*

do /duː/ [n C] British spoken a party **a bit of a do** *A friend of mine's having a bit of a do in town tomorrow night.* | **leaving do** (=for someone who is leaving the place where they work) *Are you going to Darren's leaving do?*

shower /ˈʃaʊəʳ/ [n C] American a party at which presents are given to a woman who is getting married or having a baby: *We're giving a shower for Beth next week.* | *I want to thank both of you again for your beautiful shower gifts.* | **bridal/wedding shower** (=for a woman who is getting married) *What did you give Chris for her wedding shower?* | **baby shower** (=for a woman who is going to have a baby) *We didn't play any of the usual games at the baby shower.*

bash /bæʃ/ [n C] informal a big party: *The band are flying out to Ibiza tonight for a huge four-day celebrity bash.*

2 a formal or official party

- function
- reception

function /ˈfʌŋkʃən/ [n C] a large formal or official party, usually for important people: *The Lavender Room can be booked for functions or parties.* | **corporate function** (=for a company) *His specialist service is in constant demand for big corporate functions.* | **state function** (=official government party) *Part of her duties is attending official state functions.*

reception /rɪˈsepʃən/ [n C] a large formal or official party, usually held to welcome someone or to celebrate something: *On the second night, the captain always holds a formal reception for the crew and passengers.* | *The pair were spotted together at a champagne reception at the Imperial Hotel.* | **attend a reception** *Two hundred guests attended an evening reception, held in honor of the Chancellor's visit.* | **wedding reception** (=a big party held after a wedding) *The wedding reception will take place at the Lennox Hotel, starting at 3.30 pm.*

3 to have a party

- have
- throw a party
- hold
- give
- host
- entertain

have /həv/ [v T] **have a party/get-together/reception etc** *We used to have a big Christmas party every year.* | *The couple had their wedding reception at the Museum of Modern Art.* | *Mark, my boss, had a surprise party to welcome me home.*

throw a party /ˌθrəʊ ə ˈpɑːʳti/ [v phrase] to have a party at your home, often a big or expensive one, especially in order to celebrate something: *He threw a huge party to celebrate making his first million dollars.* | **+ for** *The staff and patients threw a going-away party for Dr Rogers.* | *The Krugers threw an impromptu cocktail party for him in the backyard.*

hold /həʊld/ [v T] **hold a party/dinner/reception/function etc** to have a formal or official party: *The anniversary dinner was held Wednesday night at the Washington Hilton.* | *They are holding a fund-raising reception on Friday in the City Hall.*

give /gɪv/ [v T] **give a party/dinner party/lunch party etc** to be the person who organizes a party: *I'm giving a dinner party on Thursday night. Would you like to come?* | *On Maggie's last night in the house, Jo gave a little farewell party.* | **give a party for sb** *The prospect of giving a dinner party for my boyfriend's snobbish parents filled me with gloom.* | *The last show of the tour was in Atlanta, and I decided to give a party for the singers and musicians.*

host /həʊst/ [v T] **host a party/dinner party/reception etc** to be the person who organizes a formal party and officially welcomes the guests: *Colette will be hosting a cocktail reception at 6.00 pm in the Grosvenor Suite.* | *Last year, the city hosted a three-day gay pride festival.*

Section heading
takes you to the part of the keyword that will help you

Collocation information
shows words that are commonly used with the word you're looking at

Examples
The *Activator* has thousands of natural examples from the Longman Corpus Network, which show how the word is typically used and help you to get a 'feel' for the word

Grammar information
shows which prepositions and grammar patterns to use

Parts of speech
tells you whether the word is a countable noun, transitive verb, etc

Aa

about

RELATED WORDS

- talk about *see* **discuss**
- ask about *see* **ask**
- approximately a number or amount *see* **about/approximately**
- around a place or thing *see* **around/round**
- connected with something or someone *see* **connected/related**

1 about a subject or person

- about
- on
- concerning/regarding
- on the subject of
- re
- with regard to
- wrt

about /əˈbaʊt/ [prep] *Toby talks about you all the time.* | *This leaflet should answer all the questions you have about switching to digital TV.* | *I'm reading a really good book at the moment – it's about the French Revolution.* | *What's all the fuss about?* | **+ what/how/where etc** *I've been thinking about what you said, and I've decided that you're right.*

on /ɒn‖ɑːn, ɔːn/ [prep] about a particular subject: *Lucia Piatti has written several books on the subject.* | **advice/opinions/ideas etc on** *If you want any advice on where to stay, Jan should be able to help you.* | *His views on women are really old-fashioned.* | **+ what/how/where etc** *Do you have any ideas on where to eat tonight?* | **book/programme/film etc on** *a book on 19th century English Literature* | *a lecture on Native American customs and folklore* | *Did you see that programme on South Africa last night?*

concerning/regarding /kənˈsɜːʳnɪŋ, rɪˈɡɑːʳdɪŋ/ [prep] formal about something or someone – use this especially to talk about information, ideas, or questions: *For any details concerning a particular country you should check with the embassy.* | *Richard was called in by the police to answer questions concerning the disappearance of Thomas Ripley.* | *If you have any questions regarding any of our services, please feel free to call me.* | *Thank you for your letter regarding the annual subscription to our magazine.*

on the subject of /ɒn ðə ˈsʌbdʒɪkt ɒv / [prep] if you talk or write **on the subject of** someone or something, you talk or write about them: *Marie said nothing at all on the subject of Mr Bertram.* | **while we're on the subject** (=used when you are talking about a subject and want to say more about it) *While we're on the subject of money, do you have that $10 you owe me?*

re /riː/ [prep] used in short business letters, messages etc: *Re planning meeting on Friday, please bring sales figures.* | *To: John Deacon. From: Maria Soames. Re: computer system.*

with regard to /wɪð rɪˈɡɑːʳd tuː/ [prep] formal used especially to introduce a subject that you want to talk about in a speech, formal report, meeting etc: *With regard to the proposed new shopping mall, I would like to add a few remarks to those of the previous speaker.* | *With regard to your letter concerning my January payment, this matter has now been settled.*

wrt use this in e-mails to introduce the subject you want to talk about. **Wrt** is an abbreviation of 'with regard to': *Wrt your looking out for a new computer, I saw a good offer in the paper yesterday.* | *I'll be contacting Jean tomorrow wrt the Christmas party – is there anything you'd like me to suggest to her?*

2 to have something as the main subject

- be about
- deal with/be concerned with
- concern
- focus on

be about /biː əˈbaʊt / [v phrase] *The play is about life in the Deep South in the 1930s.* | *What's tonight's documentary about?* | *Have you ever read 'Hideous Kinky'? It's about an English woman and her daughter travelling in Morocco.*

deal with/be concerned with /ˈdiːl wɪð, biː kənˈsɜːʳnd wɪð / [phr v T/v phrase] to be about a particular subject, especially a serious one, and examine it carefully and in detail. **Deal with** is much more common than **be concerned with**: *The story deals with the psychological conflicts between mother and son.* | *The earliest films made in India dealt with mythological subjects.* | *Elton's books are often concerned with environmental issues.*

concern /kənˈsɜːʳn/ [v T] if a story, report etc **concerns** someone or something, it is about them and especially about what happens to them: *Much of the material in her early letters concerns events which happened some years before.*

focus on ALSO **centre on** British **/center on** American /ˈfəʊkəs ɒn, ˈsentər ɒn / [v phrase] if something such as a book, article, or discussion **focuses on** a subject or problem, it is mainly about it and examines it in detail: *The next chapter will focus on this problem in greater detail.* | *a weekly magazine mainly focusing on business-related issues* | *The controversy centred on the question of illegal arms sales.*

about/approximately

RELATED WORDS

opposite: **exact**

- *see also* **guess**

1 approximately a number or amount

- about
- approximately
- roughly
- or so
- odd
- give or take
- at a guess

about /əˈbaʊt/ [adv] a little more or a little less than a number, amount, distance, or time: *It should cost about $1500.* | *The church is about a mile away.* | *It's been about five years since I've seen Linda.* | *The chance of men being born colour blind is about 1 in 12.*

approximately /əˈprɒksɪ̇mɪ̇tli‖əˈprɑːk-/ [adv] a little more or a little less than a number, amount, distance, or time. **Approximately** is a little more formal than **about** and is used especially in written English: *Approximately 30% of the community is Polish.* | *Each disk stores approximately 144 pages of text.*

roughly /ˈrʌfli/ [adv] approximately – used especially when you are trying to give someone a general idea of the number or amount: *A new kitchen would cost roughly $6,000.* | *The man was roughly my own age.* | *There were roughly 50 people there.*

or so /ɔːʳ ˈsəʊ/ [adv] **3 days/a minute/fifteen people etc or so** approximately 3 days, a minute etc, or perhaps even more: *The baby usually sleeps for an hour or so after breakfast.* | *He suggested that I take a week or so off work.* | *There must be thirty people or so in the class.*

odd /ɒd‖ɑːd/ [adv] informal spoken **a hundred/forty/thirty etc odd** use this after numbers in tens, hundreds, or thousands: *'How old do you think he is?' 'Oh, I don't know. Seventy odd.'* | *It's been 30 odd years since I last saw him.*

give or take /ˌgɪv ɔːʳ ˈteɪk/ [adv] spoken **give or take a few miles/a couple of minutes/a pound etc** use this when saying approximately what a number or amount is, when it may be a few miles more or less, a few minutes more or less etc: *The village is about fifty miles north of here, give or take a few miles.* | *He's said to be worth $26 million, give or take a few million.* | *'How long will the meeting last?' 'A couple of hours, give or take.'*

at a guess /ət ə ˈges/ [adv] spoken approximately, especially when you do not know the correct number or amount and are guessing what it is: *At a guess, I'd say around 3000 people took part in the demonstration.* | *It was a cold night. About two or three degrees at a guess.* | *'How much will it cost?' 'A hundred and twenty pounds, at a guess.'*

2 approximately a large number or amount

- something/somewhere in the region of
- something like
- an estimated
- some
- or more

something/somewhere in the region of /ˌsʌmθɪŋ, ˌsʌmweər ɪn ðə ˈriːdʒən ɒv/ [adv] *The business is worth something in the region of $25m.* | *The universe is estimated to be somewhere in the region of eleven billion years old.* | *A typical price would be somewhere in the region of £2,500 per person.*

something like /ˈsʌmθɪŋ laɪk/ spoken *Smith is already something like $10,000 in debt.* | *In the USA something like 4000 such accidents occur each year.*

an estimated /ən ˈestɪmeɪtɪd/ [adj phrase] **an estimated 3000 people/one million pounds/90% of profits etc** approximately that number or amount – use this when you have no exact or detailed figures on which to calculate the exact number: *The event was seen on television by an estimated 250 million people worldwide.* | *An estimated 10% of new mothers suffer from severe depression.* | *By the end of the month an estimated 1000 people had been killed and 42,000 left homeless.*

some /səm, (*strong*) sʌm/ [adv] **some 100 people/50 years/2000 establishments etc** approximately that number or amount – use this especially when you think it is impressive or surprising: *Among the 11 factory sites across Europe, some 2,600 jobs are to be eliminated this year.* | *He lectured at the Institut Pasteur for some 50 years.*

or more /ɔːʳ ˈmɔːʳ/ [adv] **5000 people/20%/9 days etc or more** use this when the total may be a lot more, and you want to emphasize that this is a large number or amount: *How can you be tired? You slept for ten hours or more last night.* | *There were a thousand or more fans at the airport to welcome the band.*

3 at approximately a particular time or date

- about
- approximately
- some time
- or thereabouts
- circa

about ALSO **around** /əˈbaʊt, əˈraʊnd/ [adv] especially American a little later or a little earlier than a particular time or date: *It's two-thirty. They should be arriving about now.* | *The cathedral was completed in about the middle of the 16th century.* | *About six months ago he suffered a major heart attack.* | *I picked Sue up around eight o' clock.* | *I don't remember the exact date of the party, but it must have been around the first of December.* | **round about** especially British *He left the house round about four o'clock.* | *The job should be finished round about March next year.*

approximately /əˈprɒksɪmɪtli‖əˈprɑːk-/ [adv] a little later or a little earlier than a particular time or date. **Approximately** is a little more formal than **about** or **around** and is used especially in written English: *The gate will close approximately two minutes before the train leaves.* | *Tours start approximately every 15-20 minutes in summer.*

some time /ˌsʌm ˈtaɪm/ [adv] **some time after/before/around/between/in etc** at a time in the past – use this when you do not know exactly when or it is not important exactly when: *The burglary must have happened some time after 8:00 p.m.* | *His third symphony was written some time between 1750 and 1753.* | *The clinic was closed some time in the early nineties.*

or thereabouts /ɔːʳ ˌðeərəˈbaʊts/ **at 10 o'clock or thereabouts/in the 1950s or thereabouts etc** use this after a time, date etc that is not exact, especially when it is not important to know the exact time, date etc: *They're old apartments, built in the 1930s or thereabouts.* | *The book will be published in May or thereabouts.*

circa /ˈsɜːʳkə/ [prep] **circa 1920/1850/1492 etc** use this when you are saying when something happened in history: *The manuscripts date from circa 400 B.C.* | *a Robert Adam mansion, built circa 1778* | *The picture shows Tsar Nicholas, circa 1914.*

4 approximately correct

- roughly
- more or less
- kind of/sort of
- be in the right ballpark

roughly /ˈrʌfli/ [adv] *Yes, that's roughly the right answer.* | *As long as you know roughly how to do it, that's fine.*

more or less /ˌmɔːr ɔːʳ ˈles◂/ [adv] if something is **more or less** correct, it is good or correct enough to be accepted even if it is not perfect: *What she says is more or less true.* | *'Did they have what you were looking for at the hardware store?' 'Yes, more or less.'*

kind of/sort of /ˈkaɪnd əv,ˈsɔːʳt əv/ informal spoken said when you think something is approximately right or true, but not exactly: *It's kind of circular-shaped, but not exactly.* | *'Did you finish your homework?' 'Well, sort of.'*

be in the right ballpark /biː ɪn ðə ˌraɪt ˈbɔːlpɑːʳk/ [v phrase] informal if you **are in the right ballpark**, what you have guessed is not exactly correct, but is close to being correct: *'I'd think a project like this would take at least five years to complete.' 'Not quite as long as that, but you're in the right ballpark.'*

5 a number or amount that is approximately right

- approximate
- rough
- ballpark figure
- approximation

approximate /ə'prɒksɪ̊mɪ̊t‖ə'prɑːk-/ [adj] *The measurements are approximate, but I think they'll do.* | *An expert could give you the approximate value of the painting.* | *Approximate journey time to London is four hours.*

rough /rʌf/ [adj only before noun] **rough guess/calculation/estimate/indication** approximately correct, and therefore not to be used for detailed or important work: *The report should give you a rough indication of the company's stock market performance over the past year.* | *I'd say that the whole thing would cost you around $1000, but that's just a rough estimate.*

ballpark figure /'bɔːlpɑːʳk ˌfɪgəʳ‖-ˌfɪgjər/ [n C] a number or amount that is approximately correct – used especially in business: *A ballpark figure for the cost of the construction is $4.5 million.* | *A firm price hasn't been set yet, but the ballpark figure under discussion is $3 million.* | **give sb a ballpark figure** *Could you give me a ballpark figure?*

approximation /əˌprɒksɪ̊'meɪʃən‖əˌprɑːk-/ [n C] formal a number or amount that is approximately correct **a reasonable approximation** *Five thousand dollars seems to be a reasonable approximation of the actual cost.*

above

in a higher position than something

RELATED WORDS

opposite: —— **under/below**

- above someone in a company/organization etc *see* **position/rank (3)**
- *see also* **up**

- above
- over
- overhead
- up
- upstairs
- overhang

above /ə'bʌv/ [prep/adv] *There was a light above the table.* | *Above his bed is a picture of two old men sitting on a park bench.* | *During my last year of college, I lived in a little apartment above a grocery store.* | **directly above** *We looked up and saw a helicopter hovering directly above us.* | **the floor/apartment above** (=above where you are) *We could hear noises in the room above.* | **from above** (=seen from above) *The light came from above them and to their right.* | **above sea level** (=used when describing how high a place is) *Mexico City is 2400 metres above sea level.*

over /'əʊvəʳ/ [prep/adv] directly above something or moving in the air above it: *The sign over the door said 'Employees Only'.* | *A thick layer of smoke hung over the city.* | *About 400 fans jumped over barricades and invaded the playing field.* | *As the planes flew over, Selim could see the Russian markings on their wings.* | *Riot police fired over the heads of the demonstrators.*

overhead /ˌəʊvəʳ'hed/ [adv] in the sky directly above your head: *A flock of birds passed overhead.* | *Suddenly, they heard the rumble of thunder overhead.* —**overhead** /'əʊvəʳhed/ [adj only before noun] *Please put your luggage in the overhead compartment.*

up /ʌp/ [adv] **up in/on/there etc** in a higher position than where you are: *I found some old pictures of my mother up in the attic.* | *Are you able to see up there or do you need a flashlight?*

upstairs /ˌʌp'steəʳz◂/ [adv] on a higher floor of a building, above where you are: *The bathroom is upstairs on your left.* | *Don't you think the woman upstairs is kind of strange?*—**upstairs** [adj only before noun] *The thieves got in through an upstairs window.*

overhang /ˌəʊvəʳ'hæŋ/ [v I/T] if something such as a tree or a rock **overhangs** something, it sticks out over it: *The bird was sitting on a branch overhanging the water.* | *An ancient vine overhangs the terrace.* —**overhanging** /'əʊvəʳhæŋɪŋ/ [adj] *Julian waited under an overhanging rock until the rain stopped.* | *We rowed down the river beneath overhanging branches.*

accept

RELATED WORDS

opposite: —— **refuse, reject**

- *see also* **yes, let/allow, invite**

1 to accept an offer, invitation, or request

- accept
- take
- say yes
- agree
- take sb up on/take up sb's offer
- jump at the chance/opportunity

accept /ək'sept/ [v I/T] to say yes to an offer, an invitation, or a chance to do something: *I decided to accept the job.* | *The president has accepted an invitation to visit Beijing.* | *If they offered you a place on the course, would you accept it?* | *We've invited Professor Shaw to come and give a talk and she's accepted.* —**acceptance** [n U] formal when you officially accept something, such as a job offer: *She phoned the personnel department to confirm her acceptance of the job offer.*

take /teɪk/ [v T] if you **take** an opportunity or a job that someone offers you, you accept it: *Stephen says he'll take the job if the money's right.* | *This is a wonderful opportunity – I think you should take it.*

say yes /seɪ 'jes/ [v phrase] spoken if someone **says yes**, they agree to do what you have asked or invited them to do: *We'd really like you to come to France with us this summer. Please say yes!* | *David doesn't usually lend his car to anyone, so I was surprised when he said yes.* | **say yes to (doing) sth** *Do you really think your parents will say yes to letting you stay out late this Friday night?*

agree /ə'griː/ to say you will do what someone has asked you to do, especially something that may be difficult, inconvenient etc: *They've asked Tina to work overtime this week, and she's agreed.* | **+ to do sth** *I wish I had never agreed to teach Paul how to drive.* | *I've agreed to help Sarah move this weekend.*

take sb up on/take up sb's offer /ˌteɪk (sb) 'ʌp ɒn, ˌteɪk ʌp (sb's) 'ɒfəʳ‖-'ɔːf- / [v phrase] to accept someone's offer to do something for you, especially when you accept the offer some time after it was made: *'If you ever need a babysitter, let me know.' 'Thanks, I might take you up on that some time.'* |

take up sb's offer of sth *In the end, Rick took up his parents' offer of a loan.*

jump at the chance/opportunity /ˈdʒʌmp ət ðə ˌtʃɑːns‖ˌtʃæns, ɒpəˌtjuːnəti‖-ɑːpərˌtuː-/ to eagerly accept an offer to do something: *Marla jumped at the chance to spend a year working in her company's UK office.*

2 to take money or a gift that someone offers you

- take/accept

take/accept /teɪk, əkˈsept/ [v T/v I/T] to take something someone offers you, especially money or a gift. **Accept** is more formal than **take**: *Mark gave us a lot of helpful advice, but he refused to take any payment for it.* | *We hope you'll accept this small gift.* | **take sth from sb** *My mother always warned us never to take candy from strangers.* | **take bribes** *Ochoa was formally accused of taking bribes.* | **take it or leave it** (=said when telling someone that you will not change your offer) *I'll give you $500 for the car. Take it or leave it.* | **accept sth from sb** *A Senate candidate can accept up to $2,000 from individual campaign donors.*

3 to accept that something is right

- accept
- agree
- welcome
- go with
- take on board
- embrace

accept /əkˈsept/ [v T] to agree that a suggestion or idea is right, especially when you did not previously think so: *People are beginning to accept the idea that higher taxes may be necessary.* | **+ that** *The judge accepted that Carter did not mean to harm anyone.* —**acceptance** [n U] *These theories have not found much acceptance among professional psychiatrists* (=they do not accept that the theories are true).

agree /əˈgriː/ to accept that a plan or suggestion is good, especially when you have the power to decide whether it will be allowed to happen: *I spoke to my boss yesterday about postponing the meeting and she agreed.* | **+ to** *We want to have a big party, but I don't think my parents will agree to it.* | **+ that** *The music teacher agreed that Dave should play at the school concert.*

welcome /ˈwelkəm/ [v T] to think that a plan, suggestion, or decision is very good, and eagerly accept it: *Some companies have welcomed the idea of employees working from home.* | *The university's cafeteria welcomes any suggestions for improvement of its menu or service.* | **be warmly welcomed** *The proposal was warmly welcomed by the German Chancellor.*

go with /ˈgəʊ wɪð/ [phr v T] especially spoken use this to say that you are willing to accept and support a plan or suggestion that someone has made: *'What do you think of Jo's idea?' 'I think we should go with it – I can't think of anything better.'*

take on board /ˌteɪk ɒn ˈbɔːʳd/ [v phrase] British to realize that a new idea or suggestion is important and that it needs to be thought about seriously **take sth on board** *The local government says it has taken much of the public's criticism on board and it promises to make changes.* | **take on board sth** *The management says that it will take on board suggestions from employees about child-care facilities.*

embrace /ɪmˈbreɪs/ [v T] formal to eagerly accept ideas, opinions etc: *By the end of the last century, Americans had embraced the idea of the right to free public education for all children.* | **embrace sth wholeheartedly/wholeheartedly embrace sth** (=embrace it completely) *The President said he wholeheartedly embraced the need for further talks on the refugee crisis.*

4 to accept something after first refusing or opposing it

- accept
- give in
- back down
- bow to
- accede to
- cave in

accept /əkˈsept/ [v T] to **accept** someone's suggestion, offer, or demand, after refusing it for some time **finally accept sth** *After a three week strike, the company has finally accepted the workers' pay demands.* | *The owners finally accepted our offer of £62,000.* | **(finally) have to accept sth** *The President finally had to accept that there was little support for his health care initiatives.*

give in /ˌgɪv ˈɪn/ [phr v I] to unwillingly agree to accept someone's demands after they have argued with you, asked you repeatedly, or threatened you: *Jenny kept begging me for a new bicycle, and I finally gave in.* | **+ to** *The President said he would never give in to demands by terrorists.* | *You shouldn't always give in to other people – stick up for yourself more.*

back down /ˌbæk ˈdaʊn/ [phr v I] to agree to stop saying that you are right or that other people obey you: *Even though it was obvious Emma's demands were unrealistic, she wouldn't back down.* | **+ on** *Congress has backed down on its demand for an increase in defense spending.*

bow to /ˈbaʊ tuː/ [phr v T] **bow to sb's wishes/opinions/demands/pressure etc** to agree to do something because many people want you to, even though you do not want to do it: *The government finally bowed to public opinion and abolished the unpopular tax.* | *McDonald's finally bowed to consumer pressure and announced that it would no longer use styrofoam boxes to package its hamburgers.*

accede to /əkˈsiːd tuː/ [phr v T] **accede to sb's demands/request/wishes** formal to accept someone's demands etc: *The Democrats have finally acceded to Republican demands to cut taxes.* | *Meyer acceded to the President's request that he continue as education secretary until a replacement could be found.*

cave in /ˌkeɪv ˈɪn/ [phr v I] to finally accept what someone has suggested or to finally agree to something that they want – use this when you think someone should not accept something and are being weak if they do: *Strike leaders are privately saying they would like an end to the dispute, but don't want to be seen to be caving in.* | **+ to** *It's unlikely that the government will cave in to the rebels' demands.*

5 to accept a situation that you do not like

- accept
- put up with sth
- tolerate
- resign yourself to/be resigned to
- make the best of it/make the best of a bad situation
- bite the bullet
- beggars can't be choosers
- that's the way the cookie crumbles
- grit your teeth

accept /əkˈsept/ [v T] to **accept** a situation that you do not like but you cannot change: *Divorce is hard* *on children, but they have to accept it.* | **learn/come to accept** (=eventually accept) *In the US, people have come to accept that they will probably have several different jobs over the course of their career.* | **accept the fact (that)** *It was difficult for Paul to accept the fact that he was going bald.* | **+ that** *Steptoe finally accepted that his son didn't want to continue working in the family business.* —**acceptance** [n U] when you accept an unpleasant situation that cannot be changed: *Her husband had been ill for some time, and she received the news of his death with calm acceptance.*

put up with sth /pʊt 'ʌp wɪð (sth)/ [phr v T] to accept an annoying situation or someone's annoying behaviour, without trying to stop it or change it: *I don't know how you put up with this noise day after day.* | *The kind of treatment that you have to put up with as a new army recruit is pretty horrible.*

tolerate /'tɒləreɪt‖'tɑː-/ [v T] to accept an unpleasant situation, without trying to change it: *For years the workers have had to tolerate low wages and terrible working conditions.* | *I told him I wasn't going to tolerate his drinking any longer.*

resign yourself to/be resigned to /rɪ'zaɪn jɔːʳself tuː, biː rɪ'zaɪnd tuː/ [v phrase] to realize that you must accept an unpleasant situation, because you cannot prevent it or avoid it: *The children have had to resign themselves to being without their father.* | **resign yourself to the fact (that)** *I'm resigned to the fact that I'm not going to get the job.* —**resignation** /ˌrezɪg'neɪʃən/ [n U] when you accept a situation that you cannot change, although you do not like it: *Sharon accepted the bad news with resignation.*

make the best of it/make the best of a bad situation /ˌmeɪk ðə 'best əv ɪt, meɪk ðə ˌbest əv ə ˌbæd sɪtʃu'eɪʃən/ [v phrase] to accept a situation that you do not like, and try to enjoy it or make it less bad: *It's not the university that I really wanted to go to, but I suppose I'll just have to make the best of it.* | *Six months after the earthquake, city residents continue to make the best of a bad situation.*

bite the bullet /ˌbaɪt ðə 'bʊlɪ̣t/ to accept an unpleasant or difficult situation and say that you will deal with it: *It's not easy, but as a manager, sometimes you have to bite the bullet and fire people.*

beggars can't be choosers /ˌbegəʳz kɑːnt bi 'tʃuːzəʳz‖-kænt-/ spoken said when you have to accept something you do not like because you do not have the money or power to choose anything else: *It would be nice to have a suit with a better fit, but as they say, beggars can't be choosers.*

that's the way the cookie crumbles /ðæts ðə ˌweɪ ðə ˌkʊki 'krʌmbəlz/ spoken said when telling someone that a difficult situation must be accepted, especially because there is no way to prevent it or there is nothing anyone can do about it: *'Sorry you didn't get the job, Mike.' 'Yeah, thanks. I guess that's the way the cookie crumbles.'*

grit your teeth /ˌgrɪt jɔːʳ 'tiːθ/ [v phrase] to accept a situation or job you do not like and try to deal with it in a determined way: *Rescue workers here have little choice but to grit their teeth and get on with the grim task of recovering the bodies.* | *I was desperately unhappy in that job, but had to grit my teeth and stay smiling for the sake of my children.*

6 to officially accept a new law or proposal

- pass
- approve
- ratify
- be carried
- uphold
- rubber-stamp

pass /pɑːs‖pæs/ [v T] if a parliament or similar group **passes** a law or proposal, the members vote to accept it: *The State Assembly passed a law which banned smoking in public places.* | **+ by** *The bill was passed by 197 votes to 50.*

approve /ə'pruːv/ [v T] to officially accept something that has been planned to happen: *The Medical Research Council said it could not approve the use of the new drug without further tests.* | *Congress voted not to approve the President's plans for cutting the arms budget.* —**approval** [n U] when a suggestion or plan is officially accepted: *The government recently gave its approval to several US companies to sell satellite and other hi-tech equipment on the open market.*

ratify /'rætɪ̣faɪ/ [v T] **ratify an agreement/treaty** to officially agree to accept an agreement that someone else has already agreed to accept: *The US Senate refused to ratify the agreement on weapons reduction.* | *A 1961 treaty ratified by 125 nations outlawed the production of cocaine.* —**ratification** /ˌrætɪ̣fɪ̣'keɪʃən/ [n U] when an agreement is officially signed or agreed upon: *Without ratification the agreement cannot be implemented.*

be carried /biː 'kærid/ [v phrase] if a suggestion, proposal etc **is carried**, most of the people at an official meeting vote in favour of it and it is accepted: *Chao's proposal for a new downtown parking facility was carried at yesterday's council meeting.* | **be carried by 20 votes/100 votes etc** *The motion to restrict handgun sales was carried by 76 votes* (=76 more people voted for it than voted against it).

uphold /ˌʌp'həʊld/ [v T] if a court or a judge **upholds** a legal decision made by another court, they decide that it is right and they accept it: *The court's decision upheld state laws prohibiting doctor-assisted suicide.* | **+ by** *The decision was upheld by the US Supreme Court late last year.*

rubber-stamp /ˌrʌbəʳ 'stæmp/ [v T] if an official committee or someone in authority **rubber-stamps** a decision, they approve it immediately without thinking about it or discussing it because they have no real power of their own: *The town council usually rubber-stamped anything the mayor sent their way.*

7 to accept that something has legal or official authority

- accept
- recognize
- acknowledge

accept /ək'sept/ [v T] *The president refused to accept the authority of the state court when it tried to keep black students out of the University of Alabama.* | *The idea of a common defence force has been accepted by some EU governments.* —**acceptance** [n U] **widespread acceptance** (=general acceptance) *Authorities hope that the new regulations on smoking in public places will meet widespread acceptance.*

recognize ALSO **recognise** British /'rekəgnaɪz, 'rekən-/ [v T] **recognize a court/government/qualification** to officially accept that it has legal or official authority: *Papua New Guinea was the first country* *to recognize the new military regime in Fiji.* | *British medical qualifications are recognized in many countries throughout the world.* —**recognition** /ˌrekəgˈnɪʃən/ [n U] when a government, organization etc is officially accepted: *It was many years before the Communist government gained official recognition from the US government.*

acknowledge /əkˈnɒlɪdʒ‖-ˈnɑː-/ [v T] to officially accept that a government, court, organization, or person has legal or official authority: *Zaire was forced to acknowledge the authority of the Congolese state.* | **be acknowledged as** *In 1932 De Valera was elected as Prime Minister, and was acknowledged as leader of the Irish people.*

8 to accept something as payment

- take/accept

take/accept /teɪk, əkˈsept/ [v T] *Will you take a cheque?* | *The hotel accepts all major credit cards.* | *I'm afraid we only accept cash.*

accident

an event in which someone is hurt or killed, or something is damaged

RELATED WORDS

- by accident or not deliberately *see* **accidentally**
- *see also* **disaster, mistake, damage, destroy, break, kill, hurt/injure, pain, fall, drive, recover, unconscious**

1 at work, at home, when doing a sport etc

- accident
- mishap

accident /ˈæksɨdənt/ [n C] *She has been in almost constant pain since her accident.* | **have an accident** *Robert had an accident in the lab. He was opening a bottle of acid and he spilt some on his hands.* | **serious accident** *Most serious accidents in the home involve electrical equipment or hot liquids.* | **fatal accident** *The number of fatal accidents in the construction industry has dropped dramatically in recent years.* | **climbing/riding/skiing etc accident** *His best friend was killed in a skiing accident.*

mishap /ˈmɪshæp/ [n C] an accident that does not have very serious results, especially one caused by someone making a mistake: *We managed to reach our destination, despite one or two mishaps earlier on in the day.* | **minor/slight mishap** *Josh had just had a slight mishap with the breadknife, and was trying to find a Band-Aid.*

2 in a car, train, plane etc

- accident
- crash
- wreck
- pile-up
- disaster
- collision

accident /ˈæksɨdənt/ [n C] *The accident happened on Interstate 84, during the evening rush hour.* | *Brussels airport was closed today after an accident on the runway.* | **have an accident** *Teenage boys tend to drive wildly and often have accidents.* | **bad/nasty/serious accident** *As usual, the fog and icy roads had led to several very nasty accidents.* | **fatal accident** *Men have twice as many fatal accidents as women do for every mile they drive.* | **car/road/traffic accident** *Both her parents had been killed in a car accident.* | **auto/automobile accident** American *She was in an automobile accident, but she's not seriously hurt.*

crash /kræʃ/ [n C] an accident in which a vehicle or plane hits something violently and is damaged or destroyed: *Ira Louvin was killed in a crash in Montana that also took the lives of six other people.* | **car/plane/train crash** *Her husband died in a plane crash in 1981.*

wreck /rek/ [n C] American an accident involving cars or other vehicles: *Nobody could have survived the wreck.*

pile-up /ˈpaɪl ʌp/ [n C] a serious road accident in which many cars or other vehicles crash into each other: *The pile-up happened in thick fog and caused a seven-mile tailback on the motorway.* | **multiple pile-up** British (=a pile up involving a large number of cars) *a multiple pile-up involving a minibus and five cars*

disaster /dɪˈzɑːstəʳ‖dɪˈzæs-/ [n C] a very serious accident involving a train, plane, or ship, in which many people are killed: *The city has emergency plans for dealing with a major disaster such as a rail crash.* | **air/rail disaster** *At least 264 people died, in one of the worst civilian air disasters of all time.* | **the Lockerbie disaster/the Challenger disaster etc** *The Challenger disaster cost the lives of seven astronauts, and set back the nation's space program for years.*

collision /kəˈlɪʒən/ [n C] an accident in which two or more vehicles, planes, or ships hit each other **+ with** *A school bus has been involved in a collision with a fuel tanker.* | **mid-air collision** (=between two planes in the air) *The risk of a mid-air collision over central London has increased dramatically.* | **head-on collision** (=between two vehicles moving directly towards each other) *These airbags are designed to protect car drivers in head-on collisions.*

3 to have an accident

- have an accident
- crash
- be involved in an accident

have an accident /ˌhæv ən ˈæksɨdənt/ [v phrase not in progressive or passive] *You shouldn't go so fast on that motorcycle, you'll have an accident!* | *Jack's had an accident at school! They've taken him to the hospital.*

crash /kræʃ/ [v I/T] to have a serious accident in a car, train, plane etc by violently hitting another vehicle or something such as a wall or the ground: *He lost control of his car at the first bend and crashed.* | *The plane crashed shortly after take-off.* | **+ into/onto** *The bus crashed into an embankment before bursting into flames.* | **crash a car/bike/plane etc** *Rick crashed his bike before he'd finished paying for it.*

be involved in an accident /biː ɪnˌvɒlvd ɪn ən ˈæksɨdənt‖ -ˌvɑːlvd-/ [v phrase] formal to have an accident – used in official written documents and in news reports: *If you are involved in an accident, wearing a seat belt will halve the risk of death.* | *Stolen cars are more likely to be involved in accidents.*

accidentally

RELATED WORDS

opposite: ——— **deliberately**

- something happens by chance *see* **chance**
- *see also* **mistake, break, damage, hurt/injure**

1 when you do something without intending to do it

- **accidentally/by accident**
- **accidental**
- **by mistake**
- **mistakenly**
- **not mean to do something**
- **be an accident**
- **unintentionally**
- **unintended/unintentional**

accidentally/by accident /ˌæksǝ̇ˈdentl-i, baɪ ˈæksǝ̇dǝnt/ [adv] *I accidentally burnt a hole in her sofa with my cigarette.* | *An 11-month-old baby died after accidentally swallowing several of the tablets.* | *Fleming discovered the drug by accident, when he was researching something else.* | **completely by accident** ALSO **quite by accident** British *I met the man quite by accident, and we began a conversation.*

accidental /ˌæksǝ̇ˈdentl◂/ [adj] happening without being planned or intended: *She touched his elbow so timidly that he thought it must have been accidental.* | *an accidental discharge of toxic waste* | **purely accidental** (=completely accidental) *They believe that miscalculations made on the tax forms were purely accidental.*

by mistake /baɪ mǝ̇ˈsteɪk/ [adv] if you do something **by mistake**, you intend to do one thing, but you accidentally do something else instead: *Michelle must have picked up my keys by mistake.* | *I opened this by mistake, Paula, but I think it's for you – sorry.* | *Gary wandered into the wrong hotel room by mistake.*

mistakenly /mɪˈsteɪkǝnli/ [adv] if you **mistakenly** do something, you intend to do one thing, but you accidentally do something else instead, especially because you are confused: *The crew had mistakenly shut down the engine, and the plane went out of control.* | *A handful of people die each year from mistakenly eating poisonous fungi.*

not mean to do sth /nɒt ˌmiːn tǝ ˈduː (sth)/ [v phrase not in progressive] especially spoken to do something accidentally – use this especially when expressing the idea that you are sorry for something that you have done, or when you think you are being unfairly blamed for something: *I'm sorry, I didn't mean to hurt your feelings.* | *I'm sure he didn't mean to yell at you – he was just angry.* | *Sorry folks, I don't mean to interrupt your dinner.* | *If we've offended you in some way, we didn't mean to.*

be an accident /biː ǝn ˈæksǝ̇dǝnt/ [v phrase usually in past not in progressive] if you say that something was an accident, you mean that you are sorry it happened, but it was not done deliberately: *Marris told the police the killing was an accident* | *Don't blame yourself – it was an accident.*

unintentionally /ˌʌnɪnˈtenʃǝnǝli/ [adv] if you do something **unintentionally**, especially something bad, you do it even though you do not intend to do it: *Teachers often unintentionally favor certain students.* | *The advertisement unintentionally offended Scottish people.* | *Several scenes in the movie are unintentionally funny.*

unintended/unintentional /ˌʌnɪnˈtendǝ̇d◂, ˌʌnɪnˈtenʃǝnǝl◂/ [adj] use this about something you do without intending to, especially something that annoys, upsets, or causes problems for someone else: *The senator apologised, saying any offense his remarks had caused had been completely unintentional.* | *One originally unintended consequence of the discussions was the setting up of an official inquiry into the department's funding.*

2 when you do something without realizing that you are doing it

- **inadvertently**
- **unconsciously**
- **unconscious**
- **involuntary**

inadvertently /ˌɪnǝdˈvɜːʳtǝntli/ [adv] if you **inadvertently** do something, you do it without realizing you are doing it, because you are not careful enough – use this especially to talk about someone's behaviour or movements: *In a panic, I inadvertently pushed the accelerator instead of the brake.* | *The Finance Minister inadvertently revealed budget secrets to reporters.* | *The problem was caused by a worker who inadvertently contaminated the coffee machine by cleaning it with a toxic substance.*

unconsciously /ʌnˈkɒnʃǝsli‖-ˈkɑːn-/ [adv] if you **unconsciously** do something, you do it without realizing you are doing it – use this especially to talk about someone's behaviour or movements: *Martha watched the program in silence, unconsciously rubbing her hand on her dress.* | *In conversation, some people unconsciously imitate the people they are speaking with.*

unconscious /ʌnˈkɒnʃǝs‖-ˈkɑːn-/ [adj only before noun] an action, choice etc that is **unconscious** is not done deliberately but it may show your true feelings: *Many women are the victims of unconscious discrimination by men.* | *His comments were an unconscious insult to Irish people.*

involuntary /ɪnˈvɒlǝntǝri‖ɪnˈvɑːlǝnteri/ [adj] **involuntary** movements or actions are ones that you do accidentally and that you cannot control: *Her teeth were chattering and she gave an enormous involuntary shudder.* | *With an involuntary yell of alarm, she tumbled forward.*

accuse

RELATED WORDS

- *see also* **blame, judge, law, prison, court, trial, guilty, innocent, suspect**

1 to say that you think someone has done something bad

- **accuse**
- **accusation**
- **allege**
- **allegation**
- **confront**
- **point the finger at**
- **accusingly**

accuse /ǝˈkjuːz/ [v T] **accuse sb of doing sth** *Human rights lawyers have accused the police of beating Murkett to death.* | *The man accused of kidnapping Lucy Pohl has been found guilty.* | **accuse sb of sth** *Protesters angrily accused the police of violence and intimidation.* | *A former businessman has gone on trial accused of a two million pound investment fraud.* | **accuse sb** *How can you accuse me without knowing all the facts?*

accusation /ˌækjʊ̈ˈzeɪʃən/ [n C] a statement saying that someone has done something bad **make an accusation** *You've made a lot of accusations but you haven't come up with any evidence to support them.* | **+ against** *A spokesman said the accusations against Mr Fallon would be investigated.* | **+ of** *There have been accusations of racism in the Los Angeles Police Department.* | **level an accusation against sb/sth** formal (=make an accusation) *A number of accusations have been levelled against Hutchinson by his former colleagues.* | **wild accusation** (=an accusation made without thinking carefully first) *You shouldn't make any wild accusations if you're not absolutely sure that Wilkins stole the money.*

allege /əˈledʒ/ [v T] to say publicly that someone has done something bad or illegal, even though this has not been proved – used especially in newspapers and news reports **(+ that)** *In a statement to the press, Massey alleged that her husband had planned to kill her.* | **be alleged to have done sth** *Taylor is alleged to have used public money to buy expensive presents for her friends.* | **it is alleged that** *It has been alleged that senior officials were involved in a $20 million drugs deal.* —**alleged** [adj only before noun] *When questioned about the alleged incident, he claimed to know nothing.* —**allegedly** /əˈledʒɪ̈dli/ [adv] *Prosecutors have arrested Johnson for allegedly accepting bribes from a property developer.* | *A gang of Merseyside men were allegedly involved in smuggling £500,000-worth of cannabis.*

allegation /ˌælɪˈgeɪʃən/ [n C usually plural] a public statement saying that someone has done something bad or illegal, even though this has not been proved **make an allegation** *The newspaper made several allegations, none of which turned out to be true.* | **+ of** *There were allegations of corruption in the police department.* | **+ about** *The book contains shocking allegations about the senator's private life.* | **+ that** *There have been allegations in the press that the fire was started deliberately.* | **serious allegation** *These are serious allegations. Do you have any evidence to support them?* | **deny an allegation** (=say it is false) *Weimar denied allegations of financial mismanagement.*

confront /kənˈfrʌnt/ [v T] to accuse someone of doing something by showing them the proof against them **confront sb with the evidence/proof etc** *The FBI confronted Schmidt with the evidence of his part in the murder plot.*

point the finger at /ˌpɔɪnt ðə ˈfɪŋgər æt/ [v phrase] to say that you think someone is probably responsible for something bad that has happened, although you do not have definite proof: *Someone's lost the letter and the boss is pointing the finger at me.*

accusingly /əˈkjuːzɪŋli/ [adv] if you look at, point at, or speak to someone **accusingly**, you do it in a way that shows you think they have done something bad: *Janet suddenly pointed at me, and everyone looked at me accusingly.* | *'You did it, Tom,' she said accusingly. 'I know you didn't mean to, but you did do it.'* —**accusing** [adj only before noun] *'Where have you been?' Mick asked in an accusing tone of voice.*

2 when someone is officially accused of a crime

- charge
- press charges
- prosecute
- put sb on trial/bring sb to trial
- indict
- impeach

charge /tʃɑːʳdʒ/ [v T usually in passive] if the police **charge** someone, they tell that person that they believe he or she is guilty of a crime, and that the person must appear in court so that it can be proved whether they are guilty or not **charge sb with murder/theft/assault etc** *The man they arrested last night has been charged with murder.* | *They're going to charge him with dangerous driving.* | **charge sb with doing sth** *Police have charged a 22-year-old man with robbing two Japanese tourists.* | **be charged** *Twelve people involved in the demonstration have been arrested and charged.*

press charges ALSO **bring charges** British /ˌpres ˈtʃɑːʳdʒɪ̈z, ˌbrɪŋ-/ [v phrase] to make an official statement accusing someone of a crime or an offence, so that they will be judged in a court of law: *He's in trouble this time. The police have said they're going to press charges.* | **+ against** *Curran decided to bring charges against the man who attacked him.* | *Charges have been brought against the demonstrators.*

prosecute /ˈprɒsɪkjuːt‖ˈprɑː-/ [v I/T] if the authorities **prosecute** someone, they try to prove that the person is guilty of a crime in a court of law so that they can be punished: *The shopkeeper is unlikely to prosecute if the stolen goods are returned.* | *People who give the police false information will be prosecuted.* | **prosecute sb for sth** *Winstanley was prosecuted for criminal damage of property.* —**prosecution** /ˌprɒsɪˈkjuːʃən‖ˌprɑː-/ [n U] *evidence that could lead to the arrest and prosecution of car thieves*

put sb on trial/bring sb to trial /ˌpʊt (sb) ɒn ˈtraɪəl, ˌbrɪŋ (sb) tə ˈtraɪəl/ [v phrase] to send someone to a court of law where they will be officially accused of a serious crime and will be judged: *Blake was brought to trial and sentenced to seven years in prison.* | **put sb on trial for sth** *A Glasgow girl was put on trial for poisoning her lover.* | **bring sb to trial for sth** *These men were brought to trial for a crime they did not commit.*

indict /ɪnˈdaɪt/ [v I/T] to officially accuse someone of a crime, so that they will be judged in a court of law – used especially in the American legal system **be indicted** *A leading cocaine trafficker has been indicted by the United States government.* | **indict sb for sth** *He was indicted for perjury before a grand jury.* —**indictable** [adj] *Drug trafficking is an indictable offense* (=a crime for which someone can be indicted).

impeach /ɪmˈpiːtʃ/ [v T] to officially accuse an important public official or politician of a crime when they are in a position of authority – used especially in the American legal system: *Congress voted to impeach the President, but he resigned before any action was taken.* | **impeach sb for doing sth** *The governor was impeached for accepting bribes.* —**impeachment** [n U] *Richard Nixon was forced to resign the presidency in 1974 to avoid impeachment.*

3 an official statement accusing someone of a crime

- charge
- indictment

charge /tʃɑːʳdʒ/ [n C] an official statement made by the police accusing someone of a crime or an offence **a charge of burglary/theft/fraud etc** *He faces a charge of armed robbery.* | **+ against** *What are the charges against the accused?* | **on a charge** British *He appeared in court on a murder charge.* | **drop (the) charges** (=decide to stop accusing someone) *Police have dropped the charges due to lack of evidence.*

indictment /ɪnˈdaɪtmənt/ [n C] an official written statement accusing someone of a crime or an offence – used especially in the American legal system: *A 15-page indictment was placed before the panel of judges.* | *Hancock pleaded not guilty to a federal indictment accusing him of four bombings.*

4 someone who is accused of a crime in a trial

- the accused
- defendant
- be on trial
- in the dock
- be up/be had up/end up in court

the accused /ði əˈkjuːzd/ [n singular or plural] especially British the person or group of people who are officially accused of a crime or offence in a court of law: *The witness told the court that she had never seen either of the accused before.* | *The judge asked the jury if they found the accused guilty or not guilty.* | *The accused, Dorothy Jackson, was being held in the Tarrant County Jail on a charge of assault.*

defendant /dɪˈfendənt/ [n C] someone who is officially accused of a crime or offence in a court of law: *The police officer said the defendant had resisted arrest.* | *Each of the three defendants was convicted of conspiracy to commit murder.*

be on trial /biː ɒn ˈtraɪəl/ [v phrase] if someone **is on trial**, they have been accused of a serious crime in a court of law, and the court will judge whether they are guilty: *There were four defendants on trial, all sitting together in a line.* | **+ for** *Hollins is on trial for corruption after admitting he accepted bribes.*

in the dock /ɪn ðə ˈdɒk‖-ˈdɑːk/ British if someone is **in the dock**, they are in a court of law because they have been accused of a crime: *In the dock at Craigavon Crown Court was Richard Ellis (21) who denies the murder.*

be up/be had up/end up in court /biː ˌʌp, biː hæd ˌʌp, end ˌʌp ɪn ˈkɔːʳt/ [v phrase] to have been accused of a crime and be judged in a court of law: *He's been up in court several times before on charges of robbery with violence.* | *Anyone who's been had up in court will find it more difficult to get a job afterwards, even if they are innocent.* | *We need to be very careful about how we play this – we don't want to end up in court.*

5 someone who officially tries to prove that someone is guilty

- the prosecution
- prosecutor
- District Attorney/D.A.

the prosecution /ðə ˌprɒsɪˈkjuːʃən‖-ˌprɑː-/ [n singular with singular or plural verb in British English] the group of lawyers in a court of law who try to prove that the person accused of a crime is guilty: *The prosecution alleged that the men took part in a plot to kill the President.* | *McFarlane will appear as a witness for the prosecution.*

prosecutor /ˈprɒsɪˌkjuːtəʳ‖ˈprɑː-/ [n C] the lawyer who officially accuses someone of a crime or offence in a court of law and tries to prove that they are guilty: *The chief prosecutor told the court that Johnson was guilty of a horrible crime and asked for the maximum sentence.* | *A special prosecutor was appointed to deal with that particular case.*

District Attorney/D.A. /ˌdɪstrɪkt əˈtɜːʳni, ˌdiː ˈeɪ/ [n C] a government lawyer in the US who works with the police and in the courts on legal cases against people who have been charged with a crime: *the District Attorney's office* | *Richards was pictured on the front page, shaking the D.A.'s hand.*

across

RELATED WORDS

- to go across a place *see* **go**
- on the other side of something *see* **opposite (6, 7)**

- across
- over
- through
- trans-
- cross
- cut across
- cut through
- crossing

across /əˈkrɒs‖əˈkrɔːs/ [prep/adv] from one side of something to the other: *The children ran across the road.* | *I've always wanted to sail across the Atlantic.* | *We gazed across the valley.* | *The traffic was heavy so it took a long time to get across.* | **+ to** *He walked across to the window.*

over /ˈəʊvəʳ/ [prep] going from one side of something to the other, especially by flying, jumping, climbing, or using a bridge: *A cat jumped over the fence.* | *the road over the mountains* | *one of the bridges over the Rhine*

through /θruː/ [prep/adv] from one side or end of something to the other – use this about going **through** a town, a forest, or a crowd, or looking **through** a hole, window etc: *I pushed my way through the crowd.* | *walking through the forest* | *We drove through Baltimore on our way to Washington.* | *I could see her through the window.* | *The trip through the tunnel takes about 40 minutes.* | *We found a gap in the fence and climbed through.*

trans- /trans-, trænz-/ [prefix] **transatlantic/transcontinental/trans-European etc** going a long distance across a large area of land or water: *transatlantic flights* | *the first transcontinental railroad*

cross /krɒs‖krɔːs/ [v I/T] to go from one side of something to the other, for example to cross a river or road, or to cross a field or room: *Antonia went to cross the street to buy us some sodas.* | *He plans to cross the Himalayas on foot.* | *How are we going to cross the river?* | *Before you cross, make sure there are no other cars coming.*

cut across /ˌkʌt əˈkrɒs‖-əˈkrɔːs/ [phr v T] to go straight across something such as a field or road to save time, instead of going around it or by a longer way: *Farmers have begun putting up fences to prevent visitors from cutting across their land.* | *They moved south along the edge of a field, then cut across Highway 18.*

cut through /ˌkʌt ˈθruː/ [phr v T] to go across an area such as a garden, a wood, or a group of buildings, instead of going around it on a path or road, because it is quicker: *Instead of taking the main road I cut through the churchyard and jumped over the wall at the bottom.* | *Her house wasn't far, if he cut through the woods.*

crossing /ˈkrɒsɪŋ‖ˈkrɔː-/ [n C] a journey across an area of water or group of mountains: *The Atlantic crossing took nearly three months.* | *His party made the first east-west crossing of the Sierra Nevada in 1833.*

actor/actress

RELATED WORDS

- to practise for a play *see* **practise/practice**
- *see also* **perform/performance, film/movie, television/radio**

1 someone who performs in plays, films etc

- actor
- actress
- star
- film star/movie star
- luvvie
- cast

actor /ˈæktəʳ/ [n C] someone who performs in plays, films etc: *Leonardo DiCaprio is my favourite actor – he's so good-looking!* | *Actor Sidney Poitier was honoured with a Life Achievement Award.* | *Ben Chaplin is an English actor who had a small part in 'Remains of the Day'.*

actress /ˈæktrɪs/ [n C] a woman who performs in plays, films etc: *Julia Roberts is one of the most famous actresses in Hollywood.* | *Capucine, the French movie actress whose leading roles included one with Peter Sellers in 'The Pink Panther', died after falling from a window.* ▸ **USAGE** You can use ***actor*** about a man or a woman. Some women do not like the word ***actress*** and prefer to be called ***actors***.

star /stɑːʳ/ [n C] a famous actor or actress: *Eddie Murphy is one of the most successful stars in Hollywood.* | **big star** *James Caan was a big star in the '70s.*

film star British **/movie star** American /ˈfɪlm stɑːʳ, ˈmuːvi stɑːʳ/ [n C] a famous actor or actress who acts in films: *Her real ambition is to be a movie star, not just an actress on the stage.* | *Film stars like Michael Caine are trying to revive the British film industry by making movies in England.*

luvvie /ˈlʌvi/ [n C] British informal an actor or actress – used especially about groups of actors who behave towards each other in a very friendly way that is not sincere: *There's nothing worse than watching a bunch of luvvies giving speeches at some awful awards ceremony.*

cast /kɑːst‖kæst/ [n C with singular or plural verb in British English] all the people who act in a play or film: *Films like 'Ben Hur' were made with a cast of thousands.* | *The entire cast of the play deserves praise for this performance.*

2 to perform in plays, films etc

- act
- play
- go on the stage

act /ækt/ [v I] *In recent years Lewis has been acting in television dramas.* | *He learned to act when he was in high school.* | *That woman just can't act!* (=is bad at acting)

play /pleɪ/ [v T] to **play** the part of a particular character: *Milla Jovovich plays Joan of Arc in 'The Messenger'.* | *The roles of Vladimir and Estragon were played by Paul Whitworth and Ken Grantham.*

go on the stage /ˌgəʊ ɒn ðə ˈsteɪdʒ/ [v phrase] to become an actor in the theatre as a job: *Jane's parents didn't want her to go on the stage.*

3 the activity or study of acting

- acting
- theatre
- drama
- amateur dramatics

acting /ˈæktɪŋ/ [n U] the job or skill of being an actor: *You shouldn't take up acting as a career; it's a very risky business.* | *Gloria Reuben quit acting to join Tina Turner on stage as a backing singer and dancer.*

theatre British **/theater** American /ˈθɪətəʳ/ [n U] the business and activity of arranging, acting in, and performing plays in theatres: *She does some TV work, but theatre remains her first love.* | *the use of theatre in primary school education* | **the theatre/the theater** *Shakespeare's plays were written for the theater, but many people study them as literature.*

drama /ˈdrɑːmə‖ˈdrɑːmə, ˈdræmə/ [n U] the study of acting and plays as a subject at school, college, or university: *He studied English and Drama at Manchester University.* | *a drama student* | *I was never much good at drama when I was a kid – probably because I was very shy.*

amateur dramatics /ˌæmətəʳ drəˈmætɪks/ [n U] acting in plays as an activity that you do in your free time for enjoyment, not as a job you get paid for: *Jonathan once appeared in a local amateur dramatics production of 'Death of a Salesman'.* | *Her hobbies include amateur dramatics and horse riding.*

4 the most important actor in a play, film etc

- star
- co-star

star /stɑːʳ/ [n C] *Peter Fonda is best known as the star of 'Easy Rider' and other 1960s biker films.* | *'Blair Witch' star Heather Donahue has landed a new role in a college reunion film called 'Seven and a Match'.*

co-star /ˈkəʊ stɑːʳ/ [n C] one of two or more actors who are equally important in a play or film: *Stan Laurel appeared in many comedies with his co-star Oliver Hardy.* | *Hepburn was Humphrey Bogart's co-star in the movie 'African Queen'.*

5 when a play, film etc has a particular actor in it

- star
- co-star
- play the lead
- be/appear/perform in
- feature
- with
- as

star /stɑːʳ/ [v T not in passive] if an actor **stars** in a play or film, he or she is one of the most important actors in it; if a play or film **stars** an actor, he or she plays one of the most important characters in it: *The film stars Patricia Arquette and is directed by Steven Brill.* | *Director Jane Campion's latest film, which stars Kate Winslet and Harvey Keitel, was one of the highlights of the New York Film Festival.* | **+ in** *Danny Aiello stars in this comedy about New York's first big lottery winner.* | *Hollywood heart-throb Keanu Reeves is set to star in a true story based on a newspaper article from the Times.*

co-star /ˈkəʊstɑːʳ/ [v T not in passive] if two or more actors **co-star** in a play or film, they are equally important actors in it; if a play or film **co-stars** two or more people, they play the most important characters in it: *The movie co-stars Sarah Jessica Parker,*

Elle Macpherson and Ben Stiller. | **+ in** *Annette Bening co-starred in movies such as 'Valmont', 'Postcards from the Edge' and 'Regarding Henry'.*

play the lead /ˌpleɪ ðə 'liːd/ [v phrase] to act the most important part in a play or film: *Calloway played the lead in the New Federal Theater's production of 'The Louis Armstrong Story'.* | *He got an unexpected chance to play the lead after the film's original star fell ill.*

be/appear/perform in /'biː, ə'pɪər, pəʳ'fɔːʳm ɪn/ [v T not in passive] to act in a film or play, especially as one of the most important actors: *More than 60 youngsters will perform in the play at Old Town Theater in Los Gatos.* | *Clark Gable and Vivien Leigh appeared together in 'Gone with the Wind'.*

feature /'fiːtʃəʳ/ [v T not in passive] if a play or film **features** an actor, they are in it: *The play features two young actresses.* | *The original 'Star Trek' series, featuring William Shatner as Capt. Kirk and Leonard Nimoy as Mr. Spock, lasted three years.*

with /wɪð, wɪθ/ [prep] used when saying who is in a play, film etc: *Have you seen 'The Sixth Sense' with Bruce Willis?* | *Dawson is now producing a stage version of the story with a cast of young actors from New York.*

as /əz, (*strong*) æz/ [prep] if someone is in a play or film **as** a particular character, they act the part of that character: *Clint Eastwood was excellent as the strong, silent hero in his many westerns.* | *Paul McGann will star as a middle-class Jewish lawyer in a new BBC drama called 'Fish'.*

6 the person that an actor pretends to be in a play, film etc

- character
- part/role

character /'kærɪ̈ktəʳ/ [n C] *Jed is one of most likeable characters in the play.* | **central/main character** *Carmen Maura plays the passionate, beautiful Pepa, the central character of director Pedro Almodovar's movie.*

part/role /pɑːʳt, rəʊl/ [n C] the job of acting as a particular character in a play or film: *She knew she wanted the part as soon as she read the movie script.* | **play the part/role of** *She played the part of the Wicked Stepmother in 'Snow White'.*

actually

RELATED WORDS

- *see also* **true, real**

1 when the real situation is different from what people think

- actually
- in fact
- really
- in reality/the reality is
- the truth/fact is
- in practice
- in effect/effectively

actually /'æktʃuəli, -tʃəli/ [adv] especially spoken used to tell or ask someone what the real situation is, when they think it is something different: *'Here's the $10 I owe you.' 'Actually, you owe me 20.'* | *Did he actually hit you or just threaten you?* | *It turns out that one of the children I thought was a girl was actually a boy.*

in fact /ɪn 'fækt/ [adv] used to tell someone what the real situation is, when they think it is something different. **Actually** is more informal and is used more in conversation than **in fact**. **Actually** is also used more in questions than **in fact**. **Actually** is often used at the beginning of a sentence that answers a question, but **in fact** is not.: *He said it would be cheap but in fact it cost over £200.* | *No, I'm not offended at all. In fact, I'm glad you asked the question.* | **in actual fact/in point of fact** *They seem to think that building a new road will improve the traffic problem, whereas in point of fact it will make it worse.* | *There are almost 200,000 possible combinations of symbols. In actual fact, only a small number of these are used.*

really /'rɪəli/ [adv] spoken used to say what the truth is, especially because something about the situation may make people believe something that is wrong: *He failed his tests, but he's quite a bright guy, really.* | *Are you sure she's really a lawyer? She doesn't act like one.* | *They're asking £600,000 for the house. That's more than it's really worth.*

in reality/the reality is /ɪn ri'ælɪ̈ti, ðə ri'ælɪ̈ti ɪz/ [adv/n phrase] used to introduce the second part of a statement when you want to show that the first part is not true or exact: *It seems like just yesterday, but in reality it was five years ago.* | *Nowadays owning a car may appear to be a necessity, but in reality it isn't.* | *They say that the economy is already coming out of the recession, but the reality is that there has been no improvement at all.* | **the reality of the situation is** *The reality of the situation is that by sending drug users to jail, the government may be discouraging people from seeking treatment.*

the truth/fact is /ðə 'truːθ, 'fækt ɪz/ used to show what the real truth or fact is in a situation, when this is surprising or different from what people believed was true: *The truth was that she did not enjoy getting together with the rest of her family.* | *The fact is he was murdered. He didn't commit suicide at all.* | *I may make it all look easy, but the truth is I work very hard.*

in practice /ɪn 'præktɪ̈s/ [adv] used to show the difference between what is supposed to happen according to a rule or law, and what does happen: *Teenagers are not allowed to drink in bars, but in practice they often do.* | *Economic predictions are highly theoretical. It's what they mean in practice that is important.* | **in theory ... in practice** *The law seemed like a good idea in theory, but in practice it has proved far too expensive.*

in effect/effectively /ɪn ɪ'fekt, ɪ'fektɪvli/ [adv] used to show what really happens, even though this was not clear from what was said or done: *Foreign companies have been effectively running the country for decades.* | *Management seems to be saying, in effect, that if we don't like the offer, we can all quit.*

2 when what really happens is different from stories, films etc

- really/actually
- in the real world
- in real life

really/actually /'rɪəli, 'æktʃuəli/ [adv] *Does Santa Claus really exist?* | *There are many stories which describe wolves as dangerous, blood-thirsty animals, but actually they prefer to avoid human beings.*

in the real world /ɪn ðə 'rɪəl ˌwɜːʳld/ [adv] in the world in which people really live, not in the world which exists in people's imagination: *Romances of that kind don't happen in the real world.* | *In the real* *world no one actually dies of a broken heart, but it happens in operas all the time.* | *His sudden success is something you never really expect to happen in the real world.*

in real life /ɪn ˌrɪəl 'laɪf/ [adv] **in real life**, as opposed to what happens in films or stories: *In real life there's no magic wand to make all our problems disappear.* | *On TV he plays a teenager, but in real life he's married with two children.*

3 when you want to add something surprising or interesting to what you are saying

- actually/as a matter of fact/in fact

actually/as a matter of fact/in fact /'æktʃuəli, əz ə ˌmætər əv 'fækt, ɪn fækt/ [adv] spoken *Robert's an old friend of mine. We were at school together, actually.* | *The company is doing very well. As a matter of fact, we've doubled our sales budget.* | *Of course I know your mother. We go to the same church, in fact.* | *The performance was excellent. In fact, it was probably the best I've seen.*

add

to put another part or piece together with something that already exists

RELATED WORDS

- to add numbers or amounts together *see* **count/calculate**
- to take a number from another number *see* **count/calculate**
- to make something increase *see* **increase**
- *see also* **reduce, total**

1 to add a new part or piece to something

- add
- add on

add /æd/ [v T] to **add** a new part or piece to something, especially in order to improve it **add sth** *If you need more storage space it's possible to add more shelves.* | *The book would look a lot more attractive if they added a few color pictures.* | **add sth to sth** *Adding fertilizer to the soil will help the plants to grow more quickly.*

add on /ˌæd 'ɒn/ [phr v T] to add something to a building in order to improve it or make it larger **add on sth** *We're having a bedroom added on to the back of the house.* | **add sth on** *By adding a garage on, you can increase the value of your home.*

2 to add more to an amount or cost

- add
- put sth on
- supplement

add /æd/ [v I/T] *They seem to have added a 10% service charge.* | **add sth to sth** *New fire-safety equipment had to be installed, adding thousands of dollars to the cost of the repairs.* | **add to sth** *Catherine won't mind if you add to her workload* (=give her more work) *– she needs the extra money.*

put sth on /ˌpʊt (sth) 'ɒn / [phr v T] British to add an amount of money, especially a tax, to the cost of something: *There are rumours that the government plans to put 20p on the cost of a packet of cigarettes.* | *The new tax could put ten cents on the price of gas.*

supplement /'sʌpləment/ [v T] to add more to something so that you have enough – used especially about someone adding to an amount of money, or someone eating more of a particular type of food to make them healthy: *Tracy gives her children vitamin pills to supplement their diet.* | *Mary found it necessary to supplement her earnings by writing articles for magazines.*

3 to add something to something you are cooking or mixing

- add

add /æd/ [v T] *I think you need to add a little more salt.* | **add sth to sth** *Add milk to the mixture before heating it.* | *John added some water to the paint to make it thinner.*

4 to add a quality or characteristic to something

- add
- give

add ALSO **lend** formal /æd, lend/ [v T not in progressive] to **add** a quality or feature to something, for example by making it more interesting, attractive, or enjoyable: *The car chase isn't really necessary to the story, but it adds an element of excitement.* | *Using actual furniture from the 1920s should help lend some authenticity.* | **add/lend sth to sth** *Fine champagne always adds glamour to an occasion.* | *The strange music lends an air of mystery to the movie.* | *The two new members added nothing to the band's sound.* | *The fresh chilies add a spicy flavor to the sauce.*

give /gɪv/ [v T not in progressive] to add a quality or feature to something or someone **give sth sth** *The new sponsor gives the theatre some respectability.* | **give sb sth** *His uniform gave him an air of authority.*

5 to add something to what has already been said or written

- add
- tack on

add /æd/ [v T] *That's my report. Is there anything you'd like to add, Peter?* | *'Finally,' she added, 'I would like to thank my family for all their help.'* | **+ that** *Barker refused to answer more questions, adding that he had already said too much.* | **I might add** spoken (=used especially when you are complaining about something) *The bus was two hours late and, I might add, they tried to charge my children the full adult fare!*

tack on /ˌtæk 'ɒn/ [phr v T] to add something at the end of something else – use this especially when you think someone has added something carelessly and without enough thought **tack on sth** *The company gave a very long and confusing explanation, and just tacked on a short apology right at the end.* | **tack sth on** *It looks like the director ran out of ideas and tacked the last part of the film on.*

6 something that is added

- addition
- additive
- supplement
- extra
- add-on
- extension

addition /ə'dɪʃən/ [n C] *Additions are made to the list* *from time to time.* | **+ to** *There has been a last minute addition to the programme for the President's visit.* | **a new addition** (=a new person or thing in a group or list) *In the last three months there has been a new addition to the family – our daughter, Rachel.*

additive /ˈædɪ̈tɪv/ [n C] something added to food in order to make it last longer, taste better, or look more attractive: *This product contains no artificial additives.* | *Foods sold under this label are guaranteed to be free from additives and preservatives.*

supplement /ˈsʌplɪ̈mənt/ [n C] something that is added to something else in order to improve it or make it complete: *Doctors believe that vitamin supplements are largely unnecessary.* | **+ to** *He sometimes eats fish as a supplement to his vegetarian diet.* | *The current supplement to the encyclopedia 'Growing Up with Science' has a new section on cycles in nature.*

extra /ˈekstrə/ [n C] something which is added to a basic product or service which improves it and also costs more: *A wide range of extras are also available.* | **optional extra** British *Tinted windows and a sunroof are optional extras.*

add-on /ˈæd ɒn/ [n C] as a piece of equipment that can be added or connected to a computer, car etc to make it do more things or make it more useful: *Add-ons such as modems and DVD drives can easily cost you hundreds of dollars.*

extension ALSO **addition** American /ɪkˈstenʃən, əˈdɪʃən/ [n C] another room or rooms that are added to a building: *The Simpsons built a big addition onto the back of their house.* | *You'll find the Picasso collection in the extension to the museum.*

addicted

when you cannot stop taking drugs, drinking alcohol, smoking cigarettes etc

RELATED WORDS

- when you enjoy something very much and do it a lot *see* **like**
- to stop doing something because it is harmful or unhealthy *see* **stop**
- *see also* **drug, drink, smoke, obsession**

1 addicted to drugs, alcohol, tobacco etc

- addicted
- dependent
- hooked

addicted /əˈdɪktɪ̈d/ [adj not before noun] if you are **addicted** to drugs, alcohol, tobacco etc, you need to take them regularly and feel that you cannot stop: *I tried to give up smoking several times before I realized I was addicted.* | **+ to** *By the time he was 16, he was addicted to heroin.* | *The children of mothers who use crack or cocaine are often born addicted to the drug.*

hooked /ˈhʊkt/ [adj not before noun] informal addicted to drugs, tobacco etc **+ on** *She's been hooked on heroin since she was 15.* | **get hooked** *Don't let your children start smoking – it's so easy for them to get hooked.*

dependent /dɪˈpendənt/ [adj not before noun] addicted to alcohol or drugs, especially legal drugs that a doctor gives you, so that you feel you cannot live without them: *It's almost impossible to take tranquilizers for long without becoming dependent.* | **+ on** *About 10% of the population is dependent on some form of drug.* | *Far more people are dependent on alcohol than we realize.*

2 someone who is addicted to a drug

- addict
- junkie
- drug user

addict /ˈædɪkt/ [n C] *It's difficult for most smokers to admit that they are addicts.* | **drug/heroin/morphine etc addict** *A lot of women drug addicts become prostitutes in order to get money to buy drugs.* | *Heroin addicts run an increased risk of getting AIDS.*

drug user ALSO **user** /ˈdrʌg ˌjuːzəʳ, ˈjuːzəʳ/ [n C] someone who regularly takes an illegal drug: *The city has proposed a plan to register all drug users at a special clinic.* | *Once a user himself, Gary now works as a counsellor helping other addicts.*

junkie /ˈdʒʌŋki/ [n C] informal someone who is addicted to a strong illegal drug such as heroin – use this to show disapproval: *It is a dangerous part of town – there are thieves and junkies everywhere.* | *The toilets are often used by junkies who leave their needles lying around on the floor.*

3 when a drug or other substance makes people addicted

- addictive

addictive /əˈdɪktɪv/ [adj] *Most addictive drugs are illegal.* | *Humphrey claims that the tobacco industry hid evidence that cigarettes were addictive.* | **highly addictive** (=very addictive) *Crack is a highly addictive form of cocaine.* | **mildly addictive** (=slightly addictive) *The caffeine in coffee is mildly addictive.*

4 the need to have a drug etc regularly

- addiction
- dependence
- habit

addiction /əˈdɪkʃən/ [n C/U] **drug addiction** *Drug addiction is now the biggest social problem in American cities.* | **+ to** *Eventually she managed to overcome her addiction to alcohol.*

habit /ˈhæbɪ̈t/ [n C usually singular] an addiction to an illegal drug or to tobacco **drug/cocaine/heroin etc habit** *His cocaine habit was ruining his life.* | **kick the habit** (=give up the habit) *Some smokers use chewing gum containing nicotine to help them kick the habit.*

dependence /dɪˈpendəns/ [n U] addiction to alcohol or drugs, especially legal drugs that a doctor gives you, so that you feel you cannot continue to live without them **+ on** *Dependence on alcohol can have a serious effect on your relationships and career.* | **drug/alcohol dependence** *The clinic treats people affected by drug dependence.*

admire

RELATED WORDS

opposite: ———————————— **hate**

- *see also* **like, approve, support, good**

1 to admire someone

- admire
- respect
- look up to
- highly regarded/respected
- think highly of
- have a high opinion of
- be an admirer of

admire /əd'maɪəʳ/ [v T not in progressive] to have a very good opinion of someone, either because they have achieved something special or because they have skills or qualities that you would like to have: *Corbin is a superb musician. I really admire him.* | *I admire the way Sarah has brought up the children on her own.* | *What I admire most about Lee is his patience.* | **admire sb for sth** *People admired her for her beauty and intelligence.* | *Rollins is most admired for her poetry, but she also writes fiction.* | **be greatly/much admired** *Morrow's new production of 'The Nutcracker' has been greatly admired.*

respect /rɪ'spekt/ [v T not in progressive] to have a good opinion of someone, even if you do not agree with them or want to be like them, because they have high standards and good personal qualities: *He's a very strict teacher, but the students respect him.* | *Logan, a long-serving Congressman, was both feared and respected by his political opponents.* | **respect sb for sth** *She always told me exactly what she thought, and I respected her for that.* —**respected** [adj] *The speakers will include Anthony Lewis, the respected political analyst.*

look up to /ˌlʊk 'ʌp tuː / [v phrase not in progressive] to respect and admire someone who is older than you or who has authority over you: *I've always looked up to my older brother, Jerry.* | *The children need someone they can look up to.*

highly regarded/respected /ˌhaɪli rɪ'gɑːʳdɪ̣d, rɪ'spektɪ̣d / [adj] if someone is highly regarded or respected, they are admired very much because they are very good at what they do: *a highly respected surgeon* | **+ by** *Dr. Franklin was highly regarded by his colleagues at Syracuse University.*

think highly of /ˌθɪŋk 'haɪli ɒv / [v phrase not in progressive] to admire someone very much, especially because they do their job very well and always work hard: *Most of the students and staff think very highly of Dr. Smith.* | **be highly thought of** *Sally is an excellent administrator. She is highly thought of here.*

have a high opinion of ALSO **hold sb in high regard/esteem** formal /hæv ə ˌhaɪ ə'pɪnjən ɒv, həʊld (sb) ɪn ˌhaɪ rɪ'gɑːʳd, ɪ'stiːm / [v phrase not in progressive] to admire a person or their abilities very much, especially because they have special skills or very high standards in their work: *Film critics continue to hold Bergman in high esteem.* | **have a high opinion of sb as sth** *Croft had a high opinion of Marx as a political thinker.*

be an admirer of /biː ən əd'maɪərər ɒv / [v phrase] to admire someone and the work that they do, especially a leader, writer, artist etc: *I've always been an admirer of Potter's work, and was very sad to hear of her death.* | **be a great/real admirer of sb** *My tutor was a great admirer of Shakespeare, and often quoted him.*

2 to admire someone very much

- idolize
- revere
- worship
- put sb on a pedestal
- hero-worship

idolize ALSO **idolise** British /'aɪdəl-aɪz/ [v T not in progressive] to admire someone very much, especially a famous person, so that you think everything about them is perfect: *Monroe was idolized by movie fans all over the world.* | *As a child, Ted idolized his father.*

revere /rɪ'vɪəʳ/ [v T not in progressive] formal to respect someone greatly for their achievements or personal qualities, especially someone in public life **+ by** *Collins was revered by his fellow countrymen.* | **revere sb as sth** *Ondaatje is revered as one of Canada's best writers.* —**revered** [adj] *India's most famous and revered musician*

worship /'wɜːʳʃɪp/ [v T not in progressive] to admire and love someone so much that you cannot see any faults in them: *She absolutely worships Elvis Presley.* | **worship the ground sb walks on** (=to admire absolutely everything about a person) *Garvey worshipped the ground his wife walked on.*

put sb on a pedestal /ˌpʊt (sb) ɒn ə 'pedɪ̣stəl/ [v phrase] to admire someone so much that you treat them or talk about them as though they are perfect – used especially when you think someone is wrong to do this: *You shouldn't put him on a pedestal. He doesn't deserve it.* | *I used to put Sarah on a pedestal. Now I don't even like to be in the same room with her.*

hero-worship /'hɪərəʊ ˌwɜːʳʃɪp/ [v T not in progressive] to greatly admire someone and want to be like them: *His fans hero-worshipped him.* | *The brother Ian had once hero-worshipped was now an unemployed drug addict.*

3 someone that you greatly admire

- hero/heroine
- idol

hero/heroine /'hɪərəʊ, 'herəʊɪ̣n/ [n C] someone who you admire very much because of what they have done. Use hero about a man, use heroine about a woman: *I used to love David Bowie – he was my hero.* | *baseball hero, Babe Ruth* | *Mother Teresa has always been one of my heroines.*

idol /'aɪdl/ [n C] a famous actor, actress, musician, or sports player that a lot of people admire: *The former President, once the idol of the nation, now leads a quiet life in the countryside.* | *Jones continues to be a major pop idol.*

4 the feeling of admiring someone

- admiration
- respect
- adulation

admiration /ˌædmə'reɪʃən/ [n U] the feeling that someone is very good, very intelligent etc, either because of something special they have achieved or because they have skills or qualities you would like to have **+ for** *Linda had tremendous admiration for her boss.* | **feel admiration for sb** *For the first time that he could recall, Chris felt some admiration for his stepfather.* | **watch in/with admiration** *Mel watched in admiration as the goalkeeper leaped for the ball.* | **be full of admiration for sb** *I'm full of admiration for Terry – she's really achieved a lot in her life.*

respect /rɪ'spekt/ [n U] the feeling that someone is good because they have high standards and good personal qualities **respect for** *My respect for my teacher grew as the months passed.* | **have great respect for sb/have a lot of respect for sb** *I have great respect for Tom's judgement.* | **win/earn/gain sb's respect** (=get someone's respect) *With his firm handling of the dispute, he had earned the respect of his opponents.* | **mutual respect** (=when two people respect each other) *a relationship built on trust and mutual respect*

adulation /ˌædʒʊ̣'leɪʃən/ [n U] formal great love and admiration for someone, especially for someone famous: *Harley wasn't prepared for the fame and adulation that came with being a star athlete.* | **+ of** *Cuba's adulation of its aging communist leader*

admit

RELATED WORDS

- to deny that something is true *see* **say**
- *see also* **crime, mistake, guilty, accuse**

1 to admit that you have done something wrong or illegal

- admit
- confess
- own up
- come clean
- fess up

admit /əd'mɪt/ [v T] to say that you have done something wrong or illegal, especially when someone asks or persuades you to do this **+ (that)** *Rachel admitted that she had made a mistake.* | *Blake finally admitted he had stolen the money.* | **admit (to) doing sth** *Richard Maldonado admitted accepting bribes.* | *He admits to stealing the car.* | **admit it** spoken *Admit it! You lied to me!* | **admit responsibility/liability/negligence** (=admit publicly that something is legally your fault) *The hospital refused to admit liability for the deaths of the two young children.*

confess /kən'fes/ [v I/T] to tell the police or someone in a position of authority that you have done something very bad, especially after they have persuaded you to do this: *After two days of questioning, he finally confessed.* | **+ (that)** *She confessed that she had killed her husband.* | **confess to a crime/robbery/murder etc** *McCarthy confessed to the crime shortly after his arrest.* | **confess to doing sth** *Edwards eventually confessed to being a spy.*

own up /ˌəʊn 'ʌp/ [phr v I] to admit that you have done something wrong, especially something that is not serious. Own up is more informal than admit or confess: *Unless the guilty person owns up, the whole class will be punished.* | **own up to (doing) sth** *No one owned up to breaking the window.* | *I made a few mistakes, but I owned up to them.*

come clean /ˌkʌm 'kliːn/ [v phrase] informal to finally tell the truth or admit that you have done something wrong: *The bank eventually came clean and admitted they had made a mistake.* | **+ about** *It's time the government came clean about its plans to raise income tax.*

fess up /ˌfes 'ʌp/ [phr v I] especially American, informal to admit that you have done something wrong, but not something that is very serious: *Come on, fess up – you must have been the one who told her because no-one else knew!* | *If none of you guys fesses up, you're all grounded for a week.*

2 a statement admitting that you have done something wrong

- confession
- admission

confession /kən'feʃən/ [n C] an official statement that someone makes to the police, admitting that they have done something illegal and explaining what happened: *Sergeant Thompson wrote down Smith's confession and asked him to sign it.* | **make a confession** *In a confession made to police shortly after his arrest, Davis said he had killed the victim with a kitchen knife.* | **full confession** *By making a full confession, Reeves hoped he would be more kindly treated by the authorities.*

admission /əd'mɪʃən/ [n C usually singular] when you admit that you were wrong or that you have done something bad or illegal **+ (that)** *The Senator's admission that he had lied to Congress shocked many Americans.* | **What an admission (to make)!** *You only married him for his money? What an admission!* | **admission of guilt** (=when you admit that you are guilty) *The court may assume that your silence is an admission of guilt.*

3 to admit something that you feel embarrassed or ashamed about

- admit/confess
- to be honest/to tell the truth

admit/confess /əd'mɪt, kən'fes/ [v T] *'I've always hated flying,' Lisa confessed.* | **+ (that)** *She admits that she occasionally bets on horses.* | *Dave confessed he didn't visit his parents as often as he should.* | **admit/confess (to) doing sth** *Monica admitted playing rather badly in her last match.* | *He confesses to being afraid of the dark.* | **I must admit/confess** (=say this when you do not know something or cannot do something) *I must admit I was never very good at dancing.* | *I don't really like kids, I must confess.*

to be honest/to tell the truth /tə biː 'ɒnəst, tə ˌtel ðə 'truːθ‖-'ɑːn-/ say this when you admit something that other people might disagree with or disapprove of: *'What do you think of John?' 'To be honest, I don't like him at all.'* | *To tell the truth, I wasn't really listening to what everyone was saying.* | *To be perfectly honest, I don't think she should have married him.*

4 to admit that something is true

- admit
- acknowledge

admit ALSO **concede** formal /əd'mɪt, kən'siːd/ [v T] to accept that something is true, especially when you do not want to: *'Well, I suppose there is some truth in what you say,' she admitted.* | **+ (that)** *In the end he had to admit that I was right.* | *You may not like her, but you have to admit that she's good at her job.* | *Jackson conceded that higher taxes on big cars would have a harmful effect on the UK's motor industry.* | *Janis was forced to concede that much of her argument was based on prejudice.* | **admit it** spoken *You were wrong, weren't you? Come on, admit it!*

acknowledge /ək'nɒlɪdʒ‖-'nɑː-/ [v T] formal to admit that something is true or that a situation exists, even though you may not like it, it is not completely satisfactory, may be a problem etc: *You have to acknowledge the truth of what she says.* | **+ (that)** *He acknowledges it's going to be a tough job, but he's going to try it anyway.* | *The committee acknowledges that mentally ill people in the community are not receiving the care and treatment they need.* —**acknowledgment/acknowledgement** [n C/U] *The report contained no acknowledgment that the police used excessive violence when arresting demonstrators.*

5 what you say when you admit that something is true

- it's true that
- admittedly

it's true that /ɪts 'truː ðət/ say this when you admit that what someone has said is true, but you want to add something new or different that is also important: *Of course it's true that a lot of men like beer and football, but this doesn't mean that they all* *do.* | *It's true that there have been some very serious train accidents recently, but it's generally quite a safe way to travel.*

admittedly /əd'mɪtɨdli/ [adv] *Admittedly I didn't get as much work done as I'd hoped this morning, but it should be finished soon.* | *Yes, I have studied Japanese – though not for long, admittedly.*

6 what you say when you think someone should admit something

- let's face it
- there's no getting around sth
- you can't escape the fact that

let's face it /lets 'feɪs ɪt/ say this when you want other people to admit that something, especially an unpleasant fact, is true: *Let's face it, the England team are not good enough to beat Holland.* | *People are basically selfish, let's face it.*

there's no getting around sth /ðeəʳz ˌnəʊ getɪŋ ə'raʊnd (sth)/ say this when you want other people to admit that something, especially an unpleasant fact, is true and that it cannot be changed **there's no getting around it** *There's no getting around it – we'll have to start again from the beginning.* | **there's no getting around the fact that** *There's no getting around the fact that most people prefer to travel to work in their own cars, rather than by bus or train.*

you can't escape the fact that /juː ˌkɑːnt ɪ'skeɪp ðə fækt ðət‖-ˌkænt-/ say this when you want other people to admit that something, especially an unpleasant fact, is true and that it cannot be changed: *We cannot escape the fact that Mr. Mireki's death arose from a job-related activity.* | *You can't escape the fact that we all have to die some day.*

7 to admit that what you said or believed was wrong

- take back
- climb down
- eat your words
- eat humble pie

take back /ˌteɪk 'bæk/ [phr v T] to say that a criticism you previously made was wrong **take back sth** *I take back everything I said.* | **take sth back** *'You will take that remark back and apologize immediately!' he roared.* | **take it back** *She had no right to talk to you like that. You should go in there and make her take it all back.*

climb down /ˌklaɪm 'daʊn/ [phr v I] British if one side in an argument climbs down, they agree to accept the other side's demands, especially after admitting that they were wrong: *Neither side in the dispute has been willing to climb down.* | *European Court decisions have forced several employers to climb down and change their policy on women's pay.* —**climbdown** /'klaɪmdaʊn/ [n C] *a humiliating climbdown by the government over their economic policies*

eat your words /ˌiːt jɔːʳ 'wɜːʳdz/ [v phrase] informal to be forced to admit that you were wrong because what you said would happen did not in fact happen: *I never thought Clare would be any good at this job, but I've had to eat my words.* | **make sb eat their words** *When Tottenham went to the top of the league early in the season, people said it wouldn't last. They have had to eat their words.*

eat humble pie informal ALSO **eat crow** American informal /iːt ˌhʌmbəl 'paɪ, iːt 'krəʊ/ [v phrase] to be forced to admit that you were wrong and say that you are sorry: *Taylor's victory in the semi-final has forced many of her critics to eat humble pie.* | *Martinez had to eat crow when he bragged that the Red Sox would win the division and they came in last.*

adult

RELATED WORDS

opposite: **child, baby**

- young person who is almost an adult *see* **young (4)**
- films, books about sex *see* **sex**
- *see also* **old/not young, young**

1 adult

- adult
- grown-up
- grown man/woman
- full-grown/fully grown

adult /'ædʌlt, ə'dʌlt/ [n C] someone who is no longer a child – use this to talk about someone who is at least 18: *The cost of the trip is $59 for adults and $30 for children.* | *Since I left school, my parents have started to treat me like an adult.* | *Children cannot be admitted to the museum unless they are accompanied by an adult.* —**adult** [adj only before noun] *The book is intended for adult readers.* | *Over 30% of the adult population were illiterate.* | *The government has announced plans to increase spending on adult education.*

grown-up /ˌgrəʊn 'ʌp◂/ [n C] an adult – used especially by children or when you are talking to children: *Grown-ups are so boring! All they ever do is talk!* | *At home there was always a grown-up to turn to if you were in trouble.* —**grown-up** /'grəʊn ʌp/ [adj] *She has three grown-up sons.* | *Our children are all grown-up now.* | *This was the first grown-up party she'd ever been to.*

grown man/woman /ˌgrəʊn 'mæn, 'wʊmən/ [n C] an adult man or woman – used especially when you think someone is not behaving in the way an adult should behave: *Elsie had never seen a grown man cry before.* | *He' s a grown man – he should be able to cook for himself!* | *She's crazy – a grown woman letting a girl order her around like that.*

full-grown/fully grown /ˌfʊl 'grəʊn◂, ˌfʊli-/ [adj] a **full-grown** or **fully grown** animal has reached its full adult size: *A full-grown blue whale may be up to 30 metres long.* | *Many of these animals die before they are fully grown.* | *Will my tank be big enough for all these fish when they are fully grown?*

2 to become an adult

- grow up
- mature
- come of age

grow up /ˌgrəʊ 'ʌp/ [phr v I] *What do you want to be when you grow up?* | *We plan to go and live in Florida when the children have all grown up.*

mature /mə'tʃʊəʳ/ [v I] to become fully grown or developed: *Girls tend to mature more quickly than boys, both physically and emotionally.* | *The fly matures in only seven days.*

come of age /ˌkʌm əv 'eɪdʒ/ [v phrase] to reach the age when you have the legal rights and responsibilities of an adult, usually 18 or 21 – used in legal contexts: *Emma will inherit a fortune when she comes of age.* | *They planned to marry as soon as she came of age.*

3 the time when someone is an adult

- adult life
- adulthood
- maturity

adult life /ˌædʌlt ˈlaɪf/ [n U] the part of someone's life when they are an adult: *He has spent most of his adult life in the States.*

adulthood /ˈædʌlthʊd, əˈdʌlthʊd/ [n U] the time when someone is an adult – use this especially to talk about people reaching this time: *Children with the disease have little chance of surviving to adulthood.* | **reach adulthood** *Nowadays young people want to leave home as soon as they reach adulthood.*

maturity /məˈtʃʊərəti/ [n U] if a person, animal, or plant reaches **maturity**, they have grown or developed completely **reach maturity** *The plant reaches maturity after two years.* | *Sharks take 10 years to reach maturity.*

advanced

using the most modern equipment, ideas, and methods

RELATED WORDS

opposite: —— **old-fashioned, poor**

▸ *see also* **modern, new**

1 machines, systems etc

- advanced
- sophisticated
- high-tech/hi-tech
- smart
- state-of-the-art
- be ahead of its time
- at the leading edge of/cutting edge of

advanced /ədˈvɑːnst‖ədˈvænst/ [adj] *The factory has installed advanced machinery at enormous cost.* | *Modern armies consist of fewer soldiers and more advanced weapons systems.* | *The bomb-detection equipment now used in most airports is very advanced.*

sophisticated /səˈfɪstəkeɪtəd/ [adj] very advanced, and better designed or more skilfully made than other things of the same type, and often working in a complicated way: *The missile has a sophisticated guidance system.* | **highly sophisticated** (=very sophisticated) *Eye operations often involve the use of highly sophisticated equipment, such as lasers.*

high-tech/hi-tech /ˌhaɪ ˈtek◂/ [adj] **high-tech industry/company/equipment etc** using very advanced electronic equipment and machines, especially computers: *Northern California remains a popular location for high-tech firms.* | *On display at the exhibition will be a range of 'hi-tech homes of the future'.* | *Prices of computers, electronics, and other high-tech products have fallen at a rapid pace.*

smart /smɑːʳt/ [adj only before noun] a **smart** machine, bomb, weapon etc has a computer system that makes it able to control itself and make decisions for itself about how to operate: *The US used smart weapons in Iraq and Kosovo.* | *Smart machines and other appliances are operated via the Internet.*

state-of-the-art /ˌsteɪt əv ði ˈɑːʳt◂/ [adj] using the most advanced and recently developed methods, materials, or knowledge: *The new phone system uses state-of-the-art technology.* | *The movie was made with state-of-the-art computer graphics.* —**the state of the art** [n phrase] *Opus III represents the state of the art* (=the most advanced type)*in word-processing packages.*

be ahead of its time /biː əˌhed əv ɪts ˈtaɪm/ [v phrase] if something **is ahead of its time**, it is new and very different from other things of a similar type – use this especially about things that people do not understand or like at first, but later realize how good they are: *The Vortex graphics system was ahead of its time. Few were sold but it strongly influenced later designs.* | *Bonner's research in particle physics was ahead of its time and widely misunderstood.*

at the leading edge of/cutting edge of /ət ðə ˌliːdɪŋ ˈedʒ ɒv, ˌkʌtɪŋ ˈedʒ ɒv/ [prep] in a more advanced position than other organizations or companies in developing and using new methods, systems, or equipment: *The company is trying to regain its position at the leading edge of biomedical research.* | *Developments in computer chip design are at the cutting edge of the technological revolution.* —**leading-edge/cutting-edge** /ˈliːdɪŋ edʒ, ˈkʌtɪŋ edʒ/ [adj only before noun] *an exciting new project, using cutting-edge technology*

2 countries

- advanced
- developed

advanced /ədˈvɑːnst‖ədˈvænst/ [adj] **advanced** countries use **advanced** industrial methods, equipment etc, and have a modern economic and political system: *Many of the nations of southeast Asia will one day be as advanced as Japan or South Korea.* | *Social problems such as teen pregnancy, drug abuse, and high divorce rates are often common in the most advanced countries.*

developed /dɪˈveləpt/ [adj only before noun] a **developed** country has modern industrial, health, and education systems – use this when comparing these countries with poorer countries: *Birthrates in developed countries are generally very low.* | *This disease has mostly been eliminated, at least in the developed nations.*

advantage

RELATED WORDS

opposite: —— **disadvantage**

1 a good feature of something

- advantage
- the good thing about sth
- benefit
- merit
- a plus
- the beauty of

advantage /ədˈvɑːntɪdʒ‖ədˈvæn-/ a good feature of something, for example a way in which it is useful or better than other things of the same kind: *There are different ways of saving money for retirement, but this one has several advantages.* | **+ of** *The advantage of walking to work is that I get some exercise.* | **big advantage** *One of the big advantages of the course is that it helps students develop their writing skills in English.*

the good thing about sth /ðə ˈgʊd ˌθɪŋ əbaʊt (sth)/ spoken use this when you are talking about one of the main advantages of something: *The good thing about this job is that I can work at home whenever I want.*

benefit /ˈbenəfɪt/ [n C] a feature of something that has a good effect on people's lives: *Tourism has brought many benefits to the area.* | **+ of** *the benefits* *of a healthy lifestyle* | *What are the benefits for Britain of belonging to the European Union?*

merit /ˈmerɪ̈t/ [n C] one of the good characteristics of something such as a plan, system, or way of doing something: *The merits of the new health programme are gradually being recognized.* | *The committee is still considering the merits of the new proposals.*

a plus /ə ˈplʌs/ an additional quality that helps to make something more useful, valuable, or attractive than other things of the same type **be a plus** *The hotel's closeness to the beach is definitely a plus.* | **plus point** British *The plus point of this area is its school system, which is considered one of the best in the city.*

the beauty of /ðə ˈbjuːti ɒv/ a particularly good quality that makes something especially useful, suitable, or likely to be successful **that's the beauty of it** spoken *Our new generator runs entirely on recycled fuel. That's the beauty of it.* | **the beauty of sth is that** *The beauty of the plan is that it only requires a small investment.*

2 the only good feature of something

- saving grace
- redeeming feature

saving grace /ˌseɪvɪŋ ˈɡreɪs/ [n C] *I can't really play baseball. My one saving grace is that I can pitch.* | *I hate this house. Its only saving grace is that it's near the centre of town.*

redeeming feature /rɪˌdiːmɪŋ ˈfiːtʃəʳ/ the one good quality that something or someone has that saves it from being completely bad, useless, or unacceptable: *The heroine of the novel is cruel and evil, with no redeeming features.* | *Coal is relatively expensive but its redeeming feature is that it is in plentiful supply.*

3 the good and bad features of something

- advantages and disadvantages
- the pros and cons
- the pluses and minuses

advantages and disadvantages /ədˌvɑːntɪdʒɪ̈z ən ˈdɪsədˌvɑːntɪdʒɪ̈z‖-ˌvæn-/ [n phrase] the good and bad features of something – use this especially when you are comparing what is good and what is bad about something: *Being an only child has both advantages and disadvantages.* | **the advantages and disadvantages of sth** *the advantages and disadvantages of owning a car in the city* | **weigh the advantages and disadvantages of sth** (=to consider the advantages and disadvantages of something) *Politicians should carefully weigh the advantages and disadvantages of committing US troops to this conflict.*

the pros and cons /ðə ˌprəʊz ən ˈkɒnz‖-ˈkɑːnz/ [n phrase] the advantages and disadvantages of something that you need to think about in order to make a decision **the pros and cons of** *There has been a lot of discussion about the pros and cons of making certain types of drugs legal.* | *Your doctor should explain the pros and cons of the different treatments available.* | **weigh up the pros and cons** (=think about the advantages and disadvantages) *Karen and David weighed up the pros and cons of having another child and decided against it.*

the pluses and minuses /ðə ˌplʌsɪ̈z ən ˈmaɪnəsɪ̈z/ [n phrase] the advantages and disadvantages of something such as a plan or method that you consider before you do something, or that you notice after it has been done **+ of** *She talked about some of the pluses and minuses of being self-employed.*

4 something that makes you more likely to be successful

- advantage
- asset
- privilege

advantage /ədˈvɑːntɪdʒ‖ədˈvæn-/ [n C] something that makes someone more likely to be successful, especially compared to other people **have an advantage** *People who have been to university have a big advantage when it comes to finding jobs.* | **+ over** *I had already lived in France for a year, so I had a big advantage over the other students.* | **give sb an advantage** *Taxes on imports gave Japanese companies an unfair advantage.*

asset /ˈæset/ [n C] something or someone that is valuable because they help you to succeed: *A sense of humour is an important asset for any teacher.* | **be an asset to sth** *Laney continues to be a great asset to the company.*

privilege /ˈprɪvɪ̈lɪdʒ/ [n C] a special advantage or right that only a few people have, for example because their family is rich or because they have an important job: *Foreign diplomats have all kinds of special privileges.* | *Countries within the European Community grant certain commercial privileges to each other.* | **the privilege of sth** *Not everyone has the privilege of a private education.*

5 to have an advantage

- have an advantage
- be at an advantage
- the odds are stacked in sb's favour
- have a head start
- have everything going for you
- have youth/experience etc on your side
- hold all the cards
- have the upper hand
- be in a strong position/a position of strength

have an advantage /hæv ən ədˈvɑːntɪdʒ‖-ˈvæn-/ [v phrase not in progressive] to have something that makes you more likely to succeed than other people: *The American team seemed to have all the advantages – better training, better facilities, and much better financial support.* | **+ over** *The winning boxer had an advantage over his opponent because he was several pounds heavier.*

be at an advantage /biː ət ən ədˈvɑːntɪdʒ‖-ˈvæn-/ [v phrase not in progressive] if someone **is at an advantage**, they have experience or qualities which make them more likely to succeed in doing something or more likely to do something well: *Students with a strong math background will be at an advantage next year when the statistics course starts.* | **+ over** *Children have several advantages over adults when it comes to learning another language.* | **distinct advantage** (=definite advantage) *Mitchell's height gives him a distinct advantage over the other players.*

the odds are stacked in sb's favour British **/the odds are stacked in sb's favor** American /ði ˌɒdz ɑːʳ stækt ɪn (sb's) ˈfeɪvəʳ‖-ˌɑːdz-/ used to say that someone has a big advantage in a competition, election etc so that they are very likely to win: *Everyone knows that you can't win at gambling because the odds are stacked in the dealer's favour.* |

The odds were stacked in the Labour Party's favour, so it was a great surprise when they were not elected.

have a head start /hæv ə ˌhed 'stɑːʳt/ [v phrase not in progressive] to have a big advantage over others in a particular activity, especially because you started doing it before them **+ on** *The British have a head start on many other countries in areas such as genetic engineering.* | **give sb a head start** *Sending your children to nursery school clearly gives them a head start.*

have everything going for you /hæv ˌevriθɪŋ 'gəʊɪŋ fəʳ juː/ [v phrase not in progressive] to have all the qualities that are likely to make you succeed in whatever you decide to do: *She was bright and pretty and had everything going for her.* | *Barry had everything going for him – charm, looks, intelligence, but still he was unemployed.*

have youth/experience etc on your side /hæv 'juːθ ɒn jɔːʳ ˌsaɪd/ [v phrase not in progressive] to have an advantage over others because you are young, have a lot of experience etc: *He is a strong player but his opponent will have youth on his side.* | *With knowledge of the company on her side, she was more likely to get the job than any of the external candidates.*

hold all the cards /həʊld ˌɔːl ðə 'kɑːʳdz/ [v phrase] to have all the advantages in a particular situation so that you can control what happens: *It seemed that he held all the cards and that there was nothing she could do but say 'yes'.*

have the upper hand /hæv ði ˌʌpəʳ 'hænd/ [v phrase not in progressive] to have more power than someone, especially someone who is fighting against you or who does not agree with you, so that you are likely to defeat them: *Although the rebels control areas in the south, the government still has the upper hand.* | **+ against** *Police finally have the upper hand against the drug dealers in the area.*

be in a strong position/a position of strength /biː ɪn ə ˌstrɒŋ pə'zɪʃən, ə pəˌzɪʃən əv 'streŋθ‖-ˌstrɔːŋ-/ [v phrase] to be in a position where you have an advantage over someone and are likely to win, especially in discussions to get something from them: *The government claims that as long as they have nuclear weapons, they can negotiate from a position of strength.* | *At the end of the war, the US was in a strong position to influence the future of Europe.*

6 when something gives someone an advantage

- give sb an advantage
- give sb the edge
- be to sb's advantage
- be in sb's favour
- favour

give sb an advantage /ˌgɪv (sb) ən əd'vɑːntɪdʒ‖-'væn-/ [v phrase] *The fact that Liverpool had only ten men playing for them gave the other team an advantage.* | **+ over** *What gives the company an advantage over its competitors is its location.*

give sb the edge /ˌgɪv (sb) ði 'edʒ/ [v phrase] to give someone a slight advantage, for example in a competition or election: *His ten years' experience will give him the edge in tomorrow's fight.* | **+ over** *He tried to find out as much as he could about the company, believing that it would give him the edge over the other interviewees.*

be to sb's advantage /biː tə (sb's) əd'vɑːntɪdʒ ‖ -'væn-/ [v phrase] if something is to your advantage, it will help you to succeed: *It will be to your advantage to start preparing for the exam now. Don't wait until the last minute.* | **could/would/might be to sb's advantage** *I think you should accept Steve's offer to help you with the presentation – it could be to your advantage.*

be in sb's favour British **/be in sb's favor** American /biː ɪn (sb's) 'feɪvəʳ/ [v phrase] if a situation or conditions **are in someone's favour**, they will help that person succeed: *Investors are hoping that the new regulations will operate in their favor.* | **tip the balance in sb's favour** (=to give someone a slight advantage) *It will be a closely fought match, but Corgan's greater physical strength is likely to tip the balance in his favour.*

favour British **/favor** American /'feɪvəʳ/ [v T] if a situation or conditions such as the weather **favour** someone, they make that person more likely to succeed than other people: *The weather favours the Australians, who are used to playing in the heat.* | *German negotiators denied that economic circumstances had favored their companies and given them an export advantage.*

advertising

▸ *see also* **persuade, buy, sell, newspapers, television/radio**

1 to advertise something

- advertise
- promote
- publicize
- market
- hype/hype up
- plug
- sell
- push

advertise /'ædvəʳtaɪz/ [v I/T] to tell people publicly about a product or service in order to try to persuade them to buy it, for example by showing short films on television, or by showing pictures with words in newspapers and magazines: *There was a big poster advertising a well-known brand of cola.* | *We are a small business so we can only afford to advertise in the local press.* | **be advertised on TV/on the radio** *'How did you find out about the new software?' 'It was advertised on TV.'* | **be advertised in a newspaper/magazine etc** *The concert was advertised in all the national newspapers.* | **be heavily advertised** (=be advertised a lot) *Young smokers tend to buy the brands that are most heavily advertised.*

promote /prə'məʊt/ [v T] to try to make people buy a new product, see a new film etc, for example by selling it at a lower price or talking about it on television: *Meg Ryan is in Europe to promote her new movie.* | *To promote their new shampoo, they are selling it at half price for a month.* | **promote sth as sth** *They're trying to promote Dubai as a tourist destination.*

publicize ALSO **publicise** British /'pʌblɪsaɪz/ [v T] to tell the public about a situation, event, organization, problem by advertising, writing, or speaking about it on television, in newspapers etc: *Hollywood gossips were saying that the studio lacked the funds to publicize its new film properly.* | *A good estate agent will know the best ways to publicize the fact that your home is for sale.* | *A series of articles and television shows publicized concerns that the chemical Alar, used to keep apples red and firm, could cause cancer.* | **well-/highly/widely/much publicized** (=publicized a lot) *Jurors were asked what they knew about the highly publicized case.*

market /ˈmɑːʳkɪ̥t/ [v T] to try to sell a product or service by deciding which type of people are likely to buy it and by making it attractive and interesting to them: *In order to market a product well, you need to be aware of public demand.* | *The company has exclusive European rights to market the new software.*

hype/hype up /haɪp, ˌhaɪp ˈʌp/ [v T] informal to try to make people interested in a product, entertainer, film etc, using television, radio, and newspapers – use this to show that you do not trust this kind of information: *Like most Hollywood movies it was so hyped up that when I saw it I was completely disappointed.* | *The cosmetics industry is usually quick to hype its new products.* —**hyped** [adj] **heavily/greatly/much etc hyped** *Douglas Kennedy's hugely hyped first novel 'The Big Picture'*

plug /plʌg/ [v T] informal ALSO **give sth a plug** /ˌgɪv (sth) ə ˈplʌg/ [v phrase] especially British informal to try to persuade people to buy a book, see a film etc, by talking about it publicly, especially on television or radio: *The only reason she agreed to be interviewed was to plug her new record.* | *The author used the opportunity of appearing on TV to give his latest book a plug.*

sell /sel/ [v T] to encourage people to buy something: *There's no question about it – scandal sells newspapers.* | **sell sth to sb** *It's not just a question of making a good product – we also have to go out and sell it to people.*

push /pʊʃ/ [v T] informal to try to sell more of a product or service by advertising it a lot: *Revlon is really pushing its new range of beauty creams.*

2 the activity of advertising

- advertising
- promotion
- marketing
- publicity
- hype

advertising /ˈædvəʳtaɪzɪŋ/ [n U] the business of trying to persuade people to buy things, using pictures, words, songs etc on television and radio, large public notices, and magazines: *The big cigarette manufacturers spend billions of dollars a year on advertising.* | *CBS/FOX said that its advertising was mostly aimed at young adults between the ages of 18 and 23.* | *Sara is looking for a job in advertising or the media.* | **advertising agency** (=a company that advertises other companies' products) *Deutsch is the biggest advertising agency in the world.*

promotion /prəˈməʊʃən/ [n C/U] an attempt to make people buy a new product, see a new film etc, for example by selling it at a lower price or talking about it on television: *Robbie Williams arrived in New York to do a week of promotion for his new record.* | *The author was signing copies of his new book as a part of the publisher's promotion campaign.* | **sales promotion** *They ran a sales promotion scheme in which a World Cup coin was given away with every four gallons of petrol purchased.* —**promotional** [adj only before noun] **promotional video** *a promotional video made by the Apple Computer Company* | **promotional copy** *I managed to get hold of a promotional copy of the Manic Street Preachers' latest album.*

marketing /ˈmɑːʳkɪ̥tɪŋ/ [n U] the business of trying to sell a product or service by deciding which type of people are likely to buy it and making it attractive and interesting to them: *The business course includes classes on marketing.* | **marketing strategy/campaign** *The reason their cars sold so well was that they had a brilliant marketing strategy.*

publicity /pʌˈblɪsɪ̥ti/ [n U] the business of making sure that people know about a new product, a new film, a famous person etc, for example by talking about them on TV or writing about them in magazines: *The show's organizers spent over $500,000 on publicity alone.* | **good/bad publicity** *The band appeared on Larry King's show, which was good publicity for their US tour.*

hype /haɪp/ [n U] informal attempts to make people interested in a product, entertainer, film etc, using television, radio, and newspapers – use this to show that you do not trust this type of information: *Despite all the hype, I thought the book was pretty boring.* | **media hype** *Is it really Kevin Costner's best film performance, or is that just media hype?*

3 an advertisement

- advertisement
- commercial
- ad
- campaign/advertising campaign
- slogan
- hoarding/billboard
- junk mail/direct mail
- infomercial
- banner ad

advertisement /ədˈvɜːtɪ̥smənt‖ˌædvərˈtaɪz-/ [n C] something such as a large public notice, a short film on television, or a picture with words in a newspaper, that is designed to persuade people to buy something: *Most car advertisements are aimed at men.* | **+ for** *At this time of year, the papers are full of advertisements for skiing holidays.*

commercial /kəˈmɜːʳʃəl/ [n C] an advertisement on television or radio: *Have you seen the new Levi jeans commercial?* | **+ for** *a commercial for low-alcohol lager* | **commercial break** (=when there are commercials in the middle of a programme) *We'll be right back with you after a commercial break.*

ad informal ALSO **advert** British informal /æd, ˈædvɜʳt/ [n C] an advertisement: *She had started her acting career by doing shampoo ads on TV.* | **+ for** *I saw an advert for some cheap furniture in our local paper.* | **put an ad in a newspaper/magazine** *We put an ad in 'The Times' and got a terrific response.*

campaign/advertising campaign /kæmˈpeɪn, ˈædvəʳtaɪzɪŋ kæmˌpeɪn/ [n C] a planned series of advertisements for a new product or service: *The company got into a lot of trouble over its last advertising campaign.* | **launch a campaign/an advertising campaign** (=start a campaign) *Nissan is about to launch a nationwide campaign for its new range of cars.*

slogan /ˈsləʊgən/ [n C] a short clever phrase used in an advertisement: *a dry-cleaning company that used the slogan 'We know the meaning of cleaning'*

hoarding British **/billboard** American /ˈhɔːʳdɪŋ, ˈbɪlbɔːʳd/ [n C] a large flat board in a public place, where large printed advertisements are shown: *Beside the freeway was a huge billboard showing an ad for Ben & Jerry's ice cream.*

junk mail/direct mail /ˈdʒʌŋk ˌmeɪl, dɪ̥ˈrekt ˌmeɪl/ [n U] advertisements you receive in the mail from different companies, often with special deals or sales in them. **Direct mail** is the word used by the companies who send out these advertisements: *Statistics show that 44% of junk mail is thrown away and never read.*

infomercial /ˈɪnfəʊmɜːʳʃəl/ [n C] a television or radio advertisement made to look and sound like a real programme, often a financial news report or an advice show: *Cable channels began broadcasting the 30-minute infomercial in April.*

banner ad /ˈbænər æd/ [n C] an advertisement that appears at the top of a web page (=a page on the Internet), that you click on to find out more about the company, product, or service: *A banner ad for NewsPage, a personalized Internet news service, appeared on part of the screen.*

advise

RELATED WORDS

▸ *see also* **suggest, tell, ask, should/ought to (2)**

1 to advise someone

- advise
- say sb should do sth/ought to do sth
- tell
- suggest
- recommend
- urge
- give advice

advise /ədˈvaɪz/ [v T] to tell someone what you think they should do, especially when you have more knowledge or experience than they have **advise sb to do sth** *I advise you to think very carefully before making any decision.* | *All US citizens in the area have been advised to return home.* | **advise sb against doing sth** (=advise them not to do it) *Her lawyers have advised her against saying anything to the newspapers.* | **advise sb on/about sth** *Your teacher will be able to advise you about what qualifications you will need.* | **strongly advise** *I strongly advise you to get medical insurance if you're going skiing.* | **advise caution/restraint/patience etc** *Health experts advise extreme caution when handling these materials.*

say sb should do sth/ought to do sth /ˌseɪ (sb) ʃʊd ˈduː (sth), ˌɔːt tə ˈduː (sth)/ [v phrase] to tell someone what you think they should do, especially when this is your own personal opinion and not the result of particular information or knowledge: *My friends keep saying I ought to learn to drive.* | *Her mother said she should call the police immediately.* | *They say you should drink at least eight glasses of water a day.*

tell /tel/ [v T] to **tell** someone that you think they should do something, especially in order to avoid problems **tell sb to do sth** *I told him to go and see a doctor if he was worried.* | **tell sb (that) they should do sth** *Jimmy has told him he should keep away from the gang for the next couple of weeks.*

suggest /səˈdʒest‖səg-/ [v T] to tell someone your ideas about what they should do, where they should go etc: *'Why not ask Dad?' he suggested.* | *I'm not sure which is the best wine to order. What would you suggest?* | **+ (that)** *Sarah suggested that I should apply for this job.*

recommend /ˌrekəˈmend/ [v T] to advise someone to do something, especially when you have special knowledge of a particular subject or situation: *The Forsyth Report recommended stricter supervision of the trade in live animals.* | *Ask your tour guide to recommend the best places to eat.* | **+ that** *Doctors recommend that all children be immunized against polio and tuberculosis.* | **recommend doing sth** *I would always recommend buying a good quality bicycle rather than a cheap one.* | **strongly recommend** *I strongly recommend that you get your brakes checked before you go on a long drive.*

urge /ɜːʳdʒ/ [v T] to strongly advise someone to do something because you think it is very important: *The company's bosses are urging full cooperation with the trade union.* | **urge sb to do sth** *Police are urging drivers not to come into London this weekend.* | **+ that** *He gave copies of the report to all those present at the meeting, urging that they read and digest its contents.*

give advice /ˌgɪv ədˈvaɪs/ [v phrase] to advise someone about a problem or subject, especially something that they have asked you about: *I'm afraid that's the only advice I can give you.* | **give advice to sb** *The centre gives free advice to young people who have drug problems.* | **give sb advice** *Can you give me some advice? I'm thinking of buying a computer.* | **+ on/about** *Ask your bank to give you some advice about special student packages.*

2 what you say when you are advising someone

- you should do sth/you ought to do sth
- if I were you
- you'd be better off
- take my advice
- take it from me
- you'd be well advised to do sth/you would do well to do sth
- on no account/not on any account
- make sure (that) you ...
- the best thing is to ...
- a word of advice ...

you should do sth/you ought to do sth /juː ʃʊd ˈduː (sth), juː ˌɔːt tə ˈduː (sth)/ spoken *You should go to the doctor with that cough.* | *I think you should stay here until you've sobered up.* | *That new restaurant's great – you really ought to try it.* | *Do you know what you ought to do? You ought to tell her exactly what you think of her.*

if I were you /ɪf ˌaɪ wəʳ ˈjuː/ spoken say this when you are giving someone friendly advice: *I wouldn't do that if I were you.* | *Here's your money – if I were you I'd put it in the bank right now.*

you'd be better off /juːd biː ˌbetər ˈɒf/ spoken say this when you are advising someone how to do something in a better way: *The ferry takes about eight hours! You'd be better off going by plane.* | *I think you'd be better off using a knife rather than scissors for that job.*

take my advice /teɪk ˌmaɪ ədˈvaɪs/ spoken say this when you think that someone should do something because you know from your own experience how unpleasant or difficult something can be: *Take my advice – don't go into teaching unless you're absolutely committed.* | *Divorces are a nightmare. Take my advice and stay single.*

take it from me /ˌteɪk ɪt frəm ˈmiː/ spoken say this when you are telling someone that they should trust the advice you are giving them because it is based on your personal experience: *Take it from me, you'll regret it if you waste your time at school.* | *Love affairs with colleagues never work out – take it from me.*

you'd be well advised to do sth/you would do well to do sth /juːd biː ˌwel ədˌvaɪzd tə ˈduː (sth), juː wʊd duː ˌwel tə ˈduː (sth) / especially written use this when you are strongly advising someone to do something, especially because they may have trouble if they do not do it: *Before your interview you'd be well advised to have another look at what you put on the application form.* | *There are parts of Detroit you'd be well advised to avoid.*

on no account/not on any account /ɒn ˈnəʊ əˌkaʊnt, nɒt ɒn ˈeni əˌkaʊnt/ [adv] formal use this when you are strongly advising someone not to do something because it would be dangerous or stupid: *On no account should you attempt this exercise if you're pregnant.* | **not on any account** *You shouldn't sign the contract unless you are sure you understand it. Not on any account.*

make sure (that) you ... /meɪk 'ʃʊəʳ ðət juː/ spoken say this when you do not want someone to make a mistake, for example by forgetting to do something or losing something: *Make sure that you take your passport.* | *Make sure you lock all the doors and windows at night.*

the best thing is to ... /ðə 'best θɪŋ ɪz tuː/ spoken say this when you are telling someone what you think the best way of dealing with a particular situation is, based on your own experience: *The best thing is to just ignore her. She'll soon take the hint.*

a word of advice ... /ə ˌwɜːʳd əv əd'vaɪs / spoken say this especially when you are warning someone to be careful about something: *A word of advice: when you're at the interview don't mention that you used to work in a bar.*

3 to ask someone for their advice

- ask sb's advice
- get/obtain advice
- seek advice
- consult

ask sb's advice /ˌɑːsk (sb's) əd'vaɪs‖ˌæsk-/ [v phrase] to ask someone to advise you about something: *Can I ask your advice? I need to find somewhere to stay in London.* | **+ on/about** *I always ask my brother's advice about computers.*

seek advice /ˌsiːk əd'vaɪs/ [v phrase] written to ask someone to advise you or to try to find someone to advise you, especially someone who has special or professional knowledge **seek advice from sb** *The best thing to do is to seek advice from an expert.* | **seek sb's advice on** *Carla sought her grandmother's advice on all personal matters.*

get/obtain advice ALSO **take advice** British /ˌget, əbˌteɪn əd'vaɪs, ˌteɪk əd'vaɪs/ [v phrase] **get legal/medical/professional etc advice** to ask someone who has special knowledge to advise you about a problem that you cannot deal with by yourself: *If the debt is not paid within seven days, we will take legal advice.* | *Pregnant women should get medical advice before taking any kind of drug.* | **get legal etc advice on** *She had told her employers that she would be getting professional advice on her rights.*

consult /kən'sʌlt/ [v T] formal to get advice from someone who is trained in a particular profession, for example a lawyer or a doctor: *If the symptoms persist, consult your doctor.* | *I want to consult my lawyer before I say anything.* | **consult sb about sth** *Tonight the President will consult his military observers about the likelihood of an attack.*

4 to do what someone advises you to do

- take sb's advice/follow sb's advice
- do what sb says
- listen to
- on sb's advice/on the advice of sb

take sb's advice/follow sb's advice /ˌteɪk (sb's) əd'vaɪs, ˌfɒləʊ-‖ˌfɑː-/ [v phrase] to do what someone advises you to do: *I've decided to take your advice and go to art school.* | *If she had followed my advice, this would never have happened.*

do what sb says /ˌduː wɒt (sb) 'sez/ especially spoken to do what someone has told or advised you to do: *If you'd done what I'd said, none of this would have happened.*

listen to /'lɪsən tuː/ [phr v T not in progressive] to do what someone advises you to do, especially because you respect them and trust their judgement: *You tell him Dad – I'm sure he'll listen to you.* | *Bob warned us about this. I wish I'd listened to him.*

on sb's advice/on the advice of sb /ɒn (sb's) əd'vaɪs, ɒn ði əd'vaɪs əv (sb)/ [adv] if you do something **on someone's advice**, you do it because they have advised you to do it: *On her doctor's advice, she took a few days off work.* | *He decided not to take the exam, on the advice of his professor.*

5 someone's advice about what you should do

- advice
- tip
- recommendation
- guidance
- counselling

advice /əd'vaɪs/ [n U] what someone advises you to do: *Get some advice from the people in the tourist office.* | **+ on/about** *For advice on AIDS, phone this free number.* | **give sb advice** *I decided to ask Laura what she thought I should do. She always gives me good advice.* | **a piece of advice** (=some advice) *Years ago, my father gave me a piece of advice that I've never forgotten.* | **medical/legal/professional etc advice** *You should get legal advice before you sign the contract.* | **sound advice** (=good advice) *That's sound advice – I'll definitely bear it in mind.*

tip /tɪp/ [n C] a simple but useful piece of advice about how to do something more easily or effectively: *Here's a good tip: if you spill red wine on your carpet, pour salt on it to remove it.* | **+ on** *a leaflet containing some tips on how to take better photos*

recommendation /ˌrekəmen'deɪʃən/ [n C usually plural] advice about how to deal with a problem, especially given by a group of people who have made a detailed study of it: *The railway companies seem to completely ignore safety recommendations.* | **make a recommendation** *The committee made a number of recommendations for improving standards in schools.* | **recommendation** *Unless the report's recommendations are implemented soon, the future for industry could be very bleak indeed.*

guidance /'gaɪdəns/ [n U] advice about what to do in your job, your education, or your private life – use this about advice you get from someone whose job is to advise and help people: *practical guidance and support for people working abroad* | **give guidance on sth** *Your teacher can give you guidance on choosing a career and writing a job application.*

counselling British **/counseling** American /'kaʊnsəlɪŋ/ [n U] advice and support given by a specially trained person who can help people with personal problems or people who have had a very unpleasant experience: *The college will provide counselling for students who have problems with alcohol or drugs.* | *Victims of violent crimes often need counseling.*

6 someone who advises people

- adviser
- consultant
- counsellor
- guru
- focus group
- think-tank

adviser British **/advisor** American /əd'vaɪzəʳ/ [n C] someone whose job is to give advice, especially in business, law, or politics **financial/legal/careers etc adviser** *Talk to an independent financial adviser* *before you invest your money.* | **+ on** *the Prime Minister's personal adviser on economic affairs* | **adviser to sb** *She's been appointed as scientific advisor to the President.* —**advisory** [adj usually before noun] existing for the purpose of giving advice: *The Science Council is mainly an advisory body.* | *I will be present at committee meetings, but purely in an advisory capacity.*

consultant /kən'sʌltənt/ [n C] someone who gives special technical advice to companies or other organizations: *He's left his job as a computer programmer and is working as a consultant for a German firm.* | **consultant on** *Booth is a consultant on language with one of the national press agencies.* | **consultant to sb** *As a consultant to NASA, Cockburn had access to confidential details of the US space program.*

counsellor British **/counselor** American /'kaʊnsələʳ/ [n C] someone who gives professional advice and emotional support to people, especially about personal problems: *I never realized you were so depressed. Have you been to see a counselor?* | *Children in the summer camp can see a trained counselor if they have any problems.* | *The hospice is appealing for more people to work as bereavement counsellors.*

guru /'gʊruː/ [n C] informal someone who is highly respected within their area of work, and to whom people go for advice: *Peter Drucker, the management guru, has just published a new book.* | *It soon became apparent that Colin was the guru of the whole department.*

focus group /'fəʊkəs gruːp/ [n C] a group of ordinary people who are brought together and asked for their opinions about a particular subject or product by a company, political party etc, in order to help them plan what to do or produce in the future: *The government's excessive use of focus groups to sound out public opinion has come under a lot of criticism.* | *A focus group gave its responses to the proposed advertising campaign.*

think-tank /'θɪŋk tæŋk/ [n C] a committee of people with experience in a particular subject that an organization or government establishes to produce ideas and give advice: *a right-wing political think-tank*

after

RELATED WORDS

opposite: ——— **before**

- immediately after something *see* **immediately (2)**
- one after another *see* **series**
- *see also* **later, future**

1 after a particular time or event

- after
- afterwards
- next
- later
- then
- subsequently

after /'ɑːftəʳ‖'æf-/ [prep/adv/conjunction] **after** something happens or **after** someone does something: *We went for a walk after lunch.* | *Gingrich won election to the House in 1978, after Flynt retired.* | *What did you do after leaving school?* | **an hour/two days/a year etc after** *My father died two days after I was born.* | **soon after/not long after** *He joined the army in 1914, and soon after was promoted to the rank of captain.* | **right after** ALSO **straight after** British (=immediately after) *Paul rushed home right after school.* | **just after** *My sister and her husband moved west just after their wedding.* | **+ that** *The Pirates jumped to a 22-2 lead, and Georgetown never got closer than 16 points after that.* | *It was terrible: first the gearbox seized and after that the radiator burst.*

afterwards ALSO **afterward** American /'ɑːftəʳwəʳd(z)‖'æf-/ [adv] after an event or a time that you have just mentioned: *The operation was rather painful, but I felt a lot better afterwards.* | *Afterward, Nick said he'd never been so nervous in his life.* | **two years/three months etc afterwards** *A couple of years afterwards I bumped into her in a supermarket.* | **soon/shortly afterwards** *His wife fell ill in June and died soon afterwards.*

next /nekst/ [adv] after something happens or after someone does something – use this when you are describing a series of events in the order they happened: *Can you remember what happened next?* | *First, chop up two large onions. Next, fry them until they are golden brown.*

later /'leɪtəʳ/ [adv] some time after now or after the time you are talking about: *I'll tell you about it later when I'm not so busy.* | *Ronald Reagan joined the Republican Party in 1962 and later became Governor of California.* | **three months/two years/ten days etc later** *A couple of days later I saw her in a downtown bar.* | **+ on** *The first part of the film is really boring but it gets better later on.* | **much later** (=a long time later) *I found out much later that some of the children I taught had become teachers themselves.* | **later that day/month/year etc** *Later that month we got another letter from them asking for more money.*

then /ðen/ [adv] after you have done something – use this when you are describing a series of things you did, or when you are giving instructions: *First we played tennis, and then we went swimming.* | *Add a cup of sugar. Then beat in three eggs.*

subsequently /'sʌbsɪ̇kwəntli/ [adv] formal after an event was finished in the past: *The book was published in 1954 and was subsequently translated into fifteen languages.* | *The six men were subsequently acquitted of all charges, but only after they had served 17 years in prison.*

2 after a particular period of time has passed

- after
- within
- in
- from now

after /'ɑːftəʳ‖'æf-/ [prep] **after a week/several hours/a long time/a while etc after** a period of time has passed: *After half an hour we got tired of waiting and went home.* | *At first I was very nervous, but after a while I began to feel more confident.* | **after a week/a year etc of (doing) sth** *The war ended after another six months of fighting.*

within /wɪð'ɪn‖wɪð'ɪn, wɪθ'ɪn/ [prep] **within a month/two weeks/a year etc** less than a month etc after something happens, especially when this is an unusually short time: *He was bitten by a snake. Within three hours he was dead.* | *The fire alarm went off and within minutes the building had been cleared.* | **within a month/a few days etc of doing sth** *Within six years of joining the company he was Managing Director.* | **within a short period/space** British **of time** (=surprisingly quickly) *Within a short space of time, Gerry had managed to offend everyone in the group.*

in /ɪn/ [prep] **in a minute/a few hours/a month etc** a minute, a few hours after the present time: *She'll be* *here in a few minutes.* | *I'll see you again in a day or two.* | **in an hour's time/a few minutes' etc time** *In a few weeks' time I'll be off to university.*

from now /frəm ˈnaʊ/ [adv] **24 hours/a week/ six months/100 years from now** at a future time 24 hours, six months etc from now: *A week from now we will be in Paris.* | *What do you think you'll be doing six months from now?* | *Four hundred years from now people will still be listening to Mozart.*

3 starting to happen after now or after a particular time

- from now on
- from/as from/as of/starting
- after
- after that
- from then on
- thereafter
- past

from now on ALSO **from here on (out)** American /frəm ˌnaʊ ˈɒn, frəm ˌhɪər ɒn ˈaʊt/ [adv] use this to talk about a new arrangement that is going to start now and then continue in the future: *You'll be working with me from now on.* | *From here on out I'll come to every meeting, I promise.* | *From now on Neil is responsible for publicity and marketing.*

from/as from/as of/starting /frəm, ˈæz frəm, ˈæz əv, ˈstɑːʳtɪŋ/ [prep] **from tomorrow/next week etc** use this to say that a new rule or arrangement will start at a particular time and will continue from then: *As of the first of July, all back seat passengers must wear seat belts.* | *The new timetable will come into effect from January 2003.* | *Starting today Miss Carey will be in charge of the Sales Department.*

after /ˈɑːftəʳ‖ˈæf-/ [prep] **after** a particular time or date: *I'm busy right now. Could you come back sometime after 4 o'clock?* | *After 1800, more and more people worked in factories.* | **just after** (=a short time after) *If they left just after twelve, they should be here soon.*

after that /ˌɑːftəʳ ˈðæt‖ˌæf-/ [adv] used when a situation starts to exist after something happens, especially if the situation is caused by what has happened: *He found out that I had lied to him, and after that he never trusted me again.* | *The company started a big new advertising campaign, and business really improved after that.* | *I'm going to help you for the first two weeks, but after that you'll be working on your own.*

from then on /frəm ˌðen ˈɒn/ [adv] use this to talk about something that starts to happen at a time in the past or future, and continues from that time: *The latest sunrise of the winter is Friday; from then on, the dark winter mornings get brighter earlier.* | *He went to his first football game when he was four, and from then on he was crazy about it.*

thereafter /ðeərˈɑːftəʳ‖-ˈæf-/ [adv] formal after that – used especially in written instructions, rules, or agreements: *The plants should be watered every day for the first week and twice a week thereafter.* | *On retirement each employee will receive a lump sum of £10,000 and a regular annual pension thereafter.*

past ALSO **gone** British /pɑːst‖pæst, gɒn‖gɔːn/ [prep] **past 3 o'clock/midnight etc** use this when someone is late for something, or when something happens at a later time than it should happen or usually happens: *When we got home it was gone midnight.* | *We have to get you home. It's past your bedtime.*

4 coming after someone or something else

- next
- after
- following
- later
- subsequent
- succeeding
- ensuing
- follow-up
- future

next /nekst/ [adj only before noun] the **next** person, thing, or time comes just after the one you have just been talking about, or just after the most recent one: *Who was the next president of the United States after Ronald Reagan?* | *When's the next flight to Miami?* | **the next day/week/month/year** *I finished my classes on the 5th, and the next day I went home to Cleveland.* | **next Thursday/week/August etc** (=the one after this Thursday, this week, this August etc) *Next week I'm going on a training course in Seaford.*

after /ˈɑːftəʳ‖ˈæf-/ [adv/prep] **the day after/the Saturday after/the week after etc** the day etc that comes **after** the time or event that you are talking about: *Helen arrived on July 20th and I arrived the week after.* | *The party's not this Thursday but the Thursday after.* | *The weather changed the morning after we arrived.* | *I felt rather tired the day after the party.* | **the one after** (=the next one) *If we miss the ten o'clock train we'll just have to catch the one after.*

following /ˈfɒləʊɪŋ‖ˈfɑː-/ [adj only before noun] **the following day/month/year etc** the next day, month etc – use this when you are describing something that happened in the past: *The following day she woke up with a splitting headache.* | *They agreed to meet the following week in the Cafe Rouge.*

later /ˈleɪtəʳ/ [adj only before noun] happening some time **later**, not immediately afterwards **a later date/time/stage etc** *We can sort out the final details at a later stage.* | **in later years/months/centuries etc** *In later centuries Venice lost its former importance and began to go into decline.*

subsequent /ˈsʌbsɪkwənt/ [adj only before noun] formal coming after something you have just mentioned – used especially before plural nouns: *These skills were then handed down to subsequent generations of craftsmen.* | *Many of Marx's theories were disproved by subsequent events.* | *The first meeting will be in the City Hall, but all subsequent meetings will be held in the school.*

succeeding /səkˈsiːdɪŋ/ [adj only before noun] **succeeding weeks/months/years/generations etc** in every week, month, year etc that comes after something: *The government started to borrow money in 1961, and the national debt has steadily increased with each succeeding year.* | *The effects of exposure to atomic radiation at Hiroshima have been passed on to succeeding generations.*

ensuing /ɪnˈsjuːɪŋ‖-ˈsuː-/ [adj only before noun] formal **the ensuing battle/fight/confusion/panic/days/months etc** the battle etc that happens immediately after the events or period of time that you have just mentioned: *Someone shouted 'Fire!' and in the ensuing panic several people were injured.* | *They met each other several times over the ensuing six months.*

follow-up /ˈfɒləʊ ʌp‖ˈfɑː-/ [adj only before noun] **follow-up meeting/visit/interview/treatment etc** something that is done after something else in order to check it or make sure that it is successful: *Once you have installed solar heating you will receive regular follow-up visits from our experts.* | *After each training programme everyone has a follow-up interview with their manager.*

future /'fju:tʃəʳ/ [adj only before noun] **future generations/years/events/work/employees etc** the people, years etc that will come in the future: *It is our duty to preserve our culture for future generations.* | *In future years some of you will regret the decision you have made today.* | *The company is building apartment buildings for future employees.*

5 to happen after something else

- follow
- come after
- ensue
- on the heels of sth
- in the wake of sth

follow /'fɒləʊ‖'fɑ:-/ [v I/T not in progressive] especially written if an event or period **follows** another event or period, it happens after it: *We saw each other a lot in the months that followed.* | *the long period of stability that followed the war* | **be followed by sth** *The wedding was followed by a big party at the Chelsea Hotel.* | *Suddenly there was a shout from above, immediately followed by a loud bang.* | **be closely followed by sth** (=be followed very soon by) *China's first nuclear test in October 1964 was closely followed by a second in May 1965.* | **there followed/follows** (=after that there was) *There then followed a long and painful silence.*

come after /ˌkʌm 'ɑ:ftəʳ‖-'æf-/ [phr v T] to happen after something else and often as a result of something else **come after sth** *The agreement came after six months of negotiations.* | *The Napoleonic Wars came after the French Revolution.* | **come three weeks/five days etc after sth** *My first chance to talk to her came three days after our quarrel.* | **come after** *The New Stone Age lasted about 1200 years in Britain. The period which came after is known as the Bronze Age.*

ensue /ɪn'sju:‖ɪn'su:/ [v I] formal if something such as an argument or a fight **ensues**, it happens after something else, often as a result of it: *I objected to what he had just said and a heated argument then ensued.* | *The police were called in to quell the riot that ensued.*

on the heels of sth /ɒn ðə 'hi:lz əv (sth)/ especially American if something comes **on the heels of** something else, it happens very soon after it – used especially in news reports **come on the heels of sth** *The news comes on the heels of the FBI's announcement that last week's crash was caused by mechanical failure.* | **hot/hard on the heels of sth** British (=immediately after something) *Tuesday's victory came hard on the heels of last week's shock defeat by Manchester United.*

in the wake of sth /ɪn ðə 'weɪk əv (sth)/ if something, especially something bad, happens **in the wake of** an event, it happens after it and usually as a result of it: *In the wake of Thailand's economic troubles, Malaysia's currency also sank.*

6 the person who does a particular job after someone else

- successor
- succeed
- next in line
- the next

successor /sək'sesəʳ/ [n C] someone who takes a position previously held by someone else **sb's successor** *In January 1947, Secretary of State Byrnes resigned; his successor was General Marshall.* | *Two weeks after the death of Pope John Paul, the cardinals met to elect his successor.* | **+ to** *Many people regard him as a likely successor to the current managing director.*

succeed /sək'si:d/ [v I/T] to be the next person to take an important position or rank after someone else: *Eisenhower was succeeded by John F. Kennedy.* | **succeed to the throne/the presidency/the championship etc** (=become the next king, president etc) *Louis XIII succeeded to the throne when he was only nine years old.* | **succeed sb as King/President/Secretary General etc** *Bailey will succeed Fuller as Director of Operations.*

next in line /ˌnekst ɪn 'laɪn/ [adj phrase] the person who will be the next leader, when the present one dies, or the person who is most likely to be chosen for an important job, when the present person leaves: *Who is next in line when the current leader of North Korea dies?* | **+ for** *Tom's next in line for the boss's job.* | **next in line to the throne** (=next in line to become king or queen) *Edward VIII was succeeded by his younger brother, who was next in line to the throne.*

the next /ðə 'nekst/ [n phrase] **the next** leader, queen, president etc is the one that gets that position after someone else: *Who do you think will be the next prime minister?* | *The next boss was better than the old one.*

7 a book, film etc that comes after an earlier one

- sequel

sequel /'si:kwəl/ [n C] a book, play or film that continues the story of an earlier book, play or film, usually by the same writer, film-maker etc: *'Batman 2' was a rare example of a sequel being better than the original.* | *After the unexpected success of his first film, Rodriguez is making plans for a sequel.* | **+ to** *the sequel to 'Gone with the Wind'*

8 after someone or something in a list, series, line of people etc

- after
- next
- later

after /'ɑ:ftəʳ‖'æf-/ [prep] *My name is after yours on the list.* | *You'll find a reference number after each item in the catalogue.* | *There were several people after me who didn't manage to get into the game.*

next /nekst/ [adj/adv] the **next** person or thing is the one that comes just after the present one: *Could you ask the next patient to come in, please?* | *Look at the diagram on the next page.* | *Turn left at the next traffic light.*

later /'leɪtəʳ/ [adj only before noun] in a part of a book, speech that comes later: *This topic will be discussed more fully in a later chapter.*

9 to be the next person or thing after another in a list, series etc

- be/come after
- be/come next
- follow

be/come after /ˌbi:, ˌkʌm 'ɑ:ftəʳ‖-'æf-/ [v phrase not in progressive or passive] *My name should be after yours if the list is alphabetical.* | *In British and American addresses, the name of the town always comes after the name of the street.* | *The first line of the poem is 'I wandered lonely as a cloud'. What comes after that?*

be/come next /ˌbi:, ˌkʌm 'nekst/ [v phrase] to be the next person or thing in a list, series, line of people etc: *This book's called 'The Third Dimension'. Which book comes next in the series?* | *The nurse came out of her office and called out, 'Who's next?'* | **next comes sth** spoken *The first three sections of the course are just an introduction. Next comes the difficult bit.*

follow /ˈfɒləʊ‖ˈfɑː-/ [v I/T not in progressive] to come after something in a book, series, or list: *Taylor explains his theory in the pages that follow.* | **be followed by sth** *In English the letter Q is always followed by a U.* | *Each chapter is followed by a set of exercises.*

again

RELATED WORDS

- to say something again *see* **repeat**
- to use something again *see* **use sth (11)**
- to happen again *see* **happen**
- *see also* **start (7), (16)**

1 again

- again
- once again/once more
- yet again
- one more time/once more
- fresh
- not again!

again /əˈgen, əˈgeɪn‖əˈgen/ [adv] *If you're late again we'll leave without you.* | *The floor needs cleaning again.* | *It was nice to see you again.* | *Julie! It's your sister on the phone again.* | *The fresh mountain air soon made Jennifer feel strong again.* | *When I was safely back in my apartment again, I took out the letter and read it.*

once again/once more /ˌwʌns əˈgen, ˌwʌns ˈmɔːʳ/ [adv] formal use this especially about something worrying or serious that has happened before: *Once again, the French army were totally humiliated.* | *The crops had failed, and once more, famine threatened the region.* | *Once again, I must remind you of the seriousness of the problems we face.* | *The cost of living is once more on the increase.* | *Once again, the City Council has decided to ignore the interests of the taxpayers.*

yet again /ˌjet əˈgen/ [adv] use this when something has happened too many times before in a way that is very annoying: *Yet again, I was forced to ask my parents for money.* | *The opening of the new museum has been delayed yet again.* | *Yet again, you're late turning in your assignment.* | *It was the last day of their vacation and it was raining yet again.*

one more time/once more /ˌwʌn mɔːʳ ˈtaɪm, ˌwʌns ˈmɔːʳ/ [adv] again, and usually for the last time: *Can we practise the last part just once more?* | *I'm going to ask you just one more time: where did you get this money?* | *She wanted to see her grandfather once more before he died.*

fresh /freʃ/ [adj only before noun] **fresh attempt/look/start** one that is done again from the beginning in a new way, after you have been unsuccessful in the past: *I think we need to take a fresh look at the problem.* | *The army is planning a fresh attempt to regain control of the capital.*

not again! /nɒt əˈgen/ spoken say this when something annoying happens again or happens too many times: *'Sue, Steve's on the phone asking for you.' 'Oh, not again!'* | *'Not again!' said Anna, as the word CANCELLED appeared next to her flight number for the third time.*

2 to do something again

- do sth again
- repeat
- redo
- retake
- all over again
- here we go again

do sth again ALSO **do sth over** American /ˌduː (sth) əˈgen, ˌduː (sth) ˈəʊvəʳ/ [v phrase] to do something again, for example in order to practise it or because it was not done well enough the first time: *I'd like you to do this exercise again.* | *She spilt coffee on the application form and had to do it all again.* | *I'm afraid you'll have to do it over.*

repeat /rɪˈpiːt/ [v T] to do something again, especially many times, in order to achieve something useful: *Holmes repeated the experiment several times and got the same results.* | *Repeat this exercise ten times every day, and you'll soon have firmer, more muscular thighs.*

redo /riːˈduː/ [v T] to do something such as an examination, test, or piece of work again because it was not done well enough the first time: *I can't read a word of this – you'll have to redo it.* | *The wallpaper came off and we had to redo the whole thing.*

retake /riːˈteɪk/ [v T] to do a written examination or other kind of test again because you have failed it: *Julie's had to retake her driving test at least three times.* | *He decided to retake the course and try to get a higher grade.* —**retake** /ˈriːteɪk/ [n C] *The exam is in June. Retakes will be held in September.*

all over again /ɔːl ˌəʊvər əˈgen/ [adv] especially spoken if you do something long and difficult **all over again** you repeat it from the beginning: *At the police station they asked me the same questions all over again.* | *The prospect of writing the report all over again made me feel completely depressed.* | **start sth all over again** *The computer crashed and deleted all my work – I had to start the essay all over again.*

here we go again /ˌhɪəʳ wi ˌgəʊ əˈgen/ spoken said when you are annoyed because something that has happened or been done too many times before is happening again – use this especially before an argument that you frequently have with someone: *'You've been drinking again, haven't you!' 'Oh God, here we go again.'*

3 to start doing something again

- go back to/return to

go back to/return to ALSO **get back to** /gəʊ ˈbæk tuː, rɪˈtɜːn tuː, get ˈbæk tuː/ [phr v T] *After she hung up the phone, she went back to her knitting.* | *He took a drink, wiped his forehead and returned to his digging.* | *OK, lunch break's over – time to get back to work.*

4 to start talking about something again

- go back to/get back to

go back to/get back to ALSO **return to** /gəʊ ˈbæk tuː, get ˈbæk tuː, rɪˈtɜːʳn tuː/ [phr v T] especially spoken to start talking about something again, after a period when you stopped talking about it: *I'll go back to your question in a few minutes.* | *But getting back to what the real estate agent said, do you think we could get more for the house if we had it painted first?* | *I think we can return to this argument later.*

5 happening or doing something many times

- again and again
- repeated
- recurrent/recurring
- over and over again

again and again /əˌgen ənd əˈgen/ *I've told you again and again – don't play ball near the windows.* | *They hit him again and again until he was unconscious.* | *This kind of ignorance is something that I see again and again.*

repeated /rɪˈpiːtɪ̣d/ [adj only before noun] **repeated attempts/efforts/requests/warnings etc** attempts, efforts, that someone tries to make many times but without getting the result they want: *Motorists used the roads despite repeated warnings of snow.* | *Repeated attempts to fix the satellite have failed.*

recurrent/recurring /rɪˈkʌrənt‖-ˈkɜːr-, rɪˈkɜːrɪŋ/ [adj usually before noun] **recurrent** or **recurring** problems, illnesses, ideas etc happen repeatedly, especially in a way that is difficult to stop or control: *Flooding is a recurrent problem in countries such as Bangladesh.* | *a recurrent infection* | *Men trying to escape from the women who love them is a recurrent theme in Greene's novels.* | **recurring dream/nightmare** *I have this recurring dream in which my teeth are black and rotted.*

over and over again /ˌəʊvər ənd ˌəʊvər əˈgen/ [adv] use this to say that something happens a lot of times or when you have to do something a lot of times, especially when this makes you annoyed or impatient: *I've told him over and over again not to call me at work, but he won't listen.* | *She practised the lines over and over again until they were word perfect.*

against/oppose

when you think that something is wrong and should not be allowed

RELATED WORDS

opposite: —— **support**

- to play against someone in a game or sport *see* **play a game or sport**
- *see also* **disagree, disapprove, fight (7-9), opinion**

1 to think something is wrong

- be against/be opposed to
- oppose
- not agree with sth
- not believe in sth
- anti-
- hostile
- antagonistic

be against/be opposed to /biː əˈgenst, biː əˈpəʊzd tuː/ [v phrase] to think that something is wrong and that it should not be allowed: *Lundgren is against abortion.* | *Most people are opposed to the privatization of the city's public transportation system.* | **be strongly against** *There are two or three groups that are strongly against construction of the dam.* | **be dead set against** (=be very much against something) *She wants to marry him, but her parents are dead set against it.* | **be strongly/totally/opposed to** *Senator Thompson remains totally opposed to any form of gun control.*

oppose /əˈpəʊz/ [v T] to think that a plan, idea etc is wrong, and to try to prevent it from happening or succeeding: *Conservative MPs say they will oppose the new bill.* | **strongly/vigorously oppose** *The Church strongly opposes same-sex marriage.*

not agree with sth /nɒt əˈgriː wɪð (sth)/ especially spoken to be against something, for example because it is new or different and you do not like things to change: *My grandmother doesn't agree with divorce.* | *There are many people in the US who do not agree with capital punishment.*

not believe in sth /nɒt bɪ̣ˈliːv ɪn (sth)/ to not support something, because you think something is wrong or immoral: *Fiona doesn't believe in having sex before marriage.* | *I don't believe in hitting children for any reason.*

anti- /ˈænti/ [prefix] **anti-war/-smoking/-American etc** against war, smoking, America etc: *Anti-war demonstrators gathered in the city's main square.* | *The anti-smoking laws seem ridiculous to me.* | *Anti-American sentiment remains high in the region.*

hostile /ˈhɒstaɪl‖ˈhɑːstl, ˈhɑːstaɪl/ [adj] someone who is **hostile** to a plan or idea opposes it very strongly, and expresses this in an angry way: *A hostile audience refused to listen to Senator Drummond's reply.* | **+ to/towards** *Local people are hostile towards the plan, which would involve a significant tax increase.* | **openly hostile** (=showing very clearly that you are hostile) *Lydon was openly hostile to any kind of criticism of the project.*

antagonistic /ænˌtægəˈnɪstɪk◂/ [adj] behaving in a way that shows that you strongly disapprove of someone or something: *A lot of people refuse to work with Paula. Her manner is just too antagonistic.* | **+ to/towards** *The right-wing press has always been deeply antagonistic towards the Labour party.*

2 a person or group that opposes something

- opponent
- the opposition
- enemy

opponent /əˈpəʊnənt/ [n C] a person or group that opposes something **+ of** *In some countries, any opponent of the government is likely to lose their job.* | *One notable opponent of the proposal was the mayor.*

the opposition /ði ˌɒpəˈzɪʃən‖-ˌɑːp-/ [n singular with singular or plural verb in British English] a group that is opposing another group, especially the political party or parties whose elected representatives oppose the official government: *Opinion polls showed the opposition pulling ahead in some areas.* | *Newspapers must reflect the views of the opposition as well as those of the government.*

enemy /ˈenəmi/ [n C] a person or group that opposes something very strongly and tries to stop it or destroy it – used especially when you disapprove of this person or group **+ of** *the enemies of democracy* | *an enemy of the Jewish people*

3 words or behaviour that show that you oppose something

- objection
- opposition
- hostility
- antagonism

objection /əbˈdʒekʃən/ [n C] something that you say because you oppose one particular detail of a plan, course of action etc **have an objection** *If anyone has any objections, please let us know as soon as possible.* | **raise an objection** (=state an objection) *When I told him about my plans, my father raised one objection after another.* | **have no objection** *If you have no objection, I would like to use your name as a reference when I start applying for jobs.*

opposition /ˌɒpəˈzɪʃən‖ˌɑːp-/ [n U] things that people say or do in order to show that they are against something: *Widespread opposition to the military government led to violence in the streets.* | **+ to** *Opposition to the war grew rapidly.* | **face opposition** *Plans for the new stadium will no doubt face a lot of opposition.* | **express opposition** *Thousands of people plan to gather on Sunday to express their opposition to the government's handling of the crisis.* | **strong opposition** *Despite strong opposition, the law was passed.*

hostility /hɒˈstɪlǝti‖hɑː-/ [n U] angry remarks or behaviour that shows someone opposes a plan or idea very strongly: *The announcement was greeted with hostility from some employees.* | **+ to/towards** *Recently there has been hostility towards the Prime Minister from members of his own party.* | **open hostility** (=obvious or public hostility) *Given his open hostility, it seemed pointless to try and continue to persuade him.*

antagonism /ænˈtæɡənɪzəm/ [n U] angry and unpleasant feelings or behaviour that show someone dislikes or disagrees very strongly with a person, organization, plan, or idea **+ to/towards** *Hines made no effort to conceal his antagonism towards his supervisor.* | **+ between** *Mitchell sees no clear way to end the antagonism between the two groups.*

4 to say that you oppose something

- object
- raise objections

object /əbˈdʒekt/ [v I not in passive] to say something to show that you oppose a plan or action because you think it is unfair or morally wrong: *His supporters will certainly object if he is fired.* | **+ to** *Rebecca objects to being told what to do.* | **strongly object to** *The committee strongly objected to the report's recommendations.*

raise objections /ˌreɪz əbˈdʒekʃənz/ [v phrase] to give specific reasons for opposing a plan or action: *None of the committee members raised any objections, so we took a vote.* | **+ to** *Several church members raised objections to the way the money had been spent.*

age

RELATED WORDS

- *see also* **young, old, adult (2), baby, modern, old-fashioned**

1 how long someone has lived or something has existed

- age
- how old

age /eɪdʒ/ [n C/U] the number of years that someone has lived or something has existed **the age of sb/sth** *The average age of the students here is eighteen.* | *The amount you pay for license tags and registration depends on the age of the vehicle.* | **sb's age** *I tried to guess her age but couldn't.* | *Their children's ages range from twelve to seventeen.* | **be sb's age** (=be the same age as someone) *When I was your age I was already working.* | **of my age/her age etc** (=about the same age as me, her etc) *I'm surprised someone of your age didn't know that.* | **at the age of 10/20 etc** written (=use this to say how old someone was when something happened) *Dewhurst died at the age of seventy-three.* | **over/under the age of** (=older or younger than) *Anyone over the age of fourteen has to pay the full fare.* | **be small/tall etc for your age** (=be small, tall etc compared with other people of the same age) *Jimmy's very tall for his age.* | *She's in her seventies, but very fit for her age.*

how old /haʊ ˈəʊld/ [adj phrase] use this to ask or talk about the age of a person or thing: *How old is Paul?* | *I'm not sure how old the cat is – three or four, I suppose.*

2 ways of saying how old someone is

- be 5/10/35 etc
- be 5/10/35 etc years old
- be 5/10/35 etc years of age
- aged 5/10/35 etc
- 5-year-old/10-year-old etc
- of 5/10/35 etc
- in your teens/20s/thirties/40s etc
- have turned 20/30 etc
- twenty-/thirty-/forty-something

be 5/10/35 etc /biː ˈfaɪv/ [v phrase] *Julie's going to be thirty next month.* | *When I was eighteen, I thought I knew everything.* | *Luke is three and Marie is seven.*

be 5/10/35 etc years old /biː ˌfaɪv jɪəʳz ˈəʊld/ [v phrase] *Simone is nearly fifteen years old.* | *My sister got married when she was thirty-eight years old.*

be 5/10/35 etc years of age /biː ˌfaɪv jɪəʳz əv ˈeɪdʒ/ [v phrase] formal *He was tall, well-dressed and appeared to be about thirty-five years of age.* | *Elephants do not become sexually active until they are fifteen to eighteen years of age.*

aged 5/10/35 etc /eɪdʒd ˈfaɪv/ [adj phrase] used especially in written descriptions: *The child, aged ten, was last seen in a park on Bishop Street.* | *A recent survey of youths aged thirteen to eighteen shows that twelve percent are smoking regularly.* | *Females aged eighteen to thirty-four have an increased risk of contracting the disease.*

5-year-old/10-year-old etc /ˈfaɪv jɪər ˌəʊld/ [adj only before noun] (=aged 5/10/35 etc) used especially in written descriptions: *His ninety-five-year-old great-grandfather still rides his bike every day.* | *She has to pick up her twelve-year-old son from school at 3:30.* | *Twenty-one-year-old Elizabeth Parker will be the soloist in tonight's concert.* —**5/10/35-year-old** [n C] *The competition was won by a seventeen-year-old from Vestavia High School.*

of 5/10/35 etc /əv ˈfaɪv/ [adj phrase] use this especially to say what someone who is a particular age can do: *If a man of fifty-five loses his job, he'll never get another.* | *It's so simple, a child of four could use it.*

in your teens/20s/thirties/40s etc /ɪn jɔːʳ ˈtiːnz/ use this to give a general idea of how old someone is: *He was tall, with brown hair and dark eyes – I'd say he was in his forties.* | **early twenties/30s etc** *In my early twenties, I applied for my first job as a teacher.* | **mid-twenties/30s etc** *She's retired, but she's only in her mid-50s.* | **late twenties/30s etc** *A lot of women in their late twenties start thinking about having a family.*

have turned 20/30 etc /həv ˌtɜːʳnd ˈtwenti/ [v phrase] to have recently become 20, 30 etc: *McClelland recently turned forty.*

twenty-/thirty-/forty-something /ˈtwentiˌsʌmθɪŋ/ [adj only before noun] informal between the ages of 20 and 29, 30 and 39 etc: *a forty-something couple from Orlando*

3 to be almost a particular age

- be getting on for
- be pushing

be getting on for /biː ˌgetɪŋ ˈɒn fɔːʳ/ [v phrase] British used to say that someone is nearly a particular age: *Old Willis must be getting on for sixty-five.* | *The Queen was getting on for eighty and only the elderly could remember her coronation.*

be pushing /biː ˈpʊʃɪŋ/ [v phrase] **be pushing 40/50/65 etc** to be almost a particular age, especially when this is quite old or be doing a particular activity: *When you're pushing seventy it's not surprising when you start forgetting things.* | *What astonishes me is the ease with which this man, pushing seventy-five, can play his trumpet for hours at a time.*

4 ways of saying how old a building, car, machine etc is

- be 5/50/100 etc years old
- 5-year-old/100-year-old etc

be 5/50/100 etc years old /biː ˌfaɪv jɪəʳz ˈəʊld/ [v phrase] *Their home is over 100 years old.* | *The fossils are over 100 million years old.* | *The pyramids were already 2000 years old when the Greek historian Herodotus visited them.*

5-year-old/100-year-old etc /ˈfaɪv jɪər ˌəʊld/ [adj phrase only before noun] used especially in written descriptions: *A 500-year-old church in Leipzig is being threatened with demolition.* | *a 1500-year-old Latin manuscript*

5 to be the same age as someone or something else

- the same age

the same age /ðə ˌseɪm ˈeɪdʒ/ [n phrase] **be the same age** *Cliff and Jeremy are the same age.* | **be the same age as** *Cleo is the same age as me.* | **of the same age** (=the same age as each other) *Blood samples were taken from a group of patients of the same age.*

6 people who are the same age

- generation
- age group
- the under-5s/11s/25s etc
- the over-30s/40s/50s etc
- twenty-/thirty-/forty-something
- peer group/peers

generation /ˌdʒenəˈreɪʃən/ [n C usually singular] all the people in a society who are about the same age **sb's generation** *People of his generation often have a hard time with computers.* | *Many people consider her among the best writers of her generation.* | **generation-gap** (=large differences in attitude between different generations) *There's still a pretty wide generation-gap in German society.*

age group /ˈeɪdʒ gruːp/ [n C] all the people who are between two particular ages, considered as a group: *Pregnant women in the 40-45 age group are more likely to suffer complications.* | *The vacations are designed for the 20-30 age group.*

the under-5s/11s/25s etc /ði ˌʌndəʳ ˈfaɪvz/ [n plural] British a group of people, especially children or young people, who are all below a certain age – used especially in education or sport: *Sally teaches the under-5s.* | *He is one of the best of the under-18s in his football club.*

the over-30s/40s/50s etc /ði ˌəʊvəʳ ˈθɜːʳtiz/ [n plural] British a group of people, but not usually children or young people, who are all above a certain age – used especially to talk about groups of middle-aged or old people: *Many agencies provide special vacations for the over-50s.* | *The tennis club has a section for the over-40s.*

twenty-/thirty-/forty-something /ˈtwenti ˌsʌmθɪŋ/ [n C] informal someone between the ages of 20 and 29, 30 and 39 etc: *Howard's book is an entertaining book filled with tips on money management for twenty- and 30-somethings.* | *The show is about a group of twenty-somethings living in New York City.*

peer group/peers /ˈpɪəʳ gruːp, pɪəʳz/ [n C/n plural] a group of people who are the same age, especially children or young people – use this to talk about how people of the same age influence and relate to each other: *By the age of about 10, children will be much more interested in the approval of their peer group than that of their parents or teachers.* | *She learned to read late, and by the age of 13 was way behind her peers in almost every aspect of school work.* | **peer group pressure** (=the strong influence of a peer group) *Kids should be taught to resist peer group pressure to become sexually active too early.*

agree

RELATED WORDS

opposite: **disagree**

▸ *see also* **accept, let/allow, think, yes**

1 to have the same opinion as someone else

- agree
- be in agreement
- be of the same opinion
- share the view that
- subscribe to
- concur

agree /əˈgriː/ [v I/T not in progressive] to have the same opinion: *I think it's too expensive. Do you agree?* | *'Yes, I'm sure you're right,' agreed Tony.* | **+ with** *Mr Johnson thinks it's too risky, and I tend to agree with him.* | *Lee agreed with Jackson that more opportunities should be created for minorities in film.* | **+ that** *Most experts agree that drugs like heroin can cause permanent brain damage.* | **+ on/about** *I agree with you about the color – it looks awful.* | *The one thing all the parties agreed on was the need for fair elections.* | **I quite agree** British (=I agree completely) *Yes, I quite agree. Why should poor people pay so much tax?* | **I couldn't agree more** (=I agree completely) *'I wish it was time to go home.' 'I couldn't agree more.'*

be in agreement /biː ɪn əˈgriːmənt/ [v phrase] formal if people are in agreement, they have the same opinion about something, especially after discussing it a lot and trying to agree: *No decision can be made until everyone is in agreement.* | **+ on** *The two sides are in agreement on the need for arms reduction.* | **+ with** *I found myself in agreement with the lawyer, for once.*

be of the same opinion /biː əv ðə ˌseɪm əˈpɪnjən/ [v phrase] formal to have the same opinion as someone on a particular subject: *Both teachers were of the same opinion – she should be expelled from school immediately.* | *Mrs Ford clearly disapproved, and her sister appeared to be of the same opinion.*

share the view that /ˌʃeəʳ ðə 'vjuː ðət/ [v phrase not in progressive] formal to have the same opinion as someone, especially about something important, in politics, business, science etc: *I share the view that peace can only be achieved through dialogue.* | **share sb's view** *Many people shared Duvald's view, and thought the plan should be stopped.* | **share this/that view** *This view is shared by many doctors.*

subscribe to /səb'skraɪb tuː/ [phr v T not in progressive] to have the same opinion or belief as a lot of other people: *She has always subscribed to the view that children should be given responsibility from an early age.* | *There is a business philosophy I subscribe to, which says that if you are not making mistakes, you are not doing it right.*

concur /kən'kɜːʳ/ [v I not in progressive] formal to say that you have the same opinion as someone else: *'My opinion exactly', he concurred.* | **+ with** *He resigned three years later, because he did not concur with the division of the country into separate republics.*

2 to agree to someone else's plan or suggestion

- agree
- go along with
- fall in with
- go with

agree /ə'griː/ [v I not in progressive] to say yes to someone else's plan or suggestion: *Charles suggested going for a picnic, and we all agreed.* | *The project can't go ahead until the finance committee agrees.* | **+ to** *The Council of Ministers would never agree to such a plan.* | *Few people expect the rebels to agree to the peace plan.* | **agree wholeheartedly** (=agree completely and very willingly) *When I proposed that in future we should hold our meetings in the bar, the others agreed wholeheartedly.*

go along with /ˌgəʊ ə'lɒŋ wɪð‖-ə'lɔːŋ-/ [phr v T not passive] to agree with someone else's plan or suggestion, even if you are not sure if it is the right thing to do: *We went along with Eva's idea, since no one could think of a better one.* | *Usually it was easier just to go along with him, rather than risk an argument.* | *The bank decided to go along with our proposal and lent us the two million pounds we needed.*

fall in with /ˌfɔːl 'ɪn wɪð/ [v T not in passive] British to accept someone's plan or suggestion and do what they want you to do: *She expects her friends to fall in with everything she wants to do.* | *He was irritated by her refusal to fall in with his plans.*

go with /'gəʊ wɪð/ [v T not in passive] American to accept someone's plan or suggestion: *We considered all the options and decided to go with John's original proposal.*

3 when everyone agrees on a decision, plan etc

- agree
- reach agreement/ come to an agreement
- make a deal
- strike/make a bargain

agree /ə'griː/ [v I/T not in progressive] if two or more people **agree**, they reach a decision about what to do, and they are all satisfied with it: *Ultimately the two sides could not agree, and negotiations were abandoned.* | **+ on** *We've finally agreed on a date for the party.* | **+ to do sth** *They agreed to meet up later in the week.* | **agree that** *Finally, after some tough negotiating, it was agreed that the workforce would be reduced by 10%.* | **agree a price/plan/strategy etc** *After a few minutes' discussion we had agreed a price and the car was mine.* | **the agreed price/date/figure etc** *We refused to pay because the goods were not delivered by the agreed date.* | **it is agreed** (=a group of people have agreed about something) *It was agreed that the price should be fixed at $200.* | **we are (all) agreed** (=say this when everyone in a group has agreed about something) *Right then, are we all agreed?*

reach agreement/come to an agreement /ˌriːtʃ ə'griːmənt, ˌkʌm tʊ ən ə'griːmənt/ [v phrase not in progressive] to finally agree on something, by discussing it until everyone is satisfied with the decision: *After two years of talks, the Russians and the Americans finally reached an agreement.* | **+ with** *We are determined to reach agreement with the IMF before the end of the year.* | *Danvers had come to a private agreement with the owners of the land which secured his right to purchase it.* | **+ on** *After a week of talks, Britain and Iceland reached agreement on fishing limits.* | **come to some agreement** (=find a way to agree) *If you can't pay all the money now, I'm sure we can come to some agreement.*

make a deal ALSO **do a deal** British **/cut a deal** American /ˌmeɪk ə 'diːl, ˌduː ə 'diːl, ˌkʌt ə 'diːl/ [v phrase] to make an agreement with someone so that you get what you want, and they get what they want: *If he's willing to argue about the price, then he must want to do a deal.* | **+ with** *The government denied making a deal with the kidnappers.* | *He looked at me suspiciously. 'Have you made a deal with them?'* | *The administration is showing a willingness to cut a deal with Congress on gun-control legislation.*

strike/make a bargain /ˌstraɪk, ˌmeɪk ə 'bɑːʳgən/ [v phrase] to agree to do something for someone else if they will do something for you: *Let's make a bargain. I'll tell you what you want to know provided you don't breathe a word of it to anyone else.* | **+ with** *Eventually she struck a bargain with him. She would get him a job if he would help her with her singing.* | **+ that** *They made a bargain that they would stick together no matter what.*

4 to finish making a business agreement or plan

- settle
- conclude
- wrap up
- sew up
- finalize
- close a deal

settle /'setl/ [v T] *In the end we settled the deal on very favorable terms.* | *So that settles it. We'll pay you half the purchase price now, and the rest over two years.* | *We talked to the carpenter to settle plans for the expansion of the restaurant.*

conclude /kən'kluːd/ [v T] **conclude a deal/treaty agreement** successfully finish an agreement, especially one that is important and involves a large number of people: *The British car industry has just concluded a deal with the Japanese government.* | *European governments are trying to conclude a treaty to ban certain atmospheric tests.* —**conclusion** /kən'kluːʒən/ [n U] *The future of the prisoners will be decided on the conclusion of the armistice* (=when the armistice is concluded).

wrap up /ˌræp 'ʌp/ [phr v T] informal to finish a meeting, a business agreement, or a plan by settling everything quickly in a satisfactory way **wrap up sth** *If they accept our price we can wrap up the deal right away.* | **wrap sth/it/them up** *I want to wrap* *this meeting up as quickly as possible. I have another appointment in an hour.*

sew up /ˌsəʊ ˈʌp/ [phr v T] informal to settle a business agreement or plan in a satisfactory way, especially in a way that is favourable to you **sew sth/it/them up** *I called the real estate agent. The contract's been sewn up, and we can move into the apartment next week.* | **sew sth up** *Bob reckons he can sew up the deal quite quickly but I'm not so sure.*

finalize ALSO **finalise** British /ˈfaɪnəl-aɪz/ [v T] to do the last things that are necessary in order to settle an agreement, plan, or arrangement in a satisfactory way: *Mr Samuels is flying to Detroit to finalize the details and sign the contract.* | *Don't proceed any further with any plans or finalize any arrangements until you have proper authority.*

close a deal /ˌkləʊz ə ˈdiːl/ [v phrase] to finish making a business agreement, especially where a large amount of money is involved: *The oil company has just succeeded in closing a deal for the land.*

5 to agree by accepting less than you originally wanted

- compromise
- meet sb halfway
- make concessions

compromise /ˈkɒmprəmaɪz‖ˈkɑːm-/ [v I] to reach an agreement with someone in which both of you accept less than you really want: *The employers will have to be ready to compromise if they want to avoid a strike.* | *Critics accused the mayor of compromising too easily.* | **+ on** *Stalin refused to compromise on any of his demands.* | *The President might be willing to compromise on defense spending.*

meet sb halfway /ˌmiːt (sb) hɑːfˈweɪ‖-hæf-/ [v phrase] to do or pay part of what the other person in an agreement wants if they will do or pay part of what you want: *Democrats plan to meet the Governor halfway on welfare cuts.* | *They won't pay all our expenses, but they might be prepared to meet us halfway.*

make concessions /ˌmeɪk kənˈseʃənz/ [v phrase] if someone in authority **makes concessions**, they let their opponents have something that they are asking for, in order to reach an agreement: *We will have to make concessions if we want the talks to continue.* | **+ on** *The government has already made significant concessions on pay and conditions.* | **+ to** *Our policy of not making concessions to terrorists remains intact.*

6 something that has been agreed

- agreement
- treaty
- pact
- contract
- understanding
- compromise

agreement /əˈgriːmənt/ [n C] an arrangement that is made when two or more people, countries, or organizations agree to do something: *Eventually all the parties signed the agreement.* | **+ on** *Congress could not come up with an agreement on a spending plan for next year.* | **make an agreement** *They made a secret agreement not to tell anyone about their plans.* | **have an agreement that** *I thought we had an agreement that you would keep me informed about any changes in the programme.* | **under an agreement** *Under the Geneva agreement, a French force was supposed to remain in South Vietnam until July 1956.*

treaty /ˈtriːti/ [n C] a written agreement between two or more countries, especially to end a war: *The Treaty of Versailles ended the First World War.* | **sign a treaty** *Some countries are still refusing to sign a treaty banning chemical weapons.* | **peace treaty** (=a treaty that ends a war) *After months of negotiations, he eventually persuaded them to sign a peace treaty.*

pact /pækt/ [n C] a written agreement between two or more countries or political parties in which they promise to support each other or defend each other: *Officials at IBM and Apple declined to comment on a possible pact between the two personal computer makers.* | *Mexico's Defense Ministry this month signed a pact that allows Mexican troops to train at American bases.*

contract /ˈkɒntrækt‖ˈkɑːn-/ [n C] a written legal agreement with all the details of a job or business arrangement, for example what someone must do and how much they will be paid: *My contract says I have to work 35 hours per week.* | **sign a contract (with sb)** *Baltimore officials have confirmed that Olson will sign a two-year contract with the club.* | **break a contract** (=to break the rules of a contract) *The company was prosecuted for breaking the contract.*

understanding /ˌʌndərˈstændɪŋ/ [n C] an informal agreement between two people or organizations that is not written down **have an understanding** *Adams and the police have an understanding – he gives them information and they don't ask any questions about his activities.* | **come to an understanding (that)** (=agree after a discussion) *We came to an understanding that I would find a job and my husband would stay home with the baby.* | **+ between** *It was an unspoken understanding between Stu and me that I was going to be a lawyer and he was going to be an engineer.*

compromise /ˈkɒmprəmaɪz‖ˈkɑːm-/ [n C] an agreement in which both people or groups accept less than they really want **reach/find a compromise** *After several hours of discussions, they managed to reach a compromise.* | **+ between** *Officials hope to find a compromise between Britain and other EU members.*

7 when people have the same opinion about something

- agreement
- consensus
- unanimous

agreement /əˈgriːmənt/ [n U] a situation in which two or more people, groups etc have the same opinion about something **+ that** *There is general agreement among doctors that pregnant women should not smoke.* | **+ on** *Officials said there was widespread agreement on the need to promote growth by cutting government spending.* | **in agreement** *Tara nodded her head in agreement.*

consensus /kənˈsensəs/ [n U] general agreement among most of the people in a group, especially an official group that makes important decisions **+ on/about** *There is still no general consensus on what our future policy should be.* | **consensus of opinion** *The consensus of opinion seems to be that the Prime Minister should resign.* | **reach a consensus** (=achieve agreement) *The delegates will continue to meet until a consensus is reached.*

unanimous /juːˈnænɪməs/ [adj] if a group of people is **unanimous**, they all have the same opinion about something, especially about what should be done or who should be chosen or elected: *The decision of the committee was unanimous.* | **unanimous agreement/choice/decision/vote etc** *Mr Harada* *was elected by a unanimous vote.* | *Ryan needed unanimous agreement to bring his proposal up for a vote.* — **unanimously** [adv] *The union members voted unanimously for a strike.*

air

RELATED WORDS

- to travel by air *see* **travel**
- *see also* **breathe, hot, weather, feelings (8)**

1 the air that we breathe

- air
- fresh air

air /eəʳ/ [n U] the **air** that surrounds us, which we breathe in order to live: *Alex stood shivering in the cold, damp air.* | *the clean air of the countryside* | **air pollution** *Cars are a major cause of air pollution.* | **in the air** *There was a strong smell of burning in the air.*

fresh air /ˌfreʃ ˈeəʳ/ [n U] clean air that you get outdoors, considered to be more pleasant and healthy than air that you get inside buildings, in busy cities etc: *Open the window and let's get some fresh air in here!* | *I'm just going outside for a breath of fresh air.* | *Fresh air isn't necessarily better for you, but it will certainly make you feel better.*

2 when there is not enough fresh air

- stuffy
- airless
- stifling

stuffy /ˈstʌfi/ [adj] a room or building that is **stuffy** does not have enough fresh air, often because it is small or there are too many people in it: *The hotel room was hot and stuffy, and I woke up with a terrible headache.* | *It's getting stuffy in here – shall I open the window?* | *I wish I could escape from this stuffy little office.*

airless /ˈeəʳləs/ [adj] a room or building that is **airless** feels like it does not have enough air in it for you to breathe properly: *The classroom was airless and uncomfortably hot.* | *Hales lived in a tiny, airless room with one small window that wouldn't open.*

stifling /ˈstaɪflɪŋ/ [adj] very hot and uncomfortable, and without enough air for you to breathe properly: *It was stifling in there; I was glad to get out.* | *The heat in the narrow packed streets was stifling.* | **stifling hot** *The room was stifling hot.*

3 to let fresh air into a place

- air
- ventilated

air /eəʳ/ [v T] British **/air out** /ˌeər ˈaʊt/ [phr v T] American to let fresh **air** into a room or building, especially one that has been closed or not used for a while: *She was opening windows and shutters to air the empty rooms.* | *The bedrooms are aired and cleaned every morning.* | **air out sth/air sth out** *I opened all the windows, hoping that I could air the place out before the guests came.*

ventilated /ˈventəleɪtəd‖-tl-eɪt-/ [adj] **well/badly/poorly/adequately etc ventilated** if a room or building is well **ventilated**, fresh air can come in and bad air, smoke etc can go out. If a room or building is badly **ventilated**, not enough fresh air can come in and bad air, smoke etc cannot go out: *Workrooms must be adequately ventilated by the circulation of fresh air.* | *Store the potatoes in a cool, dark, well-ventilated space.* | *Working in a poorly ventilated area will affect your health.*

4 to fill something with air

- blow up
- inflate
- pump up

blow up /ˌbləʊ ˈʌp/ [phr v T] to fill something with air or gas, for example a tyre or a balloon **blow up sth/blow sth up** *Come and help me blow up the balloons.* | *This tyre's really flat – could you blow it up for me?*

inflate /ɪnˈfleɪt/ [v I/T] formal if you **inflate** something such as a tyre or balloon or it **inflates**, you fill it with air: *Tyres should always be inflated to the correct pressure.* | *You can inflate the mattress in 30 seconds, using a foot pump.* | *Her life jacket failed to inflate.*

pump up /ˌpʌmp ˈʌp/ [phr v T] to fill something with air using a pump (=a machine that forces air into something) **pump up sth/pump sth up** *Your back tire was a little flat so I pumped it up.*

5 to let the air out of something

- let the air out of
- let down
- deflate

let the air out of /ˌlet ði ˈeər aʊt əv/ [v phrase] British to let the air come out of sth, for example a tyre or a balloon: *Lisa let the air out of the balloon.*

let down /ˌlet ˈdaʊn/ [phr v T] to deliberately let the air come out of something, especially a tyre **let sth down** *Someone let the tires down on my bike!* | *The boys let his tyres down while he was in the headteacher's office.*

deflate /ˌdiːˈfleɪt, dɪ-/ [v I/T] if something filled with air **deflates**, the air comes out of it; if you **deflate** something, you let the air out of it: *The balloon gradually lost altitude as we deflated it and came in to land.* | *He woke up aching all over – somehow his airbed had deflated in the night and there was nothing to cushion him from the cold ground.*

alive

RELATED WORDS

opposite: **dead**

- to not die in an accident, war etc *see* **survive**
- *see also* **live, life, exist, die**

1 not dead

- alive
- living
- animate
- life

alive /əˈlaɪv/ [adj not before noun] not dead **still alive** *Are all your grandparents still alive?* | **keep sb alive** (=to prevent someone from dying by giving them food, medicine etc) *Paramedics fought for an hour by the roadside to keep him alive.* | **barely alive** *The police found them lying on the kitchen floor. Mr Wilkins was dead and his wife was barely alive.* | **alive and well** (=alive and not injured or ill) *The children were found alive and well after being missing for several days.* | **see sb alive** *She was the last person to see him alive.*

living /ˈlɪvɪŋ/ [adj only before noun] still **living** now: *A brother in Australia is Mary's only living relative.* |

greatest living poet/composer/painter etc *Seamus Heaney is Ireland's greatest living poet.*

animate /ˈænəmət/ [adj] formal something that is **animate** is alive and able to move, and is therefore not an object **animate objects** *At this age, children are still unable to distinguish between animate and inanimate objects.*

life /laɪf/ [n U] the fact or state of being alive: *Do you believe in life after death?* | *Unfortunately it's usually the worst experiences that remind us how precious life is.* | **fight/struggle for life** *She sat beside the hospital bed, holding his hand as he struggled for life.* | **cling to life** (=to struggle to stay alive) *An 18-year-old San José man clung to life late Wednesday after being shot in the head during a robbery.*

2 to continue to be alive

- live
- stay alive
- outlive
- survive

live /lɪv/ [v I] to continue to be alive: *The baby was born with a serious heart defect and not expected to live.* | **live for two years/three months/a long time etc** *My father only lived for a few years after his heart attack.* | *Cats normally live for about twelve years.* | **the will to live** (=the desire to live) *The will to live can be a vital factor in recovery.*

stay alive /ˌsteɪ əˈlaɪv/ [v phrase] to not die, even though you are in a dangerous situation: *The ship's crew eventually resorted to eating rats and even sawdust to stay alive.* | *Krasner, who has cancer, vowed she would stay alive until her brother was set free.*

outlive /aʊtˈlɪv/ [v T] to remain alive longer than someone else, especially a relative or friend who has died: *Judith outlived two of her three children.* | **outlive sb by 10 years/six months etc** *Women, on average, outlive men by 1.9 years.*

survive /səʳˈvaɪv/ [v T] to live longer than someone else, usually someone closely related to you – used especially in newspaper articles **survive sb by 10 years/six months etc** *Charles survived his wife by three months.* | **be survived by** *Monroe is survived by his wife, Regina, and two sons, Stanley and John.*

3 something that is alive

- living thing
- life form
- organism
- life
- wildlife

living thing /ˌlɪvɪŋ ˈθɪŋ/ [n C] a human, animal, plant, or anything that is alive: *An ocean is full of living things.* | *The tree, at 368 feet, is considered the world's tallest living thing.* | *Ecology is the study of how living things relate to their environment.*

life form /ˈlaɪf fɔːʳm/ [n C] a living thing or one type of living thing – used in scientific or technical contexts: *Hobart is convinced that there are life forms on other planets.* | *Some scientists estimate that at least one third of the life forms that exist in deep oceans have not yet been discovered.* | *strange life forms in the Galapagos Islands*

organism /ˈɔːʳgənɪzəm/ [n C] a living thing, especially an extremely small one – used in scientific and technical contexts: *Food poisoning is caused by a bacterial organism.* | **living organism** *Genetic engineers manipulate living organisms such as cells or bacteria to create products which fight disease.*

life /laɪf/ [n U] any living things, for example people, animals, plants, or all of these things together: *Oxygen is necessary to sustain life on Earth.* | *The new evidence seemed to indicate that life existed on Mars billions of years ago.* | **animal/plant life** (=all the animals or plants in a place) *Many species of plant life continue to be eradicated in South American rain forests.*

wildlife /ˈwaɪldlaɪf/ [n U] animals and plants growing in natural conditions: *The Sea of Cortez is rich with wildlife.* | *The organization was set up to protect wildlife across Europe.*

4 something that is not living and never has been living

- inanimate

inanimate /ɪnˈænəmət/ [adj] **inanimate object** *How can you get angry with a car? It's an inanimate object!* | *Some languages categorise not only living things as masculine or feminine, but inanimate objects as well.*

all/everything

RELATED WORDS

opposite: **none/nothing**

- throughout a period of time *see* **always (2-3)**
- *see also* **completely, everyone, everywhere**

1 all of a group of things or people

- all
- everything
- everyone/everybody
- the lot
- every
- each
- without exception
- the works
- the whole enchilada/shebang

all /ɔːl/ [predeterminer/quantifier] **all** the things or people in a group: *There was no one in the office – they were all having lunch.* | *The new government has banned all political parties.* | **we/you/them etc all** *He thanked us all for coming.* | *I've read five of his books, and I'm not going to stop until I've read them all.* | **all the/these/their/my etc** *Did you take all these pictures yourself?* | *All his clothes were spread around the room.* | *All the teachers in my school are women.* | **all of** *I've used up all of my traveler's checks.* | *She invited all of her friends to the party.* | **almost/nearly all** *The Prime Minister's plan would cut almost all subsidies to state-run industries.* | *Nearly all news organizations have refused to broadcast the victim's name during the trial.* | **all dogs/cars/children etc** (=use this to make a general statement about things or people of the same kind) *All mammals are warm-blooded.* | *All cars over 5 years old must have a test certificate.*

everything /ˈevriθɪŋ/ [pron] all the things in a group, or all the things that someone says or does: *The customs officer asked us to take everything out of our suitcases.* | *Don't believe everything you read in the newspapers.* | *Everything in the store costs less than $10.* | **everything else** (=all other things) *I have a tent and a sleeping-bag, and Ben said he'd lend me everything else I need for the camping trip.*

everyone/everybody /ˈevriwʌn, ˈevribɒdi‖-bɑːdi/ [pron] all people or all the people in a particular group: *I think everyone enjoyed the party.* | *If everybody is ready, I'll begin.* | *Why is everyone so excited about this tax cut?*

the lot /ðə ˈlɒt‖-ˈlɑːt/ [n singular] British informal all the things in a group or set, considered together: *I left* *my purse with my cheque book and car keys on the kitchen table and thieves broke in and stole the lot.* | *Janine bought four cream cakes, but her friends didn't turn up for dinner so she ate the lot herself.*

every /ˈevri/ [determiner] all – used only with singular nouns: *Every room in the house was painted white.* | *She bought presents for every member of her family.* | **every single** (=use this to emphasize that you really mean everyone or everything, especially when this is surprising) *It rained every single day of our vacation.* | **every single one/every last one** *The police questioned every single one of the passengers on the plane.*

each /iːtʃ/ [determiner/pron] all – use this to emphasize that you mean every separate person or thing in a group: *She had a ring on each finger of her right hand.* | *They read through each job application very carefully.* | *The president shook hands with each member of the team.* | **+ of** *We will consider each of these questions in turn.* | *She gave each of them a plate of food.* | **each one** *George and Elizabeth had visited 15 apartments and had found something wrong with each one.* | **in/for/to etc each** *She dug several tiny holes in the soil, planting a seed in each.* | **we/they/us etc each** *My brother and I each have our own room.* | *She gave us each a pen and a piece of paper.*

without exception /wɪðˌaʊt ɪkˈsepʃən/ [adv] formal use this to say that something is true of every single one of the people or things in a large group: *Every department in this city, without exception, has experienced cutbacks.* | **almost without exception** *Economists agreed on the President's proposal, almost without exception.*

the works /ðə ˈwɜʳks/ spoken informal everything in a group of similar things or all the things that are needed for a particular activity: *'What would you like on your hotdog – mustard, ketchup, relish?' 'Give me the works.'* | *The school needs new computers, calculators, chairs, cooking utensils ... basically, the works.*

the whole enchilada/shebang ALSO **the whole nine yards** /ðə ˌhəʊl ˌentʃəˈlɑːdə, ʃəˈbæŋ, ðə ˌhəʊl naɪn ˈjɑːʳdz / American spoken informal everything that you could possibly want, or expect to have: *He bought the computer, the printer, and the modem – the whole shebang.* | *It sounds like a great job offer – benefits, retirement, the whole enchilada.* | *The guy in immigration wanted to see the whole nine yards – passport, birth certificate, driver's license.*

2 all of something

- all
- whole
- entire
- every (last) bit/inch/ounce/drop
- from start to finish
- lock, stock, and barrel

all /ɔːl/ [predeterminer/quantifier] **all** of something – used especially with uncountable nouns **all the/this/that/my etc** *He spends all his money on beer and cigarettes.* | *I've seen all her movies.* | *Did you eat all that bread?* | **all of the/this/that/my etc** *I enjoyed the book although I didn't understand all of it.* | **it all** *Where's my change? You didn't spend it all, did you?* | **all day/week/year etc** (=the whole of a period of time) *I spent all day cleaning the house.*

whole /həʊl/ [adj only before noun] all of something that is large, long, or has a lot of parts, for example a large area of land, a long period of time, or a large group of people: *I didn't see her again for a whole year.* | *'I want the whole area searched!' said the chief of police.* | *She was so frightened, her whole body was shaking.* | *Nora had spent her whole life trying to find happiness.* | **the whole of sth** (=all of a particular thing, time, or place) *She spent the whole of the journey complaining about her boyfriend.* | *The Romans conquered almost the whole of Western Europe.*

entire /ɪnˈtaɪəʳ/ [adj only before noun] all of something – use this especially to show that you are annoyed or surprised by this: *I wasted an entire day waiting at the airport.* | *We realized that our entire conversation had been recorded.* | *This function of the word processor allows you to correct the entire document before printing.*

every (last) bit/inch/ounce/drop /ˌevri (lɑːst‖læst) ˈbɪt, ˈɪntʃ, ˈaʊns, ˈdrɒp‖ˈdrɑːp/ [quantifier] the whole of something – use this to emphasize that someone uses all of something, or that something covers all of an area: *Every inch of my niece's wall is covered with posters of pop groups.* | *We had to use every last bit of our savings.* | *I watched him drain every last drop out of the bottle.*

from start to finish /frəm ˌstɑːʳt tə ˈfɪnɪʃ/ [adv] including all of something such as an event, process, or piece of writing: *I've read the book three times from start to finish.* | *The whole case was badly handled from start to finish.*

lock, stock, and barrel /ˌlɒk stɒk ənd ˈbærəl‖ˌlɑːk stɑːk-/ spoken including every part of something – use this about someone moving, buying or selling all of something: *He moved the whole company, lock, stock, and barrel, to Mexico.* | *The Knolls have owned the town lock, stock, and barrel for 15 years.*

3 affecting or including all of something

- total/complete
- blanket
- overall
- global
- all-embracing

total/complete /ˈtəʊtl, kəmˈpliːt/ [adj only before noun] affecting everything or every part of a situation: *They want a total ban on cigarette advertising.* | *My parents had complete control over my life.* | *The satellite TV station is providing total coverage of the Olympic Games.*

blanket /ˈblæŋkət/ [adj only before noun] **blanket decision/statement/term etc** one that affects every part of a situation: *A blanket requirement was announced by education officials – all schools had to cut their budgets by 25%.* | *Dementia is a blanket term for various types of psychiatric disorder.*

overall /ˈəʊvərɔːl/ [adj only before noun] including or involving all or almost all the parts of a situation: *Even though some of the details are badly done, the overall effect of the painting is very dramatic.* | *His attitude towards his job seemed consistent with his overall approach to life.* | *Conference members agreed on an overall approach to drug abuse that focuses on prevention, treatment, and rehabilitation.* —**overall** /ˌəʊvərˈɔːl/ [adv] *One or two products didn't do so well, but overall we've had a highly successful year.*

global /ˈgləʊbəl/ [adj usually before noun] involving all possible parts of an idea or system: *We've done a global study on the company's weaknesses.* | *Simon & Schuster said it no longer wanted the smaller company because it did not fit into its global strategy.*

all-embracing /ˌɔːl ɪmˈbreɪsɪŋ◂/ [adj usually before noun] **all-embracing concept/statement/term etc**

(=one in which all features of a situation have been thought of and included) *The prison governor now has all-embracing powers to deal with any situation in the way he thinks fit.* | *Physicists are searching for one all-embracing theory that covers matter, energy, radiation, and gravity.*

almost

RELATED WORDS

▸ *see also* **most**

1 almost a number, time, or amount

- ▸ almost/nearly
- ▸ not quite
- ▸ close to
- ▸ approaching/nearing
- ▸ getting on for
- ▸ be pushing 40/50 etc

almost/nearly /'ɔːlməʊst, 'nɪəʳli/ [adv] use this to say that something is a little less than a number or amount, or a little before a particular time. **Almost** and **nearly** have the same meaning, but **almost** is much more common than **nearly** in American English. In British English both words are common: *I've been a teacher for nearly 10 years now.* | *We had money and almost $1000 in traveler's checks.* | *John is three years old and Sally is almost six.* | **very nearly** *It's very nearly time to go home.*

not quite /nɒt 'kwaɪt/ [adv] use this when you want to emphasize that something is a little less than a number or amount, or a little before a particular time: *'Is he 60?' 'Not quite!'* | *It's not quite time to go yet.*

close to ALSO **close on** British /'kləʊs tuː, 'kləʊs ɒn/ [adv] almost a particular number, amount, especially a surprisingly large one, or almost a particular time, especially a very late time: *The government spends close to $100 billion a year on education.* | *There must be close to a hundred people in the hall.* | *We drove close on 500 miles Saturday.* | *It was close on midnight by the time they got home.*

approaching/nearing /ə'prəʊtʃɪŋ, 'nɪərɪŋ/ [adv] almost a particular number, amount, time etc, and still increasing or getting nearer to that number, amount, time etc: *In the North East, the unemployment rate is now nearing 20 percent.* | **be fast approaching** (=very nearly a particular time) *By now the winter was fast approaching, and further travel would soon be inadvisable.*

getting on for /ˌgetɪŋ 'ɒn fɔːʳ/ British informal to be almost a particular time, age, or period of time **it's getting on for sth** *It's getting on for 10 years since we last saw each other.* | *It must be getting on for lunch time. I'm starving.* | **sb is getting on for 40, 50 etc** (=use this when guessing an older person's age) *'How old's Diane?' 'She must be getting on for 50.'*

be pushing 40/50 etc /biː ˌpʊʃɪŋ 'fɔːʳti / [v phrase] informal to be almost forty, fifty etc – use this when you are guessing an older person's age: *Burt's probably pushing 50 by now.*

2 almost all

- ▸ almost/nearly
- ▸ practically/virtually
- ▸ just about/more or less/pretty much

almost/nearly /'ɔːlməʊst, 'nɪəʳli/ [adv] **almost all/every/everything/everyone** *Almost all the wine had been drunk.* | *The burglars took nearly everything in the house that was of any value.* | *Almost everyone in the office has had the flu this year.*

practically/virtually /'præktɪkli, 'vɜːʳtʃuəli/ [adv] **practically all/everything/everyone etc** very nearly all: *The frost killed practically every plant in the garden.* | *Virtually everyone had gone home.*

just about/more or less/pretty much /ˌdʒʌst ə'baʊt, ˌmɔːr əʳ 'les, 'prɪti mʌtʃ/ [adv] especially spoken **just about all/everything/everyone etc** very nearly all – use this when saying that the difference is not important: *I've packed pretty much everything I need for the trip.* | *It rains more or less every day here in November.* | *Sonya knew more or less everyone at the party.* | *She's travelled in just about every country in Europe.* | *The second-hand shop on the corner sells just about anything.*

3 when something is almost true

- ▸ almost/nearly
- ▸ not quite
- ▸ practically/virtually
- ▸ more or less/just about/pretty much
- ▸ be close

almost/nearly /'ɔːlməʊst, 'nɪəʳli/ *His hair was almost white.* | *The moon was almost full that night.* | *Persuading Paul to change his mind is nearly impossible.*

not quite /nɒt 'kwaɪt/ [adv] not completely, but almost – use this to say that something is not true, but it is almost true: *That's a good answer but it's not quite correct.* | *It's not quite red, it's more like a maroon color.* | *The orbits of the planets are almost circular, but not quite.*

practically/virtually /'præktɪkli, 'vɜːʳtʃuəli/ [adv] very nearly: *The cupboard was practically empty.* | *Carbon fibre tennis racquets are virtually unbreakable.* | *She looks practically the same as his last girlfriend.*

more or less/just about/pretty much /ˌmɔːr əʳ 'les, ˌdʒʌst ə'baʊt, 'prɪti mʌtʃ/ [adv] especially spoken very nearly – use this when saying that the difference is not important: *All the rooms are more or less the same size.* | *His jacket was pretty much the same colour as his trousers.* | *Until the 18th century, the region remained more or less independent.*

be close /biː 'kləʊs/ [v phrase] if a guess at a number, amount etc **is close**, it is almost correct but not exactly right: *'I reckon he's about 65.' 'You're close – he's 67.'*

4 when you have almost done something or something has almost happened

- ▸ almost/nearly
- ▸ just about/more or less/pretty much
- ▸ practically/virtually
- ▸ not quite
- ▸ all but
- ▸ nearing/approaching/close to
- ▸ be on the verge/brink of

almost/nearly /'ɔːlməʊst, 'nɪəʳli/ [adv] *I've almost finished reading the newspaper.* | *It was early 1945, and the war had nearly ended.*

just about/more or less/pretty much /ˌdʒʌst ə'baʊt, ˌmɔːr əʳ 'les, 'prɪti mʌtʃ/ [adv] especially spoken not completely or exactly, but almost – use this when the difference is not important: *Hanson's acting career appears to be pretty much over.* | *I had more or less convinced her that I was telling the truth.*

practically/virtually /ˈpræktɪkli, ˈvɜːʳtʃuəli/ [adv] almost completely: *Communist parties have practically disappeared in Europe.* | *Mexico's rainforest has been virtually destroyed.*

not quite /nɒt ˈkwaɪt/ [adv] not completely, but almost – use this to say that something has not happened, but that it almost has **not quite done/finished etc** *She hasn't quite finished her homework yet.* | *Give me five minutes – I'm not quite ready.*

all but /ˈɔːl bət/ [adv] **all but over/finished/done** very nearly finished or done: *By now the war was all but over.* | *'Can we go home now?' 'Just one moment – I've all but finished my work.'*

nearing/approaching/close to /ˈnɪərɪŋ, əˈprəʊtʃɪŋ, ˈkləʊs tuː/ [adv] almost at or in a particular situation, especially an extreme one: *The police describe the situation as approaching crisis proportions.* | *Dr Dunstable was in a state nearing nervous collapse.* | *I felt close to tears as I read Vera's letter.*

be on the verge/brink of /biː ɒn ðə ˈvɜːʳdʒ, ˈbrɪŋk ɒv/ [v phrase] to be very close to an extremely bad situation: *The two countries are on the brink of war.* | **be on the verge of tears/death/hysteria etc** *Kerry is on the verge of a nervous breakdown.*

5 when something almost happens but does not

- almost/nearly
- come close to/come near to
- come within an inch/inches of
- narrowly
- close shave
- be a near thing/close thing
- that was close

almost/nearly /ˈɔːlməʊst, ˈnɪəʳli/ [adv] *I was laughing so hard I almost fell out of my chair.* | *The terrorists almost succeeded in blowing up the President's limousine.* | **very nearly** *She was very lucky. She very nearly lost her life.*

come close to/come near to /kʌm ˈkləʊs tuː, kʌm ˈnɪəʳ tuː/ [v phrase] to almost do something or almost be in a particular state **come close/near to doing sth** *She was so angry that she came very close to walking out of the meeting.* | *Dad came near to changing his mind about lending me the car.* | **be close/near to sth** *The negotiations were very near to breaking down.*

come within an inch/inches of /ˌkʌm wɪðɪn ən ˈɪntʃ, ˈɪntʃɪ̈z ɒv/ [v phrase] to very nearly do something, especially something dangerous or unpleasant **come within inches of death** *Coulson came within inches of death on a climbing trip in the Himalayas last year.* | **come within an inch of doing sth** *Manchester United came within an inch of losing the game.*

narrowly /ˈnærəʊli/ [adv] **narrowly avoid/miss/escape etc** to avoid something unpleasant or dangerous, although you almost do not avoid it: *Flying into the airport at Lima, we narrowly avoided a collision with another plane.* | *The article says Meyers narrowly escaped arrest in Rome last month.* —**narrow** [adj only before noun] *A woman and child had a very narrow escape* (=they were almost killed) *when their car hit a tree near Hartford last night.*

close shave /ˌkləʊs ˈʃeɪv/ [n C] a situation in which someone is almost killed or injured: *Mike's had two motorcycle accidents, plus a few other pretty close shaves.*

be a near thing/close thing /biː ə ˌnɪəʳ ˈθɪŋ, ˌkləʊs ˈθɪŋ/ [v phrase] British if something that you succeed in doing **is a near thing** or **a close thing** you succeed in doing it, but only at the last moment: *The Labour party won the election, but it was a very near thing.* | *Security forces managed to free the hostages, but it was a very close thing.*

that was close /ˌðæt wəz ˈkləʊs/ spoken say this when something bad very nearly happens but does not, especially when this is the result of good luck: *The guard began to search the pile of leaves where we were hiding, but then got distracted by a noise from the house. 'Phew, that was close!' said John. 'C'mon, let's get out of here!'*

alone

RELATED WORDS

- not married *see* **marry**
- *see also* **only, independent**

1 when there are no other people with you

- alone/on your own/by yourself
- unaccompanied
- solitude

alone/on your own/by yourself /əˈləʊn, ɒn jɔːr ˈəʊn, baɪ jɔːʳˈself/ [adj/adv] if you are alone, on your own, or by yourself, you are in a place and no-one else is there with you: *She was sitting alone on a park bench.* | *I don't really like walking home on my own at night.* | *Do you share the apartment, or do you live by yourself?* | **all alone/on your own/by yourself** (=completely alone) *Wendy was frightened, all alone in that big old house.* | **leave sb alone/on their own/by themselves** *The first time his parents left him alone in the house, he set fire to the kitchen.* | *Mark's not well. I can't go out and leave him on his own.*

unaccompanied /ˌʌnəˈkʌmpənid◂/ [adj/adv] if you go somewhere **unaccompanied,** you go there alone, especially when it is more usual to be with someone else: *Children flying unaccompanied are looked after by the cabin crew.* | *Some parts of town are not safe for an unaccompanied woman.*

solitude /ˈsɒlɪ̈tjuːd‖ˈsɑːlɪ̈tuːd/ [n U] when you are alone, especially when you want to be alone because this gives you time to think, work etc: *I need solitude in order to paint my pictures.* | *Ella loved the quiet solitude of her weekends.* | **in solitude** *He spent his free time in solitude, reading or walking in the hills.*

2 when you do something without help from someone else

- on your own/by yourself
- unaided
- single-handedly/single-handed
- solo
- self-made
- self-starter

on your own/by yourself /ɒn jɔːr ˈəʊn, baɪ jɔːʳˈself/ [adv] if you do something **on your own** or **by yourself**, you do it without anyone helping you: *I managed to fix the car on my own.* | *He's old enough to get dressed by himself, isn't he?* | **all on your own/ all by yourself** (=use this when it is surprising that someone has done something without anyone's help) *How did you manage to prepare so much food all by yourself?* | **you're on your own** (=use this to tell someone that you will not help them) spoken *I can get an application for you, but after that you're on your own.*

unaided /ʌnˈeɪdɪ̈d/ [adv] if you do something difficult **unaided** you do it without the help of anyone or anything: *After his illness he was unable to walk unaided.* | *With no one else in the office I had to deal with the problem unaided.*

single-handedly/single-handed /ˌsɪŋgəl ˈhændɪ̈dli, ˌsɪŋgəl ˈhændɪ̈d/ [adv] if you do something very difficult or very impressive **single-handedly** or **single-handed**, you succeed in doing it without the help of anyone else: *In 1992, he rowed across the Atlantic single-handed.* | **almost single-handedly/single-handed** *Sanger almost single-handedly founded the birth control movement in the early 1900s.*

solo /ˈsəʊləʊ/ [adv] if you do something **solo**, especially a sports or musical activity, you do it alone: *By the end of the course, all students will fly solo.* | **go solo** (=start doing something on your own instead of in a group) *John played with the band for five years before going solo.* —**solo** [adj usually before noun] *Albert wants to take a solo sailing trip around the world.*

self-made /ˌself ˈmeɪd◂/ [adj usually before noun] someone who started without much money but has become rich and successful simply through their own efforts and work **self-made man/businesswoman/millionaire etc** *C.J. Walker became one of black America's first self-made millionaires.*

self-starter /ˌself ˈstɑːʳtəʳ/ [n C] someone who is able to do things on their own without being told what to do by other people, especially in their job: *We're looking for creative self-starters with at least three years' experience.*

3 someone who spends a lot of time alone

- solitary
- loner
- recluse
- prefer your own company

solitary /ˈsɒlɪ̈təri‖ˈsɑːlɪ̈teri/ [adj] a **solitary** person spends a lot of time alone, especially because they like being alone: *She was a very solitary woman who didn't make friends easily.* | *Ed enjoys the solitary life of a rancher.*

loner /ˈləʊnəʳ/ [n C] someone who prefers to do things alone and has few friends: *I had always been a loner, and I hated sharing an apartment when I went to college.* | *Joe is one of our best workers but he's too much of a loner to be a good leader.*

recluse /rɪˈkluːs‖ˈrekluːs/ [n C] someone who lives alone and avoids meeting other people: *Old Mr Grimes was a bad-tempered recluse, rarely seen in the town.* | *If you don't get out more, you're going to turn into a recluse.* —**reclusive** /rɪˈkluːsɪv/ [adj] *The author has grown even more reclusive* (=he avoids meeting people) *in recent years.*

prefer your own company /prɪˌfɜːʳ jɔːr əʊn ˈkʌmpəni/ [v phrase] someone who **prefers their own company** prefers to be alone rather than being with other people: *We asked him to come and eat with us, but he said he preferred his own company.*

4 alone and unhappy

- lonely
- isolated
- alienated

lonely ALSO **lonesome** American /ˈləʊnli, ˈləʊnsəm/ [adj] unhappy because of being alone or without friends: *Tammy felt very lonely when she first arrived in New York.* | *Our neighbor George is a very lonely man.* | *I get so lonesome here with no-one to talk to.* —**loneliness** [n U] the feeling you have when you are lonely: *Many old people complain of loneliness.*

isolated /ˈaɪsəleɪtɪ̈d/ [adj] feeling that there is no one you can talk to or have as a friend, because your situation makes it difficult for you to meet people: *Young, single parents often feel isolated and unhappy.* | **+ from** *Children of very rich parents can grow up isolated from the rest of society.* —**isolation** /ˌaɪsəˈleɪʃən/ [n U] when you are alone and unhappy, for example because you have no-one to talk to or no-one to help you **+ of** *At first I couldn't stand the isolation of living in a foreign country.*

alienated /ˈeɪliəneɪtɪ̈d/ [adj] feeling alone and as if you are not wanted or understood by other people: *We're making a special effort to help alienated members feel more part of the group.* | **+ from** *In high school she felt somehow different and alienated from other students.* —**alienation** /ˌeɪliəˈneɪʃən/ [n U] **+ from** *Ray spoke of his daughter's growing alienation from the Church.*

5 to feel lonely because someone that you love is not there

- miss
- be pining (away) for

miss /mɪs/ [v T] to feel lonely because someone that you like very much is not with you: *When are you coming home? I miss you.* | *It was great living in Prague, but I really missed all my friends.*

be pining (away) for /biː ˌpaɪnɪŋ (əˈweɪ) fɔːʳ/ [phr v T] to feel unhappy because you cannot be with someone you love – often used humorously: *'What's wrong with Dan?' 'I think he's pining for his girlfriend.'*

although

RELATED WORDS

- *see also* **but**

1 when it is surprising that two different things are both true

- although/though
- while
- may be ... but ...

although/though /ɔːlˈðəʊ, ðəʊ/ [conjunction] *I really need some time alone, although I know I'll miss the kids while I'm gone.* | *He won several medals, though he was only 15 years old.* | *You've been here before, though you might not remember because you were pretty little.* | *Although Milan is an industrial city, it still has enormous charm.* | **even though** (=use this when you want to emphasize what you are saying) *We bought tickets to go to France, even though this isn't really the best time of year to go.* | **though old/tired/brief etc** *The marriage, though brief, was a happy one.*

while ALSO **whilst** /waɪl, waɪlst/ British formal [conjunction] use this to introduce a statement that makes your main statement seem surprising or says something different from it: *While I like Carter personally, I don't think what he's doing is right.* | *Whilst a Rolls Royce is a very nice car, it is extremely expensive to maintain.* | *While six percent of ordinary homes were damaged in the earthquake, only three percent of mobile homes were damaged.*

may be ... but ... /'meɪ biː ... bət .../ use this when you are telling someone that although what they have said may be true, something else that seems very different is a fact: *He may be intelligent but he has no common sense.* | *Bechler may be behind some of the problems, but he is not the only person responsible.*

2 when a particular fact does not prevent something from happening

- although/though
- in spite of/despite

although/though /ɔːl'ðəʊ, ðəʊ/ [conjunction] *Although I missed my train, I still arrived at work on time.* | *Although we are a small company, we produce over 10,000 cars a year.* | **even though** (=use this when you want to emphasize what you are saying) *She always buys us expensive presents, even though she can't really afford them.*

in spite of/despite /ɪn 'spaɪt ɒv, dɪ'spaɪt/ [prep] even though something happens or is true, especially something bad: *In spite of everything, I still enjoyed the trip.* | *He wore a black leather jacket, despite the heat.* | *The stock price has remained strong, in spite of the problems the company is having.* | *In spite of the language difficulty, we soon became friends.* | *Despite my misgivings, I took the job.* | **despite yourself** (=despite efforts to behave or feel differently) *At the end of the movie, Liz began to cry despite herself.* | **in spite of the fact that/despite the fact that** *Many poor people give quite a bit of money to charities, despite the fact that they do not have that much themselves.*

always

RELATED WORDS

opposite: **never**

- too often, in a way that is annoying *see* **often (2)**
- *see also* **continue, usually, sometimes**

WHAT'S HERE

• **always/every time**	see **1**
• **always/all the time**	see **2 to 3**
• **always/forever**	see **4 to 6**

always/every time

1 when someone always does something or something always happens

- always
- every time
- whenever
- every
- without fail

always /'ɔːlwɨz, -weɪz/ [adv] *I always say my prayers before I go to bed.* | *She was always ready to listen to my problems.* | *Why do you always blame me for everything?* | *He always has sandwiches for his lunch.* | *My dad's always telling me I should get my hair cut.* | **almost always** *My brother is almost always late.*

every time /ˌevri 'taɪm/ [adv/conjunction] on every occasion – use this to say that when one thing happens, something else always happens: *My neck hurts every time I turn my head.* | *Every time we talk about money, we get into an argument.* | *It seems like every time I play basketball, I get hurt.*

whenever /wen'evəʳ/ [conjunction] every time that something happens: *He calls Nancy whenever he's in town.* | *Feel free to use my computer whenever you need to.* | **whenever possible** (=whenever you can) *I try to use public transport whenever possible.*

every /'evri/ [determiner] **every day/week/Monday etc** use this to say that something happens regularly on each day, each week etc: *Thousands of tourists visit Spain every year.* | *We go to the movies almost every Saturday night.* | *Every year on her birthday, Jackie throws a big party at the Vineyard House.*

without fail /wɪðˌaʊt 'feɪl/ [adv] **every day/week/year etc without fail** if you do something **without fail** you always do it: *My mother goes to church every week without fail.* | *You must take the medication every day without fail.*

always/all the time

2 happening all the time, without stopping or changing

- always
- all the time
- the whole time
- at all times
- constantly
- permanently
- perennial
- unfailing
- incessant
- day in, day out
- morning, noon, and night
- 24/7

always /'ɔːlwɨz, -weɪz/ [adv] all the time without changing: *The temperature of the lake is always below fifty-five degrees.* | *Ron is always in a bad mood in the morning.* | *Our upstairs neighbor always keeps to himself. We hardly know him at all.*

all the time /ˌɔːl ðə 'taɪm/ [adv] *Gabrielle talks about her kids all the time.* | *The couple upstairs argue all the time.* | *I don't have to wear my glasses all the time – just for reading.*

the whole time /ðə ˌhəʊl 'taɪm/ [adv] all the time while something is happening – use this about something annoying or surprising: *He talked about himself the whole time I was with him.* | *We realized that Duncan had been standing there the whole time.*

at all times /ət ˌɔːl 'taɪmz/ [adv] all the time – used especially in official notices and rules: *Carry your passport with you at all times.* | *Keep your hotel door locked at all times.*

constantly /'kɒnstəntli‖'kɑːn-/ [adv] all the time, continuously: *Shelly constantly tries to impress her boss.* | *She constantly criticizes my cooking.* —**constant** [adj] *The patient must be kept under constant supervision.* | *The rains are constant in winter.*

permanently /'pɜːʳmənəntli/ [adv] all the time and never likely to change: *Hardy was permanently banned from professional figure skating.* | *It's such a dangerous neighborhood that the windows of some stores are permanently barricaded.* —**permanent** [adj] *The country seems to be in a permanent state of crisis.*

perennial /pə'reniəl/ [adj only before noun] **perennial problem/concern/struggle etc** one which people are concerned with all the time, and have been concerned with for a long time: *High unemployment rates are a perennial problem in several European* *countries.* | *Severe and unpredictable weather is a perennial danger for mountain climbers.*

unfailing /ʌnˈfeɪlɪŋ/ [adj only before noun] **unfailing support/loyalty/good humour etc** support, loyalty etc that you can depend on because it never changes or grows weaker even when there is trouble or difficulty: *I'd like to thank you all for your unfailing love and support.* | *Peter's unfailing humour made him popular with his fellow workers.*

incessant /ɪnˈsesənt/ happening or done all the time without stopping, in a way that is very annoying: *Julia became irritated by the child's incessant talking.* | *The incessant buzz of conversation filled the student cafeteria.* —**incessantly** [adv] *Michael smokes incessantly.*

day in, day out /deɪ ˌɪn, deɪ ˈaʊt/ every day for a long time – use this especially to say that someone keeps doing something difficult, tiring, or boring for a long time, or that something keeps happening for a long time: *Henry did the same thing, day in and day out, for over thirty years.* | *Investigators are working day in, day out to determine the cause of the crash.*

morning, noon, and night /ˌmɔːnɪŋ ˌnuːn ən ˈnaɪt/ spoken said in order to emphasize that something happens all the time, especially something that is annoying: *It seems like we've been going to meetings morning, noon, and night lately.*

24/7 /ˌtwentifɔːʳ ˈsevən/ [adv] informal all the time without stopping: *We're here to help you 24/7.* | *The deadline is next week, so everyone in the office is working 24/7.*

3 during the whole of an event or period of time

- all the time
- throughout/all through
- all day/night/summer etc long
- all along
- from start to finish/from beginning to end

all the time /ˌɔːl ðə ˈtaɪm/ [adv] **all the time (that)** *I couldn't really enjoy my holiday because I was sick all the time I was there.* | *All the time I was talking to him he just sat and stared at the television.*

throughout/all through /θruːˈaʊt, ˈɔːl θruː/ [prep] during all of a particular period of time, especially when this is a long time: *Lester was sickly all through his childhood.* | *Yvonne lived in Switzerland throughout the war.*

all day/night/summer etc long /ˌɔːl deɪ ˈlɒŋ ‖-ˈlɔːŋ/ [adv] during all of the day, night, summer etc: *It often rains here all day long.* | *The music coming from the apartment upstairs kept me awake all night long.*

all along /ɔːl əˈlɒŋ‖-əˈlɔːŋ/ [adv] if a particular situation has existed **all along**, it has existed all the time right from the beginning, although you may not have known about it: *I spent over an hour looking for my keys, and they were in my purse all along.* | **be right all along** *He realized that she'd been right all along.*

from start to finish/from beginning to end /frəm ˌstɑːʳt tə ˈfɪnɪʃ, frəm bɪˌgɪnɪŋ tʊ ˈend/ [adv] if an event or something that you do is good, bad etc **from start to finish**, it is like that from the time it begins until it ends: *It was an awful day at work – problems from start to finish.* | *The whole thing was a disaster from beginning to end.*

always/forever

4 when something will always happen or always continue

- always
- forever
- permanently
- for ever and ever
- for good
- for keeps
- for all time
- for life
- to/until your dying day

always /ˈɔːlwɨz, -weɪz/ [adv] *I'll always remember the day we first met.* | *She said she would always love him.*

forever /fərˈevəʳ/ [adv] if something lasts or continues **forever**, it remains or continues for all future time: *I'd like to stay here forever.* | *The memory of that awful day is forever etched in my mind.*

permanently /ˈpɜːʳmənəntli/ [adv] a word meaning forever, for a very long time, or for the rest of your life – use this especially to talk about changes that you expect to last forever: *The accident has left Hanson permanently disabled.* | *Thirteen students were permanently expelled from the school.*

for ever and ever /fər ˌevər ənd ˈevəʳ/ [adv] for all future time – used especially by children or in children's stories when someone feels extremely happy: *It was a beautiful day, and Ellie wanted it to go on for ever and ever.*

for good /fəʳ ˈgʊd/ [adv] if someone leaves, comes back etc **for good**, they leave or come back permanently: *The injury may keep him out of football for good.* | *I'd like to stay in Colorado for good.*

for keeps /fəʳ ˈkiːps/ [adv] spoken informal if you have something **for keeps**, you have it forever: *He's given it to me for keeps.*

for all time /fər ˌɔːl ˈtaɪm/ [adv] formal forever, used especially when saying that something will last or be remembered forever because it is very good, special etc: *The actions of those who died in the Great War will be remembered for all time.*

for life /fəʳ ˈlaɪf/ [adv] for the rest of your life: *There's no such thing as a job for life any more.* | **scarred/maimed/crippled/blind etc for life** *The abuse left him scarred for life.*

to/until your dying day /tuː, ənˌtɪl jɔːʳ ˌdaɪ-ɪŋ ˈdeɪ/ [adv] for the rest of your life – used especially in stories, plays etc: *You will regret this until your dying day.* | *I will remember your kindness to my dying day.*

5 when something has always happened or always been true

- always
- for as long as you can remember
- since/from time immemorial

always /ˈɔːlwɨz, -weɪz/ [adv] *I've always admired Sean Connery.* | *Sylvia has always hated her nose.*

for as long as you can remember /fər əz ˌlɒŋ əz juː kən rɪˈmembəʳ‖-ˌlɔːŋ-/ [adv] during all the time that you can remember: *The Watsons have lived on our street for as long as I can remember.* | *The recipe is one that my mom has been making for as long as I can remember.*

since/from time immemorial /sɪns, frəm ˌtaɪm ˌɪmɨˈmɔːriəl/ use this to emphasize that something has always happened or someone has always done something: *The Agaw people have inhabited that region since time immemorial.*

6 remaining or continuing forever

- permanent
- eternal
- everlasting
- perpetual
- never-ending
- infinite

permanent /ˈpɜːʳmənənt/ [adj] continuing forever, for a very long time, or for the rest of your life: *The car accident has caused permanent damage to her eyesight.* | *Most police departments keep a permanent record of all violent crimes committed in their area.*

eternal /ɪˈtɜːʳnl/ [adj] **eternal life/youth/salvation etc** life etc which continues forever: *The possibility of eternal life is a principal belief of many religions.* | *the search for eternal youth* — **eternally** [adv] *If you can do this for me I will be eternally grateful.*

everlasting /ˌevəʳˈlɑːstɪŋ◂‖-ˈlæ-/ [adj] a word used especially in religious contexts, meaning continuing forever: *life everlasting* | *the Buddhist's search for everlasting peace*

perpetual /pəʳˈpetʃuəl/ [adj only before noun] a state or feeling that is **perpetual** seems to be there all the time and is very annoying, upsetting, worrying etc: *For many working mothers, balancing the demands of children and job is a perpetual challenge.* | *Her husband's perpetual jealousy strongly affected their marriage.*

never-ending /ˌnevər ˈendɪŋ◂/ [adj] having no end, or continuing so long that you think it will never end: *To Miguel, the boredom of married life seemed never-ending.* | *Keeping the house neat and clean is a never-ending battle.*

infinite /ˈɪnfənət/ [adj] continuing forever and never ending or stopping: *It's difficult to really imagine an infinite universe.* | *She was a woman of seemingly infinite patience.*

ambitious

determined to be successful in your life or job

RELATED WORDS

- *see also* **succeed/successful, determined, want, no matter what/how much etc**

- ambitious
- ambition
- power-hungry/power-mad
- go-getter
- competitive

ambitious /æmˈbɪʃəs/ [adj] determined to be successful and to become rich, powerful, or famous: *Hutchings, like many ambitious young lawyers, became interested in politics.* | *The main candidate for the position is Robert Lutz, age 59, an ambitious former Ford Motor Co. executive.* | *Women have to be more ambitious than men if they want to get anywhere in the business world.*

ambition /æmˈbɪʃən/ [n U] determination to be successful and to become rich, powerful, or famous: *Eric wasn't particularly intelligent but he had plenty of ambition.* | *'Your problem,' said Arthur, 'is that you have no ambition.'*

power-hungry/power-mad /ˈpaʊəʳ ˌhʌŋgri, ˈpaʊəʳ ˌmæd/ [adj] very determined to get power and control in business or politics even if you harm other people by doing this: *Most politicians are power-hungry people who serve only themselves.* | *The article described the company's vice-president, Victor Rowan, as deceitful and power-hungry.*

go-getter /ˌgəʊ ˈgetəʳ/ [n singular] informal someone who is very ambitious and hard-working, in a way that you admire: *George was a go-getter; he wasn't afraid to take a risk.* | **sb's a real go-getter** *You can't help admiring Debbie – she's a real go-getter.*

competitive /kəmˈpetətɪv/ [adj] determined to be more successful than other people in work, sport etc: *Beth's very competitive, even with her friends.* | **fiercely/intensely competitive** (=very competitive) *Fiercely competitive at all times, Ravi is a difficult man to work with.*

amount

RELATED WORDS

- an amount of food *see* **food**
- an amount of a drug or medicine *see* **drug**
- an amount of something that an organization or country has and is available to be used *see* **available/not available**
- how often something happens *see* **often**
- when an amount reaches a particular level *see* **reach (2)**
- *see also* **number, count/calculate, total, level, increase, reduce**

1 an amount of something such as money, time, or a substance

- amount
- how much
- quantity
- volume
- level
- sum
- 100 pounds' worth/ten dollars' worth etc

amount /əˈmaʊnt/ [n C] **the amount of sth** *The amount of tax you pay depends on how much you earn.* | *Try to reduce the amount of fat in your diet.* | *The amount of calories a person needs each day is determined by the type of work they do.* | **a small/tiny amount** *The water here contains small amounts of calcium and other minerals.* | **a large/enormous/considerable amount** *He knows an enormous amount about Italian paintings.*

how much /ˌhaʊ ˈmʌtʃ/ use this to ask or talk about the size of an amount of something: *How much did your jeans cost?* | *I'll get you some paint if you tell me how much you need.* | **how much money/time/food etc** *How much money do I owe you?* | *Do you realize how much trouble you caused?* | *How much nitrogen is there in the air?* | **+ of** *You received $50,000. How much of that money is still in your bank account?*

quantity /ˈkwɒntəti‖ˈkwɑːn-/ [n C] use this, especially in written descriptions or instructions, to talk about amounts of food, liquid, or other substances that can be measured **+ of** *Make sure that you add the correct quantity of water.* | *Use equal quantities of flour and butter.* | **a large/small/enormous etc quantity** *An enormous quantity of chemical waste has been dumped in the river.* | **in large/small quantities** *Expensive spices, like saffron, are only produced in small quantities.*

volume /ˈvɒljuːm‖ˈvɑːljəm/ [n singular] use this to talk about the total amount of something such as business activity or traffic, especially when it is large or increasing **the volume of trade/sales/traffic/business** *The volume of traffic on our roads has* *risen by 50% in the past three years.* | *After 1998, there was a rapid fall in the volume of trade.*

level /ˈlevəl/ [n C] use this to talk about the exact amount of something at one time, even though this amount may go up or go down at other times **the level of sth** *a device that measures the level of carbon monoxide in the air* | **a high/low level** *The company continues to enjoy a high level of sales.* | *People who suffer heart attacks tend to have a high level of cholesterol in the blood.*

sum /sʌm/ [n C] an amount of money **a large/enormous sum** *The apartment cost over $25,000, which was an enormous sum in those days.* | **a sum of money** *She left a small sum of money to her two granddaughters.* | *A purse containing a small sum of money was found at Guildhall Square on March 20.* | **a lump sum** (=an amount of money given in a single payment) *Instead of paying him a regular pension, they gave him a lump sum when he retired.*

100 pounds' worth/ten dollars' worth etc /ə ˌhʌndrɨ̆d ˈpaʊndz wɜːʳθ/ an amount of something that is worth £100, $10 etc **+ of** *Over £10 million worth of heroin was seized in the raid.* | *The company owns millions of dollars' worth of real estate in downtown Tokyo.*

2 a number of people or things

- number
- how many
- quantity

number /ˈnʌmbəʳ/ [n singular with singular or plural verb in British English] **the number of** *We need to know the number of students in each class.* | *By next year, the number of homes with either cable or satellite television is expected to be just over 10 million.* | *The number of working days lost through strikes has continued to rise.* | **a large/small number** *A large number of reporters had gathered outside the house.* | *Thousands of men apply to join the Marines but only a small number are accepted.*

how many /ˌhaʊ ˈmeni/ use this to talk about or ask about the number of people or things that there are **how many people/things/years etc** *How many cars do you have?* | *He wouldn't tell us how many girlfriends he'd had.* | **+ of** *How many of you can swim?* | *It is not known how many of the people arrested in last Saturday's protests have been freed.*

quantity /ˈkwɒntɨ̆ti‖ˈkwɑːn-/ [n C] a number of things – used especially in written reports about stolen or illegal goods **a quantity of** *A quantity of cocaine was found in Larsson's apartment.* | **a large/small quantity** *Police are investigating a burglary in which a small quantity of jewellery was stolen.* | *Thieves escaped with a large quantity of cigarettes after breaking into a shop in Cramlington, Northumberland.*

3 an amount that is compared with another amount

- percentage
- proportion
- ratio
- rate
- fraction

percentage /pəʳˈsentɪdʒ/ [n C usually singular] a number or amount that is calculated as part of a total of 100, and is shown using a % sign **+ of** *The percentage of women students at the university has increased steadily.* | **a high/large percentage** *Most of the coffee we produce is for export – a high percentage goes to the US.* | *A high percentage of businesses fail because of the collapse of a major customer or supplier.* | **a low/small percentage** *The disease is serious, and in a small percentage of cases it can be fatal.* | *The writer only receives a small percentage of the profits from each book sold.*

proportion /prəˈpɔːʳʃən/ [n C usually singular] the number or amount of something, compared with the whole number or amount that exists **+ of** *The new law is intended to reduce the proportion of road accidents caused by drunk drivers.* | *a program to increase the proportion of women and black people in the police service* | **proportion of sth to sth** *What is the proportion of men to women in your office?* | **a high/low/large/small proportion** *A high proportion of the products tested were found to contain harmful chemicals.*

ratio /ˈreɪʃiəʊ‖ˈreɪʃəʊ/ [n C usually singular] a set of numbers, such as '20:1' or '5:1', that shows how much larger one quantity is than another **ratio of sth to sth** *a school where the ratio of students to teachers is about 5:1*

rate /reɪt/ [n C] a measurement showing the number of times that something happens during a particular period or the number of examples of something within a certain period: *Refugees were crossing the border at the rate of 1000 a day.* | **success/failure rate** *Penicillin has a high success rate in treating bacterial infections.*

fraction /ˈfrækʃən/ [n singular] a very small part of an amount or number **a (small, tiny etc) fraction of sth** *The disease affects only a tiny fraction of the population.* | **at a fraction of the cost** *Computers can now do the same job at a fraction of the cost.* | **in a fraction of the time** *A microwave oven cooks food in a fraction of the time required by a normal oven.*

4 a measured amount of goods

- quota
- yield

quota /ˈkwəʊtə/ [n C] an official limit on the amount of something that can be produced, sold, brought into a country etc: *An agreement on fishing quotas was reached by EU ministers yesterday.* | *a meeting of OPEC countries to discuss production quotas* | **impose a quota on/for sth** *Several countries imposed quotas on imports of Japanese cars.*

yield /jiːld/ [n C] the amount of something that is produced, especially crops: *a 22% fall in this year's cotton yield*

5 an amount that is carried in something

- load
- -ful

load /ləʊd/ [n C] the amount or number of things or people that can be carried in a vehicle **+ of** *The first load of supplies will be arriving at the camp next week.* | *Evans was jailed for hijacking a lorry with a £30,000 load of spirits, tobacco and groceries.* | **carload/vanload/truckload etc** *a truckload of sheep* | *a vanload of furniture* | *A carload of American tourists pulled up in the street beside him and asked for directions.*

-ful /fʊl/ [suffix] **spoonful/bagful etc** the amount that is contained in a spoon, bag etc: *We bought three bagfuls of coal.* | *She added a spoonful of olive oil to the boiling water, then threw in the pasta.*

6 the amount of something bad such as crime, poverty etc

- amount
- level
- rate
- extent
- incidence

amount /əˈmaʊnt/ [n singular] use this when you are talking generally about how often something bad happens **+ of** *There is growing alarm at the amount of violence on the streets of our city.* | *The amount of car crime seems to be on the increase.*

level /ˈlevəl/ [n C] use this to talk about the exact amount of a particular problem at one time, even though this amount may go up or down at other times: *Pollution levels in some rivers are already dangerous.* | **the level of sth** *the rising level of crime in the inner cities*

rate /reɪt/ [n C] use this to talk about the number of times something happens within a certain period of time, especially when talking about crime, social problems etc **the crime/divorce/suicide/murder etc rate** *Nassau now has the third highest crime rate in the world.* | *There is a 40% unemployment rate in the region.*

extent /ɪkˈstent/ [n singular] use this to talk about how large and how serious a problem is **the extent of sth** *Government inspectors will assess the extent of the damage.* | *Considering the extent of his injuries, he's lucky to be alive.* | **to such an extent** (=to such a large degree) *Discontent had grown to such an extent that the government had to withdraw the new tax.* | **to what extent** *To what extent were politicians responsible for the high unemployment which Britain experienced between the wars?*

incidence /ˈɪnsədəns/ [n singular] formal use this to talk about the number of times something bad happens, for example how many people have a particular illness, or how many crimes or accidents there are **the incidence of sth** *Since the early 1970s the incidence of breast cancer has increased by about 1% per year.* | **high/low incidence** *Poverty is one of the reasons for the high incidence of crime in this district.* | *a neighborhood with a high incidence of drug and alcohol abuse*

and/also

RELATED WORDS

- including something or someone *see* **include/not include (4)**
- *see also* **with/together, add**

1 and/also

- and
- also
- too
- besides
- as well
- in addition (to)

and /ənd, ən, (*strong*) ænd/ [conjunction] use this to join two things, actions, ideas etc in one sentence or in one part of a sentence: *We had coffee and hot buttered rolls.* | *Come in and sit down.* | *Maria finally turned around and confronted the man.* | *'We've got about ten friends coming to the party.' 'And half of your family.'* | *This is a flexible and user-friendly system suitable for beginners and advanced users alike.*

also /ˈɔːlsəʊ/ [adv] use this when you are adding another fact about someone or something, or when mentioning another person or thing: *François speaks perfect English. He also speaks German and Italian.* | *Sugar is bad for your teeth. It can also contribute to heart disease.* | *Chris came from England. Martin also.* | **not only .... but also** *Meissner was not only commander of the army but also a close friend of the President.*

too /tuː/ [adv] use this when you are adding another fact about someone or something. **Too** is usually used at the end of a sentence: *Gary and Martha and the kids are coming to visit. They're bringing grandmother, too.* | *It's fast and comfortable. It's economical, too.*

besides /bɪˈsaɪdz/ [prep/adv] in addition to what you are mentioning: *Besides being my doctor, he's a really good friend of mine.* | *Martina's got other things to think about besides work.* | *She's bought a fridge, a freezer, a microwave, and lots of other things besides.* | *Besides going to aerobics twice a week, she rides horses on Saturdays.*

as well /əz ˈwel/ [adv] at the same time as something else: *While you're at the store, could you get a few things for me as well?* | *Our vacation was a disaster: not only was the food terrible, the weather was awful as well.* | **as well as** *As well as being a community worker, he's a fully qualified nurse.*

in addition (to) /ɪn əˈdɪʃən (tuː)/ [adv] use this when you are adding a fact that makes an amount of money, work, information etc even larger: *We'll have to pay $800 travel insurance in addition to the air fare.* | *In addition to their normal teaching duties, teachers these days have stacks of paperwork to do.* | *Our survey will produce the essential statistics. In addition, it will provide information about people's shopping habits.*

2 ways of adding something to what you have just said

- what's more
- besides
- by the way/incidentally
- btw
- not to mention
- furthermore/moreover
- on top of
- and another thing

what's more /ˌwɒts ˈmɔːʳ/ [adv] spoken use this to add something, especially something that gives more force to what you have just said: *What's more this stuff is cheap to manufacture so we should make a big profit.* | **and what's more** *The prisoner has a gun, and what's more he's prepared to use it.*

besides /bɪˈsaɪdz/ [adv] spoken use this especially when you are giving another reason for something: *I don't mind picking up your things from the store. Besides, the walk will do me good.* | *Sonya says she couldn't get here through all the snow. Besides, her car's broken down.*

by the way/incidentally /ˌbaɪ ðə ˈweɪ, ˌɪnsəˈdentəli/ [adv] use this when you want to change the subject and talk about something else you have thought of or remembered. **Incidentally** is more formal than **by the way**: *How is she, by the way? I hear she's been ill.* | *I'll meet you at eight o'clock. Oh, by the way, could you ask John to come too?* | *The course is organized by Sheila Dean who, by the way, is head of marketing now.* | *Incidentally, these products can be dangerous if used carelessly.* | *He was offered a raise of 18% which, incidentally, is double what the rest of us got.*

btw [adv] informal an abbreviation for 'by the way', used especially in e-mail messages when you want to add some news at the end of a message: *BTW, I got a message from Andy. He's getting married in June.*

not to mention /ˌnɒt tə ˈmenʃən/ [prep] use this to introduce something that makes the situation more interesting, more surprising, worse etc: *There will be live music and food, not to mention games and prizes for the whole family!* | *Climbers have to carry all their equipment on their backs, not to mention their tents and bedding.* | *Several rare South American mammals escaped from the zoo, not to mention a three-metre-long python.*

furthermore/moreover /ˌfɜːðəˈmɔːʳ‖ˈfɜːrðər-mɔːr, mɔːrˈəʊvəʳ/ [adv] formal use this especially to introduce more information that will help persuade people to agree with what you are saying: *This new equipment will be very expensive to set up. Furthermore, more machines will mean fewer jobs.* | *The drug has powerful side effects. Moreover, it can be addictive.*

on top of /ɒn ˈtɒp ɒv‖-ˈtɑːp-/ [adv] as well as other problems or bad things you have just mentioned: *On top of all this the management has decided to make us come in on Saturdays.* | *... and on top of everything else my TV's broken.*

and another thing /ənd əˈnʌðəʳ θɪŋ/ [adv] spoken use this at the beginning of a sentence to show you are going to add something else to what you have just said, especially when you are complaining about something: *And another thing! Where's the fifty dollars you owe me?*

3 ways of saying 'and others' at the end of a list

- etc
- and so on
- or/and whatever
- and suchlike

etc British **/etc.** American /et ˈsetərə/ an abbreviation for **et cetera** used at the end of a short list to mean 'and others of a similar kind'. When you say **etc** you pronounce it 'et cetera': *Near the exit was a stand selling sandwiches, hot dogs etc.* | *Please bring pens, pencils, rulers etc to the exam.*

and so on /ənd səʊ ˈɒn/ informal used when you expect someone to guess what the other things are: *When you leave, make sure you lock the doors and windows, turn off the heating and so on.* | **and so on and so forth** *Jake does odd jobs around the house – mowing the lawn, cleaning the windows and so on and so forth.*

or/and whatever /ɔːʳ, ənd wɒtˈevəʳ‖-wɑːt-/ informal used when someone is making a choice and can have what they want: *Please help yourselves to tea or coffee or whatever.* | *The canteen isn't bad, you can have a salad, some soup and whatever.* | *If I buy him a gift voucher for his birthday he can get what he likes, a record or whatever.*

and suchlike /ənd ˈsʌtʃlaɪk/ British and other things of a similar kind: *You could spend the day doing the garden, cleaning the windows and suchlike.* | *A fertilizer ideal for trees, bushes and suchlike.*

angry

RELATED WORDS

opposite: —— **calm**

- to talk to someone in an angry way *see* **shout, tell sb off**
- *see also* **disappointed, fed up, upset, violent, insult, offend, revenge, hate**

1 feeling angry

- angry
- mad
- annoyed
- irritated
- cross
- be in a temper
- pissed off
- frustrated
- hacked off/ticked off

angry /ˈæŋgri/ [adj] *My dad gets really angry if anyone keeps him waiting.* | *Stone's new book is sure to make a lot of women angry.* | *Hundreds of angry students gathered to protest the tuition increase.* | *After the programme, the TV station received hundreds of angry phone calls.* | **+ with** *Sue's still very angry with me for forgetting our anniversary.* | **+ about** *My folks were really angry about my grades.* | **+ that** *Mary's angry that we didn't save her any pizza.* | *Local people are angry that they weren't told about plans to expand the airport.* —**angrily** [adv] *Robert slammed the door angrily on his way out.* | *'Shut your mouth!' exclaimed Tom angrily.*

mad /mæd/ [adj not before noun] especially American angry: *Ernie was mad because we woke him up.* | *Don't get mad. It was an accident.* | *Sheila's mad at me because I forgot to feed the cats yesterday.* | *Sally was mad at the children for making so much noise.* | **+ about** *Don seems really mad about something.*

annoyed /əˈnɔɪd/ [adj not before noun] a little angry: *Sandra was very annoyed that I was late.* | *Mike gets annoyed if anyone goes in his room when he's out.* | *Professor Johnson was annoyed when I told her my paper was going to be late.* | **+ with/at** *Meg was annoyed with me because I forgot to stop and buy bread on my way home.* | **+ by/about** *Everyone is annoyed by the constant noise of the construction project.* —**annoyance** [n U] formal *Uncle Ted didn't come to the dinner party, much to my mother's annoyance* (=it made her very annoyed). **in/with annoyance** *Randle looked in annoyance at the flight attendant.* (=he looked at her with an annoyed expression)

irritated /ˈɪrəteɪtəd/ [adj not before noun] a little angry and impatient about something, especially an annoying situation that you think has continued for too long **+ with/by** *Paul was irritated with the children because he was tired.* | **+ at** *The teacher was clearly irritated at having his class interrupted.* | *Margot gets irritated if people leave dirty dishes in the sink.*

cross /krɒs‖krɔːs/ [adj] British a word used especially by children or to children meaning a little angry: *Mum will be cross when she finds out about the broken vase.* | **+ with** *I'm sorry I was cross with you.* —**crossly** [adv] *'Just leave me alone,' said Lucy crossly.*

be in a temper /biː ɪn ə ˈtempəʳ/ [v phrase] British to be very angry for a short time, especially when other people think you have no real reason to be: *Jeff was in a temper this morning, so I left the house as early as possible.* | **be in a bad/foul temper** *Donna's been in a foul temper all day.*

pissed off ALSO **pissed** American /ˌpɪst ˈɒf, pɪst / [adj phrase not before noun] informal an impolite expression meaning angry, especially about something that someone has done: *I don't know why you're so pissed off – I told you I might be late.* | *Darren got really pissed when I told him that.* | **+ with** *Wendy's pissed off with me for not returning her call.* | **+ about** *I'm really pissed off about the schedule changes – it messes everything up.* | **+ at** American *Why are you pissed at him?*

frustrated /frʌˈstreɪtəd‖ˈfrʌstreɪtəd/ [adj] a little

angry and impatient because of an unpleasant or difficult situation that you feel unable to change or control: *Stacy got so frustrated that she stood up and walked out of the room.* | *Frustrated parents were calling the school to complain.* | **+ with** *My boss is frustrated with me for coming in late.*

hacked off British **/ticked off** American /ˌhækt ˈɒf, ˌtɪkt ˈɒf/ [adj phrase not before noun] a little angry about something that annoys you, especially something that happens a lot: *Mick was hacked off when he saw his girlfriend dancing with another guy.* | **+ with** *Lee's ticked off with me for not inviting him to the party.*

2 feeling extremely angry

- furious
- livid
- seething
- incensed
- be on the warpath

furious /ˈfjʊəriəs/ [adj] *Don't tell Jan I read her letter – she'll be furious.* | *I've never been so furious in all my life.* | *A furious clerk chased the children out of the store.* | **+ with** *Gina was furious with him for leaving the baby alone in the house.* | **+ at/about** *Walter came home furious at something his boss had said.* —**furiously** [adv] *'Stop it!' Jesse shouted furiously.*

livid /ˈlɪvɨd/ [adj not before noun] so angry that it is difficult for you to think clearly or speak properly: *'Was she angry when you arrived so late?' 'She was livid!'* | *I know I shouldn't have spoken to Suzanne like that, but I was absolutely livid.*

seething /ˈsiːðɪŋ/ [adj not before noun] especially written extremely angry, but unable or unwilling to show it: *Bobby drove home seething after his terrible humiliation at the party.* | **seething with anger/rage/indignation** *Seething with anger, Polly pushed back her chair and stood up from the table.*

incensed /ɪnˈsenst/ [adj] especially written extremely angry about something someone has done, and ready to react very strongly or violently: *Colonel Monroe became incensed when two of the junior officers did not treat him with respect.* | **+ by/at** *Perry was incensed by the committee's recommendations.*

be on the warpath /biː ɒn ðə ˈwɔːʳpɑːθ‖-pæθ/ [v phrase] informal to be very angry about something and to be planning to criticize and argue with the person you think has caused it: *After two accidents in the same week outside the school, the Parents' Association is on the warpath.*

3 angry for a short time

- be in a bad mood
- be in a huff
- be in one of his/her moods
- get up on the wrong side of the bed

be in a bad mood /biː ɪn ə ˌbæd ˈmuːd/ [v phrase] *I had to wait two hours for the train, which really put me in a bad mood.* | *Why were you in such a bad mood this morning?* | **be in a foul mood** (=be in a very bad mood) *Darnell came home from work in a foul mood.*

be in a huff /biː ɪn ə ˈhʌf/ [v phrase] if someone **is in a huff** they are feeling bad-tempered, especially because someone has just offended, upset, or annoyed them: *Kate is in a huff right now because we wouldn't let her go to the beach with her friends.* | **go off/leave in a huff** (=go away in a huff) *Dad started to give the waiter a hard time and Mom got up and left the table in a huff.*

be in one of his/her moods /biː ɪn ˌwʌn əv hɪz, ˌhɜːʳ ˈmuːdz/ [v phrase] if someone **is in one of his** or **her moods** they are bad-tempered at the moment and you know that they often get bad-tempered for no good reason: *It's no use trying to reason with Karen right now; she's in one of her moods.* | *When Kurt was in one of his moods, he took it out on everyone around him.*

get up on the wrong side of the bed ALSO **get out of bed on the wrong side** British /get ˌʌp ɒn ðə ˌrɒŋ ˌsaɪd əv ðə ˈbed, get ˌaʊt əv ˌbed ɒn ðə ˌrɒŋ ˈsaɪd‖-ˌrɔːŋ-/ [v phrase] spoken you say someone has **got out of bed on the wrong side** when you think they have been behaving in a bad-tempered way all day: *'What's Sarah's problem?' 'I don't know. She must have got up on the wrong side of the bed.'*

4 angry because something is unfair or wrong

- indignant
- be up in arms
- be disgusted
- outraged
- resentful
- be sickened

indignant /ɪnˈdɪgnənt/ [adj] formal *Grandfather's always writing indignant letters to the newspaper.* | **+ at/over** *Eric was indignant at being told he would have to wait two weeks for an appointment.* —**indignantly** [adv] formal *'It's not fair,' the child shouted indignantly.* —**indignation** /ˌɪndɪgˈneɪʃən/ [n U] formal *I certainly understand the public's indignation over the recent tax increase.*

be up in arms /biː ˌʌp ɪn ˈɑːʳmz/ [v phrase] if a group of people **are up in arms**, they are protesting angrily about something that has been done or decided, especially by the government or some other official group: *Pine Valley residents are up in arms about plans to build a prison in the area.*

be disgusted /biː dɪsˈgʌstɨd/ [v phrase] to feel very angry and disappointed because you think that someone's actions are very wrong, dishonest, or immoral: *Many voters are disgusted with the way Congress spends their money.* | *I'm disgusted. How could you be so rude to our guests?* | **+ at/with** *Disgusted with the political corruption in her homeland, Stepanowicz left for good in 1982.*

outraged /ˈaʊtreɪdʒd/ [adj] extremely angry about something wrong, immoral, or unfair, especially something violent: *Thousands of outraged citizens took to the streets to protest against the actions of the police.* | **+ at/by** *The whole community has been shocked and outraged at the bombing.*

resentful /rɪˈzentfəl/ feeling very angry and upset about something unfair that someone has done to you **+ of** *Robert was resentful of the fact that Forbes had been given the promotion.* | **+ about** *Harvey feels bitter and resentful about the way he's been treated.*

be sickened /biː ˈsɪkənd/ [v phrase] to feel that a situation or someone's behaviour is terrible or wrong, and wish that you could stop it: *In 1991, the world was sickened by the brutal beating of a California man at the hands of several police officers.* | **be sickened to hear/see/learn etc** *We were sickened to learn that such well-known companies were dealing with the drug kingpin.* | **+ about** *I am sickened about the destruction of the downtown area.*

5 words for describing an angry meeting, argument etc

- angry
- furious
- stormy
- heated
- furore
- uproar
- feelings run high

angry /ˈæŋgri/ [adj only before noun] *I could hear my parents having an angry argument downstairs.* | *There were more angry protests outside the Republican convention Friday.*

furious /ˈfjʊəriəs/ [adj only before noun] a **furious** argument, discussion, disagreement etc is one in which people express very angry feelings: *A furious argument was taking place outside the pub.* | *The new import laws have provoked furious complaints from business groups.*

stormy /ˈstɔːʳmi/ [adj] something such as a discussion or relationship that is **stormy** is one in which angry feelings are often expressed: *The December peace talks are likely to be stormy.* | *After a long and sometimes stormy discussion, a decision was finally reached.* | *Their relationship could be stormy at times.*

heated /ˈhiːtɪ̈d/ **heated argument/debate/discussion etc** angry and excited: *The gun control issue continues to be the subject of heated debate.* | *Ed and I used to stay up all night, drinking wine and having heated arguments about politics.* | *Things got very heated as I demanded he pay me full compensation.*

furore British **/furor** American /fjʊˈrɔːri, ˈfjʊərɔːʳ‖ ˈfjʊərɔːr/ [n singular] a situation in which a lot of angry feelings are expressed, especially about something that a lot of people care about: *Addison's theory caused a furore in the academic world.* | **+ over** *There was a furor over a recent exhibit at the Museum of Contemporary Art.*

uproar /ˈʌp-rɔːʳ/ [n singular] a situation in which a lot of people express angry feelings, shock, or disappointment at something they think is very wrong or unfair: *There was an immediate uproar when the company talked about cutting holiday time.* | **set off an uproar** *The court's decision set off an uproar among religious activists.*

feelings run high /ˌfiːlɪŋz rʌn ˈhaɪ/ if **feelings run high** a lot of people are feeling very angry and excited about something, especially something that affects them personally, or that they have very strong opinions about: *Feelings always run high in games between the two teams.* | *With the economy in ruins, feelings against the Prime Minister are running high.*

6 to get angry

- get angry
- lose your temper
- blow your top/hit the roof/go crazy/go nuts/have a fit
- go ballistic/go bananas/go berserk
- get stroppy

get angry ALSO **get mad** American /get ˈæŋgri, get ˈmæd/ [v phrase] *Mike gets very angry when he loses at tennis.* | **+ at** *You have no right to get mad at me. It's not my fault.*

lose your temper /ˌluːz jɔːʳ ˈtempəʳ/ [v phrase] to suddenly become angry, especially after you have been trying not to: *As the argument escalated, Mason lost his temper completely.* | **lose your temper with** *You should never lose your temper with the students – it'll only make things worse.*

blow your top/hit the roof/go crazy/go nuts/have a fit ALSO **go mad** British /ˌbləʊ jɔːʳ ˈtɒp‖-ˈtɑːp, ˌhɪt ðə ˈruːf, gəʊ ˈkreɪzi, gəʊ ˈnʌts, ˌhæv ə ˈfɪt, gəʊ ˈmæd/ [v phrase] informal to suddenly become very angry: *My father blew his top when I told him I was quitting medical school.* | *'What happened when you told him you wrecked the car?' 'Oh, he hit the roof.'* | *Mom would go crazy if she found out you had started smoking.* | *I'm going to go nuts if that phone doesn't stop ringing.* | *When Tommy's new bike was stolen, he had a fit.*

go ballistic/go bananas/go berserk ALSO **go ape** American /gəʊ bəˈlɪstɪk, gəʊ bəˈnɑːnəz ‖-bəˈnæ-, gəʊ bɜːʳˈsɜːʳk, gəʊ ˈeɪp / [v phrase] informal to suddenly become very angry: *If my wife ever finds out about this, she'll go berserk.* | *Joe went ape when we tried to take the car keys away from him outside the bar.*

get stroppy /get ˈstrɒpi‖-ˈstrɑːpi/ [v phrase] British informal to start behaving and talking to people in an angry way, especially when other people think this is unreasonable: *She's the sort of boss who gets really stroppy if things aren't done her way.* | *Mel got a bit stroppy when the maitre d' put us at a table he didn't like.*

7 to make someone angry

- make sb angry
- annoy
- irritate
- piss sb off
- infuriate
- anger
- bug
- get on sb's nerves
- it makes me sick
- be like a red rag to a bull

make sb angry ALSO **make sb mad** especially American /ˌmeɪk (sb) ˈæŋgri, ˌmeɪk (sb) ˈmæd/ [v phrase] *Sophie tried not to do anything that would make Henry angry.* | *It always makes me mad when people drive up behind me and start flashing their lights.*

annoy /əˈnɔɪ/ [v T] to make someone fairly angry: *The only reason she went out with Charles was to annoy her parents.* | *Jane's constant chatter was beginning to annoy me.* | *Are you doing that just to annoy me?* | **it annoys sb that/when** *It annoys me that Kim never returns the books she borrows.* | **I find it annoying when ...** *I find it annoying when people eat smelly foods on public transport.*

irritate /ˈɪrɪ̈teɪt/ [v T] to keep annoying someone: *That silly smile of hers always irritated me.* | *After a while, the loud ticking of the clock began to irritate me.* | *Jean Paul's attempts to apologize just irritated me even more.*

piss sb off ALSO **tick sb off** American /ˌpɪs (sb) ˈɒf, ˌtɪk (sb) ˈɒf / [phr v T] informal an impolite expression meaning to annoy someone: *Shut up, Bernie, before you really start to piss me off.* | **it pisses sb off the way** *Doesn't it piss you off the way your husband sits in front of the TV every night while you cook dinner?*

infuriate /ɪnˈfjʊərieɪt/ [v T] to make someone very angry especially by doing something that they cannot control or change: *Her racist attitudes infuriated her co-workers.* | *Kramer's stubborn refusal to answer any questions infuriated the officers.*

anger /ˈæŋgəʳ/ [v T] formal to make someone angry: *The police department's handling of the affair has angered many in the community.* | *The decision to again allow logging in the area angered environmentalists.*

bug /bʌg/ [v T] informal if something **bugs** you, it annoys you because it is always there or is always happening, so that you cannot stop thinking about it or noticing it: *It really bugs me when I can't remember someone's name.* | *You know what bugs me? Getting a call from a telephone salesman right when I sit down to dinner.*

get on sb's nerves /ˌget ɒn (sb's) ˈnɜːʳvz/ [v phrase] if someone or something **gets on your nerves**, they annoy you, especially by continually saying or doing something that you do not like: *The noise from the apartment upstairs was beginning to get on my nerves.* | *I hope Emma isn't going to be there – she really gets on my nerves.*

it makes me sick /ɪt ˌmeɪks miː ˈsɪk/ spoken informal use this to say that something makes you very angry, especially an unfair situation: *It makes me sick, the way they treat old people here.*

be like a red rag to a bull British **/be like waving a red rag in front of a bull** American /biː laɪk ə red ˌræg tʊ ə ˈbʊl, biː laɪk ˌweɪvɪŋ ə red ˌræg ɪn ˌfrʌnt əv ə ˈbʊl/ [v phrase] if something **is like a red rag to a bull**, it will always make a particular person angry: *Whatever you do, don't mention his ex-wife. It's like a red rag to a bull.*

8 to deliberately make someone angry

- provoke
- wind sb up
- antagonize

provoke /prəˈvəʊk/ [v T] *The dog wouldn't bite you for just petting her. You must have provoked her.* | **provoke sb into (doing) sth** *Paul tried to provoke Fletcher into a fight.* —**provocation** /ˌprɒvəˈkeɪʃən‖ˌprɑː-/ [n U] *Orson claims that the man attacked him without provocation.* —**provocative** /prəˈvɒkətɪv‖-ˈvɑː-/ [adj] likely to make people angry: *The book's provocative statements have led to it being banned in some schools.* (=its statements are likely to make people angry).

wind sb up /ˌwaɪnd (sb) ˈʌp/ [phr v T] especially British informal to deliberately say or do something in order to make someone angry, especially because you enjoy making them angry: *She's married again? You're winding me up!* | *He only pretends to be sexist in order to wind me up.*

antagonize /ænˈtægənaɪz/ [v T] to make someone feel angry with you by doing something that they do not like: *The White House does not want to antagonize Beijing.* | *The police department antagonizes the black community here on an almost regular basis.*

9 making you angry

- annoying
- irritating
- infuriating
- be a pain in the neck
- stupid
- frustrating

annoying /əˈnɔɪ-ɪŋ/ [adj] *Jason is one of the most annoying people I have ever met.* | *Just as I stepped into the shower the phone rang. It was so annoying.* —**annoyingly** [adv] *My boss's instructions are always annoyingly vague.*

irritating /ˈɪrɪ̈teɪtɪŋ/ [adj] annoying, especially because something keeps happening that makes you a little angry: *Sammy has an irritating habit of leaving the refrigerator door open while he's fixing something to eat.* | *It's so irritating how Ellen always tries to finish people's sentences for them.*

infuriating ALSO **maddening** especially British /ɪnˈfjʊərieɪtɪŋ, ˈmædənɪŋ/ [adj] making you very angry and impatient: *Jill's attitude towards the people who work under her is infuriating.* | *I can't believe she's been reading our mail. How infuriating!*

be a pain in the neck ALSO **be a pain in the ass/butt** especially American /biː ə ˌpeɪn ɪn ðə ˈnek, biː ə ˌpeɪn ɪn ði ˈæs, ˈbʌt/ [v phrase] informal to be very annoying. **Be a pain in the ass/butt** are impolite expressions: *It's such a pain in the neck to have to drive downtown every day.* | *Bobby's being a real pain in the butt today. I wish he'd just go home.*

stupid /ˈstjuːpɪ̈d‖ˈstuː-/ [adj only before noun] informal used when you are talking about something that makes you feel very annoyed or impatient, for example because it does not work properly: *I have to stay late and finish this stupid report.* | *The stupid gate won't open properly.*

frustrating /frʌˈstreɪtɪŋ‖ˈfrʌstreɪtɪŋ/ [adj] a situation that is **frustrating** is annoying and makes you feel very impatient by making it impossible for you to do what you want: *It's so frustrating when you're in a hurry and the traffic isn't moving.* | *Learning a new language can be a frustrating experience.*

10 to behave in a very angry way

- have/throw a tantrum
- make a scene
- outburst
- shake your fist
- stamp your foot

have/throw a tantrum /ˌhæv, ˌθrəʊ ə ˈtæntrəm/ [v phrase] if someone, especially a child, **has** or **throws a tantrum**, they shout angrily and cry, especially because they cannot have what they want: *Whenever it's time for bed she throws a tantrum.* | *Almost all two-year-olds have tantrums from time to time.*

make a scene /ˌmeɪk ə ˈsiːn/ [v phrase] to start a loud angry argument with someone, especially in a public place and in a way that is embarrassing: *Please don't talk so loudly. You're making a scene.* | *I hate it when people make a scene in public.*

outburst /ˈaʊtbɜːʳst/ [n C] a sudden expression of very strong angry feelings, especially because you cannot control your anger any longer: *I was embarrassed by my husband's outburst.* | *Corbin apologized for his outburst at the meeting.*

shake your fist /ˌʃeɪk jɔːʳ ˈfɪst/ [v phrase] to hold up your hand with the fingers tightly closed and shake it in order to show that you are angry: *The old man shook his fist angrily at the nurse.*

stamp your foot /ˌstæmp jɔːʳ ˈfʊt/ [v phrase] to bring your foot down hard on the ground because you are angry about something: *'Louis, get over here!' Margret demanded, stamping her foot.*

11 often behaving in an angry, unfriendly way

- bad-tempered
- grumpy/grouchy
- disagreeable
- moody
- uptight
- cantankerous
- misery
- surly

bad-tempered /ˌbæd ˈtempəʳd◂/ [adj] *Her father was a bad-tempered man who sat alone drinking beer and watching TV most nights.* | *As Aunt Matilde's pain grew worse, she became too bad-tempered to see anyone.*

grumpy/grouchy /ˈgrʌmpi, ˈgraʊtʃi/ [adj] angry and unfriendly, and often complaining about things: *a grumpy old man* | *Sandy is always grouchy in the mornings.*

disagreeable /ˌdɪsəˈgriːəbəl/ [adj] especially British someone who is **disagreeable** is bad-tempered and very unfriendly and behaves in an unpleasant way towards people: *It's impossible to have a normal conversation with your father – he's always so disagreeable.* | *The landlord is an extremely disagreeable man. Have as little to do with him as possible.* —**disagreeably** [adv] written *Joe scowled disagreeably.*

moody /ˈmuːdi/ [adj] often becoming annoyed or unhappy, especially when there seems to be no good reason to: *Tammy's been moody and emotional all day.* | *a moody teenager*

uptight /ˈʌptaɪt, ʌpˈtaɪt/ [adj] behaving in a bad-tempered way towards other people, especially because you are always nervous or worried about something: *I wish you would stop being so uptight.* | **+ about** *My parents have always been uptight about me dating boys.*

cantankerous /kænˈtæŋkərəs/ [adj] an old person who is **cantankerous** is bad-tempered and complains and quarrels a lot: *As Ethel grew older, she became more cantankerous.* | *Brooks is the committee's cantankerous chairman.* —**cantankerously** [adv] *'There's no way you're putting me in a nursing home,' said Grandad, cantankerously.*

misery /ˈmɪzəri/ [n singular] British spoken use this about someone who is always complaining and never seems to enjoy anything: *Stop grumbling, you old misery.* | *Don't invite her. She's such a misery!*

surly /ˈsɜːʳli/ [adj] someone who is **surly** behaves in a bad-tempered, rude, and unhelpful way when dealing with people: *Passengers complained about the dirty lavatory and surly staff.* | *Kevin can be really surly sometimes.* | *I declined to tip the porter, who left with a surly expression.*

12 unfriendly and quiet because you are angry

- sullen
- sulky
- sulk

sullen /ˈsʌlən/ [adj] someone who is **sullen** behaves in a bad-tempered, unfriendly way and does not smile or talk much to people: *Dick just sat there with a sullen expression on his face, refusing to speak.* | *The secretary was sullen and uncooperative.* —**sullenly** [adv] *The girl behind the counter looked at me sullenly, waiting for me to order.*

sulky /ˈsʌlki/ [adj] someone who is **sulky** has an angry, unhappy look on their face and does not talk much, especially because they think they have been treated unfairly: *On the drive home, Maria was sulky and said very little.* | *William was a sulky little boy who seemed to care for nothing except his video games.* —**sulkily** [adv] *She just looked at him sulkily and refused to say anything more.*

sulk ALSO **be in a sulk** British /sʌlk, biː ɪn ə ˈsʌlk/ [v I] if someone **sulks**, they are deliberately silent and bad-tempered for a period of time, because something has annoyed them, or because they think that they have been treated unfairly: *Cindy always sulks when I won't buy her any candy.* | *You can't sit around sulking all day.* | **sulk about sth** *What are you sulking about now?*

13 easily annoyed

- irritable
- touchy
- crotchety
- short-tempered/quick-tempered
- have a short fuse

irritable /ˈɪrɪ̣təbəl/ [adj] easily annoyed by unimportant things, especially because you already feel bad-tempered about something: *Since Steve quit smoking, he's been really irritable.* | *Zoe hadn't had much sleep and was feeling tired and irritable.* | *You're turning into an irritable old man.* —**irritably** [adv] *'Do you think you could turn the music down?' asked Eric irritably.*

touchy /ˈtʌtʃi/ [adj not before noun] someone who is **touchy** is easily offended and made angry by things, so you have to be careful what you say to them: *Saiid's a little touchy about how you pronounce her name.* | **+ about** *Try not to look at his scars – he can be really touchy about it.*

crotchety /ˈkrɒtʃɪ̣ti‖ˈkrɑː-/ [adj] an old person who is **crotchety** becomes angry about unimportant things and complains a lot: *a crotchety old man* | *When we were in Germany, we rented a room from a crotchety old woman named Brunhilde.*

short-tempered/quick-tempered /ˌʃɔːʳt ˈtempəʳd◂, ˌkwɪk ˈtempəʳd/ [adj] someone who is **short-tempered** gets angry quickly and easily: *Jackie can be very short-tempered when she's hungry.* | *Her father is a quick-tempered man.*

have a short fuse /hæv ə ˌʃɔːʳt ˈfjuːz/ [v phrase not in progressive] informal to often get angry quickly and easily: *They say the judge has a very short fuse.*

14 angry feelings

- anger
- annoyance
- temper
- rage
- frustration
- resentment
- outrage
- irritation
- exasperation

anger /ˈæŋgəʳ/ [n U] *He was finding it difficult to control his anger.* | *Sandra helped us deal with the grief and anger we felt over Patrick's death.* | **feel anger towards** *Andrea still feels a lot of anger towards her mom, who left when she was a little girl.* | **do sth in anger** *I've said some things in anger that have almost cost my marriage.*

annoyance /əˈnɔɪəns/ [n U] slight anger or impatience: *It's such an annoyance to have to drive you everywhere.* | **much to the annoyance of sb** *I like to stay up late most nights, much to the annoyance of my girlfriend.* | *The meetings were held in secret, much to the annoyance of some members of Congress.*

temper /ˈtempəʳ/ [n C usually singular] someone who has a **temper** has a tendency to become very angry suddenly: *Jill needs to learn to control her temper.* | *His wife left him because of his violent temper.* | **bad temper** *There's one thing about Don that you should know – he's got a really bad temper.*

rage /reɪdʒ/ [n U] a very strong feeling of anger that someone has that is either very difficult for them to control or is expressed very suddenly or violently **fly into a rage** (=to suddenly became very angry) *When we accused him of lying, he flew into a rage.* | **shake with rage** (=to be so angry, you shake) *Vera's hands shook with rage as she read the letter.* | **in a blind/jealous/terrible rage** *Brown killed his wife in a jealous rage.*

frustration /frʌˈstreɪʃən/ [n U] the feeling of being annoyed, caused especially by a difficult or unpleasant situation that you are unable to change or control: *Students have spoken of their growing frustration with school administrators.* | *The discussion sessions help patients deal with some of the frustrations they may be feeling.*

resentment /rɪ'zentmənt/ [n U] a feeling of anger because you feel that you are being treated badly or unfairly, and cannot do anything about it: *Patricia stared at the other girls with resentment.* | *Resentment and jealousy can often build up in relationships.* | **+ at/against/of** *She couldn't let go of her resentment over the divorce.*

outrage /'aʊtreɪdʒ/ [n U] a feeling of extreme anger at something wrong, unfair, or immoral, especially among members of the public: *Several parents of affected children have written to the Prime Minister to express their outrage.* | *Any attempts to lessen his prison sentence will cause public outrage.*

irritation /ˌɪrɨ'teɪʃən/ [n U] the feeling of being annoyed, caused especially by someone or something that is repeatedly annoying **+ with** *Bailey expressed irritation with the inaccurate reports in the media.* | **a source of irritation** (=something that causes irritation) *The heavy traffic is a constant source of irritation.*

exasperation /ɪgˌzɑːspə'reɪʃən‖-ˌzæs-/ [n U] the feeling of being very annoyed because you cannot control a situation, learn to do something, or understand something, even though you are trying very hard **+ with** *Many people express exasperation with the National Health Service, but most seem to prefer it to a private system.* | **in exasperation** *He pounded the desk in exasperation.*

15 to try to make someone less angry

- pacify
- calm sb down

pacify /'pæsɨfaɪ/ [v T] to make someone less angry and more calm: *It was no use trying to pacify him; he was simply too upset.* | *As I drove home, I tried to think how I was going to pacify my wife, who was sure to be angry.*

calm sb down /ˌkɑːm (sb) 'daʊn/ [phr v T] to make someone less angry and upset when they have been very angry or upset: *They had to use drugs to calm him down.* | *When he was really upset, only his wife could calm him down.*

another

one more of the same kind

RELATED WORDS

- *see also* **more, add, different**

- another
- one more
- extra
- spare
- additional

another /ə'nʌðəʳ/ [determiner/pron] use this to talk about one person or thing that is similar to the one you already have: *'I've lost my pencil.' 'Don't worry, here's another.'* | **another person/thing/glass etc** *Would you like another drink?* | *She got another chance to see him after the show.* | **another one** *'That was a good cup of coffee.' 'Would you like another one?'* | **+ of** *This is just another of his crazy ideas. Ignore it.*

one more /ˌwʌn 'mɔːʳ/ another – use this to emphasize that this will be the last one: *One more drink and then I really have to go.* | *I'll give you one more chance to tell the truth.*

extra /'ekstrə/ [adj only before noun] in addition to the usual amount or number – use this about something useful that you may need: *Bring an extra set of clothes in case you decide to stay overnight.* | *Do you want to earn some extra cash?*

spare /speəʳ/ [adj only before noun] **spare room/key/tyre etc** another room, key etc that you do not usually use but you can use if you need to: *I always leave a set of spare keys with my neighbor.* | *All cars have to carry a spare tyre by law.*

additional /ə'dɪʃənəl/ [adj only before noun] formal more than the usual or expected amount: *There will be an additional charge for any extra baggage.* | *Additional security was provided for the President's visit.*

answer

RELATED WORDS

- to find the answer to a problem *see* **solve**
- *see also* **ask, react**

1 to answer when someone asks you a question or speaks to you

- answer
- reply
- respond
- give sb an answer
- in reply (to)/ in answer to/ in response to
- get back to
- retort

answer /'ɑːnsəʳ‖'æn-/ [v I/T] to say something to someone when they have asked you a question or spoken to you: *Julie thought for a long time before answering.* | *I said hello to her, but she didn't answer.* | *'Why don't you just leave?' 'I'd like to,' she answered, 'but I have nowhere else to go.'* | *How much did you spend? Come on, answer me!* | **answer a question** *You don't have to answer the question if you don't want to.* | **+ that** *When questioned about the robbery, Hughes answered that he knew nothing about it.*

reply /rɪ'plaɪ/ [v I/T] to answer someone when they have asked you a question or spoken to you – used especially in written English to report what someone said: *I waited for Smith to reply, but he said nothing.* | *'I'm so sorry,' he replied.* | **+ to** *The jailers refused to reply to the prisoners' questions about where they were being taken.* | **+ that** *We asked Jane to help, but she replied that she was too busy.*

respond /rɪ'spɒnd‖-'spɑːnd/ [v I/T] to answer someone, especially someone who has criticized you or disagreed with you, in a clear and detailed way: *The waitress waited a moment and then responded.* | *'I'd be there if I could,' Bill responded.* | **+ to** *How do you respond to the allegation that you deliberately deceived your employers?* | *The meeting will give administrators a chance to respond to the community's questions and concerns.* | **+ by saying/telling/asking etc** *His father usually responds by telling him to be quiet.*

give sb an answer /ˌgɪv (sb) ən 'ɑːnsəʳ‖-'æn-/ [v phrase] to answer someone by telling them what you have decided or by providing them with the particular piece of information that they have asked for: *They're offering us a new contract and we have to give them a definite answer by the end of the month.* | *He didn't give me a very satisfactory answer*

in reply (to)/in answer to/in response to /ɪn rɪ'plaɪ (tuː), ɪn 'ɑːnsəʳ tuː‖-'æn-, ɪn rɪ'spɒns tuː‖-rɪ'spɑːns-/ [adv] if you say or do something **in reply to** what someone has said, you say or do it as a way of answering their question, request, remark etc: *'Where are we going?' Jill asked. The driver only lifted his hand in reply, as if to silence her.* | *'That won't be necessary,' Wilson said in reply to the question.* | *In response to your question, no, I don't think a meeting is necessary.*

get back to /ˌget ˈbæk tuː/ [phr v T] to answer someone at a later time especially by telephoning them, usually because you need to think about their question or find out more information before you can give an answer: *She's promised to get back to me as soon as she hears any more news from the hospital.* | *Tell you what, let me talk it over with the guys and I'll get back to you.*

retort /rɪˈtɔːʳt/ [v T not in progressive] written to answer someone angrily, especially because they have annoyed you or criticized you: *'You're not afraid?' Brenda asked. 'Of course not,' he retorted angrily.* | **+ that** *Republicans retorted that the amendment is necessary to balance the budget.*

2 to answer a letter, invitation, e-mail etc

- reply
- answer
- write back
- acknowledge
- RSVP/R.S.V.P.
- in response/answer/reply to sth

reply /rɪˈplaɪ/ [v I] to write a letter to someone who has written to you, or to someone who has put an advertisement in a newspaper: *I wrote to Franca three weeks ago but she hasn't replied yet.* | **+ to** *Becky hasn't replied to our invitation, so I assume she isn't coming.*

answer /ˈɑːnsəʳ‖ˈæn-/ [v T] if you **answer** a letter or advertisement, you write a letter to the person who has written it: *I got the job by answering an advertisement in the paper.* | *Miss Millar hired a secretary to answer her mail while she was on vacation.* | *Think carefully before answering that memo.*

write back /ˌraɪt ˈbæk/ [phr v I/T] to write a letter to someone who has written a letter to you: *Sara wrote asking if she could help, so I wrote back and said yes.* | **+ to** *Josh, have you written back to Grandma yet?* | **write sb back** American *She didn't really expect him to write her back.*

acknowledge /əkˈnɒlɪdʒ‖-ˈnɑː-/ [v T] formal to write a letter telling someone that you have received a letter, parcel etc that they have sent you: *I have just sent off a letter acknowledging their message.* | **acknowledge receipt of sth** (=officially acknowledge that you have received something) *Please acknowledge receipt of this document by signing and returning the enclosed form.*

RSVP/R.S.V.P. /ˌɑːr es viː ˈpiː/ written please answer this invitation – used at the end of formal invitations when asking someone to say if they can definitely come to a wedding, formal dinner etc: *Dr Fischer requests your company at a dinner to celebrate his retirement at the Dorchester Hotel on November 30th at 10 pm. RSVP.*

in response/answer/reply to sth /ɪn rɪˈspɒns, ˈɑːnsəʳ, rɪˈplaɪ tə (sth) ‖-rɪˈspɑːns-, -ˈæn-/ [adv] if you say or do something **in response to** what someone has written, you say or do it as a way of answering their question, request, advertisement etc: *She said she'd come to the office in response to an ad she'd seen in the paper.* | *In answer to recent criticism the President has issued a statement explaining his policies.*

3 to answer the telephone/the door

- answer
- get
- take a call
- pick up

answer /ˈɑːnsəʳ‖ˈæn-/ [v I/T] to pick up the telephone and speak when it rings, or go to the door and open it when someone knocks: *I knocked on the door for a long time, but no one answered.* | **answer the telephone/a call/the door** *A strange man answered the door.* | *She still isn't answering my calls.*

get /get/ [v T] to answer the telephone, or go to the door when someone knocks **get the phone/door** *I'll get the phone. I think it's for me.* | *Can someone get the door – I'm in the shower!* | **get it** spoken (=answer the phone/door) *The phone's ringing. Do you want me to get it?*

take a call /ˌteɪk ə ˈkɔːl/ [v phrase] to speak to someone on the telephone because the person that they want to speak to is not available: *I was out that day, and my mother took the call.* | *Do you want to take the call in your office?* | **+ for** *Someone wants to speak to Professor Welch, but I can't find him. Would you take the call for him please.*

pick up /ˌpɪk ˈʌp/ [phr v I/T] spoken to answer a phone and talk to the person who is calling: *Come on Bob, pick up! I know you're there.* | **pick up the phone** *Just pick up the phone and tell her to stop calling you here.* | **pick it/the phone up** *After the phone had rung twice, Joyce picked it up and said hello.*

4 to answer a teacher, parent etc in a rude way

- answer back/talk back
- back talk

answer back/talk back /ˌɒːnsəʳ ˈbæk‖-ˌæn-, ˌtɔːk ˈbæk / [phr v I/T/phr v I] to answer someone rudely, especially a teacher, parent etc when they criticize you or tell you to do something: *Don't talk back. It's rude.* | **answer sb back** *We were all scared of Mr Williams, but here was a girl who actually answered him back.* | **talk back to sb** *Don't talk back to your mother like that!*

back talk ALSO **back chat** British /ˈbæk tɔːk, ˈbæk tʃæt/ [n U] rude remarks that someone makes when they answer their teacher, parent etc: *I don't want any excuses, complaints, or back talk.* | *Any more of your back chat and you'll have to stay behind after school.*

5 something you say as an answer

- answer
- reply
- response
- retort

answer /ˈɑːnsəʳ‖ˈæn-/ [n C] something you say when someone asks you a question or speaks to you: *Each time I ask him when the work will be done, I get a different answer.* | *I've asked Yvonne to come on vacation with us, but I'm still waiting for her answer.* | **the answer is no/yes** *If you're asking me for money, the answer's no!* | **answer to a question** *The answer to your question is very simple: you failed the exam because you didn't do any work.* | **the answer is (that)** *Why don't people complain? The answer is that they are frightened of losing their jobs.*

reply /rɪˈplaɪ/ [n C] something you say when someone asks you a question or speaks to you – use this especially in written English to report what someone has said: *Dr Kleinert murmured a reply, but I* *couldn't hear what it was.* | *'I'm just borrowing your black dress, OK?' said Maxine, without waiting for a reply.* | **+ to** *Railway officials say it isn't their fault – which is their standard reply to customers' complaints.*

response /rɪ'spɒns‖rɪ'spɑːns/ [n C] an answer that clearly shows your reaction to a question, suggestion etc: *Wagner's responses showed that he had thought carefully about the issues.* | **+ to** *'Sure. Why not?' was his response to most of Billie's suggestions.*

retort /rɪ'tɔːʳt/ [n C] written an angry or cleverly humorous answer, especially to someone who has made you angry: *Ellie's angry retort surprised Max.* | *She could never think of a clever retort to counter Ben's string of jokes and witticisms.*

6 something you write as an answer

- reply
- answer
- acknowledgement
- response

reply /rɪ'plaɪ/ [n C] a written answer to a letter, invitation, or advertisement: *We advertised for a secretary in the local paper and got 24 replies.* | *I wrote to them three weeks ago and I haven't had a reply back yet.* | **+ to** *It is usual to send a formal reply to a wedding invitation.*

answer /'ɑːnsəʳ‖'æn-/ [n C] a letter that you write back to someone who has asked you for something: *We've written to the bank requesting a loan, and we're expecting an answer in this morning's mail.* | **+ to** *Did you ever get an answer to your last letter?*

acknowledgement /ək'nɒlɪdʒmənt‖-'nɑː-/ [n C] a formal letter or note stating that a letter, parcel etc has been received: *I received an acknowledgement from Toshiba yesterday telling me that they were considering my application for the job.* | **letter of acknowledgement** *He's still waiting for a letter of acknowledgement of the last cheque he sent them.*

response /rɪ'spɒns‖rɪ'spɑːns/ [n C] an answer that clearly shows your reaction to a question, suggestion etc: *I mailed the letter on Monday and had a response already on Friday.* | **+ to** *Write your responses to the questions on the back of the sheet.*

7 to not answer someone

- not answer
- no answer/reply/response
- make no reply/response/answer

not answer /nɒt 'ɑːnsəʳ‖-'æn-/ [v phrase] *'What are you doing here?' The child's mouth trembled a little, but he did not answer.* | **not answer sb/sth** *I'm afraid I can't answer that question.* | *I knew there was something wrong when she didn't answer me.*

no answer/reply/response /nəʊ 'ɑːnsəʳ, rɪ'plaɪ, rɪ'spɒns‖-'æn-, rɪ'spɑːns/ [n phrase] **there is no answer/reply/response** *I called Stevie's name but there was no answer.* | **get no answer/reply/response** *He's written three letters to the mayor, but he's gotten no response.*

make no reply/response/answer /meɪk ˌnəʊ rɪ'plaɪ, rɪ'spɒns, 'ɑːnsəʳ‖-rɪ'spɑːns, -'æn-/ [v phrase] to deliberately remain silent when someone asks you a question or talks to you: *I greeted Minna, but she made no reply.* | *Alan tried to start a conversation, but when Lockwood made no response, he gave up.*

8 the answer to a question in a test, competition etc

- answer
- result
- solution

answer /'ɑːnsəʳ‖'æn-/ [n C] an **answer** to a question in a test or competition: *Write your answers on the form and send it to this address.* | **the answer** (=the correct answer) *And the answer is ... Budapest!* | **+ to** *What's the answer to question 4?* | **give your answer** *Think carefully before you give the answer.* | **the right/wrong answer** *The first person to call with the right answer will win 10 CDs of their choice.*

result /rɪ'zʌlt/ [n C] an answer that you have found after calculating or doing tests: *I've tried three different ways of adding these figures and each time I get a different result.* | *We have completed our experiments and we are now analyzing the results.* | *The results of our accountant's calculations show that we are on the verge of bankruptcy.*

solution /sə'luːʃən/ [n C] the correct answer to a complicated problem in a test or competition: *It was a difficult equation, but it took her only five minutes to work out the solution.* | **+ to** *The solution to this week's puzzle will be published in next week's magazine.*

9 to give an answer to a question in a test, competition etc

- answer

answer /'ɑːnsəʳ‖'æn-/ [v I/T] **answer a question** *You have 20 minutes to answer all the questions.* | **answer correctly** *If you answer correctly, you could win a video camera.*

10 to find or calculate the answer to a question

- solve
- work out/figure out

solve /sɒlv‖sɑːlv, sɔːlv/ [v T] to find the correct answer to a question, problem, or sum by thinking about it carefully or doing calculations: *I'm never going to solve this puzzle – it's impossible.* | *According to Greek legend, it was Oedipus who solved the riddle of the Sphinx.*

work out/figure out /ˌwɜːʳk 'aʊt, ˌfɪgər 'aʊt‖ˌfɪgjər-/ [phr v T] to find the answer, usually a number or amount, to a calculation **work/figure sth out** *It's all right, I don't need a calculator. I can work it out in my head.* | *I'm sure they owe me more money than that – I'll have to sit down and figure it out.* | **work out/figure out sth** *Using a calculator, work out the answers to the following questions.*

anything/anybody

RELATED WORDS

- nothing *see* **none/nothing**
- nobody *see* **person/people (7)**
- *see also* **all, everyone, some**

1 any of a group of things

- any
- anything
- whatever
- you name it

any /ˈeni/ [determiner/pron] use this to talk about each one of the things in a group, when it is not important to say exactly which one: *You can buy the magazine at any good bookstore.* | *This remote control can be used with any television set.* | **any of the/these/my/them etc** *I told Debbie she could borrow any of my books.* | *So, do you like any of your new classes?*

anything /ˈeniθɪŋ/ [pron] everything that you may want, need etc, especially when there is a very big choice: *I was going to throw all these things away anyway, so please take anything you like.* | *Do you know anything about computers?* | *Paul goes to all the auctions in the area looking for anything in Art Deco style.* | **anything else** *The one thing he wanted more than anything else was a glass of cold water.* | **anything at all** *If you have any questions, feel free to ask me anything at all.*

whatever /wɒtˈevəʳ‖wɑːt-/ [pron] anything at all – use this to emphasize that it does not matter which object, action, idea etc: *'Can I have a cake, Mummy?' 'You can have whatever you want, darling.'* | *We'll do whatever we can to help.* | *You should find whatever you need in the cupboard under the sink.* | *Here was an audience eager to listen to whatever I had to say.*

you name it /ˌjuː ˈneɪm ɪt/ informal you say **you name it** when you are telling someone that there is everything that they want, or need, or can think of: *World-class museums, great theater, outdoor sports – you name it, this city's got it.* | *I had so many different jobs while I was a student: waiter, sales clerk, bartender – you name it.*

2 any one of the people in a group or in the world

- any
- anyone/anybody
- any Tom, Dick or Harry
- whoever/no matter who
- any fool/idiot

any /ˈeni/ [determiner/pron] use this to talk about each person in a group of people when it is not important to say exactly which one **any/man/child/teacher etc** *Ask any teacher and they'll tell you I'm right.* | *Any student who wishes to go on the trip should sign this list.* | **any of the men/their children/my teachers etc** *Have any of the guests arrived?* | *Jan decided not to invite any of her relatives to her graduation.* | **any of you/them/us** *Have any of you seen my glasses?*

anyone/anybody /ˈeniwʌn, ˈeniˌbɒdi‖-ˌbɑːdi/ [pron] *Don't worry about it. It can happen to anybody.* | *Did anyone call while I was out?* | *If anybody needs more information, come and see me after class.* | *Sarah liked him more than anyone else she knew.* | *This would be an ideal job for anyone who speaks French and Italian.*

any Tom, Dick or Harry /eni ˌtɒm ˌdɪk ɔːʳ ˈhæri‖-ˌtɑːm-/ [n phrase] informal anyone in the world, used especially when you mean that you should be more careful about who you choose or allow to do something: *Any Tom, Dick, or Harry could have written something just as good.* | *If you don't have someone at the door, any Tom, Dick or Harry could turn up at the party and walk straight in.*

whoever/no matter who /huːˈevəʳ, nəʊ ˌmætəʳ ˈhuː/ [pron] any person – use this when the identity of the person is not important or is not known: *Whoever you ask, you will get the same answer.* | *Sam wanted to feel that others, no matter who they were, agreed with him.* | *If someone comes to your door you should always ask for some form of identification, no matter who they say they are.*

any fool/idiot /eni ˈfuːl, ˈɪdiət/ [n phrase] if you say that **any fool** or **any idiot** can do something, you mean that anyone can do it because it is extremely easy, and if someone cannot do it they must be very stupid: *Any fool could see that the child was unhappy.*

appear

to start to be seen

RELATED WORDS

opposite: —— **disappear**

- to seem to be something *see* **seem**
- to start to exist *see* **start (10)**
- when the sun appears in the morning *see* **up (8)**
- to arrive unexpectedly *see* **arrive**

- appear
- become visible
- come into view/come into sight
- come out
- emerge
- loom/loom up
- reappear

appear /əˈpɪəʳ/ [v I] to start to be seen or to suddenly be seen: *A face appeared at the window.* | **+ from** *The manager suddenly appeared from his office.* | **appear from behind/under etc** *A spider appeared from under the sofa.* | *Lois was about to knock when a woman appeared from around the side of the house.* | **appear out of nowhere** (=suddenly appear) *The dog appeared out of nowhere and began running alongside me.* —**appearance** [n U] **+ of** *The sudden appearance of several reporters at the hospital caused a lot of confusion.*

become visible /bɪˌkʌm ˈvɪzəbəl/ [v phrase] to gradually start to be able to be seen – use this when you just start to see something, especially when it looks very small and difficult to see: *We had been on the boat for several hours when I noticed the coastline slowly becoming visible.* | *As the fog became thinner, the edges of buildings slowly became visible.*

come into view/come into sight /ˌkʌm ɪntə ˈvjuː, ˌkʌm ɪntə ˈsaɪt/ [v phrase] if something **comes into view/sight**, you can see it as you get closer to it or it gets closer to you – use this about things that are far away: *As the station came into sight, the train began to slow down.* | *Astronomers say that over the next few weeks the comet will be coming into view.*

come out /ˌkʌm ˈaʊt/ [phr v I] if the sun, the moon, or a star **comes out**, it appears in the sky: *The moon came out from behind a cloud.* | *As the sky grew darker, the stars came out one by one.*

emerge /ɪˈmɜːʳdʒ/ [v I] especially written to come out from a room, building or other enclosed space and start to be seen **+ from** *Baxter emerged from the building and walked across the parking lot to a waiting car.* | *Brian, emerging from the bathroom, heard his wife speaking to someone at the front door.* | *At the airport, people stood behind a metal fence waiting for passengers to emerge from customs.*

loom/loom up /luːm, ˌluːm ˈʌp/ [v I] if a large person or thing **looms** or **looms up**, they suddenly appear in a way that makes you feel nervous or frightened, especially in a situation in which you cannot see clearly: *As we rounded the curve, the* *mountain loomed up in front of us.* | *They were walking through the alley when a man suddenly loomed out of the shadows.*

reappear /ˌriːəˈpɪəʳ/ [v I] to appear again after a short time of not being there or not being able to be seen: *Baines went back inside and reappeared a few moments later carrying an umbrella.* —**reappearance** [n U] *Her sudden reappearance startled me.*

approve

to think that something is good or right

RELATED WORDS

opposite: —— **disapprove**

- to officially accept something *see* **accept**
- words meaning it is right to do something *see* **right (6-8)**
- *see also* **like, agree, support**

1 to approve of something or someone

- approve
- think sth is right
- agree with
- believe in
- condone

approve /əˈpruːv/ [v I not in progressive] *Don will only buy the motorcycle if his parents approve.* | **+ of** *I was surprised that Mom seemed to approve of Tracy's new boyfriend.* | *Bob doesn't approve of alcohol.* | *Forty percent of registered voters approved of Senator Campbell.* | **approve of (sb) doing sth** *Do you approve of doctors using human embryos for research?*

think sth is right /ˌθɪŋk (sth) ɪz ˈraɪt/ [v phrase] spoken to approve of something – used especially when you are talking about something other people might not agree with: *My mother made me get a part-time job when I was sixteen, and I think that's right.* | **think it is right (for sb) to do sth** *The bank invests a lot of money in the tobacco industry: do you think it's right for them to do that?* | *He doesn't think it's right for someone so young to be learning about sex at school.*

agree with /əˈgriː wɪð/ [phr v T not in progressive] to approve of something such as a decision, a way of doing something, or a plan: *Mr. Senator, do you agree with the court's decision?* | *I have never agreed with animal experimentation.*

believe in /bǝ̍ˈliːv ɪn/ [phr v T not in progressive] to approve of a type of behaviour or way of doing something, especially because you think there are important principles involved: *Hilary doesn't believe in sex before marriage.* | **believe in doing sth** *We believe in letting everyone have the right to see their own medical records.*

condone /kənˈdəʊn/ [v T] to say or show that you approve of something that most people think is wrong: *The state appears to condone police brutality.* | *I'm not condoning his behaviour, but I can understand why he wanted revenge on his daughter's attacker.*

2 to strongly approve of something

- strongly/totally/wholeheartedly etc approve
- be all for/be all in favour of
- be a great/firm believer in

strongly/totally/wholeheartedly etc approve /ˌstrɒŋli əˈpruːv‖ˌstrɔːŋ-/ [v phrase] *My son wants to leave school to concentrate on his acting career and I totally approve.* | **+ of** *He strongly approves of his wife's decision not to work until the children are old enough to go to school.*

be all for/be all in favour of ALSO **be all in favor of** American /biː ˌɔːl ˈfɔːʳ, biː ˌɔːl ɪn ˈfeɪvər ɒv/ [v phrase] spoken if you **are all for something** or **all in favour of something**, you strongly approve of it – used especially when you do not approve of something else that is often connected with it: *The priest is all in favour of music in church, but he doesn't think rock music is appropriate.* | **be all for (sb) doing sth** *I'm all for people going out and enjoying themselves, as long as they don't drive when they're drunk.* | *Don't get me wrong – I'm all for cutting taxes if we can do it without hurting the poor.*

be a great/firm believer in /biː ə ˌgreɪt, ˌfɜːʳm bǝ̍ˈliːvər ɪn / [v phrase] to approve of a particular way of living or of doing things because you think it brings good results: *Alan is a firm believer in a healthy diet and regular exercise.* | *I've never been a great believer in private schools.*

3 to say that you approve of something or someone

- endorse
- be an advocate of

endorse /ɪnˈdɔːʳs/ [v T] to say publicly or officially that you approve of something or someone and will support it or them: *Aides say Ames plans to endorse the proposed budget.* | *In today's edition, the paper endorsed Mayor Riley, who is running for re-election.* | *Huntley refused to endorse any candidate who did not share his views on gun control.*

be an advocate of /biː ən ˈædvəkǝ̍t ɒv / [v phrase] to think that a way of doing something is right, and often try to persuade other people to agree with you: *She has always been an advocate of women's rights.* | **be a strong advocate of sth** *Gandhi was a strong advocate of non-violent protest.*

4 when someone approves of something or someone

- approval
- blessing

approval /əˈpruːvəl/ [n U] *Ben needs to have his wife's approval before he'll do anything.* | **win/earn sb's approval** *By doing well at school he hoped to win his parents' approval.* | **nod/smile/watch etc with approval** *The children played quietly in the back yard as Frances looked on with approval.*

blessing /ˈblesɪŋ/ [n C] if someone gives their **blessing** to something, they say that they will allow it to happen and will not try to stop it **give your blessing to sth/give sth your blessing** *Mayor Wharton gave the proposal his blessing.* | **with sb's blessing** *Darren and Teresa planned to live together before they got married, with their parents' blessing.*

area

WHAT'S HERE

- **an area of the world, a country, a surface etc** see **1 to 8**
- **an area of knowledge** see **9**

an area of the world, a country, a surface etc

RELATED WORDS

▸ *see also* **space, place, land/ground, country, town**

1 an area of the world or a country

- area
- region
- zone
- country
- locality

area /ˈeəriə/ [n C] an **area** of land that is part of the world or part of a country: *Police think the crime was committed by someone from outside the area.* | **+ of** *There is a shortage of water in many areas of the world.* | *Hannah grew up in a beautiful area of Ireland.* | **sb's area** (=the area where someone lives) *The cost of electricity has risen in our area.*

region /ˈriːdʒən/ [n C] a large area that is part of a country or of the world: *There have been reports of fighting in the region.* | **+ of** *For several years they lived in a remote region of Kenya.* | *Severe winter weather is expected in the northeast region of the country.*

zone /zəʊn/ [n C] an area that is in some way special or different from the areas around it, for example because it has a particular type of problem: *San Francisco and Tokyo are both located in earthquake zones.* | *Half of the community lies in a flood zone.* | **war/battle zone** *UN troops are unwilling to enter the battle zone.*

country /ˈkʌntri/ [n U] an area of land that is of a particular type or that is used for a particular activity, lived in by particular people etc: *The Midwest is largely farming country.* | *Not many people live in the hill country any more.*

locality /ləʊˈkælɪ̈ti/ [n C] formal a small area of a country: *In some localities the price of housing has risen by more than fifty percent in the last decade.* | *The city council is responsible for providing police protection in each locality.*

2 an area in or around a town or city

- area
- district
- neighbourhood
- quarter
- zone
- block
- suburb
- precinct

area /ˈeəriə/ [n C] an **area** in or around a town or city **+ of** *The family lives in Roxbury, a working-class area of Boston.* | **poor/rich area** *Raul grew up in a poor area of Buenos Aires.*

district /ˈdɪstrɪkt/ [n C] one of the areas that a town or city is officially divided into, or one of the areas of a town or city where a particular group of people live or a particular activity happens **+ of** *Their apartment is in the Chongwen district of Peking.* | **business/financial/historical etc district** *Blaine works in the financial district.*

neighbourhood British **/neighborhood** American /ˈneɪbəʳhʊd/ [n C] one of the parts of a town or city: *The Cranstons live in a very wealthy neighbourhood.* | **+ of** *I grew up in a quiet neighborhood of Birmingham.* | **in the neighbourhood/neighborhood** *Are there any good restaurants in the neighborhood?*

quarter /ˈkwɔːʳtəʳ/ [n C] an area in a town or city that is lived in by people of a particular type or nationality **+ of** *We rented a house in the Creole quarter of New Orleans.* | *The Dahdah palace is in the old Jewish quarter of Damascus.*

zone /zəʊn/ [n C] part of a city that is officially divided from other parts because it is of a particular type **residential/commercial zone** *This is a residential zone – no commercial buildings are allowed.* | **pedestrian zone** (=a zone where cars, motorcycles etc are not allowed) *Most of the town centre is now a pedestrian zone.*

block /blɒk‖blɑːk/ [n C] especially American a group of buildings in a city, with four streets around it – often used as a way of talking about distances in the city: *She lived three blocks away from me when we were kids.* | *Many of the families on our block are Hispanic-Americans.*

suburb /ˈsʌbɜːʳb/ [n C] an area away from the centre of a city, where people live, especially an area where there are houses with gardens **+ of** *Amy teaches at a primary school in a suburb of Atlanta.* | **the suburbs** *My family moved to the suburbs when I was ten.*

precinct /ˈpriːsɪŋkt/ [n C] American an area in an American town or city that is officially divided from other parts and that has its own police department etc: *the fourteenth precinct* | *The mayor has lost support in many precincts of the city.*

3 the area around a building or place

- surroundings
- surrounding area

surroundings /səˈraʊndɪŋz/ [n plural] the objects, buildings, natural things etc that are around a building, around the place where you live, work etc: *The house is set in beautiful surroundings near Lake Coniston.* | *The mountaintop provides a spectacular view of Innsbruck and its surroundings.* | *It took me a few weeks to get used to my new surroundings.*

surrounding area /səˌraʊndɪŋ ˈeəriə/ [n C] the area around a building, street, city etc: *The city is not very attractive, but the surrounding area is lovely.* | *Police are still searching the town and surrounding areas for the child.*

4 an area used for a particular purpose

- area
- lot

area /ˈeəriə/ [n C] an **area** in a house, garden, office etc that is used for a particular purpose, although it is not completely separate: *Their apartment has a large kitchen area.* | *The boat has a sleeping area at one end.* | **smoking/non-smoking area** *There's a smoking area behind the building.*

lot /lɒt‖lɑːt/ [n C] American an area outdoors that is used for a particular purpose, for example selling a particular type of thing: *The car stopped outside a used-car lot at the end of the street.* | **parking lot** (=for parking cars)

5 a large area of land

- expanse
- stretch
- tract

expanse /ɪkˈspæns/ [n C] a large continuous area of land, water, or sky **+ of** *We traveled across a broad expanse of desert.* | **vast expanse** (=extremely large area) *the vast expanse of the Pacific Ocean*

stretch /stretʃ/ [n C] an area of land or water, especially one that is long and narrow **+ of** *an empty stretch of highway* | *The stretch of coastline between Barcelona and the French border is called the Costa Brava.*

tract /trækt/ [n C usually plural] a very large area of land of a particular type, for example, an area of forest or farming country **vast/huge/large tracts of sth** *Vast tracts of Brazilian rain forest continue to be cut down every year.* | *There are large tracts of vacant land near the river, which could be used for farming.*

6 an empty area

- space
- clearing
- vacant lot

space /speɪs/ [n C] a small empty area which is available for you to sit down in, stand in, leave your car in, etc: *There's a space over there by the bar where we can sit down.* | *I couldn't find an empty space in the car park.*

clearing /ˈklɪərɪŋ/ [n C] a small empty area of land in the middle of a forest or wood, especially where the trees have been cut down: *A small deer stood on the edge of the clearing.* | *In the clearing, there was a small cottage.*

vacant lot /ˌveɪkənt ˈlɒt ‖-ˈlɑːt/ [n C] American an empty outdoor area in a town or city where nothing has been built yet and that is not being used for any particular purpose at the moment: *A bunch of kids were playing basketball in a vacant lot.* | *With real estate prices rising, vacant lots in the area are selling for as much as $75,000.*

7 an area belonging to a country or person

- territory
- turf
- patch

territory /ˈterɪ̈təri‖-tɔːri/ [n C/U] an area that officially belongs to a particular country, or an area that a person, group, or animal controls and will defend against others: *The island of Guam is a US territory.* | *Many birds will attack other birds that enter their territory.* | *a salesman's territory* | **neutral territory** (=an area which no-one controls) *The negotiations will be held on neutral territory.*

turf /tɜːʳf/ [n U] the area that a person or group controls and defends against anyone competing for it: *Ten years ago the city was paralyzed by gang battles over turf.*

patch /pætʃ/ [n C usually singular] British informal the area that someone controls or is responsible for: *Detective McCready had taken over; he didn't want us on his patch.*

8 an area that is part of a surface

- area
- patch
- spot

area /ˈeəriə/ [n C] part of a surface that has a particular size or shape: *There were several damp areas on the living room ceiling.* | **+ of** *After an hour's work, I had only cleaned a small area of the carpet.*

patch /pætʃ/ [n C] a small area that is different from the parts around it: *a white kitten with black patches* | **+ of** *I noticed a patch of dirt in the middle of the rug.* | **damp/dirty/icy etc patch** *The car hit an icy patch on the road and went out of control.*

spot /spɒt‖spɑːt/ [n C] a small area that has been changed, especially because it is damaged or dirty, and looks different: *Do you mind cleaning the grease spots behind the stove?* | *Oh no, I've got a spot on my new shirt!*

an area of knowledge, activity, or responsibility

9 an area of knowledge, duties, study etc

- area
- field
- branch
- world
- domain
- realm
- sphere

area /ˈeəriə/ [n C] an **area** of knowledge, activity, or responsibility: *They fund research in areas like information technology.* | **+ of** *The President has won new support because of his reforms in the areas of health and education.* | *Nordstrom does research in the area of heart disease.*

field /fiːld/ [n C] a subject or area of study, especially one that you know a lot about: *Keith has a degree in engineering, but couldn't find a job in his field.* | **the field** *Laycock is one of the most brilliant psychiatrists in the field.* | **+ of** *There are good employment opportunities in the field of healthcare, particularly nursing.*

branch /brɑːntʃ‖bræntʃ/ [n C] one part of a large area of study or knowledge **+ of** *Trigonometry is a branch of mathematics.* | *He's interested in the branch of international law that deals with war crimes.*

world /wɜːʳld/ [n C usually singular] an area of activity or work – use this especially when talking about all the people who work in that area **business/fashion/hi-tech etc world** *Jaffrii is now one of the richest and most successful men in the business world.* | *the fashion world* | **the world of sth** *the fast-paced world of technology*

domain /dəˈmeɪn, dəʊ-/ [n C] formal an area of activity, interest, or knowledge to which something belongs: *The abortion issue has shifted from the political to the religious domain.* | **male/female domain** *In the US, manual labor remains a male domain.*

realm /relm/ [n C] formal a general area of thought, interest, or knowledge: *the spiritual realm* | **the realm of sth** *new discoveries in the realm of science*

sphere /sfɪəʳ/ [n C] an area of activity, interest, knowledge etc, especially one that people consider should be respected or admired: *Mitchell's greatest achievements have been in the diplomatic sphere.* | **in scientific/political etc spheres** *She has a solid reputation in scientific spheres.*

argue

RELATED WORDS

- when people who have argued do not talk to each other *see* **talk (17)**
- *see also* **disagree, shout, fight**

1 to argue

- argue
- quarrel
- fight
- have a fight
- fall out with
- be at each other's throats
- clash

argue /ˈɑːʳgjuː/ [v I] if people **argue**, they speak angrily to each other because they disagree about something: *Jim and Beth seem to spend all their time arguing.* | **+ with** *Don't argue with me, John. Just do what I tell you.* | **+ about/over** *The two men at the bar were arguing about politics.* | *My kids spend more time arguing over the rules than they do playing the game.*

quarrel /ˈkwɒrəl‖ˈkwɔː-, ˈkwɑː-/ [v I] if two people **quarrel**, they argue angrily and may stop being friends with each other: *Whenever my sisters meet they always end up quarrelling.* | **+ with** *She left home after quarrelling with her parents.* | **+ about/over** *The two brothers had quarreled over ownership of the farm.*

fight /faɪt/ [v I] to argue in an angry and violent way, especially with someone you know well: *Kerry's parents are always fighting – I'm not surprised she left home.* | **+ over/about** *Two men fighting over a parking space were arrested earlier today.* | *If you two don't stop fighting about what to watch I'm going to send you to your room.*

have a fight ALSO **have a row** British /hæv ə ˈfaɪt, hæv ə ˈraʊ/ [v phrase] informal if two people **have a fight** or **have a row**, they argue very angrily and noisily **+ with** *April had a fight with her boyfriend and doesn't want to come out of her room.* | **+ about/over** *Kelvin and his wife have endless rows over money.*

fall out with /ˌfɔːl ˈaʊt wɪð/ [v phrase] British to stop having a friendly relationship with someone, because you have disagreed with them: *I think she's fallen out with her boyfriend.* | **+ about/over** *Murray left the company after he fell out with the chairman over his salary.* —**falling out** [n] **have a falling out (with sb)** *We had a falling out after he asked me to lie for him.*

be at each other's throats /biː ət iːtʃ ˌʌðəʳz ˈθrəʊts/ [v phrase] if two people or groups **are at each other's throats**, they are always arguing in a very angry way because they cannot agree about something: *Congress and the President have been at each other's throats for so long that it's a wonder they can agree on anything.*

clash /klæʃ/ [v I] if two groups of people **clash**, they argue publicly with each other about a particular subject – used in news reports **clash with sb** *Democrats clashed with Republicans last night in a heated debate about unemployment.* | **clash over sth** *France and Britain are likely to clash over the proposed space programme.*

2 to argue about something very unimportant

- squabble
- bicker
- quibble
- split hairs

squabble /ˈskwɒbəl‖ˈskwɑː-/ [v I] to argue noisily about something that is not really important – use this especially about children or when you think someone is behaving like a child: *Oh, for goodness sake, stop squabbling, you two!* | **+ about/over** *The kids always squabble about who should do the dishes.*

bicker /ˈbɪkəʳ/ [v I] to continually argue about something unimportant in a way that annoys other people: *Whenever we go shopping together we always start bickering.* | **+ about/over** *The mayor and the town council spent most of Thursday bickering over how to balance next year's budget.* —**bickering** [n U] *She never visits her parents because she can't stand the constant bickering.*

quibble /ˈkwɪbəl/ [v I] to argue in an annoying way about unimportant details, especially about whether something is exactly correct: *She said I owed her twenty dollars. I thought it was twenty-five but I wasn't going to quibble.* | **+ over** *Why quibble over whose turn it is to buy lunch? Split it, and forget about it.*

split hairs /ˌsplɪt ˈheəʳz/ [v phrase usually in progressive] to say that there is a difference between two things and argue about this, when really the difference is too small to be important: *Batard is a little sweeter than Chevalier but perhaps that's splitting hairs; both these wines are excellent.*

3 to deliberately start an argument

- start an argument
- pick a fight
- stir things up
- make an issue (out) of

start an argument /ˌstɑːʳt ən ˈɑːʳgjəmənt/ [v phrase] *I didn't want to start an argument, so I kept quiet.*

pick a fight ALSO **pick a quarrel** British /ˌpɪk ə ˈfaɪt, ˌpɪk ə ˈkwɒrəl‖ -ˈkwɔː-/ [v phrase] to deliberately start an argument with someone by saying something that you know will make them angry: *Just ignore him, he's always picking fights.* | **+ with** *Burton was at the bar, trying to pick a quarrel with a stranger.*

stir things up /ˌstɜːʳ θɪŋz ˈʌp/ [v phrase] to deliberately do or say something to make other people argue because you want to cause problems for them: *Just as we were beginning to get on with each other again, Jackie came and stirred things up.* | *Ignore him – he's just trying to stir things up because he's jealous.*

make an issue (out) of /ˌmeɪk ən ˈɪʃuː (aʊt) ɒv/ [v phrase] especially spoken to argue about something because you think it is important, even though other people may think you are being unreasonable: *I don't want to make an issue out of it, but that's the second time you've been late this week.* | *Although she was annoyed that Ian had given her secret away, she decided not to make an issue of it.*

4 an argument

- argument
- row
- quarrel
- disagreement
- dispute
- bust-up
- exchange
- showdown
- feud

argument /ˈɑːʳgjəmənt/ [n C] when people speak angrily to each other because they disagree about something **have an argument** *My sister and I had a terrible argument last night.* | **+ about/over** *A 29-year-old man was shot and killed today after an argument over a gambling debt.* | **+ with** *I'm sorry I'm not in a good mood. I had an argument with my husband this morning.* | **get into an argument** (=to start arguing, without intending to) *Phil got into an argument with a guy at the bar.*

row /raʊ/ [n C] British a loud angry argument that continues for a short time between people who know each other well. **Row** is also used about a serious disagreement between politicians concerning important public matters: *There were always rows when my dad got home.* | *The World Trade Organization will give the two countries 60 days to end their row.* | **+ over** *The newspapers are full of stories about the continuing row over private education.* | **blazing row** (=a very angry, noisy argument) *The couple in the house next door were having a blazing row.* | **big row** *A few months ago they had a big row, and Steve drove off and spent the weekend in London.*

quarrel /'kwɒrəl‖'kwɔː-, 'kwɑː-/ [n C] an angry argument between people who know each other well: *a family quarrel* | **+ with** *I was tired of these stupid quarrels with my parents.* | **have a quarrel** *They had some sort of quarrel years ago, and they haven't spoken to each other since.*

disagreement /ˌdɪsə'griːmənt/ [n C] a situation in which people disagree with each other, but without shouting or getting angry **+ about/over** *There were the occasional disagreements about money, but mostly we got on well.* | **+ with** *Ginny had left the company after a disagreement with her boss.* | **+ between** *This bill will never be passed if disagreements between Democrats and Republicans aren't settled soon.*

dispute /dɪ'spjuːt, 'dɪspjuːt/ [n C] formal when two people, organizations, or countries publicly disagree and argue with each other about something important **+ over/about** *The dispute over weapons inspections is likely to be the main topic of tomorrow's meeting.* | **+ with** *Morris has been involved in a long legal dispute with his publisher.* | **+ between** *Representatives from both sides met late last night in an attempt to settle the budget dispute between Congress and the President.* | **settle a dispute** (=end it by agreement) *All efforts to settle the dispute have so far failed.*

bust-up /'bʌst ʌp/ [n C] British informal a very bad quarrel or fight: *After the bust-up, I didn't see Rick for several weeks.* | **have a big bust-up** *She and her boyfriend had a big bust-up over who was supposed to look after the kids.* | **+ with** *Christie was involved in an angry bust-up with reporters and photographers outside the courtroom.*

exchange /ɪks'tʃeɪndʒ/ [n C] a very short argument between people or groups, especially in a formal or official situation such as a political meeting: *During angry exchanges in Parliament the Prime Minister said he would not change existing policies.* | **heated exchange** (=an angry exchange) *A series of heated exchanges between the two governments followed.*

showdown /'ʃəʊdaʊn/ [n C usually singular] a serious argument that comes at the end of a period of time during which there has been a lot of disagreement and angry feelings: *Everyone in the office knew that there would be a showdown sooner or later, the way things were going.* | *The Senate moved toward another showdown with the President over the budget.*

feud /fjuːd/ [n C] an unpleasant and often violent situation between two groups, especially families, in which people have been arguing for so long that they cannot remember the cause of it: *The feud between the Hatfields and the McCoys raged for 20 years.* | *He has been accused of letting personal feuds affect his judgement.*

5 an argument about something unimportant

- squabble
- tiff
- spat

squabble /'skwɒbəl‖'skwɑː-/ [n C] a noisy argument about something that is not important, especially between children: *Uncle Matt bought them a computer game to share, which led to endless squabbles.* | **+ about/over** *The kids are having their usual squabble over which TV show they're going to watch.*

tiff /tɪf/ [n C] a short argument about something unimportant, especially between two people who are in love **have a tiff (with sb)** *Whenever she and Bernard had a tiff, Ari would go for a long drive to think about things.* | **lover's tiff** *It was just a silly lovers' tiff – we couldn't even remember why it had started.*

spat /spæt/ [n C] a short angry argument, usually about something unimportant: *The girls were having a spat in the back of the car over who got to use the armrest.* | *It was just a little spat over who did the dishes last.*

6 someone who likes arguing

- argumentative/quarrelsome
- confrontational

argumentative/quarrelsome /ˌɑːrgjə'mentətɪv, 'kwɒrəlsəm‖'kwɔː-, 'kwɑː-/ [adj] someone who is argumentative seems to like arguing and starting arguments. **Quarrelsome** is less common than **argumentative** and is used especially in written English: *When he drinks too much he becomes argumentative.* | *She had had enough of all her quarrelsome relatives.*

confrontational /ˌkɒnfrən'teɪʃənəl‖ˌkɑːn-/ [adj] speaking to people in a very direct way that is likely to cause an angry argument – use this when you think someone is behaving unreasonably: *Some are worried that Beier's confrontational style will upset his staff.* | *In an attempt to improve his image, Stevens has decided to be less confrontational.*

7 to stop arguing

- make up
- patch up your differences/settle your differences
- bury the hatchet
- clear the air
- conciliatory
- reconciliation

make up ALSO **make it up** British /ˌmeɪk 'ʌp, ˌmeɪk ɪt 'ʌp/ [phr v I] especially spoken if two people who know each other well **make up** or **make it up**, they stop arguing and start being friendly to each other again: *I'm glad to see you two have made up.* | **+ with** *Have you made it up with your sister yet?*

patch up your differences/settle your differences /ˌpætʃ ʌp jɔːr 'dɪfərənsɨz, ˌsetl jɔːr 'dɪfərənsɨz/ [v phrase] if two people or organizations **patch up** or **settle their differences**, they stop arguing and discuss things in a sensible way until they come to an agreement: *Their final attempt to settle their differences ended in disappointment and separation.* | **+ with** *Gary's first priority on his return home was to patch up his differences with his sister.*

bury the hatchet /ˌberi ðə 'hætʃɨt/ [v phrase] to agree to stop arguing and forgive each other, especially a long time after you first had the argument: *It's about time they buried the hatchet after all these* *years.* | *Since those two buried the hatchet, life in the office has been much quieter.*

clear the air /ˌklɪəʳ ði 'eəʳ/ [v phrase] to talk calmly and seriously with someone about what you have been arguing about, in order to end the disagreement and feel better: *I think it's about time you called her to clear the air.* | *In an attempt to clear the air, Mills has planned a meeting with employees to discuss the issue.*

conciliatory /kən'sɪliətəri‖-tɔːri/ [adj] behaving in a way that shows that you want to end an argument with someone: *The tone of my letter had been friendly and conciliatory, so I was disappointed by the cold reply I received.* | **conciliatory gesture/message/tone etc** *American intelligence flights over Cuba had been stopped as a conciliatory gesture.*

reconciliation /ˌrekənsɪli'eɪʃən/ [n C/U] when two people, countries etc agree to stop arguing or fighting after a long period of disagreement, and have a friendly relationship again: *After years of fighting, there was now a spirit of national reconciliation in South Africa.* | **+ with** *Giles is not interested in a reconciliation with his father.* | **+ between** *A large group of demonstrators stayed up all night praying for reconciliation between the two countries.*

8 when a bad situation or problem makes people argue

- cause an argument/lead to an argument
- come between
- cause a rift between

cause an argument/lead to an argument /ˌkɔːz ən 'ɑːʳgjᵿmənt, ˌliːd tʊ ən 'ɑːʳgjᵿmənt/ [v phrase] if an unpleasant situation or problem **causes** or **leads to an argument**, it makes people argue: *Don't tell him about the money. It'll only cause an argument.* | *The cleaning rota always leads to arguments in our house.*

come between /ˌkʌm bɪ'twiːn/ [phr v T] if a bad situation or a problem comes between two people, it makes them argue, usually with the result that they stop being friends: *We were such close friends that I didn't think anything could come between us.* | *I was determined not to let my career come between us.*

cause a rift between /ˌkɔːz ə 'rɪft bɪˌtwiːn/ [v phrase] if a bad situation, a problem etc causes a rift between two people, it makes them have a small argument with the result that they are not as friendly as they were before: *The street fighting has caused a slight rift between the communities involved.* | *No one is quite sure about what caused the rift between the two actors.*

army

RELATED WORDS

- leave the army, navy etc *see* **leave (26)**
- *see also* **war, weapon, attack, fight**

1 the army, navy etc

- army
- navy
- airforce
- the military
- the armed forces
- forces
- the services
- the Marines/the Marine Corps

army /'ɑːʳmi/ [n C] a large organized group of people trained to fight on land in a war **the army** *Units of the Nigerian army were quickly sent to the border.* | **in the army** *My sons are both in the army.* | **raise an army** (=collect and organize an army to fight a battle) *In 1066 William the Conqueror raised an army and invaded England.*

navy /'neɪvi/ [n C] the part of a country's military forces that is trained for fighting a war at sea **the navy** *It was an important battle for the navy.* | **in the navy** *My father was in the navy during the war.*

airforce ALSO **air force** American /'eəʳfɔːʳs/ [n C] the part of a country's military forces that is trained for fighting a war in the air: *The French have a very powerful airforce.* | **the airforce** *The airforce played a huge part in the Kosovo conflict.* | **in the airforce** *My brother and sister are both in the airforce.*

the military /ðə 'mɪlᵻtəri‖-teri/ [n singular with singular or plural verb in British English] especially American the army, navy, and air force of a country: *The military may be sent in to deal with the riots.* | *a company that supplies electronic equipment to the military*

the armed forces /ði ˌɑːʳmd 'fɔːʳsᵻz/ [n plural] the army, navy, and airforce of a country: *A new government minister is now responsible for the armed forces.* | *Measures will be taken to help modernize the country's armed forces.*

forces /'fɔːʳsᵻz/ [n plural] groups of soldiers from a country's army, navy, and airforce: *The town was captured by Italian forces under the command of General Ciano.* | *The United States placed its forces in the region on alert.* | *Ground forces were wiped out by the air attack.*

the services ALSO **the service** American /ðə 'sɜːʳvᵻsᵻ(z)/ [n plural] the army, navy, and airforce – use this especially when talking about someone having a job in the army etc **be in the service(s)** *Camp Lejune was the first place I was stationed when I was in the service.* | **go into the services** *The family has a tradition of going into the services.*

the Marines/the Marine Corps /ðə mə'riːnz, ðə mə'riːn kɔːʳ/ [n plural] a specially trained part of the US armed forces: *A special force of 500 US Marines has been sent to the area.* | *I have a 25-year-old brother who's in the Marine Corps.*

2 someone who is in the army, navy etc

- serviceman/servicewoman
- soldier
- troops
- sailor
- airman
- officer

serviceman/servicewoman /'sɜːʳvᵻsmən, 'sɜːʳvᵻsˌwʊmən/ [n C] a man or woman who is in an army, navy etc: *The ceremony was held to honour the tens of thousands of servicemen and servicewomen who lost their lives in the war.* | *Four Australian servicemen were reported missing after the ambush.* | *a tribute to the bravery of our servicemen and -women*

soldier /'səʊldʒəʳ/ [n C] a member of an army, especially someone who is not an officer: *Moore has been a soldier for most of his adult life.* | *There were several soldiers guarding the main gate.*

troops /truːps/ [n plural] soldiers – use this especially to talk about soldiers taking part in a military attack: *Thousands of French troops died in the attack.* | *The President is sending three hundred troops to the area.*

sailor /'seɪləʳ/ [n C] a member of the navy: *Janet married a sailor in the French navy.* | *Two thousand*

British sailors lost their lives when the ship went down.

airman /ˈeəʳmən/ [n C] a member of the airforce: *Three airmen were killed during the battle.*

officer /ˈɒfɪsəʳ‖ˈɒː-, ˈɔː-/ a high-ranking member of the army, navy etc, who is in charge of a group of soldiers, sailors etc: *He's an officer in the US Marines.* | **commanding officer** (=the officer in charge) *Colonel Gary G. Mahle is the commanding officer here.*

3 used by or connected with the army, navy etc

- military
- army
- naval
- air

military /ˈmɪlɪtəri‖-teri/ [adj only before noun] used by or connected with the army, navy, or airforce, especially the army: *The President visited a military cemetery at Bitburg.* | *China reportedly planned to sell military equipment to Saudi Arabia.* | *Peres said the military campaign would last as long as it took to secure the country's northern border.*

army /ˈɑːʳmi/ [adj only before noun] connected with or used by the **army**: *There's an American army base nearby.* | *An army jeep was parked outside their house.* | *Army officers have overthrown the government in a well planned coup d'état.*

naval /ˈneɪvəl/ [adj only before noun] connected with or used by the navy: *His orders were to protect the port from naval attack.* | *a huge Chinese naval base* | *Stedman spent nine months recovering in a naval hospital.*

air /eəʳ/ [adj only before noun] connected with or used by the airforce: *The island's defences have been badly damaged by recent air attacks.* | *Ground forces will be backed up by NATO air power.*

4 to join the army, navy etc

- join
- join up
- enlist

join /dʒɔɪn/ [v T] **join the army/navy/airforce/marines** to become a member of the army, navy etc: *He wants to join the air force when he finishes school.* | *Frank lied about his age in order to join the army.*

join up /ˌdʒɔɪn ˈʌp/ [phr v I] to join the armed forces, especially during a war: *My dad joined up at the beginning of the war.*

enlist /ɪnˈlɪst/ [v I] to join the armed forces, either in peace time or during a war: *By the end of 1915, over 700,000 men had enlisted.* | **+ in** *Frank enlisted in the marines at the age of 19.*

5 when people are made to join the army, navy etc

- conscription
- be conscripted
- military service
- be called up

conscription ALSO **the draft** /kənˈskrɪpʃən, ðə ˈdrɑːft‖-ˈdræft/ [n U] American when people are officially ordered to join the armed forces, especially during a war: *When was conscription introduced in Britain?* | **avoid/dodge the draft** *Many young men went abroad to avoid the draft.*

be conscripted /biː kənˈskrɪptɪd/ [v phrase] if someone **is conscripted**, they are made to join the armed forces by law: *Some of the men were volunteers, but most of them had been conscripted.* | **be conscripted into the army/the armed forces etc** *Many of the young soldiers who were conscripted into the army in World War I did not want to fight.*

military service/national service British /ˌmɪlɪtəri ˈsɜːʳvɪs‖-teri-, ˌnæʃənəl ˈsɜːʳvɪs/ [n U] the system in which everyone has to be a member of the armed forces for a period of time: *All males between the ages of 18 and 60 were liable for military service.* | *My father was exempted from military service on the grounds of ill health.* | *My father was posted to Germany during his national service, and that's where he met my mother.* | **do military service** *Did you have to do military service?*

be called up British **be drafted** American /bi ˌkɔːld ˈʌp, biː ˈdrɑːftɪd‖-ˈdræf-/ [v phrase] to be officially ordered to join the armed forces during a war: *I was called up three months after the First World War broke out.* | *Thousands of young Americans were drafted to fight in the war in Vietnam.*

around/round

around something or moving around something

RELATED WORDS

- to turn around *see* **turn**
- shaped like a ball or circle *see* **round**
- *see also* **circle**

1 around someone or something

- around
- on all sides/on every side

around ALSO **round** British /əˈraʊnd, raʊnd/ [prep/adv] completely surrounding or enclosing someone or something: *A group of students sat around the table chatting.* | *She was wearing a silver chain round her neck.* | *On the kitchen table was a package with tape wrapped around it.* | **all around/all round** *Enemy soldiers were now all around us.* | *At the bottom of the hill was a small pond with trees all round.*

on all sides/on every side /ɒn ˌɔːl ˈsaɪdz, ɒn ˌevri ˈsaɪd/ [adv] if something is around you **on all sides** or **on every side**, you see it everywhere and you may feel that you are unable to move or escape because of it: *Mountains rose steeply on all sides.* | **from all sides** *There was the sound of gunfire from all sides.*

2 to be surrounded by something

- be surrounded by
- be ringed by
- be framed by
- enclose

be surrounded by /biː səˈraʊndɪd baɪ/ [v phrase] if someone or something **is surrounded by** people or things, those people or things are around them on every side: *The tops of the hills were surrounded by clouds.* | *Jill sat on the floor surrounded by boxes.*

be ringed by /biː ˈrɪŋd baɪ/ [v phrase] if something **is ringed by** things, those things form a circle around it: *Hoover Dam is ringed by snow-capped mountains that reach high above the desert plain.* | *Fifteen minutes after the explosion, the embassy was ringed by police officers and armed guards.*

be framed by /biː ˈfreɪmd baɪ/ [v phrase] if something that you are looking at **is framed by** something, you see it within the borders of that thing: *I* *could see the church tower framed by the windows.* | *Her small face was framed by a mass of red hair*

enclose /ɪnˈkləʊz/ [v T usually in passive] to form a wall or covering around something that keeps it separate from everything outside it: *The fence enclosing the prison compound is constantly patrolled by armed guards.* | **be enclosed by sth** *The garden was completely enclosed by a high wall.* | *The fish live in a shallow tropical lagoon, which is enclosed by a coral reef.* | **be enclosed in sth** *Jerry had to spend two months enclosed in a huge plastic bubble, to prevent him from catching germs from other children.*

3 to move into a position around someone or something

- surround
- gather around
- encircle
- crowd around

surround /səˈraʊnd/ [v T] to stand in a circle around someone or something, especially to prevent someone escaping: *Football fans ran onto the field and surrounded the referee.* | *Police officers moved to surround Evans as he came out of the courtroom.*

gather around ALSO **gather round** /ˌgæðər əˈraʊnd, ˌgæðəʳ ˈraʊnd/ [v I/T] if a group of people **gathers around** someone or something, they move nearer to them, for example in order to see or hear better: *A crowd of young boys had gathered round to admire the car.* | **gather around sb/sth** *After supper we gathered around the kitchen table and listened to Grandma tell stories about her childhood.*

encircle /ɪnˈsɜːʳkəl/ [v T] if a group of people **encircle** someone or something, they move so that they are completely around them, making it impossible for them to escape: *Troops encircled the city and began firing rockets at the government buildings.* | *The photo showed the captive sitting down, encircled by several armed men.*

crowd around ALSO **crowd round** British /ˌkraʊd əˈraʊnd, ˌkraʊd ˈraʊnd/ [phr v I/T] if a group of people **crowds around** someone or something, they stand near them closely together, often pushing forward to see what is happening: *Fire officers asked the people who had crowded round to stand back.* | **crowd around sb/sth** *Dozens of journalists crowded around the Princess and started asking her questions.*

4 moving in a circle or moving around something

- around
- in circles
- circle
- orbit

around ALSO **round** British /əˈraʊnd, raʊnd/ [adv/prep] use this after verbs of movement, to show that someone or something is moving in a circle or moving **around** something **go/fly/travel/run etc around** *The Earth goes around the Sun.* | *The helicopter flew round and round above us.*

in circles /ɪn ˈsɜːʳkəlz/ [adv] if someone or something moves **in circles**, they move around in a circle several times: *Birds flew in circles above the lake.* | *As the dog got more and more excited, it started running around in circles.*

circle /ˈsɜːʳkəl/ [v I/T] especially written to move around someone or something in a circle: *The plane circled the airport several times before landing.* | **+ around/above** *As we walked along the beach, I could see seagulls circling above the cliffs.*

orbit /ˈɔːʳbɪt/ [v T] to go around the Earth, the Moon, the Sun etc in a continuous circular movement: *The satellite will orbit the Earth for the next 15 years.* | *The team confirmed the discovery of a planet orbiting the star 51 Pegasi.*

arrange

RELATED WORDS

▸ *see also* **organize, order, system**

1 to arrange a group of things or people

- arrange
- organize
- set out
- be laid out
- line up
- order
- put sth in order
- rearrange

arrange /əˈreɪndʒ/ [v T] to put a group of things or people in a particular order or position **arrange sb/sth** *Why don't you arrange the kids and I'll take their picture.* | *Coyle arranged the cushions and sat down on the sofa.* | **arrange sth in pairs/rows/groups etc** *The desks were arranged in pairs.* | **arrange sth/sb in a circle** *Can you arrange yourselves in a circle so that everyone can see me?* | **arrange sth alphabetically** (=according to the letters of the alphabet) *The books are arranged alphabetically, according to author.* | **arrange sth in order of height/importance etc** *If you have a lot of things to do, just make a list and arrange them in order of importance.*

organize ALSO **organise** British /ˈɔːʳgənaɪz/ to arrange in order information, ideas etc according to a system, so that they will be more effective or easier to use: *Organize your notes very carefully before giving a speech.* | *You might find that writing an outline will help you to organize your thoughts.* | **organize sth into piles/groups etc** *The book is organized into three sections.*

set out /ˌset ˈaʊt/ [phr v T] to arrange a group of things on the floor, on a table, on a shelf etc for people to use, take, or look at **set out sth** *If we set out the chairs now, they'll be ready for tonight's meeting.* | **set sth out** *A waiter brought drinks and sandwiches, and set them out on a low table beside the pool.*

be laid out /biː ˌleɪd ˈaʊt/ [v phrase] if a town, building etc **is laid out** in a particular way, it is arranged in that way according to a particular plan: *I like the way your new office is laid out.* | **+ according to** *Kyoto is laid out according to a grid system.*

line up /ˌlaɪn ˈʌp/ [phr v T] to arrange people or things in a line **line up sb/sth** *'Line up your men,' said the police inspector.* | **line sb/sth etc up** *He lined the dolls up from tallest to shortest.*

order /ˈɔːʳdəʳ/ [v T] to arrange a group of things so that one comes after the other in a particular order: *The psychology books are ordered according to title, not according to author.*

put sth in order /ˌpʊt (sth) ɪn ˈɔːʳdəʳ/ [v phrase] to arrange things so that they are in the correct order: *He cleaned his desk and put his papers in order before locking up the office.* | **put sth in alphabetical/numerical order** *We need to put all the names in alphabetical order.*

rearrange /ˌriːəˈreɪndʒ/ [v T] to arrange a group of things in a different way from before: *'This room looks different. Have you painted it?' 'No, I just rearranged the furniture.'* | *This program allows* *you to create and rearrange images on-screen with the click of a mouse button.*

2 the way that things or people are arranged

- arrangement
- layout
- order
- formation

arrangement /ə'reɪndʒmənt/ [n C] a group of things that are arranged according to a pattern in order to look attractive **+ of** *Our chef was never happy until the arrangement of vegetables on each plate was just right.* | **flower arrangement** (=flowers that have been cut and arranged attractively) *A small flower arrangement on the kitchen table can brighten up the room.*

layout /'leɪaʊt/ [n C] the way that a building, town, garden, book etc is arranged according to a plan, so that it looks attractive: *a computer program to help you design page layout* | *Many of the golfers complained about the course layout.* | **+ of** *He was one of the architects who planned the layout of the hospital.*

order /'ɔːʳdəʳ/ [n U] the way that events happen or that information is arranged, showing which is first, which is second, and so on **in this/that/what/any order** *It doesn't matter which order you answer the questions in.* | *Put it into a large mixing bowl and add, in this order, the milk, the honey, the melted butter, and the salt.* | **+ of** *We were given a programme showing the order of events for the day.* | **in order of importance/difficulty/size etc** (=when the most important thing is first, then the next most important etc) *Their main exports, in order of importance, are copper, coal, and maize.* | *The subjects that students enjoyed most were, in order of popularity, music, history, and art.* | **in alphabetical order** (=with 'a' first, then 'b', then 'c' etc) *This index lists each one of the 5 million books in the library, in alphabetical order by title.*

formation /fɔːʳ'meɪʃən/ [n C/U] the way in which a group of planes, ships, soldiers etc are arranged: *Formations of tanks were lined up along the border.* | **in formation** (=in a particular pattern or order when flying, marching, or sailing together) *Three small planes flying in formation collided this afternoon, killing four people.*

3 to arrange to do something or arrange for something to happen

- arrange
- organize
- fix/fix up
- set a time/date/place
- pencil in
- make the arrangements/take care of the arrangements

arrange /ə'reɪndʒ/ [v I/T] to make preparations for a meeting, party, journey etc, for example by choosing a suitable time and place and telling people about it: *Ann's arranging a surprise party for Russell's birthday.* | *We're going on Friday – it's all arranged.* | **+ to do sth** *They arranged to meet the following day.* | **arrange for sb to do sth** *He arranged for Andi to leave on the next flight home.* | **it is arranged that** *It was arranged that our visitors should stay at a nearby hotel.*

organize ALSO **organise** British /'ɔːʳgənaɪz/ [v T] to make preparations for an event, especially a big public event that needs a lot of preparation and planning: *I've been asked to organize this year's Summer Carnival.* | *an exhibition organised by the local camera club* —**organizer** also **organiser** British [n C] someone who organizes a large public event: *The organisers will give all profits from the show to charity.* | *Chief festival organizer Josephine Barnfield insists that the concert will go ahead despite the ban.*

fix/fix up /fɪks, ˌfɪks 'ʌp/ [v T] especially British, spoken to arrange something, especially for someone else, in order to help them or because they cannot arrange it for themselves **fix sth/fix up sth** *Don't worry, Jean has already fixed everything.* | *We have done our best to fix up a meeting but they haven't shown any interest.* | **fix sth/it/them up** *We need to get all the sales staff together for a conference – could I leave it to you to fix it up, Jane?* | **fix it for sb to do sth** *She can fix it for you to see the show free if you want.*

set a time/date/place ALSO **fix a date/time/place** British /ˌset ə 'taɪm, 'deɪt, 'pleɪs, ˌfɪks ə 'deɪt, 'taɪm, 'pleɪs/ [v phrase] to arrange for something to happen on a particular date etc: *I'll have my secretary set a date and we'll meet for lunch.* | *We need to meet with Elaine this afternoon but I'm having trouble fixing a time.*

pencil in /ˌpensəl 'ɪn/ [phr v T] especially British to arrange for something to happen on a particular date or time knowing that the arrangements may have to be changed later **pencil sb/sth/it/her etc in** *I'll pencil you in but we might have to change the meeting to Thursday.* | **pencil in sb/sth** *Let's pencil in the 19th for now, and you get in touch later if you can't make it.* | **pencil sb/sth in for** *Dates for the concerts are pencilled in for late next year.* | *You can pencil him in for the 8th but I'm afraid I might be out of town that day.*

make the arrangements/take care of the arrangements /ˌmeɪk ði ə'reɪndʒmənts, teɪk ˌkeər əv ði ə'reɪndʒmənts/ [v phrase] to arrange all the details of an event after you have decided what you are going to do: *Uncle Bill has made all the funeral arrangements.* | **+ for** *Margot and Paul went up to London to make the arrangements for the wedding.* | *The marketing people will take care of all the arrangements for the presentation.* | **make arrangements to do sth** *I made arrangements to see Alec while he was in town.*

4 to arrange to use a plane, train, hotel room, restaurant etc

- reserve/book
- reservation
- booking

reserve/book /rɪ'zɜːʳv, bʊk/ [v T/v I/T] *I'd like to reserve a seat on the next plane to Atlanta.* | *Marge and I are thinking of booking a holiday in Malaysia this year.* | *You'd better book now while they still have a vacancy.* | **be booked up/be fully booked** (=all the tickets, seats etc have been booked) *The lady at the bed and breakfast says she's booked up till February.* | **booked solid** (=all the tickets for a play, show etc have been completely booked for a long period of time and it is impossible to get any) *The show was booked solid for months to come.* —**reserved** [adj] *I'm afraid this table is reserved, sir.*

reservation /ˌrezəʳ'veɪʃən/ [n C] an arrangement you make with a hotel, airline, restaurant etc so that they will keep a room or seat for you to use at a later time or date: *There might be trouble getting hotel reservations the week of the festival.* | **have a reservation** *'I'd like a table for two please.' 'Do you have a reservation, madam?'* | **make a reservation** *She packed her bags, then called the airport and made a reservation on the last flight out of Los*

Angeles. | **cancel a reservation** *I have to work late tonight, so I cancelled our dinner reservations.*

booking /ˈbʊkɪŋ/ [n C] especially British an arrangement you make with a hotel, theatre, etc so that they will keep a room or seat for you to use at a later time or date: *I'd like to cancel my booking, please.* | *Advance bookings for the show currently total more than £100,000.* | **make a booking** *You can make a provisional booking over the phone.*

5 to carefully or secretly arrange something

- orchestrate
- stage-manage
- engineer
- contrive

orchestrate /ˈɔːʳkəstreɪt/ [v T] written to carefully and often secretly arrange for something to happen, especially so that people do not realize that it was a planned event: *Treasury officials are trying to orchestrate a sharp decline in the dollar.* | *The so-called 'revolution' was in fact orchestrated by the CIA.* —**orchestrated** [adj] *The newspaper article is part of a carefully orchestrated campaign to persuade people to stop smoking.*

stage-manage /ˈsteɪdʒ ˌmænɪdʒ/ [v T] to carefully and secretly arrange for something, especially a political event, to happen in exactly the way that you want, but without giving the appearance that it was planned – use this to show disapproval: *Most of the 'spontaneous demonstrations' supporting the President are stage-managed.*

engineer /ˌendʒəˈnɪəʳ/ [v T] to arrange for something to happen without anyone knowing that you have planned it: *The socialist party secretly engineered the defeat of the government.* | *Before they could engineer an escape, they had to be sure that none of the guards were suspicious.*

contrive /kənˈtraɪv/ [v T] to arrange an event or situation in a clever way, especially secretly and by tricking or deceiving people: *He contrived a meeting between his mother and her ex- husband.* | *In the play Amos contrives a scheme to make Paul pay back the money he owes him.*

6 things that must be arranged for something to happen

- arrangements

arrangements /əˈreɪndʒmənts/ [n plural] all the preparations that must be made for something to happen and be successful **+ for** *Who is in charge of the arrangements for the President's visit?* | **make arrangements** *We need to make arrangements for the neighbors to take care of the cats while we're away.* | **take care of the arrangements** *Don't worry about finding a place to stay. My department will take care of the arrangements.* | **travel/seating/sleeping arrangements** *Lena wasn't very happy about the travel arrangements.*

arrive

RELATED WORDS

opposite: **leave**

see also **late, early, on time, appear**

1 to arrive somewhere

- arrive
- get to
- come
- reach
- be here
- turn up/show up
- make it
- roll in
- get in

arrive /əˈraɪv/ [v I] if someone or something **arrives**, they get to the place they were going to: *What time do you think we'll arrive?* | *Did my package arrive?* | *Give me a call to let me know you've arrived safely.* | **+ at** *It was already dark by the time they arrived at their hotel.* | **+ in** *The British Prime Minister arrived in Tokyo today.* | **+ from** *When Uncle Guy arrived from Dublin he brought them an enormous box of chocolates.* | **arrive here/there/back/home** *When I first arrived here none of the other students would talk to me.*

get to /ˈget tuː/ [v phrase not in progressive] informal to arrive at a place: *It'll take us about half an hour to get to the airport.* | *Turn left, and walk down the street until you get to some traffic lights.* | **get back to** (=return to) *I'll call her when I get back to Chicago.* | **get there/here/home** *What time do you usually get home in the evening?* | *I want to get there before the store closes.*

come /kʌm/ [v I] if someone or something **comes**, they arrive at the place where you are waiting for them: *When the visitors come, send them up to my office.* | *Has the mail come yet?* | *My mother's saying she won't come if Richard's here.* | **come home/back** *What time is Dad coming home?*

reach /riːtʃ/ [v T not in progressive] to arrive at a place, especially after a long or difficult journey: *It took more than three days to reach the top of the mountain.* | *Snow prevented workers from reaching the broken pipeline.*

be here /biː ˈhɪəʳ/ [v phrase] spoken use this to say that someone has arrived at the place where you are waiting for them: *Susan, your friends are here.* | *Is Andy here yet?* | *Here they are. Go and open the door, will you?*

turn up/show up /ˌtɜːʳn ˈʌp, ˌʃəʊ ˈʌp/ [phr v I not usually in progressive] informal to arrive – use this about someone you are expecting to arrive, especially when they arrive late: *Steve turned up half an hour late as usual.* | *Some of the people I invited never showed up.* | *If Tina shows up, tell her we waited as long as we could.*

make it /ˈmeɪk ɪt/ [v phrase not in progressive] informal to arrive somewhere in time for something, when you were not sure you would: *If we don't make it on time, start without us.* | **+ to** *We just made it to the hospital before the baby arrived.*

roll in /ˌrəʊl ˈɪn/ [phr v I] informal if someone **rolls in**, they arrive somewhere later than they should and do not seem worried about it – often used humorously: *Chris finally rolled in at about 4:00 am.* | *Rebecca usually rolls in around noon.*

get in /ˌget ˈɪn/ [phr v I] to arrive home, especially when you are later than expected or usual: *What time did you get in last night?* | *Mark just got in a few minutes ago.*

2 a plane, ship, train, bus etc arrives

- arrive
- get in
- land
- come in
- dock
- pull in
- be in
- incoming

arrive /əˈraɪv/ [v I] *What time does his flight arrive?* | *The train isn't due to arrive until 4.30.* | **+ at/in/from** *Our flight arrived in Osaka two hours ahead of schedule.* | *Supply ships have started arriving at ports along the East coast.* —**arrival** [n U] *Would passengers awaiting the arrival of flight 405 from Honolulu please make their way to Gate 14.*

get in /ˌget ˈɪn/ [phr v I not usually in progressive] to arrive – use this when you are talking about the time when a train, ship, or plane arrives: *What time does your flight get in?* | *Hopefully the bus will get in by 8 o'clock.* | **+ to** *The ferry gets in to Harwich around noon.*

land /lænd/ [v I] if a plane **lands**, it arrives at an airport: *Despite severe weather conditions, the Boeing 727 landed as scheduled.* | **+ at** *When the plane landed at JFK, it was three hours late.* | **+ in** *Before landing in Algiers, we circled the airport several times.* | **come in to land** (=go down towards the ground at an airport) *There's a plane coming in to land now.*

come in /ˌkʌm ˈɪn/ [phr v I] if a plane, ship, or train **comes in**, it arrives in the place where you are waiting: *Has the Air India flight come in yet?* | *Crowds had gathered at the harbour to watch the ship come in.*

dock /dɒk‖dɑːk/ [v I] if a ship **docks**, it arrives at a port **+ at/in** *When the ship docked at Southampton its cargo was immediately inspected.* | *We finally docked in Portland, Maine, happy to be on dry land again.*

pull in /ˌpʊl ˈɪn/ [phr v I] if a train, car, or bus **pulls in**, it arrives at the station or the place where you are waiting: *Finally the bus pulled in, forty minutes late.* | *Just as the train was pulling in, there was a shout and someone fell onto the track.*

be in /biː ˈɪn/ [phr v I] if you say that a plane, train or ship **is in**, it has arrived at the airport, station etc where you are waiting: *Their plane's in, but it'll take them a little while to get through customs.* | *As her train wasn't in yet, she went to the bookstall and flipped through the magazines.*

incoming /ˈɪnkʌmɪŋ/ [adj only before noun] **incoming plane/flight/train etc** a place, train etc that is arriving somewhere rather than leaving: *All incoming flights are being delayed by fog.* | *The crash occurred when a freight train collided with an incoming passenger train.*

3 when something or someone arrives

- arrival

arrival /əˈraɪvəl/ [n U] **sb's arrival** *Let me know the date and time of your arrival.* | *Joe's sudden arrival spoiled all our plans.* | **the arrival of** *The show begins with the arrival of the Europeans in the New World.* | **+ at/in** *TV crews from around the world filmed President Mandela's arrival at the airport.* | **on arrival** (=when someone arrives) *On arrival in Addis Ababa please report to the Ministry of Education.* | **dead on arrival** (=dead before arriving at the hospital – used especially in news or medical reports) *She was rushed to the hospital but was pronounced dead on arrival.*

4 to arrive somewhere without intending to

- end up/fetch up
- come to
- find yourself in/at etc

end up/fetch up British /ˌend ˈʌp, ˌfetʃ ˈʌp/ [phr v I] to arrive in a place that you did not intend to go to **+ in/at** *I fell asleep on the bus and ended up in Denver.* | *I thought we were going straight home, but we all ended up at Tom's place.*

come to /ˈkʌm tuː/ [phr v T] to arrive at a place during a journey without knowing that you would arrive there: *We were walking through the woods when we came to a waterfall.* | *Ian stopped at the next house he came to and asked to use the phone.*

find yourself in/at etc /ˈfaɪnd jɔːʳself ɪn/ [v phrase] to realize that you have arrived somewhere without intending to: *After wandering around, we found ourselves back at the hotel.* | *Sammler opened a big glass door and found himself in an empty lobby.*

5 to arrive unexpectedly

- appear
- turn up/show up
- come along
- talk of the devil

appear /əˈpɪəʳ/ [v I not in progressive] *We were just having breakfast when Amy appeared.* | **+ at/in/from** *Neil appeared at my house around 9 o'clock.* | *All these people seem to have appeared from nowhere.*

turn up/show up /ˌtɜːʳn ˈʌp, ˌʃəʊ ˈʌp/ [phr v I] to arrive without warning, especially when it is difficult or not convenient for other people: *Brian has a habit of turning up just at the wrong moment.* | *At midnight Joanne's boyfriend showed up drunk.*

come along /ˌkʌm əˈlɒŋ‖-əˈlɔːŋ/ [phr v I not in progressive] if someone or something comes along, it arrives, especially in a way that is unexpected or slightly unusual: *We were having a good time until Ronnie came along.* | *Bill and I waited an hour for a bus, and then four of them came along at once.*

talk of the devil British **/speak of the devil** American /ˌtɔːk əv ðə ˈdevəl, ˌspiːk əv ðə ˈdevəl/ say this when someone you are talking about or have just mentioned comes into the room or arrives unexpectedly: *Talk of the devil! I was just telling everyone about your promotion.* | *Let's ask Amy what she thinks – speak of the devil, here she is!*

art/culture

RELATED WORDS

- *see also* **draw, paint, picture, design, dance, music, perform/performance, actor/actress, film/movie**

1 art and culture

- art
- the arts
- fine art
- culture
- art form

art /ɑːʳt/ [n U] a way of representing things or expressing ideas, using pictures, sculpture, and other objects that people can look at: *I studied art at school.* | *The statue is a fine example of early Christian art.* | *Is a pile of bricks in a museum really art?* | **modern art** *There was an exhibition of Adams' paintings at the Museum of Modern Art.* | **abstract art** (=art that does not show people or objects as they really look, but represents ideas or feelings in other ways) *Many people find it difficult to understand abstract art.* | **art critic** (=someone who's job is to write about how good or bad a piece of art is) *Art critics were not impressed by the collection.*

the arts /ði ˈɑːʳts/ [n plural] art, music, theatre, film, literature etc, all considered together: *The government should provide more money for the arts.* | *They have drama classes at the arts centre every Thursday night.* | *I've always been interested in the arts even though I didn't have much talent myself.* | **(the) performing arts** (=music, dance, and theatre considered as a group) *Under the new government much of the funding for the performing arts would be cut.* | **(the) visual arts** (=painting, drawing, sculpture, photography etc considered as a group) *Granston is a graphic artist who now teaches visual arts and journalism at the college.*

fine art ALSO **the fine arts** /ˌfaɪn ˈɑːʳt, ðə ˌfaɪn ˈɑːʳts/ [n U/n plural] art, especially painting, sculpture, drawing etc that is concerned with making beautiful things or expressing important ideas rather than with making useful objects: *Pitt worked as a medical illustrator before turning to fine art.* | *Sales of fine art on the Internet are not booming, but many experts feel that the net will play a significant role in the market.* | *Morris and other artists sought to close the chasm between the decorative or 'minor' arts and the fine arts.*

culture /ˈkʌltʃəʳ/ [n C/U] art, music, theatre, film, literature etc especially produced by a particular society or a particular group in society: *The magazine is devoted to rock music, fashion, and other aspects of youth culture.* | *Johnson's mother stressed intellectual and artistic achievement, while his father considered intellect and culture to be unmanly.*

art form /ˈɑːʳt fɔːʳm/ [n C] one of the ways that people express themselves through art: *Ballet is a 400-year-old art form, born in the courts of Europe.* | *Lehr tries to help her students understand that theater is an expressive art form.*

2 something that an artist has produced

- work
- work of art
- masterpiece

work /wɜːʳk/ [n C] a picture, sculpture, piece of music etc: *The collection contains works by Kahlo and Picasso.* | *Her later works reflected her growing depression.* | *Some of the director's best works were created during his neo-realist period.*

work of art /ˌwɜːʳk əv ˈɑːʳt/ [n C] something produced by an artist, especially something that most people agree is of very high quality: *From a single lump of clay, Torrence had produced a work of art.* | *The sketches were never meant to be works of art but are beautiful nonetheless.* | *The best works of art deal with man's struggle with the human condition.*

masterpiece /ˈmɑːstəʳpiːs‖ˈmæs-/ [n C] a picture, sculpture, film etc that is of extremely high quality, especially one that is believed to be the best work of a particular artist: *Adam Smith's masterpiece 'The Wealth of Nations' was written in the 18th century.* | *Thirteen people helped Michelangelo create his masterpiece on the ceiling of the Sistine Chapel.* | *The Davis-Evans recording of 'Porgy and Bess' has been rightly called a jazz masterpiece.*

3 relating to art or culture

- artistic
- cultural

artistic /ɑːʳˈtɪstɪk/ [adj only before noun] relating to art: *The Czech Republic has a long artistic tradition.* | *In 1881 when the first moving pictures were shown to the public, it was hailed as an 'artistic revolution'.* | *The director feared that business decisions would affect the film's artistic quality.*

cultural /ˈkʌltʃərəl/ [adj usually before noun] relating to culture: *The Principal feels that cultural education is very important.* | *Baroque music was part of a broader cultural movement that affected all the arts.*

4 someone who produces art

- artist

artist /ˈɑːʳtɨst/ [n C] someone who produces paintings, sculptures, or any kind of art: *Leonardo was the greatest artist of his time.* | *I bought some post cards of prints by Japanese artists.* | *The obituary described Nureyev as 'a great dancer and a true artist'.*

5 good at producing art

- artistic
- creative

artistic /ɑːʳˈtɪstɪk/ [adj] someone who is **artistic** is very good at drawing, painting, or sculpture: *She described her mother as 'very intelligent and artistic'.* | *That's a lovely picture – I never realized you were so artistic.*

creative /kriˈeɪtɪv/ [adj] having a lot of imagination and able to think of new and original ideas in art, music, or literature: *We encourage the children to use their creative abilities.* | *Ed, you are so creative – where did you learn to draw like that?* | *Davis was one of the most creative jazz musicians of our time.*

6 someone who is very interested in the arts

- cultured
- patron of the arts
- culture vulture
- arty/artsy

cultured /ˈkʌltʃəʳd/ [adj] knowing a lot about art, literature, music etc: *Sempaio is a highly cultured lawyer with a love of classical music.* | *The Art Nouveau Cafe is a popular meeting place for the city's cultured classes.*

patron of the arts /ˌpeɪtrən əv ði ˈɑːʳts/ [n C] someone who supports the arts, especially with money: *A genuine culture lover, the Prime Minister was a patron of the arts on a grand scale.* | *Performances are sponsored by fast food restaurants and other unlikely patrons of the arts.*

culture vulture /ˈkʌltʃəʳ ˌvʌltʃəʳ/ [n C] informal someone who is very interested in all the arts – use this to talk about people like this: *While the culture vultures looked round the ruined temples, the rest of us headed straight for the beach.* | *He's a bit of a culture vulture – he goes to the theatre just about every week.*

arty British **/artsy** American /ˈɑːʳti, ˈɑːʳtsi/ [adj] someone who is interested in or knows about art and culture – use this when you do not approve of people like this: *Jake's having a party for all his arty friends.* | **arty-farty/artsy-fartsy** *He thought of the band as just an artsy-fartsy bunch of students pretending to play rock 'n' roll.*

7 someone who does not like art

- philistine

philistine /ˈfɪlɨstaɪn‖-stiːn/ [n U] someone who does

not like or understand art, literature, music etc – used by people who disapprove of people who do not have this knowledge: *I wouldn't expect a philistine like you to understand my paintings.* | *The American desire for material goods caused Europeans to dismiss them as philistines.*

8 a place where art is shown

- gallery
- museum
- exhibition
- show

gallery /ˈgæləri/ [n C] a building or room where you can go to look at paintings, sculptures etc: *One of the rooms has been made into a small modern art gallery.* | *We spent the afternoon looking at paintings in the National Gallery.* | *Dale is showing some of his work in one of the galleries downtown.*

museum /mjuːˈziːəm‖mjʊ-/ [n C] American a large building where you can go to look at paintings, sculptures etc: *The museum has a few of Van Gogh's early paintings.* | **+ of** *Baldesaro is in New York preparing a showing at the Museum of Modern Art.*

exhibition /ˌeksəˈbɪʃən/ [n C] a collection of paintings, sculptures etc, often the work of one artist or a group of similar artists, which you can go to see – use this especially when they are only being shown for a limited period of time: *Have you seen the O'Keefe exhibition yet?* | **+ of** *The exhibition of works by Hans Memling opens next week.* | **on exhibition** *Many of the photographs on exhibition were taken by artists who worked primarily in other media.*

show /ʃəʊ/ [n C] an event at which the work of one artist or a group of artists is shown and is often for sale to the public: *Tomorrow is the opening night of her show in Cork Street, London.* | *a show of new work by young artists*

artificial

RELATED WORDS

opposite: ———— **real, natural**

- something that is intended to deceive people *see* **false**
- *see also* **pretend**

1 not made of natural materials or substances

- artificial
- synthetic
- man-made
- processed

artificial /ˌɑːʳtəˈfɪʃəl◂/ [adj usually before noun] *The juice contains no artificial coloring or flavors.* | *I usually use artificial sweetener in my coffee instead of sugar.* | *The plants can grow just as well in artificial light.*

synthetic /sɪnˈθetɪk/ [adj usually before noun] **synthetic** materials or products are made using chemical processes: *The rug is made from a mixture of wool and synthetic fibres.* | *Many old herbal remedies have disappeared and been replaced by synthetic drugs.* | *synthetic rubber*

man-made /ˌmæn ˈmeɪd◂/ [adj] made or caused by humans, rather than existing naturally: *The amusement park is built around a man-made lake.* | *The coat is 80% wool and 20% man-made fibers.* | *Current weather problems may actually be man-made, a direct result of environmental damage.*

processed /ˈprəʊsest‖ˈprɑː-/ [adj only before noun] **processed** food has not been left in its natural state, but has been chemically treated, especially in order to preserve it or make it look more attractive: *Processed foods may lack the vitamins and minerals found in fresh produce.* | *processed cheese* | *Fully processed canned hams will not spoil and can be kept on the shelf.*

2 made to look real or natural

- artificial
- false
- fake
- imitation
- simulated

artificial /ˌɑːʳtəˈfɪʃəl◂/ [adj usually before noun] not real or natural, but made to look real or do the job of something real: *On the table was a vase filled with artificial flowers.* | *We have one of those electric heaters with artificial logs.* | *It took Frank a while to learn to walk with the artificial leg.*

false /fɔːls/ [adj usually before noun] not real – use this about teeth, nails, beards etc: *Nearly a third of adults in the UK have false teeth.* | *She was heavily made up, with false eyelashes and bright red lipstick.*

fake /feɪk/ [adj usually before noun] **fake fur/jewellery/antiques etc** (=made to seem like real fur, jewellery etc, especially in order to make people think it is more valuable than it really is) *Her coat had a fake fur collar and cuffs.* | *You can buy fake Gucci bags all over the city.*

imitation /ˌɪməˈteɪʃən◂/ [adj usually before noun] use this about materials that look like something valuable, but are actually made of something less expensive: *Ted was wearing an imitation leather jacket.* | *The dark blue sweater had imitation pearls sewn across the front.*

simulated /ˈsɪmjəleɪtəd/ [adj usually before noun] not real, but made to look, feel etc like a real thing, situation, or feeling: *It was one of those horrible simulated-leather 'executive' chairs.* | *Models of the bridge have been tested under simulated earthquake conditions.*

ashamed

RELATED WORDS

opposite: ———— **proud**

- *see also* **embarrassed, guilty (6-10), regret/not regret, bad (5)**

1 ashamed

- ashamed
- humiliated
- can't look sb in the face/not be able to look sb in the face
- shamefaced
- hang/bow your head (in shame)
- shame on you!

ashamed /əˈʃeɪmd/ [adj] someone who is **ashamed** feels very sorry about something they have done or embarrassed by something relating to them, so that they think people may no longer respect them: *I didn't want anyone to know I'd been fired because I felt ashamed.* | **+ of** *She was so ashamed of cheating on the test that she went and told the teacher.* | *For a long time I was ashamed of my father and the fact he never finished school.* | **+ about** *There's nothing to be ashamed about – lots of people have money problems.* | **+ (that)** *I realize now that you were telling the truth, and I'm ashamed that I didn't believe you.* |

+ to do sth *She really needed me but – I'm ashamed to admit it – I didn't help her.* | **ashamed of yourself** *You ought to be ashamed of yourself – coming home drunk like that!* | **bitterly/deeply ashamed** *The knowledge that I had caused him to lose his job made me bitterly ashamed.*

humiliated /hjuːˈmɪlieɪtɪ̇d/ [adj not usually before noun] feeling very ashamed and upset, especially because you have been made to look weak or stupid and you think that no one will respect you: *Ross yelled at me in front of the whole office – I've never been so humiliated in my life!* | *Many women who have been assaulted feel too frightened and humiliated to report their ordeal.*

can't look sb in the face/not be able to look sb in the face /kɑːnt ˌlʊk (sb) ɪn ðə ˈfeɪs‖kænt-, nɒt bi ˌeɪbəl tə ˌlʊk (sb) ɪn ðə ˈfeɪs / [v phrase] to be so ashamed about something you have done to someone that you find it difficult to be with them or talk to them: *I'm so embarrassed – I'll never be able to look her in the face again.* | *After the layoffs were announced, I couldn't look any of the people on the shop floor in the face.*

shamefaced /ˌʃeɪmˈfeɪst◂/ [adj] showing in the expression on your face that you are ashamed about something and you know you have behaved badly: *He came to my office, shamefaced, to apologize.* | *A shamefaced spokesperson admitted that mistakes had been made.*

hang/bow your head (in shame) /ˌhæŋ, ˌbaʊ jɔːʳ ˌhed (ɪn ˈʃeɪm)/ [v phrase] to look ashamed: *He bowed his head in shame as the details of his arrest were read out in court.*

shame on you! /ˈʃeɪm ɒn juː/ spoken use this to tell someone that they should feel shame because of something they have done: *Shame on you for lying to your grandmother!*

2 the feeling of being ashamed

- shame
- disgrace
- humiliation
- indignity
- lose face
- stigma

shame /ʃeɪm/ [n U] the feeling that you have when you know that you have behaved badly or that you have lost other people's respect: *She remembered her angry words with a deep sense of shame.* | *'Please don't tell my dad about this,' he said, blushing with shame.* | **+ of** *She never overcame the shame of having abandoned her children.* | **in shame** *Following the scandal, Garrison resigned in shame.*

disgrace /dɪsˈgreɪs/ [n U] when you have completely lost other people's respect because of something bad you have done: *While the father was in jail, the whole family suffered his disgrace.* | **+ of** *Garton killed himself because he could not bear the disgrace of a public scandal.* | **in disgrace** *Browne was caught using drugs, and was sent home from the private school in disgrace.*

humiliation /hjuːˌmɪliˈeɪʃən/ [n U] a situation in which you are made to look weak or stupid that makes you ashamed and upset: *Her attackers seemed to take special pleasure in her humiliation.* | **+ of** *What really upset me was the humiliation of having to ask her for money.* | **public humiliation** *The Senator's public humiliation is almost punishment enough for what he did.*

indignity /ɪnˈdɪgnɪ̇ti/ [n C/U] a situation in which you feel that you have no pride or self-respect, because people treat you as if you were completely unimportant: *He suffered insult and indignity in silence.* | *Being accused of theft was just one of the indignities I suffered under my last employer.* | **+ of** *I had to endure the indignity of being strip-searched for drugs.*

lose face /ˌluːz ˈfeɪs/ [v phrase] to lose other people's respect for you, especially by doing something that makes you look weak, immoral, or stupid: *The leaders need to find a way of compromising without losing face among their supporters.* | *Rather than giving in and losing face, she carried on her needless quarrel with her father.* —**loss of face** /ˌlɒs əv ˈfeɪs‖ˌlɔːs-/ [n phrase] *The government suffered a severe loss of face when details of the scandal emerged.*

stigma /ˈstɪgmə/ [n C usually singular] a strong feeling of being hated by society and being ashamed because of your situation or your actions: *Even when someone has been found innocent of a crime, the stigma often remains.* | **+ of** *At first I found the stigma of being unemployed very difficult to cope with.* | **a stigma attached to sth** *In many countries there is still a strong social stigma attached to homosexuality.*

3 to make someone feel ashamed

- make sb (feel) ashamed
- shame sb
- humiliate
- disgrace
- bring shame on
- humiliating
- degrading

make sb (feel) ashamed /ˌmeɪk (sb) fiːl əˈʃeɪmd/ [v phrase] *At first the neighbor's generosity made her feel ashamed.* | *What I saw in the schools made me ashamed of my views – it was clear to me that most students really want to learn.*

shame sb /ˈʃeɪm (sb)/ [v T] to make someone feel ashamed: *People with leprosy were shamed and driven out of their communities.* | **shame sb into (doing) sth** *Many people have been shamed into silence when it comes to discussing their sex lives.* | **it shames sb to do sth** *It shamed her to realize how long she had been involved with Claude.*

humiliate /hjuːˈmɪlieɪt/ [v T] to make someone feel very ashamed and upset, especially by making them look weak or stupid: *Why do you always have to humiliate me in front of your friends?* | *The invading army took every opportunity to humiliate the local peasants.*

disgrace /dɪsˈgreɪs/ [v T] if you **disgrace** yourself or **disgrace** your family, your school etc, you behave very badly so that other people lose respect for you or for your family or school: *She didn't tell anyone that she was pregnant for fear of disgracing her family.* | *My grandmother thought I was disgracing myself, following Tim around like a love-sick puppy.*

bring shame on /brɪŋ ˈʃeɪm ɒn / [v phrase] to make people lose respect for yourself, your family, country etc because you have behaved badly: *The MP was accused of bringing shame and humiliation on the whole party.* | *The shooting of an innocent man has brought shame on the entire police department.*

humiliating /hjuːˈmɪlieɪtɪŋ/ [adj] causing a complete loss of self-respect, especially because you have been made to look weak or stupid: *I had to apologize in front of everyone – it was so humiliating.* | *Prisoners are subjected to humiliating treatment and frequent beatings.* | *Anderson suffered a humiliating defeat in the last election.*

degrading /dɪˈgreɪdɪŋ/ [adj] a situation or way of treating someone that is **degrading** makes them lose all their self-respect and makes them feel that they are completely worthless: *These poor people live in the most degrading conditions.* | **+ to** *Many of the remarks were degrading to women and minorities.*

4 not feeling ashamed

- shameless
- unabashed
- unashamed
- brazen
- unrepentant

shameless /ˈʃeɪmləs/ [adj] someone who is **shameless** or whose behaviour is **shameless** does not seem to feel ashamed about something that most people would be very ashamed about: *Lewis is shameless in making promises he doesn't intend to keep.* | *This is just another shameless attempt by the Opposition to gain power at any cost.*

unabashed /ˌʌnəˈbæʃt◂/ [adj] not feeling embarrassed or ashamed about something that most people disapprove of or consider silly: *Kendall is a nasty unabashed racist.* | *'I'd love to go!' she said with unabashed enthusiasm.*

unashamed /ˌʌnəˈʃeɪmd◂/ [adj] not feeling embarrassed or ashamed about something that people might disapprove of: *It's amazing how unashamed people are to discuss their problems on TV.* | **+ of/about** *She was raised in a strict Catholic household but seems completely unashamed and relaxed about sex.*

brazen /ˈbreɪzən/ [adj] behaving in a very confident way that shows that you do not feel shame that you are doing something wrong: *His wife could no longer tolerate his brazen love affairs.* | *At first they were careful to keep their illegal practices secret, but as time went by, they grew more brazen.*

unrepentant /ˌʌnrɪˈpentənt◂/ [adj] not feeling sorry for behaviour or ashamed of beliefs that most other people disapprove of: *Even after the rape conviction, Thayer remained unrepentant.* | *Many consider the general an unrepentant and brutal tyrant.*

ask

RELATED WORDS

opposite: **answer**

- to ask if you can do something *see* **let/allow (2)**
- *see also* **invite, advise, suggest, tell, find out**

WHAT'S HERE

- **to ask questions** see **1 to 8**
- **to ask for sth** see **9 to 17**

to ask questions

1 to ask someone a question

- ask
- consult
- want to know
- inquire
- sound out
- put sb on the spot

ask /ɑːsk‖æsk/ [v I/T] *If you have any questions, don't be afraid to ask.* | *For information about the new drug, ask your doctor.* | **ask (sb) if/whether** *I was a little surprised when he asked me if I was married.* | **ask (sb) about sth** *They'll probably just ask you about your education and work experience.* | **ask (sb) what/how/why etc** *What should I tell people if they ask me why you didn't come to the party?* | **ask (sb) a question** *At the end of the presentation you'll all have a chance to ask questions.* —**questioner** /ˈkwestʃənəʳ/ [n C] British *A questioner in the studio audience asked the Labour MP to defend his party's recent statement.*

consult /kənˈsʌlt/ [v I/T] to ask for information or advice from someone, because it is their job to know about it: *Before starting any exercise program, you should consult your doctor.* | **+ with** *The President is going to consult with European leaders before making his decision.* | **consult sb about sth** *We've consulted with several engineers about the best way to support the bridge.* —**consultation** /ˌkɒnsəlˈteɪʃən‖ˌkɑːn-/ [n U] *Baring accepted the offer after consultation with his lawyers.*

want to know /ˌwɒnt tə ˈnəʊ‖ˌwɑːnt-/ [v phrase] to ask something – use this especially when you are reporting what someone else has asked: *'Why didn't you write to me?' Barbara wanted to know.* | *The policeman wanted to know their names, but they wouldn't tell him.* | **+ about** *Everybody in the office wanted to know about my trip.* | **+ where/how/why etc** *Jason wants to know where you keep the kitchen scissors.*

inquire ALSO **enquire** /ɪnˈkwaɪəʳ/ [v I/T] especially British formal to ask someone for information about something, especially someone whose job is to know about it: *'Where is the director's office?' he enquired.* | *We inquired at all the hotels in town, but we couldn't find Carol anywhere.* | **+ about** *Several people have phoned the personnel department to inquire about the position.* | **+ if/whether** *She stopped a guard and enquired whether the train went to Evesham.* | **+ how/when etc** *We rang the hospital again to inquire how the old man was.*

sound out /ˌsaʊnd ˈaʊt/ [phr v T not in passive] to find out what someone thinks about your plan or idea by asking them questions, especially because you want their help or support **sound sb out** *I think she'll like the idea, but you'd better sound her out first.* | **sound out sb** *Before launching the project, they sounded out a number of leading experts.* | **+ about/on** *The board of directors have sounded him out about taking the CEO position.*

put sb on the spot /ˌpʊt (sb) ɒn ðə ˈspɒt‖-ˈspɑːt/ [v phrase] to deliberately ask someone a question that they find difficult or embarrassing to answer: *The reporter's questions were clearly designed to put the Senator on the spot.* | *I don't want to put you on the spot, but I'm really curious about how you know Tim.*

2 to ask several people questions

- ask around
- make inquiries
- poll
- poll
- survey
- survey
- canvass

ask around /ˌɑːsk əˈraʊnd‖ˌæsk-/ [phr v I] to ask several people, especially people that you know, in order to get information from them: *I'm not sure where you can find a babysitter – I'll ask around.* | **+ about** *Stephen's been asking around about the best places to go in the evenings.*

make inquiries ALSO **make enquiries** /ˌmeɪk ɪnˈkwaɪəriz / [v phrase] especially British to try to get information about something by asking several people, especially people whose job is to know about it: *After making a few inquiries, we decided not to* *hire her.* | **+ about** *We graduate next month and most of my classmates are already making enquiries about jobs.* | *The bank made inquiries about her financial situation before agreeing to the loan.*

poll /pəʊl/ [v T] to ask a lot of people a set of questions about a subject that is important to the public, especially politics, in order to find out the general opinion about it: *Nearly 60% of the voters who were polled did not recognize Bronson's name.* | *For its study the company polled 150 randomly selected physicians.*

poll /pəʊl/ [n C] an attempt to find out about a subject that is important to the public, especially politics, by asking many people a set of question about how they feel about it: *According to the polls, a huge majority of citizens oppose bilingual education.* | **+ of** *A poll of 700 female registered voters found that 56% favor full abortion rights.* | **opinion poll** (=a poll to find out people's political opinions) *Recent opinion polls show that the President's popularity has slipped.* | **carry out/take a poll** *In a nationwide poll carried out in January, only one person in ten said they were happy with the tax reforms.*

survey /ˈsɜːʳveɪ/ [v T] to ask a lot of people a set of questions about their opinions, the way they live, what they like and dislike etc in order to find out general opinions: *A large segment of the population that was surveyed was taking vitamin supplements.* | *Researchers surveyed 10,000 customers about the quality of companies that they used.*

survey /ˈsɜːʳveɪ/ [n C] an attempt to find out people's opinions, the way they live, what they like and dislike etc, by asking a large number of people a set of questions: *A recent survey found that 36% of the women asked did not feel safe walking alone at night.* | **+ of** *According to a survey of 606 city residents, garbage collection was the city service people liked most.* | **+ on** *Many parents were surprised by the survey on teenage drug use.* | **carry out/conduct a survey** *The survey on consumer confidence was conducted in late December.*

canvass /ˈkænvəs/ [v I/T] to go to the houses of a lot of people or phone a lot of people up in order to find out their political opinions or to get their political support: *Party members were out canvassing as soon as the election was announced.* | *We canvassed over half the constituency by phone or text-message.*

3 to ask someone a lot of questions

- question
- fire/shoot questions at
- grill
- give sb the third degree
- pump sb for
- quiz
- pick sb's brains

question /ˈkwestʃən/ [v T] to ask someone a lot of questions, in order to get information or find out what they think: *We all wondered where Sylvia got the money, but no one dared question her.* | **question sb about sth** *Liz was very well informed and questioned me about the political situation in Africa.* | **question sb closely** (=carefully, asking a lot of difficult questions) *The interviewer questioned Miss Jarvis closely about her computer experience.* —**questioner** [n C] *Jim Lehrer was the only questioner of the candidates in the debate.*

fire/shoot questions at /ˌfaɪəʳ, ˌʃuːt ˈkwestʃənz æt/ [v phrase] to ask someone a lot of questions very quickly in order to confuse them or make them admit to something: *The lawyer fired questions at me so quickly I didn't have time to think.* | *The teacher kept shooting questions at the frightened girls until they confessed everything.*

grill ALSO **give sb a grilling** British /ˈgrɪl, ˌgɪv (sb) ə ˈgrɪlɪŋ/ [v T] to ask someone a lot of difficult questions in order to make them explain their actions, plans, or opinions: *I stood in the hall and listened as the interviewers grilled the next candidate.* | *Hilda's teacher gave her a real grilling about why she'd missed so many classes.* | **grill sb about/on sth** *Maxine started grilling me on why I'd been spending so much time alone.* —**grilling** [n C] *The meeting turned out to be a grilling by Democrats of the Republican senator about his proposal.*

give sb the third degree /ˌgɪv (sb) ðə ˌθɜːʳd dɪˈgriː/ [v phrase] informal to ask someone a lot of difficult questions in order to make them explain their actions, plans, or opinions: *I was just out with friends – you don't have to give me the third degree.* | *Whenever one of my boyfriends came to the house, Dad would give them the third degree.*

pump sb for /ˈpʌmp (sb) fɔːʳ/ [v phrase] to ask someone a lot of questions about a particular subject or event in order to get as much information as possible **pump sb for information/details** *Viktor sat with Vassily and me and pumped me for information about hockey teams.* | *He wants to pump Jody for the details of some job her company is advertising.*

quiz /kwɪz/ [v T] to ask someone a lot of questions, especially because you want to find out what they have been doing, and often in a way that annoys them: *When Stan eventually came home from the party, his wife quizzed him for hours.* | **quiz sb about/on sth** *My parents never stop quizzing me about where I go at night.* | *Reporters quizzed the President on tax policy and Central America.*

pick sb's brains /ˌpɪk (sb's) ˈbreɪnz/ [v phrase] to ask someone for information about something because you think they know more about it than you: *You know all about tax law – can I pick your brains for a minute?* | *The workshop is designed so that new managers can pick the brains of managers with more experience.*

4 when the police, a court etc asks someone about a crime

- question
- interrogate
- cross-examine
- carry out door-to-door inquiries
- be helping police with their inquiries

question /ˈkwestʃən/ [v T] to ask someone a lot of questions to find out what they know about a crime: *They questioned her for three hours before releasing her.* | **question sb about sth** *The lawyer questioned me about how money was transmitted to Mexico.* | **question sb closely** (=carefully, asking a lot of difficult questions) *After questioning the suspect closely, investigators decided he was not a part of the drug operation.* —**questioning** [n U] *The lawyer's questioning of the witness did not go on as long as expected.* | **keep/hold sb for questioning** *Mr Hayes is being kept at Newham police station for questioning.* —**questioner** [n C] *Eventually his questioners realized he was not the man they wanted and let him go.*

interrogate /ɪnˈterəgeɪt/ [v T] to keep asking a lot of questions for a long time, sometimes using threats, in order to get information: *The police interrogated Waters for 24 hours until he confessed.* | *Army officers have been accused of using unorthodox methods when interrogating enemy prisoners.* | **interrogate sb about sth** *I was interrogated at length about my* *conversation with the two men.* —**interrogation** /ɪnˌterəˈgeɪʃən/ [n C/U] *Most of the information about the bombings came from the interrogation of terrorist suspects.* —**interrogator** [n C] *The report concludes that military interrogators routinely use torture to find out what they want.*

cross-examine ALSO **cross-question** British /ˌkrɒs ɪgˈzæmɪn, ˌkrɒs ˈkwestʃən‖ˌkrɔːs-/ [v T] if a lawyer **cross-examines** or **cross-questions** someone in a law court, they ask them a series of questions about their previous statements in order to find out whether they have been telling the truth: *The first lawyer cross-examined the defendant for over three hours.* | *When the witness was cross-questioned, it became clear that his earlier testimony was not entirely true.* —**cross-examination/cross-questioning** /ˌkrɒs ɪgˌzæmɪˈneɪʃən, ˌkrɒs ˈkwestʃənɪŋ‖ˌkrɔːs-/ [n C/U] **during/under/in cross-examination** *Under cross-examination, the psychiatrist admitted that he could not be sure of his diagnosis.*

carry out door-to-door inquiries /ˌkæri aʊt ˌdɔːʳ tə ˌdɔːr ɪnˈkwaɪəriz/ [v phrase] British if the police **carry out door-to-door inquiries,** they go to all the houses in a particular area to ask the people living there what they know about a crime: *Police are carrying out door-to-door inquiries on the Hazelwood Estate.*

be helping police with their inquiries /biː ˌhelpɪŋ pəˌliːs wɪð ðeər ɪnˈkwaɪəriz/ [v phrase] to be formally being asked questions by the police about a crime – used especially in news reports about someone who the police think is guilty of a crime but who has not been officially charged: *A man is helping police with their inquiries after a mother and her young baby were found dead at their home last night.*

5 to ask someone questions for a newspaper, TV programme etc

- interview
- interview

interview /ˈɪntəʳvjuː/ [v T] *At the end of the race the winner was interviewed by NBC news.* | *She has interviewed celebrities and political leaders on her radio programme for over 25 years.* —**interviewer** [n C] *Browning told one interviewer that he is considering running for office again next year.*

interview /ˈɪntəʳvjuː/ [n C] a meeting in which one person asks another person questions for a newspaper, TV programme etc: *During a recent interview Rohr said the renovations will cost $38 million.* | **+ with** *An interview with the actress appears in next week's 'People' magazine.* | **TV/radio/newspaper interview** *In his latest TV interview the lead singer talks about his drug problem.* | **give an interview** (=allow someone to interview you) *The new Prime Minister gave his first full-length TV interview last night.*

6 to ask someone questions to decide whether to offer them a job etc

- interview
- interview

interview /ˈɪntəʳvjuː/ [v T] to ask someone a lot of questions as part of a formal process, so that you can decide whether they are suitable for a job, a chance to study at a college etc: *I'll be interviewing two candidates today and three others tomorrow.* | *All prospective students are interviewed by alumni before a final decision is made.* | **interview sb for a job/post etc** *We've interviewed a woman for the job already, but she wasn't very well qualified.*

interview /ˈɪntəʳvjuː/ [n C] a formal meeting in which a person or group of people ask someone questions in order to find out whether they are suitable for a job, a chance to study at college etc: *I always get nervous before interviews.* | *Ron's going to Tufts University next week for an interview and a tour of the campus.* | **+ for** *She had an interview last week for a job at an Internet company.* | **job interview** *Kyle went out and bought a new suit for his job interview.*

7 something that you ask someone

- question
- query
- inquiry
- leading/loaded question
- trick question

question /ˈkwestʃən/ [n C] what you say or write when you are asking for information: *That's a very difficult question to answer.* | *Does anyone have any further questions?* | *There were several questions Melanie wanted to ask the interviewer.* | **+ about** *I hate it when strangers ask me questions about my private life.*

query /ˈkwɪəri/ [n C] British a question that you ask when you have not completely understood something or you are not sure that something is true or correct: *If anyone has a query I'll deal with it at the end of the meeting.* | *I would be happy to answer people's queries if they write to me at my home address.* | **+ about** *Since the TV programme the advice bureau has received lots of queries about maternity rights.* | **raise a query** (=ask a question) *One of the students raised a query about the marking system.*

inquiry ALSO **enquiry** /ɪnˈkwaɪəri‖ ɪnˈkwaɪəri, ˈɪŋkwəri/ [n C] especially British a question you ask in order to get information or find out the details about something: *We have only just put the house up for sale, and we've already received lots of enquiries.* | **+ about** *For all inquiries about flight schedules, please call the following number.*

leading/loaded question /ˌliːdɪŋ, ˌləʊdɪd ˈkwestʃən/ [n C] a question that deliberately tricks someone, so that they give you the answer that you want or say something that they do not intend to say: *You don't expect me to answer a loaded question like that, do you?* | *The jurors said interviewers used leading questions and coached the children on how they should answer.*

trick question /ˌtrɪk ˈkwestʃən/ [n C] a question that seems easy to answer but has a hidden difficulty: *'Did you have a good time while I was gone?' 'That's a trick question, right? If I say yes, you'll be angry that I didn't miss you.'*

8 a set of questions

- questionnaire
- form

questionnaire /ˌkwestʃəˈneəʳ, ˌkes-/ [n C] a piece of paper with a set of questions on it, which is given to a large number of people to find out what they think: *Of nearly 5,000 questionnaires that were sent out, only 428 were returned.* | *The questionnaire asks students how they feel about services on campus.* | **complete/fill out a questionnaire** *Please complete the questionnaire and return it in the envelope provided.*

form /fɔːʳm/ [n C] a piece of paper with a set of questions that you answer in order to provide information about yourself for an organization, employer etc: *Make sure you sign and date the form before you return it.* | **application form** (=a form with questions you must answer if you want a job, a chance to study etc) *The visa requires an application form and two photos.* | **fill out/in a form** ALSO **fill up a form** British (=write the answer to the questions on a form) *Just fill in the form and take it along to your local bank.*

to ask for sth

9 to ask for something, or to ask someone to do something

- ask
- order
- send out for
- seek
- invite

ask /ɑːsk‖æsk/ [v I/T] *If you ever need any help with anything, you only have to ask.* | *She might be willing to babysit, but you won't know till you ask her.* | **ask (sb) for sth** *A lot of people don't like asking for help.* | *He can't pay the rent, but he still doesn't want to ask his parents for money.* | **ask sth of sb** *All I've ever asked of you is to try to be polite to my mother.* | **ask sb to do sth** *I've asked Mary to water the plants for me while I'm away.* | **ask to do sth** (=ask to be allowed to do something) *The man on the phone wasn't very helpful, so I asked to speak with the manager.* | **ask if you can do sth** *Letty's been asking me if she can take the dog out for a walk.*

order /ˈɔːʳdəʳ/ [v T] to ask for something you are going to pay for – use this about asking for food or drink in restaurants, or asking companies to send you goods: *Would you like to order a drink before dinner?* | *We had ordered a pale blue armchair but the one that was delivered was dark green.* | *I'm afraid we don't have that book in stock, but we can order it for you.* —**order** [n C] *I'm very sorry, but we seem to have lost your order.*

send out for ALSO **order out for** /ˌsend ˈaʊt fɔːʳ, ˌɔːʳdər ˈaʊt fɔːʳ/ American [phr v T] to ask a restaurant or a food shop to deliver food to you at home or work: *During the meeting we sent out for some coffee.* | *I don't feel like cooking tonight. Let's order out for a pizza.*

seek /siːk/ [v T] formal to ask for advice, help, or money from someone who has the knowledge, right, or power to provide it: *The Carsons sought advice from their lawyer.* | *Take two tablets every four hours. If symptoms persist, seek medical advice.* | *In his lawsuit, Wyman is seeking $12 million in damages from his former employers.*

invite /ɪnˈvaɪt/ [v T] formal to politely ask someone to ask questions, or give their answers, opinions, or suggestions: *Applications for this position are invited from all individuals with relevant experience.* | **invite sb to do sth** *At the end of the lecture, Dr. Bosch invited the audience to ask questions and share their ideas.*

10 ways of asking someone to do something or to let you have something

- would/do you mind?
- (would/could you) do me a favour?
- I would be grateful if ...
- could you/would you/can you ... ?
- excuse me/pardon me

would/do you mind? /ˌwʊd, ˌduː jʊ ˈmaɪnd/ use this to ask someone politely to do something for you or to let you do something: *I'd like to ask you a couple of questions – do you mind?* | **+ if** *Would you mind if I held the baby?* | *Do you mind if I just turn down the volume a little?* | **would/do you mind doing something?** *Would you mind stopping at the Post Office on the way home?* | *Dinner won't be on the table for another half hour – do you mind waiting?*

(would/could you) do me a favour? British **/(would/could you) do me a favor?** American /(ˌwʊd, ˌkʊd jʊ) ˌduː mi ə ˈfeɪvəʳ/ use this to ask someone to do something for you or help you with something. Using **do me a favour** alone is more informal than saying **would** or **could you do me a favour**: *Would you do me a favour and call Tom to tell him I'm on my way home?* | *Do me a favor – in that box over there, there's a screwdriver – can you hand it to me?* | *Could you do me a favour and lock everything up at five?*

I would be grateful if ... ALSO **I would appreciate it if ...** /aɪ wʊd bi ˈgreɪtfəl ɪf, aɪ wʊd əˈpriːʃieɪt ɪt ɪf/ use this in formal language or business letters to ask someone to do something for you: *I would be grateful if you could send this information to me at the address below.* | *I would appreciate it if you could let me know when you will be making your decision.*

could you/would you/can you ... ? /ˈkjʊd juː, ˈwʊd juː, ˈkæn juː/ use this to ask someone to do something for you. **Could you** and **would you** are more polite than **can you**: *Could you hold these while I get my keys?* | *Would you get me a towel, please?* | *Can you babysit for us Friday night?*

excuse me/pardon me /ɪkˈskjuːz miː, ˈpɑːʳdn miː/ use this to politely get someone's attention or to interrupt what they are doing when you want to ask them something. **Pardon me** is slightly old-fashioned and is more formal than **excuse me**: *Excuse me, could I borrow your pen for a minute?* | *Pardon me, do you know what time it is?*

11 to ask strongly for something or for someone to do something

- demand
- beg
- plead
- press for/push for
- call for
- call on/upon

demand /dɪˈmɑːnd‖dɪˈmænd/ [v T] to ask for something, or ask someone to do something, in a firm or angry way that shows you expect them to do it: *I demand an explanation for your appalling behaviour.* | *The laboratory was surrounded by protesters demanding an end to the animal experiments.* | *The chief demanded a thorough investigation into the murder.* | **+ to do sth** *The police officer made Neil get out of the car and demanded to see his driver's licence.* | **+ that** *Just go to the dry cleaners, show them the dress, and demand that they pay for the damage.*

beg /beg/ [v I/T] to ask for something, or ask someone to do something, in an anxious way that shows you want it very much: *All right, all right, I'll come! Just stop begging.* | *He said he wouldn't give me the money unless I got down on my knees and begged him.* | **beg (sb) for sth** *The prisoner was in so much pain all he could do was scream and beg for mercy.* | *It's the same old story – one night he beats her up, and the next day he begs her for forgiveness.* | **beg sb to do sth** *We all begged him not to drive in the storm, but he wouldn't listen to us.*

plead /pliːd/ [v I/T] to ask for something that you want very much, in a sincere and emotional way: *'Please forgive me,' she pleaded 'I'll never do it again.'* | **+ for** *The wife of one of the hostages appeared on TV last night to plead for her husband's life.* | **plead with sb** *Parker pleaded with his supporters in the crowd to remain calm.*

press for/push for /'pres fɔːʳ, 'pʊʃ fɔːʳ/ [phr v T] to ask strongly and repeatedly for something important such as a change in the law or the rules, because you think it is necessary: *People in the medical profession are pressing for genuine reforms in policy.* | *The team is pushing for a new stadium to be built downtown.* | *Women have been pressing for equal rights and pay for years.*

call for /'kɔːl fɔːʳ / [phr v T] if someone, especially a group of people, **calls for** something such as justice, equality etc they ask for it strongly and publicly because they think an unfair situation needs to be changed: *Amnesty International has consistently called for the release of political prisoners.* | *The Football Association is likely to call for a ban on alcohol at football games.* | *Leaders in both parties are calling for changes in campaign finance laws.*

call on/upon /'kɔːl ɒn, əpɒn / [phr v T] if someone, especially an organization in a bad situation, **calls on** someone to do something, they ask strongly and urgently for that person to do it because their help is needed **call on/upon sb to do sth** *We are calling upon the government to release all political prisoners.* | *The Secretary called on all Americans to help stop the abuse and neglect of children.* | **call on/upon sb for sth** *The dance company has called on ballet-lovers everywhere for financial support.*

12 to keep asking for something in an annoying way

- nag
- go on
- pester

nag /næg/ [v I/T] to keep asking someone to do something, in a very annoying way: *Oh, stop nagging – I'll do it later.* | *Look, I don't want to keep nagging you, but would you please take your stuff out of the living room?* | **nag sb to do sth** *My children are always nagging me to get new videos.*

go on /gəʊ 'ɒn/ [phr v I] British informal to keep asking someone to do something that you think they should do, so that they become annoyed **+ about** *Mick went to have his hair cut just to stop his wife going on about it.* | **go on at sb** *Look, I'll do the dishes when I've finished writing this letter. Just stop going on at me!* | **go on at sb to do sth** *Mum was always going on at me to do something with my musical talent, but I was more interested in sport.*

pester /'pestəʳ/ [v T] to keep asking someone to do something or asking them for something in an annoying way: *She used to pester her father until she got exactly what she wanted.* | **pester sb to do sth** *The kids are always pestering us to take them to the beach.* | **pester sb for sth** *One of the guys at work kept pestering her for a date, so she finally reported him.*

13 to ask for something officially

- apply
- claim
- request
- approach
- put in for
- applicant
- claimant

apply /ə'plaɪ/ [v I] to write to someone asking for something such as a job, an opportunity to study at a university, or permission to do something: *'I still haven't received my passport.' 'When did you apply?'* | **+ for** *How many jobs had you applied for before you were offered this one?* | **+ to do sth** *Finland did not apply to join the EC until 1992.*

claim /kleɪm/ [v T] especially British to ask for something, especially money, from a government, company etc, because you believe you have a legal right to have it: *Thousands of people who should get welfare payments never even bother to claim them.* | **claim sth from sb** *The two companies are claiming $500 million each in damages from the government.* | **claim damages/compensation** *Because the accident had not been her fault, Barbara was able to claim damages.*

request /rɪ'kwest/ [v T] formal to officially ask someone for something or ask someone to do something: *The pilot requested permission to land the plane at O'Hare airport.* | *Officials in Seoul are requesting the drug dealer's extradition from Bahrain.* | **+ that** *We request that all cell phones and pagers be turned off for the duration of the performance.* | **be requested to do sth** *Anna was requested to make the necessary arrangements for the convention.*

approach /ə'prəʊtʃ/ [v T] to officially ask someone that you do not know well for something or ask them to do something, especially when you are not sure if they will do it: *Will you be approaching the bank for a loan?* | *They had approached Barlow to see if he would participate in the charity event.* | *I have been approached regarding the possibility of selling the building to a startup company.*

put in for /ˌpʊt 'ɪn fɔːʳ / [phr v T] to ask someone for something such as a job, government money etc that is available, by officially writing to them to say that you want it: *I've put in for a transfer to one of our overseas branches.* | *All those who lost their jobs put in for compensation.* | *Students must put in for grants at least six months before their course begins.*

applicant /'æplɪkənt/ [n C] someone who officially asks for something such as a job, official document etc by writing or answering the questions on a form: *Ten women were selected from over 30 applicants.* | **+ for** *Applicants for teacher-training courses need to have at least one year's experience.* | **job/grant etc applicant** *Many job applicants do not know how to write an appealing cover letter.*

claimant /'kleɪmənt/ [n C] someone who asks for something, especially money, from the government, a court etc, because they believe they have a legal right to it: *The company will settle the lawsuit and provide compensation for claimants.* | *Garcia is representing three Spanish-speaking claimants in their case against the state.*

14 to ask for money or food because you do not have any

- scrounge
- cadge
- bum
- mooch off
- beg

scrounge /skraʊndʒ/ [v I/T] to ask someone for food, cigarettes etc especially because you do not have enough money or would prefer not to pay for them **scrounge sth off/from** *Nigel scrounged a drink off us before we left.* | **scrounge sth** *We managed to scrounge some cigarettes because we had no money left.* | **scrounge** *When I was a kid I never had enough money for the bus, so I had to scrounge.*

cadge /kædʒ/ [v T] British informal to ask someone for something such as food, cigarettes etc because you do not have enough money or would prefer not to pay for them: *Sonia is always cadging lifts home and she never offers any money for petrol.* | *The two boys moved around the bar, cadging free drinks and cigarettes.*

bum /bʌm/ [v T] informal to ask someone for something such as food or cigarettes, in a way that annoys or embarrasses people: *I think Steve managed to bum a lift home.* | **bum sth off sb** *He's always bumming drinks off people and it really gets on my nerves.*

mooch off /ˈmuːtʃ ɒf/ [phr v T] American informal to ask someone for something such as food or cigarettes in a way that annoys or embarrasses people **mooch sth/it/them off** *This old guy was trying to mooch a beer off Dave.* | **mooch off sb** *He never pays for anything – he'd even mooch off his own mother.*

beg ALSO **panhandle** American /beg, ˈpænˌhændl/ [v I] to ask people in the street for money or food because you do not have any: *Things got so bad that at one point she thought she'd have to go out and beg.* | *He just sits there on the street all day, but he doesn't panhandle.* | **+ for** *Just a few years ago, Tanya was homeless and begging for money in front of the supermarket.* | **+ from** *Sad-looking men of all ages beg from tourists at the corner of the square.* —**beggar** ALSO **panhandler** American [n C] *The streets of the capital are full of beggars.* | *I'm so sick of the panhandlers always asking for money.*

15 to ask a professional person to do some work for you

- call in
- send for
- get in
- bring in

call in /ˌkɔːl ˈɪn/ [phr v T] to ask someone who has special skills or knowledge to come and deal with a problem **call in sb** *They called in a private investigator to help them find their son.* | *Eventually the teenager's behaviour got so bad that the police had to be called in.* | **call sb in** *When she threatened to sue, we had to call our own lawyer in.*

send for /ˈsend fɔːʳ/ [phr v T] formal to ask a professional person or professional service to come and help you do something because you do not have the knowledge yourself: *You'll have to send for the plumber to mend this leak.* | *When he started vomiting blood, they sent for the doctor.* | *The women refused to cooperate with store detectives, and we had to send for the police.*

get in /ˌget ˈɪn/ [phr v T] British informal to ask someone who provides a professional service to come to your home to do something **get sb in** *They got the electrician in because the central heating had stopped working.* | *It would be much easier if we got somebody in to do all the catering.* | **get in sb** *After the party we can get in professional carpet-cleaners to do the job.*

bring in /ˌbrɪŋ ˈɪn/ [phr v T] if someone, especially an organization, **brings in** a particular service or professional person, they ask them to come and help with a difficult situation or process **bring sb in** *Everyone was a little surprised by the board's decision to bring Bob Rice in as CEO.* | *As the crisis worsened, the government had no choice but to bring troops in.* | **bring in sb** *Many schools are now bringing in private contractors to do the cleaning.*

16 to ask for help or kindness

- ask a favour
- turn to
- call on
- appeal

ask a favour British **/ask a favor** American /ˌɑːsk ə ˈfeɪvəʳ‖ˌæsk-/ [v phrase] to ask someone to be kind or generous by helping you do something or by doing something for you: *Could I ask a favour? I need someone to collect the children from school tonight. Are you free?* | **ask sb a favour** *I need to ask you a big favor. Could you lend me $1000 till I get my tax refund?*

turn to /ˈtɜːʳn tuː/ [phr v T] if someone in a very bad situation **turns to** someone, they ask that person for help, comfort, sympathy etc: *After my wife died I didn't know who to turn to.* | *Eventually I turned to an organization that helps people with drug and alcohol problems.* | **turn to sb for sth** *When things got really bad, I turned to my family for help.*

call on ALSO **call upon** formal /ˈkɔːl ɒn, ˈkɔːl əpɒn/ [phr v T] to ask someone for help when you have a problem and especially when they have offered to help you when they can **call on/upon sb** *If you ever have a problem, you know that you can always call on us.* | **call on/upon sb for sth** *Members of the religious sect are very reluctant to call on outsiders for help.* | **call on/upon sb to do sth** *Being the only person in the office who speaks German, I'm often called upon to translate.*

appeal /əˈpiːl/ [v I] to make a public request, for example on television or in the newspapers, for money, food, information etc, especially in order to help someone who is in a very bad situation **+ for** *The Red Cross is appealing for donations of food and clothing following the earthquake.* | **appeal to sb for sth** *The Murrays have appealed to the public for any information about their missing daughter.* | **appeal to sb to do sth** *The speaker had appealed to the miners to vote for their union.*

17 a statement, letter, message etc in which you ask for something

- request
- demand
- claim
- petition
- application
- appeal
- approach
- plea

request /rɪˈkwest/ [n C] a statement, letter etc in which you ask for something politely or formally: *My grandfather's last request was that there should be no flowers at his funeral.* | **+ for** *She refused all requests for an interview.* | **+ that** *My request that everyone remain seated was ignored.* | **+ to do sth** *Davis's request to do research rather than teach this semester is being considered.* | **at sb's request** (=because someone makes a request) *Cummings eventually resigned at the governor's request.* | **on/upon request** (=when it is requested) *Information about our testing procedure is available on request.* | **make a request** *Ray made a formal written request to meet with Douglas.* | **grant sb's request** formal (=say yes to it) *The board has granted your request for funding.*

demand /dɪˈmɑːnd‖dɪˈmænd/ [n C] a strong request saying very clearly what you want, especially when you are asking for something that someone does not want to give you: *A list of the students' demands was presented to the dean of the law school.* | **+ for** *The union's demand for an 8% across-the-board increase is still under consideration.* | **+ that** *A demand from* *your boss that you babysit his children is clearly unreasonable.* | **+ to do sth** *The government has refused the rebels' demand to release their leader from prison.* | **make a demand** *The kidnappers made several demands in their telephone call to police.*

claim /kleɪm/ [n C] a request for something, especially money, that someone thinks they have a legal right to have **+ for** *The local people's claims for compensation from the chemical factory have so far been ignored.* | **make a claim** *After the fire we made a claim to our insurance company.*

petition /pə̇ˈtɪʃən/ [n C] a document signed by many people that is given to a government or other organization asking them to do something that until now they have been unwilling to do: *A petition signed by 1000 hospital doctors will be handed to the Minister of Health at lunchtime today.* | *Local groups have collected 17,000 votes on a petition to recall the mayor.*

application /ˌæplɪˈkeɪʃən/ [n C] a letter or form that someone sends when they are asking for something such as a job, official document etc: *Since I left university I've sent off nearly fifty job applications.* | **+ for** *We're pleased to announce that your application for membership has been accepted.* | *The first two banks Williams visited denied her application for a loan.*

appeal /əˈpiːl/ [n C] an urgent request for something important such as freedom, money etc, especially in order to help someone in a bad situation: *Dozens of relief agencies have responded to the drought-stricken country's appeal.* | **+ for** *The war continues as a fresh UN appeal for a ceasefire has been rejected.*

approach /əˈprəʊtʃ/ [n C] especially British an official request for someone that you do not know well to do something, especially when you are not sure if they will do it **+ from** *The footballer said he'd received an approach from another team, and that he was considering the offer.* | **make an approach** *An official approach has been made but the hostages are unlikely to be released.*

plea /pliː/ [n C] a strong emotional request for someone to help you or be kind to you: *Ignoring the man's pleas, the soldier shot him in the head.* | **+ for** *A homeless mother of six made a tearful plea for a home for her family.*

attach

RELATED WORDS

- *see also* **fasten/unfasten**

1 to attach one thing to another so that it stays in position

- attach
- fasten
- fix
- nail
- pin

attach /əˈtætʃ/ [v T] to join one thing to another, especially something larger, using glue, string, wires etc to keep it there: *Get your receipt, attach it, and send it in.* | **attach sth to sth** *A copy of my resumé is attached to this letter.* | *The doctor will attach a monitor to your stomach so that she can listen to the baby's heart.*

fasten /ˈfɑːsən‖ˈfæ-/ [v T] to attach one thing to another firmly, but in a way that makes it easy to remove again: *Passengers should keep their seat belts fastened until the warning light is extinguished.* | **fasten sth to sth** *Christine fastened the brooch to her dress.* | *Make sure the wires are properly fastened to the unit.* | **fasten sth on/around/over etc** *Divers fasten weights around their waists to help them stay under water.* | *She fastened her broad hat beneath her chin.*

fix /fɪks/ [v T] British to attach one thing to another so that it will stay permanently in this position, for example by using nails, screws, or strong glue **fix sth to sth** *He fixed the lamp to the wall above the bed with a couple of screws.* | *I don't think it's fixed to the ceiling very securely.* | **fix sth on sth** *I tried to fix them on the door, but they wouldn't stay.*

nail /neɪl/ [v T] to attach one thing to another using nails **nail sth to sth** *A large American flag is nailed to the wall above the bed.* | *The desks in all the classrooms were nailed to the floor.* | **nail sth on/together/down etc** *We watched as Dad nailed the fence panels together.* | *I got a hammer and nailed down the floorboards.* | *The windows had been nailed shut.*

pin /pɪn/ [v T] to attach something using a **pin**, especially to your clothes **pin sth to** *He had pinned a red rose to his jacket.* | *Each delegate wore a name tag pinned to their lapel.* | **pin sth on/up/together etc** *One of the straps was pinned in place with two safety pins.* | *A note was pinned on the door of his office.*

2 to attach something to a wall etc, especially so that it can be seen

- put up
- hang

put up /ˌpʊt ˈʌp/ [phr v T] to attach something to a wall, such as a picture or notice, so that it can be seen **put sth up** *Sarah had put posters up all around her room.* | *Shall I put it up opposite the mirror?* | **put up sth** *Someone's put up a notice in the library offering childcare for $11 an hour.* | *We want to put up an art display at the end of the year to show off the students' work.*

hang /hæŋ/ [v T] to attach something to a wall, tree etc so that it can be seen, especially by using string or wire: *Where do you think we should hang it?* | **hang sth on** *When are we going to hang the lights on the Christmas tree, Mommy?* | **hang up sth/hang sth up** *The children are hanging up the decorations for the party.* | *She hung it up on the bulletin board in the staff room.*

attack

RELATED WORDS

opposite: **defend, protect**
- to criticize someone *see* **criticize**
- to hit someone *see* **hit**
- to attack someone and force them to have sex *see* **sex**
- *see also* **shoot, threaten, crime, army, war, violent**

1 to attack someone

- attack
- mug
- assault
- stab
- go for
- lay into

attack /əˈtæk/ [v I/T] to use violence against someone and try to hurt them: *A woman was attacked by three youths while she was out jogging in Central Park.* | *Police dogs are trained to attack in certain* *circumstances.* | *He was badly injured when one of his own bulls attacked him.* | **attack sb with sth** *Her husband attacked her with a knife.*

mug /mʌg/ [v T usually in passive] to attack someone and take money from them in a public place such as a street: *Since moving to New Jersey, he has been mugged at gunpoint twice.* | *If anyone ever tried to mug me, I would throw my bag and run.* | **get mugged** *I was scared I would get mugged or raped.*

assault /ə'sɔːlt/ [v T] to attack and hurt someone – use this especially to talk about the crime of attacking someone: *He assaulted a female flight attendant who refused to serve him more drinks.* | *Some supporters ran onto the field and assaulted the referee.* | **sexually assault sb** *She was kidnapped and sexually assaulted at gunpoint.*

stab /stæb/ [v T usually in passive] to attack someone by pushing a knife into them: *The victim had been stabbed six times.* | **stab sb in sth** *Meyers was stabbed once in the abdomen and once in the neck.* | **+ at** *Her assailant lunged, stabbing at her again and again.*

go for /'gəʊ fɔːʳ/ [phr v T] to attack someone with a sudden violent movement **go for sb** *Charlie went for Murray as soon as he entered the room, pushing him up against the wall.* | **go for sb with sth** *One day Grandma got so mad she went for Grandpa with the kitchen knife.* | **go for sb's throat/ears/eyes etc** *The dog went straight for my throat, without warning.* | *If you are attacked, go for your attacker's eyes as they are the most vulnerable part of the face.*

lay into /'leɪ ɪntuː/ [phr v T] to attack someone very violently, hitting them repeatedly and without control **lay into sb** *From the moment the bell rang, Tyson laid into his opponent.* | **lay into sb with sth** *The video shows a policeman repeatedly laying into a protestor with his baton.*

2 to attack someone suddenly and unexpectedly

- ambush
- be set upon by
- turn on
- strike
- pounce
- jump

ambush /'æmbʊʃ/ [v T] if a group of people **ambush** someone, they hide and wait for them and then suddenly attack them: *The rebel group successfully ambushed a regiment of American reinforcements.* | *He was afraid he would be stopped by government troops or, even worse, ambushed by the Vietcong.* | *Parker ambushed a school bus on a field trip and held 17 children and their teacher hostage.*

be set upon by /biː 'set əpɒn baɪ/ [v phrase] to suddenly be attacked by people or animals, especially when you are going somewhere – used especially in written or literary contexts: *He had been set upon by bat-wielding racists, so he understood how I felt.* | *The drivers were set upon by a mob, including several women, which showered them with stones.*

turn on ALSO **turn upon** /'tɜːʳn ɒn, 'tɜːʳn əpɒn/ [phr v T] to suddenly attack someone you are with, especially when it is very unexpected: *Red with rage, Frank turned on Anna, grasping her arm in a vice-like grip.* | *Then the warriors turned upon each other, for a fight to the death.*

strike /straɪk/ [v I] to make a quick sudden attack especially on someone who is not expecting to be attacked: *They felt sure the killer would strike again, but could not say when.* | *The police struck at dawn in a carefully timed operation to catch the bombers.*

pounce /paʊns/ [v I] to suddenly jump on another person from a place where you have been hiding, in order to catch or attack them **be ready/waiting/set to pounce** *He crouched on the ground, like an animal ready to pounce.* | **+ on** *Before he could rescue it, the cat pounced on the bird and carried it to the bushes.*

jump /dʒʌmp/ [v T] informal to attack someone suddenly and usually from behind, in order to injure them or to rob them: *Two guys tried to jump me in the park last night.* | *He climbed over the wall and jumped the guard, easily overpowering him.*

3 to attack a place or country

- attack
- invade
- raid
- launch an attack/ mount an attack
- storm
- besiege

attack /ə'tæk/ [v I/T] to **attack** a place or country using weapons, aircraft, soldiers etc: *On 25 April, British and Australian troops attacked the enemy at Gallipoli.* | *The village had been attacked by enemy warplanes.* | *The special unit attacked at dawn, inflicting heavy losses.* | *General Powell consulted with the President before giving the order to attack.* —**attacking** [adj only before noun] **attacking army/forces** *Almost two-thirds of the attacking force had been wiped out.*

invade /ɪn'veɪd/ [v I/T] if a country's army **invades** another country, it enters it and tries to control it: *Enemy forces were almost certainly preparing to invade.* | *Sicily was invaded by the Normans, and later by the Saracens.* | *In his latest film, super-intelligent aliens invade Earth and try to take over.* —**invading** [adj only before noun] **invading army/forces etc** *The villagers headed for the mountains to escape the invading army.*

raid /reɪd/ [v T] if a group of soldiers **raids** a place or town belonging to an enemy, they attack it suddenly and without any warning and cause a lot of damage in a short time: *The rebels raided the tiny mountain town early on Tuesday.* | *Again, the tribe had raided a neighbouring village, inflicting many casualties.*

launch an attack/mount an attack /ˌlɔːntʃ ən ə'tæk, ˌmaʊnt -/ ALSO **launch an invasion/ mount an invasion** /ˌlɔːntʃ ən ɪn'veɪʒən, ˌmaʊnt -/ [v phrase] to start to attack an enemy's army, country, or property, in a planned way: *A fresh attack was mounted on the last remaining rebels.* | *The Huns, normally a peaceful race, launched an invasion into Europe via the Caspian Steppes.*

storm /stɔːʳm/ [v T] to suddenly attack a city or building that is well-defended by getting inside it and taking control: *Heavily armed and masked gunmen stormed an ammunitions store in Co. Mayo.* | *an attempt by government forces to storm the hijacked airplane*

besiege /bɪ'siːdʒ/ [v T] to surround a city or building with soldiers in order to stop the people inside from getting out or from receiving supplies such as food and water: *The capital has been besieged by the opposition militia for two months now.* | *Federal agents besieged the compound in Waco in 1993.* —**besieged** [adj only before noun] **besieged city/town/castle etc** *Hundreds of Serbs managed to flee the besieged city.*

4 to attack someone because they attacked you

- retaliate
- hit back/strike back
- counter-attack
- tit-for-tat

- *see also* **revenge**

retaliate /rɪ'tælieɪt/ [v I] to attack someone because they have attacked you first: *The government wants peace, but will not hesitate to retaliate if attacked.* | *She decided not to retaliate physically, because it would put her in even greater danger.* | **retaliate by doing sth** *When police tried to push back the crowd, a few youths retaliated by throwing stones at them.* | *Later that day, whites retaliated by killing a young black delivery driver.* | **+ against** *He has promised to take tough measures to retaliate against extremists.* | **+ for** (=because of what someone has done to you) *In an interview, Tyson claimed he was retaliating for Holyfield's attack on him.* | **+ with** *I fully accept that it was wrong of the guards to retaliate with blows and kicks.* —**retaliation** /rɪˌtæli'eɪʃən/ [n U] *America stopped short of military retaliation, but issued a strong statement condemning the invasion.* | *the threat of retaliation* | **in retaliation (for sth)** *They plotted the attack in retaliation for the attack by federal agents on the camp.* | *Three inmates were killed in retaliation.*

counter-attack /'kaʊntərəˌtæk/ [n C] an attack that an army makes after it has been attacked by an enemy: *The enemy had started a vicious counter-attack, forcing the French into the woods.* | **launch/mount a counter-attack** *Allied forces were regrouping in order to launch a counter-attack.* —**counter-attack** [v I] *Once the harvest was in, the peasants were free to counter-attack.*

hit back/strike back /ˌhɪt 'bæk, ˌstraɪk 'bæk/ [phr v I] to attack a person or army that has attacked you first, especially in order to try and show that you are very strong and cannot be defeated: *The tanks and artillery will hit back hard if the ceasefire is broken.* | **+ with** *Less than 24 hours after this cross-border raid, army jets hit back with a devastating air strike.* | **+ at** *He suspected that the US would take the opportunity to strike back at the Axis forces.*

tit-for-tat /ˌtɪt fəʳ 'tæt/ [adj only before noun] **tit-for-tat killings/murders/response etc** a killing, reaction etc done because someone has done something similar to someone in your group: *Any hope of peace is destroyed by these endless tit-for-tat attacks.* | *The murder is thought to have been a tit-for-tat response by the Mafia to an earlier gangland killing.*

5 an attack against a person

- attack
- assault
- mugging

attack /ə'tæk/ [n C] when someone uses violence against another person and tries to hurt them: *The attack took place as she was walking home.* | **racial/sexual/physical attack** *Fong did not suffer a physical attack, but he was humiliated by the three men.* | *victims of racial attacks* | *There was no indication of a sexual attack.* | **+ on** *They finally caught the gang responsible for the armed attacks on foreigners in Dakar.* | *New statistics show a further increase in attacks on women.* | **vicious/nasty/unprovoked etc attack** *Police say it was a particularly nasty attack.* | *a number of brutal and unprovoked attacks on gays*

mugging /'mʌgɪŋ/ [n C] an attack on someone in a public place such as a street, in order to steal something from them: *Preston was a victim of a mugging three months ago.* | **a spate/series of muggings** (=several muggings in a short period of time) *Police are investigating a spate of muggings that took place on the campus last week.*

assault /ə'sɔːlt/ [n C/U] an attack on someone – use this especially when talking about the crime of attacking someone: *The charges against the prisoner include criminal damage and assault.* | **indecent/sexual/violent assault** *He was convicted of adultery and indecent assault.* | *the problem of domestic violence and sexual assault within the home* | **+ on** *Assaults on public transportation workers have doubled in the last 10 years.*

6 a military attack

- attack
- assault
- invasion
- strike
- raid
- offensive
- ambush
- aggression

attack /ə'tæk/ [n C] when a military force attacks a place or country, using weapons, aircraft, soldiers etc: *The attack began at dawn.* | *The caller warned that the attacks will continue until the demands are met.* | **+ on** *missile attacks on civilian targets* | **naval/air/artillery/terrorist etc attack** *The city is exposed and vulnerable to air attack.* | *Eleven people were injured in a rocket attack on Sunday night.* | **launch/mount an attack** *International terrorists have mounted an attack aimed at disrupting the huge tourist industry here.* | **go on the attack** (=start to attack someone or something) *To my horror, the soldiers went on the attack, killing men, women and children indiscriminately.*

invasion /ɪn'veɪʒən/ [n C] when an army from one country enters another country and tries to control it: *The fear of an invasion by rebels is always present.* | **foreign/military etc invasion** *Some analysts fear that increasing desperation could lead to a military invasion of the country's southern neighbors.* | *the Soviet invasion of Czechoslovakia*

raid /reɪd/ [n C] a short quick attack by a group of soldiers, planes, or ships on a place that belongs to an enemy **military/bombing/aerial etc raid** *He led a commando raid in the desert.* | *a surprise raid* | *NATO bombing raids* | **air raid** (=one carried out by planes dropping bombs) *Some of the most beautiful architecture in the city was destroyed in the air raids.* | *air-raid sirens* | **+ on/against** *Sixty people are thought to have been killed in the raid on the village just west of the capital.* | *John Brown's raid on Harper's Ferry* | *As a teenager, he was involved in a raid against a village of Omaha Indians.*

ambush /'æmbʊʃ/ [n C] a sudden attack by a group of soldiers who have been hiding and waiting for someone **be killed/shot etc in an ambush** *Six or seven of the passengers were killed in an ambush on the narrowest part of the road.* | **lie/wait in ambush** (=wait in order to ambush) *They moved slowly, knowing that in the next clump of trees enemy soldiers might be lying in ambush.*

assault /ə'sɔːlt/ [n C] a military attack to take control of a place controlled by the enemy **aerial/military/naval etc assault** *a massive armed assault on the city* | **+ on/against** *Only a successful assault on the rebels' headquarters could have ended the civil war.*

strike /straɪk/ [n C] a sudden attack, especially one from the air, using bombs: *The rebels launched a retaliatory strike.* | **air/nuclear/missile etc strike**

The bomb strike took place on a camp near Krek. | *nuclear strike capability*

offensive /ə'fensɪv/ [n C] a planned attack involving large forces and often taking place over several weeks or months, especially as part of a plan to win a war **military/nuclear/air etc offensive** *The great military offensive had failed, and it seemed victory was escaping them.* | *The rebel offensive resumed on Thursday, leaving 12 dead and many injured.* | **launch/mount an offensive** *Government troops launched an offensive against UNITA positions in the north.* | **+ on/against** *The President announced a counter-offensive on the rebels.*

aggression /ə'greʃən/ [n U] the act of attacking a country, especially when that country has not attacked first – used especially in political contexts: *The invasion was condemned as 'blatant aggression' by the British Prime Minister.* | *The President promised to use all his powers to prevent further aggression.* | **armed/foreign/military etc agression** *another example of communist aggression* | **+ against** *As our older generation knows from experience, unchecked aggression against a small nation is a prelude to international disaster.* | **an act of aggression** *Any eastward expansion would be regarded by the government as an act of aggression.*

7 a person or place that attacks another person or country

- attacker
- aggressor

attacker ALSO **assailant** formal /ə'tækəʳ, ə'seɪlənt/ [n C] someone who attacks another person: *Unknown assailants stabbed a British tourist and wounded his wife.* | *The attacker fled empty-handed.* | **your/his/her etc attacker** (=the person who attacked you/him/her etc) *Her attacker is described as white, in his mid-fifties and with medium-length dark hair.* | *Mrs Lundy's alleged assailants were aquitted of all charges.*

aggressor /ə'gresəʳ/ [n C] a country that attacks another country, especially when that country has not already attacked first: *The situation is complex and it is not easy to determine exactly who is the aggressor in this case.* | **military/foreign etc aggressor** *a call for united action against the foreign aggressor* | *The USSR scored valuable propaganda points against its Western aggressors.*

8 a person or place that is attacked

- victim
- target
- be under attack

victim /'vɪktɨ̱m/ [n C] someone who has been attacked: *In most sexual offences, the attacker is known to the victim.* | *The victim was shaken, but physically unharmed.* | **murder/rape/torture etc victim** *The program was grossly insensitive to Holocaust victims.* | *One of the bombing victims was dead on arrival in hospital.* | **+ of** *She had been the victim of a particularly vicious attack.* | *victims of domestic abuse*

target /'tɑːʳgɨ̱t/ [n C] a person or place that someone, especially a military group, has chosen to attack: *The bomb missed its target by several kilometres.* | **military/civilian target** *The GIA continued its attacks on civilian targets.* | **target zone/area** *When the plane gets to the target area, it drops the missile and returns to base.* | **+ of** *The Institution has been the target of terrorist attack several times.* | *The commonly used roads are the targets of heavy fire.* | **prime target** (=very obvious and probable target) *Holding a US passport makes these tourists a prime target for terrorists.*

be under attack /biː ˌʌndər ə'tæk/ [v phrase] if an army or place **is under attack**, it is being attacked: *The rebels are under attack and may surrender at any time.* | **+ from** *At first, he thought the Pacific Fleet was under attack from German forces.* | **come under attack** (=begin to be attacked) *We were united by a sense of national pride when our country came under attack.*

9 easy to attack

- vulnerable
- sitting duck
- be an easy target

vulnerable /'vʌlnərəbəl/ [adj] easy to attack, damage, or enter by force: *His victims are vulnerable young women.* | *Ground floor windows are particularly vulnerable and secure locks should be fitted.* | **+ to** *The tanks' positions made them vulnerable to enemy gunfire.*

sitting duck /ˌsɪtɪŋ 'dʌk/ [n C] someone who is very easy to attack because they cannot move or they can only move very slowly: *The troops in their bunkers were sitting ducks for enemy missiles.* | *We were like sitting ducks, our only defense a small shed surrounded by a few concrete blocks.*

be an easy target /biː ən ˌiːzi 'tɑːʳgɨ̱t/ [v phrase] to be very easy to see or find and therefore easy to attack: *I knew that in our current position, we were an all-too-easy target for thieves and bandits.* | **make an easy target** *Women living alone make easy targets for robbers.*

attention

RELATED WORDS

- *see also* **notice/not notice, famous, interested, ignore**

1 to listen and watch carefully

- pay attention
- concentrate
- concentration
- keep your mind on
- keep your eyes on
- take notice/note
- attentive
- attention span

pay attention /ˌpeɪ ə'tenʃən/ [v phrase] to listen to and watch carefully what you are doing, what is happening, or what someone is saying: *Judith never pays attention in class.* | **+ to** *The TV was on, but Jamal wasn't really paying attention to it.* | **pay sb/sth attention** *I often find myself nodding and smiling at my children without really paying them much attention.* | **pay close/careful attention** *Lawyers around the country were paying close attention to the trial.*

concentrate /'kɒnsəntreɪt‖'kɑːn-/ [v I] to think very carefully about something that you are doing, without being interrupted: *I tried to read a few pages, but I found it hard to concentrate.* | **+ on** *There were so many people talking that I couldn't concentrate on the music.* | *Sherman sat hunched forward and staring through the windshield, trying to concentrate on the traffic.*

concentration /ˌkɒnsən'treɪʃən‖ˌkɑːn-/ [n U] your ability to think carefully about what you are doing without being interrupted: *His face was solemn with* *concentration.* | **+ on** *Plummer said she plans to continue her concentration on the 3,000 meter race.*

keep your mind on /ˌkiːp jɔːʳ ˈmaɪnd ɒn/ [v phrase] to continue to pay attention to something especially when you are very excited or worried about something else: *Just keep your mind on the driving – I'll figure out where we are.* | *Bill couldn't keep his mind on anything but the verdict.*

keep your eyes on /ˌkiːp jɔːr ˈaɪz ɒn / [v phrase] to keep watching something carefully, so that you do not make any mistakes: *We had to keep our eyes on the sandy path to avoid the roots and rocks in the way.* | *Keep your eyes on the ball – now swing!*

take notice/note /ˌteɪk ˈnəʊtɪ̇s, ˈnəʊt/ [v phrase] to pay attention to and think about something, often allowing it to affect a decision – used especially in writing: *There is a lot of criticism of the new law and a number of politicians are beginning to take notice.* | **+ of** *No one took notice of me until I pulled out my notebook and started writing.* | *The organization began to take note of its public image.* | **sit up and take note/notice** *As usual, Greenspan's announcement made the financial world sit up and take notice.*

attentive /əˈtentɪv/ [adj] someone who is **attentive** pays careful attention to someone that they are listening to, watching or looking after: *Hecke's new work has something of interest for both the casual and attentive viewer.* | **+ to** *The crew were extremely attentive to the passengers' safety.*

attention span /əˈtenʃən spæn/ [n U] the amount of time that you are able to carefully listen or watch something that is happening without getting tired or bored **have a short/limited attention span** *Kids of his age typically have a very short attention span.*

2 to pay particular attention to a subject or person

- pay attention to
- concentrate/focus on
- turn your attention to
- give sth/sb your undivided attention

pay attention to /ˌpeɪ əˈtenʃən tuː/ [v phrase] *The government never pays any attention to pre-school education.* | **pay special/particular attention to sth** *The investigators at the crash site are paying particular attention to the weather data.* | **pay more attention to sth** *Previously the company payed much more attention to its investors than it did to its customers.* | **not pay enough attention to sth** *Not enough attention is paid to the role of diet in illnesses such as cancer and heart disease.*

concentrate/focus on /ˈkɒnsəntreɪt, ˈfəʊkəs ɒn/ [v phrase] to spend your time considering a particular subject, group etc, especially because you think it is more important than others: *Concentrate on the content of your report. You can worry about its format or appearance when you've finished writing.* | *The conference will focus on the issue of population control.*

turn your attention to /ˌtɜːʳn jɔːr əˈtenʃən tuː/ [v phrase] to begin to pay attention to someone or something different or new – used especially in written and formal contexts: *Amelia next turned her attention to finding herself a place to live.* | *Having dealt with the problem of energy sources, let's now turn our attention to the question of nuclear power.*

give sth/sb your undivided attention /gɪv (sth/sb) jɔːr ʌndɪˌvaɪdɪ̇d əˈtenʃən/ [v phrase] to give all your attention to something or someone and not do anything else at the same time: *I worry about how Quincy's going to do in school – he can't sit still long enough to give anything his undivided attention.* | **give your undivided attention to sth** *Once I had finished my exams, I could give my undivided attention to looking for a job.*

3 to pay so much attention to something that you do not notice other things

- be engrossed in
- be wrapped up in
- be absorbed in
- immerse yourself in
- preoccupied

be engrossed in /biː ɪnˈgrəʊst ɪn/ [v phrase] to be paying so much attention to something you are doing, that you do not notice what is happening around you: *Helen was sitting up in bed, engrossed in a novel.* | *The two women huddled together like schoolgirls, happily engrossed in their conversation.* | *He was so engrossed in what he was doing he didn't even hear the doorbell ring.*

be wrapped up in /biː ˌræpt ˈʌp ɪn/ [v phrase] to be so involved in something that you do not notice or seem to care about other things: *Hazel's totally wrapped up in the new baby.* | *'Some novelists get wrapped up in their celebrity status,' he acknowledged. 'I hope that doesn't happen to me.'*

be absorbed in /biː əbˈsɔːʳbd ɪn/ [v phrase] to pay a lot of attention to something, especially when you are reading or watching something you enjoy and want to know what happens next: *I was so absorbed in the game on TV that I didn't hear Alexis come in.* | *The little boy sat at the edge of the pond, totally absorbed in watching the fish.*

immerse yourself in /ɪˈmɜːʳs jɔːʳself ɪn/ [v phrase] give all your attention to something such as studying or work so that you do not want to think about anything else: *He immersed himself in his work and tried to forget about Julia.* | *For the first time, I had the chance to really immerse myself in Lenin's writings.* | **be immersed in sth** *The possibility of computer addiction occurred to her when she missed a class she was teaching, because she was immersed in the Internet.*

preoccupied /priːˈɒkjɪ̈paɪd‖-ˈɑːk-/ [adj not before noun] someone who is **preoccupied** is worried or thinking about other things, and tends to forget about someone or something else: *Parents are often too busy, tired, or preoccupied to give their children the time and attention they need.* | **+ with** *Most Russians are preoccupied with matters close to home, their economic conditions in particular.*

4 not paying attention to what is happening

- not pay attention
- daydream
- switch off
- be miles away
- your mind wanders
- inattentive
- lose (your) concentration

not pay attention /nɒt ˌpeɪ əˈtenʃən/ [v phrase] *What did the announcers just say? I wasn't paying attention.* | **+ to** *When you're young, you don't pay attention to what your parents are saying half the time.*

daydream /ˈdeɪdriːm/ [v I] to not pay attention because you are thinking about pleasant things or imagining things that you would like to happen: *Blackthorne was sitting alone in a corner of the gar-*

den, daydreaming. | **+ about** *Almost anyone who has ever read a good book has daydreamed about writing his or her own best-seller.*

switch off /ˌswɪtʃ ˈɒf/ [phr v I] British informal to stop paying attention to something because you are bored, or to stop thinking about your work after you have finished in the evening and relax: *In the end I got sick of the conversation and switched off.* | *It's difficult for teachers to switch off when they go home at night.*

be miles away /biː ˈmaɪlz əˌweɪ/ [v phrase] British spoken to not be paying attention to anything or anyone around you and seem to be thinking about something very different: *Sorry, I was miles away. What did you say?* | *I don't mean to disturb you, you looked miles away – but there's a call for you.*

your mind wanders /jɔːʳ ˌmaɪnd ˈwɒndəʳz‖-ˈwɑːn-/ if **your mind wanders** you are no longer paying attention, usually because you are bored or because something is worrying you: *I tried hard to concentrate, but my mind kept wandering.* | **+ to/from** *His mind wandered to the things he was trying not to think about.* | **let your mind wander** *Corrinne let her mind wander back to the days when they first met.*

inattentive /ˌɪnəˈtentɪv◂/ [adj] someone who is **inattentive** does not pay attention to something when they are expected to: *Roger was hyperactive and inattentive as a child.* | *In spite of the inattentive servers and the bad decor, it's worth eating at Leon's for the great cheap food.* | **+ to** *The government is still being accused of being inattentive to the plight of the Health Service.*

lose (your) concentration /ˌluːz (jɔːʳ) ˌkɒnsənˈtreɪʃən‖-ˌkɑːn-/ [v phrase] if you **lose your concentration**, you stop being able to think carefully about what you are doing, for example because you are suddenly interrupted: *Sensing that the team was losing their concentration, Barret called a time out.* | *With too much homework, children may lose concentration and stop progressing.*

5 not paying attention to a particular subject or person

- not pay attention
- take no notice/not take any notice

not pay attention /nɒt ˌpeɪ əˈtenʃən/ [v phrase] *Don't pay attention to anything they say – they're just trying to get money out of you.* | *More than half the people in the study said they do not pay attention to election campaigns.* | *A high-level military official warned people not to pay attention to rumours about invasion.*

take no notice/not take any notice /ˌteɪk nəʊ ˈnəʊtɪ̆s, nɒt ˌteɪk eni ˈnəʊtɪ̆s/ [v phrase] to not pay attention to something – used especially in writing: *The conflict continued in the small African state, but the world took no notice.* | *My parents didn't seem to take any notice of my wails as we drove down the motorway.*

6 to make someone pay attention to you

- get/attract attention
- draw attention to yourself

get/attract attention /ˌget, əˌtrækt əˈtenʃən/ [v phrase] to try to make someone notice you, by doing something that they will notice: *Young children sometimes behave badly simply in order to get attention.* | *With all the competition, a website really has to give away something good to get people's attention.* | **get/attract sb's attention** *He was waving his hand wildly, trying to attract Kovitsky's attention.*

draw attention to yourself /ˌdrɔː əˈtenʃən tə jɔːʳˈself/ [v phrase] to make people notice you – used especially when you are trying to avoid doing this, or you think someone should try to avoid doing this: *I did a few of the usual idiotic things as a teenager to try to draw attention to myself.* | *Carney knew he would draw attention to himself if he rented a boat in the middle of winter.*

7 to make people pay attention to a subject or problem

- draw/call attention to
- highlight
- focus attention on
- bring sth to sb's attention
- point out

draw/call attention to /ˌdrɔː, ˌkɔːl əˈtenʃən tuː/ [v phrase] *The group is willing to use terrorism in order to draw attention to their desire for independence.* | *Fox was one of the first US scientists to call attention to the rising levels of carbon dioxide in the atmosphere.*

highlight /ˈhaɪlaɪt/ [v T] to show that something is important and make people notice it, especially so that they start to do something about it: *The report highlighted the need for prison reform.* | *The Association's first project was to publish a 35-cent brochure highlighting nine historic sites.*

focus attention on /ˌfəʊkəs əˈtenʃən ɒn/ [v phrase] to make a large group of people, especially the public, pay attention to one particular problem or bad situation because it needs their help: *The publicity campaign helped to focus attention on the needs of elderly people in the community.* | **focus sb's attention on** *The media's efforts often focus public attention on government incompetence, forcing government to do the right thing.*

bring sth to sb's attention /ˌbrɪŋ (sth) tə (sb's) əˈtenʃən/ [v phrase] to inform someone in a position of power or authority about a problem, bad situation etc so that they can do something to help or stop it: *It was one of the other students who brought your misbehaviour to my attention.* | *The reviews provide a way for companies to bring their trade concerns to the attention of the government.*

point out /ˌpɔɪnt ˈaʊt/ [phr v T] to tell someone about a mistake they have made, something they have forgotten etc: *He pointed out the danger of a mountain trek at this time of year.* | **+ that** *I pointed out that changing the date would mean rescheduling the press conference.* | **point sth/it out** *I didn't realise I'd made a mistake. Thank you for pointing it out.* | **as sb points out** *As Palermo pointed out, Peruvian university students tend to be highly political.*

8 when someone or something gets a lot of attention

- get/attract/receive attention
- be the centre of attention
- be the focus of attention
- attention

get/attract/receive attention /ˌget, əˌtrækt, rɪˌsiːv əˈtenʃən/ [v phrase] *The young Senator is getting a lot of attention.* | *The film has attracted considerable attention since it was released last week.*

be the centre of attention British **/be the center of attention** American /biː ðə ˌsentər əv əˈtenʃən/ [v phrase] if someone or something **is the centre of attention** everyone is very interested in them and gives them a lot of attention: *I loved talking and being the centre of attention, so I was chosen to be spokesperson.* | *Eliot argued that it should be the poetry, not the poet's personality, that is the center of attention.*

be the focus of attention /biː ðə ˌfəʊkəs əv əˈtenʃən/ [v phrase] if someone or something, often a bad situation, **is the focus of attention**, everyone is paying it a lot of attention: *The earthquake has made skyscrapers the focus of attention.* | *The Airline became the focus of attention yesterday after its stock fell dramatically to 31 cents.* | *Suddenly Carmichael, the shy lead singer, was the focus of millions of young girls' attention.*

attention /əˈtenʃən/ [n U] the interest that people show in someone or something: *Jerry loves the attention he gets when he's performing* | **media attention** (=attention from newspapers, television etc) *The intense media attention surrounding the case, has made it very difficult for the family to cope.*

9 to avoid attention or take attention away

- not draw attention
- draw attention away from
- divert/distract attention
- put sb off
- keep a low profile

not draw attention /nɒt ˌdrɔː əˈtenʃən / [v phrase] to make a special effort to be normal, inoffensive, or quiet, so that people will not pay attention to you **+ to** *It was obvious that Jackson didn't want to draw attention to himself.* | **without drawing attention** *The city's wealth allows drug traffickers to live a comfortable lifestyle without drawing attention to themselves.* | **avoid drawing attention** *Aides to the Prime Minister tried to avoid drawing public attention to the speech.*

draw attention away from /ˌdrɔː əˌtenʃən əˈweɪ frɒm / [v phrase] to make someone pay attention to one thing or person, either deliberately or without intending to, so that they do not pay attention to another: *The government was hoping to draw attention away from the current economic crisis.* | *His 'bad-boy' behaviour tends to draw attention away from many of the good things he is doing in his community.*

divert/distract attention /daɪˌvɜːʳt, dɪˌstrækt əˈtenʃən/ [v phrase] to make someone stop paying attention to something important, either deliberately or without intending to: *The debate is diverting attention from the urgent need to improve the way the medical system cares for terminally ill patients.* | **+ from** *The bomb could have been planted in order to distract attention from the robbery.* | **distract/divert sb's attention** *Before we could explore the matter further, some new evidence diverted our attention.*

put sb off /ˌpʊt (sb) ˈɒf/ [phr v T] British informal to make someone stop paying attention to what they are doing, especially so that they make a mistake: *Stop staring at me, it's putting me off.* | **put sb off their game/stroke** *All the noise from the crowd put Alison off her game.*

keep a low profile /ˌkiːp ə ˌləʊ ˈprəʊfaɪl/ [v phrase] to try not to make anyone notice you for a period of time, for example because you have done something bad: *She's keeping a low profile until the scandal is forgotten.* | *Many of the exiles have married, taken jobs, and generally kept a low profile.*

attract/ attraction

RELATED WORDS

- attractive/good looking *see* **beautiful**
- sexually attractive *see* **sexy**
- to talk to someone in a way that shows you are sexually attracted to someone *see* **talk (9)**
- attract someone's attention *see* **attention**
- to make someone like something *see* **like**
- to make someone dislike something *see* **dislike (4)**
- *see also* **interested, good, nice, want**

1 to make someone like or want to do something

- attract
- tempt
- seduce

attract /əˈtrækt/ [v T] *The drug's low price attracts school- and college-age users.* | **attract sb to sth** *What attracts me to the job is the salary and the possibility of foreign travel.* | **attract interest/support/attention etc** *Politicians still risk having affairs, knowing the massive media attention they attract.*

tempt /tempt/ [v T] to make someone want to have or do something, even though they know they really should not: *The Parisian shops have things to tempt even the strongest of wills.* | *Too many investors are tempted by the idea of making a quick fortune.* | **tempt sb into (doing) sth** *Most infomercials try to tempt television viewers into buying beauty aids, kitchen gadgets and other products.* | **be tempted to do sth** *I'm tempted to take a nice long vacation before I start the new job.*

seduce /sɪˈdjuːs‖-ˈduːs/ [v T] to attract someone to buy a particular product, support a particular political party etc, by making it seem very attractive – used especially in order to show disapproval: *The government has been accused of bringing down taxes simply as a means of seducing voters.* | *Hunt was seduced by the lure of fame and show business.* | **seduce sb into doing sth** *TV advertisements seduce people into buying a particular kind of chocolate bar, washing powder or car.*

2 to make someone want to go to a place

- attract
- draw
- bring in
- lure

attract /əˈtrækt/ [v T] *Leftover food attracts flies.* | **attract sb into/to/towards etc** *The special low rent is designed to attract new businesses to the area.*

draw /drɔː/ [v T] if an event or place **draws** a large number of people, it attracts them, because it is very popular: *The football game is expected to draw a crowd of around 50,000.* | **draw sb from** *Such was the reputation of the school that it drew boys from all over the south of England.* | *It was an unparalleled gathering of black artists from around the world, drawing delegates from fifty countries.*

bring in /ˌbrɪŋ ˈɪn/ [phr v T] to make people want to go to a place or event, take part in something, or join an organization **bring in sb/sth** *Officials know that fixing up the area will bring in more visitors, and eventually new businesses.* | **bring sb/sth in** *The police force introduced a new advertising campaign, in an attempt to bring more recruits in from ethnic minorities.*

lure /lʊəʳ, ljʊəʳ‖lʊər/ [v T] to make someone come to a place by offering or showing them something they want, often in order to harm them or deceive them **lure sb to/into/away etc** *The burglary was set up in order to lure the police officer into an ambush.* | *Ever since I left the company they have been making attempts to lure me back.*

3 making you like someone or something, or to want to do something

- attractive
- appealing
- tempting
- irresistible
- enticing

attractive /əˈtræktɪv/ [adj] *The houses were situated in an attractive spot, near the river.* | *an attractive personality* | *The staff includes many top scientists who left attractive jobs elsewhere to join the hard-driving CEO.* | *Lower rates have made other currencies, such as the dollar, more attractive.* | **+ to** *Improvements to public infrastructure is one way of making depressed areas more attractive to private industry.*

appealing /əˈpiːlɪŋ/ [adj] someone or something that is **appealing** has qualities that make people like them: *Having someone to do all my cleaning for me was an appealing prospect.* | *He decided to follow the example of his one-time political mentor, Nixon, and make himself a more appealing candidate.* | *Although a warmer climate may sound appealing, the effects of the heat can be difficult to cope with.*

tempting /ˈtemptɪŋ/ [adj] something that is **tempting** is something that you want to do or have very much, but which you have doubts about doing or having: *I've recently received a very tempting job offer from IBM.* | *Inside you'll find tempting recipes from around the world, all beautifully illustrated.* | *It was very tempting – only £50 for a ticket to the fight – but I decided to save the money.*

irresistible /ˌɪrɪˈzɪstəbəl/ [adj] so good or attractive that you feel you must have it or do it: *The table was covered with irresistible chocolate desserts of all descriptions.* | **+ to** *High interest rates have made these saving plans irresistible to small investors.* | *To my parents, the pull of this beautiful country town must have seemed irresistible.*

enticing /ɪnˈtaɪsɪŋ/ [adj] something that is **enticing** attracts you very strongly, especially because it is interesting and you want to find out more about it: *enticing smells coming from the kitchen* | **+ to** *The advertisers have been accused of trying to make the alcoholic drinks enticing to teenagers.*

4 something that attracts people

- attraction
- appeal
- the lure of sth
- temptation
- charm

attraction /əˈtrækʃən/ [n C] the quality that something has, which makes people like it, want it, or feel interested in it. **Attraction** is also used about places or things to do that people like, find interesting, or want to visit: *A lot of young people take drugs. Personally, I can't see the attraction.* | **+ of** *For many mothers, one of the attractions of childcare in the workplace is the chance to be near their children.* | **a tourist attraction** *The Galapagos Islands are one of Ecuador's main tourist attractions.*

appeal /əˈpiːl/ [n U] a quality that someone or something has that makes people like it, want it, or feel interested in it: *Much of Corfu's appeal lies in its lively night life.* | *Fink writes with eloquence about the appeal of the Jewish faith for her.* | *The film is flawed, although it has a certain nostalgic appeal.* | **have popular/universal/mass appeal** (=be interesting to most people) *While animation has universal appeal, audiences have become increasingly insistent on high standards.*

the lure of sth /ðə ˈlʊər əv (sth)/ [n phrase] a strongly attractive quality that makes you want something very much, even though you know it may be bad for you: *It's hard to escape the lure of credit cards and the access they provide.* | *In public housing projects, the lure of gangs is strong for teenagers.* | *I tried hard to settle down, but the lure of travel and adventure was too much for me.*

temptation /tempˈteɪʃən/ [n C/U] something that makes you want to do or have something, even though you know you should not: *Life in New York has so many temptations.* | **temptation to do sth** *When life was hard, the temptation to start drinking again was strong.* | **resist (the) temptation** (=not do something that you would really like to do) *She thought of taking a day off work, but resisted the temptation.* | **give in to (the) temptation** (=do something that you would really like to do) *I finally gave in to temptation and ate a huge piece of cheesecake.*

charm /tʃɑːʳm/ [n U] a pleasant quality that someone has that makes people like them, feel attracted to them, or be easily persuaded by them. **Charm** is also used about the special qualities that a place or thing has that make people like it: *With her charm and good looks, she's sure to be a success.* | *She was a leader of great character and tremendous personal charm.* | *The book captures Savannah's old Southern charm and its eccentric citizens perfectly.*

available/ not available

RELATED WORDS

- when someone is not available *see* **busy (9)**
- *see also* **get, buy**

1 available for someone to have or use

- available
- free
- spare
- empty
- vacant
- to be had/found
- be going
- at your disposal
- be on tap

available /əˈveɪləbəl/ [adj] if something is **available**, you can get it, buy it, or use it: *There's no room for more books – we've used up all the available space.* | **+ to** *Grants are available to students who have high grades.* | **+ from** *The publication is available from the U.S. Department of Agriculture.* | **+ at/in** *Tickets are available at all Ticketmaster locations.* | **have sth available** *Do you have a room available for this weekend?* | **readily/freely available**

(=very easy to get) *Drugs like heroin are readily available on the streets.* | **make sth available** *These statistics are never sold or made available to the public.*

free /friː/ [adj] a room or seat that is **free** is not being used by anyone now, and no one has asked for it to be kept for them to use later: *Is this chair free?* | *The only free seats on the train were in a smoking compartment.* | **have sth free** *The hotel never has any rooms free over the Christmas period.*

spare /speəʳ/ [adj] something that is **spare** is not being used now, but it can be used if someone needs it: *I need 50 cents for the parking meter – do you have any spare change?* | *We're using the spare bedroom as a storage space.* | *a spare tyre*

empty /ˈempti/ [adj] something such as a room or seat that is **empty** has no one using it at the moment and is therefore available for someone else to use: *They have three empty rooms now that the kids have moved out.* | *I think there's an empty seat in the back row.* | *The house was empty for two months before it was sold.*

vacant /ˈveɪkənt/ [adj] a building, home, room, or office that is **vacant** is available because it is not owned or rented by anyone: *There don't seem to be any vacant rooms in the whole of London!* | *If you're looking for somewhere to rent, I think there's a vacant apartment in my building.* | *Of the buildings the company owns, only 3% are vacant.* —**vacancy** [n C] a room in a hotel, rented house etc that no one is staying in now, and is available for people to pay to stay in: *All we saw for miles were 'no vacancy' signs.*

to be had/found /tə biː ˈhæd, ˈfaʊnd/ [adj phrase] something that is **to be had** or **to be found** is available to anyone who knows where to get it from: *When no work was to be had, he borrowed money from friends.* | *We looked all over, but there were no fast food restaurants to be found.* | *She knew of a place where designer clothes were to be had at bargain prices.*

be going /biː ˈgəʊɪŋ/ [v phrase] British informal if something **is going**, it is available for anyone who wants it: *Is there any more wine going?* | *There aren't many jobs going in this part of the country.*

at your disposal /ət jɔːʳ dɪˈspəʊzəl/ [adj phrase] if something is **at your disposal**, someone has provided it for you to use whenever you want or in any way that you want: *We have ample money at our disposal to do this job right.* | *A limousine and driver were put at her disposal for the entire week.*

be on tap /biː ɒn ˈtæp/ [v phrase] informal if something that you like or enjoy **is on tap**, it is available to you all the time so that you can have it whenever you want it: *It's a great place for a rest: food, music, alcohol – everything's on tap.* | *Some three hundred free outdoor shows are on tap during the weekend festival.*

2 when a job is available

- vacant
- vacancy
- open
- opening
- unfilled

vacant /ˈveɪkənt/ [adj] not being done by anyone at the moment and therefore available: *Our company only has one or two vacant positions at the moment.* | *When the post became vacant it was offered to Wendy Brooks.* | **fall vacant** (=become vacant) British *He applied for the job of Eliot's personal secretary, which had just fallen vacant.*

vacancy /ˈveɪkənsi/ [n C] an available job: *There are over 3 million people unemployed and only 400,000 vacancies.* | *I'm sorry, the firm has no vacancies at the moment.* | **fill a vacancy** *Barnhart will fill a vacancy on the Planning Commission.*

open /ˈəʊpən/ [adj not before noun] a job that is **open**, especially a job that needs a lot of skill, is still available because it has not yet been given to anyone else: *Is that job you told me about last week still open?* | **+ to** *The position is open to graduates in any subject.* | **come open** *When the job finally came open, I was the first to apply.*

opening /ˈəʊpənɪŋ/ [n C] an available job: *I was wondering if there were any job openings at your company.* | **fill an opening** *We expect to fill most of the openings through internal promotion.*

unfilled /ˌʌnˈfɪld◂/ [adj] a job or position that is **unfilled** is available because an employer has not yet decided who should do it, or cannot find someone suitable for it: *About 13,000 of the unfilled positions are for software engineers.* | *It's hard to understand the unemployment figures when so many jobs go unfilled.*

3 when someone is not busy and is available to do something

- available
- free

available /əˈveɪləbəl/ [adj] someone who is **available** is not doing anything now and is therefore **available** to do something, especially a piece of work for someone else: *We need someone to work on this job immediately. Who's available?* | *Most of the staff is away today so you'll have to use whoever is available.* | *None of the witnesses were available for comment.* —**availability** /əˌveɪləˈbɪləti/ [n U] *It is the hospital manager who should match the availability of staff with the needs of the patients.*

free /friː/ [adj] someone who is **free** is available because they are not doing anything now or have finished what they were doing: *I'll be free in about five minutes. Can you wait?* | **+ to do sth** *Are you free to talk for a couple of minutes?*

4 an amount of something that you have available to use

- supply
- stock
- reserves
- pool

supply /səˈplaɪ/ [n C] *More donors are needed as blood supplies run low.* | **+ of** *The supermarket donated a year's supply of groceries to one needy family.*

stock /stɒk‖stɑːk/ [n C] an amount of something that you keep and can use when you need to: *The government has said it has no need for chemical weapons and will destroy its stocks entirely.* | **+ of** *Jodie always had a large stock of brandy in her cupboard.*

reserves /rɪˈzɜːʳvz/ [n plural] an amount of money, goods etc that a country or organization has available to be used if they are needed: *The government has exhausted almost all its foreign currency reserves.* | **+ of** *Kuwait has large reserves of oil.*

pool /puːl/ [n C] an amount or number of workers, cars, money etc that can be shared or used by a number of people: *Most countries have a pool of surplus labour.* | *There is a much smaller pool of houses to rent than there used to be.*

5 when something is not available

- unavailable/not available
- unobtainable
- not to be had/found
- taken

unavailable/not available /ˌʌnəˈveɪləbəl, nɒt əˈveɪləbəl/ [adj not before noun] *She took a temporary job because a permanent job was not available.* | *In many Russian cities basic foodstuffs are unavailable.* | **+ to** *This type of diet pill should be made unavailable to minors.*

unobtainable /ˌʌnəbˈteɪnəbəl/ [adj not usually before noun] goods or products that are **unobtainable** are impossible to get or buy: *Fresh fruit is unobtainable at certain times of the year.* | *Good apartments to rent had become almost unobtainable.*

not to be had/found /nɒt tə biː ˈhæd, ˈfaʊnd/ [adj phrase] if something that you really want is **not to be had** or **not to be found** you know it is not available at all because you have tried to get it everywhere: *At the moment warm woollen socks are not to be found anywhere in Bucharest.* | *Good legal advice is simply not to be had because of the shortage of lawyers.*

taken /ˈteɪkən/ [adj not before noun] if something such as a seat, room, or place is **taken**, someone has already arranged to use it and it is not available for other people to use: *I'm sorry – that seat is taken.*

avoid

RELATED WORDS

- to prevent something from happening *see* **prevent**
- when something bad almost happens to you *see* **almost (5)**
- *see also* **hide**

1 to avoid something bad that could happen to you

- avoid
- get around sth
- escape

avoid /əˈvɔɪd/ [v T] to make sure that something bad does not happen to you, either by doing something or by deliberately not doing something: *You can avoid a lot of problems if you use travellers' cheques.* | *The book is intended to help students avoid common errors.* | *The driver of the car said he tried to brake to avoid the accident, but it was already too late.* | *Police were anxious to avoid any ugly scenes when the two boys made their first appearance in court nine days ago.*

get around sth ALSO **get round sth** British /ˌget əˈraʊnd (sth), ˌget ˈraʊnd (sth)/ [phr v T] informal to find a way of avoiding a difficult or unpleasant situation, so that you do not have to deal with it: *There's no way of getting around it – you're going to have to tell her the truth.* | *If we can get round these difficulties, we'll be able to discuss the really important points.*

escape /ɪˈskeɪp/ [v T] **escape death/injury/punishment** to avoid being killed, hurt, or punished: *Somehow he managed to escape serious injury.* | *Many young offenders escape punishment completely.* | **narrowly escape sth** (=almost not escape) *The train ran out of control, and the passengers narrowly escaped death.*

2 to avoid doing something that you should do

- avoid
- get out of sth
- duck out of
- wriggle out of/worm (your way) out of
- get around
- evade
- dodge

avoid /əˈvɔɪd/ [v T] *You can't go on avoiding your responsibilities forever.* | *Import duties on some goods can be avoided if you know how.* | **avoid doing sth** *Do you think he's gone away to avoid talking to the police?* | *She's a good manager, because she never avoids dealing with the problems of her staff.* | *You may be able to avoid paying income tax on the money that you save.* —**avoidance** [n U] *Your avoidance of the issue is probably not helping the relationship much.*

get out of sth /ˌget ˈaʊt əv (sth)/ [phr v T] informal to avoid doing something that you should do or that you have promised to do: *I was supposed to stay at home with my baby sister today, but I'll try to get out of it.* | **get out of doing sth** *He always manages to get out of paying for the drinks.*

duck out of /ˌdʌk ˈaʊt ɒv / [phr v T] informal to avoid doing something that you have to do or have promised to do especially in a way that makes people not like or respect you: *It's illegal for these companies to duck out of their responsibilities by changing their names.* | **duck out of doing sth** *Miller has been widely criticized for trying to duck out on paying back the loans.*

wriggle out of/worm (your way) out of ALSO **weasel (your way) out of** American /ˌrɪgəl ˈaʊt ɒv, ˌwɜːʳm (jɔːʳ weɪ) ˈaʊt ɒv, ˌwiːzəl (jɔːʳ weɪ) ˈaʊt ɒv/ [v T] to avoid doing something you should do by making up excuses: *He's somehow managed to wriggle out of watching the kids again.* | *Beth's trying to worm her way out of helping with the party.* | *You promised you'd take me, so don't try to weasel out of it.*

get around ALSO **get round** British /get əˈraʊnd, get ˈraʊnd/ [phr v T] **get around a law/rule/regulation etc** to find a legal way of not obeying a law or rule that prevents you from doing what you want to do: *Isn't there any way of getting round these regulations?* | *He gets around the fire codes by claiming the building is a private club and not a business.*

evade /ɪˈveɪd/ [v T] informal to avoid paying tax or obeying a law, in a way that is illegal or dishonest, or to avoid doing something that it is your duty to do: *Clever businessmen often manage to evade taxes.* | *Politicians have come up with many tricks to evade campaign spending limits.* —**evasion** /ɪˈveɪʒən/ [n U] *The authorities are becoming stricter about tax evasion.*

dodge /dɒdʒ‖dɑːdʒ/ [v T] informal to avoid paying something or doing something, especially in a dishonest way: *Through the help of powerful Senators, the firm has successfully dodged most federal environmental regulations.* | *During the Vietnam war, he moved to Canada to dodge the draft.* —**dodge** [n C] *He always knew about the latest tax dodge* (=the latest way to avoid paying taxes).

3 to keep away from a person or place

- avoid
- stay away/keep away
- steer clear of
- make a detour

avoid /ə'vɔɪd/ [v T] to keep away from a person, because you do not want to talk to them, or keep away from a place, because there are problems there: *I'm sure Sarah's been avoiding me recently.* | *Drivers are advised to avoid Elm Street today due to heavy traffic and long delays.* | **avoid sb/sth like the plague** informal (=try very hard to avoid them) *Except when they were filming, the two actors avoided each other like the plague.*

stay away/keep away /ˌsteɪ ə'weɪ, ˌkiːp ə'weɪ/ [phr v I] to not go near a person or place, because they may be dangerous or may cause problems **+ from** *That evening he received a note warning him to stay away from the camp.* | *Keep away from my children, or I'll call the police.* | **stay/keep well away** (=completely avoid) *She walked along the path, keeping well away from the edge of the cliff.*

steer clear of /ˌstɪəʳ 'klɪər ɒv/ ALSO **give sb/sth a wide berth** /gɪv (sb/sth) ə ˌwaɪd 'bɜːʳθ/ [v phrase] informal to make an effort to avoid a person or place, because there could be serious problems if you do not: *We were told to steer clear of the main roads where we might be recognized.* | *She advised me to steer clear of Matthew – she said he couldn't be trusted.* | *Passersby gave the old man on the sidewalk a fairly wide berth.*

make a detour /ˌmeɪk ə 'diːtʊəʳ/ [v phrase] to travel around a place instead of through the centre of it, especially to avoid a traffic problem: *We had to make a long detour because of the floods.*

4 to avoid a difficult question or subject

- avoid
- evade
- evasive
- dodge/duck/sidestep
- beat about the bush
- shy away from

▸ *see also* **talk (16)**

avoid /ə'vɔɪd/ [v T] to not talk about a subject or not answer a question, because you do not want to cause embarrassment or problems for yourself: *Try to avoid subjects like sex or religion that might offend people.* | *Typical politician! He just kept avoiding the question.*

evade /ɪ'veɪd/ [v T] to avoid a particular subject or a question because you are trying to hide something: *Steve evaded the question when I asked him why he had left work so early.* | *The best interviewers make it impossible for politicians to evade the questions.*

evasive /ɪ'veɪsɪv/ [adj] someone who is **evasive** tries to avoid answering questions or explaining their plans, because they want to hide something: *When we asked him where his wife was, O'Hare suddenly became evasive.* | *All their questions were met with vague, evasive answers.*

dodge/duck/sidestep /dɒdʒ‖dɑːdʒ, dʌk, 'saɪdstep / [v T] informal to avoid answering a question or talking about a subject, especially by talking about something else instead: *Once again the management dodged the issue of salary increases.* | *Even if you don't agree with him, you have to admit Senator Connors never ducks a question.* | *He sidestepped the question, and talked instead about plans for the future.*

beat about the bush British **/beat around the bush** American /ˌbiːt əbaʊt ðə 'bʊʃ, ˌbiːt əraʊnd ðə 'bʊʃ/ [v phrase] to avoid talking about the most important detail of something and talk about other details instead, because you are embarrassed, not confident etc: *Don't beat about the bush – get to the point.* | *If you want to leave, just say so instead of beating around the bush.*

shy away from /ˌʃaɪ ə'weɪ frɒm / [v phrase] to avoid a subject or problem, especially because you are afraid, embarrassed, or do not want to offend other people: *Parents often shy away from discussing sex with their children.*

5 to avoid being hit or seen

- avoid
- get out of the way
- duck
- dodge

avoid /ə'vɔɪd/ [v T] to move so that you do not hit something or get hit by it: *I had to swerve to avoid the truck.* | **avoid doing sth** *Penny jumped out of the way to avoid being hit by the falling branch.*

get out of the way /get ˌaʊt əv ðə 'weɪ/ [v phrase] to move quickly in order to avoid something dangerous that is moving towards you: *'Get out of the way!' he yelled, as the truck rolled down the hill.* | **+ of** *She had to run to the sidewalk to get out of the way of the car.*

duck /dʌk/ [v I] to move your head and the top part of your body down in order to avoid something: *I forgot to duck and hit my head on the branch.* | *Josie ducked and the vase smashed against the wall.*

dodge /dɒdʒ‖dɑːdʒ/ [v I/T] to avoid something or someone by moving sideways: *We had to run across some open ground, dodging the bullets.* | *He almost caught me, but I dodged and ran across the road.* | **+ behind/into/through** *When Kevin saw the soldiers, he dodged into an alley.*

Bb

baby

RELATED WORDS

▸ *see also* **child, family, father, mother**

1 a baby

- baby
- infant
- child
- newborn

baby /'beɪbi/ [n C] a very young child, especially one who has not yet learned to speak or walk: *Would you mind looking after the baby for us on Saturday afternoon?* | **baby girl/boy** *a four-day-old baby girl* | **baby clothes/food/milk etc** (=for babies) *Let's see if there are any nice baby clothes in the sales.*

infant /'ɪnfənt/ [n C] a baby: *Her parents both died when she was an infant.* | *There are clear differences in speed of learning between infants at this early stage.* | **infant son/daughter** *The couple have a three-year-old son and an infant daughter.* | **infant mortal-**

ity (=the number of babies that die in a society) *There has been a sharp rise in infant mortality since the drought began.*

child /tʃaɪld/ [n C] formal a baby at the time when it is born or before it is born: *Medical staff, seeing that the child was in danger, decided to perform an operation.* | **sb's first/second etc child** *Michael and Ronda had their first child last year.* | *Roberta's second child weighed over four kilos at birth.*

newborn /ˈnjuːbɔːʳn‖ˈnuː-/ [adj] **newborn baby/child/infant** a baby etc that has just been born: *Relatives and friends all wanted to see the newborn baby.* | *Newborn infants spend a lot of time sleeping.* | *The average weight of a newborn baby is about seven pounds.* — **newborn** [n C] *It is normal for newborns* (=newborn babies) *to have very large heads.*

2 a baby animal

- young
- baby
- newborn
- litter

young /jʌŋ/ [n plural] the babies of an animal or bird: *The mother bird's main concern is to provide food for her young.* | *Kangaroos carry their young in a pouch.*

baby /ˈbeɪbi/ [adj only before noun] **baby animal/rabbit/elephant etc** a very young animal, rabbit etc – used especially by or to children: *In the zoo there is a small farm where children can look at the baby animals.* | *Baby monkeys cling to their mother's backs.*

newborn /ˈnjuːbɔːʳn‖ˈnuː-/ [adj] a **newborn** animal is one that has just been born: *Newborn kittens cannot open their eyes.* | *a mother sheep with her newborn lamb*

litter /ˈlɪtəʳ/ [n C] a group of several baby animals that are born at the same time and have the same mother: *The vet asked how many litters the dog had had.* | *Our cat, Elsie, just had a litter of six kittens.*

3 a baby that is still developing in its mother's body

- unborn child/baby
- fetus/foetus
- embryo

unborn child/baby /ˌʌnbɔːʳn ˈtʃaɪld, ˈbeɪbi/ [n C] *Doctors do not know what the long-term effects of the drug will be on the unborn child.* | *Petra could feel her unborn baby moving inside her.*

fetus/foetus /ˈfiːtəs/ [n C] British a baby that is developing in its mother's body – used especially by doctors: *By the end of the third month of pregnancy the foetus is a miniature human being.* | *The research focuses on how alcohol may harm the fetus.*

embryo /ˈembriəʊ/ [n C] a baby that is in the very early stage of development inside its mother's body: *When first formed, the embryo is only half a millimetre long.* | *The government has banned all scientific research using human embryos.*

4 when a baby is born

- be born
- birth
- arrive
- come along

be born /biː ˈbɔːʳn/ [v phrase] *Karen's baby was born six weeks early.* | *All our children were born in the same hospital.*

birth /bɜːʳθ/ [n C/U] the fact or process of being born: *It was a very difficult birth.* | *There have been three births in our family this year.* | **+ of** *It's quite common now for fathers to be present at the birth of their babies.* | **at birth** (=at the time when someone is born) *Most birds cannot identify their parents at birth and simply follow the first moving object they see.*

arrive /əˈraɪv/ [v I] to be born – use this especially to talk about the time a baby is born: *The baby arrived at five minutes past midnight.* | *Has your sister's baby arrived yet?* — **arrival** [n U] *The arrival of our first child brought new joy into our lives.*

come along /ˌkʌm əˈlɒŋ‖-əˈlɔːŋ/ [phr v I] a word meaning to be born – use this especially to talk about how the baby's birth affects its parents' lives: *I was studying to be an accountant, but then the baby came along and I had to give it all up.* | *By the time her third child came along, Mrs Jones had strong ideas on how children should be brought up.*

5 to have a baby

- have a baby/have twins/have kittens etc
- give birth
- become a mother
- childbirth
- labour
- delivery

have a baby/have twins/have kittens etc /ˌhæv ə ˈbeɪbi/ [v phrase] *Having a baby changes your life completely.* | *After my wife had the twins, we were struggling financially for a while.* | *Our dog had six puppies while we were away on vacation.*

give birth /ˌgɪv ˈbɜːʳθ/ [v phrase] to have a baby – use this especially to talk about the actual process of doing this: *Zelda was admitted to the hospital at one o'clock, and gave birth two hours later.* | **give birth to a child/daughter etc** *When Pablo was three, his mother gave birth to a daughter.*

become a mother /bɪˌkʌm ə ˈmʌðəʳ/ [v phrase] to have a baby for the first time: *Rachel was looking forward to becoming a mother.* | **become the mother of a son/twins etc** *Nine months later she became the mother of a son, who was named George.*

childbirth /ˈtʃaɪldbɜːʳθ/ [n U] the process of giving birth: *Most women have some kind of pain relief during childbirth.* | **die in childbirth** (=die while giving birth) *Samuel's mother died in childbirth, and he was brought up by his aunt.* | **natural childbirth** (=without drugs, medical operations etc) *Natural childbirth has become more popular over the last 20 years.*

labour British **/labor** American /ˈleɪbəʳ/ [n U] the whole process of giving birth, from the time when the baby starts to be pushed out of its mother's body: *When Connie realized that her labor was starting, she quickly phoned both her husband and doctor.* | **in labour** *Sara was in labor for sixteen hours with our first child.* | **go into labour** (=begin the process of giving birth) *One of the horses had gone into labour while the farmer was away.*

delivery /dɪˈlɪvəri/ [n C] the process of giving birth, especially when the birth is helped by doctors and nurses: *A hospital is usually the best place for a safe delivery.* | *Meg was recovering from a particularly complicated delivery.*

6 to help with the birth of a baby

- deliver

deliver /dɪˈlɪvəʳ/ [v T] *Our family doctor delivered the baby.* | *The birth was so quick that my husband had* *to deliver the baby himself. | Julia's third child had to be delivered by caesarean section.*

7 having a baby developing in your body

- pregnant
- be going to have a baby/be having a baby
- be expecting
- expectant mother
- mother-to-be

pregnant /ˈpregnənt/ [adj] *The health centre provides milk and vitamins for pregnant women. | When our cat was pregnant she looked like a round, furry ball.* | **get pregnant** *We can't stop teens from having sex, but we can help them to avoid getting pregnant.* | **pregnant with sb** *When I was pregnant with Mandy, I felt fat and unattractive.* | **twenty weeks/three months etc pregnant** *When Janette was three months pregnant, she caught flu.* | **heavily pregnant** British (=when the baby is almost ready to be born) *By this time I was heavily pregnant and could hardly get into any of my clothes.*

be going to have a baby/be having a baby /biː ˌgəʊɪŋ tə hæv ə ˈbeɪbi, biː ˌhævɪŋ ə ˈbeɪbi/ [v phrase] to have a baby developing in your body – used especially when you are telling someone that you or another person is going to have a baby: *Isn't it wonderful that Susie's going to have a baby? | My boss is having a baby in March, but she's only taking two months maternity leave. | The doctor told Ellie that the tests were positive and she was going to have a baby.*

be expecting /biː ɪkˈspektɪŋ/ [v phrase] spoken informal to have a baby developing inside you: *They'd only been married a couple of months and already Rebecca was expecting.*

expectant mother /ɪkˌspektənt ˈmʌðəʳ/ [n C] a woman who is going to have a baby: *Expectant mothers are entitled to free healthcare. | Expectant mothers sometimes have cravings for unusual foods.*

mother-to-be ALSO **mum-to-be** British informal /ˌmʌðəʳ tə ˈbiː, ˌmʌm tə ˈbiː/ [n C] a woman who is going to have a baby: *I hear you are now a mother-to-be. | For first time mothers-to-be, the importance of regular check-ups cannot be stressed enough.*

8 for or relating to a woman who is going to have a baby

- maternity
- prenatal

maternity /məˈtɜːʳnɪ̥ti/ [adj only before noun] **maternity care/ward/leave etc** for women who are going to have a baby or have just had a baby: *Maternity clothes are more stylish than they used to be. | Most women who take maternity leave look forward to returning to their jobs. | Which way to the maternity ward?*

prenatal ALSO **antenatal** British /ˌpriːˈneɪtl◂, ˌæntɪˈneɪtl◂/ [adj only before noun] **antenatal classes/clinic/care etc** classes etc that provide special care for women who are going to have a baby: *Pregnant teenagers often do not want to attend antenatal classes. | Towards the end of a pregnancy, doctors recommend more frequent prenatal check-ups.*

9 the period in which a baby is developing inside its mother

- pregnancy
- gestation period

pregnancy /ˈpregnənsi/ [n C/U] *Many women find their skin is at its best during pregnancy. | This drug should not be taken during pregnancy. | She's had a difficult pregnancy.*

gestation period /dʒeˈsteɪʃən ˌpɪəriəd/ [n C] the length of time a human or animal baby develops in its mother's body: *An elephant's gestation period is almost two years.*

10 when a baby is not born alive

- lose the baby
- have a miscarriage
- stillborn
- be born dead
- abortion
- terminate a pregnancy

lose the baby /ˌluːz ðə ˈbeɪbi/ [v phrase] *'Am I going to lose the baby?' she asked the doctor. | Patricia lost the baby after six months.*

have a miscarriage /ˌhæv ə ˌmɪsˈkærɪdʒ/ [v phrase] if a woman **has a miscarriage** the baby comes out of her body far too early for it to be able to live: *She was pregnant during her first marriage, but had a miscarriage.*

stillborn /ˈstɪlbɔːʳn, ˌstɪlˈbɔːʳn/ [adj] a baby that is **stillborn** is born dead but fully developed: *Sadly, the baby was stillborn. | Libby had still not recovered from the shock of giving birth to a stillborn child.*

be born dead /biː ˌbɔːʳn ˈded/ [v phrase] if a baby **is born dead**, it is not alive when it is born: *The doctor told them that there was a danger their baby would be born dead or brain damaged.*

abortion /əˈbɔːʳʃən/ [n C/U] a medical operation to deliberately end a pregnancy so that the baby is not born alive: *The Catholic Church remains strongly opposed to abortion.* | **have an abortion** *One of my friends got pregnant when she was fifteen and had an abortion.* | **backstreet abortion** (=a secret illegal abortion by someone who is not trained) *Backstreet abortions left many women unable to have children later.*

terminate a pregnancy /ˌtɜːʳmɪ̥neɪt ə ˈpregnənsi/ [v phrase] formal to perform the operation that prevents a baby from being born alive, often because the mother's life is in danger – used especially by doctors: *Doctors may terminate a pregnancy when the life of the mother is at risk.*

11 methods used to prevent a woman becoming pregnant

- contraception
- birth control/family planning

contraception /ˌkɒntrəˈsepʃən‖ˌkɑːn-/ [n U] methods that are used to prevent a baby starting to develop inside a woman's body when a man and woman have sex: *Today there are more women using modern contraception than ever before. | For advice on contraception, talk to your doctor or local family planning clinic.* | **methods of contraception** *There are several reliable methods of contraception.* —**contraceptive** [adj] *Women who take a contraceptive pill and who also smoke cigarettes dramatically increase their chances of heart disease.*

birth control/family planning /ˈbɜːʳθ kənˌtrəʊl, ˌfæməli ˈplænɪŋ/ [n U] the practice of deliberately controlling the number of babies that are born: *Government attempts to encourage family planning have failed in many parts of the third world. | a reliable method of birth control*

12 to be able to have babies

- be able to have children
- fertile

be able to have children /biː ˌeɪbəl tə hæv ˈtʃɪldrən/ [v phrase] to be physically able to have a baby: *After the operation will I still be able to have children?*

fertile /ˈfɜːtaɪl‖ˈfɜːrtl/ [adj] able to have a baby or be the father of a baby: *While most men remain fertile into old age, women do not.* —**fertility** /fəʳˈtɪlɪ̣ti/ [n U] *Certain drugs have been found to put women's fertility at risk* (=make them less fertile).

13 to be unable to have babies

- not able/unable to have children
- infertile
- sterile

not able/unable to have children /nɒt ˌeɪbəl, ʌnˌeɪbəl tə hæv ˈtʃɪldrən/ [v phrase] *The doctor told the couple that they were unable to have children.*

infertile /ɪnˈfɜːtaɪl‖-ˈfɜːrtl/ [adj] unable to have babies – used especially about women: *New medical techniques provide hope for infertile couples.* —**infertility** /ˌɪnfəʳˈtɪlɪ̣ti/ [n U] *It took Helen a long time to come to terms with her infertility.*

sterile /ˈsteraɪl‖-rəl/ [adj] unable to have babies or to be the father of a baby, especially when this is a permanent condition: *Susan thought that her illness had made her sterile.* —**sterility** /stəˈrɪlɪ̣ti/ [n U] *Sterility in men seems to be on the increase.*

14 the process of people or animals producing babies

- reproduction
- reproduce
- breed

reproduction /ˌriːprəˈdʌkʃən/ [n U] *These insects have two different methods of reproduction.* | *Dr Weiss's research has focused mostly on human reproduction.* | *Evolution depends absolutely on the survival and reproduction of the species.*

reproduce /ˌriːprəˈdjuːs‖-ˈduːs/ [v I] to produce babies – use this especially to talk about the method by which this is done or the rate at which it happens: *People have a natural instinct to both reproduce and to care for their young.* | *Jellyfish reproduce by releasing eggs and sperm into the sea.*

breed /briːd/ [v I] if animals **breed**, they produce babies: *Rabbits breed very quickly.* —**breeding** [n U] *Birds make nests in preparation for breeding.*

back

RELATED WORDS

- to give something back to someone *see* **give (11)**
- to go back to a place *see* **return**
- to get something back from someone *see* **get (11)**

WHAT'S HERE

- **back/backwards** see **1 to 3**
- **the back of sth** see **4 to 6**

back/backwards

RELATED WORDS

opposite: —— **forward**

1 moving backwards

- back
- backwards

back /bæk/ [adv] moving or looking towards a place behind you: *He looked back over his shoulder.* | *I stepped back to let them pass.*

backwards ALSO **backward** /ˈbækwəʳdz, ˈbækwəʳd/ [adv] moving back and away from the direction in which you are facing: *Sarah fell backwards in the snow.* | *Can you skate backward?* | *Stepping backwards, Harry trod on the foot of the woman behind him.* | **backwards and forwards** *She gently rocked the baby backwards and forwards.*

2 to move backwards

- back out of/through/towards etc
- back away
- back up
- retreat
- step back
- recoil
- pull away

back out of/through/towards etc /ˌbæk ˈaʊt ɒv / [v T] to walk backwards in a particular direction, especially in order to leave a room or building: *Hardy backed slowly toward the door.* | *Simms quietly backed out of the office, his face red with embarrassment.* | *When she was sure the baby was asleep, she backed softly through the bedroom door.*

back away /ˌbæk əˈweɪ/ [phr v I] to walk slowly backwards, especially to get further away from someone or to avoid a dangerous situation: *'Are you crazy?' she cried, backing away.* | **+ from** *We slowly backed away from the rattlesnake.*

back up /ˌbæk ˈʌp/ [phr v I] especially American to move backwards a little, for example in order to give someone enough space to move: *Back up a bit so that everyone can see.* | *Can you back up a few steps so that I can open the door?*

retreat /rɪˈtriːt/ [v I] to walk backwards or away from the direction you were walking before, especially in order to avoid an embarrassing or unpleasant situation: *Jim saw me approaching and quickly retreated down a side street.* | **+ from/into/to etc** *'You haven't heard the last of this!' shouted Spencer, retreating up the stairs.*

step back /ˌstep ˈbæk/ [v phrase] to take one step or a few steps backwards: *Myers quickly stepped back into the house when he caught sight of us.* | *As the lights of a car approached he stepped back into the shadows.*

recoil /rɪˈkɔɪl/ [v I] to suddenly move part or all of your body backwards, away from something that is unpleasant or frightening: *She looked at the dead body and recoiled.* | **+ from** *She recoiled from his touch.*

pull away /ˌpʊl əˈweɪ/ [phr v I] to move quickly and suddenly backwards in order to get away from someone, especially because you are upset, angry, or frightened: *When Helen took his arm he tried to pull away.* | *I tried to kiss her but she pulled away.*

3 to make a vehicle go backwards

- reverse
- back up
- back

reverse /rɪˈvɜːʳs/ [v I/T] especially British to drive a car or other vehicle backwards: *You'll have to reverse to let them pass.* | *He slowly reversed the van into the parking place.* | **reverse out of/into/round etc** *As I approached the house a car reversed out of the driveway and sped off down the road.*

back up /ˌbæk ˈʌp/ [phr v I/T not usually in passive] especially American to drive a car or other vehicle backwards: *The car stopped and then began to back up.* | *Back the truck up a little more, will you?* | **back up sth** *Cindi backed up the car and stopped in front of the door.*

back /bæk/ [v I/T] to drive a car or other vehicle backwards, especially in order to get into or out of a space **back out/in/into** *I wouldn't park there – it's going to be very difficult to back out again.* | **back sth out/in/into** *Morris carefully backed the truck into the shed.*

the back of sth

RELATED WORDS

opposite: **front**
- *see also* **behind**

4 the back part of something

- the back
- the rear

the back /ðə ˈbæk/ [n singular] the part that is furthest from the front: *Someone crashed into the back of my car.* | *You can leave your bike around the back.* | *They walked past the back of the cottage.* | *Did you know you have paint on the back of your skirt?* | *'How do I turn the computer on?' 'There's a switch at the back.'*

the rear /ðə ˈrɪəʳ/ [n singular] formal the back part of a building or vehicle: *Access to the kitchen is from the rear.* | *There are more seats at the rear of the theater.*

5 the back of something flat

- the back
- the other side
- the reverse side

the back /ðə ˈbæk/ [n singular] *I wrote down her address on the back of an envelope.* | *He was trying to scrape the wax off with the back of a knife.* | **on the back** *If you look on the back, you'll see the artist's signature.* | *'I can't see the wine list.' 'It's on the back.'*

the other side /ði ˌʌðəʳ ˈsaɪd/ [n phrase] *Write your name here and on the other side put your phone number.*

the reverse side /ðə rɪˌvɜːʳs ˈsaɪd/ [n singular] the back side of something – used especially in written instructions or descriptions: *Sign the check on the reverse side.* | *The reverse side of the coin has the president's head on it.*

6 at the back of something

- at the back
- at the rear
- in the back
- back

at the back British **/in the back** especially American /ət ðə ˈbæk, ɪn ðə ˈbæk/ [adv] *I couldn't see very well because we were seated in the back.* | *There's something rotting at the back of the refrigerator.* | *I found your passport – it was at the back of the drawer.*

at the rear /ət ðə ˈrɪəʳ/ [adv] at the back of a building, room, or vehicle – used especially in instructions and written descriptions: *Passengers for Birmingham should sit at the rear of the train.* | *Brenda sat at the reception desk at the rear of the main hall.* | *A VW's engine is at the rear of the vehicle.*

in the back /ɪn ðə ˈbæk/ [adv] at the back of a car or other vehicle: *Just throw all your bags in the back.* | *Don't let the dog sit in the front – he has to go in the back.* | *She couldn't see out of the rear window because of all the junk in the back of the truck.*

back ALSO **rear** formal /bæk, rɪəʳ/ [adj only before noun] at the **back** of something, for example a building or car: *The burglars broke into the house through the back door.* | *The rear brakes are completely worn out.* | *You can put your suitcase on the back seat of the car.* | *They made their way toward the rear exit.* | *The rear carriage of the train is reserved for non-smokers.*

bad

RELATED WORDS

opposite: **good**
- bad at doing sth *see* **bad at doing sth**
- bad condition *see* **condition**
- serious situation *see* **serious**
- have a bad effect on something *see* **harm**
- to think something is bad or wrong *see* **disapprove**
- looking or tasting very bad *see* **horrible**
- when a situation is so bad that you cannot accept it *see* **stand (7)**
- to accept a bad situation *see* **stand (5-6)**
- *see also* **worse, cruel, dishonest**

1 bad films/books/methods/food etc

- bad
- no good
- awful/terrible/appalling/lousy
- dreadful
- rubbish/garbage
- crap
- suck

bad /bæd/ [adj] something that is **bad** is of a low standard, because it has been done badly, designed badly, performed badly etc: *The movie was so bad that we left before it finished.* | *It's the worst book she's ever written.* | *Opponents of the plan say it is a bad way of managing city traffic.* | *In the 1980s, their cars had a bad reputation for reliability.* | *Their latest album is even worse than their last one.*

no good /nəʊ ˈgʊd/ spoken not good at all: *I wouldn't go there – the food's no good.* | *I've tried that diet, and it's no good.*

awful/terrible/appalling/lousy /ˈɔːfəl, ˈterɪ̈bəl, əˈpɔːlɪŋ, ˈlaʊzi/ [adj] very bad: *That's such an awful programme! How can you watch it?* | *Your handwriting is appalling.* | *The food was lousy and the service was terrible.*

dreadful /ˈdredfəl/ [adj] especially British very bad: *The coffee tasted dreadful!* | *'How did you like the film?' 'I thought it was dreadful.'*

rubbish British informal **/garbage** especially American /ˈrʌbɪʃ, ˈgɑːʳbɪdʒ/ [n U] use this to describe something you think is very bad: *'What did you think of his speech?' 'I thought it was rubbish!'* | *Most of the food in these fast food joints is garbage.* | **a load of**

rubbish/garbage *I don't know why you're watching that film, it's a load of old rubbish.* | *I've never read such a load of garbage in my life.*

crap /kræp/ [n U] informal use this to describe something you think is very bad – some people think this word is offensive: *There's nothing but crap on television these days.* | *The stereo's great but the rest of the car is crap.* | **a load of crap** *Someone told me it was a really interesting museum, but I thought it was a load of crap.*

suck /sʌk/ [v I] especially American, informal if you say that something **sucks**, you think it is very bad – some people think this word is offensive: *Let's not go there – the food sucks.*

2 products that are badly made or of bad quality

- poor quality
- low-quality
- badly made
- cheap
- shoddy
- inferior

poor quality /ˌpʊəʳ ˈkwɒlɨti‖-ˈkwɑː-/ [adj/n phrase] **poor quality** products have been made badly: *Poor quality housing often leads to health problems.* | **be of poor quality** *Investigators believe the bridge collapsed because the concrete was of poor quality.*

low-quality /ˌləʊ ˈkwɒlɨti‖-ˈkwɑː-/ [adj usually before noun] **low-quality** products have been made badly: *It's not worth building with low-quality materials just to save money.* | *The company wants to change its image as a producer of low-cost, low-quality clothes.*

badly made /ˌbædli ˈmeɪd◂/ [adj] made without care or skill: *Her clothes looked cheap and badly made.*

cheap /tʃiːp/ [adj] **cheap** furniture, jewellery, clothes etc look unattractive and badly made, and seem to have been produced using low quality materials: *The room was depressing, with dim light and cheap furniture.* | *Hungry-looking men in cheap suits hung around the streets all day.*

shoddy /ˈʃɒdi‖ˈʃɑː-/ [adj] badly and cheaply made, using low quality materials: *You have a right to return any shoddy goods you might buy.* | **shoddily made** *Police officials blamed the deaths on the shoddily made apartment building.*

inferior /ɪnˈfɪəriəʳ/ [adj] **inferior** products are not as good as other similar ones because they have been cheaply and badly made: *Consumers buy foreign goods because they believe that British-made goods are inferior.* | *I want the best – I don't want some inferior model that's going to break down the first time I use it.*

3 not very bad, but not very good

- not very good
- mediocre
- nothing special
- all right/OK, but ...
- so-so
- second rate/third rate
- not be up to scratch
- patchy
- lacklustre

not very good /nɒt veri ˈgʊd/ [adj phrase] especially spoken not good – use this when you are disappointed because you were expecting something better: *'What was the movie like?' 'It was OK but the ending wasn't very good.'* | *He's been learning English for five years, but his pronunciation isn't very good.*

mediocre /ˌmiːdiˈəʊkəʳ◂/ [adj] something that is **mediocre** is of a lower standard than it should be, and does not show much quality or skill: *The team gave another mediocre performance last night.* | *Tourists crowd the gift shops to buy mediocre products at high prices.*

nothing special /ˌnʌθɪŋ ˈspeʃəl/ [adj phrase not before noun] spoken not very bad, but not especially good: *'Was the food good?' 'It was okay, but nothing special.'* | *The town's nice, but the beach is nothing special.*

all right/OK, but ... /ɔːl ˈraɪt, ˌəʊ ˈkeɪ bət/ spoken say this when you think that something is good in some ways but there are some bad parts of it too: *My grades were OK, but I thought I should have gotten an 'A' in chemistry.* | *The game was all right, but it wasn't worth what I paid to watch it.*

so-so /ˈsəʊ səʊ/ [adj not before noun] informal not very good, but not very bad either: *'How is your meal?' 'So-so.'* | *The hotel was in a lovely location, but the facilities were only so-so.*

second rate/third rate /ˌsekənd ˈreɪt◂, ˌθɜːʳd ˈreɪt◂/ [adj usually before noun] not as good as other things of the same kind: *People are not willing to pay a lot of money for second-rate works of art.* | *All they could afford was a room in a second-rate hotel about a mile from the beach.*

not be up to scratch /nɒt biː ʌp tə ˈskrætʃ/ [v phrase] especially British something that **is not up to scratch**, is not as good as it should be: *The hotels and transport system in this city are not up to scratch at the moment.*

patchy /ˈpætʃi/ [adj] a performance, piece of work etc that is **patchy** is good in some parts, but bad in others and in general is not good: *The film is patchy, despite one or two good performances.* | *Many department stores reported patchy sales over Christmas.*

lacklustre British **/lackluster** American /ˈlækˌlʌstəʳ/ [adj usually before noun] **lacklustre performance** not very bad, but not as good as was expected: *The corporation's profits increased dramatically this year, after a rather lacklustre performance last year.*

4 bad events/experiences/weather etc

- bad
- awful/terrible/dreadful
- appalling/atrocious
- horrendous
- horrific
- be a nightmare

bad /bæd/ [adj] not at all pleasant, enjoyable, or successful: *If the weather's bad, we could go to the museum instead.* | *bad housing conditions* | **bad news** (=news of a bad event) *I'm afraid I have some bad news.* | **a bad day/year/time etc** (=when a lot of unpleasant things happen) *This was a very bad year for the banking industry.* | *It had been a bad day, and I just wanted to go home.*

awful/terrible/dreadful /ˈɔːfəl, ˈterɨbəl, ˈdredfəl/ [adj] very bad: *The weather has been terrible lately.* | *Traffic in the downtown Boston area is awful.* | *Conditions in the hospital were dreadful. The place was falling apart and it was understaffed.*

appalling/atrocious /əˈpɔːlɪŋ, əˈtrəʊʃəs/ [adj] so bad that you are shocked: *Living conditions in the refugee camps were atrocious.* | *The appalling weather continued, with harsh winds, fogs and heavy rain.*

horrendous /hɒˈrendəs‖hɑː-, hɔː-/ [adj] extremely bad, unpleasant, and often frightening: *It was a horrendous storm.* | *She is still recovering from a horrendous car accident.*

horrific /hɒˈrɪfɪk‖hɔː-, hɑː-/ [adj] extremely bad, especially in a way that is frightening or upsetting: *It was a horrific experience. We really thought we were going to die.* | *The race was stopped after a horrific accident in which two drivers were killed.*

be a nightmare /biː ə ˈnaɪtmeəʳ/ [v phrase] spoken informal use this to talk about an extremely bad experience or situation: *The traffic coming in to work this morning was a nightmare.* | *The President's trip turned out to be a nightmare for his security staff.* | **be a complete nightmare** *Our vacation was a complete nightmare. The weather was awful and our hotel was worse.*

5 words for describing bad people or behaviour

- bad
- immoral
- evil/wicked
- no good
- sinister
- twisted
- depraved
- perverted

bad /bæd/ [adj] use this about behaviour that is morally wrong, or about people who do things that are morally wrong: *In most movies, the bad guy gets caught in the end.* | *He had a bad influence on his younger brother.* | *Is there any crime worse than murdering a child?* | *It never occurred to Sally that the man had any bad intentions.*

immoral /ɪˈmɒrəl‖ɪˈmɔː-/ [adj] use this about actions that you believe are morally wrong and unacceptable, even if they are not illegal: *Many people think that testing cosmetics on animals is immoral.* | *To spend £23 billion on nuclear weapons is immoral, and a terrible waste of money.* | *Critics complain that the lyrics of the song encourage anti-social and immoral behavior.*

evil/wicked /ˈiːvəl, ˈwɪkɪ̈d/ [adj] deliberately very bad and very cruel to other people: *Police described the crime as wicked and inhuman.* | *He was an evil man who felt no sympathy for his victims.*

no good /nəʊ ˈgʊd/ [adj] informal use this about someone who is not at all honest, helpful, or kind: *That friend of yours is no good. I want you to stay away from her.* | *My first husband was a no-good, low-down son-of-a-bitch.*

sinister /ˈsɪnɪ̈stəʳ/ [adj] someone who is **sinister** looks bad or evil, so that other people are frightened of them: *Her dark eyes and evil laugh made her seem sinister.* | **something sinister about sb** *The man was dressed in a black suit and wore dark glasses. There was something sinister about him.*

twisted /ˈtwɪstɪ̈d/ [adj] behaving in an unusually cruel and shocking way, that is not at all normal: *What kind of sick and twisted person would do such a thing?* | *Whoever sent you these disgusting letters must be twisted.*

depraved /dɪˈpreɪvd/ [adj] completely evil and morally unacceptable: *He was described as dangerous and depraved and a menace to society.* | *The film is about a psychiatrist who helps the police capture a depraved serial killer.*

perverted /pəʳˈvɜːʳtɪ̈d/ [adj] involving sexual behaviour or intentions that are considered immoral, unnatural, and harmful: *The newspaper has described the killer as perverted and sexually deviant.* | *They saw the affection she had for such an old man as unnatural and possibly perverted.*

6 a bad person

- villain
- monster
- pervert
- sicko

villain /ˈvɪlən/ [n C] the bad person in a story, film, play etc, especially someone who breaks the law or who is cruel to others: *At the end of the story, the villain is caught and punished.* | *'Speed 2' stars Willem Dafoe as the villain who takes over a luxury cruise ship.*

monster /ˈmɒnstəʳ‖ˈmɑːn-/ [n C] someone who is so violent and dangerous that people think their behaviour is impossible to understand or forgive: *A monster like that should not be allowed to live!* | *He argued that unless these monsters were put in prison immediately, they would continue to terrorize the public.*

pervert /ˈpɜːʳvɜːʳt/ [n C] someone who is thought to be bad or evil, especially because his sexual behaviour is unnatural or offensive: *What are you, some kind of pervert?* | *She took him to court, accusing him of being a pervert who was unfit to raise a child.*

sicko /ˈsɪkəʊ/ [n C] spoken informal especially American someone who gets pleasure from things that most people think are upsetting, cruel, or unpleasant: *What kind of sicko would write something like that?*

7 words for describing a bad child

- naughty
- badly behaved
- bad
- mischievous
- spoiled
- brat

naughty /ˈnɔːti‖ˈnɔːti, ˈnɑːti/ [adj] a child who is **naughty** behaves badly, for example by being rude or by doing things that are not allowed: *We've been looking for you everywhere, you naughty boy!* | *I don't believe in hitting children, no matter how naughty they've been.*

badly behaved /ˌbædli bɪˈheɪvd◂/ [adj phrase] a **badly behaved** child behaves badly and causes a lot of trouble: *Two or three badly behaved children are causing all the problems in the class.*

bad /bæd/ [adj] spoken used especially to speak angrily to a child who has done something bad: *You've been a bad girl – you know you're not allowed in my room when I'm not there.*

mischievous /ˈmɪstʃɪ̈vəs/ [adj] a child who is **mischievous** behaves badly, but in a way that makes people laugh rather than making them angry: *She was a mischievous little girl who was always playing tricks on people.* —**mischievously** [adv] *'It wasn't me who broke the window,' she replied, grinning mischievously.*

spoiled ALSO **spoilt** British /spɔɪld, spɔɪlt/ [adj] children who are **spoiled** or **spoilt** behave badly because their parents always let them do what they want and have what they want: *You're a spoilt, ungrateful little girl!* | *Those kids are definitely spoiled – they need to learn some manners.*

brat /bræt/ [n C] informal a child that you do not like, who behaves badly and is rude: *The school is full of rich brats.* | **spoiled/spoilt brat** (=a child who behaves badly because they have always been allowed to do whatever they want) *Should I tell him his kid is a spoiled brat?*

8 bad in a clever way

- calculating
- scheming

calculating /'kælkjəleɪtɪŋ/ [adj] making careful and clever plans in order to get what you want, without caring about what happens to other people: *She was a cold, calculating criminal.* | *Over the years his experiences had turned him into someone who was both calculating and ruthless.*

scheming /'skiːmɪŋ/ [adj only before noun] always trying to cleverly control situations in order to get what you want, especially by deceiving other people: *Blakemore was a cold, scheming man who could not be trusted.* | *Collins is best-known as the scheming Alexis Colby from the television series, 'Dynasty.'*

9 having a bad way of life

- immoral
- decadent
- degenerate

immoral /ɪ'mɒrəl‖ɪ'mɔː-/ [adj] *My parents think my lifestyle is both dangerous and immoral.* | *In many such stories, women are portrayed as untrustworthy and immoral.*

decadent /'dekədənt/ [adj] a way of living that is **decadent** is concerned mainly with pleasure and enjoyment, and not with hard work or serious activities: *We spent the whole summer drinking, smoking and lying around. It must sound totally decadent.* —**decadence** [n U] *The decadence of Berlin in the early 1930s had a definite charm.*

degenerate /dɪ'dʒenərət/ [adj] formal not keeping to many of society's accepted moral standards – use this especially about someone who behaves in a way that is sexually immoral: *He was labelled a degenerate youth by his teachers, and left the town before he was 16.*

10 bad or immoral behaviour

- immorality
- wrongdoing
- misconduct
- wickedness

immorality /ˌɪmə'rælɪti/ [n U] bad or immoral behaviour, especially relating to sex: *Chicago is a dangerous city and she felt surrounded by corruption and immorality.* | *Religious leaders campaigned against immorality in the film and music industry.*

wrongdoing /'rɒŋˌduːɪŋ‖ˌrɔːŋ'duːɪŋ/ [n U] bad or immoral behaviour, especially involving crimes or not being fair or just: *The investigators found no evidence of wrongdoing and the company's managers were cleared of all charges.*

misconduct /mɪs'kɒndʌkt‖-'kɑːn-/ [n U] formal bad behaviour by someone in a position of authority or trust, who is expected to behave according to the rules of their profession: *The commission decided there was no evidence of misconduct.* | **professional misconduct** *At present, therapists cannot be found guilty of professional misconduct.* | **gross misconduct** (=very serious misconduct) *The police officer found guilty of being drunk on duty was dismissed for gross misconduct.*

wickedness /'wɪkɪdnɪs/ [n U] a quality in someone that makes them enjoy behaving in a very bad or immoral way: *We sensed a wickedness in him that made us feel sick inside.*

11 an extremely bad action

- atrocity
- outrage

atrocity /ə'trɒsɪti‖ə'trɑː-/ [n C] an unusually cruel and violent action, usually against someone who has done nothing wrong, that is unacceptable even during a time of war: *The brutal destruction of an entire village was one of the worst atrocities of the Vietnam war.*

outrage /'aʊtreɪdʒ/ [n C] an extremely bad, and often cruel and unfair action that people think is shocking: *It's an outrage that men who didn't finish high school sometimes earn more than women with college educations.* | *The terrorist attack, in which two innocent tourists were murdered, is the third outrage of its kind this year.*

12 to influence someone in a bad way

- lead sb astray
- set a bad example/be a bad example
- corrupt
- be a bad influence

lead sb astray /ˌliːd (sb) ə'streɪ/ [v phrase] to encourage someone to do bad or immoral things that they would not normally do: *They're afraid their son will be led astray by the older boys.* | *Parents complained that teachers were leading students astray by discussing contraception and abortion in the classroom.*

set a bad example/be a bad example /ˌset ə bæd ɪg'zɑːmpəl, biː ə ˌbæd ɪg'zɑːmpəl‖-'zæm-/ [v phrase] if someone in a position of authority, such as a parent or teacher **sets a bad example**, they influence others to behave in a bad or immoral way because they themselves behave in a bad or immoral way: *Doctors who smoke set a bad example.* | **+ to** *Not only was it wrong of him to steal from the shop, he was setting a very bad example to his younger brother.* | **be a bad example for/to sb** *Waters doesn't drink or curse because he doesn't want to be a bad example for young people.*

corrupt /kə'rʌpt/ [v T] to make someone who would not normally behave badly behave in an immoral way, especially by having some influence over them over a long period of time: *The Senate will form a committee to determine if violence on television is corrupting young people.* | *The prison system does not work because many of the younger offenders are being corrupted by older, long-term prisoners.*

be a bad influence /biː ə ˌbæd 'ɪnfluəns/ [v phrase] someone who **is a bad influence** encourages someone else, especially a young person or someone who is easily influenced, to behave in the same bad or immoral way as themselves: *My parents don't want me to be friends with you any more. They think you're a bad influence.* | **+ on** *Her new boyfriend has been a very bad influence on her.*

13 a situation that you think is wrong or immoral

- bad
- wrong
- disgusting
- shocking/scandalous
- outrageous
- be a disgrace
- be a crime/be a sin
- criminal
- deplorable

bad /bæd/ [adj only after noun] *It's very bad that tons of food are going to waste while people are starving.* |

What's really bad is the way the government promises new housing and never provides it.

wrong /rɒŋ‖rɔːŋ/ [adj not before noun] morally unacceptable, unfair, and against accepted ideas about what should be allowed to happen: *I was taught that abortion is wrong, even though it's not illegal.* | *It's wrong the way they treat that poor animal.*

disgusting /dɪsˈgʌstɪŋ, dɪz-/ [adj] something that is **disgusting** makes people feel shocked and angry, because it is completely immoral, evil, or unfair: *The attitude toward immigrants and racial minorities in this country is disgusting.* | *It's disgusting the way politicians use their position to their personal advantage.*

shocking/scandalous /ˈʃɒkɪŋ‖ˈʃɑː-, ˈskændələs/ [adj] very immoral, unfair, or cruel, in a way that people think is unnecessary and unacceptable: *The state of the country's health system is scandalous.* | *a shocking waste of human life* | *The amount of money spent on nuclear weapons is shocking.* | *It's scandalous that a lawyer who holds a position of trust would be involved in this kind of embezzlement.*

outrageous /aʊtˈreɪdʒəs/ [adj] a situation that is **outrageous** is extremely bad and unfair in a way that makes people very angry: *I've always thought it outrageous that the poor have to pay for tax cuts for the rich.* | *The President accused the writer of an outrageous personal attack on his wife.*

be a disgrace /biː ə dɪsˈgreɪs/ [v phrase] if you say something **is a disgrace**, you think it should not be allowed to happen, because it is very unfair or unkind: *The way they treat their workers is a disgrace.* | **it's a disgrace (that)** *It's a disgrace that the only hospital in the town has been closed.* —**disgraceful** [adj] *The way children speak to their parents nowadays is disgraceful.* | *It's disgraceful that rapists are given such short sentences for such awful crimes.*

be a crime/be a sin /biː ə ˈkraɪm, biː ə ˈsɪn/ [v phrase] you say that a situation **is a crime** or **is a sin** when you mean it is very bad, especially because it is not fair and could easily be prevented: *No one should be in such a bad way that they have to beg. It's a sin.* | *The condition of the inner cities in this country is nothing short of a crime.* | **it's a crime/sin to do sth** *Mrs Clark said it would be a sin to evict them just because they hadn't paid their rent.* | *It would be a crime not to take this opportunity to reconstruct our educational system.*

criminal /ˈkrɪmɪ̈nəl/ [adj] a situation that is **criminal** is morally wrong, but not illegal: *I think keeping animals locked up in cages is criminal.* | *Having such beautiful paintings and not letting the public see them is a criminal waste of the nation's art treasures.*

deplorable /dɪˈplɔːrəbəl/ [adj] formal a situation that is **deplorable** is very bad, especially when it is unnecessary and could easily be prevented: *Something must be done about the deplorable state of our roads.* | *In addition to their harsh sentences, the prisoners have been exposed to deplorable prison conditions.*

bad at doing sth

RELATED WORDS

opposite: ——— **good at doing sth**

▸ *see also* **bad, can/can't, careless, fail**

1 not good at doing something

- bad
- badly
- not very good
- no good at sth
- second-rate/third-rate
- weak/poor

bad /bæd/ [adj] not able to do something well, for example a job, sport, or activity: *He's the worst driver I've ever seen.* | *Critics blame the students' poor test performances on bad teaching.* | **+ at** *I was always really bad at French!* | **+ at doing sth** *I'm very bad at remembering people's names.*

badly /ˈbædli/ [adv] if you do something **badly**, you do it carelessly, not skilfully, or you do it in the wrong way: *Adams admitted that he had played badly.* | *The company had been badly managed from the start.* | *Lorna speaks Spanish so badly that no one in our class can understand her.*

not very good ALSO **not much good** /ˌnɒt veri ˈgʊd, ˌnɒt mʌtʃ ˈgʊd/ British [adj phrase not before noun] especially spoken not able to do something well **+ at** *I'm afraid I'm not very good at math.* | *I'm not much good at speeches but I'll do my best.* | **+ at doing sth** *She's not very good at communicating with other people.* | *He has never been much good at dealing with people.* | **not very well** *'Do you play the piano?' 'Yes, but not very well.'* | **+ as** *She's a nice person, but not much good as a boss.*

no good at sth /nəʊ ˈgʊd ət (sth)/ spoken bad at a skill or activity: *I'm no good at tennis.* | *Cait freely admits that she's no good at anything except singing.* | **+ at doing sth** *Leo's no good at lying – his face always turns red when he's not telling the truth.*

second-rate/third-rate /ˌsekənd ˈreɪt◂, ˌθɜːʳd ˈreɪt◂/ [adj] not very good, especially not as good as other people who do the same thing: *She's a second-rate singer.* | *We spent the evening listening to third-rate writers read their poetry in a seedy nightclub.*

weak/poor /wiːk, pʊəʳ/ [adj] not having much ability or skill in a particular activity or subject: *This is Boston's weakest team in years.* | *When managers' leadership skills are poor, productivity suffers.* | *I wouldn't trust her. She's always been a poor judge of character.* | **+ at science/history etc** *She's weak at mathematics, and this affects her physics results as well.*

2 very bad at doing something

- terrible/awful/hopeless
- lousy
- pathetic
- incompetent
- can't do sth to save your life

terrible/awful/hopeless /ˈterɪ̈bəl, ˈɔːfəl, ˈhəʊpləs/ ALSO **useless** /ˈjuːsləs/ British [adj] very bad at doing something, or doing something very badly: *Poor Daniel. He loves football but he's a terrible player.* | *She'll never pass the exam – she's an awful student.* | *Make sure you bring a map – Erin has a hopeless sense of direction.* | **+ at** *My brother's a computer genius but he's useless at everything else.* | **+ at doing sth** *The manager made John a barman as he was obviously hopeless at waiting on tables.*

lousy /ˈlaʊzi/ [adj] especially spoken very bad at doing something: *I'm such a lousy cook that I usually eat out.* | **+ at** *I was lousy at biology in school.*

pathetic /pəˈθetɪk/ [adj] use this about someone who is so bad at doing something that you have no respect for them: *She's clever, but as a teacher she's* *pathetic.* | *I can't believe we wasted our money on that pathetic comedian last night.*

incompetent /ɪnˈkɒmpətənt‖-ˈkɑːm-/ [adj] use this about someone who cannot do their job at all and should not be doing it: *This government is totally incompetent.* | *Legislators are planning a new bill that will protect patients from incompetent doctors.*

can't do sth to save your life /ˌkɑːnt duː (sth) tə ˌseɪv jɔːʳ ˈlaɪf‖ˌkænt-/ [v phrase] informal to be very bad at something even though you would like to be able to do it properly **can't draw/paint/cook/act etc to save your life** *Adrian can't draw to save his life.* | *You don't expect me to take part in the play, do you? I can't act to save my life.* | *The truth is I couldn't write poetry to save my life.*

balance

when someone or something remains steady and does not fall

RELATED WORDS

- to make two things equal *see* **equal/not equal (5)**

1 to remain steady and not fall

- balance
- keep your balance
- steady

balance /ˈbæləns/ [v I] to remain steady and not fall, especially when this is difficult to do: *The beam is very narrow – you may find it difficult to balance.* | **+ on** *Balancing awkwardly on one leg, he lowered himself into his wheelchair.* | **balance precariously** (=balance in a very dangerous position) *An angel was balancing precariously on top of the Christmas tree.*

keep your balance /ˌkiːp jɔːʳ ˈbæləns/ [v phrase] to manage to remain steady and not fall, especially when something happens to nearly make you fall: *The horse tried to throw her off but she managed to keep her balance.* | *It's hard enough just keeping my balance on ice, let alone actually skating on it.*

steady /ˈstedi/ [adj] completely balanced so that there is no chance of falling: *She held on to hand rails to keep herself steady.* | *We need a steady platform above the waves before we can start drilling.*

2 to make something balance on a point or surface

- balance
- steady

balance /ˈbæləns/ [v T] *Balancing my cup of coffee in one hand, I managed to open the door.* | **balance sth on sth** *His favourite party trick is balancing tin cans on his head.* | *We tried to balance the aerial on top of the TV set, but it kept falling over.*

steady /ˈstedi/ [v T] to make something or someone become balanced again, especially when they were falling over: *When she looked as though she was going to fall, Eddie's arm immediately went out to steady her.* | *He stood up, holding on to the desk to steady himself.*

3 the ability to remain steady and not fall

- balance

balance /ˈbæləns/ [n U] *A walking stick is good for balance on rough trails.* | **sense of balance** *You need a great sense of balance to be an acrobat.*

4 to become unsteady and start to fall

- lose your balance
- totter/teeter
- wobble

lose your balance /ˌluːz jɔːʳ ˈbæləns/ [v phrase] to suddenly become unsteady and start to fall: *Put your arms out to the side so that you don't lose your balance.* | *She ran after the dog, lost her balance, and fell flat on her face.*

totter/teeter /ˈtɒtəʳ‖ˈtɑː-, ˈtiːtəʳ/ [v I] if someone or something **totters** or **teeters** they move unsteadily from side to side and look as if they are going to fall: *I could feel the tray tottering and suddenly all the drinks crashed to the floor.* | *His chair teetered back dangerously on two legs.*

wobble /ˈwɒbəl‖ˈwɑː-/ [v I] to move unsteadily from side to side: *She bumped the table and the glasses wobbled.* | *'Who could that be?' the old man said as he wobbled toward the door.*

5 unsteady and likely to fall

- unsteady
- unstable
- precarious

unsteady /ʌnˈstedi/ [adj] someone who is **unsteady** is unable to balance properly, for example because of illness, old age or too much alcohol: *For a few moments he was pale and unsteady but his colour gradually returned.* | *He walked with the unsteady gait of an old man.* | **unsteady on your feet** *She'll be a little unsteady on her feet until the anaesthetic wears off.* —**unsteadily** [adv] *She moved unsteadily towards the table, everyone expecting her to fall into a drunken heap.*

unstable /ʌnˈsteɪbəl/ [adj] something that is **unstable** is unsteady because it is too big for the thing supporting it or not properly fastened to something, so that it is dangerous: *That scaffolding looks unstable – get all the building workers off the site immediately.*

precarious /prɪˈkeəriəs/ [adj] not safe and likely to fall down – use this especially about things or people that are in high places: *The bottle was in a precarious position on the edge of the table.* | *Are you sure he's safe on that ladder? It looks very precarious up there.* —**precariously** [adv] *When we found the girl she was perched precariously on the window ledge, twelve floors up.*

6 feeling unsteady and unable to balance

- dizzy
- giddy
- sb's head is swimming

dizzy /ˈdɪzi/ [adj not before noun] feeling as if everything is spinning around you and unable to balance: *Sometimes I get dizzy at the top of staircases and escalators.* | *If you feel dizzy or short of breath, stop exercising immediately.* —**dizziness** [n U] *A fall in glucose levels results in nausea, dizziness, and faintness.*

giddy /ˈgɪdi/ [adj] feeling unsteady and unable to balance, sometimes with the result that you want to be sick: *She suddenly felt giddy and had to find somewhere to sit down.*

sb's head is swimming /(sb's) ˈhed ɪz ˌswɪmɪŋ/ if **someone's head is swimming** they feel unsteady, unable to see properly, and as though the room is spinning around them very quickly, for example because they are ill or drunk: *My head was swimming, and the floor seemed to be moving up and down.*

basic

RELATED WORDS

▸ *see also* **need, main, necessary**

1 more important or necessary than anything else

- ▸ **basic**
- ▸ **fundamental**
- ▸ **essential**
- ▸ **central**
- ▸ **underlying**

basic /ˈbeɪsɪk/ [adj] more important or necessary than anything else: *The government regards housing as a basic need.* | *The basic ingredients of this cake are eggs, flour, and butter.* | *I can't really speak Spanish, I just know a few basic words.* | *basic human rights* | *In addition to teaching basic academic skills, we offer a large variety of activities for students.* | **+ to** *Water – indeed, everything basic to life here – must be brought in by truck.*

fundamental /ˌfʌndəˈmentl◂/ [adj] more important or necessary than anything else – use this especially about things such as principles, duties, or beliefs: *the fundamental beliefs of Christianity* | *Raising your child to tell the difference between right and wrong is one of the fundamental tasks of parenthood.* | **+ to** *Water is fundamental to survival.*

essential /ɪˈsenʃəl/ [adj] **essential difference/feature/point etc** the most important difference, feature etc people should pay most attention to: *The essential difference between this class and other French classes is that this is intended for business people.* | *The essential point is that you both need to treat each other with much more respect.*

central /ˈsentrəl/ [adj] a subject, idea etc that is **central** gets more attention, time etc than others because it is more important than them: *The central theme of this novel is the desire for money.* | *Political rights have always been the central concern of feminism.* | *The use of weapons became the central issue dividing the tribes.* | **+ to** *The right to vote is central to our democratic system of government.*

underlying /ˌʌndərˈlaɪ-ɪŋ◂/ [adj only before noun] **underlying reason/cause/aim etc** the most important reason, aim etc but one that is not easy to see: *When treating any health problem, it's always important to consider the underlying causes.* | *The underlying factor in almost all suicides is the feeling of hopelessness.*

2 the feature or part of something that everything else depends on

- ▸ **basis**
- ▸ **foundation**
- ▸ **the cornerstone**
- ▸ **the key**

basis /ˈbeɪsɪs/ [n singular] **the basis of sth** *The basis of his argument was that people who sell drugs should be jailed for life.* | *Sugar has always been the basis of the Cuban economy.* | **the basis for sth** *Expert advice and support are the basis for the rehabilitation programme.* | **form the basis of sth** *Roman law still forms the basis of our own legal system.*

foundation /faʊnˈdeɪʃən/ [n C] the **foundation** for something is the thing on which it is based – use this to talk about something important that continues a long time, for example a relationship, career, or system **+ for** *Good eating habits and regular exercise are the foundation for a healthy life.* | *Teaching experience is a good foundation for a career in just about anything.* | **lay the foundations for sth** *Copernicus's findings laid the foundations for the later work of Galileo.*

the cornerstone /ðə ˈkɔːrnərstəʊn/ [n singular] the thing that something else depends on in order to be successful – use this especially to talk about things that are very important in business and politics **+ of** *The treaty of 1946 has been the cornerstone of European harmony.* | *Increased sales to the under-25s will be the cornerstone of our marketing strategy in the coming year.*

the key /ðə ˈkiː/ [n singular] the most important thing that makes it possible to do or understand something **+ to** *Nixon saw the improvement of relations with China as the key to his foreign policy.* | *The theory of natural selection remains the key to our understanding of the natural world.*

3 basic ideas or principles

- ▸ **basics**
- ▸ **the fundamentals**
- ▸ **first principles**

basics /ˈbeɪsɪks/ [n plural] the basic ideas, principles, rules etc, on which something is based **the basics (of sth)** *I still haven't mastered the basics of English grammar.* | *You need to learn the basics before you can start writing your own music.* | **get back to basics** *Unless we get back to basics in teaching, the standard of literacy will fall.*

the fundamentals /ðə ˌfʌndəˈmentlz/ [n plural] formal the most basic ideas, principles etc on which a subject is based **+ of** *This course provides an opportunity to learn more about the fundamentals of film-making.* | *Police have launched a campaign to educate children about the fundamentals of traffic safety.*

first principles /ˌfɜːrst ˈprɪnsɪpəlz/ [n plural] the most basic ideas, principles etc on which a subject is based, and which you need to understand first or consider first before you can learn any more: *No one can become a scientist without a knowledge of the first principles of mathematics.* | **return/go back to first principles** *To understand Keynesian theory we have to return to first principles.*

4 what you say to explain the most basic facts, reasons etc

- ▸ **basically**
- ▸ **at the end of the day**
- ▸ **essentially**
- ▸ **in the final/last analysis**

basically /ˈbeɪsɪkli/ [adv] spoken say this when you want to talk about the most basic facts, reasons etc about something: *Basically we're looking for someone who can work three afternoons a week.* | *We only took a few shirts and a pair of jeans. That's basically it, really.* | *The film appears to be quite complicated but it's basically a love story.*

at the end of the day /ət ði ˌend əv ðə ˈdeɪ/ [adv] British spoken say this when you are saying what you think is basically true about a situation after considering all the facts: *At the end of the day, the best team won.* | *You may be working for yourself but at the end of the day you still have to pay tax on what you earn.*

essentially ALSO **in essence** /ɪˈsenʃəli, ɪn ˈesəns/ [adv] formal use this when you are explaining what the basic truth about something is: *She's added a few characters and changed some names but essentially this is a true story.* | *The theory of relativity is, in essence, very simple.*

in the final/last analysis /ɪn ðə ˌfaɪnl, ˌlɑːst əˈnæləsɪ̇s‖-ˌlæst-/ use this to say what you think is the basic truth about a situation after considering all the facts carefully: *In the final analysis Stalin was just as much a dictator as Hitler.* | *The responsibility for the accident must, in the last analysis, rest with the captain.*

be

RELATED WORDS

- *see also* **consist of, meaning**

1 to be something

- **be**
- **represent**
- **form**
- **make**
- **constitute**

be /bi, (*strong*) biː/ [v] *Sacramento is the capital of California.* | *Laurence Olivier was the greatest actor of his generation.* | *The state of the economy is our biggest problem.* | *The Somme was the bloodiest battle of the First World War.* | *When it's finished, it will be the biggest office development in Europe.*

represent /ˌreprɪˈzent/ [v T not in progressive] **represent an improvement/an obstacle/a challenge etc** formal used to say that something, especially something important or serious, should be thought of as a particular thing: *There is no doubt that this new type of tyre represents a major advance in road safety.* | *Einstein's theory represented a significant departure from previous theories.*

form /fɔːʳm/ [v T] if something **forms** something else, it has physical qualities that gives it a particular purpose or makes it have a particular effect: *The river formed a natural boundary between the two countries.* | *Oils produced by the skin form a protective barrier against infection and disease.*

make /meɪk/ [v] to have the necessary qualities to be a particular thing or a particular type of person: *He'll make a good father.* | *This sofa doesn't make much of a bed.* | *You're quick but you'll never make a football player.*

constitute /ˈkɒnstɪ̇tjuːt‖ˈkɑːnstɪ̇tuːt/ [v T] formal if actions or behaviour **constitute** something, they are officially or legally considered as being that thing: *The local authority decided that the present housing conditions constituted a risk for the mother and baby.* | *The spread of international crime and corruption constitutes a major threat to the global economy.*

2 when a group of people or things form something together

- **make up/form**
- **constitute**
- **add up to**

make up/form /ˌmeɪk ˈʌp, fɔːʳm/ [v] to be part of a particular group of people or to be the thing on which something else is based: *The six states that make up New England are Maine, Vermont, New Hampshire, Massachusetts, Connecticut and Rhode Island.* | *These seven people made up the entire population of Oakminster.* | *The results of these studies formed the basis of state education policy in the 1960s.*

constitute /ˈkɒnstɪ̇tjuːt‖ˈkɑːnstɪ̇tuːt/ [v T not in progressive] formal if a number of people or things together **constitute** something, they are the parts that together form that thing: *Alaska is the largest of the fifty states that constitute the USA.* | *It is sometimes difficult to believe that the different groups living within our borders constitute a single society.* | *Because journalists don't think the congressman constitutes much of a threat, they don't write or broadcast stories about him.*

add up to /ˌæd ˈʌp tuː/ [phr v T not in progressive] if a group of different things **add up to** something, together they are that thing or they provide what is needed for the thing to exist: *Good wine, excellent food, and interesting company – it all added up to a splendid evening.* | *It adds up to a recipe for financial disaster.*

3 to form a particular part or amount of something

- **account for/represent**
- **constitute**

account for/represent /əˈkaʊnt fɔːʳ, ˌreprɪˈzent/ [phr v T not in progressive/v T not in progressive] to be a particular amount or part of something: *In Japan, firms employing over 1000 people accounted for 50% of total employment.* | *This project alone represents half of the department's budget.* | *Women now represent 48% of the workforce.*

constitute /ˈkɒnstɪ̇tjuːt‖ˈkɑːnstɪ̇tuːt/ [v T not in progressive] to be a particular part of something – use this especially to talk about scientific or official facts and figures: *Children constitute four out of every ten poor people in the United States.* | *Nitrogen constitutes 78% of the earth's atmosphere.*

beat/defeat

RELATED WORDS

- to win a game or competition *see* **win**
- to hit someone or something *see* **hit**
- *see also* **compete with, fight, war**

1 to beat someone in a game, competition, election etc

- **beat**
- **defeat**
- **get the better of**
- **be more than a match for**

beat /biːt/ [v T] to get more points, votes etc than an opposing team or political party: *Do you think the Socialists will beat the Liberals in the election?* | *Brazil beat Italy in the final.* | *Lewis was a tough boxer, and a hard man to beat.* | **beat sb at sth** *My Father used to let me beat him at chess.* | **beat sb by 20 points/5 seconds/50 votes etc** *The Swedish runner beat the Canadian by just under two seconds.* | **beat sb 3-1/84 to 61/etc** *The Red Sox beat the Yankees 6-3.*

defeat /dɪ'fiːt/ [v T] especially written to get more points, votes etc than an opposing team, person, or political party. **Defeat** is more formal than **beat**.: *For the sixth consecutive year, Oxford defeated Cambridge today in the annual boat race.* | *Polk of California was defeated by a Democratic challenger in the last election.* | **defeat sb by 20 points/two goals to one etc** *Sanchez defeated Dornan by just 984 votes.*

get the better of /ˌget ðə 'betər ɒv/ [v phrase] especially British, spoken to defeat an opponent or team in a game – use this especially about opponents or teams of a similar ability: *She's determined not to let Smith, her fiercest rival, get the better of her.*

be more than a match for /biː ˌmɔːʳ ðən ə 'mætʃ fɔːʳ/ [v phrase] to easily beat your opponent in a game, especially when people were not expecting you to: *I thought I might beat Tracy at tennis but she was more than a match for me.* | *The Russian president has once again proved more than a match for his political adversaries.*

2 to beat someone very easily in a game, competition, election etc

- crush/slaughter/massacre/annihilate
- clobber/hammer
- rout
- wipe the floor with sb
- outplay

crush/slaughter/massacre/annihilate /krʌʃ, 'slɔːtəʳ, 'mæsəkəʳ, ə'naɪəleɪt/ [v T] informal to completely beat someone in a game, competition, election etc: *Wow, the Raiders just slaughtered the Seahawks again.* | *The party strategy was to form an alliance to crush the communists.*

clobber/hammer /'klɒbəʳ‖'klɑː-, 'hæməʳ/ [v T] informal ALSO **cream** /kriːm/ American spoken to beat someone very easily in a game, competition, election etc: *We've been clobbered twice now by Central High's basketball team.* | *Chicago hammered Boston in an away game on Saturday.* | *'How'd the game go?' 'We creamed 'em!'*

rout /raʊt/ [v T not in progressive] especially British to beat an opposing team or political party easily and completely: *The Australians have once again routed the English cricket team.*

wipe the floor with sb /ˌwaɪp ðə 'flɔːʳ wɪð (sb)/ informal to defeat someone completely in an argument or competition: *I'd think twice before I started a fight with him – he'd wipe the floor with me!*

outplay /aʊt'pleɪ/ [v T not usually in progressive] to play much better than an opponent or team in a game and beat them easily: *Ohio outplayed Michigan, especially in the fourth quarter, winning by 14 points.*

3 to defeat an enemy in war

- defeat
- overwhelm
- annihilate
- rout
- bring sb to their knees
- conquer

defeat /dɪ'fiːt/ [v T] to completely **defeat** an enemy's army because your armed forces are much larger, have better equipment etc: *The army was well-trained and well-armed, and had little difficulty defeating the rebels.* | **heavily defeat** *The Republicans were heavily defeated in the Spanish Civil War.*

overwhelm /ˌəʊvəʳ'welm/ [v T] to completely defeat an enemy's army because your armed forces are much larger, have better equipment etc: *Napoleon's army was strong enough to overwhelm nearly any potential enemy.* | *With its greatly superior technology, the government forces completely overwhelmed the rebels.*

annihilate /ə'naɪəleɪt/ [v T] to completely defeat an enemy's army in a war and to destroy all their armed forces: *After a long and bloody battle the army succeeded in annihilating Seged's forces.* | *In 1945 Japan was helpless, with its military power annihilated.*

rout /raʊt/ [v T not in progressive] to completely defeat an enemy's army in battle: *The general was killed and his armies were routed in a magnificent cavalry charge.*

bring sb to their knees /ˌbrɪŋ (sb) tə ðeəʳ 'niːz/ [v phrase] to cause the final defeat of an enemy, especially after a long war, so that they are too weak to fight back: *The disastrous Battle of the Boyne finally brought the Catholics to their knees.* | *After years of trench warfare, the Kaiser's army had finally been brought to its knees.*

conquer /'kɒŋkəʳ‖'kɑːŋ-/ [v I/T] to completely defeat the armed forces of an enemy country, with the result that you have complete control over it: *Sailors travelled to the New World with the urge to conquer and explore.* | *Julius Caesar conquered Gaul, which we know today as France.*

4 to beat someone by using your intelligence

- outwit/outsmart
- be too clever for

outwit/outsmart /aʊt'wɪt, aʊt'smɑːʳt/ [v T] to get an advantage over someone that you are fighting or competing against, by using clever tricks and planning rather than by force: *We can't fight them. We'll just have to try and outsmart them.* | *None of the thieves wanted to admit that they had been outwitted by a couple of teenagers.*

be too clever for /biː tuː 'klevəʳ fɔːʳ/ [v phrase] ALSO **be too smart for** /biː tuː 'smɑʳt fɔːʳ/ especially American if you **are too clever** or **too smart for** someone, they have tried to trick you but you realized what they were doing and stopped them succeeding: *Molly tried to hide the presents but the children were too clever for her and found them within minutes.*

5 when someone is beaten

- defeat
- rout
- drubbing

▸ *see also* **lose**

defeat /dɪ'fiːt/ [n C/U] a situation in which a person, army, political party etc is defeated: *After his third successive election defeat he decided to retire from politics.* | **suffer a defeat** *In the last game of the season they suffered a humiliating defeat, losing 7-0 to Real Madrid.*

rout /raʊt/ [n C] a situation in which a person, army, political party etc is easily defeated: *The game was a rout, with the home team winning by 10 goals to nil.*

drubbing /'drʌbɪŋ/ [n C] a situation in which a person, team, political party etc is defeated badly: *Gramm's drubbing by Davis in the California primary has badly hurt his campaign.* | **take a drubbing** *The Lions took a drubbing from the Eagles last night, losing 58-37.*

beautiful

RELATED WORDS

opposite: **ugly**

▸ *see also* **attract/attraction, sexy, impress**

1 woman

- beautiful
- good-looking
- pretty
- attractive
- nice-looking
- cute
- gorgeous
- glamorous
- stunning
- elegant
- striking
- lovely
- ravishing
- a woman of great beauty

beautiful /'bju:tɪ̈fəl/ [adj] use this about a woman who is extremely attractive in a way that is fairly unusual and special, so that people notice and admire her: *Standing in the doorway was a beautiful woman with long black hair and green eyes.* | *Karen was even more beautiful than I had remembered.* | *She has a beautiful smile.* | *You look beautiful tonight.*

good-looking /ˌgʊd 'lʊkɪŋ◂/ [adj] use this about a woman who is nice to look at and has an attractive face and body: *Ginny was tall and good-looking.* | *A good-looking young woman in a business suit came into the room.* | *She seems to get better-looking the older she gets.*

pretty /'prɪti/ [adj] use this about a young woman or girl who has an attractive face and is good-looking, but not in an unusual way: *Maureen's really pretty, isn't she?* | *A pretty girl like you should have a boyfriend.* | *She has a pretty face.* | *Doesn't she look pretty with her hair up?*

attractive /ə'træktɪv/ [adj] use this about a woman who is good-looking, especially in a way that makes people sexually interested in her: *Frances was a charming and attractive girl.* | *Bob's wife is a very attractive woman* | **find sb attractive** *A lot of men find plump women attractive.*

nice-looking /ˌnaɪs 'lʊkɪŋ◂/ [adj] especially spoken use this about a woman who looks pleasant and friendly but is not extremely pretty: *My mother was always a nice-looking woman.*

cute /kju:t/ [adj] especially American, spoken use this about a girl or young woman who is pretty and sexually attractive: *Do you like Jill Anderson? I think she's cute!* | *Heidi is the cutest girl in my class.*

gorgeous /'gɔ:ʳdʒəs/ [adj] especially spoken use this to emphasize that a woman is extremely attractive, in a sexual way: *That woman on 'Baywatch' – I think she's gorgeous.* | *You look absolutely gorgeous in that dress!*

glamorous /'glæmərəs/ [adj] use this about a woman who looks like a beautiful actress or as if she is very rich, and has an attractive body and wears expensive clothes: *The picture showed a glamorous young woman sitting in a sports car.* | *glamorous Hollywood movie stars of the 1950s*

stunning /'stʌnɪŋ/ [adj] use this about a woman who is extremely beautiful and sexually attractive, in a way that everyone notices and admires: *Men always stared when she looked good, and today she was stunning.* | *Mother came out of her room, looking stunning in her silk dressing gown.*

elegant /'elɪ̈gənt/ [adj] use this about a woman who is tall and attractive, and wears clothes that are simple but have a lot of good style: *An elegant young woman sat at the next table, sipping a cocktail.* | *Jody manages to look elegant, even in a simple pantsuit.*

striking /'straɪkɪŋ/ [adj] use this about a woman who is very attractive, especially because she has a particular feature that is beautiful and unusual: *Even at 75, Alice is still a striking woman.* | *Celia had striking brown eyes like some Russian icon.* | *With her mass of black hair and pale skin she looked very striking.*

lovely /'lʌvli/ [adj] especially British if a woman looks **lovely**, she looks very attractive: *He told his wife that evening that she had never looked lovelier.* | *Claire was young and lovely, but rather shy.*

ravishing /'rævɪʃɪŋ/ [adj] very good-looking and sexually attractive – used especially in humorous descriptions: *The farmer had three daughters, all three blonde and ravishing.* | *Cynthia looked positively ravishing this evening.*

a woman of great beauty /ə ˌwʊmən əv ˌgreɪt 'bju:ti/ [n C] written a very beautiful woman: *In her youth she had been a woman of great beauty.*

2 man

- good-looking
- handsome
- attractive
- cute
- gorgeous
- nice-looking
- hunky
- rugged
- striking
- be a fine figure of a man
- dashing

good-looking /ˌgʊd 'lʊkɪŋ◂/ [adj] use this about a man who is nice to look at but in a fairly ordinary way: *Paul is very good-looking, but he's too arrogant.* | *She showed me a photo of a good-looking young soldier.*

handsome /'hænsəm/ [adj] especially written use this about a man who is good-looking, especially one who is tall and looks strong: *Lena had fallen in love with a rich, handsome Frenchman.* | *My brother was two years older than me, taller, and more handsome.* | *He looks really handsome in his uniform, doesn't he?*

attractive /ə'træktɪv/ [adj] use this about a man who is good-looking, especially in a way that makes people sexually interested in him: *He was a tall attractive man in his mid-forties.* | **find sb attractive** *I don't find those body-builders with huge muscles attractive at all.*

cute /kju:t/ [adj] especially American, spoken use this about a young man who looks nice and is sexually attractive **kind of cute** spoken *I don't know why she won't go out with him. I think he's kind of cute.*

gorgeous /'gɔ:ʳdʒəs/ [adj] especially spoken use this to emphasize that a man is extremely attractive in a sexual way: *Look at that guy over there. Isn't he gorgeous?*

nice-looking /ˌnaɪs 'lʊkɪŋ◂/ [adj] especially spoken use this about a man who looks pleasant and friendly but is not extremely attractive: *I suppose he's quite nice-looking, but he's not really my type.* | *Chris is a nice-looking guy with a good sense of humor.*

hunky /'hʌŋki/ [adj] informal very attractive and strong-looking: *Have you seen the new sports instructor? He's really hunky.* | *The show stars hunky Kevin Sorbo as Hercules.*

rugged /'rʌgɪ̈d/ [adj] good-looking with strong features that are often not perfect: *Ann admired his* *rugged good looks.* | *He was solidly built and looked like a rugged quarterback.*

striking /ˈstraɪkɪŋ/ [adj] very attractive, especially because you have a particular feature that is attractive and unusual: *He had a striking profile, with a large nose that reminded people of a Roman statue.*

be a fine figure of a man /biː ə ˌfaɪn ˈfɪgər əv ə ˌmæn‖-ˈfɪgjər-/ [v phrase] to be a strong-looking, attractive man – used especially in humorous descriptions: *Her husband was a fine figure of a man – tall, broad-chested and with a bushy black moustache.*

dashing /ˈdæʃɪŋ/ [adj] good-looking and well-dressed in a way that makes people notice you – used especially in literature: *She left her family to move to Argentina with her lover, a dashing polo player.* | *Steve was looking very dashing in a light-coloured suit.*

3 child

- beautiful
- lovely
- cute

beautiful /ˈbjuːtəfəl/ [adj] use this about a child who is so good-looking that everyone notices and admires him or her: *Parents always believe that their baby is the most beautiful baby in the world.* | *How did two people like Sara and Rob have such beautiful children?*

lovely /ˈlʌvli/ [adj] especially British use this about a child who looks nice and has a pleasant, friendly character: *They've got three lovely kids.* | *Rosie's a lovely baby.* | *Don't the Schultz sisters look lovely?*

cute /kjuːt/ [adj] informal use this about a child who looks attractive and has a happy or amusing character: *He's really naughty, but he's so cute.* | *You were such a cute baby!* | *Doesn't he look cute in that baseball cap!*

4 animal

- beautiful
- pretty
- cute
- magnificent

beautiful /ˈbjuːtəfəl/ [adj] use this about an animal that looks extremely attractive and impressive: *a beautiful bird with bright blue feathers* | *That's a beautiful dog. What kind is he?*

pretty /ˈprɪti/ [adj] use this about an animal that is attractive, especially because it is small or is brightly coloured **pretty bird/fish/cat/feathers/fur etc** *They had an aquarium with lots of pretty little fish.*

cute ALSO **sweet** especially British /kjuːt, swiːt/ [adj] use this about a pet or a baby animal that looks nice in a way that makes people want to look after it: *cute little kittens* | *She has a funny old dog – he's really sweet!*

magnificent /mægˈnɪfəsənt/ [adj] use this about an animal or a large bird that is very beautiful and impressive because it is large and strong or beautifully coloured: *The horse was a magnificent creature with a gleaming jet black coat.* | *a magnificent golden eagle* | *The Siberian Tiger is a magnificent animal.*

5 thing/building

- beautiful
- pretty
- magnificent
- superb
- gorgeous
- exquisite
- elegant
- attractive
- lovely
- splendid
- stunning
- artistic

beautiful /ˈbjuːtəfəl/ ALSO **lovely** /ˈlʌvli/ especially British [adj] use this about a thing or building that looks extremely good, and gives you a feeling of pleasure: *'Do you like the house?' 'Like it? It's beautiful!'* | *Thanks for the flowers – they're lovely!* | *This is one of Europe's loveliest churches.*

pretty /ˈprɪti/ [adj] use this about an object that is small and delicate, or things in your home such as curtains and carpets: *The room was decorated with pretty wallpaper with yellow flowers on it.* | *What a pretty watch!*

magnificent /mægˈnɪfəsənt/ [adj] very beautiful and very impressive – use this about a large and impressive building or piece of furniture, especially an old one: *The room was dominated by a magnificent four-poster bed.* | *a magnificent 15th century castle*

superb /sjuːˈpɜːʳb, suː-‖suː-/ [adj] extremely beautiful and of the highest quality: *The lilies we got from the flower market were absolutely superb.* | *a superb collection of Chinese porcelain* | *In the center of the crown is a superb diamond.*

gorgeous /ˈgɔːʳdʒəs/ [adj] especially British, spoken use this about a beautiful thing that you admire very much: *I love your dress! It's such a gorgeous colour!* | *The apartment had been furnished in rich, deep colors and gorgeous fabrics.*

exquisite /ɪkˈskwɪzət, ˈekskwɪ-/ [adj] very beautiful – use this about jewellery or other things that have been designed with a lot of care and made with a lot of skill: *an exquisite handcarved ivory brooch* | *The sets and costumes for the dance performance were exquisite.*

elegant /ˈeləgənt/ [adj] use this about a building, a piece of furniture, or a piece of clothing that is beautifully designed in a simple but usually expensive way: *We first met him at an elegant hotel in the uptown district of Manhattan.* | *an elegant rosewood dining table* | *She was wearing an elegant black suit.*

attractive /əˈtræktɪv/ [adj] pleasant to look at: *Kitchen utensils should be attractive as well as functional.* | *This attractive book is an ideal gift for any young baseball fan.*

lovely /ˈlʌvli/ [adj] especially British pleasant to look at: *The dress was such a lovely colour, a deep blue that really suited her.* | *It was a lovely big house with a big garden out the back.*

splendid /ˈsplendəd/ [adj] written something such as a building, piece of furniture, or work of art that is **splendid** is beautiful and impressive: *In the centre of the room was a splendid 18th century oak table.* | *Wealthy nobles inhabited splendid villas in the surrounding countryside.*

stunning /ˈstʌnɪŋ/ [adj] something that is **stunning** is very beautiful so that everyone notices and admires it: *Rafaella wore a stunning white satin wedding gown.* | *Knox's metal statues are stunning.*

artistic /ɑːʳˈtɪstɪk/ [adj] an arrangement, design etc that is **artistic** looks attractive and has been done with skill and imagination: *I love your Christmas decorations – they're very artistic.* | *The food was presented in an artistic way.*

6 place/countryside/view

- beautiful
- lovely
- stunning/ breathtaking
- magnificent
- picturesque
- scenic
- pretty
- beauty spot

beautiful /'bju:tɪ̈fəl/ [adj] use this about a place that everyone admires and likes to visit: *Florence is such a beautiful city.* | *Cornwall has some of the most beautiful stretches of coastline in Britain.* | *a restaurant with beautiful views over Sorrento and the Gulf of Naples*

lovely /'lʌvli/ [adj] especially British use this about a place that is beautiful in a way that makes you feel relaxed and gives you a lot of pleasure: *The hills will be lovely at this time of year.* | *You are so lucky to live here with all this lovely countryside around you.* | *The garden was looking lovely.*

stunning/breathtaking /'stʌnɪŋ, 'breθˌteɪkɪŋ/ [adj] use this about a view that is extremely beautiful and extremely impressive: *The view from the top of the mountain was stunning.* | *We got a breathtaking view of the Golden Gate Bridge.* | *The ruins of Angkor Wat are truly breathtaking.*

magnificent /mæg'nɪfɪ̈sənt/ [adj] use this about an area where there are beautiful, large, and impressive mountains, valleys, rivers etc: *The location of the town along the river is magnificent.* | *the magnificent mountains around Lake Titicaca*

picturesque /ˌpɪktʃə'resk◂/ [adj] use this about a village or town that is pretty in an old-fashioned way: *We visited the picturesque fishing village of Lochinver.* | *He rents a small house in the picturesque old quarter of town.*

scenic /'si:nɪk/ [adj] use this about a road that goes through beautiful countryside: *We travelled to the coast by a very scenic route.* | *a scenic road through the Welsh mountains*

pretty /'prɪti/ [adj] pleasant to look at but not really impressive: *We walked down the pretty, tree-lined avenue.* | *a pretty village on the Suffolk border*

beauty spot /'bju:ti spɒt‖-spɑ:t/ [n C] British an area or place that people visit because it is especially beautiful: *There are several beauty spots to visit in Crete.* | *People were protesting because the council planned to build a new road through Burleigh Wood, a local beauty spot.*

7 a beautiful appearance

- beauty
- good looks

beauty /'bju:ti/ [n U] the beautiful appearance of a place or person: *the beauty of the countryside in spring* | *He had written a poem about Sylvia, praising her charm and beauty.* | **of great beauty** (=very beautiful) formal *I found the temple a place of great beauty.*

good looks /gʊd 'lʊks/ [n plural] someone's attractive appearance: *With his dark good looks, Jason could have been a TV star.*

8 dressed, arranged, decorated etc in a beautiful way

- beautifully
- prettily
- attractively
- elegantly
- exquisitely
- artistically

beautifully /'bju:tɪ̈fəli/ [adv] *This is a beautifully illustrated book.* | *The flowers were placed in a beautifully decorated vase.* | *'What do you think about the garden?' 'You've done it beautifully!'*

prettily /'prɪtɪli/ [adv] in a way that is pleasant to look at: *Helen is always prettily dressed.* | *Marie arranged the radishes prettily on a plate.*

attractively /ə'træktɪvli/ [adv] in a way that makes something very pleasant to look at, especially in order to make people want it: *We hope to sell goods by packaging them attractively.* | *All her friends were younger, prettier and more attractively dressed.*

elegantly /'elɪ̈gəntli/ [adv] in a beautiful way that is simple, but usually expensive: *Tom's mother was an elegantly dressed gray-haired woman.* | *The bedroom was elegantly decorated with deep-blue and gold wallpaper.*

exquisitely /ɪk'skwɪzɪ̈tli/ [adv] in a very delicate, careful, and beautiful way: *In the box was a pair of exquisitely shaped old earrings.* | *The tiny china doll was exquisitely ornate.*

artistically /ɑ:ʳ'tɪstɪkli/ [adv] in a way that looks attractive and has been done with a lot of skill and imagination: *Red and blue flowers were artistically arranged to form a pattern.*

because

what you say when you are giving the reason for something

RELATED WORDS

- *see also* **cause, reason, result, purpose, so/therefore**

- because
- since
- due to/owing to
- thanks to
- as a result of
- the reason ... is
- through
- out of
- on account of
- seeing as

because /bɪ'kɒz, bɪkəz‖bɪ'kɔ:z, bɪkəz/ [conjunction] use this when you are explaining the reason why something happens or why you do something: *She's in a bad mood because her father won't let her go to the party tonight.* | *'This photograph doesn't look like you.' 'That's because it isn't me – it's my sister'.* | *Because you've done such a good job, I'm giving everyone a 10% bonus.* | **just because** (=used when you think an explanation is not a good enough reason for something) *You mean you dumped him just because he forgot your birthday?* | **simply because** (=used when there is a very simple reason for something) *We're not going on holiday this year, simply because we can't afford it.* | **because of sth** *I had to move because of my job.* | *Because of the increase in street crime, many old people are afraid to leave their homes.*

since ALSO **as** British /sɪns, æz/ [conjunction] use this to give the reason why someone decides to do something: *We had planned to play tennis but since it was raining we decided to go swimming instead.* | *Since you're going to be in the area anyway, you can pick up the order for me.* | *As he wasn't well, I offered to do the shopping.*

due to/owing to /'dju: tu:‖'du:-, 'əʊɪŋ tu:/ [prep] formal used especially in official statements to explain what causes a particular problem: *Our flight was delayed due to poor weather conditions.* | *Owing to circumstances beyond our control, we regret to inform customers that this store will close early.* | *In* *the end I was unable to attend the conference, owing to financial difficulties.* | **be due to** *The accident was due to a concrete block thrown from a bridge.*

thanks to /ˈθæŋks tuː/ [prep] use this to explain that something has been possible because of someone's actions or because something is very good, very effective etc: *Today thanks to the Internet, you can do all your Christmas shopping from home.* | *The play was a great success thanks to the effort and commitment of everyone involved.* ▸ **USAGE** ***Thanks to*** is also used when you want to criticize or complain about someone, when you are annoyed with them because they have caused something bad to happen. ***thanks to sb's carelessness/stupidity etc:*** *Thanks to your carelessness, the documents have been lost.* ***thanks to you:*** *Thanks to you the whole thing was a complete disaster.*

as a result of /əz ə rɪˈzʌlt ɒv/ [prep] use this when you are explaining what made something happen, especially something unpleasant: *Many people are now homeless as a result of the civil war.* | **as a direct result of** *Mr Logan died as a direct result of the injuries he received in the accident.*

the reason ... is /ðə ˈriːzən ɪz/ use this when you are explaining something carefully, especially when you have been asked to explain why something happened: *The reason we didn't consider her for the job was that she didn't have enough experience.* | *The reason we are here this evening is to say thank you to Brian for all his hard work.*

through /θruː/ [prep] use this when you are explaining why someone or something has succeeded or failed: *We succeeded through sheer hard work.* | *Hundreds of working days have been lost this year through illness.* | *The Community Association collapsed through lack of support.*

out of /ˈaʊt ɒv/ [prep] use this when someone does something because of a particular feeling **out of interest/curiosity/desperation etc** *She opened the letter, just out of curiosity.* | *I came to you out of desperation – you've got to help me.*

on account of /ɒn əˈkaʊnt ɒv/ [prep] use this when you want to give the reason why something is necessary, impossible, or true: *We had to move to London on account of my job.* | *They're called the Black Hills on account of their color.*

seeing as /ˈsiːɪŋ æz/ [conjunction] spoken informal use this to give a reason for what you are suggesting or deciding: *Seeing as it's your birthday, why don't we go out for a meal?* | *I'd better do it myself, seeing as no one else wants to do it.*

become

RELATED WORDS

▸ *see also* **change, develop, increase, less**

1 with adjectives

- ▸ become
- ▸ get
- ▸ grow
- ▸ go
- ▸ turn

become /bɪˈkʌm/ [v] if you **become** rich, famous, worried etc, you start to be rich, famous, worried etc: *Julian's book was a big success and he quickly became rich and famous.* | *The weather was becoming warmer.* | *After a while my eyes became accustomed to the dark.* | **become aware/certain/convinced etc that** *Slowly she became aware that there was someone else in the room.* | **it becomes clear/evident/obvious etc that** *It soon became clear that the fire was out of control.*

get /get/ [v] to become: *It normally gets dark at about 8.30 p.m.* | *The man in the shop got annoyed and started shouting at me.* | *The situation doesn't seem to be getting any better.* | *I think I'm getting too old for this kind of thing.* | *You'll need to take out insurance, in case anything gets damaged in the move.* ▸ **USAGE** ***Become*** and ***get: Become*** is more formal than ***get*** and is used mainly in written English. ***Get*** is the usual word to use in conversation. Don't use ***get*** with these words: ***available, calm, clear, famous, happy, important, necessary, obvious, poor, powerful, proud, sad, silent, successful, useful.*** But you can use ***get*** with comparatives, such as: ***clearer, happier, more famous, more important.*** You can also use ***get*** with past participles, such as: ***annoyed, bored, damaged, lost, broken.***

grow /grəʊ/ [v] **grow old/tired/worse/larger etc** to slowly and gradually become old, tired etc: *As we grow old, we worry more about our health.* | *I'd been waiting for forty minutes and I was beginning to grow uneasy.* | *The sound of footsteps grew louder.* | *Fiona was growing tired of being treated in this way.*

go /gəʊ/ [v] to become – only use **go** with these words **go grey/white/red/dark etc** *Her face went bright red with embarrassment.* | **go mad/wild/crazy** *Your dad'll go crazy when he finds out.* | **go quiet/silent** *As soon as the band started playing, the crowd went silent.* | **go bad/sour/cold** *My coffee's gone cold.*

turn /tɜːʳn/ [v] to become – only use **turn** with these words **turn red/white/blue etc** *It was late autumn and the leaves were slowly turning golden.* | **turn nasty/mean** *When I said that I was not prepared to help him, he suddenly turned nasty.* | **turn sour** *Their friendship was beginning to turn sour.* | **turn cold/warm** *Just when we were all getting our summer clothes out, it turned cold again.*

2 with nouns

- ▸ become
- ▸ change into/turn into
- ▸ grow into
- ▸ develop into

▸ **USAGE** Don't use ***get*** with nouns.

become /bɪˈkʌm/ [v] *Since winning all that money he's become a very unpleasant person.* | *Mobile phones have now become fashion accessories for schoolkids and teenagers.*

change into/turn into /ˈtʃeɪndʒ ɪntuː, ˈtɜːʳn ɪntuː/ [phr v T] if someone or something **changes** or **turns** into someone or something else, they become completely different: *The little brown caterpillar will eventually turn into a beautiful butterfly.* | *She's changed into a much gentler person since she had her own kids.* | *During the brewing process all the sugar turns into alcohol.* | **change from sth into sth** *When I went back, the countryside had changed from farmland into housing estates and factory sites.*

grow into /ˈgrəʊ ɪntuː/ [phr v T] to gradually change over a long time and become a different type of person, place, or thing: *Leo had grown into a slim blond young man since she last saw him.* | *In recent years the town has grown into a city of about 500,000 people.* | *The crowd's cheers slowly grew into a loud crescendo of noise.*

develop into /dɪˈveləp ɪntuː/ [v phrase] to gradually change and become something or someone that is better or worse than before: *Over the years the college developed into one of the finest language institutions in all of South East Asia.* | *Joe had no athletic ability, and was developing into an overweight* *child. | 3000 troops were sent to prevent the disturbances from developing into a full-scale civil war.*

3 to become a teacher, manager, student, etc

- become
- get to be

become /bɪˈkʌm/ [v] *Even when I was a kid, I wanted to become a psychologist. | My friend Kyle stayed with the company and became a departmental manager. | Bradley went on to become chairman of the Joint Chiefs of Staff. | Every time you open the newspaper these days someone else has just become a millionaire.*

get to be /ˈget tə biː/ [v phrase] informal to succeed in getting an important job: *She got to be a lawyer through sheer hard work and determination. | I wanted to ask him how he got to be boss of such a big company.*

before

RELATED WORDS

opposite: **after**

- the time before now *see* **past**
- *see also* **early, first, prepare**

1 before you do something or before something happens

- before
- beforehand
- first
- in advance
- pre-
- prior to
- on the eve of/in the run-up to
- advance
- prior

before /bɪˈfɔːʳ/ [prep/conjunction] **before** you do something or **before** an event happens: *The family left France just before the war. | Think carefully before you give your final answer. | Before I had a chance to say anything, David walked away.* | **before doing sth** *Before joining IBM, Frank worked for Toshiba. | You should check the oil before beginning a long car journey.* | **before that** *We spent two years in Thailand, and before that we lived in China. | I was a waiter for six months, and before that I worked in a supermarket.* | **a week/two days/five years etc before** *I was born just eleven months before my brother.*

beforehand ALSO **ahead of time** American /bɪˈfɔːʳhænd, əˌhed əv ˈtaɪm/ [adv] if you do something **beforehand** or **ahead of time**, you do it before you do something else, especially to make the situation easier: *Let me know ahead of time if you need a ride to the airport. | We had agreed beforehand not to tell anyone else about our plans.*

first /fɜːʳst/ [adv] before you do something else: *Add the onions and garlic first, then the mushrooms. | 'Shall we go for some lunch?' 'Yeah, great, let me just make a quick call first.'*

in advance /ɪn ədˈvɑːns‖-ˈvæns/ [adv] if you do something **in advance**, you do it before another event happens, especially so that you are prepared: *Pasta salad is a dish that you can easily prepare in advance. | I wish you'd told me in advance that you were going to be late.* | **+ of** *Your passport application should be submitted well in advance of your departure.* | **three days/six months/a year etc in advance** *Preparations for the president's visit had been made several months in advance.*

pre- /priː/ [prefix] **pre-war/pre-Christmas/pre-Roman etc** before the war, Christmas etc: *Life in pre-war Britain was simpler and less fast-paced. | As usual, the government seems to have forgotten most of its pre-election promises.*

prior to /ˈpraɪəʳ tuː/ [prep] formal before, especially before a particular event or date: *I spoke with Sarah prior to the meeting.* | **prior to doing sth** *The doctor should have told you about the possible side effects prior to starting you on the medication.*

on the eve of/in the run-up to /ɒn ði ˈiːv ɒv, ɪn ðə ˈrʌn ʌp tuː/ [prep] the time before an important event: *On the eve of the election, some of the candidates were showing signs of strain. | No-one claimed responsibility for the bombing, which occurred on the eve of the Prime Minister's visit. | Another round of TV debates will be held in the run-up to the referendum.*

advance /ədˈvɑːns‖ədˈvæns/ [adj only before noun] given or done before the time that a particular event takes place or before the time that something is expected to happen: *Aid workers say the village had no advance warning of the floods. | Advance bookings for the concert start today. | Airport visas may be obtained if forty-eight hours advance notice has been provided.*

prior /ˈpraɪəʳ/ [adj only before noun] formal taking place before something else happens or before someone is allowed to do something: *The airline says that some flights may be cancelled without prior warning. | The phone company is required to give you prior notice before disconnecting your service. | The tenant must get the prior consent of the landlord before doing any redecorating in the flat.*

2 before a particular time or date

- before
- by
- no later than

before /bɪˈfɔːʳ/ [prep] *Call me back before 5.30. | You should go, before John gets back.* | **just before** *Our daughter was born just before Christmas.*

by /baɪ/ [prep] **by 6 o'clock/Friday/next winter etc** at some time before 6 o'clock, Friday etc, and certainly not later than this: *I'll be home by 6.30, I promise. | By 9.00, most of the guests had arrived. | Please try to have this done by Friday.*

no later than ALSO **by sth at the latest** /nəʊ ˈleɪtəʳ ðən, baɪ (sth) ət ðə ˈleɪtɪ̣st/ [prep] before or at a particular time but definitely not after it – used especially to tell someone the time by which they must have done something: *I want your essays back no later than Wednesday, nine o'clock. | Jenny should be back by Monday at the latest. | Entry forms for the competition should arrive no later than Friday, November 1st. | The dinner party will be over by ten-thirty at the very latest.*

3 before now

- before
- ago
- earlier
- previously
- formerly

before /bɪˈfɔːʳ/ [adv] **before** now or **before** the time you are talking about: *I had never seen such an ugly baby before. | Wendell had never been on a plane before.* | **the day/week/year etc before** *Sheila and I became friends in 1995, although we had actually met several years before.*

ago /əˈgəʊ/ [adv] **five minutes/two weeks/20 years**

etc ago five minutes, two weeks, twenty years etc before now: *George went out half an hour ago. Can I have him call you back?* | *Lucy's aunt died a few months ago.* | **a long time ago** *'When did you live in Germany?' 'Oh, it was a long time ago.'* | **ages ago** spoken (=a very long time ago) *Pauline wrote to me once, but that was ages ago.*

earlier /'ɜːʳliəʳ/ [adv] at some time, date, year etc before now or before the time you are talking about: *Didn't I give you the key earlier?* | **earlier in the day/year etc** *I saw Barbara earlier in the day – she looked pretty upset.* | **20 years earlier/10 minutes earlier/moments earlier etc** *Three years earlier, Miller had been happily married, with a good job.*

previously /'priːviəsli/ [adv] before a time or event in the past: *Hastings previously worked for a software company in Richmond.* | *The bombing is being blamed on a previously unknown group of terrorists.* | **two days/three weeks/six months etc previously** *She had met Atwood at a conference a few weeks previously.*

formerly /'fɔːʳməʳli/ [adv] formal during a period in the past but not now: *Milligan, 43, was formerly a deputy foreign minister.* | *Peru was formerly ruled by the Spanish.* | *Watkins was formerly editor of the Express, a local weekly newspaper.*

4 someone or something that existed before or that you had before

- previous
- last
- ex-
- old
- the one before
- former
- predecessor
- precursor
- forerunner

previous /'priːviəs/ [adj only before noun] the **previous** person or thing is the one that existed just before now or before the time you are talking about: *The car's previous owner didn't take very good care of it.* | *Please ignore my previous instructions.*

last /lɑːst‖læst/ [adj only before noun] the **last** thing or person is the one that you had just before now, or the one that existed just before now: *The last apartment we lived in was much smaller than this one.* | *Beth broke up with her last boyfriend because he drank too much.*

ex- /eks/ [prefix] **ex-wife/ex-boyfriend/ex-soldier etc** someone who used to be someone's wife, used to be a soldier etc, but is not any more: *Her dad's an ex-policeman.* | *Lydia is still friends with her ex-husband.*

old /əʊld/ [adj only before noun] **sb's old job/car/girlfriend/boss etc** the job, car etc that someone had before the one they have now: *The new stadium is much bigger than the old one.* | *I saw Phil with one of my old girlfriends.* | *We all liked the old teacher better.*

the one before /ðə ˌwʌn bɪ'fɔːʳ/ [pron] the person or thing that existed before the one you have just mentioned: *I didn't enjoy Spielberg's last film but I thought the one before was all right.* | *Each year, the convention is a little larger than the one before.*

former /'fɔːʳməʳ/ [adj only before noun] formal use this especially to talk about someone who used to have a particular job or position but does not any more: *Her former husband now lives in Houston.* | *Weinberger was an advisor to former president Ronald Reagan.*

predecessor /'priːdəsesəʳ‖'pre-/ [n C] formal someone's **predecessor** is the person who had the same job before them: *Vandenberg has been a more active director than his predecessor.* | *Sally's predecessor had warned her about Nick, one of the company vice-presidents.*

precursor /prɪ'kɜːʳsəʳ/ [n C] formal someone whose ideas or style are later used by another more famous person, or an organization, movement or machine that later develops into one that is more important **+ of/to** *The abacus was the precursor of the modern electronic calculator.* | *The Office of Strategic Services was the precursor of the CIA.*

forerunner /'fɔːˌrʌnəʳ/ [n C] the first person, organization, machine etc that existed before the one that exists now and that the one that exists now is based on **+ of** *The P-50 is a forerunner of today's supersonic jet.* | *Hansen played in the American Basketball League, a forerunner of the NBA.*

5 before someone or something else in a list, line, series etc

- before
- come before/precede
- in front of/ahead of
- previous
- earlier
- the one before
- preceding
- above

before /bɪ'fɔːʳ/ [prep] **before** something or someone else in a list, series, or set: *I think you were before me in line, weren't you?* | *Islington station is one stop before Finsbury Park on the Victoria Line.*

come before/precede /ˌkʌm bɪ'fɔːʳ, prɪ'siːd/ [v phrase/v T] to happen or exist before something or someone else: *Churchill was a much stronger leader than the man who came before him.* | *A planning session at eleven-thirty will precede the noon lunch discussion.* | **be preceded by sth** *Witnesses say the fire was preceded by a loud explosion.* | *In most cases the illness is preceded by vomiting and chills.*

in front of/ahead of /ɪn 'frʌnt ɒv, ə'hed ɒv/ [prep] before another person in a group of people who are waiting to do something: *The man in front of me looked very familiar.* | *There were about fifty people ahead of us waiting for tickets.*

previous /'priːviəs/ [adj only before noun] coming before the one that you are dealing with now: *The previous chapter examined how children learn language.* | *Each number in the series 2 – 4 – 8 – 16 is twice as large as the previous number.*

earlier /'ɜːʳliəʳ/ [adj only before noun] coming at some time before the one you have just mentioned – use this especially about something that is very different from what is happening now: *He used a lot more color in his earlier paintings.* | *The play lacks the wit and energy of Jergen's earlier work.*

the one before /ðə ˌwʌn bɪ'fɔːʳ/ [pron] the thing that comes before another in a series: *When you're in prison, every day feels just like the one before.*

preceding /prɪ'siːdɪŋ/ [adj only before noun] formal coming before the thing you have just mentioned, or the part of a book where you are now: *The preceding chapters have described several key events in recent French history.* | *In the preceding section of the poem, Whitman is talking about how important it is to live in the present.*

above /ə'bʌv/ [adj only before noun] written use this to talk about a person or thing that was mentioned earlier: *Write to the above address for more information.* | *The above diagram shows a diesel car engine.* | **the above** [n singular] (=the people or things mentioned earlier) *Contact any of the above for* *more details.* —**above** [adv] *None of the organizations mentioned above answered our inquiries.*

6 a time, day, month etc that comes before another one

- previous
- yesterday morning/afternoon/evening etc
- last week/year/Monday etc
- the day/week/month/year before
- preceding

previous /ˈpriːviəs/ [adj only before noun] *The company recorded a 50% increase in profits over the previous year.* | *Kirsty's baby had been born the previous October, while she was still in England.*

yesterday morning/afternoon/evening etc /ˌjestəʳdi ˈmɔːʳnɪŋ/ [adv] the morning, afternoon, or evening of the day before today: *My sister and I went shopping yesterday lunchtime.* | *We met yesterday morning to discuss plans for the conference.*

last week/year/Monday etc /ˌlɑːst ˈwiːk‖ˌlæst-/ [adj only before noun] the week, year etc before this one: *I spoke to Neil and Sandra last weekend.* | *We still haven't paid last month's rent.*

the day/week/month/year before /ðə ˌdeɪ, ˌwiːk, ˌmʌnθ, ˌjɪəʳ, bɪˈfɔːʳ/ [adv/prep] the day, week, month, year before the one in the past that you have just mentioned: *The day before the exam, I felt worried and unprepared.* | *Last week she was in Paris, and the week before she was in Rome.*

preceding /prɪˈsiːdɪŋ/ [adj only before noun] formal the **preceding** months, years etc are the ones just before the time in the past that you are talking about: *The company made more profit in that one month than it made in the whole of the preceding year.* | *He had been arrested at least fifteen times in the preceding five years.*

7 to happen or exist before someone or something else

- come before
- precede
- predate
- lead up to
- come first
- be a prelude to sth

come before /ˌkʌm bɪˈfɔːʳ/ [v phrase not in progressive or passive] *The paragraph says basically the same thing as the one that came before.* | **come before sth** *The salad usually comes before the main course.* | *In the Greek alphabet, the letter delta comes before the letter epsilon.*

precede /prɪˈsiːd/ [v T] formal to come just before something else in a pattern or series: *In English, the subject precedes the verb.* | *On vehicle licence plates in the UK, the numbers are preceded by a single letter.*

predate /priːˈdeɪt/ [v T] if one historical event or object **predates** another, it happened or existed before it: *Many economic systems predate capitalism.* | **predate sth by 10/50/200 etc years** *The steam engine predates the internal combustion engine by at least 100 years.*

lead up to /ˌliːd ˈʌp tuː/ [phr v T not in passive] if an event **leads up to** another event, it comes before it and often causes it to happen: *Monroe still refuses to talk about the events which led up to his resignation.* | *The book describes some of the events leading up to the First World War.*

come first /ˌkʌm ˈfɜːʳst/ [v phrase] if one of two events **comes first**, it happens before the other event: *The rains came first, then the storms.*

be a prelude to sth /biː ə ˈpreljuːd tə (sth)/ [v phrase] formal or written if an event **is a prelude to** a more important event, it happens just before it and often makes people expect it: *The air-strike was just a prelude to the invasion.* | *The revolution of 1789 was a prelude to a more just and equal society.*

8 to do something before someone else does it

- do sth first
- be the first/be first
- beat sb to it
- ahead of
- be ahead of your time

do sth first /ˌduː (sth) ˈfɜːʳst/ [v phrase] if you do something, go somewhere, see something etc **first**, you do it before someone else: *It's mine – I saw it first.* | *Who wants to go first?* | *Sandy finished the puzzle first.*

be the first/be first /biː ðə ˈfɜːʳst, biː ˈfɜːʳst/ [v phrase] to be the first person to do a particular thing: *Many people have copied her style, but she was definitely the first.* | **be the first/first to do sth** *Of the four of us, my sister was the first to get married.*

beat sb to it /ˌbiːt (sb) ˈtuː ɪt/ [v phrase] informal to get or do something before another person who is trying to do the same thing: *I was going to have that last piece of pie but somebody beat me to it.* | *When Charlie finally got down there to buy the car, he discovered that someone else had beaten him to it.*

ahead of /əˈhed ɒv/ [prep] if you arrive somewhere or finish something **ahead of** someone, you arrive there or finish it before them: *Carrie got to the pub ahead of us.* | *Cole finished the race ahead of Jewison.*

be ahead of your time /biː əˌhed əv jɔːʳ ˈtaɪm/ [v phrase] if someone **is ahead of their time** they do something before other people do it, especially by having new ideas before anyone else: *As an architect, Sir John Soan was ahead of his time.* | **way ahead of your time** *Ashton's educational theories were way ahead of their time.*

beginning

RELATED WORDS

opposite: **end**

- to start happening or doing something *see* **start**
- *see also* **first, come from**

1 the beginning of something

- the beginning
- start
- origin
- starting point
- the onset

the beginning /ðə bɪˈgɪnɪŋ/ [n singular] the first part of an event, period of time etc **the beginning of sth** *I haven't seen her since the beginning of last year.* | *It was the beginning of a long friendship.* | *This fall's presidential election could mean the beginning of a new era in American politics.* | **back to the beginning** *It's so long since I spoke German, I'd have to go right back to the beginning if I took a class in it now.*

start /stɑːʳt/ [n singular] the beginning of something, or the way that something begins **the start of sth** *The runners are now lining up for the start of the race.* | *Tomorrow marks the start of the presidential* *election campaign. | They had an exotic meal to celebrate the start of the Chinese New Year.* | **a good/bad start to sth** *A pint of vodka at eight o'clock in the morning was not a good start to the day.* | **get off to a good/bad start** *If we get off to a good start this season, I think the team has a real chance to win the championship.*

origin /'ɒrɪ̈dʒɪ̈n‖'ɔː-, 'ɑː-/ [n C] the **origin** of something is where it came from or how it first started to exist: *AIDS became widespread in the 1980s, but no-one is certain of its origin.* | **+ of** *He's writing a dictionary that explains the origin of words.* | *Hughes's book 'The Fatal Shore' is a study of the origins of Australia as a British penal colony.* | *Advanced computer systems could trace the origin of every gun used in a violent crime.* | **have your/its origins in sth** *Today's ceremony is a modern version of a tradition which has its origins in medieval times.* | **country/place of origin** *The magazines were organized by country of origin.*

starting point /'stɑːʳtɪŋ pɔɪnt/ [n C usually singular] the **starting point** of something is where it begins or develops from: *If you want to learn about working overseas, this book would be a good starting point.* | **+ for/of** *Duffy's difficult relationship with her mother was the starting point for her fiction.* | *The assassination of Archduke Ferdinand is seen as the starting point of the war.*

the onset /ði 'ɒnset‖-'ɑːn-, -'ɔːn-/ [n singular] the time when something begins, especially something unpleasant such as an illness **the onset of sth** *Make sure to check your air conditioning before the onset of hot weather.* | *The onset of the Depression meant starvation and suffering for millions of people.* | *DiPietro's research shows that an active lifestyle can delay the onset of many diseases common with aging.*

2 at the beginning

- at the beginning/start
- at first/initially
- to start with/to begin with
- originally
- at the outset

at the beginning/start /ət ðə bɪ'gɪnɪŋ, 'stɑːʳt/ [adv] *At the start it looked as though Italy would win, but Argentina improved as the game went on.* | *She was nervous at the beginning but she settled down as she got further into her speech.* | **+ of** *We pay our rent at the beginning of the month.* | *For homework tonight, start at the beginning of chapter three and read up to page 98.* | *At the start of the century, barely 3% of the population was literate.*

at first/initially /ət 'fɜːʳst, ɪ'nɪʃəli/ [adv] use this to say what happened at the beginning, especially when something different happened later. **Initially** is more formal than **at first**: *Barney was quiet at first, but gradually he became more confident.* | *At first I didn't think Nancy and I would get along.* | *They offered her the job, initially on a temporary basis but later as a full member of the staff.* —**initial** [adj only before noun] *My initial impression of Sadie was that she was shy and a little unhappy.*

to start with/to begin with /tə 'stɑːʳt wɪð, tə bɪ'gɪn wɪð/ [adv] especially spoken use this to talk about what happens at the beginning, especially when something different may happen later: *Our employees receive health benefits and $28,000 a year to start with.* | *Even children who are healthy to begin with wouldn't survive long in these terrible conditions.*

originally /ə'rɪdʒɪ̈nəli, ə'rɪdʒənəli/ [adv] at the beginning – use this to talk about the situation at the time in the past when something first started: *Originally, they told me I was only going to work 35 hours a week.* | *Two hundred people showed up for the wedding, about 50 more than we originally planned.*

at the outset /ət ði 'aʊtset/ [adv] formal if something is known, believed, decided etc **at the outset**, it is known etc from the very earliest point in a period of time or activity: *Sylvia knew at the outset what her ultimate goals were.* | *It had been decided at the outset that Theresa would be our spokesperson.*

3 done or happening at the beginning

- initial
- early
- preliminary
- introductory
- opening

initial /ɪ'nɪʃəl/ [adj only before noun] **initial feelings/costs/reaction etc** feelings, costs etc that exist or are experienced at the beginning of an event or process: *Simon's initial feeling when he heard about the wedding was surprise.* | *After initial delays, construction on the new library is due to start in two weeks.* | *The initial cost of the computer system is more than made up for in terms of eventual profit.*

early /'ɜːʳli/ [adv] close to the beginning of an event, story, period of time etc: *I'll be seeing him early next week.* | **early in the game/story/century etc** *Rangers scored early in the game but fell behind within ten minutes.* —**early** [adj only before noun] *We're planning to go to Barcelona in early September.* | *He was described as a man in his early thirties* (=between 30 and 33 years old). | *the story of her early life in India*

preliminary /prɪ'lɪmɪ̈nəri‖-neri/ [adj only before noun] happening at the beginning of a process or event, especially in order to prepare for the rest of it: *The architect's plans are still in the preliminary stages.* | *Preliminary market research has shown that most Americans prefer environmentally-friendly products.*

introductory /ˌɪntrə'dʌktəri/ [adj only before noun] **introductory remark/paragraph/chapter etc** something someone says or writes at the beginning of a book, speech etc to explain what it is about: *Williams cleared his throat, made a few introductory remarks welcoming everyone, then began his speech.* | *The text has been revised and a new introductory essay has been added for the second edition.*

opening /'əʊpənɪŋ/ [adj only before noun] said or written at the beginning of a speech, book, play etc: *In the opening chapter, Ramona sits at the breakfast table thinking about the first day of school.* | *The audience strongly objected to the opening remarks of the president's speech.* | *Hilary makes a brief appearance in the opening scene, but doesn't have a major part.*

4 the time when something is first used or discovered

- the arrival of
- the coming of
- the birth of
- the dawn of

the arrival of /ði ə'raɪvəl ɒv/ [n phrase] the time when an important new idea, method, or product is first used or discovered, especially one that will lead to important changes: *With the arrival of the railroads after the Civil War, more and more people began moving west to California.* | *The arrival of convenience foods took much of the hard work out of preparing meals.*

the coming of ALSO **the advent of** formal /ðə 'kʌmɪŋ ɒv, ði 'ædvent ɒv/ [n phrase] the time when an important new system, idea, product, or method begins to exist or be used, causing important changes in society: *The Middle East changed dramatically with the coming of Islam 600 years after Christ.* | *Before the coming of the railways in the late 1860s these old roads were the only link between towns.* | *The advent of TV led to major changes in our social and family life.* | *Women workers tended to lose their jobs with the advent of new technology.*

the birth of /ðə ˈbɜːʳθ ɒv/ [n phrase] the beginning of something, for example a new political movement, that will become more and more important, and will change the way many people behave or think: *More than anyone else, Elvis Presley was responsible for the birth of rock and roll.* | *The birth of modern science was to fundamentally change people's attitudes towards religion.*

the dawn of /ðə ˈdɔːn ɒv/ [n phrase] the beginning of an important period of time in history – used especially in literature: *People have worshipped gods since the dawn of civilization.* | *Ordinary life would never be the same again after the dawn of the Industrial age.* | *A small group of poets and writers ushered in the dawn of the Romantic era in literature.*

5 from the beginning

- from the beginning/start
- from the word go
- since/from day one
- from the outset

from the beginning/start /frəm ðə bɪˈgɪnɪŋ, ˈstɑːʳt/ [adv] *Tell me everything that happened, from the beginning.* | *Their marriage has been in trouble from the start.* | **right from the beginning/ start** (=from the very earliest time) *Right from the start I could tell she didn't like me.* | *Mark felt very comfortable in his new job, right from the beginning.* | **from start to finish** (=from the beginning to the end) *This project has been a complete nightmare from start to finish.*

from the word go /frəm ðə ˌwɜːʳd ˈgəʊ/ [adv] informal from the beginning – used especially when something has happened or existed continuously since the beginning: *Eva's been very supportive from the word go.* | *The Elfin Theatre Company was doomed to failure from the word go.*

since/from day one /sɪns, frəm ˌdeɪ ˈwʌn/ [adv] if something has been the situation or has been someone's purpose **since** or **from day one**, it has clearly been the situation or their purpose ever since the beginning: *From day one I knew we'd have a strong team this year.* | *We've opposed this amendment since day one and we'd be stupid to change our minds now.*

from the outset /frəm ði ˈaʊtset/ [adv] from the time when a continuing activity or process began: *The new group had, from the outset, campaigned for an improvement in childcare provision.* | *I was determined from the outset to make the most of going to university.*

6 the first part of a story, book, film etc

- beginning
- the start
- the first part
- opening

beginning /bɪˈgɪnɪŋ/ [n singular] *Schoolchildren are taught that stories should have a beginning, a middle and an end.* | **the beginning of sth** *The beginning of the movie is very violent.* | *The author tells us who the killer is at the very beginning of the novel.*

the start /ðə ˈstɑːʳt/ [n singular] the point where a film, book, story etc begins: *I tried to read 'Tristram Shandy' but I couldn't get past the start.* | **the start of sth** *Not much happens at the start of the film – don't worry if you're late.* | *Speakers often give an overview at the start of a lecture and a summary at the end.*

the first part /ðə ˈfɜːʳst ˌpɑːʳt/ [n phrase] **the first part** of a piece of writing that has several parts, especially parts that can be studied separately: *Children will enjoy this movie, though they may be confused during the first part.* | **the first part of sth** *The first part of this textbook deals with mechanics.* | *Please turn to the first part of the report, which relates to safety matters.*

opening /ˈəʊpənɪŋ/ [n singular] the first words or phrases of a book or play which are very important because they tell you about the scene, the characters, and the writer's ideas: *After a slow dream-like opening, the play explodes into life.* | **the opening of** *The opening of Charles Dickens' 'Bleak House' describes a thick London fog.*

7 something that comes at the beginning of a book, speech etc

- introduction
- preamble
- prologue
- preface

introduction ALSO **intro** informal /ˌɪntrəˈdʌkʃən, ˈɪntrəʊ/ [n C] a short explanation, description, or discussion at the beginning of a book, piece of music etc: *After an introduction by the chairperson, we'll get on with the day's discussions.* | *None of us know anything about this subject, so we'd appreciate it if you give us a brief intro before you start.* | *The drummer gave a four-bar intro before the other musicians joined in.* | **+ to** *In the introduction to her fascinating book, O'Brien explains how she first became interested in music.*

preamble /priːˈæmbəl‖ˈpriːæmbəl/ [n C] an introduction to a speech or piece of writing, especially one that is boring or too long: *There's a big difference between the document's lengthy preamble and the actual content.*

prologue /ˈprəʊlɒg‖-lɔːg, -lɑːg/ [n C] an introduction to a piece of writing, for example a play or a long poem: *The brief prologue sets the scene for what is to follow.* | **+ to** *In his prologue to 'Faust', Goethe said some very interesting things about art.*

preface /ˈprefɪ̱s/ [n C] a part of a book that comes before the main part and explains what it is about: *This edition contains a new preface by the author.* | **+ to** *Murray agreed to write the preface to Baker's book, as a favor to his old friend.*

behave

RELATED WORDS

- someone who behaves badly *see* **bad (5-10)**
- someone who behaves well *see* **good (8-15)**
- to react to someone or something in a particular way *see* **react**
- the way that someone behaves *see* **way (7-8)**
- *see also* **polite, rude, sensible, stupid, conventional**

1 to behave in a particular way

- behave
- act
- be
- conduct yourself
- react

behave /bɪˈheɪv/ [v I] the way someone **behaves** is the things that they do and say, and the effects these things have on other people: *How does Sam behave at school?* | **+ towards** *William was behaving very strangely towards me.* | **behave well/badly/unreasonably etc** *I'm not going to talk to him until he starts behaving reasonably.* | **+ like** *Oh, be quiet! You're behaving like a two-year-old.* | **+ as if** *The next time I saw him, Frank behaved as if nothing had happened.*

act /ækt/ [v I] to behave in a particular way, especially in a way that seems unusual, surprising, or annoying to other people **+ like** *He has been accused of acting like a dictator.* | **+ as if** *She acts as if she owns the place and we're her servants.* | **act strangely/strange/stupid etc** *Tina's been acting very strangely lately.* | *You're acting stupid and I don't want to talk to you anymore.*

be /biː/ [v] **be rude/helpful/silly etc** to behave in a rude, helpful, silly etc way: *Don't be so rude!* | *The waiter was really friendly and helpful.* | *Stop being silly!* | *Why is she being so nice to us?*

conduct yourself /kənˈdʌkt jɔːʳˌself/ [v phrase] to behave in a particular way, especially in a situation where people will notice and judge the way you behave: *Public figures have a duty to conduct themselves responsibly, even in their private lives.* | *By the end of the course, you should be able to conduct yourself with confidence in any meeting.*

react /riˈækt/ [v I] to say or do something because of what another person has said or done, or because of something that has happened: *How did she react when you told her the news?* | **react angrily/violently/calmly** *Ned reacted angrily to Bill's comments.*

2 to behave well

- behave
- well-behaved
- good
- be on your best behaviour
- stay out of trouble
- keep your nose clean
- orderly

behave /bɪˈheɪv/ [v I] especially spoken to do what people tell you and not cause any trouble – use this especially about children: *If you two don't behave, I'm taking you straight home.* | **behave yourself** (=behave well) *Make sure you behave yourselves when we visit Grandma.*

well-behaved /ˌwel bɪˈheɪvd◂/ [adj] someone who is **well-behaved** does not cause any trouble and does what other people tell them to do – use this especially about children, pets, or large groups of people: *Can I bring my dog? She's very well-behaved.* | *a well-behaved child* | *The crowd was noisy but well-behaved.*

good /gʊd/ [adj] if a child is **good**, he or she does not cause trouble and does what he or she is told to do: *I was always very good at school.* | *He's a good little boy.* | **be good!** (=used to tell a child to behave well) *Bye now, Jessie. Be good.*

be on your best behaviour British **/behavior** American /biː ɒn jɔːʳ ˌbest bɪˈheɪvjəʳ/ [v phrase] to make a special effort to behave well by doing and saying the right things and being very polite, because you know other people are watching you: *Dinner was very formal, with everyone on their best behaviour.*

stay out of trouble /ˌsteɪ aʊt əv ˈtrʌbəl/ [v phrase] to try not to behave badly, especially because you do not want to be noticed or caught: *Have a good time, boys, but try to stay out of trouble.* | *If I stay out of trouble till June, my parents will take me to Florida.*

keep your nose clean /ˌkiːp jɔːʳ ˈnəʊz ˌkliːn/ [v phrase] informal to behave well, especially by not doing anything wrong or illegal: *It's not a great job, but if you keep your nose clean, you should be promoted by the end of the year.* | *He's been sentenced to seven years in prison, but he'll be out in four if he keeps his nose clean.*

orderly /ˈɔːʳdəʳli/ [adj] **an orderly crowd/demonstration/march etc** well-behaved and not violent or out of control: *Police said it was an orderly demonstration and there were no arrests.* | *The crowd were orderly and in good spirits.*

3 to behave badly

- behave badly
- badly behaved
- misbehave
- get into trouble
- be up to no good
- act up
- mess around
- try it on
- step out of line

behave badly /bɪˌheɪv ˈbædli/ [v phrase] to be rude, unhelpful, or unpleasant and not do what you are told to do: *I knew I'd behaved very badly, and I was sorry.* | *The kids behaved so badly that I was embarrassed.*

badly behaved /ˌbædli bɪˈheɪvd/ someone who is **badly behaved** behaves badly – use this especially about children: *The hotel was full of badly behaved celebrities.*

misbehave /ˌmɪsbɪˈheɪv/ [v I] if children **misbehave**, they deliberately behave badly by being noisy, rude etc: *Kids often misbehave when they are bored or tired.* | *We never dared to misbehave in Miss Dill's classes.*

get into trouble /ˌget ɪntə ˈtrʌbəl/ [v phrase] if someone **gets into trouble**, they do something that is illegal or against the rules, especially something not very serious, and get caught doing it: *Tony is always getting into trouble at school.* | *Don't copy my work or we'll both get into trouble.* | **+ with** *He first got into trouble with the police at the age of 15.*

be up to no good /biː ˌʌp tə nəʊ ˈgʊd/ [v phrase] if someone **is up to no good**, they are secretly doing something that they should not do – use this especially when you think someone may be doing something bad, but you are not completely sure: *She knew that her brother was up to no good but she didn't tell anyone.*

act up ALSO **play up** British /ˌækt ˈʌp, ˌpleɪ ˈʌp/ [phr v I] informal to behave badly by being very active and noisy – use this especially about children: *During his parents' divorce, Robert began acting up in class.* | *The kids have been playing up all afternoon. They're driving me mad.*

mess around ALSO **muck about** British /ˌmes əˈraʊnd, ˌmʌk əˈbaʊt/ [phr v I] informal to behave in a silly way when you should be working or paying attention: *Stop messing around and pay attention!* | *They just mucked about all afternoon and went home early.* | **+ with** *Paul blew off his fingers messing around with homemade rockets.*

try it on /ˌtraɪ ɪt ˈɒn/ [v phrase] British informal to behave badly in order to find out how bad you can be before someone gets angry with you or punishes you: *For your first few days' teaching, the kids will probably try it on just to see how you react.* | *At home she's allowed to tell everyone what to do, but she wouldn't dare try it on at work.*

step out of line /ˌstep aʊt əv ˈlaɪn/ [v phrase] to behave badly by breaking rules or disobeying orders, especially in a situation where everyone is expected to be very obedient: *The prisoners were warned that if they stepped out of line they would be severely punished.* | *The boss is very tough on anyone who steps out of line.*

4 to start to behave better

- mend your ways
- turn over a new leaf
- clean up your act
- straighten up
- a reformed character
- go straight

mend your ways /ˌmend jɔːʳ ˈweɪz/ [v phrase] to change the way you behave, and start being obedient, hard-working etc, after behaving badly for a long time: *It's possible the college might take you back, but first you'll have to convince them you've mended your ways.* | *If he doesn't mend his ways he'll be in jail by the time he's eighteen.*

turn over a new leaf /ˌtɜːʳn əʊvər ə ˌnjuː ˈliːf‖-ˌnuː-/ [v phrase] to decide that you will change the way you behave, because you really want to stop behaving badly, breaking the law etc: *I know I've done some bad things in the past, but now I'm turning over a new leaf.* | *After being released from jail, Tony decided to turn over a new leaf.*

clean up your act /ˌkliːn ʌp jɔːr ˈækt/ [v phrase] to start behaving better after a situation in which people did not trust you because you were behaving illegally or dishonestly: *She told her son to clean up his act or move out.* | *Tish has really cleaned up her act – she doesn't drink or smoke pot any more.*

straighten up /ˌstreɪtn ˈʌp/ [phr v I] American to start to behave well after you had been behaving badly: *You'd better straighten up or you'll never make it out of high school.*

a reformed character /ə rɪˌfɔːʳmd ˈkærəktəʳ/ [n singular] British someone who has changed completely and no longer behaves badly or does things they should not do – often used humorously: *'Does Alex still drink as much as he used to?' 'No, he's a reformed character now.'*

go straight /ˌɡəʊ ˈstreɪt/ [v phrase] to stop being a criminal and decide to obey the law and live an honest life: *He's been going straight for about six months now.* | *You can't expect these people to go straight when no one's ever going to give them a job.*

5 the way someone behaves

- behaviour
- manner
- conduct
- antics
- demeanour

behaviour British **/behavior** American /bɪˈheɪvjəʳ/ [n U] the way someone behaves: *His behaviour in school is beginning to improve.* | *That kind of behavior is not acceptable.* | **+ towards** *Eric's behaviour towards his family surprised me.*

manner /ˈmænəʳ/ [n singular] the way someone behaves when they are talking to or dealing with other people: *The driver's manner was very unfriendly.* | *She impressed everyone with her businesslike manner.*

conduct /ˈkɒndʌkt‖ˈkɑːn-/ [n U] the way someone behaves in public, in their job etc, especially in matters where moral principles are involved – used especially in legal or official contexts: *A middle-aged banker has been fined £200 for violent conduct on a train.* | *The Medical Committee found the doctor guilty of unethical conduct towards three of his patients.* | **code of conduct** (=rules of professional behaviour) *A new code of conduct for civil servants will be issued next week.*

antics /ˈæntɪks/ [n plural] behaviour that some people think is stupid or not responsible but other people think is funny: *The Queen is said to disapprove of the antics of some of the younger members of the Royal Family.*

demeanour British **/demeanor** American /dɪˈmiːnəʳ/ [n U] the way someone looks and behaves, that gives you a general idea of their character: *He was a small round man with a cheerful demeanor.* | *When you mention Polly's ex-husband, her entire demeanour changes.*

6 to behave towards someone in a particular way

- treat
- behave towards
- handle
- deal with

treat /triːt/ [v T] to behave towards someone or deal with someone in a particular way **treat sb well/badly** *Amy's treated him really badly – no wonder he's upset.* | **treat sb like sb/sth** *I'm sick of my parents treating me like a child.* | **treat sb like dirt** (=treat someone very badly) *I don't know what she sees in him – he treats her like dirt.* | **treat sb with respect/contempt/kindness etc** *Douglas was treated with much more respect after his promotion.* | **treat sb with kid gloves** (=be very careful how you deal with someone so that they do not become upset, angry etc.) *After my nervous breakdown, everyone kept treating me with kid gloves.*

behave towards British **/toward** American /bɪˈheɪv təˌwɔːʳd(z)/ [v phrase] to behave in a particular way when you are with someone: *Sometimes he behaves very strangely towards me.*

handle /ˈhændl/ [v T] especially British to treat someone in a particular way in order to avoid problems and to get them to do what you want: *I knew I would have to be very careful how I handled Odette – she was so emotional.* | *Francis is a natural leader. He's very good at handling people.*

deal with /ˈdiːl wɪð/ [phr v T] to treat someone in a particular way, especially someone who has a problem or someone who has behaved very badly: *There's only one way to deal with naughty children and that's to be strict with them.* | *The police received training in how to deal with families of crime victims.* | *I try to deal with everyone in an honest, ethical way.*

7 the way you treat someone else

- treatment
- behaviour towards sb

treatment /ˈtriːtmənt/ [n U] the way that a person, organization etc treats someone: *Harper described the treatment he had received in prison.* | **+ of** *We're shocked by the government's treatment of young homeless people.* | **special/preferential treatment** (=when one person is treated better than everyone else) *Although I was the boss's daughter, I didn't get preferential treatment.*

behaviour towards sb British **/behavior toward sb** American /bɪˈheɪvjəʳ təˌwɔːʳd(z) (sb)/ [n phrase] the way in which one person behaves towards someone else: *Your behaviour towards Lilly was disgusting.* | *I was confused by her behavior toward me – one minute she was cold and unfriendly, the next she was all smiles.*

behind

RELATED WORDS

opposite: —— **front**

- the back of something *see* **back (4-8)**
- behind someone in a race, competition etc *see* **lose (5)**

1 at the back of something and usually hidden by it

- **behind**
- **at the back**
- **at/to the rear**
- **round the back**

behind /bɪˈhaɪnd/ [prep/adv] at or towards the back of something, and often hidden by it: *The sun went behind a cloud.* | *Put a cushion behind you. You'll feel more comfortable.* | *I got stuck behind a truck on the way to the airport.*

at the back British **/in (the) back** American /ət ðə ˈbæk, ɪn (ðə) ˈbæk / [prep] behind something, especially a building: *There's a small garden at the back.* | *You can park your car in back.* | *Their house has a pool in the back.* | **+ of** *The tennis courts were at the back of the main school building.*

at/to the rear /ət, tə ðə ˈrɪəʳ/ [prep] written behind something, especially something large **+ of** *They parked in a small carpark at the rear of the hotel.* | *To the rear of the house is an old shed.*

round the back /ˌraʊnd ðə ˈbæk/ [prep] British informal to or in a place behind a building: *We need to go round the back. I don't have keys to the front door.*

2 the area behind the things or people in a picture, on a stage etc

- **background**
- **in the background**
- **backdrop**

background /ˈbækgraʊnd/ [n C] the area behind someone or something in a picture, on a stage etc: *The invitations had red lettering on a white background.* | **against a background** *The flag's five orange stripes stand out against a silver background.*

in the background /ɪn ðə ˈbækgraʊnd/ [adv] if someone or something is **in the background**, it is behind the place where the main activity is happening: *In the photograph, a statue of St. Andrew stood in the background.* | *Palm trees swayed in the background.* | *While I was on the phone with Julie, I could hear the sound of a television in the background.*

backdrop /ˈbækdrɒp‖-drɑːp/ [n C usually singular] the things such as buildings, hills or mountains that are behind something that you are looking at: *The snow-covered Rocky Mountains made a wonderful backdrop for the concert.*

believe

- to believe that someone is able to do something and can be trusted *see* **trust**
- words for describing strong beliefs *see* **strong (6)**
- *see also* **sure/not sure, think, opinion, true, lie, religion, moderate, extreme**

1 to believe that something is true

- **believe**
- **accept**
- **take sb's word for it**
- **give sb the benefit of the doubt**
- **take sth on trust**
- **take/accept sth at face value**
- **buy**

believe /bəˈliːv/ [v T not in progressive] to be sure that something is true or that someone is telling the truth: *Did the police believe his story?* | *I told them I didn't do it, but no one believed me.* | *You shouldn't believe everything you read in the papers.* | **+ (that)** *People used to believe that the sun moved around the earth.* | **believe it or not** (=it may be hard to believe this) *I asked them for a $10,000 loan, and believe it or not they said yes.* | **firmly/strongly believe** *I firmly believe that we are responsible for what happens to us in our lives.*

accept /əkˈsept/ [v T not in progressive] to believe something because someone has persuaded you to believe it: *I finally accepted the fact that I would die if I didn't stop smoking.* | *She succeeded in persuading the jury to accept her version of the events.* | **+ that** *She'll never accept that her husband has been unfaithful.* —**acceptance** [n U] *The late nineteenth century saw an increasing acceptance of Darwin's theories.*

take sb's word for it /ˌteɪk (sb's) ˈwɜːʳd fər ɪt/ [v phrase] to believe what someone tells you even though you have no proof of it: *When he told me he'd been in the army, I took his word for it.* | *'Do you want to check for yourself?' 'No, I'll take your word for it.'*

give sb the benefit of the doubt /ˌgɪv (sb) ðə ˌbenəfɪt əv ðə ˈdaʊt/ [v phrase] to believe what someone says even though you think they might not be telling the truth: *Something didn't seem quite right, but I decided to give him the benefit of the doubt.* | *She claimed she wasn't trying to commit suicide, and doctors gave her the benefit of the doubt.*

take sth on trust /ˌteɪk (sth) ɒn ˈtrʌst/ [v phrase] to accept that what someone tells you is true without asking for any proof, because you have decided to trust them: *I'm afraid I can't let you see the letter, so you'll just have to take what I'm saying on trust.* | *He said he'd never been in trouble before, which I was content to take on trust.*

take/accept sth at face value /ˌteɪk, əkˌsept (sth) ət ˌfeɪs ˈvæljuː/ [v phrase] to believe what someone says or what you read, without thinking that it may have another meaning: *Netta accepted Amelia's explanation at face value and didn't ask any more questions.* | *The letter, if we take it at face value, suggests that Richard is quite happy in his job.*

buy /baɪ/ [v T] informal to believe a reason or explanation, especially one that is not very likely to be true – use this especially in negatives and questions: *We could tell him it was an accident, but he'd never buy it.* | *'He said he was with friends last night.' 'Are you going to buy that?'*

2 to believe something that is not true

- swallow
- fall for
- be taken in
- gullible
- hook, line, and sinker

swallow /ˈswɒləʊ‖ˈswɑː-/ [v T] to believe a story, explanation etc that is not actually true, in a way that makes people think you are stupid: *You mean to tell me you swallowed a story like that?* | *Her explanation of where the money went is a little hard to swallow.* | **swallow sth whole** (=completely believe it) *The company has been telling lies for years, but local media has swallowed them whole.*

fall for /ˈfɔːl fɔːʳ/ [phr v T] to believe something that is not true, that someone tells you to trick you: *They told me I'd earn over a thousand dollars a week and I fell for it.* | *She should know better than to fall for that old excuse.*

be taken in /biː ˌteɪkən ˈɪn/ [v phrase] to believe that someone is telling the truth, when in fact they are lying in order to trick you: *He told me that it was a genuine diamond, and I was completely taken in.* | **+ by** *Don't be taken in by products claiming to make you lose weight quickly.*

gullible /ˈɡʌl$_{\vartheta}^{\text{I}}$bəl/ [adj] too willing to believe what other people tell you, so that it is easy to cheat you: *How can you be so gullible! He's not really French.* | *He seemed to treat me as if I were a gullible schoolgirl.*

hook, line, and sinker /ˌhʊk ˌlaɪn ənd ˈsɪŋkəʳ/ [adv] if you believe something **hook, line, and sinker**, you believe it completely even though it is so silly that it could not possibly be true: *What an idiot! He believed the whole story hook, line, and sinker!* | *The people seem to have swallowed the government's promises hook, line, and sinker.*

3 when you do not believe something

- not believe
- disbelieve
- doubt
- take sth with a pinch of salt
- disbelief
- sceptical
- cynical
- incredulous

not believe /nɒt bɪˈliːv/ [v T not in progressive] to **not believe** that something is true or that someone is telling the truth: *She doesn't believe anything he tells her.* | *I told her it was an accident, but she didn't believe me.* | **+ (that)** *I don't believe you meant half the things you said.* | **not believe a word of it** (=not believe it at all) *They say they're going to send me the money, but I don't believe a word of it.*

disbelieve /ˌdɪsbɪˈliːv/ [v T not in progressive] formal to not believe something, especially something that someone has told you: *He had nothing to gain from lying so we saw no reason to disbelieve him.* | *Kim, of course, disbelieved every word the boy said.*

doubt /daʊt/ [v T not in progressive] to think that something may not really be true or that someone may not really be telling the truth, even though you are not completely sure: *In all the years I knew him I never once doubted his story.* | *He wondered how he could ever have doubted her.* | **+ (that)** *He doubted that the car was hers because everyone knew she had no money.* | **+ whether/if** *They seriously doubted whether the letter had ever existed.* | **I doubt it** spoken *He may be able to do a good job, but I doubt it.* | **doubt very much/seriously doubt** (=think something is almost certainly not true) *She says she'll leave him, but I doubt very much that she will.* —**doubter** /ˈdaʊtəʳ/ [n C] someone who thinks that something is probably not true: *I hope to convince any doubters in the audience that our policies will work.*

take sth with a pinch of salt British **/take sth with a grain of salt** American /ˌteɪk (sth) wɪð ə ˌpɪntʃ əv ˈsɔːlt, ˌteɪk (sth) wɪð ə ˌɡreɪn əv ˈsɔːlt/ [v phrase] to not completely believe what someone says to you because you know that they do not always tell the truth: *It's best to take what he says with a pinch of salt – he's always exaggerating.* | *Every once in a while I go to a psychic, but I take everything she says with a grain of salt.*

disbelief /ˌdɪsbɪˈliːf/ [n U] the feeling that you cannot believe someone or something, especially because it is very surprising: *When people hear tragic news their first reaction is usually one of disbelief.* | *My story was met with a mixture of disbelief and contempt.* | **do sth in disbelief** *I stared at him in utter disbelief.*

sceptical ALSO **skeptical** American /ˈskeptɪkəl/ [adj] someone who is **sceptical** about something is not sure whether it is true, or does not really believe it: *When I started this investigation I was sceptical.* | *His attitude towards all religion is sceptical.* | **+ about** *I wish him luck, but I'm skeptical about his chances of success.* —**scepticism** also **skepticism** /ˈskeptɪsɪzəm/ American [n U] *His latest theories have met with a lot of scepticism.* —**sceptic** also **skeptic** American [n C] *There are a lot of skeptics out there, but I think the women's basketball program will be a success.*

cynical /ˈsɪnɪkəl/ [adj] someone who is **cynical** is not willing to believe that people have good or honest reasons for doing something: *I think movie stars just do charity work to get publicity – but maybe I'm too cynical.* | *an author with a cynical view of life* | **+ about** *Since her divorce, she's become very cynical about men.* —**cynicism** /ˈsɪnɪsɪzəm/ [n U] *The public's cynicism about politics is at an all time high.* —**cynic** [n C] *Cynics say that Christmas is nothing more than a way for stores to make money.*

incredulous /ɪnˈkredjʊləs‖-dʒə-/ [adj] unable to believe something because it is so surprising that it seems impossible: *Everyone looked incredulous when I said I used to drive a taxi.* | *'A millionaire!' she was incredulous. 'Like hell he is!'* | *The announcement was met by incredulous laughter.*

4 what you say to someone when you do not believe them

- you're kidding/you're joking
- come off it
- yeah, right
- (a) likely story
- pull the other one
- get out of here!
- I wasn't born yesterday

you're kidding/you're joking /jɔːʳ ˈkɪdɪŋ, jɔːʳ ˈdʒəʊkɪŋ/ spoken informal say this when you are very surprised by what someone has just said and cannot believe that it is true: *They got married! You're kidding!* | *'When he sat down, the chair just collapsed.' 'You're joking.'*

come off it/come on /kʌm ˈɒf ɪt, kʌm ˈɒn/ spoken informal say this when you cannot believe what someone has said, and you think they do not really believe it themselves: *'He kind of reminds me of myself at that age.' 'Oh come off it. When you were that age all you wanted to do was have fun.'* | *Oh come on Keith – do you really expect me to believe that?*

yeah, right /jeə, raɪt/ spoken informal say this when you do not believe something that someone has said, and you think they are deliberately telling you something that is not true: *'I really wanted to come, but I overslept.' 'Yeah, right. Then why didn't you set your alarm?'*

(a) likely story /(ə) 'laɪkli ˌstɔːri/ spoken say this when you think someone is telling you something that they know is not true: *'I was going to pay the money back as soon as I saw you.' 'Yeah. Likely story!'*

pull the other one /ˌpʊl ði 'ʌðəʳ wʌn/ British spoken say this when it is very clear that someone is not telling you the truth or that they are trying to trick you: *Oh, pull the other one, John. You can't seriously expect me to believe that!*

get out of here! /get 'aʊt əv ˌhɪəʳ/ American spoken say this when you think that something is very surprising or that someone is not telling you the truth or is trying to trick you: *'I got the car for just $350 dollars.' 'Get out of here!'*

I wasn't born yesterday /aɪ ˌwɒznt bɔːʳn 'jestəʳdi‖ -ˌwɑːznt-/ spoken say this when you think someone is lying to you and you want to show them that you are not stupid enough to believe it: *You can't expect me to trust you after all the other promises you've broken, you know. I wasn't born yesterday.*

5 when something seems likely to be true

- believable
- convincing
- plausible
- credible
- have a ring of truth

believable /bə̇'liːvəbəl/ [adj] if a story, explanation etc is **believable**, you can believe it because it seems possible or likely: *The plot is believable, but the characters aren't very interesting.* | *Hardly anything they put on the news programs these days is believable.*

convincing /kən'vɪnsɪŋ/ [adj] a **convincing** explanation, argument, reason etc seems likely to be true: *I didn't find any of their arguments very convincing.* | *There is no convincing evidence that the tax cut will produce new jobs.*

plausible /'plɔːzə̇bəl/ [adj] something that is **plausible** seems reasonable and likely to be true, even though it may actually be untrue – use this especially about an explanation, excuse, or idea: *His explanation sounds fairly plausible to me.* | *I need to think of a plausible excuse for not going to the meeting.*

credible /'kredə̇bəl/ [adj] something that is **credible** can be believed because it seems likely or because you trust the person who is saying it: *Her story is completely credible – she doesn't usually exaggerate.* | *The complaint would be more credible if he could remember more specific details.* —**credibility** /ˌkredə̇'bɪlə̇ti/ [n U] *Your story lends credibility to one of the witnesses' statements* (=makes it seem credible).

have a ring of truth /hæv ə ˌrɪŋ əv 'truːθ/ [v phrase not in progressive] a story or explanation that **has a ring of truth** contains something that makes you believe it, even though it does not at first seem true: *I don't really trust her, but some of what she says has a ring of truth.* | *Lies by their nature have a ring of truth – otherwise, people wouldn't believe them.*

6 when something seems very unlikely to be true

- unbelievable
- unlikely
- improbable
- implausible
- incredible
- inconceivable
- unconvincing
- far-fetched
- preposterous
- lame

unbelievable /ˌʌnbə̇'liːvəbəl/ [adj] difficult or impossible to believe: *The things he had heard about her were almost unbelievable.* | **it is unbelievable how/that** *It's unbelievable how nasty people can be.* | *I find it unbelievable that Mr. Carey does not remember the meeting at all.*

unlikely /ʌn'laɪkli/ [adj] a story, explanation, or excuse that is **unlikely** cannot be believed because it is so unusual: *That sounds a pretty unlikely story to me!* | *Students invent all sorts of unlikely explanations as to why they can't do their homework.* | **it is unlikely (that)** *I think it's unlikely that the police had anything to do with it.* | **highly unlikely** *It's highly unlikely that Burton will be the party's nominee.*

improbable /ɪm'prɒbəbəl‖-'prɑː-/ [adj] a statement or event that is **improbable** is difficult to believe, even though it may in fact be true or may actually have happened: *The Rockets managed an improbable victory in last night's game.* | **it is improbable that** *It's improbable that she would have been so successful without famous parents.* | **highly improbable** *It's highly improbable that someone would win the lottery twice.*

implausible /ɪm'plɔːzə̇bəl/ [adj] a statement or explanation that is **implausible** is difficult to believe because it is not like the way things usually happen: *Jill says she can earn $50,000 from the job, but this is an implausible figure.* | *The idea that a virus could wipe out an entire city so quickly seems a little implausible.*

incredible /ɪn'kredə̇bəl/ [adj] something that is **incredible** is so surprising or strange that it is difficult to believe, even though it is probably true: *This factory was capable of producing an incredible 100 cars per hour.* | **it is incredible that** *It is incredible that the police still haven't caught him.*

inconceivable /ˌɪnkən'siːvəbəl/ [adj] something that is **inconceivable** is so surprising or strange that it seems you cannot believe that it could possibly happen or be true: *The amount of time and money they have wasted on the project is inconceivable.* | **it is inconceivable that** *It's inconceivable that university officials would fire someone as talented and loyal as Professor Schultz.*

unconvincing /ˌʌnkən'vɪnsɪŋ◂/ [adj] ideas, statements, and excuses that are **unconvincing** do not seem to be true or right and you cannot be persuaded to believe that they are: *Peter came to me with a rather unconvincing apology.* | *Their denial was unconvincing in view of the physical evidence linking them to the bombing.*

far-fetched /ˌfɑːʳ 'fetʃt◂/ [adj] an idea, story, or explanation that is **far-fetched** is difficult to believe because it sounds so surprising, unusual, or impossible: *The idea of travelling to other solar systems may sound far-fetched but scientists now see it as a real possibility.* | *His lawyers argue that the charges are based on a far-fetched conspiracy theory.*

preposterous /prɪ'pɒstərəs‖-'pɑːs-/ [adj] formal an idea, story, or explanation that is **preposterous** is impossible to believe because it sounds completely unreasonable: *It's a preposterous claim that the gov-*

ernment is trying to poison its citizens. | **it is preposterous that** *It is preposterous that Bruce did not know that we were there.*

lame /leɪm/ [adj] an excuse or explanation that is **lame** is difficult to believe, because the person who says it has not tried hard enough to make it sound true: *She's always got some lame excuse for being late.* | *It sounded lame but I really had lost my ticket.*

7 when you believe or do not believe that God, ghosts etc exist

- believe in
- atheist
- agnostic

believe in /bɪ'liːv ɪn/ [phr v T not in progressive] *Do your kids still believe in Santa Claus?* | *According to one survey, 94% of Americans believe in God or a universal spirit.*

atheist /'eɪθi-ɪst/ [n C] someone who does not believe in any god: *A lot of young people in England these days are atheists.* —**atheism** [n U] *Christianity still flourished there, despite the official state doctrine of atheism.*

agnostic /æg'nɒstɪk, əg-‖-'nɑː-/ [n C] someone who believes that it is impossible to be certain whether God exists or not: *She likes to keep an open mind in religious matters and so refers to herself as an agnostic.* —**agnosticism** /æg'nɒstɪsɪzəm, əg-‖-'nɑː-/ [n U] *Despite their arguments, I still saw no reason to abandon my agnosticism.*

8 something that someone believes

- belief
- faith
- superstition

belief /bɪ'liːf/ [n C/U] *We need to learn to accept people who have different beliefs from ours.* | **+ that** *Their experiments were based on the belief that you could make gold from other metals.* | **+ in** *She never lost her belief in God.* | **political/religious beliefs** *They were put in prison because of their political beliefs.* | **belief system** *People with a strong spiritual or philosophical belief system are more likely to remain healthy.* | **contrary to popular belief** (=despite what most people believe) *Contrary to popular belief, cold weather does not make you ill.*

faith /feɪθ/ [n U] a strong belief that something is true or can be trusted, especially religious belief **+ in** *It was her faith in God that helped her survive the long years in prison.* | *He places a great deal of faith in people's honesty.* | **shake sb's faith** (=make someone doubt what they believe) *The judge's decision shook her faith in the legal system.*

superstition /ˌsuːpəʳ'stɪʃən, ˌsjuː-‖ˌsuː-/ [n C/U] a belief that some objects or actions are lucky and some are unlucky, based on old ideas of magic: *Some scientists view all religion as superstition.* | **+ that** *It's an old superstition that walking under a ladder is unlucky.* —**superstitious** /ˌsuːpəʳ'stɪʃəs◂, ˌsjuː-‖ˌsuː-/ [adj] too ready to believe old-fashioned ideas about particular objects or actions being lucky or unlucky: *He won't go anywhere near the cemetery because he's so superstitious.* | *Don't listen to what she says about birds in the house being bad luck – it's just superstitious nonsense.*

9 something that someone believes that is definitely not true

- illusion
- fallacy
- myth
- delusion
- mistaken belief
- misconception
- old wives' tale

illusion /ɪ'luːʒən/ [n C] a belief or idea that is false, especially a belief in something good about yourself or about the situation you are in: *She thought he loved her but it was just an illusion.* | *Alcohol gives some people the illusion of being witty and confident.* | **+ that** *There seems to be a widespread illusion that there are no class barriers anymore.* | **under an illusion** *People had bought these houses under the illusion that their value would just keep on rising.*

fallacy /'fæləsi/ [n C] something that a lot of people believe but which is completely untrue: *The idea that a good night's sleep will cure everything is a complete fallacy.* | *It's a fallacy that all fat people are fat simply because they eat too much.*

myth /mɪθ/ [n C] something a lot of people believe because they want to believe it, not because it is based on fact: *The first myth about motherhood is that new mothers instantly fall in love with their babies.* | *It is a myth that battered women deserve or want to be beaten.*

delusion /dɪ'luːʒən/ [n C] a completely mistaken idea about yourself or the situation you are in, especially one that everyone else knows is wrong: *She now had to finally forget the dreams and delusions of her youth* | **under a delusion** *I was still under the delusion that everyone was trying to cheat me.*

mistaken belief /mɪˌsteɪkən bɪ'liːf/ [n C] a belief you have that is wrong, although you do not realize it is wrong at the time when you have it: *When I started as a teacher I had the mistaken belief that all kids are interested in learning.*

misconception /ˌmɪskən'sepʃən/ [n C] something that is not true but which people believe because they do not have all the facts or they have not properly understood the situation: *No, it's not actually true that rail travel is more expensive – that's a misconception.* | **+ that** *Employers seem to share the general misconception that young people are more efficient than older workers.*

old wives' tale /ˌəʊld 'waɪvz ˌteɪl/ [n C] a popular belief or piece of advice that has existed for a long time but which you think is stupid: *It's not true that if trees have a lot of fruit in the autumn it will be a cold winter – that's just an old wives' tale.*

bend

RELATED WORDS

▸ *see also* **fold, straight**

1 to bend something

- bend
- twist
- coil/coil up

bend /bend/ [v T] to make something have a curved shape, or to fold something at an angle, by pushing or pressing it: *Someone had bent the aerial.* | *He bent the wire into an 'S' shape.* | **bend sth back/down etc** *We had to bend the branches back so we could get through the bushes and back onto the path.*

twist /twɪst/ [v T] to bend and turn something several times, such as a piece of wire, cloth, or rope, especially in order to tie it to something or make something with it: *Laura twisted the handkerchief in her hands nervously.* | *We twisted a wire coathanger and used it to open the car door.* | **twist sth into/around/through etc** *Her long blonde hair was twisted into a knot on the back of her head.*

coil/coil up /kɔɪl, ˌkɔɪl ˈʌp/ [v I/T/phr v I/T] to wind or twist into a round shape, or to wind or twist something in this way: *The snake had coiled itself in a corner of the cage.* | **coil up sth/coil sth up** *They coiled up the rope and put it away.*

2 to bend your body or part of your body

- bend
- bend over
- bend down
- bow
- crouch
- stoop
- curl up
- double up/over

bend /bend/ [v I/T] to move your body forwards or move it downwards, so that you can lift something, touch something etc: *He bent and kissed the child on the head.* | *The doctor says no bending or lifting for at least six weeks.* | **+ across/towards** *She bent towards me and whispered in my ear.* | **bend your arm/knee/finger etc** *'Bend your knees!' shouted the ski instructor.*

bend over /ˌbend ˈəʊvəʳ/ [v phrase] to bend your body from the waist, usually in order to pick something up: *Lenny bent over to pick up the coins.* | **bend over sth** *My earliest memories are of my mother bending over my cot to kiss me goodnight.*

bend down /ˌbend ˈdaʊn/ [phr v I] to bend your body low enough to pick something up, touch the floor etc: *Sheila bent down to pick up the cat.* | *He was bending down tying his shoelaces.*

bow /baʊ/ [v I] to bend your head and upper body slightly, as a formal greeting or as a sign of respect or obedience: *Archer bowed and left the stage.* | *All the men turned and bowed as the Emperor passed.*

crouch /kraʊtʃ/ [v I] to bend your legs under you, in a sitting position, and lean forwards, especially in order to hide from someone: *I crouched behind a bush as the soldiers marched by.* | *There were six people in the clearing, crouching around the campfire.* | **+ down** *The plumber crouched down and looked under the sink.*

stoop /stuːp/ [v I] to bend down low, especially to pick something up and then stand up again: *There were two letters by the door. He stooped and picked them up.* | *She stooped and hugged the little dog.*

curl up /ˌkɜːʳl ˈʌp/ [phr v I] to lie down and bend your legs, arms, back, and neck into a circular position, so that you feel warm and comfortable: *She curled up in her bed that night, thinking of Michel.* | *The two cats curled up together in the armchair.* | *I was so tired all I wanted to do was curl up and watch TV.*

double up/over /ˌdʌbəl ˈʌp, ˈəʊvəʳ/ [phr v I] to suddenly bend your body at the waist, especially because you are laughing or in pain: *We doubled over, laughing so hard it hurt.* | **be doubled up/over with** *He was doubled up with cramps from the greasy stew.*

3 when something bends

- bend
- curl
- buckle
- warp

bend /bend/ [v I] *The branches of the tree bent over into the water.* | *I tried opening it with the knife but the blade bent.*

curl /kɜːʳl/ [v I] if a leaf or piece of cloth **curls**, it gradually bends, starting at its edges, especially as a result of heat or dryness: *I threw the letter into the fire. It curled, darkened, and then burst into flames.* | **+ inward** *The document was yellow and its edges had curled inward.*

buckle /ˈbʌkəl/ [v I] if something strong and hard **buckles**, it bends in the middle, usually because of very strong pressure or great heat: *The aluminium chair buckled under Charles's weight.* | *Windows shattered with the heat from the blaze and metal doors buckled like cardboard.*

warp /wɔːʳp/ [v I] if something made of wood **warps**, it bends and twists slightly as a result of too much heat, dryness, age etc, so that it is no longer flat or straight: *The wooden fence had warped in the hot sun.* | *To prevent the violin body from warping, there is a strong wooden brace along its whole length.*

4 easy to bend

- flexible
- pliable

flexible /ˈfleksə̇bəl/ [adj] something that is **flexible** is able to bend easily or can be bent easily, especially because it has been made like this to do a particular job: *The better tennis racquets are made out of tough but extremely flexible graphite.* | *Designers have come up with a technique for making skis more flexible.*

pliable /ˈplaɪəbəl/ [adj] able to bend without breaking or cracking: *High quality leather is firm yet pliable.*

5 not easy to bend

- stiff
- rigid

stiff /stɪf/ [adj] a substance such as cloth or paper that is **stiff** is hard and is difficult to bend: *The leaves of the plant are very stiff.* | *a stiff piece of cardboard* | **frozen stiff** *In the extreme cold my wet shoes became frozen stiff.*

rigid /ˈrɪdʒə̇d/ [adj] an object or structure that is **rigid** is strong and will not bend or change its shape: *The framework of the aircraft must be rigid yet light.* | *About a dozen large rigid plates make up the Earth's crust.*

6 when something is not straight

- bent
- twisted
- warped
- curved
- crooked
- wavy
- wiggly

bent /bent/ [adj] something that is **bent** has lost its original shape and is not flat or straight: *The nail was bent.* | *How did this spoon get bent?* | *The hinge was bent and the lid wouldn't shut properly.* | *Stand with your legs slightly bent.*

twisted /ˈtwɪstə̇d/ [adj] something that is **twisted** has been bent in many directions so that it has lost its original shape and may be impossible to recognize: *Pieces of twisted metal and rusted pipe lay scattered around the yard.* | *Investigators sifted through the twisted wreckage of the plane.*

warped /wɔːʳpt/ [adj] a wooden object that is **warped** has bent and twisted because of heat or dryness, so that it is no longer flat or straight: *The window frames on the front of the house were badly warped.* | *An old man was sweeping the warped boards of the front porch.*

curved /kɜːʳvd/ [adj] something that is **curved** has a long, smooth bend in it, usually because it has been made that way: *The knife had a heavy curved blade.* | *The temple's roof is curved, in the Thai style.* | *An airplane wing is curved on top and flat on the bottom.*

crooked /ˈkrʊkᵻd/ [adj] something such as a line, row, pipe, or tree that is **crooked** is not straight but bends sharply in one or more places: *Smoke rose out of the crooked chimney.* | *They moved down the narrow crooked streets of the old town.*

wavy /ˈweɪvi/ [adj] a line or edge that is **wavy** has smooth bends in it in a regular pattern: *A series of wavy lines appeared on the video monitor.* | *The flag's stripes are wavy and alternate in color.*

wiggly /ˈwɪgəli/ [adj] a **wiggly** line is one that has a lot of small curves in it: *She wrote with large wiggly letters.*

7 when a road, path, river etc bends

- **bend**
- **curve**
- **wind**
- **twist**
- **zigzag**
- **winding**
- **tortuous**

bend /bend/ [v I] *The road bends right then left, before passing a petrol station.* | *At the top of the hill, the path bends sharply left and enters a small woodland.*

curve /kɜːʳv/ [v I] if a road, track, coast etc **curves**, it has a long smooth bend in it **curve away/round/towards etc** *The dusty white road curved away towards the mountains.* | *a sandy beach curving gently around the bay*

wind /waɪnd/ [v I] if a road, track, or river **winds**, it has many smooth bends and is usually very long **+ through/along/around etc** *The trail winds through the hills and then down towards Ironhorse Falls.* | *Route 101 winds along the coastline for several hundred miles.* | **wind its way** *We decided to take the Blueridge Parkway, which winds its way through the Smoky Mountains.*

twist /twɪst/ [v I] if a track, road, or stream **twists** it has many sharp bends and changes direction many times **+ around/along/through etc** *The path twisted back and forth up the side of the mountain.* | **twist and turn** *The streets are narrow and twist and turn and it is not advisable to take a car up them.*

zigzag /ˈzɪgzæg/ [v I] if a road, track, or path **zigzags** it has many sharp bends going in opposite directions: *The path zigzagged from side to side through the steep gully.* | *ski routes zigzagging down the mountainside*

winding /ˈwaɪndɪŋ/ [adj only before noun] a **winding** road, river etc is long and has a lot of bends in it: *The car climbed the winding road up into the hills.* | *a quiet little town on the banks of a peaceful, winding river*

tortuous /ˈtɔːʳtʃuəs/ [adj usually before noun] a **tortuous** path, stream, road etc has a lot of bends in so that it is very difficult to travel along: *Most of the villages are accessible only by boat or along tortuous jungle trails.* | *a twisting, tortuous track through the Snake Mountains*

8 the place where something bends

- **bend**
- **curve**
- **twist**
- **kink**
- **joint**

bend /bend/ [n C] the place where something bends, especially a road or river: *The plane flew low, following the bends of the river.* | *You go around a bend and the farm is on the right.* | **sharp bend** (=a sudden extreme bend) *He rounded a sharp bend, and suddenly the deep blue Mediterranean lay before him.* | **hairpin bend** (=an extremely sharp bend) *The bus creaked slowly round the hairpin bend.*

curve /kɜːʳv/ [n C] a long smooth bend in a surface, line, or object: *From the balcony, you could see the long curve of the shoreline.* | *Morgan was killed when he lost control of his car in a curve.*

twist /twɪst/ [n C] a sudden sharp bend in something: *The path has a lot of twists and turns.*

kink /kɪŋk/ [n C] a small sharp bend in something, especially something that is straight for the rest of its length: *If there's a kink in the hose, you won't get any water.* | *There was a kink in the path just before the bridge.*

joint /dʒɔɪnt/ [n C] the place where two parts of someone's body or two parts of a machine are joined, so that they can bend at this place: *I've had a lot of pain in my joints recently, especially in my wrists and shoulders.* | *The balljoint connects the driveshaft to the gearbox.*

best

RELATED WORDS

- words meaning worst *see* **worse**
- *see also* **good, better, perfect, suitable, win**

1 better than all others

- **best**
- **greatest**
- **finest**
- **ideal**
- **top**
- **number one**
- **the**
- **ultimate**
- **optimum**
- **definitive**
- **unsurpassed**
- **record-breaking**

best /best/ [adj] better than anything or anyone else: *The best ice cream in the world is made in Italy.* | *What's the best way to cook sweet potatoes?* | **by far the best/easily the best** (=much better than any others) *It was by far the best vacation I've ever had.* | **sb's best** *I've read most of his books, but 'Mosquito Coast' is easily his best.* —**best** [adv] *What kind of wine do you like best?* | *It was the best-organized conference I've ever attended.*

greatest /ˈgreɪtᵻst/ [adj] the best and most important that there has ever been: *New Yorkers think they live in the greatest city on earth.* | *Picasso is generally regarded as the greatest artist of the 20th century.* | *Gorbachev's greatest achievement was ending the Cold War.*

finest /ˈfaɪnᵻst/ [adj] the best and highest quality, or the best and most skilful: *Hemingway was the finest American writer of his generation.* | *The Silver Pavilion is one of the finest examples of Japanese architecture.* | *Many people regard Beethoven's Fifth Symphony as his finest work.* | *The gallery's collection of early Impressionist paintings is one of the world's finest.*

ideal /ˌaɪˈdɪəl◂/ [adj] the best and most suitable: *The ideal candidate will have a degree and at least two years' experience.* | *I'm afraid the accommodation here is far from ideal.* | **+ for** *The conditions are ideal for a day's skiing.* | **+ for doing sth** *The town makes an ideal base for exploring the surrounding countryside.*

top /tɒp‖tɑːp/ [adj only before noun] the most skilful, most successful, and most famous: *He is definitely one of the world's top golfers.* | *The prize is to have your hair done at a top New York salon.*

number one /ˌnʌmbəʳ ˈwʌn/ [adj only before noun] the person who is most successful in their company or in the type of work that they do: *For three years, he was the company's number one salesman.* | *Sweden's number one model has married American actor Tommy Haines.*

the /ðiː/ [determiner] **the place/shop/person/authority etc** use this to say that something is **the** best one of its kind. Pronounce it as 'thee' instead of 'thuh': *Manhattan's East Village is the place for exciting nightlife.* | *Our guest speaker today is the authority on Chinese politics.*

ultimate /ˈʌltəmət/ [adj usually before noun] the **ultimate** person or thing is the very best of their type that there has ever been, and it is hard to believe that anything could ever be better: *Monroe was the ultimate Hollywood movie star.* | *For many people, the Rolling Stones will always be the world's ultimate rock and roll band.* | **the ultimate in** *Our first-class passengers enjoy the ultimate in luxury and service.*

optimum /ˈɒptəməm‖ˈɑːp-/ [adj only before noun] the best that can be achieved or the best for a particular purpose – used especially in scientific contexts: *The optimum temperature for producing steel is around 1200C.*

definitive /dɪˈfɪnətɪv/ [adj] the **definitive** description, study etc is considered to be the best and cannot be improved – use this about a book or piece of work that is the best of its kind: *Griffin is the author of the definitive travel guide 'France at Your Fingertips'.* | *This may be the definitive book on the Scarlatti trial.* | *Many people regard it as the definitive interpretation of 'War and Peace'.*

unsurpassed /ˌʌnsəʳˈpɑːst◂‖-ˈpæst◂/ [adj] formal if something is **unsurpassed**, nothing else has ever been better – use this about qualities or achievements: *His genius as a dramatist is unsurpassed.* | *Venice is a city of unsurpassed beauty.*

record-breaking /ˈrekɔːd ˌbreɪkɪŋ‖ˈrekərd-/ [adj only before noun] a **record-breaking** result, temperature, time etc is the highest, largest, fastest etc that has ever been achieved: *A record-breaking five hundred thousand people attended the festival.* | *Record-breaking temperatures are being forecast for the weekend.*

2 the best people or things in a group

- the best
- star
- the cream of
- elite
- the best of the bunch

the best /ðə ˈbest/ [n singular] *She was the best in her class at college.* | *I chose a Japanese camera because I wanted to have the best.* | **the best in his/her field** (=the person who knows most about a particular subject) *When it comes to cancer research, Professor Williams is probably the best in her field.*

star /stɑːʳ/ [n C] the best player in a team, the best student in a class etc: *Sonya's the class star.* | **+ of** *They're all strong players, but Laura's undoubtedly the star of the team.* | **star player/performer/student/pupil etc** *Woodward continues to be the Post's star reporter.*

the cream of /ðə ˈkriːm ɒv/ [n phrase] the small number of people who are the very best in a particular group, because they are the most intelligent or the most highly skilled: *The cream of India's scientists are being attracted abroad by highly paid jobs.* | **the cream of the crop** (=the best people or things in a particular group) *Universities such as Harvard accept only the cream of the crop.*

elite /eɪˈliːt, ɪ-/ [adj only before noun] **elite troops/group/college etc** a group of people who are the best, and most highly trained or educated: *The palace is guarded by elite troops loyal to the president.* | *In 1978 he joined the CRS, France's elite corps of riot police.* —**the elite** [n singular] *The Parachute Regiment are the elite of the British armed forces.*

the best of the bunch ALSO **the pick of the bunch** /ðə ˌbest əv ðə ˈbʌntʃ, ðə ˌpɪk əv ðə ˈbʌntʃ/ [n phrase] British informal the one that you think is the best among a group of people or things, especially a small group: *This last poem's my favorite – definitely the pick of the bunch.* | *They've come out with several good wines this year, but in my opinion the chardonnay is the best of the bunch.*

3 the best part of something

- the best part
- highlight
- the high point
- pièce de résistance

the best part ALSO **the best bit** British informal /ðə ˈbest ˌpɑːʳt, ðə ˈbest ˌbɪt/ [n phrase] **the best part** of something such as an occasion, event etc: *The best part of the movie is the ending.* | *What was the best part of your vacation?*

highlight /ˈhaɪlaɪt/ [n C] the best and most exciting part of something such as a journey, a film, or a period of time: *When I was young, Christmas was the highlight of the year.* | *We were looking forward to seeing the pyramids, which promised to be the highlight of our trip.*

the high point /ðə ˈhaɪ pɔɪnt/ [n phrase] the best part of something, or the best moment of something: *The two days we spent in Granada were the high point of our trip.* | *Winning the 1994 World Championship was probably the high point of his career.*

pièce de résistance /piˌes də reziːˈstɑːns/ [n phrase] the best and most impressive part of something that someone has made, especially a meal: *And now for my pièce de résistance – wild mushrooms cooked in red wine.*

4 when you do something better than you have ever done before

- at your best
- be on top form
- be at your peak
- be at the height of your powers

at your best /ət jɔːʳ ˈbest/ [adv] when you are **at your best** you are performing at your highest level of skill: *At his best, he's one of the most exciting tennis players in the world.* | *This recording captures Grappelli at his very best.*

be on top form /biː ɒn ˌtɒp ˈfɔːʳm‖-ˌtɑːp-/ British **/be in top form** /biː ɪn ˌtɒp ˈfɔːʳm‖-ˌtɑːp/ American [v phrase] if someone who is good at doing something **is on top form**, they are doing it as well as they can:

'Sue gave a really good speech last night.' 'Yes, she was on top form.' | If the Yankees are in top form there is no one that can beat them.

be at your peak /biː ət jɔːʳ 'piːk/ [v phrase] if someone, especially a sports person, **is at their peak**, they are at the time in their life when they are playing best, running best etc: *Long-distance runners are usually at their peak in their mid-30s. | When he was at his peak, Nicklaus was one of the best golfers there has ever been.*

be at the height of your powers /biː ət ðə ˌhaɪt əv jɔːʳ 'paʊəʳz/ [v phrase] if someone such as a great writer or musician **is at the height of their powers**, they are doing the best work of their whole life: *When Orwell wrote 'Animal Farm', he was at the height of his powers. | The film shows Jimi Hendrix, at the height of his powers, giving a brilliant version of 'All Along the Watchtower'.*

betray

to be disloyal to someone or something

RELATED WORDS

- not faithful to someone you have a sexual relationship with *see* **sex (7)**
- *see also* **loyal/not loyal, trust/not trust**

1 to betray a friend or someone who trusts you

- betray
- stab sb in the back
- sell sb down the river
- treachery

betray /bɪ'treɪ/ [v T] to be disloyal to your friends or to someone who trusts you, often causing serious harm to them as a result: *He betrayed his friends in order to save his own life.* | **betray sb to the police/government etc** (=give the police etc information about someone) *Olga's best friend betrayed her to the secret police.* | **betray sb's trust/confidence/friendship etc** (=betray someone who trusts you) *I still have bitter feelings for Robert. What can I say? He completely betrayed my trust.* | **feel betrayed** (=feel that someone you trust has betrayed you) *When I heard what she had said about me I felt angry and betrayed.* —**betrayal** [n singular/U] when someone betrays another person: *a powerful story of love and betrayal set in the tranquil world of Cambridge University | The family regard her marriage to a non-Muslim as a betrayal.* | **betrayal of sb's trust/friendship/confidence etc** *What Evans did amounts to a betrayal of the trust placed in him by the company.*

stab sb in the back /ˌstæb (sb) ɪn ðə 'bæk/ [v phrase] to betray someone who trusts you, especially someone that you work with, by saying or doing something that will cause them a lot of harm and get you an advantage: *He seems friendly, but he wouldn't hesitate to stab you in the back if he thought it would help him get your job. | Thatcher was stabbed in the back by her former friends and colleagues in the Conservative Party.* —**backstabbing** /'bækˌstæbɪŋ/ [n U] *I'm not sorry to be away from the gossip and backstabbing of the office.*

sell sb down the river /ˌsel (sb) daʊn ðə 'rɪvəʳ/ [v phrase] to betray a group of people who trusted you to help them, in order to gain money or power for yourself: *The workers were promised that they would not lose their jobs as a result of the merger. Later they found out that they had been sold down the river.*

treachery /'tretʃəri/ [n U] great disloyalty to someone who trusts you, for example by secretly tricking them, or helping their enemies: *When the king learned of his brother's treachery, he quickly ordered his execution. | After a furious argument during which he accused the prime minister of treachery, he announced that he would resign his Cabinet position.*

2 to betray your country

- betray
- collaborate
- treason

betray /bɪ'treɪ/ [v T] to be disloyal to your country, for example by helping its enemies or giving them secret information: *The former federal agent betrayed his country and gave away vital military secrets.* —**betrayal** /bɪ'treɪəl/ [n C/U] **act of betrayal** *Paisley described government plans to separate Northern Ireland from the United Kingdom as an act of betrayal.*

collaborate /kə'læbəreɪt/ [v I] to betray your country by helping its enemies when they have defeated your country and taken control of it: *Those suspected of collaborating during the occupation were tried and shot* | **+ with** *He was imprisoned in 1945 for collaborating with the enemy.* —**collaboration** /kəˌlæbə'reɪʃən/ [n U] *Newly-released records show there was extensive collaboration with the occupying army.*

treason /'triːzən/ [n U] the crime of betraying your country by helping its enemies: *Fleming was flown to Washington and tried for treason.* | **commit treason** *All five of the men will be charged with committing treason against the state.*

3 to betray your beliefs or principles

- betray
- sell out

betray /bɪ'treɪ/ [v T] to behave in a way that is completely against your beliefs or principles, so that people think you have given them up completely: *The new government has betrayed the ideals of the revolution. | Greene was denounced for betraying his Catholic beliefs and siding with the Communists.*

sell out /ˌsel 'aʊt/ [phr v I] to behave in a way that is completely against what you have said are your beliefs or principles, especially in order to get advantages for yourself in politics: *When the Socialists changed their policy on nuclear weapons they were accused of selling out. | Many of the radicals of the 1960s sold out – they became accountants and salesmen.* —**sell-out** /'sel aʊt/ [n singular] *Anti-nuclear campaigners are calling the president's acceptance of nuclear testing a complete sell-out. | The settlement of the dispute was a sell-out, leaving the miners worse off than they were before.*

4 someone who betrays their country

- traitor
- collaborator

traitor /'treɪtəʳ/ [n C] someone who helps the enemies of their country, for example by giving them secret information: *At the end of the war Mata Hari was hanged as a traitor.* | **+ to** *When he left Nicaragua for the US, he was denounced as a traitor to the revolution.* | **turn traitor** (=become a traitor) *Zaragoza turned traitor when he thought the Republicans would lose the war.*

collaborator /kəˈlæbəreɪtəʳ/ [n C] someone who helps their country's enemies, especially when the enemy has taken control of that country: *Women who were suspected of collaborating had their heads shaved in public.* | **+ with** *His father had been accused of collaborating with the CIA.*

better

RELATED WORDS

opposite: —————— **worse**

- better after an illness *see* **recover**
- to make someone better when they are ill *see* **cure**
- better than someone in a game or competition *see* **beat/defeat**
- to make someone feel better *see* **comfort**
- *see also* **best, good, improve, perfect, suitable, convenient**

1 better than someone or something else

- better
- superior
- of a higher standard/of higher quality
- beat
- a cut above
- have the edge on/over
- have an advantage over
- be more than a match for
- special

better /ˈbetəʳ/ [adj] *We could either go to Florida or California – which do you think is better?* | **+ than** *Your job is better than mine.* | *My sister is a better student than me.* | *The sales figures were better than we expected.* | **better at sth/doing sth** *Lucy's better at mathematics than I am.* | **far better/much better/a lot better** *His latest novel is far better than anything he's written before.* | **better quality** *Consumers are demanding lower prices, better quality, and a larger selection of goods.* —**better** [adv] *You can see much better from up here.* | *Ralph would be able to explain this a lot better than I can.*

superior /suːˈpɪəriəʳ, sjuː-‖sʊ-/ [adj] products, skills, or services that are **superior** are better than those that they are competing against: *Our aim is to provide our clients with a superior service at all times.* | *The company has a reputation for superior technology and customer loyalty.* | **+ to** *They claimed that a vegetarian diet was superior to a meat diet.* —**superiority** /suːˌpɪəriˈɒrɪ̈ti, sjuː-‖sʊˌpɪəriˈɔː-, -ˈɑː-/ [n U] *Its chief selling point is the undoubted superiority of its after-sales service.*

of a higher standard/of higher quality /əv ə ˌhaɪəʳ ˈstændəʳd, əv ˌhaɪəʳ ˈkwɒlɪ̈ti‖-ˈkwɑː-/ [adj phrase] written goods or services that are **of a higher standard** or **higher quality** are better than they were previously or better than goods or services of a similar kind: *In the mid-eighties, American consumers began to purchase more and more Japanese products, believing they were better value and of higher quality.* | **+ than** *Government officials are claiming that the health care available here is of a much higher standard than in neighbouring countries.*

beat /biːt/ [v T not in progressive] informal to be much better and more enjoyable than something else: *Jake's home-made burgers beat anything you can get at fast-food restaurants.* | **beat doing sth** *It's not a particularly good job, but it certainly beats being unemployed.*

a cut above /ə ˌkʌt əˈbʌv◂/ [adj phrase] informal clearly better than others of the same type: *Musicians of the time admitted that the Ellington Orchestra was a cut above all others.* | **a cut above the rest** *The first applicant we interviewed was definitely a cut above the rest.*

have the edge on/over /hæv ði ˈedʒ ɒn, əʊvəʳ/ [v phrase not in progressive] to be slightly better than something or someone else **have the edge on/over sth** *Their new laptop computer seems to have the edge on the competition.* | **have the edge on/over sb** *Having spent a year in Brazil, she hoped she would have the edge over the other language students.*

have an advantage over /hæv ən ədˈvɑːntɪdʒ əʊvəʳ‖ -ˈvæn-/ [v phrase not in progressive] to be better, more effective, and more useful than something else, especially because of a particular feature **have an advantage over sth** *The fact that this computer is so simple to use means that it has an advantage over most other systems.* | **have a distinct advantage over sth** (=have a clear advantage over something) *For certain types of work, natural wood has distinct advantages over plastics.*

be more than a match for /biː ˌmɔːʳ ðən ə ˈmætʃ fɔːʳ/ [v phrase] to be much more skilful and more successful at doing something than someone else **be more than a match for sb** *When it comes to TV debates, Senator Murphy's more than a match for any of his rivals.* | **be more than a match for sth** *The rebel army's tactics are more than a match for the nation's military forces.*

special /ˈspeʃəl/ [adj] better than something of the usual type, for example by being more enjoyable, more useful, or of higher quality: *I don't want an ordinary wedding. I want something special.* | *Of my nine gold medals, this one is the most special.* | *Some aides privately complain that the Senator receives special treatment.*

2 very much better than someone or something

- be/stand head and shoulders above
- there's no comparison
- put sb/sth in the shade
- eclipse
- be in a different league
- put sb/sth to shame
- run rings around
- be streets ahead
- leave sb standing

be/stand head and shoulders above /biː, stænd ˌhed ənd ˈʃəʊldəʳz əbʌv/ [v phrase] informal to be clearly doing very much better at something than someone else: *Winger's stands head and shoulders above every other restaurant in town.* | *Kander and Ebb are head and shoulders above the others writing for the musical theater these days.*

there's no comparison /ðeəʳz ˌnəʊ kəmˈpærɪ̈sən/ spoken use this to emphasize that one person or thing is clearly much better than someone or something else: *'Which apartment do you prefer?' 'Well, there's no comparison. The first one we saw is bigger, quieter, and has much nicer furniture.'*

put sb/sth in the shade /ˌpʊt (sb/sth) ɪn ðə ˈʃeɪd/ [v phrase] British to be so much better than others that their achievements are made to seem ordinary: *Coca Cola's prize-winning advertising campaign has put all others in the shade.* | *The generous response of the public to the disaster puts the government's contribution somewhat in the shade.*

eclipse /ɪˈklɪps/ [v T] written to be so much better than someone or something else that they are made to seem unimportant and not worth paying any attention to: *Channel 5's tremendous line-up of TV programmes has eclipsed its competitors' best efforts.* | *Eclipsed by the US champion at last year's Olympic Games, Schofield has decided to retire.*

be in a different league /biː ɪn ə ˌdɪfərənt 'liːg/ [v phrase] if someone **is in a different league**, they are so much better and more skilful than someone who does similar work that it would be stupid even to compare them: *You can't possibly compare Thomas Hardy and Wilkie Collins – Hardy is in a different league.*

put sb/sth to shame /ˌpʊt (sb/sth) tə 'ʃeɪm/ [v phrase] to be so much better than someone else that they feel slightly embarrassed by their own lack of skill or quality: *The elegant way she was dressed put the rest of us to shame.* | *Acapulco is a cosmopolitan city with a nightlife that puts Rio to shame.*

run rings around /ˌrʌn 'rɪŋz əraʊnd/ [v phrase] informal to perform with much greater skill than someone else in a competitive activity such as a sport or an argument **run rings around sb** *It's no use arguing with Sophie – she can run rings around anyone who disagrees with her.* | *Tottenham Hotspur are running rings around Arsenal in the most exciting cup final in years.*

be streets ahead /biː 'striːts əˌhed/ [v phrase] British informal to be very much better than something of the same type or than someone you are competing with **+ of** *The script is original and funny, streets ahead of any other situation comedy.* | *We don't need to worry about this year's sales figures – they're streets ahead of the competition.*

leave sb standing /ˌliːv (sb) 'stændɪŋ/ [v phrase] British to be so much better at something than other people that they cannot possibly compete successfully with you: *It seems that in this campaign the Labour candidate has left the opposition standing.* | *Julie's an excellent typist – her speed and accuracy leave the rest of us standing.*

3 to reach a higher standard than someone or something else

- do better
- outdo
- outshine
- outclass
- outstrip
- overtake

do better /ˌduː 'betəʳ/ [v phrase] *The British champion has completed the course in three minutes – let's see if his Canadian rival can do better.* | **+ than** *If you are saving 5 percent of your income each year, you're doing better than most people.* | *Harris argued that the economy is doing better than it was five years ago.*

outdo /aʊt'duː/ [v T] to do better than someone you are competing with, especially because you want to prove that you are better: *Kids always try to outdo each other in attracting the teacher's attention.* | *Western Europe and Japan managed to outdo their American competitors in some economic areas.*

outshine /aʊt'ʃaɪn/ [v T] written to be clearly more attractive, popular, or skilful than someone else: *The young Japanese violinist outshone every other musician at the concert.* | *Kelly was outstanding and outshone every other player on the field.*

outclass /aʊt'klɑːs‖-'klæs/ [v T] to perform with much greater skill or success than someone or something else: *For the third time this season, Celtic outclassed their local rivals, Rangers, last night.* | *There's never been a jet engine to outclass the Rolls Royce Avon.*

outstrip /aʊt'strɪp/ [v T] to do very much better than someone or something else, especially when the person or thing you are competing with used to be of the same standard: *The new magazine's circulation of 210,000 outstrips that of all of its closest competitors.* | *Girls are now outstripping boys in all school subjects.*

overtake /ˌəʊvəʳ'teɪk/ [v T] to develop or increase more quickly than someone or something else and become bigger, better, or more advanced than them: *The Clippers played better in the second half but couldn't overtake the Rockets and lost by eight points.* | *Some are predicting that India could overtake China as the world's most populous country before 2050.*

4 better than before

- better
- improved
- be an improvement on
- that's more like it

better /'betəʳ/ [adj] *The following day, the weather was a little better.* | **+ than** *People's general health is a lot better these days than it used to be.* | **get better** *Your Spanish is definitely getting better.* | **far better/much better/a lot better** *Angie spent last week painting her bedroom – it looks much better.* —**better** [adv] *This country's people are wealthier, healthier, and better educated than ever before.* | *Relief agencies are hoping to cope better with the famine than they did in 1990.*

improved /ɪm'pruːvd/ [adj usually before noun] better than before as a result of changes that have been made – used especially when selling or advertising a product: *Perhaps you'd like to have a look at our new improved model?* | *Garrett believes the new system will allow him to lower prices and provide improved service to customers.* | **much/greatly/vastly improved** *This vastly improved information system means that doctors can see patients' medical histories at the flick of a switch.*

be an improvement on /biː ən ɪm'pruːvmənt ɒn/ [v phrase] to be better than something similar, such as a product or method, that existed before **be an improvement on sth** *The new heating system is certainly an improvement on the old one.* | **be a big improvement on sth** *I wouldn't say it was my favorite show, but it's a big improvement on her last series.*

that's more like it /ˌðæts mɔːʳ 'laɪk ɪt/ spoken say this when something that is not happening or being done in the way that you want suddenly gets better: *Faster, faster – good, that's more like it.* | *What's wrong with this TV set? It doesn't seem to be working – ah, that's more like it.*

5 to do something better than before

- do better
- improve on/upon

do better /ˌduː 'betəʳ/ [v phrase] to reach a higher standard than you reached before: *I was convinced that many of the students could have done better if they'd tried.* | *Mark ran the distance in 30 minutes in the fall, but we're hoping he'll do better this season.*

improve on/upon /ɪm'pruːv ɒn, əpɒn/ [phr v T] to do something better than before or make it better than before, especially by working harder **improve on/upon sth** *I'm sure you could improve on your assignment if you spent a little more time on it.* | *Hughes is anxious for the chance to improve upon last year's 11th place finish.*

between

between two or more people or things

RELATED WORDS

- *see also* **middle, next to**

- **between**
- **in between**
- **among**
- **in the middle**
- **be sandwiched between**

between /bɪ'twiːn/ [prep/adv] if someone or something is **between** two or more people or things, the people or things are on either side of it: *The ball rolled between the goalkeeper's legs.* | *I had to sit between my two little brothers at dinner.* | *The house is somewhere between here and the airport.* | *Between the trees and the river, the slope was covered with beautiful daffodils.* | **halfway between** *Barnegat Books is situated on Eleventh Street, about halfway between Broadway and University Place.*

in between /ɪn bɪ'twiːn/ [prep/adv] in the space that separates two or more things or people: *She found a small pool in between the rocks.* | *Why don't you put the television in between the bookcase and the window?* | *Rachel got in between Rob and Chris for a better view.* | *The farmer knocked off the lumps of earth in between the blades of his plough.*

among /ə'mʌŋ/ [prep] in a group of people or things that are all around you: *I saw him standing among a group of students.* | *The house was hidden among the trees.* | *We helped Mom search for her wedding ring among the rocks below the boardwalk.*

in the middle /ɪn ðə 'mɪdl/ [adv] if someone or something is **in the middle**, they are in the centre of a group or row with one or more people or things on either side of them: *Cindy and Marcia sat at either end of the sofa with me in the middle.* | *Here's a photo of my brother's baseball team – that's Sean in the middle.* | **+ of** *Just over the hill we saw a pond in the middle of the pines.*

be sandwiched between /biː 'sænwɪdʒd bɪˌtwiːn‖-'sændwɪtʃt-/ [v phrase] to be between two people or things that are so close that there is not enough space to move: *I spent a very uncomfortable evening at the concert sandwiched between two very large ladies.* | *Alan got back to the parking lot only to find his car sandwiched between a pick- up and a big truck.*

big

RELATED WORDS

opposite: **small**

- a tall person *see* **tall**
- a fat person *see* **fat**
- a high building, tree etc *see* **high**
- *see also* **wide, thick, lot**

1 big objects/buildings/organizations etc

- **big**
- **large**
- **biggish**
- **bulky**
- **cumbersome**

big /bɪg/ [adj] of greater than average size: *He lives in a big house in upstate New York.* | *'Which is your car?' 'The big red one next to the wall.'* | *The wind got louder and the waves grew bigger and bigger.* | *She struggled up the hill, carrying the baby and her big black bag.*

large /lɑːʳdʒ/ [adj] big. **Large** is more formal than **big**, and is more common in written English: *On the other side of the fence there was a large bull.* | *The hotel was quite large and very cold.* | *large agricultural corporations* | *Take the larger cushion to sit on – you'll be more comfortable.* | *The largest urban areas in Britain lost population and employment in the 1950s and 60s.*

biggish /'bɪgɪʃ/ [adj] especially British, spoken fairly big, but not very big: *These chocolates cost £2 for a biggish box.* | *'What's the house like?' 'Well, it has a biggish kitchen but all the other rooms are quite small.'*

bulky /'bʌlki/ [adj] a **bulky** object is big and difficult to carry or move around, or difficult to fit into a normal-sized space: *The men were carrying bulky packages under their arms.* | *The room was full of bulky old furniture.* | *a bulky camera from the 1950s*

cumbersome /'kʌmbəʳsəm/ [adj] too big and heavy to carry or move easily: *I used to have one of those old sewing machines, but it was too cumbersome.* | *The room was dominated by an enormous, cumbersome leather armchair.*

2 very big

- **huge/enormous**
- **great**
- **great big**
- **massive**
- **gigantic**
- **colossal**
- **giant**
- **extra large**
- **be a whopper**

huge/enormous /hjuːdʒ, ɪ'nɔːʳməs/ [adj] very big and impressive: *She wears an engagement ring set with a huge diamond.* | *My grandmother was wearing an enormous hat.* | *She looked at the huge motorcycle. 'I'll never be able to ride that!'* | *There was an enormous spider in the bottom of the bath.* | *By the time of his death the company had grown into an enormous multi-national operation.*

great /greɪt/ [adj only before noun] very big and impressive – used especially in literature: *Like great sailing ships, the clouds sped across the sky.* | *As far as the eye could see, there stretched a great herd of buffalo.*

great big /'greɪt bɪg/ [adj only before noun] spoken extremely big: *They've built a great big shopping mall in the centre of town.* | *There are fish in the pool, great big ones.* | *She was given a great big bunch of flowers.*

massive /'mæsɪv/ [adj] use this about things that are extremely big and impressive, especially when they are solid and heavy: *Her house is massive.* | *The ancient temple's massive stone pillars had begun to crumble.* | *The bell is massive, weighing over forty tons.*

gigantic /dʒaɪ'gæntɪk/ [adj] much bigger than other things of the same type, often in a slightly strange or frightening way: *Gigantic waves more than 40 feet high crashed against the boat.* | *These gigantic creatures became extinct in the Jurassic period.*

colossal /kə'lɒsəl‖kə'lɑː-/ [adj] extremely and surprisingly big – used especially about structures, buildings, and other things that have been built: *There was a colossal statue of the King in the middle of the square.* | *A crane arrived, its colossal arm reaching out of the sky toward the building.*

giant /'dʒaɪənt/ [adj only before noun] use this about a plant or animal that has grown to an unusually large size, or is of a type that is always much larger than ordinary plants or animals: *Giant cabbages grew in the garden.* | *Be careful. The forest is full of giant snakes and spiders.* | *... and then this giant green monster appeared from the cave.*

extra large /ˌekstrə ˈlɑːʳdʒ◂/ [adj only before noun] use this about packets, bottles, or other products that are much bigger than the size that is usually sold: *an extra large packet of cornflakes* | *Extra large eggs are generally a better buy than medium or large.*

be a whopper /biː ə ˈwɒpəʳ‖-ˈwɑː-/ [v phrase] spoken informal to be extremely big compared to the usual size: *Look at the size of that pumpkin – it's a whopper.*

3 big places, areas, cities

- big
- large
- spacious/roomy
- be a fair size
- huge/enormous
- immense
- vast
- palatial

big /bɪg/ [adj] *The nearest big town is twenty miles away.* | *Which is bigger, Tokyo or London?* | *We've got a big park fairly near our house.* | *Germany is much bigger than Britain.*

large /lɑːʳdʒ/ [adj] use this about an area that is bigger than average size: *He lived alone on the edge of a large forest.* | *The farm buildings are spread over a large area.* | *Philip found himself in a large playground surrounded by high brick walls.*

spacious/roomy /ˈspeɪʃəs, ˈruːmi/ [adj] use this about a room, building, or car that has a lot of space inside: *The holiday villas are spacious, airy, and close to the sea.* | *Spacious and luxurious apartments are available to company employees.* | *The new Toyota saloon is both roomy and comfortable.* | *Their new apartment's very roomy.*

be a fair size /biː ə ˌfeəʳ ˈsaɪz/ [v phrase] spoken to be fairly big, especially big enough or bigger than you expect: *Braintree is a fair size but it isn't exactly a lively town.* | *I'm sure it would hold 500 cars. It's quite a fair size.* —**fair-sized** [adj only before noun] *The house has a fair-sized yard at the back and a smaller one in front.*

huge/enormous /hjuːdʒ, ɪˈnɔːʳməs/ [adj] extremely big: *Archeologists have found the remains of a huge city in the middle of the desert.* | *The drawing room looked out over a huge lawn.* | *The farm is huge, stretching for over fifteen miles.* | *The distances between cities in Russia are simply enormous.*

immense /ɪˈmens/ [adj] extremely large: *Migrating birds cover immense distances every winter.* | *60 million years ago, the whole area was an immense desert.*

vast /vɑːst‖væst/ [adj] use this about areas of land, deserts, distances etc that are extremely large and usually have very few people in them: *Vast areas of the Amazon rainforest have been destroyed.* | *Vast distances separate one isolated community from another.* | *a vast area of waste land*

palatial /pəˈleɪʃəl/ [adj] use this about houses or rooms that are extremely big and impressive: *a palatial residence with a fine collection of 18th century paintings* | *She lives in a palatial New York apartment.*

4 big people

- big/large
- huge/enormous
- well-built

big/large /bɪg, lɑːʳdʒ/ [adj] use this about someone who is tall and has a large body: *My father was a big man, with legs like tree trunks.* | *A large woman in her early 50s answered the door.*

huge/enormous /hjuːdʒ, ɪˈnɔːʳməs/ very big and tall, in a way that is impressive or frightening: *The other wrestler was enormous – he must have weighed over 250 pounds.* | *A huge policeman stood outside the gate.*

well-built /ˌwel ˈbɪlt◂/ [adj] use this about someone who is big and strong and has a lot of muscles: *He was handsome and well-built, like a Hollywood movie star.*

5 large numbers/amounts

- large
- high
- considerable/sizeable/sizable
- substantial/significant
- generous
- handsome
- hefty

large /lɑːʳdʒ/ [adj usually before noun] *She's used to working with large sums of money.* | *Large numbers of seabirds have been killed by pollution following the oil spillage.* | *A large proportion of the audience consisted of teenaged girls.*

high /haɪ/ [adj usually before noun] use this about rates, levels, measurements etc that are bigger than is usual or than is acceptable: *Someone on such a high salary shouldn't have to borrow money.* | *High levels of radiation have been reported near the nuclear plant.* | *I always try to avoid foods with a high fat content.*

considerable/sizeable/sizable /kənˈsɪdərəbəl, ˈsaɪzəbəl/ [adj usually before noun] fairly large: *£1000 is a considerable sum for most people.* | *She receives a sizable income from her investments.* | *A considerable number of voters changed their minds at the last minute.* | *Sugar is added in considerable quantities to most soft drinks.*

substantial/significant /səbˈstænʃəl, sɪgˈnɪfɪkənt/ [adj] large enough to be useful or to have an important effect: *The survey showed that substantial numbers of 15-year-olds were already smoking twenty cigarettes a week.* | **in substantial/ significant numbers** *Women began to enter the British Parliament in significant numbers in the 1990s.* | **a substantial/significant proportion of** *A significant proportion of drivers fail to keep to speed limits.*

generous /ˈdʒenərəs/ [adj] use this about an amount, especially of food or money, that is larger than what is needed or expected: *He heaped the plate with a generous serving of meat and potato pie.* | *I usually stir a generous quantity of rum into the cake mixture.* | *The company offers bonuses, stock options, and a generous benefit package.*

handsome /ˈhænsəm/ [adj usually before noun] use this about an amount of money someone gets or is paid that is surprisingly large: *Ozzie left a very handsome tip on the plate.* | *She received a handsome reward for finding the wallet.* | *The big oil companies made a handsome profit out of the fuel crisis.*

hefty /ˈhefti/ [adj only before noun] use this about a surprisingly large amount of money, especially one that someone has to pay: *The other driver received a hefty fine for his role in the accident.* | *hefty admission fees* | *It was a $350,000 contract, plus hefty bonuses and expenses.*

6 very large numbers or amounts

- huge/enormous
- vast
- massive
- colossal
- whopping

huge/enormous /hjuːdʒ, ɪˈnɔːʳməs/ [adj] *A huge number of people turned up for the demonstration.* | *Their profits are enormous.* | *Joan had very little money, and her hotel bill was huge.* | *Enormous sums of money were spent on the construction of the Channel Tunnel.*

vast /vɑːst‖væst/ [adj usually before noun] use this about an amount, number etc that is so large that it cannot be easily measured: *The refugees arrived in vast numbers from villages all along the border.* | *Vast quantities of food and drink were consumed at the wedding.*

massive /ˈmæsɪv/ [adj] extremely large: *The system is capable of recording massive amounts of information.* | *Union leaders are warning of massive job losses.* | *The sums involved are massive – over £12 billion in the first year alone.*

colossal /kəˈlɒsəl‖kəˈlɑː-/ [adj] use this about numbers or amounts, especially of money, that are extremely and surprisingly large: *Children are failing exams and dropping out of school in colossal numbers.*

whopping /ˈwɒpɪŋ‖ˈwɑː-/ [adj only before noun] spoken informal a **whopping** sum of money or number is extremely large: *He managed to get a TV celebrity to open the theatre – but at a whopping fee.* | *In the divorce proceedings, she demanded the car and a whopping two-thirds of the family business.*

7 having a big effect

- big
- major
- considerable
- great
- huge/enormous/immense
- tremendous
- large scale/large-scale

▸ *see also* **serious**

big /bɪg/ [adj only before noun] *The city has a big problem with drugs.* | *If you think I'm coming with you, you're making a big mistake.*

major /ˈmeɪdʒəʳ/ [adj only before noun] having a serious and important effect, especially on a lot of people, places, situations etc: *Heavy traffic is a major problem in most cities.* | *Think carefully before you decide on such a major undertaking.* | *Nuclear weapons are a major obstacle on the road to peace.*

considerable /kənˈsɪdərəbəl/ [adj usually before noun] formal having a fairly large or important effect: *The recent slowdown in the US economy is likely to have a considerable impact on the rest of the world.* | *There was a considerable delay in the processing of our application.*

great /greɪt/ [adj only before noun] use this to emphasize how much of an effect something has, especially a good effect: *Thanks. You've been a great help.* | *It would be of great assistance if customers could have the exact money ready.* | *I have great difficulty in reading without my glasses.*

huge/enormous/immense /hjuːdʒ, ɪˈnɔːʳməs, ɪˈmens/ [adj] use this to emphasize that something is extremely big, important, or serious: *The city of Detroit has a huge crime problem.* | *Enormous changes are taking place in the way we communicate with each other.* | *The difference between living in the country and living in the city is immense.* | *His contribution to the team's success has been immense.*

tremendous /trɪˈmendəs/ [adj] use this to emphasize how big, important, and often exciting an effect will be: *My new job will be a tremendous challenge.* | *Your advice has been a tremendous help to us.* | *It was a tremendous thrill, meeting her in person.*

large scale/large-scale /ˌlɑːʳdʒ ˈskeɪl◂/ [adj] involving a lot of money or effort, or a lot of people or places: *Large-scale development has given new life to the inner city.* | *We need large-scale investment in the industry's future.* | **on a large scale** *Developing countries will need help on a large scale for many years to come.*

8 how big something is

- size
- how big
- scale
- magnitude

size /saɪz/ [n U] *He was incredibly aggressive – it was only his size that stopped me from hitting him.* | *The sheer size of the building was amazing.* | *I hadn't realized the size of the problem until now.* | **of that size** *They shouldn't keep a dog of that size in such a small apartment.*

how big /ˌhaʊ ˈbɪg/ use this to talk about or ask about the size of something: *I'm not sure how big the house is.* | *How big do these fish grow?*

scale /skeɪl/ [n singular] the size of something such as a problem or a change, not of an object, vehicle etc **on a scale** *We were not expecting a public response on such a scale.* | **the scale of sth** *Rescue workers are trying to assess the scale of the disaster.* | *Scientists are only just beginning to realize the scale of the problem.*

magnitude /ˈmægnɪ̈tjuːd‖-tuːd/ [n U] formal **the magnitude of a problem/disaster/decision etc** how big and important or serious something is: *I cannot emphasize too strongly the magnitude of this problem.* | **of this/such magnitude** *Decisions of this magnitude should not be taken by one person alone.* | *The oil spillage in the Gulf was of such magnitude that its effects will last for decades.*

9 to become bigger

- get bigger
- grow
- expand
- swell up
- stretch

get bigger /ˌget ˈbɪgəʳ/ [v phrase] to become bigger: *The hole in the ozone layer is getting bigger all the time.* | *More workers were taken on as the organization got bigger.* | *Teachers are reporting higher stress levels as class sizes get bigger.* | **get bigger and bigger** (=continue to become bigger) *The cloud of dust and debris was getting bigger and bigger as the wind grew stronger.*

grow /grəʊ/ [v I] use this especially about amounts, organizations, and places: *Mark's business grew rapidly in the first year.* | *Tandem's annual profits grew by 24% in one year.* | *Tokyo has grown a lot over the last ten years.*

expand /ɪkˈspænd/ [v I] to become bigger in size or amount. If a business, organization, or system **expands**, it becomes bigger and more successful: *Metals expand when they are heated.* | *The universe is constantly expanding.* | *Medical insurance companies expanded rapidly during the 1980s.* | *The sports and leisure market is expanding more quickly than ever before.*

swell up /ˌswel ˈʌp/ [phr v I] if a part of your body **swells up**, it becomes larger than usual, especially because of an illness or injury: *I dropped a brick on my foot, and it swelled up like a balloon.* | *His face had swollen up because of the operation.* —**swollen** /ˈswəʊlən/ [adj] *a swollen ankle*

stretch /stretʃ/ [v I] if something such as a piece of clothing **stretches**, it gets bigger and changes its shape especially because it has been pulled: *Your jeans will stretch a little once you start wearing them.* | *The elastic stretches so that the shoe can be slipped on and off.* | *This fabric will stretch if you wash it in hot water.*

10 to make something bigger

- expand
- grow
- stretch
- blow up/enlarge
- magnify
- extend

▸ *see also* **increase, grow**

expand /ɪkˈspænd/ [v T] to make something bigger – use this especially about increasing numbers or amounts, or about increasing the size of a company or organization: *She intends to expand the company's operations in the US.* | *The university is planning to expand the number of students to over 20,000.*

grow /grəʊ/ [v T] to make a company or economy bigger and increase the amount of business that it does – used especially in business English: *All this is necessary if we are to grow the business.*

stretch /stretʃ/ [v T] to pull cloth, plastic, leather, etc so that it gets bigger and changes its shape: *Stretch the canvas so that it covers the whole frame.*

blow up/enlarge /ˌbləʊ ˈʌp, ɪnˈlɑːʳdʒ/ [v T] to make something bigger, for example a photograph or an image on a computer. **Enlarge** is more formal than **blow up**.: *That's a nice photo, why don't you get it enlarged?* | *If the opening is too small, you can always enlarge it later.* | *The new photocopier will enlarge documents by up to 100%.* | **blow sth up** *You should blow that picture up and frame it.* | **blow up sth** *This section of the print has been blown up so that the enemy's tanks can be clearly seen.* —**enlargement** [n C] *an enlargement of the wedding photo*

magnify /ˈmægnɪ̇faɪ/ [v T] to make an image or detail bigger, especially by using a microscope: *This microscope can magnify an object up to forty times.* | *The image is magnified by a series of lenses within the telescope.*

extend /ɪkˈstend/ [v T] British to make a building bigger by adding more rooms or more space: *The hotel has been recently renovated and extended.* | *We're thinking of extending the kitchen.*

bite

RELATED WORDS

▸ *see also* **eat, food**

1 to bite something

- bite
- take a bite
- bite off
- bite into

bite /baɪt/ [v T] *I sometimes bite my fingernails when I'm nervous.* | *Barry bit the corner of the packet to open it.* —**bite** [n C] *After two bites I realised the apple was rotten.*

take a bite /ˌteɪk ə ˈbaɪt/ [v phrase] to bite off a piece of food and eat it: *She took a bite of doughnut, and chewed it slowly.* | *'This looks delicious,' he said, taking a bite.*

bite off /ˌbaɪt ˈɒf / [phr v T] to remove something by biting it **bite off sth** *The dog's bitten off the heel of my shoe.* | **bite sth off** *He took out a cigar and bit the end off.* | *Kenny's favourite party trick is to bite the caps off beer bottles.*

bite into /ˈbaɪt ɪntuː/ [phr v T] to bite a piece of food **bite into sth** *Earl picked up his sandwich and bit into it.* | *Henry cracked a tooth biting into a piece of hard candy.*

2 to bite someone

- bite
- sink your teeth into
- snap at
- nip
- give sb a bite

bite /baɪt/ [v I/T] *Don't worry about the dog – he won't bite.* | *She fought off her attacker, scratching and biting him.* | **bite sb on the face/hand/leg etc** *On just the second day of the trip, I was bitten on the leg by a snake.*

sink your teeth into /ˌsɪŋk jɔːʳ ˈtiːθ ɪntuː/ [v phrase] to bite a part of someone's body very hard so that your teeth go into their flesh: *The dog leapt at him, sinking its teeth into his arm.* | *The shark sank its teeth into the soft flesh of his thigh.*

snap at /ˈsnæp æt/ [v phrase] to try to bite someone by making quick biting movements: *Sean came running around the corner of the house with a small dog snapping at his heels.* | *Every time your puppy snaps at someone, give him a smack on the butt with a rolled up newspaper.*

nip /nɪp/ [v I/T] to bite someone or something with small sharp bites, or to try to do this: *When I took the hamster out of his cage, he nipped me.* | **+ at** *A school of fish swam around her feet, some nipping at her ankles.*

give sb a bite /ˌgɪv (sb) ə ˈbaɪt/ [v phrase] especially British to bite someone, not very hard: *Don't try to pet the parrot – he could give you a really nasty bite.*

3 a wound caused by an animal or insect biting you

- bite

bite /baɪt/ [n C] *Animal bites should be treated immediately.* | *We woke up to find ourselves covered in mosquito bites.*

4 to bite something several times, especially food

- chew
- gnaw
- peck

chew /tʃuː/ [v I/T] to keep biting something that is in your mouth: *Chew your food. Don't eat so quickly.* | *Helen sat there, chewing a piece of gum.* | **+ on** *I gave the baby my key ring to chew on.*

gnaw /nɔː/ [v I/T] if an animal **gnaws** something, it bites it repeatedly in order to eat it or destroy it: *The dog lay in the yard and gnawed its bone.* | **+ at** *The cat began to gnaw at the skin of the dead snake.* | **+ through** *A rat's teeth are strong enough to gnaw through lead pipes.*

peck /pek/ [v I/T] if a bird **pecks** something, it makes quick repeated movements with its beak to try to bite it: *There was a red mark where the pigeon had pecked her hand.* | *The woodpecker's long beak is specially designed for pecking.* | **+ at** *Hens pecked at the corn scattered on the ground.* —**peck** [n C] *It takes several pecks for the chick to make a hole in the eggshell.*

blame

RELATED WORDS

- to be responsible for something bad that has happened *see* **fault**
- *see also* **accuse, criticize, tell sb off, guilty, forgive/not forgive**

1 to blame someone for something

- blame
- say it's sb's fault
- put/lay/place the blame on
- accuse
- apportion blame
- hold sb responsible
- reproach yourself
- shoot the messenger

blame /bleɪm/ [v T] to say or think that someone is responsible for something bad that has happened: *It's your idea – don't blame me if it doesn't work.* | *Everyone wants to blame the referees when their team loses.* | **blame sb for sth** *Democrats have blamed Republicans for the failure to reach an agreement.* | **blame sth on sb/sth** *Some of the women blamed their husbands' violence on drinking.* | **blame yourself** *For many years I blamed myself for her death.*

say it's sb's fault /ˌseɪ ɪts (sb's) 'fɔːlt/ [v phrase] especially spoken to say that someone is responsible for something bad that has happened: *Everyone is saying it's my fault, but I didn't have anything to do with it.* | **+ (that)** *How can you say it's my fault that you lost your job?*

put/lay/place the blame on /ˌpʊt, ˌleɪ, ˌpleɪs ðə 'bleɪm ɒn/ [v phrase] to say who you think is responsible for something bad that has happened, often unfairly or wrongly: *Don't try to put the blame on me!* | *Subsequent investigations placed the blame squarely on city officials.* | **put/lay the blame for sth on sb/sth** *Farmers have laid the blame for their problems entirely on EU policies.*

accuse /ə'kjuːz/ [v T] to say that someone is guilty of a crime or of doing something bad: *They're accusing me without any proof.* | **accuse sb of doing sth** *Are you accusing her of lying?* | *The woman was accused of having beaten her four-year-old daughter.* | **be accused of murder/armed robbery etc** *West has been accused of first-degree murder.*

apportion blame /əˌpɔːʳʃən 'bleɪm/ [v phrase] formal to officially say which people are responsible for something bad that has happened: *It is not easy for the Committee of Inquiry to apportion blame in such a complicated case.*

hold sb responsible /ˌhəʊld (sb) rɪ'spɒnsəbəl‖-'spɑːn-/ [v phrase] to say that it is someone's fault that something bad has happened because you think it was their duty to prevent this from happening: *It's your decision – you can't hold me responsible if it goes wrong.* | **+ for** *Alex still holds his mother responsible for the divorce.* | **hold sb partly/largely/entirely responsible** *The shipment never arrived, and we are holding the freight company entirely responsible.* | **hold sb personally responsible** (=blame one person only) *If anything happens to Donny, I'll hold you personally responsible.*

reproach yourself /rɪ'prəʊtʃ jɔːʳˌself/ [v phrase] to feel that something is your fault and wish that you had done more to prevent it from happening: *There's no point in reproaching yourself – there's nothing you could have done.* | **+ for** *He reproached himself for not having called the police sooner.*

shoot the messenger /ˌʃuːt ðə 'mesəndʒəʳ/ [v phrase] to become angry at someone who tells you bad news even though they are not responsible for what has happened: *If you don't listen and instead shoot the messenger, you're not going to learn about the problems you need to deal with.*

2 to be blamed for something, especially unfairly

- get the blame/get blamed
- be in the firing line
- take the blame
- take the rap
- carry the can
- take the fall

get the blame/get blamed /ˌget ðə 'bleɪm, get 'bleɪmd/ [v phrase] to be blamed for something, especially something that you did not do: *Hurry up! It's me who'll get the blame if we're late.* | *The crowds cause the problems, but the police get blamed for it.* | **+ for** *Television often gets blamed for the decline in family life.* | **+ for doing sth** *Karen got blamed for losing the deal.*

be in the firing line /biː ɪn ðə 'faɪərɪŋ laɪn/ [v phrase] if a person, group, or organization **is in the firing line**, they are publicly blamed for something bad that has happened because people think they are officially responsible: *Rail bosses are in the firing line again following last week's accident.* | *Trimble may find himself on the firing line for not responding to the escalating violence.*

take the blame /ˌteɪk ðə 'bleɪm/ [v phrase] to accept that people will blame you for something, either because it is your fault or because they think it is your fault: *The coach took the blame for his team's loss.* | **+ for** *My wife didn't want me to take the blame for something we were both involved in.* | *I took the blame for Butch because I was afraid of him.*

take the rap /ˌteɪk ðə 'ræp/ [v phrase] informal to be blamed and punished for a crime or a mistake, even if you did not do it: *I'm not going to take the rap for management's mistakes.* | **+ for** *The police will make sure someone takes the rap for this, and they don't care who it is.*

carry the can /ˌkæri ðə 'kæn/ [v phrase] British informal to be the only person blamed and punished for something that is someone else's fault as well as your own: *Alan's senior colleagues decided to let him carry the can.* | **+ for** *As chairman I was left to carry the can for a decision that made no sense and was not of my doing.*

take the fall /ˌteɪk ðə 'fɔːl/ [v phrase] American to be blamed and punished for a mistake or a crime, even if you did not do it: *He won't go to jail, he'll get one of his associates to take the fall.* | **+ for** *If you think I'm going to take the fall for the scandal just to protect the Senator, you're crazy.*

3 someone who is unfairly blamed for something

- scapegoat
- fall guy

scapegoat /'skeɪpgəʊt/ [n C] someone who is unfairly blamed or punished for something, because people want to see that someone is blamed or punished for it: *The captain was just a scapegoat. The real villains were the people in charge of the shipping company.* | *The public is looking for a scapegoat, but no one will be accused until a full inquiry has been held.*

fall guy /ˈfɔːl gaɪ/ [n C] especially American someone who is punished for someone else's crime or mistake, because people have deliberately made it look as if he or she is responsible: *Journalists asked if the Secretary of State was going be the fall guy for the President's secret arms deal.* | *Benson made it clear he does not intend to be the fall guy.*

4 to blame someone else for something that is your fault

▸ shift the blame
▸ pass the buck

shift the blame /ˌʃɪft ðə ˈbleɪm/ [v phrase] **+ onto** *You can't always shift the blame onto your secretary.* | **+ for** *Lawyers for the doctor have tried to shift the blame for the child's death onto the parents.*

pass the buck /ˌpɑːs ðə ˈbʌk‖ˌpæs-/ [v phrase] informal to try to blame someone else for a problem at work that you are responsible for: *You were in charge of that project, so don't try to pass the buck.* | **+ to** *It was his mistake but he tried to pass the buck to another manager.*

5 to prove that someone should not be blamed

▸ exonerate/clear

exonerate/clear /ɪgˈzɒnəreɪt‖ɪgˈzɑː-, klɪəʳ/ [v T] to officially show that someone who has been blamed for something is not in fact responsible for it. **Exonerate** is more formal than **clear**.: *Simmons was tried and cleared of all charges.* | *False accusations were made, but he was eventually exonerated.*

6 when people blame each other

▸ recriminations

recriminations /rɪˌkrɪməˈneɪʃənz/ [n plural] a situation in which people are blaming each other: *Family life had become unbearable for her – the arguments, the recriminations, the accusations – so she left.* | *Smith's widow and son have traded recriminations since his death in August.*

boast

to talk too proudly about your abilities, achievements, possessions etc

RELATED WORDS

opposite: — **modest**

▸ to behave in a way that attracts attention in order to impress people *see* **show off**

▸ *see also* **proud**

1 to boast about something

▸ boast
▸ brag
▸ blow your own trumpet
▸ crow
▸ name-drop

boast /bəʊst/ [v I/T] to talk too proudly about your abilities, achievements, or possessions because you want other people to admire you **+ about** *She's always boasting about how clever her children are.* | *Scott was boasting about winning the game against Melrose High.* | **+ (that)** *Hank was boasting that he could drink a case of beer by himself.* —**boast** [n C] *During the campaign, he made a ridiculous boast that 30 million new jobs would be created if he won the election.*

brag /bræg/ [v I/T] to boast in a way that annoys other people **+ about** *I wish she'd stop bragging about how rich her parents are.* | **+ (that)** *Kevin used to brag that he'd had dozens of girlfriends.*

blow your own trumpet British spoken **/horn** American spoken /ˌbləʊ jɔːr əʊn ˈtrʌmpət, ˈhɔːʳn/ [v phrase] to talk a lot about your achievements – used especially to say that you do not want to do this: *I don't want to blow my own trumpet, but it was me who came up with the idea for the project in the first place.* | *Garrison has plenty of reasons to blow his own horn – his company has just shown record profits.*

crow /krəʊ/ [v I] to boast about something you have achieved, especially when other people have been less lucky or successful **+ about/over** *Nordstrom and his supporters are still crowing about winning the lawsuit.* | *The crowd was crowing over Brazil's easy victory in the match.*

name-drop /ˈneɪm drɒp‖-drɑːp/ [v I] to frequently mention the names of famous or important people that you have met or spoken to, to make people think that you know them very well: *'I found the Prince of Wales to actually be quite witty and charming,' said Edwina, name-dropping.* —**name-dropping** [n U] *The book is full of name-dropping and gossip, but not much else.*

2 someone who boasts a lot

▸ boastful
▸ big-headed
▸ be all talk
▸ name-dropper

boastful /ˈbəʊstfəl/ [adj] someone who is **boastful** boasts a lot: *After they had drunk more wine, they started to become loud and boastful.* | *In the weeks before the game, Ogden gave a number of boastful interviews to the press.* —**boastfully** [adv] *'Yes, we just bought a new Rolls Royce,' said Jay boastfully.*

big-headed /ˌbɪg ˈhedəd◂/ [adj] British informal someone who is **big-headed** thinks that they are very important and shows this by often boasting about their abilities or achievements: *I don't want to sound big-headed, but I thought my picture was the best.* —**bighead** /ˈbɪghed/ British [n C] *Morris is a bighead; he was a bighead even before he became a supervisor.*

be all talk /biː ˌɔːl ˈtɔːk/ [v phrase] spoken if you say that someone **is all talk**, you mean that they make all their plans and their achievements seem more impressive than they really are, and people should not believe them: *Ralph's all talk. I wouldn't take him too seriously if I were you.*

name-dropper /ˈneɪm ˌdrɒpəʳ‖-ˌdrɑːp-/ [n C] someone who often mentions the names of famous or important people that they have met or spoken to, in order to make people admire them: *Anna is a distant relative of the prime minister, and she's one of the worst name-droppers I've ever met.*

body

RELATED WORDS

▸ *see also* **fat, thin, tall, strong, weak, healthy/unhealthy, disabled, exercise, move**

1 the body of a person or animal

▸ **body**

body /ˈbɒdi‖ˈbɑːdi/ [n C] your **body** is your head, arms, chest, waist, legs, feet, and all the other physical parts of you: *By the time I got home my body ached all over and I knew I was getting the flu.* | *If you don't start taking care of your body, you're going to have a heart attack one of these days.* | **the human body** *There are over 1000 muscles in the human body.*

2 the shape, size, or strength of a person's body

▸ **body** ▸ **build** ▸ **figure** ▸ **physique**

body /ˈbɒdi‖ˈbɑːdi/ [n C] the shape, size, and appearance of someone's body: *Calvin was not happy with his body, no matter how much he exercised.* | *Jane Fonda has an amazing body for a woman of her age.*

build /bɪld/ [n singular] the natural size and shape of someone's body: *You're exactly the right build for a rugby player – you've got good strong broad shoulders.* | *He looks rather like me – we both have the same build.* | **of medium/slim/large/small etc build** *The man the police are looking for is about thirty years old, blond, and of medium build.*

figure /ˈfɪgəʳ‖ˈfɪgjər/ [n C usually singular] the shape of someone's body, especially a woman's body: *When she was younger, Margaret was good-looking and charming, and had a lovely figure.* | *Susie wore a close-fitting black dress which made the most of her figure.* | **keep your figure** (=keep your body an attractive shape) *She eats enormous meals but still manages to keep her figure.* | **get your figure back** (=make your body an attractive shape again after having a baby etc) *Exercise and a sensible diet will help you get your figure back after having a baby.*

physique /fɪ̈ˈziːk/ [n singular] the shape of someone's body, especially a man's body – used especially to say how strong they look: *William was tall and handsome and had a slim, muscular physique.* | *Brad had a superb physique and the looks of a young Marlon Brando.*

3 a part of the body

▸ **part of the body** ▸ **body** ▸ **torso** ▸ **limb** ▸ **organ**

part of the body /ˌpɑːʳt əv ðə ˈbɒdi‖-ˈbɑːdi/ [n phrase] *The cancer may have spread to other parts of her body.* | *More heat is lost through the head than through any other part of the body.* | *Each exercise is designed to build up muscles in a different part of your body.*

body /ˈbɒdi‖ˈbɑːdi/ [n C] someone's **body**, not including the head, legs, or arms: *Mr Price's long body and short arms and legs gave him a rather strange appearance.* | *The black widow spider has red-orange markings on its body.* | *Baby monkeys cling to their mothers' bodies until they are old enough to start climbing by themselves.*

torso /ˈtɔːʳsəʊ/ [n C] the main part of a person's body, but not including the head, arms, or legs: *Kevin liked to walk around the house in nothing but a pair of jeans, showing off his muscular torso.* | *The search led to the discovery of a headless torso in the woods.*

limb /lɪm/ [n C] formal an arm or a leg: *When babies are born they have very little control over their limbs.* | *Hundreds of children have lost limbs after stepping on mines.* | *The calf stood up slowly, with trembling limbs and took its first, uncertain steps.*

organ /ˈɔːʳgən/ [n C] a part of a body, for example the heart or lungs, that does a particular job: *The liver is an extremely complex organ.* | *This diagram shows the position of the main organs of speech.* | **vital organs** (=the most important organs such as the heart) *Her vital organs are intact and she has a good chance of recovery.*

4 the body of a dead person or animal

▸ **body** ▸ **corpse** ▸ **remains** ▸ **ashes**

body /ˈbɒdi‖ˈbɑːdi/ [n C] the **body** of someone who has recently died: *Police found the body of a young boy in Epping Forest last night.* | *The woman fell to her knees beside her son's body and began crying and wailing.* | *The bodies of the two soldiers were buried with full military honors at Arlington National Cemetery.* | **dead body** *The first time I ever saw a dead body was at my grandfather's funeral.*

corpse /kɔːʳps/ [n C] the body of a dead person, used when you consider the body as an object and not as a person: *Thieves are digging up corpses in order to steal jewellery and gold teeth.* | *The streets were filled with the stench of decaying corpses.*

remains /rɪˈmeɪnz/ [n plural] the parts of someone's body that remain after they die, especially after their body has been dead for a long time: *They found the remains of a young woman under the floor boards.* | *These rocks contain the fossilised remains of extinct animals.* | *The architect's remains are interred in St Paul's cathedral.*

ashes /ˈæʃɪ̈z/ [n plural] the white powder that is left after a body has been burned as part of a funeral ceremony: *They burned Gandhi's body and scattered the ashes on the waters of the Jumna river.* | *Kay kept her father's ashes in an urn on the mantelpiece.*

5 relating to the body

▸ **physical** ▸ **bodily**

physical /ˈfɪzɪkəl/ [adj] relating to the body, not the mind: *Your son appears to be in good physical health.* | *She has suffered terrible physical as well as emotional abuse for over 12 years.* | *A lot of British people avoid physical contact with strangers.* | *Man's primary needs are physical – food, drink and sleep.* | **physical fitness** *Nearly three quarters of the women surveyed said they were satisfied with their physical fitness.* —**physically** [adv] *At the end of the race she was completely exhausted, both mentally and physically.* | *At the age of 70 he's still physically very active.*

bodily /ˈbɒdəli‖ˈbɑː-/ [adj only before noun] relating to the body or produced by the body **bodily fluids** *Albert agreed to turn over samples of his hair and bodily fluids to the court.* | **bodily harm** (=damage to the body) *Parretti had a lengthy criminal record that included fraud and conspiracy to commit bodily harm.* | **perform your bodily functions** (=go to the toilet, wash yourself etc) *The villagers have to go down to the lake to perform most of their bodily functions.*

books

RELATED WORDS

- part of a book *see* **part (3)**
- *see also* **read, write, story, newspapers**

1 a book

- **book**
- **paperback**
- **hardback**
- **best-seller**

book /bʊk/ [n C] *I think Muriel Spark is a great writer, I love her books.* | *What book are you reading at the moment?* | **+ by** *a book by Charles Dickens* | **+ about** *I'm reading a book about a little girl who was a slave in 19th century Atlanta.* | **book on sth** (=a book giving information about a particular subject) *Do you have any books on astronomy?* | **book of sth** (=a book containing several examples of the same kind of writing) *She wrote a book of short stories, but it never got published.* | **library book** (=a book that you borrow from a library) *I went and got a library book about it.* | **secondhand book** (=a book that has already been owned by someone else) *a secondhand book dealer*

paperback /ˈpeɪpəʳbæk/ ALSO **softback** /ˈsɒftbæk‖ˈsɔːft-/ [n C] a book with a cover made of stiff paper: *Usually the hardback comes out first and the paperback comes out after.* | *a softback romantic novel* | **in paperback** (=published as a paperback) *The two books you need for the regular assignment are both inexpensive and in paperback.*

hardback /ˈhɑːʳdbæk/ [n C] a book with a hard cover: *The hardback version spent three weeks on the Times bestseller list.* | **in hardback** (=published as a hardback) *The book is published by HarperCollins, and costs $15 in hardback and $4.95 in paperback.*

best-seller /ˌbest ˈseləʳ/ [n C] a very popular book that a lot of people buy: *Already a best-seller in Japan, Quovis comes out in English later this year.* | *Her book has been an international best-seller for over a decade.* | *Nader's book, 'Unsafe at Any Speed', became a surprise best-seller.* | **best-seller list** (=an official list of books that people are buying the most) *J K Rowling's 'Harry Potter' books were number one on the best-seller list for months.*

2 a book about imaginary people and events

- **novel**
- **fiction**
- **literature**
- **science fiction**
- **whodunnit**
- **thriller**
- **short story**

novel /ˈnɒvəl‖ˈnɑː-/ [n C] a book about people and events that the writer has imagined: *The new Sidney Shelton novel is to be adapted for film later in the year.* | *This is the study where Hemingway wrote the legendary novels 'Death in the Afternoon' and 'For Whom the Bell Tolls'.* | **+ by** *The movie is based on a novel by Anne Tyler.* | **historical novel** (=about people and events in the past) *Butler has also written several historical novels under the pen-name of Jenny Melville.* | **romantic novel** (=about love) *Johnston's nudes look like cover art for romantic novels.* | **first/debut novel** (=the first novel that someone writes) *Keller's debut novel is about a Korean woman who was sold into prostitution during World War II.*

fiction /ˈfɪkʃən/ [n U] books about imaginary people and events: *His first novel won a prize for modern fiction.* | *I'm taking a class in Victorian fiction.* | **romantic fiction** (=about love) *This small band of women writers dominated the romantic fiction market for a number of years.* | **historical fiction** (=about people and events in the past) *Anthony's first books were historical fiction.* | **crime/detective fiction** *Why is Miami such a ripe setting for crime fiction?* | *Chandler remains the greatest exponent of detective fiction.*

literature /ˈlɪtərətʃəʳ‖-tʃʊər/ [n U] books, plays, and poems, especially famous and serious ones that people think are important: *the Nobel Prize for Literature* | *She is a professor of language and literature at Arizona State University.* | *Mitterrand's oratory and writings displayed a wide grasp of history, philosophy, religion and literature.* | **French/Hispanic/Hebrew etc literature** *I teach Japanese literature.* | *She's studying European literature at the University of Illinois.*

science fiction /ˌsaɪəns ˈfɪkʃən/ [n U] ALSO **sci-fi** /ˌsaɪ ˈfaɪ◂/ informal stories about things that happen in the future or in other parts of the universe: *Science fiction is often wrongly regarded as a 'lesser' form of literature.* | *Joanne says she is not a fan of science fiction, and has never read her husband's book.* | *Such developments sound like science fiction, but they're not.* —**science fiction** [adj] **science fiction writer/movie/book etc** *the sci-fi writer William Gibson*

whodunnit /huːˈdʌnɪt/ [n C] informal a book about an imaginary murder case, in which you do not find out who did the murder until the end: *If you enjoy a whodunnit, you'll lap up Janet Laurence's 'Hotel Morgue'.* | *an Agatha Christie whodunnit*

thriller /ˈθrɪləʳ/ [n C] an exciting story, for example about a crime or war, in which surprising events happen suddenly and you never know what will happen next: *They discovered a mutual love of mysteries and thrillers.* | **political/psychological/spy etc thriller** *Stephen King's new psychological thriller* | *He has written a spy thriller that recalls Fleming's James Bond series.* | *His latest work is a legal thriller set in Boston.*

short story /ˌʃɔːʳt ˈstɔːri/ [n C] a short piece of writing in which the writer tells a story: *She started out writing short stories for the magazine 'Black Mask'.* | *I understand your novel was inspired by a short story by Katherine Mansfield.* | *a collection of American short stories*

3 a book about real people, places, or events

- **non-fiction**

non-fiction /ˌnɒn ˈfɪkʃən‖ˌnɑːn-/ [n U] books about real events, people, or places: *The books in the library are divided into fiction and non-fiction.* | *He also produced works of non-fiction.* —**non-fiction** [adj] *a disturbing non-fiction account of events in Vietnam*

4 a book about someone's life

- biography
- autobiography
- memoirs
- diary
- journal

biography /baɪˈɒgrəfi‖-ˈɑːg-/ [n C] a book about someone's life, written by another person: *She's the author of three acclaimed biographies.* | *This is a competent and well-researched biography.* | **+ of** *Boswell's biography of Dr Johnson* | **authorized biography** (=approved by the person being written about) *'Paul McCartney: Many Years from Now' is an authorized biography of the former Beatle by Barry Miles.* | **unauthorized biography** (=not approved by the person written about) *He has slammed an unauthorised biography which he claims contains 'factual errors'.*

autobiography /ˌɔːtəbaɪˈɒgrəfi‖-ˈɑːg-/ [n C] a book in which someone writes about their own life: *Although she has written three novels, this autobiography is her first published work.* | **sb's autobiography** *In her autobiography, Doris Lessing writes about her childhood in Zimbabwe.* | *The incident is recounted in his autobiography.*

memoirs /ˈmemwɑːʳz/ [n plural] the story of your own life which you have written yourself, especially about your involvement in important political or military events **sb's memoirs** *The duke's memoirs will be serialised in The Sunday Times.* | *Reading Bready's unpublished memoirs, I was struck by her courage and resilience.* | *'I felt lost, abandoned,' she wrote in her memoirs.*

diary /ˈdaɪəri/ [n C] a book in which you write down the things that happen to you each day, and your private thoughts: *I wouldn't really show anyone my diary, not even you.* | **keep a diary (of sth)** (=write in a diary each day) *During his illness, David kept a diary, which his family hopes to publish.* | *I decided to keep a diary of our trip to Toronto.*

journal /ˈdʒɜːʳnl/ [n C] a diary, especially one written by a famous or important person: *In the 1837 journal, Darwin gives an account of his voyage to South America.* | *Her book draws on letters, diaries, journals and historical sources.* | **sb's journal** *I was given access to his private papers and journals.* | *Jewish life is poignantly described in Wiesel's journal, 'The Jews of Silence'.*

5 a book that gives you information about a subject

- reference book
- encyclopedia
- textbook

reference book /ˈrefərəns ˌbʊk/ [n C] a book that you look at in order to get information, for example a dictionary or encyclopedia: *Do not remove reference books from the library.* | *'The Elements of Style' is a classic reference book written by the late E.B. White.* | *Talk to the career counselors and check out the reference books on career choices.*

encyclopedia ALSO **encyclopaedia** British /ɪnˌsaɪkləˈpiːdiə/ [n C] a large book or set of books containing facts about a lot of different subjects, usually arranged in alphabetical order: *'Does anyone know when Mozart was born?' 'Look it up in the encyclopedia.'* | *a thirty-volume encyclopaedia* | *the Encyclopedia of Science*

textbook /ˈtekstbʊk/ [n C] a book that contains information and ideas about a subject, that you use when you are studying that subject: *The grant covers the costs of tuition, fees and textbooks.* | **geography/biology etc textbook** *Most economics textbooks skip over the subject of investing and financial markets.* | **academic/college textbook** *I can't get hold of any of the college textbooks he recommended.*

6 someone who writes books

- writer
- author
- novelist

writer /ˈraɪtəʳ/ [n C] someone who writes books, stories, or articles in as a job: *When I was young, I wanted to be a famous writer.* | *Greene was one of the finest writers of his generation.* | **American/German etc writer** *Do you have any books by modern American writers?* | **(the) writer George Eliot/Arthur C. Clarke etc** *Among his influences, he places Wynton Marsalis and writer Stanley Goode.* | **+ of** *Rush is a poet and writer of fiction.* | **ghost writer** (=someone who is paid to write a book for a person, as if it was their own work) *It seems likely that Campbell's book is almost wholly attributable to a ghostwriter.*

author /ˈɔːθəʳ/ [n C] someone who writes books, or who wrote a particular book, especially a literary book: *Balzac was one of her favourite authors.* | *A little gentle encouragement is all that is needed to put this promising author into the ranks of the high-flyers.* | **German/French etc author** *The prize was won by the German author, Heinrich Böll.* | **(the) author Marcel Proust/Steven King etc** *Among the guests was the author Salman Rushdie.* | **+ of** *Who was the author of 'Catch 22'?* | *We will be interviewing Lisa Mainero, author of 'Office Romance'.* | **co-author** (=someone who writes a book with another person) *With co-author Eyre, Barlow has produced a book charting the history of African music.*

novelist /ˈnɒvəlɪst‖ˈnɑː-/ [n C] someone who writes books about imaginary people or events: *Charles Dickens was one of the greatest 19th century novelists.* | **French/Hispanic etc novelist** *Japanese novelists deal with the question of old age in a way few other writers can aspire to.* | **(the) novelist Barbara Cartland/Carlos Fuentes etc** *The book quotes from the diaries of novelist Evelyn Waugh.* | *Budding gay novelist Larry Kramer is enjoying success at last.*

7 the people in a book

- character
- hero/heroine

character /ˈkærɪktəʳ/ [n C] a person in a story: *Her female characters often have strong, important relationships with other women.* | **+ from** *She reminds you of a character from Dickens.* | *Sisyphus, the character from Greek mythology* | **main character** (=the most important one) *The main character is a soldier in the First World War.* | *He writes Westerns in which the main characters are gay.* | **title character** (=an important character whose name is mentioned in the title of the book) *King Henry is the name given to a donkey, the title character in the children's book, 'King Henry Saves Christmas'.* | **fictional character** (=not a real one) *Ancient literature uses fictional characters to illustrate moral dilemmas.*

hero/heroine /ˈhɪərəʊ, ˈherəʊɪn/ [n C] the most important man or woman in a book: *By the story's end, the heroine finds herself in the hero's arms, and all ends well.* | *'Cinderella' is the story of a downtrodden heroine who wins out over her sisters.* | **+ of** *Paul Morel is the hero of 'Sons and Lovers'.*

8 to produce a book

- publish
- bring out

publish /ˈpʌblɪʃ/ [v T] to arrange for a book that has been written to be made available for people to buy: *'Moby Dick' was first published in London in 1851.* | *'I've had a remarkable life,' says the 60-year-old author, who has published 35 books.* | *King has made history by publishing a novel on the World Wide Web.* —**publication** /ˌpʌblɪˈkeɪʃən/ [n U] *A lot of work goes on behind the scenes to prepare a book like this for publication.* —**publisher** [n C] *She sent off the completed manuscript to 34 publishers before getting it accepted.* —**publishing** [n U] *How long have you worked in publishing?* | *Electronic publishing is a rapidly expanding field.*

bring out /ˌbrɪŋ ˈaʊt/ [phr v T] to produce a new book: *Fay Weldon has just brought out a new collection of stories.* | *Scribner will bring out a memoir by Candace Gringritch in the autumn.* | *He phoned to say they want to bring out a second edition.*

boring/bored

RELATED WORDS

- someone who is boring and conventional *see* **conventional/not conventional**
- *see also* **fed up**

1 jobs/books/films/activities etc

- boring
- not very interesting
- dull
- monotonous
- tedious
- banal
- mundane
- repetitive
- uninspiring
- humdrum
- soul-destroying
- send you to sleep

boring /ˈbɔːrɪŋ/ [adj] something that is **boring** is not interesting in any way and makes you feel tired and annoyed: *I don't want some boring job in an office!* | *a long boring lecture on economic planning* | *What a boring way to spend an evening!* | *Most people who see a baseball game for the first time think it's pretty boring.*

not very interesting /ˌnɒt veri ˈɪntrɪstɪŋ/ [adj phrase] especially spoken very ordinary and not really interesting or enjoyable: *Did you watch that TV show about Prince Charles? It wasn't very interesting, was it?* | *There was nothing very interesting in the local newspaper – just the usual stuff.*

dull /dʌl/ [adj] especially written boring because nothing different, interesting, or exciting happens: *We spent a dull afternoon with some of Harold's business associates.* | *This kind of mindless work can become very dull very quickly.*

monotonous /məˈnɒtənəs‖məˈnɑː-/ [adj] something that is **monotonous** is boring because it always continues in the same way and it never changes: *Life on the farm was slow and monotonous.* | *The teacher's low monotonous voice almost put me to sleep.*

tedious /ˈtiːdiəs/ [adj] something that is **tedious** is boring and tiring because it continues for too long: *It was one of the most tedious plays I've ever had to sit through.* | *Doing all those calculations without a computer would be extremely tedious.*

banal /bəˈnɑːl, bəˈnæl/ [adj] stories, books, remarks etc that are **banal**, are ordinary and uninteresting, especially because they do not contain anything new, exciting, or original: *It was just another banal newspaper story.* | *I was expecting an interesting interview but he only asked a few banal questions about the weather.*

mundane /mʌnˈdeɪn/ [adj] a job, event, or activity that is **mundane** is boring and ordinary and gives you very little pleasure, especially because you do it every day: *The play is about the mundane existence of factory workers.* | *My initial job was pretty mundane, but later I was given more responsibility.*

repetitive /rɪˈpetɪtɪv/ [adj] if something such as a job, speech, or a piece of writing or music is **repetitive**, it is boring because parts of it keep repeating again and again: *As children we suffered through schoolwork that was dull and repetitive.* | *He has some good ideas, but his lectures can get a little repetitive.*

uninspiring /ˌʌnɪnˈspaɪərɪŋ◂/ [adj] something that is **uninspiring** has nothing exciting or new about it, and makes you feel bored: *The restaurant's dessert selection was somewhat uninspiring.* | *Both candidates turned in uninspiring performances in last night's debate.*

humdrum /ˈhʌmdrʌm/ [adj] **humdrum existence/life/job** one in which nothing interesting or exciting ever happens and nothing changes: *Occasional holidays abroad were the only things that brightened up her otherwise humdrum life.* | *Going to night school might improve your chances of getting out of that humdrum job.*

soul-destroying /ˈsəʊl dɪˌstrɔɪ-ɪŋ/ [adj] especially British a job or an experience that is **soul-destroying** is extremely boring and makes you very unhappy because you feel that you are a useless person and your life has no meaning: *They spend all day sticking paper labels on toy cars – it's soul-destroying.* | *Going to the unemployment office and having to wait there for hours is a soul-destroying experience.*

send you to sleep /ˌsend juː tə ˈsliːp/ [v phrase] British informal **/put you to sleep** /ˌpʊt juː tə ˈsliːp/ American informal if a speech, performance etc **sends** or **puts you to sleep**, it is extremely boring so you completely stop paying attention to it and want to sleep: *All his talk about his financial problems just sends me to sleep.* | *Isn't there anything else to watch? This movie's putting me to sleep.*

2 place

- boring
- dead
- nothing ever happens
- dreary
- drab
- featureless

boring /ˈbɔːrɪŋ/ [adj] not at all interesting or exciting to live in: *This is such a boring town – there's nothing to do in the evenings.* | *It's so boring here. I wish we lived in L.A.*

dead /ded/ [adj not before noun] a town that is **dead** is boring because nothing interesting happens, and there is nothing interesting to do: *In summer we get a few visitors, but most of the time this place is dead.* | *It's absolutely dead here when all the students go away for the summer vacation.*

nothing ever happens /ˌnʌθɪŋ evər ˈhæpənz/ spoken if you say **nothing ever happens** in a place, you mean nothing interesting or exciting happens there: *Nothing ever happens around here. Why do you like it so much?*

dreary /ˈdrɪəri/ [adj] a **dreary** place is one where there is nothing attractive or cheerful to see: *I was* *living in a dreary apartment in a run-down part of town.* | *Laurie gazed out over a dreary landscape of factories and parking lots.*

drab /dræb/ [adj] buildings and places that are **drab** are not colourful or interesting to look at: *When I came to Manchester from Brazil everything seemed so drab and colourless.* | *You enter the drab office building half-expecting it to be abandoned.*

featureless /ˈfiːtʃəʳləs/ [adj] **featureless landscape/plain/coast etc** a large area of land that has no interesting or unusual features: *It was flat, featureless coastline.* | *In the middle of these otherwise featureless plains is a striking range of mountains.*

3 person

- boring
- dull
- bore

boring /ˈbɔːrɪŋ/ [adj] someone who is **boring** never says or does anything interesting: *He's so boring – all he ever talks about is football.* | *The professor was so boring, hardly anyone came to class.* | *Pam's parents are nice, but they're very boring.*

dull /dʌl/ [adj] someone who is **dull** is not unpleasant, but their life and their conversation is never interesting or exciting.: *Our neighbours are OK, I suppose, but they're so dull!* | *I'm afraid I must seem very dull compared with all those interesting people you meet.*

bore /bɔːʳ/ [n C] a boring person who talks too much about themselves and about the things that they are interested in: *At parties she always gets stuck with some bore who wants to tell her the story of his life.*

4 to make someone feel bored

- bore

bore /bɔːʳ/ [v T] to make someone feel bored, especially by talking too much about something they are not interested in: *Am I boring you?* | **bore sb with sth** (=bore someone by talking about a particular subject) *He bores everyone with his stories about his girlfriends.* | **bore sb to death/tears** (=make someone very bored) *Being alone with a baby all day bored her to tears.*

5 bored

- bored
- fed up
- be tired of/be sick of
- have had enough
- sb's eyes glaze over

bored /bɔːʳd/ [adj] tired and annoyed, either because you are doing something that you are not interested in, or because you have nothing to do: *Dad, can we go home now? I'm bored!* | *The game isn't great, but it might provide some amusement for bored teenagers.* | **get bored** *She seems to get bored very easily.* | **+ with** *Kelly gets a new job, and two weeks later he's bored with it.* | **bored with doing sth** *Julia soon got bored with lying on the beach.* | **bored to tears/bored to death/bored stiff** (=extremely bored) **informal** *There's nothing to do here – I'm bored stiff!*

fed up /ˌfed ˈʌp/ **especially spoken** bored and annoyed with something that has continued for too long: *Her husband's out working all the time, and she's really fed up.* | **+ with** *I'm fed up with health food – I'm going to have a hamburger.* | **fed up with doing sth** *We were all fed up with listening to her complaints the whole time.* | **get fed up** *When you have to stay in and study every night you just get fed up with it.*

be tired of/be sick of /biː ˈtaɪəʳd ɒv, biː ˈsɪk ɒv/ [v phrase] **spoken** to feel very annoyed and bored with a situation that has continued for too long, or with a person who has done something for too long: *We're always arguing, and I'm just tired of it.* | *I'm really sick of him – he's always criticizing me.* | **be tired/sick of doing sth** *People are tired of hearing politicians make promises that they never keep.* | *Do it yourself – I'm sick of cleaning up after you!* | **get tired/sick of (doing) sth** *I get tired of eating the same food day after day.* | **be sick and tired of (doing) sth** *I'm sick and tired of your whining.*

have had enough /həv ˌhæd ɪˈnʌf/ [v phrase] **spoken** to be so bored with something that has continued for a long time that you decide to leave, do something different, or change the situation: *After 10 years of teaching, Allan has had enough.* | **have had enough of (doing) sth** *By January I'd had enough of shoveling snow and decided to take a trip to Mexico.*

sb's eyes glaze over / (sb's) ˌaɪz gleɪz ˈəʊvəʳ/ if **someone's eyes glaze over**, they look as if they are going to fall asleep, because they are very bored, especially by what someone is telling them: *I could see her eyes were glazing over, so I quickly suggested a break.* | *When you start talking about important political issues, most people's eyes glaze over.*

6 the feeling of being bored

- boredom
- monotony

boredom /ˈbɔːʳdəm/ [n U] *Boredom is one of the main reasons kids get into trouble.* | **+ of** *She could no longer stand the boredom of having nothing to do.* | **sheer boredom** (=complete boredom) *Can you imagine the sheer boredom of doing the same job day in, day out for fifty years?* | **out of boredom** (=because you are bored) *I sit around all day and eat junk food out of boredom.*

monotony /məˈnɒtəni‖məˈnɑː-/ [n U] the feeling of being bored because you do the same things all the time, see the same people etc, and never do anything different **+ of** *The monotony of prison life is enough to drive anyone insane.* | **sheer monotony** (=complete monotony) *The sheer monotony of the work is itself exhausting.*

7 to try to make a situation less boring

- relieve the boredom/monotony

relieve the boredom/monotony /rɪˌliːv ðə ˈbɔːʳdəm, məˈnɒtəni‖-məˈnɑː-/ [v phrase] *Sometimes she would try out different routes to relieve the monotony of her daily journey.* | *Harry tried to relieve the boredom by singing and whistling.*

8 ways of saying that something becomes boring after a time

- the novelty wears off

the novelty wears off /ðə ˌnɒvəlti weəʳz ˈɒf‖-ˌnɑːv-/ if **the novelty wears off**, something that was new and interesting for a short time is no longer interesting: *After the novelty wears off, the*

Internet can be a very dull place. | *Once the novelty has worn off, most of these kitchen gadgets just sit in the cupboard, unused for years.*

borrow

RELATED WORDS

opposite: —— **lend**

▸ to owe money to someone because you have borrowed from them *see* **owe**

1 to borrow something

▸ **borrow** ▸ **be on loan**
▸ **have the use of**

borrow /ˈbɒrəʊ‖ˈbɑː-, ˈbɔː-/ [v T] if you **borrow** something from someone, they let you have it, and you agree to give it back to them later: *Can I borrow your pen for a second?* | *I wish Steve would buy himself a bike. He's always borrowing mine.* | **borrow sth from/off sb** *She found the poem in a book she'd borrowed off Mrs Parsons.* | *I borrowed this dress from my sister.* —**borrowed** [adj] *After I graduated from college, I moved into a borrowed apartment in Brooklyn Heights.*

have the use of ALSO **have the loan of** /ˌhæv ðə juːs ɒv, ˌhæv ðə ˈləʊn ɒv/ [v phrase] British to have someone's permission to borrow something, especially something large or expensive such as a car or boat for a particular length of time: *Could we have the loan of your video camera this weekend?* | **let sb have the use of sth** *Dad usually lets me have the use of his car when he's away on business.*

be on loan /biː ɒn ˈləʊn/ [v phrase] if something **is on loan** from a library, art collection etc, it has been borrowed from it: *These pictures are on loan from the Paul Getty Collection.* | **be out on loan** (=not be available because it has been borrowed) *The librarian phoned to say the book you want is out on loan until next week.*

2 to borrow money

▸ **borrow** ▸ **take out a loan**

borrow /ˈbɒrəʊ‖ˈbɑː-, ˈbɔː-/ [v I/T] if you **borrow** money from someone, they give it to you, and you agree to pay it back later: *Companies normally expect to borrow at cheaper rates than ordinary people have to pay.* | **borrow sth from/off sb** *Can I borrow five pounds off you till next week?* | *By the end of the war the Canadian government had borrowed over $5 billion from its own citizens.* | **borrow heavily** (=borrow a lot of money) *Maxwell had borrowed heavily to finance his business projects.* —**borrowed** [adj] *The takeover bid was financed mainly with borrowed cash.* —**borrower** [n C] *The fall in interest rates is bad news for savers but good news for borrowers.*

take out a loan /ˌteɪk aʊt ə ˈləʊn/ [v phrase] to borrow a large amount of money from a bank or company: *Three years ago, we took out a loan to buy our car and we're still paying it off.* | **+ from** *If you take out a loan from the company you have to pay it back within two years.*

3 to pay money so that you can borrow and use something

▸ **rent** ▸ **lease**
▸ **rent** ▸ **charter**

rent /rent/ [v I/T] to pay a particular amount of money regularly for the use of a house, office, telephone etc over a period of months or years: *Many young couples rent an apartment until they've saved enough money to buy a house.* | *I can't afford to rent an office in this part of town.* | *Do you own your home or are you renting?* | **rent sth from sb/sth** *Did you know you can rent a fax machine from the telephone company?* | **for rent** (=available to be rented) *Vicky put the house up for rent a month ago, but changed her mind the next day.* —**rented** [adj] *We've lived in rented accommodation since we were married so we're desperate to get our own place.*

rent especially American **hire** British /rent, haɪəʳ/ [v T] to pay money to a company to use a car, or a piece of equipment or clothing for a period of days or hours: *Should we rent a video tonight?* | *Let's hire a car for the weekend and go and visit Jenny and Steve.* | *You rented a tuxedo for two hundred dollars? Are you crazy?* | **hire/rent sth from sb/sth** *When she got to Dallas she rented a Ford convertible from the Avis desk.* —**rented** ALSO **hired** British [adj] *No, the skis aren't mine. They're hired.* | *The bride arrived at the church in a rented limousine.*

lease /liːs/ [v T] to pay rent for the use of buildings, land, equipment, or a vehicle for a long time, especially for business purposes: *The Cider Press Company leases the machinery and buildings for $1000 a month.* | *It would work out cheaper overall to lease the computers for the project.* | **lease sth from sb/sth** *The building is actually owned by the government – we're leasing it from them.*

charter /ˈtʃɑːʳtəʳ/ [v T] to pay money to a company for the use of one of their planes or ships: *A group of journalists chartered an airplane to fly them to Addis Ababa.* | *International Aid Agencies have chartered ships to transport supplies to the disaster area.*

4 money that is borrowed

▸ **loan** ▸ **interest**
▸ **mortgage**

loan /ləʊn/ [n C] an amount of money that is borrowed, especially from a bank or company, which you agree to pay back by the end of a period of time: *If you need more money, we can arrange a loan.* | **a £5000/$20,000 loan** *The organization asked for a $2 million loan to plant new trees in the rainforest.* | **take out a loan** (=get a loan) *We took out a loan to buy a new car.* | **pay off/repay a loan** (=finish paying back what you borrowed) *I can't afford to buy a new sofa until I pay off this loan.* | **bank loan** (=money you borrow from a bank) *Cox specialized in assisting borrowers who didn't qualify for bank loans.*

mortgage /ˈmɔːʳgɪdʒ/ [n C] a large amount of money that is borrowed from a bank or company in order to buy a house: *The bank says we have to buy a life insurance policy before we can get a mortgage.* | **+ on** *Nick told me the mortgage on his apartment is worth about $90,000.* | **take out a mortgage** (=arrange to get a mortgage) *Anyone taking out a mortgage should be aware that interest rates can go up at any time.* | **pay off a mortgage** (=pay all of it back) *It took my parents nearly thirty years to pay off their mortgage.*

interest /'ɪntrəst/ [n U] money that you pay for borrowing money, especially that you pay every year or every month at a fixed rate: *Credit companies charge huge amounts of interest.* | **+ on** *What's the interest on the loan?*

both

what you say to talk about two people or things

- both
- the two of them/us/you
- the pair of them/us/you
- each
- each other/one another
- either
- neither
- mutual
- share

both /bəʊθ/ [predeterminer/quantifier] use this to talk about two people or things together: *Paul and I are both scared of spiders.* | *I can't decide which dress to buy. I like them both.* | *Both drivers were injured, but not seriously.* | **both the/these/my etc** *Both the robbers were wearing masks.* | *Both their parents are doctors.* | **+ of** *Both of us felt a little sick after dinner.* | *Both of the windows had been broken.*

the two of them/us/you /ðə 'tuː əv ðəm, ʌs, juː/ [pron] spoken both the people that you are talking about: *While the two of them talked about cars, I went into the kitchen to make coffee.* | *We're taking a romantic vacation – just the two of us.* | *I want the money to be shared equally between the two of you.*

the pair of them/us/you /ðə 'peəʳ əv ðəm, ʌs, juː/ [pron] British spoken both the people that you are talking about – used especially when you are angry or disappointed with them: *Get out of here, the pair of you!* | *There we were, stranded in the middle of nowhere with no money between the pair of us.*

each /iːtʃ/ [determiner/pron] use this to talk about two people or things when you think of them as separate: *My wife and I each have our own bank account.* | **+ of** *Each of the teams has already won two games.*

each other/one another /iːtʃ 'ʌðəʳ, wʌn ə'nʌðəʳ/ [pron] use this to say that each of two people does the same thing to the other, or has the same feeling about the other: *My boyfriend and I don't talk to each other very much anymore.* | *The twins looked at one another and giggled.* | **each other's/one another's** *Ron and Joe didn't like each other's girlfriends.*

either /'aɪðəʳ‖'iː-/ [determiner/pron] use this to talk about one of two people, places, or things, especially when it does not matter which one: *'Would you like tea or coffee?' 'Either – I don't mind.'* | *You can operate the controls with either hand.* | **+ of** *If you see either of these men, contact the police immediately.* | *She says she never met either of them before.* | **either sb/sth or sb/sth** *I usually drink either coke or beer with pizza.*

neither /'naɪðəʳ‖'niː-/ [determiner/pron] not one or the other of two people, places, or things etc: *'Do you want milk or lemon in your tea?' 'Neither, thanks.'* | *The game wasn't very exciting, and neither team played well.* | **+ of** *Luckily, neither of the passengers was hurt in the crash.* | **neither sb/sth nor sb/sth** *Neither her mother nor her father knew about her boyfriend.*

mutual /'mjuːtʃuəl/ [adj] **mutual feelings/friends/interest etc mutual** feelings etc are ones that both people have at the same time: *The couple were introduced to each other by a mutual friend.* | *An investment in my company would be to our mutual benefit.* | *They would meet every week to discuss matters of mutual interest.*

share /ʃeəʳ/ [v T] to both have the same opinion, attitude, interest etc: *They share an interest in 16th century architecture.* | *My husband and my mother share the same birthday.*

bottom

RELATED WORDS

opposite: **top**
- *see also* **under/below, down**

1 the lowest part of something

- the bottom
- base

the bottom /ðə 'bɒtəm‖-'bɑː-/ [n singular] the lowest part of something **+ of** *The bottom of the mountain was strewn with rocks and debris.* | **on/around/at etc the bottom of sth** *There's a small creek at the bottom of the hill.* | *The answers are at the bottom of page 62.* | *Your account number is the last set of numbers on the bottom of your cheque.*

base /beɪs/ [n singular] the lowest part or the wide bottom part on which something stands: *The lamp has a square base.* | **the base of** *The base of the column was cracked.*

2 the lowest one of two or more things that are on top of each other

- bottom
- lower

bottom /'bɒtəm‖'bɑː-/ [adj only before noun] **bottom drawer/shelf/layer etc** the one at the bottom: *The bottom layer of the cake is made of chocolate and strawberries.* | *She looked in the bottom drawer of the chest.*

lower /'ləʊəʳ/ [adj only before noun] **lower deck/edge/lip etc** the one at the bottom when there is one at the bottom and one at the top: *We drove onto the lower deck of the ferry.* | *The dentist filled two teeth in my lower jaw.* | *The baby's lower lip quivered and then she began crying.*

3 the bottom part of something such as a box, cup, or lake

- the bottom
- the floor
- bed

the bottom /ðə 'bɒtəm‖-'bɑː-/ [n singular] **the bottom of sth** *The bottom of the pond was dark and dirty.* | **at the bottom of** *Susan found the keys at the bottom of her handbag.* | **in the bottom of** *Heavy objects should be packed in the bottom of your suitcase.*

the floor /ðə 'flɔːʳ/ [n singular] the wide area of flat ground at the bottom of a valley, the ocean etc **+ of** *The boys found some bones on the floor of the cave.* | *the floor of the Mediterranean* | **the ocean/valley floor** *They're still attempting to recover the plane's wreckage from the ocean floor.*

bed /bed/ [n C] **river/lake/sea etc bed** the flat ground at the bottom of a river, lake or sea: *Smooth stones covered the creek bed.*

4 the flat bottom surface on the outside of an object

- the bottom
- the underside

the bottom /ðə 'bɒtem‖-'bɑː-/ [n singular] *I flipped over the rock and saw that the bottom was covered with insects.* | **+ of** *The bottom of the glass is wet. You'd better put a napkin under it.* | *There are some markings on the bottom of the vase.*

the underside /ði 'ʌndərsaɪd/ ALSO **the underneath** /ði ˌʌndər'niːθ/ informal [n singular] the bottom surface on the outside of something large **+ of** *When she drove over the curb, she damaged the underside of the car.* | *Workers are repairing the underside of the bridge.* | *They used to put chalk dust on the underneath of the horse's saddle.*

5 next to the bottom of a mountain etc

- at the bottom
- at the foot of

at the bottom /ət ðə 'bɒtəm‖-'bɑː-/ [adv] next to the bottom of something such as a hill, mountain, stairs, or a ladder **+ of** *Jordan waited for her at the bottom of the stairs.* | *At the bottom of the ladder there was a large tin of paint.*

at the foot of /ət ðə 'fʊt ɒv/ [prep] an expression used especially in British English meaning next to the bottom of something such as a hill, mountain, stairs, or a tree: *The inn is situated in a beautiful village at the foot of Mt. Mitchell.*

brave/not brave

RELATED WORDS

- *see also* **confident/not confident, frightened/frightening**

1 not afraid when you are in a dangerous or frightening situation

- brave
- courageous
- heroic
- hero/heroine

brave /breɪv/ [adj] someone who is **brave** does not show that they are afraid in a frightening situation or when they have to do something dangerous, painful, or unpleasant: *You have to be very brave to be a fireman.* | *a brave rescue attempt* | *No matter how hard I tried to be brave and strong, I couldn't stop myself from crying.* | *I wasn't sure if I was being brave or stupid.* | **it is brave of sb to do sth** *It was very brave of you to tell her the truth.* | **be brave** (=used to tell someone to behave bravely) *Come on, be brave. Just grit your teeth and it will all be over in no time.* —**bravely** [adv] *Most of the soldiers who fought so bravely in the war were no older than twenty.*

courageous /kə'reɪdʒəs/ [adj] especially written someone who is **courageous** behaves very bravely, often for a long period, and especially when they are fighting for something they believe in or suffering great pain: *After a courageous struggle against cancer, Garcia died at the age of thirty.* | *Few will forget her courageous stand against inequality and injustice.* | *But for the actions of a few courageous individuals, we might all have died.* —**courageously** [adv] *This was a triumph for all those who had courageously demanded reform.*

heroic /hɪ'rəʊɪk/ [adj] extremely brave and admired by a lot of people: *Amy Johnson is famous for her heroic solo flight from Britain to Australia in 1930.* | *Although the nationalists put up heroic resistance, the revolt was crushed in three days.* | *The film is a warm tribute to the heroic pilots of C Division.* —**heroism** /'herəʊɪzəm/ [n U] heroic behaviour: *Nelson's heroism in battle won him many honours.*

hero/heroine /'hɪərəʊ, 'herəʊɪn/ [n C] someone who does something extremely brave and is admired by a lot of people. Use hero about a man or a woman, use heroine about a woman: *A famous World War Two hero, he later became a U.S. senator.* | *Don't try to be a hero. You'll only get hurt.* | *a heroine of the Resistance*

2 not afraid to do possibly dangerous things

- daring
- adventurous
- fearless
- daredevil

daring /'deərɪŋ/ [adj] not afraid of taking risks or doing dangerous things, or involving a lot of risks: *He would often do very foolish things just to prove how daring he was.* | *Three inmates fled the prison in a daring tunnel escape.* | *It is a particularly daring stunt, involving being tied up and suspended in mid-air.*

adventurous /əd'ventʃərəs/ [adj] someone who is **adventurous** enjoys going to new places and having new, possibly dangerous experiences: *The higher slopes are for the more adventurous skier.* | *She was naturally adventurous and loved the wild landscape of Colombia with all its beauty and danger.*

fearless /'fɪərləs/ [adj] not at all afraid of doing dangerous things, so that other people admire you: *The Comanches were great and fearless warriors.* | *Her fearless opposition to the military dictatorship has won admiration from around the world.* —**fearlessly** [adv] *He dived fearlessly into the sea, ignoring the rocks below.* —**fearlessness** [n U] *It is essential that bullfighters give an impression of fearlessness.*

daredevil /'deərdevəl/ [n C] someone who enjoys doing extremely dangerous things and taking a lot of risks: *World famous daredevil Evel Knievel will attempt to cross the Grand Canyon on a rocket-powered motorcycle.* —**daredevil** [adj only before noun] *Many consider Ormer Locklear to have been the greatest of all daredevil pilots.*

3 not afraid to do something new and different

- daring
- adventurous
- bold

daring /'deərɪŋ/ [adj] not afraid to do something new and unusual that many people will find shocking: *When she was young, everybody thought my grandmother was terribly daring because she smoked.* | *a daring new production of 'Hamlet'*

adventurous /əd'ventʃərəs/ [adj] someone who is **adventurous** enjoys trying new things or taking risks: *I'm not very adventurous when it comes to trying new food.* | *Le Corbusier was the most adventurous architect of modern times, always experimenting with new forms and structures.*

bold /bəʊld/ [adj] not afraid of taking risks, saying what you think and making difficult decisions: *What we need is a strong leader, someone who is bold* *enough to make tough decisions.* | *He was one of the boldest and most innovative composers of his day.* —**boldly** [adv] *Overcoming her instinctive shyness, she boldly stepped forward to speak to the crowd.*

4 the ability to behave bravely

- courage
- bravery
- guts
- nerve

courage /ˈkʌrɪdʒ‖ˈkɜːr-/ [n U] the ability to behave bravely when you are in danger, suffering illness, or pain, or when other people are opposing you: *She showed great courage during her long illness.* | *Nelson Mandela will be remembered for his courage and integrity in the struggle against apartheid.* | **take courage** (=need courage) *Driving again after his accident must have taken a lot of courage.*

bravery /ˈbreɪvəri/ [n U] the ability to behave bravely in a dangerous situation, for example during a war: *After the war, my uncle was awarded a medal for bravery.* | *Gina surprised us all with her bravery and endurance.* | *It was an act of the utmost bravery and disregard for personal safety.*

guts /gʌts/ [n plural] informal the ability and determination to do something difficult or dangerous that other people are afraid to do: *I don't think he can possibly win, but you've got to admire his guts.* | **have guts** *Whatever else you may say about Sally, she certainly has guts.* | **it takes guts to do sth** (=you need guts to do something) *It took guts and determination to overcome such a severe handicap.*

nerve /nɜːʳv/ [n U] the ability to remain calm and confident in a dangerous, difficult, or frightening situation: *In a scary situation like that you need someone with plenty of nerve.* | *After a three day siege the kidnapper's nerve failed and he gave himself up to the police.* | **it takes a lot of nerve to do sth** (=you need a lot of nerve to do something) *It takes a lot of nerve to report a colleague for sexual harassment.*

5 to be brave enough to do something

- be brave enough to do sth
- dare
- have the guts to do sth
- have the nerve to do sth
- find/get up/pluck up the courage to do sth

be brave enough to do sth /biː ˌbreɪv ɪnʌf tə ˈduː (sth)/ [v phrase] *None of the other people were brave enough to stand up to him.* | *Maybe if you were brave enough to ask her out she'd go to a movie with you.* | *Anyone brave enough to get this far would then find an electrified fence blocking their way.*

dare /deəʳ/ [v I not in progressive] to be brave enough to do something that is dangerous or that you are afraid of doing – used in questions, negatives, and sentences beginning with 'if': *My sister used to steal things from stores, but I would never dare.* | **not dare (to) do sth** *No one dared to go into the old house at night.* | *She was so high up now that she didn't dare look down.* | **dare do sth** *Dare we take this decision without consulting the Prime Minister?*

have the guts to do sth /hæv ðə ˌgʌts tə ˈduː (sth)/ [v phrase not in progressive] to be brave enough to do something unpleasant or difficult that other people are afraid to do spoken *I know he made a mistake, but at least he had the guts to admit it!* | *Sarah's the only one who has the guts to speak her mind.*

have the nerve to do sth /hæv ðə ˌnɜːʳv tə ˈduː (sth)/ [v phrase not in progressive] to be calm and confident enough to do something that is frightening or dangerous: *Not many people have the nerve to stand up and speak in front of a large audience.* | *I can't believe he had the nerve to show up at the party after what he said about Janet.*

find/get up/pluck up the courage to do sth /ˌfaɪnd, ˌget ʌp, ˌplʌk ʌp ðə ˌkʌrɪdʒ tə ˈduː (sth)‖-ˌkɜːr-/ [v phrase] to force yourself to be brave and do something that you are afraid of doing, after thinking about it for a long time: *I eventually plucked up the courage to tell my parents that I was going to go and live in Canada.* | *David loves Julie but he can't get up enough courage to ask her to marry him.*

6 not brave

- cowardly
- coward
- spineless
- wimp

cowardly /ˈkaʊəʳdli/ [adj] not brave: *He was too cowardly to say what he meant.* | *It was a cowardly attack on unarmed civilians.* | *NATO today condemned the incident, calling it a senseless and cowardly act.* —**cowardice** /ˈkaʊəʳdɪ̈s/ [n U] cowardly behaviour: *The movie is a true account of the only American soldier to be shot for cowardice since the Civil War.*

coward /ˈkaʊəʳd/ [n C] someone who is not brave enough to do something dangerous or unpleasant that they should do: *He called me a coward, because I wouldn't fight.* | *Perhaps I should have turned back but I didn't want to be known as a quitter and a coward.* | **be a coward about sth** *She knew she was an awful coward about going to the dentist.*

spineless /ˈspaɪnləs/ [adj] someone who is **spineless** is too weak to say what they really think because they are afraid of what might happen or what other people might say – use this to show disapproval: *Don't be spineless – you have to stand up to people like that.* | *The President has been accused of being spineless in the face of naked aggression.*

wimp /wɪmp/ [n C] informal someone who is afraid to do something you want them to do or think they should do, so that you think they are annoying or do not respect them – often used humorously: *Don't be such a wimp, Simon. Tell her you want to break up.* | *Because they don't risk money, corporate financiers are considered wimps by traders.*

7 to decide not to do something because you are too frightened

- lose your nerve
- not dare
- chicken out/wimp out
- not have the guts
- not have the nerve

lose your nerve /ˌluːz jɔːʳ ˈnɜːʳv/ [v phrase] to suddenly lose the confidence and calmness that you need in order to do something dangerous or frightening: *Dan wanted to ask his boss for a day off but he lost his nerve at the last minute.* | *I stood at the top of the ski-slope for a minute then lost my nerve.*

not dare /nɒt ˈdeəʳ/ [v phrase] to not be brave enough to do something because you are afraid of what might happen if you do it **not dare do sth** *The older boys used to bully me but I didn't dare complain.* | **not dare to do sth** *Billy stood on top of the rock, not daring to jump down.* | **not dare** *I wanted to ask Dad for the money but I didn't dare.*

chicken out/wimp out /ˌtʃɪkən ˈaʊt, ˌwɪmp ˈaʊt/ [phr v I] spoken informal to not be brave enough to do something that you intended to do or said you would do: *I was supposed to make the introductory speech, but I chickened out at the last minute.* | **chicken/wimp out of doing sth** *She chickened out of telling her father that she and David were going to live together.*

not have the guts /nɒt hæv ðə ˈgʌts/ [v phrase not in progressive] spoken to not be brave enough to do something that people think you should do: *He wouldn't have the guts to say that to me.* | *I planned to ask my boss for a raise but in the end I didn't have the guts.* | **not have the guts to do sth** *Peg has done all the things I never had the guts to try.* | **be without/lack guts** *Joe's a weak character, without guts or ambition.* | *She's intelligent enough, but she lacks guts.*

not have the nerve /nɒt hæv ðə ˈnɜːʳv/ [v phrase not in progressive] to not be brave or confident enough to do something because you think it is too difficult, dangerous or embarrassing: *I'd love to quit my job and go back to college but I don't have the nerve.* | **not have the nerve to do sth** *He doesn't have the nerve to tell the boss what he really thinks of her.*

break

RELATED WORDS

▸ *see also* **broken/not broken, damage, tear, destroy, squash, repair, accident**

1 to break something into pieces

- break
- bust
- crack

break /breɪk/ [v T] to **break** something, either accidentally or deliberately: *She fell off her bike and broke her glasses.* | *If you break it you'll have to pay for it out of your allowance.* | *I broke one of her platters once, and I swear she's never forgiven me.* | *He once broke a window of his grandfather's greenhouse with a football.*

bust /bʌst/ [v T] spoken informal to break something: *The ball hit him in the face and bust his glasses.* | *He busted the side window with a bat.* | **bust sth up/bust up sth** *Dean got really drunk and started busting up the bar.* | **bust sth down/bust down sth** *The police had to bust down the door.*

crack /kræk/ [v T] to break or damage something so that cracks appear in its surface: *A stone hit the windshield and cracked it.* | *I cracked one of the wine glasses when I was washing it.* | *The earthquake cracked walls and driveways and knocked out electricity and communications.*

2 to break into pieces

- break
- get broken
- crack
- give way
- bust

break /breɪk/ [v I] *She dropped a plate and it broke.* | *My watchband has broken.* | *The ice broke and they both fell through.* | *The cam belt broke and ruined the engine.*

get broken /get ˈbrəʊkən/ [v phrase] if something **gets broken**, someone breaks it accidentally: *If you leave your toys on the floor, they'll get broken.* | *A few of the cups got broken while we were moving house.* | *When her grandchildren visit, she puts away anything she doesn't want to get broken.*

crack /kræk/ [v I] if something **cracks**, it breaks slightly so that lines appear in its surface: *The bell cracked after many years of use.* | *A few windows cracked from the heat during the fire.* | *The pipeline had cracked a long time before the oil spill occurred.* —**crack** [n C] *There are a few cracks in the plaster.*

give way /ˌgɪv ˈweɪ/ [v phrase] if something such as a floor, wall, or bridge **gives way**, it finally breaks because there is a lot of pressure or weight on it: *He was changing a light bulb when the ladder gave way.* | *The crowd surged forward and the fence gave way.* | *The whole side of the hill gave way after a week of heavy rain.*

bust /bʌst/ [v I] informal if something **busts**, it breaks: *The toy is made of a balloon in a cloth sack that can be hit without busting.* | **bust open** (=break in such a way that what is inside can come out) *His suitcase busted open, and everything went all over the floor in the hotel lobby.*

3 to break something into two pieces

- break sth in two/in half
- snap
- split

break sth in two/in half /ˌbreɪk (sth) ɪn ˈtuː, ɪn ˈhɑːf‖ -ˈhæf/ [v phrase] to break something into two, fairly equal pieces: *The explosion broke the ship in two.* | *David broke the chocolate bar in half and gave a piece to Sue.*

snap /snæp/ [v T] to break something, usually a long thin object, so that it makes a sudden, short loud noise: *He hit a rock and snapped the truck's axle.* | *High winds snapped power lines in the city, leaving more than 9000 people without power.* | **snap sth in two/in half** *He accidentally snapped his putter in half during one tournament.* | **snap off** *The tip of the tree snapped off when it fell.*

split /splɪt/ [v T] to break something such as wood into two parts along a straight line: *She learned to split logs and stack a woodpile.* | **split sth in two/in half** *Split the leek in half lengthwise, and cut it into 1/4-inch pieces.*

4 to break into two pieces

- break in two/in half
- snap
- split

break in two/in half /ˌbreɪk ɪn ˈtuː, ɪn ˈhɑːf ‖-ˈhæf/ [v phrase] *The ship broke in two when it ran aground, and 900 tons of fuel oil leaked out.* | *When I pulled at the board, it broke in two and fell down.*

snap /snæp/ [v I] if something **snaps**, especially something long and thin, it breaks into two pieces making a short loud noise: *A twig snapped under his foot.* | *Power lines snapped in the high winds.* | *One of the strings on my guitar snapped when I was tuning it.* | **snap off** *The tip of the Christmas tree snapped off when it fell.*

split /splɪt/ [v I] if wood, bone etc **splits**, it breaks into two parts along a straight line: *The window frames are old and the wood is starting to split.* | *When it crashed, the plane's fuselage split behind the wings.* | **split in two/half** *The back of the chair had split in two.* | **split open** (=split so that there is a hole) *A metal tube split open in the steam generator of the nuclear power plant.*

5 to break something into a lot of pieces

- smash
- shatter
- crumble

smash /smæʃ/ [v T] to break something into a lot of small pieces, especially in a violent way, by dropping, throwing, or hitting it: *Firefighters smashed a bedroom window and rescued a two-year-old girl.* | *Her camera was smashed by soldiers when she tried to take photographs.* | **smash sth to pieces/to bits** *The boat hit the rocks and was smashed to pieces by the waves.*

shatter /ˈʃætəʳ/ [v T] to break something, especially glass, into a lot of very small pieces: *The explosion shattered office windows 500 metres away.* | *Protesters shattered a glass door and tossed red dye around the entrance.*

crumble /ˈkrʌmbəl/ [v T] to break something, especially food, into very small pieces: *Beat the eggs, crumble the cheese, and mix together.* | *Mrs. Suggs crumbled the bread into hot milk.*

6 to break into a lot of pieces

- break into pieces/bits
- break up
- fall to bits/pieces
- fall apart/come apart
- disintegrate
- shatter
- smash
- splinter
- crumble
- burst
- blow

break into pieces/bits /ˌbreɪk ɪntə ˈpiːsɪ̈z, ˈbɪts/ [v phrase] *One of the mugs rolled off the table and broke into bits on the stone floor.* | *Investigators are not sure what caused the plane to break into pieces and plunge into the ocean.*

break up /ˌbreɪk ˈʌp/ [phr v I] if a large object **breaks up**, it breaks into a lot of pieces especially as a result of natural forces, or serious damage: *The ice breaks up quicker near the shore.* | *Two of the missiles apparently broke up in flight.* | *The comet was formed when a planet broke up at some time in the distant past.*

fall to bits/pieces British **go to pieces** American /ˌfɔːl tə ˈbɪts, ˈpiːsɪ̈z, ˌgəʊ tə ˈpiːsɪ̈z/ [v phrase] to break into a lot of small pieces, especially because of being weak, old, or badly made: *The book had been read again and again, until it finally fell to pieces.* | *I picked the bag up, and it went to pieces in my hands.* | *The trunk was full of old dresses, some of which were falling to pieces.*

fall apart/come apart /ˌfɔːl əˈpɑːʳt, ˌkʌm əˈpɑːʳt/ [phr v I] to break easily into pieces, especially because of being badly made or very old: *I only bought these shoes last week, and they're falling apart already.* | *His jacket started coming apart at the seams.*

disintegrate /dɪsˈɪntɪ̈greɪt/ [v I] if something **disintegrates**, it breaks into a lot of small pieces so that it is completely destroyed or so that it completely changes its form: *A 50-foot section of the roadway began to disintegrate after only a few cars had passed over it.* | *The plane disintegrated in midair.* | *The mummified man's clothes had disintegrated almost completely, but appeared to be mainly of leather and fur.*

shatter /ˈʃætəʳ/ [v I] if something, especially glass, **shatters**, it breaks suddenly into a lot of very small pieces because it has been dropped or hit: *The glass had shattered, but the photograph itself was undamaged.* | *Storefront windows shattered and roofs blew off during the hurricane.* | *Don't try to drive nails into the bricks, they may shatter.* —**shattered** [adj only before noun] *There was shattered glass all over the floor.*

smash /smæʃ/ [v I] to noisily break into pieces as a result of being dropped or hit: *I heard something smash. What broke?* | **smash to pieces/bits** *The bottle rolled off the table and smashed to pieces on the floor.*

splinter /ˈsplɪntəʳ/ [v I] if something such as wood **splinters**, it breaks into thin, sharp pieces: *These types of wood splinter more easily than redwood or cedar.* | *The coating helps prevent the glass from splintering if it is hit by a rock while you are driving.* —**splintered** [adj] *the splintered remains of an old fence*

crumble /ˈkrʌmbəl/ [v I] to break easily into a powder or into small pieces, especially as a result of being old or dry: *The autumn leaves crumbled in my fingers.* | *Some of the tiles are crumbling around the edges.* —**crumbling** [adj] *Nestling amongst the magnificent hills were the crumbling ruins of an old monastery.*

burst /bɜːʳst/ [v I] if something such as a tyre or a pipe **bursts**, the force of the air, water etc inside makes it break into many pieces: *The Concorde disaster was caused by a tyre bursting.* | *Thousands of gallons of oil flowed into the river when an oil pipeline burst.* —**burst** [adj only before noun] *The flood was caused by a burst pipe.*

blow /bləʊ/ [v I] especially American if a tyre **blows**, it breaks open suddenly and all the air comes out of it: *One of the tires blew and they skidded into the center divider.*

7 to break a piece from the main part of something

- break off
- chip

break off /ˌbreɪk ˈɒf/ [phr v T] to **break off** a piece of something **break off sth** *She broke off a bit of bread and dipped it in the soup.* | **break sth off** *When the dough is chilled, break pieces of the dough off with your fingers, and roll into small balls.* | **break sth off sth** *Break a leaf off the bush, rub it between your fingers, and smell the lemony scent.*

chip /tʃɪp/ [v T] to accidentally break off a small piece from the edge of something, such as a cup, plate, or piece of wood: *He fell off his bike and chipped his front tooth.* | *If you don't load the dishwasher right, it might chip some of the cups.*

8 to break, so that one piece becomes separated from the main part

- break off
- come off
- come away

break off /ˌbreɪk ˈɒf/ [phr v I] if a part of something **breaks off**, it breaks and becomes separated from the main part of it: *I gave it a tug and the zipper broke off.* | *A military cargo plane made an emergency landing when one of the propellers broke off.* | *Icebergs break off from the ice sheets and float southwards.*

come off /ˌkʌm ˈɒf/ [phr v I/T] if part of something **comes off** it becomes separated from the main part of it because it is not fastened to it firmly enough:

Can you fix the door? The handle's come off. | **come off sth** *A wheel had come off a car, and rolled to the side of the road.*

come away /ˌkʌm əˈweɪ/ [phr v I] to easily become separated from a surface when touched, pulled etc: *The switch was attached to the plate and came away with it when I pulled.* | **+ from** *Mix until the dough comes away from the side of the bowl.* | **come away in sb's hand** (=become separated very easily or without you realising it) *Ralph pulled, and the lock came away in his hand.*

9 to break a bone in your body

- break
- crack
- fracture
- shatter
- bust

▸ *see also* **hurt/injure (2)**

break /breɪk/ [v T] *I broke my leg last time I went skiing.* | *She slipped on the floor, it'd just been washed, and broke her hip.* | *They thought he'd broken his back, but the X-ray showed it was okay.*

crack /kræk/ [v T] to partly break a bone: *She slipped and cracked a rib.* | *Freeman cracked his skull in the accident.* —**crack** [n C] *The X-ray showed several cracks in the bone of her left leg.*

fracture /ˈfræktʃəʳ/ [v T] to break or partly break a bone in your body – used especially by doctors: *My grandmother fell down the stairs and fractured her ankle.* | *He fractured both his legs in the car accident.* —**fracture** [n C] *More elderly women than men suffer hip fractures.* —**fractured** [adj only before noun] *He had a fractured skull.*

shatter /ˈʃætəʳ/ [v T] to break a bone in someone's body into a lot of small pieces, especially by shooting or hitting them: *The nine-year-old boy was hit by a car and shattered his skull on the pavement.* | *The bullet shattered a bone in her left forearm.*

bust /bʌst/ [v T] especially American, informal to break one of the bones in your body: *She fell and busted her knee.*

10 easily broken

- breakable
- fragile
- delicate
- brittle
- crisp

breakable /ˈbreɪkəbəl/ [adj] objects that are **breakable** break easily because they are made of glass or another thin, hard material, and must be handled carefully: *Put breakable objects out of the reach of children.* | *Many laboratories spend thousands of dollars a year on breakable glass equipment.*

fragile /ˈfrædʒaɪl‖-dʒəl/ [adj] not strong and therefore very easily broken or damaged: *The parcel was marked FRAGILE – HANDLE WITH CARE.* | *The museum sends fragile porcelain objects to specialists to be restored.*

delicate /ˈdelɪkɪ̥t/ [adj] something that is **delicate** is easily broken or damaged, especially because it is made of very thin material, and is attractive to look at: *The tea was served in delicate china cups.* | *a delicate gold necklace*

brittle /ˈbrɪtl/ [adj] hard and easily broken, especially because of being old and dry: *Perming makes your hair more brittle.* | *The building's electrical wiring was worn and brittle, causing a fire hazard.*

crisp /krɪsp/ [adj] something that is **crisp** is hard, thin, and breaks easily when you press on it: *The crisp, dry leaves rustled underneath her feet.* | *Brush the tops of the loaves with cold water, which helps form the crisp crust for which French bread is famous.*

breathe

RELATED WORDS

▸ to kill someone by preventing them from breathing *see* **kill**

▸ *see also* **air**

1 to take air into your lungs and send it out again

- breathe

breathe /briːð/ [v I/T] to take air into your lungs and send it out again through your nose or mouth: *The air was so smoky it was difficult to breathe.* | *The boy was unconscious, but he was still breathing.* | **breathe air/fumes** *People nowadays are becoming more and more concerned about the quality of the air they breathe.* | **breathe deeply** (=take a lot of air into your lungs as you breathe) *I want you to breathe deeply and relax.*

2 to take air, smoke etc into your lungs

- breathe in
- take a breath
- inhale

breathe in /ˌbriːð ˈɪn/ [phr v I/T] to take air, smoke etc into your lungs, through your nose or mouth: *Every time I breathe in I get a pain in the left side of my chest.* | **breathe in sth** *I put my handkerchief over my nose to avoid breathing in the smoke.* | *They stood on the cliff breathing in the fresh sea air.*

take a breath /ˌteɪk ə ˈbreθ/ [v phrase] to breathe in once: *Sherman stopped, took a breath, and opened the door.* | *It was so quiet that I was afraid to take a breath.* | **+ of** *Every time you took a breath of that foul air you could feel it burning your lungs.* | **take a deep breath** (=take a lot of air into your lungs) *Taking a deep breath she dived into the cool water.*

inhale /ɪnˈheɪl/ [v I/T] to take air, smoke, or gas into your lungs, through your nose or mouth – used especially in technical and medical contexts: *It is dangerous to inhale the fumes produced by these chemicals.* | *Every time he inhaled, his lungs made an awful wheezing sound.* | **inhale deeply** (=inhale a lot of air or smoke) *Stella lit up a cigarette and inhaled deeply.*

3 to send air, smoke etc out of your lungs

- breathe out
- exhale
- blow

breathe out /ˌbriːð ˈaʊt/ [phr v I/T] to send air out of your lungs, through your nose or mouth: *The doctor told her to breathe out slowly.* | *Ballet dancers are taught to breathe in before they leap, and to breathe out after they land.*

exhale /eksˈheɪl/ [v I/T] to send air or smoke out of your lungs through your nose or mouth – used especially in medical or technical contexts: *Hold your breath for 5 seconds, then exhale slowly.* | *She took a* *long pull on her cigarette, exhaled and coughed loudly.*

blow /bləʊ/ [v I/T] to breathe out strongly, especially while making a circle with your lips: *I put the balloon to my lips and blew as hard as I could.* | *He blew smoke rings across the table.* | **+ on/into etc** *'This coffee's too hot to drink.' 'Blow on it – that'll cool it down.'*

4 the action of breathing

- breathing
- breath

breathing /'bri:ðɪŋ/ [n U] the process of **breathing** air in and out: *The disease in his lungs made breathing very painful.* | *Breathing became more difficult as we got higher up the mountain.* | **deep breathing** (=breathing a lot of air into your lungs) *Deep breathing is good for relaxing your mind and your body.* | **heavy breathing** (=loud breathing) *When I picked up the phone all I heard was heavy breathing.*

breath /breθ/ [n U] the air that you breathe in or out: *It was so cold they could see their breath.* | *I could feel the horse's breath on the back of my neck.* | **hold your breath** (=stop yourself from breathing for a short time) *How long can you hold your breath underwater?* | **bad breath** (=breath that smells unpleasant) *His teeth were rotten and he had bad breath.*

5 to breathe noisily

- sniff
- sigh
- gasp
- snore
- snort

sniff /snɪf/ [v I] to breathe in noisily through your nose, for example because you have a cold or because you are crying: *Stop sniffing! Use your handkerchief.* | *'I'm sorry I got so upset,' she sniffed.* | *The dog raised its nose in the air, sniffed, and then started to follow the scent.* —**sniff** [n C] *His mother gave a sniff and asked if he had been smoking in his bedroom.*

sigh /saɪ/ [v I] to breathe in and out noisily, because you are disappointed, tired, or sad, or because you can begin to relax after worrying about something: *Frank sighed deeply and stared out of the window.* | *'That's life, I suppose,' she sighed.* | *Sighing wearily, she began her routine of getting ready for bed.* —**sigh** [n C] **with a sigh** *'Oh no!' he said with a sigh, 'Not again!'* | **breathe/give a sigh of relief** (=because you are no longer worried about something) *Irene closed the door behind her and breathed a big sigh of relief.*

gasp /gɑ:sp‖gæsp/ [v I] to suddenly breathe in noisily, because you are surprised, shocked, or in pain: *I gasped when I heard how much the ring had cost.* | *The crowd gasped as the plane burst into flames.* | **gasp with amazement/shock/pain etc** *One of the boys hit him in the face, and he gasped with pain.* —**gasp** [n C] the sound you make when you gasp **gasp of astonishment/pain/disbelief etc** *There were gasps of astonishment from the audience.*

snore /snɔ:ʳ/ [v I] to breathe noisily while you are asleep: *My husband snores so loudly that I find it difficult to get to sleep.* | *If you snore, it's better not to sleep on your back.* —**snoring** [n U] *Isn't there something you can do about your snoring?*

snort /snɔ:ʳt/ [v I] to breathe out very noisily through your nose, especially to show that you are amused or annoyed: *My sister snorts when she laughs.* | *The horse lowered its head, and snorted at them.* —**snort** [n C] *From the other side of the library came a loud unmistakable snort – it was the professor.*

6 to breathe with difficulty

- short of breath
- breathless/out of breath
- gasp
- puff
- pant
- be stuffed up
- wheeze

short of breath /ˌʃɔ:ʳt əv 'breθ/ [adj phrase] unable to breathe easily, especially because you are unhealthy: *When I wake up in the morning I'm often very short of breath.* | *She got short of breath very easily because she was so overweight.* | *The fog irritated his lungs and made him short of breath.*

breathless/out of breath /'breθləs, aʊt əv 'breθ/ [adj] having difficulty breathing, especially because you have just been running, climbing stairs etc: *She sounded a little breathless, as if she had been running.* | *We were all a little out of breath when we got on the train.* | *Can we have a rest? – I'm a bit out of breath.* —**breathlessness** [n U] *The poor lady, judging by her breathlessness and flushed cheeks, was exhausted.*

gasp /gɑ:sp‖gæsp/ [v I] to breathe very quickly and deeply because you are having difficulty breathing normally, for example after running fast or because you have been injured: *The hill was very steep and they were all gasping by the time they got to the top.* | *'Do you think you can walk?' I asked. 'I'll try,' he gasped.* | **gasp for breath** (=because you can hardly breathe) *His mother was coughing and gasping for breath.*

puff /pʌf/ [v I] to breathe loudly and with difficulty, because you are doing something which needs a lot of physical effort: *You could see her puffing as she carried the heavy washing basket.* | *'Sorry I'm so late Maxie,' he said, puffing breathlessly.*

pant /pænt/ [v I] to breathe quickly and noisily with your mouth open, for example, because you have just been running: *Matt was still panting after his run.* | *When I reached the top of the stairs I was puffing and panting like an old steam engine.* | *A strange brown dog suddenly jumped all over him, panting, its tongue out.*

be stuffed up ALSO **be bunged up** British /bi: ˌstʌft 'ʌp, bi: ˌbʌŋd 'ʌp/ [v phrase] spoken to have difficulty breathing through your nose because you have a cold: *She doesn't want to go to school. She says her throat is sore and she's stuffed up.* | **be all bunged up** *I couldn't sleep last night because I was all bunged up.*

wheeze /wi:z/ [v I] to breathe with a whistling noise in your throat and chest because you are ill or unhealthy: *When she coughed she made a terrible wheezing sound.* | *His asthma was acting up and he wheezed throughout the show.*

7 to breathe normally again after running, playing sport etc

- get your breath back/catch your breath

get your breath back/catch your breath /ˌget jɔ:ʳ 'breθ bæk, ˌkætʃ jɔ:ʳ 'breθ/ [v phrase] *It took me a few minutes to get my breath back after climbing the stairs.* | *Once you've got your breath back we can do a few more lengths of the pool.*

8 to be unable to breathe

- can't breathe
- choke
- suffocate

can't breathe /ˌkɑːnt ˈbriːð‖ˌkænt-/ [v phrase] *It's so hot in here! I can't breathe!* | *The worst thing about asthma is feeling that you can't breathe.*

choke /tʃəʊk/ [v I] to be unable to breathe because your throat is blocked or because there is not enough air: *Do something – he's choking!* | *At last I reached the shore and fell onto the sand, choking and spluttering.* | **+ on** *The old king died after choking on a chicken bone.*

suffocate /ˈsʌfəkeɪt/ [v I] to die because you are unable to breathe because you cannot get any air: *Many of the birds had suffocated in their boxes.* | *It was very hot inside the car, and I felt as though I was suffocating.* —**suffocation** /ˌsʌfəˈkeɪʃən/ [n U] when someone dies by suffocating: *Glue-sniffing carries the risk of suffocation.*

9 to make it impossible for someone to breathe

- choke
- suffocate

choke /tʃəʊk/ [v T] if a person or smoke, gas etc **chokes** someone, they make it very difficult or impossible for them to breathe: *Don't hold so tight, you're choking me.* | *I felt myself being choked by thick, yellow fumes.* | **choke sb to death** *He grabbed her around the neck and choked her to death.*

suffocate /ˈsʌfəkeɪt/ [v T] to kill someone by preventing them from getting any air: *They pushed a plastic bag over his head and almost suffocated him.* | *They found her half-suffocated from the poisonous gases given off by the burning furniture.*

bright

RELATED WORDS

opposite: — **dark**

- bright colour *see* **colour**
- *see also* **shine/shiny, light**

1 bright light

- bright
- strong
- good
- harsh

bright /braɪt/ [adj] a **bright** light shines strongly: *From the top of the hill they could see the bright lights of the city below them.* | *After so long indoors the bright sunshine hurt Jack's eyes.* | *There was a flash of bright light beyond the forest and the thunder exploded again.* —**brightly** [adv] *The fire was burning brightly now.* —**brightness** [n U] *She closed her eyes against the brightness of the sun.*

strong /strɒŋ‖strɔːŋ/ [adj] a **strong** light is very bright and helps you to see things clearly: *The light from the flashlight wasn't strong enough to read by.* | *The colors had faded after years of being exposed to strong sunlight.* —**strongly** [adv] *Daylight shone strongly through the cracks in the blinds.*

good /gʊd/ [adj] **good** light in a place where you are working is strong enough for you to see what you are doing: *The windows in the roof gave us a good light to work by.* | *The light isn't good here. Go stand by the window.*

harsh /hɑːʳʃ/ [adj] **harsh** light is very bright and unpleasant: *In the harsh light of the street lamps Michelle looked tired and old.* | *The lighting in these offices is so harsh, it gives me a headache.*

2 extremely bright

- brilliant
- blinding
- dazzling
- blazing

brilliant /ˈbrɪljənt/ [adj] extremely bright and strong, but also attractive and pleasant: *All of a sudden the stage was flooded with brilliant light.* | *A shaft of brilliant sunlight shone through the dusty attic window.* | *Suddenly, I looked up and saw a point of light that was more brilliant than any star I had ever seen.* —**brilliance** [n U] *The brilliance of the sun on the lake was quite breathtaking.*

blinding /ˈblaɪndɪŋ/ [adj] a **blinding** light is so bright that you cannot see for a short time after you have looked into it: *There was a blinding flash and then a loud bang.* | *The sun on the snow is blinding.* | *The blinding glare of our headlights frightened the deer.*

dazzling /ˈdæzlɪŋ/ [adj] a **dazzling** light is so bright that it hurts your eyes and makes it difficult for you to see: *We walked out of the cinema into dazzling sunshine.* | *The sun was so dazzling that it was impossible to even look at its reflection in the water.* —**dazzlingly** [adv] *The room was so dazzlingly bright that we had to look away.*

blazing /ˈbleɪzɪŋ/ [adj only before noun] extremely bright – use this about the sun, or about lights that you can see from a long way away: *The blazing lights of the casino shone out across the bay.* | *At twilight, the blazing orange sunset turned into a muted pink.*

3 when a place has plenty of light

- bright
- light
- well-lit

bright /braɪt/ [adj] a **bright** place is full of light, especially in a way that seems pleasant and attractive: *The big windows in this room make it nice and bright.* | *Claire had a lovely bright bedroom which was decorated in yellow and white.* | *We emerged from a dark corridor into a bright, airy courtyard.* —**brightness** [n U] *The colored lights in the distance grew in brightness as I got closer.*

light /laɪt/ [adj] a **light** building or room has plenty of **light** in it, especially because it has big windows: *The kitchen is light and airy, with a fantastic view.* | *The hallway led to a light and spacious studio.*

well-lit /ˌwel ˈlɪt◂/ [adj phrase] a place that is **well-lit** is bright because there electric lights, so it is easy for you to see what you are doing: *I always try to park in a well-lit area at night.* | *To avoid eye problems, make sure that your desk is well-lit.*

4 not bright

- pale
- dim
- weak
- poor/bad
- soft
- low

pale /peɪl/ [adj] light that is **pale** is not bright and has very little colour in it: *I couldn't get to sleep until I saw the first pale light of dawn.* | *The sunlight through the thick clouds was pale and cool that morning.* | *The banks of the river are bathed in pale moonlight.*

dim /dɪm/ [adj] a **dim** light or lamp is not bright and makes it difficult for you to see – use this about lights inside rooms or buildings, not the light outside: *It was impossible to read by the dim light of the fire.* | *There was nothing in the room but a table, a chair, and a dim lamp.* | *Dying embers gave out a dim glow in the hearth.* —**dimly** [adv] *a dimly-lit corridor* —**dim** [v I/T] if the lights dim or if you dim the lights, they become less bright: *The lights dimmed, and the audience went quiet as the curtain rose.* | *She dimmed the lights to create a more romantic atmosphere.*

weak /wiːk/ [adj] **weak** light is not bright, especially when you need it to be brighter, or when it was brighter before: *In the weak light inside the bus Tom couldn't see to read.* | *the weak glow of the dashboard lights* —**weakly** [adv] *A candle flickered weakly at the end of the table.*

poor/bad /pʊəʳ, bæd/ [adj] **poor** or **bad** light is not bright enough, so that it is difficult for you to work or see what you are doing: *Reading in poor light is very bad for the eyes.* | *It was difficult to find our way down the mountain in the mist and bad light.*

soft /sɒft‖sɔːft/ [adj only before noun] **soft light** is not bright, in a way that is pleasant and relaxing: *In the soft evening light Sonya looked ten years younger.* | *The restaurant has a romantic atmosphere with soft lights and background music.* —**softly** [adv] *Coloured lanterns shone softly in the trees and bushes.* —**softness** [n U] *The softness of candlelight added atmosphere to the evening.*

low /ləʊ/ [adj] **low** lighting is fairly dark, so that a place seems pleasant and relaxing – use this about the light in rooms or buildings, not the light outside: *For our anniversary, let's go to a restaurant with low lights and soft music.* | *It was a while before Samuel's eyes got used to the low lighting of the intensive care unit.*

broken/ not broken

RELATED WORDS

- something wrong with a machine, system etc *see* **fault (1)**
- when a machine, system etc works well without any problem *see* **working**
- *see also* **break, damage, tear, repair**

1 objects/cups/furniture etc

- broken
- chipped
- cracked
- bust/busted

broken /ˈbrəʊkən/ [adj] something that is **broken** has become separated into pieces, for example by being hit or dropped: *The floor was covered in broken glass.* | *This suitcase is no good – the handle's broken.* | *The birds had gotten into the cabin through a broken window.* | *In the corner of the room were a broken chair and a rickety old desk.*

chipped /tʃɪpt/ [adj] a cup, plate etc that is **chipped** has a small piece broken off the edge of it: *Why do I always get the chipped cup?* | *Don't use that plate – it's chipped.*

cracked /krækt/ [adj] something that is **cracked** is not completely broken, but has cracks on its surface as a result of damage: *Throw that jug away. It's cracked.* | *The tiles were old and cracked.* | *He's been driving around with a cracked windshield for months.*

bust /bʌst/ [adj not before noun] British informal **/busted** /ˈbʌstᵻd/ [adj] especially American, informal broken: *I can't carry all the shopping home in this bag – it's bust.* | *The door's bust again. Can you get it fixed?* | *In the yard, Miguel found a writing table with a busted leg.*

2 bones

- broken
- fractured
- busted

broken /ˈbrəʊkən/ [adj] a **broken** bone has been cracked or separated into pieces: *One little boy had a broken arm.* | *I think my ankle's broken.*

fractured /ˈfræktʃəʳd/ [adj] a **fractured** bone has been cracked, but it has not completely separated: *The X-ray revealed that she had several fractured ribs.*

busted /ˈbʌstᵻd/ [adj] American informal broken: *Julie's arm is busted and she can't take care of herself.*

3 machines, cars, phones etc that do not work

- is not working/doesn't work
- there's something wrong with
- broken
- be out of order
- be out of action
- be down
- be on the blink
- temperamental
- has gone
- has had it
- bust

is not working/doesn't work /ɪz ˌnɒt ˈwɜːʳkɪŋ, ˌdʌzənt ˈwɜːʳk/ [v phrase] if a machine or piece of equipment **is not working** or **doesn't work**, it does not do the job it is supposed to do: *The phone's not working.* | *Our car isn't working at the moment, so I've been taking the bus.* | *The elevator doesn't seem to be working – let's take the stairs.* | *The headlights don't work and the brakes need fixing.* | *This camera doesn't work – I'll have to take it back to the store.*

there's something wrong with /ðeəʳz ˌsʌmθɪŋ ˈrɒŋ wɪð‖-ˈrɔːŋ-/ [v phrase] if **there is something wrong with** a machine, car etc, it does not work properly, but you do not know exactly why: *There's something wrong with my car: I think it might be the battery.* | *There was something wrong with the photocopier, so we called in the service company.* | **have something wrong with sth** *If the VCR has something wrong with it, take it back to the store.*

broken /ˈbrəʊkən/ [adj] not working – use this especially about a small machine or a small piece of equipment: *'What's the time?' 'I don't know, my watch is broken.'* | *I think the doorbell must be broken – I didn't hear anything.* | *a broken dishwasher*

be out of order /biː ˌaʊt əv ˈɔːʳdəʳ/ [v phrase] if a machine, especially one used by the public, **is out of order** it is not working for a temporary period: *Every phone I tried was out of order.* | *The toilets are almost always out of order.*

be out of action /biː ˌaʊt əv ˈækʃən/ [v phrase] especially British if a vehicle or machine **is out of action**, it cannot be used at the moment because it is broken: *Three of our tanks are out of action.* | *These planes may be out of action for a week, just for regular maintenance.* | *Our washing machine's out of action at the moment, so we use the laundry down the road.*

be down /biː 'daʊn/ [v phrase] if a computer system **is down**, it is not working: *The computer system was down all afternoon so we went home.* | **go down** (=stop working) *The network went down at 11:00 and we lost the whole morning's work.*

be on the blink /biː ɒn ðə 'blɪŋk/ informal ALSO **be on the fritz** /biː ˌɒn ðə 'frɪtz/ American informal [v phrase] if a piece of electrical equipment such as a television or washing machine **is on the blink** or **on the fritz**, it sometimes works and sometimes does not: *My TV's on the blink again.* | **go on the blink/fritz** *The car's air conditioning went on the fritz just as we reached Dallas.*

temperamental /ˌtempərə'mentl◂/ [adj] informal a machine, car etc that is **temperamental** works some of the time but not all the time: *Jo's car is very temperamental in the mornings. Sometimes it starts and sometimes it doesn't.* | *The only heating was from a temperamental iron stove in the centre of each hut.*

has gone British **is gone** American /həz 'gɒn, ɪz 'gɒn‖-'gɔːn/ [v phrase] if you say that part of a machine, especially a car, **has gone** or **is gone**, you mean that it has stopped working properly: *I'm not sure what's wrong with my car – I think the clutch has gone.* | *If the gearbox is gone it'll cost you a fortune.* | *'What's that noise?' 'It sounds like the suspension's going.'*

has had it /həz 'hæd ɪt/ [v phrase] if you say that a machine **has had it** you mean that it is completely broken and cannot be repaired: *I'm afraid the stereo's had it.*

bust /bʌst/ [adj not before noun] British **busted** /'bʌstɪ̈d/ [adj] especially American broken or badly damaged: *Our television's bust, and so's the radio.* | *There's no point in trying to mend it, it's completely bust.* | *You can't record anything – the VCR's busted.* | *a busted air-conditioner*

4 to stop working

- something goes wrong
- break down
- crash
- cut out
- fail
- malfunction
- pack up

something goes wrong /ˌsʌmθɪŋ gəʊz 'rɒŋ‖-'rɔːŋ/ [v phrase] if **something goes wrong** with a machine, it stops working normally – use this especially about complicated equipment, when you do not know what the problem is: *Who'll fix my computer if something goes wrong?* | **+ with** *Occasionally something went wrong with the projector and the movie was canceled.* | *Something's gone wrong with my washing machine.*

break down /ˌbreɪk 'daʊn/ [phr v I] if a car, bus, train, or large machine **breaks down**, it stops working completely: *She was late for the meeting because her car broke down.* | *The elevators in this building are always breaking down.* —**breakdown** /'breɪkdaʊn/ [n C/U] *A mechanical breakdown during the race would mean defeat.*

crash /kræʃ/ [v I] if a computer **crashes**, it suddenly stops working, and information is often lost because of this: *I installed the new program and my computer crashed.* | *Hundreds of hospital records were wiped out when the network crashed.*

cut out /ˌkʌt 'aʊt/ [phr v I] if an engine **cuts out**, it suddenly stops working: *Every time Mark slowed down the engine cut out.* | *I started to go up the hill and the engine just cut out on me.*

fail /feɪl/ [v I] especially written if a part of a machine or of a piece of electrical equipment **fails**, it stops working: *The driver of the car claims that his brakes failed and he was unable to stop.* | *In the last ten minutes of the game, one of the television cameras failed.* | *One of the engines failed at 30,000 feet.* —**failure** /'feɪljəʳ/ [n U] **mechanical/equipment/engine failure** *Investigators traced the cause of the crash to engine failure.*

malfunction /mæl'fʌŋkʃən/ [v I] formal to stop working properly: *This is a sign that the computer's hard disk is malfunctioning.* | *Both satellites entered orbit but quickly malfunctioned.* —**malfunction** [n C] *Someone at the plant has to be ready to deal with equipment malfunctions at any time.*

pack up /ˌpæk 'ʌp/ [phr v I] British informal if a machine **packs up**, it stops working, especially because it is old: *When this record player packs up, I'll buy a CD player.* | *They won't know what to do if a pipe bursts or if the heater packs up.*

5 to stop a machine from working

- break
- disable
- put sth out of action
- immobilize

break /breɪk/ [v T] to stop a machine from working by damaging it, especially by damaging it so badly that it cannot be used again: *One of the kids put some rocks in the blender and broke it.* | *I don't know what she did, but she managed to break the sewing machine.*

disable /dɪs'eɪbəl/ [v T] written to make a machine or a system unable to work: *The robbers had disabled the bank's security system.* | *The tank's navigational system had been disabled during a grenade attack.*

put sth out of action /ˌpʊt (sth) aʊt əv 'ækʃən/ [v phrase] to deliberately stop a machine or piece of equipment from working properly by damaging it, especially because you want to stop an enemy from using it: *An electronic mine exploded under the ship and put it out of action.* | *Reporting from the area was difficult even before terrorists put all the telephone lines out of action.*

immobilize ALSO **immobilise** British /ɪ'məʊbɪ̈laɪz/ [v T] to stop a vehicle from working, especially a military vehicle: *Demonstrators immobilized tanks using gasoline bombs.* | *Kendrick had only a few minutes to immobilize the aircraft.*

6 not broken or damaged

- intact
- in one piece

intact /ɪn'tækt/ [adj not before noun] not broken or damaged, in spite of being hit, dropped etc: *Despite the bombing, the house was still intact.* | *The toys have to be intact in their original boxes or they're not worth anything.* | *Our furniture survived the long journey more or less intact.*

in one piece /ɪn ˌwʌn 'piːs/ [adv] if something arrives or is moved **in one piece**, it does not get broken in spite of being moved: *I don't know how we got the piano down in one piece!* | *The china arrived all in one piece, thank God.*

build/building

RELATED WORDS

▸ *see also* **make, house, design**

1 to build something

- ▸ build
- ▸ put up
- ▸ construct
- ▸ go up
- ▸ erect

build /bɪld/ [v I/T] to make a house, road, wall, bridge etc using bricks, stone, wood or other materials: *Are they going to build on this land?* | *His ambition is to build his own house.* | *The cost of building the new football stadium was over $40 million.* | *The road was originally built by the Romans.* | **be built of concrete/stone/wood etc** *Only about 3% of houses in the US are built of concrete.* —**builder** [n] someone whose job is to build and repair buildings: *Builders say that new home construction is slowing down.*

put up /ˌpʊt ˈʌp/ [phr v T] to build a wall, fence, or a tall building **put up sth** *They're planning to tear down these apartments and put up an office building.* | **put sth up** *Isobel and Peter have put a stone wall up along the side of the garden.*

construct /kənˈstrʌkt/ [v T] to build a large public building, a bridge, road etc: *The city council has plans for constructing two new schools and a hospital.* | *This elegant two-storey stone building was constructed in 1889.* | *New freeway ramps are being constructed in San Bruno.*

go up /ˌgəʊ ˈʌp/ [phr v I] **especially spoken** if buildings are **going up** in a place, they are being built: *It seems like new beachfront hotels are going up every week.* | *Whenever a new mall goes up, I ask myself how many of these things we need.*

erect /ɪˈrekt/ [v T] **formal** to build a public building or structure: *The first lighthouse was erected on the island in 1912.* | *The group hopes to erect a statue of Fleming next year.*

2 the process of building houses, roads etc

- ▸ construction
- ▸ building

construction /kənˈstrʌkʃən/ [n U] the process or method of building large public buildings, bridges, roads etc: *The firm deals mainly in road construction.* | **+ on** *Construction on the tunnel will begin in April.* | **+ of** *Construction of the dam is nearly complete.* | **under construction** *About 3,000 housing units are under construction in the city.* | **construction industry** *The construction industry has been severely affected by the recession.*

building /ˈbɪldɪŋ/ [n U] the process or business of **building** houses: *There has been an increase in new-home building in recent months.* | *It was the invention of pre-stressed concrete that really transformed building techniques.* | **building industry** *Thousands of workers in the building industry will lose their jobs as a result of cutbacks.*

3 the design of buildings

- ▸ architecture
- ▸ architect

architecture /ˈɑːʳkətektʃəʳ/ [n U] the way in which buildings are designed, or the work of designing buildings: *We spent most of our time in Barcelona just looking at the architecture.* | *City Hall is a fine example of Gothic architecture.* | *She's studying architecture at college.* —**architectural** /ˌɑːʳkəˈtektʃərəl◂/ [adj only before noun] *The building has won several awards for its architectural design.*

architect /ˈɑːʳkətekt/ [n C] someone whose job is to design buildings: *St Paul's Cathedral was designed by the famous architect, Sir Christopher Wren.*

4 a building or group of buildings

- ▸ building
- ▸ block
- ▸ development
- ▸ structure

building /ˈbɪldɪŋ/ [n C] *Brewer Hall is a red-brick building with white trim.* | *The whole building shook when a train went past.* | *There's a plan to convert the farm buildings into private apartments.*

block /blɒk‖blɑːk/ [n C] a large building divided into smaller parts **+ of** *The house at Number 14 was replaced by a block of flats.* | **office/apartment block** *There's another new office block going up behind the station.* | *His studios are on the tenth floor of an office block overlooking the river.* | **high-rise/tower block** (=very tall block) **British** *To the east is a landscape of concrete tower blocks.*

development /dɪˈveləpmənt/ [n C] a group of new buildings that have all been planned and built together on the same piece of land: *The new development at the edge of town is aimed at first-time buyers.* | *The former cropland has been turned into housing developments and shopping malls.*

structure /ˈstrʌktʃəʳ/ [n C] a large building or a part of a building – used especially to say what it is made of or how strong it is: *The station building was a high wooden structure with a curved roof.* | *The stone arch is one of the town's oldest existing structures.*

burn

RELATED WORDS

▸ *see also* **fire, hot, explode**

1 to burn something

- ▸ burn
- ▸ burn down
- ▸ incinerate
- ▸ scorch
- ▸ singe
- ▸ charred

burn /bɜːʳn/ [v T] to damage or destroy something with fire or heat: *She lit a fire and burned his letters one by one.* | **burn a hole in sth** (=make a hole by burning it) *Someone had dropped a cigarette and burned a hole in the carpet.* | **burn sth to a crisp/cinder** (=destroy something completely by burning it) *Most of his possessions had been burnt to a cinder.* —**burnt/burned** /bɜːʳnt, bɜːʳnd/ [adj] *The cake is slightly burnt, I'm afraid.*

burn down /ˌbɜːʳn ˈdaʊn/ [phr v T] to completely destroy a building by burning it **burn down sth** *Police believe students are responsible for burning down the school.* | **burn sth down** *Her ex-husband threatened to burn the house down with her and the kids inside.*

incinerate /ɪnˈsɪnəreɪt/ [v T usually in passive] to destroy unwanted things by burning them in a special machine: *Household waste is usually incinerated after it has been collected. | All the clothes that were affected by radiation had to be incinerated.*

scorch /skɔːʳtʃ/ [v T] to burn the surface of something and leave a dark mark on it: *The heater was left on all night and it scorched the wall. | Having the iron on a very high heat can scorch the fabric.* —**scorch mark** /ˈskɔːʳtʃ mɑːʳk/ [n C] *This shirt is ruined – there's a big scorch mark on the back.*

singe /sɪndʒ/ [v T] to damage something such as hair, wool, or paper by burning it slightly so that the ends or edges are burnt: *The flames were hot enough to singe your eyebrows. | The rug was singed by a piece of burning coal that had fallen from the fire.*

charred /tʃɑːʳd/ [adj usually before noun] wood, sticks, bones etc that are **charred** are black because they have been damaged by burning: *In the cave they found some charred animal bones. | It was nearly impossible to recognize the charred bodies.*

2 to burn yourself

- burn
- scald

burn /bɜːʳn/ [v T] if you **burn** yourself, you hurt yourself by accidentally touching something hot **burn yourself** *Don't touch the iron. You'll burn yourself.* | **burn your mouth/fingers/arm etc** *She burnt her arm on a camping stove.* | **be badly/severely/seriously burned/burnt** *Jerry was badly burned in the explosion.* —**burn** [n C] a mark on your skin where you have been burned: *The child had cigarette burns on his arms and legs.* | **severe/serious burns** *Billy was taken to the hospital with severe burns.* | **minor burns** (=not serious) *Jones suffered only minor burns when her house was set ablaze last week.*

scald /skɔːld/ [v T] to burn yourself with very hot liquid or steam **scald yourself** *If you're not careful you'll scald yourself on/with that kettle.* | **scald your arm/leg/hand etc** *The hot coffee nearly scalded his tongue.*

3 to make something start burning

- set fire to sth/set sth on fire
- light
- torch
- ignite

set fire to sth/set sth on fire /set ˈfaɪəʳ tə (sth), ˌset (sth) ɒn ˈfaɪəʳ/ [v phrase] to make something start to burn, so that it gets damaged: *Vandals set fire to an empty warehouse near the docks last night. | Teresa wondered if the burning log might set fire to the curtains. | The Vikings attacked villages along the coast and set them on fire. | The heat from the stove almost set the wallpaper on fire.*

light /laɪt/ [v T] **light a cigarette/fire/candle etc** to make a cigarette, fire etc start to burn: *Ricky sat down and lit a cigarette. | We searched around for twigs and fallen branches, so we could light a fire.*

torch /tɔːʳtʃ/ [v T] informal to deliberately make something start to burn in order to destroy it: *It looked to me like someone had torched the place.*

ignite /ɪgˈnaɪt/ [v T] to make something start to burn, especially something that burns easily such as a gas or chemical: *The gas is ignited by an electrical spark. | If the mixture proves difficult to ignite, increase the proportion of ethylene.*

4 to make something stop burning

- put out
- extinguish
- blow out
- smother
- stub out

put out /ˌpʊt ˈaʊt/ [phr v T] to make a fire stop burning, or make a cigarette, pipe etc stop burning **put out sth** *It took firefighters four hours to put out the blaze. | I put out my cigarette and went back into the house.* | **put sth out** *She threw sand on the fire to put it out.*

extinguish /ɪkˈstɪŋgwɪʃ/ [v T] formal to make a fire stop burning, or make a cigarette stop burning – used especially in official notices or statements: *Would all passengers please extinguish their cigarettes? Thank you. | He managed to extinguish the flames with his coat.*

blow out /ˌbləʊ ˈaʊt/ [phr v T] to make a flame or fire stop burning by blowing on it **blow out sth** *You have to blow out all the candles or your wish won't come true.* | **blow sth out** *We tried to light a fire but the wind kept blowing it out.*

smother /ˈsmʌðəʳ/ [v T] to cover a fire with something in order to stop it burning: *I grabbed a blanket and tried to smother the flames.*

stub out /ˌstʌb ˈaʊt/ [phr v T] to stop a cigarette from burning by pushing it against something hard **stub out sth** *She stubbed out her cigarette on the edge of the table.* | **stub sth out** *Don't stub your cigarette out on the floor!*

5 to stop burning

- go out
- die down
- burn itself out

go out /ˌgəʊ ˈaʊt/ [phr v I] if a fire, match, flame etc **goes out**, it stops burning, especially because there is nothing left to burn or something has stopped it burning: *When I got back the fire had gone out. | Suddenly the candle went out. | Don't let the campfire go out.*

die down /ˌdaɪ ˈdaʊn/ [phr v I] if a fire or flame **dies down**, it starts to burn less and less strongly: *The fire slowly died down during the night. | The barbecue won't be ready until the flames have died down and the charcoal is glowing.*

burn itself out /ˌbɜːʳn ɪtself ˈaʊt/ [v phrase] if a fire **burns itself out**, it burns until there is nothing left to burn, so that it stops: *Firefighters are hoping the blaze will burn itself out before dawn. | It's only a small fire – we can leave it to burn itself out.*

6 when something is burning

- burn
- be on fire
- be in flames
- blazing
- smoulder
- flicker

burn /bɜːʳn/ [v T] to produce flames and heat: *A pile of branches was burning in the yard. | At one end of the room a coal fire burned brightly. | The candle flickered briefly, then burned with a steady flame.* —**burning** /ˈbɜːʳnɪŋ/ [adj only before noun] *The smell of burning rubber filled the air. | He was 200 yards from the burning ship when it exploded.*

be on fire /biː ɒn ˈfaɪəʳ/ [v phrase] if a building, vehicle, or piece of clothing **is on fire**, it is burning: *Large areas of the forest are reported to be on fire. | Before long the neighboring houses were on fire too.*

be in flames ALSO **be ablaze** /biː ɪn ˈfleɪmz, biː əˈbleɪz/ [v phrase] to be on fire with a lot of flames, causing serious damage: *When the fire department arrived the whole school was in flames.* | *Twelve hours after the bombing raid, many parts of the city were still ablaze.*

blazing /ˈbleɪzɪŋ/ [adj only before noun] burning very brightly with a lot of flames and heat: *They sat on the sofa in front of a blazing fire.* | *The heat from the blazing car could be felt several metres away.*

smoulder British **/smolder** American /ˈsməʊldəʳ/ [v I] to burn slowly, producing smoke but no flames: *The fire in the chemical factory was so intense that it was still smouldering a week later.* | *A cigarette smoldered in the ashtray.* | *a pile of smoldering leaves*

flicker /ˈflɪkəʳ/ [v I] if a fire or flame **flickers**, it burns unsteadily: *A welcoming fire flickered in the grate.* | *Inside the shrine candles flicker next to statues of saints.*

7 when something starts burning

- catch fire
- burst into flames
- go up (in flames)
- break out
- flare up
- ignite

catch fire /ˌkætʃ ˈfaɪəʳ/ ALSO **catch on fire** /ˌkætʃ ɒn ˈfaɪəʳ/ especially American [v phrase] to start burning accidentally: *Two farm workers died when a barn caught fire yesterday.* | *The car turned over, but luckily it didn't catch fire.* | *There was an explosion, and the whole garage caught on fire.*

burst into flames /ˌbɜːʳst ɪntə ˈfleɪmz/ [v phrase] to suddenly start burning and produce a lot of flames that cause serious damage: *The plane crashed into the side of the mountain and burst into flames.* | *Without warning the toaster burst into flames.*

go up (in flames) /ˌgəʊ ʌp ɪn ˈfleɪmz/ [phr v I] if a building or vehicle **goes up** or **goes up in flames**, it starts burning very quickly and usually is destroyed by fire: *Be careful with those matches, or the whole place will go up in flames!* | *The fire spread slowly until it reached the gas cylinders, then the factory went up in flames.* | *If the oil tanker goes up, it could burn for weeks.*

break out /ˌbreɪk ˈaʊt/ [phr v I] if a fire **breaks out**, it starts burning accidentally and spreads very quickly: *Over £20,000 worth of damage was caused when a fire broke out in the cellar.* | *Would you know what to do if a fire broke out in your school?*

flare up /ˌfleər ˈʌp/ [phr v I] to suddenly begin to burn, or suddenly burn much more strongly than before, with a strong, bright flame: *The spilled gasoline suddenly flared up in a sheet of flame.* | *They threw some dry wood onto the bonfire and it flared up, showering sparks into the night sky.*

ignite /ɪgˈnaɪt/ [v I] to start burning: *Scientists could not explain why the gas had suddenly ignited.* | *The compound ignites at 450 degrees Celsius.*

8 to be destroyed by fire

- burn down
- gutted
- burnt-out

burn down /ˌbɜːʳn ˈdaʊn/ [phr v I] if a building **burns down**, it is completely destroyed by fire: *Charlene has lived with relatives since her house burned down.* | *The hotel burnt down in 1990.*

gutted /ˈgʌtɪ̈d/ [adj not usually before noun] a building that is **gutted** is still standing, but its inside has been completely destroyed by fire: *'Was there anything worth saving after the fire?' 'No, the place is completely gutted.'* | *a street full of gutted buildings* — **gut** [v T] *A blaze gutted the dance hall last April.*

burnt-out especially British **/burned-out** especially American /ˌbɜːʳnt ˈaʊt◂, ˌbɜːʳnd ˈaʊt◂/ [adj usually before noun] a building or a vehicle that is **burnt-out** or **burned-out** has had everything inside it destroyed by fire: *In the main square the burnt-out shell of the Palace of Justice still smouldered.* | *The van was burned-out and completely blackened by smoke.*

9 something that burns easily

- burn
- flammable

burn /bɜːʳn/ [v I] to be able to be burned: *Does styrofoam burn?* | **burn well/easily/badly etc** *Hard woods generally don't burn well.*

flammable ALSO **inflammable** /ˈflæməbəl, ɪnˈflæməbəl/ [adj] materials, chemicals, or gases that are **flammable** or **inflammable** will start burning very easily and quickly, so they can be dangerous: *The report stated that inflammable substances were found near the building's heating system.* | **highly inflammable/flammable** (=extremely flammable) *Hydrogen is a highly flammable gas.*

10 something that does not burn easily

- fireproof
- flameproof/flame-resistant

fireproof /ˈfaɪəʳpruːf/ [adj] not easily damaged by flames: *Theatre curtains have to be fireproof.*

flameproof/flame-resistant /ˈfleɪmpruːf, ˈfleɪm rɪˌzɪstənt/ [adj] clothes or substances such as glass that are **flameproof** or **flame-resistant** have been specially made so that they are not damaged by fire: *Heat the mixture in a flameproof dish.* | *Children's pajamas are usually made from flame-resistant material.*

business

RELATED WORDS

- when a business fails *see* **fail (8)**
- *see also* **company, manager, money, profit, sell, buy, job, shop/store**

1 the work that companies do

- business
- trade
- commerce
- industry
- e-commerce
- operations
- dealings
- venture

business /ˈbɪznɪ̈s/ [n U] the work that companies do when they buy and sell goods and services: *Business in Europe has been badly affected by economic conditions in Asia.* | **on business** (=for business reasons) *She'll be back next week – she's in Korea on business.* | **the advertising/computer/insurance business** (=the work of companies that are involved in advertising, computers etc) *He's been in the advertising business for over 20 years now, and he wants to get out.* | **have a head for business** (=have a good understanding of business) *Spending a year working for a big company will be good for him – at the moment he has no head for business at all.*

trade /treɪd/ [n U] the buying and selling of goods and services, especially between countries **+ with/between** *The introduction of the Euro should make trade between European countries much easier.* | **trade in sth** (=the buying and selling of a particular kind of goods) *The trade in data processing between countries is likely to grow faster than the trade in goods.* | **trade agreement** *South Korea and Japan have signed an important trade agreement.* | **trade deficit** (=when a country buys more goods from another country than it sells to that country) *The trade deficit with China remains high.* | **trade embargo** (=when a country refuses to buy goods from another country or sell goods to that country) *The U.S. has maintained a trade embargo against Cuba since 1962.* | **balance of trade** (=the difference between the amount a country buys and the amount it sells) *Strong exports of services helped the overall balance of trade.* | **world/international/overseas trade** *After agriculture, overseas trade accounts for the largest portion of the economy.* | **the fur/arms/diamond etc trade** (=the buying and selling of fur, weapons etc) *The war has created favorable conditions for the illegal arms trade.*

commerce /ˈkɒmɜːʳs‖ˈkɑː-/ [n U] the buying and selling of goods and services, especially between companies or countries – use this to talk about these activities in general: *One of the roles of the federal government is to regulate interstate commerce.* | *He had a genuine talent for commerce and soon had a brilliant career working for the World Bank.*

industry /ˈɪndəstri/ [n C/U] the production of large quantities of goods to sell to people, or the companies and people that are involved in this process: *The region has tried to attract new industry in order to reduce unemployment.* | **the textile/motor/engineering etc industry** *Many people moved from Asia to work in the British textile industry, where jobs were plentiful.* | **in industry** *She was looking for a management position in industry.* | **heavy industry** (=the production of steel, cars, ships etc) *The Ruhr valley has always been the centre of German heavy industry.* | **light industry** (=the production of goods such as electronic and electrical goods) *Ireland is now a European center for light industry, like computer assembly.*

e-commerce /ˈiː ˌkɒmɜːʳs‖-ˌkɑː-/ [n U] the buying and selling of goods and services on the Internet: *E-commerce is still a small but fast-growing part of the U.S. economy.* | *a conference to debate the future of e-commerce*

operations /ˌɒpəˈreɪʃənz‖ˌɑːp-/ [n plural] a company's **operations** are all its activities, especially in one country or one area of business **UK/US/overseas/international etc operations** *Salco may have to close down its UK operations with the loss of 1500 jobs.* | *He was an important decision maker in terms of GM's overseas operations.*

dealings /ˈdiːlɪŋz/ [n plural] business activities, especially those that involve the movement of money between companies, countries, banks etc: *The company had to pay a lot of tax on its financial dealings during the past tax year.* | **+ with** *Mr Stockwell's dealings with several Third World banks are currently under investigation.*

venture /ˈventʃəʳ/ [n C] a new business activity which involves risking money: *The group is planning to risk everything to get their next venture off the ground.* | **business venture** *His bankruptcy was the result of several reckless business ventures.* | **joint venture** *Ford has invested $125 million in a joint venture to build engines in China.*

2 the amount of business a company is doing

- business
- turnover
- sales

business /ˈbɪznɪ̈s/ [n U] (=a company is successful/not successful) *Business is really bad at the moment. They may have to sell some of their factories overseas.* | *Business was good until June and then sales fell because people were on vacation.* | **business is booming** (=business is very good) *In the old days, when business was booming, he used to fly to New York twice a week.* | **sth is good for business** *Building the new highway will be good for business.*

turnover /ˈtɜːʳnəʊvəʳ/ [n singular] the amount of goods or services that a company sells in a particular period of time: *Our corporation has an annual turnover of $3.2 billion.* | *Turnover is expected to double now that the recession is over.*

sales /seɪlz/ [n plural] the amount of goods or services that a company sells: *Sales have been far better than expected.* | *These firms report sales of between 10 and 20 million dollars a year.* | **sales figures** (=information about how much has been sold) *December sales figures will be released on Thursday.*

3 relating to business

- business
- commercial
- industrial

business /ˈbɪznɪ̈s/ [adj only before noun] *During the first week of the secretarial course we learned how to write business letters.* | *Most of the women there were wearing business suits.* | **business trip/lunch/meeting** (=a trip, meal etc arranged for business reasons not pleasure) *He's in Tokyo on a business trip.* | **business associate** (=someone you do business with) *I've known Mr Henry for years. He's one of my father's old business associates.*

commercial /kəˈmɜːʳʃəl/ [adj only before noun] a **commercial** activity or organization is concerned with the business of buying and selling goods and services: *His first commercial venture was opening a small corner shop.* | *The British Empire was established for commercial as well as political reasons.* | *The space shuttle is being used more and more for commercial purposes.* —**commercially** [adv] relating to whether something is successful and makes a profit: *Commercially, the movie was a disaster.*

industrial /ɪnˈdʌstriəl/ [adj usually before noun] relating to the production of goods in factories: *The government is giving high priority to industrial development.* | *industrial waste*

4 to do business

- do business
- be in business
- deal with
- deal in
- trade
- operate

do business /ˌduː ˈbɪznɪ̈s/ [v phrase] if a company **does business** with another company, it buys things from them or sells things to them: *I hope you'll think about my offer. I'm sure we can do business.* | **+ with** *They do a lot of business with Italian companies.* | *She's very efficient – the kind of person you want to do business with.* | **do good business** (=do a lot of successful business) *They've been doing very good business lately. They'll probably even expand their operations.*

be in business /biː ɪn ˈbɪznɪs/ [v phrase] if someone **is in business** they own a company or shop: *In all the twenty years I've been in business this is the worst period I've seen for sales.* | *The insurance companies are in business to make money, not waste it.* | **set up in business** British (=start a company, shop etc) *When I qualified I set up in business as a financial consultant.*

deal with /ˈdiːl wɪð/ [phr v T] to buy goods from another company or person, or sell goods to them: *I deal with farmers, selling them things like cattle feed and insecticides.* | *They don't buy their office supplies from a store – they only deal with the manufacturers.* | *We don't deal with the actors directly – we usually have to go through their agents.*

deal in /ˈdiːl ɪn/ [phr v T] to do business buying or selling a particular product: *Companies that deal in oil should prepare themselves for a price drop.* | *The main commodities he dealt in were rice and lentils.*

trade /treɪd/ [v I] if a country or large organization **trades** with another country or large organization, they buy, sell, or exchange goods with each other **+ with** *The two nations have not traded with each other for over 30 years.* | **trading partner** (=a country that regularly does business with another country) *Japan is one of our major trading partners.*

operate /ˈɒpəreɪt‖ˈɑː-/ [v I] if a company or organization **operates** it takes part in business activities, especially in one country or in one kind of business: *Olivetti operates in all the major computer markets in the world.* | *Screenview are a small company operating from a converted barn in a village near Norwich.*

5 a business agreement

- deal
- transaction

deal /diːl/ [n C] a business agreement between two companies, especially when one company agrees to provide goods or services, and another company agrees to buy them: *Wickes lost a lot of money on two large property deals.* | **+ with** *They agreed a $55 million deal with a leading Japanese automobile company.* | **sign a deal** *Taylor recently signed a deal to lease her three-bedroom home for $14,000.* | **finalize a deal** (=complete it) *It is expected that the deal will be finalized before the end of May.*

transaction /trænˈzækʃən/ [n C] a business deal between two or more people or companies in which money is given and something is bought or sold: *When the transaction is complete it will be at least two weeks before you receive your copy of the contract.* | *Most transactions are processed by computer at our Head Office.*

6 someone who works in business

- businessman/businesswoman/business person
- entrepreneur

businessman/businesswoman/business person /ˈbɪznɪsmən, ˈbɪznɪsˌwʊmən, ˈbɪznɪsˌpɜːʳsən/ [n C] someone who works in business, especially as the owner or manager of a company: *Tim Knight is a high-powered businessman who runs his own electronics company.* | *A successful businesswoman, she had made her first million before she was 21.*

entrepreneur /ˌɒntrəprəˈnɜːʳ‖ˌɑːn-/ [n C] someone who is willing to risk their money in order to make a profit or start a new company: *The Bay Area is full of entrepreneurs hoping to make money on the Internet.* | *A few months ago a young property entrepreneur bought a vacant house, redecorated it and sold it for twice the original value.*

busy/not busy

RELATED WORDS

- when you do not have enough time to do something *see* **time (23-24)**
- *see also* **work/work hard**

WHAT'S HERE

busy/have a lot to do

RELATED WORDS

- time when you can do what you want *see* **free (10-11)**

1 a busy person

- busy
- have a lot to do
- have a lot on
- be rushed/run off your feet
- be up to your ears/neck in
- be under (a lot of) pressure
- be snowed under
- be on the go
- have your hands full

busy /ˈbɪzi/ [adj] having a lot of things you should do: *She's very busy – it's her daughter's wedding next week.* | *Angela was becoming more and more unhappy, but her husband was too busy to notice.* | *Not now, Stephen, I'm busy.* | **busy doing sth** *Critics say the mayor is too busy campaigning to do his job properly.* | **+ with** *She was busy with business matters so we decided not to burden her with our problems.* | **keep sb busy** *He's retired now, but his work for the youth club keeps him busy.* —**busily** [adj] *The chefs were busily preparing hundreds of tantalizing dishes for the banquet.*

have a lot to do /hæv ə ˌlɒt tə ˈduː‖-ˌlɑːt-/ [v phrase not in progressive] to have to do a lot of things, and need to hurry or work hard: *I'm sorry I can't talk – I have a lot to do before my wife gets home.* | **an awful lot to do** (=used to emphasize you have a lot to do) *Let's get started. We have an awful lot to do and not much time to do it.*

have a lot on British **have a lot going on** American /hæv ə ˌlɒt ˈɒn, hæv ə ˌlɒt gəʊɪŋ ˈɒn‖-ˌlɑːt-/ [v phrase not in progressive] to be busy, especially because you have arranged to do a lot of things during a short period: *He says he'll try and see you as soon as possible, but he has a lot going on this afternoon.* | *We've got so much on at work I couldn't possibly go on holiday now.*

be rushed/run off your feet /biː ˌrʌʃt, ˌrʌn ɒf jɔːʳ ˈfiːt/ [v phrase] especially British, spoken to be very busy and always in a hurry, because you have a lot of things to do: *It's my son's birthday party tomorrow. I've been absolutely rushed off my feet getting ready for it.* | *All the sales assistants are run off their feet. The shop ought to take on more staff.*

be up to your ears/neck in /biː ˌʌp tə jɔːr ˈɪəʳz, ˈnek ɪn/ [v phrase] especially spoken to be extremely busy because you have a lot of work to do in your job: *I'm sorry I can't talk to you now – I'm up to my neck in paperwork.* | *Teachers nowadays are up to their ears in administration and don't have much time for teaching.*

be under (a lot of) pressure /biː ˌʌndər (ə lɒt‖lɑːt əv) ˈpreʃəʳ/ [v phrase] to be very busy, especially because other people are making you work hard, or because you have to do something by a particular time: *Jerry says he's under a lot of pressure at the moment from his boss.* | **work under pressure** *Some people don't work well under pressure.*

be snowed under /biː ˌsnəʊd ˈʌndəʳ/ [v phrase] especially British to be extremely busy and hardly able to deal with all the work you have to do: *Don't expect any help from them – they're snowed under at the moment.* | **+ with** *Since the hurricane, builders and roofers have been snowed under with work.*

be on the go /biː ɒn ðə ˈgəʊ/ [v phrase] spoken to be very busy for a period of time, especially when this makes you tired: *I've been on the go all week – I'm looking forward to a relaxing weekend now.* | *She's always on the go. I don't know how she does it.*

have your hands full /hæv jɔːʳ ˌhændz ˈfʊl/ [v phrase not in progressive] to be busy because you have to deal with a lot of different jobs or problems, so that you do not have time to do anything else: *I'm sorry I can't help you – I have my hands full right now.* | **+ with** *You must have your hands full with all this work to do and the children to look after.* | **have your hands full doing sth** *The Mexican government had its hands full fighting a war on three fronts.*

2 a busy time

- busy
- full
- hectic
- it's all go

busy /ˈbɪzi/ [adj] *I'm going to bed. We have a busy day ahead of us tomorrow.* | *When you are in the police force, the night shift is always busiest.* | *Restaurant managers often employ temporary staff at busy times of the year.*

full /fʊl/ [adj usually before noun] **full day/morning/week etc** a day, morning etc in which you have arranged to do a lot of things: *Tomorrow will be a very full day. You have several clients to see and two meetings in the afternoon.*

hectic /ˈhektɪk/ [adj] a time or situation that is **hectic** is extremely busy and you are always rushing and often excited or worried: *It was really hectic at work today.* | *He'd just returned from a hectic 10-day trip to New York.* | *I know you have a hectic schedule, but could you pick something up for me on your way home?*

it's all go /ɪts ˌɔːl ˈgəʊ/ British spoken say this when you are very busy and have no time to relax, especially because a lot of things are happening: *It's all go around here this morning. Ten new orders, all marked 'URGENT'.*

3 not busy

- be not busy
- not have much to do

be not busy /biː nɒt ˈbɪzi/ [v phrase] *Let's find a time when you're not so busy, and talk about this calmly.* | *Hopefully by March we won't be so busy.*

not have much to do /nɒt hæv mʌtʃ tə ˈduː/ [v phrase] especially spoken to not be busy – use this especially to say that you have enough time to do other things: *I could help if you want – I don't have much to do this weekend.*

busy place

RELATED WORDS

- crowded with people *see* **crowd (2)**
- a peaceful place *see* **peaceful**

4 a busy place

- busy
- lively
- bustling

busy /ˈbɪzi/ [adj] *Even though it was eight o'clock the market was still busy.* | *Paris nowadays is a busy and crowded metropolis.* | *The main road is busy, so be careful when you try to cross it.* | *This is a very busy area, what with the school, the bus station, and the new shopping mall.*

lively /ˈlaɪvli/ [adj] a bar, restaurant, club etc that is **lively** is noisy and full of people who are enjoying themselves: *We got to the disco at about 10 o'clock and it was already quite lively.* | *It's the liveliest bar in town, very popular with the tourists.*

bustling /ˈbʌslɪŋ/ [adj usually before noun] a **bustling** town, street, area etc is busy and noisy, with a lot of people walking about, going in and out of shops etc: *The bustling downtown area of Chicago is dotted with massive new office developments.* | *The old market is a busy, bustling place, full of local colour.*

5 a time when a place is busy

- busy
- hectic
- rush hour
- peak
- the rush
- the hustle and bustle
- the season

busy /ˈbɪzi/ [adj] *The morning is our busy time here. It's quieter in the afternoon.* | *July is our busiest month, when all the tourists come.*

hectic /ˈhektɪk/ [adj] extremely busy, so that you are always in a hurry, and often feel worried or excited: *In the last hectic weeks before the show started we were practically living in the theatre to get it ready on time.* | *There are two hundred guests arriving in one hour! That's why things are so hectic!*

rush hour /ˈrʌʃ aʊəʳ/ [n singular] the time in the morning and evening when a lot of people are travelling to or from work at the same time: *The rush hour in most British cities does not start until about 8 o'clock.* | *The buses are so crowded during the rush hour, you never get a seat.*

peak /piːk/ [adj only before noun] the **peak** time or period is the time when shops, roads, trains etc are busiest: *There should be more buses to cope with the extra passengers at peak times.* | *We usually have two people working in the shop, but at peak periods we employ extra staff.* | *In the peak month of July the market sold three hundred tons of melons a day.*

the rush /ðə ˈrʌʃ/ [n singular] a very busy time when a lot of people are shopping or travelling: *Buy your tickets early and avoid the rush.* | **the Christmas/summer/weekend etc rush** *We're building up our stocks of books and toys to get ready for the Christmas rush.*

the hustle and bustle /ðə ˌhʌsəl ən ˈbʌsəl/ [n phrase] when there are a lot of people moving around and doing things, especially in a busy town or city: *Relax on the beach or enjoy the hustle and bustle of the busy fishing port.* | *It's hard to imagine that the park is only a few minutes' walk from the hustle and bustle of midtown Manhattan.*

the season /ðə 'si:zən/ [n singular] the time of year when a tourist area is busy and a lot of people go there: *The season begins in May, and most of the hotels open then.* | *This place gets so crowded during the season. It's much nicer in the winter when the tourists have gone.* | **in season** (=during the season) *Don't travel to Benidorm in season. The hotels are crowded.* | **high season/low season** (=when a place is busiest or least busy) *They put their prices up considerably during the high season.*

6 a place that is not busy

- quiet
- sleepy

quiet /'kwaɪət/ [adj] *The house is quiet now that the kids are gone.* | *Madison Plains, Ohio, is a quiet community of 1200 inhabitants.*

sleepy /'sli:pi/ [adj usually before noun] a **sleepy** place, especially a small town or village, is never busy and very little happens there: *Sticklepath is a sleepy little town right in the heart of the Devonshire countryside.* | *It was a sleepy provincial hotel, not used to having more than two people staying there at any one time.*

7 a time when a place is not busy

- quiet
- slow
- off-peak
- in the off-season

quiet /'kwaɪət/ [adj] a **quiet** day, weekend etc is one in which there is very little business or activity and very few people: *It's been a very quiet morning so far. Only two people came in, and neither of them bought anything.* | *Even on a quiet weekend there are plenty of people on the beach.* | *This time of the year is always quiet. It gets busy again after winter.*

slow /sləʊ/ [adj] a **slow** period of time in a shop or business is one in which there are very few customers and there is very little business: *Things have been slow, real slow, for months now.* | *February is the slowest month in the tourist trade.*

off-peak /ˌɒf 'pi:k◂/ [adj] especially British the **off-peak time**, period etc is the time when trains, hotels, tourist areas etc are not busy: *At off-peak times senior citizens can use the sports centre at reduced rates.* | *Take advantage of off-peak reductions for package holidays.* —**off-peak** [adv] *If you can travel off-peak it will be cheaper and the trains will be less crowded.*

in the off-season ALSO **out of season** British /ɪn ði 'ɒfˌsi:zən, ˌaʊt əv 'si:zən/ [adv] if you go to a tourist area in the **off-season** or **out of season**, you go there during that part of the year when it is not busy and is usually cheaper: *We had arrived in Biarritz out of season and most of the hotels were closed.* | *If you go for a holiday in the off-season, you'll find some real bargains.* | **during the off-season** *During the off-season, rates start at $75 per night for a cabin that sleeps two.*

busy/not available

RELATED WORDS

- a busy telephone line *see* **telephone**
- when someone is not busy and is available to do something *see* **available/not available (3)**

8 busy

- be busy
- have something on
- not available
- have a previous/prior engagement
- be tied up

be busy /bi: 'bɪzi/ [v phrase] when you cannot do something because you have already arranged to do something else: *'Can I speak to Nigel?' 'I'm sorry, he's busy right now. Can he call you back later?'* | *I kept asking her to come out for a drink but for some reason she was always busy.*

have something on /hæv ˌsʌmθɪŋ 'ɒn/ [v phrase not in progressive] British spoken to have already arranged to do something, for example to meet someone or to go to a party, so that you are unable to do something else that someone has invited you to do: *Do you have anything on Saturday night?* | *If you're not doing anything tomorrow, you could come to the beach with us.*

not available /nɒt ə'veɪləbəl/ [adj] if you are told that someone is **not available** when you ask to see them or to speak to them on the telephone, you cannot see them or speak to them because they are busy doing something else: *I'm sorry, Mrs Evans isn't available at the moment. Shall I get her to call you back?*

have a previous/prior engagement /hæv ə ˌpri:viəs, ˌpraɪər ɪn'geɪdʒmənt/ [v phrase not in progressive] formal to have already made a definite arrangement to do something, so that you cannot do something else – used especially when you are replying to an invitation: *I'll just check her diary, she may have a prior engagement.* | *Mr Lewis regrets that he is unable to attend, owing to a previous engagement.*

be tied up /bi: ˌtaɪd 'ʌp/ [v phrase] to be busy in your job, for example because you have a lot of work to do or you have an important meeting, and therefore unable to do anything else: *I'm sorry, he's tied up at the moment. Could you call back later?* | *I can't see you tomorrow, I'm tied up all day.*

but

- but
- however/nevertheless/nonetheless
- on the other hand
- still/all the same/then again
- yet
- whereas/while
- though/although
- though
- even so
- only/except

but /bət; (*strong*) bʌt/ [conjunction] use this to join two words or phrases when the second one has the opposite meaning to the first one, or when the second one is surprising after the first one, or when one is negative and one is positive: *I called but there was no one there.* | *He's short and not really handsome, but women still find him attractive.* | *They struggled in the first half, but still won 98-82.* | *She tried to read the message, but couldn't.* | *Tom's grandfather is* *over 80, but he still plays golf.* | *'Gone with the Wind' was a great movie, but it was a little long.* | *In the US it is normal for the police to carry guns, but not in Britain.*

however/nevertheless/nonetheless /haʊ'evəʳ, ˌnevəʳðə'les, ˌnʌnðə'les/ [adv] formal use this when saying something that is surprising after what you have just said, or that is very different from it: *It was a terrible accident. Nevertheless, air travel is still the safest form of transport.* | *December saw a more than average rainfall; however, the possibility of a drought is still strong.* | *War is never welcome, nonetheless, I believe that we must defend our country.* | **but nevertheless/nonetheless** *The leaves aren't particularly dangerous, but nevertheless they are not something you'd want your child or pet to eat.*

on the other hand /ɒn ði 'ʌðəʳ ˌhænd/ [adv] use this at the beginning of a sentence when you have just mentioned one side of an argument or situation and you are going to mention the opposite side: *Nuclear power is relatively cheap. On the other hand, you could argue that it's not safe.* | *The hamburger was tough and overcooked. The fries, on the other hand, were terrific, and well worth the money.* | **but on the other hand** *You want to help your kids as much as you can, but on the other hand, you've got to be careful to help them learn on their own.*

still/all the same/then again /stɪl, ˌɔːl ðə 'seɪm, ˌðen ə'gen/ ALSO **mind you** /ˌmaɪnd 'juː/ British spoken use this when you have just said one thing and you now want to say something very different about it, for example when you give an advantage and then a disadvantage: *Teaching is an interesting job. Then again, it can be very stressful too.* | *This trip is going to be very expensive. Still, we don't go away very often.* | *I'd love to travel around the world. Mind you, I wouldn't want to go on my own.* | *My parents are happy to lend me the money. All the same, I do feel guilty about it.*

yet /jet/ [conjunction] formal use this to introduce a fact that seems surprising after what you have just said: *The sun was shining, yet it was quite cold.* | *Last summer there was a drought, yet some people were still watering their lawns every day.*

whereas/while /weər'æz, waɪl/ [conjunction] written use this to say that although something is true of one person, thing, or situation, it is not true of another: *Some house plants thrive if placed near a window with plenty of sunlight while others prefer to be in a more shaded spot.* | *American cars are generally too large for the Japanese market, whereas Japanese cars are popular in the US.*

though/although /ðəʊ, ɔːl'ðəʊ/ [conjunction] use this to introduce a fact or opinion that makes what you have just said less strong or definite: *Dan's been very ill, although he's better now.* | *I don't really like classical music, though I did enjoy that Pavarotti concert.* | *They're a very nice couple, although I very seldom see them these days.*

though /ðəʊ/ [adv] use this at the end of a sentence to add a fact or opinion that makes what you have just said seem less important, or to add a different fact or opinion: *I think she's Swiss. I'm not sure, though.* | *George did say one nice thing, though.*

even so /ˌiːvən 'səʊ/ [adv] use this to say that something is true in spite of the fact that you have just mentioned: *Try to run on a soft surface, such as grass. Even so, you may start having knee problems.* | **but even so** *She had only seen Matthew Godden once before, but even so she recognized him instantly.* | *The fines for speeding are large, but even so, they are not always a deterrent.*

only/except /'əʊnli, ɪk'sept/ [conjunction] spoken use this for introducing the reason why something is not possible: *I'd like to come and live here, only it's too expensive.* | *I would have asked them to stay with us, except we don't have enough room.*

buy

RELATED WORDS

opposite: — **sell**

▸ *see also* **pay, cost, spend, money/time, shop/store, expensive, cheap**

1 to buy something

- buy
- get
- purchase
- snap up
- pick up
- splash out on
- acquire

buy /baɪ/ [v I/T] to pay money for something so that you can own it: *I bought a new dress today at Macy's.* | *John makes his living buying and selling used cars.* | *The painting was bought by a museum in New York.* | **buy sb sth** *Keith was going to buy me a ring, but now he says he wants to buy me a watch instead.* | **buy sth for sb** *If you don't have enough money for the pen, I'll buy it for you.* | **buy sth from sb** *I wouldn't buy anything from him – I don't trust him.* | **buy sth for $10/£200 etc** *The ranch, which was originally bought for $20,000, is now valued at over $2 million.*

get /get/ [v T not in passive] especially spoken to buy something, especially ordinary things such as food, clothes, or things for your house: *Let me get the drinks. It's my turn to pay.* | *Did you remember to get the bread?* | **get sb sth** *Guess what he got her for her birthday – an iron!* | **get sth for sb** *I'm going to get one of those video games for Hillary.* | **get sth for £20/$50 etc** *What do you think of this leather jacket? I got it for $40 on sale.*

purchase /'pɜːʳtʃɪs/ [v T] formal to buy something – used in business and legal contracts: *Foreign investors are not permitted to purchase land.* | *If this product does not give complete satisfaction, please return it to the manufacturer stating when and where it was purchased.* —**purchase** [n U] **+ of** *The loan was supposed to be used for the purchase of a house.*

snap up /ˌsnæp 'ʌp/ [phr v T] to buy something immediately, especially because it is very cheap or you want it very much, and you are worried that someone else might buy it first **snap up sth** *Readers have snapped up nearly 200,000 copies of the book.* | *The best bargains tend to be snapped up immediately.* | **snap sth up** *If you see one for under $100, snap it up!*

pick up /ˌpɪk 'ʌp/ [phr v T] to buy something that you have found by chance, especially something that is unusually cheap **pick up sth** *He's hoping to pick up a few bargains at the sales.* | *It's just a little thing I picked up when I was in Kathmandu.* | **pick sth up** *That picture? Oh, I picked it up last week at a little shop downtown.*

splash out on British [phr v T not in passive] **splurge (on sth)** American [v I] /ˌsplæʃ 'aʊt ɒn, 'splɜːʳdʒ ɒn (sth)/ to buy something you want such as an expensive meal, dress etc, which you would not usually buy because it is too expensive: *We splashed out on a bottle of champagne to celebrate her promotion.* | *Let's splurge and have the steak.*

acquire /ə'kwaɪəʳ/ [v T] formal to become the owner of something such as land, a company, or a valuable object: *In 1998 the business was acquired by a Dutch company.* | *The statue was acquired at great expense by the City Corporation.* | *Robinson spent $20 million to acquire the symphony hall.* —**acquisition** /ˌækwɪ̈'zɪʃən/ [n U] **+ of** *The National Gallery has set aside £10 million for the acquisition of the painting.*

2 to buy a lot of something

- buy a lot of/lots of
- stock up
- buy (sth) in bulk
- wholesale
- buy up
- import
- buy in

buy a lot of/lots of /ˌbaɪ ə 'lɒt ɒv, 'lɒts ɒv‖-'lɑːt-/ [v phrase] *You've been buying a lot of clothes recently. Have you decided to change your image?* | *We've bought lots of food and drink, so it should be a really good party.*

stock up /ˌstɒk 'ʌp‖ˌstɑːk-/ [phr v I] to buy a large quantity of something you use regularly because you may not be able to buy it later, or because you are planning to use more of it than usual: *The supermarkets are full of people stocking up for the New Year's holiday.* | *We might as well stock up while we're here – it'll save us having to come back.* | **+ on** *We always stock up on cheap cigarettes when we go to Holland.*

buy (sth) in bulk /ˌbaɪ (sth) ɪn 'bʌlk/ [v phrase] to buy a large quantity of something, especially because it is cheaper to buy a lot of it at one time: *We always buy in bulk. It is so much more economical.* | *Today more shoppers are using coupons and buying items in bulk.* | **bulk buying** (=buying goods in large quantities) *Bulk buying has enabled the company to cut costs.*

wholesale /'həʊlseɪl/ [adv] if you buy something **wholesale**, you buy a large quantity of it directly from the company that makes it: *Mark buys the earrings wholesale and then sells them for a profit.* | *Let's see if we can get them wholesale and save ourselves a few dollars.* —**wholesale** [adj] *The shopkeeper buys his fruit and vegetables at wholesale prices.*

buy up /ˌbaɪ 'ʌp/ [phr v T] to quickly buy all of something such as land, tickets, food etc, when there is only a limited amount available **buy up sth** *In the last five years development agencies have bought up almost all the land in the area.* | **buy sth up** *There weren't any good seats left for the game – some big company had bought them all up.*

import /ɪm'pɔːʳt/ [v T] to buy goods from another country to be sold, used etc in your country, especially in large quantities: *The United States has to import some of its oil.* | **import sth from sth** *Most of the wines served in this restaurant are imported from France.* —**imports** /'ɪmpɔːʳts/ [n plural] *In 1999 our imports* (=goods that were imported)*greatly exceeded exports.*

buy in /ˌbaɪ 'ɪn/ [phr v T] British to buy enough of something to last for a long time, for example because it may be difficult to buy later **buy in sth** *People had to buy in candles during the electricity strike.* | **buy sth in** *Villagers join together to buy enough food in to last throughout the winter.*

3 to buy something for someone else

- treat
- sth is on me/John etc
- buy/get a round

treat /'triːt/ [v T] to buy something such as a meal for someone because you like them or you want to celebrate something: *As it's your birthday, I thought I'd treat you.* | **treat sb to sth** *Glen treated Cathy to dinner at one of the best restaurants in town.* —**my treat** /ˌmaɪ 'triːt/ spoken say this when you are offering to pay for someone's meal or drinks: *Let's all go to a movie – my treat.*

sth is on me/John etc / (sth) ɪz ɒn 'miː / [v phrase] spoken use this to say that you will pay for drinks, food etc or that a particular person will pay for them: *Don't worry about the price – this meal's on me.* | **be on the house** (=the bar or restaurant you are in will pay for your meal, drinks etc) *The manager apologized and told us our drinks would be on the house for the rest of the evening.*

buy/get a round /ˌbaɪ, ˌget ə 'raʊnd/ [v phrase] to buy a drink for everyone in the group that you are with, in a place which sells alcoholic drinks: *I'll get this round. What would you like?* | *Jack always leaves when it's his turn to buy a round.*

4 to go to shops in order to buy things

- go shopping
- do the shopping
- go to the shops
- shop
- shop around
- window shopping

go shopping /ˌgəʊ 'ʃɒpɪŋ‖-'ʃɑː-/ [v phrase] to go to shops to look at and buy things: *Let's meet in town. We can have lunch and go shopping.* | *I'm going shopping now. Do you want anything?*

do the shopping /ˌduː ðə 'ʃɒpɪŋ‖-'ʃɑː-/ [v phrase] to go to shops in order to buy the things that you need regularly such as food: *On Saturdays we usually do the shopping and clean the house.* | *She sent her husband out to do the week's shopping.* | **do my/your etc shopping** *I did all my shopping yesterday.* | **grocery shopping** American (=shopping for food) *We need to go grocery shopping – do you have the check book?*

go to the shops British **go to the store** American /ˌgəʊ tə ðə 'ʃɒps ‖-'ʃɑːps, ˌgəʊ tə ðə 'stɔːʳ/ [v phrase] to go out to the local shop or shops in order to buy something, especially the things that you need regularly such as food: *'Where's Julie?' 'She's gone to the shops.'* | *If you go to the store, could you get some milk?* | *Mr Parker, my next-door neighbour, is getting old and I sometimes go to the shops for him.*

shop /ʃɒp‖ʃɑːp/ [v I not in progressive] to regularly use a particular **shop**, especially to buy things that you need regularly such as food **+ at/in** *I usually shop at Safeway. It's just around the corner from my house.* | *When she moved here, she had never shopped in a supermarket before.*

shop around /ˌʃɒp ə'raʊnd‖ˌʃɑːp-/ [phr v I] to go to several different shops comparing goods and their prices before deciding which ones to buy: *If you shop around you could probably get the camera a lot cheaper.* | **+ for** *I spent a couple of weeks shopping around for the lowest insurance rates.*

window shopping /'wɪndəʊ ˌʃɒpɪŋ‖-ˌʃɑːp-/ [n U] when you look at things in shop windows without intending to buy anything: *We spent the morning window shopping at all the antique stores.*

5 someone who buys goods or services

- customer
- shoppers
- client
- buyer
- consumers
- clientele
- market

customer /'kʌstəməʳ/ [n C] someone who buys goods from a particular shop, restaurant, or company: *We don't get many customers on Mondays – Saturday is our busiest day.* | *The barman was serving the last customer of the evening.* | *Ford has launched a big sales campaign in an effort to bring in new customers.* | **biggest customer** (=the customer who buys the most goods) *The Defense Department is one of Lockheed's biggest regular customers.*

shoppers /'ʃɒpəʳz‖'ʃɑːp-/ [n plural] the people in a shop or town who are buying things: *The streets were crowded with Christmas shoppers.*

client /'klaɪənt/ [n C] someone who pays for services or advice from a professional person or organization: *Mr Langston normally meets with clients in the afternoon.* | *Elkins assured the judge that neither of his clients had a criminal record.* | *The firm is one of our oldest clients – we don't want to lose them.*

buyer /'baɪəʳ/ [n C] someone who buys something expensive such as a house, company, or painting, usually from another person, not a shop or company: *We couldn't find a buyer for our house, so we weren't able to move after all.* | *They've had a lot of enquiries about the company – there's no shortage of potential buyers.*

consumers /kən'sjuːməʳz‖-'suː-/ [n C] someone who buys and uses goods and services – use this especially to talk about people who buy things in general: *Consumers are demanding more environmentally friendly products.* | *The consumer is interested in high quality goods, not just low prices.*

clientele /ˌkliːən'tel‖ˌklaɪən'tel, ˌkliː-/ [n singular with singular or plural verb in British English] the people who regularly use a particular shop, restaurant etc, or the services of a professional person: *The hotel's clientele includes diplomats and Hollywood celebrities.* | *Madame Zara caters for a very select clientele.*

market /'mɑːʳkɪ̵t/ [n singular] the number of people who want to buy a product, or the type of people who want to buy it: *The magazine is aimed at the youth market.* | *Without research we can't be sure of the size of our market or even who our market is.* | **+ for** *The market for Internet-based products has grown dramatically in recent years.*

Cc

call/describe as

RELATED WORDS

- to call someone a particular name *see* **name**
- to say something loudly *see* **shout**
- *see also* **describe**

1 to describe something or someone in a particular way

- describe sb/sth as
- say (that) sth/sb is
- call
- label
- brand
- hail sth/sb as

describe sb/sth as /dɪ'skraɪb (sb/sth) æz/ [v phrase] *Olsen described herself as a campaign manager for the organization.* | *Critics have described the book as 'garbage'.* | *Eliot was described by Lewis as arrogant, sly and insincere.* | *How would you describe your relationship with your parents?*

say (that) sth/sb is /'seɪ ðət (sb/sth) ɪz/ [v phrase] to describe someone or something in a particular way, especially when this is your opinion and other people might disagree: *People say she's too ambitious.* | *They say that Tokyo is one of the most expensive cities in the world.* | *It is an over-simplification to say that Britain is a democracy.*

call /kɔːl/ [v T] to use a particular word or phrase to describe someone or something in order to give your opinion of them **call sb sth** *Are you calling me a liar?* | *'She's a fraud.' 'I wouldn't call her that.'* | *Already his followers were calling him a saint.* | **call sth sth** *What he did was wrong, but I wouldn't call it a crime.*

label /'leɪbəl/ [v T usually in passive] to describe someone, usually unfairly or incorrectly, as being a particular type or person, especially one that you disapprove of **label sb (as) lazy/stupid/uncooperative etc** *The unemployed are often labelled as lazy or unreliable.* | **label sb (as) a troublemaker/alcoholic/dissident etc** *When we're ready to label them as suspects, we'll release their descriptions.* | *She lashed out at her critics who had labelled her a bimbo.*

brand /brænd/ [v T] to describe someone or something as a bad type of person or thing, usually unfairly **brand sb/sth (as) unreliable/incompetent/foolish etc** *Brown's assistant has been branded in the papers as incompetent.* | **brand sb/sth (as) a racist/traitor/coward etc** *Stalin's opponents were branded as spies and traitors.* | *Government posters from the 1930s branded marijuana a 'killer drug.'*

hail sth/sb as /'heɪl (sth/sb) æz/ [phr v T] to describe someone or something as being very good, especially in newspapers, magazines, on television etc: *This new drug is being hailed as a major breakthrough in the treatment of cancer.* | *Many still hail Elvis Presley as the King of Rock 'n' Roll.*

2 to give someone or something a name that describes them

- call
- christen
- dub

call /kɔːl/ [v T] **call sth sth** *They call Chicago 'The*

Windy City'. | **call sb sth** *People call her 'The Duck Lady of Lake Murray' because she been feeding the ducks there daily for five years.*

christen /ˈkrɪsən/ [v T] to invent a name for someone or something, and use it whenever you talk about them, especially because you think it suits them or is funny **christen sb/sth sth** *The band christened her 'Mutti' after the German word for mother.* | *The engine was affectionately christened 'Puffing Billy'.*

dub /dʌb/ [v T] to give someone or something a name, often a humorous name, that describes their character – used especially in newspapers **dub sb/sth sth** *The two men had such a reputation for drug abuse that they were dubbed 'The Toxic Twins.'* | *The program to distribute Thanksgiving turkeys was dubbed 'Operation Gobble.'*

3 a name that people call someone or something

- nickname
- label
- tag

nickname /ˈnɪkneɪm/ [n C] a name given to someone, especially by their friends or family, that is not their real name, and that often describes their character or what they look like: *She got the nickname 'Sis' because her brother couldn't pronounce her name when they were kids.* | *His fondness for rings had already earned him the nickname Ringo.* —**nickname** [v T] *Mona – nicknamed Mo – had two teenage sons.*

label /ˈleɪbəl/ [n C] a word used regularly as a description of someone or something, showing that people think of them, often unfairly, as belonging to a particular type: *He objects to the sexist label – he doesn't think he's sexist at all.* | *At one time he was given the label 'communist' for his opposition to the Vietnam war.*

tag /tæg/ [n C] a word or phrase used regularly in connection with a particular person's name to describe their character, behaviour etc, especially in a way the person does not like: *During one game I accidentally scored against my own side and acquired the tag 'wrong way' Jones.* | *I didn't blame her for hating the 'mayor's ex-girlfriend' tag.*

calm

RELATED WORDS

- a calm, quiet place *see* **peaceful**
- *see also* **quiet, relax/relaxed**

1 calm in a difficult situation

- calm
- stay cool/keep cool
- keep your head
- composed
- presence of mind
- unfazed/not fazed
- level-headed

calm /kɑːm‖kɑːm, kɑːlm/ [adj] not getting angry or upset, even in a difficult situation: *I was trying to sound calm even though I was very upset.* | *Everyone praised Douglas for the calm way in which he handled the situation.* | **keep/stay calm** *Keep calm and try not to panic.* —**calmly** [adv] *'You can't make me leave,' he said calmly.*

stay cool/keep cool /ˌsteɪ ˈkuːl, ˌkiːp ˈkuːl/ [adj] to stay calm and not show your emotions, especially when other people are getting excited or angry: *Sampras is the kind of player who always manages to stay cool, even under pressure.* | **keep your cool** (=not become angry) *He managed to keep his cool and ignore her last comments.* —**coolly** [adv] *She walked coolly up to the front of the hall and picked up the microphone.*

keep your head /ˌkiːp jɔːʳ ˈhed/ [v phrase] to manage to stay calm and to behave in a sensible way when something is likely to make you feel frightened or worried: *Paul's good at keeping his head in a crisis.* | *They were looking for a coach who could stay enthusiastic and keep his head at the same time.*

composed /kəmˈpəʊzd/ [adj] in control of your emotions so that you look and feel calm in a difficult or upsetting situation: *I could see that she was angry but trying to remain composed.* | *It was several minutes before he felt composed enough to speak to anyone.*

presence of mind /ˌprezəns əv ˈmaɪnd/ [n phrase] the ability to stay calm that makes someone able to do the right thing immediately even in a dangerous or difficult situation: *His presence of mind prevented a serious accident.* | **+ to do sth** *I'm still amazed that a terrified 19-year-old would have the presence of mind to reason with her kidnapper.*

unfazed/not fazed /ʌnˈfeɪzd, nɒt ˈfeɪzd/ [adj] informal calm in a difficult situation, especially one in which someone is trying to confuse or upset you: *Barton seemed unfazed by the accusations of corruption.* | *A few traders are concerned by the recent drop in the stock market, but most are not fazed.*

level-headed /ˌlevəl ˈhedɪd◂/ [adj] able to behave sensibly, think clearly, and remain calm, even in a difficult situation: *A good pilot needs to be calm and level-headed.* | *He had a level-headed approach to financial matters.*

2 usually calm

- calm
- relaxed
- laid-back
- placid

calm /kɑːm‖kɑːm, kɑːlm/ [adj] always sensible and relaxed, rather than getting angry, excited, or upset in a difficult situation: *Joe is a very calm and competent flying instructor.* | *My sister was always calm and careful, whereas I would get excited and upset by the slightest thing.* | *He has such a calm soothing voice – I could listen to him all night.*

relaxed /rɪˈlækst/ [adj] someone who is **relaxed** is calm and does not seem to be worried about anything, and it is pleasant for other people to be with them: *George greeted us in his friendly relaxed way.* | *You seem much more relaxed since you changed jobs.*

laid-back /ˌleɪd ˈbæk◂/ [adj] informal always relaxed and never seeming to worry about things that other people worry about: *Sue's always had a laid-back attitude toward life.* | *He's very laid-back and lets the kids do whatever they want.*

placid /ˈplæsɪd/ [adj] always calm and satisfied and not often getting upset, angry, excited etc about anything: *She's a sweet, placid child who rarely gets upset or angry.* | *There was a worried look on her normally placid face.*

3 to become calm

- calm down
- cool down/off
- compose yourself
- steady your nerves

calm down /ˌkɑːm ˈdaʊn/ [phr v I] to become calm

again after you have been angry or upset: *I waited for him to calm down before I said anything.* | *He sat down and exhaled slowly, trying to calm down.*

cool down/off /ˌkuːl ˈdaʊn, ˈɒf / [phr v I] to calm down after you have been very angry: *Leave her alone until she cools down a bit.* | *I think you should both cool off, and maybe then you can sit down and discuss it rationally.*

compose yourself /kəmˈpəʊz jɔːʳself/ [v phrase] to deliberately make yourself look and feel calm after you have been upset: *She took several deep breaths to compose herself before going downstairs.* | *He waited a moment outside the door so that Philip would have time to compose himself.*

steady your nerves /ˌstedi jɔːʳ ˈnɜːʳvz/ [v phrase] especially British if you do something, especially have an alcoholic drink, to **steady your nerves**, you do it to make yourself calm: *They finally found him in the bar, where he had gone to steady his nerves.*

4 to make someone calmer

- calm down
- calm
- *see also* **comfort/make sb feel better**

calm down /ˌkɑːm ˈdaʊn/ [phr v T] to make someone calm, especially after they have suddenly become angry or excited **calm sb down** *Lois spent about an hour trying to calm him down.* | *I laid my hands on her shoulders to calm her down, but she pushed me away.* | **calm down sb** *The coach called a time-out to calm down the players.*

calm /kɑːm‖kɑːm, kɑːlm/ [v T not in passive] to make someone **calm** when they are worried and upset: *We were all very concerned and did our best to calm her.* | *His lawyer's assurances that he would be found not guilty did little to calm him.*

5 what you say to someone when you want them to be calm

- calm down
- relax
- take it easy
- it's okay/it's all right
- chill out/chill

calm down /ˌkɑːm ˈdaʊn/ spoken say this when someone is angry, upset, or excited and you want them to think calmly or speak calmly again: *Calm down! Everything's going to be OK.* | *If you don't calm down, Mom's going to know something's wrong.*

relax /rɪˈlæks/ spoken say this to someone who is worried or frightened about something, in order to stop them worrying: *Relax! This won't hurt at all.* | *You can relax now – it's all over.*

take it easy /ˌteɪk ɪt ˈiːzi/ spoken informal say this when someone is angry or upset, and you want to stop them saying or doing anything stupid: *Hey, take it easy! Nobody's saying you're not good at your job.*

it's okay/it's all right /ɪts əʊˈkeɪ, ɪts ˌɔːl ˈraɪt/ spoken say this to someone to make them stop being worried: *It's okay, Chris, he's gone now.* | *It's all right, don't cry, Mummy's here.*

chill out/chill /ˌtʃɪl ˈaʊt, tʃɪl/ spoken informal say this when someone is getting very nervous or worried, especially in a way that is annoying or unreasonable, and you want them to be calm – used especially by young people: *OK, it's all right – just chill out!* | *Just chill for a second – I'll figure something out.*

can/can't

RELATED WORDS

- be allowed to do something *see* **let/allow (4)**
- to succeed in doing something *see* **succeed/successful**
- *see also* **possible, impossible, fail, prevent, bad at doing sth**

1 to be able to do something

- can
- be able to do sth
- be capable of sth
- have the ability to do sth
- be equipped to do sth
- have it in you
- know how to do sth
- be in a position to do sth

can /kən (*strong*) kæn/ [modal verb] *'I don't think Mike can type.' 'Yes, he can.'* | **can do sth** *He can run faster than me.* | *Can you see the TV, or should I move?* | *This program can translate your e-mail into other languages.* | *How many hamburgers do you think you can eat?* | *Adrian could read when he was four.* | *If we had a boat we could row across to the island.* | *Why didn't they ask me? I could have done it for them for half the price.*

be able to do sth /biː ˌeɪbəl tə ˈduː (sth)/ [v phrase] if you are able to do something, you can do it – use this especially about something that needs a lot of effort, skill, or knowledge: *Those bags look really heavy – are you sure you'll be able to carry them on your own?* | *After the accident it was a long time before she was able to walk again.* | *To take the class, you have to be able to use a computer.* | **be able to** *My grandpa's getting old now and he can't do all the things he used to be able to.*

be capable of sth /biː ˈkeɪpəbəl əv (sth)/ [v phrase] to have the ability, energy, or qualities needed to do something, especially something very difficult or unusual – use this about people or machines: *He's a very angry kid, but he's not capable of murder.* | **be capable of doing sth** *The missiles are capable of travelling about 700 miles.* | *Around 7 or 8, children are already capable of making their own moral evaluations.* | **be perfectly capable of doing sth** (=used to emphasize that you are definitely capable of doing something) *Leave the boy alone, I'm sure he's perfectly capable of fixing it himself.*

have the ability to do sth /hæv ði əˌbɪlɨti tə ˈduː (sth)/ [v phrase not in progressive] to be able to do something, especially something that is unusual or that most people cannot do: *She seemed to have the ability to make people do anything she wanted.* | *I believe the team definitely has the ability to win the championship.*

be equipped to do sth /biː ɪˌkwɪpt tə ˈduː (sth)/ [v phrase] to be able to do something, especially to deal with a particular problem, because you have been properly prepared or had the right training: *By the end of the course, students should be equipped to deal with any business situation.* | *The emergency services are well equipped to cope with disasters of this kind.*

have it in you /ˌhæv ɪt ˈɪn juː/ [v phrase not in progressive] to have the ability and the qualities of character needed to do something difficult, especially when you or other people doubt that you can do it: *I admired the way you refused to let him bully you – I didn't think you had it in you.* | **+ to do sth** *No one* *thought I would win, but I knew I had it in me to do it if I really tried.*

know how to do sth /ˌnəʊ haʊ tə ˈduː (sth)/ [v phrase not in progressive] to be able to do something, because you know a way of a doing it, especially something practical such as operating a machine: *Do you know how to use this computer?* | *I'd turn the thing off if only I knew how.*

be in a position to do sth /biː ɪn ə pəˌzɪʃən tə ˈduː (sth)/ [v phrase] to have enough knowledge, money, or equipment to do something: *Once the loan is paid off, Jones will be in a position to run the casino himself.* | *We will have to run more tests before we are in a position to say whether the document is authentic or not.* | **be in a good/excellent/better position to do sth** *When I've read the whole report I'll be in a better position to comment.*

2 when a situation makes it possible for you to do something

- can
- be able to do sth
- it is possible for sb to do sth
- get to do sth

can /kən (*strong*) kæn/ [modal verb] *I'll call you if I can, but I'm going to be pretty busy.* | **can do sth** *Can you come to my place tomorrow and help me move some furniture?* | *I don't have an appointment, but I wonder if the dentist could see me today.* | *I hope we can find a parking space.* | *You can probably get most of the information you need from the Internet.*

be able to do sth /biː ˌeɪbəl tə ˈduː (sth)/ [v phrase] *She was able to get her watch repaired the same day.* | *Because of the drop in stock prices, investors were able to find some bargains this week.*

it is possible for sb to do sth /ɪt ɪz ˌpɒsɪ̈bəl fəʳ (sb) tə ˈduː (sth)/ spoken use this especially when you are making an arrangement with someone in order to ask or say what someone will be able to do: *Would it be possible for you to come to a meeting on Tuesday?* | *It might be possible to use the school library on Saturdays.*

get to do sth /ˌget tə ˈduː (sth)/ [v phrase not in progressive] to be able to do something that you have wanted to do for a long time, or something that you are not usually allowed to do: *We actually got to meet the president when he was here last week.* | *Do I get to stay up late when Dad comes home from his business trip?*

3 to be allowed to do something or have the power to do it

- can
- be able to do sth
- have the power to do sth
- be in a position to do sth

can /kən; (*strong*) kæn/ [modal verb] *If you want to come with us, you can.* | **can do sth** *It's my house and I can do whatever I want here.* | *Can I use your computer?* | *At that time, the king could simply have his enemies imprisoned or shot.*

be able to do sth /biː ˌeɪbəl tə ˈduː (sth)/ [v phrase] use this especially when a law or rule makes it possible for someone to do something: *You might be able to get a temporary passport.* | *Consumers are now able to buy the drug without a prescription.*

have the power to do sth /hæv ðə ˌpaʊəʳ tə ˈduː (sth)/ [v phrase not in progressive] to be able to do something because your official position gives you the authority to do it: *The judge has the power to order a witness to give evidence.* | *Each state had the power to make its own laws.*

be in a position to do sth /biː ɪn ə pəˌzɪʃən tə ˈduː (sth)/ [v phrase] to have the official authority to do something or have the moral right to do something: *Only the governor is now in a position to stop the execution.* | *Well, given her appalling record, she's not in any position to criticize my work.*

4 the ability to do something

- ability
- capability
- capacity
- skill
- competence
- power
- powers
- faculties
- resources
- aptitude

ability /əˈbɪlɪ̈ti/ [n C/U] the physical or mental skill or knowledge that makes you able to do something: *The course material depends on the level of ability of the student.* | **+ to do sth** *Our ability to think and speak makes us different from other animals.* | *Luckily, she had innate ability to judge people quickly and accurately.* | **sb's abilities as a teacher/doctor etc** *Harmon decided to create a business out of his abilities as a speaker.*

capability /ˌkeɪpəˈbɪlɪ̈ti/ [n C/U] the ability of a person, machine etc to do something, especially something difficult that needs a lot of knowledge, skill, advanced equipment etc: *Man Ray explored the capabilities of the camera to their fullest extent.* | **+ to do sth** *It is unclear whether the country has the capability to produce nuclear weapons.* | **+ of doing sth** *This computer system gives the user the capability of accessing huge amounts of data.*

capacity /kəˈpæsɪ̈ti/ [n singular] use this especially about a very great ability to do something or to behave in a particular way **+ for** *He has an enormous capacity for hard work.* | *Cheryl's capacity for understanding and compassion is impressive.* | **+ to do sth** *Children have a remarkable capacity to learn language.*

skill /skɪl/ [n C] a special ability that you need to learn in order to do a particular job or activity: *These exercises develop the student's reading and writing skills.* | *You need computer skills for most office jobs.* | *Being a good manager requires a number of highly specialized skills.*

competence /ˈkɒmpɪ̈təns‖ˈkɑːm-/ [n U] the ability and skill to do what is needed: *The level of competence among hospital staff was not as high as expected.* | *Understanding the instructions requires a ninth grade reading competence.*

power /ˈpaʊəʳ/ [n C] a natural ability to do something, especially to see, hear, speak etc **the power of sight/speech/hearing etc** *She was so surprised that for a few seconds she lost the power of speech.* | *The ostrich is a bird that no longer has the power of flight.* | **+ to do sth** *Doctors cannot explain why some people lack the power to fight off the disease.*

powers /ˈpaʊəʳz/ [n plural] **powers of judgement/reasoning/persuasion etc** the ability to do something that involves mental effort or skill, such as persuading, forming an opinion, thinking etc: *This problem is designed to test your powers of observation.* | *Teachers have the responsibility to develop students' powers of critical thinking.* | *She impressed us all with her dazzling intellectual powers.*

faculties /ˈfækəltiz/ [n plural] the natural abilities that everyone normally has, for example the ability to think, see, hear, and speak: *As we age we begin to lose some of our faculties.* | **in full possession of your faculties** *Although he was dying, he remained in full possession of his faculties.*

resources /rɪˈzɔːʳsɨ̈z/ [n plural] qualities such as courage and a strong mind that you need in order to deal with a difficult situation: *She's tough – I'm sure she has the emotional resources to handle it.* | *The new work stretches the physical resources of the company's dancers.*

aptitude /ˈæptɨ̈tjuːd‖-tuːd/ [n C usually singular] the natural ability that someone has to learn a new subject or activity and become good at it: *A trainee with normal aptitude can learn these techniques in a few months.* | **+ for** *At an early age Susan showed an aptitude for languages.* | **aptitude test** *All applicants are given aptitude tests before being invited for interview.*

5 to make someone able to do something

- enable sb to do sth
- make it possible
- allow sb to do sth/let sb do sth
- equip

enable sb to do sth /ɪˌneɪbəl (sb) tə ˈduː (sth)/ [v phrase not in passive] *The money from my grandmother enabled us to buy the house.* | *The programme is designed to enable young people to find work.*

make it possible /ˌmeɪk ɪt ˈpɒsɨ̈bəl‖-ˈpɑː-/ [v phrase] to provide the conditions in which someone is able to do something **make it possible to do sth** *The direct flight makes it possible to get from London to Tokyo in 12 hours.* | **make it possible for sb to do sth** *The loan made it possible for him to continue his education.* | **make sth possible** *I'd like to thank everyone – my family, my friends – who helped to make the whole thing possible.*

allow sb to do sth/let sb do sth /əˌlaʊ (sb) tə ˈduː (sth), ˌlet (sb) ˈduː (sth)/ [v phrase] if a piece of equipment or a service **allows you to do something** or **lets you do** it, it provides what you need to be able to do it: *The web site allows you to order groceries over the Internet.* | *The telephone service lets users see who is calling before they pick up the phone.*

equip /ɪˈkwɪp/ [v T] if education or training **equips** you to do something, especially something such as a particular kind of job, it prepares you and makes you able to do it **equip sb to do sth** *The school aims to equip students to deal with the kind of problems they will face in the outside world.* | **equip sb for** *Her privileged upbringing had not equipped her for hard work in the fields.*

6 to be unable to do something

- can't/cannot
- not be able to do sth
- be unable to do sth
- inability to do sth
- be incapable/not be capable
- not be in a position to do sth/be in no position to do sth
- not be equipped/be ill-equipped
- not know how to do sth

can't/cannot /kɑːnt‖kænt, ˈkænət, -nɒt‖-nɑːt/ [modal verb] *'Will you help me move this?' 'I'm sorry, I can't – my back's still giving me trouble.'* | **can't/cannot do sth** *Louise can't see anything without her glasses.* | *He couldn't remember where he had left the car.* | *I could never have climbed that ridge – I'm too out of shape.* | *Scientists still cannot explain exactly how the virus reproduces.* | *Sarah could not understand why anyone would want to hurt her.*

not be able to do sth /ˌnɒt biː ˌeɪbəl tə ˈduː (sth)/ [v phrase] – use this especially in the past or future tense: *Unfortunately, I wasn't able to help them.* | *I'm afraid I won't be able to come to the meeting after all.* | *The doctor told Tina she wouldn't be able to have children.* | *I've looked all over the house but I haven't been able to find my keys anywhere.*

be unable to do sth /biː ʌnˌeɪbəl tə ˈduː (sth)/ [v phrase] especially written to not be able to do something, especially something important that you want to do or need to do: *He lay awake all night, unable to sleep.* | *The surgery left her unable to walk for nearly three months.*

inability to do sth /ɪnəˌbɪlɨ̈ti tə ˈduː (sth)/ [n phrase] the fact that someone is unable to do something, used especially when you are annoyed with them because you think they are too weak, lazy etc to do it: *Her actions show an inability to distinguish between fantasy and reality.* | **sb's inability to do sth** *He even blamed his parents for his inability to make friends.* | *Voters are becoming frustrated at the inability of the administration to do anything about the debt crisis.*

be incapable/not be capable /biː ɪnˈkeɪpəbəl, nɒt biː ˈkeɪpəbəl/ [v phrase] to not have the physical or mental ability to do something – often used when you are criticizing someone **+ of** *Matthew seemed to be incapable of keeping a job.* | *She's no longer capable of taking care of herself.* | *Nero was a cruel man, utterly incapable of pity or sympathy.*

not be in a position to do sth/be in no position to do sth /nɒt biː ɪn ə pəˌzɪʃən tə ˈduː (sth), biː ɪn ˌnəʊ pəˌzɪʃən tə ˈduː (sth)/ [v phrase] informal to not be able to do something because you do not have enough knowledge, money, or authority: *I'm afraid I'm not in a position to answer your questions.* | *Local school boards are in no position to pay for the extra cost of the curriculum.* | **scarcely/hardly in a position to do sth** *The US is hardly in a position to criticize other countries for wasting energy supplies.*

not be equipped/be ill-equipped /nɒt biː ɪˈkwɪpt, biː ˌɪl ɪˈkwɪpt/ [v phrase] to be unable to do something because you do not have the right training or experience **+ to do sth** *The young teacher wasn't equipped to deal with such a difficult class.* | *The organization is ill-equipped to deal with the problems it may encounter.* | **+ for** *After so many years in prison, Victor was not equipped for life on the outside.*

not know how to do sth /nɒt nəʊ ˌhaʊ tə ˈduː (sth)/ [v phrase not in progressive] to be unable to do something, especially something practical, because you have not learned how to do it: *I didn't know how to drive a car till I was 28.* | *A lot of the doctors here still don't know how to use the new equipment.*

7 when a situation makes it impossible for you to do something

- can't/cannot
- not be able to do sth
- be unable to do sth
- it is not possible for sb to do sth

can't/cannot /kɑːnt‖kænt, ˈkænət, -nɒt‖-nɑːt/ [modal verb] *Look, I know I said I'd come, but I can't.* | **can't/cannot do sth** *I can't go out to lunch today, I have too much work to do.* | *The doctor cannot see you without a prior appointment.*

not be able to do sth /ˌnɒt biː ˌeɪbəl tə ˈduː (sth)/ [v phrase] – use this especially in the past or future tense: *She has a meeting with her boss tomorrow, so she won't be able to come.* | *With everything that's been happening at the office lately, I haven't been able to spend much time at home.*

be unable to do sth /biː ʌnˌeɪbəl tə ˈduː (sth)/ [v phrase] use this especially when you want to be polite about the fact that someone cannot do something: *I'm sorry, but Mrs Jones is unable to see you now. Please come back at 6 o'clock.* | *The Pope was unable to attend, due to illness.*

it is not possible for sb to do sth /ɪt ɪz nɒt ˌpɒsəbəl fəʳ (sb) tə ˈduː (sth) ‖-ˌpɑː-/ [v phrase] used especially when you want to give an excuse or reason for not doing something: *I have a full schedule all next week, so I'm afraid it won't be possible for me to see you then.* | *We had so many other orders that it wasn't possible to deliver yours any earlier.*

8 when you are not allowed or do not have the power to do something

- can't/cannot
- not be able to do sth
- not have the power to do sth/it is not in your power to do sth
- not be in a position to do sth
- be out of sb's hands/be no longer in sb's hands
- sb's hands are tied
- powerless
- ineligible

can't/cannot /kɑːnt‖kænt, ˈkænət, -nɒt‖-nɑːt/ [modal verb] *'I really want to see that movie.' 'You can't. You're not old enough.'* | **can't/cannot do sth** *The manager can't fire you for being pregnant.* | *Members of the public cannot enter the building unless they have an identity card.* | *In those days a woman could not divorce her husband except in the most extreme cases.*

not be able to do sth /ˌnɒt biː ˌeɪbəl tə ˈduː (sth)/ [v phrase] use this when a law or rule does not allow someone to do something: *If you don't have a library card, you won't be able to borrow any books.* | *You won't be able to get back into the country without your passport.*

not have the power to do sth/it is not in your power to do sth /nɒt hæv ðə ˌpaʊəʳ tə ˈduː (sth), ɪt ɪz nɒt ɪn jɔːʳ ˌpaʊəʳ tə ˈduː (sth)/ [v phrase not in progressive] to be unable to do something because your job does not give you the authority or right to do it: *It is not in her power to increase your salary, but she can recommend it.* | *Individual states do not have the power to declare war.*

not be in a position to do sth /nɒt bi ɪn ə pəˌzɪʃən tə ˈduː (sth)/ [v phrase] to be unable to do something because you do not have the authority or the moral right to do it: *The agency is not in a position to negotiate or make decisions.*

be out of sb's hands/be no longer in sb's hands /biː ˌaʊt əv (sb's) ˈhændz, biː nəʊ ˌlɒŋgər ɪn (sb's) ˈhændz‖-ˌlɔːŋ-/ [v phrase] if a problem or situation **is out of someone's hands**, they are no longer responsible for dealing with it because it has been taken over by someone with more power, or because it must now be decided according to the law: *The matter is out of our hands now – we'll just have to wait to see what the judge decides.* | *It's no longer in my hands, I'm afraid – I've sent a report about your son's behaviour to the police.*

sb's hands are tied / (sb's) ˌhændz əʳ ˈtaɪd/ if someone's **hands are tied** they cannot do what they want because of particular conditions or rules made by someone else: *The company's hands are tied because of government regulations.* | *I'd like to help you, but you missed the deadline. I'm afraid my hands are tied.*

powerless /ˈpaʊəʳləs/ [adj] unable to control or stop something because you do not have the power or legal right to do this: *The average citizen feels completely powerless faced with the rising tide of crime and violence.* | **+ to do sth** *Although we all thought the decision was unfair, we were powerless to change it.* | **+ against** *Citizens imprisoned for their political beliefs are powerless against the government.* —**powerlessness** [n U] *For many, feelings of powerlessness lead to complete apathy or depression.*

ineligible /ɪnˈeləd͡ʒəbəl/ [adj] if you are **ineligible** to take part in something or to receive something, you do not have the legal right to do this: *Police found that many of the people on the list were ineligible voters.* | **+ for** *People with higher incomes are ineligible for the government benefits.* | **+ to do sth** *Because he no longer lives in the district, he is ineligible to run for re-election.*

cancel

to decide that a planned event will not now happen

RELATED WORDS

- to arrange to do something at a better time *see* **later (2)**

- cancel
- call off
- be off
- scrub
- shelve

cancel /ˈkænsəl/ [v T] to change a previous arrangement, so that a meeting, concert, game etc that was planned will not happen: *Classes were canceled for the day.* | *I forgot to cancel my doctor's appointment.* | *They were forced to cancel the concert when the conductor became ill.* —**cancellation** /ˌkænsəˈleɪʃən/ [n C/U] *Bad weather led to the cancellation of most flights out of Chicago's O'Hare Airport.* | *The fighting in the region could lead to the cancellation of next month's elections.*

call off /ˌkɔːl ˈɒf / [phr v T] to stop a meeting or event that you have organized **call off sth** *The game was called off due to heavy rain.* | **call sth off** *Linda may call the wedding off.*

be off /biː ˈɒf / [phr v I] if an event or activity **is off**, it has been cancelled because of a sudden problem or change in someone's plans: *I'm afraid the party's off. Nick won't let us use his apartment.* | *Myers called me yesterday to tell me that the deal was off.*

scrub /skrʌb/ [v T] British informal to decide not to do something that you have planned because there is a problem: *We haven't really got enough money for the trip – let's just scrub it.*

shelve /ʃelv/ [v T usually in passive] **shelve a project/plan/idea/proposal etc** to decide not to continue with a plan, although it may be considered again at some time in the future: *Plans for a new stadium have been shelved for now.* | *The city shelved the project due to lack of funding.*

careful

RELATED WORDS

opposite: —————— **careless**

- too careful about small details *see* **detail (8)**
- *see also* **sensible**

1 careful to avoid risks or danger

- careful
- cautious
- with care/with caution
- wary
- vigilant

careful /ˈkeəʳfəl/ [adj] someone who is **careful** tries to avoid danger, risks, or accidents: *You'll be OK with Jane – she's a very careful driver.* | *Paints today are getting safer as companies remove harmful chemicals, but you still need to be careful.* | **+ (that)** *We had to be careful that we didn't tip the raft over.* —**carefully** [adv] *Bye, Sarah – drive carefully!*

cautious /ˈkɔːʃəs/ [adj] someone who is **cautious** does not like taking risks and is always very careful to avoid them: *If we're too cautious, we might lose a good business opportunity.* | *Phil's a very cautious driver – it'll take at least an hour to get there.* | **+ about** *I've always been cautious about giving people my phone number.* —**cautiously** [adv] *Slowly and cautiously, we made our way along the edge of the cliff.*

with care/with caution /wɪð ˈkeəʳ, wɪð ˈkɔːʃən/ [adv] if you do something **with care** or **with caution**, you do it carefully in order to avoid accidents: *Some roads may be icy and motorists are advised to drive with caution.* | **handle sth with care** *These antiques are fragile and must be handled with care.*

wary /ˈweəri/ [adj] someone who is **wary** does not easily trust people and thinks very carefully before getting involved in any situation that might be dangerous or cause problems **+ of** *She had become extremely wary of relationships as a result of her childhood experiences.* | *Wary of becoming entangled in her friend's family quarrels, Eileen made an excuse and left.* | **+ about** *The problems with selling the house had made her much more wary about financial matters.* | **keep a wary eye on sb/sth** (=watch something or someone carefully) *One of the guards was fiddling with his radio, all the time keeping a wary eye on the five prisoners.* —**warily** [adv] *He made his way up the stairs, glancing warily over his shoulder and keeping close to the wall.*

vigilant /ˈvɪdʒələnt/ [adj] formal always paying attention to what is happening, so that you notice any danger or illegal activity: *Be vigilant on public transport and at tourist sites, as pickpockets operate in these areas.* | **+ about** *We have to be vigilant about protecting our right to privacy.* | **remain vigilant** *The terrorist threat is still real, and the public should remain vigilant.* | **ever vigilant** (=always vigilant) *We must be ever vigilant. Don't think that Fascism can never rise again. It can.* —**vigilance** [n U] *'This case has reminded all Americans about the need for vigilance in guarding against racial discrimination,' Relman said.*

2 to try to avoid risks or danger

- take care
- take precautions
- be on your guard
- keep/have your wits about you
- play safe
- take no chances

take care /ˌteɪk ˈkeəʳ/ [v phrase] to do something in a sensible way, in order to avoid risks: *Of course you don't have to spend all your time worrying about possible health hazards, but you still need to take care.* | **+ how/when etc** *Take care how you cross the road. Most drivers ignore the traffic lights and just drive through.* | **+ with** *I always take great care with diets, so I don't lose too much weight too quickly.*

take precautions /ˌteɪk prɪˈkɔːʃənz/ [v phrase] to make preparations before you do something, in order to avoid the risk of something unpleasant happening: *Tourists should take precautions as they would in any large city, and should avoid traveling alone at night.* | **+ against** *The villagers had already taken precautions against random raids by the militia.* | **take the precaution of doing sth** *Bennet had taken the precaution of transferring his house into his wife's name before his company collapsed.*

be on your guard /ˌbiː ɒn jɔːʳ ˈgɑːʳd / [v phrase] to pay careful attention to what is happening and not easily trust people, in order to avoid getting into danger, being tricked etc: *Drivers have to be on their guard, as faults or signal failures can occur at any time.* | **+ against** *'We would like to warn everybody to be on their guard against unsolicited 'tradesmen',' he said.*

keep/have your wits about you /ˌkiːp, ˌhæv jɔːʳ ˈwɪts əˌbaʊt juː/ [v phrase] to watch and listen very carefully when you are in a situation that might be dangerous, or in which people might try to cheat you: *It was only because John kept his wits about him that the boys managed to get home safely.* | *Buying a second-hand car can be very tricky. You really have to have your wits about you.*

play safe /ˌpleɪ ˈseɪf/ [v phrase] to choose a careful way of doing something instead of a way that could have more risks or danger: *My friends keep advising me to invest my money in stocks and shares but I've decided to play safe and leave it in the bank.* | *The Film Club could have played safe by starting the season with one of the ever-popular Hitchcock movies, but instead they chose to show an avant-garde documentary.*

take no chances /ˌteɪk nəʊ ˈtʃɑːnsəz‖-ˈtʃæn-/ [v phrase] to organize something in a very careful way, because you want to avoid any possible risks: *This time we're taking no chances. Everything will be planned down to the last detail.* | *Weather forecasters have warned about the possibility of severe storms, and city officials are taking no chances.*

3 what you say when warning someone to be careful

- be careful
- take care
- look out/watch out!
- watch it/watch what you're doing
- mind out

be careful /biː ˈkeəʳfəl/ [v phrase] spoken **careful!/be careful!** *There's ice on the roads tonight so be careful.* | *Careful! That's hot.* | **+ with** *Hey! Careful with that cigarette!* | **be careful with sth** *You be careful with that knife.* | **be careful (not) to do sth** *Be careful not to get any of that bleach on your clothes.* | **be careful (that) you do sth** *You'll have to be careful you* *don't lose your balance.* | **be careful what/where/how etc** *The whole interview will be recorded so you'd better be careful what you say.*

take care /ˌteɪk ˈkeəʳ/ spoken say this to warn someone to be careful, especially when you think they may not realize there are dangers or risks: *Take care. That gun's loaded.* | *Take care when you open the van door, sometimes it springs open suddenly.* | **take care (not) to do sth** *Take care not to leave any money in the changing rooms.*

look out/watch out! /ˌlʊk ˈaʊt, ˌwɒtʃ ˈaʊt ‖ˌwɑːtʃ-/ spoken say this to warn someone that they are going to have an accident and they must do something quickly to avoid it: *Watch out – you're going to spill paint over my new carpet!* | *Look out, Phil – there's a car coming!*

watch it/watch what you're doing /ˈwɒtʃ ɪt‖ˈwɑːtʃ-, ˌwɒtʃ wɒt jɔːʳ ˈduːɪŋ‖ˌwɑːtʃ-/ spoken say this when someone has just done something dangerous, and you want to tell them to be careful: *Watch it! You nearly knocked my head off with that stick!*

mind out /ˌmaɪnd ˈaʊt/ British spoken say this when you want someone to move to one side to avoid possible danger: *Mind out – there's a snowball coming towards you!*

4 careful to do things correctly

- careful
- with care
- conscientious
- thorough
- meticulous
- methodical

careful /ˈkeəʳfəl/ [adj] someone who is **careful** tries not to make mistakes, and tries to do everything correctly: *She's a careful, hard-working student.* | **+ with** *Try to be more careful with your punctuation.* | **careful (not) to do sth** *They were careful not to touch anything until the police arrived.* | *Fry the garlic, being careful not to let it burn.* —**carefully** [adv] *Check your essay carefully for spelling mistakes.*

with care /wɪð ˈkeəʳ/ [adv] formal if you do something **with care** you do it carefully in order to make sure that you do not make any mistakes: *She has to work slowly and with great care in order to get the picture just right.* | *Her room is beautifully furnished, with a great deal of care and attention to detail.* | *Aunt Beryl's presents were well-received, and had obviously been chosen with a lot of care.*

conscientious /ˌkɒnʃiˈenʃəs◂‖ˌkɑːn-/ [adj] someone who is **conscientious** has a serious attitude to their work or their duties and tries hard to do everything they have been asked to do in the way that it should be done: *She was a very conscientious student and attended all her lectures.* | *His previous employer describes him as honest, hard-working and conscientious.* | **+ about** *I wish everyone was as conscientious as you are about getting to work on time.* —**conscientiously** [adv] *She can be trusted to carry out her duties conscientiously and effectively.*

thorough /ˈθʌrə‖ˈθʌrəʊ, ˈθʌrə/ [adj not usually before noun] someone who is **thorough** is careful that all the work they do is complete and correct: *Our mechanics will check everything – they're very thorough.* —**thoroughly** [adv] *All the equipment has been thoroughly tested.*

meticulous /məˈtɪkjələs/ [adj] someone who is **meticulous** pays a lot of attention to every detail in order to make sure that everything is done correctly: *This beautiful piece of jewellery is the work of a meticulous craftsman.* | *My mother was extremely meticulous and always made sure that every room in the house was spotlessly clean.* | **meticulous about** *Our accountant is very meticulous about his work. I can't imagine him ever making a mistake.* —**meticulously** [adv] *The investigators worked meticulously through the evidence for several months, but found no real evidence to connect Murray with the crime.*

methodical /məˈθɒdɪkəl‖məˈθɑː-/ [adj] someone who is **methodical** always does their work in a carefully planned way and is careful to check everything they do: *Poirot, always deliberate and methodical, made a list of all the possible suspects.* | *Barnes is a conscientious and methodical journalist who would have checked all of the facts before writing the story.*

5 careful work/checks/actions

- careful
- thorough
- systematic
- rigorous
- painstaking
- close
- scrupulous

careful /ˈkeəʳfəl/ [adj only before noun] a **careful** test, study, piece of work etc is done carefully and correctly, with a lot of attention to detail: *A careful inspection showed cracks in the foundation of the building.* | *Her book is the result of years of careful research.*

thorough /ˈθʌrə‖ˈθʌrəʊ, ˈθʌrə/ [adj] a **thorough** search, check, examination etc is one that is done carefully so that no detail is missed: *The doctor gave me a thorough check-up.* | **thorough search/check/examination etc** *The police have made a thorough search of the area.*

systematic /ˌsɪstəˈmætɪk◂/ [adj] a **systematic** way of doing something uses a fixed plan, so that everything gets done thoroughly – use this especially about activities that are dishonest or harmful: *the systematic destruction of the country's education system* | *Ex-prisoners talked of systematic cruelty within the jail.* —**systematically** [adv] *They went through the documents systematically, removing every reference to his former wife.*

rigorous /ˈrɪgərəs/ [adj] **rigorous tests/checks/examination etc** checks etc that are done very carefully to make sure that something is safe, suitable etc or of the right quality or standard: *Every new drug has to pass a series of rigorous safety checks before it is put on sale.* | *The entrance tests for people wishing to enter the diplomatic service are particularly rigorous.* —**rigorously** [adv] *The plane had been rigorously checked before taking off on its last flight.*

painstaking /ˈpeɪnzˌteɪkɪŋ/ [adj only before noun] very careful and thorough, and taking a lot of time and effort: *They began the long and painstaking task of compiling a bibliography.* —**painstakingly** [adv] *The poet's house has been painstakingly restored.*

close /kləʊs/ [adj only before noun] **close look/examination** paying very careful attention to details: *Take a close look at this photograph.* | *On closer examination of the facts it became clear that the boy was innocent.* —**closely** [adv] *The police questioned him closely about his involvement in the robbery.*

scrupulous /ˈskruːpjələs/ [adj only before noun] very carefully making sure that every detail is exactly right, so that it cannot be criticized: *Scrupulous cleanliness is necessary when preparing food in a restaurant.* | *The investigation was carried out with scrupulous fairness.* | *Outstanding hospitality and scrupulous attention to detail make The Oceanic one* *of the finest hotels in the resort.* —**scrupulously** [adv] *You must keep the wound scrupulously clean to avoid infection.*

6 to try to do something correctly and not make mistakes

- take care
- pay attention to
- take pains to do sth

take care /ˌteɪk 'keəʳ/ [v phrase] to do a piece of work carefully because you want it to be right, and you do not want to make mistakes: *Look at all these typing errors! Can't you take more care?* | **+ with** *Sally doesn't take nearly enough care with her accounts.* | **take care to do sth** *Take care to label all the disks with the correct file names.*

pay attention to /ˌpeɪ ə'tenʃən tuː/ [v phrase] to be careful that a particular thing is done in the right way: *You need to pay more attention to your grammar if you want to get a better grade.* | *Trainees are taught to pay attention to details and to strive for perfection.*

take pains to do sth /teɪk ˌpeɪnz tə 'duː (sth)/ [v phrase] to make a special effort to do something carefully and well: *Take pains to present a smart, efficient appearance, and to show that you are keen to progress in the company.* | *He had taken great pains to make the setting attractive: green candles stood waiting to be lit and in the centre was a bowl of white miniature roses.*

7 careful about what you say to other people

- careful
- tactful
- guarded
- discreet

careful /'keəʳfəl/ [adj] **+ what/how etc** *You have to be careful what you say to her, she's very easily offended.* | *They were both aware that there might be listening devices in the room, and she wanted to be careful what she said.* | **careful (not) to do sth** *'Failing your exams isn't the end of the world,' said Kay's mother, careful not to sound disappointed.* | *She is careful not to criticize the president, but makes it clear that she thinks the government's policies should be far more radical.*

tactful /'tæktfəl/ [adj] careful not to do or say anything that will hurt or embarrass other people: *I wish you'd be more tactful – didn't you realize she was divorced?* | **+ about** *My parents tried to be tactful about my new boyfriend, but I knew they didn't like him.*

guarded /'gɑːʳdɪ̵d/ [adj] if you make a **guarded** statement, remark etc you are careful not to let other people know much about your thoughts or intentions: *Michael Fallon, MP for Darlington, has given the scheme a guarded welcome.* | *Their message was expressed in very guarded language.*

discreet /dɪ'skriːt/ [adj] formal very careful about what you say or do, so that you do not make people feel angry, upset, or embarrassed: *A private detective was sent to make discreet inquiries about Miss Hutton's financial situation.* | *People might gossip if we arrived together. It would be much more discreet for us to go there separately.* —**discreetly** [adv] *The maid entered after knocking discreetly.* —**discretion** /dɪ'skreʃən/ [n U] *I should stress that this affair must be handled with the utmost discretion* (=in a very discreet way).

careless

RELATED WORDS

opposite: careful

▸ *see also* **clumsy, accident, mistake, stupid/silly, risk**

1 careless, so that you make mistakes or do something badly

- careless
- clumsy
- sloppy

careless /'keəʳləs/ [adj] someone who is **careless** makes mistakes because they do not think carefully enough about what they are doing: *I made a few careless mistakes.* | *Don't be so careless.* | **+ about** *After a few weeks, he started getting careless about taking his medication.* | **+ in** *Katz argued that the police used too much force and were careless in making arrests.* | **+ with** *Terence has always been careless with his money.* | **it is careless of sb (to do sth)** *It was very careless of you to leave your purse lying on the desk.* —**carelessly** [adv] *She opened the bottle quickly and carelessly, breaking the cork.* —**carelessness** [n U] *Most accidents are entirely due to carelessness.*

clumsy /'klʌmzi/ [adj] someone who is **clumsy** often drops things or breaks things because they move around in a careless way: *I was tall and clumsy as a child, so I avoided sports.* | *Paula always felt clumsy when she had to serve food to people.* | *a large man with big clumsy hands* —**clumsily** [adv] *I got up, clumsily knocking against the table.*

sloppy /'slɒpi‖'slɑː-/ [adj] doing something in a careless and lazy way – used especially about the way someone does their work, or the way they behave generally: *As a student, he was brilliant but sloppy.*

2 careless, so that you or other people are in danger

- careless
- reckless
- irresponsible
- negligence

careless /'keəʳləs/ [adj] not taking enough care in what you are doing because you do not think about the possible danger or risks: *Some careless idiot forgot to lock the door and the dog got out.* | *Pryce accused the other driver of being careless and negligent.* —**carelessly** [adv] *Cigarettes thrown carelessly from cars can cause forest fires.* —**carelessness** [n U] *Anna is lying in the hospital, and all because of your carelessness.*

reckless /'rekləs/ [adj] especially written someone who is **reckless** does dangerous or stupid things without thinking that they or someone else might get hurt: *The driver of the car was arrested for reckless driving.* | *a reckless disregard for human life* —**recklessly** [adj] *young men recklessly risking their lives in dangerous sports*

irresponsible /ˌɪrɪ'spɒnsɪ̵bəl‖-'spɑːn-/ [adj] someone who is **irresponsible** does not do the things they should do, or does things they should not do, usually with harmful results: *Police blame higher crime rates on irresponsible parents who allow their teenage children to stay out all night.* | *Critics accused the governor of being irresponsible, and claimed that his new proposal would put thousands of US troops at risk.*

negligence /ˈneglɪdʒəns/ [n U] when someone does not do an important job carefully enough, especially with the result that there is an accident and they are punished for causing it: *Dr. Atkins was found guilty of negligence and practising medicine without a license.* | *You can claim compensation if your injury is a result of your employer's negligence.* —**negligent** [adj] *The jury determined that the school had been negligent, and awarded the student $450,000.*

3 done in a careless way

- careless
- sloppy
- slapdash/slipshod
- haphazard

careless /ˈkeəʳləs/ [adj] *Investigators are still not sure whether the damage was intentional or due to careless work.* | *The building had been finished in a very careless way, with loose wires and unpainted ceilings.* | *Careless handling of pesticides causes dozens of accidents on farms every year.*

sloppy /ˈslɒpi‖ˈslɑː-/ [adj] done in a careless and lazy way – use this about someone's work or the way someone writes or speaks: *The carpenter I hired did such a sloppy job that I finally had to fix the roof myself.* | *The company's failure was blamed on sloppy management.* | *How can you expect an 'A' in this class when you turn in an essay as sloppy as this?*

slapdash/slipshod /ˈslæpdæʃ, ˈslɪpʃɒd‖-ʃɑːd/ [adj] done extremely carelessly and quickly, without paying any attention to the correct ways of working: *We complained to the airline that the in-flight service was hurried and slapdash.* | *The entire investigation had been conducted in an unsystematic, almost slipshod, manner.*

haphazard /ˌhæpˈhæzəʳd◂/ [adj] done without any clear plan or system: *According to the report, most Americans have a distinctly haphazard approach to saving for the future.* —**haphazardly** [adv] *Dirty plates and cups were stacked haphazardly in the sink.*

4 said without thinking carefully enough

- careless
- tactless
- indiscreet

careless /ˈkeəʳləs/ [adj only before noun] **careless remarks/talk/words etc** said without thinking about what effect they might have, and so often causing trouble or embarrassment: *You say a few careless words to a neighbour and suddenly everyone knows about it.* | *Witnesses say the argument started after a careless remark about the victim's wife.* —**carelessly** [adv] *The newspaper had carelessly described him as an 'Indian chief'.*

tactless /ˈtæktləs/ [adj] carelessly saying something that upsets or embarrasses someone, especially by mentioning something that it would be kinder or more polite not to talk about: *How could he be so tactless as to make jokes about funerals when her father's just died?* | **it is tactless to do sth** *I wanted to know about her divorce but thought it would be tactless to ask.* —**tactlessly** [adv] *'Would you like to come and have dinner with me?' asked Eddie, and then added tactlessly, 'Someone I invited has cancelled.'*

indiscreet /ˌɪndɪˈskriːt◂/ [adj] careless about what you say, especially by talking about things that should be kept secret: *I wouldn't trust him with anything personal – he can be very indiscreet.* | **it is indiscreet of sb to do sth** *I did hear them talking about sales figures but it would be indiscreet of me to say any more.*

5 not thinking carefully enough before doing something

- rash
- hasty
- impulsive
- impetuous

rash /ræʃ/ [adj] if you do something **rash**, you do not think carefully about the effect it will have, and you wish later you had not done it: *Stay where you are and don't do anything rash – I'll be over in five minutes.* | *Don't make any rash promises that you may regret later.* —**rashly** [adv] *I rashly offered to lend her the money.*

hasty /ˈheɪsti/ [adj] too quick to do or say something, without taking time to think about it first: *I think I may have been a little hasty about firing him.* | *Go home and think about whether you really want to have the operation – I don't want you to make any hasty decisions.*

impulsive /ɪmˈpʌlsɪv/ [adj] doing things as soon as you think of them, without considering the possible dangers or problems: *She's so impulsive – she saw the house for the first time and said she'd buy it straight away.* | *Although she comes across as impulsive, Harper is actually very cautious and indecisive.* —**impulsively** [adv] *He kissed her impulsively.* —**impulsiveness** [n U] *His impulsiveness surprised her. He was normally so careful.*

impetuous /ɪmˈpetʃuəs/ [adj] doing something without thinking carefully first, especially because you have an emotional character and easily get angry, excited etc: *If you weren't so impetuous you wouldn't have lost your job.* | *He says she's impetuous and emotional.*

carry

RELATED WORDS

- *see also* **take/bring, hold, lift, pull**

1 to carry something or someone

- carry
- bear
- tote
- lug
- cart

carry /ˈkæri/ [v T] to take something from one place to another, by holding it in your hands, lifting it on your back etc: *A porter helped me carry my bags.* | **carry sth to/out of/around etc** *The women have to carry water from the well to the village.* | *I've been carrying this tape-recorder around with me all day.*

bear /beəʳ/ [v T] formal or written to carry something, especially something important: *A messenger arrived, bearing a letter from the ambassador.* | *At the head of the procession a group of dark-suited men bore the coffin into the church.*

tote /təʊt/ [v T] American informal to carry something: *My job was to tote their golf bags and wash their cars.* | *a gun-toting cowboy*

lug ALSO **schlep** American /lʌg, ʃlep/ [v T] informal to carry something heavy with difficulty: *We lugged our suitcases up the hotel steps.* | *I've got enough to carry without lugging your bags as well.*

cart /kɑːʳt/ [v T] informal to carry something that is awkward or heavy **cart sth down/out etc** *Madge picked up the box and carted it out to the back yard.* | *I'm not going to cart your shopping around all afternoon.*

2 carrying a lot of things

- be loaded (down) with
- be weighed down with/by
- under the weight of
- overloaded

be loaded (down) with ALSO **be laden with** /biː ˌləʊdɪ̥d (ˈdaʊn) wɪð, biː ˈleɪdn wɪð/ [v phrase] to be carrying a lot of things, so that you cannot carry any more: *Cora was loaded down with two 70-pound suitcases.* | *A van loaded with newspapers was parked in front of the store.* | *She was carrying a tray laden with dishes.* | **be heavily loaded/laden with sth** *The bus was heavily laden with passengers and baggage.*

be weighed down with/by /biː ˌweɪd ˈdaʊn wɪð, baɪ/ [v phrase] to be carrying or holding so many things that it is difficult to move or impossible to hold any more: *The branches of the trees were weighed down with fruit.* | *She struggled along the street, weighed down by bags.*

under the weight of /ˌʌndəʳ ðə ˈweɪt ɒv/ [prep] if someone or something falls or moves unsteadily **under the weight of** of something, they do this because they are carrying something that is too heavy for them to support: *Paul staggered under the weight of two backpacks.*

overloaded /ˌəʊvəʳˈləʊdɪ̥d◂/ [adj] if a vehicle is **overloaded**, it is holding or carrying too many things, with the result that it can only move slowly and it may not be safe: *The plane was dangerously overloaded.* | *The car was so overloaded the bumpers were almost touching the ground.*

3 to regularly carry something in your pocket, bag etc

- carry

carry /ˈkæri/ [v T] **carry money/a chequebook/a gun etc** to regularly **carry** something valuable or something that you need in your pocket or bag: *The new mobile phones are slim enough to carry in your pocket.* | *You should always carry at least a little cash with you in case of an emergency.*

4 designed to be carried

- portable

portable /ˈpɔːʳtəbəl/ [adj usually before noun] **portable TV/typewriter/CD player** a television, computer etc that is specially designed so that you can carry it around with you: *There's a portable CD player in the kitchen.* | *Greenaway still writes his novels on an old portable typewriter.*

catch

RELATED WORDS

- catch a bus, train etc *see* **get on or off a bus, plane etc**
- catch an illness *see* **illness/disease (3)**

1 to catch a ball or other moving object

- catch

- *see also* **throw, sport/game**

catch /kætʃ/ [v T] to get hold of a ball or other object that is moving through the air: *Ted caught the ball and threw it back to his brother.* | *Jenny tried to catch the frisbee with her left hand but dropped it.* — **catch** [n C] when you get hold of a ball or other object that is moving through the air: *That was a great catch!*

2 when the police catch a criminal

- catch
- arrest
- get
- nail
- take sb into custody

- *see also* **follow, escape, run, crime**

catch /kætʃ/ [v T] *Police say they are determined to catch the killer.* | *A lot of thieves never get caught.*

arrest /əˈrest/ [v T] if a police officer **arrests** someone they catch them, tell them officially that they have done something illegal, and take them away: *Police arrested twenty-six demonstrators.* | *Nine men were arrested in drug raids, Saturday.* | **arrest sb for sth** *Wallace was arrested for assault.* | *Dwayne has been arrested for drunk driving again.* — **arrest** [n U] *Kramer's confession led to the arrests of six others.* | **under arrest** (=arrested) *Guzman, twenty-five, was placed under arrest at his parents' home, Friday.* | **make an arrest** (=arrest someone) *Police made several arrests over the weekend in connection with last year's courthouse bombing.*

get /get/ [v T] especially British to catch and punish someone for something illegal they have done: *They still haven't got the man who did it.*

nail /neɪl/ [v T] informal to catch someone and prove that they are guilty of a crime: *Police use radar to nail speeding drivers.* | **nail sb for sth** *Myers was nailed for selling marijuana.*

take sb into custody /ˌteɪk (sb) ɪntə ˈkʌstədi/ [v phrase usually in passive] if the police **take someone into custody**, they take that person and put them in prison until they appear in court, because they think the person is guilty of a crime: *Officers took three suspects into custody Friday morning.* | *As soon as the plane landed, the men were taken into custody by waiting FBI agents.*

3 to catch someone doing something wrong

- catch
- catch sb red-handed/ catch sb in the act
- catch sb with their fingers in the till

catch /kætʃ/ [v T] to find or see someone while they are actually doing something wrong **catch sb doing sth** *Pat caught her daughter stealing money from her purse.* | *Brooks was caught smoking in an airplane lavatory and fined $750 dollars.*

catch sb red-handed/catch sb in the act /ˌkætʃ (sb) red ˈhændɪ̥d, ˌkætʃ (sb) ɪn ði ˈækt/ [v phrase usually in passive] to catch someone who is in the middle of doing something bad or illegal, especially stealing, when they are not expecting it: *Sperling was caught red-handed attempting to break into a house.* | *Several graffiti artists were caught in the act* *on the Brown River bridge.* | **catch sb in the act of doing sth** *He caught Wendy in the act of looking through his personal papers.*

catch sb with their fingers in the till /ˌkætʃ (sb) wɪð ðeəʳ ˌfɪŋgəʳz ɪn ðə ˈtɪl/ [v phrase] British to catch someone stealing money from the place where they work: *The article says that at least five government officials have been caught with their fingers in the till.*

4 to catch someone and make them a prisoner

- capture
- round up
- take sb prisoner
- recapture

capture /ˈkæptʃəʳ/ [v T] to catch a person in order to make them a prisoner: *They've captured twenty enemy soldiers.* | *Cole was captured after his plane was shot down outside Hanoi.* —**capture** [n U] *They are offering a reward for information leading to his capture.*

round up /ˌraʊnd ˈʌp/ [phr v T] to catch several people by bringing them together from different places **round up sb** *Officers succeeded in rounding up most of the gang members.* | **round sb up** *People are saying that the civil guard rounded several of the protestors up and shot them.*

take sb prisoner /ˌteɪk (sb) ˈprɪzənəʳ/ [v phrase] to catch someone, especially in a war, and keep them as a prisoner: *Ellison was taken prisoner by the Germans during the retreat to Dunkirk.* | *Military police took Kilby prisoner and locked him in a barn.* | *350 soldiers were killed and another 300 taken prisoner.*

recapture /riːˈkæptʃəʳ/ [v T] to catch someone for a second time when they have escaped after being caught once: *Viet Cong forces quickly recaptured the soldiers.* | *The prisoners were recaptured a few hours after their escape.*

5 to catch someone after chasing them

- catch
- corner
- catch up with
- hunt down
- trap

catch /kætʃ/ [v T] to stop someone from escaping, especially by running after them and then catching them – used especially by children when playing games: *'I bet you can't catch me!' yelled Katie, skipping away.* | *You choose sides, and one team hides and the other team tries to catch them.*

corner /ˈkɔːʳnəʳ/ [v T] to catch someone by forcing them into a room or space etc that they cannot escape from: *Douglas was cornered by the killers in the back bedroom of a seventh-floor apartment.* | *The boys cornered him on a subway platform and began beating him.*

catch up with /ˌkætʃ ˈʌp wɪð/ [phr v T] to catch someone that you have been chasing or trying to catch for some time: *Agents finally caught up with Danvers in Mexico City.*

hunt down /ˌhʌnt ˈdaʊn/ [phr v T] to catch someone in order to kill, hurt, or punish them, after chasing them or trying very hard to catch them **hunt down sb** *Army troops are hunting down the guerrillas.* | **hunt sb down** *The agency was created to hunt down war criminals and bring them to justice.*

trap /træp/ [v T] to catch someone by using your skill and intelligence, or by forcing them into a place where they cannot escape: *The men were trapped at a road block near the junction of I-95 and Route 128.* | *Police have the man trapped inside a bar on the city's southside.* —**trap** [n C] a plan that is intended to catch someone **fall into someone's trap** *If we're lucky, the thief will fall right into our trap.*

cause

RELATED WORDS

- *see also* **reason, because, so/therefore**

1 to make something happen

- make sth do sth
- cause
- be the cause
- be responsible
- result in sth
- lead to sth
- give rise to
- bring about
- create
- make for

make sth do sth /ˌmeɪk (sth) ˈduː (sth)/ [v phrase] *I wish you wouldn't slam the door. It makes the floor shake.* | *Accidents don't always just happen – people can make them happen.* | *Gravity is the force that makes the planets move around the sun.*

cause /kɔːz/ [v T] to make something happen, especially something unpleasant: *Heavy traffic is causing long delays on the roads.* | *About half of the chemicals that were tested caused cancer in rats.* | *The autopsy showed that her death was caused by liver failure.* | **cause sb trouble/problems/anxiety etc** *As children we were always causing our parents trouble.* | *Try to isolate the problems that are causing you the most difficulty.* | **cause sth to do sth** *The power failure caused the whole computer system to shut down.*

be the cause /biː ðə ˈkɔːz/ [v phrase] to be the particular reason for a problem or difficulty: *After a long investigation into the fire, faulty wiring was found to be the cause.* | **+ of** *It's too early to say whether this virus is actually the cause of the disease.* | *An explosion on board appears to be the cause of the crash.* | **be the leading/main cause of sth** *The study showed that drug use is the leading cause of crime and violence.*

be responsible /biː rɪˈspɒnsəbəl‖-ˈspɑːn-/ [v phrase] to be the person or thing that causes something bad to happen, for example a mistake, a problem, or a serious accident: *The number of workplace accidents is increasing, but it is not clear who or what is responsible.* | **+ for** *Heart disease was responsible for most of the deaths.* | *He was clearly responsible for the deaths and must be punished.* | **be largely/mainly responsible for sth** *Inflation was largely responsible for the economic crisis.*

result in sth /rɪˈzʌlt ɪn (sth)/ [phr v T not in passive] if an action or event **results in** something, it makes something happen: *Workers fear that the company's reorganization will result in layoffs.* | *Months of secret talks with the rebels finally resulted in the release of the hostages.* | *If left untreated, the condition will eventually result in blindness.*

lead to sth /ˈliːd tə (sth)/ [phr v T not in passive] to start a process that finally makes something happen: *His research eventually led to the development of a vaccine.* | *The new regulations should lead to an improvement in our water supply.* | *The bank has offered a reward for information leading to the arrest of the robbers.*

give rise to /ˌgɪv ˈraɪz tuː/ [v phrase] formal if a situation, event, or action **gives rise to** a particular feeling, situation etc, it starts the process that makes it happen: *The canal project gave rise to a malaria epidemic in the region.* | *The President's frequent cancellations have given rise to concerns about his health.*

bring about /ˌbrɪŋ əˈbaʊt/ [phr v T] to make something happen, especially a change or an improved situation **bring about sth** *The President will support any efforts to bring about a ceasefire.* | *Education is the best method of bringing about economic development.* | **bring sth about** *A lot of hard work by ordinary citizens eventually brought the changes about.*

create /kriˈeɪt/ [v T] to make a particular condition that did not exist at all suddenly exist: *The white walls and mirrors helped to create an illusion of space.* | *Margot's outburst created an unpleasant atmosphere and most of the guests left early.* | *The end of the cold war helped create a situation in which more countries than ever have access to nuclear weapons.* —**creation** /kriˈeɪʃən/ [n U] *The government's main economic aim has been the creation of wealth.*

make for /ˈmeɪk fɔːʳ/ [phr v T] if something **makes for** a particular situation, it makes it easier or more likely for that situation to exist: *The stormy weather made for a very bumpy landing.* | *Delicious food and wonderful company made for a very enjoyable evening.*

2 to make someone do something

- make sb do sth
- cause sb to do sth
- lead sb to do sth
- motivate
- induce sb to do sth
- prompt sb to do sth

make sb do sth /ˌmeɪk (sb) ˈduː (sth)/ [v phrase] *Sarah's very funny. Her jokes always make me laugh.* | *The things she said make me wonder if she is in some kind of trouble.* | *The smell was so bad it almost made me throw up.* | **be made to do sth** *I was made to wait for over an hour.*

cause sb to do sth /ˌkɔːz (sb) tə ˈduː (sth)/ [v phrase] to make someone or something do something. **Cause** is more formal than **make**: *A dog ran into the road, causing the cyclist to swerve.* | *The parents' fear of gang activity caused them to move the family to a safer neighborhood.* | *No-one understands what could have caused her to hate him so much.*

lead sb to do sth /ˌliːd (sb) tə ˈduː (sth)/ [v phrase] to be the thing that makes someone do something, especially when this process takes some time: *What led you to take up teaching as a career?* | *It was my interest in gardens that led me to study biology.* | **lead sb to believe** *The negative publicity has already led many to believe that Tompkins is guilty.*

motivate /ˈməʊtɪ̈veɪt/ [v T] if something **motivates** someone to do something, it makes them want to do it – use this especially to talk about the reasons why people do things that are very good, very bad, or very dangerous **motivate sb to do sth** *I don't know what motivates people to commit such crimes.* | **be motivated by sth** *He was motivated by a desire to help his fellow man.* | *Many in the Asian community feel that the police actions were motivated by racial bias.*

induce sb to do sth /ɪnˌdjuːs (sb) tə ˈduː (sth) ‖ɪnˌduːs-/ [v phrase] formal to make someone choose to do something: *Whatever induced her to buy such an expensive car?* | *The state advertises a great deal to induce its citizens to buy lottery tickets.*

prompt sb to do sth /ˌprɒmpt (sb) tə ˈduː (sth) ‖ˌprɑːmpt-/ [v phrase not usually in progressive] to be the thing that makes you to do something, especially something you have been thinking of doing for some time: *It was reading his book that prompted me to write to him.* | *What exactly prompted him to call you in the middle of the night?*

3 to make something bad suddenly happen

- set off
- trigger/spark
- precipitate

set off /ˌset ˈɒf/ [phr v T] if someone or something **sets off** a fight, war etc, it makes it start happening **set off sth** *The army's invasion set off a major international crisis.* | **set sth off** *Nobody knows what set the riot off.*

trigger/spark /ˈtrɪgəʳ, spɑːʳk/ [v T] if a small action or event **triggers** or **sparks** serious trouble or changes, it causes them to happen very quickly: *Even the smallest diplomatic incident can trigger a major international conflict.* | *The assassination of Archduke Francis Ferdinand sparked the First World War.* | **trigger/spark off sth** *Riots, sparked off by the arrest of seven student leaders, have spread to other universities.*

precipitate /prɪ̈ˈsɪpɪ̈teɪt/ [v T] formal to make something serious happen, especially more quickly than was expected: *The 1929 stock market crash precipitated the collapse of the American banking system.* | *Both countries claimed the same area, precipitating a border war.*

4 to be the first or basic cause of something

- be at the root/bottom of
- underlying

be at the root/bottom of /biː ət ðə ˈruːt, ˈbɒtəm ɒv‖-ˈbɑː-/ [v phrase] to be the basic cause of a problem or serious situation: *Simple greed is at the root of most white-collar crime.* | *At the bottom of the country's economic problems is its overwhelming debt.* | **lie at the root/bottom of sth** *Difficulties with the company's overseas subsidiaries lie at the root of last year's losses.*

underlying /ˌʌndəʳˈlaɪ-ɪŋ◂/ [adj only before noun] **underlying cause/reason/factor etc** a cause, reason etc that is one of the most basic and important, but which is not easy to notice: *They were treating only the symptoms of the disease rather than its underlying cause.* | *Climate and geography are the underlying reasons for the region's low level of economic development.*

5 to make someone have a particular feeling

- make
- have
- excite
- arouse
- evoke
- generate
- whip up
- reduce sb to

make /meɪk/ [v T] **to make sb worried/nervous/happy etc** *Stop staring at me – you're making me nervous.* | *Money is the only thing that seemed to make him happy.* | *Standing up all day really makes me tired.* | **make sb want to do sth** *The whole thing was so depressing – it made me want to give up and go home.*

have /hæv/ [v T not in passive] **have sb worried/confused/interested etc** to make someone worried, confused etc, especially only for a short time: *You had me worried for a minute – I thought you weren't going to show up.* | *The film was so full of suspense, it had the audience on the edge of their seats.*

excite /ɪk'saɪt/ [v T not in passive] formal make people feel interested, jealous etc **excite interest/jealousy/suspicion etc** *Arthur's enormous wealth excited the envy of his rivals.* | *Recent fossil finds in Africa have excited interest among palaeontologists.*

arouse /ə'raʊz/ [v T] written to make people have a strong interest in something or strong feelings, such as anger, fear, dislike etc **arouse anger/suspicion/fear etc** *His strange behavior aroused my suspicions.* | *The resignation of the managing director is certain to arouse new fears about the future of the company.* | **arouse interest/curiosity** *The success of the recent TV series has aroused young people's curiosity about nature in general.*

evoke /ɪ'vəʊk/ [v T] written to make someone have a particular emotion, thought, or reaction: *She tried everything in an attempt to evoke sympathy and pity from her parents.* | *Her speech today evoked surprise and outrage from many French officials.* | *The names Witches Well, Candlemaker Row and Grassmarket Square evoke visions of another era.*

generate /'dʒenəreɪt/ [v T] to make something such as a feeling exist and grow: *The murder trial has generated enormous public interest.* | *Realistic programmes about crime only serve to generate fear among the public.* | *Completing the project on time and under budget generated a feeling of pride and accomplishment among the team.*

whip up /ˌwɪp 'ʌp/ [phr v T] to deliberately make a lot of people feel interested, excited, angry etc about something that you think is important **whip up sth** *It's difficult to whip up people's interest in the environment.* | *She's been giving speeches all over the state to whip up support for her campaign.* | **whip sb/sth up** *Rylan has been accused of whipping crowds up into frenzies of violent hatred.*

reduce sb to /rɪ'dju:s (sb) tu:‖rɪ'du:s-/ [phr v T] **reduce sb to tears/silence/a bag of nerves etc** to treat someone in such an unkind or unfair way, that they cry, are silent etc: *He would often yell at his wife until he had reduced her to tears.* | *One look from him was enough to reduce anyone to absolute silence.* | *Her outbursts in the classroom have the effect of reducing her students to gibbering wrecks.*

6 to cause someone or something to be in a particular situation or condition

- make
- have
- render
- plunge sth into
- put sb in/into sth

make /meɪk/ [v T] **make sb late/ill etc** *Hurry up – you're going to make me late for work.* | *Something I ate last night really made me sick.* | **make sth safe/interesting/dirty etc** *He could make things very difficult for us.* | *Engineers have been working throughout the night to make the bridge safe.* | *We gave the house a coat of paint to make it more attractive.* | **make it easy/impossible/necessary etc (for sb) to do sth** *The regulations should make it easier for patients to receive the treatment they need.* | *The increased costs made it impossible to continue producing the computers in the U.S.*

have /hæv/ [v T not in passive] to make something be in a particular condition, especially so that it is ready to be used **have sth ready/organized/prepared etc** *We'll have your car ready by 3 o'clock.* | *I'm going to have the roof fixed as soon as I can afford it.* | *My parents had the little train all laid out under the tree on Christmas morning.*

render /'rendəʳ/ [v T] formal to make someone or something unable to do something, work properly, cause any damage etc **render sth useless/impossible/harmless etc** *Both runways have been rendered useless by enemy bombings.* | *The angry exchange rendered future compromise impossible.* | **render sb unconscious/helpless etc** *Suddenly Packer struck a blow that rendered his victim unconscious.*

plunge sth into /'plʌndʒ (sth) ɪntu:/ [v phrase] to cause someone or something to suddenly be in a very bad situation **plunge sb/sth into debt/war/depression etc** *The government's uncontrolled spending has plunged the country into debt.* | *The growing hostility between the two parties is threatening to plunge the country into civil war.*

put sb in/into sth /'pʊt (sb) ɪn, ɪntə (sth)/ [v phrase] **put sb in a difficult/awkward/impossible situation/position** to do something that causes someone difficulties, embarrassment etc: *The minister's comments have put the prime minister into a very awkward position.* | *I'm afraid I've been put into a rather embarrassing position.*

7 to deliberately try to cause trouble, arguments etc

- incite
- provoke
- stir up

incite /ɪn'saɪt/ [v T] formal to deliberately encourage people to cause trouble, fight, argue etc: *Four men were arrested for inciting the riot.* | **incite sb to sth** *She was charged with inciting the crowd to violence.* | **incite sb to do sth** *Tribal leaders are accused of inciting their followers to attack rival tribes.* —**incitement** [n U] *By publishing the book they were guilty of incitement to racial hatred.*

provoke /prə'vəʊk/ [v T] if something **provokes** an angry situation or a reaction, they cause it, usually deliberately: *The new laws have provoked violent demonstrations in some towns.* | *The ambassador's offensive remarks provoked widespread criticism.* | **provoke sb to sth** *The judge ruled that Becker provoked her husband to attack her so she could shoot him.*

stir up /ˌstɜ:r 'ʌp/ [phr v T] to deliberately try to cause arguments, fighting etc between people **stir up sth** *I hope you're not trying to stir up trouble.* | *His series of articles on party leaders has stirred up a great deal of public controversy.* | **stir sth up** *He was accused of trying to stir rebellion up among the peasants.*

8 to be one of the causes of something

- play a part
- contribute to
- contributory

play a part /ˌpleɪ ə 'pɑ:ʳt/ [v phrase] if something **plays a part** in something, it is one of several things that makes it happen or be successful: *Many cases of breast cancer have genetic causes, but environmental substances may also play a part.* | **+ in** *It is not yet known if weather conditions played a part in the accident.* | *The genius of the two designers has played a big part in the company's recent success.*

contribute to /kən'trɪbju:t tu:‖-bjət-/ [phr v T not in

passive] if something **contributes to** a situation or event, it is one of the things that make it happen: *An increase in the price of drugs has contributed to the rising cost of medical care.* | *It is thought that the pilot's negligence may have contributed to the disaster.*

contributory /kənˈtrɪbjətəri‖-tɔːri/ [adj only before noun] formal **contributory cause/factor** one of several causes of something that happens, but not the main cause: *Malnutrition was considered to have been a contributory cause of death.* | *Alcohol is a contributory factor in at least 50% of the violent crimes reported.*

9 to believe that something is caused by a particular thing

- put sth down to
- attribute sth to

put sth down to /ˌpʊt (sth) ˈdaʊn tuː/ [phr v T] to explain a situation, event, or behaviour by saying that it is the result of something else: *Charlie's been drinking a lot lately, which I put down to stress at work.* | *Authorities put the acts of vandalism down to 'festive high spirits' after the team's victory.* | *Her restlessness was put down to excitement, and nobody realised she was seriously ill.*

attribute sth to /əˈtrɪbjuːt (sth) tuː‖-bjət-/ [phr v T] formal to explain a situation or fact by saying that it is the result of something else: *Over 1,000 deaths a year can be attributed to drunk driving.* | *The low crop yields are attributed to changes in climate.* | *The management attributed the success of the company to the new Marketing Director.*

10 something that makes something else happen

- cause
- factor
- reason
- origins
- root
- stimulus
- impetus

cause /kɔːz/ [n C] *Doctors cannot find a cure for the illness until they have identified the cause.* | **+ of** *Investigators are still trying to determine the cause of the accident.* | **root cause** (=basic cause) *The root cause of the current energy crisis is that we simply use too much energy.*

factor /ˈfæktəʳ/ [n C] one of several causes of a situation or condition: *The price of insurance depends on several factors, including the age of the car.* | **+ in** *His girlfriend lives in London and I'm sure that was a factor in his decision to move there.* | **key factor** (=very important factor) *Money will be the key factor when we decide to buy a new house.* | **deciding/determining factor** (=the thing that finally makes something happen) *Race should never be a deciding factor in a hiring decision.*

reason /ˈriːzən/ [n C] the thing or one of the things that makes you decide to do something or makes something happen: *'Why are you helping her?' 'She asked me to. That's the only reason.'* | *The main reason she quit is that she was not being paid enough.* | **+ for/behind** *Can anyone explain the reason for the delay?* | *There were two reasons behind the company's failure.* | **+ why/(that)** *The reason why the economy is growing more slowly is a lack of workers.* | **+ to do sth** *There's no reason to doubt what she says.*

origins /ˈɒrədʒənz‖ˈɔː-, ˈɑː-/ [n plural] the first causes from which a situation, condition etc has developed **+ of** *The origins of the crisis were very complex.* | *Other cultures' beliefs about the origins of disease often differ from our own.* | **have origins in** *Many of our attitudes to the issue of race have their origins in the colonialism of days gone by.*

root /ruːt/ [n C] the main or most important cause of a situation or condition **+ of** *The roots of the wars in the Balkans go back hundreds of years.* | **get to the root of sth** (=discover the most important cause) *We need to get to the root of the problem.*

stimulus /ˈstɪmjələs/ [n C/U] an event, action, or situation that helps a process to develop more quickly: *The appointment of a new director gave the project immediate stimulus.* | **+ to** *The surge in new housing construction ought to provide a stimulus to the economy.*

impetus /ˈɪmpətəs/ [n singular/U] an event, action, or situation that helps something to develop more quickly **+ for/behind** *The impetus for change in the industry was provided by a new management team.* | *Press criticism has been the main impetus behind the government reforms.* | **give impetus to sth** *The Surgeon General's speech will give new impetus to the anti-smoking campaign.*

celebrate

RELATED WORDS

- *see also* **party, meal**

1 to celebrate something

- celebrate
- commemorate
- do sth in sb's honour
- mark
- in celebration of

celebrate /ˈseləbreɪt/ [v I/T] to do something, for example to have a party or special meal, because it is someone's birthday, wedding, or because of some other special event: *Congratulations on your promotion – we must go out and celebrate!* | *What do you want to do to celebrate our anniversary this year?* | **celebrate sth with sth** *Harry celebrated his thirtieth birthday with a meal in a fancy restaurant.*

commemorate /kəˈmeməreɪt/ [v T] to do something to show that you remember and respect an important event in the past or someone who did something important in the past, especially someone who is now dead: *The annual parade commemorates the soldiers who died in the two World Wars.* | *The book will be published in October to commemorate the 100th anniversary of Morris's death.* —**in commemoration of** /ɪn kəˌmeməˈreɪʃən ɒv/ [prep] in order to commemorate someone or something: *Candles were lit in commemoration of Hiroshima's dead.*

do sth in sb's honour British **/honor** American /ˌduː (sth) ɪn (sb's) ˈɒnəʳ‖-ˈɑːn-/ [v phrase] to do something in order to show your respect for someone, for example because they have been very brave or have achieved something very special: *A parade was organised in honour of Madame Blier, who had risked her life to save the villagers from enemy soldiers.* | *When Mr Johns retired after 45 years' service, the company held a party in his honour.* | *The home stadium is named in Robinson's honor.*

mark /mɑːʳk/ [v T] if you do something to **mark** a particular occasion, you do something special to show that it is important and should be remembered: *A firework display was organized to mark the*

Queen's birthday. | *The celebration marked the 100th anniversary of the staging of the modern Olympic Games.*

in celebration of /ɪn ˌseləˈbreɪʃən ɒv/ [prep] in order to celebrate an important event or achievement: *In celebration of the store's grand opening, we're offering free balloons for the kids.* | *A retrospective film festival is being planned in celebration of the actor's 86th birthday.*

2 a special event at which you celebrate something

▸ **celebration**

celebration /ˌseləˈbreɪʃən/ [n C] an event such as a party or a special public occasion that is held because people want to celebrate something: *New Year celebrations in Scotland go on for three days.* | *There is a two-day citywide celebration each year at the end of June.* | **+ of** *The hospital is planning a huge celebration of its 50th anniversary.* | **birthday/anniversary/New Year's etc celebration** *Janine had her birthday celebration a week early.*

certainly/ definitely

RELATED WORDS

opposite: **doubt**

▸ when you feel sure that something is true *see* **sure/not sure**

▸ to think that something is true but not be sure *see* **think**

▸ *see also* **possible, maybe, probably**

1 when something is definitely true

▸ **certainly/definitely**
▸ **undoubtedly/ unquestionably/ without doubt/ without a doubt**
▸ **there's no doubt/ there's no question**
▸ **beyond a shadow of a doubt**
▸ **surely**
▸ **be beyond dispute**

certainly/definitely /ˈsɜːʳtnli, ˈdefənətli/ [adv] use this to emphasize that something is definitely true. **Definitely** is more common in spoken English than **certainly**: *Incredible as they seem, these events certainly took place.* | *We don't know exactly when the house was built, but it's certainly over 200 years old.* | *I definitely posted the cheque last week, so it should have arrived by now.* | *'I think it would be a great opportunity.' 'Yeah, definitely.'* | **definitely/certainly not** *'She's not thinking of going back out with Simon again?' 'No, definitely not.'*

undoubtedly / unquestionably / without doubt/without a doubt /ʌnˈdaʊtədli, ʌnˈkwestʃənəbli, wɪðˌaʊt ˈdaʊt, wɪðˌaʊt ə ˈdaʊt/ [adv] use this to say that, in your opinion, something is definitely true about someone or something: *The years my parents spent in Kenya were undoubtedly the happiest of their lives.* | *Japan has unquestionably one of the most successful economies in the world.* | *Without a doubt, taxation is going to be the key issue in the President's campaign.*

there's no doubt/there's no question /ðeəʳz ˌnəʊ ˈdaʊt, ðeəʳz ˌnəʊ ˈkwestʃən/ use this to say that, in your opinion, something definitely is true about someone or something **+ that** *There's no doubt that he completely dominates her.* | *There is no question that Maridan had known all about the deal.* | *There was no doubt that, without the peacekeeping force, the civil war would have continued.* | **+ about it/about that** *You can see they're short of staff – there's no doubt about it.* | *'We made some mistakes. No question about that,' Glavine said.*

beyond a shadow of a doubt /bɪˌjɒnd ə ˌʃædəʊ əv ə ˈdaʊt‖bɪˌjɑːnd-/ [adv] use this to say that, in your opinion, there is definitely no doubt at all that something is true: *The evidence proves, beyond a shadow of a doubt, that this man was in the victim's apartment on the day of the murder.*

surely /ˈʃʊəʳli/ [adv] spoken say this when you want to emphasize that something must be true and you want the person you are talking to to agree with you: *Surely he must have realized that the money was stolen.* | *'I'm not sure how the heating system works.' 'Surely it can't be that complicated.'* | *Your car must be worth more than $500, surely!*

be beyond dispute /biː bɪˌjɒnd dɪˈspjuːt‖-ˌjɑːnd-/ [v phrase] if something **is beyond dispute** it certainly happened or exists and no one thinks differently: *Her professionalism is beyond dispute.* | *That the reports were stolen is beyond dispute. What we need to know is who took them.*

2 when something will definitely happen

▸ **certainly/definitely**
▸ **for sure**
▸ **be bound to/be sure to/be certain to**
▸ **it's only/just a matter of time**
▸ **cut and dried**
▸ **be a certainty**
▸ **be a foregone conclusion**

certainly/definitely /ˈsɜːʳtnli, ˈdefənətli/ [adv] use this to say that you are completely sure that something will happen or that someone will do something. **Definitely** is more common in spoken English than **certainly**: *I'll certainly be glad when this course is over.* | *Roger and Andy are definitely coming, but I'm not sure about Nancy.* | *We'll certainly be back by 7 o'clock.* | *Owen is injured and will definitely miss the game on Saturday.*

for sure /fəʳ ˈʃʊəʳ/ [adv] informal if you say that something will happen **for sure**, you mean it will certainly happen: *Yeah, you'll see him. He'll be there for sure.* | *Milan are going to win the cup for sure. They're just such a strong team.* | **that's for sure** *She'll come home when she runs out of money, that's for sure.*

be bound to/be sure to/be certain to /biː ˈbaʊnd tuː, biː ˈʃʊəʳ tuː, biː ˈsɜːʳtn tuː/ [v phrase] if something **is bound to** happen it is certain to happen, especially because that is what always happens: *The kids are bound to be hungry when they get home – they always are.* | *My car broke down today. It was bound to happen sooner or later.* | *Have you asked Ted? He's sure to know.* | *The drop in prices and lack of demand are certain to affect the manufacturing industry.*

it's only/just a matter of time /biː ˌəʊnli, ˌdʒʌst ə ˌmætər əv ˈtaɪm/ [v phrase] use this to say that something is certain to happen but no one knows exactly when: *You'll learn how to do it eventually – it's only a matter of time.* | *Your father is dying and there's nothing we can do. I'm afraid it's just a matter of time.* | **+ before** *It was only a matter of time before Lynn found out Phil's secret.*

cut and dried /ˌkʌt ən ˈdraɪd◂/ [adj phrase] if something is **cut and dried**, it is certain to happen in a particular way because it has already been planned or decided, and nothing can be done to change it: *My future was cut and dried. I would join my father's firm, and take it over when he retired.* | *We made the arrangements weeks ago. It's all cut and dried.*

be a certainty /biː ə ˈsɜːʳtnti/ [v phrase] if something **is a certainty**, it is certain to happen, especially because the situation has changed and made it certain: *Johnson was the fastest man on earth, and a gold medal seemed a certainty.* | *Being left alone in her old age, the fate she had always feared, now became a certainty.*

be a foregone conclusion /biː ə ˌfɔːʳgɒn kənˈkluːʒən‖-gɔːn-/ [v phrase] if something, especially a result, **is a foregone conclusion,** it is certain to happen even though it has not yet been officially decided: *Ian's bound to get the job – it's a foregone conclusion.* | *The outcome of the battle was a foregone conclusion.*

3 certain or definite

- certain
- definite
- conclusive

certain /ˈsɜːʳtn/ [adj] *Computer prices will continue to fall – that's certain.* | **it is certain (that)** *Nobody knows exactly who built the manor, but it is certain that an architect called John Sturges supplied the drawings.* | **almost certain** *As the results came in, it was now almost certain that Ken Livingstone would be the new Mayor of London.* | **certain death/failure/disaster etc** *Ignoring all warnings, the general led his men to certain death.*

definite /ˈdefɪnɪ̇t, ˈdefənɪ̇t/ [adj] if something is **definite**, it is certain because someone has officially stated that it will happen, is true etc: *I've got a good chance of getting the job, but it's not definite yet.* | *We have some statistics, but we really need something more definite before we can make any firm decisions.* | **definite answer** *I don't know what time she's coming. She won't give me a definite answer.*

conclusive /kənˈkluːsɪv/ [adj] **conclusive proof/evidence/argument etc** proof etc that is certainly true and cannot be doubted: *We still have no conclusive proof that Walters was at the scene of the crime.* | *They have been able to collect some data, but as yet nothing really conclusive.* —**conclusively** [adv] *The documents show conclusively that Pickering was aware of, and took part in, corrupt deals.*

4 certain to win or succeed

- be destined to
- be assured of
- sb/sth is a dead cert
- can't go wrong
- it's in the bag
- it's a safe bet/it's a sure bet/it's a sure thing
- foolproof

be destined to /biː ˈdestɪ̇nd tuː/ [v phrase] if someone **is destined to** do or become something, they will certainly do it or become it, especially something that will make them famous or admired: *She was convinced that her little boy was destined to become President.* | *Clara worked in a factory and sang in clubs at weekends – but even then you could tell that she was destined to become a star.*

be assured of /biː əˈʃʊəʳd ɒv/ [v phrase] formal to be certain to get something good or to be successful: *After the success of its recent single, the band is now assured of a contract with a major record company.* | *Our clients are assured of comfortable accommodation and the attention of our trained staff.*

sb/sth is a dead cert / (sb/sth) ɪz ə ˌded ˈsɜːʳt/ spoken informal use this to say that someone or something will definitely win or succeed: *I'm betting on Sceptre. He's a dead cert to win the Gold Cup.*

can't go wrong /ˌkɑːnt gəʊ ˈrɒŋ‖ˌkænt gəʊ ˈrɔːŋ/ [v phrase] spoken use this to say that something or someone will definitely be successful: *We've been through the plan a dozen times. It can't go wrong.* | *Just follow the instructions and you can't go wrong.*

it's in the bag /ɪts ˌɪn ðə ˈbæg/ spoken informal use this to say that you will certainly get something you want, or something you want will certainly happen, because you have almost got it or it has almost happened already: *You're bound to get Bill's job when he leaves – it's in the bag.* | **be in the bag** *If we win the next game, the championship's in the bag.*

it's a safe bet/it's a sure bet/it's a sure thing /ɪts ə ˌseɪf ˈbet, ɪts ə ˌʃʊəʳ ˈbet, ɪts ə ˌʃʊəʳ ˈθɪŋ/ use this to say that it is almost certain something will happen because of what you know of the situation: *I told my friends it was a sure thing, and they bet every last penny on that horse of yours.* | **+ (that)** *If the President supports him it's a sure bet that he'll get a seat in Congress.* | *As it was the first concert of the season it was a safe bet all the critics would be there.*

foolproof /ˈfuːlpruːf/ [adj] a **foolproof** plan or method is one that is certain to work and be successful: *A pasta book is a foolproof gift for anyone who cooks.* | **foolproof method/system/plan etc** *The new speech recognition system is not absolutely foolproof, but it is a huge breakthrough.* | *The gang hit on a seemingly foolproof way of getting drugs into the country.*

5 certain to fail or end in a bad way

- doomed
- be fated to do sth

doomed /duːmd/ [adj] if someone or something is **doomed**, it is certain that they will die, fail, or end in a very bad way: *The film is about a set of aliens living on a doomed planet.* | **+ to** *Without his job, his family would be doomed to a life of deprivation.* | **doomed to do sth** *Marx taught that capitalist economies are eventually doomed to collapse.* | **doomed to failure/disappointment/extinction etc** *In the novel, Jude's marriage is doomed to failure from the start.*

be fated to do sth /biː ˌfeɪtɪ̇d tə ˈduː (sth)/ [v phrase] if something, especially something bad, **is fated to** happen, it seems that it is certain to happen because of some mysterious force that you cannot control: *It seems that she was fated to be alone in life.* | *Achilles was kept back by his mother. She knew that if he went to Troy he was fated to die there.*

6 when something is certain and impossible to avoid

- inevitable
- whether you like it or not
- predestined
- be meant to be
- the inevitable

inevitable / ɪˈnevɪ̇təbəl/ [adj] *War now seems inevitable.* | *Nina could never escape the inevitable comparisons that people made between her and her twin.* | **inevitable result/consequence** *If the population continues to expand, Ehrlich argues, mass starvation and ecological disaster will be the inevitable* *consequence.* | *The price of bread was doubled, with the inevitable result – riots in the streets of Paris.* | **it is inevitable (that)** *It was inevitable that he'd find out her secret sooner or later.* —**inevitably** [adv] *Tax cuts for the rich inevitably lead to worse provision for the poor.*

whether you like it or not /weðəʳ juː ˌlaɪk ɪt ɔːʳ ˈnɒt/ use this to tell someone that something is certain to happen and that they cannot prevent it even if they do not like it: *You're going to have to face him one day, whether you like it or not.* | *Whether she likes it or not, she's got to accept that her kids are grown up now.*

predestined /prɪˈdestɪ̇nd/ [adj] something that is **predestined** will certainly happen and cannot be changed because it has been decided in advance by a power or force beyond our control: *Life isn't a series of predestined events: we have some control over what happens.* | **+ to do sth** *Many religions teach that man is predestined to suffer.*

be meant to be /biː ˌment tə ˈbiː/ [v phrase] if you know that a situation **is meant to be** you know it is certain to happen, especially because it is right and suitable: *We tried to be happy together but it was never meant to be.* | *Although saying goodbye was painful, she knew it was meant to be.*

the inevitable /ði ɪˈnevɪ̇təbəl/ [n singular] something that is definitely going to happen and cannot be avoided or prevented: *It's time they accepted the inevitable and got a divorce.* | **bow to the inevitable** (=accept something that cannot be prevented) *Week after week the papers were full of revelations about the minister's alleged corrupt dealings, until eventually he bowed to the inevitable and resigned.*

7 to make certain that something will happen

- make sure/make certain
- insure/ensure
- see that/see to it that

make sure/make certain /meɪk ˈʃʊəʳ, meɪk ˈsɜːʳtn/ [v phrase] **Make sure** is more common in spoken English than **make certain**: *I think Harry knows the way, but I'll go with him just to make sure.* | **+ (that)** *Make sure you lock your car.* | *You must make sure that your dog is vaccinated against illness.* | *The producer must make certain there is enough material to fill the one-hour programme.*

insure ALSO **ensure** British /ɪnˈʃʊəʳ/ [v T] to do something in order to be certain that something will happen in the way you want it to: *To insure accuracy, three consultants worked closely with the producer during filming.* | **+ that** *It is important to insure that universities have enough funds to carry out important research.* | *A new television campaign has been launched to ensure that the victims are not forgotten.*

see that/see to it that /ˈsiː ðət, ˈsiː tʊ ɪt ðət/ [v phrase] especially spoken to make sure that something someone has asked you to do is done: *I'll see that Jason isn't late for school again!* | *Will you please see to it that this work is finished by the end of the week.* | **see to it** *'This letter must be posted today.' 'Don't worry, I'll see to it.'*

chance

WHAT'S HERE

- **when sth happens by chance** see **1 to 3**
- **when you have the chance to do sth** see **4 to 6**

when sth happens by chance

RELATED WORDS

opposite: **deliberately**

- when you do something without intending to *see* **accidentally**
- *see also* **intend/not intend, lucky, unlucky**

1 when something happens without being planned

- by chance
- by accident
- happen to do sth
- as luck would have it
- coincidence
- luck/chance
- fate
- accident
- as it happens

by chance /baɪ ˈtʃɑːns‖-ˈtʃæns/ [adv] if something happens **by chance**, it happens unexpectedly and seems to have no particular cause: *I met an old friend by chance on the train.* | *If by chance I'm not in when she calls, can you take a message?* | **quite/purely/entirely by chance** (=completely by chance) *Quite by chance, a TV crew was filming in the area when the accident happened.*

by accident /baɪ ˈæksɪ̇dənt/ [adv] if you do something **by accident**, you do it by chance and without intending to do it: *Fleming discovered penicillin almost by accident.* | *We ended up by accident on the wrong train and had to ride all the way to Montreal.* | *The trigger of the gun is locked so that it cannot be fired by accident.* | **quite by accident** (=completely by chance) *Lombardi heard about their plan quite by accident.*

happen to do sth /ˌhæpən tə ˈduː (sth)/ [v phrase not in progressive] if you **happen to do something**, you do it by chance and not because of any particular reason or plan: *Justin forgot the map but I happened to have another one in the glove compartment.* | **just happen to do sth** *I'm sorry I didn't phone first – I just happened to be passing and thought I'd drop in.* | *We're not related – we just happen to have the same name.*

as luck would have it /əz ˌlʌk wʊd ˈhæv ɪt/ [adv] use this to say that something happened by chance, when this is connected with what you have just been talking about: *This was the first time I had ever seen a panda, and as luck would have it, I had my camera with me.* | *As luck would have it, it rained the next day and the game was canceled.*

coincidence /kəʊˈɪnsɪ̇dəns/ [n C/U] a surprising situation in which two things happen that are similar or seem connected, but no-one planned or intended this to happen: *Hi Phil. What a coincidence – we were just talking about you.* | **by coincidence** *My mother is called Anna, and by coincidence my wife's mother is called Anna too.* | **just a coincidence**

It was just a coincidence that we were in Paris at the same time. | **by a strange/sad/happy etc coincidence** *By a strange coincidence the king was assassinated on the very spot where his grandfather had been killed.*

luck/chance /lʌk, tʃɑːns‖tʃæns/ [n U] the way in which good or bad things seem to happen to people by chance: *There's no skill in a game like roulette, it's all luck.* | *Success is not a matter of chance – it takes a lot of hard work.* | **pure luck/chance** *It was pure chance that we ran into each other on the street.* | **leave sth to chance** (=let things happen by chance) *You must plan ahead. You can't leave these things to chance.*

fate /feɪt/ [n U] the power or force that is supposed to control the way everything happens, so that people cannot completely control their own lives: *It was fate that brought us together.* | *They saw themselves as victims of fate.* | **by a twist of fate** (=because fate made things happen in an unexpected way) *By a strange twist of fate the judge died on the very day that Cordell was executed.*

accident /ˈæksɪdənt/ [n C] something that happens by chance with no plan or intention: *I only met her again through a fortunate accident.* | *It is no accident that most of the country's outstanding public schools are in wealthy communities.*

as it happens /əz ɪt ˈhæpənz/ [adv] use this when you are talking about a situation that is surprising because by chance it is connected with something else that has been noticed or mentioned: *We've just seen a really beautiful house and, as it happens, it's for sale.* | *I needed to borrow a car, and as it happened Andrew wasn't using his.*

2 happening by chance

- chance
- accidental
- fortuitous

chance /tʃɑːns‖tʃæns/ [adj only before noun] **chance meeting/remark/discovery etc** a meeting etc that happens unexpectedly and was not planned or arranged: *Their friendship was the result of a chance meeting.* | *A chance encounter at the conference gave him the opportunity to tell the professor about his work.* | *Wilson hoped his chance discovery would benefit poor families in developing nations.*

accidental /ˌæksɪˈdentl◂/ [adj] happening by chance, without being planned or intended, especially in a way that has a bad result: *Are you insured against accidental damage to your property?* | *A system of valves limits accidental releases of the substance.* —**accidentally** [adv] *Don't tell Sue about our plan. She might accidentally mention it to the wrong person.* | *He claims he opened my mail accidentally but I'm not sure I believe him.*

fortuitous /fɔːʳˈtjuːɪtəs‖-ˈtuː-/ [adj] formal happening by chance, especially in a way that has a good result: *A fortuitous fire destroyed all evidence of his wrongdoing.*

3 when things are done, chosen etc by chance

- at random
- random
- arbitrary

at random /ət ˈrændəm/ [adv] if you do or choose things **at random**, you do or choose them without using any plan or system: *The forms were distributed at random to people passing by.* | *While he waited, he picked up a magazine, turned to a page at random, and started reading.* | *Twenty students were chosen at random to take part in the experiment.*

random /ˈrændəm/ [adj] something that is **random** is done or chosen without using any plan or system: *The union believes that the random drug testing of employees is an invasion of their privacy.* | *A few random shots were fired, but the battle was over.* —**randomly** [adv] *Participants for the show are randomly selected from a long list.*

arbitrary /ˈɑːʳbɪtrəri, -tri‖-treri/ [adj] something that is **arbitrary** is decided or arranged without any reason, plan, or system, especially in a way that seems unfair: *The way the programme of events is organized seems completely arbitrary to me.* | *The fans complained about the apparently arbitrary distribution of tickets for the next game.* —**arbitrarily** /ˈɑːbɪtrərɪli‖ˌɑːrbɪˈterɪli/ [adv] *Protesters accused the military of arbitrarily arresting Pereira and forty others.*

when you have a chance to do sth

RELATED WORDS

▸ *see also* **advantage (4-6)**

4 when you have the chance to do something

- chance
- opportunity
- break
- golden opportunity
- chance of a lifetime
- room/scope
- prospects
- possibility
- open doors for/ open the door for

chance /tʃɑːns‖tʃæns/ [n C] a situation in which it is possible for you to do something enjoyable, useful, or exciting, or something that you want to do **+ to do sth** *I never got the chance to thank him for all his help.* | *It's a beautiful building – you should go and see it if you have a chance.* | **give sb a/the chance to do sth** *I wish he'd just give me the chance to explain.* | **take the chance to do sth** (=use a chance when you have it) *You should take the chance to travel while you are still young.* | **chance for sb to do sth** *'Back to School Night' will be a chance for parents to meet their child's teacher.* | **sb's last chance** (=when you will not have another chance) *It was her last chance to see him before she left town.*

opportunity /ˌɒpəˈtjuːnɪti‖ˌɑːpərˈtuː-/ [n C] a chance to do something, especially something that is important or useful to you, or something that you want to do very much: *It was too good an opportunity to pass up.* | **+ to do sth** *All he needs is an opportunity to show his ability.* | **opportunity of doing sth** *After they had refused him the opportunity of improving his position, he resigned.* | **opportunity for sb to do sth** *We see this as an exciting opportunity for our companies to work together.* | **have an/the opportunity (to do sth)** *She was delighted to have an opportunity to talk with someone who shared her interest in classical music.* | **equal opportunities** (=the same opportunities as other people) *All over the world women are demanding equal opportunities.*

break /breɪk/ [n C] informal a sudden or unexpected chance to do something, especially to be successful in your job: *Gary wants to work in television. He's just waiting for a break.* | **lucky break** *Seeing that advertisement in the paper was a lucky break for* *me.* | **big break** *Nimoy's big break in television came in the mid-'60s, when he won the role of Spock on 'Star Trek'.*

golden opportunity /ˌgəʊldən ɒpəˈtjuːnɪ̇ti‖ -ɑːpərˈtuː-/ [n C] *I got a grant from my university to study in the USA for a year. It's a golden opportunity!* | **a golden opportunity (for sb) to do sth** *The management course is being paid for by the company and it's a golden opportunity to improve your skills.*

chance of a lifetime /ˌtʃɑːns əv ə ˈlaɪftaɪm◂‖ ˌtʃæns-/ [n phrase] the chance to do something very exciting or important that you might never be able to do again: *This job is the chance of a lifetime. You'd be a fool not to take it.* | *If you don't hurry up and make a decision, you could miss the chance of a lifetime.*

room/scope /ruːm, skəʊp/ [n U] a chance to do things you want to do, in the way that you want to do them. **Scope** is more formal than **room**: *He refused the post because he felt it didn't offer him much scope.* | **+ for** *There will always be room for debate and disagreement in this class.* | *I have two jobs, which doesn't leave much room for socializing.* | *Despite our recent success, there is still scope for improvement.* | **+ to do sth** *We've left the course deliberately vague, so there's room to concentrate on your particular areas of interest.* | *Better paid labour means greater scope to increase the company's profits.*

prospects /ˈprɒspekts‖ˈprɑː-/ [n plural] the chance of being successful at something in the future, especially your job: *He had no job, no family, no home, no prospects.* | *Employers are now offering more jobs with quality training and excellent career prospects.* | **+ for** *The prospects for an alliance between the two nations do not look good.*

possibility /ˌpɒsɪ̇ˈbɪlɪ̇ti‖ˌpɑː-/ [n C] the chance to do something **+ for** *The possibilities for improvement are endless.* | *We need to investigate all possibilities for helping these children.*

open doors for/open the door for /ˌəʊpən ˈdɔːʳz fɔːʳ, ˌəʊpən ðə ˈdɔːʳ fɔːʳ/ [v phrase] to give someone an opportunity to do something, for example the opportunity to do a particular job: *My experience in the Peace Corps really opened doors for me when I started looking for a job.* | *Alice Coachman's Olympic success opened the door for generations of African-American track athletes.*

5 to use an opportunity

- take the opportunity
- grab the chance
- jump at the chance/opportunity
- strike while the iron is hot
- make hay while the sun shines
- opportunist

take the opportunity /ˌteɪk ði ɒpəˈtjuːnɪ̇ti‖ -ɑːpərˈtuː-/ [v phrase] **+ to do sth** *I would like to take this opportunity to thank you all for your help.* | **+ of doing sth** *I'm going to take every opportunity of going to see Brian while he's living in Germany.*

grab the chance /ˌgræb ðə ˈtʃɑːns‖-ˈtʃæns/ [v phrase] informal to quickly use an opportunity to do something, especially when you think you might not get another chance: *It may be the last time he offers you the job so I'd grab the chance while you can.* | **+ to do sth** *Knowing how difficult it is to find a job I grabbed the chance to be trained as an electrician.*

jump at the chance/opportunity /ˈdʒʌmp ət ðə ˌtʃɑːns, ɒpəˌtjuːnɪ̇ti‖-ˌtʃæns, -ɑːpərˌtuː-/ [v phrase] to eagerly and quickly use an opportunity to do something: *The early retirement plan is excellent and I'm surprised that people haven't jumped at the opportunity.* | **+ to do sth** *When the resort was put up for sale, the Millers jumped at the chance to buy it.* | *She thought Lewis would jump at the opportunity to make some extra money on weekends.* | **+ of doing sth** *Who wouldn't jump at the chance of spending a month in Australia?*

strike while the iron is hot /ˌstraɪk waɪl ði ˌaɪəʳn ɪz ˈhɒt‖-ˈhɑːt/ [v phrase] to do something quickly, while you are in a situation in which you are most likely to be successful: *Don't wait until tomorrow before you tell him, strike while the iron is hot!*

make hay while the sun shines /meɪk ˌheɪ waɪl ðə ˈsʌn ˌʃaɪnz/ [v phrase] spoken to take the opportunity to do something now while the conditions are good, because you might not be able to do it later: *Let's make hay while the sun shines and finish this project before I start falling asleep.*

opportunist /ˈɒpətjuːnɪ̇st‖ˌɑːpərˈtuː-/ [n C] someone who always looks for and takes opportunities that might make them more successful – used to show disapproval: *It is difficult to tell whether he really wants to help May or whether he is just an opportunist.* | *As the finance company started to fail a few opportunists managed to make more money out of it.*

6 to not use an opportunity

- miss a chance/an opportunity
- miss out on
- blow it/blow your chance
- miss the boat
- let sth slip through your fingers
- lost opportunity

miss a chance/an opportunity /ˌmɪs ə ˈtʃɑːns, ən ˌɒpəˈtjuːnɪ̇ti‖-ˈtʃæns, -ˌɑːpərˈtuː-/ [v phrase] **+ of** *Denise never misses the chance of a free meal.* | **+ to do sth** *Don't miss this great opportunity to fly for half price.* | *Dan never misses an opportunity to remind me that I still owe him money.* | **miss your chance/opportunity** *Jerry's already sold the car to someone else. You've missed your chance.*

miss out on /ˌmɪs ˈaʊt ɒn/ [phr v T] to not use the chance to do something enjoyable or useful, especially when this is not a good thing: *If you don't come to the picnic you'll miss out on all the fun.* | *I don't want to be the type of father who is so busy he misses out on his daughter's childhood.*

blow it/blow your chance /ˈbləʊ ɪt, ˌbləʊ jɔːʳ ˈtʃɑːns‖-ˈtʃæns/ [v phrase] informal to waste a chance that you had to do or get something good: *Don't panic and talk too much in the interview or you'll really blow it.* | *I was afraid I'd blown my chance but she agreed to go out again on Saturday night.* | **blow your chances of doing sth** *She started running much too fast at the beginning and blew her chances of winning the race.*

miss the boat /ˌmɪs ðə ˈbəʊt/ [v phrase] informal to be too late to use an opportunity to do something good: *Buy your shares in the company now or you'll miss the boat.* | *He didn't get his application in early enough so he missed the boat.*

let sth slip through your fingers /let (sth) ˌslɪp θruː jɔːʳ ˈfɪŋgəʳz/ [v phrase] to not use a good opportunity when you are able to, especially an opportunity that you will not get again: *We had an opportunity to win the championship last season and we let it slip through our fingers.*

lost opportunity /ˌlɒst ɒpəˈtjuːnɪ̇ti‖ˌlɔːst ɑːpərˈtuː-/ [n phrase] an opportunity that you wasted by not using it to become successful, enjoy yourself etc: *If you don't take the job it'll just be another lost opportunity in your life.*

change/ not change

RELATED WORDS

- *see also* **develop, improve, become**

WHAT'S HERE

to become different

1 to become different

- **change**
- **changing**
- **alter**
- **turn into sth**
- **turn cold/nasty/violent etc**
- **go from ... to ...**

change /tʃeɪndʒ/ [v I] *She's changed a lot since she went to college.* | *It's amazing how much things have changed since we were young.* | *Her expression did not change, and she answered me calmly.* | *'The telecommunications industry is changing at lightning speed,' said Richard Miller, the company's chief financial officer.* | **+ into** *The caterpillar eventually changes into a beautiful butterfly.* | **change from sth to/into sth** *In the 18th century, Britain changed from a mainly agricultural society to an industrial one.* | **+ to** *The lights changed to green, and the motorbike sped off.* | **change colour** British **change color** American *It was the end of September, and the leaves on the trees were starting to change color.* | **change out of all recognition** (=change completely) *The town I grew up in has changed out of all recognition.*

changing /ˈtʃeɪndʒɪŋ/ [adj] becoming different: *I find it hard to keep up with changing fashions.* | *His book is concerned with the changing role of fathers.* | *Ansel Adams loved wide landscapes and changing light.* | **constantly/rapidly changing** *Businesses need to be flexible enough to adapt to changing conditions in a rapidly changing world.* | **fast-changing/ever-changing** (=changing quickly or frequently) *Job insecurity is widespread in the fast-changing American workplace.*

alter /ˈɔːltəʳ/ [v I] to change – use this especially about someone's feelings or behaviour, or about a situation: *His mood suddenly altered and he seemed a little annoyed.* | *His defence lawyer said that Wilson's lifestyle had altered dramatically since the offences three years ago.* | *Her face hadn't altered much over the years.*

turn into sth /ˈtɜːʳn ɪntə (sth)/ [phr v T] to become something completely different: *In fairy tales when the princess kisses a frog, it turns into a handsome prince.* | *A trip to the beach turned into a nightmare for a local family yesterday.*

turn cold/nasty/violent etc /ˌtɜːʳn ˈkəʊld/ [v phrase] to suddenly become cold, unpleasant etc: *The ink-black nights were turning cold, and the stars were frosty and fewer.* | *The protest turned violent when groups of demonstrators stormed the parliament building.*

go from ... to ... /ˈgəʊ frɒm ... tuː .../ [v phrase] especially spoken to stop being one thing and start being something else, especially something very different: *In less than five years, he went from being a communist to being a member of the military government.* | *His face went from pink to bright red.* | *The Mexican economy went from boom to bust very quickly, with disastrous results for the people.* | **go from bad to worse** (=change from being bad to being even worse) *After Kathy lost her job, things went from bad to worse, and eventually she and Ed split up.*

2 to change all the time or often

- **keep changing**
- **vary**
- **fluctuate**
- **be in flux/be in a state of flux**

keep changing /kiːp ˈtʃeɪndʒɪŋ/ [v phrase not in progressive] especially spoken *His ideas about what he wants keep changing.* | *I'll check the regulations for you – they keep changing.* | *The police strongly suspected that she had been involved – her story kept changing and was filled with inconsistencies.*

vary /ˈveəri/ [v I] to change often: if something **varies**, it changes according to what the situation is: *Ticket prices to New York vary, depending on the time of year.* | **vary from ... .to** *Driving regulations vary from state to state.* | **vary considerably/enormously/greatly** (=change a lot) *Her income varies considerably from one month to the next.* | **vary in price/quality/size etc** *Vegetables vary in quality according to the season.* | **it varies** *'How much milk do you use a day?' 'Oh, it varies.'* | **vary from day to day/week to week etc** *It hadn't been established where we'd all sleep – the location seemed to vary from night to night.*

fluctuate /ˈflʌktʃueɪt/ [v I] if something such as a price or amount **fluctuates**, it changes very often from a high level to a low one and back again: *The car industry's annual production fluctuates between 5.1 million and 9.2 million vehicles.* | *Cholesterol levels in the blood fluctuate in the course of a day.* | **fluctuate wildly** *Share prices on the New York Stock Exchange often fluctuate wildly.* —**fluctuating** [adj] *Your savings will earn fluctuating rates of interest.* —**fluctuation** /ˌflʌktʃuˈeɪʃən/ [n C/U] *Is there any way of avoiding fluctuations in coffee and tea prices?*

be in flux/be in a state of flux /biː ɪn ˈflʌks, biː ɪn ə ˌsteɪt əv ˈflʌks/ [v phrase] if something such as a system or a set of ideas **is in flux** or **in a state of flux**, it is changing a lot all the time, especially in a confusing way, so that you do not know what it will finally be like: *The computer industry is in constant flux, responding all the time to changes in technology.* | *Our education programme is in a state of flux, as new approaches are being developed.*

3 often changing or likely to change

- **changeable**
- **erratic**
- **volatile**
- **unstable**
- **variable**
- **inconsistent**
- **unsettled**

changeable /ˈtʃeɪndʒəbəl/ [adj] feelings or conditions that are **changeable** change frequently so that it is difficult to know what they will be like in a short time: *You love him now, but at your age feelings are changeable.* | *I'm a changeable sort of person.* | *changeable weather*

erratic /ɪ'rætɪk/ [adj] behaviour, processes, or services that are **erratic** change suddenly in an unexpected and surprising way, when it would be better if they remained the same: *Her behaviour was becoming more and more erratic.* | *Heating was difficult owing to erratic supplies of gas, electricity and water.* | *The company's erratic performance is a cause for some concern.* —**erratically** [adv] *My car has been performing very erratically – some days it's fine and other days it won't even start.*

volatile /'vɒlətaɪl‖'vɑːlətl/ [adj] a **volatile** situation or character is likely to change suddenly and unexpectedly: *The political situation in the Balkans is still extremely volatile.* | *She formed enduring friendships with women and more intense, volatile ones with men.*

unstable /ʌn'steɪbəl/ [adj] a person, situation, or system or government that is **unstable** is likely to change suddenly and become worse, because there is something wrong with their character or the way things are organized: *Regimes governed by violence are always unstable.* | *Was it safe to trust someone who was so emotionally unstable?* —**instability** /ˌɪnstə'bɪlɨti/ [n U] *The area is going through a period of instability and social crisis.* | *Government policies have resulted in higher inflation and financial instability.*

variable /'veəriəbəl/ [adj] changing according to the situation – use this about amounts, prices, speeds, temperatures etc: *Demand for the company's products is variable.* | *The weather here is likely to be very variable.*

inconsistent /ˌɪnkən'sɪstənt/ [adj] **inconsistent** behaviour or work changes too often from good to bad, and you cannot trust it to be good all the time: *People feel threatened when decision-making is inconsistent and arbitrary.* | *A succession of injuries produced an inconsistent season for one of our best players.* —**inconsistency** [n U] *The inconsistency of her work makes a really good result unlikely.*

unsettled /ʌn'setld/ [adj] conditions or situations that are **unsettled** change frequently so that it is impossible to make plans or know what will happen: *It is dangerous to visit there while the political situation is so unsettled.* | *The weather has been very unsettled lately.* | *Eliot led a strangely unsettled life, drifting from place to place and job to job.*

4 someone who has changed completely

- a changed man/woman
- reformed

a changed man/woman /ə ˌtʃeɪndʒd 'mæn, 'wʊmən/ [n phrase] use this to say that someone has changed a lot from what they were like before because of an important or powerful experience: *My father came back from the war a changed man.* | *She returned from her travel a changed woman.*

reformed /rɪ'fɔːʳmd/ [adj] someone who is **reformed** has completely changed their behaviour and stopped doing things that other people disapprove of, for example stealing or drinking too much: *Since the birth of his baby, Mark has totally reformed.* | *Al Pacino plays a reformed crook who gets pulled back into a life of crime.*

to make sth different

5 to change something or someone

- change
- alter
- make changes
- revise

change /tʃeɪndʒ/ [v T] to make someone or something different: *They've changed the timetable, and now there's only one bus an hour.* | *Going to college changed him a lot. It made him much more mature.* | *Having a baby changes your life completely, whatever your age.*

alter /'ɔːltəʳ/ [v T] to change something so that it is better or more suitable: *You can alter the color and size of the image using a remote control.* | *The border was closed, and they were forced to alter their plans.*

make changes /ˌmeɪk 'tʃeɪndʒɨz/ [v phrase] to change some parts of a system or the way something is done, but not all of it: *Don't make any major changes yet.* | *I've analysed the system and made changes where I thought they were needed.* | **+ to/in** *You'll have to make some changes in your life – stop smoking and eating fatty food, and stop working so hard.* | *The manufacturer has agreed to make one or two changes to the computer's design.*

revise /rɪ'vaɪz/ [v T] to change an idea or plan because of new information: *This discovery made them revise their old ideas.* | *You should review and revise the plan in the light of events as they unfold.* | *By the time the President arrived at Keflavik, the revised speech was ready.*

6 to make something completely different

- transform
- turn sth/sb into
- revolutionize
- reverse
- overturn

transform /træns'fɔːʳm/ [v T usually in passive] to completely change something, especially so that it is much better: *Well, you've certainly transformed this place – it looks great!* | **transform sth into sth** *In the last 20 years, Korea has been transformed into a major industrial nation.* | **totally/completely transform** *When she smiled, her face was completely transformed.*

turn sth/sb into /'tɜːʳn (sth/sb) ɪntuː/ [v phrase] to make something become a completely different thing or make someone become a completely different kind of person: *We're planning to turn the spare bedroom into a study.* | *The war had turned Cassidy into a violent thug.* | *Edwards saved the Tivoli, an elegant 1920s art deco hotel, and turned it into a movie theatre.*

revolutionize ALSO **revolutionise** British /ˌrevə'luːʃənaɪz/ [v T] to completely and permanently change the way people do something or think about something, especially because of a new idea or invention: *Computers have revolutionized the way we work.* | *This important discovery has revolutionized our understanding of the universe.* | *The new technology is revolutionising the way music is played, composed and studied.*

reverse /rɪ'vɜːʳs/ [v T] to change a process or decision so that it is the opposite of what it was before: *The longer the economic decline is allowed to go on the more difficult it will be to reverse it.* | *Cities are* *expanding and using up more and more of the desert. Our aim is to reverse this trend and to protect our open spaces.* | *The court of appeal reversed the original verdict and set the prisoner free.* | *Many of the former administration's policies were reversed by the new president.*

overturn /ˌəʊvəʳˈtɜːʳn/ [v T] to change a previous official decision or order so that it is the opposite of what it was before or so that it can no longer have its original effect: *The execution ended a 14-year battle to have Bannister's death sentence overturned.* | *Wolf was found guilty of treason, but the conviction was overturned by Germany's highest court in 1995.*

7 to change something for a particular use or purpose

- adapt
- modify
- convert
- customize

adapt /əˈdæpt/ [v T] to change something so that it can be used in a different way: *They have adapted their house so they can look after their disabled son more easily.* | *The movie was adapted by Forsyth from his own bestselling novel.* | **+ for** *The materials in the book can be adapted for use with older children.* | **adapt sth to do sth** *These recipes can be easily adapted to suit vegetarians.*

modify /ˈmɒdɪfaɪ‖ˈmɑː-/ [v T] to make small changes to something such as a piece of equipment, a set of ideas, or a way of behaving in order to improve it or to make it more suitable for a particular purpose: *We can modify the design to make it suitable for commercial production.* | *We all modify our speech when speaking to people in authority.* | **genetically modify** (=change the genes of plants or animals) *The biotech corporations argue that genetically modified crops will put an end to food shortages in the developing world.*

convert /kənˈvɜːʳt/ [v T] to change something completely so that it has a different form and can be used for a different purpose: *We've converted the basement to give the children more room to play.* | **convert sth into sth** *A Swiss company has found a way to convert animal waste into fuel.* | *This computer system converts typed words into speech.* —**converted** [adj] *The nightclub is in a converted church.*

customize ALSO **customise** British /ˈkʌstəmaɪz/ [v T] to change something, such as a car or a piece of equipment, to suit a particular person or group of people: *General Motors will customize Cadillacs for special clients.* | *The computer programs can be customised for individual users.* | *customized software*

8 to make small changes to something in order to improve it

- adjust
- make adjustments
- amend
- revise

adjust /əˈdʒʌst/ [v T] to make small changes in the position or level of something in order to improve it or make it more suitable: *Check and adjust your brakes regularly.* | *I don't think the color control on this TV is properly adjusted.* | *The amount of any of these ingredients can be adjusted according to your taste.* | *'You don't have to come,' Lewis said, as he adjusted his tie in a mirror.*

make adjustments /ˌmeɪk əˈdʒʌstmənts/ [v phrase] to make small changes to something such as a machine, a system, or the way something looks: *You can use this tool to make adjustments in all kinds of machines.* | **+ to** *Scientists were able to locate the star by making a few minor adjustments to their original calculations.*

amend /əˈmend/ [v T] to make small changes to something written, for example a law or legal agreement: *Programs written in languages such as BASIC are very easy to edit and amend.* | **amend a bill/rule/law/act etc** *Congress amended the Social Security Act in 1967 to help the disabled.* | *The law was amended so that profits from drug dealing could be seized by the government.* | **amend the Constitution** *To amend the Constitution voters must approve the measure in a referendum.*

revise /rɪˈvaɪz/ [v T] to check a piece of writing from beginning to end and make any changes that are necessary to improve it: *He gave his work to his friend to revise, because he found it hard to see his own mistakes.* | *The publisher will not accept your manuscript until it has been thoroughly revised.* —**revised** [adj] *a revised edition of the novel*

9 to change the way something is done or organized

- change
- reorganize
- restructure
- reform

change /tʃeɪndʒ/ [v T] *The government is considering changing the local voting system.* | *Agriculture must be changed to reduce damage to the environment.*

reorganize ALSO **reorganise** British /riːˈɔːʳgənaɪz/ [v T] to change the way that a system or organization works: *During the 1980s, the government reorganized the civil service.* | *The proposals for reorganizing the company have made many people in the workforce feel very insecure.*

restructure /ˌriːˈstrʌktʃəʳ/ [v T] to completely change the way something is organized, especially a large political or economic system or a big company, in order to make it more effective: *Mr Gorbachev's attempt to restructure the Soviet economy met with criticism from traditional communists.* | *In the coming years a lot of money will go into restructuring the education system.*

reform /rɪˈfɔːʳm/ [v T] to change a law, system, or organization, so that it is fairer or more effective: *They reformed the voting system, and introduced a secret ballot.* | *We are working to reform the nation's prisons.*

10 to change facts or information in a dishonest way

- twist
- misrepresent
- distort
- falsify
- put words into sb's mouth
- cook the books
- rewrite history

twist /twɪst/ [v T] to dishonestly change the meaning of a piece of information or of something that someone has said, in order to get some advantage for yourself or to support your own opinion: *The lawyers twisted everything I said to make it look as if I was guilty.* | *Every time I try to talk to him about it, he just twists everything I say.* | *Write very clearly so that no one can twist your meaning.*

misrepresent /ˌmɪsreprɪˈzent/ [v T] to give people a wrong idea about someone or their opinions, by what you write or say: *Your reporter has completely misrepresented my opinions about immigration.* | *Many women feel that the history books either ignore or misrepresent them.*

distort /dɪˈstɔːʳt/ [v T] to explain facts, statements etc in a way that makes them seem different from what they really are: *Newspaper readers are usually given a simplified and often distorted version of events.* | *These incidents were grossly distorted by police witnesses.* | **distort the truth/the facts** *Journalists were accused of sensationalizing the story and distorting the facts.*

falsify /ˈfɔːlsɪ̈faɪ/ [v T] to dishonestly change official documents or records so that they contain false information: *She falsified her birth certificate to get the job.* | *A whole team was kept busy falsifying official government records.* | *Their accounts had been falsified over a long period of time*

put words into sb's mouth /pʊt ˌwɜːʳdz ɪntə (sb's) ˈmaʊθ/ [v phrase] to pretend that you think someone has said something that is not what they actually said or meant: *I didn't mean that at all – you're just putting words into my mouth!* | *You're putting words into her mouth. You don't know what she thinks.*

cook the books /ˌkʊk ðə ˈbʊks/ [v phrase] informal to dishonestly change a company's financial records, in order to steal money: *We've just found out Alec's been cooking the books.* | *The directors of the company made millions from cooking the books before the fraud investigators caught them.*

rewrite history /riːˌraɪt ˈhɪstəri/ [v phrase] if a government, film company etc rewrites history, it deceives people by pretending that particular historical events did not really happen or that they happened differently: *Hollywood has been accused of rewriting history, by once again denying the role played by African Americans.*

11 easy to change

- flexible
- adaptable

flexible /ˈfleksɪ̈bəl/ [adj] methods, systems, or rules that are **flexible** can easily be changed if necessary: *We need a flexible management system, able to meet the changing needs of our customers.* | *Unions would like more flexible working hours to replace the nine-to-five, forty-hour week.* | *The rules are deliberately left flexible as each case is different.*

adaptable /əˈdæptəbəl/ [adj] a system or way of doing something that is **adaptable** can be changed so that it is suitable for very different uses and very different situations: *In this job you need to be adaptable and able to cope with unexpected situations.* | **highly adaptable** (=very adaptable) *Young children are highly adaptable – I'm sure they won't mind moving to a different area.* —**adaptability** /əˌdæptəˈbɪlɪ̈ti/ [n U] *All the recent changes had tested the limits of her adaptability.*

to change sth you have for another one

RELATED WORDS

- move from one place or home to another *see* **move (6-8)**
- *see also* **exchange**

12 to change what you do or use

- change
- switch
- move
- transfer
- go over to
- convert to

change /tʃeɪndʒ/ [v I/T] to **change** from one thing to another so that you have something different from what you had before: *They've changed their phone number.* | *We had to change the tyre because we had a flat.* | **+ to** *Japanese industry is changing to alternative marketing techniques.* | **change from sth to sth** *We've changed from traditional ways of working to an automated system.* | **change jobs/cars etc** (=move from one to another) *Women have to be ambitious and willing to change jobs frequently if they want to get to the top of their profession.* | **change direction/course** (=start moving in a new direction) *I tried to follow him but he kept changing direction.* | **change channels** (=change from one programme on television to another) *If you don't like the programme you can always change channels.*

switch /swɪtʃ/ [v I/T] to change, especially suddenly, from one thing to another **+ to** *I used to play golf but I switched to tennis to get more exercise.* | *It took a long time for Americans to switch to smaller cars.* | **switch from sth to sth** *He switched easily and fluently from speaking English to French to German.*

move /muːv/ [v I] to change, especially gradually, from one thing to another **+ from** *The book follows the life of Ann Pollock, as she moves from the optimism of young love, through the disastrous years of World War II.* | **move from sth to sth** *The bank has moved from private client work to banking for large corporations.* | **move away from sth** *Many socialists were moving away from faith in revolution towards a fight for reform.*

transfer /trænsˈfɜːʳ/ [v T] **transfer your affection/allegiance/support etc** to change from loving or supporting one person, group etc to loving or supporting another **+ to** *The generals are transferring their allegiance to their new leader.* | *Fed up with the disastrous performances of the team he'd been watching for years, he transferred his support to their rivals.*

go over to /ˌgəʊ ˈəʊvəʳ tuː/ [phr v T not in passive] to change from one system to a new one, especially a more modern one: *Britain went over to decimal currency in 1971.* | *The factory is going over to computerised machinery and many workers are losing their jobs.*

convert to /kənˈvɜːʳt tuː/ [v phrase] to change to a different religion: *In 1976 he converted to Islam.* | *Large numbers of people are converting to Eastern religions such as Buddhism and Hinduism.*

13 to keep changing from one thing to another

- alternate
- vary
- rotate
- chop and change

alternate /ˈɔːltəʳneɪt/ [v I/T] to change repeatedly from one thing or condition to a different one and back again **alternate between sth and sth** *His mother would alternate inexplicably between kindness and cruelty.* | *The guide explained the situation, alternating between Spanish and German.* | **+ with** *He has periods of depression, which alternate with frenzied activity.* | **alternate sth with sth** *Leroy alternated aerobic exercises with weight training to improve his stamina.*

vary /ˈveəri/ [v T] to regularly change what you do or the way you do it so that you are more effective or do not become bored: *Teachers can keep students' interest by varying their classes.* | *One of Dickens' great skills as a writer is the way he varies his style.* | *If you're bored with the trip to work, try varying your route.*

rotate /rəʊ'teɪt‖'rəʊteɪt/ [v I/T] if people **rotate**, they each do something such as a piece of work once, then another person does it, then another, and then the first person again: *We rotate – I teach French grammar one week, and she teaches it the next.* | **rotate a job/task etc** *We usually rotate the worst jobs so that no one gets stuck with them.*

chop and change /ˌtʃɒp ən 'tʃeɪndʒ‖ˌtʃɑːp-/ [v phrase] British informal to keep changing from one thing to another, in a way that annoys people: *Don't chop and change from one style to another. It confuses the reader.* | *I wish they wouldn't keep chopping and changing. There's a different team on the field every week.*

14 to change your clothes

- get changed
- change

get changed /get 'tʃeɪndʒd/ [v phrase] to take off your clothes and put on different clothes: *The first thing I do when I get home from school is get changed.* | *Are you going to get changed before the party?*

change /tʃeɪndʒ/ [v I/T] to take off all or some of your clothes and put some different clothes on: *I'll just change my shirt and I'll be with you in a minute.* | *'Have you got your bathing suit on?' 'No, I'll change when we get there.'* | **+ into** *She changed into a sweater and some jeans.*

15 to change from one vehicle to another during a journey

- change
- transfer

change /tʃeɪndʒ/ [v I/T] to get out of one train, bus, or plane and get into another in order to complete your journey: *Is this a direct flight or do we have to change?* | *Passengers for York change at Leeds.* | **change trains/planes/buses etc** *We stopped at Los Angeles, just to change planes.*

transfer /træns'fɜːʳ/ [v I] to change from one vehicle to another, as part of a journey, especially when all the other people in the vehicle do the same: *I must have lost my luggage when we transferred.* | **+ from/to** *The train broke down so we transferred to a bus.*

a change

16 when things change

- change
- alteration
- turnaround
- upheaval
- revolution
- transformation

change /tʃeɪndʒ/ [n C/U] *There have been so many changes around here lately that I'm not sure what's happening any more.* | *A lot of people are frightened of change.* | **+ in** *There was a sudden change in the weather.* | *House plants are often sensitive to changes in temperature.* | *The delay was the result of a change in the way that we administer the grants.* | **social/economic/political etc change** *1989 was a year of great political change in eastern Europe.* | **big change/major change** *There have been big changes in the way languages are taught in schools.* | **a change for the better/worse** *For most ordinary workers, the new tax laws represent a change for the worse.*

alteration /ˌɔːltə'reɪʃən/ [n C] a change in something, especially one that has happened gradually or naturally: *The relationship between the United States and China has altered in recent years.* | **+ in** *She noticed the alteration in his looks and manner.* | *Max walked past her, without acknowledging her presence by the slightest alteration in his expression.*

turnaround ALSO **turnround** British /'tɜːʳnəˌraʊnd, 'tɜːʳnraʊnd/ [n C usually singular] a complete change from a bad economic situation to a good one, or a change from failing to succeeding: *BRITCON's turnround has been achieved by drastic reductions in manpower.* | *The team's dramatic turnaround is attributed to their new coach Bill Snyder.* | **+ in** *The expected turnaround in the beer industry has, for various reasons, not yet occurred.*

upheaval /ʌp'hiːvəl/ [n C/U] a big change in your life or in the way things are organized, especially when this causes problems and anxiety: *Moving to a different school can be a big upheaval for young children.* | **political/social/economic etc upheaval** *The company managed to survive the economic upheavals of the last 20 years.* | **emotional upheaval** *Changing jobs can be an exciting challenge, but it can also be a time of great emotional upheaval.*

revolution /ˌrevə'luːʃən/ [n C] a complete change in the way of doing things or thinking, because of new ideas or methods: *They argue that our schools are failing our children, and that the education system needs a revolution.* | **+ in** *Einstein's General Theory of Relativity started a revolution in scientific thinking.* | **scientific/technological/social etc revolution** *The 1970s saw the beginnings of a new technological revolution, based on microelectronics.*

transformation /ˌtrænsfəʳ'meɪʃən/ [n C usually singular] a complete change in something or someone, especially so that there is a great improvement **+ of** *The transformation of the Inner Harbor included new office buildings, and a marketplace of small shops and food stalls.* | **transformation from sth to sth** *Her friends and neighbors watched her transformation from shy local girl to famous movie actress.* | **+ in** *The last great overall transformation in American business took place between 1890 and 1910, when the modern corporation was forged.* | **+ into** *Today, spruced-up Times Square is in the midst of a surprising transformation into a family-oriented entertainment center.* | **undergo a transformation** *It is rare for a person to undergo a dramatic transformation in his political thinking, but it does happen.*

17 a change made in order to improve something

- change
- alteration
- reform
- revision
- shake-up
- reorganization

change /tʃeɪndʒ/ [n C] *We need some changes if we are going to make this company successful.* | *I can't get used to all these changes.* | **+ to** *He hates all changes to his routine.* | *The computers will record any changes to the system.* | **+ in** *We are working to bring about changes in the laws concerning the rights of children.* | **make a change** *The producer wants to make some changes to the script before we get the director on board.* | **big/major change** *Labor Secretary Lynn Martin recommended major changes in the management operations of the company.*

alteration /ˌɔːltə'reɪʃən/ [n C] a change made to something, especially a small change which makes it different but not completely different: *I've sent the suit to a tailor for alterations.* | **+ to** *We're having some alterations made to our house.* | **minor alter-**

ations (=small changes) *Your essay looks fine – I've suggested one or two minor alterations here and there in the margin.*

reform /rɪˈfɔːʳm/ [n C] a change made to a system, especially a political system, in order to improve it or make it more fair: *Feminists sought legal reforms to ensure that women had genuinely equal opportunities.* | **economic/educational/welfare etc reform** *The Socialists have promised a programme of radical political and economic reform.* | **+ in** *Reforms in agriculture, although slow, are beginning to have an impact.* | **+ of** *the reform of local government* | **radical reform** *The revival in the island's economy has come about because of radical reforms introduced over the past three years.*

revision /rɪˈvɪʒən/ [n C/U] the process of changing something, especially a piece of writing, by correcting it or including new information: *I've written the article, but it needs a lot of revision.* | *The book went through several revisions before the publisher was finally satisfied with it.* | **+ of/to** *These amendments constitute the most significant revision of U.S. asylum law since the Refugee Act of 1980.*

shake-up /ˈʃeɪk ʌp/ [n C] a situation in which a lot of changes are very quickly made in a system, company, or organization in order to make it more effective: *The department has not performed well and is badly in need of a shake-up.* | **+ of** *The Administration is planning a thorough shake-up of the welfare system.*

reorganization /riːˌɔːʳgənaɪˈzeɪʃən ‖-gənə-/ [n U] a complete change in the way a system or a group of people is organized: *The company is bringing in a team of consultants to oversee the reorganization.* | **+ of** *Next came the total reorganization of the Mexican Attorney General's Office.*

18 a small change that is made to improve or correct something

- modification
- amendment
- adjustment

modification /ˌmɒdəfəˈkeɪʃən‖ˌmɑː-/ [n C] a small change made to something in order to improve it or to make it more suitable for a particular purpose: *The new modifications made it the finest of aircraft.* | **+ to** *The editor suggested a few modifications to the text.* | *We need to make some modifications to our teaching program.*

amendment /əˈmendmənt/ [n C] a change to a law or rule in order to improve it: *Congress passed an amendment ensuring that the law was fairer to everyone.* | **+ to** *The committee proposed some amendments to the rules.*

adjustment /əˈdʒʌstmənt/ [n C] a small change made to something such as a machine, a system. or the way something looks **make adjustments to sth** *The room was full of dancers, all making last-minute adjustments to their costumes.* | *We've had to make some adjustments to our original calculations.* | **slight/minor adjustments** *I've made a few very minor adjustments to the decor, but in general it was excellent.*

19 a change made in order to use something for another purpose

- conversion
- adaptation

conversion /kənˈvɜːʳʃən‖-ʒən/ [n U] the process of changing something from one form or system to another one so that it can be used for a different purpose **+ into** *The company buys raw material such as wool for conversion into cloth.* | **+ of** *Local people are protesting about the proposed conversion of a church into a late-night bar.*

adaptation /ˌædæpˈteɪʃən/ [n U] the process of changing something in particular ways so that it can be used for a different purpose **+ of** *She was responsible for the adaptation of the book 'The Witches of Eastwick' into a stage play.*

20 a change from one thing to another

- change
- switch
- move
- reversal
- U-turn

change /tʃeɪndʒ/ [n C] *After a number of career changes, she settled into a job with a major bank.* | **+ of** *The police must be notified of any change of address.* | *There are even more broken promises with every change of government.* | **+ to** *If you are thinking about a change to a different part of the country you will need to use your vacation to look for accommodation.* | **change from sth to sth** *French people were asked how they felt about the change from the franc to the Euro.*

switch /swɪtʃ/ [n C] a complete, and usually sudden, change from one thing to another **+ to** *A switch to completely different new foods may cause stomach upsets.* | **switch from sth to sth** *The switch from political activity to family life was hard to handle.* | **+ of** *His sudden switches of mood are difficult to deal with.*

move /muːv/ [n C] a change from one job or type of work to another: *Let's face it – going from an academic life to the world of business is never an easy move.* | **+ to** *It's probably time to think about a move to a new job.* | *This picture marks the move to the big screen of some of our best television comedians.*

reversal /rɪˈvɜːʳsəl/ [n C usually singular] a change to an opposite process or effect: *The profits of supermarkets declined until 1975 when a reversal began.* | **+ of** *This appears to be a complete reversal of government policy.* | *The Second World War saw a dramatic reversal of traditional attitudes towards women.* | **reversal**

U-turn /ˈjuː tɜːʳn/ [n C] a complete change in the plans of a government or political party so that it decides to do the opposite of what it originally said it would do: *The party lost all public support after a series of U-turns and policy failures.* | **do a U-turn** *The government was forced to do a U-turn after angry protests about their taxation policy.*

21 a gradual change from one thing to another

- transition
- shift
- trend
- move
- movement

transition /trænˈzɪʃən, -ˈsɪ-/ [n C/U] the process of change, especially gradual change, from one state or situation to another **transition from sth to sth** *The transition from a communist system to a free market economy will be difficult.* | **+ to** *It's difficult for someone who's been a stage actor to make the transition to television.* | **make a transition** *a scheme to help families making the transition from welfare to work* | **be in transition** (=be changing at the moment) *The textile industry is currently in transition.* | **transition period** *The new system will be introduced gradually over a six month transition period.*

shift /ʃɪft/ [n C] a gradual but important change in the way people think about something **shift in attitude/approach/policy etc** *There has been a big shift in attitudes towards sex during the past 50 years.* | **marked shift** (=a very clear shift) *We've seen a marked shift in our approach to the social issues.* | **+ away from** *The new emphasis on human rights was a shift away from the policies of Nixon.* | **+ towards** *He is very worried about the shift towards free market thinking in Eastern Europe.*

trend /trend/ [n C] a general change in the way people think or behave, especially one that is happening at the moment: *If present trends continue, the earth will be considerably warmer in fifty years.* | *Our managers are very alert to new trends in the industry.* | **+ towards** *There is a growing trend towards payment by credit card.* | *The current trend in this area is towards part-time employment.*

move /muːv/ [n C] the gradual change of a country or society towards something different **+ towards/to** *There is a move towards greater equality for women in the workplace.* | *Planners hope to encourage the move towards increased use of public transport.* | *The United Nations was supposed to supervise the move to independence.* | **+ away from** *Public sector unions are likely to oppose Blair's move away from government investment in health and transport.*

movement /ˈmuːvmənt/ [n C/U] a gradual change, especially a political or social change, in which a lot of people are involved **+ towards** *There is a gradual movement towards tolerance and understanding.* | *The modern age of movement towards democracy began with the French Revolution in 1789.*

not changing

RELATED WORDS

- *see also* **same**

22 not changing and always the same

- constant
- steady
- stable
- fixed
- unchanging

constant /ˈkɒnstənt‖ˈkɑːn-/ [adj] use this about an amount or level that remains the same over a long period: *We live next door to a busy street and there is always a constant level of noise in the background.* | **remain/stay constant** *Unemployment is likely to remain more or less constant for the next two years.*

steady /ˈstedi/ [adj] use this about an amount that remains the same or a process that continues in the same way over a long period, especially when this is a good thing: *We drove all day at a steady 65 miles an hour.* | *It's important to keep the temperature of the oven at a steady high heat.* | **a steady increase/decrease/decline etc** *The study also notes a steady decline in the number of college students taking science courses.* | **steady growth/progress** *Economists say they expect continued steady growth throughout the year.* | **at a steady rate** *Larger families were being rehoused at a steady rate.* | **a steady stream of visitors/enquiries etc** *A steady stream of refugees arrived at the camp.*

stable /ˈsteɪbəl/ [adj] use this about prices, amounts, or levels that are no longer changing, after a period when they were changing a lot: *Fuel prices have become more stable after several increases last year.* | **remain stable** *His temperature remained stable throughout the night.*

fixed /fɪkst/ [adj] use this about amounts, prices, or times that cannot be changed: *The lessons began and ended at fixed times.* | *In Communist Russia prices of all common commodities used to be fixed.* | **fixed income/price/rate etc** *Workers are paid a fixed rate per hour.* | *a fixed-rate mortgage* | *'I'm retired and on a fixed income,' Marson said. 'I can't handle this myself, financially.'* | **fixed penalty** *The policeman told me there was a fixed penalty of $20 for driving without a rear light.*

unchanging /ʌnˈtʃeɪndʒɪŋ/ [adj] not changing even when conditions change: *the unchanging nature of God* | *The road ran through an unchanging desert landscape.* | *Here, you seem to be immersed in an unchanging rural way of life, seemingly unaffected by progress and the modern world.*

23 difficult or impossible to change

- rigid
- inflexible

rigid /ˈrɪdʒɪ̈d/ [adj] a system that is **rigid** is extremely difficult or impossible to change and is therefore annoying: *People naturally get very frustrated with rigid bureaucracies.* | *The rigid class distinctions which characterised British society are beginning to break down.* | *The President will not be able to meet enough people if he is kept to an unnaturally rigid schedule.* | *The government had centralized political power and imposed rigid controls on economic activity.*

inflexible /ɪnˈfleksɪ̈bəl/ [adj] difficult or impossible to change, even when a change would be better: *The regulations are precise and inflexible in such matters.* | *It is a huge, inflexible and impersonal organization.*

to change/not change your plans, opinions, or decisions

RELATED WORDS

- not willing to change your mind *see* **determined**
- *see also* **decide, sure/not sure**

24 to change your decisions, intentions, or plans

- change your mind
- have second thoughts
- get cold feet
- backtrack

change your mind /ˌtʃeɪndʒ jɔːʳ ˈmaɪnd/ [v phrase] *No, I'm not going out tonight. I've changed my mind.* | *What if she changes her mind and doesn't turn up?* | **+ about** *If you change your mind about the job, just give me a call.* | *Barry hadn't changed his mind about leaving.*

have second thoughts /hæv ˌsekənd ˈθɔːts/ [v phrase] to feel less sure about something that you intended to do, and begin to think that it may not be a good idea: *Couples contemplating divorce often have second thoughts when they realize how it will affect their children.* | **+ about** *It was obvious that the* *company was having second thoughts about the whole project.*

get cold feet /get ˌkəʊld ˈfiːt/ [v phrase] informal to suddenly feel that you are not brave enough to do something that you intended to do: *A month before the wedding Rose seemed nervous and anxious, and I wondered if she was getting cold feet.* | *Some investors got cold feet, and pulled out of the project at the last minute.*

backtrack /ˈbæktræk/ [v I] to change your mind about something you have publicly promised to do, by saying that you will only do part of it or that you might not do it at all: *If union leaders start to backtrack now, they'll lose their supporters.* | **+ on** *The President seems to be backtracking on some of his election promises.* | *There is increased pressure on Congress to backtrack on some of the welfare cuts imposed last year.*

25 to change your opinion or belief about something

- change your mind
- revise your opinion
- change your tune
- change of heart
- come around
- recant

change your mind /ˌtʃeɪndʒ jɔːʳ ˈmaɪnd/ [v phrase] to change your opinion about something or someone: *At first the doctor said I was suffering from a virus, but now he's changed his mind.* | *Everyone has a right to change their mind.* | **+ about** *I'm hoping Dad will change his mind about Louise after he meets her tonight.* | *I've changed my mind about the Riviera. I do like it after all.*

revise your opinion /rɪˌvaɪz jɔːr əˈpɪnjən/ [v phrase] formal to change your opinion because something has happened that has made you realize that you were wrong before **+ about/of** *Mrs Pemberton revised her opinion of her future son-in-law when he was accepted into law school.* | *Since visiting the refugee camps, I have revised my opinion about immigration quotas.*

change your tune /ˌtʃeɪndʒ jɔːʳ ˈtjuːn‖-ˈtuːn/ [v phrase] to change your mind about something and talk about it in a very different way from how you did before: *She used to be a Communist, but she changed her tune when her parents left her all that money.* | *You've changed your tune all of a sudden! Only yesterday you were saying you thought Christmas presents were a waste of money.*

change of heart /ˌtʃeɪndʒ əv ˈhɑːʳt/ [n phrase] when you begin to feel differently about something or someone so that your attitude completely changes: *It's hard to explain this apparent change of heart.* | **have a change of heart** *He didn't want kids at first, but he's had quite a change of heart.* | **+ about** *We can only hope Congress may have a radical change of heart about welfare benefits.*

come around ALSO **come round** British /ˌkʌm əˈraʊnd, ˌkʌm ˈraʊnd/ [phr v I] to change your mind so that you gradually begin to agree with someone else's idea or opinion, especially after they have persuaded you that they are right: *He'll come around eventually. He doesn't have any choice, does he?* | *My mother stopped speaking to me when I first married Tom, but she's slowly coming around now.* | **come around to sb's view/way of thinking** *We had to talk to Sam for a long time before he came round to our way of thinking.* | **come around to the idea/view that** *A lot of employers are coming around to the idea that older employees have a lot to offer a company.* | **come around to doing sth** *We're hoping that they'll eventually come round to accepting our offer.*

recant /rɪˈkænt/ [v I] formal to say publicly or formally that you have changed your mind and stopped believing what you used to believe, especially about religion or politics: *During the Moscow Show Trials in the 1930s, prisoners were forced to publicly recant.* | *After the Reformation, many Catholics recanted to avoid punishment.*

26 to keep changing your mind

- vacillate
- fickle
- blow hot and cold

vacillate /ˈvæsɪleɪt/ [v I] to keep changing your mind about what you believe or what you are going to do, especially when you have two choices and you cannot decide which one is best: *The longer you vacillate the less time you'll have to do anything worthwhile.* | **+ between** *The writer seems to vacillate between approving of Collins' actions and finding them disgusting.*

fickle /ˈfɪkəl/ [adj] someone who is **fickle** is always changing their mind about the people or things that they like so you cannot depend on them: *She had been a great star once, but the fickle public now ignored her movies.*

blow hot and cold /bləʊ ˌhɒt ən ˈkəʊld‖-ˌhɑːt-/ [v phrase] especially British, informal if someone **blows hot and cold** about something, they keep changing their attitude so that sometimes they are eager to do it and at other times they are unwilling: *I can't tell what he wants – he keeps blowing hot and cold.* | *In our dealings with the police we have found that they can blow hot and cold. Sometimes they are keen to have media help in solving a crime, other times they are more reluctant.*

27 willing to change the way you do something

- flexible
- adaptable

flexible /ˈfleksɪbəl/ [adj] willing to change your ideas, plans, or methods according to the situation: *If you're looking for a job you need to be flexible about where you're prepared to work.* | *He said the key to his business success was not forgetting to stay flexible.*

adaptable /əˈdæptəbəl/ [adj] someone who is **adaptable** does not get upset or annoyed if they have to change the way they do things, and easily gets used to new situations: *Children are often more adaptable than adults.* | *I'm not sure Ken's adaptable enough to take a job abroad.*

28 to refuse to change your mind

- stubborn
- stand firm
- stand your ground
- intransigent

stubborn /ˈstʌbəʳn/ [adj] determined not to change your mind, even when people think you are being unreasonable: *We need to do something about Craig, but he's so stubborn I just know he wouldn't listen if we tried to talk to him.* | **a stubborn streak** (=a stubborn part of your character) *I've got a very stubborn streak and I discovered that I couldn't bear people telling me what I could and couldn't eat.* | **stubborn as a mule** (=very stubborn) *Jean-Paul can be as a stubborn as a mule.*

stand firm /ˌstænd ˈfɜːʳm/ [v phrase] to refuse to change your opinions or plans even though other people are trying to make you: *When you know that you are right, you have to stand firm and defend your principles.* | **+ against** *We stood firm against any deal with the terrorists.* | **+ on** *The president has failed to stand firm on his promise to allow gays to serve in the military.*

stand your ground /ˌstænd jɔːʳ ˈɡraʊnd/ [v phrase] to refuse to change your position in an argument even though other people are trying to persuade you to change it: *They tried to make him change his mind, but he stood his ground.* | **+ against** *Richard always went along with Ella's plans, never once daring to stand his ground against her.*

intransigent /ɪnˈtrænsɪ̇dʒənt/ [adj] formal refusing to do what other people want you to do, even if this is unreasonable: *For many years the South African government remained intransigent, despite mounting world opposition to apartheid.* | **+ on** *The Church has been criticized for being intransigent on the issues of abortion and birth control.*

29 unwilling to accept changes or new ideas

- have fixed ideas
- reactionary
- entrenched
- stick in the mud
- diehard
- hidebound

have fixed ideas /hæv ˌfɪkst aɪˈdɪəz/ [v phrase not in progressive] someone who **has fixed ideas** has opinions and attitudes that never change, and often seem unreasonable: *These old teachers tend to have very fixed ideas.* | **+ about** *He has very fixed ideas about the way a wife should behave.*

reactionary /riˈækʃənəri‖-ʃəneri/ [adj] strongly opposed to change, especially social or political change, in a way that you think is unreasonable: *The seventy-year-old president has been condemned as reactionary by his radical opponents.* | *He is known for his reactionary views on immigration and the reintroduction of the death penalty.* | *Cultural attitudes to women were more reactionary than in most of Western Europe.* —**reactionary** [n C] *a bunch of right wing reactionaries*

entrenched /ɪnˈtrentʃt/ [adj usually before noun] **entrenched** attitudes are ones that people have had for a long time and are very difficult to change **+ in** *The unequal treatment of men and women in the labour market is deeply entrenched in our culture.* | **firmly/deeply entrenched** *In the small towns racial prejudice was deeply entrenched.* | **entrenched attitudes/habits/beliefs etc** *The attitudes of adults to the mentally handicapped tend to be firmly entrenched, and difficult to change.*

stick in the mud /ˈstɪk ɪn ðə ˌmʌd/ [n phrase] informal someone who has old-fashioned attitudes and is unwilling to change or try something new: *Come on, don't be such an old stick in the mud.* | *She accused him of being a stick in the mud.*

diehard /ˈdaɪhɑːʳd/ [n C] someone who still refuses to change their beliefs even when most other people have changed them: *Apart from a few union diehards most of the men have accepted the new productivity agreement.* —**diehard** [adj] *Diehard opponents of the scheme say that they will appeal against the court's decision.* | *The attempted coup was staged by a group of the ex-president's most diehard supporters.*

hidebound /ˈhaɪdbaʊnd/ [adj] a group of people or an institution that is **hidebound** has very old-fashioned ideas and attitudes and is unwilling to change them: *It was predictable that the medical establishment, so hidebound and reactionary, would reject Dr Stone's ideas.* | *The hidebound attitudes of Russia's powerful aristocracy made any kind of progress impossible.*

30 unwilling to change the way you do things

- inflexible
- be set in your ways
- rigid

inflexible /ɪnˈfleksɪ̇bəl/ [adj] not willing to change the way you think or the way you do something: *Although many students adored Albers, others found him inflexible and stifling.* | *Union negotiators criticized the employers for being too inflexible on the issues of pay and working conditions.*

be set in your ways /biː ˌset ɪn jɔːʳ ˈweɪz/ [v phrase] to be unable to change the way you do things because you have done them that way for a long time: *I'm too old and set in my ways to try living in a foreign country now.*

rigid /ˈrɪdʒɪ̇d/ [adj] someone who is **rigid** will never change their mind about what is right or wrong or about how things should be done: *Our manager was so rigid, he'd never listen to our ideas.* | *Any major changes were prevented by the rigid conservatism of the Church.* | **rigid in your ideas/opinions/attitudes etc** *Andrew was even more rigid in his attitudes towards child-rearing than his father, who was himself quite strict.*

31 when something that has been decided cannot be changed

- final
- irrevocable
- there is no going back

final /ˈfaɪnl/ [adj] a decision that is **final** cannot be changed, especially because it has been made officially by someone in authority: *They thought carefully before making a final commitment to buy.* | **final approval/decision etc** *The judges' decision is final.* | *The officials have final authority when making decisions.* | **and that's final!** spoken (=used to say that you will not change your mind about something, and do not want to hear any more about it) *You're not going out, and that's final!* | **have the final say** (=be the person who makes the final decision) *My boss has approved the project, but it's the Chief Executive who has the final say.* —**finally** [adv] *The new school timetable has not been finally decided yet.*

irrevocable /ɪˈrevəkəbəl/ [adj] formal a decision or choice which is **irrevocable** cannot be changed after it has been made: *Her decision was immediate and irrevocable.* | *I posted the letter, then realized that what I had done was irrevocable, and that I couldn't change my mind now.* —**irrevocably** [adv] *Britain could be irrevocably tied to a single European currency.*

there is no going back /ðeər ɪz ˌnəʊ ɡəʊɪŋ ˈbæk/ use this to say that what you have decided or done is permanent and cannot be changed: *You've committed your time and money to the project now – there's no going back.* | *It had started as a casual affair but they both knew that now there was no going back.*

character

RELATED WORDS

- the way that someone behaves or does something *see* **way (7-8)**
- *see also* **person/people, typical (2), nice, horrible**

1 someone's character

- character
- personality
- nature
- temperament
- a nervous/jealous etc disposition
- make-up
- what makes sb tick

character /ˈkærəktəʳ/ [n C usually singular] the combination of qualities that makes someone a particular kind of person, for example a good or bad, honest or dishonest person: *Her behavior last night revealed a lot about her character.* | *A candidate's character and qualifications are more important than past experience.* | *What strikes me most about Hamlet is his noble character.*

personality /ˌpɜːʳsəˈnæləti/ [n C] someone's character – use this especially about how someone behaves towards other people, for example whether they are friendly or unfriendly, confident or easily frightened etc: *It's true he can be emotional at times but that's just part of his personality.* | *This election should be about issues and policies, not about the personalities of the candidates!* | **friendly/nice/warm etc personality** *Yun has a lovely, warm personality.*

nature /ˈneɪtʃəʳ/ [n C/U] someone's character – use this especially to say whether someone is naturally good or bad, gentle or severe etc: *Kindness and sympathy were in his nature.* | *My girlfriend has a rather unforgiving nature so I don't think that I'll tell her.* | *She was surprised to learn he had a romantic side to his nature.* | **by nature** (=use this when saying what someone's usual character is) *She's generous by nature.* | *I am not by nature a violent man, but these insults were more than I could bear.* | **it's not in sb's nature** *It was not in his nature to take risks.*

temperament /ˈtempərəmənt/ [n C/U] the emotional part of someone's character, especially how likely they are to become angry, happy, sad etc: *His calm, quiet temperament made him popular with his colleagues.* | *My father and I got along very well, having very similar temperaments.* | **the right temperament** *I'm not sure if she has the right temperament for the job.*

a nervous/jealous etc disposition /ə ˌnɜːʳvəs dɪspəˈzɪʃən/ [n singular] formal a character that makes it likely that you will behave nervously, jealously etc: *This program may not be suitable for people with a nervous disposition.* | **be of a nervous/jealous etc disposition** *He's considerate and sweet-tempered but of a very nervous disposition.* | **have a nervous/jealous etc disposition** *Sue had a sunny disposition and a warm smile.*

make-up British **/makeup** American /ˈmeɪk ʌp/ [n singular] someone's character – use this especially to say that someone's character is completely fixed and they cannot change it or control it: *It's not in their make-up to accept defeat.* | *Her constant attempts to justify her actions tell the reader a lot about her emotional make-up.* | *This behaviour is part of our genetic make-up rather than our cultural conditioning.* | **be part of sb's make-up** *Stubbornness has always been a significant part of his makeup.*

what makes sb tick /wɒt ˌmeɪks (sb) ˈtɪk/ informal if you know **what makes someone tick**, you understand their character, desires, and what makes them behave in the way they do: *After working with him for five years, I still don't know what makes him tick.* | *As a teacher, you need to get to know your students, find out what makes them tick.*

2 one part of someone's character

- quality
- attribute
- characteristic
- trait
- side
- part of me/her
- streak
- thing
- good points/bad points
- quirk
- there's something about sb

quality /ˈkwɒləti ‖ ˈkwɑː-/ [n C] something such as an ability or a way of behaving that is part of someone's character: *Besides intelligence and charm, Bella had some less desirable qualities.* | *The essential quality of a good parent is patience.* | *Among his other endearing qualities, Ralph was an exceedingly patient man.*

attribute /ˈætrəbjuːt/ [n C] a part of someone's character, especially a part that is thought by other people to be good and useful: *The attribute that people found most attractive in Sharon was her optimism.* | *Hope is one of mankind's most enduring and rewarding attributes.* | *He had all the attributes of a great leader: charisma, energy, discipline, and resourcefulness.*

characteristic /ˌkærəktəˈrɪstɪk◂/ [n C usually plural] someone's **characteristics** are the qualities that are typical of them and which make them easy to recognize: *All great leaders share certain characteristics which must be seen as the key to their success.* | *Ralph can be very mean sometimes. It's one of his less endearing characteristics.*

trait /treɪ, treɪt ‖ treɪt/ [n C] one type of feeling or behaviour that is particularly noticeable in a person or group of people: *It's a human trait to joke about subjects that make us uncomfortable.* | **family trait** (=a trait shared by members of a family) *Pride seems to be one of our family traits.* | **personality trait** *Certain personality traits make people more likely to become victims of violent crime.*

side /saɪd/ [n C] **romantic/serious/funny etc side** a part of someone's character, especially one that is very different from the rest of their character: *Canning was a very traditional Englishman but he had a surprisingly romantic side to him as well.* | *Val revealed her wild side at the office party.* | *After his arrest people realized that there had always been a darker side to his nature.*

part of me/her /ˈpɑːʳt əv miː, hɜːʳ/ [n C] one part of someone's character, which makes them behave or feel in particular ways: *Part of me loves going to parties but there's another part that prefers staying at home.* | *There is a part of her that I just don't understand.*

streak /striːk/ [n C] a part of someone's character that is quite different from the rest of their character, especially one that makes them behave badly **mean/nasty/violent etc streak** *She had a mean streak that she didn't bother to hide.* | *The District Attorney argued that Johnson has a violent streak and is a danger to society.*

thing /θɪŋ/ [n C] informal a part of someone's character, especially one that you like or dislike: *One of the things I like about Susan is the way she always keeps* *smiling, even when there are problems.* | *The nicest thing about Richard is that he doesn't mind being criticized.*

good points/bad points /ˈgʊd ˌpɔɪnts, ˈbæd pɔɪnts/ good or bad things about someone's character: *Fred was a bad manager but he had his good points.* | *She always tried to be fair with her students and not just stress their bad points.* | *When you're dead people don't remember your faults – only your good points.*

quirk /kwɜːʳk/ [n C] a strange or unusual habit or part of someone's character: *Although on the outside he was quiet and shy, Albert had more than his share of quirks.* | *She took pride in her children's quirks and individuality, and made no effort to try to change them.*

there's something about sb /ðeəʳz ˈsʌmθɪŋ əbaʊt (sb)/ you say this when there is something about a person's character that you like or dislike, but you're not sure exactly what it is: *I don't know what it is, but there's something about that man which really irritates me.*

3 someone's real character

- true colours
- underneath
- deep down
- at heart

true colours British **/true colors** American /ˌtruː ˈkʌləʳz/ [n plural] if someone shows their **true colours** they do something that shows what they are really like, when they have been pretending to be something different: *With the elections safely behind him, Hitler began to show his true colours.* | *He was friendly to me at first but he showed his true colors when we were both up for the same promotion.*

underneath /ˌʌndəʳˈniːθ/ [adv/prep] if someone is nice, jealous, frightened etc **underneath**, they really are nice, jealous, or frightened even though their behaviour shows a different character: *I know that she seems very aggressive, but underneath she's really quite shy.* | *Underneath all that boastful talk you'll find that he's actually a very nice guy.* | **underneath it all** *She laughed as if she was joking but underneath it all, I knew she meant it.*

deep down /ˌdiːp ˈdaʊn/ [adv] if someone is cruel, dishonest, good etc **deep down**, that is their true character even though they hide this in their usual behaviour: *Deep down, I think she's really very ambitious.* | *Yeah, sometimes he can be really nice and polite but, I tell you, deep down he's an animal!*

at heart /ət ˈhɑːʳt/ [adv] if you are a particular type of person **at heart**, that is your true character even though you may sometimes think you are different: *She's a traveller at heart. You'll never get her to settle down.* | *Paul was an easy-going fellow at heart who wanted only to enjoy himself.*

4 a definite character that makes someone different from other people

- identity
- individuality
- personality

identity /aɪˈdentəti/ [n U] the definite character that a person or group sees themselves as having, which lets them feel different and separate from everyone else: *She was afraid marriage would cause her to lose her identity.* | *The islanders are proud of their strong regional identity.* | **sense of identity** (=the feeling that you have a strong identity) *Many teenagers play sports to gain a sense of identity.*

individuality /ˌɪndəˌvɪdʒuˈæləti/ [n U] the quality of being clearly different from other people and having your own personal character: *It's difficult to be part of a highly organized group such as the armed forces without losing some of your individuality.* | *We have a close working relationship while retaining our individuality and separate interests.*

personality /ˌpɜːʳsəˈnæləti/ [n U] the quality of being interesting, friendly, and enjoyable to be with, that makes someone seem very different from most other people: *Everyone loves her for her cheerful personality.* | *Yes, he's got plenty of talent and ambition, but he's got no personality.* | *Billie Holiday or Bessie Smith had more personality than a hundred of today's pop singers.*

5 the character of something

- character
- nature
- essence

character /ˈkærəktəʳ/ [n singular/U] the combination of qualities that a particular kind of place, thing etc has **the character of** *The whole character of the school had changed.* | *We'll find out about the true character of this team after these next few games.* | **character** *Marx's view of society stressed its dynamic character.* | **in character** *Liquids are different in character from both solids and gases.*

nature /ˈneɪtʃəʳ/ [n singular/U] the true character of something, which you must understand in order to know what it is really like **the nature of** *The doctor admitted that he didn't yet understand the nature of Julie's illness.* | *Monnens spends his days explaining the nature of Internet advertising to clients.* | **by its nature** (=because of its nature) *Computers, by their nature, tend to change the way offices are organized.* | **be in the nature of sth** (=be a permanent part of its nature) *It's in the nature of elections that campaigning sometimes gets quite tough.*

essence /ˈesəns/ [n singular] the most basic and important quality of something that make it different from anything else **the essence of** *This is the essence of the problem, as I see it.* | *The movie brilliantly captures the essence of Calcutta's street life.* | *Sharing is the essence of friendship.* | **in essence** (=most importantly) *His speech was, in essence, a plea for understanding and conciliation.*

6 one part of the character of something

- characteristic
- quality
- property
- feature
- attribute
- thing
- good points/bad points
- there's something about sth

characteristic /ˌkærəktəˈrɪstɪk◂/ [n C usually plural] a part of the character of something that makes it clearly different from or similar to other things: *One of the characteristics of this species is the dark blue markings on its back.* | *The main characteristics of capitalism are private ownership of capital and freedom of enterprise.* | **share characteristics/have characteristics in common** (=have similar characteristics) *The UK shares many characteristics with other European countries.* | *The two diseases have a number of characteristics in common.*

quality /ˈkwɒlᵻti‖ˈkwɑː-/ [n C] an important part of the character of something, especially a part that is good: *There are certain qualities in Orwell's prose that I greatly admire.* | *Despite its many qualities, the school simply isn't getting results.* | *This wine possesses a unique quality.* | **a quality of** *There is a wonderful quality of innocence in these paintings.*

property /ˈprɒpəʳti‖ˈprɑː-/ [n C] a characteristic that a particular substance or chemical has: *The properties of the soil influence the growth of the plants.* | *We test the chemical and biological properties of the samples.* | *The conducting properties of solids vary widely.*

feature /ˈfiːtʃəʳ/ [n C] an important, noticeable, or interesting characteristic of something: *The hotel's most attractive feature is its magnificent view of Mount Hood.* | *Patriotism was a prominent feature in Bush's election campaign.* | **a feature of** *Information on employment is a central feature of this training course.*

attribute /ˈætrᵻbjuːt/ [n C] a characteristic of an organization or system, especially a good characteristic: *He possesses the essential attributes of a journalist.* | *She spent most of the interview describing the company's attributes to me.*

thing /θɪŋ/ [n C usually singular] informal a characteristic of something, especially one that you like or dislike: *The thing that I really hate about this job is having to work late at night.* | *All that lovely fresh air – that's the best thing about living in the country.*

good points/bad points /ˈgʊd pɔɪnts, ˈbæd pɔɪnts/ [n plural] the good or bad things about a place or thing: *The city is big and noisy, but it does have its good points too.*

there's something about sth /ðeəʳz ˈsʌmθɪŋ əbaʊt (sth)/ you say this when there's something about a thing, a place, someone's behaviour etc that you like or dislike, but you're not sure exactly what it is: *There's something very strange about this whole affair.* | *There was something about the place that gave me the creeps.*

cheap

RELATED WORDS

opposite: **expensive**

▸ *see also* **cost, buy, pay, reduce, spend money/time, shop/store, free**

1 not costing much money

- ▸ cheap
- ▸ inexpensive
- ▸ not cost much
- ▸ economical
- ▸ affordable
- ▸ low-cost
- ▸ be low in price
- ▸ low-budget
- ▸ budget
- ▸ it won't break the bank

cheap /tʃiːp/ [adj] something that is **cheap** costs very little money, or costs less than you expected: *My shoes were really cheap – they only cost $15.* | *The cheapest way to get to Chicago is to take the bus.* | **it is cheap to do sth** *It's cheaper to phone after six o'clock.* | **relatively cheap** (=cheap compared with other things) *Wooden houses are relatively cheap to build.* —**cheaply** [adv] *You can buy electronic diaries fairly cheaply nowadays.*

inexpensive /ˌɪnɪkˈspensɪv◂/ [adj] not expensive – use this especially about things that are of good quality, even though they do not cost a lot: *The furniture is inexpensive but well-made.* | *a simple, inexpensive meal* | *Beans and lentils are an inexpensive source of protein.* | **relatively inexpensive** (=not expensive compared to something similar) *a hotel that offers air-conditioned rooms at relatively inexpensive prices*

not cost much /nɒt ˈkɒst ˌmʌtʃ‖-ˈkɔːst-/ [v phrase not in progressive] especially spoken to not be expensive: *We stayed in a very nice hotel in Vienna and it didn't cost much.* | **it doesn't cost much to do sth** *It doesn't cost much to rent an apartment here.*

economical /ˌekəˈnɒmɪkəl◂, ˌiː-‖-ˈnɑː-/ [adj] cheap to use or cheap to do – use this about cars, machines, or ways of doing things that do not waste money, fuel etc: *We have a very economical heating system, so the bills aren't too high.* | **be economical to use/run/operate** *This is a well-designed car that is also very economical to run.* | **it is more economical to do sth** *It's more economical to buy the big packet – it's only 50p more than the small one.*

affordable /əˈfɔːʳdəbəl/ [adj usually before noun] cheap enough for most people to be able to buy: *Single mothers often have trouble finding affordable child care.* | *We have a vast range of cars to choose from at affordable prices.*

low-cost /ˌləʊ ˈkɒst◂‖-ˈkɔːst◂/ [adj only before noun] **low-cost housing/heating/transport etc** intended to be cheap to use, buy, rent etc: *If you want low-cost transport and regular exercise, a bike is ideal.* | *If elected, he promised to build more low-cost housing in the city.* | *The US is giving low-cost loans to help under-developed countries in the region.*

be low in price /biː ˌləʊ ɪn ˈpraɪs/ [v phrase] especially written if a product is **low in price**, it is cheap to buy: *Nikon's latest camera is low in price and easy to use.* | *The 'Pocket-Pack' range of toys are very low in price and will provide hours of pleasure for the kids.*

low-budget /ˌləʊ ˈbʌdʒᵻt◂/ [adj only before noun] **low-budget film/movie/ production etc** one that has been made very cheaply: *My first acting job was in a low-budget horror movie with a terrible plot.*

budget /ˈbʌdʒᵻt/ [adj only before noun] **budget hotel/flight/accommodation etc budget** hotels, flights etc are very low in price: *The Tourist Information Office will give you a list of budget hotels in the area.*

it won't break the bank /ɪt ˌwəʊnt breɪk ðə ˈbæŋk/ spoken use this to say that you have enough money to buy or do something, and you should buy or do it: *'I'm not sure if I should buy this suit.' 'Come on! It won't break the bank!'* | **without breaking the bank** (=without having to pay a lot of money) *This guide lists 900 of the best places in which to eat without breaking the bank.*

2 cheap but bad in quality

- ▸ cheap
- ▸ cheap and nasty

cheap /tʃiːp/ [adj usually before noun] something that is **cheap** does not cost much, and is clearly of bad quality: *The tourist shops were full of cheap souvenirs.* | *The hotel room was very small, with cheap furniture and a bumpy bed.* | *Oh look – a present from Rob. I bet it's another bottle of cheap perfume.*

cheap and nasty /ˌtʃiːp ən ˈnɑːsti‖-ˈnæs-/ [adj phrase not before noun] British furniture, jewellery, or clothes that are **cheap and nasty** look cheap and of very bad quality: *What do you think of these bracelets? They look really cheap and nasty to me.* | *I don't like plastic shoes. They always seem cheap and nasty.*

3 when you get something for a good price

- be good value
- value for money
- be a good buy
- a good deal
- bargain

be good value /biː ˌgʊd 'væljuː/ [v phrase] to be worth the price that you pay, especially a price that is not high: *The meals at Charlie's Pizza are really good value.* | **be a good value** American *The CD-ROM encyclopedia is a good value because the printed encyclopedia set sells for twice as much.*

value for money /ˌvæljuː fəʳ 'mʌni/ [n phrase] especially British if something that is being sold is **value for money**, it is worth the price that you pay – use this about something that is fairly cheap but is of a reasonable standard or quality **be (good) value for money** *Sainsbury's cookbooks are generally considered to be value for money.* | *There's a special ticket that means you can see six concerts, which is definitely good value for money.* | **get value for money** (=get something that is worth the price you paid) *The show was less than one hour long and we didn't really get value for money.*

be a good buy /biː ə ˌgʊd 'baɪ/ [v phrase] something that **is a good buy** is worth the price you pay for it, because it is not expensive but is still good: *The Brazilian white wine is a good buy at only $2.99 a bottle.* | *College officials insist that higher education is a good buy despite rising tuition costs.*

a good deal /ə ˌgʊd 'diːl/ [n phrase] if something is **a good deal**, it is worth the price you pay, because it includes a lot of additional things or services **be a good/excellent/great etc deal** *The price of the holiday includes free use of the tennis courts, the pool, and the gym. It's a very good deal.* | **give sb a good deal** *They gave me a really good deal on my camera.* | **get a good deal** *Cowpland said he was willing to buy the company if he got a good deal.*

bargain /'bɑːʳgɪ̈n/ [n C] something that costs a lot less than you expect or a lot less than it usually costs: *Did you get any bargains at the market?* | *I got this shirt when I was in Indonesia. It was a real bargain.*

4 not too expensive when compared to other prices

- reasonable
- competitive

reasonable /'riːzənəbəl/ [adj] **reasonable** prices seem fair because they are not too high: *They sell good-quality computer equipment at reasonable prices.* | *Only £15 a night? That sounds reasonable.*

competitive /kəm'petɪ̈tɪv/ [adj] as low as or lower than the prices charged by other shops or companies: *I think you'll find our prices are extremely competitive.* | *The hotel offers a high standard of service at very competitive rates.* —**competitively priced** /kəmˌpetɪ̈tɪvli 'praɪst/ [adj phrase] *Call this number for our free catalogue of competitively priced software.*

5 very cheap

- dirt cheap
- be a snip
- at rockbottom prices
- for very little money
- for nothing

dirt cheap /ˌdɜːʳt 'tʃiːp◂/ [adj not before noun] informal extremely cheap: *You can get beautiful leather jackets in the markets and they're dirt cheap.* —**dirt cheap** [adv] *She buys all her clothes dirt cheap in charity shops.*

be a snip /biː ə 'snɪp/ British informal /**be a steal** /biː ə 'stiːl/ American informal [v phrase] to be extremely cheap at a particular price: *She says her new outfit was a steal.* | *The new computer package is a snip at only £599 plus tax.*

at rockbottom prices /ət ˌrɒkbɒtəm 'praɪsɪ̈z‖ˌrɑːkbɑː-/ ALSO **at giveaway prices** /ət 'gɪvəweɪ ˌpraɪsɪ̈s/ British [adv] if a shop is selling goods **at rockbottom prices** or **at giveaway prices**, it is selling them at extremely low prices – used especially in advertisements: *Fox Hi-Fi specialize in selling top quality CD players at rockbottom prices.* | *In our summer sale, we have clothes from top designers at giveaway prices.*

for very little money /fəʳ ˌveri lɪtl 'mʌni/ [adv] *You can pick up video recorders for very little money if you know where to look.*

for nothing /fəʳ 'nʌθɪŋ/ [adv] especially American very cheaply: *We got the car for nothing because the woman wanted to get rid of it fast.*

6 to reduce the price of something

- reduce/cut
- knock £1/$20/20p etc off
- be marked down
- slash

reduce/cut /rɪ'djuːs‖rɪ'duːs, kʌt/ [v T] to make prices, charges etc lower: *There is a lot of pressure on electricity companies to reduce their prices.* | *The company needs to cut costs drastically if it's going to survive.* | *Unless they can reduce their prices, they will soon be unable to compete on the American market.* | **reduce sth by 10%/£20 etc** *Continental Airlines are to reduce fares by up to 10% in some areas.* —**reduction/cut** /rɪ'dʌkʃən, kʌt/ [n C] *If there was a reduction in fares more people would ride the train to work.* | *Further cuts in oil prices seem unlikely.*

knock £1/$20/20p etc off /ˌnɒk ə ˌpaʊnd 'ɒf‖ˌnɑːk-/ [phr v T] informal to reduce the price of something that you are selling: *I expect if you ask him he'll knock a couple of pounds off.* | *Knock fifty bucks off and I'll buy it.*

be marked down /biː ˌmɑːʳkt 'daʊn/ [v phrase] to be reduced in price – use this about goods in shops: *Their prices are usually marked down after Christmas.* | *To celebrate the store's 100th anniversary, all merchandise has been marked down by 20 percent.*

slash /slæʃ/ [v T] to reduce the price of something by a very large amount – used especially in news reports and advertisements: *Sony has slashed the price of its new CD player, the D50.* | *Final Sale. All prices slashed. Everything must go!* | **slash sth by 50%/£50/$100 etc** *British Airways have slashed fares by over 50%.*

7 when the price has been reduced

- sale
- on sale
- reduced
- £1/$20/10% etc off
- discount
- special offer
- cut-price
- be going cheap
- special

sale /seɪl/ [n C] a time when a shop sells things more cheaply than usual: *There's going to be a sale at Macy's next week.* | *Amelia bought her jacket at a sale for twenty dollars.* | **have a sale** *The bookstore across the street is having a sale.* | **the sales** British

(=when a lot of shops sell things at reduced prices) *I got this coat for half price in the January sales.*

on sale /ɒn 'seɪl/ American **/in the sales** /ɪn ðə 'seɪlz/ British [adv] something that is **on sale** is being sold at a specially low price in a shop: *'How much was your jacket?' 'I got it on sale in Montgomery Wards. It only cost $45.'* | *His suit was bought in the sales for £100.* | **go on sale** *I need a new pair of shoes but I want to wait until they go on sale.*

reduced /rɪ'dju:st‖-'du:st/ [adj not before noun] goods that are **reduced** are being sold at a lower price than usual: *Everything is reduced because the store's closing down next month.* | **+ from ... to ...** *The CDs were reduced from $10 to $5.*

£1/$20/10% etc off /ə ˌpaʊnd 'ɒf/ [n phrase] if there is **£1, $20, 10% etc off** something, its usual price has been reduced by that amount: *20% off all computers in Dixon's summer sale* | *We got $10 off the chair because it had a small mark on it.*

discount /'dɪskaʊnt/ [n C] a reduction in the price you pay for something, which is given for a special reason **get a discount** (=pay less) *Do you get a discount if you pay in cash?* | **+ on** *Workers at the store get a discount on books and records.* | **30%/£50 etc discount** *There's a 30% discount on all electrical goods.* | **at a discount** (=at a reduced price) *Air UK are currently offering tickets to students at a special discount.*

special offer /ˌspeʃəl 'ɒfər‖-'ɔ:f-/ [n C] a very low price that a shop sells something for, in order to persuade more people to buy things there: *They've got a special offer for seniors – five nights for the price of three.* | *Take advantage of our special offer between now and Oct 30 this year.*

cut-price /ˌkʌt 'praɪs◂/ [adj only before noun] **cut-price** goods or services are sold at prices that are much lower than the usual price, either because they have been specially reduced or because they are being sold by someone who always sells things cheaply: *Tottenham Court Road is the best place for cut-price stereo equipment.* | *Fruit is fairly inexpensive in Japan because they buy cut-price oranges and apples from South Africa.*

be going cheap /bi: ˌgəʊɪŋ 'tʃi:p/ [v phrase] spoken if something **is going cheap**, it is being sold more cheaply than usual: *If they have any bicycle lamps going cheap, can you get me one?* | *Have a look in the travel agent's and see if there are any flights to Toronto going cheap.*

special /'speʃəl/ [n C] a product that is sold at a low price for a short time – used especially about food, drink, or meals: *Today's lunch special is smoked salmon with rice.* | **on special** American (=being sold as a special) *We have Bud beer 6-packs on special at $5.*

8 to persuade someone to reduce the price of something

- haggle
- bargain with
- beat sb down

haggle /'hægəl/ [v I] to try to persuade someone to reduce the price of something by arguing with them about what it is worth: *If you go to a street market, you'd better be prepared to haggle.* | **haggle over sth** *The passenger haggled over the fare before she got into the taxi.* | **haggle with sb** *My mother used to spend hours haggling with the market traders.*

bargain with /'bɑ:rgɪ̂n wɪð/ [v phrase not in passive] to try to persuade someone to reduce the price of something by discussing it with them: *She bargained with the woman who was selling the plates and managed to get them for half the usual price.*

beat sb down /ˌbi:t (sb) 'daʊn/ [phr v T] to persuade someone to reduce the price of something by arguing with them about it **beat sb down to $50/£20 etc** *The owners originally wanted $1000 for the horse, but George managed to beat them down to $850.* | **beat sb down** *I beat him down and got the bracelet for $2.*

cheat

RELATED WORDS

- to make someone believe something that is not true *see* **trick/deceive**
- to tell a lie *see* **lie (3-5)**
- *see also* **dishonest**

1 to get money or possessions from someone dishonestly

- cheat
- swindle
- con
- fiddle
- defraud
- fleece
- trick sb out of
- do sb out of
- you've been had

cheat /tʃi:t/ [v T] *He doesn't trust car mechanics – he thinks they're all trying to cheat him.* | **cheat sb out of sth** *She says she was cheated out of $10,000 she paid to a modeling agency.* | *Cohen claimed that criminals posing as salesmen cheat Americans out of billions of dollars each year.*

swindle /'swɪndl/ [v T] to get money from a person or organization by cheating them, especially using clever and complicated methods: *He was jailed in 1992 for attempting to swindle the insurance company he worked for.* | **swindle sb out of sth** *Investors have been swindled out of millions of pounds.*

con /kɒn‖kɑ:n/ [v T] especially spoken to persuade someone to buy something or to give you money by telling them lies: *By the time she realized she had been conned, she had lost more than $3000.* | **con sb out of sth** *The old lady was conned out of her life savings by a crooked insurance dealer.* | **con sth out of sb** *A man pretending to be a faith healer has conned around £20,000 out of desperate sick people.* | **con sb into doing sth** *She was too embarrassed to admit that they had conned her into buying 100 acres of worthless land.*

fiddle /'fɪdl/ [v T] British informal to give false information or make dishonest changes to financial records, in order to get money or avoid paying money: *My boss thinks I've been fiddling my travel expenses.* | **fiddle the books/fiddle the accounts** (=change a company's financial records) *The company secretary has been fiddling the books for years.*

defraud /dɪ'frɔ:d/ [v T] to get money from a company or organization, especially a very large one, by deceiving it: *Trachtenberg is charged with attempting to defraud his business partner.* | **defraud sb (out) of sth** *Between them they defrauded the company out of hundreds of thousands of dollars.*

fleece /fli:s/ [v T] informal to get a lot of money from someone by tricking them: *She fleeced him for everything he had.* | *Authorities estimate at least 300 elderly couples were fleeced in the scheme.* | **fleece sb of sth** *She estimates he fleeced her of about £50,000 by tricking her into buying fake antiques.*

trick sb out of /ˌtrɪk (sb) 'aʊt ɒv/ [v phrase] to get money or possessions from someone, by tricking or deceiving them: *Police are warning residents to be on their guard after two men tricked a pensioner out of several hundred pounds.* | *Megan was tricked out of her life savings by a smooth-talking handsome man who had promised to marry her.*

do sb out of /ˌduː (sb) ˈaʊt ɒv/ [v phrase] especially British, informal to cheat someone by not giving them money that they deserve or that they are owed: *The way I see it, they've done me out of three weeks' wages.* | *She's convinced the sales assistant did her out of £15.*

you've been had /juːv bɪn ˈhæd/ spoken use this to say that someone has been cheated but they do not realize it: *I hate to tell you this but you've been had. The antique clock you bought is a phoney.*

2 to make someone pay too much money for something

- overcharge
- rip off
- a rip-off
- fleece

overcharge /ˌəʊvərˈtʃɑːrdʒ/ [v I/T] to make someone pay too much for something in a shop, restaurant, taxi etc: *Garage mechanics are twice as likely to overcharge women car owners as men.* | **overcharge sb for sth** *The cab driver tried to overcharge us for the ride from the airport.* | *The university was accused of overcharging the government millions of dollars for research-related costs.*

rip off /ˌrɪp ˈɒf/ [phr v T] spoken informal to make someone pay much more for something than it is worth **rip sb off** *Don't buy a watch from those guys, they'll just rip you off.* | **rip off sb** *The bars by the sea make huge profits by ripping off tourists.*

a rip-off /ə ˈrɪp ɒf/ [n singular] spoken informal if something is a **rip-off**, it costs much more than it is worth – use this when you think that someone is trying to cheat you: *'It cost £200 to get it fixed.' 'What a rip-off!'* | **a complete/total rip-off** *The meal cost me $80 – it was a total rip-off.*

fleece /fliːs/ [v T] informal to get a lot of money from someone by charging far too much for goods or services: *Some airport shops are accused of fleecing their customers, who don't have any choice but to use them.*

3 to cheat in an examination or game

- cheat
- copy

cheat /tʃiːt/ [v I] to use dishonest methods in order to pass an examination or win a game: *Studies indicate about 20 to 30 percent of college students cheat.* | **+ at** *Jenny always cheats at cards.* —**cheating** [n U] when someone cheats in an examination or game: *Their teacher suspected them of cheating when they both missed the same question on the test.*

copy /ˈkɒpi‖ˈkɑː-/ [v I/T] to cheat in an examination, schoolwork etc by copying someone's work: *If I see anyone copying I'll send you straight to the principal's office.* | **+ off** *The only way I made it through high school was by copying off my best friend.* | **copy sth from sth** *She was expelled for handing in an essay that she had copied directly from a newspaper article.*

4 to dishonestly arrange the result of a game, election etc

- fix
- rig
- ballot-rigging
- throw

fix /fɪks/ [v T] to dishonestly arrange the result of something, especially of a sports game, so that it is to your advantage: *He was convicted of fixing college basketball games in the 1950s.* | *Many people believe that the outcome of wrestling matches are fixed.* —**fix** [n C] *Supporters of the losing team protested that the whole thing was a fix.*

rig /ˈrɪg/ [v T usually in passive] if something **is rigged**, especially a vote or an election, it is dishonestly arranged so that a person or group gets the result they want: *The senator resigned after accusations that the vote had been rigged.* | *They would never have got into power if the whole thing hadn't been rigged.* | *Many Labour Party members believed that the ballot to elect a mayoral candidate was rigged.*

ballot-rigging /ˈbælət ˌrɪgɪŋ/ [n U] when someone dishonestly arranges an election or other vote so that they get the result they want: *The MP resigned after charges of fraud and ballot-rigging.*

throw /θrəʊ/ [v T] if a player or team **throw** a game, they deliberately lose it, especially in order to get money: *Joe Jackson was one of eight Chicago White Sox accused of throwing the 1919 World Series.*

5 when people are dishonest in order to get money

- fraud
- scam
- swindle
- fiddle
- con
- racket

▸ *see also* **steal**

fraud /frɔːd/ [n C/U] the crime of getting money dishonestly from a big organization, for example by giving false information or changing documents, especially over a long time: *Big losses due to theft and fraud forced the company to close.* | *Landale is calling for more laws to protect consumers against fraud.*

scam /skæm/ [n C] informal a method, usually used by several people working together, who cheat someone by making them believe something that is not true: *I spent more than $4000 before I realized the whole thing was a scam.* | **scam to do sth** *She and her boyfriend were involved in a scam to get $5 million from the company.* | **tax scam** (=a way of dishonestly avoiding paying tax)

swindle /ˈswɪndl/ [n C] a well-planned and often complicated arrangement to cheat people: *Young was convicted for his participation in a $2 million stock swindle.* | *The whole property development proposal was a swindle. They never intended to build anything.*

fiddle /ˈfɪdl/ [n C] British a situation in which people are cheated, especially in small ways over a long period of time: *The firm realised some sort of fiddle was going on, but they had no idea how much they were losing.* | **work a fiddle** (=do a fiddle) *Managers don't really get paid much here, but most of them are working a few fiddles.*

con /kɒn‖kɑːn/ [n C] a method or process of persuading someone to buy something or to give you money by telling them lies: *A lot of people gave money to the charity collectors, not realising it was a con.* | **con trick** British *She wanted me to visit a fortune-teller but I thought it was all a big con trick.*

racket /ˈrækɪ̈t/ [n C] an illegal business that is used by criminals to make a large profit for themselves: *The FBI believe they have found the real criminals behind a big gambling racket.* | *The Mafia runs a highly sophisticated drugs racket.*

6 someone who cheats

- cheat
- con-man/con artist
- swindler

cheat ALSO **cheater** American /tʃiːt, 'tʃiːtəʳ/ [n C] *Don't pretend you can't afford to pay me that money back – you're nothing but a cheat and a liar!* | *My grandmother thinks all car salesmen are cheats.* | *I'll never play cards with you again, you cheater!*

con-man/con artist /'kɒn mæn, 'kɒn ˌɑːʳtɪst ‖'kɑːn-/ [n C] spoken informal someone who gets money by cheating people or lying to them: *a handsome con-man who charms women into giving him money, then simply disappears from their lives* | *She gave $11,000 to two con artists who pretended to be bank officials.*

swindler /'swɪndləʳ/ [n C] someone who regularly cheats people or organizations to get money: *That firm is a bunch of swindlers. Don't pay them anything until the goods have been delivered and checked.* | *I wasn't going to let any kid of mine work among those swindlers on Wall Street.*

check

to make sure that something is true or correct

RELATED WORDS

- to examine something or someone *see* **examine**
- *see also* **test 9-10, sure/not sure**

- check
- check out
- make sure/make certain
- double-check
- verify
- confirm
- ascertain

check /tʃek/ [v I/T] to do something in order to find out whether something is really true or correct: *'Are you sure this is the right phone number?' 'Yes, I've just checked.'* | *You'd better check the figures one more time – we don't want any mistakes.* | **+ that** *I'll just check that I locked the door.* | *Check that the meat is cooked thoroughly before serving it.* | **+ if/whether** *Before your trip, check if your insurance covers you abroad.* | **check to see if/whether** *Let's check to see if she's OK.*

check out /ˌtʃek 'aʊt/ [phr v T] to make sure that something, especially something that someone else has told you, is actually true **check out sth** *We got in touch with the bank to check out the suspect's story.* | **check sth out** *What he said didn't seem quite right, so I decided to check it out.*

make sure/make certain /ˌmeɪk 'ʃʊəʳ, ˌmeɪk 'sɜːʳtn/ [v phrase] to check that a situation is really the way you want or expect it to be: *I don't think Jo's back yet, but you can knock on her door just to make sure.* | **+ (that)** *Make certain the car is in good condition before you sign the rental agreement.* | *I phoned the hotel to make sure that they had reserved a room for us.*

double-check /ˌdʌbəl 'tʃek/ [v I/T] to check something a second time, so that you are completely sure: *'Did you switch the heating off?' 'Yes, I double-checked.'* | *I don't think I made a mistake. I checked and double-checked all my calculations.* | **+ that** *Double-check that the computer file was properly copied.*

verify /'verɪfaɪ/ [v T] formal to officially check a fact or statement and show that it is correct: *You can verify the facts in the report by calling his office.* | **+ that** *Doctors have verified that the injury was indeed work-related.* —**verification** /ˌverɪfɪ'keɪʃən/ [n U] *The documents are being sent to the State Department for verification.*

confirm /kən'fɜːʳm/ [v T] to check that an arrangement you have made has happened or is still going to happen: *Have you called to confirm your flight yet?* | **+ that** *Let me just confirm that the money has arrived in your account.* —**confirmation** /ˌkɒnfəʳ'meɪʃən‖ˌkɑːn-/ [n U] *We're waiting for written confirmation of the reservations.*

ascertain /ˌæsəʳ'teɪn/ [v I/T] formal to find out if a fact that you think is true is really true **ascertain sth** *The case remains a mystery. The police were never able to ascertain the true facts.* | **ascertain that** *The pathologist ascertained that the victim had died from a gunshot wound.* | **ascertain how/when/why etc** *A doctor should examine the patient to ascertain where the pain is localized.* | **ascertain** *As far as we have been able to ascertain, our client is not involved in anything illegal.*

child

RELATED WORDS

- a young person aged 11-18 *see* **young**
- *see also* **adult, baby, father, mother**

1 a child

- child
- kid
- boy
- girl
- toddler

child /tʃaɪld/ [n C] a young person from the time they are born until they are aged about 14 or 15: *How many children are there in your class?* | *Children under 14 travel free.* | *Every child was given a present.* | **as a child** *As a child, she preferred playing football with the boys to playing with dolls.* | **child prodigy** (=a child who is extremely good at doing something, for example playing music or speaking languages, from a very young age) *While growing up in North Carolina, Amos was considered a child prodigy on the piano.* | **child development** (=the way a child grows and learns new skills) *After her first baby was born, Barb read child development books constantly.* | **child care** (=when someone looks after children while their parents work) *The state will provide child care when both parents participate in the training program.* | **child abuse** (=cruel or violent treatment of children by adults) *Nationwide, only one in four cases of child abuse and neglect is reported.*

kid /kɪd/ [n C] informal a child: *Jamie's a bright kid.* | *I really enjoy working with kids.* | *When we were kids, we used to spend practically the whole summer outdoors.* | **just a kid** *Don't be so hard on him – he's just a kid.*

boy /bɔɪ/ [n C] a male child: *I used to live in Spain when I was a boy.* | *Harry teaches in a boys' school in Glasgow.* | *He put a hand on the boy's shoulder and walked with him down the hall.* | **little boy** (=a very young boy) *Why don't you go play with that little boy over there?*

girl /gɜːʳl/ [n C] a female child: *What's that girl's name?* | *More girls play sports now than when I was younger.* | *Beth is one of the most popular girls in her class.* | **little girl** (=a very young girl) *A little girl was sitting on the front doorstep.*

toddler /ˈtɒdləʳ‖ˈtɑːd-/ [n C] a very young child who has just learned to walk: *As a toddler, he was attacked and injured by the family's pet dog.* | *A toddler was squatting in the middle of the carpet, thumb in mouth.*

2 someone's son or daughter

- ▸ **child**
- ▸ **kid**
- ▸ **son**
- ▸ **daughter**
- ▸ **little boy/little girl**
- ▸ **offspring**

child /tʃaɪld/ [n C] someone's son or daughter, of any age: *She named her first child Katrin.* | *One of her children lives in Australia now.* | *The house seems very quiet now that all the children have left home.* | **an only child** (=a child that has no brothers or sisters) *Alexandra was an only child and the centre of her mother's world.*

kid /kɪd/ [n C] **informal** someone's son or daughter – use this about children aged up to 14 or 15: *All I ever wanted was to get married and have kids.* | *Could you look after the kids this evening?*

son /sʌn/ [n C] someone's male child: *We have two teenage sons.* | *Her son used to work in Texas.* | *The family business has now been taken over by Anderson's eldest son.*

daughter /ˈdɔːtəʳ/ [n C] someone's female child: *Our youngest daughter is getting married next month.* | *My aunt has five daughters and three sons.* | *In traditional societies, parents were often reluctant to send their daughters to school.*

little boy/little girl /ˌlɪtl ˈbɔɪ, ˌlɪtl ˈgɜːʳl/ [n C] **spoken** someone's young son or daughter: *Paula had to go home – her little girl's sick.* | *'How old's your little boy?' 'He's three.'*

offspring /ˈɒfˌsprɪŋ‖ˈɔːf-/ [n singular or plural] a person's or animal's baby or babies – used humorously or in formal contexts about someone's children **sb's offspring** *Parents with the disease are likely to pass it on to their offspring.* | *Hardly a day goes by without Mrs Molt or one of her offspring calling around to borrow something.*

3 a child whose parents have died

- ▸ **orphan**

orphan /ˈɔːʳfən/ [n C] *Pepino was a ten-year-old orphan. His parents had been killed in the war.* | *Dr Barnardo founded homes for orphans in the late nineteenth century.* —**orphaned** [adj] *Orphaned at the age of six, Laura grew up with her father's relatives.*

4 the time when someone is a child

- ▸ **childhood**
- ▸ **in infancy/during infancy**

childhood /ˈtʃaɪldhʊd/ [n C/U] *Since childhood Margot had longed to be a dancer.* | *Steven had happy memories of his childhood on the farm.* | **childhood illness/experiences/dream etc** (=that you have when you are a child) *Of course, I had all the usual childhood illnesses, like measles and mumps.* | *It was his childhood dream to play professional baseball.* | **early childhood** *Much of my early childhood was spent with my aunt in California.*

in infancy/during infancy /ɪn ˈɪnfənsi, ˌdjʊərɪŋ ˈɪnfənsi‖ˌdʊər-/ [n U] **formal** while someone is a baby or a very young child – use this especially to talk about children dying or getting diseases: *Three of her children died in infancy.*

choose

RELATED WORDS

- ▸ choose to do something *see* **decide**
- ▸ *see also* **vote**

1 to decide which one you want

- ▸ **choose**
- ▸ **pick**
- ▸ **select**
- ▸ **go for**
- ▸ **make a choice**
- ▸ **take your pick**

choose /tʃuːz/ [v I/T] to decide which one of several things or possibilities you want: *I can't decide what I want. You choose.* | *Will you help me choose a present for Warren?* | **+ to do sth** *Why do so few women choose to become engineers?* | **+ whether/which/when etc** *It took her three hours to choose which dress to wear.* | **+ between** (=choose one of two things) *We have to choose between doing geography or studying another language.* | **+ from** (=choose from among several things) *Import restrictions will reduce the number of cars buyers have to choose from.*

pick /pɪk/ [v T] **informal** to choose something, especially without thinking very carefully about it: *Pick a number from one to five.* | *Let me pick the movie tonight – I don't want to see another comedy.*

select /sə̇ˈlekt/ [v T] **formal** to choose something by carefully thinking about which is the best or most suitable: *It's very important that parents select the right school for a child with learning difficulties.* | *Our wines have been carefully selected from vineyards throughout Europe.* | **select sth from sth** *The team's name was selected from more than 1,700 suggestions.*

go for /ˈgəʊ fɔːʳ/ [phr v T] **spoken informal** to choose something because you think it is the most attractive, interesting, or enjoyable: *I don't usually go for horror movies.* | *Whenever we eat out, she always goes for the most expensive thing on the menu.*

make a choice /ˌmeɪk ə ˈtʃɔɪs/ [v phrase] to make a decision, especially a difficult decision, about which thing to choose: *I felt I was being forced to make a choice between my family and my job.* | *It had been difficult to leave her unhappy marriage, but she had made her choice.* | **make the right/wrong choice** *Sean's decided to study law – I hope he's made the right choice.*

take your pick /ˌteɪk jɔːʳ ˈpɪk/ [v phrase] if someone can **take their pick**, they can choose exactly the thing that they want without anything limiting their choice: *She showed me the box of kittens and told me I could take my pick.* | *With so many houses for sale, buyers with cash can take their pick.* | **+ of** *The program's top graduate took her pick of five job offers.*

2 to finally choose something after considering all the possibilities

- ▸ **decide on**
- ▸ **settle on**
- ▸ **plump for**
- ▸ **opt**

decide on /dɪˈsaɪd ɒn/ [phr v T] to finally choose something, especially when making the decision has been difficult or has taken a long time: *Have you decided on a name for the baby yet?* | *We couldn't* *decide on a new color for the kitchen, so we left it white.*

settle on /ˈsetl ɒn / [phr v T] if someone, especially a group of people, **settles on** something, they finally agree to choose that thing after considering all the possibilities, discussing it etc: *Hiroaki wanted white and I wanted black, so we settled on grey.* | *Can we at least settle on a date for our next meeting?* | *We finally settled on Miami as the site of our next conference.*

plump for /ˈplʌmp fɔːʳ/ [phr v T not in passive] British informal to choose one of two or more things after thinking carefully about it, especially if you have had difficulty in deciding: *They thought of going to Madeira or mainland Spain, but finally plumped for the Canary Islands.* | *She looked at every sweater in the shop before plumping for a red mohair one.*

opt /ɒpt‖ɑːpt/ [v I] to choose something after thinking carefully about all the possibilities **+ for** *After college, Ruffin opted for the Army over college.* | **+ to do sth** *When her parents divorced, Mary Ann opted to live with her father.*

3 to choose one person or thing from among a lot of similar things

- single out
- pick out

single out /ˌsɪŋgəl ˈaʊt/ [phr v T] to choose someone or something from among a group of similar people or things, especially in order to praise them or criticize them **single out sb/sth** *Could you single out one factor that is more important than the others?* | **single sb/sth out** *His teacher was always singling him out, calling on him when his hand wasn't even raised.* | **single sb/sth out for sth** *Captain Withers was singled out for special mention and was awarded the Military Cross.*

pick out /ˌpɪk ˈaʊt/ [phr v T] to consider a group of similar people or things and to choose the one that you like most **pick out sb/sth** *He looked through the tourist guide and picked out a few exhibitions to see while he was in town.* | **pick sb/sth out** *The editor looked through the file, picking the best models out for the fashion shoot.*

4 to choose someone for a job or team

- choose
- select
- appoint
- pick
- name
- nominate
- be shortlisted
- tap

choose /tʃuːz/ [v T] to decide who is the best person for a job, team, prize etc: *Companies are now using computers to help them choose new workers.* | **choose sb as sth** *The board has unanimously chosen Cole as Gray's temporary replacement.* | **choose sb to do sth** *Eventually, Jane was chosen to deliver the message.*

select /sə̇ˈlekt/ [v T] formal to choose someone for a particular job, team, place at school etc, after considering a lot of different people who might be suitable: *The college selects only twelve students a year from the thousands who apply.* | **select sb for sth** *We selected four applicants for interview.* | **select sb to do sth** *Ernst had been selected to play in the game against Belgium.*

appoint /əˈpɔɪnt/ [v T] to officially choose someone to do an important job: *The company has appointed a new sales director.* | **appoint sb to sth** *Simpson has been appointed to the Memphis Branch board for a three-year term.* | **appoint sb as sth** *They have appointed Jane Staller as their new East Coast manager.* | **appoint sb to do sth** *A committee was appointed to consider changes to the Prison Service.*

pick /pɪk/ [v T] to choose someone for a sports team or an important job: *The class was divided into four teams, and each group was asked to pick a leader.* | **pick sb to do sth** *Joe picked Steve and Terry to be on his team.* | **pick sb for sth** *Do you think he might pick another woman for the Supreme Court?*

name /neɪm/ [v T] to publicly say who has been chosen for an important job in an organization: *The editor of 'The Times' has resigned amid a political storm. His successor has not yet been named.* | **name sb to sth** *McCarthy was recently named to the Small Business Committee.* | **name sb as sth** *The magazine has named Bonnie Fuller as deputy editor.* | **name sb sth** *We are naming Dr Bob McClure head of the IRC in China.*

nominate /ˈnɒmə̇neɪt‖ˈnɑː-/ [v T] if someone, especially a group of people, **nominates** someone, they officially choose that person to be considered for a particular job **nominate sb to sth** *Mills is expected to be formally nominated to the board next month.* | **nominate sb to do sth** *Lee was the first Chinese American nominated to head the Civil Rights Division.* | **nominate sb as sth** *They nominated her as the British spokesperson at the International Arms Conference.*

be shortlisted /biː ˈʃɔːʳtlɪstə̇d/ British **/be on the short list** /biː ɒn ðə ˈʃɔːʳt lɪst/ [v phrase] if you **are shortlisted** or **on the short list** for a job or a position, you are one of a small group of people who have been chosen from other people who want the job, and from that small group one person will be chosen: *Three applicants have been shortlisted and will be invited for interview next week.* | **+ for** *He's been on the President's short list for the job twice.*

tap /tæp/ [v T] American to officially choose someone for an important job **tap sb for sth** *Reinhardt was tapped for the federal bench in 1980 by former President Carter.*

5 to choose someone or something for a particular purpose

- choose

choose /tʃuːz/ [v T] *A committee will be selected to choose the new leader.* | **choose sb/sth as sth** *Seattle has been chosen as the venue for next year's conference.* | **choose sb/sth for sth** *Many of the industries chosen for government investment have in fact already gone bankrupt.* | **choose sb/sth to do sth** *The fabric that she chose to be made into a dress is a combination of silk and cotton.*

6 the decision you make when you choose

- choice

choice /tʃɔɪs/ [n C/U] *It was a difficult choice, but we finally decided that Hannah should have the prize.* | *The board denied that financial considerations had influenced their choice.* | *Patients are demanding greater choice in the type of treatment they get.* | **freedom of choice** (=when you can choose for yourself) *I don't believe in fate – we all have freedom of choice.* | **by choice** (=without being influenced by other people) *He says he lives on the street by choice.*

7 something or someone that has been chosen

- choice
- selection
- chosen
- selected
- handpicked/hand-picked
- of your choice

choice /tʃɔɪs/ [n singular] something or someone that has been chosen: *Maria was very pleased with her choice.* | **first/second/third choice** (=the thing you wanted most, the thing you wanted most after that etc) *Greece was our first choice for a vacation, but all the flights were full.* | **sb's choice of** *I don't like his choice of friends.*

selection /sə̇ˈlekʃən/ [n C usually singular] a small group of the best things that have been chosen from a larger group **+ of** *She showed me a selection of her drawings.* | *a selection of songs from 'West Side Story'*

chosen /ˈtʃəʊzən/ [adj only before noun] use this about the person or thing that has been chosen: *I want my children to be successful in their chosen careers.* | *You have two minutes to answer questions on your chosen subject.* | **well-chosen** (=carefully and successfully chosen) *The flavorful vegetables require only melted butter and some well-chosen herbs.*

selected /sə̇ˈlektə̇d/ [adj only before noun] carefully chosen from a larger group, usually for a particular purpose: *There is a discount of 10% off selected items in this store.* | *The book is a collection of selected essays by D.H.Lawrence.* | **specially/carefully selected** *A small and carefully selected group of friends has been invited to the wedding.*

handpicked/hand-picked /ˌhændˈpɪkt◂/ [adj] people who are **hand-picked** have been specially chosen by someone because they are the best or most suitable people for a particular job, position etc: *The school is staffed with handpicked educators and psychiatric specialists.* | *With a small, hand-picked squad of ex-paratroopers, Collins managed to get through the defences.*

of your choice /əv jɔːʳ ˈtʃɔɪs/ [adj phrase] something **of your choice** has been chosen by you, with nothing limiting which one you choose: *The magician told her to hold up three cards of her choice.* | *You could win a fabulous weekend break at a luxurious hotel of your choice.*

8 the things or people that you can choose from

- choice
- option
- alternative
- selection
- to choose from

choice /tʃɔɪs/ [n singular/U] **+ of** *The school seems OK, but there isn't a great choice of courses.* | **have a choice** (=be able to choose from several things) *With her high grades and athletic skill, Celeste had her choice of colleges.* | **have no choice but to do sth** (=to be forced to do something because there is nothing else you can choose) *Spooner says he had no choice but to file for bankruptcy.* | **wide choice** (=a lot of things to choose from) *There is a wide choice of hotels and hostels in the town.*

option /ˈɒpʃən‖ˈɑːp-/ [n C] one of the things that you can choose to do in a particular situation: *He basically has two options: he can have the surgery, or he can give up playing football.* | **keep/leave your options open** (=delay choosing so that you continue to have several things to choose from) *I haven't signed any contracts yet – I want to keep my options open.*

alternative /ɔːlˈtɜːʳnətɪv‖ɔːl-, æl-/ [n C] one of two or more ways of doing something: *Did you consider other alternatives before you moved in with Lucy?* | **+ to** *There is no practical alternative to our current policy.* | **have no alternative** (=to not have a choice) *He says he doesn't want to see a doctor, but I'm afraid he has no alternative.*

selection /sə̇ˈlekʃən/ [n singular] a lot of things of a similar type for you to choose from, especially in a shop **+ of** *A wonderful selection of cakes and pastries was displayed in the window.* | **wide/large selection** *The restaurant offers a wide selection of local dishes.*

to choose from /tə ˈtʃuːz frɒm/ [adj phrase] if there is a particular range of things or people **to choose from**, you can choose what you want from that range: *There are a lot of good restaurants downtown to choose from.* | *Portland has so many theaters to choose from.*

9 when you are very careful about choosing things

- choosy
- fussy/picky
- be particular about
- selective
- shop around

choosy /ˈtʃuːzi/ [adj] informal someone who is **choosy** chooses things carefully and only wants the things they think are the best: *I get offered a lot of work now, so I can be more choosy.* | **+ about** *She's very choosy about what airline she travels on.*

fussy/picky /ˈfʌsi, ˈpɪki/ [adj] informal someone who is **fussy** or **picky** is difficult to please because they only like a few things and will only accept exactly what they want: *Maybe I'm too picky, but all the guys I meet seem so boring.* | **+ about** *She was always very fussy about her clothes.* | **picky/fussy eater** (=someone who will only eat the few things they like) *We're not really picky eaters, but we don't eat much fast food.*

be particular about /biː pəʳˈtɪkjə̇lər əbaʊt/ [v phrase] to be very careful about choosing only the very best of something, or only exactly what you like, usually with the result that people think you are too careful about it **+ about** *He's very particular about the clothes he buys.* | **be particular about what/where etc** *Monica is particular about what she eats – no meat, and only organic vegetables.*

selective /sə̇ˈlektɪv/ [adj] someone who is **selective** chooses things very carefully because they want to choose the best, most suitable etc: *You've got to be very selective when choosing a roommate.* | **+ about** *People are becoming more and more selective about the food they eat these days.*

shop around /ˌʃɒp əˈraʊnd‖ˌʃɑːp-/ [phr v I] informal to look at or try several different possibilities before choosing the one which is the best, cheapest etc: *Never buy the first car you see. Always shop around.* | *Shop around a little bit before you choose a therapist.* | **+ for** *You should shop around for a better price.*

circle

RELATED WORDS

- go around, move in a circle *see* **around/round**
- shaped like a ball *see* **round**
- *see also* **shape**

1 a circle

- **circle**
- **ring**
- **loop**

circle /'sɜːʳkəl/ [n C] an area or line that is in the shape of a circle: *The teacher drew a circle on the blackboard.* | *The circle of stones at Stonehenge is thought to have originally been a temple.* | *The flashlight threw a dim circle of light onto the wall.* | **in a circle** (=in a shape like a circle) *We all stood in a circle and tossed the ball to each other.* | **form a circle** (=to make a group of people or things in the shape of a circle) *I want you to form two circles, one inside the other. Boys on the outside, girls on the inside.*

ring /rɪŋ/ [n C] a line that is in the shape of a circle, especially of people or things surrounding something: *The cottage was surrounded by a ring of trees.* | *The cup left a dark ring on the table.* | *The hostage's wrists had red rings on them where the ropes had been pulled tight.* | **in a ring** (=in a shape like a circle) *The children sat around him in a ring, eager to hear his story.*

loop /luːp/ [n C] a shape like a curve or a circle made by a line curving back towards itself: *The road goes round in a loop and rejoins the main road about 2 kilometres past the town.*

2 shaped like a circle

- **round**
- **circular**

round /raʊnd/ [adj] shaped like a circle: *In the kitchen there was a round table with a vase of flowers on it.* | *Violet stared at him with her huge round eyes.* | *The moon was perfectly round that night.*

circular /'sɜːʳkjᵊləʳ/ [adj] shaped like a circle, or moving in the shape of a circle: *The cattle are kept in a large enclosure surrounded by a circular fence.* | *The villa has a circular courtyard with rooms leading off it in all directions.* | *The procession follows a circular route through the town, and finishes back in the park.*

3 shaped like a circle but with two slightly flat sides

- **oval**
- **egg-shaped**
- **elliptical**

oval /'əʊvəl/ [adj] *In the dining room is a highly polished oval table with matching chairs.* | *She was a pretty woman with an oval face.*

egg-shaped /'eg ʃeɪpt/ [adj] shaped like an egg, slightly wider at one end: *The chocolates are egg-shaped and full of nuts.*

elliptical /ɪ'lɪptɪkəl/ [adj] shaped like a circle but with two slightly flat sides: *The earth moves around the sun in an elliptical orbit.* | *A striking feature of this architectural style is the elliptical windows.*

4 something that is shaped like a circle

- **ring**
- **disk**
- **loop**

ring /rɪŋ/ [n C] an object that is in the shape of a circle with a large round space in the middle: *Cut the onion into rings and fry in a little oil.* | *You have to throw the wooden rings so that they land around the bottles.* | *He sat in a corner blowing smoke rings.*

disk ALSO **disc** British /dɪsk/ [n C] an object that is in the shape of a flat circle: *He gazed up at the pale yellow disk of the moon.* | *Each player chooses a coloured disk and places it on the board in the space marked 'go'.*

loop /luːp/ [n C] something such as a piece of string or wire that is curved round to make a shape almost like a circle: *The gate was attached to the post by a loop of rusty wire.* | *Pull the end of the string through the loop and tighten.*

5 to draw a circle around something

- **circle/ring**

circle/ring /'sɜːʳkəl, rɪŋ/ [v T] to draw a **circle** around something that is written or drawn on a page, especially in order to make it easier to see or notice: *Two of the advertisements in the paper had been circled.* | *Someone had ringed all the important landmarks on the map in pencil.*

6 half a circle

- **semicircle**

semicircle /'semɪˌsɜːʳkəl/ [n C] *Behind the beach is a huge semicircle of limestone cliffs.* | **in a semicircle** *The teacher had arranged the desks in a semicircle.* —**semicircular** /ˌsemɪ'sɜːʳkjᵊləʳ◂/ [adj] *We ate at a small semicircular table which stood against the wall.*

clap

to hit your hands together to show how much you like someone or something

RELATED WORDS

- *see also* **watch, perform/performance, praise**

1 to clap

- **clap**
- **applaud**
- **cheer**
- **applause**
- **standing ovation**

clap /klæp/ [v I/T] to hit your hands together loudly and quickly to show that you approve of and are pleased with a play, someone's performance, someone's actions etc: *The audience cheered and clapped as the curtain came down.* | *Fans usually clap the batsman when he leaves the field.* | **clap your hands** *A crowd gathered to watch the runners, clapping their hands and urging them on.* —**clapping** [n U] *After a while the clapping died down.*

applaud /ə'plɔːd/ [v I/T] if people **applaud**, they clap excitedly, and often for a long time, in order to show how much they liked something or to show their support for someone: *The crowd applauded when Evans promised to cut taxes.* | *A group of supporters applauded the strikers as they were led into court.*

heer /tʃɪəʳ/ [v I/T] to give a loud, happy shout expressing admiration, approval, and often excitement, for example at a sports event or after a speech: *The audience were now on their feet, cheering wildly.* | *Thousands of people lined Broadway to cheer the Yankees and celebrate their World Series triumph.* —**cheer** [n C] *A great cheer went up when the first goal was scored.* | *Three cheers for the next Governor of Nebraska!* —**cheering** [n U] *The cheering went on for ages as the victorious athletes ran around the track.*

pplause /əˈplɔːz/ [n U] the sound of a crowd of people clapping and cheering someone, to show their approval and admiration: *There was loud applause when the band members ran onto the stage.* | **a round of applause** (=a short period of applause) *The candidate's promise to improve public schools was greeted with a loud round of applause.* | **applause dies down** (=gradually stops) *The conductor waited for the applause to die down before signalling for the orchestra to begin.*

tanding ovation /ˌstændɪŋ əʊˈveɪʃən/ [n C] if someone receives a **standing ovation** at the end of a performance or speech, the people who are watching or listening to them stand up, clap, and cheer, to show their approval and admiration: *Miller got a standing ovation when he entered the game.* | **give sb/sth a standing ovation** *The speech was given a standing ovation.*

2 what you say when you want someone to clap

- give sb a (big) hand
- give it up for sb
- put your hands together

ive sb a (big) hand /ˌgɪv (sb) ə ˌbɪg ˈhænd/ [v phrase] spoken if people **give** a performer **a big hand**, they clap at the end of their performance, to encourage them and to show their approval – use this especially to ask people to do this: *Let's give young Suzy a big hand for the marvellous dancing display!*

ive it up for sb /ˌgɪv ɪt ˈʌp fəʳ (sb)/ [v phrase] spoken informal use this to tell people to clap in order to show that they have enjoyed something, or approve of someone: *Come on everyone, let's give it up for Tom Jones!*

ut your hands together /ˌpʊt jɔːʳ ˈhændz təˌgeðəʳ/ [v phrase] spoken use this to tell people to clap to show their approval for someone who is being introduced or a performance: *Ladies and gentlemen, put your hands together and give a warm welcome to Ricardo Montalban!*

3 to show that you dislike a person or a performance

- boo
- hiss
- jeer

oo /buː/ [v I/T] to shout 'boo' to show that you do not like a speaker, performance etc: *Some people in the crowd booed when she walked on stage.* | *Taylor was booed as he left the field.* —**boo** [n C] *Keough denied that the boos affected his performance.*

iss /hɪs/ [v I/T] to make a noise which sounds like 'ssss' to show that you do not like a speaker, performance etc: *Relatives of the victim hissed as the killer was led from the courtroom.* | **+ at** *Hundreds of people shouted and hissed at the prime minister.* —**hiss** [n C] *This announcement was greeted with boos and hisses.*

jeer /dʒɪəʳ/ [v I/T] to shout rude remarks at someone or laugh unkindly at them to show that you strongly disapprove of them or their performance: *The fans jeered as it became obvious that their team was going to lose.* | *The mayor was jeered and booed as he tried to speak to the crowd.* —**jeer** [n C] *The audience interrupted the candidate's speech with jeers and shouts.*

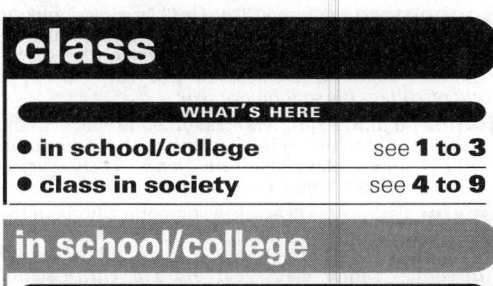

class

WHAT'S HERE

- **in school/college** see **1 to 3**
- **class in society** see **4 to 9**

in school/college

RELATED WORDS

- *see also* **teach, learn, study, school/university**

1 a group of students in a school, college etc

- class
- grade
- form
- year
- set
- freshman
- sophomore
- junior
- senior

class /klɑːs‖klæs/ [n C] a group of students or schoolchildren who are taught together: *There are twenty kids in the class.* | *She gets along well with the other children in her class.* | *I'm going out with some friends from my dance class.* | *I graduated in 1999. What class were you in?*

grade /greɪd/ [n C] a class or group of classes for children of a particular age in an American school **third/seventh/twelfth etc grade** *She's in the fifth grade.* | *I really liked my eighth grade math teacher.* | *The second grade class is doing a play about the Pilgrims.* —**third-/fourth-/fifth- etc grader** /ˌθɜːʳd ˈgreɪdəʳ/ [n C] a child in the third, fourth, fifth etc grade: *According to the test, 40% of fourth-graders are not reading at the basic level.*

form /fɔːʳm/ [n C] a class or a group of classes for all the children of the same age in a British school for children between 11 and 18: *She's by far the brightest pupil in the form.* | **third/fourth/fifth etc form** *I'm in the third form.* | *Mrs Davies took the fifth form to the science museum.* —**third-/fourth-/fifth- etc former** /ˈθɜːʳd ˌfɔːʳməʳ/ [n C] a child in the third, fourth, fifth etc form: *Some of the fifth-formers have started a rock band.*

year /jɪəʳ, jɜːʳ‖jɪər/ [n C] all the classes for children of a particular age in a British school or for students in a particular **year** of study at a British university: *He works a lot harder than most of the students in his year.* | **third/fourth/fifth etc year** *There are 130 children in the second year.* | *I hated teaching the fifth year. They were always causing trouble.* —**third-/fourth-/fifth- etc year** /ˈθɜːʳd jɪəʳ/ [n C] a student in the third, fourth, fifth etc year: *A group of fourth-years are collecting money for food aid to Africa.*

set /set/ [n C] a class for children with a particular level of ability in a British school: *She's in set one for* *maths and English and set two for history.* | *I was useless at school – always in the bottom set in every subject.* | *We think you've improved sufficiently to go up to a higher set.*

freshman /ˈfreʃmən/ [n C] American someone who is in the first year at a high school or university: *We were only freshmen, so the older kids liked to pick on us.* | **freshman class/year/course etc** *Chris remembers his freshman year at UCLA as if it were yesterday.*

sophomore /ˈsɒfəmɔːʳ‖ˈsɑː-/ [n C] American someone who is in the second year at a high school or university: *This class is mainly for freshmen and sophomores.* | **sophomore class/year etc** *George dropped out of college his sophomore year.*

junior /ˈdʒuːniəʳ/ [n C] American someone who is in the third year at a high school or university: *a junior at NYU* | **junior class/year etc** *Donna spent spring semester of her junior year in Paris.*

senior /ˈsiːniəʳ/ [n C] American someone who is in the fourth and final year at a high school or university: *I can't believe that Cari is a high school senior already.* | **senior class/year etc** *The entire senior class took a trip to Disneyworld.*

2 the period of time during which a class is taught

- class
- lesson
- period
- session
- lecture
- seminar
- tutorial

class /klɑːs‖klæs/ [n C/U] a period of time, usually about 30 minutes to one hour, in which a teacher teaches a group of students: *Heidi fainted during French class today!* | *Let's go – I have my first class in 10 minutes!*

lesson /ˈlesən/ [n C] a period in which someone teaches one person or a group of people – use this especially about practical skills such as music, swimming, or driving, or in British English about a class in a school: *Dominic will be having his first driving lesson this Thursday.* | *She gives English lessons to business people in the evenings.*

period /ˈpɪəriəd/ [n C] one of the periods of time that a school day is divided into: *At our school we have four periods in the morning and three in the afternoon.* | **double period** British (=one class which lasts for two periods) *On Monday mornings there was French, English, and then a double period of maths.*

session /ˈseʃən/ [n C] the period of time in which a particular subject or a particular area of a subject is taught, especially when this is one of a fixed number of classes: *We have 5 hours of English a week, including one session in the language laboratory.*

lecture /ˈlektʃəʳ/ [n C] a long talk on a subject, given by a teacher at a college or university, and listened to by a large number of students **+ on** *a lecture on the causes of the Russian Revolution* | **give a lecture** *Professor Blair is giving a series of lectures on Einstein's theories.*

seminar /ˈseməˌnɑːʳ/ [n C] a class, usually at a college or university, where a teacher and small group of students discuss a subject **+ on** *Every week we have a seminar on modern political theory.*

tutorial /tjuːˈtɔːriəl‖tuː-/ [n C] a regular class at a British college or university during which a teacher discusses a particular subject with one student or with a small group of students: *Small group tutorials are used to discuss problems which come up in lectures.* | *Oxford's one-to-one tutorials are a effective but also costly way of teaching.*

3 a series of lessons in one subject

- course

course /kɔːʳs/ ALSO **class** /klɑːs‖klæs/ [n C] *Are yo enjoying the course?* | **+ in/on** *a course in music jou nalism* | **language/computer/history etc cours class** *The college is offering three basic comput courses this year.* | **take a course/class** ALSO **do course** British informal *She's taking a class in art histor*

class in society

RELATED WORDS

- political, legal, or social rights *see* **right 9-12**
- *see also* **come from, poor, rich, position/rank, person/people**

4 someone's social class

- class
- background
- status
- caste

class /klɑːs‖klæs/ [n C/U] the social group that yc belong to because of your job, the type of family yc come from, or the amount of money you have: *Su cess in this country seems to be based on class rath than on ability.* | *the professional and manageri classes* | **the class system** (=the system by whic society is divided into classes) *The old class syste is slowly disappearing.* | **social class** (=the class society you come from) *There is a clear link betwe social class and educational achievement.* | **class di tinctions** (=differences between social classe *Some people argue that class distinctions do not exi in the U.S., but this is untrue.*

background /ˈbækgraʊnd/ [n C] the type of hon and family you come from, and its social class: *T school takes kids from all sorts of backgrounds.* | *V come from the same town and share a similar bac ground.* | **working-class/middle-class etc bac ground** *The organization helps children fro working-class backgrounds to go to university.*

status /ˈsteɪtəs‖ˈsteɪtəs, ˈstæ-/ [n U] someone's pos tion in society, according to how much other peop respect them, especially because of the kind of jc they have: *Now that he was a bank manager, wanted a car that would reflect his status.* | **high/lo status** *Many mothers feel that they have very low st tus in today's society.* | **status symbol** (=somethir that someone owns in order to show their high st tus) *The latest mobile phones have become stat symbols among teenagers.*

caste /kɑːst‖kæst/ [n C] a fixed division of people society according to the family they are born int especially within the Hindu religion: *In the south India there are up to 20 different castes.* | **caste sy tem** *Buddha was a social reformer who condemn India's caste system.*

5 belonging to the highest class

- upper-class
- aristocracy
- privileged
- elite
- posh

upper-class /ˌʌpəʳ ˈklɑːs◂‖-ˈklæs◂/ [adj] belongi to the class of people who originally had most of t money and power, especially families that own a l of land: *Most senior politicians in the UK are from upper-class families.* | *He spoke with an upper-class accent.* —**the upper class/the upper classes** [n singular or plural] people who are upper class: *In South America, the upper classes tend to be of European origin.*

aristocracy /ˌærɪ̇ˈstɒkrəsi‖-ˈstɑː-/ [n singular] the people who belong to families that own a lot of land, and used to have a lot of power, and have special titles before their names, like 'Lord' or 'Lady' – used especially when you are talking about the past **the aristocracy** *Daughters of rich merchants would often marry into the aristocracy.* —**aristocratic** /ˌærɪstəˈkrætɪk◂, əˌrɪ-‖əˌrɪ-/ [adj] *old aristocratic families*

privileged /ˈprɪvɪ̇lɪdʒd/ [adj] having a high position in society that has special, and usually unfair, advantages such as power, money and the best education: *In many countries today only a privileged minority get the chance of going to university.* —**privilege** [n U] *Her comments about immigrants revealed an astonishing sense of privilege and arrogance.*

elite /eɪˈliːt, ɪ-/ [n C with singular or plural verb in British English] a small group of rich and powerful people who have special, unfair advantages that other people do not have: *The President has been accused of developing policies in favor of a small elite.* | *The sort of goods once reserved for the elite are now available to everyone.* —**elitist** [adj] *The British House of Lords is seen by many as an elitist institution.*

posh /pɒʃ‖pɑːʃ/ [adj] British spoken use this about someone who behaves and speaks in a way in which upper-class people usually behave or speak: *Will your posh university friends be coming tonight?* | **posh school/hotel/restaurant etc** (=one that is very expensive, that rich people go to) *She went to a posh girls' school in Switzerland.*

6 the middle class

- middle-class
- bourgeois
- the bourgeoisie
- white-collar

middle-class /ˌmɪdl ˈklɑːs◂‖-ˈklæs◂/ [adj] belonging to the class of people who are usually well educated, fairly rich, and who work in jobs which they have trained to do. For example, doctors, lawyers, and managers are middle-class: *The newspaper's readers are mostly middle class.* | *They live in a middle-class neighbourhood on the edge of town.* —**the middle class/the middle classes** [n singular or plural] people who are middle class: *The government needs the support of the middle classes to win the next election.*

bourgeois /ˈbʊəʒwɑː‖bʊərˈʒwɑː/ [adj] typical of richer middle-class people and their attitudes or way of life, especially their concern with money, property, and correct social behaviour: *She rejected her parents' conventional bourgeois lifestyle.* | *They never married because they believed that marriage was a bourgeois institution.*

the bourgeoisie /ðə ˌbʊəʳʒwɑːˈziː/ [n singular with singular or plural verb in British English] the class that owns most of the wealth, property, and industry – use this especially when you are talking about politics or history: *The poor viewed with envy the increasing wealth of the bourgeoisie.* | *A revolution would be a threat to the nation's bourgeoisie.*

white-collar /ˌwaɪt ˈkɒləʳ◂‖-ˈkɑː-/ [adj only before noun] **white-collar worker/job/employee** someone who works in an office, not a factory, mine etc: *The economic recession has put many white-collar workers in danger of losing their jobs.*

7 the lowest class

- working-class
- lower-class
- the masses
- blue-collar
- humble
- underclass

working-class /ˌwɜːʳkɪŋ ˈklɑːs◂‖-ˈklæs◂/ [adj] belonging to the class of people who do not have much money or power, and who have jobs where they do physical work. For example, factory workers, builders, and drivers are **working-class**: *Most of the people who live round here are working class.* | *I come from a working-class family – I'm the first one to graduate from college.* —**the working class/the working classes** [n singular or plural] people who are working class: *Cuts in welfare spending affect the working class most.*

lower-class /ˌləʊəʳ ˈklɑːs◂‖-ˈklæs◂/ [adj] an impolite word meaning belonging to the class that has less money, power, and education than anyone else: *It has been shown that children of lower-class parents are less likely to do well at school.* | *My mother's parents thought my father was terribly lower-class.* —**the lower class/the lower classes** [n singular or plural] *There was a time when tequila was a cheap product drunk only by the lower classes.*

the masses /ðə ˈmæsɪ̇z/ [n plural] all the ordinary people in society who do not have power or influence, especially when they are thought of as not being very educated: *Television has brought cheap entertainment to the masses.* | *Lenin's position depended on the support of the masses.*

blue-collar /ˌbluː ˈkɒləʳ◂‖-ˈkɑː-/ [adj only before noun] **blue-collar worker/job/employee** someone who does physical work, for example in a factory or a mine, and does not work in an office: *His political support comes mainly from blue-collar workers.*

humble /ˈhʌmbəl/ [adj] **of (a) humble background/family/origins etc** from a low social class and without much money, but often with a lot of determination to work hard and succeed: *The school had originally provided a good education for children of humble backgrounds.* | *Eisenhower, Nixon, and Ford were all men of humble origins and no inherited wealth.*

underclass /ˈʌndəʳklɑːs‖-klæs/ [n singular] the lowest social class, who are very poor and may not have jobs, homes etc: *The government has created an underclass who do not feel they have any rights in society.*

8 to move into a higher social class

- move/go up in the world
- upwardly mobile
- social climber

move/go up in the world /ˌmuːv, ˌgəʊ ˈʌp ɪn ðə ˌwɜːʳld/ [v phrase] *Hillary was bright and ambitious and wanted to move up in the world.* | *Education, he believed, was the only way that anyone could move up in the world.*

upwardly mobile /ˌʌpwəʳdli ˈməʊbaɪl‖-ˈməʊbəl/ [adj phrase] someone who is **upwardly mobile** is in the process of moving into a higher class, especially because they have a well-paid job: *a highly educated, upwardly mobile young woman* | *The dating agency specializes in finding partners for the young and upwardly mobile.*

social climber /ˌsəʊʃəl ˈklaɪməʳ/ [n C] someone who wants very much to move into a higher social class, and tries to do this by becoming friendly with people who have more money and power than they do: *The new private schools cater for the children of social climbers rather than those of the old upper classes.* | *The hotel lobby was full of the usual hangers-on and social climbers.*

9 someone who thinks they are better than people from a lower social class

- snobbish
- snob
- stuck-up

snobbish /ˈsnɒbɪʃ‖ˈsnɑːb-/ [adj] someone who is **snobbish** thinks that they are better than people from a lower social class: *Snobbish home-owners are protesting about a refugee family moving into their street.* | *Aunt Harriet was very rich and very snobbish.*

snob /snɒb‖snɑːb/ [n C] someone who thinks that they are better than people from a lower social class, and does not want to talk to them or be friends with them: *My mother was such a snob she wouldn't let me play with the local children.* | *They're just a bunch of snobs – you wouldn't want to be friends with them anyway.*

stuck-up /ˌstʌk ˈʌp/ [adj] informal proud and unfriendly because you think you are better and more important than other people: *Tanya is so stuck-up. She won't go out with anyone who went to a state college.* | *the spoiled, stuck-up daughter of a millionaire*

clean

RELATED WORDS

opposite: **dirty**

- clean something with water, soap etc *see* **wash**
- to remove dirt, marks etc from something *see* **remove (3-4, 7)**
- *see also* **tidy, shine/shiny**

1 not dirty

- clean
- spotlessly clean/spotless
- immaculate
- spick and span

clean /kliːn/ [adj] not dirty: *He changed into a clean shirt.* | *I'll put some clean sheets on the bed.* | *A large house is difficult to keep clean.* | **nice and clean/lovely and clean** British (=very clean) *Our hotel room was lovely and clean.*

spotlessly clean/spotless /ˌspɒtləsli ˈkliːn‖ˌspɑːt-, ˈspɒtləs‖ˈspɑːt-/ [adj] completely clean – use this especially about clothes, rooms, or houses: *Nina keeps the kitchen absolutely spotless.* | *He was wearing a spotlessly clean white shirt.*

immaculate /ɪˈmækjələt/ [adj] things that are **immaculate** are completely clean and look new: *She wore an immaculate grey suit and a tasteful, blue woven hat.* | *The house was absolutely immaculate.*

spick and span /ˌspɪk ən ˈspæn/ [adj phrase] a room or house that is **spick and span** is very clean and tidy: *Every room in the house was spick and span.* | *We'll have the place spick and span in no time.*

2 completely clean so that diseases cannot spread

- clean
- pure
- hygienic
- sterile

clean /kliːn/ [adj] *Three out of five people in develo[p]ing countries have no easy access to clean water.* *The department is responsible for maintaining th[e] bedrooms and public rooms in a clean and sanitar[y] condition.*

pure /pjʊəʳ/ [adj] water or air that is **pure** is com[-]pletely clean and does not contain anything harm[-]ful such as dirt or bacteria: *It felt good to get awa[y] from the city and breathe in some pure mountai[n] air.* | *The water in the lake is so pure you can drink i[t]* —**purity** /ˈpjʊərəti/ [n U] *There is concern about th[e] purity of our tap water.*

hygienic /haɪˈdʒiːnɪk‖-ˈdʒe-, -ˈdʒiː-/ [adj] extremel[y] clean so that diseases are unlikely to spread[:] *Cleansall kills germs as well, leaving your kitche[n] clean and hygienic.* | **hygienic conditions** *Meat prod[-]ucts must always be kept in hygienic conditions.*

sterile /ˈsteraɪl‖-rəl/ [adj] completely clean, fre[e] from bacteria, and safe for medical or scientific pu[r]poses: *Red Cross officials say they are running shor[t] of disinfectant and sterile bandages.* | *Giving bloo[d] is perfectly safe. All equipment is sterile, used onc[e] and thrown away.*

3 when you keep things clean to prevent disease

- hygiene
- disinfect
- sterilize

hygiene /ˈhaɪdʒiːn/ [n U] the practice of keepin[g] yourself and the place where you live or work clea[n] so that diseases cannot spread: *Restaurants may b[e] closed down if they fail to maintain minimum stan[-]dards of hygiene.* | *Schools should have policies t[o] ensure good hygiene in kitchen areas.* | **persona[l] hygiene** (=the practice of keeping your body clean[)] *A healthy lifestyle includes having a nutritious di[et] and good personal hygiene.*

disinfect /ˌdɪsənˈfekt/ [v T] to use chemicals to clea[n] a place, a piece of equipment, or a wound, in orde[r] to prevent disease: *The nurse cleaned and disin[-]fected the cuts on his hands.* | *Disinfect the toilet reg[-]ularly using bleach.*

sterilize ALSO **sterilise** British /ˈsterəlaɪz/ [v T] t[o] make something safe to use by heating it or usin[g] chemicals, in order to kill all bacteria and preven[t] disease – use this about medical or scientific equip[-]ment, or babies' bottles: *Has the needle been steri[l]ized?* | *Babies' bottles can be sterilized simply b[y] boiling them in water.*

4 to clean a room, house etc

- clean
- clean out
- spring-clean
- housework

clean /kliːn/ [v I/T] to make something **clean** b[y] removing the dirt, dust etc: *I clean the window[s] every Saturday.* | *Tony was cleaning the inside of hi[s] car.* | *How often do you clean the kitchen?* | **clean st[h] up/clean up sth** (=remove dirt by cleaning, espe[-]cially in a room, from a floor etc) *There was mud a[ll] over the carpet, and it took me a long time to clean [it] up.* | **clean your teeth** British *I always clean my teet[h]* *last thing at night.* | **+ behind/under etc** *Make sure you clean behind the stove.* —**cleaning** [n U] when you clean things, especially in a room, or a house: *I spent the whole weekend cleaning.* | **do the cleaning** *Her husband does most of the cleaning.*

clean out /ˌkliːn ˈaʊt/ [phr v T] to completely clean a room, cupboard etc, especially by taking everything out and putting it back in neatly **clean out sth** *The apartment needs to be cleaned out before a new tenant can move in.* | *I think it's time we cleaned out the garage.* | **clean sth out** *We really need to clean the refrigerator out.*

spring-clean /ˌsprɪŋ ˈkliːn/ [v I/T] to clean your whole house very thoroughly, including things that you do not clean very often: *Barry spent the day spring-cleaning.* | *I want to spring-clean the whole apartment before Easter.*

housework /ˈhaʊswɜːʳk/ [n U] the things that you do to keep your house clean and tidy: *Housework takes up most of my time in the evenings.* | **do (the) housework** *I hate doing housework so I pay someone to do it for me.*

5 to make something clean with a cloth

- wipe
- dust
- polish
- shine

wipe /waɪp/ [v T] to remove dirt or liquid from something using a slightly wet cloth: *The waiter was wiping the tables.* | **wipe sth up** *If you spill any paint, wipe it up immediately.* | **wipe up sth** *Wipe up all that mess before you begin cooking.*

dust /dʌst/ [v T] to remove **dust** from furniture, shelves etc using a soft cloth: *She decided to dust the dining room furniture again.* | **+ behind/under etc** *A thorough cleaning includes dusting under the wardrobes.* | *She didn't often dust behind the pictures.*

polish /ˈpɒlɪʃ‖ˈpɑː-/ [v T] to make something clean and shiny, for example your shoes or a piece of furniture, by rubbing it with a cloth or brush: *He polished the piano until the wood shone.* | *a polished wooden floor*

shine /ʃaɪn/ [v T] to make shoes clean and shiny by rubbing or polishing them with a brush or cloth and shoe polish: *If you're coming, you'd better shine your shoes and put on a clean shirt.* | **have/get your shoes shined** *You should have your shoes shined before the interview.* —**shine** [n singular] *Those shoes need a shine* (=to be shined).

6 to clean something with a brush

- brush
- scrub
- sweep
- scour

brush /brʌʃ/ [v T] to clean something with a brush: *You should brush your jacket – it's covered in dust.* | **brush sth off** *I brushed the crumbs off the sofa.* | **brush your teeth** *Have you brushed your teeth yet?*

scrub /skrʌb/ [v T] to clean something by rubbing it hard with a brush and some water or soap: *Part of my job was to wash the dishes and scrub the floors.* | *Scrub the potatoes and boil them for 5-10 minutes.*

sweep /swiːp/ [v T] to clean the floor or the ground using a brush with a long handle: *When everyone had left, Ed swept the floor.* | **sweep up sth/sweep sth up** (=remove something from a floor by sweeping) *Can you help me sweep up all the pieces of glass?*

scour /skaʊəʳ/ [v T] to rub a cooking pan or hard surface with a piece of rough material in order to clean it: *I scoured the pots and pans.* | *Scour the bowl with a mixture of vinegar and baking soda.*

7 to clean something with a special cleaning machine

- vacuum

vacuum ALSO **hoover** British /ˈvækjuəm, -kjʊm, ˈhuːvəʳ/ [v I/T] to clean something using a special machine that sucks dirt up off the floor etc: *Have you vacuumed the carpets?* | *You do the hoovering and I'll finish the kitchen.*

8 someone whose job is to clean things

- cleaner
- cleaner's/dry cleaner's

cleaner /ˈkliːnəʳ/ [n C] someone who is paid to clean a house or office: *We finish work at six, and then the cleaners come in.* | *a window cleaner*

cleaner's/dry cleaner's /ˈkliːnəʳz, ˌdraɪ ˈkliːnəʳz/ [n C] a shop where you can take your clothes to be cleaned, especially with chemicals, not water: *My suit is at the dry cleaner's.* | *Can you collect my dress from the cleaner's?*

clear/not clear

WHAT'S HERE

- clear and easy to understand — see **1 to 5**
- clear and easy to see — see **6 to 8**

clear and easy to understand

RELATED WORDS

- easily noticed or understood *see* **obvious**
- *see also* **understand/not understand, confused**

1 clear and easy to understand

- clear
- plain
- unambiguous
- explicit
- unequivocal
- expressly

clear /klɪəʳ/ [adj] *The instructions aren't really clear.* | **+ on/about** *Children need clear rules about what is allowed and what isn't* | *You're not allowed to use a dictionary in this exam. The rules are quite clear on this point.* | **clear to sb** *It may be clear to you, but I haven't got a clue what it means.* | **crystal clear** (=extremely clear) *Though he didn't say anything directly his meaning was crystal clear.* —**clearly** [adv] *The contract says quite clearly that the landlord must pay for all repairs to the house.* | *Procedures for making insurance claims need to be more clearly defined.* —**clarity** /ˈklærəti/ [n U] *The opera was sung with brilliant clarity and precision.*

plain /pleɪn/ [adj usually before noun] language, instructions etc that are **plain** are easy to understand because there is nothing difficult or unnecessary in them that might be confusing: *She spoke slowly and carefully, using plain simple language.* | *The document is written in plain English.* —**plainly** [adv] *Tell me plainly what you want.* | *The leaflet plainly states what the party's position is on immigration.*

unambiguous /ˌʌnæmˈbɪgjuəs/ [adj] having only one possible meaning and therefore clear: *Safety guidelines need to be plain and unambiguous.* | *In last night's speech, the president finally made an unambiguous statement on the issue of taxes.* —**unambiguously** [adv] *The wording of the policy is written clearly and unambiguously.* | *Congressman Phillips clearly and unambiguously expressed regret for his actions.*

explicit /ɪkˈsplɪsɪ̥t/ [adj] **explicit instructions/account/warning etc** expressed very clearly and including every detail, so that no part of your meaning is hidden: *Mr Beazley left explicit instructions that he wasn't to be disturbed.* | *I don't quite understand – could you be a bit more explicit?* | **+ about** *He's not being very explicit about his plans, is he?* —**explicitly** [adv] *Students are explicitly forbidden to smoke in the dorm rooms.*

unequivocal /ˌʌnɪˈkwɪvəkəl/ [adj] formal so clear that the meaning or intention cannot be mistaken or doubted: *The European Parliament has given the plan its unequivocal support.* | *The answer to our request was an unequivocal 'no'.* | *This time his father was unequivocal: 'You're getting no more money from me, and that's final.'* —**unequivocally** [adv] *She unequivocally rejects any moves towards conciliation.*

expressly /ɪkˈspresli/ [adv] formal if you **expressly** state something, you state it very clearly and firmly, usually in writing **expressly state sth** *Although it's not expressly stated in your contract, you are expected to attend weekend training sessions.* | *It is expressly stated in the sales agreement that the buyer is to pay for any home inspection.* | **expressly forbid sth** *The new law expressly forbids the importation of radioactive waste.*

2 to make something completely clear

- make clear/make it clear
- clarify
- spell out
- lay it on the line
- in no uncertain terms

make clear/make it clear /ˌmeɪk ˈklɪəʳ, ˌmeɪk ɪt ˈklɪəʳ/ [v phrase] *I tried to make clear exactly what I meant.* | **make it clear (that)** *The teacher made it clear that she would not allow talking in class.* | **make sth clear** *We want to make the rules clear from the beginning.* | **make yourself clear** (=make it clear what you mean) *Am I making myself clear?*

clarify /ˈklærɪ̥faɪ/ [v T] formal to make something clearer, especially because people have not completely understood it: *I hope this statement has helped to clarify a few points.* | **clarify your position** (=make it clear what you think about something and what your intentions are) *The senator tried to clarify his position on abortion.* —**clarification** /ˌklærɪ̥fɪ̥ˈkeɪʃən/ [n U] *Parts of the document are ambiguous and in need of clarification.*

spell out /ˌspel ˈaʊt/ [phr v T] to explain something in the clearest possible way, especially when you think it should be unnecessary to make things so simple or to give so many details: *Do I have to spell out to you how important this is to me?* | *Andrews was asked to spell out exactly how pensions would be affected.* | *Campbell spelled out the reasons why staff reductions were necessary.*

lay it on the line /ˌleɪ ɪt ɒn ðə ˈlaɪn/ [v phrase] informal to state something clearly and strongly, especially something that other people may be unwilling to listen to or accept: *I'm going to lay it on the line. If you don't quit drinking, I'm going to leave you.*

in no uncertain terms /ɪn ˌnəʊ ʌnˌsɜːʳtn ˈtɜːʳmz/ [adv] if you say something **in no uncertain terms** you make your meaning very clear, especially when you are annoyed with someone about something: *The president of the university condemned racism on campus in no uncertain terms.* | *You've got to let him know, in no uncertain terms, that you will no longer tolerate his abuse.*

3 not clear

- unclear/not clear
- ambiguous
- imprecise
- vague
- confusing
- muddled/garbled
- unintelligible

unclear/not clear /ʌnˈklɪəʳ, nɒt ˈklɪəʳ/ [adj] *It is unclear how the man died.* | *The instructions aren't very clear.* | *The terms of our tenancy agreement are somewhat unclear.* | *The reasons for his resignation are still not clear.* | **+ about** *His ideas are good, but he's very unclear about how he's going to achieve them.* | **+ whether/what/why etc** *It's not clear why Parks didn't go straight to the police.* | *It is unclear whether the she will agree to the new arrangements.*

ambiguous /æmˈbɪgjuəs/ [adj] having more than one possible meaning and therefore confusing and unclear: *The document's ambiguous wording makes it very difficult to follow.* | **deliberately ambiguous** (=intended to be difficult to understand) *The last part of her letter was deliberately ambiguous.* —**ambiguously** [adv] *The contract was worded ambiguously.* —**ambiguity** /ˌæmbɪ̥ˈgjuːɪ̥ti/ [n C/U] *The report is full of ambiguities.*

imprecise /ˌɪmprɪˈsaɪs◂/ [adj] words or statements that are **imprecise** are unclear because they do not describe or explain something in an exact way when this is necessary: *Many of the terms used in this book are imprecise.* | *She gave me directions to the hotel, but they were, shall we say, somewhat imprecise.*

vague /veɪg/ [adj] unclear, especially because not enough details are given: *There have been vague rumours of a coup.* | **vague idea** *I only had a vague idea of where the place was.* | **+ about** *He was rather vague about the reasons why he never finished school.* —**vaguely** [adv] *The man is described vaguely as 'medium build with brown hair'.*

confusing /kənˈfjuːzɪŋ/ [adj] a **confusing** situation, story, explanation, etc is difficult to understand because there does not seem to be any clear pattern or order to it: *The kidnappers issued a series of confusing demands.* | *I found the book really confusing. I kept forgetting who the characters were.* | *Cricket can be a pretty confusing game for non players.*

muddled/garbled /ˈmʌdld, ˈgɑːʳbəld/ [adj] if something that someone tells you is **muddled** or **garbled**, it is very unclear and confusing because they themselves have not really understood it very well: *I heard a garbled version of the story from one* *of my students.* | *Conroy made some muddled statement about how company policy has to be observed in these situations.* | *The old woman's directions were so garbled that I just rolled up the window and drove on.*

unintelligible /ˌʌnɪnˈtelɪdʒɪbəl◂/ [adj] **unintelligible** speech or writing is impossible to understand, for example because the words are not clear or it is written very badly: *Her note was practically unintelligible.* | *I liked the music but the lyrics were completely unintelligible.*

4 when it is not clear what is happening or why something happens

- unclear/not clear
- confused

unclear/not clear /ʌnˈklɪəʳ, nɒt ˈklɪəʳ/ [adj] *It is not clear why the disease affects some people and not others.* | *The circumstances surrounding his death are still unclear.*

confused /kənˈfjuːzd/ [adj] a situation that is **confused** is difficult to understand because a lot of things are happening at the same time and you do not have enough information about it: *Newspaper reports give a rather confused picture of the state of the economy.* | *US policy towards China has always seemed mixed and confused.* | *The situation in the city centre is getting increasingly confused, and riot police have been told to stand by.*

5 to make something unclear

- confuse
- blur
- cloud/confuse the issue

confuse /kənˈfjuːz/ [v T] to make a situation unclear by making it more complicated: *The instructions just confused me even more.* | *The Press Secretary gave a completely different version of events, which greatly confused the situation.* | **confuse matters further** (=make things more confused) *I think my explanation only confused matters further.*

blur /blɜːʳ/ [v T] to make the difference between two ideas or subjects unclear: *The difference between male and female roles within the house has become blurred.* | *The show blurs the difference between education and entertainment.* | *His novels tend to blur the distinctions between reality and fantasy.* —**blurred** [adj] *In the US, the dividing line between political and business interests has always been blurred.*

cloud/confuse the issue /ˌklaʊd, kənˌfjuːz ði ˈɪʃuː/ [v phrase] to make a subject or problem unclear by bringing in ideas, information, etc that are not really connected with it: *The Supreme Court's latest decision has only clouded the issue of gun control.* | *I'm talking about social problems. My opponent is just confusing the issue when he keeps referring to family values.*

clear and easy to see

RELATED WORDS

- something that can or cannot see through *see* **see (8-9)**
- *see also* **notice/not notice**

6 clear and easy to see

- clear
- distinct

clear /klɪəʳ/ [adj] *He had left clear footprints in the wet sand.* | *Even after two thousand years the writing is quite clear.* | *Most of the photos were very sharp and clear.* —**clearly** [adv] *I could clearly see a row of cottages at the top of the hill*

distinct /dɪˈstɪŋkt/ [adj] an object, line, or shape that is **distinct** is very clear so that you can easily see that it is separate from the things around it: *The sign's lettering was crisp and distinct.* | *As night fell, the outline of the mountain became less distinct.* —**distinctly** [adv] *Many of the stars that we see quite distinctly actually died millions of years ago.*

7 photographs/images/pictures

- clear
- sharp
- in focus

clear /klɪəʳ/ [adj] *High-definition television is amazing. The picture is so clear.* | *The images of Mars sent back by the Voyager satellite are amazingly clear.*

sharp /ʃɑːʳp/ [adj] very clear, especially because the edges of objects are very easy to see: *'Clear, sharp photos every time,' the advertisement promised.* | *Lichtenstein's paintings are full of colours and sharp outlines – almost like children's comics.*

in focus /ɪn ˈfəʊkəs/ [adj phrase] photographs, films, or images that are **in focus** have been photographed or filmed from the correct distance or with the camera correctly set, so that everything in the pictures is clear: *Several of the photos weren't in focus.* | *Roy adjusted the TV set so that the picture was in sharper focus.*

8 not easy to see clearly

- unclear/not clear
- faint
- blurred
- fuzzy
- hazy

unclear/not clear /ʌnˈklɪəʳ, nɒt ˈklɪəʳ/ [adj] *I'll try and read this, but the handwriting's pretty unclear.* | *The photos were not very clear.*

faint /feɪnt/ [adj] a picture, shape, image etc that is **faint** is unclear because it is a long way away, there is not enough light, or it was very lightly drawn: *There were a few faint pencil lines on the page.* | **faint outline** *On the wall you could see the faint outline of where a picture had once hung.*

blurred /blɜːʳd/ [adj] unclear so that only the general shape can be seen, and not small details: *Without my glasses, anything more than a few feet away looks blurred.* | *All I have to remind me of Albert are a few letters and a blurred photo.*

fuzzy /ˈfʌzi/ [adj] a photograph, television picture etc that is **fuzzy** is not clear, and it is difficult to see separate edges and objects, often because there is something wrong with your equipment or with the way the pictures were taken: *Police have only a fuzzy videotape of the bank robbery.* | *a fuzzy snapshot*

hazy /ˈheɪzi/ [adj] a view that is **hazy** is not clear because there is a slight mist caused by heat, smoke etc: *The view to the west was hazy.* | **+ with** *The room was hazy with smoke.*

climb

RELATED WORDS

- see also **up, down**

1 to climb up or down something

- climb
- scale
- clamber
- shin up/down
- ascent

climb /klaɪm/ [v I/T] to move up towards the top of a wall, mountain, tree etc, using your hands and feet: *Most kids love climbing trees.* | *Trying not to look down, Alan began to climb.* | **+ up/over/onto etc** *Several fans climbed onto the roof of the arena to get a better view.* | *One of the boys lost his footing as he was climbing up the steepest part of the cliff.* | **climb down** (=go down a wall, tree etc using your hands and feet) *The burglar escaped by climbing down a drainpipe.*

scale /skeɪl/ [v T] especially written to climb to the top of something very high, especially something that is very difficult or dangerous to climb: *Somehow the men had scaled the twenty-foot wall without setting off the alarm.* | *Rescuers had to scale a one-thousand-foot cliff before they could reach the injured climber.*

clamber /ˈklæmbəʳ/ [v I] to climb in an awkward way or with difficulty, but moving fairly quickly **+ up/down/to etc** *At last we saw the two girls clambering down the slope to safety.* | *Hundreds of people clambered to the roof of the building to watch the fire spread.*

shin up/down British **/shinny up/down** American /ˌʃɪn ˈʌp, ˈdaʊn, ˌʃɪni ˈʌp, ˈdaʊn / [phr v T not in passive] to climb up or down something tall and narrow such as a pipe, tree, or rope, by wrapping your legs around it and pulling yourself up with your arms: *I locked myself out of the house and had to shinny up a drainpipe to get in.* | *We watched as small boys shinned up palm trees and brought coconuts down.* | *Craig shinned down the rope to where we were standing.*

ascent /əˈsent/ [n C usually singular] the act of climbing something, especially a mountain: *The men began their final ascent at six o'clock the next day.* | *He wrote a best-selling book about the first ascent of Everest.*

2 someone who climbs hills or mountains as a sport

- climber
- mountaineer

climber /ˈklaɪməʳ/ [n C] someone who climbs hills or rocks as a sport, especially using special equipment: *The search is still continuing for a group of climbers reported missing in the Scottish highlands.* | *an experienced climber*

mountaineer /ˌmaʊntəˈnɪəʳ/ [n C] someone who climbs high mountains using special equipment: *Most mountaineers dream of climbing Everest.* | *Sports equipment stores in Alpine towns cater for the needs of walkers, hikers and mountaineers.*

3 climbing hills or mountains as a sport

- climbing
- mountaineering

climbing /ˈklaɪmɪŋ/ [n U] the sport of **climbing** hills or mountains: *Eva's hobbies are horse-riding, climbing, and aerobics.* | *strong climbing boots* | **rock climbing** (=the sport of climbing up steep rocks and cliffs) *Accident insurance does not cover you for dangerous activities such as rock climbing.*

mountaineering /ˌmaʊntəˈnɪərɪŋ/ [n U] the sport of climbing high mountains using special equipment: *I joined the mountaineering club when I went to university.*

clothes

RELATED WORDS

- wearing good clothes *see* **well-dressed**
- *see also* **fashionable/not fashionable, material (2), fasten/unfasten, loose, tight, fit/not fit (1-4), simple 5, style/elegance, suit/look good together, taste in clothes, music etc**

1 clothes

- clothes
- clothing
- something/anything/nothing to wear
- garment
- wardrobe
- wear

clothes /kləʊðz, kləʊz/ [n plural] things that you wear, for example coats, shirts, and dresses: *I need to go buy some new clothes.* | *The temperature should be around freezing tonight – it's time to get the winter clothes out.* | *My mother always made us wear our good clothes for travelling.* | *There are lots of clothes shops on Newbury Street.* | **baby/school/dance etc clothes** (=for babies, for school etc) *You can pick up second-hand baby clothes very cheaply.*

clothing /ˈkləʊðɪŋ/ [n U] clothes in general – use this either to talk about a particular type of clothes, or to talk about a large quantity of clothes: *Charities have been delivering food and clothing to the disaster area.* | **warm/light/outdoor etc clothing** *Because of the heat, officials are asking people to wear light, loose-fitting clothing and to drink plenty of water.* | **piece/item/article of clothing** (=one thing that you wear, for example a shirt or a dress) formal *There was nothing in the chest except for a few items of clothing.*

something/anything/nothing to wear /ˌsʌmθɪŋ, ˌeniθɪŋ, ˌnʌθɪŋ tə ˈweəʳ/ [n phrase] spoken clothes, especially clothes for a particular event or occasion: *I must buy something to wear at Julie's wedding.* | *You're always saying you have nothing to wear, but you've got a whole closet full of clothes.* | *I can't find anything to wear!*

garment /ˈgɑːʳmənt/ [n C] formal a single piece of clothing – used especially by people who make or sell clothes: *The garment industry has grown by 20% in this area in the past five years.* | *Only two garments may be taken into the changing room.*

wardrobe /ˈwɔːʳdrəʊb/ [n singular] all the clothes that you own – used especially by people who write about fashion or by people who sell clothes: *Enter our simple fashion quiz and win a whole new wardrobe.* | *We have everything you need to update your business wardrobe.* | **winter/summer etc wardrobe** (=the clothes you have that are suitable to wear in the winter, summer etc) *By adding a few bright buttons or belts to your old clothes you can have a new summer wardrobe.*

wear /weəʳ/ [n U] **evening/casual/sports/children's etc wear** the clothes worn for a particular occasion or activity or by a particular group of people – used especially by people who make or sell clothes: *a shop that specializes in evening wear | You'll find a nice range of silk ties in the menswear department on the fourth floor. | The company's line of casual wear is primarily sold in large discount chain stores.*

2 clothes that you wear together as a set

- suit
- costume
- outfit

suit /suːt, sjuːt‖suːt/ [n C] a pair of trousers or a skirt, that you wear with a short coat made of the same material: *She wore a black suit for the interview. | Bob was wearing a business suit. | The restaurant seemed to be filled with men in grey suits.*

outfit /ˈaʊtˌfɪt/ [n C] a set of clothes that look attractive together, that you wear for a special occasion – use this especially about women's clothes: *That's a beautiful outfit you're wearing. | She went out and spent $200 on a new outfit for the party.*

costume /ˈkɒstjʊm‖ˈkɑːstuːm/ [n C/U] a set of clothes for acting in a play or performance or that you wear for a party to make you look like someone or something else: *My daughter wore a witch costume in the Hallowe'en parade. | I didn't like the play much but the costumes were amazing.*

3 special clothes worn by a group or profession

- uniform

uniform /ˈjuːnɪ̈fɔːʳm/ [n C/U] a set of clothes that are worn by all the people who belong to a particular organization, for example soldiers, police officers, or schoolchildren: *Do you have to wear a uniform if you work at McDonald's?* | **school uniform** *I used to hate wearing a school uniform.* | **in uniform** (=wearing uniform) *Some of the policemen walking amongst the crowds were not in uniform.*

4 clothes that you wear for sport

- things
- strip
- kit
- gear

things British ALSO **stuff** American /θɪŋz, stʌf/ [n plural] **swimming/football/tennis etc things** spoken the clothes that you wear for swimming, playing football etc: *Don't forget to bring your swimming things when we go to Brighton. | I left my gym stuff in the car.*

kit /kɪt/ [n U] British a set of clothes that that you wear when you play football, tennis etc: *I told the children to put on their gym kit and go outside. | Roz keeps her squash kit at the office and plays at lunchtime.*

strip British **/uniform** American /strɪp, ˈjuːnɪ̈fɔːʳm/ [n C] the set of clothes that a particular team wears in sport: *The uniform of the New York Yankees is white with a fine blue stripe. | Charlie wasn't allowed to play because he'd forgotten his strip.*

gear /gɪəʳ/ [n U] informal the set of clothes and other equipment that are used for a sport or activity: *Did you pack my hiking gear? | Now that I've got all the gear, I'm ready to come out riding with you.*

5 clothes that used to belong to someone else

- cast-offs/castoffs
- hand-me-down

cast-offs/castoffs /ˈkɑːst ɒfs‖ˈkæst-/ [n plural] clothes that you no longer wear and have given to someone else: *I'm not interested in wearing other people's castoffs. | Our mother kept a box of old castoffs and we spent hours dressing up, pretending to be princesses or pirates.* —**cast-off** [adj only before noun] *castoff clothes and shoes*

hand-me-down /ˈhænd miː ˌdaʊn/ [n C usually plural] a piece of clothing that is given to a younger child in a family when their older brother or sister has grown too big for them or stopped wearing them: *The youngest child in the family usually gets all the hand-me-downs. | This sweater is a hand-me-down from my sister, but I love it.* —**hand-me-down** [adj only before noun] *Diego wore a hand-me-down jacket, still too big for him.*

6 to wear a particular piece of clothing or set of clothes

- wear
- be dressed up
- in
- dress down
- have on
- be bundled up
- be dressed
- be kitted out in

wear /weəʳ/ [v T] to have clothes, shoes, glasses, jewellery etc on your body: *She was wearing shorts and a T-shirt. | Were you wearing your jacket when we got on the bus?* | **wear black/red/green etc** (=wear black clothes, red clothes etc) *Carolyn always wore bright colors like red.* | **sb wears sth** (=someone usually wears a particular type of clothes) *She wears sandals, even in the winter. | I wear a lot of black.*

in /ɪn/ [prep] **in a suit/in a red dress etc** wearing a suit, a red dress etc: *a couple of boys in baseball caps | There was a man in a linen suit standing at the bar.*

have on /ˌhæv ˈɒn / [phr v T not in progressive] to be wearing clothes, shoes, glasses, or jewellery **have a coat/jacket/suit etc on** *That's Jenny Salton over there; she has a blue dress on. | Could you read this for me? I don't have my glasses on.* | **have on a coat/jacket/suit etc** *'What was she wearing?' 'I think she had on a dark suit.'*

be dressed /biː ˈdrest/ [v phrase] to be wearing clothes: *Are you dressed yet? We have to leave now!* | **+ in** *They were all dressed in T-shirts and jeans. | a woman dressed in green* | **be dressed as sb** (=wearing clothes that make you look like someone else) *Some of the children were dressed as soldiers.*

be dressed up /biː ˌdrest ˈʌp/ [v phrase] American to be wearing formal clothes or your best clothes, for example on a special occasion: *Look at you – you're all dressed up! | Harvey arrived, dressed up in his only business suit.*

dress down /ˌdres ˈdaʊn/ [phr v I] British to wear clothes that are more informal than you usually wear: *We dress down at work these days, unless we're going to a client meeting.*

be bundled up /biː ˌbʌndld ˈʌp/ [v phrase] to be wearing a lot of warm clothes because it is cold **+ in** *The old man sat on his porch bundled up in old sweaters and scarves.* | **+ against the cold/rain/wind etc** *Spectators, bundled up against the cold, stood and listened to the President speak for an hour.*

be kitted out in /biː ˌkɪtɪ̈d ˈaʊt ɪn/ [v phrase] British to be wearing a particular kind of clothes, especially to do an activity: *Anna was kitted out in her riding gear, waiting by the car.*

7 to put on clothes

- put on
- get dressed
- try on
- slip on
- wrap up
- dress up

put on /ˌpʊt ˈɒn / [phr v T] to **put on** a piece of clothing **put sth on** *Put your coat on if you're going out.* | **put on sth** *She put on her bathrobe and went downstairs.*

get dressed /ˌget ˈdrest/ [v phrase] to put on the clothes that you usually wear during the day or to go out in clothes: *I got dressed quickly and ran outside.* | *Sandra's in the bedroom getting dressed.*

try on /ˌtraɪ ˈɒn/ [phr v T] to put on a piece of clothing, to see if it fits you and if it looks nice on you **try sth on** *If you like the shoes, why don't you try them on?* | **try on sth** *I tried on a beautiful coat, but it was too big.*

slip on /ˌslɪp ˈɒn / [phr v T] to put a piece of clothing on quickly and easily **slip sth/it/them on** *I took out my old cardigan and slipped it on.* | *The girls got out their party dresses, giggling as they slipped them on.* | **slip on sth** *She slipped on a pair of white jeans and a black sleeveless top.*

wrap up /ˌræp ˈʌp/ [phr v I/T] to put on warm clothing, especially because you are going out in cold weather **wrap up warm** *You ought to wrap up warm – I think it's going to snow.* | **be wrapped up against the cold** *The kids, wrapped up in layers against the cold, waddled out to play.*

dress up /ˌdres ˈʌp/ [phr v I/T] to wear clothes that you do not normally wear so that you look like someone else for fun: *Most kids love dressing up.* | **dress up in** *They were dressed up in old sheets, pretending to be ghosts.* | **dress up as** *One of the students dressed up as a rabbit and marched around campus carrying a sign.* | **dress yourself up** *I came in to find that my daughter had dressed herself up in my clothes.*

8 to put on clothes for a special occasion

- dress up/get dressed up
- doll yourself up/get dolled up

dress up/get dressed up /ˌdres ˈʌp, get ˌdrest ˈʌp/ [phr v I/v phrase] to put on clothes that are suitable for a special or formal occasion: *Do we have to get dressed up to go to this restaurant?* | *It's an informal party, so you don't need to dress up.*

doll yourself up/get dolled up /ˌdɒl jɔːʳself ˈʌp ‖ˌdɑːl-, get ˌdɒld ˈʌp‖-ˌdɑːld-/ [v phrase] informal to put on your best clothes and pay a lot of attention to your appearance, usually for a special occasion – used especially about women: *You don't need to doll yourself up. It's only my sister who's coming to dinner.*

9 to put someone else's clothes on for them

- dress sb/get sb dressed

dress sb/get sb dressed /ˈdres (sb), ˌget (sb) ˈdrest/ [v T/v phrase] *Honey, can you get the kids dressed, please?* | *The nurses have to wash and dress the patients before the doctor comes to see them.*

10 to take off your clothes

- take off
- get undressed
- undress
- get changed
- change
- strip off
- strip
- tear off

take off /ˌteɪk ˈɒf/ [phr v T] **take off sth** *'It's warm i here,' said Michael, taking off his jacket.* | **take sth it/them off** *Take your shoes off before you come in.* *Mom, I hate this tie. Can I take it off?*

get undressed /ˌget ʌnˈdrest/ [v phrase] to take o all your clothes, especially before going to bed: *Sh got undressed and went to bed.*

undress /ʌnˈdres/ [v I] written to take off all you clothes, especially before going to bed: *Paul wer into the bathroom to undress.*

get changed /get ˈtʃeɪndʒd/ [v phrase] to take o your clothes and put on different clothes: *The boy ran up the stairs to get changed.* | *I'll be ready in second, I just have to get changed.*

change /tʃeɪndʒ/ [v I/T] to take off all or some c your clothes and put different clothes on: *Do yo mind waiting while I change my clothes?* | **+ into** *Sh changed into a sweater and some jeans.* | **+ out of** *E went into the bedroom to change out of his wor clothes.*

strip off /ˌstrɪp ˈɒf / [phr v I/T] to quickly take off a your clothes or a piece of clothing: *We stripped o and dived into the pool.* | **strip off sth** *She ra upstairs, stripped off her jeans and sweater an pulled on a dressing gown.*

strip /strɪp/ [v I] to take off all your clothes, esp cially because someone has told you to, or in a wa that is deliberately sexually exciting: *The women i the club screamed and clapped as the male dancer began to strip.* | **strip to the waist** (=take off all th clothes on the top half of your body) *'I'd like you strip to the waist so I can listen to your chest,' said th doctor.* | **strip (down) to your shorts, underwear et** (=take off everything except your shorts, unde wear etc) *The prisoners were ordered to strip down t their underwear and wait for the guards.*

tear off /ˌteər ˈɒf / [phr v T] to take off your clothes o a piece of clothing very quickly and roughly **tear o sth** *I tore off the plastic gloves and threw ther away.* | **tear sth off** *James began to undress wildl tearing his clothes off as if he was on fire.*

11 to take off someone else's clothes

- undress/get sb undressed
- strip
- tear sb's clothes off
- strip search

undress sb/get sb undressed /ʌnˈdres (sb ˌget (sb) ʌnˈdrest/ [v T/v phrase] to take off all som one's clothes for them, especially because they ar unable to do it themselves: *I'll get the childre undressed and ready for bed.* | *Two nurses undresse the old woman and lifted her on to the bed.*

strip /strɪp/ [v T] to take off all someone's clothe because you are going to punish or search then *One of the guards stripped the prisoner and beat hi with a chain.* | *I was taken to police headquarte where I was stripped and searched.* | **strip sb nake** *The men were stripped naked and herded into small prison cell.*

tear sb's clothes off /ˌteəʳ (sb's) ˈkləʊðz ɒf/ phrase] to very quickly and roughly take off som one's clothes: *Molly tore off the child's clothing looking for more marks and bruises.*

strip search /ˈstrɪp ˌsɜːʳtʃ/ [v T] to make someone remove their clothes in order to check their body for hidden drugs or weapons: *We cannot open every piece of baggage and strip search every passenger on every flight.* | *Hicks was taken to the police station, strip searched, and put in a holding cell.* —**strip search** [n C] *Are strip searches legal?*

12 not wearing any clothes

- have nothing on/not have anything on
- naked
- undressed
- bare
- nude
- in the nude
- in your birthday suit
- nudist/naturist

have nothing on/not have anything on /hæv ˌnʌθɪŋ ˈɒn, nɒt hæv ˌeniθɪŋ ˈɒn/ [v phrase] especially spoken to not be wearing any clothes: *Don't come in yet – I don't have anything on!* | *I didn't want to walk near the windows with nothing on.*

naked /ˈneɪkɪ̈d/ [adj] wearing no clothes – use this especially when it is surprising that someone is not wearing clothes: *He was lying on the bed, completely naked.* | *The magazine was full of pictures of naked men.* | **stark naked** ALSO **buck naked** American (=completely naked) *I walked in, and Mr Tolifero was standing there buck naked.*

undressed /ʌnˈdrest/ [adj] wearing no clothes because you have just taken them off, for example to have a bath or go to bed: *When you're undressed, the nurse will come back and explain the procedure.*

bare /beəʳ/ [adj] a part of your body that is **bare** is not covered by any clothes: *bare feet* | *The dress tied around her neck, leaving her shoulders bare.*

nude /njuːd‖nuːd/ [adj] a word meaning naked, used especially when talking about images of naked people in paintings, films etc: *At the front of the painting is a nude figure carrying a torch.* | **nude photograph/scene/drawing etc** (=showing someone wearing no clothes) *On the wall was a nude drawing of her husband.* —**nudity** /ˈnjuːdɪ̈ti‖ˈnuː-/ [n U] *Attitudes to nudity in films have changed in recent years.* —**nude** [n C] *He showed me a beautiful painting of a nude* (=a picture of a nude person).

in the nude /ɪn ðə ˈnjuːd‖-ˈnuːd/ [adv] if you do something **in the nude**, you do it wearing no clothes at all, especially when this is unusual, exciting, or shocking: *He told me he cleans his house in the nude!* | *The pictures show Collier on top of a New York skyscraper in the nude.*

in your birthday suit /ɪn jɔːʳ ˈbɜːʳθdeɪ ˌsuːt/ [adv] informal without any clothes on – used humorously: *Martin's threatened to turn up for the wedding in his birthday suit.*

nudist/naturist /ˈnjuːdɪ̈st‖ˈnuː-, ˈneɪtʃərɪ̈st/ [n C] someone who enjoys not wearing any clothes because they believe it is natural and healthy: *A close friend who is a nudist, convinced Michelle to visit the community with him.* —**nudist/naturist** [adj] *There are naturist beaches on most of the Greek islands.*

clumsy

doing things carelessly or moving awkwardly

RELATED WORDS

opposite: **graceful**
see also **careless, nervous, confident**

1 doing things in a careless and awkward way

- clumsy
- be all thumbs
- accident-prone
- klutz

clumsy /ˈklʌmzi/ [adj] someone who is **clumsy** does things in a careless way and often breaks things or has accidents: *I was so shy and clumsy when I was seventeen.* | *Andrew made a clumsy attempt to kiss her, but she pushed him away.* | *You clumsy idiot! Look what you've done to my car.* —**clumsily** [adv] *Sam took a cigarette, lit it clumsily and sat down.* —**clumsiness** [n U] *He apologized for his clumsiness and offered to pay for the damage.*

be all thumbs ALSO **be all fingers and thumbs** British /biː ɔːl ˈθʌmz, biː ɔːl ˌfɪŋgəʳz ən ˈθʌmz/ [v phrase] to have difficulty doing something with your hands, especially because you are in a hurry or feel nervous: *Can you sew this button on for me? I'm all fingers and thumbs this morning.* | **go/become all fingers and thumbs** *I can't type at all when people are watching me. I go all fingers and thumbs.*

accident-prone /ˈæksɪ̈dənt ˌprəʊn/ [adj] someone who is **accident-prone** often has accidents or breaks things: *Lots of kids are accident-prone but they soon grow out of it.* | *Studies have shown women to be less accident-prone than men.*

klutz /klʌts/ [n C] American informal someone who annoys you because they do things in a careless way and often break things or have accidents: *'Look what you've done, you silly klutz!' Nathan said angrily.* | *Tom's a real klutz when it comes to baseball – even if he hit the ball he'd trip on the way to first base.*

2 moving in an awkward way

- uncoordinated
- awkward
- ungainly

uncoordinated /ˌʌnkəʊˈɔːʳdɪ̈neɪtɪ̈d/ [adj] not able to control your movements skilfully, and therefore not usually good at sports and other physical activities: *I can't play tennis very well – I'm too uncoordinated.* | *There was Thomas, walking towards me in his strange uncoordinated way.*

awkward /ˈɔːkwəʳd/ [adj] moving in a way that looks clumsy and uncomfortable: *She felt awkward in her high-heeled shoes.* | *Bud turned round and gave an awkward wave out of the car window.* —**awkwardly** [adv] *I fell really awkwardly and twisted my ankle.*

ungainly /ʌnˈgeɪnli/ [adj] moving in an ungraceful way – use this about people or things that are very big: *Dinosaurs were huge ungainly animals with tiny brains.* | *She was old, fat and ungainly, and had to struggle to get to her feet.*

cold

RELATED WORDS

opposite: **hot**

▸ *see also* **weather, wet, dry**

1 cold weather

- ▸ **cold**
- ▸ **the cold**
- ▸ **chilly**
- ▸ **nippy**
- ▸ **frosty**
- ▸ **wintry**
- ▸ **cold spell**
- ▸ **cold snap**

cold /kəʊld/ [adj] *This is the coldest winter we've had in years.* | *a cold January evening* | **it's cold** (=the weather is cold) *Put your gloves on – it's cold outside today.* | **it gets cold** *It gets really cold here at night.* | **cold weather** *The layer of fat below a goose's skin protects it from cold weather.*

the cold /ðə ˈkəʊld/ [n U] cold weather – use this to emphasize how unpleasant and uncomfortable it is outside: *Come in. Don't stand out there in the cold.*

chilly /ˈtʃɪli/ [adj] cold, but not extremely cold: *a chilly morning in April* | **it's chilly** (=the weather is chilly) *It's a little chilly out here – I think we'll go inside.* | **it gets/turns chilly** *Temperatures were in the 80s on Tuesday, but it turned chilly Wednesday afternoon.*

nippy /ˈnɪpi/ [adj] informal a little cold: *The weather's getting warmer, but the mornings are still nippy.* | **it's nippy** (=the weather is nippy) *I'm going indoors. It's a little nippy out here.*

frosty /ˈfrɒsti‖ˈfrɔːsti/ [adj] very cold, when everything is covered in a thin white layer of ice, and the sky is often bright and clear: *They were both shivering slightly from the frosty air.* | *It was a frosty autumn morning with spiders' webs glistening in the frozen grass.*

wintry /ˈwɪntri/ [adj] cold with snow or rain, and typical of the weather you often have in winter: *We can expect a few wintry showers on the northern hills.* | *Outside it was a cold wintry day, but Anne felt safe and warm inside by the fire.*

cold spell /ˈkəʊld ˌspel/ [n C] a period of several days or weeks when the weather is much colder than usual: *Last month's cold spell was responsible for the deaths of hundreds of old people.* | *The price of firewood usually shoots up during cold spells.*

cold snap /ˈkəʊld ˌsnæp/ [n C] a sudden short period of very cold weather: *It was a wintry day in April in the middle of an unexpected cold snap.*

2 extremely cold weather

- ▸ **freezing/freezing cold**
- ▸ **bitterly cold/bitter**
- ▸ **arctic**
- ▸ **subzero temperatures**

freezing/freezing cold /ˈfriːzɪŋ, ˌfriːzɪŋ ˈkəʊld◂/ [adj] extremely cold, so that water turns to ice: *The freezing weather continued all through February.* | **it's freezing/freezing cold** *How can you stand to be out here without a coat? It's freezing!*

bitterly cold/bitter /ˌbɪtəʳli ˈkəʊld◂, ˈbɪtəʳ/ [adj] extremely cold so that it almost hurts you to be outdoors: *We arrived in Chicago during the bitterly cold winter of 1935.* | *a bitter east wind* | **it's bitterly cold** *Don't go out tonight. It's bitterly cold.*

arctic /ˈɑːʳktɪk/ [adj only before noun] **arctic conditions/winds/chill** extremely cold, usually with ic and snow: *I wouldn't take the car out in these arcti conditions.* | *He could feel the arctic chill creepin into the cabin.*

subzero temperatures /ˌsʌbzɪərəʊ ˈtempəɪ ətʃəʳz‖ -ziːrəʊ-/ [n plural] temperatures that are ver cold and below the point at which water freezes *Subzero temperatures can be expected for the nex few days.* | *Thousands of refugees are spendin tonight on a mountainside in subzero temperatures.*

3 pleasantly cold weather

- ▸ **cool**
- ▸ **fresh**
- ▸ **crisp**
- ▸ **bracing**

cool /kuːl/ [adj] cold in a pleasant way, especiall after the weather has been hot: *a cool sea breeze Although the days are very hot, it's much cooler a night.*

fresh /freʃ/ [adj] especially British pleasantly cold an windy: *We walked towards the sea with a fresh breez blowing in our faces.* | *The hot weather will continu today, but tomorrow will be fresher with cool, wes erly winds.*

crisp /krɪsp/ [adj] pleasantly cold, dry, and clear: *love to be out of doors on these bright, crisp autum mornings.* | *The weather was crisp and clear an you could see the mountains fifty miles away.*

bracing /ˈbreɪsɪŋ/ [adj] cold, fresh and clear in a wa that makes you feel healthy and cheerful: *Han loved the feel of the bracing sea air against his face. Tourists are attracted by the beautiful scenery an bracing mountain climate.*

4 person

- ▸ **cold**
- ▸ **freezing**
- ▸ **shiver**
- ▸ **be blue with cold**
- ▸ **have goosepimples**
- ▸ **sb's teeth are chattering**

cold /kəʊld/ [adj not before noun] feeling cold: *Dad, I'n cold. Can I put the heater on?* | *Your hands are reall cold!* | **feel cold** *He woke up in the middle of the nigh feeling cold.* | **look cold** *Come and sit by the fire. Yo look cold.*

freezing ALSO **frozen** British /ˈfriːzɪŋ, ˈfrəʊzən/ [adj nc before noun] spoken feeling very cold and uncomfort able: *How much longer do we have to wait out her I'm freezing.* | *You look absolutely frozen.*

shiver /ˈʃɪvəʳ/ [v I] to shake a little because you ar cold: *I was shivering in my thin sleeping bag.* **shiver with cold** *They were forced to wait outside fo hours, shivering with cold.* —**shiver** [n C] *A shiver o cold ran through him when he stepped outside.*

be blue with cold /biː ˌbluː wɪð ˈkəʊld/ [v phrase] t be so cold that your skin turns slightly blue: *He wa huddled into his coat, his face blue with cold.* | *Loo at her. The poor girl's quite blue with cold.*

have goosepimples British **/have goose bumps** American /hæv ˈguːsˌpɪmpəlz, hæv ˈguːs bʌmps/ [n plural] to have small raised areas on you skin because you are cold: *She was shivering, he arms and legs covered in goosepimples.* | *Why don' you put something else on? You've got goosebumps.*

sb's teeth are chattering / (sb's) ˈtiːθ ɑː ˌtʃætərɪŋ/ if **your teeth are chattering** you are s cold that your teeth keep knocking together and yo cannot stop them: *Her teeth were chattering wit cold.*

5 place/room

- cold
- cool
- chilly
- draughty
- freezing

cold /kəʊld/ [adj] *I love being in a warm bed in a cold room.* | *He waited an hour for the train on a cold platform.* | **it's cold** *Why is it always so cold in here?*

cool /kuːl/ [adj] cold in a pleasant way, especially when the weather is hot: *Medicine should always be stored in a cool place.* | **it's cool** *It's much cooler over here in the shade.*

chilly /ˈtʃɪli/ [adj] a little too cold for you to feel comfortable: *They have to get washed and dressed in a chilly bathroom.* | **it's chilly** *It's chilly in the house, even when it's sunny outside.*

draughty British **/drafty** American /ˈdrɑːfti‖ˈdræf-/ [adj] a room that is **draughty** has cold air blowing into it from outside: *The two women live in a drafty old farmhouse.* | **it's draughty/drafty** *It's so draughty in here. Is there a window open?*

freezing /ˈfriːzɪŋ/ [adj] extremely cold, so that you feel very uncomfortable: *The little children sat in rows in the freezing classroom.* | **it's freezing** *It's absolutely freezing in the basement.*

6 liquid/object/surface

- cold
- freezing
- cool

cold /kəʊld/ [adj] having a low temperature: *I wanted to swim, but the water was too cold.* | *a cold stone floor*

freezing /ˈfriːzɪŋ/ [adj] extremely cold: *His friends pulled him from the freezing water.* | **freezing cold** *The river is freezing cold this time of year.*

cool /kuːl/ [adj] pleasantly cold but not very cold: *Ruth put her cool hand on my burning forehead.* | *I slid into bed between cool white sheets.*

7 food/drink

- cold
- cold
- cool
- chilled
- ice-cold
- frozen

cold /kəʊld/ [adj] *I want something cold like an ice cream bar.* | *Most white wine tastes best when served very cold.*

cold /kəʊld/ [adj] cooked food that is **cold** is cooked but no longer hot: *They provided a selection of cold meats.* | *You can serve the quiche hot or cold.* | **get cold/go cold** *Come eat your dinner before it gets cold.* | **stone cold** (=completely cold) *By the time I got off the phone, my coffee was stone cold.*

cool /kuːl/ [adj] pleasantly cold to eat or drink but not very cold: *Can I interest you in a nice, cool drink?* | *Summer is the time for cool, refreshing fruit salads.*

chilled /tʃɪld/ [adj] food and drinks that are **chilled** have been made very cold, especially by putting them on ice: *a bottle of chilled champagne*

ice-cold /ˌaɪs ˈkəʊld◂/ [adj] **ice-cold** drinks have been made extremely cold so that they are pleasant to drink, especially when you are very hot: *The kids were rewarded with ice-cold lemonade.* | *I could do with an ice-cold beer.*

frozen /ˈfrəʊzən/ [adj] **frozen** food is stored at a very low temperature so that it freezes and can be kept for a long time: *frozen vegetables* | *All I had in the freezer was a couple of frozen pizzas.*

8 to make food and drink cold

- cool
- chill
- freeze
- refrigerate

cool /kuːl/ [v T] to make food cold when it has been hot or warm: *Blow on the soup first to cool it.* | *Cool the jam by stirring it before putting it into jars.*

chill /tʃɪl/ [v T] to make food or drink very cold, without freezing it: *Chill the salad for an hour or two before serving.* | *Put some ice in the sink, and we'll chill the drinks in there.*

freeze /friːz/ [v T] to make something extremely cold so that it freezes, in order to preserve it for a long time: *You can make a big batch and freeze some of it for later.* | *Don't freeze the rolls for longer than three weeks.*

refrigerate /rɪˈfrɪdʒəreɪt/ [v T] to put food or drink in a refrigerator in order to keep it cold and fresh: *Cover the bowl and refrigerate the dough overnight.* | *Poultry, fish, and seafood should be kept refrigerated.*

9 to get cold or colder

- get cold/colder
- turn cold/colder
- drop/fall
- cool down
- cool

get cold/colder /get ˈkəʊld, ˈkəʊldəʳ/ [v phrase] *It's getting colder – I guess winter's on its way.* | *Hey, John, your soup's getting cold.*

turn cold/colder /ˌtɜːʳn ˈkəʊld, ˈkəʊldəʳ/ [v phrase] if the weather or the wind **turns cold** or **colder**, it becomes much colder, usually suddenly: *I need to finish fixing the roof before the weather turns cold.* | *The wind had turned cold and Billy took off his coat and gave it to the girl.*

drop/fall /drɒp‖drɑːp, fɔːl/ [v I] if the temperature **drops** or **falls** it becomes colder, often much colder in a short period of time: *Fortunately the temperature never dropped low enough to freeze the pipes.* | **drop 10/20/30 etc degrees** *The temperature dropped 10 degrees during the night.*

cool down /ˌkuːl ˈdaʊn/ [phr v I] if something **cools down**, it becomes colder after being hot: *It's been hot all summer, but it's finally starting to cool down a little.* | *If the engine overheats, switch it off and do not start it again until it has cooled down.*

cool /kuːl/ [v I] if hot food or some other hot substance **cools**, it becomes colder: *She took the cake out of the oven and left it on the kitchen table to cool.* | *Most liquids contract steadily as they cool.*

collect

to get and keep objects because you think they are attractive or interesting

RELATED WORDS

▸ *see also* **thing**

1 to collect things

- collect

collect /kəˈlekt/ [v T] *Arlene collects teddy bears.* | *Nigel's hobby is collecting rare books.* | *Anyone who* *collects jazz records should buy this book. It's full of information on old recordings.*

2 someone who collects things

- collector

collector /kəˈlektəʳ/ [n C] **coin/stamp/antiques etc collector** *He's been a coin collector for years.* | *The gallery was full of art collectors and dealers.* | **+ of** *He's an avid collector of Beatles memorabilia.*

3 things that have been collected

- collection
- set

collection /kəˈlekʃən/ [n C] a group of things that someone has collected because they are attractive or interesting **coin/stamp etc collection** *Have you seen Alvin's stamp collection?* | **+ of** *On the shelf was his mother's collection of crystal vases.* | *The museum has one of the world's finest collections of Impressionist paintings.*

set /set/ [n C] a complete collection of one type of object: *The head teacher was presented with a set of the Encyclopaedia Britannica, worth more than £1,600.* | **complete set** *For sale – 'The Guitarist' magazine – complete set, 1984-1992.* | **+ of** *a set of commemorative gold coins*

colour

RELATED WORDS

- *see also* **paint**

1 a colour

- colour
- shade
- tint
- vivid
- hue
- colouring

colour British **/color** American /ˈkʌləʳ/ [n C/U] *What's your favourite colour?* | *I like nice bright colours like yellow and pink* | *What colour is his hair?* | *Look carefully at the rear door. It's not quite the same colour as the rest of the car.* | *The chameleon is able to change colour to protect itself.*

shade /ʃeɪd/ [n C] a particular type of one colour, which is darker or lighter than other types of the same colour: *When buying make-up, choose the right shade to match your skin.* | **shade of blue/green etc** *Valerie's eyes are a beautiful shade of blue.* | *In the fall, the woods are full of countless shades of brown, yellow and orange.*

tint /tɪnt/ [n C] a small amount of a particular colour in something that is mostly another colour: *The sun shining on her head gave her hair an attractive red tint.* | *The glass had a bluish tint to it, like ice.* | *It was October, and the leaves had begun to take on their warm autumn tints.*

vivid /ˈvɪvɪ̈d/ [adj] a **vivid** colour is very bright and noticeable, especially in a way that is attractive: *a vivid blue sky* | *a cloud of vivid yellow butterflies*

hue /hjuː/ [n C] a colour or a shade of a colour: *The Prince wore majestic robes of a rich purple hue.*

colouring British **/coloring** American /ˈkʌlərɪŋ/ [n U] the colour of a person's or animal's hair, skin, or eyes: *This lipstick is perfect for your coloring.* | *People with very light colouring need to protect themselves from the sun as they burn easily.* | *Many poisonous animals have distinctive coloring that is easily recognized.*

2 to be a particular colour

- be
- coloured
- tinted

be /bi (*strong*) biː/ [v] **be red/green etc** *The Japanese flag is white with a red circle in the middle.* | *Frogs are green, toads are brown. That's how you tell the difference.* | *'What colour is your car?' 'It's black.'*

coloured British **/colored** American /ˈkʌləʳd/ [adj usually before noun] having one or more colours and not black or white: *The front door was painted blue and had a coloured glass panel in it.* | *You can make Christmas decorations from almost anything – beads, colored ribbons, sea shells – anything.* | **brightly coloured** *The cages were full of brightly-coloured tropical birds.*

tinted /ˈtɪntɪ̈d/ [adj] glass that is **tinted** has a slight colour, so that people cannot see through it, so that light does not shine too brightly through it: *The limousine had tinted windows, so we couldn't see who was inside.* | **blue-tinted/green-tinted etc** *She wore a pair of pink-tinted glasses.*

3 brightly coloured

- bright
- colourful
- brilliant
- multicoloured
- gaudy
- garish
- vibrant
- lurid

bright /braɪt/ [adj] a **bright** colour is strong and very easy to notice: *The artist clearly loved bright colours.* | *If you are cycling at night, always wear something bright.* | **bright blue/red/yellow etc** *The front door was painted bright red.* | *a bright yellow van* —**brightly** [adv] *a brightly painted boat* | *brightly coloured balloons*

colourful British **/colorful** American /ˈkʌləʳfəl/ [adj] having a lot of different colours, especially bright colours: *The garden was full of colourful and fascinating flowers.* | *That's a really colourful tie you're wearing.* | *Stunning tropical fish swim in and out of the colorful rock formations.*

brilliant /ˈbrɪljənt/ [adj usually before noun] **brilliant white/blue/green etc** so bright that it almost hurts your eyes to look at it: *a brilliant blue sky* | *The room was painted a brilliant white.*

multicoloured British **/multicolored** American /ˈmʌltiˌkʌləʳd/ [adj usually before noun] having several different colours, especially bright colours: *A giant multicoloured flag waved in the midday sun.* | *A group of women sat around talking, their multicoloured dresses radiant.*

gaudy /ˈgɔːdi/ [adj] something that is **gaudy** has too many different colours or is too brightly coloured, with the result that it looks cheap and in bad taste: *I didn't like the decorations – they looked rather gaudy.* | *She smelled of cheap perfume and wore gaudy clothing and fake costume jewellery.*

garish /ˈgeərɪʃ/ [adj] too brightly coloured in a way that is unpleasant to look at: *Her hair had been dyed a garish shade of red.* | *The streets are lined with garish neon signs.* | *The traditional designs have been replaced by much more garish colours.*

vibrant /ˈvaɪbrənt/ [adj] **vibrant** colours are very bright and strong – used when you like these colours very much: *the vibrant reds and oranges of* *the leaves in autumn* | *The streets of the capital are vibrant with color.*

lurid /ˈlʊərɨd, ˈljʊərɨd‖ˈlʊərɨd/ [adj] **lurid** colours are too bright and look very unattractive – used when you dislike these colours: *The carpets were a lurid shade of green.*

4 light colours

- light
- pale
- fair
- pastel
- faded

light /laɪt/ [adj] **light** colours are closer to white than to black: *They both have brown hair, but Tina's is slightly lighter.* | **light blue/green/orange etc** *This is a nice jacket and we also do it in a light green.*

pale /peɪl/ [adj] very light in colour: *There were dark rings under her eyes and her skin was paler than usual.* | **pale pink/green/blue etc** *Her dress is pale pink, with a small flowery pattern.* | *The old man's pale blue eyes moved from the dartboard to the bar and then back again.*

fair /feəʳ/ [adj] use this about the colour of people's hair and skin: *Someone with fair skin like you should probably use a stronger sunscreen.* | **fair-haired/fair-skinned** *The Indians were at first frightened of the fair-skinned Europeans.*

pastel /ˈpæstl‖pæˈstel/ [adj only before noun] **pastel** colours, especially pink, yellow, green or blue, are soft and light and not at all bright: *Before the baby was born Jenny bought some pretty, pastel baby clothes.* | *Mrs Singh preferred saris in pastel colours, such as salmon pink.* —**pastels** [n plural] pastel colours: *White, cream, and pastels suit me better than dark colours.*

faded /ˈfeɪdɨd/ [adj] if something is **faded**, it is a lighter colour than it was originally because of being affected by the sun, washing, or age: *The woman wore a faded blue dress and old brown sandals.* | *Joe dropped a faded newspaper picture on Woodward's desk.*

5 dark colours

- dark
- deep
- rich

dark /dɑːʳk/ [adj] **dark** colours are closer to black than to white: *She has beautiful dark brown eyes.* | *If you're going to have such dark walls I really think you should have a pale carpet.* | *'What do you think of this blouse?' 'It's a bit dark – navy doesn't really suit you.'*

deep /diːp/ [adj usually before noun] **deep** colours are strong, dark, and attractive: *I'm looking for a deeper shade of purple to paint the bedroom.* | **deep blue/red/purple etc** *She looked into his eyes. They were deep blue.* | *In the lounge hung long curtains of luxurious deep red velvet.*

rich /rɪtʃ/ [adj] dark and giving a pleasant feeling of comfort and warmth: *I admired the warm, rich colors of her Persian rugs.* | *The horse had a rich chestnut coat.*

6 having no colour

- colourless

colourless British **/colorless** American /ˈkʌləʳləs/ [adj] *Carbon monoxide is a colourless, odourless gas.* | *He stared out the window at the colorless sky.*

7 photograph/film/television

- colour
- black and white
- monochrome

colour British **/color** American /ˈkʌləʳ/ [adj] showing pictures in all colours, not just in black, white, and grey: *You need a colour television to fully appreciate nature programmes.* | *Does your new computer have a colour monitor?* | *The outstanding feature of this book is its 45 full-page color photographs.* | **in colour** (=showing all the colours) *All the pictures are in color.*

black and white /ˌblæk ən ˈwaɪt/ [adj phrase usually before noun] **black and white television/photograph/film etc** one that has a black, white, and grey picture, not colours such as blue, red and yellow: *Black and white TV sets are now very cheap to buy.* | *I love the old black-and-white movies.* | *an exhibition of black and white photos* | **in black and white** (=showing only black, white, and grey) *'Is the film 'Casablanca' in colour?' 'No, it's in black and white.'*

monochrome /ˈmɒnəkrəʊm‖ˈmɑː-/ [adj] **monochrome** pictures have no colour, and use only black, white, and shades of grey: *There were some beautiful monochrome pictures of Yosemite.* | **in monochrome** *McCullin still prefers to shoot in monochrome.*

8 to change the colour of something

- colour
- dye
- bleach

colour British **/color** American /ˈkʌləʳ/ [v T] to put **colour** into something: *Last time I tried to colour my hair it turned red!* | *Marigold petals were once used for colouring butter and cheese.* | **colour/color sth in** (=colour inside the lines of a picture) *Josie sat at the table coloring in her picture while her father made the dinner.*

dye /daɪ/ [v T] to change the colour of material or hair by using a special coloured liquid: *I'm bored with this skirt. I'm going to dye it.* | *Wool and silk are the materials that are easiest to dye.* | **dye sth blue/yellow/red etc** *She's dyed her hair red – it looks so unnatural.* —**dyed** [adj] *The boy wore a headdress of dyed ostrich feathers.*

bleach /bliːtʃ/ [v T] to use chemicals to make the colour of material or hair lighter: *To play the part, Kensit had to bleach her hair and gain 20 pounds.* | *I'm going to bleach these curtains and see if I can get the stains out.* —**bleached** [adj] *The beach was full of bleached blondes.*

9 to lose colour

- fade
- lose its colour
- run

fade /feɪd/ [v I] if a colour or coloured material **fades**, its colour becomes paler, for example because it has been in sunlight for a long time: *Over the years the green paint had faded.* | *Your natural hair colour begins to fade as you grow older, and eventually you go grey.* —**faded** [adj] *The curtains that were at one time bright and cheerful were now faded and torn.*

lose its colour British **/lose its color** American /ˌluːz ɪts ˈkʌləʳ/ [v phrase] if a material or object **loses its colour**, the colour comes out of it, especially because of the effects of washing or sunlight: *Will* *this shirt lose its colour if you wash it? | Red onions lose their color when cooked.*

run /rʌn/ [v I] if the colours **run** on a piece of clothing when you wash it, some of the colour goes from one part of it and onto another part of it because the water is too hot: *It is usually advisable to wash new clothes separately as they tend to run.*

come from

to have something or somewhere as a starting point or place

RELATED WORDS

▸ *see also* **start, beginning, cause, country, class (2)**

1 to come from a particular country, town etc

- ▸ **come from/be from**
- ▸ **be a native of**
- ▸ **be American/French/Japanese etc by birth**
- ▸ **be of Scottish/Russian etc ancestry**

come from/be from /ˈkʌm frɒm, biː ˈfrɒm/ [phr v T not in progressive/v phrase not in progressive] if you **come from** or **are from** a particular place, that is where you were born or where you lived for a long time: *She comes from Japan. | Where are you from? | My wife's parents and my parents come from the same town.*

be a native of /biː ə ˈneɪtɪv ɒv/ [v phrase] **be a native of Tokyo/London/Wales etc** to have been born in and to have spent the early part of your life in that place – used especially when you are writing about someone's life: *Hughes, who is a native of Belfast, often uses the city as a setting for his novels. | DeParle is a native of Rockwood, Tennessee.*

be American/French/Japanese etc by birth /biː əˌmerɪkən baɪ ˈbɜːʳθ/ [v phrase] to have been born in a particular country or to be a citizen of that country because your parents come from there, especially when you now live somewhere else: *She's lived in Australia for a long time, but she's Welsh by birth. | They're Russian by birth but they've lived in America for so long that they feel little attachment to their homeland.*

be of Scottish/Russian etc ancestry /biː əv ˌskɒtɪʃ ˈænsestri‖-ˌskɑː-/ [v phrase] if you **are of Scottish/Russian etc ancestry**, relatives of yours that are now dead came from that country a long time ago: *There are roughly 40 million Americans of Irish ancestry. | Her fine features suggested she was of Arabic or Indian ancestry.*

2 the place you come from

- ▸ **home town**
- ▸ **birthplace**
- ▸ **place of birth**
- ▸ **home**

home town /ˌhəʊm ˈtaʊn/ [n C] the town where you live now, where you were born, or where you spent most of your early life: *I haven't been back to my home town since my mother died. | She hated her home town so much she would never admit where she was from.*

birthplace /ˈbɜːʳθpleɪs/ [n C] the place where someone, especially someone famous, was born: *We visited the birthplace of Lenin in Ulyanovsk. | Muslims are expected to make at least one pilgrimage to Mecca, Muhammad's birthplace.*

place of birth /ˌpleɪs əv ˈbɜːʳθ/ [n phrase] the place where you were born – used especially in official documents: *Forms usually ask you your name, address, nationality and place of birth. | She hoped that one day she would return to her place of birth.*

home /həʊm/ [n C usually singular] the place where you usually live or the place that you come from, especially when that is the place where you feel you belong and where you would most like to live: *It took us about ten years to think of Atlanta as home. | Her home, she said, was in Southern China, but she hadn't been there since she was a child.*

3 to come from a particular family or social group

- ▸ **come from/be from**
- ▸ **be descended from**
- ▸ **background**
- ▸ **origins**
- ▸ **roots**

come from/be from /ˈkʌm frɒm, biː ˈfrɒm/ [phr v T not in progressive/v phrase not in progressive] *Most of the people here come from very poor families. | She comes from a family of seven kids. | He's from a very upper class background.*

be descended from /biː dɪˈsendəd frɒm/ [v phrase] if you **are descended from** someone, especially someone famous or a group of people who lived a long time ago, you are related to them: *She always claimed her family was descended from the ancient Kings of Egypt. | The Japanese are thought to be descended from tribes from the north of China.*

background /ˈbækgraʊnd/ [n C] the particular type of family or social group that you come from: *How quickly kids learn to read will often depend on both their ability and their backgrounds. | Sylvie had always expected that she would marry someone of a similar background to herself. |* **working class/Jewish etc background** *Gary always tried to hide his working class background.*

origins /ˈɒrədʒənz‖ˈɔː-, ˈɑː-/ [n plural] the social position that you were born into and in which you spent the early part of your life, for example who your parents were or whether they were rich or poor: *Miller questioned her closely, about her present job, her family and her origins. |* **humble origins** (=a poor social position that someone comes from) *Politicians love to talk about their humble origins because they think it will make them popular with voters.*

roots /ruːts/ [n plural] your connection with a place or group in society because you were born there, or your family used to live there: *Rizzo was a man who never forgot his roots. | Beth went to Israel in search of her roots.*

4 to be grown or made in a particular place

- ▸ **come from/be from**
- ▸ **be made in**

come from/be from /ˈkʌm frɒm, biː ˈfrɒm/ [phr v T not in progressive/v phrase not in progressive] *Try this bread – it comes from the bakery on Central Avenue. | U.S. officials say some 60 percent of the heroin on the streets comes from Myanmar. | All the medical equipment here is from France.*

be made in /biː ˈmeɪd ɪn/ [v phrase] to have been made in a particular country: *These shoes were* *made in Italy.* | *About 57 percent of the cars and trucks sold in Colombia are made in Colombia.* | *The label on the bottle said the wine was made in Germany.*

5 when a sound, smell etc comes from somewhere

- come from
- emanate from
- source

come from /ˈkʌm frɒm/ [phr v T not in passive] *The wind was coming from the west.* | *Coming from outside in the street was the sound of children playing.* | *There was an awful smell coming from under the sink.*

emanate from /ˈeməneɪt frɒm/ [phr v T not in passive] formal to come from somewhere: *Smoke emanated from the kitchen window.* | *The President argued that accusations emanating from Congress were not accurate.* | *Just as the audience grew quiet, the unmistakable ring of a cellular phone emanated from the last row of the theater.*

source /sɔːʳs/ [n C] the place that a sound, a smell, smoke, gas etc comes from: *In the case of an electric shock, turn the power off at its source.* | **an unknown source** *The sound came from an unknown source, far away in the distance.* | **+ of** *The tank's losing water, but we can't find the source of the leak.*

6 to have developed from something

- come from
- be based on
- originate
- go back to
- have its origins in
- have its roots in
- derive from/be derived from
- be founded on
- grow out of
- develop from/evolve from

come from /ˈkʌm frɒm/ [phr v T not in progressive or passive] use this to say that something that exists now developed from something else that existed before: *My idea for the film came from an article I read about West Virginia coal miners.* | *The name 'terrier' comes from the Latin word 'terra' meaning the earth.*

be based on /biː ˈbeɪst ɒn/ [v phrase] if a film, story, idea, plan etc **is based on** something else, that is where its basic ideas or facts come from: *The film is based on a popular Bengali novel.* | *Overtime pay will be based on the number of hours you work each week.* | *Your test questions will be based on the work you have done in the past year.*

originate /əˈrɪdʒᵻneɪt/ [v I not in progressive] to have developed in a particular place or from a particular situation: *How did the tradition of wearing costumes on Hallowe'en originate?* | **+ in** *Welfare is a program that originated in the 1930s to help widows.* | *Buddhism originated in India and came to China in the first century A.D.*

go back to /gəʊ ˈbæk tuː/ [phr v T not in progressive or passive] to have developed from something that happened or existed a long time ago: *Many phrases in the language go back to early religious writings.* | *Our friendship goes back to our freshman year in college.* | *Jo just refuses to get into a car – it all goes back to when she had that accident.*

have its origins in /hæv ɪts ˈɒrᵻdʒɪnz ɪn‖-ˈɔːr-/ [v phrase not in progressive] if something **has its origins in** something that existed a long time ago, that is where it comes from and is the reason for it being as it is: *Modern medicine often has its origins in ancient ways of doing things.* | *Vaudeville had its origins in French street culture.*

have its roots in /hæv ɪts ˈruːts ɪn/ [v phrase not in progressive] if something such as a belief or attitude **has its roots in** conditions that existed earlier, it developed from them and is still influenced by them: *Many music historians believe that jazz has its roots in blues music.* | *Economic policy in the US has its roots in the free market system.*

derive from/be derived from /dɪˈraɪv frɒm, biː dɪˈraɪvd frɒm/ [v phrase not in progressive/v phrase] to have developed from something else, especially by a long or complicated process: *Much of the English language is derived from Latin and Greek.* | *About a quarter of the drugs in prescription medicines today are derived from plants.*

be founded on /biː ˈfaʊndᵻd ɒn/ [v phrase] to have one main idea, belief etc that something else develops from: *The constitution in this country is not written. It's founded on tradition and precedent.* | *White resistance to Civil Rights was founded on age-old fears of democracy.*

grow out of /ˈgrəʊ aʊt ɒv/ [v T not in progressive or passive] to develop from something small or simple by becoming bigger or more complicated: *Socialist ideals grew out of an earlier idea that all men are created equal.* | *The skill of writing grew out of a wish to put speech into a permanent form.*

develop from/evolve from /dɪˈveləp frɒm, ɪˈvɒlv frɒm‖ɪˈvɑːlv-/ [v phrase] to come from an original idea or form and change into something bigger, more important, or more advanced: *The whole basis of her novel evolved from a chance meeting she had with an old friend.* | *Within years, the site developed from an area of waste ground into a thriving farm.*

7 the place, situation etc that something comes from

- origin/origins
- source
- cradle
- birthplace
- root

origin/origins /ˈɒrᵻdʒᵻn(z)‖ˈɔː-, ˈɑː-/ [n C] the situation, ideas, events etc that something else developed from: *The rumour is now so widespread, it's difficult to be certain of its origin.* | **+ of** *Astronomers hope new instruments will give them further clues to the origins of the universe.* | *a book that tries to explain the origin of words and phrases*

source /sɔːʳs/ [n C] the point or place where something comes from or where people get something from: *They get their money from various sources.* | **+ of** *Beans and lentils are a very good source of protein.* | *Most Americans rely on television as their chief source of information.*

cradle /ˈkreɪdl/ [n C usually singular] **cradle of democracy/civilization/human society etc** the place or situation in which democracy etc first started: *Ancient Athens is generally thought of as the cradle of democracy.* | *Baghdad, the cradle of civilization*

birthplace /ˈbɜːʳθpleɪs/ [n C] the place where something first started to exist **+ of** *New Orleans, the birthplace of jazz* | *Walden Pond has been called the birthplace of modern environmentalism.*

root /ruːt/ [n C] the most important reason for or cause of something else happening or existing, especially a problem or something bad **+ of** *Low taxation of the rich is the root of the economic problems in this country.* | **the root of all evil** *The love of money is said to be the root of all evil.*

comfortable/uncomfortable

WHAT'S HERE

comfortable

RELATED WORDS

▸ *see also* **relax/relaxed**

1 feeling comfortable

▸ **comfortable** ▸ **in comfort**
▸ **snug** ▸ **comfort**

comfortable /'kʌmftəbəl, 'kʌmfət-‖'kʌmfərt-, 'kʌmft-/ ALSO **comfy** /'kʌmfi/ [adj] **spoken informal** feeling physically relaxed, for example because you are sitting on a soft chair or lying on a soft bed: *I was so warm and comfortable in bed that I didn't want to get up.* | *You'll probably be more comfortable if you tilt the seat back.* | *'Comfy?' 'Yes, thanks.'* | **make yourself comfortable** *Sit down and make yourselves comfortable while I get us some coffee.* —**comfortably** [adv] *He was sitting comfortably in an armchair by the window.*

snug /snʌg/ [adj] feeling comfortable and happy when you are sitting down or in bed because you are in a warm place: *She looks really snug under all those blankets.* —**snugly** [adv] *It was freezing outside but we were soon sitting snugly by the fire.*

in comfort /ɪn 'kʌmfərt/ [adv] if you do something **in comfort**, you are comfortable while you are doing it: *Travelling first class allows you to enjoy your journey in comfort.* | *Now you can watch your favorite movies in the comfort of your own home.*

comfort /'kʌmfərt/ [n U] *The hotel staff made sure nothing disturbed our comfort or enjoyment.* | *After he became rich, he lived a life of idleness and comfort.*

2 chairs/places/clothes

▸ **comfortable** ▸ **snug**
▸ **comfy** ▸ **luxurious**
▸ **cosy**

comfortable /'kʌmftəbəl, 'kʌmfət-‖'kʌmfərt-, 'kʌmft-/ [adj] use this about clothes, furniture, or rooms that make you feel comfortable: *Thomas can sleep on the sofa, but I'm afraid it's not as comfortable as a bed.* | *She has a big comfortable apartment overlooking Central Park.* | *Can you wait for a moment while I change into something more comfortable?* —**comfortably** [adv] *Make sure you're comfortably dressed before you start the walk.*

comfy /'kʌmfi/ [adj] **informal** a piece of furniture or clothing that is **comfy** is comfortable and makes you feel relaxed: *Grandpa likes to sit in the comfy chair beside the fire.* | *These old shoes are so comfy. I don't want to get rid of them.*

cosy British **cozy** American /'kəʊzi/ [adj] a **cosy** room, chair, or situation is very pleasant and makes you feel warm, relaxed, and comfortable: *The fire had been lit and the room looked bright and cosy.* | *I wis I was at home in a nice cozy bed.* | *There was a coz atmosphere in the bar.* —**cosily/cozily** [adv] *The bec room was cosily furnished in bright warm colours.*

snug /snʌg/ [adj] a room or space that is **snug** i small, warm, and comfortable and makes you fe happy and protected from the cold outside: *a snu little cabin*

luxurious /lʌg'zjʊəriəs, ləg'ʒʊəriəs‖ləg'ʒʊəriəs [adj] a **luxurious** house, hotel, apartment etc make you feel very comfortable because it has larg rooms and expensive furniture, carpets etc: *Th hotel we stayed in was really luxurious.* | *a luxur ous yacht*

3 journey/ride

▸ **comfortable** ▸ **smooth**

comfortable /'kʌmftəbəl, 'kʌmfət-‖'kʌmfərt 'kʌmft-/ [adj] *'Did you have a good flight?' 'Yes, ver comfortable thank you.'* | *The truck gives you a sur prisingly comfortable ride.* —**comfortably** [adv] *always go by boat – it's the only way to travel con fortably.*

smooth /smu:ð/ [adj] a **smooth** journey is comfor able because your car or plane does not shake, c the sea is not rough: *It was one of the smoothe flights I've ever had.* | *The car has excellent susper sion and the journey was really smooth.*

4 things that make you feel comfortable

▸ **comforts**

comforts /'kʌmfərts/ [n plural] things that mak your life more pleasant and comfortable, especiall things that are not completely necessary but whic you are used to having in your home: *She was star ing to miss the familiar comforts of her home i Massachusetts.* | **material comforts** (=comfort such as money and possessions) *We enjoyed th material comforts of the booming economy.*

uncomfortable

RELATED WORDS

▸ *see also* **embarrassed/embarrassing**

5 not feeling comfortable

▸ **uncomfortable** ▸ **discomfort**

uncomfortable /ʌn'kʌmftəbəl, -'kʌmfə ‖-'kʌmfərt-, -'kʌmft-/ [adj] not comfortable: *The hea was making us all uncomfortable.* | *They were force to spend another uncomfortable night at the airpo waiting for their plane.*

discomfort /dɪs'kʌmfərt/ [n U] *There's a limit to th amount of discomfort anyone can put up with.* **acute discomfort** (=great discomfort) *The diseas causes acute physical discomfort.*

6 chairs/places/clothes

▸ **uncomfortable** ▸ **spartan**
▸ **cramped**

uncomfortable /ʌn'kʌmftəbəl, -'kʌmfət- ‖ -'kʌn fərt-, -'kʌmft-/ [adj] *She was dressed in a very tigh* *skirt and uncomfortable-looking shoes.* | *These chairs may look good, but they're very uncomfortable to sit on.*

cramped /kræmpt/ [adj] a **cramped** room, apartment, car etc is uncomfortable because there is not enough space: *cramped living conditions* | *They worked from cramped offices near the main station.*

spartan /ˈspɑːʳtn/ [adj] a room, building, or conditions that are **spartan** are very simple and without comfortable furniture or unnecessary decorations: *The students' rooms are spartan but clean, with no carpets or central heating.* | *The hotel was like a different world compared to the spartan accommodation I'd had in the army.*

7 journey/ride

- uncomfortable
- rough
- bumpy

uncomfortable /ʌnˈkʌmftəbəl, -ˈkʌmfət- ‖-ˈkʌmfərt-, -ˈkʌmft-/ [adj] *I hate travelling by train – the carriages are always so dirty and uncomfortable.* | *In those days visiting the island meant a long uncomfortable voyage across choppy seas.*

rough /rʌf/ [adj] a sea journey that is **rough** is uncomfortable because bad weather makes the boat go up and down a lot: *It was a rough crossing and most of the passengers were seasick.*

bumpy /ˈbʌmpi/ [adj] a journey by car or plane that is **bumpy** is uncomfortable because bad road conditions or bad weather make the car or plane shake a lot: *After a bumpy landing, all the passengers cheered and thanked the pilot.* | *To get to Agra we had to endure a long bumpy ride in an old bus.*

8 things that make you feel uncomfortable

- discomforts

discomforts /dɪsˈkʌmfəʳts/ [n plural] conditions that make you feel uncomfortable, for example lack of rest, nowhere to wash yourself, or very hot or cold weather: *I wasn't prepared for the discomforts of living in a place with no electricity or running water.* | *the discomforts of pregnancy*

comfort/make sb feel better

RELATED WORDS

- *see also* **upset, disappointed, fed up, worried/worrying, sad, calm, happy**

1 to make someone feel less upset, sad, worried, etc

- comfort
- make sb feel better
- cheer sb up
- console
- reassure
- soothe
- cheer up
- don't worry

comfort /ˈkʌmfəʳt/ [v T] to **comfort** someone, for example by telling them there is nothing to worry about or putting your arms around them: *He tried to comfort her by telling her that everything would be all right.* | *Joyce did her best to comfort him, assuring him that it was not his fault.* | *The two sisters hugged each other, sharing their grief and comforting one another.*

make sb feel better /ˌmeɪk (sb) fiːl ˈbetəʳ/ [v phrase] to say something to someone or give them something that makes them feel less upset, sad, worried etc: *What can I do to make you feel better?* | *It might make you feel better to eat something.* | *Why don't you tell me what's troubling you? It'll make you feel better.*

cheer sb up /ˌtʃɪəʳ (sb) ˈʌp/ [phr v T] to make someone feel happier when they are disappointed or sad about something: *Thanks for the card. It really cheered me up.* | *I'm taking Jenny out tonight to cheer her up.* | *I tried to think of something to say to cheer him up.*

console /kənˈsəʊl/ [v T] written to comfort someone when they feel unhappy or disappointed, especially by saying something that makes them realize the situation is not so bad: *A priest was called in to console victims' families.* | *I wanted to console her, but I didn't know how.* | **console yourself with sth** *Archer consoled himself with the thought that at least he had done his best.*

reassure /ˌriːəˈʃʊəʳ/ [v T] to make someone feel less worried or frightened about a situation, for example by being friendly to them or by telling them there is nothing to worry about: *My mother did her best to reassure me, but I still felt nervous and insecure.* | **reassure sb about sth** *The company tried to reassure shareholders about the safety of their stocks.* | **reassure sb that** *The doctor did his best to reassure us that Cindy would be all right.* | *The president reassured voters that there would be no tax increase.* | *I tried to reassure her that she had made the right decision in turning down the job.*

soothe /suːð/ [v T] to make someone feel more calm and relaxed when they are upset, anxious, or nervous: *When the baby cried, his mother soothed him by stroking his hot little head.* | *Maybe a drink would help soothe your nerves.*

cheer up /ˌtʃiːr ˈʌp/ [v phrase] spoken say this to tell someone to stop feeling disappointed or sad and try to be more cheerful: *Cheer up! It's not that bad.* | *Cheer up, Phil. You'll find another job.*

don't worry /ˌdəʊnt ˈwʌri‖-ˈwɜːri/ spoken say this when you want to make someone less worried or nervous, because you do not think there is anything to be worried or nervous about: *Don't worry. The doctor says it's just a bad cold.* | *Don't worry! The flight's not until 9:30. We have plenty of time.*

2 making you feel less upset, sad, worried etc

- comforting
- soothing
- reassuring
- consoling

comforting /ˈkʌmfəʳtɪŋ/ [adj] *It was comforting to see the lights of home.* | *Stefan tried to think of something comforting to say.* | *She laid a comforting hand on my arm.* —**comfortingly** [adv] *She squeezed his shoulder comfortingly.*

soothing /ˈsuːðɪŋ/ [adj] something that is **soothing** makes you feel calm and relaxed when you are upset, anxious, or nervous: *My mother had a gentle, soothing voice.* | *I love Mozart's music. I find it very soothing.* | *The shower was wonderfully soothing.* —**soothingly** [adv] *She rocked the baby soothingly in her arms.*

reassuring /ˌriːəˈʃʊərɪŋ◂/ [adj] making you feel less worried or frightened about something: *The teacher gave him a reassuring smile.* | *My dad tried to sound calm and reassuring.* | **enormously reassuring** (=very reassuring) *I found his words enormously reassuring.* —**reassuringly** [adv] *Bill squeezed her hand reassuringly.*

consoling /kənˈsəʊlɪŋ/ [adj] especially written something that is **consoling**, especially something that someone says, makes you feel better when you are unhappy or disappointed: *What you said about George was very consoling.* | *I didn't find his words very consoling.* | *He nodded and put a consoling arm around her shoulders.*

3 a happier feeling after you have been upset, worried, etc

- comfort
- consolation
- relief

comfort /ˈkʌmfəʳt/ [n U] *Emily goes to a women's group for comfort and emotional support.* | **bring/give comfort** *Your letter brought me great comfort after John died.* | *Her faith gave her comfort during a very difficult time.* | **take/draw comfort from** *The family has taken some comfort from the fact that her condition has stabilized.*

relief /rɪˈliːf/ [n singular/U] the feeling you have when something worrying or frightening has ended or has not happened: *When the plane finally landed, we all felt a tremendous sense of relief.* | *It was a great relief to know that the children were safe.* | **that's a relief!/what a relief!** *What a relief! We were so worried about you.* | *What a relief to finally get away from the office.* | **to your relief** (=making you feel relief) *To our relief, the deal went through without any problems.* | **heave/breathe a sigh of relief** (=breathe loudly to show your relief) *She breathed a sign of relief when he finally answered the phone.*

consolation /ˌkɒnsəˈleɪʃən‖ˌkɑːn-/ [n singular/U] a thought or fact that makes you feel less disappointed or sad, for example when someone has died or when you have just heard some disappointing news: *It was some consolation to know that he could take the exam again.* | *My one consolation is that she died peacefully.* | **take (some) consolation** *It was difficult to say goodbye, but I took some consolation from the fact that I would see her again at the end of the year.*

common

RELATED WORDS

opposite: **rare/rarely, unusual**

▸ *see also* **usually, lot, often, typical, conventional, normal/ordinary, unusual, special**

1 when there are a lot of something

- common
- commonplace
- be everywhere
- be ten a penny

common /ˈkɒmən‖ˈkɑː-/ [adj] if something is **common**, there are a lot of them and they are not unusual: *Jones is a very common name in Great Britain.* | *Foxes are common in the area.* | *Personal computers are nearly as common in American homes as televisions.*

be everywhere /biː ˈevriweəʳ/ [v phrase] to be extremely common and be seen in many different places: *Images of the dictator were everywhere.* | *Microchips seem to be everywhere these days – even in washing machines.* | *One of the first things you notice in Beijing are the bicycles – they're everywhere.*

commonplace /ˈkɒmənpleɪs‖ˈkɑː-/ [adj not before noun] things that are **commonplace** exist in large numbers so that they are not considered to be special or unusual even though in other places they may be much less common: *Superstores such as Wal-Mart are now commonplace in America's small towns.* | *Expensive foreign cars are commonplace in this Chicago suburb.*

be ten a penny British **/be a dime a dozen** American /biː ˌten ə ˈpeni, biː ə ˌdaɪm ə ˈdʌzən/ [v phrase] informal to be very common in a particular area and therefore not be considered special or unusual: *Jobs like this are a dime a dozen.*

2 when something happens a lot

- common
- be rife
- widespread
- prevalent
- commonplace
- pervasive

common /ˈkɒmən‖ˈkɑː-/ [adj] happening often or in a lot of places: *It's a common mathematical error.* | *Petty theft and pickpocketing are becoming increasingly common in the city centre.* | *Many of the more common forms of cancer can be treated successfully if detected early.* | **+ among** *The condition is most common among women aged 18 to 24.* | **it is common for sth to happen/sb to do sth** *It's very common for older children to feel jealous after the birth of a baby.* —**commonly** [adv] *Computers are now commonly used in language learning.*

widespread /ˈwaɪdspred/ [adj] happening in a lot of places or done by a lot of people: *Racism is much more widespread than people imagine.* | *The report claimed that the problem of police brutality was widespread.* | *Thanks to the widespread availability of antibiotics diseases such as typhoid have largely been eradicated.*

commonplace /ˈkɒmənpleɪs‖ˈkɑː-/ [adj not before noun] happening very often, and therefore not considered to be special or unusual: *Nudism on beaches has long been commonplace in Europe.* | *Organ transplants are now commonplace.* | **increasingly commonplace** *It used to be rare to see young people sleeping on the streets of London – these days it's become increasingly commonplace.*

be rife /biː ˈraɪf/ [v phrase] if bad behaviour such as stealing or violence **is rife** in a particular area it happens very often there: *Political corruption was rife in those days.* | **sth is rife with sth** *A place like Hollywood is always rife with gossip.* | *The schools are rife with drug abuse.*

prevalent /ˈprevələnt/ [adj] formal a problem, idea, or type of behaviour that is **prevalent** in one place, time, or group of people is common there: *Flu is most prevalent during the winter months.* | *Depression remains one of the most prevalent health disorders in the US.* | *This belief is more prevalent among men than women.*

pervasive /pəʳˈveɪsɪv/ [adj] problems, behaviour, or situations that are **pervasive** are very common and are spreading to more and more people or areas so that they are impossible to prevent: *Violence and crime are pervasive features of city life.* | *She argues that sexual discrimination remains a pervasive ele-*

ment in corporate culture. | **all-pervasive** (=extremely pervasive) *the all-pervasive influence of television*

company

a business organization

RELATED WORDS

- part of a company *see* **part (4)**
- when a company reduces its activities, costs etc *see* **reduce (4)**
- *see also* **business, manager, position/rank, job, work, work for sb, in charge of**

1 a company

- company
- firm
- business
- subsidiary
- dotcom
- start-up

company /ˈkʌmpəni/ [n C] an organization, that produces goods or provides services in order to make a profit: *The company employs over 10,000 people worldwide.* | **oil/insurance/phone etc company** *It is the second largest insurance company in Germany.* | **work for a company** *My father used to work for one of the big oil companies.* | **join a company** (=start to work there) *Davis joined the company as vice-president of sales nine months ago.* | **set up/start a company** *The company was set up in 1975.*

firm /fɜːʳm/ [n C] a company, especially one that provides services rather than producing goods, for example financial or legal services: *Hanson decided to start his own management consulting firm.* | **law/electronics/building etc firm** *She works for a law firm in Amsterdam.* | **firm of lawyers/accountants etc** *Edward got a job with a firm of accountants in London.* | **join a firm** (=start working for a firm) *Harris joined the firm in 1992.*

business /ˈbɪznɪ̈s/ [n C] a company that sells or produces goods or provides services, especially one that employs only a small number of people or only one person: *Jack's thinking of starting his own business.* | *Several small businesses have folded* (=closed) *in recent months.* | **manage/run a business** *Don and his wife run their own business.* | **set up/start a business** *Profits have slowly increased since we started the business three years ago.* | **small business** (=one that employs only one person or very few people) *His oldest daughter, 31, owns a small printing business in Fresno.* | **family business** (=one that was started by and employs members of the same family) *His sons have worked in the family business for years.*

subsidiary /səbˈsɪdiəri‖-dieri/ [n C] a company that is owned and controlled by a larger company: *Sharp Electronics is the U.S. subsidiary of Japan's Sharp Corporation.* | **subsidiary company** *Relco plans to establish a subsidiary company in the UK with a capital of around $4m.*

dotcom /ˈdɒtkɒm‖ˈdɑːtkɑːm/ [n C] a company that sells its goods and services on the Internet: *Many dotcoms fail in their first year of trading.* —**dotcom** [adj] *Investment analysts are predicting another dotcom boom.*

start-up /ˈstɑːʳtʌp/ [n C] a small company that has just been started, often one concerned with computing or the Internet: *She works for a small internet start-up.* —**start-up** [adj] *start-up companies*

2 a very big company

- multinational
- corporation
- conglomerate

multinational /ˌmʌltɪˈnæʃənəl◂/ [adj only before noun] **multinational company/corporation/business** a very large company that has offices or factories in many different countries: *The recording business is now controlled by multinational corporations.* —**multinational** [n C] *the power of the big multinationals*

corporation /ˌkɔːʳpəˈreɪʃən/ [n C] a large company that employs a lot of people, especially one that includes several smaller companies: *IBM is one of the biggest corporations in the world.* | *U.S. corporations sold nearly $6.2 billion in new stock in May – the highest monthly volume in history.*

conglomerate /kənˈglɒmərɪ̈t‖-ˈglɑː-/ [n C] a very large business organization that consists of several different companies which have joined together: *A vast American conglomerate has announced plans to buy the site at a cost of well over a billion dollars.* | *In the mid-1980s the big financial conglomerates muscled into the market.* | *The German media conglomerate Kronstadt AG reported record earnings last year.*

3 when a company operates in many different parts of the world

- globalization

globalization /ˌgləʊbəlaɪˈzeɪʃən‖-bələ-/ [n U] when companies, especially from rich countries, employ people and trade in many different parts of the world: *Globalization has brought very little real benefit to developing countries.* | *The history of capitalism has been a history of the globalization of production.* | *a demonstration against globalization*

4 relating to a company

- company
- corporate

company /ˈkʌmpəni/ [adj only before noun] *Company profits have more than doubled in the last four years.* | *One of the benefits of the job is the use of a company car.* | *A spokesman said company policy doesn't allow comment on mergers and acquisitions.*

corporate /ˈkɔːʳpərɪ̈t/ [adj only before noun] relating to a large company: *Ad campaigns are used to both bolster sales and improve corporate image.* | *Fisher, 37, will be responsible for corporate planning.* | *The company is moving its corporate headquarters from Philadelphia to New York.*

5 abbreviation for different types of company

- Ltd
- Corp.
- Co.
- plc

Ltd British **/Inc.** American the written abbreviations of 'Limited' and 'Incorporated' – used after the name of a company to show that it is legally established and that its owners are legally responsible for only a limited amount of money if the company gets into debt: *Stevenson Securities Ltd* | *Syquest Technology Inc.*

Corp. the written abbreviation of 'Corporation' – used after the name of a large company, especially in the US: *Federal Express Corp.*

Co. /kəʊ/ the abbreviation of 'Company': *Henry Butt and Co. Ltd | Imperial Life Assurance Co. of Canada*

plc /ˌpiː el ˈsiː/ the abbreviation of 'Public Limited Company' – used in Britain after the name of a large company that ordinary people can buy shares in: *Marks & Spencer plc*

compare

RELATED WORDS

- *see also* **different, same**

1 to compare things

- compare
- liken
- make a comparison
- draw an analogy
- draw a parallel
- contrast

compare /kəmˈpeəʳ/ [v T] to think about two or more things or people, in order to see how similar or different they are: *You should compare at least three or four computers before buying one.* | **compare sth/sb with** *I hate the way you always compare me with your ex-boyfriend.* | *If you compare rents in London with those in New York, you'll find they are about the same.* | *You can't compare Charlie Parker with John Coltrane. They were completely different musicians.*

liken /ˈlaɪkən/ [v T usually in passive] to describe someone or something as being similar to someone or something else, especially in order to make it easier to understand **liken sb/sth to** *Critics have likened the new city hall building to a barn.* | *Morris has often been likened to Bobby Kennedy.* | *He likened today's stockmarket to that of the 1920s.*

make a comparison /ˌmeɪk ə kəmˈpærɪsən/ [v phrase] to compare two or more situations or ideas, people etc **+ between** *The article makes a comparison between the novels 'Anna Karenina' and 'Madame Bovary'.*

draw an analogy /ˌdrɔː ən əˈnælədʒi/ [v phrase] to compare two similar situations or ideas in order to explain or prove something about one of them **+ between** *He drew an analogy between mathematics and language.* | *Joe drew an analogy between the Soviet Union of 1946 and Germany of 1938.*

draw a parallel /ˌdrɔː ə ˈpærəlel/ [v phrase] to compare two different situations in order to show that they are similar in some ways **+ between/with** *One could draw a parallel between the professions of acting and politics.* | *He was drawing parallels between events leading up to the last war and current political problems.* | *You could draw parallels with the old Samson and Delilah story.*

contrast /kənˈtrɑːst‖-ˈtræst/ [v T] to compare two things, situations, ideas etc in order to show how they are different from each other: *The guide was contrasting the styles of Monet and Manet.* | **+ with** *In the film, the peaceful life of a monk is contrasted with the violent life of a murderer.* | *It is interesting to contrast life in Spain now with what it was like prior to 1975.* | **compare and contrast** (=show the similarities and differences) *The book compares and contrasts the various methods used in language teaching.*

2 when one thing is being compared with another

- compared to/with
- in comparison/by comparison
- in contrast/by contrast
- beside
- as against
- in proportion to
- relative
- comparative
- than

compared to/with /kəmˈpeəʳd tuː, wɪð/ [prep] *The British are good drivers compared to those in the rest of the EU.* | *Statistics show that there has been a 20% reduction in burglary compared with last year.* | *Women visit their doctors six times a year compared to the three or so visits that men make.*

in comparison/by comparison /ɪn kəmˈpærɪsən, baɪ kəmˈpærɪsən/ [adv] as shown when compared with another situation, idea, person etc: *My car is so slow that it makes a bicycle look fast in comparison.* | **+ with** *We employ far fewer staff in comparison with similar-sized companies.* | **pale in/by comparison** (=to look worse or much less important in comparison) *Forecasters say this year's drought could make that of 1991 pale by comparison.* | *The Yankees' problems pale by comparison with those of the Dodgers.*

in contrast/by contrast /ɪn ˈkɒntrɑːst, baɪ ˈkɒntrɑːst‖ -ˈkɑːntræst/ [adv] use this to talk about the difference between the things, situations, people etc that you are comparing: *I read a lot as a child, but my daughter, by contrast, just seems interested in television.* | **in contrast to** *In contrast to the hot days, the nights are bitterly cold.*

beside /bɪˈsaɪd/ [prep] use this to say that something seems more or less impressive, important etc when compared to something else: *Tom's efforts seemed so weak beside Martin's.* | *Delhi is so old that many European cities actually look young beside it.*

as against /æz əˈgenst/ [prep] use this when you are comparing two pieces of information, facts, etc in order to show how they are different: *Last year there were 443 industrial accidents as against 257 in 1985.* | *With only 57 inhabitants per square mile, as against a world average of over 70, the country is far from overcrowded.*

in proportion to /ɪn prəˈpɔːʳʃən tuː/ [prep] use this to say that something does not seem correct, suitable, impressive etc compared with the things that surround it: *Ricky's head is small in proportion to the rest of his body.* | *I've always thought that my problems were very minor in proportion to those of many other people.*

relative /ˈrelətɪv/ [adj usually before noun] having a particular quality when compared with something else: *Kim lived a life of relative ease and privilege.* | **relative strength/weakness** *the relative strength of the dollar against the Mexican peso* | **relative advantages (and disadvantages)** *She was terrified of flying. The relative advantages of air travel didn't tempt her at all.* | **relative merits** (=what is good about them compared with each other) *The two men stood at the bar discussing the relative merits of various sports cars.* | **it is all relative** (=it can not be judged on its own, but must be compared with others) *It's all relative, isn't it? Someone who is poor in this country might be considered well off in another.*
—**relatively** [adv] *Once you've mastered the basic strokes of squash, the rest is relatively simple.*

comparative /kəmˈpærətɪv/ [adj only before noun] **comparative happiness/comfort/safety etc** happiness, comfort, safety etc that is fairly satisfactory when compared to another: *After a lifetime of poverty, his last few years were spent in comparative comfort.* | *Fresh fruit and vegetables have become a comparative rarity in the region.* | *During the bombings, families sheltered in the comparative safety of the underground rail stations.* —**comparatively** [adv] *We were absolutely broke in those days. Now we're comparatively well off.*

than /ðən; (*strong*) ðæn/ [prep/conjunction] **more/less/ bigger etc than** *Geographically, Canada is bigger than the US.* | *My sister earns a lot more than I do.*

compete with

RELATED WORDS

▸ *see also* **against/oppose, competition, play a game or sport, sport/game, game, win, lose, take part/be involved**

1 to take part in a competition, sports event etc

- ▸ compete
- ▸ contest
- ▸ race

compete /kəm'piːt/ [v I] *Any child between the ages of 8 and 12 is allowed to compete.* | **+ in** *Athletes from 197 countries competed in the Olympic Games in Atlanta.* | **+ against** *Bailey has competed against athletes half his age and won.*

contest /kən'test/ [v T] British **contest the final/the US Open/the election etc** to compete in a sporting event or election – used especially in newspapers and television reports: *In 1991 White contested the US Open and the J G Scott Trophy.* | *The leadership election will be contested by four candidates.* —**contested** [adj] **hotly contested** *a hotly contested Democratic primary*

race /reɪs/ [n C] a competition in which people try to run, drive, ride a horse, etc faster than other people in order to finish first: *It's a 10-kilometer race from downtown to the river.* | *the Breeder's Cup races at Churchill Downs* | **win a race** *He's won three races in a row, using the same car and the same engine.* | **qualify for a race** (=to have run, driven etc fast enough to take part in a particular race) *Krystal has already qualified for the hundred-metre race in the Olympics next year.*

2 to try to do better than another person or organization

- ▸ compete
- ▸ fight
- ▸ vie
- ▸ pit yourself against

compete /kəm'piːt/ [v I] to try to do better than another person or organization, for example in business or politics **+ with** *Nowadays we have to compete more and more with foreign companies.* | **+ against** *The cities are competing against each other to attract and retain business.* | **+ for** (=in order to get something) *Children will always compete for their parents' attention.* | **can't compete with sb/sth** (=not have enough skill, money etc to compete with another person, company etc) *Small independent bookstores just can't compete with national chains and online retailers.* | **+ to do sth** *Fujitsu, Hitachi, and NEC are competing with US firms to build the world's fastest supercomputer.*

fight /faɪt/ [v I/T] to try extremely hard to get an important job or political position that other people are also trying to get **+ for** *If you want the job, you'll have to fight for it.* | **fight sb for sth** *Williams fought several rivals for the leadership of the party.*

vie /vaɪ/ [v I] written if two people, organizations etc **vie** with each other in order to do something, they compete in order to try to do it **+ for** *The two political factions are vying for control of the school board.* | **vie with sb for sth** *Paris and Milan vie with each other for the title of world fashion capital.*

pit yourself against /'pɪt jɔːʳself əˌgenst/ [v phrase] to compete with someone in a fight or competition, especially someone who is stronger, more powerful etc than you: *The company had pitted itself against the giants of the computer industry in an attempt to increase its share of the market.* | **pit your wits against sb** (=compete with someone in a test of knowledge) *On the quiz show ordinary people pit their wits against a panel of celebrities.*

3 a situation in which people try to do better than each other

- ▸ competition
- ▸ competitive
- ▸ rivalry
- ▸ battle/fight
- ▸ race
- ▸ rat race

competition /ˌkɒmpɪ'tɪʃən‖ˌkɑːm-/ [n U] when people or organizations try hard to get something that they all want but only one of them can get **+ for** *Competition for these jobs is very tough – we had over 200 applicants.* | **+ between** *There's a lot of competition between the big supermarket chains.* | **face competition** *Today television networks face increasing competition from cable programming.* | **fierce/strong/ tough/stiff competition** (=when a lot of people are all trying very hard to get something) *There is fierce competition for places on the Olympic team.* | **be in competition with sb/sth** (=to be in the situation where you are competing with someone else) *Hotels in the downtown area were in direct competition with each other.* | **cut-throat competition** (=very strong competition) *Weak management and cut-throat competition put the company out of business.*

competitive /kəm'petɪtɪv/ [adj] a **competitive** situation is one in which people try hard to do better than each other, for example in business or at school: *Amanda hated working in advertising – it was so competitive.* | **highly/fiercely competitive** (=very competitive) *The atmosphere at our school was highly competitive.* | *In such a fiercely competitive environment, it's inevitable that some companies will go out of business.*

rivalry /'raɪvəlri/ [n C/U] when two people, teams, or companies, especially when they are similarly successful or skilled, try to do better than each other over a long period of time **+ between** *Holmes says that the rivalry between the two companies has been exaggerated.* | **fierce/intense rivalry** (=very strong rivalry) *There was an intense rivalry between the Brazilian and Italian teams.* | **sibling rivalry** (=when brothers and sisters try to do better than each other) *Just because sibling rivalry is normal doesn't mean you should ignore it.*

battle/fight /'bætl, faɪt/ [n C] a situation in which people or organizations fight against each other to get power or control of something, and they are all very determined to win **+ for** *The President's advisors were engaged in a fierce battle for power.* | *The fight for the construction contract is getting more bitter by the day.* | **straight fight** British (=a competition involving only two people or groups, especially after other people or groups have stopped taking part) *The Socialist candidate beat the Liberal in a straight fight.*

race /reɪs/ [n C] a situation in which people or groups compete to get or achieve something: *He lost to Pfeiffer in last year's mayoral race.* | *the arms race* | **+ for** *In the race for the White House, candidates will promise almost anything.* | **the race is on** (=the competition has started) *The race is on to find a cure for AIDS, and drug companies have already invested millions in research.*

rat race /'ræt reɪs/ [n singular] a situation or way of life in which everyone is competing strongly all the time, especially at work, with the result that they always feel worried and they do not enjoy their lives: *I'm tired of the rat race – I'm tired of never getting ahead.* | *Sunday I just try to relax because Monday morning, it's back to the rat race.*

4 someone who takes part in a competition

- competitor
- contestant

competitor /kəm'petɪtəʳ/ [n C] someone who takes part in a competition: *Two of the competitors failed to turn up for the first race.* | *Each of these competitors has their eye on the £50,000 prize money.*

contestant /kən'testənt/ [n C] someone who takes part in a contest, a television game, test of knowledge etc: *The next contestant is Alice Myers from Vancouver.* | *Each contestant has to answer questions on a variety of subjects.*

5 people who are trying to do better than each other

- competitor
- rival
- the competition

competitor /kəm'petɪtəʳ/ [n C] a person or company that tries to do better than another that offers similar goods or services: *Their major competitors are IBM and Sun Microsystems.* | *If we're going to succeed, we'll have to provide something that our competitors don't.*

rival /'raɪvəl/ [n C] a person, team, or company that tries to do better than another similar one, especially over a long period: *The two teams have always been rivals.* | **rival group/school/gang etc** *The fight started as an argument between rival gang members.*

the competition /ðə ˌkɒmpɪ'tɪʃən‖-ˌkɑːm-/ [n singular] all the people or groups that are trying to do better than you, especially in business: *Our sales figures are 10% ahead of the competition.* | **strong competition** (=when the people you are competing against are very good) *The team overcame strong competition to gain their place in the finals.*

6 someone who likes competing

- competitive

competitive /kəm'petɪtɪv/ [adj] someone who is **competitive** enjoys competing with other people and is always trying to do better than them: *I hate playing tennis with Stephen – he's too competitive.*

competition

RELATED WORDS

- *see also* **against/oppose, compete with, game, take part/be involved, win, lose, game, sport/game, result**

- competition
- championship
- tournament
- contest

competition /ˌkɒmpɪ'tɪʃən‖ˌkɑːm-/ [n C] an organized event in which people try to do an activity or sport better than other people, especially in order to win a prize: *He was awarded first prize in the National Poetry Competition.* | *A spelling bee is a competition in which people try to correctly spell words.* | **win a competition** *A student from St. Paul won the speechwriting competition.* | **enter a competition** (=be in a competition) *Enter our free competition and win a weekend in Paris.* | **competition to do sth** *They're holding a competition to come up with a name for the new bridge.* | **hold/have a competition** *The company developing the site had held a competition to find a master-planner.*

championship /'tʃæmpiənʃɪp/ [n C] an important sports event in which players or teams play against each other to decide who is the best in an area, the country, or the world: *The sixth game of the World Chess Championship will be broadcast tonight on Channel 6.* | **win a championship** *At 17, he was the youngest player to win the Men's Tennis Championship.* | **state/national/world etc championship** *Gutierrez said he has a plan he hopes will carry him through to his first world championship.*

tournament /'tʊəʳnəmənt/ [n C] a competition in a sport or game in which each player or team plays a series of games until one person or team wins: *an international golf tournament* | *There's a volleyball tournament at Sunset Park which begins today.* | **win a tournament** *Telford won the local five-a-side football tournament.*

contest /'kɒntest‖'kɑːn-/ [n C] a competition in which a person or team does an activity, and a group of judges decide which of them is the best: *The event, held every four years in Fort Worth, Texas, is the country's leading piano contest.* | **enter a contest** *Jake always enters the arm-wrestling contest at the local fair.* | **enter sb in/for a contest** *Harriet decided to enter Henry in the cute baby contest.* | **win a contest** *Jack always wins the pub's karaoke contest.* | **beauty contest** (=a contest in which judges decide who is the most beautiful woman) *She won several beauty contests when she was in her early twenties.*

complain

RELATED WORDS

- *see also* **protest, criticize, satisfied/not satisfied**

1 to say that you are annoyed or not satisfied about something

- complain
- make a complaint
- lodge a complaint
- protest
- object
- take it up with/take the matter up with
- air your grievances

complain /kəm'pleɪn/ [v I/T not in passive] to say that

you are annoyed and not satisfied about something or someone: *We had to remove the advertisement because so many people complained.* | *Residents are complaining because traffic in the area has increased.* | **+ about** *Their neighbours complained about their constant loud music.* | **+ that** *Jenny's always complaining that her boss gives her too much work.* | **+ to** *If the hotel isn't satisfactory, you should complain to the Tourist Office.* | **constantly complain** *He constantly complains about how he's treated at work.* | **complain bitterly** (=complain very strongly) *Workers who had lost their jobs complained bitterly about the way they had been treated.*

make a complaint /ˌmeɪk ə kəmˈpleɪnt/ [v phrase] to formally complain about something to someone in authority: *Write to this address if you wish to make a complaint.* | **+ to** *Parents made a complaint to the principal about bullying in the school.*

lodge a complaint British **/file a complaint** American /ˌlɒdʒ ə kəmˈpleɪnt‖ˌlɑːdʒ-, ˌfaɪl ə kəmˈpleɪnt/ [v phrase] to make an official complaint, usually in writing, to someone in authority: *She went to the city council and lodged a complaint.* | **+ with** *The company said it plans to file a complaint with the International Trade Commission.* | **+ against** *Conyers said she had been blocked from promotion after filing a complaint against a male co-worker.*

protest /prəˈtest/ [v I/T not in passive] to complain about something, especially publicly or officially, because you are annoyed or think it is unfair: *He was carried away in a police van, protesting loudly.* | **+ about** *Passengers protested angrily about increased rail fares.* | **+ to** *The journalists have protested to government officials about the way they were treated.* | **+ (that)** *Dan protested it wasn't him who had caused the problems.* | **protest your innocence** (=say that you are innocent) *Mills, who has been in prison since 1987, has always protested his innocence.*

object /əbˈdʒekt/ [v I/T] to say that you do not agree with something or you do not approve of it, because it annoys you or offends you: *'My name's not Sonny,' the child objected.* | **+ to** *Does anyone object to these proposals?* | **+ if** *Will she object if I use her laptop?*

take it up with/take the matter up with /ˌteɪk ɪt ˈʌp wɪð, ˌteɪk ðə ˌmætər ˈʌp wɪð/ [v phrase] to speak or write to someone in authority complaining about something: *I told her she should take it up with her local council.* | *Alton said he was prepared to take the matter up with the Ministry of Health if necessary.*

air your grievances /ˌeəʳ jɔːʳ ˈgriːvənsɪ̈z/ [v phrase] to talk about the things you are unhappy or annoyed about, especially in public to people in authority so that they can do something about them: *The meeting gave employees an opportunity to air their grievances.* | *The uprising at Southport prison ended after inmates were allowed to air their grievances to the media.*

2 to complain a lot in an annoying way

- moan
- grumble
- make a fuss
- go on about
- nag
- whinge
- whine

moan /məʊn/ [v I/T] especially British, informal to keep complaining in an annoying way – use this about someone who complains all the time, even about things that are not important: *I'm fed up with hearing you moaning the whole time!* | **+ about** *Why do people always moan about the weather?*

grumble /ˈgrʌmbəl/ [v I] to keep complaining in a bad-tempered way, especially when you think you have been treated unfairly: *The old man turned away, grumbling as he went.* | **+ about** *She was grumbling about having to work so late.* | *The people standing beside me were grumbling about not being able to find a place to park.*

make a fuss especially British ALSO **kick up a fuss** British /ˌmeɪk ə ˈfʌs, ˌkɪk ʌp ə ˈfʌs/ [v phrase] to complain angrily and noisily about something, so that everyone hears you or notices you: *I don't understand why you're making such a fuss. It's not that important.* | **+ about** *The couple sitting next to us made a big fuss about their bill.*

go on about /gəʊ ˈɒn əbaʊt/ [v phrase] British informal to keep complaining about something or someone's behaviour in an annoying way: *Our neighbours are always going on about the noise we make.* | **go on and on about** (=for a long time) *Look, I'm sorry I kept you waiting, but there's no need to go on and on about it.*

nag /næg/ [v I/T] to keep complaining to someone, especially in order to make them do something that they do not want to do: *I wish you'd stop nagging me.* | **+ about** *My mom's always nagging me about my room.* | **+ at** *Jane's boss nags at her all the time.* —**nagging** [n U] **constant/incessant etc nagging** *I don't know how you put up with Claire's constant nagging.*

whinge /wɪndʒ/ [v I] British informal to keep complaining in an annoying way – use this when someone is complaining about something that is not important or is something they could change if they really wanted to **+ about** *He's always whinging about being underpaid.* | *Nick was a pain in the neck. He did nothing but whinge the whole trip.*

whine /waɪn/ [v I] to keep complaining about something unimportant, especially in a sad, annoying voice: *'What did you do that for?' he whined.* | *For heaven's sake stop whining. Nobody has touched your precious records.* | **+ about** *He's always whining about how much everything costs.*

3 someone who is always complaining

- grouch
- misery/misery guts
- whinger

grouch /graʊtʃ/ [n C] someone who is always complaining: *Her dad's a terrible grouch.* | *You're such a grouch in the morning.*

misery/misery guts /ˈmɪzəri, ˈmɪzəri ˌgʌts/ [n singular] British informal someone who is always complaining, is never happy, and does not like other people to enjoy themselves: *Emma is a real misery guts.* | *Stop being such a misery. It's not the end of the world.*

whinger /ˈwɪndʒəʳ/ [n C] British informal someone who keeps complaining in an annoying way – use this when someone is complaining about something that is not important or is something they could change if they wanted to: *This place is full of whingers. It's just pathetic.*

4 a complaint

- complaint
- protest
- outcry
- grievance
- gripe

complaint /kəmˈpleɪnt/ [n C/U] something that you say or write when you are complaining, especially to someone in an official position: *If you have any complaints, please contact our customer relations department.* | *Our main complaint is the poor standard of service.* | *If you have a complaint, you should write to the manager.* | **make a complaint** *Some employees are worried about what will happen to them if they make a complaint.* | **+ about** *Keating was dismissed after complaints about the quality of his work.* | **formal complaint** *Mr Kelly has made a formal complaint against the police.* | **letters of complaint** *The commission has so far received nearly 10,000 letters of complaint.*

protest /'prəʊtest/ [n C/U] when someone complains publicly about something that they think is wrong or unfair and should not be allowed to happen: *Despite their protests, the students' fees were increased.* | **in protest** (=as a way of making a protest) *When two members of the team were dismissed, the rest of them walked out in protest.* | **+ against** *The ambassador lodged a formal protest against the proposals.* | **ignore sb's protests** *Ignoring my protests, he took off his jacket and wrapped it around my shoulders.*

outcry /'aʊtkraɪ/ [n C usually singular] an angry protest by a lot of people about something that they think is very wrong or unfair: *Despite an outcry, the university refused to change its admission policies.* | **public outcry** *The shooting of an unarmed teenager by police caused a public outcry.* | **+ about/over** *There was a widespread outcry over the increase in fuel tax.* | **+ against** *The public outcry against the executions made little difference.*

grievance /'gri:vəns/ [n C] something that you feel unhappy about because you think that you have been treated unfairly – use this especially about an official complaint you make about the place where you work **file a grievance** (=officially complain) *She filed a grievance last year after her supervisor refused to promote her.* | **+ against** *Anyone who has a legitimate grievance against the company can take it to the arbitration committee.* | **air a grievance** (=discuss a grievance publicly) *The meetings give employees the opportunity to express their views or air grievances.*

gripe /graɪp/ [n C] informal something unimportant that you keep complaining about or feel unhappy about: *Students' main gripe is the poor quality of the dorm food.* | *I left the house because I wasn't in the mood to listen to Maude's gripes.*

completely

completely and in every way

RELATED WORDS

opposite: —————— **partly**

▸ *see also* **complete/not complete, all/everything, very**

- ▸ completely
- ▸ absolutely
- ▸ fully
- ▸ totally
- ▸ entirely
- ▸ wholly
- ▸ utterly
- ▸ positively
- ▸ complete/total/absolute/utter
- ▸ in every way/respect/detail
- ▸ in every sense
- ▸ through and through
- ▸ whole-heartedly

completely /kəm'pli:tli/ [adv] *The carpet is completely ruined.* | *She felt completely relaxed.* | *Keith's dad was completely different from what I'd expected.* | *I intended to give you the card on Saturday but I completely forgot.* | *Sometimes the UK seems completely isolated from the main stream of European culture.* —**complete** [adj only before noun] *He needs complete rest for a few weeks.* | *The whole thing's a complete waste of time.*

absolutely /'æbsəlu:tli, ˌæbsə'lu:tli/ [adv] especially spoken say this when you strongly agree with something or approve of something, or to emphasize strong adjectives **absolutely right/correct** *You're absolutely right – we can't all fit in one car.* | **absolutely marvellous/amazing/brilliant** *That's an absolutely brilliant idea.* | **absolutely certain/sure** *Are you absolutely sure you don't mind?* | **absolutely exhausted/soaked/ruined etc** *By the end of the day, I was absolutely exhausted.* —**absolute** /'æbsəlu:t/ [adj only before noun] *They have no absolute proof that he is the murderer.* | *What absolute nonsense.*

fully /'fʊli/ [adv] use this especially to say that you have completely understood something or have everything that you need **fully understand/realize/appreciate** *I can fully understand your concern.* | **fully aware/informed** *Please keep me fully informed of any developments.* | **fully furnished/equipped** *The house is fully furnished, including washer and dryer.*

totally /'təʊtl-i/ [adv] use this especially to show that you completely disagree with something or that you are very annoyed about it **totally refuse/ignore/reject etc** *He totally ignored my advice.* | **totally impossible/unacceptable/ridiculous etc** *What you're saying is totally ridiculous.* | *Myers said that a two-year prison sentence for rape was totally unacceptable and inadequate.*

entirely /ɪn'taɪəʳli/ [adv] completely and in every possible way – use this especially in negative sentences, or with 'almost': *At the very beginning of the project, Paul made it clear that he would be entirely in control.* | **not entirely** *I'm not entirely sure what she meant.* | *The reasons for his departure weren't entirely clear.* | **consist entirely of** *The audience consisted almost entirely of journalists.* | **depend entirely on** *The foundation depends entirely on voluntary contributions.*

wholly /'həʊl-li/ [adv] in every possible way – use this especially in negative sentences **not wholly responsible/reliable/committed etc** *The evidence we have is not wholly reliable.* | *The commission found that the officer on duty at the time was not wholly responsible.* | **wholly unacceptable/unexpected/unfounded etc** *The city council's proposals are wholly unacceptable.* | *Help came from a wholly unexpected source.*

utterly /'ʌtəʳli/ [adv] use this especially to describe things that are completely wrong, untrue, impossible etc **utterly impossible/useless/worthless etc** *Without their help it would have been utterly impossible to arrange the conference.* | *Whether you like her or not is utterly irrelevant.* | **utterly reject/spoil/destroy etc** *We utterly reject the philosophy of compulsory wage control.* —**utter** [adj only before noun] *We all watched in utter amazement.* | *The government is demonstrating utter stupidity in pursuing such a policy.*

positively /'pɒzətɪvli‖'pɑ:-/ [adv] use this to talk about an extreme situation or something extreme that someone has done **positively disgusting/harmful/dangerous etc** *The food in this place isn't just bad, it's positively disgusting.* | *Her performance was positively marvellous.*

complete/total/absolute/utter /kəm'pli:t 'təʊtl, 'æbsəlu:t, 'ʌtəʳ/ [adj only before noun] use this to emphasize how strong a feeling or quality is or how bad a situation is: *It was a complete surprise* –

I didn't have any idea they were planning a party. | *Don't pay any attention to him – the guy's a total idiot!* | *Nobody can say with absolute certainty how much oil there is in Alaska.* | *By any measurement, our corrections program is an utter failure.*

in every way/respect/detail /ɪn ˌevri ˈweɪ, rɪˈspekt, ˈdiːteɪl‖-dɪˈteɪl/ [adv] use this to say that something is true in every detail or part: *The two drawings are identical in every way.* | *The plans are unworkable in every respect.*

in every sense /ɪn ˌevri ˈsens/ [adv] use this when a word or phrase that you say is true in every possible way that it could be understood: *There are still men who want to be in every sense, the 'head of the household'.* | **in every sense of the word** *She was a true sportswoman – a professional in every sense of the word.*

through and through /ˌθruː ən ˈθruː/ [adv] if someone is good, bad etc **through and through**, every part of their character and behaviour shows that they are like that: *Don't trust him. He's rotten through and through.* | *Einstein was a realist through and through.* | *After 30 years in Queensland, he felt he was an Australian through and through.*

whole-heartedly /ˌhəʊl ˈhɑːʳtə̇dli/ [adv] **whole-heartedly agree/approve/support etc** completely and willingly: *Her father whole-heartedly approved of their decision to get married.* | *Rowan whole-heartedly agreed that the company needed to do more to improve its ties to the community.* —**whole-hearted** [adj] *The government has agreed to give the plan its whole-hearted support.*

complete/ not complete

RELATED WORDS

- finish doing something *see* **finish**
- *see also* **completely, all/everything, full**

1 with all its parts included and nothing missing

- complete
- full
- whole
- in full
- in its entirety
- be all there

complete /kəmˈpliːt/ [adj] use this to say that something includes all the parts it should have, with nothing missing: *Scientists have unearthed a complete dinosaur skeleton in Montana.* | **complete set** *When my grandmother died, I inherited a complete set of Dresden china.* | **the complete works of sb** (=everything that an author has written) *We gave Vicki the complete works of Shakespeare.*

full /fʊl/ [adj only before noun] complete: *Please write your full name and address at the top of the form.* | *Sidney got married in full army uniform.* | *Connors made a full confession to the police.* | **the full story** *We're not being told the full story here.*

whole /həʊl/ [adj only before noun] complete, especially when this is very good, impressive, or unusual: *I drank a whole bottle of wine by myself.* | *After spending years piecing together fragments, we now have the whole original manuscript.*

in full /ɪn ˈfʊl/ [adv] if something is written, described, explained etc **in full**, everything necessary is included and nothing is left out; if you pay an amount of money **in full**, you pay the full amount: *The text of the president's speech will be published in full in tomorrow's papers.* | *The bill had been stamped 'Paid in Full'.* | *Taped testimony will be heard in full at the opening of the trial.*

in its entirety /ˌɪn ɪts ɪnˈtaɪərə̇ti/ [adv] if something is read, performed, seen etc **in its entirety**, the whole of it is read etc, especially when it is something very big or complicated: *Bach's great masterpiece, the Mass in B minor, was never performed in its entirety during his lifetime.*

be all there /biː ˌɔːl ˈðeəʳ/ [v phrase] to be complete with the parts that should be there: *It's an old set, but you'll find it's all there – the dice, cards, everything.* | *You can count it if you want to, but it's all there.*

2 examining, considering, or including every detail or part

- complete
- thorough
- full
- comprehensive
- exhaustive
- in-depth

complete /kəmˈpliːt/ [adj] *Police made a complete search of the area.* | *A complete safety check was performed on the aircraft prior to takeoff.* | *This is a complete list of educational publishers in Britain.* —**completely** [adv] *He had the engine completely rebuilt.* —**completeness** [n U] *For the sake of completeness we should add these figures to the report.*

thorough /ˈθʌrə‖ˈθʌrəʊ, ˈθʌrə/ [adj] a **thorough** search, examination, check etc includes everything that can be included: *Congress is demanding a thorough investigation.* | *Have you had a thorough medical check-up within the last year?* | *His assessment of the situation was quite thorough.* | **thorough understanding** *The position requires a thorough understanding of web page design software.* —**thoroughly** [adv] *A teacher must thoroughly understand his or her subject.* —**thoroughness** [n U] *The study was carried out with both thoroughness and objectivity.*

full /fʊl/ [adj only before noun] including all the necessary facts, or a lot of details: *The atlas contains full statistical descriptions of each country.* | *Full details of the travel arrangements will be published as soon as possible.* | *David wants a full report of the accident first thing in the morning.* —**fully** [adv] *The airline says the complaints will be fully investigated.* | *Schatz pledged that the parents would be fully informed of the inquiry's findings.*

comprehensive /ˌkɒmprɪˈhensɪv◂‖ˌkɑːm-/ [adj] very thorough, especially because it is important that nothing is left out and that every possible problem is dealt with: *The factory was given a comprehensive safety inspection three months ago.* | *This is the largest and most comprehensive study ever made of the city's public transportation system.* —**comprehensively** [adv] *The service had not been comprehensively reviewed since the Seventies.*

exhaustive /ɪgˈzɔːstɪv/ [adj] so complete that not even the smallest detail or possibility is missed: *As a result of exhaustive inquiries the police are at last able to issue a description of the murderer.* | *The list shown here is by no means exhaustive.* —**exhaustively** [adv] *The report has been exhaustively examined for errors.*

in-depth /ˌɪn ˈdepθ◂/ [adj only before noun] an **in-depth** study, discussion, report etc is thorough and complete and considers all details: *See chapter 6 for an* *in-depth discussion of this topic.* | *The study is based on in-depth interviews with a nationally representative sample of 1,500 US households.*

3 to make something complete

- complete
- make up

complete /kəmˈpliːt/ [v T] *Brown lace leggings and black leather shoes completed the outfit.* | *I only need one more volume to complete the collection.* | *Complete the sentences using either the simple past or present perfect tense of the verbs.*

make up /ˌmeɪk ˈʌp/ [phr v T] to complete a group, set, or amount by adding something or someone to it: *We need two more players to make up the team.* | *If you haven't got enough to pay for that, I can make up the difference.*

4 not complete

- incomplete
- partial
- patchy

incomplete /ˌɪnkəmˈpliːt◂/ [adj] *Historical records for this time are incomplete.* | *an incomplete job application* | *For many, a good meal is incomplete without a fine wine.*

partial /ˈpɑːʳʃəl/ [adj only before noun] only containing or including part of what is necessary to be complete: *From where I was standing, I had a partial view of the house.* | *This is only a partial solution to the problem.* | *At best, the mission was a partial success.* | *Wade received only partial compensation for her injuries.*

patchy /ˈpætʃi/ [adj] if something is **patchy**, it does not include enough information, or important details are missing: *The records are patchy and incomplete.* | *A patchy picture began to emerge of what happened that night.* | *My knowledge of the subject is pretty patchy.*

complicated

RELATED WORDS

opposite: simple

▸ *see also* **difficult, problem**

1 having a lot of different parts and difficult to understand

- complicated
- complex
- intricate
- elaborate
- involved
- tortuous
- convoluted

complicated /ˈkɒmplɪkeɪtɪd‖ˈkɑːm-/ [adj] consisting of a lot of different parts or details and therefore difficult to understand: *I didn't realize programming the VCR would be so complicated.* | *The brain is like a very powerful, very complicated computer.* | *the complicated problem of bringing peace to the Middle East*

complex /ˈkɒmpleks‖ˌkɑːmˈpleks/ [adj] a **complex** process or system is difficult to understand because it has a lot of parts that are all connected in different ways: *The chemical processes involved in the experiment are extremely complex.* | *The seminar focuses on the complex relationship between government, the military, and the media.* —**complexity** /kəmˈpleksɪti/ [n U] *I don't think you fully understood the complexity of his argument.*

intricate /ˈɪntrɪkɪt/ [adj] having a lot of small parts or details – use this especially about something that is cleverly designed or made: *Lasers are used to cut intricate designs in wood.* | *The farmers use an intricate system of drainage canals.* | *the intricate workings of a watch* | *intricate patterns of coloured marble*

elaborate /ɪˈlæbərɪt/ [adj] having a lot of parts or details and very carefully planned, but often more complicated than is necessary: *Mike had worked out an elaborate system for categorizing his collection of CDs.* | *Sociologists have been coming up with increasingly elaborate theories to explain unsafe sexual practices.*

involved /ɪnˈvɒlvd‖-ˈvɑːlvd/ [adj usually before noun] very long and complicated – use this about a system, description, or explanation that you think should be made simpler: *The system for choosing candidates is very involved, and I won't go into it here.* | *Adopting a child can be a long involved process.*

tortuous /ˈtɔːʳtʃuəs/ [adj] much too long and complicated, and therefore confusing and annoying: *The book begins with a long, tortuous introduction.* | *At last, an end to the tortuous negotiations was in sight.*

convoluted /ˌkɒnvəˈluːtɪd◂‖ˌkɑːn-/ [adj] too complicated and difficult to understand – use this especially about someone's language or arguments, or about a system: *He always uses a lot of convoluted arguments to support his theories, but no one's ever impressed.* | *James's books are full of long paragraphs and convoluted sentences, which many people do not find appealing.*

2 a complicated official system

- bureaucracy
- bureaucratic
- red tape

bureaucracy /bjʊəˈrɒkrəsi‖-ˈrɑː-/ [n U] a complicated, official system in which there are a lot of rules and processes that you have to complete, especially one that employs a lot of people: *The EU bureaucracy in Brussels has grown in size and authority.* | *We need less bureaucracy in the school system – teachers should be allowed to make more decisions.*

bureaucratic /ˌbjʊərəˈkrætɪk◂/ [adj] involving a lot of complicated official rules and processes: *The procedure for getting funding approval is so bureaucratic!* | **bureaucratic nightmare** (=official system that is extremely complicated and annoying) *Trying to enforce the law regulating the length of passenger buses has been a bureaucratic nightmare.*

red tape /ˌred ˈteɪp/ [n U] complicated and annoying official rules that you have to obey before you can do or have something: *There's so much red tape involved in getting a work permit.* | **cut through red tape** (=avoid it) *There must be a way to cut through all this red tape.*

computers/ Internet/email

WHAT'S HERE

computers

RELATED WORDS

▸ *see also* **machine, fault 1, working, switch on or off**

1 hardware

▸ **hardware** ▸ **computer** ▸ **PC** ▸ **machine** ▸ **workstation** ▸ **laptop** ▸ **network**

hardware /'hɑːʳdweəʳ/ [n U] computer equipment, rather than the programs that make it work: *The company has spent millions of dollars replacing outdated computer hardware.*

computer /kəm'pjuːtəʳ/ [n C] an electronic machine that uses programs to store and deal with large amounts of information quickly, and which is used for a wide range of different jobs **by computer** *The information from the survey is being processed by computer.* | **on a computer** *I can't get the program to work on my computer.* | *How long are you going to be on the computer? I need to type something.* | **computer literate** (=able to use a computer fairly well) *It is important that all children become computer literate while they are in school.*

PC /ˌpiː 'siː/ [n C] personal computer; a computer that is usually used by one person in an office, at home, or in a school: *Sales of PCs were down for the second year running.*

machine /mə'ʃiːn/ [n C] especially spoken a computer: *I think there's something wrong with my machine – would you take a look at it?*

workstation /'wɜːʳkˌsteɪʃən/ [n C] a computer – used especially by computer manufacturers for the names of particular models of computer: *I have to share my workstation with two other people in the office.*

laptop /'læptɒp‖-tɑːp/ [n C] a small computer that you can carry with you and use when you are travelling: *Her boss's laptop got stolen from her car.*

network /'netwɜːʳk/ [n C] a group of computers that are connected to each other, and are able to exchange information and messages: *Most workplaces have a local network as well as access to the Internet.*

2 software

▸ **software** ▸ **program/computer program** ▸ **file** ▸ **application** ▸ **interactive** ▸ **multimedia**

software /'sɒftweəʳ‖'sɔːft-/ [n U] the sets of programs that tell a computer what to do: *You need special software to view the information in the file.* | *The company develops interactive software for schoolchildren.* | *India's software industry barely existed 15 years ago but is growing rapidly today.*

program/computer program /'prəʊgræm, kəmˌpjuːtəʳ 'prəʊgræm/ [n C] a set of instructions used to tell a computer what to do: *I didn't have enough memory on my computer to run the program.* | *She was writing simple computer programs when she was eight years old.*

file /faɪl/ [n C] a collection of information on a computer that is stored under a particular name: *I seem to have lost the file with all my personal records on it.* | *Just click on the icon to open the file.* | *It's a good idea to save your files to a floppy disk as a backup.*

application /ˌæplɪ'keɪʃən/ [n C] a piece of software for a particular use or job: *a graphics application*

interactive /ˌɪntər'æktɪv◂/ [adj] **interactive** software allows the person using it to affect what happens on the computer screen: *an interactive education package for 7-10-year-olds* | *When designing your site, think about whether it needs to be interactive or informational.*

multimedia /ˌmʌltɪ'miːdiə/ [adj] using a mixture of sound, pictures, video, and writing to give information: *The virtual tour includes multimedia displays demonstrating how the market works.*

3 people

▸ **user/computer user** ▸ **programmer/computer programmer** ▸ **techie** ▸ **hacker** ▸ **software developer/engineer/designer** ▸ **systems analyst** ▸ **IT support**

user/computer user /'juːzəʳ, kəm'pjuːtəʳ ˌjuːzəʳ/ [n C] someone who uses a computer: *Most computer users do not realize how much their computers can do.* | *Users often complain that the Internet is slow and unreliable.* | **user-friendly** (=easy to use) *The program is remarkably user-friendly and can be learned by anyone.*

programmer/computer programmer /'prəʊgræməʳ, kəmˌpjuːtəʳ 'prəʊgræməʳ/ [n C] someone whose job is to write programs: *Computer programmers are in great demand, and a good one can earn a very high salary.*

techie /'teki/ [n C] informal someone who works in computing or who knows a lot about computers: *I don't even bother trying to fix things that go wrong on my computer – I leave that to the techies.*

hacker /'hækəʳ/ [n C] someone who secretly and often illegally gets into another person's or company's computer system: *Hackers broke into the Pentagon's security system last night.*

software developer/engineer/designer /'sɒftweəʳ dɪˌveləpəʳ, endʒɪˌnɪəʳ, dɪˌzaɪnəʳ/ [n C] someone whose job is to make software: *Software developers need to be aware that not all users are technical experts.*

systems analyst /'sɪstəmz ˌænəlɪst/ [n C] someone whose job involves studying business or industrial systems, and who uses computers to plan improvements or changes: *His first job as a systems analyst was to reorganize they way the store's stock was recorded.*

IT support British **/tech support** American /aɪ 'tiː səˌpɔːʳt, 'tek səˌpɔːʳt/ [n U] people whose job involves making sure that the computers in an organization are working properly: *If you're not prepared to pay* *for adequate IT support, it's no wonder you lose so much time through computer problems.*

4 things you do with a computer

- enter
- copy
- save
- delete
- select
- scroll
- search
- open
- close
- click on
- cut and paste
- highlight
- drag
- hack into

enter /ˈentəʳ/ [v T] to put information into a computer by pressing the keys: *When you have entered your credit card information, go to the next screen.*

copy /ˈkɒpi‖ˈkɑː-/ [v T] to make a file, program etc that is exactly the same as another one: *Copy the files into a new folder.*

save /seɪv/ [v T] to make a computer keep the work that you have done in its memory or on a disk: *Save your work and close down any applications that are open.*

delete /dɪˈliːt/ [v T] to remove a piece of information from a computer's memory: *Delete any files that end in '.tmp'.*

select /sɪˈlekt/ [v T] to use the mouse to choose words or pictures on a computer screen, usually making them change colour: *To create parallel columns, press Alt-F7 and select option 4.*

scroll /skrəʊl/ [v I] to move up or down through a document on a computer **scroll up/down** *Scroll down to see when the website was last updated.*

search /sɜːʳtʃ/ ALSO **do a search** /ˌduː ə ˈsɜːʳtʃ/ [v I/T] to look for information on a computer or on the Internet **+ for** *I did a search for any articles by Varenqe on the web, and I found quite a few.* | **+ by** *To find a book on our site, you can search by author, title, or subject.* | **search sth for sth** *You can search the document for particular words or phrases, in order to get directly to the information you need.*

open /ˈəʊpən/ [v T] to make a document or computer program ready to use: *Open the file called Templates.*

close /kləʊz/ [v T] to do the things you have to do when you want to stop using a document or a computer program: *Close all applications before shutting down your computer.*

click on /ˈklɪk ɒn/ [phr v T] to press a button on a mouse in order to choose something on the screen and make the computer perform a particular action: *Click on 'next' when you have finished filling out the form.*

cut and paste /ˌkʌt ən ˈpeɪst/ [v phrase] to remove a piece of information from one place in a computer program or document and put it in a different place instead: *It's easier if you just cut and paste the information from one page to another.*

highlight /ˈhaɪlaɪt/ [v T] to mark words in a computer document in a different colour so that you can see them easily or to separate it from the rest of the document: *To delete a block of text, highlight it and then press Del.*

drag /dræg/ [v T] to move something on a computer screen by pulling it along with the mouse: *You can delete the files by dragging them into your 'trash' folder.*

hack into /ˈhæk ɪntuː/ [phr v T] to secretly and often illegally find a way to reach the information on someone else's computer system so that you can use, change, or damage it: *A criminal gang hacked into a credit card company's most secure files.*

5 starting and finishing

- log on/log in/ sign in
- log out/log off/ sign out
- start up
- boot up
- reboot
- shut down
- username
- password

log on/log in/sign in /ˌlɒg ˈɒn, ˌlɒg ˈɪn‖ˌlɔːg-, ˌsaɪn ˈɪn/ [phr v I] to do the actions that will allow you to begin using a computer system, for example by typing a special word or giving a particular command: *Log on to our website and find out about the latest travel deals to the Far East.*

log out/log off/sign out /ˌlɒg ˈaʊt, ˌlɒg ˈɒf‖ˌlɔːg-, ˌsaɪn ˈaʊt/ [phr v I] to do the actions you have to do when you finish using a computer system: *When I logged off, the whole system froze up.*

start up /ˌstɑːʳt ˈʌp/ [phr v I/T] if you **start up** a computer, or it **starts up**, you turn it on: *The anti-virus icon should appear whenever you start up your computer.*

boot up /ˌbuːt ˈʌp/ [phr v I/T] if a computer **boots up**, it becomes ready to use by getting all the programs it needs into its memory. If you **boot up** a computer, you turn it on so that it is ready to use: *Just wait a couple of minutes while the computer boots up.*

reboot /riːˈbuːt/ [v I/T] if you **reboot** a computer, or if it **reboots**, you make it turn itself off and then back on again, especially because it has not been working correctly: *If a program crashes you usually have to reboot the computer.*

shut down /ˌʃʌt ˈdaʊn/ [phr v I/T] if you **shut** a computer **down** or it **shuts down**, you turn it off: *I'm always forgetting to shut down my computer before I go home.*

username /ˈjuːzəʳneɪm/ [n C] the name that you type into a computer, system, website etc. before typing your password: *Please enter your username and password.*

password /ˈpɑːswɜːʳd‖ˈpæs-/ [n C] a series of secret letters or numbers that you must type into a computer before you can use a system or a program: *Don't let anyone know your password.*

6 to put information or a program into a computer

- put sth in/into
- input
- enter
- load

put sth in/into /ˌpʊt (sth) ˈɪn, ˈɪntuː/ [phr v T] *We put all these details into our computer, and it chooses a suitable partner for you.* | *The quality of output data will depend on the data you have put in.*

input /ˈɪnpʊt/ [v T] to put information into a computer: *The user inputs the data, and the computer stores it in its memory.* | *We're currently inputting the names and addresses of all our customers into a database.*

enter /ˈentəʳ/ [v T] to put information into a computer by pressing the keys: *Enter the amount of money you wish to take out of your account.* | *If a word is entered incorrectly the machine refuses to obey the command.*

load /ləʊd/ [v I/T] to put a program into a computer so that it is ready to be used: *LOAD is a command which loads a new program from the file.* | **+ into** *The* *program can be encoded on the disk's surface and then loaded into the microprocessor.*

7 computer problems

- crash
- freeze/freeze up
- down
- bug
- virus
- error
- corrupt

crash /kræʃ/ [v I/T] if a computer or a piece of software **crashes**, or if you **crash** it, it suddenly and unexpectedly stops working: *My computer crashed, and we couldn't get it working again.*

freeze/freeze up /friːz, ˌfriːz ˈʌp/ [v T] if a computer screen **freezes**, the computer will not accept any instructions because of a fault and everything on the screen is fixed in position: *The screen froze up, it crashed, and I lost all my work.*

down /daʊn/ [adj not before noun] if a computer system is **down**, it has stopped working because of a fault or a problem: *Our computers are down right now, could you call back in an hour?* | **go down** *The whole network went down without any warning.*

bug /bʌg/ [n C] a small fault in a computer program which prevents it from working properly: *Some bug in the program meant when I typed in a letter I got a number instead.*

virus /ˈvaɪərəs/ [n C] a set of instructions that have been secretly put on a computer or a computer program, that can destroy or change information stored there. Viruses spread easily from one computer or computer program to another: *A warning has gone out about a new virus that could wipe everything off your hard disk.* | *You cannot get a virus from an email message alone.*

error /ˈerəʳ/ [n C] a problem with a piece of hardware or software, especially when the user gives the computer an instruction which it will not accept: *Whenever I try to enter the data the computer gives me an error window.*

corrupt /kəˈrʌpt/ ALSO **corrupted** /kəˈrʌptɪ̥d/ [adj] information on a computer that is **corrupt** has been damaged and can no longer be read or used by the computer: *a corrupted file* | *Some segments of your hard drive are corrupt.*

Internet

8 the Internet and places on the Internet

- (the) Internet/ (the) Net
- e-
- cyber-
- dotcom
- website
- web page
- home page
- chat room
- link/hyperlink
- search engine
- browser
- FAQ, faq
- online
- hit

(the) Internet/(the) Net /(ðiː) ˈɪntəʳnet, (ðə) ˈnet/ [n singular] a network of computer connections that allows computer users around the world to exchange information: *The Internet makes it possible for people all over the world to keep in touch.* | *In theory, the Net should make things quicker, but that isn't always the case.* | **on the Internet/Net** *She spends nearly all her free time on the Internet.* | *The couple met on the Internet.* | **Internet/Net access** *The city's libraries provide free Internet access.*

e- ALSO **E-** /iː/ [prefix] used to form words that relate to activities involving use of the Internet, especially those connected with business.: *E-commerce was then seen as a booming economic area.*

cyber- /ˈsaɪbəʳ/ [prefix] used to form words that relate to activities involving the use of computers, especially the Internet: *Cyber-crime, for example the fraudulent use of credit cards on the net, presents particular problems for the police.* | *He seems to spend all his time in cyberspace!*

dotcom /ˈdɒtkɒm‖ˈdɑːtkɑːm/ [adj only before noun] relating to a company whose business involves the Internet: *The business world was shaken by the huge drop in dotcom shares.* | *dotcom jobs* — **dotcom** [n C]

website /ˈweb saɪt/ [n C] a place on the Internet where you can find information about a particular company, organization, or person: *Visit our website on www.stellamary.UK.*

web page /ˈweb peɪdʒ/ [n C] one of the areas you can go to on a website: *Do you want me to print off this web page?*

home page /ˈhəʊm peɪdʒ/ [n C] the first place you go to on a website: *You can reach all the other pages on a website from its home page.*

chat room /ˈtʃæt ruːm/ [n C] an area on the Internet where people can talk to each other by sending messages that can be read or heard immediately: *Children should be taught to be careful about who they talk to in chat rooms.*

link/hyperlink /lɪŋk, ˈhaɪpəʳˌlɪŋk/ [n C] writing or pictures on a web page which you can click on if you want to immediately go to another website or to another web page on the same website: *For more info, click on this link.*

search engine /ˈsɜːʳtʃ ˌendʒɪ̥n/ [n C] a computer program that helps you find information on the Internet: *This search engine will only find sites that originate in Europe.*

browser /ˈbraʊzəʳ/ [n C] a program, such as Internet Explorer or Netscape Navigator, that allows you to find and read documents on the Internet: *My browser really is incredibly slow.*

FAQ, faq /ˌef eɪ ˈkjuː, fæk/ [n C] frequently asked question(s); on websites, a list of questions that users often ask about the website, and answers to them: *Before e-mailing us, it might be advisable to click on FAQ first.*

online /ˈɒnlaɪn‖ˈɔːn-/ [adj] connected to other computers through the Internet, or available through the Internet **go online** *I'll just go online and look up her address.*

hit /hɪt/ [n C] an occasion when someone uses a website, a web page, or part of a web page. Companies count the number of hits their websites, advertisements, etc receive to find out how well they are doing: *The official World Cup website scored a record number of hits last week.*

9 things you do on the Internet

- surf the Internet/Net/Web
- download
- upload
- visit
- chat
- instant-message/IM

surf the Internet/Net/Web /ˌsɜːʳf ði ˈɪntəʳnet, ˈnet, ˈweb / [v phrase] to look at information on the Internet, especially when you look quickly in order to find something that interests you: *People caught surfing the Net at work are liable to be dismissed.*

download /'daʊnləʊd/ [v I/T] to copy a file from the Internet onto your own computer: *Download your favorite songs by clicking here.* —**download** [n C]

upload /'ʌpləʊd/ [v I/T] to copy something from your computer onto the Internet: *Take great care when uploading personal information such as your address or credit card number.* —**upload** [n C]

visit /'vɪzət/ [v T] to use a website on the Internet: *For more information on how you can help, visit our website.*

chat /tʃæt/ [v I] to communicate with several people by computer, using a special Internet program that allows you to exchange written messages very quickly: *You can chat to Brad Pitt live this evening.* —**chat** [n C]

instant-message/IM /ˌɪnstənt 'mesɪdʒ, ˌaɪ 'em/ [v I/T] to communicate with someone by computer, using a special Internet program that allows you to exchange written messages very quickly: *Teenagers are the group most likely to IM each other.* —**instant message/IM** [n C] **instant-messaging** [n U]

email

RELATED WORDS

▸ *see also* **message, contact, write**

10 email

- email
- email
- snailmail
- mailing list
- attachment
- attach
- flame
- spam
- bounce

email ALSO **e-mail** /'iːmeɪl/ [n C/U] electronic mail; the system that allows people to send messages and documents to each other by computer, or a message or file that has been sent using this system: *Email has revolutionized the way we all think and work.* | **email address** *Give me your email address and I'll send you directions to the party.* | **send an email** *I sent him an email two weeks ago, but I haven't heard anything back.*

email ALSO **e-mail** /'iːmeɪl/ [v T] to send someone a message or a computer file by email: *We'd been emailing each other for six months before we actually met.* | **email sb sth** *I'll email you my résumé when I get home.*

snailmail /'sneɪlmeɪl/ [n U] the traditional system of collecting and delivering letters, packages etc – use this when you are comparing this system to email: *Sorry about the snailmail – my email's not working.*

mailing list /'meɪlɪŋ ˌlɪst/ [n C] a discussion group on the Internet, which consists of a list of people who can each send messages to the rest of the list by email

attachment /ə'tætʃmənt/ [n C] a document or file, for example a document from a word processor or spreadsheet, which is sent with an email so that it can be read and used by the person who receives the email: *I'm sending the document as an attachment. Please let me know if you have trouble reading it.*

attach /ə'tætʃ/ [v T] to connect a document or a file to an email: *I've attached the latest spreadsheet for you to look at.*

flame /fleɪm/ [v T] to send someone a message that criticizes them on the Internet, especially in a rude or angry way: *Flaming your boss really isn't a good idea, however angry you are.*

spam /spæm/ [n U] email messages that a computer user has not asked for and does not want to read, for example, messages from advertisers: *I was getting so much spam mail that I changed my email address.* —**spamming** [n U]

bounce /baʊns/ [v I/T] if an email message that you send **bounces** or is **bounced**, it is automatically returned to you because of a technical problem: *She tried to mail him several times but the message always bounced.*

condition

RELATED WORDS

▸ the conditions you live in *see* **situation**

WHAT'S HERE

- **the condition that sth is in** see **1 to 6**
- **a condition that sth depends on** see **7 to 10**

the condition that sth is in

RELATED WORDS

▸ *see also* **damage, decay, broken/not broken, tear**

1 the condition of something

- condition
- state

condition /kən'dɪʃən/ [n C/U] whether something is broken or not broken, damaged or not damaged, dirty or clean etc: *The price of used cars varies according to their condition.* | *How well your plants will grow depends on the quality and condition of the soil.* | **be in (a) good/bad/reasonable etc condition** *The basic structure of the house is in very good condition.* | *Our science laboratories were in such a terrible condition we've had to close them.* | *I'm not buying anything until I see what kind of condition it's in.*

state /steɪt/ [n C] the condition of something – use this especially when something is in bad condition because it has not been well looked after **the state of sth** *One of the things people complain of most is the state of the sidewalks.* | *Given the general state of his health, it may take him a while to recover from the operation.* | **in a good/bad/reasonable etc state** *When I got back home, I was horrified to see what a terrible state the kitchen was in.* | **in a sorry state** (=in very bad condition) *Most of the country's existing schools are in a sorry state of disrepair.*

2 in a good condition

- in good condition
- in good shape
- in good nick
- in perfect/mint condition
- as good as new

in good condition /ɪn ˌgʊd kən'dɪʃən/ [adj phrase] something that is **in good condition** is not broken and has no marks or other things wrong with it: *The car hadn't been used much, and was in very good condition.* | *The charity is accepting toys and clothing in good condition.* | *The 3,000-year-old tools are* *still in such good condition it looks almost as if they were made yesterday.*

in good shape /ɪn ˌgʊd ˈʃeɪp/ [adj phrase] something that is **in good shape** is in good condition – use this especially when you do not really expect it to be or when it was not always in such good condition: *Doctor Morrissey told her that her leg was healing well, and was now in very good shape.* | *To avoid accidents, it's important to check that all your tools are in good shape before starting.*

in good nick /ɪn ˌgʊd ˈnɪk/ [adj phrase] British informal use this especially about something such as a car or a piece of equipment that is old or used, but is still in good condition and working well: *She keeps her car in really good nick.* | *My stereo's quite old but it's still in pretty good nick.*

in perfect/mint condition /ɪn ˌpɜːʳfɪkt, ˌmɪnt kənˈdɪʃən/ [adj phrase] something that is **in perfect** or **mint condition** looks as good or works as well as when it was new, especially because it has not been used or touched very much: *The book is over 100 years old, but it's still in perfect condition.* | *I can't believe it. She's selling me her car for only £800 and it's still in mint condition.*

as good as new /əz ˌgʊd əz ˈnjuː‖-ˈnuː/ [adj phrase] especially spoken something that is **as good as new** is almost as good as when it was new – use this about things that have recently been cleaned or repaired: *I've just had the bike serviced, and it looks as good as new.*

3 buildings or places in bad condition

- in bad condition
- dilapidated
- run-down
- derelict
- ramshackle
- crumbling
- tumbledown

in bad condition ALSO **in a bad state** especially British /ɪn ˌbæd kənˈdɪʃən, ɪn ə ˌbæd ˈsteɪt/ [adj phrase] *It's a lovely city, but most of the buildings are in very bad condition.* | *Considering the bad condition the place is in, the price seems much too high.* | *The inspectors said the bridge was in a bad state and potentially dangerous.* | **be in a terrible/dreadful etc condition** *The house really is in an awful condition – it would cost far too much to repair.*

dilapidated /dəˈlæpədeɪtəd/ [adj] a building that is **dilapidated** is in very bad condition because it has not been looked after or has not been repaired for a long time: *We stayed in an old, dilapidated hotel with a leaky roof.* | *Jesse was raised in a large, dilapidated house on the East Side.* | *Some of the old homes in Newville are well kept, but others are dilapidated.*

run-down /ˌrʌn ˈdaʊn◂/ [adj] a **run-down** area of a town is one in which the buildings and roads are all in bad condition, especially because the people who live there do not have enough money to look after them properly: *Since the textile company moved out, the area's gotten very run-down.* | *The men were hiding in an abandoned theater in a run-down part of the city.*

derelict /ˈderəlɪkt/ [adj] something, such as a house or piece of land, that is **derelict** is in very bad condition because it has been empty and not used for a very long time: *In the middle of town is a derelict building that used to be the school.* | *The land behind the factory is stony and derelict.*

ramshackle /ˈræmʃækəl/ [adj only before noun] a building that is **ramshackle** is in very bad condition and looks as though it is likely to fall down, especially because it was badly built, with cheap materials: *No one had lived in the ramshackle farmhouse for years.*

crumbling /ˈkrʌmblɪŋ/ [adj only before noun] a **crumbling** building or wall is breaking into pieces because it is very old and damaged by the weather: *Tourists wandered through the crumbling remains of an ancient Greek temple.* | *Elvira lived on a street of old townhouses with crumbling façades.*

tumbledown /ˈtʌmbəldaʊn/ [adj only before noun] especially British **tumbledown building/ house/cottage etc** use this about a building that is old and beginning to fall down, especially in a way that seems attractive: *We arrived at a tumbledown cottage, surrounded by overgrown rose bushes and a broken fence.* | *The college was a collection of tumbledown old buildings in Paddington.*

4 furniture, cars, or machines that are in bad condition

- in bad condition/shape
- rickety
- battered
- be falling apart
- be on its last legs
- has seen better days
- clapped-out

in bad condition/shape ALSO **in a bad state** especially British /ɪn ˌbæd kənˈdɪʃən, ˈʃeɪp, ɪn ə ˌbæd ˈsteɪt/ [adj phrase] *When I bought the chairs they were in very bad condition.* | *The car's in pretty bad shape, but I'll give you $300 for it.* | **be in terrible/dreadful etc condition/shape** *It's a nice piece of furniture, but in such terrible condition you won't get much money for it.*

rickety /ˈrɪkəti/ [adj] furniture and other structures that are **rickety** are in such bad condition that they look as if they would break if you tried to use them: *The staircase was old and rickety.* | *They sat around the card table on rickety old chairs.* | *a rickety bamboo fence*

battered /ˈbætəʳd/ [adj] something that is **battered** is old and in bad condition because it has been used a lot and treated roughly: *There was nothing in his office except for a few battered chairs.* | *Alex and Lisa used to drive around town in a battered old Fiat Uno.*

be falling apart /biː ˌfɔːlɪŋ əˈpɑːʳt/ [v phrase] especially spoken if something **is falling apart**, it is gradually breaking into pieces, because it is old or badly made: *I need some new shoes. These are falling apart.* | *San Diego's public buildings are falling apart, but the city refuses to do anything about it.*

be on its last legs /biː ɒn ɪts ˌlɑːst ˈlegz‖-ˌlæst-/ [v phrase] if something **is on its last legs**, it has been used so much and is in such bad condition that you will soon not be able to use it any more: *The old car was on its last legs, and Renee knew she wouldn't be able to afford a new one.*

has seen better days /həz siːn ˌbetəʳ ˈdeɪz/ [v phrase] if something **has seen better days** it is not in the good condition it once was in, because it is old or has been used a lot: *The carpets, curtains, and cushions had all seen better days but still looked quite pretty.* | *She lived in a rambling Victorian house that had certainly seen better days.*

clapped-out /ˌklæpt ˈaʊt◂/ British informal **/beat-up** /ˌbiːt ˈʌp◂/ American informal [adj usually before noun] use this about a vehicle or machine that is so old that it does not work properly: *Of course the carpet's a mess – all we've got is a clapped-out old vacuum cleaner.* | *She drives an old beat-up Ford.*

5 things made of paper or cloth that are in bad condition

- shabby
- worn
- tattered
- threadbare
- tatty
- battered
- dog-eared

shabby /ˈʃæbi/ [adj] clothes, books etc that look **shabby** are no longer in good condition because they are old and have been used a lot: *John was standing in the doorway in his shabby blue suit.* | *She wore shabby black clothes, with holes in the elbows of her jacket.* —**shabbiness** [n U] *She tried to ignore the faded carpet and the shabbiness of the curtains.*

worn /wɔːʳn/ [adj] something such as material or cloth that is **worn** is thinner or weaker in particular parts as a result of being used a lot over a long time: *There was a worn Persian rug on the parquet floor.* | *We used to cut up worn blankets to make sleeping bags for the children.* | *The brake pads are very worn.*

tattered /ˈtætəʳd/ [adj] clothes or books that are **tattered** are old and torn: *The old man clutched a tattered copy of 'War and Peace'.* | *The shirt was now tattered beyond recognition.* —**tatters** [n plural] **in tatters** *Her clothes were in tatters, but she held two bottles of expensive whiskey under her arms.*

threadbare /ˈθredbeəʳ/ [adj] clothes, curtains, carpets etc that are **threadbare** have become extremely thin and weak because they have been used so much: *She stood shivering in her threadbare dress.* | *There was a clean but threadbare rug on the floor beside the bed.*

tatty /ˈtæti/ [adj] British clothes or books that are **tatty** are in bad condition and slightly torn because they have been used a lot: *At the window of the cottage hang tatty, faded curtains.* | *Some of our textbooks are starting to look rather tatty.*

battered /ˈbætəʳd/ [adj] something that is **battered** is in bad condition and looks old especially because it has been used a lot: *He carried the same battered green journal with him on all his travels.* | *a battered old suitcase*

dog-eared /ˈdɒg ɪəʳd‖ˈdɔːg-/ [adj] a book, page, photograph etc that is **dog-eared** is torn and bent at the edges because it has been used a lot: *Professor Brightly walked into the lecture hall with a pile of dog-eared notes under his arm.* | *On the other wall was a dog-eared calendar with faded pictures.*

6 to get into bad condition

- fall into disrepair
- go to rack and ruin

fall into disrepair /ˌfɔːl ɪntə ˌdɪsrɪˈpeəʳ/ [v phrase] if a building, structure, or machine **falls into disrepair**, its condition gradually becomes worse because no one looks after it: *Dave and Sally couldn't afford to get anything done to the house and it fell into disrepair.* | *Standing in the fields were pieces of farm machinery that had long since fallen into disrepair.*

go to rack and ruin /gəʊ tə ˌræk ənd ˈruːɪ̯n/ [v phrase] if something **goes to rack and ruin**, its condition gets worse and worse and no one tries to repair it until it becomes impossible to save or repair **let sth go to rack and ruin** *He's let his father's old house go to rack and ruin.* | *It seems that the government is prepared to let all our hospitals and schools go to rack and ruin.*

a condition that sth depends on

RELATED WORDS

- *see also* **if, depend/it depends, agree**

7 something that must happen before something else can happen

- condition
- precondition
- prerequisite

condition /kənˈdɪʃən/ [n C] **+ for/of** *Finance ministers claimed that all the conditions for economic revival were already in place.* | *In her view, women's full participation in the labor market is a necessary condition of equality.* | **meet a condition** *The Chancellor says that five conditions have to be met before the UK joins the Euro.*

precondition /ˌpriːkənˈdɪʃən/ [n C] formal a situation that has to exist before something else can happen **+ to/for/of** *The president has demanded that the rebels turn in their weapons as a precondition to any talks.* | *One of the most obvious preconditions for economic growth is a stable government.*

prerequisite /priːˈrekwɪ̯zɪ̯t/ [n C] formal something that you must have before something else is possible **+ for/of** *Adequate food and shelter are the minimum prerequisites of a decent life.* | *Some knowledge of the French language is a prerequisite for employment there.*

8 in an agreement or contract

- condition
- terms
- requirements
- proviso
- stipulation

condition /kənˈdɪʃən/ [n C] something that is stated in an agreement or contract as being necessary before something else can happen or be allowed: *After two weeks of negotiations the two sides still cannot agree on the conditions.* | **+ of** *One of the conditions of the agreement was that both sides would call an immediate ceasefire.* | *It is a condition of my contract with the university that I spend half of the summer vacation doing research.* | **meet/satisfy a condition** (=do what is demanded by a condition) *The World Bank will only agree to make this loan if certain conditions are met.* | **lay down/impose a condition** (=state what must be done) *The Pentagon laid down strict conditions regarding the export of these weapons.* | **under the conditions of sth** (=according to what is stated in an agreement) *Under the conditions of the GATT trade agreement, farm subsidies would be gradually phased out.*

terms /tɜːʳmz/ [n plural] the conditions that are stated in a written agreement, contract, or legal document **+ of** *The president refused to reveal the terms of the peace agreement to the press.* | *The lawyers think we should alter the terms of our contract with the computer company.* | **under the terms of sth** (=according to the terms of an agreement) *Under the terms of the will, Mallory could only inherit the family home if he agreed to continue living there.*

requirements /rɪˈkwaɪəʳmənts/ [n plural] a set of things that you must do or must achieve in order to be officially allowed to do or have something: *A high grade in mathematics is one of the requirements for entry to medical school.* | **meet/satisfy/fulfil require-**

ments (=do what is necessary) *The company's child safety seats did not meet the standards for crash safety.* | *The business does not satisfy all the requirements necessary to qualify for tax concessions.*

proviso /prə'vaɪzəʊ/ [n C] a single condition that you make before you agree to do something: *He agreed to do the work, but there was one proviso – he wanted to be paid in cash.* | **with the proviso that** *Bill had left the money to his grandson, with the proviso that it should be spent on his education.*

stipulation /ˌstɪpjəˈleɪʃən/ [n C] a particular condition that is clearly stated as part of an agreement: *The union is pressing for higher pay but has made no stipulations about the numbers of workers to be employed.* | **with the stipulation that** *The company agreed to hire the law firm, with the stipulation that they hire more women lawyers.*

9 when you agree to do something if something else happens

- on condition that
- be conditional on/upon

on condition that /ɒn kən'dɪʃən ðət/ [conjunction] if you agree to do something **on condition that** something else happens, you will only do it if this thing happens: *Ron lent me the money on condition that I paid it back within three weeks.* | *General Motors agreed to supply trucks to the Chinese government on condition that they altered their pricing policy on cars.* | **on one condition** (=if this one thing is done) *You can borrow the car on one condition – that you promise to be back before midnight.*

be conditional on/upon /kən'dɪʃənəl ɒn, əˌpɒn/ [v phrase] if an offer, agreement, or someone's permission **is conditional on** something else, it will only be given if something else happens: *Offers of financial aid were conditional upon the company changing its management structure.* | *Permission to use firearms is conditional on the consent of the Chief of Police.* —**conditional** [adj] *They have made us a conditional offer*

10 without any conditions

- unconditional
- no strings attached

unconditional /ˌʌnkən'dɪʃənəl◂/ [adj usually before noun] **unconditional surrender/release/agreement etc** an agreement or offer that is **unconditional** is made without any conditions: *The general said he would fight on until the enemy agreed to an unconditional surrender.* | *They are campaigning for the unconditional release of all political prisoners.* —**unconditionally** [adv] *If you are not completely satisfied with our service, we will unconditionally refund your money.*

no strings attached /nəʊ ˌstrɪŋz ə'tætʃt/ [n phrase] if you offer something or ask for something with **no strings attached**, you offer it or ask for it without stating any conditions and without trying to get an advantage for yourself: *Emergency food aid should be given with no strings attached.* | *Before you accept the loan you'd better make sure that there are no strings attached.*

confident/ not confident

RELATED WORDS

- sure that something good will happen *see* **sure**
- *see also* **independent, proud, brave/not brave, shy**

1 confident

- confident
- self-confident
- self-assured
- assertive
- sure of yourself
- extrovert

confident /'kɒnfɪdənt‖'kɑːn-/ [adj] sure that you have the ability to do something well, and not worried about failing: *It's a difficult test, but she seems fairly confident.* | *He gave his speech in a strong, confident voice.* | **+ about** *After living in France for a year, I felt much more confident about my French.* | **be/feel confident about (doing) sth** *I'm not very confident about going back to work.* | **+ of** *Baldwin is confident of victory in this year's senate race.* —**confidently** [adv] *She answered each question confidently.* | *'It'll all work out in the end,' said Brown confidently.*

self-confident /self 'kɒnfɪdənt‖-'kɑːn-/ [adj] someone who is **self-confident** is very confident about their own abilities and is not shy or nervous in social situations: *Jess was only 12, but she was very self-confident.* | *I eventually became more self-confident as a public speaker.* | **supremely self-confident** (=extremely self-confident) *She was supremely self-confident, with the gift of being able to talk on any subject whenever the camera was rolling.*

self-assured /ˌself ə'ʃʊəʳd◂/ [adj] very confident in your own abilities and able to deal calmly with other people, especially in public situations: *Having done this many times before, she was self-assured and spoke without notes.* | *On the surface Dana was calm and self-assured, but I knew that this wasn't completely the case.*

assertive /ə'sɜːʳtɪv/ [adj] someone who is **assertive** behaves confidently so that they get what they want: *Jack has a very assertive personality.* | *The course helps women learn how to be more assertive in the workplace.* —**assertively** [adv] *Try to communicate assertively – not aggressively.* —**assertiveness** [n U] *The group has been given training in public speaking and assertiveness.*

sure of yourself /'ʃʊər əv jɔːʳself/ [adj phrase] very sure that what you think is right, even when other people do not agree with you: *He sounded so sure of himself that I didn't bother to argue.* | *Jenny was younger than her sister but seemed much more sure of herself.*

extrovert /'ekstrəvəʳt/ [n C] someone who enjoys being with other people and getting a lot of attention from other people: *Jan says her twin babies are completely different: Kelly is a real extrovert while Jessie is quiet and thoughtful.* | *Most actors are natural extroverts.* | *He's a total extrovert who will talk to any stranger.* —**extrovert** [adj] *The Signore was extrovert and jolly and his wife was a wonderful cook.*

2 too confident

- overconfident
- cocky
- brash

overconfident /ˌəʊvərˈkɒnfɪ̈dənt‖-ˈkɑːn-/ [adj] too sure that you will succeed or win, often when you do not have the ability to do this: *Murray worried that the team was becoming overconfident.* | *As drivers, teenage boys are often overconfident and take stupid risks.*

cocky /ˈkɒki‖ˈkɑːki/ [adj] informal too confident about yourself and your abilities, especially in a way that annoys other people: *a cocky young lieutenant* | *My brother can be a little bit cocky sometimes.* | *She didn't come off well in the interview – she was a bit too cocky, a bit too sure of herself.*

brash /bræʃ/ [adj] someone who is **brash** is very confident in an annoying way, for example because they talk too loudly and never listen to other people: *The hotel bar was full of brash, noisy journalists.* | *a brash young salesman from New York*

3 a confident feeling

- confidence
- self-confidence
- morale
- assurance/self-assurance
- belief in yourself
- self-esteem

confidence /ˈkɒnfɪ̈dəns‖ˈkɑːn-/ [n U] the feeling that you have the ability to do things well, and to not make mistakes or be nervous in new situations: *You need patience and confidence to be a good teacher.* | **have the confidence to do sth** *'We have the confidence to beat Brazil,' said Sampson.* | *After the accident it took a long time before she had the confidence to get back in a car again.* | **full of confidence** (=very confident) *I went into the test full of confidence, but it was more difficult than I had imagined.*

self-confidence /self ˈkɒnfɪ̈dəns‖-ˈkɑːn-/ [n U] a strong belief that you can do things well and that other people will like you, which means you behave confidently in most situations: *He's new in the job but he has plenty of self-confidence.* | *Studies show that girls tend to lose some of their self-confidence in their teenage years.* | *Students who get some kind of work experience develop greater self-confidence and better communication skills.*

morale /məˈrɑːl‖məˈræl/ [n U] the level of confidence, satisfaction, and hope that people feel, especially a group of people who work together **low/high morale** *Morale among the soldiers has been low.* | **keep up morale** (=keep it at a high level) *They sang songs to keep up their morale until the rescuers arrived.*

assurance/self-assurance /əˈʃʊərəns, ˌself əˈʃʊərəns/ [n U] a feeling of calm confidence in your own abilities, especially because you have a lot of experience: *She envied the older woman's assurance.* | *Danby spoke to the committee with the self-assurance of an expert.*

belief in yourself /bɪ̈ˈliːf ɪn jɔːrˌself/ [n phrase] confidence in your own abilities, value, and judgment, which makes it likely that you will be successful at something: *You must have belief in yourself if you want to make it as an actor.* | *To acquire that level of skill requires years of training and an unfailing belief in yourself.*

self-esteem /ˌself ɪˈstiːm/ [n U] the feeling that you are someone who deserves to be liked and respected: *Getting a job did a lot for her self-esteem.* | *Sports should build a child's self-esteem, not damage it.*

4 to make someone feel more confident

- give sb confidence
- boost sb's confidence
- build/build up (sb's) confidence
- boost morale/raise morale
- boost sb's ego
- give sb a boost/a lift

give sb confidence /ˌgɪv (sb) ˈkɒnfɪ̈dəns‖-ˈkɑːn-/ [v phrase] *Teaching abroad was good for me. It gave me a lot of confidence.* | *'The activities,' said Harris, 'are designed to give children confidence in their reading abilities.'* | **give sb the confidence to do sth** *The country needs the backing of the international community to give it the confidence to rebuild its war-battered economy.*

boost sb's confidence /ˌbuːst (sb's) ˈkɒnfɪ̈dəns‖ -ˈkɑːn-/ [v phrase] an event or action that **boosts someone's confidence** quickly makes them feel more confident: *Winning this game will really boost the team's confidence.* | *To boost my confidence I went for a haircut and bought some new clothes.*

build/build up (sb's) confidence /ˌbɪld, ˌbɪld ʌp (sb's) ˈkɒnfɪ̈dəns‖ˈkɑːn-/ [v phrase] to gradually make someone feel more confident: *The games are designed to make maths fun and build up youngsters' confidence.* | *Build confidence by assigning tasks which draw on an employee's areas of strength.*

boost morale/raise morale /ˌbuːst məˈrɑːl, ˌreɪz məˈrɑːl‖-məˈræl/ [v phrase] to raise the level of confidence and satisfaction among a group of people: *A pay raise would boost employee morale a great deal.* | *Visits by celebrities and politicians were meant to boost morale among the troops.*

boost sb's ego /ˌbuːst (sb's) ˈiːgəʊ/ [v phrase] to make someone feel more confident about themselves, for example by saying good things about their appearance, character, or work: *It was nice to have my work praised for once – it really boosted my ego.* | *The fact that Jane was attracted to him boosted his ego quite a bit.*

give sb a boost/a lift /ˌgɪv (sb) ə ˈbuːst, ə ˈlɪft/ [v phrase] to make someone feel happier or more confident: *Nothing could have given the team a bigger boost than the victory over Canada.* | *When I was feeling down, talking to Marion always gave me a lift.*

5 not confident

- lack confidence/be lacking in confidence
- lose confidence
- unsure of yourself
- insecure
- demoralized
- discouraged

lack confidence/be lacking in confidence /ˌlæk ˈkɒnfɪ̈dəns, biː ˌlækɪŋ ɪn ˈkɒnfɪ̈dəns‖-ˈkɑːn-/ [v phrase] to not be confident about your abilities or appearance: *Francine lacks confidence and needs a lot of encouragement and support.* | *I was fat, had no friends, and lacked confidence.* | *While girls lack confidence, boys often overestimate their abilities.*

lose confidence /ˌluːz ˈkɒnfɪ̈dəns‖-ˈkɑːn-/ [v phrase] to stop feeling confident, especially after making a mistake: *'How was your driving test?' 'Terrible – I made one small mistake, and then I just lost* *confidence.' | People tend to lose confidence if they've been out of work for a while.*

unsure of yourself /ʌn'ʃʊər əv jɔːʳself/ [adj phrase] to not be confident, especially because you are young or you do not have much experience: *At first, Chris seemed nervous and unsure of herself. | He was only 21 and still very unsure of himself with girls.*

insecure /ˌɪnsɪ'kjʊəʳ/ [adj] not confident about making decisions, trying new experiences, or forming new relationships, especially because you are worried that you are not good enough: *Ben's parents' divorce left him lonely and insecure.* | **+ about** *Even though she's a model, she's very insecure about how she looks.*

demoralized /dɪ'mɒrəlaɪzd‖-'mɔːr-/ [adj] if a person or a group of people are **demoralized**, they have lost all their confidence that they can succeed at something and are unwilling to continue with it: *a demoralized work force | Many employees became demoralized and cynical when the company announced another round of job cuts.* | **utterly/thoroughly demoralized** *The team was a wreck – thoroughly demoralized after a humiliating season.*

discouraged /dɪs'kʌrɪdʒd‖-'kɜː-/ [adj] not confident about something you are trying to achieve, because you have had difficulty achieving it: *I was very discouraged at the time, but I still hoped we could find a solution.* | **get/become discouraged** *Students with learning difficulties who do not have a dedicated teacher can become discouraged very easily.* | **+ by** *Discouraged by her failed marriages, she gradually withdrew from the world.* | **+ about** *Hartman was so discouraged about the way his performing career was going, that he gave up acting for writing.*

6 to make someone feel less confident

- shake/damage (sb's) confidence
- demoralizing
- take the wind out of sb's sails
- discourage
- discouraging

shake/damage (sb's) confidence /ˌʃeɪk, ˌdæmɪdʒ (sb's) 'kɒnfɪ̇dəns‖ -'kɑːn-/ [v phrase] if something **shakes** or **damages someone's confidence**, it makes them feel unsure of their abilities and less confident: *Being fired really shook his confidence.* | **badly shaken** *Her confidence was badly shaken when she was involved in a car accident a few years ago.*

demoralizing /dɪ'mɒrəlaɪzɪŋ‖-'mɔːr-/ [adj] making people feel that they cannot be successful at something they are trying to do, so that they become unwilling to continue with it: *the demoralizing effects of unemployment | Many of the teachers found the school board's criticism unfair and demoralizing. | Rivas says being on welfare was a demoralizing and humiliating experience.*

take the wind out of sb's sails /teɪk ðə ˌwɪnd aʊt əv (sb's) 'seɪlz/ [v phrase] informal to make someone lose their confidence, especially by saying or doing something unexpected: *Last night's defeat has taken some of the wind out of the team's sails.*

discourage /dɪs'kʌrɪdʒ‖-'kɜː-/ [v T] to make someone feel less confident about something they are trying to achieve: *What discouraged me most was our lack of progress in the pay negotiations. | Although the troubles in the financial markets have made him cautious, Reid said they haven't discouraged him.*

discouraging /dɪs'kʌrɪdʒɪŋ‖-'kɜː-/ [adj] making someone feel less confident about something they are trying to achieve: *My father made a few discouraging remarks about my academic abilities that have stayed with me to this day. | Despite discouraging viewing figures for their movie 'For the Boys', Paramount decided to try to make another similar film.* | **be discouraging to do sth** *It's very discouraging to find out that your own team members have been lying to you.* | **+ that** *It is deeply discouraging that the government can struggle with the nation's budget for nearly a year and still fail to achieve anything.*

confused

RELATED WORDS

▸ *see also* **understand/not understand, organize, sure/not sure, clear/not clear (1-6)**

1 confused

- confused
- confusion
- be in a muddle
- bewildered
- bemused
- mixed-up

confused /kən'fjuːzd/ [adj] not able to understand what is happening, what someone is saying etc, especially when this makes you feel worried: *I'm a little confused – could you explain it again? | She felt hurt and confused when her husband left her.* | **+ about** *We're a little confused about what we're supposed to be doing.* | **get confused** *Every time someone tries to explain the Internet to me, I get even more confused.*

confusion /kən'fjuːʒən/ [n U] the feeling you have when you are confused, or a situation in which people are confused: *The new rules have caused a lot of confusion.* | **+ about/over** *There is still confusion over who is responsible for the accident.* | **throw sb/sth into confusion** (=make them feel confused) *The final scene of the play threw much of the audience into confusion.*

be in a muddle /biː ɪn ə 'mʌdl/ [v phrase] British informal confused, especially because you are trying to do something complicated or because you have a lot of things to do: *I wonder if you could help Emma sort out the papers – she's in a bit of a muddle.* | **+ about** *There were four phone calls at once and the secretary was in a muddle about who wanted to talk to who.* | **get into a muddle** *It's best to paint the background first and then the pattern. That way you don't get into a muddle.*

bewildered /bɪ'wɪldəʳd/ [adj] very confused and surprised when something unusual and unexpected happens to you: *He was bewildered to find three policemen at the front door. | Police took a burglary report from a bewildered resident.* | **+ by/at** *At first she was bewildered by all the noise and activity of the city.*

bemused /bɪ'mjuːzd/ [adj] confused, surprised, and slightly annoyed by what has happened, or by what someone has said: *She told him to leave, but he just sat there with a bemused expression on his face.* | **+ by** *Shop-owners and residents alike seem bemused by the recent arrival of so many tourists.*

mixed-up /ˌmɪkst 'ʌp◂/ [adj] informal confused, especially over a long period of time, and unable to decide what to do, especially because of personal or emotional problems: *Carol wrote poems about her feelings to try and figure out why she felt so mixed-*

up. | *With parents like that, it's no wonder he's a mixed-up kid.*

2 confused because something is difficult to understand

- puzzled
- baffled
- perplexed
- mystified

puzzled /ˈpʌzəld/ [adj] completely unable to understand why or how something happened, especially because it is very different from what you expect: *I'm a little puzzled – why did you call her yourself when I specifically told you I would do it?* | *After my explanation, Mandy still had a puzzled expression on her face.* | **+ by/at** *The doctor was puzzled by the man's symptoms and ordered several further tests.*

baffled /ˈbæfəld/ [adj] very confused and unable to understand something, even though you have tried hard for a long time: *'I still can't figure this out,' said Dane, baffled.* | **+ by/at** *At times the old man seemed baffled by his surroundings.* | **+ as to/about** *Detectives admit they are baffled about the killer's motive.*

perplexed /pərˈplekst/ [adj] formal confused and worried by an event or situation that you do not understand: *Mr Rice was staring at the report with a perplexed expression on his face.* | *The sudden ups and downs of the stock market have left analysts perplexed.* | **+ by** *Julie, perplexed by her boyfriend's sudden outburst, kept out of his way.*

mystified /ˈmɪstɪfaɪd/ [adj] if someone is **mystified** by something, they are completely unable to understand it, and they are often very surprised by it: *'How could you possibly have known that?' he asked, totally mystified.* | **+ by** *Army officials are mystified by the illnesses that have struck veterans of the Gulf War.*

3 something that makes you feel confused

- confusing
- puzzling
- baffling
- bewildering

confusing /kənˈfjuːzɪŋ/ [adj] **confusing** instructions, explanations, situations etc make you feel confused, because it is not clear what they mean or what you should do: *The road signs were very confusing and we ended up getting lost.* | *I found some of the questions really confusing.* | **+ for** *The procedure can be a little confusing for beginners.*

puzzling /ˈpʌzəlɪŋ/ [adj] a **puzzling** action or situation is very confusing, especially because it is strange or new, or because a lot of different things are happening at the same time: *Jan's decision not to take part in the race was very puzzling.* | *Don't you think it's puzzling that no-one noticed them leave?* | **+ to** *Some of the results of the experiments were puzzling to researchers.*

baffling /ˈbæflɪŋ/ [adj] extremely difficult or impossible to understand, and therefore making you feel extremely confused: *I found his sudden refusal to come to the wedding completely baffling.* | *New evidence has provided a clue to one of the most baffling crimes the police have had to deal with.*

bewildering /bɪˈwɪldərɪŋ/ [adj] a **bewildering** situation is very confusing, especially because it is strange or new, or because of lot of different things are happening at the same time: *Changes in society are happening so fast, they sometimes seem bewildering.* | **a bewildering number/variety/range etc** (=so many things that is difficult for you to choose) *There was a bewildering variety of styles to choose from.*

4 to make someone feel confused

- confuse
- puzzle
- baffle
- throw
- do your head in

confuse /kənˈfjuːz/ [v T] *His sudden change in mood completely confused her.* | *Don't show him the other way of doing it – it'll only confuse him.*

puzzle /ˈpʌzəl/ [v T] if something **puzzles** you, you are completely unable to understand it, or why it has happened: *Her unwillingness to answer any of his questions puzzled him.* | **what puzzles me is** *What puzzles me is why she doesn't just leave him.*

baffle /ˈbæfəl/ [v T] if something **baffles** you, you cannot understand it at all, even though you try very hard to: *The exact nature of black holes continues to baffle scientists.* | *The fact that none of the neighbors ever reported the abuse has baffled authorities.*

throw /θrəʊ/ [v T] if something **throws** you, it makes you suddenly feel confused because it is unexpected and surprising: *I could answer most of the questions but the last one really threw me.* | **throw sb for a loop** American informal (=completely confuse someone) *Rick was Kitty's boyfriend, you know, and his death threw her for a loop.*

do your head in /ˌduː jɔːʳ ˈhed ɪn/ [v phrase] British spoken if someone or something is **doing your head in**, they are making you feel very confused and often very annoyed or worried: *He's so fussy about how he wants things done, it really does my head in.* | *I've got to do an essay on Kant and it's doing my head in.*

5 to think one person or thing is another person or thing

- confuse
- mix up

confuse /kənˈfjuːz/ [v T] to wrongly think that one person or thing is another person or thing: *Try not to confuse 'your' and 'you're'.* | **confuse sb/sth with sb/sth** *I always confuse Anthea with her sister – they're so alike.* | **get sb/sth confused** *You don't write a résumé to get a job; you write it to get an interview – don't get the two things confused.*

mix up /ˌmɪks ˈʌp/ [phr v T] to make a mistake and think that one person or thing is another person or thing **mix up sb/sth** *Children often mix up 'b' and 'd' when they're learning to write.* | **mix sb/sth up with sb/sth** *Is Stan the guy you work with or am I mixing him up with somebody else?* | **get sb/sth mixed up** *Which one's Jane and which one's Jen? I always get their names mixed up.*

connected with/related

RELATED WORDS

- relationships between people *see* **relationship**
- to join things together *see* **join**

1 to be connected with a fact, event, idea etc

- be connected/be related
- be linked
- associated
- have/be something to do with
- be bound up with sth/go hand in hand

be connected/be related /biː kəˈnektɪ̈d, biː rɪˈleɪtɪ̈d/ [v phrase] if two things **are connected** or **related**, there is a relationship between them: *It seems likely that the western diet and high levels of heart disease are connected.* | *It's fairly obvious that pollution and heavy car use are related.* | **be connected with sth** *Changes in moral values tend to be connected with changes in a society's economic standing.* | *The most common illnesses among VDU operators are connected with the eyes and vision.* | **be closely connected/related** *Diet and exercise are closely connected with overall health.* | *Studies suggest that cigarette advertising is closely related to adolescents' smoking behavior.* | **be related to sth** *Each country has its own problems, which are related to its economic and political position.* | *Families reported widespread hardship directly related to absentee or alcoholic fathers.* | **related issues/problems etc** *Leaders will meet to discuss the debt crisis, investment and other related issues.*

be linked /biː ˈlɪŋkt/ [v phrase] if two things **are linked**, one affects or causes the other, although the connection is not always easy to see and cannot always be proved: *Drug dealing and prostitution are often linked.* | **+ with/to** *Aluminium in water is now being linked with premature ageing.*

associated /əˈsəʊʃieɪtɪ̈d, əˈsəʊsi-/ [adj] problems that are **associated** with a particular situation or event, are likely to happen because of it: *The group tours schools, talking to kids about drug abuse and its associated problems.* | *I was warned by the doctor about the associated side effects of the new treatment.* | **be associated with sth** *Low educational achievement is strongly associated with poverty and disadvantage.*

have/be something to do with /hæv, biː ˌsʌmθɪŋ tə ˈduː wɪð/ [v phrase] especially spoken to be connected in a way that you do not understand clearly: *I don't know much about his job, but it has something to do with finance.* | *'What's wrong with your car?' 'I'm not sure. I think it's something to do with the starter motor.'*

be bound up with/go hand in hand /biː ˌbaʊnd ˈʌp wɪð, gəʊ ˌhænd ɪn ˈhænd/ [v phrase] especially British if something **is bound up with** or **goes hand in hand with** something else, the two things are very closely connected and need to be considered together: *His problems are all bound up with his relationship with his parents.* | *In most societies, wealth and power go hand in hand.* | *According to Marx, the decline of feudalism was bound up with the growth of towns in the twelfth century.* | **go hand in hand with sth** *Scientists have noticed that climate changes seem to go hand in hand with sea-level changes.*

2 to be connected with an organization

- be connected with
- have links/connections with
- be linked with

be connected with /biː kəˈnektɪ̈d wɪð/ [v phrase] *She's not a professor but she's connected with the university in some way.* | *Senators are demanding to know whether the vice-president is in any way connected with the arms suppliers.*

have links/connections with /hæv ˈlɪŋks, kəˈnekʃənz wɪð/ [v phrase] to have a relationship with an organization, group, or country: *He is believed to have connections with extremist fundamentalist groups.* | **have close links/connections with sth** *South Korea continues to have close military links with the US.* | **sever/cut/break off links with sth** (=end your relationship with them) *Lipman called for the U.S. to sever links with countries known to support terrorists.*

be linked with /biː ˈlɪŋkt wɪð/ [v phrase] to be connected with an organization, activity or event – use this especially when you do not approve of the connection: *Police are still saying the Mafia may be linked with the shooting.*

3 when two facts, events, or situations are connected

- connection
- relationship
- link
- correlation

connection /kəˈnekʃən/ [n C] *The two incidents might have something to do with each other, but I can't see the connection.* | **connection between sth and sth** *Students need to realize that there is a connection between education and their future.* | **close connection** *Sheldon revealed the close connection between poverty and bad health.*

relationship /rɪˈleɪʃənʃɪp/ [n C] the way in which two things are connected and affect each other, or the way in which the connection can be explained: *Interest rates and government spending are connected, but the relationship is quite a complex one.* | **relationship to/with sth** *These accusations against me have no relationship to the truth.* | **relationship between sth and sth** *She was worried that the company wouldn't see any relationship between her work experience and the job she was applying for.*

link /lɪŋk/ [n C] a connection between two facts or events, especially when one causes or affects the other **+ between** *Some scientists believe there may be a link between caffeine and heart disease.* | **+ with** *Police are investigating the scene to determine if there are any links with last week's bombing.*

correlation /ˌkɒrɪ̈ˈleɪʃən‖ˌkɔː-/ [n C/U] if there is a **correlation** between two things, they happen or exist together and it seems likely that one causes or influences the other **+ between** *One of the students asked whether there was any correlation between rainfall and temperature.* | *In tests, no correlation was found between diet and intelligence.* | **+ with** *The study examines the correlation of violence on television with children's behavior.* | **strong correlation** *Dawson argued that there is a strong correlation between teenage crime and low educational achievement.*

4 connected with the subject that is being talked about

- relevant
- pertinent

relevant /ˈrelɪ̈vənt/ [adj] directly connected with the subject you are discussing or considering: *We can't make a decision until we have all the relevant information.* | *The judge ruled that the defendant's previous conviction was relevant and could be* *discussed during the case.* | **+ to** *I don't think your arguments are relevant to this discussion.*

pertinent /ˈpɜːʳtənənt/ [adj] formal something that is **pertinent** to a subject is directly concerned with it and is important when considering it: *That's a very pertinent question.* | *I think it may be pertinent at this point to raise the question of how the new department will be funded.* | **+ to** *The police department is appealing for any information that may be pertinent to this inquiry.*

5 to say, believe, or prove that there is a connection between two facts, events, or people

- link
- associate
- make a connection
- establish a link

link /lɪŋk/ [v T] to say or believe that there is a connection between two things, even though the connection may not be easy to see or prove **link sth and sth** *Police are linking the availability of alcohol and a recent rise in the number of teenage arrests.* | **link sb/sth with sb/sth** *His name has been linked with several famous actresses since he and his wife separated last year.* | *The health department has linked several cases of food poisoning with contaminated shellfish.* | **link sth to sth** *For centuries farmers have linked the behavior of animals and plants to changes in the weather.*

associate /əˈsəʊʃieɪt, əˈsəʊsi-/ [v T] if you **associate** something with something else, the two things are always connected in your mind **associate sth with sth** *Shoppers tend to associate certain brand names with high quality.* | *People associate the old days with good times, and seem to forget the hardship they endured.* | **associate sth and sth** *I've always associated the smell of paint and my first grade art class.*

make a connection /ˌmeɪk ə kəˈnekʃən/ [v phrase] to realize that two things are connected: *At least 24 women who took the diet pills developed heart disease before doctors made the connection.* | **+ between** *Young children quickly make a connection between the pictures in books and the real objects they see.*

establish a link /ɪˌstæblɪʃ ə ˈlɪŋk/ [v phrase] to prove or discover that something is connected with something else **+ between** *Police have so far failed to establish a link between the two murders.* | *Sir Austin Bradford Hill led one of the first research teams to establish a link between smoking and lung cancer.*

6 not connected with something or someone

- not connected/not related
- unrelated/unconnected
- have no connection with
- be/have nothing to do with

not connected/not related /nɒt kəˈnektəd, nɒt rɪˈleɪtəd/ [n phrase] *The two diseases seem similar, but they are not related in any way.* | **+ with** *The group is not connected with any political party.*

unrelated/unconnected /ˌʌnrɪˈleɪtəd◂, ˌʌnkəˈnektəd◂/ [adj] formal not connected in any way: *The two robberies are said to be unconnected.* | **unrelated to sth/unconnected with sth** *A spokesperson claimed that Hoyle's dismissal was completely unrelated to his recent criticism of the club.*

have no connection with /hæv ˌnəʊ kəˈnekʃən wɪð/ [v phrase] especially written to not be connected with something in any way: *His comment had absolutely no connection with what we were talking about.*

be/have nothing to do with /biː, hæv ˌnʌθɪŋ tə ˈduː wɪð/ [v phrase] to not be connected with something or someone in any way: *Those boxes are nothing to do with me. Sally left them there.* | *Your age has nothing to do with your ability to do the job.*

7 not connected with the subject you are talking about

- irrelevant
- that's beside the point
- be/have nothing to do with
- what has that got to do with ... ?
- doesn't come into it/doesn't enter into it
- be neither here nor there
- have no bearing on sth
- red herring

irrelevant /ɪˈreləvənt/ [adj] *Chris continued to annoy her with questions on totally irrelevant subjects.* | *'But I didn't know it was illegal to park here.' 'That's completely irrelevant.'* | **+ to** *To many young people, the church seems outdated and irrelevant to modern times.* —**irrelevantly** [adv] *'In this light,' I said, irrelevantly, 'my hand looks blue.'*

that's beside the point /ðæts bɪˌsaɪd ðə ˈpɔɪnt/ spoken say this when you think that what someone has said does not have any real connection with what you are arguing about: *'Is she married or single?' 'That's completely beside the point – the question is, does she have the ability to do the job?'*

be/have nothing to do with /biː, hæv ˌnʌθɪŋ tə ˈduː wɪð/ [v phrase] if something **has nothing to do with** a subject, it is not connected with it in any way: *My back was bothering me a little bit, but that had nothing to do with how badly I played.* | *I don't know what's the matter with Billy – he says it's nothing to do with school.* | *My father was a remote figure who had nothing to do with my every-day life.*

what has that got to do with ... ? British spoken **/what does that have to do with ... ?** especially American, spoken /wɒt həz ˈðæt gɒt tə duː wɪð‖-gɑːt-, wɒt dəz ˈðæt hæv tə duː wɪð/ say this when someone has mentioned something and you cannot understand how it is connected with the subject you are talking about: *I realize you didn't get home until after midnight but what does that have to do with coming in late for work?*

doesn't come into it/doesn't enter into it /ˌdʌzənt kʌm ˈɪntʊ ɪt, ˌdʌzənt entər ˈɪntʊ ɪt/ [v phrase] spoken say this about something that someone has mentioned that does not influence or affect what you are talking about: *Whether the applicant is a man or a woman doesn't come into it.* | *I'm afraid this is company policy, and your own views on the matter simply don't enter into it.*

be neither here nor there /biː ˌnaɪðəʳ ˌhɪəʳ nɔːʳ ˈðeəʳ/ [v phrase] spoken say this when someone has mentioned something that they think is important but you do not agree: *What I think about your husband is neither here nor there.* | *It's true we're not friends but that's neither here nor there. We're still able to work together.*

have no bearing on sth /hæv ˌnəʊ ˈbeərɪŋ ɒn (sth)/ if something **has no bearing on** the situation that you are talking about, it does not affect that situation or help to explain it: *The president's* *age has no bearing on whether or not I will vote for him.* | *A suspect's previous criminal record should have no bearing on the trial.*

red herring /ˌred 'herɪŋ/ [n C] facts or information that are not connected with the subject that is being discussed or considered, and take people's attention away from what is really important: *Concerns about the cost of the project are a red herring.*

conscious

awake and able to understand what is happening around you

RELATED WORDS

opposite: —— **unconscious**
- not sleeping *see* **sleep**
- *see also* **wake up/get up, ill/sick, hurt, accident**

1 conscious

- conscious
- awake

conscious /'kɒnʃəs‖'kɑːn-/ [adj not before noun] awake and able to understand what is happening around you – use this especially about someone who is ill or has had an accident or operation: *The driver was still conscious when the ambulance reached her.* | *Frank was found lying beside the road, covered in blood but still conscious.* | **barely conscious** *The man was so drunk that he was barely conscious.*

awake /ə'weɪk/ [adj not before noun] especially spoken conscious again after having been given a drug that made you unconscious: *They won't allow us to see her until the anesthesia has worn off and she's fully awake.* | *Will I be awake by the time I get back to the ward?*

2 to become conscious again after being unconscious

- regain consciousness
- come round
- come to

regain consciousness /rɪˌgeɪn 'kɒnʃəsnəs‖-'kɑːn-/ [v phrase] formal to become conscious again after being unconscious: *The doctors don't know when he'll regain consciousness.* | *She died without regaining consciousness.*

come round British **/come around** American /ˌkʌm 'raʊnd, ˌkʌm ə'raʊnd/ [phr v I] to become conscious again gradually, especially after an accident or injury: *Sue was coming around, but she still felt dizzy.* | *The police are waiting for him to come round so they can question him about the attack.*

come to /ˌkʌm 'tuː/ [phr v I] to become gradually conscious again after being made unconscious, especially by being hit on the head: *He came to a few minutes later, unable to remember anything about the accident.*

3 to make someone conscious again

- bring sb round

bring sb round British **/bring sb around** American /ˌbrɪŋ (sb) 'raʊnd, ˌbrɪŋ (sb) ə'raʊnd/ [phr v T] to make someone conscious, especially someone who has been unconscious for a short time: *Paramedics eventually brought the man around.* | *Elsie had fainted in the heat, and they were having difficulty bringing her round.*

consist of

RELATED WORDS

- *see also* **be, contain, include/not include**

1 to consist of a number of parts or substances

- consist of/be made up of
- be made of
- be made out of
- be composed of
- comprise

consist of/be made up of /kən'sɪst ɒv, biː ˌmeɪd 'ʌp ɒv/ [v phrase not in progressive] if something **consists of** or **is made up of** several parts, those parts form the whole of it: *Lorna's whole wardrobe consisted of jeans, tee shirts, and sweaters.* | *Up to 70% of your total body weight is made up of water.* | *The executive board is made up of public officials, citizens, and businesspeople.*

be made of /biː 'meɪd ɒv/ [v phrase] if something **is made of** a particular substance, that substance was used for making it: *The candlesticks are made of brass.* | *She mixed a batter made of flour, eggs, and water.* | *What's this carpet made of?*

be made out of /biː ˌmeɪd 'aʊt ɒv/ [v phrase] if something **is made out** of something else, it was made by changing a substance or object into something different: *The eight-string 'guitar' he played was made out of a roasting pan.* | *Tyra Banks wore a bikini made out of toilet paper.* | *At my grandparents' we would take turns riding on a swing made out of an old tire.*

be composed of /biː kəm'pəʊzd ɒv/ [v phrase] to be naturally formed from a group of substances or parts: *The earth's atmosphere is composed mainly of nitrogen, oxygen, and carbon dioxide.* | *The human body is composed of billions of tiny cells.* —**composition** /ˌkɒmpə'zɪʃən‖ˌkɑːm-/ [n U] the way in which something is made up of different parts or members: *What is the chemical composition of lava?*

comprise /kəm'praɪz/ [v T not in progressive] formal to consist of a number of parts, groups, organizations etc: *The house comprises 2 bedrooms, a kitchen, and a living room.* | *The city's population comprises mainly Asians and Europeans.*

2 to have or include something as a part

- have sth in it
- contain

have sth in it /ˌhæv (sth) 'ɪn ɪt/ [v phrase] *Does this fish have bones in it?* | *I can't find a pen that has any ink in it.*

contain /kən'teɪn/ [v T not in progressive or passive] formal if something **contains** a particular part or substance, that part or substance is in it but does not form the whole of it: *It is important to eat meat or eggs, as they contain protein and vitamins.* | *The film was banned because it contained a number of extremely violent scenes.*

contact

to communicate with someone

RELATED WORDS

▸ *see also* **talk, write, telephone, letter, message, computer/Internet/email**

1 to write to, talk to, telephone etc someone

- ▸ get in touch with
- ▸ contact
- ▸ get onto
- ▸ make contact with
- ▸ approach

get in touch with /ˌget ɪn ˈtʌtʃ wɪð/ [v phrase not in passive] to write to, telephone, email etc someone, especially someone you do not see very often: *I really ought to get in touch with Paula. It's been months since we last spoke.* | *I've been trying to get in touch with my sister for several days.* | *You can get in touch with me at home, or at the office if necessary.*

contact /ˈkɒntækt‖ˈkɑːn-/ [v T] to write to, phone, email etc someone especially for the first time, in order to give or ask for information: *I was given the names of three government officials to contact.* | *After they received the bomb threat, school officials immediately contacted the police.*

get onto /get ˈɒntuː / [phr v T not usually in progressive] British spoken to phone, write to, email etc someone in order to complain, explain, or ask for something: *I'm afraid I can't help you. You'd better get onto the foreign office.* | *I'll get onto Eddy and see if I can find out what's going on.*

make contact with /ˌmeɪk ˈkɒntækt wɪð‖-ˈkɑːn-/ [v phrase] to succeed in contacting someone, especially when this is difficult: *The pilot finally managed to make contact with the control tower.* | *I've managed to make contact with most of the people on the list.*

approach /əˈprəʊtʃ/ [v T] to contact someone that you do not know or have not contacted before, in order to offer them something or ask them for something: *Nash has already been approached by several pro football teams.* | **approach sb about sth** *The company confirmed that it had been approached about a merger.*

2 to regularly telephone, write to, email etc someone

- ▸ be in contact
- ▸ keep in touch/stay in touch
- ▸ keep in contact
- ▸ communicate

be in contact /biː ɪn ˈkɒntækt‖-ˈkɑːn-/ [v phrase] to regularly telephone, write to, email etc someone so that you quickly find out about any news: *Harrison maintains that the pair were not in contact for over 10 years.* | **+ with** *We're in close contact with the Italian division of the company.* | *John is no longer in contact with his family.*

keep in touch/stay in touch /ˌkiːp ɪn ˈtʌtʃ, ˌsteɪ ɪn ˈtʌtʃ/ [v phrase] to continue to see, speak to, or write to someone when you are no longer working with them, living near them etc: *Linda and I stay in touch by sending occasional postcards.* | *Have a safe trip back. Don't forget to keep in touch.* | **+ with** *I haven't kept in touch with any of the people I went to school with.*

keep in contact /ˌkiːp ɪn ˈkɒntækt‖-ˈkɑːn-/ [v phrase] to continue to write to, telephone, email etc someone although you are far away from them: *We keep in contact, but I rarely see them.* | **+ with** *I've kept in contact with several of my army buddies.* | **+ by** *Teenagers keep in contact by text messaging on their mobile phones.*

communicate /kəˈmjuːnɪ̥keɪt/ [v I] to exchange information or have a conversation with someone, by telephone, letter etc, or by seeing them **communicate by phone/email/letter etc** *Now that we live in different cities, we communicate by e-mail.* | **communicate in writing** *They couldn't communicate in writing, because William was illiterate.*

3 to succeed in contacting someone by telephone

- ▸ get hold of
- ▸ get through
- ▸ reach

get hold of /ˌget ˈhəʊld ɒv/ [v phrase] to succeed in contacting someone by telephone after trying several times: *Where have you been? I've been trying to get hold of you all week.* | *It's no use trying to phone Linda at work – she's impossible to get hold of.*

get through /ˌget ˈθruː/ [phr v I] to succeed in contacting someone by telephone, especially after a delay or technical problem: *I finally got through, but it took several minutes.* | **get through to sb** *By the way, did you get through to Sharon?* | *I hate dealing with the bank over the phone. It takes ages to get through to the right person.*

reach /riːtʃ/ [v T] to contact someone by telephone – use this especially when you are saying whether you can or cannot contact them: *You can reach me here through Friday. I leave for Denver Saturday.* | *Have you been able to reach Neil?*

4 when people write, speak etc to each other

- ▸ communication
- ▸ contact

communication /kəˌmjuːnɪ̥ˈkeɪʃən/ [n U] the activity or process of speaking, writing, or sending messages to other people: *Good communication is vital in a large organization.* | *There were some communication problems during the first phase of the project.* | **means of communication** *Radio was the pilot's only means of communication.*

contact /ˈkɒntækt‖ˈkɑːn-/ [n U] communication between two people or groups – use this especially when you are talking about people who do not speak to each other very often **+ between** *We need better contact between staff and management.* | **+ with** *'Have you had any other contact with him?' asked the lawyer.*

5 to no longer speak to or write to someone

- ▸ lose touch
- ▸ lose contact

lose touch /ˌluːz ˈtʌtʃ/ [v phrase not in passive] to not speak to, write to, or see someone for a long time, so that finally you do not know where they are or what they are doing: *It's sad, but Wendy and I have lost touch.* | **+ with** *After Jason moved to Utah, I lost touch with him.*

lose contact /ˌluːz ˈkɒntækt‖-ˈkɑːn-/ [v phrase] to no

longer be able to contact someone by radio or electronic signals, as a result of technical problems **+ with** *Air traffic control say they've lost contact with the plane.*

contain

RELATED WORDS

▸ *see also* **include/not include, consist of**

1 to have something inside

▸ **contain** ▸ **have sth in it**

contain /kən'teɪn/ [v T not in progressive] to have something inside, or to have something as a part – used especially on packages or in written descriptions: *He opened the bag, which contained a razor, soap, and a towel.* | *Some paints contain lead, which can be poisonous.* | *Cigarettes containing less than 0.8 mg can be classified as 'light'.* | *The drawer contained various odds and ends.* | *a pewter box containing Spanish coins from the 1540s*

have sth in it /hæv (sth) 'ɪn ɪt/ if a container, room, food or drink **has something in it**, something has been put into it: *Does this coffee have sugar in it?* | *Carol can't eat anything that has nuts in it.* | *The hallway had a huge grandfather clock in it.*

2 to be able to contain a particular amount

▸ **hold** ▸ **take** ▸ **can carry**

hold /həʊld/ [v T] if something **holds** 50 people, 10 litres etc, that is the amount it can contain: *This jug holds about two litres.* | *The lecture theatre can hold up to 200 students.* | *A blank data disk can hold about 360,000 characters.*

take /teɪk/ [v T not in progressive or passive] especially British to only have enough space to contain a particular number or amount, but no more: *The car can only take five people.* | *The bookshelves won't take any more books.*

can carry /kən 'kæri/ if a vehicle or ship **can carry** a particular number of things or people, it has enough space inside for them to go in it: *The helicopters can carry eight soldiers each.* | *The ferry can carry 300 passengers, plus 100 vehicles.*

continue

WHAT'S HERE

- **continue/not stop** see **1 to 7**
- **continue after stopping** see **8 to 10**
- **to continue to be the same as before** see **11 to 12**

continue/not stop

RELATED WORDS

opposite: —— **stop**

▸ *see also* **last (5-7)**

1 to continue doing something

▸ **continue** ▸ **go on** ▸ **keep doing sth/keep on doing sth** ▸ **drive on/play on/read on etc** ▸ **keep up** ▸ **go on** ▸ **get on with** ▸ **pursue** ▸ **persist**

continue /kən'tɪnjuː/ [v I/T] to not stop doing something that you are already doing: *The project's organizers hope the government will continue funding it next year.* | *Sometimes she just couldn't see the point of continuing.* | *NASA continues its efforts to communicate with intelligent beings in outer space.* | **continue doing sth** *They continued arguing long after everyone else had gone to bed.* | *Turn the steaks over and continue broiling for 4 to 5 more minutes.* | **+ to do sth** *She continued to live in the same house after the death of her husband.* | *Despite all the warnings, many people continue to smoke.* | **+ with** *My teacher advised me to continue with my studies.*
—**continuation** /kən,tɪnju'eɪʃən/ [n U] *There is no justification for the continuation of the war* (=for continuing it).

go on ALSO **carry on** British /,gəʊ 'ɒn, ,kæri 'ɒn/ [phr v I] to continue doing something that you have started without allowing anything to stop you: *The baby started crying at ten and went on all night.* | *It was almost too dark to see properly, but he carried on anyway.* | **go on/carry on doing sth** *When I tried to interrupt, he ignored me and went on speaking.* | *If you have been taking malaria tablets while abroad, you should carry on taking them for a month after you return.* | **+ with** *The delegates decided to go on with the meeting instead of breaking off for lunch.* | *Don't stop! Carry on with your work.*

keep doing sth/keep on doing sth /,kiːp 'duːɪŋ (sth), ,kiːp ɒn 'duːɪŋ (sth)/ [v phrase not in progressive] to continue to do something for a long time – use this especially when it happens for so long that it is tiring or annoying: *That man keeps staring at me. I wish he'd stop it.* | *We were all tired, but we knew that we had to keep moving.* | *If you keep on trying, you'll get better at it.* | *Keep going till you come to a crossroads.*

drive on/play on/read on etc /,draɪv 'ɒn/ [phr v I] to continue doing something when you could have stopped: *We drove on, passing fewer and fewer houses.* | *Jones had injured his foot, but played on despite the pain.* | *Paul grabbed her hand and they ran on, hand in hand.*

keep up /,kiːp 'ʌp/ [phr v T] an expression meaning to continue to do something as well or with as much effort as you have been doing until now, used especially to encourage someone **keep it up** *You're doing a good job, boys. Keep it up.* | **keep up sth** *The enemy kept up the attack all through the night.* | *Scott kept up a constant barrage of calls and faxes until he got the answers he wanted.* | **keep up the good work** spoken *'Keep up the good work,' Harry said, patting Davy's shoulder.*

go on /,gəʊ 'ɒn/ [phr v I] especially British to continue talking about something, especially in a boring or annoying way **+ about** *I wish you'd stop going on about work all the time.* | **go on and on** *He went on and on until we were all half asleep.*

get on with /get 'ɒn wɪð / [phr v T] especially British, spoken to continue doing a piece of work and avoid talking or doing anything else: *Get on with your work, please. There's a lot to do.* | *Get on with it! We don't have all day.* | *I need to get on with my homework.*

pursue /pəʳ'sjuː‖-'suː/ [v T] formal to continue doing an activity or trying to achieve something over a long period of time: *The US intends to pursue vigorous programs in space science.* | *A good reporter will pursue a story until he or she knows all the facts.*

persist /pəʳ'sɪst/ [v I] formal to continue to do something, especially something bad that you have been warned not to do, or something difficult that other people do not want you to do **persist in doing sth** *He persisted in smoking even after having a heart attack.* | *American students of Spanish often persist in pronouncing words such as 'presidente' in the same way as similar English words.* | **+ in** *The White House persisted in its efforts to pass the bill, despite the opposition of Congress.*

2 when something continues to happen

- continue
- last
- go on
- carry on
- persist
- proceed
- progress
- drag on

continue /kən'tɪnjuː/ [v I] to happen without stopping: *The good weather seems likely to continue.* | *Unless there are serious negotiations, the fighting will continue.* | *Some people have lost work, and this will continue to happen until the computer system is fixed.* | **continue for three months/a long time/several weeks etc** *The review process is expected to continue for several weeks.* —**continuation** /kənˌtɪnju'eɪʃən/ [n U] *The continuation of the ceasefire now seems to be in danger.*

last /lɑːst‖læst/ [v I] to continue – use this to say how long something continues for **last two hours/six months/a long time etc** *The concert lasted all day.* | *It's not certain how long the ceasefire will last.* | **last for two hours/six months/a long time etc** *The discussion lasted for no more than thirty minutes.* | **+ from/until** *The meeting lasted until lunchtime.* | *The training period lasted from July 2 to August 25.*

go on /ˌgəʊ 'ɒn / [phr v I] to continue, especially for a long time: *The discussion went on for another four hours before agreement was reached.* | *The applause went on for ten minutes after the actors left the stage.* | **go on and on** (=continue for a very long time) *The noise from next door went on and on.*

carry on /ˌkæri 'ɒn/ [phr v I] British to continue, especially in spite of problems or opposition: *The celebrations carried on as if nothing had happened.* | *The struggle for liberation will carry on long after I am dead.*

persist /pəʳ'sɪst/ [v I] formal if a problem or bad conditions **persist**, they continue to exist because you cannot stop them: *See your doctor if the symptoms persist.* | *If adverse weather conditions persist, the game will be cancelled.*

proceed /prə'siːd/ [v I] formal to continue in the way that has been planned: *Work on the new tunnel is proceeding very well.* | *According to the newspaper the negotiations are proceeding smoothly.*

progress /prə'gres/ [v I] to continue to happen or develop gradually over a period of time **as sth progresses** *As the meeting progressed Jack became more and more bored.* | *As the war progressed, it became increasingly difficult to buy fresh food.*

drag on /ˌdræg 'ɒn/ [phr v I] if something that is happening **drags on**, it is boring and seems to continue for much longer than necessary: *The talks dragged on, with no apparent hope of achieving a peaceful solution.* | **drag on for an hour/weeks/years etc** *The history lesson dragged on for another hour.*

3 to continue doing something in a determined way

- persevere
- stick to it
- keep at
- press on
- undaunted
- soldier on

persevere /ˌpɜːʳsə̇'vɪəʳ/ [v I] to continue trying to do something in a very patient and determined way, in spite of difficulties: *He didn't know any English, but he persevered and became a good student.* | **+ with** *When a country is able to persevere with reforms, the result can be a return to economic stability.* | **+ in** *Stevenson persevered in his efforts to discover what had really happened.* | **persevere in the face of sth** *Children today seem less willing to seek out challenges and persevere in the face of adversity.*

stick to it spoken ALSO **stick at it** British spoken /ˌstɪk 'tuː ɪt, ˌstɪk 'æt ɪt/ [v phrase] to continue working or studying in a very determined way in order to achieve something **stick at/to it** *If you stick at it, I'm sure you'll pass your examinations.* | *It was hard to follow the diet plan at first, but I stuck to it and eventually lost 20 pounds.*

keep at /ˌkiːp 'æt/ [phr v T] to force yourself to continue working, practising etc in order to achieve something, even though it needs a lot of effort **keep at it** *You'll have to keep at it if you want to play the piano as well as your father does.* | **keep at sth** British *I wish I'd kept at my language lessons when I was at school.*

press on /ˌpres 'ɒn / [phr v I] British to continue doing something or going somewhere in spite of difficulties, because you are determined to finish your work, journey etc without delay: *I was finding the book hard to understand, but I pressed on.* | *We're nearly there, so let's press on while it's still daylight.* | **+ with** *Despite opposition,the government is pressing on with its welfare reforms.* | **press on regardless** (=ignoring all difficulties) *It started to rain and a strong wind blew, but he pressed on regardless.*

undaunted /ʌn'dɔːntə̇d/ [adj/adv] someone who is **undaunted** or does something **undaunted** does not give up because of difficulties, dangers etc, but continues to do what they intended to do: *Undaunted, he said he would take the test again.* | **+ by** *Undaunted by the low pay and lack of respect, she feels teaching is the most rewarding job she can do.* | **remain undaunted** *The policy changes she wants have not happened, but Banyan remains undaunted.*

soldier on /ˌsəʊldʒər 'ɒn / [phr v I] British to continue doing something in a steady determined way even though it is very difficult: *The team were all feeling seasick but they soldiered on valiantly.* | *Charles was asked to soldier on as Sayle's assistant.*

4 to make something continue

- continue/carry on
- maintain
- perpetuate
- keep up
- preserve

continue/carry on /kən'tɪnjuː, ˌkæri 'ɒn / [v T/phr v T] to **continue** something, often something that has been started by someone else: *Who's going to carry on the project when she leaves?* | *Immigrant families often try to continue cultural traditions.* | *In* *the eighteenth century, his research was carried on by Dubois.*

maintain /meɪnˈteɪn‖mən-/ [v T] to make something continue in the same way or at the same high standard as before: *Air France has maintained a high level of service for many years.* | *It is best if divorced parents can maintain friendly relations for the sake of the children.* —**maintenance** /ˈmeɪntənəns/ [n U] *At first a newly independent country relies heavily on the maintenance of existing links with the former colonial power.*

perpetuate /pəʳˈpetʃueɪt/ [v T] to make something bad continue to exist, especially a situation that is not fair or involves false ideas: *This new book perpetuates all the old myths about the Kennedy assassination.* | *The proposed law will perpetuate existing economic and class inequalities.*

keep up /ˌkiːp ˈʌp/ [phr v T] to make something continue, especially when it is difficult and a lot of effort is needed: *She and Laura keep up their friendship through frequent telephone calls and lunch dates.* | *Environmental groups intend to keep up the pressure until the government changes the law.*

preserve /prɪˈzɜːʳv/ [v T] to make something good continue because you think it should not be allowed to disappear: *As a family, we want to preserve the traditions of Jewish culture and religion.* | *All the names in the book have been changed to preserve the victims' anonymity.* —**preservation** /ˌprezəʳˈveɪʃən/ [n U] *The government is committed to the preservation of law and order.*

5 continuing for a long time

- continuous
- constant
- uninterrupted
- on-going
- non-stop
- without a break
- for days/hours/miles etc on end
- at a stretch
- solid
- day after day/week after week etc
- day in, day out

continuous /kənˈtɪnjuəs/ [adj only before noun] continuing for a long time without stopping: *Although we nearly always need extra drivers, we cannot guarantee continuous employment.* | *CNN provided continuous coverage of the trial.* | *The campsites have had three decades of continuous use.* —**continuously** [adv] *Shake the pan continuously until the almonds are lightly browned.*

constant /ˈkɒnstənt‖ˈkɑːn-/ [adj usually before noun] continuous and seeming to be there all the time: *He suffered constant pain in the months before his death.* | *A newborn baby needs constant care and attention.* | *The refugees lived in constant fear of being attacked.* —**constantly** [adv] *The country is very unstable and the government is constantly in danger of being overthrown.*

uninterrupted /ˌʌnɪntəˈrʌptɪ̣d◂/ [adj only before noun] something good or pleasant such as peace or sleep that is **uninterrupted** continues for a long time with no interruptions: *On average, two-year-old children need ten to twelve hours of uninterrupted sleep a night.* | *Banks need uninterrupted, 24-hour computer systems.*

on-going /ˈɒn gəʊɪŋ / [adj only before noun] an **on-going** activity, situation, or piece of work is not intended to end at a definite time, but will continue into the future: *The police refused to comment on the on-going investigation.* | *We have a major on-going research programme into North Sea pollution.*

non-stop /ˌnɒn ˈstɒp◂‖ˌnɑːn ˈstɑːp◂/ [adv] continuing without stopping: *She's been driving non-stop for hours.* | *Make sure he does some homework – he'll watch TV non-stop if you let him.* —**nonstop/non-stop** [adj only before noun] *There has been 48 hours of nonstop rain.*

without a break /wɪðˌaʊt ə ˈbreɪk/ [adv] without stopping for a rest: *Victor talked for forty minutes without a break.* | *On average, the human mind cannot concentrate on spoken information for more than six minutes without a break.*

for days/hours/miles etc on end /fəʳ ˌdeɪz ɒn ˈend/ [adv] if something unpleasant or unusual continues for hours, days, miles etc **on end**, it continues for that time, distance etc without stopping: *The rain had been falling for days on end.* | *In Siberia the temperature can stay more than twenty below freezing for months on end.*

at a stretch /ət ə ˈstretʃ/ [adv] if someone works or does something for ten hours, three days etc **at a stretch**, they do it for that time without stopping, although this may be difficult or unusual: *A lion can lie on the same spot, without moving, for twelve hours at a stretch.* | *Doctors who are forced to work 36 hours at a stretch cannot possibly be fully efficient.*

solid /ˈsɒlɪ̣d‖ˈsɑː-/ [adj only before noun] if you do something for two **solid** hours, three **solid** weeks etc you do it continuously for that period with no breaks at all: *After eight solid hours of driving, I was exhausted.* | *Nobody really wants to sit through four solid hours of someone else's wedding video.*

day after day/week after week etc /ˌdeɪ ɑːftəʳ ˈdeɪ‖-æf-/ [adv] every day, every week etc for a long time: *The fighting went on week after week and there seemed no end to it.* | *She sits at home day after day, waiting for a message from her husband.*

day in, day out /deɪ ˌɪn deɪ ˈaʊt/ [adv] if something happens **day in, day out**, it happens every day and is always the same, with the result that it becomes very boring: *Working in a factory involves the same routine day in, day out.* | *He wears an old brown jacket day in, day out.*

6 not stopping, even at night

- day and night/night and day
- around the clock
- twenty-four-hour/24-hour
- 24/7

day and night/night and day /ˌdeɪ ən ˈnaɪt, ˌnaɪt ən ˈdeɪ/ [adv] continuously, all day and all night: *During his illness, his wife was by his side day and night.* | *The printing presses run day and night.* | *My next-door neighbor's dog barks continually, day and night.*

around the clock ALSO **round the clock** British /əˌraʊnd ðə ˈklɒk, ˌraʊnd ðə ˈklɒk‖-ˈklɑːk/ [adv] if you work **around the clock**, you work all day and all night without a break, especially because there is something very urgent that you have to do: *Since the outbreak of war, journalists have been working round the clock.* | *Rescuers are working round the clock to find survivors of the blast.* —**round-the-clock** /ˈraʊnd ðə klɒk‖-klɑːk/ [adj only before noun] *We want a round-the-clock guard on the murder witnesses for their protection.*

twenty-four-hour/24-hour /ˌtwenti fɔːr ˈaʊəʳ/ [adj only before noun] **twenty-four-hour service/guard/care etc** a service etc that is done or provided continuously, all day and all night: *Twenty-four-hour medical care is provided.* | *The police cannot provide 24-hour protection for everyone.*

24/7 /ˌtwenti fɔːʳ ˈsevən/ [adv] informal happening, done, or existing 24 hours a day and seven days a week and never stopping: *The hotline is open 24/7 to teenagers who need someone to talk to.* | *Do you think about this guy 24/7?*

7 when something unpleasant continues for a long time

- continual
- constant
- perpetual
- incessant
- nagging
- endless/ unending/ never-ending
- persistent
- unrelenting

continual /kənˈtɪnjuəl/ [adj only before noun] use this about something annoying or unpleasant that continues for a long time without stopping: *The deadline was getting closer and we were under continual pressure to reach our targets.* | *The exhaustion felt by new parents comes from the continual disturbance of their sleep patterns.* —**continually** [adv] *Her knee is continually sore..*

constant /ˈkɒnstənt‖ˈkɑːn-/ [adj] use this about an unpleasant or frightening situation that continues for a long time without stopping: *She has learned to put up with the constant roar of trucks and cars whizzing by.* | *People under the regime lived in constant fear.* | *Lehman is in constant pain, and suffers from a severe form of arthritis.*

perpetual /pəʳˈpetʃuəl/ [adj] use this about an unpleasant or upsetting situation that is always there and does not change: *For many working mothers, balancing the demands of children and job is a perpetual strain.* | *Those who remain in the city are in perpetual danger of being hit by bullets and shells.*

incessant /ɪnˈsesənt/ [adj only before noun] something unpleasant and annoying, especially a noise, that is **incessant** continues over a long period of time and never stops: *Outside the window is the incessant noise of cars and buses.* | *She gave two- or three-word answers to reporters' incessant questions.* | *The incessant rain has meant that many matches had to be cancelled.* —**incessantly** [adv] *Mike smoked incessantly.*

nagging /ˈnægɪŋ/ [adj only before noun] **nagging doubt/fear/worry/suspicion etc** a doubt etc that is probably unnecessary but that stays with you all the time and does not go away: *She had a nagging worry that she hadn't done enough to prepare.* | *I have a nagging feeling that I forgot to do something.* | *There are still some nagging doubts about the future of the company, though for now it is doing well.*

endless/unending/never-ending /ˈendləs, ʌnˈendɪŋ, ˌnevər ˈendɪŋ◂/ [adj] use this about something unpleasant, boring, or tiring that continues for so long that you think it will never end or change: *How can I stop my children's endless quarrelling?* | *The wet winter days seemed at times unending.* | *His immune system failed, and he caught a never-ending series of viruses and infections.*

persistent /pəʳˈsɪstənt/ [adj] a **persistent** problem or illness is not very serious but it continues to exist even though you try to get rid of it: *He has a persistent cough because of his smoking.* | *The country has suffered from persistent economic problems.*

unrelenting /ˌʌnrɪˈlentɪŋ◂/ [adj] formal an unpleasant situation or feeling that is **unrelenting** continues for a long time without stopping: *The unrelenting pressures of the job started to affect her health.* | *The relief efforts have been hindered by unrelenting bad weather.* | *The unrelenting air attack on the country continued.*

continue after stopping

RELATED WORDS

- *see also* **start, again, pause**

8 to continue doing something after stopping

- continue
- start again
- go on
- go back to/return to
- resume
- take sth up again
- pick up/take up where you left off
- reopen
- renew

continue /kənˈtɪnjuː/ [v I/T] if you **continue** doing something, or it continues, it starts again after stopping: *After a while the rain stopped, allowing the game to continue.* | *He has decided to go back to Cambridge to continue his medical studies.* | *The tour continued after a rest day in Bordeaux.* | **continue doing sth** *Have a rest before you continue driving.* | *He's not sure whether he'll be able to continue skiing competitively after the operation.*

start again /ˌstɑːʳt əˈgen/ [v phrase] to **start again**, continuing the same thing that you were doing before you stopped, or continuing to happen in the same way as before: *He stopped exercising after the injury, but recently he's started again.* | **start sth again** *I've had a good vacation and I'm not exactly looking forward to starting work again.* | **start doing sth again** *After a two-week rest I was ready to start running again.* | *Billy was afraid to say anything in case she started crying again.* | **start to do sth again** *Marian stared through the window. It was starting to snow again.*

go on ALSO **carry on** British /ˌgəʊ ˈɒn, ˌkæri ˈɒn / [phr v I] to continue doing something after stopping for a short time: *Occasionally he would stop writing, read through what he had written, and then go on.* | *It's one o'clock now. Shall we carry on after lunch?* | **go on/carry on doing sth** *After a short break for coffee, they went on working until 3 o'clock.* | *She decided to carry on working after having the baby.* | **+ with** *Let's stop now. We'll go on with this tomorrow.* | *As soon as Mr Saunders gets back, we'll carry on with the meeting.*

go back to/return to /gəʊ ˈbæk tuː, rɪˈtɜːʳn tuː/ [phr v T not in passive] to start doing a particular job again after a period when you were doing something else. **Return to** is more formal than **go back to**: *Melanie made herself a cup of tea and then went back to her reading.* | *Some mothers return to full-time work only a few weeks after their baby is born.* | **go back to/return to doing sth** *If he can't get work as an actor, he can always go back to being an electrician.*

resume /rɪˈzjuːm‖-ˈzuːm/ [v I/T] formal if you **resume** something or it **resumes**, it continues after a pause or interruption: *Collins was so seriously injured that he was unable to resume his career.* | *The jurors are anxious to resume their normal lives again.* | **resume doing sth** *He said no more, and resumed reading his newspaper.*

take sth up again /ˌteɪk (sth) ˈʌp əgen/ [v phrase] to start doing something such as a sport or activity again after a long period of time when you were not doing it **take sth up again** *I stopped playing the guitar when I was fifteen, but now I'd like to take it up again.* | **take up sth again** *Now that I don't have to work in the evenings, I'd like to take up sketching again.*

pick up/take up where you left off /pɪk ˌʌp, teɪk ˌʌp weəʳ juː left ˈɒf/ [v phrase] to start something again at exactly the same point where you stopped: *After a long absence I went back to college, hoping to pick up where I'd left off.* | *The team has picked up where they left off last spring.* | *Negotiators will meet again after the holidays and take up where they left off.*

reopen /riːˈəʊpən/ [v I/T] if someone **reopens** a formal discussion, trial etc, or it **reopens**, it starts again after stopping, especially because new information has been found: *The two sides are prepared to reopen peace talks.* | *The action is likely to reopen debates about affirmative action.* | *Police have decided to reopen the investigation in the light of important new evidence.*

renew /rɪˈnjuː‖-ˈnuː/ [v T] to start to do something again – use this especially about activities done by governments and military organizations: *The rebels waited until nightfall to renew their attack on the city.* | *Iceland has no immediate plans to renew commercial whaling.*

9 to continue talking about something after stopping

- continue
- go on
- go/get back to
- return to

continue /kənˈtɪnjuː/ [v I/T] to **continue** talking about something after stopping or after talking about something else: *Continuing in a quieter voice, she asked how long he'd been married.* | *Nate didn't answer, so Murphy continued, 'All of this happened before I was hired.'* | *Before they could continue their conversation, Frank Gordon came over to speak to Oliver.*

go on /ˌgəʊ ˈɒn / [phr v I] to continue talking after stopping, especially when you need to say more about something: *He went on in a soft voice, 'I love you, Jane.'* | *She started crying and couldn't go on.* | **+ with** *Once everyone was quiet, Michael went on with his story.* | **go on to say sth** *He went on to say that there would be times when she would be expected to attend evening or weekend meetings.*

go/get back to ALSO **return to** /ˌgəʊ, ˌget ˈbæk tuː, rɪˈtɜːʳn tuː/ [phr v T] to start talking about a subject that you have already talked about earlier: *Finally, I'd like to go back to the point I made at the beginning of the lecture.* | *Getting back to what we were talking about earlier, do you think it's a realistic goal?*

return to /rɪˈtɜːʳn tuː/ [phr v T not in passive] to start talking about a subject again having already talked about it earlier: *During the interview, they kept returning to the question of why he had left his previous job.* | **return to what sb said/talked about etc** *Returning to what you said earlier, do you really think there is a chance of a complete ceasefire?*

10 to start doing something again

- start again
- go back to/revert to
- slip back into

start again /ˌstɑːʳt əˈgen/ [v phrase] to start doing something again, especially something bad that you had decided not to do: *She's quit smoking four or five times, but she always starts again.* | **start doing sth again** *He started drinking again when he lost his job.* | **start to do sth again** *She attended school regularly for a while, then started to miss classes again.* | **start that again** *'I didn't do it!' 'Oh, don't start that again. I saw you.'*

go back to/revert to /ˌgəʊ ˈbæk tuː, rɪˈvɜːʳt tuː/ [phr v T] to start behaving in a particular way again, after you had decided not to or when you are not supposed to; **revert** is more formal than **go back to**: *I went to a school where we had to speak French all the time, but outside school hours I reverted to English.* | *He's been in the hospital a couple of times, but he keeps going back to drinking.* (=starts drinking alcohol again) | **go back to/revert to doing sth** *Do you think she'll go back to using drugs?* | *We go home for Christmas and revert to being children again.*

slip back into /ˌslɪp ˈbæk ɪntuː/ [v phrase not in passive] to gradually start doing something bad again after you had stopped, because you are not determined enough to prevent yourself from doing it: *Children will often slip back into babyish ways to get what they want.* | **slip back into doing sth** *to slip back into having a few drinks after work*

to continue to be the same as before

RELATED WORDS

opposite: ———————— **change**

- *see also* **same**

11 to continue to be the same as before

- stay
- remain
- keep
- continue to be
- still

stay /steɪ/ [v] to continue to be the same as before: *The library stays open until 8pm on Fridays.* | *It will stay cold for the next few days.* | *They stayed friends after their divorce.* | *The details of her death have stayed a closely guarded secret.*

remain /rɪˈmeɪn/ [v] written to continue to be the same as before: *She remained calm and waited till he had finished shouting at her.* | *Would the audience please remain seated.* | *The details of his death remain a closely guarded secret.* | **remain the same** *His doctors say this his condition remains the same.*

keep /kiːp/ [v] **keep quiet/awake/silent etc** to continue to be awake, calm, quiet etc – use this especially to say someone has to make an effort to do this: *Paul managed to keep awake by drinking lots of strong black coffee.* | *Try to keep calm and let me know if anything changes.* | *We kept quiet and very still until the footsteps had passed.*

continue to be /kənˈtɪnjuː tə biː/ [v phrase] to be the same as in the past, especially when you expected there might have been a change: *Inflation continues to be one of the government's main problems.* | *UN soldiers continue to be killed for nothing.* | *Peanut growing continues to be the main industry in Senegal.*

still /stɪl/ [adv] use this to emphasize that something or someone has not changed and continues to be the same: *At the age of 50, Marlene was still a beautiful woman.* | *She still has that rusty old car.* | *I'm still confused. Would you explain it again?*

12 to continue to be in the same place or situation

- stay
- remain
- linger
- still

stay /steɪ/ [v I] to continue to exist or still be in the same place: *The car was abandoned in a field, and there it stayed until police towed it back.* | **stay with** *He stayed with the company for over thirty years.* | *The memory of his father's death stayed with him all his life.*

remain /rɪˈmeɪn/ [v I not usually in progressive] written to continue to exist or still be in the same place: *The computers remained in their boxes until enough money was found to buy the software needed to operate them.* | **+ with** *Her unhappy face remained with me throughout the rest of my journey.* | *The picture remained with the artist's family for a number of years.*

linger /ˈlɪŋgəʳ/ [v I] if a sight, smell, or taste **lingers** you can still see it, smell it, or taste it even after a long time: *Garlic has a taste which tends to linger in your mouth.* | *The faint smell of cigar smoke lingered on in the room.*

still /stɪl/ [adv] use this to emphasize that someone or something **still** exists or is **still** in the same place, especially when this is unusual or surprising: *After two hours the dog was still there, just sitting and staring at our door.* | *Soloviov returned to the town where he was born after more than forty years and found his old house still standing.*

control/ not control

RELATED WORDS

- see also **in charge of, limit, manager, leader, power/powerful**

1 to control people or to control what happens

- control
- control
- be in control
- what sb says, goes
- call the tune/shots
- be in the driving seat
- be the boss
- wear the trousers
- keep/hold sb/sth in check

control /kənˈtrəʊl/ [v T] to make things happen or make people behave in the way that you want, by using your authority, skill, money etc: *Miss Weston is having difficulty controlling the children in that class.* | *The area is now controlled by rebels.* | *The head of department controls the budget.* | *Oloco is a huge company, controlling over half the world's oil trade.*

control /kənˈtrəʊl/ [n U] the ability or power to make things happen or make people behave in the way that you want **have control** *Heads of department can make some decisions, but the chairman has overall control within the company.* | **+ over** *They seem to have no control over their children.* | **+ of** *Who has control of the budget?*

be in control /biː ɪn kənˈtrəʊl/ [v phrase] to control a situation, organization, country etc – use this especially about someone who got their power by using force or by clever planning, but not by being elected: *The President has been arrested, and the rebel forces are now in control.* | **+ of** *Mr Howard questioned whether the police were still in control of the situation.*

what sb says, goes /wɒt (sb) ˌsez ˈgəʊz/ spoken used to say that someone has the power to make all the decisions and tell other people what to do: *Mrs Earnshaw is in charge, and what she says, goes.*

call the tune/shots /ˌkɔːl ðə ˈtjuːn, ˈʃɒts‖-ˈtuːn, -ˈʃɑːts/ [v phrase] informal to control a situation so that everyone else has to do what you say, agree with you etc: *It's definitely my mother who calls the shots in my family.* | *It's always been our policy that the customer should call the tune.*

be in the driving seat British **/be in the driver's seat** American /biː ɪn ðə ˈdraɪvɪŋ siːt, biː ɪn ðə ˈdraɪvəʳz siːt/ [v phrase] informal to have more power than anyone else in a particular organization or situation, so that you control everything: *The Conservatives say they are looking forward to the election, and are confident that they will soon be back in the driving seat.* | **be firmly in the driving seat** *This is how the government is now made up, with the Socialists firmly in the driving seat.*

be the boss /biː ðə ˈbɒs‖-ˈbɔːs/ [v phrase] if you say someone **is the boss** within a family or group, you mean they have the most power over the other people in it: *You'd better ask Mom – she's the boss around here.* | **show sb who's boss** (=show them that you are in control) *He gave the dog a slap round the head, just to show him who was boss.*

wear the trousers /ˌweəʳ ðə ˈtraʊzəʳz/ [v phrase] informal to be the person who has most power in a relationship – use this especially to say that the woman in a relationship controls the man: *I think you should talk to Pat – she's the one who wears the trousers in that household.*

keep/hold sb/sth in check /ˌkiːp, ˌhəʊld (sb/sth) ɪn ˈtʃek/ [v phrase] if you keep people **in check**, you control their behaviour, especially so that they cannot behave badly; if you keep a situation, especially a bad one, **in check**, you stop it developing any further: *The court heard that the general was unable to keep his troops in check.* | *The disease is held in check by weekly injections of a power drug.*

2 to secretly control people or events

- manipulate
- be pulling the strings
- have sb in your pocket

manipulate /məˈnɪpjəleɪt/ [v T] to make someone do what you want them to do by cleverly influencing them, especially when they do not realize what you are doing: *He accused the environmentalists of trying to manipulate public opinion in their favour.* —**manipulative** /məˈnɪpjələtɪv‖-leɪ-/ [adj] clever at manipulating people: *She's a devious and manipulative young woman.*

be pulling the strings /biː ˌpʊlɪŋ ðə ˈstrɪŋz/ [v phrase] to secretly control an organization, country or situation, by controlling the person or group that is officially in charge of it: *There is little doubt now who is pulling the strings behind this government.*

have sb in your pocket /hæv (sb) ɪn jɔːʳ ˈpɒkət‖-ˈpɑː-/ [v phrase not in progressive] to be able to control someone such as a policeman or politician so that they do what you want, for example because you know something bad about them, or you are illegally paying them money or threatening them: *Most drug dealers have a few cops in their pocket.* | *Jackson got these plans approved very easily – it makes you wonder if he had the local council in his pocket.*

3 to completely control someone's behaviour

- dominate
- domineering
- walk all over
- have a hold on/over
- have sb in your power

dominate /ˈdɒmɪ̈neɪt‖ˈdɑː-/ [v T] to have a very powerful influence on another person and control the way that they behave: *It was obvious that her husband completely dominated her.* | *a very self-confident man with a dominating manner*

domineering /ˌdɒmɪ̈ˈnɪərɪŋ◂‖ˌdɑː-/ [adj] someone who is **domineering** always wants to control what other people do and never considers what they want themselves: *Hattie was struggling to break free from her domineering father.* | *He's arrogant and domineering and never listens to anyone.* | *My mother has a very domineering personality.*

walk all over /ˌwɔːk ɔːl ˈəʊvəʳ/ [v phrase] informal to treat someone very badly by doing whatever you want to do, without caring about what they want or feel: *Why do you let him just walk all over you, have you no pride?* | *It's important not to let colleagues walk all over you at work.*

have a hold on/over /ˌhæv ə ˈhəʊld ɒn, əʊvəʳ/ [v phrase] to be able to control someone because you have some emotional power over them, for example, because you know their secrets or weak points: *He seems to have a very powerful hold over the women in his life.* | *It's been two years since we divorced, but he still has a hold on me.*

have sb in your power /hæv (sb) ɪn jɔːʳ ˈpaʊəʳ/ [v phrase] to be able to control someone because you have emotional power over them – used especially in literature: *At last she had McAdams in her power!*

4 to completely control the people in a country

- oppress
- oppressive
- keep sb down
- repress

oppress /əˈpres/ [v T] to use force to control large groups of people – use this especially about governments and people in authority: *Since colonial times, black people in South Africa have been oppressed by the white minority.* | *Marxists have studied the role of the family in oppressing women.* —**oppressed** [adj] *Gay people suffer just as much discrimination as any other oppressed minority.* | *the oppressed nations of Latin America* —**oppression** /əˈpreʃən/ [n U] *He's spent a lifetime fighting oppression and injustice.*

oppressive /əˈpresɪv/ [adj] **oppressive** laws or governments control people so tightly that they have very little freedom left: *The country is in the grip of an extremely oppressive regime.* | *New, oppressive laws were brought in to restrict the freedom of the press.*

keep sb down /ˌkiːp (sb) ˈdaʊn/ [phr v T] to control people by not allowing them to use their natural abilities, intelligence, or energy to improve their situation **be kept down** *The population is kept down by poverty and fear of the secret police.* | **keep sb down** *In Marlowe's opinion, religion was invented in order to keep people down.*

repress /rɪˈpres/ [v T] to control people: *It's a cruel and vicious regime that represses all opposition.* | *For years the inhabitants of these islands have been repressed by the colonizers.* —**repressive** [adj] *a violent and repressive regime* —**repression** /rɪˈpreʃən/ [n U] *Most of the refugees are fleeing from repression in their homeland.*

5 to be able to control someone because they like you

- have sb eating out of your hand
- can wrap/twist sb round your little finger

▸ *see also* **use (20-21)**

have sb eating out of your hand /hæv (sb) ˌiːtɪŋ aʊt əv jɔːʳ ˈhænd/ [v phrase] to be able to control someone because you have made them like you so much that they will do whatever you want: *I introduced Mr Wilkinson to my mother, and within minutes she had him eating out of her hand.* | *He's brilliant in job interviews – he always manages to get the panel eating out of his hand.*

can wrap/twist sb round your little finger /kən ˌræp, ˌtwɪst (sb) raʊnd jɔːʳ ˌlɪtl ˈfɪŋgəʳ/ [v phrase] to be able to control someone so that they do what you want, especially because they love you and want to make you happy: *Get Rebecca to ask Dad for the money – she can wrap him round her little finger.* | *Mary knew she could twist Henry round her little finger.*

6 to completely control a situation

- dominate
- monopolize
- monopoly
- stranglehold
- have total/complete control
- hold sway

dominate /ˈdɒmɪ̈neɪt‖ˈdɑː-/ [v I/T] to be the most powerful or important person or thing in a situation and therefore able to control it completely: *Men still tend to dominate the world of law – hardly any top judges are women.* | *You shouldn't allow your job to dominate your life like that.* | *A handful of multinational companies dominate the economy.* —**domination** /ˌdɒmɪ̈ˈneɪʃən‖ˌdɑː-/ [n U] *There have so far been few attempts to end the domination of one or two companies in the computing industry.*

monopolize ALSO **monopolise** British /məˈnɒpəlaɪz‖məˈnɑː-/ [v T] to completely control an activity, situation etc and unfairly prevent other people or organizations from having any control over it at all: *All night he monopolized the conversation, not letting anyone else get a word in.* | *The company has monopolized the building market in this area.*

monopoly /məˈnɒpəli‖məˈnɑː-/ [n C usually singular] a situation in which one person or organization unfairly has complete control **have a monopoly** *It is not good for consumers if one company has a monopoly in any area of trade.* | **+ of** *It was not easy to persuade the monarchy to let go of its monopoly of power.* | **+ over** *Within a few years, the company had a virtual monopoly over all trade with India.*

stranglehold /ˈstræŋgəlhəʊld/ [n singular] total power and control over a situation, organization etc – use this especially when you think this is not fair or right **have a stranglehold on sth** *For years, two giant recording companies have had a stranglehold on the CD market.* | **break the stranglehold** (=to stop someone having complete control) *Satellite TV* *should at last break the stranglehold of the big national TV channels.*

have total/complete control /hæv ˌtəʊtl, kəmˌpliːt kən'trəʊl/ [v phrase] to control a situation completely: *In modern politics, no one political group can expect to have total control.* | **+ over** *The head of department has complete control over the budget.*

hold sway /ˌhəʊld 'sweɪ/ [v phrase] if a person or group **holds sway**, they have the most power or influence over the people in a particular situation, place, or organization: *The old communist party still holds sway in many rural areas.* | **+ over** *This all happened long ago, when priests held sway over the majority of the Irish people.*

7 methods, laws etc that are used to control situations or people

- controls
- restraints

controls /kən'trəʊlz/ [n plural] **+ on** *Within months, most of the wartime controls on trading were abandoned.* | **rigid controls** (=strict controls) *Rigid rent controls ensured that no one paid too much for housing.* | **tight controls** (=strict controls) *The government is proposing to introduce even tighter controls on immigration.*

restraints /rɪ'streɪnts/ [n plural] laws, beliefs, or customs that control an activity or situation, especially by not allowing people to do exactly what they want to do **+ on** *Every society has its own restraints on moral behaviour.* | **+ of** *The economy is beginning to grow again after the restraints of the war.* | **impose restraints** (=introduce rules in order to control someone or something) *As they grow older, kids begin to rebel against the restraints imposed by their parents.*

8 to be controlled by someone else

- be under sb's control
- be in sb's power
- be under sb's spell
- be at sb's mercy
- doormat

be under sb's control /biː ˌʌndəʳ (sb's) kən'trəʊl/ [v phrase] *The whole town seems to be under the control of one family.* | *Almost three thousand troops are under Captain Marsh's control.* | *Roughly a quarter of the area came under Soviet control.*

be in sb's power /biː ɪn (sb's) 'paʊəʳ/ [v phrase] if you **are in someone's power** you have to do whatever they want you to do, especially because they have some emotional power over you – used especially in literature: *He'll do whatever I tell him to do. He's completely in my power.*

be under sb's spell /biː ˌʌndəʳ (sb's) 'spel/ [v phrase] if you **are under someone's spell** they have almost complete power over how you feel, the way you behave etc especially because you love or admire them very much: *Harry knew that he was in love with Susie, completely under her spell.* | **come/fall under sb's spell** (=start to be under someone's spell) *She loves the company of showbiz personalities, and many have fallen under her spell.*

be at sb's mercy /biː ət (sb's) 'mɜːʳsi/ [v phrase] if you **are at someone's mercy** they have the power to decide whether good or bad things happen to you: *Once in prison, inmates are at the guards' mercy.* | *Children often find themselves at the mercy of other kids who are older and bigger.* | **to be at the mercy of sb** *Small firms are completely at the mercy of the banks.*

doormat /'dɔːʳmæt/ [n C] informal someone who lets other people treat them badly and who does not complain or try to change their situation: *Fiona was determined that she would be nobody's doormat.* | *Make sure he doesn't treat you like a doormat.*

9 to get control of a situation, organization, country etc

- take control
- bring sth under control
- regain control
- take over
- seize
- take

take control /ˌteɪk kən'trəʊl/ [v phrase] to get control of a situation, organization, or place: *He's invested a lot of money in the company since he took control last May.* | **+ of** *Following requests from the police, the army has now taken control of the area.* | *Anne Williams will take control of the research division on August 5th.*

bring sth under control /ˌbrɪŋ (sth) ʌndəʳ kən'trəʊl/ [v phrase] to get control of a situation that is out of control: *The agriculture ministry is struggling to bring the latest outbreak of the disease under control.* | *Rioting broke out again last night, and police and soldiers are still struggling to bring the situation under control.* | *Government attempts to bring the drug problem under control have so far failed.*

regain control /rɪˌgeɪn kən'trəʊl/ [v phrase] to get control of a situation again after you had lost control of it: *It took several hours for the police to regain control after a demonstration in the city centre turned violent.* | **+ of** *The extremists have managed to regain control of the party.* | *At last she seemed to regain control of the situation, and started to speak.*

take over /ˌteɪk 'əʊvəʳ/ [phr v I/T] to get control of a company or organization, or become the leader, president etc after someone else: *People are wondering who's going to take over when the old dictator dies.* | **take over sth/take sth over** *The company was taken over by Sony in 1989.* | **+ from** *She took over from Barton as Managing Director in 1994.*

seize /siːz/ [v T] if an army or group **seizes** power or an area of land, they get control of it by using force to suddenly take political control: *The General has been Head of State since he seized power in 1982.* | *Rebel soldiers attacked the island, seizing the capital and arresting government officials.*

take /teɪk/ [v T] to get political and military control of a country or part of a country, especially during a war: *Rebel forces have taken the northern part of the region.*

10 when you cannot control something

- lose control
- out of control
- get out of hand
- be beyond sb's control
- lose your grip (on sth)
- runaway
- rampant
- run wild

lose control /ˌluːz kən'trəʊl/ [v phrase] to no longer be able to control a situation, vehicle, group of people etc: *The car skidded on the ice, and I lost control.* | **+ of** *She felt as if she was losing control of her children.* | *O'Connor recently lost control of the company he had run for seven years.*

out of control /ˌaʊt əv kən'trəʊl/ [adj phrase] a situation that is **out of control** has got much worse and can no longer be controlled: *The fire was out of control.* | *Teenage crime was now out of control.* | **get out of control** *It's easy to let spending on credit cards get out of control.*

get out of hand /get ˌaʊt əv ˈhænd/ [v phrase] if something, especially a situation, **gets out of hand**, it gets so serious or difficult that it can no longer be controlled: *The costs have continued to increase, and now seem to be getting out of hand.* | *Police were called in when the situation began to get out of hand.*

be beyond sb's control /biː bɪˌjɒnd (sb's) kənˈtrəʊl‖-ˌjɑːnd-/ [v phrase] a situation or force that **is beyond your control** is one that you are not able to control, especially if someone else is controlling it or because no one can control it: *Some of the kids there were beyond any teacher's control.* | **circumstances beyond our control** (=a situation that we cannot control) *Due to circumstances beyond our control, we have had to cancel tonight's performance of 'Carmen'.*

lose your grip (on sth) /ˌluːz jɔːʳ ˈgrɪp (ɒn (sth))/ [v phrase] to no longer be able to control a situation that you have had difficulty controlling for a long time: *By 1965, US troops in the area were beginning to lose their grip.* | **lose your grip on sth** *I was worried that Clive seemed to be losing his grip on things.*

runaway /ˈrʌnəweɪ/ [adj only before noun] increasing or spreading in an unexpected way that cannot be controlled: *Some economists are now predicting the danger of runaway inflation.* | *They see technology as a runaway force that humans can no longer control.*

rampant /ˈræmpənt/ [adj] growing, spreading or continuing very quickly, in a way that is impossible to stop – used especially in literature: *It wasn't military action but rampant disease that finally caused the population to surrender.* | *Corruption soon became rampant.*

run wild /rʌn ˈwaɪld/ [v phrase] to grow or develop in a completely uncontrolled way: *Organized crime has been running wild since the collapse of the old regime.* | *She allowed her imagination to run wild.*

11 to control the temperature, speed, or amount of something

- control
- keep sth under control
- regulate

control /kənˈtrəʊl/ [v T] to make the temperature, speed, or amount of something stay at the level you want: *A valve controls the flow of water into the main tank.* | *The finance committee controls the club's budget.*

keep sth under control /ˌkiːp (sth) ʌndəʳ kənˈtrəʊl/ [v phrase] to prevent an amount of something from becoming too large: *He's been trying for years to keep his drinking under control.* | *The administration has certainly succeeded in keeping inflation under control.*

regulate /ˈregjəleɪt/ [v T] to keep the temperature, speed, or amount of something at exactly the right level: *Sweating helps regulate body temperature.* | *A hand-operated switch is used to regulate the gas flow.*

12 to control machines, equipment, or vehicles

- control
- operate
- work
- be at the controls

control /kənˈtrəʊl/ [v T] to make a vehicle work: *She's a good driver and controls the car very well.* | *He was having trouble controlling the heavy truck on the slippery road surface.*

operate /ˈɒpəreɪt‖ˈɑː-/ [v T] formal to control a large or complicated machine or piece of equipment: *Don't worry – everyone will be shown how to operate the new machines.* | *Do you know how to operate the air conditioning?* | *They passed a cement mixer that was being operated by two men in dusty overalls.*

work /wɜːʳk/ [v T] to make a complicated machine or piece of equipment do what it is meant to do: *Does anyone here know how to work this microwave?* | *Simon showed me how to work the video player.*

be at the controls /biː ət ðə kənˈtrəʊlz/ [v phrase] if someone **is at the controls** of a large vehicle or plane, they are driving it, flying it etc **+ of** *The pilot remained at the controls of his plane even when it became clear that a crash was inevitable.* | *When we were kids we used to sit in a cardboard box, pretending to be at the controls of a spaceship.*

13 to control your feelings

- control
- self-control
- keep your temper
- self-discipline
- restrain yourself
- snap out of it
- get a grip on yourself
- pull yourself together

control /kənˈtrəʊl/ [v T] if you **control** yourself or **control** your feelings, you continue to behave calmly and sensibly and do not become too angry, excited, or upset **control yourself/himself etc** *She was really annoying me, but I managed to control myself and not say anything.* | **control your temper** *I wish he'd learn to control his temper.*

self-control /ˌself kənˈtrəʊl/ [n U] the ability to behave calmly and sensibly and not become too angry, excited, or upset, even when you have a good reason to: *The German team showed amazing self-control throughout the game.*

keep your temper /ˌkiːp jɔːʳ ˈtempəʳ/ [v phrase] to manage to stay calm and not become angry, especially when someone is trying to make you angry: *I knew they were trying to annoy me but I was determined to keep my temper.* | *Police officers are expected to keep their tempers whatever people say to them.* | *It took all her patience just to keep her temper.*

self-discipline /self ˈdɪsəplən/ [n U] the ability to make yourself work hard, take a lot of exercise, not eat the wrong foods etc because you know it is good for you to do so: *I don't know if I've enough self-discipline to work full-time and go to night school.* | *We try to teach the children self-reliance and self-discipline.*

restrain yourself /rɪˈstreɪn jɔːʳˌself/ [v phrase] to stop yourself doing or saying something, especially something that might have a harmful result: *I was tempted to stay for another drink, but in the end I restrained myself and went home.* | **+ from** *So far I have managed to restrain myself from phoning up to complain.*

snap out of it /ˌsnæp ˈaʊt əv ɪt/ [v phrase] to suddenly start to control yourself after you have been very sad or upset and make yourself feel better again: *You've been in this mood for days now – I wish you'd snap out of it.* | *He's so depressed. He doesn't seem able to snap out of it at all.*

get a grip on yourself /ˌget ə ˈgrɪp ɒn jɔːʳself/ spoken say this when you want someone to stop behaving in a very emotional way, especially when they are so frightened or upset that they cannot control the way they are behaving: *Come on, calm down,* *get a grip on yourself.* | *Occasionally Georgie would find Tommy crying, and he'd tell him to get a grip on himself.*

pull yourself together /ˌpʊl jɔːʳself təˈgeðəʳ/ spoken say this when you want someone to stop behaving emotionally, especially when you are a little annoyed or embarrassed at the way they are behaving: *Pull yourself together. It's ridiculous to get upset about such a silly little thing.* | *His father was not one to hand out sympathy, but would simply tell him to 'pull himself together'.*

14 unable to control your feelings

- lose control
- uncontrollable
- get carried away
- go to pieces
- snap
- give in to
- lose it

lose control /ˌluːz kənˈtrəʊl/ [v phrase] to become unable to control your feelings and become very angry or upset: *He made her so angry that she lost control and hit him.*

uncontrollable /ˌʌnkənˈtrəʊləbəl◂/ [adj] **uncontrollable** emotions or actions are difficult or impossible to control: *Barbara was shaking with uncontrollable laughter.* | *At the mention of Hannah's name, he flew into an uncontrollable rage.*

get carried away /get ˌkærid əˈweɪ/ [v phrase] especially spoken to feel so excited, interested etc that you cannot control what you are saying or doing: *It's easy to get carried away and buy a lot of things that you don't need.* | *A few of the younger men got a bit carried away and started dancing on the tables.*

go to pieces /ˌgəʊ tə ˈpiːsəz/ [v phrase] especially spoken to be so upset or nervous that you cannot control what you are doing and cannot think sensibly: *I was so nervous in my driving test I just went to pieces.* | *Keeping busy was the only thing that kept her from going to pieces during the divorce.*

snap /snæp/ [v I] to suddenly become very angry or upset, after you have been trying to stop yourself getting angry or upset for a long time: *Leroy finally snapped and attacked his tormentors.* | *Melanie Smithson, who is accused of murdering her husband, has claimed that she snapped after years of violence and abuse.* | **sb's patience snaps** *Charlotte's patience suddenly snapped.*

give in to /gɪv ˈɪn tuː/ [phr v T] if you **give in to** an emotion such as anger or unhappiness, you can no longer control that emotion: *She was determined not to give in to despair.* | *Miles struggled not to give in to his feelings of anger and hopelessness.*

lose it /ˈluːz ɪt/ [v phrase] informal to suddenly get very angry or upset, so that you are no longer able to control what you say or do: *Pete just lost it completely and started shouting and screaming at us.*

convenient

RELATED WORDS

▸ *see also* **useful, suitable, near**

1 a time or arrangement that is convenient

- convenient
- a good time
- suit
- be OK/be okay
- fit in with
- be good for

convenient /kənˈviːniənt/ [adj] a **convenient** time to do something is a time that does not cause you any problems, for example because you were not planning to do anything else: *I'd like to talk to the manager – can you suggest a convenient time?* | **+ for** *We need to arrange a meeting. Would 11 o'clock on Tuesday be convenient for you?*

a good time /ə ˌgʊd ˈtaɪm/ especially spoken a convenient time to do something: *'I'm too busy to talk to you now.' 'When would be a good time?'* | **a good time to do sth** *A good time to reach me is in the evening after 7:00.* | **+ for** *I'm afraid Friday isn't a good time for me – I've got a dance class.*

suit /suːt, sjuːt‖suːt/ [v T] if a time or date **suits** you, it is convenient for you: *Which day would suit you best?* | *Finding a time that suits everyone is going to be difficult.*

be OK/be okay /biː əʊ ˈkeɪ/ spoken informal if a time or date **is OK** or **is okay**, it is convenient for you: *I'll pick you up by the front gate. Is 10 o'clock OK?* | **+ for** *Friday's probably okay for me, but I'll check with Jean.*

fit in with /ˌfɪt ˈɪn wɪð/ [phr v T not in progressive or passive] if something **fits in with** your plans, you do not need to change your plans in order to do it: *We'd like to go out for a meal on Thursday evening – does that fit in with your plans?*

be good for /biː ˈgʊd fɔːʳ/ [v phrase] spoken if something, especially an arrangement, time, date etc **is good for you**, it is convenient because you do not need to change your plans in order to do it: *Ten o'clock is good for me. How about you?* | *OK, we'll meet at my house tomorrow night. Is that good for everyone?*

2 a thing or way of doing something that is easy and quick

- convenient
- handy

convenient /kənˈviːniənt/ [adj] a **convenient** thing or way of doing something is useful because it is quick, easy, and does not cause you any problems: *Credit cards are probably the most convenient way of paying for concert tickets.* | **it is convenient to do sth** *I could take the train, but it's more convenient to go by car.* —**convenience** [n C/U] *Many parents prefer the convenience of working at home while their children are small.*

handy /ˈhændi/ [adj] a **handy** object or method is easy to use or easy to do: *Many fruit juices are now available in handy little cartons.* | *It's a handy way of keeping a record of your spending.*

3 a place that is good because it is near to other places

- convenient

▸ *see also* **near**

convenient ALSO **handy** informal /kənˈviːniənt, ˈhændi/ [adj] close to a particular place so it is easy to go there: *I leave my umbrella in a convenient spot by the door so I don't forget it on the way out.* | *Our daycare center, located right here in the building, is convenient for parents with young children.* | **+ for the school/shops/station etc** (=close to the school etc, so it is easy to get there) British *The hotel is very convenient for the station – it's only a two-minute walk.* | *Our house is very handy for the shops.* —**conveniently** [adv] *My new place is conveniently located across from a supermarket.*

4 a time or arrangement that causes difficulties

- inconvenient/not convenient
- a bad time
- be bad for/be no good for
- awkward/difficult

inconvenient/not convenient /ˌɪnkənˈviːniənt◂, nɒt kənˈviːniənt/ [adj] *I'm afraid he's come at an inconvenient time.* | **+ for** *I can call you back later if it's not convenient for you to talk now.* | *They discussed moving the office to a new building downtown but it wasn't convenient for most of the staff.* | **it is inconvenient to do sth** *If you find it inconvenient to come to the office, we can email the files to you.*

a bad time /ə ˌbæd ˈtaɪm/ [n phrase] especially spoken a time that is not convenient because you are busy or you have made other plans: *Sorry – have I come at a bad time?*

be bad for/be no good for /biː ˈbæd fɔːʳ, biː nəʊ ˈgʊd fɔːʳ/ [v phrase] spoken if something, especially an arrangement, time, date etc **is bad for** or **is no good for** you, it is not convenient because you have other plans: *Saturdays are no good for me. Could we play Fridays instead?* | *Would it be bad for you if we met at my house instead of yours?*

awkward/difficult /ˈɔːkwəʳd, ˈdɪfɪkəlt/ [adj] if something is **awkward** or **difficult**, it is inconvenient to do it, especially because it would interrupt something else: *Robson's resignation comes at an awkward time for the company.* | *Things are a bit difficult at the moment. Can I call you back this afternoon?*

conventional/ unconventional

behaving and thinking in a way that most people think is right and socially acceptable

RELATED WORDS

- *see also* **normal/ordinary, tradition, old-fashioned, crazy, strange**

1 conventional

- conventional
- conformist
- straight
- conservative
- suburban
- traditional

conventional /kənˈvenʃənəl/ [adj] **conventional** people, behaviour, and opinions are the type that most people in society think are normal and socially acceptable, although some people think they are boring and old-fashioned: *Rosemary led a quiet, conventional life until she went to college.* | *Her outrageous stage act is seen as a challenge to conventional morality.* | *Acupuncture may work, but I still believe in a more conventional approach to medicine.* —**conventionally** [adv] *She was dressed very conventionally in a dull grey suit.* | *Dickinson was very spiritual but not conventionally religious.*

conformist /kənˈfɔːmɪ̈st/ [adj] thinking and behaving like everyone else, because you do not want to be different: *Your problem is that you are too conformist in your thinking.* | *Our children's creativity is being beaten down by the conformist educational system.* —**conformist** [n C] *He'd never dream of trying something like that – he's too much of a conformist.* —**conformity** [n U] *The system seems to value conformity over originality.*

straight /streɪt/ [adj not usually before noun] informal conventional and often fairly boring: *Paul's quite nice but he's awfully straight.* | *I can't stand it when your friends come to visit – they're so straight.*

conservative /kənˈsɜːʳvətɪv/ [adj] a **conservative** person is fairly old-fashioned in their attitudes, beliefs, styles of clothes etc, and does not like change or new ideas. Old-fashioned attitudes, beliefs, styles etc can also be called **conservative**: *June's parents were very conservative and wouldn't allow her to date till she was 18.* | *middle-aged men in conservative business suits* —**conservatively** [adv] *She was in her mid-thirties, attractive, and conservatively dressed.*

suburban /səˈbɜːʳbən/ [adj] especially British typical of the attitudes and way of life of people who are conventional and ordinary, and who disapprove of anyone who does not live or behave like them: *She hated her parents' suburban attitudes.* | *Despite her suburban clothes and appearance she was popular at college.*

traditional /trəˈdɪʃənəl/ [adj] doing things in a way that have existed for a long time, and not interested in anything new or different: *Many traditional teachers still think of computers as useless toys.* | *His critics objected to the way he broke many of the traditional rules of art.*

2 unconventional

- unconventional
- alternative
- unorthodox
- nonconformist
- drop out

unconventional /ˌʌnkənˈvenʃənəl◂/ [adj] very different from the way people usually behave, think, dress etc: *His business methods were unconventional but successful.* | *Her unconventional opinions finally cost her her job.* | *The two never lived in the same house, but their unconventional marriage lasted over 30 years.*

alternative /ɔːlˈtɜːʳnətɪv/ [adj only before noun] **alternative** methods, ideas, ways of living etc are completely different from the ones that most people think are normal, and are based on different principles **alternative medicine/lifestyle/music etc** *Alternative medicine can cure many problems but not diseases like cancer.* | *San Francisco has a long history of accepting the city's many alternative lifestyles.*

unorthodox /ʌnˈɔːʳθədɒks‖-dɑːks/ [adj] ideas, behaviour, or methods that are **unorthodox** are original and different from what is usual or the accepted principles of a profession, religion etc: *There was no tolerance of unorthodox political views.* | *Treating the disease with a diet rather than with medicine is an unorthodox approach that few doctors recommend.*

nonconformist /ˌnɒnkənˈfɔːʳmɪ̈st◂‖ˌnɑːn-/ [adj] not wanting to think or behave in the same way as most ordinary people, or to follow accepted ways of doing things: *As a writer he remained nonconformist all his life, always searching for new means of expression.* —**nonconformist** [n C] *She prided herself on being a nonconformist, on getting results by breaking the rules.*

drop out /ˌdrɒp ˈaʊt‖ˌdrɑːp-/ [phr v I] to decide not to work or take part in normal society because you want to be different and live life your own way: *He advised young people to 'turn on, tune in, and drop* *out'.* | **+ of** *She decided to drop out of the rat race because she couldn't stand working 60 hours a week.* —**dropout/drop-out** /'drɒpaʊt‖'drɑːp-/ [n C] *He was a dropout and a hippy back in the '60s.*

cook

RELATED WORDS

- to prepare food by cutting it *see* **cut (2)**
- to prepare food by mixing it *see* **mix**
- *see also* **food, meal, drink, taste, eat, delicious**

1 to cook something

- cook
- make
- get
- fix
- rustle up
- prepare
- do
- concoct
- mix
- put sth on
- be on

cook /kʊk/ [v I/T] to prepare food or a meal by heating it, boiling it, frying it etc: *I'm just too tired to cook after work.* | *Prick the potatoes with a fork before cooking them.* | **cook lunch/supper/a meal etc** *I usually cook a big meal on Sundays.* | **cook (sth) for sb** (=cook a meal for someone) *The last time she cooked a meal for us we really enjoyed it.* —**cooked** [adj] *Mix the vegetables with the cooked rice.* | *Is the pasta cooked yet?*

make /meɪk/ [v T] to **make** a meal or dish or type of food, either by cooking it or by preparing it in some other way: *My mother used to make delicious strawberry jam.* | *I think I'll make fish pie for supper.* | *I'll make the salad if you'll make the pasta.* | **make lunch/dinner/supper etc** *When I got home, Martin was in the kitchen making lunch.* | **make sb sth** *I'll make you some sandwiches to take with you.*

get /get/ [v T not in passive] especially British, spoken to cook or prepare a meal: *Sit down and let me get dinner.* | *Joey was downstairs getting the kids their breakfast.*

fix /fɪks/ [v T] especially American to make a meal or dish – use this about meals you make quickly, not about big, formal meals **fix breakfast/lunch/dinner etc** *I have to fix lunch now.* | **fix sb sth** *If you're hungry, I can fix you some scrambled eggs.*

rustle up /ˌrʌsəl 'ʌp/ [phr v T] to make a meal quickly using whatever food you have available: *She managed to rustle up a delicious meal with just a little salad and some eggs.* | **rustle something up** *'I don't think there's any food in the house.' 'Don't worry, I'm sure we can rustle something up.'*

prepare /prɪ'peəʳ/ [v T] written to make a meal, especially something that needs time, effort, or skill: *Prepare a vinaigrette dressing with olive oil, white wine vinegar, and mustard.* | *Some French dishes take hours to prepare.* | *Mrs Fujimoto prepared a delicious meal for them.*

do /duː/ [v T] spoken informal to make a particular kind of food **do sth** *I was thinking of doing fish tonight.* | **do sb sth** *I could do you an omelette.*

concoct /kən'kɒkt‖-'kɑːkt/ [v T] to make an unusual or unpleasant drink, dish, or medicine, by mixing together several different things **concoct sth** *For the party, they had concocted a special cocktail containing, among other things, rum and vodka.* | **concoct sth out of** *Whenever I had a cold, my grandmother would concoct a remedy out of herbs, ginger, lemons and garlic.* —**concoction** /kən'kɒkʃən‖-'kɑːk-/ [n C] *In the glass was a greenish concoction with pieces of ice and fruit floating in it.*

mix /mɪks/ [v T] to make a drink by mixing two or more liquids or substances together: *If they sell cocktails would you ask the bartender to mix a Harvey Wallbanger?* | *You can leave the meal cooking while you mix a drink for your guests.*

put sth on /ˌpʊt (sth) 'ɒn/ [phr v T] **put the dinner/potatoes/vegetables etc on** to start cooking something: *Can we put the dinner on? I'm starved.* | *They'll be here soon. You'd better put the steaks on.*

be on /biː 'ɒn / [phr v I] if food **is on**, it is being cooked: *The soup is on, so dinner will be ready in about twenty minutes.* | *Okay, the chicken is on. What can I do now?*

2 ways of cooking

- cook
- boil
- simmer
- fry
- stir-fry
- bake
- roast
- grill/broil
- steam

cook /kʊk/ [v I/T] *In a large sauté pan, cook the bacon until crisp.* | *Cover and cook slowly until beets are tender, stirring occasionally.*

boil /bɔɪl/ [v I/T] to cook food in very hot water: *Boil the potatoes until they are soft.* | *The beans should be boiled rapidly for at least twenty minutes.* —**boiled** [adj only before noun] *boiled eggs*

simmer /'sɪməʳ/ [v I/T] to cook food slowly in water that is boiling very gently: *Simmer the macaroni in lightly salted water.* | *Cover the pan and let it simmer for fifteen minutes.* | **simmer gently/slowly** *Combine all ingredients and simmer gently for 30 to 45 minutes.*

fry /fraɪ/ [v I/T] to cook food in hot oil, butter, or fat: *Fry the onions gently for five minutes.* | *Mushrooms are best when fried in olive oil.* —**fried** [adj only before noun] *the smell of fried bacon*

stir-fry /'stɜːʳ fraɪ/ [v T] to cook something by mixing it in hot oil for a short time and keeping it moving in the pan: *Add the garlic, ginger and onions and stir-fry for 30 seconds.* | *Water chestnuts can be eaten straight from the tin or stir-fried.* | *Chinese peanut oils are perfect for stir-frying.*

bake /beɪk/ [v I/T] to cook food in an oven, for example bread, cakes, or potatoes: *My grandmother baked her own bread.* | *Bake at 190C for 20-25 minutes.* | *Bake the soufflés for 12 minutes.* | *Place on a baking sheet and bake in a very low oven until crisp.* —**baked** [adj] *I love baked potatoes with cheese and broccoli.*

roast /rəʊst/ [v I/T] to cook meat or vegetables in an oven or over a fire: *Roast the chicken for three hours in a hot oven.* | *the smell of roasting meat* —**roast** [adj only before noun] *There's some cold roast beef in the fridge.*

grill/broil /grɪl, brɔɪl/ [v I/T] to cook food by putting it directly underneath a flame or a heated electric object: *Grill the steak for about five minutes on each side.* | *Brush the kebabs lightly with oil and broil them.* | *Broil until cheese melts and edges of bread are crusty.* —**grilled/broiled** [adj] *I like grilled sole.* | *I ordered broiled steak, French fries and salad.*

steam /stiːm/ [v I/T] to cook food in steam: *Steam the courgettes for 3-4 minutes.* | *The broccoli, peppers and squash should be steamed.* —**steamed** [adj only before noun] *a steamed pudding*

3 not cooked

- raw
- uncooked
- underdone/ undercooked/ not cooked

raw /rɔː/ [adj] **raw** food has not been cooked: *Sushi consists of raw fish and rice.* | *a salad made with nuts, raisins and raw carrots* | *If you can't resist snacking between meals, eat something healthy such as fruit or raw vegetables.*

uncooked /ˌʌnˈkʊkt◂/ [adj usually before noun] **uncooked** food has not yet been cooked, but should be cooked before it is eaten: *Uncooked meat should be stored separately.* | *Spoon the sauce into large uncooked pasta shells.*

underdone/undercooked/not cooked /ˌʌndəʳˈdʌn◂, ˌʌndəʳˈkʊkt◂, nɒt ˈkʊkt/ [adj] informal not cooked for long enough: *It can be dangerous to eat undercooked pork.* | *The potatoes were underdone.* | *The poultry wasn't cooked and the fish was practically raw.*

4 cooked too much

- overcooked/ overdone
- burn

overcooked/overdone /ˌəʊvəʳˈkʊkt◂, ˌəʊvəʳˈdʌn◂/ [adj] food that is **overcooked** or **overdone** has been cooked too much and does not taste nice: *The steak's a little overdone.* | *I hate overcooked vegetables.*

burn /bɜːʳn/ [v T] to cook food for too long, or too close to the heat, so that it becomes black on the outside: *Oh, no! I've burnt the chicken!* | *The muffins are a little burned on the bottom.* —**burned/burnt** British [adj] *the smell of burnt hamburger*

5 the activity of cooking

- cooking
- cookery

cooking /ˈkʊkɪŋ/ [n U] the activity of cooking: *His hobbies include cooking and wine-making.* | **do the cooking** *Who does the cooking in your house?*

cookery /ˈkʊkəri/ [n U] British the activity or study of cooking: *My favourite subject at school was cookery.* | *Ken Lowery, a cookery expert, will be giving free demonstrations from 4.30 until 7.00.* | *She studied at a vegetarian cookery school in London.*

6 a style of cooking

- cooking
- cookery
- cuisine

cooking /ˈkʊkɪŋ/ [n U] the way food is cooked by a particular person or in a particular place: *I can recommend that new Greek restaurant. Their cooking is excellent.* | *Stop criticizing my cooking!* | **French/Chinese/Italian etc cooking** *Karen loves Italian cooking.* | *Maybe you should take a Chinese cooking class.* | **home cooking** (=cooking that you do at home) *There's nothing like home cooking.*

cookery /ˈkʊkəri/ [n U] British the way food is cooked in a particular place: *Annatto is a small seed used in Latin American cookery.* | *Puddings are a great speciality of British cookery.*

cuisine /kwɪˈziːn/ [n U] formal the style of cooking of a particular country or place, especially when the food is very good: *Hungary has an excellent and internationally recognised cuisine.* | **French/Italian/Chinese etc cuisine** *Trompe Le Monde features classic French cuisine served amid sumptuous surroundings.* | *Venetian cuisine is based on seafood and rice.*

7 instructions for cooking

- recipe
- cookbook

recipe /ˈresəpi/ [n C] a set of instructions for cooking a particular meal or type of food: *I'm not a great cook, but I can follow a recipe pretty well.* | *rabbit pie made to a traditional country recipe* | **+ for** *Could you give me the recipe for that chocolate cake?*

cookbook ALSO **recipe/cookery book** British /ˈkʊkbʊk, ˈresəpi,ˈkʊkəri bʊk/ [n C] a book that has instructions for preparing various dishes: *Peters is the author of the popular cookbook 'Doing it in the Kitchen'.* | *an illustrated cookbook* | **French/Italian/Japanese etc cookbook** *We have several French cookbooks in stock.*

8 something that is used in cooking

- cooking
- culinary

cooking /ˈkʊkɪŋ/ [adj only before noun] **cooking utensils/oil/salt etc** used for or in **cooking**, and not usually for anything else: *We keep all the cooking utensils on the bottom shelf.* | *That's cooking chocolate – you shouldn't really eat it on its own.*

culinary /ˈkʌlənəri‖ˈkʌləneri, ˈkjuːl-/ [adj] formal used for or in cooking: *Mint is perhaps the best-known of culinary herbs.* | *The use of garlic, whether for medicinal or culinary purposes, dates back several centuries.*

9 someone who cooks

- cook
- chef

cook /kʊk/ [n C] someone who cooks food, either as their job or for pleasure: *Jane used to work as a cook in an Italian restaurant.* | **a good/excellent/terrible cook** (=someone who is very good or very bad at cooking) *Frank's a very good cook.*

chef /ʃef/ [n C] a cook in a restaurant or hotel, especially one who has been trained in a special school to do this work: *Marco's ambition had been to become a chef in one of the big hotels.* | *Sagin is a 31-year-old French chef living and working in Montreal.*

copy

WHAT'S HERE

- **to copy sth** see **1 to 5**
- **to do the same as sb else** see **6 to 10**

to copy sth

1 to copy something

- copy
- make a copy
- photocopy
- reproduce
- clone
- forge
- back up

copy /ˈkɒpi‖ˈkɑːpi/ [v T] to produce something that is exactly the same as something else or that is very similar to it: *Would you go down to the print room and copy these documents for me?* | *They were arrested for illegally copying video recordings.* | *Each artist was asked to copy the scene exactly as he or she saw it.* | **copy sth from/into/onto sth** *The drawings had been copied from photographs.* | *Copy all the files onto disk.*

make a copy /ˌmeɪk ə ˈkɒpi‖-ˈkɑːpi/ [v phrase] to copy something using a machine: *Can you make some extra copies for the staff?* | **+ of** *John said he'd make a copy of the will and send it over to the house.* | *The program does not automatically make backup copies of your files.*

photocopy ALSO **copy** /ˈfəʊtəkɒpi‖-kɑːpi, ˈkɒpi‖ˈkɑːpi/ [v T] to copy a piece of paper with writing or pictures on it, using a special machine that makes a photograph of the original: *Photocopy the application before sending it.* | *This form needs to be copied and sent to Paul with the letter.*

reproduce /ˌriːprəˈdjuːs‖-ˈduːs/ [v T usually in passive] to print a copy of a picture, document etc especially in a book or newspaper: *We'll need to ask the New Yorker for permission to reproduce the cartoon.* | *Letters and rare maps are handsomely reproduced in the book.*

clone /kləʊn/ [v T] to make an exact copy of a plant or animal by taking a cell from it and developing it artificially: *The process allowed Scottish scientists to clone the sheep named Dolly.* | *It is only a matter of time before we are able to clone human beings.*

forge /fɔːʳdʒ/ [v T] to illegally copy something written or printed, such as a bank note or official document, for dishonest purposes: *Marino obtained the drugs by forging his doctor's signature on a prescription.* | *He entered the country using a forged passport.* —**forgery** [n U] the crime of forging a document: *Spearman is now serving a three-year prison sentence for forgery.* —**forger** [n C] *Mason is a convicted forger from Rialto.*

back up /ˌbæk ˈʌp/ [phr v T] to copy information from a computer onto a disk, so that it can be used if something goes wrong with the computer **back up sth** *Don't forget to back up all the new files you create.* | **back sth up** *I didn't back the document up and lost the whole lot.*

2 to write down exactly what someone has said or written

- copy
- copy out
- copy down
- transcribe

copy /ˈkɒpi‖ˈkɑːpi/ [v T] to write down exactly what someone else has written: *Can I copy your notes?* | **copy sth from sth** *She copied the poem from an old book of Grandma's in the attic.* | **copy sth into/onto sth** *I need to copy these phone numbers into my address book.*

copy out /ˌkɒpi ˈaʊt‖ˌkɑː-/ [phr v T] to copy the whole of a piece of writing using exactly the same words as the original **copy out sth** *At school we often had to copy out whole chapters from the Bible.* | **copy sth out** *As a kid, I used to copy song lyrics out and keep them in notebooks.*

copy down /ˌkɒpi ˈdaʊn‖ˌkɑː-/ [phr v T] to copy a short piece of written information such as a list or an address **copy down sth** *The witness had copied down the license plate number of the taxi the suspect used to get away.* | **copy sth down** *Roger copied the train times down on the back of an envelope.*

transcribe /trænˈskraɪb/ [v T] to write an exact copy of a piece of writing or a speech: *I record my business letters, and my secretary transcribes them.* | **transcribe sth into sth** (=transcribe something using special signs or a different alphabet) *The conversation had been transcribed into phonetic script.*

3 to copy someone else's work or ideas

- copy
- plagiarize
- lift
- steal
- derivative

copy /ˈkɒpi‖ˈkɑːpi/ [v I/T] to **copy** something that someone else has written or thought of and pretend it is your own work: *Any student caught copying will fail the test.* | *The company has been accused of copying software ideas from larger competitors.* | **copy sth straight from sth** (=copy it without changing anything) *Most of his answers had been copied straight from the student who sat next to him.*

plagiarize ALSO **plagiarise** British /ˈpleɪdʒəraɪz/ [v I/T] to illegally copy words, ideas etc from something written by someone else, and pretend that they are your own: *He got kicked out of school because he plagiarized a term paper.* | *She claimed that she didn't plagiarize – she just paraphrased.* —**plagiarism** [n U] *Donahue's reputation was damaged when he was accused of plagiarism.*

lift /lɪft/ [v T usually in passive] informal to copy someone else's words or ideas and pretend that they are your own: *One paragraph of his essay has been lifted from an economics textbook.* | **be lifted straight from/out of sth** (=use exactly the same words or ideas) *The plot of the play had been lifted straight out of an old episode of 'The Honeymooners'.*

steal /stiːl/ [v T] to take someone else's ideas and use them without their permission in order to make money from them: *Professional designers and architects steal ideas from each other all the time.* | *She claims that the director stole ideas from her historical novel and used them in the movie.*

derivative /dɪˈrɪvətɪv/ [adj] formal not original, but strongly influenced by someone else's work or partly copied from it: *a derivative artistic style* | **+ of** *This relatively new style of music is derivative of ragtime and blues.*

4 something that has been copied from something else

- copy
- photocopy
- duplicate
- model
- replica
- reproduction
- imitation
- facsimile
- backup copy/backup
- clone

copy /ˈkɒpi‖ˈkɑːpi/ [n C] something that has been copied and made to look exactly like something else: *I don't have my original birth certificate. Will you accept a copy?* | **+ of** *Connie left copies of the document on everybody's desk.* | *a 19th century copy of the popular Rembrandt painting*

photocopy ALSO **copy** /ˈfəʊtəˌkɒpi‖-ˌkɑːpi, ˈkɒpi‖ˈkɑːpi/ [n C] a copy of a piece of paper or a picture that has been made using a machine: *Please send a photocopy of your passport.* | **make a copy** *Can you make seven copies of this, please?*

duplicate /ˈdjuːplɪkɪt‖ˈduː-/ [n C] an exact copy of something that can be used in the same way, especially when the original one has been lost: *I only have one house key, but I'll have a duplicate made for when you visit.* —**duplicate** [adj only before noun] *It's a good idea to keep duplicate files on floppy disk.*

model /ˈmɒdl‖ˈmɑːdl/ [n C] a small copy of a building, vehicle, or machine, made to look exactly like the original building, vehicle etc **+ of** *White's team made a model of the new ballpark to show the public.* | **model ship/airplane etc** *There was a shelf in his bedroom full of model planes.* | **scale model** (=a model with the same size and distance relationships as the real thing) *The 1957 photo shows him holding a scale model of an ocean liner he built entirely by hand.*

replica /ˈreplɪkə/ [n C] a copy of a well-known vehicle, building, or weapon, especially one that is the same size as the original: *a replica fire truck from the 1920s* | **+ of** *A replica of the space shuttle is parked at the center's entrance.* | *The building is an exact replica of the original Globe theatre.*

reproduction /ˌriːprəˈdʌkʃən◂/ [n C] a copy of an old or valuable work of art or piece of furniture: *The store sells a range of reproduction furniture in Colonial style.* | **+ of** *a reproduction of a beautiful Ming vase*

imitation /ˌɪmɪ̯ˈteɪʃən◂/ [adj only before noun] **imitation** jewellery, furniture, fur etc are copies of expensive things that are made of cheaper material so that they look similar but cost much less: *an imitation sheepskin seat cover* | *The original wood-frame house had been covered with imitation brick siding.* —**imitation** [n C] *The necklace was a cheap imitation, but she was obviously very proud of it.*

facsimile /fækˈsɪmɪ̯li/ [n C] an exact copy of an old or valuable document or piece of writing, that is done on the same kind of paper or material it was originally written or printed on: *A facsimile of the 1896 book was published in February.*

backup copy/backup /ˈbækʌp ˌkɒpi‖-ˌkɑːpi, ˈbækʌp/ [n C] a copy of computer information that you save on a separate disk, so that if something goes wrong with your computer, you will still have the information: *Make sure to make backup copies of all your data.* | *Don't store the backups near the computer, where someone could easily steal them both.*

clone /kləʊn/ [n C] an animal or plant that is an exact copy of another one, and is produced by taking a cell from another plant or animal and developing it artificially: *These plants are all clones of the same original plant.*

5 a copy of something that is intended to deceive people

- forgery
- fake
- counterfeit
- pirate

forgery /ˈfɔːʳdʒəri/ [n C] an illegal copy of something official such as a bank note, legal documentation or work of art: *Three paintings now thought to be forgeries are included in the show* | *Further investigation showed that the so-called 'Hitler Diaries' were a forgery.*

fake /feɪk/ [adj] made to look like the product of a particular company or the work of a particular artist in order to trick people in to buying them: *They were selling fake Rolex watches on the street.* | *His I.D. is obviously fake.* —**fake** [n C] a copy of a valuable object or painting that is intended to deceive people: *Three months after I bought it, a friend who works at the museum told me it was probably a fake.*

counterfeit /ˈkaʊntəʳfɪt/ [adj] **counterfeit** money looks exactly like real money but has been produced illegally: *Police have warned stores to look out for counterfeit $50 bills.* —**counterfeiting** [n U] the crime of making counterfeit money: *The new twenty-dollar bills contain features designed to prevent counterfeiting.* —**counterfeiter** [n U] *Counterfeiters are now able to produce almost perfect notes.*

pirate British **/pirated** especially American /ˈpaɪərət, ˈpaɪərətɪ̯d/ [adj only before noun] **pirate copies/videos/CDs** copies of books, records, films etc that have been made illegally and are sold without the permission of the people who originally produced them: *The government has closed a factory that was producing pirate CDs.* | *It's pretty easy to get pirated copies of the software.*

to do the same as sb else

RELATED WORDS

▸ *see also* **make fun of**

6 to do the same as someone else does

- copy
- imitate
- impersonate
- ape
- do what sb does
- follow sb's example
- follow in sb's footsteps
- follow suit/follow sb's lead

copy /ˈkɒpi‖ˈkɑːpi/ [v T] to do the same things that someone else does, especially in order to look like them or be like them: *Children learn swearing from copying their parents and siblings.* | *Martin often claimed he copied Bing Crosby's singing style, but there was much more to his music than that.*

imitate /ˈɪmɪ̯teɪt/ [v T] to copy the way someone behaves, speaks, writes, or moves, especially because you admire them or want to be like them: *'Don't you talk to me like that!' she said imitating her mother's high-pitched voice.* | *A lot of writers have tried to imitate Lawrence's style.*

impersonate /ɪmˈpɜːʳsəneɪt/ [v T] to pretend to be someone else by copying the way they talk, walk, dress etc, especially in order to make people think you are really the other person: *Harmon is charged with impersonating a police officer.* | *She makes a living out of impersonating Tina Turner in shows and films.* —**impersonation** /ɪmˌpɜːʳsəˈneɪʃən/ [n C/U] **+ of** *Katy does a great impersonation of Grandpa when he's annoyed.*

ape /eɪp/ [v T] to imitate someone's behaviour, in a way that other people think is stupid or silly: *His music attempts to ape classical styles, but the results are not very original.* | *California wine makers are trying to do new things with Sauvignon blanc instead of just aping French styles.*

do what sb does /duː wɒt (sb) ˈdʌz/ [v phrase] informal to do the same things as someone else, especially in order to learn from them: *Just watch and do what I do. It's pretty easy.*

follow sb's example /ˌfɒləʊ (sb's) ɪɡˈzɑːmpəl‖ˌfɑːləʊ (sb's) ɪɡˈzæm-/ [v phrase] to copy what someone else has done because you think that their behaviour or actions were a good idea: *Brian persuaded his brothers to follow his example and join the navy.* | *Following the example of Nixon, a politician* *he greatly admired, he decided to try to make himself more appealing to voters.*

follow in sb's footsteps /ˌfɒləʊ ɪn (sb's) ˈfʊtsteps ‖ ˌfɑː-/ [v phrase] to do something that someone else has done before you, especially someone in a more powerful position than you: *My father was always disappointed that Joey didn't follow in his footsteps and take over the farm.* | *We will watch with interest what happens to these two women officers and to the young women who wish to follow in their footsteps.*

follow suit/follow sb's lead /ˌfɒləʊ ˈsuːt, ˌfɒləʊ (sb's) ˈliːd‖ˌfɑː-/ [v phrase] to do what someone else has just done because it seems the correct thing to do: *We're hoping that Europe will follow the US's lead and ban all use of these poisonous gases.* | *Because the Black community has long experience with civil rights issues, other minority groups may follow its lead.* | *Other oil companies are expected to follow suit and raise prices before the end of the month.*

7 to copy someone you admire

- emulate
- model yourself on

emulate /ˈemjɡ̈leɪt/ [v T] formal to copy someone else because you admire something that they have done very much: *There is much in Cheng's work that we can admire and emulate.* | *Developing countries often try to emulate experiences of developed countries, but this is not always a good idea.*

model yourself on /ˈmɒdl jɔːʳself ɒn‖ˈmɑːdl-/ [v phrase] to copy someone's behaviour and character as closely as you can because you want to be like them: *The junior Wimbledon champion said that she tried to model herself on Martina Navratilova.* | *Pender says his show models itself on the old-style talk shows.*

8 to do the same things as other people in a group

- follow the crowd/go (along) with the crowd
- jump on the bandwagon

follow the crowd/go (along) with the crowd /ˌfɒləʊ ðə ˈkraʊd‖ˌfɑː-, ˌɡəʊ (əlɒŋ) wɪð ðə ˈkraʊd/ [v phrase] to do the same as the rest of a group of people because you have not really thought about what you want or because you do not want to disagree with what most people think: *That experience taught me never to follow the crowd blindly.* | *It's hard, as an investor, to resist the urge to go along with the crowd, but that isn't where the money is.*

jump on the bandwagon /ˌdʒʌmp ɒn ðə ˈbændwæɡən/ [v phrase] to do the same as a lot of other people are doing because you think there will be some advantage for you or because it is fashionable: *When they realized there was money to be made from games such as snooker, sportswear advertisers soon jumped on the bandwagon.* | *Opposition leaders have accused the government of jumping on the asylum seeker bandwagon.*

9 someone who other people copy

- example
- set an example
- role model

example /ɪɡˈzɑːmpəl‖ɪɡˈzæm-/ [n C usually singular] **an example to** *As the eldest in the family, she was expected to be an example to her younger brothers and sisters.* | **a shining example** (=someone or something that should be admired and copied) *The school is a shining example of what parent-teacher cooperation can achieve.*

set an example /ˌset ən ɪɡˈzɑːmpəl‖-ˈzæm-/ [v phrase] if someone **sets an example** they behave correctly, work hard etc because other people are expected to copy them: *If Saunders is sincere about reform, he should set an example by taking a pay cut.* | **set a (good) example for sb** *Senior officers should be setting a good example for the men.*

role model /ˈrəʊl ˌmɒdl‖-ˌmɑːdl/ [n C] someone that you try to imitate because they are successful and have good qualities that you would also like to have: *He's a wonderfully kind man and an excellent role model for the children.* | *There aren't enough positive role models for young people today, especially for minority groups.*

10 to copy someone or something to make people laugh

- imitate
- do an impression/imitation
- mimic
- a take-off of sb/sth

imitate /ˈɪmɡ̈teɪt/ [v T] to copy what someone says or does, in order to make people laugh: *She's really good at imitating our teacher's Scottish accent.*

do an impression/imitation /ˌduː ən ɪmˈpreʃən, ɪmɡ̈ˈteɪʃən/ [v phrase] to copy the way someone famous moves, talks etc, in order to make people laugh: *He made her laugh hysterically during their walks, with his impression of Gene Kelly doing 'Singin' in the Rain.'*

mimic /ˈmɪmɪk/ [v I/T] to unkindly copy the way someone talks or moves in order to make people laugh: *'Hmm,' Phil said. 'Hmm,' Graham mimicked.* | *Yolanda mimicked their father opening the letter.*

a take-off of sb/sth ALSO **a take-off on sb/sth** American informal /ə ˈteɪk ɒf əv (sb/sth), ə ˈteɪk ɒf ɒn (sb/sth)/ [n phrase] a copy of the way someone moves or talks, or of the style of a movie, book, etc that is done to make people laugh: *A local television reporter dubbed him StyroCop – a take-off on the movie 'RoboCop'.* | **do a take-off of/on sb** *Karen can do a hilarious take-off of Bette Davis.*

cost

RELATED WORDS

- reduce the price of something *see* **reduce (1, 7)**
- *see also* **pay, value, cheap, expensive, free, money**

1 what you have to pay for something

- cost
- price
- charge
- fee
- rate
- fare
- toll
- rent
- rental

cost /kɒst‖kɔːst/ [n C usually singular] the amount of money you have to pay for services, activities, or things you need all the time such as food and electricity: *We'll make sure you have the operation, whatever the cost.* | **+ of** *The cost of electricity has fallen in the last twelve months.* | *Internet banking will considerably reduce the cost of doing business.* | **high/low cost** *The high cost of health care in the US is causing a great deal of concern.* | **building/legal/transportation etc costs** *If you lose the case, you will face substantial legal costs.* | **cost of living** (=the amount of money you need for things such as food, clothes, or rent) *Many old people have to live in poverty because of the steady rise in the cost of living.* | **cut costs** (=reduce the cost of something) *IBM is continuing to cut costs in an effort to be more competitive.* | **at no extra cost** (=without having to pay more) *We will deliver and install your computer at no extra cost.* | **running costs** (=the amount of money that a business or organization regularly spends on things such as salaries, electricity, and rent) *£650,000 will be needed to cover the hospital's running costs during its first year.*

price /praɪs/ [n C/U] the amount of money you have to pay for something that is for sale, especially in a shop: *There's a great new clothes store on Main Street, and its prices seem very reasonable.* | **+ of** *What's the price of a pack of cigarettes nowadays?* | **high/low price** *Microsoft chairman Bill Gates said it was impossible to build a good computer for such a low price.* | **house/food/oil etc prices** *House prices rose by around 12% in the south-east last year.* | **charge a price** *They charge the same price for a take-away as they do for eating in the restaurant.* | **half price** (=half the usual price) *I bought these jeans half price in a sale.* | **reduce/cut prices** *Apple was forced to cut prices sharply, reducing its profit margin.* | **increase/raise prices** *The Japanese have raised prices just $8 a vehicle on average.* | **price rise** (=increase in the price of something) *Experts say they expect price rises to be gradual but persistent.* | **the asking price** (=the price that someone wants for something they are selling) *The asking price for the 60-acre estate in Atlanta is $27 million.*

charge /tʃɑːʳdʒ/ [n C] the amount of money that you pay for a service, or for being allowed to use something **+ for** *There's no charge for telephoning the operator.* | **bank/delivery/electricity etc charges** *If your order comes to over $30, we will not make a delivery charge.* | **admission charge** (=the amount of money you must pay to go into a public place) *There's an admission charge for adults, but children get into the museum free.* | **at no extra charge** (=without having to pay more) *Members and their guests are welcome to use the club's facilities at no extra charge.* | **additional charge** (=an amount that is added to the usual price) *An additional charge of 15% will be added to your bill for service.*

fee /fiː/ [n C] the amount of money that you pay to someone for a professional service, or the amount that you pay in order to do something **+ of** *Some actors can ask a fee of around $1,000,000 a movie.* | **charge a fee** *The doctor I saw charged a £100 fee for an initial consultation.* | **school/legal/medical etc fees** *An accident on vacation can cost you a lot in medical fees.* | **entrance fee** (=the amount of money you pay to go in somewhere) *The entrance fees to the park have gone up by 50%.*

rate /reɪt/ [n C] the usual cost of a service or job: *We are able to offer a whole range of services at very reasonable rates.* | **hourly/weekly/daily rate** *Our shop assistants are paid an hourly rate of £5.50* | **the going rate** (=the rate that people are willing to pay at the present time) *£150 is the going rate for tickets for the concert.* | **fixed rate** (=one that is always the same) *There is a fixed rate for the job, regardless of how long it takes.*

fare /feəʳ/ [n C] the cost of a journey on a bus, train, plane etc: *I had to walk home because I didn't have enough money for the fare.* | **coach/train/air etc fare** *How much is the train fare from Toronto to Montreal?* | *A one-week stay in Majorca costs $779 including air fare.* | **fare increases** *The biggest fare increases were on the Kansas City to Minneapolis line.*

toll /təʊl/ [n C] money that you have to pay in order to drive over some bridges or roads: *You have to pay tolls on many of the major roads in France.* | **toll bridge/road/lane** (=one that you have to pay to use) *In 1871 they built a toll bridge from the mainland to the island.*

rent /rent/ [n C/U] the amount of money that you pay to live in or use a place that you do not own **pay rent** *She pays £350 a month rent for a one-bedroomed apartment.* | **high/low rent** *Office rents are highest in the city centre.* | **put up the rent/raise the rent** (=increase it) *If my landlord raises the rent again, I'll have to look for somewhere smaller.*

rental /ˈrentl/ [n C usually singular] the amount of money that you pay to use a car, television, tools etc over a period of time: *The rental on the TV includes maintenance and repairs.* | **car/television/video etc rental** *Car rental is $200 a week and you need a clean driving licence.*

2 ways of saying or asking how much something costs

- cost
- how much
- be
- at a cost of
- set sb back
- be priced at
- sell for/go for
- fetch
- what's the damage

cost /kɒst‖kɔːst/ [v] if something **costs** £10, $100 etc, that is what you have to pay in order to buy it: *How much does a house like that cost in America?* | **cost £10/$20/a lot etc** *Tickets for the show cost £15 or £20.* | **cost sb £10/$20 etc** *I stayed in a hotel in Paris which cost me $150 a night.* | **cost a fortune** informal (=cost a lot of money) *Look at Frank's new Mercedes – it must have cost a fortune.* | **it costs £10/$20/a lot etc to do sth** *The Department of Education estimates that it will cost $17 billion to build the new schools.*

how much /ˌhaʊ ˈmʌtʃ/ [adv] spoken say **how much** to ask what the price or cost of something is: *That's a beautiful rug – how much did you pay for it?* | *By the way, how much does it cost to use the swimming pool?*

be /bi (*strong*) biː/ [v] if something **is** £100, $1000 etc, that is how much it costs – use this especially when you are asking or replying to a question about the cost of something: *'I like your new shirt – how much was it?' 'It was only fifteen pounds.'* | *I can't remember how much the flight cost. I think it was around $400.*

at a cost of /ət ə ˈkɒst ɒv‖-ˈkɔːst-/ [prep] if something is done, sold etc **at a cost of** a particular amount, that is how much it costs – used especially in news reports: *Surveys are being conducted in 10 European States at a cost of £50 million.*

set sb back /ˌset (sb) ˈbæk/ [phr v T] if something that you buy **sets you back** a particular amount of money, usually a large amount, that is how much it costs, especially when you think that it is very expensive **set sb back £200/$400 etc** *A good quality saxophone will set you back at least £1000.* | **set sb back** *If she's hoping to buy a new sportscar, it's going to really set her back!*

be priced at /biː ˈpraɪst æt/ [v phrase] if a product **is priced at** a particular price that is how much the person who makes or sells it has decided it should cost: *The book, which is priced at £38, will be available in the shops from September.* | *I watched a demonstration of their new cordless phone, priced at $350.*

sell for/go for /ˈsel fɔːʳ, ˈgəʊ fɔːʳ/ [phr v T] to cost a particular amount of money – use this especially when you think this is more than it is worth **sell for £400/$600 etc** *Clothes with designer labels sell for ridiculous prices nowadays.* | *Houses in this area are selling for over $400,000.* | **go for £100/$250 etc** *Watches like that are going for about £15 in the market.* | **go to sb for £100/$250 etc** *The painting finally went to a private collector for $60 million.*

fetch /fetʃ/ [v T not in progressive or passive] if something **fetches** a particular price, it is sold for that price or someone receives that amount of money by selling it, especially at a public sale **fetch £40/$500 etc** *It's a very old car, but I'm still hoping it'll fetch around £200.* | *Van Gogh's 'Sunflowers' was expected to fetch more than $20 million.*

what's the damage /ˌwɒts ðə ˈdæmɪdʒ/ British spoken use this to ask what the total cost of something is, especially a job someone has already done for you or something you have already received: *'The mechanic's just about finished working on your car, sir.' 'Thanks, and what's the damage?'*

3 to calculate how much something costs

- cost
- price
- estimate
- quotation

cost /kɒst‖kɔːst/ [v T usually in passive] to calculate the total **cost** of a plan or process – used especially in business contexts **be costed** *The project had been incorrectly costed and the money ran out before it could be completed.* | **get/have sth costed** *It would be a good idea to get the plan costed before presenting it to the board.*

price /praɪs/ [v T usually in passive] to decide how much a product should cost **be priced** *Porsche said its new 911 Carrera 4s would be very competitively priced.* | *Please get your fruit and vegetables weighed and priced before you take them to the checkout.*

estimate /ˈestᵻmᵻt/ [n C] a statement that says how much money it will probably cost to build or repair something: *The final cost was £2000 higher than the original estimate.* | **+ for** *I've asked the builders to give us an estimate for fixing the roof.*

quotation ALSO **quote** informal /kwəʊˈteɪʃən, kwəʊt/ [n C] a written statement of exactly how much money something will cost, especially a service: *Get a few quotations from different firms so that you can compare prices.*

4 to take or ask for an amount of money in return for something you are selling

- charge
- want £20/$40 etc for

charge /tʃɑːʳdʒ/ [v T] if someone **charges** an amount of money for a service or product, that is how much you pay for it: *Lawyers charge such high fees, but they never seem short of clients.* | **charge £5/$60 etc for** *My piano teacher charges £9 for a half hour class.* | *Small shops charge much higher prices for the same products.* | **charge sb £5/$60 etc** *The cheapest doctor we could find charged us four hundred francs for a five minute examination.*

want £20/$40 etc for /wɒnt ˌtwenti ˈpaʊndz fɔːʳ‖wɑːnt-/ [phr v T] informal to ask for or expect to be paid a particular amount of money for something that you are selling to another person: *I might be interested in your TV. How much do you want for it?* | *Bob said he'd give Frank private guitar lessons, but he wanted $60 an hour.*

count/calculate

RELATED WORDS

▸ *see also* **amount, number, cost, total**

1 to count numbers, objects etc in order to find the total

- count/count up
- add up
- keep track
- keep a tally of
- at the last count

count/count up /kaʊnt, ˌkaʊnt ˈʌp/ [v T] to find the total number of things or people in a group by counting them all: *Katherine counted her money. There was almost $50 left.* | *Count up the number of calories you have each day.* | *Count the kids as they get on the bus and make sure they're all here.*

add up ALSO **tot up** British informal /ˌæd ˈʌp, ˌtɒt ˈʌp‖ˌtɑːt-/ [phr v T] to put several numbers or amounts together and calculate the total **add up sth** *When we added up the receipts we realized we had spent too much.* | **tot up sth** *Just tot up the total and write it at the bottom.* | **add sth up** *Five percent may not sound like much but it's a lot of money when you add it all up.* | **tot sth up** *Tot the whole lot up to make sure you'll have enough money to pay.*

keep track ALSO **keep count** especially British /ˌkiːp ˈtræk, ˌkiːp ˈkaʊnt/ [v phrase] to keep a record, either on paper or in your memory, of numbers or amounts that increase over a period of time, so that you always know what the total is: *I don't know what the score was. I wasn't keeping count.* | **+ of** *She was trying to keep count of how many stations they'd passed.* | *He kept a notebook in the car to keep track of how much money he was spending on gas.*

keep a tally of /ˌkiːp ə ˈtæli ɒv/ [v phrase] British to keep a record of numbers that are to be added up, for example by writing or marking them on paper: *Steve kept a tally of the days he spent in prison by scratching marks on the wall.* | *The plastic rings help the sales assistants to keep a tally of the number of garments customers have taken into the changing rooms.*

at the last count British **/at last count** American /ət ðə ˌlɑːst ˈkaʊnt, ət ˌlɑːst ˈkaʊnt‖-ˌlæst-/ [adv] if there is a particular total **at the last count,** this is what the total was the last time anyone checked: *At the last count, only 18 Japanese firms were making car parts in America.* | *There are a lot of professional athletes living in the Orlando area – more than 100 at last count.*

2 to calculate an amount or price

- calculate
- work out
- make
- figure
- estimate
- assess

calculate /ˈkælkjᵿleɪt/ [v T] to find out how much

something will cost, how long something will take etc by using numbers: *Their accountant calculated the total cost of the project.* | **calculate how much/how many/how far etc** *I began calculating how long it would take to get to the airport if I left at 4:00.* | **+ that** *Sally calculated that she needed $300 to pay all her bills.* —**calculation** /ˌkælkjəˈleɪʃən/ [n C] a process by which you calculate a total, price, time etc: *NASA calculations put the cost of the space program at $118 billion.*

work out ALSO **figure out** American /ˌwɜːrk ˈaʊt, ˌfɪgər ˈaʊt‖ˌfɪgjər-/ [phr v T] especially spoken to calculate an answer, amount, price, or value **work/figure out sth** *I always use a calculator to work out percentages.* | *Has anyone been able to figure out the answer to number seven?* | **work/figure sth out** *'How much do I owe you?' 'I haven't worked it out yet.'* | **+ how much/how many/how far etc** *We need to work out how much food we'll need to take with us.* | *I spent all of last night trying to figure out how much this wedding is going to cost me.*

make /meɪk/ [v T not in passive] British informal to calculate a particular total **make it 250/20 kilos/$50 etc** *'How much do I owe you for the meal?' 'I make it $10.50.'* | *Will you count these figures again? I make the total 248, but Chris made it 249.*

figure /ˈfɪgər‖ˈfɪgjər/ [v T] American to calculate an amount: *He needs to sit down and figure out how many people are coming.* | *There has been criticism about the current method for figuring social security retirement benefits.*

estimate /ˈestəmeɪt/ [v T] to guess an amount, price, or number as exactly as you can: *Analysts estimate the business earned about $135 million last year.* | **+ that** *The police department estimates that the number of violent crimes will increase this year by about 15%.* | **estimate sth to be sth** *At that point, the public sector deficit was estimated to be around £45 billion.* | **estimate sth at sth** *Industry sources estimate the value of the ranch at $7 million.* | **+ how much/how many/how far etc** *Our staff will help you estimate how much fabric you will require.*

assess /əˈses/ [v T] to calculate what the value or cost of something is, especially before buying it or selling it: *This computer program will assess how much is spent on each student within the school.* | *I took the ring to a jeweller to have its value assessed.* | **assess sth at sth** *The total value of the paintings is assessed at $20 million.*

3 to say numbers in order

- count
- countdown

count /kaʊnt/ [v I] *Most children know how to count by the time they start kindergarten.* | **count to 3/10/20 etc** *Shut your eyes, count to twenty, then come and find us.*

countdown /ˈkaʊntdaʊn/ [n singular] when seconds are counted backwards to show how much time is left until something happens, especially when a rocket is sent into space: *NASA has stopped the countdown for the space shuttle mission because of technical problems.*

4 to add one number to another

- add
- add up to
- plus

add /æd/ [v I/T] to put two or more numbers together and calculate the answer **add sth and sth** *If you add 11 and 31, you get 42.* | **add sth to sth** *Add 10% to the total.* —**addition** /əˈdɪʃən/ [n U] when you add a number

plus /plʌs/ [prep] spoken use **plus** between numbers or amounts to show that you are adding one to another.: *Twelve plus eight is twenty.* | *The cost is £45 plus £5 for delivery.*

add up to /ˌæd ˈʌp tuː/ [phr v T] if amounts **add up to** a total, they are that total when added together: *Just 200 extra calories each day add up to one-half pound of extra body fat each week.* | *The three angles of a triangle always add up to 180 degrees.*

5 to take one number away from another

- take/take away
- minus
- subtract
- deduct

take/take away /teɪk, ˌteɪk əˈweɪ/ [v T/phr v T] especially spoken to take one number from another and calculate the answer **take sth (away) from** *If you take 37 from 94 you get 57.* | *Take 19 away from 48 and then add 15.*

subtract /səbˈtrækt/ [v I/T] to take one number from another and calculate the answer: *To convert the temperature into Celsius, subtract 32, then multiply by 5 and divide by 9.* | **subtract sth from sth** *Subtract 12 from 32.* —**subtraction** /səbˈtrækʃən/ [n U] when you subtract a number

minus /ˈmaɪnəs/ [prep] use **minus** between numbers or amounts to show that you are taking one figure from another: *30 minus 5 leaves 25.* | *Here's the twenty dollars I owe you, minus seven dollars for the movie.*

deduct /dɪˈdʌkt/ [v T] to take away an amount of money, points etc from a total, especially when following official rules or an official system: *Marks may be deducted for illegible handwriting.* | **deduct sth from sth** *Your employer will deduct income tax from your salary.* | *Your monthly repayments will be deducted from the total amount that you owe.*

6 to multiply one number by another

- multiply
- times

multiply /ˈmʌltəplaɪ/ [v I/T] to add a number to itself a particular number of times **multiply sth by sth** *If you multiply ten by seven you get seventy.* | **+ by** *To find the price in yen, you multiply by 86.* | **multiplied by** *11 multiplied by 10 is 110.* —**multiplication** /ˌmʌltəpləˈkeɪʃən/ [n U] when you multiply a number

times /taɪmz/ [prep] spoken use **times** between numbers or amounts to show that you are multiplying one figure by another: *Five times six equals thirty.* | *What is eight times twelve?*

7 to divide one number by another

- divide
- go into

divide /dəˈvaɪd/ [v I/T] to **divide** one number by another, usually smaller, number **+ by** *It is easier to divide by 10 than by 12.* | **divide sth by sth** *If you divide twenty by four, you get five.* | **divided by** *36 divided by 2 is 18.* —**division** /dɪˈvɪʒən/ [n U] when you divide a number

go into /ˌgəʊ ˈɪntuː/ [phr v T not in progressive or passive] if one number **goes into** a larger number a particular number of times, the larger number can be divided that many times by the smaller number: *13 goes into 78 six times.* | *How many times will nine go into eighty-one?*

8 to calculate or count something wrongly

- miscalculate
- miscount
- lose count
- overestimate
- underestimate

miscalculate /ˌmɪsˈkælkjəleɪt/ [v I/T] *We have too many chairs. I must have miscalculated.* | *The city miscalculated the cost of earthquake repairs for the Bay Bridge.* | **miscalculate how much/how many/how long etc** *Sorry we're late – we miscalculated how long it would take to get here.*

miscount /ˌmɪsˈkaʊnt/ [v I/T] to count something wrongly: *I thought everyone was here, but I must have miscounted.* | **miscount sth** *Census Bureau officials announced that they miscounted the nation's official population by 5 million people.*

lose count /ˌluːz ˈkaʊnt/ [v phrase] to forget how many things or people you have already counted, when you are counting a lot of things over a long period: *I've been trying to keep a record of how many tickets we've sold, but I've lost count.*

overestimate /ˌəʊvərˈestəmeɪt/ [v I/T] to wrongly guess an amount, price or number by making the total too high: *I made enough food for forty people but it looks like I overestimated.* | *A Harvard University survey found that Americans significantly overestimate the cost of higher education.*

underestimate /ˌʌndərˈestəmeɪt/ [v I/T] to wrongly guess an amount, price, or number by making it too low: *We saved about $1000 for our trip but we underestimated and may have to wait until next year to go.* | *Early mapmakers often underestimated the earth's circumference.*

9 a calculation

- calculation
- sum
- estimate
- estimated

calculation /ˌkælkjəˈleɪʃən/ [n C] *This type of calculation would take several hours without a computer.* | *According to our calculations, 2000 jobs will be lost.* | **do/make a calculation** *Mickey sat at the kitchen table doing calculations on a scratch pad.* | *Once all the necessary calculations have been made the experiment can proceed.*

sum /sʌm/ [n C] especially British a simple calculation, especially one done by children as an exercise in school: *It'll be quicker if I use a calculator for these sums.* | *We had to do some really hard sums today.*

estimate /ˈestəmət/ [n C] what you think the number, price, or value of something probably is, after calculating it quickly: *I'm allowing $300, but that's only an estimate.* | **+ of** *Officials said Huntcor's estimate of building costs was about $3 million more than expected.* | **rough estimate** (=not exact but good enough to be useful) *This proposal represents a rough estimate of the cost of materials and labor.* | **conservative estimate** (=an estimate that is probably too low, so you can be sure that the true amount will not be less than this) *The paintings have been valued at $3.5 million, which is probably a conservative estimate.*

estimated /ˈestəmeɪtəd/ [adj only before noun] **an estimated number/cost/value etc** a number, cost etc that is not exact but has been roughly calculated: *The tunnel is being constructed at an estimated cost of £15 million.* | *An estimated 1 million Irish people died from starvation and disease during the Famine.*

country

WHAT'S HERE

- **country/nation** see **1 to 12**
- **country/countryside** see **13 to 14**

country/nation

RELATED WORDS

- come from a country *see* **come from**
- leave a country *see* **leave**
- an area of a country *see* **area (17-18)**
- *see also* **land/ground, world**

1 a country

- country
- nation
- state
- power
- superpower
- land

country /ˈkʌntri/ [n C] a separate independent area of land whose people have their own government, president, king etc: *Brazil is one of the biggest countries in the world.* | *The northeast of the country will experience heavy rainfall and high winds.* | *Most people in this country are worried about the economy.* | **all over/all around the country** *Riots and demonstrations broke out all over the country after the assassination of Martin Luther King.*

nation /ˈneɪʃən/ [n C] a country considered especially in relation to its people and its social and economic conditions and structures: *Japan has become one of the richest nations in the world.* | *Representatives from the world's leading industrial nations will meet in Geneva.* | **+ of** *We are a nation of both great wealth and terrible poverty.*

state /steɪt/ [n C] a country considered especially as a political unit that has a particular type of political organization: *In 1830, Greece became an independent state.* | *The state of Israel was created in 1948.* | **a democratic/one-party etc state** (=with that type of government) *For more than 70 years, the former Soviet Union was a one-party state.* | **member state** (=a country belonging to an international organization) *the member states of the European Union*

power /ˈpaʊəʳ/ [n C] a strong country that is able to influence other countries politically or economically: *The western powers hardly knew how to react to this threat.* | *France was the only European power not to sign the treaty.* | **world power** (=having influence all over the world) *Germany's strong industrial base has helped maintain its status as a major world power.*

superpower /ˈsuːpəʳˌpaʊəʳ, ˈsjuː-‖ˈsuː-/ [n C] a nation that has very great military and political power: *The book traces the emergence of China as a superpower in the 21st century.*

land /lænd/ [n C] country – use this especially in stories and in formal speeches: *His travels in foreign lands provided him with the inspiration for many of his poems and songs.* | *Our story takes place in a far-off land, long, long ago.*

2 a country that is partly or completely controlled by another

▸ colony

colony /ˈkɒləni‖ˈkɑː-/ [n C] a country that has no independent government of its own and is controlled by another, more powerful country: *The United States was once a colony of Great Britain.* | *In 1980, the former British colony of Rhodesia gained independence as the Republic of Zimbabwe.* —**colonial** /kəˈləʊniəl/ [adj] *The people of Africa have successfully fought against colonial rule.*

3 land that belongs to a particular country

▸ territory ▸ soil

territory /ˈterɪtəri‖-tɔːri/ [n U] *Colombian guerrillas had reportedly been operating in Venezuelan territory.* | *Ecevit campaigned in May 1991 to have foreign troops removed from Turkish territory.*

soil /sɔɪl/ [n U] **on British/French/US etc soil** on land that belongs to Britain, France, the US etc – use this to talk especially about important events: *The treaty will be signed on US soil.* | *This was the first time that the Pope had set foot on Cuban soil.*

4 all the people who live in a particular country

▸ the people ▸ population
▸ the nation/the country

the people /ðə ˈpiːpəl/ [n singular] all **the people** of a country: *It was a fair election, the people have made their decision, and we must all accept it.* | **the American/British/Thai etc people** *UK Prime Minister Tony Blair said the British should stand shoulder to shoulder with the American people.* | **my/our people** *'Millions of our people are still victims of poverty,' said Mandela.* | **+ of** *To what extent did the people of Italy support the new government?*

the nation/the country /ðə ˈneɪʃən, ðə ˈkʌntri/ [n singular] all the people of a country, considered together as a group – use this especially to talk about important events that affect everyone in the country: *The President will make a radio broadcast to the nation this evening.* | *When Churchill died, the whole nation went into mourning.* | *The president seems to no longer care what the country thinks.* | *People think our country has lost its sense of purpose and direction.*

population /ˌpɒpjʊˈleɪʃən‖ˌpɑː-/ [n C usually singular] the total number of people who live in a particular country or the total number of a particular group of people: *In many Western European countries the population is no longer increasing.* | **+ of** *The population of Germany is about 80 million.* | **the Jewish/Russian/Asian etc population** *The country's Jewish population was angered by the prime minister's remarks.*

5 someone from a particular country

▸ citizen ▸ a native of
▸ national

citizen /ˈsɪtɪzən/ [n C] someone from a particular country, especially someone who has rights in that country, such as the right to vote and the right to live there permanently: *Noriko's a Japanese citizen, but her parents are originally from South Korea.* | *Fahd became a British citizen after living there for several years.* | **+ of** *Claire is now a citizen of the US.*

national /ˈnæʃənəl/ [n C] someone who is a citizen of a particular country – use this about someone who is living in another country **Polish/American etc national** *There are many Russian nationals living in Frankfurt.* | **foreign national** *During the war, foreign nationals were forced to leave the country.*

a native of /ə ˈneɪtɪv ɒv/ [n phrase] formal someone who was born in a particular country, used especially to talk about the life of a famous person who moved to another country **a native of Spain/France/Scotland etc** *Picasso was a native of Spain, although he spent much of his life in France.*

6 the legal right to live in a particular country

▸ nationality ▸ citizenship

nationality /ˌnæʃəˈnælɪti/ [n C/U] *The application form asks you to state your name, age, and nationality.* | **French/German/British etc nationality** *Despite being born in Germany, these children do not have an automatic right to German nationality.* | **dual nationality** (=nationality of two countries) *Jeanne has dual nationality because her mother is French and her father is English.* | **+ of** *The nationalities of the plane crash victims have not yet been released.*

citizenship /ˈsɪtɪzənʃɪp/ [n U] the legal right to live in a country, use this especially when this right is given to someone who comes from another country: *After five years in the US, foreign nationals can apply for full US citizenship.* | **grant sb citizenship** (=officially give someone citizenship) *Krebs was granted French citizenship in 1992.*

7 the country where you were born

▸ home country ▸ native land

home country /ˌhəʊm ˈkʌntri/ [n C] *Many of the refugees are keen to return to their home countries now that the fighting has stopped.* | *Jesper Parnevik became the first Swedish golfer to win a European Tour event in his home country.* | *After spending seven years in Japan, Claude returned to his home country of France.*

native land /ˌneɪtɪv ˈlænd/ [n C] formal or written the country where you were born: *Connery is a nationalist and fiercely proud of his native land.* | *Thousands of Irish families left their native land and went to America in search of a better life.*

8 having a great love of your country

▸ patriotic ▸ nationalistic

patriotic /ˌpætriˈɒtɪk◂, ˌpeɪ-‖ˌpeɪtriˈɑːtɪk◂/ [adj] *At Llewellyn's funeral service, she was remembered as a patriotic American who had served her country well.* | **patriotic duty** (=something you must do if you love your country) *Voting is part of your patriotic duty.* —**patriot** /ˈpætriət, -triɒt, ˈpeɪ-‖ˈpeɪtriət, -triɑːt/ [n C] someone who has a great love for their country: *De Gaulle will always be remembered as a great French patriot.* —**patriotism** /ˈpætriətɪzəm, ˈpeɪ-‖ˈpeɪ-/ [n U] great love for your country: *One of*

McCarthy's most evil tactics was to question the patriotism of his opponents.

nationalistic /ˌnæʃənəˈlɪstɪk◂/ [adj] someone who is **nationalistic** is very proud of their own country, but often has no respect for people from other countries because they believe that their own country is much better: *The senator's strong nationalistic views are frightening to many liberals.* | *As nationalistic feelings grew, life became increasingly difficult for immigrants.*

9 people who want their country or area to be independent

▸ nationalist

nationalist /ˈnæʃənəl̩ɪst/ [n C] *His father was a nationalist during the civil war.* | *Indian nationalists finally won independence for their country in 1947.* —**nationalist** [adj only before noun] *The Scottish Nationalist Party wants Scotland to be independent of the UK.* | *Nationalist candidates managed to win only one seat in the elections.* | *The newspaper has campaigned vigorously for the nationalist cause.* —**nationalism** [n U] nationalistic feelings: *The end of the Cold War was followed by an increase in nationalism in Eastern Europe.*

10 happening in, or relating to a particular country

▸ national ▸ internal
▸ domestic ▸ at home

national /ˈnæʃənəl/ [adj only before noun] happening in or relating to all of a particular country, not just part of it: *The national news comes on at 18:30.* | *Winners of the regional competitions compete in the national finals.*

domestic /dəˈmestɪk/ [adj only before noun] happening in or relating to your own country, not other countries **domestic issue** *The President's speech covered a range of foreign and domestic issues.* | **domestic market** (=when a company sells goods in the country where it is based) *Volkswagen produce cars both for the domestic market and for export.* | **domestic flight** (=within a country) *Security on domestic flights in the US has been stepped up considerably.*

internal /ɪnˈtɜːnl‖-ɜːr-/ [adj only before noun] **internal affairs/problems/matters** things that concern a particular country – use this especially to say that foreign countries should not become involved in them: *Each country has the right to control its own internal affairs.* | *Western countries have been accused of interfering in Brazil's internal problems.*

at home /ət ˈhəʊm/ [adv] events that happen **at home** happen within your own country and do not involve any other countries, used especially when you are comparing what is happening in your country with what is happening in foreign countries: *Sales of electrical goods have increased, both at home and abroad.* | *Shocked by the events at home, the president cut short his trip to Europe.*

11 belonging to, provided by, or involving a particular country

▸ national ▸ federal

national /ˈnæʃənəl/ [adj only before noun] *Alitalia is the national airline of Italy.* | *a national policy for energy* | *the National Museum of Film and Photography in Bradford*

federal /ˈfedərəl/ [adj only before noun] controlled by or involving the central government, rather than the governments of the separate states that make up a large country: *Medicaid is a large federal health care program for the poor.* | *Several federal officials have been charged with corruption.* | *Most people want to see new federal gun laws introduced.*

12 happening in or involving a lot of countries

▸ international ▸ multilateral
▸ multinational

international /ˌɪntəʳˈnæʃənəl◂/ [adj] *This is CNN, bringing you all the latest international news.* | *an international agreement on the disposal of toxic waste* | *The goal of the program is to increase international understanding and good will.*

multinational /ˌmʌltɪˈnæʃənəl◂/ [adj only before noun] **multinational company/firm/corporation etc** a big company that trades and employs people in several different countries: *The government is attempting to stimulate the economy by attracting multinational corporations.* | *Multinational companies have often been accused of employing cheap labour in developing countries.* —**multinational** [n C] *Several multinationals were fined for environmental pollution.*

multilateral /ˌmʌltɪˈlætərəl◂/ [adj only before noun] **multilateral agreement/treaty/negotiations etc** involving or done by the governments of several different countries: *EU ministers proposed a multilateral agreement on arms control.*

country/countryside

RELATED WORDS

▸ *see also* **land/ground, town, natural**

13 the area away from towns and cities

▸ the country ▸ countryside

the country /ðə ˈkʌntri/ [n singular] *They've gone to the country for the weekend.* | **in the country** *Clarisa didn't care for New York, she wanted to live in the country.* | *We've found a lovely little cottage in the country.* | *Living in the country, you feel much closer to nature.*

countryside /ˈkʌntrisaɪd/ [n U] use this especially when you are talking about the beauty or good qualities of this kind of area: *Somerset is famous for its rolling hills and beautiful countryside.* | **the countryside** *She went to an expensive girls' school situated deep in the heart of the countryside.* | **+ of** *The countryside of Tuscany is a wonderful landscape of fields and valleys, with many historic monuments.* | **the French/Sussex/German etc countryside** *The Provençal countryside provided the inspiration for many artists.*

14 in or from the area away from towns or cities

▸ country ▸ rustic
▸ rural

country /'kʌntri/ [adj only before noun] *It took us an hour to reach the farm house, driving along winding country roads.* | *Old country churches are a big tourist attraction.* | *Brattleboro offers all the pleasures of a small country town.* | *Umbria is a wonderful region where life is simple and the people are decent country folk.*

rural /'rʊərəl/ [adj usually before noun] use this especially to talk about social problems or conditions that exist in the country: *a rural development program* | *There continues to be a shortage of jobs for young people in many rural areas.* | *The committee will investigate ways of recruiting doctors and nurses for rural communities.* | *At that time, much of rural Ireland was desperately poor.*

rustic /'rʌstɪk/ [adj] use this especially to talk about things or people in the countryside that are interesting, attractive, or old-fashioned **rustic charm/beauty/simplicity** *American tourists are fascinated by the village's rustic charm.* | *The rustic beauty of the countryside attracted many prominent citizens to Marin County.* | **rustic scene** *The picture showed a typical rustic scene.*

court/trial

RELATED WORDS

▸ *see also* **crime, punish, accuse, prove, prison, law, judge, guilty, innocent**

1 the place where crimes or legal problems are judged

▸ court ▸ courtroom

court ALSO **courthouse** especially American /kɔːʳt, 'kɔːʳthaʊs/ [n C] a building where legal cases are officially judged: *A group of photographers and reporters gathered outside the court.* | *the United States Supreme Court* | **appear in court/appear before a court** *Benton appeared in court yesterday on three charges of assault.* | **go to court** (=officially ask to have a legal problem dealt with in a law court) *She says she will go to court to try to prove that she was unfairly dismissed from her job.*

courtroom /'kɔːʳtrʊm, -ruːm/ [n C] a room where legal cases are officially judged: *A fight broke out in a London courtroom yesterday.* | **packed courtroom** (=full of people) *Roberts told a packed courtroom of the events that occurred on the night of the murder.*

2 the parts of the legal process

▸ trial ▸ evidence
▸ case ▸ verdict
▸ charge ▸ sentence

trial /'traɪəl/ [n C] a legal process in a court, in which people try out find out whether or not someone is guilty of a crime: *The trial is due to take place next month at Wood Green Crown Court.* | **be on trial (for sth)** (=to be judged in a court) *A man from Seattle is on trial for the murder.* | **go on trial** (=to begin being judged in a court) *A man was due to go on trial at Liverpool Crown Court later today accused of murdering his wife.* | **awaiting trial** (=to be waiting for your trial to start) *Drake is in a federal prison in Houston, awaiting trial on charges of cocaine trafficking.* | **face trial** (=wait for your trial to start) *Perelli faces trial later in the year on corruption and perjury charges.* | **murder/rape/robbery etc trial** *On Tuesday, a judge rejected requests to televise the murder trial of Robert Caine.*

case /keɪs/ [n C] a particular crime or legal problem that is judged in court: *They lost their case in the High Court and had to pay damages.* | **murder/robbery/rape etc case** *Mathers called it the worst multiple murder case in the city's history.*

charge /tʃɑːʳdʒ/ [n C] an official statement made by the police, saying someone has done something illegal **criminal charges** (=official statements saying that someone has done something illegal) *Criminal charges were filed in October against Sorvino by the District Attorney's office.* | **file charges (against sb)** (=start a legal process against someone) *On Tuesday, the police officially filed charges against Jeffers.* | **murder/burglary/rape etc charges** *San Francisco police have arrested a 39-year-old man on murder charges.*

evidence /'evɪ̱dəns/ [n U] the information, objects, documents etc that are used in a court to help to prove what really happened in a legal case: *Prosecutors believe they have enough evidence to convict Smith.* | *The government's case was based on evidence gathered over a two-year investigation.* | *The evidence proves clearly and beyond a reasonable doubt that the defendant is guilty.* | **piece of evidence** *The most important piece of evidence, the murder weapon, has not been found.* | **give evidence** (=tell a court what you know about a crime) *His former girlfriend was called to give evidence.* | **give evidence against sb** (=tell the court things that help to prove someone is guilty) *Husbands and wives cannot be forced to give evidence against each other.*

verdict /'vɜːʳdɪkt/ [n C] the decision that a judge or jury makes about whether someone is guilty of a crime or not **guilty/not guilty verdict** *The jury's not guilty verdict was criticized all over the country.* | **reach a verdict** (=finally decide whether someone is guilty or not) *Jurors were unable to reach a verdict after deliberating two hours Friday afternoon.* | **return/hand down a verdict** (=officially say whether someone is guilty or not) *The judge will hand down a verdict in January, the newspaper reported.*

sentence /'sentəns/ [n C] the official punishment that someone is given by a judge when a court decides that they are guilty of a crime, especially a period of time in prison **a 7 year/6 month etc sentence** (=when someone has to go to prison for 7 years, 6 months etc) *Neale is finishing a three-month sentence for petty theft.* | **maximum/minimum sentence** (=the longest or shortest time that someone can be sent to prison for a crime) *If convicted of the charges against him, Blackburn could receive a maximum sentence of 30 years.* | **pass sentence** (=officially say what a criminal's punishment will be) *Judge Evans will pass sentence on the three men tomorrow.* | **life sentence** (=when someone is sent to prison for a very long time or for the rest of their life) *Croy is currently serving a life sentence for the 1992 rape and murder of an Iowa woman.* | **death sentence** (=when the punishment is death) *Richardson was convicted of murder and given a death sentence.*

3 the people in the legal process

▸ judge ▸ the accused
▸ jury ▸ the defence
▸ lawyer ▸ the prosecution
▸ defendant ▸ witness

judge /dʒʌdʒ/ [n C] the person in charge of a court, who knows a lot about the law and makes the official decision about what the punishment for a crime should be: *Everyone stood up as the judge entered the courtroom.* | *Judge Butler gave the defendant a six-month jail sentence.* | *The judge advised the governor that the law violated the First Amendment rights of teachers.*

jury /ˈdʒʊəri/ [n C] a group of ordinary people, who listen to the people speaking at a trial, and then decide whether or not someone is guilty of a crime: *The jury was made up of seven women and five men.* | *Have you ever been on a jury?* | *The jury awarded Hayes $3.5 million in damages.* | **jury duty/service** (=a period of time during which you must be ready to be part of a jury if necessary) *I have been called for jury duty twice.* | **hung jury** (=a jury that cannot make a decision about whether someone is guilty or not) *Broderick's first trial last year ended in a hung jury.* | **sit on a jury** (=be a member of a jury) *Are people with criminal records allowed to sit on a jury?*

lawyer ALSO **attorney** especially American /ˈlɔːjəʳ, əˈtɜːʳni/ [n C] someone who is trained in the law and who represents people in court: *You have to study for a long time to become a lawyer.* | *He refused to answer any questions until his lawyer came.* | **defence lawyer** British **/defense lawyer** American (=a lawyer who tries to prove that a person is not guilty of a crime) *Defense lawyer Charles Grieshammer said he was not surprised by the verdict.*

defendant /dɪˈfendənt/ [n C] the person in a trial who is being judged guilty or not guilty of a crime: *The defendant pleaded not guilty.* | *According to the defendant, the heroin was destined for the New York City area.*

the accused /ði əˈkjuːzd/ [n singular] someone who is trying to prove that they are not guilty of a crime that they are on trial for: *The accused is being held in the Pelham County Jail on charges of assault and battery.* | *According to the sixth amendment, the accused has the right to a fair and public trial.*

the defence British **/the defense** American /ðə dɪˈfens/ [n singular] the lawyers in a court who try to prove that someone is not guilty of a crime: *The defence plans to call only one witness to testify.* | *Today, the defence makes its final presentation to the jury.* | *Peres said the defense team would appeal the sentencing by Judge Bernardo Tirado.*

the prosecution /ðə ˌprɒsɪˈkjuːʃən‖-ˌprɑː-/ [n singular] the lawyers in a court who try to prove that someone is guilty of a crime: *The prosecution's first witness is expected to be one of the defendant's co-workers.* | *Speaking for the prosecution, Lipscomb said that both men should go to prison for the rest of their lives.*

witness /ˈwɪtnɨs/ [n C] someone who tells what they know about a crime in court: *Police have appealed for witnesses to come forward.* | *The witness was asked to identify the defendant in the courtroom.* | **call sb as a witness** *The congressman was called as a witness for the prosecution today.*

4 to bring someone to court to be judged

- prosecute
- put sb on trial

prosecute /ˈprɒsɪkjuːt‖ˈprɑː-/ [v I/T] to officially say that someone has broken the law and bring them to a court of law to be judged: *Shoplifters will be prosecuted.* | *The Prime Minister pledged to do everything possible to prosecute those who carried out the bombing.* | **prosecute sb for sth** *Baldwin was prosecuted in 1998 for distributing child pornography online.* | **prosecute a case** American *Last year, Napolitano's office prosecuted 115 child abuse cases, the highest number in the nation.* —**prosecution** /ˌprɒsɪˈkjuːʃən‖ˌprɑː-/ [n U] *Failure to pay the tax may result in prosecution and imprisonment.*

put sb on trial /ˌpʊt (sb) ɒn ˈtraɪəl/ [v phrase] to officially bring someone to a court of law to be judged: *A month after the murder, a man was arrested by police and put on trial.* | **+ for** *The couple were put on trial for fraud and found guilty.*

5 to be judged in a court of law

- be tried
- be on trial
- stand trial

be tried /biː ˈtraɪd/ [v phrase] *The suspect will be tried within the next few weeks.* | *Patterson is being tried for the murder of a 30-year-old Oakland hairdresser.* | **+ for** *The two women are being tried for drug smuggling.*

be on trial /biː ɒn ˈtraɪəl/ [v phrase] if someone is **on trial**, a court of law is trying to decide whether they are guilty or a crime or not: *Three men are now on trial after a series of terrorist attacks.* | *The accused was extradited to Miami earlier this year, and is currently on trial there.* | **+ for** *Three men are on trial for illegally smuggling tropical birds into the country.*

stand trial /ˌstænd ˈtraɪəl/ [v phrase] formal to be judged in a court of law: *The judge ruled that Pinochet was too ill to stand trial in Spain.* | **+ for** *Brady stood trial for the killings late last year.* | **+ on** *An employee of the bank is due to stand trial on embezzlement charges in February.*

6 when a legal case is judged in court

- come to trial
- come/be brought before the court
- be heard

come to trial /ˌkʌm tə ˈtraɪəl/ [v phrase] if a serious legal case **comes to trial**, it is judged in a court of law: *The case won't come to trial until next summer.* | *The British press is not permitted to comment on a case until it comes to trial.*

come/be brought before the court /ˌkʌm, biː ˌbrɔːt bɪˌfɔːʳ ðə ˈkɔːʳt/ [v phrase] if a legal case or a criminal **comes** or **is brought before the court**, they go to a court of law so it can be officially decided what further legal action should be taken: *He thinks his case will come before the court within the next few months.* | *The case was brought before the court by farmer Brad Morgan.*

be heard /biː ˈhɜːʳd/ [v phrase] if a court case, a problem, or a complaint **is heard**, a judge or lawyer listens to it to decide what legal action should be taken: *Last year 2,047 cases were heard in the Hillbrow small claims court.* | *Yesterday counsel for both parties agreed the case should be heard on March 12.*

cover

RELATED WORDS

- to deliberately hide facts or information *see* **hide (8-10)**

1 to put something over, on, or around something else

- cover/cover up
- put sth over
- wrap up/wrap
- coat

cover/cover up /ˈkʌvəʳ, ˌkʌvər ˈʌp/ [v T] to put something over, on, or around something else, in order to hide it, protect it, or improve its appearance: *Prepare the salad, and cover it until it's time to serve.* | **cover sth with sth** *She covered her face with her hands and ran upstairs.* | **cover up sth** (=cover something completely) *She always wears a lot of make-up to cover up her spots.* | **cover sth up** *They used special paint to cover up the cracks in the wall.*

put sth over /ˌpʊt (sth) ˈəʊvəʳ/ [phr v T] to put a cloth, piece of material loosely over the top of something in order to cover it: *The stewardess gave him a blanket to put over his legs.* | *Before you paint the walls, put some old sheets over the furniture.*

wrap up/wrap /ˌræp ˈʌp, ræp/ [v T] to put paper, plastic, cloth etc tightly around something in order to protect, decorate, or post it: *Have you wrapped up all your Christmas presents yet?* | **wrap sth (up) in sth** *Ruth caught a sea bass and wrapped it up in paper to bring home to her cat.* | *He wrapped the uneaten half of his sandwich in foil and put it in the refrigerator.*

coat /kəʊt/ [v T] to thinly cover the whole surface of something with something soft or liquid **coat sth with/in sth** *A special machine coats the nuts with chocolate.*

2 to be on top of something

- cover
- envelop

cover /ˈkʌvəʳ/ [v T] *Posters of Elvis covered practically the whole wall.* | *Tropical rain forests cover 7 percent of the world's surface.* | *As you can see from the weather map, huge rain clouds are completely covering the South East.* | *He was about fifty, with strands of fair hair covering a receding hair line.*

envelop /ɪnˈveləp/ [v T] written to cover something completely so that it is difficult to see or touch: *The mist and rain enveloped the forest so that we could only see the nearest trees.* | *At sunset, darkness enveloped the town.*

3 to be covered with something

- be covered in/with/by
- be coated in/with
- be encrusted in/with
- be plastered in/with
- be caked in/with
- be shrouded in mist/smoke etc

be covered in/with/by /biː ˈkʌvəʳd ɪn, wɪð, baɪ/ [v phrase] if something **is covered in**, **with**, or **by** something, it has that substance lying all over the top of it or spread all over it: *The ground was covered with snow.* | *Look at your clothes! They're covered in mud.* | *His face was covered by a thick black beard with tiny flecks of gray in it.*

be coated in/with /biː ˈkəʊtɪ̈d ɪn, wɪð/ [v phrase] if an object **is coated in** or **is coated with** a liquid or soft substance, it has a layer of that substance all over its surface: *Serve the chicken with new potatoes coated in butter.*

be encrusted in/with /biː ɪnˈkrʌstɪ̈d ɪn, wɪð/ [v phrase] especially written to be covered with something thick and hard that is difficult to remove: *He took off his gloves, which were deeply encrusted with dirt.* | **mud/dirt/blood etc encrusted** (=covered with mud, dirt, blood etc) *Evan reached into the pocket of his mud-encrusted jacket and drew out a map.*

be plastered in/with /biː ˈplɑːstəʳd ɪn, wɪð ‖-ˈplæs-/ [v phrase] to be covered thickly with something such as mud, especially in a way that looks unpleasant: *He looked at his garden tools, old and plastered with mud.* | *Her face was plastered in make-up.*

be caked in/with /biː ˈkeɪkt ɪn, wɪð/ [v phrase] to be covered with something thick and hard, especially mud: *The children were caked in mud from head to toe.* | *When the police found him, his shoes were missing and his hands were caked with dried blood.*

be shrouded in mist/smoke etc /biː ˌʃraʊdɪ̈d ɪn ˈmɪst / [v phrase] be covered and hidden in mist etc – used especially in literature: *I looked back, but the shore was shrouded in mist.*

4 something that is used to cover something else

- cover
- covering
- lid
- top/cap
- wrapper
- wrapping

cover /ˈkʌvəʳ/ [n C] a piece of paper, plastic, cloth etc that is used to **cover** something: *It's a good idea to buy a cover for your computer keyboard.* | *She took the card out of its plastic cover.* | **record/book/CD etc cover** *There were old record covers scattered all over the floor.* | **covers** (=the sheets, blankets etc on a bed) *Patrick threw back the covers and hopped out of bed.*

covering /ˈkʌvərɪŋ/ [n C/U] something that is used to cover a large flat area, especially in order to protect it from damage, dirt etc: *The insect's shell gives it a tough protective covering.* | *The prison cells have no electricity and no floor coverings.*

lid /lɪd/ [n C] a flat part that fits on top of a container, a pan, a box etc in order to close it: *a saucepan lid* | *Annie, do you know where the lid for the garbage can is?* | **+ of** *Sam lifted the lid of his desk and took out a calculator.*

top/cap /tɒp‖tɑːp, kæp/ [n C] a thing that fits on the top of a bottle, pen, or narrow container, that you press on or turn in order to close it: *Why don't you ever put the top back on the toothpaste?* | *I can't get the top off this bottle.* | *Remove the gas cap by turning it twice to the left and then back to the right.*

wrapper /ˈræpəʳ/ [n C] a piece of paper, or very thin plastic or metal, that covers food, chocolate etc when you buy it: *chewing-gum wrappers* | *The empty stadium was littered with burger wrappers and empty cans.*

wrapping /ˈræpɪŋ/ [n C/U] cloth, paper, or plastic that is wrapped around something to protect it: *He undid the ribbons and tore at the paper wrapping.* | *Torn Christmas wrapping littered the floor.*

5 a thin flat layer that covers a surface

- layer
- film
- coating

layer /ˈleɪəʳ/ [n C] a thin flat quantity of something that covers the whole of a surface **+ of** *A layer of dust covered everything in the room.* | *Sprinkle a layer of soil over the seeds.*

film /fɪlm/ [n C] a very thin clear layer, especially of something liquid, that has formed on a surface **film of oil/grease/sweat etc** *She wiped away the light film of sweat that had formed on her upper lip.*

coating /ˈkəʊtɪŋ/ [n C] a layer of a liquid or soft substance that has been put on the surface of something, for example in order to protect it or make it taste better: *Cassette tapes have a magnetic oxide coating.* | **+ of** *ice-cream with a thick coating of chocolate*

crazy

RELATED WORDS

opposite: ———————— **sensible, calm**

- someone who is mentally ill *see* **mentally ill**
- *see also* **angry, careless, strange, stupid/silly**

1 people

- crazy
- be nuts
- mad/barmy
- be insane/be out of your mind
- need your head examined/have taken leave of your senses
- nutty
- be out to lunch/be out of your tree
- flaky
- be one sandwich short of a picnic
- have a screw loose

crazy /ˈkreɪzi/ [adj] someone who is **crazy** does things that are extremely strange or stupid: *My dad told me I was crazy to leave my job.* | *You agreed to marry him? Are you crazy?* | *crazy drivers who cause accidents* | *His friends thought he was crazy when he told them he was going to spend his entire vacation exploring a cave.* | **completely/totally crazy** *Put that gun down! Are you totally crazy?* | **crazy to do sth** *You're crazy to lend him all that money – you'll never get it back.*

be nuts ALSO **be crackers** British /biː ˈnʌts, biː ˈkrækəʳz/ spoken informal to be crazy: *People will think you're crackers if you go around talking to yourself like that.* | *The guy's completely nuts! He goes around in nothing but a pair of shorts in the middle of winter.*

mad/barmy /mæd, ˈbɑːʳmi/ [adj] British spoken crazy: *You spent $190 on a pair of shoes? You must be mad!* | **completely mad/barmy** *Monica's new boyfriend is completely barmy. He calls her almost every day from Australia.* | **mad/barmy to do sth** *She's mad to turn down an offer like that.* | *I must have been mad to let myself become involved with someone like Dennis.*

be insane/be out of your mind /biː ɪnˈseɪn, biː ˌaʊt əv jɔːʳ ˈmaɪnd/ [v phrase] especially spoken you say someone is **insane** or **out of their mind** if they do something or intend to do something that is completely crazy: *Anyone who would take a boat out in this weather must be insane.* | *Tell the police? Are you out of your mind?*

need your head examined/have taken leave of your senses /ˌniːd jɔːʳ ˈhed ɪɡˌzæmɨnd, həv teɪkən ˌliːv əv jɔːʳ ˈsensɨz/ [v phrase not in progressive] say this when you think someone is crazy because they have done something that you do not approve of or agree with: *A man who would give his fourteen-year-old son a motorcycle has obviously taken leave of his senses.* | *If you ask me, anyone who believes in UFOs needs their head examined.*

nutty informal ALSO **dotty/batty** /ˈnʌti, ˈdɒti‖ˈdɑː-, ˈbæti/ [adj] British informal crazy – use this to describe someone, especially an old person, who behaves in a slightly strange but often amusing way: *Grandma can act kind of nutty at times.* | *My uncle frequently wore shoes which didn't match, and everyone thought he was a bit dotty.* | *Next door to us lived a batty old lady who used to have long conversations with her plants.*

be out to lunch/be out of your tree /biː ˌaʊt tə ˈlʌntʃ, biː ˌaʊt əv jɔːʳ ˈtriː/ [v phrase] informal someone who **is out to lunch** or **out of their tree** behaves in a strange, confused way and does not seem to know what is happening around them: *Our English teacher's really out to lunch – the class started five weeks ago and she hasn't even asked our names yet.* | *He is quoted as saying privately that he thinks the former prime minister is 'out of her tree'.*

flaky /ˈfleɪki/ [adj] especially American, informal someone who seems unable to think clearly or do what they should do, and behaves in a strange but often amusing way: *Christy was kind of flaky, but everyone liked her.* | *You couldn't trust Sam to do anything important. He was too flaky.*

be one sandwich short of a picnic ALSO **be a couple of cans short of a six-pack/be a few clowns short of a circus etc** /biː wʌn ˌsænwɪdʒ ʃɔːʳt əv ə ˈpɪknɪk, biː ə ˌkʌpəl əv ˌkænz ʃɔːʳt əv ə ˈsɪks pæk, biː ə fjuː ˌklaʊnz ʃɔːʳt əv ə ˈsɜːʳkəs/ strange and slightly crazy: *I always thought Toby was one sandwich short of a picnic. Do you remember how he would sometimes work naked in the garden?* | *Come on. Let's face it – nobody trusts the guy because he's at least one clown short of a circus.*

have a screw loose /hæv ə ˈskruː ˌluːs/ [v phrase] informal slightly crazy, often in an amusing way: *'Fernando can be really weird sometimes.' 'Yeah, he's got a screw loose, no question.'*

2 crazy things/ideas/situations

- crazy
- screwy
- insane
- madness/lunacy

crazy ALSO **mad** British /ˈkreɪzi, mæd/ [adj] especially spoken ideas, actions, or situations that are **crazy** or **mad** are not at all sensible and are likely to cause problems or danger: *Jade wants to build a swimming pool in the garden, which I think is a mad idea.* | *You see drivers do some crazy things.* | **it's/that's crazy** *It's crazy to have an expensive, elaborate judicial system handling parking tickets and minor traffic violations.* | *The farmers get more money from the government if they don't plant crops, and I think that's just crazy.*

screwy /ˈskruːi/ [adj] especially American, spoken crazy and making no sense, especially in an amusing way: *She has these screwy theories about how crystals can cure all kinds of illnesses.* | *Warren Brigs, president of the Illinois State Chamber of Commerce, calls the proposal a 'screwy idea'.*

insane /ɪnˈseɪn/ [adj] something that is **insane** is completely crazy, because it cannot possibly succeed or is very dangerous: *For some insane reason he decided to do the whole journey in one day.* | **it is insane to do sth** *It would be insane to try to go camping in this kind of weather.*

madness/lunacy /ˈmædnɨs, ˈluːnəsi/ [n U] behaviour that it is completely crazy: *Coppola's film shows the madness of war.* | **it's madness/lunacy** *They can't build a motorway through all that beauti-*

ful parkland – it's madness! | **it is madness/lunacy to do sth** *It is madness for a country to spend that much on its military.*

3 to start to feel crazy because you are extremely bored, worried, etc

- go crazy/go nuts/go mad
- go out of your mind/lose your mind
- go round the bend

go crazy/go nuts ALSO **go mad** British /ˌgəʊ ˈkreɪzi, ˌgəʊ ˈnʌts, ˌgəʊ ˈmæd/ [v phrase] informal to start feeling as if you are crazy, especially when you are in a very unpleasant or very boring situation: *I wouldn't last a month in a desk job. I'd just go crazy.* | *I'd go nuts if I had to get up that early every morning.* | *If the neighbors don't turn down that music, I'm going to go mad.*

go out of your mind/lose your mind /gəʊ ˌaʊt əv jɔːʳ ˈmaɪnd, ˌluːz jɔːʳ ˈmaɪnd/ [v phrase] to become unable to think clearly or sensibly, especially because you are extremely bored or worried: *If I have to wait in one more line, I'm going to go out of my mind.* | *I'm with the kids all day, and I feel like I'm losing my mind.*

go round the bend British **/go around the bend** American /gəʊ ˌraʊnd ðə ˈbend, gəʊ əˌraʊnd ðə ˈbend/ [v phrase] informal to start feeling as if you are crazy, for example because you have so much work to do, you are extremely worried about something, or you hate the situation you are in so much: *I had such a heavy workload last semester that I almost went round the bend.* | *We hadn't heard from our daughter in days, and we were practically going round the bend.*

4 to start to behave in a crazy and excited way

- go crazy/go nuts/go mad
- go berserk

go crazy/go nuts ALSO **go mad** British /ˌgəʊ ˈkreɪzi, ˌgəʊ ˈnʌts, ˌgəʊ ˈmæd/ [v phrase] to start behaving in a crazy, uncontrolled way, especially when you are very excited: *The fans went crazy when the band came onto the stage.* | *During Carnival the entire city goes crazy for a week.* | *As soon as the dog hears anyone at the door he goes completely nuts.* | *When Italy scored the winning goal the crowd went mad.*

go berserk /ˌgəʊ bɜːʳˈsɜːʳk/ [v phrase] to suddenly start behaving in an extremely wild, violent, and often frightening way: *When they tried to arrest him, he suddenly went berserk.* | *She went berserk and began shouting at everybody on the platform.*

5 to make someone feel crazy

- drive sb crazy/nuts/mad/insane
- drive sb round the bend/twist
- drive sb up the wall

drive sb crazy/nuts/mad/insane /ˌdraɪv (sb) ˈkreɪzi, ˈnʌts, ˈmæd, ɪnˈseɪn/ [v phrase] to make someone feel crazy or behave in a crazy way: *I've just got to get another job – this one's driving me nuts.* | *I can't wait to get my exam results. All this waiting is driving me insane.* | *I hate doing crossword puzzles – they drive me mad.* | *Those kids are enough to drive anyone crazy. I'll be glad when they go back to school.*

drive sb round the bend/twist /ˌdraɪv (sb) ˌraʊnd ðə ˈbend, ˈtwɪst/ [v phrase] especially British, informal if something such as a lot of work, worry, or doing something you hate **drives you round the bend** or **drives you round the twist**, it makes you feel completely crazy: *I have so much to do at the moment. It's driving me round the twist.* | *She was really glad when she gave up teaching. It was driving her right round the bend.*

drive sb up the wall /ˌdraɪv (sb) ʌp ðə ˈwɔːl/ [v phrase] to make someone feel crazy, especially by repeatedly doing something annoying: *Can you turn down that TV? It's driving me up the wall!* | *I love my husband, but he's driving me up the wall.*

6 a crazy person

- nut
- nutcase/loony
- maniac/lunatic
- nutter

nut /nʌt/ [n C] *A lot of people think he's a complete nut, but he's actually quite harmless.* | *The woman sounds like a real nut.* | **sb is some kind/type of nut** *He started asking me a lot of questions about my personal life. I think the guy's some kind of nut.*

nutcase/loony /ˈnʌtkeɪs, ˈluːni/ [n C] someone who behaves in a crazy and often amusing way and who has strange ideas: *Our old maths teacher was a real nutcase – he used to eat chalk because he said it was good for your bones.* | **a bunch of loonies** *In the 1960s, people thought that vegetarians were a bunch of loonies.*

maniac/lunatic /ˈmeɪniæk, ˈluːnətɪk/ [n C] especially spoken someone who behaves in a stupidly dangerous way: *Ken drives like a maniac.* | *Some lunatic threw a can of lighter fluid on the fire.*

nutter /ˈnʌtəʳ/ [n C] British informal someone who has strange ideas or who behaves in a strange and often frightening way: *Sometimes you get these nutters calling you at 3 o'clock in the morning.* | *Burns can be a nutter – especially when he's had a few drinks.* | **complete nutter** *He's a complete nutter. He's got no sense whatsoever.*

crime

RELATED WORDS

- against the law *see* **illegal**
- *see also* **kill, steal, attack, threaten, violent, court/trial, punish, suspect, accuse, guilty, innocent, prove, law**

1 a crime

- crime
- offence
- felony
- misdemeanor

crime /kraɪm/ [n C] an action that is against the law, for example stealing something, taking drugs, or deliberately hurting someone: *The number of crimes reported in the New York City area has decreased dramatically over the last ten years.* | **commit a crime** (=do something that is a crime) *Investigators believe that the crime was committed at around 7.30 p.m.* | **+ against** *He was sentenced to 25 years in prison for rape and other sexual crimes against women.* | **serious crime** *Not surprisingly, the police say that 50% of serious crimes are drug-related.* | **solve a crime** (=find out who did it) *The demonstrators called on the governor to make solving the crime a priority.*

offence British **/offense** American /ə'fens/ [n C] an action that can be punished by law: *Tarrant is now in jail for various offenses, including rape.* | **commit an offence** (=do something that is an offence) *Bates is being tried for offences committed in the early 1990s.* | **criminal offence** *Driving under the influence of alcohol is a criminal offense.* | *The bill seeks to make it a criminal offence to inflict cruelty on any animal.* | **serious offence** *Possession of an unregistered firearm is a serious offense.* | **minor offence** (=not very serious) *Hewson was arrested for a number of minor offences.* | **speeding/parking etc offence** *Speeding offences are usually punishable by a fine.*

felony /'feləni/ [n C] a serious crime such as murder or a violent attack – used especially in the legal system in the US: *Leach was charged with sexual assault, which is a felony in Connecticut.* | *Johnson was preparing his defense against felony charges of armed robbery and assault.* | **commit a felony** *She denied that she had committed any kind of felony.*

misdemeanor /ˌmɪsdɪ'miːnəʳ/ [n C] a crime that is not very serious – used especially in the legal system in the US: *By the time he was 14, Horowitz already had several misdemeanors on his file.* | *McFarlane pleaded guilty to four federal misdemeanor charges that he had lied to Congress.* | **commit a misdemeanor** *The court also processes cases of children and youth who have committed misdemeanors or felonies.*

2 crimes in general

- crime
- criminal
- delinquency

crime /kraɪm/ [n U] crimes in general – use this to talk generally about the reasons for **crime**, the problems it causes, and the number of crimes: *Crime is a complex social problem with no single cause or solution.* | *the growing problem of crime in the inner cities* | **violent crime** *Violent crime increased by 11% last year.* | **serious crime** *Increasing the number of patrol cars on the street has not had any effect on the level of serious crime.* | **petty crime** (=crime that is not serious) *Reynolds became involved in petty crime at a very young age.*

delinquency /dɪ'lɪŋkwənsi/ [n U] formal criminal behaviour that seems to have no reason, such as fighting or destroying things, especially when this is done by young people: *Delinquency and drug addiction are more common in areas of high unemployment.* | **juvenile delinquency** (=among young people) *The study clearly demonstrates the link between juvenile delinquency and child abuse.*

criminal /'krɪmɪnəl/ [adj only before noun] connected with crimes: *He denies that he was ever involved in any criminal activities.* | *an expert on criminal law* | **criminal charges** *The former president could face criminal charges.* | **criminal investigation** *Scottish police are carrying out a criminal investigation into the affair.*

3 someone who is guilty of a crime

- criminal
- lawbreaker
- offender
- felon
- delinquent
- wanted

criminal /'krɪmɪnəl/ [n C] someone who is guilty of a serious crime or of several crimes: *Grimes is considered to be one of the most dangerous criminals in the US.* | *Sending children to adult prisons just means they learn to be 'better' criminals from the adult inmates.* | **common criminal** (=not someone who commits crimes for political reasons or because of their principles) *The British government maintains that Donavan is a common criminal who should be brought to justice.*

offender /ə'fendəʳ/ [n C] someone who has broken the law and is punished for doing this: *The courts should impose tougher punishments on offenders.* | **young offender** British **/juvenile offender** American (=under 18 years old) *The committee will investigate more effective ways of dealing with young offenders.*

delinquent /dɪ'lɪŋkwənt/ [n C] someone, especially a young person, who is guilty of criminal behaviour such as fighting or destroying things: *He blames most of the town's problems on local delinquents.* | **juvenile delinquent** (=one who is still a child) *More than half of all juvenile delinquents currently in state institutions have disturbed family backgrounds.* —**delinquent** [adj only before noun] *delinquent children*

lawbreaker /'lɔːbreɪkəʳ/ [n C] someone who does something illegal – used especially in newspapers or on television: *The penalties must be severe enough to deter lawbreakers.* | *Police say lawbreakers are encouraged by the slowness of the judicial system.*

felon /'felən/ [n C] someone who is guilty of a serious crime – used especially in the legal system in the US: *Oakdale Prison holds over 600 dangerous felons.* | *Stevens said his plan would keep guns out of felons' hands.*

wanted /'wɒntɪd‖'wɑːn-/ [adj] someone who is **wanted** is being looked for by the police because they are thought to be guilty of a crime **+ for** *Richards is wanted for the murder of a security guard at the City Bank in December of last year.* | **most wanted man/criminal/fugitive etc** *The mass murderer known as the 'Yorkshire Ripper' was for a long time the most wanted man in Britain.*

4 a group of criminals

- gang
- organized crime
- ring
- underworld
- syndicate

gang /gæŋ/ [n C] a group of criminals who work together: *Warning: gangs of pickpockets operate in this area.* | *Police say an armed gang stole nearly $1.9 million in a bank robbery over the weekend.*

ring /rɪŋ/ [n C] a group of people who work together and organize an illegal trade, especially in something such as drugs or weapons: *Drug rings operate in most large cities of the world.* | *Corvino was the sixth member of the spy ring to be arrested for stealing high-tech secrets from several Silicon Valley firms.*

syndicate /'sɪndɪkɪt/ [n C] a large and powerful organization that controls illegal businesses and criminal activities: *The syndicates see these women as easy candidates to force into the sex trade.*

organized crime /ˌɔːʳgənaɪzd 'kraɪm/ [n U] large criminal organizations that plan and control serious crime such as robbing banks or selling drugs: *The police need more resources to combat organized crime.*

underworld /'ʌndəʳwɜːʳld/ [n singular] the group of secret organizations that plan and organize crime in a particular city: *Owen has been active in the Las Vegas underworld for years.* | *He's accused of having connections with Japan's criminal underworld.*

5 to do something that is a crime

- commit
- break the law
- get into trouble
- turn to crime
- have a criminal record

commit /kəˈmɪt/ [v T] **commit a crime/offence/murder etc** do something that is a crime, especially a serious or violent crime: *Brady committed a series of brutal murders.* | *Women commit far fewer crimes than men.* | *It now seems likely that Mason was sent to prison for an offence he never committed.*

break the law /ˌbreɪk ðə ˈlɔː/ [v phrase] to do something that is illegal: *I didn't realize that I was breaking the law.* | *Hamer acknowledges that what he did was wrong, but denies breaking the law.* | *Should journalists ever break the law in order to get a story?*

get into trouble /ˌget ɪntə ˈtrʌbəl/ [v phrase] to get into a situation in which you are blamed or punished for doing something illegal: *Logue got into trouble for drug violations.* | **+ with** *When he was a teenager, Wayne got into a lot of trouble with the police.*

turn to crime /ˌtɜːʳn tə ˈkraɪm/ [v phrase] to begin a way of life that involves crime: *He claims that when he could not find work, he was forced to turn to crime.* | *Kramer said that he turned to crime in a bid to pay off his debts.*

have a criminal record /hæv ə ˌkrɪmɪnəl ˈrekɔːd‖-ərd/ [v phrase] if someone has a criminal record, they have been found guilty of a crime in the past, and this information is officially recorded by the police or the courts: *A background check confirmed that he had a criminal record.* | *Loman has a lengthy criminal record.*

criticize

RELATED WORDS

opposite: —————— **praise, defend (3)**

- to angrily tell someone that they should not have done something *see* **tell sb off**
- *see also* **accuse, blame, complain, disapprove, judge, offend**

1 to say what you think is bad about someone or something

- criticize
- be critical
- be a critic of sb/sth

criticize ALSO **criticise** British /ˈkrɪtɪsaɪz/ [v I/T] *Stop criticizing my driving!* | *People are always criticizing the Royal family, but I think they do a good job.* | *Jackson declined to criticize his opponent, choosing instead to focus on his own message.* | *It's easy to criticize, but managing a football team can be an extremely difficult job.* | **criticize sb for doing sth** *The United Nations was criticized for failing to react sooner to the crisis.* | **criticize sb/sth as** *The President criticized the proposal as expensive and impractical.*

be critical /biː ˈkrɪtɪkəl/ [v phrase] to strongly criticize a plan, system, or way of doing something, especially when you give detailed reasons why you think it is wrong: *Don't be so critical – we're doing our best.* | **+ of** *Miller was critical of the way the company was managed.* | **be highly critical** (=very critical) *Environmental groups were highly critical of the government's new transportation policy.*

be a critic of sb/sth /biː ə ˈkrɪtɪk əv (sb/sth)/ if someone **is a critic of** the government, a person in authority etc, they regularly and publicly criticize them: *She is one of the most well-known critics of the American private school system.* | **be an outspoken critic of sb/sth** (=not afraid to critize strongly and publicly) *He is regarded as one of Congress's most outspoken critics of television violence.* | **be sb's greatest/biggest etc critic** (=criticize them more than anyone else does) *Mr Levy has established a reputation as the committee's biggest, most vehement critic.*

2 to strongly criticize someone or something

- attack
- slam
- pan
- tear sth to shreds
- pillory
- do a hatchet job on
- lay into

attack /əˈtæk/ [v T] to strongly and publicly criticize a person, plan, or belief that you completely disagree with: *Several actors have attacked proposals to cut the theatre's budget.* | **attack sb for (doing) sth** *Union leaders attacked management for eliminating employee health benefits.*

slam /slæm/ [v T] to criticize someone or something very strongly in a public statement – used especially in newspapers: *Sullivan never misses a chance to slam the tobacco industry.* | **slam sb for doing sth** *Police slammed drivers for ignoring safety warnings.*

pan /pæn/ [v T usually in passive] to strongly criticize something such as a film, play, or a performance by writing about it in a newspaper, talking about it on television etc: *The movie was panned by all the critics.*

tear sth to shreds /ˌteəʳ (sth) tə ˈʃredz/ [v phrase] to find a lot of faults in someone's ideas or arguments and criticize them very severely: *After the prosecutor had presented his case, the defence lawyer tore his arguments to shreds.*

pillory /ˈpɪləri/ [v T usually in passive] if someone is **pilloried**, they are criticized very strongly and publicly by a lot of people: *Harper was pilloried in the press after his team's sixth consecutive defeat.* | *Middleton suffered the ultimate humiliation of being pilloried by his colleagues in front of the television cameras.*

do a hatchet job on /duː ə ˈhætʃɪt dʒɒb ɒn ‖-dʒɑːb-/ [v phrase] informal to criticize every part of someone's character or work: *Field did a complete hatchet job on his former colleague at a cabinet meeting last week.*

lay into /ˈleɪ ɪntuː/ [v T] informal to criticize someone very strongly for something they have done: *The teacher really laid into us this morning – told us we'd all fail if we didn't start doing some work.* | **+ about** *You should have heard my wife laying into me about coming home late last night.*

3 to be criticized

- come in for criticism
- be under attack/fire
- get/take a lot of flak
- be open to criticism
- be in the firing line
- target

come in for criticism /ˌkʌm ɪn fəʳ ˈkrɪtɪsɪzəm/ [v phrase] *The unions came in for strong criticism from the government after the strike.* | *Caro came in for a* *lot of criticism for his biography of the late president.*

be under attack/fire /biː ˌʌndər əˈtæk, ˈfaɪəʳ/ [v phrase] to be severely criticized, especially in public: *Banks are under attack for their refusal to reduce interest rates on loans to small businesses.* | **come under attack/fire** *His theories came under attack from other scientists.* | *The police department has come under fire for the recent rise in violent crime.*

get/take a lot of flak /ˌget, ˌteɪk ə lɒt əv ˈflæk‖-lɑːt-/ [v phrase] informal to be criticized a lot for something: *Ferguson's been getting a lot of flak for the team's poor performance recently.* | *The immigration department is taking a lot of political flak for not moving faster to help the refugees.*

be open to criticism /biː ˌəʊpən tə ˈkrɪtɪsɪzəm/ [v phrase] if someone or something **is open to criticism**, there are good reasons for criticizing them: *The general is open to criticism for his handling of the war.* | *Current reforms in the legal system may be open to criticism if they appear to be undemocratic.*

be in the firing line British **/be on the firing line** American /biː ɪn ðə ˈfaɪərɪŋ laɪn, biː ɒn ðə ˈfaɪərɪŋ laɪn/ [v phrase] to be the person who is most likely to be criticized for something, even if you are not the only person who is responsible for it: *As head of the police department, Hall is constantly on the firing line.* | *When you're in the firing line, it's tempting to avoid making difficult decisions.*

target /ˈtɑːʳgɪt/ [n C] an organization, person in authority etc that is criticized, especially by a lot of people **+ of** *Kay was the target of a noisy demonstration in which 54 people were arrested.* | **+ for** *The Communist Party has become the main target for critical attack among left-wing intellectuals.*

4 to criticize someone or something unfairly

- find fault with
- pick holes in
- knock
- put down
- slag off
- bitch about
- get at
- nit-picking

find fault with /ˌfaɪnd ˈfɔːlt wɪð/ [v phrase] to criticize things that are wrong with someone or something, especially small and unimportant things: *No-one enjoys working for a boss who always finds fault with their work.* | **find fault with sb for sth** *The report found fault with the police department for its handling of the case.*

pick holes in /ˌpɪk ˈhəʊlz ɪn/ [v phrase] especially British, informal to criticize small details in someone's ideas or plans – use this about someone who seems to be deliberately looking for problems and mistakes: *As soon as she stopped talking, Janet's colleagues began to pick holes in the idea.*

knock /nɒk‖nɑːk/ [v T] to criticize someone, their work, or their performance in an unfair and annoying way: *It's hard to knock Gordon because he always works so hard.* | *Critics knocked his latest film for its portrayal of women.* | **don't knock it!** *Hey, don't knock it! It's the only suit I've got!*

put down /ˌpʊt ˈdaʊn/ [phr v T] to make someone feel unimportant or stupid especially by criticizing them in public **put down sb** *Television programs always seem to put down people from the South.* | **put sb down** *She enjoys putting me down in front of other people.*

slag off /ˌslæg ˈɒf/ [phr v T] British informal to criticize someone, especially in a nasty and unfair way **slag off sb** *She spent the whole evening slagging off her ex-boyfriend.* | **slag sb off** *When the team isn't winning everyone starts slagging them off.*

bitch about /ˈbɪtʃ əbaʊt/ [v phrase] informal to make nasty remarks about someone when that person is not there: *People in our office are always bitching about each other.*

get at /ˈget æt/ [phr v T] informal to keep criticizing someone by making remarks about their behaviour or habits, especially in an unkind or annoying way: *I try not to take it personally – he gets at everyone on the team.* | **+ about** *My mother keeps getting at me about the state of my room.*

nit-picking /ˈnɪt ˌpɪkɪŋ/ [n U] informal the annoying habit of criticizing someone about unimportant details, especially in someone's work: *I've had enough of your constant nit-picking. Why can't you say something encouraging?* —**nitpicking** [adj only before noun] *nitpicking remarks*

5 something you say or write in order to criticize

- criticism
- attack
- slur
- put-down

criticism /ˈkrɪtɪsɪzəm/ [n C/U] what you say or write when you criticize someone or something: *Bill's very sensitive to any kind of criticism.* | **+ of** *The report makes many criticisms of the nation's prison system.* | **severe/strong criticism** *The government faces severe criticism for its slow response to the disaster.* | **come in for criticism** (=be criticized) *Taylor has come in for a lot of criticism for his part in the affair.*

attack /əˈtæk/ [n C] a statement that criticizes someone publicly, especially in politics or business **+ on** *O'Brien promised to continue his attacks on the film industry.* | **come under attack from sb** (=be criticized by someone) *Once again the oil companies have come under attack from environmentalists.* | **launch an attack on sb/sth** *France launched a bitter attack on EU proposals to reduce farm subsidies.*

slur /slɜːʳ/ [n C] unfair criticism that reduces the good opinion that people have about someone: *Your accusation of bribe-taking is a slur which I shall never forgive.*

put-down /ˈpʊt daʊn/ [n C] spoken informal something that someone says to someone, especially when other people are there, that criticizes them and makes them feel stupid or unimportant: *She was a master of the sarcastic put-down.* | *I didn't mean it as a put-down but I could tell from her response that she took my criticism personally.*

6 intended to criticize someone or something

- critical
- scathing
- negative

critical /ˈkrɪtɪkəl/ [adj] a **critical** statement, report, or description criticizes someone or something: *Critical remarks by a teacher can damage the confidence of children.* | **highly critical** (=very critical) *The government has just published a highly critical report on the state of the education system.*

scathing /ˈskeɪðɪŋ/ [adj] criticizing someone or something very strongly, because you think they are completely wrong or of very low quality **scathing attack/comments/report etc** *Her new book* *is a scathing attack on American imperialism in Central America.* | *The health department issued a scathing report on conditions in local hospitals.* | **+ about** *'The New York Times' was particularly scathing about his performance.*

negative /ˈnegətɪv/ [adj] a **negative** comment, report etc is intended to criticize someone or something, especially in a way that is unnecessary or unfair; a **negative** person has a tendency to criticize or complain about everything, especially when this is annoying or unfair: *The portrayal of working women in the media tends to be very negative.* | *You shouldn't let his negative comments get you down – he doesn't know what he's talking about.* | *I wish you'd stop being so negative all the time!*

7 someone who criticizes

- critic

critic /ˈkrɪtɪk/ [n C] someone who criticizes someone or something especially in public: *The Prime Minister answered his critics in a televised speech.* | **+ of** *Daley accused critics of the city's Police Department of lying.*

crowd

RELATED WORDS

- when there are a lot of people travelling, shopping etc *see* **busy/not busy**
- *see also* **full (5)**

1 a large number of people together in a public place

- crowd
- horde/hordes
- mob
- mass
- swarm
- throng
- the crush

crowd /kraʊd/ [n C] a large number of people together in one place: *I don't go to football games because I don't like big crowds.* | **+ of** *a crowd of angry protesters* | **crowds of people/visitors/tourists etc** *The exhibition is expected to attract large crowds of visitors.*

horde/hordes /hɔːʳd, hɔːʳdz/ [n C] a large crowd of people who are behaving in a way that you disapprove of or that annoys you **+ of** *She was chased down the steps of the courthouse by a horde of reporters and camera crews.* | *This time of year is perfect to visit New York because it isn't overrun with the hordes of tourists.*

mob /mɒb‖mɑːb/ [n C] a crowd of noisy and violent people who are difficult to control: *The mob set fire to cars and buildings.* | **+ of** *A mob of fans caused millions of pounds worth of damage in the area surrounding the stadium.*

mass /mæs/ [n singular] a very large crowd which is not moving and which is very difficult to move through **+ of** *A mass of people stood before the courthouse.* | **seething mass** (=when there are far too many people all pushing and trying to go somewhere) *The bus station was a seething mass of people.*

swarm /swɔːʳm/ [n C] a large crowd of people who are moving quickly in many directions in a very uncontrolled way **+ of** *Outside the school a swarm of small children ran around shouting and laughing.*

throng /θrɒŋ‖θrɔːŋ/ [n C] a very large crowd: *The throng greeted Sutter with cheers and applause.* | **+ of** *a throng of reporters* | *Animals and carts moved along the dusty road with the throng of refugees.*

the crush /ðə ˈkrʌʃ/ [n singular] a crowd of people who are all pressed close together so that it is very difficult to move between them: *Unable to get out of the crush, Chris began to panic.* | *A number of people fainted in the crush.* | *There was chaos as people tried to escape the flames and two children were badly injured in the crush.*

2 when a place is full of people

- crowded
- packed
- overcrowded
- be swarming with
- teeming

crowded /ˈkraʊdɪ̈d/ [adj] so full of people that it is difficult to move or find a place to sit or stand: *The train was really crowded.* | *a crowded elevator* | **+ with** *It was two weeks before Christmas and the mall was crowded with shoppers.*

packed ALSO **packed out** /pækt, ˌpækt ˈaʊt/ [adj] informal so full of people that there is almost no space left: *The club is so popular that it's usually packed by 9 o'clock.* | **+ with** *St Peter's Square was packed with tourists.* | **jam-packed** (=completely full) *The football ground was absolutely jam-packed.*

overcrowded /ˌəʊvəʳˈkraʊdɪ̈d◂/ [adj] a place that is **overcrowded** has too many people in it and is unpleasant and uncomfortable: *The buses are filthy and overcrowded.* | *overcrowded prisons*

be swarming with /biː ˈswɔːʳmɪŋ wɪð/ [v phrase] if a place **is swarming with** people it is so crowded with them that it is difficult to move around – use this especially when a place is full of people you disapprove of or when you are annoyed that a place is so crowded: *The place was swarming with noisy schoolkids.*

teeming /ˈtiːmɪŋ/ [adj] very full of people and activity: *the teeming streets of Cairo* | **+ with** *It was the start of the new semester, and the campus was teeming with students.*

3 when a crowd fills a place

- crowd
- fill
- mill around/about
- swarm

crowd /kraʊd/ [v I/T] if people **crowd** a place, they fill it and move around in it: *Shoppers crowded the town market.* | **+ around** ALSO **round** British *A large group of people crowded around the screaming child.* | *Fans crowded around the rear entrance of the concert hall, hoping to catch a glimpse of the band.*

fill /fɪl/ [v T] if a lot of people **fill** a place, there are so many of them that there is no room left for any more: *An audience of over 5,000 had filled the hall that night.* | *Visitors fill Brighton's streets during the summer.*

mill around/about /ˌmɪl əˈraʊnd, əˈbaʊt/ [phr v I] if a lot of people **mill around**, they move around a place in different directions, without any particular aim, especially while waiting for something: *People were milling around in the corridor, waiting for the show to start.* | *About 40 onlookers milled about while detectives examined the scene.*

swarm /swɔːʳm/ [v I] if a lot of people, especially people that you do not like or approve of, **swarm**

around a particular place, they fill it and move around it **+ across/along etc** *Every day tourists swarm through the narrow streets of the old city.* | *Hundreds of troops swarmed across the border.*

4 when people come together to make a crowd

- gather
- form
- congregate
- converge
- collect

gather /ˈgæðəʳ/ [v I] if people **gather**, they meet or come together and form a crowd: *By the time the president arrived, a large crowd had gathered.* | **+ around/at/in etc** *Angry workers were gathering on the steps of City Hall.* | *A crowd gathered around to watch the fight.*

form /fɔːʳm/ [v I] if a crowd **forms**, more and more people join a group of people who are already watching or listening to something: *A crowd was beginning to form at the scene of the accident.*

congregate /ˈkɒŋgrɪgeɪt‖ˈkɑːŋ-/ [v I] if people **congregate** in a particular place, a large number of them meet there, especially regularly in the same place, and at the same time **+ at/in/around etc** *On Friday evening, teenagers congregate outside the bars on Greene Street.* | *Marchers were due to congregate at Market Square for an open-air meeting.*

converge /kənˈvɜːʳdʒ/ [v I] formal if groups of people **converge** in a particular place, they come there from many different places and meet together with others to form a large crowd, in order to do something or go somewhere **+ on** *The two groups of demonstrators converged on Hyde Park.* | *About 20,000 motorcyclists will converge on Milwaukee this weekend, to celebrate the 90th birthday of the Harley Davidson bike company.*

collect /kəˈlekt/ [v I] if a crowd **collects**, people gradually come together so that there is a crowd, usually because they stop to watch or listen to something: *An hour or so before the press conference, a crowd began to collect outside the building.* | *A crowd was starting to collect outside the theatre to await the arrival of the prime minister.*

5 when a crowd separates

- disperse
- break up
- thin out
- melt away

disperse /dɪˈspɜːʳs/ [v I] if a crowd **disperses**, people begin to move away from it: *Once the ambulance had left, the crowd began to disperse.*

break up /ˌbreɪk ˈʌp/ [phr v T] if a crowd **breaks up**, people start to leave and move away in small groups: *When the police arrived, the crowd broke up very quickly.*

thin out /ˌθɪn ˈaʊt/ [phr v I] if a crowd **thins out**, people gradually leave so that there are fewer of them in the crowd: *By midnight, the crowds outside the concert hall were beginning to thin out.* | *I decided to wait until the crowd thinned out a bit before trying to leave.*

melt away /ˌmelt əˈweɪ/ [phr v I] if a crowd **melts away**, the people leave gradually and quietly, hoping that no one will notice: *The excitement of the arrest was over and the crowd began to melt away.*

6 to make a crowd separate

- disperse
- break up

disperse /dɪˈspɜːʳs/ [v T] if the police or the army **disperses** a crowd, they make it separate, and people leave in different directions: *National Guard troops were called in to disperse the crowd.*

break up /ˌbreɪk ˈʌp/ [v T] if someone, especially the police, **breaks up** a crowd, they make it separate, and people go away in small groups: *The police had to use tear gas to break up the protest.*

cruel

RELATED WORDS

opposite: **kind**

- to treat someone badly and use them for your own advantage *see* **use (20-21)**
- *see also* **unkind, violent, bad, strict/not strict**

1 words for describing people who are cruel

- cruel
- ruthless
- heartless
- tyrannical
- sadistic
- sadist
- bully
- tyrant

cruel /ˈkruːəl/ [adj] someone who is **cruel** deliberately causes pain or makes people suffer: *Children can sometimes be very cruel.* | *Brand was a cruel and intimidating man who abused his children and his wife.* | **+ to** *Her parents were very cruel to her when she was young.* —**cruelly** [adv] *The prisoners were so cruelly beaten that some even died in captivity.*

ruthless /ˈruːθləs/ [adj] so determined to get what you want that you do not care how much you harm other people: *These men are ruthless terrorists and will kill anyone who tries to stop them.* | *Father could be quite ruthless about getting his own way.* | *the ruthless dictator, Joseph Stalin* —**ruthlessly** [adv] *All political opponents were ruthlessly executed.*

heartless /ˈhɑːʳtləs/ [adj] not feeling any pity and not caring about other people or their problems: *How can you be so heartless?* | *In his autobiography, he portrays his father as cold and heartless.* | *She was a heartless, money-grabbing woman who made her fortune from the misery and desperation of others.*

tyrannical /tɪˈrænɪkəl/ [adj] using your power to cruelly force other people to do what you want: *Lewis was a tyrannical boss who frightened and humiliated his employees.* | *Thousands of refugees fled the tyrannical regime in search of political freedom.*

sadistic /səˈdɪstɪk/ [adj] someone who is **sadistic** gets pleasure from making other people suffer: *The principal was a sadistic man who enjoyed tormenting his students.* | *In the film, Khan portrays a murderer who gets a deep sadistic thrill out of killing.* | *'I'm afraid you will never see your children again,' he said with a sadistic smile.* —**sadistically** [adv] *The man was taken deep into a Mississippi forest by a local gang and sadistically murdered.*

sadist /ˈseɪdɪst/ [n C] someone who enjoys being cruel to other people: *Andrea's father was an absolute sadist. It's not surprising she hates him.*

bully /ˈbʊli/ [n C] someone who uses their authority or strength to frighten or hurt someone who is weaker: *A group of kids stood by and watched the school bully beat up a smaller boy.* | *Critics describe the mayor as an arrogant bully who hates to be contradicted.*

tyrant /'taɪərənt/ [n C] someone in a position of power who treats other people very cruelly: *She was a tyrant who had absolutely no tolerance for mistakes.*

2 cruel behaviour/punishments/ treatment

- cruel
- barbaric
- inhuman
- inhumane
- cold-blooded
- in cold blood

cruel /'kruːəl/ [adj] intended to upset someone or make them suffer: *Lyle was always playing cruel jokes on his little sister.* | *The electric chair is possibly the cruellest method of execution.* | **it is cruel to do sth** *I think it's cruel to keep dogs locked up inside all day.*

barbaric /bɑːʳ'bærɪk/ [adj] extremely cruel, in a way that shocks people: *We consider the death penalty to be barbaric.* | *the barbaric treatment of civilians in the concentration camps*

inhuman /ɪn'hjuːmən/ [adj] very cruel and not showing any of the pity or concern that normal people feel when they see other people suffering: *The prison conditions in this country are inhuman.* | *The government has been accused of using artificial and inhuman criteria to decide which refugees should be deported.*

inhumane /ˌɪnhjuː'meɪn/ [adj] **inhumane treatment/conditions/methods etc** actions or conditions that are not considered acceptable because they cause too much suffering: *Amnesty International is protesting against the inhumane treatment of these political prisoners.* | *This method of slaughtering chickens is now regarded by many as inhumane.*

cold-blooded /ˌkəʊld 'blʌdɪ̇d◂/ [adj usually before noun] **cold-blooded murder/killing/attack** a murder etc done without showing any feeling or pity for the person who is attacked: *The entire nation has been shocked by the cold-blooded murder of the two girls.*

in cold blood /ɪn ˌkəʊld 'blʌd/ [adv] if you kill someone **in cold blood**, you kill them in a cruel and deliberate way without showing any emotion: *The killers hunted Pedro down like an animal and murdered him in cold blood.*

3 deliberately cruel in order to upset someone

- malicious
- spiteful
- spite
- vindictive

malicious /mə'lɪʃəs/ [adj] deliberately cruel and unkind to someone because you really want to upset them and enjoy doing so: *Miss Simms took a malicious pleasure in other people's misfortunes.* | *Mr Jameson dismissed the allegations as malicious rumours.* | *Nixon's family called Stone's depiction of the late President 'erroneous and malicious'.* —**maliciously** [adv] *Beatrice maliciously delighted in Catherine's dismay.* —**malice** /'mælɪ̇s/ [n U] *Heard told the court that he had acted out of love and not malice.* | *'I see,' she said, and her small eyes glimmered with malice.*

spiteful /'spaɪtfəl/ [adj] deliberately nasty to someone in order to hurt or upset them, especially because you are jealous of them or are angry with them: *On the rare occasions when he was angry, Lowry could be spiteful and petty.* | **+ to** *You shouldn't be so spiteful to your sister.* | *I tried to like Julie but I couldn't forget how spiteful she'd been to me in the past.* —**spitefully** [adv] *'Doreen never liked you,' Rob said spitefully.*

spite /spaɪt/ [n U] a feeling of wanting to hurt or upset other people by saying or doing cruel things, especially if you feel jealous or think you have been unfairly treated: *Gerald's feelings of injustice turned to bitterness and spite.* | **pure/sheer spite** (=spite and nothing else) *Ignore what Martin says. It's pure spite.* | **out of spite** (=because of spite) *She quit college and worked as a waitress out of spite towards her parents.*

vindictive /vɪn'dɪktɪv/ [adj] deliberately cruel and unfair because you want to harm someone who has harmed you: *'I'll pay her back for this.' 'Don't be so vindictive. It doesn't help anyone.'* | *Doug could be nasty and vindictive when he was drinking.* —**vindictiveness** [n U] *Tom's generosity to his friends was matched by vindictiveness to those who fell out of his favour.*

4 cruel behaviour

- cruelty
- abuse
- bullying
- mistreatment/ ill-treatment/ maltreatment
- persecution
- atrocities
- sadism
- inhumanity

cruelty /'kruːəlti/ [n U] cruel treatment or behaviour: *What kind of person could treat a fellow human being with such cruelty?* | *Her black eye and bruises were undeniable evidence of his cruelty.* | **+ to** *Burnett has campaigned against cruelty to animals for more than 20 years.*

abuse /ə'bjuːs/ [n U] deliberately cruel treatment of someone, especially someone in your family that you are supposed to care for: *Doctors believed that there was no evidence of abuse, despite the woman's claims.* | **child abuse** (=cruel treatment of children) *There has been an increase in the number of cases of child abuse.* | **sexual abuse** (=when someone forces another person to take part in sexual activities) *a victim of sexual abuse*

bullying /'bʊliɪŋ/ [n U] cruel treatment of someone who is smaller, younger, or weaker – use this especially about children being cruel to other children: *The government has become involved in the effort to solve the problem of bullying in schools.*

mistreatment/ill-treatment/maltreatment /mɪs'triːtmənt, ɪl 'triːtmənt, mæl'triːtmənt/ [n U] cruel treatment of people or animals, especially those you have some control over: *There can be no good reason for the ill-treatment of factory-farm animals.* | *Jailers singled out certain prisoners for maltreatment.* | *There can be no excuse for the mistreatment of people seeking asylum in this country.*

persecution /ˌpɜːʳsɪ̇'kjuːʃən/ [n U] cruel treatment of people because of their religious or political beliefs, or because of the race they belong to: *Many Jews fled to America to escape persecution in Europe.* | *Katya asked the United States to protect her from persecution in her home country.* | **+ of** *the relentless persecution of American Communists in the 1950s*

atrocities /ə'trɒsɪ̇tiz‖ə'trɑː-/ [n plural] extremely cruel and shocking actions against people, especially during a war: *Survivors from the concentration camps had witnessed unspeakable atrocities.* | **commit atrocities** *Retreating soldiers told stories of awful atrocities committed by the enemy.*

sadism /ˈseɪdɪzəm/ [n U] taking pleasure in cruel acts: *Sadism may stem from a desire to dominate.* | *Mzukwa grew quiet as he recalled the brutality and sadism of the prison guards.*

inhumanity /ˌɪnhjuːˈmænəti/ [n U] cruelty that includes violence and a complete lack of sympathy for people's suffering: *Reformists were appalled by the immorality and inhumanity of the slave trade.* | *The novel focuses on the inhumanity of prisons and labour camps.*

5 to treat a person or animal in a cruel way

- be cruel to
- mistreat/ill-treat
- bully
- abuse
- persecute
- treat sb like dirt
- pick on
- victimize

be cruel to /biː ˈkruːəl tuː/ [v phrase] *My father drank too much and was often very cruel to my mother.* | *It is unspeakably cruel to the prisoners to house them in such conditions.*

mistreat/ill-treat /mɪsˈtriːt, ɪl ˈtriːt/ [v T] to deliberately treat a person or animal in a cruel way, especially when you are responsible for looking after them: *It looks as though this dog has been mistreated by its owner.* | *Neighbours were sure that the young couple had been ill-treating their children.*

bully /ˈbʊli/ [v T] to be cruel to someone who is weaker, younger, or has less authority than you: *A group of girls would bully the younger kids, and force them to give them money.* | *The court heard that the head of department would routinely bully and humiliate workers.*

abuse /əˈbjuːz/ [v T] to treat someone in your family or someone you are responsible for in a cruel way, especially violently or sexually: *My father abused us for years.* | *Erica runs a hostel for women who have been abused by their husbands.* | **sexually abuse** (=force someone to take part in sexual activities) *Erik testified he was sexually abused by his father since the age of 6.*

persecute /ˈpɜːʳsɪkjuːt/ [v T] to be cruel to a person or group of people over a period of time, because of their race or their religious or political beliefs: *Countries all over Europe have persecuted gypsies for centuries.* | *Human rights advocates say racial minorities continue to be persecuted.* —**persecution** /ˌpɜːʳsɪˈkjuːʃən/ [n U] *They left the country to escape religious persecution.*

treat sb like dirt /ˌtriːt (sb) laɪk ˈdɜːʳt/ [v phrase] informal to treat someone as if they were completely worthless and not care about their feelings: *She treats him like dirt but he still loves her.* | *I wanted us to be friends again, but I wasn't prepared to be treated like dirt to achieve it.*

pick on /ˈpɪk ɒn/ [phr v T] informal to choose someone from a group to treat cruelly and unfairly especially by repeatedly criticizing them: *Bullies usually pick on younger children.* | *Why don't you pick on someone your own size?* | *Older members of staff often pick on an apprentice and make his life a misery.*

victimize ALSO **victimise** British /ˈvɪktəmaɪz/ [v T usually passive] if a person or group is **victimized**, they are treated unfairly, for example because of their beliefs, their race, or because they are weak: *He wasn't happy at the school and said he was victimized because of his colour.* | *The company says she was not dismissed because of her political activities but she claims she was victimized.*

6 not cruel

- humane

humane /hjuːˈmeɪn/ [adj] treating people or animals in way that is not cruel and causes them as little pain or suffering as possible: *Imprisonment is not a humane form of punishment.* | *French revolutionaries considered death by guillotine to be a more humane method of execution.* —**humanely** [adv] *We must all try to treat farm animals more humanely.*

cry

RELATED WORDS

opposite: **laugh**

- to say something loudly *see* **shout**
- *see also* **sad, upset**

1 to cry

- cry
- weep
- sob
- bawl
- snivel/sniffle
- whimper
- be in tears
- your eyes water
- tears

cry /kraɪ/ [v I] if you **cry**, tears come from your eyes, for example because you are sad or upset, or because you have hurt yourself: *I could hear the baby crying in the next room.* | *Kim's eyes were red and she looked as though she'd been crying.* | *Don't cry, I didn't mean to upset you.* | **+ about** *Jenny won't tell me what she's crying about.* | **make sb cry** *The film was so sad, it made me cry.* | **cry and cry** (=cry for a long time) *I sat alone in my room and cried and cried.* | **cry your eyes out** (=cry a lot because you are very upset) *The poor kid's so miserable, he's upstairs crying his eyes out.* | **cry with happiness/joy/relief etc** *She cried with joy when she heard that the children were safe.* | **cry yourself to sleep** (=cry until you fall asleep) *At night I'd cry myself to sleep, thinking about you.* —**cry** [n singular] *You'll feel better when you've had a good cry.*

weep /wiːp/ [v I] especially written to cry quietly and for a long time because you are very sad or you feel a strong emotion: *She sat beside her dying father and wept.* | **weep openly** (=without trying to stop or hide it) *Thousands of French citizens, many weeping openly, bade a silent farewell to Mitterand.* | **weep with emotion/grief/joy etc** *I remember weeping with pride when my first son was born.* | **weep bitterly** (=cry strongly) *His mother wept bitterly and his father sat grim-faced.*

sob /sɒb‖sɑːb/ [v I] if you **sob**, you cry noisily and your body shakes, because you are very sad or because someone has upset you: *The sound of her sobbing kept them awake all night.* | *'Please don't leave me,' he sobbed.* | *The child covered her face with her hands and started to sob uncontrollably.*

bawl /bɔːl/ [v I] to cry loudly – use this especially about young children or people you do not have any sympathy for: *'Stop, bawling,' Dad said crossly, 'and come over here.'* | *The baby was sitting in his high chair, red in the face and bawling.*

snivel/sniffle /ˈsnɪvəl, ˈsnɪfəl/ [v I] to cry in a weak, complaining way and at the same time breathe in air noisily through your nose: *'What are you snivelling about, Jake?'* | *She kept sniffling into her handkerchief and saying how unfair everything was.*

whimper /ˈwɪmpəʳ/ [v I] to make a quiet, continuous, unhappy sound like an animal in pain, or to say something with this sound in your voice: *'I'm sorry,' she whimpered, but Richard wasn't listening.* | **+ with** *Pat whimpered with the pain of the bullet wound in his shoulder.* —**whimper** [n C] *The boy's crying died down to a whimper.*

be in tears /biː ɪn ˈtɪəʳz/ [v phrase] crying because someone has upset you, or because something is very sad: *Everyone started to laugh and Frank ran out of the room in tears.* | *Most of us were in tears by the time he'd finished his story.*

your eyes water / jɔːr ˈaɪz ˌwɔːtəʳ/ if your **eyes water**, you have tears in your eyes, usually because of something such as wind or smoke going into them: *Jo's eyes were watering from the smoke that filled the room.* | **make your eyes water** *An icy wind blew into my face, making my eyes water.*

tears /tɪəʳz/ [n plural] drops of water that come from your eyes when you are crying – this is often used to represent the idea of crying: *Grandpa wiped the tears from his eyes.* | **have tears in your eyes/with tears in your eyes** (=be nearly crying) *Yusuf had tears in his eyes, and I knew he was thinking of home.* | *She turned to me with tears in her eyes and begged me to help her.* | **tears roll/run down sb's cheeks** (=someone cries a lot) *He stood silently, tears rolling down his cheeks, while the music played.* | *Mum showed us the letter with tears running down her cheeks.* | **be close to tears** (=almost crying) *Howell was close to tears as he told the court what had happened.*

2 to start to cry

- start crying/start to cry
- burst into tears
- break down
- turn on the waterworks

start crying/start to cry /ˌstɑːʳt ˈkraɪ-ɪŋ, ˌstɑːʳt tə ˈkraɪ/ [v phrase] *Jim turned away from me and started to cry.* | *'I want Daddy to come home,' Anna said, starting to cry.* | *Just at that moment, the baby started crying.*

burst into tears /ˌbɜːʳst ɪntə ˈtɪəʳz/ [v phrase] to suddenly start to cry because you are upset about something: *Laura burst into tears and ran out of the room.*

break down /ˌbreɪk ˈdaʊn/ [phr v I] to suddenly start to cry a lot, after trying not to cry: *I broke down when he'd gone, knowing that I might never see him again.* | **break down and cry** *As the funeral service began, Frances broke down and cried.* | **break down in tears** *All the worry and anxiety had been too much for her, and she suddenly broke down in tears.*

turn on the waterworks /ˌtɜːʳn ɒn ðə ˈwɔːtəʳwɜːʳks/ [v phrase] British informal to deliberately start to cry in order to get someone's sympathy or persuade them to do something: *She was one of those people who could turn on the waterworks in order to get what they want.*

3 almost crying

- be close to tears/be on the verge of tears
- have a lump in your throat
- fight back tears

be close to tears/be on the verge of tears /biː ˌkləʊs tə ˈtɪəʳz, biː ɒn ðə ˌvɜːʳdʒ əv ˈtɪəʳz/ [v phrase] *The lesson was going very badly and the student teacher was close to tears.* | *Fiona was on the verge of tears as the train pulled out of the station.*

have a lump in your throat /hæv ə ˈlʌmp ɪn jɔːʳ ˌθrəʊt/ [v phrase not in progressive] to have a tight feeling in your throat and feel that you might start crying: *I had a lump in my throat watching Rick go up to get his prize.* | **bring a lump to sb's throat** *The sight of the soft green hills of her homeland brought a lump to her throat.*

fight back tears /ˌfaɪt bæk ˈtɪəʳz/ [v phrase] to try very hard not to cry even though you are almost crying: *Bill fought back his tears and tried to comfort Sarah's mother.* | *I quickly left the room, fighting back tears of rage and frustration.*

4 to make someone cry

- make sb cry
- reduce sb to tears
- bring tears to sb's eyes/bring a lump to sb's throat

make sb cry /ˌmeɪk (sb) ˈkraɪ/ [v phrase] *David often teases his little sister and makes her cry.* | *She was so unhappy that the slightest thing made her cry.*

reduce sb to tears /rɪˌdjuːs (sb) tə ˈtɪəʳz‖-ˌduːs-/ [v phrase] to make someone cry by behaving unkindly or by making them feel sad: *He shouted at Louise and in the end reduced her to tears.* | *Sam was almost reduced to tears by the sight of his mother in a hospital bed.*

bring tears to sb's eyes/bring a lump to sb's throat /brɪŋ ˌtɪəʳz tə (sb's) ˈaɪz, brɪŋ ə ˌlʌmp tə (sb's) ˈθrəʊt/ [v phrase] to make someone start to cry, or nearly start to cry: *Just the thought of saying goodbye to Craig brought tears to her eyes.* | *Outside the sharpness of the cold made him cough and brought tears to his eyes.* | *This movie is guaranteed to bring a lump to your throat.*

5 to stop crying

- stop crying
- dry your eyes/tears
- wipe the tears from your eyes/wipe your tears
- don't cry

stop crying /ˌstɒp ˈkraɪ-ɪŋ‖ˌstɑːp-/ *The little girl, who was very thin with a pale face, couldn't stop crying.* | *'Now stop crying,' Marilla said, 'and tell me what's the matter.'*

dry your eyes/tears /ˌdraɪ jɔːr ˈaɪz, ˈtɪəʳz/ especially written to stop crying, especially because someone has done or said something to make you feel happier: *Harry didn't mean to upset you. Now dry your eyes and come back downstairs.* | *At the thought of an ice-cream, Zoe dried her tears and began to smile.*

wipe the tears from your eyes/wipe your tears /waɪp ðə ˌtɪəʳz frəm jɔːr ˈaɪz, ˌwaɪp jɔːʳ ˈtɪəʳz/ [v phrase] to stop crying and use your hand or something else to dry your face – used especially in literature: *'Do you really mean that?' Jane said, wiping the tears from her eyes.* | *'Wipe your tears, dear,' Mrs Bristow said. 'It's not as bad as all that.'*

don't cry /ˌdəʊnt ˈkraɪ/ spoken say this when someone is crying, especially when you want to comfort them: *Please don't cry! You'll make me want to cry as well.* | *It's alright, he won't hurt you – don't cry.*

cure

RELATED WORDS

- to give someone medical treatment *see* **medical treatment**
- to get better after an illness *see* **recover**
- *see also* **drug, hospital, illness/disease, ill/sick, doctor**

1 to cure someone

- **cure**
- **make sb (feel) better**
- **heal**

cure /kjʊəʳ/ [v T] to make someone who has an illness completely well again or to stop a disease making someone ill: *It is possible that in the near future we will be able to cure AIDS.* | | **cure sb** *Many cancer victims can be cured if the disease is detected early enough.* | **cure sb of sth** *Eventually we found a doctor who was able to cure her of her depression.* —**curable** [adj] able to be cured: *Breast cancer is curable when caught in the early stages.*

make sb (feel) better /ˌmeɪk (sb) fiːl ˈbetəʳ/ [v phrase] to make someone who is ill well again, especially when they have an illness that is not very serious: *Take this – it'll make you feel a lot better.* | *I've had all kinds of medicines from the chemist, but nothing seems to make me any better.* | **make a headache/cold/pain etc better** *She refuses to take anything to make her headache better.*

heal /hiːl/ [v T] to cure someone of a physical or mental illness, especially using methods that do not involve the usual drugs or forms of medical treatment: *This cream is good for healing minor cuts and bruises.* | *Madame Bernice claimed to be able to heal people simply by laying her hands on their bodies.*

2 something that cures someone

- **cure**
- **remedy**
- **antidote**

cure /kjʊəʳ/ [n C] *I can give you some tablets that will ease the symptoms, but they're not a cure.* | **+ for** *What's the best cure for a hangover?* | *As yet there's no known cure for the disease.*

remedy /ˈremɪ̈di/ [n C] a way to treat a health problem, especially a small problem such as a cold, using plants or other natural methods **herbal remedies** *I tried some herbal remedies such as drinking camomile tea, but none of them worked.* | **+ for** *Salt water is a good home remedy for a sore throat.*

antidote /ˈæntɪdəʊt/ [n C] a medicine that will stop the effects of a poison or dangerous drug: *Unless an antidote is given immediately the patient could die.* | **+ to** *There is no known antidote to a bite from this snake.*

3 when a disease cannot be cured

- **incurable**
- **chronic**
- **terminal**

incurable /ɪnˈkjʊərəbəl/ [adj] *My doctor told me that the cancer was incurable.* | *Patients with incurable illnesses are brought to the hospice, where they are given the best possible care.*

chronic /ˈkrɒnɪk‖ˈkrɑː-/ [adj usually before noun] a **chronic** illness continues for a very long time or is permanent: *He suffers from chronic asthma.*

terminal /ˈtɜːʳmɪ̈nəl/ [adj] a **terminal** illness is one that cannot be cured, and the person who has it will die from it: *Two years ago, his mother developed terminal cancer.* | *St Helen's Hospice cares for people with terminal illnesses.* | **the terminal stages** (=the last stages of a disease that is killing them) *Many of the patients are in the terminal stages of the disease.* —**terminally** [adv] *Her father is terminally ill.*

cut

RELATED WORDS

- to reduce a price or amount *see* **reduce**
- *see also* **sharp, piece**

1 with scissors, a knife, or a sharp object

- **cut**
- **snip**
- **slit**
- **slash**
- **stab**
- **hack**

cut /kʌt/ [v T] to divide something into two or more pieces, using a knife or scissors: *He cut the string and carefully unwrapped the parcel.* | **cut sth in two/cut sth in half** *Mandy cut the paper in half and gave a piece to each child.* | **cut sth up/cut up sth** (=into several pieces) *Tommy sat on the floor, cutting up old magazines.* | **cut sth open/cut open sth** *Rescue workers had to use special equipment to cut open the steel doors.*

snip /snɪp/ [v T] to cut something with scissors using quick small cuts: *She snipped the thread which held the two pieces of cloth together.*

slit /slɪt/ [v T] to make a long narrow cut through something, especially skin or cloth: *He killed the goat by slitting its throat.* | **slit sth open/slit open sth** *Diane slit the envelope open with a knife.* | **slit your wrists** *Graham slit his wrists in a suicide attempt.*

slash /slæʃ/ [v T] to cut something quickly and violently with a knife, because you want to damage it or cause an injury: *The painting had been slashed with a knife.* | *Someone had slashed the tyres on Bayle's car.* | **slash your wrists** *She slashed her wrists with a razor blade.*

stab /stæb/ [v T] to push a knife into someone's body in order to kill or seriously injure them: *Betty Carroll was stabbed 61 times and left to die on the floor of her Escondido home.* | **stab sb in the heart/arm etc** *Luca stabbed her in the thigh with a breadknife.* | **stab sb to death** (=kill someone by attacking them a knife) *Kitty Davison was found stabbed to death one night in 1997.*

hack /hæk/ [v I/T] to cut something very roughly or violently **hack at sth** *He picked up an axe and began hacking at the door.* | **hack sb to death** *All of the victims had been hacked to death.* | **hack sb/sth to pieces** *The two women were hacked to pieces by their attackers.*

2 to cut food

- **cut**
- **chop/chop up**
- **slice**
- **carve**
- **mince**
- **grate**
- **shred**
- **dice**

cut /kʌt/ [v T] *Do you want me to cut the cake?* | **cut sth into pieces/chunks** *Cut the fish into four pieces and serve hot or warm.*

chop/chop up /tʃɒp, ˌtʃɒp ˈʌp‖ˌtʃɑːp-/ [v T/phr v T] to cut something such as vegetables or meat into small pieces when you are preparing a meal: *Chop two onions for the stew.* | *Elsa was in the kitchen chopping up vegetables.* | **chop sth into pieces/chunks/cubes** *Could you chop the eggplant into cubes for me?* —**chopped** [adj only before noun] *Next, sprinkle some chopped walnuts on the salad.*

slice /slaɪs/ [v T] to cut food such as bread, meat, or vegetables into thin flat pieces: *Wash and slice the mushrooms.* —**sliced** [adj only before noun] *sliced white bread*

carve /kɑːʳv/ [v I/T] to cut a large piece of cooked meat into pieces: *You start carving while I fetch the vegetables.* | *Who's going to carve the turkey?*

mince British **/grind** American /mɪns, graɪnd/ [v T] to cut raw meat into very small pieces, usually in a machine: *Mince the meat and mix in the remaining ingredients.* —**minced/ground** /mɪnst, graʊnd/ [adj only before noun] *minced beef*

grate /greɪt/ [v T] to cut cheese or vegetables into small thin pieces by rubbing them against a metal surface with holes in it: *I always like to grate some cheese over the potatoes before serving them.* —**grated** [adj only before noun] *grated orange peel*

shred /ʃred/ [v T] to cut food, especially vegetables with leaves, into long thin pieces: *Remove the outside leaves and shred the cabbage finely.* —**shredded** [adj only before noun] *a salad consisting of a few bits of shredded lettuce*

dice /daɪs/ [v T] to cut food, especially raw vegetables, into small square pieces: *Dice the potatoes and cook them in salted water.* —**diced** [adj only before noun] *Melt three tablespoons of butter in a saucepan and add the diced vegetables.*

3 to cut part of your body, especially accidentally

- cut
- scratch
- graze/scrape
- gash
- nick

cut /kʌt/ [v T] *She cut her hand trying to open a can of sardines.* | **cut sth on sth** *One of the children had cut her foot on some glass.* | **cut yourself shaving** *Phil cut himself shaving this morning.* —**cut** [n C] *Several passengers were treated for cuts and bruises.*

scratch /skrætʃ/ [v T] to cut part of your body very slightly leaving a long very thin cut: *The cat scratched me while I was playing with her.* | *She found her friend, Felicia Moon, bruised and scratched after a fight with her husband.* —**scratch** [n C] a slight cut that is not at all deep: *His face was covered in scratches.* | *It's just a scratch – nothing serious.*

graze/scrape /greɪz, skreɪp/ [v T] to slightly break the surface of your skin by rubbing against something, for example when you fall on the ground: *Oliver fell down on the path and grazed his knee.* | *I wasn't really hurt – I scraped my elbows a bit, that's all.* —**graze/scrape** /greɪz, skreɪp/ [n C] a slight wound on your skin where it has been rubbed against something hard and rough: *He had a bit of a graze on his elbow, but otherwise he was fine.*

gash /gæʃ/ [n C] a large, deep cut in someone's skin: *The accident left her with an ugly gash above the left eye.*

nick /nɪk/ [v T] to accidentally make a small cut in the surface of your skin: *I must have nicked myself when I was shaving this morning.*

4 when a doctor or scientist makes a cut in someone's body

- make an incision
- dissect

make an incision /ˌmeɪk ən ɪnˈsɪʒən/ [v phrase] to cut into someone's body, using a special knife, during a medical operation: *The surgeon began by making an incision about six inches long.*

dissect /dɪˈsekt, daɪ-/ [v T] to cut a dead animal or person into pieces in order to study it: *The specimens were carefully dissected and examined under a microscope.*

5 to cut someone's hair, beard, or fingernails

- cut
- haircut
- shave
- trim

cut /kʌt/ [v T] *My sister usually cuts my hair.* | *I wish you wouldn't cut your fingernails in the living room.* | **have your hair cut** (=pay someone to cut it for you) *Beth's at the salon having her hair cut.*

haircut /ˈheəʳkʌt/ [n C] when someone cuts your hair: *Isn't it about time you had a haircut?*

shave /ʃeɪv/ [v I/T] to cut the hair on your face or body so that your skin feels smooth: *Have you shaved today?* | *I didn't have time to shave my legs.* | **shave off sth/shave sth off** *I wish he'd shave off that awful beard!* —**shave** [n singular] *He went upstairs and had a quick shave.*

trim /trɪm/ [v T] to cut a small amount off someone's hair or beard, so that it looks neater: *Could you just trim my hair at the back?* —**trim** [n singular] *Ian gave Sue's hair a trim before shampooing it.* (=he quickly cut her hair)

6 to cut wood, plants, or grass

- cut down/chop down
- fell
- chop/chop up
- cut
- mow
- saw
- prune
- trim
- hack

cut down/chop down /ˌkʌt ˈdaʊn, ˌtʃɒp ˈdaʊn‖ˌtʃɑːp-/ [phr v T] to make trees or bushes fall down by cutting them **cut/chop sth down** *The tree was blocking the view from our window, and we asked a neighbour to chop it down.* | **cut/chop down sth** *Cutting down vast areas of the rainforests has created serious ecological problems.*

fell /fel/ [v T] to cut down trees, especially a large number of them, using special equipment: *63 percent of trees felled in Guatemala are used for fuel.* | *More trees are being felled annually now than ever before.*

chop/chop up /tʃɒp, ˌtʃɒp ˈʌp‖ˌtʃɑːp-/ [v T/phr v T] to cut wood into pieces using an axe (=a tool with a long handle and a sharp blade): *Ivan spent the day chopping wood and sawing logs.* | **chop sth up/chop up sth** *I chopped up the old fence and used it for firewood.*

cut /kʌt/ [v T] to **cut** grass or **cut** off leaves, in order to make a place or plant look tidy: *She had to stand on a ladder to cut the top of the hedge.* | **cut the**

lawn/grass *My dad used to cut the grass every Sunday morning.*

mow /məʊ/ [v T] to cut grass using a special machine, in order to make it look tidy **mow the lawn/the grass** *It took me two hours to mow the lawn.*

saw /sɔː/ [v T] to cut wood using a **saw** (=sharp tool that you push backwards and forwards across the surface of the wood) *We had to saw the wood to the right length, and then nail the pieces together.* | **saw sth up/saw up sth** (=into several pieces) *It took all morning to saw up the logs.*

prune /pruːn/ [v T] to cut off some of the branches of a tree or bush to make it grow better: *Miniature roses do not need much pruning and are ideal for planting in pots.* | *What's the best time of the year for pruning apple trees?*

trim /trɪm/ [v T] to cut small amounts off something, especially a bush, in order to make it have a neat shape or surface: *Do you think the hedge needs trimming?*

hack /hæk/ [v I/T] to cut trees, plants etc by hitting them with a heavy knife or other sharp tool using short violent movements **+ at** *Robert was hacking at the base of the tree with an axe.* | **hack your way through/hack a path through** (=make a path by cutting down plants and trees) *They managed to hack their way through the jungle.*

7 to remove something by cutting

- cut off
- chop off
- snip off
- lop off
- amputate
- sever
- gouge sb's eyes out

cut off /ˌkʌt ˈɒf / [phr v T] to cut part of something away from the rest of it **cut off sth** *Cut off the stalks of the broccoli.* | **cut sth off** *She took the cheese and cut a big piece off.*

chop off /ˌtʃɒp ˈɒf‖ˌtʃɑːp-/ [phr v T] to cut something off by hitting it hard or cutting it with a sharp tool **chop off sth** *Chop off the tops of the carrots.* | **chop sth off** *Careful you don't chop your fingers off!*

snip off /ˌsnɪp ˈɒf/ [phr v T] to quickly remove something using scissors **snip sth off/snip off sth** *Snip the ends of the beans off before you cook them.* | *After the plant finishes blooming, snip off the dead flowers.*

lop off /ˌlɒp ˈɒf ‖ˌlɑːp-/ [phr v T] to cut a part of something off, especially a branch of a tree **lop off sth/lop sth off** *Workmen have lopped off some of the branches in an effort to save the tree.*

amputate /ˈæmpjəteɪt/ [v I/T] to cut off someone's arm, leg, or foot as a medical operation: *He damaged his leg so badly that it had to be amputated.* —**amputation** /ˌæmpjəˈteɪʃən/ [n C/U] *If the infection spreads quickly, amputation may be necessary.*

sever /ˈsevəʳ/ [v T usually passive] to cut off a part of someone's body in an accident or an attack: *The victim's head had been severed in the accident.* —**severed** [adj only before noun] *Surgeons were able to sew the severed finger back on.*

gouge sb's eyes out /ˌgaʊdʒ (sb's) ˈaɪz aʊt/ [v phrase] to remove someone's eyes with a pointed weapon or object **gouge sb's eyes out/gouge out sb's eyes** *McLaren accused Roberts of trying to gouge his eyes out during the fight.*

8 to make a shape by cutting

- cut
- carve
- whittle

cut /kʌt/ [v T] **cut sth into a square/circle etc** *First cut the paper into a triangle.* | **cut out sth/cut sth out** *Stella stood at the kitchen table, cutting out the pattern for a new dress.* | *The children drew Christmas trees on their pieces of paper and cut them out carefully.*

carve /kɑːʳv/ [v T] to cut shapes out of solid wood or stone: *Michelangelo carved this figure from a single block of marble.* —**carved** [adj] *The church has intricately carved doors.*

whittle /ˈwɪtl/ [v I/T] to cut a piece of wood into a particular shape by cutting off small pieces with a small knife: *He took out his penknife and began whittling a piece of wood.*

Dd

damage

RELATED WORDS

- to have a bad effect on something *see* **harm**
- to damage something so badly it cannot be repaired *see* **destroy**
- to hurt or injure someone *see* **hurt/injure**
- damage to the environment *see* **environment (5)**
- *see also* **break, broken, spoil, tear, mark, repair, condition (1-6)**

1 to damage something

- damage
- do/cause damage
- break
- scratch

damage /ˈdæmɪdʒ/ [v T] to break part of something or spoil its appearance: *The goods were damaged during transport.* | *Don't put any hot things on the table – you'll damage the surface.* | **badly/severely damaged** *The building had been severely damaged by fire.* —**damaged** [adj] *I was lucky to escape from the accident with nothing but a damaged windscreen.*

do/cause damage /ˌduː, ˌkɔːz ˈdæmɪdʒ/ [v phrase] if one thing or person **does** or **causes damage** to another, it damages that person or thing – use this especially to say how much damage there is: *The explosion caused over £50,000 worth of damage.* | *In the end, the Internet virus did little permanent damage.* | **+ to** *Too much sun can do serious damage to your skin.*

break /breɪk/ [v T] to damage a machine or piece of equipment so that it does not work or cannot be used: *Leave that clock alone – you'll break it!* | *We used to have a remote control for the TV, but my brother broke it.* —**broken** /ˈbrəʊkən/ [adj] *One of the car's rear lights is broken.*

scratch /skrætʃ/ [v T] to damage a painted or polished surface by making long thin marks on it with something sharp or rough: *Be careful not to scratch the table with those scissors.* | *I scratched the side of the car as I was backing it into the driveway.*

—**scratched** [adj] *The kitchen has a beautiful wooden floor, but it's badly scratched.*

2 to damage something deliberately

- vandalize
- smash up
- trash
- sabotage
- tamper with
- deface
- desecrate

vandalize ALSO **vandalise** British /'vændəl-aɪz/ [v T usually in passive] to deliberately damage buildings, vehicles, or public property: *All the public telephones in the area had been vandalized.* | *No-one is really sure why people vandalize their own neighbourhoods.* —**vandal** [n C] someone who vandalizes things: *Vandals broke into the school and wrecked two classrooms.* —**vandalism** [n U] the criminal activity of vandalizing things: *In recent years, there has been an increase in vandalism in inner-city areas.*

smash up /ˌsmæʃ 'ʌp/ [phr v T] British to deliberately damage a room or building by breaking windows, furniture etc **smash sth up** *They didn't only rob the house, they smashed it up too.* | **smash up sth** *About 400 rioters had seized control and were smashing up the jail.* | **smash the place up** *Some of the men got drunk and smashed the place up.*

trash /træʃ/ [v T] especially American, informal to cause a lot of damage to a thing or place, either deliberately or by using it carelessly: *That kid of yours has trashed my VCR.* | **trash the place** spoken (=cause a lot of damage to a room or building) *Dad says it's OK to have the party here, as long as we don't trash the place.*

sabotage /'sæbətɑːʒ/ [v T] to secretly damage machines or equipment so that they cannot be used, especially in order to harm an enemy: *The railway line had been sabotaged by enemy commandos.* | *Security lighting was sabotaged before the theft took place.* —**sabotage** [n U] when people secretly damage machines or equipment: *Armed soldiers patrol the airbase to guard against sabotage.*

tamper with /'tæmpəʳ wɪð/ [phr v T] to deliberately and illegally damage or change a part of something in order to prevent it from working properly: *Someone had tampered with the lock on my door.* | *After the accident, police discovered that the car's brakes had been tampered with.*

deface /dɪ'feɪs/ [v T] to deliberately spoil the appearance of something by writing on it, spraying paint on it etc: *Several of the gravestones had been defaced and were impossible to read.* | **deface sth with sth** *The Central Bank issued a statement warning against defacing bank notes with what it called 'indecent expressions'.*

desecrate /'desɪkreɪt/ [v T] to damage a church or other holy place: *The church had been desecrated by vandals.* | *Most of the Egyptian tombs were desecrated and robbed.* —**desecration** /ˌdesɪ̥'kreɪʃən/ [n U]

3 when weather/water/chemicals etc slowly damage something

- wear away
- erode
- corrode
- rust/rust away

wear away /ˌweər ə'weɪ/ [phr v T] if the wind, rain, sea etc **wears** something **away**, it very gradually destroys its surface until there is nothing left **wear away sth** *The action of the sea is constantly wearing away the cliff face.* | **wear sth away** *Environmentalists are concerned that rock climbers are wearing the crags away in some places.* | **get worn away** *The cathedral steps were getting worn away by the feet of thousands of visitors.*

erode /ɪ'rəʊd/ [v T] if water, wind, air etc **erodes** rock, land, soil etc, it gradually damages it over a long time by removing little pieces of it: *Caves are formed by water eroding rock.* | *If the river is not controlled, it will erode its banks as well as the surrounding farmland.* —**erosion** /ɪ'rəʊʒən/ [n U] *the erosion of the coastline* | *soil erosion on hillsides*

corrode /kə'rəʊd/ [v T] if a chemical **corrodes** something metal, it damages it and makes it gradually disappear or become weaker: *Salt corrodes metal.* | *If the batteries leak, they can corrode the case of your flashlight.* | *The pipework was badly corroded in places.* —**corrosion** /kə'rəʊʒən/ [n U] *The problem is how to protect the metal surface from corrosion.* —**corrosive** /kə'rəʊsɪv/ [adj] *a bottle of corrosive acid*

rust/rust away /rʌst, ˌrʌst ə'weɪ/ [v I/T/phr v I] if something made of iron **rusts**, it is gradually damaged by a chemical reaction with water and turns red-brown in colour: *The iron crosses that marked the graves had rusted badly over the years.* | *The underside of the car had virtually rusted away.* —**rust** [n U]

4 to damage something by using it

- wear out
- wear
- wear and tear

wear out /ˌweər 'aʊt/ [phr v T] to damage clothes, material, or equipment by wearing them or using them a lot **wear out sth** *After only a month Terry had worn out the soles of his shoes.* | **wear sth out** *If you drive as fast as this all the time, you'll wear the brakes out.* | **get worn out** *The carpet on the stairs is getting worn out.*

wear /weəʳ/ [n U] damage caused by continuous use over a long period: *Excessive tyre wear may be caused by faulty brakes.* | **heavy wear** (=a lot of wear) *Dalton said that the machine showed signs of heavy wear and had not been well-maintained.*

wear and tear /ˌweər ən 'teəʳ/ [n phrase] the normal amount of damage that is caused to furniture, cars, pieces of equipment etc, by using them **+ on** *Having a large family obviously increases the wear and tear on your furniture.* | **normal/everyday wear and tear** (=the degree of wear and tear you expect) *Allowing for normal wear and tear, a washing machine should last at least ten years.*

5 physical damage caused by something

- damage

damage /'dæmɪdʒ/ [n U] the physical **damage** that spoils the way something looks or the way it works: *It will take many years to repair the damage caused by the floods.* | *The vandals did over £20,000 worth of damage.* | **+ to** *New ways of reducing the damage to the environment are urgently needed.* | **severe/serious damage** *Acid rain has caused serious damage to the pine forests of northern Europe.*

dance

RELATED WORDS

▸ *see also* **music, perform/performance, sing**

1 to dance

▸ **dance**
▸ **dancing**
▸ **do**

dance /dɑːns‖dæns/ [v I] to move your body in time to music, for example at a social event or as part of a performance: *Everyone got up and danced.* | **+ with** *Will you dance with me?* | **+ to** *If you like dancing to drum and bass, come to the Coven on Saturday night.* | **dance the night away** (=dance all night) *The disco starts at 11pm so you can dance the night away.* | **dance the waltz/the tango/the twist etc** (=dance a particular kind of dance) *I have an old photo of my parents dancing a waltz.*

dancing /ˈdɑːnsɪŋ‖ˈdæn-/ [n U] the activity of moving your feet and body to music: *My boyfriend doesn't like dancing.* | *There was music, Scottish dancing, and lots of food.* | **go dancing** (=go somewhere in order to dance) *Mum and Dad used to go dancing every Friday night.*

do /duː/ [v T] to **do** a particular kind of dance: *She got up and did a little dance.* | *The tribespeople did a special dance, which they said would bring rain.* | **do the waltz/the tango/the twist etc** *Can you do the twist?*

2 a set of movements performed to a particular type of music

▸ **dance**
▸ **steps**

dance /dɑːns‖dæns/ [n C] a set of movements that you do to a particular kind of music: *I prefer old-fashioned dances like the waltz or the tango.* | **folk dance** (=a traditional dance) *Hungarian folk dances* | **dance craze** (=a style of dance that is very popular for a short time) *The surprise hit of that summer was 'Macarena', which was also a dance craze.*

steps /steps/ [n plural] the movements you make with your feet as part of a particular dance: *Can you show me the right steps for this dance?* | *I'd like to dance but I don't know the steps.* | **dance steps** *It took me ages to get right some of the more complicated dance steps.*

3 someone who dances

▸ **dancer**
▸ **partner**

dancer /ˈdɑːnsəʳ‖ˈdæn-/ [n C] someone who dances, either because it is their job or for enjoyment: *I'm not a very good dancer.* | *a world famous dancer* | **ballet/belly/break etc dancer** *The ballet dancer, Rudolph Nureyev, died at the age of fifty-four.*

partner /ˈpɑːʳtnəʳ/ [n C] another person that you dance with: *When I saw her again, she was dancing with a different partner.* | *Try not to step on your partner's toes.*

4 a social event where people dance

▸ **dance**
▸ **club**
▸ **disco**
▸ **ball**
▸ **prom**

dance /dɑːns‖dæns/ [n C] an organized social event where people go to dance: *Do you want to go to the dance on Saturday night?* | **hold a dance** (=organize a dance) *Dances used to be held in the church hall at least once a month.* | **dinner dance** (=a formal event with dinner and dancing) *The Society are holding their 15th anniversary dinner dance at the Broomshill Hotel.*

club /klʌb/ [n C] a place where people go at night to dance to loud popular music: *I met some friends at a party and then we went on to a club.* | **go clubbing** (=go to one or more clubs) *If you want to go clubbing, London's the place to be.*

disco /ˈdɪskəʊ/ [n C] a place or fairly informal social event where people dance to popular music: *Nick met Rachel at a disco when she was 17 years old.* | *It was a small seaside town with a couple of bars and one shabby-looking disco.*

ball /bɔːl/ [n C] a formal social event at which people dance and wear formal clothes: *It was the first time I'd ever been invited to a ball.* | **hold a ball** *The University holds a summer ball at the end of June.*

prom /prɒm‖prɑːm/ [n C usually singular] a social event for high school students in the US where there is music and dancing, and that people usually go to with a partner: *Joey walked me home after the prom.* | **high school prom** *The band first played together at a high school prom.*

5 to invent a set of movements or steps to be used in a dance

▸ **choreograph**
▸ **choreography**
▸ **choreographer**

choreograph /ˈkɒriəgrɑːf, ˈkɔː-‖ˈkɔːriəgræf/ [v T] *She has been asked to choreograph a modern ballet for the National Dance Theatre.* | *There were some fabulous, beautifully choreographed dance routines.*

choreography /ˌkɒriˈɒgrəfi, ˌkɔː-‖ˌkɔːriˈɑːg-/ [n U] the art of inventing steps and movements and combining them into a dance: *She studied choreography at the Royal School of Ballet.* | *The splendid choreography was by Ann-Marie Brady.*

choreographer /ˌkɒriˈɒgrəfəʳ, ˌkɔː-‖ˌkɔːriˈɑːg-/ [n C] someone who invents the movements or steps to be used in a dance: *McKayle was considered the leading black modern dance choreographer of his day.*

dangerous

RELATED WORDS

opposite: ——— **safe**

▸ *see also* **risk, warn**

1 dangerous

▸ **dangerous**
▸ **risky**
▸ **poisonous**
▸ **hazardous**
▸ **high-risk**
▸ **treacherous**
▸ **perilous**

dangerous /ˈdeɪndʒərəs/ [adj] someone or something that is **dangerous** is likely to cause death or serious harm: *Snow and ice are making driving conditions very dangerous.* | *dangerous drugs such as heroin and crack* | *It's dangerous work but for men like Clement, summer firefighting is an important source of income.* | **highly/extremely dangerous** (=very dangerous) *Police described the three escaped* *prisoners as highly dangerous.* | **it is dangerous (for sb) to do sth** *The pilot says it's too dangerous to try to land the plane in this weather.* | *It's too dangerous for the kids to play in the street.* —**dangerously** [adv] *The plane was flying dangerously low.*

risky /ˈrɪski/ [adj] if you do something **risky**, it is easy to make a mistake that might cause death or serious harm – use this about things that you decide to do although you know they may be dangerous: *He'll have to land the aircraft in a field. It's risky, but there's no alternative.* | *Personal insurance is expensive if you plan to take part in a risky sport such as parachuting.* | **+ to do sth** *The State Department advised its employees that fighting near the borders made it too risky to leave the country.* | **risky business** (=something you do that is risky) *the risky business of putting a space vehicle into orbit*

poisonous /ˈpɔɪzənəs/ [adj] something that is **poisonous** will make you ill or kill you if you swallow it or breathe it: *The boy died after eating poisonous berries.* | *Many of our rivers are full of poisonous chemicals.* | **highly poisonous** *Carbon monoxide is a highly poisonous gas.*

hazardous /ˈhæzəʳdəs/ [adj] especially written a **hazardous** activity or journey is one that is dangerous. **Hazardous** chemicals or substances are dangerous – used especially on warning signs: *All of us knew that the expedition was likely to be extremely hazardous.* | *Being the President's bodyguard is obviously a hazardous occupation.* | *In 1820, a voyage to Australia was a hazardous undertaking.* | *Employees who were exposed to hazardous substances are now claiming compensation.*

high-risk /ˌhaɪ ˈrɪsk◂/ [adj only before noun] a **high-risk** job, situation, place, or type of behaviour is likely to be dangerous: *A polio vaccine is recommended before travelling to high-risk areas.* | *We are getting the message across to drug users that sharing needles is a high-risk behaviour.*

treacherous /ˈtretʃərəs/ [adj] places or conditions that are **treacherous** are very dangerous for anyone who is walking, driving, climbing etc in them: *Strong winds and heavy rain are making driving conditions treacherous in some areas.* | *There are treacherous underwater currents along this stretch of coast.*

perilous /ˈperɪ̈ləs/ [adj] written a **perilous** journey, situation etc is very dangerous – used especially in literature: *Refugees cross the rugged San Ysidro mountains, and it is always a perilous trip.* | *Blondin soon became famous as a rope-dancer. Nothing was too perilous for him to attempt.*

2 to be likely to be dangerous to people or things

- be a danger to sb/sth
- pose a threat
- threaten
- be a menace
- be a hazard
- a fire risk/health risk
- death trap

be a danger to sb/sth /biː ə ˈdeɪndʒəʳ tə (sb/sth)/ to be likely to harm other people or things: *People who drink and drive are a danger to themselves and to others.* | *The judge described Thomas as 'a danger to the public'.* | *Extreme nationalism is the single greatest danger to peace in the modern world.*

pose a threat /ˌpəʊz ə ˈθret/ [v phrase] formal if a situation or the existence of something **poses a threat**, it is dangerous to people: *Supplies of food were so low that this posed a threat as serious as invasion.* | **+ to** *Chemicals in our drinking water could pose a serious threat to public health.* | **pose no threat** *Scientists feel that present levels of radiation pose no threat.*

threaten /ˈθretn/ [v T] if an activity or a problem **threatens** something such as a place, animal, or way of life, it could cause it to no longer exist: *Illegal hunting threatens the survival of the African elephant.* | *By August, it was clear that the volcano could threaten the whole island.*

be a menace /biː ə ˈmenɪ̈s/ [v phrase] someone **who is a menace** behaves in a dangerous way, without thinking about the safety of other people: *Drivers like that are a menace. They shouldn't be allowed on the road.* | **+ to** *We consider drug trafficking to be a menace to the security of our nation.*

be a hazard /biː ə ˈhæzəʳd/ [v phrase] to be likely to kill people, cause accidents etc: *Ice on the road is a major hazard at this time of the year.* | **+ to** *The residents of Hollyhurst Road complained that cars parked there were a hazard to pedestrians.* | **be a fire/health/environmental etc hazard** *Garbage that is left uncollected becomes a serious health hazard.*

a fire risk/health risk /biː ə ˈfaɪəʳ ˌrɪsk, ˈhelθ ˌrɪsk/ [n phrase] a situation or object that is likely to cause a fire or to damage people's health: *Litter problems and a high fire risk mean that there is now restricted camping on the route.* | *Cigarettes are acknowledged as a serious health risk and the main cause of lung cancer.*

death trap /ˈdeθ træp/ [n C] informal if a building, road, car etc is a **death-trap**, it is very dangerous to enter or use, for example because it is in very bad condition, or is badly designed: *Fire-safety inspectors described the basement night-club as a death trap.* | *The ancient bridge was described as a potential death trap for the tourists that flock there.*

3 to be in a dangerous situation

- be in danger
- be at risk
- be in trouble
- be in peril

be in danger /biː ɪn ˈdeɪndʒəʳ/ [v phrase] *Mr and Mrs Watkins are worried that their daughter may be in danger.* | **be in danger of sth** (=be in a situation when it is possible you may be killed or injured by something dangerous) *Some of the children were in danger of starvation.* | **sb's life is in danger** *Even a small accident in these mountains can mean that your life is in danger.* | **be in grave/serious danger** (=be in a very dangerous situation) *The ship was in grave danger of being sunk by enemy aircraft.*

be at risk /biː ət ˈrɪsk/ [v phrase] if someone **is at risk**, they are in a dangerous situation, especially because they are weak and are more likely to be harmed than other people: *Accidents in the home are extremely common, and elderly people are most at risk.* | **+ from** *The vaccine is available for those who are most at risk from the flu epidemic.* | **+ of (doing) sth** *The hospital refused to move her, implying she was still at risk of committing suicide.*

be in trouble /biː ɪn ˈtrʌbəl/ [v phrase] to be in a dangerous and difficult situation, especially because of an unexpected problem: *Scott said nothing, but I knew from his face that we were in trouble.* | **be in serious trouble** *It was clear from the storm reports that the fishing boat must be in serious trouble.*

be in peril /biː ɪn ˈperɪ̈l/ [v phrase] to be in a dangerous situation – used especially in literature **be in great/grave peril** (=be in serious danger) *It soon* *became clear that the ship was in grave peril.* | **put sb/sth in peril** *Anything that slows down the operation, immediately puts the patient in peril.*

4 to do something that may hurt or kill you

- risk your life
- at your own risk
- risk your neck
- play with fire
- take your life in your hands
- dice with death
- at your peril

risk your life /ˌrɪsk jɔːʳ ˈlaɪf/ [v phrase] to do something very dangerous, especially in order to help someone, when you know that you may get killed because of your action: *Every day firefighters risk their lives in the course of their duty.* | **+ to do sth** *She risked her life to save the drowning child.*

at your own risk /ət jɔːr ˌəʊn ˈrɪsk/ [adv] if you do something **at your own risk**, you must accept that it is dangerous and that it is your own fault if you are injured or killed: *Anyone who swims in this part of the river does it at their own risk.*

risk your neck /ˌrɪsk jɔːʳ ˈnek/ [v phrase] informal to do something very dangerous in order to help someone – use this especially when you think the action is unnecessary: *Don't do it. It's not worth risking your neck.* | **+ to do sth** *'Come back!' Ned shouted. 'You can't risk your neck to save a dog!'*

play with fire /ˌpleɪ wɪð ˈfaɪəʳ/ [v phrase] to do something that could have a very dangerous or harmful result: *Failure to stick to the safety rules is simply playing with fire.* | *These men are criminals. If you get involved with them, you'll be playing with fire.*

take your life in your hands /ˌteɪk jɔːʳ ˌlaɪf ɪn jɔːʳ ˈhændz/ [v phrase] informal to put yourself in a situation in which you may get killed, especially when it is a situation which you cannot control: *The teenager took his life in his hands in trying to avoid being caught by police.* | *You'll be taking your life in your hands if you let Eric drive you home!*

dice with death /ˌdaɪs wɪð ˈdeθ/ [v phrase] to deliberately do something that is so dangerous that you may easily get killed, especially when you do it for excitement: *When young people experiment with drugs, they're dicing with death.*

at your peril /ət jɔːʳ ˈperəl/ [adv] formal if you warn someone that they do something **at their peril**, you mean that it would be very dangerous for them to do it: *Any climber who neglects these simple precautions does so at their peril.* | *Ignore this warning at your peril.*

5 to put someone else in a dangerous situation

- endanger
- put sb's life at risk

endanger /ɪnˈdeɪndʒəʳ/ [v T] formal **endanger someone's life/health/safety etc** to put someone in a dangerous situation that would badly affect their health, safety etc: *Smoking during pregnancy endangers your baby's health.* | *The city authorities complained that low-flying aircraft were endangering public safety.* | *Any raid or rescue operation would endanger the lives of the hostages.*

put sb's life at risk /ˌpʊt (sb's) ˈlaɪf ət ˌrɪsk/ [v phrase] to put someone in a dangerous situation in which they could be killed, especially by not obeying safety rules: *If an ambulance crew goes on strike, it is putting people's lives at risk.* | *By not dealing with the problem of radioactive waste, we are putting the lives of future generations at risk.*

6 danger of death or serious harm

- danger
- risk
- hazard
- peril

danger /ˈdeɪndʒəʳ/ [n C usually plural] the possibility that someone or something will be harmed or killed: *Danger! Keep out.* | *I stood at the side of the road and waved my arms to warn other drivers of the danger.* | **+ of** *The organization ran a national campaign about the dangers of cigarettes and other tobacco products.*

risk /rɪsk/ [n C/U] the possibility of serious harm if you do something dangerous – use this especially when you want to say how great the possibility is: *How much risk is there with this kind of operation?* | *A lot of children start smoking without realizing what the risks are.* | **+ of** *What exactly is the risk of an ordinary aircraft crashing?* | **high/low risk** *There is a high risk of injury in contact sports such as rugby.* | *It is possible to get malaria in this area, but the risk is pretty low.* | **reduce/increase the risk** *Wearing a seatbelt can reduce the risk of serious injury.* | **+ to/for** *The disease affects cats but there is no risk to humans.* | **carry a risk** *Many of these beaches are not clean, and they carry a high risk of viral infection for swimmers.*

hazard /ˈhæzəʳd/ [n C] something that may be dangerous, cause accidents etc: *Flashing signs on the motorway warn drivers of hazards ahead.* | **+ of** *Despite the hazards of working 50 storeys above the ground, my grandfather loved his job.* | **present/represent a hazard (to sb)** *Steep stairs can present a particular hazard to older people.*

peril /ˈperəl/ [n C usually plural] something that can cause danger, especially during a journey – used especially in literature: *None of us who set off on that calm September morning could have foreseen the perils that lay ahead.* | **+ of** *the perils of a life at sea*

dark

RELATED WORDS

opposite: light

- dark colour *see* **colour/color**

1 dark and with little or no light

- dark
- pitch dark/pitch black
- gloomy
- dingy
- darkened
- dimly-lit
- unlit

dark /dɑːʳk/ [adj] if a place is **dark**, there is little or no light: *Thick curtains covered the windows and the room was very dark.* | *I shrank back into the darkest corner of the room, and prayed that the soldiers would not see me.* | *No, you can't play outside, it's too dark.* | *It was a dark night and he was afraid they might get lost if they went across the fields.* | *Anyone who disobeyed him ran the risk of getting beaten up in a dark alley, or even killed.*

pitch dark/pitch black /ˌpɪtʃ ˈdɑːʳk◂, ˌpɪtʃ ˈblæk◂/ [adj not usually before noun] completely dark, so that nothing can be seen: *It's pitch dark in there. I can't see a thing.* | *Inside the cellar it was pitch black.*

gloomy /'glu:mi/ [adj] a **gloomy** place or room is not at all bright or cheerful – use this especially in stories or written descriptions: *The bar was gloomy and smelled of stale cigar smoke.* | *I never liked visiting Dr Allen in his gloomy old study.*

dingy /'dɪndʒi/ [adj] a room, street, or place that is **dingy** is fairly dark and usually dirty and in bad condition: *He ate lunch in a dingy little cafe next to the station.* | *The room was damp and dingy.*

darkened /'dɑːʳkənd/ [adj only before noun] a **darkened** room or building is darker than usual, especially because its lights have been turned off or there are no lights: *The prisoner lay in a darkened room.* | *The production opens with a darkened stage, and the sound of a woman singing softly.*

dimly-lit /ˌdɪmli 'lɪt◂/ [adj] an area or building that is **dimly- lit** is fairly dark because the lights there are not very bright: *a long, dimly-lit corridor* | *Madame Gloriana led the way into a dimly lit back room.*

unlit /ˌʌn'lɪt◂/ [adj] an area, building, or room that is **unlit** is dark because there are no lights on there: *The path was unlit, and she needed a torch to find her way.* | *Behind the gasoline pumps the unlit garage stood like a huge black shadow.*

2 to become dark

- it gets dark
- the light fades
- darken
- fall
- be plunged into darkness

it gets dark /ɪt ˌgets 'dɑːʳk/ when **it gets dark**, the sky becomes dark, usually because it is night: *It was getting dark, and we were worried that we wouldn't make it back to the village before nightfall.* | *When we were camping we used to go to sleep as soon as it got dark.* | *It's getting very dark out there – there's going to be a storm.*

the light fades /ðə ˌlaɪt 'feɪdz/ if natural light **fades**, it gradually becomes weaker, because night is coming: *The light slowly began to fade and the trees became mere shadows.* | *I want to take some photographs before the light fades.*

darken /'dɑːʳkən/ [v I] if the sky **darkens**, it gradually becomes darker than before, often because of bad weather: *In a few minutes the sky darkened and heavy rain began to fall.* | *We walked along the shore as the sun's last rays winked over the darkening sea, then headed for home.*

fall /fɔːl/ [v I] **night/evening/darkness falls** use this especially in stories to say that the night begins and it becomes dark: *We got back home just as night was falling.* | *Darkness fell on the town and the streetlights came on one by one.*

be plunged into darkness /biː ˌplʌndʒd ɪntə 'dɑːʳknɪ̈s/ [v phrase] if a room, building etc **is plunged into darkness** it is suddenly made dark because all the lights have been turned off: *Suddenly the light went out and the narrow stairs were plunged into darkness.* | *Lightning struck the power lines, plunging half the city into darkness.*

3 darkness

- darkness
- the dark
- the shadows
- the half-light
- the gloom

darkness /'dɑːʳknɪ̈s/ [n U] a place or time where there is no light: *A voice came from out of the darkness, but she couldn't see anyone.* | *As my eyes became used to the darkness I could make out a bed in the corner of the room.* | *The city was a violent place at that time, and it was not safe to walk the streets during the hours of darkness.* | **in complete darkness** *Colour films must be developed in complete darkness.*

the dark /ðə 'dɑːʳk/ [n singular] when there is no light, especially in a room: *Children who are afraid of the dark need to be reassured.* | **in the dark** *Why are you sitting there in the dark? Put the light on.*

the shadows /ðə 'ʃædəʊz/ [n plural] the place near a building, trees etc where it is darker than everywhere else because it is hidden from the sun's light: *Someone was hiding in the shadows at the end of the garden.* | *Two figures moved out of the shadows into the moonlit street.*

the half-light /ðə 'hɑːf laɪt‖-'hæf-/ [n singular] dull, grey light like the light of the early morning or early evening – use this especially in stories and written descriptions: *He urged the mule forward through the half-light of the forest.* | **in the half-light** *It was difficult to see who was standing there in the dim half-light of the hall.*

the gloom /ðə 'gluːm/ [n singular] when a place or room does not have enough light to see properly and is not at all cheerful – use this especially in stories and written descriptions: *I stepped through the doorway and peered into the gloom.* | *Jon could hear her voice but was unable to see anything in the gloom.*

dead

no longer alive

RELATED WORDS

opposite: **alive**

- body of a dead person *see* **body**
- *see also* **die, kill, ghost**

- dead
- late
- stone-dead/dead as a doornail
- lifeless
- the dead
- the deceased
- posthumous
- be pushing up daisies

dead /ded/ [adj] someone or something that is **dead** has stopped living: *She's no longer breathing – I think she's dead.* | *The dead man's wife was questioned by police.* | *The doctor told him that unless he stopped drinking he would be dead within a year.* | *It was autumn, and the path was covered in dead leaves.* | *These flowers look dead – shall I throw them away?* | *Following the shoot-out six people were dead and three were wounded.* | **dead on arrival** (=already dead when arriving at a hospital) *One of the gunshot victims was pronounced dead on arrival at City Hospital.*

late /leɪt/ [adj only before noun] formal use this as a polite way of talking about someone who has died, especially someone who died recently **sb's late husband/wife/mother/father** *She set up the fund in memory of her late husband.* | **the late President Marcos/John Lennon etc** *He is a big fan of reggae music and the late Bob Marley.*

stone-dead/dead as a doornail /ˌstəʊn 'ded, ˌded əz ə 'dɔːʳneɪl/ [adj not before noun] informal completely dead – use this when you are completely certain that someone or something is dead: *By the time we found him he was stone-dead.* | *Tom poked the bird with a stick. 'Yeah, it's as dead as a doornail.'*

lifeless /'laɪfləs/ [adj] something that is **lifeless** shows no sign of life – use this about someone's body, or someone's hand or face: *He took the dead girl's hand. It felt cold and lifeless.* | *The men found Dunlap's lifeless body slumped in the front seat of his car.*

the dead /ðə ˈded/ [n plural] especially written people who have died – use this especially about people who died in wars or accidents: *a religious service to commemorate the dead of two World Wars* | *Four of the dead had been travelling in the same car.* | *Ordinary Americans are beginning the heart-breaking task of counting their dead.*

the deceased /ðə dɪˈsiːst/ [n] formal a dead person, especially one who has died recently – used especially in news reports and legal contexts: *The deceased died from an overdose of diet pills.* —**deceased** [adj] dead – use this especially when talking about someone's relative who has died recently: *The President was an old friend of her deceased father, Dr. Bernstein.*

posthumous /ˈpɒstjʊməs‖ˈpɑːstʃə-/ [adj usually before noun] given to someone or done for someone after they die: *Bentley's relatives are demanding a posthumous pardon from the government.* —**posthumously** [adv] *She was posthumously awarded the Queen's medal for bravery.*

be pushing up daisies /biː ˌpʊʃɪŋ ʌp ˈdeɪziz/ [v phrase] spoken if someone **is pushing up daisies**, they are dead – used humorously: *He talks about spending his parents' money as if they were already pushing up daisies.*

deal with

RELATED WORDS

- solve a problem *see* **solve**
- *see also* **problem**

1 to do things that need doing

- deal with
- see to/attend to
- take care of
- leave it to me
- process
- follow up

deal with /ˈdiːl wɪð/ [phr v T] to decide what needs to be done and make sure that it is done: *Who is dealing with the accommodation arrangements for the conference?* | *I spend most of my working day dealing with customer inquiries.* | *I'm sorry I'm late. I had an urgent call to deal with.*

see to/attend to /ˈsiː tuː, əˈtend tuː/ [phr v T] to deal with all the practical details of something that needs to be done or organized: *I'll join you later – there are a few things I need to see to at the office first.* | *My brother attended to all the funeral arrangements.* | *You'd better get someone to see to that leaking pipe.* | **see to it that** *I'll see to it that everything is ready on the day.*

take care of /ˌteɪk ˈkeər ɒv/ [v phrase] to make sure that arrangements are made or work is completed, especially when you do this for someone else so that they do not need to worry about it: *My secretary will take care of the details.* | *Shall I take care of your mail for you while you are away?* | **it/everything is taken care of** (=someone has dealt with it for you) *Don't worry about your passport and visa – it's all taken care of.*

leave it to me /ˌliːv ɪt tə ˈmiː/ spoken say this to tell someone that you will be responsible for making arrangements or for doing something that needs doing: *'We need to make sure the others know where we'll be meeting.' 'Leave it to me. I'll phone them when I get home.'*

process /ˈprəʊses‖ˈprɑː-/ [v T usually in passive] if an organization such as a government department **processes** a letter, an official document, or formal process etc, it deals with it: *You should allow two weeks for your visa application to be processed.* | *Computers have given banks the power to process millions of transactions a day.*

follow up British /**follow up on** American /ˌfɒləʊ ˈʌp, ˌfɒləʊ ˈʌp ɒn‖ˌfɑː-/ [phr v T] to take further action in order to deal with a complaint, request, letter etc: *I got your e-mail but I'm afraid I forgot to follow it up.* | *Our rule is that the complaints department must follow up a letter within two days.* | *Following up on recommendations made last year, the president called for the more efficient use of resources.*

2 to deal with a problem or difficult situation

- tackle
- handle
- sort out
- grapple with
- take the bull by the horns

tackle /ˈtækəl/ [v T] to begin to deal with a problem in a determined way, especially a big or complicated problem: *Many schools are now trying to tackle the problem of drug abuse.* | *The new laws are aimed at tackling unemployment.* | **tackle sth head on** (=deal with something in a direct and determined way) *Police forces in the area are trying to tackle car crime head on.*

handle /ˈhændl/ [v T] to deal with a problem or a difficult situation, especially in an effective or confident way: *There were a few problems, but nothing I couldn't handle.* | *A lot of people find it difficult to handle criticism.* | **handle sth well/badly** *The whole situation has been very badly handled.* | *It's her first year as a doctor, but she is handling the pressures of the job very well.*

sort out /ˌsɔːrt ˈaʊt/ [phr v T] especially British to deal with small but difficult problems that are causing trouble or preventing you from doing something: *I spent the weekend sorting out my tax affairs.* | *We'll have to sort your immigration status out before we can offer you a job.* | **sort yourself out** (=deal with any personal problems you have) *I decided to take a week's holiday to try and sort myself out.*

grapple with /ˈgræpəl wɪð/ [phr v T not in passive] to try hard to deal with a difficult problem or situation, especially for a long time: *The authorities have been grappling with the problem for a decade, but cars still choke the streets in the rush hour.* | *There is no environmental policy in a country that is still grappling with increasing poverty.*

take the bull by the horns /teɪk ðə ˌbʊl baɪ ðə ˈhɔːrnz/ [v phrase] to deal with a difficult situation or problem in a quick, confident, and determined way: *Helena decided to take the bull by the horns and organize the show herself.*

3 to deal successfully with a difficult situation

- manage
- cope
- get through
- have sth under control
- get over
- come/get to grips with
- rise to the occasion/challenge
- take sth in your stride
- rise above

manage /ˈmænɪdʒ/ [v I/T] to deal successfully with a fairly difficult but ordinary situation: *'How did you manage while you were unemployed?' 'Luckily, I had some savings.'* | *I'll be away for a week, do you think you can manage on your own?* | *Helen was always a difficult child. None of her teachers knew how to manage her.* | *The seminar discusses typical work-related problems and strategies to manage them.*

cope /kəʊp/ [v I] to succeed in dealing with difficult problems in your life, your job, or your relationships: *It's a tough job but I'm sure he'll cope.* | **+ with** *When I got back from holiday, I had an enormous backlog of work to cope with.* | **cope emotionally/financially/psychologically etc** *The kids were very young and it was difficult to cope financially.* | **cope well/successfully/nicely etc** *People who cope successfully with difficult situations usually look ahead and anticipate the circumstances.*

get through /ˈget θruː/ [phr v T] to live through an unhappy or unpleasant time in your life, and deal with the problems that it brings: *Her friends helped her to get through the first awful weeks after Bill died.*

have sth under control /hæv (sth) ˌʌndəʳ kənˈtrəʊl/ [v phrase not in progressive or passive] to be dealing successfully with a difficult situation at the moment: *The police have the situation under control.* | **be under control** *The flight was very bumpy but the pilot assured us that everything was under control.* | **bring sth under control** (=start to deal with it successfully) *The disease is spreading so fast that it is going to take years to bring it under control.* | **keep sth under control** *During the 1990s low oil prices helped to keep inflation under control.*

get over /ˌget ˈəʊvəʳ/ [phr v T] especially spoken **/overcome** /ˌəʊvəʳˈkʌm/ [v T] especially written to deal successfully with a problem so that it no longer exists or is not as bad: *I've always wanted to overcome my fear of spiders.* | *It's perfectly normal to be a bit nervous. I'm sure you'll get over it once you start your presentation.* | *The school overcame the problem of funding by getting local firms to sponsor them.*

come/get to grips with /ˌkʌm, ˌget tə ˈgrɪps wɪð/ [v phrase] to consider, understand, and deal with a very difficult or important problem or situation: *The residents of the small town are still struggling to come to grips with the tragedy.* | *Teachers must be prepared to spend time getting to grips with new technology.* | *No country has really got to grips with the problem of nuclear waste.*

rise to the occasion/the challenge /ˌraɪz tə ði əˈkeɪʒən, ðə ˈtʃæləndʒ/ [v phrase] to deal successfully with a sudden, unexpected situation or problem by trying especially hard: *We are calling on all our employees to rise to the occasion and become more efficient and productive.* | *The team rose to the challenge and fought back to produce another goal.* | **rise to the challenge of sth** *Naylor was one of those men who rise to the challenge of danger.*

take sth in your stride /ˌteɪk (sth) ɪn jɔːʳ ˈstraɪd/ [v phrase] to deal with an unexpected or difficult problem calmly and confidently: *Liz seems to be taking the divorce in her stride.* | *Most kids get teased a bit at school – they have to learn to take it in their stride.* | *Nigel smiled and took the criticism in his stride.*

rise above /ˌraɪz əˈbʌv/ [phr v T not in passive] to deal with a problem or difficult situation, by being able to ignore or forget about it: *Kate rose above all the trouble at home and did well in her classes.* | *Immigrants to the country were struggling to survive and rise above the poverty that surrounded them.*

4 to deal with a difficult situation in a particular way

- treat
- play/play it
- approach

treat /triːt/ [v T] to deal with something or someone in a particular way and with a particular attitude: *The school are treating this matter very seriously.* | **treat sth/sb lightly** (=not seriously or severely) *No one would suggest that sex offenders should be treated lightly.* | **treat sth as sth** *The company treats training as a continuous part of career development.* | *Police say that her death is being treated as suspicious.*

play/play it /ˈpleɪ (ɪt)/ [v T/v phrase] to deal with a situation by behaving in the way you think will be best in order to achieve the result that you want: *Have you decided how you want to play it?* | **play it well/carefully/steady etc** *You can get exactly what you want if you play it carefully.* | **play (it) safe** (=not take any risks) *In the run-up to the election, politicians in both parties just wanted to play it safe.* | **play (it) straight** (=do something or deal with someone in a direct honest way) *Some of the people involved in the competition, were not playing it straight.* | *'Play straight with me or I'll kill you,' he hissed.* | **play it cool** (=behave as though you do not care about something or someone) *She would not show him how upset she was. It was always smarter to play it cool.* | **play it by ear** (=decide what to do as the situation develops) *'What'll you do if he asks you?' 'I'm not sure, I'll play it by ear.'*

approach /əˈprəʊtʃ/ [v T] to begin to deal with a difficult situation in a particular way or with a particular attitude: *I don't think refusing to negotiate is the right way to approach this problem.* | *Try to relax before the exam, and you'll approach it in a better frame of mind.*

5 when there are difficult problems that you must deal with

- face
- be confronted with/by
- have to contend with
- face up to
- have sb/sth to reckon with

face /feɪs/ [v T] if you **face** a difficult problem or duty, or it **faces** you, you must deal with it: *Latin America faces a growing debt problem.* | *McManus knew he was facing the biggest challenge of his career.* | *This report highlights some of the problems faced by learners of English.* | *The new administration faces the difficult task of rebuilding the country's economy.* | **be faced with/by sth** *He was faced with the task of breaking the bad news to the boy's relatives.* | *Today's violence highlights the problems faced by the government here.*

be confronted with/by /biː kənˈfrʌntəd wɪð, baɪ/ [v phrase usually in passive] if you are **confronted with/by** a difficult problem, you must deal with it: *Nurses are confronted with life-or-death situations on a daily basis.* | *He remembered when he was first confronted by the racial realities of living in South Africa.*

have to contend with /hæv tə kənˈtend wɪð/ [v phrase] to have to deal with a problem or several problems, especially when you are already in a difficult situation: *The chairman also had to contend with divisions among the committee members.* | *Rescuers* *were having to contend with cold weather, snow and ice.*

face up to /ˌfeɪs ˈʌp tuː/ [phr v T] to accept and deal with an unpleasant fact or something difficult instead of ignoring it: *The Principal accused parents of not facing up to their responsibilities.* | *It's only by facing up to her addiction that she can hope to live a normal life again.* | **face up to doing sth** *It's time the government faced up to spending more on health and education.* | **face up to things** *You should face up to things, not just pretend that nothing's happening.*

have sb/sth to reckon with /hæv (sb/sth) tə ˈrekən wɪð/ [v phrase] to be in a position where you must deal with something or someone so difficult or powerful that you might not succeed: *You'll have the boss to reckon with if you go home this early.* | *Anyone attempting to invade the country will have to reckon with the peacekeeping force.*

6 a particular way of dealing with something

- course of action/course
- approach
- option
- your best bet

course of action/course /ˌkɔːʳs əv ˈækʃən, kɔːʳs/ [n phrase] an action or several actions which could be taken in order to deal with a particular situation: *The best course of action would be to speak to her and tell her the whole story.* | *One possible course of action is to increase taxes on alcohol and tobacco.* | *Jim didn't want to start an argument, so agreeing seemed to be the safest course.*

approach /əˈprəʊtʃ/ [n C] a particular way of dealing with a problem, difficult situation, or job: *The company needs to adopt a much more radical approach.* | **+ to** *Each of the delegates suggested a different approach to the problem.* | *the government's aggressive approach to the question of homelessness*

option /ˈɒpʃən‖ˈɑːp-/ [n C] one of several ways that you could choose in order to deal with a problem or a difficult situation: *Working full-time may not be your best option.* | *What other options do I have?* | **only option** (=the only thing you can do) *Our only option now is to contact the police.* | **no option** (=no other way of dealing with something) *These people have no option but to take low-paid unattractive work.* | **environmental/nuclear/political etc option** *As for replacement fuels, many people do not like to contemplate the nuclear option.*

your best bet /jɔːʳ ˈbest ˌbet/ [n phrase] spoken the best way of dealing with something: *For getting around the city centre, a bicycle's your best bet.* | **sb's best bet is to do sth** *We decided that our best bet was to leave him where he was and go and get help.*

decay

to be gradually destroyed by a natural process

RELATED WORDS

- food that is not fresh *see* **fresh/not fresh**

1 to decay

- decay
- rot
- decompose
- go mouldy
- rust
- corrode

decay /dɪˈkeɪ/ [v I] if something **decays**, it is gradually destroyed by chemical changes – use this about dead plants or flesh, fruit or wood, or teeth: *Freezing conditions will stop most things from decaying.* | *Some of the apples lying on the ground had already begun to decay.* | *In a warm climate where flesh decays rapidly, there is more risk of infection from dead animals.* | *If you eat too many sweets, it'll make your teeth decay.* —**decaying** [adj only before noun] *the decaying remains of a dead sheep* | *The stream was blocked by decaying vegetation.*

rot /rɒt‖rɑːt/ [v I] to decay – use this especially about wood, vegetables, plants etc: *If water gets inside the woodwork, it causes it to rot.* | **leave sth to rot** *In some countries food is left to rot, while in others people are dying from hunger.* | **rot away** (=rot until it becomes extremely weak or gradually disappears) *The roof had fallen in and the floor had completely rotted away.* —**rotting** [adj] *If you lift up a rotting log you will find all sorts of insects underneath.*

decompose /ˌdiːkəmˈpəʊz/ [v I] to decay and gradually break up – use this about dead plants or flesh: *As household refuse decomposes, it produces an explosive gas, methane.* | *A dead fish in the aquarium will decompose rapidly, fouling the water badly.* —**decomposing** [adj only before noun] *The men's decomposing bodies were found in a shallow grave in Epping forest.*

go mouldy British **/go moldy** American /gəʊ ˈməʊldi/ [v phrase] if food goes **mouldy**, a soft green or black substance starts to grow on the surface, and it is not good to eat any more: *Throw that bread away. It's gone mouldy.* | *If you don't keep cheese in the fridge, it goes mouldy very quickly.*

rust /rʌst/ [v I] if something made of iron **rusts**, it decays by becoming brown and rough, losing its strength, especially because it has not been protected from the damaging effects of water: *Several of the pipes have rusted and will need to be replaced.* | **rust away** (=rust until something begins to break into pieces) *Parts of the floor of the car had simply rusted away.* —**rusting** [adj only before noun] *The barn was full of rusting old farm machinery.*

corrode /kəˈrəʊd/ [v I] if metal **corrodes**, it decays by becoming weak and changing its colour, especially because it has not been protected from the damaging effects of chemicals: *By the time they found the wreckage of the plane, it had already started to corrode.* —**corroding** [adj only before noun] *Corroding radiators are a problem because they may start to leak.*

2 something that has decayed

- rotten
- decayed
- decomposed
- mouldy
- rusty
- corroded

rotten /ˈrɒtn‖ˈrɑːtn/ [adj] something that is **rotten** has decayed badly and often smells unpleasant – use this especially about wood, fruit, vegetables, plants etc: *There was a disgusting smell in the house – a bit like rotten eggs.* | *I wouldn't climb that tree if I were you – some of the branches look rotten.* | *a pile of rotten apples*

decayed /dɪˈkeɪd/ [adj usually before noun] **decayed** objects and materials are ones that are gradually being destroyed by natural chemical changes: *Bees will often build their nests in decayed wood.* | *Sixty years ago, the average 4 year old had 7 decayed or missing teeth.* | *Even the stonework on the old house was decayed and crumbling.*

decomposed /ˌdiːkəmˈpəʊzd◂/ [adj usually before noun] **decomposed** flesh or plants are dead and are gradually being broken up and destroyed by natural chemical changes **decomposed body/remains** *The girl's decomposed body had been in the water for a long time.* | **badly/partially/half decomposed** *Coal is the partially decomposed remains of forests that covered the earth millions of years ago.* | *Both men's bodies were badly decomposed.*

mouldy British **/moldy** American /ˈməʊldi/ [adj] something that is **mouldy** has a soft green or black substance growing on its surface: *All there was in the fridge was a piece of mouldy cheese and some tomatoes.* | *The cupboards were damp and full of moldy old clothes.* | **go mouldy** *This pizza's so old it's gone mouldy!*

rusty /ˈrʌsti/ [adj] **rusty** metal has become rough and brown because it is decaying, especially because it has not been protected from the damaging effects of water and air: *A rusty old car had been abandoned at the side of the road.* | *I opened the rusty iron gate and walked up the path.* | *The bicycle looked a bit rusty, but it worked.* —**rust** [n U] *You must remove all traces of rust before repainting the windows.*

corroded /kəˈrəʊdɪ̇d/ [adj] metal that is **corroded** has become weak and has changed colour, especially because it has not been protected from the damaging effects of chemicals, water, and air: *You should never use leaking or corroded batteries.* | *Badly corroded metal gutters and downpipes should be replaced by the plastic type.*

3 to make something decay

- rot
- corrode

rot /rɒt‖rɑːt/ [v T] *Bedtime drinks aimed at helping children to sleep may be rotting their teeth.* | **rot sth away** *If you leave any water in the bottom of the boat, it'll slowly rot it away.*

corrode /kəˈrəʊd/ [v T] if a chemical or chemical process **corrodes** a metal, it makes it decay: *Acid can corrode most metals.* | *Over the years, rain, wind, and sun had corroded the statue, turning the bronze a bright green.* —**corrosive** /kəˈrəʊsɪv/ [adj] *That chemical is highly corrosive, so be careful.*

4 the process of decaying

- decay
- corrosion

decay /dɪˈkeɪ/ [n U] *Tiny organisms that live in the soil assist the process of decay.* | **tooth decay** *Brushing your teeth regularly helps to fight against tooth decay.*

corrosion /kəˈrəʊʒən/ [n U] when a chemical or a chemical process makes a metal decay: *The crash happened as a result of corrosion to the airplane's fuselage.*

decide

RELATED WORDS

- *see also* **judge, choose, think, opinion, determined**

1 to decide to do something

- decide
- make up your mind
- choose
- make a decision
- arrive at/come to/reach a decision
- resolve
- come down in favour of
- take it into your head to do sth

decide /dɪˈsaɪd/ [v I/T] to make a choice that you are going to do something: *We'll support you whatever you decide.* | **decide to do sth** *She decided to tell her mother all about it that evening.* | **decide not to do sth** *If you decide not to accept our offer, let me know.* | **+ (that)** *I've decided that I really must stop smoking.* | **decide what/how/which etc** *Martha took hours deciding which dress to wear.* | *Have you decided whether to apply for that job?* | **decide against (doing) sth** (=decide not to do something) *For a second he thought about using his gun, but decided against it.* | *I was so tired that I decided against going to the party after all.* | **you decide** spoken (=used to tell someone to decide) *I don't mind which restaurant we go to. You decide.*

make up your mind /ˌmeɪk ʌp jɔːʳ ˈmaɪnd/ [v phrase] to finally decide that you will definitely do something, after thinking about it **make up your mind what/how/which etc** *I couldn't make up my mind which college I wanted to go to.* | **make your mind up** *You'll have to make your mind up soon, or there won't be any tickets left.* | **make up your mind to do sth** *John had made up his mind to forget the past and make a fresh start.* | **+ (that)** *She's finally made up her mind that she wants to study Law.*

choose /tʃuːz/ [v T] to decide to do something because you want to, without worrying about what other people think **choose to do sth** *More and more young couples today are choosing not to marry.* | *I told him to drive more slowly, but he chose to ignore my advice.*

make a decision /ˌmeɪk ə dɪˈsɪʒən/ [v phrase] to decide after thinking carefully about something, especially about something that is very important: *After weeks of sleepless nights, I finally made a decision.* | **make a decision to do sth** *I think you should make the decision to marry him – he's great!* | **+ about** *We don't have to make a decision about that now, let's think about it for a day or two.*

arrive at/come to/reach a decision /əˌraɪv ət, ˌkʌm tʊ, ˌriːtʃ ə dɪˈsɪʒən/ [v phrase] to officially decide about something important after discussing and carefully considering it: *Before reaching a decision the chairman usually talks to senior managers.* | *Let me know as soon as you arrive at a decision.* | **+ on/about** *After two hours the committee had still not come to a decision on any of the proposals.*

resolve /rɪˈzɒlv‖rɪˈzɑːlv, rɪˈzɔːlv/ [v T not in progressive or passive] formal to decide that you will definitely do something and will not change your mind about it, especially because you have learned from your past experiences **resolve to do sth** *I resolved to keep quiet about what I had heard, since it would only cause trouble.* | *After the divorce she resolved never to marry again.*

come down in favour of British **/come down in favor of** American /kʌm ˌdaʊn ɪn ˈfeɪvər ɒv/ [v phrase] to decide finally to support one plan or action instead of another: *Following a heated debate, the House of Commons came down in favour of the treaty.* | *The Senate came down in favor of the appointment of Judge Thomas to the US Supreme Court.*

take it into your head to do sth /ˌteɪk ɪt ɪntə jɔːʳ ˌhed tə 'duː (sth)/ [v phrase not in progressive] spoken if someone **takes it into their head to do something**, they suddenly decide to do something that you think is stupid or strange: *He took it into his head to borrow his Dad's car without asking.* | *For some reason they took it into their heads to go swimming at midnight.*

2 to decide that something is true

- decide
- come to/reach the conclusion
- conclude
- jump to conclusions
- judge
- deduce
- infer

decide /dɪ'saɪd/ [v T not in progressive] to think that something is true, after thinking about it, checking it, or looking at it **+ (that)** *I listened to his story and decided he was probably telling the truth.* | **decide whether/which/what etc** *She couldn't decide whether the dress suited her or not.*

come to/reach the conclusion /ˌkʌm tə, ˌriːtʃ ðə kən'kluːʒən/ [v phrase] to decide that something is true after thinking carefully about all the facts **+ (that)** *I came to the conclusion that there was only one way of tackling the problem.* | *Scientists were gradually coming to the conclusion that the disease was hereditary.*

conclude /kən'kluːd/ [v T not in progressive] to decide that something is true or to make a judgment about it after carefully considering all the facts **+ (that)** *The jury listened carefully to the evidence and concluded that the man was guilty.* | *It seems reasonable to conclude that people's behaviour is influenced by what they see on TV.* | **conclude from sth that** *Davis concludes from an analysis of traffic accidents that the speed limit should be lowered.*

jump to conclusions /ˌdʒʌmp tə kən'kluːʒənz/ [v phrase] to decide too quickly that something is true, without considering all the facts: *Don't jump to conclusions! Just because he's late doesn't mean he's had an accident.*

judge /dʒʌdʒ/ [v T] formal to decide that something is true after examining a situation carefully and using your knowledge and experience **+ that** *Kaldor judged that the moment was exactly right to call an election.* | **judge whether/which/what etc** *It's difficult to judge whether this is the right time to tell him.*

deduce /dɪ'djuːs‖dɪ'duːs/ [v T not in progressive] to decide that something must be true because of other facts that you know – used to talk about scientific or technical decisions **+ (that)** *Darwin's observations led him to deduce that plants and animals could adapt to their surroundings.* | **deduce sth from sth** *The police surgeon was able to deduce the probable time of death from the temperature of the body.*

infer /ɪn'fɜːʳ/ [v T not usually in progressive] to form an opinion or decide that something is probably true because of other information you already know **+ that** *It is easy to infer that the marriage was not a very happy one.* | **infer from sth that** *From archaeological evidence we can reasonably infer that these people used stone cutting tools.*

3 something that has been decided

- decision
- judgment
- verdict

decision /dɪ'sɪʒən/ [n C] *They're going to close the school, but I think that's the wrong decision.* | **make/take a decision** *As chief executive, I often have to take difficult decisions.* | **decision to do sth** *My decision to leave school when I was only 15 was the worst mistake I ever made.* | **+ on** *The board is expected to make a decision on the merger by August.* | **big decision** (=a difficult and important decision) *It's a big decision. Go home and discuss it with your wife.* | **sb's decision is final** (=cannot be changed) *The referee's decision is final.*

judgment /'dʒʌdʒmənt/ [n C] an official decision given by a judge or court of law: *Another opposition newspaper was suspended for three months in a court judgement on Thursday.*

verdict /'vɜːʳdɪkt/ [n C] an official decision made by a jury in a court of law about whether someone is guilty or not guilty of a crime **reach a verdict** (=make a decision) *It took the jury 24 hours of deliberations to reach their verdict.* | **return a verdict** (=officially say what your verdict is) *A second inquest in February returned a verdict of death by misadventure.* | **a verdict of guilty/not guilty** *The foreman read the verdict of guilty fourteen times, one for each defendant.*

4 when someone has the right or responsibility to decide

- it is up to sb
- be for sb to decide
- the ball is in your court
- rest with

it is up to sb /ɪt ɪz 'ʌp tə (sb)/ especially spoken if you say it's up to someone, you mean that that person should make the decision about something, and no one else: *'Where would you like to go this evening?' 'It's up to you – it's your birthday.'* | **it is up to sb what/when/whether etc** *It's up to them what they do with their money.* | **it is entirely up to sb** *I think you should take the job, but of course it's entirely up to you.*

be for sb to decide /biː fəʳ (sb) tə dɪ'saɪd/ [v phrase] formal use this when only one person or group has the right or authority to make a decision about something important: *We cannot say if he's guilty or not. That is for the court to decide.* | **it is for sb to decide what/whether/when etc** *It's for you to decide whether you go to university or not – not your parents.*

the ball is in your court /ðə ˌbɔːl ɪz ɪn 'jɔːʳ ˌkɔːʳt/ if **the ball is in your court**, it is your turn to make a decision and other people are waiting for that decision: *I've told you what I think of your idea – the ball's in your court now.* | *The terrorists had made their demands clear and the ball was in the government's court.*

rest with /'rest wɪð/ [phr v T] if a decision **rests with** someone, they have the authority to decide what should be done: *The committee has made certain recommendations, but the final decision rests with the President.* | *Responsibility for any military operation always rested with the commander.*

5 able to make decisions quickly and firmly

- decisive

decisive /dɪ'saɪsɪv/ [adj] someone who is **decisive** can make decisions firmly and confidently, without needing too much time to talk about them or think about them: *We are still waiting for Jim to make up* *his mind. I wish he would be more decisive. | This country needs strong, decisive leadership.* —**decisively** [adv] *The police responded to the crisis quickly and decisively.*

6 when someone has not yet decided

- have not decided/have not made up your mind
- be undecided
- keep your options open

have not decided/have not made up your mind /hæv ˌnɒt dɪˈsaɪdɪ̆d, hæv ˌnɒt meɪd ʌp jɔːʳ ˈmaɪnd/ [v phrase] *'Are you selling your house?' 'We haven't decided yet.'* | **have not decided what/how/whether etc** *I haven't decided what I'm going to get my brother for his birthday.* | *Steve hasn't made up his mind whether he's in favour of the idea or not.*

be undecided /biː ˌʌndɪˈsaɪdɪ̆d/ [v phrase] someone who is **undecided** has not yet decided about something, especially something important: *'Is Fred going to take the job?' 'He's still undecided.'* | **+ about/as to** *A third of the voters remain undecided about how they will vote.* | **be undecided what/which/whether etc** *He hesitated, undecided whether to go or stay.*

keep your options open /kiːp jɔːr ˈɒpʃənz ˌəʊpən‖-ˈɑːp-/ [v phrase] to deliberately avoid or delay making an important decision so that you are free to decide later: *New technology's getting cheaper and better all the time, so if I were you I'd keep my options open for a while.* | *Some presidential candidates keep their options open about policy issues in order to avoid losing any voters.*

7 unable to decide about something

- can't decide/can't make up your mind
- be in two minds
- dither

can't decide/can't make up your mind /ˌkɑːnt dɪˈsaɪd, ˌkɑːnt meɪk ʌp jɔːʳ maɪnd‖ˌkænt-/ [v phrase] to not be able to make a decision: *What colour are you going to paint your room?' 'I can't make up my mind.'* | **can't decide what/whether/how etc** *It was time to go and I still couldn't decide what to wear.* | *We can't decide whether to go to Greece or Italy this year.*

be in two minds /biː ɪn ˌtuː ˈmaɪndz/ [v phrase] informal to be unable to decide whether or not to do a particular thing **+ about** *My parents want me to study medicine, but I'm still in two minds about it.* | *Des was in two minds about buying the car, but the salesman persuaded him.* | **be in two minds whether to do sth** *I'm in two minds about whether to get a dog or not – it's such a responsibility.*

dither /ˈdɪðəʳ/ [v I] informal to keep changing your mind – use this when you think someone is weak or stupid because they cannot decide about something: *Stop dithering and make up your mind.* | **+ over** *Marcia was still upstairs, dithering over what she should pack.*

8 not good at making decisions quickly and firmly

- indecisive

indecisive /ˌɪndɪˈsaɪsɪv/ [adj] *I'm sorry to be so indecisive, but can I let you know tomorrow?* | *An indecisive commander is unlikely to win the confidence of his men.* —**indecisiveness** [n U] *The report criticized the chairman for his indecisiveness and lack of leadership.*

decorate

RELATED WORDS

▸ *see also* **paint, design, pattern, simple**

1 to decorate something

- decorate
- garnish
- tart up

decorate /ˈdekəreɪt/ [v T] to improve the way something looks by painting it or adding something attractive to it: *The children always enjoy decorating the Christmas tree.* | **decorate sth with sth** *Tom had decorated his room with a series of photos of Naples.*

garnish /ˈgɑːʳnɪʃ/ [v T] to make food look nice or to add taste to it by adding a small amount of another type of food, often of a different colour: *Before serving the pie, add a little parsley to garnish it.* | **garnish sth with sth** *Garnish the salad with tropical fruits and sautéed wild mushrooms.*

tart up /ˌtɑːʳt ˈʌp/ [phr v T] British informal to decorate a place so that it looks bright and new, but often in a way that looks cheap and unpleasant **tart up sth** *I don't like the way they've tarted up our office. It looked better the way it was before.* | **tart sth up** *'The Waggon and Horses' used to be a really rough pub but now they've tarted it up.*

2 decorated in a particular way

- decorated
- be decked out
- adorn
- be festooned with
- decor

decorated /ˈdekəreɪtɪ̆d/ [adj] *On the table was an ancient book with a decorated cover.* | **+ with** *The little mirror was decorated with shells and beads.* | *She wore a wide-brimmed straw hat decorated with colored ribbons.* | **richly/elaborately decorated** *Sabina stood in the centre of an elaborately decorated living room.*

be decked out /biː ˌdekt ˈaʊt/ [v phrase] to be specially and colourfully decorated, especially for a celebration or party **+ with** *The whole street was decked out with flags and streamers to celebrate the wedding.* | **+ for** *Behind the door was another table, all decked out for the party.*

adorn /əˈdɔːʳn/ [v T] formal or written to decorate something in a beautiful or artistic way: *Rings and gems adorned the fingers of both her hands.* | **adorn sth with sth** *The bridesmaids had adorned their heads with flowers.* | **be adorned with sth** *The walls of the church were richly adorned with carvings and pictures.*

be festooned with /biː feˈstuːnd wɪð/ [v phrase] if a place **is festooned with** something, it has long chains of flowers, flags, or material hanging all around it, giving a bright and cheerful appearance: *On the day of the festival the streets were festooned with flags and banners.*

decor /ˈdeɪkɔːʳ‖deɪˈkɔːr/ [n U] the particular way that a room or building is decorated, including all the colours, furniture, pictures etc: *It was a comfortable enough room, but I didn't like the decor very much.* | *The hotel's decor is dark and museum-like.*

3 used to decorate something

- decorations
- decoration
- ornament
- garnish
- decorative
- ornamental

decorations /ˌdekəˈreɪʃənz/ [n plural] things that you use to decorate a place, object, piece of furniture etc especially for a special occasion: *Have you put up your Christmas decorations yet?* | *The bride's mother had made all the table decorations.*

decoration /ˌdekəˈreɪʃən/ [n U] designs and patterns used to decorate buildings, clothes, or furniture: *The only decoration in the room was a picture above the fireplace.* | *The building was very plain with hardly any decoration at all.* | **for decoration** *These plants are grown mainly for decoration.*

ornament /ˈɔːʳnəmənt/ [n C] an object, often something fairly small, that is used in a room or house to make it look more attractive: *I bought a new Christmas tree ornament – do you want to see it?* | *Thieves stole all the silver and gold ornaments from the palace.*

garnish /ˈgɑːʳnɪʃ/ [n C] a small amount of food, often of a different colour, that is used to make a dish look nice or to add taste to it: *Serve the fish with a garnish of lemon.* | *Fresh parsley is often used for garnishes.*

decorative /ˈdekərətɪv‖ˈdekərə-, ˈdekəreɪ-/ [adj] something that is **decorative** is intended to make a place, object, piece of furniture etc look attractive – use this especially about designs and patterns: *The poem had been embroidered on a pretty decorative pillow.* | **purely/highly decorative** *Many of the nature books are purely decorative, but a few are very informative.*

ornamental /ˌɔːʳnəˈmentl◂/ [adj usually before noun] something **ornamental**, especially in a garden or building, is intended to make a place look more attractive, and usually does not have a useful purpose: *A gardener comes in each week to trim the ornamental trees and bushes.* | *an ornamental pond*

4 having a lot of decoration

- fancy
- ornate
- elaborate

fancy /ˈfænsi/ [adj] **fancy** clothes, patterns etc have a lot of decoration or bright colours – use this especially when you think something has too much decoration: *a velvet jacket with fancy buttons* | *The Web site has a lot of fancy graphics.*

ornate /ɔːʳˈneɪt/ [adj] an **ornate** object, picture, or part of a building has a lot of expensive or complicated decoration on it: *A pair of ornate gold candlesticks stood on the altar.* | *The ornate interior of the opera house was almost overwhelming.*

elaborate /ɪˈlæbərə̇t/ [adj] carefully and skilfully decorated with a lot of small details: *Nick examined the elaborate carvings on the tomb.* | *Elaborate murals had been painted on three of the four walls.*

5 someone who decorates

- decorator
- interior designer/decorator

decorator /ˈdekəreɪtəʳ/ [n C] British someone who paints houses and puts paper on the walls as their job: *We've had the decorators in all week.* | *My uncle Bill's been a painter and decorator all his life.*

interior designer/decorator /ɪnˌtɪəriəʳ dɪˈzaɪnəʳ, ˈdekəreɪtəʳ/ [n C] someone whose job is to plan and choose the colours, materials, furniture etc for the inside of people's houses: *They hired an interior designer to redo the entire office.*

deep/not deep

RELATED WORDS

- a deep colour *see* **colour/color**
- a deep sound or voice *see* **low**
- *see also* **thick**

1 water/hole/snow/sand

- deep
- bottomless
- the depths

deep /diːp/ [adj] use this about water, holes, snow etc where the bottom is a long distance from the top: *Be careful. The water's quite deep here.* | *The hole was deeper than they thought.* | *Larry had a deep cut on his left leg.* | **get deeper** *The pond gets much deeper in the middle.*

bottomless /ˈbɒtəmləs‖ˈbɑː-/ [adj] extremely deep and seeming to have no bottom: *To the child the hole seemed like a bottomless pit.* | *In the dream, I was falling and falling in a bottomless abyss.*

the depths /ðə ˈdepθs/ [n plural] **the depths** of the sea, a lake, the Earth etc are the very deepest parts of the sea, a large lake, or the Earth: *Who knows what creatures live in the depths of the ocean?* | *As I hiked around the volcano, clouds of steam rose up from the depths of the Earth.*

2 a long distance below the surface

- deep
- deeply

deep /diːp/ [adv] *As we dug deeper, we uncovered a large wooden chest.* | **deep in/down/below etc sth** *Turtles lay their eggs deep in the sand and leave them there until they hatch.* | *Earthquakes are caused by movements deep below the Earth's surface.* | **deep underground** *Crews are working deep underground to build the tunnel.*

deeply /ˈdiːpli/ [adv] **deeply buried/submerged/embedded etc** (=a long way down from the surface) *They found rock with gold in it deeply buried beneath the earth's surface.* | *It is said that there is an ancient city deeply submerged in this part of the ocean.* | *The road followed the deeply cut river valley.*

3 how deep something is

- how deep
- 40 metres/100 feet etc deep
- depth

how deep /haʊ ˈdiːp/ *How deep was the snow?* | *I wasn't sure how deep the water was and I didn't want to swim out too far.*

40 metres/100 feet etc deep /ˌfɔːʳti miːtəʳz ˈdiːp/ [adj phrase] use this to say exactly how deep something is: *The pool is only five feet deep.* | *The snow is over two metres deep.* | **ankle-deep/knee-deep etc** (=deep enough to reach your ankles, knees, etc) *After the floods, the streets had become ankle-deep streams.*

depth /depθ/ [n C/U] the distance from the surface to

the bottom of a hole, river, sea etc **+ of** *The depth of the pond varies with the rainfall.* | *The plants need sand with a depth of at least 10 to 15 cm to grow.*

4 not deep

- shallow
- not very deep

shallow /ˈʃæləʊ/ [adj] not very deep – use this especially about the water in a river, lake, swimming pool etc: *The babies splashed around at the shallow end of the pool.* | *The river is too shallow for our boat.*

not very deep /nɒt veri ˈdiːp/ [adj] if a river, lake, hole, etc is **not very deep**, the distance from the surface to the bottom is not very large: *Come on in – the water isn't very deep.* | *The wound isn't very deep so it shouldn't take long to heal.*

defend

RELATED WORDS

opposite: **attack, criticize**

- unable to defend yourself *see* **weak**
- *see also* **protect, safe, look after**

1 to defend a person, place, or country from attack

- defend
- hold off
- come to sb's defence
- in defence of sth

defend /dɪˈfend/ [v T] to use physical or military force to protect a person or place that is being attacked: *Hundreds of soldiers died while defending the town.* | *US troops in Panama will only be used to defend the Canal.* | **defend sth against/from sb** *The castle was built in 1549 to defend the island against invaders.* | **defend yourself** *Carson claims he was defending himself when he struck the other man.*

hold off /ˌhəʊld ˈɒf/ [phr v T] to prevent someone who is attacking you from coming any closer **hold off sb/sth** *The bunkers were built on the cliffs to hold off the enemy's landing forces.* | **hold sb/sth off** *At that point our troops were too weak to hold them off.*

come to sb's defence British **/defense** American /ˌkʌm tə (sb's) dɪˈfens/ [v phrase] to defend another person or country that is being attacked: *Things seemed to be going badly until NATO forces came to their defence.* | **come to the defence/defense of sb** *Rhonda came to the defense of her brother by swinging a chain at his attacker.*

in defence of sth British **/defense of sth** American /ɪn dɪˈfens əv (sth)/ [prep] if you do something **in defence of** a place, especially your country, you do it in order to defend that place: *Would you be prepared to fight in defence of your country?* | *These brave young men have given their lives in defence of freedom.*

2 used for defence against attack

- defence
- self-defence
- defences
- defensive

defence British **/defense** American /dɪˈfens/ [n U] all the weapons, soldiers, systems, or activities that a country uses to defend itself against attack by an enemy: *Defense is expected to be a big issue during the next election.* | **defence/defense spending** (=money spent on defence) *Defence spending has risen by 10% in the current budget.* | **defence/defense system** *The military is continuing to work on its missile defense system.* | **the defence/defense industry** (=all the companies that make weapons) *The defence industry relies heavily on sales of weapons to foreign countries.*

self-defence British **/self-defense** American /ˌself dɪˈfens/ [n U] methods used by countries or people to stop themselves from being attacked or harmed: *All nations have the right to self-defence.* | *self-defence classes* | **in self-defence/defense** (=in order to protect yourself) *She claims she shot him in self-defence.*

defences British **/defenses** American /dɪˈfensɨz/ [n plural] all the soldiers and equipment that are available for defending a country or place: *The new radar system is an important part of the country's defences.* | *The country has responded to threats of invasion by strengthening its defenses.*

defensive /dɪˈfensɪv/ [adj] used only for protecting your country or group, not for attacking someone else: *Police officers claimed that their actions during the riots were purely defensive.* | **defensive weapons/position/measures** *According to the report, only defensive weapons had been supplied to Iran.*

3 to defend an idea or person when they are criticized

- defend
- stand up for
- stick up for
- come to sb's defence
- in sb's defence
- in defence of sth
- defence

defend /dɪˈfend/ [v T] to say something to support an idea or person when other people are criticizing them: *It's difficult to defend a sport that involves hurting animals.* | *Her speech defended the workers' right to strike.* | *The Fire Chief defended his staff and said that they had done everything possible to save the girl's life.* | **defend sb against/from sth** *She has repeatedly tried to defend her husband against hostile criticism in the press.* | **defend yourself** *Everyone was shouting at me, and I never got a chance to defend myself.* | **vigorously defend sb/sth** (=defend them very strongly) *Carey vigorously defended his fund-raising methods.*

stand up for /ˌstænd ˈʌp fɔːʳ/ [phr v T] to strongly defend someone who is being criticized, or strongly defend your ideas or your rights: *You have to be ready to stand up for the things you believe in.* | *Didn't anyone stand up for James and say it wasn't his fault?* | **stand up for yourself** *Don't let her get away with that – stand up for yourself.*

stick up for /ˌstɪk ˈʌp fɔːʳ/ [phr v T] spoken to strongly defend someone who is being criticized, especially when no one else will defend them: *The only person who stuck up for me was Sarah.* | *You're her husband – you should stick up for her.*

come to sb's defence British **/defense** American /ˌkʌm tə (sb's) dɪˈfens/ [v phrase] to say something to defend someone who is being criticized: *Dad seemed to think the accident was my fault, but Judy came to my defence and told him what had happened.* | *A large group of supporters have come to Robinson's defense.* | *Surprisingly, Major came to the defence of his old enemy.*

in sb's defence British **/defense** American /ɪn (sb's) dɪˈfens/ [adv] if you say something **in some-**

one's defence, you say it in order to defend them from criticism: *As far as I'm concerned, there is nothing you can say in her defence.* | *I ought to say, in Jim's defence, that he only heard about the meeting half an hour ago.* | **in defence/defense of sb** *No one spoke up in defense of Principal Blackman during the entire meeting.*

in defence of sth British **/defense of sth** American /ɪn dɪˈfens əv (sth)/ [prep] if you do or say something **in defence of** something, you do or say it to defend something that is very important to you, such as your rights or principles: *The miners went on strike in defence of their jobs.* | *She spoke bravely and defiantly in defence of human rights.*

defence British **/defense** American /dɪˈfens/ [n singular] a written or spoken statement that defends something against criticism, especially something that is very important to you **+ of** *The article was a rather unconvincing defence of her economic record.* | **strong/robust/spirited/vigorous defence** (=strong defence) *Pacheco gave a vigorous defense of the state's affirmative action laws.*

delay

RELATED WORDS

- arrange to do something later than planned *see* **later**
- *see also* **late, later, cancel**

1 to make someone or something arrive late

- **be delayed**
- **make sb late**
- **hold up**
- **keep**
- **detain**

be delayed /biː dɪˈleɪd/ [v phrase] to make someone or something late – use this especially about a problem or something unexpected: *Mr Evans has been delayed but will be joining us shortly.* | *Our plane was delayed by fog.* | *I mustn't delay you any longer.* | **get delayed** *There was an accident on the freeway and we got delayed.*

make sb late /ˌmeɪk (sb) ˈleɪt/ [v phrase not in passive] to delay someone or something so that they arrive somewhere late **+ for** *The accident made us late for work.* | *I'll let you go – I don't want to make you late for your appointment.* | **make sb late doing sth** *Catching a later train made Frank late getting to the office.*

hold up /ˌhəʊld ˈʌp/ [phr v T] to make someone or something stop or go more slowly when they are going somewhere **hold sb up** *I won't hold you up – I can see you're in a hurry.* | **hold up sb/sth** *Get a move on, you two! You're holding up the whole queue!* | **be/get held up** *We got held up in traffic and missed the show.*

keep /kiːp/ [v T not in passive] informal to delay someone when they are trying to go somewhere: *He should be here by now. What's keeping him?*

detain /dɪˈteɪn/ [v T] formal to delay someone, especially by keeping them talking or working: *I won't detain you for much longer, Miss Reid. There are just a few more questions that I need to ask you.* | **be unavoidably detained** (=by something that you cannot prevent) *Mr Jones should be here, but I'm afraid he's been unavoidably detained.*

2 to make something happen later or take longer than it should

- **delay**
- **hold up**
- **set back**
- **get bogged down**

delay /dɪˈleɪ/ [v T usually in passive] to make something happen later than it should, or take longer than it should: *The President's visit had to be delayed because of security problems.* | *This latest terrorist attack is bound to delay the peace talks even further.* | **+ by** *The plane's departure was delayed by mechanical problems.* | **be delayed for 5 hours/2 months etc** *The opening of the new bridge may be delayed for several months.*

hold up /ˌhəʊld ˈʌp/ [phr v T] to make something happen late, or make it happen more slowly than it should **hold up sth** *Protesters held up work on the new road.* | **be held up by sth** *The peace talks are being held up by continued fighting on the border.* | **hold sb/sth up** *They should have finished that job on Friday – what's holding them up?* | *Her stubbornness on this one issue is holding the whole deal up.*

set back ALSO **put back** British /ˌset ˈbæk, ˌpʊt ˈbæk/ [phr v T] to delay the progress or development of something by a number of weeks, months etc **set sb/sth etc back** *Your mistake has set us back several weeks.* | *The Transportation Department first announced that the expressway would be completed by 2002, but it has since set the timetable back.* | **set back sb/sth** *The start date kept being put back, for a variety of reasons.*

get bogged down /get ˌbɒgd ˈdaʊn‖-ˌbɑːgd-/ [v phrase] informal if a person or planned piece of work **gets bogged down**, they are delayed and prevented from continuing because of complicated or difficult problems **+ in** *The project got bogged down in a series of legal disputes.* | **+ by** *Keep the document simple and avoid getting bogged down by complicated formatting.*

3 to deliberately delay someone or something

- **stall**
- **play for time**
- **delaying tactics**
- **procrastinate**

stall /stɔːl/ [v I/T] to deliberately delay doing something, or to deliberately stop someone else from doing something until a later time, either because you are not ready or to give yourself an advantage: *Quit stalling and tell me where she is.* | *I'm not ready to talk to him yet – go out there and see if you can stall him.* | *City officials have slowed the development by stalling building permits for the area.*

play for time /ˌpleɪ fəʳ ˈtaɪm/ [v phrase] to deliberately try to delay doing something or making a decision, because you are not ready or want more time to think about it: *Stop playing for time and give us an answer.* | *The rebel's current ceasefire doesn't amount to much more than playing for time.*

delaying tactics /dɪˈleɪ-ɪŋ ˌtæktɪks/ [n plural] methods used, especially by politicians, in order to delay a plan or decision so that something can be done during the delay: *Some politicians are prepared to use delaying tactics to block the bill.* | *The peace negotiations were being held up by the delaying tactics of France and Great Britain.*

procrastinate /prəˈkræstəneɪt/ [v I] to delay doing something that you ought to do, usually because you do not want to do it – used especially to show disapproval: *He hesitated and procrastinated for weeks* *before he finally told her he wanted their relationship to end.* | **+ about/over** *Certain players are procrastinating over their contracts in order to see how much money they can squeeze out of their clubs.* —**procrastination** /prəˌkræstɪ̇ˈneɪʃən/ [n U] *She finally agreed to take the job after months of procrastination.*

4 a situation in which someone or something is delayed

- delay
- hold-up/holdup
- bottleneck

delay /dɪˈleɪ/ [n C/U] when someone or something is delayed: *Any delay in the production process is costly to a company.* | **long delay** *The strike is causing long delays at the airport* | **three months'/several weeks' etc delay** *After three months' delay, work finally began on the new building.* | **delay in doing sth** *There have been a lot of complaints about delays in issuing passports.*

hold-up/holdup /ˈhəʊld ʌp/ [n C] a delay, especially one caused by an unexpected problem, that interrupts a journey or a piece of work: *An accident on the London–Brighton road has caused a major hold-up.* | *There's been a hold-up with the builders, so the new office won't be ready for several months.*

bottleneck /ˈbɒtlnek‖ˈbɑː-/ [n C] a delay in one stage of a process that stops it making progress and makes the whole process take longer: *There's always going to be a bottleneck because only two people review all the applications.* | *If we don't hire more people in production we're going to have a huge bottleneck in a few months.*

deliberately

RELATED WORDS

opposite: —— **accidentally**

see also **intend/not intend**

1 deliberately

- deliberately
- on purpose
- intentionally
- knowingly
- consciously
- wilfully
- pointedly
- make a point of

deliberately /dɪˈlɪbərətli/ [adv] if you do something **deliberately**, you do it because you want to do it, and you hope it will have a particular result or effect: *She left the letter there deliberately so that you'd see it.* | *Police believe the fire was started deliberately.* | *Rogers was dismissed from the army for deliberately disobeying an order.* | *I think he was deliberately ignoring me.*

on purpose /ɒn ˈpɜːʳpəs/ [adv] spoken if you do something **on purpose**, you do it deliberately, for example in order to annoy people or to get an advantage for yourself – use this especially about things that are not very important: *I spilled my drink on purpose – I needed an excuse to leave the room.* | *Will always pronounces my name wrong. Do you think he does it on purpose?* | *Is he really that dumb or is he acting that way on purpose?*

intentionally /ɪnˈtenʃənəli/ [adv] if you do something **intentionally**, you do it deliberately – use this especially about actions that are wrong or illegal: *The jury had to decide whether he killed John Bishop intentionally or whether it was an accident.* | *The mayor denied intentionally misleading the public and proclaimed his innocence.* | *The article is intentionally provocative and looks likely to cause a stir.*

knowingly /ˈnəʊɪŋli/ [adv] if you **knowingly** do something wrong or illegal, you do it even though you know it is wrong: *If any employee knowingly breaks the terms of this contract they will be dismissed immediately.* | *Stansfield would never have knowingly become involved in political espionage.*

consciously /ˈkɒnʃəsli‖ˈkɑːn-/ [adv] if you do something **consciously**, you do it carefully and you think about it as you are doing it, especially because you know what the result of your actions might be: *I don't think she was consciously trying to hurt your feelings.* | *Most school teachers do not consciously discriminate between their students.*

wilfully British **/willfully** American /ˈwɪlfəli/ [adv] if you **wilfully** do something, you do it deliberately or do not try to stop it even though you know it is wrong or it will cause harm – used especially in legal contexts: *The mother could face a charge of wilfully neglecting her children.* | *The defendants were convicted of wilfully promoting racial hatred.* | *The new evidence was either not available or was wilfully ignored.*

pointedly /ˈpɔɪntɪ̇dli/ [adv] said or done in a way that will make other people notice you, especially to show them that you think they should do something: *Miss Phillips looked at the clock pointedly and I realized that it was time for me to leave.* | *The shopkeeper made a rude comment about shoplifters and looked pointedly at the boy standing next to me.* —**pointed** [adj] *My father has been asking some pointed questions about how I spend my money.*

make a point of /ˌmeɪk ə ˈpɔɪnt ɒv/ [v phrase] to deliberately do something because you think it is important to do it, or because you want other people to notice that you have done it **make a point of doing sth** *Kramer made a point of looking very bored while the colonel was speaking.* | *You should make a point of arriving fifteen minutes early at the office every morning – show that you're keen.* | **make a point of sth** *'Did you complain about it?' 'Yes, I made a point of it.'*

2 deliberate

- deliberate
- intentional
- conscious
- calculated
- premeditated

deliberate /dɪˈlɪbərɪ̇t/ [adj] use this about things that you do or say deliberately **deliberate attempt** *It was a deliberate attempt to prevent the truth from being known.* | **deliberate act of sth** *FBI agents believe Thursday's power failure was a deliberate act of sabotage.* | **quite deliberate** British *He definitely meant to be rude – it was quite deliberate.*

intentional /ɪnˈtenʃənəl/ [adj] use this about things that you do or say deliberately, especially about things that are wrong or illegal: *The damage was not intentional but I was still annoyed.* | *The jury has to decide whether the killing was an intentional act.* | *If their advertisements are shocking, this is entirely intentional.*

conscious /ˈkɒnʃəs‖ˈkɑːn-/ [adj only before noun] **conscious decision/effort/attempt etc** a decision, effort that you decide to make after thinking carefully about what the result would be: *Julia made a conscious effort to appear unconcerned, even though she was very upset.* | *Dylan's latest record is a conscious* *attempt to break away from his old image and try out a new style.*

calculated /ˈkælkjəleɪtəd/ [adj] deliberately and carefully planned – use this about something that is morally wrong or dishonest: *a calculated attempt to deceive the American public* | *The cruelty with which Mengele's orders were carried out was ruthless and calculated.* | *Statements made by Mr. Lyman were just a calculated scare tactic designed to frighten consumers.* | **cold and calculated** (=deliberate and without any pity) *She got rid of her victims one by one, with cold and calculated precision.*

premeditated /priːˈmedəteɪtəd‖prɪ-/ [adj] a **premeditated** crime or act of violence is one that is deliberate and has been planned – used especially in legal contexts: *The defense claim that the killing was not premeditated.* | *The maximum penalty for premeditated murder is death or life imprisonment.*

delicious

RELATED WORDS

opposite: **horrible**

▸ *see also* **taste, food, drink, meal, cook**

1 having a very good taste

▸ **delicious** ▸ **tasty** ▸ **good**

delicious /dɪˈlɪʃəs/ [adj] something that is **delicious** tastes very good, and you enjoy eating or drinking it: *Thank you, that was a delicious meal.* | *The apple pie is delicious with vanilla ice cream.* | *Mmm. This wine is delicious.*

tasty /ˈteɪsti/ [adj] food that is **tasty** has a strong taste that you like: *These sausages are really tasty – where did you buy them?* | *She makes a really tasty dish with chicken and rice.*

good ALSO **nice** British /gʊd, naɪs/ [adj] tasting nice and **good** to eat or drink: *This is a really good pizza. I think I'll have another slice.* | *That's good coffee – are you sure it's decaffeinated?* | *You can get some very nice bread at Walker's bakery.* | **taste good/nice** *The vegetables tasted surprisingly good.* | *This casserole tastes nice. How did you make it?* | **good/nice to eat** *Everyone has the capability of making themselves something good to eat when they get home in the evening.*

2 delicious and full of juice

▸ **juicy** ▸ **succulent**

juicy /ˈdʒuːsi/ [adj] **juicy** food contains a lot of juice and tastes good – use this especially about meat or fruit: *I like my steaks to be tender, juicy, and full of flavour.* | *As a starter, we had delicious juicy tomatoes stuffed with rice.*

succulent /ˈsʌkjələnt/ [adj] written **succulent** food contains a lot of juice and tastes good – use this especially about meat, fish, fruit, or vegetables: *This part of the country is famous for its fine wines and succulent peaches.* | *The chicken was golden and crispy on the outside and juicy and succulent inside.*

3 looking or smelling delicious

▸ **appetizing** ▸ **tempting** ▸ **mouth-watering** ▸ **make your mouth water**

appetizing ALSO **appetising** British /ˈæpətaɪzɪŋ/ [adj] food that looks or smells **appetizing** makes you feel that you want to eat it: *An appetizing smell of baked apples filled the house.* | *The soup didn't look very appetizing but it tasted delicious.* | *The average hospital serves meals that are neither appetizing nor nutritious.*

tempting /ˈtemptɪŋ/ [adj] food or drink that is **tempting** looks or smells so good that it is difficult to stop yourself from eating or drinking it, especially when you think you should not have it: *The chocolate cake was tempting but I couldn't have any because of my diet.* | *Contained in the pages of the book are tempting recipes from around the world.*

mouth-watering /ˈmaʊθ ˌwɔːtərɪŋ/ [adj] food that is **mouth-watering** smells or looks delicious, especially in a way that persuades you to buy or eat it: *The waitress came round with a tray of mouth-watering cream cakes.* | *The delicatessen sells a mouth-watering variety of cooked meats and cheeses.*

make your mouth water /ˌmeɪk jɔːʳ ˈmaʊθ ˌwɔːtəʳ/ [v phrase] if food or drink **makes your mouth water**, it makes you feel very hungry and ready to eat because it looks or smells so good: *The thought of bacon and eggs made her mouth water.*

depend/ it depends

when what happens is influenced by other facts or events

RELATED WORDS

▸ depend on someone *see* **need**

▸ *see also* **condition, necessary (2), if**

▸ **depend** ▸ **according to** ▸ **depending on sth** ▸ **be determined by** ▸ **be dictated by** ▸ **be based on** ▸ **be dependent on** ▸ **hinge on/hang on** ▸ **be riding on** ▸ **be decided by**

depend /dɪˈpend/ [v I] if something **depends** on a fact, result, decision etc, it is not fixed or decided because it will change if the fact, result, decision etc changes **it depends how/where/what etc** *I might not be able to go to France – it depends how much it costs.* | **it depends/that depends** spoken (=say this when your decision may change according to what happens) *'Are you going to apply for that job?' 'Well, it depends.'* | **it all depends** spoken (=say this to emphasize that you cannot be certain about something) *We still don't know whether we'll have to move to a new house or not – it all depends.* | **+ on** *The amount I earn depends on the kind of work I'm doing.*

according to /əˈkɔːʳdɪŋ tuː/ [prep] if something is done **according** to particular facts, a particular situation etc, these affect the way it is done: *Telephone charges vary according to the time of day.* | *The students were grouped according to age and ability.*

depending on sth /dɪˈpendɪŋ ɒn (sth)/ [prep] use this to say that what will happen or what you do will change according to what happens in another situation: *Inflation goes up and down depending on the state of the economy.* | *In many languages there are different words for 'you' depending on who you are talking to.* | *I kept getting different answers depending on who I asked.*

be determined by /biː dɪˈtɜːʳmɪnd baɪ/ [v phrase] if the quality or nature of something **is determined by** other things, it depends on those things for how it is made: *The colour of the rock is determined by the type of mineral present in it.* | *The ultimate flavor of the cheese variety is determined by the length of time it is allowed to mature.* | *An individual's metabolism is generally determined by his or her genetic make-up.*

be dictated by /biː dɪkˈteɪtə̇d baɪ/ [v phrase] if a decision, choice, or result **is dictated by** something, it depends very strongly on it, and leaves no choice for the people involved: *A country's choice of export products is dictated by geography, climate, and natural resources.* | *Any development in the city center is dictated by the city's historic preservation laws.*

be based on /biː ˈbeɪst ɒn/ [v phrase] if one decision, situation, calculation etc **is based on** another, the second is the main thing upon which the first decision etc depends: *Your pension will be based on the amount that you are earning when you retire.* | *This year's funding for the program is based on the number of applications that we received last year.* | *The jury's decision must be based on the evidence heard in court.*

be dependent on /biː dɪˈpendənt ɒn/ [v phrase] formal to depend on something: *The speed of the plane is dependent on the efficiency of the engines.* | *Benefits paid will be dependent on length of service with the company.*

hinge on/hang on /ˈhɪndʒ ɒn, ˈhæŋ ɒn / [phr v T] if a result, especially an important result, **hinges on** or **hangs on** something happening, it depends on it completely: *The future prospects of a student can hinge on his or her performance in these exams.* | *The case hinged on whether the jury believed the defendants had planned to kill anyone when they broke into the house.*

be riding on /biː ˈraɪdɪŋ ɒn/ [v phrase] if something important such as money or success **is riding on** the result of something else, it depends on it: *It's really stressful when you know that your whole future may be riding on this one interview.* | *Boxing has become big business, with a huge amount of money riding on the outcome of a fight.*

be decided by /biː dɪˈsaɪdə̇d baɪ/ [v phrase] if what someone does or what happens **is decided by** something else, it depends on it: *The future of the school will be decided by the results of this survey.* | *Your choice of tool will be decided by the hardness of the wood you are working on.*

describe

RELATED WORDS

▸ *see also* **detail, tell, write**

1 to describe someone or something

- describe
- give a description of
- talk about
- write about
- what sb/sth is like
- give an account of
- tell of

describe /dɪˈskraɪb/ [v T] to talk or write about a person, place, event etc, saying what they are like and giving details about them: *Could you try and describe the man you saw?* | *In her book, she describes her journey across the Sahara.* | **describe sb/sth as** *Police described the attack as particularly violent.* | **describe sb/sth to sb** *I tried to describe the feeling to my doctor, but she didn't understand.* | **describe how/what** *It's difficult to describe how I felt.*

give a description of /ˌɡɪv ə dɪˈskrɪpʃən ɒv/ [v phrase] to describe someone or something, especially by giving details about what they look like: *King gave a detailed description of a dark-haired muscular man to police.* | *The brochure gives a general description of the island and some of the things you can do there.*

talk about /ˈtɔːk əbaʊt/ [phr v T] to describe something that you have seen or experienced by talking to people about it: *Grandma always talks about the way they used to live on the farm.* | *You should talk about your problems with someone – maybe they can help you.*

write about /ˈraɪt əbaʊt/ [phr v T] to describe a person, place, event, situation etc by writing about it: *Have the children write about what they did last summer.* | *Purcell wrote about his son's illness for a popular magazine.*

what sb/sth is like /wɒt (sb/sth) ɪz ˈlaɪk/ spoken use this when you are asking someone to describe someone or something to you or when you are describing someone or something to them: *'I've just met Anna's new boyfriend.' 'What's he like?'* | *I'll try and explain to you what being in prison was like.*

give an account of /ˌɡɪv ən əˈkaʊnt ɒv/ [v phrase] to describe something that happened, giving only the facts and not adding your own feelings or opinions: *Please give a brief account of your previous work experience.* | *The second witness gave a similar account of what happened.*

tell of /ˈtel ɒv/ [phr v T] written to describe an event, situation etc, especially as though it was a story, in order to make it sound more exciting or impressive: *Many of the prisoners have told of the terrible conditions they were kept in and how they were beaten.* | **tell sb of** *In the evenings Morris would tell us of his youth spent in Europe.*

2 to describe someone or something in a way that shows your opinion

- describe sth/sb as
- characterize sb/sth as
- label
- portray/represent
- depict
- paint a picture

describe sth/sb as /dɪˈskraɪb (sth/sb) æz/ [v phrase] to describe someone or something in a particular way that shows your opinion of them: *I wouldn't describe the job as boring, just a little repetitive sometimes.* | *John describes himself as the intelligent but shy type.* | *De la Cruz is described as Mexico's greatest woman poet.*

characterize sb/sth as /ˈkærə̇ktəraɪz (sb/sth) æz/ [v phrase] to describe the character of someone or something in a particular way, especially with the result that people believe it to be true when it may not be: *A reporter characterized Mrs. Clinton as the most controversial first lady in modern history.* | *She grew up in a small Wisconsin community which she characterizes as conservative.*

label /ˈleɪbəl/ [v T] to describe someone or something in a negative way, especially incorrectly or unfairly: *Children who are labelled 'slow' usually get less attention from teachers.* | *Critics have unfairly labelled Young a racist.* | **label sb/sth as** *Campbell has labelled the commission's recommendations as sheer nonsense.*

portray/represent /pɔːʳˈtreɪ, ˌreprɪˈzent/ [v T] formal to describe someone or something in a particular way, especially in a way that makes people have an untrue idea of what they are like: *The magazine has been criticized for the way it portrays women.* | **portray/represent sb/sth as** *The treatment has been portrayed as a painless way of curing cancer, which is untrue.* | *Police have represented her as a willing participant in the crimes.*

depict /dɪˈpɪkt/ [v T] to describe someone or something, especially in writing, by providing a lot of details which give a very true idea of what they are like: *His stories depict life in Trinidad as seen through the eyes of a young boy.* | **depict sb/sth as** *In this new biography she is depicted as a lonely and unhappy woman.*

paint a picture /ˌpeɪnt ə ˈpɪktʃəʳ/ [v phrase] **paint a bleak/grim/rosy etc picture** to describe in a very pleasant or very unpleasant way, which may be very different from the truth **+ of** *My uncle's letters generally painted a rosy picture of how things were.* | *He went on to paint a discouraging picture of the problems facing the state.*

3 a written or spoken description

- description
- report
- account
- commentary
- portrayal
- descriptive
- profile

description /dɪˈskrɪpʃən/ [n C] what you say or write when you are describing a person, place, or thing **+ of** *Write a description of someone you know well.* | **give sb a description** *Tom gave the police a description of his car.* | **a full/detailed description** (=containing all the important details) *You can read a detailed description of the products on their Web site.*

report /rɪˈpɔːʳt/ [n C] a description of a situation or event, based on a study of the facts, that provides people with information about it and also tries to explain it: *The report is based on visits to schools in five cities.* | **+ on** *Amnesty International released another report on the government's use of torture.* | **newspaper/news/television report** *News reports suggest that over 300 people may have died.*

account /əˈkaʊnt/ [n C] a written or spoken description of something that happened **+ of** *The newspaper printed a detailed account of the trial.* | **give an account** *In the magazine, Cook gives a colorful account of his first meeting with Hamilton.*

commentary /ˈkɒməntəri‖ˈkɑːmənteri/ [n C] a spoken description of an event such as a race or sports event which is given while it is happening, especially on the radio or television: *Joe Garagiola will provide the commentary tonight on Channel 7.* | **+ on** *Now let's go over to our London studio for commentary on the wrestling.* | **running commentary** (=a continuous commentary all the time that something is happening) *Sarah was looking out the window and giving us a running commentary on what was happening in the street.*

portrayal /pɔːʳˈtreɪəl/ [n C] a description of a person, thing, place etc that deliberately chooses particular details about them in order to make people form a particular opinion about them, especially a bad opinion **+ of** *Many have criticized Hollywood for its unrealistic portrayal of life in America.* | **portrayal of sb/sth as** *I cannot accept the article's portrayal of these men as bloodthirsty terrorists.*

descriptive /dɪˈskrɪptɪv/ [adj] a piece of writing that is **descriptive** contains a lot of details describing what someone or something is like, rather than telling a story or describing events: *The book contains many fine descriptive passages about everyday life in China.* | *When you write your paragraph, include as many descriptive details as possible.*

profile /ˈprəʊfaɪl/ [n C] a short description of someone's life, work, and character, especially of someone famous, that is written in a newspaper, shown on television etc **+ of** *Every week the magazine presents the profile of a well-known sports personality.* | *I heard a fascinating profile of Madeleine Albright on the radio yesterday.*

deserve

RELATED WORDS

▸ *see also* **earn, praise, give**

1 to deserve something good

- deserve/be owed
- well-deserved/well-earned
- have earned

deserve/be owed /dɪˈzɜːʳv, biː ˈəʊd/ [v T/v phrase] if you **deserve** something, it is right that you should have it, because you have worked hard, done something well etc: *Well done. I think we all deserve a drink after that.* | *Jill was awarded first prize, and she thoroughly deserved it.* | *After all that hard work, you deserve a rest.* | **deserve to do sth** *The team have trained hard and they deserve to do well.* | *Chang played better than Sampras, and he deserved to win.* | **deserve a medal** (=used humorously about someone who has worked very hard or done something very difficult) *Anyone who can work with that man deserves a medal.*

well-deserved/well-earned /ˌwel dɪˈzɜːʳvd◂, ˌwel ˈɜːʳnd◂/ [adj] a **well-deserved** or **well-earned** rest, win, drink etc is one that you deserve to have, because you have worked hard: *The game ended in a well-deserved victory for the German team.* | *At 9 o'clock, she settled down for a well-earned rest.*

have earned /həv ˈɜːʳnd/ [v phrase] to deserve something such as reward, success, or someone's respect etc because you have worked very hard or done something impressive: *I think Paul should get first prize – he's certainly earned it.* | *Let's have a break now – we've definitely earned it.*

2 to deserve something bad

- deserve
- serve sb right
- get what you deserve
- be asking for it
- had it coming
- get your comeuppance
- get your just deserts

deserve /dɪˈzɜːʳv/ [v T not in progressive] if you think that someone **deserves** something bad that happens to them, you think it is fair that it happens because they have done something wrong or stupid **deserve to do sth** *Anyone who drives like that deserves to lose their licence.* | **deserve it** (=deserve the bad things that happen) *'You really weren't very nice to her.' 'Well, she deserved it!'* | **get what you deserve** (=when something bad happens to you and you deserve it) *He was a bully, and in the end he got what he deserved.*

serve sb right /ˌsɜːʳv (sb) ˈraɪt/ [v phrase not in progressive] spoken use this to say you think someone deserves something bad that happens to them because they have been unkind or done something stupid **+ for** *'I feel terrible.' 'Serves you right for drinking so much last night.'* | **it serves sb right** *It'd serve him right if Jo walked out on him.*

get what you deserve /ˌget wɒt juː dɪˈzɜːʳv/ [v phrase] especially spoken use this when you think someone deserves a punishment or bad experience, because it is a result of their own actions: *'Do you feel sorry for him?' 'No, he shouldn't have hit that guy – he got what he deserved.'*

be asking for it /biː ˈɑːskɪŋ fər ɪt‖-ˈæsk-/ [v phrase] spoken say this when something bad happens to someone and you think they deserve it because their behaviour made it very likely to happen: *Anyone who invites a complete stranger into their house is asking for it.*

had it coming /ˌhæd ɪt ˈkʌmɪŋ/ [v phrase] spoken use this to say you think someone deserves something bad that happens to them, and this is what you expected to happen: *I don't feel sorry for her at all. She had it coming.* | **had it coming to you/her etc** *'Terry's very upset about his wife leaving him.' 'Well he's had it coming to him for years.'*

get your comeuppance /ˌget jɔːʳ kʌmˈʌpəns/ [v phrase] to finally get the punishment or something bad that you deserve because of the way you have behaved: *The evil Mr Grove gets his comeuppance at the end of the story.* | *She's callous and snobbish and it's time she got her comeuppance.*

get your just deserts /get jɔːʳ ˌdʒʌst dɪˈzɜːʳts/ [v phrase] to finally get the punishment you deserve, especially after having avoided it for a long time: *Tobin finally got his just deserts, and was sentenced to 8 years' imprisonment.* | *This is a movie in which everyone gets their just deserts in the end.*

3 to deserve an explanation/answer/apology etc

▸ deserve

deserve /dɪˈzɜːʳv/ [v T] ALSO **be owed** [v phrase] **deserve/be owed an explanation/apology/answer** use this to say that someone should have an explanation etc, especially from someone who does not want to explain or apologize: *She feels she deserves an apology after all the cruel things you said about her.* | *Why didn't you turn up for the meeting? I think I'm at least owed some kind of explanation.* | *Why did ministers fail to inform the public of these dangers? The people of Britain deserve answers.*

4 to deserve attention

▸ deserve/merit

deserve/merit /dɪˈzɜːʳv, ˈmerɪ̇t/ [v T not in progressive] if a suggestion, idea, or plan **deserves** or **merits** consideration, attention etc, it is good enough to be considered or examined in more detail: *Neal's book explores some interesting ideas which deserve attention.* | *This is a complex problem, that deserves closer consideration.* | *It's an interesting idea and it certainly merits another look.*

design

the way that something has been planned to look or work

RELATED WORDS

- building design *see* **build**
- *see also* **pattern, plan, invent, draw, decorate, simple**

1 the design of something

▸ design

design /dɪˈzaɪn/ [n C/U] the way something has been planned and made, including its appearance and the way it works – use this about things like furniture, clothes, buildings, or cars: *Conran's furniture was based on simple, modern designs.* | *The success of the product was largely due to good design.* | **+ of** *The basic design of the vehicle has been improved.* | **in design** *The new hockey rink is similar in design to the one in San José.*

2 to plan how something new will look or work

▸ design ▸ plan

design /dɪˈzaɪn/ [v T] to make drawings or plans of something new that will be made or built: *Sally designs and makes all her own clothes.* | *The car was designed and built in Korea.* | **be well/badly/poorly designed** *The offices weren't very well designed – the rooms are too small and it's much too hot in summer.* | **be designed to do sth** *Airbags are currently designed to protect average-sized adult males.*

plan /plæn/ [v T] to design a large area, such as a town or a park, and decide how all the different parts should be arranged and what it should look like: *It took them years to plan and build the plaza downtown.* | *The town was originally planned in the 1950s, when there were fewer cars.* | *We planned the building very carefully with special facilities for the disabled.*

3 someone whose job is designing things

▸ designer ▸ planner
▸ architect

designer /dɪˈzaɪnəʳ/ [n C] someone whose job is to design new machines, furniture, clothes etc: *Designers at Ford say the car's soft shape is supposed to be attractive to women.* | **fashion/furniture/software etc designer** *The show features clothes by famous fashion designers like Jean-Paul Gaultier.* | *Anyone with experience as a Web page designer can easily get a job.*

architect /ˈɑːʳkɪ̇tekt/ [n C] someone whose job is to design buildings: *The Imperial Hotel in Tokyo was designed by the famous architect Frank Lloyd Wright.* | *We're working with a team of architects on the plans for the new building.*

planner /ˈplænəʳ/ [n C] someone who is responsible for planning something large such as a city, park, or large public building: *City planners have been working for years on a new design for the plaza.* | *Planners expect the new segment of the subway to carry as many as 3,000 people per day.*

destroy

RELATED WORDS

- to gradually be destroyed by a natural process *see* **decay**
- *see also* **damage, explode, spoil, disaster, break, broken/not broken**

1 to destroy an area or place

- destroy
- devastate
- wreck
- be flattened
- obliterate
- be ravaged by
- reduce sth to rubble/ashes etc
- trash

destroy /dɪ'strɔɪ/ [v T] to damage something so badly that it cannot be repaired: *The earthquake destroyed much of the city.* | *In Brazil the rainforests are gradually being destroyed.* | *The factory was almost completely destroyed by fire.*

devastate /'devəsteɪt/ [v T] to cause so much damage over a large area that most of the buildings, trees, and crops there are destroyed: *A huge explosion devastated the downtown area last night.* | *The country has been devastated by floods.* | *Years of war have devastated this island nation.*

wreck /rek/ [v T] to deliberately damage a building or room very badly: *He came home drunk again, threatening to wreck the apartment.* | *Bulldozers were brought in to wreck the tents and shacks that protesters had put up.*

be flattened /bi: 'flætnd/ [v phrase] if an area such as a town or forest **is flattened** all the buildings or trees there are destroyed by bombs, storms etc: *It will cost $400 million to rebuild the houses that were flattened in the fighting.* | **be flattened by** *Thousands of miles of woodland were flattened by storms last month.*

obliterate /ə'blɪtəreɪt/ [v T] to destroy a place so completely that nothing remains, and it is difficult to see or imagine what was once there: *Entire sections of the city were obliterated by the repeated bombing.* | *Frequent flooding eventually obliterated all traces of the community that used to live there.*

be ravaged by /bi: 'rævɪdʒd baɪ/ [v phrase] if a place or an area **is ravaged by** war, fire etc, it is very badly damaged and a lot of it is destroyed – used especially in newspapers and news reports: *The country has been ravaged by civil war for the last 10 years.* | *North Africa and the Middle East are regularly ravaged by plagues of locusts.*

reduce sth to rubble/ashes etc /rɪˌdju:s (sth) tə 'rʌbəl‖rɪˌdu:s-/ [v phrase] to completely destroy a building: *Their new two-storey house had been reduced to ashes in the fire.* | *We won't stand by while developers reduce the historic remains of the city to rubble.*

trash /træʃ/ [v T] informal to deliberately destroy a lot of the things in a room, house, etc: *Someone had broken in and trashed her apartment.* | *Band members have been accused of trashing their hotel rooms.*

2 to deliberately destroy a building

- demolish
- knock down
- tear down

demolish /dɪ'mɒlɪʃ‖dɪ'mɑ:-/ [v T] to destroy a building using special equipment, because it is old or not safe: *Eventually, in 1997, the apartment block was demolished.* | *When they demolished the church, a cave was discovered beneath it.*

knock down ALSO **pull down** British /ˌnɒk 'daʊn‖ˌnɑ:k-, ˌpʊl 'daʊn/ [phr v T] to deliberately destroy a building or wall because it is not now needed, not safe etc **knock/pull down sth** *If you knocked down this wall, the living room would be a lot bigger.* | *She was brought up in a tatty little house that has since been pulled down.* | **knock/pull sth down** *They'll have to knock down these houses when they build the new road.*

tear down /ˌteəʳ 'daʊn/ [phr v T] to deliberately destroy a building or other structure, especially in order to put something else in its place – use this especially when you do not approve of this action **tear down sth** *We need laws to keep people from tearing down these beautiful old buildings.* | **tear sth down** *I'll be really upset if they tear the old theater down.*

3 to completely destroy a vehicle

- wreck
- write off

wreck /rek/ [v T] to damage a car, boat etc very badly in an accident so that it cannot be used again: *They had stolen a car and wrecked it on the freeway.* | *Glen drove right into a tree and wrecked his car.* —**wrecked** [adj] *Wrecked vehicles lay abandoned at the roadside.*

write off /ˌraɪt 'ɒf/ [phr v T] British **/total** /'təʊtl/ American [v T] to damage a vehicle, especially a car, so badly in an accident that it cannot be repaired or used again: *I totaled my car in a blizzard once, and I won't drive in the snow anymore.* | **write off sth/write sth off** *She wrote her mother's car off the first time she drove it.*

4 to destroy someone's relationships, hopes, happiness etc

- destroy
- wreck
- break sb's spirit/resolve/will etc
- ruin

destroy /dɪ'strɔɪ/ [v T] to **destroy** someone's relationships, hopes, happiness etc: *Even close relationships can be destroyed by alcoholism.* | *Few things destroy trust more than telling a friend's secrets.* | *Chandler worried that the scandal would destroy his chances for a respectable career.*

wreck /rek/ [v T] to completely destroy someone's relationships, hopes, chances etc, especially by doing or saying something without thinking of the likely results: *Ron's affair wrecked our marriage.* | *His confrontational speech has wrecked any chances of a peace settlement.*

break sb's spirit/resolve/will etc /ˌbreɪk (sb's) 'spɪrɪ̈t/ [v phrase] to destroy someone's determination although they have tried hard to keep it: *Years in prison did not break Mr Mandela's spirit.* | *Her captors used violence and psychological torture to try to break her will.*

ruin /'ru:ɪ̈n/ [v T] to completely spoil or destroy someone's chances, hopes, relationship etc: *Phelps's mistake has ruined her chances of winning the championship.* | *Patty's ex-boyfriend is ruining our relationship.*

5 likely to destroy something

- destructive
- devastating

destructive /dɪˈstrʌktɪv/ [adj] likely to destroy something or cause serious damage to it: *The border war has been wasteful and destructive.* | *The destructive side-effects of pesticides are now well known.* | *Alcoholics often tend to have stormy and destructive relationships.*

devastating /ˈdevəsteɪtɪŋ/ [adj] causing very serious damage to all the buildings, trees, crops etc in an area, so that they are almost completely destroyed: *The palace was rebuilt in 1832 after a devastating fire.* | **have a devastating effect** *The oil spill had a devastating effect on sea birds and other wildlife.*

6 when something is destroyed

- destruction
- devastation
- demolition
- be/lie in ruins

destruction /dɪˈstrʌkʃən/ [n U] when something is destroyed: *The war caused widespread death and destruction.* | **+ of** *The destruction of forests for timber, fuel, and charcoal increased during the 18th century.*

devastation /ˌdevəˈsteɪʃən/ [n U] the result of an area being completely and violently destroyed: *Few buildings in the city had escaped devastation.* | **utter devastation** (=complete devastation) *The scene after the explosion was one of utter devastation.*

demolition /ˌdeməˈlɪʃən/ [n U] the deliberate destruction of a building, because it is in bad condition or in order to build a new one: *The old factory will be knocked down by demolition experts.* | **+ of** *Building the new freeway is going to mean the demolition of an entire housing complex.*

be/lie in ruins /biː, laɪ ɪn ˈruːɪnz/ [v phrase] if a town or building **is in ruins** or **lies in ruins**, it has been completely destroyed: *After the war entire neighborhoods lay in ruins.* | **leave sth in ruins** *Four days and nights of continuous bombing had left the city in ruins.*

7 a place or thing that is destroyed

- wreckage
- ruins
- wreck
- write-off

wreckage /ˈrekɪdʒ/ [n U] the broken parts of a car, plane etc that has crashed: *Wreckage from the plane was scattered over a large area.* | *Investigators are looking through pieces of the wreckage for any clues about the crash.*

ruins /ˈruːɪnz/ [n plural] the parts of a building or town that remain after it has been destroyed: *The tour will visit ancient monasteries and Roman ruins in Merida.* | **+ of** *Gunfire still echoed through the ruins of the city.*

wreck /rek/ [n C] a ship that has been sunk, or a car that has been very badly damaged in a crash: *Divers went down to search the wreck.* | *The car was a complete wreck, but the driver escaped with minor injuries.*

write-off /ˈraɪt ɒf/ [n C] British a car that has been so badly damaged that it cannot be used again: *The car was a complete write-off – I was lucky I wasn't killed.*

detail

RELATED WORDS

- see also **information, describe**

1 a single piece of information

- detail
- point
- thing

detail /ˈdiːteɪl‖dɪˈteɪl/ [n C usually plural] a single fact or piece of information about something: *The story's very complicated – I can't remember the exact details.* | **+ of** *The student advice office provides details of all the university courses in the country.* | *Baker advises the President on the details of foreign policy.* | **personal details** (=details such as someone's age, their address, whether they are married etc) *To apply for a loan, first fill in the section marked 'Personal Details'.* | **full details** *For full details of this exclusive offer, just send in a stamped addressed envelope.* | **further details** *The donated liver came from the UK, but the hospital is giving no further details.*

point /pɔɪnt/ [n C] a detail that you need to talk about when you are discussing a plan, statement, or written agreement: *There's one point in your letter that is not quite clear.* | *Almost everything has been agreed. There is just one final point that needs to be settled.* | **small/minor point** (=one that is not very important) *We only have a few small points left to discuss.*

thing /θɪŋ/ [n C] spoken a detail in something such as a plan, statement, or written agreement: *There's one thing I'm not clear about, and that's how we are going to get to the airport.* | *In the new version of the story, a few things have been changed.*

2 details about something

- particulars
- specifics
- the ins and outs of sth
- the nitty-gritty
- technicalities
- the minutiae

particulars /pəʳˈtɪkjələʳz/ [n plural] the exact details about a particular person, plan, agreement etc: *I gave him all the particulars he needed: my name, address, and the name of the hospital where I work.* | **+ of** *The treaty was signed despite some haggling over the particulars of each country's stock of weapons.* | **take down sb's particulars** (=write down their personal details, for example their name and address) *After the police officer had taken down their particulars, the two men explained what had happened.*

specifics /spəˈsɪfɪks/ [n plural] all the separate facts and details about something, especially an official proposal, contract, or statement: *It ought to be possible for partners to disagree on specifics while agreeing in general terms.* | **+ of** *Few of the specifics of James' proposals were implemented.* | **get down to specifics** (=consider or talk about the details) *Now that we've agreed on the general principles of our policy, let's get down to specifics.*

the ins and outs of sth /ði ˌɪnz ənd ˈaʊts əv (sth)/ [n phrase] informal all the exact details of something complicated: *I can't tell you all the ins and outs of the situation over the phone, I'll write to you next week.* | *I found I needed to spend quite a while learning all the ins and outs of the system.*

the nitty-gritty /ðə ˌnɪti ˈgrɪti/ [n phrase] informal the most important basic facts about something **get down to the nitty-gritty** (=consider or discuss the most important basic facts) *You've got to get down to the nitty-gritty: how the stage will look, what the lighting will be like, and who designs the costumes.* | **the nitty-gritty details/issues** *Kennedy immersed himself in the nitty-gritty details of the prosecutions.*

technicalities /ˌteknɪˈkælɪtiz/ [n plural] technical details of something such as a system, process, or skill that you can only understand if you have special knowledge or training: *He got a job at a printer's and quickly learned the technicalities such as paper sizes and the processes involved.* | **+ of** *They discussed the technicalities of this delicate operation for some time.* | *Although most of us do not know much about the technicalities of surveys, we have a broad idea of what they are about.*

the minutiae /ðə maɪˈnjuːʃiaɪ‖-mɪˈnuː-/ [n plural] formal very small and exact details that are not really important: *Don't get bogged down in factual minutiae.* | **+ of** *He carefully recorded the minutiae of his social life in his diary.*

3 small details in a contract or set of rules

- the small print
- technicality

the small print /ðə ˈsmɔːl ˌprɪnt/ [n phrase] details that are included in a contract or agreement and are written in small print, with the result that people do not always notice them: *I'm afraid you can't cancel your contract now. You should have read the small print.* | *A close study of the small print will reveal that many of these insurance policies do not cover the cost of repairing storm damage.*

technicality /ˌteknɪˈkælɪti/ [n C usually singular] a small detail in a set of rules or a law, especially one on which a decision is based: *The vote was declared invalid because of a technicality.* | **on a technicality** (=because of a technicality) *Baxter was released on a technicality because his 'offence' was committed in the city, and only a city judge had the authority to sign the warrant.*

4 with a lot of details

- detailed
- in detail
- elaborate
- go into detail/details
- specify
- blow-by-blow account
- in-depth

detailed /ˈdiːteɪld‖dɪˈteɪld/ [adj] a **detailed** description, explanation, picture etc contains a lot of details: *The police have issued a detailed description of the man they are looking for.* | *Do you have a more detailed map of the area?* | *Her biography is clear, detailed, and illuminating.*

in detail /ɪn ˈdiːteɪl‖-dɪˈteɪl/ [adv] if you discuss or consider something **in detail**, you discuss or consider all the details: *I haven't had time to look at the plans in detail yet.* | **in more/greater detail** *This problem is discussed in more detail in Chapter 7.* | **in great detail** *Fortunately, she was able to describe her attacker in great detail.* | **in some detail** *The layout of the house had been described to me in some detail.*

elaborate /ɪˈlæbərət/ [adj] carefully produced and full of details: *The diaries have been published in one volume, with elaborate biographical notes by Professor Emson.* | *The lawyer had concocted an elaborate defence that gave a totally false impression of what happened.* | **an elaborate excuse** *She had prepared an elaborate excuse for her absence.*

go into detail/details /ˌgəʊ ɪntə ˈdiːteɪl(z)‖-dɪˈteɪl(z)/ [v phrase] to include a lot of details when you are describing or explaining something: *Without going into detail, I can tell you that we have had a very successful year.* | *Be brief. If you go into too much detail people will get bored.* | *Chapter 1 is a brief outline of the process, then the next chapter goes into all the technical details.*

specify /ˈspesɪfaɪ/ [v T] to state something exactly and with full details, so that what you want, what must be done etc is completely clear: *The order specifies a December deadline for completion of the work.* | **+ that** *The rules clearly specify that competitors are not allowed to accept payment.* | **+ which/where/ how etc** *Architects usually specify which particular hardwood they want to use.*

blow-by-blow account /ˌbləʊ baɪ bləʊ əˈkaʊnt/ [n phrase] a full and detailed description of an event, in which everything that happened is described in correct order – use this especially when you want to say that this is boring and unnecessary: *His memoirs are simply a blow-by-blow account of battles, and contain very little personal comment or reflection.*

in-depth /ˌɪn ˈdepθ◂/ [adj] thorough, and giving as much detail as possible: *The committee has ordered an in-depth study of juvenile crime.* | *We shall be conducting a series of in-depth interviews with economic experts.* | *The aim of the neighbourhood studies was to obtain in-depth information from a number of selected communities.*

5 not containing many details

- general
- rough
- broad
- outline
- not go into detail

general /ˈdʒenərəl/ [adj only before noun] a **general** description or explanation of something contains the most basic information but does not include all the details: *The course is called 'A General Introduction to Computing'.* | *This general description of the countryside oversimplifies what is really a very complicated pattern of soils and climate.* | **a general idea** (=basic knowledge) *This guidebook will give you a good general idea of the city.*

rough /rʌf/ [adj only before noun] not exact or complete, but with enough details for you to understand something **rough plan/outline etc** *We've drawn up a rough plan but we haven't worked out all the costs.* | *I have not been able to do more than suggest the rough outline of this approach.* | **a rough idea** (=a basic explanation or understanding) *Give us a rough idea of what you're trying to do.*

broad /brɔːd/ [adj only before noun] **broad outline/generalization etc** giving you basic information, so that you can understand a situation, but not giving many details: *Can you give me a broad outline of what the speech was about?* | *It's only a short course, but it's enough to give you a broad understanding of the subject.* | *To say that people are healthier than they used to be is a broad generalization – the reality is a little more complex.*

outline /ˈaʊtlaɪn/ [adj only before noun] **outline knowledge/agreement/approval etc** based on general principles, not on exact details: *Students taking this course need to have at least an outline knowledge of computing.* | *The two leaders have reached an out-*

line agreement on controlling short range nuclear weapons.

not go into detail /nɒt gəʊ ɪntə 'di:teɪl‖-dɪ'teɪl/ [v phrase] if you do **not go into detail** when you are telling someone about something, you only give them the basic facts, without any details: *It was only a quick explanation – he didn't really go into detail.*

6 not containing enough details

- vague
- sketchy
- thin

vague /veɪg/ [adj] something that is **vague** is not clear because it does not provide enough details: *Dave's instructions were rather vague.* | *I had heard vague rumours that they were getting married.*

sketchy /'sketʃi/ [adj] something that is **sketchy** is not thorough or complete enough because it lacks details: *It would be very unwise to change our policy on the basis of such a sketchy report.* | *I'm afraid my knowledge of the subject is rather sketchy.*

thin /θɪn/ [adj not before noun] a piece of information or a description that is **thin** is not detailed enough to be useful or effective: *I was disappointed with your history essay, it seemed a little thin in terms of content.* | *I'm afraid the evidence is really too thin as it stands. We need to investigate further.*

7 to add details to what you have said

- give (sb) more details
- expand on/ enlarge on
- go into more/ greater detail
- be more specific/be more explicit
- elaborate
- specifically

give (sb) more details /ˌgɪv (sb) mɔ:ʳ 'di:teɪlz‖-dɪ'teɪlz/ [v phrase] to give more information about something by adding details to what you have already said or written: *Can you give me more details about the cost of these courses, please?* | *The press officer was unable to give any more details about the assassination attempt.*

expand on/enlarge on /ɪk'spænd ɒn, ɪn'lɑ:ʳdʒ ɒn/ [phr v T] formal to provide more information about something in order to make it easier for someone to understand: *Could you expand on your last comment, please?* | *When asked to expand on his accusations of injustice, the journalist refused to say any more.* | *I was unsure whether this was meant as an insult or a compliment, but he didn't choose to enlarge on his remark.*

go into more/greater detail /ˌgəʊ ɪntə ˌmɔ:ʳ, ˌgreɪtəʳ 'di:teɪl‖-dɪ'teɪl/ [v phrase] to give someone more details about something than you have already said or written: *I don't have time to go into more detail. Perhaps we could talk about this tomorrow.* | *I would like you to tell your story to my colleagues, and they may want you to go into greater detail.* | **+ about** *Her talk was interesting, but I wish she'd gone into more detail about the early part of her career.*

be more specific/be more explicit /bi: ˌmɔ:ʳ spə'sɪfɪk, bi: ˌmɔ:r ɪk'splɪsət/ [v phrase] to give much clearer and more detailed information about something, especially when you have been asked to do this: *I don't understand what your plan is exactly. Could you be a little more specific?* | **+ about** *The main political parties need to be much more explicit about their policies for the environment.*

elaborate /ɪ'læbəreɪt/ [v I/T] formal to provide more details about something that you have said or written, especially in order to make it easier to understand: *What exactly do you mean by 'traditional education'? Would you care to elaborate?* | **+ on/upon** *I would like now to elaborate upon the points raised in my introduction.* | **elaborate an argument/point etc** *This argument will be elaborated more fully in the next chapter.*

specifically /spə'sɪfɪkli/ [adv] use this to add a particular detail or example to what you are already saying, so that people know exactly what you are going to talk about: *In the next chapter I want to explore the question of the cultural boundaries between different subjects. Specifically I will look at what we mean by the terms 'art' and 'science'.*

8 too concerned with small details

- pedantic
- fussy

pedantic /pɪ'dæntɪk/ [adj] too concerned with rules and details that most people do not think are important: *Don't be so pedantic – does it really matter if I don't pronounce it right?* | *The papers were stacked with pedantic neatness on his desk.* | *The booklet that accompanies the CD is informative and scholarly, without being pedantic.*

fussy /'fʌsi/ [adj] someone who is **fussy** is too concerned with unimportant details of correctness, neatness, comfort etc and is hard to please: *My grandmother was a notoriously fussy housekeeper.* | *Although he spent three years writing these songs, the album does not sound fussy or labored.* | **+ about** *He's very fussy about his drinks being served in the right kind of glass.*

determined

when you have definitely decided to do something, and you will not let anyone stop you

RELATED WORDS

- *see also* **no matter what/how much, insist, confident/not confident, ambitious, brave/not brave**

1 determined to do something

- determined
- be set on
- set your mind on
- be intent on
- adamant
- purposefully
- be resolved
- mean business
- play hardball
- tenacious

determined /dɪ'tɜ:ʳmənd/ [adj] if you are **determined** to do something, you have decided that you are definitely going to do it, and you will not let anything stop you: *There's no point in trying to stop her – it'll only make her more determined.* | **+ to do sth** *I was determined to be a professional dancer, and practised for hours every day.* | *Both sides in the dispute seemed determined not to compromise.* | **+ (that)** *She was determined that her children should have the best possible education.*

be set on /bi: 'set ɒn/ [v phrase] to be determined to do something, especially something important that will affect your whole life, even if other people think you should not do it **be set on (doing) sth** *Nina seems to be set on marrying him.* | **be dead set on sth** (=extremely determined to do something) *I didn't* *particularly want to go to Africa, but Bob was dead set on the idea.*

set your mind on /ˌset jɔːʳ ˈmaɪnd ɒn/ [v phrase] if you **set your mind on** something, you decide that that is what you definitely want to do or have, especially something that you will have to work hard to achieve **set your mind on (doing) sth** *Once Tammy's set her mind on something, she doesn't rest until she's done it.* | *She's set her mind on having a big posh wedding.*

be intent on /biː ɪnˈtent ɒn/ [v phrase] to be determined to do something, especially something that other people do not approve of or think you should do: *Michael left school at fifteen, intent on a career in showbusiness.* | **be intent on (doing) sth** *He's always seems intent on stirring up trouble among his colleagues.*

adamant /ˈædəmənt/ [adj not before noun] determined not to change your opinion or decision, especially when other people are trying to persuade you to change it: *The man in the shop was adamant. 'Definitely not,' he said.* | **+ that** *Taylor was adamant that she was not going to quit.* | **be adamant in your belief/refusal/own mind** *Nicolson was always adamant in his belief that his films did not encourage drug-taking.* | **+ about** *To this day, Matthews is adamant about his innocence.*

purposefully /ˈpɜːʳpəsfəli/ [adv] in a way that shows that you are determined to do something: *She strode purposefully up to the door and rang the bell loudly.*

be resolved /biː rɪˈzɒlvd‖-ˈzɑːlvd/ [v phrase] formal to be determined to do something because you are sure that it is the right thing to do **+ to do sth** *The new President is resolved to impose a number of reforms.* | **+ that** *Our city authorities are resolved that the new school will be built within six months.*

mean business /ˌmiːn ˈbɪznɪ̈s/ [v phrase not in progressive] to be determined to do something and show other people that you are determined to do it, even if it involves harming someone: *And to prove we mean business, our members will stage a one-day strike next week.* | *Firm action would show both sides that the EU and the UN really meant business.*

play hardball /pleɪ ˈhɑːʳdbɔːl/ [v phrase] American informal to be very determined to get what you want, especially in business or politics: *Toymaker Mattel is getting ready to play hardball in an effort to persuade Hasbro to reconsider a merger.* | **+ with** *The Deputy Prime Minister told reporters that Canada was ready to play hardball with the US.*

tenacious /tɪ̈ˈneɪʃəs/ [adj] refusing to stop trying to do something even though the situation is difficult or people are opposing you: *As a reporter, David was tougher and more tenacious than the other three.* | *He was the most tenacious politician in South Korea.* —**tenaciously** [adv] *The company tenaciously insisted on their right to pay tax at the lower level.* | **cling/hold on etc tenaciously to sth** *Rose clung tenaciously to her original idea.*

2 someone who has a determined character

- determined
- single-minded
- strong-willed
- uncompromising
- feisty
- tough

determined /dɪˈtɜːʳmɪ̈nd/ [adj] someone who is **determined** works very hard to achieve what they want to achieve, and will not let problems stop them: *Not many women went to university in those days, but Dorothy was a very determined woman.* | *I was immediately impressed by how determined he was.*

single-minded /ˌsɪŋgəl ˈmaɪndɪ̈d◂/ [adj] someone who is **single-minded** works very hard in order to achieve one particular thing, and thinks that everything else is much less important: *During a war, a leader must be single-minded and, if necessary, ruthless.* | **sb's single-minded pursuit of sth** *Many athletes withdraw from the world in their single-minded pursuit of their sport.* | **single-minded determination/ambition/commitment** *Her single-minded commitment to the job meant that she had little time left for her family.*

strong-willed /ˌstrɒŋ ˈwɪld◂‖ˌstrɔːŋ-/ [adj] always very determined to do what you want to do, even if other people think it is not a good idea to do it: *At seventy-nine, she is as strong-willed as she ever was.* | *Sally was only 14, but Nick no longer knew how to handle his strong-willed young daughter.*

uncompromising /ʌnˈkɒmprəmaɪzɪŋ‖-ˈkɑːm-/ [adj] unwilling to change your opinions or intentions because you are sure you are right, even when other people think you are being unreasonable: *At work, George was known as an uncompromising businessman.* | *The District Officers were uncompromising in their opposition to the proposals of the wildlife conservationists.*

feisty /ˈfaɪsti/ [adj] someone who is **feisty** is determined to get what they want, and is not afraid of stating their opinion, or fighting for it: *Davis was known in Hollywood as the feistiest actress of her day.* | *Pavlov was feisty in his opposition to the Soviets, but, aware of his fame, they were forced to ignore his insults.* | *Riordan frequented the restaurant for 40 years, coming back for the food and the feisty attitude of the staff.*

tough /tʌf/ [adj] someone who is **tough** is determined to succeed at anything they do, and does not let difficult or frightening situations stop them: *My grandmother was a tough old lady, who lived through some very hard times.* | *In games like this it is more important to be mentally tough, than physically fit.* | *Voters traditionally believe that women are not as tough as men on crime and defense issues.*

3 determined in a way that is annoying or silly

- stubborn
- obstinate
- pig-headed
- headstrong
- wilful
- not listen

stubborn /ˈstʌbəʳn/ [adj] someone who is **stubborn** refuses to change their mind about something, even when people think they are wrong or are being unreasonable: *I told him it was a bad idea, but Dave's so stubborn that he just never listens.* | *a stubborn old man* —**stubbornly** [adv] *My grandmother stubbornly refuses to eat any 'foreign' foods.*

obstinate /ˈɒbstɪ̈nɪ̈t‖ˈɑːb-/ [adj] someone who is **obstinate** always does what they want and refuses to change their mind, even when this is annoying and unreasonable: *How do you deal with an obstinate teenager who always says she isn't hungry?* | *You know I'm right really. You're just being obstinate.* —**obstinately** [adv] *She obstinately refused to admit she was wrong.*

pig-headed /ˌpɪg ˈhedɪ̈d◂/ [adj] informal use this about someone who refuses to change their mind when you think that what they want to do is stupid: *He really was the most pig-headed man I've ever had* *the misfortune to meet.* | *Don't be so pig-headed! You can't possibly drive home after the amount you've had to drink.*

headstrong /'hedstrɒŋ‖-strɔːŋ/ [adj] someone who is **headstrong** is very independent and wants to do things in the way that they want, without listening to other people's advice or thinking about the results of their actions: *Leo's parents soon found that they were completely unable to control their headstrong son.* | *Suzie was headstrong, and sometimes thoughtless of other people's feelings.*

wilful British **/willful** American /'wɪlfəl/ [adj] someone who is **wilful**, especially a child or young person, deliberately behaves badly by continuing to do what they want to do, even after they have been told to stop: *Billy is a very wilful little boy who's constantly being punished for not doing as he's told.* | *Sometimes kids who are described as difficult or wilful just need a little extra love and attention.*

not listen /nɒt 'lɪsən/ [v phrase] if you say that someone **will not listen**, you mean that they refuse to accept other people's helpful advice or opinions: *I've told him again and again what I think, but he won't listen.* | **not listen to reason** *Wait until she calms down. She's far too upset at the moment to listen to reason.*

4 extremely determined to do something, even if it is wrong

- go to any lengths/stop at nothing
- be hellbent on
- whatever the cost
- come hell or high water
- ruthless

go to any lengths/stop at nothing /gəʊ tʊ ˌenɪ 'leŋθs, ˌstɒp ət 'nʌθɪŋ‖ˌstɑːp-/ [v phrase not in progressive] to be willing to do anything, even if it is cruel, dishonest, or illegal, in order to get what you want: *He's prepared to go to any lengths to find the men who killed his daughter.* | *Lawrence would stop at nothing to achieve power and wealth.*

be hellbent on /biː ˌhel'bent ɒn/ [v phrase] informal to be extremely determined to do something, especially something dangerous or something that may have a bad result **+ on doing sth** *Bob's hellbent on going through with the plan, even though it's sure to end in disaster.* | **be hellbent on revenge/destruction** *Gangs of youths rampaged through the streets, hellbent on destruction.*

whatever the cost /wɒtˌevəʳ ðə 'kɒst‖-'kɔːst/ [adv] if you do something **whatever the cost**, you are determined to do it even if it causes a lot of problems or you have to spend a lot of money, use a lot of effort etc: *I want him back here as soon as possible, whatever the cost.* | *They are determined to win back the disputed territories, whatever the cost in human terms.*

come hell or high water /kʌm ˌhel ɔːʳ haɪ 'wɔːtəʳ/ [adv] spoken use this to emphasize that you are determined to do something in spite of any problems or difficulties: *I'll be there in time. Don't worry. Come hell or high water.* | *Come hell or high water, he'd never missed a race and he wasn't going to miss this one.*

ruthless /'ruːθləs/ [adj] someone who is **ruthless** is so determined to get what they want, especially in business or politics, that they do not care if they harm other people: *You should be careful of Ian – he can be pretty ruthless if anyone gets in his way.* | *a ruthless and pitiless dictator* —**ruthlessly** [adv] *She was an unfeeling, ruthlessly ambitious woman.*

5 the ability to be determined

- determination
- ambition
- willpower
- will
- resolve
- drive
- spirit
- perseverance
- tenacity

determination /dɪˌtɜːʳmə̇'neɪʃən/ [n U] the ability to continue trying to achieve what you want, even when this is difficult: *After the accident, Bill learned to walk again through sheer hard work and determination.* | **+ to do sth** *A spokesman stressed the police's determination to find the girl's killer.* | **dogged determination** (=strong determination) *Success requires dogged determination, as well as ability.*

ambition /æm'bɪʃən/ [n U] determination to become successful, rich, powerful, or famous: *Eric wasn't particularly intelligent but he had plenty of ambition.* | *My teachers always told me that I lacked ambition, and would never get anywhere.* | **burning ambition** *Getting to the top hadn't been easy, in spite of his burning ambition and will to succeed.*

willpower /'wɪlˌpaʊəʳ/ [n U] the ability to control your mind and body in order to achieve whatever you decide to do: *It takes a lot of willpower to give up smoking.* | **by/through sheer willpower** (=by willpower alone) *She made herself get better by sheer willpower, when everyone else had given up hope.*

will /wɪl/ [n U] the strong desire to do or achieve something **the will to live/recover/get better, etc** *When her husband died, she seemed to lose the will to live.* | **the will to do sth** *They weren't the best side in the European Cup, but they possessed the will to win.*

resolve /rɪ'zɒlv‖rɪ'zɑːlv, rɪ'zɔːlv/ [n U] formal a strong determination to succeed in doing something especially because you are sure that it is a good thing to do **sb's resolve to do sth** *He restated his firm resolve to become president, and achieve clean and honest government.* | **strengthen/harden/stiffen sb's resolve** (=make it stronger) *The latest unemployment figures should strengthen the government's resolve to do something about it.*

drive /draɪv/ [n U] the determination and energy that makes you successfully achieve something: *Without my mother's drive and energy, our family would have starved.* | *He's clever enough, but he lacks drive.*

spirit /'spɪrə̇t/ [n U] the courage and energy that someone shows when they are determined to achieve something or determined not to let a difficult situation make them stop trying: *The fact that they reached the semi-final is a reflection of their spirit and commitment.* | **fighting spirit** (=brave determination to keep trying or fighting in a difficult situation) *She never once thought of giving up. Everyone admired her fighting spirit.* | **break sb's spirit** (=make them lose their determination to fight, be brave etc) *The hours of interrogations and beatings were designed to break his spirit.*

perseverance /ˌpɜːʳsə̇'vɪərəns/ [n U] the ability to keep on trying to achieve something over a long period, even when this is difficult: *The job requires perseverance and, above all, patience.* | **+ to do sth** *Some of the girls did not have the perseverance to train to his standards of precision.*

tenacity /tə'næsə̇ti/ [n U] formal the determination to never stop trying to succeed in something or to allow anyone to stop you from doing something: *I admired him for his tenacity and his courage in confronting problems that other people might avoid.* | **show/exhibit tenacity** *The tenacity and ingenuity* *shown by these women's groups during the war was remarkable.*

6 behaviour that shows determination

- determined
- stubborn
- steadfast
- resolute
- dogged

determined /dɪˈtɜːʳmɪ̈nd/ [adj usually before noun] **determined effort (to do sth)** *The world must make a more determined effort to stop the flow of arms to trouble spots.* | **determined resistance/opposition etc (from sb)** *The proposal met with determined opposition from the government.*

stubborn /ˈstʌbəʳn/ [adj usually before noun] **stubborn opposition/resistance/defence etc** when the people involved are very determined to get what they want in a difficult situation and refuse to let anyone change their mind: *Despite stubborn opposition, the President managed to raise interest rates.* | *The oil companies face stubborn resistance from environmentalists.* —**stubbornly** [adv] *A small minority remained stubbornly opposed to the idea.*

steadfast /ˈstedfɑːst‖-fæst/ [adj] **steadfast** actions or behaviour show that you are determined not to change your beliefs or your support for someone, especially because you want to be loyal to them **steadfast belief/refusal/support etc** *Malta's steadfast defence from 1940-43 played an important part in the course of the war.* | *the steadfast support of America's allies* | **remain steadfast in your belief/loyalty/determination etc** *As a politician, you have to show resilience – the ability to remain steadfast in your beliefs.* —**steadfastly** [adv] *The town remained steadfastly loyal to the King.*

resolute /ˈrezəluːt/ [adj] **resolute** actions or behaviour show that you are strongly determined not to change your opinions or intentions, even though other people want you to change them: *Tough policies and resolute leadership always create enemies.* | **resolute action/measures/opposition etc** *In the face of resolute opposition, the bill was withdrawn in November.* | **stand resolute** *The players stood resolute in the hope of having their former agreement renewed.* —**resolutely** [adv] *Theirs is a resolutely nomadic culture.*

dogged /ˈdɒgɪ̈d‖ˈdɔː-/ [adj usually before noun] **dogged** actions or behaviour show that you are very determined to continue doing something, even though it is difficult or takes a long time, and refuse to let others prevent you **dogged determination/persistence/insistence etc** *In the end we succeeded, through dogged determination plus a bit of good luck.* | *The dogged persistence of the police finally paid off when Hooper told them what he knew.* —**doggedly** [adv] *For ten years the men doggedly maintained that they were innocent.*

develop

RELATED WORDS

- *see also* **change/not change, grow, progress/make progress, increase, advanced**

1 to change over a period of time and become bigger, stronger etc

- develop
- evolve

develop /dɪˈveləp/ [v I] *In some patients, the disease develops very slowly.* | *The interesting part of the movie is how the two women's relationship develops.* | *The Internet has developed at a remarkable rate.* | **+ from/into** *She developed from a shy child into an international star.*

evolve /ɪˈvɒlv‖ɪˈvɑːlv/ [v I] to develop and change gradually over a long period of time: *The city's importance as a financial centre has evolved slowly.* | **+ from** *Many scientists now believe that birds evolved from dinosaurs.* | **+ into** *Brooks's original idea has now evolved into an official NASA program.*

2 in the process of developing

- developing
- embryonic
- emerging

developing /dɪˈveləpɪŋ/ [adj only before noun] *Good nutrition is very important to a developing child.* | *These drugs are effective in the developing stages of the disease.*

embryonic /ˌembriˈɒnɪk◂‖-ˈɑːn-/ [adj] plans, activities etc that are **embryonic** are in a very early stage of development, so that the details have not yet been fully planned or decided: *The program is still in the embryonic stage, but we are confident of its success.* | *Online gambling as an industry is still illegal and embryonic.*

emerging /ɪˈmɜːʳdʒɪŋ/ [adj only before noun] in an early stage of development and only just beginning to be noticed: *In 1911 the newly emerging car industry faced a crisis.* | *The program is designed to help identify emerging trends in drug use.*

3 a process or period during which someone or something develops

- development
- evolution
- progression

development /dɪˈveləpmənt/ [n U] *The country has experienced impressive economic development in the past decade.* | *A child's emotional development may be severely damaged by a traumatic experience in its early years.* | **+ of** *Climate was an important factor in the development of classical Greek culture.* —**developmental** /dɪˌveləpˈmentl◂/ [adj] *A new form of the drug is still in the developmental stage.*

evolution /ˌiːvəˈluːʃən, ˌevə-‖ˌevə-/ [n U] a long, gradual process during which something develops and changes, usually becoming more advanced: *The process of biological evolution has taken billions of years.* | **+ of** *The next chapter describes the evolution of the International Monetary System.*

progression /prəˈgreʃən/ [n U] a development from one situation or state to a better or more advanced one **+ of** *The exhibit is arranged to show the progression of Picasso's work.* | **+ from sth to sth** *The progression from school to university is difficult for many students.*

4 to develop a new plan, idea, method

- develop
- evolve

develop /dɪˈveləp/ [v T] to make something change over a period of time and become bigger, stronger, better etc: *The department is developing a strategy to fight unemployment.* | *We need to help young people develop a sense of responsibility while they're still at school.*

evolve /ɪˈvɒlv‖ɪˈvɑːlv, ɪˈvɔːlv/ [v T] to change something gradually over a long period so that it becomes better: *If you want to be a poet, you must evolve your own style of writing.*

5 to help something to develop

- nurture
- foster

nurture /ˈnɜːʳtʃəʳ/ [v T] written to spend a lot of time and effort thinking about and helping a plan, idea, feeling etc to develop: *The goal of the economic policies is to create jobs and nurture new industries.* | *It is important to nurture potential in your employees.*

foster /ˈfɒstəʳ‖ˈfɔː-, ˈfɑː-/ [v T] written to help a skill, feeling, idea etc to grow and develop over a period of time: *These classroom activities are intended to foster children's language skills.* | *Recent studies show that advertising usually fosters competition and therefore lower prices.*

die

RELATED WORDS

opposite: —— **living/alive**

- not die despite an accident, illness etc *see* **survive**
- *see also* **dead, kill**

1 to die because you are old or ill

- die
- pass away
- drop dead
- kick the bucket

die /daɪ/ [v I] to stop being alive, as a result of old age or illness: *I want to see Ireland again before I die.* | *Many people are worried about growing old and dying alone.* | *No wonder your plants always die – you don't water them enough.* | **+ of** *His son died of liver cancer three years ago.* | **die in your sleep** (=die while you are sleeping) *In the spring of her 93rd year, Miss Grantley died in her sleep.* | **die a natural death/die of natural causes** (=die as a result of illness or old age) *The autopsy said he had died of natural causes, but his family is not convinced.*

pass away /ˌpɑːs əˈweɪ‖ˌpæs-/ [phr v I] to die – use this when you want to avoid using the word 'die', because you think it might upset someone: *Have you heard? Carl passed away last night.* | *My wife had just passed away, and I didn't want to be around people.*

drop dead /ˌdrɒp ˈded‖ˌdrɑːp-/ [v phrase] spoken if someone **drops dead**, they die very suddenly and unexpectedly, especially when they are in the middle of doing something: *One of their neighbors just dropped dead on the tennis court.* | *McSherry dropped dead of a heart attack in the middle of a baseball game.*

kick the bucket spoken informal ALSO **snuff it** British /ˌkɪk ðə ˈbʌkɪ̵t, ˈsnʌf ɪt/ [v phrase not in progressive] to die – use this humorously when you are not being serious: *When I kick the bucket you'll be able to live on my life insurance.* | *I feel like I've done everything I wanted to – I might as well snuff it.*

2 to die in an accident, war, fight etc

- die/be killed
- to death
- lose your life
- come to a sticky end
- perish
- suffer heavy losses

die/be killed /daɪ, biː ˈkɪld/ [v I/v phrase] *The firefighters died when the warehouse floor collapsed.* | **+ in an accident/explosion/the war etc** *Two people were killed and four injured in a gas explosion this morning.* | **die/be killed in action** (=be killed in a war) *His brother was killed in action in Vietnam.*

to death /tə ˈdeθ/ [adv] **starve/freeze/bleed etc to death** to die because of having no food, being too cold, losing blood etc: *The baby starved to death.* | *He bled to death after being stabbed repeatedly.*

lose your life /ˌluːz jɔːʳ ˈlaɪf/ [v phrase] to be killed in a terrible event – used especially in news reports and descriptions of past events: *Hundreds of people lost their lives when the ship overturned in a storm.* | *Supporters continue to visit the site where Colosio lost his life to an assassin's bullet.*

come to a sticky end /ˌkʌm tʊ ə ˌstɪki ˈend/ [v phrase not in progressive] British informal to die in a violent or unpleasant way – use this especially when you think the person who died deserved this: *At the end of the film the prisoners are rescued, and the pirates come to a sticky end.*

perish /ˈperɪʃ/ [v I] to die in a terrible event – used especially in literature and news reports: *Everyone aboard the ship perished when it sank off the coast of Maine.* | *Five children perished before firefighters could put out the blaze.*

suffer heavy losses /ˌsʌfəʳ ˌhevi ˈlɒsɪ̵z‖-ˈlɔːsɪ̵z/ [v phrase] if a military force **suffers heavy losses**, a very large number of its soldiers die while fighting: *US forces withdrew after suffering heavy losses.* | *The troops suffered heavy losses fighting their way through the Italian countryside.*

3 to die when you are still young

- die young
- be cut off/down in your prime
- untimely death

die young /ˌdaɪ ˈjʌŋ/ [v phrase] to die when you are young: *Like so many other pop stars, Jim Morrison died young.* | *a memorial to tens of thousands of allied soldiers, many of whom died so young*

be cut off/down in your prime /biː kʌt ˌɒf, ˌdaʊn ɪn jɔːʳ ˈpraɪm/ [v phrase] to die when you are still young, strong, and active, as a result of an accident, sudden illness etc: *The movie tells the story of a popular athlete cut down in his prime.* | **+ by** *Dolly was an energetic woman who was suddenly cut off in her prime by scarlet fever.*

untimely death /ʌnˌtaɪmli ˈdeθ/ [n singular] someone's death that happens before it would normally be expected: *James Dean had made just three movies before his untimely death in 1955.*

4 to die for your country or for something you believe in

- die for
- give your life/lay down your life
- martyr
- suicide bomber/pilot/killer

die for /ˈdaɪ fɔːʳ/ [v phrase] *These brave men were*

ready to fight and die for their country. | *How many of you would be willing to die for your religion?*

give your life/lay down your life /ˌgɪv jɔːʳ ˈlaɪf, ˌleɪ daʊn jɔːʳ ˈlaɪf/ [v phrase] formal to die in order to save someone, or because of something that you believe in: *We want to pay special tribute to the men and women who have given their lives in service of their country.* | **+ for** *He was ready to lay down his life for his comrades.*

martyr /ˈmɑːʳtəʳ/ [n C] someone who is killed because of their religious or political beliefs, and becomes very famous because of this: *The early Christian martyrs were killed by the thousands.* | **make sb a martyr/make a martyr out of sb** (=make people think someone is a martyr) *His death in police hands made him a martyr among the people.* —**martyrdom** [n U] *His martyrdom encouraged the people to resist.*

suicide bomber/pilot/killer /ˈsuːɪsaɪd ˌbɒməʳ, ˌpaɪlət, ˌkɪləʳ‖-ˌbɑːm-/ [n C] someone who attacks and kills people with a bomb etc even though they know they will die as well: *FBI agents found the passport of one of the suicide bombers among the wreckage.* | *Suicide pilots are brainwashed into believing they will go straight to paradise when they die.*

5 when someone is going to die very soon

- dying
- be close to death/ near (to) death
- on your deathbed
- be at death's door

dying /ˈdaɪ-ɪŋ/ [adj] if someone is **dying**, they will die very soon because they are very ill or very badly injured: *He gave the dying man a drop of water from his flask.* | *The priest was killed as he was giving the last rites to a dying man.* | **lie dying** *Even as she lay dying in a hospital bed, she was still thinking of her children.*

be close to death/near (to) death /biː ˌkləʊs tə ˈdeθ, ˌnɪəʳ (tə) ˈdeθ/ [v phrase] formal to be going to die very soon: *When the fisherman spotted the boat, its crew were already close to death.* | *Davis had suffered a stroke and was near death.*

on your deathbed /ɒn jɔːʳ ˈdeθbed/ [adv] to be lying in your bed, about to die: *My grandmother gave me that ring when she was on her deathbed.* | *Thirty years later, on her deathbed, she confessed to the crime.*

be at death's door /biː ət ˌdeθs ˈdɔːʳ/ [v phrase] spoken to be extremely ill and likely to die soon: *His skin was so pale, he looked like he was at death's door.*

6 when someone dies

- death
- fatalities
- loss of life

death /deθ/ [n C/U] *After her husband's death, she moved back to California.* | *The bomb caused at least one death, and several serious injuries.* | **+ from** *The number of deaths from AIDS is still increasing in many parts of the world.* | **the death of sb** formal *A comet appeared at the time of the death of Julius Caesar in 44 B.C.* | **the death toll** (=the number of deaths in one terrible event) *The latest death toll in the Turkish earthquake is over 2000.* | **accidental death** (=death resulting from an accident – used in official contexts) *The policy provides full insurance in the case of accidental death.* | **untimely death** (=death that comes earlier than is normally expected) *Basquiat's work had become well known even before his untimely death at age 27.* | **on sb's death** (=when they die) *Catherine will inherit a large sum of money on her father's death.*

fatalities /fəˈtælɪtiz/ [n plural] the number of people who have died in accidents or from illnesses, especially when this is being calculated officially: *A fifth of all road fatalities are caused by people not wearing seatbelts.* | *An attack on the city would cause tens of thousands of civilian fatalities.*

loss of life /ˌlɒs əv ˈlaɪf‖ˌlɔːs-/ [n phrase] formal the deaths of people in an accident or a war: *The plane managed to crash-land on St. Lawrence Island with no loss of life.* | *The Bishop condemned what he called 'this futile and tragic loss of life'.*

7 when one of your relatives or friends dies

- lose
- be widowed
- be orphaned
- bereaved

lose /luːz/ [v T] if you **lose** a close relative or friend, they die: *Sharon lost her mother when she was very young.* | *It's a terrible thing to lose someone very close to you.*

be widowed /biː ˈwɪdəʊd/ [v phrase] if you **are widowed**, your husband or wife dies: *Tony's mother was widowed at the age of 23 with three children.* —**widowed** [adj only before noun] *He's gone to stay with his widowed mother in Florida.*

be orphaned /biː ˈɔːʳfənd/ [v phrase] if you **are orphaned**, both your parents die when you are still young: *Ben was orphaned at an early age and raised by an uncle.* —**orphaned** [adj only before noun] *a home for orphaned children*

bereaved /bɪˈriːvd/ [adj] formal used about someone whose close relative or friend has died: *The bereaved mother stood by her son's grave.* | *Bereaved family members are demanding more information about the plane crash.* —**bereavement** [n U] *Jim's depression had been brought on by the bereavement he had suffered earlier in the year* (=when a close relative or friend of yours dies). | *Bereavement counsellors* (=people trained to help people who have been bereaved) *have been flown to the city.*

8 an illness or accident that you die from

- fatal
- terminal

fatal /ˈfeɪtl/ [adj] a **fatal** accident or medical condition kills the person who has it, usually immediately: *a fatal heart attack* | *Meyer's car was involved in a fatal accident on the freeway.* —**fatally** [adv] **fatally injured/wounded** *His father had been fatally injured in an explosion in the mine where he worked.*

terminal /ˈtɜːʳmɪnəl/ [adj] a **terminal** illness cannot be cured, and the person who has it will soon die: *Is the disease terminal?* | *She was recently told she has terminal cancer.* —**terminally** [adv] **terminally ill** *We need to improve the way we treat terminally ill patients.*

different

RELATED WORDS

opposite: ——— **like/similar, same**

- different kinds of *see* **various/of different kinds**
- *see also* **unusual, special, opposite, conventional/unconventional, strange**

1 not like someone or something else

- different
- not like
- not the same
- vary
- differ
- contrast with
- be a departure from
- diverse

different /ˈdɪfərənt/ [adj] if something or someone is **different**, they are not like something or someone else, or they are not like they were before: *You look different. Have you had your hair cut?* | *People are all so different. You can never tell how they will react.* | *Things are different now, since John left.* | *We've painted the door a different colour.* | **different from sth/sb** ALSO **different than sth/sb** American *This computer's different from the one I used in my last job.* | *Life today is different than ten, fifteen years ago.* | **completely/totally different** *I'd like a totally different look in the kitchen – something brighter and more modern.* —**differently** [adv] *The two words sound the same, but they're spelled differently.*

not like /nɒt ˈlaɪk/ [prep] different from – use this especially when two things or people are not at all similar: *Walking in the hills isn't like walking down the street – it can be very dangerous.* | **not at all like/nothing like** (=completely different from) *She's very shy – not at all like her sister.* | *James was nothing like I'd expected, from what I had heard.* | **not look/sound like** *The voice on the answering machine didn't sound like Anna's at all.*

not the same /nɒt ðə ˈseɪm/ [adj phrase not before noun] different – use this especially when two things are similar but are not exactly like each other, or when one of them is not as good as the other: *The two designs are similar but not the same. Which do you prefer?* | *I prefer having my own house. Living in a rented flat really isn't the same.* | **+ as** *I've tried Mexican food here in London, but it just isn't the same as in Mexico.*

vary /ˈveəri/ [v I] if things of the same type **vary**, they are all different from each other: *Methods of treatment vary according to the age and general health of the patient.* | **vary considerably/greatly/widely** *Prices of video cameras vary considerably.* | **vary in price/quality/size etc** *The hotel rooms vary in size, but all have televisions and telephones.*

differ /ˈdɪfəʳ/ [v I] formal if two things **differ**, they have different qualities or features: *People's abilities differ, but their rights and opportunities should be the same.* | **+ from** *Scottish law has always differed from English law.* | **differ in cost/size/appearance etc** *A lot of painkillers are basically the same, differing only in cost.* | **differ greatly/widely** *Opinions on the subject differ greatly.*

contrast with /kənˈtrɑːst wɪð ‖-ˈtræst-/ [v phrase] if one thing **contrasts with** another thing, the difference between them is very easy to see and is sometimes surprising: *His extrovert personality contrasts with his sister's quiet, shy character.* | *The snow was icy and white, contrasting with the brilliant blue sky.* | **contrast sharply/markedly with sth** (=to be extremely different) *These results contrast sharply with those of similar tests carried out in Australia.*

be a departure from /biː ə dɪˈpɑːʳtʃəʳ frɒm/ [v phrase] a method, way of behaving etc that **is a departure from** the usual one is different, new, and unusual: *Such methods are, of course, a departure from traditional medical practice.* | **mark/represent/signal a departure from sth** *The move represented a departure from the government's commitment to finding a peaceful solution to the crisis.*

diverse /daɪˈvɜːʳs‖də-, daɪ-/ [adj] things that are **diverse** are different from each other and cover a wide range of possible styles, types etc: *The music college aims to encourage talents as diverse as members of symphony orchestras and pop groups.* | *diverse political views* | **a diverse range of sth** *People enter the organisation from a diverse range of social, economic, and educational backgrounds.*

2 very different from something or someone else

- have nothing in common
- bear no relation to
- worlds apart/poles apart
- be a far cry from
- there's a world of difference between
- be a whole new ball game
- be like chalk and cheese

have nothing in common /hæv ˌnʌθɪŋ ɪn ˈkɒmən‖-ˈkɑː-/ [v phrase not in progressive] if two or more people or things **have nothing in common**, they do not have the same qualities, opinions, or interests: *Apart from the fact that we went to the same school, we have absolutely nothing in common.* | **+ with** *Batavia was a completely new modern city, having very little in common with other Indonesian towns.*

bear no relation to /beəʳ ˌnəʊ rɪˈleɪʃən tuː/ [v phrase not in progressive] to be completely different from and not connected in any way with another person or thing: *Everyone complains that the national tests bear no relation to what children have learnt in class.* | *I was astonished when I read the press release, which bore no relation to what I had told them.*

worlds apart/poles apart /ˈwɜːʳldz əˌpɑːʳt, ˈpəʊlz əˌpɑːʳt/ [v phrase] people, beliefs, or ideas that are **worlds** or **poles apart** are so completely different that there is almost nothing about them that is similar: *I don't know why Max took an interest in me. We were always worlds apart.* | **+ from** *The children were on holiday, enjoying a lifestyle worlds apart from the one they had to put up with at home.*

be a far cry from /biː ə ˌfɑːʳ ˈkraɪ frɒm/ [v phrase] if a situation **is a far cry from** another situation or place, it is so different that it is almost the opposite: *We had dinner at the Ritz, a far cry from our usual hamburger and fries.* | *The first Olympic Games in 1896 were a far cry from the slick spectacle of today.*

there's a world of difference between /ðeəʳz ə ˈwɜːʳld əv ˌdɪfərəns bɪtwiːn/ if you say **there is a world of difference between** two activities or situations, you mean that they are completely different from each other and people should not expect them to be the same: *There is a world of difference between home-made bread and the tasteless substance that many people buy today.*

be a whole new ball game /biː ə ˌhəʊl njuː ˈbɔːl geɪm‖-nuː-/ [v phrase] especially American, informal to be very different from what you have done or experienced before: *Being married is one thing, but having children is a whole new ball game.*

be like chalk and cheese /biː laɪk ˌtʃɔːk ən ˈtʃiːz/ [v phrase] British informal if two people who are related or good friends **are like chalk and cheese**, they are completely different in a way that surprises you: *It's hard to believe that they're brothers – they're like chalk and cheese!*

3 completely different from anyone or anything else

- unique
- distinctive
- be the only one of its kind
- be one of a kind
- individual
- be a one-off

▸ *see also* **new**

unique /juːˈniːk/ [adj] different, special, or unusual and the only one of its kind: *The book is certainly very rare, and possibly unique.* | *the unique wildlife of the Galapagos Islands* | **+ among** *The power of speech makes the human race unique among animals.*

distinctive /dɪˈstɪŋktɪv/ [adj] something that is **distinctive** has a special feature or appearance that makes it different from other things, and makes it easy to recognize: *Male birds have distinctive blue and yellow markings.* | *Whatever you think of Larkin's poetry, it's certainly distinctive.* | **distinctive feature (of sth)** *The most distinctive feature of the building is its enormous dome-shaped roof.*

be the only one of its kind /biː ði ˌəʊnli wʌn əv ɪts ˈkaɪnd/ [v phrase] if something **is the only one of its kind**, it is the only one that exists: *The 22-bedroomed clinic will be the only one of its kind in Ireland.*

be one of a kind /biː ˌwʌn əv ə ˈkaɪnd/ [v phrase] someone or something that **is one of a kind** is different because they are the only one to exist or be made: *Marilyn Monroe was one of a kind. There's no such thing as 'the new Monroe'.* | *Each tile is a work of art, guaranteed one of a kind by the handprint of its maker.*

individual /ˌɪndɪ̇ˈvɪdʒuəl◂/ [adj] an **individual** style, way of doing things etc is different from anyone else's and is often fairly unusual: *Every baby has its own, individual personality.* | *a tennis player with a completely individual style* | **highly individual** *She dresses in a highly individual way.*

be a one-off /biː ə ˌwʌn ˈɒf/ [v phrase] especially British to be so different or unusual that people cannot expect to find anything or meet anyone like them again: *I was really upset when I lost that hat. It was a one-off – I'll never find another like it.* | *Doug's achieved a lot with very limited resources. There's no doubt that he's a one-off.*

4 when someone is different from other people

- be different
- not belong/not fit in
- be on a different wavelength
- stick/stand out like a sore thumb
- be out of step/sync

▸ *see also* **strange**

be different /biː ˈdɪfərənt/ [v phrase] to think or behave in a way that is unusual: *It's a small community and anyone who shows any signs of being different just isn't made to feel welcome.* | *For teenagers, it's important to speak and dress like their friends. They really don't want to be different.*

not belong/not fit in /nɒt bɪˈlɒŋ‖-ˈlɔːŋ, nɒt fɪt ˈɪn/ [v I not in progressive] someone who **does not belong** or **does not fit in** is so different that people do not like them, do not help them to become one of the group etc: *From the moment she first joined the company, Sally just didn't belong.* | *Until we learnt the language, we felt that we didn't fit in. But after that the people seemed to accept us.*

be on a different wavelength /biː ɒn ə ˌdɪfərənt ˈweɪvleŋθ/ [v phrase] if two people **are on a different wavelength**, they have very different ideas and attitudes from each other, with the result that they do not understand each other: *My dad doesn't understand me. He's on a completely different wavelength.* | *We'd been married for twenty years, but we just weren't on the same wavelength anymore.*

stick/stand out like a sore thumb /stɪk, stænd ˌaʊt laɪk ə ˌsɔːʳ ˈθʌm/ [v phrase not in progressive] to be very different from the people around you especially in the way you dress or look, so that people notice you and look at you: *You can't come to the restaurant dressed in jeans. You'd stick out like a sore thumb.*

be out of step/sync /biː ˌaʊt əv ˈstep, ˈsɪŋk/ [v phrase] to be different from the other people in a group because you behave in a different way and have different ideas: *In my school, anyone who was out of sync was ignored or ridiculed.* | **+ with** *The Prime Minister has been criticized for being out of step with the British people.*

5 when something is of the same type, but not the same one

- another
- other
- different
- new
- else
- alternative
- variation
- variant

another /əˈnʌðəʳ/ [determiner/pron] one more of the same kind of thing or person: *Louise has a house in New York, and another in Florida.* | *The blue suitcase is broken. Have we got another I could use?* | *creatures from another planet* | **another one** *I decided I didn't like the dress after all, so I changed it for another one.*

other /ˈʌðəʳ/ [determiner/pron] different ones from the ones that you already have, or that you have already mentioned: *I'm afraid we don't have these jeans in any other sizes.* | *Of course, my train was late, but the others seemed to be on time.* | *Maria's blond, but all my other children have dark hair.*

different /ˈdɪfərənt/ [adj only before noun] use this about several people or things of the same general type, when you are comparing them with each other and noticing the differences between them: *Let's compare the prices of five different detergents.* | *a drug that affects different people in different ways*

new /njuː‖nuː/ [adj only before noun] use this about something or someone that replaces the one that was there before: *Have you met Keith's new girlfriend?* | *She's really enjoying her new job.*

else /els/ [adv] use this after a noun to talk about another thing, place, or person instead of this one: *Go and play somewhere else. I'm trying to work.* | *Andrea's obsessed with money – she never thinks about anything else.* | *Jamie's special. There's really no one else like him.*

alternative ALSO **alternate** American /ɔːlˈtɜːʳnətɪv, ɔːlˈtɜːnɪ̇t‖ˈɔːltɜːrnɪ̇t/ [adj usually before noun] an **alternative** plan, arrangement, or system can be used instead of the usual or main one: *For vegetarian* *guests there is an alternative menu.* | *The bridge is closed so we advise you to use an alternate route.* | *Do you have any alternative suggestions to make?*

variation /ˌveəriˈeɪʃən/ [n C] something that is done in a way that is different from the way it is usually done **+ on** *This recipe makes an interesting variation on the traditional Christmas cake.* | **a variation on the theme of sth** *The new movie is a variation on the theme of the original 'Blue Lagoon'.* | **+ in** *There are at least ten styles of Apple Mac computers, and countless variations in those models.*

variant /ˈveəriənt/ [n C] something that is slightly different from the usual form of something or has developed from it: *The English and Americans often spell words differently, but both variants are acceptable.* | *The name Lloyd and its variant Floyd are Celtic in origin.* | **+ of** *There is evidence that a new variant of the disease has recently been found in Britain.*

6 clearly different from other things of the same type

- special
- specially
- particular
- distinct

special /ˈspeʃəl/ [adj] designed for one particular purpose, and therefore different from other things of its type: *Bob's been on a special diet since his heart attack.* | *The fish will be kept in special tanks that mimic the natural currents in rivers.*

specially /ˈspeʃəli/ [adv] **specially designed/made/built/chosen etc** designed, made, built etc for a special purpose: *Customs officers use specially trained dogs to search for drugs.* | *We're introducing a new range of beauty products specially designed for teenagers.*

particular /pəʳˈtɪkjᵊləʳ/ [adj only before noun] clearly different from others of the same kind: *The lights were arranged to give a particular effect.* | *Is there a particular type of car that you are looking for?* | *I didn't have any particular plan in mind.*

distinct /dɪˈstɪŋkt/ [adj] two or more things that are **distinct** from each other belong to the same general type, but are clearly different from each other in an important way: *The European Union is made up of 15 nations with distinct cultural, linguistic and economic roots.* | **+ from** *The mammoth was related to, but distinct from, modern elephants.*

7 a fact or quality that makes someone or something different

- difference
- distinction
- distinguishing feature/mark/characteristic

difference /ˈdɪfərəns/ [n C/U] a detail, fact, or quality that makes one person or thing different from another: *We should think about the similarities between cultures, not the differences.* | **+ between** *Try and spot the differences between these two pictures.* | *The difference between the two cheeses is that one is made from goat's milk.* | **+ in** *I don't think there's any difference in the way you pronounce these two words.* | **know the difference** *He's speaking Italian, not Spanish. Don't you know the difference?*

distinction /dɪˈstɪŋkʃən/ [n C] a clear, but usually small, difference between similar things: *Pablo insists that he is Basque, not Spanish – an important distinction.* | **+ between** *There is a clear distinction between lawful protest and illegal strike action.*

distinguishing feature/mark/characteristic /dɪˈstɪŋgwɪʃɪŋ ˌfiːtʃəʳ, ˌmɑːʳk, kærᵻktəˌrɪstɪk/ [n C] a feature of a particular person or thing that makes them look different from other similar people or things: *The distinguishing feature of the African elephant is the size of its ears.* | *The melodies of most composers have distinguishing characteristics which make them instantly identifiable.*

8 the difference between two people or things

- difference
- contrast
- gap
- gulf
- divide
- disparity

difference /ˈdɪfərəns/ [n singular/U] the amount by which one person, thing, or amount is different from another **+ between** *Calculate the difference between the amount you started with and what you have left.* | **a big/huge etc difference** *There is a vast difference between daytime and night-time temperatures in the desert.* | **+ in** *There was fifteen years difference in age between the two women.* | **age/height/price etc difference** (=between one amount and another) *I prefer the Peugeot 406 to the 405. What's the price difference?* | **pay the difference** *If you put all your savings towards the cost of a bike, your Dad and I will pay the difference.*

contrast /ˈkɒntrɑːst‖ˈkɑːntræst/ [n singular/U] a very clear difference that you can easily see when you compare two things or people **contrast between sth/sb and sth/sb** *What surprised me was the contrast between Picasso's early style and his later work.*

gap /gæp/ [n C] a big difference between two amounts, two ages, or two groups of people **+ between** *There's a ten-year gap between Kay's two children.* | *The gap between rich and poor is wider in the South than in the rest of the country.* | **age/gender/income etc gap** *The age gap between us didn't seem to matter until we decided to have children.*

gulf /gʌlf/ [n C usually singular] a very big difference and lack of understanding between two groups of people, especially in their beliefs, opinions, and way of life **gulf between sb and sb** *More riots led to a growing gulf between the police and the communities in which they worked.* | **bridge/cross the gulf** (=improve understanding and communication) *The central problem was how to bridge the gulf between the warring factions of the party.*

divide /dᵻˈvaɪd/ [n C usually singular] a difference between two groups of people, especially in their beliefs, opinions, and way of life which means they will never be friends, become the same etc **+ between** *Recently the divide between the two sides has widened.* | **a cultural/political etc divide** *There is still a great economic and political divide between the east and the west of the country.*

disparity /dɪˈspærᵻti/ [n C/U] formal a big difference between two groups of people or things – use this especially when you think the difference is unfair or may cause problems **+ between** *It is not easy to explain the disparity that still exists between the salaries of men and women.* | **+ in** *the disparity in wealth between the highest and the lowest employees* | **the economic/income etc disparity** *The economic disparity between the area's black and white citizens is a serious problem.*

9 in a different way

- differently/in a different way
- along different lines
- otherwise

differently/in a different way /ˈdɪfərəntli, ɪn ə ˌdɪfərənt ˈweɪ/ [adv/adv] *The words 'through' and 'threw' sound the same, but they are spelled differently.* | *These three chemicals react to heat in slightly different ways.* | *He started to treat me in a different way once we got married.* | **+ from** *I always felt that my parents treated me differently from my brothers and sisters.* | **see/look at sth differently** (=have a different opinion) *I believe you, but I think the police might see it differently.*

along different lines /əlɒŋ ˌdɪfərənt ˈlaɪnz‖ əlɔːŋ-/ [adv] using a different method or system: *Their organization was run along different lines to ours.*

otherwise /ˈʌðəʳwaɪz/ [adv only after verb] if you do, say, or think **otherwise**, you do, say, or think something different from what has already been mentioned: *The situation was very serious indeed, even if the government tried to pretend otherwise.* | *The police stressed that Straskow would be considered innocent until proved otherwise.*

10 to notice that two things or people are different

- can tell the difference
- can tell sb/sth apart
- distinguish
- differentiate
- draw/make a distinction
- discriminate

can tell the difference /kən ˌtel ðə ˈdɪfərəns/ [v phrase] to be able to notice that two things or people are different, even though they seem to be similar: *It looked just like a real diamond – I couldn't tell the difference.* | **+ between** *Can you tell the difference between a really good wine and the sort that you might drink every day?*

can tell sb/sth apart /kən ˌtel (sb/sth) əˈpɑːʳt/ [v phrase] to be able to see that two very similar people or things are different – use this especially in questions and negative statements: *The twins are identical – even their parents can't always tell them apart.*

distinguish /dɪˈstɪŋgwɪʃ/ [v I/T] to be able to recognize and understand the difference between two or more similar people or things: *Several thousand minerals can be distinguished, each defined by its own set of properties.* | **+ between** *Even a expert would find it hard to distinguish between the original painting and the copy.* | **+ from** *A tiny baby soon learns to distinguish its mother's face from other adults' faces.*

differentiate /ˌdɪfəˈrenʃieɪt/ [v I/T] to know, see, or show the difference between a group of people or things **+ between** *As journalists, we have to differentiate between facts and opinions.* | **+ from** *Part of the management course was teaching us how to differentiate essential tasks from less important ones.*

draw/make a distinction /ˌdrɔː, ˌmeɪk ə dɪˈstɪŋkʃən/ [v phrase] to say what the difference is between two or more similar people or things **+ between** *The law draws a distinction between different types of killing, according to whether it was intended or not.* | *In the government's education proposals there is a clear distinction made between academic and practical training.*

discriminate /dɪˈskrɪmɪ̈neɪt/ [v I/T] to be able to find differences between similar people or things in order to make a choice **+ between** *The monkeys were easily able to discriminate between the different objects, according to their visual appearance.* | **+ from** *A test is useful for discriminating those students who have reached a higher level from those at a lower level.*

11 to be the thing that makes someone or something different

- distinguish
- set sb/sth apart

distinguish /dɪˈstɪŋgwɪʃ/ [v T] to be the thing that makes someone or something different from other people or things: *What really distinguishes the proposal?* | **+ from** *There's not a lot that distinguishes her from the other candidates.* | *What distinguishes this approach from previous attempts to deal with HIV?*

set sb/sth apart /ˌset (sb/sth) əˈpɑːʳt/ [phr v T] if a quality **sets someone** or **something apart**, it makes you notice them because they are so different or unusual: *Such seriousness and ambition in a very young man set him apart.* | **+ from** *The new software was a unique tool that set the Microsoft Network apart from other commercial online services.*

12 when one statement, idea etc makes a different one seem untrue

- contradict
- conflicting
- be inconsistent with
- discrepancy
- go against
- be at odds with

contradict /ˌkɒntrəˈdɪkt‖ˌkɑːn-/ [v T] if one statement or fact **contradicts** another one, it is so different that it makes the other one seem untrue or impossible: *The two newspaper reports totally contradict each other.* | *Recent experiments seem to contradict earlier results.* | *O'Brien's later statement contradicted what he had told Somerville police on the night of the murder.* —**contradictory** /ˌkɒntrəˈdɪktəri◂‖ˌkɑːn-/ [adj] ideas, statements, results etc that are contradictory are different from each other, especially when you would expect them to be the same: *The two boys gave contradictory accounts of the accident.* | *A lot of the information we receive from historical sources is contradictory, inaccurate, or incomplete.*

conflicting /kənˈflɪktɪŋ/ [adj only before noun] very different from each other – use this especially when two things should be the same: *At first we received conflicting information about the number of children who were seriously hurt.* | *Researchers tend to offer conflicting advice on which vitamin and mineral supplements might keep us healthy.*

be inconsistent with /biː ˌɪnkənˈsɪstənt wɪð/ [v phrase] if a statement, story, fact etc **is inconsistent with** what you expect or already know of the situation, it is completely different from it: *IBM said that the £37 million payment had been made in a way that was inconsistent with company policy.* | *Wolff, an economics professor at New York University, said that the results were inconsistent with all the other data they had.*

discrepancy /dɪˈskrepənsi/ [n C] a small fact or detail that is different from what you expected, especially one that makes you think that something is wrong: *Whenever he works out his accounts there are always discrepancies.* | **+ between** *Apparently* *there were discrepancies between police reports taken from the same witnesses at different times.* | **+ in** *She always refused to discuss the discrepancies in her biography.*

go against /ˌgəʊ əˈgenst/ [v phrase] if something **goes against** what you think or what someone has told you, it is different from the opinions, attitudes etc that you have learnt: *What the teacher was saying went against everything his parents had taught him.* | *She couldn't explain what had made her go against her upbringing and character and behave so recklessly.*

be at odds with /biː ət ˈɒdz wɪð ‖-ˈɑːdz-/ [v phrase] if a statement, story, fact etc **is at odds with** another, the two things are so completely different that one of them must be untrue: *John Nelson has been re-examining the evidence, and his conclusions are greatly at odds with the story so far.* | *The government decision to raise taxes was at odds with their policies on inflation.*

difficult

RELATED WORDS

opposite: **easy**

▸ *see also* **problem, complicated**

1 difficult to do or understand

- difficult
- hard
- tough
- be a tall order
- easier said than done
- not the easiest
- not an easy ... /be no easy ...
- a pain (in the neck)

difficult /ˈdɪfɪkəlt/ [adj] *That's a good question, but it's a difficult one to answer.* | **+ for** *The reading exercise was very difficult for most of the children.* | **difficult to see/hear/describe etc** *The insects are so small that they are difficult to see without using a microscope.* | **it is difficult (for sb) to do sth** *It's very difficult to find people who are willing to do the job.* | **find it difficult to do sth** *Until now, patients often found it difficult to get information about their rights.* | **make it difficult for sb to do sth** *My mother's illness makes it difficult for her to walk.*

hard /hɑːʳd/ [adj] not easy to do or understand. **Hard** is less formal than **difficult**: *I thought the exam was really hard.* | *The hardest thing about moving to a new place was meeting new people.* | **it is hard (for sb) to do sth** *It's hard to see the stage from here.* | *It was hard for me to understand her – her accent was very strong.* | **find it hard to do sth** *I find it hard to believe that he didn't know the gun was loaded.*

tough /tʌf/ [adj] very difficult to do or deal with – use this about jobs, decisions, questions, or problems: *The judge asked the lawyers on both sides some very tough questions.* | *The governor is trying to show voters that he's able to deal with the toughest issues facing Ohio today.*

be a tall order /biː ə ˌtɔːl ˈɔːʳdəʳ/ [v phrase] spoken use this about something difficult you have been asked to do, especially when you do not think it is likely you will be able to do it: *'Can you finish the work by Friday?' 'Sounds like a tall order to me, but I'll see what I can do.'*

easier said than done /ˌiːziəʳ ˌsed ðən ˈdʌn/ [adj phrase] spoken use this to tell someone that something is much more difficult than they think it is: *Talking calmly to a screaming child sounds like a good idea, but any parent will tell you it's easier said than done.*

not the easiest /nɒt ði ˈiːziˌst/ [adj phrase] **not the easiest ... to do** spoken use this to say that it is difficult to do something: *I'll drive you there – it's not the easiest place to get to if you don't have a car.* | *I tried to explain it to him, but he's not the easiest person to talk to.*

not an easy ... /be no easy ... /nɒt ən ˈiːzi..., biː nəʊ ˈiːzi.../ [v phrase] use this to say that something is difficult to do or make: *Finding a solution to the present crisis in the region is no easy task.* | **not an easy task/job/decision** *The roads are often dangerous, and getting food to the villages has not been an easy task.*

a pain (in the neck) /ə ˌpeɪn (ɪn ðə ˈnek)/ [n phrase] spoken something that is difficult and annoying to do or deal with: *It was a pain – I had to read more than 200 articles – but I learned a lot from it.* | *Getting across town at rush hour is a real pain in the neck.*

2 needing a lot of skill, hard work, and determination

- challenging
- be a challenge
- demanding
- daunting
- take some doing
- taxing
- exacting
- stretch

challenging /ˈtʃælˌndʒɪŋ/ [adj] a **challenging** job or activity needs a lot of hard work and skill, but it is also interesting and enjoyable: *The job wasn't challenging enough for me – I wanted something more creative.* | *Bowden called the piece 'one of the most challenging pieces of music I've ever played.'*

be a challenge /biː ə ˈtʃælɪndʒ/ [v phrase] if a new job or activity **is a challenge**, it is difficult, but you are determined to do it because it is interesting and exciting: *You may find your first couple of months in the job quite a challenge.* | *Getting the two groups to work together was a challenge, but we did it.*

demanding /dɪˈmɑːndɪŋ‖dɪˈmæn-/ [adj] a **demanding** job or activity is very difficult and tiring, because it needs all your effort and skill: *Being a nurse in a busy hospital is a demanding job – you don't get much free time.*

daunting /ˈdɔːntɪŋ/ [adj] if something is **daunting**, it seems almost impossible, and the idea of doing it makes you feel nervous: *Climbing Everest is a daunting challenge for any mountaineer.* | **daunting task** *I was faced with the daunting task of learning the whole script in 24 hours.*

take some doing /ˌteɪk sʌm ˈduːɪŋ/ [v phrase not in progressive] spoken use this about something that needs a lot of effort, skill, or determination, and you admire someone who does it: *Winning 3 gold medals in the Olympic Games takes some doing.* | *It took some doing, but I finally persuaded Jim to give me a few more days off.*

taxing /ˈtæksɪŋ/ [adj] formal difficult for someone because of needing more mental or physical effort than they are able to give: *The job was taxing, but there were some good moments.* | *Later in the pregnancy when the drive to work was getting too taxing, I worked at home two days a week.*

exacting /ɪgˈzæktɪŋ/ [adj] needing hard work and a lot of attention given to the details of a job, in order to make sure that it is done well: *Film-editing is a difficult and exacting job.* | *The article is based on the institute's exacting study of wages in the health care professions.*

stretch /stretʃ/ [v T] if an activity, job etc **stretches** you, it is difficult enough to make you use all your skill, ability etc, and this helps you become better at it: *The exercises are designed to stretch the abilities of even the most advanced students.* | *I was disappointed with the course – I didn't feel I was being stretched enough.*

3 needing a lot of energy or physical effort

- hard
- strenuous
- backbreaking/back-breaking
- gruelling
- arduous
- punishing
- be murder
- be a slog

hard /hɑːʳd/ [adj] tiring and needing a lot of work, energy, or physical effort: *Let your mother sit down. She's had a hard day at work.* | *Their car broke down, and they were suddenly faced with a long hard walk back to the nearest town.*

strenuous /ˈstrenjuəs/ [adj] needing a lot of physical effort: *The doctors advised against any strenuous activity for six weeks.* | *Last season his trainers put him through a strenuous running program.*

backbreaking/back-breaking /ˈbækbreɪkɪŋ/ [adj] **backbreaking** work, especially work that involves carrying and lifting heavy things, is extremely hard and needs a lot of physical effort: *After four hours of backbreaking work, we had finally pulled the wall down.*

gruelling British **/grueling** American /ˈgruːəlɪŋ/ [adj] something that is **gruelling** is extremely tiring because it continues for a long time and you have to use a lot of effort continuously: *The Le Mans 24-hour race is the most gruelling event in the motor-racing calendar.* | *Before they join the army, young recruits are put through a particularly grueling endurance course.*

arduous /ˈɑːʳdjuəs‖-dʒuəs/ [adj] written work or a journey that is **arduous** is long and tiring and needs a lot of strength and effort: *In those days, long-distance travel was slow and arduous.* | *Today, Corbett will continue his arduous climb to the top of the park's highest peak.*

punishing /ˈpʌnɪʃɪŋ/ [adj] extremely difficult in a way that damages or weakens something or makes someone feel very tired: *The transatlantic flight was a punishing task for the plane's old engines.* | *He set himself a punishing schedule of talks, lectures and conferences all over America.*

be murder /biː ˈmɜːʳdəʳ/ [v phrase] spoken use this when something is extremely difficult and needs a lot of effort or skill: *Traveling five days a week is murder. I can't do it anymore.* | **it is murder doing sth** *It's murder trying to park in this town!*

be a slog /biː ə ˈslɒg‖-ˈslɑːg/ [v phrase] British informal if something **is a slog,** it takes a lot of time and effort and is often boring: *He didn't become famous overnight – it's been a long hard slog.* | *The first half of the book was quite interesting but the last part was a bit of a slog.*

4 complicated and needing a lot of care

- tricky
- fiddly

tricky /ˈtrɪki/ [adj] a **tricky** job is difficult to do because it is complicated and you have to do it very carefully: *Getting the two sides of the mobile to balance is tricky.* | **be (a) tricky business** (=be difficult to do) *Refuelling a plane in mid-air is a tricky business.*

fiddly /ˈfɪdli/ [adj] British difficult to do because you have to handle very small objects: *He managed to fix the television, but it was a time-consuming and fiddly job.* | **fiddly to eat/mend/open etc** *I don't like shrimps – they're so fiddly to eat.*

5 a situation that is difficult to deal with or talk about

- difficult
- awkward
- tricky
- delicate
- sensitive
- touchy
- hot potato

difficult /ˈdɪfɪkəlt/ [adj] a **difficult** situation or subject is not easy to deal with or talk about, and it makes you feel nervous or unhappy: *Things at home have been very difficult since my father died.* | **be in a difficult position** (=to have problems that are difficult to deal with) *Officials say they are in the difficult position of having to implement a law they strongly disagree with.*

awkward /ˈɔːkwəʳd/ [adj] an **awkward** situation or subject is difficult to deal with or talk about, especially because it might be embarrassing: *He's at an age when kids start asking awkward questions – like 'Where do babies come from?'*

tricky /ˈtrɪki/ [adj] a **tricky** situation is one that you have to deal with very carefully, because there are a lot of things that could easily go wrong: *Teachers often have to deal with tricky situations such as interviews with angry parents.* | **it could/would be tricky to do sth** *It would be very tricky to try to stabilize the region without the support of other countries.*

delicate /ˈdelɪkɨt/ [adj] a **delicate** matter, subject, situation etc is one that you must be very careful talking about or dealing with because you risk offending or upsetting people: *I am seeking your professional advice on a very delicate matter.* | *Madeline was wondering how to approach the delicate question of her salary with her new boss.*

sensitive /ˈsensɨtɪv/ [adj] something that is **sensitive**, such as a political or social problem or a document, is likely to cause trouble or be likely to upset someone: *The team is gathering information on the sensitive subject of child abuse.* | *The administration claims that the documents contain information of a highly sensitive political nature.*

touchy /ˈtʌtʃi/ [adj] a **touchy** subject or situation is one that you must be very careful talking about or dealing with because you risk upsetting or offending someone: *Until now both candidates have avoided talking about the touchy subject of health care reform.*

hot potato /ˌhɒt pəˈteɪtəʊ‖ˌhɑːt-/ [n singular] informal a political problem that is very difficult for the government to deal with because there is a lot of disagreement about it: *Fortunately for the government, this issue has drawn attention away from the hot potato of funding the London Underground.*

6 to make a situation more difficult

- make sth more difficult/make sth harder
- complicate

make sth more difficult/make sth harder /meɪk (sth) mɔːʳ ˈdɪfɪkəlt, meɪk (sth) ˈhɑːʳdəʳ/ [v phrase] to make a situation worse or harder to deal with: *The differences in languages made the negotiations more difficult.* | *Changes in the bus service will make it harder for people to get to the hospital and other medical facilities.* | *The new job means more hours at work, which makes it harder for me to see my kids.*

complicate /'kɒmplɪkeɪt‖'kɑːm-/ [v T] to make a situation, problem etc more difficult by making it more complicated: *I don't need a boyfriend – they just complicate your life.* | **complicate matters/things** *Far from helping the situation, the new regulations are likely to complicate matters.* | **greatly complicate** *A student who has no desire to learn greatly complicates the teacher's job.*

7 someone who is unhelpful and causes problems

- difficult
- awkward
- impossible
- be a pain (in the neck)
- problem child
- not the easiest ...
- bolshy/bolshie

difficult /'dɪfɪkəlt/ [adj] someone who is **difficult** is not easy to live with or work with because they do not behave in a helpful, friendly way: *When Darren was a little boy, he was very difficult at times.* | *Campbell has the reputation of being difficult to work with.*

awkward /'ɔːkwərd/ [adj] someone who is **awkward** is deliberately unhelpful and unfriendly, and seems to like causing problems for people: *Do you have to be so awkward about everything?*

impossible /ɪm'pɒsɪbəl‖ɪm'pɑː-/ [adj] spoken someone who is **impossible** makes you annoyed and impatient, for example because they are never satisfied or they keep changing their mind: *She's impossible! Even when I offer to help her she always finds some reason to complain.* | *Dan's impossible to live with when he's sick.*

be a pain (in the neck) /biː ə ˌpeɪn (ɪn ðə 'nek)/ [v phrase] someone who **is a pain** is annoying and difficult to deal with: *Carla can be a pain sometimes, but she's been a good friend to me.* | *Little brothers are such a pain in the neck!*

problem child /'prɒbləm ˌtʃaɪld‖'prɑː- / [n phrase] a child who is always behaving badly and often gets into trouble: *In my years as a teacher, I've seen plenty of problem children come and go.*

not the easiest ... /nɒt ði 'iːziɪst .../ [adj phrase only before noun] very difficult to deal with, live with, work with etc: *I'm not surprised you've had problems with Diane. She's not the easiest person to work with, is she?*

bolshy/bolshie /'bɒlʃi‖'bəʊlʃi/ [adj] British informal someone who is **bolshy** behaves in an unhelpful, bad-tempered way and argues with the people that they are supposed to obey: *Stop being so bolshie and just get on with it, will you?*

8 a time when you have a lot of problems

- difficult/hard
- bad
- tough

difficult/hard /'dɪfɪkəlt, hɑːrd/ [adj] use this about a period of time when you have a lot of problems or a lot of bad things happen to you: *The last few months have been especially hard for her.* | *Those few days were so difficult that I decided to leave my job.* | *1996 was perhaps the worst year the automobile industry has faced so far.* | **have a difficult/hard time** *Most families have a very difficult time dealing with a family member's drug addiction.*

bad /bæd/ [adj] use this about a period of time when there are a lot of problems, especially when these are very serious: *It seemed that the bad years were finally behind me.* | **(have a) bad time** *He had an especially bad time at boarding school.*

tough /tʌf/ [adj] spoken use this about a situation or period of time when you have had a lot of problems or a lot of bad things have happened to you: *He's a good person to be with if ever you're in a tough situation.* | *Many of the veteran players had a tough time adjusting to the coach's style.*

9 difficult conditions

- difficult
- unfavourable
- adverse
- hostile

difficult /'dɪfɪkəlt/ [adj] **difficult** conditions are ones that make what you are doing more difficult: *Heavy snow will mean difficult driving conditions in some areas.* | *I'd like to thank the staff for working very hard in these difficult conditions.*

unfavourable British **/unfavorable** American /ʌn'feɪvərəbəl/ [adj] **unfavourable** conditions make it difficult for someone to do something, or for something to exist: *Bloom states clearly that he believes that many schools provide unfavorable learning conditions.* | *Despite an unfavourable business environment, the stock market remained steady.* | **+ for** *Weather forecasters said winds and 13-foot waves may make conditions unfavorable for clean-up and salvage operations.*

adverse /'ædvɜːrs/ [adj only before noun] **adverse** conditions make it difficult for someone to do something, or for something to exist: *Planes are being kept on the ground because of the adverse weather.* | *In spite of adverse public opinion, the plan to privatize the railways continued.*

hostile /'hɒstaɪl‖'hɑːstl, 'hɑːstaɪl/ [adj] use this to describe severe conditions or weather that make it difficult for people to live or travel: *The Antarctic survey team will be using vehicles specially designed to cope with the hostile environment.*

10 to have problems when you are trying to do something

- have difficulty/trouble
- find sth difficult
- with difficulty
- have a hard time
- can hardly/barely
- be too much for sb
- be a struggle
- be hard put to do sth/be hard pressed to do sth
- have your work cut out for you
- be thrown in at the deep end
- have a job doing sth

have difficulty/trouble /hæv 'dɪfɪkəlti, 'trʌbəl/ [v phrase] if you **have difficulty** when you are trying to do something, you cannot easily do it **have difficulty/trouble (in) doing sth** *It was obvious the patient was having great difficulty breathing.* | **have difficulty/trouble with sth** *A lot of Japanese students of English have trouble with the pronunciation of 'b's and 'v's.*

find sth difficult /ˌfaɪnd (sth) 'dɪfɪkəlt/ [v phrase] to not be able to do something easily, especially because you do not have enough ability or skill: *I* *found the course difficult at first, but it gradually got easier.* | **find it difficult to do sth** *She always found it difficult to keep up with the rest of the class.*

with difficulty /wɪð ˈdɪfɪkəlti/ [adv] if you do something **with difficulty**, you can do it, but only by using all your strength, all your determination etc: *She spoke with difficulty, choking back her tears.*

have a hard time /hæv ə ˌhɑːʳd ˈtaɪm/ [v phrase] to find it difficult to do something, especially because there are unexpected problems or because you have difficulty persuading other people: *I tried to find the house but I had such a hard time, I decided to give up.* | **have a hard time doing sth** *I'm still having a hard time getting the company to pay me.*

can hardly/barely /kən ˈhɑːʳdli, ˈbeəʳli/ if you **can hardly** or **can barely** do something, especially something physical, it is so difficult that you almost cannot do it: *By the end of the day she could hardly walk.* | *The smell was so bad that I could barely force myself to stay in the room.*

be too much for sb /bi tuː ˈmʌtʃ fəʳ (sb)/ [adj phrase] if a situation or job **is too much for someone**, it is too difficult for them to deal with: *All the bullying and back-stabbing in the office was simply too much for him.* | *The job was too much for any single manager to cope with.*

be a struggle /biː ə ˈstrʌgəl/ if something **is a struggle** you have to try very hard and even suffer in order to do it: *Clark lived 112 days on the artificial heart, and each day was a struggle.* | *She managed to get her money out of the welfare office, but only after a struggle.* | **it is a struggle (for sb) to do sth** *It was a struggle for my mother to understand our lifestyle, but she tried very hard.* | **it is a struggle doing sth** *It was a struggle trying to feed a family of five on my salary.*

be hard put to do sth/be hard pressed to do sth /biː ˌhɑːʳd ˌpʊt tə ˈduː (sth), biː ˌhɑːʳd ˌprest tə ˈduː (sth)/ [v phrase] if you say someone **would be hard put** or **hard pressed** to do something, you doubt that they would be able to do it because you think it is too difficult: *The two girls look so similar that you'd be hard put to tell the difference between them.* | *The governor will be hard pressed to find more money for schools while dealing with a $6 billion budget deficit.*

have your work cut out for you ALSO **have your work cut out** /hæv jɔːʳ ˌwɜːʳk kʌt ˈaʊt (fəʳ juː)/ [v phrase not in progressive] informal to have to work very hard if you are going to succeed in doing something: *I'll have my work cut out to get this design finished by this afternoon.* | *Rice hopes to break the record during tonight's game, but he'll have his work cut out for him.*

be thrown in at the deep end /biː ˌθrəʊn ɪn ət ðə ˈdiːp end/ [v phrase] informal to have to start doing something difficult such as a new job without people making it easier for you because you are new: *When I first started teaching I was really thrown in at the deep end – I had a class of forty six-year-olds all on my own.*

have a job doing sth /hæv ə ˌdʒɒb ˈduːɪŋ (sth) ‖-ˌdʒɑːb-/ [v phrase] British spoken if you **have a job doing sth**, it takes a lot of time or a lot of effort, and you may not be able to do it: *You'll have a job persuading him to give you any more money.* | *There was some kind of festival going on, and we had a job finding somewhere to park the car.*

11 to pretend that something is more difficult than it really is

- make a meal (out) of

make a meal (out) of /ˌmeɪk ə ˈmiːl (aʊt) ɒv/ [v phrase] British to pretend that a piece of work you have to do is more difficult than it really is, especially so that other people will notice and feel sorry for you: *Whenever I ask my husband to do the washing he always makes a real meal of it.* | *There's no need to make such a meal of it – here, give it to me.*

dig

RELATED WORDS

▸ *see also* **hole**

1 to dig earth out of the ground

- dig
- excavate
- tunnel
- burrow
- plough

dig /dɪg/ [v I/T] to make a hole in the ground, using your hands, a tool, or a machine: *I found two dogs digging in the garden, looking for bones.* | *He was paid twelve dollars an hour to dig ditches and mix cement.* | **dig for sth** (=in order to find something) *There were two fishermen on the beach digging for worms.* | **dig a hole/ditch/grave etc** *The workmen began digging a hole in the middle of the road.* | *Some of the prisoners escaped through a tunnel they had dug under the wall.*

excavate /ˈekskəveɪt/ [v T] formal **excavate a hole/chamber/trench etc** to dig a deep or large hole, especially as a preparation for building something: *The turtle excavates a hole in the sand and then lays its eggs in it.* | *Workers had already begun excavating the foundations for the house.*

tunnel /ˈtʌnl/ [v I/T] to dig a long passage under the ground, especially one that people or vehicles can go through **tunnel under/beneath/through etc** *Special drilling equipment is being used to tunnel beneath the sea bed.* | *worms tunnelling through the mud* | **tunnel your way out/through/under etc** *After days of digging, the prisoners finally tunnelled their way out of the camp and escaped.*

burrow /ˈbʌrəʊ‖ˈbɜːrəʊ/ [v I/T not in passive] if an animal **burrows**, it makes a passage under the ground by digging through the earth as it moves forward **+ into/under/through** *Toads burrow into the earth to hide from their enemies.* | **burrow a hole** *The rabbits had burrowed a hole under the fence.*

plough British **/plow** American /plaʊ/ [v I/T] to turn over the earth in a field using a special tool or machine in order to prepare it for growing crops: *The fields are ploughed as soon as the winter crop is removed.* | *Farmers were plowing their land and planting cotton seeds.*

2 to remove something from the ground by digging

- dig out
- dig up
- excavate
- mine

dig out /ˌdɪg ˈaʊt/ [phr v T] to remove something that is just below or partly below the surface of the ground by digging **dig sb/sth out** *What do we do with* *these trees after we've dug them out?* | *The spade was missing, and we had no choice but to dig the weeds out by hand.* | **dig out sth** *A couple of local people helped us dig out the car, which was by now completely stuck in the mud.*

dig up /ˌdɪg ˈʌp/ [phr v T] to dig, and remove something from the ground that is buried or that is growing there **dig up sth** *Thieves came in the night and dug up the body.* | *I don't know why archaeologists get such a thrill from digging up broken pots.* | **dig sth up** *Squirrels bury hundreds of nuts, then dig them up in winter when food is scarce.*

excavate /ˈekskəveɪt/ [v T] to remove ancient objects from the ground or uncover ancient houses, villages etc, by taking away the earth carefully: *Archaeologists are excavating a Bronze Age settlement on the outskirts of the village.* | *The mosaics excavated in 1989 have now been fully restored.* —**excavation** /ˌekskəˈveɪʃən/ [n C] *The excavation revealed layer after layer of ancient fortifications.*

mine /maɪn/ [v I/T] to take minerals such as coal, iron, or diamonds out of the ground, especially by digging a deep hole and a series of passages: *Lead has been mined in this area for hundreds of years.* | *The church was built by Don José de la Borda, who made his fortune mining silver.* | **mine for gold/silver etc** *Most of the new settlers came here to mine for gold.* —**mine** [n C] *Before World War I more than a million workers labored in the coal mines of Great Britain.*

direction

RELATED WORDS

▸ *see also* **way (9-10), road, path, travel**

1 the direction in which someone or something is moving, aimed etc

- direction
- way
- course

direction /dɪ̵ˈrekʃən, daɪ-/ [n C] *The moons all move around the planet in the same direction.* | *Frightened by the sound of footsteps, the rabbits ran off in all directions.* | **in sb's direction** (=towards someone) *I was hoping he wouldn't look in our direction and notice us sitting there.* | **in the direction of sth** (=towards something) *The two young men headed off in the direction of Central Park.* | **from the direction of sth** (=from something) *The sound of shots came from the direction of the compound, a quarter of a mile away.* | **in the right/wrong direction** *We're going in the right direction now – I can see the main road up ahead.* | **in the opposite direction** *Bill marched off angrily in the opposite direction.* | **from opposite directions** *Tornadoes usually form when rising warm, moist air rotates, as winds from opposite directions collide.* | **in a southerly/easterly etc direction** *The plane was traveling in a northeasterly direction when it was hit by lightning.*

way /weɪ/ [n C usually singular] the general direction in which someone or something is moving, is aimed etc: *The bear went that way – you can see its tracks in the snow.* | *It is important to consider which way the house faces, as that determines how much sun it gets.* | **the right/wrong way** *Are you sure we're going the right way? I don't remember seeing that church before.*

course /kɔːʳs/ [n C usually singular] the direction in which something such as a ship or aircraft is moving, which has been previously planned: *The captain decided to change the ship's course to avoid the storm.* | **on/off course** (=following the correct or incorrect course) *Investigators say the plane was over 800 miles off course when it crashed.*

2 ways of asking about direction

- which way
- which direction
- ask sb how to get to/ask sb the way/ask the way
- ask for directions
- can you tell me the way to/do you know the way to
- how do I get
- is this the way to

which way /ˌwɪtʃ ˈweɪ/ [adv] spoken use this to ask someone the general direction that something is in, that someone is travelling in etc: *Which way are you going? Maybe we can share a cab.* | *'Excuse me, which way is the Natural History Museum?' 'That way. Keep walking and you'll see it on the left.'*

which direction /ˌwɪtʃ dɪ̵ˈrekʃən/ [n phrase] use this when you when you want to know exact details about **which direction** something is in, about **which direction** someone is travelling in etc: *Which direction do we take once we reach the top of the hill?*

ask sb how to get to/ask sb the way/ask the way /ˌɑːsk (sb) haʊ tə get tuː, ˌɑːsk (sb) ðə ˈweɪ, ˌɑːsk ðə ˈweɪ‖ˌæsk-/ [v phrase] to ask someone the way to a place, especially when you have already started your journey: *He looked suspicious when we asked him how to get to the border.* | *Maggie stopped the first person she saw and asked them the way to the hospital.* | *I've got no idea where we are – we'll have to stop and ask the way.*

ask for directions /ˌɑːsk fəʳ dɪ̵ˈrekʃənz‖ˌæsk-/ [v phrase] to ask for instructions on how to get somewhere, either before you start a journey or after you have started it: *Some people stopped as they passed, asking for directions.* | **+ to** *I asked for directions to the town hall and made my way there on foot.*

can you tell me the way to/do you know the way to /kən juː ˌtel miː ðə ˈweɪ tuː, duː juː ˌnəʊ ðə ˈweɪ tuː/ spoken use this to ask the way to somewhere: *Can you tell me the way to the harbor, please?* | *Excuse me, buddy – do you know the way to the beach?*

how do I get /ˌhaʊ duː aɪ ˈget/ spoken used especially when you know that someone knows the way to that place **how do I get to** *How do I get to the station from here?* | **how do I get there/back/home etc** *I've got her address but how do I get there?*

is this the way to /ɪz ðɪs ðə ˈweɪ tuː/ spoken used especially when you have already started going somewhere and want to know if you are going the right way: *'Is this the right way to the Science Museum?' 'No, you're going in the wrong direction.'*

3 to tell someone the way to a place

- tell sb how to get to/tell sb the way
- give directions
- show sb the way
- direct

tell sb how to get to/tell sb the way /ˌtel (sb) haʊ tə ˈget tuː, ˌtel (sb) ðə ˈweɪ/ [v phrase] *He knows how to get here. I told him the way myself.* | **tell sb the way to sth** *Graham can tell you the way to Yvonne's house.* | **tell sb the way out/here/there etc** *Excuse me, could you tell me the way out, please?*

give directions /ˌgɪv dɪ̵ˈrekʃənz/ [v phrase] to give someone written or spoken instructions about how to get to a place: *He got into the car and began to give directions.* | **give sb directions/give directions to sb** *I'm not surprised you couldn't find your way here if Peter gave you directions!*

show sb the way /ˌʃəʊ (sb) ðə ˈweɪ/ [v phrase] to show someone how to get to a place, especially by going there with them: *I'll send someone with you to show you the way.* | **+ to** *She asked a scruffy-looking little boy to show her the way to the police station.*

direct /d½ˈrekt, daɪ-/ [v T] formal to show someone the way to a place, especially by telling them where it is or pointing to it **direct sb behind/towards/out etc** *A steward directed us behind the stage and towards the dressing rooms.* | **direct sb to sth** *Go and ask the patrolman – he'll direct you to the freeway.*

4 the ability to guess or find the right direction

- sense of direction

sense of direction /ˌsens əv d½ˈrekʃən/ [n singular] *When night came we lost all sense of direction and were soon completely lost.* | **good/bad/excellent etc sense of direction** *I can't believe you got us back to the hotel – you've got a really good sense of direction.*

dirty

RELATED WORDS

opposite: clean

▸ *see also* **wash, mark**

1 dirty

- dirty
- muddy
- dusty
- greasy
- grubby
- grimy
- mucky

dirty /ˈdɜːrti/ [adj] not clean: *Look how dirty your hands are!* | *Take off those dirty jeans.* | *We were hot and dirty after working in the garden all afternoon.* | *Do you have any dirty clothes you need me to wash?* | **get dirty** (=become dirty) *How did the floor get so dirty?*

muddy /ˈmʌdi/ [adj] covered in mud: *Your shoes are really muddy – take them off before you come in.* | *They moved slowly along the muddy footpath.* | *She left a trail of muddy footprints behind her.*

dusty /ˈdʌsti/ [adj] a **dusty** room, piece of furniture etc is covered in dust, especially because no one has cleaned it or moved it for a long time: *The room was dark and dusty.* | *dusty shelves* | *The journal was dusty and beginning to fall apart.*

greasy /ˈgriːsi, -zi/ [adj] something that is **greasy** looks dirty because it has an oily substance on it: *greasy pots and pans* | *Dick wiped his hands on a greasy rag.* | *Her long greasy hair hung down to her shoulders.*

grubby /ˈgrʌbi/ [adj] something that is **grubby** is fairly dirty, usually because it has been used a lot and not washed: *He blew his nose with a grubby handkerchief.* | *Her coat was grubby and one of the sleeves was torn.* | *From his back pocket Robert took out a grubby scrap of paper.*

grimy /ˈgraɪmi/ [adj] something that is **grimy** has a covering of dirt on its surface, especially because it has not been cleaned for a long time: *Chris was in a grimy apron, sweeping up.* | *The whole town was grimy from smoke and coal-dust.* | *It was difficult to see through the grimy windows of the cafe.*

mucky /ˈmʌki/ [adj] especially British, informal dirty: *Don't wear your best shoes – you'll only get them all mucky.* | *The cafeteria was self-service, and guests had to carry their food on little plastic trays to mucky tables.*

2 very dirty

- filthy
- foul
- squalid

filthy /ˈfɪlθi/ [adj] extremely dirty: *The inside of the oven was filthy.* | *We didn't go swimming because the water looked filthy.* | *filthy sheets* | **absolutely filthy** *You ought to wash that sweatshirt – it's absolutely filthy.*

foul /faʊl/ [adj] very dirty – use this especially about air or water: *the foul air of the factory* | *A foul haze of pollution hung over the city.*

squalid /ˈskwɒl½d‖ˈskwɑː-/ [adj] very dirty and unpleasant – use this about the place or conditions in which someone lives: *Dalmer lived in a squalid little room above a shop.* | *Her childhood was spent in the squalid slums east of the city.* | **squalid conditions** *After the squalid conditions of the refugee camps even this place seems preferable.*

3 dirty and bad for your health

- unhygienic
- polluted
- contaminated
- insanitary

unhygienic /ˌʌnhaɪˈdʒiːnɪk◂‖-ˈdʒen-, -ˈdʒiːn-/ [adj] likely to cause disease – use this about dirty conditions in kitchens, restaurants, and hospitals: *It is unhygienic to store raw meat at that temperature.* | *Hospital cleaners were criticized for the unhygienic conditions of the central kitchens.*

polluted /pəˈluːt½d/ [adj] water or air that is **polluted** has a lot of harmful waste or poisonous chemicals in it: *Sayers said that if he's elected his administration will make a priority of cleaning up the region's polluted rivers.* | *Central London is the most polluted spot in Britain.* | **+ with/by** *Large parts of the Mediterranean are still polluted with toxic waste.* | **heavily polluted** (=very badly polluted) *The air was heavily polluted with exhaust fumes.*

contaminated /kənˈtæm½neɪt½d/ [adj] food, water, or land that is **contaminated** is not safe to use or be in because dangerous chemicals or bacteria have come into it: *contaminated drinking water* | **+ with/by** *Several people became ill after eating hamburger meat contaminated with the E.coli bacteria.* | **heavily contaminated** (=very badly contaminated) *The soil around the plant is heavily contaminated.*

insanitary /ɪnˈsæn½təri‖-teri/ [adj] **insanitary** conditions are dirty and likely to cause disease, especially because there is no effective way of getting rid of waste: *Amnesty claims the prisoners are being kept in overcrowded and insanitary conditions.*

4 to make something dirty

- get sth dirty
- dirty
- soil

get sth dirty /ˌget (sth) ˈdɜːrti/ [v phrase] use this especially in negative statements: *Try not to get the floor dirty.* | *I don't want to get my new shoes dirty.*

dirty /ˈdɜːʳti/ [v T] to make something **dirty**, especially clothes: *You can borrow my gloves, but please try not to dirty them.* | *As he stood on the pavement, muddy water splashed up and dirtied his trousers.*

soil /sɔɪl/ [v T] formal to make clothes, sheets, etc dirty, especially with sweat, waste from your body, or other liquids: *The baby had soiled her diaper again.* | *His shirtfront was soiled with blood and his hair was wild.* | *Many of the pages had been soiled by the old man's dirty fingers.*

5 to make something dirty and dangerous

- **pollute**
- **contaminate**

- *see also* **environment**

pollute /pəˈluːt/ [v T] to make air, water, the ground etc dirty by putting chemicals or waste products into it, so that it is unsafe for use by people or animals: *An investigation revealed that the mine was polluting both the air and the groundwater.* | *The company is charged with polluting the River Mersey by allowing crude oil to enter the river.* | **pollute sth with sth** *The factory explosion, which polluted the surrounding area with dioxin, was reportedly caused by negligence.*

contaminate /kənˈtæmɪneɪt/ [v T] to accidentally make a place or a substance dirty and dangerous by adding something to it, for example chemicals or bacteria: *Lead pipes can contaminate drinking water.* | *The food was contaminated during the production process.* —**contamination** /kənˌtæmɪˈneɪʃən/ [n U] *contamination of air, food and water*

6 something that makes things dirty

- **dirt**
- **dust**
- **mud**
- **pollution**
- **muck**
- **grime**

dirt /dɜːʳt/ [n U] dust, mud, or anything else that makes things dirty: *Why is there dirt all over the back seat of the car?* | *She swept the dirt off the back porch.* | *He took off his glasses, which were covered with dirt.* | **speck of dirt** (=small piece of dirt) *The rooms were cleaned until every speck of dirt and grit was gone.*

dust /dʌst/ [n U] dry powder that forms a layer on furniture, floors, clothes etc, especially when they have not been cleaned or moved for a long time: *Max brushed the dust off his coat.* | **layer of dust** *There was a thick layer of dust on the furniture.*

mud /mʌd/ [n U] wet earth that sticks to your shoes, clothes, car, tyres etc: *There's mud all over the carpet.* | *Hayley scraped the dried mud off her boots.* | *Their expensive riding jackets were covered in mud.*

pollution /pəˈluːʃən/ [n U] the harmful effects on water, air, or land of chemicals and waste from factories, cars, modern farming methods etc: *Industrial pollution has killed much of the river's wildlife.* | *Pollution from cars is the main cause of global warming.* | *The convention, signed by the six states bordering the Black Sea, aims to reduce current pollution levels.*

muck /mʌk/ [n U] British informal dirt or mud: *I'll just clean the muck off the windscreen and wing mirrors.* | **be covered in muck** *His hands and fingernails were filthy, his face and legs covered in muck.*

grime /graɪm/ [n U] thick, dark dirt that covers a surface over a period of time and is difficult to remove: *On one wall of the entryway hangs a large oil painting, covered with grime.* | *His hands were black with grime from working on the car.*

disabled

RELATED WORDS

- unable to see *see* **see (11-12)**
- unable to hear *see* **hear (6)**
- *see also* **hurt/injure**

1 disabled

- **disabled**
- **handicapped**
- **special needs**
- **learning difficulties**

disabled /dɪsˈeɪbəld/ [adj] someone who is **disabled** cannot use a part of their body, for example their legs or their arms: *David goes to a special school for disabled children.* | *Her son is disabled and she has to take care of him all the time.* | **the disabled** *The governor has guaranteed health care for pregnant women, preschool children, and the disabled.* | **disabled toilets/parking etc** (=for disabled people)

handicapped /ˈhændɪkæpt/ [adj] someone who is **handicapped** has serious difficulty using part of their body or mind: *She works with handicapped teenagers.* | **mentally handicapped** (=handicapped in the mind) *a school for mentally handicapped children*

special needs /ˌspeʃəl ˈniːdz/ [n plural] people with **special needs** need different teaching methods, special equipment etc because they are physically or mentally disabled **have special needs/with special needs** *a school for children with special needs*

learning difficulties /ˈlɜːʳnɪŋ ˌdɪfɪkəltiz/ [n plural] people with **learning difficulties** have difficulty learning at the same rate as most other people: *He's studying to teach children who have learning difficulties.*

2 a physical or mental problem that makes someone disabled

- **disability**
- **handicap**

disability /ˌdɪsəˈbɪlɪti/ [n C/U] a problem with part of your body which makes it difficult for you to walk, talk, see etc: *There are special courses for people with disabilities.* | *Because of his disability, he depended on his wife to dress him, feed him and bathe him.* | **learning disability** *Studies say exposure to loud continuous noise can cause learning disabilities and behavioral problems in children.*

handicap /ˈhændɪkæp/ [n C/U] a mental or physical problem that makes someone disabled: *We help people with mental or physical handicaps to find work.* | *Babies of alcoholic mothers can be born with a severe degree of handicap.*

3 not disabled

- **able-bodied**

able-bodied /ˌeɪbəl ˈbɒdid◂‖-ˈbɑː-/ [adj] not disabled – use this when you are comparing disabled people with people who are not disabled: *Disabled students face different problems from their able-bodied friends.*

disadvantage

RELATED WORDS

opposite: **advantage**

▸ *see also* **poor**

1 a bad feature of something

- disadvantage
- drawback
- liability
- limitations
- the downside

disadvantage /ˌdɪsədˈvɑːntɪdʒ‖-ˈvæn-/ [n C] a bad feature of something, for example a way in which it causes problems or is worse than other things of the same kind: *The proposal has some major disadvantages.* | **+ of** *The main disadvantage of being a nurse is working irregular hours.*

drawback /ˈdrɔːbæk/ [n C] a disadvantage of something, that makes it seem less attractive – use this especially when something seems good in other ways: *It's a good-looking car – the only drawback is the price.* | **+ of** *One of the major drawbacks of being famous is the lack of privacy.* | **+ to** *High house prices are one drawback to economic growth.*

liability /ˌlaɪəˈbɪlɪ̈ti/ [n C] someone or something that is a disadvantage because they are likely to make you less successful: *In those days, a politician's wife who did not hold traditional views could be a liability.* | **+ to** *The product that was once so popular is now a liability to the company.* | **serious liability** *The bank realized that the dispute was becoming a serious liability in doing business*

limitations /ˌlɪmɪ̈ˈteɪʃənz/ [n plural] the limits on how good someone or something can be or what they are able to do: *I think we've done a wonderful job, considering the limitations we've had to work under.* | *We made an inspection of the building's resources and limitations.*

the downside /ðə ˈdaʊnsaɪd/ [n C usually singular] the disadvantage of a plan or situation that in most other ways seems good: *The band sounds great. The only downside is the quality of the recording.* | **+ of** *The downside of the New Economy is the forced resettlement of villagers.*

2 something that makes it more difficult for someone to succeed

- disadvantage
- handicap

disadvantage /ˌdɪsədˈvɑːntɪdʒ‖-ˈvæn-/ [n C/U] something that makes it more difficult for you to succeed or to do what you want, especially compared to other people: *Like many other black families, his family had to struggle to overcome social and economic disadvantage.* | *Our goal is to try to provide financial help people in our community with a lot of disadvantages.*

handicap /ˈhændɪkæp/ [n C] something that prevents you from doing something as well as you could: *Not being able to drive is a real handicap if you live in the country.* | **+ of** *The team had a good season despite the handicap of having 5 new players.* | **be a handicap to sb** *His lack of height has not been a handicap to him. He is as good an athlete as anyone else in the school.*

3 to have a disadvantage compared to other people or things

- have a disadvantage
- be at a disadvantage
- disadvantaged
- be handicapped
- the odds are stacked (heavily) against you
- be to sb's/sth's disadvantage
- be against
- count against

have a disadvantage /hæv ə ˌdɪsədˈvɑːntɪdʒ‖-ˈvæn-/ [v phrase not in progressive] *She has the same qualifications as the other candidates, but has one big disadvantage – lack of experience.* | *Their restaurant has the disadvantage of being located south of town, a little too far from the tourist routes.*

be at a disadvantage /biː ət ə ˌdɪsədˈvɑːntɪdʒ‖-ˈvæn-/ [v phrase] to have a disadvantage, especially because you do not have the experience or qualities that make you more likely to succeed in doing something: *Women are still at a disadvantage when it comes to getting jobs in the military.* | *People with previous convictions are always at a disadvantage when on trial in a court of law.* | **put/place sb at a disadvantage** *The test put candidates whose first language was not English at a disadvantage.*

disadvantaged /ˌdɪsədˈvɑːntɪdʒd‖-ˈvæn-/ [adj] if someone is **disadvantaged**, they are suffering social or economic disadvantages such as lack of money or bad education, so that they have less chance of being successful than other people: *The club runs programs for disadvantaged children in the inner city areas.* | **the disadvantaged** (=disadvantaged people) *Booth invented schemes to help the disadvantaged in the community.*

be handicapped /biː ˈhændɪkæpt/ [v phrase] to have a disadvantage that makes it very difficult for you to do something **be handicapped by sth** *The Republican candidate was handicapped by his heavy schedule.* | *In all its ambitious plans the company has been handicapped by an outdated system of management.*

the odds are stacked (heavily) against you /ði ˌɒdz ɑːʳ ˌstækt (hevɪ̈li) əˈgenst juː‖-ˌɑːdz-/ use this to say that someone has a big disadvantage so that they are very unlikely to be successful: *With every big company in town trying to stop them, the odds are stacked against them.* | *Most people who go into casinos know the odds are stacked heavily against them, but it doesn't stop them from trying.*

be to sb's/sth's disadvantage /biː tə (sb's/sth's) ˌdɪsədˈvɑːntɪdʒ‖ -ˈvæn-/ [v phrase] to give someone or something a disadvantage: *Her height could be to her disadvantage if she wants to be a dancer.* | *To its disadvantage, the book contains a lot of material that is difficult for the average person to understand.* | **to the disadvantage of** *The government has reorganized the taxation system to the disadvantage of low-paid workers.*

be against /biː əˈgenst/ [v T] if particular conditions **are against** someone or something, they make it unlikely or impossible for them to succeed in doing something: *Time is against us. The longer we wait to find a solution to the crisis, the worse it will get.* | *He wanted to become a pilot but his bad eyesight was against him.*

count against /ˌkaʊnt əˈgenst/ [phr v T] if something counts against you, it makes people have a worse opinion of you, and often makes people decide not to choose you, or makes them decide that you are guilty: *We believe Caroline Connely is inno-*

cent, but her silence could count against her in a court. | *He was a child when he committed the crime. Should that count against him as an adult with a clean record?*

disagree

RELATED WORDS

opposite: ——— **agree**

▸ *see also* **argue, opinion, criticize, reject**

1 to have a different opinion from someone else

- ▸ **disagree**
- ▸ **not agree**
- ▸ **not see eye to eye**
- ▸ **take issue with**
- ▸ **differ**
- ▸ **agree to disagree**
- ▸ **dissent**

disagree /ˌdɪsəˈgriː/ [v I not in progressive] to have a different opinion about something from someone else: *A lot of people think that capitalism is the only system that works, but I disagree.* | **+ with** *I showed my article to the editor. He disagreed with almost everything I'd written.* | **+ about** *Throughout their marriage my parents disagreed about whether to stay in their hometown or not.* | **+ that** *The company's lawyers disagreed that the complaint was a criminal matter.* | **strongly disagree** *The court decision represents an issue on which the president and the Justice Department strongly disagree.*

not agree /nɒt əˈgriː/ [v phrase] to disagree with someone about a subject or about what to do: *He thinks we'd have a better chance of finding work if we moved house, but I don't agree.* | **+ with** *I'd never vote for Davies. He has too many policies I don't agree with.* | **+ on/about** *Before long, they realized that they couldn't agree about anything.* | *We couldn't agree on what to do in the afternoon, so we just stayed at home.* | **+ that** *The doctor did not agree that the only solution was to operate.*

not see eye to eye /nɒt siː ˌaɪ tʊ ˈaɪ/ [v phrase] if two people **do not see eye to eye**, they have very different opinions and ideas, so that it is difficult for them to be friends or to work together **+ on/about** *Unfortunately, Julie and I don't see eye to eye on money matters.* | **+ with** *Donato doesn't see eye to eye with several of the other committee members.*

take issue with /teɪk ˈɪʃuː wɪð/ [v phrase] formal to disagree strongly with someone about something they have said or done, and to argue with them about it **take issue with sb over sth** *I took issue with Meeker over the way he was running the company.*

differ /ˈdɪfəʳ/ [v I] especially written if a group of people **differ** about something, they have a range of different opinions on it **+ about/over** *Critics differed about the importance of Osborne's new play.* | *All politicians agree that inflation must be beaten but they differ over methods of achieving this.* | **differ widely** (=differ a lot) *Scholars differ widely about when the two manuscripts were written.*

agree to disagree ALSO **agree to differ** British /əˌgriː tə ˌdɪsəˈgriː, əˌgriː tə ˈdɪfəʳ/ [v phrase not in progressive] to stop arguing with someone about something and accept that they cannot be persuaded to agree with you: *The two sides had agreed to differ.* | *After two days, the negotiators had done little more than agree to disagree.*

dissent /dɪˈsent/ [v I] formal to say publicly that you disagree with an official opinion or belief, or one that is accepted by most people: *The decision was supported by almost everyone. Baldwin was the only one to dissent.* | **+ from** *No one dared dissent from the official party line.* | **dissenting voices** (=people who say they disagree) *Blair would be wise to listen to some of the dissenting voices in his party.*

2 to disagree strongly with someone

- ▸ **be at loggerheads**
- ▸ **be at odds**
- ▸ **fall out**
- ▸ **be in conflict with**
- ▸ **irreconcilable**
- ▸ **nonsense**

be at loggerheads /biː ət ˈlɒgəʳhedz‖-ˈlɔːg-/ [v phrase] if two people or groups **are at loggerheads**, they strongly disagree with each other and argue, usually about how to deal with a problem or decision: *As a result of the strike, neighbours and even families were soon at loggerheads.* | **+ over/about** *Congress and the President are still at loggerheads over how to balance the federal budget.*

be at odds /biː ət ˈɒdz‖-ˈɑːdz/ [v phrase] to disagree with a person, organization, or way of thinking and be opposed to them – used especially in news reports **+ with** *Britain and France were constantly at odds with each other throughout the negotiations.* | **+ over** *The two sides are still at odds over a pay increase for airline pilots.*

fall out /ˌfɔːl ˈaʊt/ [phr v I not in progressive] British to disagree strongly with someone and argue with them about it so that your good relationship with them is damaged: *Jung and Freud fell out when Jung disagreed with some of Freud's central theories.* | **+ with** *Maria fell out with some of her colleagues and decided to look for a new job.* | **fall out (with sb) over** *They fell out over some stupid little issue.* —**falling-out** [n singular] *She was fired from the Broadway production after a highly-publicized falling-out with Weber.*

be in conflict with /biː ɪn ˈkɒnflɪkt wɪð ‖-ˈkɑːn-/ [v phrase] to strongly disagree with someone and to be continuously opposing them and arguing against their actions and intentions: *Rather than be in continual conflict with his boss, Bruce moved to another job.* | *Union leaders are again in conflict with management, this time over job losses.*

irreconcilable /ɪˌrekənˈsaɪləbəl◂/ [adj] having or resulting from such completely different aims or opinions that agreement is impossible: *The split in the Liberal party seems to be irreconcilable.* | **irreconcilable differences** *When irreconcilable differences exist between two people, it is better that they should separate.* | **+ with** *Both these ways of looking at the world are valid but utterly irreconcilable with each other.*

nonsense spoken ALSO **rubbish** British spoken /ˈnɒnsəns‖ˈnɑːnsens, ˈrʌbɪʃ/ use this when you strongly disagree with something someone has said: *'You always think you're right!' 'Nonsense!'*

3 when members of a group disagree with each other

- ▸ **be divided/split**
- ▸ **division**
- ▸ **split**
- ▸ **rift**

be divided/split /biː dəˈvaɪdəd, ˈsplɪt/ [v phrase] if a group of people **is divided** or **split** over something, some of them support one opinion and others support a completely different one **+ over/on** *The country's leaders appear to be split on the question of tax cuts.* | *Foreign aid agencies were split over whether to resume their operations in the troubled country.*

division /dɪ̈'vɪʒən/ [n C/U] disagreement among the members of a group that causes it to separate into smaller groups, each with a different opinion: *There are signs of growing division within the administration about the best strategy to adopt.* | **+ over** *There was a deep division in the Republican Party over policy on Central America.*

split /splɪt/ [n C] a serious disagreement that divides an organization or group into two smaller groups: *There is great danger of a split in the party if a competent leader is not found soon.* | **+ over** *There is a deep split in the country over the best way to move forward the peace process.*

rift /rɪft/ [n C] a serious disagreement that divides a group for a very long time or prevents two people or organizations from continuing to live or work together: *It took a good five years for the rift within the party to mend.* | **+ between** *The family arguments finally caused a rift between the mother and daughter that has not yet healed.*

4 when people disagree

- **disagreement**
- **difference of opinion**
- **controversy**
- **deadlock/stalemate**
- **friction**
- **discord**
- **dissent**

disagreement /ˌdɪsə'griːmənt/ [n C/U] when people disagree with each other: *The party is seriously split by internal rivalries and disagreements.* | **+ about/over** *Disagreement over who should produce the next album caused the band to split.* | **+ between/among** *There is some disagreement among medical experts about the best treatment for back pain.*

difference of opinion /ˌdɪfərəns əv ə'pɪnjən/ [n phrase] when people are unable to agree, especially about something important – use this as a way of avoiding more direct words like 'argument' and 'disagreement' **+ about/over** *There were major differences of opinion over who should command the UN forces.* | **+ between/among** *There is a difference of opinion between the chairman and the board as to the best way to handle the takeover.*

controversy /'kɒntrəvɜːsi, kən'trɒvəsi‖'kɑːntrəvɜːrsi/ [n C/U] a serious disagreement about a decision, plan, or action, that causes arguments for a long time in newspapers, on television etc: *Controversy surrounds the TV show, which many consider to be racist, sexist, and homophobic.* | **+ over** *There has been a huge controversy over where to put the city's new sports stadium and who should build it.*

deadlock/stalemate /'dedlɒk‖-lɑːk, 'steɪlmeɪt/ [n singular] a situation in which two groups disagree, and no agreement is possible because each group refuses to change its mind even slightly: *Parents believe that pressure from city hall could force an end to the stalemate with the school board.* | **+ over** *the political deadlock over allowable levels of greenhouse emissions* | **break the deadlock/stalemate** (=end the situation) *US negotiators met with representatives from both countries today in an attempt to break the deadlock.*

friction /'frɪkʃən/ [n U] continuous disagreement and angry feelings or unfriendliness between people: *Teenage children begin to assert their independence and this can lead to a good deal of friction in the family.* | **+ between** *There has been serious friction between the two army commanders.*

discord /'dɪskɔːʳd/ [n U] formal strong disagreement that makes people feel unfriendly towards each other: *Money is the single biggest cause of discord in marriage.* | **+ over** *There has always been discord over NATO's role in world conflict.*

dissent /dɪ'sent/ [n U] a refusal to accept an official opinion or an opinion that most people accept: *During the Prime Minister's speech there were several murmurs of open dissent from the crowd.* | *Anti-war dissent was increasing by the time Nixon took office.*

5 to cause disagreement

- **give rise to/lead to/cause disagreement**
- **divide**
- **split**

give rise to/lead to/cause disagreement /gɪv ˌraɪz tuː, ˌliːd tuː, ˌkɔːz dɪsə'griːmənt/ [v phrase] *The issue of organ cloning has given rise to some disagreement among doctors.* | *It was Garcia's plan to redistribute land that caused the most disagreement.* | *His speech is bound to lead to some disagreement, but I think most people will accept it.*

divide /dɪ̈'vaɪd/ [v T] to cause strong disagreement among a group of people so that they separate and form different groups with different opinions: *The election campaign was bitter, dividing the city.* | *The issue dividing the Church was the question of women priests.*

split /splɪt/ [v T] to cause strong disagreement among a group of people so that it is divided into two smaller groups – use this especially about political groups or political ideas: *When the book appeared just before the end of the century, it almost split the feminist movement.* | **split the country/party etc down the middle** (=split it into two equal and opposing groups) *Feelings about the war split the country right down the middle.*

6 causing disagreement

- **controversial**
- **contentious**
- **bone of contention**

controversial /ˌkɒntrə'vɜːʳʃəl◂‖ˌkɑːn-/ [adj] something that is **controversial** causes a lot of disagreement and angry argument, especially in the newspaper, on television etc: *A recent government paper on education contains some controversial new ideas.* | *Rossellini's controversial film, 'The Miracle'* | *The decision to use the bomb remains the most controversial question of the Second World War.*

contentious /kən'tenʃəs/ [adj] **contentious issue/subject/problem etc** one that is likely to cause a lot of disagreement and argument: *Abortion has always been a contentious subject.* | *the contentious issue of arms sales to non-democratic countries*

bone of contention /ˌbəʊn əv kən'tenʃən/ [n phrase] a subject that people strongly disagree about for a long time and often argue about: *The new tax on property is likely to become a serious bone of contention.* | **+ between** *The way we manage money has been the only real bone of contention between us.*

disappear

RELATED WORDS

▸ *see also* **leave, see, lose, find, look for**

1 to become impossible to find

- ▸ disappear
- ▸ vanish
- ▸ go missing
- ▸ disappear/vanish without trace

disappear /ˌdɪsəˈpɪəʳ/ [v I] if someone or something **disappears**, you do not know where they are and cannot find them: *Where are my keys? They seem to have disappeared.* | *By the time of the trial, the tape had mysteriously disappeared.* | **+ from** *Thirteen-year-old Nicola disappeared from her home on Saturday night.* | **disappear with sth** *When I turned round, I discovered the man had disappeared with my bag.* —**disappearance** [n U] *The mysterious disappearance of Lord Lucan has never been solved.*

vanish /ˈvænɪʃ/ [v I] if someone or something **vanishes**, they disappear and you cannot understand what has happened to them: *When she returned, her car had vanished.* | **+ from** *Smith vanished from Heathrow Airport in 1969 and is believed to be living in Florida.* | **vanish into thin air** (=vanish quickly, leaving no sign) *The company that supplied the missing cargo seems to have vanished into thin air.*

go missing /gəʊ ˈmɪsɪŋ/ [v phrase] British if an object **goes missing**, it is no longer in the place where it should be and may have been stolen; if a person **goes missing**, they cannot be found, and may be in danger: *Security was tightened up at the embassy after a number of important files went missing.* | *He's a strange man – sometimes he goes missing for days and doesn't tell a soul.* | **+ from** *Stock has been going missing from the stock room, and we're trying to find out who is responsible.*

disappear/vanish without trace British/ **without a trace** American /dɪsəˌpɪəʳ, ˌvænɪʃ wɪðˌaʊt (ə) ˈtreɪs/ [v phrase not in progressive] **disappear/vanish/sink without trace** to disappear completely without leaving any sign of what happened: *A father and son have disappeared without trace while on a walking expedition in the mountains.* | *Several aircraft and ships have vanished without trace in the notorious Bermuda Triangle.*

2 to become impossible to see

- ▸ disappear
- ▸ vanish
- ▸ out of sight
- ▸ fade away
- ▸ blend into/blend in with

▸ *see also* **clear/not clear**

disappear /ˌdɪsəˈpɪəʳ/ [v I] if someone or something **disappears**, you cannot see them any more **+ behind/under/into/over etc** *The sun disappeared behind a cloud.* | *She watched the boat sail out to sea until it disappeared over the horizon.* | **disappear from view/sight** *Sheila's car turned the corner and disappeared from view.*

vanish /ˈvænɪʃ/ [v I] if someone or something **vanishes**, you suddenly cannot see them any more – used especially when this is unexpected or strange: *The snowflakes vanished as they touched the ground.* | **+ into/behind/under etc** *The last of the police cars sped past and vanished into the storm.* | **+ from** *The plane vanished from radar screens soon after taking off.*

out of sight /aʊt əv ˈsaɪt/ [adv] if something or someone goes **out of sight**, they gradually move away from you until you cannot see them any more: *Just as she went out of sight, he remembered he hadn't given her his number.* | *The yacht sailed away into the distance and out of sight.* | *We watched his car as it rounded the bend and sped off out of sight.*

fade away /ˌfeɪd əˈweɪ/ [phr v I] if a mark or light **fades away**, it slowly becomes less clear or less bright until you cannot see it any more: *The light faded away and the tunnel became completely black.* | *The bruises will fade away over time.*

blend into/blend in with /ˌblend ˈɪntuː, ˌblend ˈɪn wɪð/ [v T not in passive] if something or someone blends into the place where they are they are like it in appearance, and you cannot see them easily: *These creatures can change colour in order to blend into their surroundings.* | *Bruno was hoping to blend in with the crowd and escape unnoticed.*

3 to stop being heard, felt etc

- ▸ disappear
- ▸ fade away
- ▸ wear off
- ▸ go away
- ▸ die away

disappear /ˌdɪsəˈpɪəʳ/ [v I] if a feeling **disappears**, you stop feeling it: *Drugs won't make the pain disappear altogether, but they will help.* | *Your grief won't disappear overnight. It takes time to get over the death of someone close to you.*

fade away /ˌfeɪd əˈweɪ/ [phr v I] if a sound, a feeling, or a memory **fades away**, it gradually becomes less loud, less strong, or less clear, until you cannot hear, feel, or remember it any longer: *As the last notes of the song faded away, the audience began to applaud.* | *For the first two years after the divorce, he was permanently angry, but then the anger faded away.* | *The memory of the attack will fade away in time.*

wear off /ˌweər ˈɒf/ [phr v I] if something, especially the effect of something, **wears off**, it gradually disappears: *The pain got worse as the anaesthetic wore off.* | *The effects of child abuse never wear off.* | *Once the initial shock has worn off you'll realize that things aren't as bad as you first thought.*

go away /ˌgəʊ əˈweɪ/ [phr v I] if an unpleasant feeling, situation etc **goes away**, it disappears, especially when you have been trying to get rid of it for a long time: *I wish I could make this headache go away.* | *His shyness soon went away when he started school.*

die away /ˌdaɪ əˈweɪ/ [phr v I] if a sound **dies away**, it gradually becomes less loud and less clear until you cannot hear it any longer: *The sound of his footsteps grew fainter and eventually died away.* | *As the rhythm of the music died away, screams could be heard in the distance.*

4 to stop existing

- ▸ disappear
- ▸ vanish
- ▸ become extinct
- ▸ extinction
- ▸ die out
- ▸ cease to exist

▸ *see also* **die, environment**

disappear /ˌdɪsəˈpɪəʳ/ [v I] if something **disappears**, it stops existing, and cannot be seen any more: *Thousands of square miles of rainforest are disappearing each year.* | *The dolphin has just about* *disappeared from the coasts of Britain.* | *Once you start drinking too heavily, the beneficial effects of alcohol disappear.* —**disappearance** [n U] **+ of** *The increase in tourism may result in the disappearance of the islanders' traditional way of life.*

vanish /ˈvænɪʃ/ [v I] to stop existing, especially because of a sudden or quick process: *All hopes of finding the boy alive have vanished.* | *The Shatin rice fields have long vanished beneath a new town of skyscrapers and motorways.* | **vanish without a trace** (=so that nothing remains) *Like so many dance crazes, the 'moonwalk' was popular for a while in the clubs, then vanished without a trace.*

become extinct /bɪˌkʌm ɪkˈstɪŋkt/ [v phrase] if a type of animal or plant **becomes extinct**, all the animals or plants of that type die, so that the type does not exist any more: *Dinosaurs became extinct millions of years ago.* | *If nothing is done to save the whales now, the species will soon become extinct.*

extinction /ɪkˈstɪŋkʃən/ [n U] when all the animals or plants of a particular type die, so that the type no longer exists: *The Scarlet Macaw is in imminent danger of extinction.* | **face/be threatened with extinction** (=likely to soon become extinct) *Out of 329 parrot species, 30 now face extinction.* | *Large numbers of rare and beautiful Alpine plants are threatened with extinction.* | **save sth from extinction** *attempts to save the elephant from extinction*

die out /ˌdaɪ ˈaʊt/ [phr v I] to gradually become rarer and then stop existing – use this about a type of animal or plant, a disease, or a custom: *Diseases such as leprosy and polio have almost completely died out.* | *The country is changing very quickly and many of the old traditions are dying out.* | *The nearest common ancestor of man and the modern great apes died out about 30 million years ago.*

cease to exist /ˌsiːs tʊ ɪɡˈzɪst/ [v phrase] to stop existing: *The town which Joyce wrote about has long since ceased to exist.* | *As of 1991, the Russian Communist Party effectively ceased to exist.*

disappointed

unhappy because things did not happen in the way that you hoped

RELATED WORDS

▸ *see also* **fed up, sad, satisfied/not satisfied**

1 disappointed

- ▸ disappointed
- ▸ feel let down
- ▸ disillusioned
- ▸ crestfallen
- ▸ disenchanted

disappointed /ˌdɪsəˈpɔɪntɪ̈d◂/ [adj] unhappy because things did not happen in the way you hoped they would, or were not as good as you expected them to be: *I felt a little disappointed when she didn't come to the party.* | *The hall was already full, and hundreds of disappointed fans were turned away at the door.* | **+ in** *I'm very disappointed in both of you – I guess I expected better behavior.* | **+ with/by** *Were you disappointed with the way you played today?* | **+ that** *The children were very disappointed that we couldn't go to the zoo.* | **disappointed to find/learn/hear/see** *We were disappointed to find that the museum was closed.* | **bitterly disappointed** (=very disappointed) *Backley was bitterly disappointed when an injury prevented him from competing in the Olympic Games.* —**disappointment** [n U] the feeling of being disappointed: *She couldn't hide her disappointment when David told her he wasn't coming.* | **bitter disappointment** *Davis expressed bitter disappointment with Carlson's resignation.*

feel let down /fiːl ˌlet ˈdaʊn/ [v phrase] to feel disappointed because someone did not do what they promised to do, or did not help you when you needed them: *No wonder the nurses feel let down – they were promised a big pay increase, but nothing has happened.* | *They were ashamed of their daughter's behaviour, and felt badly let down.*

disillusioned /ˌdɪsɪ̈ˈluːʒənd◂/ [adj] disappointed because you realize that a person, belief, way of life etc is not as good as you thought they were: *Disillusioned voters are turning against the government.* | **+ with/by** *As David grew older he became increasingly disillusioned with socialism.* | *Japanese college students in particular are disillusioned by the restrictions placed on them by society.* —**disillusionment** [n U] **+ with** *Public disillusionment with government promises is at an all time high.*

crestfallen /ˈkrestˌfɔːlən/ [adj] looking very disappointed and sad: *Steve looked crestfallen as he returned from the mailbox empty-handed.* | *She ripped open the package but found nothing in it but shoes. She was crestfallen.*

disenchanted /ˌdɪsɪ̈nˈtʃɑːntɪ̈d◂‖-ˈtʃænt-/ [adj] disappointed with something that you used to enjoy or believe in, or with someone you used to have great respect for: *The party's greatest problem is trying to win back the support of its own disenchanted members.* | **+ with** *After three divorces he must be pretty disenchanted with married life.* —**disenchantment** [n U] **+ with** *There seems to be a growing disenchantment with work in the high-tech world.*

2 making you feel disappointed

- ▸ disappointing
- ▸ be a disappointment
- ▸ not live up to (sb's) expectations
- ▸ be a letdown
- ▸ be an anticlimax/be anticlimactic
- ▸ be a non-event
- ▸ be a bummer
- ▸ sth is not all it's cracked up to be

disappointing /ˌdɪsəˈpɔɪntɪŋ◂/ [adj] something that is **disappointing** makes you feel unhappy or dissatisfied, because it is not as good as you hoped it would be: *The team had a disappointing season.* | *Company profits this year have been very disappointing.*

be a disappointment /biː ə ˌdɪsəˈpɔɪntmənt/ [v phrase] something that **is a disappointment** does not happen in the way you hoped, or is not as good as you expected: *The holiday was a bit of a disappointment – it rained the whole time.* | **+ to** *The election results were a disappointment to civil rights groups.* | **be a great/major disappointment** *It was a great disappointment to my parents that I didn't go to university.*

not live up to (sb's) expectations /nɒt lɪv ˌʌp tə (sb's) ekspekˈteɪʃənz/ if an event or person **does not live up to expectations**, you expected them to be very good but in fact they are not: *I'm afraid as a husband I never really lived up to Kelly's expectations.* | *Despite the enormous cost of making it, the film didn't live up to expectations.* | **fail to live up to (sb's) expectations** *I failed to live up to my parents' expectations, particularly at school.*

be a letdown /biː ə ˈletdaʊn/ [v phrase] spoken if something **is a letdown**, you do not enjoy it as much as you expected: *The party was a real letdown.* | *After months of planning and anticipation, the Florida trip was kind of a letdown.*

be an anticlimax/be anticlimactic /biː ən ˌæntɪˈklaɪmæks, biː ˌæntɪklaɪˈmæktɪk/ [v phrase] something that **is an anticlimax** or **is anticlimactic** does not seem very exciting or interesting because it comes after something that was much better: *Going back to work after a month travelling in China is bound to be an anticlimax.* | *Compared to the excitement of the earlier parts of the film, the ending was a little anticlimactic.*

be a non-event /biː ə ˌnɒn ɪˈvent‖-ˌnɑːn-/ [v phrase] an event or occasion that **is a non-event** is disappointing because nothing interesting or exciting happened: *Sue's party was a total non-event. Only five people turned up.*

be a bummer /biː ə ˈbʌməʳ/ [v phrase] spoken informal if you say that a situation or event **is a bummer**, you mean it is very disappointing: *'I heard Reggie's going to quit the team.' 'That's a bummer.'* | **bummer!** American *'The party was last Saturday.' 'Oh, bummer! I always miss those things.'*

sth is not all it's cracked up to be / (sth) ɪz nɒt ˌɔːl ɪts krækt ˈʌp tə biː/ informal use this to say that something is not as good as people say it is: *Northbourne Leisure Centre isn't all it's cracked up to be, they don't even have a sauna.* | *Being a fashion model isn't all it's cracked up to be. It is extremely hard work.*

3 to make someone feel disappointed

- disappoint
- let sb down
- dash (sb's) hopes

disappoint /ˌdɪsəˈpɔɪnt/ [v T] *The band disappointed thousands of fans by cancelling at the last minute.* | *I'm sorry to disappoint you, but there aren't any tickets left.*

let sb down /ˌlet (sb) ˈdaʊn/ [phr v T] to not do what you promised to do for someone, or not behave as well as they expected: *I said I would help them – I can't let them down.* | **let sb down badly** *Many disabled soldiers feel the government has let them down very badly.*

dash (sb's) hopes /ˌdæʃ (sb's) ˈhəʊps/ [v phrase] to disappoint someone very badly by doing or telling them something that is the opposite of what they hoped for or what they needed to happen: *Renewed fighting has dashed all hopes of an early settlement.* | *The family's hopes that their daughter would be found alive were cruelly dashed this morning.*

disapprove

RELATED WORDS

opposite: **approve**

▸ *see also* **criticize, bad, opinion, judge**

1 to think that someone or something is bad or morally wrong

- disapprove
- do not approve
- disapproval
- think sth is wrong
- frown on/upon
- take a dim view of
- have a low opinion of
- think badly of
- not hold with

disapprove /ˌdɪsəˈpruːv/ [v I] to think that someone or something is bad, morally wrong, or very stupid: *I could tell from my mother's face that she disapproved.* | **+ of** *A lot of church leaders disapproved of the book when it was first published.* | **disapprove of sb doing sth** *My friends disapprove of me smoking.* | **strongly disapprove** (=disapprove very much) *I strongly disapprove of any form of gambling.*

do not approve /duː nɒt əˈpruːv/ [v phrase] to think that someone or something is bad, morally wrong, or very stupid **+ of** *His mother clearly did not approve of Sophie.* | **do not approve of sb doing sth** *You know I don't approve of you smoking.*

disapproval /ˌdɪsəˈpruːvəl/ [n U] how you feel when you think someone's ideas, behaviour, or actions are bad or morally wrong **do sth with disapproval** *She looked at our clothes with obvious disapproval.* | **sb's disapproval/the disapproval of sb** *Peter was determined to go to art school, despite his parents' disapproval.*

think sth is wrong /ˌθɪŋk (sth) ɪz ˈrɒŋ‖-ˈrɔːŋ/ [v phrase] to think that something is morally wrong and should not happen: *A lot of people now think that killing animals for food is wrong.* | **think it is wrong to do sth** *I think it's wrong to hit a child, whatever the circumstances.*

frown on/upon /ˈfraʊn ɒn, əpɒn/ [phr v T] if a group of people **frown on** or **upon** a particular kind of behaviour, they think that it is not the right way to behave: *The people who went to church frowned on those who spent Sunday mornings in bed.* | *Romantic relationships between teachers and students are frowned upon by the college authorities.*

take a dim view of /teɪk ə ˌdɪm ˈvjuː ɒv/ [v phrase] to disapprove of someone's behaviour – use this especially about someone in authority or someone who could take action to stop the behaviour: *The school takes a very dim view of this behaviour.* | *The electorate took a dim view of the tax increase.*

have a low opinion of /hæv ə ˌləʊ əˈpɪnjən ɒv/ [v phrase not in progressive] to think that a particular person or group of people has a bad character, so that you do not respect them: *I'm afraid I have a rather low opinion of Mr Evans.* | *He had a very low opinion of insurance salesmen.*

think badly of /ˌθɪŋk ˈbædli ɒv/ [v phrase not in progressive] to disapprove of someone because of a particular thing they have done: *I didn't want my parents or teachers to think badly of me.* | *Please, Harry, you mustn't think badly of me. I had no choice.*

not hold with /nɒt ˈhəʊld wɪð/ [v phrase not in progressive] informal to strongly disapprove of a particular kind of behaviour, attitude, or idea: *I don't hold with racism. Never have, never will.* | *Many of the older generation simply don't hold with mixed marriages.*

2 to say that you disapprove of something or someone

- voice/express/show etc your disapproval
- condemn
- denounce
- deplore

voice/express/show etc your disapproval / ˌvɔɪs jɔːʳ dɪsəˈpruːvəl/ [v phrase] to say, write, or show publicly that you disapprove of someone or something: *The president expressed his disapproval of protest groups that break the law.* | *Thousands of people have voiced their disapproval of the government.* | *Nurses plan to show their dis-*

approval by organizing a series of one-day strikes. | *How can dissatisfied taxpayers register disapproval of government policies?*

condemn /kənˈdem/ [v T] to clearly and publicly say that you strongly disapprove of someone or something: *Politicians and religious leaders have universally condemned this act of terrorism.* | *Lawyers were quick to condemn the new legislation.* | **condemn sth as sth** *The destruction of rainforests has been condemned as a disaster for the environment.* | **condemn sb for doing sth** *Local authorities have been condemned for failing to tackle the problem of homelessness.* —**condemnation** /ˌkɒndəmˈneɪʃən, -dem-‖ˌkɑːn-/ [n U] **+ of** *His speech contained a strong condemnation of last week's bomb attack.* | **widespread condemnation** *The government's action has brought widespread condemnation from teachers.*

denounce /dɪˈnaʊns/ [v T] to say publicly that you strongly disapprove of something or someone and think that they are morally bad: *The Republicans denounced the waste of public money involved in the new program.* | *Community leaders were quick to denounce the police for reacting too violently to the disturbances.* | **denounce sb/sth as sth** *Darwin's theories about evolution were denounced by many people.*

deplore /dɪˈplɔːʳ/ [v T] **formal** to say that you strongly disapprove of a particular kind of behaviour or something that has happened, because it is morally wrong: *We deplore the use of violence against innocent people.* | *The United Nations has issued a statement deploring the continued fighting.*

3 to look at someone in a disapproving way

- give sb a dirty look
- glare at
- frown

give sb a dirty look /ˌgɪv (sb) ə ˌdɜːʳti ˈlʊk/ [v phrase] **informal** to look quickly and angrily at someone in a way that shows you disapprove strongly of what they have said or done: *Frank turned round and gave me a really dirty look.*

frown /fraʊn/ [v I] to look slightly unhappy or annoyed, because you disapprove of something: *Mr Bonner frowned and pursed his lips, but said nothing.* | **frown at** *Mrs Gold frowned at the children, who were getting mud all over their clothes.*

glare at /ˈgleər æt/ [v phrase] to look at someone in a way that shows that you are very angry with them: *Roger glared angrily at her across the dinner table.*

4 showing disapproval

- disapproving
- pejorative
- derogatory

disapproving /ˌdɪsəˈpruːvɪŋ◂/ [adj] if someone speaks to you or looks at you in a **disapproving** way, they show by the way they talk or look that they disapprove of you: *The announcement of a further pay increase for politicians provoked disapproving comments from the leader of the opposition party.* | **disapproving glance/look/stare** *John gave me a disapproving look when I suggested another drink.*

derogatory /dɪˈrɒgətəri‖dɪˈrɑːgətɔːri/ [adj] a **derogatory** remark expresses disapproval of something or someone and is often also insulting: *I wish you wouldn't make derogatory remarks about members of my family.* | *I didn't like the way he made derogatory comments about his colleagues.*

pejorative /pɪˈdʒɒrətɪv‖-ˈdʒɔː-, -ˈdʒɑː-/ [adj] **formal** a **pejorative** word expresses disapproval, often in an offensive way: *He used the word 'girl' in the pejorative sense when referring to the women who worked for him.* —**pejoratively** [adv] *The word 'liberal' seems to be used pejoratively by both the left and the right.*

disaster

a terrible event or accident that causes death and destruction

RELATED WORDS

▸ *see also* **accident, environment**

1 a disaster

- disaster
- tragedy
- catastrophe
- calamity

disaster /dɪˈzɑːstəʳ‖dɪˈzæ-/ [n C/U] an extremely bad accident or natural event in which a lot of people are killed: *The disaster killed more than 200 people.* | *The crash on Monday is the latest in a long line of air disasters in West Africa.* | *The local people are used to coping with disaster.* | **natural disaster** (=caused by wind, rain, or other natural forces) *Natural disasters such as floods and earthquakes are common occurrences in California.* | *The governor said the earthquake was the worst natural disaster to hit India for over 50 years.* | **disaster area** *The Los Alamos area was officially declared a disaster area after the forest fires there in May.*

catastrophe /kəˈtæstrəfi/ [n C/U] a terrible event that causes a lot of deaths, damage, and destruction over a wide area: *The blizzard was a catastrophe that affected 17 states, ranging from New Hampshire to Tennessee.* | **environmental/ecological/nuclear etc catastrophe** *Scientists say the oil spill is an ecological catastrophe.* | *Most people now accept that global warming could result in an environmental catastrophe.*

tragedy /ˈtrædʒɪ̈di/ [n C/U] a terrible and very sad event or situation, usually resulting in suffering or death: *Investigators still do not know what caused the tragedy, which killed all 278 people on board.* | *the worst tragedy in the history of space flight* | *Unless the world deals with the AIDS threat now, the African continent could suffer 'a tragedy of historic proportions'.*

calamity /kəˈlæmɪ̈ti/ [n C/U] a terrible and unexpected event that causes great damage and loss: *Hurricane George was just the latest calamity to hit the state.* | *The flood was a calamity from which Bangladesh has never fully recovered.* | *Singh told reporters that he had not seen such human suffering in any previous natural calamity.*

2 causing a lot of destruction or suffering

- disastrous
- tragic
- catastrophic

disastrous /dɪˈzɑːstrəs‖dɪˈzæs-/ [adj] *A disastrous fire destroyed much of the city in the early 1900s.* | *Much of the damage wrought by the disastrous three-day storm was still apparent.* | **disastrous consequences** *There was a fault in the engine design, which had disastrous consequences.* —**disastrously**

[adv] **go disastrously wrong** *Things went disastrously wrong when the craft's navigational system failed.*

catastrophic /ˌkætəˈstrɒfɪk◂‖-ˈstrɑː-/ [adj] causing terrible destruction and suffering and many deaths, over a wide area: *The flooding was catastrophic, killing hundreds of people and leaving thousands homeless.* | *The destruction of the world's rain forests could have a catastrophic influence on the earth's climate.*

tragic /ˈtrædʒɪk/ [adj] causing great suffering and sadness: *The President referred to Friday's air disaster as a 'tragic loss of life'.* —**tragically** [adv] *Fourteen schoolchildren were tragically killed in the accident.*

discuss

RELATED WORDS

▸ *see also* **talk, argue, tell, opinion**

1 to talk about something with someone

- discuss
- talk
- talk over
- debate
- kick around
- put your heads together
- have it out

discuss /dɪˈskʌs/ [v T] to talk about and exchange ideas about something in order to come to an agreement, understand it better, or to make plans: *The two families got together to discuss the wedding arrangements.* | *The report will be discussed at next week's meeting.* | **discuss sth with sb** *Don't make any plans yet – I want to discuss this with Jamie first.* | **discuss what/how/where etc** *We need to discuss what kind of food we want at the party.*

talk /tɔːk/ [v I] *I think we need to talk.* | **+ about** *If you have a problem at school, sit down and talk about it with your parents.* | **+ to** *Gerry wants to talk to his girlfriend before he makes a decision.* | **+ with** American *If you need more money you should talk with Richard.*

talk over /ˌtɔːk ˈəʊvəʳ/ [phr v T] to talk to someone about all the details of a serious problem or difficult situation, in order to understand it better **talk sth/it over** *If you're worried about your work, come and see me and we'll talk it over.* | **talk over sth** *The girls were talking over the events of the day.* | **talk sth over with sb** *It's often useful to talk things over with a trained counsellor.*

debate /dɪˈbeɪt/ [v T] to discuss different possible choices of what to do before choosing the best one: *We were debating the best way to reach the river, when a passing ranger kindly pointed it out.* | **+ where/what/whether etc** *We debated whether to fly or go by train, finally deciding on the train.* | *They had already debated where to go on vacation, Yosemite or Lake Tahoe.*

kick around /ˌkɪk əˈraʊnd/ [phr v T] informal to discuss an idea with a group of people in order to decide whether it is good or not: *These meetings are useful for kicking around preliminary ideas.* | *Academics have been kicking around the idea for three decades.*

put your heads together /ˌpʊt jɔːʳ ˈhedz təˌgeðəʳ/ [v phrase] informal if two or more people **put their heads together**, they discuss something together in order to solve a problem: *We'll put our heads together after work and see if we can come up with a solution.* | **+ to do sth** *150 government leaders are putting their heads together to discuss how to curb the production of greenhouse gases.*

have it out /ˌhæv ɪt ˈaʊt/ [v phrase] to settle a disagreement or difficult situation by talking to the person involved, especially when you are angry with them: *We've had it out and I've told John exactly what I think.* | **+ with** *I've a good mind to have it out with him here and now.*

2 to try to reach an agreement in politics or business

- negotiate
- bargaining
- thrash out
- hammer out
- debate

negotiate /nɪˈgəʊʃieɪt/ [v I/T] to discuss a political problem or business arrangement in order to try to reach an agreement – use this especially about political or business leaders: *If we corner him, he won't negotiate.* | **+ with** *The government says it will not negotiate with terrorists.* | **negotiate an agreement/deal/price etc** *Colombia and Venezuela are currently negotiating a trade agreement.*

bargaining /ˈbɑːʳgənɪŋ/ [n U] a discussion in politics or business during which each group tries to gain for themselves as many advantages as possible but has to give something or do something in return: *After much bargaining, we agreed to share the profits 50-50.* | *Effective bargaining by their union has gained clothing workers a 9% pay rise.*

thrash out /ˌθræʃ ˈaʊt/ [phr v T] to discuss the details of a problem or plan thoroughly and argue about them until an agreement is reached **thrash out sth** *Her lawyers have been ruthless in thrashing out a divorce settlement.* | *Differences over EU policy were left to be thrashed out at a later date.* | **thrash it out** *If that's going to cause you a problem, we'll have to thrash it out before we get started.*

hammer out /ˌhæmər ˈaʊt/ [phr v T] if two people or groups **hammer out** an agreement, plan etc, they reach agreement about it after discussing it and arguing about it a lot: *Canada and the US have hammered out a final form for their trade agreement.* | *Before an advertising strategy can be hammered out, the agency must understand the client's true needs.*

debate /dɪˈbeɪt/ [v I/T] to discuss a political or social problem publicly or officially, especially in a parliament or committee: *The new law was debated in Parliament on 14 February.* | *The government clearly refuses to give us an opportunity to debate any longer.* | **be hotly debated** (=to be discussed by a lot of people who have strong feelings) *Few areas of nutrition are more hotly debated than whether or not people should take vitamin supplements.* —**debate** [n U] *This matter has been the subject of intense public debate in recent weeks.*

3 when something is discussed

- be discussed
- be under discussion
- be on the agenda

be discussed /biː dɪˈskʌst/ [v phrase] *The issues have been widely discussed, but so far no one has drawn any conclusions.* | *Healthy eating is much discussed these days, and several books have been published on the subject.* | **be widely discussed** *Questions about how to raise children have been widely discussed.*

be under discussion /biː ˌʌndəʳ dɪˈskʌʃən/ [v phrase] if something such as a situation, plan, or proposal **is under discussion**, people are discussing it with the intention of deciding what to do about it: *A proposal to reduce the size of the army has been under discussion for some time now.* | *A title for the new book is still under discussion.*

be on the agenda /biː ɒn ði əˈdʒendə/ [v phrase] if something affecting the public or society **is on the agenda**, most people have heard of it and are talking about it: *The recent riots have put the problem of unemployment back on the agenda.* | **be high on the agenda** *The prevention of ordinary crime has been high on the agenda for ten years.*

4 when something can be discussed before a decision is made

- negotiable
- be open to discussion/negotiation

negotiable /nɪˈgəʊʃiəbəl, -ʃə-/ [adj] an offer, price, agreement etc that is **negotiable** can be discussed and changed before being agreed on: *We are looking for an experienced journalist to join the news team. The salary is negotiable.* | *The offer is negotiable, so feel free to suggest changes.* | *The contract is for a period of six months, and is not negotiable.*

be open to discussion/negotiation /biː ˌəʊpən tə dɪˈskʌʃən, nɪˌgəʊʃiˈeɪʃən/ [v phrase] if something **is open to discussion** or **negotiation**, it has not yet been officially decided and you are allowed to discuss it and suggest changes: *Which company gets the franchise is open to negotiation.* | *My father's orders were not open to discussion.*

5 a meeting where people discuss something

- discussion
- negotiations
- talks
- debate
- forum

discussion /dɪˈskʌʃən/ [n C/U] when people talk about and exchange ideas about something, especially in order to make a decision: *The committee, after much discussion, had decided to go ahead with the proposal to ban cigarette advertising.* | **+ about** *Most people find honest discussions about sex a little awkward.* | **+ with** *After a long discussion with her father, she decided not to take the job.*

negotiations /nɪˌgəʊʃiˈeɪʃənz/ [n plural] when people who represent governments, companies, workers' groups etc meet to discuss a problem or business arrangement and try to reach an agreement: *The trade negotiations between the US and Japan are going very well.* | **+ with** *Negotiations with the Turkish government are due to begin tomorrow.*

talks /tɔːks/ [n plural] a series of discussions between political or business leaders, which may continue for several days or weeks and are intended to solve a difficult problem: *the Strategic Arms Limitation Talks, known as 'SALT'* | **hold talks** *The peace talks are being held in Geneva.* | **+ with** *The company's managers have begun talks with union leaders.* | **be in talks** *Russia's main diamond producer has also been in talks with the mining company.* | **peace/trade talks** *a tough negotiator in international trade talks*

debate /dɪˈbeɪt/ [n C] a formal public discussion, for example in parliament or on television, in which two or more groups of people make speeches giving different opinions about a subject, and people vote on it afterwards: *The law was passed, after a long and sometimes angry debate.* | **+ on/about** *There will be a televised debate between those in favour of military action and those who are against.*

forum /ˈfɔːrəm/ [n C] an organization, meeting, or television programme where people have a chance to discuss an important subject in public **+ for** *The association began as a forum for sharing ideas about management problems.* | **+ to do sth** *I want a forum to address the most serious problem facing the people of this state.*

dishonest

RELATED WORDS

opposite: —— **honest**

- to take part in something dishonest *see* **take part/be involved (7)**
- *see also* **cheat, illegal, lie, steal, crime**

1 dishonest

- dishonest
- corrupt
- crooked
- crook
- bent
- unscrupulous

dishonest /dɪsˈɒnɪ̈st‖-ˈɑː-/ [adj] someone who is **dishonest** tells lies or tries to trick people or steal things: *A few dishonest dealers give the used car trade a bad name.* | *a dishonest politician* | *People on welfare are often wrongly characterized as lazy or dishonest.* | **it is dishonest of sb to do sth** *It was dishonest of him to suggest that he actually had a degree from Oxford – he was just there for one term.*

corrupt /kəˈrʌpt/ [adj] a **corrupt** politician, official, or police officer uses their power in a dishonest way for their own advantage, for example by accepting money from people in return for helping them: *In the 1970s, the city's police force was among the most corrupt in the nation.* | *Corrupt customs officials have helped the drug trade to flourish.* | *Perez said that there were virtually no procedures in place to weed out corrupt officials.*

crooked /ˈkrʊkɪ̈d/ [adj] someone who is **crooked** is involved in illegal or dishonest business activities: *A crooked civil servant sold hundreds of British passports on the black market, a court heard yesterday.* | **crooked (business) deal** *The land was obtained in a crooked business deal between politicians and an Arizona savings and loans association.*

crook /krʊk/ [n C] someone who is involved in dishonest and usually criminal activities, especially someone who gets money by cheating people: *Collins called the governor a crook and said he should be removed from office.*

bent /bent/ [adj] British spoken use this about someone in an official position, who uses their power illegally or dishonestly: *Half the inspectors here are bent.* | *A few bent coppers can give the whole police force a bad name.*

unscrupulous /ʌnˈskruːpjɪ̈ləs/ [adj] someone who is **unscrupulous** uses dishonest and unfair methods to get what they want, and does not care if they harm other people: *Isn't it time we did something to protect the elderly from unscrupulous business people?* | *Morgan admitted that some of his actions may have been unscrupulous, but he denied doing anything illegal.*

2 secretly dishonest

- devious
- sneaky
- sly
- underhand

devious /ˈdiːviəs/ [adj] someone who is **devious** tries to get what they want by secretly using clever plans to trick people, so you can never be sure what their real intentions are: *You have to be pretty devious to be successful in that sort of business.* | *In the film, he plays a devious defence lawyer named Richard Adler.*

sneaky /ˈsniːki/ [adj] someone who is **sneaky** does things secretly and tricks people in order to get what they want: *You never know what's going on in that sneaky mind of his.* | *Watch out for Andy. He can be really sneaky.*

sly /slaɪ/ [adj] someone who is **sly** deliberately and cleverly hides their real intentions and feelings in order to get what they want, without other people realizing what they are doing: *Children of that age can be very sly.* | **sly smile/look/expression etc** *A sly look crossed his face when Patsy mentioned the money.* —**slyly** [adv] *They had slyly arranged to have the party while we were away.*

underhand British /**underhanded** American /ˌʌndəʳˈhænd◂, ˌʌndəʳˈhændəd◂/ [adj] **underhand** methods or ways of doing things involve secretly deceiving people in an unfair way in order to get what you want without them knowing your intentions: *In a series of very smart, underhand moves, Browne gradually gained control of the company.* | *A federal judge criticized U.S. immigration officials for 'underhanded tactics' to deny asylum to Haitians.* | *She accused the council of behaving in an 'underhand' manner and said residents should have been consulted.*

3 when someone or something seems dishonest

- suspicious
- shady
- shifty
- dodgy
- dubious/questionable
- be up to no good

suspicious /səˈspɪʃəs/ [adj] use this about behaviour or a situation that makes you think that someone is doing something dishonest: *It all seems very suspicious to me. Where did he get all that money from?* | *The circumstances surrounding McBain's death are suspicious.* | *He glanced around, satisfied that nobody was taking any notice of his suspicious behaviour, then opened the door.* | **suspicious-looking** *There was a suspicious-looking man standing in a doorway across the street.* —**suspiciously** [adv] **behave/act suspiciously** *The victim was attacked after spotting the men acting suspiciously outside his house in Bracknell, Berkshire.*

shady /ˈʃeɪdi/ [adj] use this to describe business deals or the people involved in them, when they seem dishonest or illegal, especially because the business is secret: *His acceptance of an interest-free £125,000 loan from a shady businessman looks suspicious to say the least.* | **shady deal** *He has been mixed up in a number of shady deals in the Cayman Islands.*

shifty /ˈʃɪfti/ [adj] someone who is **shifty** looks or behaves as if they are doing or planning something dishonest: *There's something shifty about that guy.* | *a shifty, fast-talking lawyer*

dodgy /ˈdɒdʒi‖ˈdɑː-/ [adj] British informal probably dishonest, although you are not sure of the facts – use this especially to say that you do not want to be involved with someone or something: *Don't buy a car from him, he's a real dodgy character.* | *The whole thing looks distinctly dodgy to me.*

dubious/questionable /ˈdjuːbiəs‖ˈduː-, ˈkwestʃənəbəl/ [adj] use this about someone's behaviour or a business arrangement that does not seem completely right or correct, so that you think it is probably dishonest: *He had been involved in some questionable business activities at one time.* | *Marantz resigned after discovering that dubious business deals were being negotiated by his fellow officials.* | **highly dubious/questionable** *The whole deal seems highly dubious to me.*

be up to no good /biː ˌʌp tə nəʊ ˈgʊd/ [v phrase] informal use this about someone you think is doing or planning something dishonest, even though you do not know exactly what it is: *If you ask me, that husband of hers is up to no good.* | *Anyone waiting around on street corners at night must be up to no good.*

4 dishonest behaviour

- dishonesty
- corruption
- bribery
- graft
- sharp practice
- dirty tricks

dishonesty /dɪsˈɒnəsti‖-ˈɑː-/ [n U] dishonest behaviour: *Are you accusing me of dishonesty?* | *The report accuses both politicians of dishonesty and of misrepresenting the facts.*

corruption /kəˈrʌpʃən/ [n U] when someone who works for the government, the police etc uses their power dishonestly to get money or gain an advantage: *The chief of police was forced to resign after allegations of corruption.* | *The administration has frequently been accused of corruption and abuse of power.* | **widespread corruption** *Corruption has become so widespread there that you almost can't imagine the system working without it.*

bribery /ˈbraɪbəri/ [n U] when someone offers money to a politician or government official in order to persuade them to do something: *Officials said the bribery investigation would continue.* | *US firms are alleged to have used bribery to win contracts.* | *Several politicians are linked to the bribery and sex scandal.* | **bribery and corruption** *One of Murrow's chief campaign promises was to do something about bribery and corruption.*

graft /grɑːft‖græft/ [n U] American dishonest behaviour by politicians who accept money from companies in return for helping them: *Stevens was in court yesterday facing charges of graft and tax evasion.* | *A major investigation is underway to root out graft there, he said.*

sharp practice /ˌʃɑːʳp ˈpræktəs/ [n U] British business activities or ways of making money that are clever and dishonest, though not actually illegal: *We couldn't discover anything specific, but there was definitely some sharp practice going on.* | *His grandfather had made a fortune out of a piece of commercial sharp practice in the 19th century.*

dirty tricks /ˌdɜːʳti ˈtrɪks/ [n plural] dishonest activities that are designed to gain political advantage, for example by spreading false information about your opponents: *Burrows denied that members of his election staff had been involved in dirty tricks.* | *The book focuses on the dirty tricks, break-ins, and illegal campaign contributions of the 1972 presidential election.* | **dirty tricks campaign** *They had car-*

ried out a dirty tricks campaign to discredit opposition leaders.

dislike

RELATED WORDS

opposite: **like, enjoy**

- to dislike someone or something very much *see* **hate**
- *see also* **unfriendly, disapprove**

1 to not like something or someone

- not like
- dislike
- don't think much of sth/sb
- not be very keen on sth/not be very fond of sth
- not be sb's type
- not be sb's kind of thing
- not be to your taste/liking
- have no time for
- not take kindly to

not like /nɒt 'laɪk/ [v phrase] *John doesn't like garlic.* | *Why did you invite Claire? You know I don't like her.* | **not like doing sth** *My girlfriend doesn't like camping.* | *I don't like walking home alone at night.* | **not like sth/sb very much** *Mum didn't like Mark very much when she first met him.*

dislike /ˌdɪs'laɪk/ [v T] written to think someone or something is very unpleasant: *Eldridge was a quiet man who disliked social occasions.* | *She now seriously disliked her former friend.* | **dislike doing sth** *I dislike having to get up so early in the morning.* | **dislike sb/sth intensely** (=dislike them very much) *Muriel disliked Paul intensely.*

don't think much of sth/sb /ˌdaʊnt θɪŋk 'mʌtʃ əv (sth/sb)/ spoken to think that something is not very good or that someone is not very good at something: *You don't think much of Carol, do you?* | *The hotel was okay, though I didn't think much of the food.* | *I don't think much of The Beatles, to be quite honest.*

not be very keen on sth/not be very fond of sth /nɒt bi: veri 'ki:n ɒn (sth), nɒt bi: veri 'fɒnd əv (sth) ‖-'fɑ:nd-/ British informal to not like something, although you do not think it is very bad or very unpleasant: *Actually, I'm not very keen on modern art.* | *George had never been particularly fond of small children.*

not be sb's type /nɒt bi: (sb's) 'taɪp/ [v phrase] if someone is **not your type**, they are not the kind of person you usually like or enjoy being with: *Rob isn't her type at all.* | *'What do you think of Michael?' 'He looks a bit rough – he's not really my type.'*

not be sb's kind of thing ALSO **not be sb's cup of tea** British informal /nɒt bi: (sb's) ˌkaɪnd əv 'θɪŋ, nɒt bi: (sb's) ˌkʌp əv 'ti:/ [v phrase] to not be the kind of thing that you enjoy – use this about activities, films, books etc: *Tennis is not my thing.* | *Horror films aren't really my cup of tea.*

not be to your taste/liking /nɒt bi: tə jɔ:ʳ 'teɪst, 'laɪkɪŋ/ [v phrase] use this to say that something is not the type of thing that you like or that you think is good: *It seems that the music wasn't exactly to his taste.* | *The food wasn't really to my liking – it all tasted rather salty.*

have no time for /ˌhæv nəʊ 'taɪm fɔ:ʳ/ [v phrase not in progressive] to dislike a person, their attitude, or their behaviour and have no respect for them: *I've no time for that kind of attitude.* | *My father had no time for complainers.* | *He has no time for players who aren't completely dedicated.*

not take kindly to /nɒt teɪk 'kaɪndli tu:/ [v phrase not in progressive] to be unwilling to accept a particular situation, suggestion, or type of behaviour, because you think it is annoying: *Nancy doesn't take kindly to being corrected.* | *He didn't take very kindly to being disturbed in the middle of the night.*

2 to not like someone because of something they have done

- have something against
- have it in for
- bear a grudge
- there is no love lost between sb

have something against /hæv ˌsʌmθɪŋ ə'genst/ [v phrase not in progressive] to dislike someone for a particular reason, although the reason is not clear: *Sam has something against me.* | *Your brother's got something against me. God knows what.* | *She probably has something against men.*

have it in for /ˌhæv ɪt 'ɪn fɔ:ʳ/ [v phrase not in progressive] informal if someone **has it in for** you, they dislike you and are always looking for ways to hurt you, especially because of something you have done in the past: *I don't know why anybody would have it in for Eddy. He's a really nice guy.* | *Sometimes I think my supervisor has it in for me.*

bear a grudge /ˌbeər ə 'grʌdʒ/ [v phrase not in progressive] to continue to dislike someone and feel angry with them, because you believe they harmed you in the past and you have not forgiven them: *She bore a grudge for a long time.* | *It isn't in that woman's nature to bear grudges.* | **+ against** *He bore a grudge against my father for years.*

there is no love lost between sb /ðeər ɪz ˌnəʊ 'lʌv ˌlɒst bɪtwi:n (sb) ‖-ˌlɔ:st-/ if **there is no love lost** between two people, they dislike each other and do not have a friendly relationship: *Sounds like there's not a lot of love lost between the two of you.* | *It is clear from these letters that there was no love lost between the Princess and her stepmother.*

3 to stop liking something or someone

- go off

go off /ˌgəʊ 'ɒf/ [phr v T] British spoken use this to say that you have stopped liking someone or something that you used to like: *I used to drink tea all the time, but I've gone off it lately.* | *Many women go off coffee and alcohol during pregnancy.* | *I used to think he was really funny, but now I've gone off him.*

4 to make someone stop liking a person, thing, or activity

- put sb off
- turn sb against

put sb off /ˌpʊt (sb) 'ɒf/ [phr v T] informal to stop someone from liking or being interested in someone or something: *Don't let her put you off, it's a really good movie.* | *When you know an artist used to abuse his wife and children it does tend to put you off his work.* | *That weekend put me off camping for the rest of my life!* | *When she told me she worked in an abattoir it rather put me off her.*

turn sb against /ˌtɜ:ʳn (sb) ə'genst/ [phr v T] to deliberately change someone's feelings, so that they stop liking someone that they used to like: *My ex-wife is trying to turn the children against me.* | *Brenda even tried to turn my sister against me.*

5 a feeling of not liking someone or something

- dislike
- distaste
- aversion

dislike /ˌdɪsˈlaɪk/ [n U] a feeling of not liking someone or something **+ for/of** *She could not hide her personal dislike of the man.* | *Churchill was said to have a dislike for unnecessary formality.* | **intense dislike** (=very strong dislike) *My intense dislike for him seemed to grow day by day.*

distaste /dɪsˈteɪst/ [n U] a feeling of dislike that you have for someone or something because you think they are very unpleasant or offensive: *Oliver looked with distaste at my clothes.* | *Gina moved away from me with a look of distaste on her face.*

aversion /əˈvɜːʳʃən‖-ʒən/ [n C/U] a strong, sometimes unreasonable, dislike of something **have an aversion to sth** *Most people have a natural aversion to anything associated with death or dying.*

disobey

RELATED WORDS

opposite: **obey**

- *see also* **law, rule, regulation, illegal**

1 to not obey a person

- disobey
- not do as you're told
- defy
- go against sb's wishes
- rebel

disobey /ˌdɪsəˈbeɪ, ˌdɪsəʊ-/ [v I/T] to not do what you are told to do by someone in authority: *It was unfair of the teacher to make us stay after school, but no one dared disobey.* | *My father was very strict and old-fashioned, but I never disobeyed him.* | *Black had disobeyed the judge's ruling, and continued to harass his ex-wife.* —**disobedience** /ˌdɪsəˈbiːdiəns, ˌdɪsəʊ-/ [n U] *Her parents never allowed disobedience to go unpunished.*

not do as you're told /nɒt ˌduː əz jɔːʳ ˈtəʊld/ [v phrase] if someone, especially a child, does **not do as they are told**, they refuse to obey a parent, teacher, etc: *'Daddy, why?' 'Don't ask, just do as you're told.'* | *If she doesn't do as she's told, send her to her room.*

defy /dɪˈfaɪ/ [v T] to deliberately disobey someone in authority, even though you know this will make them angry: *Billy defied his mother, and smoked openly in the house.* | *She said she would defy the party leader and vote against him.* —**defiance** [n U] *There wasn't much he could do about his daughter's defiance.*

go against sb's wishes /ˌgəʊ əgenst (sb's) ˈwɪʃɪ̈z/ [v phrase] to not do what someone has asked you to do, or what you know they want you to do: *They went against their parents' wishes and got married secretly.* | *Sacha went against her family's wishes by leaving school at 16.*

rebel /rɪˈbel/ [v I] to deliberately behave in a way that is completely different from the way that your parents and people in general expect you to behave: *Her parents wanted her to go to university, but she rebelled and went to live on a commune.* | **+ against** *Teenagers tend to rebel against people in authority.*

2 to not obey a rule or law

- disobey
- break a rule/law
- violate
- disregard
- contravene
- flout

disobey /ˌdɪsəˈbeɪ, ˌdɪsəʊ-/ [v T] to not obey a law or rule: *Protesters disobeyed the law and blocked the city's main roads.* | *Troops openly disobeyed orders, refusing to use force against their own people.*

break a rule/law /ˌbreɪk ə ˈruːl, ˈlɔː/ [v phrase] to not do what a rule or law says you must do: *Students who break the rules and smoke in school will be suspended.* | *I do not want my sons' TV role models to be tough, cool guys, who break laws and kill people.* | **break the law** *If you fail to buy a ticket before you get on the train, you are breaking the law.*

violate /ˈvaɪəleɪt/ [v T] formal to disobey or do something that is against a rule, agreement, principle etc: *This action violated the constitution and the Civil Rights Act.* | *Police have arrested twenty people, accused of violating a ban on demonstrations.* —**violation** /ˌvaɪəˈleɪʃən/ [n C/U] *The movement of troops was in violation of the peace treaty.* | *Excessive workloads can lead to the violation of health and safety rules.*

disregard ALSO **ignore** /ˌdɪsrɪˈgɑːʳd, ɪgˈnɔːʳ/ [v T] to pay no attention to a law, rule, or to what someone has told you to do, and behave as if it does not affect you. **Disregard** is more formal than **ignore**: *Many cyclists ignore the law and ride around at night without lights.* | *I tell her to come home by 10 o'clock, but she just ignores me.* | *Marlow sometimes disregards the law, but his aim is always justice.* | *By disregarding speed limits and passing red lights, we somehow got to the airport in time.* —**disregard** [n U] *You have shown a total disregard for the law and for public safety.*

contravene /ˌkɒntrəˈviːn‖ˌkɑːn-/ [v T] formal to break a particular written law, rule, or agreement: *The sale of untreated milk may contravene public health regulations.* | *If a licence holder contravenes any of these conditions, their licence will be withdrawn.* —**contravention** /ˌkɒntrəˈvenʃən‖ˌkɑːn-/ [n C/U] **a contravention of** *Driving faster than the speed limit is a contravention of the Road Traffic Act.* | *The Security Council ruled that the country had acted in contravention of international law.*

flout /flaʊt/ [v T] **flout a rule/law etc** to deliberately break a law or a rule, especially because you think it is unnecessary or stupid: *Many bar owners flout the laws on under-age drinking.* | *Thousands of people are killed on our roads every year, yet a majority of us insist on flouting speed limits.*

3 someone who refuses to obey people, rules, laws etc

- disobedient
- defiant
- rebellious
- rebel

disobedient /ˌdɪsəˈbiːdiənt◂, ˌdɪsəʊ-/ [adj] someone, especially a child, who is **disobedient** does not do what he or she is told to do by a parent, teacher etc: *Lee stood before her like a disobedient schoolboy.* | *She said that if we were disobedient she would send us home immediately.* —**disobedience** [n U] *Any act of disobedience was severely punished.*

defiant /dɪˈfaɪənt/ [adj] not obeying people in authority and showing that you have no respect for them: *Her reply was clear and defiant.* | *Defiant party members openly challenged the leadership.* |

defiant of sb/sth *Demonstrators became increasingly defiant of police controls.* —**defiantly** [adv] *The prisoners defiantly sang a revolutionary song as they were led away.* —**defiance** [n U] *She looked up at him with open defiance. | In defiance of the law, the building was knocked down.*

rebellious /rɪˈbeljəs/ [adj] someone, especially a young person, who is **rebellious** deliberately disobeys people in authority such as their parents or teachers: *Such extremist groups may well attract rebellious teenagers. | Maria was headstrong and rebellious.*

rebel /ˈrebəl/ [n C] someone, especially a young person, who behaves in a completely different way from the way people are expected to behave by society and by people in authority: *In his black leather jacket and chains he looked every inch the young rebel. | She was a rebel, who horrified her family by rejecting a promising career in law to become an actor.*

distance

RELATED WORDS

- a long distance *see* **far**
- a short distance *see* **near**

1 the distance between one place or point and another

- distance
- how far
- from
- away
- off
- apart
- a long/short way

distance /ˈdɪstəns/ [n C/U] how far it is from one place to another **distance from sth to sth** *What is the distance from New York to Miami?* | **the distance between sth and sth** *Measure the distance between the window and the door. | the distance between the earth and the sun*

how far /ˌhaʊ ˈfɑːʳ/ [adv] use this to ask what the distance is between where you are and another place: *'How far is Newark?' 'It's about 200 miles.'* | **how far is it to ... ?** *How far is it to the nearest gas station?*

from /frəm, (*strong*) frɒm‖frəm, (*strong*) frʌm, frɑːm/ [prep] if one place is 10 kilometres/30 miles/20 minutes etc **from** another place, that is the distance between the two places, or the time it takes to get **from** one to the other: *Seattle is about 100 miles from the Canadian border. | The junior high school is five minutes from our house. | She was standing just a couple of metres from the edge of the cliff.*

away /əˈweɪ/ [adv] if a place or person is 10 kilometres/30 miles/20 minutes etc **away**, they are that distance from where you are, or it takes that amount of time to travel there: *The nearest village was about 20 miles away. | Toronto's only about an hour and a half away by car.* | **+ from** *The station is about two miles away from the city centre. | He was standing three metres away from the bomb when it exploded.*

off /ɒf‖ɔːf/ [adv] if something is 10 kilometres/30 metres etc **off**, that is how far it is from you or from the place you are talking about: *The nearest town is fifteen kilometres off. | The robbers must be a long way off by now. | We were still several miles off, but you could already see a glow in the sky from the lights of the city.*

apart /əˈpɑːʳt/ [adv] if two places, objects, or peopl are three miles, two centimetres etc **apart**, that i the distance between them: *The seeds should b planted a few inches apart. | The two towns are fi teen miles apart. | We were standing a few feet apar from each other.* | **well apart** (=wide apart) *Stand o the skis with your feet well apart.* | **far apart** (=a lon way apart) *The National Weather Service is forecas ing snow in cities as far apart as Atlanta, Bostor and Cleveland.*

a long/short way /ə ˌlɒŋ, ˌʃɔːʳt ˈweɪ‖-ˌlɔːŋ-/ us this to say how far one place is from another or fron where you are **+ from** *California is a long way fron Georgia. | Only a short way from the buildings is th impressive entrance to Bruntscar Cave.* | **+ awa** *Oxford is just a short way away. You can make th drive in under an hour.*

2 to continue for a particular distance

- extend/stretch
- range

extend/stretch /ɪkˈstend, stretʃ/ [v I] to continu over a particular distance, especially a long dis tance **+ around/over/through etc** *The deser stretches over five different countries. | From the cor ner of the terrace the path extended down to the sea.* **stretch from sth to sth** *The valley stretches from Vas sai in the north to Momere in the southwest.* | **+ fo** *The estuary stretches for over 100 miles.*

range /reɪndʒ/ [n C/U] the distance that somethin can travel over or reach **+ of** *The rockets have range of 4000 km. | A typical radio signal has range of about 100 miles.* | **within range** (=at a dis tance that is less than the range) *As soon as th tanks came within range, the soldiers opened fire.* **out of range** (=at a distance greater than the range *The enemy were just out of range of our cannon. The demonstrators were hurling rocks but the polic stayed out of range.*

disturb

RELATED WORDS

- to say something when someone else is talking *see* **interrupt**

1 to disturb someone so that they cannot continue what they are doing

- disturb
- interrupt
- bother
- distract
- put sb off
- break sb's train of thought

disturb /dɪˈstɜːʳb/ [v T] to stop someone when the are working, talking, or having a meeting, espe cially because you want to ask a question or te them something: *Sorry to disturb you, but could ask a quick question? | Try not to disturb your dad he's working. | Before closing the door to his office, h told his secretary that he was not to be disturbed.*

interrupt /ˌɪntəˈrʌpt/ [v I/T] to stop someone whe they are working, talking, or having a meeting especially because you want to ask them a questio or tell them something: *Don't interrupt – I haven finished yet. | I'm sorry to interrupt your meeting but may I speak with Michael for a moment? | Whil*

I was giving my report, some guy in the back kept interrupting me every two minutes. —**interruption** /ˌɪntəˈrʌpʃən/ [n C] when someone interrupts you: *It's hard to study with so many interruptions.*

bother /ˈbɒðəʳ‖ˈbɑː-/ [v T] to disturb someone who is doing something, especially in a way that is annoying: *Will you stop bothering me? I'm trying to watch a program.* | *Sorry to bother you, but could you help me one more time with the copier?* | *Don't bother Ellen while she's reading.*

distract /dɪˈstrækt/ [v T] to stop someone who is trying to work, study, or read, by making them look at or listen to something else: *Don't distract your father while he's driving.* | *The couple behind us kept distracting everyone by talking during the movie.* | *I was distracted by the sound of a car alarm in the street.*

put sb off /ˌpʊt (sb) ˈɒf/ [phr v T] British to make it difficult for someone to do something, by preventing them from paying attention and thinking clearly about what they are doing: *Seles couldn't concentrate on the game – the photographers were putting her off.*

break sb's train of thought /ˌbreɪk (sb's) ˌtreɪn əv ˈθɔːt/ [v phrase] to disturb someone so that they forget what they were thinking about: *The phone rang, breaking my train of thought.* | *I sat very still, not wanting to break her train of thought.*

2 to disturb a situation or event

- disrupt
- upset
- break up
- disturb

disrupt /dɪsˈrʌpt/ [v T] to disturb a situation, system, event etc, so that it cannot happen or work in its usual way: *The aim of the strike was to disrupt rail services as much as possible.* | *The protest disrupted the Democratic convention Saturday, nearly forcing its cancellation.* | *Moving schools frequently can disrupt a child's education.* | *Hecklers repeatedly disrupted Duke's news conference, calling him a liar and a fascist.* —**disruption** /dɪsˈrʌpʃən/ [n U] *The storm has caused serious disruption to road and rail travel.*

upset /ʌpˈset/ [v T] to disturb a plan, situation, relationship etc, especially so that people feel confused or angry: *Young children don't like anything which upsets their daily routine.* | *The closing of the plant threatens to upset the local economy.* | *Rowan said this latest outbreak of violence could upset the peace talks.*

break up /ˌbreɪk ˈʌp/ [phr v T] **break up a meeting/demonstration/march etc** deliberately disturb it or prevent it from continuing, especially in a violent way **break up sth** *Police broke up the demonstration with tear gas.* | *The conference was broken up by animal rights campaigners.* | **break sth up** *Breaking meetings up and harassing party members are just some of the tactics our opponents have used.*

disturb /dɪˈstɜːʳb/ [v T] to **disturb** an organized event or a peaceful situation, for example by making a lot of noise or arguing with someone: *Loud frogs are disturbing the sleep of local home owners.* | *It is thought that the intruder was disturbed by a barking dog.*

divorce

RELATED WORDS

opposite: **marry**

▸ *see also* **separate, leave, relationship**

1 to get divorced

- get divorced
- divorce
- divorce
- separate
- split up

get divorced /ˌget dɪ̇ˈvɔːʳst/ [v phrase] to legally end your marriage: *My parents got divorced last year.* | *Before getting divorced, you should think carefully about the effect it will have on the children.*

divorce /dɪ̇ˈvɔːʳs/ [v I/T] if someone **divorces** their husband or wife, or if two people **divorce,** they legally end their marriage: *Finally, after years of unhappy marriage, Eva divorced Stanley.* | *He kept promising her that he would divorce his wife, but he never actually did it.* | *Petra's parents divorced when she was about seven years old.*

divorce /dɪ̇ˈvɔːʳs/ [n C/U] the legal process of ending a marriage: *I've only seen my ex-wife once since the divorce.* | *Gwen has just been through a bitter divorce.* | **get a divorce** *It's much too easy to get a divorce nowadays.* | **ask (sb) for a divorce** *Caroline's husband asked her for a divorce and she agreed.* | **end in divorce** *A third of all marriages in Britain end in divorce.* | **divorce rate** (=the number of divorces each year) *The divorce rate has risen steadily since the 1950s.*

separate /ˈsepəreɪt/ [v I] if a husband and wife **separate**, they no longer live together, usually because they intend to get divorced: *Linda and George have only been married for a year and they're already thinking of separating.* | *Anne and I separated for three months, but we are now together again.*

split up /ˌsplɪt ˈʌp/ [phr v I] informal if two people **split up**, they end their marriage or they stop having a romantic relationship: *They're always arguing but I don't think they'll ever split up.* | **+ with** *Have you heard? Katie's splitting up with Andrew!*

2 someone who is divorced

- divorced
- divorcee
- separated
- ex-husband/ex-wife

divorced /dɪ̇ˈvɔːʳst/ [adj] someone who is **divorced** has officially ended their marriage: *Sue's parents are divorced.* | *At twenty-five Maria is now divorced, and lives with her three children.* | *More than 80% of divorced men, and 75% of divorced women, go on to remarry.* | **get divorced** *They got divorced only three years after they got married.*

divorcee /dɪ̇ˈvɔːʳsiː/ [n C] a woman who is legally no longer married to her former husband: *Pam is a divorcee who has to bring her baby daughter up on her own.* | *Most of the people on the holiday seemed to be divorcees.*

separated /ˈsepəreɪtɪ̇d/ [adj] if a husband and wife are **separated**, they do not live with each other, because they are not happy together any more, but they are not divorced: *David and I have been separated for the last six months, but we're not legally divorced yet.* | *I didn't know Linda and Mike were separated.* | **+ from** *Victoria's separated from her husband and caring for her children alone.*

ex-husband/ex-wife ALSO **ex** /ˌeks ˈhʌzbənd, ˌeks ˈwaɪf, eks/ [n C] spoken informal the man or woman that someone was once married to: *I had a letter from my ex-wife yesterday.* | *Women who are attacked by their husbands or ex-husbands often fail to report them to the police.* | *My ex and I haven't spoken in years.*

doctor

RELATED WORDS

- *see also* **illness/disease, ill/sick, medical treatment, hospital, mentally ill, drug, cure, recover, healthy/unhealthy, pain**

1 a doctor

- doctor
- physician
- GP
- specialist
- consultant
- surgeon
- intern
- the medical profession

doctor /ˈdɒktəʳ‖ˈdɑːk-/ [n C] someone whose job is to treat people who are sick or injured: *Doctor, I keep getting a pain in my throat.* | *Tracy is interested in journalism, but Sarah wants to be a doctor.* | *She looks very ill – you'd better call a doctor.* | **see a doctor** (=visit a doctor so that they can examine you) *I went to see the doctor about my cough but she said there was nothing wrong with me.* | **the doctor's** (=the place where the doctor works) *'Where's Karen?' 'She's at the doctor's.'* | **Doctor Smith/Jones etc** *I'd like to make an appointment to see Doctor Patel some time this morning.* | **Dr Smith/Jones etc** written abbreviation *Dr Harrington has warned that the NHS is in serious need of greater funding.*

physician /fɪ̆ˈzɪʃən/ [n C] American formal a doctor: *People with heart problems should talk to their physician before making the trip.*

GP /ˌdʒiː ˈpiː/ [n C] British a doctor who is trained in general medicine and treats the people who live in a local area: *If your GP can't help you he will refer you to a specialist.* | *A lot of GPs are too quick to prescribe drugs, instead of letting the body get better on its own.*

specialist /ˈspeʃəlɪ̆st/ [n C] a doctor who has special knowledge of a particular illness, part of the body, or type of medical treatment: *The doctor arranged for Marcel to see a top specialist in Paris.* | **eye/heart/cancer etc specialist** *Professor Holloway, an eye specialist, organized a national survey of eye diseases in children.* | **+ in** *Professor Williams is one of the world's leading specialists in radiotherapy.*

consultant /kənˈsʌltənt/ [n C] British a doctor who has special knowledge of a particular area of medicine and is in charge of a hospital department: *The consultant told Jean that an operation was necessary to save her life.* | **consultant psychologist/paediatrician etc** *Dr Jamieson is the consultant psychologist at St Andrew's hospital.*

surgeon /ˈsɜːʳdʒən/ [n C] a doctor who does operations in a hospital: *The surgeon told reporters that Sara was making good progress after the heart transplant.* | **heart/brain/eye etc surgeon** *A famous brain surgeon from Boston performed the operation.*

intern /ˈɪntɜːʳn/ [n C] American someone who has nearly finished their training as a doctor and works in a hospital: *She refused to be treated by an intern and demanded to see a qualified doctor.*

the medical profession /ðə ˈmedɪkəl prəˌfeʃən/ [n phrase] doctors, nurses etc considered as a group: *The magazine's chief function is to keep the medical profession up to date with the latest advances and drugs.* | *These proposals are unpopular with most of the medical profession.*

2 a doctor who treats mental illnesses

- psychiatrist
- analyst/therapist/psychotherapist
- psychologist
- counsellor
- shrink

psychiatrist /saɪˈkaɪətrɪ̆st‖sə-/ [n C] a doctor who treats people with mental illnesses, using drugs or other forms of medical treatment: *Her psychiatrist told her she no longer needed to take tranquillizers.* | *Child psychiatrist Dr Goldman has written a book on anorexia in young girls.* | **see a psychiatrist** (=go to be treated by a psychiatrist) *I made an appointment to see a psychiatrist the following week.*

analyst/therapist/psychotherapist /ˈænəlɪ̆st, ˈθerəpɪst, ˌsaɪkəʊˈθerəpɪst/ [n C] a doctor or other trained person who treats people with mental or emotional problems, especially by talking with them about their thoughts, feelings, and past experiences: *I don't think her analyst has really helped her very much.* | *My therapist has been working with me on my anger.*

psychologist /saɪˈkɒlədʒɪ̆st‖-ˈkɑː-/ [n C] someone who is trained to understand people's behaviour and help them with mental or emotional problems, but who is not a medical doctor: *He admitted to his psychologist that he had been too shy to talk to women.* | **child/educational/occupational etc psychologist** *She told us she worked as an educational psychologist in Athens.*

counsellor British **/counselor** American /ˈkaʊnsələʳ/ [n C] someone who helps people with mental or emotional problems by talking with them and giving them advice: *Blau has been a counselor at the school since 1987.* | *Maybe we should see a marriage counsellor.*

shrink /ʃrɪŋk/ [n C] informal a doctor who treats people with mental illnesses and problems: *The shrinks at the hospital said they think Gary needs therapy.* | *That guy's crazy – he ought to see a shrink.*

3 a doctor who treats people's teeth

- dentist

dentist /ˈdentɪ̆st/ [n C] *My dentist told me I shouldn't eat so much chocolate.* | **see/visit the dentist** (=go to the dentist and be examined or treated) *You should visit the dentist twice a year.* | **the dentist's** (=the place where the dentist works) *I hate going to the dentist's.*

4 a doctor who treats animals

- vet

vet ALSO **veterinarian** American /vet, ˌvetərɪ̆ˈneəriən/ [n C] *Jane's taking her kitten to the vet on Friday.* | *Could you call the vet and ask him to come to the farm? I'd like him to have a look at one of the horses.* | *Gina has wanted to be a veterinarian since she was a little girl.*

do/not do

WHAT'S HERE

to do sth

RELATED WORDS

- to start doing something *see* **start**
- *see also* **take part, make, job, work**

1 to do something

- **do**
- **make**
- **give**
- **go about**
- **perform**
- **conduct**
- **dabble in**

do /duː/ [v T] *I do half an hour of exercises every morning.* | *What is Carla doing? She's been in the garage for a half an hour.* | *Howard did some rapid calculations on the back of an envelope.* | *Listen, I'm only trying to do my job – don't yell at me.* | **do work/housework/homework etc** *She does a lot of work for charity.* | *I want you to do your homework before you start watching TV.* | **do the washing/cooking/shopping etc** *You wash the dishes, and I'll do the drying.* | **do a test/exam/course etc** British *He's doing an art course at Wrexham College.*

make /meɪk/ to do something – use this with these words **make an effort/decision/start** *We can't wait any longer. You need to make a decision now.* | *Archie doesn't even make an effort to help out around the house.* | **make a speech/suggestion/remark/complaint/joke** *At school the other kids always made jokes about my name.* | *I'd like to make a suggestion if that's all right.* | *The governor will be making a speech here next week.*

give /gɪv/ [v T] **give a talk/speech/performance etc** talk, speak, sing, perform etc in front of a group of people: *Mr Banks gave a short talk about his travels in Africa.* | *Professor Williams will be giving a series of lectures on environmental pollution.* | *Davis gives a wonderful performance as an 81-year-old man.*

go about /ˌgəʊ əˈbaʊt/ [phr v T] to start or continue doing a job – use this when someone does a job in their usual way, or when you are talking about the way they do it: *The old man hummed to himself as he went about his gardening.* | *I'm thinking about changing careers, but I don't quite know how to go about it.* | **go about doing sth** *How would you go about reorganizing the kitchen?* | **go about your business** (=continue doing what you were doing or always do) *The next morning, she went about her business as if nothing out of the ordinary had happened.*

perform /pəʳˈfɔːʳm/ [v T] **perform a duty/operation/task etc** to do a duty, operation, or piece of work: *The ship's captain performed the wedding ceremony.* | *The operation was performed by a team of surgeons at Addenbrookes Hospital.* | *Students perform increasingly difficult tasks as the course continues.*

conduct /kənˈdʌkt/ [v T] **conduct an experiment/survey/inquiry etc** to do something, especially in order to find out or prove something: *All the children in the class have to conduct their own science experiments.* | *The committee will conduct a thorough investigation of the bribery charges.* | *The data comes from a survey conducted by the company last fall.*

dabble in /ˈdæbəl ɪn/ [phr v T] to do something that you are interested in or enjoy, but not very often or regularly, or not in a very serious way: *When he was younger he used to dabble in astronomy.* | *Beck has dabbled in poetry over the years, but this is her first published book of poems.*

2 to do something that has already been planned or ordered

- **carry out**
- **execute**
- **implement**
- **put sth into practice**
- **deliver the goods/come up with the goods**

carry out /ˌkæri ˈaʊt/ [phr v T] to do something that has been planned or that someone has asked you to do **carry out tests/research/a search etc** *Police are carrying out a thorough search of the area.* | *Technicians carried out extensive tests on the equipment.* | **carry out sb's orders/instructions/wishes** *If my instructions had been carried out, the accident would not have happened.* | **carry out a threat/promise** *The terrorists carried out their threat and shot two of the hostages.*

execute /ˈeksɪ̈kjuːt/ [v T] formal to do something that you have carefully planned or that you have agreed to do – used especially in official, legal, or business contexts: *We will not be able to execute the programs without more funding.* | *The directors make the decisions, but it's the managers who have to execute them.* | *The goal of landing people on Mars will not be an easy one to execute.* —**execution** /ˌeksɪ̈ˈkjuːʃən/ [n U] **+ of** *The department is responsible for the planning and execution of military operations.*

implement /ˈɪmplɪ̈ment/ [v T] formal to do something after an official decision has been made that it should be done **implement a plan/a proposal/recommendations/policy etc** *We need a strategy that can be implemented quickly.* | *Very few parties in government ever want to implement major political reform.* | *An international team has been set up to implement recent UN recommendations.* —**implementation** /ˌɪmplɪ̈menˈteɪʃən/ [n U] *A clear timetable for the implementation of new city programs is lacking.*

put sth into practice /ˌpʊt (sth) ɪntə ˈpræktɪ̈s/ [v phrase] if you **put** an idea or something you have learned **into practice**, you use it in your work or in your life, and you find out if it is effective: *The office has been slow to put the new proposals into practice.* | *A lot of these modern theories about teaching sound really good until you actually try and put them into practice.*

deliver the goods/come up with the goods /dɪˌlɪvəʳ ðə ˈgʊdz, kʌm ˌʌp wɪð ðə ˈgʊdz/ [v phrase] informal to successfully do what other people have asked you to do or expect you to do – used especially in business: *What the country needs is an economic and political system capable of delivering the goods.* | *When the company's director failed to come up with the goods, he was out.*

3 to do something after a delay or pause

- get on with
- get around to
- get going

get on with /get 'ɒn wɪð / [phr v T not in passive] especially British, spoken to start doing something that you should have started already, or continue doing something that you have stopped doing for a short time: *I'm glad the guests are gone so I can get on with my work.* | *Heavy rain is preventing rescue teams from getting on with the search.* | **get on with it** *Stop messing around – just get on with it!*

get around to ALSO **get round to** British /get ə'raʊnd tuː, get 'raʊnd tuː/ [phr v T not in passive] to finally do something that you have been intending to do for a long time, but have been too busy or too lazy to do: *I was going to fill out an application, but I never got around to it.* | **get around/round to doing sth** *I must get round to painting the kitchen some day.*

get going /get 'gəʊɪŋ/ [v phrase] spoken to start doing something, especially when you should have started already: *We've got so much to do – let's get going.* | **+ on** *You need to get going on that report. It's due tomorrow.*

4 to do something that is bad or wrong

- be up to
- get up to
- commit
- indulge in
- stoop to

be up to /biː 'ʌp tuː/ [v phrase] informal if someone **is up to something** they are probably doing something bad, but you do not know exactly what: *I know he's lying – what do you think he's up to?* | **be up to something** *The kids have been whispering and giggling all day – I think they're up to something.* | **be up to no good** (=be doing something bad) *She was beginning to suspect that the handsome stranger was up to no good.*

get up to /get 'ʌp tuː/ [v phrase] British to do something that other people disapprove of, especially because you think it is funny or because you enjoy it: *She peeped into the bedroom to see what mischief her grandson was getting up to.* | *When we were students, we used to get up to all sorts of things.*

commit /kə'mɪt/ [v T] to do something that is a crime, especially a serious crime **commit a crime/murder/robbery etc** *Women commit far fewer crimes than men.* | *The murder must have been committed between 7 and 10pm.*

indulge in /ɪn'dʌldʒ ɪn/ [phr v T] to do something that you enjoy, even though there is a reason you should not do it: *I was downtown, so I decided to indulge in a little shopping.* | *Most people indulge in harmless fantasies to relieve the boredom of their lives.*

stoop to /'stuːp tuː/ [phr v T] to do something that you know is morally wrong because you think it is the only way that you can achieve what you want to achieve: *'She even tried to get him fired.' 'I can't believe she'd stoop to that.'* | **stoop to doing sth** *They ended up stooping to hair-pulling and name-calling.* | *His lawyers even stooped to using the children to gain public sympathy.*

5 ways of asking what someone is doing

- what is sb doing?
- what is sb up to?
- what is sb playing at?

what is sb doing? /ˌwɒt ɪz (sb) 'duːɪŋ/ spoken *What are you two doing?* | *He's been in the yard a long time – what's he doing out there?*

what is sb up to? /ˌwɒt ɪz (sb) 'ʌp tuː/ spoken say this when you think someone is secretly doing something bad: *You look guilty, Stuart. What have you been up to?* | *They've been locked in there all morning – what are they up to?*

what is sb playing at? /ˌwɒt ɪz (sb) 'pleɪ-ɪŋ æt/ British spoken say this when you are angry and think someone has done something wrong or stupid: *She shouldn't have told him what I said. What was she playing at?* | *You boys! What on earth do you think you're playing at? Stop it at once!*

6 when someone is doing something

- active
- in action

active /'æktɪv/ [adj] always doing things or ready to do things, especially physical activities or activities within an organization: *They're both in their seventies, but they're still very active.* | **+ in** *In Washington Harriman quickly became active in Democratic Party affairs.* | **active member** *Today there are over 5,000 active members in the Accra church.*

in action /ɪn 'ækʃən/ [adv] if you see someone **in action**, you see them doing the job or activity that they are trained to do or usually do: *I've heard a lot about his dancing – I'd love to see him in action.* | *The advertisement shows two firefighters in action putting out a blaze.* | *I had seen him in action during the San José strike, and I was very impressed.*

7 something that someone does

- thing
- action
- activities
- activity
- act
- deed
- feat
- exploits

thing /θɪŋ/ [n phrase] something that someone does – always use this with the verb **do**: *The first thing you should do is connect the printer to the computer.* | **a nice/stupid/nasty etc thing to do** *That was a really nice thing to do – I know Leona enjoys your visits.* | *I know I shouldn't have hit him – it was a dumb thing to do.* | **the right/best/smart/only etc thing to do** *He gave her half the money because it was the right thing to do.*

action /'ækʃən/ [n C] something that someone does: *You can't be blamed for the actions of your parents.* | *Bedell's financial problems do not excuse his actions.* | **course of action** (=something that you could do in order to deal with a situation) *There was only one possible course of action – he had to resign.*

activities /æk'tɪvətiz/ [n plural] things that people do, especially as an organized group – use this especially about illegal things that people do: *The FBI is investigating the company's business activities.* | *There is growing evidence of drug-smuggling activities in and around the port.* | *Alberts created false documents to hide his activities from his employers.*

activity /æk'tɪvəti/ [n U] when people are doing things, moving around, and looking busy: *There's a* *lot of activity downstairs – do you know what's going on?* | *Military activity was secretly taking place for weeks before the invasion.*

act /ækt/ [n C] a particular kind of action **act of courage/stupidity/cruelty/kindness etc** *Saving the boys from the river was an act of great courage.* | *We condemn all acts of violence, no matter what the reason.* | *The whole nation is very grateful for the numerous acts of kindness rendered in this time of crisis.*

deed /diːd/ [n C] something very brave, very good or very bad that someone does – used especially in literature: *One day he will pay for his evil deeds.* | *He grew up reading the tales and legends of heroic deeds.* | **good deed** *Well, that's my good deed for the day.*

feat /fiːt/ [n C] something that someone does that is admired because it is very difficult and you need a lot of skill or strength to do it **+ of** *Using the code requires incredible feats of memory.* | **perform/accomplish/achieve a feat** *The circus acrobats perform amazing feats on the trapeze.* | *He led his team to victory for the tenth time, a feat no captain had achieved before.*

exploits /ˈeksplɔɪts/ [n plural] brave or exciting actions that people are told about and admire: *The children loved to hear their father tell stories of his wartime exploits.* | *Powell's exploits on the Colorado River made him a hero of the old West.*

8 something that people do for enjoyment

- activity
- pursuits
- pastime
- something to do
- hobby

activity /ækˈtɪvəti/ [n C] *What kind of activities do you enjoy?* | **outdoor/indoor activities** *Rebecca has always loved hiking and other outdoor activities.* | **leisure/social/cultural etc activities** *The retirement home arranges social and cultural activities for its seniors.* | **lay on activities** British (=provide them) *In the afternoon, there will be plenty of activities laid on for the kids.*

pursuits /pəʳˈsjuːts‖-ˈsuːts/ [n plural] formal things that people do because they enjoy them **leisure/outdoor/artistic etc pursuits** *Her husband never gave her much support in her artistic pursuits.* | *After he retired, my grandfather was able to devote his time to literary pursuits.*

pastime /ˈpɑːstaɪm‖ˈpæs-/ [n C] an activity that is pleasant, relaxing and usually not very difficult, that you do when you are not working, because you enjoy it: *Our cat's favourite pastime is sitting at the window and watching the people walk by.* | *Watching talk shows has become a national pastime in this country.*

something to do /ˌsʌmθɪŋ tə ˈduː/ [n phrase] something that you can do and that will stop you feeling bored when you have nothing to do: *I don't mind helping – it'll give me something to do.* | *He really needs something to do in his spare time to keep him out of trouble.*

hobby /ˈhɒbi‖ˈhɑː-/ [n C] something that you do for interest and enjoyment regularly over a long period of time, for example, collecting things or making models: *My hobbies are wind-surfing and playing the guitar.* | *I never saw my song-writing as anything more than a hobby until recently.*

to do sth in order to deal with a situation

RELATED WORDS

▸ see also **deal with, interfere**

9 to do something in order to deal with a bad situation

- do something
- take action
- act
- take steps/take measures
- move
- intervene/step in

do something /ˈduː ˌsʌmθɪŋ/ [v phrase] to **do something** to deal with a problem, especially one that is urgent: *Quick, do something – there's water all over the kitchen floor.* | *We need to do something before everyone gets fed up and quits.* | **+ about** *When are you going to do something about this broken window?* | *Teenagers were dropping out of school in huge numbers, until a group of parents and teachers decided to do something about it.*

take action /ˌteɪk ˈækʃən/ [v phrase] to do something to stop a bad situation from happening or continuing – use this to talk about people who have a clear plan for dealing with a problem: *Unless governments take action, the Earth's atmosphere will continue to heat up.* | **+ against** *The school will take strong action against any students using illegal drugs.* | **+ on** *Congress is expected to take action on campaign finance reform soon.* | **+ to do sth** *The President may step in and take action to lower energy prices.*

act /ækt/ [v I] to use your power or authority to deal with an urgent problem: *We must act before the situation gets out of control.* | *Despite the crisis, the Commission seems unwilling to act.* | *Critics accuse the company of acting too slowly in notifying residents of the chemical leak.*

take steps/take measures /ˌteɪk ˈsteps, ˌteɪk ˈmeʒəʳz/ [v phrase] if a government or someone in a position of power **takes steps** or **measures**, they do what is necessary to improve a situation or to deal with a problem: *The governor has not yet decided what measures should be taken.* | **+ to do sth** *All departments must take measures now to reduce costs.* | *We apologize for the error and have taken steps to see that it does not happen again.* | **take drastic measures** *Drastic measures will be taken against those who engage in terrorism.*

move /muːv/ [v I] if a person or organization **moves** to do something, they start to take action, especially in order to deal quickly with an urgent matter: *If anyone wants to put in a bid on the property they'll have to move quickly.* | **+ to do sth** *Airport authorities are moving fast to improve security following a series of bomb threats.* | *In the past year the leadership has moved to strengthen their control over the party.*

intervene/step in /ˌɪntəʳˈviːn, ˌstep ˈɪn/ [v I/phr v I] to get involved in a difficult situation in order to stop a fight or deal with someone else's problem: *The referee intervened when two of the players started to fight.* | *The situation was allowed to continue for several months before the local authorities stepped in.* | **intervene in sth** *The UN was not authorized to intervene in a country's internal affairs.* | **+ to do sth** *Soldiers intervened to prevent further bloodshed.* | *Thomas had listened to the argument for long enough and he stepped in to defend Miss*

Price. —**intervention** /ˌɪntəʳˈvenʃən/ [n U] *We don't need more government intervention in private industry.*

10 something that someone does in order to deal with a situation

- action
- step
- measure
- move

action /ˈækʃən/ [n U] what someone does when they use their power to deal with a problem or to achieve something: *Strong action is needed to restore law and order.* | *It's been politics as usual – all talk and no action.* | **+ on** *The agency has promised action on the pollution problem for years, but nothing has happened.*

step /step/ [n C] one of a series of things that someone does in order to deal with a problem or to achieve success: *Her first big step towards a career in movies was her move to Hollywood.* | *Now that we've identified the problem, what's the next step?* | *These steps are necessary if the company is to succeed in the European market.*

measure /ˈmeʒəʳ/ [n C usually plural] an action taken by a government or someone in authority to deal with a problem or improve a situation, for example by making a new law or rule: *Government officials refused to say what measures were being planned to deal with the refugee crisis.* | **+ to do sth** *Lawmakers are searching for the best measures to strengthen Social Security.* | **drastic measures** *Drastic situations require drastic measures.*

move /muːv/ [n C] something that you decide to do in order to achieve a particular result, especially as one of a series of planned actions **sb's move** *The management have offered less money than we wanted so what's our next move?* | *His first move after taking office was to appoint four communists to his cabinet.* | **+ to do sth** *The UN's latest move to stop the fighting has ended in failure.*

to do sth well

RELATED WORDS

- *see also* **good, succeed/successful, careful (4-6), praise**

11 to do something skilfully or carefully

- do (sth) well
- do a good job
- make a good job of
- excel
- outdo
- distinguish yourself

do (sth) well /ˌduː (sth) ˈwel/ [v phrase] *Don't worry about the test – I'm sure you'll do well.* | *She enjoys her job and does it very well.* | *If a firm does a job well, we use them again.*

do a good job /duː ə ˌgʊd ˈdʒɒb‖-ˈdʒɑːb/ [v phrase] especially spoken to do something well, especially a job that you have been asked to do: *You can always rely on Brian to do a good job.* | *You're doing a good job there, Sally. I don't know what we'd do without you.* | **+ of doing sth** *They did a really good job of decorating my bathroom.*

make a good job of /ˌmeɪk ə gʊd ˈdʒɒb ɒv‖-ˈdʒɑːb-/ [v phrase] British to do something well, especially a piece of practical work, so that it looks good or works well: *The hairdresser made a good job of your hair. It looks lovely.* | *We've just had a new heating system installed, but unfortunately they didn't make a very good job of it.*

excel /ɪkˈsel/ [v I not in progressive] to do something much better than most other people, especially because you have a natural ability to do it well: *I didn't exactly excel academically and I left school as soon as I had the chance.* | **+ at/in** *He played cricket for Middlesex but it was football that he really excelled at.* | *Many parents put too much pressure on their children to excel in school.* | **excel yourself** British (=do even better than usual) *Costner has excelled himself in this movie – definitely his best performance yet.*

outdo /aʊtˈduː/ [v T] to be better or more successful than someone else at doing something: *The Canadian hockey team has outdone all its rivals.* | **outdo sb in sth** *Each state seems to be trying to outdo its neighbors in cutting health services.* | **outdo yourself** (=do even better than usual) *The singer outdid himself at the festival, singing for almost three hours to noisy applause.* | **not to be outdone** (=so that no one else does better than you) *Not to be outdone, Stern went on television and made a speech of his own.*

distinguish yourself /dɪˈstɪŋgwɪʃ jɔːʳself/ [v phrase] to do something very well, so that people notice you, praise you, and remember you: *Bradley has distinguished himself as the top scorer on the team.* | *After joining the newspaper, she quickly distinguished herself with a series of hard-hitting exposés.*

to do sth badly

RELATED WORDS

- *see also* **bad at doing sth, careless, clumsy, mistake**

12 to do something in a careless or unskilful way

- do (sth) badly
- mess up
- make a mess of
- screw up
- do a bad job
- bungle
- botch/botch up
- mismanage
- fluff
- not do yourself justice

do (sth) badly /ˌduː (sth) ˈbædli/ [v phrase] *I think I did pretty badly in the exam today.* | *They packed the glass and china for us, but they did it very badly and a lot of stuff got broken.*

mess up /ˌmes ˈʌp/ [phr v I/T] informal to do something badly because you have made mistakes, often so that you do not get the result you wanted: *I've practiced all week, but I'm still afraid I'll mess up.* | **mess sth up** *Don't ask Terry to do it – she'll probably just mess it up.* | **mess up sth** *Danny messed up three plays and made us lose the game.*

make a mess of ALSO **make a hash of** British /ˌmeɪk ə ˈmes ɒv, ˌmeɪk ə ˈhæʃ ɒv/ [v phrase] informal to do something badly and make a lot of mistakes, especially when it is important that you do it well: *Let's be honest. Most people make a mess of handling money.* | *She picked herself up and started the dance again, determined not to make a hash of it this time.* | **make a complete hash of sth** *I made a complete hash of the interview – I don't stand a chance of getting the job.*

screw up /ˌskruː ˈʌp/ [phr v I/T] informal to spoil something you are trying to do, by making stupid mistakes: *If you screw up too many times, they'll kick you off the team.* | **screw sth up** *I was so nervous about the driving test that I screwed the whole thing up.* | **screw up sth** *My audition was going really well until I screwed the last part up.*

do a bad job /duː əˌbæd ˈdʒɒb‖-ˈdʒɑːb/ [v phrase] to do something badly, especially a job you have been asked to do: *Most people think the mayor is doing a pretty bad job.* | **+ of doing sth** *He did such a bad job of labeling these envelopes I don't think I'll ask for his help again.*

bungle /ˈbʌŋɡəl/ [v T] if an organization or someone in authority **bungles** what they are trying to do, they fail to do it successfully because of stupid or careless mistakes: *The plan seemed simple enough, but the CIA managed to bungle the operation.* | *Analysts agree that the company bungled its response to the crisis.* —**bungling** [n U] *Because of bureaucratic bungling the hospital had never been built.* —**bungled** [adj] *a bungled rescue attempt*

botch/botch up /bɒtʃ, ˌbɒtʃ ˈʌp‖ˌbɑːtʃ-/ [v T/phr v T] to do something badly, especially a practical job such as making or repairing something, as a result of being too careless or not having enough skill: *They were supposed to fix the roof, but they completely botched the job.* | **botch sth up** *We hired someone to fix the computer system, but he botched it up even more.* | **botch up sth** *I wouldn't take your car to that garage – they botch up the simplest jobs.* —**botched** [adj] *He was killed by burglars in a botched robbery at his mansion.*

mismanage /ˌmɪsˈmænɪdʒ/ [v T] if someone who is in charge **mismanages** a system or planned piece of work, they do it badly because they did not organize and control it properly: *The whole project was seriously mismanaged from the beginning.* | *Many people accused the government of mismanaging the environment and indirectly causing the flooding.*

fluff /flʌf/ [v T] informal to do something badly because you are not paying enough attention, especially when it is your turn to do something in a play or in a game: *I was so nervous that I fluffed my lines.* | *It should have been an easy catch, but he fluffed it.*

not do yourself justice /nɒt ˌduː jɔːʳself ˈdʒʌstɪ̇s/ [v phrase] British to do something less well than you could, in an examination, game etc: *My grandfather was very intelligent, but he never did himself justice at school.* | *There were a couple of good performances, but most of the players didn't really do themselves justice.*

to not do sth

RELATED WORDS

- not do something now because you can do it later *see* **later**
- *see also* **avoid, stop, delay**

13 to not do something that you should do

- not do
- do nothing/not do anything
- take no action
- fail to do sth
- neglect to do sth
- omit to do sth
- stand by/sit by
- just stand there/just sit there

not do /nɒt ˈduː/ [v phrase] *I haven't done my taxes yet and they're due next week.* | *The electrician came round yesterday, but he didn't do all the jobs I asked him to do.* | *She was afraid that if she didn't do what her boss told her she would be fired.*

do nothing/not do anything /ˌduː ˈnʌθɪŋ, ˌnɒt duː ˈeniθɪŋ/ [v phrase] to not try to help someone or prevent a bad situation, even though you know it is happening: *How could neighbors listen to her scream and do nothing?* | **+ about** *We told the police months ago, but they still haven't done anything about it.* | **+ to do sth** *No one did anything to stop the purse snatcher.*

take no action /ˌteɪk nəʊ ˈækʃən/ [v phrase] formal to do nothing, especially when this is a deliberate decision: *If you have already paid the amount shown on this bill, you need take no further action.* | **+ to do sth** *Local police took no action to protect the family from the attacks.*

fail to do sth /ˌfeɪl tə ˈduː (sth)/ [v phrase not usually in progressive] formal to not do something that you should do, especially when this has serious results: *The driver of the car failed to stop in time, and the boy was killed.* | *If you fail to provide all the information, we will be unable to process your application.*

neglect to do sth /nɪˌglekt tə ˈduː (sth)/ [v phrase not in progressive] to not do something because you do not pay enough attention or forget, especially when this could have serious results: *Marie decided not to move, but she neglected to inform the rental agency.* | *The public are demanding to know why the government neglected to warn them of the oil shortages.*

omit to do sth /əʊˌmɪt tə ˈduː (sth)/ [v phrase not in progressive] formal to not do something, either because you forget to do it or because you deliberately choose not to do it: *Mrs Hobbs told me about the meeting but she omitted to tell me where it was.* | *Starr's account omits to mention that it was his own actions that caused the fire.*

stand by/sit by /ˌstænd ˈbaɪ, ˌsɪt ˈbaɪ/ [phr v I] to not do anything to stop something bad from happening, when you should do something to show that you care about the situation: *Why did people just stand by while she was attacked?* | *We can't afford to just sit by and watch more of our local industry shut down.*

just stand there/just sit there /dʒʌst ˈstænd ðeəʳ, dʒʌst ˈsɪt ðeəʳ/ [v phrase] spoken to not even move or start to do something when there is an urgent situation: *Don't just stand there – help me catch the cat!* | *When the fire alarm went off she just sat there as if she hadn't heard a thing.*

14 to decide it is better not to do something

- refrain
- abstain
- stop short of
- hold back
- keep from doing sth
- forget
- think twice

refrain /rɪˈfreɪn/ [v I not in progressive] formal to not do something that you want to do or usually do, especially because you do not want to offend or upset someone: *Kate wanted to slap Keith round the face but she refrained.* | **+ from** *Rand refrained from comment on the scandal involving his opponent.* | **+ from doing sth** *Please refrain from smoking in the restaurant.*

abstain /əbˈsteɪn/ [v I] to decide not to do something, especially something enjoyable, because it is considered to be bad for your health or morally wrong: *Most of the church members drink only moderately or abstain completely.* | **+ from** *You should abstain from food and caffeinated drinks before the operation.* | **+ from doing sth** *Junior politicians are supposed to abstain from criticizing the government.* —**abstinence** /ˈæbstɪ̇nəns/ [n U]

stop short of /ˌstɒp ˈʃɔːʳt ɒv‖ˌstɑːp-/ [v phrase not in progressive or passive] to not do something extreme, even though what you have been doing or saying until now makes this very likely to be the next thing you do: *The US was willing to support sanctions, but stopped short of military intervention.* | **stop short of doing sth** *Morris has strongly criticized Paulson's writings but stops short of calling him a racist.*

hold back /ˌhəʊld ˈbæk/ [phr v I] to not do something, especially because you are worried about what will happen if you do: *He wanted to tell her everything, but something made him hold back.* | **+ from doing sth** *Republicans have expressed interest in the plan but have held back from making a commitment.*

keep from doing sth /ˌkiːp frəm ˈduːɪŋ (sth)/ [v phrase not in progressive] to stop yourself from doing something you want to do, because you do not want to offend someone, spoil a secret etc: *It was all I could do to keep from hitting him.* | **keep yourself from doing sth** *Sara was so excited, she could hardly keep herself from giving away the whole plan.*

forget /fəʳˈget/ [v T] to decide or agree not to do something, especially because it is likely to be unsuccessful or is unnecessary: *Look, we aren't making any progress – let's just forget the whole idea.* | **forget it** spoken *If you're not going to take this project seriously we might as well forget it.*

think twice /ˌθɪŋk ˈtwaɪs/ [v phrase not in progressive] to not do something that you were going to do, or to think very carefully before you do it, because you know it could have a bad result: *Anyone thinking about having unprotected sex should think twice.* | **+ about** *I hope this latest attack will make people think twice about mindless violence towards ethnic minorities.* | **+ before doing sth** *The heavy penalties are designed to make people think twice before committing a crime.*

15 to not do something because it does not seem important

- not bother
- give sth a miss
- skip

not bother /nɒt ˈbɒðəʳ‖-ˈbɑː-/ [v phrase] especially spoken to not do something because you do not think it is important or necessary, or because you want to do something else: *'Shall I come get you at the station?' 'Don't bother – I can walk.'* | **+ to do sth** *Most people don't bother to make a will while they're still young.* | *I don't even bother to open most of the junk mail I get.*

give sth a miss /ˌgɪv (sth) ə ˈmɪs/ [v phrase not in passive] British to decide not to do something that you had planned to do, for example because you are too tired: *I think I'll give my exercise class a miss tonight – I'm worn out.* | *'Do you want to come to the cinema?' 'No thanks, I'll give it a miss this time.'*

skip /skɪp/ [v T] to not do something that you usually do or that you should do, especially because you would prefer to do something else: *Bill likes to leave work early, so he skips lunch sometimes.* | *The weather's so nice today – let's skip class and go to the beach.*

16 to not do anything because there is nothing to do

- have nothing to do/not have anything to do
- sit around/stand around
- be at a loose end

have nothing to do/not have anything to do /hæv ˌnʌθɪŋ tə ˈduː, nɒt hæv ˌeniθɪŋ tə ˈduː/ [v phrase not in progressive] if you **have nothing to do** there is nothing interesting for you to do, and you feel bored: *I get depressed if I have nothing to do.* | *The kids are always complaining that they don't have anything to do.* | **with nothing to do/without anything to do** *She was sick of sitting around at home with nothing to do.*

sit around/stand around /ˌsɪt əˈraʊnd, ˌstænd əˈraʊnd/ [phr v I] to sit or stand somewhere for a long time, feeling bored, when you are waiting for something to happen or when you are just being lazy: *I spent the whole morning sitting around waiting for him to call.* | *A group of teenagers were standing around outside the station.* | *If you're just standing around, why don't you come help me?*

be at a loose end British **/be at loose ends** American /biː ət ə ˌluːs ˈend, biː ət ˌluːs ˈendz/ [v phrase] to be unable to think of anything to do: *After her husband died, Mildred found herself suddenly at loose ends.* | *I felt rather at a loose end at the end of the term so I decided to take a trip to London.*

17 not doing anything

- idle
- inactive
- passive

idle /ˈaɪdl/ [adj not usually before noun] not doing anything, especially work, because there is nothing to do: *Almost half the skilled workers in this country are now idle.* | **sit/stand idle** *Hundreds of workers sat idle on the factory floor waiting for the assembly line to start again.*

inactive /ɪnˈæktɪv/ [adj] not doing anything, for example, because you are old or ill: *She dreaded becoming old and inactive.* | *Very shy people often become socially inactive.* —**inactivity** /ˌɪnækˈtɪvəti/ [n U] *Failing health is the biggest reason for Herman's long period of inactivity.*

passive /ˈpæsɪv/ [adj] not making decisions or taking control of situations yourself but allowing other people to do it for you, especially in a situation where other people are trying to control or influence you: *Emma plays far too passive a role in group discussions.* | *You're too passive, Harry. You should just tell her you don't want to go.* —**passively** [adv] *The majority of people will passively accept what newspapers tell them.*

don't care

RELATED WORDS

- when you care about someone or something a lot *see* **important**

1 when you do not care about something because it is not important to you

- not care
- couldn't care less
- not give a damn
- be past caring
- for all I care
- who cares?/so what?/what do I care?
- let him/her/them (do sth)
- tough!

not care /nɒt ˈkeəʳ/ [v phrase] if you **don't care** about something, it is not important to you: *'Wha* *do you think I should do?' 'I don't care. Do what you want.'* | **+ what/whether/if etc** *I like George, and I don't care what anyone else thinks about him.* | *I don't care what my parents say – I am going to the party.* | **+ about** *She doesn't care about anything except money.*

couldn't care less /ˌkʊdnt keəʳ 'les/ [v phrase not in progressive] informal to not care at all about something: *The politicians are making a big deal out of the issue, but most voters couldn't care less.* | **+ about** *Shelley couldn't care less about what other people thought of her.* | **+ whether/if** *To be perfectly honest with you, I couldn't care less whether he comes or not.*

not give a damn /ˌnɒt gɪv ə 'dæm/ [v phrase not in progressive] spoken to not care at all about something – use this when you are very annoyed with someone or something **+ about** *You're so selfish. You don't give a damn about anyone except for yourself.* | **+ what/who/why etc** *I don't really give a damn what the press says.*

be past caring /biː ˌpɑːst 'keərɪŋ‖-ˌpæst-/ [v phrase] to no longer care about something that you were worried about for a long time, because you realize that the situation cannot be changed: *I used to worry a lot about my weight when I was young, but now I'm past caring.* | *The company wrote and apologized for their mistake, but by then Sarah was past caring.*

for all I care /fər ˌɔːl 'aɪ ˌkeəʳ/ [adv] spoken say this when you do not care at all what someone does or what happens to them, especially when you are annoyed with them: *I don't want to hear any more about her. She can drop dead for all I care.*

who cares?/so what?/what do I care? /ˌhuː 'keəʳz, ˌsəʊ 'wɒt, ˌwɒt duː 'aɪ keəʳ/ spoken informal say this when you do not care about something, because you do not think it is important at all: *So your house isn't perfectly clean. Who cares?* | *'Phil was really angry when he heard what you had done.' 'So what? It's none of his business.'* | *'He says he's depressed and really short of money.' 'What do I care? It's his own fault.'*

let him/her/them (do sth) /ˌlet hɪm ('duː (sth))/ spoken say this when you do not care if someone does what they have threatened to do: *'Brenda says she's going to quit unless we give her a raise.' 'Let her quit then. It's not as if we can't find another nanny.'* | *'They're threatening to disconnect the phone unless we pay the bill.' 'Let them!'*

tough! /tʌf/ spoken informal say this when someone tells you about a problem they have and you do not have any sympathy for them, especially because you feel angry with them: *'Mom, I don't want to go to school today.' 'Tough! You're going anyway.'* | *'Can't we stop? I'm hungry.' 'That's tough. I told you to eat something before we left the house.'*

2 when you do not care because you will be happy whatever happens

opposite: —— **complain (2), worried/worrying**
▸ *see also* **relax/relaxed**

- ▸ **don't mind**
- ▸ **be not fussy**
- ▸ **it makes no difference to me/it doesn't bother me/it's all the same to me**
- ▸ **I'm easy**
- ▸ **it's no skin off my nose**
- ▸ **suit yourself**

don't mind British **/don't care** American /dəʊnt 'maɪnd, dəʊnt 'keəʳ/ to not care because you will be happy with whatever happens or with whatever someone decides: *'What would you like to do tonight?' 'I don't mind. You decide.'* | *'Do you want white bread or wheat?' 'I don't care. Either one is fine.'* | **+ where/what/how etc** *Honestly, I don't mind whether Linda comes with us or not.* | *They won't care if we're a few minutes late.*

be not fussy /biː nɒt 'fʌsi/ [v phrase] especially British, spoken to not care what happens or what is decided, especially when someone has asked you what you would prefer: *'Do you want to sit in the front seat or the back?' 'I'm not fussy.'* | **+ where/what/which etc** *I'm not fussy where I stay, as long as it's cheap.* | **+ about** *She's not fussy about what kind of car she drives.* | *He's not very fussy about his appearance, is he?*

it makes no difference to me/it doesn't bother me/it's all the same to me /ɪt meɪks nəʊ ˌdɪfərəns tə 'miː, ɪt dʌzənt ˌbɒðəʳ 'miː‖-ˌbɑː-, ɪts ɔːl ðə ˌseɪm tə 'miː/ spoken say this when you do not mind what happens because it does not affect you or cause you any problems: *You can come on Thursday or Friday – it makes no difference to me.* | *We can go out to eat if you want – it's all the same to me.* | *Mamet says it makes no difference to him what a movie costs, as long as it's a good movie.*

I'm easy /aɪm 'iːzi/ spoken informal say this when someone asks you which one of two things you would prefer, and you want to tell them that you do not mind what is decided: *'Do you want to watch the news or the late night film?' 'I'm easy.'*

it's no skin off my nose /ɪts nəʊ ˌskɪn ɒf 'maɪ nəʊz/ spoken say this when you do not care what someone else does because it does not affect you in any way: *It's no skin off our nose if they don't want to come along.* | *If my sister wants to throw her money away, then fine. It's no skin off my nose.*

suit yourself /ˌsuːt jɔːʳ'self/ spoken say this when someone has told you what they are going to do, and even though you do not think it is a good idea, you do not care whether they do it or not: *'I think I'll just stay home tonight.' 'Suit yourself.'* | *'Do you mind if I sit here?' 'Suit yourself,' she said, without looking up.*

3 not caring about something

- ▸ **unconcerned**
- ▸ **indifferent**
- ▸ **apathetic**
- ▸ **blasé**
- ▸ **casual**
- ▸ **offhand**
- ▸ **nonchalant**

unconcerned /ˌʌnkən'sɜːʳnd/ [adj not before noun] not worried or not caring about something, especially when you would normally expect someone to care: *It was strange. They threatened to fire him, but he seemed quite unconcerned.* | **+ about** *She seemed unconcerned about the risk of violence.* | *They appeared completely unconcerned about the shelling going on around them.*

indifferent /ɪn'dɪfərənt/ [adj not before noun] not seeming to care about what is happening, especially about other people's problems or feelings: *Her father was quite friendly, but her mother seemed somewhat cold and indifferent.* | **+ to** *His opponents have tried to characterize him as indifferent to the concerns of the working class.*

apathetic /ˌæpə'θetɪk◂/ [adj] not interested in anything or not caring about anything, and not making any effort to change or improve things: *The voters have become increasingly apathetic over the last several years.* | **+ about** *Parents are completely apathetic about their children's education and show little interest in it.* —**apathy** /'æpəθi/ [n U] a feeling of not being interested and not caring about something:

'There's a growing sense of apathy and cynicism about the whole democratic process here,' one Western diplomat said.

blasé /ˈblɑːzeɪ‖blɑːˈzeɪ/ [adj not usually before noun] not caring or worrying about something that other people think is important: *She used to be very meticulous about her work but she's becoming very blasé.* | *I was surprised by Carol's blasé attitude.* | *Despite his air of blasé, there was something childlike and curious about Andy Warhol.* | **+ about** *People have become blasé about the violence they see on their TV screens.*

casual /ˈkæʒuəl/ [adj] seeming not to care or pretending not to care about something: *She hurried into the room with no more than a casual glance in our direction.* | **casual attitude (+ toward/about sth)** *He had a casual attitude toward studying and grades.* —**casually** [adv] *'I was wondering if maybe you'd like to get together sometime,' he said casually.*

offhand /ˌɒfˈhænd◂‖ˌɔːf-/ [adj] not caring or seeming not to care about something or someone **+ with** *The store manager was rather offhand with us at first.* | *She said you were a bit offhand with her this afternoon.* | **offhand reply/manner/ attitude etc** *I didn't like his offhand manner.*

nonchalant /ˈnɒnʃələnt‖ˌnɑːnʃəˈlɑːnt/ [adj] seeming not to care about something, especially when you really do care but are trying to pretend that you do not: *a nonchalant attitude* | *'I'm sorry I'm so late. Have you been waiting long?' he asked. She gave a nonchalant shrug.* | **try to appear/look nonchalant** *When Peter came in, she glanced up, trying to appear nonchalant.* —**nonchalantly** [adv] *'Oh, come on, Dick – you're just imagining things,' she said nonchalantly.* —**nonchalance** [n U] *I was surprised by her nonchalance. We hadn't seen each other in over fifteen years, yet she acted like it was no big deal.*

doubt

when you think something is unlikely to happen or be true

RELATED WORDS

opposite: **certainly/definitely**

- not believe someone or something *see* **believe**
- *see also* **sure/not sure, uncertain, disagree**

- **don't think**
- **doubt**
- **be doubtful**
- **be dubious**
- **I'd be surprised if**
- **I wouldn't have thought**
- **I'm not sure (about that)**

don't think /ˌdəʊnt ˈθɪŋk/ [v phrase not in progressive] **don't think (that)** *At first I didn't think that Jim was going to reply.* | *I don't think many people will come to the meeting, do you?* | **don't think so** *'Do we have any coffee left?' 'I don't think so – I'll have a look.'* | *'Is Mr Brown there?' 'No, I don't think so, I saw him go out earlier.'*

doubt /daʊt/ [v T not in progressive] to think that something will probably not happen or is probably not true **+ if/whether** *We'd better go to the party, but I doubt if it'll be very exciting.* | *I doubt whether I'll be able to find a decent car for the price I can afford.* | **+ (that)** *Some people doubted that the attacks on the American ships had actually taken place.* | **very much doubt/doubt very much** *I very much doubt whether we'll get someone for the job by September.* | **seriously doubt** *At the time we seriously doubted that the doctor had got the diagnosis right.* | **doubt it** *It was possible that Maggie had been delayed, but he doubted it.*

be doubtful /biː ˈdaʊtfəl/ [v phrase] if you **are doubtful** about something, you do not believe that it will happen or should be done: *Mick felt optimistic about going to work in Hong Kong, but Sue was doubtful.* | *My brother looked doubtful when I asked him if he'd mind looking after the baby.* | **+ about** *A lot of us felt doubtful about the project at the beginning.* | **+ (that)** *The doctor said she was doubtful that antibiotics would work.* | **it is doubtful whether/ that/if** *It is doubtful that life could survive under such extreme conditions as these.*

be dubious /biː ˈdjuːbiəs‖-ˈduː-/ [v phrase] if you **are dubious** about something, you do not think it is a good idea or that it is true: *'Do you think they'll let us in?' Gabby looked dubious.* | **+ about** *Marian is still dubious about whether any of the government's 'solutions' will work.*

I'd be surprised if /aɪd biː səʳˈpraɪzd ɪf/ spoken say this when you think something is very unlikely to happen or is very unlikely to be true: *I'd be surprised if they get here in time for the show.* | *I'd be very surprised if Ronnie got the job – he just doesn't have enough experience.*

I wouldn't have thought /aɪ ˌwʊdnt əv ˈθɔːt/ spoken say this when you think that something is unlikely to happen or be true, especially when you are not completely sure that you are right **+ (that)** *I wouldn't have thought that there would be much traffic on a Sunday morning.* | **I wouldn't have thought so** *'Will John and Carmen be coming tonight?' 'I wouldn't have thought so. They're very busy at the moment.'*

I'm not sure (about that) /aɪm nɒt ˈʃʊər (əbaʊt ˌðæt)/ spoken use this in order to say politely that you think what someone has said is unlikely: *'I think Kate and Eddie will end up getting married.' 'Really? I'm not sure about that.'*

down

RELATED WORDS

opposite: **up**

- prices, numbers, amounts etc go down *see* **less, reduce**
- *see also* **under/below**

1 moving down

- **down**
- **downwards**
- **downhill**
- **earthwards**
- **downward**
- **face down**

down /daʊn/ [adv/prep] to a lower position or place: *I told you not to climb on that table. Get down!* | **+ into/to/from etc** *He's gone down to the basement to get some more beer.* | *The accident happened when we were coming down off the mountain.* | **roll/fall/jump etc down** *Tears began to roll down her cheeks.* | *The heat of the fire brought ceilings crashing down onto the floor.* | **look/glance/stare etc down** *She gazed down at the ring on her finger.* | *The doctor glanced down at the notepad on his desk.*

downwards British ALSO **downward** American /ˈdaʊnwəʳd(z)/ [adv] moving, looking, or pointing towards a lower level or towards the ground: *We came to a path winding downwards through the trees.* | *He was gazing downward into the pit.*

downhill /ˌdaʊnˈhɪl◂/ [adv] if you move, walk, drive etc **downhill**, you go down a slope: *We set off downhill towards the lake.* | *After we get to the top it'll be downhill all the way to Kendal.*

earthwards British ALSO **earthward** American /ˈɜːʳθwəʳd(z)/ [adv] formal down towards the ground from the sky or from a high place: *Moments later he tripped and was falling earthwards.* | *Flight 427 suddenly rolled and plunged earthward as it approached Pittsburgh.*

downward /ˈdaʊnwəʳd/ [adj only before noun] going or moving towards a lower level or towards the ground: *He managed to pull himself free with a sudden downward movement of his hands.* | *She gave the bell-rope a swift downward tug.* | *The downward pressure on my chest became more intense.*

face down /ˌfeɪs ˈdaʊn/ [adv] if someone is lying **face down**, they are lying with their face on the ground or a surface **lie face down** *Douglas found her lying face down on the floor.* | **collapse/land/fall etc face down** *She was flung violently forward, to land face down in a heap of blankets.*

2 to go down

- go down
- come down
- drop
- fall
- descend
- dive
- land
- touch down

go down /ˌgəʊ ˈdaʊn/ [v I/T] to **go down** some stairs, a ladder, a slope etc: *You go down a steep slope, then turn left at the bottom of the hill.* | *Right, here's the ladder. Who's going down first?* | **+ to** *I'll go down* (=downstairs) *to the kitchen and get you a glass of water.*

come down /ˌkʌm ˈdaʊn/ [phr v I] if a plane, bomb etc **comes down** somewhere, it comes down to the ground there, especially by accident: *Airline officials believe that the plane came down somewhere in the Andes mountains.* | *One of the missiles came down in a heavily populated suburb of Beirut.*

drop /drɒp‖drɑːp/ [v I] to fall straight downwards through the air: *When I let go of her hand, it dropped like a stone.* | **+ onto/from/off etc** *The bottle rolled across the table, dropped onto the floor, and smashed.* | *One of your buttons has dropped off.*

fall /fɔːl/ [v I] to come down through the air from a higher place: *Just as we were about to leave the house, rain began to fall.* | **+ from/down/on etc** *Leaves were falling from the trees.* | *Bombs fell on the streets, destroying neighbouring homes, but leaving the school intact.*

descend /dɪˈsend/ [v I/T] written to go down a slope, a mountain etc slowly and carefully: *Slowly the two climbers descended the cliff face.* | **+ into/from etc** *We descended into the cave by a rope ladder.*

dive /daɪv/ [v I] if a plane or a bird **dives**, it moves quickly down through the air: *The engine did not restart, and the plane dived to the ground.* | *The hawk stopped in mid-flight before diving down on its prey.* —**dive** [n C] *Two BF109 planes flashed past in a steep dive.*

land /lænd/ [v I] if a plane or a bird **lands**, it comes down to the ground in a controlled way: *He loves watching planes take off and land at the airport.* | **+ in/on/at** *We will be landing at Singapore airport at 3 am local time.* | *A flock of Canada geese landed on the river in front of us.* —**landing** [n C] *Captain Edwards brought the plane in for a perfect landing.*

touch down /ˌtʌtʃ ˈdaʊn/ [phr v I] if a plane **touches down**, it arrives safely on the ground at an airport but has not yet stopped moving: *The King's private plane touched down at Heathrow airport at exactly 12.15 this afternoon.* | *We will be touching down in about an hour's time.*

3 when the sun goes down

- go down/set
- sink
- sunset

go down/set /ˌgəʊ ˈdaʊn, set/ [phr v I/v I] if the sun **goes down** or **sets** at the end of the day, it moves downwards in the sky until it cannot be seen: *We sat on the balcony and watched the sun go down.* | *The sun usually sets at about 6pm at this time of year.* | *The setting sun cast a deep red glow over the city's rosy stone.*

sink /sɪŋk/ [v I] if the sun **sinks**, it goes down slowly – used especially in descriptions or stories: *The sun sank and darkness fell on the island.* | *As the sun sank lower and lower, the sky first turned pink and then orange.*

sunset /ˈsʌnset/ [n C/U] the time when the sun goes down or the way the sun looks when it goes down: *We sat and watched the glorious sunset from across the Mekong river.* | **at sunset** (=at the time when the sun is setting) *You may prefer to sit on the terrace sipping a cocktail at sunset.*

4 to go down under the surface of water, mud etc

- sink
- dive
- plunge
- submerge
- go under

sink /sɪŋk/ [v I] to go down below the surface of water, mud, sand etc, without being able to control or prevent it: *Hundreds of passengers tried desperately to escape from the boat as it sank.* | **+ into** *The guns sank deeper and deeper into the mud.* | *With the car sinking into a marsh, there wasn't a moment to spare.* | **sink without trace** (=sink and disappear completely) *There was a sucking noise, and then the branch sank without trace.* —**sinking** [adj only before noun] *He swam away from the sinking ship.*

dive /daɪv/ [v I] to jump down into water with your head first: *She stood at the edge of the pool waiting to dive.* | **+ into/in** *Ralph dived into the icy water.* | *A woman dived in to rescue the boy.* —**dive** [n C] *She did a perfect dive from the top board.*

plunge /plʌndʒ/ [v I] to jump into a river, lake etc quickly, making a lot of noise **+ into/in** *Colin plunged into the icy water.* | *I plunged in fully-clothed and pulled her to the river bank.*

submerge /səbˈmɜːʳdʒ/ [v I/T] to deliberately go under the surface of water or make something do this: *Peter pulled on the mask and submerged again.* | **submerge sth in sth** *elephants submerging themselves in cooling water* —**submerged** [adj only before noun] *The divers explored the submerged wreck.*

go under /ˌgəʊ ˈʌndəʳ/ [phr v I] if a ship or person **goes under**, they sink below the surface of water, usually after an accident: *By the time the sea rescue service arrived, the ship had gone under.* | *According to the only survivor, his comrades went under one by one.*

5 to make a plane, boat, etc go down

- sink
- shoot down/bring down

sink /sɪŋk/ [v T] **sink a ship/boat/submarine etc** to damage a ship, boat etc so badly that it goes under the water: *Submarines were used to sink the enemy's supply ships.* | *One battleship was sunk and two were badly damaged in last night's fighting.*

shoot down/bring down /ˌʃuːt ˈdaʊn, ˌbrɪŋ ˈdaʊn/ [phr v T] to deliberately shoot at or damage a plane while it is flying so that it falls to the ground and crashes **shoot/bring down sth** *In May 1960 the Russians shot down an American U2 spy plane.* | **shoot/bring sth down** *He followed the dive-bomber round in a very tight turn and shot it down into the sea.* | *One helicopter gunship had been brought down by small-arms fire.*

6 to move something down or let it move down

- drop
- put down
- lower

drop /drɒp‖drɑːp/ [v T] if you **drop** something that you are holding, it suddenly falls from your hands, especially accidentally: *You've dropped your handkerchief.* | *Be careful not to drop that bowl, it's very valuable.* | **drop sth onto/on/in sth** *I nearly dropped my glass on the floor when they said I'd won.*

put down /ˌpʊt ˈdaʊn/ [phr v T] if you put an object **down**, you put it on the ground or another surface; if you put your hand, head etc **down**, you move it into a lower position: *Put the gun down.* | *OK, you can all put your hands down now.*

lower /ˈləʊəʳ/ [v T] to move an object or your body into a **lower** position: *We need to lower the mirror in the bathroom.* | **lower your head/arms/body** *Lowering its head, the bull charged at him.* | **lower sth into/onto/over etc sth** *The coffin was lowered slowly into the ground.* | **lower yourself into/onto sth** (=sit down slowly and carefully) *The old man lowered himself wearily into his chair.*

7 when something hangs down

- hang
- dangle
- be suspended
- swing

hang /hæŋ/ [v I] *He stood very still, his arms hanging loosely, his feet apart.* | **+ from** *In the corner of the room was a large lamp, hanging from the ceiling.* | *The watch was on a gold chain that hung from his belt.* | **+ down** *Hold one end of the rope in your hand and let the other end hang down.* | **+ on/under/next to etc** *The keys are hanging on a nail by the door.* | *A picture of their parents hangs over the bedroom door.*

dangle /ˈdæŋgəl/ [v I] to hang loosely, moving slightly from side to side **+ from** *Dangling from her ears were two large gold earrings.* | *He dangled helplessly from the cliff, trying not to look down.* | **+ in/over/next to etc** *We sat on the edge of the pool with our legs dangling in the water.*

be suspended /biː səˈspendɪ̱d/ [v phrase] to be hanging from a high position **+ by** *A row of hares were suspended by their feet outside the butcher's shop.* | **+ from** *All sorts of artefacts were suspended from the ceiling.*

swing /swɪŋ/ [v I] to move from side to side while hanging from a higher position, or to make something do this **+ from** *A lantern swung from a hook in the roof.* | *A small jewelled cross swung from a gold chain around her neck.*

8 to move down to a lower position in a list

- fall
- slip

fall /fɔːl/ [v I] to move down to a lower position in a list of people or things that are competing with each other: *The pound fell against the Euro again today.* | **fall (from sth) to sth** *Within the space of a few minutes, the British song fell from top to bottom position.* | **fall (by) 3 places/6 points etc** *Aston Villa fell 3 places in the league after their defeat by Barnsley.*

slip /slɪp/ [v I] to gradually move to a lower position in a list, competition etc **slip (from sth) to sth** *Mansell has now slipped to third position.* | *The American slipped from second place to fourth.* | **+ down** *The team has been slipping down the league table and really needs some new players if it is to improve.*

draw

RELATED WORDS

- *see also* **paint, picture, design, art/culture, pattern**

1 to draw a picture, pattern, line etc

- draw
- sketch
- doodle
- scribble
- trace

draw /drɔː/ [v I/T] to make a picture, pattern, line etc using a pen or pencil: *What are you drawing?* | *She can draw really well.* | *I'm good at drawing animals, but I can't draw people.* | **draw a picture of sb/sth** *Mike was sitting outside, drawing a picture of the trees at the bottom of the garden.* | **draw a line/circle/square etc** *Someone had drawn a line under my name.*

sketch /sketʃ/ [v I/T] to make a quick, simple drawing of a person, place etc, without many details: *Maggie grabbed a piece of paper and quickly sketched the bird before it flew away.* | *He sat by the river, sketching.*

doodle /ˈduːdl/ [v I] to draw shapes, lines, or patterns without really thinking about what you are doing, for example when you are thinking about something else or when you feel bored: *I always doodle while I'm talking on the phone.* | **+ on** *Simon was lying on the floor, doodling on a sheet of paper.*

scribble /ˈskrɪbəl/ [v I/T] to quickly draw lines and shapes without making any particular pattern, shape, or picture – use this especially about what small children do before they have learnt to draw or write: *Katie can't draw a real picture yet but she enjoys scribbling with crayons.* | **scribble all over/on sth** *Oh no! One of the kids has scribbled all over my report!* — **scribble** [n C]

trace /treɪs/ [v T] to copy a picture by putting transparent paper over it and then drawing along the lines of the picture: *The children traced the map of France and then wrote in the names of the places they had visited.*

2 something that you draw

- drawing
- doodle
- sketch
- scribble

drawing /'drɔːɪŋ/ [n C] a picture that you draw with a pen or pencil: *Leonardo da Vinci's drawings show an immensely inventive and inquiring mind.* | **do a drawing of sth** *I did a drawing of the church.*

sketch /sketʃ/ [n C] a quick, simple drawing that does not show many details **+ of** *She opened her folder and took out a sketch of her mother.* | **do/draw a sketch** *Phil drew a sketch to show us what the new school would look like.* | **rough sketch** (=a sketch that is not very exact or detailed) *I've done a rough sketch of how to get to the church.*

doodle /'duːdl/ [n C usually plural] a drawing of shapes, lines, or patterns that you do when you are thinking about something else or when you are bored: *By the end of the lecture the back of my book was covered in little doodles.*

scribble /'skrɪbəl/ [n C usually plural] a drawing of lines, shapes etc that look untidy and have no particular pattern, shape, or picture – use this especially about what small children do before they can draw or write properly: *How am I going to get all these scribbles off the wallpaper?*

dream

RELATED WORDS

- something that you want very much *see* **want(4,8)**
- imagine something pleasant *see* **imagine (2)**
- *see also* **sleep, wake up/get up**

1 a dream

- dream
- daydream
- nightmare
- reverie

dream /driːm/ [n C] a series of events that you seem to experience while you are asleep: *I never remember my dreams when I wake up.* | *When she woke, she found that it was all a dream.* | **+ about** *None of my dreams are about work.* | **have a dream** *I had a strange dream last night – you and I were in some sort of tropical forest.* | **bad dream** (=an unpleasant or frightening dream) *The events of the past few days seemed like a bad dream.* | **recurring dream** (=a dream that you keep having) *When I was younger, I had recurring dreams in which I was constantly pursued by soldiers.*

nightmare /'naɪtmeəʳ/ [n C] a very unpleasant and frightening dream: *He woke from a nightmare, trembling with fear.* | **have a nightmare** *Years after the accident I still have nightmares about it.*

daydream /'deɪdriːm/ [n C] a series of pleasant thoughts that you experience when you are awake, so that you do not notice what is happening around you: *Ingrid was brought out of her daydream by a shout from her mother.* | **in a daydream** *Neil seemed lost in a daydream, and didn't hear what I said.*

reverie /'revəri/ [n C/U] a state of imagining or thinking about pleasant things, that is like dreaming: *The doorbell rang, shaking me from my reverie.* | *Sometimes he would drift off into reverie, and gaze out of the window for hours.*

2 to have a dream

- have a dream
- daydream
- dream

have a dream /ˌhæv ə 'driːm/ [v phrase] *He had a dream in which he was running through the forest, being chased by a bear.* | **+ about** *I keep having the same dream about trying to get across a deep river.*

dream /driːm/ [v I/T] PAST TENSE AND PAST PARTICIPLE **dreamt** /dremt/ British OR **dreamed** American to have a **dream** or have dreams: *Do animals dream?* | *I hoped that someone would wake me up, that I had only been dreaming.* | **+ about/of** *I dreamt about you last night.* | *Stephanie often dreams of long sea journeys.* | **+ (that)** *I dreamed that I was lying on a beach in the Caribbean.* | *Last night I dreamt I went to Manderley again.*

daydream /'deɪdriːm/ [v I] to think pleasant thoughts when you are awake and when you should be paying attention to something else: *At school, he was always being told to 'stop daydreaming'.* | **+ about** *Colin began to daydream about what he would do if he won the lottery.*

drink

RELATED WORDS

- *see also* **thirsty, drunk, eat, taste, delicious**

1 to drink something

- drink
- quench your thirst
- have
- slurp
- take
- lap/lap up
- sip

drink /drɪŋk/ [v I/T] to take liquid into your mouth and swallow it: *Drink your coffee before it gets cold.* | *Is this water safe to drink?* | *He was drinking vodka straight from the bottle.* | *She picked up the cup and began to drink thirstily.*

have /hæv/ [v T not in passive] to **have** a drink of something: *We always have tea in the morning.* | *Robin was driving, so he just had a glass of orange juice.* | *We had a couple of beers and talked about old times.* | **have a drink (of sth)** *Can I have a drink of water, please?* | *Sit down and have a drink.*

take /teɪk/ [v T] to drink a small amount or a single mouthful of something: *He was very weak, but managed to take a mouthful of water from my bottle.* | *Jody took another sip of wine.*

sip /sɪp/ [v I/T] to drink something slowly, in very small amounts: *Sue sat at the bar sipping a Martini.* | *She sipped water all the way through the interview.* —**sip** [n C] *Can I just try a sip, to see if I like it.* | **+ of** *Jenny cautiously took a couple of sips of the liquid.*

quench your thirst /ˌkwentʃ jɔːʳ 'θɜːʳst/ [v phrase] written to drink something in order to stop being thirsty: *We stopped in a small village to quench our thirst and refuel the jeep.* —**thirst-quenching** [adj] *Ice-cool, thirst-quenching beers on sale here!*

slurp /slɜːʳp/ [v I/T] to drink liquid while making a noisy sucking sound: *He bent his face over the steaming bowl and slurped loudly.* | *The old man started to slurp his beer.*

lap/lap up /læp, ˌlæp 'ʌp/ [v T/phr v T] if an animal **laps** or **laps up** a liquid, it drinks it with quick movements of its tongue: *We spotted the cubs lap-*

ping water from a stream in the forest. | **lap sth up** *The tiny creature started to lap the milk up eagerly.* | **lap up sth** *A large dog lapped up the gravy that had spilt on the floor.*

2 to drink very quickly

- gulp/gulp down
- swig

gulp/gulp down /gʌlp, ˌgʌlp 'daʊn/ [v T/phr v T] to drink something quickly, taking large mouthfuls: *I gulped down my tea and dashed out of the house.* | *Rodney gulped his wine nervously.* | **gulp sth down** *Manny gulped his beer down and followed me.* —**gulp** [n C] *She finished the drink in a single gulp.*

swig /swɪg/ [v I/T] to drink something quickly, especially from a bottle, taking large mouthfuls: *The soldiers took it in turns to swig vodka.* | *Jack swigged the last of his tea and got up to leave.* | **+ from** *The old man wandered along, swigging occasionally from a whiskey bottle.* —**swig** [n C] *He took a swig of brandy from a small metal flask.*

3 to drink all of something

- drink up
- knock back
- down
- drain
- polish off

drink up /ˌdrɪŋk 'ʌp/ [phr v I/T] *Come on, drink up. I want to go home.* | **drink sth up** *Come on, drink your milk up.* | **drink up sth** *She drank up her brandy and signalled to the waiter to bring another.*

knock back /ˌnɒk 'bæk‖ˌnɑːk-/ [phr v T] informal to quickly drink large quantities of an alcoholic drink **knock back sth** *Two bored-looking businessmen were knocking back glasses of schnapps.* | *He knocked back the last of the bourbon, then lit his last cigarette.* | **knock sth back** *When his whisky arrived, he knocked it back in a single gulp.*

down /daʊn/ [v T] to drink all of a drink fairly quickly, especially an alcoholic drink: *The servant brought a glass of water, which I downed in a single mouthful.* | *After downing a whole bottle of tequila, she swallowed several dozen sleeping tablets.*

drain /dreɪn/ [v T] **drain a bottle/glass/cup etc** to drink everything that is in a bottle etc, including the last few drops: *Jim drained his glass then offered to buy everyone another one.* | *Hurriedly draining her cup, she reached for her purse.*

polish off /ˌpɒlɪʃ 'ɒf‖ˌpɑː-/ [phr v T] to finish something that you enjoy drinking, especially quickly or before someone else can drink it **polish sth off** *I think I'll polish that last beer off before George gets in.* | **polish off sth** *Did you polish off all the wine last night?*

4 something that you drink

- drink
- something to drink
- beverage

drink /drɪŋk/ [n C] something that you drink: *'Would you like a drink?' 'Yes, I'll have a lemonade please.'* | *a nice cool drink* | *She tipped her drink over his head and stormed out.* | **a drink of sth** *Give the children a drink of milk and something to eat.* | **food and drink(s)** *You can bring your own food and drink to the picnic.* | *It's under $10 for lunch and drinks at the Ivy Bush.*

something to drink /ˌsʌmθɪŋ tə 'drɪŋk/ [n phrase] especially spoken a drink: *I'm really thirsty. Let's stop for something to drink.* | *Can I get you something to drink?*

beverage /'bevərɪdʒ/ [n C] written a word meaning something that you drink – used especially in restaurants and by people in the food and drinks business: *Non-alcoholic beverages will be on sale in the foyer.*

5 drinks that contain gas or do not contain gas

- carbonated
- sparkling
- still
- flat

carbonated ALSO **fizzy** British /'kɑːʳbəneɪtɪ̈d, 'fɪzi/ [adj] **carbonated** or **fizzy** drinks have gas in them: *fizzy lemonade* | *I don't like fizzy drinks much.* | *I'd like a glass of carbonated mineral water, please.*

sparkling /'spɑːʳklɪŋ/ [adj] **sparkling** water or wine has gas in it: *a sweet, sparkling wine* | *a bottle of sparkling mineral water*

still British **/uncarbonated** American /stɪl, ʌn'kɑːʳbəneɪtɪ̈d/ [adj] **still** or **uncarbonated** drinks, especially water, do not have gas in them: *Would you like that still or sparkling, madam?*

flat /flæt/ [adj] if a drink that should contain gas is **flat**, there is no gas left in and it is not pleasant to drink: *I don't know why some English people prefer flat beer.* | **go flat** *That champagne must have gone flat by now.*

6 drinks that contain alcohol

- alcohol
- drink
- liquor
- booze

alcohol /'ælkəhɒl‖-hɔːl/ [n U] drinks that contain **alcohol** – used especially in rules and warnings about alcoholic drinks: *We're not allowed to serve alcohol to people under 18.* | *low-alcohol wines* (=not containing a lot of alcohol) | *He doesn't drink alcohol or smoke.* | *She could smell alcohol on his breath.* —**alcoholic** /ˌælkə'hɒlɪk◂‖-'hɔː-/ [adj] containing alcohol: *You can't sell alcoholic drinks unless you have a licence.*

drink /drɪŋk/ [n C/U] a **drink** that contains alcohol. In British English, **drink** can also be an uncountable noun, meaning alcoholic drinks in general: *'Can I get you a drink?' 'I'll have a gin and tonic, please.'* | *After a few drinks, Rick began to feel better.* | *They've always got loads of drink in the house.* | **go (out) for a drink** (=go somewhere such as a bar to drink alcohol) *Do you feel like going out for a drink tonight?* | *They all went for a drink together after the film.*

liquor /'lɪkəʳ/ [n U] American drinks that contain alcohol, especially strong alcoholic drinks: *The man was holding a bottle of liquor in one hand and a cigarette in the other.* | *a liquor store* | **hard liquor** (=strong alcoholic drinks) *He got used to drinking hard liquor at an early age.*

booze /buːz/ [n U] informal alcoholic drinks: *The doctor told Jimmy to stay off the booze for a while.* | *The prince is known for his love of women, gambling, and booze.*

7 drinks that do not contain alcohol

- soft drink
- non-alcoholic
- low-alcohol

soft drink /ˌsɒft 'drɪŋk‖ˌsɔːft-/ [n C] a cold drink,

such as fruit juice, which does not contain alcohol: *Do you want a beer, or would you prefer a soft drink?* | *a soft drinks manufacturer*

non-alcoholic /ˌnɒn ælkəˈhɒlɪk◂‖-ˈhɔː-/ [adj] a **non-alcoholic** drink does not contain alcohol – use this especially about drinks that are normally alcoholic: *We got some non-alcoholic wine for Lisa because she doesn't drink.* | *non-alcoholic beer*

low-alcohol /ˌləʊ ˈælkəhɒl◂‖-hɔːl◂/ [adj] **low-alcohol** beer or wine contains very little alcohol: *There is a growing market for low-alcohol beers.* | *There's quite a variety of low-alcohol drinks available now.*

8 to drink alcohol

- have a drink
- drink

have a drink /hæv ə ˈdrɪŋk/ [v phrase] to drink something alcoholic: *We had a few drinks to celebrate.* | *You can't have a drink if you're driving Mary home.* | *Cliff wanted us all to go and have a drink after the show.*

drink /drɪŋk/ [v I] to **drink** alcohol, especially regularly: *He's been depressed, and drinking a lot more recently.* | *Did you drink a lot over Christmas?* | *It was obvious that Jimmy had been drinking.* | **drink and drive** (=drink alcohol before driving your car) *I think people who drink and drive should be banned from driving permanently.* | **drink heavily** (=drink a lot) *It was clear that Malone had been drinking heavily.* | *She's been drinking more heavily recently.* | **drink like a fish** informal (=regularly) *My uncle drinks like a fish, and has done for years.* —**drinking** [n U] *His family life is beginning to be affected by his drinking.* | *We went out drinking last night.*

9 someone who never drinks alcohol

- don't drink/doesn't drink
- teetotaller
- not touch

don't drink/doesn't drink /ˌdəʊnt ˈdrɪŋk, ˌdʌzənt ˈdrɪŋk/ [v I] *I'll have orange juice please. I don't drink.* | *Ben is the only one of my friends who doesn't drink.*

teetotaller British **/teetotaler** American /tiː-ˈtəʊtələʳ/ [n C] someone who never drinks anything containing alcohol, often for religious or moral reasons: *He's recently become a strict teetotaller.* | *We're not teetotalers, but we recommend sensible drinking limits.* —**teetotal** /ˌtiːˈtəʊtl◂/ [adj] *He's a teetotal, non-smoking vegetarian yoga teacher.*

not touch /nɒt ˈtʌtʃ/ [v phrase not in progressive] to not drink even a little of anything alcoholic, usually because you have decided to stop drinking alcohol: *I used to drink a bottle of whisky a week but I never touch it these days.* | **not touch a drop** *'Rick hasn't touched a drop in years,' said Mrs Marsden proudly.*

10 to stop drinking alcoholic drinks

- give up drinking/stop drinking
- be on the wagon

give up drinking/stop drinking /ˌgɪv ʌp ˈdrɪŋkɪŋ, ˌstɒp ˈdrɪŋkɪŋ‖-ˌstɑːp-/ [v phrase] to stop drinking anything alcoholic, especially because it is becoming a problem: *Sam's been told that unless he stops drinking, he could be dead within a year.* | *I didn't realize I had a problem until I tried to give up drinking but couldn't.*

be on the wagon /biː ɒn ðə ˈwægən/ [v phrase] informal no longer drink alcohol, or to have stopped drinking alcohol for a short time: *Do you want a beer, Harry, or are you still on the wagon?* | *I thought you were on the wagon!*

11 what people say when they drink alcohol together

- cheers
- here's to ...

cheers /tʃɪəʳz/ spoken say this as you raise your glass when you are drinking with someone: *They all clinked glasses and said 'Cheers!'*

here's to ... /ˈhɪəʳz tuː/ spoken say this when you want other people to drink with you to wish someone happiness or success: *Here's to Clare and Malcolm! May they have a long and happy marriage!*

drive

RELATED WORDS

- *see also* **travel, road/path, accident, get on or off a bus, train etc**

1 to drive a car, train, or other vehicle

- drive
- driving
- ride
- steer
- be behind the wheel/at the wheel
- be at the controls
- joyriding

drive /draɪv/ [v I/T] to **drive** a car, bus, train etc: *Drive carefully – the roads are very icy.* | *They drive on the left in the UK.* | **learn to drive** *I'm learning to drive. In fact, I take my test next week.* | **drive a car/bus/truck etc** *We need someone to drive the school bus.* | *'What car do you drive?' 'A Fiat Brava.'* | *Driving a Rolls Royce into a swimming pool was one of the most dangerous stunts Crawford had to perform.*

driving /ˈdraɪvɪŋ/ [n U] the activity of **driving** a car or other road vehicle: *Driving in central London is pretty unpleasant.* | **dangerous/reckless/bad/careless driving** *She was arrested for dangerous driving.* | **driving lesson** *I got driving lessons for my 18th birthday.* | **driving offence** *The man was stopped by police for an alleged driving offence.*

ride /raɪd/ [v I/T] to drive a vehicle with two wheels, for example a bicycle or motorcycle: *I ride a bicycle to work every day.* | *Riding a motorcycle is safer than riding a scooter.* | *After you've been riding a bike all day, you're really glad to reach your campsite.*

steer /stɪəʳ/ [v I/T] to control the direction that a vehicle is going in by turning the wheel: *Even the children had a go at steering the boat.* | *Steer slightly to the right as you enter the bend.* | **steering wheel** (=the part of a car that you turn to change direction) *You can adjust the height of the steering wheel.*

be behind the wheel/at the wheel /biː bɪˌhaɪnd ðə ˈwiːl, ət ðə ˈwiːl/ [v phrase] to be the person who is driving a car, bus etc: *An old Pontiac pulled up, with a young Mexican man at the wheel.* | *Seymour was glad to be behind the wheel again after his two-year ban.*

be at the controls /biː ət ðə kənˈtrəʊlz/ [v phrase] to be the person who is driving or controlling a large vehicle such as a plane: *The King himself was* *at the controls when his helicopter landed.* | *The power boat, with Don at the controls, swept around the bay.* | **+ of** *When I was a child I used to imagine myself at the controls of a fighter plane.*

joyriding /ˈdʒɔɪraɪdɪŋ/ [n U] the activity of driving a stolen car very fast and dangerously for excitement: *Joyriding is the most common type of crime among boys under 18.* | **go joyriding** *A group of youths went joyriding in stolen cars, causing three accidents before the police caught them.* —**joyrider** [n C] *Joyriders are becoming a serious problem in the inner cities.*

2 to go somewhere in a car or other vehicle

- drive
- by car/bike etc
- cycle
- go for a drive
- go for a ride

drive /draɪv/ [v I] to go somewhere in a car: *'How do you get to work?' 'I drive.'* | **+ to/from/into/through etc** *We drove to the airport, but couldn't find anywhere to park.* | *They drove home in silence.* | **+ off/away** (=leave somewhere in a car) *She drove off without saying goodbye.* | **drive 50 kilometres/100 miles etc** *Was the restaurant worth driving 50 miles for?* —**drive** [n C] a journey in a car: *It's a two-hour drive to Hamilton from here.*

by car/bike etc /baɪ ˈkɑːʳ/ [adv] to go somewhere in a car, on a bicycle etc – use this especially when you are comparing different methods of travelling: *One group went by car and the others took a taxi.* | *I can get to work in about 20 minutes by bike.* | *I went by boat the first time I went to Tahiti.*

cycle /ˈsaɪkəl/ [v I] to go somewhere on a bicycle: *Cycling isn't only good for the environment – it's a great form of exercise too.* | **+ to/from/through etc** *I usually cycle through the park to get to school.* | **cycle 50 kilometres/10 miles etc** *It took about 20 minutes for her to cycle the 5 miles to her home.*

go for a drive ALSO **take a drive** American /ˌgəʊ fər ə ˈdraɪv, ˌteɪk ə ˈdraɪv/ [v phrase] to go somewhere in a car, especially for enjoyment: *We'll go for a drive after lunch and see if we can find this park.* | *We took a drive down to the ocean.*

go for a ride ALSO **take a ride** American /ˌgəʊ fər ə ˈraɪd, ˌteɪk ə ˈraɪd/ [v phrase] to go somewhere in a car or on a bicycle especially for enjoyment: *When you've finished your work, shall we take a ride?* | *It was unusual that someone should be taking a ride on a stormy night like this.*

3 when you take someone somewhere in a car etc

- take/drive sb somewhere
- lift
- carpool

take/drive sb somewhere /ˈteɪk, ˈdraɪv (sb) sʌmweəʳ/ [v phrase] *Could you take me to the station, please?* | *The President was driven away in a big black limousine.* | **drive sb home/back** *He always expected his girlfriend to drive him home at the end of the night.*

lift /lɪft/ especially British **/ride** /ˈraɪd/ American [n C] if you give someone a **lift** or a **ride**, you take them somewhere in your car: *Never accept lifts from strangers.* | **give sb a lift/ride** *Pedro stopped to give me a lift.* | **+ to** *Do you need a ride to school?* | **a lift/ride home** *I accepted her offer of a lift home.*

carpool /ˈkɑːʳpuːl/ [n C] a group of car owners who agree to drive everyone in the group to work on different days, so that only one car is used at a time: *I've been in a carpool with the same three women for ten years.* | **carpool lane** (=part of a road that only people who share cars can use) *a proposal to open up a new network of carpool lanes* —**carpool** [v I] American *We should encourage more people to carpool.* —**carpooling** [n U] the practice of driving everyone in a group to work on different days: *Despite efforts to promote carpooling, 70% of all commuters drive to work alone.*

4 someone who drives a car, train etc

- driver
- motorist
- motorcyclist
- rider
- cyclist

driver /ˈdraɪvəʳ/ [n C] someone who regularly drives or is driving a car, train, etc: *Many drivers suffer from backache.* | *The car was almost torn in half in the crash but amazingly the driver was unhurt.* | *Car drivers now pay more than ever for fuel.* | *Some women drivers are concerned about their personal safety.* | **driver's seat/door/side etc** *He got into the driver's seat and started the engine.*

motorist /ˈməʊtərɪ̣st/ [n C] someone who drives a car – use this especially to talk about the costs of driving or the laws that affect driving: *Motorists are developing the habit of buying a new car every other year.* | *Safety needs to be improved, not only for motorists but also for pedestrians.* | **the motorist** (=all motorists) *The countryside is being destroyed for the benefit of the motorist.*

motorcyclist /ˈməʊtəʳˌsaɪklɪ̣st/ [n C] someone who rides a motorcycle: *Three motorcyclists dressed in black rode past.* | *The President's car arrived with its escort of police motorcyclists.*

rider /ˈraɪdəʳ/ [n C] someone who rides a bicycle or motorcycle: *The rider wasn't badly hurt, but his bicycle was all smashed- up.* | *The leading rider in this year's motorcycle championship is Wayne Rainey.*

cyclist /ˈsaɪklɪ̣st/ [n C] especially British someone who rides a bicycle: *Most cyclists in London have their bikes stolen eventually.* | *Cyclists are demanding more and safer cycle paths in the city.* | **a keen cyclist** *Heather, a keen cyclist, is hoping to raise £10,000 by riding her bike across Europe.*

5 someone whose job it is to drive a car, train, etc

- driver
- chauffeur

driver /ˈdraɪvəʳ/ [n C] *The limousine pulled up outside the church and the driver got out.* | **truck/lorry etc driver** *A lot of truck drivers stop at this restaurant because it's open all night.* | **cab/taxi/bus etc driver** *Harry asked the cab driver to stop outside the store for a couple of minutes while he bought a paper.*

chauffeur /ˈʃəʊfəʳ, ʃəʊˈfɜːʳ/ [n C] someone whose job is to drive a car for someone else: *I'll learn to drive and be some film star's chauffeur.* | *a chauffeur-driven Rolls Royce*

drug

RELATED WORDS

- someone who often takes illegal drugs and cannot stop *see* **addicted**
- *see also* **medical treatment, unconscious, smoking**

1 legal drugs used to treat illnesses, pain etc

- **drug**

drug /drʌg/ [n C] a chemical substance used for treating illnesses or to stop people feeling pain: *Morphine is a very powerful drug.* | *The drugs I take for hay fever make me feel very drowsy.* | *One disadvantage of the drug is that it is very expensive.* | **drug company/maker** *The New Jersey drug maker will begin marketing its new anti-balding medication in April.* | **prescription drug** (=a drug that you can only get with the permission of a doctor) *The article says that Ware tried to commit suicide by combining prescription drugs and alcohol.*

2 an illegal drug

- **drug**
- **narcotics**
- **illegal substance**

drug /drʌg/ [n C] an illegal substance that people take for pleasure, or because they cannot stop taking it: *Thompson was arrested for selling drugs in the fall of 1992.* | *a new campaign to warn teens about the danger of drugs* | **illegal drugs** *The agency's efforts to reduce the flow of illegal drugs into the United States has largely failed.* | **hard drug** (=a powerful illegal drug that can make you very ill or kill you) *Dewey said that legalizing marijuana would encourage people to experiment with hard drugs such as cocaine or heroin.* | **soft drug** (=an illegal drug that is less dangerous than a hard drug) *Seven out of ten teenagers said they had tried soft drugs.* | **drug abuse** (=the use of illegal drugs, especially in a way that is very bad for your health) *She has been treated for alcohol and drug abuse.* | **drug addiction** *The organization tries to deal with the widespread problems of drug addiction and alcoholism.*

narcotics /nɑːʳˈkɒtɪks‖-ˈkɑː-/ [n plural] especially American illegal drugs – used especially in news reports and in legal contexts: *Laws governing the sale of narcotics vary from state to state.* | *Police are investigating a recent spate of narcotics offenses in Miami.*

illegal substance /ɪˌliːgəl ˈsʌbstəns/ [n C usually plural] an illegal drug of any type – used especially in legal and official contexts: *Tucker was charged with the possession of an illegal substance.* | *Drug tests taken 24 hours after the crash showed no trace of illegal substances in either of the drivers.*

3 to take a drug

- **take**
- **be on**
- **use**
- **do drugs**
- **inject**
- **come down**

take /teɪk/ [v T] to put a drug into your body – use this about legal or illegal drugs: *I can't take penicillin; I'm allergic to it.* | *She took a couple of aspirins before going to bed.* | **take drugs** (=use illegal drugs) *Sinclair admitted that she had taken drugs several years before.* | *He neither drinks nor takes drugs.*

be on /biː ˈɒn/ [v T] to take a drug regularly, especially because you cannot stop taking it **be on heroin/cocaine/speed etc** *How long has she been on heroin?* | **be on drugs** (=regularly take illegal drugs) *Our 28-year-old son is on drugs.*

use /juːz/ [v T] to regularly take illegal drugs: *She first started using drugs when she was thirteen.* | *Morgan stopped using drugs and alcohol six years ago when he entered a long-term treatment program.* —**drug user** /ˈdrʌg ˌjuːzəʳ/ [n C] *Herring, 55, is a former drug user who started the foundation in San José in 1980.*

do drugs /duː ˈdrʌgz/ [v phrase] informal to take illegal drugs, especially regularly: *I did a lot of drugs when I was at university.* | *Davis said he quit doing drugs when he became a parent.*

inject /ɪnˈdʒekt/ [v I/T] to put a drug into someone's body using a needle: *Most heroin users prefer to inject the drug.* | *A drug that is injected reaches the brain faster than if it is smoked or sniffed.* | *Two years ago I was both smoking and injecting.*

come down /ˌkʌm ˈdaʊn/ [phr v I] to stop being affected by a powerful drug that you have taken: *I think I'm starting to come down. Let's smoke another joint.*

4 when someone's mind has been affected by illegal drugs

- **high**
- **stoned**
- **wired**
- **be out of your head/be out of it**

high /haɪ/ [adj not before noun] feeling very excited, happy, and full of energy because of the effects of a drug: *God, I got so high last night.* | **high on drugs/ecstasy/LSD etc** *Newton died at age 47 while high on crack cocaine.* | **as high as a kite** (=very high) *She was as high as a kite.*

stoned /stəʊnd/ [adj not before noun] informal feeling very relaxed or happy and not able to behave normally because of the effect of a drug: *The guy playing lead guitar was completely stoned.* | **get stoned** *'What did you guys end up doing last night?' 'Not much. We got stoned and watched TV – that's about it.'*

wired /waɪəʳd/ [adj not before noun] informal feeling very excited and nervous as a result of taking a drug: *I was still way too wired to go to bed.*

be out of your head/be out of it /biː ˌaʊt əv jɔːʳ ˈhed, biː ˈaʊt əv ɪt/ [v phrase] informal to not know what you are doing or what is happening around you, because you have taken an illegal drug: *Can Sally go back in your room and lie down? She's really out of it.* | *They had taken some mushrooms and were completely out of their heads by the time they got to the party.*

5 to take too much of a drug

- **take an overdose**
- **overdose on**
- **OD**

take an overdose /ˌteɪk ən ˈəʊvəʳdəʊs/ [v phrase] to take a dangerously large amount of a drug, usually deliberately: *Can someone call an ambulance? I think he's taken an overdose.* | **+ of** *The woman apparently tried to commit suicide by taking an overdose of a prescription drug.* —**overdose** [n C] *Mari-*

lyn Monroe was 36 when she died of an overdose of sleeping pills in August 1962.

overdose on /ˈəʊvəʳdəʊs ɒn/ [v phrase] to take a dangerously large amount of a particular drug, usually by accident: *He overdosed on heroin.*

OD /ˌəʊ ˈdiː/ [v I] spoken informal to take a dangerously large amount of a drug, usually deliberately: *'How did she die?' 'She OD'd.'* | **+ on** *Brody OD'd on a mixture of cocaine and heroin.*

6 to stop taking drugs

- come off
- be in rehab

come off /kʌm ˈɒf/ [phr v T] especially British to gradually stop taking a drug that you have been taking for a long time – use this about legal or illegal drugs: *It was ten years before she managed to come off morphine.*

be in rehab /biː ɪn ˈriːhæb/ [v phrase] if someone is **in rehab**, they are getting treatment to help them stop taking drugs or drinking too much alcohol: *He's been in rehab for over three months.* | *Danny was recently arrested for cocaine, but he's kept his job and he's in rehab.* —**rehab** [adj only before noun] *a rehab center*

7 buying and selling drugs

- drug trafficking
- drug dealer/dealer
- pusher/drug pusher

drug trafficking /ˈdrʌg ˌtræfɪkɪŋ/ [n U] the illegal activity of taking drugs from one country to another and selling them: *He's wanted in the US on charges of drug trafficking.* | *The government's efforts to limit drug trafficking have mostly failed.* —**drug trafficker** [n C] someone who takes drugs illegally from one country to another and sells them: *a suspected drug trafficker*

drug dealer/dealer /ˈdrʌg ˌdiːləʳ, ˈdiːləʳ/ [n C] someone who sells illegal drugs, especially to someone that they know: *He was accused of purchasing cocaine from an Indianapolis drug dealer.* | *Police arrested a dealer yesterday who was selling marijuana to 12-year-olds.*

pusher/drug pusher /ˈpʊʃəʳ, ˈdrʌg ˌpʊʃəʳ/ [n C] someone who sells illegal drugs, especially in order to encourage people to start taking drugs: *A pusher approached us, asking if we wanted to buy any crack.* | *Being a university city, Oxford is an obvious target for the pushers.*

drunk

RELATED WORDS

- *see also* **drink, drug, unconscious**

1 drunk

- drunk
- pissed
- have had too much to drink/have had one too many
- drunken
- intoxicated
- have been drinking

drunk /drʌŋk/ [adj] someone who is **drunk** has **drunk** too much alcohol and cannot think clearly or behave sensibly: *She was so drunk she could hardly stand up.* | *Gary was too drunk to remember what had happened that night.* | **get drunk** (=become drunk) *I just hope they don't get too drunk and start fighting.*

pissed /pɪst/ [adj not before noun] British spoken drunk – many people consider this to be an impolite word: *Every time she goes to a party she gets pissed.* | *Don't listen to him – he's pissed.*

have had too much to drink/have had one too many /həv hæd ˌtuː mʌtʃ tə ˈdrɪŋk, həv hæd ˌwʌn tuː ˈmeni/ [v phrase] to have drunk too much alcohol so that you feel very drunk or sick: *I'd better take Tanya home – she's had too much to drink.* | *He usually has one too many and starts making a fool of himself.*

drunken /ˈdrʌŋkən/ [adj only before noun] written a **drunken** person is drunk and their **drunken** behaviour shows that they are drunk: *A couple of drunken sailors were arguing with a policeman outside the bar.* | *The place was full of noise and drunken shouting.* | **drunken brawl** (=a fight between people who are drunk) *Many of their beer parties ended in a drunken brawl.* | **in a drunken stupor** (=almost unconscious as a result of being drunk) *We found him lying by the roadside in a drunken stupor.* —**drunkenness** [n U] *She hated Morel because of his constant drunkenness and his violent temper.*

intoxicated /ɪnˈtɒksɪ̈keɪtɪ̈d‖-ˈtɑːk-/ [adj usually not before noun] formal drunk – use this especially in legal, official, and medical contexts: *Jensen was found guilty of driving while intoxicated.* | *Our policy is not to serve alcohol to anyone who is already intoxicated.* —**intoxication** /ɪnˌtɒksɪ̈ˈkeɪʃən‖-ˌtɑːk-/ [n U] formal *He's already been arrested twice for public intoxication.*

have been drinking /həv biːn ˈdrɪŋkɪŋ‖-bɪn-/ [v phrase] use this about someone who you know has been drinking alcohol because they are behaving as if they were drunk or because you can smell alcohol on their breath: *Have you guys been drinking all day?* | *She answered the door in her bathrobe and I could tell she'd been drinking.*

2 a little drunk

- tipsy
- mellow
- merry
- buzzed

tipsy /ˈtɪpsi/ [adj] *After the second glass of wine I was feeling a little tipsy.* | *We went out to dinner, got a little tipsy, and ended up at my place.*

mellow /ˈmeləʊ/ [adj] pleasantly friendly and ready to talk because you are slightly drunk: *She wasn't drunk yet, but she was feeling nice and mellow and happy.* | *She poured him another glass of brandy to keep him in a mellow mood.*

merry /ˈmeri/ [adj not before noun] British feeling happy and friendly because you are slightly drunk: *We were all very merry by the time the party broke up.* | *Some of the officers got quite merry celebrating our recent victory.*

buzzed /bʌzd/ [adj not before noun] American spoken feeling slightly drunk: *This stuff is strong – I'm already a little buzzed.*

3 very drunk

- blind drunk
- roaring drunk
- smashed/plastered/trashed
- bombed/loaded/wasted
- paralytic/legless

blind drunk /ˌblaɪnd ˈdrʌŋk/ [adj not before noun] *Every Saturday night he came home blind drunk.* | *Don't give him anything more to drink. He's already blind drunk.*

roaring drunk /ˌrɔːrɪŋ ˈdrʌŋk/ [adj not before noun] very drunk and very noisy: *They were all roaring drunk and kept singing bawdy songs.*

smashed/plastered/trashed /ˈsmæʃt, ˈplɑːstəʳd‖ˈplæs-, træʃt/ [adj not before noun] spoken informal very drunk: *We went to a nightclub in town last night and got absolutely plastered.* | *She came home completely smashed at about 2 o'clock this morning.* | *Man, you were so trashed. How much did you have to drink?*

bombed/loaded/wasted /bɒmd‖bɑːmd, ˈləʊdɪ̈d, ˈweɪstɪ̈d/ [adj not before noun] American spoken very drunk: *Did you see Kim at Rob's party? She was totally wasted.* | *He's loaded. Somebody better call him a cab.* | *I was so bombed, I can't even remember half of what I did.*

paralytic/legless /ˌpærəˈlɪtɪk◂, ˈlegləs/ [adj not before noun] British spoken extremely drunk: *Don't give Dave any more to drink – he's already legless.* | *The day I got my exam results we went out and got absolutely paralytic.*

4 to get drunk

- get drunk
- drown your sorrows
- hit the bottle

get drunk /ˌget ˈdrʌŋk/ [v phrase] *Their idea of a good time is to go out and get drunk.* | *I can't remember the last time I got drunk.* | **+ on** *She sometimes gets drunk on two glasses of wine.*

drown your sorrows /ˌdraʊn jɔːʳ ˈsɒrəʊz‖-ˈsɑː-/ [v phrase] to drink a lot of alcohol with the purpose of getting drunk, in order to forget your problems: *After his girlfriend left he spent the evening drowning his sorrows in a local bar.* | **+ in** *You can't just sit around day after day drowning your sorrows in whiskey.*

hit the bottle /ˌhɪt ðə ˈbɒtl‖-ˈbɑːtl/ [v phrase] informal to start to drink a lot of alcohol regularly, especially in order to forget your problems: *When his wife died he hit the bottle again.* | *My sister's been hitting the bottle a lot lately and her work is starting to suffer.*

5 to drive while you are drunk

- drink and drive
- drink driving
- be over the limit
- under the influence
- DUI/DWI

drink and drive /ˌdrɪŋk ən ˈdraɪv/ [v phrase] an expression meaning to drive after you have been drinking alcohol, used especially in warnings about the dangers of doing this: *Val's not the kind of person who would drink and drive.* | *I don't care if people who drink and drive kill themselves – what worries me is that they might kill someone else.*

drink driving British **/drunk/drunken driving** American /ˌdrɪŋk ˈdraɪvɪŋ, ˌdrʌŋk, ˌdrʌŋkən ˈdraɪvɪŋ/ [n U] the act of driving while under the influence of alcohol: *Drink driving causes over 800 deaths a year on the roads.* | *He was convicted of drunk driving and had his license suspended.* —**drunk/drunken driver** /ˌdrʌŋk, ˌdrʌŋkən ˈdraɪvəʳ/ [n C] someone who drives while they are drunk: *Her husband was nearly killed by a drunk driver.*

be over the limit /biː ˌəʊvəʳ ðə ˈlɪmɪ̈t/ [v phrase] especially British to have drunk more alcohol than is legal and safe for driving: *He was caught driving over the limit and had to pay a large fine.* | *In a large proportion of fatal accidents it is found that one driver is over the limit.*

under the influence /ˌʌndəʳ ði ˈɪnfluəns/ [adv] formal if someone drives **under the influence**, they drive when they are drunk – used especially by the police and in news reports: *Driving under the influence is a very serious offense.* | *Witnesses claimed that Jones was under the influence of alcohol at the time of the accident.*

DUI/DWI /ˌdiː juː ˈaɪ, ˌdiː dʌbəlju: ˈaɪ/ American the crime of driving while you are drunk: *It was his first DUI offense.* | *I've never had a DUI or any kind of drugs record.*

6 someone who is often drunk

- alcoholic
- drunk
- drinker
- have a drink problem
- lush
- drunkard

alcoholic /ˌælkəˈhɒlɪk◂‖-ˈhɔː-/ [n C] someone who drinks too much alcohol and cannot stop: *Many alcoholics do not realize that they have a problem until it is too late.* | *I usually have a drink or two after work, but I don't think I'm an alcoholic.*

drunk /drʌŋk/ [n C] someone who is **drunk** or who often gets **drunk** – use this especially about someone you see in a public place such as a street or a bar: *A couple of drunks were passed out on the sidewalk.* | *I don't like to take the bus at night. It's full of drunks and crazy people.*

drinker /ˈdrɪŋkəʳ/ [n C] someone who often drinks a lot of alcohol: *He had the watery eyes and swollen nose of a drinker.* | **heavy drinker** (=someone who regularly drinks a lot of alcohol) *Paul and Jane were both heavy drinkers and spent most of their time in the local bar.* | **hard drinker** (=someone who regularly drinks a lot of alcohol) *He quickly earned the reputation as a hard drinker and hell-raiser.*

have a drink problem British **/have a drinking problem** American /hæv ə ˈdrɪŋk ˌprɒbləm, hæv ə ˈdrɪŋkɪŋ ˌprɒbləm‖ -ˌprɑːb-/ [v phrase not in progressive] to be unable to stop the habit of drinking too much alcohol, so that it has a bad effect on your life: *My sister has a drink problem but she won't admit it.* | *From everything you tell me, it sounds as if your husband may have a drinking problem.*

lush /lʌʃ/ [n C] American informal someone who is often drunk – often used humorously: *You'll see her sitting at the bar all day. She's a real lush.* | *What are you drinking, you big lush?*

drunkard /ˈdrʌŋkəʳd/ [n C] someone who is drunk very often – used especially in literature: *They were all drunkards, but Arthur was the worst of them all.* | *Unfortunately she had married an incurable drunkard.*

7 an occasion when people get drunk

- booze-up
- drunken
- boozy

booze-up /ˈbuːz ʌp/ [n C] British informal a party or other occasion where people drink a lot of alcohol: *We usually get together with our friends for a booze-up at Christmas.*

drunken /ˈdrʌŋkən/ [adj only before noun] **drunken party/night/orgy etc** where people drink a lot of alcohol: *The two met at a drunken party in college.*

boozy /ˈbuːzi/ [adj only before noun] especially British, informal a **boozy** occasion is one on which people drink a lot of alcohol: *She's going for a boozy night out with her friends.*

8 when you feel ill the day after you have been drinking

- hangover

hangover /ˈhæŋəʊvəʳ/ [n C] the feeling you have the morning after you have drunk too much alcohol, when your head hurts and you feel sick: *Kevin woke up the next day with a terrible hangover.* | **have/have got a hangover** *Could you try to keep the noise down? I've got a hangover.* | *After all you had to drink last night, I'm surprised you don't have a hangover.*

9 not drunk

- sober
- sober up

sober /ˈsəʊbəʳ/ [adj not before noun] not drunk: *I don't think I've ever seen Bill sober.* | *I'll drive you home – I think I'm the only one here that's sober.*

sober up /ˌsəʊbər ˈʌp/ [phr v I] if someone who has been drunk **sobers up**, they gradually become less drunk until they are not drunk at all: *He didn't sober up till he'd had a cup of strong coffee.* | *Give her a little time to sober up.*

10 able to drink a lot of alcohol

- can hold your drink

can hold your drink British **/can hold your liquor/alcohol** American /kən ˌhəʊld jɔːʳ ˈdrɪŋk, kən ˌhəʊld jɔːʳ ˈlɪkəʳ, ˈælkəhɒl‖-hɔːl/ [v phrase] if you **can hold your drink**, you are able to drink a large amount of alcohol without getting drunk: *He can really hold his drink. I've seen him drink seven whiskies and still play a good game of billiards.* | *Debra giggled again – she'd never held her liquor very well.*

dry

RELATED WORDS

opposite: **wet**

- *see also* **weather, water, thirsty**

1 not wet

- dry

dry /draɪ/ [adj] *You should change into some dry clothes.* | *Keep the apples stored in a cool, dry place.* | *The wood was dry and it burned easily.* | *Can you check to see if the laundry's dry?* | **bone dry/dry as a bone** (=completely dry) *I forgot to water the plants and the soil has gone bone dry.*

2 when there is not much rain

- dry
- drought
- dusty
- arid
- parched

dry /draɪ/ [adj] if the weather is **dry**, there is not much rain: *It was a very dry summer.* | *The weather tomorrow will be sunny and dry.* | *Tunisia has a hot, dry climate.* | *In Arizona, the air is often extremely dry.*

drought /draʊt/ [n C/U] a long period when there is little or no rain, so that people and animals do not have enough water and plants die: *Central Africa is suffering one of the worst droughts of the century.* | *A severe drought has caused most of the corn crop to fail.*

dusty /ˈdʌsti/ [adj] a **dusty** road, town, track etc is dry and covered with dust, because the weather is hot and there is not much rain: *The road to Bangalore was hot and dusty.* | *Samandari lives in a small dusty village on the edge of the desert.*

arid /ˈærɪ̈d/ [adj] land that is **arid** is extremely dry and produces low quality crops because there is very little rain: *Much of Namibia is arid country and only fit for raising goats.* | *The region is an arid wasteland.*

parched /pɑːʳtʃt/ [adj] ground that is **parched** is completely dry because the weather has been very hot and there has been no rain for a long time: *The earth was so parched that there were huge cracks in it.* | *The parched yellow landscape of Death Valley stretched out for miles in front of us.*

3 to become dry

- dry
- dry out
- dry up
- shrivel up

dry /draɪ/ [v I] to become dry: *This should only take a few minutes to dry.* | *Wet clothes dry quickly on a sunny day.* | *Leave the dishes on the draining board to dry.* | **hang sth out to dry** (=hang clothes outside, so that they are dried by the sun or wind) *I like to hang the sheets out to dry. It gives them a fresh smell.*

dry out /ˌdraɪ ˈaʊt/ [phr v I] to become completely dry – use this about something that dries naturally in the air, sun etc: *Hang your towel over the chair to dry it out.* | *Cover the pastry with a damp cloth to prevent it from drying out.* | *Farmers will have to wait for fields to dry out before they can harvest their soybeans.*

dry up /ˌdraɪ ˈʌp/ [phr v I] if a river or lake etc **dries up**, it becomes completely dry because there has not been any rain: *Last summer the river dried up and you could walk right across it.* | *The town's reservoir has nearly dried up and many homes are without water.* | *Lake Elizabeth will not dry up, but its water level could drop.*

shrivel up /ˌʃrɪvəl ˈʌp/ [v I] if a plant or a fruit **shrivels up** it becomes smaller and deep lines form on its surface, because it has become very dry: *There was so little rain that most of the crops shrivelled up and died.*

4 to make something dry or make yourself dry

- dry
- dry off
- dry yourself off

dry /draɪ/ [v T] to make something dry: *Could you wait ten minutes while I dry my hair?* | *We built a fire to get ourselves warm and dry our clothes.*

dry yourself off /ˌdraɪ jɔːrself ˈɒf/ [v phrase] to use a towel to make yourself dry, for example after a bath or a swim: *Evan got out of the pool and dried himself off.* | *She began to dry herself off, talking to me over her shoulder.*

dry off /ˌdraɪ ˈɒf/ [phr v T] to dry the surface of something **dry off sth** *He dried off his bicycle seat with a towel.* | **dry sth off** *Clean the plastic cover with a damp sponge, then dry it off with a soft cloth.*

5 something that has had liquid removed from it

- dried

dried /draɪd/ [adj] **dried** food or plants have been allowed to become dry, or have had the liquid taken out of them in order to preserve them: *Dried herbs are convenient but I think fresh ones have more flavour.* | *My friend Minu loves dried flowers.* | *Add four tablespoons of dried milk to a pint of cold water, and stir until dissolved.*

during

RELATED WORDS

- at the same time *see* **time**

1 during

- during
- in
- within
- through
- all through/throughout
- over
- in the course of/during the course of
- by day/by night

during /ˈdjʊərɪŋ‖ˈdʊ-/ [prep] at one point in a period of time, or through the whole of a period of time: *Terry's work has improved a lot during the last three months.* | *Henry died during the night.* | *During the summer we spend a lot more time out of doors.* | *At some time during the weekend someone broke into the building.* | *This place was an air-raid shelter during the war.*

in /ɪn/ [prep] between the beginning and end of a period of time: *The long vacation is in August.* | *In the last six years, Carol has moved three times.* | *In 1982 Paget was living in Geneva.* | *I always feel drowsy early in the morning.*

within /wɪðˈɪn‖wɪðˈɪn, wɪθˈɪn/ [prep] during a period of time or before the end of a period – use this to emphasize that it is a short or limited period of time: *There have been five serious accidents within the last few days.* | *If we do not hear from you within 14 days, we will contact our solicitors.*

through /θruː/ [prep] during the whole of a period of time, continuing until the end: *The party continued through the night until dawn.* | *We'll have to see how he copes through the next couple of months.*

all through/throughout /ɔːl ˈθruː, θruːˈaʊt/ [prep] through – use this to emphasize that something continues from the beginning to the end of a long period: *It's closed all through the winter, and opens again in April.* | *Throughout her career she has worked hard and maintained high standards.*

over /ˈəʊvəʳ/ [prep] during a particular period of time: *She's been a great help to me over the past year.* | *They plan to redecorate their house over the Christmas period.* | *They met in 1962 and wrote each other several letters over the next few years.*

in the course of/during the course of /ɪn ðə ˈkɔːʳs ɒv, ˌdjʊərɪŋ ðə ˈkɔːʳs ɒv‖ˌdʊərɪŋ-/ [prep] formal during a process or particular period of time: *In the course of a few years, Lambert built up a highly successful export business.* | *We expect to see some important political developments during the course of the next week or two.*

by day/by night /baɪ ˈdeɪ, baɪ ˈnaɪt/ [adv] if you do something **by day** or **by night** you do it during the day or night: *By day they relied on the sun for direction, and by night they followed the stars.* | *By day he works at a construction company, but by night he's a bartender.* | *They attacked by night, hoping to surprise their enemy.*

2 happening during the time that something else happens

- while
- meanwhile
- in the meantime

while /waɪl/ [conjunction] during the same period of time that something is happening: *I bought a magazine while I was waiting for the train.* | *I'll just make a phone call while you finish the dishes.*

meanwhile /ˈmiːnwaɪl/ [adv] while something else is happening: *They're still working on our bedroom. Meanwhile, we're sleeping out back in tents.* | *People keep complaining about the service at hospitals, and meanwhile more and more nurses are losing their jobs.*

in the meantime /ɪn ðə ˈmiːntaɪm/ [adv] during the period of time between now and a future event or between two events in the past: *We'll meet again on April 21st, and in the meantime I'll collect some more information for you.* | *I came back to work after just a month, but in the meantime, all my things had been moved to a smaller office.*

Ee

each other

ways of saying that two or more people do something to each other

- each other/one another
- exchange
- mutual
- reciprocal
- two-way
- trade

each other/one another /iːtʃ ˈʌðəʳ, wʌn əˈnʌðəʳ/ [pron] use this to say that each of two or more people do the same thing to the other person or people, or have the same feelings towards them: *The twins looked at one another and giggled.* | *You can tell that George and Hannah like each other, can't you?* | *By the end of the holiday we were all beginning to annoy each other.* | **each ... the other** *When Kerry and Sam met again two years later, each was equally pleased to see the other.* | *The brothers started to quarrel, each accusing the other of being responsible for the mistake.*

exchange /ɪksˈtʃeɪndʒ/ [v T] **exchange looks/glances/insults etc** look at each other, insult each other etc: *Danny and his lawyer exchanged uneasy looks.* | *As Sally approached wearing her new dress, the others exchanged glances and tried not to laugh.* | *The two men were exchanging insults and accusing each other of mismanagement.*

mutual /ˈmjuːtʃuəl/ [adj] **mutual respect/hatred/support etc** respecting, hating etc each other equally: *A good marriage should be based on mutual love and respect.* | *The meeting broke up in an atmosphere of mutual irritation.* | **the feeling is mutual** (=both people feel the same) *He was very much in love with Hilda and the feeling appeared to be mutual.* —**mutually** [adv] *After weeks of discussion the two sides have reached a mutually acceptable agreement* (=one that both sides can accept).

reciprocal /rɪˈsɪprəkəl/ [adj only before noun] formal **reciprocal agreement/arrangement/visit etc** an agreement etc in which one person or country does or gives the same thing to another, as they have officially agreed to do: *The French students come to our school in November, and we then make a reciprocal visit to theirs.* | *In countries which do not have reciprocal health agreements with your own, you will need to take out health insurance.* | **on a reciprocal basis** (=with the understanding that both people, countries etc will do the same) *Senior officials from both countries make regular visits on a reciprocal basis.*

two-way /ˈtuː weɪ/ [adj only before noun] **two-way communication/exchange/contact etc** when two people or groups have an equal chance to express their opinions and are listening to or helping each other: *It was impossible to have a two-way conversation with Derek, because he never stopped talking.* | *Managers who want two-way communication with their staff must be prepared to listen to what they have to say.*

trade /treɪd/ [v T] **trade insults/threats/blows etc** to insult, threaten etc each other in an argument or fight, especially in public: *The prime minister and his chancellor exchanged insults on the front pages of the national newspapers last week.* | *The debating chamber is often simply used as a platform for trading verbal abuse.*

early

RELATED WORDS

opposite: —— **late**

▸ *see also* **before, beginning, first, soon**

1 before the usual or expected time

- ▸ **early**
- ▸ **ahead of time**
- ▸ **ahead of schedule**
- ▸ **in good time**
- ▸ **with time to spare**

early /ˈɜːʳli/ [adj/adv] if something happens **early**, it happens before the usual time or the most suitable time; if someone is **early**, they arrive before the time they are expected to: *I finished work early today.* | *If you plant the seeds too early they won't grow.* | *After an early lunch, we started the meeting at one o'clock.* | *Everyone was deeply shocked by his early death at the age of forty-five.* | **be early (for sth)** (=arrive early) *You're early – I wasn't expecting you till seven.* | *I'm sorry, I'm a bit early for my appointment.* | **seven months/three days etc early** (=seven months/three days etc earlier than expected) *Our first child was born eight weeks early.*

ahead of time /əˌhed əv ˈtaɪm/ [adv] earlier than the time when you have arranged or expect to do something: *We will try to complete the building ahead of time.* | *Visas must be obtained ahead of time, and it may take several weeks to get them in order.* | *You can always prepare the salad ahead of time and refrigerate it.*

ahead of schedule /əˌhed əv ˈʃedjuːl‖-ˈskedʒʊl/ [adv] earlier than the officially agreed time: *Due to the economy's strong recovery, Mexico will repay ahead of schedule the last installment of a $13.5 billion loan.* | **six months/two weeks/a year etc ahead of schedule** *The renovation of the school has just been completed three months ahead of schedule.*

in good time /ɪn ˌgʊd ˈtaɪm/ [adv] early enough, so that you do not have to rush, or so that you have time to get ready: *I like to get all my Christmas presents bought and sent in good time.* | **+ for** *It is important to arrive in good time for your interview.*

with time to spare /wɪð ˌtaɪm tə ˈspeəʳ/ [adv] if you arrive somewhere or finish something **with time to spare**, you arrive or finish before the time when you have to arrive or finish: *In spite of the bad traffic, we reached London with plenty of time to spare.* | **with ten minutes/half an hour etc to spare** *I finished the test with just two minutes to spare* (=two minutes before the end).

2 too early

- ▸ **too early**
- ▸ **too soon**
- ▸ **untimely**
- ▸ **premature**
- ▸ **jump the gun**
- ▸ **it's early days**

too early /tuː ˈɜːʳli/ [adv] *Too much success too early can cause you to grow overconfident.* | **+ to do sth** *It's still too early to tell if the treatment is going to be effective.* | **+ for** *There aren't any raspberries in the stores yet. It's too early for them.* | **far/way too early** (=much too early) *We arrived far too early and had to wait outside for an hour.*

too soon /tuː ˈsuːn/ [adv] happening too early after something else, or doing something much earlier than you should: *I don't think you should go back to work too soon after having the baby.* | **+ to do sth** *It's too soon to say what effect the merger will have on the company's 1500 employees* | **+ for** *I knew it was too soon for any likely resolution of the problem.* | **far/way too soon** (=much too soon) *You can't get married next week! That's far too soon.* | *Lendl hit the ball way too soon.*

untimely /ʌnˈtaɪmli/ [adj usually before noun] written **untimely death/end** much earlier than usual or expected, so that people are surprised by it: *Before his untimely death in 1991, Freddie Mercury was a brilliant singer and performer.* | **meet an untimely end** (=die early) *His grandfather had met an untimely end as the result of too much whisky.*

premature /ˈpremətʃəʳ, -tʃʊəʳ, ˌpreməˈtʃʊəʳ‖ˌpriːməˈtʃʊər◂/ [adj] happening before the normal or natural time **premature death/birth/ageing** *Alcoholism is one of the major causes of premature death.* | *It has been proved that sunbathing causes premature ageing of the skin.* | **premature baby** (=a baby that is born before the normal time) *Her baby was premature and weighed only 2kg.* —**prematurely** [adv] *Hannah's hair went prematurely grey when she was only 24.*

jump the gun /ˌdʒʌmp ðə ˈgʌn/ [v phrase] informal to do or say something too early, before you know what is going to happen next, so that you risk making a mistake: *I think it would be jumping the gun to sign the agreement at this stage.* | *Surely it's jumping the gun to buy the ring before you've even asked her to marry you?*

it's early days /ɪts ˌɜːʳli ˈdeɪz/ British if you say **it's early days**, you mean that it is still too early in a process or event to know what will happen: *It's still early days, but all the signs are that the operation has* *been a success.* | **it's early days yet** *'It looks like Liverpool are going to win the championship.' 'Oh I don't know. It's early days yet.'*

3 early in the morning

- early
- first thing
- at the crack of dawn
- bright and early

early /ˈɜːʳli/ [adj/adv] **early** in the morning: *I always wake up early when the weather's warm.* | *Early the next day, Jamie received a call from his mother.* | **make an early start** (=start an activity or journey early in the morning) *If we make an early start we should avoid the worst of the traffic.* | **in the early hours** (=during the first hours of the day, when most people are asleep) *The robbery took place in the early hours of Sunday morning.* | **early bird** (=someone who gets up early in the morning) *Jack was always an early bird; he did a lot of his work before dawn.*

first thing /ˌfɜːʳst ˈθɪŋ/ [adv] especially spoken if you do something **first thing**, you do it immediately after you get up or as soon as you start work: *I'll telephone her first thing, I promise.* | **first thing tomorrow/Wednesday/in the morning etc** *Leave it on my desk and I'll deal with it first thing tomorrow.*

at the crack of dawn /ət ðə ˌkræk əv ˈdɔːn/ [adv] informal use this to emphasize that something happens very early in the morning, when most people are still in bed: *My Dad used to get up at the crack of dawn every Sunday to go fishing.*

bright and early /ˌbraɪt ənd ˈɜːʳli/ [adv] if you get up **bright and early**, you get up very early in the morning, especially because there is something that you want to do: *Geoffrey was up bright and early on Saturday morning, and had everything packed before breakfast.* | *Waking bright and early, I went for a swim and took the dog for a walk.*

earn

RELATED WORDS

- *see also* **pay, work, job, spend, money, profit**

1 to get money for your work

- earn
- make
- get
- be paid/get paid
- be on
- gross

earn /ɜːʳn/ [v T] to be paid a particular amount of money for your work, especially over a period of time – **earn** is more formal than **make** or **get**: *At the peak of his career, Rogers was earning more than seven million dollars a year.* | *It's not uncommon nowadays for women to earn more than their husbands.* | **earn £15,000 per year/$15 an hour etc** *Alan earns $30,000 a year.*

make /meɪk/ [v T] to be paid a particular amount of money for your work, especially a lot of money: *Ella makes a lot of money.* | *How much to you think he makes?* | **make $500 a week/£25,000 per year etc** *Some models make millions of dollars a year.*

get /get/ [v T] informal to earn a particular amount of money every hour, week etc **get £10 per hour/$350 dollars a week etc** *My sister gets $22 an hour at her new job.* | *How much are you getting a week?* | **get $25/£15 etc for doing sth** *I got £5 for washing Nick's car.*

be paid/get paid /biː ˈpeɪd, get ˈpeɪd/ [v phrase] to earn money when you work for an employer and not for yourself **be paid £50/$200 etc** *City maintenance workers are paid around $250 a week.* | *We get paid every two weeks.*

be on /biː ˈɒn / [v phrase] British informal to earn a particular amount of money each year: *Claire's on a very good salary.* | *In January, I'll be on £23,350.* | *How much were you on in your last job?*

gross /grəʊs/ [v T] especially American to earn a particular amount of money each year, before tax has been taken away – use this especially to talk about companies or businesses making money: *Jack grosses $58,000 a year, but he has to pay taxes and health insurance out of that.* | *Walmax, a California superstore, grosses more than eight million dollars annually.* | **+ over/more than** *If you gross over $100,000, you should consult a good tax accountant.*

2 to earn an amount of money after tax etc has been taken away

- take home
- net
- clear

take home /ˌteɪk ˈhəʊm/ [v phrase] to earn a certain amount of money, after tax etc has been taken away from your pay: *Lidia takes home only about $150 a week.* | *Did you know that plumbers can take home as much as $40,000 a year?* — **take-home pay** /ˈteɪk həʊm ˌpeɪ/ [n phrase] the pay remaining after tax has been taken away: *My dad's take-home pay was around £50 a week when he first started out.*

net /net/ [v T] to earn a particular amount of money as a profit after tax has been paid – use this especially to talk about companies or businesses making money: *For the first three months of 1990, Starcorp netted $547 million.* | *Donna got a raise in February, but she's still only netting $19,000 a year.*

clear /klɪəʳ/ [v T] to earn a particular amount of money after tax etc has been taken away, especially in a job where you work for yourself: *Sandra cleared £50,000 last year.* | *A good lawyer can clear $250,000 a year easily.*

3 to earn enough money to pay for the things that you need

- earn/make a living
- support yourself/your family
- earn your keep

earn/make a living /ˌɜːʳn, ˌmeɪk ə ˈlɪvɪŋ/ [v phrase] to earn enough money to pay for the things that you or your family need **earn/make a living by doing sth** *As an engineer, you can earn a living anywhere in the world.* | *It's difficult to make a living as a writer.* | *Nordstrom earned his living by teaching violin.* | **earn a good/decent living** (=earn more than enough) *A programmer earns a pretty decent living.*

support yourself/your family /səˌpɔːʳt jɔːʳˈself, jɔːʳ ˈfæməli/ [v phrase] to pay for the things that you or your family need out of the money that you earn, especially when you are the only person in the family who is earning money: *After his father died, Peter had to quit school and support the family.* | *Hank supported himself for years by doing construction work.* | *I have no idea how he's supporting himself.*

earn your keep /ˌɜːʳn jɔːʳ ˈkiːp/ [v phrase] to earn enough money to pay for your food and other needs, especially when someone has been supporting you until now: *It's time you got a job and started earning your keep.*

4 to earn a lot of money

- make a fortune
- earn/make good money
- highly-paid/well-paid
- rake it in
- be overpaid

make a fortune ALSO **make a bomb** British /ˌmeɪk ə ˈfɔːʳtʃən, ˌmeɪk ə ˈbɒm‖-ˈbɑːm/ [v phrase] to earn a very large amount of money: *The person who invented Post-It notes must have made a fortune.* | **make a fortune (by) doing sth** *Roger makes a fortune buying and selling real estate.* | **make your fortune** (=become rich) *Jules made his fortune in the liquor business.*

earn/make good money /ˌɜːʳn, ˌmeɪk gʊd ˈmʌni/ [v phrase] to be paid a lot of money by the person or company you work for, or a lot of money from your own business: *Milos earns good money as a foreman.* | *Dan is making good money now, but for years we really struggled.*

highly-paid/well-paid /ˌhaɪli ˈpeɪd◂, ˌwel ˈpeɪd◂/ [adj] earning a lot of money: *Most engineers are very well-paid.* | *Dr. Singh is one of the most highly-paid surgeons in Britain.*

rake it in /ˈreɪk ɪt ɪn/ [v phrase] informal to earn a lot of money quickly: *Athletes rake it in these days.* | **sb must be raking it in** *What a car! Jasper must be raking it in.*

be overpaid /biː ˌəʊvəʳˈpeɪd/ [v phrase] to be paid more money for your work than you should be paid: *In my opinion, lawyers are overpaid and underworked.*

5 words for describing a job that you earn a lot from

- well-paid/highly paid
- pay well
- lucrative

well-paid/highly paid /ˌwel ˈpeɪd◂, ˌhaɪli ˈpeɪd◂/ [adj] *There are not enough women in well-paid, responsible jobs.*

pay well /ˌpeɪ ˈwel/ [v phrase] if work or a job **pays well**, the workers are paid a lot of money for doing it: *Boring jobs often pay well.* | *Modelling usually pays very well but the work is not very regular.*

lucrative /ˈluːkrətɪv/ [adj] work or a particular type of business that is **lucrative** earns a lot of money for the people who do it: *Transferred from Barcelona to Naples, Maradona signed a highly lucrative three-year contract.* | *An increase in consumer demand has made sports shoe retailing a lucrative business.*

6 not earning much money

- low-paid
- be badly-paid
- get peanuts/work for peanuts
- not pay well
- slave labour

low-paid /ˌləʊ ˈpeɪd◂/ [adj usually before noun] **low-paid** workers do not earn much money for their work. **Low-paid** work is work that people do not get paid much money for: *a low-paid mechanic* | **low-paid job** *The jobs centre seems to list only low-paid temporary jobs.*

be badly-paid /biː ˌbædli ˈpeɪd/ [v phrase] if someone is badly paid, they do not earn much money for their work – use this when you think someone should earn much more money: *A lot of people think that nurses are badly-paid.*

get peanuts/work for peanuts /get ˈpiːnʌts, ˌwɜːʳk fəʳ ˈpiːnʌts/ [v phrase] informal to be paid very little money: *Jobs are so hard to find that people are willing to work for peanuts.*

not pay well /nɒt ˈpeɪ wel/ [v phrase] if work or a job **does not pay well**, the people who do it do not receive much money, especially considering the amount of work they have to do, the amount of knowledge they need to have etc: *It used to be accepted that teaching didn't pay very well, but things have changed a lot.*

slave labour British **/slave labor** American /ˌsleɪv ˈleɪbəʳ/ [n U] if you say that what someone is paid is **slave labour**, you mean that they are paid very little money even though they have to work extremely hard, and this is unfair: *£50 a week? That's slave labour!* | *Working for them is slave labor – they only pay five bucks an hour.*

7 pay that is too low

- low pay
- a pittance
- peanuts

low pay /ˌləʊ ˈpeɪ/ [n U] *Low pay is one of the disadvantages of working in publishing.* | *These jobs are unattractive because of low pay and inadequate training.*

a pittance /ə ˈpɪtəns/ [n singular] an unfairly small amount of money paid to someone for their work: *In the 19th century, children worked long hours in factories for a pittance.* | *Compared to what some people earn, my salary is a pittance.*

peanuts /ˈpiːnʌts/ [n plural] informal an unfairly small amount of money paid to someone for their work: *'It's not fair,' she said. 'He pays me peanuts, and he expects me to work late as well.'*

8 the money that you earn

- pay
- salary
- wage
- income
- earnings
- fee

pay /peɪ/ [n U] the money that you earn by working: *'What's the pay?' 'About $10 an hour.'* | *The worst thing about being a nurse is the low pay.* | **sick pay** (=pay that you get when you are ill and cannot work) *Joe's been receiving sick pay since the accident.*

salary /ˈsæləri/ [n C] the money that someone is paid every month by their employer, especially someone who is in a profession, such as a teacher or a manager **a salary of £100,000/$10,000 etc** *The university provides a salary of $3,000 a month plus benefits.* | *Johansen reportedly earns an annual salary of $4 million.* | **be on a salary** (=be earning a salary) *I joined the company in 1985, on a salary of $22,000 a year.* | **a good/high salary** *Our daughter makes a good salary, but she really works for it.*

wage ALSO **wages** /weɪdʒ, ˈweɪdʒɪ̵z/ [n singular/n plural] the money that someone is paid every week by their employer, especially someone who works in a factory, shop etc: *Elvina earns an hourly wage of $11.* | *Without qualifications it's nearly impossible to get a job with decent wages.* | **minimum wage** (=the lowest amount of money that can legally be paid per hour to a worker) *Most of the new jobs in the area only pay the minimum wage.*

income /ˈɪŋkʌm, ˈɪn-/ [n C/U] all the money that you receive regularly, for work or for any other reason: *Braund's annual income is just over $40,000.* | *The amount of tax you have to pay depends on your income.* | **be on a low income** (=receive very little money) *Families on low incomes are eligible for state benefits.* | **+ from** *Richard has a comfortable income from his salary and his investments.*

earnings /ˈɜːʳnɪŋz/ [n plural] the total amount of money you earn from any work you do: *Most single mothers spend a large part of their earnings on childcare.* | *The average worker's earnings have not kept up with inflation.*

fee /fiː/ [n C] money paid to a professional person such as a doctor or lawyer for a piece of work: *Dr Allison charges a fee of $90 for a consultation.* | *Last year IBM paid $12 million in legal fees to a single law firm.* | *The fee for the standard structural survey is £175.*

9 money that you earn in addition to your usual pay

- overtime
- bonus
- commission
- tip
- fringe benefits
- perk

overtime /ˈəʊvəʳtaɪm/ [n U] money that is paid to someone for additional hours that they have worked: *Last week Alex earned $300, including ten hours of overtime.* | *Teachers never get paid overtime.*

bonus /ˈbəʊnəs/ [n C] money added to someone's pay, especially as a reward for good work: *Liz earned a £1000 bonus for being the best salesperson of the year.* | *The management offered a large bonus to those workers who stayed to the end of the contract.*

commission /kəˈmɪʃən/ [n U] money earned by someone whose job is to sell things, based on the value of what they sell: *His basic salary is low, but he gets 20% commission on everything he sells.* | **be on commission** (=receive commission every time you sell something) *Most insurance agents are on commission, and some earn a lot of money.*

tip /tɪp/ [n C] a small amount of money in addition to the ordinary payment, which you give to someone such as a waiter or taxi-driver: *The boy carried my suitcases up to my room and then stood waiting for a tip.* | *We finished our lunch and left a tip on the table for the waiter.* —**tip** [v T] give someone a tip: *She tipped the taxi-driver.*

fringe benefits /ˌfrɪndʒ ˈbenɪ̇fɪts/ [n plural] the additional things such as holiday pay, free food, or free health insurance, which a worker receives in addition to their pay: *The salary isn't very high, but fringe benefits include free health insurance and a company car.*

perk /pɜːʳk/ [n C] something valuable or enjoyable that you get from your work apart from pay, especially something you get unofficially: *One of the perks of working for a fashion designer is that you get to wear lots of nice clothes.* | *It's not always fun being an air hostess, but the perks are good.* | *The professors regard foreign travel as a perk, and they go to all the international conferences.*

10 someone who earns money

- the breadwinner
- wage-earner

the breadwinner /ðə ˈbredwɪnəʳ/ [n singular] the person in a family who earns most of the money that the family needs: *Many people still expect the man to be the breadwinner.*

wage-earner /ˈweɪdʒ ˌɜːʳnəʳ/ [n C] someone who has a job and earns wages: *Jim is the family's main wage earner.* | *Families without wage-earners must seek relief from government social security programs.*

11 not earn anything for work that you do

- unpaid
- voluntary

unpaid /ˌʌnˈpeɪd◂/ [adj] an **unpaid** worker does not get paid for the work that he or she does; **unpaid** work is work that you do but do not get paid for: *Amir worked as an unpaid informant for the internal security service* | *Coburn works 20 to 25 unpaid hours a week for the organization.*

voluntary ALSO **volunteer** American /ˈvɒləntəri‖ˈvɑːlənteri, ˌvɒlənˈtɪəʳ‖ˌvɑː-/ [adj] **voluntary** work is done by people who want to do it, without expecting to be paid for it: *Since retiring Martha has been doing voluntary work for the Red Cross.* | **voluntary worker/helper etc** *Most charities depend on the services of volunteer workers.*

easy

RELATED WORDS

opposite: ———— **difficult**

▸ *see also* **simple, complicated**

1 easy to do, use, or understand

- easy
- not difficult/hard
- simple
- straightforward
- user-friendly

easy /ˈiːzi/ [adj] not difficult to do, use, or understand: *The questions were really easy.* | *It's an easy journey – we just drive to the station, then take the direct train to Paris.* | *Our new computer system should make the work a lot easier.* | **easy to read/use/learn etc** *All the instructions are in large print to make them easy to read.* | **it is easy to do sth** *It is easy to see why she didn't marry him.* | **easy for sb to do sth** *Was it easy for you to find a job?* | **find sth easy/find it easy to do sth** *Susan's always found school work easy.* | *He doesn't find it easy to talk about his personal feelings.* —**easily** [adv] *E-mail enables people to communicate easily and inexpensively with each other on a regular basis.*

not difficult/hard /nɒt ˈdɪfɪkəlt, ˈhɑːʳd/ [adj] easy **not hard** is more informal than **not difficult**: *'Did you make this pizza yourself?' 'Yes, it's not difficult.'* | **it's not difficult to do sth** *It's not difficult to see why she's unhappy all the time.* | *The reason for the problem is not hard to find.*

simple /ˈsɪmpəl/ [adj] easy to understand or do because it is not complicated – use this about things like explanations or instructions, or about machines or systems: *She drew us a simple map so that we wouldn't get lost.* | *I like this recipe because it's so simple.* | **be simple to use/make/prepare etc** *The new photocopier is much simpler to use than the one we had before.*

straightforward /ˌstreɪtˈfɔːʳwəʳd◂/ [adj] easy to understand and easy to do, so someone should not have any problems – use this especially about a method or process: *It is very straightforward – you just type the file name, then press 'Enter'.* | *There's a straightforward calculation for working out how much tax you have to pay.*

user-friendly /ˌjuːzəʳ ˈfrendli◂/ [adj] spoken easy to use or understand – use this especially about computers or written information: *We are trying to develop software that is more user-friendly.* | *The booklet is intended to be a user-friendly guide to pension schemes.*

2 to be very easy to do

- **be a cinch/a piece of cake**
- **be a doddle**
- **be child's play**
- **there's nothing to it**
- **anyone can do sth**
- **be a pushover**
- **like taking candy from a baby**

be a cinch/a piece of cake /biː ə ˈsɪntʃ, ə ˌpiːs əv ˈkeɪk/ [v phrase] spoken informal *If you can learn Japanese, learning French should be a piece of cake.* | *Don't worry about the exam. It'll be a cinch!* | **be a cinch to learn/drive/use etc** *My new car's a cinch to drive, compared to the old one.*

be a doddle British informal **/be a snap/a breeze** American informal /biː ə ˈdɒdl‖-ˈdɑːdl, biː ə ˈsnæp, ə ˈbriːz/ [v phrase] *'You passed your driving test?' 'Yes – it was a doddle!'* | *Managing a team of businessmen is a snap compared to a team of twelve-year-olds.* | **a doddle/snap/breeze to do sth** *It's a snap to make this sauce if you have a few basic ingredients in the cupboard.*

be child's play /biː ˈtʃaɪldz pleɪ/ [v phrase] use this when saying that something is surprisingly easy for someone to do, or that something is very easy compared to something else: *Persuading people to give away their money is child's play when you know how.* | *Life today is child's play compared to how it was 100 years ago.*

there's nothing to it /ðeəʳz ˌnʌθɪŋ ˈtuː ɪt/ spoken say this when it is easy for you to do something, even though other people think it is difficult: *'Oh, great! You've fixed the washing machine.' 'Yeah, there was nothing to it, really.'*

anyone can do sth /ˈeniwʌn kən duː (sth)/ use this to say that something is so easy that everyone could do it: *Anyone can learn to cook.* | *I don't know why you think you're so clever – anyone can do that.* | *Politicians insist that there are plenty of jobs and that anyone can get one if they really try.*

be a pushover /biː ə ˈpʊʃəʊvəʳ/ [v phrase] someone who **is a pushover** is very easy to defeat, persuade etc: *The kids all think their new English teacher's a real pushover.* | **be no pushover** (=not be easy to defeat, persuade etc) *Colonel Moore was no pushover. He wouldn't let anyone tell him what to do.*

like taking candy from a baby /laɪk teɪkɪŋ ˌkændi frəm ə ˈbeɪbi/ spoken extremely easy: *Sally smiled to herself. It was easy to attract men. Like taking candy from a baby.*

3 an easy job or way of life

- **easy**
- **cushy**
- **coast**

easy /ˈiːzi/ [adj] *He has lived an easy life in college for the last few years.* | *Being a teacher isn't easy.* | **have it easy** (=have a very easy life) *Lawyers really have it easy – lots of money for very little work.*

cushy /ˈkʊʃi/ [adj] informal very easy – use this especially when you think that someone has an extremely easy job or life and you are jealous of them or do not approve of them: *Eventually he got a cushy job as a newspaper correspondent in Madrid.* | *Being a stewardess is not a cushy lifestyle – it's very hard work.* | **a cushy number** British (=a cushy job or way of life) *What a cushy number, living rent-free in return for taking the dog out once a day!*

coast /kəʊst/ [v I] to not have to make much effort in your job or school work because the work is easy for you to do: *If you feel that you've been coasting in your job, perhaps it's time for a change.* | **coast along** *Laura was a bright kid and she could coast along at school without too much effort.*

4 when someone can do something easily

- **easily**
- **effortless**
- **come naturally**
- **can do sth with your eyes shut/ standing on your head/ blindfolded**
- **think nothing of**
- **breeze/breeze through**

easily /ˈiːzəli/ [adv] *A burglar could easily climb in through that window.* | *When I went to college, I made friends very easily.* | **easily recognized/damaged/done etc** (=when something can be recognized, damaged etc easily) *These plates are easily damaged, so please be careful with them.* | *Lizzie and Jane are so alike that they're easily mistaken for each other.*

effortless /ˈefəʳtləs/ [adj] something that is **effortless** is done in a way that makes it seem very easy, although in fact it is very skilful: *The way she dances makes it seem so effortless.* | *Other musicians were amazed by Parker's effortless improvisational skill.* —**effortlessly** [adv] *Greg's a great cook, and he does it all so effortlessly!*

come naturally /ˌkʌm ˈnætʃərəli/ [v phrase not in progressive] if something **comes naturally** to you, you seem to have a natural ability to do it, so that you can do it well without having to try hard: *Her family are all actors, so it probably comes naturally.* | **+ to** *Speaking in public seems to come quite naturally to her.* | *Looking after babies doesn't come naturally to all new mothers.*

can do sth with your eyes shut/standing on your head/blindfolded /kən duː (sth) wɪð jɔːr ˈaɪz ˌʃʌt, ˌstændɪŋ ɒn jɔːʳ ˈhed, ˈblaɪndˌfəʊldəd/ [v phrase] to be able to do something very easily, especially because you have done it so many times before: *He's a really good mechanic – he could change a tyre standing on his head.* | *Don't worry. I've driven to the Bronx so many times, I could do it standing on my head.*

think nothing of /ˌθɪŋk ˈnʌθɪŋ ɒv/ [v phrase not in progressive] to think that something is a very easy and normal thing to do, although most people think it is difficult and unusual: *Emily thinks nothing of preparing a meal for twenty people.* | *Before cars were invented, people thought nothing of walking six miles to work.*

breeze/breeze through /briːz, ˈbriːz θruː/ [v T/phr v T] informal to win or succeed in something easily: *McKenzie breezed the first three rounds of the tournament.* | *She's likely to breeze through this game, but the next might not be so easy.*

5 the easiest way to do something

- the easy way
- easy option

the easy way /ðiˈiːzi ˌweɪ/ [n phrase] *The easiest way of making money is to get other people to do it for you.* | **do things the easy way** *As a student, Louise was lazy, and always did things the easy way.* | **take the easy way out** (=avoid the difficult or best way by doing something that is easier) *I decided to take the easy way out and take a different class.*

easy option /ˌiːzi ˈɒpʃən‖-ˈɑːp-/ ALSO **soft option** /ˌsɒft ˈɒpʃən‖ˌsɔːft ˈɑːp-/ British [n C] if someone takes the **easy option** they choose to do the easiest thing they can, rather than something that is better but more difficult, because they are lazy **take the easy/soft option** *Instead of working to keep their marriages, more and more people are taking the easy option and getting divorced.* | **be an easy/soft option** *Some people think that studying languages instead of sciences is a soft option.*

6 to make something easier for someone to do

- make sth easier
- simplify
- facilitate
- smooth the way
- ease
- spoonfeed

make sth easier /ˌmeɪk (sth) ˈiːziəʳ/ [v phrase] *The new system will make buying and selling houses much easier.* | **make it easier for sb to do sth** *Health authorities want to make it easier for patients to be treated at home.* | **make things/life easier** *We've got a new secretary starting tomorrow – that should make things easier.* | *It would make life a lot easier if there was a reliable train service.*

simplify /ˈsɪmplɪ̇faɪ/ [v T] to make something easier to understand, by removing the parts that cause difficulty or problems: *The whole university admissions procedure has been simplified.*

facilitate /fəˈsɪlɪ̇teɪt/ [v T] formal to make it easier for a process to happen or for someone to do something: *Both centers are electronically linked to facilitate communication.* | *Legislation is urgently needed to facilitate police counterterrorist operations.*

smooth the way /ˌsmuːð ðə ˈweɪ/ [v phrase] to make it easier for someone to do something or for something to happen, by dealing with any problem that might prevent it: *Our representatives will be waiting for you to arrive, and ready to help smooth the way.* | **+ for** *It is hoped that the negotiations will smooth the way for an agreement later this year.*

ease /iːz/ [v T] to make it easier for a process to happen or move forward, especially by officially changing something that has previously been making it difficult: *The help of UN experts eased the transition to independence.* | *We need to get rid of Africa's long-term debt burden, and ease trade and commerce.*

spoonfeed /ˈspuːnfiːd/ [v T] to make it too easy for someone to do something by giving them too much information and help, so that they do not learn for themselves: *Don't spoonfeed him – he's got to learn how to do things for himself!* | *Spoonfeeding students is never a good idea – they always fail when it comes to exams.*

eat

RELATED WORDS

- someone who eats too much *see* **greedy**
- *see also* **drink, taste, hungry/not hungry, food, cook, meal, delicious**

1 to eat

- eat
- have
- chew
- swallow
- lick
- consume
- dig in/tuck in
- feed
- chow down

eat /iːt/ [v I/T] *Don't eat so fast – you'll get sick.* | *I'm so full. I couldn't eat another thing.* | *She was sitting on the wall, eating an apple.* | *Hey! – Someone's eaten all my chocolates.*

have /hæv/ [v T] to eat a particular thing: *I wasn't very hungry, so I just had a sandwich.* | *I think I'll just have one more piece of cake.* | **have sth for lunch/dinner/breakfast** *What shall we have for dinner?* | *I usually just have fruit for breakfast.*

chew /tʃuː/ [v I/T] to bite food several times and turn it around in your mouth: *I chewed the toffee slowly.* | *There was a cow in the field, slowly chewing a mouthful of grass.*

swallow /ˈswɒləʊ‖ˈswɑː-/ [v I/T] to make something go down your throat towards your stomach: *If you drink some water it will make the pills easier to swallow.* | *I threw a piece of meat to the dog and he swallowed it in one go.*

lick /lɪk/ [v T] to eat something soft by moving your tongue across its surface: *The children sat licking their ice creams.* | **lick sth off sth** *Nina licked the melted chocolate off her fingers.*

consume /kənˈsjuːm‖-ˈsuːm/ [v T] to eat or drink something – used especially in scientific or technical contexts: *In order to survive human beings need to consume food and water.* | *People who consume large amounts of animal fats are more likely to get cancer and heart disease.* —**consumption** /kənˈsʌmpʃən/ [n U] *Food products have dates printed on them to show if they're safe for consumption* (=safe to be consumed).

dig in/tuck in /ˌdɪg ˈɪn, ˌtʌk ˈɪn/ [phr v I] to eat eagerly and with enjoyment: *Dinner's ready everyone. Dig in!* | *Nick was already at the table, tucking in.* | **tuck into** *'This is delicious!' he said, tucking into his steak and kidney pudding.*

feed /fiːd/ [v I] if animals or babies **feed**, they eat or drink: *Most new babies will want to feed every few hours.* | *The pigs were feeding from a trough in the middle of the yard.* | **+ on** *The larvae feed on the young shoots of water-lilies.*

chow down /ˌtʃaʊ ˈdaʊn/ [phr v I] American informal to eat, especially in a noisy way or in a way that shows you are very hungry: *We each grabbed a container of ice cream and chowed down.* | **+ on** *The kids were chowing down on a large pizza.*

2 to have a meal

- have
- eat
- have something to eat
- grab something/a bite to eat
- have a snack
- snack
- dine

have /hæv/ [v T] to eat a meal **have breakfast/lunch/dinner** *Have you had lunch?* | *Make sure you have a good breakfast because lunch isn't until two o'clock.* | **have a meal** *We had an excellent meal in a Thai restaurant.*

eat /iːt/ [v I/T] to **eat** a meal: *We usually eat at seven o'clock.* | *I'm not hungry, thanks – I've already eaten.* | **eat out** (=eat a meal in a restaurant) *We eat out about once a month.* | **eat breakfast/lunch/dinner** *We ate dinner at around six, then went out.*
▸ **USAGE** ***Have*** is the usual word to use when talking about eating a particular meal such as lunch or dinner, and is much more common than ***eat***. ***Have*** is always transitive but ***eat*** can be transitive or intransitive.

have something to eat /hæv ˌsʌmθɪŋ tʊ ˈiːt/ [v phrase] to eat something such as a small meal or a sandwich: *Shall we stop here and have something to eat?* | *Halfway to Berlin we stopped to have something to eat.* | *The movie didn't start for another hour, so we had something to eat in the cafe across the street.*

grab something/a bite to eat /ˌgræb sʌmθɪŋ, ə ˌbaɪt tʊ ˈiːt/ [v phrase] informal to eat something quickly, such as a small meal or a sandwich, because you are in a hurry: *Let's grab something to eat before we go out.* | *Do you want to grab a bite to eat, or can you wait until we get home?*

have a snack /ˌhæv ə ˈsnæk/ [v phrase] to eat a small meal in the time between your main meals: *I usually have a snack at about 3 o'clock.* | *Dinner wouldn't be ready for a couple hours, so we had a snack while we watched television.* —**snack** [n C] *They stopped for a snack at a roadside cafe.*

snack /snæk/ [v I] to eat small amounts of food between main meals or instead of a meal: *Children who snack often develop poor eating habits.* | **+ on** *Tim was always snacking on potato chips and popcorn.*

dine /daɪn/ [v I] formal to eat a meal, often a formal or official meal, especially in the evening **+ with** *I have received an invitation to dine with the Mayor.* | **dine alone** *Dining alone this evening?* | **+ on** *Guests dined on sea bass and saffron potato mousseline.* | **dine out** (=have a meal in a restaurant) *It's a place where the famous can dine out and not be bothered.*

3 to eat a lot or too much

- stuff/gorge yourself
- pig out
- make a pig of yourself
- overeat

stuff/gorge yourself /ˈstʌf, ˈgɔːʳdʒ jɔːʳself/ [v phrase] to eat so much food that you cannot eat anything else **+ with** *Having stuffed himself with burgers, Terry was unable to finish his dessert.* | **+ on** *The Romans would gorge themselves on grapes and plums.*

pig out /ˌpɪg ˈaʊt/ [phr v I] informal to eat a lot of food – used humorously: *Last night we pigged out and ate three pizzas.* | **+ on** *When he's depressed he always pigs out on ice cream.*

make a pig of yourself /meɪk ə ˈpɪg əv jɔːʳself/ [v phrase] informal to eat too much food – used especially humorously, and used to say that someone has behaved in an embarrassing way when eating with other people: *I had four pieces of cake and made a real pig of myself.* | *Don't make such a pig of yourself; you've eaten enough.*

overeat /ˌəʊvərˈiːt/ [v I usually in progressive] to regularly eat too much in a way that is bad for your health: *You need to watch your weight – have you been overeating?* | *A woman who overeats during pregnancy can cause health problems for her child.* —**overeating** [n U] *We're constantly being reminded of the dangers of overeating.*

4 to eat something very quickly

- wolf down
- bolt down
- gobble up/down
- scoff

wolf down /ˌwʊlf ˈdaʊn/ [phr v T] informal to eat food quickly and eagerly, especially because you are very hungry or are in a hurry **wolf down sth** *I wolfed down my breakfast but still felt hungry.* | *They were already late so they wolfed down their lunch and caught the 2.30 train.* | **wolf sth down** *When the food finally came she wolfed it down immediately.*

bolt down /ˌbəʊlt ˈdaʊn/ [phr v T] British to eat something too quickly, especially because you are in a hurry **bolt down sth** *He bolted down two hamburgers then washed them down with Coca-Cola.* | **bolt sth down** *Don't bolt your food down! Chew it up slowly.*

gobble up/down /ˌgɒbəl ˈʌp, daʊn‖ˌgɑː-/ [phr v T] to eat something quickly and noisily, especially because you are taking a lot of food into your mouth **gobble sth up/down** *Mike gobbled his lunch down then dashed off to meet his next client.* | **gobble up/down sth** *The cat leapt onto the kitchen counter and gobbled up the smoked salmon intended for dinner.*

scoff /skɒf‖skɔːf/ British informal **/scarf** /skɑːʳf/ American informal [v T] to eat something very quickly: *I left three pies in the fridge and someone's scoffed the lot!* | **scarf up/down sth** *I scarfed down breakfast in my car on the way to work.* | **scarf sth up/down** *Wow, you two really scarfed those cookies up.*

5 to eat noisily

- munch
- crunch

munch /mʌntʃ/ [v T] to eat something with continuous movements of your mouth, especially when you are enjoying your food: *Jamie came out of the store munching a bag of potato chips.* | **+ on** *We sipped black coffee and munched on homemade biscuits.*

crunch /krʌntʃ/ [v T] to noisily eat something hard: *He drank his orange juice and crunched a half burnt piece of toast.* | *Jill was reading the paper, crunching a raw carrot as she read.* | **+ on** *Miguel, crunching on a mouthful of chips, wiped the cheese from his beard.*

6 to eat all of something

- eat up
- finish
- finish off/up
- polish off
- demolish
- devour

eat up /ˌiːt ˈʌp/ [phr v T] to eat all of something and not leave anything: *Come on, boys – eat up your supper and get to bed.* | **eat sth/it/them up** *Margaret ate it all up and then asked for more.* | *We were always taught to eat our vegetables up.*

finish /ˈfɪnɪʃ/ [v I/T] to **finish** eating something: *Are you finished?* | *You may not leave the table until you've finished your supper.* | *I finished my lunch, repacked my back pack, and set off again.* | *Hurry up and finish so we can make the 7 o'clock show.*

finish off/up /ˌfɪnɪʃ ˈɒf, ˈʌp/ [phr v T] to finish eating the rest of the food that is still on the plate, in the pan etc **finish off/up sth** *Who finished off the cake that was left after the party? | Can someone finish up these strawberries so I don't have to throw them away?* | **finish sth/it/them off** *Finish those carrots off and you can have dessert.*

polish off /ˌpɒlɪʃ ˈɒf‖ˌpɑː-/ [phr v T] to eat everything that is available, with great enjoyment, until there is none left **polish off sth** *At dinner he polished off six fudge brownies and then asked for some more.* | **polish sth/it/them off** *If anyone wants more pizza, come and get it before Dan polishes it all off.*

demolish /dɪˈmɒlɪʃ‖dɪˈmɑː-/ [v T] to eat all of something very quickly – used humorously: *The kids demolished the cake and then ran back outside to play. | I've seen Marian demolish a big box of chocolates in one sitting!*

devour /dɪˈvaʊəʳ/ [v T] especially written to eat all of something quickly because you are very hungry: *After the tennis match the boys devoured the sandwiches in seconds. | Wendell devoured a large piece of gingerbread, then licked his fingers greedily.*

7 to eat small amounts of food

- nibble
- pick at
- hardly touch your food/dinner/meal etc

nibble /ˈnɪbəl/ [v I/T] to eat something by biting very small pieces: *The horse lowered his head and began to nibble the grass.* | **+ on/at** *We stood around drinking wine and nibbling on little snacks.*

pick at /ˈpɪk æt/ [v T] to eat only a small part of a meal, especially because you feel ill or unhappy: *I sat picking at my dinner, wishing I were somewhere else.*

hardly touch your food/dinner/meal etc /ˌhɑːʳdli ˈtʌtʃ jɔːʳ fuːd/ [v phrase] to eat almost none of your dinner, meal etc: *Are you feeling okay? You've hardly touched your dinner. | We were so full by the time dessert came that we hardly touched it.*

8 to eat less in order to lose weight

- diet
- diet

diet /ˈdaɪət/ [v I] to eat less in order to lose weight: *I've been dieting for two months and I've lost 6 kilos. | She dieted and went on exercise programs but nothing seemed to work.*

diet /ˈdaɪət/ [n C] when you eat less food over a period of time because you want to become thinner or healthier: *I've tried all the diets and they never work. | This new diet involves eating very small amounts throughout the day.* | **go on a diet** *The doctor told Tom to quit smoking and go on a diet.* | **be on a diet** *Since his heart attack, Brice has been on a salt-free diet.*

9 to stop eating or refuse to eat

- fast
- go on (a) hunger strike
- be off your food

fast /fɑːst‖fæst/ [v I] to stop eating food for a fixed period of time, especially for religious reasons: *Muslims fast during Ramadan.* —**fast** [n C] *At the end of their fast, the people have a big party to celebrate.*

go on (a) hunger strike /ˌgəʊ ɒn (ə) ˈhʌŋgəʳ straɪk/ [v phrase] if someone **goes on a hunger strike**, they refuse to eat for days or weeks in order to protest about something or bring public attention to a political problem: *More than 300 prisoners went on hunger strike in February in protest against the living conditions.* | **be on (a) hunger strike** *67 men had been on hunger strike since August 13th.*

be off your food /biː ˌɒf jɔːʳ ˈfuːd/ [v phrase] British especially spoken if someone is **off their food**, they do not want to eat, for example because they feel sick or ill: *What's wrong with Billy? He seems to be off his food.*

10 when you have eaten enough or too much food

- have had enough
- be full
- couldn't eat another thing
- bloated
- on a full stomach

have had enough /həv ˌhæd ɪˈnʌf/ [v phrase] to have eaten enough food, so that you do not want any more: *'Would you like some dessert?' 'No thanks, I've had enough.' | Leave the rest if you've had enough.*

be full /biː ˈfʊl/ [v phrase] spoken if you **are full**, you have eaten so much food that you cannot eat any more: *'Would you like some more pie?' 'No thanks, I'm full.'*

couldn't eat another thing /kʊdnt iːt əˌnʌðə ˈθɪŋ/ you say **I couldn't eat another thing** when you have eaten a lot, especially because you enjoyed the food, and are very full: *The apple pie is delicious, but I won't have another slice – I couldn't eat another thing.*

bloated /ˈbləʊtɪ̣d/ [adj] having eaten so much that your stomach feels very full and uncomfortable: *I feel really bloated. I wish I hadn't eaten so much.* | **+ with** *He fell onto the sofa, his stomach bloated with food.*

on a full stomach /ɒn ə ˌfʊl ˈstʌmək/ [adv] if you do something **on a full stomach**, you do it soon after eating a meal, when you are still feeling full: *It isn't wise to go swimming on a full stomach.*

11 someone who enjoys eating a lot

- big eater
- like your food
- gourmet
- foodie

big eater /ˌbɪg ˈiːtəʳ/ [n C] someone who usually eats a lot of food: *Don't give me such a large portion. I'm not a big eater. | What can I cook for them? They're such big eaters.*

like your food /ˌlaɪk jɔːʳ ˈfuːd/ [v phrase not in progressive] informal to enjoy food and to usually eat a lot: *Give him a big plate of spaghetti. He likes his food. | 'Now there's a man who likes his food,' she said, as her brother took a third helping of pie.*

gourmet /ˈgʊəmeɪ‖ˈgʊər-, gʊərˈmeɪ/ [n C] someone who knows a lot about food and drink and likes good quality food and drink: *They're real gourmets and buy only the best cuts of meat. | Many gourmets say that Camembert should never be kept in a fridge.* | **gourmet food/cooking etc** (=very good and usually expensive) *The shop only sells gourmet food, at astronomical prices.*

foodie /ˈfuːdi/ [n C] British informal someone who is interested in food, and likes going to restaurants and trying new and unusual foods: *a new magazine for foodies | Michael Caine is an avid foodie who owns a string of restaurants.*

12 someone who only eats certain types of food

- be a fussy/picky eater

be a fussy/picky eater /biː ə ˌfʌsi, ˌpɪki ˈiːtəʳ/ [v phrase] to refuse to eat particular types of food and only eat food that you especially like: *Stan's such a picky eater; it's impossible to know what to cook for him.*

13 when something can be eaten

- edible

edible /ˈedəbəl/ [adj] food, plants, and animals that are **edible** are suitable for people to eat and will not cause illness or death: *Are these mushrooms edible?* | *There are many edible fruits growing wild in the coastal forest.*

14 when something cannot be eaten

- inedible
- unfit for human consumption

inedible /ɪnˈedəbəl/ [adj] food, plants, and animals that are **inedible** cannot be eaten, especially because they have a bad taste: *Onondaga Lake is now so polluted that the fish are inedible.* | *Mark hadn't realized that the leaves of the rhubarb plant were inedible.*

unfit for human consumption /ʌnˌfɪt fəʳ ˌhjuːmən kənˈsʌmpʃən/ [adj phrase] not suitable for people to eat – used especially in official contexts: *Most of this meat is so old it is unfit for human consumption.* | *Warning: Animal Feed only – Unfit for human consumption.*

edge

RELATED WORDS

- *see also* **side, middle, around/round**

1 the edge of an object, surface, or place

- edge
- side
- margin
- border
- rim

edge /edʒ/ [n C] the part of something that is nearest to its outside or end: *The plates have blue lines around the edges.* | *Don't put your glass so close to the edge of the table.* | **at the edge (of)** *There's an enormous oak tree at the edge of the garden.*

side /saɪd/ [n C] the part of an object that is near its left or right edge: *The stage was lit from the side.* | **on the side (of)** *Mike always puts his feet on my side of the bed.* | **left-hand/right-hand side of sth** (=on the left or right) *The new five-dollar bills have shifted the president's head toward the left-hand side.*

margin /ˈmɑːʳdʒən/ [n C] the empty space at the side of a printed page: *The program sets the margins automatically.* | **in the margin** *There were notes pencilled in the margin.*

border /ˈbɔːʳdəʳ/ [n C] a narrow band that goes around the edge of something such as a picture or a piece of material, especially one that is for decoration: *The tablecloth had a brightly patterned border.* | *Samantha was wearing a knee-length skirt with a green border.* | **+ of** *Jill wants to plant a border of flowers around the lawn.*

rim /rɪm/ [n C] the circular edge of something, especially the edge at the top of a glass or cup, or the outside edge of a wheel or a pair of glasses: *The china set was blue with a gold rim.* | *John's glasses had small lenses and steel rims.* | **+ of** *Her lipstick left a red mark on the rim of the cup.*

2 the edge of a country, place or area of land

- edge
- outskirts
- border
- frontier
- boundary
- perimeter

edge /edʒ/ [n C] the part of a town, city etc that is farthest from the centre **on the edge (of)** *My uncle's house is on the edge of town, near the airport.* | *Gretel lives in a simple cottage on the edge of the forest.*

outskirts /ˈaʊtskɜːʳts/ [n plural] the areas of a city furthest away from the centre **on the outskirts (of)** *Her parents lived in a big house on the outskirts of Manchester.* | *We stayed on the outskirts of the capital.* | **the outskirts of sth** *We heard gunshots as we drove through the outskirts of the city.*

border /ˈbɔːʳdəʳ/ [n C] the official line that separates two countries, or the area of land near this line **the Italian/Brazilian/Nigerian etc border** (=the border between Italy, Brazil etc and another country) *Isn't Manto near the Italian border?* | *Jeumont is a small town on the French-Belgian border.* | **cross the border** *Refugees have been warned not to attempt to cross the border.* | **on the border (with sth)** *The talks were held in the northeastern state of Nuevo Leon, on the border with the US.* | **the border with** (=the border separating one country from another) *It is a mountainous region, occupying a large area near the border with Nepal.* | **border town/area/patrol** *We spent the night in, a miserable little border town.* | **border dispute** (=arguments and fighting between countries about where a border should be) *Fighting in border disputes has killed at least 25 people.*

frontier /ˈfrʌntɪəʳ‖frʌnˈtɪər/ [n C] especially British the border of a country, where people cross from one country to another: *Many of the cars crossing the frontier were stopped and searched.* | *They settled in Ronco, a picturesque village near the Italian frontier.* | **frontier post** (=place where soldiers guard a border) *He was questioned by soldiers at a frontier post.*

boundary /ˈbaʊndəri/ [n C] the official line that marks the edge of an area of land, for example of a farm or a part of a country: *A fence marks the property's boundaries.* | **+ of** *the easternmost boundary of Greater Manchester* | **+ between** *The Mississippi River forms a natural boundary between Iowa and Illinois.*

perimeter /pəˈrɪmətəʳ/ [n C] the outside edge around an enclosed area of land such as a military camp or a prison: *Security guards patrol the perimeter.* | *the perimeter of the airfield* | **perimeter fence/wall/road etc** (=one that goes around the perimeter) *A secure perimeter fence should be at least two metres high.*

effect/affect

RELATED WORDS

- *see also* **change/not change, effective/not effective, result**

1 to have an effect on someone or something

- have an effect
- have an impact
- affect
- take effect
- make a difference
- impact

have an effect /ˌhæv ən ɪˈfekt/ [v phrase] to make someone or something change in some way, for example by making them better or worse: *For some patients, the treatment has an immediate effect.* | **+ on** *What you eat when you are pregnant can have an effect on your baby.* | *No one knows yet what effects genetically modified foods will have on the environment.* | **have little/no effect** *The government's policies have so far had little effect in reducing the level of inflation.*

have an impact /ˌhæv ən ˈɪmpækt/ [v phrase] if an event, invention, or new idea **has an impact** on something, it affects it in important ways and causes big changes: *The new management team has clearly had an impact.* | **+ on** *It is unlikely that the storms will have much impact on this year's harvest.* | *the impact of the Internet on all our lives* | **have a great/enormous/major etc impact** *Einstein's work on relativity had an enormous impact on the way physics developed.* | **have little/no impact** *At first, the revolution had little impact on the lives of ordinary people.*

affect /əˈfekt/ [v T] to produce a change, for example in the way that something develops or in someone's situation: *The new tax law doesn't affect me because I'm a student.* | *Scientists are investigating the ways in which climate changes affect the ozone layer.*

take effect /ˌteɪk ɪˈfekt/ [v phrase] if something **takes effect**, especially a medicine or drug, or a new plan or system, it starts to have an effect: *It will be a while before the government's new economic policy takes effect.* | *The dentist gave me an injection that took effect almost immediately, and I didn't feel a thing.*

make a difference /meɪk ə ˈdɪfərəns/ [v phrase] to have a noticeable effect on a situation: *If everybody helps a little, it really makes a difference.* | *You can call and complain, but I don't think it will make any difference.* | **make a big difference** *Just getting a new hairstyle and new outfit made a big difference to my confidence.*

impact /ˈɪmpækt/ [v T] to affect something such as sales or profits – used especially in business and journalism: *How is the growth of e-commerce likely to impact the retail sector?* | **+ on** *Child care is an issue that impacts on a broad cross-section of working women.*

2 to have a bad effect

- have a bad/serious/harmful etc effect
- badly/seriously etc affect
- be bad for
- take a toll/take its toll
- leave a mark/leave its mark
- tell
- have a negative impact on

have a bad/serious/harmful etc effect /hæv ə ˌbæd ɪˈfekt/ [v phrase] *The drug can have a serious effect on the body's immune system.* | **have a devastating/disastrous effect** (=have an extremely bad effect) *The war is having a devastating effect on people's lives.*

badly/seriously etc affect /ˌbædli əˈfekt/ [v phrase] to have a bad effect on someone or something: *Late nights and lack of sleep can seriously affect your performance at work.* | *Rescue officials have gone to three villages badly affected by the earthquakes.*

be bad for /biː ˈbæd fɔːʳ/ [v phrase] to have a bad effect on someone or something: *Changing schools too often can be bad for a child's social development.* | **it's bad for sb to do sth** *I think it's bad for her to spend so much time worrying about him.*

take a toll/take its toll /ˌteɪk ə ˈtəʊl, ˌteɪk ɪts ˈtəʊl/ [v phrase] to have a serious and harmful effect on something or someone, especially after continuing for a long time: *Years of civil war and drought have taken their toll, and the population of the region is greatly reduced.* | **+ on** *Bad working conditions eventually take a toll on staff morale.*

leave a mark/leave its mark /ˌliːv ə ˈmɑːʳk, liːv ɪts ˈmɑːʳk/ [v phrase] to have an important and permanent effect on something: *She was only here for a few months, but she certainly left her mark.* | **+ on** *The long dispute has left its mark on the mining industry.*

tell /tel/ [v I] to have a noticeable and often harmful effect on a person or on a situation **+ on** *The strain of living with her violent husband was telling on Judy.* | **start/begin to tell** *The power of the mayor's cronies began to tell as the election drew closer.*

have a negative impact on /hæv ə ˌnegətɪv ˈɪmpækt ɒn/ [v phrase] to affect something in a way that harms it or makes it worse than it was before: *We need to be assured that the new development will not have a negative impact on the local environment.* | *Last year's attacks have continued to have a negative impact on the tourist industry this year.*

3 to have an effect on the way people think or behave

- influence
- have an influence
- sway
- play a part
- come into/enter into
- colour

influence /ˈɪnfluəns/ [v T] to affect the way someone behaves or thinks: *Don't let him influence you – make up your own mind.* | *How much does TV advertising really influence what people buy?* | *The jury's verdict was clearly influenced by their sympathy for the defendant.* | **influence sb to do sth** *The prisoner claims he was influenced by his older friends to carry out the crime.*

have an influence /ˌhæv ən ˈɪnfluəns/ [v phrase] to have a continuing effect on the way that people think or behave: *His ideas are too complicated to have much real influence.* | **+ on** *Clearly, the cost of fuel has an influence on what sort of car someone buys.* | **have a great/important/profound etc influence** *Descartes' ideas have had a profound influence on modern science.*

sway /sweɪ/ [v T] to influence someone when they have not yet definitely decided about something, so that they change their mind: *The court is unlikely to be swayed by those arguments.* | *Ed's parents never tried to sway him, but they are happy with the decision he's made.* | **be easily swayed** *Insecure people are often easily swayed by flattery.*

play a part /ˌpleɪ ə ˈpɑːʳt/ [v phrase] to be one of the things that has an effect on what someone decides or on what happens **+ in** *Of course, the pay played some part in my decision to take the job.* | **play a big/major part** *He was to go on to play a major part in the success of the new government.*

come into/enter into /ˌkʌm ˈɪntuː, ˌentər ˈɪntuː/ [phr v T] if something **comes into** or **enters into** a decision, it is one of the things that influences you when you decide or choose something – use this especially in negative sentences: *Try not to let your personal feelings enter into the decision.* | *An applicant's age or sex doesn't come into it – we simply choose the best candidate for the job.*

colour British **/color** American /ˈkʌləʳ/ [v T] to influence someone's opinions or decisions, usually in a way that makes them less fair: *Foster's early experiences in Hollywood colored his views of the entire film industry.* | *How can he make fair and impartial decisions when political loyalties colour his judgement?*

4 the effect that something has

- effect
- side effect
- impact
- influence
- what sth does to
- the implications

effect /ɪˈfekt/ [n C/U] a change that is caused by something that happens or by something that someone does **+ of** *the harmful effects of smoking* | *Gail was still recovering from the effects of her operation.* | **+ on** *The study measured the effect of fertilizers on the size of crops.* | **without much effect** *I tried using bleach to remove the stain, but without much effect.* | **feel the effects of sth** *I was starting to feel the effects of two nights without much sleep.*

side effect /ˈsaɪd ɪˌfekt/ [n C] a bad effect that something can have in addition to its good effects – use this especially about harmful effects that a drug can have: *At higher doses, the most common side effects are nausea and vomiting.* | **+ of** *One possible side effect of the drug is loss of memory.*

impact /ˈɪmpækt/ [n singular/U] a big and permanent change that happens as a result of something important **+ of** *the lasting impact of improved education on the country's economic success* | **+ on** *The Internet's impact on the way we do business has been remarkable.* | *The company is trying to lessen the impact of the oil spill on marine life.*

influence /ˈɪnfluəns/ [n singular/U] the continuing effects that something has on the way that people think or behave, or on the way that things develop **+ of** *The authorities were worried about the influence of Western films and TV programmes.* | **influence of sth on sth** *The book is about the influence of feminist ideas on American society.*

what sth does to /ˌwɒt (sth) ˈdʌz tuː/ especially spoken use this to talk about a bad effect that something has on someone or something: *Do you ever think about what those cigarettes must be doing to your lungs?* | *Look what the storm has done to the flowers.*

the implications /ði ˌɪmplɨˈkeɪʃənz/ [n plural] the possible effects that something is likely to have in the future **+ for** *What do you think the implications of the new law will be for small businesses?* | **have implications** *The new treatment will have implications for anyone suffering from an allergy.* | **wider implications** (=more important implications, especially ones that people have not yet considered) *The case is likely to have wider implications, for example those affecting press freedom.* | **+ of** *The implications of the committee's decision are many.*

5 something or someone that has an effect on people's ideas or behaviour

- influence
- influential

influence /ˈɪnfluəns/ [n C] something that has an effect, especially on the way people think or behave: *The two main influences in a child's development are the family and the school.* | **good/bad influence** *I think the boys that Todd is hanging around with are a bad influence.*

influential /ˌɪnfluˈenʃəl◂/ [adj] having an important effect on people's ideas: *Marx was clearly the most influential of all the socialist writers.* | **highly influential** *It is a highly influential art magazine that is widely read by dealers.* | **influential in doing sth** *Although she was not a professional politician, her views were influential in shaping government policy.*

6 having a big effect

- far-reaching

far-reaching /ˈfɑːʳ ˌriːtʃɪŋ/ [adj] **far-reaching effects/implications/changes/consequences etc** effects, changes etc that are likely to have a big and continuing effect on something: *The court's decision will have far-reaching implications for the health care industry.*

effective/ not effective

RELATED WORDS

- *see also* **succeed/successful, fail, useless, purpose, effect/affect**

1 method/plan/system

- effective
- work
- have/achieve the desired effect
- successful
- do the job/do the trick
- work wonders
- make a difference

effective /ɪˈfektɪv/ [adj] a method, system etc that is **effective** succeeds in achieving the result that you want: *The advertisement was simple but remarkably effective.* | *Our training programme covers a range of effective management techniques.* | **an effective way of doing sth/to do sth** *There are many effective ways of using videos in language teaching.* | **highly effective** *The new system has proved to be a highly effective way of extending trading hours.* —**effectively** [adv] *Children have to learn how to communicate effectively.* —**effectiveness** [n U] *Surveys were conducted in eight cities to determine the effectiveness of this approach.*

work /wɜːʳk/ [v I] if a plan or method **works**, it produces the result that you want: *'I can't open the jar.' 'Try putting it in hot water. That sometimes works.'* | **work well** *The recipe works just as well if you cook the fish in the microwave.* | **work with sb** (=make someone react in the way you want) *That type of sales talk doesn't work with me.* | **work like magic/like a charm/like a dream** (=have exactly the result that you want, especially when this is surprising) *I bought a bottle of stain remover, and it worked like magic.*

have/achieve the desired effect /ˌhæv, əˌtʃiːv ðə dɪˌzaɪəʳd ɪ'fekt/ [v phrase] to produce the result or effect that is intended: *You may have to take two pills in order to achieve the desired effect.* | **have the desired effect of doing sth** *The meetings had the desired effect of driving home the urgent need for change.*

successful /sək'sesfəl/ [adj] an action, or piece of work that is **successful** produces very good results: *Their new advertising campaign has been very successful.* | *Did you have a successful shopping trip?* | *It was one of the President's most successful speeches.* | **highly successful** *Freire introduced highly successful literacy programs in Brazil.*

do the job/do the trick /ˌduː ðə 'dʒɒb‖-'dʒɑːb, ˌduː ðə 'trɪk/ [v phrase] spoken say this about a tool or method you think will be effective: *An electric saw will do the job at twice the speed.* | *Exercise and a low-calorie diet should do the trick.*

work wonders /ˌwɜːʳk 'wʌndəʳz/ [v phrase not in progressive] to be extremely effective in dealing with a difficult problem or situation: *Many elderly people need to get out more, and often a new hobby works wonders.* | **+ for** *The team's recent successes have worked wonders for their morale.*

make a difference /ˌmeɪk ə 'dɪfərəns/ [v phrase] if the way you do something or the methods or people you use **make a difference**, they make something much more effective and successful: *If you're a young energetic college graduate who wants to make a difference in the world of media, this is the job for you!* | **make all the difference** *The kind of technology you choose will make all the difference to the success of your business.*

2 medicine/treatment

- effective
- work
- powerful/potent
- miracle drug/cure

effective /ɪ'fektɪv/ [adj] if a medicine, treatment etc is **effective**, it achieves the result that you want: *Antibiotics are only effective if you finish the whole course of treatment.* | **effective in doing sth** *Doctors soon realized that this drug was also effective in relieving the symptoms of arthritis.* | **+ against** *Penicillin can be taken in various forms and is effective against a wide range of infections.* | **highly effective** *Malarone is a new drug that has already proved highly effective.* —**effectiveness** [n U] *Recent studies have questioned the effectiveness of current AIDS treatments.*

work /wɜːʳk/ [v I] if a medicine, treatment etc **works**, it has the effect that you want it to have: *I've tried several different diets, but none of them seem to work.* | *It's too late for surgery, but chemotherapy might just work.*

powerful/potent /'paʊəʳfəl, 'pəʊtənt/ [adj] a medicine or drug that is **powerful** or **potent** is very strong and works very quickly so that it should be used very carefully: *Little is known about the long-term effects of powerful drugs such as Duromine.* | *Nicotine is a powerful appetite suppressant.* | *Alcohol is much less potent than opium, because it works in an entirely different way.*

miracle drug/cure /'mɪrəkəl ˌdrʌg, ˌkjʊəʳ/ [n C] a drug or type of treatment that will completely cure a painful or serious illness – use this especially when you do not really think that such a drug or treatment exists: *Unfortunately there's no miracle cure for a hangover.* | *Some alternative practitioners seem to regard the herb as some kind of miracle drug, but conventional doctors are warning them to be careful.*

3 always effective

- reliable
- surefire
- foolproof
- infallible
- never fails/can't fail/works every time

reliable /rɪ'laɪəbəl/ [adj] *The system is new, but so far it seems to be reliable.* | **a reliable way/method etc of doing sth** *Eating sensibly and taking regular exercise is a fairly reliable method of losing weight.* | *In Africa, cellular phones are often the only reliable way of communicating.* —**reliability** /rɪˌlaɪə'bɪl̥ti/ [n U] *The advantages of the computerized process are speed and reliability.*

surefire /'ʃʊəʳfaɪəʳ/ [adj only before noun] certain to be effective or successful: *Thursday night's line-up includes such surefire attractions as 'The Simpsons' and 'Friends'.* | **a surefire way to do sth/of doing sth** *I know a surefire way to get a car started on a freezing winter morning.* | **a surefire solution to sth** *There's no surefire solution to the problem of improving the company's performance.* | **a surefire recipe for success/disaster** (=something that is certain to be successful or not successful) *Going on holiday with my parents would be a surefire recipe for disaster.*

foolproof /'fuːlpruːf/ [adj] a method, system, or plan that is **foolproof** is always effective, because it is simple to understand and operate, and cannot go wrong: *I thought this method was foolproof until four customer orders went missing.* | *Each article goes through a foolproof system of checking which ensures that there are no mistakes in the final text.* | **a foolproof way to do sth/of doing sth** *There's no foolproof way to judge whether someone is the right person for the job.*

infallible /ɪn'fæl̥bəl/ [adj] a method or system that is **infallible** always produces the right result and never goes wrong: *Banks claim their cash-dispensing computers are infallible.* | **an infallible way to do sth/of doing sth** *There is no infallible way of predicting exactly what the weather will be like.* —**infallibly** [adv] *Even experts were not able to distinguish infallibly between the two artists' work.*

never fails/can't fail/works every time /ˌnevəʳ 'feɪlz, ˌkɑːnt 'feɪl‖ˌkænt-, ˌwɜːʳks evri 'taɪm/ [v phrase] spoken use this to tell someone that a method is always effective, especially when you have used it successfully before: *It's a very simple technique, but it never fails.* | *If I'm having trouble sleeping, having a hot bath at night works every time.* | *You should try this recipe. It's so easy that you can't fail.*

4 not effective

- not effective
- useless
- be a waste of time
- not work
- have no effect
- fail
- be dead in the water

not effective ALSO **ineffective** /nɒt ɪ'fektɪv, ˌɪnɪ'fektɪv/ [adj] having very little effect, so that it does not achieve what it is meant to achieve: *Studies have shown that this is not effective as a teaching technique.* | *The German tactics were so ineffective that Brazil had complete control in midfield.* | **ineffective in doing sth** *The government's approach has been ineffective in reducing unemployment.* —**ineffectiveness** [n U] *the ineffectiveness of the prison system*

useless /ˈjuːsləs/ [adj] informal not having any useful effect and not helping you get the result you want: *This book is useless! I can't find any of the information I need.* | *I reminded myself that worrying is a useless activity.* | **+ against** *Antibiotics are useless against viral infections such as influenza.* | **it is useless to do sth** *Jenny decided to say nothing. It was useless to argue.* | **worse than useless** (=used to emphasize that something has no useful effect and may make a situation worse) *Of course we need to test children's ability, but some of these exams are worse than useless.*

be a waste of time /biː ə ˌweɪst əv ˈtaɪm/ [v phrase] spoken say this when you have been trying to do something, but you realize that what you are doing is never likely to be effective: *This whole project's a waste of time, if you ask me.* | **be a big/complete waste of time** *I came to the conclusion that therapy was a complete waste of time.*

not work /nɒt ˈwɜːʳk/ [v phrase] if something does not work, it does not produce the result that you want: *My doctor recommended several different creams for dry skin, but none of them worked.* | *If stain remover doesn't work, you'd better send your dress to the dry cleaners.* | *I tried ignoring his unpleasant remarks, but it didn't work.*

have no effect /hæv ˌnəʊ ɪˈfekt/ [v phrase] if something **has no effect**, it produces no results at all or is completely unsuccessful: *The drugs had no effect.* | *Paul realized that his words were having no effect; Karen was not going to change her mind.*

fail /feɪl/ [v I not usually in progressive] if an attempt to do something **fails**, you do not achieve the result that you want: *My attempt to lose weight failed completely.* | *Our plan to go into business failed when the bank refused to lend us enough money.*

be dead in the water /biː ˌded ɪn ðə ˈwɔːtəʳ/ [v phrase] never likely to be effective – used especially by newspapers about political activities, plans etc: *They're saying that the democratic campaign is dead in the water just two days after its launch.* | *I think you should admit that the government's plans for higher education are now dead in the water.*

5 to prevent something from being effective

- neutralize
- cancel out/negate

neutralize ALSO **neutralise** British /ˈnjuːtrəlaɪz‖ˈnuː-/ [v T] to prevent something from being effective or stop the effect that it was having: *Congress can try to neutralize new legislation by modifying it or delaying it.* | *Recent events have done much to neutralize the influence of the right-wing.*

cancel out/negate /ˌkænsəl ˈaʊt, nɪˈgeɪt/ [phr v T/v T] to prevent something from being effective by having an equal but opposite effect: *Increases in rent cancel out any rise in wages.* | *He treated me so badly at the end, it cancelled out the good times we'd had.* | *The side effects of the drug negate any possible benefit.* | **cancel each other out** *The two arguments simply cancel each other out.*

efficient/ not efficient

RELATED WORDS

see also **organize**

1 organization/system/method

- efficient
- well-organized
- well-run
- well-oiled machine
- smooth

efficient /ɪˈfɪʃənt/ [adj] an **efficient** organization, method, or system is one in which all the parts work well together and good results are achieved without any money or time being wasted: *The passport office seems very efficient – I got a new passport in just 48 hours.* | *We need more efficient methods of transporting goods.* —**efficiently** [adv] *Under the new management, the business is working much more efficiently.*

well-organized ALSO **well-organised** British /ˌwel ˈɔːʳgənaɪzd◂/ [adj] organized in a careful and efficient way, and therefore likely to be successful: *The exhibition was very well-organized.* | *It was a well-organized demonstration, in which about 1000 people took part.* | *More employers now have well-financed and well-organized health promotion programs within the workplace.*

well-run /ˌwel ˈrʌn◂/ [adj] use this about an organization or business that is successful and efficient because the people in charge organize it well: *The Klausner is a comfortable, well-run hotel.* | *Public transport in this country is well-run and inexpensive.*

well-oiled machine /ˌwel ɔɪld məˈʃiːn/ [n singular] an organization or system that is very efficient and operates easily, without any problems **run/work like a well-oiled machine** *The administration runs like a well-oiled machine.*

smooth /smuːð/ [adj] efficient and without problems or difficulties: *To ensure a smooth change-over, we'd like you to start work one week before your predecessor leaves.* | *FrontPage is a software program that helps to organize the entire web site so that it works in a smooth fashion.* | *The main responsibility of the Project Co-ordinator is to ensure the smooth running of the department.* —**smoothly** [adv] *The rescue was carried out smoothly and with the minimum of fuss.*

2 machine

- efficient
- economical

efficient /ɪˈfɪʃənt/ [adj] use this about a machine that works well and produces good results without any money or time being wasted: *This is the most efficient and economical washing machine on the market.* | *My new computer's much faster and more efficient than the old one was.* | **energy efficient** (=using less gas, oil etc than other systems, machines etc) *Modern houses are much more energy efficient* | *an energy efficient heating system* —**efficiently** [adv] **work/run efficiently** *The shower doesn't seem to be working very efficiently at the moment.*

economical /ˌekəˈnɒmɪkəl, ˌiː-‖-ˈnɑː-/ [adj] a machine or vehicle that is **economical** is not expensive to use or run because it does not use much electricity, oil, gas etc: *People should be encouraged to* *buy smaller, more economical cars with fewer toxic emissions.* | *The Unipot does the work of several saucepans, and is very economical.* | **+ on** *I'd like to buy a car that is more economical on petrol.*

3 person

- efficient
- efficiency
- effective
- capable
- well-organized
- businesslike
- run a tight ship
- productive

efficient /ɪˈfɪʃənt/ [adj] someone who is **efficient** works well and does what needs to be done without wasting time: *For a successful business, friendly and efficient staff are essential.* | *The doctor was cheerful and efficient, which immediately made me feel more relaxed.* —**efficiently** [adv] *The secretary dealt with all our inquiries very efficiently.*

efficiency /ɪˈfɪʃənsi/ [n U] an efficient way of working: *I was impressed by her speed and efficiency.* | *The management seems to expect staff to be constantly achieving higher levels of efficiency and productivity.*

effective /ɪˈfektɪv/ [adj] someone who is **effective**, especially someone in a position of authority, deals quickly and successfully with the work they have to do: *An effective teacher will always produce better exam results.* | *What we need is a tough and effective leader with a sense of direction.* —**effectively** [adv] *It's the responsibility of the head teacher to deal effectively with any behavioural problems.* —**effectiveness** [n U] *The course is designed to help you improve your effectiveness* (=how effective you are) *in managing people.*

capable /ˈkeɪpəbəl/ [adj] someone who is **capable** does things well and confidently and does not need anyone else's help or advice: *All the staff at the nursing home seemed very capable.* | *They've got a very capable lawyer working on the case.* | *Rebecca was, without question, the most capable technician on the team.* —**capably** [adv] *Mr Stevenson chaired the meeting firmly and capably.*

well-organized ALSO **well-organised** British /ˌwel ˈɔːʳgənaɪzd◂/ [adj] someone who is **well-organized** plans things well so that they achieve what they want to achieve: *If you work as a personal assistant, you need to be well-organized.* | *Well-organized rebel forces have succeeded in recapturing the town.*

businesslike /ˈbɪznɪ̈s-laɪk/ [adj] someone who is **businesslike** deals with people effectively and does not waste time on things that are not important: *As a lawyer, you have to be controlled and businesslike at all times.* | *Gates gave a brief, businesslike explanation of his plans for the company.*

run a tight ship /rʌn ə ˌtaɪt ˈʃɪp/ [v phrase] to manage a business or company very efficiently, especially by having strict rules and by not allowing the people working there to have much freedom: *We run a very tight ship here, and we expect all our employees to be at their desks by nine o'clock.*

productive /prəˈdʌktɪv/ [adj] someone who is **productive** does a job efficiently and with good results, because they work faster than most people or do more work than most people: *Studies show that if screen workers have short but frequent breaks they become much more productive.* | *The most productive members of staff are rewarded by financial bonuses.*

4 to make a business or system more efficient

- improve/increase efficiency
- streamline
- rationalize

improve/increase efficiency /ɪmˌpruːv, ɪnˌkriːs ɪˈfɪʃənsi/ [v phrase] *We must increase efficiency and reduce costs if we are to make a profit this year.* | *The company has concentrated on encouraging worker involvement and improving efficiency.* | *Less complex business processes can reduce costs and improve efficiency and quality.*

streamline /ˈstriːmlaɪn/ [v T] to make the processes of a business or system simpler so that it operates more quickly and more efficiently: *We have streamlined the whole business by introducing a new computer system.* | *People are calling for steps to reform the juvenile justice system, including streamlining the process of prosecuting young offenders.*

rationalize especially British ALSO **rationalise** British /ˈræʃənəlaɪz/ [v T] to make a business or system more efficient by making it quicker, more modern, and less wasteful: *Since the administrative side of the business has been rationalized, all departments have become more efficient.* | *The budget proposed selling off $1,300 million worth of state-run enterprises and rationalizing the tax structure.* —**rationalization** /ˌræʃənəlaɪˈzeɪʃən‖-lə-/ [n U] *Rationalization within the industry means that some workers may lose their jobs.*

5 not efficient

- inefficient
- ineffectual
- ineffective
- badly-run

▸ *see also* **waste**

inefficient /ˌɪnɪ̈ˈfɪʃənt◂/ [adj] something or someone that is **inefficient** does not work as well as they should or could, in a way that wastes time, money, or effort: *The postal service in this country is very inefficient.* | *Inefficient management leads to poor employee performance.* —**inefficiency** [n U] *Because of our lawyer's inefficiency, we had to wait another month before moving into our new house.*

ineffectual /ˌɪnɪ̈ˈfektʃuəl◂/ [adj] a person or organization that is **ineffectual** is not able to get things done because they are not good enough or do not have a strong character: *The police were completely ineffectual in this matter.* | *He's a nice enough man, but rather ineffectual as a team captain.* | *The problems were made worse by the ineffectual political leadership of the coalition.*

ineffective /ˌɪnɪ̈ˈfektɪv/ [adj] someone who is **ineffective**, especially someone in a position of authority, is not able to deal successfully with the work they have to do: *I sometimes feel that she is just totally ineffective in this job.* | *A combination of ineffective management and inadequate investment brought about this collapse.*

badly-run /ˌbædli ˈrʌn◂/ [adj] an organization that is **badly-run** produces bad results because it is badly managed: *The club was badly run and had to close after only six months.* | *a badly-run company*

embarrassed/ embarrassing

feeling uncomfortable, shy or nervous about what people think of you

RELATED WORDS

▸ *see also* **ashamed**

1 words meaning embarrassed

- ▸ embarrassed
- ▸ self-conscious
- ▸ uncomfortable
- ▸ awkward
- ▸ sheepish
- ▸ mortified
- ▸ squirm
- ▸ I could have died/ I almost died
- ▸ egg on your face

embarrassed /ɪmˈbærəst/ [adj] feeling uncomfortable or shy and worrying about what people think of you, for example because you have made a stupid mistake or because you have to talk about your feelings, about sex etc: *Tony spilled red wine all over their carpet. He was so embarrassed!* | *The teachers are supposed to teach us about 'safe sex', but most of them are too embarrassed.* | **get/feel embarrassed** *Kids get embarrassed if their Mums kiss them in front of their friends.* | **+ about** *I got very drunk at the party, and I feel really embarrassed about it.* | **+ by/at** *Marlon was always embarrassed by his lack of education.* | **acutely embarrassed** (=very embarrassed) *'I'm not sure if I actually want to marry her,' Harry said, feeling acutely embarrassed.*

self-conscious /self ˈkɒnʃəs‖-ˈkɑːn-/ [adj] shy and embarrassed about your body, or about the way you look or talk **feel self-conscious** *I always feel really self-conscious in a bikini.* | **+ about** *Teenagers are often very self-conscious about their appearance.* —**self-consciously** [adv] *He got up rather self-consciously and walked towards the stage.*

uncomfortable /ʌnˈkʌmftəbəl, -ˈkʌmfət-‖-ˈkʌmfərt-, -ˈkʌmft-/ [adj] feeling embarrassed because you cannot relax with the people around you: *All this talk about love and romance was making me uncomfortable.* | **feel uncomfortable** *Jim always felt uncomfortable on such formal occasions.* | *an uncomfortable silence* —**uncomfortably** [adv] *Rhys shuffled his feet uncomfortably, trying to think of an excuse to leave.*

awkward /ˈɔːkwəʳd/ [adj] feeling so shy, nervous, and embarrassed that you cannot behave in a natural way **feel awkward** *I didn't know anyone at the party, and I felt really awkward at first.* | **an awkward moment/silence etc** (=when you or other people feel awkward) *For one awkward moment I thought I had said something terribly wrong.* | *Carrie laughed out loud, and there was an awkward silence.* —**awkwardly** [adv] *David felt too shy to say anything, and looked at them awkwardly.* —**awkwardness** [n U] *There was an awkwardness in her manner which made it difficult to talk to her.*

sheepish /ˈʃiːpɪʃ/ [adj usually before noun] looking or feeling a little embarrassed because you feel guilty about something: *He gave her a sheepish look and said, 'I'm very sorry, I forgot it was your birthday.'* | **look sheepish** *Debbie arrived late for work looking a bit sheepish.* —**sheepishly** [adv] *'I only have one or two cigarettes now and then,' he said sheepishly.*

mortified /ˈmɔːʳtɪ̈faɪd/ [adj not before noun] very shocked, embarrassed, or ashamed because you realize that you have done something wrong, or because of something unpleasant that happens to you **+ by** *Deaver was mortified by his mistake and immediately admitted that he was wrong.* | **mortified at the thought of sth** *Carla felt mortified at the thought of having to repeat another year at school.* | **mortified to find/see etc sth** *I was mortified to find that everyone else was wearing evening dress.*

squirm /skwɜːʳm/ [v I] to feel extremely embarrassed and uncomfortable because of something stupid that you did or said, or because of something that someone else does: *Whenever I think back to what I said at the party it makes me want to squirm.* | **squirm with embarrassment** *The little boy squirmed with embarrassment when his mother told him off in front of his friends.*

I could have died/I almost died /aɪ ˌkʊd həv ˈdaɪd, aɪ ˌɔːlməʊst ˈdaɪd/ spoken say this when you are telling someone about a time when you felt extremely embarrassed: *When I realized that Sally had heard every word I said about her, I could have died.*

egg on your face /ˈeg ɒn jɔːʳ ˌfeɪs/ if someone, especially someone in authority has egg on their face, they have done something wrong or embarrassing in a way that makes them look stupid: *Don't underestimate this club or you'll be left with egg on your face. I've got one of the best squads ever in the Premier League.* | *The government ended up with egg on its face when it was found to have withheld documents for political purposes.*

2 to make someone feel embarrassed

- ▸ embarrassing
- ▸ embarrass
- ▸ cause embarrassment
- ▸ be an embarrassment
- ▸ excruciating

embarrassing /ɪmˈbærəsɪŋ/ [adj] something that is **embarrassing** makes you feel embarrassed: *It was so embarrassing – I couldn't remember his name!* | *The doctor asked me a lot of embarrassing questions about my sex life.* | **+ to/for** *The revelations about the President's university life were to prove deeply embarrassing to him.*

embarrass /ɪmˈbærəs/ [v T] to make someone feel embarrassed: *I hope I didn't embarrass you in front of your friends.* | *One woman was trying to embarrass me by asking me questions I couldn't answer.*

cause embarrassment /ˌkɔːz ɪmˈbærəsmənt/ [v phrase] if a situation or an action **causes embarrassment** to someone, it makes them feel embarrassed in front of a lot of people: *If you want I'll leave – I don't want to cause any embarrassment.* | **cause sb embarrassment** *His wife's frequent affairs with other men had caused him acute public embarrassment.* | **cause embarrassment to sb** *The article was intended to cause the greatest possible embarrassment to the government.*

be an embarrassment /biː ən ɪmˈbærəsmənt/ [v phrase] if someone or something **is an embarrassment** to someone, they make them feel embarrassed or ashamed to be connected with them: *Look at the way he's dressed. It's an embarrassment.* | **+ to** *His heavy drinking was an embarrassment to his friends and family.*

excruciating /ɪkˈskruːʃieɪtɪŋ/ [adj] use this about something that makes you feel extremely embarrassed: *The ambassador opened the gift in front of all his guests – and the box was empty! It was the* *most excruciating moment of my life.* | *There followed an excruciating silence that lasted for at least a minute.*

3 the feeling you have when you are embarrassed

▸ embarrassment

embarrassment /ɪmˈbærəsmənt/ [n U] the feeling you have when you are embarrassed: *He looked down at the floor in an attempt to hide his embarrassment.* | **I almost/nearly died of embarrassment** spoken (=a humorous way of saying you felt very embarrassed about something) *She read my poem out to the whole class – I almost died of embarrassment.*

4 when your face goes red because you are embarrassed

▸ blush/turn red

blush/turn red ALSO **go red** especially British /blʌʃ, ˌtɜːʳn ˈred, ˌgəʊ ˈred/ [v I/v phrase] if you **blush** or **turn red**, your face becomes red because you are embarrassed: *As soon as Mark came into the room, she blushed and looked away.* | *David's really shy – he always turns red when the teacher asks him a question.* | **go/turn as red as a beetroot** British (=become very red) *I can't wait to see his face when you tell him – he'll go as red as a beetroot.*

emphasize

to show that something is particularly important

RELATED WORDS

▸ *see also* **important**

1 to emphasize something

▸ emphasize/stress
▸ highlight
▸ underline/underscore
▸ drive the point home/drive home the point
▸ play up
▸ accentuate
▸ point up

emphasize/stress /ˈemfəsaɪz, stres/ [v T] to say or show that you think something is especially important: *Mann stressed the need to educate people about the risks of AIDS.* | *She said smoking was not permitted anywhere in the school – emphasizing the word 'anywhere'.* | **+ (that)** *The County Sheriff emphasized that there was no evidence to show that the driver had been drinking.* | **I can't emphasize enough** spoken (=this needs to be emphasized a lot) *I can't emphasize enough how grateful we are for your donations.*

highlight /ˈhaɪlaɪt/ [v T] to emphasize something such as a problem or a fact, especially by providing new information about it: *This report highlights some of the problems faced by old people in winter.* | *The slump in the car industry was highlighted by Ford's offer of a $600 rebate on new cars.*

underline/underscore /ˌʌndəʳˈlaɪn, ˌʌndəʳˈskɔːʳ/ [v T] if something that happens **underlines** or **underscores** a fact, especially one that is already known, it helps to emphasize that it is true: *Yesterday's shelling of a Red Cross hospital underlines the difficulties faced by rescue teams.* | *The recent rioting in South Africa has underlined the government's lack of control.* | *The dire state of child health in the country was underscored in a report by UNICEF.*

drive the point home/drive home the point /ˌdraɪv ðə ˌpɔɪnt ˈhəʊm, ˌdraɪv həʊm ðə ˈpɔɪnt/ [v phrase] to emphasize a fact or idea by giving additional, often surprising or shocking, information about it: *After the talk, the students were shown a video about heroin addiction to drive the point home.* | **+ that** *The reconstruction of the accident certainly drove home the point that drink-driving can kill.*

play up ALSO **make great play of** British /ˌpleɪ ˈʌp, meɪk ˌgreɪt ˈpleɪ ɒv/ [phr v T] to emphasize a fact or idea, by giving it more attention than anything else, especially if you are trying to make it seem more important than it really is: *At the interview, remember to play up your experience of teaching in Japan.* | *On TV last night the Democratic candidate was clearly playing up his caring image.* | **make great play of (doing) sth** *The Prime Minister made great play of environmental issues, considering how little the government has done.*

accentuate /əkˈsentʃueɪt/ [v T] to emphasize something, especially the differences between two things or situations: *In Britain, the choice between state and private schools accentuates the differences between rich and poor.* | *The director uses music to accentuate the rising dramatic tension.*

point up /ˌpɔɪnt ˈʌp/ [phr v T] to make something, especially the true facts of a situation, clearer and more noticeable: *Recent protests in the north of the country point up the dilemma the opposition forces are in.* | *Low literacy rates among the women in this area point up the need for much greater investment in girls' education.*

2 to emphasize something too strongly

▸ overemphasize
▸ labour the point

overemphasize /ˌəʊvərˈemfəsaɪz/ [v T] to emphasize something too much: *I think the book overemphasizes the importance of religion in the history of the US.*

labour the point British **/belabor the point** American /ˌleɪbəʳ ðə ˈpɔɪnt, bɪˌleɪbəʳ-/ [v phrase] to emphasize an idea or a fact too strongly, especially by repeating it often so that people get bored: *I understand what you're saying – there's no need to labour the point.* | *I don't want to keep belaboring the point, but the Barnes Foundation is an educational institution, not a museum.*

3 when something is particularly emphasized

▸ emphasis/stress
▸ with the accent on

emphasis/stress /ˈemfəsɪs, stres/ [n singular/U] special attention that is given to a particular activity, subject etc, because it is believed to be more important than other things **+ on** *There is a greater emphasis on environmental issues nowadays.* | **put emphasis on sth** *The school puts a lot of emphasis on discipline and respect for authority.* | **with the emphasis on sth** *an exciting new French course for beginners, with the emphasis on fun*

with the accent on /wɪð ði ˈæksənt ɒn‖-ˈæksent-/ [prep] if something is done **with the accent**

on a particular quality or feature, that quality or feature is emphasized – used especially in written descriptions of products and services: *Toptours Travel is now offering numerous special vacation packages with the accent on choice.* | *a new range of children's toys with the accent on creativity*

empty

RELATED WORDS

opposite: —— **full**

1 container/bottle/glass

- **empty**
- **empties**
- **there's nothing in it**

empty /ˈempti/ [adj] a container, bottle, or glass that is **empty** has nothing inside it: *There were two empty beer bottles on the table.* | *I noticed her glass was empty, and offered her some more wine.* | *There was nothing at all in the room except an empty cupboard.* | **half empty** (=used to say that half of the contents of a packet. bottle etc have been used) *We've only got one bottle of milk left, and that's half empty.*

empties /ˈemptiz/ [n plural] informal empty containers, especially empty bottles: *The bartender picked up the crate of empties and took it down to the cellar.* | *You can get some money back if you return the empties to the shop.*

there's nothing in it /ðeəʳz ˌnʌθɪŋˈ ɪn ɪt/ use this to say that a container is empty: *I looked in her bag, but there was nothing in it.*

2 building/room/seat

- **empty**
- **free**
- **vacant**
- **bare**
- **unoccupied**

empty /ˈempti/ [adj] a building, room, or seat that is **empty** has nothing or no-one in it: *My footsteps echoed across the empty room.* | *We were a little worried to find that half the seats in the theatre were empty.* | *Police say the shot was fired from an empty office building across the street.* | **half empty** (=used to say that a room, building etc has not got many people in it) *I was surprised that the train was half empty at that time of day.*

free /friː/ [adj not usually before noun] a seat, space, or room that is **free** is not being used and is available for people to use: *Is this seat free?* | *There are never any parking spaces free at this time of day.* | *The meeting room won't be free until at least 3.30, I'm afraid.*

vacant /ˈveɪkənt/ [adj] a building, room, or seat that is **vacant** is not being used and is available for people to use: *The police had set up a temporary station in a vacant apartment across the street.* | *The next guesthouse we tried had a couple of rooms vacant.* | *Brunton went into the bar, but he couldn't spot a single vacant seat.*

bare /beəʳ/ [adj] a room or building that is **bare** has very little furniture or other things in it: *The room was completely bare except for a bed against the wall.* | *We spent a long time walking through the bare rooms, remembering the games we used to play there.*

unoccupied /ʌnˈɒkjəpaɪd‖-ˈɑːk-/ [adj] especially written an **unoccupied** house, room, office etc is not being lived in or used: *Many of the old houses that back onto the railway are now unoccupied.* | *It's a scandal that there are so many unoccupied buildings in this city, and so many homeless people.*

3 place/area of land

- **empty**
- **deserted**
- **uninhabited**
- **desolate**
- **ghost town**
- **wasteland**

empty /ˈempti/ [adj] a place that is **empty** has no-one in it: *It was 2 o'clock in the morning and the streets were completely empty.*

deserted /dɪˈzɜːʳtəd/ [adj] a place that is **deserted** is empty and quiet because there is no one there, or the people who are usually there have left: *The beach was deserted and unsafe for bathing according to the guidebook.* | *We passed through several deserted villages whose inhabitants had fled.*

uninhabited /ˌʌnɪnˈhæbətəd◂/ [adj] an area or place that is **uninhabited** has no people living in it: *Most of the islands in Clear Bay are uninhabited.* | *Access to this remote uninhabited Himalayan mountain is via high snow-covered passes.*

desolate /ˈdesələt/ [adj] an area that is **desolate** is empty and sad-looking, because there are no people there, no trees or plants growing, and nothing attractive to see: *We looked out over a desolate landscape of bare trees and stony fields.* | *The little mining town was desolate and ugly.* | *the desolate terrain of the moon*

ghost town /ˈgəʊst taʊn/ [n C] a town that is empty because all the people have left **become/turn into a ghost town** *Since the closing of the coal mines the place has become a ghost town.* | *By March the population had been evacuated, and Verdun had become a ghost town.*

wasteland /ˈweɪstlænd, -lənd/ [n C/U] an area of land, especially in a city, that is empty, ugly, and unused: *The area down by the docks is just a wasteland.* | *Detectives discovered the man's body dumped on wasteland near the railway.*

4 paper/tape/screen

- **blank**
- **space**
- **empty**

blank /blæŋk/ [adj] a **blank** screen, tape, or piece of paper has nothing written or recorded on it: *Ian stared at the blank sheet of paper in front of him.* | *I want to record the late-night movie. Do we have any blank video cassettes?*

space /speɪs/ [n C] a place that has been left empty in a piece of writing, especially so that you can write something in it: *There's a space for you to sign your name.* | *Write your address in the space provided.* | **empty space** *The students were told to fill in the empty spaces with suitable adjectives.*

empty /ˈempti/ [adj] a page or piece of paper that is **empty** has nothing written or drawn on it: *He stared at the empty page. The test was nearly over, and he hadn't managed to answer any of the questions.* | *an empty canvas with a few red blobs in the centre*

5 to make something empty

- **empty**
- **drain**
- **clear out**
- **turn out**

empty /ˈempti/ [v T] to make something **empty** by removing what was in it: *The garbage cans are emp-*

tied once a week. | **empty your pockets** *The police made us stand against the wall and told us to empty our pockets.* | **empty your glass** (=drink everything that is in it) *'See you,' he called, emptying his glass and making for the door.*

drain /dreɪn/ [v T] to remove all the liquid from a large container or a machine: *The police even drained the lake in their search for the body.* | **drain off sth/drain sth off** *To remove algae from your aquarium, drain off the water and wash the tank thoroughly.*

clear out /ˌklɪər ˈaʊt/ [phr v T] to empty a room, cupboard, house etc, especially because you no longer want the things that are in it **clear out sth** *I found a pile of her old letters while I was clearing out my desk.* | **clear sth out** *We have to clear the garage out this weekend.* —**have a clear-out** [v phrase] British when you empty your cupboards, a room etc and get rid of things: *I decided to have a clear-out and throw out all my old clothes.*

turn out /ˌtɜːʳn ˈaʊt/ [phr v T] British to empty a cupboard, a drawer, pockets etc, especially when you are looking for something **turn out sth/turn sth out** *The headteacher told them to turn out their pockets.* | *The thieves had turned out the drawer, scattering the contents on the floor.*

6 to make everyone leave a place

- clear
- evacuate

clear /klɪəʳ/ [v T] to empty a place by asking the people in it to leave: *Police cleared the building and carried out a controlled explosion.* | *The area around the palace had been cleared for the parade.*

evacuate /ɪˈvækjueɪt/ [v T] if the police or the authorities **evacuate** a place, they order everyone in it to leave, especially because it may be dangerous: *A five-block area had to be evacuated following the discovery of 500 pounds of dynamite in a house.* | *Terra, 60 miles southwest of Salt Lake City, was evacuated as the fires threatened to spread.*

7 a room or place becomes empty

- empty

empty /ˈempti/ [v I] to become **empty** because all the people leave: *On Saturday night, most of the clubs empty at around 3 am.* | *By the autumn, the hotels along the sea front were emptying, and the town became quiet again.* | *When we reached Dortmund the carriage emptied, and I was left alone.*

end

the end of something, or the part at the end of an object

RELATED WORDS

opposite: —— **beginning, start**

- to finish *see* **finish**
- to finish something *see* **finish**
- to make something stop happening *see* **stop**
- in the end/finally *see* **finally/eventually**
- *see also* **last**

1 the last part of an event or period of time

- the end
- close
- conclusion

the end /ði ˈend/ [n singular] the last part of an event or period of time **the end of sth** *The end of the game was really exciting.* | **at/by/towards the end** *He left New York at the end of December.* | *Towards the end of the interview, I was beginning to feel that I might have got the job.* | **come to an end** (=finish) *It was a difficult project and I was glad when it came to an end.* | **there's an end/no end in sight** (=use this to say that something is nearly finished or that you do not know when it will finish) *The current housing crisis is more serious than ever, and there doesn't seem to be an end in sight.* | **to/until the bitter end** (=until the time when a very difficult event or situation finally finishes) *She remained loyal to her unfaithful husband right to the bitter end.* | *The company's board vowed to fight to the bitter end, rather than submit to the takeover.*

conclusion /kənˈkluːʒən/ [n singular] the end of an event or piece of work, especially one that has several different stages or has continued for a long time: *Introducing the changes has been a long process, and it's still nowhere near its conclusion.* | **the conclusion of sth** *At the conclusion of the trial, the jury returned with a verdict of guilty.* | **bring sth to a conclusion** (=make something reach an end) *The talks are aimed at bringing the dispute to a conclusion.*

close /kləʊz/ [n singular] formal the end of a period of time or an activity **the close of sth** *The beginning of April usually marks the close of the skiing season.* | *At the close of trading on the stock market, Ciena shares were up to $37.* | **draw/come to a close** (=finish) *Several hours later, the meeting drew to a close and the board members filed out of the room.*

2 the last part of a book, film, show etc

- the end
- finale
- ending
- conclusion

the end /ði ˈend/ [n singular] the last part of a book, film, show etc: *It was such a terrible movie, half the audience walked out before the end.* | **+ of** *The end of the book was so sad that I almost cried.* | **at/by/towards etc the end** *By the end of the play, the main characters have all either died or gone mad.* | **the very end** (=the most final part of something) *You don't find out who the killer is until the very end.*

ending /ˈendɪŋ/ [n C] the way a story or film ends: *In the Spanish version of this story, the ending is completely different.* | **happy/sad ending** (=an ending in which something good or bad happens) *I love those old Hollywood movies with happy endings.*

finale /fɪˈnɑːli‖fɪˈnæli/ [n C usually singular] the exciting or impressive last part of a piece of music, show, ceremony etc **the finale of sth** *The finale of Beethoven's ninth symphony is really magnificent.* | **the grand finale** (=one that is very impressive) *For the grand finale there was a marching band and fireworks.*

conclusion /kənˈkluːʒən/ [n C] formal the last part of a book, play, report etc **the conclusion of sth** *At the conclusion of the book, the reader is still not certain whether Markham is guilty or not.* | **come to a conclusion** *There was complete silence in the room as the play came to its tragic conclusion.*

3 happening at the end of an event, time, book, film etc

- at the end
- closing
- final
- late
- latter
- end/finish with

at the end /ət ði 'end/ [adv] **at the end** of an event, period of time, book, film etc: *If you have any questions, can you ask them at the end, please.* | **+ of** *At the end of the first half, the score was 2-0.*

closing /'kləʊzɪŋ/ [adj only before noun] done or coming at the end of a meeting, film, book, race etc: *In his closing speech, he thanked the organizers of the conference.* | *In the closing shot of the film, Hoffman walks away from the camera without looking back.* | *The closing paragraphs were very moving.* | **the closing stages/minutes etc of sth** *I turned on the TV just in time to catch the closing minutes of the race.*

final /'faɪnl/ [adj only before noun] happening at or near the end of an event or process: *The war reached its final stages in July.* | *The Board is expected to make its final decision on the merger by August 12th.*

late /leɪt/ [adj/adv] if something happens in **late** August, **late** spring etc, it happens near the end of that time: *Can you come round late morning – at about 11.30?* | *It was late summer, and the evenings were already getting cooler.* | **late in August/the evening/1918 etc** *We don't usually expect to have a frost so late in the spring.*

latter /'lætəʳ/ [adj only before noun] **the latter part/half of sth** the part that comes fairly near the end or after the middle of something: *This point is explained more fully in the latter part of the chapter.* | *The house became known as Fields Mill during the latter half of the 17th century.*

end/finish with /'end, 'fɪnɪʃ wɪð/ [v phrase not in passive] if an event or period of time ends with something, that thing happens at the end of it: *The concert ended with a laser light show.* | *The coming term finishes with an exhibition in the Arts Centre on December 12th.*

4 the part at the end of an object

- end
- point
- tip
- nose
- head

end /end/ [n C] the part at the **end** of something long and narrow **the end of sth** *She chewed the end of her pencil thoughtfully.* | **the end of the road/street/passage etc** (=the furthest part of the road etc) *Go to the end of the street and turn left.* | **at one end** *You need a long pole with a hook at one end.* | **at both ends/at either end** *We sat in silence at either end of a long wooden table.*

point /pɔɪnt/ [n C] the thin, sharp end of something such as a needle, stick, or sword **the point of sth** *Ben carved his name in the tree trunk, using the point of his knife.* | *the point of a needle* | **sharp point** *It has small white flowers, and leaves that taper to a sharp point.*

tip /tɪp/ [n C] the narrow part at the end of something such as a finger, a branch, or a piece of land **the tip of sth** *Doctor Gordon felt my neck with the tips of his fingers.* | *The village is on the southern tip of the island.*

nose /nəʊz/ [n C] the rounded part at the front of a vehicle such as a plane **+ of** *The nose of the plane dipped as we came in to land.* | **sth's nose** *Each missile carries 150 kilos of high explosive in its nose.*

head /hed/ [n C] the rounded end part of a small object, especially something such as a nail or pin which also has a pointed end **+ of** *There was a hole in the pipe, no bigger than the head of a matchstick.* | *I picked up a hammer and hit the head of the nail as hard as I could.*

enemy

RELATED WORDS

opposite: ——— **friend**

- someone who opposes something *see* **against/oppose**
- someone who is trying to beat you in a game or sport *see* **play a game or sport**
- a person or organization that is competing against you *see* **compete with**
- *see also* **hate, unfriendly**

1 someone you are fighting against, especially in a war

- enemy
- foe
- adversary
- hostile

enemy /'enəmi/ [n C] someone you are fighting against, especially in a war: *You cannot attack an enemy unless you have precise information about their numbers and position.* | **the enemy** (=the army or country that your army or country is fighting against in a war) *They accused him of giving secret information to the enemy.* | **common enemy** (=an enemy you share with another person, country etc) *Britain and France decided to unite and fight against their common enemy.* | **enemy/aircraft/soldiers/ tanks etc** *One man was ordered to observe enemy aircraft and to warn when danger was imminent.*

foe /fəʊ/ [n C] formal or written a person or country that wants to attack and defeat you or your country: *Mitterrand drew France closer to the European union and to Germany, its former foe.* | **friend or foe** *As we approached the camp a guard called out: 'Who goes there – friend or foe?'*

adversary /'ædvəʳsəri‖-seri/ [n C] formal or written a country or person that you are fighting against: *The peace talks proved that even great adversaries were capable of cooperation.* | *Symes grabbed his adversary by the throat and wrestled him to the ground.*

hostile /'hɒstaɪl‖'hɑːstl, 'hɑːstaɪl/ [adj only before noun] **hostile** areas, soldiers etc are those belonging to a country or group that wants to attack and defeat your country, and are therefore dangerous: *Hostile forces have taken control of cities in the north of the country.* | *The ships had travelled thousands of miles through hostile waters to converge in the Atlantic.*

2 someone who hates you and wants to harm you

- enemy

enemy /'enəmi/ [n C] *Did your husband have any enemies?* | *My parents sometimes seem to treat me as if I was their enemy.*

energetic

RELATED WORDS

opposite: ——— **tired, lazy**

1 very active and full of energy

- energetic
- be full of energy/ bursting with energy
- active
- dynamic
- tireless
- hyperactive
- boisterous

energetic /ˌenəʳˈdʒetɪk◂/ [adj] very active and able to work hard or do an activity for a long time: *If you're feeling energetic, we could go out for a run.* | *My mother was a bustling, energetic woman.* | *The club has the support of an energetic and enthusiastic management committee.*

be full of energy/bursting with energy /biː ˌfʊl əv ˈenəʳdʒi, ˌbɜːʳstɪŋ wɪð ˈenəʳdʒi/ [v phrase] to have a lot of energy and be ready to work hard and do a lot of things: *William raced up the stairs, full of energy and excitement.* | *You have to be bursting with energy and health to do the top jobs, so they usually go to younger men.*

active /ˈæktɪv/ [adj] always doing things: *She may be over 80, but she's still very active!* | *Aaron seemed like a normal active baby until he was about ten months old.*

dynamic /daɪˈnæmɪk/ [adj] very energetic, determined to succeed, and full of new ideas: *She is clearly a dynamic young woman with big ambitions.* | *What this country needs is dynamic and inspiring leadership!*

tireless /ˈtaɪəʳləs/ [adj usually before noun] **tireless worker/campaigner etc** someone who keeps on working hard for a long time without getting tired: *Martin was a very popular teacher and a tireless worker for the school.* | *She has been a tireless peace campaigner for many years.*

hyperactive /ˌhaɪpərˈæktɪv◂/ [adj] someone who is **hyperactive** is too active and often nervous, so that they are unable to relax or work calmly: *Our youngest daughter was hyperactive, and it had a damaging effect on the whole family.* | *The City is full of hyperactive executives who never stop rushing around.*

boisterous /ˈbɔɪstərəs/ [adj] very energetic and noisy in a way that annoys other people – used especially about children: *Dan's a nice boy, but rather boisterous.* | *A large, boisterous crowd poured into the bar, singing and shouting noisily.* —**boisterously** [adv] *The kids were out in the backyard playing and fighting boisterously.*

2 happy and energetic

- lively
- vivacious
- animated
- be full of life
- be full of beans
- feel alive

lively /ˈlaɪvli/ [adj] cheerful and active: *She was a lively and adventurous girl – not one for a quiet life.* | *As a speaker, he was articulate, lively, and funny.*

vivacious /vəˈveɪʃəs/ [adj] a woman or girl who is **vivacious** has a lot of energy and a happy and attractive manner: *Laura was an all-American type – cute, blonde, vivacious.* | *He married a vivacious girl called Sarah who he met at university.* —**vivaciously** [adv] *'It's so wonderful to see you all!' she said vivaciously.*

animated /ˈænəmeɪtəd/ [adj] full of interest and energy, especially when talking to someone: *Mike tends to be more animated in the presence of women.* | **become animated** *As the evening went on she became quite animated, talking and laughing with the other girls.*

be full of life /biː ˌfʊl əv ˈlaɪf/ [v phrase] to feel happy and lively, and to show this by the way you behave: *Stephen was a normal boy of seven, full of life and fun.* | *Before the accident he had been a cheerful, confident man, full of life.*

be full of beans /biː ˌfʊl əv ˈbiːnz/ [v phrase] informal to feel happy, energetic, and eager, and to show this by the way you behave: *I wish I was one of those people who are full of beans first thing in the morning.* | *You'd never think she'd been ill – she came bouncing in this morning, full of beans.*

feel alive /ˌfiːl əˈlaɪv/ [v phrase] to feel full of energy, happy, and free: *After the divorce she felt really alive for the first time in her life.* | *I only feel truly alive when I'm outside, in the open air.*

3 energetic activities, behaviour etc

- energetic
- vigorous
- tireless
- lively
- animated

energetic /ˌenəʳˈdʒetɪk◂/ [adj] involving a lot of physical activity: *Pete was lying on his bed, resting after an energetic game of tennis.* | *I don't feel like doing anything very energetic this evening. I've had a tiring day.* —**energetically** [adv] *A group of cyclists passed us, pedalling energetically up the hill.*

vigorous /ˈvɪgərəs/ [adj] using a lot of energy and strength: *Next there was a vigorous Russian dance, with plenty of stamping of feet and clapping.* | **vigorous exercise** *According to a recent survey, a quarter of people over twelve get no vigorous exercise at all.* —**vigorously** [adv] *He seized me by the shoulders and shook me vigorously.*

tireless /ˈtaɪəʳləs/ [adj usually before noun] **tireless efforts/work etc** work that always involves the same high level of effort: *The prisoners were finally released, thanks to the tireless efforts of their families and friends.* —**tirelessly** [adv] *Rescuers worked tirelessly to free the survivors from the rubble.*

lively /ˈlaɪvli/ [adj] full of quick, energetic movement and therefore exciting or enjoyable: *A group of children entertained us with a lively dance called a tarantella.* | *Any question about taxation is likely to produce a lively debate in parliament.*

animated /ˈænəmeɪtəd/ [adj] full of excitement and strong feelings – use this especially about conversations **animated conversation/discussion etc** *The two Americans were having an animated discussion about basketball.* | *Peter was engaged in an animated conversation at the bar.*

4 energy

- energy
- vigour
- get-up-and-go
- vitality

energy /ˈenəʳdʒi/ [n U] the physical and mental strength that allows you to do things: *Certain vitamins can give you more energy, if you're always feeling tired.* | *She's got tremendous energy and a huge* *capacity for hard work.* | *I don't have the time or the energy to go out in the evenings.*

vigour British **/vigor** American /ˈvɪgəʳ/ [n U] physical and mental energy, determination, and strength **with vigour** *His new job was certainly a challenge, but Edward tackled it with vigour and imagination.* | **renewed/new vigour** *Holidays make it possible for you to return to your normal routine with renewed vigour and enthusiasm.*

get-up-and-go /ˌget ʌp ən ˈgəʊ/ [n U] an energetic determination to get things done without delay: *Fred got the job because he seemed to have more get-up-and-go than the other applicants.* | **get-up-and-go feeling/approach etc** *Golden Crunchies will help you start the day with that get-up-and-go feeling.*

vitality /vaɪˈtæləti/ [n U] healthy energy and cheerfulness: *He was a small man with enormous vitality.* | *Gail was someone who needed the stimulus of a big city to maintain her mental vitality.*

enjoy

RELATED WORDS

opposite: **dislike**

▸ *see also* **like, happy, enthusiastic/unenthusiastic**

1 to enjoy doing something

- enjoy
- like
- love
- have a good/great/wonderful etc time
- live it up/whoop it up
- have fun
- have a blast/have a ball
- have the time of your life/have a whale of a time
- get a kick out of doing sth

enjoy /ɪnˈdʒɔɪ/ [v T] to get pleasure from doing something: *Did you enjoy the party?* | **enjoy doing sth** *My father always enjoyed playing golf at weekends.* | **enjoy yourself** (=do things that make you feel happy) *The park was full of people enjoying themselves in the sunshine.* | **thoroughly/greatly enjoy** *Thanks for a lovely evening. I thoroughly enjoyed it.* | *Most of the students said that they had really enjoyed the day out.* | **enjoy every minute/moment of sth** *It was a wonderful vacation – we enjoyed every minute of it.* | **enjoy sth immensely** especially British *Parts of the play were extremely funny. I enjoyed it immensely.*

like /laɪk/ [v T not in progressive or passive] to enjoy doing something, especially something that you do regularly or for a long time: *I don't like meetings, especially if they go on for too long.* | **like doing sth** *We liked living abroad. It was a wonderful experience.* | **like to do sth** (=do something often or regularly because you enjoy it) *Nick likes to relax and read a book in the evenings.*

love /lʌv/ [v T not in progressive or passive] especially spoken to enjoy doing something very much and get a lot of pleasure out of it: *Cassie works in the theatre, and she really loves it.* | **love doing sth** *Ben loves swimming, playing tennis, those kinds of thing.* | **love to do sth** (=do something often or regularly because you enjoy it a lot) *She loved to sit in the park and feed the ducks.*

have a good/great/wonderful etc time /hæv ə ˌgʊd ˈtaɪm/ [v phrase] especially spoken to enjoy yourself very much when you are with other people: *We had a great time last night – you should have come.* | *Did you have a good time at the beach?* | **have a good/great etc time doing sth** *The kids all had a wonderful time meeting up at each other's houses.*

live it up/whoop it up /ˌlɪv ɪt ˈʌp, ˌwuːp ɪt ˈʌp/ [v phrase] informal to enjoy yourself very much by going out a lot and spending a lot of money on social activities: *Pat spent most of his time at college going to parties and living it up.* | *I had saved about two thousand dollars, so I decided to whoop it up in Vegas before going home.*

have fun /ˌhæv ˈfʌn/ [v phrase] to enjoy yourself with other people, for example by relaxing, talking, or laughing with them: *I was having so much fun I forgot how late it was.* | **have fun doing sth** *We had fun trying to guess who Mike's new girlfriend was.*

have a blast/have a ball /ˌhæv ə ˈblɑːst‖-ˈblæst, ˌhæv ə ˈbɔːl/ [v phrase] especially American, informal to have a very good time: *We went down to the Gulf Coast of Florida for spring break – we had a blast!*

have the time of your life/have a whale of a time /hæv ðə ˌtaɪm əv jɔːʳ ˈlaɪf, hæv ə ˈweɪl əv ə ˌtaɪm/ [v phrase] informal to enjoy yourself very much: *'Your vacation sounds fantastic.' 'We had the time of our lives!'* | **have the time of your life/have a whale of a time doing sth** *Alan was having the time of his life, playing to an admiring audience.* | *The kids all had a whale of a time, in and out of the pool all day.*

get a kick out of doing sth /get ə ˌkɪk aʊt əv ˈduːɪŋ (sth)/ [v phrase] to enjoy doing or seeing something: *I get a real kick out of watching my son learning to speak.* | *Jody got a kick out of trying some of the new video games.*

2 to enjoy something, especially something bad or wrong

- revel in
- get a kick out of
- relish
- gloat
- wallow in
- take pleasure in
- delight in

revel in /ˈrevəl ɪn/ [phr v T] to enjoy something that most people would not like: *Her job is very stressful, but she seems to revel in it.* | **revel in doing sth** *Tom seems to revel in disagreeing with everything I say.*

get a kick out of /get ə ˈkɪk aʊt ɒv/ [v phrase] to enjoy doing something, especially something that is difficult, dangerous, or unkind: *I love speaking to a large audience. I get a real kick out of it.* | **get a kick out of doing sth** *Maggie seems to get a big kick out of flirting with other people's husbands.*

relish /ˈrelɪʃ/ [v T] to very much enjoy doing something that is difficult or hurts other people: *Setting up your own business is never easy, but Frank relished the challenge.* | **relish doing sth** *The interviewer seemed to relish asking her personal questions.* | **relish the chance/opportunity to do sth** *I stayed with an Israeli family, and relished the chance to soak up their culture at ground-level.* | **relish the thought/prospect/idea of doing sth** (=relish the idea of doing something in the future) *She clearly relished the prospect of breaking the news to them.* | *I really didn't relish the idea of being alone for two weeks.*

gloat /gləʊt/ [v I] to get pleasure from someone else's failure or bad luck, especially when you have been more successful or luckier than them: *'I told you that idea wouldn't work.' 'Well, there's no need to gloat.'* | **+ about/at/over** *Jane used to gloat over other people's misfortunes.* | *'What are you gloating about?' he said in an irritated voice.*

wallow in /ˈwɒləʊ ɪn‖ˈwɑː-/ [phr v T] to enjoy being sad, feeling sorry for yourself etc, especially in order to make people notice you and pay attention to you **wallow in grief/guilt/pity etc** *Since his girlfriend left him, he's been wallowing in self-pity.* | *Wallowing in angst at the unfairness of it all will only make the problem worse.*

take pleasure in /ˌteɪk ˈpleʒər ɪn/ [v phrase] to enjoy doing something bad to other people: *Charlie's always bullying the smaller kids. He seems to take pleasure in it.* | **take pleasure in doing sth** *He appears to take pleasure in hurting her feelings.*

delight in /dɪˈlaɪt ɪn/ [phr v T] to enjoy doing something that makes other people feel a little uncomfortable or embarrassed: *Most people delight in a bit of scandal, especially when it involves public figures.* | **delight in doing sth** *She's the kind of woman who delights in pointing out other people's mistakes.*

3 experiences and activities that you enjoy

- enjoyable
- fun
- pleasurable
- pleasure
- be a delight
- be a blast
- be a good laugh

enjoyable /ɪnˈdʒɔɪəbəl/ [adj] an **enjoyable** activity, especially something you do with other people, is pleasant and interesting: *We spent an enjoyable evening playing cards.* | *I try to make my lessons more enjoyable by using games.*

fun /fʌn/ [n U] especially spoken if something is **fun**, you enjoy it because it is very interesting and exciting: *The course was really hard work but it was fun.* | **have fun** (=enjoy yourself with other people) *On Saturday night, all I want to do is relax and have some fun.* | **it is fun to do sth/it is fun doing sth** *It's fun to eat out sometimes, instead of cooking at home.* | *It'll be fun seeing all my old friends again.* | **good/great fun** (=very enjoyable) *Have you ever been windsurfing? It's really good fun.* | **sb's idea of fun** (=what someone enjoys doing, although other people might not) *Running around a freezing hockey field isn't my idea of fun.* | **half the fun (of it)** (=almost as enjoyable as the experience itself) *Planning a vacation is half the fun of it.* —**fun** [adj] *Hundreds of people were there and it was a really fun day out.*

pleasurable /ˈpleʒərəbəl/ [adj] formal giving you a lot of pleasure, enjoyment and satisfaction: *The pleasurable effects of any drug quickly wear off.* | *Once you are reasonably fit, you will find the exercise satisfying and pleasurable.*

pleasure /ˈpleʒə^r/ [n C] an experience or activity that makes you feel happy and satisfied: *One of her greatest pleasures was walking in the mountains.* | **the simple pleasures (of life)** *Ted enjoyed the simple pleasures of life: his family, his home, and his garden.* | **be a pleasure to look at/watch/read etc** *A really good game of basketball is a pleasure to watch.*

be a delight /biː ə dɪˈlaɪt/ [v phrase] formal an event or activity that **is a delight** is extremely enjoyable, especially when you did not expect it to be: *Sarah found that work was a delight compared to motherhood.* | *The story's really funny and the illustrations are a delight.* | **be a delight to hear/look at/ see etc** *Anna's piano playing is a delight to listen to.*

be a blast /biː ə ˈblɑːst‖-ˈblæst/ [v phrase] American informal to be very enjoyable and exciting: *The party was a blast. We didn't stop dancing till three in the morning.*

be a good laugh /biː ə ˌgʊd ˈlɑːf‖-ˈlæf/ [v phrase] British informal to be enjoyable and amusing: *We went skating on Saturday. I kept falling over, but it was a good laugh.*

4 someone who enjoys something very much

- avid
- keen
- great

avid /ˈævəd/ [adj only before noun] **avid reader/collector/listener** someone who enjoys reading, collecting something etc, and does it with great interest: *Tim's father is an avid collector of old blues and jazz records.* | *As a keen writer and avid newspaper reader, Jenny had always wanted to be a journalist.*

keen /kiːn/ [adj only before noun] British **keen gardener/sportsman/golfer/painter etc** someone who enjoys gardening, sport etc so much that they spend a lot of their free time doing it: *Goethe was a keen amateur geologist.* | *Paul, a keen sportsman, prided himself on his level of fitness.*

great /greɪt/ [adj only before noun] **great traveller/reader/talker etc** someone who has an eager, lively interest in travelling, reading etc, so that they do it as often as they can: *Thesiger was a great traveller, especially in Arabia and Africa.* | **be a great one for sth** British *I was never really a great one for sport as a child.*

5 someone who people enjoy being with

- be good company
- fun
- be a good laugh

be good company /biː ˌgʊd ˈkʌmpəni/ [v phrase] if someone **is good company**, people enjoy spending time with them: *Harry was such good company – always joking and full of fun.*

fun /fʌn/ [adj] spoken use this about people who are always cheerful, interesting, and amusing: *Let's invite Margot – she's always fun.* | **be good/great fun** British **be a lot of fun** *I like Sam a lot – he's good fun.* | **be fun to be with** *The O'Brien boys were always fun to be with.* | **a fun person/guy/girl** *Oh yes, I know Eddie – he's a really fun guy.*

be a good laugh /biː ə ˌgʊd ˈlɑːf‖-ˈlæf/ [v phrase] British informal to be amusing and cheerful when you are with other people: *I'm glad Sylvia's coming too – she's a good laugh.*

6 when you do something for enjoyment

- for fun
- for a laugh
- just (for) a bit of fun
- (just) for the hell of it
- (just) for kicks

for fun /fə^r ˈfʌn/ [adv] if you do something **for fun**, you do it because you enjoy it and not for any other reason: *I only really started the shop for fun, but it's been a huge success.* | **just for fun** *When we started our band we played music in restaurants just for fun.*

for a laugh /fər ə ˈlɑːf‖-ˈlæf/ [adv] British in order to enjoy yourself and to make people laugh: *I only entered the contest for a laugh, so I couldn't believe it when I won!* | *In the end Kelly admitted that she'd invented the story for a laugh.*

just (for) a bit of fun /ˌdʒʌst (fə^r) ə bɪt əv ˈfʌn/ [n phrase/adv] British spoken if something is **just a bit of**

fun, it is done as a joke or for enjoyment, especially when other people do not approve: *The two boys told the court that they stole the car – 'just for a bit of fun'.* | *Don't get upset Mum – it was only a bit of fun.*

(just) for the hell of it /(ˌdʒʌst) fəʳ ðə ˈhel əv ɪt/ [adv] informal if you do something **for the hell of it**, you do it only because you enjoy it and for no other reason, especially something bad: *We used to go out every Saturday night and get drunk, just for the hell of it.* | *A lot of rich kids are turning to crime just for the hell of it.*

(just) for kicks /(ˌdʒʌst) fəʳ ˈkɪks/ [adv] informal for enjoyment – use this when someone does something that you strongly disapprove of, for example hurting another person, for enjoyment: *Detectives say that the murderer is a 'lunatic who kills for kicks'.* | *Some kids steal from shops just for kicks.*

7 a feeling of enjoying something

- enjoyment
- ecstasy
- pleasure

enjoyment /ɪnˈdʒɔɪmənt/ [n U] the feeling you get when you enjoy doing something **get enjoyment out of sth** *I get a lot of enjoyment out of working with young children.* | **+ of** *A really good wine will add to your enjoyment of the meal.*

pleasure /ˈpleʒəʳ/ [n U] the happy feeling you get when you are enjoying something **get pleasure from sth** *My father always got a lot of pleasure from being with his grandchildren.* | **do sth for pleasure** (=because it gives you pleasure) *I don't very often read for pleasure.* | **with pleasure** *I noticed with pleasure how much happier he seemed.* | **give/bring pleasure to sb** (=make someone happy) *Her singing has given pleasure to so many people over the years.* | **take pleasure in (doing) sth** *His French was excellent, and he took pleasure in speaking it.*

ecstasy /ˈekstəsi/ [n U] a feeling of extreme enjoyment, happiness and satisfaction **the ecstasy of (doing) sth** *I remember the ecstasy of opening the letter and finding that I'd passed my exam.* | **in ecstasy** (=with great happiness and enjoyment) *The ball flew out of the stadium, and the Boston fans hugged each other in ecstasy.* | **sheer/pure ecstasy** (=complete ecstasy) *Just let the chocolate melt in your mouth. It's sheer ecstasy!*

8 to enjoy getting a lot of praise, attention etc

- bask in
- lap up
- revel in

bask in /ˈbɑːsk ɪn‖ˈbæsk-/ [phr v T] to enjoy a situation where people are saying how good or successful you are: *The group were clearly basking in the crowd's adoration and applause.* | **bask in the glory/glow (of sth)** *It was a tremendous victory for the team, and they sat back and basked in the glory.* | *For several months I'd been basking in the glow of graduation, but now it was time to get a job.*

revel in /ˈrevəl ɪn/ [phr v T] to enjoy a situation where you get a lot of attention or praise: *Barrymore clearly revels in the joy of entertaining an audience.* | *During his visit, the President seemed to revel in the limelight.*

lap up /ˈlæp ʌp/ [phr v T] to enjoy getting a lot of attention or praise **lap up sth** *We all lapped up the five-star treatment on the ship.* | **lap sth up** *Fred was in the middle of a group of girls, and was obviously lapping it up.*

9 things you do for enjoyment

- recreation
- leisure

recreation /ˌrekriˈeɪʃən/ [n U] activities, especially physical activities and games, that you do to enjoy yourself: *The afternoons at the conference were left free for recreation.* | *Vancouver is a city more in tune with outdoor recreation than cultural institutions.* —**recreational** [adj] *The town's recreational facilities were totally inadequate until the new sport center was built.*

leisure /ˈleʒəʳ‖ˈliː-/ [n U] the time when you are not working, when you can enjoy yourself, especially by doing something relaxing: *Your standard of living depends on your income and also on the amount of leisure you have.* | **leisure time/activity/facilities** *The reduction in average working hours has led to an increase in leisure time.* | *A wide range of leisure activities such as swimming, fishing, and sailing are also available.*

enough/ not enough

RELATED WORDS

▸ *see also* **full**

1 when there is enough of something you need

- enough
- suffice
- sufficient
- cover
- adequate
- last
- will/should do
- meet sb's needs

enough /ɪˈnʌf/ [quantifier] *Here's $20. Is that enough?* | *Have you got enough drivers? I can help if you need me.* | **enough sth to do sth** *I make enough money to pay the bills and keep food on the table.* | **enough (sth) for sth** *Will there be enough room for Joey in the car?* | *This recipe makes enough for eight people.* | **more than enough** (=more than you need) *I've given you more than enough time to make up your mind.* | **I've had enough** (=say this when you have eaten enough food) *'Would you like some more pizza?' 'No thanks, I've had enough.'*

sufficient /səˈfɪʃənt/ [adj] formal enough: *It was decided that there was sufficient evidence to convict Marconi.* | **+ for** *The money should be sufficient for one month's travel.*

adequate /ˈædɪkwɪ̣t/ [adj] formal enough in amount, and good enough in quality: *None of his workers received adequate safety training.* | **+ for** *The heating system would only be adequate for a much smaller house.*

will/should do /wɪl, ʃʊd ˈduː/ [v phrase not in progressive] spoken use this to say that a particular number or amount will be enough for what you need: *'I can't find any more envelopes.' 'That's OK – these should do.'* | **will do** *I can lend you some money – will £10 do?* | **sth should do for sth/sth ought to do for sth** *Ten bottles of wine should do for the party.* | **That should do it/That ought to do it/That'll do it** *Take a few more for the kids. There, that should do it.* | **sth**

should do/ought to do/will do sb *Here's £20 for the shopping – that should do you.*

suffice /səˈfaɪs/ [v I not in progressive] formal to be enough **will/would suffice** *A doctor's certificate will suffice as a form of permission.* | **should suffice to do sth** (=will probably be enough to do it) *These few examples should suffice to illustrate how social attitudes are changing.*

cover /ˈkʌvəʳ/ [v T not in progressive] if an amount of money **covers** the cost of something, it is enough to pay for it: *$29.90 a month covers the cost of all your insurance.* | *Western aid to Third World countries barely covers the interest on their loans.*

last /lɑːst‖læst/ [v] if an amount of food or money **lasts** for a period of time, there is enough of it for that period **+ until** *I still have $100, but that won't last until the end of the vacation.* | **last (sb) 2 years/3 days etc** *A can of baby formula costing $6.00 will last you three to four days.*

meet sb's needs /ˌmiːt (sb's) ˈniːdz/ [v phrase] if an amount of something **meets someone's needs**, there is as much of it as that person needs – use this especially in formal or official contexts: *In many parts of the world, there is not enough food to meet everyone's needs.*

2 big enough, strong enough, old enough etc

- enough
- sufficiently
- adequately

enough /ɪˈnʌf/ [adv] **big/old/strong enough etc** *Will that box be strong enough?* | **+ for** *The sled is big enough for three children to ride on it safely.* | **+ to do sth** *The pole was just long enough to reach the top window.* | *Raphael is probably the only one crazy enough to try it.*

sufficiently /səˈfɪʃəntli/ [adv] formal enough: *I had recovered sufficiently by the end of the week to give two more speeches.* | **sufficiently large/easy etc to do sth** *I don't think the candidate is sufficiently skillful to do the job.* | **sufficiently large/easy etc for sth** *The measurements are sufficiently accurate for our purposes.*

adequately /ˈædɪkwə̇tli/ [adv] formal enough or well enough: *There are no plans to change the current system, which is performing adequately.* | *We're trying to encourage parents to make sure their children are adequately protected against childhood diseases.*

3 to have enough of something

- have enough
- have the time/money/help etc
- can afford
- can spare
- run to
- be OK for/be all right for
- be well off for

have enough /ˌhæv ɪˈnʌf/ [v phrase not in progressive] to **have enough** of something to do what you want: *I'll come and see you if I have enough time.* | **have enough time/money etc to do sth** *We didn't have enough room to lie down, so we couldn't really sleep.*

have the time/money/help etc /hæv ðə ˈtaɪm/ [v phrase not in progressive] to have enough of something to do what you want: *I know I should exercise, but I just never seem to have the time.* | *I'm sure Jonathan would be willing to help, if he had the money.* | **+ to do sth** *A small company like ours just doesn't have the resources to compete with the big corporations.*

can afford /kən əˈfɔːʳd/ [v phrase] to have enough money to do something or to buy something: *I love the apartment, but I don't think we can afford the rent.* | **+ to do sth** *These days more and more people can afford to fly, which means the airways become increasingly crowded.*

can spare /kən ˈspeəʳ/ [v phrase] informal to have enough time, money etc for a particular purpose, because you do not need it all for other purposes: *Can you spare a couple of minutes to talk about next week's programme?* | *The firm has agreed to improve the toilet facilities as soon as they can spare the money.* | *The records show that the city has a few acres of land to spare.*

run to /ˈrʌn tuː/ [v T not in progressive or passive] British informal if someone's money **runs to** something, they have enough money to pay for it, especially when it is something expensive: *I don't think my salary quite runs to holidays in the Caribbean!* | *The company budget wouldn't run to a Mercedes, so I had to make do with a Ford instead.*

be OK for/be all right for /biː əʊ ˈkeɪ fɔːʳ, biː ɔːl ˈraɪt fɔːʳ/ [v phrase] informal to have enough of something that you need, such as time, money, or food: *'Do you have to rush off?' 'No, I'm OK for time.'* | *We're all right for vegetables, but we need to buy some more fruit.* | *'Are we ok for little plates?' 'Yeah, Matthew washed them all.'*

be well off for /biː ˌwel ˈɒf fɔːʳ/ [v phrase] British informal to have plenty of something that is needed or that makes life easier or more pleasant: *We're quite well off for public transport in this part of the country.* | *The school's reasonably well off for books and equipment but there is a shortage of staff.*

4 enough and more

- more than enough
- plenty
- ample

more than enough /ˈmɔːʳ ðən ɪˌnʌf/ [quantifier] *I've given you more than enough money to pay for everything.* | *There were more than enough people to set up the stage.* | *The software provides more than enough tools to make just about any object you might imagine.*

plenty /ˈplenti/ [quantifier] more than enough – use this when you do not need any more of something: *'Do you need any more paper?' ' No, thanks, I have plenty here.'* | **+ of** *There's plenty of time. We don't have to hurry.* | *At that time of year there will still be plenty of daylight at 8:00 in the evening.*

ample /ˈæmpəl/ [adj] if an amount of something is **ample**, there is more than enough of it – use this in writing or formal speech: *The hotel's main dining room has ample room for both dining and dancing.* | *He was given ample opportunity to express his opinion.*

5 not enough

- not enough
- too little/few
- scarce
- inadequate
- insufficient
- be in short supply
- lack of sth
- be short

not enough ALSO **insufficient** /nɒt ɪˈnʌf, ˌɪnsəˈfɪʃənt◂/ [quantifier/adj] **not enough** for what you need. **insufficient** is much more formal than **not enough**: *You're not getting enough sleep.* | **not enough (sth) to do sth** *We didn't win enough games to get to the championship.* | *No matter how much* *money they offer me, it wouldn't be enough to make me like the job.* | *There was insufficient evidence to prove their allegations.* | **not enough (sth) for sth** *There weren't enough apples for a pie, but they're good for eating.* | *Officials were worried that supplies would be insufficient for the long winter that was being predicted.* | **not nearly enough/nowhere near enough** (=much less than enough) *£1 million is not nearly enough to clean up the water in the bay.* | *The time they've given us is nowhere near enough.*

too little/few /ˌtuː ˈlɪtl, ˈfjuː/ [quantifier] less than you need or fewer than you need – use this especially when you are criticizing or complaining about something: *Some churches are in danger of closing because there are too few priests.* | *There is too little cooperation between the opposing parties to get anything done in government.* | **too little/few to do sth** *There's too little time to do everything.* | *There were some police officers there, but too few to control the crowd.* | **far too little/few** (=much too little or few) *Most of the students explained far too little about their research methods.*

scarce /skeəʳs/ [adj not before noun] if something is **scarce**, there is not enough of it, so it is very difficult to get or buy: *During the war, things like clothes and shoes were scarce.* | *Cheap, clean hotel rooms are scarce in this city, especially in the summer.*

inadequate /ɪnˈædɪkwɪt/ [adj] an amount of something that is **inadequate** is not enough for a particular purpose: *The state pension is wholly inadequate – no one can live on £50 a week.* | *Inadequate lighting made it difficult to continue the work after dinner.* | **+ to do sth** *The amount of fertilizer used was inadequate to ensure a good harvest.*

insufficient /ˌɪnsəˈfɪʃənt◂/ [adj] formal not enough: *The bank charged me for having insufficient funds in my account.* | *There has been insufficient rainfall over the past two years, and farmers are having trouble.* | **+ to do sth** *The data we have is insufficient to draw any conclusions.*

be in short supply /biː ɪn ˌʃɔːʳt səˈplaɪ/ [v phrase] if a product **is in short supply** people cannot buy or get enough of it: *Health workers reported that medicines and basic equipment were in short supply.* | *The unemployment rate was at 2.5%, and talented job seekers were in short supply.*

lack of sth /ˈlæk əv (sth)/ [n singular] if there is a **lack of** something there is not enough of it, or none at all: *Fernando's eyes were red through lack of sleep.* | *It's lack of confidence, not lack of ability, that makes most people fail.* | *They threw the case out of court because of a lack of evidence.*

be short /biː ˈʃɔːʳt/ [v phrase] if time or money **is short**, there is not as much of it as you would like: *Money's a little short this month – we'd better be careful about spending.* | *The military authorities considered that the need for action was great, and time was short.*

6 not good enough, important enough etc

- not ... enough
- not sufficiently

not ... enough /nɒt ... ɪnʌf/ *'Can you read the sign?' 'No, we're not close enough.'* | **+ for** *This room isn't large enough for public meetings.* | **not ... enough to do sth** *Dana isn't strong enough to survive the operation at this time.*

not sufficiently /nɒt səˈfɪʃəntli/ [adv] formal not good enough, not important enough, etc **not sufficiently ... to do sth** *Frasier's right foot has not healed sufficiently to allow him to play tonight.* | *The report is not sufficiently detailed to give us all the information we require.*

7 to not have enough of something

- not have enough
- can't afford
- be short of/be low on
- be short on
- be running out/short of
- be stretched
- be strapped for cash
- deficient
- be starved of

not have enough /nɒt hæv ɪˈnʌf/ [v phrase not in progressive] *The computer doesn't have enough memory – it just crashes all the time.* | **not have enough time/money etc to do sth** *We don't have enough time to go shopping now.* | **not have enough to do/eat/drink etc** *The number of children in the cities that do not have enough to eat is rising daily.*

can't afford /ˌkɑːnt əˈfɔːʳd‖ˌkænt-/ [v phrase] to not have enough money to do something: *We can't afford a really good printer right now.* | *I know I can't really afford it, but I want to buy her something nice.* | **can't afford to do sth** (=not have enough money to do it) *I can't afford to fly, so I'm renting a car.* | *I can't afford to have any more unpaid days off.*

be short of/be low on /biː ˈʃɔːʳt ɒv, biː ˈləʊ ɒn/ [v phrase] to not have enough of something that is necessary, such as money or food: *I was short of money, so George lent me $20.* | *The county is short of affordable housing, and the situation is getting worse.* | *The pilot knew the plane was low on fuel.*

be short on /biː ˈʃɔːʳt ɒn/ [v phrase] informal to have less than you should have of a useful or important quality: *Warren is a good worker, but short on new ideas.* | *I sometimes felt our evenings together were a little short on fun.*

be running out/short of /biː ˌrʌnɪŋ ˈaʊt, ˈʃɔːʳt ɒv/ [v phrase] to be using so much of something that you will soon not have enough of it left: *We're running out of time – can you finish up quickly?* | *Is the world running out of natural resources?* | *The refugees are running short of supplies and winter is approaching.*

be stretched /biː ˈstretʃt/ [v phrase] to have only just enough money or just enough of a supply of something, so that you have to be very careful about how you use it: *With a hundred thousand new people in the area, city resources are stretched.* | **be stretched to the breaking point/the limit** (=to have so little of something that you are likely to fail) *If this cut in resources occurs, it could severely damage a social fabric that is already stretched to the breaking point.* | **be stretched thin** American *The army's supply lines in the area along the southern border were stretched dangerously thin.*

be strapped for cash /biː ˌstræpt fəʳ ˈkæʃ/ [v phrase] informal to not have enough money at the present time: *We sold the restaurant when we were strapped for cash a few years ago.* | *If you are seriously strapped for cash, I'm sure Robert could give you a job.*

deficient /dɪˈfɪʃənt/ [adj] not containing as much of a particular substance or not having as much of a particular quality as is necessary – used especially in scientific contexts **+ in** *Your diet is deficient in vitamins.* | **protein/nutrient/iron etc deficient** *Only hormone-deficient children are allowed to use the drug.*

be starved of /bi: ˈstɑːʳvd ɒv/ [v phrase] to be given much less of something than is needed: *Most of the animals are just starved of attention.* | *She admitted that living on the island she had been starved of conversation and ideas.* | *Starved of foreign aid money, the country collapsed into war last year.*

8 an amount, quantity etc that is less than is needed

- shortage
- shortfall
- deficiency

shortage /ˈʃɔːʳtɪdʒ/ [n C] a situation in which there is not enough of something very basic and important that people need in order to live or work **+ of** *There is a shortage of nurses and doctors in this area.* | **water/food/housing etc shortage** *Parts of Britain are suffering water shortages after the unusually dry summer.* | **acute/severe shortage** (=a very bad shortage) *The drop in the birth rate 20 years ago has created a severe shortage of workers.*

shortfall /ˈʃɔːʳtfɔːl/ [n C] the amount by which there is not enough of something: *a 3% production shortfall* | *The center had projected a $38,000 shortfall for its $6.47 million budget.* | **+ in** *We've had to trim our budget to compensate for a $1.5 million shortfall in revenue.* | **+ of** *The districts affected by the drought will face a predicted shortfall of 7.5 million gallons a day.*

deficiency /dɪˈfɪʃənsi/ [n C/U] when there is not enough of an important or necessary substance or quality: *Women suffering from iron deficiency can take supplements in the form of tablets.* | *One of the symptoms of vitamin C deficiency is extreme tiredness.* | **+ of** *A deficiency of soil nutrients can cause the resulting crop to be disease-ridden and of very poor quality.*

enter

RELATED WORDS

opposite: **leave**

- to enter a competition, race etc *see* **take part/be involved**
- *see also* **arrive, get on or off a bus, plane, etc**

1 to enter a place

- go in
- come in
- enter
- get in
- gain admission
- burst in
- barge in
- make an entrance/make your entrance
- breeze in

go in /ˌgəʊ ˈɪn/ [phr v I/T] *It was getting cold, so we went in.* | *There was a man at the door trying to stop people from going in.* | *Don't go in my room – it's a mess.* | **go into sth** *Make sure you wipe your feet before you go into the house.*

come in /ˌkʌm ˈɪn/ [phr v I/T] if someone **comes in**, they enter a room or building that you are in: *That must be Nina coming in right now.* | *As soon as Adrian came in, everyone stopped talking.* | *Why don't you come in the house for a little while and get warmed up.* | **come into sth** *When you first come into the building, you'll see the elevators just across the lobby.*

enter /ˈentəʳ/ [v I/T] formal to go or come into a room, building, or area: *You need a ticket to enter.* | *The army entered the city from the north.* | *As soon as he entered the room, he knew there was something wrong.*

get in /ˌget ˈɪn/ [phr v I/T] to succeed in entering a place, especially when this is difficult or takes a long time: *We queued in the rain for two hours and still didn't get in.* | *You usually have to wait a while before you can get in the club.* | **get into sth** *You shouldn't have any trouble getting into the concert – they've only sold half the tickets.*

gain admission /ˌgeɪn ədˈmɪʃən/ [v phrase] formal to succeed in entering a place or being allowed to enter, especially when this is difficult or takes a long time: *Brown gained admission by claiming to be a newspaper photographer.* | **+ to** *We had to talk to several guards to gain admission to the courtyard.*

burst in /ˌbɜːʳst ˈɪn/ [phr v I] to suddenly and noisily enter a room: *Two men with guns burst in and told us to lie on the floor.* | **+ on** *I ran back to Iris's and burst in on Polly who was ironing in the kitchen.* | **burst into sth** *Lotty burst into the room waving a letter in the air.*

barge in /ˌbɑːʳdʒ ˈɪn/ [phr v I] to suddenly enter a room where you are not wanted, for example because you are interrupting someone: *I was studying when Ben suddenly barged in.* | **+ on** *It's impossible to concentrate when people keep barging in on you.* | **barge into sth** *Some of the strikers came barging into the meeting and demanded to speak with the directors.*

make an entrance/make your entrance /ˌmeɪk ən ˈentrəns, ˌmeɪk jɔːr ˈentrəns/ [v phrase] to enter somewhere in a way that makes the people who are already there notice you: *I waited until everybody was sitting quietly before making my entrance.* | **make a grand entrance** *She walked slowly down the staircase, making a grand entrance.*

breeze in /ˌbriːz ˈɪn/ [phr v I] to enter a place confidently and calmly, especially when other people would be a little nervous or embarrassed to enter: *Katie breezes in at eleven o'clock each morning, two hours late.* | **breeze into sth** *Giles just breezed into the office, used the phone, and then breezed out again.*

2 to tell someone that they can come into your house, room etc

- come in
- ask sb in/invite sb in
- come on in

come in /ˌkʌm ˈɪn/ spoken say **come in** when you want someone to come into your room, home, or office: *Come in and sit down. I'll be ready in a minute.* | *Marge, it's so good to see you! Come in! Come in!* | *'Come in,' she said in answer to my second knock.*

ask sb in/invite sb in /ˌɑːsk (sb) ˈɪn‖ˌæsk-, ɪnˌvaɪt (sb) ˈɪn/ [phr v T] to ask someone if they want to come into your home: *Stella didn't know whether to ask him in or not.* | *A salesman came around this morning and I made the mistake of inviting him in.* | **+ for** *She seemed so upset, I felt I had to ask her in for a cup of tea.*

come on in /ˌkʌm ɒn ˈɪn/ spoken say **come on in** when you want someone to come into your room, home, or office, especially when you want to be friendly and make the other person feel welcome: *Hi! Come on in! Can I fix you something to drink?* | *'Mike, could I talk with you a minute?' 'Sure, come on in.'*

3 to enter somewhere quietly or secretly

- sneak in
- slip in

sneak in /ˌsniːk ˈɪn/ [phr v I] to enter a place secretly, hoping that no one will notice you: *When he was drunk he would sneak in late, hoping his wife was asleep.* | **sneak into sth** *He had a passion for bebop and was sneaking into jazz clubs at age 14.* | **sneak sb in** (=help someone else sneak in) *We wanted to sneak my dad in, so my mom wouldn't see.*

slip in /ˌslɪp ˈɪn/ [phr v I] to enter a place quietly and quickly without being noticed: *Maggie opened the door silently and slipped in.* | **slip into sth** *A few latecomers had slipped into the room and were standing at the back of the audience.*

4 to enter a place illegally or by using force

- enter
- get in
- break in
- gain entry/gain access
- force your way in
- breaking and entering
- trespass
- penetrate

enter /ˈentəʳ/ [v I/T] *A man was arrested for trying to enter the actress's Beverly Hills home.* | **+ through/by etc** *It appears the burglars entered through a back window.*

get in /ˌget ˈɪn/ [phr v I/T] to succeed in entering a room, building, or area which is locked or difficult to enter, especially by using force or by finding an unusual way in: *How did you get in? I thought the door was locked.* | *Some animals had gotten in the shed and made a mess.* | **get into sth** *Thieves had apparently got into the apartments by posing as electricians.*

break in /ˌbreɪk ˈɪn/ [phr v I] to enter a building by using force, in order to steal something: *If anyone tries to break in, the alarm will go off.* | **break into sth** *Thieves broke into the gallery and made off with paintings valued at over $2 million.*

gain entry/gain access /ˌgeɪn ˈentri, ˌgeɪn ˈækses/ [v phrase] if someone, especially criminals or the police **gain entry** or **gain access**, they succeed in entering a locked building or room, especially by using force: *The police gained entry by smashing down the door.* | **+ to** *Somehow the woman had gained access to his dressing room and was waiting there when he came off the stage.*

force your way in /ˌfɔːʳs jɔːʳ weɪ ˈɪn/ [v phrase] to enter a building or room by using force, especially when someone is trying to stop you: *They've blocked the door. We'll have to force our way in.* | **force your way into sth** *Police eventually forced their way into the building and arrested the gunman.*

breaking and entering /ˌbreɪkɪŋ ənd ˈentərɪŋ/ [n U] the crime of entering a place illegally, especially with the intention of stealing something: *You can't just go into his apartment when he's not there – that's breaking and entering.* | *He was caught in the school at night and has been charged with breaking and entering.*

trespass /ˈtrespəs, -pæs/ [v I] to illegally enter or be on someone's land or in a building without permission from the owner: *Get out of the yard! Can't you see the sign? It says 'No Trespassing.'* | **+ on** *Carlson was fined $1000 for trespassing on government property.* —**trespasser** [n C] *Trespassers will be prosecuted.*

penetrate /ˈpenətreɪt/ [v T] to enter an area that is well guarded or dangerous to enter – used especially in a military context: *The barbed wire fences and security shields made the air base very difficult to penetrate.*

5 to enter a country

- enter
- cross the border
- immigrate

enter /ˈentəʳ/ [v I/T] *Everyone entering the country must show a passport.* | *The barbed wire fences and mine fields are designed to stop people leaving or entering.* | *Congress is considering raising the number of skilled workers who may enter the country each year.*

cross the border /ˌkrɒs ðə ˈbɔːʳdəʳ‖ˌkrɔːs-/ [v phrase] to enter a country from another country which is next to it, and is not separated from it by the sea: *Many people cross the border illegally in search of work.* | **+ into** *Every day more and more desperate refugees were crossing the border into Kenya.*

immigrate /ˈɪməgreɪt/ [v I] to enter another country in order to live there permanently **+ to** *Her father immigrated to America from China in 1947.* | *Born in Jamaica, Rigby had immigrated to England 30 years before.* —**immigration** /ˌɪməˈgreɪʃən/ [n U] **+ to/into** *Most immigration to New York City has been from the Caribbean, Europe, and Asia.*

6 someone who enters another country

- immigrant
- refugee
- asylum-seeker
- immigration

immigrant /ˈɪməgrənt/ [n C] someone who enters another country in order to live there permanently: *The new immigrants come mainly from Asia and Latin America.* | **+ from** *Jae Min's parents are immigrants from South Korea.* | **+ to** *The winery was started by an Italian immigrant to California.* | **legal/illegal immigrant** *The bill would have cut off government aid even to legal immigrants.*

refugee /ˌrefjʊˈdʒiː/ [n C] someone who enters another country because they are not safe in their own country, for example because there is a war there: *The government has been unable to provide enough tents for all the refugees.* | **+ from** *Most of the refugees from the former war zone have now been sent back.* | **political refugee** *Britain has traditionally been a safe haven for political refugees.*

asylum-seeker /əˈsaɪləm ˌsiːkəʳ/ [n C] someone who asks to be allowed to enter another country because they are not safe in their own country, especially because of their political beliefs or activities: *Too often asylum-seekers are treated like criminals.* | *Officially recognized asylum-seekers cannot be deported.*

immigration /ˌɪməˈgreɪʃən/ [n U] when people enter a country in order to live there permanently: *Most people in the UK believe that immigration has enriched the economy and national culture.* | *Immigration reached its peak in the 1950s.* | *Immigration officials stopped and arrested the man at JFK airport.*

7 when a large number of people enter a country, place, city etc

- pour in/flood in
- crowd in
- troop in
- trickle in
- influx
- flood

pour in/flood in /ˌpɔːr ˈɪn, ˌflʌd ˈɪn/ [phr v I] if a lot of people **pour in** or **flood in**, they all enter a place at the same time: *Once the region was declared safe, tourists started flooding in again.* | **pour/flood into sth** *An estimated 50,000 people poured into London over the weekend for the opening of the Commonwealth Games.*

crowd in /ˌkraʊd ˈɪn/ [phr v I] if a lot of people **crowd in**, they all enter a place, especially a place that is not big enough for so many people: *People kept crowding in, and one woman started to panic.* | **crowd into sth** *More than 100 people crowded into the fire station for Thursday night's council meeting.*

troop in /ˌtruːp ˈɪn/ [phr v I] if a group of people **troop in** they enter a place, often in a tired or unwilling way: *After the game they all trooped in to eat.* | **troop into sth** *Every morning we had to troop into the school hall for roll call.*

trickle in /ˌtrɪkəl ˈɪn/ [phr v I] if people **trickle in**, they enter a place gradually and not all at the same time: *A few fans had already started to trickle in.* | **trickle into sth** *The bell rang, and the students trickled into the class.*

influx /ˈɪnflʌks/ [n U] the sudden or unexpected arrival of a large number of people **+ of** *The influx of migrants to the city is estimated at 1,000 per week.* | *The sudden influx of families needing work and housing caused some problems at first.*

flood /flʌd/ [n singular] a large number of people entering a place at the same time **+ of** *The company has employed a number of new staff to cope with the flood of visitors to the site.* | *A flood of refugees poured over the bridge to escape the fighting.*

8 to let someone enter a place

- let sb in
- admit

let sb in /ˌlet (sb) ˈɪn/ [phr v T] *Let me in! It's freezing out here.* | *There's Ryan at the door. Let him in, would you?* | *Who let those guys in? They don't belong here.* | *Don't let anybody in the house while I'm gone.* | **let sb into sth** *His girlfriend was there and let me into the apartment.*

admit /ədˈmɪt/ [v T] to officially allow someone to enter a public place in order to watch a game, performance etc: *Children under 17 will not be admitted.* | **admit sb to sth** *They refused to admit Paul to the performance because of what he was wearing.*

9 to not let someone enter

- keep out
- shut out
- lock out
- refuse entry
- turn away
- bar/ban

keep out /ˌkiːp ˈaʊt/ [phr v T] to prevent someone from entering a place, for example by locking doors and windows, or building fences **keep out sb** *He bought a new security system to keep out intruders.* | **keep sb out** *Family members can go in to visit him, but we need to keep everyone else out.* | **keep sb out of sth** *Try to keep Ed out of the bedroom while I finish wrapping his present.*

shut out /ˌʃʌt ˈaʊt/ [phr v T] to shut a door, window etc in order to prevent someone from entering, especially because they would be interrupting you or annoying you **shut out sb** *He slammed the door, shutting out the dogs.* | **shut sb out (of sth)** *John shut everybody out of the kitchen so that he could prepare his grand surprise.*

lock out /ˌlɒk ˈaʊt‖ˌlɑːk-/ [phr v T] to stop someone from entering a place by locking a door **lock sb out/lock out sb** *Her husband threw her out of the trailer without shoes or clothes and locked her out.* | **lock sb out of sth** *I can't believe I locked myself out of the house again.*

refuse entry /rɪˌfjuːz ˈentri/ [v phrase] to refuse to allow someone to enter a country or a public place **refuse sb entry** *Immigration officials refused her entry because they thought she was planning to stay.* | **refuse entry to sb** *The management reserves the right to refuse entry to anyone who is improperly dressed.*

turn away /ˌtɜːʳn əˈweɪ/ [phr v T] to refuse to let someone into a place where a public event is happening, especially because it is full **turn sb away/turn away sb** *Hundreds of disappointed fans were turned away at the gates.* | *The club's so popular, we have to turn people away every night.*

bar/ban /bɑːʳ, bæn/ [v T] to officially forbid someone from entering a building or area, especially because they have caused trouble or because it is dangerous for them to go there: *The tavern banned Ted for starting a fight.* | **bar/ban sb from sth** *We've had to bar visitors from the garden because some of the pathways aren't safe.* | **bar/ban sb for life** (=forbidden from entering for the rest of your life) *After the incident at the country club, Chuck was banned for life.*

10 somewhere where you enter

- entrance
- entry/entryway
- way in
- access

entrance /ˈentrəns/ [n C] **+ to** *It took us ages to find the entrance to the park.* | **back/front/side entrance** *Davis used a side entrance to avoid the waiting reporters.*

entry/entryway /ˈentri, ˈentriweɪ/ [n C] American the door or space you go through to enter a place: *Over the entryway was an inscription in Latin.* | **+ to/of** *We stopped at the entry to the church to admire the architecture.*

way in /ˌweɪ ˈɪn/ [n C] the entrance to a large public building: *We walked all the way around the museum looking for the way in.* | *There's a red flashing sign above the door saying 'Way In' – you can't miss it.*

access /ˈækses/ [n U] the way things are arranged so that the public can enter somewhere: *The entrance has been widened to give improved access for disabled people.* | **+ to** *City officials are considering building a path to give the public access to the ruins.*

11 when something enters a space, especially through a surface

- enter
- penetrate
- seep in
- permeate

enter /ˈentəʳ/ [v I/T] *The bullet entered his rib cage from the left side.* | **+ through/by etc** *Bacteria can enter through a cut or graze on the skin.*

penetrate /ˈpenə̍treɪt/ [v T] if something **penetrates** an object or substance, it fully enters it, or goes through it: *The sun's rays can penetrate the sea to a depth of twenty metres.* | *He threw a grenade that penetrated the wall of the building and exploded inside.*

seep in /ˌsiːp ˈɪn/ [phr v I] if liquid **seeps in**, it gradually enters a substance or a place: *Despite all our efforts to stop it, the floodwater was still seeping in.* | **seep into sth** *Chemicals from the plant have seeped into the city's water supply.*

permeate /ˈpɜːʳmieɪt/ [v T] if a liquid or gas **permeates** an object or substance it enters it and spreads through it: *Toxic chemicals may permeate the soil, threatening the environment.*

enthusiastic/ unenthusiastic

RELATED WORDS

▸ *see also* **excited/exciting, willing, like, enjoy, don't care, dislike**

1 enthusiastic

- ▸ enthusiastic
- ▸ keen
- ▸ eager
- ▸ be full of enthusiasm
- ▸ be/get excited about sth
- ▸ be raring to go
- ▸ zealous

enthusiastic /ɪnˌθjuːziˈæstɪk‖-ˌθuː-/ [adj] behaving in a way that shows how much you like, enjoy, or approve of something: *A small but enthusiastic crowd cheered as the players ran onto the field.* | *Several enthusiastic young teachers have just started working at the school.* | **+ about** *He's still really enthusiastic about his new job.* —**enthusiastically** [adv] *The public has responded very enthusiastically to our appeal.*

keen /kiːn/ [adj] especially British very enthusiastic about an activity or job: *She hasn't much experience but she's very keen.* | **+ on** *There are plenty of after-school opportunities for people who are keen on athletics.* | **keen on doing sth** *My parents have always been keen on travelling, whenever they get the chance.* | **a keen golfer/photographer/gardener etc** *Chris is a keen photographer – he's won several competitions.* | **+ to do sth** *Gabby was obviously anxious to do well, and Jane was keen to help her.*

eager /ˈiːgəʳ/ [adj] wanting very much to do, get, or see something soon: *A crowd of eager fans were waiting outside the hotel.* | **+ to do sth** *She hurried home from college, eager to hear Tom's news.* | **+ for** *Simon was an ambitious man, eager for power and prestige.* —**eagerly** [adv] *He jumped up eagerly and ran to answer the phone.*

be full of enthusiasm /biː ˌfʊl əv ɪnˈθjuːziæzəm‖-ˈθuː-/ [v phrase] to be very enthusiastic about an idea or plan, and talk about it with great excitement: *We've discussed the idea and she seems to be full of enthusiasm.* | **+ for** *Roger was full of enthusiasm for Tony's plan.*

be/get excited about sth /biː, get ɪkˈsaɪtə̍d əbaʊt (sth)/ [v phrase] to be enthusiastic about something that is going to happen: *It was a great opportunity, and I began to get really excited about it.* | *Astronomers are very excited about a comet that will pass close to Earth later this month.*

be raring to go /biː ˌreərɪŋ tə ˈgəʊ/ [v phrase] to be extremely enthusiastic and excited about something that you are going to do, so that you cannot wait to begin: *Come on, hurry up. The kids are raring to go.* | *It's going to be a tough game, but the whole team's ready and raring to go.*

zealous /ˈzeləs/ [adj] extremely enthusiastic about something such as a political or religious idea which you believe in very strongly, and behaving in a way that shows this **a zealous believer/opponent/supporter etc** *Only the most zealous supporters of Thatcherism were in favour of the tax.* | **zealous in doing sth** *Some of the officers were more zealous than others in enforcing the disciplinary code.* —**zealously** [adv] *Until now the Democrats have zealously opposed any reduction in the Healthcare budget.*

2 to talk about something in an enthusiastic way

- ▸ enthuse
- ▸ be full of it

enthuse /ɪnˈθjuːz‖-ˈθuːz/ [v I] written *'You should have seen the match. It was so exciting,' Gerry enthused.* | **+ about/over** *She was enthusing over my English essay, which I didn't think was very good.*

be full of it /biː ˈfʊl əv ɪt/ [v phrase] British informal to talk a lot about something because you feel enthusiastic about it: *She's really pleased with her new job – she was full of it when I saw her last night.*

3 enthusiastic feelings or behaviour

- ▸ enthusiasm
- ▸ eagerness

enthusiasm /ɪnˈθjuːziæzəm‖ɪnˈθuː-/ [n U] enthusiastic feelings or behaviour **the enthusiasm of sb/sb's enthusiasm** *The company has had another successful year, thanks to the enthusiasm and energy of our workforce.* | **+ for** *I'd forgotten about Jim's enthusiasm for going on 20-mile walks.* | **full of enthusiasm** (=very enthusiastic) *Greta was full of enthusiasm for the plan.* | **with great enthusiasm** *She plays tennis with great enthusiasm, but not very well.*

eagerness /ˈiːgəʳnə̍s/ [n U] a great and excited desire to do, get, or see something soon: *He could see the eagerness in her face.* | **+ for** *the President's obvious eagerness for an arms-control agreement* | **in sb's eagerness to do sth** *Mark spoke quickly in his eagerness to explain his ideas.*

4 to make someone feel enthusiastic about something

- ▸ inspire
- ▸ motivate
- ▸ fire sb with enthusiasm
- ▸ rousing

inspire /ɪnˈspaɪəʳ/ [v T] to make someone feel enthusiastic about something and make them feel that it is worth doing: *When I actually visited the university, it inspired me and made me want to go there.* | **inspire sb to do sth** *The lecture today really inspired me to read more poetry.* —**inspiring** [adj] *After hearing Joe's inspiring story, I was determined to raise as much money as I could for Cancer Research.*

motivate /ˈməʊtə̍veɪt/ [v T] to make someone feel enthusiastic about their work or their studies, and work hard: *It's often more difficult to motivate boys than girls.* | *Every good teacher knows that criticism* *does not motivate learners.* | **motivate sb to do sth** *Only one third of workers said their supervisors know what motivates them to do their best work.*

fire sb with enthusiasm British ALSO **fire sb up** especially American /ˌfaɪəʳ (sb) wɪð ɪnˈθjuːziæzəm‖-ˈθuː-, ˌfaɪəʳ (sb) ˈʌp/ [v phrase] to make someone extremely enthusiastic so that they want to work very hard to achieve something: *His speech fired the audience with enthusiasm.* | **be (all) fired up** *Brown was fired up about being back on the field again after his injury.* | *By the end of the meeting the sales team were all fired up and eager to start selling.*

rousing /ˈraʊzɪŋ/ [adj] a **rousing** song, speech etc makes people feel excited and eager to do something: *His rousing speeches soon created a massive following.* | *Rousing organ music was coming from the church.*

5 not enthusiastic

- unenthusiastic/not enthusiastic
- half-hearted
- your heart's not in it
- lukewarm
- lack of enthusiasm
- muted

unenthusiastic/not enthusiastic /ˌʌnɪnθjuːziˈæstɪk◂, nɒt ɪnˌθjuːziˈæstɪk‖-ˌθuː-/ [adj not before noun] *Are you sure you want to come? You don't sound very enthusiastic.* | **+ about** *She had never been very enthusiastic about her job as a designer.* | **distinctly unenthusiastic** (=definitely unenthusiastic) *The staff were distinctly unenthusiastic about the whole idea.*

half-hearted /ˌhɑːf ˈhɑːʳtɪ̈d‖ˌhæf-/ [adj] without much enthusiasm or effort: *Her apology was very half-hearted.* | *People are starting to criticize the government for its half-hearted approach to reform.* | **half-hearted attempt** *Yves had made a half-hearted attempt to be friendly.*

your heart's not in it /jɔːʳ ˌhɑːʳts nɒt ˈɪn ɪt/ if you say **your heart's not in it**, you mean you are not enthusiastic about something you are doing, especially because you are not interested in it any more or because you do not think it is worth doing: *I really loved teaching at first but my heart's not in it any more.* | *My heart's not in this job. In fact I hate it.*

lukewarm /ˌluːkˈwɔːʳm◂/ [adj] not enthusiastic about something that someone has suggested or done, especially because you do not think it is very good: *Their response to my idea was only lukewarm.* | **+ to/towards** *Research chief, Michael Greenall, said 'I'm lukewarm toward the whole deal.'* | **+ about** *Investment fund managers are a little lukewarm about the prospects of these bonds.* | **lukewarm response/reaction etc** *Lester finished speaking, and there was a ripple of rather lukewarm applause.*

lack of enthusiasm /ˌlæk əv ɪnˈθjuːziæzəm‖-ˈθuː-/ [n phrase] if someone shows a **lack of enthusiasm** about something, they are not as enthusiastic about it as people expect them to be **a clear/distinct/marked lack of enthusiasm** (=very definite and clear lack of enthusiasm) *Sam showed a distinct lack of enthusiasm when I told him my holiday plans.* | **+ for** *Many people displayed a lack of enthusiasm for the proposal.*

muted /ˈmjuːtɪ̈d/ [adj usually before noun] **muted response/enthusiasm/reaction etc** expressions of feelings which are not as enthusiastic as usual or as expected: *There was rather a muted response to the speech.* | *The Air Transport Association expressed muted support for the action.*

environment

RELATED WORDS

▸ *see also* **weather, world, natural**

1 the natural world that people, animals, and plants live in

- the environment
- ecosystem
- ecology
- habitat
- food chain

the environment /ðə ɪnˈvaɪərənmənt/ [n singular] the air, water, and land where people, animals, and plants live, and the way all these things depend on each other so that life can continue: *Many modern farming methods are highly damaging to the environment.* | *Young people between 18 and 30 tend to be much more concerned about the environment than the older generation.* | *Ask your local MP what he or she intends to do to help protect the environment.*

ecosystem /ˈiːkəʊˌsɪstɪ̈m/ [n C] the animals, plants etc that exist in a particular area or type of area and the way they all depend on each other in order to live, considered as a single separate part of the environment: *The bay has a very complex and delicate ecosystem.* | *The rainforest is a self-supporting ecosystem.* | **a marine/forest/riverbank etc ecosystem** *Many species of burrowing insects are essential for maintaining a healthy soil ecosystem.*

ecology /ɪˈkɒlədʒi‖ɪˈkɑː-/ [n U] the way in which plants, animals, and the natural features of a place affect and depend on each other, or the scientific study of this: *Plans to build a new airfield could threaten the delicate ecology of the island.* | *She is giving a lecture about the natural history and ecology of the sea shore.*

habitat /ˈhæbɪ̈tæt/ [n C/U] the place and natural conditions that a plant, animal, etc lives or grows best in: *Further building development would threaten valuable badger and red squirrel habitats.* | *Suburban gardens can provide habitats for many forms of wildlife.* | *Ancient habitats such as grasslands, bogs, and wetlands are rapidly disappearing.*

food chain /ˈfuːd tʃeɪn/ [n singular] the natural system in which plants, animals, insects etc feed on each other, for example when a particular bird feeds on a particular insect, which feeds on a particular plant etc: *The oil spill has killed off billions of microscopic sea plants, thus threatening marine life further up the food chain.* | *Pesticides destroy insects that are an important part of the food chain for several species of songbird.*

2 relating to the environment

- environmental
- green
- ecological

environmental /ɪnˌvaɪərənˈmentl◂/ [adj, usually before noun] *The explosion in the nuclear plant led to one of the most serious environmental catastrophes in history.* | *We want to stress the environmental benefits of a cheap, efficient public transport system.* | *environmental pollution* | **environmental group** (=a group of people whose aim is to protect the environment) *Environmental groups and residents have united to protest against plans for a new shopping mall.* —**environmentally** [adv] *The group claims that flying is one of the most environmentally dam-*

aging forms of travel. | *Car manufacturers worldwide are working to develop environmentally cleaner vehicles.*

green /griːn/ [adj usually before noun] **green** methods, products, practices etc are intended not to cause damage to the environment. **Green** political groups are concerned with the protection of the environment: *A government committee is considering a proposal for a green energy policy.* | *More money needs to be invested in developing greener fuel sources.* | *a conference attended by representatives of all the Green parties of Europe*

ecological /ˌiːkəˈlɒdʒɪkəl◂‖-ˈlɑː-/ [adj] relating to the way plants, animals, people, and the natural creatures of a particular place affect and depend upon each other – used especially by scientists or groups that try to protect the environment: *The government is to provide incentives for people to protect natural ecological assets such as forests.* | *There are warnings that the building of the dam will upset the ecological balance of the river basin.* —**ecologically** [adv] *ecologically sound methods of pest elimination*

3 protecting the environment

- environmentally friendly
- eco-
- organic
- renewable
- sustainable
- recycling
- conservation

environmentally friendly /ɪnˌvaɪərənˌmentəli ˈfrendli/ [adj] **environmentally friendly** products and methods do not damage the environment: *Many shoppers will buy environmentally friendly washing powders even if they are slightly more expensive.* | *Of course public transportation is more environmentally friendly than cars, but it needs to be efficient or people won't use it.* | *an environmentally friendly alternative to the aerosol spray*

eco- /ˈiːkəʊ/ [prefix] involved with or relating to the protection of the environment – used before some adjectives and nouns: *eco-friendly agriculture* | *Activists want the government to invest in low-impact eco-tourist facilities.* | *Officials see a role for sophisticated eco-technology to help eradicate pollution sweeping across the region.*

organic /ɔːʳˈgænɪk/ [adj] **organic** fruit, vegetables, grains etc are grown naturally without the use of chemicals that can harm the insects, birds, bacteria etc that depend on them to live. **Organic** meat, eggs etc come from animals or birds that are fed on natural food and contain no harmful artificial chemicals: *Worried by repeated food scares, more and more people are buying organic products.* | *For this recipe, use a free-range, organic chicken.* | **organic farming** (=the production of organic vegetables, meat etc) *Several farmers in the county have moved to organic farming recently.*

renewable /rɪˈnjuːəbəl‖rɪˈnuː-/ [adj] **renewable** forms of energy, fuel, materials etc can be replaced naturally, so that they are never completely used up: *The 'green' housing community uses renewable energy sources such as solar power.* | *The problem with fossil fuels is that they are not renewable.*

sustainable /səˈsteɪnəbəl// [adj] farming methods, methods of managing forests, hunting practices etc that are **sustainable** do not use up more land or trees or kill more animals than can be replaced, and therefore do not damage the environment: *All wood used in our furniture comes with a certificate saying it comes from sustainable forests.* | *Traditional agricultural methods employed by the local people are highly sustainable.* —**sustainability** /səˌsteɪnəˈbɪlɪ̇ti/ [n U] *The bill is an EU attempt to ensure the sustainability of cod fishing groups in the North Sea.*

recycling /ˌriːˈsaɪklɪŋ/ [n U] when waste made of materials such as paper, metal, glass, and plastic is not thrown away, but is put through a special process so that it can be used again: *School students collected tons of drinks cans and bottles for recycling.* | *The recycling program involves every household in the neighborhood.* —**recycled** [adj] *recycled paper/glass/plastic* —**recycle** [v I/T] *We aim to recycle at least 50% of household waste by 2005.* | *Can computers be recycled?* —**recyclable** [adj] able to be recycled: *Some plastics aren't recyclable, though many are.* | *recyclable packaging*

conservation /ˌkɒnsəʳˈveɪʃən‖ˌkɑːn-/ [n U] the practice of protecting animals, plants, forests etc, for example by officially not allowing building on the areas where they live or by not allowing them to be hunted: *The group is mainly concerned with bird conservation in coastal areas.* | **+ of** *the conservation of several species of dolphin* | **conservation area** (=a place where plants, wild animals etc are officially protected) *The flower now exists only in a small conservation area in Essex.*

4 people who are concerned about the environment

- environmental activist/group
- eco-warrior

environmental activist/group /ɪnˌvaɪərənmentl◂ ˈæktɪ̇vɪ̇st, ˈgruːp/ [n C] a person or group who works to protect the environment, especially by trying to influence the government and large companies: *Three environmental activists came to speak at the conference.*

eco-warrior /ˈiːkəʊ ˌwɒriə‖-ˌwɔː-/ [n C] informal someone who does extreme and often illegal things in order to protest against governments, companies etc who damage the environment: *One of the young eco-warriors had to be pulled from a tree by police.*

5 damage to the environment

- pollution
- global warming
- greenhouse gases
- acid rain
- climate change
- hole in the ozone layer
- deforestation
- endangered species

pollution /pəˈluːʃən/ [n U] harmful chemicals, gases, or waste materials from factories, houses etc that enter the air, water, or land and kill or damage the things that live or grow there: *Pollution levels in the area shot up as soon as the factory started operating.* | *What pollution controls will the state authorities put in place?* | **air/marine/land etc pollution** *She says that transporting goods by rail instead of road would cut air pollution dramatically.* —**pollutant** [n C] a chemical, gas etc that harms the environment: *carbon monoxide and other pollutants in traffic fumes*

global warming /ˌgləʊbəl ˈwɔːʳmɪŋ/ [n U] a general increase in the temperature of the world caused by harmful chemicals and gases from cars, factories etc entering the air: *Scientists estimate that global warming could cause a six degree rise in temperatures by 2100.* | *One of the most devastating consequences of global warming could be the melting of the polar ice caps.*

greenhouse gases /ˈgriːnhaʊs ˌgæsɪz/ [n plural] gases from cars, factories, machines etc that form a layer around the earth and keep the heat in. These are a cause of global warming: *International controls are needed to reduce emissions of greenhouse gases.* | *Western countries are overwhelmingly responsible for current levels of greenhouse gases.*

acid rain /ˌæsɪd ˈreɪn/ [n U] rain that is harmful to trees and buildings because it contains pollution from factories, power stations etc: *Typical symptoms of acid rain include deformed and dying trees, and trees with vastly reduced numbers of leaves.*

climate change /ˈklaɪmɪt tʃeɪndʒ/ [n U] changes in the weather across large areas of the world caused by damage to the natural environment, for example increases in temperature, more storms, or more or less rain: *People will have to get used to more flooding and droughts as climate change becomes a reality.* | *an international conference on Climate Change*

hole in the ozone layer /həʊl ɪn ði ˈəʊzəʊn ˌleɪəʳ/ [n phrase] a hole in the layer of natural gases around the earth that protects people, animals etc from damage from the sun. This is thought to be caused by harmful gases from cars, household products, factories etc entering the earth's atmosphere: *The increase in the incidence of skin cancer is directly due to the hole in the ozone layer.*

deforestation /diːˌfɒrɪˈsteɪʃən‖-ˌfɔː-,-ˌfɑː-/ [n U] when too many trees are cut down in an area, so that the environment is badly damaged: *Some parts of tropical America have seen over 70% deforestation.* | *The land is severely eroded as a result of widespread deforestation and intensive farming.*

endangered species /ɪnˌdeɪndʒəʳd ˈspiːʃiːz/ [n C] a type of animal, plant etc that might soon stop existing because of damage to the environment it lives in or because too many of them have been killed by humans: *Environmentalists say that the area includes the habitats of at least 20 endangered species.* | *Although the tiger is an endangered species, it is still hunted in some areas.*

equal/not equal

RELATED WORDS

▸ *see also* **same, fair, unfair**

1 the same in number, amount, level etc as something else

- equal
- as old/strong/long etc as
- be the same
- equivalent
- equal
- match
- keep pace with

equal /ˈiːkwəl/ [adj] *You should spend an equal amount of time on each question in the test.* | *Dilute the syrup with an equal volume of water, stir and serve with ice.* | **+ to** *The alcohol in a pint of beer is equal to that in two glasses of wine.* | *The distance between A and B in the diagram is equal to the diameter of the circle, C.* | **of equal size/length/weight/power/strength etc** *When facing an opponent of equal strength, Barker's speed gives her a big advantage.* —**equally** [adv] **divide/share sth equally** *The money was divided equally between their three children.*

as old/strong/long etc as /əz ˈəʊld əz/ something that is **as old, strong, long etc as** something else is of equal age, strength, length etc: *At fourteen Jeremy was already as tall as his father.* | *The nation was once more as strong as the other major powers in Europe.* | *Harry was lively and intelligent, but not as good-looking as his older brother.*

be the same /biː ðə ˈseɪm/ [v phrase] if two amounts, levels etc **are the same** they are equal: *The northern route is longer than the southern one, but the fare is the same.* | *The experiment was repeated by Professor Schwartz, and the results were the same.* | **be the same size/weight/power etc** *The two cars are roughly the same size, and have similar engines.* | **be the same height/age etc as** *Her sister is the same age as me.* | **exactly/roughly the same** *We're both exactly the same height.*

equivalent /ɪˈkwɪvələnt/ [adj] something such as an amount, level, or quantity that is **equivalent** to something else has an equal effect or result but is not completely the same as it: *If these prizes are not in stock we will send you an equivalent gift of the same value.* | **+ to** *The volcanic eruption on Krakatoa had an explosive power equivalent to 20,000 tons of TNT.* | *Unemployed workers receive welfare payments and rent assistance equivalent to 50% of their usual income.*

equal /ˈiːkwəl/ [v T not in progressive] to be exactly **equal** to a number, amount, or level – used especially in technical or scientific contexts: *Air pressure at sea level equals 1.03kg per square centimetre.* | *The most efficient basis for the trade of goods is when demand equals supply.*

match /mætʃ/ [v T] to be equal in number or amount to something that is itself already very high or very great: *The only cars which could match the acceleration of the Ferraris were the Shelby Cobras and Aston Martins.* | *Forming alliances with other countries was the only way to match the power of the enemy.*

keep pace with /kiːp ˈpeɪs wɪð/ [v phrase] to increase quickly enough to remain equal to something else which is also increasing quickly: *There has been a constant expansion of the city boundaries to keep pace with a growing population.* | *Working-class incomes have generally kept pace with increases in the cost of living.*

2 having equal rights

- equal
- equality
- on an equal footing
- equal
- peer
- parity

equal /ˈiːkwəl/ [adj] people who are **equal** have the same rights as each other and are treated in the same way as each other; if people get **equal** treatment, pay etc, they are all treated in the same way or get paid the same money: *Democracy is based on the idea that all members of society are equal.* | **equal rights** (=the idea that all types of people in society should have the same rights and should be treated fairly and equally) *Black protestors campaigned for equal rights throughout the 1960s.* | **equal opportunities** (=the idea that all types of people in society should have the same chances of employment) *Companies are being urged to do more to promote equal opportunities in the workplace.* | **equal pay** *The Treaty of Rome states that men and women shall receive equal pay for equal work.* —**equally** [adv] *People should be treated equally, regardless of their race or sex.*

equality /ɪˈkwɒlɪti‖ɪˈkwɑː-/ [n U] when all people have the same rights and opportunities in society and are treated equally: *Greater equality was one of* *the aims of the post-war government.* | **racial/sexual equality** *the struggle for sexual equality* | *It will take more than laws to bring about genuine racial equality.*

on an equal footing /ɒn ən ˌiːkwəl ˈfʊtɪŋ/ [adj phrase] people, countries, or organizations that are **on an equal footing** in a particular situation are being treated as equal, even though this would not happen in other places or situations: *It's the beginning of the course, so you're all on an equal footing.* | **place/put sb on an equal footing** (=treat them in the same way) *It wasn't until 1928, that divorce laws were reformed to put men and women on an equal footing.*

equal /ˈiːkwəl/ [n C usually plural] someone who has the same rights, advantages, and position in society as someone else, with the result that they can have **equal** respect for each other: *Most women these days want marriage to be a partnership of equals.* | **treat people as equals** (=show equal respect to all people) *The police have a duty to treat all members of the community as equals.*

peer /pɪəʳ/ [n C] someone who has the same background or position in society as you – used especially in technical or official contexts: *The jury system gives you the basic right to be judged by your peers.* | *Everyone wants to be successful in the eyes of their peers.* | *At about three years old, children begin to take an interest in their peers.*

parity /ˈpærəti/ [n U] formal the state of being measurably equal, for example by receiving equal wages or having equal numbers of jobs as another group – used especially in political contexts **+ with** *Part-time workers are demanding parity with their full-time colleagues.* | *Middle class blacks in the US have not yet achieved parity with whites in graduate school entries.*

3 equal in quality, standard, or ability

- be as good as
- be equal to
- equally
- equal/match
- rival
- be on a par with
- be evenly matched
- there's nothing to choose between

be as good as /biː əz ˈgʊd əz/ [v phrase] *I don't think she ever recorded a song as good as 'Stormy Weather'.* | *They say that the new Argentinian striker will be as good as Maradona.* | *'How's the strawberry flavor?' 'It's OK, but not as good as the chocolate one.'*

be equal to /biː ˈiːkwəl tuː/ [v phrase] to be as good or as important as all the other things that are available **+ anyone/anything** *There's no doubt that she can produce work that is equal to anyone else's in her class.* | *The architecture here is equal to anything found in Florence or Rome.*

equally /ˈiːkwəli/ [adv] **equally strong/good/difficult etc** equal in strength, quality etc: *Chantal Johnson was brought up in Canada, and is equally fluent in French and English.* | *The meat can then be baked, grilled, or sautéed with equally good results.* | *Danny has great skill as a football player, and, equally important, the determination that you need to succeed.*

equal/match /ˈiːkwəl, mætʃ/ [v T usually in negative sentences] to be as good as something else or equal in size, speed, power etc: *No one has ever equalled her performance as Juliet.* | *The cloth dyers of ancient Tyre produced beautiful colours that have never been equalled by even the finest synthetic dyes.* | **be matched/equalled only by sth** *The facilities at the club were only matched by one or two other clubs in Europe.*

rival /ˈraɪvəl/ [v T] to be almost as good, impressive, or successful as something that is very good, impressive etc: *The college's facilities rival those of Harvard or Yale.* | **rival sth in sth** *The new aeroplane would rival its competitors in terms of noise, range and versatility.* | *The prince built a vast palace, rivalling Versailles in size and opulence.*

be on a par with /biː ɒn ə ˈpɑːʳ wɪð/ [v phrase] to be as good or almost as good as something that is very good: *The acquisition of Walker puts the company on a par with its rivals in France and Germany.* | *Donald showed up with a woman called Pandora, whose beauty was on a par with any film star.*

be evenly matched /biː ˌiːvənli ˈmætʃt◂/ [v phrase] if competitors or opponents **are evenly matched** they have almost equal ability, so a game or competition between them will be very even: *The two wrestlers were evenly matched.* | *It seems that the teams are pretty evenly matched, but the French players are probably more experienced.*

there's nothing to choose between /ðeəʳz ˌnʌθɪŋ tə ˈtʃuːz bɪtwiːn/ British you say **there's nothing to choose between** two things or people when they are both equally good and you cannot say which is better: *After the interviews we had to admit there was nothing to choose between the two candidates.* | *There's really nothing to choose between the performance of these two cars.*

4 to be in an equal position in a game, competition etc

- tie
- be level
- be neck and neck
- draw
- draw
- be two all/be four all etc
- photo finish
- be too close to call

tie /taɪ/ [v I/T] if two of the competitors in a game or competition **tie**, they get the same number of points **be tied** *The two teams are tied with two games a piece.* | **+ for** *Woosnam and Lyle tied for fourth place on 264.* | **+ with** *I won the first competition and tied with Wilson in the second.* —**tie** [n C] *If there is a tie* (=if two competitors get the same score) | *the prize money will be split.*

be level /biː ˈlevəl/ [adj not before noun] British two teams or competitors that **are level** at a particular moment in a game or competition have the same number of points: *They scored in the eighth minute but four minutes later we were level.* | *If the scores are level after 90 minutes, extra time will be played.* | **+ with** *Thanks to today's victory they are level with their main rivals, AC Milan, at the top of the Italian league.* | **draw level** (=get enough points to be level) *Brazil were in the lead, until Argentina drew level at the half-time whistle.*

be neck and neck ALSO **be level pegging** British /biː ˌnek ən ˈnek, biː ˌlevəl ˈpegɪŋ/ [v phrase] informal use this when two people, horses etc are doing equally well in a race or competition, so that it is impossible to guess who will win: *The two horses are running neck and neck.* | *For three miles now both yachts have been neck and neck.* | *The Republicans and Democrats are neck and neck in the opinion polls.* | *The poll shows the two main parties level pegging, with 33% of the vote each.*

draw /drɔː/ [n C] especially British a game in which both opponents or teams have equal points at the end, so that neither wins: *Neither side has scored. It looks as if it's going to be another draw.* | *Last week's draw was a bad result for Arsenal, putting Manchester United ahead of them in the league.* | **end in a draw** (=finish with scores equal) *If the final ends in a draw, the game will be decided on penalties.*

draw /drɔː/ [v I/T] British to finish a game with the same number of points as your opponent, so that neither of you wins: *'Did you win?' 'No, we drew.'* | **+ with** *Real Madrid drew with Barcelona in the last game of the season.* | **draw a game/match** *The Australian rugby team drew the first game of their European tour, sixteen-all against France at Lyon.*

be two all/be four all etc /biː ˌtuː ˈɔːl/ [v phrase] spoken say this when both players or teams have two points, four points etc in a game: *It's two all at the moment, but Germany seems the better team.* | *'What was the final score?' 'One all.'*

photo finish /ˌfəʊtəʊ ˈfɪnɪʃ/ [n C] a finish to a race between horses, dogs, or people that is very nearly equal so that it is extremely difficult to say who has won: *It's a photo finish – we'll have to bring in the judges to decide the winner.* | *After a very close-run race, it ended in a photo finish.*

be too close to call /tuː ˌkləʊs tə ˈkɔːl/ [v phrase] if the result of a competition, election, race etc **is too close to call**, the people taking part in it are equally successful, so there is no clear winner: *The exit polls suggest that the election may well be too close to call.*

5 to make two numbers, amounts, situations etc equal

- balance
- equalize
- balance out
- even out
- strike a balance
- redress the balance
- make up for
- compensate for

balance /ˈbæləns/ [v T] *As a parent trying to balance home and career, it's very difficult to find time for a social life.* | **balance sth with sth** *No government so far has been able to balance the number of jobs available with the number of people out of work.*

equalize ALSO **equalise** British /ˈiːkwəlaɪz/ [v T] to change things so that people are treated equally, especially in their employment: *The Association of Women Teachers in New York fought to equalize male and female pay.* | *Miners demanded a standard rate throughout the country to equalize wages.*

balance out /ˌbæləns ˈaʊt/ [phr v I] if two amounts, numbers etc **balance out**, they become equal or have an equal effect, especially if this happens over a fairly long period of time: *Sometimes we have a slight loss and sometimes a slight surplus, but over time they balance out.* | *Sometimes I do the cooking and sometimes John does – so in the end it all balances out.*

even out /ˌiːvən ˈaʊt/ [phr v I] if two amounts, or levels **even out** or you **even** them **out**, the differences between them gradually become smaller **even out sth** *On cold days the device periodically provides a burst of hot air, to even out the air temperature.* | **even sth out** *We want to even the workload out a little, so that no one has more than they can handle.*

strike a balance /ˌstraɪk ə ˈbæləns/ [v phrase] to achieve a situation in which you give the correct amount of attention and importance to two opposing activities or ideas: *Most reporters are either violently for or violently against the government, but some try to strike a balance.* | **+ between** *School children have to learn to strike a balance between work and play.* | *Prison reformers are trying to strike a balance between punishing offenders and helping them to avoid repeating their offences.*

redress the balance /rɪˌdres ðə ˈbæləns/ [v phrase] to make a situation equal or fair again after it has not been fair or equal: *Eventually, if the population of one species rises too much a new epidemic will come along to redress the balance.* | *Gypsies have often been portrayed as lawless savages, and the film tries to redress the balance by showing their culture as it really is.*

make up for /ˌmeɪk ˈʌp fɔːʳ/ [phr v T] to replace or balance something good that has been lost or something bad that has been done, by providing or doing something: *Nothing they can do will make up for the damage they have caused.* | *He had to work twice as hard as the other children to make up for his lack of natural ability.* | **more than make up for** (=make up for something very well) *The weather was a bit cold, but the beautiful scenery more than made up for it.*

compensate for /ˈkɒmpənseɪt fɔːʳ‖ˈkɑːm-/ [v phrase] to replace or balance something good that has been lost or is lacking, by providing or doing something equally good: *Ray tries to compensate for his shyness by telling a lot of jokes.* | *It is hoped that the new car's style and design will compensate for its lack of speed.* | *Failures in this area will have to be compensated for by successes in other areas.*

6 when two amounts, levels, etc are equal

- balance
- equilibrium

balance /ˈbæləns/ [n singular] **+ between** *Take care to achieve a balance between career and home life.* | *Migration plays a crucial role in maintaining the balance between population and resources.* | **strike a balance/strike the right balance** (=succeed in finding a balance) *When dealing with his staff, Mr Allen somehow managed to strike the right balance between being sympathetic and businesslike.* | **upset the balance** (=change and harm the balance) *The biological balance is upset by over-intensive farming.*

equilibrium /ˌiːkwəˈlɪbriəm/ [n singular] a state in which two or more forces, such as temperature and pressure, remain at a particular level, but would all change if any one of them were changed – used especially in technical or scientific contexts **maintain an equilibrium** *The operation of the free market maintains an equilibrium between supply, demand and price.* | **be in equilibrium** (=be balanced, equal etc) *The temperature at which the solid and liquid are in equilibrium is called the freezing point.*

7 when something has an equal but opposite effect

- cancel out
- offset
- counterbalance
- it's swings and roundabouts/it cuts both ways

cancel out /ˌkænsəl ˈaʊt/ [phr v T] if one thing **cancels out** another, it has an opposite effect to it, so that the situation does not change: *The new tuition fees mean that increases in student grants are effectively cancelled out.* | **cancel each other out/cancel one another out** *Two waves coming from opposite directions will cancel each other out.* | *Capital gains and losses can be expected to cancel one another out.*

offset /ˈɒfset, ˌɒfˈset‖ˈɔːfset, ˌɔːfˈset/ [v T] if something such as a cost or a sum of money **offsets**

another cost, sum etc, it has an opposite effect so that the situation remains unchanged: *The savings on staff wages are offset by the increased maintenance costs.* | *$3000 was spent in US schools to offset the disadvantages of about 6 million school children.*

counterbalance /ˌkaʊntəʳˈbæləns/ [v T] to have an equal and opposite effect to something such as a change, an influence, or a feeling: *Fortunately there are strong democratic forces in the country that counterbalance any extremist influences.* | *His fear of his father is counterbalanced by a genuine respect for him.*

it's swings and roundabouts/it cuts both ways /ɪts ˌswɪŋz ənd ˈraʊndəbaʊts, ɪt ˌkʌts bəʊθ ˈweɪz/ British spoken use this to say that although a particular method, decision, situation etc might give you an advantage, it will also involve an equal disadvantage: *Well, it's a case of swings and roundabouts really. You win some, you lose some.* | *The global economy can cut both ways, as some of a country's industries benefit from increased opportunity, and others lose to overseas competition.*

8 not equal in number, amount, level etc

- unequal
- imbalance
- disproportionate

unequal /ʌnˈiːkwəl/ [adj] *People are paid unequal amounts because they have unequal talents.* | **of unequal size/length etc** *two pieces of wood of unequal length* | **unequal in size/length etc** *The boxers were so unequal in size that it was never really a true contest.*

disproportionate /ˌdɪsprəˈpɔːʳʃənɪ̥t◂/ [adj] a **disproportionate** share of something is higher than it should be because the thing has not been shared equally: *Children who disrupt lessons at school take up a disproportionate amount of the teacher's time.* | *The report shows that a disproportionate number of black women do unskilled, low-paid work.* | *The richest areas of the country are getting a disproportionate share of government grants.* —**disproportionately** [adv] *The poorer cities of the industrial north have disproportionately high rates of child mortality.*

imbalance /ɪmˈbæləns/ [n C/U] a state in which two things are not equal, especially if this is unfair or causes problems: *Eighty per cent of our wealth belongs to five per cent of the people, and there's no legislation to counter this imbalance.* | *At the higher levels of management, there's definitely a gender imbalance.* | **+ between** *The economy is failing because of the great imbalance between imports and exports.* | **+ in/of** *the imbalance of power between women and men in nineteenth-century America* | *The company was ordered to remedy the racial imbalance in its workforce.*

9 not having equal rights

- inequality
- unequal
- discrimination

inequality /ˌɪnɪˈkwɒlɪ̥ti‖-ˈkwɑː-/ [n C/U] when people do not have the same rights or opportunities in their education, their jobs etc, because of their sex, race, or social class: *The report looks at inequality in education.* | *There are still a lot of inequalities in society.* | **social/sexual/racial inequality** *Social inequality tended to increase rather than lessen in the 1980s.*

discrimination /dɪˌskrɪmɪ̥ˈneɪʃən/ [n U] when people are treated unfairly because of their race, sex, age etc: *Federal law forbids discrimination on the basis of race, sex, or color.* | *Immigrants faced harassment and discrimination, and were paid considerably less than their white colleagues.* | **+ against** *Laws have got to be tougher to stop discrimination against the disabled.* | *In 1974 IBM became the first American company to bar discrimination against gay workers.* | **+ in** *They managed to reform American law, and ban racial and religious discrimination in housing, schools, and the workplace.* | **racial/sex/age discrimination** *The most common victims of age discrimination are employees in their mid-50s.* | *The company was found guilty of racial discrimination, and was ordered to renew Ms. Jayalalitha's employment contract.* | **anti-discrimination law/legislation/policy** (=a law etc that forbids discrimination) *An insurance company is being investigated under federal anti-discrimination laws for refusing home insurance to a black Ohio couple.*

unequal /ʌnˈiːkwəl/ [adj] **unequal** treatment, relationships, conditions etc are unfair to some of the people involved because they do not have equal rights or advantages: *The unequal distribution of wealth is a feature of our system of government.* | *When people are forced to compete on unequal terms they become resentful.* | *It was an unequal relationship. He was rich, powerful and experienced – I was very young and naive.*

equipment

things you use for doing something

RELATED WORDS

- *see also* **machine, tool, computers/Internet/email**

- equipment
- gear
- tools
- kit
- apparatus
- stuff
- things

equipment /ɪˈkwɪpmənt/ [n U] the machines, tools, or objects that you use for doing something: *You should check all your electrical equipment regularly.* | **+ for** *high technology equipment for policing and traffic control* | **office/video/sports etc equipment** *Thieves stole all the video equipment from the college.* | *We were told to keep all our sports equipment in the lockers downstairs.* | **a piece of equipment** *It's much easier if you have the right piece of equipment for the job.*

tools /tuːlz/ [n plural] equipment, especially simple things, that you use to make something or do something useful: *The plumber went back out to the van to get his tools.* | *As a writer, I don't need any tools, apart from my computer and the internet.* | **tools of the trade** (=equipment necessary for a particular job) *For a salesman, a cheap suit and a Ford Escort are the traditional tools of the trade.*

apparatus /ˌæpəˈreɪtəs‖-ˈræ-/ [n C/U] tools and machines used especially for scientific, medical, and technical purposes: *This experiment can be performed using the apparatus shown in the diagram.* | **breathing/gym/surgical etc apparatus** *Astronauts have special breathing apparatus.* | *There's a shop in town which sells all the latest photographic apparatus.*

things /θɪŋz/ [n plural] especially British, spoken the pieces of equipment or clothes that you need for a particular activity: *Now, have you got all your things* *ready?* | **swimming/painting/sewing etc things** *Don't forget to bring your swimming things with you.*

gear /gɪəʳ/ [n U] informal the equipment and special clothes that you need to do something, especially an activity that you do in your free time: *At 8.30 we loaded all our gear into the boat, and cruised out to a spot a few miles offshore.* | **camping/skiing/fishing etc gear** *Have you got all your football gear?* | *The soldiers were wearing heavy combat gear and travelling in convoys.*

kit /kɪt / [n C] **shaving/sewing/repair etc kit** a set of small things that you use to do something: *Always take a first-aid kit with you when you go camping.* | *You should never go cycling without a basic repair kit.*

stuff /stʌf/ [n U] spoken informal the equipment that you use to do something: *The builders have left all their stuff round the back of the house.* | **camping/painting etc stuff** *Our camping stuff alone took up most of the space in the back of the car.*

escape

RELATED WORDS

- to avoid being killed or injured *see* **avoid**
- *see also* **run, free, tie/untie, prison, follow, catch**

1 to escape from somewhere where you are in danger

- escape
- get out
- run away/run off
- bolt
- run for it/make a run for it
- flee
- make your escape
- take to your heels
- break free/break away
- bail out

escape /ɪ'skeɪp/ [v I/T] to get away from a place, country etc where you are in danger, especially when it is difficult to do this because someone is trying to catch you or stop you leaving: *Only four people managed to escape before the roof collapsed.* | *The refugees have crossed miles of desert to escape civil war and famine.* | **+ from** *Josie managed to escape from her attacker and call the police.* | **+ into/through/over etc** *Some people were able to escape over the border into Tanzania.* | *When the army began killing civilians in the town, he was able to escape through the jungle.*

get out /ˌget 'aʊt/ [phr v I] to escape from a place or country when there is a serious risk that something bad will happen very soon: *Eventually we realized there was no way of getting out.* | *A few people managed to get out before the government crackdown.* | **+ of** *All US tourists and journalists are being advised to get out of the country as soon as possible.* | **get out alive** *The whole building was on fire – we were lucky to get out alive!*

run away/run off /ˌrʌn ə'weɪ, ˌrʌn 'ɒf/ [phr v I] to try to escape from someone by running away: *Don't run away – I'm not going to hurt you.* | *Delia managed to get away from the man and ran off screaming.* | **+ from** *If you run away from the bull, it's almost certain to attack you.* | **+ into/down/ across etc** *He jumped out of the car and ran off into the woods.*

bolt /bəʊlt/ [v I] to suddenly run away very quickly, as soon as you have a chance, especially because you are very frightened: *One of the horses got into a panic and bolted.* | *When police approached him to ask him some questions, he bolted.* | **+ across/into/out etc** *Before I could say a word, she turned and bolted out the front door.*

run for it/make a run for it /'rʌn fər ɪt, meɪk ə 'rʌn fər ɪt/ [v phrase] informal to suddenly run away very quickly because you are in danger of being caught, especially when you are doing something illegal: *Somebody's coming. Quick, run for it.* | *There's no way we can beat them – we're going to have to make a run for it.*

flee /fliː/ [v I/T] to escape as quickly as possible because you are in great danger – used especially in newspapers: *When police arrived, the two men fled.* | **+ from/to/into etc** *Most of the women there were Somalis fleeing from the civil war.* | *Up to five million political refugees have fled to other countries.* | **flee the country/the city etc** *Rollins tried to flee the country but was stopped at the airport.*

make your escape /ˌmeɪk jɔːr ɪ'skeɪp/ [v phrase] to escape from a place or a dangerous situation, especially when you do this quickly and secretly, as soon as you have a chance: *He made his escape by climbing through the window and down the fire escape.* | *The hostages spent days waiting for the opportunity to make their escape.*

take to your heels /ˌteɪk tə jɔːʳ 'hiːlz/ [v phrase] to escape by running away very quickly – used especially in stories: *The kids immediately took to their heels as Mrs Brewster appeared around the corner.* | *He jumped off the train, took to his heels, and was quickly out of sight.*

break free/break away /ˌbreɪk 'friː, ˌbreɪk ə'weɪ/ [v phrase] to escape from someone who is holding you: *She wanted to break away, but his grip was too strong.* | *With a violent twist he broke free and ran out of the room.* | **+ from** *Then Tammy broke free from Judd and ran for the door screaming.*

bail out /ˌbeɪl 'aʊt/ [phr v I] to escape from an aircraft that is going to crash: *The pilot bailed out of the aircraft just in time and was only slightly injured.*

2 to escape from a prison or from where someone is keeping you

- escape
- break out/get out

escape /ɪ'skeɪp/ [v I] to **escape** from a prison or from a place where someone is keeping you: *Guards have been ordered to shoot anyone trying to escape.* | **+ from** *He escaped from prison in June, but was re-arrested by police a month later.* | **+ into/through/ out etc.** *Grant had escaped through a bathroom window while in police custody.*

break out/get out /ˌbreɪk 'aʊt, ˌget 'aʊt/ [phr v I] to escape from a prison or from a building or room where you are being kept: *Some of the men were planning to break out.* | *The doors and windows are all firmly locked – I don't know how we're going to get out.* | **+ of** *In 1998 the two men broke out of jail and murdered a police officer.* | *No one has ever managed to get out of this prison alive.*

3 to succeed in escaping from someone who is chasing you

- escape
- get away
- give sb the slip
- throw sb off the scent
- shake off
- make your getaway/make a getaway
- elude

escape /ɪ'skeɪp/ [v I/T] to succeed in escaping from someone who is trying to catch you: *It looks as if* *they've escaped. They're probably over the border by now.* | *So far the terrorists have managed to escape the police.* | **+ from** *He ducked down an alley to escape from the mob that was chasing him.* | **+ into/across/over etc** *Criminals generally know their neighborhood well, so it's not difficult for them to escape into the back streets.*

get away /ˌget əˈweɪ/ [phr v I] to escape from someone who is chasing you, especially when there is no chance that you will be caught afterwards: *How could you let him get away!* | *Police believe the gunmen got away in a white Ford pickup.* | **+ from** *Follow that car and don't let it get away from you.* | **get clean away** (=get away completely) *Detectives followed the man as far as the harbour, but then he jumped into a speedboat and got clean away.*

give sb the slip /ˌgɪv (sb) ðə ˈslɪp/ [v phrase] informal to escape from someone who is chasing you by tricking them or doing something unexpected: *Watch him very carefully – he might try and give us the slip.* | *I wanted to talk to her before she left the hotel, but she gave me the slip.*

throw sb off the scent /ˌθrəʊ (sb) ɒf ðə ˈsent/ [v phrase] to escape from someone who is chasing you or trying to find you by cleverly doing something that makes it impossible for them to know where you are: *He made the calls from different pay phones around the city to throw the police off the scent.*

shake off /ˌʃeɪk ˈɒf/ [phr v T] to escape from someone, especially someone who has been chasing you for a long time, for example by hiding or by going faster than them **shake off sb** *Mailer disappeared into a dark basement, hoping to shake off the gang.* | **shake sb off** *You're going to have to drive faster if you want to shake them off.*

make your getaway/make a getaway /ˌmeɪk jɔːʳ ˈgetəweɪ, ˌmeɪk ə ˈgetəweɪ/ [v phrase] to successfully escape after a crime, leaving no signs to show where you are: *Police have found the helicopters that the terrorists used to make their getaway.* | **make a clean getaway** (=to escape leaving no signs to show where you are) *The robbers hopped into a waiting car and made a clean getaway.*

elude /ɪˈluːd/ [v T] formal to cleverly avoid being found or caught by someone, especially for a long time: *Despite a $25,000 reward on his head, he continues to elude the authorities.* | **elude capture** *Lt. Forney managed to elude capture by enemy forces for several weeks.*

4 when someone escapes

- escape
- breakout

escape /ɪˈskeɪp/ [n C] when someone escapes from prison, from danger, or from someone who is chasing them: *They had planned their escape very carefully.* | *'Tunnel to Tanto Grande' is the story of a daring escape staged by political prisoners in Peru.* | **+ from** *Until his escape from the camps, he was beaten nearly every day by his captors.* | **narrow escape** (=when you only just escape from danger) *It was a narrow escape – a couple of minutes later the whole place went up in flames.*

breakout ALSO **jailbreak** American /ˈbreɪkaʊt, ˈdʒeɪlbreɪk/ [n C] an escape from a prison, especially one that involves several prisoners and is done using violence: *Prison governors met today to discuss ways of preventing similar breakouts in the future.* | *As many as 20 guards may have been involved in the jailbreak.* | **+ from** *There was a mass breakout from a city center prison yesterday.*

5 someone who has escaped

- escaped
- be on the loose/be at large
- be on the run
- fugitive

escaped /ɪˈskeɪpt/ [adj only before noun] use this to describe someone who has **escaped**, especially from a prison: *Police are on the lookout for three escaped prisoners.* | *Sherwood, an escaped convict, hunted down his ex-girlfriend and killed her.*

be on the loose/be at large /biː ɒn ðə ˈluːs, biː ət ˈlɑːʳdʒ/ [v phrase] someone who is **on the loose** or **at large** has escaped from the police or from a prison and is likely to be dangerous: *There's a killer on the loose, and we've got to find him.* | *Carillo's murderer remained at large yesterday as investigators continued their search.*

be on the run /biː ɒn ðə ˈrʌn/ [v phrase] someone who **is on the run** is trying to hide or escape from someone who is chasing them, especially the police: *After the train robbery he spent three years on the run.* | **+ from** *Dean was a drug addict who was constantly on the run from the police.*

fugitive /ˈfjuːdʒətɪv/ [n C] someone who has escaped from the police or from danger, who has to keep moving from one place to another so that they will not be caught: *Porter escaped in 1995 and remains a fugitive.* | **+ from** *a fugitive from Stalin's oppressive regime*

6 to escape from a difficult/embarrassing/boring situation

- escape/get away
- extricate yourself
- talk your way out of

escape/get away /ɪˈskeɪp, ˌget əˈweɪ/ [v] to get out of a difficult, embarrassing, or boring situation: *He decided to tell me all about his trip to Majorca, and I just couldn't get away.* | *Let's see if we can escape before the speeches start.*

extricate yourself /ˈekstrəkeɪt jɔːʳself/ [v phrase] formal to escape from an embarrassing or difficult situation: *Once they realized that I had been lying, it was almost impossible to extricate myself.* | **+ from** *At that time, the US was on the verge of extricating itself from the unpopular war.*

talk your way out of /ˌtɔːk jɔːʳ weɪ ˈaʊt ɒv/ [v phrase] to escape from an unpleasant or embarrassing situation by giving explanations, making excuses etc: *I don't know how she's going to talk her way out of this one.* | *Phil never does his homework, but he always manages to talk his way out of it.*

7 unable to escape

- can't escape/can't get out
- trapped
- be stuck
- be cooped up
- there is no escape
- be imprisoned
- be a prisoner

can't escape/can't get out /ˌkɑːnt ɪˈskeɪp, ˌkɑːnt get ˈaʊt‖ˌkænt-/ [v phrase] *I've locked all the doors and windows – he can't get out.* | *Two of the children couldn't escape, and died in the fire.*

trapped /træpt/ [adj] unable to escape from a dangerous place or an unpleasant situation: *The miners have been trapped underground for three days.* | *He was beginning to feel trapped in his job.* | *The two trapped firefighters were rescued on the second day.*

be stuck /biː ˈstʌk/ [v phrase] especially spoken to be unable to escape from an unpleasant or boring situation **+ in/with/here** *I don't want to be stuck in an office all my life.* | *I'm tired of being stuck here with the kids all day.*

be cooped up /biː ˌkuːpt ˈʌp/ [v phrase] informal to be unable to leave a place, so that you feel bored or very impatient **+ in** *I didn't want to be cooped up in a small hotel room, while everyone else enjoyed the sea.* | **+ with** *I don't know how she survives being cooped up with three screaming kids all day!*

there is no escape /ðeər ɪz ˌnəʊ ɪˈskeɪp/ used to say that there does not seem to be any way of escaping from a dangerous or unpleasant place or situation: *Don't even try to get out of here – there's no escape.* | **+ from** *There seems to be no escape from the noise and confusion of city life.*

be imprisoned /biː ɪmˈprɪzənd/ [v phrase] to be unable to escape, or feel too frightened to escape, from the place where you are or from an unpleasant situation: *Some of these old people are imprisoned in their own homes by the threat of violence on the streets.*

be a prisoner /biː ə ˈprɪzənəʳ/ [v phrase] to be unable to escape, for example from a place, an unpleasant situation, or your own thoughts and opinions, so that you feel you cannot do anything to change things: *The door was locked from the outside, and suddenly they realized they were prisoners.* | **+ of** *In some respects I'm a prisoner of my past – I don't feel I can just start over.*

especially

more than usual or more than others

RELATED WORDS

▸ see also **special, unusual**

- especially/particularly
- specially
- in particular
- above all
- most of all
- least of all
- notably
- of all people
- more than anyone
- special/particular

especially/particularly /ɪˈspeʃəli, pəʳˈtɪkjələʳli/ [adv] use this to emphasize that something is more important or happens more with one particular thing than any others: *This disease mostly affects women, particularly women over 50.* | *Paris is always full of tourists, especially during the summer months.* | **+ if/when** *Allow plenty of time for your visa to be processed, especially if you are applying by mail.* | **+ good/important/difficult etc** *This is a particularly good example of the problem we've been discussing.*

specially /ˈspeʃəli/ [adv] spoken especially – used in conversation: *I bought it specially for you.* | *We specially wanted to see the Eiffel Tower and Montmartre.* | **+ if/when** *You really need a car – specially when you live a long way from the nearest town.*

in particular /ɪn pəʳˈtɪkjələʳ/ [adv] use **in particular** to mention one person or thing that is more important or more interesting than all similar things: *Mary loves most classical music, in particular Bach and Vivaldi.* | *Kids in particular will love the rides and shows.* | **anything/anyone/anywhere etc in particular** *Was there anything in particular that you wanted to talk about?*

above all /əˌbʌv ˈɔːl/ [adv] use **above all** to emphasize that something is more important than all the other things you have mentioned: *Get plenty of sleep, eat lots of good food, and above all try to relax.* | *John felt sad, embarrassed, but above all angry that Anna could treat him like this.*

most of all /ˌməʊst əv ˈɔːl/ [adv] more than anything or anyone else: *Swimming and soccer are fun, but I like dancing most of all.* | *He was friendly and intelligent, but most of all he was a good worker.* | *Out of everybody at school she was the person who helped me most of all.*

least of all /ˌliːst əv ˈɔːl/ [adv] especially not: *She told no one, least of all her husband, what she planned to do.* | *Nobody wants to stop you from following the career of your choice, least of all me.*

notably /ˈnəʊtəbli/ [adv] formal use this to say that someone or something is an important example of what you are talking about: *The use of illegal drugs – notably marijuana – has increased in recent years.* | **most notably** *A number of respected philosophers, most notably Leibniz, criticized Newton's theories.*

of all people /əv ˈɔːl ˌpiːpəl/ [adv] spoken more than anyone else – use this when someone has said or done something you think is very surprising or unlikely for them to do or say: *You of all people shouldn't be calling him worthless.* | *Why is Jennifer Stern, of all people, so important?*

more than anyone /ˌmɔːʳ ðən ˈeniwʌn/ [adv] more than any other person: *You more than anyone should know how difficult it is to raise a child alone.* | *Freud, more than anyone, was responsible for the establishment of psychology as a science.*

special/particular /ˈspeʃəl, pəʳˈtɪkjələʳ/ [adj only before noun] if you give **special** or **particular** care, attention, or interest to something, you give it more attention than usual or more attention than you give anything else **+ care/attention/interest** *You should pay particular attention to spelling.* | *Special care must be taken to reward children appropriately for good behavior.*

ever

at any time in the past or future

RELATED WORDS

▸ see also **always, never, past, before**

- ever
- at any time
- in history
- in your life
- of all time

ever /ˈevəʳ/ [adv] *Have you ever bought any of their products?* | *When he left, Bartlett didn't know if he'd ever see Alaska again.* | *I don't think I'll ever get used to that feeling of excitement before a show.* | **ever ... (before)** *Have you ever been on a ship like this before?* | **best/biggest/worst ever etc** *That was the biggest mistake I ever made.* | **more/better/worse etc than ever (before)** *Within a few years of the two World Wars, the standard of living of Western European countries was higher than ever before.*

at any time /ət ˈeni taɪm/ [adv] used especially in formal questions and statements: *'Of course, no one should have to suffer at any time,' said the general gruffly, 'but things are different in times of war.'* | *Have you at any time met with the defendant?* | **at any time in history/in our existence etc** *There are more single parents today than at any time in history.*

in history /ɪn ˈhɪstəri/ [adv] at any time in the past, since humans have kept records of events: *Robin-*

son has won more matches than any coach in history. | *His arrest ended the longest manhunt in history.* | *Spielberg then went on to direct 'Close Encounters of the Third Kind', which became one of the highest earning films in history.* | *It was the first attempt in history to assemble representatives of all the major regions.*

in your life /ɪn jɔːʳ ˈlaɪf/ [adv] at any time during your life: *I've never owned a gun in my life.* | *Susan felt she had never worked so hard in her life as she did that day.* | *He knew that this was one of the saddest things he'd ever have to do in his life.* | *For the first time in his life, Yossarian prayed.*

of all time /əv ˌɔːl ˈtaɪm/ [adv] at any time in history or in someone's life: *Fleetwood Mac's 'Rumours' is one of the best-selling rock albums of all time.* | *My favourite joke of all time is the one about the donkey who goes to the doctor and says ...* | *a list of the 100 Most Influential Women of All Time*

everyone

RELATED WORDS

- everything *see* **all/everything**
- anyone *see* **anything/anybody**
- no one *see* **person/people**

1 all the people in a group

- everyone/everybody
- all
- the whole world/town/office etc
- the lot of them/us/you etc
- all and sundry
- all round

everyone/everybody /ˈevriwʌn, ˈevriˌbɒdi‖-ˌbɑːdi/ [pron] all the people in a group, or people in general. **Everyone** is slightly more formal than **everybody**: *I think everyone enjoyed the party.* | *Everybody knows that too much fatty food is bad for you.* | *Help yourselves, there's plenty of food for everyone.* | **everyone/everybody else** (=all the other people) *I take lots of photographs of everybody else, but I don't have many of me.* | **everyone but Ann/Mark/me etc** (=all the people except Ann, Mark etc) *He blames everyone but himself for his problems.*

all /ɔːl/ [predeterminer/quantifier] every person in a group: *There was no-one in the office – they were all having lunch.* | **+ the/these/their/my etc** *John spoke for all the workers.* | *All my friends like my boyfriend.* | **we all/you all/them all/us all** *We all felt tired so we didn't go out.* | *I decided to give them all another chance.* | **+ of** *Come in, all of you.* | *All of our great leaders have had reputations for being difficult to work with.* | **all children/teachers etc** (=used for making a general statement about people of the same kind) *All children love candy.* | **almost/nearly all** *Nowadays, almost all employers will expect to see your CV before they call you for an interview.*

the whole world/town/office etc /ðə ˌhəʊl ˈwɜːʳld/ [n phrase] everyone in the world, town, office etc – use this to emphasize that everyone is included: *On 13th May, Churchill spoke from London and the whole world listened.* | *Keep your voice down, you don't have to tell the whole office.* | *The whole town has been affected by this disaster. Everyone knows someone who died.*

the lot of them/us/you etc /ðə ˈlɒt əv ðəm‖-ˈlɑːt-/ [n phrase] British spoken all the people in a group – use this especially when you do not like those people: *I hate the lot of them.* | *'Outside, the lot of you!' he shouted.* | *Those two have tricked the lot of us.*

all and sundry /ˌɔːl ən ˈsʌndri/ [n phrase] use this to mean everyone in a group of people when you want to show that none of the people are important in any way: *Her sister told her mother, who then told all and sundry.* | *After the book signing Clancy stood around talking to all and sundry.*

all round British **all around** American /ˌɔːl ˈraʊnd, ˌɔːl əˈraʊnd/ [adv] if there are smiles, tears etc **all round**, everyone in the group smiles, cries etc: *There were smiles all round as he stood up to make his speech.* | *There were tears all round when the time came for him to leave.* | *It was compliments all around as security operators celebrated a virtually trouble-free day.*

2 every individual person in a group

- each
- every
- each and every person/child/member etc

each /iːtʃ/ [determiner/pron] **each person/member/student etc** *Each member of the winning team received a medal.* | **we each/they each/you each/us each** *She gave us each a piece of paper.* | *There were six of us in the expedition and we each had different reasons for taking part.* | **+ of** *He is always there for each of us when we need him.* | *Each of our staff has their own strengths and weaknesses.* | **each one** *Children follow the same pattern of physical development but each one at a different pace.* | **one/two/ three etc each** *There are six sweets left; that means we can have three each.*

every /ˈevri/ [determiner] use this to say that all members of a group do something or are involved in something: *She brought presents for every member of the family.* | *Every teacher knows the problems that difficult children can cause.* | **every single** (=use this to emphasize that you really mean everyone, especially when this is surprising) *Fire regulations state that every single child should be out of the building in three minutes.*

each and every person/child/member etc /ˌiːtʃ ənd ˌevri ˈpɜːʳsən/ [pron] use this to emphasize that every member of a group is included: *Each and every guest is given the highest level of personal attention.* | **each and every one** *There were over two hundred children in the hospital but each and every one was given a Christmas present.* | **each and every one of us/them/you** *Each and every one of us saw him take the money and are prepared to say so in court.*

3 for everyone or affecting everyone

- for everyone/everybody
- all round
- across the board
- for all

for everyone/everybody /fər ˈevriwʌn, ˈevriˌbɒdi‖-ˌbɑːdi/ [adv] *Don't worry. There's plenty of food for everyone.* | *Inflation is falling, and that's good news for everyone.* | **be better for everyone** *Sometimes I think it would be better for everybody if I wasn't here.*

all round British **all around** American /ˌɔːl ˈraʊnd, ˌɔːl əˈraʊnd/ [adv] if people get something **all round** or **all around**, someone gives something to everyone: *Bernie ordered drinks all round.* | *After presents all around, we all tucked into our Christmas dinner.*

across the board /əˌkrɒs ðə ˈbɔːʳd/ [adv] if something, especially a change, happens **across the board**, it affects or involves everyone, especially in a company or organization: *They decided on a pay increase of 10% across the board.* | *Jobs will be lost across the board, in manufacturing, marketing, and administration.* | **right/all across the board** *The changes will cause problems right across the board.*

for all /fər ˈɔːl/ [adv] an expression meaning for everyone – use this especially when talking about something that everyone deserves to have, such as a job, or freedom: *In an ideal society there would be jobs for all.* | *In his acceptance speech the President promised civil rights for all.*

4 feelings that everyone has, something that everyone does etc

- universal
- unanimous
- collective
- common
- share

universal /ˌjuːnəˈvɜːʳsəl◂/ [adj] done, felt, used etc by all the people in a group or all the people in the world: *There does not appear to be universal agreement on the future of the British monarchy.* | *Support for the government is by no means universal.* | **have universal appeal** (=be liked by everyone) *It is not easy to write a song that has universal appeal.* —**universally** [adv] *These arguments have never been universally accepted.*

unanimous /juːˈnænəməs/ [adj] if a group of people or a decision they make is **unanimous**, all the members of the group agree about something: *Many party members agreed with their leader, but they certainly weren't unanimous.* | **sb is unanimous that** *Medical opinion is unanimous that John's condition is unlikely to improve.* | **sb is unanimous in (doing) sth** *The meeting was unanimous in adopting the proposals.* | **unanimous decision/agreement/verdict etc** (=a decision that everyone in a group agrees on) *The committee made a unanimous decision to expel the three students.* | *The resolution was affirmed by a unanimous vote.*

collective /kəˈlektɪv/ [adj usually before noun] **collective** decisions, responsibilities, guilt etc, are shared or made by every member of a group: *Unless we act now to protect the environment, we shall have failed in our collective responsibility to future generations.* | *The present crisis is a result of the collective failure of the political parties to put forward a plausible economic programme.*

common /ˈkɒmən‖ˈkɑː-/ [adj] something that is **common** to everyone is something that everyone shares: *Luckily we all had a common language, English, which meant we could communicate with each other.* | *Monkeys and apes are so similar that it is reasonable to say they have a common ancestor.* | **+ to** *These problems are common to all modern societies.*

share /ʃeəʳ/ [v T not in progressive or passive] if people **share** a feeling, belief etc, they all have that feeling, belief etc: *None of us are close friends but we all share an interest in sport.* | *One thing united all three men – they shared a burning hatred of the political regime under which they lived.* —**shared** [adj] *All of us felt a shared responsibility towards our widowed mother.*

everywhere

RELATED WORDS

- *see also* **world, country**

1 everywhere in the world

- everywhere
- worldwide
- all over the world
- global
- the world over
- globalization

everywhere /ˈevriweəʳ/ [adv] in or to every country or area of the world: *Everywhere, even in the Antarctic, there are signs that the Earth is getting warmer.* | *Women everywhere are beginning to assert their rights.* | *Poverty affects children everywhere – not just in developing countries, but in Europe and North America as well.* | **everywhere else** (=in every other place) *We deliver goods the next day in the UK and within a week everywhere else.*

worldwide /ˌwɜːʳldˈwaɪd◂/ [adj] in every part of the world: *There has been a worldwide decrease in the number of whales.* | *Campaigners are calling for a worldwide ban on the use of land mines.* | *a worldwide TV audience of over a billion people* —**worldwide** [adv] *The company employs about 20,000 worldwide.* | *On the Internet, people can send messages worldwide in seconds.*

all over the world /ɔːl ˌəʊvəʳ ðə ˈwɜːʳld/ [adv] in every part of the world – use this especially to say how much a particular idea, organization etc has spread: *The Red Cross is a large organization with members all over the world.* | *Teams from all over the world will compete in next week's tournament.* | *All over the world people's lives are being changed by the new technology.*

global /ˈgləʊbəl/ [adj usually before noun] involving or including the whole world – used especially in newspapers: *The new global economy is exciting and full of possibilities.* | *Only the UN can tackle global problems like pollution of the atmosphere.* | **on a global scale** *Anything the US does is likely to have an impact on a global scale.* —**globally** [adv] *The goal of the treaty is to reduce the number of nuclear weapons globally.*

the world over /ðə ˌwɜːʳld ˈəʊvəʳ/ [adv] in every country or area of the world – use this to say that something is the same in each country: *Hollywood films are popular the world over.* | *Children the world over love a good story.*

globalization ALSO **globalisation** British /ˌgləʊbəlaɪˈzeɪʃən‖-lə-/ [n U] when companies and businesses operate all over the world and have factories, workers, shops etc in many different countries: *Globalization can often lead to the destruction of local customs and cultures.* | *Thanks to globalization, the burger you buy in Moscow is exactly the same as the one you buy in New York.* | *Anti-globalization protesters clashed with police on the streets of Geneva today.*

2 everywhere in a place or country

- everywhere
- all over
- throughout
- wherever you go/look
- here, there and everywhere
- nationwide
- widespread

everywhere ALSO **every place** American informal /ˈevriweəʳ, ˈevri pleɪs/ [adv] in or to every part of a place or country: *The whole street was flooded – there was water everywhere.* | *Where did you find my keys? I've been looking everywhere for them.* | *You see bank machines everywhere nowadays.* | *They go every place together.* | **+ in** *There were beautiful rice fields everywhere in the region.* | **everywhere else** (=in every other place) *Doctors in Colorado, like doctors everywhere else, did not have enough of the vaccine.*

all over /ɔːl 'əʊvəʳ/ [prep/adv] in or to many different parts of a town, country etc, especially when you want to say that you have been to many places: *We spent two weeks in Mexico and traveled all over.* | *The choir has sung in concerts all over the country.* | *Katie's toys were spread out all over the floor.* | **all over the place** *He went all over the place looking for a shop selling corkscrews but couldn't find one.*

throughout /θruː'aʊt/ [prep/adv] in every part of an area or place: *You could hear their laughter throughout the building.* | *The house is in excellent condition with fitted carpets throughout.*

wherever you go/look /weərˌevəʳ juː 'gəʊ, 'lʊk/ [adv] if you find a particular thing **wherever you go** or **look**, you find it in all the different places that you go to or look in: *There seem to be fountains wherever you look in this park.* | *He seems to make friends wherever he goes.*

here, there and everywhere /ˌhɪəʳ ˌðeər ənd 'evriweəʳ/ [adv] informal in many different places, without any particular plan or pattern: *We lived here, there, and everywhere as I was growing up.* | *The adults sat on the porch while the children ran here, there, and everywhere.*

nationwide /ˌneɪʃən'waɪd◂, 'neɪʃənwaɪd/ [adj only before noun] in every part of a country **nationwide strike/demonstration/campaign** *Workers held nationwide strikes and demonstrations all over Spain.* | **nationwide search/hunt/study/survey** *A nationwide hunt was launched yesterday for the killer of 13-year-old Nicola Jones.* —**nationwide** [adv] *We have a total of 96 stores nationwide.*

widespread /'waɪdspred/ [adj] happening in many places – use this especially about problems or bad situations that affect many areas or many countries: *There has been widepread flooding in Germany, and the rivers are still rising.* | *Government corruption is widespread in the country.*

3 in or to any place

- anywhere

anywhere ALSO **any place** American /'eniweəʳ, 'eni pleɪs/ [adv] in or to any place: *You can buy them anywhere, and they're very cheap.* | *We never go any place or do anything interesting.* | **+ in** *Is there any place in the neighborhood where I can get a quick lunch?* | **anywhere else** *I'm so happy here. I couldn't possibly imagine living anywhere else.* | **anywhere near** *I don't want that man anywhere near my house.*

exact/not exact

1 an exact number/amount/time

- exact
- precise
- exactly
- on the dot
- sharp
- on the stroke of seven/nine etc/at the stroke of seven/nine etc
- bang on six/midnight etc/dead on six/midnight etc

exact /ɪg'zækt/ [adj usually before noun] an **exact** number, amount, or time is completely correct and is no more and no less than it should be: *'Can you tell me the exact time?' 'It's 6.37.'* | *The exact weight of the baby at birth was 3.2 kg.* | *I don't suppose you have the exact amount of money, do you?* | *You need to give me the exact measurements of the room.* | **to be exact** (=used after a number to give an exact answer, statement etc) *It took her about an hour – 58 minutes to be exact.*

precise /prɪ'saɪs/ [adj usually before noun] **precise** information is based on clear and exact figures or measurements, especially when it is important that no mistakes are made: *We need to know your precise location.* | *Each plane has to follow a precise route.* | **to be precise** (=to give precise information or figures) *It's difficult to be precise about the number of deaths caused by smoking.* —**precisely** [adv] *At 3 o'clock precisely, the ceremony began.* | *She couldn't describe the car very precisely.*

exactly /ɪg'zæktli/ [adv] use this to emphasize that a number, amount, or time is no more or less than a particular time or figure: *It's exactly 5 o'clock.* | *The bill came to exactly $1000.*

on the dot /ɒn ðə 'dɒt‖-'dɑːt/ [adv] informal at an exact time, no earlier and no later: *She always leaves the office at 5.30 p.m. on the dot.*

sharp /ʃɑːʳp/ [adv] **at nine o'clock/six/ten-thirty sharp** at exactly nine o'clock etc – used especially to emphasize that something will not be delayed or that someone should not be late: *The performance starts at 8 o'clock sharp.*

on the stroke of seven/nine etc/at the stroke of seven/nine etc /ɒn ðə ˌstrəʊk əv 'sevən, ət ðə-/ at exactly seven o'clock, nine o'clock etc: *On the stroke of midnight, the British flag was lowered for the last time over Delhi.* | *The judge entered the courtroom at the stroke of nine.*

bang on six/midnight etc/dead on six/midnight etc /ˌbæŋ ɒn 'sɪks, ˌded ɒn-/ British informal use this to emphasize that it is exactly a particular time or at exactly the right time: *'What time is it?' 'Bang on midnight.'* | *We finished dead on eight, and we were back home for nine.* | *Luckily, he arrived dead on time.*

2 an exact description/translation/copy

- accurate
- exact
- literal
- word for word
- faithful
- strict
- verbatim

▸ *see also* **copy**

accurate /'ækjərət/ [adj] completely correct because all the details are true: *The witness tried to* *give an accurate description of what she had seen.* | *accurate financial forecasts* —**accuracy** [n U] *We double checked the figures to ensure their accuracy.*

exact /ɪg'zækt/ [adj] an **exact** copy, model etc of something is like it in every possible way: *an exact replica of a 900-year-old Buddhist shrine* | *I can't remember her exact words, but this is the gist of what she said.* | **exact likeness** (=use this about a painting or drawing of someone that looks very much like that person) *It's not an exact likeness, but it's recognisable as my father.* | **exact same** spoken *She's wearing the exact same dress I bought last week!*

literal /'lɪtərəl/ [adj usually before noun] a **literal** translation gives the exact meaning of a word, or each word in a sentence, instead of translating the word or whole sentence in a natural way: *The literal meaning of the Yiddish word 'mensch' is 'person'.* | *It's rare to use a literal translation of a film title when it is sold abroad.* —**literally** [adv] *'Vino de tavola' literally means 'table wine'.*

word for word /ˌwɜːʳd fəʳ 'wɜːʳd/ [adv/adj] if you repeat, copy, or translate something **word for word**, you use the exact words that are in it: *He asked me to repeat word for word the instructions he'd just given me.* | *The footnote gave a word for word translation of the quotation.*

faithful /'feɪθfəl/ [adj usually before noun] a **faithful** copy of something is as close as possible to the original: *His model cars are faithful copies of the originals.* | *This is a faithful interpretation of Shakespeare's original text.* | *a faithful reconstruction of an Anglo-Saxon village* —**faithfully** [adv] *The TV version follows the original novel faithfully.*

strict /strɪkt/ [adj usually before noun] exact and correct according to accepted rules or an accepted system: *Dates must be listed in strict chronological order.* | *Under a strict interpretation of the rules, she would be suspended.* | *In the strictest sense of the word, all popular fiction is 'romantic'.*

verbatim /vɜːʳ'beɪtəm/ [adj/adv] formal repeating the exact words that were spoken or written: *The government released a verbatim transcript of the pilot's last words.* | *He lifted passages almost verbatim from an earlier essay he had written.*

3 exactly how, what, where etc

- exactly
- just
- precisely

exactly /ɪg'zæktli/ [adv] use this to give or ask for exact details or information: *Glue the pieces together, exactly as shown in the diagram.* | *It took us exactly two hours to get here.* | **exactly who/what/where etc** *The police want to know exactly when you left the building.* | *The doctors can't say exactly what's wrong with my mother.* | **exactly the same** *It tastes exactly the same as meat.* | **who/what/where exactly?** *Where exactly are you from?* | *What exactly did you want to see?*

just /dʒʌst/ [adv] especially spoken use this to say exactly how, what, where etc something is: *That's just the right place for the painting, don't you think?* | **just what/how/where etc** *A new handbag! That's just what I wanted.* | *Just who does he think he is, coming in here and shouting like that?* | **just the same** *He and his brother are just the same – lazy.*

precisely /prɪ'saɪsli/ [adv] exactly – use this when it is important to describe something very carefully or to get very exact information **precisely what/where/who etc** *We need to know precisely how much this is going to cost.* | *Can you tell us more precisely what happened?* | **where/what/who precisely?** *What precisely do you mean by 'relativity'?*

4 exactly in a particular place

- right
- smack in the middle of sth/smack in front of sth
- bang

right /raɪt/ [adv] **right in/on/up etc** use this when something is in an exact position or place: *That hit me right in the eye!* | *I got a mosquito bite right on the end of my nose.* | *There's the house, right in front of you.* | *He sat down right beside her.*

smack in the middle of sth/smack in front of sth /ˌsmæk ɪn ðə 'mɪdl əv (sth), ˌsmæk ɪn 'frʌnt əv (sth)/ [adv] informal use this to say that something is exactly in a place, especially when this is unpleasant in some way: *They live smack in the middle of a huge housing estate.* | *A garbage truck had parked smack in front of our house.* | **smack dab** American (=use this to emphasize that you are being exact) *The ball hit me smack dab in the middle of my forehead.*

bang /bæŋ/ [adv] British informal **bang in/on/up etc** use this when something is in an exact point or position, especially if it falls there: *He landed bang in the middle of the roof, and it collapsed.* | *The eraser hit him bang on the top of his head.* | **right/slap bang** *The arrow hit the target right bang in the middle.* | *They've put an ornamental fountain slap bang in the middle of the roundabout.*

5 doing something in exactly the right way

- exactly
- strictly
- religiously

exactly /ɪg'zæktli/ [adv] use this to talk about doing something in **exactly** the right way: *Assemble the table exactly as shown in the diagram on the left.* | *I don't exactly know how to dry herbs, could you show me?* | *You must do exactly as I say.*

strictly /'strɪktli/ [adv] done exactly according to a set of rules or instructions: *The work is strictly on a volunteer basis.* | *The immigration laws have been strictly implemented.* | *Martha and Joan kept strictly to their part of the house.*

religiously /rɪ'lɪdʒəsli/ [adv] if you do something **religiously**, you do it in exactly the way that you are supposed to do it: *He counted his money up religiously every night.* | *Julia has been sticking religiously to her diet.*

6 exactly the right thing

- exactly
- precisely
- just

exactly /ɪg'zæktli/ [adv] use this to emphasize that something is the particular thing that you want or mean: *This is exactly the kind of job that computers are good at.* | *That's exactly the sort of material I'm looking for.* | **exactly what** *The earrings are beautiful! They're exactly what I wanted.* | *That's exactly what happened to me!*

precisely /prɪ'saɪsli/ [adv] exactly – use this to emphasize exactly what the situation is, exactly what happened, exactly what you meant etc: *That is precisely the point I was trying to make earlier.* | *The* *new legislation won't solve the problem – it will do precisely the opposite.*

just /dʒʌst/ [adv] informal use this to talk about exactly the thing, person, or place you mean, want etc: *We want just the same rights as everyone else.* | *He said he was leaving her and proceeded to do just that!* | **just who/what/how etc** *I'm not sure just who you mean.* | *Mallorca? That's just where we want to go.*

7 not exact

- rough
- approximate
- vague
- hazy
- loose

rough /rʌf/ [adj only before noun] not exact, or not containing exact details: *He gave us a rough outline of the course.* | **rough estimate/guess** *I've got a rough estimate here of what it might cost.* | **rough idea** *She had a rough idea of where Harry lived, but she didn't know the exact street.*

approximate /əˈprɒksɨmɨt‖əˈprɑːk-/ [adj] formal an **approximate** number, amount, or time is close to the true number, amount, or time but does not need to be completely correct: *Our approximate time of arrival will be 10.30.* | *Please state on the form the approximate value of all your household goods.*

vague /veɪg/ [adj] an explanation, promise, reason etc that is **vague** is not exact, but you think that it should be: *The doctor's vague explanations only increased Clara's fears.* | *I've only got a vague idea of what he wants for this project.* | **be vague about** (=explain something in a vague way) *Officials were vague about the number of weapons that were uncovered.* —**vaguely** [adv] *They murmured something vaguely when I asked how long they had been there.*

hazy /ˈheɪzi/ [adj] a **hazy** memory, understanding, idea etc is not clear and not exact: *She had a hazy recollection of being carried out of the room.* | *The details are still a little hazy.*

loose /luːs/ [adj usually before noun] **loose translation/interpretation/sense etc** a record, explanation etc of something that includes parts that are not exactly like what was said, written, or decided originally: *This is only a loose translation of the original paper.* | *A looser interpretation of the law would lead to more convictions.* —**loosely** [adj] *The term 'empire' is often loosely applied to a federation of states.*

exaggerate

to say that something is much better, worse, more important etc than it really is

1 to exaggerate something

- exaggerate
- blow sth (up) out of all proportion
- make too much of
- overrated
- overemphasize
- overstate
- be melodramatic
- lay it on

exaggerate /ɪgˈzædʒəreɪt/ [v I/T] to say that something is much bigger, better, worse, more important etc than it really is: *'He said you walked 30 miles.' 'No – he's exaggerating. It was only about 15.'* | *Newspapers tend to exaggerate their influence on the way people vote.* | *The grass in the garden was about three feet high – I'm not exaggerating.*

blow sth (up) out of all proportion /ˌbləʊ (sth) ʌp aʊt əv ˌɔːl prəˈpɔːʳʃən/ [v phrase] to say that a situation or event is a lot worse or much more serious than it really is, especially with the result that people become very worried or annoyed: *The whole thing has been blown out of all proportion by the media.* | *It was just a simple disagreement. Don't blow it up out of all proportion.*

make too much of /ˌmeɪk tuː ˈmʌtʃ ɒv/ [v phrase] to treat something that has happened as though it were more important or serious than it really is: *The press made too much of his stupid remark. He was only joking.* | *She loved the fact that he'd sent her flowers, but she didn't want to make too much of it in case it meant nothing.*

overrated /ˌəʊvəˈreɪtɨd◂/ [adj] if someone or something is **overrated**, people say they are much better than they really are: *I think her books are very overrated.* | *Critics claim that many soccer players are overpaid, overrated and out of touch.*

overemphasize ALSO **overemphasise** British /ˌəʊvərˈemfəsaɪz/ [v T] to say that a part of something is more important than it really is, especially in relation to other things: *The report overemphasizes the role of the teacher. Children also learn from their parents and from each other.* | *The importance of strict hygiene in the preparation of food cannot be overemphasized.*

overstate /ˌəʊvərˈsteɪt/ [v T] to describe something in a way that makes it sound more important or serious than it really is, especially in order to persuade people about something: *The company says that the dangers of driving while using cell phones have been overstated.* | *Politicians typically overstate their case in order to get their point across.*

be melodramatic /biː ˌmelədrəˈmætɪk/ [adj] behaving as if a situation is much worse or more serious than it really is, especially with the result that you seem silly: *Oh, don't be so melodramatic! You're not the only one who has ever failed an exam.* | *She said she'd kill herself if he left her. She's always so melodramatic!*

lay it on /ˌleɪ ɪt ˈɒn/ [v phrase] informal to say that your situation is much worse or you feel much more upset than is really true, in order to make someone feel sorry for you: *She really laid it on – saying that her kids would starve if we didn't give you a job.* | **lay it on thick** *Most charities lay it on so thick it's hard to know what the truth is.*

2 something that is exaggerated

- exaggeration
- exaggerated
- extravagant
- overstatement

exaggeration /ɪgˌzædʒəˈreɪʃən/ [n C/U] a statement that makes something seem better or worse, bigger or smaller etc than it really is: *Jim's not fat exactly – that's an exaggeration. He's just a little overweight.* | *How much of the story was exaggeration is impossible to say.* | **gross exaggeration** (=a big exaggeration) *It would be a gross exaggeration to describe the film as a masterpiece, but it has some good moments.* | **it is an exaggeration to say that** *It is an exaggeration to say that he earns more money than anyone I know, but he is certainly very well paid.*

exaggerated /ɪgˈzædʒəreɪtɨd/ [adj] making something seem much worse, better, more important etc than it really is: *The numbers killed in the massacre are probably exaggerated.* | **wildly/grossly exaggerated** *Some wildly exaggerated claims have been made about this so-called 'wonder-drug'.*

extravagant /ɪkˈstrævəgənt/ [adj] exaggerated a lot and therefore difficult to believe: *Extravagant* *claims have been made for some herbal remedies including the curing of baldness.*

overstatement /ˈəʊvəʳsteɪtmənt/ [n singular] a statement that is exaggerated and therefore probably not true – use this especially as a polite way of saying that a statement is exaggerated: *He said she was really beautiful – a slight overstatement I thought.* | *To say the company was going bankrupt is an overstatement. We have one or two financial problems, that's all.*

examine

to look at someone or something carefully

RELATED WORDS

- an exam or test *see* **test**
- *see also* **look for**

1 to examine something

- examine
- look carefully/closely
- take/have a look at
- analyze
- study
- check
- check over
- inspect
- go through/go over
- look over
- scrutinize

examine /ɪgˈzæmɪn/ [v T] to look at something carefully and thoroughly because you want to find out more about it: *Experts who examined the painting believe it is genuine.* | *Her new book examines the causes of social discontent.* | *A team of divers was sent down to examine the wreckage.* | **examine sth for sth** (=in order to find something) *The police will examine the weapon for fingerprints.*

look carefully/closely /ˌlʊk ˈkeəʳfəli, ˈkləʊsli/ [v phrase] to look carefully at something in order to see small details: *If you look carefully, you can see the artist's name in the corner of the picture.* | **+ at** *I had to look closely at the two fish to tell them apart.*

take/have a look at /ˌteɪk, ˌhæv ə ˈlʊk æt/ [v phrase] especially spoken to look carefully at something in order to find out what is wrong with it or to find out something about it: *'You'd better take a look at this,' she said, passing me a letter.* | *I've asked Ken to have a look at the car – it's been making strange noises.* | **take/have a good look at sth** (=look very carefully and thoroughly) *Take a good look at the photograph and see if you recognize anyone*

analyze ALSO **analyse** British /ˈænəlaɪz/ [v T] to examine something closely and in detail, especially a problem or a piece of information, in order to understand it: *Scientists use computers to help analyse the data.* | *One of the problems in analyzing the situation is that we do not have all the information yet.*

study /ˈstʌdi/ [v T] to spend a lot of time examining something very carefully, for example a document, a plan, or a problem: *I won't comment till I've had time to study the proposals.* | *A team of scientists has been studying the effects of acid rain over a twenty-year period.*

check /tʃek/ [v T] to look at something carefully and thoroughly to make sure that it is correct, safe, or working properly: *Their passports were checked by immigration officers at the airport.* | **check sth for sth** (=in order to find something) *We need to check the building for structural damage.*

check over /ˌtʃek ˈəʊvəʳ/ [phr v T] to quickly examine every part of something to make sure that it is correct or safe **check over sth** *The editor always checks over what I've written.* | **check sth over** *I'm going to take the car in and ask the mechanic to check it over before we go on vacation.*

inspect /ɪnˈspekt/ [v T] to look at something carefully and thoroughly to make sure that it is correct, safe, or working properly, especially when it is your job to do this: *The building is regularly inspected by a fire-safety officer.* | *Russian and American teams will have the right to inspect each other's missile sites.* | *Some insurance people have already been here to inspect the damage caused by the storm.* | **inspect sth for sth** (=in order to find something) *All trucks coming through are inspected for mechanical violations.* —**inspector** [n C] an official whose job is to check that something is correct, safe, or working properly: *a health and safety inspector*

go through/go over /ˌgəʊ ˈθruː, ˌgəʊ ˈəʊvəʳ/ [phr v T] to examine something such as a document or plan thoroughly from beginning to end, especially in order to check that it is correct: *I'd like to go over last month's accounts with you.* | *You should still go through the contract with a lawyer before you sign.*

look over /ˌlʊk ˈəʊvəʳ/ [phr v T] to look at every part of something in order to see if it is satisfactory, but fairly quickly and without paying much attention to detail **look over sth** *I've looked over all the records and they seem okay.* | **look sth over** *The book is expensive, so look it over to make sure it's what you really want.*

scrutinize ALSO **scrutinise** British /ˈskruːtɪnaɪz/ [v T] to examine something very closely and carefully in order to find out whether there is anything wrong, especially because it is your official duty to do this: *The coach's assistants stood along the field and scrutinized every move we made.* | *The Federal Trade Commission is scrutinizing the proposed merger of the two companies.*

2 to examine someone

- examine
- inspect
- check up on

examine /ɪgˈzæmɪn/ [v T] if a doctor examines you, he or she looks at your body to find out if there is anything wrong: *I'm going to the hospital tomorrow to have my knee examined again.* | *The doctor examined her, but didn't find anything wrong.*

inspect /ɪnˈspekt/ [v T] to officially check someone or make sure that they are doing their job properly – used especially about soldiers and about teachers in Britain: *General Allenby arrived to inspect the troops.* | *The school will be inspected in May.*

check up on /ˌtʃek ˈʌp ɒn/ [phr v T] informal to check, especially secretly, that someone is doing what they are supposed to do: *Some companies use hidden cameras in order to check up on their employees.* | *I just want to call home and check up on the kids.*

3 when something is examined

- examination
- analysis
- check
- inspection
- study
- scrutiny

examination /ɪgˌzæmɪˈneɪʃən/ [n C/U] when someone looks at something carefully and thoroughly to find out more about it **+ of** *Mandelbaum's new book is an examination of US foreign policy.* | **careful/close/detailed/thorough examination** *A detailed* *examination of population statistics reveals a steady decline in the birth rate.* | **be under examination** (=be in the process of being examined) *The committee's latest proposals are still under examination.* | **on closer examination** (=when examined more carefully) *On closer examination the vases were found to be cracked in several places.*

analysis /ə'næləsɪ̵s/ [n C/U] a detailed examination of something in order to understand it better, especially when this involves studying a large amount of information: *Our analysis shows that the proposed cost for the new highway is unrealistic.* | **+ of** *An analysis of data from Australia shows that skin cancer is on the increase.* | **detailed analysis** *The article provides a detailed analysis of various research designs.* | **in the final analysis** (=after all other ideas have been considered) *In the final analysis, it is the better organized party that will probably win.*

check /tʃek/ [n C] an examination of something to make sure that it is correct, safe, or satisfactory **+ on** *There are regular checks on the quality of goods leaving our factory.* | **carry out/run/do a check** (=make a check) *All routine safety checks were carried out before the flight.* | **spot check** (=an unplanned check on a thing or person that is chosen from a group by chance) *Spot checks by customs officers led to the arrest of several drug smugglers.* | **background check** (=a check on what someone has done in the past) *The agency does background checks on all the nannies it hires.*

inspection /ɪn'spekʃən/ [n C/U] a thorough examination of something, especially by someone in an official position, in order to find out more about it or find out if it is satisfactory **+ of** *There are regular inspections of the prison by government health officers.* | **carry out an inspection** *Admiral Naumenko personally carried out an inspection of the fleet.* | **on/upon closer inspection** (=when you look at something more carefully) *The bundle, on closer inspection, turned out to be a small child.*

study /'stʌdi/ [n C] a careful examination of or research into a particular subject or problem in which the process and results are reported in a written document **+ of** *Studies of dolphins have shown that they are able to communicate information to each other.* | **make a study** *A series of studies was made to discover the relationship between diet and behavior.*

scrutiny /'skru:tɪ̵ni/ [n U] formal careful and thorough examination of something: *The company's plans for expansion have attracted scrutiny from consumer groups.* | **+ of** *Airlines have increased their scrutiny of the size and amount of carry-on luggage.* | **under scrutiny** *The city's elections department has been under scrutiny since last year.* | **close/intense/careful scrutiny** *Closer scrutiny of the document revealed a number of interesting facts.* | **come under public scrutiny** (=begin to be closely examined by people) *Once you become famous your private life comes under public scrutiny.*

4 when a doctor examines someone

- examination
- physical (examination)
- check-up
- post-mortem

examination /ɪgˌzæmɪ̵'neɪʃən/ [n C] when a doctor examines someone's body to find out if there is anything wrong with them: *After a brief examination by a local doctor, I was taken to the city's main hospital.* | **give sb an examination** *Each of the prisoners was given a thorough medical examination.*

physical (examination) /ˌfɪzɪkəl (ɪgˌzæmɪ̵'neɪʃən)/ [n C] a thorough examination of someone's body and general health by a doctor, especially to decide whether they are fit to do a particular job: *My insurance plan covers one complete physical per year.* | **get a physical (examination)** *Bobby has to get a physical before he can join the football team.* | **give sb a physical (examination)** *Prior to the study all test subjects were given physical examinations.*

check-up /'tʃek ʌp/ [n C] a medical examination to make sure that someone is healthy – especially one that is done regularly: *I see my dentist every six months for a check-up.* | **give sb/sth a check-up** *The vet gave both our horses a thorough check-up and pronounced them fit to race.*

post-mortem especially British **/autopsy** especially American /pəʊst 'mɔːʳtəm, 'ɔːtɒpsi‖-tɑːpsi/ [n C] a medical examination of a dead body in order to find out how the person died: *A post-mortem revealed that the woman had died of blood poisoning.* | **carry out/do/perform/ conduct a post-mortem** *A police pathologist carried out a post-mortem on the body.* | **do/perform/conduct an autopsy** *Officials would not release the results of the autopsy that had been performed on Gallagher.*

example

RELATED WORDS

- *see also* **typical**

1 a typical example of something

- example
- case
- instance
- exemplify

example /ɪg'zɑːmpəl‖ɪg'zæm-/ [n C] something that you mention because it is typical of the kind of thing that you are talking about: *There are many ways in which technology has changed our lives. The car is an obvious example.* | **+ of** *The church is an interesting example of the Gothic style.* | *This painting is a typical example of Picasso's work in his Blue Period.* | **give an example** *Attitude problems? Can you give me an example?* | **a good/typical/classic example** *Some activities are too expensive for poorer children to take part in. Horseriding is a good example.* | *Max is a classic example of a man who can't control his ambition.* | **a prime example** (=an example of something or someone you do not like) *Hitler, Mussolini, Franco: all prime examples of men hungry for power.* | **a shining example** (=an example of something you admire) *The school is a shining example of what parent-teacher co-operation can achieve.*

case /keɪs/ [n C] an example of something that happens, especially something bad **+ of** *There have been some cases of women employees being fired because they are pregnant.* | **in one case/in some cases/in every case** *In one case a man was charged $2000 for a simple medical check-up.* | **a classic case** (=a very typical case) *Recent government spending on schools is a classic case of too little, too late.* | **in sb's case** *Seat belts are supposed to prevent serious injury, but they didn't work in my case.*

instance /'ɪnstəns/ [n C] an example of a particular kind of situation or event: *Some users of Ecstasy have actually died, but such instances are very rare.* | **+ of** *Another instance of Charles's outspokenness was his attack on his sister's choice of husband.* | **in some instances** *The grey suit has been* *replaced in some instances with pink trousers and sandals.*

exemplify /ɪg'zemplɨfaɪ/ [v T not in progressive] if a particular person, situation, or type of behaviour **exemplifies** something, it is a typical example of it: *This court exemplifies the values of fairness and justice.* | *The modern spirit of revolt was best exemplified by the work of Kafka and Freud.*

2 to give an example

- give (sb) an example
- cite

give (sb) an example /ˌgɪv (sb) ən ɪg'zɑːmpəl‖-'zæm-/ [v phrase] to mention something as an example in order to explain what you mean, prove you are right etc: *I don't really understand what you mean. Could you give me an example?* | *I think my theory could be best explained by giving an example from everyday life.* | *To illustrate his point, he gave the example of the Amazonian tribe that had no contact with civilization.*

cite /saɪt/ [v T] formal to name a person, situation etc as a typical example of what you are talking about: *I can cite several recent racial attacks which prove my point.* | *The report contained details of the poison gas and cited examples of accidents involving it.* | **be cited as sth** *Britain is often cited as an example of a declining industrial power.*

3 what you say when you give an example

- for example/for instance
- e.g./eg
- such as
- like
- take
- be a case in point
- by way of illustration
- to name but a few

for example/for instance /fər ɪg'zɑːmpəl, fər 'ɪnstəns‖-'zæm-/ [adv] use this when you are giving an example: *There are lots of famous buildings in Kyoto, for example the Golden Pavilion and the Tyoanyi Temple.* | *There are some tasks which are your responsibility. For instance, it's up to you to dismantle furniture and take down curtains.*

e.g./eg /ˌiː 'dʒiː/ written use this when you are giving an example or a series of examples. In British English, people usually write **eg**; in American English people usually write **e.g.**: *Make sure you eat foods that contain protein, e.g. meat, cheese, fish, milk, or eggs.* | *This course includes a study of basic language skills (eg speaking and listening).*

such as /'sʌtʃ æz/ [prep] especially written used when you want to give one or two typical examples of something but not all the examples that are possible: *It is difficult to get even basic foods such as sugar and bread.* | *People's ability to do the tests is influenced by factors such as age, sex, and ethnic background.*

like /laɪk/ [prep] especially spoken used in spoken English when you are giving a example which is typical of what you mean: *We could cook something easy, like pasta.* | *We still haven't settled a number of problems, like who is going to be in charge here while I'm away.*

take /teɪk/ [adv] spoken say this when you are talking about something and you want to give an example of a certain type of situation, person etc, in order to prove what you are saying is correct: *I can think of lots of people who got worse grades than you and still have good jobs. Take Julie.* | **take sb/sth for example** *Take me for example. I've never relied on other people for help.*

be a case in point /biː ə ˌkeɪs ɪn 'pɔɪnt/ [v phrase] a particular person, situation etc that **is a case in point**, is a very good or typical example of what you have just mentioned: *Some birds have returned to England after once being extinct here. The return of the osprey is a case in point.* | *Some women have managed to achieve success in football. A case in point is Anne Spencer.*

by way of illustration /baɪ ˌweɪ əv ɪlə'streɪʃən/ [adv] formal if you name a particular situation, person etc **by way of illustration**, you want to use them as a way of explaining what you mean: *Other countries have totally different laws on abortion. By way of illustration let us look at the cases of Germany and Japan.*

to name but a few /tə ˌneɪm bət ə 'fjuː/ [adv] if you say **to name but a few** after giving several examples of something, you mean that these are just a few examples of what you mean and there are many more: *So many industries have been hit in the recession. Steel, coal, construction, to name but a few.*

except

RELATED WORDS

- see also **but, include/not include**

1 not including someone or something

- except/except for
- except
- apart from
- but
- other than
- with the exception of
- bar
- but for

except/except for /ɪk'sept, ɪk'sept fɔːʳ/ [prep] not including the person or thing that you mention. At the beginning of a sentence, always use **except for**, not just **except**: *Everyone's going except Donald.* | *The house was silent except for a clock chiming in the living room.* | *Except for a small part in an obscure movie years ago, Depardieu had never before acted in an English-language picture.*

except /ɪk'sept/ [conjunction] use this when you have made a statement that is true, but then you want to introduce a fact that does not match what you have said **except (that)** *Celia looks just like her sister, except that her sister has shorter hair.* | *It's similar to Paris, except the people look a lot poorer.* | **except do sth** (=that is the only thing it cannot do) *a computer that can do everything except talk*

apart from ALSO **aside from** American /ə'pɑːʳt frɒm, ə'saɪd frɒm/ [prep] use this when you mention one or two things that do not fit the main thing that you are saying: *This is an excellent piece of work, apart from a couple of spelling mistakes.* | *Aside from its mineral resources, Mongolia's major assets are its 25.5 million livestock.* | **apart from doing sth** *Apart from going swimming occasionally, I don't get much exercise.*

but /bət; (*strong*) bʌt/ [prep] use this especially after the words **any, none, nothing, all, anyone,** or **everyone** to show that you mean everything except the thing, person etc you are mentioning: *I can come and see you any day but Tuesday.* | *There was nothing left but a few dried up sandwiches.* | *Anyone* *but Tommy would have realized I was trying to apologize.*

other than /ˈʌðəʳ ðən/ [prep] use this in a negative sentence to show that the thing, person etc that you mention is the only person or thing that is not included in your statement: *Other than at football matches, people sing less than they used to.* | **+ to do sth** *Sam refused to discuss the argument, other than to say that Diane had called him 'gutless'.* | **other than that** *You should get a little stiffness, but other than that, there should be no side effects.*

with the exception of /wɪð ði ɪkˈsepʃən ɒv/ [prep] formal not including one thing, person, or group – use this when saying something about the whole of a group: *The whole school, with the exception of the youngest class, had to attend the ceremony.* | **with the possible exception of** (=but possibly not that person or thing) *I think they should all pass the test, with the possible exception of Fauzi.*

bar /bɑːʳ/ [prep] use this to introduce the only thing, person, or group about which your statement is not true: *I get hardly any mail, bar the occasional postcard from my mother.* | *He died with no possessions bar a small piece of land in Ireland.*

but for /ˈbʌt fɔːʳ/ [prep] use this to introduce the only thing that makes a description of something not completely true – used especially in writing: *There was complete silence but for the occasional sound of distant traffic.*

2 someone or something that is not included

- exception

exception /ɪkˈsepʃən/ [n C] someone or something that is not included in a general statement, or does not do what most others in the same situation do: *Most of the students did well, though there were one or two exceptions.* | **notable exception** (=one that is very famous or special) *Women do not usually get to the top in politics, but there have been a few notable exceptions.* | **major/minor exception** (=an important/not very important one) *With a few minor exceptions, the legal system in the two countries is very similar.* | **exception to the rule** *Most couples who break up seem to find it hard to remain friends. Kim and Gerry are exceptions to that rule.*

exchange

to give something to someone, and receive something similar from them

RELATED WORDS

- *see also* **give, get**

1 to exchange one thing for another

- exchange
- swap
- trade
- do a swap
- trade in
- change
- barter
- switch
- change places
- change partners

exchange /ɪksˈtʃeɪndʒ/ [v T] to give something to someone and receive a similar thing from them at the same time **exchange addresses/telephone numbers** *We exchanged addresses and phone numbers.* | **exchange sth for sth** *Foreign currency can be exchanged for sterling at any bank.*

swap /swɒp‖swɑːp/ [v I/T] informal to exchange something with someone, especially with someone you know well, so that you each get something that you want: *Jacky had the book I wanted, but wasn't willing to swap.* | **swap sth with sb** *Taylor offered to swap jobs with me.* | **swap sth for sth** *I'm trying to sell my bike, or swap it for a slightly bigger one.*

trade /treɪd/ [v I/T] especially American to exchange something that you have for something that someone else has: *We liked each other's clothes, so we traded.* | **trade sth for sth** *The West is accused of trading weapons for hostages.* | **I'll trade you** spoken (=say this when you want to exchange something) *I'll trade you my baseball for those two cars.*

do a swap /ˌduː ə ˈswɒp‖-ˈswɑːp/ [v phrase] British an informal expression: if two people **do a swap** with each other they exchange things so that they each get what they want **do a swap with sb** *If you can't work a particular shift, you can always do a swap with a colleague.*

trade in /ˌtreɪd ˈɪn/ [phr v T] to give your old car, washing machine etc to the shop that you are buying a new one from, so that they will let you buy the new one for a slightly lower price **trade in sth** *You can get quite good price reductions on new cars if you trade in your old one.* | **trade sth/it/them in** *My car was now six years old, so I traded it in and got a newer one.* | **trade in sth for** *They traded in their Porsche for a family car.*

change British **/exchange** American /tʃeɪndʒ, ɪksˈtʃeɪndʒ/ [v T] to exchange something you have bought or chosen because you have decided you want something different or because there is something wrong with it: *If the trousers are the wrong size you can always change them.* | **change sth for sth** *Can I exchange this sweater for a black one?*

barter /ˈbɑːʳtəʳ/ [v I/T] to exchange something that you have for something that you want or need without giving or taking money for it **barter sth for sth** *In the local market, meat and vegetables are bartered for electrical goods.* | **+ with** *She had some success in bartering with her guards.* —**barter** [n U] *In the mountain areas, most of the trade is still done by barter* (=people barter to get what they need).

switch /swɪtʃ/ [v I/T] to exchange something so that two or more things or people change the places that they are in: *He was accused of switching the price labels on goods.* | *Professor Rigby's talk may be switched to the main hall.* | **switch seats/places** *We switched seats halfway through the show.*

change places /ˌtʃeɪndʒ ˈpleɪsɪ̇z/ [v phrase] to exchange the place you are standing or sitting on with another person **change places with** *Would you mind changing places with me?*

change partners /ˌtʃeɪndʒ ˈpɑːʳtnəʳz/ [v phrase] if a group of people who are dancing **change partners**, they stop dancing with one person and dance with another person in the group: *We agreed to change partners after a couple of dances.*

2 when you exchange one thing for another

- exchange
- interchange
- swap

exchange /ɪksˈtʃeɪndʒ/ [n C usually singular] when you give something to someone and receive a similar thing from them at the same time: *Sale goods can be brought back to the store for an exchange or store credit.* | **+ of** *The exchange of prisoners took place on* *a bridge over the Mekong river.* | *In any negotiations there must be an honest exchange of information.*

interchange /ˈɪntəʳtʃeɪndʒ/ [n C usually singular] the useful exchange of ideas or information between people or organizations, especially when this happens continuously over a long period of time **+ of** *The conference provides a forum for the interchange of ideas and information.* | **data/document interchange** (=the exchange of information by computer) *The new program should help solve some of the problems of data interchange between companies with different computer systems.*

swap /swɒp‖swɑːp/ especially British **/trade** /treɪd/ especially American [n C usually singular] informal when you give something to someone and receive a similar thing from them, usually someone you know: *If you are unable to sell your house, it is sometimes possible to arrange a swap.* | *After a brief discussion we agreed a trade.*

3 ways of saying what you give or get when you exchange things

- in exchange/in return
- for

in exchange/in return /ɪn ɪksˈtʃeɪndʒ, ɪn rɪˈtɜːʳn/ [adv] if you give something or do something **in exchange** or **in return** for something else, you give it in order to get something else back: *He is always willing to help people out, without expecting anything in return.* | **+ for** *In exchange for giving evidence in court, Jacobs was granted freedom and allowed to leave the country.*

for /fəʳ; (*strong*) fɔːʳ/ [prep] in exchange for **give/offer sb sth for sth** *They gave me £200 for my old car.* | *She offered me $30 for my bike.* | *I get £35 for each shift, plus tips.*

excited/exciting

RELATED WORDS

- *see also* **energetic, enjoy, enthusiastic/unenthusiastic**

1 feeling excited about something

- excited
- look forward to
- can't wait
- thrilled
- exhilarated
- be pumped (up)
- be buzzing (with excitement)
- be on the edge of your seat
- be on tenterhooks
- be at/reach fever pitch

excited /ɪkˈsaɪtɪ̈d/ [adj] feeling happy and full of energy, especially about something good that has happened or is going to happen: *Steve's coming home tomorrow – we're all really excited.* | *crowds of excited football fans* | **+ about** *How can you be so excited about a stupid computer game?* | **get excited** *When Mattie gets excited, she starts talking really fast.* | **+ by** *Doctors are very excited by the discovery.* | **+ to do sth** *When we get home, the dogs are always excited to see us.* ▸ **USAGE** Be careful not to confuse ***excited*** (=used about how someone feels) and ***exciting*** (=used about things or situations that make you feel excited).

look forward to /lʊk ˈfɔːʳwəʳd tuː/ [phr v T] to feel excited about something good that is going to happen and to think about it a lot: *The kids are looking forward to their vacation – they've never been to California before.* | **look forward to doing sth** *She's really looking forward to meeting him.*

can't wait /ˌkɑːnt ˈweɪt‖ˌkænt-/ [v phrase] spoken if you **can't wait** for something to happen, you want it to happen soon because you are very excited about it: *'We'll see you next week.' 'I know – I can't wait!'* | **+ for** *The kids can't wait for Christmas.* | **+ to do sth** *He couldn't wait to get home and tell Dean the news.* | **can't wait for sb/sth to do sth** *I can't wait for the football season to start.*

thrilled /θrɪld/ [adj not before noun] very excited, happy, and pleased **+ to do sth** *I'm thrilled to be here tonight.* | **+ with** *Chester's absolutely thrilled with his baby daughter.* | **+ at/by** *She was thrilled at the idea of flying to Europe.* | **thrilled to bits** British spoken **thrilled to death/pieces** American spoken (=very thrilled) *Paul is thrilled to death that I'm finally learning to cook.*

exhilarated /ɪgˈzɪləreɪtɪ̈d/ [adj not before noun] feeling very excited and full of energy because you are experiencing something that you have never experienced before, especially something dangerous or unusual: *The first time I flew a plane alone, I felt both exhilarated and scared.* | **+ by** *She felt exhilarated by her new sense of power.*

be pumped (up) /biː ˌpʌmpt (ˈʌp)/ [v phrase] American informal to be excited and full of energy, especially when this makes you ready to compete or play sport: *After the coach's pep talk, we were all really pumped and ready to play.* | **get sb pumped (up)** (=make some excited and full of energy) *Nothing gets the crowd or the players pumped up more than a good slam dunk.*

be buzzing (with excitement) /biː ˌbʌzɪŋ (wɪð ɪkˈsaɪtmənt)/ [v phrase] if a place is **buzzing with excitement**, people are very excited, especially because something is about to happen: *The crowd was buzzing as everyone waited for the band to come on stage.* | *The new stadium has sports fans buzzing with excitement.*

be on the edge of your seat /biː ɒn ði ˌedʒ əv jɔːʳ ˈsiːt/ [v phrase] to be excited and slightly nervous when you are watching something because you do not know what will happen next: *I was on the edge of my seat from the beginning of the movie to the end.* | **keep sb on the edge of their seat** (=make someone very excited because they do not know what will happen next) *The final ten minutes of the game kept everyone on the edge of their seats.*

be on tenterhooks /biː ɒn ˈtentəʳhʊks/ [v phrase] to be nervous and excited because you are anxiously waiting to hear the result of something, or to know what happens at the end of a story: *After the interview Fran was on tenterhooks, wondering if she'd got the job.* | **keep sb on tenterhooks** (=make someone feel nervous and excited by not telling them something) *Agatha Christie keeps the reader on tenterhooks until the final pages of the story.*

be at/reach fever pitch /biː ət, riːtʃ ˈfiːvəʳ pɪtʃ/ [v phrase] if the feeling among a large group of people **is at** or **reaches fever pitch**, they are all extremely excited: *The anticipation surrounding the band's arrival is now at fever pitch.*

2 too excited

- overexcited
- hysterical
- in a frenzy
- excitable
- hyper

overexcited /ˌəʊvərɪkˈsaɪtɪ̈d◂/ [adj] someone, especially a child, who is **overexcited** has become too excited to behave calmly: *The kids are getting overexcited and won't go to sleep.* | *'Does it bite?' asked one of an overexcited group of boys.*

hysterical /hɪˈsterɪkəl/ [adj] unable to stop shouting, crying etc because you are extremely excited: *Hysterical fans tried to stop Damon's car at the airport.* | *He got a hysterical phone call from his mother in the middle of the night.* | **get/go hysterical** (=become hysterical) *The crowd went hysterical as Juventus scored in the last minute of the game.*

in a frenzy /ɪn ə ˈfrenzi/ [adj phrase] in a state of great and uncontrollable excitement: *There are just two minutes to go of this game, and the crowd is in an absolute frenzy.* | **work yourself into a frenzy** (=become more and more excited until you are in a frenzy) *Supporters of Hodge have worked themselves into a frenzy over the latest polls.*

excitable /ɪkˈsaɪtəbəl/ [adj] someone who is **excitable** gets excited too easily: *Puppies are naturally affectionate and excitable.* | **highly excitable** (=very excitable) *On my first day's teaching, I had a class of highly excitable 5-year-olds.*

hyper /ˈhaɪpəʳ/ [adj] spoken too excited and too full of energy, so that you do not feel comfortable: *The kids are really hyper today – I think I'm going to send them outside.* | **get hyper** *Sometimes he gets so hyper you can't talk to him.*

3 to make someone feel excited

- excite
- get sb excited
- thrill
- give sb a thrill
- get the adrenaline going/flowing/pumping

excite /ɪkˈsaɪt/ [v T not usually in progressive or passive] especially written to make someone feel excited: *Being part of the crowd at a ball game had always excited me.* | *She was at a point in her life where her work didn't really excite her anymore.*

get sb excited /ˌget (sb) ɪkˈsaɪtɨd/ [v phrase not in passive] informal to make someone excited: *We've chosen some fairly controversial topics to try to get the students excited.* | **get sb excited about sth** *Looking through all those cook books has gotten me excited about cooking again.*

thrill /θrɪl/ [v T not usually in progressive] especially written to make someone feel very happy and excited: *Her first sight of the African landscape thrilled her enormously.* | **it thrills sb to do sth** *It thrilled Sara to learn that the visitor was a member of the Royal Family.*

give sb a thrill /ˌgɪv (sb) ə ˈθrɪl/ [v phrase] if something **gives someone a thrill**, it makes them feel happy and excited, although it is very simple or may seem unimportant: *Catching small animals used to give the boys a thrill.* | *It gives me a thrill to see kids that I have taught succeed in life.*

get the adrenaline going/flowing/pumping /get ði əˈdrenəlɪn ˌgəʊɪŋ, ˌfləʊɪŋ, ˌpʌmpɪŋ/ [v phrase] to make you feel nervously excited and full of energy. **Adrenaline** is a chemical produced in your body that makes your heart beat faster when you are afraid or excited: *Performing for the President really gets your adrenaline going.* | *At the end of a long race, it's the sight of the finish line that gets the old adrenaline pumping.*

4 exciting

- exciting
- thrilling
- gripping
- exhilarating
- dramatic
- nailbiting
- action-packed
- heady

exciting /ɪkˈsaɪtɪŋ/ [adj] making you feel excited: *You're going to India? How exciting!* | *I've got some exciting news for you.* | *Hockey is a fast, exciting game to watch.* | **find sth exciting** *Stuart found life in Paris exciting.* ▸ **USAGE** Be careful not to confuse ***exciting*** (=used about things or situations that make you feel excited) and ***excited*** (=used about how someone feels): *The movie was very **exciting**.* | *We were all **excited**.*

thrilling /ˈθrɪlɪŋ/ [adj] making you feel very excited and slightly nervous: *The helicopter trip over the mountains was a thrilling end to a fantastic holiday.* | *In a thrilling victory over Arizona, Bailey scored four straight points.*

gripping /ˈgrɪpɪŋ/ [adj] use this about books or films that are so exciting that you cannot stop reading or watching them: *a gripping detective story* | *The author describes in gripping detail the accident on the icy highway.*

exhilarating /ɪgˈzɪləreɪtɪŋ/ [adj] an **exhilarating** experience or activity makes you feel excited and full of energy: *Learning to surf is exhausting but exhilarating.* | *I still remember the exhilarating freedom of driving my first car.*

dramatic /drəˈmætɪk/ [adj] a **dramatic** part of a story, film etc has a lot of exciting and unexpected things happening in it: *The movie starts with a dramatic car chase across the desert.* | *'Voice of the Heart' is a dramatic story of two women that sweeps from New York to Europe and back again.*

nailbiting /ˈneɪlˌbaɪtɪŋ/ [adj only before noun] extremely exciting because you do not know what is going to happen next: *The movie's rescue scene makes a nice nailbiting finish.* | *The Minutemen managed another nailbiting win to remain undefeated.*

action-packed /ˌækʃən ˈpækt◂/ [adj usually before noun] an **action-packed** film, book etc has a lot of exciting action in it: *Kids will love this action-packed adventure movie.* | *The book has an action-packed plot dealing with life during the Civil War.*

heady /ˈhedi/ [adj only before noun] formal **heady days/atmosphere/excitement etc** a time, feeling etc that makes you feel very excited, hopeful, and full of energy: *the heady excitement of being in love* | *He often wished he could relive the heady days of his youth.*

5 the most exciting part of something

- climax
- high point/spot
- highlight

climax /ˈklaɪmæks/ [n C] the most exciting or important part of a story or event, usually near the end **+ of** *A parade through the streets marks the climax of the festival.* | **reach a climax** *The opera reaches its climax with Violetta's death in the third act.*

high point/spot /ˈhaɪ pɔɪnt, spɒt‖-spɑːt/ [n C] the most exciting, enjoyable, or important moment of an event or activity, especially one that continues for a long time **+ of** *For Amelia, a high point of the trip was riding with her father on a Ferris wheel.* | *The 1972 election was the high spot of her political career.*

highlight /ˈhaɪlaɪt/ [n C] the part of an event or activity such as a holiday or a game that is the most exciting or enjoyable, and that you remember most clearly **+ of** *Highlights of the ball game will be shown later.* | *A highlight of most Alaska cruises is a day spent among the glaciers.*

6 the feeling of being excited

- excitement
- thrill
- exhilaration
- high spirits
- hysteria
- fever

excitement /ɪkˈsaɪtmənt/ [n U] *If you're looking for excitement, you won't find it here.* | **+ of** *He missed the excitement of working with so many intelligent people.* | **in/with excitement** (=in an excited way) *In the stands, the crowd was shouting with excitement.* | **great/tremendous excitement** *There's an atmosphere of tremendous excitement here in the stadium.*

thrill /θrɪl/ [n C usually singular] a sudden very strong feeling of excitement, mixed with pleasure and sometimes fear **+ of** *Most of the researchers are motivated by the simple thrill of discovery.* | **get a thrill out of sth** *Even though I've been acting for 40 years, I still get a thrill out of going on stage on opening night.* | **give sb a thrill** *Using a gun always gave me a strange thrill.*

exhilaration /ɪgˌzɪləˈreɪʃən/ [n U] a feeling of happy excitement, for example that you get from an exciting physical activity or from something you have achieved: *She was filled with exhilaration when she first saw her newborn baby.* | **+ of** *Nothing can compare with the exhilaration of riding a motorcycle as fast as you can.*

high spirits /ˌhaɪ ˈspɪrɪ̈ts/ [n plural] excited and cheerful feelings or behaviour, especially of a group of young people: *They didn't mean to cause any damage – it was just high spirits.* | **in high spirits** *It was the last day of term and everyone was in high spirits.*

hysteria /hɪˈstɪəriə‖-ˈsteriə/ [n U] extreme excitement that makes people cry, laugh, shout etc uncontrollably: *The hysteria of the screaming girls was somewhat frightening.* | **mass hysteria** (=hysteria in a crowd of people) *The pushing and grabbing at yesterday's sales bordered on mass hysteria.*

fever /ˈfiːvəʳ/ [n singular] when a lot of people are very excited about a particular thing **World Cup/Harry Potter/ election etc fever** *For a few months after its introduction, lottery fever swept the nation.* | *Football fever has always been widespread in Thailand, but this year perhaps more than ever before.*

7 an exciting experience

- thrill
- adventure
- excitement
- blast

thrill /θrɪl/ [n C usually singular] an event or experience that gives you a feeling of excitement and pleasure: *Flying is still a tremendous thrill for me.* | **the thrills and spills/chills** (=the exciting experiences, moments etc in a film, race etc) *Don't miss all the thrills and spills of Formula 1 Grand Prix racing on Channel 26!*

adventure /ədˈventʃəʳ/ [n C/U] an exciting experience in which something dangerous or unusual happens: *He always used to tell us about his adventures at sea.* | **sense/spirit of adventure** (=a desire to do unusual or dangerous things) *All right, I'll go without you – you guys have no sense of adventure at all!*

excitement /ɪkˈsaɪtmənt/ [n C] something unexpected or unusual that happens and makes you feel excited and unable to relax: *Gerry found it difficult to sleep after all the excitements of the day.* | *The biggest excitement of the day was when Joe accidentally set off the fire alarm.*

blast /blɑːst‖blæst/ [n C] American informal an exciting experience that you enjoy very much: *You should try water-skiing – it's a blast.* | **have a blast** *Thanks for taking us camping – Miranda had a blast!*

8 to do something just for excitement

- do sth for kicks
- do sth for the thrill of it

do sth for kicks /ˌduː (sth) fəʳ ˈkɪks/ [v phrase] to do something, especially something dangerous or harmful, in order to get a feeling of excitement and not for any other reason: *He was a nasty man who mistreated people for kicks.* | **just for kicks** *He says he started stealing just for kicks, not because he didn't have the money.*

do sth for the thrill of it /ˌduː (sth) fəʳ ðə ˈθrɪl əv ɪt/ [v phrase] to do something just to get a feeling of excitement or because you are bored, and not for any more serious reason: *Gina would gamble away thousands of dollars in casinos just for the thrill of it.* | *Sometimes I walk very close to the edge of the cliffs for the thrill of it.*

9 to make someone feel sexually excited

- excite
- turn sb on
- titillate

excite /ɪkˈsaɪt/ [v T] *She excites me in a way that no other woman can.* | **get sb excited** (=make them excited) *Some of those Internet chat rooms can get you pretty excited.* —**exciting** [adj] *I suppose some men might find pictures like this sexually exciting.*

turn sb on /ˌtɜːʳn (sb) ˈɒn/ [phr v T] informal to make someone feel sexually excited: *It's difficult telling your partner what actually turns you on.* | *Men with long hair really turn me on.* —**turn-on** [n singular] something that makes you sexually excited: *My last boyfriend always found nurses' uniforms a real turn-on.*

titillate /ˈtɪtɪ̈leɪt/ [v T] if pictures, stories etc in newspapers and books **titillate** people, they are deliberately intended to make people feel slightly sexually excited: *Details of the sex scandal are being revealed just to titillate the public, not inform them.* —**titillation** /ˌtɪtɪ̈ˈleɪʃən/ [n U] *The play has been condemned as just an excuse for sexual titillation.* —**titillating** [adj] *The titillating advertisements suggested more nudity than actually was in the film.*

exercise

to walk, do sports etc to stay healthy and become stronger

RELATED WORDS

- an activity that is designed to make you practice a skill *see* **practise/practice**
- *see also* **fit/not fit, sport/game, play a game or sport, sweat**

1 to exercise your body

- exercise
- do exercise
- get exercise
- work out
- keep fit
- get into shape
- warm up
- train

exercise /ˈeksəʳsaɪz/ [v I] to walk, do sports etc in order to stay healthy and become stronger: *You should exercise every day and get plenty of fresh air.* | *Even people who start exercising quite late in life notice considerable benefits.* | *A lot of managers spend long hours in their cars and exercise very little.*

do exercise ALSO **take exercise** British /ˌduː ˈeksəʳsaɪz, ˌteɪk ˈeksəʳsaɪz/ [v phrase] to exercise, especially regularly: *You should do at least fifteen minutes' exercise each day.* | *Doctors are always telling us that we should do more exercise.* | *Most of the people here never take any exercise at all.*

get exercise /ˌget ˈeksəʳsaɪz/ [v phrase] to do exercise, especially as part of your daily work or daily life: *A lot of children these days don't get enough exercise.* | *Try to increase the amount of exercise you get, perhaps by walking to work.*

work out /ˌwɜːʳk ˈaʊt/ [phr v I] to exercise regularly, using all the important muscles in your body, especially in a gym or exercise class: *Professional footballers spend at least an hour every day working out in the gym.* | *I go jogging every morning and work out with weights twice a week.*

keep fit /ˌkiːp ˈfɪt/ [v phrase] British to exercise regularly in order to stay healthy and young: *Jim gave up drinking and took up tennis in an attempt to keep fit.* | *Many older people find that keeping fit can be fun as well as good for their health.*

get into shape ALSO **get fit** British /ˌget ɪntə ˈʃeɪp, ˌget ˈfɪt/ [v phrase] to do regular exercise because you are not healthy or strong enough: *It's not too late to get into shape before the summer holidays.* | *If you want to get fit quickly, jogging is one of the best ways.*

warm up ALSO **limber up** especially British /ˌwɔːʳm ˈʌp, ˌlɪmbər ˈʌp/ [phr v I] to do gentle physical exercises just before playing a sport, dancing etc, so that you do not injure your muscles: *It's important to warm up properly before you do any sport.* | *The runners are now limbering up as they get ready for the race.*

train /treɪn/ [v I] to prepare for a sporting event, especially by exercising: *We train twice a week at the local gym.* | *I'm not as fit as I should be. I don't train enough.*

2 to exercise a particular part of your body

- exercise
- firm/tone up

exercise /ˈeksəʳsaɪz/ [v T] if an activity or movement exercises the muscles in your body, it keeps them strong and healthy: *Swimming exercises all the major muscle groups.* | *Raise your knee to exercise the upper leg and hip.*

firm/tone up /ˌfɜːʳm, təʊn ˈʌp/ [phr v I/T] to make your body or part of your body firmer: *I'd like to tone up my hips, thighs, and stomach*

3 activities for exercising your body

- exercise
- workout
- aerobics
- keep fit
- training

exercise /ˈeksəʳsaɪz/ [n C/U] a physical movement that you do to keep a part of your body strong and healthy. Physical activities such as sports that you do in order to keep your body strong and healthy are also called exercise: *The doctor recommended a diet and a programme of exercises to help her lose weight.* | *Try a few gentle exercises once or twice a day.* | *Thirty minutes of squash gives you as much exercise as an hour of any other game.* | **do exercises** *Most people find it more fun doing exercises to music.* | **regular exercise** *A new medical report has again highlighted the health benefits of regular exercise.* | **strenuous exercise** (=very hard exercise) *Do not start a programme of strenuous exercise if you have any heart problems.*

workout /ˈwɜːʳkaʊt/ [n C] a series of exercises that you do regularly in order to keep fit and healthy: *Start your workout with some gentle stretching exercises.* | *I always feel better after a good workout.*

aerobics /eəˈrəʊbɪks/ [n U] a very active type of physical exercise done to music, usually in a class, which makes your heart and lungs stronger: *Have you ever tried aerobics?* | *My mum's started going to an aerobics class.* | **do aerobics** *I do aerobics twice a week.*

keep fit /ˌkiːp ˈfɪt/ [n U] British a class in which you do exercises to keep yourself healthy **do keep fit** *I started doing keep fit a couple of years ago.* —**keep-fit** [adj only before noun] *keep-fit classes for the over 60s*

training /ˈtreɪnɪŋ/ [n U] regular exercise that you do to prepare for a sport or competition; in British English, **training** also means regular exercise that you do to stay strong and healthy **do training** *I do two hours' training every evening – an hour running or swimming, and an hour in the gym.* | **football/rugby etc training** (=training in which a team prepares for a sport together) *All the children do football training at least once a week.* | **in training** (=doing training for a particular event) *She's in training for the New York Marathon.* | **weight training** (=training which involves lifting weights) *The sports centre offers such activities as dance classes, aerobics and weight training.*

exist

RELATED WORDS

- *see also* **alive, dead**

1 to exist

- exist
- there is/are
- be found
- occur
- existence

exist /ɪgˈzɪst/ [v I not in progressive] to be something that is really present or living: *Do you think ghosts really exist?* | *The blue whale is the largest creature that has ever existed on earth.* | *We can't continue to pretend that the problem of homelessness doesn't exist in this city.* | **there exists/there exist** *There now exists a significant body of scientific research on the subject.*

there is/are /ðeər ɪz, ɑːʳ/ if you say **there is** something, you mean that it exists: *Is there life on other planets?* | *There's no evidence to prove that Gray is the murderer.* | *There are hundreds of different computer programs designed specifically for children.* | *I didn't know there was Chinese restaurant in your neighborhood.*

be found /biː ˈfaʊnd/ [v phrase] to exist in a particular place, or inside a particular thing: *Otters are still found in some parts of Britain.* | *Vitamin C is found in green vegetables and fresh fruit.* | **can be found** *Other examples of this type of romantic poem can be found throughout history.*

occur /əˈkɜːʳ/ [v I not in progressive] if something such as a particular type of substance or illness **occurs** in a particular place, it exists there – used especially in scientific contexts **+ in** *The disease occurs mainly in children, but can also occur in adults.* | *Chromium and nickel occur commonly in areas which are also rich in magnesium.* | *The Japanese 'f' sound does not occur in European languages.*

existence /ɪɡˈzɪstəns/ [n U] when something exists **the existence of sth** *For the first time she began to doubt the existence of God.* | **in existence** *Today there are less than 100 copies of the book still in existence.* | *The organization has been in existence for only 18 months.*

2 to not exist

- **not exist**
- **there's no such thing**
- **nonexistent**

not exist /nɒt ɪɡˈzɪst/ [v phrase] *The Atlantic Ocean did not exist 150 million years ago.* | *She looked right through me as if I didn't exist.* | *The village the old man mentioned doesn't exist on any of my maps.*

there's no such thing /ðeəʳz ˌnəʊ sʌtʃ ˈθɪŋ/ spoken use this to tell someone that you are sure something does not exist: *I don't believe in vampires – there's no such thing.* | **+ as** *I've come to the conclusion that there's no such thing as perfect happiness.*

nonexistent /ˌnɒn ɪɡˈzɪstənt◂‖ˌnɑːn-/ [adj] something that is **nonexistent** does not exist: *Steady jobs are almost nonexistent in remote parts of the country.* | *It turned out that many of the letters of recommendation were from nonexistent companies.*

3 when something no longer exists

- **no longer exist/not exist any more**
- **extinct**
- **die out**
- **disappear**

no longer exist/not exist any more /nəʊ ˌlɒŋɡər ɪɡˈzɪst‖-ˌlɔːŋ-, nɒt ɪɡˈzɪst eni mɔːʳ/ [v phrase] *Many of the old birth and death records do not exist any more.* | *The system that guaranteed lifetime employment no longer exists.* | *The ideal is to build a society in which racism no longer exists.*

extinct /ɪkˈstɪŋkt/ [adj] if a type of animal is **extinct**, none of them are alive anymore: *The white rhino is now almost extinct.* | *There are several theories as to why the dinosaurs became extinct.* | *The valley contains fossils of many extinct species.*

die out /ˌdaɪ ˈaʊt/ [phr v I] if something such as a type of plant or animal **dies out**, there are fewer and fewer of them until finally there are none left: *Many of the old village traditions are dying out.* | *Unless we do something now, hundreds of plant and animal species will die out.*

disappear /ˌdɪsəˈpɪəʳ/ [v I] if something **disappears**, it stops existing and can no longer be seen or felt: *Thousands of miles of rainforest are disappearing every year.* | *As the economy improves, workers' fears of being laid off have disappeared.*

expect

RELATED WORDS

- when something happens before you expect it to *see* **ready/not ready**
- wait for something to happen *see* **wait**
- *see also* **hope, surprised/surprising**

1 to expect something

- **expect**
- **think**
- **anticipate**

expect /ɪkˈspekt/ [v T] if you **expect** something to happen, you think it probably will: *I'm expecting a fax from Korea. Has anything arrived yet?* | *Drivers should expect long delays on all roads out of town today.* | **+ to do sth** *I expected to find him in the bar, but he wasn't there.* | **+ (that)** *We all expected she'd get the job – it was a real shock when she didn't.* | **expect sb/sth to do sth** *Economists expect the economy to grow by 5% next year.* | **fully expect** (=confidently expect that something will definitely happen) *Perkins fully expects to be back in Boston by July 1.*

think /θɪŋk/ [v T not in progressive] to believe that something is likely to happen **+ (that)** *Do you think they'll come to the party?* | *I never thought her business would be so successful.* | **think sth is likely** *The builders said the job would be finished tomorrow, but I don't think that's likely.*

anticipate /ænˈtɪsɪ̵peɪt/ [v T] to expect that something will happen, and be prepared for it – use this especially to say that something was different from what you had expected: *The journey took a lot longer than we had anticipated.* | **+ that** *We had anticipated that interest rates would have fallen further by now.* | **anticipate doing sth** *I think we've fixed everything, and I don't anticipate finding any more problems.* —**anticipation** /ænˌtɪsɪ̵ˈpeɪʃən/ [n U] *They started off on the trip with a sense of nervous anticipation.*

2 what you say when you expect something to happen

- **I expect**
- **I bet/my bet is**
- **I suspect**
- **I would think**
- **I wouldn't be surprised**
- **my expectation is**

I expect /aɪ ɪkˈspekt/ especially British **/I guess** /aɪ ˈɡes/ especially American *Hasn't Tony arrived yet? He'll be here soon, I expect.* | **+ (that)** *I expect your mother will be overjoyed when she hears you're having a baby.* | **I expect/guess so** *'Is Alan going to drive tonight?' 'Yeah, I guess so.'*

I bet/my bet is /aɪ ˈbet, maɪ ˈbet ɪz/ informal use this to introduce something that you expect to happen because of what you know about someone or about the way things usually happen. **I bet** is more common than **my bet is + (that)** *I bet you'll miss your boyfriend when you go away for college.* | *Sandra says she's never going to have any children, but my bet is she has at least three.*

I suspect /aɪ səˈspekt/ use this when you have a feeling that something is going to happen, especially something bad or unpleasant: *You'll find Rick's parents rather hard to talk to, I suspect.* | **+ (that)** *I suspect that 10 years after the book is published, nobody will even remember the name of the author.*

I would think especially British ALSO **I should think** British /aɪ wʊd 'θɪŋk, aɪ ʃʊd 'θɪŋk/ use this when you think something is likely to happen although you are not really sure: *It'll be cooler down by the lake, I would think.* | **+ (that)** *I should think Sarah and Greg will be going to the party.* | **I would/should think so** *'Will you have finished work by 6.30?' 'Oh yes, I should think so.'*

I wouldn't be surprised /aɪ ˌwʊdnt biː səʳ'praɪzd/ say this when you think something may happen, even though other people think it is unlikely: *'Do you think they'll get married?' 'I wouldn't be surprised.'* | **+ if** *You know, I wouldn't be surprised if some of the top executives lose their jobs.*

my expectation is /maɪ ˌekspek'teɪʃən ɪz/ formal use this to introduce something that you expect to happen because of information that you have: *My expectation is that the two companies will eventually come to an agreement.*

3 to do something because you expect something to happen

- figure on/reckon on
- count on
- in expectation/anticipation of
- don't count your chickens (before they're hatched)

figure on/reckon on /'fɪgər ɒn‖'fɪgjər-, 'rekən ɒn/ [phr v T not in passive] especially spoken to expect something to happen, so that you make plans or take actions that depend on it happening: *We had expected it to take about an hour to get home, but we hadn't reckoned on the traffic.* | **reckon/figure on doing sth** *Visitors to the city should figure on spending about $150 a day for food and lodging.* | **reckon/figure on sb doing sth** *We can reckon on about 100 people coming to the meeting.*

count on /'kaʊnt ɒn/ [phr v T] to expect something so much that your plans depend on it happening or you are completely prepared for it when it happens: *We're counting on good weather for the picnic – if it rains, we'll have to cancel.* | **count on doing sth** *The automaker is planning on earning large profits with this new model.* | **count on sb doing sth** *Don't count on Congress passing the bill anytime soon.*

in expectation/anticipation of /ɪn ˌekspek'teɪʃən, ænˌtɪsə̇'peɪʃən ɒv/ [prep] especially written if you make plans or take actions **in expectation** or **anticipation** of something happening, you do this because you expect it to happen and you want to be prepared: *The workers have called off their strike in expectation of a pay settlement.* | *Residents are buying supplies and stacking wood in anticipation of the coming storms.*

don't count your chickens (before they're hatched) /ˌdaʊnt kaʊnt jɔːʳ ˌtʃɪkə̇nz (bɪˌfɔːʳ ðeəʳ 'hætʃt)/ use this to tell someone not to be too sure that what they are hoping for will happen: *If you want to go on a date sometime, you can ask me. But don't count your chickens.* | *Getting an Oscar would be wonderful, but I think it's too early to count my chickens.*

4 to make someone expect something

- lead sb to expect
- raise/arouse expectations

lead sb to expect /ˌliːd (sb) tʊ ɪk'spekt/ [v phrase] to encourage someone to expect something, especially something that does not actually happen: *The hotel was horrible – not at all what we'd been led to expect.* | *I think his campaign promises led us all to expect he'd be a much more honest politician.*

raise/arouse expectations /reɪz, əˌraʊz ekspek'teɪʃənz/ [v phrase] if something that someone says **raises** or **arouses expectations**, it makes people begin to expect something good or interesting: *A good manager raises expectations among employees.* | **+ of** *The prime minister's remarks aroused expectations of tax cuts.*

5 expecting something good to happen

- optimistic
- optimist
- upbeat

optimistic /ˌɒptə̇'mɪstɪk◂‖ˌɑːp-/ [adj] someone who is **optimistic** expects good things to happen: *In spite of all her problems she manages to remain optimistic.* | *an optimistic economic forecast* | **+ about** *I'm pretty optimistic about our chances of winning here today.* | **+ that** *Are you still optimistic that the climbers can be rescued?* | **cautiously/guardedly optimistic** (=expecting good things to happen but knowing that they might not happen) *We are cautiously optimistic that the trade deal will go through.* | **overly optimistic** (=more optimistic than you should be) *The company was overly optimistic in its sale projections.* —**optimistically** [adv] *Fisher speaks optimistically about the possibility of a vaccine.*

optimist /'ɒptə̇mə̇st‖'ɑːp-/ [n C] someone who always expects good things to happen: *Optimists still believe we can resolve the problem without going to war.*

upbeat /'ʌpbiːt/ [adj] expressing a cheerful attitude and showing that you expect to succeed, even though the situation may not be encouraging: *The senator took an upbeat view of the Republicans' chances in the next election.* | **+ about** *Analysts are more upbeat about the long-term outlook for the economy.*

6 expecting something bad to happen

- pessimistic
- pessimist
- downbeat
- gloomy
- fear the worst

pessimistic /ˌpesə̇'mɪstɪk◂/ [adj] someone who is **pessimistic** always expects bad things to happen: *Don't be too pessimistic – we may still win the game.* | **+ about** *He's quite pessimistic about his chances of getting another job.* | **+ that** *Beron is pessimistic that a peaceful solution can be found.* —**pessimistically** [adv] *In his book, Miller writes pessimistically about the future of American cities.*

pessimist /'pesə̇mə̇st/ [n C] someone who always expects bad things to happen: *Don't be such a pessimist – I'm sure you'll pass your driving test!*

downbeat /'daʊnbiːt/ [adj] expressing an attitude that is not at all hopeful and showing that you do not expect success: *The latest economic surveys are more downbeat as a result of the recent decline in world trade.*

gloomy /'gluːmi/ [adj] not having or offering much hope for the future: *A year ago it seemed that a peace treaty looked possible, but now the outlook is much gloomier.* | *The world's largest chip maker gave a gloomy forecast for the first quarter.* | **+ about** *Most* *political analysts are gloomy about the country's future.* —**gloomily** [adv] *He spoke gloomily about the prospect of a long civil war.* —**gloom** [n U] *The bad forecast brought gloom to the struggling retail industry.* | **gloom and doom** *I'm not paying much attention to their predictions of gloom and doom.*

fear the worst /ˌfɪəʳ ðə 'wɜːʳst/ [v phrase] formal to expect a situation to have the worst possible result because you know how bad the situation could be: *After I hadn't heard from him for several hours, I began to fear the worst.* | *Fearing the worst, police have called in reinforcements to help control the crowds.*

7 when things happens in the way you expected

- as expected
- be no surprise/come as no surprise
- predictable
- be only to be expected
- be par for the course
- I'm not surprised

as expected /æz ɪk'spektɪ̈d/ [adv] if something happens **as expected**, it happens exactly in the way that people expected it to happen: *As expected, the three men were sentenced to life imprisonment.* | *Tulsa beat New Mexico as expected in last night's game.* | **as was/had been expected** *Yesterday, as had been expected, the government announced its intention to launch a public enquiry.*

be no surprise/come as no surprise /biː ˌnəʊ səʳ'praɪz, ˌkʌm əz ˌnəʊ səʳ'praɪz/ [v phrase not in progressive] if something that happens **is no surprise** or **comes as no surprise**, it is exactly as you expected, so you are not surprised by it: *After a series of scandals, Fleischman's resignation comes as no surprise.* | **+ to** *Tina was shocked when she heard she was not being promoted, but it came as no surprise to the rest of us.* | **be/come as no great surprise** *The fact that Brown has decided to run for reelection comes as no great surprise.* | **it is/comes as no surprise that** *It's no surprise that Jeff and his wife are getting divorced.* | **+ to hear/discover/find etc** *It was no surprise to hear that Joel had messed the whole thing up again.*

predictable /prɪ'dɪktəbəl/ [adj] happening as you expect – use this especially about someone's behaviour, when you think they are boring or stupid because they always do exactly what you expect: *My dad's so predictable – every evening he comes home, has two beers, and falls asleep in front of the TV.* | *The movie was completely predictable – I couldn't wait for it to end.* —**predictably** [adv] as you would expect: *Predictably, a crowd gathered to watch the fire.*

be only to be expected /biː ˌəʊnli tə biː ɪk'spektɪ̈d/ [v phrase] if something, especially something bad or unpleasant, **is only to be expected**, it is what you should expect in that situation: *A few mistakes were only to be expected when you're cooking something for the first time.* | **it is only to be expected that** *When you're over 60, it's only to be expected that you can't do as much as you used to.*

be par for the course /biː pɑːʳ fəʳ ðə kɔːʳs/ [v phrase] to be what you would normally expect to happen in a particular situation: *If you want to be a politician, a little criticism is par for the course.* | *It seems in some of those countries that political torture and assassination are par for the course.*

I'm not surprised /aɪm ˌnɒt səʳ'praɪzd/ spoken say this when something happens that you expected to happen: *I'm not surprised she left him – look at the way he treated her!* | *Of course I'm disappointed that we lost, but I'm not really surprised.*

8 when something happens that you did not expect

- unexpected
- unforeseen
- be a surprise/come as a surprise
- out of the blue
- the last person/thing/place (that) you would expect
- catch sb off guard/catch sb unawares
- contrary to expectations
- unannounced
- in your wildest dreams
- more than you (had) bargained for

unexpected /ˌʌnɪk'spektɪ̈d◂/ [adj] something that is **unexpected** surprises you because you did not expect it: *There have been unexpected delays on the freeway because of an accident.* | **completely/totally unexpected** *Bobby's decision to leave the band was totally unexpected.* —**unexpectedly** [adv] *Dunbar died unexpectedly of a stroke on Thursday.*

unforeseen /ˌʌnfɔːʳ'siːn◂/ [adj] **unforeseen circumstances/problems/changes etc** situations, problems, changes etc that you did not expect or prepare for, and which usually cause you difficulty: *We had to cancel our visit to Egypt because of unforeseen problems.* | *Once you have started the training you will not be allowed to leave, unless unforeseen circumstances arise.*

be a surprise/come as a surprise /biː ə səʳ'praɪz, ˌkʌm əz ə səʳ'praɪz/ [v phrase, not in progressive] if something that happens **is a surprise** or **comes as a surprise**, you did not expect it to happen, and so you are surprised by it: *Winning the award was a total surprise.* | **+ to** *Fazio's announcement came as a surprise to most political observers.*

out of the blue /ˌaʊt əv ðə 'bluː/ [adv] informal if something happens **out of the blue**, you did not expect it, and you are very surprised or shocked by it: *Out of the blue, he asked me to come with him to Europe.* | *One evening, Angela phoned me out of the blue and said she was in some kind of trouble.*

the last person/thing/place (that) you would expect /ðə 'lɑːst ˌpɜːʳsən, ˌθɪŋ, ˌpleɪs (ðət) jʊ wʊd ɪkˌspekt‖-ˌlæst-/ [v phrase] informal one that you did not expect, so that you are very surprised: *Mary's the last person you'd expect to be stopped for drunk driving* | *It's such a quiet little village – it's the last place you'd expect something like this to happen.*

catch sb off guard/catch sb unawares /ˌkætʃ (sb) ɒf'gɑːʳd, ˌkætʃ (sb) ˌʌnə'weəʳz/ [v phrase] to happen or do something when someone is not expecting it and not ready to deal with it: *I was caught unawares by the hug and the kiss he gave me.* | *Her rude comments really caught me off guard.*

contrary to expectations /ˌkɒntrəri tʊ ekspek'teɪʃənz‖ˌkɑːntreri-/ [adv] formal if something happens **contrary to expectations**, it is the opposite of what people expected to happen: *Contrary to expectations, the play was a big success.* | **contrary to sb's expectations** *Michael won the competition, contrary to everyone's expectations.*

unannounced /ˌʌnə'naʊnst◂/ [adj] happening unexpectedly, because no one was told about it: *Investigators from the health department made unannounced visits to the hospital in March.* | **arrive unannounced/show up unannounced** *My brother is famous for showing up at our houses unannounced, usually around dinner time.*

in your wildest dreams /ɪn jɔːʳ ˌwaɪldɨst ˈdriːmz/ [adv] if something happens that you did not expect **in your wildest dreams**, it is so good that you never thought that there was any possibility that it could happen: *In our wildest dreams, we could not have expected how successful this program would be.* | **never in sb's wildest dreams** *Never in her wildest dreams had she imagined she would win the gold medal.*

more than you (had) bargained for /ˌmɔːʳ ðən juː (həd) ˈbɑːʳgɨnd fɔːʳ/ if you get **more than you had bargained for**, you have more problems or difficulties while doing something than you had expected or prepared for: *Their summer vacation turned out to be much more expensive than they'd bargained for.* | *We got more than we bargained for when we bought the house. There's so much work to be done!*

9 when someone or something is expected

- expected
- long-awaited
- be due

expected /ɪkˈspektɨd/ [adj only before noun] *An expected crowd of 200,000 will take part in the march.* | *The expected increase in interest rates has already had an effect on stock prices.*

long-awaited /ˈlɒŋ əˌweɪtɨd‖ˈlɔːŋ-/ [adj only before noun] a **long-awaited** event, book, film etc is one that people have been expecting for a long time: *Band members were celebrating the long-awaited release of their first album.* | *The court's long-awaited decision was unpopular with groups on both sides of the issue.*

be due /biː ˈdjuː‖-ˈduː/ [v phrase] to be expected to happen, arrive, or be finished at a particular time: *When is your baby due?* | **+ at** *The flight from New York is due at 10:30.* | **+ in** *I've ruined the meal and our guests are due in half an hour!* | **+ on** *The report is due on Monday, so we'll have to work over the weekend.* | **+ to do sth** *Federal employees are due to return to work on January 8.*

expensive

RELATED WORDS

opposite: —— **cheap**
- worth a lot of money *see* **value**
- *see also* **cost, pay, buy, spend, shop/store, rich**

1 expensive

- expensive
- cost a lot (of money)
- high
- costly
- it's going to cost you/it'll cost you
- not come cheap
- pricey
- dear

expensive /ɪkˈspensɪv/ [adj] something that is **expensive** costs a lot of money, more than other things of the same type: *She spends most of her money on expensive clothes.* | *Do you have any less expensive cameras?* | *Taxis are so expensive – that's why I usually take the bus.* | **expensive to make/run/buy etc** *Movies are incredibly expensive to make these days.*

cost a lot (of money) /ˌkɒst ə ˌlɒt (əv ˈmʌni)‖ˌkɔːst ə ˌlɑːt-/ [v phrase] especially spoken if something, especially something you do, **costs a lot** it is expensive: *I managed to find the bike I wanted but it cost a lot.* | *It costs a lot of money to go to medical school, you know.* | **+ to do sth** *Did it cost a lot to fly to Rio?*

high /haɪ/ [adj] if the price or cost of something is **high**, it costs a lot: *Rents in central London are very high.* | *The cost of living is higher in Denmark than in Germany.* | *Increased production costs will mean higher prices for consumers.*

costly /ˈkɒstli‖ˈkɔːstli/ [adj] a plan, activity etc that is **costly** is too expensive and wastes money – used especially about plans carried out by governments or companies: *The finance committee rejected their plan because they said it was too costly.* | *Caring for the park's swans is a costly business – roughly $26,600 per year.* | **costly mistake** *Buying all those computers was a costly mistake.*

it's going to cost you/it'll cost you /ɪts ˌgəʊɪŋ tə ˈkɒst juː, ɪtl ˈkɒst juː‖-ˈkɔːst-/ spoken informal if you say **it's going to cost you** or **it'll cost you** when someone wants to buy something, you mean it will be expensive for them: *You can get new parts specially made for these, but it'll cost you.* | *There are some places that can mend the suit in a couple of hours, but it's going to cost you.*

not come cheap /nɒt kʌm ˈtʃiːp/ [v phrase not in progressive] informal to be expensive – use this especially when you think that even though something is expensive, it is still worth buying: *Gibson guitars sound great, but they don't come cheap.* | *It would be great if we could hire her, but with all her experience, she won't come cheap.*

pricey /ˈpraɪsi/ [adj not usually before noun] informal very expensive or too expensive – use this especially when you are deciding whether or not to buy something: *Let's not eat here – it's too pricey.* | *The tickets were kind of pricey, but the show was good.*

dear /dɪəʳ/ [adj not before noun] British expensive – use this especially about things you buy in shops: *Those strawberries look a bit dear.* | *The blue jacket is slightly dearer, but it's much better material.* | *No, you can't have an ice-cream – they're too dear.*

2 extremely expensive

- cost a fortune
- cost a bomb/the earth
- astronomical
- cost an arm and a leg

cost a fortune /ˌkɒst ə ˈfɔːʳtʃən‖ˌkɔːst-/ [v phrase] especially spoken, informal if something **costs a fortune**, it is very expensive: *What a beautiful car – it must have cost a fortune.* | **cost sb a fortune** *We had to eat out every night – it ended up costing us a fortune.* | **+ to do sth** *It'll cost a fortune to get that old car of his repaired.* | **cost an absolute fortune** *The hotel was great, but it cost an absolute fortune.*

cost a bomb/the earth /ˌkɒst ə ˈbɒm, ði ˈɜːʳθ‖ˌkɔːst ə ˈbɑːm-/ [v phrase] British informal to be very expensive: *I can't imagine how she affords to send her kids to that school – it must cost a bomb.* | *Good shoes needn't cost the earth.* | **cost sb a bomb/the earth** *The divorce cost me a bomb.*

astronomical /ˌæstrəˈnɒmɪkəl◂‖-ˈnɑː-/ [adj] a price or cost that is **astronomical** is extremely high: *The painting was sold for an astronomical price.* | *Tuition at private universities has become astronomical.*

cost an arm and a leg /kɒst ən ˌɑːʳm ənd ə ˈleg‖kɔːst-/ [v phrase] spoken to be very expensive: *That carpet must have cost an arm and a leg.* | **cost sb an**

arm and a leg *Getting good health insurance these days costs an arm and a leg.*

3 expensive and fashionable

- expensive
- exclusive
- luxurious
- fancy
- posh
- upmarket
- classy
- plush

expensive /ɪk'spensɪv/ [adj] an **expensive** hotel, restaurant, area etc is very fashionable and it is **expensive** to stay, eat, or live there: *My uncle took us out to dinner at an expensive restaurant.* | *The house is on West Boston Avenue, Detroit's most expensive residential area.*

exclusive /ɪk'skluːsɪv/ [adj] an **exclusive** area, school, shop, club etc is very expensive, and only a few very rich people have enough money to live there or use it: *They live in Bel Air, an exclusive suburb of Los Angeles.* | *The country club is very exclusive – you have to be invited to join.*

luxurious /lʌg'zjʊəriəs, ləg'ʒʊəriəs‖ləg'ʒʊəriəs/ [adj] a **luxurious** building or room is large, very comfortable, and has expensive decorations and furniture: *a room in a luxurious New York hotel* | *Atlantis is one of the world's most luxurious cruise ships.*

fancy /'fænsi/ [adj] especially American, spoken a **fancy** house, car, hotel, restaurant etc is expensive and fashionable: *You'd think a fancy restaurant like this would have better service.* | *We stayed in a fancy Victorian hotel in San Francisco.*

posh /pɒʃ‖pɑːʃ/ [adj] especially British, spoken a **posh** restaurant, house, car etc is expensive and looks as if it is used or owned by rich people: *When I'm famous I'm going to stay in a posh hotel and drink champagne all day.* | *She goes to a posh girls' school near Brighton.*

upmarket especially British **/upscale** American /ˌʌp'mɑːʳkɨt◂, 'ʌpskeɪl/ [adj] used or bought by people who belong to a higher social class or have more money than ordinary people, and therefore more expensive: *I was surprised when I saw her apartment – I'd have expected a lawyer to have something a little more upmarket.* | *New upscale shops and restaurants are driving some of the older businesses out of the neighborhood.*

classy /'klɑːsi‖'klæsi/ [adj] fashionable, expensive, and used by people who have a lot of money or belong to a high social class: *She took us to a very classy seafood restaurant in the old part of the city.* | *The cafe's interior has been redone and looks very classy.* | *The Grand Union Hotel is one of the classiest hotels in this part of the country.*

plush /plʌʃ/ [adj] **plush hotel/office/apartment etc** a hotel, office etc that looks expensive because it contains a lot of nice furniture, decorations etc: *The firm's headquarters is a plush $2.5 million office building on Woodside Road.* | *the plush lobby of a four-star hotel*

4 when something is too expensive

- can't afford
- exorbitant/ extortionate
- be a rip-off
- prohibitive/ prohibitively expensive
- inflated prices
- steep
- be daylight robbery
- price sth out of the market

can't afford /ˌkɑːnt ə'fɔːʳd‖ˌkænt-/ [v phrase] if you **can't afford** something, you do not have enough money to buy it or pay for it: *I really need a new coat, but I can't afford one.* | **+ to do sth** *We couldn't afford to go on holiday last year.* | **can't afford it** *Hiring a lawyer would be expensive, and she just couldn't afford it.*

exorbitant/extortionate /ɪg'zɔːʳbɨtənt, ɪk'stɔːʳʃənɨt/ [adj] prices, charges, rents etc that are **exorbitant** or **extortionate**, are very much higher than they should be, and you think they are unfair: *The restaurant charges exorbitant prices for very ordinary food.* | *Interest rates for some of the credit cards are extortionate.*

be a rip-off /biː ə 'rɪp ɒf/ [v phrase] spoken informal you say something is **a rip-off** when you think someone is unfairly charging too much money for it: *Eighty dollars for a pair of jeans? What a rip-off!* | **a complete/total rip-off** *The vacation package we bought ended up being a total rip-off.*

prohibitive/prohibitively expensive /prə'hɪbɨtɪv, prəˌhɪbɨtɪvli ɪk'spensɪv‖prəʊ-/ [adj] prices or costs that are **prohibitive** or **prohibitively expensive** are so high that people cannot pay them or decide not to pay them because they are too expensive: *For most people, the cost of living in the centre of town is prohibitive.* | *The computer was superior to other models, but it was prohibitively expensive.*

inflated prices /ɪnˌfleɪtɨd 'praɪsɨz/ [n plural] prices that are much higher than usual and much higher than they should be, so that the person who charges them can make a big profit: *Nightclubs often charge inflated prices for drinks.* | **at inflated prices** *Some people buy large blocks of tickets and then try to sell them at vastly inflated prices.*

steep /stiːp/ [adj not before noun] informal prices, charges, rents etc that are **steep** seem unusually or surprisingly high: *I think £7 for a drink is a bit steep, don't you?* | *It's hard to find an apartment around here, and when you do the rents are pretty steep.*

be daylight robbery British **/be highway robbery** American /biː ˌdeɪlaɪt 'rɒbəri, biː ˌhaɪweɪ 'rɒbəri‖-'rɑː-/ [v phrase] informal if you say that a price or charge **is daylight robbery** or **highway robbery** you mean it is very much higher than it should be: *I'm not paying £5 for an ice-cream – that's daylight robbery!* | *We knew it was highway robbery, but we had no choice but to pay.*

price sth out of the market /ˌpraɪs (sth) aʊt əv ðə 'mɑːʳkɨt/ [v phrase] to make something so expensive that people will no longer buy it because they can buy something similar at a lower price **be priced out of the market** *British electrical equipment is likely to be priced out of the market by cheap imports.* | **price yourself out of the market** *Ford don't want to raise its prices any more – it's worried about pricing itself out of the market.*

experience

RELATED WORDS

- experienced in a job, activity etc *see* **experienced**

1 something that happens to you

- experience
- adventure
- fortunes

experience /ɪk'spɪəriəns/ [n C] something that happens to you or something that you do, especially something unusual or important that you remember and learn from: *After she retired, Hannah wrote a book about her experiences as a war reporter.* | **have an experience** *I'm glad I had this experience but I wouldn't want to do it again.* | **good/great/bad/awful experience** *Living alone has been a good experience for her.* | **+ of** *Tonight on Channel 4, young people will be discussing their experiences of racism.* | **the experience of doing sth** *Simulators are very realistic, but they don't compare to the actual experience of flying an airplane.*

adventure /əd'ventʃəʳ/ [n C/U] a situation in which exciting and dangerous things happen to you: *My grandfather used to tell us about his adventures as a sea captain during the war.* | *As a young man he went off to Africa, looking for adventure.*

fortunes /'fɔːʳtʃənz/ [n plural] the experiences that happen to you over many years, and how happy or successful you are, especially when this is told in a story, film etc **sb's fortunes/the fortunes of sb** *It's a documentary about the fortunes of a group of musicians during the 1920s.* | *After he left London, his fortunes improved.* | **changing fortunes** *The movie traces the changing fortunes of a poor family in Southern Australia.*

2 something bad that happens to you

- bad/terrible/dreadful etc experience
- nightmare
- ordeal
- trauma

▸ *see also* **horrible (2)**

bad/terrible/dreadful etc experience /ˌbæd ɪk'spɪəriəns/ [n C] *You shouldn't let one bad experience affect your decision.* | *Being arrested was one of the worst experiences of my life.* | *My passport was stolen and the police said they couldn't help me. It was a terrible experience.*

nightmare /'naɪtmeəʳ/ [n C usually singular] a very unpleasant or frightening experience when you feel that you have no control over what is happening: *Starting school can be a nightmare for some children.* | *As the ship went down, people were rushing around in the dark screaming and yelling. It was an absolute nightmare.* | **+ of** *The hostages described life in the prison camp as a nightmare of fear and uncertainty.*

ordeal /ɔːʳ'diːl, 'ɔːʳdiːl/ [n C] a painful, frightening, or worrying experience, especially one that continues for a long time: *The three week trial turned out to be an emotional ordeal for everyone involved.* | *The hostages were relieved that their long ordeal was finally over.*

trauma /'trɔːmə, 'traʊmə/ [n C/U] a very bad experience or shock that has an effect on you: *June never recovered from the trauma of her husband's violent death.* | *Multiple-personality disorder is usually caused by early childhood trauma.*

3 when something happens to you

- happen to
- experience
- go through
- live through
- know

happen to /'hæpən tuː/ [phr v T] if something **happens to** you, it affects you and you are involved in it, but you did not do anything to make it happen: *The crash wasn't your fault. It could have happened to anyone.* | *Winning this award is the greatest thing that's ever happened to me.*

experience /ɪk'spɪəriəns/ [v T] if you **experience** something, especially an emotion, a physical feeling, or an unpleasant situation, it happens to you: *When you first tried a cigarette, you probably experienced a feeling of dizziness.* | *It was the first time she had ever experienced real poverty.*

go through /'gəʊ θruː/ [phr v T] to experience a period of time that is difficult or unhappy: *Kevin's going through a painful divorce.* | **sb's been through a lot** *Betty's been through a lot recently – I think you ought to try and be nice to her.*

live through /'lɪv θruː/ [phr v T] to experience a period of time when there are important historical events happening which affect people's lives: *His new book is a collection of essays and fiction by writers who lived through the Great Depression.*

know /nəʊ/ [v T not in progressive] **know hardship/joy/sorrow etc** to experience problems, joy, sorrow etc – used especially in literature: *In his seven short years, he has known war, famine and death.* | *I don't think I've ever known true happiness.*

experienced/ not experienced

experienced in a job or activity, or experienced about life and dealing with people

RELATED WORDS

▸ *see also* **good at**

1 experienced in a particular job or activity

- experienced
- seasoned
- practised
- veteran
- old hand
- know a thing or two
- know the ropes
- pro

experienced /ɪk'spɪəriənst/ [adj] someone who is **experienced** knows a lot about a job or activity because they have done it for a long time: *Ms Carter is one of our most experienced teachers.* | **experienced in (doing) sth** *This job would suit someone experienced in dealing with the public.* | **highly experienced** (=very experienced) *Highly experienced cost estimators for construction projects earn around $80,000 a year.*

seasoned /'siːzənd/ [adj only before noun] **seasoned traveller/politician/professional etc** someone who has done something regularly for a long time and knows all the problems involved: *Being a seasoned traveller, he was fully prepared for the long delay at the airport.* | *We need a seasoned manager to run this project.*

practised British **/practiced** American /'præktɪst/ [adj] someone who is **practised** in a particular job or skill has become good at it through experience: *A practised observer would quickly notice changes in the birds' behaviour.* | **+ in** *Morris is a skilful salesman, practiced in the art of persuasion.*

veteran /'vetərən/ [n C usually before noun] someone who has been doing something important in public life for a very long time and is respected by other people **+ of** *Chiles, a three-term veteran of the U.S. Senate, won the governorship of Florida.* | **veteran campaigner/statesman/broadcaster etc** *Millett is a veteran campaigner for women's rights.* | *Veteran diplomat Richard Murphy is heading the commission.*

old hand /ˌəʊld ˈhænd/ [n C] someone who has been doing something for a long time and knows all the best ways of doing it: *Charlie will show you what to do – he's one of our old hands.* | **+ at** *Nurse Baker is an old hand at dealing with difficult patients.*

know a thing or two /ˌnəʊ ə ˈθɪŋ ɔːʳ tuː/ [v phrase] informal to have a lot of knowledge about something, gained from experience: *You may not want to believe me, but I do know a thing or two.* | **+ about** *I think he knows a thing or two about football – he's been playing for 15 years.*

know the ropes /ˌnəʊ ðə ˈrəʊps/ [v phrase] to know how to do all the parts of a job or to be able to deal with a system because you have had a lot of experience: *The best way to learn is to spend some time with someone who knows the ropes.* | *People who shop at thrift stores regularly know the ropes.*

pro /prəʊ/ [n C] informal someone whom you admire because of their great skill and experience in a particular job, profession, or activity: *My accountant knows his stuff – he's a real pro.* | **old pro** *If there's a fish down there he'll catch it – he's a old pro.*

2 the knowledge and skill that you get from doing something

- experience

experience /ɪkˈspɪəriəns/ [n U] the knowledge and skill you get from doing something, especially for a long time **have experience** *She's very bright and ambitious but she doesn't have much experience.* | **experience of (doing) sth** British *She has plenty of experience of dealing with difficult situations.* | **experience doing sth** American *I have a little bit of experience working in a hotel.* | **teaching/secretarial/political etc experience** *The job requires five years' secretarial experience.* | **previous experience** (=experience you have gained already in a job before this) *Have you had any previous experience as a construction worker?* | **gain experience** *Fran is gaining valuable experience working for her father's firm.*

3 not experienced in a particular job or activity

- inexperienced
- lack experience
- be new to sth
- untrained
- rookie
- novice
- the uninitiated

inexperienced /ˌɪnɪkˈspɪəriənst◂/ [adj] someone who is **inexperienced** does not know much about a job or activity, either because they have not done it at all or because they have done it for only a short time: *Inexperienced managers often have problems with their staff.* | *There are a lot of young, inexperienced players on the team.*

lack experience /ˌlæk ɪkˈspɪəriəns/ [v phrase not in progressive] to not have enough experience of doing a particular job or activity: *I know Sally lacks experience, but she's tremendously enthusiastic.* | **+ of** British *If Glover lacks experience of management, why was he put in charge?* | **lack experience doing sth** American *He clearly lacked experience speaking before large groups.*

be new to sth /biː ˈnjuː tə (sth)‖-ˈnuː-/ [v phrase] if you **are new to** a job or activity, you do not have much experience of doing it because you have only just started it: *As you are new to the job, we don't expect you to work as fast as the others.* | **be new to the game** (=to have no experience of an activity or a business) *They're new to the software game, so they're spending a lot on advertising.*

untrained /ˌʌnˈtreɪnd◂/ [adj] someone who is **untrained** is doing a job or activity that they have not yet been officially taught to do: *Untrained nurses are not allowed to treat patients who are seriously ill.* | **+ in** *The records are confusing to anyone untrained in accounting.*

rookie /ˈrʊki/ [n C] American someone who is still new and inexperienced in an activity or job, especially in a sport, the army, or the police: *Don't be too hard on the guy, he's just a rookie.* | **rookie pitcher/quarterback/agent/coach etc** *Mariucci is the first rookie coach in NFL history to win 11 games in a row.*

novice /ˈnɒvɪ̈s‖ˈnɑː-/ [n C] someone who has just started doing a particular job or activity and has very little or no experience: *The Eiger is a difficult mountain to climb. Novices should not attempt it.* | **+ to** *If you're a novice to working with computer graphics, you should buy this CD-ROM.* | **novice skier/user/driver etc** *Novice drivers are responsible for a large portion of all accidents.*

the uninitiated /ði ˌʌnɪˈnɪʃieɪtɪ̈d/ [n plural] people who have no experience or knowledge of a difficult subject or skill – used in formal or humorous situations **to/for the uninitiated** *To the uninitiated, most computer systems seem complex and difficult to understand.* | *The classes are designed for the uninitiated, starting with the basics of car mechanics.*

4 lack of experience

- inexperience
- lack of experience

inexperience /ˌɪnɪkˈspɪəriəns/ [n U] the fact of having little or no experience in a job or activity: *Because of my inexperience in the business, I think I trusted other people too much.* | *The inexperience of the teaching staff has taken its toll on student test scores.*

lack of experience /ˌlæk əv ɪkˈspɪəriəns/ [n phrase] the fact of not having enough experience in a job or activity: *I'm not worried about her lack of experience – we can easily train her.* | *Mallory's lack of political experience shows in some of the decisions he's made.*

5 knowing about life, people, and the world

- experienced
- have been around
- be a man/woman of the world
- sophisticated
- streetwise
- worldly
- hardened
- hard-bitten

experienced /ɪkˈspɪəriənst/ [adj] *Paul liked to turn to more experienced people for advice.* | **+ in** *My elder brother was a lot more experienced in these matters than I was.*

have been around /həv ˌbiːn əˈraʊnd‖-ˌbɪn-/ [v phrase] informal if you say that someone **has been around**, you mean that they have had experience of many different situations and many different types of people and so they can deal with new situations confidently and easily: *When you've been around as long as I have you realize some things aren't worth getting upset about.* | **have been around the block (a few times)** *I've been around the block a few times, and I think I know when someone's trying to cheat me.*

be a man/woman of the world /biː ə ˌmæn, ˌwʊmən əv ðə ˈwɜːʳld/ [v phrase] to be someone who knows a lot about life, has had a lot of different experiences etc and is not easily shocked by things: *Look, Ray, you're a man of the world – I'm sure you've been in situations like this before.*

sophisticated /sə'fɪstɪkeɪtɪd/ [adj] someone who is **sophisticated** has a lot of knowledge and experience of clever, fashionable things, and shows this by the way they talk and behave: *Everyone at the party was sophisticated and well-educated.* | *The play is intended for a sophisticated audience.*

streetwise /'striːtwaɪz/ [adj] someone who is **streetwise** has had enough experience of life in big cities to know how to deal with difficult or dangerous people and situations: *Kids these days are much more streetwise than we ever were at their age.* | *Copeland is a streetwise cop who knows how to take care of himself.*

worldly /'wɜːʳldli/ [adj] having a lot of experience and knowledge about life and the practical rather than the moral reasons for people's actions: *For a priest he was surprisingly worldly.* | *She was much older and more worldly than I was.*

hardened /'hɑːʳdnd/ [adj only before noun] **hardened criminal/ cynic etc** someone who has had a lot of experience dealing with difficult situations and is therefore less affected by them: *Even the most hardened criminal would have been shocked by the brutality of the crime.* | *Hardened foes of abortion are unlikely to be persuaded by her arguments.*

hard-bitten /ˌhɑːʳd 'bɪtn◂/ [adj] someone who is **hard-bitten** has developed a hard, unsympathetic character because their experience of life has been difficult and unpleasant: *Miss Davies is not really the tough, hard-bitten businesswoman that she appears to be.* | *Jensen's experience in prison left him hard-bitten, cynical, and ruthless.*

6 not knowing very much about life, people, and the world

- inexperienced
- innocent
- naive
- unsophisticated
- green
- babe in the woods

inexperienced /ˌɪnɪk'spɪəriənst/ [adj] *She's too young and inexperienced to go abroad on her own.* | *I'm not going to take orders from some foolish inexperienced young man.*

innocent /'ɪnəsənt/ [adj] having very little experience of the world, especially because you are young so that you do not realize that some people might want to cause others harm: *He's so innocent that anyone can take advantage of him.* | *Don't get her mixed up in your plan – she's just an innocent girl.* —**innocence** [n U] *He'll lose his innocence pretty fast, living in New York.*

naive /naɪ'iːv‖nɑː'iːv/ [adj] having little experience of life, so that you believe that life is simple and are too ready to trust people: *I was so naive – I believed everything the military told me.* | *He held onto the naive belief that Marxism would solve all the world's problems.* —**naively** [adv] *She naively believed that he would send her a check as soon as he got home.* —**naivety** /naɪ'iːvəti‖nɑː-/ [n U] *Through naivete, she signed over the rights to all her music to her manager.*

unsophisticated /ˌʌnsə'fɪstɪkeɪtɪd◂/ [adj] having little knowledge or experience of clever, fashionable things, and showing this by the way you talk and behave: *When she arrived in the city, she was just an unsophisticated country girl.* | *I felt very ignorant and unsophisticated when I was with my brother and his university friends.*

green /griːn/ [adj] having very little experience of an activity or job: *Even when I was 21 I was so green, I had no idea that my best friend was on drugs.* | *Pike was a grizzled combat veteran in charge of fifteen green recruits.*

babe in the woods /ˌbeɪb ɪn ðə 'wʊdz/ [n C] someone who does not have much experience, and can easily be deceived: *Stop worrying about Lucia – she's no babe in the woods anymore.*

explain

RELATED WORDS

- explain what you are thinking or feeling *see* **express**
- information about how to use something or what to do *see* **instructions**
- *see also* **clear/not clear, understand/not understand, learn, teach**

1 to explain something

- explain
- tell
- say what/why/where etc
- show
- demonstrate
- go through
- throw/shed light on
- set out

explain /ɪk'spleɪn/ [v I/T] to give someone the information they need to understand something: *It's not so complicated – let me explain.* | *We listened carefully while Pam explained the process.* | *Let me show you – it's too difficult to explain.* | **explain sth to sb** *If you don't get the joke, I'll explain it to you later.* | *Could you explain the rules of the game to me, please?* | **+ how/what/why etc** *Can you explain what the poem means?* | *The doctor explained how the clinic operates.*

tell /tel/ [v T] especially spoken to explain to someone how something works or how to do something **tell sb how/what/why etc** *Can you tell me how to log on to the Internet?* | *The leaflet tells you what to do if you get malaria.*

say what/why/where etc /'seɪ wɒt‖-wɑːt/ [v phrase] spoken to explain the reasons for something or give detailed information about something: *He didn't say where he was going or who he was going with.* | *Did Caroline say why she needed the tape recorder?*

show /ʃəʊ/ [v T] to explain to someone how to do something by doing it while they watch you: *'How do you change the speed of the drill?' 'Let me show you.'* | **show sb sth** *I'll show you an easier way to get down from there.* | **show sb how to do sth** *Can you show me how to use your camera?* | **show sb what to do** *If you show him what to do, I'm sure he'll do a good job.*

demonstrate /'demənstreɪt/ [v I/T] to show someone how to do something by doing it while they watch you, especially when it is your job to show people how to do things: *The ski instructor began by demonstrating the correct way to turn.* | *If you still don't understand, Marcia will be happy to demonstrate.* | **+ how** *A trainer came in to demonstrate how the new computer system worked.*

go through /'gəʊ θruː/ [phr v T] to explain all the details about something in the right order, to help someone understand it: *I'll go through the instructions once more in case you missed anything.* | *If you stay after class, I'll go through the theory with you again.*

throw/shed light on /ˌθrəʊ, ˌʃed ˈlaɪt ɒn/ [v phrase] written to provide new information which makes something easier to understand, especially something which has been studied, but which is still not well understood: *These discoveries may shed light on the origins of the universe.* | *Scientists working in the Gobi desert have thrown new light on the life of dinosaurs.*

set out /ˌset ˈaʊt/ [phr v T] to explain facts, arguments, reasons etc by stating them clearly and in a carefully planned order **set out sth** *She set out the reasons for her resignation in a confidential letter to her boss.* | *The Republicans' goals for the year are clearly set out in the party platform.* | **set sth out** *The facts, as you have set them out, seem convincing enough.*

2 what you say when you are going to explain something

- (you) see
- I mean
- in other words
- the thing is
- that is
- let me explain
- to put it another way
- put it like this/put it this way
- let me rephrase that

(you) see /(jʊ) ˈsiː/ spoken say this when you are explaining something to someone, and you want to check that they are listening and that they understand you: *This fits on here, see, where the arrow is.* | *Simon's car broke down, you see, and neither of us knew how to fix it.*

I mean /aɪ ˈmiːn/ spoken say this when you are explaining something you have said or giving an example of something: *Ted seems kind of lazy. I mean, he never offers to help and he just lies in front of the TV.* | **what I mean (to say) is** *I'm afraid I can't help you. What I mean is that I'm not a detective, and I don't solve crimes.*

in other words /ɪn ˌʌðəʳ ˈwɜːʳdz/ use this when you are saying something in a different way in order to explain it more clearly: *What we need is a more sustainable transport system, in other words, more buses and trains, and fewer cars.* | *This is supposed to be a democracy – in other words, one person one vote.*

the thing is /ðə ˈθɪŋ ɪz/ spoken use this when you are explaining a problem or the reason for something: *I really don't want to leave yet. The thing is, I have an appointment in 15 minutes.* | *I do have a computer, but the thing is, it's really old and I can't use it for email.*

that is /ˈðæt ɪz/ use this to explain the meaning of the previous word or phrase by giving more information about it: *The fare is reduced for children, that is, anyone under 15 years old.* | *All documents are printed in the two official languages – that is, English and French.*

let me explain /ˌlet miː ɪkˈspleɪn/ spoken say this when you want to explain something to someone because you think they have not understood: *I can see you're getting confused. Let me explain.* | *I know the plan seems a little crazy at first, but it's really not. Let me explain.*

to put it another way /tə ˌpʊt ɪt əˈnʌðəʳ ˌweɪ/ used when you have explained something in one way and you are going to try to make it clearer by explaining it in a different way: *Money makes money. To put it another way, the more you invest, the greater your potential profit will be.* | *The problem demands a global solution. To put it another way, local regulations will have very little effect.*

put it like this/put it this way /ˌpʊt ɪt laɪk ˈðɪs, ˌpʊt ɪt ˈðɪs weɪ/ spoken say this when someone is not sure what you mean and you are going to try to explain in a way that will help them to understand, especially by saying something humorous or direct: *'Does he get many dates?' 'Put it like this – you don't have to feel sorry for him.'* | *Put it this way, honey – what the boss doesn't know isn't going to bother him.*

let me rephrase that /ˌlet miː riːˈfreɪz ðæt/ spoken used when you are going to use different words to say something again, because you have just said it in an unsuitable way and it may not have been understood correctly: *I'm sorry, let me rephrase that. That wasn't what I meant to say at all.* | *Most of the people there were incredibly old. Let me rephrase that – we were the youngest couple there.*

3 to explain something in a simpler way

- simplify
- demystify
- in plain English

simplify /ˈsɪmplɪ̈faɪ/ [v T] to explain something difficult in simple language so that it is easier to understand: *We have done everything we can to simplify the procedure.* | *She took a complex topic and simplified it in a way that we could all understand.*

demystify /ˌdiːˈmɪstɪ̈faɪ/ [v T] to give a simple, clear explanation of an important but difficult subject so that it is easier for ordinary people to understand: *This new book demystifies some of the computer language currently in use.* | *The course seeks to demystify the loan application process for people buying a home for the first time.*

in plain English /ɪn pleɪn ˈɪŋglɪʃ/ [adv] if you explain something or tell someone something **in plain English**, you explain it simply and clearly, without using difficult words or technical language: *I just wish someone would explain to me in plain English what is wrong with my computer.* | *It says 'the children lack the ability to mobilize self and commit' – what does that mean in plain English?*

4 the words you write or say to explain something

- explanation
- instructions
- account

explanation /ˌekspləˈneɪʃən/ [n C] something that you say or write in order to make something clearer or to explain why something happened: *Each diagram is followed by a simple explanation.* | **+ for** *What was their explanation for their decision?* | **+ of** *Our guide gave us a detailed explanation of the system of government.* | **give/offer (sb) an explanation** *Can you give us a quick explanation of how it works?* | *She offered no explanation as to why she had left so suddenly.*

instructions /ɪnˈstrʌkʃənz/ [n plural] written or spoken information that explains exactly how to do something: *Read the instructions carefully before using the machine.* | *The cooking instructions are on the back of the box.* | **give (sb) instructions** *They gave us detailed instructions explaining how to get to their house.* | **follow instructions** (=do what they tell you) *if you had followed my instructions, none of this would have happened.*

account /əˈkaʊnt/ [n C] a detailed description of a process which also explains how it happens and what makes it possible **+ of** *So far no linguist has* *given us a satisfactory account of how children learn language.* | *Her account of the events of that day was wildly different from the first witness's.*

explode

RELATED WORDS

- *see also* **weapon, war, kill, hurt/injure, destroy**

1 to explode

- **explode/go off**

explode/go off /ɪk'spləʊd, ˌgəʊ 'ɒf/ [v I/phr v I] if a bomb **explodes** or **goes off**, it bursts suddenly and violently with a loud noise, causing a lot of damage: *A bomb exploded in a crowded metro station this morning, killing five people.* | *The building was still being evacuated when the bomb went off.* | *As many as ten bombs went off across the city, most of them car bombs.*

2 to make something explode

- **set off**
- **detonate**
- **let off**
- **let off**

set off /ˌset 'ɒf/ [phr v T] to make a bomb explode either deliberately or accidentally **set off sth** *The group set off a bomb outside a crowded cafe in Izmir last September.* | **set sth off** *Police say radio signals were probably used to set the bomb off.*

detonate /'detəneɪt/ [v T] to make a bomb explode, especially by using special equipment. **Detonate** is a more technical word than **set off**: *Army experts detonated the bomb safely in a nearby field.* | *The 200 kg bomb was detonated by terrorists using a remote-control device.*

let off /ˌlet' ɒf/ [phr v T] British to deliberately make a bomb explode: *Terrorists let off a bomb in the city centre.* | *The bomb was let off shortly before 3pm.*

let off British **/set off/shoot off** American /ˌlet 'ɒf, ˌset 'ɒf, ˌʃuːt 'ɒf/ [phr v T] to make fireworks explode. A firework is a thing which explodes in the air and produces lots of noise or coloured lights, and is used in celebrations: *They're going to let off fireworks in the park.* | *A group of teenagers were in the parking lot shooting off fireworks.* | *Somebody set off a firecracker in the cafeteria.*

3 when a building/plane etc explodes

- **blow up**
- **explode**

blow up /ˌbləʊ 'ʌp/ [phr v I] if a building, car, plane etc **blows up**, it bursts suddenly and violently into pieces, causing a lot of damage: *The plane blew up in mid-air, killing all the passengers and crew.* | *In early 1986, a US space shuttle blew up shortly after launch.*

explode /ɪk'spləʊd/ [v I] if a container of chemicals, oil, or gas **explodes**, it bursts suddenly and violently into pieces: *Seconds after the car crashed, its fuel tank exploded.* | *Investigators still don't know what caused the storage tanks to explode.*

4 to destroy something using a bomb

- **blow up**

blow up /ˌbləʊ 'ʌp/ [phr v T] to destroy a building, car, plane etc using a bomb: *Two of the ships were blown up while they were still in the harbour.* | *Extremists blew up a mosque on the outskirts of the city.*

5 an explosion

- **explosion**
- **blast**

explosion /ɪk'spləʊʒən/ [n C] the loud noise and violent force that is produced when something explodes: *The noise of the explosion could be heard all over the city.* | *Murray was killed instantly by the explosion.*

blast /blɑːst‖blæst/ [n C] an explosion – used especially in news reports: *The blast killed 168 people and wounded hundreds.* | *Every window in the building had been shattered by the force of the blast.*

6 an exploding weapon

- **bomb**
- **device**
- **explosives**

bomb /bɒm‖bɑːm/ [n C] a weapon that explodes: *The bomb exploded on a bus in Jerusalem during the city's morning rush hour.* | *The protesters were armed with rocks and petrol bombs.* | **letter bomb** (=a small bomb hidden in a package and sent to someone in order to hurt or kill them) *Morrow was convicted in 1998 of sending four letter bombs to government officials.*

device /dɪ'vaɪs/ [n C] especially British a bomb – used especially in news reports: *Police found the device hidden in a suitcase.* | *Four of the victims received serious injuries when the device ripped through one of the station's lavatories.*

explosives /ɪk'spləʊsɪvz/ [n plural] bombs or substances that can cause explosions: *The bomb, containing 150 grams of explosives, was placed outside the house shortly before 1 am.* | *Traces of explosives were found on the clothing of the three men accused of the bombing.* | *a bomb packed with 1,000 lbs of explosives*

express

to let people know what you are feeling or thinking

RELATED WORDS

- stop people from expressing their opinions *see* **stop (27)**
- *see also* **show, feel, say, tell, explain**

1 to express what you think or feel

- **express**
- **convey**
- **communicate**
- **say**
- **get sth over**
- **put sth into words/find the words to say**

express /ɪk'spres/ [v T] to let someone know what you are thinking or feeling, by using words, by your behaviour or the look on your face, or through art, music, films etc: *Many of his films express the fears and anxieties of the post-war years.* | **express concern/satisfaction/annoyance/sympathy etc** *Parents have expressed concern about the amount of violence in some children's shows.* | **express your feelings** *My grandfather found it hard to express his feelings about the war.* | **express sth by/through sth** *It is the* *story of a middle-aged businessman, who starts going to tango lessons, and learns to express himself through dance.* | *Workers traditionally express their discontent by going on strike.* —**expression** /ɪk'spreʃən/ [n C] *His poems were a desperate expression of his loneliness and isolation.*

convey /kən'veɪ/ [v T] to express something about what you or other people are feeling or thinking, especially without stating it directly, but using touch, the sound of your voice, the way something looks etc: *His tone conveyed an unmistakable warning.* | *I tried to convey my sympathy by touching her hand.* | *His office conveyed an impression of efficiency and seriousness.*

communicate /kə'mju:nəkeɪt/ [v T] to manage to express what you think or feel with words, movements, or by the way you behave: *Andrea smiled at Jamie, communicating her affection for him with her eyes.* | **communicate sth to sb** *She tried to communicate her fears to her mother.* | *You can communicate your mood to your baby without realising it.*

say /seɪ/ [v T] if someone's behaviour, appearance, or something they produce **says** something, it expresses their feelings, attitudes etc: *This painting says so much in such a simple way.* | *What do you think the writer is saying in this passage?* | **say it all** (=to explain something in a very short form) *One look said it all – Richard knew that Sally wouldn't marry him.* | *When Joshua walked across the room for the first time, the smile on his face said it all.* | **say a lot about** (=express something very clearly) *The fact she didn't invite her mother to her wedding says a lot about their relationship.*

get sth over British **/get sth across** American /ˌget (sth) 'əʊvəʳ, ˌget (sth) ə'krɒs‖-ə'krɔ:s/ [phr v T] to express an idea or feeling to someone, especially something that is difficult to explain, so that they can understand: *I always try to get this idea over to my students.* | **get sth over to sb** *Gina felt trapped and insecure but found it difficult to get this over to her husband.*

put sth into words/find the words to say /ˌpʊt (sth) ɪntə 'wɜ:ʳdz, ˌfaɪnd ðə ˌwɜ:ʳdz tə 'seɪ/ [v phrase] to express your feelings or ideas clearly in words, especially when this is very difficult to do, and you have to try very hard to think of the right words: *She tried to put these feelings into words, but it all came out wrong.* | *He could not find the words to say that he was leaving.*

2 expressing your ideas clearly and well

- communicate
- express yourself
- articulate
- eloquent
- expressive
- project yourself

communicate /kə'mju:nəkeɪt/ [v I/T] to make your feelings or thoughts clear to others, especially by talking or writing about them: *The course is designed to enable people to communicate effectively in speech and writing.* | *She's clever, but she can't communicate her ideas.* | **+ with** *Many parents find it difficult to communicate with their teenage sons or daughters.* —**communication** /kəˌmju:nə'keɪʃən/ [n U] *Lack of communication, not lack of caring, often causes marriages to break up.*

express yourself /ɪk'spres jɔ:ʳself/ [v phrase] to make your feelings or thoughts about something known clearly, so that other people are able to understand: *The children were encouraged to express themselves freely and openly.* | **+ in** *Payne also expresses himself in poetry, which he began writing in college.* | **express yourself in words/writing** *I find it hard to express myself in writing.*

articulate /ɑ:ʳ'tɪkjələt/ [adj] able to talk or write easily and effectively about what you think and feel: *He is handsome, confident and articulate, like many of the students at this college.* | *You have to be articulate to be good at debating.*

eloquent /'eləkwənt/ [adj] expressing ideas and feelings in very clear, beautiful language, especially in a way that persuades people to agree with you, or fully understand what you are saying: *She was an eloquent speaker, able to move and inspire audiences.* | *The poem is full of eloquent phrases about the beauty of nature.* | *Few will forget his eloquent defence of individual freedom.* —**eloquently** [adv] *Stein eloquently describes the pain of losing someone you love.* —**eloquence** [n U] *Despite his charm and eloquence, there was something about him that made him unpopular.*

expressive /ɪk'spresɪv/ [adj] showing very clearly what a person thinks or feels **expressive eyes/face/eyebrows/features/voice/hands etc** *She is a wonderful actress, with striking, expressive features.* | *He had a quiet but expressive voice.* —**expressively** [adv] *She had tiny hands which she waved around expressively when she spoke.*

project yourself /prə'dʒekt jɔ:ʳself/ [v phrase] to express what you think or feel in a confident way that other people admire: *Sam projects himself well – he should stand a good chance in the interview.* | *Your problem is presentation – you don't project yourself very well.*

3 not good at expressing your ideas clearly

- inarticulate
- be at a loss/be lost for words

inarticulate /ˌɪnɑ:ʳ'tɪkjələt/ [adj] unable to express what you are feeling or thinking because you cannot think of the right, or best, words to use: *Maisie had always thought of herself as being uneducated and inarticulate, and was surprised that anyone should ask her opinion.* | *Footballers are famous for being inarticulate when they are interviewed on TV, and Danny Lord was no exception.*

be at a loss/be lost for words /bi: ət ə 'lɒs‖-'lɔ:s, bi: ˌlɒst fəʳ 'wɜ:ʳdz‖-ˌlɔ:st-/ [v phrase] to be unable to express yourself clearly or properly, especially because you are nervous, upset, or embarrassed: *Jenna looked around the room, completely at a loss.* | *Howard was so shocked that he was lost for words.* | **be at a loss for words** *Mrs Miller seemed at a loss for words. She sank down into a chair and took off her hat.* | **be at a loss to explain** *I was at a loss to explain my sudden fit of rage.*

4 when it is difficult to express ideas or feelings in words

- can't express
- be difficult/hard to describe
- indescribable
- inexpressible

can't express /ˌkɑ:nt ɪk'spres‖ˌkænt-/ [v phrase] *She couldn't express how happy and relieved she was.* | *I cannot express my gratitude for your kindness.* | **words can't express** *Words can't express the terrible grief I felt on losing my daughter.*

be difficult/hard to describe /bi: ˌdɪfɪkəlt, ˌhɑ:ʳd tə dɪ'skraɪb/ [v phrase] to be difficult to express what a feeling, experience, taste etc is like in words: *The atmosphere of tension and nervousness here is hard to describe.* | *The sound the bird makes is difficult to describe – it's a bit like scissors opening and closing rapidly.*

indescribable /ˌɪndɪsˈkraɪbəbəl/ [adj] if emotions, situations etc are **indescribable**, they are so terrible, so good, or so strange that you cannot describe them properly: *The chaos and confusion was indescribable.* | **indescribable joy/peace/horror/sadness etc** *I woke up on the day after my wedding with a feeling of indescribable joy.* —**indescribably** [adv] *A long, low moan, indescribably sad, swept over the moor.*

inexpressible /ˌɪnɪkˈspresəbəl◂/ [adj] formal an **inexpressible** emotion is one that is too strong to be described in words: *Looking up into his concerned brown eyes, I had felt an inexpressible sense of relief.* | **inexpressible anger/gratitude/joy/longing etc** *And then, to her almost inexpressible joy, she saw the familiar tall, broad-shouldered figure across the station.*

expression on sb's face

the way someone shows in their face what they are thinking or feeling about something

1 the expression on someone's face

- expression
- look
- -faced

expression /ɪkˈspreʃən/ [n C] *His expression became serious as he listened to her story.* | **+ of** *'I'm not eating it,' Maria said, with an expression of disgust on her face.* | **wear an expression** (=have an expression) *Wearing an expression of utter boredom, Harry turned back to his book.* | **expression on sb's face** *The expression on her face told me that she didn't want to discuss it.*

look /lʊk/ [n C] an expression on your face that shows what you are feeling: *She has a pensive, almost sad look about her.* | **+ of** *A look of relief crossed his face.* | **give sb a look** *Sheila nodded and gave him a sympathetic look.* | **a look of sth on sb's face** *After winning, she had a look of pure joy on her face.* | **the look on sb's face** (=someone's expression, especially an angry, shocked or disappointed expression) *You should have seen the look on his face when I told him I was leaving.* | **look in sb's eyes** *Mrs. Moody had it in for me – I could tell by the look in her eyes.* | **dirty look** (=an expression of disapproval or anger) *She's been giving me dirty looks all morning. What have I done wrong?* | **wear a look** (=have a particular expression) *He normally wore a slightly amused look on his round face.*

-faced /feɪst/ [suffix] showing a particular expression on your face **sad-faced/grim-faced/solemn-faced** *A grim-faced doctor gave Marge the bad news.* | **stony-faced/stone-faced/stern-faced** (=with a very serious expression that shows little emotion) *Mr. Tanaka sat stone-faced, as if he could not hear the complaints.* | **straight-faced** (=without smiling, especially when you are lying or saying something funny) *He told us straight-faced that he was thinking of running for president.* | **ashen-faced/gray-faced/white-faced** (=looking very pale and upset, ill, or frightened) *He returned from the meeting ashen-faced and shaken, saying he had to go home.* | **red-faced** (=having a red face because you are embarrassed or angry) *Myra still gets red-faced when she remembers the speech.*

2 a face that shows a lot of feeling

- expressive
- animated
- mobile

expressive /ɪkˈspresɪv/ [adj] showing very clearly what a person thinks or feels: *She is a wonderful actress, with striking, expressive features.* | *He would use his expressive face to bring the stories to life.* —**expressively** [adv] *Anthony said nothing, but rolled his eyes expressively.*

animated /ˈænəmeɪtəd/ [adj] showing a lot of lively interest or excitement: *As he talked about her, his face became animated.* | *Stephan's animated eyes widened at the mention of Patricia.*

mobile /ˈməʊbaɪl‖-bəl, -biːl/ [adj] British a **mobile** face is one that can change its expression quickly in a way that is attractive: *She has an extraordinarily mobile face and an infectiously comic manner.*

3 a face that does not show any feelings or opinions

- expressionless
- blank
- deadpan
- inscrutable
- poker-faced
- impassive

expressionless /ɪkˈspreʃənləs/ [adj] *Oswini was watching her with expressionless eyes.* | *Terry's face was expressionless as he listened to the report.*

blank /blæŋk/ [adj] showing no emotion, interest, or understanding in your expression, for example because you are bored, or have not been paying attention to what is being said: *Maria could tell by the blank look in my eyes that I didn't understand.* | *The children's faces were blank with sleepiness.* —**blankly** [adv] *Charlie looked at her blankly, and she patiently repeated everything she had said.*

deadpan /ˈdedpæn/ [adj only before noun] deliberately showing no humour in your expression, even though what you are saying or doing is meant as a joke: *'We're out of gas, so I guess you'll have to walk home,' he said, giving me a deadpan expression.* —**deadpan** [adv] *They look at each other deadpan, and then look at me.*

inscrutable /ɪnˈskruːtəbəl/ [adj] someone who has an **inscrutable** expression shows no emotion or reaction, so it is impossible to guess what they are thinking or feeling: *She looked for some response, but Jean's expression remained inscrutable.* | *The inscrutable gaze of the palace guards made me a little nervous.* —**inscrutably** [adv] *The man just stood there grinning inscrutably.*

poker-faced /ˈpəʊkər feɪst/ [adj] someone who is **poker-faced** does not show at all what they are thinking or feeling, either because they do not want other people to know or because they disapprove of something: *Not even Will Rogers could make the poker-faced President laugh.* | *Albert, normally poker faced, wore a look of shock.*

impassive /ɪmˈpæsɪv/ [adj] not showing any emotion, especially in a situation where you would normally expect someone to be sad, shocked, upset, etc: *Russell struggled to keep an impassive face as she continued.* | *The defendant remained impassive as the judge announced the guilty verdict.* —**impassively** [adv] *Adams was staring impassively at the death and destruction caused by the blast.*

extreme

words for describing strong opinions and beliefs, especially political or religious beliefs, that most people regard as unreasonable or unacceptable

RELATED WORDS

- *see also* **politics, opinion**

1 words for describing extreme opinions or people

- **extreme**
- **extremist**
- **far-left/far-right**
- **hardline**
- **ultra**

extreme /ɪk'striːm/ [adj usually before noun] **extreme** opinions or beliefs about politics, religion etc are too strong and most people regard them as unreasonable: *Buchanan's political views are too extreme for most Americans.* | *extreme left-wing groups* | *We like to present an extreme position to get people to react to it.*

extremist /ɪk'striːmɪst/ [adj only before noun] **extremist** ideas or political organizations involve actions or aims that are very strong and most people think are unreasonable: *The military is expecting a violent response from extremist groups.* | *extremist elements within the party* | *Neither of these extremist solutions seemed very popular with the voters.*

far-left/far-right /ˌfɑːʳ 'left, ˌfɑːʳ 'raɪt/ [adj only before noun] relating to the most extreme left wing or right wing of a political organization or among followers of a set of political beliefs: *Both the far-left Communists and the far-right National Alliance are calling for new elections.* | *Observers are disturbed by the rise in the number of far-right militias.*

hardline /'hɑːʳdlaɪn/ [adj only before noun] having very definite and extreme political opinions and aims, and completely unwilling to accept or support anything different or less extreme: *The army is run by a few hardline generals.* | *Hardline separatists have rejected the proposed constitution.*

ultra /'ʌltrə/ [prefix] **ultra-right-wing/left-wing/radical etc** far more right-wing, left-wing etc than usual: *He spoke before the ultra-right-wing Heritage Foundation on Thursday.* | *The Socialist party has been infiltrated by members of the ultra-radical 'True Path' group.*

2 someone who has extreme opinions

- **extremist**
- **fanatic**
- **hardliner**
- **militant**
- **fundamentalist**
- **hardcore/hard-core**
- **zealot**
- **diehard**
- **lunatic fringe**

extremist /ɪk'striːmɪst/ [n C] someone who has extreme opinions, especially about politics or religion: *The government condemns anyone who disagrees with it as extremists.* | *The regime has been accused of supporting extremists in other countries in the region.* | *Left-wing extremists have threatened to disrupt the political convention.*

fanatic /fə'nætɪk/ [n C] someone who agrees with and supports very extreme religious or political aims, is completely certain that their opinions are right, and who is thought to be dangerous: *His parents were religious fanatics who didn't allow him to play with other children.* | *Pro-Fascist fanatics have continued their attacks on foreigners.* —**fanatical** [adj] *His government has supplied weapons to fanatical separatist groups abroad.* —**fanaticism** /fə'nætɪsɪzəm/ [n U] *Her religious fanaticism has alienated most of her old friends.*

hardliner /ˌhɑːʳd'laɪnəʳ/ [n C] someone who believes very deeply in a set of political aims and ideas, and will not accept or support any changes to them, even if this is unreasonable or unhelpful: *Cuban-American hardliners continue to reject any dealings with Castro.* | *The Prime Minister has been criticized by hardliners in his party for giving away too much in the treaty.*

militant /'mɪlɪtənt/ [n C] someone who is willing to work outside usual political structures, and use illegal or violent methods if necessary, in order to achieve political change: *He is one of the militants convicted of the World Trade Center bombing.* | *A crowd of militants took to the streets to protest the government's policies.* —**militant** [adj] *Yassin is the founder of the militant Islamic movement Hamas.*

fundamentalist /ˌfʌndə'mentəl-ɪst/ [n C] someone who follows the rules of their religion very strictly, in a way that seems very unusual to people who do not believe in the same way **Christian/Muslim/Jewish/Hindu etc fundamentalist** *an organized Christian fundamentalist movement* | **fundamentalist group/leader/party/church etc** *They belong to a fundamentalist church.*

hardcore/hard-core /'hɑːʳdkɔːʳ/ [adj only before noun] the **hardcore** members of a political organization are the small group of people who have the strongest beliefs and who do the most work: *The organization has only about 30 hardcore supporters.* | *Dole at least had the support of loyal hard-core Republicans.*

zealot /'zelət/ [n C] someone who has very extreme beliefs about something, especially about religion, and who thinks that everyone else should live their lives according to religious rules and beliefs: *A few zealots strongly objected to the proposed sale of alcohol at the local store.* | *Anti-abortion zealots are responsible for the bombing of the clinic.*

diehard /'daɪhɑːʳd/ [n C] someone who completely refuses to accept new ideas, especially political ideas, even after most other people have accepted them: *Salisbury, Walton, and a few other diehards still refused to join the coalition.* | *Taylor is one of the diehards willing to push the development program at any price.* —**diehard** [adj only before noun] *The government supported Burnell to keep his diehard supporters happy.*

lunatic fringe /ˌluːnətɪk 'frɪndʒ/ [n singular with singular or plural verb in British English] a small number of people within a larger organization or movement, whose ideas are so extreme or unusual that most people think they are stupid or a little crazy: *Many think the lunatic fringe has really harmed the public image of gays among the middle class.* | *Animal rights campaigners blame the latest set of bomb attacks on the lunatic fringe within the movement.*

Ff

fail

RELATED WORDS

opposite: —— **succeed/successful**

- lose a game, argument, election, war etc *see* **lose**
- *see also* **test, business**

1 when you do not succeed

- fail
- failure
- not make it
- get nowhere
- for nothing
- in vain
- draw a blank

fail /feɪl/ [v I] *We tried to make her change her mind, but we failed.* | **+ to do sth** *I failed to convince him that I was right.* | *Having failed to find her friend, she decided to return home.* | **fail completely** *If they were trying to put us out of business, they have failed completely.* | **fail miserably** (=fail completely, in a way that is embarrassing) *Millions of people have tried to quit smoking and failed miserably.*

failure /ˈfeɪljəʳ/ [n C/U] when you fail in something you are trying to do: *She never tries anything because she's terrified of failure.* | *His ability has been called into question after a number of recent failures.* | **+ to do sth** *The failure of the international community to deal effectively with the problem has cost thousands of lives.*

not make it /nɒt ˈmeɪk ɪt/ [v phrase] informal to fail in your job, especially because you do not earn a lot of money or do not become well known and respected **+ as** *No one was surprised when he didn't make it as a rock star.* | **+ in** *She soon realized she'd never make it in the cut-throat world of journalism.*

get nowhere /ˌget ˈnəʊweəʳ/ [v phrase] to fail after trying hard for a long time: *Unless you compromise, you'll get nowhere.* | **+ with** *Realizing she was getting nowhere with Paul, she approached John.*

for nothing /fəʳ ˈnʌθɪŋ/ [adv] if all your work, preparation etc is **for nothing**, you have tried to achieve something and spent a lot of time on it, but failed: *If we don't get the contract all our hard work will have been for nothing.* | *I don't want to struggle all my life for nothing.*

in vain /ɪn ˈveɪn/ [adv] if you tried to do something **in vain**, or if your efforts were **in vain**,you completely failed after a lot of effort **try/search/battle etc in vain** *Doctors tried in vain to save him but he died just before dawn.* | *Police have spent hours searching in vain for the missing teenager.* | **be in vain** *It took a great deal of courage to admit that all her efforts had been in vain.*

draw a blank British **/come up empty-handed** American /ˌdrɔː ə ˈblæŋk, ˌkʌm ʌp ˌempti ˈhændɪd/ [v phrase] informal fail to find or discover information or a person or thing you are looking for: *Once again police investigators have drawn a blank.* | *The private detective she hired to look for him had come up empty-handed.*

2 when a plan or attempt fails

- fail
- failure
- not succeed
- unsuccessful
- vain
- fruitless
- unproductive
- be a failure
- go wrong
- not work
- do no good
- fall through
- be dead in the water

fail /feɪl/ [v I] if a plan or attempt **fails**, it does not achieve what you want it to achieve: *They said the latest space mission was bound to fail.* | *Try changing the spark plugs, but if that fails take the car to a mechanic.* | **+ to do sth** *The investigation failed to establish the cause of the accident.* | **sth never fails** *The only way I can make her help me is to pretend I don't want her help. It never fails.*

failure /ˈfeɪljəʳ/ [n C/U] when a plan or attempt fails **+ of** *The failure of the peace talks has led to increased tension on the streets.* | **end/result in failure** *Their first attempt to climb Mount Everest ended in failure.*

not succeed /nɒt səkˈsiːd/ [v phrase] to fail: *Hoover's attempts to boost the economy did not succeed.* | *I argued that neither strategy could succeed.* | **not succeed in doing sth** *The campaign might not succeed in eliminating the disease, but it would make people think about health and hygiene.*

unsuccessful /ˌʌnsəkˈsesfəl◂/ [adj] an **unsuccessful** attempt to do something does not have the result that you wanted: *The army made an unsuccessful attempt to end the rebellion.* | *I regret to inform you that your application was unsuccessful.*

vain /veɪn/ [adj only before noun] **vain attempt/effort/search** a serious attempt, effort etc that is completely unsuccessful: *I remembered all my vain attempts to change his mind.* | *He stretched up his arms in a vain effort to reach the top of the embankment.*

fruitless /ˈfruːtləs/ [adj] **fruitless attempt/search/effort etc** one that fails completely to bring the result that you want: *I spent the next three hours in a fruitless search of her room.* | *After weeks of fruitless argument they finally agreed to go their separate ways.* | *Their attempt to settle the dispute by peaceful negotiations proved fruitless.*

unproductive /ˌʌnprəˈdʌktɪv◂/ [adj] a meeting, discussion etc that is **unproductive** produces very few good results: *The meeting was long and noisy, but unproductive.* | *It was one of those unproductive confrontations between students and senior members of the university.*

be a failure /biː ə ˈfeɪljəʳ/ [v phrase] to be unsuccessful – use this especially about something that fails even though it was very carefully planned: *The government's expensive election campaign had been a failure.* | **be a complete/total failure** *There was a 5-year plan to modernize the economy, but it was a complete failure.*

go wrong /ˌgəʊ ˈrɒŋ‖-ˈrɔːŋ/ [v phrase] if a planned attempt to do something **goes wrong**, it fails after it has started well: *The experiment went wrong when the chemicals combined to form a poisonous gas.* | **go badly wrong** British (=fail completely) *The rescue attempt went badly wrong when the building collapsed.*

not work /nɒt ˈwɜːʳk/ [v phrase] if a method or attempt does **not work**, it fails because it is not suitable or not right for the situation you are in: *I tried to fix it with glue, but that didn't work.* | **+ with** *Teaching methods that work with adults do not always work with children.*

do no good /ˌduː nəʊ ˈgʊd/ [v phrase] if something you do to try to help or deal with a problem **does no good, it** does not have any useful effect: *Calm down Robyn. Getting hysterical will do no good.* | *You can try and persuade her to change her mind, but I don't think it'll do any good.* | **do no good whatsoever** (=have no useful effect at all) *Judges expect a certain level of competence, so staging a little-girl-lost act in court will do no good whatsoever.*

fall through /ˌfɔːl ˈθruː/ [phr v I not in progressive] if a plan, arrangement, or deal **falls through**, something stops it from happening, with the result that people are disappointed: *The deal fell through because they couldn't get enough money from the bank.* | *It was unbelievable – it took two years to set the whole thing up and it fell through at the last minute!*

be dead in the water /biː ˌded ɪn ðə ˈwɔːtəʳ/ [v phrase] if a business or political plan is **dead in the water**, it has failed completely, almost before it has even started – used especially in newspapers: *Their election campaign now appears to be dead in the water.*

3 to have the opposite effect to what was intended

- backfire
- self-defeating
- counterproductive

backfire /ˌbækˈfaɪəʳ‖ˈbækfaɪər/ [v I] if a plan or action **backfires**, it is intended to do one thing but instead does the opposite: *His plan to get attention backfired, and instead of being promoted he lost his job.* | **+ on** *Trying to make your partner jealous by flirting with other people can easily backfire on you.*

self-defeating /ˌself dɪˈfiːtɪŋ◂/ [adj] an action or plan that is **self-defeating** is not well planned or is badly done, so that it produces the opposite effect from the one intended: *Taxing poor people to pay for hospitals is always self- defeating.* | *Attempts to stir up nationalistic feeling at such times are bound to be self-defeating.*

counterproductive /ˌkaʊntəʳprəˈdʌktɪv◂/ [adj not usually before noun] intended to make something better, but actually making it worse: *Putting very young offenders in prison can be counterproductive.* | *Constant correction by a teacher is often counterproductive, as the student may become afraid to speak at all.*

4 certain to fail

- pointless
- be a waste of time
- there's no point/what's the point
- doomed
- lost cause
- non-starter

pointless /ˈpɔɪntləs/ [adj] something that is **pointless** is unlikely to have a very useful or successful result, so it would be better not to do it or try it: *The argument was completely pointless.* | *Most people think the project is a pointless waste of money.* | **pointless exercise** *Speculating like that was always a pointless exercise, but he did it nevertheless.* | **it is pointless to do sth** *It's pointless to take notes and then never look at them again.* | **it is pointless doing sth** *She decided it was pointless trying to work while her mind was on other things.*

be a waste of time /biː ə ˌweɪst əv ˈtaɪm/ [v phrase] especially spoken something that is a **waste of time** is unlikely to achieve any useful result, so you would be wasting your time if you tried to do it: *Many people think that complaining about bad service is a waste of time.* | **a complete/total waste of time** *These meetings are a complete waste of time. Nothing ever gets decided.* | **it is a waste of time doing sth** *It's a waste of time going to the doctor – he'll just tell you to get plenty of rest.*

there's no point/what's the point /ðeəʳz ˌnəʊ ˈpɔɪnt, ˌwɒts ðə ˈpɔɪnt/ spoken say this when you think that it is useless to do something because you will not achieve anything useful by doing it: *'Why don't you try to explain things to him?' 'There's no point, he never listens.'* | *I was going to buy a new car, but what's the point when my old one's perfectly all right?* | **there's no point (in) doing sth** *There's no point getting a new carpet until the decorating's done.* | **what's the point in/of doing sth?** *What's the point of giving a signal when there are no other cars around to see it?*

doomed /duːmd/ [adj] not having any chance at all of succeeding: *Attempts to clean up the environment are doomed unless businesses take a leading role.* | *Within a few months she realized that her marriage was doomed.* | **doomed to failure** *If you refuse to provide any information to the user, then your computer program is doomed to failure.* | **doomed from the start** *Their business venture was doomed from the start, as they did not have the necessary capital.*

lost cause /ˌlɒst ˈkɔːz‖ˌlɔːst-/ [n C] something that you try to make successful, although it seems very clear to other people that it cannot succeed: *At first it seemed the attempt to save the species was a lost cause.* | *The miners' strike of 1984 turned out to be a lost cause.*

non-starter /nɒn ˈstɑːʳtəʳ / [n C] British an idea or plan that will definitely not be successful: *Everybody would prefer a lower rate of tax, but that that is a non-starter economically.* | *The project would have been a non-starter without the help of Judith Glyn.*

5 when an event or product is unsuccessful

- be a failure
- be a fiasco
- be a disaster
- be a shambles
- flop/be a flop
- bomb

be a failure /biː ə ˈfeɪljəʳ/ [v phrase] *The latest model seems likely to be a failure since cheaper versions are now available.* | **be a complete/total failure** *It takes a little while for an author to realize that his book has been a complete failure.* | **be a commercial failure** (=to not make enough profit) *Her first film was praised by the critics, but was a commercial failure.*

be a fiasco /biː ə fiˈæskəʊ/ [v phrase] to be completely unsuccessful, in a way that makes people feel disappointed and embarrassed: *It was a fiasco! Nobody knew what they were doing and everything went wrong.* | *The show turned into a fiasco when members of the audience invaded the stage.* | **be a complete/total fiasco** *Lamont's attempts to prop up the pound were a complete fiasco.*

be a disaster /biː ə dɪˈzɑːstəʳ‖-ˈzæs-/ [v phrase] if an event, especially a social event, **is a disaster**, it makes people feel angry, disappointed, or embarrassed, instead of being enjoyable: *Our first date was a disaster.* | *The whole visit was something of a disaster, and he was still recovering from it months later.* | **be a total/complete disaster** *Even the host would have to admit that the evening had been a complete disaster.*

be a shambles /biː ə ˈʃæmbəlz/ [v phrase] if a situation or event **is a shambles**, it is completely unsuccessful because it has been very badly planned or organized: *The whole conference was a shambles because half the speakers did not come.* | *The way this school is run is a shambles.* | **be a complete/total shambles** *Let's hope this year's celebrations aren't a complete shambles like last year's.*

flop/be a flop /flɒp, biː ə 'flɒp‖-'flɑːp/ [v I/v phrase] if a product, play, or performance **flops** or **is a flop**, it is not successful because people do not like it: *The movie flopped and Laughton never got the chance to direct again.* | *It was just another so-called 'wonder product' that flopped when people failed to buy it.* | *Despite all the publicity, the show was a flop.* | *It is the public who decide whether a film will be a hit or a flop.*

bomb /bɒm‖bɑːm/ [v I] informal if a product, play, or performance **bombs**, it is not successful because people do not like it: *Although the show was a hit in London it bombed on Broadway.* | *She has had few offers of work since her last movie bombed so spectacularly.*

6 to fail an exam or test

- fail
- flunk
- flunk out
- bomb

fail /feɪl/ [v I/T] to not succeed in an examination or test: *Jonathan failed his law exams at the end of the year.* | *If I fail my driving test again, I'm going to give up.* | *'How did you do in accountancy?' 'I failed'.* | **fail by 2 marks/5% etc** *We expected her to pass easily, but she failed by 15 marks.*

flunk /flʌŋk/ [v I/T] especially American, informal to fail an examination or test: *He thought he was going to flunk chemistry, but he got a D.* | *I flunked, and had to do the test again.*

flunk out /ˌflʌŋk 'aʊt/ [phr v I] especially American, informal to fail a course at college or university and be forced to leave: *You either pass and get your degree or flunk out.* | **flunk out of college/school etc** *It was extremely humiliating to flunk out of law school like that.*

bomb /bɒm‖bɑːm/ [v T] American informal to fail very badly: *I bombed the English test yesterday.*

7 when a relationship or marriage fails

- fail
- go wrong
- be on the rocks

fail /feɪl/ [v I] *If your marriage fails it can be difficult to make a new start in life.* | *She was trapped in a failing relationship.* —**failed** [adj only before noun] *He was 50, in bad health and with two failed marriages behind him.*

go wrong /ˌgəʊ 'rɒŋ‖-'rɔːŋ/ [v phrase] British if a marriage or other relationship **goes wrong**, or something about it **goes wrong**,something happens or changes to make it fail after it had started well: *It was soon after the birth of their first child that their relationship started to go wrong.* | *Only the two of you know what went wrong.*

be on the rocks /biː ɒn ðə 'rɒks‖-'rɑːks/ [v phrase] informal if a marriage **is on the rocks**, it is in difficulties and likely to fail: *There had been signs that their marriage was on the rocks for years.*

8 when a company, shop, or business fails

- fail
- go out of business
- go under
- close down
- closure
- go bankrupt/go bust
- fold
- go to the wall

fail /feɪl/ [v I] *A large number of businesses failed when interest rates rose.* | *Several thousands of small businesses fail each week.* —**failure** /'feɪljəʳ/ [n C] *Company failures have led to massive job losses.*

go out of business /gəʊ ˌaʊt əv 'bɪznɪ̈s/ [v phrase] if a company **goes out of business**, it stops existing because it is no longer making a profit: *Many small farms are going out of business.* | **be put/forced out of business** *As the recession hit, many traders were forced out of business.*

go under /ˌgəʊ 'ʌndəʳ/ [phr v I] if a business, bank, or company **goes under**, it fails – used especially in newspapers and business contexts: *When the company went under, some of our workers found positions with Ford.*

close down /ˌkləʊz 'daʊn/ [phr v I] if a shop, factory, or business **closes down**, it stops making or selling goods: *If the factory closes down, 600 people will lose their jobs.* | *Coal mines are closing down all over the country.* | *Not long ago, the orchestra was the pride of the city. Now it is on the verge of closing down.*

closure British **/closing** American /'kləʊʒəʳ, 'kləʊzɪŋ/ [n C/U] when a shop, factory, or business fails and closes: *Further factory closures have been announced.* | **+ of** *The closing of the Minton Savings and Loan was a great loss to the town.* | **face/be threatened with closure** (=to be going to close down) *Penrhyn is now the largest quarry in the world, yet 5 years ago it faced closure.*

go bankrupt/go bust /ˌgəʊ 'bæŋkrʌpt, ˌgəʊ 'bʌst/ [v phrase] informal if a person or company **goes bankrupt**, they are legally forced to sell their property and possessions to pay their debts: *Her father went bankrupt in 1984.* | *He bought a small printing firm that had gone bankrupt.* | *The company went bust last year, owing £12 million.*

fold /fəʊld/ [v I] informal to fail and be unable to continue in business: *Most of the companies dependent on the steelworks folded within weeks.*

go to the wall /ˌgəʊ tə ðə 'wɔːl/ [v phrase] informal to fail and be unable to continue in business, especially because of difficult economic conditions: *Over 300 small firms have gone to the wall in the past year.* | *High interest rates will force many businesses to go to the wall.*

9 a time when an economy is not successful

- recession
- slump
- depression
- crash

recession /rɪ'seʃən/ [n C/U] a period when a country's economic growth stops and there is less trade, so that many companies have to reduce the number of workers they employ: *The car industry, like most other industries, is feeling the effects of the recession.* | **severe recession** (=very bad recession) *In times of severe recession companies are often forced to make massive job cuts in order to survive.* | **in recession** (=suffering from a recession) *The economy is in recession and will remain so for at least another year.*

slump /slʌmp/ [n C] a period when there is a big reduction in trade so that many companies fail and a lot of people lose their jobs: *The post-war slump sent the unemployment figures to twice the expected level.* | **+ in** *The slump in the property market is making it difficult for people to sell their homes.*

depression /dɪˈpreʃən/ [n C] a period of time continuing for several years when greatly reduced business activity severely affects a country's economic growth, and a lot of people lose their jobs – use this especially when this affects many countries across the world: *In Germany the depression in the late 1920s helped Hitler's rise to power.* | *Hartnell blamed his financial difficulties on the worldwide depression.*

crash /kræʃ/ [n C] a sudden and unexpected fall in the value of shares in companies, with the result that many companies have to close and a lot of people lose their jobs: *Luckily, I sold my shares just before the crash.* | *The Wall Street Crash was disastrous for many American businessmen.* | **stock market crash** (=crash in the organizations that buy and sell shares in companies) *The stock market crash made me suspicious of those types of insurance schemes.*

fair

RELATED WORDS

opposite: **unfair**

▸ *see also* **equal/not equal, right**

1 treating people in a way that is reasonable and equal

- ▸ fair
- ▸ just
- ▸ reasonable
- ▸ balanced
- ▸ even-handed
- ▸ fair's fair
- ▸ play fair

fair /feəʳ/ [adj] treating everyone equally, or treating people in a way that most people think is right: *The old system of student funding seemed much fairer.* | *Everyone has the right to a fair trial.* | *Observers will be present to ensure a free and fair election.* | **it is fair that** *Do you think it's fair that she gets paid more money than me?* | **it's only fair** spoken *Her husband should help take care of the baby – it's only fair.* | **be fair to sb** *In order to be fair to everyone, ticket sales are limited to two for each person.* | **to be fair** spoken (=say this when you are giving a reason why someone should not be criticized too strongly) *To be fair, these are complicated, serious issues, and the department has only been discussing them for a short time.* —**fairly** [adv] *Her job is to make sure that the money is distributed fairly.*

just /dʒʌst/ [adj] a situation, decision etc that is **just** gives someone what they rightly deserve or have a right to expect: *Many of us did not feel that the court's decision was just.* | *a just and lasting peace* | **just decision/punishment/settlement etc** *The Attorney General called the sentence a fair and just punishment for someone who had committed such a dreadful crime.*

reasonable /ˈriːzənəbəl/ [adj] if an agreement, offer, or what someone does is **reasonable**, most people would agree that it is fair and sensible: *The company made every reasonable effort to correct the problem.* | *The students' goals in the protest seem so reasonable that the university is setting up a committee to consider them.* | **it is reasonable to do sth** *Do you think it's reasonable to expect people to work more than 60 hours a week?*

balanced /ˈbælənst/ [adj usually before noun] giving fair and equal treatment to all sides of an argument or subject: *'Newsweek' gave a reasonably balanced report on the crisis.* | *Recently historians have taken a far more balanced view of the Irish question.*

even-handed /ˌiːvən ˈhændɪ̈d◂/ [adj] treating everyone equally and not showing special favour to anyone: *Local magistrates are expected to respect the law and provide even-handed justice.* | *The BBC has the reputation of being even-handed in its coverage of election news.*

fair's fair /ˌfeəʳz ˈfeəʳ/ spoken use this to tell someone that they should do something because it is right and fair, especially after you have done something for them: *Come on, fair's fair. It's your turn to mind the kids.*

play fair /ˌpleɪ ˈfeəʳ/ [v phrase] to do something in an honest and fair way: *The film company says that it played fair in all its contract dealings with the actors' unions.* | *A mystery novel should play fair with the reader, providing all the clues necessary to solve the crime.*

2 words for describing someone who is always fair

- ▸ fair
- ▸ just
- ▸ fair-minded

fair /feəʳ/ [adj not usually before noun] *Kelson has a reputation as a fair and compassionate judge.* | *Despite the discrimination they suffered, my grandparents remained fair, decent, good people.* | **be fair to sb** *I've always tried to be fair to all my children.* —**fairly** [adv] *I believe I acted fairly when I expelled those students.*

just /dʒʌst/ [adj] written someone who is **just** treats people in a way that is fair and right – use this especially about leaders, rulers, and other people in authority, especially in historical descriptions: *He was the perfect choice for Emperor – just, patient, merciful and of royal blood.* | *No just government would allow this kind of treatment of its own citizens.*

fair-minded /ˌfeə ˈmaɪndɪ̈d◂‖ˈfeər ˌmaɪndɪ̈d/ [adj] someone who is **fair-minded** is able to see situations in a fair and reasonable way and always considers other people's opinions: *The Chairman is a fair-minded man, so will listen to any criticism of his proposals.* | *She remained maddeningly fair-minded, even about her greatest opponents.*

3 able to be fair because you are not involved in a situation

- ▸ objective
- ▸ impartial
- ▸ neutral
- ▸ not take sides
- ▸ unbiased
- ▸ disinterested

objective /əbˈdʒektɪv/ [adj] not influenced by personal opinions or emotions, especially when you have to make a decision about something: *I could use an objective opinion on this problem.* | *It's always difficult to be objective about such a sensitive issue as abortion.* | *The selection board, which decides on promotions, should be strictly objective.* —**objectively** [adv] *If you're worried, get the advice of someone who can look at the problem objectively.* —**objectivity** /ˌɒbdʒekˈtɪvɪ̈ti‖ˌɑːb-/ [n U] *Most quality newspapers aim at objectivity, but few achieve it.*

impartial /ɪmˈpɑːʳʃəl/ [adj] able to make fair judgements or decisions about a situation because you do not support anyone who is involved in it: *Historians try to be impartial, but they cannot free themselves entirely from their own opinions.* | *Our representative attended the peace negotiations as an impartial observer.* —**impartiality** /ɪmˌpɑːʳʃiˈæləti/ [n U] *After the trial, people questioned the impartiality of the jury.* —**impartially** [adv] *I'm not sure we can trust this court to consider the evidence impartially.*

neutral /ˈnjuːtrəl‖ˈnuː-/ [adj] not supporting any side in a disagreement, argument, war etc: *Switzerland remained neutral during World War II.* | *Civil servants are supposed to be politically neutral.* —**neutrality** /njuːˈtræləti‖nuː-/ [n U] *In 1917, U.S. neutrality ended when two of their ships were torpedoed.*

not take sides /nɒt teɪk ˈsaɪdz/ [v phrase] especially spoken to deliberately not support either side in an argument: *Teachers shouldn't take sides when students argue.* | **+ in** *It is important that social workers don't take sides in family disputes.*

unbiased /ʌnˈbaɪəst/ [adj] not influenced by personal opinions or a tendency to support a particular person or side, and therefore able to make a fair judgment: *This murder case has had so much media publicity that it will be difficult to find an unbiased jury.* | *Women need accurate, unbiased information about their options when they become pregnant.*

disinterested /dɪsˈɪntrəstəd/ [adj] able to be fair in considering a particular situation because you are not involved in it and do not expect to gain any personal advantage from it: *Find a financial consultant who can offer completely independent and disinterested advice.*

4 when a situation or decision is fair

- fairness
- justice
- fair play

fairness /ˈfeəʳnəs/ [n U] when something is done or decided in a way that is fair and right: *News reports should be held to a high standard of accuracy and fairness.* | *The judge has a record of fairness and non-discrimination.*

justice /ˈdʒʌstəs/ [n U] when a situation is dealt with in a way that is fair and right, especially as the result of an official or legal decision: *It's up to the courts to uphold justice – you can't take the law into your own hands.* | *It is clear that 'liberty and justice for all' is still a goal rather than a reality in the U.S.*

fair play /ˌfeəʳ ˈpleɪ/ [n U] if there is **fair play** in a situation, activity, game etc, people behave fairly and no one tries to cheat: *We need to instil in our children a strong sense of fair play.* | *A high level of sportsmanship and fair play is a tradition in the game.*

fairly/quite

more than a little, but not very

RELATED WORDS

see also **very**

- fairly
- quite
- pretty
- moderately
- rather
- somewhat
- reasonably

fairly /ˈfeəʳli/ [adv] if something is **fairly** heavy, **fairly** easy etc, it is more than a little heavy or easy, but it is not very heavy or very easy: *The house has a fairly big living room.* | *She was fairly certain that she had been there before.* | *The disease is still fairly common in many countries.*

quite /kwaɪt/ [predeterminer/adv] especially British if something is **quite** heavy, **quite** easy etc, it is more than a little heavy or easy, but it is not very heavy or very easy: *The hotel was quite expensive.* | *Geoffrey was young, handsome and probably quite wealthy.* | *I quite like it here but I'd rather live in Manchester.* | **quite a long way/a nice day/a good book etc** *It's quite a long way to the church from here.* | *I thought it was quite an interesting movie.* | **quite a lot** *Mick and Carla have been together quite a lot recently.*

pretty /ˈprɪti/ [adv] spoken more than a little, but not very: *It's pretty cold today.* | *'It's pretty tough work,' he wearily confessed.* | *'Hi Beth, how are you?' 'Pretty good. And you?'* | *I felt pretty nervous going into the exam, but after I got started I loosened up some.*

moderately /ˈmɒdərətli‖ˈmɑː-/ [adv] formal more than a little, but not very: *The food was only moderately good – nothing special.* | *The guidebook describes the climb as 'moderately difficult'.* | *While his career as a pro football player was moderately successful, he certainly wasn't famous.* | *She did moderately well in her final examinations.*

rather /ˈrɑːðəʳ‖ˈræ-/ [predeterminer/adv] especially British much more than a little, but not very – use this especially to describe something bad, unsuitable etc: *Gail seems rather unhappy today.* | *The attendance figures for this year's festival were rather disappointing.* | **rather a long way/a short dress etc** *Unfortunately, we're rather a long way from the airport.* | **rather a lot** *She was wearing rather a lot of make-up.*

somewhat /ˈsʌmwɒt‖-wɑːt/ [adv] formal use this especially to talk about something that is in fact more than a little annoying, big, high etc but you do not want to say this directly: *The ambassador looked somewhat irritated by the interruption.* | *My husband has a somewhat higher opinion of Mr Jones than I do.* | *This year's celebrations should be somewhat larger than last year's.*

reasonably /ˈriːzənəbli/ [adv] to a satisfactory level or degree: *She speaks Spanish reasonably well.* | *Kevin is a hard worker and reasonably intelligent but he has never been promoted.* | *Chao is still in reasonably good health.*

fall

RELATED WORDS

see also **down, accident, hit, jump**

1 when someone accidentally falls from a standing position

- fall
- fall over/down
- have a fall
- tumble
- fall flat on your face
- collapse
- keel over
- go head over heels

fall /fɔːl/ [v I] to accidentally **fall** from a standing position: *She was going up the stairs when she fell.* | *George held on tightly, afraid that he might fall.* | **fall down the stairs/steps etc** *There was concern for the Queen Mother yesterday after she fell down a short flight of steps at the airport.*

fall over/down /ˌfɔːl ˈəʊvəʳ, ˈdaʊn/ [phr v I] to fall onto the ground from a standing position: *Ben fell* *down and scraped his knee.* | *Beginning skiers can expect to fall down a lot.* | *The pavement was slippery and it was easy to fall over.*

have a fall /ˌhæv ə ˈfɔːl/ [v phrase not in progressive] British if someone, especially an old person, **has a fall**, they fall and hurt themselves: *My neighbour has had a fall and broken a rib.* | *Grandma had a bad fall in the snow that winter.*

tumble /ˈtʌmbəl/ [v I] to fall quickly down a slope or down stairs, rolling over and over and unable to stop **+ down/off/into etc** *She tumbled down the stairs and landed in a heap at the bottom.* | *A bus veered off the road and tumbled down the hill into the river below.*

fall flat on your face /fɔːl ˌflæt ɒn jɔːʳ ˈfeɪs/ [v phrase] to fall over suddenly so that you are lying on your front on the ground, especially in a way that makes you look funny: *She fell flat on her face getting out of the car.* | *The last time I wore high-heeled shoes I fell flat on my face outside a restaurant.*

collapse /kəˈlæps/ [v I] to fall suddenly and heavily onto the ground, into a chair etc, because of tiredness, illness, or injury: *One of the horses collapsed from exhaustion after the race.* | **+ on** *Cohen was hospitalized after he collapsed on the floor and briefly lost consciousness.* | **+ into** *Milligan collapsed into a chair, sighing deeply.* —**collapse** [n singular] *After Stephen's sudden collapse during the meeting, he was rushed to the hospital.*

keel over /ˌkiːl ˈəʊvəʳ/ [phr v I] to suddenly fall to the ground, because you are ill or have had a shock: *She'd been complaining of a headache all morning, and suddenly she just keeled over.* | *Carson keeled over and died in front of the nightclub after taking a number of illegal drugs.*

go head over heels /gəʊ ˌhed əʊvəʳ ˈhiːlz/ [v phrase] to fall forward with so much force that you roll over: *She slipped on the polished floor and went head over heels.* | *Shelly's horse stepped into soft sand and went down, horse and rider going head over heels in a cloud of dust.*

2 to almost fall from a standing position

- trip
- slip
- stumble
- lose your balance
- lose your footing

trip ALSO **trip over** British /trɪp, ˌtrɪp ˈəʊvəʳ/ [v I] to accidentally hit something with your foot when you are walking or running, so that you fall or nearly fall: *I didn't push him – he tripped.* | *She'd had quite a lot to drink and kept tripping over.* | **+ over** *Pick up that box – someone might trip over it.* | **+ on** *Her medical problems began when she tripped on a rug and broke her hip.* | **trip and fall** *One boy tripped and fell into the water.*

slip /slɪp/ [v I] to accidentally slide on a wet or smooth surface, so that you fall or nearly fall: *Be careful you don't slip – the floor's wet.* | **+ on** *She slipped on the icy sidewalk and grabbed Will's arm to steady herself.* | **slip and fall** *I walked slowly through the mud, trying not to slip and fall.*

stumble /ˈstʌmbəl/ [v I] to nearly fall down when you are walking or running, because you do not put your foot down carefully or because something is in the way: *In her hurry, Eva stumbled and dropped the tray she was carrying.* | **+ on/over** *Mason headed towards the house, stumbling on the rough ground.*

lose your balance /ˌluːz jɔːʳ ˈbæləns/ [v phrase] to fall or nearly fall, when you need to balance carefully to remain in an upright position, for example when you are standing on a ladder or riding a bicycle: *I tried to help Gina up, but I lost my balance and we both fell into the stream.* | *Bill was leaning over to watch, and lost his balance.*

lose your footing /ˌluːz jɔːʳ ˈfʊtɪŋ/ [v phrase] to lose your balance because your foot slips, especially when you are walking or climbing over an uneven or slippery surface: *I lost my footing on the snowy bank and fell into the river.* | *A climber who lost his footing was taken to hospital with serious injuries.*

3 when an upright object, a building, a wall, etc falls

- fall
- fall over
- fall down
- collapse
- fall in
- cave in
- topple over
- tip over

fall /fɔːl/ [v I] *She was playing just yards from where the building fell.* | **+ across/onto/on top of** *A tree had fallen across the road and blocked it.* | **+ off/out of/from** *The days were getting shorter and the leaves had started falling from the trees* | *I can't find my passport – it must have fallen out of my pocket.* —**fallen** [adj only before noun] *Fallen trees blocked the railway tracks.*

fall over /ˌfɔːl ˈəʊvəʳ/ [phr v I] if a tall object **falls over**, it falls onto its side from an upright position: *That bookcase looks as if it's about to fall over.* | *There was no wind; the tree just fell over.*

fall down /ˌfɔːl ˈdaʊn/ [phr v I] if a building, wall, or fence **falls down**, part or all of it falls to the ground, because it is in bad condition or because it has been damaged: *A boy was injured yesterday when part of a wall fell down near to where he was playing.* | *A large tree fell down during a windstorm and damaged our car.*

collapse /kəˈlæps/ [v I] if a building, wall etc **collapses**, it suddenly falls down, especially because of a sudden pressure: *Our tent collapsed in the middle of the night.* | *The building was badly damaged in the explosion, and rescue workers are worried that it may collapse.* | *Minutes later the second tower collapsed.*

fall in /ˌfɔːl ˈɪn/ [phr v I] if a roof **falls in**, it falls to the ground inside the building: *During the hurricane the roof fell in.* | **+ on** *We need to fix the ceiling before it falls in on us.*

cave in /ˌkeɪv ˈɪn/ [phr v I] if a roof, wall etc **caves in**, it suddenly and heavily falls inwards especially because it is weak and in bad condition: *The roof has caved in, so the whole building has been declared unsafe.* | **+ on** *Wooden beams support the roof, preventing it from caving in on the miners.*

topple over /ˌtɒpəl ˈəʊvəʳ‖ˌtɑː-/ [phr v I] if something **topples over**, it moves unsteadily backwards and forwards then falls to the ground: *The little boy put one more brick on the tower and it toppled over.* | *That plant's going to topple over if you don't put it in a bigger pot.*

tip over /ˌtɪp ˈəʊvəʳ/ [phr v I] to suddenly turn and fall to the ground as a result of not being properly balanced: *I sat on the edge of the table, and the whole thing tipped over.* | *The fire started when a lamp tipped over and ignited a cloth sofa.*

4 to fall through the air to the ground

- fall
- fall off
- plunge
- plummet
- drop
- tumble
- come down

fall /fɔːl/ [v I] *One of the climbers fell fifty feet.* | *A light rain was falling.* | **+ out/into/from etc** *She opened the cupboard and everything fell out.* | *There should be spaces between the boards of the deck to allow debris to fall through.* | *Fred fell out of the tree and broke his arm.* | *The girl had fallen from a fourth-floor window, but was not badly hurt.* | **+ on** *Careful that box doesn't fall on you, Charlotte!*

fall off /ˌfɔːl ˈɒf/ [phr v I/T] to accidentally fall from something in a high position to the ground: *Jim was laughing so hard he fell off his chair.* | *A bag of groceries fell off the table onto the floor.*

plunge /plʌndʒ/ [v I] to suddenly fall a long way from somewhere high up: *The aeroplane's engines failed and it plunged into the ocean.* | **+ off/down/into etc** *Their car swerved to avoid a truck, and plunged off the cliff.* | **plunge to your death** (=fall a long way and be killed) *A skydiver plunged to his death yesterday when his parachute failed to open.*

plummet /ˈplʌmɪ̥t/ [v I] to fall from somewhere high up, very quickly and very directly: *The rope snapped, causing the climber to plummet several hundred feet down the mountain.* | *Two aircraft on a training flight collided and plummeted to the ground.*

drop /drɒp‖drɑːp/ [v I] to fall suddenly from a high place straight down onto or towards the ground **+ onto/to/from etc** *Two bottles rolled across the table, dropped onto the floor, and smashed.* | *A few pine cones had already dropped to the ground.*

tumble /ˈtʌmbəl/ [v I] to fall quickly through the air, rolling over and over **+ down/off/from etc** *A little girl tumbled about 30 feet from the window of her family's third-floor apartment.*

come down /ˌkʌm ˈdaʊn/ [phr v I] if rain, snow etc **comes down**, it falls heavily: *We can't go out now – the rain's really coming down.* | *Snow was coming down so thickly I could barely see through the window.*

5 to fall off a horse, bicycle etc

- fall off
- be thrown

fall off /ˌfɔːl ˈɒf/ [v I/T] to accidentally fall from something you are riding on, for example a horse or a bicycle: *He fell off his bike and broke his wrist.* | *A bolt broke on an amusement park ride, and several children who fell off were seriously injured.*

be thrown /biː ˈθrəʊn/ [v phrase] to fall off a horse or similar animal because of a violent or sudden movement: *Rodeo riders can suffer appalling injuries after being thrown by bulls and steers.* | **+ from** *He broke his neck when he was thrown from a horse.*

6 to deliberately make someone fall

- knock sb over/ knock sb down
- trip
- push sb over
- knock sb to the ground

knock sb over/knock sb down /ˌnɒk (sb) ˈəʊvəʳ, ˌnɒk (sb) ˈdaʊn‖ˌnɑːk-/ [phr v T] to push or hit someone hard, so that they fall to the ground **knock sb over/down** *Careful where you're going! You nearly knocked me over!* | *In the rush to get out of the building, she was knocked down.* | **knock down/over sb** *Some of the bigger boys purposely knock over the smaller ones.*

trip ALSO **trip up** /trɪp, ˌtrɪp ˈʌp/ British /trɪp, ˌtrɪp ˌʌp/ [v T/phr v T] to make someone fall or almost fall by putting your foot or another object in their way: *One of the runners claimed she had been tripped.* | **trip sb up** *One man tripped me up and the other one grabbed my handbag.*

push sb over /ˌpʊʃ (sb) ˈəʊvəʳ/ [phr v T] to deliberately push someone with your hand so that they fall to the ground: *Another little kid came and pushed him over onto the grass.*

knock sb to the ground /ˌnɒk (sb) tə ðə ˈgraʊnd ‖ ˌnɑːk-/ [v phrase] to hit someone so hard that they lose their balance and fall to the ground: *A teenage boy knocked him to the ground and ran off with his briefcase.*

7 to let something fall or make something fall

- drop
- knock over
- spill
- tip over
- overturn
- upset

drop /drɒp‖drɑːp/ [v T] to stop holding something so that it falls, especially accidentally: *Watch you don't drop that box – it's very heavy.* | *Her hands shake constantly and she keeps dropping things.* | *You dropped your toy. Do you want it back?* | **drop sth on/onto sth** *Margaret dropped the letters onto her desk.*

knock over /ˌnɒk ˈəʊvəʳ‖ˌnɑːk-/ [phr v T] to hit something so that it falls onto its side from an upright position, especially when you do this accidentally **knock sth over** *Be careful or you'll knock the vase over.* | **knock over sth** *He bumped into the table and knocked over the candle.*

spill /spɪl/ [v T] to accidentally let liquid, powder, or small pieces of something fall onto a surface and spread out over it: *Oops, I just spilled my water.* | **spill sth down/all over/onto sth** *'How was the party?' 'OK, but some idiot spilled wine all over my new dress.'* | *Aaron spilled all the popcorn on the floor.*

tip over /ˌtɪp ˈəʊvəʳ/ [phr v T] to make something fall over, usually accidentally, by making it lose balance **tip sth over** *The cat managed to tip the Christmas tree over.* | **tip over sth** *He accidentally tipped over a candle, and the tablecloth caught fire.*

overturn /ˌəʊvəʳˈtɜːʳn/ [v T] to make something fall on its side or turn something over completely, especially by pushing it very hard: *The wind was so strong that it overturned dustbins and wrecked fences.* | *Protestors overturned cars and set fire to them.*

upset /ʌpˈset/ [v T] to accidentally knock or push something over, so that its contents fall out and spread over a wide area: *One of the kids upset a bottle of water on the table.*

false

RELATED WORDS

opposite: ——— **real**

- not natural *see* **artificial**
- not true *see* **untrue**
- not sincere *see* **pretend**
- *see also* **true**

1 made to look real for dishonest purposes

- false
- fake
- forged
- phoney/phony

false /fɔːls/ [adj only before noun] not real, but made to look real in order to deceive people: *He gave the clerk a false name and address in case the police were looking for him.* | *Her suitcase had a false bottom, containing 2 kilos of heroin.*

fake /feɪk/ [adj only before noun] use this about objects or documents that are not real, but are intended to look like something more important or valuable: *They were selling fake Rolex watches on the market stall.* | *a fake driver's license* | *Whitehorn pleaded guilty to possession of equipment to make fake identification documents.*

forged /fɔːʳdʒd/ [adj] a **forged** official document or bank note has been illegally made to look like a real one: *He came into the country using a forged visa.* | *a forged £50 note*

phoney/phony /ˈfəʊni/ [adj usually before noun] informal something that is **phoney** is false, but usually in an obvious way so that people realize it is not real: *I left a phoney name but the right telephone number.* | *Ever since he came back from London, John's been talking with a phony British accent.*

2 an object that is made to look real for dishonest purposes

- fake
- forgery
- dummy

fake /feɪk/ [n C] a copy of a valuable object or painting that is intended to make people think it is real: *Is the vase a genuine antique or a fake?*

forgery /ˈfɔːʳdʒəri/ [n C] a copy of a document, painting, or banknote that is made to look real for dishonest purposes: *The painting, believed to be by Renoir, turned out to be a very clever forgery.*

dummy /ˈdʌmi/ [adj only before noun] a **dummy** object is one that is made to look like the real object but cannot be used: *dummy rifles* | *Semionov threatened the pilot with a dummy hand grenade and forced him to land the plane.*

family

RELATED WORDS

▸ *see also* **mother, father, child, baby, relationship, home**

1 a group of people who are related to each other

- family
- parents
- folks
- background

family /ˈfæməli/ [n C] a group of people who are related to each other, especially a mother, father, and their children all living together: *He comes from a family of eight children.* | *A lot of the families living in this area are very poor.* | **member of a family** *Pearl is the last surviving member of her family.* | **the Armstrong/Mitchell/Jones family** (=the family with this name) *Various members of the Kennedy family were at the funeral.* | **immediate family** (=your closest relatives) *Only her immediate family knew she had heart disease.* | **nuclear family** (=a family consisting of a mother, a father, and their children) *Having an intact nuclear family does not guarantee that a child will turn out well.* | **extended family** (=including cousins, grandparents etc) *My extended family usually gets together at holidays.* | **one-parent family/single-parent family** (=a family in which there is only one parent) *Single-parent families are much more common these days.* | **big/large/small family** *I grew up in a large family in the South.* | *The cost of sending kids to college – even for a small family – is extremely high.*

parents /ˈpeərənts/ [n plural] someone's mother and father: *Do you get on well with your parents?* | *Parents need to become more involved in their children's school activities.*

folks /fəʊks/ [n plural] informal your family, especially your parents: *She's gone back home to see her folks.* | *My folks were waiting for me at the station.*

background /ˈbækgraʊnd/ [n C] the type of family and social class that you grew up in: *Most of his friends were from similar middle-class backgrounds.* | *In our class we have children of all different religious and ethnic backgrounds.*

2 things that happen in a family or belong in a family

- family
- domestic
- run in the family

family /ˈfæməli/ [adj only before noun] **family home/business/argument etc** something that belongs to a **family** or happens in a family: *I stopped going on family holidays when I was 15.* | *When her parents died, she took over the family business.* | *We're planning a big family celebration when my cousin gets married.*

domestic /dəˈmestɪk/ [adj only before noun] **domestic violence/trouble/argument etc** fighting, arguments, or problems between members of the same family: *Victims of domestic violence are often reluctant to tell the police.* | *I'm worried about Jim – I think he may be having some domestic problems.*

run in the family /ˌrʌn ɪn ðə ˈfæməli/ [v phrase not in progressive] if an illness or type of behaviour **runs in the family**, it is common in that family: *Asthma seems to run in our family.* | *Good looks must run in the family.*

3 someone who belongs to your family

- relative/relation
- family member/member of the family
- next of kin

relative/relation /ˈrelətɪv, rɪˈleɪʃən/ [n C] someone who is a member of your family although they do not live with you: *Over a hundred friends and relatives came to the wedding.* | **+ of** *Some relatives of the victims are planning to sue.* | **close relative/relation** (=someone who is closely related to you) *When he died, there were no children or close relatives to contact.* | **distant relative/relation** (=someone who is not closely related to you) *We have some distant relations in Australia that we've never met.* | **no relation to sb** (=used to say someone is not related to someone else with the same name) *Marty Rogers (no relation to Governor Rogers) is one of the governor's biggest critics.*

family member/member of the family /ˌfæməli ˈmembəʳ, ˌmembər əv ðə ˈfæməli/ [n C] someone who is part of your family: *Only close family members are allowed to visit her.* | *Woods says she's not sure if any of the members of her family have read the book.*

next of kin /ˌnekst əv ˈkɪn/ [n phrase] the person or people who are most closely related to you, for example your husband or mother, and who need to be told when you die or if you have a serious accident: *The college need to know your next of kin in case something happens to you.* | *The police will not release the dead man's name until his next of kin have been informed.*

4 to belong to the same family

- be related
- be descended from

be related /biː rɪˈleɪtɪ̈d/ [v phrase] if two people **are related**, they are both members of the same family – use this about cousins, grandparents etc, but not about your parents or your brothers and sisters: *'I didn't know you and Ted were related.' 'Yes, Ted's wife is my sister.'* | **+ to** *John told me he was related to Mel Gibson – is that true?*

be descended from /biː dɪˈsendɪ̈d frɒm/ [v phrase] to be related to someone who lived a long time ago, especially someone famous or important: *She is descended from the Duke of Marlborough.* | *Many of the plantation owners were descended from American missionaries.*

5 people who are related to you because of marriage

- mother-in-law/son-in-law etc
- stepmother/stepson/stepsister etc
- half-brother/half-sister
- by marriage
- in-laws

mother-in-law/son-in-law etc /ˈmʌðər ɪn ˌlɔː, ˈsʌn ɪn ˌlɔː/ [n C] someone who is related to you because of a marriage, for example, your **mother-in-law** is the mother of your wife or husband, and your **sister-in-law** is the sister of your wife or husband, or the wife of your brother: *Surprisingly, my mother-in-law and I get along very well.* | *My sister and brother-in-law are coming to visit next week.*

stepmother/stepson/stepsister etc /ˈstepmʌðəʳ, ˈstepsʌn, ˈstepsɪstəʳ/ [n C] someone who becomes your mother, sister, son etc when you or a person you are related to marries for a second time: *After my mother got remarried, it took a while to get used to having a stepfather.* | *She has two sisters and a stepbrother.*

half-brother/half-sister /ˈhɑːf brʌðəʳ, ˈhɑːf sɪstəʳ ‖ ˈhæf-/ [n C] someone who is the child of one of your parents but not both of them: *Alyssa has a half-brother she's never met because her parents don't speak to each other any more.*

by marriage /baɪ ˈmærɪdʒ/ [adv] if you are related to someone **by marriage**, they are married to someone in your family or you are married to someone in their family: *John's my cousin by marriage.*

in-laws /ˈɪn lɔːz/ [n plural] informal the parents of your husband or wife: *We lived with my in-laws until we had enough money to buy a house of our own.*

6 people who were in the same family as you a long time ago

- ancestor
- family
- descendant
- forefathers

ancestor /ˈænsəstəʳ, -ses-‖-ses-/ [n C] a member of your family who lived a long time ago, especially hundreds of years ago: *My ancestors originally came from Ireland.* | *During the festival of Obon, Japanese show respect to their dead ancestors.*

family /ˈfæməli/ [n C] people that you are related to who lived a long time ago: *Her family came to America from Scotland in about 1750.* | *Our family has lived around here for hundreds of years.*

descendant /dɪˈsendənt/ [n C] someone who is a relative of a person who lived and died a long time ago, especially a famous or important person: *Frederick and Bertha moved to Iowa in 1852, and their descendants still live in the area.* | **+ of** *Paul claims to be a descendant of King Charles I.*

forefathers /ˈfɔːʳˌfɑːðəʳz/ [n plural] people in your family who lived a long time ago: *His forefathers helped settle this area a century and a half ago.*

famous

RELATED WORDS

- *see also* **important, succeed/successful, actor/actress, television/radio, film/movie**

1 famous

- famous
- well-known/well known
- legendary
- celebrated
- noted
- renowned
- eminent
- notorious
- infamous

famous /ˈfeɪməs/ [adj] **famous** people, places, books etc are known about and talked about by a lot of people in a lot of places: *Famous stars like Keanu Reeves and Demi Moore attended the party.* | *The package includes a tour of Sydney's famous Opera House.* | *'David Copperfield' is one of Dickens' most famous books.* | **+ for** *Manchester is famous for its nightlife and for its football teams.* | **world-famous** (=famous all over the world) *Rio's world-famous carnival* — **the rich and famous** /ðə ˌrɪtʃ ən ˈfeɪməs/ [n plural] people who are rich and famous: *The night club is popular among the rich and famous.*

well-known/well known /ˌwel ˈnəʊn◂/ [adj] famous, especially in a particular place or among a particular group of people: *She works in local radio, and is quite well known in the Houston area.* | *Large companies have an advantage because of their well-known brand names.* | **+ for** *The island is well-known for its beautiful beaches.* | **better-known/best-known** *Pat Boone is one of America's best-known Christian entertainers.*

legendary /ˈledʒəndəri‖-deri/ [adj usually before noun] someone or something that is **legendary** is famous for being very special or interesting, and people like to talk or read about them: *The studio was owned by Sam Goldwyn, the legendary Hollywood producer.* | *The album was recorded at the legendary Abbey Road studios.*

celebrated /ˈselɪ̈breɪtɪ̈d/ [adj] very well known, admired, and talked about by a lot of people, especially because of some special success or achievement: *Martin Luther King Jr. gave his celebrated speech before the Lincoln Memorial in 1963.* | *Van Gogh, perhaps Holland's most celebrated artist, died in poverty.*

noted /ˈnəʊtɨ̣d/ [adj only before noun] **noted musician/scientist/surgeon etc** well known and respected because of a special ability or achievement: *The picture was taken in the mid-1880s by the noted photographer C.S. Fly.* | *The author quotes Stephen Jay Gould, the noted Harvard scientist, to support his theories.*

renowned /rɪˈnaʊnd/ [adj] famous for a particular quality or activity: *Jesse Jackson, the renowned civil rights leader, was in the city again last night.* | **+ for** *Barbados is renowned for the marvellous cricket players it produces.* | **+ as** *Renowned as a newspaper editor, Greeley ran against Grant for president in 1872.*

eminent /ˈemɪnənt/ [adj usually before noun] an **eminent** doctor, lawyer, scientist etc is famous for being extremely successful in his or her profession and is admired and respected for this: *She's an eminent psychiatrist at the Harvard Medical School.* | *While he lived, Nehru remained the most eminent spokesman for the Third World.*

notorious /nəʊˈtɔːriəs, nə-/ [adj] someone who is **notorious** is famous because of something bad they have done: *One of Britain's most notorious criminals has escaped from prison.* | *Davis is a notorious woman-hater.* | **+ for** *English soccer fans are notorious for their drunkenness.*

infamous /ˈɪnfəməs/ [adj only before noun] famous for being bad, especially for being immoral or evil: *He was a member of the regime's infamous secret police.* | *The night club is named after New Orleans' infamous red light district.*

2 receiving a lot of attention in newspapers etc

- be in the public eye
- be in the spotlight/limelight
- much/most talked about
- sb's name is on everyone's lips
- high-profile

be in the public eye /biː ɪn ðə ˌpʌblɪk ˈaɪ/ [v phrase] to receive a lot of attention, so that a lot of what you do is reported in newspapers, on television etc: *The President's family is constantly in the public eye.* | *Marks has kept himself in the public eye for years by filing bizarre lawsuits.*

be in the spotlight/limelight /biː ɪn ðə ˈspɒtlaɪt, ˈlaɪmlaɪt‖-ˈspɑːt-/ [v phrase] to receive a lot of attention in newspapers, on television etc, but often only for a short period of time: *The band is in the spotlight again because of its recent hit single.* | *How do her children feel about having a mother who's constantly in the limelight?*

much/most talked about /ˌmʌtʃ, ˌməʊst ˈtɔːkt əbaʊt/ [adj phrase] receiving a lot of attention from newspapers, television etc, and talked about by a lot of people: *The much talked about new museum is somewhat disappointing.* | *She is Australia's most talked about TV actress.*

sb's name is on everyone's lips / (sb's) ˌneɪm ɪz ɒn ˌevriwʌnz ˈlɪps/ if someone's **name is on everyone's lips** they are very well known and talked about for a short time, usually as a result of a news story: *As a result of the scandal, the tall Texan millionaire's name was on everyone's lips.*

high-profile /ˌhaɪ ˈprəʊfaɪl◂/ [adj] often attracting a lot of attention because of your position in society or your job: *a high-profile civil rights lawyer* | *a high-profile position as Chief Executive*

3 to become famous

- become famous/well known
- make your name/make a name for yourself
- rise to fame/shoot to fame/win fame (as)
- achieve notoriety
- hit the headlines/make (the) headlines
- rising star

become famous/well known /bɪˌkʌm ˈfeɪməs, wel ˈnəʊn/ [v phrase] *Many people dream of becoming famous.* | *The brand name has become well known in Britain through clever advertising.* | **become famous overnight** (=very suddenly) *With the success of their first record, they became famous overnight.*

make your name/make a name for yourself /ˌmeɪk jɔːʳ ˈneɪm, ˌmeɪk ə ˈneɪm fər jɔːʳself/ [v phrase] to become well known, especially as a result of hard work or an unusual achievement: *Clint Eastwood first made a name for himself in the TV series 'Rawhide'.* | **+ as** *By the time he was 30, Evans had made his name as the editor of 'The Sunday Times'.* | *She is beginning to make a name for herself as a fashion designer.*

rise to fame/shoot to fame/win fame (as) /ˌraɪz tə ˈfeɪm, ˌʃuːt tə ˈfeɪm, ˌwɪn ˈfeɪm (æz)/ [v phrase] to become famous, especially suddenly: *John Lydon shot to fame in the mid-1970s as Johnny Rotten of the Sex Pistols.* | *She won fame as the youngest-ever Olympic champion gymnast.* —**rise to fame** [n phrase] *The movie focuses on Stern's rise to fame.*

achieve notoriety /əˌtʃiːv nəʊtəˈraɪəti/ [v phrase] to become famous for something bad: *The director's films have achieved notoriety for their graphic depiction of violence.* | **achieve a certain notoriety** (=become slightly famous for something) *The club has achieved a certain notoriety as a meeting place for criminals and drug dealers.*

hit the headlines/make (the) headlines /ˌhɪt ðə ˈhedlaɪnz, ˌmeɪk (ðə) ˈhedlaɪnz/ [v phrase] to suddenly become very famous and receive a lot of attention from the newspapers, television etc, sometimes only for a short time: *The island hit the headlines last year when huge tidal waves killed 2,000 people.* | *The bizarre court case was shown on TV and made headlines around the world.*

rising star /ˌraɪzɪŋ ˈstɑːʳ/ [n C] someone, especially a young person, who is quickly becoming more and more famous: *She's one of the rising stars of politics and an excellent public speaker.*

4 when someone is famous

- fame
- stardom
- renown

fame /feɪm/ [n U] the success and attention people get when they are famous: *She came to Hollywood in search of fame.* | **at the height of sb's fame** (=when someone is most famous) *At the height of his fame, it is estimated that 500 million people watched his show.* | **fame and fortune** (=fame and money) *He never really achieved the fame and fortune he dreamed of.* | **of television/movie/baseball etc fame**

(=famous because of television, films etc) *The book is about Bonnie Parker of Bonnie and Clyde fame.*

stardom /ˈstɑːʳdəm/ [n U] when someone is very famous, especially in music, films, or sport: *Stardom is the ultimate ambition of most young singers and actors.* | *She feared that by having a baby she had sacrificed her chances of stardom.*

renown /rɪˈnaʊn/ [n U] written fame and admiration that someone has because of something good such as great skill, knowledge, or bravery: *The general's victories won him renown throughout the country.* | **of great/international/high etc renown** *Speakers of international renown will attend the conference.*

5 a famous person

- star
- celebrity
- superstar
- personality
- big name
- legend
- household name

- *see also* **actor/actress**

star /stɑːʳ/ [n C] a very famous and successful actor, entertainer, or sports player: *Hollings' latest movie role could make her a big star.* | **movie/rock/tennis etc star** *John Cusack is one of my favourite movie stars.* | *She was once married to a well-known football star.* | **big star** *If he becomes a big TV star, we'll probably never hear from him again.*

celebrity ALSO **celeb** informal /sə̇ˈlebrə̇ti, sə̇ˈleb/ [n C] someone who is well known, for example as an entertainer or sports player, and who is often seen on television or written about in newspapers: *People waited outside for the chance to see some celebrities.* | *The bar is a good place to go if you want to spot some celebs.* | **TV/showbusiness/media etc celebrity** *The club is popular with media celebrities and literary types.* | **celebrity interview/photograph/biography etc** *Mattie reads mainly tabloids and celebrity biographies.* | **celebrity golf tournament/game show** (=in which celebrities take part) *Nash played in a celebrity golf tournament while in Canada.* | **minor celebrity** (=not extremely famous, popular, or successful) *Six minor celebrities took part in the charity 'Big Brother' programme.*

superstar /ˈsuːpəʳstɑːʳ, ˈsjuː-‖ˈsuː-/ [n C] an actor, musician, or sports player who is famous all over the world: *Janet Jackson became a superstar largely because of her exciting music videos.* | **radio/TV/basketball etc superstar** *Hockey superstar Wayne Gretzky played for L.A. before retiring.*

personality /ˌpɜːʳsəˈnælə̇ti/ [n C] someone who is well known because they often appear on television and at public events: *For years she was one of the best-loved personalities in the newspaper gossip columns.* | **TV/radio/sports etc personality** *Radio personality Don Imus has gotten in trouble again for what he said on the air.*

big name /ˌbɪg ˈneɪm/ [n C] informal a famous and successful performer: *Eric Hawkins, one of the big names of modern American dance* — **big-name** /ˈbɪg neɪm/ [adj] *The stadium has managed to attract a number of big-name entertainers.*

legend /ˈledʒənd/ [n C] someone who has become very famous over a long period of time, especially because they are very good at a particular activity: *Among Mexican music fans, Fernandez is a legend.* | **living legend/legend in sb's own lifetime** (=someone who has become a legend while still alive) *Michael Jordan is a living legend of basketball.*

household name /ˌhaʊshəʊld ˈneɪm/ [n C] a person, company, or product that is a **household name** is so famous that everyone knows their name: *Coca-Cola is a household name all over the world.* | **make sb/sth a household name** *Ralph Nader's consumer activism has made him a household name in the U.S.*

6 not famous

- unknown
- obscure
- a nobody

unknown /ˌʌnˈnəʊn◂/ [adj] not at all famous: *As an unknown author, it isn't easy to get your work published.* | *Horn was beaten by a relatively unknown politician in the last election.* — **unknown** [n C] *a movie made with a cast of complete unknowns*

obscure /əbˈskjʊəʳ/ [adj] someone or something that is **obscure** is known about only by a few people, because they belong to a group, place, or subject that not many people know about or are interested in: *He's using an obscure old law to try to stop the new road being built.* | *The lines were written by an obscure English poet named Mordaunt.* — **obscurity** [n U] *After the accident he retired from acting and died in relative obscurity.*

a nobody /ə ˈnəʊbədi/ [n singular] someone who is very ordinary and not at all famous or important: *After all her hard work, she didn't want to end up just a nobody.* | *A lot of the rich people who come in here treat us like nobodies.*

far

RELATED WORDS

opposite: —— **near**

- how far *see* **distance**
- *see also* **long**

1 a long distance

- far
- far away
- a long way
- a fair way/quite a way/a good way
- some distance/quite a distance/a good distance
- miles
- nowhere near
- far afield

far /fɑːʳ/ [adv] a long distance – use this especially in negatives and questions: *Have you driven far?* | *We won't be able to go much farther because of the snow.* | *Who do you think can jump the farthest?* | **+ from** *Cleveland isn't very far from here.* | *We were sitting too far from the stage to hear what the actors were saying.* | **+ above/below/behind etc** *I was now far behind the others and knew I couldn't catch up.*

far away /ˌfɑːr əˈweɪ/ [adv] a very long distance from where you are: *The ship was so far away that we could hardly see it.* | **+ from** *She wanted to get as far away from New York as possible.* | **as far away as sth** *Because of the snowstorm on the east coast, flights for Boston were sent as far away as Montreal.* | **from far away** *Thousands of people had come from far away for a chance to see the Pope.*

a long way ALSO **a long ways** American spoken /ə ˌlɒŋ ˈweɪ, ə ˌlɒŋ ˈweɪz‖-ˌlɔːŋ-/ [adv] a long distance: *You must be tired – you've come a long way.* | **+ from** *The farm is a long way from the highway.* | **a long way away/a long way off** (=a long way from where you are now or from the place you are talking about) *We could hear them shouting from a long way away.* | *From the map, it looked as if the lake was* *still a long way off.* | **+ ahead/below/behind etc** *It's a long way down – hold on tight.*

a fair way/quite a way/a good way British ALSO **quite a ways** American spoken /ə ˌfeəʳ ˈweɪ, ˌkwaɪt ə ˈweɪ, ə ˌgʊd ˈweɪ, ˌkwaɪt ə ˈweɪz/ [adv] fairly far, used especially to warn someone that a distance is longer than they think: *Look at the map. It's a fair way to drive in one day.* | *The children will have to walk quite a way if we take them into the woods.*

some distance/quite a distance/a good distance /ˌsʌm ˈdɪstəns, ˌkwaɪt ə ˈdɪstəns, ə ˌgʊd ˈdɪstəns/ [adv] further than usual or further than you expected: *José accompanied us for some distance until we reached the highway.* | *Their house is actually quite a distance from the edge of town.*

miles /maɪlz/ [adv] informal a very long way: *We hiked miles yesterday.* | **+ away** *I don't see Jane much any more – she lives miles away.* | **+ from** *The hotel is miles from the station – I'll come and get you.* | **miles from anywhere** (=a long way from the nearest town) *They live up in the mountains, miles from anywhere.* | **miles and miles** *Around here you can walk miles and miles and never see anyone.*

nowhere near /ˌnəʊweəʳ ˈnɪəʳ/ [prep] a very long way from somewhere, further than you expect to be, or further than someone else says you are: *The car was parked in the middle of the street, nowhere near the curb.* | *After eight hours climbing, we were still nowhere near the top of the mountain.*

far afield /ˌfɑːr əˈfiːld/ [adv] formal if you travel **far afield**, you travel a very long way from the place where you usually live: *With the car they could travel far afield each summer.* | **as far afield as sth** *His work took him as far afield as Moscow and Delhi.* | **further/farther afield** *The next day we ventured farther afield and sailed out to one of the islands.*

2 when something you can see or hear is far away

- in the distance
- distant
- on the horizon
- from a distance/at a distance
- a long way off/far off/far away
- way off
- at long range

in the distance /ɪn ðə ˈdɪstəns/ [adv] if you can see or hear something **in the distance**, it is a long way from where you are, so it looks small or does not sound loud: *In the distance, he could see the tall chimneys of the factory.* | *Dogs were barking somewhere in the distance.*

distant /ˈdɪstənt/ [adj only before noun] especially written a **distant** thing or noise is very far away, so that it looks small or sounds quiet: *By now, the plane was just a distant speck in the sky.* | *There was a flash of lightning and then the rumble of distant thunder.*

on the horizon /ɒn ðə həˈraɪzən/ [adv] at the place far away where the land or sea seems to meet the sky: *Another ship appeared on the horizon.* | *Storm clouds on the horizon were rapidly blowing in our direction.*

from a distance/at a distance /frəm ə ˈdɪstəns, ət ə ˈdɪstəns/ [adv] from a place that is a fairly long way away: *From a distance, the two birds look similar.* | *He followed her at a distance, making sure she didn't see him.*

a long way off/far off/far away /ə ˌlɒŋ weɪ ˈɒf‖-ˌlɔːŋ-, ˌfɑːr ˈɒf, ˌfɑːr əˈweɪ/ [adv] in a place very far from where you are now, so that it is difficult to see or hear what is there: *Then, from a long way off, I heard high-pitched laughing.* | *There was a sound of a car backfiring far off in the night.* | *Far away, to the east, you can just see the spire of the cathedral.*

way off /ˌweɪ ˈɒf/ [adv] American far from where you are: *He could hear voices from way off in another part of the house.* | *Way off in the distance I could see a light shining.*

at long range /ət ˌlɒŋ ˈreɪndʒ‖-ˌlɔːŋ-/ [adv] if you do something **at long range**, especially shoot someone or something, you do it from far away: *The police officer fired one shot at long range and hit the man.* | *The guns are not nearly as accurate at long range.*

3 far away from other places

- distant/far-off
- faraway
- remote
- isolated
- secluded
- in the middle of nowhere/miles from anywhere/in the back of beyond
- in the boondocks/boonies
- out of the way
- off the beaten track
- way out
- far-flung

distant/far-off /ˈdɪstənt, ˈfɑːr ɒf/ [adj usually before noun] a **distant** or **far-off** town or country is a long way from where you are: *Food at the fair comes from such far-off places as Brazil and Lithuania.* | *How can we send our young men off to distant lands to die in foreign wars?*

faraway /ˈfɑːrəweɪ/ [adj only before noun] written a **faraway** country, especially one that you have been told about or have read about, is very far away, and different from your own country: *Ed told us stories of all the faraway countries he had visited.* | *Avis always dreamed of an exotic vacation in some faraway place.*

remote /rɪˈməʊt/ [adj] **remote** places are far away from other places or people, and very few people go there: *They moved to a remote farmhouse in North Wales.* | *The helicopter crashed in a remote desert area.*

isolated /ˈaɪsəleɪtɪ̣d/ [adj] a long way from other towns, buildings, or people, especially in a quiet place where you are alone: *If you travel to isolated areas, make sure you have a good guide.* | *The area is extremely isolated because of the hills that surround it.* —**isolation** /ˌaɪsəˈleɪʃən/ [n U] *The community was protected from change by its isolation* (=because it was isolated).

secluded /sɪˈkluːdɪ̣d/ [adj] a **secluded** place is private and quiet because it is a long way from other people – use this about a place where people can do what they want without being disturbed: *They drove to a secluded spot in the country to have their picnic.* | *We rented a little cabin on the edge of a secluded lake.*

in the middle of nowhere/miles from anywhere/in the back of beyond /ɪn ðə ˌmɪdl əv ˈnəʊweəʳ, ˌmaɪls frəm ˈeniweəʳ, ɪn ðə ˌbæk əv bɪˈjɒnd‖-ˈjɑːnd/ [adv] informal in a lonely place a long way from towns or villages, where you do not expect to find any houses: *Amazingly, we found a really nice motel in the middle of nowhere.* | *We were miles from anywhere and had no idea how to get back.*

in the boondocks/boonies /ɪn ðə ˈbuːndɒks, ˈbuːniz‖-dɑːks/ [adv] American informal in a part of the country that is a long way from any town: *I'm not moving to that place – it's out in the boondocks.* | *Gayle lives out in the boonies – it would take at least an hour to get there.*

out of the way /ˌaʊt əv ðə ˈweɪ◂/ [adv] fairly far away from any town or from where other people live, and a little difficult to find and travel to: *The house is a little out of the way, but you should be able to find it.* —**out-of-the-way** [adj only before noun] *This must be one of the most out-of-the-way places in Scotland.*

off the beaten track ALSO **off the beaten path** American /ˌɒf ðə ˌbiːtn ˈtræk, ˌɒf ðə ˌbiːtn ˈpɑːθ‖-ˈpæθ/ [adv] a place that is **off the beaten track** or **path** is a long way from the places where people usually go, which usually makes it more interesting to visit: *The little restaurant was so far off the beaten track that we almost didn't find it.* | *Greg likes to get off the beaten path and discover places that other tourists don't find.*

way out /ˌweɪ ˈaʊt/ [adv] a long way from where you are now or far away from the nearest town **+ in/past/beyond etc** *I live way out in Laurel Canyon.* | *We drove way out past Reno to the old Fielding place.*

far-flung /ˌfɑːʳ ˈflʌŋ◂/ [adj usually before noun] **far-flung** places are all connected with a particular organization, country etc but they are all very far away from it: *Our job is to organize the company's far-flung offices.* | *Participants come from nations as far-flung as Iceland and Japan.*

4 too far away to reach

- out of reach
- out of range

out of reach /ˌaʊt əv ˈriːtʃ/ [adv] too far away to pick up or touch: *Gary jumped for the ball but it was just out of reach.* | **+ of** *Put the food somewhere out of reach of the dog.* | **out of sb's reach/out of reach of** *All medicines should be kept out of children's reach.*

out of range /ˌaʊt əv ˈreɪndʒ/ [adv] too far away to be hit by a shot from a gun: *We'd better shoot now before the trucks get out of range.* | **+ of** *Villagers are moving south, out of range of enemy gunfire.*

5 travelling or reaching over a long distance

- long-range
- long-haul
- long-distance

long-range /ˌlɒŋ ˈreɪndʒ◂‖ˌlɔːŋ-/ [adj only before noun] **long-range missile/gun/bomber etc** a weapon that can hit something far away: *There are fears that the country has produced long-range missiles capable of reaching across the border.*

long-distance /ˌlɒŋ ˈdɪstəns◂‖ˌlɔːŋ-/ [adj only before noun] **long-distance trade/transport/telephone call etc** between places that are a long way away from each other: *Long-distance phone calls have gotten so much cheaper.* | *A long-distance bus service now links the cities.* | *The development of long-distance commerce led to greater cultural contacts between continents.*

long-haul /ˈlɒŋ hɔːl‖ˈlɔːŋ-/ [adj only before noun] **long-haul flight/aircraft etc** travelling long distances: *It's so much nicer to fly business class on long-haul flights.* | *long-haul routes between Europe and Asia*

6 not travelling or reaching a long distance

- short-range
- short-haul

short-range /ˌʃɔːʳt ˈreɪndʒ◂/ [adj only before noun] **short-range missile/gun etc** a weapon that can only hit something that is a short distance away: *Short-range missiles in Asia do not pose a direct threat to the U.S.*

short-haul /ˈʃɔːʳt hɔːl/ [adj only before noun] **short-haul flight/aircraft etc** only travelling short distances: *The airline plans to increase the number of short-haul flights between European capitals.*

fashionable/ not fashionable

RELATED WORDS

▸ *see also* **clothes, taste in clothes, music etc, old-fashioned, smart/well-dressed, style/elegance, suit/look good together, design**

1 fashionable

- fashionable
- cool
- hot
- trendy
- stylish
- chic
- cult
- in
- hip
- happening

fashionable /ˈfæʃənəbəl/ [adj] clothes, styles, places or activities that are **fashionable** are popular at the present time, but will probably only be popular for a short time: *The store sells fashionable clothes at prices you can afford.* | *a style of painting that was fashionable in the 1930s* | *Kate spent her summers in Cape Cod working in a fashionable resort.* | *They recently opened a cafe on Manhattan's fashionable East Side.*

cool /kuːl/ [adj] spoken informal said to show approval of something that is fashionable, interesting, or attractive – used especially by young people: *He was wearing these really cool sunglasses.* | *Many young people start smoking because they think it looks cool.*

hot /hɒt‖hɑːt/ [adj] informal very fashionable now: *one of the hot young writers of the decade* | *They're supposed to be the hottest thing since the Beatles.*

trendy /ˈtrendi/ [adj] informal very fashionable, often for a short time – used especially humorously or to show disapproval: *a trendy street market in the centre of Paris* | *Delgado predicts that blonde hair will become trendy this summer.* | *Trendy bars and restaurants are opening and inexpensive apartments in the area are getting hard to find.*

stylish /ˈstaɪlɪʃ/ [adj] well designed, and attractive in a fashionable way: *She was wearing a stylish black woollen dress.* | *stylish modern furniture*

chic /ʃiːk/ [adj] very fashionable in an expensive way, and showing a lot of good judgement about good style: *They live in a chic apartment overlooking the Seine.* | *a chic restaurant in Boston* | *The east side of the city has become very chic in the past few years.*

cult /kʌlt/ [adj only before noun] fashionable and only known about by a small group of people – use this especially about things or people that later become very famous: *Alex Garland's cult novel 'The Beach' was later made into a film starring Leonardo di Caprio.* | *60s cult band The Velvet Underground* | *Frankie Knuckles is a cult figure in dance music.*

in /ɪn/ [adj] informal fashionable at the present time: *Purple seems to be in this year.* | **be the in place**

Gstaad is the in place to go skiing in winter. | **the in thing to do** *Cycling to work has become the in thing to do.*

hip /hɪp/ [adj] informal doing things or done according to the latest fashion: *The South Side is becoming a really hip place to live.* | *I hate old people who dress like teenagers and think they're hip.*

happening /ˈhæpənɪŋ/ [adj] informal fashionable and exciting: *In four to five years, this will be a happening film festival.* | *The town's OK, but not what you'd call a happening place.*

2 to be fashionable

- be in fashion
- be the fashion
- be the latest thing/ be the in thing
- be in
- be all the rage
- be in vogue

be in fashion /biː ɪn ˈfæʃən/ [v phrase] if clothes, music, places, or activities **are in fashion**, they are fashionable and popular with many people at the present time: *Latin music is very much in fashion.* | *Surprisingly, flared trousers are in fashion again.* | *Country cottage furniture has been in fashion for a long time now.*

be the fashion /biː ðə ˈfæʃən/ [v phrase] to be fashionable: *I thought it looked ugly, but Iris said white suits were the fashion so I tried it on.* | **be the fashion among sb** *Wearing coats hanging off one shoulder is the fashion among schoolchildren at the moment.*

be the latest thing/be the in thing /biː ðə ˌleɪtɪ̈st ˈθɪŋ, biː ði ˌɪn ˈθɪŋ/ [v phrase] informal to be the most recent and most popular fashion now: *When I was growing up, the video game 'Pong' was the latest thing.* | *I know cigars are the in thing, but you'll never see me smoke one.* | **be the latest thing in sth** *Herbert's house looks like a factory, but it's the latest thing in modern architecture.* | **be the in thing to do** *Having a holiday in Ibiza seems to be the in thing to do at the moment.*

be in /biː ˈɪn/ [adj] informal to be fashionable at the present time: *Long skirts are in at the moment.*

be all the rage /biː ˌɔːl ðə ˈreɪdʒ/ [v phrase] if something, especially an activity, **is all the rage**, it is very fashionable, and popular with a lot of people, especially for a short time: *Before the war, ragtime was all the rage in the dancehalls.* | *Buying a cabin in the mountains may be all the rage at the moment, but is it really a sound investment?*

be in vogue /biː ɪn ˈvəʊg/ [v phrase] if something, especially a style of music, decoration, art etc, **is in vogue**, it is fashionable at that time with a particular group of people: *Do you remember when New Wave music was in vogue?* | *His photographs, stark and sometimes shocking, are very much in vogue with young intellectuals.*

3 ways of saying that something becomes fashionable

- come into fashion
- come in
- make a comeback

come into fashion /ˌkʌm ɪntə ˈfæʃən/ [v phrase] *When did baseball caps come into fashion?* | *When mini-skirts first came into fashion, women said they'd never wear them.* | **come back into fashion** *Short haircuts for men went out for a time, and then they came back into fashion.*

come in /ˌkʌm ˈɪn/ [phr v I] to become fashionable, especially for a short period of time: *Skateboarding first came in during the early 1980s.* | *New fashions seem to come in and go out again much more quickly these days.*

make a comeback /ˌmeɪk ə ˈkʌmbæk/ [v phrase] to become fashionable and popular again, after having been unfashionable for a long period of time: *Who'd have thought platform soles would ever make a comeback?* | *Games like 'Ludo' and 'Snakes and Ladders' are really making a comeback.*

4 to make something fashionable

- set the trend

set the trend /ˌset ðə ˈtrend/ [v phrase] to make something that is new fashionable, by doing, using, or wearing it, so that a lot of people copy you: *Young backpackers set the trend, and now people of all ages are looking for cheap ways to travel around South-east Asia.* | **+ of** *To save the planet we must set the trend of caring for the environment.*

5 fashionable people

- fashionable
- trendy
- sophisticated
- fashion victim

fashionable /ˈfæʃənəbəl/ [adj] someone who is **fashionable** wears **fashionable** clothes, owns **fashionable** things, and goes to **fashionable** places: *This is the latest style of hat worn by fashionable women in Milan.* | *I've never been very fashionable. I'd rather wear what feels comfortable.*

trendy /ˈtrendi/ [adj] informal fashionable – use this especially about someone who you think tries too hard to be fashionable: *stylish South Beach cafés filled with trendy young couples* | *She only talks like that because she wants to sound trendy.*

sophisticated /səˈfɪstɪ̈keɪtɪ̈d/ [adj] someone who is **sophisticated** knows a lot about fashionable things and feels confident about being with fashionable people: *a sophisticated woman whose friends included many rich and famous people* | *a play that will appeal to a sophisticated audience*

fashion victim /ˈfæʃən ˌvɪktɪ̈m/ [n C] someone who wears clothes that are fashionable, but that make them look silly: *a new designer who will appeal to fashion victims everywhere*

6 fashionable activity, product, style etc

- fashion
- trend
- craze/fad
- the latest thing
- vogue

fashion /ˈfæʃən/ [n C] a style of clothes, hair, behaviour etc that is fashionable **latest fashion** (=the newest styles of clothes) *I always find it hard to keep up with the latest fashions.* | **fashion in clothes/music etc** *changing fashions in popular music* | **fashion for doing sth** *Who started this fashion for wearing old army clothes?*

trend /trend/ [n C] a way of doing something or a way of thinking that is becoming fashionable: *A lot of the students here don't think for themselves, they just follow the latest trends.* | **+ in** *Today we'll be examining the latest trends in kitchen design*

craze/fad /kreɪz, fæd/ [n C] a fashion, activity, type of music etc that suddenly becomes very popular, but only remains popular for a short time: *A new fit-*

ness craze from Australia is rapidly catching on. | *To no one's surprise, the macarena proved to be a short-lived fad.*

the latest thing /ðə ˌleɪtɪ̈st ˈθɪŋ/ [n phrase] the most fashionable and newest thing to do, wear, or have: *The latest thing is to wear only white clothes.* | *No matter how expensive, he always has to do the latest thing.* | **+ in** *I can remember when eight-track tapes were the latest thing in music.*

vogue /vəʊg/ [n C] a style of music, clothes, art etc that is fashionable with a particular group of people: *People's fondness for wearing black and other dark colours was a vogue I never really liked.* | *a vogue for the paintings of Claude Lorraine*

7 the business of making and selling fashionable clothes

- fashion

fashion /ˈfæʃən/ [n U] *He's one of the best-known designers in the world of fashion.* | *a fashion designer* | *a fashion show*

8 not fashionable

- out of fashion
- go out
- unfashionable
- uncool
- date

out of fashion /ˌaʊt əv ˈfæʃən/ [v phrase] no longer fashionable – use this especially about clothes and music: *It seems like all the clothes I buy are out of fashion by the time I wear them.* | **go/fall out of fashion** *Rock'n'Roll began in the fifties and has never really gone out of fashion.*

go out /ˌgəʊ ˈaʊt/ [phr v I] especially British to stop being fashionable: *Jogging went out when it was found to be harmful for the joints.* | *I can't believe you're wearing those shoes – they went out years ago!*

unfashionable /ʌnˈfæʃənəbəl/ [adj] not fashionable – use this especially about people's ideas, beliefs, and way of life: *She lives in an unfashionable part of West London.* | *Socialism became unfashionable after the collapse of the Berlin Wall.*

uncool /ʌnˈkuːl/ [adj] spoken informal not fashionable, interesting, or attractive – used especially by young people: *a really uncool place for a holiday* | **it's uncool to do sth** *Nowadays it's considered very uncool to wear fur.*

date /deɪt/ [v I] to gradually become unfashionable, and be replaced with more modern styles, methods, ideas etc: *The trouble with high fashion clothes is that they date very quickly.* | *Certain styles of music will never date, and will always be popular.* —**dated** [adj] fashionable in the past but looking or seeming old-fashioned now: *I loved that album when I bought it a few years ago but it sounds really dated today.* | *The production was excellent but the costumes looked dated.*

fast

RELATED WORDS

opposite: **slow**

▸ *see also* **speed, hurry, run, time**

1 moving or travelling fast

- fast
- quick
- swift
- at high speed
- at top speed
- at breakneck speed
- flat out
- like lightning
- at speed

fast /fɑːst‖fæst/ [adv] *Don't drive so fast – there's ice on the road.* | *The new fighter aircraft flies almost twice as fast as the old one.* | *She walked faster and faster, then started to run.* | **as fast as you can** *He ran home as fast as he could.* —**fast** [adj] able to go fast: *When I was a kid, I was the fastest boy in my class.*

quick /kwɪk/ [adv] spoken use this to tell someone to come or go somewhere quickly: *Come quick, your brother's on TV.* | *You'll have to walk quicker than that if you want to keep up with me.*

swift /swɪft/ [adj] written moving fast with a continuous, flowing movement – used especially in literature: *The horses ran along the track at a swift trot.* | *We had to steer our ship through the swift currents of the Bering Straits.* —**swiftly** [adv] *White clumps of cloud were moving swiftly across the sky.* —**swiftness** [n U] *These animals are unrivalled for their grace and swiftness.*

at high speed /ət ˌhaɪ ˈspiːd/ [adv] moving or working very fast – use this about cars, trains, machines etc: *Two cars raced past him at high speed.* | *a metal disk revolving at high speed* —**high-speed** [adj] *You can travel by high-speed train from Paris to Brussels.* | *a high-speed drill*

at top speed /ət ˌtɒp ˈspiːd‖-ˌtɑːp-/ [adv] if a vehicle moves **at top speed**, it moves as fast as it can go – use this especially when a situation is urgent and someone has to get somewhere very fast: *They headed east at top speed in pursuit of the enemy ship.* | *At top speed, the Pave Hawk helicopter can travel 221 miles per hour.*

at breakneck speed /ət ˌbreɪknek ˈspiːd/ [adv] travelling dangerously fast: *It took us an hour to get there, driving at breakneck speed.* | *Jenny stepped onto her skis and sped off at breakneck speed down the glistening, white mountain.*

flat out /ˌflæt ˈaʊt/ [adv] at the fastest speed possible when using all the strength or power there is: *Going flat out, the BMW 325 will reach a speed of 140 miles per hour.* | *The exercise involved running flat out for two minutes and then resting for one minute.*

like lightning /laɪk ˈlaɪtnɪŋ/ [adv] moving extremely fast, often with a single sudden movement: *Somewhere a dog barked and, like lightning, the cat darted into some bushes.* | *Her foot slipped on the smooth tiles but Mitch moved like lightning and caught her before she fell.*

at speed /ət ˈspiːd/ [adv] formal if a car or train is travelling **at speed**, it is travelling fast: *The train was already travelling at speed when she tried to open the carriage door.*

2 fast cars/planes/trains

- fast
- high-speed
- supersonic

fast /fɑːst‖fæst/ [adj] *Dean always loved fast cars and expensive clothes.* | *Rosa caught the fast train to London.* | *Boeing's new plane is faster and more luxurious than anything else they have ever produced.*

high-speed /ˌhaɪ ˈspiːd◂/ [adj only before noun] **high-speed train/computer/drill etc** a train, computer etc that moves or operates very fast: *The era of high-speed jet travel began after the end of World War II.* | *Journey times have been reduced considerably since the introduction of high-speed trains.*

supersonic /ˌsuːpəˈsɒnɪk◂, ˌsjuː-‖ˌsuːpərˈsɑː-/ [adj usually before noun] **supersonic aircraft/travel/flight etc** faster than the speed of sound: *Concorde is capable of travelling at supersonic speeds.* | *Thanks to supersonic travel, busy executives can attend meetings in New York and be back in London the same day.*

3 doing things quickly or happening quickly

- quickly
- quick
- fast
- rapid
- swift
- speedy
- prompt
- meteoric
- at an alarming rate
- in a flash

quickly /ˈkwɪkli/ [adv] doing things **quickly** or happening **quickly**, without taking much time: *She undressed quickly and got into bed.* | *It's important to realize how quickly this disease can spread.* | *Quickly fry the onions, then add the meat.*

quick /kwɪk/ [adj] a **quick** movement or action is one that you do quickly or one that only takes a short time: *I'll just take a quick shower.* | *That was quick – have you finished already?* | *I had to make a quick decision.* | **be quick** (=use this when you are telling someone to hurry) *You'll have to be quick – we don't have much time.*

fast /fɑːst‖fæst/ [adv] if you work, talk, or write **fast**, you do it quickly: *Don't talk so fast – I can't understand what you're saying.* | *We're working as fast as we can.*

rapid /ˈræpɪ̈d/ [adj usually before noun] a **rapid** change, increase, or improvement is one that happens much more quickly than usual: *a rapid increase in the population* | *She made a rapid recovery after her operation.* | *Adolescence is a period of great and rapid change.* —**rapidly** [adv] *the rapidly changing world of computer technology*

swift /swɪft/ [adj] happening or done very quickly and without any delay: *Punishment of the protesters was swift and severe.* | *Swift fashion changes mean that the shop has to change its stock every six to eight weeks.*

speedy /ˈspiːdi/ [adj only before noun] a **speedy** return, reply, reaction, etc is one that is done or made successfully, as quickly and efficiently as possible: *We are working to ensure the safe and speedy return of all the refugees to their homes.* | *Thousands of letters and telegrams arrived wishing Nikolai a speedy recovery from his surgery.* —**speedily** [adv] *The mayor's proposal was speedily approved by the town council.*

prompt /prɒmpt‖prɑːmpt/ [adj usually before noun] a **prompt** action, reply, delivery etc is one that is done without delay because quick action is needed: *A major disaster was prevented by the prompt action of the safety officer.* | *It is important to ensure prompt delivery of goods that customers order.* —**promptly** [adv] *Store the shellfish in a covered container and refrigerate them promptly.*

meteoric /ˌmiːtiˈɒrɪk◂‖-ˈɔːrɪk◂, -ˈɑːrɪk◂/ [adj] **meteoric rise/career** achieving success extremely quickly and suddenly: *The film tells the story of Lee's meteoric rise from North Dakota radio singer to jazz legend.*

at an alarming rate /ət ən əˌlɑːʳmɪŋ ˈreɪt/ [adv] if something happens **at an alarming rate**, it happens so quickly that it makes people very worried: *The Amazonian rainforest is disappearing at an alarming rate.* | *The number of people dying from lung cancer has increased at an alarming rate.*

in a flash /ɪn ə ˈflæʃ/ [adv] use this to say that something happens extremely quickly and suddenly, so that you almost do not notice what is happening: *He was gone in a flash.* | *In a flash Atticus was up and standing over him.* | *Joel slipped but was on his feet in a flash.*

4 to move very fast in a particular direction

- race/tear
- rush/dash
- fly
- dart
- streak
- whizz
- zoom
- speed
- be really moving

race/tear /reɪs, teəʳ/ [v I] to go somewhere as fast as you can **race back/up/into etc** *Hearing the children's screams, she raced back to the house.* | *A police car came racing down the road.* | **tear away/up/across etc** *She tore across the lobby, then up three flights of stairs.* | *Just before the explosion, a man came tearing across the street.*

rush/dash /rʌʃ, dæʃ/ [v I] to go somewhere very quickly because you are in a hurry **rush out/around/into etc** *Everyone rushed out into the street to see what was happening.* | *People were rushing past me on their way to work.* | **dash into/around/to etc** *Pam dashed into the store just as it was closing.* | *The boys dashed across the road and disappeared into the woods.*

fly /flaɪ/ [v I] to travel or go somewhere extremely quickly **fly past/up/along etc** *As I slowed down another car flew past me and turned to the left.* | *The bus was flying along when suddenly the driver slammed on the brakes.*

dart /dɑːʳt/ [v I] to run, fly, or swim with a sudden quick movement **dart through/back/across etc** *I could see small silvery fish darting through the water.* | *As the rain began to fall harder, I darted into the first shop I could find.*

streak /striːk/ [v I] written if someone or something **streaks** somewhere, they run or fly there so fast that you can hardly see them **streak across/past/away etc** *Two aircraft streaked across the sky.* | *I caught a glimpse of a man streaking away into the shadows.*

whizz /wɪz/ [v I] to move extremely quickly through the air or along a road, making a loud high noise **whizz past/by/through etc** *A bullet whizzed past my ear.* | *I stared out the window, watching as kids on bicycles and skateboards whizzed by.*

zoom /zuːm/ [v I] if a car, bus, plane etc **zooms** somewhere, it moves there extremely fast, making a loud noise with its engine **zoom past/through/over etc** *The plane zoomed low over the airfield.* | *A fire engine zoomed past us.*

speed /spiːd/ [v I] to move somewhere very quickly, especially in a vehicle **speed along/by/towards etc** *An ambulance sped by on its way to an accident.* | *Small patrol boats sped along the shore.*

be really moving /biː ˌrɪəli ˈmuːvɪŋ/ [v phrase] use this to say that someone or something is going extremely fast: *That car must have been really moving when it hit the van.*

5 to move or work faster

- go faster
- speed up
- pick up/gather speed
- accelerate
- quicken your pace
- gain/gather momentum

go faster /ˌgəʊ ˈfɑːstəʳ‖-ˈfæs-/ [v phrase] *Could you go a little faster? We don't want to miss our plane.* | **move/work etc faster** *You'll have to work a lot faster than this.* | **faster and faster** (=more and more quickly) *I could feel my heart beating faster and faster.*

speed up /ˌspiːd ˈʌp/ [phr v I/T] to make something happen more quickly: *Nancy, if you don't speed up we'll be here until midnight.* | **speed sth up** *I'll phone the manager and get them to speed things up.* | **speed up sth** *The company announced they're speeding up plans to expand the site.*

pick up/gather speed /ˌpɪk ʌp, ˌgæðəʳ ˈspiːd/ [v phrase] if a vehicle, especially a large vehicle **picks up speed** or **gathers speed**, it starts to gradually move faster: *Francis leaned back in his seat as the plane picked up speed.* | *The truck was already moving, gathering speed with a deep-throated roar.*

accelerate /əkˈseləreɪt/ [v I] if a vehicle or driver **accelerates**, they go faster, especially suddenly: *The Ferrari Mondial can accelerate from zero to 60 mph in 6.3 seconds.* | *The truck's wheels skidded on the snow as the driver accelerated forward.*

quicken your pace /ˌkwɪkən jɔːʳ ˈpeɪs/ [v phrase] written to begin to walk faster – use this especially in stories or descriptions of events: *Suddenly realizing he was late, he quickened his pace towards the hotel.* | *'I have some questions to ask you, Mr Murray,' said the reporter, quickening his pace to keep up with me.*

gain/gather momentum /ˌgeɪn, ˌgæðəʳ məʊˈmentəm/ [v phrase] if something **gains** or **gathers momentum**, it travels faster and faster, especially going down a hill, because it is pushed forward by the force of its own weight: *Gradually the train gathered momentum, and within seconds it was moving at top speed.* | *The slope was getting steeper and their sledge was gaining momentum all the time.*

6 to move as fast as someone else

- catch up
- be gaining on
- keep up

catch up /ˌkætʃ ˈʌp / [phr v I/T] to move forward fast enough to reach someone who was in front of you going in the same direction: *We need to start cycling faster or we'll never catch up.* | **+ with** *Go on ahead. I'll catch up with you later.* | *The police car caught up with the stolen van after a long chase.*

be gaining on /biː ˈgeɪnɪŋ ɒn/ [v phrase] to be getting closer and closer to someone that you are chasing or trying to pass, because you are moving faster than they are: *Run faster – they're gaining on us!* | *Seeing the van was gaining on him, he turned suddenly onto a dirt road.*

keep up /ˌkiːp ˈʌp / [phr v I] to succeed in moving as fast as someone else, when they are moving very quickly: *Maggie had a stone in her shoe and was finding it hard to keep up.* | **+ with** *Slow down! I can't keep up with you.* | *She had difficulty keeping up with J.D.'s long, quick strides.*

7 to move faster than someone or something else

- pull ahead
- leave sb behind
- leave sb standing

pull ahead /ˌpʊl əˈhed/ [phr v I] to pass another vehicle on the road and move in front of it because you are going faster: *I turned around and saw that, out of the dust and the crowd, another car was pulling ahead to join us.* | **+ of** *With the finish line in sight, Wallace pulled ahead of the pack and drove to victory.*

leave sb behind /ˌliːv (sb) bɪˈhaɪnd/ [phr v T] to move far in front of someone who cannot run, walk, drive etc as fast as you: *We were all running to catch the bus, but the others had longer legs and gradually left me behind.* | **leave sb way behind** (=a long way behind) *Dinah urged her horse on until she had left all the other riders way behind.*

leave sb standing /ˌliːv (sb) ˈstændɪŋ/ [v phrase] informal to move very far in front of someone, especially in a race, because you are much faster than them: *Collins accelerated around the final turn and left the other runners standing.*

8 a course of study that you do quickly

- rapid
- intensive
- crash course

rapid /ˈræpɪ̈d/ [adj only before noun] *The college offers a rapid programme of training for librarians.* | *Rapid learning: Learn to speak a new language in 12 weeks!*

intensive /ɪnˈtensɪv/ [adj] an **intensive** course of study is one in which you are taught a lot in a short time: *Before moving to Paris, Michael went on an intensive course to improve his French.* | *After a brief period of intensive training, I was allowed to make my first parachute jump.*

crash course /ˈkræʃ kɔːʳs/ [n C] a course of study in which you learn a particular skill in a very short time in order to prepare yourself for a job **+ in** *We offer crash courses in word processing.* | **crash course** *Students lacking math and science skills take a seven-week crash course during the summer.*

fasten/unfasten

RELATED WORDS

- *see also* **tight, tie/untie, attach, join, stick, clothes**

1 to fasten something

- fasten
- button/button up
- zip up
- do up
- tie
- buckle up

fasten /ˈfɑːsən‖ˈfæ-/ [v T] to join together the two sides of a piece of clothing, bag, belt etc, so that it is closed: *Fasten your coat – it's cold outside.* | *He fastened the bracelet for her.* | *Ella fastened her blouse with shaking fingers.* —**fastened** [adj not before noun] *Please keep your seat belts fastened.*

button/button up /ˈbʌtn, ˌbʌtn ˈʌp/ [v T/phr v T] to fasten the buttons on a piece of clothing: *He began buttoning his shirt and putting on his tie.* | *Stone buttoned up his heavy jacket.* | **button sth up/button**

up sth *She buttoned her cardigan up all the way to her neck.* | *I adjusted my tie and buttoned up my coat.* —**buttoned up** [adj] *It was cold and his coat was completely buttoned up.*

zip up [phr v T] ALSO **zip** [v T] especially American /ˌzɪp ˈʌp, zɪp/ to fasten clothes, bags etc with a zip: *I can't zip up these jeans – they're too tight.* | *Can you zip my dress for me?* | **zip sth up** *She took some money out of her purse and quickly zipped it up again.* | **zip up sth** *Roger zipped up the battered black case he carried his guitar in.* —**zipped up** [adj not before noun] *My sleeping bag was fully zipped up.*

do up /ˌduː ˈʌp/ [phr v T] British especially spoken to fasten clothes, or the buttons, zips etc on clothes **do up sth** *Come on then, do up your coat and let's go.* | *When I walked into the room, Allen was doing up his trousers.* | **do sth up** *I can't do this zip up – it's stuck.* | *Are your shoelaces done up properly?* —**done up** /ˌdʌn ˈʌp/ [adj not before noun] *The toggles on his duffel coat were done up wrongly.*

tie /taɪ/ [v T] to fasten something by making a knot: *She tied a scarf around her neck.* | *Do you know how to tie a bow tie?*

buckle up [phr v I] ALSO **buckle** [v T] American /ˌbʌkəl ˈʌp, ˈbʌkəl/ to fasten your seatbelt in a car: *Eighty percent of motorists now buckle up, studies show.* | *Nancy got behind the wheel and buckled up.* | *The new law will require passengers in the rear seats of automobiles to buckle their seatbelts.*

2 to unfasten something

- unfasten
- undo
- unbutton
- unzip
- untie
- loosen
- open

unfasten /ʌnˈfɑːsən‖-ˈfæ-/ [v T] to open the two sides of a piece of clothing, bag, belt etc: *It was hot in the waiting-room, so I unfastened my coat.* | *Jack unfastened his seatbelt and stepped out of the car.* —**unfastened** [adj not before noun] *The back of her dress was unfastened.*

undo /ʌnˈduː/ [v T] to unfasten clothes or unfasten buttons, zips etc on clothes: *My fingers were so cold that I couldn't undo the buttons.* | *Rosie undid her necklace and put it on the bedside table.* —**undone** /ʌnˈdʌn/ [adj not before noun] *Your zip's undone!* | **come undone** (=become unfastened) *One of his shoelaces had come undone.*

unbutton /ʌnˈbʌtn/ [v T] to unfasten the buttons on a piece of clothing: *She slowly unbuttoned her blouse.* | *Father Poole began to unbutton his overcoat.* —**unbuttoned** [adj not before noun] *His shirt was completely unbuttoned.*

unzip /ʌnˈzɪp/ [v T] to unfasten clothes, bags etc by unfastening a zip: *She unzipped the case and took out a thick file.* | *He unzipped his jacket and flung it on a chair.* —**unzipped** [adj] *An unzipped bag was sitting on one of the benches.*

untie /ʌnˈtaɪ/ [v T] to unfasten the knot that fastens shoes, a tie, a scarf etc: *He untied his right shoe first.* | *Amy untied her apron and folded it neatly.* —**untied** [adj] *He's always walking around with his shoelaces untied.*

loosen /ˈluːsən/ [v T] to unfasten clothes a little in order to make yourself more comfortable: *I'd eaten so much that I had to loosen my belt.* | *Carter took off his jacket and loosened his tie.*

open /ˈəʊpən/ [adj] a shirt, bag etc that is **open** is not fastened: *It was very hot and the men had their shirts open to the waist.* | *Emily realised that her handbag was open and her money gone.* | **come open** (=become open accidentally) *Her blouse came open in front of a nationwide TV audience!*

fat

RELATED WORDS

opposite: **thin**

▸ *see also* **weigh, strong, big, wide, thick, eat, greedy**

1 words for describing someone who is fat

- fat
- overweight
- big/large
- plump
- chubby
- portly
- hefty
- beefy
- burly
- fatty/fatso

fat /fæt/ [adj] having too much flesh on your body. It is rude to tell someone that they are fat: *Peter was a fat little boy.* | *I'm getting too fat for my clothes.* | *After thirty years, Teddy looked just the same, only a little fatter.* | *Most fat people simply eat too much by normal standards.* | *Though she weighed only six stone, she thought she was fat.*

overweight /ˌəʊvəʳˈweɪt◂/ [adj] too fat, especially so that you need to lose some weight in order to be more healthy or attractive: *The doctor said I was slightly overweight and that I needed more exercise.* | *The majority of overweight people who diet tend to gain the weight back within a few years.* | **5 kilos/10 pounds etc overweight** *My mother is about 50 pounds overweight.* | **grossly overweight** (=extremely overweight) *People who are grossly overweight are more likely to suffer from high blood pressure.*

big/large /bɪg, lɑːʳdʒ/ [adj] fat – use this especially when you do not want to say 'fat' because it would be impolite: *Even though she's big, Rosemary is an attractive woman.* | *It's often difficult for large people to find fashionable clothes that fit them.* | *Mrs. Medlock is a large woman, with a very red face and bright black eyes.* | *He runs quite fast for a big man.*

plump /plʌmp/ [adj] fat, especially in a pleasant and attractive way: *Stevie is a plump healthy-looking child.* | *Frieda's mother was a plump, cheerful woman, quick with a laugh.* | *He's a little on the plump side, but nevertheless quite handsome.*

chubby /ˈtʃʌbi/ [adj] someone, especially a small child, who is **chubby**, is fat in a pleasant, healthy-looking way: *The baby was pink and chubby.* | *Who's that chubby little girl with the dark hair?*

portly /ˈpɔːʳtli/ [adj] someone, especially a fairly old man, who is **portly** is fat and round – used especially in literature: *The bishop was a dignified, portly man, with thinning white hair.* | *the portly figure of General von Hindenburg*

hefty /ˈhefti/ [adj] big and fat, but also tall and strong: *Both of Myra's sons were hefty, energetic boys.* | *The mechanic was a big hefty man who could lift up the front of a truck with his bare hands.*

beefy /ˈbiːfi/ [adj] strong but also a little fat and unattractive: *The second prisoner was a fat-faced beefy fellow who smelled of sweat.* | *Amanda and Tina were both beefy, sporty types.*

burly /ˈbɜːʳli/ [adj] a **burly** man is big, strong, and heavy, in a way that may make you feel nervous: *The farmer was a big, burly man with a red face.*

fatty/fatso spoken informal ALSO **lard ass** American spoken /ˈfæti, ˈfætsəʊ, ˈlɑːʳd æs/ [n C] a rude word used for a fat person: *Hey! Fatso! Pull up a couple of chairs!*

2 extremely fat

- obese
- obesity

obese /əʊˈbiːs/ [adj] extremely fat in a way that is dangerous to your health: *Glenda is not just fat, she's obese.* | *a special summer camp for obese children and teens* | **clinically obese** (=obese according to medical measurements) *He may not be clinically obese, but he certainly needs to lose a lot of weight.*

obesity /əʊˈbiːsəti/ [n U] the condition of being too fat in a way that is dangerous to your health – used especially in medical contexts: *Obesity can lead to heart disorders and other health problems.* | *The program is aimed at reducing obesity among women.*

3 fat and not very tall

- dumpy
- tubby
- stout

dumpy /ˈdʌmpi/ [adj] someone, especially a woman or child, who is **dumpy**, is short and fat: *Clara was a plain, dumpy woman, several years older than her husband.* | *In his youth, William had been a dumpy little boy who ate too many sweets.* | *I think this skirt makes me look dumpy.*

tubby /ˈtʌbi/ [adj] someone who is **tubby** is short and has a fat, round stomach: *The banker was a tubby, jolly-looking man.* | *He's getting a bit tubby – too much of his wife's cooking I expect.*

stout /staʊt/ [adj] someone, especially a middle-aged person, who is **stout** is short and fat: *A stout woman in a tweed coat was standing outside the door.* | *Amy was now stout and matronly, the mother of three children.*

4 a part of the body that is fat

- fat
- plump
- chubby
- podgy/pudgy
- flabby
- full

fat /fæt/ [adj] *Sally hates going swimming – she thinks her legs are too fat.* | *The colonel rubbed his fat stomach, reaching for something from the table to put into his mouth.* | *My stomach's much fatter than yours.*

plump /plʌmp/ [adj] pleasantly fat: *The doctor's wife had a plump face and a small mouth.* | *Paula had silver bracelets on her plump arms.*

chubby /ˈtʃʌbi/ [adj] fat and round in an attractive way: *The baby reached out with its chubby little fingers.* | *Mark's cheeks were slightly chubby.*

podgy/pudgy /ˈpɒdʒi‖ˈpɑː-, ˈpʌdʒi/ [adj] small and fat, especially in an amusing way: *His pudgy little fingers were covered in chocolate.* | *Elsie had a large body and a podgy face.*

flabby /ˈflæbi/ [adj] covered in soft loose fat in a way that looks unattractive: *Her body was getting old and flabby.* | *John's flabby white thighs wobbled as he walked across the beach.*

full /fʊl/ [adj usually before noun] fat and round in an attractive way: *Joanna's full red lips were fixed in an inviting smile.* | *A black necklace hung down over her full breasts.*

5 a fat stomach

- paunch
- pot belly
- beer gut
- spare tyre
- middle-age spread

paunch /pɔːntʃ/ [n C] a man who has a **paunch** has a large stomach: *You're getting a paunch, did you know that?* | *Merv lay back in his chair with his hands crossed above his paunch, listening to the radio.* | *Wally crossed the mirrored lobby, sucking in his paunch as he caught sight of himself.*

pot belly /ˈpɒt ˌbeli‖ˈpɑːt-/ [n C] a round stomach that sticks out at the front, especially when this is the result of eating or drinking too much: *Larry was just a regular guy: short, with a pot belly and moustache.* | *You really should do something about that pot belly of yours.* —**pot-bellied** [adj] *Our history teacher was a balding, pot-bellied man of about 50.* | *pot-bellied politicians, puffing cigars*

beer gut /ˈbɪəʳ ˌgʌt/ [n C] informal a fat stomach caused by drinking too much beer: *His beer gut was popping the buttons on his shirt.* | *At only seventeen, Lonny already had the beginnings of a beer gut.*

spare tyre /ˌspeəʳ ˈtaɪəʳ/ [n C] British informal a ring of fat around the waist: *You should go on a diet – look at that spare tyre!*

middle-age spread /ˌmɪdl eɪdʒ ˈspred/ [n phrase] the fat around the waist that people gradually get as they grow older: *A lot of people start to get middle-age spread once they pass 30.*

6 to become fatter

- put on weight
- gain weight
- fill out

put on weight /ˌpʊt ɒn ˈweɪt/ [v phrase] to get fatter and heavier: *John's put on a lot of weight recently, hasn't he?* | **put on 5 kilos/2 lbs etc** *I put on several pounds while I was on holiday, so now I'm on a strict diet.*

gain weight /ˌgeɪn ˈweɪt/ [v phrase] to become fatter and heavier, especially until you reach the weight you should be: *When I was young, I could eat all I wanted without gaining weight.* | **gain 2 kilos/4 lbs etc** *Ben's gained at least five kilos since he was born.*

fill out /ˌfɪl ˈaʊt/ [phr v I] to start getting fatter after being too thin: *Gerry was terribly thin when he came out of hospital, but he's filled out a lot since then.* | *Sue looks much healthier now and her face has started to fill out.*

7 to make someone fat

- fatten sb up
- fattening

fatten sb up /ˌfætn (sb) ˈʌp/ [phr v T] to make someone fatter because they are too thin – often used humorously: *The women in his family were always trying to fatten him up.*

fattening /ˈfætnɪŋ/ [adj] food that is **fattening** makes you fat: *I shouldn't have any more of this cake. It's way too fattening.* | *Grill the fish instead of frying it. It's less fattening that way.* | *Avoid fattening desserts – eat a piece of fruit instead.*

8 to make an animal fatter

- fatten up

fatten up /ˌfætn ˈʌp/ [phr v T] to make an animal fatter so that it will produce more meat **fatten up sth/fatten sth up** *The farmers are fattening up their cattle and getting them ready for market.*

father

RELATED WORDS

- *see also* **mother, child, baby, family, man**

1 father

- father
- dad
- daddy
- pop
- old man

father /ˈfɑːðəʳ/ [n C] *My father's a doctor.* | **+ of** *He's now the proud father of a three-week-old baby girl.* | *Larry Blake, a father of three children, was shot dead outside his home last night.*

dad /ˈdæd/ [n C] informal a name you use to talk to your father or to talk about someone else's father: *Was your dad angry when you got home?* | *Can I borrow your car, Dad?* | *My dad retired ten years ago.*

daddy /ˈdædi/ [n C] a name for a father – used especially by young children or when you are talking to young children: *Where's your daddy?* | *Daddy, can I have a drink, please?* | *Go and ask Daddy if he'll give you a ride to school.*

pop /pɒp‖pɑːp/ [n singular] American informal a name you call your father: *I helped Pop fix the gate this morning.* | *Relax, Pop, I'll have the car back by midnight.*

old man /ˌəʊld ˈmæn/ [n singular] informal father – use this to talk about your father or someone else's father: *My old man never could understand why I married Doris.* | **the old man** (=my father) *I'm going to visit the old man next week.*

2 when someone is a father

- fatherhood
- become a father
- father

fatherhood /ˈfɑːðəʳhʊd/ [n U] *Jerry doesn't take the responsibilities of fatherhood very seriously.* | *Fatherhood has been the greatest challenge of my life.*

become a father /bɪˌkʌm ə ˈfɑːðəʳ/ [v phrase] if a man **becomes a father**, a woman has his baby: *I didn't really care about what was going on in the world until I became a father.* | *Just think about it – you don't really want to become a father while you're still in your teens, do you?*

father /ˈfɑːðəʳ/ [v T] written if a man **fathers** a child, a woman has his baby: *He fathered eight daughters and three sons.* | *Bill was told he would never be able to father children.*

3 like a father

- paternal
- fatherly

paternal /pəˈtɜːʳnl/ [adj] **paternal** feelings are like the feelings that a good father has for his children: *Although he had no children of his own, he took a kind of paternal interest in Katie's progress at school.*

fatherly /ˈfɑːðəʳli/ [adj] behaving in a kind way towards someone who is younger than you, which shows you care about them a lot, as if you were their father: *Do you mind if I give you some fatherly advice?* | *From the plane window he could still see the two young women, and gave them a fatherly wave.*

fault

WHAT'S HERE

- **sth wrong** see **1 to 2**
- **when sb causes sth bad to happen** see **3 to 4**

sth wrong

RELATED WORDS

opposite: **working**

- *see also* **problem, broken/not broken**

1 something wrong with a machine, system, plan etc

- fault
- defect
- problem
- trouble
- flaw/weakness
- bug
- glitch
- virus
- be sth wrong with/be sth the matter with

fault /fɔːlt/ [n C] something wrong with one of the parts of a machine that prevents it from working properly: *Quality control staff are employed to check for any faults.* | **+ in** *I think there's a fault in one of the loudspeakers.* | *The fault could be either in the tape or in the VCR.* | **electrical/mechanical/technical etc fault** *The rocket launch was delayed because of a technical fault.*

defect /ˈdiːfekt, dɪˈfekt/ [n C] something wrong with a product or machine, especially caused by a mistake in the way it was made or designed: *All the computers are checked for defects before they leave the factory.* | **+ in** *A defect in the braking system caused several accidents before the car was recalled.* | *Investigators found a defect in the design of the ship.*

problem /ˈprɒbləm‖ˈprɑː-/ [n C] something that stops a machine or system from working normally: *Please call 5326 if you have any computer problems.* | **+ with** *There seems to be some kind of problem with the heaters.* | **+ in** *Engineers were unable to find the source of the problem in the spacecraft's cooling system.*

trouble /ˈtrʌbəl/ [n U] something wrong with a machine, car etc, especially when you do not know exactly what is causing it: *If you have engine trouble, park as far to the side of the road as possible.* | **have trouble** *If you used the same tape later and had no trouble with the picture, the problem is probably* *in the VCR.* | **+ with** *We've been having some trouble with the air-conditioning.* | **the trouble** (=the particular thing causing the problem) *I think we've found out what the trouble is.*

flaw/weakness /flɔː, 'wiːknɪ̆s/ [n C] something wrong with a plan, system, or set of ideas, which may make the whole thing useless or not effective: *His plan seemed foolproof, but I was sure there was a flaw somewhere.* | *The program has serious weaknesses, and I would avoid using it.* | **+ in** *There are several obvious flaws in his argument.* | *One major weakness in the study is that it is based on a very small sample.*

bug /bʌg/ [n C] a small problem in a computer or a computer system: *The program suffers from some minor bugs, but is still better than the first version.* | *Some chips contained a bug that caused computers to crash frequently.*

glitch /glɪtʃ/ [n C] a small fault in the way something works, that can usually be corrected easily: *As the glitches are found and corrected, the process is speeding up.* | **+ in** *A glitch in the system shut down the telephone service to nearly 6 million customers.* | **technical/mechanical etc glitch** *NASA officials found a way to work around the technical glitch on the Galileo spacecraft.*

virus /'vaɪərəs/ [n C] a set of instructions that someone puts secretly into other people's computers, that can destroy information stored in them or stop them working correctly: *The disk was accidentally infected with a virus called 'Stoned III'.* | *Computer users from around the world reported that the virus had invaded their systems.* | *an anti-virus program*

be sth wrong with/be sth the matter with /biː (sth) 'rɒŋ wɪð‖-'rɔːŋ-, biː (sth) ðə 'mætəʳ wɪð/ [v phrase] spoken say this when there is a problem in a machine, part of a car etc, but you do not know exactly what it is: *I think there's something wrong with the clutch in my car.* | *I don't know what's the matter with it, but I can't get it to work.* | *There are programs that will help you figure out what's wrong with your PC, and help you correct it.*

2 a fault in someone's character

- fault
- flaw/weakness
- shortcomings

fault /fɔːlt/ [n C usually plural] a bad point in someone's character: *The secret of a good relationship is to accept the other person's faults, and not try to make them change.* | **have his/her/their faults** *She's my best friend and I love her dearly, but she has her faults.* | **for all his/her/their faults** (=even though they have these faults) *For all his faults, he was a good father.*

flaw/weakness /flɔː, 'wiːknɪ̆s/ [n C] a small fault in someone's character or a lack of a good quality such as courage or good judgement: *The flaw that leads to Othello's downfall is his jealousy.* | *The biographer believes that flaws in Kennedy's character weakened his leadership of the nation.* | *Despite his weaknesses, he was a fair man.*

shortcomings /'ʃɔːʳtkʌmɪŋz/ [n plural] the faults in someone's character – use this especially when you are saying that the person has good qualities too: *He acknowledged his own shortcomings, including at times being stubborn and a little vain.* | *Whatever his shortcomings, Hamilton was one of the great men in American history.*

when sb causes sth bad to happen

RELATED WORDS

see also **blame, accuse, criticize**

3 when something bad is someone's fault

- be sb's fault
- be to blame
- be responsible
- be at fault
- only have yourself to blame
- blame yourself

be sb's fault /biː (sb's) 'fɔːlt/ [v phrase] if something **is someone's fault**, they are responsible for it, especially because they made a mistake: *He played very well, and it is not his fault we lost.* | **be sb's own fault** (=when someone is responsible for something bad that happens to them) *Marie failed the exam, but it was her own fault – she didn't do any work.* | **+ (that)** *I'm so sorry. It's my fault that we're so late.* | **+ for doing sth** *Of course she was angry – but it's your fault for telling her about the whole thing in the first place.* | **the fault of sb** *Suggesting that our problems are the fault of someone else won't solve anything.*

be to blame /biː tə 'bleɪm/ [v phrase] if someone or something **is to blame** for a bad situation, they caused it: *When kids do badly at school, it's not always the teachers who are to blame.* | **+ for** *Some people think television is to blame for a lot of the problems in modern society.* | *She was as much to blame for the breakup of their marriage as he was.*

be responsible /biː rɪ'spɒnsɪ̆bəl‖-'spɑːn-/ [v phrase] if someone **is responsible** for an accident, crime etc, they caused it and they should be punished for it: *The police are trying to find out who was responsible.* | **+ for** *There is a reward for information leading to the arrest of the people responsible for the explosion.* | **feel responsible** (=think that something is your fault) *I knew the accident wasn't really my fault, but I can't help feeling a little responsible.*

be at fault /biː ət 'fɔːlt/ [v phrase] if someone, especially a group of people or an organization, **is at fault**, they are responsible for something bad that has happened because they did not behave correctly or did not take enough care: *The accident report found both drivers to be at fault.* | **+ for doing sth** *With regard to the chaos after the earthquake, many people believe the government is at fault for not responding quickly enough.*

only have yourself to blame /ˌəʊnli hæv jɔːʳ'self tə ˌbleɪm/ [v phrase not in progressive] if you **only have yourself to blame** for something bad that has happened, it is your own fault that it happened and you should not feel sorry for yourself: *His wife's left him but he only has himself to blame.* | **+ for doing sth** *I've only got myself to blame for losing the race.*

blame yourself /ˌbleɪm jɔːʳ'self/ [v phrase] to think that it is your fault that something bad has happened, so that you feel very upset or ashamed: *You mustn't blame yourself – it wasn't your fault.* | *Children sometimes feel responsible for their parents divorcing and blame themselves.* | **+ for** *He never stopped blaming himself for his wife's death.*

4 when something is not someone's fault

- be not sb's fault
- through no fault of your own
- not be to blame
- can't help it

be not sb's fault /biː nɒt (sb's) ˈfɔːlt/ [v phrase] if something **is not someone's fault**, they did not make it happen and they should not be blamed for it: *Try not to worry about it too much – it's not your fault.* | *She felt guilty, even though the accident wasn't her fault.* | **+ (that)** *It wasn't the builders' fault that the work wasn't finished on time.*

through no fault of your own /θruː nəʊ ˌfɔːlt əv jɔːr ˈəʊn/ [adv] if something bad happens **through no fault of your own**, it is not your fault that it happens but you suffer because of it: *The center exists to help those who have lost their jobs through no fault of their own.* | *Because of the budget cuts, some students, through no fault of their own, may have a hard time paying their way.*

not be to blame /nɒt biː tə ˈbleɪm/ [v phrase] to not be responsible for something bad that happens – use this especially when other people think you might have done something to make it happen: *The press won't leave him alone, but he wasn't really to blame.* | **+ for** *Hospital workers were not to blame for a nine-year-old's death, a court decided yesterday.* | *The report said that no one was to blame for the accident.*

can't help it /ˌkɑːnt ˈhelp ɪt‖ˌkænt-/ [v phrase] especially spoken use this to say that someone should not be blamed for something because they cannot stop it from happening: *'Stop walking up and down like that!' 'I can't help it – I'm really nervous.'* | *I tried not to cry but I just couldn't help it.* | **+ if** *He can't help it if they didn't understand what he was telling them to do.*

favourite

RELATED WORDS

- *see also* **like, best, prefer, delicious**

1 the one you like better than any others

- favourite
- like best
- preferred
- first choice
- preference

favourite British **/favorite** American /ˈfeɪvərɪ̈t/ [adj only before noun] your **favourite** colour, food, teacher etc is the one you like more than all other colours, types of food etc: *My favourite colour is purple.* | *Who is your favorite singer?* | *Proceeds from the concert will go to the singer's favorite charities.* —**favourite/favorite** [n C] the one thing that you like more than other things of the same kind: *I love all his films but 'Rashomon' is my favourite.* | *I made lasagna for dinner – your favorite.*

like best /ˌlaɪk ˈbest/ [v phrase] especially spoken to like something better than other things – use this especially when you are asking someone to choose or when you are choosing: *Which of these dresses do you like best?* | **like sth best** *I think I like the red one best.*

preferred /prɪˈfɜːʳd/ [adj only before noun] formal the **preferred** method, plan etc is the one that people think is the best: *Steaming is the preferred method of cooking in Central Asia.* | *Seventeen percent of likely voters picked Stark as their preferred candidate.*

first choice /ˌfɜːʳst ˈtʃɔɪs/ [n C] the thing or person you like best and would choose first when you have several to choose from: *Frances was our first choice as a name for the baby.* | *Parents choosing schools for their children are rarely given their first choice.* | **+ for** *Atkins was the producers' first choice for the part of the maid.* | **+ of** *Twenty-six percent of the students said that teaching was their first choice of occupations.*

preference /ˈprefərəns/ [n C] when someone likes one thing or person rather than another: *There are definite regional preferences amongst our clients.* | *Oil or vinegar may be added for a more bland or sharp sauce, according to your preference.* | **+ for** *Adams expressed her preference for New York, despite the fact that she's lived in California for six years.*

2 someone who is liked more than other people

- favourite
- teacher's pet
- blue-eyed boy/girl
- the darling of

favourite British **/favorite** American /ˈfeɪvərɪ̈t/ [n C] someone who is liked better, especially by someone in authority, than the others in a group, and who is often treated better: *Admit it, you were always Mom's favourite.* | *Of all my customers, Sherman was easily my favorite.*

teacher's pet /ˌtiːtʃəʳz ˈpet/ [n C usually singular] informal someone who is their teacher's favourite student, and who the other students do not like because of this: *By his own account, Huggins was a teacher's pet whose life revolved around his schoolwork.*

blue-eyed boy/girl /ˌbluː aɪd ˈbɔɪ, ˈgɜːʳl/ [n C usually singular] British informal someone who is treated better than anyone else by their teacher, employer, parent etc, because they think he is perfect and do not notice his faults: *Tom Cruise is Hollywood's blue-eyed boy at the moment.*

the darling of /ðə ˈdɑːʳlɪŋ ɒv/ [n phrase] written the person who a group of people like most, for example a political party or people who write for a particular newspaper: *For some strange reason Livingstone became the darling of the right-wing press.*

fed up

feeling tired, bored, or annoyed

RELATED WORDS

opposite: —— **excited/exciting, happy**

- *see also* **sad, boring/bored, angry, disappointed**

- be fed up
- be tired of
- be sick of
- have had enough
- have had it
- be pissed off
- be at the end of your tether
- jaded

be fed up /biː ˌfed ˈʌp/ [v phrase] to feel tired, bored, and annoyed, especially because something annoying keeps happening or something has continued for too long **+ with** *He tells me he's fed up with school. Maybe that's why his grades have been so bad.* | **be fed up with doing sth** *I'm fed up with watching what I eat.* | **get fed up** *He waited for two hours, then he got* *fed up and left.* | *I'm getting fed up with this cold weather.*

be tired of /biː ˈtaɪəʳd ɒv/ [v phrase] to be fed up because you have been doing something or have experienced something boring, annoying etc for too long: *He just seems to be tired of the whole thing.* | **be tired of doing sth** *Gabrielle was tired of staying at home with the children.* | **get tired of sth** *Well, if you get tired of life in the city, you can always come back home.* | *I'm getting tired of chicken for dinner every night.*

be sick of /biː ˈsɪk ɒv/ [v phrase] to be very fed up and annoyed, especially with a situation or someone's behaviour that has continued for much too long: *After living here for ten years, we're sick of Los Angeles.* | **be sick of doing sth** *I'm sick of living with my parents.* | **be sick and tired of sth/be sick to death of sth** (=use this when something is extremely annoying or boring) *You must be sick and tired of having to deal with other people's problems all day.* | *I'm sick to death of all these stupid questions about my private life.*

have had enough /həv ˌhæd ɪˈnʌf / [v phrase] if you **have had enough** of someone's behaviour, the way someone is treating you etc, you are very fed up with it and will not accept it any longer: *The work was boring and the office was depressing. By the end of the first week she had had enough.* | **+ of** *Stop interrupting. I've had just about enough of you and your stupid remarks.* | *After thirty years, MacMillan had had enough of management.*

have had it /həv ˈhæd ɪt/ [v phrase] spoken say this when you are so fed up with someone's behaviour or a situation that you cannot accept it any longer: *I've had it. I'm taking the kids and going to Mom's.* | **+ with** *She's looking for another job – she's just about had it with this place.* | **have had it up to here** *I tell you, I've just about had it up to here – what with all the staffing problems and now the computer breaking down. I feel like quitting.* | **have had it up to here with sb/sth** *Dave's had it up to here with the kids. They've been complaining and arguing all day.*

be pissed off /biː ˌpɪst ˈɒf/ [v phrase] informal to be very fed up – use this only in informal situations and to people you know well: *I think you'd better try and cheer her up. She's really pissed off.* | **+ with** *She's pissed off with him for calling her all the time.*

be at the end of your tether British **/be at the end of your rope** American /biː ət ði ˌend əv jɔːʳ ˈteðəʳ, biː ət ði ˌend əv jɔːʳ ˈrəʊp/ [v phrase] to be so worried, tired, and unhappy that you feel you can no longer deal with a difficult, unpleasant, or upsetting situation: *I had no money, my husband was sick, and I couldn't get a job. I was at the end of my tether.* | *She didn't know what to do to stop the baby crying – she was at the end of her rope.*

jaded /ˈdʒeɪdɪ̈d/ [adj] fed up with an activity or job because you have been doing it for a very long time and you no longer find it interesting or exciting: *After two years of the same routine I was feeling jaded.* | *The beauty of St. Petersburg will impress even the most jaded tourist.* | *Mick Jagger arrived at the airport looking jaded after almost a year of touring.*

feel

RELATED WORDS

- to stop yourself from having or showing a feeling *see* **stop (28)**
- *see also* **touch, expression on sb's face**

1 to feel hot/tired/hungry etc

- feel/be
- come over all
- experience

feel/be /fiːl, biː/ [v] **feel/be tired/hot/hungry etc** *I was very tired and I just wanted to sleep.* | *Stop the car – Ben feels sick!* | *I know you're hungry but you'll just have to wait until dinner.* | *If you're feeling hot, go ahead and open the window.* | **feel well/better** *'How do you feel?' 'I feel much better now I've had some sleep.'*

experience /ɪkˈspɪəriəns/ [v T] formal to have a feeling of pain, sickness etc: *He said that he had never experienced such pain before.* | *Many cancer patients experience nausea following chemotherapy.*

come over all /kʌm ˈəʊvər ɔːl/ [v phrase] British informal **come over all funny/weak/dizzy etc** to suddenly feel weak, tired, ill etc: *I was standing at the bus stop when suddenly I came over all dizzy.* | *I'm sorry. I missed what you said. I just came over all funny for a minute.*

2 a physical feeling of heat, cold, tiredness, hunger etc

- feeling
- sensation

feeling /ˈfiːlɪŋ/ [n C] a physical **feeling** of heat, cold, tiredness etc: *When he woke up, he was aware of a tight feeling in his chest.* | **+ of** *One symptom of this illness is a general feeling of ill-health and tiredness.*

sensation /senˈseɪʃən/ [n C] a physical feeling, especially one that is unclear or difficult to describe: *She felt a cold sensation as the icy water dripped down her back.* | *A common sign of brain tumours is a tingly, numb sensation in the toes and fingertips.* | **+ of** *The fear of pain can be worse than the sensation of pain.*

3 how something feels when you touch it

- feel

feel /fiːl/ [v] if something **feels** hot, soft, wet etc, this is the feeling it gives you when you touch it: *Your forehead feels very hot – let's check your temperature.* | *The marble felt cold and smooth against her cheek.* | **feel like sth** (=feel the same as) *The material feels just like silk.*

4 experiencing physical feelings more than most people

- feel the heat/cold

feel the heat/cold /ˌfiːl ðə ˈhiːt, ˈkəʊld/ [v phrase] to be affected by heat or cold more easily than most people, especially because you are old or because you are not used to it: *As I get older I feel the cold more and more.* | *It can get very hot in Spain at this* *time of year – those English tourists must really be feeling the heat.*

5 when you cannot feel anything in a part of your body

- numb
- have no feeling
- can't feel anything
- go to sleep

numb /nʌm/ [adj] if part of your body is **numb**, it does not feel anything, for example because it is very cold or because your blood is not reaching it: *His legs grew so numb he couldn't move.* | **go numb** (=become numb) *It was so cold my fingers had gone numb.*

have no feeling /hæv ˌnəʊ ˈfiːlɪŋ/ [v phrase not in progressive] to be unable to feel anything in a part of your body, usually permanently, and often because of an accident or illness: *After the stroke, he had no feeling in his left side.* | *When they found her the next morning, she had no feeling in her toes.*

can't feel anything /ˌkɑːnt fiːl ˈeniθɪŋ‖ˌkænt-/ [v phrase] to not be able to feel pain, heat, touch etc in part of your body especially because it is hurt in some way: *Since her motorbike accident, she can't feel anything below the neck.* | *The doctor pricked his toe with a pin, but he couldn't feel anything.*

go to sleep /ˌgəʊ tə ˈsliːp/ [v phrase] informal if a part of your body, such as your arm or foot **goes to sleep**, you have no feeling in it, especially because it has been in the same position for a long time: *Can you stop leaning on me please? My arm's gone to sleep.*

6 to feel happy/frightened/bored etc

- feel/be
- experience
- be overcome with/by
- be burning with
- give way to
- harbour
- nurse

▸ *see also* **sad, angry, happy, boring/bored, fed up, excited/exciting, comfort/make sb feel better**

feel/be /fiːl, biː/ [v] **be happy/frightened/bored etc** *Don't be scared – the dog won't bite.* | *Hazel was furious when I lost her camera.* | **feel happy/frightened/bored etc** *She's feeling a little nervous about the wedding.* | *I couldn't help feeling a little sad when he left.* | *You shouldn't feel guilty – it wasn't your fault.*

experience /ɪkˈspɪəriəns/ [v T] formal to feel a strong emotion such as joy, pride, or sorrow: *I experienced a great sense of loss when my father died.* | *When she was younger, my mother experienced a depression so severe she had to be hospitalized.*

be overcome with/by /biː əʊvəʳˈkʌm wɪð, baɪ/ [v phrase] to feel an emotion such as sadness or disappointment so strongly that you are unable to remain calm or think clearly: *When Diana met the starving children she was overcome with pity and outrage.* | *Suddenly, I was overcome by a feeling of panic.* | *Receiving the prize in honour of her dead father, she was overcome with emotion.*

be burning with /biː ˈbɜːʳnɪŋ wɪð/ [v phrase] **be burning with curiosity/desire/anger etc** to have an emotion that is so strong that it is very difficult to control: *Martha was burning with curiosity but realized that now wasn't the time to ask questions.*

give way to /ˌgɪv ˈweɪ tuː/ [v phrase] to let a strong emotion show or affect you, especially after you have been trying not to feel it or show it: *Giving way to her grief, Anna burst into tears.* | *He was ashamed to have given way to such feelings of self-pity.*

harbour British **/harbor** American /ˈhɑːʳbəʳ/ [v T] to have feelings, especially bad ones, in your mind for a long time: *Parker is believed to harbor political ambitions.* | *Some commuters still harbor resentment toward the protesters for blocking traffic and creating chaos.* | **harbour a grudge** *Taylor denied harbouring a grudge against his former boss.*

nurse /nɜːʳs/ [v T not in passive] formal **nurse resentment/anger/a grievance/a grudge** to have angry feelings for a long time but not express them: *Police believe the suspect nursed a grudge against women.* | *She never nurses a grievance or plans revenge.*

7 a feeling of happiness, anger, fear etc

- feeling
- emotion
- a sense of
- passion

feeling /ˈfiːlɪŋ/ [n C] something that you feel, for example happiness, anger, or fear: *It was a wonderful feeling to be home again.* | **express your feelings** *Many men find it hard to express their feelings.* | **a feeling of horror/sadness/accomplishment etc** *Regular exercise gives a feeling of accomplishment.* | *After less than a week away, he began to have feelings of homesickness.*

emotion /ɪˈməʊʃən/ [n C/U] a strong serious feeling such as love, hate, or anger that is often difficult to control: *She stared at him, overcome by emotion.* | *Parents feel a mixture of emotions when their first child starts school.*

a sense of /ə ˈsens ɒv/ [n phrase] a particular kind of feeling, especially one that affects your behaviour: *He felt a huge sense of relief after he finished his last exam.* | *Children need to be given a sense of security.* | *Both sides admitted there was a sense of urgency to end the strike quickly.* | *He hated working for his father-in-law but he did it out of a sense of duty to his wife.*

passion /ˈpæʃən/ [n C/U] a strong and deeply felt emotion, especially a strong feeling of sexual love for someone or a strong belief in an idea or principle: *He throws himself into his art with a creative passion.* | *There is a common prejudice in this country that Italians display their passions more readily than the English.* | **+ for** *Despite his passion for Carolyn, Mark never seriously considered leaving his wife for her.* | **with a passion** *She hated her ex-husband with a passion.*

8 a general feeling among a group of people

- atmosphere
- mood
- ambience

atmosphere /ˈætməsfɪəʳ/ [n singular/U] the general feeling among the people in a place, or the feeling you get from being in a particular place: *The atmosphere in the meeting was tense.* | *The new owners have tried to give the restaurant a more family-friendly atmosphere.* | **+ of** *We're trying to create an atmosphere of trust between management and staff.* | **heated atmosphere** (=when people in a place have very strong and often angry feelings) *the heated atmosphere of the House of Commons*

mood /muːd/ [n singular] the way a group of people feels about something at a particular time: *Pes-*

simism replaced the mood of democratic optimism that existed before World War I. | *Mondovi provoked severe unrest, contributing to the rebellious mood of the entire region.* | **the political/religious etc mood** *Labor leaders figured that given the political mood of the time, Truman was the best candidate.* | **the general/public/popular/national mood** (=one felt by most people in a country or region) *In keeping with the general mood of the time, these novels tended to sentimentalize the past.*

ambience /ˈæmbiəns/ [n singular/U] the feeling you get from a particular place, because of the way it looks, sounds, smells etc, and because of the way people treat you when you are there: *The restaurant's ambience makes you feel you're sitting down to dinner in the dining room of an old friend.* | *Winnetka has that small-town ambience of tree-lined streets and a one-street shopping district that you can't find in suburbia.* | *Ambience is as important to a business's success as the product you sell.*

9 behaving in a way that shows strong feelings

- emotional
- passionate
- with feeling
- impassioned

emotional /ɪˈməʊʃənəl/ [adj] behaving in a way that shows that you have strong feelings about something, for example by crying or shouting: *Grandpa gets very emotional when he talks about the war.* | **emotional outburst** (=a sudden powerful expression of strong emotion) *In an emotional outburst, Shahidi told reporters she now had no life worth living.* —**emotionally** [adv] *Imran shook my hand and said emotionally, 'I'll miss you, my friend.'* | *One of his problems is he always reacts too emotionally to things.*

passionate /ˈpæʃənˌt/ [adj] use this about people who openly show very strong feelings about something, especially love or anger: *She was a handsome Spanish woman with a passionate nature and a warm, generous heart.* | *Sometimes I wish he was more passionate, not so rational about everything.* —**passionately** [adv] *She wrapped her arms around him and kissed him passionately.* | *The new MP argued passionately for better housing, education, and welfare services for the poor.*

with feeling /wɪð ˈfiːlɪŋ/ [adv] if you say, do, or write something **with feeling**, you do it in a way that shows you have strong feelings about it: *I want you to sing it once more, this time with feeling.* | *She writes with great feeling about the fate of the refugees, having been a refugee herself in the last year.*

impassioned /ɪmˈpæʃənd/ [adj] an **impassioned** speech, request, argument etc is full of strong feeling and emotion: *Robins criticized the investigation during an impassioned speech outside police headquarters.* | *Moore gave an impassioned defense of the government's role in the affair.* | **an impassioned supporter/defender/champion of sth** *Muir was an impassioned and persuasive champion of wilderness preservation.*

10 events and situations that make people have strong feelings

- emotional
- moving
- touching
- emotive
- poignant

emotional /ɪˈməʊʃənəl/ [adj] an **emotional** event or situation makes people feel strong emotions: *The council's vote came after nearly six hours of emotional debate.* | *Newspaper reporters were there to record the emotional reunion between the woman and her children.* | **highly emotional** *Most couples remember the arrival of their first baby as a highly emotional time.*

moving /ˈmuːvɪŋ/ [adj] a **moving** account, experience, or event makes people feel strong emotions of pity, sadness, or joy: *The book is a very moving account of life in the refugee camps of Thailand.* | *After the final game there was a moving tribute to one of the players, who died tragically during the season.* | *The scene at the end of Act III is very moving, when Rafaella finds out that her husband has betrayed her.*

touching /ˈtʌtʃɪŋ/ [adj] a **touching** event or moment makes people feel a little sad and happy at the same time, and makes them like the people involved: *It was a touching scene when old Mr Adams received his leaving present.* | *It was touching to see them together. They were obviously still in love after thirty years of marriage.*

emotive /ɪˈməʊtɪv/ [adj] **emotive issue/area/phrase etc** a subject, statement, use of language etc that makes people have very strong feelings or emotions, especially of anger: *The candidates agreed to avoid emotive issues like abortion and child abuse.* | **highly emotive** (=very emotive) *The documentary deliberately uses highly emotive language, talking about 'exploitation' and 'blackmail'.*

poignant /ˈpɔɪnjənt/ [adj] especially written a **poignant** event, image, remark etc makes you feel great sadness and pity: *This is one of her most beautiful and poignant works.* | *In a poignant moment, Richter interrupted his speech to thank his mother and father.* —**poignantly** [adv] *His remarkable life and tragic death poignantly express the hopes and disappointments of a whole generation.*

11 too easily influenced by emotions

- sentimental
- sentimentality
- soppy
- gooey
- drama queen

sentimental /ˌsentɪˈmentl◂/ [adj] someone who is **sentimental** is too easily affected by emotions such as sympathy, love, or sadness: *My father became increasingly sentimental as he got older and his friends died off.* | **+ about** *Ramos admitted he was sentimental about his old school and was sad to see it torn down.*

sentimentality /ˌsentɪmenˈtælɪti/ [n U] a tendency to become emotional and to enjoy feelings such as sadness, sympathy, and self-pity, especially in a way that other people think is silly: *The film is flawed by moments of melodrama and sentimentality.* | *He talked about his homeland with all the sentimentality of an expatriate.* | **+ about** *He has no sentimentality about firing unproductive employees, even those who have worked for the company for years.*

soppy /ˈsɒpi‖ˈsɑːpi/ [adj] informal someone who is **soppy** seems silly to other people, because they express feelings of love or sympathy too strongly: *After a few drinks, he got all soppy and started talking about the 'good old days'.* | **+ about** *I was heartbroken when our dog died but I was determined not to be soppy about it.*

gooey /ˈguːi/ [adj] British informal expressing your love for someone, especially a baby, in a way that other people think is silly: *Babies make her go all gooey.*

drama queen /'drɑːmə kwiːn/ [n C] informal someone who becomes very excited, upset, or angry about things that are not important, especially in order to make people notice them or feel sympathy for them: *Stop being such a drama queen! It's not the end of the world!*

12 a story, film, song etc that is full of feelings of love or sadness

- sentimental
- soppy
- tearjerker

sentimental /ˌsentɪ'mentl◂/ [adj] dealing with emotions such as love and sadness in a way that seems silly and insincere: *I quite enjoyed the movie but I thought the ending was a little sentimental.* | *From the living room came the sound of a deep male voice singing a sentimental ballad.*

soppy /'sɒpi‖'sɑːpi/ [adj] informal a song, poem etc that is **soppy** seems silly to people because it expresses feelings of love and sympathy too strongly but in a way that does not seem serious: *She never tired of listening to soppy love songs.* | *I couldn't think of anything else so I just bought her a soppy card and some flowers.*

tearjerker /'tɪəʳˌdʒɜːʳkəʳ/ [n C] informal a story, play, film etc that is intended to make people feel sad and cry: *His latest movie is a typical Hollywood tearjerker.*

13 not showing your feelings

- unemotional
- cold
- clinical
- matter-of-fact
- detached
- impassive
- unmoved

unemotional /ˌʌnɪ'məʊʃənəl◂/ [adj] not showing your feelings: *Police were shocked at the unemotional way the murderer described the killings.* | *Pat's father was a distant, unemotional man who couldn't really talk to his children.* —**unemotionally** [adv] *The witness answered most questions unemotionally with a simple 'yes' or 'no'.*

cold /kəʊld/ [adj] not showing any feelings and especially not showing friendliness, humour, or pleasure: *She accused me of being cold and uncaring towards her.* | *The officers were cold and aloof in their dealings with other ranks.* | *The English are often unfairly stereotyped as cold, reserved people.* —**coldly** [adv] *The woman coldly told us to mind our own business.*

clinical /'klɪnɪkəl/ [adj] not showing the feelings that people usually show in an upsetting situation, because you have to do a job or because you really have no feelings about the situation: *His words were harsh and clinical – 'I don't love you any more. It is over. I am leaving you.'* —**clinically** [adv] *'Are you Mrs Wood?' the officer asked clinically. 'Your son Thomas is dead.'*

matter-of-fact /ˌmætər əv 'fækt◂/ [adj] showing no emotion when you are talking about something that is very frightening, embarrassing etc: *We were surprised at the matter-of-fact way Judith described her husband's death.* | *A spokesman listed the casualties in a detached, matter-of-fact tone of voice.* | *The condom advertising campaign is going to be very straightforward and as matter-of-fact as possible.*

detached /dɪ'tætʃt/ [adj] trying not to react in an emotional way, so that you can do your job properly or make the correct decisions about something: *You'll never be a good lawyer until you learn to be more detached.* | *Witnessing all the pain and suffering, it is sometimes difficult for relief workers to remain detached.*

impassive /ɪm'pæsɪv/ [adj] not allowing your feelings to show on your face, so that it is very difficult for people to guess how you feel: *Mr Deacon remained impassive throughout the performance.* | *Her impassive face showed no sign of reaction to the verdict.* —**impassively** [adv] *The three men sat impassively watching their captors.*

unmoved /ʌn'muːvd/ [adj] feeling no pity, sadness, or sympathy, in a situation where most people would feel this: *The defendant's claims of self-defense left the jury unmoved.* | *How can anyone remain unmoved by pictures of starving children on our TV screens?* | **+ by** *Unmoved by his pleas, Lucy strolled out of the room.*

few/not many

RELATED WORDS

opposite: —— **lot, common**

- when only a few of something exist *see* **rare/rarely (1)**
- *see also* **little, less, only**

1 a small number of people or things

- a few
- a small number
- not many
- one or two
- a couple
- a handful
- a minority
- sparse

a few /ə 'fjuː/ [quantifier] a small number of people, things, places etc: *Most of the trees were destroyed by the fire, but a few survived.* | **a few people/days/things etc** *She's gone to stay with her father for a few days.* | *Can I borrow a few dollars until I get paid?* | *I invited a few friends around on Saturday night.* | **a few of** (=a small number from a larger group) *Sean left the gate open and a few of the cows got out.*

a small number /ə ˌsmɔːl 'nʌmbəʳ/ [quantifier] formal a few people, things, places etc, especially when they are part of a much bigger number: *Hundreds of people begin the training programme, but only a small number complete it successfully.* | **+ of** *Only a small number of people still speak Gaelic.* | *The new system is being tested in a small number of schools.* | *A relatively small number of industrially advanced countries control the world economy.*

not many /nɒt 'meni/ [quantifier] a smaller number than you expected or wanted: *'Were there many people at the show?' 'No, not many.'* | **not many people/places etc** *There weren't many people at the party, but we still had a good time.* | *Not many restaurants stay open after midnight.* | **+ of** *I think I'm quite a good cook but not many of my friends agree with me.*

one or two /ˌwʌn ɔːʳ 'tuː◂/ [quantifier] spoken a small number of people or things: *'Do you have any Bob Dylan albums?' 'Yes, one or two.'* | **one or two people/places/questions etc** *We've had one or two problems with the car but nothing serious.* | *There are one or two things I'd like to ask you about.* | **+ of** *I only know the names of one or two of the new students.*

a couple /ə 'kʌpəl/ [quantifier] especially spoken two, or a small number: *'How many drinks did you have?' 'Just a couple.'* | **+ of** *A couple of kids were playing in the street.* | *I saw her a couple of days ago.*

a handful /ə 'hændfʊl / [quantifier] a very small number of people or things, especially when this number is disappointing or surprising: *We offer a gym for our employees but only a handful ever use it.* | **+ of** *Only a handful of artists in Britain can make a living from painting.* | *A handful of people stayed after the concert to help clear the chairs away.*

a minority /ə maɪ'nɒrɪ̥ti‖-mɪ̥'nɔː-, -'nɑː-/ [quantifier] a small group of people or things from within a larger group, usually forming much less than half of the larger group **+ of** *Only a minority of union members voted in favour of continuing the strike.* | **a small/tiny etc minority** *Joyce is among the tiny minority of arthritis sufferers who experience these symptoms.* | *Every year more than three hundred students enter this program but only a small minority will go on to become lawyers.*

sparse /spɑːʳs/ [adj] if something is **sparse**, there are only very small amounts of it, especially spread over a large area: *sparse traffic* | *Trees are sparse in this part of the world because of the continuous wind that blows across the plains.* —**sparsely** [adv] *This is one of the most sparsely populated areas of Asia* (=there are only a few people living there).

2 very few

- few/very few
- almost no
- hardly any/scarcely any
- be able to count sth on (the fingers of) one hand

few/very few /fjuː, ˌveri 'fjuː/ [quantifier] a very small number of people, things, places etc: *At that time, few people had televisions.* | *Very few new restaurants survive for more than two years.* | **+ of** *Very few of the students we asked said they were interested in politics.*

almost no /ˌɔːlməʊst 'nəʊ/ [quantifier] so few people or things that there are almost none: *There are almost no black students at the college.* | *My grandmother received almost no education as she was growing up.* | *Except for a lone seagull flying overhead, there are almost no signs of animal life.*

hardly any/scarcely any /ˌhɑːʳdli 'eni, ˌskeəʳsli 'eni/ [quantifier] so few people or things that there are almost none – use this especially when this number is disappointing or surprising: *There are supposed to be a lot of teachers at the conference, but I've met hardly any.* | **hardly/scarcely any people/things/places etc** *Although it was Monday morning there were hardly any people around.* | *He enjoyed his work even though he made scarcely any money.* | **hardly anyone** *We sent out over a hundred invitations but hardly anyone came.* | **+ of** *Scarcely any of the private schools replied to the researcher's questionnaire.*

be able to count sth on (the fingers of) one hand /biː eɪbl tə ˌkaʊnt (sth) ɒn (ðə ˌfɪŋgəʳz əv) ˌwʌn 'hænd/ [v phrase] spoken say this to emphasize that there is only a very small number of people, things, times when something happens etc: *I can count the number of times my son's called me on one hand.* | *Ten years ago, you could count the Korean restaurants in this city on the fingers of one hand.*

3 when a small number of people or things arrive, leave etc

- a trickle
- in dribs and drabs
- in ones and twos

a trickle /ə 'trɪkəl/ [n singular] a number of people going in small groups from one place to another, especially from one country to another, over a long period of time: *The flow of immigrants from Bosnia has slowed to a trickle.* | **+ of** *Since the rebellion there has been a steady trickle of refugees making their way across the border.*

in dribs and drabs /ɪn ˌdrɪbz ən 'dræbz/ [adv] if people or things arrive, leave etc **in dribs and drabs**, they come or go in small groups and not all together at the same time: *The wedding guests were arriving in dribs and drabs.* | *He insisted on paying me back in dribs and drabs, five or ten dollars at a time.*

in ones and twos /ɪn ˌwʌnz ən 'tuːz/ [adv] if people or things arrive, leave etc **in ones or twos**, they arrive etc on their own or in very small groups: *There were only about fifty people in the hall, standing around in ones and twos.*

fight

RELATED WORDS

- *see also* **attack, argue, war, hit, violent, weapon, unconscious**

WHAT'S HERE

- **when people fight each other** see **1 to 6**
- **when you try to change sth** see **7 to 9**

when people fight each other

1 when people fight each other

- fight
- have a fight
- struggle
- wrestle
- come to blows
- clash

fight /faɪt/ [v I/T] if people **fight**, or if one person **fights** another, they hit or kick each other in order to hurt each other: *Two men were fighting in the street outside.* | *He said he'd fight anyone who tried to stop him entering.* | **+ with** *Billy had been fighting with some kids from another school.* | **+ over/about** *Two men in the bar began fighting over a game of cards.* | *As kids, we fought about everything, but now we're pretty good friends.*

have a fight /hæv ə 'faɪt/ [v phrase] to fight with another person: *The two girls had a fist fight in the school cafeteria.* | **+ with** *He ran away from school after he had a fight with a bigger boy.*

struggle /'strʌgəl/ [v I] to fight someone who is attacking you or holding you, especially so that you can escape from them: *She tried to struggle but he put his hand over her mouth.* | **+ to do sth** *Vince struggled to free himself from the policeman's grip.* | **+ with** *It seems that he struggled with the robber and got quite seriously hurt.* | **+ against** *The victim had obviously struggled furiously against her attacker.*

wrestle /'resəl/ [v I] to fight someone by holding, pulling, or pushing them rather than hitting them: *The two boys wrestled for a while then gave up, tired.* | **+ with** *His jaw was broken while he tried to wrestle with a drunken bus driver.*

come to blows /ˌkʌm tə ˈbləʊz/ [v phrase] if two people **come to blows**, they start fighting after an argument or when both people are very angry: *Police say they don't know what the two were arguing about, only that it came to blows.*

clash /klæʃ/ [v I] if two groups of people, especially people with opposing opinions or aims, **clash**, they fight for a short time: *Animal rights activists and fox-hunters clashed at the annual Boxing Day hunt.* | *Police clashed with demonstrators for the second time in a week.*

2 to start a fight

- start a fight
- pick a fight
- be looking/spoiling for a fight/itching for a fight

start a fight /ˌstɑːʳt ə ˈfaɪt/ [v phrase] *Don't talk to him – he's just trying to start a fight.* | *The fight was started by a group of English football fans.*

pick a fight /ˌpɪk ə ˈfaɪt/ [v phrase] to deliberately start a fight with someone, especially by arguing with them or saying rude things to them: *Some of the students regularly try to pick fights in the playground.* | **+ with** *I walked into the bar and some drunk tried to pick a fight with me.*

be looking/spoiling for a fight/itching for a fight /biː ˌlʊkɪŋ, spɔɪlɪŋ fər ə ˈfaɪt, ˌɪtʃɪŋ fər ə ˈfaɪt/ [v phrase] to want to get rid of angry or violent feelings by fighting or trying to start a fight: *When he's drunk, he gets violent and starts looking for a fight.* | *The other driver came at me, obviously spoiling for a fight.* | *He's not the kind of guy that goes into a bar itching for a fight.*

3 behaving in a way that is likely to start a fight

- aggressive
- belligerent

aggressive /əˈgresɪv/ [adj] behaving in an angry and threatening way that is likely to start a fight: *The men were drunk and aggressive.* | *Some breeds of dog, such as German shepherds, were bred to be aggressive.* —**aggressively** [adv] *He glared aggressively at me.* —**aggression** /əˈgreʃən/ [n U] *When parents divorce, children often respond with anger and aggression.*

belligerent /bəˈlɪdʒərənt/ [adj] formal wanting to fight or argue, especially in order to prove that you are right, the best, the most important etc: *When police officers questioned him, he became belligerent and tried to hit one of them.* | *Harris is a belligerent man with an explosive temper.*

4 a fight

- fight
- punch-up
- brawl
- scuffle
- scrap
- altercation

fight /faɪt/ [n C] *There was a massive fight after school yesterday.* | **in a fight** *Three of his ribs were broken in a fight.* | **get into a fight** *He had been at the pub for several hours before getting into a fight with another man.* | **a fight breaks out** *A couple of fights broke out near the stadium after the game.* | **be in a fight** *How did you get that black eye? Were you in a fight?*

punch-up /ˈpʌntʃ ʌp/ [n C] British informal a fight: *He ended up in jail after a punch-up with a bloke in the pub.* | **get into a punch-up** *Some drunks began calling us names and we ended up getting into a punch-up.*

brawl /brɔːl/ [n C] a fight between a group of people in a public place, especially when they are drunk: *No one was injured in the brawl, which police quickly stopped.* | *He got his face cut in a brawl outside a nightclub.*

scuffle /ˈskʌfəl/ [n C] a short fight that is not very violent and which usually only involves people pushing each other: *There was a brief scuffle as the crowd left the football ground.* | **a scuffle breaks out** (=starts suddenly) *Rioters threw stones at the police and a few scuffles broke out.*

scrap /skræp/ [n C] a short fight, especially between children: *Scraps in the playground are a pretty frequent occurrence.* | **have a scrap** *It's normal for brothers and sisters to have a few scraps. It's part of growing up.*

altercation /ˌɔːltəʳˈkeɪʃən/ [n C] formal a short noisy argument or fight, especially one that is not serious: *There was a brief altercation and someone called the police.*

5 a fight involving a large number of people

- fighting
- riot
- battle
- clash
- confrontation
- free-for-all

fighting /ˈfaɪtɪŋ/ [n U] when a lot of people fight each other in a public place: *There was fighting on the streets of Paris yesterday when police and demonstrators clashed.* | **+ between** *Fighting between rival gangs resulted in the death of a teenage boy.* | **fighting breaks out** (=starts) *Fighting broke out between English and Dutch football fans after the game.*

riot /ˈraɪət/ [n C] an uncontrolled violent fight in a public place that involves a large number of people and usually damage to property, cars etc, especially among people who are protesting about something: *There were riots in several cities after it was announced that the price of bread would rise by 200%.* | *Four days of unrest and anti-government riots left at least three people dead.* | **a riot breaks out** (=starts) *A riot broke out after a police shooting of a local man.*

battle /ˈbætl/ [n C] a fight between two large groups of people: *He was killed in a street battle in 1998.* | **+ between** *a battle between rival gangs* | **pitched battle** (=a very violent fight) *About 200 students fought pitched battles with police during the demonstrations.*

clash /klæʃ/ [n C] a short fight between two groups of people who have opposing opinions or aims: *The clashes came as farmers blockaded roads.* | **+ between** *There were clashes last night between local residents and young people attending the rock festival.*

confrontation /ˌkɒnfrənˈteɪʃən‖ˌkɑːn-/ [n C] a situation in which there is a lot of angry disagreement between two groups, which may develop into a fight: *The police were obviously anticipating a confrontation, as they were heavily armed.*

free-for-all /ˌfriː fər ˈɔːl/ [n singular] a fight that a lot of people in a crowd join, especially when they have no particular reason to be fighting each other: *After Mathews was attacked, a free-for-all broke out in the audience.*

6 when people fight as a sport

- fight
- fight
- boxing
- wrestling

fight /faɪt/ [n C] a game in which two people hit each other or try to throw each other onto the ground: *He knocked out his opponent only five minutes into the fight.* | **the big fight** (=an important fight) *Are you going to watch the big fight tomorrow?* | **+ between** *the fight between Joe Louis and Rocky Marciano*

fight /faɪt/ [v T] to take part in a sport in which you hit your opponent or try to throw him or her onto the ground: *McCallum and Toney fought to a draw.* | *The two wrestlers have fought each other many times before.*

boxing /ˈbɒksɪŋ‖ˈbɑːk-/ [n U] a sport in which two people wearing special thick gloves hit each other and try to make the other person fall to the ground: *As a teenager, Dolittle took up boxing.* | **boxing match** *The boxing match will be held at the Arena.*

wrestling /ˈreslɪŋ/ [n U] a sport in which two people hold each other and try to throw each other onto the ground: *Sumo wrestling originated in Japan.* | **wrestling match** *He won six high-school wrestling matches in a row.* —**wrestler** [n C] someone who does wrestling: *a professional wrestler*

when you try to change sth

RELATED WORDS

- *see also* **against/oppose, protest**

7 to fight for something you think is right or against something you think is wrong

- fight
- work
- campaign
- champion/be a champion of
- combat
- wage war on

fight /faɪt/ [v T] to try hard for a long time to stop something bad from happening or to improve a situation: *We are determined to fight drug abuse in schools.* | **+ for** *Freedom of speech is something well worth fighting for.* | **fight to do sth** *Mandela fought to abolish white-only rule in South Africa.* | **+ against** *Amnesty is an organization that fights against torture and injustice.*

work /wɜːʳk / [v I] to **work** continuously and patiently to make changes that will improve society or the world **+ for** *The group has become a small but significant force working for change.* | **+ to do sth** *an organization that is working to preserve California's redwood trees* | **work tirelessly** (=work very hard) *She will be remembered as someone who worked tirelessly for educational reform.*

campaign /kæmˈpeɪn/ [v I] to work for a long time, for example making speeches, writing to newspapers and political representatives etc, in order to persuade people that something needs to be done: *After months of campaigning, local parents have persuaded the council to provide a school bus service.* | **+ for** *Women campaigned for equal pay and equal rights throughout the 1960s.* | **+ to do sth** *He was one of the people who campaigned to change the law on homosexuality.* —**campaigner** [n C] *During his years as a human rights campaigner he was arrested seven times.*

champion/be a champion of /ˈtʃæmpiən, biː ə ˈtʃæmpiən ɒv/ [v T/v phrase] to publicly fight for and defend an aim or principle such as the rights of a group of people: *Martin Luther King championed the rights of all black Americans.* | *Throughout her political career she was a champion of prison reform.*

combat /ˈkɒmbæt, kəmˈbæt‖kəmˈbæt, ˈkɑːmbæt/ [v T] to take action effectively in order to oppose something bad such as injustice, crime, or illness: *The police are looking for more effective ways to combat drugs gangs in the city.* | *Measures to combat pollution within the city have been introduced.* | *The government sees price controls as a way to combat inflation.*

wage war on /ˌweɪdʒ ˈwɔːr ɒn/ [v phrase] if a government or organization **wages war on** something such as an illness, bad conditions, or crime, they fight against it for a long time in a very determined way: *The World Health Organization is constantly waging war on malaria.* | *We need a comprehensive strategy to wage war on poverty in our inner cities.*

8 to fight against someone powerful or something bad

- fight/fight against
- resist
- resistance
- fight back
- stand up to
- put up a fight
- hold out against
- make a stand
- oppose

fight/fight against /faɪt, ˈfaɪt əgenst/ [v T/v phrase] *Residents are fighting the local council over plans for a new road.* | *The community is struggling to fight against drug dealers and prostitution, in their effort to make the area a safer place to live.*

resist /rɪˈzɪst/ [v T] to fight in a very determined way against changes that you think will be unfair or could take people's freedom away: *By resisting the Mafia's attempts to control the region, he was putting his own life in danger.* | *The unions have resisted attempts to change the pay structure.*

resistance /rɪˈzɪstəns/ [n U] when people fight in a very determined way against changes or a government that they think will be unfair or could take people's freedom away: *She became one of the symbols of resistance both at home and abroad.* | **+ to** *There has been a lot of resistance to tax increases, even those designed to benefit education.* | **meet with resistance** (=cause resistance) *Any policy that creates unemployment is likely to meet with strong resistance.*

fight back /ˌfaɪt ˈbæk/ [phr v I] to fight against someone who is doing something that harms you: *Children are often powerless to fight back when they are treated unfairly.* | *You must fight back if you become a victim of discrimination.* | *This nation has been oppressed for too long, and it's time we fought back.*

stand up to /ˌstænd ˈʌp tuː/ [phr v T] to refuse to accept bad or unfair treatment from someone, especially someone who is stronger or more powerful than you are: *Aggressive bosses are less likely to criticize workers who stand up to them.* | *He is respected as a leader who is willing to stand up to the West.*

put up a fight /ˌpʊt ʌp ə ˈfaɪt/ [v phrase] to fight in order to show that you are against something that you think is bad or unfair, even though you are not likely to succeed in stopping it: *Although parents and local residents put up a fight, they couldn't stop* *the school being closed.* | *People are not going to accept being sent back to the war zone without putting up a fight.*

hold out against /ˌhəʊld 'aʊt əgenst/ [v T] to fight for as long as possible against a change that someone powerful is trying to make, because you think it is wrong or unfair: *The workers held out for several months against the closure of the mine, but they were eventually defeated.*

make a stand /ˌmeɪk ə 'stænd/ [v phrase] to show publicly that you think something is wrong, and take action to stop it: *If you're not prepared to make a stand yourself, you can't expect anyone else to.* | **+ against** *Gandhi and his followers made a determined stand against the racist and imperialist policies of the government.*

oppose /ə'pəʊz/ [v T] to fight against something such as a law or system that you think is wrong: *Those who opposed the regime were put into prison or even executed.* | *There will be a rally on September 22 for all those who oppose direct military action.* —**opposition** /ˌɒpə'zɪʃən‖ˌɑː-/ [n U] *The newspaper became well known for its fierce opposition to apartheid.*

9 when someone fights for or against something

- fight
- struggle
- battle
- campaign
- crusade
- cause
- drive

fight /faɪt/ [n singular] when people try hard for a long time to stop something bad from happening or to improve a situation **+ against** *New laws have been passed to help the police in their fight against organized crime.* | *The fight against malnutrition and preventable diseases must continue.* | **+ for** *Women's fight for equality has not ended.* | *He was a hero in the fight for independence from France.*

struggle /'strʌgəl/ [n C usually singular] when people try for many years to get freedom, independence, or equal rights, and a lot of people suffer, are killed, or are put in prison: *Many freedom fighters were imprisoned, but they never gave up the struggle.* | **+ for** *Nkrumah led the people in their struggle for independence.* | **+ against** *He devoted his life to the struggle against fascism and oppression.*

battle /'bætl/ [n C usually singular] when a person or group tries hard for a long time to change a bad situation, or deal with a problem in society **+ against** *The battle against racial discrimination is not over.* | *The President is fully committed to the battle against the drug traffickers.* | **win the battle against sth** *They now have a good chance of winning the battle against violence and drugs in the community.*

campaign /kæm'peɪn/ [n C] a planned set of actions or events, such as public meetings, letters to the government etc, that is intended to persuade the public that something is bad or unfair and should be changed **+ for** *Motoring organizations have started a campaign for safer roads in the area.* | *the Campaign for Nuclear Disarmament* | **+ against** *Our campaign against drug abuse is supported by the medical profession.* | **vigorous campaign** (=a very strong campaign) *Clark's vigorous campaign against the dumping of nuclear waste will continue.* | **launch/mount a campaign** (=start a campaign) *Environmental groups launched a campaign against the widespread production of genetically modified crops.*

crusade /kruː'seɪd/ [n C] a fight that someone continues for a long time, because they feel strongly that something is morally wrong and must be changed: *As a politician she's made the fight for women's rights into a personal crusade.* | **+ against** *She intends to continue her crusade against sex and violence on TV.* | **+ for** *He has begun a crusade for gun control.*

cause /kɔːz/ [n C usually singular] something such as a principle or political aim that people fight for – used especially by the people involved in fighting for it: *Our cause is just, and we are prepared to give our lives for it.* | **+ of** *Thousands died in the cause of freedom.* | *The cause of Socialism is not dead.*

drive /draɪv/ [n C] a planned effort by an organization, government etc to achieve a change within a short time that will improve a particular situation: *The Health Department launched an anti-smoking drive.* | **economy drive** (=a drive to reduce spending) British *The government's economy drive has failed to produce the expected savings.*

film/movie

RELATED WORDS

- part of a film *see* **part (3)**
- *see also* **actor/actress, perform, watch, television/radio, story, famous**

1 films and going to see them

- film
- cinema
- go to the cinema
- be on/be playing

film especially British **/movie** especially American /fɪlm, 'muːvi/ [n C] a story that is told using sound and moving pictures: *Are there any good movies on TV tonight?* | *What's your favourite James Bond film?* | *The film starred Tom Cruise and Nicole Kidman.* | **see a film/movie** *Have you seen any good films lately?* | *I saw an Arnold Schwarzenegger movie on the plane – I can't remember its name.* | **+ about** *It's the usual sort of film about boy meets girl.* | **film/movie director/producer/company** *Tarantino is one of the most famous film directors of our time.* | **film crew** (=the people who operate the equipment when making a film) *For months the town was full of cameras, lighting and members of the film crew.* | **feature film** (=a full-length film that has a story and is acted by professional actors) *The story of Lawrence of Arabia was made into a feature film in 1962.*

cinema British **/movie theater** American /'sɪnɪ̈mə, 'muːvi ˌθɪətəʳ/ [n C] a building where you go to see films: *the MGM cinema in Leicester Square* | *The city put $6.5 million towards a 10-screen movie theater and retail complex in Main Street.*

go to the cinema British **/go to the movies** American /ˌgəʊ tə ðə 'sɪnɪ̈mə, ˌgəʊ tə ðə 'muːviz/ [v phrase] to go to a cinema in order to see a film: *Do you want to go the movies this weekend?* | *The last time I went to the cinema was when I saw 'Stigmata'.*

be on/be playing /biː 'ɒn, biː 'pleɪ-ɪŋ/ [v phrase] if a film **is on** or **is playing** at a cinema, it is being shown there: *'Three Kings' is on at the Phoenix at the moment.* | *Spielberg's new blockbuster is currently playing at over 2000 theaters nationwide.* | **what's on?** *What's on at the cinema this weekend?*

2 types of film

- horror film/horror movie
- slasher film/movie
- comedy
- science fiction film/science fiction movie
- thriller
- western
- war film/war movie
- action film/action movie
- road movie
- romantic comedy
- cartoon/animated film/animated movie
- epic

horror film/horror movie /ˈhɒrəʳ fɪlm, ˈhɒrəʳ ˌmuːvi‖ˈhɔː-/ [n C] a film that is intended to make you feel frightened, for example one in which people get attacked by strange creatures, or in which dead people come to life

slasher film/slasher movie /ˈslæʃəʳ fɪlm, ˈslæʃəʳ ˌmuːvi/ [n C] informal a film that is intended to make you feel frightened, in which people are suddenly violently attacked and killed

comedy /ˈkɒmədi‖ˈkɑː-/ [n C] a film that is intended to make you laugh and usually has a happy ending

science fiction film/science fiction movie /ˌsaɪəns ˈfɪkʃən fɪlm, ˌsaɪəns ˈfɪkʃən ˌmuːvi/ [n C] a film about life in the future, often with people or creatures who live in other parts of the universe

thriller /ˈθrɪləʳ/ [n C] a film that tells an exciting story about murder or crime

western /ˈwestəʳn/ [n C] a film about cowboys and life in the 19th century in the American West

war film/war movie /ˈwɔːʳ fɪlm, ˈwɔːʳ ˌmuːvi/ [n C] a film about people fighting a war

action film/action movie /ˈækʃən fɪlm, ˈækʃən ˌmuːvi/ [n C] a film that has a lot of exciting events in it, for example people fighting or chasing each other in cars

road movie /ˈrəʊd ˌmuːvi/ [n C] a film about people who are on a long journey in a car, and the adventures they have while they are travelling

romantic comedy /rəʊˌmæntɪk ˈkɒmədi‖ˈkɑː-/ [n C] a film that is intended to make you laugh, about two people who meet and have a romantic relationship

cartoon/animated film/animated movie /kɑːʳˈtuːn, ˌænəmeɪtəd ˈfɪlm, ˌænəmeɪtəd ˈmuːvi/ [n C] a film made using photographs of models or drawings, which are put together to look as if they are moving

epic /ˈepɪk/ [n C] a long film in which a lot of things happen, for example one about a period in history or the whole of someone's life

finally

when something happens after a long time

RELATED WORDS

- see also **wait, hope, future**

- finally/eventually/in the end
- at last
- sooner or later
- one day
- in time
- end up

finally/eventually/in the end /ˈfaɪnəl-i, ɪˈventʃuəli, ɪn ði ˈend/ [adv] after a long period of time, especially after a lot of difficulties or after a long delay: *After a lot of questioning, James finally admitted he had taken the car.* | *In the end, I decided that the best thing to do was to ask Billy for help.* | *The plane eventually arrived at 6:30 – over three hours late.*

at last /ət ˈlɑːst ‖-ˈlæst/ [adv] use this when something good happens after you have waited for it for a long time: *I'm really glad that Ken's found a job at last.* | *At last the rain stopped and the players came back on the field.* | **at long last** (=after a very long time) *At long last he was able to see his family again.*

sooner or later /ˌsuːnər ɔːʳ ˈleɪtəʳ/ [adv] if something is going to happen **sooner or later**, it will certainly happen but you do not know exactly when: *Sooner or later this would end up in the papers, and I would be out of a job.* | *I'm sure Brian will turn up sooner or later.* | *He is worried that sooner or later his business will fail.*

one day /ˈwʌn deɪ/ [adv] use this to say that something will happen at some time in the future, especially something that you hope will happen, although you do not know exactly when: *They're bound to find a cure for cancer one day.* | *I knew that we would meet again one day.* | *One day ordinary people will be able to travel in space.*

in time /ɪn ˈtaɪm/ [adv] after a particular period of time, especially after a gradual process of change or development: *She started as an office junior, and in time became director of the whole company.* | *Jarvis was a strange man, but in time I got to like him.*

end up /ˌend ˈʌp/ [phr v I not in progressive] if someone or something **ends up** in a particular situation or condition, they eventually come to be in that situation or condition – use this especially about something bad that happens: *Forbes ended up in prison for not paying his taxes.* | *The sweater that my mum knitted ended up twice the size it should have been.* | **end up doing sth** *We ended up having to postpone our vacation.* | **+ as** *Our chess game finally ended up as a draw.*

find

RELATED WORDS

opposite: **lose**

- see also **look for, find out, invent**

1 to find someone or something that is lost

- find
- turn up
- trace
- track down

find /faɪnd/ [v T] to **find** someone or something that you have lost: *I've looked everywhere, but I can't find my sunglasses.* | *Have you found your passport yet?* | *The murder weapon was found outside the house.* | *Luis was gone, and she had no way of ever finding him again.*

turn up /ˌtɜːʳn ˈʌp/ [phr v I] if something that is lost **turns up**, someone finds it later in a place where they did not expect it to be: *Don't worry about your earrings – I'm sure they'll turn up sooner or later.* | *Have those files turned up yet?*

trace /treɪs/ [v T] to find someone or something by a careful process of asking a lot of people for information: *Police are trying to trace a red van, which several witnesses reported seeing near the scene of the crime.* | *The cash was eventually traced to a prominent Paris lawyer.* | *Philips hired a private* *detective to trace his daughter, who had been missing for two months.*

track down /ˌtræk ˈdaʊn/ [phr v T] to find someone or something that is difficult to find, by searching or by making inquiries in several different places **track down sb/sth** *The police have had a difficult time tracking down Corbin.* | *I have copies of the documents but haven't managed to track down the originals.* | *The president vowed to track down those responsible for the bombing.* | **track sb/sth down** *It took Alvin quite a while to track her down, but he eventually found her.*

2 to find something you need or want

- find
- locate
- dig out

find /faɪnd/ [v T] to **find** something that you need, such as a job or a place to live: *I really need to find a better job.* | *It took us half an hour to find somewhere to park.* | *Jenny found an apartment in Brooklyn.*

locate /ləʊˈkeɪt‖ˈləʊkeɪt/ [v T not in passive] formal or written to find out where something is – used especially in official or technical contexts: *Investigators searched through the plane's wreckage for several hours before locating the flight recorder.* | *If you have difficulty locating a particular book, please ask one of the librarians for assistance.* —**location** /ləʊˈkeɪʃən/ [n U] *Techniques for the location of tumours have improved greatly over the last twenty years.*

dig out /ˌdɪg ˈaʊt/ [phr v T] especially British to find something you have not seen for a long time, or that may not be easy to find, especially in order to give it to someone who has asked for it **dig out sth** *It seems like every time Grandma comes over we have to dig out the family photos.* | *I took the opportunity to dig out a few facts and figures about this remote island.* | **dig sth/it/them out** *I have her address somewhere – I'll dig it out for you when I get time.*

3 difficult to find

- be difficult to find/hard to find
- elusive

be difficult to find/hard to find /biː ˌdɪfɪkəlt tə ˈfaɪnd, ˌhɑːʳd tə ˈfaɪnd/ [v phrase] if someone or something that you need **is difficult to find** or **hard to find**, you cannot easily find them because there are not many of them or they are well hidden: *Taxis are hard to find at that time of night.* | *What we wanted was a house with a big garden – something that was difficult to find in the middle of a city.*

elusive /ɪˈluːsɪv/ [adj] an **elusive** person or animal is difficult to find, often because they do not want to be found: *The gray fox is a very shy elusive creature.* | *A cure for the disease has proven to be elusive.* | *We repeatedly tried to contact the manager, an elusive man who was never in his office.*

4 to find a place you are trying to get to

- find
- find your way

find /faɪnd/ [v T] to **find** a place that you are trying to go to: *Did you manage to find the house without too much trouble?* | **be easy to find** *The Blue Moon is easy to find: get off Highway 78 at 23rd Avenue and go right.*

find your way /ˌfaɪnd jɔːʳ ˈweɪ/ [v phrase] to get to a place by finding the right way to go: *I couldn't find my way out of the building.* | **+ to** *It was my first visit to New York, but I managed to find my way to their apartment without any problem.* | **find your own way** (=find your way without anyone's help) *Thanks, it's not necessary for you to get up. I can find my own way out.*

5 to find something new and important

- find
- discover
- make a discovery
- unearth
- turn up

find /faɪnd/ [v T] to **find** something important that no one knew about before, especially information or a way of doing something: *Medical researchers are determined to find a cure for cancer.* | *It's crucial that we find cleaner ways of generating electricity.* | *Bodies up to 2,000 years old have been found buried in the peat bogs of central England.*

discover /dɪsˈkʌvəʳ/ [v T] to find an object, a substance, a place, information etc, that is important and that no one knew about before: *The planet Pluto was discovered in 1930.* | *Australian researchers have discovered a substance in coffee that acts like morphine.*

make a discovery /ˌmeɪk ə dɪsˈkʌvəri/ [v phrase] to find something important, interesting, or surprising that no one knew about before: *Hawking made many discoveries about the nature of stars.* | *Carlo Rubbia, who led the team of scientists that made the discovery, received the Nobel prize in 1984.* | *Amazing discoveries have been made by anthropologists excavating in the Rift Valley.* | *An important discovery was made by Mendel in the mid-nineteenth century.*

unearth /ʌnˈɜːʳθ/ [v T] to find something that was hidden or kept secret for a long time, especially information: *Investigators have unearthed new evidence about the possible cause of the crash.* | *The incredible story was unearthed by reporters at the 'Post'.* | *His research unearthed new information about the origins of the HIV virus.*

turn up /ˌtɜːʳn ˈʌp/ [phr v T not usually in passive] to find something interesting or useful, especially information, while you are searching carefully: *After seven months on the case, the police failed to turn up any real clues.* | *A thorough examination of the company's account books turned up several interesting facts.*

6 to unexpectedly find something that you were not looking for

- find/discover
- come across
- stumble on/across
- chance upon/happen upon

find/discover /faɪnd, dɪsˈkʌvəʳ/ [v T not in progressive] *We found a lovely seafood restaurant by the harbour.* | *The body was discovered by a man walking his dog.* | *It wasn't until I got to university that I discovered poetry.*

come across /ˌkʌm əˈkrɒs‖-ˈkrɔːs/ [phr v T] to find something unexpectedly when you are not looking for it but are doing something else: *I came across an interesting news item in yesterday's 'Times'.* | *Digging in the garden, she came across some pieces of bone.*

stumble on/across /ˈstʌmbəl ɒn, əˌkrɒs‖ -əˌkrɔːs/ [phr v T] to find something by chance and unexpectedly, especially something that was secret or that no one knew before: *The officers stumbled across the drugs when they stopped Moyers for a routine traffic violation.* | *Fleming was carrying out other research when he stumbled on penicillin.* | *Some people believe that Jenkins was murdered by government agents because he stumbled across a military secret.*

chance upon/happen upon /ˈtʃɑːns əˌpɒn‖ ˈtʃæns-, ˈhæpən əˌpɒn/ [phr v T] written to find a place or thing that you were not deliberately looking for, or meet someone you did not know you would meet, especially when you consider this a good or lucky thing to have happened: *We happened upon a beautiful little hotel about an hour outside of Tours.* | *I was walking home from the station when I happened upon Richard.* | *Leafing through a magazine, I chanced upon a photo of an old high school friend, Robert Mason.*

7 something you find

- ▸ discovery
- ▸ be a real find

discovery /dɪsˈkʌvəri/ [n C] something important that has been found and that no one knew about before: *Among the discoveries of the late nineteenth century were several new chemical elements, including radium.* | *New archaeological discoveries prove the existence of an ancient civilization in the Indus Valley.* | **chance discovery** (=one that happens by chance) *The chance discovery of a blood-stained shirt led to the capture of the killer.*

be a real find /biː ə ˌrɪəl ˈfaɪnd/ [v phrase] if someone or something **is a real find**, you were lucky to find them because they are very good, useful, or interesting: *That little Greek restaurant was a real find.* | *Last month the club signed on a new player, Nate Tompkins, who has already proved to be a real find.*

find out

RELATED WORDS

▸ *see also* **know/not know, look for, learn, secret**

1 to find out about something

- ▸ find out
- ▸ discover
- ▸ see
- ▸ hear
- ▸ be told
- ▸ find
- ▸ learn
- ▸ gather
- ▸ come to sb's attention/notice
- ▸ hear through/on the grapevine

find out /ˌfaɪnd ˈaʊt/ [phr v I/T] to get information about something, either by chance or by deliberately trying to get it: *'Do you have these shoes in size 8?' 'I'm not sure – I'll just go and find out.'* | *When we found out the price we were shocked.* | **+ what/where/whether etc** *I'll go and find out which platform the train leaves from.* | *Dad was really mad at me when he found out where I'd been.* | **+ about** *He's trying to find out about Japanese classes in the area.* | **find out sth/find sth out** *Could you find out his address for me, please?* | *'John's been married twice.' 'How did you find that out?'* | **+ (that)** *She found out that her husband was having an affair.*

discover /dɪsˈkʌvəʳ/ [v T] to find something out, especially something that is surprising or something that is difficult to find out. **Discover** is more formal than **find out**: *Fire officers are still trying to discover the cause of the fire.* | **+ (that)** *I began to learn the guitar, and discovered that I was pretty good at it.* | *She discovered the job wasn't as easy as it might seem.* | **+ how/why/what etc** *They never discovered who the murderer was.*

see /siː/ [v I/T] especially spoken to get the information that you want by going somewhere to look, or by doing something and noticing what happens: *'Is he ready yet?' 'I don't know – I'll go and see.'* | **+ if/whether** *See if the rice is done while you're in the kitchen, will you?* | **+ how/where/what etc** *Can you see who's at the door?* | *Let's see what happens if we add some oil.*

hear /hɪəʳ/ [v I/T not in progressive] to know about something because someone has told you, you have read about it, seen it on television etc: *'Nina's quit her job.' 'Yes, so I've heard.'* | **+ about** *How did you hear about our company?* | *We've heard such a lot about you from our daughter.* | **+ (that)** *I hear you're moving to Toronto.* | **+ whether/if** *When will you hear whether you've got the job?* | **+ what/why/how etc** *I suppose you've heard what happened?*

be told /biː ˈtəʊld/ [v phrase] to find out about something because someone tells you **+ (that)** *He was told that Anna had left some time ago.* | *Visitors have been told the building will be used as a museum.* | **so I'm told** spoken *'Is it true that she's moving to Hollywood?' 'So I'm told.'*

find /faɪnd/ [v T] especially written to **find** out a fact or **find** out that something is true, especially by asking questions **+ that** *We found that, despite their poverty, very few people wanted to leave the area.* | *Researchers found that smokers were more likely to get depressed than non-smokers.*

learn /lɜːʳn/ [v I/T not in progressive] to find out something because someone tells you, you read it somewhere etc: *I doubt if we will ever learn the truth.* | **+ of/about** *She learned of her mother's death when it was announced on the radio.* | **+ (that)** *Several months ago, McNair learned that he had cancer.*

gather /ˈgæðəʳ/ [v T not in progressive] to know a piece of information because that is what you hear people saying and not because you have been told it directly **+ (that)** *I gather you've decided not to resign after all.* | *Despite my limited Spanish, I gathered that there was a problem with my passport.* | **from what sb can gather** (=according to what I have found out) *From what I can gather, there has been fighting further down the valley.*

come to sb's attention/notice /ˌkʌm tə (sb's) əˈtenʃən, ˈnəʊtɪ̩s/ [v phrase] formal if something such as a problem or a mistake **comes to someone's attention** or **notice**, that person finds out about it, especially because someone else tells them about it: *Illegal trading first came to the attention of top management in late April.* | **+ that** *It has come to my notice that your account is overdrawn by £200.*

hear through/on the grapevine /ˌhɪəʳ θruː, ɒn ðə ˈgreɪpvaɪn/ [v phrase] to find out about something because the information has been passed on from one person to another in conversation: *'How did you find out she was leaving?' 'I heard it through the grapevine.'* | **+ that** *I heard on the grapevine that Josie and Tom are expecting a baby.*

2 to find out something new or something that was secret

- find out
- uncover/unearth
- dig up
- get at
- get wind of
- get wise to

find out /ˌfaɪnd ˈaʊt/ [phr v I/T not in progressive] *He just had to hope he'd get away with it and that nobody would find out.* | *She doesn't want people to find out her age.* | *You read her diary? Just make sure she never finds out!* | **+ what/why/how etc** *Dad was furious when he found out where I was living.* | **+ about** *It's a surprise party, so I don't want her to find out about it.* | **+ (that)** *It was three months before my parents found out I'd been going out with Peter.* | **find sb out** (=find out someone's secret) British *It won't work. Someone's bound to find you out eventually.*

uncover/unearth /ʌnˈkʌvəʳ, ʌnˈɜːʳθ/ [v T] to find out information that has been deliberately kept secret, especially while you are studying or examining a particular subject: *Detectives have uncovered a plan to smuggle illegal weapons into the country.* | *Lawyers unearthed evidence that he held several bank accounts.*

dig up /ˌdɪɡ ˈʌp/ [phr v T] to find out information by searching carefully for it, especially information about someone's past that they have deliberately tried to keep secret **dig sth up/dig up sth** *I wanted to dig a few more facts up for my article.* | **dig up dirt on sb** (=find out something bad about someone) *Politicians try to dig up dirt on their opponents.* | **dig sth up on sb** *He wanted as much evidence as could be dug up on the girl.*

get at /ˈɡet æt/ [phr v T] to find something out, especially the truth about a situation, or facts that someone has tried to hide: *It's hard to get at the facts when people are afraid to speak out.* | *He was a good reporter, who wanted to get at the truth and present it without bias.*

get wind of /ˌɡet ˈwɪnd ɒv/ [v phrase] informal to find out about a situation or something that is going to happen, especially when it is supposed to be secret: *Reporters somehow got wind of the fact that Carr was going to be arrested.*

get wise to /ˌɡet ˈwaɪz tuː/ [v phrase] informal to find out about something such as a trick or an illegal activity: *The police parked an empty patrol car there to reduce speeding, but drivers got wise to it pretty quickly.*

3 when something is found out

- come out
- come to light/be brought to light
- emerge
- leak
- get out
- it transpires that

come out /ˌkʌm ˈaʊt/ [phr v I] if something that people knew nothing about **comes out**, people find out about it, especially as a result of an official inquiry: *The truth about the scandal came out long after he had left office.* | *A few new facts came out at the trial.* | **it comes out that** *During the hearing it came out that she had tried to commit suicide.*

come to light/be brought to light /ˌkʌm tə ˈlaɪt, biː ˌbrɔːt tə ˈlaɪt/ [v phrase] if new information or a new fact **comes to light** or **is brought to light**, people find out about it: *Fresh evidence has come to light since the report was published.* | *Some serious problems have been brought to light by the latest report on health and safety.* | **it comes to light that/it is brought to light that** *It came to light that the CIA knew he was a security risk.*

emerge /ɪˈmɜːʳdʒ/ [v I] if facts **emerge** from a meeting or an inquiry, people find out about them: *More details of the plan emerged at yesterday's meeting.* | **it emerges that** *During the court case it emerged that both men had convictions for terrorist offences.*

leak /liːk/ [v T] if someone within a government or organization **leaks** official information, they secretly tell the public or a newspaper about it: *Someone at the Pentagon leaked a letter from the Secretary of Defense.* | *Information on the merger had been leaked to the press.*

get out /ˌɡet ˈaʊt/ [phr v I] if a piece of information **gets out**, people find out about it even though other people have tried very hard to keep it secret: *If any of this gets out, we'll be in serious trouble.* | **word/news etc gets out** *If word gets out that Jordan is here, we'll be mobbed.* | **it gets out that** *If it gets out that we knew about this, we'll lose all our clients.*

it transpires that /ɪt trænˈspaɪəʳz ðət/ formal if **it transpires that** something is true, people find out that it is true: *It now transpires that the prime minister knew about the deal all along.*

4 to find out the exact cause of something

- determine
- establish
- identify
- pinpoint
- diagnose

determine /dɪˈtɜːʳmɪn/ [v T] to find out the exact details or facts about something, especially by using technical methods and equipment: *'Web police' are often able to determine the exact source of unwanted mailings on the Internet.* | **+ what/why/how etc** *Quizzes are used to determine how much material students have learned.* | **+ that** *A survey of traffic accidents determined that seat belts reduced serious injuries by up to 90%.*

establish /ɪˈstæblɪʃ/ [v T] to find out facts that will prove how something happened or what caused it: *We haven't yet established the cause of the accident.* | **+ that** *It was quickly established that several members of the crew had been negligent.* | **+ how/where/ why etc** *They are carrying out research to establish exactly why so many species of songbird are disappearing.*

identify /aɪˈdentɪfaɪ/ [v T] to find out exactly what the cause or origin of something is: *After years of research, scientists have identified the virus that is responsible for the disease.* | *Experts are examining the wreckage, but the cause of the accident has not yet been identified.*

pinpoint /ˈpɪnpɔɪnt/ [v T] to find out exactly what something is, when something happened, or what exactly is causing something: *Investigators are trying to pinpoint the cause of the fire.* | *Mechanics are having difficulty pinpointing the problem.* | **+ what/how/when etc** *The test is meant to pinpoint which types of jobs you are suited for.*

diagnose /ˈdaɪəɡnəʊz‖-nəʊs/ [v T] to find out what is wrong with someone or something, especially what illness someone has, by making a careful examination: *If cervical cancer is diagnosed in its early stages, it can be cured.* | **diagnose sb as having sth** (=find out that they have a particular disease) *Several years ago, she was diagnosed as having Alzheimer's disease.* | **diagnose sth as sth** *Programmers diagnosed the problem as a computer virus.* | **+ what/how/where etc** *There are various methods* *for diagnosing what is wrong with a sick person.* —**diagnosis** /ˌdaɪəɡˈnəʊsɪs/ [n U] *Much progress has been made in the diagnosis of genetic diseases.*

5 to find out information from someone

- find out
- get sth out of
- get information
- extract
- worm sth out of
- drag sth out of

▸ *see also* **ask**

find out /ˌfaɪnd ˈaʊt/ [phr v T] to **find out** information from someone by asking them questions or by forcing them to tell you **find out sth** *'Did you find out her views on the subject?' 'No, she wouldn't tell me.'* | **+ what/how/when etc** *He asked me to find out what your plans are after you leave.* | **find sth out** *Will you see if you can find anything out about Sandy?*

get sth out of /ˌɡet (sth) ˈaʊt ɒv/ [v phrase] informal to find out a particular piece of information from someone, especially by forcing them to tell you: *Jed admitted he'd been at the scene, but that's all I could get out of him.* | *We'll get the truth out of her sooner or later.*

get information /ˌɡet ɪnfəʳˈmeɪʃən/ [v phrase] to find out something from a person, a book, the Internet etc: *To get more information, telephone or contact us on our website.* | *You will be able to get most of the information you need from the school library.* | **+ about/on** *I've written to the tourist information centre to get some information about the area.*

extract /ɪkˈstrækt/ [v T] formal to find out information from someone who does not want to give it, by asking them questions or by using physical force: *Police questioned the prisoner for several hours, but were unable to extract any further information.* | **extract sth from sb** *The court ruled that her confession had been unlawfully extracted from her.*

worm sth out of /ˌwɜːʳm (sth) ˈaʊt ɒv/ [v phrase] to find out information from someone who is unwilling to give it, especially by being clever, making them feel they can trust you etc: *He didn't want to tell me her name but I managed to worm it out of him.*

drag sth out of /ˌdræɡ (sth) ˈaʊt ɒv/ [v phrase] to get information from someone who does not want to tell you it, especially by asking a lot of questions: *If she doesn't want to tell you, there's no point in trying to drag it out of her.*

6 to try to find out something private or personal

- snoop
- pry
- nose around

snoop /snuːp/ [v I] to try to find out about someone's private affairs, especially by secretly looking in their house, examining their possessions etc: *Bob caught her snooping through the papers on his desk.* | **+ on** *Technology is making it easier to snoop on just about anybody.* | **+ around/about** British *What are you doing snooping around in my room?*

pry /praɪ/ [v I] to try to find out about someone's private life by asking a lot of personal questions in a way that people find rude or annoying: *My son hasn't given us a reason for his divorce, and we don't want to pry.* | **+ into** *Employers shouldn't try to pry into what a person does in the privacy of their own home.*

nose around /about British /ˌnəʊz əˈraʊnd, əˈbaʊt/ [phr v I/T] informal to look around a place, especially someone's home or office, to try to find out things that do not really concern you: *The kids were nosing around in the attic and found a box of old photos.* | **nose around an office/room/house etc** *I got suspicious when I found him nosing around my office early one morning.*

7 to try and find out about an accident, crime etc

- investigate
- make inquiries/enquiries
- go into
- probe
- look into
- solve
- be under investigation

investigate /ɪnˈvestɪɡeɪt/ [v I/T] to try to find out the truth about a crime, an accident, or a problem, especially by using careful and thorough methods: *Police are investigating an explosion at the city store.* | *We sent our reporter, Michael Gore, to investigate.* | *The commission will investigate the cause of the accident, focusing especially on safety issues.*

make inquiries/enquiries /ˌmeɪk ɪnˈkwaɪəriz/ [v phrase] especially British to ask people questions about a person, crime, accident etc in order to find out information about it: *A reporter who tried to make inquiries was arrested.* | **+ into/about** *Police are making inquiries into the theft of a quantity of explosives.* | *He had made a few inquiries and learnt that she inherited the money from her father.*

go into /ˌɡəʊ ˈɪntuː/ [phr v T] to try to find out the facts of a situation in order to explain why it happened: *'How did Blake manage to escape?' 'That's something that we will have to go into.'* | *The headteacher promised the parents that he would be going into the matter of bullying very thoroughly.*

probe /prəʊb/ [v I/T] to carefully and thoroughly try to find out all the facts about a situation, especially when someone wants to keep these a secret: *The Secretary of State is probing claims of election fraud.* | **+ for** *Reporters began probing for more information.* | **+ into** *The press have been criticised for probing too deeply into the actor's private life.*

look into /ˌlʊk ˈɪntuː/ [phr v T] if someone in an official position **looks into** a problem or bad situation, they try to find out more about it so that the situation can be improved: *The manager promised to look into my complaint.* | *Police are looking into the possibility that the bomb warning was a hoax.* | *Callahan hired me to look into the accident.*

solve /sɒlv‖sɑːlv, sɔːlv/ [v T] if someone **solves** a crime or a mystery, they get all the information they need so that they can explain exactly what happened: *Detectives are trying to solve the murder of a young girl.* | *Officials hope the Navy will solve the mystery of four bombs that are missing from the wreckage of a military jet.*

be under investigation /biː ˌʌndər ɪnvestɪˈɡeɪʃən/ [v phrase] if a person, organization etc **is under investigation,** the police are trying to find out if they are involved in a crime or illegal activity: *A health club is currently under investigation by Boston detectives.* | *Several of the company's executives are under investigation.*

8 the process of finding out about something

- investigation
- inquiry
- inquest
- autopsy

investigation /ɪnˌvestɪ̇ˈgeɪʃən/ [n C] a process by which the police or another official organization tries to find out the truth about a crime or accident: *Following a major police investigation, two men have been arrested.* | **+ into** *The investigation into the cause of the air crash is continuing.* | **carry out an investigation** *Prison officials are carrying out a full investigation after two prisoners escaped from a prison vehicle.* | **full/thorough investigation** *The Senator promised a thorough investigation into the fund-raising activities of both parties.*

inquiry ALSO **enquiry** British /ɪnˈkwaɪəri‖ ɪnˈkwaɪəri, ˈɪŋkwəri/ [n C] a series of official meetings at which people try to find out why something happened: *The inquiry will be supervised by a senior judge.* | **+ into** *Local people are calling for an inquiry into the accident.* | **hold an inquiry** *An inquiry will be held to discover why the school's educational record is so bad.*

inquest /ˈɪŋkwest/ [n C] a legal process in Britain to find out why someone died: *The inquest heard that Mr Bovary was found hanging by a rope in his bedroom.* | **+ into** *an inquest into the death of a 54-year-old woman* | **hold an inquest** *An inquest will be held into the actor's death.*

autopsy /post mortem British /ˈɔːtɒpsi‖-tɑːp-, ˌpəʊst ˈmɔːʳtəm/ [n C] a medical examination of a dead person's body, done in order to officially find out why the person died: *If she died of a drug overdose, it will show up in the autopsy.* | *The post mortem revealed that the man had been shot in the back.*

9 something that you find out

- discovery
- finding

discovery /dɪsˈkʌvəri/ [n C] something such as a new fact or method that someone has found out, either accidentally or as a result of careful examination or questions: *At first I did not realize the importance of my discovery.* | **+ that** *An investigation was ordered after the discovery that $89,000 was missing from the account.* | **+ about** *The depletion of the ozone layer has been one of the most dramatic discoveries about our planet in recent years.*

finding /ˈfaɪndɪŋ/ [n C usually plural] the information that someone has found out as a result of examining something carefully: *One of the findings was that many cases of 'stomach flu' are caused by improper cooking of food.* | *The police force has had its image severely battered by the commission's findings.*

10 someone who likes to find out about things

- curious
- curiosity
- inquisitive
- nosy

curious /ˈkjʊəriəs/ [adj] wanting to find out about someone or something because you are very interested in them: *'Why do you want to know about Catherine?' 'Oh no reason. I'm just curious.'* | *Being naturally curious animals, cats often find their way into dangerous places.* | **+ about** *Even young children often become curious about drugs.* | **curious to learn/know/see etc** *It was a weird situation, and I was curious to learn more.* —**curiously** [adv] *'Why are you wearing that ring?' said Sally, looking at me curiously.*

curiosity /ˌkjʊəriˈɒsɪ̇ti‖-ˈɑːs-/ [n U] the desire to find out about things: *Events like these excite a child's natural curiosity.* | **+ about** *Olly was bursting with curiosity about the new house.* | **satisfy sb's curiosity** (=tell them about something so that they are no longer curious) *To satisfy vistors' curiosity, park officials have prepared maps on which the historical sites are clearly marked.*

inquisitive /ɪnˈkwɪzɪ̇tɪv/ [adj] always wanting to find out about what people are doing, how things work, what is happening etc: *Jenny was a very inquisitive child, always asking 'why?'* | *The crowded room was filled with lights, cameras, and inquisitive reporters.* | *The kids were wide-eyed and inquisitive.* —**inquisitively** [adv] *He peered inquisitively into the open window.*

nosy /ˈnəʊzi/ [adj] always wanting to find out things that do not concern you, especially other people's private affairs: *A nosy neighbor actually videotaped them in their own backyard.* | *At first, the children are afraid to ask questions they think might be impolite or nosy.*

11 someone whose job is to find out about something

- investigator
- private investigator/private detective
- detective

investigator /ɪnˈvestɪ̇geɪtəʳ/ [n C] someone whose job it is to find out about situations, crimes, problems etc in order to explain them: *A team of special investigators have gone to the scene of the explosion.* | *The investigator has concluded that they were making a false insurance claim.*

private investigator/private detective /ˌpraɪvɪ̇t ɪnˈvestɪ̇geɪtəʳ, ˌpraɪvɪ̇t dɪˈtektɪv/ [n C] someone who people pay to find out about such things as a person's disappearance, someone's secret activities etc, but who does not work for the police: *She hired a private detective to find her husband.* | *A private investigator had been engaged to watch Mr Hart and report on his activities.*

detective /dɪˈtektɪv/ [n C] a police officer whose job is to find out the facts about crimes and who is responsible for them: *I'm a detective with the Los Angeles Police Department. Do you mind if I ask you a few questions?* | *Detectives made a TV appeal for anyone with any information about the crime to contact them.*

finish

WHAT'S HERE

to finish doing sth

RELATED WORDS

▸ *see also* **stop, end, complete/not complete, ready/not ready**

1 to finish doing something or making something

- finish
- have done sth
- complete
- get sth finished
- be through
- conclude

finish /ˈfɪnɪʃ/ [v I/T] to **finish** doing or making something: *Have you finished your homework yet?* | *He was in London at the time, finishing a degree in economics.* | *The builders say they should have finished by Friday.* | *'To think you might have been ...' Carlos didn't finish his sentence.* | **finish doing sth** *Give me a call when you've finished unpacking.* | *Let me finish washing the dishes, then I can help you.*

have done sth /həv ˈdʌn (sth)/ [v phrase] if you **have done** a piece of work, you have finished doing it: *Ask Jane if she's done that essay yet.* | *I've done all the painting. Now all that's left is to put the pictures back up.*

complete /kəmˈpliːt/ [v T] to finish making something, writing something, or doing something that takes a long time to finish: *The building is likely to be completed in two years' time.* | *The novel wasn't published until 40 years after it was completed.* —**completion** [n U] *On completion of the course you will be given a certificate of competence.*

get sth finished /ˌget (sth) ˈfɪnɪʃt/ [v phrase] to make an effort to finish something before you do something else: *I'd like to get all these letters finished so I can mail them on my way home.* | *He doesn't think he's going to get the baby's room finished before it's born.*

be through /biː ˈθruː/ [v phrase] informal to have finished doing something: *We thought it would only take a few minutes to put up the tent but by the time we were through it was dark.* | **+ with** *The mechanic thought he'd be through with the car at about four.*

conclude /kənˈkluːd/ [v T] formal to finish a piece of work or process etc properly and completely, especially so that you are ready to use the results of it: *By July the research team had concluded the main part of its work.* | *The police have now concluded their investigations.*

2 to have nearly finished something

- be nearly finished/done/through
- be on the last lap/in the home stretch
- put the finishing touch/touches to
- finish off
- tie up the loose ends
- finalize

be nearly finished/done/through especially British ALSO **be almost finished/done/through** /biː ˌnɪəʳli ˈfɪnɪʃt, ˈdʌn, ˈθruː, biː ˌɔːlməʊst ˈfɪnɪʃt, ˈdʌn, ˈθruː/ [v phrase] *I'm nearly finished – I just want to put these files away.* | *Are you almost done in the shower?* | *Just give me a couple more minutes. I'm nearly through.*

be on the last lap/in the home stretch /biː ɒn ðə ˌlɑːst ˈlæp‖-ˌlæst-, ɪn ðə ˌhəʊm ˈstretʃ/ [v phrase] to have almost finished something, especially something that has taken a long time: *The election campaign is now on its last lap.* | *The regular season is in the home stretch, and the playoffs will soon begin.*

put the finishing touch/touches to British ALSO **put the finishing touch/touches on** American /ˌpʊt ðə ˌfɪnɪʃɪŋ ˈtʌtʃ, ˈtʌtʃɪz tuː, ˌpʊt ðə ˌfɪnɪʃɪŋ ˈtʌtʃ, ˈtʌtʃɪz ɒn/ [v phrase] to finish something by adding the last details, especially in order to make it look nice: *Sue's just putting the finishing touches to her make-up.* | *Painters are putting the finishing touches on the baseboards and railings.* | *The team are busy putting the finishing touches to the new design.* —**the finishing touch/touches** [n phrase] *Your patio is lovely. Those tubs of flowers are the perfect finishing touch.*

finish off /ˌfɪnɪʃ ˈɒf/ [phr v T] to finish something by adding the last parts or details **finish off sth** *I came to work early this morning to finish off some urgent work for the boss.* | **finish sth off** *I usually partially cook steaks in the microwave and then finish them off on the grill.*

tie up the loose ends /ˌtaɪ ʌp ðə ˌluːs ˈendz/ [v phrase] to finish a meeting, an agreement etc by dealing with all the details that remain: *If we can tie up the loose ends in the next ten minutes, we'll break for an early lunch.* | *Apart from a few loose ends that need to be tied up, everything has gone according to schedule.*

finalize ALSO **finalise** British /ˈfaɪnəl-aɪz/ [v T] to do the last things that are necessary in order to settle an agreement, plan, or arrangement in a satisfactory way: *Mr Samuels is flying to Detroit to finalize the details and sign the contract.* | *The meeting has been postponed until travel arrangements can be finalized.*

3 to finish using something

- finish with
- be through/be done

finish with /ˈfɪnɪʃ wɪð/ [phr v T not in passive] especially British *Can you pass me the scissors when you've finished with them, please?* | *'Have you finished with the Monopoly game?' 'Yes.' 'Well put it away then.'*

be through/be done /biː ˈθruː, biː ˈdʌn/ [v phrase] to have finished using something: *I need to use the computer. Can you let me know when you're done?* | **+ with** *Aren't you through with the phone yet?*

4 to finish a performance, speech, meeting etc

- finish/end
- wind up
- bring sth to an end/to a close
- conclude
- round off
- finish off/finish up

finish/end /ˈfɪnɪʃ, end/ [v T] *When Sir George finished his speech there was a moment's silence.* | **finish/end sth by doing sth** *The priest ended the service by saying a short prayer.* | **finish/end sth with sth** *She ended her recital with an old French song.*

wind up /ˌwaɪnd ˈʌp/ [phr v I/T] to gradually end an event or activity such as a meeting, making sure that it finishes at the right time: *About 40 minutes after the interview starts, the interviewer will signal to you to start winding up.* | **wind up sth** *He was fired and the board would give him no more time to wind up his affairs.* | **wind sth up** *Mark wanted to wind the meeting up quickly because he had a plane to catch.*

bring sth to an end/to a close /ˌbrɪŋ (sth) tʊ ən ˈend, tʊ ə ˈkləʊz/ [v phrase] to formally finish a meeting, lesson, process etc: *The committee has brought to a close one of the longest-running Senate investigations ever.* | *Efforts must continue to bring the conflict to an end.*

conclude /kənˈkluːd/ [v I/T] to formally or officially end a meeting, public event, speech etc by doing one final thing **conclude sth with sth** *This year, Muslims will conclude Ramadan with the usual festivities on April 15 or 16.* | **+ with** *He concluded with an appeal to everyone to support the campaign.* | **+ by doing sth** *I'd like to conclude by thanking everyone who has worked so hard to make this conference possible.*

round off /ˌraʊnd ˈɒf/ [phr v T] to do something as a way of ending an event, performance etc in a suitable or satisfactory way **round off sth** *To round off National Peace Week, a concert was organized in the park.* | **round sth off with sth** *She served us a splendid dinner, rounded off with a marvellous orange mousse.* | *They rounded off the day with a barbecue at the beach.*

finish off/finish up /ˌfɪnɪʃ ˈɒf, ˌfɪnɪʃ ˈʌp/ [phr v I/T] to complete an event, performance, piece of work etc by doing one final thing that is necessary or suitable: *Please finish off now. The test will end in three minutes.* | *You can finish up the puzzle tomorrow morning. It's time for bed now.* | **finish off/up sth by doing sth** *We finished off our vacation by spending two days in Santa Fe.* | **finish off/up sth with sth** *Dan finished up his act with a joke about the Vice-President.*

5 something that is finished

- finished
- be done
- completed
- be complete

finished /ˈfɪnɪʃt/ [adj] *All the packing was finished and we were ready to leave.* | *A young couple moved into the house three weeks after it was finished.* | *The finished book was more of a personal diary than an autobiography.* | **finished version/product/article etc** *Looking at the finished product, you wouldn't know it was made from paper.*

be done /biː ˈdʌn/ [v phrase] to be successfully finished: *Mom won't let me watch television till all my homework's done.* | *We'll send you a bill when the repairs are done.*

completed /kəmˈpliːtɪ̈d/ [adj] finished, especially after a long period of time or a lot of work: *We'll only get paid if the job is satisfactorily completed.* | *At last all the arrangements were completed and we waited impatiently for the big day to arrive.*

be complete /biː kəmˈpliːt/ [v phrase] if something that involves a number of stages **is complete**, it is finished: *You'll be paid more when your training is complete.* | *Building work should be complete within 20 weeks.* | *When the mixing process is complete, the mixture is ready to be heated.*

6 to finish something that is difficult or unpleasant

- see through
- get it over with/get it over and done with
- to the bitter end
- stick it out/stick with
- have/be done with it

▸ *see also* **determined**

see through /ˌsiː ˈθruː/ [phr v T] *The course was hard, but I wanted to see it through.* | *Cassidy, aged 83, intends to see the project through to completion.*

get it over with/get it over and done with /ˌget ɪt ˈəʊvəʳ wɪð, ˌget ɪt ˌəʊvər ən ˈdʌn wɪð/ [v phrase] to do something now, without delaying any more, so that it is finished and you can stop worrying about it: *I'm going to make an appointment at the dentist and get it over with before the holidays.* | *Let's get the clean-up over and done with.*

to the bitter end /tə ðə ˌbɪtər ˈend/ [adv] if you do something **to the bitter end**, you continue doing it in a determined way until it is finished, even though it is very unpleasant or difficult: *Campaigners vowed to carry on the struggle to the bitter end.* | *Despite his injury, Johnson carried on playing on to the bitter end.*

stick it out/stick with /ˌstɪk ɪt ˈaʊt, ˌstɪk ˈwɪð ɪt/ [v phrase/phr v T] to finish doing something in spite of great difficulty or pain: *Eleven girls joined the junior high football team, but only four stuck it out until the end of the season.* | *It's hard to stick with an exercise program you don't enjoy.*

have/be done with it /hæv, biː ˈdʌn wɪð ɪt/ [v phrase] especially British to do or finish something difficult or unpleasant now, so that you can stop thinking about it or worrying about it: *Just go pay the fine and be done with it.* | *If that's what you want to do, for heaven's sake do it and have done with it.*

to end

7 when an event, activity, situation etc finishes

- end
- be over
- come to an end
- be at an end

end ALSO **finish** British /end, ˈfɪnɪʃ/ [v I] *World War II ended in 1945.* | *What time does your class finish?* | *How does the story end?* | *The celebrations didn't finish till after midnight.* | **end in sth** (=end in a particular way, especially a bad way) *Their marriage finally ended in divorce three years later.*

be over /biː ˈəʊvəʳ/ [v phrase] if an event or an activity **is over**, it has ended and nothing more is going to happen: *By the time we arrived, the party was already over.* | *Right, that's the formal part of the interview over. Is there anything you'd like to ask us?* | **be all over** (=have completely finished) *The game should be all over by 5 o'clock.*

come to an end /ˌkʌm tʊ ən ˈend/ [v phrase] to finally end – use this about a period of time, a situation, or an activity that has continued for a long time: *Months of uncertainty came to an end when the final votes were counted.* | *It was already September, and our stay in Zurich was coming to an end.*

be at an end /biː ət ən ˈend/ [v phrase] formal if something such as a meeting or conversation **is at an end**, it has ended because someone wanted it to end: *The young man stood up, realizing that the audition was at an end.* | *It is with great sadness that I announce that our marriage is at an end.*

8 when a period of time ends

- end
- come to an end
- be over
- break up
- draw to a close/to an end
- be up
- run out
- be out of time

end /end/ [v I] *The school year ends in June.* | *Winter was finally ending, and the first flowers of spring had begun to appear.* | *The evening ended cordially with handshakes all round.*

come to an end /ˌkʌm tʊ ən ˈend/ [v phrase] if a long period of time **comes to an end**, it ends: *Autumn came to an end with the first snow.* | *A generation of civil war had finally come to an end.*

be over /biː 'əʊvəʳ/ [phr v I] if a period of time **is over**, it has ended: *The long vacation was almost over, and she hadn't done any of the things she'd planned.* | *I think I'm going to lose my temper before this evening is over.*

break up /ˌbreɪk 'ʌp/ [phr v I] British if a school or the students in a school **break up**, a part of the school year ends and the holidays begin: *When does your school break up?* | *The kids break up on Wednesday.*

draw to a close/to an end /ˌdrɔː tʊ ə 'kləʊz, tʊ ən 'end/ [v phrase] to gradually come to an end – used especially in stories or descriptions: *The long hot summer was drawing to an end.* | *As the class drew to a close, Hanson asked a student to summarize the lesson.*

be up /biː 'ʌp/ [phr v I] if the time allowed for something **is up**, it is finished: *'Time's up,' said the teacher. 'Stop writing, everyone!'* | *The chairman may be asked to resign before his four-year term is up.*

run out /ˌrʌn 'aʊt/ [phr v I] if the time available for doing something, especially something important, **runs out**, it comes to an end so that there is no more time left: *We'd almost finished solving the problem when our time ran out.* | *The desperate search for survivors continues, but time is running out.*

be out of time /biː ˌaʊt əv 'taɪm/ [v phrase] spoken use this to tell someone to stop doing something because there is no more time allowed: *I'm sorry, listeners, we have to stop there. We're out of time.*

9 when the time in which you can use tickets etc finishes

- run out
- expire

run out /ˌrʌn 'aʊt/ [phr v I] if a ticket, document, or agreement **runs out**, it can no longer be used or no longer has any legal or official value: *I want to use this train ticket before it runs out.* | *The lease on the shop runs out soon.* | *The current treaty runs out at the end of this year.*

expire /ɪk'spaɪəʳ/ [v I] if a ticket, bank card, legal document etc **expires**, the period of time during which it can legally be used has ended: *I'm afraid we can't accept this credit card – it expired last week.* | *Your passport will expire ten years from the issue date.* | *She retired six months before her contract expired.* —**expiration** /ˌekspɪ̈'reɪʃən/ [n U] *After the expiration of the trial period for the software, please contact our website.*

10 when something bad has finished

- be over/be all over
- be over and done with
- be behind
- it's all in the past
- be closed

be over/be all over /biː 'əʊvəʳ, biː ˌɔːl 'əʊvəʳ/ [v phrase] if a problem or bad experience **is over**, it has ended: *There had been a fight in the bar, but when the police got there it was all over.* | *His captors finally released him, and his long ordeal was over.* | *In 1963, the White House wrongly predicted that the military action in Vietnam would be over by 1965.*

be over and done with /biː ˌəʊvər ən 'dʌn wɪð/ [v phrase] if something unpleasant or something you have been worrying about **is over and done with**, it has finished and no longer affects you: *What happened many years ago is over and done with as far as I'm concerned.* | *They belonged to a part of her life that was over and done with.*

be behind /biː bɪ'haɪnd/ [v phrase] if an unpleasant experience **is behind** you, it is finished so that it does not affect your life or feelings any more: *Because of the measures we have taken, the worst is now behind us.* | **put sth behind you** (=deal with an unpleasant experience, so that it no longer affects you) *Counselling helped her put the experience behind her.*

it's all in the past /ɪts ˌɔːl ɪn ðə 'pɑːst‖-'pæst/ spoken use this to say that an unpleasant experience has ended and can be forgotten: *Your troubles are all in the past now.*

be closed /biː 'kləʊzd/ [v phrase] use this to say that you are not willing to discuss a subject any more, especially because it is unpleasant or upsetting: *As far as I am concerned, the matter is closed.* | *Until we can talk about this in a civil manner, I consider the discussion closed.*

11 not finished

- not finished/unfinished
- incomplete
- not over yet

not finished/unfinished /nɒt 'fɪnɪʃt, ʌn'fɪnɪʃt/ [adj] *On her desk was an unfinished letter to her mother.* | *To this day, the building remains unfinished.* | **unfinished business** (=something you have not had the chance to finish) *It is past time for Congress to attend to unfinished business.*

incomplete /ˌɪnkəm'pliːt◂/ [adj] not finished, because not all of the work has been done on something, or because it does not have all the parts that it should have: *The excavation of the tunnel is still incomplete.* | *Incomplete historical records have made the investigation more difficult.*

not over yet /nɒt ˌəʊvəʳ 'jet/ [adv] if something **is not over yet**, especially something difficult or unpleasant, it is not finished and still needs to be done or dealt with: *The struggle for equal rights is not over yet.* | *The crisis is not over yet. We are still involved in negotiations.*

to use all of sth

RELATED WORDS

see also **use, remain**

12 to use all of something

- finish
- run out of
- use up
- exhaust

finish /'fɪnɪʃ/ [v T] especially British to eat or drink all of something, so that there is none left: *The kids have finished all the ice-cream.* | *Wait till I've finished my drink and then we'll go.* | *Come on, finish your dinner.*

run out of /ˌrʌn 'aʊt ɒv/ [phr v T] if you **run out of** something that you need, there is none left: *We ran out of gas on the freeway last night.* | *By the time they got back to the camp, they had nearly run out of water.*

use up /ˌjuːz 'ʌp/ [phr v T] to use all of something, especially when it is difficult to get more of it **use up sth** *By 2100, we may have used up all our supplies of natural gas.* | **use sth up** *I thought I'd bought plenty of paint, but we used it up before the room was finished.*

exhaust /ɪg'zɔːst/ [v T] written to use up all of something, especially a supply of something that will be difficult to replace: *What will happen when we have* *exhausted all our natural resources? | The organization has exhausted all its funds. | Over-intensive farming had exhausted the supply of nutrients in the soil.*

13 when there is nothing left

- be (all) gone
- be finished
- no more/not any more
- none left/not any left
- run out
- exhausted

be (all) gone /biː (ˌɔːl) ˈgɒn‖-ˈgɔːn/ [v phrase] if something **is all gone**, there is none of it left because it has all been used, eaten, or drunk: *'Are there any cookies left?' 'No, they're all gone.' | Then Cal lost his job and soon our savings were gone. | I used to feel sorry for her, but my sympathy's all gone now.*

be finished /biː ˈfɪnɪʃt/ [v phrase] if a supply of something important **is finished**, it has all been used and there is none left: *In this area, emergency food aid is likely to be finished within days. | When that can's finished, there won't be any fuel left.*

no more/not any more /nəʊ ˈmɔːʳ, ˌnɒt eni ˈmɔːʳ/ [adj phrase] if there is **no more** of something or **not any more** of something, it has all been used or sold: *'Where are the matches?' 'We don't have any more.'* | **there's no more/there aren't any more** *There's no more sugar. You'll have to get some next time you go out.* | **+ of** *The store didn't have any more of the dolls, but they might get some in next week.*

none left/not any left /ˌnʌn ˈleft, ˌnɒt eni ˈleft/ [adj phrase] if there is **none left** or **not any left** of something, all of it has been used or sold **there is none left/there is not any left** *Don't eat any more cake or there will be none left for your dad. | There weren't any dresses left in a size 12.* | **there is no wine/milk/fruit etc left** *There's no coffee left. Shall I make some more?*

run out /ˌrʌn ˈaʊt/ [phr v I] if something that you need **runs out**, there is none of it left because it has all been used: *Our supplies had run out and all we could do was wait. | I was in a phone box and my money ran out before I'd finished.*

exhausted /ɪgˈzɔːstɪd/ [adj] if a supply of something is **exhausted**, there is none of it left; if something that produces a supply is **exhausted**, there is nothing left in it: *The oxygen supply would soon become exhausted. | All that's left are some barren hillsides and a couple of exhausted mines.*

14 to not use all of something

- not finish
- leave

not finish /nɒt ˈfɪnɪʃ/ [v phrase] *No you can't have another notepad – you haven't finished that one yet. | Try not to finish your food rations too quickly. We don't know when there will be more.*

leave /liːv/ [v T] to not use or eat all of something, especially because you do not want to, or because you want to keep some: *Is Tom all right? He left nearly all his dinner.* | **leave sth for sb** *Always leave enough fuel for the next person to build a fire with.* | **leave sb sth** *Leave me some space, will you!*

15 something that is never all used

- inexhaustible
- endless supply

inexhaustible /ˌɪnɪgˈzɔːstɪbəl◂/ [adj] an **inexhaustible** supply etc is never all used or seems impossible to use all of: *The enemy seemed to have an inexhaustible supply of ammunition. | What is the source of Armstrong's seemingly inexhaustible wealth? | Scientists are working to create a fuel that would be cheap, clean, and inexhaustible.*

endless supply /ˌendləs səˈplaɪ/ [n phrase] a supply of something that seems as if it will never all be used – use this especially when you know that it could all be used up soon: *A seemingly endless supply of fireworks lit up the clear night sky. | We don't have an endless supply of oil. | He seems to think I have an endless supply of cash.*

fire

RELATED WORDS

- *see also* **burn, hot, smoke, explode, destroy, save (4-7)**

1 a fire that damages a building, forest, etc

- fire
- blaze
- inferno
- flames

fire /faɪəʳ/ [n C] *Eleven people died in a fire in Chicago early Monday.* | **fire spreads** (=gets bigger or worse) *The fire quickly spread throughout the building.* | **fire breaks out** (=starts suddenly) *Investigators say the fire probably broke out in the hotel kitchen.* | **start a fire** *The fire was started by an electrical fault.* | **forest fire** *A forest fire had been raging in the south and the sky in that direction had a deep red glow.*

blaze /bleɪz/ [n C usually singular] a large and dangerous fire that burns very strongly: *Firefighters struggled to control the blaze. | The church was completely destroyed in the blaze.*

inferno /ɪnˈfɜːʳnəʊ/ [n C usually singular] a very large, very hot, and very dangerous fire, especially in an enclosed space such as a building – used especially in newspapers and in literature: *Eleven homes and several businesses were destroyed in the inferno. | He rushed back into the inferno to rescue his two-year-old sister, Cora, who had been trapped inside.*

flames /fleɪmz/ [n plural] the bright parts of a fire that you see burning in the air: *I saw flames coming from the engine. | She frantically sprayed the flames with a fire extinguisher.*

2 a fire for making you warm, for cooking, or for burning things

- fire
- bonfire
- campfire

fire /faɪəʳ/ [n C] a small, controlled **fire** that you make in order to provide heat or to cook food: *Could you bring in some wood for the fire? | In the evenings the whole family would gather around the fire.* | **log/coal etc fire** (=a fire that burns logs, coal etc) *There's nothing more comforting than a blazing log fire.* | **light a fire** (=make it burn) *The old man lit a fire in the stove of the front room.*

bonfire /ˈbɒnfaɪəʳ‖ˈbɑːn-/ [n C] a large outdoor fire used for burning dead leaves, wood, or things you do not need, or used for celebrations **light a bonfire** (=make it burn) *The bonfire will be lit at 7.00 p.m., with fireworks starting just 15 minutes later.* | **build/make a bonfire** *They piled up scrap wood, boxes and other junk and made a big bonfire.*

campfire /ˈkæmpfaɪə^r/ [n C] a fire made outdoors for people who are camping, used for keeping them warm and cooking: *Never leave a campfire unattended.* | **sit around the campfire** *That night we sat around the campfire telling stories.*

3 the heat and light produced by something that is burning

- fire
- flame

fire /faɪə^r/ [n U] *Most animals are afraid of fire.* | *When did humans first learn to use fire?*

flame /fleɪm/ [n C] the hot bright area of burning gas which is produced by something that is burning: *Natural gas burns with a bright blue flame.* | *You can sterilize a needle by holding it in a flame.* | *The candle flame flickered and then went out.*

4 to make or start a fire

- make/build a fire
- light a fire
- start a fire
- arson

make/build a fire /ˌmeɪk, ˌbɪld ə ˈfaɪə^r/ [v phrase] *He made a fire out of old rags and newspapers.* | *There isn't enough wood here to build a fire.*

light a fire /ˌlaɪt ə ˈfaɪə^r/ [v phrase] to deliberately make a fire start burning, especially in order to provide heat or to cook something: *It was her job to light a fire every morning before the family got up.* | *In such a strong wind it was almost impossible to light a fire.*

start a fire /ˌstɑː^{r}t ə ˈfaɪə^r/ [v phrase] to make a fire start burning, especially in a place where it might cause damage: *The kids accidentally started a fire in the garage.* | *The fire was started by a carelessly tossed cigarette.*

arson /ˈɑː^{r}sən/ [n U] the crime of deliberately starting a fire in order to damage a building or property: *Police are treating the fire as a case of arson.* | *Brooks was arrested for arson in North Carolina.*

5 to stop a fire from burning

- put out
- extinguish
- blow out
- smother

put out /ˌpʊt ˈaʊt/ [phr v T] to make a fire stop burning **put out the fire/blaze/flames** *It took firefighters four hours to put out the blaze.* | **put sth out** *She threw sand on the fire to put it out.*

extinguish /ɪkˈstɪŋgwɪʃ/ [v T] formal to stop a fire burning: *He managed to extinguish the flames with his coat.* | *It took several hours to extinguish the blaze.*

blow out /ˌbləʊ ˈaʊt/ [phr v T] to make a flame or fire stop burning by blowing on it **blow out a candle/match/fire etc** *He blew out the candle and went to sleep.* | **blow sth out** *We tried to light a fire but the wind kept blowing it out.*

smother /ˈsmʌðə^r/ [v T] to cover a fire with something in order to stop it from burning: *If the victim's clothes are burning, use a blanket to smother the flames.*

6 people whose job is to stop fires

- firefighter
- fireman
- the fire brigade

firefighter /ˈfaɪə^{r}ˌfaɪtə^r/ [n C] someone whose job is to stop fires burning: *Firefighters rescued the children, who were trapped in an upstairs room.* | *It took firefighters over two hours to put out the fire.* | *Over 300 firefighters were killed when the North Tower collapsed.*

fireman /ˈfaɪə^{r}mən/ [n C] especially British a man whose job is to stop fires burning: *Two firemen died in a blaze.* | *I wanted to be a fireman when I was a child.*

the fire brigade British **/the fire department** American /ðə ˈfaɪə^r brɪˌgeɪd, ðə ˈfaɪə^r dɪˌpɑː^{r}tmənt/ [n singular] the organization in a town or area that works to prevent fires and to stop fires burning: *The fire brigade arrived promptly and the fire was quickly brought under control.* | *Spending on police and fire departments accounts for about 55 percent of the city's general fund.*

first

RELATED WORDS

opposite: **last**

▸ *see also* **start, beginning, introduce, new, invent**

1 happening, existing, done etc first

- first
- first
- first of all
- original
- initial
- earliest
- the first time
- unprecedented

first /fɜː^{r}st/ [adj] before everyone or everything else: *Laurie's name was first on the list.* | *I still remember my first day of school.* | *She had her first baby in 1998.* | *I've only read the first chapter, but it seems like a really good book.* | *The first thing I ever had published was an article for the Boy Scout magazine.*

first /fɜː^{r}st/ [adv] before you do any other things, or before anything else happens: *I always read the sports page of the newspaper first.* | *Shall we go out now, or do you want to eat first?* | *I'll help you with your homework, but first let me finish the dishes.*

first of all /ˌfɜː^{r}st əv ˈɔːl/ [adv] at the beginning, before other events or actions – use this especially to say what you should do or what you did do first: *First of all, fry the onions.* | *First of all, let me welcome everyone to the meeting.* | *First of all I went to tell my wife and then my daughter and son-in-law what had happened.*

original /əˈrɪdʒɪnəl, -dʒənəl/ [adj only before noun] use this about something that existed at the beginning, especially before a lot of things were changed: *The house still has its original stone floors.* | *Our original plan was to go camping, but it was pouring with rain.*

initial /ɪˈnɪʃəl/ [adj only before noun] use this to talk about what happened at the beginning of a process or activity or what someone felt at the beginning, especially when this changes later **initial response/reaction/feeling etc** *My initial reaction was one of complete disbelief.* | *After the initial shock, people adjusted to the new circumstances.* | **initial difficulties/problems/setbacks etc** *Initial difficulties with the computer system were soon fixed.* | **initial stage/trial/step etc** *I was only involved in the initial stages of the planning.* | *Classes in gun handling are recommended as the initial step for those who want to own a handgun.* —**initially** [adv] *Far fewer people have applied for the visas than the government initially expected.*

earliest /ˈɜː^{r}li$_{ə}$st/ [adj usually before noun] happening or existing before all others: *'The Comedy of Errors' is one of Shakespeare's earliest plays.* | *The earliest form of transport was probably some kind of sledge.* | *Ginger was one of the earliest oriental spices known to Europeans.*

the first time /ðə ˌfɜːʳst ˈtaɪm/ **[adv]** use this to say that something happens that has never happened before **+ (that)** *The first time I went on a plane I was really nervous.* | *It was the first time that she had seen her mother cry.* | **for the first time** *For the first time, representatives from the two countries will talk at a conference table.*

unprecedented /ʌnˈpresɪ̈dentɪ̈d/ **[adj]** something that is **unprecedented** has never happened before and is usually unexpected: *An unprecedented number of cars entered the race.* | *The police took the unprecedented step of publishing the victim's photograph.* | *The depression that started in mid-1929 was a catastrophe of unprecedented dimensions for the United States.*

2 first in a race or competition

- **be first/come first/finish first**

be first/come first/finish first /biː ˈfɜːʳst, ˌkʌm ˈfɜːʳst, ˌfɪnɪʃ ˈfɜːʳst/ **[v phrase]** to be the person who wins a race or a competition: *Jones came first in the 200 metres.* | *Maryam was first to cross the line, in just 12 seconds.* | *Krzystof finished first among the 147 professional cyclists.*

3 when something is the first thing you want to say

- **firstly/first**
- **first of all**
- **to start/begin with**
- **in the first place**
- **before I start**

firstly/first /ˈfɜːʳstli, fɜːʳst/ **[adv] spoken** say this to introduce the first fact, reason, or question, when you are going to mention several more things: *I wanted to change schools, firstly because I didn't like the teacher and secondly because it was too far away.* | *First, may I say that I am extremely grateful for the trust my colleagues have put in me.* | *African leaders are worried, firstly about the official flow of aid, and also about levels of private investment.*

first of all /ˌfɜːʳst əv ˈɔːl/ **[adv] spoken** say this when the reason you are giving first is the most important one: *Freddy, first of all, I didn't flirt with him. He flirted with me.* | *I called the book 'Drum Planet' because first of all, there are drums in every culture.*

to start/begin with /tə ˈstɑːʳt, bɪˈgɪn wɪθ/ **[adv] spoken** say this when your reason or fact is the most easy to see or understand: *To start with, one of the biggest problems in the classroom is that the kids don't get enough discipline at home.* | *Working at home is a good option, because, to begin with, what's the point of driving two hours a day just to sit in front of a computer?*

in the first place ALSO **for a start** British /ɪn ðə ˈfɜːʳst pleɪs, fər ə ˈstɑːʳt/ **[adv] spoken** say this when you are arguing or discussing something with someone and you are going to give the main reason that proves that what you are saying is true: *In the first place, they have a more experienced team, so they're more likely to win.* | *We haven't made a decision, because, in the first place, we do not know enough at this point.* | *For a start, someone's sex should not matter in a job interview.*

before I start /bɪˌfɔːr aɪ ˈstɑːʳt/ **spoken** say this when you are going to say something before you start the main part of a speech or talk to a group of people: *Before I start, I'd like to thank everyone for coming.* | *All right, before I start, could everyone please stand up and introduce themselves.*

4 someone's first performance, appearance, or speech

- **debut**
- **premiere**
- **maiden**
- **inaugural**

debut /ˈdeɪbjuː, ˈdebjuː‖deɪˈbjuː, dɪ-/ **[n C usually singular]** someone's first public performance, especially in a play, a film or a sport: *'Little Man Tate' was Jodie Foster's directorial debut.* | **+ for** *This is his debut for his new club, Manchester United.* | **make your debut** *Charlie Chaplin made his film debut in 1913.*

premiere /ˈpremieəʳ‖prɪˈmɪər/ **[n C usually singular]** the first public performance of a play or film: *I've been invited to the premiere of the new Schliessman play.* | **world premiere** (=the first performance anywhere in the world) *Music-lovers gathered in Boston for the world premiere of Gershwin's opera, 'Porgy and Bess'.* | **film/movie premiere** *'Singing in the Rain' begins with its stars attending a movie premiere.*

maiden /ˈmeɪdn/ **[adj only before noun]** **maiden voyage/flight/speech** the first one that a particular ship, aircraft, or person makes: *The Titanic sank on its maiden voyage.* | *Two jets crashed on their maiden flights last year.* | *The new prime minister admitted that her maiden speech had been too long.*

inaugural /ɪˈnɔːgjɪ̈rəl/ **[adj only before noun]** **inaugural lecture/address/speech etc** one that an important person does or makes when they first start a new job: *The inaugural address drew a large audience.* | *Professor Eston gave the inaugural lecture in 1860.*

5 to do something that has never been done before

- **be the first to do sth**
- **show the way/lead the way**
- **never been done/attempted/tried before**
- **pioneer**
- **pioneering**
- **break new ground**
- **break the mould**

be the first to do sth /biː ðə ˌfɜːʳst tə ˈduː (sth)/ **[v phrase]** *The Spanish were the first to keep cattle in the American deserts.* | *She was the first to see the link between poverty and poor health.* | **be the first person to do sth** *Yuri Gagarin became the first man to fly in space.*

show the way/lead the way /ˌʃəʊ ðə ˈweɪ, ˌliːd ðə ˈweɪ/ **[v phrase]** to be the first to do something, especially something good or successful, which may encourage others to do something similar: *Once the Japanese had shown the way, manufacturers in other countries soon began to use robots on a large scale.* | **lead the way in doing sth** *The company has led the way in developing environmentally friendly products.*

never been done/attempted/tried before /ˌnevəʳ biːn ˈdʌn, əˈtemptɪ̈d, ˈtraɪd bɪˌfɔːʳ/ use this about something someone does or tries to do that no-one has ever done before: *The special effects in the movie included things that had never been done before.* | *Because of advances in technology, we are* *able to try something that has never been attempted before.*

pioneer /ˌpaɪəˈnɪəʳ/ [v T] to be the first to invent or find a new method of doing something, and make it possible or easier for others to do the same: *He pioneered techniques for photographing moving objects.* | *Heart-transplant surgery was pioneered by Professor Christiaan Barnard.* —**pioneer** [n C] *She became famous as a pioneer of* (=the person who pioneered) *prison reform.*

pioneering /ˌpaɪəˈnɪərɪŋ◂/ [adj only before noun] using new and better methods or ideas for the first time: *Her pioneering work in the field of education will be remembered.* | *Cowley's pioneering development of modern emergency medicine helped save countless lives.*

break new ground /ˌbreɪk njuː ˈgraʊnd‖-nuː-/ [v phrase] if someone or their work **breaks new ground**, their work is completely new and different from anything that existed before: *Roosevelt's social reform program broke new ground.* | *The album is enjoyable, but breaks no new ground.* | *There's a lot of new ground being broken in the field of genetic research.* —**ground-breaking** /ˈgraʊnd ˌbreɪkɪŋ/ [adj only before noun] *He won praise as governor for his ground-breaking educational reforms.*

break the mould British **/mold** American /ˌbreɪk ðə ˈməʊld/ [v phrase] to be the first to do something in a different way from the way it was usually done before: *The governor urged teachers to break the mold in establishing new ways of teaching.* | *The new party promised to break the mould of British politics.*

6 something that is the first

- a first
- prototype
- original
- first-generation

a first /ə ˈfɜːʳst/ [n singular] something that has never been done or achieved by anyone before and is therefore surprising or exciting: *If an animated film was nominated as best picture, it would be a first.* | **+ in** *Roger Bannister's four-minute mile was a notable first in the history of athletics.* | *During the 1960's, the Soviet Union achieved a series of firsts in space exploration.* | **+ for** *Delivering a baby on the job was a first for the two police officers.*

prototype /ˈprəʊtətaɪp/ [n C] the first model of something, especially of a machine or a new invention, that is often improved in later models: *No damage to the prototype aircraft was reported after its first test flight.* | **+ of** *Pilots have begun testing a prototype of the new aircraft.* | *The prototype of this particular computer was developed by an American in 1975.* | **+ for** *Within a year, the company expects to have a prototype for military use.*

original /əˈrɪdʒɪnəl, -dʒənəl/ [n C] something such as a picture or a piece of writing that is not a copy but is the one produced for the first time by the artist or writer themselves: *I wasn't sure whether the portrait was an excellent copy or the original.* | *This is a photograph of the manuscript. The original is in the city museum.* —**original** [adj] *Only a millionaire could afford to buy an original Picasso* (=a picture by Picasso that is not a copy).

first-generation /ˌfɜːʳst dʒenəˈreɪʃən/ [adj only before noun] **first-generation** computers, machines etc were the first ones of their type to be produced, and are the ones that later computers, machines etc of the same type are based on: *The first-generation digital televisions cost over $2000.* | *There were a variety of problems common to first-generation computer software programs.* —**first generation** [n singular] **+ of** *The first generation of cellular phones used analog transmitters and receivers.*

fit/not fit

WHAT'S HERE

- **to be the right size** see **1 to 4**
- **physically strong and healthy** see **5 to 6**

to be the right size

RELATED WORDS

- *see also* **clothes, tight, loose, suit/look good together, size**

1 when clothes are the right size

- fit
- be the right size
- be a good fit
- grow into

fit /fɪt/ [v I/T not in progressive or passive] if clothes **fit**, they are the right size: *He's put on so much weight that his clothes don't fit any more.* | *Do these shoes still fit you?* | **fit like a glove** (=fit perfectly) *The pants were a little tight at first, but after I wore them a few times, they fit like a glove.*

be the right size /biː ðə ˌraɪt ˈsaɪz/ [v phrase] *Why don't you try it on to see if it's the right size?* | *They had the jacket I wanted and it was just the right size too.* | **+ for** *Are you sure those shoes are the right size for Bill?*

be a good fit /biː ə ˌgʊd ˈfɪt/ [v phrase] to fit very well and be comfortable to wear: *The suit was a good fit, but I didn't like the pattern.* | *I had to guess what size she was, but fortunately the dress was a good fit.*

grow into /ˈgrəʊ ɪntuː/ [phr v T not in passive] if a child or young person **grows into** clothes, they grow big enough to be able to wear them: *I know the sweater's too big for Jenny, but she'll soon grow into it.*

2 when clothes are not the right size

- not fit
- be too big/small
- not be the right size
- tight
- can't get into

not fit /nɒt ˈfɪt/ [v I/T not in progressive or passive] *If the boots don't fit, we can return them tomorrow.* | **not fit sb** *There was nothing wrong with the coat – we took it back to the shop because it didn't fit her.*

be too big/small /biː ˌtuː ˈbɪg, ˈsmɔːl/ [v phrase] *You can't wear your father's suit, it's far too big.* | *I have to buy Tim some new sandals. The ones he's wearing are too small.* | **+ for** *Those jeans must be two sizes too big for you.*

not be the right size /nɒt biː ðə ˌraɪt ˈsaɪz/ [v phrase] *I bought him a shirt, but it wasn't the right size.* | **+ for** *That sweater won't be the right size for him – he'll need an extra-large.*

tight /taɪt/ [adj] clothes that are **tight** are uncomfortable to wear because they are too small and press into your body: *I don't wear my black dress very much. It's very tight around the waist.* | *If your shirt collar's too tight, undo your top button.*

can't get into /ˌkɑːnt get ˈɪntuː‖ˌkænt-/ [v phrase] if you **can't get into** a dress, skirt, trousers etc, you have difficulty putting them on because they are too small: *I put on five pounds over Christmas and now I can't get into these jeans.*

3 to be the right size for a particular space

- be the right size
- fit
- will go

be the right size /biː ðə ˌraɪt ˈsaɪz/ [v phrase] *We didn't know if the carpet would fit in the bedroom, but it turned out to be just the right size.* | **+ for** *Do you think this bulb is the right size for the lamp?*

fit /fɪt/ [v I/T not in progressive or passive] to be the right shape or not too big for a particular space, hole etc: *We were going to put the fridge between the stove and the washing machine, but it wouldn't fit.* | *Does your key fit the lock on the garage door?* | **+ in/into** *Will this bag fit in the trunk?* | *We've designed a computer that fits into an ordinary briefcase.*

will go /wɪl ˈgəʊ/ [v phrase] if something **will go** into a particular place or space, it is possible to put it there: *It's no good trying to force it, it just won't go.* | **+ in/into** *Do you think the car will go in that parking space?* | *I've measured the space, and with a bit of luck, the washing machine should just about go into it.*

4 to be almost too big to fit into a space

- squeeze
- be a squeeze

squeeze /skwiːz/ [v I] to get into a space with great difficulty and only by forcing your way into it because the space is almost too small for you **+ into/through/past etc** *The tunnel was so narrow that only one person at a time could squeeze into it.* | *I squeezed through a hole in the hedge into the garden.* | **+ in** *The bus was already full but someone opened the doors and another passenger squeezed in.*

be a squeeze /biː ə ˈskwiːz/ [v phrase] use this to say that there are too many people or things in a small space: *It'll be a squeeze but I think we can get everyone into Stephen's car.* | **it's a tight squeeze** *We got everything into the suitcase, but it was a tight squeeze.*

physically strong and healthy

RELATED WORDS

- *see also* **healthy/unhealthy, exercise**

5 physically strong and healthy

- fit
- be in shape
- be in good condition
- athletic

fit British **/physically fit** American /fɪt, ˌfɪzɪ̈kli ˈfɪt/ [adj] healthy and strong, especially because you play sport or do exercise regularly: *Sandy's very fit – he runs five miles every day.* | *Just because you're in your sixties doesn't mean you can't be physically fit.* | **keep fit/stay fit** (=remain fit) *Cycling is a good way to keep fit.* | *We've got a match next month, so we've got to keep ourselves reasonably fit.* | *I stay fit by swimming for an hour each morning.* —**(physical) fitness** [n U] *I began running about a month ago to improve my physical fitness.* | *The magazine contained several articles about healthy eating, fitness, and exercise.*

be in shape /biː ɪn ˈʃeɪp/ [v phrase] if you are **in shape**, you are not fat and you can play sport or do exercise without getting tired: *I'll start playing basketball with you as soon as I'm in shape.* | **be in good shape** *She's in pretty good shape but I don't know if she'll be able to run a marathon.* | **stay in shape/keep in shape** (=to exercise regularly) *Walking to and from work helps me to stay in shape.* | *He's good at badminton but plays handball to keep in shape.*

be in good condition /biː ɪn ˌgʊd kənˈdɪʃən/ [v phrase] to be generally fit and healthy, especially because you take exercise regularly: *We were both good runners and in good condition but we still found the course difficult.* | **keep yourself in good condition** *Most of the players had kept themselves in good condition over the summer months.*

athletic /æθˈletɪk, əθ-/ [adj] fit, strong, and usually also good at sports: *He can play any sport, he's naturally athletic.* | *If you want me to play, I will, but I'm not very athletic.*

6 not fit

- unfit
- not be in shape/be out of shape/be out of condition

unfit /ˌʌnˈfɪt/ [adj] British not fit and not able to do hard physical activities easily, especially because you do not take enough exercise: *I realised how unfit I was when I tried to run up the stairs.* | *The survey shows that the typical 16-year-old is unfit, lazy, and probably plays no sports at all.*

not be in shape/be out of shape/be out of condition /nɒt biː ɪn ˈʃeɪp, biː ˌaʊt əv ˈʃeɪp, biː ˌaʊt əv kənˈdɪʃən/ [v phrase] to be unfit at the present time, especially when you have been fit in the past: *He knew that he was out of condition and it would be risky to attempt the climb.* | *I've been really out of shape since I stopped running every day.*

flat/not flat

RELATED WORDS

- *see also* **squash**

1 flat and smooth

- flat
- smooth
- even

flat /flæt/ [adj] a place that is **flat** has no hills or mountains; a surface or object that is **flat** has no raised or curved parts: *Cambridge is very flat and you can see for miles.* | *a flat, sandy beach* | *We sat down on a big flat rock.* | *Focaccia, an Italian flat bread, has become very popular for sandwiches.*

smooth /smuːð/ [adj] a **smooth** surface feels completely flat and has no rough or raised parts, especially in a way that is pleasant and attractive: *The marble table felt smooth and cold against her arm.* | *She has lovely smooth skin.* —**smoothness** [n U] *She sanded the edge of the board and rubbed her hand against it to test its smoothness.*

even /ˈiːvən/ [adj] a surface such as a floor or road that is **even** is completely flat and all its parts are at the same height: *The floor must be completely even before we lay the tiles.* | *After driving for so long on the gravel I was glad to get on an even stretch of road.*

2 not sloping or vertical

- flat
- level
- horizontal
- on its side

flat /flæt/ [adj/adv] *In those days the houses all had flat roofs.* | *We lay flat on our backs and stared up at the sky.*

level /ˈlevəl/ [adj] a surface or area that is **level** does not slope in any direction: *He looked for a strip of level ground where he could land the plane.* | *These shelves aren't level.*

horizontal /ˌhɒrəˈzɒntl◂‖ˌhɑːrəˈzɑːntl◂/ [adj] a **horizontal** line, position, or surface is completely straight, flat, and not sloping, and is parallel with the ground or the bottom of something: *The cliff revealed horizontal layers of rock.* | **horizontal line** *The teacher drew a long, horizontal line across the blackboard.* | **horizontal position** *The wine bottles should be kept in a horizontal position.*

on its side /ɒn ɪts ˈsaɪd/ [adv] something that is **on its side** has been moved from its usual upright position to a horizontal position: *One of the vehicles in the accident still lay on its side, blocking all four traffic lanes.* | *Place the chicken on its side in a baking dish and roast for 20 minutes.* | *A dog was pulling garbage out of a trash can which was lying on its side in the street.*

3 to make something flat

- flatten
- level
- roll/press/squash etc sth flat
- smooth

flatten /ˈflætn/ [v T] to make something flat, especially something that is not usually flat: *The wind and rain had flattened the crops.* | *Roll the dough into a ball and then flatten it with a rolling pin.*

level /ˈlevəl/ [v T] to make a piece of land flat and stop it sloping in any direction: *It is important to level the land before planting.* | **level sth off/out** *The site of the explosion has now been levelled out and is going to be made into a memorial garden.*

roll/press/squash etc sth flat /ˌrəʊl (sth) ˈflæt/ [v phrase] to make something flat by rolling it, pressing it etc: *Roll the pastry flat and cut out two 8-inch circles.* | *Please squash all aluminum cans flat before placing them in the bin.*

smooth /smuːð/ [v T] to make the surface of something such as paper or cloth completely flat and smooth: *She removed her cap and smoothed her lush black hair.* | **smooth sth down/out** *Across the table, Tanya smoothed down her skirt and looked at her watch.* | *Every morning she smoothes the bedclothes out and dusts the room.*

4 to lay something flat on a surface

- lay sth/sb flat
- lay down

lay sth/sb flat /ˌleɪ (sth/sb) ˈflæt/ [v phrase] *Lay the skirt flat on an ironing board and cover it with a damp cloth.* | *The fish are laid flat on a board and scraped with the back of a knife to remove the scales.* | *Realizing the man had a back injury, we laid him flat on the ground and waited for the ambulance to arrive.*

lay down /ˌleɪ ˈdaʊn/ [phr v T] to carefully put something or someone into a horizontal position **lay sth/sb down** *We carried the injured child over to the bed and laid her down.* | **lay sth/sb down on/in etc** *She folded her scarf and laid it down on the seat next to her.* | **lay down sth/sb** *'That thing weighs a ton,' said Ian, laying down the marble slab on the floor.*

5 when a road, piece of land etc becomes flat

- flatten/flatten out
- level off/out

flatten/flatten out /ˈflætn, ˌflætn ˈaʊt/ [v I/phr v I] *The road widens and flattens as it nears the sea.* | *Towards the top of the hill the ground flattens out and the climb should be easier.*

level off/out /ˌlevəl ˈɒf, ˈaʊt/ [phr v I] to become flat and level, especially after sloping: *Where the path levels out you will find an old cottage.* | *After climbing steeply through woodland the lane levelled off.*

6 not flat or smooth

- rough
- bumpy
- uneven
- lumpy

rough /rʌf/ [adj] not flat – use this about roads, walls, areas, land etc where the surface is not smooth because there are a lot of stones or small raised parts: *A rough gravel trail was the only way into town.* | *rough mountain paths* | *the rough stone walls of the old castle*

bumpy /ˈbʌmpi/ [adj] a **bumpy** road, path, or area of land has a lot of holes and raised parts in it: *The field was too bumpy to play football on.* | *Neal drove the last mile down the bumpy road towards the highway.* | **bumpy ride** (=when you are travelling in a vehicle on an uneven surface) *Fasten your seatbelt, this ride may be bumpy.*

uneven /ʌnˈiːvən/ [adj] an **uneven** surface has areas that are not flat or not all at the same level: *His teeth were yellow and uneven.* | *The old uneven brick sidewalk was ripped up and replaced.*

lumpy /ˈlʌmpi/ [adj] a bed or chair that is **lumpy** has lumps under the surface so that it is uncomfortable to sit on or lie on: *Sandra lay on the lumpy mattress, unable to sleep.* | *I paid $40 a week for a tiny room with a lumpy couch and a battered old desk.*

7 not level

- sloping
- slope

sloping /ˈsləʊpɪŋ/ [adj only before noun] something that is **sloping** is higher at one end than at the other: *an old hotel with lovely sloping lawns* | *A gently sloping bank led down to the stream.*

slope /sləʊp/ [v I] if the ground or a surface **slopes**, it is not level but goes gradually upwards or downwards **slope downwards/upwards/away/into etc** *The garden sloped down gradually towards the sea.* | *Tilt the board so that it is sloping upwards away from you.*

8 with lots of hills or mountains

- hilly
- rolling
- mountainous

hilly /ˈhɪli/ [adj] an area of land that is **hilly** has lots of hills: *the hilly farmlands of New Jersey* | *The vineyards are hilly and difficult to cultivate.*

rolling /ˈrəʊlɪŋ/ [adj only before noun] **rolling hills/fields/farmland etc** with a lot of rounded, not very steep hills and valleys, especially when this looks attractive: *The castle is set in rolling hills to the north of Orvieto.* | *He stood at the top of the hill, admiring the rolling landscape.*

mountainous /ˈmaʊntənəs/ [adj] an area of land that is **mountainous** has lots of high mountains: *The mainland of Greece is mountainous and largely infertile.* | *Fog and rain are common in the mountainous regions near the border.*

flow

when liquid moves or comes out of something

RELATED WORDS

▸ *see also* **liquid, water, pour**

- ▸ **flow**
- ▸ **come out**
- ▸ **pour**
- ▸ **run**
- ▸ **leak**
- ▸ **drip**
- ▸ **ooze**
- ▸ **gush**
- ▸ **trickle**
- ▸ **squirt**
- ▸ **spurt**
- ▸ **cascade**

flow /fləʊ/ [v I] if a liquid **flows**, it moves in a steady, continuous stream from one place to another: *The river flows more slowly here and it is safe to swim.* | **+ into/out of/over** *From here, factory waste flows straight into the sea.* | *Tears flowed down her cheeks as she hugged her children.* | *Oil flowed from the tanker into the sea.*

come out /ˌkʌm ˈaʊt/ [phr v I] if liquid **comes out** of a pipe, container etc, it flows out fairly slowly and in fairly small quantities: *When I turned on the tap a brownish liquid came out.* | **+ of** *There's oil coming out of your engine.* | *I can't get the ketchup to come out of the bottle.*

pour /pɔːʳ/ [v I] if a liquid or substance **pours** out of something, large amounts flow out of it **+ out of/off/down etc** *Sweat poured down his face.* | *Water was pouring out of the release gates on the dam.* | *Rain poured through the open window, waking me again an hour later.* | *Lava from the volcano is pouring down the mountain towards the town.*

run /rʌn/ [v I] if a liquid **runs** somewhere, it flows quickly and smoothly; if a tap is **running**, water is flowing out of it: *Who left the faucet running?* | **+ along/down etc** *Tears ran down her face.* | *A stream runs along the bottom of the field.*

leak /liːk/ [v I] if a liquid **leaks** from a container or pipe, or if a container or pipe **leaks**, the liquid comes out through a small hole or crack because the container or pipe is damaged: *I think the fuel tank is leaking.* | **+ through/into/out of/from** *Water was leaking from a pipe in the bathroom.* | *Yoghurt had leaked out of the pot all over my lunchbox.*

drip /drɪp/ [v I] if a liquid **drips**, it falls slowly and steadily, in drops **+ off/out/onto etc** *The blood was still dripping from the cut on his lip.* | *We stood under a tree, with rain dripping onto our heads.* | *Wax from the candle dripped on the tablecloth.*

ooze /uːz/ [v I] if a thick liquid, or a substance such as blood or mud, **oozes** out of something, it comes out of it slowly and steadily **+ out of/from** *A mixture of mud and rainwater oozed out of the bottom of the bucket.* | *Blood was oozing from the wound.* | *Thick, sticky syrup oozes out of the tree trunk and is collected in buckets.*

gush /gʌʃ/ [v I/T] if a liquid **gushes** from something, or if something **gushes** it, it flows or pours out very quickly in large quantities: *The knife wound was gushing blood.* | **+ out/from/down etc** *Oil gushed from the hole in the ship's hull.* | *A pipe burst in one of the apartments above, and water gushed down.* —**gush** [n singular] **+ of** *A sudden gush of liquid spurted out of the plant.*

trickle /ˈtrɪkəl/ [v I] if a liquid **trickles** somewhere, it flows slowly in drops or in a thin stream **+ down/into/out** *Blood trickled down the side of her face.* | *Water trickled out of the pipe.* | *The fire spread when burning gasoline trickled from the car toward other vehicles.* —**trickle** [n singular] *The raging torrent had been reduced to no more than a trickle.*

squirt /skwɜːʳt/ [v I/T] if you **squirt** liquid or it **squirts**, it is forced out of a narrow hole in a thin fast stream: *Kids were squirting each other with water pistols.* | **squirt sth on sb/sth** *He squirted some ketchup on his fries.* | **+ from/into** *The batter is squirted into round molds, then baked.* —**squirt** [n C] **+ of** *Add a couple of squirts of lemon juice to the mixture.*

spurt /spɜːʳt/ [v I/T] if a liquid **spurts** or something **spurts** it, it comes out of something quickly and suddenly and with a lot of force: *The knife hit an artery, and the wound spurted blood.* | **+ from/out of/into** *Oil from the spill spurted into the crystal waters of Prince William Sound.* | *Water spurted from the burst pipe.* —**spurt** [n C] *The whale sent one final spurt into the air and disappeared.*

cascade /kæˈskeɪd/ [v I] to flow down something in large quantities **+ from/into/down etc** *The walls of the cave are smooth, polished by the water cascading from above.* | *Water from the broken water main cascaded into a subway station.* —**cascade** [n C] **+ of** *Rainbows glanced off the cascade of the waterfall.*

fold

1 to fold something

- ▸ **fold**
- ▸ **fold up**
- ▸ **turn down**

fold /fəʊld/ [v T] to bend a piece of paper or cloth, so that one part of it covers another: *He folded his newspaper and handed it to me.* | *Before getting into bed, I usually fold my clothes and put them on the chair.* | **fold sth in two/in half** (=across the middle) *Tom folded the letter in half and stuck it in his pocket.* | **fold sth into a square/triangle etc** (=so that it has the shape of a square or triangle) *The napkins were folded into neat triangles.* —**folded** [adj only before noun] *a pile of folded towels*

fold up /ˌfəʊld ˈʌp/ [phr v T] to fold something, usually several times, in order to make it into a smaller or neater shape **fold up sth** *Rachel folded up the ironing board and put it in the closet.* | **fold sth up** *Don't just leave your clothes on the floor like that – fold them up.*

turn down /ˌtɜːʳn ˈdaʊn/ [phr v T] **turn down a sheet/blanket/collar etc** fold it back so that the top or corner of it is pressed down **turn down sth** *I turned down a corner of the page I was reading and shut the book.* | *The maid always turns down the bedclothes and places a mint on the pillow.* | **turn**

sth/it/them down *Button up your jacket and turn the collar down.*

2 a piece of furniture or equipment that can be folded

▸ folding/collapsible ▸ fold/fold up

folding/collapsible /ˈfəʊldɪŋ, kəˈlæpsəbəl/ [adj only before noun] a **folding** or **collapsible** bed, chair, bicycle etc is one that is specially designed so that it can be folded up and easily carried or stored: *You'll have to sleep on a folding bed in the living room.* | *By the window stood a large collapsible table with drawings and pencils all over it.*

fold/fold up /fəʊld, ˌfəʊld ˈʌp/ [v I/phr v I not in progressive] able to be folded: *My umbrella folds up and fits into my handbag.* | *I want a push chair that folds easily and weighs very little.* | **fold up into sth** (=fold into the shape of something else) *This portable bath folds up into a carrying case that is perfect for storing baby clothes.*

3 the straight line where something has been folded

▸ fold ▸ crease

fold /fəʊld/ [n C] a straight line where something, especially paper or cloth, has been folded: *Cut the paper along the fold.* | *She lay there in the narrow bed, her chin resting on the fold of the sheet.*

crease /kriːs/ [n C] a straight fold made carefully, especially in clothing: *I folded the paper back into its original creases and put it into the drawer.* | **sharp crease** *The defendant wore a blue blazer, a white shirt, and gray pants with a sharp crease.*

4 when something gets folds in it

▸ crease ▸ crumpled
▸ creased

crease /kriːs/ [v I] if clothes **crease**, they get unwanted folds or lines in them when you leave them somewhere, or when you wear them: *These trousers will crease if you don't hang them up properly.* | *Linen is a beautiful fabric but it creases very easily and needs to be pressed regularly.*

creased /kriːst/ [adj] clothes that are **creased** have unwanted folds or lines in them because you have left them somewhere or been wearing them: *His shirt was creased at the back where he had been lying down on it.* | *Professor Haines finally showed up wearing a badly creased suit with stains on the front.* | **get creased** *Don't put your shirts in there – they'll get creased.*

crumpled /ˈkrʌmpəld/ [adj usually before noun] if papers or clothes are **crumpled**, they have a lot of unwanted lines and folds, and look old and untidy: *She reached into her pocket and handed the clerk a crumpled ten-dollar bill.* | *I spent the night under a bridge, using a crumpled blanket as a bed.*

5 to open something that is folded

▸ unfold

unfold /ʌnˈfəʊld/ [v T] *He took out his handkerchief, unfolded it, and blew his nose.* | *Eileen struggled to unfold a large map.* | *'I must lay the table,' she said, unfolding a clean white linen tablecloth.*

follow

RELATED WORDS

- happening after something *see* **after**
- obey a law or someone's orders *see* **obey**
- *see also* **escape, catch (3-6)**

1 to follow someone

▸ follow ▸ follow on

follow /ˈfɒləʊ‖ˈfɑː-/ [v I/T] to walk, drive, run etc behind someone else, going in the same direction as them, especially because you are going somewhere together: *Follow me and I'll show you where the library is.* | *You drive on ahead and I'll follow.* | **follow sb around** (=to follow someone wherever they go, especially when this is annoying) *My little brother's been following me around all day.* | **followed by sb** *The woman entered the room, followed by three young children.* | **follow sb out/down/across etc** *She didn't notice that Jack had followed her into the kitchen.*

follow on /ˌfɒləʊ ˈɒn‖ˌfɑː-/ [phr v I] British to follow someone to the place where they are going but at a later time: *You go ahead. I'll follow on later.* | **follow on behind** *The bus set off first and we followed on behind in the car.*

2 to closely follow a person or animal in order to watch them

▸ follow ▸ track/trail
▸ tail ▸ hound
▸ be/sit on sb's tail ▸ stalk
▸ shadow ▸ stalker

follow /ˈfɒləʊ‖ˈfɑː-/ [v T] *He followed her home to find out where she lived.* | *Did you make sure you weren't followed on the way over here?* | *She complained to the police officer that she was being followed by two strangers.*

tail /teɪl/ [v T] informal if someone such as a police officer **tails** someone, they secretly follow that person to find out where they are going or what they are doing: *That police car has been tailing us for the last 5 miles.* | *A group of photographers tailed the couple all over London.*

be/sit on sb's tail /biː, ˌsɪt ɒn (sb's) ˈteɪl/ [v phrase] to follow close behind someone, especially in order to watch or catch them: *A police car was on their tail within seconds of the alarm going off.* | *We sat on their tail for about an hour until we lost them in traffic.*

shadow /ˈʃædəʊ/ [v T] to follow someone or something very closely in order to watch all their movements without them realizing that they are being followed: *I want you to shadow him for the next three days and find out who he hangs out with.* | *Consumed with jealousy, he shadowed her for three days, hoping to catch her with her lover.*

track/trail /træk, treɪl/ [v T] to follow a person or animal closely, especially by looking for signs showing that they have gone in a particular direction: *Undercover agents have been tracking him for weeks.* | *It would be impossible to trail anyone across this type of ground.* | **track/trail sb to sth** *The police trailed the gang to their hideout.* | *Dogs are used to track the wolves to their lair in the forest.*

hound /haʊnd/ [v T usually in passive] to keep following someone and asking them questions about their activities, personal problems etc, in a way that is annoying or threatening: *After the court case she was hounded relentlessly by the press.* | *The couple found themselves hounded by photographers as they left the church.*

stalk /stɔːk/ [v T] to follow a person or animal quietly in order to catch, injure, kill them: *Polar bears stalk seals that are resting on the ice.* | *The killer would stalk his victim, overpower her and then brutally murder her.*

stalker /ˈstɔːkəʳ/ [n C] a criminal or mentally ill person who continuously follows and watches someone in a threatening way, especially someone famous or someone they are attracted to: *Women's groups are demanding that Congress toughen the law against stalkers.* | *The stalker's reappearance has led to increased security around the actress.*

3 to follow a person or animal quickly in order to catch them

- run after
- chase
- pursue
- in pursuit
- be on/at sb's heels
- go after
- give chase

run after /ˌrʌn ˈɑːftəʳ‖-ˈæf-/ [phr v T] to run or walk quickly behind someone in order to catch them or talk to them, when they are going away from you: *A group of little boys ran after him to ask for his autograph.* | *She's left her briefcase. Quick! Run after her!*

chase /tʃeɪs/ [v T] to run after someone in order to catch them, when they are trying to escape from you: *I didn't have the energy to chase him any more.* | **chase sb across/up/down etc sth** *The farmer chased the children across the field.* | **+ after** *We chased after him for about five blocks but then we lost him and had to turn back.*

pursue /pəʳˈsjuː‖-ˈsuː/ [v T] especially written to chase someone in a very determined way – used especially in stories and news reports: *Police pursued the gunman into an abandoned building.* | *The ship was being pursued by enemy submarines.*

in pursuit /ɪn pəʳˈsjuːt‖-ˈsuːt/ [adv] if you are **in pursuit** of someone, you chase them because you want to catch them – used especially in stories and news reports: *The robbers sped off in a stolen car with three police vehicles in pursuit.* | **+ of** *Cheng raced through a crowded shopping mall in pursuit of the man who had grabbed her purse.* | **in hot pursuit** *A deer suddenly sprang across the road, with a pack of hunting dogs in hot pursuit.*

be on/at sb's heels /biː ɒn, ət (sb's) ˈhiːlz/ [v phrase] written to follow very closely behind someone who is trying to escape from you, especially when you want to catch or attack them – used especially in stories: *The rebels headed for the border but government troops were still at their heels.* | **be hard/hot/close on sb's heels** *Just 15 minutes into the race Lawson was already hot on the champion's heels.* | **on/at sb's heels** *He rushed out of the theatre with a pack of reporters at his heels.*

go after /ˌgəʊ ˈɑːftəʳ‖-ˈæf-/ [phr v T] to follow someone quickly especially because you want to talk to them: *Don't go after him now. Let him calm down first.*

give chase /ˌgɪv ˈtʃeɪs/ [v phrase] to start to chase someone who is trying to escape from you – used especially in stories and descriptions: *Police spotted the car speeding on Dumbarton Bridge and quickly gave chase.*

food

RELATED WORDS

- food that is hard *see* **hard (2)**
- food that you grow *see* **grow**
- *see also* **meal, eat, cook, delicious, horrible, taste, simple (5), fresh/not fresh, drink**

1 food

- food
- something to eat
- grub
- diet
- refreshments
- nourishment

food /fuːd/ [n U] what people eat in order to grow and stay alive: *They didn't even have enough money to buy food.* | *The church program provides food and clothing for the needy.* | *Juntao refused food as a protest against prison conditions.*

something to eat /ˌsʌmθɪŋ tʊ ˈiːt/ [n phrase] especially spoken food, especially a small meal that you eat quickly: *You should have something to eat before you go out.* | *I'm not hungry – I had something to eat earlier.* | *Do you want me to fix you something to eat?*

grub informal ALSO **nosh** British spoken /grʌb, nɒʃ‖nɑːʃ/ [n U] food: *Where's the grub? I'm starving.* | *There was plenty of nosh at the party.*

diet /ˈdaɪət/ [n C] the type of food that someone usually eats: *The doctor told him to reduce the amount of fat in his diet.* | **a good/healthy/poor etc diet** *150,000 Californians die each year from diseases related to a poor diet.* | **balanced diet** (=a good mixture of healthy foods) *The secret to a longer life is a balanced diet and regular exercise.* | **low-fat/high-fibre etc diet** *a low-fat diet rich in fruits and vegetables* | **staple diet** (=a main diet consisting of one or two basic foods) *People in the coastal region live on a staple diet of rice and fish.* | **+ of** *For 27 years in the jungles of Guam, Yokoi survived on a diet of shrimp, coconuts, snails, frogs and rats.*

refreshments /rɪˈfreʃmənts/ [n plural] small amounts of food and drink that are served at a public meeting, a performance, or on a long journey: *Mrs Thompson has kindly offered to provide the refreshments for the school sports day.* | **light refreshments** (=a small quantity of food) *Light refreshments will be served during the interval.*

nourishment /ˈnʌrɪʃmənt‖ˈnɜː-, ˈnʌ-/ [n U] the different things that your body needs to grow and be healthy, that you get from food: *A growing child needs proper nourishment.* | *Calves rely on their mother's milk to provide nourishment.* | *The foetus gets nourishment via the mother's blood supply.*

2 a particular kind of food, or food that has been cooked in a particular way

- food
- dish
- speciality/specialty
- delicacy
- fare

food /fuːd/ [n C/U] *The doctor told him not to eat fatty foods.* | *Do you like spicy food?* | **French/Italian/Japanese etc food** *I've never had Indonesian food – what's it like?* | **fast food** (=food that is prepared and served quickly to customers) *the world's largest fast food restaurant chain* | **junk food** (=food that is not very healthy and is already prepared so you can eat it immediately) *You shouldn't eat all that junk food,* *it's bad for you.* | **health food** (=a special kind of food that people eat because they think it is good for their health) *A health food store is a good place to look for herbs.* | **baby food** (=specially prepared for babies) *You can quite easily make your own baby food at home.*

dish /dɪʃ/ [n C] several foods cooked together in a particular way, especially in a way that is typical of a country or place: *This dish can be served hot or cold.* | *a delicious vegetable dish with a spicy nut sauce* | *We serve a variety of Thai dishes.*

speciality/specialty /ˌspeʃiˈæləti, ˈspeʃəlti/ [n C] a type of special food that a restaurant, country, or area is famous for: *The village is famous for its seafood specialties.* | **local/regional speciality** (=from a particular area) *Fish curry is a local speciality*

delicacy /ˈdelɪkəsi/ [n C] a rare and expensive kind of food which people in a particular area think is very special: *Squid is a delicacy in this part of Italy.* | *Hasan plied us with drinks and an array of Egyptian delicacies which he brought from the kitchen.*

fare /feəʳ/ [n U] simple or healthy food – used especially in books or newspapers about the food in a restaurant: *The Elephant and Castle is known for its traditional English fare.* | *Children will be thrilled to find such simple fare as macaroni and cheese on the menu.*

3 food for animals

- food
- fodder
- feed

food /fuːd/ [n U] *New-born birds stay in their nest while their mother goes out in search of food.* | *Make sure you leave the cat plenty of food and water before you go.* | **cat/dog etc food** *Buddy won't eat the new dog food I bought.*

fodder /ˈfɒdəʳ‖ˈfɑː-/ [n U] food for animals such as cattle and horses, especially dried grass and raw vegetables: *All the left-over crops are chopped up and used as cattle fodder.* | *Beet tops were left on the ground as fodder for a small flock of sheep.*

feed /fiːd/ [n U] **chicken/hen/animal etc feed** food for birds or animals, especially in the form of grain: *A large part of our income goes on animal feed.*

4 to give food to a person or animal

- feed
- feed up
- serve
- serve up

feed /fiːd/ [v T] to give food to someone, especially a baby, animal, or a lot of people: *My sister feeds the cats when we are away.* | *How often do you have to feed the baby?* | *They hardly earn enough to feed their children.* | *The catering service feeds over 600 employees every day.* | **feed sb/sth on sth** *The horses were fed on hay and grain.*

feed up /ˌfiːd ˈʌp/ [phr v T] British to give a lot of food to a person or animal in order to make them fat or because they are not eating enough **feed sb up** *When I was young, my grandmother was always trying to feed me up with sweets and biscuits.* | **feed up sb** *We'll have to start feeding up the turkey for Thanksgiving soon.*

serve /sɜːʳv/ [v I/T] to give someone food by putting it in front of them, especially at a restaurant or a formal meal **serve sth** *Dinner will be served at eight o'clock.* | **serve sb** *The chef serves important guests himself.* | *We sat around for forty-five minutes, waiting to be served.* | **serve sb with sth** *They served us with soup and bread.* | **serve sth to sb** *Andrew, will you serve coffee to the visitors?*

serve up /ˌsɜːʳv ˈʌp/ [phr v T] to put food onto plates for people to eat, especially at home **serve up sth/serve sth up** *At dinner, Mrs. Carothers served up poached salmon and filled our glasses with white wine.*

5 an amount of food that someone is given or that someone eats

- portion
- helping
- serving

portion /ˈpɔːʳʃən/ [n C] an amount of food that is considered to be enough for one person as part of a meal: *My mother always gave the boys bigger portions than she gave me.* | **+ of** *Two portions of French fries please.*

helping /ˈhelpɪŋ/ [n C] an amount of food that is served to one person as part of a meal, use this especially when someone asks for a second similar amount: *He held out his bowl for another helping.* | **second/third etc helping** *Anyone want a second helping?* | **+ of** *She took another helping of pie when she thought no one was looking.* | **large/small helping** *They had turkey and stuffing topped off with large helpings of mashed potatoes.*

serving /ˈsɜːʳvɪŋ/ [n C] the amount of food that is cooked or prepared for each person: *This recipe makes enough minestrone soup for four to six servings.* | *The dish has about 250 calories per serving.*

6 food that makes your stomach feel full

- filling
- stodgy
- heavy
- rich

filling /ˈfɪlɪŋ/ [adj] food that is **filling** makes your stomach feel full very quickly, especially when it does not look as though it will: *I'll only give you a small amount of rice because it's quite filling.* | *Of course I like your chocolate cake, but it's so filling I couldn't possibly eat another piece.*

stodgy /ˈstɒdʒi‖ˈstɑː-/ [adj] food that is **stodgy** makes you feel full, is bad for your health, and usually has very little taste: *Stress, lack of rest and too much stodgy food had made Pauline break out in spots.* | *The food in Suzie's Café tends to be stodgy rather than fresh and light.*

heavy /ˈhevi/ [adj] food that is **heavy** makes your stomach feel full and you can feel it lying in your stomach for a long time after you have eaten it: *Some people find wholemeal bread too heavy.* | *Try to avoid heavy meals late in the evening.*

rich /rɪtʃ/ [adj] food that is **rich** contains a lot of cheese, cream, butter, or chocolate, and makes you feel full very quickly: *You mustn't eat too much rich food – it's bad for you.* | *The meat was browned to perfection and topped with a rich sauce.*

forbid

RELATED WORDS

opposite: —— **allow**

- not allowed by law *see* **illegal**
- *see also* **limit, no, rule/regulation, law, strict/not strict**

1 to tell someone that they must not do something

- not let/not allow
- tell sb not to do sth
- forbid
- say no/say sb can't do sth
- ban
- prohibit
- outlaw
- blacklist

not let/not allow /nɒt 'let, nɒt ə'laʊ/ [v phrase] to say that someone must not do something, and stop them doing it. **Not allow** is more formal than **not let** **not let sb do sth** *My parents won't let me stay out after 11 o'clock.* | **not allow sb to do sth** *The university does not allow athletes to work during the school year.* | **not allow sth** *Joan and Bill don't allow smoking in their house.*

tell sb not to do sth /ˌtel (sb) nɒt tə 'duː (sth)/ [v phrase] to tell someone that they should not do something, especially because it is dangerous or harmful: *My mother always told us not to talk to strangers.* | *His doctor told him not to drink any alcohol while he was taking the tablets.*

forbid /fəʳ'bɪd/ [v T] formal to say clearly and strongly that someone should not do something: *Their religion forbids the eating of pork.* | **forbid sb to do sth** *The management forbids employees to accept tips from customers.* | **forbid sb (from) doing sth** *They were forbidden from entering the sacred chamber.*

say no/say sb can't do sth /ˌseɪ 'nəʊ, ˌseɪ (sb) kɑːnt 'duː (sth) ‖-kænt-/ [v phrase] to tell someone that they cannot do something when they have asked for your permission to do it: *He wanted to use the car tonight but I said no.* | *She wanted to go to the conference but her boss said she couldn't take the day off from work.*

ban /bæn/ [v T] to officially forbid something – use this about activities that are forbidden by law or agreement, especially because they are dangerous: *Many doctors now say that boxing should be banned.* | *a new international treaty banning all nuclear tests* | **ban sb from (doing) sth** *Relatives of the prisoners were banned from visiting them.*

prohibit /prə'hɪbɪ̈t‖prəʊ-/ [v T] to forbid an activity by making it illegal: *International Law prohibits the use of chemical weapons.* | *The U.S. prohibited all flights to the country while the war was in progress.* | **prohibit sb from doing sth** *Mexican law prohibits the clergy from teaching in universities and schools.*

outlaw /'aʊtlɔː/ [v T] to completely forbid something by making it illegal: *Attempts to outlaw abortion have so far been unsuccessful.* | *Slavery was not officially outlawed in Australia until 1859.*

blacklist /'blækˌlɪst/ [v T usually in passive] if a government or organization **blacklists** someone, they keep a record of their name in order to forbid them doing a particular job or taking part in a particular activity: *Members of the Communist Party were blacklisted and had great difficulty finding work.* | *When she tried to get a loan she found she had been blacklisted.*

2 when you are not allowed to do something

- not be allowed to do sth
- be forbidden
- can't
- no smoking/parking etc
- be prohibited/not be permitted
- be not to do sth
- taboo

not be allowed to do sth /nɒt biː əˌlaʊd tə 'duː (sth)/ [v phrase] when a person or a rule says that you must not do something: *We're not allowed to wear jewellery at school.* | *My mom wasn't allowed to wear makeup until she was 16.* | **sth is not allowed** *Smoking is not allowed anywhere in the building.*

be forbidden /biː fəʳ'bɪdn/ [v phrase] if something **is forbidden**, you are not allowed to do it. If someone **is forbidden** to do something, they are not allowed to do it. **Be forbidden** is more formal than **not allowed**: *In Saudi Arabia, alcohol and drug use are forbidden.* | **be forbidden to do sth** *Prisoners were forbidden to speak to each other while they were working.* | **be strictly forbidden** *The use of mobile phones is strictly forbidden during take-off and landing.* | **forbidden by law** *Teachers were forbidden by law to teach Darwin's theory of evolution.*

can't /kɑːnt‖kænt/ [v phrase] spoken if you **can't** do something, you are not allowed to do it: *You can't park here.* | *Dad says I can't go out tonight.*

no smoking/parking etc /nəʊ 'sməʊkɪŋ/ used on signs and notices to say that you are not allowed to smoke, park your car etc: *There were 'no smoking' signs in every room.* | *The gate was locked and the sign said 'No Trespassing'.*

be prohibited/not be permitted /biː prə'hɪbɪ̈tɪ̈d, nɒt biː pəʳ'mɪtɪ̈d/ [v phrase] formal to be forbidden by a law or rule – used especially on official notices and warnings: *Cars are prohibited in the city centre.* | *Talking is not permitted in class.* | *Cameras are prohibited inside the cathedral.* | *The use of calculators in the test is not permitted.* | **strictly prohibited** *Smoking in the cinema is strictly prohibited.*

be not to do sth /biː ˌnɒt tə 'duː (sth)/ [v phrase] use this to tell someone that they are not allowed to do something: *You're not to tell anybody about this!* | *Employees are not to leave their cars in the company parking lot overnight.*

taboo /tə'buː, tæ-/ [adj] a subject, word, or activity that is **taboo** is not normally talked about or done because it is considered embarrassing or offensive according to social custom or accepted moral standards: *Sex before marriage is no longer taboo in western countries.* | **taboo subject** *Death is still a taboo subject for many people.* —**taboo** [n C] *Until a few years ago, there was a taboo around the subject of divorce.*

3 to forbid books, films etc

- ban
- censor
- censorship

ban /bæn/ [v T] to forbid a book, film, play etc from being sold, seen, performed etc because it is considered morally harmful or politically dangerous: *Films like that should be banned!* | *Comics were banned in my house because my parents thought they weren't a good influence.* | *'Lady Chatterley's Lover' was banned when it was first published.*

censor /'sensəʳ/ [v T] to examine films, books, letters etc and take out any parts that are considered to be morally harmful or politically dangerous: *The government censored all letters and telegrams going abroad during the war.* | *The court ruled that student newspapers could not be censored by school officials.*

censorship /'sensəʳʃɪp/ [n U] the practice of officially examining films, books, letters etc to take out any parts which are considered to be morally harmful or politically dangerous: *Any films that are shown here have to pass government censorship.* |

+ of *Angry journalists accused the government of censorship of free speech.*

4 to forbid someone from going somewhere

- be out of bounds
- be off limits
- ground

be out of bounds /biː ˌaʊt əv 'baʊndz/ [v phrase] if a place **is out of bounds**, you are not allowed to go there or enter it: *When I was younger, my parents allowed me to go anywhere except the town centre, which was out of bounds.* | **be out of bounds to sb** *The swimming pool is out of bounds to children unless they are with an adult.*

be off limits /biː ˌɒf 'lɪmɪ̈ts/ [v phrase] if a place **is off limits**, you are officially forbidden to go there: *The officer told the soldiers that the town was off limits.* | **+ to** *Much of the palace is off limits to the public.*

ground /graʊnd/ [v T] informal if a parent **grounds** their child, they do not allow them to go out with their friends for a period of time, as a punishment for behaving badly: *Mr Finkelstein grounded his kids after they were caught fighting at school.* | *I can't go to the movie with you – I'm grounded for the next two weeks.*

5 to forbid someone from taking part in an activity or sport

- suspend
- ban
- disqualify
- bar

suspend /sə'spend/ [v T] to remove someone from their job or their school for a limited period of time as a punishment or in order to find out whether they have done something wrong: *Martinez was suspended for a week because he attacked another student.* | *The teacher has been suspended while the accusation is being investigated.* | **suspend sb for doing sth** *Three police officers have been suspended for accepting bribes.*

ban /bæn/ [v T] to officially state that someone is not allowed to do something, especially as a punishment for something bad they have done **ban sb from doing sth** *She was banned from driving for 6 months.* | *The government has banned public officials from accepting gifts from foreigners.*

disqualify /dɪs'kwɒlɪ̈faɪ‖-'kwɑː-/ [v T] to officially state that someone is no longer allowed to take part in a competition or activity, because they have broken a rule **disqualify sb from sth** *Three athletes were disqualified from the championships after failing drugs tests.* | **disqualify sb from doing sth** *He was fined £500, and disqualified from holding any political office.*

bar /bɑːʳ/ [v T usually in passive] to forbid someone from entering a place or taking part in an activity, especially because they have done something wrong: *Sorry, you can't come into this club – you're barred.* | **be barred from doing sth** *The fans were barred from ever attending football matches in England again.* | **bar sb from doing sth** *In 1903 the New York School Board barred married women from teaching.*

6 forbidden political organizations

- banned
- outlawed
- illegal

banned /bænd/ [adj only before noun] a **banned** political organization is one that is forbidden to meet or exist: *The government ordered members of the banned political party to appear for questioning.* | *Leaders of the banned trade union were arrested last night.*

outlawed /'aʊtlɔːd/ [adj] a political organization that is **outlawed** is completely forbidden to operate because it is considered extremely bad or dangerous: *The government announced that the National Democratic Party had been outlawed.* | *Police were blaming an outlawed leftist group for the bombing.*

illegal /ɪ'liːgəl/ [adj] an **illegal** political organization is forbidden to operate by law: *All unions have been declared illegal by the ruling party.* | *An increasing number of racist attacks are being carried out by the NPA and other illegal organizations.*

7 an official order forbidding something

- ban
- sanctions
- embargo
- injunction

ban /bæn/ [n C] an official statement that forbids something, based on a law or a government decision **+ on** *The city has imposed a ban on smoking in all restaurants.* | *There has been worldwide protest against the ban on girls' education.* | **a total/complete ban** *The government is considering a total ban on the sale of handguns.* | **impose a ban on sth** (=ban something) *A ban has been imposed on the hunting and killing of whales.* | **lift a ban** (=stop having a ban) *The new prime minister agreed to lift the ban on opposition newspapers.*

sanctions /'sæŋkʃənz/ [n plural] official orders forbidding trade or dealings with a particular country, used as a way of punishing them or stopping them from doing something: *Economic sanctions can be as effective as military action.* | **+ against** *The Canadian foreign minister criticized U.S. sanctions against Cuba.* | **+ on** *Protesters called for sanctions on all countries that violate the human rights of their citizens.* | **impose sanctions** (=start having sanctions) *The U.S. threatened to impose sanctions on any country that used chemical or biological weapons.*

embargo /ɪm'bɑːʳgəʊ/ [n C] an official order forbidding trade in a particular product with a particular country for political or economic reasons **trade/oil/arms etc embargo** *There was a relaxation of the American trade embargo.* | **+ on** *an embargo on British beef* | *The government has imposed an arms embargo on countries involved in international terrorism.*

injunction /ɪn'dʒʌŋkʃən/ [n C] an official order made by a court forbidding someone to do something, which includes a threat of punishment if they ignore the order: *A court injunction forbade Clive Heywood to enter his wife's house.* | **take out an injunction** (=get an injunction from a court) *The government is taking out an injunction against the newspaper to try to stop it publishing a secret report.*

force sb to do sth

RELATED WORDS

▸ *see also* **must/don't have to, threaten**

1 to force someone to do something

- force
- make
- put pressure on
- pressurize
- push
- browbeat
- emotional blackmail
- be breathing down sb's neck
- be on sb's back

force /fɔːʳs/ [v T] *You don't have to come if you don't want to. Nobody's forcing you.* | **force sb to do sth** *Women's organizations are trying to force the government to appoint more women to senior positions.* | **force sb into doing sth** *Her parents are trying to force her into marrying a man she hardly knows.* | **force sb into sth** *I had never thought of buying an insurance policy, and I wasn't going to be forced into it by some young salesman.* | **force sb out of** *Eddie feels that he was forced out of his job in order to make way for a younger man.*

make /meɪk/ [v T] to force someone to do something that they do not want to do. **Make** is less formal than **force**: *I really didn't want to go, but she made me.* | **make sb do sth** *I wanted to watch the film, but Dad made me do my homework.* | *Karen made him promise never to discuss the subject again.*

put pressure on /ˌpʊt ˈpreʃər ɒn/ [v phrase] to keep trying to persuade someone to do something, for example by saying that it is their duty or that it will help other people **put pressure on sb to do sth** *Our parents were putting pressure on us to get married.* | *Advertising puts pressure on parents to work long hours, in order to buy things that their children don't need.*

pressurize ALSO **pressurise** British **/pressure** American /ˈpreʃəraɪz, ˈpreʃəʳ/ [v T] to try to make someone do something by persuading them very strongly and making them feel that they should do it: *I'll get this done as soon as I can – just don't pressure me, OK!* | *If she feels you're trying to pressurize her, she won't do it.* | **pressurize/pressure sb into doing sth** *School children are often pressurized into studying very hard from an early age by their parents.* | *The committee pressured him into resigning.* | **pressure sb to do sth** *Her boyfriend is pressuring her to have an abortion.*

push /pʊʃ/ [v T] to strongly encourage someone to do something **push sb to do sth** *My parents keep pushing me to get a good job.* | **push sb into doing sth** *Don't let them push you into a making a decision before you're ready.* | **push sb into sth** *Are you sure you want to marry me? I don't want to push you into anything.*

browbeat /ˈbraʊbiːt/ [v T] to force someone to do what you want them to do by repeatedly asking them to do it until they finally agree: *The salesman tried browbeating me but it didn't work.* | **browbeat sb into (doing) sth** *The miners were browbeaten into working in a part of the mine that the company knew to be dangerous.* | *I really didn't want to make this speech – I was browbeaten into it by my colleagues.*

emotional blackmail /ɪˌməʊʃənəl ˈblækmeɪl/ [n U] an attempt to force someone to do something, by making them feel guilty for not doing it: *She's always using emotional blackmail and playing on other people's feelings.* | *Any relationship that has to depend on emotional blackmail can't be a healthy one.*

be breathing down sb's neck /biː ˌbriːðɪŋ daʊn (sb's) ˈnek/ [v phrase] informal if someone **is breathing down your neck** about something, they keep asking you to do it in order to make you do it sooner: *I'm already really busy today, and now Paul's breathing down my neck saying he wants the Paris deal completed.* | **have sb breathing down your neck** *We'd better start sending out those letters soon – I've had the sales manager breathing down my neck about it all week.*

be on sb's back /biː ɒn (sb's) ˈbæk/ [v phrase] informal to be trying to make someone do something they do not want to do, especially by telling them several times to do it: *Nick knew that the coach would be on his back if he missed another training session.* | **+ about** *Aunt Mimi was always on his back about him 'wasting time playing that silly guitar'.*

2 to force someone do something by using threats or violence

- force
- make
- coerce
- compel
- bully
- blackmail
- use force
- strongarm tactics/methods
- under duress

force /fɔːʳs/ [v T] *If you don't comply I'm afraid we'll have to force you.* | **force sb to do sth** *Thieves had tied him up and forced him to lie on the floor.* | *All the hostages were forced to hand over their passports.* | **force sb into (doing) sth** *She claimed she was forced to take part in the robbery by her husband.*

make /meɪk/ [v T] to force someone to do something by using violence or threats: *I didn't want to take part in the attack but the soldiers made me.* | **make sb do sth** *They made sales staff open the safe.* | **be made to do sth** *The couple were made to hand over all their money and jewellery.*

coerce /kəʊˈɜːʳs/ [v T] written to force someone to do something that they do not want to do by threatening that something bad might happen to them if they do not do it: *Ray withdrew his confession, saying that he had been coerced by the police.* | **coerce sb into doing sth** *The mine owners coerced the workers into going back to work, by threatening to close down the mines completely.* | *Officials coerced peasants into voting for the government candidates.* | **coerce sb to do sth** *The company paid the workers the minimum rate of $4.86 an hour, but coerced some to give back half their pay in cash.* —**coercion** /kəʊˈɜːʳʃən ‖-ʒən/ [n U] *When peaceful methods of persuasion had failed, the government tried using coercion.*

compel /kəmˈpel/ [v T] formal to make someone do something by using force or official power **compel sb to do sth** *All the young men in the area were compelled to work in the quarries and coal mines.* | *The attorney general has the right to compel witnesses to appear in court.*

bully /ˈbʊli/ [v I/T] informal to force someone to do something by shouting at them, treating them badly, or using threats: *Don't let the salesman bully you – it's your choice.* | **bully sb into doing sth** *If you try and bully him into giving you the money he's sure to say no – you should try and persuade him gently.* | **bully sb into sth** *Ben didn't want to study law, but his father bullied him into it by threatening to cut off his allowance.*

blackmail /ˈblækmeɪl/ [v T] to force someone to give you money or do what you want, by threatening to tell embarrassing secrets about them: *Gina tried to blackmail him, by threatening to tell his wife about their affair.* | **blackmail sb into doing sth** *The FBI blackmailed her into informing on the other members of the gang.*

use force /ˌjuːz ˈfɔːʳs/ [v phrase] if someone **uses force**, they hit, shoot, or use other forms of violence against people in order to make them do something or stop them from doing something: *The regime was quite willing to use force and terror against its enemies.* | *The law permits every citizen to use reasonable force to defend themselves or their property.* | **+ against** *The police have recently had to defend their policy of using force against rioters.*

strongarm tactics/methods /ˈstrɒŋɑːʳm ˌtæktɪks, ˌmeθədz‖ˈstrɔːŋ-/ [n plural] violence or the threat of violence, used to force someone to do something: *The police have been accused of using strongarm tactics when breaking up strikes and public demonstrations.* | **use strongarm tactics/methods to do sth** *More and more credit companies are using strongarm methods to collect debts.*

under duress /ʌndəʳ djʊˈres‖-dʊˈres/ [adv] if someone does something **under duress**, they only agree to do it because they have been threatened, not because they want to do it: *The defendants claimed that their confessions were made under duress.* | *Judge Mershon ruled that the agreement was signed under duress, and was therefore null and void.*

3 to be forced to do something because of a bad situation

- force
- drive
- have no choice/ option
- compel sb to do sth
- be condemned to

force /fɔːʳs/ [v T] **force sb to do sth** *They had so little money that they were forced to sell the farm.* | *They were halfway up the mountain, when the weather became so bad that they were forced to turn back.* | **force sb into sth** *Here, girls are often forced into prostitution because they have no other means of earning money.*

drive /draɪv/ [v T] if something, especially someone else's behaviour **drives** someone to do something, it has such a bad effect on them that it forces them to take extreme action **drive sb to do sth** *At the trial, she claimed that years of abuse from her violent husband had driven her to kill him.* | **drive sb to despair/desperation etc** *Many farmers claim that they have been driven to desperation by the latest blow to the industry.* | **drive sb to drink** (=make someone drink alcohol all the time in order to forget their situation) *This job's enough to drive anyone to drink!* | **drive sb into doing sth** *Her mother's continual nagging drove her into running away from home.*

have no choice/option /ˌhæv nəʊ ˈtʃɔɪs, ˈɒpʃən‖-ˈɑːp-/ [v phrase] to be forced to do something because it is the only thing you can do even though you may not want to do it: *We had to leave them there. We had no choice.* | *Firefighters said they had to knock down the remaining walls – they have no other option.* | **leave sb with no choice/option but to do sth** *You leave me with no option but to resign.* | **leave sb with no choice/ option** *The business was failing, and in the end we had to close it down. We were left with no choice.*

compel sb to do sth /kəmpel (sb) tə ˈduː (sth)/ [v phrase] formal if a bad situation **compels someone to do something** they do not want to do, they are forced to do it because they feel there is nothing else they can do: *The high cost of materials will compel manufacturers to increase their prices.* | *These people are compelled by poverty to commit crime.*

be condemned to /biː kənˈdemd tuː/ [v phrase] to be forced to accept a very unhappy situation because there is nothing else you can do **be condemned to do sth** *The rich lived in luxury while thousands were condemned to live a life of poverty and despair.* | **be condemned to sth** *The island was condemned to centuries of colonial rule.* | *The accident condemned her to a lifetime of pain and disability.*

4 to force someone to accept something they do not want

- force sth on
- impose
- inflict sth on
- foist sth on

force sth on /ˈfɔːʳs (sth) ɒn/ [phr v T] *He thinks that just because he's the head of department he can force his opinions on everybody.* | *You shouldn't blame your father – the decision was forced on him by his situation.* | *Elaine kept forcing drinks on him all evening, and he wondered if she was trying to seduce him.*

impose /ɪmˈpəʊz/ [v T] if you **impose** your ideas and beliefs on other people, you try to force them to have the same ideas and beliefs as you: *Within days of being appointed office manager he had imposed his own working methods.* | **impose sth on sb** *Teachers should try to avoid imposing their own beliefs on their students.* —**imposition** /ˌɪmpəˈzɪʃən/ [n U] *There has been widespread protest against the imposition of religious teaching in schools.*

inflict sth on /ɪnˈflɪkt (sth) ɒn/ [phr v T] to force someone to accept something that causes them harm or suffering: *As time progressed, the king inflicted harsher and harsher measures on the people.* | *The new policy means that even higher bills will be inflicted on the taxpayer.*

foist sth on /ˈfɔɪst (sth) ɒn/ [phr v T] to get rid of a thing or piece of work that you do not want by giving it to someone else: *It's no use trying to foist your work on me.* | **foist sth off on to sb** *He's always trying to foist the children off on to me while he goes out and enjoys himself.*

foreign

RELATED WORDS

- someone who enters a country *see* **enter (5-7)**
- *see also* **country, travel, come from**

1 not from your own country

- foreign
- overseas
- from abroad

foreign /ˈfɒrɪ̣n‖ˈfɔː-, ˈfɑː-/ [adj usually before noun] not from your own country or not connected with your own country: *Can you speak a foreign language?* | *Some of the hotels accept foreign currency.* | *efforts to increase foreign investment*

overseas /ˌəʊvəʳˈsiːz◂/ [adj only before noun] especially British from or connected with a foreign country, especially one that is a long way away: *The university has a large number of overseas students.* | *There has been an increase in overseas trade during the last year.*

from abroad /frəm əˈbrɔːd/ from another country or from other countries: *There's a shortage of medical staff, so a lot of the doctors here are from abroad.* | *She seemed to receive a lot of mail from abroad.* | *Listening to radio broadcasts from abroad is still a criminal offense in this country.*

2 from a different country

- foreigner
- alien
- expatriate

foreigner /ˈfɒrɨnəʳ‖ˈfɔː-, ˈfɑː-/ [n C] someone who comes from another country – many people consider it impolite to call someone a **foreigner**: *A lot of foreigners work here illegally.* | *Saleem felt that people were suspicious of him because he was a foreigner.* | *About 40 million foreigners visited the US last year.*

alien /ˈeɪliən/ [n C] someone who lives or works in your country, but who comes from another country – used especially in legal and official contexts: *Some aliens may qualify for citizenship under the new law.* | **illegal aliens** *The law makes it easier to find and deport illegal aliens.*

expatriate especially British ALSO **expat** British informal /eksˈpætriət‖eksˈpeɪ-, ˌeksˈpæt/ [n C] someone who has gone to live in a foreign country, especially because they have a job there: *I was in Spain for over a year, but most of my friends were expatriates.* | *Schmidt was a German expatriate who had been living in Portugal since 1989.* —**expatriate** [adj] *Several expatriate families have left the country since war broke out.*

3 in or to a different country

- abroad
- overseas
- emigrate

abroad /əˈbrɔːd/ [adv] in or to a foreign country: *Katya will make her first trip abroad next month.* | **live/work/study etc abroad** *Our daughter wants to study abroad for a year.* | **be abroad** *Mr Harris is abroad on business this week.*

overseas /ˌəʊvəʳˈsiːz◂/ [adv] in or to a foreign country, especially one that is a long distance from your own: *Much of the wood harvested in the northwest is shipped overseas.* | **go/work/travel etc overseas** *Douglas often travelled overseas when he was in the army.*

emigrate /ˈemɨgreɪt/ [v I] to leave your own country in order to live permanently in another country: *The couple emigrated in 1987 and are back here on holiday to see friends and relatives.* | **+ from/to** *My grandparents emigrated from Italy.* | *Our son and his wife, Jenny, emigrated to Australia in 1988.*

forget

RELATED WORDS

opposite: **remember**

▸ *see also* **remind/make sb remember**

1 to forget something

- forget
- don't remember/can't remember
- have no recollection of
- slip your mind

forget /fəʳˈget/ [v I/T] to no longer remember information, something that happened in the past, or something that you must do: *I'm sorry, I've forgotten your name.* | *It was an experience she would never forget.* | *It's his birthday tomorrow. I hope you haven't forgotten.* | **+ what/where/how etc** *She forgot where she'd left her keys.* | **+ (that)** *I keep forgetting that you're allergic to chocolate.* | **+ to do sth** *Don't forget to call your mom tomorrow.* | **+ about** *Tom had forgotten about Tanya coming to stay.* | **forget all about sth** *I forgot all about tomorrow's exam.* | **completely forget** *I completely forgot about the meeting.* | **I forget** spoken (=I have forgotten) *She had this boyfriend – I forget his name – who was an actor.*

don't remember/can't remember /ˌdəʊnt rɪˈmembəʳ, ˌkɑːnt rɪˈmembəʳ‖ˌkænt-/ [v phrase] to not be able to remember something that you want to remember: *'How did you get home after the party?' 'I don't remember.'* | *I was going to phone you, but I couldn't remember your number.* | *Brad doesn't remember much about his mother because she died when he was small.* | **don't/can't remember doing sth** *Has she got an invitation? I don't remember inviting her.* | **+ what/where/how etc** *I don't remember exactly what happened.* | *He couldn't remember where he put his coat.*

have no recollection of /hæv ˌnəʊ rekəˈlekʃən ɒv/ [v phrase not in progressive] formal to not be able to remember something: *He claims to have no recollection of the incident.* | *I have no recollection of living in Australia, as my family left for England when I was three years old.*

slip your mind /ˌslɪp jɔːʳ ˈmaɪnd/ [v phrase] if something that you must do, especially something that is not very important, **slips your mind**, you forget to do it because you are too busy thinking about other things: *'I'm sure we agreed to meet here.' 'Maybe it's just slipped his mind.'*

2 to suddenly forget something

- it's on the tip of my tongue
- escape
- can't place
- your mind goes blank
- dry up
- go in one ear and out the other

it's on the tip of my tongue /ɪts ɒn ðə ˌtɪp əv maɪ ˈtʌŋ/ [v phrase] spoken use this to say that you know a name or word, but you are having difficulty remembering it at that moment: *That place we visited in Paris, what's it called? It's on the tip of my tongue.*

escape /ɪˈskeɪp/ [v T] spoken if a name, detail, fact etc **escapes** you, you forget it for a very short time but you know you will remember it soon: *I know I've heard this song before but its name escapes me.* | *Although I know that the novel was published in the nineteenth century, the actual date escapes me.*

can't place /ˌkɑːnt ˈpleɪs‖ˌkænt-/ [v phrase] spoken if you **can't place** someone or something, you recognize them but have forgotten their name or where you met them before: *I'm sure I've seen him before, but I just can't place him.* | *Her perfume seemed so familiar but he couldn't place it*

your mind goes blank /jɔːʳ ˌmaɪnd gəʊz ˈblæŋk/ if **your mind goes blank** you are suddenly unable to remember something at a time when you need it: *That's ... Oh, my mind's gone blank – I can't remember her name.* | *My mind goes blank when I have to take a test.*

dry up /ˌdraɪ ˈʌp/ [phr v I] British to forget what you were going to say or what you are supposed to say when speaking or acting, especially because you are nervous: *I dried up just as I was about to talk, even though I had been preparing the speech for weeks.* | *There was one worrying moment where one of the actors seemed to dry up for a few seconds.*

go in one ear and out the other /gəʊ ˌɪn wʌn ˌɪər ənd ˌaʊt ði ˈʌðər/ [v phrase] if details, a piece of information etc **go in one ear and out the other**, you forget them very quickly because you are not interested or not listening properly: *She understands nothing about football so it all goes in one ear and out the other.* | *He was trying to explain the assignment to me but it just went in one ear and out the other.*

3 to forget to bring something

- forget
- leave

forget /fərˈget/ [v T] to not bring something that you intended to bring, because you did not think of it: *Michael was at the airport before he realized he'd forgotten his passport.* | *Oh, I forgot your camera. Is it all right if I bring it to you tomorrow?* | *Don't let me forget my purse.*

leave /liːv/ [v T] to forget to take something with you when you leave: *I can't find my coat – I must have left it at work.* | **leave sth behind** *Oh no! I think I left my credit card behind at the restaurant.*

4 to try not to think about something

- forget
- put sth out of your mind
- put sth behind you
- take/keep your mind off

forget /fərˈget/ [v I/T] to deliberately try not to think about something sad or unpleasant: *I've been trying not to think about her but my friends won't let me forget.* | *a war the country was trying to forget* | *Years after they had gotten divorced, Olivia found it very difficult to forget John.* | **+ (that)** *Forget I mentioned it. I didn't mean to hurt your feelings.* | **+ about** *We can forget about the accident now and concentrate on getting on with our lives.*

put sth out of your mind /ˌpʊt (sth) aʊt əv jɔːr ˈmaɪnd/ [v phrase] to try to make yourself stop thinking about something that makes you angry, sad, or nervous: *It's time to put her out of your mind and find a new girlfriend.* | *I was nervous about flying for the first time but I tried to put it out of my mind.*

put sth behind you /ˌpʊt (sth) bɪˈhaɪnd juː/ [v phrase] to try not to think about something sad or unpleasant that happened in the past so that you can continue with your life and try to be happy: *Try and put the incident behind you and get on with normal life.* | *The team have put last night's loss behind them and are looking forward to next week's game.*

take/keep your mind off /ˌteɪk, ˌkiːp jɔːr ˈmaɪnd ɒf/ [v phrase] if an activity **takes your mind off** a worrying problem, it makes you not think about it for a short time: *Joe suggested a game of cards to take my mind off things.* | *Staying busy helped keep his mind off his troubles.*

5 someone who often forgets things

- have a bad/terrible/awful etc memory
- forgetful
- absent-minded
- have a memory like a sieve

have a bad/terrible/awful etc memory /hæv ə ˌbæd ˈmeməri/ [v phrase not in progressive] to not be good at remembering facts or information: *I'm sorry for forgetting to phone her – I have a terrible memory.* | **+ for** *I have a bad memory for names.*

forgetful /fərˈgetfəl/ [adj] someone who is **forgetful** often forgets things, especially things they have to do: *My grandfather's getting so forgetful – I have to remind him to take his medication.* | *She was easily distracted and forgetful at school.* —**forgetfulness** [n U] *Victims of the disease typically complain of dizziness, headaches, and forgetfulness.*

absent-minded /ˌæbsənt ˈmaɪndᵻd◂/ [adj] someone who is **absent-minded** often forgets things because they are thinking about other things: *He's a brilliant scientist but hopelessly absent-minded.* —**absent-mindedness** [n U] *Mrs. Chamorro was famous for her occasional absent-mindedness.*

have a memory like a sieve /hæv ə ˌmeməri laɪk ə ˈsɪv/ [v phrase not in progressive] British informal to not be able to remember facts or information, even for a short time: *You'd better remind him about the party – he's got a memory like a sieve!*

6 a medical condition that makes you forget things

- amnesia
- memory loss

amnesia /æmˈniːziə‖-ʒə/ [n U] the medical condition of not being able to remember a particular period of time or particular events or facts, caused by an injury or a very bad emotional shock: *A man suffering from amnesia was identified by his sister, who saw his picture on television.* —**amnesiac** /æmˈniːziæk/ [n C] *In his latest film he plays an amnesiac* (=someone with amnesia) *who meets his wife but doesn't recognize her.*

memory loss ALSO **loss of memory** /ˈmeməri ˌlɒs, ˌlɒs əv ˈmeməri‖ˌlɔːs-/ [n phrase] the inability to remember a particular period of time or particular events or facts, especially for a short time, caused by old age, illness, the effects of drugs etc: *Heimdal was critically injured in an accident and suffered head and back injuries, and memory loss.*

forgive/ not forgive

to decide not to blame someone or be angry with them although they have done something wrong

RELATED WORDS

- *see also* **sorry/apologize, blame, punish**

1 to forgive someone

- forgive
- excuse
- pardon
- forgive and forget
- let bygones be bygones

forgive /fərˈgɪv/ [v I/T not in progressive] to stop being angry with someone for something bad they have done, especially when they have upset you or done something unkind: *He's not the kind of person who is quick to forgive.* | *Please forgive me – it was a complete accident.* | *Hugh found his wife's behaviour hard to forgive.* | **forgive sb for sth** *He had lied to me, and I couldn't forgive him for that.* | **forgive sb sth** *I could understand her being angry, but I'll still never forgive her the way she treated me afterwards.* —**forgiving** [adj] able to forgive people easily: *He is a forgiving man who accepted the apologies of the men who attacked him.*

excuse /ɪk'skjuːz/ [v T not in progressive] to forgive a small fault such as carelessness, rudeness, lateness etc: *Excuse my brother if he talks too much, he's rather excitable.* | *I didn't realize this was a formal party, so I hope you can excuse my appearance.*

pardon /'pɑːʳdn/ [v T not in progressive] formal to forgive someone for something that is not serious, such as impolite or bad-tempered behaviour: *Pardon the mess – I got home late last night and didn't have time to clean up.* | **pardon sb for sth** *I am so sorry about that, Mr Judd. Please pardon my daughter for her little outburst.*

forgive and forget /fəʳˌgɪv ənd fəʳ'get/ [v phrase usually in infinitive] to forgive someone for something that happened in the past, usually a long time ago: *You two haven't said a word to each other for a year now. Don't you think it's time to forgive and forget?* | *Angela's father was not a man who found it easy to forgive and forget.*

let bygones be bygones /let ˌbaɪgɒnz biː 'baɪgɒnz‖-gɔːnz-/ [v phrase] spoken to forgive someone for something bad they did to you in the past, and stop being unfriendly towards them: *Why don't we let bygones be bygones and forget about the whole thing?*

2 what you say to tell someone that you forgive them

- it's all right/OK
- forget it
- never mind
- don't give it another thought
- no hard feelings

it's all right/OK /ɪts ˌɔːl 'raɪt, ˌəʊ 'keɪ/ spoken say this when someone has said that they are sorry for something they did: *'Sorry I didn't phone you last week.' 'That's OK – I know how busy you've been.'* | *'I must apologize for keeping you waiting so long.' 'That's all right.'*

forget it /fəʳ'get ɪt/ spoken informal say this to tell someone that you do not blame them for something, and that they should not worry about it any more: *'I feel so bad about upsetting your plans.' 'Oh, forget it. it really doesn't matter.'*

never mind /ˌnevəʳ 'maɪnd/ spoken say this when someone says they are sorry that they made a mistake or forgot something, and you want to tell them not to worry: *'Please forgive me for losing your book.' 'Oh, never mind. I have another copy.'*

don't give it another thought /dəʊnt ˌgɪv ɪt əˌnʌðəʳ 'θɔːt/ spoken say this when someone says they are sorry, and you want to tell them politely that there is no need to be sorry: *'I'm sorry we had to cancel the party.' 'Oh, please don't give it another thought. It wasn't your fault that you were ill!'*

no hard feelings /ˌnəʊ hɑːʳd 'fiːlɪŋz/ spoken informal say this when you want to tell someone that you are not angry with them, even though they have upset you or you have quarrelled with them: *No hard feelings, Stu. You had every right to be angry with me.*

3 behaviour that cannot be forgiven

- unforgivable/unforgiveable
- inexcusable

unforgivable/unforgiveable /ˌʌnfəʳ'gɪvəbəl◂/ [adj] behaviour that is **unforgivable** is so bad that you cannot forgive it: *The way you spoke to your mother was unforgivable.* | *It was an unforgiveable thing to do.*

inexcusable /ˌɪnɪk'skjuːzəbəl/ [adj] an action or situation that is **inexcusable** cannot be excused and someone must be blamed for it, because there is no good reason for it: *Anyone can make a mistake, but to ignore basic safety regulations is quite inexcusable.* | **it is inexcusable that** *It is inexcusable that the government has never paid a cent to the widows of these brave men.* — **inexcusably** [adv] *When you consider the cost of the meal, the service in the restaurant was inexcusably poor.*

4 to refuse to forgive someone

- never forgive
- bear/hold a grudge
- hold it against

never forgive /ˌnevəʳ fəʳ'gɪv/ [v phrase] to refuse to forgive someone, because they have done something very bad **never forgive sb for sth** *She never really forgave Roy for what he said.* | **never forgive yourself** *I'd never forgive myself if anything happened to the children while I was out.*

bear/hold a grudge /ˌbeər, ˌhəʊld ə 'grʌdʒ/ [v phrase] to continue to feel angry with someone for a long time because they treated you badly in the past: *Coughlan loved to argue but he never held a grudge.* | **+ against** *Can you think of anyone who might bear a grudge against you?* | *Police believe the suspect held a grudge against the federal government.*

hold it against /ˌhəʊld ɪt ə'genst/ [v phrase] to dislike someone because of something they did in the past, even though it is no longer important: *Look, he made one mistake – you can't hold it against him for the rest of his life.*

forward

RELATED WORDS

opposite: **back**

- to make progress when you are trying to do something *see* **progress**
- *see also* **front**

1 towards the front

- forward
- ahead
- on
- onward

forward ALSO **forwards** British /'fɔːʳwəʳd(z)/ [adv] towards the front: *She leaned forward and whispered 'I love you' in his ear.* | *I pushed my way forwards to the front of the crowd in order to get a better view.* | *Bill took two steps forward and shook Mark's hand.* | *Sit facing forward with your legs straight out in front of you.* | *She had her back towards me, her head bent forwards over a book.* | *Frank's fair hair fell forward into his eyes in a very attractive way.*

ahead /ə'hed/ [adv] if someone or something moves **ahead**, looks **ahead** etc, they move or look towards a place in front of them: *The doctor strode ahead to the end of the corridor, and waited there for the others to catch up.* | *He stuck his head out of the window but it was impossible to see ahead through the fog.* | **straight ahead** (=directly ahead) *Devraux stared straight ahead, without looking at his son.*

on /ɒn‖ɑːn, ɔːn/ [adv] if someone or something moves **on**, they continue moving forward in order to get to a particular place: *He walked on without even stopping to say hello.* | *Keep on in this direction for about*

100 metres, and you'll see the bank on your left. | **straight on** (=directly ahead) *Go straight on to the end of this road, then turn left.*

onward ALSO **onwards** British /ˈɒnwəʳd(z)‖ˈɑːn-, ˈɔːn-/ [adv] written if someone or something moves, travels etc **onward**, they move or travel forward, especially in order to continue a journey: *We wandered slowly onwards, pausing now and again to admire the view.* | *Traffic police stood at various points, waving the motorists onward.*

2 to move forward

- advance
- move up
- nose
- surge

advance /ədˈvɑːns‖-ˈvæns/ [v I] if a person or army **advances**, they move forward in a slow and determined way, for example in order to attack someone: *The plane slowly advanced down the runway and then paused, ready for take-off.* | *Villagers hid in the hills as the troops advanced.* | **+ across/into/through etc** *In early 1940 the army began to advance across France.*

move up /ˌmuːv ˈʌp/ [phr v I] if you **move up** when you are in a line of people or vehicles, you move forward into the position that is just in front of where you were before: *Could you guys at the front move up a bit?* | **move up the line** *The bank clerks seemed to be working really slowly as I moved up the line.* | **+ next to/alongside etc** *Suddenly a car moved up alongside Joseph and the driver shouted something at him.*

nose /nəʊz/ [v I] if a vehicle **noses** through or into something, it moves forward slowly and carefully in order to avoid hitting things in its way **+ through/past/in etc** *The Rolls Royce slowly nosed through the crowds, and drew up outside the hotel.* | **nose your way** *A ship was nosing its way through the small fishing boats in the harbour.*

surge /sɜːʳdʒ/ [v I] if a crowd of people **surges** forward, they suddenly move forward together **+ forward** *The new barriers are designed to give way if spectators surge forward too violently.* | **+ across/through/into** *Demonstrators surged through the streets, demanding the President's resignation.*

free

WHAT'S HERE

- **not costing any money** see **1 to 2**
- **free to do what you want** see **3 to 7**
- **not in prison** see **8 to 9**
- **free time** see **10 to 11**

not costing any money

RELATED WORDS

- *see also* **give, cheap, cost**

1 not costing any money

- free
- cost nothing/not cost anything
- for nothing/for free
- free of charge
- no charge
- be on the house
- at no cost to sb
- at no extra cost
- gratis

free /friː/ [adj] something that is **free** costs no money: *Parking is free after 6 pm.* | *'How much is it to get into the concert?' 'Oh, I think it's free.'* | *The clinic offers free advice on contraception.* | *I'm saving these tokens to get a free poster.*

cost nothing/not cost anything /ˌkɒst ˈnʌθɪŋ, ˌnɒt kɒst ˈeniθɪŋ‖ˌkɔːst-/ [v phrase not usually in progressive] to be free: *Luckily I was insured, so the treatment didn't cost anything.* | **+ to do sth** *It doesn't cost anything to get advice from them.* | *The competition costs nothing to enter, just send a postcard with your name and address.*

for nothing/for free /fəʳ ˈnʌθɪŋ, fəʳ ˈfriː/ [adv] without having to pay for something that you would normally have to pay for: *He offered to fix the car for nothing.* | *Fans were allowed into the stadium for nothing as a way of celebrating.* | *Children under five can see the show for free.*

free of charge /ˌfriː əv ˈtʃɑːʳdʒ/ [adv] without having to pay – used especially in advertisements and official notices: *Guests can park free of charge all day.* | *Copies of the leaflet can be obtained free of charge from your local library.* | *This policy ensures that you get emergency medical treatment free of charge when travelling abroad.*

no charge /ˌnəʊ ˈtʃɑːʳdʒ/ [n phrase] if there is **no charge** for a service that someone provides, you do not have to pay for it: *'How much is the prescription?' 'No charge – students are exempt from payment.'* | *Entry to the museum costs £3, but there is no charge on Wednesdays and Sundays.* | **+ for** *There is no charge for cashing these travellers' cheques.*

be on the house /biː ˌɒn ðə ˈhaʊs/ [v phrase] if drinks or meals **are on the house**, they are given to you by the owner of the bar or restaurant that you are in and you do not have to pay for them: *On New Year's Eve, he offered a glass of champagne to everyone, on the house.* | *The owner let us have the first bottle of wine on the house.*

at no cost to sb /ət ˌnəʊ ˈkɒst tə (sb) ‖-ˈkɔːst-/ [prep] if a service is provided **at no cost to** someone, they do not have to pay for it: *The Helpline provides advice on all types of personal problems at no cost to the caller.* | *Treatment at the health center is available at no cost to students.*

at no extra cost /ət ˌnəʊ ekstrə ˈkɒst‖-ˈkɔːst/ [adv] if a shop or a company provides an additional service **at no extra cost,** they do it without asking you for any more money: *Many activities are available at the hotel at no extra cost, but theatre trips and excursions are not included.* | **+ to** *The store is offering to install satellite dishes at no extra cost to the buyer.*

gratis /ˈgrætɪ̈s, ˈgreɪtɪ̈s/ [adj/adv] especially written provided without payment: *His work for the church is performed gratis.* | *You can see some local bands at local clubs absolutely gratis.*

2 something that is given free by a company

- complimentary
- free gift
- freebie

complimentary /ˌkɒmplɪ̈ˈmentəri◂‖ˌkɑːm-/ [adj only before noun] use this about things that a company, theatre, hotel etc gives people for free: *Karen's sister works at the New York Ballet and she's managed to get us some complimentary tickets.* | *Honeymooners receive a complimentary bottle of champagne in their hotel room.*

free gift /ˌfriː ˈgɪft/ [n C] something that is given free by a shop or a company, especially in order to advertise its products or to encourage you to buy something else: *Buy three skincare products and you can choose your super free gift.* | *We came back from the tour round the factory loaded down with free gifts.*

freebie /ˈfriːbiː/ [n C] informal something a company gives free with its products, or gives to the people it employs: *'Where did you get that calendar?' 'It was a freebie from work.'* | *Most airlines offer freebies to children traveling on their planes.*

free to do what you want

RELATED WORDS

- *see also* **let/allow, control/not control, busy/not busy**

3 allowed to do what you want

- free
- be at liberty to do sth
- freely
- do your own thing

free /friː/ [adj not usually before noun] allowed or able to do what you want, without being restricted by rules or by other people: *I had just left home, and was enjoying the feeling of being free and independent at last.* | **+ to do sth** *During 'Golden Time', the pupils are free to choose the activity they would like to do.*

be at liberty to do sth /biː ət ˌlɪbəʳti tə ˈduː (sth)/ [v phrase] formal to be free to do something, especially because someone has given you official permission or you have the right to do it: *The Secretary of State told reporters, 'I am not at liberty to get into the details of the proposal.'* | *You are quite at liberty to make an official complaint if you wish.*

freely /ˈfriːli/ [adv] if you can travel, speak, operate etc **freely**, you can do it as much as you like and in whatever way you like, without anyone trying to stop you: *For most of the year, farmers allow the sheep to roam freely on the hillsides.* | *In England he could write freely, without fear of arrest.* | *TV companies need the ability to operate freely, with the minimum of government interference,*

do your own thing /ˌduː jɔːr əʊn ˈθɪŋ/ [v phrase] especially spoken to do what you want to do, especially when these are not the same things as other people generally do: *As a kid, I wanted to do my own thing, but when I got older I realized I wanted to continue the family business.* | *The three women worked together on a stage play, and then each went off to do her own thing.*

4 activities or actions that are not restricted

- free
- unrestricted
- open
- open-ended

free /friː/ [adj only before noun] *This computer program assures the free movement of facts, figures, and text between files.* | *Bulgaria's first free elections were held in 1990.* | **free market** (=a system in which prices and trade are not controlled by the government) *Things like health and education cannot be left to the free market.* | **free speech** (=the right to say or write what you want) *All Americans have the right of free speech.* | **a free press** (=when newspapers are not controlled by the government) *Activists were calling for a free press and political reforms.*

unrestricted /ˌʌnrɪˈstrɪktɪ̈d◂/ [adj usually before noun] not restricted by any rules or orders: *Reporters were later given unrestricted access to the evidence in the case.* | *The U.N. demanded unrestricted searches for weapons within the country.* | *Most countries do not permit unrestricted immigration.*

open /ˈəʊpən/ [adj] if an activity or event is **open**, anyone can take part in it: *The military government has agreed to hold open elections next year.* | *We are holding an open competition to find a name for our new ship.*

open-ended /ˌəʊpən ˈendɪ̈d◂/ [adj] not restricted by time, length, subject etc: *The summit meeting was intended to be wide-ranging and open-ended.* | *As well as practice exercises, students should be encouraged to do more open-ended activities.*

5 the right to do what you want

- freedom
- liberty
- a free hand

freedom /ˈfriːdəm/ [n U] the right to do what you want without being controlled or restricted, especially by a government or by someone in authority: *There was a huge party at the Berlin Wall as East Germans celebrated their freedom.* | *Teachers in the special program have a greater amount of freedom in what they teach.* | **+ to do sth** *People here have the freedom to practise whatever religion they like.* | **freedom of speech/choice/expression etc** *In a country where freedom of speech is guaranteed, citizens should expect to hear ideas with which they disagree.* | **+ from** *The constitution guarantees freedom from persecution on grounds of race, sex, or sexuality.*

liberty /ˈlɪbəʳti/ [n U] a person's legal right to do what they want, without being unfairly controlled or restricted by the government: *They were fighting for liberty and equality.* | *Many people think that compulsory ID cards interfere with personal liberty.*

a free hand /ə ˌfriː ˈhænd/ [n phrase] when someone is allowed to do something in the way that they want, without being told what to do: *Some government agencies will be run like private companies, with a free hand when it comes to rules on hiring, buying equipment, etc.* | **give sb a free hand** *He was given a remarkably free hand in making all the arrangements.*

6 a country or system of government in which people have freedom

- free
- liberal

free /friː/ [adj] a **free** country, political system, or society is one in which people are allowed to live their lives in the way that they choose, express their opinions freely, take part in political activity etc: *We will continue our struggle until our country is free.* | *They were able to return to visit their family in a free Czech Republic.* | *Sometimes you realize how lucky you are to live in a free society.*

liberal /ˈlɪbərəl/ [adj] a **liberal** society or system is one in which people have the right to express their own opinions, live their own way of life, have their own religious beliefs etc, even if these are different from those of most other people: *In a liberal society you may have the right to express your own beliefs, but not necessarily to cause offence to other people.* | *In the 1840s, President Herrera promoted a policy of gradual liberal reform in Mexico.*

7 to make a country free

- free
- liberate

free /friː/ [v T] to remove the control or authority of a strict or unfair system of government from a country: *He joined the resistance movement in order to free his country from the enemy.* | *The allies arrived in Brussels on September 3rd and Antwerp was freed the next day.*

liberate /ˈlɪbəreɪt/ [v T] if an army **liberates** a country, it enters that country and defeats the foreign army and government that controlled it: *Algeria was liberated from France in 1962.* | *Poland, the Czech Republic, and other countries liberated from Soviet rule have done very well economically.* —**liberation** /ˌlɪbəˈreɪʃən/ [n U] *the liberation of Italy*

not in prison

RELATED WORDS

- *see also* **prison, escape, keep (8-11)**

8 not in prison

- free
- out
- at liberty
- freedom

free /friː/ [adj not usually before noun] not in prison, or not being kept somewhere by force: *He was free again, after 10 long years in jail.* | *The hostages are now free after their five-day ordeal.* | *The rapist was sentenced to five years in prison, but he could be free in 18 months.*

out /aʊt/ [adj not before noun] no longer in prison because you have been allowed to leave: *Peters could be out in as little as 3 years.* | **get out** *Her husband gets out of jail next week.*

at liberty /ət ˈlɪbəʳti/ [adj phrase] if a criminal is **at liberty**, he or she is not in prison because the police cannot catch them: *Tonight only one of the escaped prisoners remains at liberty; the other seven are now back in Central Prison.* | *Walker was at liberty for many years before the police apprehended him.*

freedom /ˈfriːdəm/ [n U] when you are not in prison or not being kept somewhere by force: *One of the protesters was arrested again after only 48 hours of freedom.* | *The negotiations led to freedom for the eight hostages.*

9 to let someone leave prison

- release
- set sb free
- let sb out
- let sb go
- free

release /rɪˈliːs/ [v T] to let someone leave prison: *McKay moved to Newcastle after being released from prison.* | *They released ten political prisoners last year.* —**release** [n U] *The four men were greeted by jubilant relatives upon their release.* | **+ of** *Thousands of people worldwide campaigned for the release of Nelson Mandela.*

set sb free /ˌset (sb) ˈfriː/ [v phrase] to let someone leave a place where they are being kept by force: *The hostages were set free last night.* | *The Emancipation Proclamation, in 1863, set the American slaves free.*

let sb out /ˌlet (sb) ˈaʊt/ [phr v T] to let someone leave a place where they are being kept, especially a prison: *Lusani hopes to be let out early.* | **+ of** *She was let out of prison to attend her daughter's funeral.*

let sb go /ˌlet (sb) ˈgəʊ/ [v phrase] to allow someone to leave a place where they have been kept by force for a short time: *Due to a lack of evidence against the suspect, the police had to let the prisoner go.* | *I just kept praying that the man would let me go.*

free /friː/ [v T] to allow someone who is a prisoner or being kept somewhere to be free: *Many of these young offenders should have been freed a long time ago.* | **+ from** *His supporters are demanding that he be freed from prison.* | **+ into** *The dolphins will be freed into the ocean once their injuries have healed.*

free time

RELATED WORDS

- *see also* **holiday, rest, enjoy, busy/not busy**

10 time when you can do what you want

- free time
- spare time
- time off
- leisure/leisure time
- time out

free time /ˌfriː ˈtaɪm/ [n phrase] time when you can do what you want, because you are not working or studying: *Now that she's retired she has plenty of free time.* | *On Wednesday afternoons most of the students have free time.* | **spend your free time (doing sth)** *Theo spends his free time doing volunteer work.* | **in your free time** *In his limited free time, Carson likes to take his family skiing.*

spare time /ˌspeəʳ ˈtaɪm/ [n phrase] time when you have finished what you have to do or are expected to do, so that you can do what you want: *Mothers with young babies rarely have much spare time.* | **in your spare time** *She's studying for a degree in her spare time.* | **spend your spare time (doing sth)** *How do you spend your spare time?* | *Penny spends her spare time writing letters and emailing friends.*

time off /ˌtaɪm ˈɒf/ [n phrase] time when you are officially allowed not to be at your place of work or study: *All employees are allowed time off for doctor's appointments.* | *She hasn't had any time off for six months.* | *I'll need some extra time off for revision.* | **time off work/school etc** *Americans get much less time off work than European workers.*

leisure/leisure time /ˈleʒəʳ, ˈleʒəʳ ˌtaɪm‖ˈliː-/ [n U] time when you are not working, studying etc and can do activities that you enjoy: *Very often, retired people need to be taught how to use and enjoy their leisure time.* | *If I have a moment of leisure, I go to the movies.* | **in your leisure time** *In his leisure time he visits museums and art galleries.* | **leisure (time) activities** *tourism, sightseeing, and other leisure time activities* | *Reading was one of the most popular leisure activities.*

time out /ˌtaɪm ˈaʊt/ [n phrase] time when you stop what you are doing, especially in order to rest: *Taking time out just to relax each day is important for busy working people.*

11 when you are not busy and have free time

- free
- not have anything planned
- at (your) leisure

free /friː/ [adj] if you are **free** at a particular time, you are not busy and there is nothing that you have to do: *Are you free this weekend?* | *I'm free on Wednesday evening, if you want to go out to dinner then.*

not have anything planned ALSO **not have anything on** British spoken /nɒt hæv ˌeniθɪŋ ˈplænd, nɒt hæv ˌeniθɪŋ ˈɒn/ [v phrase] to not have arranged to do anything at a particular time: *I don't think we have anything on next Tuesday, do we?* | *We don't have anything planned yet for Christmas; we might go to my parents'.*

at (your) leisure /ət (jɔːʳ) ˈleʒəʳ‖-ˈliː-/ [adv] if you do something **at (your) leisure**, you do it when you are not busy and have time to do it without hurrying: *Take a brochure home to read at your leisure.* | *Sixty cars will be displayed, and potential buyers will be able to inspect them at leisure.*

fresh/not fresh

RELATED WORDS

▸ *see also* **decay, smell, food, new**

1 food that is fresh

▸ **fresh**

fresh /freʃ/ [adj] **fresh** food has been produced or picked recently, and has not been frozen or put into cans: *I go to the market twice a week to buy fresh fruit and vegetables.* | *Fresh fish is much more delicious than frozen.* | *a dozen fresh eggs* | **keep sth fresh** *Put the milk in the fridge to keep it fresh.* —**freshly** [adv] *freshly-baked bread*

2 not fresh

▸ **go off/go bad**
▸ **bad**
▸ **stale**
▸ **sour**
▸ **rotten**

go off/go bad /ˌgəʊ ˈɒf, ˌgəʊ ˈbæd/ [phr v I] especially spoken if food **goes off** or **goes bad**, it starts to decay because it has been kept for too long: *Can you smell this milk and see if you think it's gone off?* | *I don't think we should eat that meat now – it's probably gone bad.*

bad /bæd/ [adj] especially British food that is **bad** is not good to eat, because it has started to decay: *She must have eaten something bad because she was really sick in the night.* | *Shall I just throw away these bad apples?*

stale /steɪl/ [adj] bread, cake etc that is **stale** is hard, dry, and unpleasant to eat: *This bread's stale – have we got another loaf?* | *All we got was a cup of tea and a bit of stale cake.* | **go stale** *Put the biscuits back in the tin or they'll go stale.*

sour /saʊəʳ/ [adj] milk, cream, wine etc that is **sour** tastes bitter and smells unpleasant: *The wine was so sour that I couldn't drink it.* | **go sour** *In these temperatures, milk goes sour very quickly.*

rotten /ˈrɒtn‖ˈrɑːtn/ [adj] fruit, vegetables, meat etc that is **rotten** is very badly decayed, has gone soft, smells unpleasant, and cannot be eaten: *There were some cheap oranges in the market but most of them were rotten.* | *the unmistakable smell of rotten eggs*

friend

RELATED WORDS

opposite: —— **enemy**

▸ *see also* **friendly, relationship, girlfriend/boyfriend, unfriendly**

1 a friend

▸ **friend**
▸ **mate**
▸ **buddy**
▸ **pal**
▸ **acquaintance**
▸ **friend of a friend**

friend /frend/ [n C] *Dad, this is my friend Steve.* | *She's going to Palm Springs with some friends.* | *I got a letter from a friend from college.* | **friend of mine** *I'm going out for a drink with a friend of mine tonight.* | **be a good friend to sb** (=to be someone's friend and help them a lot when they have problems) *John was a really good friend to me when I had all those problems last year.*

mate /meɪt/ [n C] British informal a friend – use this especially about boys or men: *He always goes to the pub with his mates on Friday night.* | **mate of mine** *Terry's an old mate of mine.*

buddy /ˈbʌdi/ [n C] American informal a friend – use this especially about men or young people: *He's one of Mike's buddies.* | **army/high school/war etc buddy** (=a friend that you met in the army, high school etc) *He's out playing basketball with some of his high school buddies.*

pal /pæl/ [n C] informal a friend. **Pal** is slightly more old-fashioned than **mate** or **buddy**: *Nicholas was a pal of William's at school.* | *Thanks for helping us out, Frankie. You're a real pal.*

acquaintance /əˈkweɪntəns/ [n C] someone that you know and sometimes see, but who is not one of your close friends: *She's just an acquaintance – I sometimes see her at aerobics.* | *I don't want to talk about religion with business acquaintances.*

friend of a friend /ˌfrend əv ə ˈfrend/ [n C] someone who is not really your friend, but is someone one of your friends knows: *I got the tickets through a friend of a friend who works in the theatre.* | *No I don't know him personally, he's a friend of a friend.*

2 a very good friend

▸ **good/close friend**
▸ **best friend**
▸ **old friend**
▸ **inseparable**
▸ **go back a long way**

good/close friend /ˌgʊd, ˌkləʊs ˈfrend/ [n C] someone that you know very well and like very much: *Helen is one of my closest friends.* | *Sam and I didn't get along very well at first but now we're really good friends.* | *They were close friends of my parents when we lived in Minneapolis.*

best friend /ˌbest ˈfrend/ [n C] the one special friend who is more important to you than any other: *We lived next door to each other when we were kids, and we've been best friends ever since.* | *Caroline and her best friend both had babies within three weeks of each other.*

old friend /ˌəʊld ˈfrend/ [n C] a good friend that you have known for a long time: *Lotte's one of my oldest friends.* | *I saw a few old friends at the reunion.*

inseparable /ɪnˈsepərəbəl/ [adj] friends who are **inseparable** are together most of the time: *My* *brother and James have been inseparable since they were at primary school.* | *The three girls were inseparable friends.*

go back a long way ALSO **go way back** /gəʊ ˌbæk ə lɒŋ 'weɪ ‖-lɔːŋ-, gəʊ 'weɪ ˌbæk/ [v phrase] informal if two people **go back a long way**, they have known each other or been working together for a very long time: *Sam and I go way back. We sat next to each other in first grade.* | *I know your aunt – in fact we go back a long way.*

3 a group of friends

- circle of friends
- the boys/the girls
- the gang
- crowd
- set
- cronies

circle of friends ALSO **circle** /ˌsɜːʳkəl əv 'frendz, 'sɜːʳkəl/ [n C usually singular] the people you know, especially a group of friends who all know each other and often meet socially: *He had a large circle of friends.* | *Since my children have started school, my circle has widened to include the mothers of other kids.*

the boys/the girls /ðə 'bɔɪz, ðə 'gɜːʳlz/ [n plural] spoken a group of male or female friends who often do things together: *Sally's having a night out with the girls from the office.* | *It's his poker night with the boys.*

the gang /ðə 'gæŋ/ [n C] informal a small group of friends who often meet socially: *I usually go out with the gang on Saturday nights.* | **one of the gang** (=accepted into the group of friends) *She's not really one of the gang, but I invited her to the party.*

crowd /kraʊd/ [n singular] informal a group of friends who often do things or go out together: *He wasn't with his usual crowd last night.* | *It may be necessary to change your child's school if they get in with a bad crowd.*

set /set/ [n singular] **the tennis/golf club/arty etc set** a group of friends who meet socially, especially because they are all interested in the same sport or activity, especially an expensive one: *She likes to mingle with the arty set.*

cronies /'krəʊniz/ [n plural] a group of people who know each other, and will help each other, even if this means being slightly dishonest: *Weiss was careful not to upset his political cronies.* | *Her father is probably in the bar, drinking with his cronies.*

4 to be someone's friend

- be friends
- get along
- be friendly with

be friends /biː 'frendz/ [v phrase] if two people **are friends**, they like each other and they enjoy doing things together: *Bill and I used to be good friends, but we don't see each other much now.* | **+ with** *I've been friends with Andrea for about 10 years.*

get along ALSO **get on** British /ˌget ə'lɒŋ‖-ə'lɔːŋ, ˌget 'ɒn/ [phr v I] if two or more people **get along** or **get on**, they find it easy to talk and agree with each other, and so they feel relaxed when they spend time together: *I used to argue a lot with my parents, but now we get along fine.* | **+ with** *Julie's nice, but I don't really get on with her brother.* | *He's a nice boy – very easy to get along with.*

be friendly with /biː 'frendli wɪð/ [v phrase] to have a good relationship with someone, even though you may not spend a lot of time together: *Her family became very friendly with their neighbors, the Mayers.* | *I used to be very friendly with a girl from Boston.*

5 to become someone's friend

- make friends
- become friends
- hit it off
- click
- strike up a friendship
- befriend
- fall in with

make friends /ˌmeɪk 'frendz/ [v phrase] to start to be someone's friend, especially when you have to make an effort to do this: *Her family moved a lot, and it wasn't always easy to make friends.* | **+ with** *The children soon made friends with the kids next door.*

become friends /bɪˌkʌm 'frendz/ [v phrase] if two people **become friends**, they begin to be friends: *They met at an art class and became friends.* | *I'd known him for years, but we really didn't become friends until high school.*

hit it off /ˌhɪt ɪt 'ɒf/ [v phrase] informal if two people **hit it off**, they immediately become friends when they meet for the first time: *I knew you and Mark would hit it off.* | *The two men ended up in the same business law class and hit it off immediately.*

click /klɪk/ [v I] informal if two people **click**, they like each other immediately when they first meet, because they have the same ideas or opinions, or laugh at the same things: *We just clicked, and we've been friends ever since.* | **+ with** *I never really clicked with my boss, and it made work a little more difficult.*

strike up a friendship /ˌstraɪk ʌp ə 'frendʃɪp/ [v phrase] to make friends with someone very quickly, especially if you do it intentionally: *The two women struck up a friendship when they met on holiday.* | *We met for the first time at a business conference, and we immediately struck up a friendship which has lasted for years.*

befriend /bɪ'frend/ [v T] to be friendly to someone who needs help, for example someone with financial or emotional problems: *His parents befriended some American soldiers who served in Wales during World War II.* | *It's fairly unusual for high school seniors to befriend freshmen.*

fall in with ALSO **get in with** spoken /ˌfɔːl 'ɪn wɪð, ˌget 'ɪn wɪð/ [v T] to begin to be friends with a group of people, especially people that other people do not approve of: *He's fallen in with a group of boys I don't like very much.* | *She used her husband's money and family to get in with a group of Hollywood's social elite.*

6 a friendly relationship with someone

- friendship
- companionship

friendship /'frendʃɪp/ [n C/U] *Our marriage is based on friendship, love, and trust.* | *We didn't see each other much during that time, but our friendship remained strong.* | **+ with** *I had no close friendships with other boys at school.* | **+ between** *Bernstein's visit to Copland's studio led to a friendship between the two composers.*

companionship /kəm'pænjənʃɪp/ [n U] a friendly and comfortable relationship with someone that you enjoy spending time with: *He was lonely and looking for companionship.* | *Older people often benefit from having a pet for companionship.*

7 to have important or rich friends who can help you

- have friends in high places
- well-connected

have friends in high places /hæv ˌfrendz ɪn haɪ ˈpleɪsɪ̈z/ [v phrase not in progressive] *He won't lose his job – he has plenty of friends in high places.*

well-connected /ˌwel kəˈnektɪ̈d◂/ [adj] having friends who have a lot of influence: *The couple were well-educated and well-connected members of an elite social class.* | *Richardson is very well-connected, both in the Democratic leadership and on political committees.*

8 to stop being friendly with someone

- fall out

▸ *see also* **argue**

fall out /ˌfɔːl ˈaʊt/ [phr v I] especially British to stop being friends because you have an argument: *It was the first time Bill and I had fallen out.* | **+ with** *She fell out with some of her school friends.* | **+ over** *I didn't think it was worth falling out over, but Emily obviously did.*

friendly

RELATED WORDS

opposite: — **unfriendly**

▸ nice person *see* **nice**

▸ *see also* **friend, polite, kind, relationship**

1 behaving in a friendly way

- friendly
- nice
- easy to get on with
- easygoing
- warm
- approachable
- welcoming
- hospitable
- affable
- amiable
- genial

friendly /ˈfrendli/ [adj] easy to talk to, and ready to behave like a friend towards people you have not met before: *Ella was very friendly, and I liked her immediately.* | *The hotel staff were very friendly and helpful.* | **+ to/towards** *One surprise was how friendly everyone was to us on our travels.* —**friendliness** [n U] *Everywhere he was treated with kindness and friendliness.*

nice /naɪs/ [adj] someone who is **nice** is friendly and very easy to like: *We met some really nice people at the party – friends of my sister.* | **+ to** *All Brad's friends were very nice to me, but I was too shy to join in their chat.*

easy to get on with British **/easy to get along with** American /ˌiːzi tə get əˈlɒŋ wɪð‖-əˈlɔːŋ-, ˌiːzi tə get ˈɒn wɪð / [adj phrase] friendly, relaxed, and not the type of person who causes unnecessary problems or arguments: *What's he like? Is he easy to get on with?* | *As a director, I'm always looking for good actors, but it's a bonus if they are easy to get along with too.*

easygoing /ˌiːziˈgəʊɪŋ◂/ [adj] friendly and relaxed, and not easily annoyed or upset: *I feel lucky to have such an easygoing and affectionate child.* | *Stein's easygoing manner is only one of the reasons he will be missed when he retires.*

warm /wɔːʳm/ [adj usually before noun] someone who is **warm** is very friendly in a sincere way, and seems to really care about other people: *She's a warm, caring person, and she'll make a wonderful nurse.* | *He welcomed us with a warm smile.* —**warmly** [adv] *The Secretary General was warmly welcomed at the White House yesterday.*

approachable /əˈprəʊtʃəbəl/ [adj] someone who is **approachable** is friendly and easy to talk to, even though they are in a more important position than you: *If you have any problems, the head teacher is very approachable* | *Olivia has a reputation as an easygoing, approachable executive who always has lunch with her employees.*

welcoming /ˈwelkəmɪŋ/ [adj] behaving in a way that shows you are glad to have other people visiting your home or your country, and doing things to make them feel relaxed and happy there: *He stood at the door with a welcoming smile.* | *Restaurant and hotel prices in the area are reasonable, and the townspeople are welcoming.*

hospitable /ˈhɒspɪtəbəl, hɒˈspɪ-‖hɑːˈspɪ-, ˈhɑːspɪ-/ [adj] someone who is **hospitable** is friendly and generous to you when you visit their home or their country: *Most of the people I met in Laos were very hospitable and kind.* —**hospitality** /ˌhɒspɪ̈ˈtælɪ̈ti‖ˌhɑː-/ [n U] someone's friendly, generous behaviour towards you when you visit their home or their country: *He was known for his hospitality and generosity.*

affable /ˈæfəbəl/ [adj] formal someone who is **affable**, especially a man, is polite, friendly, and cheerful: *She married an affable, middle-aged businessman.* | *Brown was affable and sympathetic, but also firm and decisive in dealing with the problems presented to him.*

amiable /ˈeɪmiəbəl/ [adj] formal friendly and pleasant, and not easily annoyed or worried: *The waiter was an amiable young man.* | *Cohen is soft-spoken and amiable.*

genial /ˈdʒiːniəl/ [adj] formal friendly, often laughing and making jokes, and enjoyable to be with: *Dr Saito has a warm, genial manner.* | *Our hosts were genial and friendly, and our stay was a very pleasant one.*

2 usually enjoying talking to people and being with them

- sociable
- outgoing
- extrovert

sociable /ˈsəʊʃəbəl/ [adj] *She's a friendly, sociable woman.* | *Some research has shown that people without brothers and sisters tend to be less sociable.*

outgoing /ˌaʊtˈgəʊɪŋ◂/ [adj] someone who is **outgoing** likes to meet and talk to new people and is not nervous in social situations: *She's become more outgoing since she went to college.* | *Marshall's skills and her outgoing personality made her very effective in her public relations jobs.*

extrovert British **/extroverted** American /ˈekstrəvɜːʳt, ˈekstrəvɜːʳtɪ̈d/ [adj] lively and confident and enjoying being with a lot of people: *Lisa is very extrovert, but her sister is a little shy.* | *Brass players have a reputation as the most extroverted musicians – they're the party animals of the orchestra.* —**extrovert** [n C] someone who is extrovert: *The work in sales appeals to the extrovert in me.*

3 friendly relationships/ conversations

- friendly
- amicable
- cordial

friendly /ˈfrendli/ [adj] *Friendly relations between the two countries have continued through this difficult time.* | **on friendly terms** (=in a friendly way) *Fontaine said that he was leaving the company on very friendly terms.*

amicable /ˈæmɨkəbəl/ [adj] formal an **amicable** arrangement or solution is one when people who do not agree with each other are able to solve their problems in a reasonably friendly way: *The meeting between the two leaders was very amicable.* | **amicable arrangement/divorce/solution etc** *Simons sent his attorney to meet with the ranchers in hopes that they could still come to an amicable settlement.*

cordial /ˈkɔːʳdiəl‖-dʒəl/ [adj] a **cordial** relationship between two people or groups is one in which people are polite and friendly to each other although they are not close friends: *Britain and Portugal have had cordial relations for more than four centuries.* | *Donnely was polite and cordial, but she refused to sign the contract.* —**cordially** [adv] *He greeted them cordially.*

4 friendly places/situations

- friendly
- welcoming
- convivial

friendly /ˈfrendli/ [adj] *The restaurant had good food and a friendly atmosphere.* | *You're lucky to work in such a friendly office.*

welcoming /ˈwelkəmɪŋ/ [adj] a place, room etc that is **welcoming** makes you feel relaxed and happy to be there: *A bunch of fresh flowers on the table always looks welcoming.* | *a bright, clean, welcoming room*

convivial /kənˈvɪviəl/ [adj] formal a **convivial** event or social situation is one in which people are friendly to each other and enjoy themselves: *The mood was relaxed and convivial.* | *Pubs are good places for a drink and some convivial conversation.*

5 too friendly in a way that is unpleasant

- familiar
- smarmy
- over-friendly
- obsequious
- slimy

familiar /fəˈmɪliəʳ/ [adj] talking to someone as if you know them very well although in fact you do not, especially in a way that people think is unpleasant or offensive: *I don't like it when men I've just met are too familiar.* | *She came up to me and started talking in such a familiar way that I thought I must have met her before.*

smarmy /ˈsmɑːʳmi/ [adj] informal someone who is **smarmy** behaves in a very friendly way but seems completely insincere: *He's been criticized for his smarmy behavior when interviewing celebrities.* | *a slick, smarmy public relations officer* | *He denies calling the Prime Minister 'smarmy'.*

over-friendly /ˌəʊvəʳ ˈfrendli◂/ [adj] British if someone is **over-friendly**, they are too friendly in a way that is unpleasant, for example standing or sitting too close to you: *A man in the pub was a little over-friendly, so I left early.*

obsequious /əbˈsiːkwiəs/ [adj] formal someone who is **obsequious** always tries too hard to be friendly and helpful, and always agrees with what other people say, in a way that people think is very annoying: *The waiter was polite and efficient, but not obsequious.* | *All this obsequious praise for his actions is enough to make most normal people sick.*

slimy /ˈslaɪmi/ [adj] informal someone who is **slimy** is too friendly and praises people too much in a way that is clearly dishonest and makes you think they are just trying to get an advantage for themselves: *What a slimy, horrible man.* | *They had the usual slimy politician on TV talking about 'the innate good sense of the voters'.*

6 to be too friendly to someone in authority

- suck up to sb
- grovel
- brown-nose
- creep

suck up to sb informal ALSO **creep up to sb** British informal ALSO **kiss up to sb** American informal /ˌsʌk ˈʌp tə (sb), ˌkriːp ˈʌp tə (sb), ˌkɪs ˈʌp tə (sb)/ [phr v T] to say or do a lot of nice things to someone in authority, in order to make them like you and help you in some way – use this to show disapproval: *Sucking up to the teacher doesn't mean you'll pass your exams.* | *I'm not going to kiss up to anyone for favors.* | *He was creeping up to the interviewer, trying to look good.*

grovel /ˈgrɒvəl‖ˈgrɑː-, ˈgrʌ-/ [v I] to behave in a very respectful, obedient way towards someone, because you want them to help you or forgive you: *If a police officer stops your car, be respectful to him, but don't grovel.* | **+ for** *The department is having to grovel for money again.* | **+ to** British *I grovelled to my parents and promised I wouldn't do it again.* —**grovelling** British /**groveling** American [adj] *He received a grovelling apology.*

brown-nose /ˈbraʊn nəʊz/ [v I/T] informal to be very nice to someone in authority and help them do things in order to try to make them like you and help you – use this to show disapproval: *Kids don't want other kids to think they're brown-nosing, so they don't tell teachers when they've enjoyed a class.*

creep /kriːp/ [n C] British someone who pretends to really respect or admire someone, but only in order to make the other person like them or do something for them: *She's such a creep at work.* | *Will's the class creep, and the teachers don't notice.*

frightened/ frightening

RELATED WORDS

- shake because you are frightened *see* **shake (2)**
- *see also* **nervous, brave/not brave, confident/not confident, scream, ghost, magic, strange**

1 frightened of someone or something

- frightened
- afraid
- scared
- terrified
- petrified
- panic-stricken
- live in fear
- scared stiff/scared out of your wits/ scared to death

frightened /ˈfraɪtnd/ [adj] feeling very nervous and afraid of someone or something, because you think something bad is going to happen to you because of them: *Don't be frightened, it's only thunder.* | *Two frightened children were hiding in a corner of the room.* | **+ of** *A lot of people are frightened of dentists.* | *Are you frightened of the dark?* | **frightened to do sth** *I was frightened to move in case the branch broke.* | **frightened of doing sth** *He was frightened of making mistakes.* | **+ (that)** *I was frightened my parents would get divorced, and wished that there was something I could do to make them happy again.* | *Alice kept perfectly still, frightened that the dog might attack her.*

afraid /əˈfreɪd/ [adj not before noun] frightened: *Don't be afraid. I won't hurt you.* | **+ of** *He had a terrible temper and everyone was afraid of him.* | *It's amazing how many people are afraid of spiders.* | **+ (that)** *Billy was afraid his aunt would punish him if he owned up.* | **afraid to do sth** *She was afraid to speak up in front of all these important people.* | **afraid of doing sth** *I didn't tell anyone, because I was afraid of being punished* (=afraid I might be punished).

scared /skeəʳd/ [adj not before noun] especially spoken frightened: *The first time I went on a motorcycle I was really scared.* | **+ of** *She's always been scared of heights.* | **scared to do sth** *I stood still, scared to move forward and scared to go back.* | **scared of doing sth** *I think they were all scared of offending him.* | **+ (that)** *I hate reading out my work in class – I'm scared that people are going to laugh at me.* | **scared stiff/scared to death** (=very scared) *When he came back he looked scared stiff, as if he'd seen a ghost.*

terrified /ˈterɪ̈faɪd/ [adj] extremely frightened: *The faces of the four terrified teenagers looked up at us.* | **+ of** *He's absolutely terrified of snakes.* | **terrified to do sth** *The little boy cowered behind the tree, terrified to make a sound.* | **+ (that)** *I was terrified that my father would find out I had lied to him.* | **absolutely terrified** *I couldn't move – I was absolutely terrified.*

petrified /ˈpetrɪ̈faɪd/ [adj] extremely frightened, especially so frightened that you cannot move: *She just stood there, petrified at the thought of the crowds waiting outside.* | **absolutely petrified** *He had the gun pointed at my head. I was absolutely petrified.* | **+ of** *She's a very nervous dog, and she's petrified of traffic.* | **be petrified with fear** *He was petrified with fear as I held my knife in front of him.*

panic-stricken /ˈpænɪk ˌstrɪkən/ [adj] so frightened that you cannot think clearly or behave sensibly, especially when something has suddenly frightened you: *A few seconds after the explosion the street was full of panic-stricken people, fleeing in all directions.* | *Mr Cottle dashed in, looking panic-stricken.* | *In a panic-stricken attempt to free herself from Annie's grip, she snatched the scissors off the table.*

live in fear /ˌlɪv ɪn ˈfɪəʳ/ [v phrase] to always be afraid of something unpleasant that is fairly likely to happen: *Until security can be assured, the people here will continue to live in fear.* | **live in fear of sth/doing sth** *After leaking the secret document, Sarah lived in fear of being found out.* | **live in fear (that)** *A surgeon lives in constant fear that something will go wrong in an operation when he's feeling tired.*

scared stiff/scared out of your wits/ scared to death /ˌskeəʳd ˈstɪf, ˌskeəʳd aʊt əv jɔːʳ ˈwɪts, ˌskeəʳd tə ˈdeθ/ [adj phrase] informal extremely frightened: *You must have been scared stiff when you saw the car coming straight towards you.* | *Helen had to go for an interview with the school Principal – she was scared stiff.* | *I knew a man was following me, and I was scared out of my wits.* | *Some of the prisoners were only 16 or 17, and they looked scared to death.*

2 when you do not want to do something because you are frightened

- be afraid/be frightened/be scared
- be terrified
- dread
- fear
- be fearful
- for fear of sth
- have a phobia about

be afraid/be frightened/be scared /biː əˈfreɪd, biː ˈfraɪtnd, biː ˈskeəʳd/ [v phrase] to be unwilling to do something because you are frightened about what may happen if you do it. **Be scared** is more informal than **be afraid** or **be frightened**: *I wanted to talk to you about it, but I was frightened.* | *We are urging our citizens to carry on as normal and not be afraid.* | *A lot of young children are frightened the first time they are put on a horse's back.* | **+ to do sth** *Many old people are afraid to go out at night.* | **+ of doing sth** *She asked me to come with her because she was scared of going there on her own.* | *He's frightened of flying in case there's a bomb on the plane.* | **+ (that)** *She was afraid that if she went to the police, her husband would beat her up again.*

be terrified /biː ˈterɪ̈faɪd/ [v phrase] to be unwilling to do something because you are extremely frightened about what may happen if you do it: *When my name was finally called I was terrified.* | **be terrified (that)** *I didn't tell my parents I was pregnant. I was terrified that they would throw me out of the house.* | **be terrified of doing sth** *They always travel by boat because Jimmy's terrified of flying.* | **+ to do sth** *She was too terrified to jump from the flames.*

dread /dred/ [v T] to feel worried and frightened about something you have to do: *I have to go to the dentist's tomorrow, and I'm dreading it.* | **dread doing sth** *The Wilsons were coming back from holiday today, and I was dreading telling them what had happened while they were away.*

fear /fɪəʳ/ [v T not in progressive] written to be frightened about what may happen if you do something: *Many of the gang's victims refused to give information to the police because they feared reprisals.* | **+ (that)** *The rescuers dug slowly and carefully, fearing that the wreckage might collapse on top of them.*

be fearful /biː ˈfɪəʳfəl/ [v phrase] formal to be unwilling to do something because you are worried about the possibility of trouble or danger **+ of** *The Energy Department, fearful of public reaction, has cancelled its plans to build four new nuclear reactors.* | **be fearful of doing sth** *The threats left her plagued by nightmares, and fearful of making public appearances.* | **+ (that)** *She gave up smoking when she was pregnant, fearful that it might damage her baby.*

for fear of sth /fəʳ ˈfɪər əv (sth)/ [prep] if you are unwilling to do something **for fear of** something bad happening, you are frightened that something bad will happen if you do it: *The workers are unhappy but will not complain for fear of losing their jobs.* | *I didn't turn on the light, for fear of waking the baby.* | *Women and the elderly refuse to leave their apartments, for fear of the hooligans who rule the streets.*

have a phobia about /ˌhæv ə ˈfəʊbiə əbaʊt/ [v phrase not in progressive] to have a strong and unreasonable dislike and fear of something, especially of something that is not frightening for most people: *Carol had a phobia about snakes – even talking about them made her shiver.* | *She has a phobia about telephone answering machines and will never leave a message.*

3 to be suddenly frightened

- get a fright
- panic
- jump
- go white/pale

get a fright /ˌget ə ˈfraɪt/ [v phrase not in progressive] to be suddenly frightened by something that happens: *I got a terrible fright when that dog jumped out at me.* | **get the fright of your life** informal (=be suddenly very frightened) *I got the fright of my life when he suddenly spoke from out of the darkness.*

panic /ˈpænɪk/ [v I] to suddenly become so frightened that you cannot think clearly, especially if this makes you do something dangerous or stupid: *When the parachute didn't open I just panicked.* | *The soldiers panicked and opened fire on the raiders.* | *When a plane gets into difficulty it is essential that the pilot does not panic.*

jump /dʒʌmp/ [v I] to make a sudden movement because you are surprised and frightened by something that happens very suddenly: *Something came out in front of me and I jumped.* | *Following the attacks, he now jumps every time he hears a plane.* | **jump out of your skin** *She jumped out of her skin, as something cold and snakelike was thrust into her hand.*

go white/pale /ˌgəʊ ˈwaɪt, ˈpeɪl/ [v phrase not in progressive] to suddenly feel very frightened, with the result that your face becomes very pale: *Alexander looked down the hall, and went pale with fright. It was as if he had seen a ghost.* | **go white as a sheet** *You're as white as a sheet. What's happened?* | *The nurse came in with a hypodermic needle, and Rob went white as a sheet.*

4 to make someone feel frightened

- frighten
- scare
- terrify
- give sb a fright
- alarm
- startle
- make sb jump
- give sb the creeps
- make your hair stand on end
- send shivers down your spine
- make your blood run cold

frighten /ˈfraɪtn/ [v T] *Does the thought of death frighten you?* | *Take that silly mask off – you're frightening the children.* | **it frightens sb to know/think etc** *It frightens me to know that the rapist still hasn't been caught.* | **frighten the life out of sb** (=make someone feel very frightened) *What are you doing creeping up on me like that? You frightened the life out of me!* | **frighten sb out of their wits** (=make someone feel very frightened) *Film-makers have always known that one way to capture an audience is to frighten it out of its wits.* | **frighten the (living) daylights out of sb** (=make someone feel very frightened) *Melissa spun round to see Eddie standing behind her. 'You frightened the daylights out of me!' she gasped. 'I never heard you come in.'* | **frighten sb into doing sth** (=make someone do something by frightening them) *Their lawyers tried to frighten us into signing the contract.* | **frighten sb off/frighten off sb** (=frighten someone so that they go away or stop trying to do something) *The man pulled out a gun and managed to frighten off his attackers.*

scare /skeəʳ/ [v T] especially spoken to make someone feel frightened, especially by making them think something very unpleasant might happen: *He was driving fast just to scare us.* | *We're not really going to get arrested – I think the police are trying to scare us.* | **it scares sb to know/think etc** *It scared him to think that his mother might never recover.* | **scare the hell out of sb** (=make someone feel very frightened) informal *She scared the hell out of me when she said she had to go into hospital.* | **scare the (living) daylights out of sb** (=make someone feel very frightened) *Don't creep up on me like that! You scared the living daylights out of me!*

terrify /ˈterɨfaɪ/ [v T] to make someone feel very frightened: *The idea of going down into the caves terrified her.* | *The teacher terrified her so much, that she hated going to school.* | *My uncle suffers from agoraphobia, and the idea of leaving the house terrifies him.* | **it terrifies sb to think/know etc** *It terrified him to think that, in six months' time, he would have to stand up in front of a class and teach them something.*

give sb a fright /ˌgɪv (sb) ə ˈfraɪt/ [v phrase not in progressive] to make someone suddenly feel frightened so that they make a sudden movement or their heart starts beating quickly: *He really gave me a fright when he phoned at that time of night.* | **give sb a hell of a fright** (=make someone suddenly very frightened) informal *I accidentally touched a live wire in the motor, and even though it didn't hurt me it gave me a hell of a fright.*

alarm /əˈlɑːʳm/ [v T] to make people feel very worried about a possible danger: *We don't wish to alarm people unnecessarily, but it would be wise to avoid drinking the tap water here.* | *Many women are alarmed by suggestions of a link between the contraceptive pill and breast cancer.* —**alarming** [adj] *There have been several alarming incidents where planes have almost crashed.*

startle /ˈstɑːʳtl/ [v T] if someone or something **startles** you, they frighten you because you see them suddenly or hear them when you did not know they were there: *I'm sorry. I didn't mean to startle you.* | *The noise startled him, and he dropped his glass on the floor.* | *Any unexpected movements can startle the animal, so it must be approached slowly and steadily.*

make sb jump /ˌmeɪk (sb) ˈdʒʌmp/ [v phrase] to suddenly surprise and frighten someone so that they make a sudden movement: *Sorry! I didn't mean to make you jump.* | *Something darted out from behind the hedge, and made me jump.*

give sb the creeps /ˌgɪv (sb) ðə ˈkriːps/ [v phrase] if a person or a place **gives you the creeps**, they make you feel slightly frightened and nervous because they are strange: *This house gives me the creeps – it's so dark and quiet.* | *I hate being left alone in the office with Graham – he gives me the creeps.*

make your hair stand on end /ˌmeɪk jɔːʳ ˈheəʳ stænd ɒn ˌend/ [v phrase] informal if something such as a story or account **makes your hair stand on end** it makes you very frightened: *Wait until I tell you about the murder – it'll make your hair stand on end.* | *I've heard rumours about how Captain Crayshaw disciplines his crew ... things to make your hair stand on end.*

send shivers down your spine /send 'ʃɪvəʳz daʊn jɔːʳ ˌspaɪn/ [v phrase] if a thought or experience **sends shivers down your spine**, it makes you feel very frightened especially because it involves someone or something that is very evil: *When you think of what happened in that house, it sends shivers down your spine.* | *Mere mention of his name is enough to send shivers down the spine of even the most battle-hardened fighter.*

make your blood run cold /ˌmeɪk jɔːʳ 'blʌd rʌn ˌkəʊld/ [v phrase] if a thought or experience **makes your blood run cold**, it shocks and frightens you because it is extremely cruel, violent, or dangerous: *The thought of ever returning to the prison makes his blood run cold.* | *The man stepped forward, and when Amelie saw him give a Nazi salute, it made her blood run cold.*

5 making you feel frightened

- frightening
- terrifying
- scary
- spooky
- creepy
- chilling
- hair-raising
- spine-chilling
- blood-curdling

frightening /'fraɪtnɪŋ/ [adj] making you feel frightened: *Driving in big cities can be pretty frightening for many people.* | **it's frightening** *There are so many people with guns these days, it's really frightening.* | **it is frightening to do sth** *It's frightening to think that something like this can happen in America today.* | **a frightening experience/thought/prospect** *It was the most frightening experience of my life.* | *After so many years, going back to college and studying was a frightening prospect.*

terrifying /'terᵻfaɪ-ɪŋ/ [adj] very frightening: *They stopped me, and I saw that they had a gun. It was terrifying.* | *I opened my eyes, and tried to banish the terrifying images of the plane falling from the sky, and crashing into the sea.* | **a terrifying scream/crash/sound etc** *There was a terrifying crash, and the house seemed to shake.* | **a terrifying experience/ordeal/thought** *It had been a terrifying ordeal, but now, at last, he was free.*

scary /'skeəri/ [adj] especially spoken frightening – use this especially about stories, films, or situations in which strange or frightening things happen: *She didn't like the film. It was too scary for her.* | *I had a really scary dream last night.* | **it's scary** *I don't regret my decision to start a new life, in a new country. It's scary, but it's also really exciting.* | *a big scary monster*

spooky /'spuːki/ [adj] a place or story that is **spooky** is frightening, especially because it is dark, strange etc: *The forest is really spooky in the dark.* | *Will you shut up about ghosts! You always scare me with that spooky talk!* | *I remembered that spooky feeling of being alone in the woods, and feeling that you are being watched by supernatural eyes.* | *We sat around the fire and told spooky tales.*

creepy /'kriːpi/ [adj] a **creepy** feeling or place is one that is strange and makes you feel nervous and frightened, especially because you think that someone or something frightening might be there: *The house looked OK from the outside but inside it was all dark and creepy.* | *This place is really creepy. Let's get out of here.* | *I got a real creepy feeling on the way over there, as if someone was watching me.*

chilling /'tʃɪlɪŋ/ [adj] a fact, statement or experience that is **chilling**, makes you feel frightened or shocked, because it is extremely cruel, violent, dangerous etc: *The lawyer gave a chilling demonstration of how the accused used a towel to suffocate his victim.* | *The captain's message ended with the chilling words: 'Mission completed. All prisoners disposed of.'* | *The case is a chilling reminder of how ordinary, seemingly respectable citizens still have racist and deeply intolerant views.*

hair-raising /'heəʳ ˌreɪzɪŋ/ [adj] an experience that is **hair-raising** is frightening because it is very dangerous: *We ended up making a hair-raising 200-kilometre night drive to the border.* | *After various hair-raising adventures in Afghanistan, Newcombe settled in Northern India.* | **hair-raising tale/story** *Jenny had lots of adventures, travelling all over the world and always coming home with hair-raising stories.*

spine-chilling /'spaɪn ˌtʃɪlɪŋ/ [adj] something such as a story, film, or statement that is **spine-chilling** is frightening because it clearly describes or shows frightening or evil events: *The collection includes a spine-chilling ghost story by Edgar Allan Poe.* | *The only journalist to witness the rebellion gave a spine-chilling account of atrocities carried out by both sides.*

blood-curdling /'blʌd ˌkɜːʳdlɪŋ/ [adj only before noun] **blood-curdling scream/howl/roar etc** very frightening or made by someone who is extremely frightened: *Mary went upstairs to look for Dean and seconds later I heard a blood-curdling scream.* | *the blood-curdling howls of the wolves in the forest*

6 to deliberately frighten someone

- frighten/scare sb into sth
- terrorize

see also **threaten**

frighten/scare sb into sth /'fraɪtn, 'skeəʳ (sb) ɪntə (sth)/ [phr v T] to make someone feel frightened about what will happen if they do not do something, so that they do it. **Scare sb into** is more informal than **frighten sb into** **frighten/scare sb into doing sth** *The Nationalists kept talking about the 'Communist threat' to scare people into voting for them.* | *Stapleton had tried to frighten her into keeping quiet, but she had refused to be intimidated.*

terrorize ALSO **terrorise** British /'terəraɪz/ [v T] to deliberately frighten people over a long period of time, by using violence or by threatening them, especially in order to make them do what you want: *Some of the older children dominated the playground and terrorized the smaller kids.* | *A gang of youths are roaming the city, vandalising stores, starting fires, and terrorizing people.* | **terrorize sb into doing sth** (=make someone do something by using violence, threats etc) *With threats, beatings, and even murder, the workers were terrorized into leaving their unions.*

7 someone who easily gets frightened

- scare easily
- timid
- nervous

scare easily /'skeəʳ ˌiːzᵊli/ [v phrase] informal to easily get frightened: *Being a police officer isn't a job for someone who scares easily.* | *I'll go down and see what that noise was. I don't scare easily you know.*

timid /'tɪmᵻd/ [adj] easily frightened and unwilling to do anything that might be unpleasant or dangerous: *Decker knew that the senior officer was wrong,* *but was too timid to tell him.* | *They think I'm just a timid woman, but I'll show them they're wrong.* | **+ about doing sth** *I was always timid about taking action in a crisis, but not Doris.*

nervous /ˈnɜːʳvəs/ [adj] a **nervous** person is always worried or frightened about something that may happen, so that they cannot relax: *You know what makes me nervous? When people drive really close behind you.* | *The stage is huge, you know, and I walked out there, and I was real nervous.* | **+ about** *I was so nervous about my exams that I couldn't sleep.* | **+ of** *Jill's always been a little nervous of dogs.* | **of a nervous disposition** (=with a nervous character) formal *People of a nervous disposition may be upset by some of the scenes in the following programme.*

8 the feeling of being frightened

- fear
- terror
- horror
- panic
- foreboding

fear /fɪəʳ/ [n C/U] the feeling you have when you are very frightened, or the thought that something very unpleasant will happen: *The boy's eyes were full of fear.* | **+ of** *Fears of a recession have wiped billions of dollars off share values.* | *fear of flying* | *My fear of the dentist goes back to when I was a child.* | **+ that** *There was always the fear that he might never return.* | **do sth in fear** (=do sth because you feel fear) *I glanced around in fear. Was someone following me?* | **do sth in fear of your life** (=do something because you think you are going to be killed) *People fled in fear of their lives, as mud began to pour down the mountainside.* | **shake/tremble/go white etc with fear** *Her hands were shaking with fear.* | **frozen/sick with fear** *The boat had gone. We stood frozen with fear, staring at the sea.* | **hopes and fears** (=the things that you hope will happen and the things that you are frightened will happen) *On New Year's Eve we come together, and share our hopes and fears for the coming year.*

terror /ˈterəʳ/ [n U] a very strong feeling of fear when you think that something very bad is going to happen to you, especially that you will be killed: *Denver burst from the room, terror in her eyes.* | *The men on the quivering, battered boat were mad with terror.* | *Their faces were white, and their eyes were filled with terror.* | **in terror** (=because you are very frightened) *Shots were fired, and the children fled in terror.* | **sheer terror** (=very great terror) *I will never forget the look of sheer terror on her face.* | **terror-stricken** (=feeling terror) *Terror-stricken refugees fled across the border.*

horror /ˈhɒrəʳ‖ˈhɔː-, ˈhɑː-/ [n U] a strong feeling of shock and fear that you have when you see something terrible happen, or when you think of something terrible: *Jocasta turned white, a look of horror on her face.* | **in horror** *The crowd watched in horror as the plane hit the ground and burst into flames.* | **to sb's horror** (=making someone feel very frightened) *He suddenly realized to his horror that the brakes weren't working.* | *To his horror, PC Kelly saw a handgun protruding from the man's coat.*

panic /ˈpænɪk/ [n U] a sudden, strong feeling of fear when you are in a dangerous situation, that often makes you do things that are not sensible because you cannot think clearly: *There was a sudden panic and everyone started rushing towards the door.* | **in panic** *Shoppers fled the street in panic after two bombs exploded in central London.* | **get into a panic/be thrown into a panic** *She got into a real panic when she thought she'd lost the tickets.* | **panic-stricken** (=feeling panic) *The panic-stricken crowd pushed through the exit, and 10 people were crushed to death.*

foreboding /fɔːʳˈbəʊdɪŋ/ [n U] a feeling of fear because you think something bad is going to happen although you do not have any real reason for thinking this: *'Jeanie, I have to go away,' he said, his voice full of foreboding.* | **a feeling/sense of foreboding** *As they waited at the airfield, Sara had the same feeling of foreboding that she had felt before her father died.* | *He had a sudden sense of foreboding. Something was wrong, very wrong.*

9 an event or situation that frightens people

- scare
- horror

scare /skeəʳ/ [n C] a situation in which a lot of people are frightened of something such as a serious illness, violence, or a problem that may harm them – used especially in news reports: *Aids has caused such a scare that fewer and fewer people are giving blood.* | **+ about/over** *A year after Chernobyl the scare about radioactive food had died down.* | **bomb scare** (=when there is a report that there is a bomb) *Retail sales were down due to a spate of bomb scares before Christmas.* | **food/health scare** *Some people, nervous about the health scare over cellular phones, have started using hands-free apparatus.*

horror /ˈhɒrəʳ‖ˈhɔː-, ˈhɑː-/ [n C] an event or situation which frightens and shocks people because they see terrible things happening: *Children in these famine-stricken areas simply cannot be protected from the horror all around them.* | **the horror of** *One woman cried as she told of the horror of seeing workmates killed in the lift.* | *They joined the anti- nuclear campaign after seeing a film about the horrors of Hiroshima.*

10 a film or story that is intended to frighten you

- horror
- thriller

horror /ˈhɒrəʳ‖ˈhɔː-, ˈhɑː-/ [adj only before noun] **horror film/movie/story etc** a film or story that is intended to make you feel frightened: *The movie is based on a horror story by Stephen King.* | *a low-budget horror film about a group of teenagers in a wood*

thriller /ˈθrɪləʳ/ [n C] a film or book that is intended to be exciting and frightening because you do not know what will happen next: *Kurt Russell and Steven Seagal team up in a thriller about a hijacked plane.* | **action/crime/psychological etc thriller** *'Psycho' is Hitchcock's greatest psychological thriller.* | *'Bullet to Beijing', a spy thriller, starring Michael Caine and Michael Gambon*

front

RELATED WORDS

opposite: **back**

- *see also* **towards, forward**

1 the part of something that is nearest to you or furthest away from the back

- the front

the front /ðə 'frʌnt/ [n singular] *She was wearing a T-shirt with a picture of an elephant on the front.* | *Could you cut my hair short in the back but leave it a little longer in the front?* | **+ of** *They painted the front of the house bright green.* | *He wrote her name on the front and back of the envelope.*

2 the part of a space, room, vehicle etc that is furthest forward

- **the front**

the front /ðə 'frʌnt/ [n singular] *Let's get to the concert early so we can sit near the front.* | **+ of** *The teacher was standing at the front of the classroom.* | *There's only room for two people in the front of the car.* | *At the front of the cage was a dish with a few scraps of food in it.*

3 the position at the front of a crowd or line of people, cars etc

- **the front**

the front /ðə 'frʌnt/ [n singular] *I stood in the line for two hours before I got to the front.* | **+ of** *Joseph pushed to the front of the crowd to see what was happening.* | *Halfway through the race, Cami was still at the front of the pack.*

4 at, in, or towards the front

- **front**
- **in front/in the front**
- **up front**
- **at the head of sth**
- **forward**
- **in the foreground**

front /frʌnt/ [adj only before noun] *You should have knocked on the front door.* | *The dog rested its head on its front paws.* | *Laura always sits in the front row at the movies.* | *He leaned across the front seat of the car and grabbed her arm as she tried to get out.* | *There was a large picture of Bush on the front page of the evening newspaper.*

in front/in the front /ɪn 'frʌnt, ɪn ðə 'frʌnt/ [adv] in the front part of a space, room, vehicle etc: *He sat in front beside the driver.* | *Miss Abbot led me through the classroom to an empty desk in the front.* | *We were looking for a two-storey building with a verandah in the front.*

up front /ʌp 'frʌnt/ [adv] if someone is **up front** in a room or vehicle, they are in the most forward position possible: *Why don't you sit up front with the driver so you can give him directions?* | *The only people who laughed were the American soldiers who sat up front.*

at the head of sth /ət ðə 'hed əv (sth)/ [prep] at the front of a line or group of people: *A man at the head of the line was arguing with the saleslady.* | *Two soldiers carried flags at the head of the procession.*

forward /'fɔːʳwəʳd/ [adv] if you move **forward**, you move towards the front of a room, space etc: *Mr Hoffman stepped forward to collect his prize.* | *Can we sit a little further forward? I can't see from here.*

in the foreground /ɪn ðə 'fɔːʳgraʊnd/ [adv] in the part of a picture, scene, or view that is or seems closest to you: *The figures in the foreground are painted more brightly than those farther away.* | **+ of** *'That's me,' he said, pointing to a child in the foreground of the faded photograph.*

5 at, in, or towards a position that is further forward than you

- **in front**
- **ahead**
- **up ahead**

in front /ɪn 'frʌnt/ [adv] *The car in front started to slow down.* | *Ellie walked in front, carrying the baby.* | **+ of** *Because of the fog, we could only see a few yards in front of us.*

ahead /ə'hed/ [adv] a short distance from the front or face of someone or something: *He looked ahead down the road towards the village.* | **+ of** *Let Tom walk ahead of you – he knows this path very well.* | **straight ahead** (=directly ahead) *Albert was staring straight ahead, pretending not to listen.*

up ahead /ʌp ə'hed/ [adv] in the distance but not very far in front of you: *Traffic is awfully slow – there must be an accident up ahead.* | *Up ahead we could see the bright lights of the city coming into view.*

6 directly in front of a person, building etc

- **in front**

in front /ɪn 'frʌnt/ [adv] close to the front of someone or something: *The kids are playing out in front.* | **+ of** *There was a tall man standing in front of me, so I couldn't see what was happening.* | **right in front** (=directly in front) *She parked the car right in front of the main entrance.*

full

RELATED WORDS

opposite: **empty**

- food that makes your stomach feel full *see* **food**
- feeling full of food *see* **eat**
- *see also* **tight, complete/not complete**

1 full

- **full**
- **filled with sth**
- **packed**
- **overflowing**
- **bulging**
- **be full to the brim**
- **be chock-a-block**
- **crammed/jammed**
- **be stuffed with**

full /fʊl/ [adj] if a container, room, or space is **full**, nothing more can go into it: *a full bottle of milk* | *All the parking spaces were full.* | *The lecture hall was full for MacGowan's talk.* | **+ of** *The buses were full of people going to work.* | *You can order a birthday box full of balloons, banners and party favors.*

filled with sth /'fɪld wɪð (sth)/ [adj phrase] full of something – use this about a container when a lot of things have been put into it: *Pour the mixture into a tall glass filled with ice.* | *There were lots of tiny drawers filled with screws and nails.*

packed /pækt/ [adj] completely full of people – use this about a room, theatre, train, bus etc: *a packed theatre* | *The plane was packed, because a previous flight had been cancelled.* | **+ with** *On the day of her funeral the church was packed with friends and relatives.*

overflowing /ˌəʊvəʳ'fləʊɪŋ◂/ [adj] a container that is **overflowing** is so full that the liquid or things inside it come out over the top: *Sewers were overflowing because of the rain.* | *The tables were covered with dirty coffee cups and overflowing ashtrays.* | **+ with** *a trash can overflowing with garbage*

bulging /'bʌldʒɪŋ/ [adj] something such as a bag or a pocket that is **bulging** is so full that the objects inside it push its sides outwards: *Wilson carried two bulging shopping bags from the duty-free shop.* | *a bulging wallet full of credit cards* | **+ with** *The files are bulging with letters, mailing lists, and information on the subject.*

be full to the brim British **/be filled to the brim** American /biː ˌfʊl tə ðə 'brɪm, biː ˌfɪld-/ [v phrase] if a container **is full to the brim**, it is full right to the very top, especially with liquid: *The reservoirs are filled to the brim after the spring floods.* | **+ with** *The sink was full to the brim with dirty water and dishes.*

be chock-a-block /biː ˌtʃɒk ə 'blɒk‖-'tʃɑːk ə blɑːk/ [v phrase] British informal a room, vehicle, or building that is **chock-a-block** is so full of people that you cannot move easily in it: *The train was chock-a-block and I couldn't get a seat for the whole journey.* | **+ with** *The cinema is usually chock-a-block with kids on Sunday afternoons.*

crammed/jammed /kræmd, dʒæmd/ [adj] so full of things that nothing else can possibly be put in: *How can children learn in crammed classrooms?* | **+ with** *The box was crammed with books.* | *O'Hare Airport was jammed with holiday flights.* | *The two resorts are crammed with hotels, discos, bars, and restaurants.*

be stuffed with /biː 'stʌft wɪð/ [v phrase] if a container **is stuffed with** things, it is very full of them because as much as possible has been put into it: *a huge picnic basket stuffed with food* | *The girls each had a small backpack stuffed with books, cards, crayons, paper, and games.* | *Police seized the plane and found bags stuffed with 1300 kilos of cocaine.*

2 to become full

- fill up
- fill

fill up /ˌfɪl 'ʌp/ [phr v I] to gradually become full: *About half an hour before the performance, the theatre starts to fill up.* | *The drought has ended at last, and the reservoirs are filling up again.*

fill /fɪl/ [v I] to become full: *They opened the doors and the hall quickly filled.* | **+ with** *Her eyes suddenly filled with tears.*

3 to make something full

- fill
- fill up
- stuff
- cram/jam
- load

fill /fɪl/ [v T] to put enough of something into a container to make it full: *Mix the spinach and cheese and use it to fill the pasta shells.* | **fill sth with sth** *We stood at the counter, filling our bowls with salad.* | *He had a notebook that he had filled with stories and poems.*

fill up /ˌfɪl 'ʌp/ [phr v T] to fill a container that already has a small amount of something in it: *The waiter filled up everyone's glasses.* | **fill sth up with sth** *If the oil tank is less than half full, tell them to fill it up.* | **fill up sth with sth** *I filled up the sandbox with some more sand.*

stuff /stʌf/ [v T] to quickly fill something such as a bag or pocket by pushing things into it tightly **stuff sth into sth** *She hurriedly stuffed some things into an overnight bag and left.* | **stuff sth with sth** *We had to stuff envelopes with letters and information packs.*

cram/jam /kræm, dʒæm/ [v T] to push too many things into a container or space, so that they are all pressed together **cram/jam sth into sth** *I crammed all my clothes into the suitcase and called a taxi.* | *Too many houses are crammed into too small an area.* | *Fifty-five children were jammed into a classroom designed to hold thirty.*

load ALSO **load up** /ləʊd, ˌləʊd 'ʌp/ [v T/phr v T] to fill a vehicle with goods, furniture etc: *Loading the van was hard work.* | *This giant machine can load up a 10-ton truck every few minutes.* | **load sth into sth** *A woman was loading groceries into her car.* | **load sth with sth** *Two men were loading up a truck with boxes of melons.* —**loaded** [adj] *The runway is too short for the plane to take off when it is fully loaded.*

4 to make something full again after part of what is in it has been used

- refill
- replenish
- top up

refill /ˌriː'fɪl/ [v T] to fill something again, after what was inside it has been used: *If you bring your empty bottles back to the store, we can refill them.* | *Can I refill anyone's glass?* | **refill sth with sth** *The tank was emptied, cleaned, and refilled with fresh water.* —**refill** /'riːfɪl/ [n C] *A cup of coffee is $1.20, refills are free.*

replenish /rɪ'plenɪʃ/ [v T] formal to make something full again, especially with a supply of something such as water or food: *In an emergency, water can be pumped from the well to replenish the irrigation canals.* | *Shortages of food and poor transportation mean that the stores are not able to replenish their shelves as often as they would like to.*

top up /ˌtɒp 'ʌp‖ˌtɑːp-/ [phr v T] especially British to fill a glass, cup etc that is half full or nearly empty **top sth up** *'More wine anyone?' 'Yes, please, could you top mine up?'* | **top sth up with sth** *Pour a little brandy over the sugar and top it up with champagne.* —**top up** /'tɒp ʌp‖'tɑːp-/ [n C] British *'Would you like a top up?' he said, pointing to her glass.*

5 when a place is full of animals, people etc

- be teeming with
- be swarming/crawling with
- be jammed

be teeming with /biː 'tiːmɪŋ wɪð/ [v phrase] be full of people, animals, insects etc all moving around: *The small stretch of water was teeming with wildfowl.* | *Times Square was teeming with theatergoers.* | *The tragedy is that this whole region remains teeming with desperately poor people.*

be swarming/crawling with /biː 'swɔːʳmɪŋ, 'krɔːlɪŋ wɪð/ [v phrase] to be very full of animals, people, insects etc, all moving around very quickly or busily – use this especially when you think this is unpleasant in some way: *At this time of year the town is usually crawling with tourists.* | *The campsite was filthy and swarming with flies.* | *Our hotel room was crawling with bugs and roaches.*

be jammed /biː 'dʒæmd/ [v phrase] to be full of a lot of people standing or sitting very close together: *Japanese trains may be jammed, but at least they are punctual.* | **+ with** *The room was jammed with fans trying to get his autograph.*

funny

RELATED WORDS

- unusual or strange *see* **strange**
- *see also* **joke, laugh, smile, serious**

1 when something or someone makes you laugh

- **funny**
- **make sb laugh**
- **amusing**
- **humorous**
- **witty**
- **hilarious**
- **comical**
- **light-hearted**
- **be a laugh**
- **be a hoot**

funny /ˈfʌni/ [adj] something or someone that is **funny** makes you laugh: *It was the funniest story I'd ever heard.* | *He can be pretty funny when he's had a few drinks.* | *The goat was chasing Mark round and round the field – it was so funny.* | **look funny** *You look really funny in that hat.* | **hilariously/hysterically funny** *Did you like 'Notting Hill'? I thought it was hilariously funny.*

make sb laugh /ˌmeɪk (sb) ˈlɑːf‖-ˈlæf/ [v phrase not in passive] to make someone laugh, for example by telling a joke or doing something funny: *I must tell Jerry what you said – it'll make him laugh.* | *Charlie Chaplin was a great actor with a wonderful ability to make people laugh.* | *It always makes me laugh when you look at me like that.*

amusing /əˈmjuːzɪŋ/ [adj] especially written funny and entertaining enough to make you smile: *I like a newspaper with one or two amusing articles, as well as all the serious stuff.* | *He was a really special person, gentle and amusing at the same time.* | **find sth/sb amusing** *Mrs Denton didn't find it amusing when I spilt all the paint on the floor.* | **highly amusing** *My mother was embarrassed, but I found the situation highly amusing.*

humorous /ˈhjuːmərəs‖ˈhjuː-, ˈjuː-/ [adj] intended to be amusing – use this especially about stories, descriptions, songs, and other things that people write: *The book is a humorous account of a young man's travels in South America.* | *It was a brilliant speech – clear, precise and humorous.* | *humorous birthday cards*

witty /ˈwɪti/ [adj] using words in a clever and amusing way: *Sam is intelligent, witty, and great fun to be with.* | *I enjoyed the play – it had a clever plot and a very witty script.*

hilarious /hɪˈleəriəs/ [adj] extremely funny – use this about situations, jokes, and stories, but not about people: *Our attempts at dancing were hilarious – we all kept tripping over each other.* | *the hilarious BBC comedy series 'Absolutely Fabulous'*

comical /ˈkɒmɪkəl‖ˈkɑː-/ [adj] especially written funny in a strange or unexpected way, although not always intended to be: *Carlo looked so comical, striding along in a coat which nearly touched the ground.* | *The puffin is an unusual sea bird, and there is something almost comical about the way it moves and looks.* | *Lizzie, bouncing along on the donkey, made a comical sight.* —**comically** [adv] *He bowed comically and asked my sister to dance.*

light-hearted /ˌlaɪt ˈhɑːʳtɪ̈d◂/ [adj] funny in a gentle way, and often about a subject that is usually serious: *We always try to keep our newsletter light-hearted, so that people will enjoy it.* | *The light-hearted way in which the author has approached this book should take some of the hard work out of trying to lose weight.* | **take a light-hearted look at sth** *The film takes a light-hearted look at life in prison.* —**light-heartedly** [adv] *Somehow, Moore manages to deal light-heartedly with subjects such as death and illness.*

be a laugh /biː ə ˈlɑːf‖-ˈlæf/ [v phrase] informal if a person or activity **is a laugh**, they are amusing and give you a lot of fun: *There were about 100 people there and it was a laugh from beginning to end.* | **a real laugh** spoken *Wait until you meet Tony. He's a real laugh.* | **be a laugh a minute** (=be very amusing) *We all had to sleep in one tent and it was a laugh a minute.*

be a hoot /biː ə ˈhuːt/ [v phrase] informal if a person, situation, performance, film etc **is a hoot**, they are very funny and enjoyable: *The movie has a script that is smartly funny, and Hugh Grant is a hoot!* | *At the end of the day, there was the moms' soccer match, which was a hoot!*

2 a funny film, play etc

- **comedy**
- **comic**

comedy /ˈkɒmɪ̈di‖ˈkɑː-/ [n C] a film, play, TV programme etc that is intended to entertain people and make them laugh: *'One Fine Day' was a romantic comedy with George Clooney and Michelle Pfeiffer.* | **comedy programme/series/show** *a comedy show on Channel 4* | **black comedy** (=one that is funny about things such as death) *The movie's a black comedy about a pair of junkie musicians who are trying to kick the drug habit.*

comic /ˈkɒmɪk‖ˈkɑː-/ [adj only before noun] intended to entertain people and make them laugh: *Streep provided one of the best comic performances of her career.* | **comic writer/actor/performer etc** (=one who writes or performs things that make you laugh) *Like all comic writers, Shaw was fascinated by the gap between appearance and reality.* | **comic verse/song** (=that entertains you and makes you laugh) *Then Gertie got up on the stage and delighted us all by singing a comic song.* | **comic relief** (=something funny in a serious story) *In Shakespeare's Henry IV, the character of Falstaff provides us with a little comic relief.*

3 when the opposite of what is expected happens

- **ironic**
- **irony**

ironic /aɪˈrɒnɪk‖-ˈrɑː-/ [adj] something that is **ironic** is funny, but in a sad or strange way, because it is the opposite of what you would expect: *'I've heard that Dan's really upset about the divorce.' 'How ironic. He was always the one who was against them getting married in the first place.'* | *It was an ironic situation, the two men in her life meeting like that.* | **it is ironic that** *It's ironic that the most important people in the country often have so little understanding of how ordinary people live.* —**ironically** [adv] *Ironically, the government ended up harming the very people it was trying to help.*

irony /ˈaɪərəni/ [n C/U] something that is funny, but in a sad or strange way, because it is the opposite of what you would expect: *Life is full of ironies, some hilarious, some tragic.* | **+ of** *The irony of the situation was obvious – if I told the truth, nobody would believe me!* | **the irony is that** *The irony is that some of the poorest countries have the richest natural resources.*

4 how you feel when you think something is funny

- amused
- amusement

amused /ə'mju:zd/ [adj not usually before noun] if you are **amused** by something, you think it is funny and it makes you smile: *When I told him what had happened, he sounded amused rather than annoyed.* | **+ by/at** *They seemed amused at his embarrassment.* | **greatly/highly amused** *My grandmother seemed to be highly amused by my remarks.* | **amused expression/smile/grin** *She stood watching them with an amused expression on her face.*

amusement /ə'mju:zmənt/ [n U] the feeling that you have when you think something is funny: *This story is bound to cause some amusement in the anti-Campbell campaign.* | **watch/listen/notice etc with amusement** *Everyone was watching the little dog with interest and amusement.* | **+ at** *Gloria couldn't hide her amusement at what the children were saying.* | **in amusement** *'You must be joking!' Mum said, her lips curling in amusement.* | **(much) to sb's amusement** (=making them feel very amused) *Suddenly, the teacher's chair collapsed, much to everyone's amusement.*

5 the quality in someone or something that makes them funny

- humour
- comedy
- wit

humour British **humor** American /'hju:mər‖'hju:-, 'ju:-/ [n U] the quality or thing in a situation, book, remark etc that makes it funny: *Everyone laughed except Dad, who obviously didn't appreciate the humour of the situation.* | *The most popular children's books are ones that have plenty of humor in them.* | **black humour** (=about things such as death and violence) *Tom Lehrer's black humor offended some people, who found jokes about such subjects as nuclear war unacceptable.*

comedy /'kɒmədi‖'kɑ:-/ [n U] the quality in a book, film, television programme etc that is intended to entertain people and make them laugh: *It was a brilliant play – full of drama, and both sadness and comedy.* | *Much of the comedy in Pratchett's books comes from the clever way he plays around with words and ideas.*

wit /wɪt/ [n U] the ability to use words and express ideas in a clever and amusing way, especially when it is shown in conversation or writing: *He seemed to have everything you could want in a man – intelligence, wit, good looks and charm.* | *The wit and irony of the original novel has been lost in the film version.*

6 the ability to realize when something is funny

- sense of humour
- can take a joke
- see the funny side of
- can laugh

sense of humour British **/sense of humor** American /ˌsens əv 'hju:mər/ [n C usually singular] your ability to understand and enjoy jokes, funny situations etc: *Mr Hardman was a popular teacher, renowned for his sense of humor.* | **have a (good/great/strange etc) sense of humour** *I like Ann – she has such a good sense of humour.* | **lose your sense of humour** *Maybe I'm losing my sense of humor but I didn't find it at all funny.*

can take a joke /kən ˌteɪk ə 'dʒəʊk/ [v phrase] especially spoken to be able to laugh and not get angry when other people make jokes about you or do something that makes you look stupid: *I hope he can take a joke – have you seen what they've done to his car?* | *You may find army life difficult if you can't take a joke.*

see the funny side of /ˌsi: ðə 'fʌni saɪd ɒv/ [v phrase] to realize that a situation that seems to be bad is also funny: *I explained that it was all my fault and fortunately she saw the funny side of the situation.* | **see the funny side of it** *As a teacher, things often go wrong, and you have to be able to see the funny side of it.* | **see the funny side of life** *A cartoonist's job is all about making people see the funny side of life.*

can laugh /kən 'lɑ:f‖-'læf/ [v phrase] to be able to laugh and joke about your own mistakes and faults or about past experiences which did not seem funny when they were happening: *We can laugh now, but at the time it seemed like the end of the world.* | **can laugh at yourself** *Don't take yourself too seriously – it's a good thing if you can laugh at yourself sometimes.*

future

RELATED WORDS

opposite: —— **past**

▸ *see also* **predict, soon, after, time, past, modern, possible**

1 the time after now

- the future
- ahead
- to come
- be still/yet/more etc to come
- from now on
- in future
- in the long/short/medium term

the future /ðə 'fju:tʃər/ [n singular] the time, especially a fairly long time, after now: *Ellen's finishing college soon but she doesn't really have any plans for the future.* | *As for the future, Tucker said she intends to take a well-deserved break before deciding what to do next.* | **of the future** (=that will exist in the future) *The car of the future may run on solar-powered batteries.* —**future** [adj only before noun] **future date/time** *We agreed to consider the matter again at a future date.*

ahead /ə'hed/ [adv] in the future – used especially when you know you will have problems or difficulties in the future **the day/week/months ahead** *David had his breakfast and thought about the day ahead.* | *Unemployment in the region is expected to grow in the months ahead.* | **lie ahead** *The government faces some difficult decisions in the months which lie ahead.* | **+ of** *I know there are some big problems ahead of us, but I'm sure we can overcome them.*

to come /tə 'kʌm/ [adv] **generations/years/a long time to come** for a long time in and affecting many people in the future: *In years to come, people will look back on the 20th century as a turning point in history.* | *Nuclear power stations will still be needed for a long time to come.*

be still/yet/more etc to come /bi: ˌstɪl tə 'kʌm/ [v phrase] to not have happened yet but going to happen in the future, especially soon in the future: *The best is still to come – there's chocolate ice cream for dessert.* | *The worst of the storm was still to come.*

from now on /frəm ˌnaʊ ˈɒn/ [adv] use this to say that something will always happen in the future, starting from now: *From now on, I'm not letting anyone borrow my car.* | *From now on, you kids will have to make your own lunch.* | *From now on, homeowners will have to get a city permit if they want to build an addition onto their homes.*

in future /ɪn ˈfjuːtʃəʳ/ [adv] British starting from now – use this especially to tell someone that they must do something starting from now: *In future, I expect you to be at work no later than 9.15.* | *In future, prisoners must serve at least half of their sentence before qualifying for any type of early release.*

in the long/short/medium term /ɪn ðə ˈlɒŋ, ˈʃɔːʳt, ˈmiːdiəm ˌtɜːʳm‖-ˈlɔːŋ-/ [adv] use this to talk about what will happen over a period from now until a long, short etc time in the future: *We don't know what will happen in the long term.* | *Aid to these countries is bound to run into billions of dollars in the long term.* | *Analysts say the reports could have a major impact on the stock market in the short term.* —**long-/short-/medium-term** [adj] *The country's oil and natural gas reserves are capable only of meeting short-term needs.*

2 at some time in the future

- in the future
- some time
- one day/some day
- one of these days
- the day will come (when)

in the future /ɪn ðə ˈfjuːtʃəʳ/ [adv] at some time **in the future**, but you do not know exactly when: *It's likely that global warming will become a major problem in the future.* | *What do you think life in the future will be like?* | **in the near future** (=at a time not long from now) *The new software will be available in the UK in the near future.* | **in/for the foreseeable future** (=at a time not long from now) *It is unlikely that the company will achieve a very high profit margin in the foreseeable future.*

some time /ˌsʌm ˈtaɪm/ [adv] at a time in the future that has not been arranged yet: *Come over and see us some time.* | *We should get together some time.* | **some time next week/next year/in 2005 etc** *The project should be completed some time next year.*

one day/some day /ˌwʌn ˈdeɪ, ˌsʌm ˈdeɪ/ [adv] at some time in the future, especially a long time from now: *Perhaps one day we could all go to London together.* | *One day, I'd like to visit the Grand Canyon.* | *She always knew that some day he would leave her.*

one of these days /ˌwʌn əv ðiːz ˈdeɪz/ [adv] at some time in the future – used especially when you think that something will probably happen or that someone will probably do something: *One of these days you're going to be sorry.* | *Richard's going to have a heart attack one of these days if he doesn't slow down.*

the day will come (when) /ðə ˌdeɪ wɪl ˈkʌm (wen)/ use this to emphasize that something will definitely happen at some time in the future: *The day will finally come when a woman or a black man is elected president of the United States.* | *Let's hope that the day will come when it's no longer necessary to have such a vast amount of money spent on the military.*

3 at a specific time in the future

- from now
- then
- away/off
- come July/summer/next year

▸ *see also* **then (3)**

from now /frəm ˈnaʊ/ [adv] **an hour/10 years/2 weeks etc from now** an hour, 10 years etc from the time when you are speaking: *The package should arrive a few days from now.* | *There may be no rainforest left 30 years from now.* | *A couple of months from now, you'll probably have forgotten all about him.*

then /ðen/ [adv] at a time in the future, that you have just mentioned: *I should be finished work by noon. Would you like to get together then?* | **until then** *School starts in September, and until then I'll be staying with friends.* | *They're sending the results next week, so I won't know anything until then.* | **by then** *Tell him he has two weeks to finish the job. If he's not finished by then, he's fired.*

away/off /əˈweɪ, ɒf‖ɔːf/ [adv] **6 months/4 days/a week etc away/off** if something that you know will happen is 6 months, 4 days, a week etc **away** or **off**, it will happen after 6 months, 4 days, a week etc have passed: *The next general elections are still two years away.* | *Mary was desperately looking forward to her retirement, which was less than a year off.* | *The wedding was more than a year away but she had already bought a dress for it.* | *The exams are still a few weeks off – you've got plenty of time to prepare for them.*

come July/summer/next year etc /kʌm dʒʊˈlaɪ/ spoken say this when something will happen at a particular time in the future: *Come Monday, we'll be in our new house.* | *A mild winter is nice, but it means that come summer you're going to have a bug problem.*

4 what will happen to someone or something in the future

- sb's future
- the future of sth
- fate
- destiny
- the outlook
- prospect

sb's future / (sb's) ˈfjuːtʃəʳ/ what will happen to someone in their job, life etc: *I'm worried about my future.* | *I had a meeting with my boss to discuss my future.* | *You really should start thinking about your future. You're not a child anymore.*

the future of sth /ðə ˈfjuːtʃər əv (sth)/ what will happen to something – use this especially to talk about whether something will be successful, will continue to exist etc: *One key issue at the talks will be the future of Taiwan and the Republic of China.* | *The memo refers to a meeting in Los Angeles, where the future of the network was discussed.*

fate /feɪt/ [n C usually singular] what will happen to someone – used about an important official decision, or about an event in which something very bad happens: *Congress will meet to discuss the fate of the US nuclear defense shield.* | **decide sb's/sth's fate** *The fate of the prisoners will be decided by a panel of three judges.* | *He urged a nationwide referendum to decide the fate of the country.* | **sb's/sth's fate is sealed** (=fixed and definite) *His fate was sealed when The New York Times learned of the situation and began preparing an article about it.* | **seal the fate of** (=decide it definitely) *This afternoon's debate is likely to seal the fate of the imprisoned aid workers.*

destiny /ˈdestɨni/ [n C usually singular] what someone is going to do in their life and what is going to happen to them during it: *The government wants to give people more control over their own destinies.* | **be sb's destiny to do sth** *Susan wondered whether it was her destiny to marry Jorge and live in Mexico.*

the outlook /ði ˈaʊtlʊk/ [n singular] a general idea of what people expect to happen in the future, and whether they expect things to go well or badly: *The economic outlook is better than it has been for several years.* | **long-range/short-range outlook** *Company officials insist the long-range outlook for share holders will be brighter.* | **+ for** *With drought conditions continuing, the outlook for farmers is not very good.*

prospect /ˈprɒspekt‖ˈprɑː-/ [n C] the idea or possibility that something will happen in the future: *I hope I never have to have a brain operation – it must be an appalling prospect.* | **the prospect of sth/doing sth** *The prospect of putting weapons in space is frightening to many people.* | *I had read a great deal about Professor Chomsky and I felt very excited at the prospect of meeting him.* | *We are facing the prospect of a very hard winter.* | **prospects for** *Prospects for a peace settlement in the region are not very hopeful at the moment.*

5 likely to happen in the future

- be on the horizon
- be in store

be on the horizon /biː ɒn ðə həˈraɪzən/ [v phrase] if something, especially an important change or event, **is on the horizon**, it seems likely to happen at some time in the future: *The prospect of real democracy is on the horizon for this Latin American country of 57 million.* | *After two weeks of talks a solution to the dispute is finally on the horizon.*

be in store /biː ɪn ˈstɔːʳ/ [v phrase] if something unexpected such as a surprise or a sudden problem **is in store** for someone, it is soon going to happen to them **+ for** *There was a surprise in store for Paul when he got to his office.* | *Russell said expulsion may be in store for some of the students involved in the fighting that broke out Friday.* | **what fate/the future holds in store (for sb)** (=what is going to happen to someone in the future) *When she first arrived in the US she was afraid of what the future might hold in store for her here.* | *None of us know what the future has in store.*

6 likely to be or do something in the future

- future
- potential
- prospective
- in the making
- have a great/bright/brilliant etc future

future /ˈfjuːtʃəʳ/ [adj only before noun] *He's an extremely talented football player – he could well be a future captain of England.* | *It was then that Milstead took the first steps toward a future career in law enforcement.* | *Before the scandal erupted, Grieg was talked about as a future presidential candidate.*

potential /pəˈtenʃəl/ [adj only before noun] **potential customer/client/witness etc** someone who might become a customer etc in the future: *Police believe they may have found a potential witness.* | *It's wrong to regard all soccer fans as potential troublemakers – it's only a small minority who are responsible for the violence.* | *By denying these people a decent education, you're losing out on potential captains of industry and political leaders.*

prospective /prəˈspektɪv/ [adj only before noun] **prospective candidate/employee/husband etc** one who wants to get or may be chosen for a job, position etc in the future: *My mother keeps introducing me to men she considers to be prospective husbands.* | *Texaco has introduced a compulsory HIV testing program for all prospective employees.*

in the making /ɪn ðə ˈmeɪkɪŋ/ [adj phrase] likely to do very well in your area of work or sport in the future: *When I first saw her play tennis I knew that she was a future Wimbledon champion in the making.*

have a great/bright/brilliant etc future /hæv ə ˌgreɪt ˈfjuːtʃəʳ/ to be likely to be very successful in the future: *She's a very talented musician, and we think she has a great future.* | *He's obviously got a bright future in this organization.*

Gg

gambling

RELATED WORDS

- *see also* **risk, win**

1 to gamble

- gamble
- gambling
- bet/have a bet
- put £10/$20 on
- back
- play for money
- have a flutter
- lose money on
- win money on

gamble /ˈgæmbəl/ [v I/T/phr v T] to try to win money, for example by playing cards or guessing which horse will win a race: *Eddie loved to gamble, and would spend most evenings at the roulette table.* | **gamble away sth/gamble sth away** (=waste a lot of money by gambling) *Roger gambled away all his money in a Las Vegas casino.* | *She inherited $50,000 but gambled it away.*

gambling /ˈgæmblɪŋ/ [n U] when you try to win money, for example by playing cards or guessing which horse will win a race: *Is gambling legal here?* | *Your Uncle Maury has a gambling problem.* | *Crane admits that he is addicted to gambling.* | *He was against the introduction of a National Lottery as he thought it might encourage gambling.*

bet/have a bet /bet, ˌhæv ə ˈbet/ [v I/T/v phrase] to try to win money by guessing who will win a race or game: *I don't bet very often.* | **bet on sth/have a bet on sth** (=gamble money on the result of a race or game) *We usually have a bet on the Grand Prix.* | *Rogers was not much of a gambler. When he bet on the horses, he almost always lost.* | **bet £10/$100 etc on sth** *Jerry bet $1000 on the game.* | **place a bet** (=say which horse, team, competition etc you want to gamble on and pay the money that you want to gamble) *I've placed a bet on a horse in the next race.* | *All bets must be placed before the start of the race.*

put £10/$20 etc on /pʊt ˌten ˈpaʊndz ɒn/ [phr v T] to gamble £10, $20 etc on the horse or team that you think will win a race or competition: *I put $20 on the Cowboys to win.* | *He put £50 on Middlesborough to beat Manchester United at odds of 3-1.* | **put a bet on sth** (=gamble on a horse, game etc) *I think I'll put a bet on the next race.*

back /bæk/ [v T] to gamble money on a particular horse, team, or person that you think will win a particular competition: *We backed a horse named Travelling Light that finished first at 10-1.* | **back sth/sb to win sth** *Uncle Barry backed Arsenal to win the FA Cup.*

play for money /ˌpleɪ fəʳ ˈmʌni/ [v phrase] to gamble money on the result of a game which you are playing, for example cards: *'Are we playing for money here, gentlemen?' he said as he approached the pool table.* | *You're allowed to play cards in the bar, but not for money.*

have a flutter /ˌhæv ə ˈflʌtəʳ/ [v phrase] British informal to gamble a small amount of money, especially on the result of a horse race – use this especially about someone who does not gamble very often: *I'm not a heavy gambler, but I like to have a flutter from time to time.* | **+ on** *I had a little flutter on the Grand National and won £5.*

lose money on /luːz ˈmʌni ɒn/ [v phrase] to lose money by not guessing correctly the result of a game, race, or competition: *He claims that he lost the money on a dice game.* | *I lost a lot of money on the dogs last night.*

win money on /wɪn ˈmʌni ɒn/ [v phrase] to win money by correctly guessing the result of a game, race, or competition: *I heard that he won a lot of money on the Superbowl a few years ago.*

2 someone who gambles

▸ gambler

gambler /ˈgæmbləʳ/ [n C] someone who gambles, especially someone who gambles a lot and cannot stop: *Jack was a great drinker and gambler.* | *De Niro plays Sam 'Ace' Rothstein, a professional gambler.* | **compulsive gambler** (=someone who cannot stop gambling) **heavy gambler** (=someone who gambles a lot) *It was rumoured that he was a heavy gambler and lost large sums in Monte Carlo.*

game

RELATED WORDS

▸ *see also* **competition, sport, gambling, score, beat/defeat, win, lose, play a game or sport**

1 an activity played by rules that you do for enjoyment

▸ game

game /geɪm/ [n C] an activity that you do for enjoyment, and that you play according to a set of rules: *Chess is such a difficult game.* | *Have you ever played Mah Jong? It's a Chinese game.* | *The women set up bingo games and bake sales to raise money for the charity.* | **the game of football/basketball/tennis** *The game of golf was invented in Scotland.* | *Chadwick suggested that baseball evolved from the English game of rounders.* | **the national game** (=the most popular game in a country) *In Wales, rugby is the national game.* | **computer game** *About 7 million households have people who play computer games.* | *'Psychic Detective' is a CD-ROM computer game from Electronic Arts Studios.* | **card game** (=a game you play using a set of playing cards) *I'm not very good at card games.* | *Harvey has devised a Spanish-English language card game.* | **board game** (=a game played on a board with pieces of wood, plastic etc that you move around) *board games like Monopoly and Ludo*

2 an occasion when people compete against each other in a game

▸ game ▸ event
▸ match

game /geɪm/ [n C] an occasion when two people or two teams compete against each other in a **game** or sport: *Sharpe had injured a knee in a football game a few weeks earlier* | **a game of chess/soccer/darts etc** *Would you be up for a game of darts at the local pub?* | *We played three games of checkers, and she beat me every time.* | **best/worst/first etc game of the season** *We were able to get seats for the last game of the season.*

match /mætʃ/ [n C] an occasion when two people or teams compete against each other in a sport or game – used especially about soccer, rugby, cricket, tennis, or chess: *Chess experts expected Kadparov to win the next match.* | **football/cricket/boxing etc match** *A cricket match was in progress on the school sports field.* | *Keith sprained his wrist in a wrestling match.*

event /ɪˈvent/ [n C] a match or competition, especially one that is important and is attended by a lot of people: *Tomorrow's match against Portugal is expected to be the big event of the season.* | **sporting event** *John rarely misses a sporting event in his town.* | *Wimbledon is one of Britain's great sporting events.*

3 to play a game

▸ play ▸ give sb a game

play /pleɪ/ [v I/T] *I used to play tennis all the time.* | *Do you know how to play backgammon?* | *Ask Alex if he wants to play.* | **play for sb** *Sweet Lou played for the Detroit Tigers.* | **play sb/play against sb** *'They played well against us,' Cooper said, 'I have to give them credit.'*

give sb a game /ˌgɪv (sb) ə ˈgeɪm/ [n phrase] British to play a game against someone, especially when it is not a serious or important game: *I'll give you a game of chess if you want.* | *No one wants to give him a game because he's too good.*

4 someone who plays a game

▸ player ▸ team
▸ opponent

player /ˈpleɪəʳ/ [n C] *a game for four players* | *Rodriguez was voted Player of the Year.* | **good player** (=good at playing a game) *I like chess, even though I'm not a very good player.* | *Wikerson is not as good a player as Phillips.*

opponent /əˈpəʊnənt/ [n C] someone who plays against another person in a game: *Brownlee regards Reaney as his most difficult opponent.* | *My opponent was much older than I was.*

team /tiːm/ [n C] a group of people who play against

another group in a game: *You're the best person on the team.* | *Pub quiz teams often have really silly names.* | **team captain/manager etc** *Nasser Hussain, the England team captain, was injured in the game against the West Indies.*

5 when children play games

▸ **play**

play /pleɪ/ [v I/T] if children **play**, they do things they enjoy, either together in a group, or with their toys: *This is the schoolground where we played as children.* | *We played card games and hide-and-seek.* | **+ with** *Ian was upstairs playing with his new train set.* | *Jimmy was playing with a little boat in the bathtub.* | **play at sth** British (=play a game in which you pretend to be someone) *We used to play at cops and robbers.*

gay

RELATED WORDS

▸ *see also* **relationship, girlfriend/boyfriend, love, sex, prejudiced**

1 gay

▸ **gay**
▸ **lesbian**
▸ **homosexual**
▸ **bisexual**
▸ **homophobia**

gay /geɪ/ [adj] sexually attracted to people of the same sex: *There are very few gay men on television.* | *The president's record with gay rights groups has been good.* | *Thousands of people attended the Gay Pride march in Brighton last weekend.* | *He didn't even realize that Elton John was gay!* | **gay community** *Kirkland is an especially popular figure in the gay community.* | **gay and lesbian** *Gay and lesbian couples should be eligible for the same health benefits as married heterosexual couples.* —**gays** [n plural] *the debate over gays in the military*

lesbian /ˈlezbiən/ [n C] a woman who is sexually attracted to other women: *I didn't realize I was a lesbian until I was in my twenties.* | *Lang was the first major pop star to come out as a lesbian.* —**lesbian** [adj] *We regularly publish a magazine that celebrates lesbian poetry and other women's literature.*

homosexual /ˌhəʊməˈsekʃuəl◂, ˌhɒ-‖ˌhəʊ-/ [adj] formal or written sexually attracted to people of the same sex: *Steve was 18 when he told his parents he was homosexual.* | *Greek literature provides evidence for homosexual activity among both males and females.* —**homosexual** [n C] someone who is homosexual – used especially by people who disapprove of this: *Most fundamentalist churches disapprove of homosexuals.* —**homosexuality** /ˌhəʊməˌsekʃuˈæləti, ˌhɒ-‖ˌhəʊ-/ [n U] the condition of being homosexual: *Homosexuality may be biologically determined.*

bisexual /baɪˈsekʃuəl/ [adj] sexually attracted to both men and women: *Although Tony's married, he's bisexual.* | *Oberlin College has a large gay, lesbian, and bisexual student group.* | *Woolf believed that all human beings are basically bisexual.*

homophobia /ˌhəʊməˈfəʊbiə, ˌhɒ-‖ˌhəʊ-/ [n U] hatred and fear of people who are gay: *There's still a lot of homophobia in American society.* | *Issues of racism, sexism, and homophobia were discussed.* —**homophobic** [adj] *Rose was criticized for the racist and homophobic lyrics in several of his songs.*

2 not gay

▸ **heterosexual**
▸ **straight**

heterosexual /ˌhetərəˈsekʃuəl◂/ [adj] sexually attracted to people of the opposite sex – use this especially when you are also talking about gay people: *Most of the people who come to the club are heterosexual, but we do get a small number of gay men.* | *The law applies to both heterosexual and homosexual employees.* —**heterosexual** [n C] a heterosexual person: *In Africa, most AIDS victims have been heterosexuals.* —**heterosexuality** /ˌhetərəsekʃuˈæləti/ [n U] the condition of being heterosexual: *Lawrence assumed that heterosexuality is 'normal'.*

straight /streɪt/ [adj] not gay – use this especially when you are comparing people who are not gay with people who are: *Straight men often feel nervous in the company of gays.* | *She's straight but she's got a lot of lesbian friends.*

3 to tell people you are gay

▸ **come out**
▸ **out**

come out /ˌkʌm ˈaʊt/ [phr v I] if someone who is gay **comes out**, they say publicly that they are gay: *John came out to his family last year.*

out /aʊt/ [v T] if you **out** someone, especially a well-known person, you say publicly that they are gay when they have tried to keep this a secret: *The Advocate, a national gay magazine, outed the congressman.* | *The Air Force pilot was afraid of being outed by his ex-lover.* —**out** [adj] someone who is out has told people that they are gay: *You will have the support of other men who are out.* | *As an out lesbian, I don't think my sexuality is any of your business.*

4 not having told people you are gay

▸ **be in the closet**

be in the closet /biː ɪn ðə ˈklɒzət‖ˈklɑː-/ [v phrase] to not have told other people that you are gay: *We provide help for young people who are in the closet and are too scared to come out.*

generous/ not generous

RELATED WORDS

▸ *see also* **give, kind, selfish/not selfish, spend, money/time**

1 generous

▸ **generous**
▸ **generosity**

generous /ˈdʒenərəs/ [adj] someone who is **generous** gives money or presents to other people, and you think it is kind and good of them to do this: *My sister's really generous. She's always buying things for her friends.* | *I am so amazed at how caring and generous people are here.* | *The Cranstons are among the museum's most generous donors.* | **+ to** *Roy was always cheerful and outgoing and generous to everyone.* | **it is generous of sb (to do sth)** *My dad offered* *to pay my plane fare, which was very generous of him.* —**generously** [adv] *These children need your help. Please give generously.*

generosity /ˌdʒenəˈrɒsɪ̈ti‖-ˈrɑː-/ [n U] generous behaviour: *The Prince was famous for his generosity.*

2 not generous

- stingy
- mean
- tight/tight-fisted
- penny-pinching

stingy ALSO **miserly** /ˈstɪndʒi, ˈmaɪzəʳli/ [adj] not generous, especially in small ways, when you could easily afford to be generous: *They are rich, but they are terribly stingy.* | *A hard, miserly woman, she left her daughters emotionally damaged.* | **+ with** *I don't know why they were so stingy with the drinks – they have plenty of money.*

mean /miːn/ [adj] British someone who is **mean** does not like spending money or sharing what they have with other people: *He's so mean, he won't even buy his wife a birthday present.* | **+ with** *Marsha has always been mean with her money.*

tight/tight-fisted /taɪt, ˌtaɪt ˈfɪstɪ̈d◂/ [adj] spoken informal someone who is **tight** or **tight-fisted** is not at all generous and tries hard to avoid spending money: *'I don't think I'll bother getting them a present.' 'Don't be so tight!'* | *Don't even ask Dad. You know how tight-fisted he is about these kinds of things.* | *a tight-fisted boss* | **tight with money** *Even as a young man, Paul was notoriously tight with his money.*

penny-pinching /ˈpeni ˌpɪntʃɪŋ/ [adj] spending very little, or always spending less than is needed, often because you do not have very much money: *His grandparents were humourless and penny-pinching.* | *She could finally tolerate no more of his coldness and penny-pinching ways.* | *Unfortunately we have a penny-pinching local government that spends as little as possible on parks and sports facilities.*

3 someone who is not generous

- miser
- skinflint
- cheapskate

miser /ˈmaɪzəʳ/ [n C] someone who hates spending money, and tries to spend as little as possible, especially someone who stores their money in a secret place: *Everyone said Mr Henny was a miser who had thousands of pounds hidden under his bed.* | *My uncle was a terrible miser – he would walk in lashing rain rather than pay a bus fare.*

skinflint ALSO **tightwad** especially American /ˈskɪnˌflɪnt, ˈtaɪtwɒd‖-wɑːd/ [n C] informal someone who hates to spend or give money: *We waited for the old skinflint to find his wallet and pay us our money.* | *Joe is such a tightwad that he won't even buy his own newspaper.*

cheapskate /ˈtʃiːpskeɪt/ [n C] informal someone who dislikes spending money, and does not care if they behave in an unreasonable way to avoid spending it: *Howard rode with us in the taxi, but the cheapskate didn't offer to pay any of the fare.* | *I'm not going out with those cheapskates again – they didn't buy a drink all night!*

get

RELATED WORDS

- to get an illness *see* **illness/disease**
- *see also* **have/not have, own, available/not available, buy, earn**

1 to get something by buying it, asking for it, or finding it

- get
- obtain
- find
- acquire

get /get/ [v T not in passive] *I don't feel like cooking – let's go get a pizza.* | *I still haven't gotten a birthday present for Sherri.* | **get sth from sb/sth** *I got a really nice coat from Hudson's.* | *We had to get permission from the landlord before painting the apartment.* | **get a job** *Did you hear? Stuart got a new job.*

obtain /əbˈteɪn/ [v T] formal to get something: *Maps and guides can be obtained at the tourist office.* | **obtain sth from sb/sth** *Scientists in Brazil are obtaining medicines from plants.*

find /faɪnd/ [v T] to get the money, time, energy etc that you need to do something: *If I can find the money, I'll come to the theatre with you.* | *I haven't found the time to read Morrison's latest novel yet.*

acquire /əˈkwaɪəʳ/ [v T] formal to get something very big or expensive, or to get more knowledge or skills: *It took him a long time to acquire the skills he needed to become a professional artist.* | *The Boston Museum of Fine Arts has recently acquired several paintings by Salvador Dali.*

2 to be given something

- get
- receive
- be given
- be awarded
- inherit

get /get/ [v T not in passive] to be given something without having to ask for it or pay for it: *What did you get for your birthday?* | *You get a free CD with this magazine.* | **get sth from sb** *Here's the card I got from Jane.*

receive /rɪˈsiːv/ [v T] formal to be given something, especially officially: *Did Caroline receive an invitation?* | *You will receive your credit card in approximately two weeks.* | **receive sth from sb/sth** *She received an honorary degree from Harvard in 1990.*

be given /biː ˈgɪvən/ [v phrase] to **be given** something, especially by someone in authority: *He was given a ten-year jail sentence.* | *Why shouldn't disabled people be given the chance to compete in the Games?* | *Sarah was given the opportunity to study at the Cooper Union School of Art.*

be awarded /biː əˈwɔːʳdɪ̈d/ [v phrase] to be given a prize, especially by an important organization, for something that you have achieved: *The restaurant was awarded four stars in the 'Good Food Guide'.* | *Yasunari Kawabata was the first Japanese writer to be awarded the Nobel Prize for literature.*

inherit /ɪnˈherɪ̈t/ [v T] to be given someone's money or property after they die: *Who will inherit the house when he dies?* | *The ten richest women in the UK all inherited their wealth.* | **inherit sth from sb** *She inherited the money from her mother.*

3 to succeed in getting something, especially something that is difficult to get

- get
- get hold of
- get/lay your hands on
- land
- win
- clinch
- wangle
- secure

get /get/ [v T not in passive] *Getting the money for the house wasn't easy.* | *If I get first prize it'll be a miracle.*

get hold of /ˌget ˈhəʊld ɒv/ [v phrase] informal to get something that is rare or difficult to find: *Do you know where I can get hold of a German–Japanese dictionary?* | *These kids have very little difficulty getting hold of illegal weapons.*

get/lay your hands on /ˌget, ˌleɪ jɔːʳ ˈhændz ɒn/ [v phrase] informal to get something that you want or need very much, or have been trying hard to get: *I bet he can't wait to lay his hands on all that money.* | *When Ted was a kid, he read every book about space that he could get his hands on.*

land /lænd/ [v T] **land a job/contract/interview etc** to get a job etc that was difficult to get – use this especially when someone was very lucky to do this: *A French company has landed a contract to supply computers to China.* | **land yourself sth** British *He's managed to land himself an amazing job in advertising.*

win /wɪn/ [v T] **win sb's support/trust/confidence etc** to get someone's support, trust etc, especially by working hard to achieve this: *It will take time to win her trust.* | *Gandhi won the support of many liberals in England.*

clinch /klɪntʃ/ [v T] **clinch a deal/contract/championship etc** to finally succeed in making a deal, winning a contract etc after trying very hard: *We finally clinched the contract by offering them a lower price.* | *Mitchell phoned from Chicago to say that he was close to clinching the deal.* | *Germany scored twice in the last ten minutes to clinch the championship.*

wangle /ˈwæŋgəl/ [v T] informal to get something, especially something that is difficult to get, by using clever and often slightly dishonest methods: *'They're sending me to Paris next weekend.' 'How did you manage to wangle that?'* | **wangle it so that** *Gail has wangled it so that we can get in without tickets.*

secure /sɪˈkjʊəʳ/ [v T] formal to succeed in getting official permission for or agreement about something, especially when this was difficult: *France was able to secure the release of two of its hostages.* | *Schiller secured funds for the special education project.*

4 to get a letter/phone call/message

- get
- receive
- come in
- pour/flood in
- on/upon receipt of

▸ *see also* **send, message, letter, telephone, computers/internet/email**

get /get/ [v T not in passive] *Did you get my message?* | **get sth from sb** *We get so many calls from salespeople.* | *I got an e-mail from a friend who lives in Bangkok.*

receive /rɪˈsiːv/ [v T not in passive] formal to get a letter, phone call, or message: *I'm sorry I didn't call earlier, but I've only just received your message.* | *We received your letter the 1st of March.* | **receive sth from sb** *He says he never received the fax from us.*

come in /ˌkʌm ˈɪn/ [phr v I] if telephone calls, messages, letters etc **come in**, they arrive at a place where people are waiting for them: *Reports are coming in of an explosion in the centre of Paris.* | *Several calls have come in from people who think they can identify the two men.*

pour/flood in /ˌpɔːʳ, ˌflʌd ˈɪn/ [phr v I] if letters, calls, messages etc **pour in** or **flood in**, a very large number of them are received: *Letters of support have been pouring in since we began our appeal.* | *According to reports, contributions to Roe's campaign are flooding in.*

on/upon receipt of /ɒn, əˌpɒn rɪˈsiːt ɒv/ [prep] formal if someone does something **on receipt of** a letter, sum of money etc, they do it when they receive it – used especially in official letters, instructions etc: *Upon receipt of a complaint, the department will investigate the problem and, if necessary, take appropriate measures.* | *The Department of Social Security can only issue benefits on receipt of your claim form.*

5 to get a score, grade etc in a game, test etc

- get
- score
- make

▸ *see also* **score, test, sport/game**

get /get/ [v T not in passive] to **get** a particular result in a test or examination: *I only got 35% in my history test.* | *Pam's really smart. She got straight A's in high school.*

score /skɔːʳ/ [v T] to get a particular number of points in a sports game, or in a test or examination: *The test was difficult, and no-one scored more than 45 points.* | *AC Milan scored a record number of goals this season.*

make /meɪk/ [v T] American to get a particular grade in a text or for a piece of work at school: *I made an A on the test today.* | *Allison's going to Auburn University? She must have made good grades in high school.*

6 to get more of something over a long period of time

- accumulate
- amass
- gain

accumulate /əˈkjuːmjəleɪt/ [v T] to gradually get more and more money, possessions, knowledge etc over a period of time: *Watkins said he has accumulated more than $100,000 in legal bills.* | *By the late 1950s scientists had already accumulated enough evidence to show a clear link between smoking and cancer.* | *I just don't know how we've managed to accumulate so much junk!*

amass /əˈmæs/ [v T] to gradually collect a very large amount of something such as money or properly: *The Lewins amassed their art collection over more than 40 years.* | *Over the years he had amassed an absolute fortune.*

gain /geɪn/ [v T] formal to gradually get more of a useful skill or a good quality: *It took her a long time to gain enough confidence to speak in public.* | *She stayed in the job for five years, gaining valuable experience.* | *His ideas are gaining a lot of support.*

7 someone who expects to get something without doing anything to earn it

- parasite
- freeloader
- scrounger

parasite /ˈpærəsaɪt/ [n C] someone who does not work, but still expects society to provide them with money, food, a home etc: *You shouldn't feel sorry for these people – they're just parasites.* | *Most government employees had become parasites, expecting to retain their positions through friendship or political favor.*

freeloader /ˈfriːləʊdəʳ/ [n C] someone who regularly takes money from another person, from the government, etc with no intention of doing anything to earn it or change the situation: *Ms. Louis' attorney characterized her ex-husband as a freeloader, looking for the easy life.* | *The freeloaders are leaving a bad impression on the public, making it hard for those who genuinely need the government's help.*

scrounger /ˈskraʊndʒəʳ/ [n C] British someone who always expects other people to give them money, food etc, especially because they are too lazy to earn money or get things for themselves: *You're such a scrounger – buy your own cigarettes!* | *Far from being 'scroungers', unemployed people are usually desperate to earn money for themselves.*

8 to get a large number of things from several different places or people

- collect
- gather
- assemble

▸ *see also* **collect**

collect /kəˈlekt/ [v T] to get things of the same type from different places and bring them together: *I've been collecting samples of the different types of rock which occur in this area.* | *Historians are skilled in collecting facts and interpreting them.* | *Organizers have already collected 650 signatures.*

gather /ˈgæðəʳ/ [v T] to search for and get things of the same type from different places: *Many of the plants in the gardens were gathered on trips to Japan and China.* | *Some of the men gathered firewood while others made a fire.* | *Computers make it far easier to gather information.*

assemble /əˈsembəl/ [v T] to get and put together something such as proof or information in an organized way: *We will let you have the report as soon as we have assembled all the data.* | *When all the evidence is assembled, it will be clear that Michael is innocent.*

9 to get so many things to do that you cannot deal with them

- be swamped with
- be inundated with

be swamped with /biː ˈswɒmpt wɪð‖-ˈswɑːmpt-/ [v phrase] *Susan is always swamped with work this time of year.* | *Since we started the advice service we have been swamped with requests from people who need help.*

be inundated with /biː ˈɪnəndeɪtɪ̮d wɪð/ [v phrase] to get so many telephone calls, offers, answers etc after a statement or request has been made, that it is difficult to deal with them all: *Cameron claims he has been inundated with film offers.* | *Our Houston office has been inundated with calls in the last few days.*

10 to get something from someone by using force or threats

- get sth out of/squeeze sth out of
- extort

▸ *see also* **threaten, force sb to do sth**

get sth out of/squeeze sth out of /ˌget (sth) ˈaʊt ɒv, ˌskwiːz (sth) ˈaʊt ɒv/ [phr v T] informal to make someone give you something such as money or information by persuading them, tricking them, or threatening them: *They won't stop till they've succeeded in squeezing every last penny out of you.* | *The police did everything they could to get the name of his accomplice out of him, but he wouldn't talk.*

extort /ɪkˈstɔːʳt/ [v T] to illegally force someone to give you money by frightening or threatening them: *The terrorist groups have been extorting hundreds of millions of dollars.* | **extort money from/out of sb** *The Mafia makes most of its money from prostitution and extorting money from small businesses.* —**extortion** /ɪkˈstɔːʳʃən/ [n U] *Barratt is charged with extortion and murder.*

11 to get back something that you had before

- get sth back
- regain
- recover
- retrieve
- recoup
- reclaim
- win back

get sth back /ˌget (sth) ˈbæk/ [phr v T not in passive] to get back something that you had before, especially something that belongs to you: *Susanna has my lecture notes – I won't be able to get them back until Monday.* | **+ from** *I need to get the tape recorder back from her.*

regain /rɪˈgeɪn/ [v T] to get back an ability or quality that you have lost, for example your authority or confidence **regain power/control** *Republicans hope to regain control of the House of Representatives.* | *The army is struggling to regain control over the southern part of the country.* | **regain your confidence/faith/trust etc** *I don't know if I can ever regain my faith in him after what he's done.* | **regain your strength** (=become healthy and strong again) *Bill spent two weeks in the hospital regaining his strength after the operation.*

recover /rɪˈkʌvəʳ/ [v T] to get back something such as an ability that you have lost, or something that has been stolen from you: *The bank is planning to sue the company in order to try and recover it's money.* | *It took the rest of the winter for her to recover her health.* —**recovery** [n U] when something is recovered: *The book tells the story of the recovery of a stolen bomb by American agents.*

retrieve /rɪˈtriːv/ [v T] formal to get back something after you have put it somewhere: *I had left my bag at the railroad station and went back to retrieve it.* | **retrieve sth from** *She bent down and retrieved the map from under the car seat.* | *If you want to retrieve a file from the computer, press FIND and then enter the name of the file you want.* —**retrieval** [n U] *The information is stored on disc for easy retrieval* (=so that it can be retrieved easily).

recoup /rɪˈkuːp/ [v T] to get back money or profits that you have spent or lost **recoup your losses** *She put $50 on the next race in an attempt to recoup her losses.* | **recoup sth from sb** *The dentist gives treatment for free and then recoups the cost from the government.*

reclaim /rɪˈkleɪm/ [v T] to get back something that belongs to you that someone else has taken or that you have let them have: *You can reclaim tax if you find you have paid too much.* | *A British woman is waiting to hear how she can reclaim a family estate inside the former Soviet Union.* | **reclaim sth from** *China reclaimed Hong Kong from Britain in 1997.*

win back /ˌwɪn ˈbæk/ [phr v T] to succeed in getting someone or something back by trying hard **win back sb/sth** *The airlines are trying to win back passengers by offering special low fares at certain times.* | *Debra sued the company and won back her job and $144,000 in damages.* | **win sb/sth back** *Jack could see no way of winning his wife back.*

12 to not get something that you could get

- lose out
- miss out
- pass sb by

lose out /ˌluːz ˈaʊt/ [phr v I] to not get something such as a job, contract etc because it is given to someone else instead: *It's simple – unless you make an effort you're going to lose out.* | **+ to** *In the end we lost out to a French company because they could do the job cheaper.* | **+ on** *Time and time again, women seem to lose out on promotions and career opportunities.*

miss out /ˌmɪs ˈaʊt/ [phr v I] to not get something or be able to enjoy something because you are not in the right place to do this: *Where were you last night? You missed out.* | **+ on** *She was so busy studying at university that she missed out on all the fun.* | *Get to the sales early to avoid missing out on all the best bargains.*

pass sb by /ˌpɑːs (sb) ˈbaɪ‖ˌpæs-/ [phr v T not in passive] if a chance or enjoyable experience **passes you by**, you do not get it because you do not make an effort or pay enough attention to it: *Sometimes I feel that all the best things in life are passing me by.* | *Seize opportunities while you can – don't let them pass you by.* | *He ended up a bitter old man who felt that life had somehow passed him by.*

get on or off a bus, plane etc

RELATED WORDS

see also **travel, drive, go**

1 to get on a bus, plane etc

- get on
- get in/into
- catch
- hop on/in/into
- board
- embark
- mount
- on board/aboard

get on /ˌget ˈɒn/ [phr v I/T] to go onto a bus, train etc at the beginning of a journey: *The train stopped in the middle of the night in Nogales. No one got on or off.* | *We got on the train at Lime Street Station.* | *Get on a number 73 bus at the corner. That will take you to Islington High Street.* | *She's old and needs help getting on and off the bus.*

get in/into /ˌget ˈɪn, ˈɪntuː/ [v phrase] to go into a small vehicle, for example a car or boat: *'Can you give me a lift into town?' 'Sure. Get in.'* | *Be careful getting into the boat.* | *I got in a taxi and went to the hospital immediately.*

catch /kætʃ/ [v T] to get on a particular bus, train, or plane in order to go somewhere: *Stephen caught the 6.15 to Birmingham.* | *If we're quick, we should still be able to catch our train.* | *Jonathan looked at his watch. 'I've got a plane to catch,' he said.*

hop on/in/into /ˌhɒp ˈɒn, ˈɪn, ˈɪntuː‖ˌhɑːp-/ [v phrase] informal to get on a bus, train, plane etc, or get into a car, taxi etc, especially after suddenly deciding to: *Karl hopped on the first plane back to Germany.* | *'Hop in,' shouted Lucy, throwing open the door of her van.* | *She hopped into a cab and told the driver to go to King's Cross.* | *'Why not hop in the car and come with us?' Myrtle asked with a sly smile.*

board /bɔːʳd/ [v T] formal to get on a ship, plane, or train: *A week later he boarded a ship bound for New York.* | *Before boarding the plane, Jenny tried once more to call home.*

embark /ɪmˈbɑːʳk/ [v I] formal to get on a ship – use this especially when a large number of people do this: *A large group had assembled at the pier, waiting to embark.* | **+ for** *Their training completed, the regiment embarked for the war zone.* —**embarkation** /ˌembɑːʳˈkeɪʃən/ [n U] *Embarkation will begin one hour before the ship is due to leave port.*

mount /maʊnt/ [v I/T] to climb onto a horse: *Can you help Shelly mount?* | *He mounted the pony and rode off.*

on board/aboard /ɒn ˈbɔːʳd, əˈbɔːʳd/ [prep/adv] if you get **on board** or **aboard** a ship or plane, you get onto it: *It was time to get on board the ship.* | *A group of men, some in military uniform, climbed aboard the plane.* | *The ship's crew saluted the President as he came aboard.*

2 to get off a bus, plane etc

- get off
- get out
- leave
- disembark
- dismount

get off /ˌget ˈɒf/ [phr v I/T] to: *Tell the driver you want to get off at Greene Street.* | *Lennox got off the plane and made his way through customs.* | *At the foot of the hill, she got off her bicycle and began to push it.* | *Do you know where we're supposed to get off?*

get out /ˌget ˈaʊt/ [phr v I] to come out of a car, boat, or train: *Most of the passengers got out at Oxford Circus.* | **+ of** *She got out of the car and slammed the door.* | *The farmer got out of his car to open the gate.*

leave /liːv/ [v T] to get off a train or ship on which you have been travelling – used especially in official notices or messages: *When you leave the train, please make sure that you have all your belongings with you.* | *Passengers leaving the ship at Alexandria should proceed to the immigration office.*

disembark /ˌdɪsəmˈbɑːʳk/ [v I] formal to get off a ship or plane – use this especially when a large number of people do this: *We weren't allowed to disembark until an hour after the ship had docked.* | *The only one to disembark at Tiree was me.*

dismount /dɪsˈmaʊnt/ [v I] to get down off a horse: *They dismounted and led their horses through the forest.*

get rid of

RELATED WORDS

▸ *see also* **remove, tidy**

1 to get rid of something that you do not want

- ▸ get rid of
- ▸ throw away
- ▸ throw out
- ▸ dispose of
- ▸ get shot of
- ▸ sth will have to go

▸ *see also* **rubbish/garbage**

get rid of /ˌget ˈrɪd ɒv/ [v phrase] to remove something that you do not want or do not use any more, for example by giving it to someone else or throwing it away: *Let's get rid of some of these old books.* | *I hate these chairs. I wish we could get rid of them.* | *We finally got rid of all that old junk we had stored in the basement.*

throw away /ˌθrəʊ əˈweɪ/ [phr v T] to get rid of something by putting it somewhere where it will be taken away and destroyed **throw away sth** *Don't throw away these boxes – I might want to use them later.* | **throw sth away** *Oh, no. I think I've accidentally thrown the invitation away.*

throw out /ˌθrəʊ ˈaʊt/ [phr v T] to get rid of something, especially when you are trying to make a place more tidy or to make space for new things **throw out sth** *My wife made me throw out my old tennis shoes.* | **throw sth out** *Can I throw these newspapers out, or are you still reading them?*

dispose of /dɪˈspəʊz ɒv/ [phr v T] formal to get rid of something that is difficult or unpleasant to get rid of: *The company has been charged with illegally disposing of hazardous wastes.* | *Police are still puzzled as to how he managed to dispose of his victim's body.* —**disposal** [n U] + **of** *We need new legislation to ensure the safe disposal of nuclear waste.*

get shot of /ˌget ˈʃɒt ɒv ‖-ˈʃɑːt-/ [v phrase] British informal to get rid of something, especially something that you have been wanting to get rid of for a long time: *I can't wait to get shot of this old car.* | *Everybody's in a rush to get shot of their shares in the company.*

sth will have to go ALSO **sth has got to go** American / (sth) wɪl ˌhæv tə ˈgəʊ, (sth) həz ˌgɒt tə ˈgəʊ‖-ˌgɑːt-/ [v phrase] spoken if you say that something **will have to go** you think it should be thrown away, especially because you do not like it: *I can't stand this carpet. I'm sorry Larry, it'll have to go.*

2 to get rid of a leader, someone in authority etc

- ▸ get rid of
- ▸ overthrow
- ▸ oust
- ▸ be deposed

get rid of /ˌget ˈrɪd ɒv/ [v T] to get rid of a leader, someone in authority etc: *He's a terrible manager – it's about time they got rid of him.* | *Local people desperately want to get rid of US troops on the island.* | *The trustees of the University are considering getting rid of him.*

overthrow /ˌəʊvəʳˈθrəʊ/ [v T] to take power away from a leader or government, especially by force: *President Kassem was overthrown and murdered in 1963.* | *The dictatorship was overthrown after a year of fighting, in which thousands of people were killed.* —**overthrow** /ˈəʊvəʳθrəʊ/ [n U] *He came to power after the overthrow of Haile Selassie.*

oust /aʊst/ [v T] written force a leader out of his or her position of power: *Nusabe was ousted in a coup late last year.* | *Reformers have expressed concern that he could be ousted by hard-liners opposed to his reforms.* —**ousted** [adj only before noun] *Supporters of the ousted dictator have been rounded up and jailed.*

be deposed /biː dɪˈpəʊzd/ [v phrase] if a political leader, king etc **is deposed**, their power is taken away from them: *He was deposed after more than 18 years in power.* | *Moreau was deposed in a military coup and fled to the US.* —**deposed** [adj only before noun] *The deposed king will set up a government in exile.*

3 to get rid of someone because you do not like or need them any more

- ▸ get rid of
- ▸ purge
- ▸ weed out
- ▸ root out
- ▸ sb will have to go
- ▸ dump

get rid of /ˌget ˈrɪd ɒv/ [v T]: *New police chief Brody promised to get rid of the city's drug dealers.* | *The company announced that it will get rid of another 500 workers by the end of the year.* | *One of the administration's first tasks will be to get rid of many of the officials appointed by the previous president.*

purge /pɜːʳdʒ/ [v T] if the leaders of a political organization **purge** a group of people from that organization, they get rid of them because they have political views that they strongly disagree with: *Many radicals were purged from the party in the early seventies.* | *In the North, Sung systematically purged those whom he considered a threat.* —**purge** [n C/U] *Stalin's purges of the 1930s*

weed out /ˌwiːd ˈaʊt/ [phr v T] to find out those people who are not suitable to belong to an organization or group, and get rid of them: *We do have procedures in place to weed out individuals who are corrupt.* | *The report claimed that there were at least 20,000 inefficient teachers that needed to be weeded out.*

root out /ˌruːt ˈaʊt/ [phr v T] to try hard to find out all the people who are not suitable to belong to a particular group or organization, especially when it is not easy to know who they are, and get rid of them: *The Ministry of Health is continuing its efforts to root out incompetent doctors.* | *At that time, a secret branch of the National Police was involved in rooting out dissidents.*

sb will have to go ALSO **sb has (got) to go** American spoken / (sb) wɪl ˌhæv tə ˈgəʊ, (sb) həz (ˌgɒt‖ˌgɑːt) tə ˈgəʊ/ say this when you no longer want to employ someone: *It's been decided. Murrow will have to go.* | *'Gates has done nothing but divide this city. He has got to go,' said one of the protesters.*

dump /dʌmp/ [v T] informal to end a relationship with a boyfriend or girlfriend: *I think the guy's a jerk. I'm glad Debbie dumped him.* | *'Why did he dump her?' 'He met somebody else.'*

4 to get rid of something that is causing problems

- ▸ get rid of
- ▸ abolish
- ▸ scrap
- ▸ ditch
- ▸ do away with
- ▸ eradicate
- ▸ eliminate
- ▸ root out

get rid of /ˌget ˈrɪd ɒv/ [v phrase] to remove or deal with something that is causing you trouble, such as an illness or a problem: *I can't seem to get rid of this cold.* | *We've cleaned the carpet twice, but still can't get rid of the smell.* | *Weedaway is a safe and natural way to get rid of weeds coming up in the garden.*

abolish /ə'bɒlɪʃ‖ə'bɑː-/ [v T] to officially end a law, legal right, or system, especially one that has existed for a long time: *The unpopular tax was finally abolished some ten years ago.* | *He served over 27 years in prison for fighting to abolish white-only rule.* —**abolition** /ˌæbə'lɪʃən/ [n U] when something is abolished: *The group is working toward the abolition of the death penalty.*

scrap /skræp/ [v T] to end a system, law etc, or to decide not to use a plan that you were intending to use: *Plans to build a new airport have been scrapped because of lack of funding.* | *The president's proposal to scrap the program has angered many members of Congress.*

ditch /dɪtʃ/ [v T] to get rid of something because you do not need it: *Investors ditched stocks that were performing badly.* | *Brumfeld apparently ditched the car near Texarkana and fled into the woods.*

do away with /duː ə'weɪ wɪð/ [phr v T] to get rid of something so that it does not exist any more: *San José State University is doing away with its business school and department of journalism.* | *All countries in the region should commit themselves to doing away with weapons of mass destruction.*

eradicate /ɪ'rædɪ̇keɪt/ [v T] to completely get rid of something such as a disease, a social problem, or something that causes these things: *The disease has been eradicated from the Western world through the use of vaccines.* | *Their aim is to eradicate child poverty in the country within 10 years.* —**eradication** /ɪˌrædɪ̇'keɪʃən/ [n U] *The eradication of the beetle has led to a five-fold increase in crop yields.*

eliminate /ɪ'lɪmɪ̇neɪt/ [v T] to completely get rid of something that is unnecessary or unwanted: *Traffic police intend to eliminate congestion caused by illegally parked vehicles.* | *Advances in medical science have eliminated the need for many patients to spend long periods of time in hospital.*

root out /ˌruːt 'aʊt/ [phr v T] to completely and thoroughly get rid of something that is causing you problems, especially by trying to make sure the causes of it are found and stopped **root out sth** *The new president has promised to root out high level corruption.* | **root sth out** *Wherever we find waste and incompetence we will root it out.*

5 to get rid of harmful ideas or influences

- rid sth of
- free sth of
- dispel

rid sth of /'rɪd (sth) ɒv/ [phr v T not usually in passive] to get rid of something bad or harmful so that they no longer exist in a place or organization: *Scientists hope to one day rid the world of this terrible disease.* | *McCarthy wanted to rid America of the 'evils of Communism'.* | *I can't seem to rid my mind of what happened on the day of the accident.*

free sth of /'friː (sth) ɒv/ [phr v T] to get rid of ideas, behaviour, influences etc that are considered bad or harmful and have been present for a very long time: *Neighbourhood Watch schemes have succeeded in virtually freeing the area of crime.* | *Aid organisations are trying to free the country of the ravages of two decades of civil war.*

dispel /dɪ'spel/ [v T] to get rid of beliefs, ideas or feelings from people's minds, especially if they are false or harmful **dispel rumours/notions/doubts etc** *The Central Bank attempted to dispel rumours of a possible financial crisis.* | *In an interview Monday, the Foreign Affairs Secretary tried to dispel doubts about his handling of the crisis.*

6 to have got rid of something or somebody

- be rid of
- be glad/happy to see the back of

be rid of /biː 'rɪd ɒv/ [v phrase] to have got rid of someone or something, so that they are not there to worry or annoy you: *At first I was glad to be rid of the extra work, but then I realized how much money I was losing.* | *The sooner we're rid of this government the better.* | *You shouldn't even think about buying a new car until you're rid of your current debts.*

be glad/happy to see the back of /biː ˌglæd, ˌhæpi tə siː ðə 'bæk ɒv/ [v phrase] British informal to be very pleased you have got rid of something or someone: *I'll be glad to see the back of this project.* | *We will be glad to see the back of Williams, that's for sure.*

ghost

RELATED WORDS

- *see also* **die, dead, body, frightened/frightening, scream, mysterious, strange, magic, imagine**

1 a ghost

- ghost
- ghostly
- spirit
- poltergeist
- phantom
- apparition
- spectre
- the supernatural
- things that go bump in the night

ghost /gəʊst/ [n C] the spirit of a dead person that some people believe they can see or hear: *'The ghost can be heard going up and down the stairs in the middle of the night,' Ackley said.* | *Do you believe in ghosts?* | *Hindus believe that ghosts are scared of fire.* | **ghost of sb** *The church is haunted by the ghost of a young man who was killed there on his wedding day.* | **ghost story** *Do you know any good ghost stories?*

ghostly /'gəʊstli/ [adj usually before noun] looking like a ghost, or making you think of ghosts: *A ghostly figure hovered at the top of the stairs.* | *In the last scene of the play, a ghostly female figure shimmers into the room, her arms laden with books.* | *She felt the touch of a ghostly hand on her shoulder.*

spirit /'spɪrɪ̇t/ [n C] the part of a person that, according to some people's beliefs, continues to live after they have died **spirit of sb** *In Japan people believe that the spirits of the dead return to visit the earth every summer during the Obon festival.* | **evil spirits** (=spirits that want to harm people) *My grandparents used to wear charms to protect themselves against evil spirits.*

poltergeist /'pɒltəʳgaɪst‖'pəʊl-/ [n C] a type of ghost you cannot see, that moves furniture and throws things around: *Clark says the poltergeist scatters pots and pans over the kitchen floor, opens locked doors and frightens the family dog.*

phantom /ˈfæntəm/ [n C] a frightening and unclear image of a dead person – used especially in literature: *Suddenly a phantom appeared out of the mist, terrifying the hikers.*

apparition /ˌæpəˈrɪʃən/ [n C] an image of a dead person that you see suddenly and only for a short time: *The women said they saw an apparition in the church, next to the altar.* | *The apparition ran silently across the lobby and disappeared through a window.*

spectre British **/specter** American /ˈspektəʳ/ [n C] a ghost, especially a frightening one – used especially in literature: *They say that the spectres of the murdered children walk through the grounds at night.* | *The spectre is reputed to be that of Frances Culpepper, daughter of Lord John Freschville.*

the supernatural /ðə ˌsuːpəʳˈnætʃərəl, ˌsjuː-‖ ˌsuː-/ [n U] the world of ghosts, spirits etc and things that cannot be explained by science: *Many of the people here continue to believe in the supernatural.* | *stories about the supernatural* —**supernatural** [adj only before noun] *supernatural forces* | *The villagers believed that she had supernatural powers.*

things that go bump in the night /ˌθɪŋz ðət gəʊ ˌbʌmp ɪn ðə ˈnaɪt/ [n phrase] ghosts and other strange frightening things in general – used humorously: *She's always been a bit scared of things that go bump in the night.*

2 when there are ghosts in a place

- haunted
- haunt
- spooky

haunted /ˈhɔːntɪ̈d/ [adj] a place that is **haunted** has ghosts in it: *The locals say the villas are haunted.* | **haunted house** *Both John and his wife Susy are convinced the house is haunted.* | *Billed as 'America's most haunted house', the Myrtles Plantation is supposedly inhabited by 14 ghosts.*

haunt /hɔːnt/ [v T not in progressive] if a ghost **haunts** a place, it appears there often: *The ghost of the murdered prince still haunts the castle.* | **be haunted by** *Legends say the building is haunted by ghosts.*

spooky /ˈspuːki/ [adj] informal a place that is **spooky** feels strange and makes you feel that there are ghosts there: *Let's get out of here, this place is really spooky!* | *a spooky castle* | *He lived in kind of a spooky place at the end of a long dirt road.*

girlfriend/ boyfriend

RELATED WORDS

- get rid of a girlfriend or boyfriend *see* **get rid of (3)**
- *see also* **friend, relationship, love, sex, marry, gay**

1 someone that you have a romantic or sexual relationship with

- girlfriend
- boyfriend
- partner
- mistress
- lover
- old flame

girlfriend /ˈgɜːʳlfrend/ [n C] a girl or woman that you have a romantic relationship with, especially for a fairly long time **sb's girlfriend** *I met my brother's new girlfriend last night.* | *Katherine is his first girlfriend since breaking up with Maggie.* | **have a girlfriend** *Does Mark have a girlfriend?* | **old/ex-/former girlfriend** (=someone who used to be your girlfriend) *Denver police said the suspect had earlier made threats to kill his ex-girlfriend and then himself.* | **serious/steady girlfriend** (=a girlfriend that you have a serious romantic relationship with) *Wendell hasn't had a steady girlfriend in years.*

boyfriend /ˈbɔɪfrend/ [n C] a boy or man that you have a romantic relationship with, especially for a fairly long time **sb's boyfriend** *Josh was my first boyfriend.* | *All she does is talk about her boyfriend.* | **have a boyfriend** *I was talking to this guy at the bar and he starting asking me whether I was married or had a boyfriend.* | **old/ex-/former boyfriend** (=someone who used to be your boyfriend) *Oh, my God! I've just seen Barry, my ex-boyfriend.* | **serious/steady boyfriend** (=a boyfriend that you have a serious romantic relationship with) *Sarah's doing well and has a serious boyfriend, Michael, whom she plans to marry next year.*

partner /ˈpɑːʳtnəʳ/ [n C] someone that you have a serious romantic and sexual relationship with, especially someone that you live with: *Sweden allows gay partners to receive many of the benefits awarded to heterosexual married couples.* | **sexual partner** *The survey found that only about one of every four men had had ten or more sexual partners over their lifetime.*

mistress /ˈmɪstrɪ̈s/ [n C] a woman who has a sexual relationship with a man who is married to someone else: *She thought that her husband had a mistress but could not prove it.* | *The former Prime Minister's wife and mistress both attended the funeral.*

lover /ˈlʌvəʳ/ [n C] someone who you have a sexual relationship with, without being married to them **sb's lover** *That night she received a call from her lover.* | **have a lover** *Over her lifetime, Catherine had many lovers.* | **become lovers** *A few nights later, they became lovers.* | **be lovers** *Kilpatrick claims that she and the congressman were once lovers.*

old flame /ˌəʊld ˈfleɪm/ [n C] informal someone who was your girlfriend or boyfriend in the past: *In a box in the closet, I found love letters from one of his old flames.* | *After 17 years of marriage, he left his wife for an old flame he ran into at a high school reunion.*

2 to have a girlfriend or boyfriend

- go out with
- be seeing
- go steady

go out with /ˌgəʊ ˈaʊt wɪð/ [phr v T] to have someone as your girlfriend or boyfriend: *She's going out with some guy she met at work.* | *Can you believe she's going out with him?* | **be going out together** *Jack and I have been going out together for four years.*

be seeing /biː ˈsiːɪŋ/ [v phrase] to have a romantic or sexual relationship with someone, especially a relationship that is not very serious and does not last very long: *Do you know if Tanya's seeing anyone at the moment?* | *Her husband, whom she adored, confessed that he had been seeing other women.*

go steady /ˌgəʊ ˈstedi/ [v phrase] to have a serious romantic relationship with someone – used especially about young people: *We've been going steady since our sophomore year.* | *Samantha went steady with her high school boyfriend for more than a year before they had sex.*

give

RELATED WORDS

opposite: **take, get**

▸ *see also* **provide/supply, share, generous/not generous, exchange**

1 to give something to someone without expecting to be paid for it

- give
- let sb have
- give away
- pass
- hand
- slip
- spare

give /gɪv/ [v T] **give sb sth** *I gave my nieces and nephews $20 each.* | *Why don't we give her some flowers for her birthday?* | *Let me give you some advice.* | *They gave me this leaflet – it's really helpful.* | *Can you give me a ride to the office tomorrow?* | **give sth to sb** *Would you give this letter to your uncle when you see him?* | *Russell was accused of giving secret information to the enemy.*

let sb have /ˌlet (sb) ˈhæv/ [v phrase not in passive] to give something to someone, especially something that they have asked for or something that they need: *She lets her kids have anything they want.* | *One of my mum's friends was getting a new sofa, and so she let us have the old one.* | *If you could let me have your suggestions, it would be very helpful.*

give away /ˌgɪv əˈweɪ/ [phr v T] to give something that you own to someone else, especially because you do not want it or need it **give away sth** *I gave away most of my old furniture because I didn't have room for it in my new apartment.* | **give sth away** *He decided to give all his money away and become a Buddhist monk.* | **give sth away to sb** *I don't need all this stuff – I'll give it away to the first person who asks for it.*

pass /pɑːs‖pæs/ [v T] to give something to someone by putting it in their hand or putting it near them, especially because they cannot reach it themselves: *Could you pass the salt, please?* | **pass sb sth** *Would you pass me my sweater? It's on the back of your chair.* | **pass sth to sb** *Ellis quickly passed the note to the woman, looking around to check that no one had noticed.*

hand /hænd/ [v T] to take something in your **hand** and give it to someone by putting it in their hand **hand sb sth** *The nurse handed me a glass of brown liquid and told me to drink it.* | *As the delegates entered the room they were each handed a name-badge.* | **hand sth to sb** *Would you please hand your ticket to the man at the door.*

slip /slɪp/ [v T] to quickly give someone something small such as money or a piece of paper, by putting it into their hand, especially so that other people do not notice **slip sb sth** *I know it's a private party, but if you slip the doorman $5, he'll let you in.* | **slip sth into sb's hand/pocket etc** *During the meeting, she reached under the table and slipped a note into my hand,*

spare /speəʳ/ [v T] if you can **spare** a particular amount of something, you can only give that amount but no more because you need the rest for yourself: *If anyone can spare a couple of hours a week to help out, it would be much appreciated.* | *Dad, can you spare a fiver?* | **spare sb sth** *We don't have very much coffee, I'm afraid, but we can spare you a little.*

2 to give something to everyone in a group

- hand out/give out
- pass around
- distribute
- share out
- hand around
- serve
- dish out/dole out

hand out/give out /ˌhænd ˈaʊt, ˌgɪv ˈaʊt/ [phr v T] to give something to all the people in a group **hand out/give out sth** *The princess plans to hand out gifts at a children's hospital tomorrow.* | *Don't start the test until I've finished giving out the question papers.* | **hand/give out sth to sb** *Outside the embassy, students were handing out leaflets to everyone who walked past.* | **hand/give sth out** *I need some volunteers to hand programs out tonight.*

pass around ALSO **pass round** British /ˌpɑːs əˈraʊnd, ˌpɑːs ˈraʊnd‖ˌpæs-/ [phr v T] if a group of people **pass** something **around**, one person takes it and gives it to the next person, who then gives it to the next person **pass around sth** *They passed around a list, and we each had to sign our name.* | **pass sth around** *Don't keep all the chocolates to yourself – pass them around!*

distribute /dɪˈstrɪbjuːt/ [v T] to give things out to a large number of people, especially in an organized way: *Aid agencies are calling for local volunteers to help them distribute food and medicine.* | **distribute sth to sb** *The Red Cross has started distributing food and blankets to villages in the flood area.* | **distribute sth among sb** *Medical supplies have been distributed among families affected by the epidemic.*

share out /ˌʃeər ˈaʊt/ [phr v T] to divide something into equal parts and give a part to each person **share out sth** *As long as they share out the profits fairly, everyone will be happy.* | **share sth out** *Take these cookies and share them out.* | **share out sth among/between sb** *We've got three pizzas to share out between five people.* | *More than $1.7 million has been shared out among victims of the disaster.*

hand around ALSO **hand round** British /ˌhænd əˈraʊnd, ˌhænd ˈraʊnd/ [phr v T] to go from person to person offering or politely giving them something such as a drink, food, etc **hand around sth** *Dorothy was handing around coffee and biscuits when we arrived.* | *I'm handing round a summary of last week's lecture.* | **hand sth around** *Would you mind helping me hand the crackers around, please?*

serve /sɜːʳv/ [v T] to give food and drinks to people, for example at a restaurant or a party: *Dinner will be served at 8.30.* | *Don't forget to serve the guests first.* | **serve sth to sb** *We don't serve alcohol to anyone under 21.* | **serve sb with sth** *As soon as they sat down, they were served with steaming bowls of soup.*

dish out/dole out /ˌdɪʃ ˈaʊt, ˌdəʊl ˈaʊt/ [phr v T] to give something, especially food or money, to people who are waiting to receive it **dish/dole out sth** *They want me to dress up as Santa Claus, and dish out presents at the kids' Christmas party.* | *The federal government doles out $58 billion in student grants every year.* | **dish/dole sth out** *Jo, would you dish the ice cream out?* | **dish/dole out sth to sb** *Air stewardesses were doling out meals to the passengers.*

3 to officially give something to someone

- award
- present
- grant
- confer
- allocate
- allotted

award /əˈwɔːʳd/ [v T usually in passive] to officially give someone something such as a prize, money etc, especially as a reward for their hard work or for something they have done **award sb sth** *She was awarded the Nobel Prize for her work in medical research.* | *The management have awarded all factory employees a 5% pay increase.* | **award sb compensation/damages etc** *A woman who suffered brain damage during an operation has been awarded $300,000 in compensation.* —**award** [n C] *The award ceremony will be held at the National Film Theatre tonight.*

present /prɪˈzent/ [v T] to give someone something at an official ceremony **present a prize/medal/trophy/certificate/award etc** *Who's going to present the prizes this year?* | *The trophy will be presented by last year's winner, Brett Butler.* | **present sth to sb** *A little girl presented a basket of flowers to the President's wife.* | **present sb with sth** *Last night Phil Donahue was presented with a Lifetime Achievement Award by the National Academy of Television Arts and Sciences.* —**presentation** /ˌprezənˈteɪʃən‖ˌpriːzenˈteɪʃən, -zən-/ [n C] *Vic Reeves and Bob Mortimer received the award at a star-studded presentation in London last night.*

grant /grɑːnt‖grænt/ [v T] to formally or officially give someone something that they have asked for, especially permission to do something: *The company's application to build a billion dollar leisure complex has been granted by city hall.* | **grant sb sth** *The authorities have refused to grant him a visa to visit the US.* | **grant sb's request** *I am pleased to inform you that your request for housing benefit has been granted.*

confer /kənˈfɜːʳ/ [v T] formal **confer a degree/honour/title etc** to officially give someone a degree, honour etc especially as a reward for something they have achieved **confer sth on sb** *The university has already conferred honorary degrees on several prime ministers.* | **confer on sb sth** *The President trusted him so much that he conferred on him the role of 'Principal Advisor'.*

allocate /ˈæləkeɪt/ [v T] if someone in authority **allocates** something such as money, a house, a job etc to someone, they decide to give that person some of the money, or one of the houses, jobs etc that are available **allocate sth to sb** *The company has allocated $1000 to the team to get the project started.* | **allocate sb sth** *Several single parent families have been allocated homes on the new site.* —**allocation** /ˌæləˈkeɪʃən/ [n U] *The allocation of places at the university is based on candidates' examination results.*

allotted /əˈlɒtəd‖əˈlɑːt-/ [adj only before noun] **allotted money/time/space etc** the money, time etc that has been officially given or allowed to someone in order for them to do something: *This department has already spent all its allotted budget.* | *David wasn't able to finish the task within the allotted time.*

4 something that you give someone on a special occasion

- gift
- present
- reward

gift /gɪft/ [n C] something that you give to someone as a sign of friendship, love, respect, or as part of a formal ceremony: *These candlesticks would make a lovely gift.* | *I got this jacket as a gift. I wouldn't have chosen this color myself.* | **+ from** *In the hall was a magnificent vase, which was a gift from a Japanese businessman.* | *It was a gift to the US from the Chinese people.* | **+ for** *I bought this CD as a gift for Jane, but she's already got it.* | **birthday/graduation/wedding etc gift** especially American *I'm going to go pick up a birthday gift for Uncle Warren, and then I'm going to go and see him.* | **gift shop** (=a shop that sells small things that are suitable for giving as gifts) *There's a gift shop in the hotel. They have jewelry and souvenirs and stuff.*

present /ˈprezənt/ [n C] something that you give to someone on a special occasion, for example on their birthday or when they leave their job: *I've bought you all a present!* | **get a present** *How many birthday presents did you get?* | **+ for** *He got a lot of expensive presents for his 21st birthday.* | *'What's this?' 'It's a present for Valerie – she needs cheering up.'* | **+ from** *The watch was a present from my mother.* | **Christmas/birthday/wedding etc present** *We can't afford to spend much on Christmas presents this year.*

reward /rɪˈwɔːʳd/ [n C] something, especially money, that you give someone because they have done something good or helpful **+ of** *The parents of the missing boy are offering a reward of £10,000.* | **+ for** *The police say there is a $50,000 reward for any information that helps them find the killer.* | *She got no reward for all the hard work she did.*

5 to give money, food etc in order to help people

- give
- donate
- make a donation
- go to
- charity
- donor
- blood/kidney etc donor
- benefactor
- philanthropist

give /gɪv/ [v I/T] to **give** money to an organization that will use it to help people who are poor, sick, in trouble etc: *The British give animal welfare organizations over £200 million per year.* | *Please give generously, these children need your help.* | *We would be grateful for any donation that you are prepared to give.* | **give sth to sb** *Local people have given over $100,000 to our Help a Child appeal.* | **+ to** *About a quarter of Britons regularly give to charity.*

donate /dəʊnˈneɪt‖ˈdəʊneɪt/ [v T] to give money, or something useful or valuable, in order to help people – use this especially about things that are given by companies or organizations: *The books were donated by a local publishing company.* | **donate sth to sth** *The concert organizers say they will donate all profits to charity.*

make a donation /ˌmeɪk ə dəʊˈneɪʃən/ [v phrase] to give an amount of money to an organization that will use it to help people: *We're collecting money to build a hostel for homeless people – would you like to make a donation?* | **+ to** *The company made several large donations to charities.*

go to /ˈgəʊ tuː/ [v T not in passive] if something such as a sum of money **goes to** someone, especially to a group of people who are poor, hungry, sick etc, it is given to them: *All the money raised will go to local charities.*

charity /ˈtʃærəti/ [n C/U] an organization that collects money or goods from people who give them, and uses them to help people who need help: *Elton John has campaigned for a number of AIDS charities.* | **give/donate sth to charity** *The corporation has donated nearly $70 million to children's charities over the past 17 years.* | *Clear out all the clothes you never wear, and give them to charity.* | **go to charity** *All profits from the show will go to charity.* | **do sth for charity** *They aim to walk 30 miles for charity.* | **a**

charity ball/lunch/concert etc (=an event organized to make money for charity) *Porter spent his retirement years organizing charity golf tournaments throughout the United States.*

donor /ˈdəʊnəʳ/ [n C] a person, organization, or country that gives something, especially money, to another organization or country so that they can use it to help other people: *Money for the new health centre has come mostly from private donors.* | *Some donor countries have criticized the way in which their aid is being distributed.*

blood/kidney etc donor /ˈblʌd ˌdəʊnəʳ/ [n C] someone who gives blood or a part of their body so that it can be used in the medical treatment of someone else: *The patient needs a liver transplant, and the search has begun for a suitable donor.* | *Unless more blood donors come forward, it may be necessary to cancel some operations.*

benefactor /ˈbenəˌfæktəʳ/ [n C] someone who gives something, especially a large amount of money, to an organization or institution such as a school, hospital or library: *Getty had been the museum's chief benefactor.* | *The painting was bought by an anonymous benefactor, and donated to the Museum of Modern Art.*

philanthropist /fəˈlænθrəpəst/ [n C] a rich person who gives a lot of money to help poorer people: *In Victorian times, factory owners were often also philanthropists.* | *the millionaire philanthropist, Graham Paulo*

6 something that is given to help people who need it

- donation
- charity
- aid
- handout

donation /dəʊˈneɪʃən/ [n C] something, especially money that is given to help people: *Any donation, however small, will be gratefully received.* | *The Famine Appeal has raised more than a million pounds through private donations and fund-raising activities.*

charity /ˈtʃærəti/ [n U] money or help given to help the poor, the sick etc: *Many homeless people are too proud to ask for charity.* | *The organization depends on charity, and on volunteer workers who are prepared to give up their time.*

aid /eɪd/ [n U] money, food, medicine etc that is given by a government or organization to the people of another country or to people who are in a very difficult situation: *Aid is not getting through to the refugees.* | **foreign/overseas aid** *The education programme is dependent on foreign aid, and the US Agency for International Development had been approached for funding.* | **aid agency** (=an organization that brings aid to people in places where there is war, not enough food etc) *Another harvest has failed, and international aid agencies warn of the threat of mass starvation.* | **aid worker** (=someone who works for an aid agency) *An Italian aid worker was kidnapped by rebels last month, and still hasn't been released.*

handout /ˈhændaʊt/ [n C] money, food etc that is given to someone who is poor – use this especially when you think they should not be given it or should not have to ask for it: *The unemployed need jobs, not government handouts!* | *She applied for a bank loan because she did not want to depend on her father for handouts.*

7 to give something to someone in authority

- hand in/give in
- turn in/turn over
- hand over
- hand sb over/turn sb over
- pass on
- surrender
- sign away
- relinquish

hand in/give in /ˌhænd ˈɪn, ˌgɪv ˈɪn/ [phr v T] to give something to someone in authority, for example to the police or a teacher **hand/give in sth** *When you leave the hotel, please hand in your key at the desk.* | *Luckily, someone gave in her purse at the lost property office.* | **hand/give sth in** *Have you given your English assignment in yet?*

turn in/turn over /ˌtɜːʳn ˈɪn, ˌtɜːʳn ˈəʊvəʳ/ [phr v T] to give something such as weapons or important documents to the police or to government officials, when you should not legally have them or you have been officially asked to give them **turn sth in/over** *Police are encouraging people to turn illegal weapons in at their local police station.* | **turn in/over sth to sb** *The government is refusing to turn over the documents to the UN inspection team.*

hand over /ˌhænd ˈəʊvəʳ/ [phr v T] to give something to someone because they have asked or forced you to **hand over sth** *The robbers forced them to hand over the money.* | *'Give us a bit of your rum,' he said. Virginia handed over the bottle.* | **hand sth over** *If you don't hand it over I'll shoot!*

hand sb over/turn sb over /ˌhænd (sb) ˈəʊvəʳ, ˌtɜːʳn (sb) ˈəʊvəʳ/ [phr v T] to give a prisoner to another group of people, especially the police or the people in authority in another country **hand/turn sb over to sb** *The terrorists were taken to the airport, where they were handed over to the French authorities.* | **hand/turn over sb** *The kidnappers promised to go to the embassy and turn over all their hostages within 24 hours.*

pass on /ˌpɑːs ˈɒn‖ˌpæs-/ [phr v T] to give information or documents to another person: *Officials admitted that they failed to pass on important information.* | **pass on sth to sb** *It was discovered that he had been passing secrets on to the Russians whilst working at the Pentagon.* | **pass sth on to sb** *He was accused of stealing secret documents and passing them on to the enemy.*

surrender /səˈrendəʳ/ [v T] formal to give your power or possessions to someone else because you have been forced to or have agreed to: *The President has indicated that he intends to surrender power on February 7th.* | **surrender sth to sb** *They promised to abide by the peace agreement and surrender all their weapons to the occupying forces.*

sign away /ˌsaɪn əˈweɪ/ [phr v T] to let someone else have your possessions or rights by officially signing a legal document: *With a stroke of the pen he signed away his claim to the family estate.* | *Her husband has tricked her into signing away her rights to the property.* | **sign sth away** *'I have no intention whatsoever of signing my inheritance away,' she informed him coldly.*

relinquish /rɪˈlɪŋkwɪʃ/ [v T] to let someone else have your position, power or rights, especially unwillingly: *The Prince was persuaded to relinquish his claim to the throne.* | *The United States is pressing the rebel army to relinquish power.*

8 to officially give control of something to someone else

- hand over
- make over
- transfer

hand over /ˌhænd ˈəʊvəʳ/ [phr v T] **hand over sth (to sb)** *In 1997 the sovereignty of Hong Kong was handed over to China.* | *It was only after many legal battles that he agreed to hand over the farm.* | **hand sth over (to sb)** *She was forced to hand executive control over to the new board.* —**handover** /ˈhændəʊvəʳ/ [n U] *Negotiations have begun in preparation for the handover of power to the new government.*

transfer /trænsˈfɜːʳ/ [v T] **transfer power/responsibility/control etc to** officially give it to another person, organization, or country **transfer sth to sb** *The military government is refusing to transfer power to a democratically elected civilian government.* | *In 1923 the ownership of the forest was transferred to a rich Dutch family.* —**transfer** /ˈtrænsfɜːʳ/ [n U] **+ of** *The transfer of power was effected swiftly and peacefully.*

make over /ˌmeɪk ˈəʊvəʳ/ [phr v T] to officially give something such as money or property by signing a legal document, so that it then belongs to someone else **make over sth to sb** *Before he died he made over the family business to his daughter.* | **make sth over to sb** *Elderly people sometimes unknowingly make huge sums of money over to unscrupulous business advisers.*

9 to arrange for something to be given to someone after you die

- leave
- bequeath
- will
- will

leave /liːv/ [v T] to arrange for something to be given to someone after you die **leave sth to sb** *He left £1000 to each of the nurses who had looked after him.* | **leave sb sth** *My aunt died last year and left me some of her furniture.*

bequeath /bɪˈkwiːð, bɪˈkwiːθ/ [v T] formal to officially arrange for something you own to be given to someone else after your death **bequeath sth to sb** *She bequeathed her collection of paintings to the National Gallery.* | **bequeath sb sth** *John Frazer made a will bequeathing his local church $5000.*

will /wɪl/ [n C] an official document that says who your money and possessions will be given to after you die **make a will** (=write a will) *He made a will just hours before he died.* | **leave sb sth in your will** *Mrs Williams left her daughter $200,000 in her will.* | **cut sb out of your will** (=change your will so that someone does not get any of your money or possessions) *When Henrietta told her father that she was going to marry Weinberger, he threatened to cut her out of his will.*

will /wɪl/ [v T] formal to give something to someone after you die, by writing it down in an official document **will sth to sb** *Wilson established a fine collection of artworks, which he willed to Peale's Museum.*

10 to give something that you have received to someone

- pass on
- be handed down

pass on /ˌpɑːs ˈɒn‖ˌpæs-/ [phr v T] to give something that has been given to you to someone else, especially after you have finished using it **pass sth on (to sb)** *There's only one copy of the leaflet, so when you've read it please pass it on.* | **pass on sth (to sb)** *When he gave up playing football, he passed on all his gear to me.*

be handed down /biː ˌhændɪ̵d ˈdaʊn/ [v phrase] if something **is handed down**, it is given to a younger person in the same family, for example to a sister or brother, or to a son or daughter **+ to** *In most big families, clothes are handed down to younger brothers and sisters.* | *The ring had been handed down to her from her grandmother.* | *traditional shipbuilding skills that have been handed down from generation to generation* | **be handed down from mother to daughter/from father to son** *ancient stories handed down from father to son*

11 to give something to someone who had it before

- give back
- hand back
- return
- restore

give back /ˌgɪv ˈbæk/ [phr v T] to give something to the person who gave it to you **give sth back** *Don't forget to give my pen back when you've finished with it.* | **give sth back to sb** *He still hasn't given that book back to me.* | **give sb sth back** *I looked at the letter, then gave her it back.* | *We'll have to cancel the show and give the audience their money back.*

hand back /ˌhænd ˈbæk/ [phr v T] to give something back to someone by hand **hand sth back (to sb)** *Here's the file you want. Please hand it back when you've finished with it.* | *The official looked at her identity card carefully and then handed it back to her.* | **hand back sth (to sb)** *Teachers will hand back student assignments after the vacation.* | *She handed back the photograph to him.*

return /rɪˈtɜːʳn/ [v T] formal to give something to the person or organization that owns it, especially after you have borrowed it from them: *You must return all your library books before the end of the year.* | **return sth to sb** *Your passport will be returned to you when you check out of your hotel.* | **return sth to its rightful owner** (=give something back to the person who has the right to own it) *Since the end of the war, many of the paintings have been found and returned to their rightful owners.*

restore /rɪˈstɔːʳ/ [v T] formal to give something valuable back to its owner, especially after it has been taken from them **restore sth to sb** *In 1905 both Japan and Russia agreed to restore Manchuria to China.* | **restore sth to its rightful owner** (=give something back to the person who has the right to own it) *After decades of colonial rule, the land was finally restored to its rightful owners.*

12 to give someone something that you would prefer to keep

- give up
- let sth go
- part with
- sacrifice
- trade away

give up /ˌgɪv ˈʌp/ [phr v T] **give up sth** *Fania was prepared to give up all her jewelry to help her father get out of debt.* | *Russia is very unlikely to give up its nuclear weapons.* | **give sth up** *Americans love their cars, and no-one is going to persuade them to give them up.*

let sth go /ˌlet (sth) ˈgəʊ/ [v phrase] to unwillingly give or sell something to someone, for example because they have won it from you or you cannot afford to keep it any longer: *They've held the world record for many years, and they're not going to let it go without a fight.* | *I've nowhere to store all this china, so I'm letting the whole lot go for $50.*

part with /ˈpɑːʳt wɪð/ [phr v T] to unwillingly give or sell something that is very important to you: *I'm reluctant to part with any of my precious books.* | *The new house was much smaller, and we had to part with things that we had been hoarding for years.*

sacrifice /ˈsækrɪfaɪs/ [v T] to agree or decide to stop having something that is valuable, especially in order to gain something more important **sacrifice sth to do sth** *He sacrificed a promising career to look after his handicapped daughter.* | **sacrifice sth for sth** *The nation is not prepared to sacrifice its independence for the sake of an alliance with a powerful neighbour.*

trade away /ˌtreɪd əˈweɪ/ [phr v T] to let someone take a right, advantage etc from you – use this when you think someone is stupid to do this **trade away sth for** (=lose one thing and gain another) *The Unions would be wrong to trade away their future for short-term financial gain.* | **trade away sth** *It's disgusting to trade away your democratic rights in this way.*

13 to give generously

- be generous
- lavish sth on
- shower

be generous /biː ˈdʒenərəs/ [v phrase] *We've received thousands of dollars to help the children – people have been incredibly generous.* | **+ to** *He was very generous to her when they divorced, and let her keep the house and the car.* | **be generous with sth** (=give a lot of something) *When it comes to training, Marion's always been generous with her time.*

lavish sth on /ˈlævɪʃ (sth) ɒn/ [phr v T] **lavish gifts/attention/affection etc on someone** to give a lot of gifts, attention etc to someone, especially in an uncontrolled or wasteful way: *When the series was first shown, the media lavished praise on its creator David Lynch.* | *Pet owners lavish love and attention on animals because they're a lot easier to deal with than their fellow human beings.*

shower /ˈʃaʊəʳ/ [v T] **shower sb with gifts/affection/praise etc** to give someone a lot of gifts, love, prizes etc: *Trudi was treated as a special guest and was showered with gifts everywhere she went.* | *His family loved him so much they showered him with affection.* | **shower sth on/upon sb** *When Elvis first became famous he had honours and awards showered upon him.*

14 when several people give some of the total money needed

- contribute
- make a contribution
- have a collection
- chip in
- pay/give towards
- have a whip-round

contribute /kənˈtrɪbjuːt/ [v I/T] to give some of the money that is needed to pay for something **+ to** *I'd like to thank all of you who contributed to the hospital appeal.* | **contribute sth to/towards sth** *My parents said they would contribute something towards the cost of my driving lessons.*

make a contribution /ˌmeɪk ə ˌkɒntrɪˈbjuːʃən‖-ˌkɑːn-/ [v phrase] to give an amount of money that when added to money given by other people, can be used to pay for something useful: *If we all make a contribution, we'll be able to get him something really nice.* | **+ to/towards** *Several local businesses have made contributions towards our new school bus.*

have a collection /ˌhæv ə kəˈlekʃən/ [v phrase] to collect money from each of the people in a group, especially in order to buy something for someone: *They had a collection at the bar and they raised over $80.* | **+ for** *We're having a collection for Jane's birthday present.*

chip in /ˌtʃɪp ˈɪn/ [phr v I/T] informal if everyone in a group **chips in** an amount of money, they each give an amount so that they can pay for something together: *We all chipped in to pay for the food and wine.* | *When Mona retired, all her co-workers chipped in and bought her a lovely dinner service.* | **+ with** *Electronics firm Compol chipped in with over $20,000.*

pay/give towards British **/give toward sth** American /ˈpeɪ, ˈɡɪv təˌwɔːʳdz, ˈɡɪv təˌwɔːʳd (sth)/ [v phrase] to give part of the money needed to pay for something **pay/give sth towards sth** *I don't mind paying something towards Samantha's wedding present.* | *She feels it's partly her fault the TV's broken, so she's ready to pay $50 toward a new one.* | **pay/give towards sth** *Although students receive government grants, parents are still expected to pay towards living costs.*

have a whip-round /ˌhæv ə ˈwɪp raʊnd/ [v phrase] British informal if a group of people **have a whip-round**, everyone in the group immediately gives some money in order to buy something with the total amount that is collected: *It's Sally's birthday tomorrow. We'd better have a whip-round so we can get her a present.*

15 to give something extra when someone buys something

- give away
- throw in
- free gift

give away /ˌɡɪv əˈweɪ/ [phr v T] if a company **gives away** something, they give it to people when they buy the company's products **give away sth (with sth)** *They're giving away free wine glasses when you spend more than $15 on gas.* | *700 concert tickets were given away to people buying CDs or cassettes.* | **give sth away (with sth)** *'Where did you get that badge?' 'They're giving them away with this week's Melody Maker magazine.'*

throw in /ˌθrəʊ ˈɪn/ [phr v T] to give someone something at no additional cost when they buy something from you **throw in sth** *The person selling the house may offer to throw in the carpets and curtains as part of the deal.* | **throw sth in** *Never mind the chairs – I'll throw them in with the table.*

free gift /ˌfriː ˈɡɪft/ [n C] something, usually something not very valuable, that is given to you when you buy something else: *Most banks offer students a free gift when they open a new account.* | *Your Free Gift From Cachet. A perfume atomiser with every 50ml Eau de Toilette purchase.*

16 to give someone something useless or that you do not want

- palm sth off on
- fob sb off with
- offload

palm sth off on /ˌpɑːm (sth) ˈɒf ɒn/ [phr v T] informal to get rid of something that you do not want by giving or selling it to someone else without telling them about its faults: *If he tries to palm that old Ford of his off on you, just tell him you're not interested.* | *I've managed to palm that early morning class off on Mary – she's desperate for work.*

fob sb off with /ˌfɒb (sb) ˈɒf wɪð‖ˌfɑːb-/ [phr v T] to make someone accept something that is not as good as or not the same as the thing that they actually wanted: *Don't let him fob you off with some cheap imported whisky – you want the real thing.* | *People are much more selective about what they watch on TV these days, and they don't want to be fobbed off with any old rubbish.*

offload /ɒfˈləʊd‖ɔːf-/ [v T] to get rid of something such as work or responsibility that you have by giving part of it to someone else: *You should try and offload some of your duties and relax more, instead of spending all day at the office.* | *The bank are trying to offload some of their US holdings.*

go

RELATED WORDS

- see also **leave, travel, move/not move**

1 to go to a meeting, party, concert etc

- go
- come
- attend
- show up/turn up
- make an appearance/put in an appearance

go /gəʊ/ [v I] *She invited me to her wedding, but I couldn't go.* | *How many of you actually went last week?* | **+ to** *Did you go to the baseball game last weekend?* | *I have to go to a meeting this afternoon.*

come /kʌm/ [v I] to go to a game, concert, meeting, party etc, either at the home of the person who invites you, or with someone who is also going there: *We're having a meal at my home tomorrow night. Do you want to come?* | **+ to** *Can you come to my party?* | *You should have come to the concert – it was really good.*

attend /əˈtend/ [v I/T] **formal** to go to an event such as a meeting: *Will you be attending the conference?* | *Employees are expected and required to attend team meetings.* | *Several people were unable to attend because of the storm.*

show up/turn up /ˌʃəʊ ˈʌp, ˌtɜːʳn ˈʌp/ [phr v I] **informal** to go to a particular event that you are expected to be at: *It's my sister's birthday party. She'll be very disappointed if I don't show up.* | *Chris turned up an hour late.* | **+ for** *She showed up twenty minutes late for class.* | *Schmidt failed to turn up for a scheduled meeting on Monday morning.*

make an appearance/put in an appearance /ˌmeɪk ən əˈpɪərəns, ˌpʊt ɪn ən əˈpɪərəns/ [v phrase] to go to an event such as a party or a meeting, but only for a short time: *The president made an appearance on 'CBS This Morning'.* | *I hate these official cocktail parties, but I suppose I'd better put in an appearance for half an hour.*

2 to regularly go to a school, work or church

- go to
- attend
- be at

go to /ˈgəʊ tuː/ [v phrase] *As a child I used to hate going to church.* | *Karen goes to Daley College.* | *He's been going to Spanish lessons for months and he still can't speak a word of it.*

attend /əˈtend/ [v I/T] **written** to regularly go to a class, school or church: *Both children attend St. Joan Church* | *Karl attended college after military service.*

be at **especially British** **/be in** **American** /ˈbiː æt, ˈbiː ɪn/ [v T] if you **are at** or **are in** a school, college, or university, you study there: *I'm at Belton School. What about you?* | *Mary is at Northwestern University.* | *Sam was an athlete in school.* | **be at school/college/university** *My husband and I met when we were both at college.*

3 to deliberately not go to school, work etc

- skive/skive off/bunk off
- play truant
- cut

- see also **avoid**

skive/skive off/bunk off /skaɪv, ˌskaɪv ˈɒf, ˌbʌŋk ˈɒf/ [v I/T/v I/T/phr v I/T] **British informal** to deliberately not go to school, work etc, when you should be there: *He says that he was so ill he had to be sent home from school. I bet he's skiving.* | *Have you been skiving off again? You'll get caught one of these days.* | *We were bunking off one day, and playing down by the canal.*

play truant **British** **/play hooky** **American** /ˌpleɪ ˈtruːənt, ˌpleɪ ˈhʊki/ [v phrase] if a child **plays truant** or **plays hooky** from school, they deliberately stay away from school without their parent's permission: *Billy was caught playing truant and has been given extra homework for a month.* | *He'd played hooky again and ridden the train out to Brooklyn.*

cut /kʌt/ [v T] **especially American, informal** if a student **cuts** classes, school etc, they deliberately do not go to the classes that they should go to: *Kids cut class and ran down the street to watch the fire.*

good

RELATED WORDS

opposite: ———————— **bad**

- to be good at something *see* **good at**
- see also **best, better, perfect, delicious, convenient, impress, enthusiastic/not enthusiastic, excited/exciting, enjoy, like**

1 something you like or enjoy very much

- good
- nice
- great
- perfect
- marvellous/wonderful/fantastic/terrific
- amazing/incredible
- brilliant
- neat
- be out of this world

good /gʊd/ [adj] *Did you have a good weekend?* | *It's one of the best books I've ever read.* | *That smells good. What are you cooking?* | *There's nothing good on TV these days.* | *This year's show was much better than last year's.* | **very/really good** *We enjoyed our trip to Canada. It was really good.*

nice /naɪs/ [adj] pleasant or enjoyable: *I hope you have a nice vacation.* | *Come over on Saturday. It would be nice to see you.* | **very/really nice** *She made us a really nice dinner.*

great spoken ALSO **excellent** /greɪt, 'eksələnt/ [adj] extremely good: *Thanks for a great afternoon.* | *'Did you have a good holiday?' 'It was great!'* | *Our local theatre has put on some excellent productions.* | *an excellent film*

perfect /'pɜːʳfɪkt/ [adj] so good that it could not be made any better: *It was a perfect day out.* | *This church is a perfect example of Gothic architecture.* | *'How was your holiday?' 'Oh, just perfect!'*

marvellous / wonderful / fantastic / terrific /'mɑːʳvələs, 'wʌndəʳfəl, fæn'tæstɪk, tə'rɪfɪk/ [adj] spoken very good in a way that makes you feel happy or excited: *The kids had a marvellous time at the carnival.* | *You get a wonderful view of the mountains from here.* | *The special effects in the movie were just fantastic.* | *Their latest album's terrific.*

amazing/incredible /ə'meɪzɪŋ, ɪn'kredəbəl/ [adj] very good in a surprising and exciting way: *Standing there on top of Mount Fuji was an amazing experience.* | *What a goal! That was just incredible!*

brilliant /'brɪljənt/ [adj] spoken extremely good: *You should come to the new sports centre – it's brilliant.* | *'How was your trip?' 'Absolutely brilliant!'*

neat /niːt/ [adj] American spoken very good or enjoyable: *That's such a neat car.* | **really neat** *The fireworks over Golden Gate Park were really neat.*

be out of this world /biː ˌaʊt əv ðɪs 'wɜːʳld/ [v phrase] spoken use this to say that something is so good, enjoyable etc, that it is almost the best you have ever experienced: *Her new apartment's out of this world!* | *This is the best soufflé I've ever tasted – it's out of this world.*

2 well made or of good quality

- good
- well
- excellent
- good quality/high quality
- first-class
- fine
- superior
- deluxe

good /gʊd/ [adj] *Lisa's work has been much better recently.* | *It's a good car, but it's very expensive.* | *It's worth paying a bit more for a good haircut.* | **very good** *There are one or two very good restaurants nearby.*

well /wel/ [adv] if something is done or made **well**, it is done with a lot of care and skill, so that it is of a high standard: *Jean's playing much better since you gave her some lessons.* | *one of the best designed cars on the market* | **very well** *Both books are very well written and enjoyable to read.* | **do well** *Don't worry about the test – I'm sure you'll do well.*

excellent /'eksələnt/ [adj] of extremely good quality or very well made: *The bank provides an excellent service for its customers.* | *They told me my English was excellent.*

good quality/high quality /ˌgʊd 'kwɒləti, ˌhaɪ 'kwɒləti‖ -'kwɑːl-/ [adj phrase] well made from good materials: *If you buy good quality shoes, they last much longer.* | *We only use the highest quality ingredients for our pizzas.* | **of good/high quality** *hand-made carpets of the highest quality*

first-class /ˌfɜːʳst 'klɑːs◂‖-'klæs◂/ [adj] a product or service that is **first-class** is much better than most others: *Jaguar has always made first-class cars.* | *The food at the restaurant is always first-class.*

fine /faɪn/ [adj only before noun] of a very high quality and often valuable, rare, or very skilfully made: *The collar is made of finest English lace.* | *The train passes near Gate Manor, a fine Victorian mock Jacobean hall.*

superior /suː'pɪəriəʳ, sjuː-‖sʊ-/ [adj] better made or of a better quality than most similar products – used especially in advertisements: *Style, comfort and superior cuisine are the most important characteristics of a good hotel.*

deluxe /də'lʌks‖-'lʊks/ [adj only before noun] **deluxe model/version/edition etc** one that is of high quality because it has more features or uses better quality materials than others made by the same company: *The deluxe model comes complete with an in-car CD player and car-phone.* | *Longman has published a deluxe, leather-bound edition of Johnson's Dictionary.*

3 good ideas/plans/suggestions

- good
- excellent
- great
- neat
- terrific/fantastic
- brilliant
- attractive

good /gʊd/ [adj] *'Why don't you write to your bank and ask for a loan?' 'That's a good idea.'* | *I thought it would be a good idea to arrive early.* | *That's the best suggestion you've made all day.* | *The best way of getting your children to learn foreign languages is to send them to stay abroad.*

excellent /'eksələnt/ [adj] extremely good: *We were given some excellent financial advice by Mr Samuel.* | *That sounds like an excellent idea to me.*

great /greɪt/ [adj] spoken informal a **great** idea is one that you like very much **great idea** *'Let's have a barbecue.' 'That's a great idea.'* | **great!** *'You want to go to a movie instead?' 'Yeah, great, why not!'*

neat /niːt/ [adj] American spoken say this when you think an idea is good because it is original and clever: *Jim and I need more time together away from the kids, so we came up with this neat idea of meeting after work.* | *'Why don't we go to the beach!' 'Yeah that sounds really neat.'*

terrific/fantastic /tə'rɪfɪk, fæn'tæstɪk/ [adj] extremely good, in a way that makes you feel happy or excited: *I've just though of a fantastic idea.* | *'What do you think of Kate's suggestion?' 'I think it's terrific.'*

brilliant /'brɪljənt/ [adj] British informal extremely good and clever: *'Maybe we should invite them over here instead of going to their place.' 'Brilliant!'* | *Joanna came up with a brilliant idea for a new book.*

attractive /ə'træktɪv/ [adj] **attractive offer/proposition/package etc** one that is very good and makes you want to accept it: *The job pays well and you get a company car and 30 days holiday a year – it's certainly an attractive offer.* | *We've put together what we think is a very attractive package, including discounts, special offers, and free credit.*

4 a good performance/piece of work/achievement

- good
- excellent
- outstanding
- brilliant
- impressive
- exceptional
- admirable

good /gʊd/ [adj] *Harry's work is always very good.* |

Rosemary does a good job here. | *It's the best performance we've seen from Giggs all season.* | *Her grades are getting better all the time.*

excellent /ˈeksələnt/ [adj] extremely good: *They complimented her on her excellent English.* | *Many studies reported excellent results with the drug.*

outstanding /aʊtˈstændɪŋ/ [adj] an **outstanding** performance or achievement is extremely good and much better than that of most other people: *It was an outstanding performance by a talented young actor.* | *Her work has been outstanding all year.*

brilliant /ˈbrɪljənt/ [adj] extremely good, and showing an unusually high level of skill or intelligence: *Michael Horden gave a brilliant performance as King Lear.* | *After a brilliant career at St Luke's Hospital, she was given her own department.* | *The decision to reorganize the company was a brilliant success.* —**brilliantly** [adv] *The team played absolutely brilliantly.*

impressive /ɪmˈpresɪv/ [adj] something that is **impressive** is of an unusually good quality and you admire it: *The school's examination results were very impressive.* | *an impressive achievement*

exceptional /ɪkˈsepʃənəl/ [adj] much better than the usual standard: *He writes good essays, but I wouldn't say that his work is particularly exceptional.* | *Merits are given as an honour for exceptional achievement.* —**exceptionally** [adv] *Only exceptionally bright students are entered for the examination.*

admirable /ˈædmərəbəl/ [adj] formal something that is **admirable** has good qualities that make you like and admire it: *It is an admirable book, the first to tell the whole truth about the war.* —**admirably** [adv] *We found the organization of the company to be admirably democratic.*

5 good literature/music/art

- good
- great
- classic
- work of art
- masterpiece

good /gʊd/ [adj] *Good music seems to be a thing of the past.* | *Students need to read a lot of good fiction in order to form their own opinions about quality.* | *Her early work is much better than her more recent stuff.* | *Which do you think is their best album?*

great /greɪt/ [adj] extremely good and skilful, and therefore admired and remembered by many people for a long time: *Many of our great works of art are being sold and exported.* | *There's some debate as to what constitutes great poetry.* | *The Renaissance period produced some of the greatest architecture of all time.*

classic /ˈklæsɪk/ [adj only before noun] **classic film/book/album etc** a film, book etc that is one of the best of its kind: *2001 is a classic science fiction movie.* | *The Rolling Stones produced a string of classic singles in the mid 60s including 'Satisfaction' and 'Brown Sugar'.* —**classic** [n C] *Movies like 'Paris, Texas' have become modern classics.*

work of art /ˌwɜːʳk əv ˈɑːʳt/ [n phrase] something produced by an artist, especially something that most people agree is of very high quality: *Several priceless works of art were badly damaged when the palace was bombed.*

masterpiece /ˈmɑːstəʳpiːs‖ˈmæs-/ [n C] a picture, sculpture etc that is of extremely high quality, especially one that is believed to be the best work of a particular artist: *one of the great Italian masterpieces* | *Many people regard this painting as Raphael's masterpiece.*

6 good weather

- good
- nice
- beautiful/glorious
- fine

good /gʊd/ [adj] *Did you have good weather in France?* | *The weather report says the weather should be good over the weekend.* | *The weather was a bit better in the second week.*

nice /naɪs/ [adj] especially British, spoken pleasantly warm and with plenty of sun: *Morning, Bill. Nice weather, isn't it?* | *It's a nice day – why don't we go for a walk?*

beautiful/glorious ALSO **lovely** especially British /ˈbjuːtɪ̆fəl, ˈglɔːriəs, ˈlʌvli/ [adj] especially spoken warm and with a lot of sun: *a beautiful sunny morning* | *a glorious summer* | *What a lovely morning!*

fine /faɪn/ [adj] British if the weather is **fine**, it is not raining and the sky is clear: *Next week will be fine but a little cooler.* | *a fine summer evening*

7 how good something is

- quality
- standard

quality /ˈkwɒlɪ̆ti‖ˈkwɑː-/ [n U] the measure of how well something is made or produced, or how good a material is: *Supermarket wines tend to vary in price and quality.* | *We always guarantee the best quality to our customers.* | **be of good/reasonable/poor etc quality** *She always insists that her writing paper is of good quality.* | *The recording is of very poor quality.*

standard /ˈstændəʳd/ [n C/U] the measure of how well someone does something: *Safety standards are simply not being maintained.* | **above/below a standard** *In reading tests, 15% of school students were found to be below the standard for their age.* | **be of a good/high standard** *All his work is of a very high standard.* | **be up to standard** (=be of an acceptable level) *I'm afraid your driving isn't yet up to standard.* | **+ of** *The standard of workmanship on this table is extraordinarily high.*

8 morally good person

- good
- decent
- respectable
- upright
- virtuous
- saint
- saintly
- be an example to

good /gʊd/ [adj] kind, honest, and helpful: *Jean's a very good person – she's always ready to help.* | *He had always tried to lead a good life.* | *I wish I could be a better person.* | *There are good and bad people wherever you go.*

decent /ˈdiːsənt/ [adj] someone who is **decent** is good and honest according to the normal standards of society: *Decent citizens have nothing to fear from the police.* | *a decent, honest, hard-working woman* | *Decent members of the public will be outraged by this decision.*

respectable /rɪˈspektəbəl/ [adj] behaving and living your life in a way that is considered morally correct by society, especially because of the family you come from: *Tony was always in trouble with the police when he was young, but now he's a respectable married man.* | *The girls in the school all come from very respectable families.* —**respectability** /rɪˌspektəˈbɪlɪ̆ti/ [n U] *Many of the worst gangsters maintained an air of respectability.*

upright /ˈʌpraɪt/ [adj usually before noun] written someone who is **upright** is honest, obeys the law, and behaves according to the moral standards of society: *Most upright, law-abiding citizens have very little contact with the police.* | *Maggie's parents set her a good example, being upright and hard-working people.*

virtuous /ˈvɜːʳtʃuəs/ [adj] formal very good and honest and always behaving according to the highest moral standards: *Father Tom was a hard-working, virtuous man, liked and respected by everyone.* | *They wanted him to marry a virtuous young woman from a respectable family.*

saint /seɪnt/ [n C] someone who is unusually kind, generous, helpful etc and is therefore considered to be very special: *Your mother's a saint. She's done so much to help us.* | *I always thought she was a selfish woman but she was an absolute saint compared to Abigail.*

saintly /ˈseɪntli/ [adj] behaving in a very good way, especially by living your life in a very pure and holy way: *He was a saintly man who always put others before himself.* | *There were aspects of her life that were not as saintly as the Victorians liked to believe.*

be an example to /biː ən ɪgˈzɑːmpəl tuː‖-ˈzæm-/ [v phrase] to be so good or to have achieved something so good that other people would improve if they tried to be like you: *You're a very brave young man. An example to all of us!* | *His discipline and organization should be an example to teachers everywhere.*

9 morally good behaviour

- good
- right
- ethical
- decent
- honourable
- be above/beyond reproach

good /gʊd/ [adj] *The nuns here do many good things for people in the local community.* | **it is good of sb to do sth** *It was very good of you to hand the money in to the police – a lot of people would have just kept it.* | **good deed** (=a good action) *Victor devoted his life to helping others and didn't expect any reward for his good deeds.*

right /raɪt/ [adj not usually before noun] morally correct: *You can't do that. It's not right.* | *I only want to do the right thing.* | *It's not right to tell lies.* | **it's only right** (=anything else would not be right) *It's only right that parents should help their children.* —**right** [n U] *She always tried to teach her children the difference between right and wrong.* —**rightly** [adv] *They've been punished for their crimes, and quite rightly.*

ethical /ˈeθɪkəl/ [adj] morally correct, especially according to a set of ideas about how people should behave in a particular profession: *Is it ethical to use this drug to control patients' behaviour?* | *There is only one ethical way to carry out this experiment.*

decent /ˈdiːsənt/ [adj] fair, honest, or kind: *Perhaps Jack wanted to do something decent, for a change.* | **it is decent of sb to do sth** *It's very decent of you to be so pleased for me – I know how much you wanted to win this competition.* —**decently** [adv] *You could at least try to behave decently towards the people you have to work with.*

honourable British **/honorable** American /ˈɒnərəbəl‖ˈɑːn-/ [adj] morally correct and showing that you have high moral standards, especially if you are doing something that you feel is your duty: *It would not be honourable for me, as a solicitor, to reveal my client's business to anyone.* | *The most honorable thing that he can do in these circumstances is to resign.* —**honourably** [adv] *Despite his anger at having been wrongly accused, Peterson behaved honourably throughout the trial,*

be above/beyond reproach /biː əˌbʌv, bɪˌjɒnd rɪˈprəʊtʃ‖-ˌjɑːnd-/ [v phrase] so good that no one can criticize or find any fault in the way you behave: *Throughout this ordeal her behaviour was beyond reproach.* | *We need a chairman whose reputation and character are above reproach.*

10 books, films, jokes etc that are not morally offensive or harmful

- wholesome
- clean

wholesome /ˈhəʊlsəm/ [adj] **wholesome** behaviour, activities, books etc are considered good and suitable for everyone, especially because they do not involve sex or swearing: *He read your new book and said it was wholesome and not at all offensive.* | *The good thing about this game is that it provides clean and wholesome fun for all the family.*

clean /kliːn/ [adj] **clean humour/jokes/language etc** not offensive to anyone, especially because of not being about sex: *Join us tomorrow night for an evening of good clean fun.* | **keep it clean** (=not do or say anything offensive) *He's been asked to tell some jokes in his speech but he's got to keep it clean.*

11 the quality of being morally good

- goodness
- good
- decency

goodness /ˈgʊdn¹̣s/ [n U] what is good in a person's character: *She had a wonderful combination of beauty and goodness.* | *His goodness shines through his every action.*

good /gʊd/ [n U] **good** actions, characteristics, or behaviour: *Everyone has a choice between good and evil.* | *I just can't see any good in these people at all.*

decency /ˈdiːsənsi/ [n U] kindness, honesty, and fairness in the way that you treat other people: *You can rely on their decency and good sense.* | **have the decency to do sth** *I think you should have the decency to tell him you are already married.* | **common decency** (=ordinary decency that most people have) *He borrowed money from me and didn't even have the common decency to pay me back.*

12 standards of good and bad behaviour

- morals
- right and wrong
- morality
- ethics
- standards
- values

morals /ˈmɒrəlz‖ˈmɔː-/ [n plural] the basic ideas that a person or a society has about what is morally good and right: *He only knew the morals, customs and beliefs of his mountain village.* | *the influence of rock music on the minds and morals of young people* | *Harry doesn't seem to have any morals at all.*

right and wrong /ˌraɪt ən ˈrɒŋ/ [n phrase] the idea or understanding that some things are morally good and some or morally bad: *They're only children, but they do know the difference between right and wrong.* | *Do we naturally have a sense of right and wrong, or are we taught it?*

morality /məˈræl¹̣ti/ [n U] ideas about what is right and what is wrong, or the degree to which something is morally acceptable: *Victorian commentators were very concerned about public morality generally.* | *I think we should question the morality of turning away refugees.* | *Anyone who carried out such an attack obviously has no morality whatsoever.*

ethics /ˈeθɪks/ [n plural] a system of rules about what is morally right or wrong, especially rules followed by a religious group or people in a particular profession: *What are the differences between Muslim and Christian ethics?* | *medical ethics* | **code of ethics** (=system of ethics) *As a therapist he has to follow a very strict code of ethics.*

standards /ˈstændəʳdz/ [n plural] personal rules of behaviour, based on an idea of what is morally good and right: *He was a good man who kept up the very highest standards throughout his life.* | *There has been a serious decline in moral standards among the young people of today.*

values /ˈvæljuːz/ [n plural] the ideas that a person or group has about what things are good, right, and important in life: *As a child he had admired his father's values and lifestyle.* | *a black identity based on black culture and black values* | *She rejected the traditional values of her society.*

13 relating to what is right or wrong

- moral
- morally
- ethical

moral /ˈmɒrəl‖ˈmɔː-/ [adj usually before noun] *We follow the moral laws laid down by our religion.* | *They live according to a deeply held moral code.* | *Everything that he writes has a high moral purpose.* | **moral obligation** (=something that you do not have to do, but your moral sense says that you must do) *You have a moral obligation to help your sister's children.* —**morality** /məˈrælɪ̈ti/ [n U] *There was a lot of public debate about the morality of the invasion.*

morally /ˈmɒrəli‖ˈmɔː-/ [adv] according to what is right or wrong, or good or evil: *We are morally opposed to capital punishment.* | *The government is morally obliged to do all it can for the refugees.* | *It is morally wrong to punish someone for something they did not do.*

ethical /ˈeθɪkəl/ [adj] morally correct according to the rules of behaviour in a particular profession: *It would not be ethical for me, as a doctor, to talk to you about my patients.*

14 your personal ideas about what is right or wrong

- conscience
- scruples
- principles

conscience /ˈkɒnʃəns‖ˈkɑːn-/ [n C/U] the inner sense of what is right or wrong that makes you feel guilty if you do something wrong: *Her conscience would not let her take all the credit for their work.* | **guilty/bad conscience** *It was a guilty conscience that made him admit stealing the money.* | **clear/good conscience** *Marie got up especially early to do all her work so that she could enjoy herself afterwards with a clear conscience.* | **social/political etc conscience** (=a moral sense of how society should be) *He was a man of strong social conscience, who actively campaigned against poverty in all its forms.* | **conscience-stricken** (=feeling guilty because you have done something wrong) *She hurried home, conscience-stricken about having left all the dishes for Natalie to do.*

scruples /ˈskruːpəlz/ [n plural] personal moral principles that stop you from doing something morally wrong – use this especially about someone who does not have moral principles: *He is very ambitious and has absolutely no scruples.* | *These large drug syndicates are not affected by moral scruples – they just want to make a profit.*

principles /ˈprɪnsɪ̈pəlz/ [n plural] strong ideas about what is morally right and wrong, that you try to follow in everything that you do: *Jimmy tried to live according to Christian principles.* | *Does she have any principles at all?* | **against sb's principles** (=morally wrong to that person) *I won't get involved in a deal like this – it's against all my principles.*

15 thinking you are morally better than other people

- self-righteous
- sanctimonious
- holier-than-thou
- moralistic
- preachy

self-righteous /ˌself ˈraɪtʃəs/ [adj] feeling very confident about how good you are and about your high moral standards, in a way that annoys other people: *His grandparents were stern and self-righteous people.* | *I've got nothing against vegetarians, but some of them are so self-righteous!* —**self-righteousness** [n U] *She sniffed, with a mixture of self-righteousness and self-pity.* —**self-righteously** [adv] *'I always give plenty of money to charity,' he boasted self-righteously.*

sanctimonious /ˌsæŋktɪ̈ˈməʊniəs◂/ [adj] behaving as if you are morally better than other people, especially in telling them what you think is right and wrong: *Don't be so sanctimonious, Helen! I'll live my life the way I want to live it.* | *The Principal reacted to the school party with an air of sanctimonious disapproval.*

holier-than-thou /ˌhəʊliəʳ ðən ˈðaʊ/ [adj] showing other people very clearly that you think you are morally better than they are: *I know he doesn't smoke or drink but I wish he wasn't so holier-than-thou.* | *She was intensely irritated by Emma's holier-than-thou attitude.*

moralistic /ˌmɒrəˈlɪstɪk◂‖ˌmɔː-/ [adj] telling other people what you think is right or wrong about their behaviour, especially in an annoying way or when you have no right to do this: *Our teachers were dull, uninspiring, and moralistic.* | *a moralistic, middle-class newspaper*

preachy /ˈpriːtʃi/ [adj] trying too hard to make people accept your ideas about what it right or wrong, especially when this is unnecessary or annoying: *It's not a bad book, but it's a bit preachy.* | *Much of the film is preachy, pretentious, and slow.*

good at

RELATED WORDS

opposite: —— **bad at**

▸ *see also* **good at, can/can't, know/not know, best, better**

1 able to do something well

- be good at
- good
- proficient
- able
- capable
- competent

be good at /bi: 'gʊd æt/ [v phrase] to be able to do something well: *When she was at school she was good at art.* | *She loves her job, and she's very good at it.* | **be good at doing sth** *You've never been much good at lying.* | *Robson is particularly good at dealing with people, and should make an excellent manager.*

good /gʊd/ [adj] able to do something well: *The school orchestra is surprisingly good.* | **good singer/player/teacher etc** *Frank had always been a good football player, and it was no surprise when he was chosen for the team.* | *I can refer you to a good dentist.* | **be good with sb/sth** (=be good at dealing with someone or something) *Mrs. Hill is very good with children.* | *The two Drew girls are unusually good with animals.* | **be good with your hands** (=be good at making or repairing things with your hands) *Jeremy's good with his hands – he built our kitchen cupboards.*

proficient /prə'fɪʃənt/ [adj] formal having reached an acceptable standard in something, by learning or practising it **+ in** *Before you can study at a British university, you have to be proficient in English.* | **proficient skier/climber/actor etc** *The black runs are for proficient skiers only.* —**proficiency** [n U] *Once children have achieved a certain proficiency in reading, they prefer to read silently rather than aloud.*

able /'eɪbəl/ [adj usually before noun] good at doing something, especially at doing a difficult or important job that involves a lot of responsibility: *Mrs Thomas is a very able teacher.* | *She was widely regarded as one of the most able members of the president's staff.*

capable /'keɪpəbəl/ [adj] someone who is **capable** can be trusted to do a job or piece of work well and without needing other people's help or advice: *Mr. Young is a very capable attorney.* | *The team desperately needs a capable quarterback.*

competent /'kɒmpətənt‖'kɑːm-/ [adj] someone who is **competent** has enough skill and knowledge to be able to do something to a high or satisfactory standard: *Competent skiers should find no difficulty with the course.* | *Though the country is poor, the doctors and nurses are qualified and competent.* | **highly competent** (=very competent) *Tomita is a highly competent translator.* | **+ in** *New students are expected to be competent in mathematics.*

2 very good at doing something

- great
- brilliant
- excellent
- outstanding

great /greɪt/ [adj only before noun] **great actor/player/scientist etc** one of the best actors, players etc in the world, and famous and respected because of this: *Olivier was a great actor.* | *Some of the world's greatest athletes will be competing in the Olympic Games.* | *McEnroe was possibly the greatest tennis player of all time.* —**the greats** [n plural] *Fitzgerald is one of the all-time jazz greats.*

brilliant /'brɪljənt/ [adj] extremely clever and skilful at something, so that people admire you a lot: *Have you seen her dance? She's absolutely brilliant.* | *Paganini was a brilliant violinist, famous for his technical skill in both playing and composing music.* | **+ at** especially British *She's brilliant at handling difficult clients.* —**brilliance** [n U] *Hendrix's brilliance as a rock guitarist remains unsurpassed, even to this day.*

excellent /'eksələnt/ [adj usually before noun] extremely good at something: *Andrew had always been an excellent student.* | *She's enthusiastic and hardworking and has the potential to be an excellent teacher.*

outstanding /aʊt'stændɪŋ/ [adj] so good at doing something that you are noticeably much better than other people who do the same thing: *Woods is an outstanding golfer.* | *The book is a series of interviews with outstanding artists and writers.* | *A lot of my teachers were good, but Farley was outstanding.*

3 good at something because you have experience or training

- skilful
- skilled
- expert
- know what you're doing
- adept
- accomplished
- have a good command of
- can do sth in your sleep

skilful British **/skillful** American /'skɪlfəl/ [adj] someone who is **skilful** does something very well because they have had a lot of training or experience: *the artist's skillful use of color* | *Success in business depends on skilful management.* | *Skilful and confident, Donaldson should become one of the game's best players.*

skilled /skɪld/ [adj] someone who is **skilled** at a particular job has the training and skill to do it well: *There is a demand for carpenters and other skilled craftsmen.* | **skilled job/work** (=requiring special skill, especially when you use your hands) *Shoeing a horse is a skilled job, and no unskilled person should try it.* | **highly skilled** (=very skilled) *Keeping highly skilled sailors in the Navy is a priority.* | **skilled at doing sth** *Our advisors are skilled at dealing with financial problems.*

expert /'ekspɜːʳt/ [adj] extremely skilful at doing something because you have gained a lot of knowledge or experience of this particular subject or activity over a long period of time: *Students learn to cook French food with the help of expert chefs.* | *My grandmother was an expert dressmaker.* | **+ at/in** *Politicians are usually expert at turning a crisis to their advantage.* | **expert help/advice/opinion etc** (=given by someone who knows a lot about it) *Tennis coaches will be available to provide expert advice.* —**expertly** [adv] *The campaign was well-publicised and expertly co-ordinated.*

know what you're doing /ˌnəʊ wɒt jɔːʳ 'duːɪŋ/ [v phrase] spoken use this to say that someone is good at doing something and you admire and trust them because of this: *Kids can tell if a teacher doesn't know what he's doing.* | *You seem to know what you're doing – I'll leave you to it.*

adept /'ædept, ə'dept‖ə'dept/ [adj] good at doing something that needs care and skill, for example dealing with people or with difficult social situations **+ at/in** *Of all our staff, Peter is the most adept at dealing with difficult customers.* | *McCrea was equally adept in comedy and drama.*

accomplished /ə'kʌmplɪʃt‖ə'kɑːm-, ə'kʌm-/ [adj] someone who is very good at writing, acting, or other artistic skills, especially as a result of a lot of practice and training, but who does not usually have a special natural ability for it: *His two daughters are both accomplished athletes.* | **highly accomplished** *Johann Sebastian Bach had three sons who all became highly accomplished musicians and composers.*

have a good command of /hæv ə ˌgʊd kə'mɑːnd ɒv‖-'mænd-/ [v phrase not in progressive] to know a subject, especially a language, well and be good at it: *Candidates should have good typing skills and a good command of English.* | *She has an excellent command of all the facts.*

can do sth in your sleep /kən ˌduː (sth) ɪn jɔːʳ ˈsliːp/ [v phrase] informal to be able to do something very easily because you have done it a lot of times before: *I've played this piece so often I can practically do it in my sleep.*

4 having a natural ability to do something well

- talented
- gifted
- a natural
- have an aptitude for
- have a gift for
- born

talented /ˈtæləntɪ̈d/ [adj] very good at doing something because you have a lot of natural ability: *The show has talented actors, but the writing is poor.* | **highly talented** (=very talented) *The Brazilian team includes some highly talented young players.* | *The musicians are talented and enthusiastic about their new venture.*

gifted /ˈgɪftɪ̈d/ [adj] very good at doing something, especially art, music, or sport, because you were born with natural ability: *Picasso was one of the most gifted artists who ever lived.* | *It's a difficult subject, even for a writer as gifted as Mathers.* | **gifted children** *Most school systems offer programs for gifted children.* | **highly gifted** (=very gifted) *He is a highly gifted young singer, who combines a beautiful voice with unusual musical sensitivity.*

a natural /ə ˈnætʃərəl/ [n singular] someone who has a natural ability to do something and thinks it is easy as soon as they start to do it: *His sense of humor made him a natural for the TV talk shows.* | **+ at** *McAvoy is a natural at public relations.* —**natural/natural-born** [adj only before noun] *She is a natural leader.* | *a natural-born story teller*

have an aptitude for /ˌhæv ən ˈæptɪ̈tjuːd fɔːʳ ‖-tuːd-/ [v phrase not in progressive] to have a natural ability to learn a particular subject or skill very easily and quickly: *The school is for children who have an exceptional aptitude for math and science.*

have a gift for /ˌhæv ə ˈgɪft fɔːʳ/ [v phrase not in progressive] **have a gift for languages/painting/music/dancing etc** have a special natural ability to do something very well, especially something artistic: *Mozart had a gift for music even when he was very young.* | *As a director, he has a gift for inspiring his actors to give their best performances.*

born /bɔːʳn/ [adj only before noun] **born leader/teacher/writer etc** someone who clearly has a natural ability to lead, teach etc well, so that it seems as if they do not need to be taught how to do it: *When I read his first essays I knew that he was a born writer.* | *He seemed to be a born leader, someone who inspired confidence and loyalty.*

5 likely to become good at something

- promising/shows promise
- potential
- have the makings of

promising/shows promise /ˈprɒmɪ̈sɪŋ‖ˈprɑː-, ˌʃəʊz ˈprɒmɪ̈s‖-ˈprɑː-/ [adj/v phrase] someone who is **promising** or **shows promise**, especially someone who is young, is good at something and seems likely to become very good and successful at it: *The new England team members show a lot of promise.* | **promising actor/musician/player etc** *Promising researchers are allowed to take time off teaching and administrative duties.*

potential /pəˈtenʃəl/ [n U] natural ability that could be developed so that you become extremely good at something: *Stephen is a player with real potential.* | **have/show potential** *He's young but he shows a lot of potential.* | *She may not be a great violinist yet but she has potential.* | **+ to do/be sth** *One of their children has the potential to be a brilliant scientist.*

have the makings of /ˌhæv ðə ˈmeɪkɪŋz ɒv/ [v phrase] to have the qualities or skills needed to become a particular type of person or thing: *They have the makings of a good team this year.*

6 good at doing a lot of different things

- versatile
- all-rounder

versatile /ˈvɜːʳsətaɪl‖-sətl/ [adj] good at doing a lot of different things and able to learn new skills quickly and easily: *Meryl Streep is a wonderfully versatile actress.* | *Few musicians are as versatile as he is: he plays, composes, arranges, and teaches.*

all-rounder /ˌɔːl ˈraʊndəʳ/ [n C usually singular] British someone who is good at doing a lot of different things: *We're looking for a good all-rounder – someone who can run the office, deal with customers' complaints, and so on.* | *At the school, children were encouraged to be 'all-rounders' – they were to aim for success in games as well as study.*

7 the ability to do something well

- skill
- ability
- talent
- flair
- have a knack
- craftsmanship

skill /skɪl/ [n C/U] the ability to do something well especially because you have learned and practised it: *Most of us learn the knowledge and skills needed to drive a car fairly easily.* | *The Australians played with great skill and determination.* | **computer/management/language etc skills** *You need good communication skills for this job.* | **+ in** *On the course you will develop skills in business management.* | **with skill** *Price handles the role of the angry wife with great skill.*

ability /əˈbɪlɪ̈ti/ [n U] the **ability** to do something well, either because you have learned how to do it or because you are naturally good at it: *Maria will be a fine musician; she shows a lot of ability.* | **+ to do sth** *No one doubts his ability to get work done quickly.* | **spelling/reading/writing etc ability** (=the level of ability in spelling, reading etc) *The children are divided into groups according to their reading ability.*

talent /ˈtælənt/ [n C/U] a natural ability to do something very well: *John Lennon's talent as a songwriter was matched by McCartney's talent as a composer.* | **have a talent for doing sth** *Porter has a talent for making a difficult subject understandable and interesting.* | **+ for** *Teachers soon recognized and encouraged his talent for sculpture.* | **hidden talents** (=ones that people do not know about) *I never knew you were so good at making speeches. Do you have any other hidden talents?*

flair /fleəʳ/ [n singular/U] a special ability to do something very well and in a way that shows a lot of imagination: *Being a good salesman requires skill, flair, and a good knowledge of your product.* | *One of the best new players, he shows flair and creativity at* *the game.* | **have a flair for sth** *If you have a flair for languages, there are some good career opportunities in Europe.*

have a knack /ˌhæv ə ˈnæk/ [n singular] to have a special skill or ability that you usually gain by practice **+ for doing sth** *She has a knack for making everyone feel comfortable and relaxed.* | **+ for** *The family seems to have a knack for success in business.*

craftsmanship /ˈkrɑːftsmənʃɪp‖ˈkræfts-/ [n U] the special skill that someone uses to make something beautiful with their hands: *Hopi baskets are beautiful in both color and craftsmanship.* | *Fabergé eggs are famous for their intricate craftsmanship.*

8 something that you are especially good at

- strength
- be sb's forte

strength /streŋθ, strenθ/ [n C] something that you are particularly good at in your job, in a sport, or in your life in general: *Before choosing a career you should spend time identifying your personal strengths and weaknesses.* | *His ability to charm people is one of his greatest strengths.*

be sb's forte /biː (sb's) ˈfɔːteɪ‖-ˈfɔːrt/ [v phrase] to be the activity that you are best at: *Love songs have become Bolton's forte.* | *She's much better in the longer races. Short distances are not her forte.*

goodbye

RELATED WORDS

opposite: hello

- *see also* **leave**

1 ways of saying goodbye

- goodbye/bye
- see you
- later/catch you later
- so long
- have a nice day/ good weekend/ great time etc
- have a good one
- take care
- take it easy
- nice to meet you/ nice meeting you

goodbye/bye /gʊdˈbaɪ, baɪ/ spoken say this when you are leaving or when someone is leaving you. **Bye** is more informal than **goodbye**: *'Goodbye, Mrs Moore.' 'Goodbye, Dr Aziz.'* | *Goodbye, Louise. See you soon.* | *Thank you for calling. Goodbye.* | *'Bye, Annie.' 'Bye, Mom,' she said, kissing her mother on the cheek.* | **bye for now** (=say this to a friend who you will see again soon) *I've got some stuff to do. Maybe we can have a drink or something later tonight. Anyway, bye for now.*

see you ALSO **see you later/see you around** /ˈsiː juː, ˌsiː juː ˈleɪtəʳ, ˌsiː juː əˈraʊnd/ spoken informal use this to say goodbye to a friend you will see again soon: *See you, Darren.* | *Bye, Dad. I'll see you later.* | *You're still coming to the party tonight, aren't you? Good. See you later then.* | *She turned at the gate and waved. 'See you around, Billy.'* | **see you tomorrow/in the morning/at the club etc** *'See you in the morning,' she said as she closed the door.* | *'We'll be back early next week.' 'Okay. See you then.'* | **see you soon** *Safe trip back guys and we'll see you soon.*

later/catch you later /ˈleɪtəʳ, ˌkætʃ juː ˈleɪtəʳ/ especially American, spoken use this to say goodbye to a friend you will see again soon. **Later** and **catch you later** are used especially by young people: *Catch you later, Matt.* | *'Later, Mike.' 'Later, Steve.'*

so long /səʊ ˈlɒŋ‖-ˈlɔːŋ/ American spoken use this to say goodbye to someone you do not expect to meet again for a long time: *'So long,' he said. 'Don't forget to write.'* | *She grabbed Nick by the shoulders and hugged him affectionately. 'So long, Nick.'*

have a nice day/good weekend/great time etc /ˌhæv ə ˌnaɪs ˈdeɪ/ spoken say this when you are saying good bye to someone to wish them a good day, a good weekend, a good holiday etc: *Have a nice weekend.* | *Have a great time at the concert, you guys!*

have a good one /ˌhæv ə ˈgʊd wʌn/ American spoken say this when you are saying goodbye to someone to wish them a nice day: *'I'm off to work.' 'Alright, have a good one.'*

take care /ˌteɪk ˈkeəʳ/ spoken use this to say goodbye to family or friends: *'All right, Pat. Take care.' 'You too, Sally. Bye bye.'* | *Take care and we'll talk to you soon.*

take it easy /ˌteɪk ɪt ˈiːzi/ American spoken use this to say goodbye to a friend or member of your family: *'See you next week.' 'Yeah, take it easy.'*

nice to meet you/nice meeting you /ˌnaɪs tə ˈmiːt juː, ˌnaɪs ˈmiːtɪŋ juː/ spoken say this when you are going to leave someone who you have just met for the first time: *Well, it was nice meeting you guys.* | *'It was nice to meet you, Paul.' 'Nice to meet you too, Joanne.'*

2 ways of saying goodnight

- goodnight/night
- night night

goodnight/night /gʊdˈnaɪt, naɪt/ spoken say this to say goodbye to someone in the evening. **Night** is more informal than **goodnight**: *Goodnight. Thanks for having us.* | *'Night, folks.' 'Goodnight, Don. Careful driving.'*

night night /ˌnaɪt ˈnaɪt/ spoken goodbye – use this especially to children: *'Night night, Timmy.' 'Night, Mommy.'*

3 to say or wave goodbye to someone

- say goodbye
- say your goodbyes
- wave goodbye
- wave sb off
- see sb off
- bid sb farewell

say goodbye /ˌseɪ gʊdˈbaɪ/ [v phrase] to say **goodbye** to someone, or to say the last things that you want to say to them before you leave each other: *I've just come to say goodbye.* | *They left so suddenly, I didn't get a chance to say goodbye.* | **+ to** *I said goodbye to the kids and got into the car.*

say your goodbyes /ˌseɪ jɔːʳ gʊdˈbaɪz/ [v phrase] if two or more people **say their goodbyes**, they say the last things they want to say to each other before leaving each other for a long time: *We delayed saying our goodbyes until the last possible moment.* | *Adam went to get the car as Billie and Jenny said their goodbyes.*

wave goodbye /ˌweɪv gʊdˈbaɪ/ [v phrase] to wave to someone as they go away from you or as you leave them: *'Come back soon!' called Mary, waving goodbye from behind the gate.* | **+ to** *She waved goodbye to him through the car window.* | *As we left, I turned to wave goodbye to Helen.*

wave sb off /ˌweɪv (sb) ˈɒf/ [phr v T] British to wave to someone as they go away from you: *She waved them off, then went slowly back inside.* | *A crowd of children had gathered on the station platform to wave him off.* | *She looked back and saw her mother waving her off from the kitchen door.*

see sb off /ˌsiː (sb) ˈɒf/ [phr v T] to go with someone to the door of your house or to a place such as a station or airport in order to say goodbye to them when they leave: *All our friends had come to the airport to see us off.* | *Mrs Carey went to the door to see him off.* | *Dee was up the next day at sunrise to see me off.*

bid sb farewell /ˌbɪd (sb) feəʳˈwel/ [v phrase] formal to say goodbye to someone, especially when you know you will not meet again for a very long time – used especially in literature: *The time has come to bid you all farewell.* | *Some 400 Pakistani soldiers turned out to bid their comrades farewell.* | **bid farewell to sb** *Queen Victoria bade farewell to her most trusted servant.*

good enough

RELATED WORDS

▸ *see also* **enough, satisfied/not satisfied, good at, bad**

1 good enough

- good enough
- satisfactory
- be all right/OK
- not bad
- adequate
- acceptable
- passable
- reasonable
- competent
- decent
- will do

good enough /ˈgʊd ɪˌnʌf/ [adj phrase] *If the weather's good enough next weekend we'll go camping.* | **+ for** *It's just a cheap wine but it's good enough for a picnic.* | **good enough to do sth** *Do you think she's good enough to be in the team?*

satisfactory /ˌsætɪ̵sˈfæktəri/ [adj] something that is **satisfactory** reaches the expected standard but is not better than it: *You won't get paid unless your work is satisfactory.* | *Lynne got satisfactory grades and was offered a place at university.*

be all right/OK /biː ˌɔːl ˈraɪt, əʊˈkeɪ/ [v phrase] spoken use this about something that is good enough but not especially good: *The children made the cakes. I hope they're all right.* | *'What did you think of the movie?' 'Oh, it was OK – nothing special.'* | *This book is OK for beginners but it's not really suitable for more advanced students.*

not bad /nɒt ˈbæd/ [adj phrase] spoken use this to say that something is fairly good, and better than you expected: *'What was the food like?' 'Oh, not bad – better than last time.'* | *You know, that's not a bad idea.* | **not too bad** *'How was the exam?' 'Oh, not too bad. I think I passed.'*

adequate /ˈædɪkwɪ̵t/ [adj] good enough for a particular purpose, especially by being of a high enough level, amount, or quality: *Employers must provide adequate training opportunities.* | *Now that we have extended the hall, those small electric heaters are no longer adequate.* | *Make sure that the lighting is adequate so that your guests can see what they are eating.* —**adequately** [adv] *Some students cannot express themselves adequately on paper.* —**adequacy** [n U] *There are doubts about the adequacy of the medical care that was provided.*

acceptable /əkˈseptəbəl/ [adj] good enough to be able to be used for a particular purpose: *We had a lot of applicants for the job but only a few of them were acceptable.* | *Some low-fat cheeses have quite an acceptable flavour but some taste like rubber.* | **+ to** *The dispute was settled in a way that was acceptable to both sides.* —**acceptably** [adv] *Their response was acceptably quick.*

passable /ˈpɑːsəbəl‖ˈpæ-/ [adj] good enough, but not very good: *There was some bread, a little cheese and a passable French wine.* | *He gave a passable imitation of Charlie Chaplin.*

reasonable /ˈriːzənəbəl/ [adj] fairly good, but not very good: *Most of her work is of a reasonable standard.* | *A reasonable number of people turned up for the meeting.* | *We had an enjoyable weekend and the weather was quite reasonable.* —**reasonably** [adv] *We want to be reasonably sure that everything's safe.*

competent /ˈkɒmpɪ̵tənt‖ˈkɑːm-/ [adj] a piece of work or a performance that is **competent** is done to a satisfactory standard but does not have any particularly good or skilful features: *Most of the essays were competent but one was really outstanding.* | *Ben took out his pen and produced a quick but very competent sketch of the building.*

decent /ˈdiːsənt/ [adj] spoken of a good enough quality or standard: *I want to provide my boys with a decent education.* | *There isn't one decent restaurant around here.* —**decently** [adv] *decently cooked food*

will do /wɪl ˈduː/ [v phrase] especially spoken to be good enough for a particular purpose: *If you don't have any butter, margarine will do.* | *I want someone to practise first aid on. You'll do, Simon.* | **will do sb** (=be good enough for someone) *Don't bother fetching me another chair. This one'll do me fine.*

2 to reach a high enough standard

- make the grade
- measure up
- come up to sb's standards/expectations etc
- live up to
- meet
- have what it takes
- pass

make the grade /ˌmeɪk ðə ˈgreɪd/ [v phrase] to succeed in reaching the necessary standard, especially in a difficult job: *She would like to become a lawyer but she's not sure whether she'll make the grade.* | *Only the talented few make the grade in professional golf.*

measure up /ˌmeʒər ˈʌp/ [phr v I] use this when you are asking or considering whether someone will be good enough to do a particular job or to reach a particular standard: *We'll give you a week's trial in the job so we can see how you measure up.* | **+ to** *How will the new General Secretary measure up to his new task?*

come up to sb's standards/expectations etc /kʌm ˌʌp tə (sb's) ˈstændəʳdz/ [v phrase] to achieve the level of quality that is necessary or expected: *The new design doesn't come up to our usual standards.* | *The computer system has certainly come up to expectations – it's great!*

live up to /ˌlɪv ˈʌp tuː/ [phr v T] to be as good as people expect – use this especially about people and their achievements, performances etc: *It was impossible to live up to my parents' expectations of me.* | *He's been under a lot of pressure to live up to his reputation as the world's best player.*

meet /miːt/ [v T] to be good enough according to a standard that has been officially established: *Does* *the tap water meet government health standards? | The building does not meet the essential safety requirements. | Only one system succeeded in meeting the main performance specifications.*

have what it takes /ˌhæv wɒt ɪt ˈteɪks/ [v phrase] to be good enough at something, especially something difficult, to be able to do it successfully: *Do you have what it takes to run this business, or shall I give someone else the chance? | If you have what it takes and can stand the pace of advertising, you can earn a very good salary.*

pass /pɑːs‖pæs/ [v T] to say officially that someone or something has reached the necessary standard: *Each car has to be passed by a team of inspectors before it leaves the factory. | His blood pressure was rather high so the doctor couldn't pass him as fit for the job.*

3 something that stops someone or something from being completely bad

- **saving grace/ redeeming feature**

saving grace/redeeming feature /ˌseɪvɪŋ ˈgreɪs, rɪˌdiːmɪŋ ˈfiːtʃəʳ/ [n phrase] something, often the only thing, that makes someone or something not completely bad: *Her only saving grace is her sense of humour. | None of the characters in her novels have any redeeming features. | The accommodation – dirty and freezing cold – had one redeeming feature. It was cheap.*

4 not good enough

- **not be good enough**
- **unsatisfactory**
- **inadequate**
- **not be up to scratch/not come up to scratch**
- **substandard**
- **not come up to/not live up to**
- **won't do**
- **not cut it**

not be good enough /nɒt biː ˈgʊd ɪˌnʌf/ [v phrase] *I'm afraid I can't translate this letter. My Italian isn't good enough. |* **+ for** *The soil here isn't good enough for arable farming. | I paid $40 for that champagne, but it wasn't good enough for your snobbish friends. |* **+ to do sth** *a good club player, but not good enough to play for his country* — **not well enough** /nɒt ˈwel ɪˌnʌf/ [adv] *She didn't play well enough to be selected for the team.*

unsatisfactory /ʌnˌsætɪ̇sˈfæktəri/ [adj] formal not good enough and likely to cause problems or make people unhappy: *People should not accept unsatisfactory products. They should complain. | It was a most unsatisfactory meeting – not a single decision was made. | Sharing my office with the two secretaries proved an unsatisfactory arrangement.*

inadequate /ɪnˈædɪ̇kwɪ̇t/ [adj] not good enough for a particular purpose or for what someone needs: *The disease spread quickly because of poor living conditions and inadequate health care. |* **hopelessly/woefully inadequate** (=extremely inadequate) *My light clothing was hopelessly inadequate for the cold Japanese winter. | The training that nurses get is woefully inadequate.*

not be up to scratch/not come up to scratch /ˌnɒt biː ʌp tə ˈskrætʃ, ˌnɒt kʌm ʌp tə ˈskrætʃ/ [v phrase] if someone's performance, work, or products **are not up to scratch**, they are not of the standard that is necessary or expected: *I wonder if Sykes is ill. His work hasn't been up to scratch lately. | Schools are being threatened with closure if exam results are not up to scratch. | If they don't come up to scratch, you can do them all again.*

substandard /ˌsʌbˈstændəʳd◂/ [adj] generally considered to be below the necessary standard: *More money should be spent on the improvement of substandard housing. | Most household goods sold here are substandard, but food is plentiful and cheap. | substandard accommodation*

not come up to/not live up to /ˌnɒt kʌm ˈʌp tuː, nɒt lɪv ˈʌp tuː/ [v phrase not in passive] to not achieve the level or quality that someone expects: *The film didn't live up to our expectations. It was too long and the acting was appalling. | Mark found that he simply could not live up to his teachers' high standards. | So far, she has not lived up to the tremendous promise she displayed earlier.*

won't do /ˌwəʊnt ˈduː/ [v phrase] British spoken use this about something that is not good enough for a particular purpose: *I need strong nylon thread. Cotton won't do. | I can't accept this quality of work. It just won't do. | Handwritten notes won't do for our purposes. You'll have to type them.*

not cut it /nɒt ˈkʌt ɪt/ [v phrase] American spoken to not have the ability, strength etc to succeed in a particular job or activity: *Most of the kids who start here are young and haven't worked before. Some just can't cut it.*

government

RELATED WORDS

- when governments use film, newspapers etc to persuade people *see* **persuade (5)**
- get rid of a leader or government *see* **get rid of (2)**
- to stop opposition to a government *see* **stop (21)**
- *see also* **politics, vote, represent, country, public services, protest, strike, power/powerful, official, rebellion/revolution, spy**

1 the people who govern a country

- **government**
- **administration**
- **the authorities**
- **the state**
- **the powers that be**
- **regime**

government /ˈgʌvəmənt, ˈgʌvənmənt‖ˈgʌvərn-/ [n C with singular or plural verb in British English] the people who govern a country, state, or local area, and who make all the important decisions about taxes, laws, relationships with other countries etc: *The government has promised to cut taxes. | Unemployment is a problem that many Western governments continue to face. |* **+ of** *the city government of Los Angeles | The newspaper, La Prensa, was shut down for nearly two years because of its criticism of government policies. |* **the French/Japanese/Russian etc government** *The French government strongly condemned the killings. |* **local/central/federal etc government** (=the government of a town or city, or a country) *The local government has been unable to meet the demand for affordable housing. | It has been difficult for the central government to conduct elections in remote areas.*

administration /ədˌmɪnɪ̇ˈstreɪʃən/ [n C] the government of a country – use this especially to talk about the national government of the United States

the administration *The new administration has been strongly criticized for its handling of the affair.* | *The administration also proposed $600 million in tax breaks for small businesses.* | **the Kennedy/Clinton etc administration** (=the government when this person is president) *The Eisenhower administration refused to take military action in Vietnam.*

the authorities /ði ɔːˈθɒrəˌtiːz‖-əˈθɔːr-/ [n plural] the people or organizations that have the power to decide what people are allowed to do in a country or area: *The country is facing famine, and the authorities are doing little to prevent it.* | **the South African/Mexican/Swiss etc authorities** *The South African authorities arrested Mandela in August 1962.* | **local/federal authorities** (=the authorities in a community, town or city, or in a whole country) *On January 12, the local authorities decided that the strike had gone on long enough.* | *Federal authorities said that no one has claimed responsibility for the bombing as of yet.*

the state /ðə ˈsteɪt/ [n singular] the government, the police, the courts etc, considered as a single group that has the power to control what people do: *At that time, the state controlled nearly every aspect of people's lives.* | *The programs are funded by the state.* | **state-run** (=owned and controlled by the state) *CBC, the state-run broadcasting company*

the powers that be /ðə ˌpaʊəʳz ðət ˈbiː/ [n phrase] informal the people in government responsible for making decisions – use this especially if you think that they have too much power or that they use their power badly: *The powers that be do not seem interested in solving the city's transportation problems.*

regime /reɪˈʒiːm/ [n C] the group of people who are in charge of the government of a country – use this especially about a government you disapprove of because it was not elected to power: *The military regime refused to recognize the elections.* | *The US supported several right-wing regimes in central America.*

2 the most powerful people in a government

- leadership
- executive
- cabinet

▸ *see also* **leader**

leadership /ˈliːdəʳʃɪp/ [n singular with singular or plural verb in British English] the leader of a government and the other people in high positions of power **+ of** *He will challenge Sinclair for the leadership of the Liberal Party.* | *The collapse of European communism in the late 1980s shocked the Chinese leadership.* | **under the leadership of sb/sth** *Under the leadership of the Conservative Party, the gap between the rich and the poor widened considerably.*

cabinet /ˈkæbənət/ [n C with singular or plural verb in British English] the group of important politicians who run the different departments in a government, for example education, health etc, and advise the leader of the government: *The Prime Minister has offered Stroud a position in the cabinet.* | **cabinet minister** (=one of the politicians in the cabinet) *The spy scandal involved two cabinet ministers and several civil servants.* | **cabinet meeting** (=a meeting when the cabinet discusses something) *The cabinet meeting broke up after four-and-a-half hours.*

executive /ɪgˈzekjətɪv/ [n singular] the part of a government that approves decisions and laws and is responsible for making them work **the executive** *In theory, the civil service is the non-political arm of the executive.* | *Power is shared between three main branches of government: the executive, the legislative, and the judiciary.*

3 the people who make the country's laws

- parliament
- Congress
- Senate

parliament /ˈpɑːʳləmənt/ [n C] the group of people who are elected to make a country's laws: *During his 28 years in Parliament, the 59-year-old Chuan has been untainted by corruption.* | *New budget measures were approved Tuesday by the Russian parliament.* | *Elections for the European parliament are set for late next year.*

Senate /ˈsenət/ [n singular] the smaller and more important of the two parts of the parliament of the USA: *Bradley was elected to the Senate in 1978.* | *If approved by the Senate, the bill would make it harder to purchase handguns.*

Congress /ˈkɒŋgres‖ˈkɑːŋ-/ [n U] the group of people elected to make laws in the US, consisting of the Senate and the House of Representatives: *Hirsch doubts Congress will accept the president's proposal.* | *Congress rejected a measure that would make it easier for low-income workers to get health insurance.*

4 a government that controls people's lives too much

- dictatorship
- tyranny
- police state
- totalitarian
- junta
- oppressive

dictatorship /dɪkˈteɪtəʳʃɪp/ [n C] a government in which one person or group has total power and uses it unfairly and cruelly: *In 1971, the country's 10 year military dictatorship came to an end.* | *Ethiopia's dictatorship was toppled by Eritrean and Ethiopian rebels.* | *How do we explain the rise in European dictatorship in the 1930s?*

police state /pəˈliːs ˌsteɪt/ [n C] a country where the police and other people who work for the government have too much power and control people's lives too much: *The country is a police state and the media is controlled by the government.* | *'Do you want a free society or a police state?' Stark asked the crowd of about 2,000 people.* | *The Home Secretary denied that the introduction of identity cards would lead to a police state.*

junta /ˈdʒʌntə, ˈhʊntə/ [n C] a government run by a small group of army officers who have not been elected but have taken power by force: *All the opponents of the junta have been murdered or imprisoned.* | **military junta** *The country was ruled by a military junta from 1974 until 1982.*

tyranny /ˈtɪrəni/ [n C/U] written a situation in which a government, especially an illegal one, rules unfairly and cruelly: *Any political system that refuses to allow people to protest becomes a tyranny.* | *the extraordinary struggle against tyranny in South Africa*

totalitarian /təʊˌtæləˈteəriən/ [adj usually before noun] a **totalitarian** country or system of government is one in which the government controls every part of people's lives and there is no freedom: *A totalitarian state must maintain complete control of the press.* | *The country held its first elections after 40 years of totalitarian rule.* | *The minister called the secret* *police 'a product and a tool of the old totalitarian regime'.*

oppressive /ə'presɪv/ [adj usually before noun] an **oppressive** government treats people in a cruel way, using military force to prevent any opposition: *the oppressive rule of Ceaucescu in Romania | A poor, uneducated people does not have the willpower or knowledge to challenge an oppressive government.*

5 different systems of government

- democracy
- democratic
- republic
- monarchy

democracy /dɪ'mɒkrəsi‖dɪ'mɑː-/ [n U] a system of government in which everyone in the country can vote to choose the government and has the freedom to oppose it, to protest against it etc: *In 1974, democracy returned to Greece after seven years of military rule. | Adolfo Suarez supervised Spain's transition to democracy in the 1970s.* —**democracy** [n C] a country in which the people vote to choose the government: *Costa Rica is a democracy. | the democracies of Western Europe*

democratic /ˌdemə'krætɪk◂/ [adj] a **democratic** country, government, or political system is one in which the people vote to choose the government: *Costa Rica is often mentioned as an example of what countries can accomplish under stable, democratic governments. | The Communist Party was voted out of power in the nation's first democratic elections in decades. | Open, free, and fair elections are the most basic element of the democratic process.*

republic /rɪ'pʌblɪk/ [n C] a country whose leader is a president, not a king or queen: *the French Republic | Moldavia, a republic of more than 4 million people, borders Romania.* | **+ of** *the People's Republic of China*

monarchy /'mɒnəʳki‖'mɑː-/ [n C/U] a system of government in a country that has a king or queen, or the members of a royal family in that country: *Many people in Britain think the country no longer needs a monarchy. | The US has close ties with the Saudi monarchy.* | **absolute monarchy** (=a monarchy with complete power) *At that time, Nepal was transformed from an absolute monarchy into a multi-party democracy.*

6 part of a government that deals with health, education etc

- department

department /dɪ'pɑːʳtmənt/ [n C] one of the separate parts of a government, that is responsible for a particular part of government activity, for example health, education, or defence **the Department of Education/Health/Transport etc** British *Ellison is now head of the Department of Education.* | **the Defense/Justice/Treasury Department** American *At that time, Robert Kennedy was head of the Justice Department.*

7 to govern a country

- govern
- run
- rule
- be in power
- be in government
- hold office

govern /'gʌvəʳn/ [v I/T] if a political party or group **governs** a country, its members make all the important decisions about laws, taxes, relationships with other countries etc: *The former Chancellor questioned the Prime Minister's ability to govern. | The PRI party has governed the country for more than seventy years.* | **governing party** (=the political party that is governing a country) *The governing party controls two-thirds of the parliament.*

run /rʌn/ [v T] to control a country – use this also about a powerful person or group that controls a country but has not been elected: *Who's running this country, the government or the trade unions? | The revolutionary council ran the country until democratic elections were held. | The country is being run by an interim prime minister, Jean-Claude Cousin.*

rule /ruːl/ [v T] if a king, queen, military leader, or a foreign government **rules** a country, they have official power over it: *Marcos ruled the Philippines for 20 years. | India was ruled by the British for a very long time.* —**rule** [n U] when a country is ruled by a king or queen, a military leader or a foreign government: *For many years Algeria was under French rule.*

be in power /biː ɪn 'paʊəʳ/ [v phrase] if a political party or a leader **is in power** at a particular time, they are the government or leader of a country at that time: *Castro has been in power for more than 30 years. | Taxes were higher when the Democrats were in power.*

be in government /biː ɪn 'gʌvəmənt‖-vərn-/ [v phrase] especially British if a political party **is in government**, it has been elected to govern the country: *The Liberal Democrats have been in government for five years now. | He thought it unlikely that the Republican party would be in government for much longer.*

hold office /ˌhəʊld 'ɒfɪs‖-'ɔːf-/ [v phrase] to have an important job in a government, for example as its leader or as head of a government department: *Jemison had previously held office as Minister of Education. | In Mexico, the president holds office for a fixed term of six years. | People convicted of certain criminal offenses are not allowed to hold office.*

8 the way a country is governed

- government

government /'gʌvəmənt, 'gʌvənmənt‖'gʌvərn-/ [n U] the way a country is governed: *Having a popular leader does not guarantee good government. | The current Liberal Party has no actual experience of government. | After years of corrupt government, people are tired of politics.* | **big government** American (=when the government controls many things) *The Republicans were elected by campaigning against big government and high taxes.*

graceful

moving in a smooth and controlled way that is attractive to look at

RELATED WORDS

opposite: **clumsy**

- *see also* **beautiful**

1 graceful

- graceful
- elegant
- lithe
- effortless
- flowing

graceful /ˈgreɪsfəl/ [adj] moving in a smooth, controlled way that is attractive to look at: *Gwyneth Paltrow is wonderful in the film, tall, graceful and elegant.* | *In recent years these graceful birds have been seen again in increasing numbers.* | *He sketched her quickly, with a few graceful strokes of his pen.* —**gracefully** [adv] *As all film stars know, it's almost impossible to get out of a car gracefully.*

elegant /ˈelɪ̆gənt/ [adj] someone who is **elegant** dresses, behaves, and moves in a graceful and attractive way: *He was a tall, elegant man, silver-haired and beautifully dressed.* | *All the dancers looked so elegant as they moved slowly round the room.* | *Her good looks and confident, elegant manner made her the centre of attention.* —**elegantly** [adv] *Simon took out a long cigar and lit it elegantly.*

lithe /laɪð/ [adj usually before noun] written someone who has a **lithe** body is able to bend, stretch, and move easily – use this especially about someone who looks young, thin, and attractive: *I felt awkward among the lithe young sun-tanned girls on the beach.*

effortless /ˈefəʳtləs/ [adj] **effortless** movements or actions are very smooth and controlled, as though they are made without any effort at all, especially because the person who makes them has a lot of skill: *She performed her dive with effortless grace.* | *Mark drew quickly and with confidence, in a way that looked completely effortless.* —**effortlessly** [adv] *The pianist's fingers ran effortlessly over the keys.*

flowing /ˈfləʊɪŋ/ [adj only before noun] **flowing** movements are made gracefully and without interruption: *Steve turned, raised his arm and threw the ball, all in one flowing movement.* | *The cheetah's long flowing strides make it faster than any other animal on earth.*

2 a graceful appearance or way of moving

- grace/gracefulness
- poise
- elegance

grace/gracefulness /greɪs, ˈgreɪsfəlnɪ̆s/ [n U] *Kim had all the grace and charm of a young woman, though she was still only a girl.* | *Rudolph Nureyev's skill and gracefulness made him a legend in his own lifetime.*

elegance /ˈelɪ̆gəns/ [n U] a graceful and attractive manner or appearance: *Francesca was impressed by the beautiful house and the elegance of the guests.*

poise /pɔɪz/ [n U] a calm and very graceful way of moving your body, or of standing or sitting: *Margerie was very beautiful, with the grace and poise of a movie star.* | *They felt that he lacked sufficient poise and confidence for the job.*

grade

RELATED WORDS

- *see also* **test, result, school/university**

1 a letter or number that shows how well a student has done

- grade
- mark
- score
- results
- grade point average/GPA

grade /greɪd/ [n C] a letter that is put on a student's work or on an exam to show how good or bad it is: *I wasn't very happy with the grade on my essay.* | *Class participation is a quarter of your final grade.* | **good/bad grade** *I need a really good grade on the final exam to pass the class.* | **get a grade** *If he gets good enough grades, he'll get a scholarship to Michigan State.*

mark /mɑːʳk/ [n C] especially British the number or letter that is put on a student's work to show how good or bad it is: *His mark on the last test gave him a final average of 88%.* | **get a mark** *'What mark did you get?' 'B.'* | **good/high mark** *She came out with the second highest marks in the class.* | **bad/low/poor mark** *You have to do the course again if you get low marks.* | **get full marks** (=get the highest possible marks) *I got full marks in the history test.*

score /skɔːʳ/ [n C] American a number which shows how well or badly a student has done in an examination, especially an important exam given to a lot of students **high/low score** *Students at King elementary generally have the highest test scores in the city.* | **+ on** *Scores on standardized tests have been steadily falling over the past ten years.*

results /rɪˈzʌlts/ [n plural] British all the marks that a student gets in a set of tests or examinations, that show whether he or she has been successful or not: *The school's 'GCSE' results had been much better the previous year.* | **get good results** *Ceri got better results than she expected.* | **exam results** *David had appaling exam results at school despite his obvious intelligence.*

grade point average/GPA /ˌgreɪd pɔɪnt ˈævərɪdʒ, ˌdʒiː piː ˈeɪ/ [n C usually singular] American the average score that a student earns based on all their grades. Usually an A is 4 points, a B is 3, a C is 2, and a D is 1, and an F is 0: *To be on the honor roll, students must have a GPA of at least 3.5.*

2 to decide how well a student has done

- mark

mark British **/grade** American /mɑːʳk, greɪd/ [v T] to look at students' work or examination papers and give them numbers or letters to show how good they are: *I have 48 English papers to grade this evening.* | *Mrs Parry, have you marked our tests yet?* | *The examiners who marked her A-level paper were very lenient and gave her a pass.* | **mark/grade sb/sth on sth** *The rough draft is graded on content, not on grammar.*

greedy

wanting more food, money, power etc than you need

1 food

- greedy
- pig
- greedy guts
- greed
- glutton
- gluttony

- *see also* **eat, food, meal, delicious**

greedy /ˈgriːdi/ [adj] someone who is **greedy** wants to eat too much food, or eats more than their share of food – use this to show disapproval: *Don't be so greedy! Leave some cake for everyone else.* | *Greedy children often tend to put on too much weight.* | *Take* *your greedy fingers off that pie – you've had more than enough already.* —**greedily** [adv] *He drank greedily, taking huge gulps from the bottle.*

pig /pɪg/ [n C] spoken informal someone who is greedy: *You pig, you've eaten it all!* | **greedy pig** *The greedy pig! He didn't leave any pizza for us.* | **make a pig of yourself** (=eat a lot of food greedily) *That's what Christmas is all about, isn't it? Making a pig of yourself.*

greedy guts /ˈgriːdi gʌts/ [n singular] British spoken someone who is very greedy – used especially by children: *Don't be such a greedy guts!* | *Hey, greedy guts, leave those sweets alone. They're mine.*

greed /griːd/ [n U] a strong desire to eat too much food: *You don't really want more ice cream – it's just greed.*

glutton /ˈglʌtn/ [n C] someone who eats too much food: *Uncle Richard was a glutton who ate everything in sight.* | *We had salmon to start, followed by a glutton's dessert of crème brûleé.*

gluttony /ˈglʌtəni/ [n U] formal when someone eats or drinks much more than necessary, usually with the result that they become ill or unhealthy – used especially in literature: *As soon as Christmas is over, people often start to regret their gluttony.* | *The level of heart disease in the western world is a measure of our gluttony.*

2 money, possessions, power etc

- ▸ greedy
- ▸ grasping
- ▸ materialistic
- ▸ greed

▸ *see also* **money, selfish/not selfish, ambitious**

greedy /ˈgriːdi/ [adj] someone who is **greedy** wants more money, possessions, power etc than they need, or wants more than their share: *He was an ambitious man, selfish and greedy.* | *the ridiculously high fees charged by greedy lawyers* | **become/get greedy** *Some landlords have become greedy and are demanding higher rents than people can afford.* | **+ for** *There were ten of us children in the family, and we were all greedy for attention.* —**greedily** [adv] *'How much money are you offering?' she asked greedily.*

grasping /ˈgrɑːspɪŋ‖ˈgræs-/ [adj only before noun] very greedy so that you are not at all generous and treat other people very badly: *He seems like a good guy to me, not at all the usual grasping political type.*

materialistic /məˌtɪəriəˈlɪstɪk◂/ [adj] believing that having a lot of money and possessions is the most important thing in life: *Kids these days are very materialistic. They only seem to be interested in expensive toys and computer games.* | *Western societies are becoming more materialistic as their wealth increases.* —**materialism** /məˈtɪəriəlɪzəm/ [n U] *They disliked the materialism of the West and went to live in Nepal.*

greed /griːd/ [n U] a strong desire for more money, possessions, power etc than you need, or for more than your share: *It's a story of lust, hatred and greed.* | *Greed got him his fancy cars and high-powered boats. And greed caused his downfall.* | **+ for** *The greed for power of local politicians is simply amazing.* | **pure greed** *No one needs to earn salaries as big as that. It's pure greed, that's all it is.*

group

WHAT'S HERE

- **a group of people** see **1 to 9**
- **a group of things** see **10 to 12**
- **to put people or things into groups** see **13**

a group of people

RELATED WORDS

▸ *see also* **crowd, together**

1 a group of people together in one place

- ▸ group
- ▸ crowd
- ▸ cluster
- ▸ knot

group /gruːp/ [n C with singular or plural verb in British English] several people who are together in the same place: *A small group had gathered outside the stage door.* | **+ of** *Outside the school, little groups of friends were talking to each other.* | *an old photograph of a group of soldiers sitting on the ground* | **in groups** (=forming separate groups) *Men stood in groups on street corners.* | **get into groups** (=make groups with other people so that you can do something together) *The teacher told us to get into groups of three.*

crowd /kraʊd/ [n C] a large number of people who are all together in the same place: *A huge crowd gathered to hear Mandela speak.* | *a football crowd* | **+ of** *A crowd of reporters were waiting for her at the airport.* | **crowds of people/tourists/shoppers etc** (=a lot of people in the same place) *I walked down Regent Street with its crowds of tourists and Christmas shoppers.*

cluster /ˈklʌstəʳ/ [n C] a group of people standing or sitting very close to each other, for example in order to see something or talk to someone **+ of** *A cluster of people, all anxious to shake his hand, formed around the speaker.* | *Some relatives were standing in a cluster around her hospital bed.*

knot /nɒt‖nɑːt/ [n C] a small group of people all sitting or standing very close to each other **+ of** *The knot of men at the bar had started talking about the elections.* | *Outside the hotel, a little knot of bystanders had gathered to see what was happening.*

2 a group of people who do things together

- ▸ group
- ▸ party
- ▸ bunch/crowd
- ▸ gang
- ▸ contingent

group /gruːp/ [n C with singular or plural verb in British English] *The tickets are expensive, but there is a discount for school groups.* | **+ of** *A group of us went out for a drink to celebrate Sonia's birthday.* | **in groups** *Robberies were common on the lonely roads, so people usually travelled in groups.* | **in groups of three/four etc** *We were warned not to walk in the mountains except in groups of three or more.*

party /ˈpɑːʳti/ [n C with singular or plural verb in British English] a group of people that someone has organized in order to go somewhere or do something: *A party of Japanese businessmen will be visiting the factory next week.* | **+ of** *John was taking a party of tourists around the museum.* | **a search/rescue party** (=a group of people trying to find and help someone who is in danger) *The climbers did not return, and a search party was sent out to look for them.*

bunch/crowd /bʌntʃ, kraʊd/ [n C usually singular] especially spoken, informal a group of people who do things together or spend time together: *The people on my French course are a really friendly bunch.* | **+ of** *There was the usual crowd of students standing at the bar.* | *Willy's band is playing tonight, and I invited a bunch of people to come along*

gang /gæŋ/ [n C with singular or plural verb in British English] a group of young people who spend time together, especially a group that causes trouble, fights with other groups etc: *Inner-city kids often join gangs for protection, and for the chance to make money by selling drugs.* | **gang of youths/kids** *There are always gangs of kids hanging around the shopping mall.* | **gang member/leader** *It is not just gang members who get into trouble – it's middle-class and upper-class kids as well.* | **rival gang** (=a gang that fights with another gang) *Fighting broke out between two rival gangs.*

contingent /kən'tɪndʒənt/ [n C with singular or plural verb in British English] a group of people representing a particular country, organization, belief etc: *Not surprisingly, there was a large student contingent at the demonstration.* | *There was a large American contingent, including the Olympic bronze medallist, Thomas Jefferson.* | **+ of** *A small contingent of English fans had made the trip to Sydney to support their team.*

3 a group of people who are similar or have similar ideas

- group
- lot
- collection/assortment
- element
- movement
- school
- circle
- batch

group /gru:p/ [n C] a number of people who are similar in some way, or who have the same ideas and aims: *Their policy was to keep demonstrators from different political groups apart.* | **+ of** *The factory was burned down by a group of animal-rights activists.*

lot /lɒt‖lɑ:t/ [n singular] British informal a group of people – use this especially about people that you do not like or do not approve of: *I don't like her new friends – they're a snobbish lot.* | **+ of** *We've got another lot of visitors coming this weekend.* | **that lot** (=use this to show disapproval) spoken *Don't take any notice of that lot, they're just ignorant.*

collection/assortment /kə'lekʃən, ə'sɔ:ʳtmənt/ [n C usually singular] a group of people, especially people who you think are strange or unusual **+ of** *There was an interesting collection of people at the wedding.* | *Jack brought an odd collection of characters home from the racetrack.* | *We shared the train compartment with an odd assortment of fellow travellers.*

element /'eləmənt/ [n C with singular or plural verb in British English] **the criminal/student/fascist etc element** a group of people who have the same ideas, aims, beliefs etc that are different from those of a larger group – use this especially about people you do not like or agree with: *The chief had been warned that there were criminal elements within the Security Police.* | *They seem to be trying to get rid of all left-wing elements in the party.* | *The committee agreed on the need to get rid of the hooligan element amongst football supporters.*

movement /'mu:vmənt/ [n C] a large group of people who share the same ideas and beliefs, and who work together to achieve something important: *She was active in a number of political movements, including the campaign to end slavery.* | **the peace /environmental/women's etc movement** *One of the leaders of the pro-democracy movement has been arrested.* | *The aim of the civil rights movement was to eliminate racial discrimination in all its forms.*

school /sku:l/ [n C] a group of artists, writers etc who share the same ideas, style of work etc: *There is no denying the influence of the Impressionist school in his painting.* | *He seems to be very much part of the Marxist school in his approach to politics.* | **school of thought** (=a group of people who believe in the same theory, idea etc) *One school of thought argues that introducing stiffer penalties would bring the crime rate down.*

circle /'sɜ:ʳkəl/ [n C usually plural] **literary/political/academic etc circles** people who work in or are interested in literature, politics etc: *By 1920 she had written two novels, and had succeeded in winning recognition in literary circles.* | *It was the 1960s, and the military had become unpopular among academic and intellectual circles.*

batch /bætʃ/ [n C] a group of people who are all dealt with together at the same time, for example because they are all starting something together **+ of** *The latest batch of new recruits had just arrived at the camp.*

4 a group of people who work together

- team
- crew
- committee
- board
- panel
- working group/working party
- unit

team /ti:m/ [n C with singular or plural verb in British English] a group of people who work together to do a job: *There will be a meeting for all members of the team next Wednesday.* | *Dr Gaultier and his medical team worked in the refugee camps for over a year.* | **+ of** *The coins were discovered by a team of archaeologists.* | *The Prime Minister works closely with a team of unelected advisers.*

crew /kru:/ [n C with singular or plural verb in British English] the people who work together on a ship or plane: *The captain and crew would like to welcome you on board Flight 381 to Geneva.* | *Everyone aboard the Montreal Queen, including the crew, died.*

committee /kə'mɪti/ [n C with singular or plural verb in British English] a small group of people in an organization who have been chosen to make official decisions: *Bill Dean has been elected chairman of the committee.* | **finance/health/housing etc committee** *The finance committee has decided to raise membership fees for next season.* | **be on a committee** (=be a member of a committee) *She's been on the Church committee for 20 years.*

board /bɔ:ʳd/ [n C with singular or plural verb in British English] a group of people in an organization or company who make rules and decisions about how the organization works, give permission for particular plans to be carried out etc: *The licensing board has refused us permission to sell alcohol on the premises.* | *In October, the school board recom-*

mended that uniforms become compulsory. | **board of examiners/governors/directors etc** *If you don't agree with the result etc, you can appeal to the board of examiners.*

panel /'pænl/ [n C with singular or plural verb in British English] a group of people who have been chosen to give advice or their opinion or to make an official decision about something, usually because they know a lot about it: *I've been invited to join the panel on a radio arts programme.* | **+ of** *All applicants are questioned by a panel of experienced interviewers.* | *He was on a panel of judges for a famous literary prize.*

working group /working party British /'wɜːʳkɪŋ ˌgruːp, 'wɜːʳkɪŋ ˌpɑːʳti/ [n C with singular or plural verb in British English] a group of people chosen to consider a particular problem in detail and to suggest how to deal with it: *A Police Force working party concluded that many people found the police intimidating.* | *A working party was set up to investigate and act on the report's findings.*

unit /'juːnɪ̇t/ [n C with singular or plural verb in British English] an official group that has been formed to work together to do a particular job or be responsible for a particular problem: *Hospital officials plan to use the donations to set up a new cardiac unit.* | *One of the policemen from the drug unit will be visiting local schools.*

5 a group of people who are the same age, have the same income etc

- group
- bracket
- band

group /gruːp/ [n C with singular or plural verb in British English] **age/income/blood etc group** a **group** of people with the same age, income, blood type etc: *The good thing about the class is that all the students belong to the same age group.* | *Families in the lowest income group could not afford to educate their children.* | *The hospital is desperate for donors from the rhesus negative blood group.*

bracket /'brækɪ̇t/ [n C] **tax/income/age etc bracket** people who are considered as a group, especially for official or financial purposes, because they have the same income, are of similar age etc: *Several companies have produced pension plans specifically for people in the higher income tax bracket.*

band /bænd/ [n C] **income/tax/age etc band** a group of people whose income, tax, or age comes within a particular range: *These changes will not affect people in the lowest tax band.* | *As you move into the higher income bands, the charges start to increase.*

6 a small group of people who are unwilling to let other people join them

- clique
- elite
- in-crowd

clique /kliːk/ [n C with singular or plural verb in British English] a small group of people who like the same things and are very friendly with each other but who do not want other people to join them: *Most of the kids were friendly, apart from a clique of girls who came from rich families.* | *a clique of literary friends who thought they were so superior* — **cliquey** [adj] spoken *The tennis club has good facilities, but it's terribly cliquey.*

elite /eɪ'liːt, ɪ-/ [n C with singular or plural verb in British English] a group of people who are the richest, most powerful, best educated etc in society, and who do not want others to share their advantages: *Only a small elite can afford to send their children to this school.* | *All the glamorous Washington elite were at the dinner that evening.* — **elite** [adj] *Anyone who studied at the college joined an elite band of well-connected lawyers, doctors and businessmen.*

in-crowd /'ɪn kraʊd/ [n singular with singular or plural verb in British English] a small group of people who are admired by others because they are very fashionable, or who know things that other people do not, and who it is difficult to become friendly with: *That's the nightclub where all the in-crowd go.* | *He wanted to be accepted, to be part of the in-crowd.* | *Within the political in-crowd are some extremely influential figures.*

7 a small group within a larger political or religious organization

- faction
- fringe
- splinter group

faction /'fækʃən/ [n C with singular or plural verb in British English] a group of people within a larger political or religious organization who have different aims from many of the other people within it: *The pro-war faction within the party condemned any attempt at negotiation.* | *The whole of the country has been taken over and destroyed by warring factions.*

fringe /frɪndʒ/ [n singular with singular or plural verb in British English] a group of people in a political or religious organization who have ideas that most people in the organization do not agree with or think are extreme: *The terrorist fringe condemned the decision and threatened to use force.* | *Crusading journalist William Lloyd Garrison represented the radical fringe.* | **lunatic fringe** (=people with very extreme, stupid ideas) *a lunatic fringe of cranks and reactionaries, who probably still believe that the earth is flat*

splinter group /'splɪntəʳ ˌgruːp/ [n C with singular or plural verb in British English] a small group of people who leave a larger political or religious group to form their own smaller group, because they do not agree with the larger group's beliefs, aims, methods etc: *They broke away and formed a splinter group that believed in revolution, not gradual change.* | *The splinter group rapidly gained support from discontented members.*

8 a group of people who have been chosen to give information, answer questions etc

- sample
- focus group

sample /'sɑːmpəl‖'sæm-/ [n C] *56% of the women in the sample said that they supported the government's policies.* | **random sample** (=one that is chosen completely by chance, not according to a plan) *These responses were drawn from a random sample of the electorate.* | **representative sample** (=one that is designed to contain a balance of different types of people) *She based her analysis on data from a representative sample of women and men aged 18-25.*

focus group /'fəʊkəs ˌgruːp/ [n C] a small group of ordinary people who are chosen to give their opinions about a particular product or idea, in order to help the organization that supplies it to know what the public wants or thinks: *We use focus groups, surveys, and questionnaires to try to gauge our customers' needs.* | *Focus groups revealed that teenagers who had higher self-confidence were more likely to use contraception.*

9 when people come together to form a group

- form a group/get into a group
- group
- assemble
- huddle
- cluster

form a group/get into a group /ˌfɔːʳm ə ˈgruːp, ˌget ɪntʊ ə ˈgruːp/ [v phrase] to stand or sit close together in order to make a group so that you can do something together: *We formed groups, and discussed the text together.* | *Several people formed a group round the speaker.* | **form/get into groups of three/four etc** *Get into groups of three for this exercise.*

group /gruːp/ [v I] to stand or sit close together so that you form a group **+ around/behind/outside etc** *Students grouped around the notice board to read their exam results.* | **group together** *Julia sat down at the piano, and the others grouped together to sing.*

assemble /əˈsembəl/ [v I] if a group of people **assemble**, they come together in one place, especially to talk about something or to plan something together: *I looked down onto the square, where a large crowd had assembled.* | **+ opposite/outside/in front of etc** *A large crowd had assembled opposite the American embassy.* | *A group of angry parents had assembled outside the head teacher's office.*

huddle /ˈhʌdl/ [v I] to form a group by moving very close to each other, especially in order to keep warm, feel safer etc: *A group of beggars were huddling in the shop entrance to keep dry.* | **huddle together** *The room didn't have any heating, and we had to huddle together for warmth.*

cluster /ˈklʌstəʳ/ [v I] to form a small group by moving very close to each other in order to look at something, talk to someone etc: *Children had clustered outside the shop window to look at the toys on display.* | **cluster together** *The nurses were clustered together in the corridor, giggling about something.*

a group of things

RELATED WORDS

see also **type, collect**

10 a number of things thought of as a group

- group
- set
- collection
- lot
- assortment
- cluster
- batch

group /gruːp/ [n C with singular or plural verb in British English] a number of separate things that are thought of as a **group** because they are close together or are all similar in some way **+ of** *The house was hidden behind a tall group of trees.* | *News International is a group of companies that produce newspapers and TV programmes.* | *A group of new houses is to be built on the old playing-field.* | *Today you will learn a new group of verbs.*

set /set/ [n C with singular or plural verb in British English] a group of similar things that are used together, or a group of ideas, facts etc: *a chess set* | *a cutlery set* | **+ of** *Amy bought him a set of tools for metal and woodworking.* | *I gave a spare set of house keys to my neighbours.* | *The first set of questions wasn't too bad, but they got really difficult after that.* | *We started the meeting by agreeing on a set of objectives.*

collection /kəˈlekʃən/ [n C] a group of similar things that have been put together because they are interesting or attractive **+ of** *a collection of ancient Greek coins* | *The museum has a superb collection of Mexican pottery.* | **art/stamp/postcard etc collection** *Have you seen her CD collection – it's enormous!*

lot /lɒt‖lɑːt/ [n singular] British informal a group of things **this lot/that lot** *She handed me a bag of old clothes. 'Could you take this lot to the charity shop for me?'* | *Right lads, let's pick up this lot and go home.* | *Bring that lot over here, will you?*

assortment /əˈsɔːʳtmənt/ [n C usually singular] a group of things of different types, or different things of one type, mixed together **+ of** *On the floor was an assortment of boxes and packages.* | *The soldier received a parcel containing an assortment of shirts, biscuits, and canned food.*

cluster /ˈklʌstəʳ/ [n C] a small group of things of the same type that are close to each other **+ of** *From the airplane we could already see little clusters of houses.* | *It's an attractive shrub with dark shiny leaves, that has clusters of white flowers in early June.* | *The adult female lays large clusters of eggs.* | **in clusters** *Most galaxies are found in clusters rather than in isolation.*

batch /bætʃ/ [n C] a group of things of the same type that are made or dealt with at the same time: *Sort the files into batches and give one batch to each secretary.* | **+ of** *The baker took a batch of freshly baked rolls out of the oven.* | *Mr Green, I have a batch of letters here for you to sign.*

11 a group of things that are tied together or fastened together

- bundle
- bunch
- wad
- sheaf

bundle /ˈbʌndl/ [n C] several things of the same type, for example papers, clothes, or sticks, that are fastened or tied together: *She keeps all his old letters, tied up in bundles.* | **+ of** *a bundle of twigs* | *He put his hand in his pocket, and pulled out a large bundle of £50 notes.*

bunch /bʌntʃ/ [n C] **bunch of flowers/keys/grapes etc** a group of flowers, keys etc fastened, tied, or held together: *He handed her a huge bunch of roses.* | *Has anyone seen a bunch of keys?* | *I bought a kilo of apples and a bunch of grapes.*

wad /wɒd‖wɑːd/ [n C] a number of sheets of paper, especially paper money, that are held or tied together **+ of** *I saw him trying to press a wad of cash into the woman's hand. She wouldn't take it.* | *She opened her handbag, and pulled out a wad of banknotes.*

sheaf /ʃiːf/ [n C] **sheaf of papers/notes etc** a lot of pieces of paper held or fastened together in a flat pile: *He had a sheaf of papers under his arm.* | *I saw her put a sheaf of notes into her briefcase.*

12 a group of things on top of each other

- pile
- heap
- stack
- mound

pile /paɪl/ [n C] several things of the same kind

placed one on top of the other: *Put those letters on the other pile.* | *Can you separate those out into two piles – A to L and M to Z, please?* | **+ of** *Greg carried the pile of ironed shirts upstairs.* | *Her office is a terrible mess – there are piles of papers all over the floor.* | *a pile of dirty dishes* | **in piles** *The books were arranged in neat piles on her desk.*

heap /hiːp/ [n C] a lot of things lying one on top of the other in an untidy way **+ of** *There was a huge heap of blankets and pillows on the bed.* | **in a heap** *The kids left all their wet towels in a heap on the bathroom floor.*

stack /stæk/ [n C] a large number of things put neatly on top of each other: *The whole stack fell over, and half the plates got broken.* | **+ of** *Next to the bottles was a tall stack of plastic cups.* | *a stack of sales brochures*

mound /maʊnd/ [n C] a large pile of something **+ of** *The Grand Hotel was now just a mound of rubble.* | *A mound of leaves is the perfect place for a hedgehog to hibernate.*

to put things or people into groups

RELATED WORDS

- *see also* **type**

13 to put things or people into groups

- sort
- categorize
- classify
- be grouped
- class
- grade

sort /sɔːʳt/ [v T] to arrange a large number of things by putting them into groups, so that you can deal with each group separately: *It takes a couple of hours to sort the mail in the morning.* | **sort sth into sth** *We sorted all the clothes into two piles – those to be kept, and those to be given away.* | *The rubbish has to be sorted into things that can be recycled and things that can't* | **sort sth according to sth** *The eggs are sorted according to size.*

categorize ALSO **categorise** British /ˈkætɪ̵gəraɪz/ [v T] to decide which group something should belong to, when there is a clear system of separate groups: *Communication involves a variety of behaviours which are difficult to categorise.* | **categorize sth according to sth** *The hotels are categorized according to the standard of the rooms and services they offer.* | **+ into** *Words can be categorised into verbs, nouns, adjectives etc.* | *Animals are categorised into three types – carnivores, herbivores and omnivores.* | **categorize sth as sth** (=say which group it is in) *The store categorizes records from Asia and Africa as 'World Music'.*

classify /ˈklæsɪ̵faɪ/ [v T] to decide what group books, plants, animals etc belong to according to an official or scientific system: *Scientists have discovered a new type of butterfly which has not yet been classified.* | **classify sth as** *43 countries are categorized as 'low-income' by the World Bank.* | *Babies walking later than 18 months were classified as slow walkers.* —**classification** /ˌklæsɪ̵fɪ̵ˈkeɪʃən/ [n U] *There is no common European standard for the classification of hotels.*

be grouped /biː ˈɡruːpt/ [v phrase] if people or things **are grouped**, they have been put into separate groups according to a system **+ according to** *The vehicles are grouped according to engine size.* | **+ together** *Non-fiction books are grouped together under different subjects.* | **+ into** *Most European languages can be grouped into two main families.* | **group sth into types/categories/classes etc** *The respondents were grouped into three categories – non-smokers, smokers, and ex-smokers.*

class /klɑːs‖klæs/ [v T] to say that people or things belong to a particular group, especially according to an official system **class sb/sth as sth** *This prison houses the most dangerous criminals in Britain, those classed as 'category A'.* | *Heroin and cocaine are classed as hard drugs.*

grade /ɡreɪd/ [v T] to separate things such as food, drinks, or products into groups according to their quality: *All the fruit is taken to the warehouse where it is graded and packed.* | *One supermarket now grades its wines on a scale of 1 to 9, from driest to sweetest.*

grow

RELATED WORDS

- to become larger in number, amount, cost etc *see* **increase**
- to change over a period of time and become bigger, stronger, better etc *see* **develop**
- *see also* **big, change/not change**

1 when people, animals, or plants get bigger

- grow
- develop
- get taller/bigger
- shoot up
- come up
- increase in size
- mature

grow /ɡrəʊ/ [v I] to become bigger and more developed over a period of time: *Tom has really grown since I last saw him.* | *The fish are kept in tanks until they have grown enough to be released into the river.* | **grow one metre/two centimetres/six inches etc** *Amy grew 6 inches last year.* | **+ into** *Within a few years, these saplings will grow into tall trees.* | **grow to ten inches/two metres/70 feet etc** *The Eastern White Pine often grows to 200 feet.* | **grow to a height/length/width etc of** *Sunflowers can grow to a height of ten feet.* —**growth** [n U] *A healthy diet is necessary for a child's normal growth.*

develop /dɪˈveləp/ [v I] if a child, plant, or animal **develops**, it gradually changes into the form it will have as an adult: *The baby develops very quickly during the first few weeks of pregnancy.* | **+ into** *In less that 12 weeks the chicks will develop into adult birds.* —**development** [n U] *All the children are weighed and measured regularly to check their development.*

get taller/bigger /ˌɡet ˈtɔːləʳ, ˈbɪɡəʳ/ [v phrase] to grow and become taller, especially in a short period of time: *Eleanor's getting bigger, isn't she? I hardly recognised her.* | **get bigger and bigger/taller and taller** *The grass got taller and taller over the summer.*

shoot up /ˌʃuːt ˈʌp/ [phr v I] to suddenly get a lot bigger – use this about children and plants that have grown quickly: *Jo's shot up since I last saw her.* | *In May the plants all start to shoot up.*

come up /ˌkʌm ˈʌp/ [phr v I] if plants **come up**, they start growing above the soil, especially in the spring: *I sowed lots of poppies, but they haven't come up yet.* | *The weeds keep coming up year after year.*

increase in size /ɪnˌkriːs ɪn ˈsaɪz/ [v phrase] if something **increases in size**, it gets bigger, especially as a result of particular conditions: *As the plant grows, the roots also increase in size.* | *If the tumour is not removed, it will increase in size and may cause a blockage.*

mature /məˈtʃʊəʳ/ [v I] if a plant **matures**, it grows to its full size: *A tree takes many years to mature.* | *In the hot weather the fruit matured quickly.*

2 someone or something that has finished growing

▸ fully grown ▸ mature
▸ adult

fully grown /ˌfʊli ˈgrəʊn◂/ [adj] a **fully-grown** person, animal, or plant has reached the size that it will stay at: *A fully grown elephant can weigh several tons.* | *Jim was six foot at the age of fourteen, even before he was fully grown.* | *The shrubs were transplanted fully grown from other parts of the country.*

adult /ˈædʌlt, əˈdʌlt/ [adj only before noun] **adult animal/insect/female etc** an animal that has developed fully and finished growing – use this especially in scientific contexts when you are comparing older and younger animals: *The disease can be very serious in adult animals.* | *It was thought that the skull was too small and light to belong to an adult male.* | *Soon the skin of the pupa splits open, and the fully-formed adult butterfly emerges.*

mature /məˈtʃʊəʳ/ [adj] a plant or animal that is **mature** has finished growing and developing: *The house has a lovely garden surrounded by mature oak trees.* | *A hen is a mature female chicken, more than ten months old.*

3 to make plants grow

▸ grow ▸ raise
▸ cultivate ▸ have green fingers

grow /grəʊ/ [v T] to plant and look after plants so that they develop and grow: *Farmers in this area grow mainly wheat.* | *It's very satisfying growing your own vegetables.* | *Wild flowers are quick and easy to grow from seed.*

cultivate /ˈkʌltɪveɪt/ [v T] to grow vegetables and other crops, especially in order to sell them: *Nearer the coast, huge areas of land are given over to cultivating tomatoes.* | *Gradually it was found more profitable to cultivate vines and olives rather than grain.* | **cultivate the land** (=use the land to grow crops) *Population growth is causing people to clear more woodland so that they can cultivate the land.* —**cultivation** /ˌkʌltɪˈveɪʃən/ [n U] **+ of** *In the mountains, the higher rainfall allows for the cultivation of some cereals.* —**cultivated** [adj] *Wild strawberries are smaller than the cultivated variety.*

raise /reɪz/ [v T] to grow plants, especially in large amounts to be used as food: *Last year we raised a good crop of onions.* | *Tomato plants can be raised from seed in a heated greenhouse.*

have green fingers British /**have a green thumb** American /hæv ˌgriːn ˈfɪŋgəʳz, hæv ə ˌgriːn ˈθʌm/ [v phrase] to be good at making plants grow: *He had green fingers, my grandfather. He could grow anything.* | *The flower show season is upon us, and whether you have a green thumb or not, you should take a look at your garden.*

4 to put seeds or young plants into the ground

▸ plant ▸ sow

plant /plɑːnt‖plænt/ [v T] to put seeds or plants into the soil so that they will grow: *Before you plant the seeds, prepare the soil carefully.* | *They planted an oak tree in the middle of the field.* | *Towards the end of March, the potatoes can be planted outside in the ground.*

sow /səʊ/ [v I/T] to plant seeds in the soil, especially in a planned way and at the best time of year for them to grow well: *If you want an early crop, you should sow in September.* | *Sow the seeds in rows about 20 centimetres apart.* | *The ground was still too waterlogged for sowing rice.*

5 the amount of something that is grown in one season

▸ crop ▸ harvest

crop /krɒp‖krɑːp/ [n C] the amount of wheat, rice, fruit etc that is produced in one season: *The rain was so bad this year that he lost the whole crop of barley.* | *With high-yield varieties of rice the farmers can grow two or three crops a year.* | **potato/cereal/rice etc crop** *Indian farmers have doubled their output of cereal crops like wheat.* | **crop failure** (=when the crop does not grow or is destroyed) *The famine was caused by drought, which led to widespread crop failure.* | **record/bumper crop** (=an unusually large crop) *Thanks to the lovely weather we had a bumper crop of peaches and nectarines this year.*

harvest /ˈhɑːʳvɪst/ [n C] the crops that are ready to be gathered or that have been gathered at a particular time of the year: *The harvest is usually ready in July or August.* | **a good/bad etc harvest** (=when you get a lot of crops or not many) *The heavy frosts had ended hopes of a good harvest that year.* | **olive/grain/grape etc harvest** *This year's olive harvest was the best since the war.* | **a bumper harvest** (=an unusually large harvest) *As a result of several bumper harvests, the country now has a grain surplus.* | **get the harvest in** (=gather the crops) *Even the youngest children would come and help to get the harvest in.*

6 land where the soil is good for growing plants

▸ fertile ▸ rich

fertile /ˈfɜːʳtaɪl‖-tl/ [adj] land or soil that is **fertile** is good for growing plants because it contains substances that plants need: *This shrub likes sun and water as well as a fertile well-drained soil.* | *Farmers left the rocky hills of New England for the fertile plains of the Middle West.* | *The valley was fertile, and a good crop was a near certainty.* —**fertility** /fɜːʳˈtɪlɪti/ [n U] *Native American tribes migrated to the region, exploiting the fertility of the soil.*

rich /rɪtʃ/ [adj] soil or land that is **rich** contains a lot of substances that help plants to grow: *Potato plants are easy to grow and do not require rich soil.* | *the rich farmland of the Ukraine* | **+ in** *The soil in this area is rich in nitrogen.*

7 land where the soil is not good for growing plants

- poor
- barren

poor /pʊəʳ / [adj] soil or land that is **poor** does not contain many substances that help plants to grow: *Most herbs grow fairly well in dry, poor soil.* | *The land around here is poor because of years of intensive farming.* | **+ in** *The soil is very poor in minerals and needs some fertilizer.*

barren /ˈbærən/ [adj] land that is **barren** is useless for growing crops on, and is usually dry and empty: *Intense heat had created a completely barren landscape, almost like the moon.* | *the rocky, barren slopes of the mountain*

guess

RELATED WORDS

- *see also* **answer/reply, think, know/not know, sure/not sure**

1 to guess something

- guess
- make a guess
- have a guess
- estimate
- put sth at
- speculate

guess /ges/ [v I/T] to give an answer or decide that something is probably true, when you do not know enough to be definitely sure: *Are you sure Linda's pregnant, or are you just guessing?* | *I'm only guessing, but I should think their house is worth over a million.* | *I didn't know all the answers so I just had to guess some of them.* | **+ who/what/how etc** *Guess who I saw in town yesterday.* | *Guess how much I paid for this watch!* | **+ at** *We can only guess at the cause of the crash.* | **+ (that)** *Sally guessed that he had been drinking for most of the afternoon.* | *Detectives guess the attacker must be aged from 25–30.*

make a guess /ˌmeɪk ə ˈges/ [v phrase] to guess something, especially when you are trying to answer a question or explain how something might have happened: *I've no idea where I lost the keys. I couldn't even make a guess.* | **+ at/about/as to** *It's possible to make a guess at who the woman in the story might be.*

have a guess British **/take a guess** especially American /ˌhæv ə ˈges, ˌteɪk ə ˈges/ [v phrase] to guess an answer, amount, or number – use this especially when you are telling someone to do this: *'How much rent do you pay for your apartment?' 'Take a guess.'* | **+ at** *Have a guess at the answer, then check it with your calculator.*

estimate /ˈestɪmeɪt/ [v T] to say how much something will cost, how many of something there are etc, partly by calculating and partly by guessing **+ (that)** *Police estimate that over 10,000 people took part in the demonstration.* | **estimate sth at $350/£400 etc** *His personal fortune is estimated at £150 million.* | *The mechanic estimated the cost of repairs at $350.* | **+ how much/how many etc** *Can you estimate how much fabric you will need for the curtains?* —**estimated** [adj] *More classrooms are urgently needed, at an estimated cost of $300,000.*

put sth at /ˈpʊt (sth) æt/ [phr v T] **put the cost/the value/sb's age etc at sth** to guess that the cost, value etc is a particular amount without trying to be very exact: *I'd put her age at around 35.* | *The cost of the war was put at more than $10 billion.*

speculate /ˈspekjɡleɪt/ [v I] to think about or discuss something in order to guess what its causes or results might be: *We don't know why the prehistoric stone circles were built. We can only speculate.* | **+ about/on/as to** *Edward began to speculate on what life would be like if he were single again.* | *People have been speculating about interstellar flight for years.*

2 what you say when you guess something

- my guess is
- I bet
- off the top of my head

my guess is /maɪ ˈges ɪz/ spoken say this when you are telling someone what you think has probably happened or will probably happen **+ (that)** *My guess is that they've been delayed in a traffic jam.* | *My guess is she'll move back to the States after the divorce.*

I bet /aɪ ˈbet/ spoken say this when you are fairly sure that something is true or something is happening, although you cannot prove this: *He'll be really pleased to see you, I bet!* | **+ (that)** *Come and sit down, I bet you're exhausted.* | *I bet that the meeting will be cancelled again.*

off the top of my head /ɒf ðə ˌtɒp əv maɪ ˈhed‖-ˌtɑːp-/ spoken say this when you are guessing a number or amount and you have not checked it exactly: *Off the top of my head, I think that the figure is about 25%.* | *'What's the painting worth?' 'Three million or so,' he said, off the top of his head.*

3 to guess correctly

- guess
- you're getting warm

guess /ges/ [v I/T not in progressive] to **guess** correctly that something is true, or **guess** the right answer to something: *'Are you Dan's brother?' 'Yes, how did you guess?'* | *Luckily, I guessed the right answer and won the prize!* | **+ what/who/where etc** *Guy looked at her face, and guessed what she was thinking.* | **+ (that)** *From their behaviour it was easy to guess that they were married.* | **guess the truth** *They had already guessed the truth about their son's disappearance.* | **guess right** *Which hand have I got the chocolate in? If you guess right you can have it.*

you're getting warm /jɔːʳ ˌgetɪŋ ˈwɔːʳm/ spoken say this when someone's guess about something is nearly correct: *'Where are you going? Egypt, Morocco?' 'You're getting warm!'*

4 to guess incorrectly

- guess wrong
- overestimate
- underestimate
- be wide of the mark

guess wrong /ˌges ˈrɒŋ‖-ˈrɔːŋ/ [v phrase] to guess incorrectly: *I guessed she was over sixteen, but I guessed wrong.*

overestimate /ˌəʊvərˈestɪmeɪt/ [v T] to guess wrongly, by thinking that the amount, level, or cost of something is bigger, more expensive etc than it really is: *People overestimated the risk of catching the disease.* | **+ how much/how long etc** *We overestimated how long the journey would take, and arrived far too early.* —**overestimate** /ˌəʊvərˈestɪmɪt/ [n singular] *We thought the job would cost $5000, but this was an overestimate.*

underestimate /ˌʌndərˈestɪmeɪt/ [v T] to guess wrongly, by thinking that the amount, level, or cost of something is smaller, less expensive etc than it really is: *They underestimated the amount of time it would take to finish the work.* | **+ how much/ how long etc** *You must never underestimate how much I love you.* | **how difficult/ how important etc** *Don't underestimate how good the other team is, or how hard they're going to play.* | **badly/greatly underestimate** *They had badly underestimated how many lifeboats would be needed.* —**underestimate** /ˌʌndərˈestɪmɪt/ [n singular] *There could be 50 people at the wedding, but this is probably an underestimate.*

be wide of the mark /biː ˌwaɪd əv ðə ˈmɑːʳk/ [v phrase] to guess incorrectly – use this when someone is not at all close to being correct: *The movie was expected to gross millions, but that forecast was wide of the mark.* | **be seriously/hopelessly wide of the mark** *All the opinion polls turned out to be hopelessly wide of the mark.*

5 an attempt to guess something

- guess
- estimate
- guesswork
- speculation
- speculative
- conjecture

guess /ges/ [n C] an attempt to **guess** something: *This is only a guess, but I think Barbara might have gone to Jan's house.* | *I didn't really know the answer. It was just a lucky guess.* | **make a guess** *I'm not sure why she left him, but I think I can make a guess.* | **good guess** spoken (=say this when someone's guess is almost correct) *'When was the house built – about 1600?' 'That's a good guess – it was 1624.'* | **I'll give you two/three guesses** spoken (=say this when you think the other person already knows the answer to the question) *'Who's her new boyfriend then?' 'I'll give you three guesses!'* | **an educated guess** *'Did Cindy tell you that she's sold the business?' 'No, it was just an educated guess.'*

estimate /ˈestɪmɪt/ [n C] an opinion about the value, size, speed etc of something that is formed partly by calculating and partly by guessing: *According to some estimates, almost two thirds of the city has been destroyed by the earthquake.* | **rough estimate** (=an estimate that is not intended to be exact) *These are the figures, but they're only a rough estimate.* | **at/as a rough estimate** (=making a rough estimate) *At a rough estimate, staff are recycling less than a quarter of the paper we buy.* | **a conservative estimate** (=an estimate that is deliberately low) *We're predicting a 10% rise in oil prices – and that's a conservative estimate.*

guesswork /ˈgeswɜːʳk/ [n U] when you try to understand something or find the answer to something by guessing, because you do not have all the information you need: *It's important to find out what consumers want to buy, rather than relying on guesswork.* | *At the beginning, the police investigation was largely based on guesswork.* | **it was pure/sheer guesswork** spoken (=use this to say that you found out something by guessing) *'How did you know where she'd gone?' 'It was pure guesswork.'*

speculation /ˌspekjʊˈleɪʃən/ [n C/U] when a lot of people, especially in newspapers and on television, try to guess what is happening or what will happen because they do not have much definite information **+ about** *There has been a lot of speculation about the date of the next election.* | *The success of the book was heightened by media speculation about who the characters were in real life.* | **+ that** *A further defeat for the government led to increasing speculation that the Prime Minister would resign.* | **amid speculation (that)** *The investigation into the crash continued amid speculation that terrorists had destroyed the plane.* | **wild speculation** (=guesses that are not sensible) *the wild speculation that surrounded Princess Diana's death* | **pure speculation** (=guesses that are not sensible based only on guessing, and not on informaion) *Any suggestion of an imminent crash in property prices is pure speculation.*

speculative /ˈspekjʊlətɪv‖-leɪtɪv/ [adj] an opinion, explanation etc that is **speculative** is based on guessing and not on facts: *Theories of the origin of life are partly speculative.* | **highly speculative** (=based almost completely on guessing and probably not correct) *Until further research has been done, any figures that I can give you are highly speculative.* | **entirely/purely speculative** (=based completely on guessing) *The papers were full of talk of Lucan's whereabouts, all of it entirely speculative.*

conjecture /kənˈdʒektʃəʳ/ [n U] formal guesses that are based on information that is not complete **a matter for/of conjecture** (=something that people can try to guess but cannot know) *It's a matter for conjecture who wrote the original text in the fifteenth century.* | **pure conjecture** (=based only on guessing, and not on facts) *The judge dismissed the evidence as pure conjecture.*

6 a guess that is based on very little information

- rough guess
- hunch
- wild guess
- a shot in the dark

rough guess /ˌrʌf ˈges/ [n C usually singular] the answer you give when you are trying to guess a number or amount but are not able to be exact: *I'd say Mrs Roberts was about 35, but that's only a rough guess.* | **make/take/have a rough guess** *It's terribly difficult to calculate, but I could make a rough guess and say the cost will be about half a million.* | **at a rough guess** *'How long will the journey take?' 'At a rough guess, about six hours.'*

hunch /hʌntʃ/ [n C] a strange feeling that you know the answer to something, even though you have very little information to help you to guess: *It's just a hunch, but it's possible the murderer may have been a woman.* | **+ that** *My hunch that he was lying turned out to be correct.* | **have a hunch** *I have a hunch that Jodie may be planning a surprise party.* | **+ about** *'How did you know the answer?' 'I just had a hunch about it.'*

wild guess /ˌwaɪld ˈges/ [n C] a guess, especially an answer, that seems stupid or is very likely to be wrong: *This is a wild guess, but is the answer Michael Jackson?*

a shot in the dark /ə ˌʃɒt ɪn ðə ˈdɑːʳk‖-ˌʃɑːt-/ [n phrase] a guess that you make when you have no information at all, so that it is almost certainly wrong: *Let's see if she's at Fiona's house. It's a shot in the dark, but we've got to start looking somewhere.*

guilty

WHAT'S HERE

- **guilty of doing sth bad** see **1 to 5**
- **to feel guilty** see **6 to 9**

guilty of doing sth bad

opposite —— **innocent**
see also **crime, court/trial, blame, accuse, fault**

1 guilty

- guilty
- responsible
- culpable

guilty /ˈgɪlti/ [adj] if someone is **guilty** of a crime, he or she is the person that did it: *The guilty were each given a life sentence.* | **find sb guilty** (=decide in a law court that someone is guilty) *The jury found Sewell guilty and he was sent to prison.* | **guilty of murder/rape/a crime etc** *A 23-year-old woman was found guilty of murder in the Central Court today.* | **+ of doing sth** *Davis was found guilty of abducting and killing Polly Klaas.* | **plead guilty** (=say in a law court that you are guilty of a crime) *Roberts pleaded guilty to driving without insurance.*

responsible /rɪˈspɒnsə̇bəl‖rɪˈspɑːn-/ [adj not before noun] if someone is **responsible** for a crime, accident, or mistake, they did it or made it happen: *The other driver was responsible for the accident, and he should pay for the damage.* | **+ for** *Police believe a local gang is responsible for the recent burglaries.* | *Mrs Williams says that the hospital was responsible for her husband's death.*

culpable /ˈkʌlpəbəl/ [adj] guilty of causing something bad to happen, especially because you did not do anything to prevent it – used especially in formal or legal contexts: *If people develop smoking-related diseases, are they or the tobacco companies culpable?* | *Lawyers are debating whether allowing a terminally ill patient to die amounts to culpable homicide* (=a legal decision that someone was criminally guilty of the death).

2 someone who is guilty

- culprit
- guilty party

culprit /ˈkʌlprə̇t/ [n C] someone who has done something wrong, especially a crime **the culprit** *Some money was taken from my desk yesterday. I think I know who the culprit is.* | *The police did everything they could to try and track down the culprit, but he was never caught.*

guilty party /ˌgɪlti ˈpɑːʳti/ [n phrase] formal the person who is considered to be responsible for a crime or for doing something wrong, especially when two people are blaming each other: *We think we know who the guilty party is, but we need your help to find the evidence.* | *It's silly to imagine that one partner in a divorce is completely innocent and that the other is the sole guilty party.*

3 to show that someone is guilty

- implicate
- incriminating
- incriminate

implicate /ˈɪmplə̇keɪt/ [v T] to show or seem to show that someone is involved in something bad or illegal: *She is claiming that the police are deliberately trying to implicate her.* | **implicate sb in sth** *New evidence implicates Mr Stapleton and his wife in the blackmail attempt.* | *The managing director of the bank was implicated in a fraud scandal.*

incriminating /ɪnˈkrɪmə̇neɪtɪŋ/ [adj] use this about documents, tapes, photographs, statements etc that seem to show that someone is guilty of a crime: *The killer left an incriminating trail of footprints across the lawn.* | *Police found incriminating letters in the suspect's home.* | **incriminating evidence** *They tried to dispose of the incriminating evidence by burning all their blood-stained clothes.*

incriminate /ɪnˈkrɪmə̇neɪt/ [v T] to make someone seem guilty of a crime: *Tape recordings of alleged conversations between the two suspects are unlikely to incriminate them.* | *These tapes incriminate a number of well-known politicians.*

4 to deliberately try to make someone seem guilty when they are not

- set up
- frame
- pin sth on
- plant

set up ALSO **fit up/stitch up** British /ˌset ˈʌp, ˌfɪt ˈʌp, ˌstɪtʃ ˈʌp/ [phr v T usually in passive] informal to deliberately make it seem that someone is guilty of a crime that they are not really guilty of **set up sb** *He wasn't guilty of the fraud. He'd been set up by his business rivals.* | **set sb up** *Cahill has always protested his innocence, and insists that someone set him up.*

frame /freɪm/ [v T] to make someone seem guilty of a crime, especially by providing something that seems like proof: *That's not my handwriting and it's not my signature! I've been framed.* | *Healey agreed to defend two young men, who were being framed in a local murder case.* | **+ for** *The accused told the court that the police tried to frame him for assault.*

pin sth on /ˈpɪn (sth) ɒn/ [phr v T] informal to say that someone is guilty of a crime or of doing something wrong, especially when this is not true: *The police pinned the murder on two men who were later proved to be innocent.* | *You're not going to pin it on me! I was a hundred miles away at the time.*

plant /plɑːnt‖plænt/ [v T] to put something such as illegal drugs or stolen goods into someone's house or into their pocket, in order to make it seem that they are guilty of a crime: *The police found the stolen cameras in his flat, but he insisted they had been planted.* | **plant sth on sb** *Someone planted the drugs on her before she left the country.*

5 to officially prove that someone is guilty

- prove sb guilty
- find sb guilty/convict

prove sb guilty /ˌpruːv (sb) ˈgɪlti/ [v phrase] to prove that someone is guilty of a crime: *Think of all the time they've wasted trying to prove me guilty, while the real killer goes free.* | **innocent until proven guilty** (=someone cannot be considered guilty until it is officially proved that they are guilty) *It is a basic principle of US law, that a person is innocent until proven guilty.*

find sb guilty/convict /ˌfaɪnd (sb) ˈgɪlti, kənˈvɪkt/ [v phrase/v T] if a court of law **finds someone guilty** or **convicts** them, they decide that that person is guilty of a crime: *If the jury finds him guilty he will face a maximum sentence of seven years.* | *No one has yet been convicted of any of the terrorist attacks.* | **find sb guilty of sth** *The two men were found guilty of the murder and jailed for life.* | **find sb guilty of doing sth** *He was found guilty of supplying drugs.* | **convict sb of sth** *Have you ever been convicted of a criminal offence?* | **convict sb of doing sth** *All four men were convicted of illegally bringing drugs into the country.*

to feel guilty

RELATED WORDS

▸ *see also* **ashamed, sorry/apologize**

6 to feel guilty

- feel guilty
- be/feel ashamed
- feel bad
- blame yourself
- feel responsible
- have a guilty conscience
- be on sb's conscience

feel guilty /ˌfiːl ˈgɪlti/ [v phrase] to feel worried and unhappy because you have done something wrong or because you have upset someone: *I felt really guilty after spending all that money.* | *Are you feeling guilty because you didn't help her?* | **+ about** *Ed felt guilty about leaving work so early.*

be/feel ashamed /ˌbiː, ˌfiːl əˈʃeɪmd/ [v phrase] to feel very guilty and disappointed with yourself because you have done something wrong or behaved in an unpleasant or embarrassing way: *She felt thoroughly ashamed when she remembered how drunk she'd been.* | **+ of** *I feel ashamed of what I did.* | **be/feel ashamed to do sth** *I'm ashamed to admit it, but I wasn't really sorry when he died.*

feel bad /ˌfiːl ˈbæd/ [v phrase] especially spoken to feel very sorry because you have upset someone or done something that you should not have done: *We had a long talk about it afterwards and I know she felt bad.* | **+ that** *I should have told Helen I was sorry. I feel really bad that I didn't.* | **+ about** *I feel bad about what I said. Things haven't been easy for either of us.* | **feel bad about doing sth** *I feel bad about not going to Debbie's party, but I've just got too much to do.*

blame yourself /ˌbleɪm jɔːʳˈself/ [v phrase] to feel that it was your fault that something bad happened: *You mustn't blame yourself. It was an accident. There was nothing you could have done.* | **+ for** *Assistant coach Rex Hughes blamed himself for the team's poor performance.*

feel responsible /ˌfiːl rɪˈspɒnsəbəl‖-rɪˈspɑːn-/ [v phrase] to feel guilty about something bad that has happened even though you did not cause it, especially when you feel you could have prevented it: *I'm sorry it didn't work out. I feel responsible.* | **+ for** *For a long time afterwards I felt responsible for his death.*

have a guilty conscience /hæv ə ˌgɪlti ˈkɒnʃəns‖-ˈkɑːn-/ [v phrase not in progressive] to feel guilty for a long time and keep thinking about something bad that you have done: *I suppose I did have a guilty conscience for a while, but not any more.* | **+ about** *Why is she being so nice to everyone all of a sudden? She's obviously got a guilty conscience about something.*

be on sb's conscience /biː ɒn (sb's) ˈkɒnʃəns‖-ˈkɑːn-/ [v phrase] if something bad that you have done **is on your conscience**, you cannot stop feeling guilty and thinking about it: *Even if you didn't get caught, the murder would be on your conscience for the rest of your life.* | *In the end Martin told his wife about his affair – he just couldn't live with it on his conscience.*

7 a guilty feeling

- guilt
- shame
- remorse
- conscience

guilt /gɪlt/ [n U] the feeling you have when you have done something that you know is wrong: *Guilt can be a very destructive emotion.* | **feeling of guilt** *People often have feelings of guilt after a divorce.*

shame /ʃeɪm/ [n U] the guilty feeling that you have when you know that you have behaved badly and lost people's respect: *Voting through cuts in benefits to the poorest people is a matter of shame for all of us.* | **+ about** *Too many women are taught to feel guilt or shame about sex.* | **+ at** *As he left the house, Mungo felt a pang of shame at telling Alice a lie.* | **almost die of shame** (=be very ashamed) *The next day I remembered how drunk I'd been, and almost died of shame.* | **bring shame on sb** *Some girls feel that refusing their parents' choice of husband will bring shame on their family.*

remorse /rɪˈmɔːʳs/ [n U] a feeling of being very sorry for something bad that you have done, so that you wish you had not done it: *He admitted killing the man but showed no sign of remorse.* | **+ for** *She was full of remorse for hurting her family.* | **+ at** *Many men are afflicted with guilt and remorse at leaving their wives.* | **twinge/pang of remorse** (=a small feeling of remorse) *The woman sounded so nice, McKee felt a twinge of remorse at what he had done to her family.*

conscience /ˈkɒnʃəns‖ˈkɑːn-/ [n U] a set of feelings that stop you from doing something wrong or that make you feel guilty when you have done something wrong: *Her murderer was a psychopath with a total lack of conscience.* | **twinge/pang of conscience** (=a sudden feeling of guilt) *He was capable of making the most ruthless decisions with no apparent pangs of conscience.*

8 to not feel guilty about something

- not feel guilty
- a clear conscience
- have no qualms
- have/feel no compunction

not feel guilty /nɒt fiːl ˈgɪlti/ [v phrase not usually in progressive] *I made her cry but I don't feel guilty – she deserved it.* | **+ about** *Working mothers shouldn't feel guilty about wanting a career.* | *I don't understand how on earth he can go on lying like that and not feel guilty about it.*

a clear conscience /ə ˌklɪəʳ ˈkɒnʃəns‖-ˈkɑːn-/ [n phrase] if you have **a clear conscience**, you feel that you have not done anything wrong, so that you do not feel guilty about anything you have done **with a clear conscience** *You can face Lionel with a clear conscience – you've done nothing to harm him.* | **have a clear conscience** *Let them say whatever they like. I have a clear conscience.*

have no qualms /ˌhæv nəʊ ˈkwɑːmz/ [v phrase not in progressive] if you **have no qualms** about doing something, you have no worries or doubts about whether what you are doing is right, even though other people may think it is wrong **+ about** *She had no qualms about sending her young children to boarding school.* | *Donald had been stealing stationery from work for years and had no qualms about it at all.*

have/feel no compunction /hæv, fiːl ˌnəʊ kəmˈpʌŋkʃən/ [v phrase not in progressive] formal to not feel guilty about doing something, even though other people may think it is wrong: *I warn you. These people have no compunction whatsoever and cannot be trusted.* | **+ about** *Eliot felt no compunction about living at the expense of his friends.*

9 to stop yourself feeling guilty

- salve your conscience
- clear your conscience

salve your conscience /ˌsælv jɔːʳ ˈkɒnʃəns‖ -ˈkɑːn-/ [v phrase] to try to stop yourself feeling guilty by doing something good or kind: *She felt guilty and tried to salve her conscience by inviting him out for a meal.* | *Don't think you can salve your consciences by giving us money. We won't forgive you that easily.*

clear your conscience /ˌklɪəʳ jɔːʳ ˈkɒnʃəns‖ -ˈkɑːn-/ [v phrase not in progressive] to stop yourself feeling guilty by telling someone about something bad that you have done: *She decided to clear her conscience and confess everything.* | *He knew he might get into trouble if he went to the police but he had to do it to clear his conscience.*

Hh

habit

something that someone does often without thinking about it

RELATED WORDS

- *see also* **usually, often, addicted**

1 something that you do very often without thinking

- habit
- mannerism
- ways

habit /ˈhæbɪ̈t/ [n C] something that you do very often and without thinking about it, because you have done it so many times before: *Peter had some pretty odd habits.* | *Patterns of behaviour develop gradually until they become unconscious habits.* | **bad habit** *Don't start smoking – it's a very bad habit.* | **have a habit of doing sth** *He has a really annoying habit of leaving his clothes all over the floor.* | **become a habit** *If you have one or two drinks each day, it soon becomes a habit.* | **be/get into the habit of doing sth** *You ought to get into the habit of planning your work at the beginning of each week.* | **eating/dating/viewing etc habits** *People need to change their eating habits and include more fruit and vegetables in their diet.*

mannerism /ˈmænərɪzəm/ [n C] a way of speaking, or a small movement of your face or body, that is part of your usual behaviour, and that other people think is strange or funny: *All the kids imitated Mr Pearce's mannerisms.* | *Before you go to an interview, ask yourself whether you have any irritating mannerisms such as saying 'you know' all the time.*

ways /weɪz/ [n plural] someone's **ways** are their habits and their usual behaviour – use this especially when you think someone's usual behaviour is slightly strange: *Rosy had a warm easy-going personality, so she was good at tolerating other people's ways and opinions.* | *It was a small rural community, and its people felt deeply suspicious of foreigners and their strange ways.*

2 when someone does something because it is a habit

- from habit/out of habit
- force of habit
- compulsive

from habit/out of habit /frəm ˈhæbɪ̈t, aʊt əv ˈhæbɪ̈t/ [adv] if you do something **from habit**, you do it just because it is your habit to do it, not because you have deliberately decided to do it: *Some people drink alcohol from habit, as much as from desire.* | *Out of habit he continued to get up at six o'clock, even after he'd retired.*

force of habit /ˌfɔːʳs əv ˈhæbɪ̈t/ [n phrase] if you do something from **force of habit**, you do it because you had often done the same thing in the past and not for any other reason: *'Why did you call her "Miss"? She's "Mrs" now, you know.' 'Sorry, force of habit.'* | **by/from/through/out of force of habit** *Most women apply the same old make-up year after year through force of habit.*

compulsive /kəmˈpʌlsɪv/ [adj] a **compulsive** activity or way of behaving is one that someone cannot stop himself or herself doing repeatedly, especially because they have a mental problem: *Her problem is compulsive over-eating.* | *compulsive hand-washing* | **compulsive liar/eater/gambler etc** *Compulsive shoppers often never even open the goods they buy.*

happen

RELATED WORDS

- when you think something is unlikely to happen *see* **doubt**
- when something happens by chance *see* **chance**
- *see also* **situation, start, finish**

1 to happen

- happen
- take place
- there is
- be
- occur
- come about
- crop up
- come up
- be coming up
- turn up
- arise
- strike

happen /ˈhæpən/ [v I] *The accident happened at two o'clock this afternoon.* | *What's happened? Why are you crying?* | *The strangest thing happened when I was in Singapore.* | *Before I realised what was happening, the man had grabbed my bag and run off with it.* | **anything can/could/might happen** (=used to say that it is uncertain what will happen) *You mustn't go there alone at night. Anything might happen!*

take place /ˌteɪk ˈpleɪs/ [v phrase] to happen – use this about events, performances, ceremonies and other things that have been planned to happen: *The wedding will take place at St Andrew's church.* | *Police are trying to prevent the demonstration from taking place.*

there is /ðeər ɪz/ [v phrase] if **there is** an event, accident, change etc, it happens: *There's a concert at the school next Saturday.* | *There has been a major accident on the Santa Monica Freeway.* | *I'll let you know if there's any change in our plans.*

be /bi, (*strong*) biː/ [v] if a planned event **is** at a particular time or place, it happens or is arranged to happen at that time or place: *Dinner is at eight, so come at about half past seven.* | *Christmas will be on a Saturday next year.* | *Last year's degree ceremony was in the main university building.*

occur /əˈkɜːʳ/ [v I] formal to happen – use this especially about things that have not been planned or that people do not expect: *Major earthquakes like this occur very rarely.* | *The court will have to decide exactly what occurred on the night Mellor died.*

come about /ˌkʌm əˈbaʊt/ [phr v I not in progressive] to happen, especially as a result of earlier events or decisions: *Our problems came about because we ignored the advice of experts.* | *A number of educational reforms have come about as a result of the report.* | **+ through** *The decrease in the number of salmon has come about through commercial overfishing.* | **how did it come about that** *How did it come about that she married an awful man like that?*

crop up /ˌkrɒp ˈʌp‖ˌkrɑːp-/ [phr v I] informal if something such as a problem **crops up**, it happens suddenly and unexpectedly: *A couple of problems cropped up while you were away.* | *If anything crops up, give me a call.* | *You have to learn to deal with difficult situations when they crop up.*

come up /ˌkʌm ˈʌp/ [phr v I] if something, especially a problem or a chance to do something **comes up**, it happens unexpectedly: *He rang to say he would be late home – something had come up at the office.* | *There are job vacancies from time to time. I'll let you know if anything comes up.* | *When the opportunity to go to the States came up, Dora took it at once.*

be coming up /biː ˌkʌmɪŋ ˈʌp/ [v phrase] if a planned event **is coming up**, it will happen soon: *Don't forget you've got exams coming up in a couple of weeks' time.* | *Our 12th annual Folk Festival is coming up again soon.*

turn up /ˌtɜːʳn ˈʌp/ [phr v I not in progressive] if something such as a job or a chance to do something **turns up**, it happens or becomes available, especially through good luck: *Ben's been looking for a job for two months, but nothing good's turned up.* | *I'd almost given up hope of finding a house I liked, and then suddenly this one turned up.*

arise /əˈraɪz/ [v I not usually in progressive] formal if a problem or difficult situation **arises**, it happens and comes to your attention: *It would be best to deal with these issues at once, before a crisis arises.* | **+ over** *Several problems have arisen recently over questions of pay.* | **+ from** (=as a result of something) *The conflict arose from tensions between the different ethnic groups.*

strike /straɪk/ [v I] if something unpleasant **strikes**, it suddenly happens: *It is always devastating when this illness strikes.* | *Most people were fast asleep when the hurricane struck at 4.05 pm.*

2 when what you want or expect happens

- happen
- come true
- be realized
- be fulfilled
- materialize

happen /ˈhæpən/ [v I] *We'd always feared that this might happen.* | *For some time there had been predictions of a major earthquake, and then on April 19, 1906, it happened.* | *I want to make things up with her, but I don't think it's going to happen.*

come true /ˌkʌm ˈtruː/ [v phrase] if your wishes, dreams etc **come true**, what you have wished for or dreamed about actually happens: *Patterson's dream came true when he won the Boston marathon on his first attempt.* | *People say that if you make a wish at the top of the hill, it always comes true.*

be realized ALSO **be realised** British /biː ˈrɪəlaɪzd/ [v phrase] if your expectations, hopes, fears etc **are realized**, what you expected or hoped for actually happens: *At thirty-five her ambition of running her own business was finally realized.* | *My worst fears were realised when I saw what was on the exam paper.*

be fulfilled /biː fʊlˈfɪld/ [v phrase] if a wish or promise **is fulfilled**, what someone wished for or was promised actually happens: *Tom decided to run the farm himself, so that his father's wish might be fulfilled.* | *We knew that the 'democratic elections' were a promise which would not be fulfilled.*

materialize ALSO **materialise** British /məˈtɪəriəlaɪz/ [v I usually in negative sentences] if an event which has been planned, expected, or promised **materializes**, it actually happens: *Even if the salary rise materialises, it won't be worth much.* | *It was rumoured that Apple would be sold to Sun Microsystems, but that deal never materialized.* | **fail to materialize** (=not happen) *The promised recovery failed to materialize and unemployment kept on rising.*

3 ways of saying something happens to someone or something

- happen to
- experience
- undergo
- meet with

happen to /ˈhæpən tuː/ [v phrase not in passive] if something **happens to** someone or something, it happens and has an effect on them, usually a bad effect: *I wonder what's happened to Dave. He should have been here by now.* | *A lot of people don't seem to care about what is happening to the environment.* | **it can happen to anyone** (=use this to emphasize that something is not someone's fault) *The crash wasn't her fault, it could have happened to anyone.* |

experience /ɪkˈspɪəriəns/ [v T] if someone **experiences** something such as a problem, a difficult situation etc, it happens to them: *Many local companies have recently been experiencing financial difficulties.* | **experience difficulties/problems etc with** *They've experienced a lot of problems with their eldest son.* | **experience sth at first hand** (=experience something personally) *It is shocking to think of boys as young as sixteen experiencing at first hand the horrors of war.*

undergo /ˌʌndəʳˈgəʊ/ [v T] if someone or something **undergoes** a change or an unpleasant event, it happens to them or it is done to them: *He has undergone tremendous emotional problems following the breakdown of his marriage.* | *In the last few years the museum has undergone extensive renovation.* | *Part* *of Mrs Galley's right arm was shattered and she underwent a five-hour emergency operation.*

meet with /ˈmiːt wɪð/ [phr v T] to get a particular reaction, especially an unpleasant one, from other people: *The initial plan to sell off part of the company met with intense criticism.* | **meet with sth from sb** *Many working women still meet with prejudice from men.* | *Rebel forces entered the town and met with no resistance from government troops.*

4 to happen with a good or bad result

- turn out
- go
- work out/pan out
- go off

turn out /ˌtɜːʳn ˈaʊt/ [phr v I] to happen so that the final result is good, bad, unexpected etc: *We were worried when only twenty people came to the party but it turned out very well.* | *How did things turn out in the end?* | **turn out to be sth** *I was a bit doubtful at first, but it turned out to be a really good idea.* | **not turn out as planned/expected** *We wanted the baby to be born at home, but it didn't quite turn out as planned.* | **as it turned out** (=used to say that this is what happened in the end) *As it turned out, James was delayed and didn't arrive until three.*

work out/pan out /ˌwɜːʳk ˈaʊt, ˌpæn ˈaʊt/ [phr v I] informal to happen with a particular result, especially a successful or unsuccessful one: *Some election campaigns work out better than others.* | *We had a few problems when Jake first gave up work, but things are panning out very well now.* | *I'm not sure if we'll decide to get married or not – we'll wait and see how things work out.*

go /gəʊ/ [v I] **go well/badly/smoothly etc** if something such as an arranged event or someone's work **goes** well, badly etc, it happens in a way that is successful, unsuccessful etc: *Did the party go well?* | *Things went badly for the company last year. Their profits are down by 50%.* | *How's the job going these days?*

go off /ˌgəʊ ˈɒf/ [phr v I not in progressive] **go off well/successfully/smoothly etc** if an arranged event **goes off** well, successfully etc, it happens and is completed without any problems: *Thanks to the helpful staff at the hotel, the conference went off very well.* | *I'm sure that everything will go off smoothly on the day.* | **go off without a hitch** (=happen without any problems) *Everyone was relieved when the ceremony at the Ambassador's residence went off without a hitch.*

5 ways of saying that something is happening

- be happening
- be on
- be going on
- be in full swing
- be in progress
- be in operation

be happening /biː ˈhæpənɪŋ/ [v phrase] *She looked out of the window to see what was happening.* | *Property prices continue to rise and we still don't understand exactly why it's happening.* | **what's happening?** *The room began to shake and we stared at each other in terror. 'What's happening?' asked Robert.*

be going on /biː ˌgəʊɪŋ ˈɒn/ [v phrase] if something **is going on** it is happening, especially if it makes you feel worried or annoyed: *It was obvious from the way they kept looking at each other that there was something going on.* | **what's going on?** *'What's going on at the town hall?' asked my mother. 'There's a huge crowd of people there.'*

be in progress /biː ɪn ˈprəʊgres‖-ˈprɑː-/ [v phrase] formal if an arranged event, game, or operation **is in progress**, it has started and has not finished yet: *By the time we got to the stadium, the match was already in progress.* | *There must be no noise in the school while examinations are in progress.* | *An emergency relief operation is already in progress in Southern Sudan.*

be on /biː ˈɒn/ [v phrase] to be happening now or to be going to happen: *The summer sales are on next week.* | *People have to learn to economize when there is a war on.* | *The presidential election was on when we arrived in the States.*

be in full swing /biː ɪn ˌfʊl ˈswɪŋ/ [v phrase] if an organized activity or an event such as a party **is in full swing**, it has already been happening for some time and people are taking part in a very active way: *By 10 o'clock the party was in full swing and everyone was dancing.* | *Barcelona was full of visitors, and preparations for the Olympic Games were in full swing.*

be in operation /biː ɪn ˌɒpəˈreɪʃən‖-ˌɑːp-/ [v phrase] if a plan or a system **is in operation**, it is being used and is working: *Over 20 training programmes are in operation, with almost 2000 trainees.*

6 to happen again

- happen again
- repeat performance
- recur
- repeat itself
- repetition/repeat

▸ *see also* **again, repeat**

happen again /ˌhæpən əˈgen/ [v phrase] *She apologized for the incident and promised it wouldn't happen again.* | *I think I've solved the problem with your computer, but let me know if it happens again.*

recur /rɪˈkɜːʳ/ [v I] formal to happen again, once or repeatedly: *Although the treatment for skin cancer is usually successful, the problem can recur later.* | *Some people find that the same dream keeps recurring over a period of many years.* —**recurrence** /rɪˈkʌrəns‖-ˈkɜːr-/ [n C/U] when something happens again: *She reported several recurrences of the same technical fault.*

repetition/repeat /ˌrepəˈtɪʃən, rɪˈpiːt/ [n C] an event or action that is the same as something that happened before **+ of** *Hopefully, the experience will help us to avoid a repetition of our mistakes.* | *A lot of the lesson was just a repetition of what we'd already done.* | *Will next Saturday's game be a repeat of Germany's triumph last season?*

repeat performance /rɪˌpiːt pəʳˈfɔːʳməns/ [n C] something that happens in exactly the same way as it happened before, usually with all the same problems: *The journey to work had taken hours that morning, and I wasn't looking forward to a repeat performance on the way home.* | **+ of** *We must try to make this summer camp a success. We don't want a repeat performance of last year's disaster.*

repeat itself /rɪˈpiːt ɪtself/ [v phrase] use this to say that things happen again in just the same way: *Stricter controls of farming methods are needed, if we want to prevent the disaster from repeating itself.* | **history repeats itself** *The Cambodian people were afraid that history would repeat itself.*

7 something that happens, that is not planned

- event
- thing
- occurrence
- incident
- happening
- phenomenon

event /ɪˈvent/ [n C] something that happens, especially something that is important or interesting: *Meeting Professor Kearney was an event which changed my life.* | *The book discusses the events leading up to the outbreak of World War Two.* | *The evening meal is a time when all the family can get together and discuss the day's events.* | **chain/sequence of events** (=the order in which events happened) *Police are attempting to reconstruct the sequence of events on the night of the killing.* | **the course of events** (=the way that events happened) *Nothing we could have done would have changed the course of events.*

thing /θɪŋ/ [n C] informal something that happens: *So many things have happened since I last saw you.* | **a funny thing happened** *A funny thing happened to me on the way to work this morning.* | **not remember a thing** (=used to emphasize that you do not remember what happened) *When I woke up the next morning, I couldn't remember a thing.*

occurrence /əˈkʌrəns‖əˈkɜː-/ [n C] formal something that happens, use this especially to say whether something happens often or not often **a common/daily/frequent etc occurrence** *Vicious fights and arguments were a daily occurrence in the shipyards.* | *Earthquakes are an unusual occurrence in England but are not totally unknown.*

incident /ˈɪnsɨdənt/ [n C] something that happens, especially something that is unusual or unpleasant or something that is part of a longer series of events: *Apart from the incident in Las Vegas our vacation was completely trouble-free.* | *One violent incident turned into a political and family tragedy.* | **a bomb/shooting/terrorist etc incident** (=used especially in news reports) *Friday's shooting incident in East London led to several arrests.* | **without incident** (=without anything unpleasant happening) *The fans were well behaved, and the game was played without incident.*

happening /ˈhæpənɪŋ/ [n C] something that happens, especially something that is strange or unusual: *The happenings of the last two days had left me feeling dazed.* | *'The X Files' is a fictional television programme about strange, unexplained happenings.*

phenomenon /fɪˈnɒmɨnən‖fɪˈnɑːmɨnɑːn, -nən/ [n C] PLURAL **phenomena** /-nə/ a natural or social process that can be seen or is known to happen, and is often studied: *We now know that our system of planets orbiting the sun is not a unique phenomenon.* | *The cell phone is a relatively recent phenomenon. It's difficult at the moment to assess its effects.* | **+ of** *the increasing phenomenon of the single parent family* | **natural phenomenon** *A thorough understanding of mathematics is sufficient to explain a wide variety of natural phenomena.*

8 something planned that happens

- event
- occasion
- proceedings

▸ *see also* **plan, organize**

event /ɪˈvent/ [n C] something that happens that has been planned and arranged, for example a party, performance, or sports competition: *Joe's party was a splendid event – about 200 people were there.* | **annual event** (=an event that takes place every year) *The town's beer festival is an annual event.* | **social/sporting event** *We have a full programme of social events that take place throughout the year.* | **a golfing/media/diplomatic etc event** *The Ryder Cup is the big golfing event this month.*

occasion /əˈkeɪʒən/ [n C] an important social event, ceremony, or celebration **big/important/special occasion** *She was saving four bottles of their best champagne for a special occasion.* | *Thanksgiving is a really big occasion in the States.* | **celebrate the occasion** *It's our wedding anniversary next month, and we're having a party to celebrate the occasion.* | **quite an occasion** (=a very exciting or important occasion) *It was quite an occasion. All the local dignitaries were there, dressed in their finest clothes.*

proceedings /prəˈsiːdɪŋz/ [n plural] all the things which happen during an official meeting or discussion, especially in a court of law or in parliament: *You can sit along the back wall of the courtroom to watch the proceedings.* | *The chairman usually takes charge of the proceedings and decides who will speak next.*

9 a series of bad things that happen at the same time

- affair
- business
- goings-on
- scenes

affair /əˈfeəʳ/ [n C usually singular] something that happens, especially something unpleasant or shocking, that usually involves several people and several events: *The court case was an awful affair that dragged on for months.* | *The whole world was waiting for the outcome of the Watergate affair.* | *Nick Leeson had to serve a prison term in Singapore for his part in the affair.*

business /ˈbɪznɨs/ [n singular] a set of connected events which you think are unpleasant, shocking, annoying etc: *It was a nasty business. In the end, she killed herself, you know.* | **the whole business (of sth)** *I don't want to argue about this any more – I'm sick of the whole business.* | *The whole business of getting a visa can take a very long time.*

goings-on /ˌgəʊɪŋz ˈɒn / [n plural] informal things that have been happening somewhere, especially ones that surprise, annoy, or amuse you: *I could hardly believe it when he told me about the goings-on in his office.* | *According to Gwen, there had been some very strange goings-on in the upstairs apartment.*

scenes /siːnz/ [n plural] things that are happening at the same time in the same place involving a lot of people, all behaving in an angry, excited etc way: *Angry scenes in Parliament followed the minister's statement.* | *The airport was full of the usual emotional scenes, and people saying 'goodbye'.*

10 when a lot of things happen

- eventful
- action-packed

eventful /ɪˈventfəl/ [adj] a period of time that is **eventful** is one during which a lot of interesting or important things happen: *It has been an eventful week in politics, with the resignations of three Presidential advisers.* | *When Marilyn Monroe died the press was anxious to uncover every aspect of her eventful career.* | **highly eventful** *The General's last two years were to prove highly eventful for him and the country.*

action-packed /ˈækʃən pækt/ [adj usually before noun] **action-packed holiday/trip/film etc** a holiday trip etc during which you do a lot of exciting things or during which a lot of exciting things happen: *We provide action-packed holidays for children including riding, sailing, rock-climbing, and canoeing.* | *another action-packed adventure movie starring Harrison Ford*

happy

RELATED WORDS

- become happy again after a period of problems or unhappiness *see* **recover (4-5)**
- *see also* **enthusiastic/unenthusiastic, enjoy, smile, laugh, satisfied/not satisfied, excited/exciting, confident/not confident**

1 feeling happy

- **happy**
- **cheerful**
- **be in a good mood**
- **content**
- **cheery**

happy /ˈhæpi/ [adj] someone who is **happy** seems relaxed and cheerful, and feels that their life is good, especially because they are in a situation, job, or relationship that they enjoy: *For the first five years of their marriage they were very happy.* | *She seems a lot happier now that she's got a new job.* | **to do sth** *I was very happy to be back home.* | **happy doing sth** *We were quite happy living in Africa.* —**happily** [adv] *The two children were playing happily in the garden.*

cheerful /ˈtʃɪəʳfəl/ [adj] behaving in a way that shows you are happy, for example by smiling, laughing, or being very friendly: *Amelia seemed a little more cheerful today than last week.* | *She greeted us with a cheerful smile.* | *'Fine, thanks,' he replied in a cheerful manner.* —**cheerfully** [adv] *'We're almost there,' Robin said cheerfully.*

be in a good mood /biː ɪn ə ˌgʊd ˈmuːd/ [v phrase] to be happy at this particular time and therefore friendly to other people: *Why are you in such a good mood this morning?* | *I was in quite a good mood till you asked me that.*

content /kənˈtent/ [adj not before noun] satisfied with what you have, so that you are happy enough and do not want anything else: *All he needs is a good book to read and he is quite content.* | **+ with** *Carla seems pretty much content with her life.* | **+ to do sth** *We were perfectly content to go on walking until it got dark.*

cheery /ˈtʃɪəri/ [adj usually before noun] happy – use this when someone's behaviour and the way they talk seems happy: *The woman behind the counter greeted us with a cheery hello.* | *'How wonderful,' he said, but his cheery tone sounded a bit forced.*

2 happy because something good has happened

- **happy**
- **pleased**
- **glad**
- **be tickled**
- **gloat**
- **gleeful**

happy /ˈhæpi/ [adj not before noun] feeling **happy** because something good has happened or is going to happen: *They returned from their vacation feeling happy and relaxed.* | *The children's happy faces were reward enough.* | **+ about** *Is she happy about being pregnant?* | **+ (that)** *Grandma is so happy that everyone will be there for Christmas.* | **+ to see/hear/learn/be etc** *I'm just happy to be home again.* | *They were happy to see Flynn looking so much better.* | **happy for sb** (=happy because something nice has happened to someone else) *I'm so happy for you – I know how much you wanted the job.*

pleased /pliːzd/ [adj not before noun] happy and satisfied that something has happened, especially something that has happened to someone else or something good they have done: *'That was quite a performance,' he said, looking pleased.* | **+ with** *We're all quite pleased with Amanda's progress.* | **+ about** *His parents were very pleased about his award.* | **+ to see/hear/learn/be etc** *You'll be pleased to hear that your application has been accepted.* | **+ (that)** *Laurie was pleased that her daughter decided to go to college.*

glad /glæd/ [adj not before noun] happy about a situation, especially because it has improved or because it is not as bad as it could have been: *We were all glad when it was time to go home.* | **+ (that)** *She was glad that the birthday party was a success.* | *'The meal was excellent.' 'I'm glad you liked it.'* | **+ to see/hear/learn etc** *Viv was glad to learn they'd reached home safely.*

be tickled /biː ˈtɪkəld/ [v phrase] informal to feel happy and pleased that something has happened or that someone has done something for you, especially when it is amusing or unusual **+ about/with** *Kurt is tickled about all the attention he's been getting.* | **+ (that)** *We're tickled that the magazine has become so popular.* | **be tickled pink/be tickled to death** (=feel very happy) *I'm sure Dick will be tickled pink to see you.*

gloat /gləʊt/ [v I] to show in an unpleasant way that you are happy about your own success or someone else's failure or problems: *He has an unpleasant habit of gloating whenever he wins at tennis.* | *I hate to gloat, you guys, but I told you it wouldn't work.* | **+ over** *It was horrible to see her gloating over her brother's misfortune.*

gleeful /ˈgliːfəl/ [adj] really enjoying the fact that something good has happened to you or that something bad has happened to someone else: *She seemed almost gleeful when I told her Hope had been fired.* | *The park was full of gleeful children playing on sleds.* —**gleefully** [adv] *'Go ahead and ask him – he won't help you either!' Phil yelled gleefully.*

3 very happy because something good has happened

- **delighted**
- **thrilled**
- **be (sitting) on top of the world**
- **be over the moon**
- **overjoyed**
- **ecstatic**
- **jubilant**
- **elated**
- **joyful**
- **radiant**

delighted /dɪˈlaɪtɪ̥d/ [adj not before noun] *When she saw the new car, she was delighted.* | **+ about** *His parents were absolutely delighted about the baby.* | **+ at** *Andrea was delighted at the chance to go to the Bolshoi ballet.* | **+ to hear/see/learn/be etc** *I was delighted to hear you were getting married.* | **+ (that)** *We are delighted that the negotiations have been completed successfully.*

thrilled /θrɪld/ [adj not before noun] very happy and excited about something that has happened: *You* *should go for a visit – my parents would be thrilled.* | **+ with** *Louise is thrilled with the changes she has seen in her son's behavior.* | **+ at/by** *She was thrilled at the possibility of being sent to Europe.* | **+ (that)** *My mother's thrilled that the new house is so close to the park.* | **+ to do sth** *She was thrilled to have her picture taken with Mel Gibson.* | **thrilled to bits** (=very thrilled) *We were thrilled to bits when our daughter appeared on TV.*

be (sitting) on top of the world /biː (ˌsɪtɪŋ) ɒn ˌtɒp əv ðə ˈwɜːʳld‖-ˌtɑːp-/ [v phrase] to feel extremely happy and confident because you are very successful or because something very good has happened to you: *Since the baby came Anna's been on top of the world.* | *After Mark got the promotion, he was sitting on top of the world.*

be over the moon /biː ˌəʊvəʳ ðə ˈmuːn/ [v phrase] British informal to be very happy about something good that has happened, especially something that makes you proud of yourself: *'How does it feel to have scored the winning goal?' 'Over the moon, Brian.'* | *When she discovered she'd got the job she was over the moon.*

overjoyed /ˌəʊvəʳˈdʒɔɪd/ [adj] written very happy about something, especially a piece of good news: *Naturally I was overjoyed when I was offered the part in the play.* | **+ to see/hear/learn/be etc** *My parents were overjoyed to see my brother again.*

ecstatic /ɪkˈstætɪk, ek-/ [adj] extremely happy and excited about something: *The kids were ecstatic when we brought home the new video game system.* | **+ about/over** *Coggan said his clients were ecstatic about the judge's ruling.* —**ecstatically** [adv] *Josie's little arms twined around the dog, hugging him ecstatically.*

jubilant /ˈdʒuːbələnt/ [adj] use this about a crowd of people who are very happy about something, for example because they have won something: *The jubilant fans lifted the players up on their shoulders.*

elated /ɪˈleɪtəd/ [adj not before noun] written very happy and excited for a short time, especially because you have achieved something that is important to you: *When I told her the news I thought she'd be elated.* | **+ by/at/with** *Jeremy felt elated by this sudden and unexpected success.* | *Elated with the election victory, the crowd waved banners and chanted.*

joyful /ˈdʒɔɪfəl/ [adj] a group of people that are **joyful** are extremely happy, especially because they are celebrating a happy event – used especially in literature: *The streets of the city were filled with joyful crowds celebrating the New Year.* | *After their election victory, party members seemed positively joyful.* —**joyfully** [adv] *The hospital released her, and her family joyfully welcomed her home.*

radiant /ˈreɪdiənt/ [adj] looking extremely happy: *He was radiant with excitement when he came off the stage.* | *She announced, with a radiant smile, that she was going to have a baby.* —**radiantly** [adv] *She smiled radiantly and gestured him toward her.*

4 happy most of the time

- happy
- cheerful
- contented
- have a happy/cheerful/sunny disposition
- jolly

happy /ˈhæpi/ [adj] *Mike was a happy child and never gave us any trouble at all.* | *Sarah's main aim in life is simply to be happy.* —**happily** [adv] *They have been happily married for 30 years.*

cheerful /ˈtʃɪəʳfəl/ [adj] usually behaving in a way that shows you are happy, by smiling, laughing, talking in a happy way, etc: *Thomas was cheerful and good-natured, and we soon became good friends.* | *She's kind of like a puppy – she's so cheerful and friendly.*

contented /kənˈtentəd/ [adj] happy and satisfied with your life: *He seems to be getting more contented as he gets older.* | *We spent ten contented years together.* —**contentedly** [adv] *The cat sat on my lap purring contentedly.*

have a happy/cheerful/sunny disposition /hæv ə ˌhæpi, ˌtʃɪəʳfəl, ˌsʌni dɪspəˈzɪʃən/ [v phrase not in progressive] to have a happy character and always behave in a happy way, even when there are problems: *Rosalind had a sunny disposition and a pleasant smile.* | *Marcia managed to keep a cheerful disposition despite her troubles at home.*

jolly /ˈdʒɒli‖ˈdʒɑː-/ [adj] British usually behaving in a cheerful, friendly way: *My uncle was a jolly man with a loud laugh.* | *Sue was always jolly and helpful.*

5 to make someone feel happy

- make sb happy
- cheer up
- make sb's day
- please
- put sb in a good mood
- raise/lift sb's spirits
- heartening

make sb happy /ˌmeɪk (sb) ˈhæpi/ [v phrase not in passive] *He would do anything to make her happy.* | *Would winning a million dollars really make you happy?* | *It made him happy to see how much they enjoyed the presents.*

cheer up /ˌtʃɪər ˈʌp/ [phr v T] to do something for someone who is sad in order to make them happy **cheer sb up** *I tried to cheer him up by telling a joke.* | **cheer up sb** *As a clown he visits local hospitals to cheer up sick children.*

make sb's day /ˌmeɪk (sb's) ˈdeɪ/ [v phrase] informal to say or do something to someone that makes them suddenly feel very happy: *Sherry's phone call really made my day.* | *Go on, tell him you like his new suit. It'll make his day!*

please /pliːz/ [v T] to do something to make someone happy, especially because they want you to do it: *I only got married to please my parents.* | *Sam is always doing little things to please her, but she hardly even notices.*

put sb in a good mood /ˌpʊt (sb) ɪn ə ˌgʊd ˈmuːd/ [v phrase] to do something that makes someone happy for a short time: *If you think buying me flowers will put me in a good mood, you're wrong.* | *Shopping for new shoes usually puts her in a good mood.*

raise/lift sb's spirits /ˌreɪz, ˌlɪft (sb's) ˈspɪrəts/ [v phrase] if something **raises** or **lifts someone's spirits**, it makes them feel happier and more hopeful after they have been unhappy and not very hopeful: *The chance to get out of the house for a few hours had clearly raised her spirits.* | *He had been tired when he arrived, but the sight of the little children playing really lifted his spirits.*

heartening ALSO **cheering** British /ˈhɑːʳtnɪŋ, ˈtʃɪərɪŋ/ [adj] making you feel happier, more hopeful, and more confident: *Kevin's school work is greatly improved, which is heartening.* | *It was about 8 o'clock when we heard the cheering news that Damien was out of danger.*

6 to feel happy again after feeling sad

- cheer up
- brighten up
- perk up
- be heartened/be cheered
- take heart

▸ *see also* **comfort/make sb feel better, feel**

cheer up /ˌtʃɪər ˈʌp/ [phr v I] *Cheer up, Mandy – the insurance will cover most of the damage.* | *You'd better get dressed and cheer up. The guests are coming any minute.*

brighten up /ˌbraɪtn ˈʌp/ [phr v I] to start to look happy again: *Mrs Verity brightened up at the news.* | *'Oh, I know the answer!' she said, brightening up.*

perk up /ˌpɜːʳk ˈʌp/ [phr v I] to start to feel a little more happy: *She wasn't feeling too good yesterday but she perked up in the evening.* | *Jessica always perks up when Richard comes over.*

be heartened/be cheered /biː ˈhɑːʳtnd, biː ˈtʃɪəʳd/ [v phrase] to feel happier and more hopeful, especially because you have received some good news, or have seen or thought something encouraging **+ by** *We are all heartened by the news that several families had already reached safety.* | **+ to see/hear/know/learn etc** *He was cheered to learn that his two attackers had been arrested.*

take heart /ˌteɪk ˈhɑːʳt/ [v phrase] to feel a little happier and more hopeful because something has happened to make a bad situation better: *Yes, the situation's pretty bad, but take heart – we'll find a way out of it.* | **+ from/in** *Company executives are taking heart from the success of recent sales.*

7 a happy feeling

- happiness
- pleasure
- joy
- delight
- contentment
- bliss
- euphoria
- elation

happiness /ˈhæpinɨs/ [n U] *Happiness is more important than money.* | *Pauline was willing to do anything for her children's happiness.* | **find happiness** (=become happy) *I doubt she'll find happiness with Gary.*

pleasure /ˈpleʒəʳ/ [n U] the feeling you have when you are doing something you enjoy or when something very nice had happened to you: *Most craftsmen get a lot of pleasure out of making things.* | **for pleasure** *Are you taking the trip for business or pleasure?* | **give/bring pleasure** *His music has brought pleasure to people all over the world.* | **take pleasure in (doing) sth** *Cooper took obvious pleasure in announcing the merger.*

joy /dʒɔɪ/ [n U] especially written a feeling of great happiness, often because something good has happened: *It's hard to describe the joy we felt, seeing each other again after so many years.* | *The time we spent together in the Bahamas was pure joy.* | **bring joy to sb** *The toys will bring great joy to countless children.* | **with joy** *People at the wedding laughed and danced with joy.* | **jump/shout/yell etc for joy** *I was so excited about getting the job, I nearly jumped for joy.* | **tears/shouts/cries etc of joy** *The sisters hugged and cried tears of joy.*

delight /dɪˈlaɪt/ [n U] great happiness and excitement, especially about something good that has happened: *Imagine our delight when we saw your article in the New Yorker.* | **+ at/in** *Paul's delight at being asked to play the piano for us was clear.* | **to sb's delight** *To the audience's delight, she agreed to do another number.* | **take delight in (doing) sth** *Horton takes great delight in learning.* | **with delight** *Robin laughed with delight as the birthday cake was carried in.*

contentment /kənˈtentmənt/ [n U] a quietly happy and satisfied feeling: *Joey sighed with contentment, snuggling down in his warm bed.*

bliss /blɪs/ [n U] a feeling of very deep happiness and extreme pleasure: *A feeling of bliss came over him as he fell asleep.* | **sheer/pure bliss** *Lying in the warm sun, listening to the sea was sheer bliss.* | **wedded/marital bliss** *After what appeared to be nine years of wedded bliss, the couple has separated.*

euphoria /juːˈfɔːriə‖jʊ-/ [n U] an extremely strong feeling of happiness and excitement that continues for a short time: *The whole country experienced a period of euphoria after winning the war.* | *The euphoria that new parents feel quickly changes to exhaustion.*

elation /ɪˈleɪʃən/ [n U] written a strong feeling of happiness, excitement, and pride: *As he spoke you could hear the elation in his voice.* | *The troops sense of elation at the victory was not to last.*

8 a happy time/situation/occasion

- happy
- blissful
- idyllic

happy /ˈhæpi/ [adj] *He had a very happy childhood.* | *Everyone thought their marriage was happy.* | *My years at college were the happiest time of my life.*

blissful /ˈblɪsfəl/ [adj] extremely happy and not worried by anything: *They were a young couple in the first blissful days of their marriage* | *She wandered deep into the forest, blissful in her freedom.* | **blissful ignorance** (=when you are happy because you do not know about something bad) *While her husband had affairs with other women, she lived in blissful ignorance.* —**blissfully** [adv] *For years they were blissfully happy.*

idyllic /ɪˈdɪlɪk‖aɪ-/ [adj] a situation or period of time that is **idyllic** is one in which you are extremely happy and that you think could not be better: *It was an idyllic life for both of them, and they hated to leave the island.* | *Lou recalled his idyllic camping trips to Maine as a child.*

9 a film, story, piece of music that makes you happy

- happy
- feel-good
- heartwarming

happy /ˈhæpi/ [adj only before noun] *I could hear the happy sound of the street musicians.* | *Well that's not a very happy story, is it?* | **happy ending** (=the end of a story or film in which everyone is happy) *Most children's stories have happy endings.*

feel-good /ˈfiːl gʊd/ [adj only before noun] a **feel-good** film, book, television programme etc makes you feel happy and cheerful because good things happen in it: *His latest film is a feel-good movie with a message.* | *There are still a few feel-good shows on TV, but most series have a harder edge.*

heartwarming /ˈhɑːʳtˌwɔːʳmɪŋ/ [adj] a **heartwarming** story or event makes you feel happy, because the people in it do well in a difficult situation, and behave in a way that shows that people are good: *The movie tells a heartwarming story about a* *boy who saves his sister's life.* | *The response to our plea for more food and blankets has been heartwarming.*

hard

RELATED WORDS

opposite: **soft**

- hard to do or understand *see* **difficult**
- having no sympathy *see* **unkind**
- treating someone strictly *see* **strict**

1 when something does not change its shape or bend

- hard
- solid
- firm
- stiff
- rigid

hard /hɑːʳd/ [adj] *That night I had to sleep on a hard stone floor.* | *I wish this chair wasn't so hard and uncomfortable.* | *Diamond is probably the hardest substance known to man.* | *As people age, their skin becomes harder and less supple.* | **rock- hard** (=very hard) *After several weeks without rain, the ground was rock-hard.* | **as hard as sth** *A tiled floor in the kitchen is as hard as stone, and very cold beneath your feet.* —**hardness** [n U] *The hardness of limestone varies depending on the area in which it is found.*

solid /ˈsɒlɪ̈d‖ˈsɑː-/ [adj] something that is **solid** is made of thick hard material, is not hollow, and is difficult to damage or break: *The door was made of solid steel.* | *During winter the lake became a solid block of ice.*

firm /fɜːʳm/ [adj] something that is **firm** is not completely hard, but does not change shape much when you press it – use this about things that are sometimes soft, for example fruit, muscles, or the ground: *I find I sleep better on a firm mattress.* | *These exercises are good for making your stomach muscles nice and firm.*

stiff /stɪf/ [adj] something that is **stiff** keeps its shape and is not easy to bend: *To make the picture, you will need a sheet of stiff card.* | *The collar of his shirt felt stiff and uncomfortable.* | **go stiff** British *The sheets outside on the washing line had gone stiff in the frost.*

rigid /ˈrɪdʒɪ̈d/ [adj] a material that is **rigid** is difficult or impossible to bend, and is often used to support something else: *The tent is made of strong canvas attached to a rigid frame.* | *Spoon the ice-cream into a rigid plastic container and freeze.*

2 food

- hard
- tough
- crunchy
- crisp
- firm

hard /hɑːʳd/ [adj] food that is **hard** is difficult to bite through and not nice to eat: *I've cooked the potatoes for half an hour but they still seem a bit hard.* | *That candy was so hard I nearly broke a tooth.* | **go hard** *Keep the cake in a tin, to prevent it from going hard.*

tough /tʌf/ [adj] food, especially meat, that is **tough** is difficult to cut or eat, for example because it is too old or has been cooked for too long: *The chicken was very tough, as though it had not been freshly cooked that day.* | *You can throw away the tough outer leaves of the cabbage.*

crunchy /ˈkrʌntʃi / [adj] food that is **crunchy** is firm and fresh, and makes a noise when you bite it: *Children love crunchy breakfast cereals and they're full of vitamins too.* | *For lunch I usually have something simple, with a fresh crunchy salad.*

crisp /crispy /krɪsp, ˈkrɪspi/ [adj] food, especially fruit or vegetables, that is **crisp** is firm and fresh, or has been cooked until it is quite hard and slightly brown: *a delicious crisp green apple* | *You can serve the chicken with a crispy stir fry of mixed vegetables.* | *Bake the pastry at 180 for about twenty minutes until crisp and golden.*

firm /fɜːʳm/ [adj] fruit or vegetables that are **firm** are not soft when you press them: *Buy peaches that are quite firm, as they ripen very quickly indoors.* | *For this recipe you will need six firm tomatoes.*

3 to become hard or make something hard

- harden
- solidify
- set
- freeze
- stiffen

harden /ˈhɑːʳdn/ [v I/T] *The glue needs about 24 hours to harden.* | *Steel is hardened by heating it to a very high temperature.* | **+ into/to** *Much of the mountain consists of volcanic ash, long since hardened to jagged rock.*

solidify /səˈlɪdɪ̈faɪ/ [v I] if a liquid such as melted metal or wax **solidifies**, it becomes hard: *Tools are made by pouring liquid metal into a mould and allowing it to cool and solidify.* | *As the lava flowed down the volcano it solidified, forming strange shapes.*

set /set/ [v I] if a liquid substance **sets**, it becomes harder – use this to talk about something that slowly becomes harder after it is mixed with water, for example, food or building materials: *Put the jelly in the fridge for an hour to set.* | *The concrete will take several hours to set, so make sure no one walks on it.*

freeze /friːz/ [v I] if a liquid **freezes**, it becomes hard because it has become very cold: *The water in the lake used to freeze most winters, and then it was good for skating.* | **be frozen solid** *Hey! The milk's frozen solid!*

stiffen /ˈstɪfən/ [v T] to make something stiffer and harder: *Point your toes and stiffen the muscles in your legs.* | *You can stiffen curtain fabric by using a special liquid solution.*

harm

RELATED WORDS

- do physical harm to someone *see* **attack, hurt/injure**
- *see also* **damage, destroy, break, spoil, suffer**

1 to harm a person, group, country etc

- harm
- damage
- be bad for/have a bad effect on
- hit
- hurt
- be/deal a blow to
- impair
- be detrimental to
- at the expense of sth
- wreak havoc/play havoc

harm /hɑːʳm/ [v T] to have a bad effect on something, in a way that makes it weaker, less effective, or less successful: *Walking out without giving any notice will only harm your career.* | *Any scandal will certainly harm the company's reputation.* | *These new export restrictions are sure to harm the economy.* | *The most important consideration is that the environment is not harmed.*

damage /ˈdæmɪdʒ/ [v T] to permanently harm something such as the success, health, or image of a person, organization etc so that they are not as effective as before: *Several recent events have damaged the government's public image.* | *This is likely to damage Scott's reputation even more.* | **seriously/badly damage sth** *Smoking can seriously damage your health.* | *The company's future prospects will be badly damaged if this deal falls through.*

be bad for/have a bad effect on /biː ˈbæd fɔːʳ, hæv ə ˌbæd ɪˈfekt ɒn/ [v phrase] to change or effect something in a harmful way: *Drinking so much is bound to have a bad effect on your health.* | *An increase in interest rates at the present time would definitely be bad for business.*

hit /hɪt/ [v T] to have a sudden bad effect on someone or something, harming them badly: *A sudden rise in inflation always hits living standards.* | **be badly hit** *Southern England has been badly hit by flooding, and many homes are now without power.* | **hit sth/sb hard** *Elderly people were the hardest hit by the increase in tax on fuel.*

hurt /hɜːʳt/ [v T] to have a bad effect on an organization or activity, by making it less successful or effective: *Most companies have been hurt by the economic slowdown.* | *This is mainly going to hurt those who already have least.*

be/deal a blow to /biː, ˌdiːl ə ˈbləʊ tuː/ [v phrase] to harm the plans, chances, confidence etc of a person or organization: *It would be stupid to pretend this was anything but a blow to the prime minister.* | **be a big/serious/severe etc blow** *The incident was a severe blow to UN peace efforts.* | *Losing the match against Rumania, dealt a huge blow to the team.*

impair /ɪmˈpeəʳ/ [v T] to harm something such as an ability or the way a body or system works – use this especially in medical or technical contexts: *If a witness is allowed to withhold evidence, it impairs the legal process.* | *Alcohol significantly impairs your ability to drive a car or operate machinery.* —**impaired** [adj] *Rubella infection can lead to impaired hearing.*

be detrimental to /biː ˌdetrɪ̈ˈmentl tuː/ [v phrase] formal to be likely to harm something: *Working in front of a computer all day may be detrimental to your eyesight.* | *Any further housing development will be detrimental to the character of this small town.*

at the expense of sth /ət ði ɪkˈspens əv (sth)/ [prep] if you do something **at the expense of** someone or something else, you do it in order to gain an advantage, even if it harms them or has a bad effect on them: *Cigarette manufacturers continue to pursue profit at the expense of our children.* | *Many people are now working a fifty or sixty hour week, at the expense of their family life.*

wreak havoc/play havoc /ˌriːk ˈhævək, ˌpleɪ ˈhævək/ [v phrase] to seriously harm something by causing a lot of harm and confusion: *A major computer failure wrought havoc on the New York Subway last night.* | **+ with** *Working so late is starting to play havoc with her social life.*

2 to harm yourself by your own actions

- harm yourself
- cut your own throat
- be your own worst enemy
- shoot yourself in the foot
- cut off your nose to spite your face

harm yourself /ˈhɑːʳm jɔːʳself/ [v phrase] **only harm yourself** *They'll only harm themselves if they decide to leave the association.* | *By making the complaint the only person he harmed was himself.*

cut your own throat /ˌkʌt jɔːr ˌəʊn ˈθrəʊt/ [v phrase] to behave in a way that is certain to cause you harm, especially because of pride or anger: *It would be silly to give up your job now – you'd just be cutting your own throat.*

be your own worst enemy /biː jɔːr ˌəʊn wɜːʳst ˈenəmi/ [v phrase] to continuously behave in a stupid way that results in you being harmed: *My mother was her own worst enemy. She knew she was ill but she did nothing to help herself.* | *Many drivers are their own worst enemy – driving too close, driving too fast, all the usual faults.*

shoot yourself in the foot /ˌʃuːt jɔːʳself ɪn ðə ˈfʊt/ [v phrase] to stupidly do something that seriously harms you, especially by saying something stupid or making plans that go badly wrong: *Once again, the government has shot itself in the foot – this time by reducing widows' pensions.*

cut off your nose to spite your face /ˌkʌt ɒf jɔːʳ ˌnəʊz tə ˌspaɪt jɔːʳ ˈfeɪs/ [v phrase] to deliberately not do something that would make an unpleasant situation better for you, because you are too angry or proud to do it: *If you love him, ask him to stay. Otherwise you'll be cutting off your nose to spite your face.*

3 harming something or someone

- harmful
- damaging
- negative
- be bad for

harmful /ˈhɑːʳmfəl/ [adj] *Pushing kids so hard from such an early age is likely to have some harmful results.* | *Scientists tend to agree that most diets don't work and can be harmful.* | *The destruction of the ozone layer will have a very harmful effect on the environment.* | **+ to** *80% of Americans think that television is harmful to society and especially to children.*

damaging /ˈdæmɪdʒɪŋ/ [adj] harmful and usually having a permanent effect: *Up to 1500 patients suffered damaging side-effects after taking the drug.* | *The publicity that followed the scandal has been extremely damaging.* | **+ to** *The British beef crisis was damaging to the livelihoods of thousands of people in the industry.*

negative /ˈnegətɪv/ [adj] likely to harm someone or something, especially in a way that is not too serious – use this especially about something that could also have a good effect if the situation was different: *Doctors have a duty to inform patients of the possible negative side-effects of the drug.* | *The school environment can be a negative force as well as a positive one.*

be bad for /biː ˈbæd fɔːʳ/ [v phrase] to have a harmful effect on something such as an activity, organization, or type of work: *When companies close down, it's bad for the town and bad for the local economy.* | *A bad marriage is bad for the kids.* | *Reading without good lighting is bad for your eyes.*

4 likely to harm people's health or the environment

- harmful
- poisonous
- hazardous
- toxic
- noxious

harmful /ˈhɑːʳmfəl/ [adj] *Scientists have recommended that new technology be used to target harmful bacteria.* | *Many of the products that we have around our homes are harmful if swallowed.* | *The protests were aimed at ending the dumping of harmful industrial waste at sea.* | **+ to** *The sun's rays can be very harmful to the skin.*

poisonous /ˈpɔɪzənəs/ [adj] something that is **poisonous** contains a chemical that makes people, animals, or plants etc very ill or could kill them if they breathe it, swallow it, or touch it etc: *Don't drink that – it's poisonous!* | *The adder is the only poisonous snake in Britain.* | **highly poisonous** *Carbon monoxide is a highly poisonous gas, mostly produced by cars.*

hazardous /ˈhæzəʳdəs/ [adj usually before noun] **hazardous chemicals/waste/substances etc** substances that are poisonous and will harm people, animals, or the environment if they are not dealt with or got rid of carefully: *Lead is one of the most hazardous substances known, causing cancer and nerve damage.* | *The building is now unoccupied, and all radioactive or hazardous materials have been removed.* | *We need better regulations regarding the transportation of hazardous waste along public roads.*

toxic /ˈtɒksɪk‖ˈtɑːk-/ [adj] chemicals, gases, or waste products that are poisonous and harmful to people, animals, or the environment – used especially in technical or scientific contexts: *Research has found that the drug contains a toxic chemical that can cause respiratory problems.* | **toxic waste** (=from factories etc) *We need more installations for the disposal of toxic waste.* | **highly toxic** *highly toxic radioactive waste products* | **+ to** *Carbon dioxide is not highly toxic to animals or humans in small amounts.*

noxious /ˈnɒkʃəs‖ˈnɑːk-/ [adj] formal a **noxious** chemical or gas harms your health and is very unpleasant: *Residents have to put up with noxious fumes from the nearby factory.* | *Increasing tax on petrol would encourage people to drive smaller cars with fewer noxious emissions.*

5 not harming anything or anyone

- harmless
- innocuous
- do no harm/not do any harm
- friendly

harmless /ˈhɑːʳmləs/ [adj] *I don't know why you're so upset – it was only a harmless bit of fun.* | *Radioactive waste needs to be stored for 25,000 years before it is harmless.* | **harmless enough** (=used to say that someone or something that may seem harmful, is in fact not harmful) *He's a little crazy, I know, but he's harmless enough.* —**harmlessly** [adv] *Fortunately the knife missed me and landed harmlessly on the floor.*

innocuous /ɪˈnɒkjuəs‖ɪˈnɑːk-/ [adj] not harmful – use this especially when people have said or believe that something or someone is harmful: *The producer dismissed the comment as quite innocuous.* | *The murder suspect was an innocuous-looking man with wire-framed glasses.* | **seemingly/apparently innocuous** (=seeming harmless, but actually intended to be harmful) *Someone stood up and asked the professor an apparently innocuous question about his laboratory work.*

do no harm/not do any harm /ˌduː nəʊ ˈhɑːʳm, ˌnɒt duː eni ˈhɑːʳm/ [v phrase] if an action, activity, experience etc **does no harm**, it does not harm someone or something and may even help: *Learning how to live on your own for a while will do you no harm at all.* | **it would do no harm to do sth** *I expect they've sold all the tickets, but it won't do any harm to ask.*

friendly /ˈfrendli/ [adj] **environment-friendly/ozone-friendly etc** used especially about products in shops, meaning that they do not harm the environment etc: *Look for aerosols which say 'ozone-friendly' on the can.* | *Tighter laws are needed to prevent manufacturers from falsely claiming their products are environment friendly.*

hate

RELATED WORDS

opposite: love

▸ *see also* **dislike, angry, revenge**

1 to feel strong dislike and anger towards someone or something

- hate
- hate sb's guts
- can't stand
- detest
- loathe
- despise
- abhor

hate /heɪt/ [v I/T not in progressive] *'Go away!' Jackie screamed. 'I hate you!'* | *I hated my first husband. He used to hit me and the children.* | *Turner was a rebel from the start. He hated authority and he hated the law.* | *He was an evil dictator who was universally hated.* | *It takes many years for kids who have suffered so much to learn to love and not to hate.*

hate sb's guts /ˌheɪt (sb's) ˈgʌts/ [v phrase not in progressive] informal to hate someone very much: *I wish she'd die tomorrow. I hate her guts.* | *The sergeant knew the men all hated his guts for the way he treated them.*

can't stand /ˌkɑːnt ˈstænd‖ˌkænt-/ [v phrase] especially spoken to have a very strong feeling of dislike for a person or for their behaviour because they make you feel very angry or uncomfortable when you are with them: *We used to be quite good friends but now I can't stand her.* | *I can't stand the way he's always telling people what they should do.* | *If there's one thing I can't stand, it's hypocrisy.* | **can't stand the sight of sb** *Don't invite Alice. Mum can't stand the sight of her.*

detest /dɪˈtest/ [v T not in progressive] to have a strong feeling of hatred, especially for a particular kind of person, or a particular type of behaviour: *He was exactly the kind of arrogant, self-satisfied man I detest.* | *I detest any form of cruelty toward animals.* | *According to Hollywood gossip, both the leading actors were detested by the rest of the cast.*

loathe /ləʊð/ [v T not in progressive] to have a very strong feeling of hatred for someone or for a type of behaviour, because you think that they are the very worst kind of person or behaviour that there is: *Mrs Morel loathed her husband when he was drunk and violent.* | *Kemp was loathed by all the other prisoners, who regarded him as a traitor.* | *I really loathe it when people make promises and then don't keep them.*

despise /dɪ'spaɪz/ [v T not in progressive] to hate someone or something and think they have no importance or value: *We were brought up to despise the people from the poor side of town. They seemed so dirty and ignorant.* | *Otis despised inherited wealth and social class.* | **despise sb for (doing) sth** *I felt that the other kids despised me for having the wrong accent and the wrong colour skin.*

abhor /əb'hɔːʳ, æb-/ [v T not in progressive] formal to hate a particular kind of behaviour or attitude, especially because you think it is morally wrong: *The great majority of the Irish people have always abhorred violence.* | *The president abhorred all forms of racism.*

2 to hate something because it is unpleasant

- hate
- can't stand/can't bear
- detest
- loathe

hate /heɪt/ [v T not in progressive] *I hate it when you speak to me like that.* | *Tony hated science when he was at school because he wasn't any good at it.* | **+ doing sth** *If you're playing against Gary, I warn you, he hates losing!* | *Don't go in now – she hates being interrupted.* | **+ to do sth** *Hurry up – I hate to be late!*

can't stand/can't bear /ˌkɑːnt 'stænd, ˌkɑːnt 'beəʳ‖ˌkænt-/ [v phrase] especially spoken to dislike something so much that you want to avoid it, because it upsets you, annoys you, or makes you feel ill: *She stopped working in the factory because she couldn't stand the smell.* | *Turn the radio off. I can't bear that noise.* | **+ doing sth** *He couldn't bear seeing her in so much pain.* | **can't stand/bear sb doing sth** *I can't stand people smoking around me when I'm eating.* | **+ to do sth** *I can't bear to think about the day she actually leaves home.*

detest /dɪ'test/ [v T not in progressive] to hate something very much, especially a particular activity, taste, or smell: *When he was at school he detested football.* | *You don't understand. It's not just that I don't like cabbage – I absolutely detest it!* | **+ doing sth** *I detested spending two hours every day travelling to work and back.*

loathe /ləʊð/ [v T not in progressive] to dislike something very much, especially because it makes you feel sick or nervous: *She loathes spiders.* | *If there's one thing I really loathe, it's long car journeys.* | **+ doing sth** *Even after years of practice, he still loathed making public speeches.*

3 a feeling of hating someone or something

- hatred
- hate
- loathing
- animosity
- abhorrence
- contempt

hatred /'heɪtrɪ̈d/ [n U] an angry feeling of deep dislike for someone or something: *I could see the jealousy and hatred in Jeff's eyes.* | **+ of** *The long cold winter had only increased his hatred of the place.* | **have a hatred of sth** *Tom had a hatred of any kind of authority.* | **+ for/towards** (=use this about a feeling of hate for people, not things) *In her autobiography, she describes her hatred for her stepfather.* | **deep hatred** *The experience left him with a deep hatred of politicians.*

hate /heɪt/ [n U] the angry feeling that someone has when they **hate** someone and want to harm them: *There was anger and hate in her voice, and I felt afraid.* | **be filled with hate** *His mind was filled with hate and the desire for revenge.*

loathing /'ləʊðɪŋ/ [n U] a very strong feeling of hatred for someone or something that you think is extremely unpleasant **+ for/of** *I felt nothing but loathing for him after the way he'd treated me.* | **fear and loathing** *Sandra didn't dare look at him, in case he saw the fear and loathing in her eyes.*

animosity /ˌænɪ̈'mɒsɪ̈ti‖-'mɑː-/ [n U] a feeling of hatred and anger that often makes people behave unpleasantly to each other **+ between** *The animosity between parents who are getting a divorce can often cause great suffering to their children.* | **+ towards** *David's brother told reporters that the family felt no animosity towards anyone over David's death.* | **personal animosity** (=for personal, not political reasons) *The two leaders have done very little to disguise their personal animosity.*

abhorrence /əb'hɒrəns‖-'hɔːr-/ [n U] formal a deep feeling of hatred towards something that you think is morally wrong or unpleasant: *The thought of marrying him filled her with abhorrence.* | **+ of** *the abhorrence of terrorism by all decent people*

contempt /kən'tempt/ [n U] a feeling of hate towards someone or something you think does not deserve any respect at all **+ for** *He never tried to hide his contempt for those who were not as intelligent as him.* | **feel/have/show contempt** *I feel nothing but contempt for people who are obsessed with fast cars and designer clothes.* | **with contempt** *The teachers were very old-fashioned, treating any new ideas with contempt and scorn.*

4 someone or something that you hate

- hated
- pet hate

hated /'heɪtɪ̈d/ [adj only before noun] *He quickly became the country's most hated man./* | **the hated sth/sb** *The students, backed by the workers, managed to bring down the hated military regime.*

pet hate British **/pet peeve** American /ˌpet 'heɪt, ˌpet 'piːv/ [n C] informal something that you do not like, because it always annoys you – use this about something that is not very important: *TV Game shows have been my pet hate for some time now.* | *Mum's particular pet peeve is people leaving their dirty clothes lying on the floor.*

5 someone who hates you and wants to harm you

- enemy

enemy /'enəmi/ [n C] *The detective wanted to know whether the dead man had had any enemies.* | **sb's enemy** *the president's political enemies were quick to denounce him.*

have/not have

RELATED WORDS

- to have an illness *see* **illness/disease**
- have to *see* **must/don't have to**
- *see also* **get, own**

WHAT'S HERE

- **to have sth** see **1 to 4**
- **to not have sth** see **5 to 10**

to have sth

1 to have something such as a television, car, house etc

- have
- with
- own
- possess

have ALSO **have got** especially British /hæv, həv ˈgɒt‖-ˈgɑːt/ [v T not in progressive] *Most families in England have a car, and over 25% of them have two cars.* | *'Have you got a garden in your new place?' 'Yes, we have.'* | *They have a houseboat out on the lake.* | *'Do you have a phone here?' 'Yes sir, we do.'* | *Have you got your own computer at home?*

with /wɪð, wɪθ/ [prep] someone **with** something has that thing: *There aren't many people with cars in this part of town – they're too poor.* | *Taking the bus across the country appeals to people with more time than money.* | *Anybody with shares in the company is urged to contact the receivers to register a claim.*

own /əʊn/ [v T] if you **own** something, especially something valuable such as a car, a house, or a company, it belongs to you legally: *Andy and his wife own a vacation home near the beach.* | *The company was previously owned by the French government.* | *American newspapers in different cities are often owned by the same company.*

possess /pəˈzes/ [v T not in progressive] formal to have or own something, especially something valuable or important: *The number of nations that possess nuclear weapons has risen.* | *Hamly admitted illegally possessing a handgun.* | *The caller claimed to possess valuable information about the boy's whereabouts.*

2 to have something with you

- have
- with
- have sth on you
- have sth with you
- have/keep sth handy
- have sth in your possession

have ALSO **have got** especially British /hæv, həv ˈgɒt‖-ˈgɑːt/ [v T not in progressive] *Excuse me, do you have change for a dollar?* | *Have you got a pen I could borrow?* | *Here, I have a map.* | *I think you've got my tickets.* | *The dancers had elaborate costumes with long embroidered skirts.*

with /wɪð, wɪθ/ [prep] someone **with** something has that thing now: *There's a man at the door with a parcel for you.* | *A woman with a baby in a stroller was looking at clothes.* | *Rob is the guy with the blue jacket.*

have sth on you /ˌhæv (sth) ˈɒn juː/ [v phrase not in progressive] to be carrying something in your pocket, bag etc: *I don't have enough change on me for the parking meter.* | *Jim is the only guy I know who always has a handkerchief on him.*

have sth with you /ˌhæv (sth) ˈwɪð juː/ [v phrase not in progressive] to have something in your pocket, bag, hand etc: *Her address is in my diary but I haven't got it with me.* | *She had her camera with her on the hike.* | *You should have your identity card with you at all times.*

have/keep sth handy ALSO **have/keep sth to hand** /ˌhæv, ˌkiːp (sth) ˈhændi, ˌhæv, ˌkiːp (sth) tə ˈhænd/ [adv] to have something near you, especially because you might need to use it **have sth handy/have sth to hand** *When you call, have your credit card handy.* | *Before you begin make sure you have all the tools you need to hand.* | **keep sth handy/keep sth to hand** *Keep a fire extinguisher handy in the kitchen.* | *Keep important telephone numbers to hand by the telephone.*

have sth in your possession /ˌhæv (sth) ɪn jɔːʳ pəˈzeʃən/ [v phrase not in progressive] formal to have something in your hand, pocket, bag etc, especially something illegal: *The man who was arrested had an illegal firearm in his possession.* | *The drugs he had in his possession had an estimated street value of $15,000.*

3 to have something that you do not want

- be stuck with

be stuck with /biː ˈstʌk wɪð/ [v phrase] *It's only a rented house, so we're stuck with the decor.* | *As a result of the financial collapse many people are stuck with worthless investments.*

4 to have a particular feature, quality, or ability

- have
- with
- there is/there are
- possess
- of
- enjoy
- be blessed with
- be endowed with
- boast

have ALSO **have got** especially British /hæv, həv ˈgɒt‖-ˈgɑːt/ [v T not in progressive] *Although she's eighty she has an excellent memory.* | *Kids have wonderful imaginations, and it is natural for them to create imaginary friends.* | *The hotel only had two double rooms and they were both occupied.* | *The jacket has two side pockets and two more pockets inside.* | *Her brother's got long dark hair and blue eyes.*

with /wɪð, wɪθ/ [prep] use this after a noun to describe the qualities or features that someone or something has: *We booked a room with a sea view.* | *The company needs more people with marketing experience.* | *Katrina's over there in front of that man with red hair.*

there is/there are /ðeər ɪz, ðeər ɑːʳ/ use this to describe the things that a place has: *It's a big house – there are five bedrooms.* | *There are lots of old temples and gardens to visit in Kyoto.* | *There's an Olympic-sized swimming pool on campus.*

possess /pəˈzes/ [v T not in progressive] formal to have a particular ability, feature, or quality: *He possessed an unusual ability to learn languages quickly.* | *Like all towns and villages on Trinidad, it possessed a cricket ground.* | *The Western Highlands possess a beauty and a majesty found nowhere else in Britain.*

of /əv, ə, (*strong*) ɒv‖əv, ə, (*strong*) ɑːv/ [prep] especially written if someone or something is of a particular feature, quality, or ability, they have that feature etc, especially if it is something good: *Father was a man of great integrity and honesty.* | *an area of outstanding beauty* | *She was an actress of great skill.*

enjoy /ɪnˈdʒɔɪ/ [v T not in progressive] formal to have special advantages, conditions, abilities etc that are better than the ones that other people or things have: *Some of the workers enjoy a relatively high degree of job security.* | *When first introduced on the market, these products enjoyed great success.*

be blessed with /biː ˈblest wɪð/ [v phrase] to have something such as a useful ability, a good feature, or an important advantage – used formally or humorously: *Londoners are blessed with some of the very best Thai restaurants in the country.* | *Justine was unfortunately not blessed with a sense of humour.* | *Few gardens are blessed with an ideal site.*

be endowed with /biː ɪnˈdaʊd wɪð/ [v phrase] formal to have something good, especially a natural ability or social advantage: *Hugh was young, handsome, and endowed with the privileges of class and education.* | *Jefferson wrote that all citizens were endowed with 'the rights to life, liberty, and the pursuit of happiness.'*

boast /bəʊst/ [v T not in progressive] if something such as a place, organization, or object **boasts** a good feature, it has that feature – used especially in advertisements and literature: *The golf course is surrounded by hills and boasts some of the finest scenery in the country.* | *Each luxury home boasts an indoor pool and three-car garage.*

to not have sth

RELATED WORDS

- *see also* **lose, poor**

5 to not have something

- **not have**
- **without**
- **be missing**

not have ALSO **haven't got** especially British /nɒt ˈhæv, ˌhævnt ˈgɒt‖-ˈgɑːt/ [v phrase not in progressive or passive] *I don't have any brothers or sisters.* | *My parents haven't got a television.* | *The store didn't have the right type of glue in stock.* | *She hasn't got anything to wear for her interview.* | *Haven't we got any more tomatoes? I need some for the salad.* | **not have sth with you** (=not have brought something with you) *I'm sorry, I don't seem to have my credit card with me – can I pay by cheque?*

without /wɪðˈaʊt‖wɪðˈaʊt, wɪθˈaʊt/ [prep] if you do something **without** something, you do not have or own that thing: *Billy came to class without his school books.* | *You can't get a passport without a birth certificate.* | *There are so many people without jobs that companies receive hundreds of applications to each advertisement.* | *The schools are having to provide programs without adequate funding.*

be missing /biː ˈmɪsɪŋ/ [v phrase] if something **is missing**, you do not have it because it has been lost, removed, or stolen: *Two of her front teeth were missing.* | *When I put my hand inside my pocket I discovered that my wallet was missing.* | **have sth missing** *The dog has part of his left ear missing.* | **what's missing is/all that's missing is** *It's such a romantic setting – all that's missing is the candles.*

6 to not have any more of something

- **not have any more/not have any left**
- **be out of sth/run out of**

not have any more/not have any left /nɒt hæv ˌeni ˈmɔː, nɒt hæv ˌeni ˈleft/ [v phrase not in progressive] *That was my last one – I don't have any more.* | *I didn't have any time left to finish.* | *The theatre didn't have any seats left when I went to get tickets.* | *He didn't have any more questions.*

be out of/run out of /biː ˈaʊt ɒv, ˌrʌn ˈaʊt ɒv/ [v phrase/phr v T] to not have something that you usually have or that you regularly use, because you have used or sold all of it: *Looks like we're out of milk again – can you go to the store for me?* | *The store was out of the paint I wanted.* | *In the end she ran out of patience and started yelling.* | *Better take plenty of water – we don't want to run out.*

7 to not have something you need

- **lack**
- **be without**
- **go without**
- **do without/manage without**
- **through lack of sth/for lack of sth/for want of sth**

lack /læk/ [v T not in progressive] to not have something that you need, especially something that you need in order to do something: *Tom lacks confidence and needs a lot of encouragement.* | *They lived in appalling conditions, lacking even the most primitive sanitation.* —**lack** [n singular] + **of** *She showed a complete lack of interest in her own baby.*

be without /biː wɪðˈaʊt/ [v phrase] if someone **is without** food, water, clothes, or other important things that they need, they do not have them: *Over a million people in the Sudan have been without supplies of food and water for several months.* | *Some towns are still without electricity after last week's storms.*

go without /ˌgəʊ wɪðˈaʊt/ [v I/T not in passive] to not have something that you usually have, for example food or sleep: *Lucas's soldiers had to go without food or water for several days.* | *New parents go without much sleep for at least the first few months.* | *There wasn't enough water to go around, and some people went without.*

do without/manage without /ˌduː wɪðˈaʊt, ˌmænɪdʒ wɪðˈaʊt/ [phr v I/T not in passive/v phrase not in passive] to live your life or do something you want to do without having something you need or without someone's help: *For three years I managed without pain-killing drugs.* | *From May to November it is very hot, but the schools do without air-conditioning.* | *Many of the young people here had never before had to do without.*

through lack of sth/for lack of sth/for want of sth /θruː ˈlæk əv (sth), fəʳ ˈlæk əv (sth), fəʳ ˈwɒnt əv (sth) ‖-ˈwɑːnt-/ [prep] if something happens **through lack of** a particular thing, it happens because there is not enough of that thing available or because there is none at all: *Crops and animals died through lack of rain.* | *The case was abandoned for lack of evidence.* | *We haven't yet quite succeeded, but not for want of trying.*

8 to not allow yourself to have something you need

- do without/go without
- deny yourself
- abstain
- forgo

do without/go without /ˌduː wɪðˈaʊt, ˌɡəʊ wɪðˈaʊt/ [phr v I/T not in passive] to choose or decide not to have something, especially because there is not enough of it, because you need to save money, or for religious reasons: *His parents often did without lunch or supper so that he could have more.* | *During the month of Ramadan, Muslims go without food and drink between the hours of sunrise and sunset.* | *Meat was expensive and a lot of people went without.* | *Cuts have to be made, and city residents need to think about what services they can do without.*

deny yourself /dɪˈnaɪ jɔːʳˈself/ [v phrase] to not do or have things you enjoy because you think this will be good for you: *Girls who constantly deny themselves food in order to get thin rarely do well at school.* | *I worked hard, lived frugally, and denied myself material goods in order to achieve financial security.*

abstain /əbˈsteɪn/ [v I] to not do something that you usually do or that you want to do, especially for health or moral reasons: *The sex education program encourages teens to abstain.* | **+ from** *Catholics are supposed to abstain from meat on Good Friday.* | **+ from doing sth** *Trial volunteers are told to abstain from watching TV for a month.* —**abstinence** /ˈæbstɪnəns/ [n U] *a season of fasting and abstinence*

forgo ALSO **forego** /fɔːʳˈɡəʊ/ [v T] formal to not have or do something good or something you enjoy, especially for moral reasons, because of your principles etc: *Senior board members have offered to forgo their annual bonuses this year.* | *Novices were expected to forgo all earthly pleasures and concentrate on the hereafter.*

9 to not have a particular substance, quality, feature etc

- not have
- lack
- without
- there isn't/there aren't
- be free from
- -free

not have ALSO **haven't got** especially British /nɒt ˈhæv, ˌhævənt ˈɡɒt‖-ˈɡɑːt/ [v phrase not in progressive or passive] *He doesn't have much of a sense of humor.* | *Her little girl doesn't seem to have any fear at all.* | *It doesn't really have any practical use.* | *She said she hasn't got as much pain in her leg as she used to.*

lack /læk/ [v T] if someone or something **lacks** a particular substance, quality, feature, or ability, they have never had it: *He lacked the energy to argue with him.* | *Many people lack adequate pension arrangements.* | *Glenn has the discipline that Forman lacks.*

without /wɪðˈaʊt‖wɪðˈaʊt, wɪθˈaʊt/ [prep] not having or containing a particular substance, feature etc: *'With or without sugar?' 'Without, please!'* | *'Gourmet Food without Salt' is aimed at people with high-blood pressure.* | *He was without any sense whatsoever.*

there isn't/there aren't /ðeər ˈɪzənt, ðeər ˈɑːʳnt/ use this to describe the things that a place or thing does not have: *There aren't enough ladies' rooms at the stadium.* | *There wasn't a decent restaurant for miles.*

be free from /biː ˈfriː frɒm/ [v phrase] if a product, food, or drink **is free from** a substance, especially one that is harmful, it does not contain that substance: *The new shampoo uses only natural products and is completely free from artificial colouring and preservatives.* | *Organic produce is free from harmful chemicals.*

-free /friː/ [adj] **sugar-free/fat-free/lead-free etc** not containing sugar, fat, lead etc – use this especially about things that have been deliberately made this way: *a sugar-free soft drink* | *It looks like wine and tastes like wine, but it's almost alcohol-free.*

10 to no longer have something important

- lose
- cost
- at the cost of
- be a high price to pay

lose /luːz/ [v T] to no longer have something important or valuable, such as your job or your home, because it has been destroyed or taken away from you: *I'll lose my job if the factory closes.* | *We lost our home and all our belongings in the fire.* | **lose your sight/hearing etc** (=lose the ability to see/hear etc) *Professor Wilkes lost his sight in an accident three years ago.*

cost /kɒst‖kɔːst/ [v T not in passive] if a mistake, accident etc **costs** you something important such as your job or your health, you lose that important thing because of it **cost sb sth** *Another mistake like that could cost you your job.* | *All this delay has cost the company an important contract.* | **cost sb his/her life** *Larry's years of hard drinking and living almost cost him his life.*

at the cost of /ət ðə ˈkɒst ɒv‖-ˈkɔːst-/ [prep] if you achieve something **at the cost of** something else, you lose something of great importance or value as a result of what you achieve: *An increase in profits was achieved, but only at the cost of hundreds of jobs.*

be a high price to pay /biː ə ˌhaɪ ˌpraɪs tə ˈpeɪ/ [v phrase] if something is **a high price to pay,** losing or damaging it is so bad that the advantage you gain as a result is not worth it **+ for** *The pollution of our rivers is a high price to pay for agricultural development* | *Most people know now that getting sunburnt is a high price to pay for a quick tan.* | **be too high a price to pay (for)** *The new road has made life easier for commuters, but some say it is too high a price to pay.*

healthy/unhealthy

RELATED WORDS

- *see also* **cure, recover, fit/not fit, strong, exercise**

1 someone who is healthy

- healthy
- well
- fine
- in good/perfect/excellent health

healthy /ˈhelθi/ [adj] someone who is **healthy** has nothing physically wrong with them: *I've been much healthier since I stopped smoking.* | *She's just had a lovely healthy baby girl.*

well /wel/ [adj not usually before noun] healthy – use this to say that someone feels or looks healthy, or that they are healthy again after an illness: *'How are you?' 'I'm very well, thank you.'* | *Clare's been much better since the operation.* | **look well** *You're looking well – have you been on holiday?* | **fit and well** *You need to eat regular nourishing meals if you want to keep yourself fit and well.*

fine /faɪn/ [adj not before noun] spoken say this when someone has asked you how you or someone else feels, and you are replying that you or the other person feels well: *'How are you?' 'Fine, thanks.'* | *'How's your wife now?' 'Oh, she's fine, thank you.'*

in good/perfect/excellent health /ɪn ˌgʊd, ˌpɜːʳfɪkt, ˌeksələnt 'helθ/ [adj phrase] formal very healthy: *The hostages arrived back in Britain yesterday, tired but otherwise in good health.* | *My grandmother remained in excellent health until she was in her nineties.*

2 someone who is usually healthy

- healthy
- strong
- have a strong/good etc constitution
- robust

healthy /'helθi/ [adj] *He's nearly 60 now but he's strong and healthy and full of energy.* | *Her death came as a terrible shock. She had always been so healthy.* | **stay/keep healthy** *Eating plenty of fresh fruit and vegetables will help you to stay healthy.*

strong /strɒŋ‖strɔːŋ/ [adj] someone who is **strong** has a healthy body that can do a lot of physical exercise, and becomes well quickly after any illnesses: *My father's over eighty now, and not very strong.* | *Only people who are physically strong and fit should consider coming on this expedition.*

have a strong/good etc constitution /hæv ə ˌstrɒŋ kɒnstɪ̈'tjuːʃən‖-ˌstrɔːŋ kɑːnstɪ̈'tuː-/ [v phrase not in progressive] to not become ill easily and easily get well again after an illness or injury: *Your husband has an excellent constitution and is likely to recover in no time.* | *Her injuries were horrifying. Only her determination and robust constitution pulled her through.*

robust /rə'bʌst, 'rəʊbʌst/ [adj] written someone who is **robust** is very healthy, strong, and active, and almost never ill: *He was a robust little boy, with curly dark hair.* | *Paul travelled north to visit his parents, who he found less robust than before.*

3 someone who looks healthy

- healthy-looking
- be a picture of health

healthy-looking /'helθi lʊkɪŋ/ [adj] looking very healthy: *Two healthy-looking suntanned kids were playing in the driveway.* | *Even the most healthy-looking person could be carrying HIV.*

be a picture of health /biː ə ˌpɪktʃər əv 'helθ/ [v phrase] use this to say that someone looks extremely healthy: *The baby lay in her father's arms, a picture of health and contentment.* | **look the picture of health** *In spite of all her complaints, Jilly looked the picture of health.*

4 how healthy or unhealthy you are

- health

health /helθ/ [n U] *Linda's one of those people who always seem to be worrying about their health.* | **health problems** *Pollution in the atmosphere causes serious health problems for many people.* | **mental/physical health** *Too much stress is likely to affect both your mental and physical health.* | **be in good/poor health** (=be healthy or unhealthy) *There's no reason why you shouldn't continue working until you're 70 or over, if you're in good health.*

5 the state of being healthy

- health
- wellbeing
- wellness

health /helθ/ [n U] *For most animals, a shiny coat is a sign of health.* | *Your health is more important than any amount of money.*

wellbeing /ˌwel'biːɪŋ‖'welbiːɪŋ/ [n U] the condition of being healthy, happy, and having no problems **the wellbeing of sb/sb's wellbeing** *A warm home is essential to the wellbeing of elderly people.* | **physical/mental/emotional etc wellbeing** *Samuel Roberts was a large man in his fifties who exuded physical wellbeing and self confidence.* | **a feeling/sense of wellbeing** *It's a relaxing treatment that should leave you calm with a sense of wellbeing.*

wellness /'welnɪ̈s/ [n U] American when someone is usually healthy and does things to take care of their health, such as exercising and eating good foods: *In Denmark, regular health visiting promotes wellness by developing healthier children.* | *The institute trains people to manage wellness programs for industries, schools, communities and hospitals.*

6 something that makes or keeps you healthy

- healthy
- be good for you/be good for your health
- do sb good
- wholesome
- nutritious
- nourishing
- healthful
- beneficial

healthy /'helθi/ [adj] *Taking plenty of exercise can be both healthy and enjoyable.* | *I'm trying to eat a healthier diet now, with less fat and sugar.* | *a healthy outdoor life*

be good for you/be good for your health /biː 'gʊd fəʳ juː, biː ˌgʊd fəʳ jɔːʳ 'helθ/ [v phrase] if something **is good for you** or **is good for your health**, it makes you more healthy or stops you getting ill: *Citrus fruits such as oranges and lemons are very good for you.* | *I can't see how gazing at a crystal is in any way good for your health.* | *I love junkfood but I know it's not good for me.*

do sb good /ˌduː (sb) 'gʊd/ [v phrase] if something **does you good**, it makes you feel better physically or emotionally, especially when you have not been feeling well: *I thought that a vacation would do me good.* | *Let's ask Jean to come tonight.. It might do her good to meet some new people.* | **do sb the world of good** (=make you feel a lot better) *What you need is a good night out – it'd do you the world of good!*

wholesome /'həʊlsəm/ [adj] food that is **wholesome** helps you stay healthy because it has nothing unhealthy added to it and is usually prepared very simply: *'Rosie's Pantry' is a small restaurant that serves good wholesome food.* | *Quality controllers ensure that all our products are safe, wholesome, and of good quality.*

nutritious /njuː'trɪʃəs‖nuː-/ [adj] food that is **nutritious** is full of natural substances that your body needs to stay healthy or to grow properly: *Brown bread is more nutritious than white.* | *I eat a lot of beans, lentils and vegetables, which are nutritious but cheap.* | *Milk is a very nutritious food, containing protein, vitamins and minerals.*

nourishing /ˈnʌrɪʃɪŋ‖ˈnɜː-, ˈnʌ-/ [adj] food that is **nourishing** helps your body to grow or to stay healthy and also gives you energy: *A simple chicken soup is both nourishing and delicious.* | *Preparing good nourishing family meals was a challenge with eight mouths to feed.* | *The Centre is open throughout the year, to ensure that homeless people can get at least one hot, nourishing meal a day.*

healthful /ˈhelθfəl/ [adj] American food or activities that are **healthful** help keep your body healthy: *The American breakfast is getting more healthful, with whole-grain breads and high-fiber cereals.* | *Our research group found that consumers want healthful food based on vegetables not meat products.*

beneficial /ˌbenəˈfɪʃəl◂/ [adj] formal something that is **beneficial** makes you more healthy or helps you to stay healthy: *The occasional glass of wine is both enjoyable and beneficial.* | **+ to** *This treatment can be very beneficial, especially to young children.*

7 someone who is not healthy

- **unhealthy**

- *see also* **ill/sick, illness/disease, mentally ill, pain, weak, doctor, medical treatment**

unhealthy /ʌnˈhelθi/ [adj] not usually healthy, so that you easily become ill: *James was a thin, pale, unhealthy child.* | *People who are very overweight tend to be more unhealthy than others.* | *At the age of 30 I was fat, unhealthy, and smoked two packs of cigarettes a day.*

8 something that is bad for your health

- **be bad for you/be bad for your health**
- **unhealthy**
- **harmful**
- **damaging**

be bad for you/be bad for your health /biː ˈbæd fəʳ juː, biː ˌbæd fəʳ jɔːʳ ˈhelθ/ [v phrase] to make you less healthy or make you ill: *Children always seem to love food that's bad for them – ice-cream, sugar, burgers.* | *Everyone knows that smoking is bad for your health.*

unhealthy /ʌnˈhelθi/ [adj] likely to make you ill or less healthy: *He has such an unhealthy lifestyle – smoking, drinking, eating too much.* | *An unhealthy diet is one that is too high in fat and sugar and too low in fibre.* | *My mother thought it was unhealthy to sleep with the windows shut at night.*

harmful /ˈhɑːʳmfəl/ [adj] likely to have a bad effect on your health: *The new air pollution controls are designed to limit harmful emissions from industry and motor vehicles.* | *You should always use sunscreen to protect your skin from the harmful effects of the sun.* | **+ to** *As yet there is no proof that genetically modified foods are harmful to humans.*

damaging /ˈdæmɪdʒɪŋ/ [adj] very harmful to your health, and usually having a permanent effect: *Avoid too much exposure to damaging ultraviolet light.* | **+ to** *X-rays can be extremely damaging to living cells.*

hear

RELATED WORDS

- to listen to what someone is saying, to music etc *see* **listen**
- *see also* **sound, loud, quiet**

1 to hear something or someone

- **hear**
- **overhear**

hear /hɪəʳ/ [v I/T not in progressive] *Did you hear that noise?* | *Suddenly we heard a knock at the door.* | *Say that again – I didn't hear you.* | *She called after him but he kept on walking and pretended not to hear.* | **hear sb/sth doing sth** *Neighbours heard the child screaming and called the police.* | *I could have sworn I heard the phone ringing.* | **hear sb/sth do sth** *I heard the front door close, and knew that Bob had left for work.* | *Did you hear them announce the result?*

overhear /ˌəʊvəʳˈhɪəʳ/ [v T not in progressive] to accidentally hear what someone is saying, when they do not realize that you can hear them: *Claire, who was outside the door, overheard their conversation.* | **overhear sb saying/talking etc** *We overheard Jenny and her friends talking about their boyfriends last night.* | **I couldn't help overhearing** (=say this when you have accidentally overheard someone saying something) *I couldn't help overhearing you and Jim last night – is something wrong?*

2 the ability to hear

- **hearing**

hearing /ˈhɪərɪŋ/ [n U] **sb's hearing** *My hearing's not very good – can you speak a little louder please?* | **sense of hearing** *Bats have a very powerful sense of hearing.* | **lose your hearing** (=become unable to hear) *Paula lost her hearing after a tragic car accident.* | **loss of hearing** *Years of playing in a rock band had resulted in a loss of hearing.*

3 when you can hear something or someone

- **can hear**
- **can make out**
- **audible**
- **within earshot**
- **carry**

can hear /kən ˈhɪəʳ/ [v phrase] *You don't have to shout, I can hear you!* | *The explosion could be heard over 10 miles away.* | *Can you hear all right or do you want me to turn the television up?* | **can hear sb/sth doing sth** *We knew he was asleep because we could hear him snoring.* | **can hear what sb says** *Could you hear what she was saying?*

can make out /kən ˌmeɪk ˈaʊt/ [v phrase] if you **can make out** what someone is saying, you can hear them but it is difficult: *She was crying and the only thing I could make out was Lou's name.* | *Sarah spoke so softly that Kathryn could hardly make out her words.* | *Now and then I could just make out George's voice above the music.* | *I could make out the sound of thunder in the distance.*

audible /ˈɔːdəbəl/ [adj] loud enough to be heard: *The signal is clearly audible up to 200 miles away.* | *When the engine finally started she gave an audible sigh of relief.* | **barely audible** (=almost not audible) *His voice was barely audible above the noise of the generator.*

within earshot /wɪðɪn ˈɪəʳʃɒt‖-ʃɑːt/ [adv] if you are **within earshot**, you are near enough to someone to be able to hear what they are saying: *You can play anywhere on the beach as long as you stay within earshot.* | **+ of** *Two of the shop assistants were complaining loudly within earshot of the customers.*

carry /ˈkæri/ [v I] if a sound **carries**, it can be heard a long distance away from where the sound was made: *Deeper sounds carry further than high-pitched ones.* | **+ across/down/through etc sth** *Their voices carried across the lake to where we were sitting.*

4 when you cannot hear someone or something

- can't hear
- didn't hear
- didn't catch
- can't make sth out
- inaudible
- out of earshot

can't hear /ˌkɑːnt ˈhɪəʳ‖ˌkænt-/ [v phrase] *Speak up a bit. I can't hear you.* | *Could you turn the radio up – I can't hear the news.* | *Let's move nearer to the front. I can't hear very well here.* | *The music was so loud that I couldn't hear what she was saying.*

didn't hear /ˌdɪdnt ˈhɪəʳ/ use this when you did not hear something at all, especially when you did not realize there was anything to hear: *I was outside in the yard, so I didn't hear the phone.* | *She was staring out of the window and didn't hear the teacher.* | **didn't hear sb do sth** *What time did you get back last night? I didn't hear you come in.* | **didn't hear sb/sth doing sth** *She didn't hear the car pulling up outside the house.*

didn't catch /ˌdɪdnt ˈkætʃ/ [v phrase] **spoken** say this when you did not hear what someone said, because they were speaking too quietly or because you were not listening carefully: *'What did he just say?' 'I didn't quite catch it.'* | *I'm sorry, I didn't catch your name.* | *He turned away from me so I didn't catch what he said.*

can't make sth out /ˌkɑːnt meɪk (sth) ˈaʊt‖ˌkænt-/ [v phrase] **spoken** to not be able to hear what someone is saying because it is very quiet or unclear: *Mat whispered something but I couldn't make out the words.* | *She knew they were arguing though she couldn't make out exactly what they were saying,*

inaudible /ɪnˈɔːdɪ̇bəl/ [adj] not loud enough to be heard: *Nick's voice was inaudible through the glass barrier.* | *Three girls were singing something but their words were almost inaudible.*

out of earshot /ˌaʊt əv ˈɪəʳʃɒt‖-ʃɑːt/ [adv] if you are **out of earshot** you are not near enough to someone or something to be able to hear them: *As soon as the guards were out of earshot, Grimes explained his plans.* | **+ of** *The social worker wanted to talk to the children out of earshot of their parents.*

5 make something impossible to hear

- drown out

drown out /ˌdraʊn ˈaʊt/ [phr v T] if something **drowns** something or someone **out**, it is so loud or noisy that you cannot hear them properly: *His voice was drowned out by the traffic.* | **drown out sth** *The applause from the audience almost drowned out the music.* | **drown sth out** *Some of the crowd were now hissing and stamping their feet in an attempt to drown him out.*

6 someone who cannot hear

- deaf
- be hard of hearing
- hearing impaired

deaf /def/ [adj] *Her second child, Oscar, was born deaf.* | *There is no reason why deaf people wouldn't lead perfectly normal lives.* | **go deaf** (=become deaf) *You'll need to speak quite loudly because my father's going deaf.* | **the deaf** (=deaf people) *More programmes these days have subtitles for the deaf.* | **stone deaf/deaf as a post** especially British (=completely deaf) *Mr Farrer, a white-haired man in his fifties, had been stone deaf since he was a child.* —**deafness** [n U] *Deafness should not be an obstacle to finding work.*

be hard of hearing /biː ˌhɑːʳd əv ˈhɪərɪŋ/ [v phrase] to be unable to hear well: *My grandfather's a little hard of hearing, so he has the TV on very loud.* | **the hard of hearing** (=people who are hard of hearing) *The library provides films with subtitles for the hard of hearing.*

hearing impaired /ˈhɪərɪŋ ɪmˌpeəʳd/ [adj only before noun] not able to hear – use this especially about things that are provided especially for people who cannot hear. **Hearing impaired** is a more polite word than **deaf**: *Each lecture will be translated by the signer for the benefit of hearing impaired students.* | *special classes for hearing impaired children*

heavy

RELATED WORDS

opposite: **light (4-5)**

- *see also* **weigh, fat**

1 weighing a lot

- heavy
- weigh a ton
- weight

heavy /ˈhevi/ [adj] *That table's too heavy for you to lift on your own.* | *Boys are usually slightly heavier than girls at birth.* | *Heat the oil in a large, heavy saucepan.*

weigh a ton /ˌweɪ ə ˈtʌn/ [v phrase] **spoken** to be very heavy or to be a lot heavier than you expected: *What on earth have you got in this suitcase? It weighs a ton!* | *That piano weighs a ton. You'll need four men to lift it.*

weight /weɪt/ [n U] use this to say that something is very heavy: *Victory was easy for a man of his weight and strength.* | **the weight of sth** *Several branches had been torn from the trees by the weight of the snow.* | *Jim was staggering along under the weight of a huge box of encyclopaedias.*

2 how heavy someone or something is

- weigh
- be 5 kilos/10 pounds etc
- how heavy
- weight

weigh /weɪ/ [v] to be a particular weight: *What do you weigh – a hundred kilos or so?* | **weigh 50 kilos/15 tons etc** *She weighs about 58 kg.* | *Each whale was about 40 feet long and weighed 45 tonnes.* | **how much sb/sth weighs** *How much does this parcel weigh?* | *She didn't tell me how much the baby weighed.*

be 5 kilos/10 pounds etc /biː ˌfaɪv ˈkiːləʊz/ [v phrase] to weigh five kilos, ten pounds etc: *Fortunately my suitcase was less than 25 kilos.* | *I've put on weight recently, so I'm probably about 120 kilos.*

how heavy /haʊ ˈhevi/ use this to ask or say how much something weighs, especially something that is very heavy: *Well, how heavy is your boat? would it go on top of the car?* | *You'd be surprised how heavy these boxes are.*

weight /weɪt/ [n singular] the amount that something or someone weighs: *If you can guess the weight of the cake, you win a prize.* | *The cost of transportation depends on the weight of the load.* | *Premature babies have a low birth weight.* | *Vehicles over a certain weight are not allowed to use the bridge.*

hello

RELATED WORDS

opposite: **goodbye**

▸ *see also* **meet**

1 ways to say hello

- **hello**
- **hi**
- **hi there**
- **how are you?/how are you doing?/how's it going?**
- **morning/afternoon/evening**
- **good morning/afternoon/evening**

hello /həˈləʊ, he-/ *Hello, Sally. How are you doing today?* | *Hello. Could I speak to someone in customer service?* | *'Hello, Mr Decker.' 'Hello, John. I didn't expect to see you here.'*

hi informal **/hiya** informal **/hey** American informal /haɪ, ˈhaɪjə, heɪ/ say this when you are greeting someone, especially a friend or relative. **Hiya** and **hey** are more informal than **hi**, and you say them to people you know very well: *Hi, Gwen – did you have a nice weekend?* | *Hi. I'm just calling to see if you'd like to come over for dinner tonight.* | *Hiya, Jake. How's it going?* | *Hey, Scott. What's up, buddy?*

hi there informal **hey there** American informal /ˈhaɪ ðeəʳ, ˈheɪ ðeəʳ/ say this when you are greeting someone, especially someone you did not expect to see: *Hi there, Mark! Did you have trouble getting here?* | *Hey there, stranger. We haven't seen you around here for a long time.*

how are you?/how are you doing?/how's it going? informal /haʊ ˈɑːʳ juː, ˌhaʊ əʳ juː ˈduːɪŋ, ˌhaʊz ɪt ˈgəʊɪŋ/ say this when you are greeting someone and starting a conversation: *How's it going, Tom? I haven't seen you for a long time.* | *Morning, Bob. How are you today?* | *Hi, Val. How are you doing? Did you get the job?*

morning/afternoon/evening /ˈmɔːʳnɪŋ, ˌɑːftəʳˈnuːn ‖ˌæf-, ˈiːvnɪŋ/ say this as a quick greeting at a particular time of day, especially when you work with the person you are greeting and see them regularly: *Morning, everyone. Sorry I'm late.* | *Afternoon, Sheila – got time for a quick cup of coffee?* | *Evening, all! Can I buy anyone a drink?*

good morning/afternoon/evening /gʊd ˈmɔːʳnɪŋ, ˌɑːftəʳˈnuːn‖-ˌæf-, ˈiːvnɪŋ/ formal say this to greet someone at a particular time of the day: *Good afternoon. I have a three o'clock appointment with Ms. Davis.* | *Good morning, class! To start with I have a couple of announcements.* | *Good evening, Raym. Let me introduce David Bruce.*

2 ways to say hello to someone when you first meet them

- **hello**
- **pleased/good/nice to meet you**
- **how do you do**

hello /həˈləʊ, he-/ *'Dad, this is Kevin.' 'Hello, Kevin. Andrea's told me a lot about you.'* | **hello, I'm ... /hello, my name's ...** *Hello, I'm Alan Simmons. I work in the production team.*

pleased/good/nice to meet you /ˌpliːzd, ˌgʊd, ˌnaɪs tə ˈmiːt juː/ say this when you meet someone for the first time and have just been told their name: *'Richard, this is my brother Ronnie.' 'Nice to meet you, Ronnie.'* | *Mrs. Parrish, it's good to meet you after hearing Lynn talk so much about you.* | *'My name is Lena Curtis.' 'Pleased to meet you, I'm David Bennet.'*

how do you do /ˌhaʊ djə ˈduː/ formal say this when you are meeting someone for the first time, especially when you have just been told their name: *How do you do, sir. My name is Greg Dunbar.* | *'Sue, this is Mr. Vance.' 'Oh, how do you do.'*

3 ways to ask someone to say hello to someone else for you

- **say hello/say hi (for sb)**
- **send your love**
- **send your regards**
- **give my love/regards to**

say hello/say hi (for sb) /ˌseɪ həˈləʊ, ˌseɪ ˈhaɪ (fəʳ (sb))/ [v phrase] *By the way, Dad says hi!* | **+ to** *I'd better go now. Say hello to Shelley for me, will you?*

send your love /ˌsend jɔːʳ ˈlʌv/ [v phrase] to ask someone to give your loving greetings to someone else when they see them, write to them etc: *Nick's sorry he couldn't be here, but he sends his love.* | **+ to** *Aunt Mary sends her love to you and the children.*

send your regards /ˌsend jɔːʳ rɪˈgɑːʳdz/ [v phrase] to ask someone to give your greetings to someone else when they see them, write to them etc: *I talked to Steven on the phone the other day and he sends his regards.*

give my love/regards to ALSO **give sb my love/regards** /ˌgɪv maɪ ˈlʌv, rɪˈgɑːʳdz tuː, ˌgɪv (sb) maɪ ˈlʌv, rɪˈgɑːʳdz/ [v phrase] use this to ask someone to give your greetings to someone else when they see them, write to them etc – use **give my love to sb** especially about family or close friends: *Give my love to your mother when you see her.* | *Have a wonderful evening and give Tim my regards.*

4 to say hello to someone

- **say hello**
- **greet**
- **greeting**
- **welcome**

say hello /ˌseɪ həˈləʊ/ [v phrase] *The two men said hello and shook hands.* | *I saw Mrs Trevors in the village, and she didn't even say hello!* | *I just wanted to call and say hello and find out how you're doing.*

greet /griːt/ [v T] to say hello to someone when they arrive, showing that you are pleased to see them: *She greeted each of the guests as they came through the door.* | *Mr Grimshaw got up from behind his desk to greet me and offer me a chair.*

greeting /ˈgriːtɪŋ/ [n plural] the words you use to say hello to someone when they arrive and show that you are pleased to see them: *Michelle shouted out a* *greeting from across the room.* | *Siegfried bustled in, muttered a greeting, and began to pour his coffee.* | **exchange greetings** (=greet someone and be greeted by them) *Jim paused next to the fence to exchange greetings with his neighbor on the other side.*

welcome /ˈwelkəm/ [v T] to greet someone who has arrived for the first time in your town, home, office etc, and show that you are glad they have come: *The visitors were welcomed at reception and shown where to go.* | *Texans tend to welcome newcomers and go out of their way to be friendly.* — **welcome** [n singular] **give sb a warm welcome** (=welcome someone in a very friendly way) *Their guests were given a very warm welcome on arrival.*

help

RELATED WORDS

▸ *see also* **comfort/make sb feel better, support, advise, advantage, disadvantage**

1 to help someone

- help
- give/lend a hand
- assist
- do sth for
- do sb a favour
- help out
- do sb a good turn
- do your bit
- come to sb's aid/assistance
- give help/ assistance/support

help /help/ [v I/T] to make it easier for someone to do something by doing part of their work, showing them what to do, or giving them something they need: *I'm ready to help. Is there something for me to do?* | *Dad, I don't understand my homework. Will you help me?* | *The money will be used to help starving children around the world.* | **+ with** *Dan's mother has been great about helping with the kids.* | **help do sth** *Warren offered to help clean up the house after the party.* | **help to do sth** *Part of the assistant's job is to help to organize conferences and keep the director informed.* | **help sb do sth** *Help me lift this, will you?* | **help sb to do sth** *Her uncle said he would help her to find a job.* | **help sb with sth** *Do you want me to help you with those bags?* | **help sb into/off/across/ down etc** (=help someone go somewhere) *'Did you enjoy the trip?' asked Jack, helping her out of the boat.*

give/lend a hand /ˌgɪv, ˌlend ə ˈhænd/ [v phrase] informal to help someone do something, especially something they have to do in their home such as carrying or lifting things: *Scott is moving Saturday and I promised to lend a hand.* | **give/lend sb a hand** *Give me a hand and let's see if we can get this box in the car.* | **+ with** *Could you give me a hand with the shopping.*

assist /əˈsɪst/ [v I/T] formal to help someone do something, especially by doing all the easier or less important things for them so that their job is easier: *Can you do the job alone, or do you want someone to assist you?* | **+ in** *In this position, you will assist in training new employees.* | **+ with** *Some of the guests assisted with the preparation of the food.* | **assist sb in/with sth** *A consultant has been brought in to assist management in restructuring the company.*

do sth for /ˈduː (sth) fɔːʳ/ [v phrase] to help someone by doing something for them that they would normally do themselves: *If you're not feeling well, I'll do the shopping for you.* | *Did you have someone do your homework for you? It doesn't look like your writing.*

do sb a favour British **/favor** American /ˌduː (sb) ə ˈfeɪvəʳ/ [v phrase] to do something to help someone, especially a friend or someone you know well: *Could you do me a favour and mail these letters for me?* | *She's always doing favours for us. The least we can do is help her out now.* | **do sb a big favour/favor** (=help someone a lot) *They did us a big favor by letting us stay there, you know.*

help out /ˌhelp ˈaʊt/ [phr v I/T] to help someone do something, especially because there are not enough people to do all the work: *Their son used to help out in the shop when it was busy.* | *Organizing the school trip will be a lot of work, so I need some volunteers to help out.* | **+ with** *The kids are always good about helping out with the chores.* | **help sb out** *While I'm gone, try to help your Mom out, OK?* | **help out sb** *No need to thank me – I was just glad to help out a friend.*

do sb a good turn /ˌduː (sb) ə ˌgʊd ˈtɜːʳn/ [v phrase] to help someone by doing something for them that they have not asked you to do, because you think they need your help and you want to help them: *She's always happy to do a stranger a good turn.* | *He did me a good turn when he advised me not to sell my house – it's worth twice as much now.*

do your bit British **/do your part** American /ˌduː jɔːʳ ˈbɪt, ˌduː jɔːʳ ˈpɑːʳt/ [v phrase] to do what you can to help in a bad or difficult situation, especially because you think you are expected to do it or that it is your duty: *I've done my bit – now it's up to you.* | **+ for** *Brown feels that she's done her part for the Democratic Party.*

come to sb's aid/assistance /ˌkʌm tə (sb's) ˈeɪd, əˈsɪstəns/ [v phrase] formal to offer to help someone who is in difficulty and who will not be able to continue without your help: *It took an ambulance 27 minutes to come to the aid of the accident victims.* | *Many expect the central government to come to the assistance of the ailing industry.*

give help/assistance/support /gɪv ˈhelp, əˈsɪstəns, səˈpɔːʳt/ [v phrase] to help a person or group **+ to** *The program gives assistance to unemployed mothers and their children.* | **give sb help/assistance/support** *My family gave me very little support when I decided to go back to college.* | *Any kind of help you can give would be greatly appreciated.*

2 to help someone by making them feel more confident and less worried

- encourage
- be supportive
- support
- give sb moral support

encourage /ɪnˈkʌrɪdʒ‖ɪnˈkɜːr-/ [v T] to say or do things that help someone feel confident enough to do something, for example by telling them they are good enough to do it, by giving them advice etc: *She was always looking for ways to encourage her students.* | **encourage sb to do sth** *I would never have won if my friends hadn't encouraged me to keep trying.*

be supportive /biː səˈpɔːʳtɪv/ [v phrase] to make someone feel less worried and more confident by talking to them in a sympathetic way and giving them practical help: *It was a difficult decision, but my family was very supportive.* | **+ of** *My husband has always been very supportive of everything that I do.*

support /səˈpɔːʳt/ [v T] to help someone by being sympathetic and kind to them during a difficult time in their life: *She is my daughter, and I will love* *and support her no matter what happens.* | *I am very grateful to members of the faculty who have supported me in so many ways.* —**support** [n U] sympathetic encouragement and help that you give to someone: *He was grateful for his friends' support during his divorce.* | **+ of** *I would not have been able to finish writing the book without the support of my husband and family.*

give sb moral support /ˌgɪv (sb) ˌmɒrəl səˈpɔːʳt‖-ˌmɔː-/ [v phrase] to help someone, especially someone who is in a difficult situation, by telling them that they are right in what they are doing, and encouraging them to be brave, confident, etc: *She was very nervous about the interview, so I went along to give her some moral support.* | *The US is giving the rebel leaders moral support, but so far no weapons.*

3 to help something to happen

- help
- encourage
- promote
- aid
- benefit
- advance/further
- be conducive to
- give sth a boost
- be favourable for/to

help /help/ [v T] to **help** something such as an improvement to happen: *The plan was intended to help development in rural areas.* | **help do sth** *Spending time in Spain should help improve her Spanish.* | **help to do sth** *It is hoped that the tax increases will help to stabilize the economy.*

encourage /ɪnˈkʌrɪdʒ‖ɪnˈkɜːr-/ [v T] to make something more likely to happen or make people more likely to do something, often something that you think they should not do: *Congress is considering tax breaks to encourage investment.* | *Damp conditions encourage the growth of the fungus.* | **encourage sb to do sth** *Cigarette machines in the streets will only encourage more teenagers to smoke.*

promote /prəˈməʊt/ [v T] formal **promote good relations/cooperation/trade etc** to help something good to happen or to develop and increase: *The aim of the meeting is to promote trade between the two countries.* | *A balanced diet promotes good health and normal development.* —**promotion** /prəˈməʊʃən/ [n U] *Government policies have focussed on the promotion of economic growth.*

aid /eɪd/ [v T] formal to help something get better, develop, grow etc: *The country's economic recovery has been aided by increased international trade.* | *The large number of Latino voters aided Garcia's victory in the last election.*

benefit /ˈbenǝ̣fɪt/ [v T] to give advantages to someone or something, so that something can improve: *Critics argue that the tax cuts will only benefit large companies.* | *Admission is $5, with proceeds benefiting a local children's charity.*

advance/further /ədˈvɑːns‖ədˈvæns, ˈfɜːʳðəʳ/ [v T] to help something you are trying to do to be successful: *Separatist rebels have used terrorism to advance their cause in the region.* | *The associations allow professionals to band together to further their interests.*

be conducive to /biː kənˈdjuːsɪv tuː‖-ˈduː-/ [v phrase] formal if a situation **is conducive to** something such as work, rest etc, it provides the conditions that make it easier: *All this noise is hardly conducive to rest and relaxation.* | *We want to create an atmosphere conducive to serious discussion.*

give sth a boost /ˌgɪv (sth) ə ˈbuːst/ [v phrase] to help something such as a business so that it suddenly begins to develop more quickly: *The recent drop in interest rates has given the economy a much needed boost.* | **+ to** *The central government also privatized farmland, giving a boost to food production.*

be favourable for/to British **/be favorable for/to** American /biː ˈfeɪvərəbəl fɔːʳ, tuː/ [v phrase] written if conditions **are favourable for** or **to** something such as an agreement or an improvement in a situation, they make it more likely to happen: *The conditions are now favorable for job creation and economic growth.* | *The conference has produced a political climate that is favourable to a peace settlement.*

4 ways of saying that something helps you to do something

- help
- assist
- aid
- be a help
- helpful
- beneficial
- be a boon
- with the aid of

help /help/ [v I/T] to make it easier for someone to do something or to make a difficult situation easier: *I took a couple of aspirin for my headache, but they didn't help.* | *The warm weather this spring has certainly helped the farmers.* | **help sb do sth** *All this arguing isn't going to help us win the election.* | **help sb to do sth** *The latest report should help us to evaluate the true benefits of the program.*

assist /əˈsɪst/ [v I/T] formal to help someone do something: *They have developed a computerized system that will greatly assist all library users.* | **assist sb in/with sth** *The guide is written to assist consumers in choosing the best insurance plan.*

aid /eɪd/ [v I/T] formal to help someone or something achieve something, by making the situation that they are in easier: *The new government grants are intended to aid small businesses.* | *Our ability to combat organized crime has been aided by our partnership with local police.* | **+ in** *The new equipment has been provided to aid in the diagnosis of liver disorders.*

be a help /biː ə ˈhelp/ [v phrase] if something **is a help**, it makes it easier for you to do something, especially something that would be difficult to do without it: *For the teachers, just having more books and equipment would be a help.* | **be a big/great/real help** *Stating your objectives clearly will be a great help in organizing the research.*

helpful /ˈhelpfəl/ [v phrase] making it likely to be easier for you to do or achieve something: *If you're looking for a good guidebook, I found this one to be very helpful.* | *She gave us some helpful advice about renting apartments.* | **+ in** *Giving the test can be helpful in deciding the best way to treat a patient.* | **it is helpful to do sth** *It's helpful to prepare a list of questions before going to an interview.*

beneficial /ˌbenǝ̣ˈfɪʃəl◂/ [adj] actions, experiences, changes etc that are **beneficial** help to improve someone's situation or give them an advantage: *The relationship between the two companies has been mutually beneficial.* | **+ to** *Recent studies show that moderate amounts of alcohol are beneficial to health.* | **beneficial effect/impact/result** *There is no evidence that the diet pills have any beneficial effect on weight loss.*

be a boon /biː ə ˈbuːn/ [v phrase] something that **is a boon** happens or is given to you, especially unexpectedly, and makes it much easier for you to do something: *Having a bicycle was a tremendous boon as our house was so far from the village.* | **+ to/for** *The current low exchange rates are a boon for exporters.* | *Increased competition among airlines will prove to be a boon to tourists.*

with the aid of /wɪð ði 'eɪd ɒv/ [prep] if you do something **with the aid of** something, especially an object, you need that thing to help you do it: *The bacteria can only be seen with the aid of a high power microscope.* | *Since the accident he's only been able to walk with the aid of a cane.*

5 someone who helps another person to do something

- assistant
- helper
- aide
- aide
- accomplice
- right-hand man

assistant /ə'sɪstənt/ [n C] someone who is employed to help someone do their job, especially by doing all the easier or less important things for them so that their job is made easier: *The dentist had her assistant sterilise the instruments.* | **+ to** *Lydia is the assistant to the Director of Finance.* | **assistant manager/director/editor etc** *Winston got a job as assistant manager at Wal-Mart.*

helper /'helpə^r/ [n C] someone who helps someone else to do something, especially when they want to do it and are not paid for it: *Ella works at the hospital once a week as a voluntary helper.* | *Helpers are needed to run the book stall and man the bar.*

aide /eɪd/ [n C] someone who is employed to help a very important person, especially someone in politics or government: *An aide confirmed this week that the President will not be running for re-election.* | **+ to** *Anderson has worked as an aide to the mayor for three years.*

aide ALSO **aid** /eɪd/ [n C] American **teacher's aid/nurse's aid** someone whose job is to help a teacher, nurse etc to do their work, especially by doing the less important jobs: *Amelia went to work as a nurse's aide in the children's wing of the hospital.* | *As a teacher's aide, I help watch the children and run errands for the teacher.*

accomplice /ə'kʌmplɪ̈s‖ə'kɑːm-, ə'kʌm-/ [n C] someone who helps someone else in a crime: *Evans could not have carried out the robbery without an accomplice.* | *One man held a gun on her while his accomplice took the money.* | **+ in/to** *She has been accused of being an accomplice in the kidnapping.*

right-hand man /ˌraɪt hænd 'mæn/ [n C] the person who someone in a position of authority depends on most to help and support them: *Beria, the head of the KGB, was Stalin's right-hand man.* | *Newman's resignation leaves his boss without a right-hand man.*

6 help that is given

- help
- assistance
- a hand
- aid
- support
- service
- back-up/backup
- encouragement

help /help/ [n U] *If I need any help I'll call you.* | *I'm having trouble paying the rent, but I don't want to ask my parents for help.* | **+ with** *Would you like some help with those suitcases?* | **with help from sb** *We managed to buy the house with a little help from Dave's parents.* | **with the help of sb/sth** *With the help of a nicotine patch she was able to quit smoking.* | **get help** (=find someone to help you) *You go get help – I'll wait here with the car.*

assistance /ə'sɪstəns/ [n U] formal something you provide in order to help someone do something: *Patients can usually walk without assistance within a week of the operation.* | *The federal agency provides assistance to families whose homes were destroyed by flooding.* | *The company has a toll-free number that offers technical assistance to anyone who needs it.* | **be of assistance** *Our tour guides will be pleased to be of assistance if you have any problems.*

a hand /ə 'hænd/ [n singular] informal practical help from someone when something needs to be done: *Everybody needs a hand now and then.* | **+ with** *I could use a hand with the yard work if you're not busy.* | **lend/give sb a hand** *Could you give me a hand moving those boxes?*

aid /eɪd/ [n U] help, especially money, that an organization or country gives to another country or to people who are in a very difficult situation: *Aid is not getting through to the refugees.* | *Each year, the U.S. sends more than $1.8 billion in aid to sub-Saharan Africa.*

support /sə'pɔː^rt/ [n U] equipment, money, or help from other people that is available for you to use when you need it: *I'd like to thank you all for your support in the upcoming election.* | *Our two company lawyers provide all the legal support we need.*

service /'sɜː^rvɪ̈s/ [n U] help given to customers of a particular business, by the people who work there: *I thought the service in the pizza place was very good.* | **provide a service** *We knew the shop would never survive if we didn't provide a good service from the minute we opened the doors.*

back-up/backup /'bækʌp/ [n U] people, equipment etc that are provided to be used if people need help: *This department needs more secretarial and clerical back-up.* | *Police had to wait for backup to arrive before making any arrests.*

encouragement /ɪn'kʌrɪdʒmənt‖-'kɜːr-/ [n U] something such as praise or advice from other people that helps give someone the confidence and determination to do something: *Children need lots of encouragement when they're learning new things.* | **words of encouragement** *After his speech, he shook hands and offered words of encouragement to people in the crowd.* | **by way of encouragement** (=in order to encourage someone) *'But you're doing a great job,' he added by way of encouragement.*

7 words for describing someone who is helpful

- helpful
- be a help
- cooperative
- obliging
- accommodating

helpful /'helpfəl/ [adj] *Thanks, Sam. You've been very helpful.* | *A helpful woman at the tourist office gave me some tips on places to visit.* — **helpfully** [adv] *She explained how the machine worked as helpfully as she could.*

be a help /biː ə 'help/ [v phrase] if someone **is a help**, they make it easier for you to do something: *Thanks for looking after the children – you've really been a help.* | **be a big/great/real help** *Jim was a big help getting the house ready for the party.*

cooperative ALSO **co-operative** British /kəʊ'ɒpərətɪv‖-'ɑːp-/ [adj] someone who is **cooperative** helps someone who has asked them to help, by working together with them and not causing any problems: *Some of the students are highly cooperative and attentive, but unfortunately, most aren't.* | *The suspect has been cooperative with investigators, but he shows little remorse.*

obliging /ə'blaɪdʒɪŋ/ [adj] formal someone who is **obliging** is always ready to help and enjoys helping people, even people who are unreasonable or difficult: *The shop assistants were very obliging, and brought me at least fifteen pairs of shoes to try on.* —**obligingly** [adv] *'Let me get that,' he said and obligingly lifted the suitcase into the trunk.*

accommodating /ə'kɒmədeɪtɪŋ‖ə'kɑː-/ [adj] someone who is **accommodating** is willing to do what someone else wants, even if this is not the best thing for themselves, in order to help them or make them more comfortable: *He was very accommodating, always asking if I needed anything.* | *She's so nice and accommodating, I'm afraid people will take advantage of her.*

8 words for describing someone or something that is not helpful

- not helpful/unhelpful
- be no help/not be any help/not be much help
- uncooperative
- useless
- not lift a finger

not helpful/unhelpful /nɒt 'helpfəl, ʌn'helpfəl/ [adj] *He bought a book on relaxation techniques but it wasn't very helpful.* | *The authorities weren't helpful at all when Rob reported his passport stolen.* | *I found the sales assistants most unhelpful.*

be no help/not be any help/not be much help /biː ˌnəʊ 'help, ˌnɒt biː eni 'help, ˌnɒt biː mʌtʃ 'help/ [v phrase] if something or someone **is no help** they do not help you do something or get something: *Clarissa was no help – she just sat around and watched TV.* | *The phrase book wasn't much help in carrying on a conversation.*

uncooperative /ˌʌnkəʊ'ɒpərətɪv‖-'ɑːp-/ [adj] not wanting to help someone who wants you to help them, especially by deliberately opposing them or stopping them doing something easily: *Many of the older patients are uncooperative and difficult for the nurses to handle.* | *Hubbel has been a very uncooperative witness.*

useless /'juːsləs/ [adj] especially spoken not giving any help – use this when you are annoyed with someone or something because they should help you but they do not: *I tried calling the tax office but they were completely useless.* | **completely/absolutely useless** *There's no point reading the instructions – they're completely useless.*

not lift a finger /nɒt ˌlɪft ə 'fɪŋgəʳ/ [v phrase] if someone does **not lift a finger**, they do not help when help is wanted or needed, especially because they are lazy: *She stayed with us for two weeks and never lifted a finger the whole time.* | *Police knew there would be a fight, but they didn't lift a finger to try and stop it.*

9 having no one to help you

- on your own/by yourself
- helpless

on your own/by yourself /ɒn jɔːr 'əʊn, baɪ jɔːʳ'self/ [adv] if you do something **on your own** or **by yourself** you do it without help from anyone else: *Peter cooked everything by himself – he wouldn't even let me in the kitchen.* | *I doubt I would have been able to find this job on my own.* | **all on your own/all by yourself** (=used to emphasize that you do not have any help) *You mean to tell me he painted the whole house all by himself?*

helpless /'helpləs/ [adj] needing help because you cannot do anything for yourself or you need protection: *Why are you so afraid of a helpless old woman?* | *Frightened and helpless, Alvin wondered if they might kill him.* | **utterly helpless** *His mother's death left the boy feeling utterly helpless and alone.* —**helplessly** [adv] *I started to cry as helplessly as a baby.*

here/not here

RELATED WORDS

- *see also* **there/not there, place**

1 in this place

- here
- in this place
- on this (very) spot

here /hɪəʳ/ [adv] in or to the place where you are: *We've lived here for over a year now.* | *I'll stay here and wait for the others.* | *I love it here – it's so quiet and peaceful near the ocean.* | **around here/round here/near here** (=near this place) *Did you grow up around here?* | *I think Jeff lives somewhere near here.* | **right here** (=in this exact place) *The keys were right here 15 minutes ago. Where did they go?* | **from here** (=from this place) *I know a good Japanese restaurant not far from here.* | **down/in/up etc here** *'Where are you?' 'I'm down here in the basement.'* | **get/come/move etc here** *They got here about 15 minutes before you did.*

in this place /ɪn ˌðɪs 'pleɪs/ [adv] in the place where you are now, especially a place that you like or dislike: *I'm sick of living in this place – there's nothing to do.* | *It's impossible to find a decent restaurant in this place.*

on this (very) spot /ɒn ðɪs (ˌveri) 'spɒt‖-'spɑːt/ [adv] in the place where you are standing, especially a place where something very important happened in the past: *It was on this very spot that President Kennedy was assassinated.* | *It's exciting to think that so many great men and women have made speeches on this spot.*

2 to be here

- be here
- be around
- be in
- be present

be here /biː 'hɪəʳ/ [v phrase] *Check the names off the list to make sure everyone is here.* | *'Have you seen the can opener anywhere?' 'Yes, it's here on the counter.'* | *I'm not going out – I want to be here when Tony arrives.* | *The monument has been here since 1876.*

be around /biː ə'raʊnd/ [phr v I] if someone or something **is around**, they are here or somewhere in this area, especially when they are needed: *Chuck must be around – I just saw him a few minutes ago.* | *Are you going to be around at Christmas or are you going on holiday?* | *Yesterday's newspaper must still be around somewhere.*

be in /biː 'ɪn/ [v phrase] to **be in** your home, the place where you work etc, especially when you are expected to be there: *Hello Mrs Baxter. Is Mark in?* | *Sonia won't be in today – she's not feeling very well.* | *You can go out for a while but make sure you're in by 11 o'clock.*

be present /biː 'prezənt/ [v phrase] formal to be here, especially because you are expected or have planned to be here: *The teacher keeps a daily record of who is present.* | *The President was not able to be present for the ceremony.* | **those present** (=the people here) *Among those present were several film and television stars.*

3 to not be here

- not be here
- not be around
- be out/not be in
- be away
- be absent
- be off
- missing

not be here /nɒt biː ˈhɪəʳ/ [v phrase] *How would she know what happened? She wasn't even here.* | *Why aren't the scissors here where they belong?* | *The supermarket hasn't been here long but it's already doing a lot of business.*

not be around /nɒt biː əˈraʊnd/ [v phrase] if someone or something **is not around** they are not here or anywhere in this area, especially when they are needed: *If Julie isn't around, maybe Maria could help you.* | *Every time I want to talk to Ted, he's not around.* | *Why isn't there ever a taxi around when you need one?*

be out/not be in /biː ˈaʊt, nɒt biː ˈɪn/ [v phrase] to not be in your home, the place where you work etc for a short time, especially when someone wants to see you: *Sally phoned while you were out. I told her to phone back later.* | *Mr Rogers isn't in at the moment. Can I help you?* | *I'm going to be out all afternoon.* | *I'm so busy. If anyone calls for me, tell them I'm not in.*

be away /biː əˈweɪ/ [v phrase] to not be at home, school, or work for several days or weeks, because you are travelling or staying somewhere else: *'We're taking a trip to California.' 'Oh, how long do you plan to be away?'* | **+ from** *My job requires me to be away from home for five months of the year.* | **be away on business** *While Kurt was away on business, his wife completely redecorated the house.*

be absent /biː ˈæbsənt/ [v phrase] formal if someone **is absent**, they are not here, especially in school or the place where they work, because they are ill, on holiday etc: *According to the personnel department you have been absent twice this week already.* | **+ from** *James was absent from school again today.*

be off /biː ˈɒf/ [v phrase] informal if someone **is off**, they are not at work, usually because they are ill or on holiday. In British English you can also use this when someone is not at school: *I'll be off all next week, so I can do some of the yard work then.* | **+ with** *Becky's been off for several days with a bad back.* | **be off sick** *Chris has been off sick a lot lately.* | **be off school/work** British *Jenkins isn't off school again, is he? What's his excuse this time?*

missing /ˈmɪsɪŋ/ [adj] a **missing** thing is lost and may have been stolen; a **missing** person cannot be found and may be in danger: *One of my earrings is missing – have you seen it?* | **+ from** *Oh no! The last page is missing from the book!*

hide

RELATED WORDS

see also **secret, show**

1 to hide something especially by putting it in a secret place

- hide
- conceal
- stash
- cover
- bury
- secrete

hide /haɪd/ [v T] to make something difficult to see or find, for example by putting it somewhere secret, or by covering it: *Where can we hide these presents so the kids don't find them?* | **hide sth in/under/behind etc sth** *They put the money in a small box and hid it under the bed.* | *Some cameras are so small they can be hidden in a reporter's baseball cap.* | **hide sth from sb** *I used to hide his cigarettes from him so he couldn't smoke.*

conceal /kənˈsiːl/ [v T] formal to hide something carefully, especially by covering it **conceal sth in/under/behind etc sth** *The secret police had concealed microphones in the walls.* | *Several kilos of drugs had been concealed in the back of the truck.*

stash /stæʃ/ [v T] informal to hide money or something that you should not have **stash sth in/under/behind etc sth** *Where did you stash the drugs?* | *The late president supposedly stashed millions of dollars in Swiss bank accounts.*

cover /ˈkʌvəʳ/ [v T] to hide something by putting something else on or over it: *Embarrassed, she reached for a towel to cover her body.* | **cover sth with sth** *When he walked into the room, she quickly covered the letter with a pillow.* | **cover sth up/cover up sth** (=cover something completely) *You could probably cover up the scratches with a little bit of paint, and no one will ever notice.*

bury /ˈberi/ [v T] to hide something by putting it in or on the ground and covering it with soil, sand etc: *Snakes usually bury their eggs.* | **bury sth in/under etc sth** *He murdered his wife and buried her body in a field.* | *The dog buried one of my slippers in the backyard.* —**buried** [adj] *There was supposed to be buried treasure somewhere on the island.*

secrete /sɪˈkriːt/ [v T] formal to carefully hide small, valuable objects: *No one knew where the old woman had secreted her jewels.* | **secrete sth in/behind/among etc sth** *He showed me the coin briefly and then secreted it in some dark corner of his house.*

2 to hide yourself

- hide
- go into hiding
- lie low
- hole up
- stow away
- conceal yourself
- lie in wait
- lurk/skulk

hide /haɪd/ [v I] to go somewhere where you cannot be easily found or seen: *Dad's coming. Quick – hide!* | **+ under/behind/in etc** *Dale hid behind some garbage cans in the alley until the men passed.* | *The cat always hides under the bed when we have visitors.* | **+ from** *Why is he hiding from us? Is he afraid?*

go into hiding /ˌgəʊ ɪntə ˈhaɪdɪŋ/ [v phrase] to go to a safe place where you can hide for a long time because you are in danger or because the police are looking for you: *He went into hiding soon after the* *government denounced him.* | *Police believe the robbers have gone into hiding.*

lie low /ˌlaɪ ˈləʊ/ [v phrase] to hide from people who are trying to catch you, and to make sure you do not attract any attention until it is safe to come out: *If you don't want to go back to jail, you'd better lie low for a while.* | *Weaver had been lying low at his sister's apartment for the past week.*

hole up /ˌhəʊl ˈʌp/ [phr v I] to hide somewhere and not go out at all, especially because the police are looking for you: *We were all planning to hole up till the trouble blew over.* | **hole up in/on etc sth** *The gang holed up in a cheap hotel for a few weeks.* | **be holed up in/on etc sth** *The FBI believes that Richards is holed up on an estate in Colombia.*

stow away /ˌstəʊ əˈweɪ/ [phr v I] to hide in a ship in order to travel to a place without being noticed and without paying: *With no money, his only hope of getting to New York was to stow away on the next ship.* | *Customs officials discovered several illegal immigrants stowed away at the front of the ship.*

conceal yourself /kənˈsiːl jɔːʳself/ [v phrase] formal to hide yourself carefully so that you cannot be seen: *When police arrived, Black made no effort to hide or conceal herself.* | **+ in/beneath/behind etc** *It was easy for the man to conceal himself in the museum before closing time.* | **+ from** *Many spiders spin special webs to conceal themselves from danger.*

lie in wait /ˌlaɪ ɪn ˈweɪt/ [v phrase] to hide in a place in order to attack or stop someone you know will come there: *The tank commander feared there might be enemy soldiers lying in wait in the hills up ahead.* | **+ for** *Aitkins lay in wait for his victims and shot them as they walked toward their front door.*

lurk/skulk /lɜːʳk, skʌlk/ [v I] to wait or move around in a particular area while trying not to be seen, especially because you are going to do something wrong or something you do not want other people to know about: *Who's that skulking over there?* | **+ around/about** *Police received reports of a man lurking around the neighborhood.* | **+ in/behind/under etc** *I'm sure I saw someone lurking in the bushes just now.* | *He skulked along the street, looking this way and that to see if anyone was following him.*

3 to hide someone or something by making them look different

- disguise
- camouflage

disguise /dɪsˈgaɪz/ [v T] to make someone or something look different in order to deceive people, for example by changing someone's clothes or hair: *The FBI say the hijackers were very likely to have been disguised.* | **disguise sb/sth as** *The men had disguised the vessel as fishing boat to escape.* | *He spent several years in the monastery disguised as a monk.* | **disguise yourself as** *She managed to get into the camp by disguising herself as a soldier.*

camouflage /ˈkæməflɑːʒ/ [v T] to hide someone or something by covering them with materials that help them to look like the surrounding area: *We camouflaged the plane by covering it with leaves.* | **camouflage sb/sth with sth** *Soldiers had camouflaged the trucks with branches and dirt.* | **camouflage yourself** *The lizards camouflage themselves by changing colour.*

4 to make something difficult to see by being in front of or over it

- hide
- conceal
- cover
- screen
- blot out

hide /haɪd/ [v T] *Low clouds hid the top of the mountain.* | *Most of his face was hidden by a beard.* | *The bushes had become overgrown and now hid the entrance to the garden.* | **hide sth from view** *A pair of mirrored sunglasses hid her eyes from view.*

conceal /kənˈsiːl/ [v T] formal to hide something by covering it: *A wide-brimmed hat concealed her graying hair.* | *Her legs were concealed to the ankle by a loose flowing skirt.*

cover /ˈkʌvəʳ/ [v T] to be over something or on top of it so that it cannot be seen: *The make-up didn't cover her bruises as well as she'd hoped.* | *He pulled back a corner of the blanket that covered the dead body.*

screen /skriːn/ [v T] to hide something completely by being in front of it: *In the back yard, a hedge neatly screens the vegetable plot.* | **screen sth (off) from sth** *The house is screened from the road by a row of tall trees.*

blot out /ˌblɒt ˈaʊt‖ˌblɑːt-/ [phr v T] to cover something so completely that you are not able to see any of it **blot out sth** *The clouds of dust grew heavier till they blotted out the desert and the moon.* | **blot sth out** *The shadow of someone in the back of the theater blotted the movie screen out for a moment.*

5 a place where you can hide

- place to hide
- hiding place
- hideout

place to hide /ˌpleɪs tə ˈhaɪd/ [n phrase] a place where someone can hide: *We were grateful for a place to hide during the raids.* | *With the police closing in, he had no one to help him and no place to hide.*

hiding place /ˈhaɪdɪŋ pleɪs/ [n C] a place where someone can hide, or a place where you can hide something: *I've found a good hiding place for the money.* | *From his hiding place in the closet, Dwayne could hear the conversation in the bedroom.*

hideout /ˈhaɪdaʊt/ [n C] a place where someone goes to hide from the police or someone dangerous: *It is believed that the guerrillas have a hideout in the southern mountains.* | *Police raided the gang's hideout on Thursday, arresting six people.*

6 hidden

- hidden
- concealed

hidden /ˈhɪdn/ [adj] *Under the lampshade Harry discovered a hidden microphone.* | **+ under/behind/in etc** *She kept the letters hidden in a box in her closet.* | **+ away** *I've got the kids' presents all hidden away ready for Christmas day.* | **+ from** *The pit was hidden from view by branches and leaves that had been laid across it.*

concealed /kənˈsiːld/ [adj] something that is **concealed** has been deliberately hidden by someone, especially by covering it with something or by putting something in front of it: *Concealed cameras help security guards spot intruders.* | **+ behind/beneath/in etc** *One of the pistols was concealed in the lining of her coat.* | **+ by** *Half-concealed by the curtain, he peered out of the window.* | **+ from** *Sacred* *paintings are screened off, concealed from public view.* | **concealed weapon** *The man said he had a permit to carry a concealed weapon.*

7 to hide your feelings

- hide
- not show
- conceal
- disguise/mask
- bottle up
- suppress
- repress
- put on a brave face/ put up a brave front

hide /haɪd/ [v T] to deliberately not show what you are feeling or thinking: *He hides his real feelings under that big smile.* | *'That's OK,' she said, trying to hide her disappointment.* | **hide sth from sb** *I tried to hide my anxiety from the rest of the family by pretending that everything was normal.*

not show /nɒt 'ʃəʊ/ [v phrase] to not show in your face, voice, or movements what you really think or feel: *If she was surprised, she didn't show it.* | *My husband never shows emotion, so I never know if he's upset.*

conceal /kən'siːl/ [v T] formal to hide your feelings or intentions especially when you have to make an effort to do this: *Kim could barely conceal her annoyance that I had arrived so late.* | *I yawned, not bothering to conceal my boredom.* | **conceal sth from sb** *Hawkins was incapable of concealing how he felt from his close friends.*

disguise/mask /dɪs'gaɪz, mɑːsk‖mæsk/ [v T] to avoid showing your true feelings or intentions by pretending to feel something else: *Kate gave a cheerful smile, somehow managing to disguise her embarrassment.* | *'That's great!' she cried, unable to disguise her excitement.* | *He often masked his feelings of guilt by becoming angry at the people he had wronged.*

bottle up /ˌbɒtl 'ʌp‖ˌbɑː-/ [phr v T] to not allow yourself to show your feelings, especially if you are angry, worried, or upset – use this especially when you think it would be better for someone to show their feelings so they can be dealt with **bottle sth up** *It's not healthy to bottle all your feelings up like that.* | *The anger that he had bottled up inside him finally exploded.* | **keep sth bottled up** *She wanted to cry but she kept it bottled up inside.*

suppress /sə'pres/ [v T] formal to not allow yourself to feel or show strong feelings such as anger, sadness, or love, especially when you have difficulty controlling these feelings: *She had had to suppress her feelings for George throughout his long marriage to her friend.* | *Finally Glen could suppress his anger no longer and he lashed out at his mother.* —**suppression** /sə'preʃən/ [n U] **+ of** *Suppression of emotions in childhood can lead to problems in later life.*

repress /rɪ'pres/ [v T] formal to deliberately stop yourself from having or expressing particular feelings, especially because you are ashamed of them, in a way that may have harmful mental effects: *Individuals who repress their sexual desires often suffer from psychological problems.* | *Denying or repressing sorrow often seems the easiest way out when confronted with death.* —**repression** /rɪ'preʃən/ [n U] *Much of his adult life has been marked by sexual repression and feelings of guilt.*

put on a brave face/put up a brave front /ˌpʊt ɒn ə ˌbreɪv 'feɪs, ˌpʊt ʌp ə ˌbreɪv 'frʌnt/ [v phrase] to pretend that you are happy or confident when in fact you are very upset about something but you do not want to show this: *When she lost her job she put on a brave face and said it didn't matter.* | *Most of his teammates put up a brave front when they talked about his departure.* | **+ on** *The speech was given to put a brave face on the president's declining popularity.*

8 to hide information

- hide
- conceal
- cover up
- suppress
- cover your tracks
- sweep sth under the carpet

hide /haɪd/ [v T] *He took off his ring to hide the fact that he was married.* | *She somehow hid the fact she couldn't read throughout her schooldays.* | **hide sth from sb** *The agency has been criticized for being too secretive and hiding information from the public.* | **have nothing to hide** *Ask me anything you want – I have nothing to hide.*

conceal /kən'siːl/ [v T] formal to hide facts or the truth about something, especially by not giving people enough information about it or by lying: *He managed to conceal the fact that he had been in prison and so got a job as a security officer.* | **conceal sth from sb** *Several drug companies are accused of concealing information from the Food and Drug Administration.*

cover up /ˌkʌvər 'ʌp/ [phr v T] to do things that prevent people from finding out mistakes or unpleasant facts **cover up sth** *Lewis asked his wife to lie in an attempt to cover up the murder.* | **cover sth up** *Kate has made some big mistakes, and she won't be able to cover them up for long.*

suppress /sə'pres/ [v T] formal to prevent important facts or information from being made known in a public or official situation: *Police were accused of suppressing evidence that might have proved that the men were innocent.* | *The CIA has often tried to suppress reports that are embarrassing to the agency.*

cover your tracks /ˌkʌvər jɔːʳ 'træks/ [v phrase] informal to make a careful and deliberate attempt to stop people finding out about something wrong or criminal that you have done, by telling lies, hiding facts etc: *She covered her tracks by saying that she'd been at a friend's house all that evening.* | *Davis covered his tracks so well that no one could prove he had received any of the money.*

sweep sth under the carpet /ˌswiːp (sth) ʌndəʳ ðə 'kɑːʳpɪ̈t/ [v phrase] informal to try to keep something wrong that has happened a secret: *All the evidence pointing to McKay's guilt has been swept under the carpet.* | *Before the scandal broke, an attempt had been made to sweep the senator's illegal activities under the carpet.*

9 words for describing feelings, attitudes etc that are hidden

- hidden
- disguised
- suppressed
- repressed
- veiled

hidden /'hɪdn/ [adj] *He's always joking around to make sure his true feelings stay hidden.* | *Even after years of psychiatric treatment, she was full of hidden anger.* | **hidden talents** (=abilities that you did not know someone had) *You can dance and sing! I never realized you had so many hidden talents.* | **hidden meaning** *The lyrics of most of his songs have some hidden meaning.*

disguised /dɪs'gaɪzd/ [adj] feelings or attitudes that are **disguised** are kept hidden, but usually not very well: *'OK, I'll do it,' she said with barely disguised hostility.* | **thinly disguised** (=hardly disguised at all) *The speech was seen by many as a thinly disguised attack on the President.*

suppressed /sə'prest/ [adj] strong feelings, such as anger, fear, or happiness, that are **suppressed** are ones that you do not allow yourself to feel or show: *He is full of suppressed anger and needs to find some way of releasing it.* | *The intensity of the trial caused her long-suppressed emotions to come out in the open.*

repressed /rɪ'prest/ [adj] feelings that are **repressed** are ones that you deliberately stop yourself from feeling, or have been taught not to feel from when you were a child, especially feelings that you are ashamed of: *The Victorian era is characterized by its strict conventions and repressed emotion.* | *I had a lot of repressed anger toward my family that I didn't realize till my father died.*

veiled /veɪld/ [adj usually before noun] a **veiled** threat, warning etc is one that you do not make directly, but deliberately do not hide well, so that the person you are dealing with understands what your real intention is: *His attempt to get us to help him is just a veiled form of blackmail.* | *Her comments were nothing more than a veiled criticism of my work.* | **thinly veiled** (=only slightly hidden) *The opposition leader has made thinly veiled threats of violence.*

10 when people try to hide the truth

- cover-up
- whitewash
- cover
- front
- smokescreen

cover-up /'kʌvər ʌp/ [n C] a deliberate plan to prevent mistakes or embarrassing information, especially about politicians or other people in official positions, from being publicly known: *The Watergate cover-up eventually led to Nixon's resignation.* | **+ of** *Some people suspect that government officials were involved in a cover-up of the incident.*

whitewash /'waɪtwɒʃ‖-wɑːʃ, -wɔːʃ/ [n singular] an attempt by a government or official committee to hide the true facts of a situation from the public, especially when there was supposed to have been an official and fair examination of these facts: *A Greenpeace spokesperson described the official report on nuclear waste disposal as a whitewash.*

cover /'kʌvəʳ/ [n singular] something that you do or say as a way of hiding your true actions or intentions, especially when these are illegal or dishonest: *The ceasefire turned out to be just a cover to gain time to prepare another attack.* | *For years he had used his position at the United Nations as a cover for his spying activities.*

front /frʌnt/ [n singular] something such as an organization or a type of behaviour that seems to be normal but is used to hide what is really happening: *She puts on this 'innocent little girl' act, but it's all a front.* | *The car rental company is actually a front for a drugs ring.*

smokescreen /'sməʊkskriːn/ [n singular] something that is done or said in order to take people's attention away from other things that could be embarrassing or less acceptable: *The administration's emphasis on the drop in inflation is just a smokescreen to divert attention from rising unemployment.*

11 when people do not try to hide the truth

- open

open /'əʊpən/ [adj] *I try to be open and honest with my employees and let them know exactly what's going on.* | *Some of her former supporters are now expressing open hostility to her leadership.* — **openly** [adv] *The family talks openly now about Bill's depression and suicide.*

high

WHAT'S HERE

- **high above the ground** see **1 to 6**
- **high sound or voice** see **7**
- **high temperature/level/cost** see **8**

high above the ground

RELATED WORDS

opposite: **low**

see also **tall, big, up**

1 a long way above the ground

- high
- upper
- up in/into the air

high /haɪ/ [adj/adv] *The shelf's too high for me to reach.* | *Cowles Mountain is the highest peak in the city of San Diego.* | *The plane flew higher to avoid the storm.* | **+ up** *We stayed in a cabin high up in the mountains.* | *You're awfully high up there – be careful.* | **+ in/into/above** *He let go and watched the balloon float high above the trees.* | *Lava from the volcano was sent high into the air.*

upper /'ʌpəʳ/ [adj only before noun] **upper room/floor/deck etc** the highest room etc when there are two or more: *People had climbed into the upper branches of the tree to escape the rising waters.* | *Gunmen were firing machine guns from the upper floor of the hospital.*

up in/into the air /ˌʌp ɪn, ɪntə ði 'eəʳ/ [adv] a long way or to a long way above the ground without being on any surface: *The force of the explosion blew the boxes straight up into the air.* | *Once the plane is up in the air, I'll let you try using the controls.* | **high up in the air** *The ride shot high up in the air and then plunged back down toward the earth.*

2 a high building/mountain/tree etc

- high
- tall
- towering
- skyscraper
- high-rise

high /haɪ/ [adj] measuring a long distance from top to bottom – use this about mountains, walls, or buildings: *The castle was surrounded by high walls.* | *Mt. McKinley is the highest mountain in North America.* | *A couple of boys had climbed the high chain-link fence to get into the park.*

tall /tɔːl/ [adj] high and narrow or long – use this about trees and plants or about buildings and parts of buildings: *Two tall marble columns stood at* *either side of the entrance.* | *The twin towers of the World Trade Center were the highest buildings in New York.* | *The cat was hiding in the tall grass in the backyard.*

towering /ˈtaʊərɪŋ/ [adj only before noun] very high especially in a way that seems frightening or impressive: *The building seems out of place among the towering redwood trees.* | *The towering Cliffs of Dover loomed in front of them.*

skyscraper /ˈskaɪˌskreɪpəʳ/ [n C] a very tall modern city building, especially one used for offices: *His office looked out on the other skyscrapers of downtown Dallas.*

high-rise /ˈhaɪ raɪz/ [adj only before noun] a **high-rise** building is a tall modern building, used either for apartments or for offices: *High-rise apartment buildings now stood where his childhood home had been.* —**high-rise** [n C] *A new high-rise is going up downtown.*

3 how high something is

- how high
- 30 metres/100 feet etc high
- height
- altitude
- level

how high /haʊ ˈhaɪ/ use this to ask about or say what the height of something is: *'How high is Mount Fuji?' 'It's almost 4000 metres.'* | *I'm not sure how high the ceiling is.*

30 metres/100 feet etc high /ˌθɜːʳti miːtəʳz ˈhaɪ/ [adj phrase] if something is **30 metres, 100 feet etc high**, the distance from its base to its top is 30 metres, 100 feet etc: *The highest mountain in Scotland is over 4000 feet high.* | *The stone fireplace was at least ten feet wide and 12 feet high.* | *He's built a 3-metre high fence between the two gardens.* | **shoulder-/waist-/knee- etc high** (=as high as your shoulder, waist, knee etc) *The corn was already knee-high and growing fast.*

height /haɪt/ [n C/U] the distance between the top and the bottom of something, or the distance that something is above the ground: *My brother and I are nearly the same height.* | **+ of** *What's the height of the average banana tree?* | **200 feet/30 metres etc in height** *Some of the pyramids are over 200 feet in height.* | **a height of 25 metres/100 feet etc** *One of the climbers fell from a height of 25 metres.*

altitude /ˈæltɪ̈tjuːd‖-tuːd/ [n C] formal the distance that something is above the ground – use this especially to talk about planes or about places in the mountains or high areas **+ of** *The altitude of Addis Ababa is eight thousand feet.* | **an altitude of 10,000 metres/30,000 feet etc** *The plane is now flying at an altitude of 30,000 feet.* | **high/low altitude** *It's very difficult to breathe at high altitudes.*

level /ˈlevəl/ [n C/U] how high something is – use this especially about the height of something in relation to something else: *The apartment is split into two different levels with a bedroom on each.* | **+ of** *Hang the picture just below the level of the window.* | **eye level** *Posters line the walls at eye level.* | **sea level** (=the height of the surface of the sea, used for measuring the height of mountains, hills etc) *The village is about 1500 metres above sea level.*

4 to be much higher than other things

- tower over/above
- dwarf
- dominate

tower over/above /ˈtaʊəʳ əʊvəʳ, əbʌv/ [phr v T] *The great cathedral towers over the rest of the main square.* | *Life-size dinosaur models tower above visitors to the Prehistoric Park.*

dwarf /dwɔːʳf/ [v T not usually in progressive] if something **dwarfs** other things, it is so big that it makes the other things around it seem very small: *The ship came slowly into the harbour, dwarfing all the surrounding boats.* | *The smaller, older houses are dwarfed by the new apartment blocks and hotels.*

dominate /ˈdɒmɪ̈neɪt‖ˈdɑː-/ [v T not usually in progressive] if a particular building, structure, or tree **dominates** an area or place, it is much higher and much easier to see than everything else, so that it seems to be the most important thing: *The fortress on top of the hill still dominates Barcelona harbour.* | *A giant Ferris wheel dominates the skyline.*

5 a surface that is higher than the area around it

- raised
- elevated

raised /reɪzd/ [adj] *There was a raised platform and a blackboard at the far end of the room.* | *His name had been put on a bronze plaque in raised letters.*

elevated /ˈelɪ̈veɪtɪ̈d/ [adj] a surface that is **elevated** has been deliberately put in a place that is higher than everything else, for example in order to protect it or to make it easier to see: *The train runs on an elevated track above the city street.* | *The judge's bench is well elevated and covered by a walnut canopy.*

6 fear of being in high places

- fear of heights
- be afraid/scared of heights
- vertigo

fear of heights /ˌfɪər əv ˈhaɪts/ [n phrase] *He refused to climb the ladder because of his fear of heights.* | *She overcame her fear of heights and did a parachute jump for charity.*

be afraid/scared of heights /biː əˌfreɪd, ˌskeəʳd əv ˈhaɪts/ [adj] to feel frightened when you are in high places: *Hiking this trail is not recommended for people who are afraid of heights.* | *She's so scared of heights we couldn't get her to go parasailing.*

vertigo /ˈvɜːʳtɪgəʊ/ [n U] formal a feeling that things are moving and that you are going to fall, that you get especially when you are on or in a high place: *Just the thought of standing on the balcony gave her vertigo.*

a high sound or voice

RELATED WORDS

opposite: **low**

- *see also* **sound, music**

7 a high sound or voice

- high
- high-pitched
- piercing
- shrill
- squeaky
- tinny

high /haɪ/ [adj] near the top range of sounds that humans can hear – use this about sounds, voices, or musical notes: *Dogs respond to sounds that are too high for humans to hear.* | *I was amazed that he* *could sing such high notes.* | *He mocked her by repeating what she said in a high, childish voice.*

high-pitched /ˌhaɪ ˈpɪtʃt◂/ [adj usually before noun] a **high-pitched** sound or voice is very high, and often unpleasant or annoying to listen to: *Above the music on the radio was an annoying, high-pitched whistle.* | *I could hear high-pitched laughter coming from the girls' bedroom.*

piercing /ˈpɪəʳsɪŋ/ [adj usually before noun] a **piercing** sound or voice is very high and loud, often with the result that it is unpleasant or painful to listen to: *Sammy put his finger and thumb in his mouth and gave a piercing whistle.* | *Maggie let out a piercing scream as she saw the truck speeding toward her.*

shrill /ʃrɪl/ [adj] very high, loud, and unexpectedly sharp, often giving the person who hears it a sudden shock: *I was suddenly woken up by the shrill ringing of the telephone.* | *As Sophie became angry her voice got shriller.*

squeaky /ˈskwiːki/ [adj] a **squeaky** sound or voice makes short high sounds, especially because there is something wrong with it: *This door needs oiling – it's very squeaky.* | *If you have a squeaky little voice, people tend not to listen to your ideas.*

tinny /ˈtɪni/ [adj] music that is **tinny** is high and unpleasant, especially because it comes from a low quality radio or musical instrument: *The music sounded tinny through the old speakers.* | *As he neared the park he could hear the tinny music from Joey's radio.*

a high temperature/level/cost

RELATED WORDS

opposite: —— **low**

▸ *see also* **increase, less, level**

8 a high temperature/level/cost

- ▸ **high**
- ▸ **rising**
- ▸ **soaring**

high /haɪ/ [adj] *In summer, the temperatures can be as high as 40°C.* | *The city has one of the highest crime rates in the world.* | *Analysts are concerned about the high level of consumer debt.* | *Gas prices are much higher here than in other parts of the country.*

rising /ˈraɪzɪŋ/ [adj] getting higher than before: *Many families are struggling to keep up with the rising costs of education.* | **rapidly rising** *Despite rapidly rising incomes, few in the country are able to afford cable TV.*

soaring /ˈsɔːrɪŋ/ [adj] getting very high, especially suddenly and quickly: *Congress seems unable or unwilling to control soaring medical costs.* | *A soaring 77% of college-educated women between 30 and 44 hope to have both children and a career.*

hit

RELATED WORDS

▸ *see also* **hurt/injure, attack, shoot, unconscious (4), kick**

1 to hit someone deliberately

- ▸ **hit**
- ▸ **punch**
- ▸ **slap**
- ▸ **strike**
- ▸ **throw a punch**
- ▸ **whack**
- ▸ **thump**
- ▸ **bash**
- ▸ **clobber**

hit /hɪt/ [v T] to **hit** someone with your hand or with something that you are holding in your hand: *Dad! Peter keeps hitting me!* | **+ with** *The victim had been hit with a baseball bat.* | **hit sb on the nose/in the stomach/over the head etc** *There was a fight, and someone had hit him over the head with a chair.* | **hit sb hard** (=with a lot of force) *He hit him hard in the stomach.* | **hit sb back** (=to hit someone when they have hit you) *Don't hit him, he'll only hit you back.*

punch ALSO **slug** informal /pʌntʃ, slʌg/ [v T] to hit someone hard with your closed hand, especially in a fight or because you are angry: *The woman claimed that she had been punched and kicked by one of the policemen.* | *The actor slugged a photographer who got too close.* | **punch sb on the nose/in the eye/in the chest etc** *Dean punched her in the ribs and pushed her against the wall.*

slap /slæp/ [v T] to hit someone, especially on their face, with the flat part of your open hand: *I was so angry I wanted to slap him.* | **slap sb across the face** *She slapped him across the face and stormed out of the room.* | **slap sb's face** *Dora slapped his face and ran home.* —**slap** [n C] *If you don't behave yourself, you'll get a slap!*

strike /straɪk/ [v T] formal to hit someone, especially on a particular part of their body: *Her husband had never struck her before.* | **+ with** *Evidence shows that the victim had been struck several times with an iron bar.* | **strike sb on the head/in the stomach etc** *The court heard that the defendant had struck Payne repeatedly in the face, causing serious bruising.*

throw a punch /ˌθrəʊ ə ˈpʌntʃ/ [v phrase] to hit or try to hit someone very hard with a closed hand in a fight: *Rogers threw a punch at Martin.* | *Foreman, once the World Heavyweight Champion, says 'I never throw a punch in anger.'*

whack /wæk/ [v T] informal to hit someone hard, with your hand or with an object: *If he said anything like that to me, I'd whack him!*

thump /θʌmp/ [v T] informal to hit someone very hard with your closed hand, especially on their body rather than on their face or head: *Mike thumped Stephanie's back several times to stop her choking.*

bash /bæʃ/ [v T] spoken to hit someone hard, especially in a fight **bash sb's head/face/teeth etc in** *I told him I'd bash his head in if he ever touched her again.*

clobber /ˈklɒbəʳ‖ˈklɑː-/ [v T] spoken to hit someone very hard, either with your hand or with a hard object: *The kids are bored, and have nothing to do but clobber each other.*

2 to hit someone repeatedly

- ▸ **beat**
- ▸ **beat up**
- ▸ **batter**
- ▸ **beat up on**
- ▸ **knock sb about**
- ▸ **club**

beat /biːt/ [v T] to hit someone hard and repeatedly with your hand or with something such as a stick: *It was clear that she had been badly beaten by her husband.* | **+ with** *Police officers had beaten the man with their batons.* | **beat sb black and blue** (=beat someone so hard that their body is covered in marks) *The child had been beaten black and blue.* | **beat the living daylights out of sb** (=beat someone very hard and violently) *Osborne wanted to beat the living daylights out of Flanagan.*

beat up /ˌbiːt ˈʌp/ [phr v T] to hit someone hard and repeatedly all over their body, leaving them badly hurt and often unable to move: *He would come home drunk, get into a fight with Mom, and beat her up.* | *Carl got beaten up outside a nightclub on Saturday night.*

batter /ˈbætəʳ/ [v T] to repeatedly hit someone in an uncontrolled and violent way: *Teachers suspect that the child is being battered regularly by his parents.* | **+ with** *There were reports of soldiers battering prisoners with their rifles.* | **batter sb to death** (=until they are dead) *The jury heard how Thompson had been maddened by what he saw and battered his wife to death.*

beat up on /ˌbiːt ˈʌp ɒn/ [phr v T] American to repeatedly hit someone weaker than yourself, for example a younger child at school: *He was a bully, a mean kid who beat up on the other kids.*

knock sb about British **/knock sb around** American /ˌnɒk (sb) əˈbaʊt, ˌnɒk (sb) əˈraʊnd‖ˌnɑːk-/ [phr v T] to hit someone several times, especially in order to frighten them: *My father used to knock my mother about when he was drunk.* | *They had been threatened with a gun, pushed, shoved, and knocked around.*

club /klʌb/ [v T] to hit someone very hard, especially on the head with a thick heavy object: *Football fans were clubbed by riot police trying to stop the violence.* | **club sb to death** (=until they are dead) *Baby seals are clubbed to death for their fur.*

3 a car/train/plane etc hits something

- hit
- run into
- run over
- crash/smash into
- ram/slam into
- plough into
- collide
- ram
- go into

hit /hɪt/ [v T] *The bus hit a tree and the driver was badly injured.* | *He pulled out of the driveway without looking, and almost hit another car.* | *Five sailors were killed when their ship hit a mine.* | **hit sth head-on** (=directly) *The driver of a Ford van lost control and hit another car head-on.*

run into /ˈrʌn ɪntuː/ [v phrase] to hit something that is directly in front of you with your vehicle, especially because you are not paying attention: *I turned too sharply and ran into the curb.* | *We almost ran into a Rolls-Royce that pulled out in front of us without signalling.*

run over /ˌrʌn ˈəʊvəʳ/ [phr v T] to hit and injure a person or animal while driving a vehicle **run over sb/run sb over** *How can you run over a child and not stop?* | **be run over by sth** *The boy's dog had been run over by a car.* | **get run over** *Make sure the lights on your bike are working. I don't want you getting run over.*

crash/smash into /ˈkræʃ, ˈsmæʃ ɪntuː/ [v phrase] to hit something or someone very hard while you are driving a vehicle, making a lot of noise and causing damage: *The driver lost control on a curve and crashed into a tree.* | *An airplane had crashed into a mountain, killing all two hundred passengers.* | **go crashing into sth** *The car skidded, then went crashing into the bus shelter.* | *An army helicopter smashed into the side of the mountain.*

ram/slam into /ˈræm, ˈslæm ɪntuː/ [v phrase] to hit something or someone very hard while you are moving in a vehicle, especially when what you hit is not moving: *The driver had been drinking when he rammed into a car waiting at a red light.* | *Some idiot slammed into me from behind.*

plough into British **/plow into** American /ˈplaʊ ɪntuː/ [v phrase] to hit a large number of vehicles or people with a vehicle, especially as a result of driving too fast, not paying attention etc: *The car went out of control and ploughed into a group of people on the sidewalk.* | *When the driver fell asleep, the bus ploughed into a line of traffic.*

collide /kəˈlaɪd/ [v I] if two vehicles **collide**, they hit each other when they are moving in opposite directions: *Four or five cars had collided in the fog.* | **+ with** *The transport helicopter he was in collided with another and crashed.*

ram /ræm/ [v T] to deliberately hit another vehicle very hard, especially when it is not moving: *The ship had been rammed by a submarine.*

go into /ˈgəʊ ɪntuː/ [v phrase] British informal to hit something or someone with a vehicle: *Someone went into the back of my bike at the traffic lights.*

4 to hit someone or something accidentally

- hit
- bump into
- bump
- strike
- crash into
- knock
- bang/bash
- collide
- crack

hit /hɪt/ [v T] *Be careful with that stick! You nearly hit me with it.* | *There's a chip on the windshield where a stone hit it.* | **hit sb on the head/knee etc** *The ball hit me in the face.* | **hit your head/knee/elbow etc** *The ceiling's very low. Mind you don't hit your head.* | **hit sth on/against sth** *I hit my elbow on the corner of that table.* | **get hit** *He ran out into the road and almost got hit.* | *Buildings that had gotten hit by bombs had still not been repaired.*

bump into /ˈbʌmp ɪntuː/ [v phrase] if you **bump into** something or someone, you hit them with part of your body accidentally when you are walking or running somewhere: *Jim turned suddenly and bumped into me.* | *The room was dark, and I bumped into the door.*

bump /bʌmp/ [v I/T] to accidentally and suddenly hit part of your body against something **bump your head/elbow/knee etc** *Babies are always bumping their heads.* | **+ against** *His right leg bumped against the parking brake.*

strike /straɪk/ [v T] formal if something, especially a heavy object, **strikes** something or someone, it hits them hard once: *A house nearby had been struck by a falling tree.* | *The ball struck him in the face.*

crash into /ˈkræʃ ɪntuː/ [v T] to hit someone or something extremely hard, especially while moving very fast: *Tyler injured his shoulder when he crashed into Jesse Lyons during practice.* | *Parts of the satellite crashed into the sea.* | **go crashing into sb/sth** *He stopped suddenly, and I went crashing into him.* | *Glasses and bottles went crashing to the floor.*

knock /nɒk‖nɑːk/ [v I/T] to hit someone or something with a short quick movement: *She knocked me with her elbow as she passed.* | **+ against** *The heavy video camera knocked against his hip as he walked.* | **+ into** *She turned and ran, knocking into bystanders as she went.* | **knock sth against/into sth** *One of the movers knocked the sofa against a doorway.*

bang/bash /bæŋ, bæʃ/ [v I/T] to hit someone or something hard, often making a noise and hurting someone or damaging something **bang your head/knee/elbow etc** *I banged my head getting into the car.* | **bang sth into/against/on etc sth** *Tom bashed his knee against the table.* | *He slipped, banging his guitar against the door.* | **+ into/against** *Kids raced around the playground, banging into each other, screaming, and letting off steam.*

collide /kəˈlaɪd/ [v I] if two people or things **collide**, they accidentally hit each other when they are moving in different directions: *Barker and Mason collided while going for the ball.* | *When the plates of land that form the earth collide or slide past each other, earthquakes result.* | **+ with** *I backed out of the door and promptly collided with someone. 'I'm sorry,' I said.*

crack /kræk/ [v T] to hit your head, knee, elbow etc hard and painfully against something **crack sth on/against sth** *He slipped and cracked his head on the steps.* | *Mary cracked her knee on the corner of her desk.*

5 to hit someone as a punishment

- beat
- spank
- smack/slap
- give sb a beating
- whip/flog
- corporal punishment

beat /biːt/ [v T] to repeatedly hit someone with your hand, with a stick etc as a punishment: *The guards used to regularly beat the prisoners.* | *Teachers are no longer allowed to beat students who misbehave.* | **+ with** *Slaves were sometimes beaten with sticks or even whipped.*

spank /spæŋk/ [v T] to hit someone repeatedly, especially a child who has behaved badly, with your open hand, on their bottom: *The two boys were spanked and sent to bed without their supper.* | *Many parents no longer spank their kids as a form of discipline.* —**spanking** [n C/U] *Just behave yourself or you'll get another spanking.* | *Child welfare groups are campaigning to get spanking made illegal.*

smack/slap ALSO **swat** American /smæk, slæp, swɒt‖swɑːt/ [v T] to hit someone, especially a child who has behaved badly, with your open hand on their hand, the backs of their legs, their face etc: *If you don't stop that, I'll smack you!* | *Slap her hand lightly when she touches something she shouldn't.* | *He grinned and I wanted to swat him, but he wasn't my son so I didn't.*

give sb a beating /ˌɡɪv (sb) ə ˈbiːtɪŋ/ [v phrase] to hit someone violently and repeatedly with something such as a stick, in order to punish them: *The guards gave the prisoner a beating.* | **give sb a good/sound beating** *His father took him into the barn and gave him a good beating.*

whip/flog /wɪp, flɒɡ‖flɑːɡ/ [v T] to hit someone very hard with a rope, **whip** etc especially on their back in order to punish them: *The hostage had terrible scars on his back where he had been whipped.* | *What kind of a society flogs women simply for saying what they think?*

corporal punishment /ˌkɔːʳpərəl ˈpʌnɪʃmənt/ [n U] the practice of punishing people, especially children at school, by hitting them with something such as a stick: *In my first year at Hendon School, I had my first taste of corporal punishment.* | *Corporal punishment is, thankfully, no longer used.*

6 to hit someone in a friendly way etc

- slap/clap sb on the back
- pat

slap/clap sb on the back /ˌslæp, ˌklæp (sb) ɒn ðə ˈbæk/ [v phrase] to hit someone on the back with the flat part of your hand, for example as a friendly greeting or in order to praise them: *'How are you? I haven't seen you for ages,' she said, slapping Jim on the back.* | *The coach said 'Well done!' and clapped each player on the back as they entered the changing room.*

pat /pæt/ [v T] to gently hit someone, usually on their back, shoulder, or head, in order to praise them or show them that you like them: *Roz reached over and patted her hand.* | *He got up, patted her on the shoulder, and gave her a quick kiss.*

7 to make someone or something fall down by hitting them

- knock out
- punch out
- knock down/over
- knock off

knock out /ˌnɒk ˈaʊt‖ˌnɑːk-/ [phr v T] to hit someone so hard that they fall down and become unconscious **knock sb out** *Jackson hit Brian hard with his left fist and knocked him out.* | **knock out sb** *He is a good boxer, a powerful puncher who has knocked out 18 of his 20 opponents to date.* | **knock sb out cold** (=so that they become completely unconscious) *The blow to Sergeant Lewis' head had knocked him out cold.*

punch out /ˌpʌntʃ ˈaʊt/ [phr v T] American to hit someone with your closed hand, so hard that they become unconscious **punch sb out** *I got so mad I just wanted to punch someone out.* | **punch sb out** *The coach threw him off the team after he punched out a teammate.*

knock down/over /ˌnɒk ˈdaʊn, ˈəʊvəʳ‖ˌnɑːk-/ [phr v T] to hit someone or something and make them fall onto the ground – use this about people or objects hitting someone or something **knock sb/sth down/over** *Jo was almost knocked down by a kid on a bicycle.* | *One boy crashed into him and knocked him over.* | **knock over sb/sth** *There was a crash as the cat knocked over something in the kitchen.* | **get knocked down/over** *As the crowd rushed towards the gate, several people got knocked over.*

knock off /ˌnɒk ˈɒf‖ˌnɑːk-/ [phr v T] to hit something so that it falls off a surface **knock off sth/knock sth off** *Part of the puzzle had been knocked off onto the floor.* | **knock sth off sth** *Ellie accidentally knocked a cup of milk off the table.*

8 to hit an object/door/table etc with something

- hit
- knock
- tap
- bang
- rap
- strike
- bash
- whack
- hammer

hit /hɪt/ [v T] *You have to try to hit the ball over the net.* | *The first time I tried archery, I couldn't even hit the target.*

knock /nɒk‖nɑːk/ [v I] to hit a door or window, especially with your closed hand, in order to attract the attention of the people inside: *Would you mind* *knocking before you come in?* | *I waited a moment, then knocked again.* | **+ on/at** *Lula knocked at the back door and he appeared, dressed in pyjamas.* | *'Mattie?' called Jerry, knocking on the door.* —**knock** [n C] **+ at/on** *I had just turned out the lights when I heard a knock at the door.* —**knocking** [n singular] the sound of someone knocking: *We were woken by a frantic knocking at the door.*

tap /tæp/ [v I/T] to hit something gently so that it makes a light noise, especially in order to get someone's attention: *Daley read the notes, tapping a pencil on the desk.* | **+ on/at** *She tapped on the window to attract his attention.* —**tap** [n C] *I was startled by a light tap at the door.*

bang /bæŋ/ [v I/T] to hit a door, table etc very hard with your hand or with an object, in order to attract attention or because you are angry: *Thomas banged his fist on the table.* | **+ on/at** *I banged at the door but nobody came.* | *He complained loudly until Val finally banged on the table and shouted at him.* | **bang sth shut** *Sherman banged the door shut.*

rap /ræp/ [v I/T] to hit something loudly and very quickly several times in order to attract attention: *The conductor rapped the music stand with his baton and the violins stopped playing.* | **+ on/at** *Seeing her son outside, Mrs Evans rapped on the window and called him back into the house.* —**rap** [n C] *There was a rap at the kitchen door.*

strike /straɪk/ [v T] formal to hit something hard, especially in a very controlled or skilful way: *Morris struck his drum, and the band started to march down the street.* | *In anger, he struck the wall with a stick.*

bash ALSO **give sth a bash** British /bæʃ, ˌgɪv (sth) ə ˈbæʃ/ [v T] informal to hit something hard with your hand or with a stick, hammer etc especially in a careless way: *If the television stops working, just bash it a couple of times – that usually helps.* | *I put the box on the floor and gave it a good bash with my hammer, but it still wouldn't open.*

whack /wæk/ [v T] to hit something hard and noisily, especially using a flat object: *Buckley whacked the ball into left field.* | *The Georgia man whacked his fist on the bar.*

hammer /ˈhæməʳ/ [v I] to keep hitting something very loudly and quickly especially with your closed hand, because you are angry, impatient etc **+ on/at/against** *The children hammered at the door to be let in out of the rain.* | *Her heart hammered against her ribs.*

9 to hit an object or surface and move away again

- bounce off
- rebound
- glance off
- ricochet

bounce off /ˈbaʊns ɒf/ [v phrase] to move a long way away from a surface or object after hitting it hard **bounce off sth** *The game of squash is played by hitting a ball that bounces off a wall.* | **bounce sth off sth** *The device works by bouncing sound waves off objects and measuring the time it takes for the sound to return.*

rebound /rɪˈbaʊnd/ [v I] to hit something and then move away again: *Summers caught the ball as it hit the wall and rebounded.* | **+ off** *Electrons move around quickly, hitting and then rebounding off each other.*

glance off /ˈglɑːns ɒf‖ˈglæns-/ [phr v T] if something **glances off** an object that it hits, it hits the surface at an angle and then moves away from it in another direction: *A shot by Best glanced off the rim of the basket.*

ricochet /ˈrɪkəʃeɪ/ [v I] if a bullet **ricochets**, it hits an object and moves away from it very quickly: *I heard the shot ricochet, then felt a sudden pain in my leg.* | **+ off** *A bullet ricocheted off the rock he was hiding behind.*

10 when something hits someone or something

- blow
- impact
- collision

blow /bləʊ/ [n C] the movement of hitting someone hard with your hand or with something held in your hand: *The blow proved fatal.* | **strike (sb) a blow** *The assailant struck several blows before he was restrained.* | *Officer Stacey was knocked over by a sharp blow to the head.*

impact /ˈɪmpækt/ [n singular] when one object hits another: *Just after the impact there was a flash as the rocket exploded.* | **on impact** *Both cars burst into flames on impact.*

collision /kəˈlɪʒən/ [n C] when something, especially a vehicle, hits something else while it is moving: *Whiplash, a neck injury, is a result of automobile collisions.* | *News of the mid-air collision reached the papers quickly.* | **head-on collision** (=when two vehicles hit each other directly) *Those who drive the road regularly say their biggest fear is a head-on collision.*

hold

RELATED WORDS

- have an amount of something inside *see* **contain**
- *see also* **lift, carry, take**

1 to have something in your hand

- hold
- in your hand

hold /həʊld/ [v T] *I held the money tightly in my hand.* | *In the photograph there was a small boy holding a flag.* | *A smiling woman holding a can of beer came over to us.* | **hold sth up/hold up sth** (=hold something high in the air) *What a lovely picture! Hold it up so everyone can see it.* | **hold sth out/hold out sth** (=hold something towards someone, especially to offer it to them) *I took a glass of champagne from the tray the waiter held out.*

in your hand /ɪn jɔːʳ ˈhænd/ [adv] if something is **in your hand**, you are holding it: *What's that in your hand?* | *He arrived at the door with an enormous bouquet of flowers in one hand and a bottle of champagne in the other.* | **in each hand** *Theo walked across the yard with a pail in each hand.*

2 to hold something tightly

- hold on/hang on
- grip
- clutch/clasp
- cling to

hold on/hang on /ˌhəʊld ˈɒn, ˌhæŋ ˈɒn/ [phr v I] to put your hand around something and hold it tightly, in order to stop yourself from falling or from losing what you are holding: *We're coming up to a bumpy bit – you'd better hold on!* | *Just hang on as best you* *can and I'll try and get some help.* | **hold/hang on to sth** *Mother's not strong. She can't walk without holding on to someone's arm.* | *People stood hanging on to the overhead straps of the swaying subway car.* | **hold on tight** *As the roller coaster turned upside down I shut my eyes and held on tight.* | *He inched across the roof, hanging on as best he could.*

grip /grɪp/ [v T] to hold something tightly, by pressing your fingers very hard against it: *David suddenly gripped my arm and pulled me away from the road.* | *His knuckles whitened as he gripped the microphone.* | *She found his hand and gripped it tightly.*

clutch/clasp /klʌtʃ, klɑːsp‖klæsp/ [v I/T] to hold something tightly, closing your fingers around it: *'Ah!' he cried, clutching his stomach.* | *A group of tourists stood clutching their phrase books.* | *A little girl stood clasping her mother's hand.* | *Sally ran out of the house, clasping her schoolbooks to her chest.*

cling to /ˈklɪŋ tuː/ [v phrase] to hold on to someone or something very tightly for comfort or support: *The baby monkey clings to its mother's back until it can climb by itself.* | *Many children will cling to a soft blanket or toy as a substitute for their mother at night.* | *Rescue workers saved a 9-year-old boy who was clinging to rocks after he was swept into the ocean by the tide.*

3 to start holding something

- get/take hold of
- grab
- clutch/grasp at

get/take hold of ALSO **get a hold of** /ˌget, ˌteɪk ˈhəʊld ɒv, ˌget ə ˈhəʊld ɒv/ [v phrase] to take something and hold it in your hand: *I took hold of the handle and pulled as hard as I could.* | *Sheila fished in her handbag until she got hold of her keys.* | *The baby got a hold of her beads and broke the string.*

grab /græb/ [v T] to quickly and roughly take something and hold it: *Brown grabbed the phone and started shouting.* | *She turned to him and grabbed his arm so hard it surprised him.* | **grab hold of sth** *The boy grabbed hold of my bag and disappeared quickly into the crowd.* | **grab sth from sb** *According to the report, Mason grabbed the gun from a friend.*

clutch/grasp at ALSO **grasp for** /ˈklʌtʃ, ˈgrɑːsp æt, ˈgrɑːsp fɔːʳ‖ˈgræsp-/ [phr v T] to take something in your hand, especially when it is very difficult to do this: *I clutched at my mother's arm to keep from falling.* | *The climber grasped at a small hold just above him.*

4 to hold something and turn it around in your hands

- handle
- fiddle with
- play with
- fumble with

handle /ˈhændl/ [v T] to hold something and turn it around in your hands, for example to examine it or use it: *Please do not handle the fruit and vegetables.* | *This violin is very old and valuable and must be handled carefully.*

fiddle with /ˈfɪdl wɪð/ [phr v T not in passive] to hold something small and keep turning it around in your hands, especially because you are nervous or bored: *Martina was fiddling nervously with her pen.* | *Stop fiddling with the remote control!*

play with /ˈpleɪ wɪð/ [phr v T not in passive] to hold something in your hands and turn it around continuously for no reason: *She played with the red roses on the table as she talked.* | *Is it worth reading to our kids when they're busy playing with their hair or their teddy bears? Yes.*

fumble with /ˈfʌmbəl wɪð/ [v phrase not in passive] to hold something with your fingers or in your hand, trying to move it in some way, but doing it carelessly or with difficulty: *She could hear someone fumbling with the handle of her door.* | *I fumbled drunkenly with the keys, dropping them to the floor.* | *He stood before them, his eyes lowered, fumbling with his hat.*

5 to hold a weapon

- wield
- brandish

wield /wiːld/ [v T] to hold a weapon such as a knife or stick and wave it around so that people can see that you are going to use it: *The rioters faced police who were wielding clubs and batons.* | **knife-wielding/gun-wielding/sword-wielding etc** *Home was a cramped two rooms in a street where gun-wielding criminals walked.*

brandish /ˈbrændɪʃ/ [v T] to hold something such as a gun, knife, or stick so that people can see it, especially while threatening them: *A man brandishing a gun had threatened staff and customers at a local bank.* | *Four horsemen dashed up at full gallop, shouting and brandishing their weapons.*

6 to put your arms around someone

- hold
- put your arms around
- hug
- cuddle
- take sb in your arms
- embrace

hold /həʊld/ [v T] to put your arms around someone and **hold** them close to you, especially to show that you love them, or in order to comfort them: *I held her until she went to sleep.* | **hold sb tight** *There was nothing I could say so I just held her tight and let her cry.* | **hold sb in your arms** *She held a baby in her arms.*

put your arms around /ˌpʊt jɔːr ˈɑːʳmz əraʊnd/ [v phrase] to hold someone especially when you want to comfort them or kiss them or show that you love them: *Mama put her arms around me and tried to comfort me.* | *She put her arms around his neck and kissed his cheek.*

hug /hʌg/ [v T] to put your arms around someone and hold them close to you, especially to show that you love them, or to comfort them: *My father hugged me affectionately when I got home.* | *'I'll never forget you,' she said, and we hugged each other for the last time.* | **hug sb close/tight** *Jane threw her arms around him and hugged him tight.* —**hug** [n C] **give sb a hug** *Give me a hug, then it's time for bed.* | **bear hug** (=a very tight hug) *His arms tightened around her in a bear hug.*

cuddle /ˈkʌdl/ [v I/T] to hold someone in your arms for a long time, especially a child, a small animal, or someone you love: *She had fallen asleep in her chair, cuddling a little teddy bear.* | **kiss and cuddle** (=when two people hold each other and kiss each other) *They were kissing and cuddling on the sofa.* —**cuddle** [n C] **give sb a cuddle** *She was giving the baby a cuddle.*

take sb in your arms /ˌteɪk (sb) ɪn jɔːr ˈɑːʳmz/ [v phrase] to gently pull someone towards you and hold them in your arms, especially someone you love: *He took Sophie in his arms and kissed her.* | *Margaret took the little boy in her arms and carried him downstairs.*

embrace /ɪmˈbreɪs/ [v I/T] formal put your arms around someone and hold them in a friendly or loving way, especially when you are meeting or leaving someone: *Phoebe ran to embrace her mother.* | *Before my flight was called we stood and embraced.* —**embrace** [n C] *The children rushed into the embrace of their father.*

7 to hold someone's hand, arm etc

- hold sb's hand
- take sb by the arm/hand etc

hold sb's hand /ˌhəʊld (sb's) ˈhænd/ [v phrase] to hold someone's hand, especially to comfort them or to make them feel safe: *Hold Mummy's hand – there's a good girl.* | *Andrew sat next to Jane and held her hand.* | *He held her hand tightly and led her across the street.* | **hold hands** (=if two or more people hold hands, they hold each other's hands) *She saw Kurt and Eileen coming back from the beach, kissing and holding hands.* | *Then we all sat in a circle and held hands.*

take sb by the arm/hand etc /ˌteɪk (sb) baɪ ði ˈɑːʳm/ [v phrase] to take hold of someone's hand, arm etc, in order to take them somewhere: *Emily took me by the hand and led me into the garden.* | *A nurse took her arm and led her to a chair.*

8 the way that someone holds something

- hold
- grip
- grasp

hold /həʊld/ [n singular] the way in which someone is holding something **sb's hold on sth** *I tightened my hold on the child as we crossed the busy road.* | **tighten/loosen/relax your hold (on)** *My mother relaxed, and loosened her hold on my hand.* | **keep/have hold of** *Prevost asked me if I still had hold of my camera.* | *In this form of wrestling there are a number of different holds, each used in a different situation.*

grip /grɪp/ [n singular] the way you hold something tightly: *The policeman had a firm grip on my arm.* | *To play this shot, you need to change your grip on the racquet slightly.* | **lose your grip** (=be unable to hold something any longer) *I lost my grip on the branch, and fell out of the tree.* | **tighten your grip** (=grip something more tightly) *She looked anxious and tightened her grip on her shoulder bag.*

grasp /grɑːsp‖græsp/ [n singular] the way you hold something tightly, especially a part of someone's body, in order to keep them close to you: *She tried to escape Moore's grasp but he was too strong for her.* | **tighten your grasp** (=grasp something more tightly) *Helen tightened her grasp on my collar and shouted 'Don't fool around with me, Mickey!'*

9 to stop holding something

- let go
- drop
- release

let go /ˌlet ˈgəʊ/ [phr v I] to stop holding something or someone: *Let go! You're hurting me.* | **let go of** *She wouldn't let go of the letter.* | *At the end of the fair, the school let go of hundreds of balloons.*

drop /drɒp‖drɑːp/ [v T] to stop holding something suddenly, especially by accident, so that it falls to the ground: *I dropped my sunglasses and they broke.* | *As soon as she saw him she dropped her suitcases and ran towards him.*

release /rɪˈliːs/ [v T] especially written to stop holding something, especially someone's hand, wrist, arm etc: *He took hold of my hand but then released it again quickly.*

hole

RELATED WORDS

- *see also* **cut, space, dig**

1 a hole that goes through something

- hole
- gap
- opening
- aperture

hole /həʊl/ [n C] *The sheet was ancient and full of holes.* | *She stuck her finger through the hole.* | **+ in** *Troy looked through a hole in the fence at the garden next door.* | *A shaft of light came in through a hole in the corrugated iron roof.* | **sth has a hole in it** *I can't wear my green shirt – it has a hole in it.* | **gaping hole** (=a big hole) *They stared at the gaping hole in the wall.*

gap /gæp/ [n C] an empty space in the middle of something such as a wall or fence, especially because part of it is missing or broken **+ in** *The gate was locked but we managed to get through a gap in the fence.* | **+ under** *The light was coming through a tiny gap under the door.* | **+ between** *Sharon has a gap between her two front teeth.*

opening /ˈəʊpənɪŋ/ [n C] a hole that something can pass through or that you can see through, especially one which is at the entrance or top of something: *Bees come and go through a small opening at the bottom of the hive.* | *We zipped up the opening of the tent to stop the mosquitoes getting in.*

aperture /ˈæpəʳtʃəʳ/ [n C] a hole, especially one that allows light to pass through – use this especially in scientific and technical contexts: *The telescope has an aperture of 2.4 metres.*

2 a hole in the ground or in the surface of something

- hole
- crater
- pothole
- pit
- abyss
- chasm

hole /həʊl/ [n C] *The old mineshaft had left a deep hole, dangerous to both people and livestock.* | **+ in** *The aim is to get the ball in a hole in the ground.* | **make a hole (in sth)** *We made a small hole in the earth, just deep enough to cover the roots of the plant.* | *Make a hole in the bottom of each plant pot to let the water drain out.* | **dig a hole** *A fox had dug a hole under our garden fence.* | *Construction workers have to dig a thousand foot hole before work can start on the tunnel.*

crater /ˈkreɪtəʳ/ [n C] a big hole in the surface of something, especially the ground, that is caused by an explosion or a large falling object: *The meteor left a crater over five miles wide.* | **+ in** *When the bomb exploded it left a huge crater in the ground.*

pothole /ˈpɒthəʊl‖ˈpɑːt-/ [n C] a hole in the surface of a road that makes driving difficult or dangerous: *He rode his bike over an enormous pothole.* | *It is going* *to cost the city at least $500,000 to patch potholes created by winter rains.*

pit /pɪt/ [n C] a large wide hole in the ground, especially one that is used for a particular purpose such as burying things: *They found a large pit where all the dead bodies had been thrown.* | *We dug a pit a yard deep in the soil.*

abyss /əˈbɪs/ [n C] an extremely deep empty space, seen from a very high point such as the edge of a mountain – used especially in literature: *Matthew found himself standing at the edge of a deep abyss.*

chasm /ˈkæzəm/ [n C] a very deep space between two high areas of rock, especially one that is dangerous: *An unsteady-looking rope bridge was the only way to get across the chasm.* | *The landscape was a series of mountains, chasms, canyons and valleys.*

3 a place on a surface that is lower than the rest

- dip
- indentation
- depression
- dent

dip /dɪp/ [n C] a place where the surface of the ground goes down suddenly **+ in** *The boy fell off his bicycle when he went over a dip in the road too fast.*

indentation /ˌɪndenˈteɪʃən/ [n C] a place or area in a hard surface that is slightly lower than the rest of the surface, especially caused by something pressing hard on it **+ in** *The X-rays showed a slight indentation in the man's skull.* | *She gently made an indentation in the centre of each cookie.*

depression /dɪˈpreʃən/ [n C] an area, especially of the ground, that is slightly lower than the area around it, caused by something heavy pressing on it **+ in** *You could see a depression in the ground where the helicopter had landed.* | *The depressions in the sand are made by turtles, that come up here to lay their eggs.*

dent /dent/ [n C] a place in the surface of something, especially metal, that is slightly lower because something has hit it accidentally: *The picture frame came with scratches, dents and marks that make it look old.* | **+ in** *Emma backed into a tree, leaving a dent in the car's rear bumper.*

4 a long narrow hole across the surface of something

- crack
- split
- slit
- slot

crack /kræk/ [n C] a long, narrow line across the surface of a hard substance such as glass or stone where it has been damaged **+ in** *This cup has a crack in it.* | *The crack in the bedroom wall seems to be widening.*

split /splɪt/ [n C] British a long straight hole caused when a material such as plastic or cloth tears: *We suddenly noticed there was a split in the side of the tent.*

slit /slɪt/ [n C] a long, narrow hole, especially one that you can see through or put things through: *Tania's skirt has a long slit up the back.* | *I covered my eyes with my hands, watching through the slits between my fingers.*

slot /slɒt‖slɑːt/ [n C] a straight narrow hole, for example on a container, made so that a particular type or size of object can fit through it: *I dropped a quarter in the slot and dialed the number.* | *The message was placed in every employee's mail slot.*

5 a hole in something that has been damaged, allowing water, air etc to escape

- hole
- leak
- puncture

hole /həʊl/ [n C] **+ in** *Water trickled in through the hole in the roof.* | *There are holes in the ozone layer above Antarctica.*

leak /liːk/ [n C] a hole where something has been damaged or broken that allows a gas or liquid to pass through when it should not: *The water pressure's right down – there must be a leak in the pipe.* | **spring a leak** (=suddenly get a leak) *The boat had sprung a leak and it was sinking fast.*

puncture /ˈpʌŋktʃəʳ/ [n C] British a small hole in a tyre through which air escapes: *I could hear the hissing sound of air escaping from the puncture.* | **slow puncture** (=a puncture from which air escapes slowly) *The tyre's gone flat again – I think we've got a slow puncture.*

6 words for describing something that has lots of holes in it

- be full of holes
- riddled with holes
- perforated
- porous
- leaky

be full of holes /biː ˌfʊl əv ˈhəʊlz/ [v phrase] *Parker's socks were so full of holes that his toes peeked through.* | *The roof was full of holes, all of which sprouted grass and moss.*

riddled with holes /ˌrɪdld wɪð ˈhəʊlz/ [adj phrase] full of a great many small holes, especially in a surface: *The old table was riddled with holes.* | *The ship returned from the war-zone riddled with bullet holes.*

perforated /ˈpɜːʳfəreɪtɪ̣d/ [adj] having a lot of small holes arranged in a regular pattern that has been made by a machine for a particular purpose: *They put the insect into a tin with a perforated lid.* | *Tear along the perforated line and return the bottom part of the form.*

porous /ˈpɔːrəs/ [adj] a substance such as rock or soil or a surface that is **porous** allows liquid or gas to pass through it: *If a garage has a porous floor, it can become extremely damp.* | *Plants in containers made of porous material, must be watered more often than those in plastic pots.*

leaky /ˈliːki/ [adj usually before noun] a **leaky** roof, pipe etc is damaged so that it has a hole or holes in it that water comes through: *The house had a leaky roof.* | *There was a pool of water in the corner where water was dripping from a leaky pipe.*

7 to make a hole in the ground or surface of something

- hollow out
- dig out
- gouge
- prick
- drill
- bore
- dent

hollow out /ˌhɒləʊ ˈaʊt‖ˌhɑː-/ [phr v T] to make a space by removing the inside part of something **hollow out sth/hollow sth out** *Carefully hollow out the pineapple and then fill it with the ice-cream.*

dig out /ˌdɪg ˈaʊt/ [phr v T] British to make a hole in the ground using a tool that is made for digging: *To* *plant the tree you need to dig out a hole about 20 cm wide and 30 cm deep.* | *The workmen were already digging out the foundations for the building.*

gouge /gaʊdʒ/ [v I/T] to make a deep cut in a surface, using something sharp, especially in order to remove something: *The blade gouged a deep wound in her leg.* | **gouge out sth/gouge sth out** (=remove something by violently cutting a hole) *In the play he tries to gouge out his own eyes.*

prick /prɪk/ [v T] to make a very small hole in something, especially accidentally, using something pointed such as a pin: *A small bead of blood formed where she had pricked her finger.* | *Prick the potatoes before baking them.*

drill /drɪl/ [v I] to make a narrow hole in something using a tool that turns round and round very quickly: *I heard the dentist start drilling, but I couldn't feel anything.* | **drill for oil/water/gas etc** *Oil companies still drill for oil off Santa Barbara.* | **+ into** *It sounds like someone's drilling into the wall.* —**drilling** [adj] *The oil engineers have already moved their drilling equipment into the area.*

bore /bɔːʳ/ [v I/T] to make a hole in a hard surface such as rock or the ground using a lot of pressure, especially in order to find or remove minerals, coal etc: *The mining company bored a 5000 foot hole.* | *The machine they used to bore the tunnel is the size of a two storey house.* | **+ into/through** *They had to bore through solid rock.*

dent /dent/ [v T] to accidentally hit the surface of something, especially something metal, so that part of the surface is bent or slightly lower than the rest: *He accidentally dented the garage door, trying to reverse in.* —**dented** [adj] *In the market I bought a beautiful but badly dented silver bowl.*

8 to make a hole through something

- make a hole in
- pierce
- puncture
- punch
- drill a hole

make a hole in /ˌmeɪk ə ˈhəʊl ɪn/ [v phrase] *Make a hole in the bottom of the plant pot to allow the water to drain out.* | *Make a hole in the surface of the pie before you put it in the oven.*

pierce /pɪəʳs/ [v T] to make a small hole through something using something long and sharp: *She pierced the lid of the can and poured the milk into a saucepan.* | *The arrow pierced his heart.* | **have your ears/nose/navel etc pierced** (=have holes made in them so that you can wear jewellery) *Shelley had her ears pierced when she was a teenager.*

puncture /ˈpʌŋktʃəʳ/ [v T] to damage something by making a hole through which air escapes: *The doctor was worried that the broken rib might puncture the woman's lung.* —**punctured** [adj] *There was an old punctured football lying between the goal-posts.*

punch /pʌntʃ/ [v T] to make a hole through paper or material with a quick strong movement using a special tool: *The conductor walked through the train, punching everyone's ticket.* | **punch a hole in sth** *I punched holes in the papers and filed them away in a binder.* | *The shoemaker was threading stitches through tiny holes he had punched in the leather.*

drill a hole /ˌdrɪl ə ˈhəʊl/ [v phrase] to make a small hole in something using a tool that turns around and around very quickly **+ in** *I drilled two holes in the shelf and attached it to the wall.* | *We drilled several small holes in the lid of the jar.*

holiday/vacation

RELATED WORDS

▸ *see also* **travel, visit, get on or off a bus, plane etc, free (10-11), stay (4-8)**

1 time when you are allowed to be away from work or school

- holiday
- vacation
- break
- day off/afternoon off etc
- time off
- leave
- half-term

holiday /ˈhɒlədi‖ˈhɑːlədeɪ/ [n C/U] British a period of time when you do not have to go to work or school: *I get four weeks' holiday each year.* | *Work has been so hectic – I really need a holiday.* | **the holidays/summer holidays/school holidays** (=the long periods when schools close) *July 20th is the first day of the summer holidays.* | **Christmas/Easter etc holiday** *Last year we spent most of the Christmas holiday at our grandma's.* | **spend your holidays** *As a boy, Luckett spent his holidays here in Ledsham.* | **in/during the holidays** *We try to do as many different activities as we can with the children during the school holidays.*

vacation /vəˈkeɪʃən‖veɪ-/ [n C] especially American a period of time when you do not have to go to work or school: *I want you to write about your vacation.* | *The company allows us 14 vacation days a year.* | **summer/Christmas etc vacation** *Under the new plan, students will have shorter summer vacations and longer winter vacations.* | **spend your vacation** *I spent part of my Christmas vacation with my dad's family.* | **during summer/winter etc vacation** *The skating rink will be open from 8 a.m. to 8 p.m. during summer vacation.* | **during sb's/a vacation** *He worked at the resort during his college vacations.*

break /breɪk/ [n C] a short holiday from your work or school: *The students get a few days' break in February.* | **spring/winter/Christmas etc break** *Daytona Beach is preparing for the thousands of college students who will arrive for spring break.* | **take a break** *Can you take a break next month?*

day off/afternoon off etc /ˌdeɪ ˈɒf/ [n phrase] a period of time when you are allowed to be away from work: *Wednesday is my only day off this week.* | **have/take a day off** *I've got a day off on Friday – I'll come and see you then.* | *Can you take the morning off tomorrow?*

time off /ˌtaɪm ˈɒf/ [n phrase] time when you are allowed to be away from your work, in order to rest or do something different **have/take time off** *Is Phyllis taking any time off when you're there?* | *I'll get some time off around Christmas.*

leave /liːv/ [n U] a period of official holiday time, especially for people who are in the army, navy, or police etc: *I get twenty-five days' leave a year.* | *Phil still has three days' annual leave owing to him.* | **be on leave** (=having a holiday) *They got married while he was on leave from the army.*

half-term /ˌhɑːfˈtɜːʳm◂‖ˌhæf-/ [n C] British a short holiday in the middle of the school term: *It rained all through half-term.* | *Half-term is the last week in October.*

2 a day's holiday when all the shops, banks etc are closed

- holiday

holiday /ˈhɒlədi‖ˈhɑːlədeɪ/ [n C] *We'd forgotten that July 14th was a holiday in France.* | **national holiday** (=a holiday for the whole country) *St Patrick's Day is a national holiday in Ireland.* | **bank holiday/public holiday** British (=an official holiday) *This shop is closed on Sundays and public holidays.* | *The roads are always busy on bank holidays.*

3 time when you travel to another place for enjoyment

- holiday
- trip
- honeymoon

holiday British **/vacation** American /ˈhɒlədi‖ˈhɑːlədeɪ, vəˈkeɪʃən‖veɪ-/ [n C] a period of days or weeks that you spend in another place or country for enjoyment: *France is the ideal place for a romantic holiday.* | **be on holiday/vacation** *Mrs Southey is on holiday in Florida.* | *Karl will take care of the house while we're on vacation.* | **have a holiday/vacation** *I had two weeks' holiday in Thailand last year.* | **take a holiday/vacation** (=go somewhere for a holiday) *We couldn't afford to take a vacation at the moment.* | **family holiday/vacation** (=with your family) *They take a two-week family vacation every summer.*

trip /trɪp/ [n C] a holiday, especially an organized holiday that you go on in order to do a particular activity: *This year we're going to Colorado on a five-day skiing trip.* | **go on a trip** *They went on a trip to Australia and loved it.* | *Every year Peter goes on a fishing trip with all his old friends.* | **take a trip** *We have enough money saved to take a trip to Cancun.*

honeymoon /ˈhʌnimuːn/ [n C] the holiday that a man and a woman have just after they are married: *We had our honeymoon in Majorca.* | **on honeymoon** *Where are you going on honeymoon?*

4 someone who is on holiday

- tourist
- holidaymaker
- honeymooner

tourist /ˈtʊərəst/ [n C] someone who visits a different place for interest and enjoyment: *More than 3 million American tourists visit Britain every year.* | *Tourists can use the colour-coded map to guide themselves on walks of the city.*

holidaymaker British **/vacationer** American /ˈhɒlədiˌmeɪkəʳ‖ˈhɑːlədeɪ-, vəˈkeɪʃənəʳ‖veɪ-/ [n C] someone who is spending time in another place or country for enjoyment – used especially in newspapers and advertising: *The town seems so empty in the autumn when all the holidaymakers have gone home.* | *In the 1950s, vacationers flocked to resorts in the Catskills.*

honeymooner /ˈhʌnimuːnəʳ/ [n C] someone who is on holiday with their new husband or wife soon after their wedding: *All the honeymooners will receive a free bottle of champagne.*

5 to go for a holiday somewhere

- go on holiday
- go away
- get away
- take off

go on holiday British **/go on vacation** American /ˌgəʊ ɒn ˈhɒlədi‖-ˈhɑːlədeɪ, ˌgəʊ ɒn vəˈkeɪʃən‖-veɪ-/ [v phrase] to go away from your home, especially for a holiday: *We used to go on holiday in Scotland when we were kids.* | *Make sure you get insurance before you go on holiday.* | *Most families go on vacation during the summer.*

go away /ˌgəʊ əˈweɪ/ [phr v I] to **go away** from your home, especially for a holiday: *We're going away for two weeks in June.* | *Martha and Tom are going away this weekend.*

get away /ˌget əˈweɪ/ [phr v I] to spend time away from your home – use this especially about someone who goes on holiday for a rest from their normally busy life: *We managed to get away for a week in August.* | **get away from it all** (=spend time away from all the things you usually have to do) *Yosemite is a great place to get away from it all.*

take off /ˌteɪk ˈɒf/ [phr v I] American informal to go on holiday, especially somewhere exciting or far away **+ for** *Carlos just took off for Venezuela for three weeks.*

6 a place where people go or stay on holidays

- resort
- tourist attraction
- tourist destination
- tourist trap
- camp
- holiday camp
- cruise
- tour
- holiday home
- timeshare
- campground
- hostel/youth hostel

resort /rɪˈzɔːʳt/ [n C] a place where a lot of people go for a holiday, especially one that has a lot of things specially provided for tourists such as hotels, swimming pools, organized activities etc: *Acapulco is one of Mexico's most popular resorts.* | *Lift tickets at most ski resorts are about $30 to $40 a day.*

tourist attraction /ˈtʊərəst əˌtrækʃən/ [n C] something such as a museum, place, event etc that tourists want to see: *Graceland, Elvis Presley's former home, is now a tourist attraction that draws more than 600,000 visitors every year.*

tourist destination /ˈtʊərəst destəˌneɪʃən/ [n C] a place where a lot of people like to go on holiday: *Amsterdam is the Netherlands' most popular tourist destination.* | *Phuket is an international tourist destination 430 miles south of Bangkok.*

tourist trap /ˈtʊərəst ˌtræp/ [n C] a place that a lot of tourists go to, but where hotels, food, gifts etc are more expensive than they should be, and that is often not as pleasant or interesting as tourists expect: *Residents are worried that the president's home town will turn into a tourist trap.*

camp /kæmp/ [n C] American a place where children go to stay for a short time and do special activities and have fun: *College students work at a camp for kids from the inner city, leading craft activities and sports competitions.* | *A girl's basketball camp is being organized by the City Recreation Department.* | **summer camp** *He's going to a Boy Scout summer camp for two weeks in August.* | **day camp** (=a camp where children go during the day, but come home at night) *The YMCA is running a day camp with crafts, sports, and water fun.*

holiday camp /ˈhɒlədi ˌkæmp‖ˈhɑːlədeɪ-/ [n C] British a place where people, especially families, go for their holidays and where there are a lot of organized activities: *She won a talent show at a holiday camp in Wales.*

cruise /kruːz/ [n C] a holiday during which you travel on a large boat that has entertainment, restaurants, swimming pools etc: *The seven-day cruise stops at Cabo San Lucas, Puerto Vallarta and other Mexican resorts.* | **cruise liner/ship** *a luxury cruise ship*

tour /tʊəʳ/ [n C] a trip in which you visit several different places with a group of other people: *The tour includes stops in Salzburg and Vienna.* | **package tour** (=a tour in which all the travel arrangements are made by the tour company) *Package tours that include tickets to Olympic events have sold well.*

holiday home British **/vacation home** American /ˈhɒlədi ˌhəʊm‖ˈhɑːlədeɪ-, vəˈkeɪʃən ˌhəʊm‖veɪ-/ [n C] a house that someone owns in a place such as the mountains or the coast where they go for their holidays: *Many Swedes have small vacation homes on a lake shore.*

timeshare /ˈtaɪmʃeəʳ/ [n C] a holiday home that you buy with other people, so that each person can spend a period of time there: *They have a timeshare in Majorca.*

campground American **/campsite** British /ˈkæmpgraʊnd, ˈkæmpsaɪt/ [n C] a place where people can bring tents or vehicles that they sleep in, to stay in while they are on holiday: *Campgrounds in Glacier National Park open in late May and early June.* | *Most French towns have a municipal campsite.*

hostel/youth hostel /ˈhɒstl, ˈjuːθ ˌhɒstl‖ˈhɑː-/ [n C] a cheap hotel where people can stay for a short time while they are travelling on their holidays: *We stayed at a cheap hostel in the centre of Prague.*

7 the business of arranging holidays for people

- travel/tourist industry
- tourism
- travel agency
- tour guide

travel/tourist industry /ˈtrævəl, ˈtʊərəst ˌɪndəstri/ [n U] all the jobs that are involved in providing services for tourists: *Restrictions introduced to control foot and mouth disease have hit the tourist industry hard.* | *In the U.S., the travel industry is the second largest employer in the nation.*

tourism /ˈtʊərɪzəm/ [n U] when people travel to another place for a holiday – use this especially when you are talking about all the services tourists need, such as hotels, food etc: *As part of a plan to increase tourism, visitors staying less than 90 days do not need a visa.* | *The country relies on tourism and the sale of raw materials for hard currency.*

travel agency /ˈtrævəl ˌeɪdʒənsi/ [n C] a business that arranges travel and holidays: *Travel agencies issue at least 80 percent of all airline tickets.* —**travel agent** [n C] someone who works in a travel agency: *Check with your travel agent for the best rates.*

tour guide /ˈtʊəʳ gaɪd/ [n C] someone who leads a tour to different places and tells people about their history, meaning etc: *Student tour guides take visitors on a one-hour tour of the campus.* | *According to our tour guide, Gibraltar is the largest fortress in the world.*

home

RELATED WORDS

- be from a country *see* **come from**
- leave your home *see* **leave (14-18)**
- *see also* **house, live**

1 where someone lives

- home
- Jerry's/my mother's/the Carters' etc
- place
- residence
- address

home /həʊm/ [n C/U] the place where you live: *People like to feel secure in their own homes.* | *Buying your first home is a very important step.* | **family home** (=the house where a family has lived for a long time) *To raise the extra money they had to sell the family home.* | **home life** (=the things you do at home) *You need to maintain a good balance between your home life and career.*

Jerry's/my mother's/the Carters' etc /ˈdʒeriz/ [n phrase] spoken the place where Jerry, my mother, the Carters etc live: *OK. I'll see you at Helen's at eight o'clock.* | *We were at the Thompsons' last Saturday for dinner.* | *You've never been to my sister's, have you?*

place /pleɪs/ [n singular] spoken informal the house, apartment etc where someone lives: *Terry's just bought himself a place over in Newgate, overlooking the harbour.* | **sb's place** *Why don't you come around to our place for a drink on Saturday?* | *Your place is too small for a party. Let's have it at mine.*

residence /ˈrezədəns/ [n C] formal someone's home, especially the home of an important person, that is sometimes used for official dinners, meetings etc: *10 Downing Street is the British Prime Minister's official residence.* | *We first met at a cocktail party at the residence of the Russian ambassador.*

address /əˈdres‖ˈædres/ [n C] the number of the house or building, and the name of the street, road and town where someone lives: *What's your address and telephone number?* | **change of address** (=when you move to a different address) *Notify your credit card company of any change of address.* | **address book** (=a list of addresses of your friends, family etc) *I checked my address book for Rick's house number.*

2 to be in your home

- be at home/be home
- be in

be at home/be home /biː ət ˈhəʊm, biː ˈhəʊm/ [v phrase] *I'll be at home tonight if you want to call me.* | *We're just going to stay at home rather than go away anywhere.* | *Jim's never home Friday nights. You should know that.* | **stay home** *It was raining, so I stayed home.* | **be home alone** (=home on your own, used especially about children) *The two-year-old girl had been left home alone.*

be in /biː ˈɪn/ [v phrase] if someone **is in**, they are in their home and you can visit them or talk to them on the phone: *'Hello, Mrs Jones. Is Sally in, please?'* | *We went to see Phil and Tony but there was nobody in.* | *No, Gerry won't be in until after eight o'clock.*

3 happening or doing something in someone's home

- at home
- domestic

at home /ət ˈhəʊm/ [adv] *The good thing about my job is that I can often work at home.* | *Earlier in the century it was normal for women to have their babies at home.* | *Darren still lives at home with his parents.*

domestic /də'mestɪk/ [adj usually before noun] happening in or relating to the home: *She likes to keep her domestic life quite separate from her work.* | *The women had all experienced some form of domestic violence.*

4 words for describing something that is used in people's homes

- home
- domestic

home /həʊm/ [adj only before noun] designed to be used in homes: *The company has decided to expand in the home computer market.* | *Home furnishings are on the second floor next to the toy department.*

domestic /də'mestɪk/ [adj only before noun] designed to be used in homes, rather than in factories, offices, or other public places: *The gas is used for domestic heating and cooking.* | *The store sells a wide range of domestic appliances.*

5 to or towards your home

- home

home /həʊm/ [adv] **go/come/arrive etc home** *He cleans the offices after all the workers have gone home.* | *Come straight home after the theatre, won't you?* | **bring/take sth home** *You can take the laptop home with you if you like.*

6 to not be in your home

- be out
- be away

be out /bi: 'aʊt/ [v phrase] especially spoken to not be in your home for a short period: *'Can I speak to Frank?' 'I'm sorry he's out right now.'* | *While they were out, someone broke in and stole their TV and VCR.*

be away /bi: ə'weɪ/ [v phrase] to not be in your home for several days, weeks, or months: *Who's going to look after your cats while you're away?* | **+ from** *Jack worked as a pilot and was often away from home.*

7 to provide someone with a place to live

- house
- accommodate

house /haʊz/ [v T] if an organization **houses** someone, it provides them with a home to live in: *The refugees have been fed, clothed and housed by welfare organizations around the world.*

accommodate /ə'kɒmədeɪt‖ə'kɑ:-/ [v T] formal to provide someone with a place to live, especially someone who is away from their own home, for example a student: *Once you have been accepted at the university they promise to accommodate you in a dormitory.* | *Migrant workers are to be accommodated near the place where they work.*

8 to have no home

- not have anywhere to live
- homeless
- be on the streets

not have anywhere to live ALSO **have nowhere to live** /nɒt hæv ˌeniweəʳ tə 'lɪv, hæv ˌnəʊweəʳ tə 'lɪv/ [v phrase not in progressive] *She was in a strange city, with no job and without anywhere to live.* | *He's staying at my house because he has nowhere to live right now.*

homeless /'həʊmləs/ [adj] having no home to live in, especially because you are very poor or have been forced to leave your old home: *The possibility that he might become homeless frightened him.* | *There is a system of shelters for homeless people.* | *The earthquake left thousands of people homeless.* —**homelessness** [n U] *The committee criticized the government's new policy on homelessness.*

be on the streets /bi: ɒn ðə 'stri:ts/ [v phrase] informal to sleep outdoors in a city because you do not have anywhere to live: *As many as 250,000 children are homeless and on the streets.* | *He ran away from home and lived rough on the streets until the police helped him get into a hostel.*

9 people who have no home to live in

- the homeless
- transient
- bum
- bag-lady
- tramp
- vagrant

the homeless /ðə 'həʊmləs/ [n phrase] *We distribute food and blankets to the homeless on the streets of London.* | *There aren't enough places in short-stay hostels, so the homeless are reduced to sleeping in cardboard boxes.*

transient /'trænziənt‖'trænʃənt/ [n C] American someone who has no home or regular work: *Empty houses attract drug users and transients.* | *Farther along the street was a transient who was carrying his belongings in a plastic bag.*

bum /bʌm/ [n C] American informal a person, usually a man, who has no home or regular job and asks people for money on the streets: *A couple of bums were passing a bottle in a doorway.*

bag-lady /'bæg ˌleɪdi/ [n C] informal a woman with no home or job who carries all her possessions around with her in a bag: *A bag lady with a shopping cart was picking through the garbage for aluminum cans.*

tramp /træmp/ [n C] someone, especially a man, who has no home or job, and who often asks people for money to live: *An old tramp was sleeping under Waterloo Bridge, his coat wrapped tight to keep out the cold.*

vagrant /'veɪgrənt/ [n C] especially written someone who has no home or regular work, and goes from place to place – used especially in legal or official contexts: *Our charity provides shelter, meals, and clothing for vagrants.* | *The number of vagrants is increasing because of the lack of affordable accommodation for rent in the capital.*

honest

RELATED WORDS

opposite: **dishonest**

see also **trust/not trust, trick/deceive, true, lie**

1 someone who does not cheat, steal, break the law etc

- honest
- reputable
- above suspicion
- can trust

honest /'ɒnɪ̵st‖'ɑ:n-/ [adj] someone who is **honest** does not lie, steal or cheat, and can be trusted: *He's one of the few honest politicians we have left.* | *As the job involves handling large amounts of money, it's essential that our workers are honest.* | **scrupulously**

honest (=very careful to always be completely honest) *She was scrupulously honest in all her business dealings.* —**honestly** [adv] *I'm not convinced that the salesman dealt with us honestly.*

reputable /ˈrepjətəbəl/ [adj] known to be honest, especially in your business activities: *She had her antique vases valued by a reputable dealer.* | *Before you buy a used car it's best to go to a reputable garage.* | *How do we know that all the firms involved in this deal are reputable?*

above suspicion /əˌbʌv səˈspɪʃən/ [adj phrase] known to be very honest – use this especially about someone who is in a position in which it is important to be trusted: *People who look after other people's money should be above suspicion.* | *During the investigation no one will be considered above suspicion.*

can trust /kən ˈtrʌst/ [v phrase] if you **can trust** someone, you are sure that they are honest and that you can depend on them: *Beth's an honest hard-working girl who I know I can trust.* | **can trust sb to do sth** *I knew I could trust Neil to look after the money.*

2 someone who tells the truth

- honest
- truthful
- sincere
- frank
- open
- direct
- up front
- straight
- candid

honest /ˈɒnəst‖ˈɑːn-/ [adj] someone who is **honest** says what they really think or what is really happening, and does not try to hide the truth or deceive people: *You can always rely on Stewart to be honest.* | **+ about** *I don't think she's being completely honest about what she knows.* | **be honest with sb** *All we are asking is that management be honest with us, even if the situation is difficult.* | **honest answer/reply etc** *Tell me where you were – and I want an honest answer.* —**honestly** [adv] *Tell me honestly, are you in love with her?*

truthful /ˈtruːθfəl/ [adj] someone who is **truthful** does not lie: *As a child she was obedient and truthful.* | *Not everyone believes the government is being truthful.* | **+ about** *He has clearly not been truthful about the nature of their relationship.* | **be truthful with sb** *I hope we can be truthful with each other.* | **truthful account/story/answer etc** *It is unlikely that a truthful account of conditions in the prison will ever be seen.* —**truthfully** [adv] *Jackson claims he answered the questions truthfully.*

sincere /sɪnˈsɪəʳ/ [adj] showing your true feelings and what you really believe: *She said she would love to come, but I wasn't sure if she was being sincere.* | *My client extends his sincere apologies to anyone who may have been hurt by his actions.*

frank /fræŋk/ [adj] talking in an honest and direct way, especially about subjects that are difficult to talk about: *I'll be frank with you – I don't think you're doing a very good job.* | *Parents should not be afraid to have frank discussions about sex with their children.* | **+ about** *Graham was surprisingly frank about his feelings.* | **be frank with sb** *The doctor was very frank with me and told me how serious my condition was.* —**frankly** [adv] *Adams frankly admitted that he was disappointed with his team's performance.*

open /ˈəʊpən/ [adj] honest, friendly, and happy to tell other people the truth, especially about things that other people might be embarrassed to talk about: *Diana's very easy to talk to because she's so open.* | *He's a nice looking young man with an open, honest smile.* | **+ about** *Greg has always been very open about his sexuality.* —**openly** [adv] *People find it difficult to talk openly about death.*

direct /dəˈrekt, daɪ-/ [adj] saying exactly what you think in an honest, clear way, even though this may sometimes annoy or upset other people: *People were often scared of my father, who was very direct.* | *With her direct manner and good head for business she was soon promoted.* —**directly** [adv] *Dole spoke directly about his age, saying it was not a liability.*

up front /ʌp ˈfrʌnt/ [adj phrase] honest and willing to tell the truth, even if the truth is unpleasant: *He's always up front and willing to admit his mistakes.* | **+ about** *The company's directors have been surprisingly up front about their financial problems.* | **be up front with sb** *Karen is always very up front with her boyfriends.*

straight /streɪt/ [adj] **especially spoken** honest and likely to tell people exactly what you think or what is happening, without trying to hide anything: *Tony Blair stated that he was 'a pretty straight kind of guy'.* | **be straight with sb** *I don't care what you've done, Mike – just be straight with me.* | **straight answer** *I've asked several people what happened, but no one will give me a straight answer.*

candid /ˈkændəd/ [adj] **especially written** honest about your opinions and feelings, even if other people disapprove of them: *Lena is amusingly candid when she talks about the men in her life.* | **+ about** *The management team has been very candid about the problems the company is now facing.* | **candid discussion/conversation/comment etc** *She led a candid discussion about race relations in the city.* —**candidly** [adv] *It can be useful to talk candidly about your feelings to someone.*

3 so honest that some people think you are rude

- forthright
- blunt

forthright /ˈfɔːʳθraɪt/ [adj] saying honestly what you think in a way that often seems rude: *She was by nature forthright and impatient.* | *Bruck's forthright comments angered several people in the audience.* —**forthrightly** [adv] *He continued to speak forthrightly about whatever was on his mind.*

blunt /blʌnt/ [adj] saying what is true or what you really think, especially in a situation in which other people would be more polite: *His response was a blunt 'no.'* | *Maria can be very blunt and sometimes shocks people who don't know her well.* —**bluntly** [adv] *'If you don't like your job here, you can leave,' she said bluntly.*

4 to speak honestly

- tell the truth
- to be honest (with you)/in all honesty
- to be frank/frankly
- level with
- tell it like it is/tell sb straight
- speak your mind
- not mince (your) words
- call a spade a spade
- pull no punches/not pull any punches

tell the truth /ˌtel ðə ˈtruːθ/ [v phrase] to be honest in what you say: *He wouldn't believe that I was telling the truth.* | *When you testify in court, you have to swear to tell the truth.* | **tell sb the truth** *Tell me the truth – does this dress make me look fat?*

to be honest (with you)/in all honesty /tə biː ˈɒnɪst (wɪð juː)‖-ˈɑːn-, ɪn ˌɔːl ˈɒnɪsti‖-ˈɑːn-/ spoken say this before giving your honest opinion, especially when your opinion may sound unkind or surprising: *To be honest, I don't really like babies.* | *I wish I'd never met him, to be quite honest.* | *To be honest with you, I never expected him to get the job.* | *In all honesty, I've got no idea where she's living now.*

to be frank/frankly /tə biː ˈfræŋk, ˈfræŋkli/ spoken you say **to be frank** or **frankly** before giving your honest opinion, especially when your opinion may sound unkind or shocking: *To be frank, George isn't very good at the job.* | *Frankly, my dear, I don't give a damn.* | *Well, frankly, I think this proves that there are a lot of people making laws in this country who don't really know what they're doing.*

level with /ˈlevəl wɪð/ [phr v T] to be honest with someone, especially when they have asked you to give them the correct story, reason etc: *I promise I won't get angry. Just level with me and tell me what happened.* | *I'm going to level with you – some of the other managers don't think you're ready for a promotion.*

tell it like it is/tell sb straight /ˌtel ɪt laɪk ɪt ˈɪz, ˌtel (sb) ˈstreɪt/ [v phrase] to be honest and give someone all the facts about a situation, even if they are unpleasant: *I told her straight that she was wrong.* | *The people who report to me have to be willing to tell it like it is.*

speak your mind /ˌspiːk jɔːʳ ˈmaɪnd/ [v phrase] to say exactly what you think even if it offends people: *She believes in speaking her mind, which makes her very unpopular.* | *Larry isn't afraid to speak his mind, even in front of the boss.*

not mince (your) words /nɒt ˌmɪns (jɔːʳ) ˈwɜːʳdz/ [v phrase not usually in progressive] to say what you think in a way that you know might offend other people: *Helmut didn't mince any words in his criticism of the department.*

call a spade a spade /ˌkɔːl ə ˌspeɪd ə ˈspeɪd/ [v phrase not usually in progressive] to say exactly what you think about someone or something, especially in a situation where other people would be more polite: *Why not call a spade a spade and say that she's incompetent, if that's what you're thinking.*

pull no punches/not pull any punches /ˌpʊl nəʊ ˈpʌntʃɪz, nɒt ˌpʊl eni ˈpʌntʃɪz/ [v phrase] to speak honestly about someone or something, especially when you are criticizing them, without thinking about their feelings: *Rollins pulled no punches in his memoir, especially when writing about the political system.*

5 when someone behaves in an honest way

- honesty
- sincerity
- openness
- candour
- integrity

honesty /ˈɒnɪsti‖ˈɑːn-/ [n U] *Are you questioning my honesty?* | *Judy answered all the panel's questions with honesty and courage.* | *As a newspaper reporter I am committed to honesty and accuracy.*

sincerity /sɪnˈserɪti/ [n U] when you say or do things in a way that shows clearly that you honestly mean them: *'I'll do anything I can to help,' she said with sincerity.* | *Nothing about his behavior leads me to doubt his sincerity.*

openness /ˈəʊpən-nɪs/ [n U] when you are honest, friendly and happy to tell people the truth about yourself, especially about things that other people might be embarrassed to talk about: *Intimacy in a relationship requires openness.* | *The public expects complete openness from the President about his health.*

candour British **/candor** American /ˈkændəʳ/ [n U] when you are honest about your opinions and feelings, even if other people disapprove of them: *Winik writes with great candor, which has won her a wide following.* | *After so many lies from politicians, Dunbar's candour is refreshing.*

integrity /ɪnˈtegrɪti/ [n U] when you are very honest and always have the same moral principles in every situation: *Councilman Hughey's integrity is unquestioned.* | **man/woman of integrity** *She is a woman of integrity who has never abandoned her principles for the sake of making money.*

hope

RELATED WORDS

▸ *see also* **want**

1 to hope that something will happen or that something is true

- hope
- hopeful
- keep your fingers crossed
- hope for the best
- in the hope that
- optimistic
- pin your hopes on
- have high hopes

hope /həʊp/ [v I/T] *See you soon, I hope!* | *Even when everyone else thought he was dead, Julie never stopped hoping.* | **+ (that)** *We hurried out of the building, hoping that no one would see us leave.* | **+ to do sth** *Bob's hoping to travel to Africa next year.* | **+ for** *I'm hoping for a better salary in my next job.* | **I hope so** spoken *'Have we got enough money for the rent?' 'I don't know. I hope so.'* | **hope and pray** *She could only hope and pray that Liza would be back to her normal self the next time she saw her.* —**hope** [n C] *Everett soon forgot all his hopes of fame and fortune.* | *My hope is that Peter will realize his mistake and apologize.*

hopeful /ˈhəʊpfəl/ [adj] hoping that something good is likely to happen: *We don't know if Gascoigne will be fit to play in Saturday's game, but we're all hopeful.* | **+ (that)** *I'm quite hopeful that I'll get the job.* | **+ about** *James felt more hopeful about his future after his chat with his professor.* | **be hopeful of (doing) sth** British *The local police are hopeful of catching those responsible for the graffiti.* —**hopefully** [adv] *'Will there be any food left over?' he asked hopefully.*

keep your fingers crossed /ˌkiːp jɔːʳ ˈfɪŋgəʳz ˌkrɒst‖-ˌkrɔːst/ [v phrase] use this to say that you hope that something will happen the way you want, when you cannot do anything to affect what happens: *'Have you had your test results yet?' 'No. I'm just keeping my fingers crossed.'* | *Let's keep our fingers crossed and hope that this idea of yours works.*

hope for the best /ˌhəʊp fəʳ ðə ˈbest/ [v phrase] to hope that a situation will end well, when it is possible that something might go wrong: *He never uses a recipe. He just throws all kinds of food into a pan and hopes for the best.* | *Every expectant mother goes into labour hoping for the best*

in the hope that British **/in hopes that** American /ɪn ðə ˈhəʊp ðət, ɪn ˈhəʊps ðət/ if you do something

in the hope that it will have a good result, you do it because you hope it will make something good happen: *He showed me a photo of his wife, in the hope that I might have seen her.* | *He was rejecting Nancy in hopes that something better might develop with Lydia.*

optimistic /ˌɒptəˈmɪstɪk◂‖ˌɑːp-/ [adj] hoping and expecting that everything will happen in the best way possible: *Although his lawyers were optimistic, they couldn't be sure about the final outcome of the trial.* | *The Democrats went into this election in an optimistic mood.* | **+ about** *I am very optimistic about the future of our company.* | **cautiously optimistic** (=optimistic, but realizing that a good result is not definite) *The patient is still in a critical condition but doctors say they are cautiously optimistic that he will make a full recovery.* —**optimistically** [adv] *Tom said rather optimistically that we could finish the job in a day or two.*

pin your hopes on /ˌpɪn jɔːʳ ˈhəʊps ɒn/ [v phrase] to hope that one particular thing will happen, because your happiness or all your other plans depend on this: *Sue is pinning all her hopes on getting this job.* | *'I do hope she remembers.' 'Don't pin your hopes on it', warned David.*

have high hopes /hæv ˌhaɪ ˈhəʊps/ [v phrase] to be very hopeful and excited about something, so that you would be very disappointed if it did not happen **+ of doing sth** *Sam has high hopes of going to university next year.* | *Despite our differences, we came here with high hopes of signing a new treaty.* | **+ for** *Japanese car manufacturers have high hopes for increased profits in Europe.*

2 what you say when you hope something will happen

- hopefully
- with any luck
- let's hope
- if all goes well

hopefully /ˈhəʊpfəli/ [adv] spoken say this when you hope something will happen: *He's been resting today, so hopefully he'll be feeling better tomorrow.* | *Hopefully we can find a way of solving this problem.*

with any luck ALSO **with a little luck** /wɪð ˌeni ˈlʌk, wɪð ə ˌlɪtl ˈlʌk/ spoken say this when you hope something will happen, even though there is a small chance it might not: *With any luck, we'll have this finished by the end of the day.* | *With a little luck, Ruth will forget all about the party.*

let's hope /lets ˈhəʊp/ spoken say this when you hope that something will happen, especially because it will be very unpleasant if it does not: *Let's hope we can find a parking space.* | *The whole thing has been nothing but heartache and worry. Let's hope nothing like it ever happens again.*

if all goes well /ɪf ˌɔːl gəʊz ˈwel/ spoken say this when you hope something will be successful, but you know that success depends on everything happening in the right way: *If all goes well, I'll be sailing from Vera Cruz in about a week.* | *The tunnel should be finished by 2010 if all goes well.*

3 a feeling of hope

- hope
- optimism

hope /həʊp/ [n U] the feeling that you have when you **hope** something will happen and you think it is likely to happen: *The Queen sent a message of hope and sympathy to the American people.* | **+ of** *We now have no hope of finding any more survivors.* | **+ for** *Most of these youths have no jobs and no hope for the future.* | **be full of hope** *Thousands of emigrants set off for the New World full of hope.* | **give/offer sb hope** *Recent reports of a ceasefire agreement have given us new hope.* | **live in hope** (=keep hoping for something) *We haven't had much success yet. but we live in hope.*

optimism /ˈɒptəmɪzəm‖ˈɑːp-/ [n U] the feeling that everything will happen in the way you want it to or that good things will happen in the future: *There is a mood of optimism among Socialist Party supporters tonight.* | *the optimism of the post-war period*

4 to hope for something even when it is unlikely

- hope against hope (that)/cling to the hope that
- get your hopes up
- on the off chance that

hope against hope (that)/cling to the hope that /ˌhəʊp əgenst ˈhəʊp (ðət), ˌklɪŋ tə ðə ˈhəʊp ðət/ [v phrase] to continue to hope very much that something is true or will happen, even when you know it is extremely unlikely: *Daniel waited all day, hoping against hope that Annie would change her mind and come back.* | *James was still clinging to the hope that Jo might have made a mistake.*

get your hopes up spoken ALSO **build up your hopes** British /ˌget jɔːʳ ˈhəʊps ʌp, ˌbɪld ʌp jɔːʳ ˈhəʊps/ [v phrase] to get excited because you hope something will happen, usually when you are later disappointed because it does not: *I would have told you about this earlier, but I didn't want to get your hopes up.* | *I may be able to arrange something, but please don't get your hopes up.*

on the off chance that /ɒn ði ˈɒf ˌtʃɑːns ðət‖-ˌtʃæns-/ [conjunction] informal if you do something **on the off chance** that another thing will happen, you do it because you hope the other thing will happen, even though it seems unlikely: *They got to the man as quickly as they could, on the off chance that he was still alive, but he was not.*

5 unreasonable hopes

- wishful thinking
- pipe-dream
- pie in the sky

wishful thinking /ˌwɪʃfəl ˈθɪŋkɪŋ/ [n U] when something you hope for or want to believe is very unlikely to happen or to be true: *I think she likes me – but maybe it's just wishful thinking on my part!* | *Hopes that scientists have found a cure for baldness now seem based more on wishful thinking than reality.*

pipe-dream /ˈpaɪp driːm/ [n C] something pleasant or exciting that you like to imagine happening, but which is very unlikely to happen: *I'd always wanted to travel around the world, but it seemed nothing more than a pipe-dream.* | *'What do you think the chances are of lasting peace in the Middle East?' 'I think it's all just a pipe-dream.'*

pie in the sky /ˌpaɪ ɪn ðə ˈskaɪ/ [n phrase] informal an idea or plan that is **pie in the sky** is one that someone wishes or hopes will happen, but is unlikely to happen because it is not very practical: *Any talk of getting a reasonable response from the terrorists is just pie in the sky.*

6 making you feel more hope

- hopeful
- encouraging
- promising
- offer hope
- raise hopes
- auspicious
- light at the end of the tunnel
- a glimmer of hope/a ray of hope

hopeful /ˈhəʊpfəl/ [adj] *The fact that the two sides have agreed to hold negotiations is an extremely hopeful sign.* | **look hopeful** *Things might get better, but it isn't looking very hopeful right now.* | **sound hopeful** *At the interview they told me I was 'the right sort of person'. I thought that sounded kind of hopeful.*

encouraging /ɪnˈkʌrɪ̇dʒɪŋ‖-ˈkɜːr-/ [adj] making you feel more confident and hopeful: *The doctor had some encouraging news – I would soon be able to walk again.* | *There are one or two more encouraging signs in the economy now.* | *So far the results of our tests have been very encouraging.*

promising /ˈprɒmɪ̇sɪŋ‖ˈprɑː-/ [adj] seeming likely to be good or successful: *The future looks promising for British companies abroad.* | *The weather outlook for the weekend isn't very promising.* | *My grandfather gave up a promising career in law to fight for his country.*

offer hope /ˌɒfəʳ ˈhəʊp‖ˌɔːf-/ [v phrase] if something such as a new situation or discovery **offers hope**, it makes it possible for people to feel more hopeful that a bad situation will improve **+ to** *The new treatment may offer hope to thousands of cancer patients.* | **+ of** *A recent UN initiative seems to offer some hope of a lasting peace settlement in the region.*

raise hopes /ˌreɪz ˈhəʊps/ [v phrase] to make people more confident than before that what they are hoping for will happen **+ that** *The latest news has raised hopes that another Western hostage might soon be released.* | **raise sb's hopes** *Speculation in the press about tax cuts has raised everyone's hopes.*

auspicious /ɔːˈspɪʃəs/ [adj usually before noun] formal making people hopeful that good things will happen: *The baseball season got off to an auspicious start with two good wins for the Tokyo Giants.* | *It is my honour to toast the bride and groom on this auspicious occasion.*

light at the end of the tunnel /ˌlaɪt ət ði ˌend əv ðə ˈtʌnl/ [n phrase] something good that gives you hope that a long and difficult period is going to end soon: *For Jane there is some light at the end of the tunnel, but many anorexia sufferers continue to suffer in silence.* | **see the light at the end of the tunnel** (=realize that there is hope) *After all the problems we've had we're finally beginning to see some light at the end of the tunnel.*

a glimmer of hope/a ray of hope /ə ˌɡlɪmər əv ˈhəʊp, ə ˌreɪ əv ˈhəʊp/ [n phrase] something that gives you a small reason to hope that a bad situation will improve: *The news gave a glimmer of hope that Michael might be released from prison early.* | *The one ray of hope seemed to be the possibility that the enemy would call off their attack because of the weather.*

7 what you say when you hope something does not happen

- I hope not
- God/heaven forbid!

I hope not /aɪ ˈhəʊp nɒt/ spoken say this when you hope that what has just been mentioned will not happen or is not true: *'Do you think she's lost?' 'I hope not!'* | *'I promise I won't do it again.' 'I certainly hope not,' replied her mother.*

God/heaven forbid! /ˌɡɒd, ˌhevən fəʳˈbɪd‖ˌɡɑːd-/ spoken use this to say very strongly that you hope something does not happen or has not happened: *'She said she was going to find out where you live and come and visit you'. 'Heaven forbid!'*

8 to stop hoping

- lose hope/give up hope
- despair
- lose heart
- hopes are fading
- dash sb's hopes

lose hope/give up hope /ˌluːz ˈhəʊp, ˌɡɪv ʌp ˈhəʊp/ [v phrase] *Some seeds take a long time to germinate, so don't lose hope if nothing happens in the first year.* | **+ of doing sth** *After his accident, Jack had almost given up hope of ever working again.* | **+ that** *We never lost hope that our son would return one day.*

despair /dɪˈspeəʳ/ [v I] to stop hoping and become extremely unhappy, because you think there is no possibility of something happening: *You mustn't despair. Nothing is impossible.* | *He glared at her, despairing.* | **+ of doing sth** *Kate despaired of ever seeing her husband again.*

lose heart /ˌluːz ˈhɑːʳt/ [v phrase] to stop hoping that you will achieve something, because you feel you have not been making much progress: *I think if he fails again he'll just lose heart and give up.* | *The tunnel had never been finished. Perhaps the builders lost heart and abandoned it.*

hopes are fading /ˌhəʊps ɑːʳ ˈfeɪdɪŋ/ [n phrase] use this to say that people are beginning to stop hoping that someone is safe, that something will succeed etc: *Hopes are fading, but the search for survivors of the earthquake continues.* | **+ for** *Hopes are fading for the missing fourteen year old.*

dash sb's hopes /ˌdæʃ (sb's) ˈhəʊps/ [v phrase] to make someone completely stop hoping that something will happen or is true: *I didn't want to dash your hopes unnecessarily.* | **+ of doing sth** *a shattering knee injury which dashed his hopes of playing in the World Cup*

9 when there is no hope of improvement or success

- hopeless
- desperate
- gloomy
- bleak
- there is no hope

hopeless /ˈhəʊpləs/ [adj] *The firemen tried to stop the flames from spreading, but it was hopeless.* | *Remember, it's just when things look hopeless that you sometimes get a lucky break.*

desperate /ˈdespərɪ̇t/ [adj] so bad that, unless you get help immediately, there is no hope: *The situation is desperate – there are just not enough beds in the hospital.* | *Another two weeks without emergency aid and I'd think things could become quite desperate.*

gloomy /ˈɡluːmi/ [adj] a **gloomy** situation is one in which there is very little hope of improvement: *This latest survey presents a gloomy picture of the Russian economy.* | *Evidence that the world's population is increasing faster than ever implies a gloomy prospect for humanity: starvation.*

bleak /bliːk/ [adj] a **bleak** situation is one in which there is very little hope of improvement and will probably get worse: *His prospects of finding another job are bleak.* | *The future looked bleak for the Democratic party.*

there is no hope /ðeər ɪz ˌnəʊ ˈhəʊp/ say this when a situation is so bad that it is useless to hope that it will improve: *The doctor has said there's no hope. She only has a few weeks to live.* | **+ of** *The prison was on a small, rocky island. There was no hope of escape.* | **+ for** *I'm afraid there's no hope for us, unless you can give us the help we need.*

10 a feeling that it is useless to hope

- hopelessness
- despair

hopelessness /ˈhəʊpləsnɪ̈s/ [n U] *After a few weeks, our confidence that our embassy had heard of our plight gave way to hopelessness.* | **+ of** *Suddenly he saw the utter futility and hopelessness of his mission.* | **sense of hopelessness** *Who can really imagine the sense of hopelessness felt by people who commit suicide?*

despair /dɪˈspeəʳ/ [n U] an extremely unhappy feeling you have when your situation is so bad that you have stopped hoping: *Separation from someone you love can bring loneliness and despair.* | *He gazed at the confusion around him and was overwhelmed by a feeling of despair.* | **be in despair** *Dan was in despair. Everything seemed to be going wrong.*

horrible

RELATED WORDS

opposite: **nice**

▸ *see also* **dislike, hate**

1 unpleasant person/behaviour

- horrible
- unpleasant
- nasty
- mean
- not very nice
- obnoxious/objectionable
- creep
- nasty piece of work

▸ *see also* **cruel, unkind, rude, unfriendly, dishonest**

horrible /ˈhɒrɪ̈bəl‖ˈhɔː-, ˈhɑː-/ [adj] especially British behaving in a very rude, unkind, or annoying way: *Her husband was a horrible man – lazy, and always drunk.* | *I really don't like her at all – she's horrible!* | **be horrible to sb** *I think I'll go out if you're just going to be horrible to me.*

unpleasant /ʌnˈplezənt/ [adj] rude or unfriendly in the way you talk to people or answer their questions: *That man in the grocery store is always so unpleasant.* | *Did she really say that? What an unpleasant person!* | **be unpleasant to sb** *You shouldn't have been so unpleasant to her – she was only trying to help.*

nasty /ˈnɑːsti‖ˈnæsti/ [adj] someone who is **nasty** has a very unpleasant character and is often unkind to people: *I'd avoid him. if I were you. He can be quite nasty.* | *My first boss was a really nasty person, who seemed to enjoy making life difficult for everyone.* | **be nasty to/towards sb** *Some of the older boys were being very nasty to him.*

mean /miːn/ [adj] American rude and unkind in the way you treat people: *We soon found out that our new teacher could be real mean.* | **be mean to sb** *Sharon and the others were really mean to me at school today.*

not very nice /nɒt veri ˈnaɪs/ [adj phrase not before noun] especially spoken unkind or unfriendly – use this especially about things people say to each other: *They just told us to shut up, which wasn't very nice.* | **not very nice of sb** *It wasn't very nice of him to have a party without inviting me.*

obnoxious/objectionable /əbˈnɒkʃəs‖-ˈnɑːk-, əbˈdʒekʃənəbəl/ [adj] rude and offensive, especially deliberately **Objectionable** is more formal than **obnoxious**: *I'd hate to be her secretary – she's so obnoxious.* | *You're behaving like a spoilt obnoxious child.* | *I'd never have employed him if I'd realized what an objectionable person he was.* | *What was most objectionable about her was her arrogance.*

creep /kriːp/ [n C] informal someone who you dislike because they are unpleasant and behave in a way that makes you feel uncomfortable: *Get out of here you little creep! You make me sick!* | *He didn't say that, did he? What a creep!*

nasty piece of work /ˌnɑːsti piːs əv ˈwɜːʳk‖ˌnæsti-/ [n phrase] informal someone who is very unpleasant and is likely to behave in a cruel or violent way: *Casey and Wyatt went round in a gang with Don, who was a nasty piece of work.* | *Why would anyone want to kill Howard, do you think?' 'It's obvious. He was a nasty piece of work.'*

2 an unpleasant experience

- horrible
- nasty
- unpleasant
- not very nice
- nightmare

▸ *see also* **experience (2)**

horrible /ˈhɒrɪ̈bəl‖ˈhɔː-, ˈhɑː-/ [adj] a **horrible** experience or situation is one that makes you feel very worried and upset: *It was really horrible coming home and finding all our things had been stolen.* | *There was a horrible moment when she thought she had left all her files on the train.*

nasty /ˈnɑːsti‖ˈnæsti/ [adj] horrible – use this especially about events where there is violence, injury, or death: *There was a nasty accident on the freeway and seven people were killed.* | *a particularly nasty murder case* | *The news of his death came as a very nasty shock.*

unpleasant /ʌnˈplezənt/ [adj] making you feel slightly worried, uncomfortable, or embarrassed: *I had an unpleasant feeling that someone was following me.* | *Phil and Jane argued the whole time, so it was a pretty unpleasant evening.* | *Then Nel lost her temper and there was an extremely unpleasant scene in Kenwood's office.*

not very nice /nɒt veri ˈnaɪs/ [adj phrase not before noun] especially spoken unpleasant: *It's not very nice being stuck in an elevator for an hour.* | *Divorce is not a very nice business.*

nightmare /ˈnaɪtmeəʳ/ [n singular] a very unpleasant or frightening experience: *We were stuck in a traffic jam for about four hours – it was a nightmare.* | *The couple's honeymoon turned into a nightmare when Martin suddenly became very ill.* | **nightmare day/journey etc** *Thousands of commuters faced a nightmare journey to work because of the strikes.* | **nightmare scenario** (=the worst possible situation) *An oil spill on this part of the coast is the conservationists' nightmare scenario.*

3 an unpleasant taste or smell

- horrible/disgusting/revolting
- unpleasant
- foul
- gross
- not very nice
- nasty
- unappetizing

opposite —— **delicious**

▸ *see also* **smell, taste**

horrible/disgusting/revolting /ˈhɒrɪ̈bəl‖ˈhɔː-, ˈhɑː-, dɪsˈgʌstɪŋ, rɪˈvəʊltɪŋ/ [adj] very bad – use this especially to talk about things that taste, smell, or look really bad: *It was the most disgusting meal I've ever eaten.* | *He smiled showing his teeth, which were a revolting yellow colour.* | *What a horrible smell!* | *Dick had cooked a special stew, which looked and smelled revolting.*

unpleasant /ʌnˈplezənt/ [adj] tasting or smelling horrible: *Undercooked potatoes taste unpleasant and can be harmful.* | *Some animals give off an unpleasant odor that deters attackers.*

foul /faʊl/ [adj] a **foul** smell or taste is extremely bad, and is caused especially by waste or things decaying: *There was a foul smell coming up from the river.*

gross /grəʊs/ [adj] informal very unpleasant – use this to talk about food, smells, or behaviour that you dislike very much: *Ooh, gross! I hate spinach!* | *Brad threw up on the floor at the party. It was really gross.*

not very nice British **/not very good/not too good** /nɒt veri ˈnaɪs, nɒt veri ˈgʊd, nɒt tuː ˈgʊd/ [adj phrase not before noun] spoken a taste or smell that is **not very nice** or **not very good** is slightly unpleasant: *This cheese isn't very good. How long have we had it?* | *The first time I smoked a cigarette it didn't taste very nice.* | *I wouldn't cook that if I were you. It doesn't smell too good.*

nasty /ˈnɑːsti‖ˈnæsti/ [adj] tasting or smelling very strong and unpleasant: *I'm not very keen on this wine. It has a nasty aftertaste.* | *Police were alerted when neighbors complained of a nasty smell coming from the basement.* | *Cheap perfume often smells nasty after a couple of hours.*

unappetizing /ʌnˈæpɪ̈taɪzɪŋ/ [adj] a meal or food that is **unappetizing** has an unpleasant appearance or smell and does not make you want to eat it: *The soup was cold and unappetizing, but it was all there was.* | *The main course was an unappetizing leg of chicken with boiled potatoes.*

4 an unpleasant sound

- harsh
- grating
- sickening

▸ *see also* **sound**

harsh /hɑːʳʃ/ [adj] a sound that is **harsh** is unpleasant, rough, and usually loud: *Cheap loudspeakers often produce a harsh metallic tone.* | *'You'll do what I tell you,' he said, his voice harsh in her ear.* | *The wind made a harsh wailing sound in the trees.*

grating /ˈgreɪtɪŋ/ [adj] a sound that is **grating** is unpleasant, and is often produced by two rough things rubbing together: *The machine began to spin faster and faster, with the grating screech of metal on metal.* | *We could hear a group of tourists, talking in loud grating voices.* —**grate** [v I] *I can't stand the sound of chalk grating on a blackboard.*

sickening /ˈsɪkənɪŋ, ˈsɪknɪŋ/ [adj] a **sickening** sound is very unpleasant and makes you feel physically sick – use this especially about the sound when someone is badly hurt or something is badly damaged: *His head hit the door with a sickening thud.* | *There was a sickening crash and the sound of broken glass as the two trains collided.*

5 the feeling you have when you think something is very unpleasant

- disgust
- revulsion
- disgusted
- sickened
- nauseated

disgust /dɪsˈgʌst, dɪz-/ [n U] *Martia gave him a look of disgust, and walked away.* | *Disgust at cruel sports has come to be a common feature of British life.* | **in disgust** (=feeling disgust) *She held the glass away from her in disgust. 'What's this awful stuff you've given me to drink?'*

revulsion /rɪˈvʌlʃən/ [n U] a strong, sudden feeling of shock and disgust: *A little boy had died and, as a mother, I felt horror and revulsion.* | **+ at** *Holly was unable to hide her revulsion at what she had just read.* | **+ against** *What we are now seeing is a public revulsion against violence in society.* | **a feeling/sense/wave of revulsion** *News of the atrocities produced a wave of anger and revulsion.*

disgusted /dɪsˈgʌstɪ̈d, dɪz-/ [adj] feeling shocked and angry at something you think is very wrong, cruel, unpleasant etc: *Ann was disgusted when she saw the dirty hotel room.* | *Disgusted onlookers claimed that the man was more concerned about his car than the victims of the crash.* | **+ at** *Many people are disgusted at the continuing slaughter of dolphins.* | **+ by** *He ate noisily and greedily. I tried hard not to be disgusted by his manners.* | **+ with** *I was absolutely disgusted with the way our fans behaved.*

sickened /ˈsɪkənd/ [adj] very shocked and angry at something such as violence or suffering: *Country vets aren't easily sickened, but I felt my stomach turning when I saw the state of the dog.* | *Sickened detectives said the old lady was lucky to be alive after such a brutal attack.*

nauseated /ˈnɔːzieɪtɪ̈d, -si-‖-zi-, -ʒi-/ [adj not before noun] if you are **nauseated** by something, it is so unpleasant that it makes you feel physically sick: *The thought of him kissing her made her feel nauseated.* | *Recognizing the dead woman's face, she turned away, nauseated.*

6 to seem very unpleasant to someone

- disgust
- revolt
- turn your stomach
- sicken

disgust /dɪsˈgʌst, dɪz-/ [v T not in progressive] *His habit of sniffing loudly really disgusted her.* | *The heat, the noise, the smell of the other passengers; everything about the subway disgusted him.* | *'Get out,' she said. 'You disgust me!'*

revolt /rɪˈvəʊlt/ [v T not in progressive] if something **revolts** you, you think it is extremely unpleasant: *I opened the door and was instantly revolted by the smell.* | *He kissed her full on the lips in a way that revolted her.*

turn your stomach /ˌtɜːʳn jɔːʳ ˈstʌmək/ [v phrase] if something **turns your stomach** it makes you feel ill because it is so unpleasant or shocking: *The sight of the dead body turned his stomach.* | *The strike has meant piles of rotting garbage in the streets. 'It's enough to turn your stomach,' said one resident.*

sicken /ˈsɪkən/ [v T] if something such as violence or suffering **sickens** you, it makes you feel ill and you wish you could stop it: *The smell of the blood sickened her and she ran out of the room.* | *'Some of the recent attacks on horses in this area are enough to sicken anyone,' a police spokesman said.*

hospital

RELATED WORDS

- *see also* **doctor, ill/sick, illness/disease, cure, recover, medical treatment, mentally ill**

1 a hospital

- **hospital**
- **medical center**
- **clinic**
- **hospice**

hospital /ˈhɒspɪtl‖ˈhɑː-/ [n C/U] a large building where sick or injured people are looked after and receive medical treatment: *Lucy works as a nurse at the local hospital.* | **be in hospital** British/**be in the hospital** especially American (=being treated in a hospital) *I was in hospital for eight weeks after the accident.* | **be admitted to (the) hospital** (=be brought into a hospital for treatment) *A man has been admitted to hospital with gunshot wounds.* | **hospital bed** (=a place in a hospital for a sick person) *There is an urgent need to make more hospital beds available for long-term patients.*

medical center /ˈmedɪkəl ˌsentəʳ/ [n C] American a very large building that contains a hospital, doctors' offices, and other medical services: *Frank is being treated at Valley Medical Center with minor injuries.* | *The test is expensive and available only at certain medical centers.*

clinic /ˈklɪnɪk/ [n C] a building, often part of a hospital, where people come for special medical treatment or advice about particular medical problems: *The Harvey Clinic specializes in the treatment of alcohol-related problems.* | *Ellen decided to go to the family planning clinic for some advice.*

hospice /ˈhɒspəs‖ˈhɑː-/ [n C] a special hospital where people who are dying are looked after: *Mary, who was suffering from terminal cancer, spent her last few months in a hospice.*

2 a hospital for people who are mentally ill

- **mental hospital**
- **psychiatric hospital**
- **mental institution**

mental hospital /ˈmentl ˌhɒspɪtl‖-ˌhɑː-/ [n C] *Shirley spent most of her adult life in a mental hospital.* | *At the age of 19 Greg had a nervous breakdown and had to be admitted to a mental hospital.* | **commit sb to a mental hospital** *Knapman was committed to a mental hospital in August.*

psychiatric hospital /ˌsaɪkiˈætrɪk ˌhɒspɪtl‖-ˌhɑː-/ [n C] a hospital for mentally ill people. **Psychiatric hospital** is more technical than **mental hospital**: *Humphrey is in a state psychiatric hospital after being convicted of beating his grandmother.* | *The judge will decide whether Barry will be sent to prison or a psychiatric hospital.*

mental institution ALSO **institution** /ˈmentl ɪnstəˌtjuːʃən, ˌɪnstəˈtjuːʃən‖-ˈtuː-/ [n C] formal a hospital for mentally ill people – use this especially when you do not think this is a good place for someone to be treated: *Sally spent several years in an institution.* | *Psychiatrists argue that closing down mental institutions will lead to more homeless people on our streets.*

3 a part of a hospital

- **unit**
- **casualty (department)**
- **ward**
- **outpatient**

unit /ˈjuːnət/ [n C] a part of a hospital where a particular type of medical problem is treated: *Funding has been approved for a 40-bed unit for the elderly at Aberdare General Hospital.* | **coronary/psychiatric/intensive care etc unit** *A new psychiatric unit will be added to the John F. Kennedy Medical Center.*

casualty (department) British **/emergency room** American /ˈkæʒuəlti (dɪˌpɑːʳtmənt), ɪˈmɜːʳdʒənsi ˌruːm/ [n C] the part of a hospital you go to for emergency treatment, for example if you have had an accident or if you suddenly become very ill: *He arrived in casualty with multiple injuries to his head.* | *Thorpe was treated in the casualty department at Middlesborough General.* | *Emergency room doctors tried to save Ryan's life.*

ward /wɔːʳd/ [n C] a large room in a hospital or a part of a hospital where a group of patients with similar medical conditions have their beds: *Linda is a doctor in a ward for premature babies.* | **psychiatry/maternity/pediatric etc ward** *When her baby was due, Barbara was admitted to the maternity ward of Mercy Hospital.*

outpatient /ˈaʊtpeɪʃənt/ [adj] **outpatient clinic/department** a part of a hospital where people come in for treatment, although they do not stay at the hospital: *Two outpatient clinics in the area are offering drug treatment programs.*

hot

RELATED WORDS

opposite: **cold**

- food that has a hot taste *see* **taste (6)**
- *see also* **weather, sweat**

1 objects/surfaces/liquids

- **hot**
- **heat**
- **boiling/boiling hot**
- **scalding/scalding hot**
- **molten**

hot /hɒt‖hɑːt/ [adj] *The sand on the beach was hot under our feet.* | *Be careful! That pan's still very hot.* | *At the end of the day all I want to do is to relax in a nice hot bath.* | *The hottest part of the engine is the cylinder head.* | **burning hot** (=hot enough to burn you) *Don't touch the barbecue – it's burning hot.* | **red/white hot** (=extremely hot – use this about metal or things that are burning) *Cook the steaks over red hot coals.* | *The white-hot metal sculptures are moved to a cooling room.*

heat /hiːt/ [n U] the high temperature that something has: *The heat of the water caused the glass to shatter.* | *The reaction gives off tremendous heat.* | *Once the coals are ready, close the lid of the barbecue to keep in the heat.*

boiling/boiling hot /ˈbɔɪlɪŋ, ˌbɔɪlɪŋ ˈhɒt◂‖-ˈhɑːt◂/ [adj] a liquid that is **boiling** or **boiling hot** is extremely hot and has bubbles coming up to its surface: *Add the pasta to 4 quarts of boiling water.* | *The mud in the pools is boiling.* | *Boiling-hot steam shoots out from underground.* | **boiling point** (=the temperature at which a particular liquid starts to boil) *Bring the milk to the boiling point over a low heat.*

scalding/scalding hot /ˈskɔːldɪŋ, ˌskɔːldɪŋ ˈhɒt◂‖-ˈhɑːt◂/ [adj usually before noun] liquid that is **scalding** or **scalding hot** is so hot that it will burn you badly if you touch it: *The factory sends scalding water into the river nearby.* | *The bathwater was scalding hot.*

molten /ˈməʊltən/ [adj only before noun] **molten** metal, rock, plastic etc is so hot that it has turned into liquid: *Molten iron is poured into huge moulds and allowed to cool.* | *Rivers of molten rock were flowing down the sides of the volcano.*

2 food/drink

- hot
- piping hot
- steaming/steaming hot
- scalding/scalding hot

hot /hɒt‖hɑːt/ [adj] *The soup's very hot. Let it cool down a bit.* | *The waitress set down a pot of hot tea and a plate of cakes.* | *Dozens of volunteers serve hot meals to 200 homeless people every night.*

piping hot /ˌpaɪpɪŋ ˈhɒt◂‖-ˈhɑːt◂/ [adj phrase] food that is **piping hot** has just been cooked and is very hot, especially in a way that makes it seem good to eat: *Heat the fish under a grill and serve piping hot.* | *She handed him a piping hot bread roll and a steaming cup of coffee.*

steaming/steaming hot /ˈstiːmɪŋ, ˌstiːmɪŋ ˈhɒt◂‖-ˈhɑːt◂/ [adj/adj phrase] a drink or a food such as soup that is **steaming** or **steaming hot** is very hot, so that you can see the steam coming from it: *Cooper held a steaming mug of coffee.* | *The soup was served steaming hot in a large bowl.*

scalding/scalding hot /ˈskɔːldɪŋ, ˌskɔːldɪŋ ˈhɒt◂‖-ˈhɑːt◂/ [adj/adj phrase] a drink that is **scalding** or **scalding hot** is so hot that it hurts your mouth if you try to drink it: *I burned my mouth on the scalding hot coffee.* | *a cup of scalding tea*

3 room/place/weather

- hot
- the heat
- boiling/boiling hot
- broiling
- baking/baking hot
- sweltering
- stifling/stifling hot
- muggy/humid
- oppressive
- like an oven
- heatwave

hot /hɒt‖hɑːt/ [adj] *The weather's been very hot lately.* | *I make a lot of salads during hot weather.* | *a hot summer's day* | *The Gobi desert is one of the hottest places on earth.* | **it's hot** *It's hot in here. Isn't the air conditioner working?* | *It was much too hot in his office to do any work.* | *It's going to be a hot, sunny day.*

the heat /ðə ˈhiːt/ [n singular] high temperatures caused by hot weather, especially when this makes you feel uncomfortable in a room or outdoors: *Don't leave food sitting out in the heat.* | *the heat and dryness of an Arizona summer* | **the heat of the day** *Avoid running or other vigorous exercise during the heat of the day.*

boiling/boiling hot /ˈbɔɪlɪŋ, ˌbɔɪlɪŋ ˈhɒt◂‖-ˈhɑːt◂/ [adj] spoken very hot: *It was a boiling hot day in August.* | **it's boiling/boiling hot** *Leave the door open, it's boiling in here.*

broiling /ˈbrɔɪlɪŋ/ [adj usually before noun] American, especially spoken very hot and uncomfortable: *a broiling summer day* | **broiling heat** *the incredible broiling heat of a Mississippi summer* | **broiling sun** *Troops stood at attention under a broiling noon sun.*

baking/baking hot /ˈbeɪkɪŋ, ˌbeɪkɪŋ ˈhɒt◂‖-ˈhɑːt◂/ [adj] weather that is **baking** or **baking hot** is very hot and dry: *The weather was baking hot and conditions at the camp became unbearable.* | **it's baking/baking hot** *It's baking in here – I need a drink.*

sweltering /ˈsweltərɪŋ/ [adj] especially written weather that is **sweltering** is very hot and makes you feel wet and uncomfortable: *Everyone headed for the beach on that sweltering summer afternoon.* | **sweltering heat** *The soldiers marched on in the sweltering heat.*

stifling/stifling hot /ˈstaɪflɪŋ, ˌstaɪflɪŋ ˈhɒt◂‖-ˈhɑːt◂/ [adj] a room or enclosed space that is **stifling** or **stifling hot** is very hot and is difficult to breathe in: *The room was stifling hot, and full of flies.* | *The subway stations are stifling, and reek of urine.* | **stifling heat** *Helen sat uncomfortably in the stifling heat of the railway carriage.*

muggy/humid /ˈmʌgi, ˈhjuːmɪd/ [adj] weather that is **muggy** or **humid** makes you feel uncomfortable because the air feels wet, warm, and heavy: *In June the weather was often muggy in the evenings and it was difficult to get to sleep.* | *The climate stays hot and humid all summer long.* | **it's muggy/humid** *It's been really muggy the last few days, so we haven't done much.*

oppressive /əˈpresɪv/ [adj] weather or heat that is **oppressive** is very hot and unpleasant, especially because it feels as if there is not enough air to breathe: *As the sun climbed higher in the sky, the heat grew gradually more oppressive.* | **oppressive heat** *Despite the oppressive heat, more than 1,000 people came to the celebration.*

like an oven /ˌlaɪk ən ˈʌvən/ [adj phrase] a room or enclosed space that is **like an oven** is extremely hot and uncomfortable: *The heat of the day made the gymnasium feel like an oven.* | **it's like an oven** *It's like an oven in here. Let's open some windows.*

heatwave /ˈhiːtweɪv/ [n C] a period of unusually hot weather: *There was a heatwave during the first part of July.* | *A long summer heatwave had turned the river into a weak trickle of water.*

4 warm, but not hot

- warm
- lukewarm
- tepid

warm /wɔːʳm/ [adj] a little hot, but not very hot, especially in a way that is pleasant: *I didn't want to get out of my nice warm bed.* | *It's nice and warm in the kitchen.* | *a warm day* | *These plants only grow in warm climates.* —**warmth** [n U] when an object, the weather, a place etc is warm: *The warmth of the sun was making them all sleepy.*

lukewarm /ˌluːkˈwɔːʳm◂/ [adj] food or drinks that are **lukewarm** are slightly warm and not as warm or cold as they should be: *The bartender handed me a mug of lukewarm beer.* | *The coffee was only lukewarm.*

tepid /ˈtepɪ̈d/ [adj] liquid that is **tepid** is only slightly warm, especially in a way that seems unpleasant: *The soup was disgusting, greasy, tepid and watery.* | *He soaked a handkerchief in some tepid water and wiped her forehead.*

5 when you feel hot

- hot
- warm
- boiling/roasting
- sweltering
- have/run a temperature
- feverish

hot /hɒt‖hɑːt/ [adj not before noun] feeling **hot**, especially when this makes you feel uncomfortable: *I'm too hot – could you open the window?* | *The travellers were hot, tired, and thirsty.*

warm /wɔːʳm/ [adj not before noun] feeling **warm** when it is cold outside, especially in a way that is pleasant and comfortable: *Are you nice and warm?* | **keep warm** (=make yourself stay warm) *We had to keep moving in order to keep warm.* | **warm as toast** (=very warm and comfortable) *It was freezing outside but in the ski lodge they were as warm as toast.*

boiling/roasting /ˈbɔɪlɪŋ, ˈrəʊstɪŋ/ [adj not before noun] spoken to feel very hot and uncomfortable: *'I'm going for a swim,' said Gary, 'I'm boiling.'* | *You must be roasting in that coat.*

sweltering /ˈsweltərɪŋ/ [adj] if you are **sweltering**, you feel very hot, wet, and uncomfortable, because the weather or the room you are in is too hot: *Hundreds of children sweltering in the heat went to the neighborhood pool.*

have/run a temperature /ˌhæv, ˌrʌn ə ˈtemprətʃəʳ/ [v phrase not in progressive] if you **have a temperature** or **run a temperature**, your body is hotter than usual because you are ill: *Liz was running a temperature of 39.8° C.* | *Victims of heat stroke have a body temperature of 104 degrees Fahrenheit or higher.* —**high temperature** /ˌhaɪ ˈtemprətʃəʳ/ [n phrase] when your body is very hot because you are ill: *Symptoms of the disease include a headache and a high temperature.*

feverish /ˈfiːvərɪʃ/ [adj not usually before noun] feeling very hot and often red in the face because you have a fever: *Hannah looked weak and feverish and we decided to call the doctor.* | *He said he felt feverish and complained of pains in his chest.*

6 clothes that make you warm

- warm
- thermal

warm /wɔːʳm/ [adj] *These gloves are lovely and warm.* | *My mother's knitted me a nice warm sweater.* | *Make sure you bring plenty of warm clothing.*

thermal /ˈθɜːʳməl/ [adj usually before noun] **thermal** clothing is made from special material to keep you warm in cold weather: *Wear thermal underwear, hat, and gloves while skiing.* | *Runners were given thermal blankets to prevent heat loss at the end of the race.*

7 to get hot or hotter

- get hot/warm/hotter/warmer
- heat up
- warm up
- overheat

get hot/warm/hotter/warmer /ˌget ˈhɒt, ˈwɔːʳm, ˈhɒtəʳ, ˈwɔːʳməʳ‖-ˈhɑːt-/ [v phrase] *If the lawnmower gets hot, turn it off.* | *As the summer got hotter, the streams began to run more slowly.* | *The rocks get warmer in the sun and the lizards come out to lie on them.* | **it gets hot/warm** (=the weather gets hot) *It got hotter and hotter throughout the day.*

heat up /ˌhiːt ˈʌp/ [phr v I] to get hotter, especially gradually as a result of being heated by something else: *The stones heated up in the sun.* | *As the gas heats up, it expands.* | *While the oven is heating up, prepare the sauce.*

warm up /ˌwɔːʳm ˈʌp/ [phr v I] if something such as a place **warms up**, it gradually becomes warmer after being cold, especially so that it reaches a more comfortable temperature: *The room began to warm up.* | *It usually takes a long time for the sea to warm up.* | *It's pretty cold outside now, but it should warm up later.*

overheat /ˌəʊvəʳˈhiːt/ [v I] if an engine or a machine **overheats**, it becomes too hot and cannot work properly: *The engine started overheating and steam poured out of the front of the car.* | *The cooling system broke down, the nuclear reactor overheated, and the plant had to be evacuated.*

8 to make something hot or hotter

- heat
- heat/warm up
- heat sth through
- warm/warm up
- take the chill off

heat /hiːt/ [v T] to make something hot by using a machine or fire: *She heated the water in a small pan.* | *Wax melts quickly when it is heated.* | *It costs a lot to heat these offices.*

heat/warm up ALSO **warm sth over** American informal /ˌhiːt, ˌwɔːʳm ˈʌp, ˌwɔːʳm (sth) ˈəʊvəʳ/ [phr v T] to heat food so that it can be eaten, especially food that was cooked earlier and has become cold **heat/warm up sth** *I heated up yesterday's chicken pie and had it for lunch today.* | **heat/warm sth up** *Do you want some soup? It'll only take a few minutes to heat it up.* | *Waffles are good warmed over in a toaster.*

heat sth through /ˌhiːt (sth) ˈθruː/ [phr v T] to heat food thoroughly so that it is completely cooked: *Add the chopped onion to the mixture and heat it through.* | *Make sure you heat that stew through before you eat it.*

warm/warm up /wɔːʳm, ˌwɔːʳm ˈʌp/ [v T] if something such as the sun or a fire **warms** a place or **warms it up**, it makes it warm: *I put the heater on to warm the bedroom.* | *The sun'll warm up the water in the lake.*

take the chill off /ˌteɪk ðə ˈtʃɪl ɒf/ [v phrase] informal to heat something slightly so that it does not feel very cold any more: *Put the heater on for long enough to take the chill off the room.* | *Don't boil the milk, just heat it enough to take the chill off.*

9 to make someone warmer

- warm up
- warm yourself

warm up /ˌwɔːʳm ˈʌp/ [phr v I/T] *Hardin stood by the fire to warm up.* | **warm sb up** *Drink some of this coffee – it'll warm you up.* | *I tried to warm her up by covering her in a blanket.*

warm yourself /ˈwɔːʳm jɔːʳself/ [v phrase] to make yourself feel warmer, for example by standing near a fire or heater: *Jim came into the living room to warm himself by the fire.* | **warm your hands/feet etc** *I put my feet near the radiator to warm them.*

10 how hot something is

- how hot
- temperature
- heat

how hot /haʊ 'hɒt‖-'hɑːt/ *No matter how hot it is outside, it's always cool in here.* | *How hot are those coals? Can I start cooking over them now?* | *I couldn't believe how hot it was by eight o'clock in the morning.*

temperature /'tempərətʃər/ [n C] a measure of how hot or how cold something is: *Temperatures in the south of the country reached 30 degrees centigrade.* | *The temperature of the water was just right for swimming.* | **room temperature** (=the normal temperature in a room) *The wine can be served at room temperature.* | **high temperature** (=one which is very hot) *Steel is produced at very high temperatures.* | **low temperature** (=one that is cold) *Professional film is stored at a low temperature to prevent it from deteriorating.* | **+ of** *The gas freezes at a temperature of 180C.* | **at a constant temperature** (=one that stays the same) *The greenhouse is kept at a constant temperature of 40C.* | **take sb's temperature** (=measure their temperature) *You feel very hot – let me take your temperature.* | **the temperature rises/goes up** *The temperature of the world's oceans has risen by more than 2 degrees in the past hundred years.* | **the temperature falls/goes down** *The temperature is expected to go down below freezing during the night.*

heat /hiːt/ [n C usually singular] how hot something is – use this especially when you can control how hot something is, for example on an electric heater: *When the oven reaches the correct heat, the light goes off.* | *At this heat, all the poisonous chemicals are changed into safe compounds.* | **turn up/turn down the heat** (=change it so that it becomes hotter or less hot) *She turned down the heat on the electric fire.* | **turn the heat down/up** *Turn the heat up, I'm cold.*

house

RELATED WORDS

- leave your house *see* **leave (14-16)**
- *see also* **home, build/building**

1 different types of house

- house
- cottage
- bungalow
- townhouse
- mansion

house /haʊs/ [n C] a building for people to live in, that may have more than one level, and may either stand separately or be joined to other buildings: *Our house is the one with the red door.* | *I went over to Barbara's house after school.* | *The street was lined with identical red-brick houses.* | **detached house** British (=a house that is not joined to another house) *a detached house in Surrey* | **semi-detached house** British (=a house that is joined to another house on one side) *a three-bedroom semi-detached house* | **terraced house** British/**row house** American (=a house that is in a row of houses that are all joined together) *The street ran between rows of dingy terraced houses.*

cottage /'kɒtɪdʒ‖'kɑː-/ [n C] a small house, especially an old house in the country – use this especially about houses in the UK: *She lives in a charming cottage deep in the Kent countryside.* | *a row of thatched cottages in a rural village*

bungalow /'bʌŋgələʊ/ [n C] a small house in which all the rooms are on the same level: *He and his wife lived in a modern bungalow on the outskirts of the city.*

townhouse /'taʊnhaʊs/ [n C] American a house in a group of houses that share one or more walls: *Old buildings were knocked down, and new apartments and townhouses built.*

mansion /'mænʃən/ [n C] a very large and impressive house: *a magnificent mansion set in 2000 acres of countryside* | *an eleven-bedroom mansion in Hancock Park*

2 different types of apartment

- apartment
- flat
- condominium

apartment /ə'pɑːrtmənt/ [n C] especially American a set of rooms that are usually all on the same level and are part of a larger building: *They went back to her apartment for a cup of coffee.* | *There was no point in paying rent for an empty apartment.* | **apartment building** (=a building that has several apartments on each level) *Small apartment buildings filled with families line the street.* | **high-rise apartment building** (=a tall apartment building with many levels) *High-rise apartment buildings have gone up where once there was open land.*

flat /flæt/ [n C] British a set of rooms that are usually all on the same level and are part of a larger building: *Stella and Keith moved into a cold, damp flat together.* | *a group of students in a shared flat* | **block of flats** (=a building that consists of different levels and has several flats on each level) *Lisa lives on the nineteenth floor of a block of flats in London.*

condominium ALSO **condo** informal /ˌkɒndə'mɪniəm‖ˌkɑːn-, 'kɒndəʊ‖'kɑːn-/ [n C] American an apartment in a building that consists of several apartments, all of which are owned by the people who live in them: *He lives in a condo in San Jose.* | *They rent out their condominium to skiers during the winter.*

3 a place for someone to live

- housing
- accommodation
- home
- somewhere to live
- a roof over your head
- estate
- housing project/projects
- development

housing /'haʊzɪŋ/ [n U] the houses, flats etc within a particular area that are available for or are provided for people to live in: *Most of the housing in the area is sub-standard and nothing is being done to improve it.* | *The council is making a great effort to provide cheap housing and more public facilities.*

accommodation /əˌkɒmə'deɪʃən‖əˌkɑː-/ [n U] formal a place where people can live or stay, including houses, flats, hotels etc: *The holiday costs about £400 for a week's accommodation and flights.* | **student/rented/holiday etc accommodation** *I've been looking in the newspapers for student accommodation but it's all so expensive.*

home /həʊm/ [n C usually plural] a house, flat etc for people to live in – used especially in advertisements or to talk about large numbers of homes: *They want to build forty luxury homes on a disused railway site.* | *Between 1945 and 1970 the government built 110,000 new homes for low-paid workers.*

somewhere to live /ˌsʌmweər tə 'lɪv/ [n phrase] a place where you can live – use this especially when this is difficult to get: *I'll stay at my grandmother's at first, until I find somewhere to live.* | *Students looking for somewhere to live can go the university accommodation service.*

a roof over your head /ə ˌruːf əʊvə jɔːʳ ˈhed/ [n phrase] informal a place to live – use this especially when you are comparing this with the possibility of not having anywhere to live at all: *It doesn't matter what kind of place it is, at least you'll have a roof over your head.* | *It's hard to be cheerful when you haven't even got a roof over your head.*

estate ALSO **housing estate** /ɪˈsteɪt, ˈhaʊzɪŋ ɪˌsteɪt/ [n C] British an area where houses have all been built together in a planned way: *Jane has her own house on a neat housing estate in the south-east.* | **council estate** (=an estate built by the local government, especially to be rented) *They live in a block of flats on a bleak council estate.*

housing project/projects /ˈhaʊzɪŋ ˌprɒdʒekt, ˈprɒdʒekts‖-ˌprɑː-/ [n C/n plural] American informal a group of houses or apartments usually built with government money for poor people to rent: *Under this proposal, Federal money will no longer go to public housing projects but will go instead directly to the people.* | *Chicago's Cabrini Green housing project* | *She says she wants something better for her kids than what she had in the projects.*

development /dɪˈveləpmənt/ [n C] a group of new buildings that have all been planned and built together on the same piece of land: *New developments are springing up all around the town.*

hungry/ not hungry

RELATED WORDS

▸ *see also* **thirsty, eat, food, meal, thin, taste, horrible, delicious**

1 wanting to eat

- ▸ **hungry**
- ▸ **feel like something to eat/want something to eat**
- ▸ **starving/ravenous/famished**
- ▸ **peckish**
- ▸ **have/get the munchies**

hungry /ˈhʌŋgri/ [adj] *We were really hungry after our long walk.* | *Are you hungry? Do you want a sandwich?* | *Hungry shoppers waited in line at the food counters.*

feel like something to eat/want something to eat /ˌfiːl laɪk sʌmθɪŋ tʊ ˈiːt, ˌwɒnt sʌmθɪŋ tʊ ˈiːt‖ˌwɔːnt-/ [v phrase] spoken to want to eat something: *It's 12 o'clock – do you feel like something to eat?* | *Do you guys want something to eat?*

starving/ravenous/famished ALSO **starved** American /ˈstɑːʳvɪŋ, ˈrævənəs, ˈfæmɪʃt, stɑːʳvd/ [adj not before noun] spoken very hungry: *Can we talk about this after dinner, please? I'm famished.* | *I missed lunch and I'm starved.* | *Normally she did not eat a lot in the morning, but today she was ravenous.* | **absolutely starving/ravenous/famished** *I've been driving for eight hours non-stop and I am absolutely starving.*

peckish /ˈpekɪʃ/ [adj not before noun] British informal a little hungry: *I'm feeling a bit peckish. What's in the fridge?* | *The kids were getting peckish so Sammy found a cafe nearby.*

have/get the munchies /ˌhæv, ˌget ðə ˈmʌntʃiz/ [v phrase not in progressive] informal to begin to feel a little hungry, and want something to eat, especially something small rather than a large meal: *If you get the munchies later on there are some cookies in the kitchen.*

2 not hungry

- ▸ **not be hungry**
- ▸ **not feel like/not want anything**
- ▸ **lose your appetite**

not be hungry /nɒt biː ˈhʌŋgri/ [v phrase] *'How about something to eat?' 'No thanks, I'm not hungry.'* | *We offered her some sandwiches but she said she wasn't hungry.*

not feel like/not want anything /nɒt ˈfiːl laɪk, nɒt ˈwɒnt ˌeniθɪŋ‖-ˈwɔːnt-/ [v phrase] spoken informal say this to tell someone that you are not hungry: *I had a really big lunch, so I don't feel like anything just now.* | *'Do you want some toast?' 'No thanks, I don't want anything.'*

lose your appetite /ˌluːz jɔːr ˈæpətaɪt/ [v phrase] to no longer want to eat anything, especially because you are upset or ill or thinking about something else: *Jane's not feeling too well and has lost her appetite.* | *I shifted the food around my plate, suddenly losing my appetite as he told me the news.*

3 the feeling you have when you are hungry

- ▸ **hunger**
- ▸ **appetite**

hunger /ˈhʌŋgəʳ/ [n U] the feeling you have when you have eaten very little food: *The baby screamed with hunger.* | *Many slimming diets don't provide enough calories to satisfy hunger.* | **hunger pangs** (=the uncomfortable feelings in your stomach that tell you are very hungry) *If you do feel hunger pangs, nibble on carrot, celery, or cucumber sticks.*

appetite /ˈæpətaɪt/ [n C/U] the feeling of wanting to eat when you have not eaten for some time – use this especially when someone does not have their normal desire to eat, for example when they are ill: *How's his appetite? Is he getting enough to eat?* | **good/healthy/big appetite** (=desire to eat a lot) *She must be growing; she's got a big appetite right now.* | **spoil/ruin your appetite** (=make you not want to eat a meal) *Don't eat any cake now. You'll spoil your appetite.*

4 to become hungry

- ▸ **get hungry**
- ▸ **work up an appetite**
- ▸ **give sb an appetite**

get hungry /get ˈhʌŋgri/ [v phrase] to start to feel hungry, especially because you have not eaten for some time: *Is it lunchtime yet? I'm getting hungry.*

work up an appetite /ˌwɜːʳk ʌp ən ˈæpətaɪt/ [v phrase] to do something to make yourself want to eat, especially by hard physical exercise: *After a long day walking across the hills they had worked up quite an appetite.* | *There's nothing like skiing to work up an appetite.*

give sb an appetite /ˌgɪv (sb) ən ˈæpətaɪt/ [v phrase not in passive] if work, exercise, etc **gives you an appetite** it makes you feel hungry: *All that exercise has given me an appetite.* | *Spending all day in the fresh air had given them all an appetite.*

5 not having enough food

- starving
- starve
- hungry
- not get enough to eat
- half-starved
- underfed
- malnourished

starving /ˈstɑːʳvɪŋ/ [adj] someone who is **starving** has not had enough food for a long time and will die soon if they do not eat: *The people are starving and they need all the food and medical supplies we can give them.* | *They have barely enough money to keep them from starving.* | *a country full of starving people* | **the starving** (=people who are starving) *The homeless and the starving, refugees of the war, were flocking to the cities.*

starve /stɑːʳv/ [v I] to have so little food to eat that you become ill or die: *The prisoners were taken out into the desert and left to starve.* | *In 1884, the crew of Young's ship nearly starved when they were blown off course.* | **starve to death** (=starve and die) *Unless these people get food in the next two weeks they will starve to death.*

hungry /ˈhʌŋgri/ [adj] if people are **hungry**, they need food but do not have enough food to eat over a long period of time: *My children are hungry, I need a job.* | *Hungry people crowded around the relief wagon for food.* | **go hungry** (=not get food to eat) *If the crops fail again this year thousands of people will go hungry.*

not get enough to eat /nɒt get ɪˌnʌf tʊ ˈiːt/ [v phrase] to not be given enough food, so that you are becoming ill: *The refugees in the camps are not getting enough to eat, and the living conditions are terrible.* | *A baby who is not gaining weight is probably not getting enough to eat.*

half-starved /ˌhɑːf ˈstɑːʳvd◂‖ˌhæf-/ [adj] thin and looking ill because you do not have enough to eat: *Poor dog! He looks half-starved.* | *The soldiers were dirty and half-starved.*

underfed /ˌʌndəʳˈfed◂/ [adj] written people or animals who are **underfed** are not being given enough food to eat: *The servants were overworked and underfed.* | *fields full of underfed cattle*

malnourished /ˌmælˈnʌrɪʃt◂‖-ˈnɜː-, -ˈnʌ-/ [adj] formal unhealthy and thin because you have not had the right kinds of food over a long period of time: *During the 1930s a large proportion of Britain's urban population was malnourished.*

6 when people are ill or dying because of not having enough food

- hunger
- starvation
- malnutrition
- famine

hunger /ˈhʌŋgəʳ/ [n U] *Many people could die from cold and hunger this winter as the war continues.* | *The slum-dwellers suffer from poverty, hunger, and disease.* | **weak with/from hunger** *Weak with hunger, she staggered up to the cabin door.*

starvation /stɑːʳˈveɪʃən/ [n U] suffering or death caused by not having enough food to eat: *The survivors were close to starvation when they were rescued.* | *A global fall in the price of rice spread hardship and even starvation to many parts of Indochina.* | **die of starvation** *30 million people die of starvation each year.* | **brink of starvation** (=almost dying because of not having enough food) *Thousands of refugees are on the brink of starvation in camps south of the capital.*

malnutrition /ˌmælnjʊˈtrɪʃən‖-nʊ-/ [n U] bad health caused by not eating enough food or by not eating enough of the right kinds of food: *Many of the children showed signs of malnutrition.* | *A survey of US households found evidence of malnutrition in those persons with the lowest incomes.*

famine /ˈfæmɪn/ [n C/U] a situation in which a large number of people in a country or area are very hungry and many die because the crops of rice, wheat etc have failed: *Millions of people in Africa continue to die because of war and famine.* | *The four-year drought has caused widespread famine across Afghanistan.*

hurry

RELATED WORDS

- *see also* **fast, slow, run, time, immediately**

1 to go somewhere or do something very quickly

- hurry
- rush
- dash
- in a hurry/in a rush
- hurry through/rush through
- hurriedly
- in haste

hurry /ˈhʌri‖ˈhɜːri/ [v I/T] to go somewhere or do something more quickly than usual, for example because you are late or because you must finish something by a particular time: *Please hurry – this is an emergency.* | *We have plenty of time, there's no need to hurry.* | *Brewing beer is a long process and should not be hurried.* | **+ across/after/away etc** *The day was cold, and students hurried across campus to warm classrooms.* | *Elizabeth disappeared into the crowd and Donald had to hurry after her.* | **+ to do sth** *In the kitchen Paul was hurrying to get the dinner ready before six o'clock.*

rush /rʌʃ/ [v I/T] to do something or go somewhere very quickly, often so quickly that you do not do it carefully or properly: *Try to do your work calmly and carefully, without rushing.* | *The book was rushed into print, and there are a lot of mistakes in it.* | *If you rush your meals, you'll get indigestion.* | **+ out/around/into etc** *Everyone rushed out into the street to see what was happening.* | *We rushed around trying to get all the information we needed before the end of the week.* | **+ to do sth** *Zack rushed to tell her what had happened.* | *I rushed over to meet him.* | **rush things** *Don't try to rush things in a new relationship.*

dash /dæʃ/ [v I] to go somewhere very quickly, usually by running, especially because there is something important or urgent you must do **+ around/out/into/across etc** *Kids were dashing across the playground chasing a ball.* | *He just dashed into the office and then dashed out again without speaking to anyone.* | *She dashed off to the airport and just managed to catch her plane.* | **+ to do sth** *I dashed downstairs to answer the phone.*

in a hurry/in a rush /ɪn ə ˈhʌri‖-ˈhɜːri, ɪn ə ˈrʌʃ/ [adv] if you do something **in a hurry** or **in a rush**, you do it too quickly because you do not have much time, usually with the result that you make mistakes: *She had left in a hurry, and had forgotten her driver's license.* | **be in a hurry/rush to do sth** *We were in a hurry to get back to the office.* | *Why are they in such a rush to sell the house?*

hurry through/rush through /ˌhʌri ˈθruː‖ ˌhɜːri-, ˌrʌʃ ˈθruː/ [phr v T] to hurry in order to finish something in time, often so that you do not do something properly: *She hurried through her breakfast with her eye on the clock.* | *Don't rush through the chapters; take notes as you read.* | *People hurried through their morning chores, wanting to get to the fair.*

hurriedly /ˈhʌrɪdli‖ˈhɜːr-/ [adv] written if you do something **hurriedly**, you do it very quickly because you do not have much time: *He dressed hurriedly and went to answer the door.* | *The official hurriedly glanced through my papers and stamped my passport.* | *'Sorry,' Alice said, as she hurriedly put out her cigarette.*

in haste /ɪn ˈheɪst/ [adv] especially written if you do something **in haste**, you do it too quickly and without taking enough care – used especially in literature: *She had married in haste and regretted it ever since.* | **in your haste to do sth** (=because you want to do something very quickly) *In his haste to leave, he almost forgot his coat.*

2 what you say to tell someone to hurry

- hurry up
- come on
- get a move on
- step on it
- get cracking
- jump to it

hurry up /ˌhʌri ˈʌp‖ˌhɜːri-/ [phr v I not in progressive or past] spoken *Hurry up or you'll be late for school.* | *If you want tickets, you'd better hurry up. There's only a few left.* | **hurry up and do sth** *Hurry up and get your things, it's time to go.*

come on /ˌkʌm ˈɒn/ say this when you want someone to hurry, especially when you are annoyed with them for being too slow: *Come on, you two, we're going to be late.* | *Oh come on! We don't have all day!*

get a move on ALSO **get moving** especially American /ˌget ə ˈmuːv ɒn, ˌget ˈmuːvɪŋ/ [v phrase not in progressive or past] spoken to start to do something or go somewhere more quickly than before: *Come on Sally, get a move on!* | *I think we'd better get moving, it's only five minutes to boarding time.*

step on it /ˈstep ɒn ɪt/ [v phrase] spoken say this when you want someone who is driving to hurry: *Step on it. We have a plane to catch.* | *You'll have to step on it if you're going to be there by eleven thirty.*

get cracking /get ˈkrækɪŋ/ [v phrase] British spoken to start working quickly: *Get cracking you people! I want the whole house cleaned by four o'clock.* | **+ doing sth** *When Alf arrives we'll get cracking moving the furniture.* | **+ with** *It's time you got cracking with your homework.*

jump to it /ˈdʒʌmp tʊ ɪt/ [v phrase] British spoken say this when you are ordering someone to do something quickly: *I need to have that job done before lunch. Come on, jump to it!*

3 to make someone hurry

- hurry sb up
- rush/hurry
- chivvy sb along

hurry sb up /ˌhʌri (sb) ˈʌp‖ˌhɜːri-/ [phr v T] *They're taking a long time to finish. Can you hurry them up a little?* | *I think she's nearly finished packing. I'll go hurry her up.*

rush/hurry /rʌʃ, ˈhʌri‖ˈhɜːri/ [v T] to make someone hurry, especially when you are impatient, and so that they do not have time to do something carefully or properly: *I wish you wouldn't hurry me. I'm being as quick as I can.* | *Don't rush me! You'll only make me get it wrong.* | *I'm sorry to rush you, but we don't have much time left.*

chivvy sb along /ˌtʃɪvi (sb) əˈlɒŋ‖ -əˈlɔːŋ/ [phr v T] British informal to try to make someone do something more quickly, by repeatedly telling them to hurry: *He'll get the job done, but you need to chivvy him along a bit.*

4 done quickly because you are hurrying

- hurried
- quick
- rushed
- hasty
- frantic
- feverish
- a rush job

hurried /ˈhʌrid‖ˈhɜːrid/ [adj usually before noun] done very quickly because you are in a hurry: *After a hurried dinner, the boys do their homework or watch TV.* | *They made a hurried search for the missing letters, but they couldn't find them.* | *Her handwriting looked shaky and hurried.*

quick /kwɪk/ [adj only before noun] a **quick** look, meal, visit, decision etc is done very quickly, because you do not have much time: *Do I have time for a quick shower?* | *Could I just make a quick phone call?* | *The house is priced for a quick sale.*

rushed /rʌʃt/ [adj] something that is **rushed** is done very quickly, often too quickly to do it carefully or properly; someone who is **rushed** does things very quickly, often so that it is not done carefully or properly: *People have complained that the doctors seem rushed, with too many patients to see in a day.* | *The actors' performances were needlessly rushed.*

hasty /ˈheɪsti/ [adj usually before noun] done very quickly and without much care or attention, because you have very little time: *He only had time for a hasty glance at the papers.* | *'I have to go now,' said Alex, bidding them a hasty goodbye.* —**hastily** [adv] *I managed to leave a hastily scribbled note for John.*

frantic /ˈfræntɪk/ [adj usually before noun] in a **frantic** situation, people are rushing around in a confused way, especially because they are worried that they will not have time to do something or get something: *Before the game there was a frantic rush to get the last few remaining tickets.* | *The staff spent three frantic days trying to get everything ready.* | *Throughout the night, everyone mopped floors and washed walls in a frantic effort to clean the place up for the inspectors.* —**frantically** [adv] *Mel was frantically trying to finish all her work before the deadline.*

feverish /ˈfiːvərɪʃ/ [adj only before noun] **feverish activity/preparations/ haste etc** when people are hurrying to finish something, in an excited way, and when there is not much time to do it in: *The show was about to begin and behind the stage there were scenes of feverish activity.* | *Feverish preparations were being made for the arrival of the President.* —**feverishly** [adv] *Negotiators worked feverishly late into the night to hammer out an agreement.*

a rush job /ə ˌrʌʃ ˈdʒɒb‖-ˈdʒɑːb/ [n phrase] informal a piece of work that is done too quickly and therefore not as well as it should be done, especially because there is not enough time: *I don't want a rush job. I want this work done right.* | *Getting back into condition after a serious injury can't be a rush job.*

5 to be in a situation in which you must hurry

- be in a hurry
- be pushed/pressed for time
- work/race against the clock
- a race against time
- rush

be in a hurry /biː ɪn ə ˈhʌri‖-ˈhɜːri/ [v phrase] *I'm sorry, I'm in a hurry. I can't stop now.* | *Some people always seem to be in a hurry.* | **+ to do sth** *Would you like to stay for a coffee, or are you in a hurry to leave?*

be pushed/pressed for time /biː ˌpʊʃt, ˌprest fəʳ ˈtaɪm/ [v phrase] to be in a situation when you must hurry because you do not have enough time for what you have to do: *I don't want to seem rude but I'm very pressed for time. Could I call you back later?* | *I can't stop right now, I'm a little pushed for time.*

work/race against the clock /ˌwɜːʳk, ˌreɪs əgenst ðə ˈklɒk‖-ˈklɑːk/ [v phrase] to work as quickly as you can because you only have a short time to finish something: *In advertising you're always working against the clock, trying to meet deadlines.* | **+ to do sth** *We really had to work against the clock to finish the report on time.*

a race against time /ə ˌreɪs əgenst ˈtaɪm/ [n phrase] a situation in which you have to work extremely quickly, especially in order to do something very important, because there is not much time to do it in: *Battleship repair crews swung into action in a race against time* | *In an urgent race against time, the Coast Guard and marine biologists struggled to rescue a whale that had beached itself on the shore.*

rush /rʌʃ/ [n singular] a situation or time in which you hurry: *I had forgotten my wallet in the usual Monday morning rush.* | *There was a furious rush to have everything ready for the opening night.*

6 what you say to tell someone not to hurry

- there's no hurry/there's no rush
- take your time
- what's the hurry?/what's the rush?

there's no hurry/there's no rush /ðeəʳz ˌnəʊ ˈhʌri‖-ˈhɜːri, ðeəʳz ˌnəʊ ˈrʌʃ/ *There's no hurry. The train never leaves on time.* | *You can hand in your report any time next week. There's no rush.*

take your time /ˌteɪk jɔːʳ ˈtaɪm/ say this when you want someone to do something more slowly and without hurrying, especially so that they do it carefully and properly: *Take your time, think the matter over carefully, and then tell me what you've decided.* | *Just take your time, and speak slowly and clearly.*

what's the hurry?/what's the rush? /ˌwɒts ðə ˈhʌri‖-ˈhɜːri, ˌwɒts ðə ˈrʌʃ/ say this when someone is trying to do something quickly and you do not think they need to hurry: *What's the hurry? The plane doesn't leave for another two hours.* | *'I'd better go.' 'Why? What's the rush?'*

7 not hurrying

- be in no hurry/not be in any hurry
- unhurried
- leisurely

be in no hurry/not be in any hurry /biː ɪn ˌnəʊ ˈhʌri, nɒt biː ɪn eni ˈhʌri‖-ˈhɜːri/ [v phrase] to not be in a hurry, because you have plenty of time: *I'm in no hurry. I can wait.* | *He wasn't in any hurry, so he decided to take a look around town.* | **+ to do sth** (=be very slow to do something, perhaps too slow) *Danny seemed in no hurry to pay me the money he owed me.*

unhurried /ʌnˈhʌrid‖-ˈhɜː-/ [adj] done slowly and calmly, without hurrying: *He swam gracefully, with easy, unhurried strokes.* | *It's a community of old trees, big houses, and an unhurried life.* | *She walked along, calm and unhurried.*

leisurely /ˈleʒəʳli‖ˈliː-/ [adj usually before noun] a **leisurely** activity or way of doing something is pleasantly slow and relaxed, and done without hurrying: *She enjoyed a leisurely breakfast and had time to read the newspaper.* | *The horse walked at a leisurely pace through the flat Fenland countryside.*

hurt/injure

RELATED WORDS

- *see also* **harm, damage, accident, shoot, hit, pain, hospital, medical treatment**

1 hurt or injured in an accident, fight etc

- be injured/be hurt
- be wounded

be injured/be hurt /biː ˈɪndʒəʳd, biː ˈhɜːʳt/ [v phrase] if someone **is hurt** or **is injured**, part of their body is damaged, especially in an accident or fight: *'Did you hear about that fire in the school?' 'Yes, thank God no one was hurt.'* | *Four people have been injured in a road accident on the Arizona highway.* | **badly/seriously injured** *One man died, and another was seriously injured when a wall on a construction site collapsed.* | **badly/seriously hurt** *Fortunately, the driver of the van was not badly hurt.* | **slightly injured/hurt** *Six soldiers were slightly injured when a grenade exploded in a nearby truck.* | **get hurt** *There were so many people at the match – it was lucky that no one got hurt.* | **be fatally injured** (=be injured so badly that someone dies) *The motorbike rider, Gregory Watts, was fatally injured in the crash.*

be wounded /biː ˈwuːndɨd/ [v phrase] to be injured in a war, a fight etc, by a weapon such as a knife, gun, or bomb: *The man, in his early 30s, was wounded in the stomach after two gunmen opened fire.* | **be badly/seriously wounded** *During the first five months of the war, 10, 000 people died and over 12,000 were seriously wounded.* | **be fatally wounded** (=be wounded so badly that someone dies) *We heard that my brother had been fatally wounded in the battle, and died two days later.*

2 to hurt a part of your body

- hurt
- injure
- bruise
- sprain
- break
- twist/wrench
- pull
- damage
- dislocate
- be bleeding

hurt /hɜːʳt/ [v T] if you **hurt** a part of your body, you accidentally damage it so that it feels painful or you cannot move it easily: *Nick's hurt his back, and the doctor says he will have to rest for a few weeks.* | *I can't go running this week – I've hurt my foot.* | **hurt**

yourself *That's a sharp knife. Be careful you don't hurt yourself.*

injure /ˈɪndʒəʳ/ [v T] to hurt a part of your body, especially seriously and in a way that takes a long time to get better: *Tom injured his shoulder playing tennis.* | **injure yourself** *Many elderly people injure themselves in their own homes, for example by slipping in the bath.*

bruise /bruːz/ [v I/T] to hurt a part of your body when you fall or hit it against something, causing a dark, painful mark to form on your skin: *Mom fell on the ice and bruised the side of her leg.* | **badly bruise** *Keller badly bruised a hip, and came off early in the second half of the match.* | *My skin bruises quite easily.* —**bruised** [adj] *Some of his teeth were damaged and his jaw was badly bruised.*

sprain /spreɪn/ [v T] to hurt your knee, wrist, or another joint by twisting or pulling it suddenly and awkwardly: *I sprained my knee while I was playing basketball.* | *You'll need strong walking boots in the mountains, if you don't want to sprain an ankle.* —**sprained** [adj] *Stadler had to withdraw from the tournament, because of a sprained wrist.*

break /breɪk/ [v T] to **break** a bone in your body: *It was such bad luck – it was our first time skiing and Nicola broke her leg.* —**broken** /ˈbrəʊkən/ [adj] *Chris escaped from the accident with no more than a broken arm.*

twist/wrench /twɪst, rentʃ/ [v T] to hurt your knee or another joint, by turning it too suddenly or strongly while you are moving: *I couldn't play, having twisted my knee in the previous night's game.* | *The doctor said that I'd wrenched my shoulder and shouldn't drive for a while.* —**twisted** [adj] *Scott insisted on coming, despite his twisted ankle.*

pull /pʊl/ [v T] **pull a muscle** to injure a muscle by stretching it too much, especially during hard physical activity: *I pulled a muscle trying to move the piano into the apartment.* | *Crawford had been ordered to take a day's rest after pulling a leg muscle.* —**pulled** [adj] *Ted was having treatment for a pulled muscle.*

damage /ˈdæmɪdʒ/ [v T] written to injure a part of your body fairly seriously, especially in a way that means it will take a long time to get better or will never get better: *Lewis damaged his knee in training and will not appear in the game.* | *When carrying out the operation, doctors have to take great care not to damage the delicate nerve endings.* —**damaged** [adj] *His damaged left foot will keep him off the field for the rest of the season.*

dislocate /ˈdɪsləkeɪt/ [v T] to injure a joint by falling on it or stretching it so that the two parts of the joint are moved out of their normal position and stay out of position: *Sam dislocated his shoulder in a riding accident.* —**dislocated** [adj] *The fall left her with several bruises and a dislocated shoulder.*

be bleeding /biː ˈbliːdɪŋ/ [v phrase] if part of your body is **bleeding**, blood is coming out of it because you have been injured: *His head was bleeding, and he'd obviously been in a fight.* | **+ from** *John saw that he was bleeding from some sort of wound on his chest.* | **+ heavily/profusely** (=a lot of blood is coming out) *The cut on her leg had opened again and was bleeding heavily.*

3 to hurt or injure someone

- hurt
- injure
- wound
- inflict pain

hurt /hɜːʳt/ [v T] to cause physical harm to someone and make them feel pain: *Let go of my arm! You're hurting me!* | *Dan was a good man. He'd never hurt anyone deliberately.* | **hurt sb with sth** *Put the stick down, Terry. You might hurt someone with it.*

injure /ˈɪndʒəʳ/ [v T] to cause physical harm to someone, for example in an accident or fight: *The bomb killed eleven people and injured 55.* | **badly/seriously/critically injure** *Several shots were fired, critically injuring three women.*

wound /wuːnd/ [v T] to injure someone with a weapon such as a knife or gun, causing cuts, bleeding etc: *Two boys were on trial for wounding a sixteen-year-old girl with a revolver.* | **wound sb in the chest/knee etc** *The bullet wounded him in the shoulder.*

inflict pain /ɪnˌflɪkt ˈpeɪn/ [v phrase] formal to deliberately hurt a person or an animal: *Inflicting pain as a means of teaching children discipline is wrong.* | **+ on** *Most drugs can be produced quite successfully without inflicting pain on helpless animals.*

4 to permanently injure someone

- cripple
- maim

cripple /ˈkrɪpəl/ [v T] to injure someone's legs or back so that they can never move or walk properly again: *The driver, who had been taking drugs, crippled the young woman for life.* | *Richard was crippled in the bombing of 1984, and had been in a wheelchair ever since.* —**crippled** [adj not usually before noun] *He came home from Africa crippled, his career in the army over.*

maim /meɪm/ [v T] to injure someone very seriously and permanently, especially in an accident or deliberate attack: *Surely terrorists cannot believe that killing and maiming ordinary people is an achievement?* —**maimed** [adj not usually before noun] *Of those who survived, most were sick, physically maimed, or mentally impaired.*

5 damage to a part of the body

- injury
- wound
- bruise
- sprain
- damage

injury /ˈɪndʒəri/ [n C/U] *The glass roof collapsed onto the crowd, causing horrific injuries.* | *Our insurance provides cover in the case of illness or injury.* | **leg/back etc injury** *Unfortunately, she had to withdraw from the game because of a leg injury.* | **serious injury** *Wearing a helmet may protect you from serious injury.* | **suffer an injury** (=be injured) *He suffered serious injuries in the car crash, and died on the way to hospital.* | **escape injury** (=not be injured) *Ten passengers were lucky to escape injury when their train was derailed last night.* | **injury to your leg/chest etc** *Morrison had to undergo surgery on an injury to his left knee.*

wound /wuːnd/ [n C] an injury caused by a weapon such as a knife, gun, or bomb **deep wound** *The wound was deep and needed eighteen stitches.* | **bullet/stab/gunshot etc wound** *Barratt was taken to the hospital with stab wounds to his chest and neck.* | **wound to the leg/chest etc** *He died of a single gunshot wound to the left side of his head.*

bruise /bruːz/ [n C] a dark, painful mark on your skin where you have fallen or been hit: *Jenny looked as though she'd been crying, and there was a nasty bruise on her cheek.* | **be covered in cuts and bruises** *Jack often comes home from rugby covered in cuts and bruises.*

sprain /spreɪn/ [n C] an injury in which you hurt a joint by twisting or pulling it suddenly and awkwardly: *It's a slight sprain – you should rest it for a few days.* | **ankle/shoulder/knee etc sprain** *Robinson is suffering from an ankle sprain, and can't train this week.*

damage /ˈdæmɪdʒ/ [n U] written an injury that will take a long time to get better or that may never get better: *Never look straight at the sun. Any damage to the retina could cause permanent blindness.* | *Rubella is a serious infection, which can cause severe physical damage to the unborn child.*

6 someone who is injured

- injured
- wounded
- paralysed
- casualty

injured /ˈɪndʒəʳd/ [adj] hurt in an accident, fight etc: *Firefighters had to cut off the roof of the car, so that the injured man could be lifted out.* | **the injured** (=people who are injured) *The injured were rushed to St Thomas's Hospital.*

wounded /ˈwuːndɪ̈d/ [adj] injured, especially in a war, by a weapon such as a knife, gun, or bomb: *a wounded soldier* | *There are over 4000 refugees in the camp, many of them wounded.* | **the wounded** (=people who are wounded) *Helicopters have been sent in to rescue the wounded from the war zone.*

paralysed ALSO **paralyzed** American /ˈpærəlaɪzd/ [adj] unable to move part or all of your body because of a serious injury or illness: *Mrs Burrows had been paralysed by a stroke, and could not move or speak.* | **leave sb paralysed** *The fall had left him permanently paralysed.* | **be paralysed from the neck/chest/waist down** *Paralysed from the neck down, Bundini could only move his eyes.*

casualty /ˈkæʒuəlti/ [n C usually plural] someone who has been injured or killed in a war, attack, or accident: *The bomb caused serious damage to the building, but there were no casualties.* | **suffer casualties** *Indian troops have suffered more than 1200 casualties.*

7 not hurt or injured

- unhurt
- unharmed
- without a scratch
- in one piece
- walk away from
- unscathed
- come to no harm/not come to any harm

unhurt /ʌnˈhɜːʳt/ [adj not before noun] to not be hurt, even though you have been in a dangerous situation such as an accident: *The driver of the car was unhurt, but his passenger was killed.* | **escape unhurt** *Six day trippers escaped unhurt when their hot air balloon hit power lines.* | **otherwise unhurt** (=apart from a condition that is not serious or physical) *The younger woman was suffering from shock but was otherwise unhurt.* | **shaken/shocked but unhurt** (=shocked, but not physically hurt) *The two youths, shaken but unhurt, declined to talk about the incident.*

unharmed /ʌnˈhɑːʳmd/ [adj not before noun] to not be hurt or harmed, even though you have been in a dangerous situation: *The hostages were released unharmed some time afterwards.* | **escape unharmed** *All fourteen people who were working inside the building when the blaze started escaped unharmed.*

without a scratch /wɪðˌaʊt ə ˈskrætʃ/ [adv] informal if you have a dangerous experience and escape from it **without a scratch**, you do not have any injury at all, because you have been very lucky **walk away/escape without a scratch** *All four people in the car were seriously hurt, but the truck driver walked away without a scratch.*

in one piece /ɪn ˌwʌn ˈpiːs/ [adj phrase not before noun] informal not seriously hurt in a war, accident etc: *Unlike Ed, Josh returned from the war in one piece.* | **all in one piece** *I was extremely relieved when my son came back from the warzone all in one piece.*

walk away from /ˌwɔːk əˈweɪ frɒm / [v phrase] to not get injured in a very dangerous situation you have been involved in, because you have been very lucky – used especially in news reports: *I can hardly believe they were able to just walk away from the crash – I thought they'd all been killed.*

unscathed /ʌnˈskeɪðd/ [adj not before noun] written not injured at all, even though you have had a dangerous experience: *The bullet grazed the side of his head, leaving him virtually unscathed.* | **escape/emerge/come out of sth unscathed** *Most of the passengers escaped from the plane unscathed.*

come to no harm/not come to any harm /ˌkʌm tə ˌnəʊ ˈhɑːʳm, nɒt ˌkʌm tʊ ˌeni ˈhɑːʳm/ [v phrase] use this to say that someone will not be hurt if they do something, or was not hurt by doing something, going somewhere etc: *If you keep quiet, you'll come to no harm.* | *I'm sure Craig's old enough to catch a train into town without coming to any harm.* | *Fortunately, none of the hostages came to any serious harm.*

Ii

idea

RELATED WORDS

- *see also* **think, opinion, invent, imagine, intelligent, suggest, logical**

1 something that you think of

- idea
- thought

idea /aɪˈdɪə/ [n C] something that you think of, such as a plan or suggestion **have an idea** *'I have an idea,' she said. 'Why don't you come with us?'* | *We're trying to think of a name for the book. Does anyone have any ideas?* | **+ for** *Here are some new ideas for quick meals that taste great.* | *an idea for a new TV game show* | **it was sb's idea** (=they thought of it) *I never wanted to go to Spain. It was Sue's idea.* | **+ to do sth** *Who's idea was it to ask him to the party?* | **the idea of (doing) sth** *The idea of an underground garage in the park has provoked a lot of anger.* | **+ that** *Nobody seemed very keen on the idea that we should all dress up for the party.*

thought /θɔːt/ [n C] an idea – use this especially when you have not yet considered it carefully: *That's an interesting thought. Let's discuss it at the meeting.* | **have a thought** *I've just had a thought – it might be quicker to go by bus.* | **thoughts on sth** *If you have any thoughts on the matter, let me know.* | **sb's thoughts about sth** *I'd like you to begin by writing down your thoughts about the play.* | **it was**

(just/only) a thought spoken (=say this when someone seems to disagree with your idea) *'That's not a very good time of year to travel.' 'Perhaps not. It was just a thought.'*

2 a good idea

- good/great/fantastic etc idea
- bright idea
- brainwave
- inspiration
- stroke of genius

good/great/fantastic etc idea /ˌgʊd aɪˈdɪə/ [n C] especially spoken *'We could go and see a movie.' 'Good idea!'* | *I think a skiing holiday is a brilliant idea.* | *That's a great idea! Let's call Madge and see if she can come too.*

bright idea /ˌbraɪt aɪˈdɪə/ [n C] a very good idea that you think of suddenly. This is sometimes also used when you think that someone's idea is not good: *Why not ask Sylvia? She's always full of bright ideas.* | **whose bright idea was it ...** (=used when you think something is a bad idea) *Whose bright idea was it to start major road repairs right at the start of the holiday season?*

brainwave British **/brainstorm** American /ˈbreɪnweɪv, ˈbreɪnstɔːʳm/ [n C] informal a sudden, very good idea: *Unless someone comes up with a brainwave soon, I can't see how we can possibly get out of this mess.* | **have a brainwave** *Then Mo had a brainstorm. She would start her own coffee bar for teenagers.*

inspiration /ˌɪnspəˈreɪʃən/ [n C/U] a sudden good idea about what to do or say, that seems to come to you from nowhere: *Of course! If he thinks it was his idea in the first place, he's bound to agree. What an inspiration!* | **+ for** *Where exactly did you get the inspiration for the movie?* | **inspiration comes to sb** *Inspiration came to him as he started to write for the second time.* | **flash of inspiration** (=a sudden good idea) *In that instant, he had a flash of inspiration: he and Tom would try and rescue Frankie themselves.*

stroke of genius /ˌstrəʊk əv ˈdʒiːniəs/ [n phrase] informal a very good and original idea about what to do or how to deal with a problem: *They named the new car 'Thunderbird.' It was a stroke of genius.* | *At first, the manager's appointment of talented but inexperienced players seemed like a stroke of genius.*

3 an idea or set of ideas that explains something

- theory
- hypothesis
- premise
- idea
- notion
- concept

theory /ˈθɪəri/ [n C/U] an idea or set of ideas that is intended to explain something, especially in science: *This theory helps to explain how animals communicate with each other.* | **+ that** *It's my theory that the murderer knew his victim quite well.* | *There's a theory that Kennedy was killed by the CIA.* | **+ about** *There have been a lot of theories about the meaning of dreams.* | **sb's theory of sth** *Darwin's Theory of Evolution* | *Einstein's theory of relativity* | **economic/political etc theory** *Atkin taught political theory at Hunter College.*

hypothesis /haɪˈpɒθəsəs‖-ˈpɑː-/ PLURAL **hypotheses** /-siːz/ [n C] formal an idea that is based on very few facts and that you cannot be sure is right: *Various hypotheses are possible regarding the nature and structure of the world.* | *The results of our experiment confirmed this hypothesis.*

premise /ˈpreməs/ [n C] a statement or idea that you accept as being true and use as a base for developing other ideas: *American justice works on the premise that an accused person is innocent until they are proved guilty.* | *I believe his whole argument is based on a false premise.*

idea /aɪˈdɪə/ [n C] a way of explaining something about life, society, etc: *Ideas and customs used to be passed on intact down the generations.* | *Do you agree generally with Marx's ideas?* | **+ about** *medieval ideas about the origins of the universe* | **+ that** *How old is the idea that there is life after death?* | **+ of** *Ideas of how society should function have changed dramatically in the last 200 years.*

notion /ˈnəʊʃən/ [n C] a way of explaining something about life, society, etc, that people often think is a little stupid or old-fashioned: *Many widely-held notions about crime have come from the cinema, magazines, or novels.* | **+ of** *Modern society does not always correspond to classical notions of democracy.* | **a vague/absurd/fanciful etc notion** *Humans still hold on to the absurd notion that we are the only intelligent beings in the Universe.*

concept /ˈkɒnsept‖ˈkɑːn-/ [n C] someone's idea of how something is done, or how it should be done: *She thinks that marriage is an old-fashioned concept.* | **+ of** *What's your concept of an ideal society?*

4 to think of an idea

- have an idea
- get an idea
- think of
- come to
- hit on/upon
- be inspired by

have an idea /ˌhæv ən aɪˈdɪə/ [v phrase] *I've had an idea. What do you think about going to Greece this summer?* | *That's the best idea you've had all day.* | **+ for** *Do you have any ideas for a birthday present for Mum?* | **have the idea of doing sth** *He had the idea of hiding Ali's shoes.*

get an idea /ˌget ən aɪˈdɪə/ [v phrase] to think of an idea – use this especially to say what made you think of it or to ask someone what made them think of it: *Where on earth did you get that idea?* | **get the idea for sth** *Mark got the idea for the novel when he was in Boston in 1969.* | **+ from** *It wasn't my own idea. I got it from a TV movie.* | **get the idea of doing sth** *She first got the idea of working with elderly people after the death of her mother.* | **+ that** *I don't know how she got the idea that she was too fat.*

think of /ˈθɪŋk ɒv / [phr v T not in progressive] to have an idea about what to do, how to do something etc: *At first, we couldn't think of a name for the band.* | *Seth decided to go home. He couldn't think of anything else to do.* | *Ask Dad. He might be able to think of a solution.*

come to /ˈkʌm tuː/ [phr v T] if an idea **comes to** someone, they have the idea suddenly and without trying hard to think of it: *The idea for the new advertising campaign came to me while I was visiting Thailand.* | **it came to sb that** *It suddenly came to me that I'd seen her somewhere before.* | **come to sb in a flash** (=very suddenly) *It came to Blake in a flash that the man was really a detective.*

hit on/upon /ˈhɪt ɒn, əpɒn / [phr v T not in progressive] informal to have a good idea after thinking about or working on a problem for a long time: *At last we hit on a way of getting Tom and Marcia to meet.* | *The architects finally hit upon a design that seemed to please everyone.*

be inspired by /biː ɪnˈspaɪəʳd baɪ/ [v phrase] if someone's plan, work of art, action etc **is inspired**

by something, that is what gave them the idea to do it: *The novel was inspired by her own experiences in India.* | *Some of Picasso's work was inspired by African art.* | *The 1911 strike was inspired by the revolutionary ideas flooding out of Europe at that time.*

5 good at thinking of new ideas

- creative
- imaginative/inventive
- full of ideas

creative /kri'eɪtɪv/ [adj] good at using your imagination to think of new ideas or to produce new things: *Tarantino is one of Hollywood's most creative directors.* | *We need someone creative and enthusiastic to take this project forward.* | **creative abilities/faculties** *Children should be allowed to develop their creative as well as their academic abilities.* —**creatively** [adv] *The aim of the course is to teach students to write creatively.* —**creativity** /ˌkriːeɪ'tɪvəti/ [n U] *Her latest work displays tremendous skill and creativity.*

imaginative/inventive /ɪ'mædʒənətɪv, ɪn'ventɪv/ [adj] use this about someone who is very good at thinking of new and unusual ways of doing things: *He was one of the most original and imaginative writers of his time.* | *Marr had a brilliant inventive mind.* | *the most inventive sculptor since Picasso*

full of ideas /ˌfʊl əv aɪ'dɪəz/ [adj phrase] informal to have a lot of new ideas and to want to tell people all about them: *Ron was full of ideas and seemed very enthusiastic about the show.* | *I don't know what's the matter. She's usually so bright and full of clever ideas.*

6 containing interesting or new ideas

- imaginative/inventive

imaginative/inventive /ɪ'mædʒənətɪv, ɪn'ventɪv/ [adj] containing new ideas that are used in interesting and original ways: *The film uses computer graphics in an unusual and highly imaginative way.* | *an imaginative solution to the city's crime problem* | *These figures are some of the most inventive of all African tribal sculptures.* | *Inside the magazine you will find plenty of inventive ideas for redecorating your home.*

if

RELATED WORDS

▸ *see also* **depend/it depends, maybe**

1 ways of saying 'if'

- if
- should
- had
- even if
- in case
- in the event of
- in case of

if /ɪf/ [conjunction] *If you do that again I'll hit you.* | *Do you think I'd be here if I had a choice?* | *I know I look tired. So would you if you had this house, a husband, and three children to look after.* | **if you like/want** *I have a drill. If you like, you can borrow it.* | **if so** formal (=if this is true) *I believe you sell video cameras. If so, please would you send me a price list?* | **if necessary/possible** (=if it is necessary or possible) *We're prepared to work all through the night if necessary.* | *Use live natural yoghurt, full-fat if possible.* | **if taken/used/needed etc** *If taken in small doses, the drug has no harmful effects.*

should /ʃʊd/ [modal verb] formal use this when something might happen in the future but it is not likely: *We've planned everything very carefully, but should there be any problems, contact me immediately.* | *Should you ever find yourself in Oxford, I'm sure Uncle Eric would be glad to see you.*

had /hæd/ [modal verb] formal use this when you are saying what the result would have been if things **had** happened differently in the past: *Had I known earlier that you wanted to join the team, I'd have put your name on the list.* | *My horse would have won had he not fallen at the final fence.*

even if /'iːvən ɪf/ [conjunction] use this when something will still happen if a situation changes or if there is a problem: *He's going to buy the farm even if they raise the price.* | *Even if the government survives this crisis, they still face enormous problems.* | *You should always exercise – even if it's only 10 minutes a day.*

in case /ɪn 'keɪs/ [conjunction] use this to say that something is done because something else might happen or be true: *I'll take an umbrella in case it rains.* | *In case you missed the first episode, here is the story so far.* | *In case you were thinking I'd lend you any money, I'll tell you now – I won't!* | **just in case** *I'm sure they haven't forgotten but let's send them a reminder just in case.*

in the event of /ɪn ði ɪ'vent ɒv/ [prep] formal use this when you are saying what will be done if at any time there is a serious problem, an accident etc – used especially in official notices, plans, or instructions: *Britain agreed to support the US in the event of war.* | *The plan outlines emergency procedures in the event of a major accident.* | **in the unlikely event of** (=if something unlikely happens) *In the unlikely event of a burglar entering the building, the alarm system will be activated.*

in case of /ɪn 'keɪs ɒv/ [prep] written used especially in official notices and instructions to tell people what to do if something unpleasant or unexpected happens: *In case of fire, leave the building by the nearest exit.* | *It is illegal to park on the hard shoulder except in case of emergency.*

2 asking what the result will be if something happens

- what if ... ?
- supposing/suppose/say

what if ... ? /'wɒt ɪf/ [conjunction] use this to ask someone what they will do if something in particular happens: *What if your plan doesn't work?* | *I sat there till lunchtime thinking, 'What if he doesn't come back?'*

supposing/suppose/say /sə'pəʊzɪŋ, sə'pəʊz, seɪ/ [conjunction] spoken use this when you are asking or imagining what the result will be if a particular thing happens: *Supposing things change and the industry becomes more important. We might make a big profit.* | *You don't expect me to join the army, do you? Suppose I get killed?* | *'I'm not a violent person.' 'No, but say someone attacked you. You wouldn't just stand there, would you?'*

3 when something will happen if something else happens first

- if
- only if
- on condition (that)
- as long as/provided (that)/providing (that)
- assuming (that)

if /ɪf/ [conjunction] *I'll give you twenty pounds if you fix my computer for me.* | *If she does well in her exams, she will be going to college in October.*

only if /ˈəʊnli ɪf/ [conjunction] use this to emphasize that something will only happen if something else happens first, but will definitely not happen if the first thing does not: *OK, I'll tell you, but only if you promise not to tell anyone else.* | *Seat belts are effective only if they are correctly adjusted.*

on condition (that) /ɒn kənˈdɪʃən (ðət)/ [conjunction] use this when you agree to do something only if someone first promises or agrees to do something else: *I'll lend you the money on condition you pay it back within three weeks.* | *Many surgeons offer patients an operation only on condition that they stop smoking.*

as long as/provided (that)/providing (that) /əz: ˈlɒŋ əz‖-ˈlɔ:ŋ, prəˈvaɪdɪ̣d (ðət), prəˈvaɪdɪŋ (ðət)/ [conjunction] use this when something will be possible or satisfactory only if something else happens or is done: *You'll be quite safe as long as you follow my instructions.* | *You can come and see the baby so long as you don't make any noise.* | *Provided we have your order by the end of March, the price will be £500.* | *Of course we'll look after your kids, providing you can drop them off at our house, that is.*

assuming (that) /əˈsju:mɪŋ (ðət)‖əˈsu:-/ [conjunction] use this when something will happen or something is possible only if what you think might be true really is true: *Assuming that this painting really is a Van Gogh, how much do you think it's worth?* | *All we have to do is to explain the problem to her, assuming of course that she's prepared to listen.*

4 if something does not happen

- if not
- unless
- otherwise
- or/or else
- without
- barring
- before
- failing that

if not /ɪf ˈnɒt/ [conjunction/adv] *Your car should be ready by 12 o'clock, but if not I'll let you know.* | *If you don't leave now, I'll call the police.* | *Try these gloves on. If they're not the right size I'll take them back.* | **if not, why not?** spoken (=used to ask why something has not happened or why someone has not done something) *Have you done your homework yet? If not, why not?*

unless /ʌnˈles, ən-/ [conjunction] use this to say that something will happen if something else does not change the situation: *Unless the weather improves, we will have to cancel the game.* | *You won't pass your examinations unless you study hard.* | *Milk quickly turns sour, unless it's refrigerated.*

otherwise /ˈʌðəʳwaɪz/ [adv] use this when there will be a bad result if someone does not do something or if something does not happen: *Stir the sauce until it cools, otherwise it will be lumpy.* | *I'm glad you told me about the show being cancelled. Otherwise I'd have travelled all the way to Glasgow for nothing.*

or/or else /ɔ:ʳ, ɔ:r ˈels/ [conjunction] use this when you are warning someone what will happen if they do not do what you are telling them to do: *Be careful or you'll bump your head.* | *Stop making so much noise or else the neighbours will start complaining.*

without /wɪðˈaʊt‖wɪðˈaʊt, wɪθˈaʊt/ [prep] use this when you cannot do something if you do not do something else first: *No one can succeed in business without taking certain risks.* | *How can you judge a book without reading it?*

barring /ˈbɑ:rɪŋ/ [prep] use this when something will happen or continue in the way that you want, if something does not happen to prevent it: *Barring unexpected delays, work on the tunnel should be completed by the end of next month.*

before /bɪˈfɔ:ʳ/ [conjunction] use this when you are saying what someone must do if they want to stop something bad from happening: *Put that money somewhere safe before it gets stolen.* | *That dog ought to be destroyed before it attacks any more children.*

failing that /ˌfeɪlɪŋ ˈðæt/ [adv] use this when you are saying what you will do if the first thing you suggested is not possible: *My mother wanted me to be a teacher or, failing that, a nurse.* | *Dr Schwabe said he could find me a room either on the campus, or failing that, in a house nearby.*

5 why something must be true

- unless
- otherwise
- or else

unless /ʌnˈles, ən-/ [conjunction] use this to say that you think something is true, because the only other possibility is very unlikely: *He must have resigned, unless they fired him.* | *Unless he's a complete idiot, he'll understand.*

otherwise /ˈʌðəʳwaɪz/ [adv] use this to say that something must be true, because if it is not true the situation would be different: *She must have missed the train, otherwise she'd be here by now.* | *It can't have been anything important, otherwise she'd have called back.*

or else /ɔ:r ˈels/ [adv] use this to say that something must be true, because if it is not, the situation would be different or something very unlikely would be true: *They must have thought everything was safe, or else they would have warned us.*

6 when the situation would be different if something had not happened

- but for sb/sth
- if it had not been for
- if it wasn't/weren't for

but for sb/sth /ˈbʌt fəʳ (sb/sth)/ [prep] use this when a situation would be different if something was not happening now or had not happened in the past: *I would have walked out of the job earlier but for the fact that I desperately needed the money.* | *But for the actions of a brave fireman, I wouldn't be alive now.* | *Whole industries would have collapsed but for a massive injection of public funds.*

if it had not been for /ɪf ɪt ˈhæd nɒt bi:n fɔ:ʳ/ [prep] use this when a situation would have been different if something had not happened or someone had not done something in the past: *If it hadn't been for the war, Larry would have stayed on the farm.* | *If it hadn't been for Christine, I would never have met Michael.*

if it wasn't/weren't for /ɪf ɪt ˈwɒzənt, ˈwɜ:ʳnt

fɔːʳ‖-ˈwɑːzənt-/ [prep] use this when you would do something different if a particular situation did not exist now: *He'd be playing in this afternoon's game if it wasn't for his injury.* | *If it weren't for the children, I'm sure she would leave her husband.*

ignore

RELATED WORDS

▸ *see also* **disobey, attention**

1 to not pay attention to what someone says or does

- ignore
- pay no attention/not pay any attention
- take no notice/not take any notice
- not listen to
- fall on deaf ears
- not want to know
- tune out

ignore /ɪgˈnɔːʳ/ [v T] to deliberately pay no attention to what someone does or says, and pretend it is not important or does not affect you: *She ignored my question and continued her story.* | *Someone made a rude noise, which the teacher decided to ignore.* | *My father's always telling me what to do, but I usually just ignore him.* | **ignore sb's advice/warning** *It was very stupid of you to ignore your mother's advice.* | *Ignoring my warnings, he dived straight into the shallow water.*

pay no attention/not pay any attention /ˌpeɪ nəʊ əˈtenʃən, nɒt peɪ ˌeni əˈtenʃən/ [v phrase] to ignore someone or something, especially by not watching or listening to them: *'What's this injection for?' he asked the nurse. She paid no attention, rolling up his sleeve in silence.* | *People living near the crash scene paid no attention when they heard the aircraft's engine cut out in mid-air.* | **+ to** *More than half the people questioned said they did not pay any attention to political broadcasts.*

take no notice/not take any notice /ˌteɪk nəʊ ˈnəʊtəs, nɒt teɪk ˌeni ˈnəʊtəs/ [v phrase] not to let someone affect what you do or the way you feel: *Stan has fired me before. I usually take no notice and turn up for work again the next day.* | **+ of** *Take no notice of him. He's just being silly.* | *He never took any notice of the baby, even when it screamed.*

not listen to /nɒt ˈlɪsən tuː/ [v phrase] to ignore someone's advice when they talk to you: *You never listen to me. You just do whatever you want.* | *It's because you didn't listen to Roger that you are in this trouble now.* | **not listen to reason** (=not listen to sensible advice) *We all warned Susan not to marry that man, but she wouldn't listen to reason.*

fall on deaf ears /ˌfɔːl ɒn ˌdef ˈɪəʳz/ [v phrase] if your request or suggestion **falls on deaf ears**, it is ignored by the people who have the power to deal with it: *The workers' demand for a wage increase has fallen on deaf ears.* | *As rioting continued, Mayor Warren appealed for calm, but his words fell on deaf ears.*

not want to know /nɒt ˌwɒnt tə ˈnəʊ‖-ˌwɑːnt-/ [v phrase not in progressive] informal to not be willing to listen to people's problems, complaints, bad news etc because you do not want to be worried by them: *You'd think the government would be concerned about people sleeping rough, but they just don't want to know.* | **+ about** *If you're going to start an argument with Alex, I don't want to know about it.*

tune out /ˌtjuːn ˈaʊt‖ˌtuːn-/ [phr v T] especially American to deliberately not listen to what someone is saying, especially because it is unpleasant or you have heard it before **tune out sth** *He had learned to tune out the kids' constant questions.* | **tune sth out** *There was a warning voice in the back of her mind, but she tuned it out.*

2 to rudely pretend not to notice someone

- ignore
- pretend not to notice/see
- look right through
- snub
- cut sb dead
- blank
- send sb to Coventry

ignore /ɪgˈnɔːʳ/ [v T] *Don't ignore me when I'm talking to you!* | *Now that she had lost all her wealth, she was ignored by former friends.* | **totally/completely ignore sb** *The waiter totally ignored Glen and served a girl who had come up beside him.*

pretend not to notice/see /prɪˌtend nɒt tə ˈnəʊtəs, ˈsiː/ [v phrase] *Henry waved but Martha pretended not to notice.* | *If people think you're a beggar, they pretend not to see you.*

look right through /ˌlʊk raɪt ˈθruː/ [v phrase] to pretend not to notice someone that you know, even though you are looking directly at them: *I saw Carrie yesterday, but when I smiled at her she just looked right through me.* | *In the lift at work, the doctors looked right through you as if you didn't exist.*

snub /snʌb/ [v T] to ignore someone deliberately, in order to show that you are angry with them or that you have no respect for them: *I couldn't believe Simon had snubbed me at the party.* | *The senator was furious. 'How would you feel if you'd been snubbed by the wife of your president?'* | **snub sb's invitation/request etc** *They snubbed his invitation to a meeting of foreign ministers at the UN in New York.* —**snub** [n C] *Her absence was not intended as a snub.*

cut sb dead /ˌkʌt (sb) ˈded/ [v phrase] to completely ignore someone when you see them, especially because you are angry with them: *I saw Josie today – she must still be angry with me because she cut me dead.* | *Where he used to cut them dead, he now helps them on with their coats.*

blank /blæŋk/ [v T] informal if someone **blanks** you, they pretend not to notice you even though your eyes are facing theirs: *I said hello to her in the street, but she just blanked me and carried on walking.*

send sb to Coventry /ˌsend (sb) tə ˈkɒvəntri‖-ˈkʌv-, -ˈkɑːv-/ [v phrase] British if a group of people **send someone to Coventry**, they all agree they will not talk to that person as a punishment: *Unfairly sent to Coventry for two weeks, Hannah decided to run away from school.*

3 to ignore something bad, even though you know it is wrong

- overlook
- let it pass
- turn a blind eye
- shut/close your eyes to
- bury your head in the sand

overlook /ˌəʊvəʳˈlʊk/ [v T] to ignore something wrong that someone has done, especially because it is unimportant: *I'll overlook your mistake this time.* | *Mrs Johnson tends to overlook any small faults the girls may have.* | *Although this is a first offence it cannot be overlooked.*

let it pass /ˌlet ɪt ˈpɑːs‖-ˈpæs/ [v phrase] to decide not to punish or criticize someone for doing something wrong, although you might do so if they do it again: *I think they've broken the rules, but I'll let it pass.* | *Howard had insulted her, but she thought it better to let it pass this time.*

turn a blind eye /ˌtɜːʳn ə ˌblaɪnd ˈaɪ/ [v phrase] if someone in authority **turns a blind eye** to illegal activity or bad behaviour, they ignore it and pretend they do not know about it: *If my sister did something wrong my mother always turned a blind eye.* | *The guards turned a blind eye when the prisoners stole food from the kitchen.* | **+ to** *The President could no longer turn a blind eye to the indiscretions of his Chief of Staff.*

shut/close your eyes to /ˌʃʌt, ˌkləʊz jɔːr ˈaɪz tuː/ [v phrase] to ignore something and pretend it does not exist because it is unpleasant or difficult to deal with: *The officials in charge of the Chernobyl power station had shut their eyes to the danger.* | *Of course, it is tempting to criticize other countries and close your eyes to all the problems of your own society.*

bury your head in the sand /ˌberi jɔːʳ ˈhed ɪn ðə ˌsænd/ [v phrase] to ignore an unpleasant situation and hope it will stop if you try not to think about it: *You'll never solve your problems if you just bury your head in the sand – you have to face them.*

illegal

RELATED WORDS

opposite: **legal**

- to take part in something illegal *see* **take part/be involved (7)**
- *see also* **crime, law, steal, court/trial, forbid, rule, regulation**

1 illegal

- illegal
- be against the law
- be a crime
- unlawful
- criminal
- illicit
- be against the rules

illegal /ɪˈliːgəl/ [adj] forbidden by law: *Scott was arrested for being in possession of illegal drugs.* | *In those days, abortion was illegal.* | *Large numbers of illegal immigrants crossed the border at night.* | **it is illegal (for sb) to do sth** *It is illegal to sell tobacco to children under 16.* | *Since 1990, it has been illegal for the US to develop or possess biological weapons.* | **make sth illegal** *Gorbachev wanted to make all strikes illegal, but the Soviet parliament refused to accept such a ban.* —**illegally** [adv] *It is possible, of course, for computer users to illegally download games for free.*

be against the law /biː əˌgenst ðə ˈlɔː/ [v phrase] to be illegal: *Driving a car without insurance is against the law.* | **it is against the law (for sb) to do sth** *In Britain, it's against the law to own a gun without having a licence.* | *Nowadays it is against the law for a teacher to hit a child in any circumstances.*

be a crime /biː ə ˈkraɪm/ [v phrase] if something **is a crime** it is illegal and you can be punished for it: *Violence in the home is a crime, just as much as violence from a stranger.* | **it is a crime (for sb) to do sth** *It should not be a crime for people to criticize their own government.*

unlawful /ʌnˈlɔːfəl/ [adj usually before noun] illegal – use this especially about something that could be legal if the situation in which it was done was different: *The court ruled that the raid had been unlawful.* | *unlawful employment practices* | **unlawful arrest/killing/imprisonment etc** (=the illegal arrest, killing etc of someone) *Anyone who has been the victim of unlawful arrest is entitled to compensation.* —**unlawfully** [adv] *The teacher claimed that his contract was terminated unlawfully.*

criminal /ˈkrɪmɪ̍nəl/ [adj only before noun] **criminal activities/behaviour/offence etc** activities, behaviour etc that can be severely punished by law: *Cruelty to animals is a criminal offence.* | *It was estimated that Walker had made around £100,000 from his criminal activities.*

illicit /ɪˈlɪsɪ̍t/ [adj usually before noun] **illicit** activities or goods are illegal and usually kept secret: *Illicit diamond exports are said to be worth over $200 million.* | *Marijuana remains the most commonly used illicit drug in the United States.*

be against the rules /biː əˌgenst ðə ˈruːlz/ [v phrase] if a type of behaviour or an activity **is against the rules**, it is not allowed by the rules of an organization, game etc: *Smoking in the school building is strictly against the rules.* | **it's against the rules to do sth** *It's against the rules to touch the ball with your hand.*

2 an illegal action

- offence
- infringement
- violation
- breach
- contravention

see also **crime**

offence British **/offense** American /əˈfens/ [n C] an illegal action for which you can be punished: *Travelling on the train without a ticket is an offence.* | **it is an offence (for sb) to do sth** *It is an offence for a shopkeeper to sell alcohol to anyone under 18.* | **commit an offence** (=do something illegal) *Davies claimed that he did not know he was committing an offence by accessing the website.* | **criminal offence** *Driving when drunk is a criminal offence.* | **serious offence** *The number of women convicted of serious offences is still relatively small.* | **minor offence** (=not serious) *Motorists can be fined on the spot for minor offences, such as speeding.*

infringement /ɪnˈfrɪndʒmənt/ [n C] an illegal action, especially one that breaks a law that protects someone's rights **+ of** *The new rule was regarded as an infringement of the free-speech rights of government employees.* | *an infringement of Article 86 of the Treaty of Rome*

violation /ˌvaɪəˈleɪʃən/ [n C] an action that breaks a law or agreement, especially one that has been agreed by several different countries – use this about a serious illegal action **+ of** *Any further fighting will be seen as a violation of the ceasefire agreement.* | **flagrant/blatant violation of sth** (=one that is done without any attempt to hide it) *The United Nations described the invasion as 'a flagrant violation of international law'.* | **gross violation of sth** (=a very serious violation) *The way they treat women there represents a gross violation of human rights.* | **in violation of sth** *The UK government was found to be in violation of the European Convention.*

breach /briːtʃ/ [n C usually singular] something that a company or government does that breaks a particular law, especially when they do not do it intentionally **+ of** *This is a clear breach of the 1994 Trade Agreement.* | **breach of contract** *Workers who have lost their jobs plan to sue the company for breach of* *contract.* | **be in breach of sth** *In future, six-monthly accounts will be required from those firms that are in breach of the rules.*

contravention /ˌkɒntrəˈvenʃən‖ˌkɑːn-/ [n C usually singular] formal something a business, organization, or government does that breaks a particular law or part of an official agreement **in contravention of sth** *Many shops and bars stayed open, in contravention of the Sunday trading laws.* | **+ of** *It was a clear contravention of EU regulations.*

3 to do something that is illegal

- break the law
- commit
- contravene
- break the rules
- infringe

break the law /ˌbreɪk ðə ˈlɔː/ [v phrase] *If you break the law, you must expect to be punished.* | *You're breaking the law if you drive without wearing a seat belt.* | *In many cases, people who have been released from prison will break the law again.*

commit /kəˈmɪt/ [v T] **commit a crime/an offence/burglary/murder etc** to do something that is a crime, or that is a particular type of crime: *Detectives believe that the crime was committed at around 7.30 pm.* | *Most violent crimes are committed by young men under the age of 25.* | *She later claimed that she did not realize she was committing an offense.*

contravene /ˌkɒntrəˈviːn‖ˌkɑːn-/ [v T] if something a company or government does **contravenes** a particular law, it breaks that law, especially unintentionally – used especially in legal or official contexts: *Penalties for contravening the laws on food hygiene have been increased.* | *Any interference in one country's domestic affairs by another country contravenes the UN charter.*

break the rules /ˌbreɪk ðə ˈruːlz/ [v phrase] to do something that is not allowed by the rules of an organization, game etc: *Any student caught breaking the school rules was immediately sent to the Principal.* | **+ on** *Athletes can be fined thousands of dollars for breaking the rules on steroid use.*

infringe /ɪnˈfrɪndʒ/ [v T] to break a law, especially one that protects someone's rights: *If a teacher makes copies of software for students, he or she is infringing copyright.* | *Arrangements for widow's pensions infringed laws on equal pay and treatment.*

illness/disease

RELATED WORDS

- *see also* **ill/sick, doctor, cure, recover, weak, pain, drug, mentally ill, pain, hospital, healthy/unhealthy, medical treatment, sick/vomit, suffer**

1 an illness

- illness
- disease
- virus
- bug
- infection
- condition
- ailment
- disorder
- complaint

illness /ˈɪlnɪs/ [n C/U] a health problem that you are suffering from which makes you feel ill: *She died yesterday after a long illness.* | **suffer from an illness** *People are often too embarrassed to admit that they have suffered from any form of mental illness.* | **recover from an illness** *80% of patients now recover completely from this illness and are able to lead perfectly normal lives.* | **contract an illness** formal (=get or begin to have an illness, especially a serious one) *Doctors believe he may have contracted the illness while he was in Africa.* | **minor illness** (=one that is not serious) *Minor illnesses such as colds are usually best left to get better by themselves.* | **terminal illness** (=one that cannot be cured and causes death) *Should doctors always tell patients that they have terminal illnesses such as cancer?* | **serious illness** (=one that makes you very ill) *You are allowed time off work only in cases of serious illness or bereavement.*

disease /dɪˈziːz/ [n C/U] a particular illness that has a medical name: *The most common symptoms of the disease are a high temperature and spots all over the body.* | *Thousands of people in this area are dying from hunger and disease.* | **catch a disease** (=get a disease from another person) *Anyone can catch the disease – not just homosexual men or drug addicts.* | **suffer from a disease** (=have a disease) *She suffers from a rare disease of the nervous system.* | **infectious disease** (=easily passed from one person to another by breathing) *Travellers to India are advised to get vaccinated against infectious diseases such as typhoid before they go.* | **contagious disease** (=easily passed from one person to another by touch) *Childhood diseases such as measles and chickenpox are highly contagious.* | **fatal disease** (=one which causes death) *Malaria is still a common disease in West Africa and is often fatal.* | **heart/lung/kidney etc disease** *Smoking is a major cause of heart disease.*

virus /ˈvaɪərəs/ [n C] a small living thing that causes infectious illnesses, or a type of infectious illness: *the virus that causes the common cold* | *He could be carrying the AIDS virus.* | *It is estimated that over thirty million people are now infected with the virus.* | *a vaccine which protects against Hepatitis B, a highly infectious virus which is transmitted sexually or by sharing infected needles.* | *She thinks she picked up some kind of mystery virus while she was on vacation.*

bug /bʌg/ [n C] informal an illness that people catch very easily from each other but that is not very serious **pick up a bug** (=get a bug) *I think I've picked up the bug that's been going round the office.* | **stomach/tummy bug** (=illness affecting the stomach) *Gemima's been off school with a tummy bug this week.* | **catch a bug** *Young schoolkids are always catching various bugs.*

infection /ɪnˈfekʃən/ [n C] an illness that is caused by bacteria and that affects one part of your body, such as your ears, throat, lungs, or skin: *If you don't clean the wound properly you could get an infection.* | **throat/ear/lung etc infection** *Roz was suffering from a throat infection and could hardly talk.*

condition /kənˈdɪʃən/ [n C] a problem that affects someone's health permanently or over a long period of time: *People with your condition should not smoke.* | **suffer from a condition** *Diane suffers from a rare heart condition which means she has to take drugs all the time.*

ailment /ˈeɪlmənt/ [n C usually plural] formal an illness of condition, especially one that affects a particular part of your body: *The medicine was supposed to cure all kinds of ailments, ranging from colds to back pains.* | *The most commonly reported ailment among VDU operators is eye-strain.* | **minor ailment** *Patients who often complain of minor ailments might have something more important on their minds.*

disorder /dɪs'ɔːʳdəʳ/ [n C] an illness that prevents part of your body from working properly or affects the way you behave, especially one that is permanent or continues for a long time **eating/personality disorder** *Children with eating disorders such as anorexia need close supervision.* | **stomach/liver/skin etc disorder** *Minor stomach disorders are common when travelling abroad.* | *Eventually after weeks of tests they discovered I had a rare liver disorder.* | **disorder of the liver/stomach/brain etc** *The hospital specializes in treating disorders of the brain.*

complaint /kəm'pleɪnt/ [n C] an illness that affects a particular part of your body, especially one that is not very serious – used especially by doctors or in medical books: *The cream is normally used for treating minor skin complaints.* | *Hay fever is a common complaint in spring and summer.*

2 to have an illness

- have
- suffer from
- there's something wrong with
- with
- complain of
- be infected with

have ALSO **have got** British /hæv, həv 'gɒt‖-'gɑːt/ [v T] to **have** an illness: *Beth has an awful cold.* | *I had all the usual childhood illnesses.* | *Have you ever had pneumonia?* | *I think Jo's got flu.*

suffer from /'sʌfəʳ frɒm/ [phr v T] to have a particular type of illness or health problem, especially one that is serious or one that you have often: *Dewey had been in hospital for several weeks suffering from malaria.* | *She suffers from asthma attacks.*

there's something wrong with /ðeəʳz ˌsʌmθɪŋ 'rɒŋ wɪð‖-'rɔːŋ-/ informal use this to say that you have a medical problem affecting part of your body, but you are not sure exactly what it is: *There's something wrong with my chest – it feels really tight.* | *We thought there might be something wrong with her hearing.*

with /wɪð, wɪθ/ [prep] use this before the name of a disease, to say that someone has this disease: *'Where's Helen?' 'She's in bed with flu.'* | *The charity provides support for people with AIDS.*

complain of /kəm'pleɪn ɒv/ [phr v T] to tell a doctor that you have a particular kind of pain or other sign of being ill – used especially to say what the person who is ill said: *He was admitted to hospital complaining of severe stomach pains.* | *Many patients complain of headaches and difficulty sleeping when they take this drug.*

be infected with /biː ɪn'fektɪ̈d wɪð/ [v phrase] to have an illness, especially a serious illness, that you caught from another person: *Figures released last week put the number of people infected with HIV at over 30,000.* | *Did you know when you first met him that he was infected with the disease?*

3 to start to have an illness

- get
- catch
- come down with
- pick up
- develop
- contract

get /get/ [v T] to start to have an illness: *I feel all hot – I think I'm getting flu.* | *Smoking increases the risk of getting cancer.* | **get sth from/off someone** (=get an infectious disease from someone else) *He thinks he got the cold from someone in the office.*

catch /kætʃ/ [v T] to get a disease from someone else: *Luke has measles. I hope I don't catch it.* | **catch sth from/off sb** *I think I must have caught the flu from Sarah.*

come down with ALSO **go down with sth** British /ˌkʌm 'daʊn wɪð, ˌgəʊ 'daʊn wɪð (sth)/ [phr v T] spoken to start to have an illness, especially one that is not serious: *I'm afraid we can't come this weekend – the baby's gone down with a sore throat.*

pick up /ˌpɪk 'ʌp/ [phr v T] to get a not very serious illness such as a cold, a stomach problem etc – use this especially to say where you got it **pick up sth** *I picked up a stomach bug on holiday in Turkey.* | **pick sth up** *Brendan has a cold. He must have picked it up at school.*

develop /dɪ'veləp/ [v T not in passive] to gradually become ill with a particular illness, but not by catching it from someone else: *After her family brought her home from hospital, she developed pneumonia.* | *It is possible to develop diabetes in adulthood.* —**development** [n U] *a vaccine to prevent the development of influenza*

contract /kən'trækt/ [v T] to get a serious illness – used especially in formal or medical contexts: *Orwell contracted tuberculosis during the war and eventually died from the disease.* | *Dr Chalmers is trying to find out how many people may have contracted the disease in her area.*

4 a short illness

- attack
- a bout of
- a touch of

attack /ə'tæk/ [n C] when you suddenly begin to have an illness that you often have, especially when this only continues for a short time: *One of my students suddenly had an attack of asthma and I didn't know what to do.* | *Malaria often doesn't go away completely, and a patient may suffer from repeated attacks over several years.*

a bout of /ə 'baʊt ɒv/ [n phrase] a short period of suffering from an illness, especially one that is not serious: *In recent months he had had several bouts of flu.* | *The patient may experience bouts of nausea as a result of the treatment.*

a touch of /ə 'tʌtʃ ɒv/ [n phrase] informal a short period of suffering from an illness that is not serious: *It's nothing serious – just a touch of indigestion.* | *I feel like I'm getting a touch of flu.*

5 when a lot of people have an illness

- outbreak
- epidemic

outbreak /'aʊtbreɪk/ [n C] when a lot of people suddenly start to get an illness at the same time **+ of** *Doctors are very concerned about an outbreak of tuberculosis in an East London School.*

epidemic /ˌepɪ̈'demɪk/ [n C] when a lot of people in an area or country get a disease, and it spreads very quickly: *AIDS has become an epidemic in some countries.* | *Doctors warn that a flu epidemic may be on the way.*

ill/sick

RELATED WORDS

▸ *see also* **illness/disease, sick/vomit, doctor, cure, recover, pain, weak, mentally ill, hospital, drug, medical treatment, suffer, healthy/unhealthy, spread (3)**

1 ill

- ill
- sick
- be not (very) well
- unwell
- poorly
- be in a bad way
- look like death warmed up

ill /ɪl/ [adj not before noun] especially British suffering from bad health or not feeling well: *Mel was so ill that she had to stay in bed for a month.* | **seriously ill** (=very ill) *Apparently Don's wife is seriously ill, and they think it might be cancer.* | **critically ill** (=extremely ill) *The baby caught a virus and became critically ill.* | **terminally ill** (=so ill that you are going to die) *psychological support for terminally ill patients* | **mentally ill** (=suffering from a mental illness) *Mentally ill patients have the same rights as anyone else.* | **lie ill** (=be ill in bed) *All that week, Catherine lay ill, drifting in and out of consciousness.* —**illness** [n U] when someone is ill: *Tuesday's game had to be cancelled because of illness.*

sick /sɪk/ [adj] especially American ill: *Where's Mary today? I hope she's not sick again.* | *Sheila spent months looking after her sick mother.* | **be off sick** (=not at work or school because of illness) *Gary phoned to say that he's off sick today.* | **be off work sick/be in bed sick** *I'm sorry I didn't reply to your e-mail. I was in bed sick for a couple of days.* | **sick with the flu/a virus etc** (=ill as a result of flu etc) *Grant Hill played despite being sick with the flu for the past ten days.* | **be sick with worry/fear/exhaustion etc** (=so worried etc that you feel sick) *We were dirty, hungry, cold and sick with exhaustion.* —**sickness** [n U] *On average, companies lose twelve days per employee per year as a result of sickness.*

be not (very) well /biː ˌnɒt (veri) ˈwel/ [adj phrase] especially spoken to be ill, but not seriously ill: *Sarah's not very well – she's got a throat infection.* | *Jed's Mum says he's not well, so he's staying at home today.*

unwell /ʌnˈwel/ [adj] formal ill: *Mrs Hedges is unwell today, so her class will be taken by Mr Collier.* | *Tom had been unwell for some time but had refused to see a doctor.*

poorly /ˈpʊəʳli/ [adj not before noun] British informal ill: *Dad was always out, Mum was often poorly, and I had to look after the rest of the kids.* | *'I'm afraid your grandmother's very poorly,' the nurse on duty said.*

be in a bad way /biː ɪn ə ˌbæd ˈweɪ/ [adj phrase] informal to be very ill, especially as a result of a serious injury or disease: *You'd better get an ambulance – she's in a pretty bad way.* | *Martin came back from Africa with malaria, and he was in a pretty bad way for months.*

look like death warmed up British **/death warmed over** American /lʊk laɪk ˌdeθ wɔːʳmd ˈʌp, ˌdeθ wɔːʳmd ˈəʊvəʳ/ [v phrase] spoken to look ill and pale, especially because you did not get enough sleep or are suffering for the effects of too much alcohol: *Kate didn't sleep a wink last night. She looks like death warmed up.* | *Boy, you look like death warmed over this morning!*

2 slightly ill

- under the weather
- off colour
- run down

under the weather /ˌʌndəʳ ðə ˈweðəʳ/ [adj phrase] informal slightly ill: *I hear you've been a bit under the weather. Are you feeling better now?* | *Mike's feeling a little under the weather so he couldn't come tonight.*

off colour /ˌɒf ˈkʌləʳ/ [adj phrase] British slightly ill: *I'm fine, thank you, but Elinor's a bit off colour at the moment.* | *Bruce went to the doctor, feeling a little off colour, and was told that he had anaemia.*

run down /ˌrʌn ˈdaʊn/ [adj phrase] feeling slightly ill and tired all the time, for example because you have been working too hard, not eating well etc: *You're run down – you need a vacation.* | *A lot of people feel run down in the winter months, when the days are short and there's very little sunlight.*

3 when someone is often ill

- sickly
- delicate
- in poor health
- infirm
- prone to sth

sickly /ˈsɪkli/ [adj] a **sickly** child is often ill: *He was a sickly child with a bad chest and a permanent cough.* | *Louise, who was often sickly, couldn't join in the other children's games.*

delicate /ˈdelɪkɪ̆t/ [adj] formal unhealthy and weak and likely to become ill easily: *Clare was more active than her brother, who had always been a delicate child.* | *Mr Humphreys' wife was delicate – the doctor was called in once or twice a week.*

in poor health /ɪn ˌpʊəʳ ˈhelθ/ [adj phrase] fairly ill all the time or over a long period of time, and generally not strong and healthy: *When he left Trinidad he was already over 60, frail, and in poor health.*

infirm /ɪnˈfɜːʳm/ [adj not before noun] formal not healthy or strong, especially because of old age: *She lives with her grandmother who is elderly and infirm.* | **the infirm** (=people who are infirm) *The 'Meals on Wheels' service delivers food to the old and infirm.*

prone to sth /ˈprəʊn tə (sth)/ [adj phrase] likely to become ill or to get a particular illness: *As a child she had always been prone to allergies.* | *The disease had left her weak and prone to all kinds of infections.*

4 someone who imagines they are ill

- hypochondriac

hypochondriac /ˌhaɪpəˈkɒndriæk‖-ˈkɑːn-/ [n C] someone who often thinks that they are ill when they are not and worries too much about their health: *Don't be such a hypochondriac – it's only a cold!* | *She's a bit of a hypochondriac – always looking up her minor illnesses in a medical book.*

5 to feel ill

- feel ill
- not feel (very) well
- feel funny
- feel rough
- feel sick
- groggy
- feel faint

feel ill British **/feel sick** American /ˌfiːl ˈɪl, ˌfiːl ˈsɪk/ [v phrase] *'Do you feel ill, darling?' asked Rosie anxiously.* | *I was feeling ill, so I went home.* | *Mark said he felt sick, so I've made an appointment with the doctor.*

not feel (very) well ALSO **not feel too good** ALSO **not feel good** American informal /ˌnɒt fiːl (veri) ˈwel, ˌnɒt fiːl tuː ˈgʊd, ˌnɒt fiːl ˈgʊd/ [v phrase] to feel slightly ill: *If you don't feel well, the best thing to do is to stay in bed.* | *'I don't feel very well,' said Jamie, suddenly going very pale.* | *Ben's not feeling good this morning. I think it's something he ate.* | *No, I don't think I'll be coming out tonight. I'm not feeling too good.*

feel funny /ˌfiːl ˈfʌni/ [v phrase] spoken informal to feel slightly ill – use this especially when you do not know what is wrong with you: *I felt a bit funny and dizzy, and then the next thing I knew I was lying on the floor.*

feel rough /ˌfiːl ˈrʌf/ [v phrase] British spoken to feel ill: *Don't get up if you're feeling rough – I'll bring you some breakfast in bed.* | *Liz said she was feeling pretty rough yesterday – I don't think she'll come to work today.*

feel sick British **/feel sick to your stomach** American /ˌfiːl ˈsɪk, fiːl ˌsɪk tə jɔːʳ ˈstʌmək/ [v phrase] to feel as if you are going to vomit (=bring food up from your stomach): *We'd only been in the car two minutes when David said he felt sick.* | *When I was pregnant, the smell of coffee made me feel sick to my stomach.*

groggy /ˈgrɒgi‖ˈgrɑːgi/ [adj not usually before noun] informal feeling weak and tired as a result of illness or drugs: *You shouldn't drive after taking these pills. They're likely to make you feel groggy.* | **+ from** *I went to see Sally in hospital, but she was still groggy from the anaesthetic.*

feel faint /ˌfiːl ˈfeɪnt/ [v phrase] to feel very weak and as if you are going to become unconscious: *It was a very hot day, and I suddenly felt faint and sick.* | *If at any time you feel faint or nauseous, stop taking the tablets.*

6 to become ill

- get/become ill
- fall ill
- be taken ill

get/become ill British **/get/become sick** American /ˌget, bɪˌkʌm ˈɪl, ˌget, bɪˌkʌm ˈsɪk/ [v phrase] *It's horrible when you get ill on holiday.* | *If you take vitamin C every day, it helps to stop you getting sick.* | *My father first became ill when I was 12, and died a few months later.* | *People were scared of becoming sick because they couldn't pay the doctor's bills.*

fall ill ALSO **fall sick** American /ˌfɔːl ˈɪl, ˌfɔːl ˈsɪk/ [v phrase] to become ill, especially with a long or serious illness: *If you live alone, you often wonder who would look after you if you fell ill.* | *New Year's Eve revellers fell sick after drinking an orange liquid at a downtown 'rave' party.* | **+ with** *It was the first time the president had been back to his office since falling ill with pneumonia in January.*

be taken ill /biː ˌteɪkən ˈɪl/ [v phrase] especially British, written to suddenly or unexpectedly become ill: *I heard that her sister had been taken ill and rushed to hospital.* | **+ with** *The band cut short their tour after singer Robert Smith was taken ill with severe stomach pains.*

7 someone who is ill

- patient
- sufferer
- invalid
- the sick

patient /ˈpeɪʃənt/ [n C] someone who is ill and is being looked after by a doctor, nurse etc: *St Dominic's Hospital treats about 10,000 patients a year.* | **cancer/leukemia/AIDS etc patients** *He gave a half million pound donation towards the care of AIDs patients.* | **patients with cancer/aids/leukemia etc** *Clinical trials show that some patients with breast cancer do better if they take the drug for five years after surgery.*

sufferer /ˈsʌfərəʳ/ [n C] someone who has a particular illness or who often has a particular illness: *Lupus is a disease of the immune system and nine out of ten sufferers are women.* | **hay fever/asthma/cancer etc sufferer** *The health centre runs a support group for Parkinson's disease sufferers.* | *Summer can be a nightmare for hay fever sufferers.* | **sufferer from hay fever/asthma/cancer etc** *Many sufferers from depression struggle on for years before seeking help.*

invalid /ˈɪnvəliːd, -ləd‖-ləd/ [n C] someone who is permanently ill and needs to be looked after, especially if they have to stay in bed: *My father's an invalid, and needs constant care.* | **sb's invalid wife/son etc** *Barbara decided to move her invalid mother to Mississippi, so that she could look after her herself.*

the sick /ðə ˈsɪk/ [n plural] people who are ill and need to be helped or treated: *At that time there were no state benefits for the old and the sick.* | *terrible wartime photographs of the sick and the dying*

imagine

RELATED WORDS

▸ *see also* **think, idea, pretend, real**

1 to have a picture or idea of something in your mind

- imagine
- visualize
- picture
- can see
- form a picture
- conceive of

imagine /ɪˈmædʒən/ [v T not in progressive or passive] to think about something and form a picture or idea in your mind about it: *Try to imagine a room as big as a football field.* | **+ (that)** *For a while she imagined that she was a rich woman, living in a beautiful house.* | **+ what/who/where** *From the description Janet gave in her letter it was easy to imagine what her new apartment was like.* | **+ doing sth** *Just imagine having to spend the rest of your life in jail.* | **imagine sb doing sth** *I can quite easily imagine you running your own business.* | **can't imagine sb doing sth** *I can't imagine anyone wearing clothes that colour.*

visualize ALSO **visualise** British /ˈvɪʒuəlaɪz/ [v T not in progressive] to form a very clear picture of something or someone in your mind, especially in order to help you prepare to do something or help you to remember something clearly: *An architect can look at a drawing and visualize a three-dimensional shape.* | *David could still visualize Polly, even though he had not seen her for ten years.* | **+ where/what/how** *He closed his eyes, trying to visualize where he had put his watch.*

picture /ˈpɪktʃəʳ/ [v T not in progressive] to have a clear **picture** of something or someone in your mind, especially because you are trying to imagine what it is like to do something or what someone looks like: *Can you picture it? Lying in the sun, sipping cocktails – it would be paradise!* | **picture sth/sb as** *I had never met Graham but I pictured him as a pale, thin young man wearing glasses.* | **picture sb doing sth** *Miguel could still picture the children laughing and joking, and chasing each other around the garden.*

can see /kən ˈsiː/ [v phrase not in progressive or in passive] to have a clear picture of something you are thinking about in your mind, especially something pleasant or funny, or something you think is likely to happen: *I'm going to Corfu next week. I can see it all now – sun, sand and sea!* | **can see sb doing sth** *Jimmy's gone skiing for the first time. I can just see him coming home with a broken leg.*

form a picture /ˌfɔːʳm ə ˈpɪktʃəʳ/ [v phrase] to form an idea of something in your mind, using the information you have about it: *The Hubble Space Telescope allows astronomers to form a more accurate picture of our solar system.*

conceive of /kənˈsiːv ɒv/ [phr v T not in progressive or in passive] formal to imagine something happening or what a particular situation is like – use this especially in questions and negative statements: *It is difficult to conceive of a society in which nobody has to work.* | **cannot conceive of sth** *I don't know about you, but I cannot conceive of a home without electricity or water.*

2 to imagine something you want to do or want to happen

- fantasize
- daydream
- dream

fantasize ALSO **fantasise** British /ˈfæntəsaɪz/ [v I] to think about something that you would like to do or that you would like to happen, especially when it is very unlikely that you will do it or that it will happen **+ about doing sth** *I often fantasize about living in a big house with tennis courts and a swimming pool.* | *Many men fantasize about sleeping with someone who is not their partner.*

daydream /ˈdeɪdriːm/ [v I] to spend a short time imagining something pleasant, so that you forget where you are and what you are doing, especially when you are bored: *Mark had begun to daydream, and didn't even hear the teacher's question.* | **+ about/of** *Carol sat at her desk, daydreaming about meeting Mel Gibson.* | *When Charles tapped me on the shoulder I was daydreaming of golden beaches and palm trees.*

dream /driːm/ [v I] to imagine something pleasant that you would like to do or to happen, especially if it is possible that it might happen **+ of/about** *When I was at college I dreamed of becoming a great novelist.* | *Going abroad for a holiday was something our grandparents could only dream about.* | **+ (that)** *Maura had never dreamt that she could feel like this.*

3 to wrongly think that something is happening

- imagine
- be seeing things
- be in the mind/be in your mind
- hallucinate
- figment of your imagination

imagine /ɪˈmædʒɪn/ [v T] to wrongly think that you can see or hear something when it is not really happening **+ (that)** *When I was a child I would lie awake imagining that there were monsters in the dark corners of my room.* | *Mary was always imagining that people were talking about her behind her back.* | **I/you/he etc must be imagining things** *'I'm sure I saw Brian in the park today.' 'No, you must be imagining things. Brian hasn't lived here for nearly fifteen years.'*

be seeing things /biː ˈsiːɪŋ θɪŋz/ [v phrase] especially spoken say this when you or someone else has imagined something that cannot be real **I/you/he etc must be seeing things** *'Did that man just wave at me?' 'Of course not, you must be seeing things.'*

be in the mind/be in your mind /biː ɪn ðə ˈmaɪnd, biː ɪn jɔːʳ ˈmaɪnd/ [v phrase] if something **is in the mind** or **in your mind**, you are imagining it and it does not really exist **all in the mind** *I don't think Martin is really ill – it's all in the mind.* | **all in your mind** *No-one is trying to kill you. It's all in your mind.*

hallucinate /həˈluːsɪneɪt/ [v I] if someone who is ill or has taken drugs **hallucinates**, they believe that they can see things that are not really there: *After two days without food and water, Voss began to hallucinate.*

figment of your imagination /ˌfɪgmənt əv jɔːr ɪˌmædʒɪˈneɪʃən/ [n phrase] something that does not really exist and that you were just imagining: *Sceptics will tell you that there is no such thing as reincarnation and that living a previous life is a figment of the subject's imagination.*

4 something that you imagine

- imaginary
- fantasy
- daydream
- hallucination
- vision

imaginary /ɪˈmædʒɪnəri‖-neri/ [adj] not real, but existing only as a picture or idea in your mind: *When Linda was a child she had an imaginary friend called Booboo.* | *He pointed an imaginary gun at me and pretended to shoot.* | *Frankie was the kind of guy who lived in an imaginary world all of his own.*

fantasy /ˈfæntəsi/ [n C] an exciting or enjoyable experience that you imagine happening to you, but which will probably never happen: *Everyone's fantasy is that one day they will win the National Lottery.* | **live in a fantasy world** (=to always be having fantasies) *My son seems to live in a fantasy world sometimes.*

daydream /ˈdeɪdriːm/ [n C] pleasant thoughts you have about something you would like to do, that make you forget where you are and what you are doing: *I began to have daydreams about us being married.* | *She was sitting at the back of the class, lost in a daydream.*

hallucination /həˌluːsɪˈneɪʃən/ [n C] something you see that does not really exist, especially something that you see because you are ill or have taken drugs: *I knew that what I had seen was a hallucination, but it was so real and frightening.* | **have hallucinations** *Jamie lost two and a half stone in the next fortnight, couldn't eat and had hallucinations.*

vision /ˈvɪʒən/ [n C] an image, especially a religious image, that you can see but which other people cannot: *Bernadette had a vision in which the Virgin Mary appeared before her.*

5 your ability to imagine things

- imagination

imagination /ɪˌmædʒɪˈneɪʃən/ [n U] *Reading is a good way to develop a child's imagination at an early age.* | *There's no-one knocking at the door – it must have been your imagination.* | **use your imagination** *I don't have a photograph with me so you'll have to use your imagination.* | **vivid imagination** (=very strong imagination) *Jack's vivid imagination often gave him bad dreams.* | **fertile imagination** (=having a lot of original ideas) *Shakespeare has the most fertile imagination of all the poets.*

immediately

RELATED WORDS

opposite: **later, delay**

▸ *see also* **now, fast, soon, hurry**

1 immediately

- immediately
- at once/right away
- this minute/right now
- without delay

immediately /ɪ'mi:diətli/ [adv] quickly and without any delay: *If your baby has a fever you should call the doctor immediately.* | *When mother saw my face, she knew immediately that something was wrong.* | *Knowing the case was urgent, I replied to her lawyer's email immediately.*

at once/right away ALSO **straight away** British /ət 'wʌns, ˌraɪt ə'weɪ, ˌstreɪt ə'weɪ/ [adv] if you do something **at once**, **right away**, or **straightaway**, you do it immediately, especially because it is urgent: *The principal wants to see you at once.* | *We're in love and we want to get married right away.* | *You said it was important so I came straight away.*

this minute/right now /ˌðɪs 'mɪnɪt, ˌraɪt 'naʊ/ [adv] spoken if someone in authority orders you to do something **this minute** or **right now**, they want you to do it immediately, and they are usually annoyed with you: *Katie, put that down this minute, or you'll go straight to bed.* | *Tell Mick that I want to see him in my office, right now.*

without delay /wɪðˌaʊt dɪ'leɪ/ [adv] formal if you do something **without delay**, you do it immediately and without wasting any time, especially because it is important to do it as soon as possible: *If you lose your passport, you should contact the embassy without delay.* | *The crew and passengers were keen to get airborne without further delay.*

2 immediately after something else happens

- immediately
- as soon as/the moment (that)
- no sooner ... than
- had hardly/barely
- lose no time
- instantly
- outright

immediately /ɪ'mi:diətli/ [adv/conjunction] *We met at a friend's party, and immediately became friends.* | *There was a loud explosion in the engine-room, and almost immediately a fire broke out.* | *I'll call you immediately we hear any news about the baby.* | **+ after/afterwards** *We'll have to leave immediately after the meeting.* | *Mrs Smith was admitted to hospital at 10 o'clock, but died immediately afterwards.*

as soon as/the moment (that) /əz 'su:n əz, ðə 'məʊmənt (ðət)/ [conjunction] immediately after something has happened or immediately after you have done something: *As soon as Stephen felt well again, he returned to work.* | *I will pay you back, I promise, the moment I get paid.* | *Honey, I swear, I'll phone you the moment I get to New York.*

no sooner ... than /nəʊ 'su:nəʳ... ðən/ [conjunction] immediately after something has happened or someone has done something – use this especially in stories or in descriptions of events **no sooner had ... than** *No sooner had they sat down to eat than the phone rang.* | *No sooner had he arrived in the city than his wallet was stolen.* | **no sooner was/were ... than** *No sooner were the words out of her mouth than she regretted them.*

had hardly/barely ALSO **hardly had** /həd 'hɑ:ʳdli, 'beəʳli, 'hɑ:ʳdli hæd/ [conjunction] immediately after an event or action has finished – use this especially in stories or in descriptions of events: *I'd done food shopping and had barely gotten to the door, when Debbie asked if I'd been listening to the radio.* | *Hardly had the film reached our screens last July than it was plagued by troubles and controversy.*

lose no time /ˌlu:z nəʊ 'taɪm/ [v phrase] to do something immediately, as soon as you have the chance to do it **+ in doing sth** *When the new manager was appointed, he lost no time in reorganizing the office.* | *Murdock lost no time in setting out for London to find work.*

instantly /'ɪnstəntli/ [adv] at almost the same time that something else happens, and happening as a direct result of it: *Sea snakes inject a poison so strong that it kills a fish instantly.* | *It was a head-on crash and both drivers died instantly.*

outright /aʊt'raɪt/ [adv only after verb] written if someone is killed **outright**, they die immediately from an attack or an accident: *He was killed outright when his car crashed at high speed.*

3 when you do something immediately

- at a glance
- on the spot
- there and then/then and there
- off the top of your head
- right off/right off the bat

at a glance /ət ə 'glɑ:ns‖-'glæns/ [adv] if you know something **at a glance**, you only need to look quickly in order to know immediately what is happening, how someone feels etc **can see/tell (sth) at a glance** *I could see at a glance that the situation was serious.* | *An expert can tell at a glance whether it's a real diamond or a fake.*

on the spot /ɒn ðə 'spɒt‖-'spɑ:t/ [adv] if you do something **on the spot**, you do it immediately, without taking time to think about the situation, without waiting for official permission etc: *I was so angry I almost resigned on the spot.* | *The police can fine motorists on the spot for driving offences.* | *Look, I can't give you a decision on the spot. I'll have to talk to my boss first.*

there and then/then and there /ˌðeər ənd 'ðen, ˌðen ənd 'ðeəʳ/ [adv] if you do something or decide something **there and then** or **then and there**, you do it immediately and without stopping to think or delaying your decision until a later time: *When Kate knew John was seeing someone else, she should have left him then and there.* | *This time I'd gone too far, and I quit drinking there and then.*

off the top of your head /ɒf ðə ˌtɒp əv jɔ:ʳ 'hed‖-ˌtɑ:p-/ [adv usually in questions or negative sentences] informal if you answer a question or provide information **off the top of your head**, you do it immediately, using information you already know, and without thinking about it or trying to find out more about it: *'How old is Chris?' 'I don't know off the top of my head.'* | *There are some good restaurants around here, but I can't tell you their names off the top of my head.*

right off/right off the bat /ˌraɪt 'ɒf, ˌraɪt ɒf ðə 'bæt/ [adv] American informal if you do or say something **right off** or **right off the bat**, you do it or say it immediately, without taking time to think about it: *I* *couldn't think of a reply right off.* | *We let them know right off the bat that we weren't going with them.*

4 happening or needing to be done immediately

- immediate
- instant
- instantaneous

immediate /ɪˈmiːdiət/ [adj usually before noun] *My immediate reaction was shock and horror.* | *This letter requires your immediate attention.* | *The immediate needs of the refugees are for warm clothing and clean drinking water.* | *One immediate worry is money.*

instant /ˈɪnstənt/ [adj usually before noun] happening immediately, without any delay or doubt: *The workers are being threatened with instant dismissal.* | **take an instant dislike to sb** *He took an instant dislike to LeRoy.*

instantaneous /ˌɪnstənˈteɪniəs/ [adj] very nearly at the same time as something else happens, and often as a result of it: *Death from a massive heart attack was almost instantaneous.* —**instantaneously** [adv] *Lightning flashed, followed almost instantaneously by the sharp crack of thunder.*

important

RELATED WORDS

opposite: **unimportant**

see also **main**

1 something that is important

- important
- major
- big
- key
- significant/of great significance
- of importance
- historic
- momentous
- critical
- landmark

important /ɪmˈpɔːʳtənt/ [adj] something that is **important** has a big effect on people's lives and on the way things will happen: *Next Thursday's game is very important – if Italy lose they will be out of the World Cup.* | *I have an important announcement to make, so please listen carefully.* | *She didn't realize how important schoolwork was until it was too late.* —**importance** [n U] how important something is **+ of** *No-one should underestimate the importance of this discovery.*

major /ˈmeɪdʒəʳ/ [adj only before noun, not in comparative or superlative] one of the most important or serious things – use this especially when there is a small number of very important things, but a larger number of less important things: *Smoking is a major cause of heart disease* | *All the world's major sporting events can be seen on HHS TV.* | *It's the chief executive who makes all the major decisions.*

big /bɪg/ [adj] **big decision/event/occasion/day etc** an important decision, event etc, especially one that will influence or affect the rest of your life: *This is a big decision – you'll have to give me time to think.* | *Graduation Day is one of those big occasions when everyone wants a souvenir photograph.* | **the big day** **especially spoken** (=a very important day in someone's life) *I hear you're getting married – when's the big day?*

key /kiː/ [adj] **key role/factor/issue etc** someone or something that has an extremely important effect on the way something develops: *Education is likely to be a key issue in the forthcoming election.* | *The key person in this project will be the design manager.* | *He held a key position in the Bush administration.*

significant/of great significance /sɪgˈnɪfɪkənt, əv ˌgreɪt sɪgˈnɪfɪkəns/ [adj] important enough to be noticed and considered and to make a difference to a situation: *There has been a significant change in people's attitude to the environment.* | *Winning the award was a significant achievement.* | *a significant new discovery, which will improve our understanding of the AIDS virus*

of importance /əv ɪmˈpɔːʳtəns/ [adj phrase] important **of some/great/major etc importance** *This battle was of great importance.* | *They suddenly became silent, listening as if what he said was of the greatest importance.* | **of no/not of any importance** *Nothing of any importance was agreed at their meeting.*

historic /hɪˈstɒrɪk‖-ˈstɔː-, -ˈstɑː-/ [adj usually before noun] a **historic** event, moment etc is remembered as a part of history because it brings important changes that affect a situation for a long time: *the historic moment when Nelson Mandela was released from prison* | *In his book, Churchill describes that historic first meeting with Roosevelt.*

momentous /məʊˈmentəs, mə-/ [adj usually before noun] **momentous event/decision/occasion etc** something that is very important because it has a very great effect or influence on future events: *At this point William made a momentous decision – he resigned from his job and joined the army.* | *The revolution taking place in eastern Europe must be counted as one of the most momentous events of this century.*

critical /ˈkrɪtɪkəl/ [adj] a time or situation that is **critical** is extremely important and possibly dangerous because your future will depend on what happens or is decided at that time: *These accusations came at a critical phase in the negotiations.* | **+ for** *The next few months could be critical for the whole mining industry.*

landmark /ˈlændmɑːʳk/ [n C] an important time or event in someone's life, in history, in the development of knowledge etc, especially one that is the beginning of great improvements: *Getting my first part in a movie was a major landmark in my life.* | *This new drug is a landmark in the treatment of cancer.*

2 important and necessary

- important
- vital
- essential
- crucial

important /ɪmˈpɔːʳtənt/ [adj] something that is **important** should be given special attention because it is very necessary: *Young children should be given a healthy diet – that's very important.* | **it's important to do sth** *It is important to read the instructions carefully before you start.* | **it is important that** *It is important that everyone understands the risks involved in this plan.* —**importance** [n U] how important and necessary something is **+ of** *Most people realize the importance of getting enough sleep.*

vital /ˈvaɪtl/ [adj] something that is **vital** is very important and necessary, and if it is not done or dealt with correctly there could be serious problems: *nurses, police officers and other workers who provide vital services* | **+ to** *His evidence was vital to the defence case.* | **it is vital that** *It is vital that leaking gas pipes are fixed immediately.*

essential /ɪ'senʃəl/ [adj] extremely important to the existence, health, safety etc of someone or something: *Emergency services such as medical supplies must be maintained at all times.* | **+ to** *The layer of fat on the baby seal's body is essential to its survival.* | **it is essential that** *It's essential that you wear protective clothing in this area.*

crucial /'kruːʃəl/ [adj] something that is **crucial** is extremely important, because everything that happens afterwards depends on it: *Crucial decisions had to be made, involving millions of dollars.* | *The crucial factor in their relationship was their unshakeable faith in each other.* —**crucially** [adv] *The test results were crucially important.*

3 most important

- the most important
- priority
- urgent
- be at the top of the agenda
- take precedence over
- overriding
- paramount

the most important /ðə ˌməʊst ɪm'pɔːʳtənt/ *This was possibly the most important scientific discovery of the 20th century.* | *For Muslims, this is the most important day of the year.* | *If there is a fire, the most important thing is to get all the students out of the building immediately.*

priority /praɪ'ɒrᵻti‖-'ɔːr-/ [n C/U] the most important thing, which needs to be dealt with before anything else or given more attention than anything else: *First, let's decide what our priorities are.* | *My main priority is get through all my exams.* | **first/top/number one priority** *Safety has always been our number one priority.* | **give priority to sth** (=decide that something is very important, and deal with it urgently) *The President promised to give priority to reducing unemployment.*

urgent /'ɜːʳdʒənt/ [adj] something that is **urgent** must be dealt with or done as soon as possible, especially because something very bad could happen if it is not: *I've got one or two urgent letters to write.* | *Your sister's been calling – I think it's urgent.* | *An international effort is required to cope with the urgent needs of the earthquake victims.* —**urgently** [adv] *Mr Van Heeren is leaving on a trip and needs those papers urgently.* —**urgency** [n U] *This is a matter of great urgency.*

be at the top of the agenda /biː ət ðə ˌtɒp əv ði ə'dʒendə‖-ˌtɑːp-/ [v phrase] to be the most important and urgent of all the things that have to be done, especially by a government or company: *Getting inflation down is at the top of the agenda.* | *The government were reluctant to put equal pay for women anywhere near the top of the agenda.*

take precedence over /ˌteɪk 'presᵻdəns əʊvəʳ/ [v phrase] if someone or something **takes precedence over** someone or something else, they are more important and need to be dealt with first: *Don't keep Mr Rawlings waiting, he takes precedence over any other client.* | *Once again, the leader's wishes have taken precedence over the students' demands.*

overriding /ˌəʊvə'raɪdɪŋ◂/ [adj only before noun] **overriding need/concern/consideration etc** the thing that is most important and must be dealt with before anything else: *The overriding need here is to end the civil war.* | *an overriding concern to secure business efficiency*

paramount /'pærəmaʊnt/ [adj] more important than anything else: *The patients' wishes and needs are paramount and they must always come before our own.* | *While some musical ability is necessary, it is not the paramount concern.* | **of paramount importance** *Public safety and security are matters of paramount importance.*

4 an important person

- important
- leading
- influential
- VIP
- prominent
- heavyweight
- dignitary
- valued

▸ *see also* **position/rank, leader, famous**

important /ɪm'pɔːʳtənt/ [adj] an **important** person has a lot of power or influence: *The school is having some very important visitors next week.* | *Several important politicians are calling for a change in the laws on gun control.*

leading /'liːdɪŋ/ [adj only before noun] **leading scientist/politician/company etc** a scientist, politician etc who is well-known and successful, and who usually has a lot of influence: *She was one of America's leading athletes.* | *Some of the world's leading politicians will be meeting in Geneva to discuss disarmament.* | **leading light** (=one of the most important and active people in an organization) *Debbie was one of the leading lights in the drama club.*

influential /ˌɪnflu'enʃəl◂/ [adj] important and having a lot of influence especially in politics or business: *Jacobson's one of the most influential people in New York.* | *The program has gained the support of several influential businessmen.* | **influential in doing sth** *Various groups were influential in shaping public policy.* | **highly influential** *a highly influential member of Hong Kong's banking community*

VIP /ˌviː aɪ 'piː/ [n C] a very important, famous, or powerful person who is treated with special attention and respect: *The First Lady is expected to be among the many VIPs attending tonight.* | *The pair had their meeting in the VIP lounge* (=room for important people) *at Heathrow airport.*

prominent /'prɒmᵻnənt‖'prɑː-/ [adj] important, well-known, and respected in politics, business, education etc: *Daguerre was a prominent Mexico City lawyer.* | *The conference was attended by both government officials and prominent academics.* | *Politicians who are prominent in public life may be at risk from terrorism.* —**prominence** [n U] *Karpati had recently risen to prominence in the communist party.*

heavyweight /'heviweɪt/ [n C] someone who is important because they have a lot of power and experience in a particular business or job: *Intellectual heavyweights will be debating what is one of the most important issues or our time.*

dignitary /'dɪgnᵻtəri‖-teri/ [n C] someone who has an important position in society or in an organization such as a church or government: *Italy's president will be there, with foreign dignitaries including the Prince of Wales.* | *Most of the local dignitaries attended the event.*

valued /'væljuːd/ [adj only before noun] **valued friend/worker/customer etc** someone who is considered important because they provide a lot of support, business, service etc – used especially in advertisements and business contexts: *I had a letter from William, one of my most valued friends.* | *The most valued workers in the factory are the technicians.* | *The company is offering discount to its valued customers.*

5 someone or something that you care a lot about

- important
- care
- mean a lot to
- be sb's whole life
- live for
- be/mean (all) the world to
- the be all and end all

important /ɪm'pɔːʳtənt/ [adj] if something is **important** to you, you care a lot about it, and it has an **important** influence on the way you think and behave: *Which is more important to you – your family or your career?* | **be important to sb** *While I was a student, my parents' support and encouragement were very important to me.* | **the important thing** (=the only important thing) *At least the children are safe – that's the important thing.*

care /keəʳ/ [v I not in progressive] if you **care** about something or someone, you think they are important and you pay attention to them, consider their feelings etc: *Thousands are dying from disease and starvation and yet no one seems to care.* | **+ about** *Of course I care about the homeless and the unemployed, but what can I do?* | **+ what/who etc** *We make a range of natural, additive-free foods for people who really care what they eat.*

mean a lot to /ˌmiːn ə 'lɒt tuː‖-'lɑːt-/ [v phrase] especially spoken if someone or something **means a lot to** you, you care about them or think about them a lot, and your happiness depends on them: *You mustn't discourage her – this job means a lot to her.* | **mean everything to sb** (=to be more important than anything else) *Karen trained day and night – winning the gold medal meant everything to her.*

be sb's whole life /biː (sb's) ˌhəʊl 'laɪf/ [v phrase] if something or someone **is your whole life**, they are so important to you that life would seem to have no meaning without them and you would be very unhappy: *I could never consider another career – making films is my whole life.* | *Paul loves you very much. You are his whole life.*

live for /'lɪv fɔːʳ/ [phr v T not in progressive] if you **live for** something or someone, they are the most important or enjoyable thing in your life: *Margot lived for ballet and was completely dedicated.* | *Bob lives for just two things – his daughters and his music.*

be/mean (all) the world to /biː, miːn (ˌɔːl) ðə 'wɜːʳld tuː/ [v phrase] especially British if someone **is** or **means (all) the world to** you, they are more important to you than anyone else because you love them so much: *My son means all the world to me. If anything happened to him I'd never forgive myself.*

the be all and end all /ðə ˌbiː ɔːl ənd 'end ɔːl/ [n phrase] the thing that someone considers to be the most important thing in their life – use this when you think that they are wrong to think that it is the most important thing: *Going to university isn't the be all and end all, you know.*

6 the most important things

- essentials
- basics

essentials /ɪ'senʃəlz/ [n plural] things that are important because they are necessary for life or for doing something: *The refugees were provided with the essentials – food and shelter, but nothing more.* | **bare essentials** (=the most necessary things) *We don't have much room for luggage so we're only taking the bare essentials.*

basics /'beɪsɪks/ [n plural] the most necessary things that you need to know, understand, have etc before you can understand or do something: *You have to understand the basics before you can move on to more advanced work.*

7 to make something seem more important than it really is

- make a fuss
- make an issue of
- make a mountain out of a molehill
- make too much of

make a fuss /ˌmeɪk ə 'fʌs/ [v phrase] to get upset or angry about something that is not really very important: *It won't cost much to repair the damage, so there's no need to make such a fuss.* | **+ about** *Be quiet. You're all making a fuss about nothing.*

make an issue of ALSO **make a big deal out of** /ˌmeɪk ən 'ɪʃuː ɒv, meɪk ə ˌbɪg 'diːl aʊt ɒv/ [v phrase] to argue about something that is not really very important, so that it seems to be important: *Hilary was upset about not being promoted, but she didn't want to make an issue of it.* | *It really was just a temporary lapse – there's no need to make a big deal out of it.*

make a mountain out of a molehill /meɪk ə ˌmaʊntɪ̵n aʊt əv ə 'məʊlhɪl/ [v phrase] to make a problem seem worse and more important than it really is: *She was only five minutes late! You're making a mountain out of a molehill.*

make too much of /meɪk tuː 'mʌtʃ ɒv/ [v phrase] to talk about something so much that it seems more important than it really is: *You're making too much of this – it's really not worth out falling out over.*

8 to have an important part in something

- play a leading part/role
- figure prominently in/be prominent in
- be the driving force
- be instrumental in

play a leading part/role /ˌpleɪ ə ˌliːdɪŋ 'pɑːʳt, 'rəʊl/ [v phrase] to be important in making important changes or achieving an important success: *The Church has played a leading role in the struggle for human rights.* | *Von Braun played a leading part in the development of space flights.*

figure prominently in/be prominent in /ˌfɪgə 'prɒmɪ̵nəntli ɪn, biː 'prɒmɪ̵nənt ɪn‖ˌfɪgjər 'prɑːm-/ [v phrase] to be important in a process, event, or situation, especially by working very hard to achieve something: *The British Prime Minister figured prominently in the peace talks.* | *The campaign, in which many celebrities figured prominently, was a great success.* | *She will be remembered as someone who was always prominent in the anti-apartheid movement.*

be the driving force /biː ðə 'draɪvɪŋ ˌfɔːʳs/ [v phrase] to be the most important person in changing or developing something because you have so much energy and determination: *James is the senior partner in the firm, but it is Peter who is the driving force.* | **+ behind** *Carlsson has been the driving force behind the bank's ambitious expansion plans.*

be instrumental in /biː ˌɪnstrʊ̵'mentl ɪn/ [v phrase] to be important in making something possible, especially because of the things you do to achieve it: *Mary had been instrumental in securing my release* *from jail.* | *Women's organizations have been instrumental in promoting women's rights.*

9 to make someone or something less important

- downgrade
- devalue
- relegate

downgrade /ˈdaʊngreɪd, daʊnˈgreɪd‖ˈdaʊngreɪd/ [v T] to make something less important, valuable, or powerful, especially by giving it less money or support: *The professor claims that the government is deliberately downgrading scientific research.* | *Economic advisers in Washington have been discussing whether to downgrade foreign loans.*

devalue /diːˈvæljuː/ [v T] to make someone or something seem less important or valuable: *They're always trying to devalue my contribution to the department.*

relegate /ˈreləgeɪt/ [v T usually in passive] to give someone or something a less important position than before **+ to** *Carlo has been relegated to a more junior position in the company.* | *Our team were relegated to a minor league.*

impossible

RELATED WORDS

opposite: possible

▸ *see also* **can/can't**

1 when something cannot be done

- impossible
- not possible
- there's no way
- impractical
- out of the question
- can't possibly
- hopeless
- not stand a chance/not have a hope
- impossibility

impossible /ɪmˈpɒsəbəl‖ɪmˈpɑː-/ [adj] something that is **impossible** cannot be done: *We're supposed to do all this work by tomorrow, but it's impossible.* | *It's a seemingly impossible task.* | **it is impossible (for sb/sth) to do sth** *The twins are so alike that it's impossible to tell them apart.* | *The street was narrow and it was impossible for the two buses to pass.* | **make it impossible** *Her back injury has made it impossible for her to play tennis anymore.* | **find it impossible** (=discover that you cannot do something) *When people leave prison, they often find it impossible to get a job.*

not possible /nɒt ˈpɒsəbəl‖-ˈpɑː-/ [adj] impossible or extremely difficult to do: *We can't buy a new computer for every student – it's just not possible.* | **it is not possible (for sb/sth) to do sth** *It is not possible, in a book of this size, to cover every aspect of the subject.* | *She's in a meeting, so I'm afraid it's not possible for you to see her now.*

there's no way /ðeəʳz ˌnəʊ ˈweɪ/ especially spoken say this when you strongly believe that something is impossible **+ (that)** *There's no way we can get to the airport in less than an hour.* | **there's no way of knowing sth** *There's no way of knowing when the volcano will erupt again.*

impractical /ɪmˈpræktɪkəl/ [adj] an idea, suggestion, or action that is **impractical** is not really possible because it would cost far too much money, waste too much time, be much too difficult etc: *Officials stated that building a dam for irrigation purposes was hopelessly impractical.* | *Telling people to avoid any exposure to the sun is impractical advice.* | **it is impractical to do sth** *It would be impractical to attempt to review all the types of multimedia technology in this study.*

out of the question /ˌaʊt əv ðə ˈkwestʃən/ [adj phrase] if an idea or suggestion is **out of the question**, it is completely impossible or it cannot be allowed: *I'd love to come with you, but with all the work I have to do it's out of the question.* | *The cost would be over $5000, which is quite out of the question.* | **it's out of the question for sb (to do sth)** *I'm afraid it's out of the question for you to go alone.*

can't possibly /ˌkɑːnt ˈpɒsəbli‖ˌkænt ˈpɑː-/ especially spoken use this in order to emphasize that you think something is impossible: *You know we can't possibly pay as much as that in rent.* | *That was delicious but I couldn't possibly eat another thing!*

hopeless /ˈhəʊpləs/ [adj] if something that you try to do is **hopeless**, there is no possibility of it being successful: *Police now face the hopeless task of trying to find the bombers.* | **it is hopeless** *'Please let me go to the party' Ali begged her mother, but she knew it was hopeless.* | **it is hopeless to do sth** *It's hopeless to try to persuade him while he's in this mood. Let's talk to him tomorrow.* | **a hopeless cause** (=something that cannot possibly succeed) *'I do not believe that working to block the movement of cocaine into the US is a hopeless cause,' McCaffrey told the panel.*

not stand a chance/not have a hope /nɒt ˌstænd ə ˈtʃɑːns‖-ˈtʃæns, nɒt ˌhæv ə ˈhəʊp/ [v phrase not in progressive] informal to not have any chance of doing what you want, for example because it is much too difficult, someone else will do it first etc: *Everyone in the town votes Republican. The Democrats don't stand a chance.* | *There's no point in me applying for the job. I wouldn't have a hope.* | **not stand a chance of doing sth** *'The driver of the train didn't stand a chance of stopping in time,' a Railtrack spokesman said.* | **not have a hope/have no hope of doing sth** *The bank said that it will no longer lend to enterprises that have no hope of making a profit.*

impossibility /ɪmˌpɒsəˈbɪləti‖ɪmˌpɑː-/ [n singular] something that is impossible to do: *At first they thought that building a bridge across to the island was an impossibility.* | *The equal division of all roles is a practical impossibility for many parents.* | *I was suddenly struck by the impossibility of achieving our aims.*

2 when something cannot happen, exist, or be true

- impossible
- be not possible
- can't/couldn't
- there's no way
- inconceivable
- unthinkable
- by any/by no stretch of the imagination

impossible /ɪmˈpɒsəbəl‖ɪmˈpɑː-/ [adj] use this to say that you are sure that something cannot happen, exist, or be true: *'Did you know that I can hold my breath for three minutes?' 'Impossible!'* | *'The police suspect John.' 'But that's impossible. He was with us the whole day.'* | **it is impossible (that)** *It was impossible that anyone could have survived the crash.*

be not possible /biː nɒt ˈpɒsəbəl‖-ˈpɑː-/ [v phrase] impossible use this especially when you are very surprised about something: *'Abigail won't give us* *the money,' said Jim. 'But that's not possible', replied Ben; 'she told me only this morning that she would.'* | **it is not possible that** *It's not possible that Kate was at the party too. I would have seen her.*

can't/couldn't /kɑːnt‖kænt, ˈkʊdnt/ [modal verb] use this to say that it is not possible for something to have happened or for someone to have done something: *They can't have gone out because all the windows are open.* | *What you're saying can't possibly be true. I don't believe it.* | *New evidence proved that the accused couldn't have been at the scene of the crime.*

there's no way /ðeəʳz ˌnəʊ ˈweɪ/ spoken say this when you strongly believe that something is impossible **+ (that)** *There's no way we can possibly get the bed up those stairs.* | *If the computer system is working properly, there's no way that it could make a mistake.*

inconceivable /ˌɪnkənˈsiːvəbəl/ [adj] impossible or very difficult to imagine: *When I was a boy, having a bath every day was an inconceivable luxury.* | *The slaughter of thousands of innocent US citizens would have been inconceivable until recently.* | **it is inconceivable that** *Many people thought it was inconceivable that the crash could have been an accident.*

unthinkable /ʌnˈθɪŋkəbəl/ [adj] if something is **unthinkable**, it seems impossible because it is so shocking, nasty, difficult etc: *The amount of sex on television that we see today would have been unthinkable in previous decades.* | **it is unthinkable that** *It is unthinkable that anyone would dare to enter the Control Area without permission.* | **unthinkable for sb to do sth** *In those days it was unthinkable for a lady to work outside the home.*

by any/by no stretch of the imagination /baɪ ˌeni, baɪ ˌnəʊ ˌstretʃ əv ði ɪmædʒəˈneɪʃən/ [adv] if something is not possible **by any** or **by no stretch of the imagination,** you cannot even imagine it being possible: *The new software program is not perfect, by any stretch of the imagination.* | *By no stretch of the imagination could Carl ever be called good-looking.*

3 impossible to get

- unattainable
- out of reach

unattainable /ˌʌnəˈteɪnəbəl/ [adj] impossible to achieve: *Television can create deep dissatisfaction by portraying lifestyles that are unattainable.* | *The new exams have been designed for weaker students who, until now, have been set unattainable targets.* | *For many young people in rural areas, a university education seems like an unattainable dream.*

out of reach /ˌaʊt əv ˈriːtʃ/ [adj phrase] impossible to get or achieve – use this about your aims and things you want very much: *A cure for the HIV virus may not be out of reach for much longer.* | *Peace in the region remained the goal, but a permanent solution still seemed out of reach.*

4 to make something impossible

- rule out
- preclude

rule out /ˌruːl ˈaʊt/ [phr v T] to make something impossible, especially something that you had already planned or decided to do: *Mark's serious physical condition ruled out our trip to Hungary that year.* | *Severe weather conditions ruled out any rescue operation until the following day.*

preclude /prɪˈkluːd/ [v T] formal to make it impossible for someone to do something: *Lack of evidence may preclude a trial.* | **preclude sb from doing sth** *These regulations may preclude newspapers from publishing details of politicians' private lives.*

impress

to do something that makes someone admire you

RELATED WORDS

- good, admire, beautiful

1 to impress someone

- impress
- make an impression
- make a good impression
- come across well/come over well

impress /ɪmˈpres/ [v T not in progressive] if someone or something **impresses** you, they are so interesting, intelligent, original etc that you like or admire them very much: *None of the people I've interviewed so far have impressed me.* | *Quinnell's fifty-yard run down the touchline with the ball in one hand impressed the Wales coach.* | *What impressed the judges most was the originality of the dancers' performance.* | **+ with** *The boy has impressed his doctors with his courage and determination.*

make an impression /ˌmeɪk ən ɪmˈpreʃən/ [v phrase] to make someone admire you the first time they see you, so that they like you or approve of you: *When you go for a job interview, you have just a few minutes to make an impression.* | *Rick looked at the pretty salesgirl and smiled. Sandy could tell that he wanted to make an impression.* | **+ on** *George, with his dark hair and blue eyes, made an impression on almost everyone he met.*

make a good impression /meɪk ə ˌgʊd ɪmˈpreʃən/ [v phrase] to make someone admire or like you the first time they see you, for example by dressing or behaving in an impressive way: *Everyone was dressed in their best clothes, eager to make a good impression.* | **+ on/with** *It's pretty important around here to make a good impression with the boss.*

come across well/come over well /ˌkʌm əkrɒs ˈwel‖-əkrɔːs-, ˌkʌm əʊvəʳ ˈwel/ [v phrase] to impress the people who are watching or listening to you by seeming intelligent, confident, skilful etc: *It was her first time on TV, but she came across very well.* | *I thought the play was rather long and slow, and the jokes didn't really come over well.*

2 to impress someone very much

- dazzle
- knock out

dazzle /ˈdæzəl/ [v T] to impress someone very much by being or doing something very exciting and unusual – used especially in news reports: *The Princess's off-the-shoulder dress dazzled the waiting crowds.* | *As a speaker he would dazzle listeners with his brilliant wordplay and witty remarks.*

knock out /ˌnɒk ˈaʊt‖ˌnɑːk-/ [phr v T] informal to impress someone very much by doing something in a way that is surprisingly good: *If this performer doesn't knock the audience out, I don't know what would.* | **really knock sb out** *Why don't you start the gig with that song you wrote yourself? That'll really knock them out.*

3 to feel impressed

- be impressed
- be overawed

be impressed /biː ɪmˈprest/ [v phrase] *It was a superb performance – even the critics were impressed.* | **+ by/with** *All of Lucy's teachers said that they were impressed with her progress.* | *I was greatly impressed by the beauty of their art and the richness of their culture.* | **+ (that)** *I'm impressed to hear that you're learning Chinese.* | **be favourably impressed** British **be favorably impressed** American (=be impressed and pleased) *UN observers said that they were very favorably impressed by the fairness of the elections.* | **be suitably/duly impressed** (=be as impressed as someone wants you to be) *The Director read through my report, and looked suitably impressed.*

be overawed /biː ˌəʊvərˈɔːd/ [v phrase] to be so impressed by a place, an occasion, or a person that you become nervous: *When I first arrived in New York, I was completely overawed.* | **be overawed by sth/sb** *Although Sheila's parents tried to put Jim at his ease, he still felt overawed by them.*

4 words for describing someone or something that impresses you

- impressive
- imposing
- dazzling
- striking
- awe-inspiring
- breathtaking
- grand
- majestic
- spectacular

impressive /ɪmˈpresɪv/ [adj] *The rich variety of animal life we found was very impressive.* | *Alan Howard has been impressive in 'Henry IV' at the National Theatre.* | *You can visit the desert as part of an impressive 5-day excursion out of the city.* | *He gave an impressive performance of Rachmaninoff's Piano Concerto No 3.*

imposing /ɪmˈpəʊzɪŋ/ [adj] a building or part of a building that is **imposing** is big and impressive: *An imposing staircase led out of the hall.* | *The show took place outside the imposing Central Library building on Fifth Avenue.* | *It's one of the most distinguished hotels in Italy, grand and imposing.*

dazzling /ˈdæzlɪŋ/ [adj] impressive, especially because of being extremely skilfully done, having an unusually beautiful appearance etc – used especially in news reports: *During his short but dazzling career he broke almost every scoring record in the National League.* | *She looked dazzling, with her long blonde hair and diamond earrings.*

striking /ˈstraɪkɪŋ/ [adj] impressive, especially because of being very unusual to look at: *From the outside, the most striking aspect of the building is its tall, slender tower.* | *It's a tall plant with striking red flowers in early spring.* | *The face in the photograph was striking – good-looking and vivacious.*

awe-inspiring /ˈɔː ɪnˌspaɪərɪŋ/ [adj] so big and impressive that you feel slightly nervous: *The pyramids at dawn were an awe-inspiring sight.* | *The canyon was so awe-inspiring that even Dan was speechless.*

breathtaking /ˈbreθˌteɪkɪŋ/ [adj] very impressive and exciting, especially as a result of great speed, size, or beauty: *The bank's new on-line service is still growing at a breathtaking pace.* | *The drive along the beach and up the mountain is truly breathtaking.* | *The guest house was on the side of the cliff, with breathtaking views of the ocean below.* —**breathtakingly** [adv] *The courtyard of the huge old building is breathtakingly beautiful.*

grand /grænd/ [adj] made or done in order to impress people: *The conferences always take place in grand hotels, away from the realities of life.* | *They always make grand promises to the biggest group of voters.*

majestic /məˈdʒestɪk/ [adj] very impressive because of being very big and beautiful: *the majestic mountains of the Himalayas* | *Tintern Abbey is noted for its majestic arches, fine doorways and elegant windows.*

spectacular /spekˈtækjᵊləʳ/ [adj] something such as a view or a performance that is **spectacular** is very impressive and exciting to look at or watch: *The campground in Emerald Bay State Park has a spectacular setting.* | *To celebrate independence day, there was a spectacular fireworks display.*

5 to not impress someone

- not impress/fail to impress
- unimpressive

not impress/fail to impress /nɒt ɪmˈpres, ˌfeɪl tʊ ɪmˈpres/ [v phrase not in progressive] *OK, so he went to Yale! That doesn't impress me!* | *The defence evidence didn't impress the judge, and he sentenced Wright to 3 years in jail.* | *I tried making a joke but it failed to impress anyone.*

unimpressive /ˌʌnɪmˈpresɪv◂/ [adj] not good enough to impress anyone: *Marie's performance in the last exam was unimpressive.* | *When you think how much has been spent on research, the results are sadly unimpressive.* | *The best the team could come up with was an unimpressive 1-1 tie.*

improve

RELATED WORDS

opposite: **worse**

▸ *see also* **good, best, better**

1 to become better

- get better
- improve
- catch up
- pick up
- things are looking up

get better /get ˈbetəʳ/ [v phrase] especially spoken *I hope the weather gets better soon.* | **get a lot better** *The first part of the book is pretty boring, but it gets a lot better as the story goes on.* | **things get better** (=a situation gets better) *If things don't get better, we may end up having to sell the house.* | **get better and better** (=continue to get better) *I don't mind training hard, because you get better and better all the time.*

improve /ɪmˈpruːv/ [v I] especially written to get better: *In the weeks that followed, his health continued to improve.* | *Some wines improve with age.* | **improve dramatically/greatly etc** *Conditions in prisons have improved dramatically in the last 20 years.*

catch up /ˌkætʃ ˈʌp/ [phr v I/T] to improve so that you reach the same standard as other people in your class, group etc: *If you miss a lot of school, it will be very difficult to catch up.* | **+ with** *Although she had never studied German before, Jane soon caught up with the others.* | **catch sb up** *The other players in the team are better than me, but I'm slowly catching them up.*

pick up /ˌpɪk ˈʌp/ [phr v I] if a business or economic

situation **picks up**, it improves after a period without much business activity: *Financial commentators think we'll see the economy starting to pick up early next year.* | *Sales were very slow in the first half of the year, but business is beginning to pick up now.*

things are looking up /ˌθɪŋz əʳ ˌlʊkɪŋ ˈʌp/ **spoken** say this when good things have started to happen to you, and your life seems much better than it was: *Things are looking up – I've got a new job and a new boyfriend.*

2 to make something better

- ▸ improve
- ▸ make sth better
- ▸ make improvements
- ▸ knock sth into shape
- ▸ upgrade
- ▸ streamline
- ▸ clean up
- ▸ brush up (on)

improve /ɪmˈpruːv/ [v T] to make something better: *I wanted to improve my French, so I got a job in Paris.* | *The funds will go towards improving road and rail services.* | *By managing natural resources more effectively, our quality of human life could be improved greatly.*

make sth better /ˌmeɪk (sth) ˈbetəʳ/ [v phrase] to improve a situation or improve someone's life: *Instead of making the traffic situation better, the new road has just made things worse.* | *You won't make things any better by worrying about them.* | *Have computers really made life better for everyone?*

make improvements /ˌmeɪk ɪmˈpruːvmənts/ [v phrase] to make changes to something or add things to it in order to make it better, more useful, or more effective: *After we've made a few improvements, the software should be fine.* | **+ to** *Several improvements have been made to the original designs.* | *They made a lot of improvements to the house after they moved in.*

knock sth into shape British **/whip sth into shape** especially American /ˌnɒk (sth) ɪntə ˈʃeɪp‖ˌnɑːk-, ˌwɪp (sth) ɪntə ˈʃeɪp/ [v phrase] informal to make changes to something in order to make it good enough: *We've only got one week left to knock the play into shape.* | *The new Chief Executive is whipping the company into shape and making it more competitive.*

upgrade /ˌʌpˈgreɪd/ [v T] to improve something such as machinery, a building, or a system by making it more modern, effective, and successful: *The city has recently spent $3 million on upgrading its sports stadium.* | *It was decided that the entire computer system should be upgraded.* | *Since July, the airport has upgraded security measures, at a cost of $560,000.*

streamline /ˈstriːmlaɪn/ [v T] to improve a system or process by making it more simple and therefore faster and more effective: *The new system is an attempt to streamline the decision-making process.* | *Apple is going to streamline its operations and concentrate development efforts on the Internet and multimedia.* —**streamlined** [adj] *The IMF has adopted a streamlined procedure for doling out emergency loans.*

clean up /ˌkliːn ˈʌp/ [phr v T] to improve standards of behaviour in a place or organization, especially by removing dishonest or criminal people **clean up sth** *It's time someone cleaned up this city; we have one of the highest crime rates in the country.* | *Most clubs have made a big effort to clean up football's image.* | **clean sth up** *The management of some our prisons has sometimes been corrupt, and it is our job to clean it up.*

brush up (on) ALSO **brush up sth** British /ˌbrʌʃ ˈʌp ɒn, ˌbrʌʃ ˈʌp (sth)/ [phr v T] especially spoken to practise doing something that you have not done for a long time in order to try to improve it: *I'd like to brush up on my Italian before our trip.* | *Public libraries frequently have computers that people can use to brush up their IT skills.*

3 to keep improving something until it is perfect

- ▸ perfect
- ▸ refine
- ▸ fine-tune

perfect /pəʳˈfekt/ [v T] to improve something such as a skill, system, or something you have designed until you make it perfect: *The best way to perfect your Spanish is to live in a country where it's spoken.* | *The Chief Executive of the company said that they had spent ten years on perfecting the product.* | **perfect the art/technique etc (of doing sth)** *Dom Perignon perfected the art of blending wines from many different vineyards.*

refine /rɪˈfaɪn/ [v T] to make something as good as possible by checking it again and again and making small changes each time until you are satisfied: *Volvo spent three years refining the design of their new car.* | *It was a four week course, aimed at refining our understanding of the managerial role.* —**refinement** [n C] *The new proposal is basically a refinement of an earlier scheme.*

fine-tune /ˌfaɪn ˈtjuːn‖-ˈtuːn/ [v T] to make small changes to a plan or system that is already good, so that it works as well as possible: *You've established the general direction you want to go in, now you need to fine-tune your plans.* | *The election campaign had to be constantly fine-tuned so that the right message got across.* —**fine-tuning** [n U] *We have developed an efficient banking service, but there is scope for further fine-tuning of the system.*

4 to add a good quality to something

- ▸ enhance
- ▸ enrich
- ▸ make

enhance /ɪnˈhɑːns‖ɪnˈhæns/ [v T not usually in progressive] to make a good quality in something even more attractive, enjoyable etc: *You can enhance the flavour of most dishes with the careful use of herbs.* | *Low lighting and soft music enhanced the atmosphere in the room.*

enrich /ɪnˈrɪtʃ/ [v T not usually in progressive] to add a quality that makes something much more interesting, valuable etc: *People who have fame and money usually search for something else to enrich their lives.* | *Most people agree that immigrant communities enrich our culture.*

make /meɪk/ [v T not in progressive or passive] informal to provide the special quality that makes something completely enjoyable, attractive, or successful: *The right curtains can make a room.* | *For me, the trip to Caracas made the holiday.*

5 when something improves

- ▸ improvement
- ▸ advance

improvement /ɪmˈpruːvmənt/ [n C/U] a change that makes something better: *I'm afraid if you don't show some improvement soon we won't be entering you for the exam.* | *You'll see that there's been a* *remarkable improvement in recent weeks.* | **+ in** *Have you noticed any improvement in his work?* | *Accidents have become less frequent, thanks to recent improvements in our safety checks.* | **a big/great/tremendous improvement** *There's been a great improvement in the team's performance over the last three games.* | **+ to** *We had to borrow money to pay for all the improvements to our home.* | **design/home/performance etc improvements** *Design improvements in the computer system have greatly increased our efficiency.*

advance /əd'vɑːns‖əd'væns/ [n C usually plural] an important new idea or way of doing something, especially in science **+ in** *Advances in medical science may make it possible for people to live for 150 years.* | **a big/enormous/major advance** *The last 20 years have seen enormous advances in communications technology.*

in charge of

RELATED WORDS

- to tell someone to do something *see* **tell (17-24)**
- *see also* **manager, leader, control/not control, responsible, position/rank, government**

1 to be in charge of an activity or group of people

- be in charge
- run
- manage
- head
- lead
- supervise
- oversee

be in charge /biː ɪn 'tʃɑːʳdʒ/ [v phrase] if you **are in charge** of an activity or a group of people, you are the person who has the authority to control what happens, tell other people what to do etc: *He's the captain. He's in charge, so he's responsible for anything that happens.* | **+ of** *Who's the officer in charge of the investigation* | **+ of doing sth** *As senior supervisor, she is in charge of training new employees.* | **put sb in charge** *Two years after joining the police force, he was put in charge of the department's records.*

run /rʌn/ [v T] to be the person who makes the important decisions about what will happen in a business, organization, country etc: *She runs a company called Sunshine Holidays.* | *a drug counselling service that is run by ex-addicts* | *Who really runs the country – the elected government or big business?* | **well/badly/poorly etc run** *The voting process was smooth and, for the most part, well-run.* | **state-run** (=run by the government) *a state-run mental hospital*

manage /'mænɪdʒ/ [v T] to be in charge of a business, especially one that is owned by someone else: *My husband manages a mill, 200 miles north of Bombay.* | *Managing four pizza outlets is extremely hard work.* | *The family business was skilfully managed by her elder brother, Michael.*

head /hed/ [v T] if you **head** a company or activity, you are in charge of it: *Levy headed an investigation into the fund mismanagement.* | *The program is headed by an expert in teaching gifted and talented children.* | **head up** American informal *Heading up the investigation into the crash is Officer Frank Foyle.*

lead /liːd/ [v T] to be the person with responsibility for a large group or team that is working together on an important activity: *The drug raid was led by top officers.* | *Dr Jenkins leads a team of researchers at the Plant Institute.* | *A group of 80 planes, led by Lieutenant Commander Egusha, was on its way to attack.*

supervise /'suːpəʳvaɪz, 'sjuː-‖'suː-/ [v T] to be in charge of a group of workers or students and be responsible for making sure that they do their work properly, especially by being with them to give instructions, answer questions etc: *At work, she supervises a production team of fifteen.* | *All volunteers are supervised by a qualified nurse.* | *The teacher's duties that morning included supervising the before-school reading program.* —**supervision** /ˌsuːpəʳ'vɪʒən, ˌsjuː-‖ˌsuː-/ [n U] *We work under the Chief Engineer's supervision.* | *Children of this age do not need constant supervision.*

oversee /ˌəʊvəʳ'siː/ [v T] formal to be in charge of a group of workers, especially when this involves planning and organizing what they should do rather than being with them or giving instructions to them directly: *Team leaders and project managers oversee groups of programming staff.* | *Administrators oversee the testing of students, to place them in the appropriate classes.*

2 someone who is in charge at work

- supervisor
- head
- foreman
- boss
- manager
- superior

supervisor /'suːpəʳvaɪzəʳ, 'sjuː-‖'suː-/ [n C] someone who is in charge of a group of workers, and makes sure they do their jobs properly: *You must receive approval from a supervisor before visiting a high-risk area.* | *Haworth, formerly a supervisor of 120 people at a printing company, left to start his own business.*

head /hed/ [n C] the person who is in charge of a company, department, or particular activity **+ of** *According to Rice, the head of the planning committee, the project is 25% completed.* | **be head of sth** *Hwang is head of the local Communist Party, and is also a farmer.*

foreman /'fɔːʳmən/ [n C] someone who is in charge of a group of factory workers or builders and is responsible for seeing that orders from managers are carried out: *Time taken in unloading should be recorded by the foreman and paid at the agreed rate.*

boss /bɒs‖bɔːs/ [n C] the person who is in charge of you at work: *As a secretary, my job includes taking my boss's phone calls.* | *She accuses her former boss of sexually harassing her.* | **immediate boss** (=the person who is directly in charge of you) *The managing director is a man but my immediate boss is a woman.* | **be your own boss** (=to run your own business and organize your own work) *I don't make as much money as I used to, but I prefer being my own boss.*

manager /'mænɪdʒəʳ/ [n C] someone whose job is to run part or all of a company or other organization and who is in charge of you at work: *He was a manager for Safeway Stores before leaving to start his own business.* | *If the sales clerk cannot help you, ask to see the manager.* | *McBride was a general manager in charge of research and development.* | **line manager** (=the person who is directly in charge of your work) *Notify your line manager if you are ill.*

superior /suː'pɪəriəʳ, sjuː-‖sʊ-/ [n C] formal someone who is in a higher position than you at work: *The report he submitted to his superiors accurately reflected the poor morale of the workers.* | **immediate**

superior (=the person in the position directly above you) *Your most important working relationship is with your immediate superior.*

3 to be in charge of a meeting

- chair
- preside over

chair /tʃeəʳ/ [v T] to be in charge of an official meeting: *The meeting was chaired by Professor Grainger of the Biology Department.* | *Her job involves chairing meetings, and producing and circulating the minutes of those meetings.*

preside over /prɪˈzaɪd əʊvəʳ/ [phr v T] formal to be in charge of an official meeting, especially an important one or one attended by a lot of people: *The meeting was held at Halling Institute and was presided over by T.H. Baker.* | *Johnson presided over a long Senate ethics committee investigation.*

4 someone who is in charge of an official meeting

- chair/chairperson
- chairman/chairwoman

chair/chairperson /tʃeəʳ, ˈtʃeəʳpɜːʳsən/ [n C] someone who is in charge of a meeting – use this when it is not important to say, or you do not know, whether the person is a man or woman: *All questions must be addressed to the chair.* | *Topics may be selected by the chairperson at the beginning of the meeting.* | **+ of** *Councillor Jones will be chair of the housing committee meeting.*

chairman/chairwoman /ˈtʃeəʳmən, ˈtʃeəʳˌwʊmən/ [n C] someone who is in charge of a meeting. Use **chairman** about either a man or a woman, and **chairwoman** only about a woman: *'Mr Chairman,' a woman's voice called from the back of the hall, 'may I ask a question?'* | **+ of** *Rogers was asked to serve as chairman of the committee.* | *The chairwoman of the committee to reform the state's welfare program says she wants a proposal drafted by June.*

include/ not include

RELATED WORDS

- *see also* **contain, consist of, have/not have**

1 to include someone or something

- include
- contain
- among
- range from sth to

include /ɪnˈkluːd/ [v T not in progressive] if a group of people, things, ideas etc **includes** someone or something, it has them as one of its parts: *Our tour party included several young families.* | *Symptoms of the disease include tiredness and loss of memory.* | *Today's programme will include a workshop on language learning games.*

contain /kənˈteɪn/ [v T not in progressive] to include particular ideas, images, or information – use this about books, films, reports etc: *The film contains some very unpleasant scenes of violence.* | *Her report contained some interesting suggestions.* | *All computer manuals should contain a list giving addresses of suppliers.*

among /əˈmʌŋ/ [prep] someone or something that is **among** a group of similar people, things, ideas etc is one of the people or things in the group: *The prime minister was among the 300 people who attended the funeral.* | *Among the collection of photographs are two taken in Hamburg in 1911.* | **among whom/which** *There were about twenty spectators, among whom were Bill, Maria and myself.*

range from sth to sth /ˈreɪndʒ frɒm (sth) tə (sth)/ [v phrase] if prices, levels, temperatures etc **range from** one amount to another amount, they include both these amounts and anything in between: *Prices range from $10 to $500,000.* | *Levels of disability may range from very slight hearing problems to total deafness.*

2 to include more than one subject, period etc

- cover
- encompass
- embrace
- span

cover /ˈkʌvəʳ/ [v T] to include or deal with more than one subject, period etc at the same time: *His book on European history covers the period from 1914 to 2001.* | *The course lasts two years and covers seven basic subjects.* | **cover a wide range/variety of sth** *The term RSI – repetitive strain injury – covers a wide variety of painful hand and arm conditions.*

encompass /ɪnˈkʌmpəs/ [v T] formal to include or deal with a very wide range of ideas, subjects etc: *The Hindu religion encompasses many widely differing forms of worship.* | *It was a fruitful discussion which encompassed several different viewpoints.*

embrace /ɪmˈbreɪs/ [v T] formal if a word or way of describing something **embraces** several things, they are all included within its meaning: *The word 'culture' embraces both artistic and sociological aspects of a society.* | *The category 'kinsmen' also embraces grandparents and grandchildren.*

span /spæn/ [v T] if a book, film, plan etc **spans** a period of time, it goes from the beginning to the end of that time: *'Heimat' is a vivid social drama spanning sixty years in the life of one small village.* | *In a career spanning four decades, Brewster had many legal triumphs.*

3 included in a price

- include
- come with
- inclusive

include /ɪnˈkluːd/ [v T] if a price you pay for something **includes** something else, you do not have to pay more for that thing: *The price of the computer includes £500 worth of free software.* | *The toy has flashing lights and a siren noise, but batteries are not included.* | **be included in sth** *You don't have to pay for your flights – they're included in the price of your holiday.*

come with /ˈkʌm wɪð/ [phr v T] if something that you buy **comes with** another thing, the second thing is always included when you buy the first: *The luxury model comes with a matching metal carrying case.* | *Most new cars now come with a driver's airbag as standard.*

inclusive especially British ALSO **all-inclusive** especially American /ɪnˈkluːsɪv, ˌɔːl ɪnˈkluːsɪv◂/ [adj] an **inclusive** price or cost includes everything: *The inclusive cost of the car, complete with tax and insurance, is £9,800.* | **£50/$100 etc inclusive** *The cost of the flights, accommodation and car rental is two* *thousand dollars all-inclusive.* | *At a cost of $25 per person per night inclusive, bed and breakfast accommodation is fairly cheap.*

4 including someone or something

- including
- counting
- with
- inclusive
- included

including /ɪn'klu:dɪŋ/ [prep] *There'll be eighteen people at the party, including you and me.* | *Including weekends, there are only twelve more shopping days until Christmas.* | *Not including cassettes, he has eight thousand albums in his collection.*

counting /'kaʊntɪŋ/ [prep] especially spoken including: *Counting the one I've just bought, I now have three hundred different sets of playing cards.* | *Counting Singapore, where we stopped to refuel, we've visited eleven countries in three weeks.*

with /wɪð, wɪθ/ [prep] including a number or amount added to a final total, list etc: *With tax, the hotel bill came to four hundred dollars.* | *With Peter and his mother, there'll be six for lunch tomorrow.* | *'Our rooms cost $30 a night.' 'Is that with breakfast?'*

inclusive /ɪn'klu:sɪv/ [adj] **April to June inclusive/15 to 20 inclusive etc** including all dates, ages, numbers etc between the two mentioned: *The library will be closed from April to June inclusive.* | *Children aged 9 to 16 inclusive are welcome to enrol on the course.*

included /ɪn'klu:dɨd/ [adj] **myself/John/the Chairman etc included** including the person you have mentioned: *We're all going to the game, Betty included!* | *Everyone, the chairman included, eats in the staff restaurant.*

5 to deliberately include something or someone

- include
- work in/into
- incorporate

include /in'klu:d/ [v T] *Even if you include the cost of food, it's still a cheap vacation.* | *The team is looking strong, especially now that they have included Roscoe.* | **include sth in/on sth** *I have included two jazz numbers in my selection.* —**inclusion** /ɪn'klu:ʒən/ [n U] *Watson's inclusion in the US athletics team has caused much controversy.*

work in/into /ˌwɜ:ʳk ˌɪn, 'wɜ:ʳk ɪntu:/ [phr v T] informal if you **work something into** a plan, speech, product etc, you include it so that it becomes part of it **work in sth** *Do you think you can work in a reference to our project?* | **work sth into sth** *Boorman was once a director able to work his obsessions into movies like 'Point Blank' and 'Deliverance'.* | *the sort of facilities currently being worked into the latest software releases*

incorporate /ɪn'kɔ:ʳpəreɪt/ [v T] to deliberately include something so that it combines well with the other parts of the thing it is in: *We have incorporated a users' guide with the software.* | **incorporate sth in/into sth** *The architect has incorporated Egyptian and Renaissance themes in the building's design.*

6 to not include someone or something

- leave out
- exclude
- omit
- miss out
- drop

leave out /ˌli:v 'aʊt/ [phr v T] to not include someone or something, either deliberately or accidentally **leave sb/sth out of sth** *Fans were shocked that Giggs had been left out of the team.* | **leave out sb/sth** *He briefly told us what had happened, leaving out the more gruesome details.* | **leave sb/sth out** *I went through a list of people to be thanked, and hoped I hadn't left anyone out.*

exclude /ɪk'sklu:d/ [v T] formal to deliberately not include someone or something, especially in a way that seems wrong or unfair: *The new law protects most workers, but excludes those on part-time contracts.* | **exclude sb from sth** *She felt they were deliberately excluding her from their plans.*

omit /əʊ'mɪt, ə-/ [v T] formal to not include something, especially a piece of information, either deliberately or because you forget: *Please do not omit any details, however trivial they may seem.* | **omit sth from sth** *Sara's name had been omitted from the list of employees.*

miss out /ˌmɪs 'aʊt/ [phr v T] British to not include someone or something that should be included, often by mistake **miss out sb/sth** *You missed out several important facts.* | **miss sb/sth out** *Those are the people I'm inviting. Did I miss anyone out?*

drop /drɒp‖drɑ:p/ [v T] informal to suddenly remove something or someone from a list, plan etc, because there is a good reason for not including them: *I don't think this article will be of interest to our readers. Let's drop it.* | **drop sth from sth** *The coach just announced that Henri will be dropped from the team.*

7 when a number, total, or price does not include something

- exclusive of sth
- excepted

exclusive of sth /ɪk'sklu:sɪv əv (sth)/ [adv] not including something – used especially on official documents, advertisements etc: *The rent is £80 a week, exclusive of bills.* | *The fully fitted kitchen costs $5,000, exclusive of tax.*

excepted /ɪk'septɨd/ [adj only after noun] formal not including: *English excepted, Peter has made good progress in all his subjects this term.* | *Gardening excepted, she does very little in the way of good regular exercise.*

increase

RELATED WORDS

opposite: —— **less**

▸ *see also* **grow, more, big**

WHAT'S HERE

numbers or amounts increase

1 to increase

- increase
- go up/rise
- grow
- climb
- gain
- escalate
- pick up
- widen
- be on the increase
- intensify
- expand
- build up

increase /ɪn'kriːs/ [v I] to become larger in number, amount, price, value etc: *Gradually the noise and traffic increased as they approached the city.* | *Hormone levels increase throughout pregnancy.* | *The use of mobile phones has increased enormously over the past two years.* | *Revenue and profits have increased dramatically this year.* | **increase by 10%/$100/2 million etc** *The price of cigarettes has increased by 30% in the last two years.* | **+ to** (=to reach a total of $1000 etc) *Wind speeds are expected to increase to 60 mph.* | *The number of high school students using LSD has increased to its highest level since 1986.* | **increase from £300/1 million etc to £400/1.5 million etc** *Health care costs increased from £1.9 billion in 2000 to £4 billion in 2001.* | **increase in number/value etc** *Major league clubs have increased in number from 26 to 28.*

go up/rise /ˌgəʊ 'ʌp, raɪz/ [phr v I/v I] to increase – use this about numbers, prices, or temperatures etc, but also about the level or standard of something: *The price of petrol is going up again, for the third time this year.* | *The jobless rate hit 9.3% last month, after rising for four months in a row.* | *With more and more cars on the road, pollution levels are rising steadily.* | *You'll need about £10, if the rail fare's gone up again, which I expect it has.* | **go up/rise by 10%/$500 etc** (=become 10% etc greater) *Personal computer sales rose by 70% in the run-up to Christmas.* | **+ to** *By mid-day, the temperature had already risen to 40 degrees.* | **go up/rise from £300/1 million etc to £400/2 million etc** *The average price of a loaf of bread has gone up from 25p to 60p.*

grow /grəʊ/ [v I] to increase gradually over a period of time – use this about numbers or amounts, or about a total amount of business activity or trade: *China's economic output continues to grow at a remarkable annual rate.* | *Demand for new cars is growing rapidly.* | *The number of openly gay rock musicians has grown steadily in recent years, and shows no signs of abating.* | **grow by 10%/5000 etc** (=become 10% etc greater) *Profits in the military aircraft business grew by 28% to a record $905 million.* | **+ to** *The personnel team has grown to 6,700 full-time employees from just 900 in 2000.*

climb /klaɪm/ [v I] if the temperature, prices, profits etc **climb**, they increase until they reach a very high level: *Demand for goods grew and imports climbed steadily.* | **+ to** *The original estimate of $500 million has now climbed to a staggering $1300 million.* | *Temperatures are expected to climb to record levels this weekend.*

gain /geɪn/ [v T] if something or someone **gains** speed, weight, or height, their speed, weight, or height increases: *The train rolled forward, gaining speed rapidly.* | *A new-born baby will gain weight at around one ounce per day.* | *The four men told the inquiry they did not know why the plane failed to gain height after it took off.*

escalate /'eskəleɪt/ [v I] to increase to a high level – use this about things you do not want to increase such as prices, crimes etc: *Gas prices are expected to continue to escalate in the short term.* | *Staff saw costs escalating and sales slumping as the effect of the recession hit the company.* | **+ to** *The cost of the new building has escalated to a worrying level.* | **escalate sharply/dramatically** *The number of attacks on foreign aid workers has escalated dramatically.*

pick up /ˌpɪk 'ʌp/ [phr v I] if trade, business, or work **picks up**, the amount of it that is available increases after it has been at a level that is too low: *Their shop was losing money, but they carried on in the hope that business would pick up soon.* | *At present the hotel is almost empty, but I'm sure things will start to pick up in the spring.*

widen /'waɪdn/ [v I] if a difference between two amounts **widens**, or the range of things available **widens**, it increases: *The range of university courses available has widened tremendously in recent years.* | *The gap between the incomes of two-carer families and lone mothers with children has widened.*

be on the increase /biː ɒn ði 'ɪŋkriːs/ [v phrase] if something bad such as a problem or illness **is on the increase**, it is happening more and more frequently: *Juvenile crime is on the increase in most parts of the country.* | *Homelessness has been on the increase for a long time.* | **+ among** *What is particularly alarming is that bullying is on the increase among even very young primary children.*

intensify /ɪn'tensɪ̈faɪ/ [v I] if an effort or an activity such as fighting **intensifies**, it increases so that more people do it or the people already doing it use more effort: *The fighting intensified and spread through the city.* | *As the season intensifies, quarterback Young will need to work on his fitness.* | *The controversy is only expected to intensify.* —**intensification** /ɪnˌtensɪ̈fɪ̈'keɪʃən/ [n U] *The decades of the 1950s and 1960s saw an intensification of the Cold War.*

expand /ɪk'spænd/ [v I] if trade or a business activity **expands**, it increases: *Trade between developing countries and industrialized countries is beginning to expand.* | *The business was growing rapidly and beginning to expand abroad.* —**expansion** /ɪk'spænʃən/ [n U] *the continued expansion of the Chinese economy* | **economic expansion** *a period of rapid economic expansion*

build up /ˌbɪld 'ʌp/ [phr v I] if the number or amount of something **builds up**, it increases gradually so that there is much more than there was before: *Traffic is building up on the southern exit of the motorway.* | *A huge backlog of work had built up during my absence.*

2 when numbers or amounts are increasing

- increasing
- rising
- growing
- mounting
- escalating

increasing /ɪn'kriːsɪŋ/ [adj only before noun] *An increasing number of Australians see the link to the British monarchy as irrelevant.* | *An increasing percentage of American property owners are taking their houses off the market.* | **ever-increasing** (=increasing all the time) *Ever-increasing numbers of science teachers are leaving their jobs to work in industry.* | *Ever-increasing amounts of land were brought under cultivation.*

rising /ˈraɪzɪŋ/ [adj only before noun] increasing – use this about prices, numbers etc or about the level or standard of something: *Rising fuel costs have forced many airlines to put up the price of air tickets.* | *Le Shuttle competes with an ever-rising number of ferries for the busy Channel crossing.* | *the rising rate of smoking among teenagers* (=when problems increase and become more serious) *We are entering a period of slow economic growth and rising unemployment.*

growing /ˈgrəʊɪŋ/ [adj only before noun] gradually increasing: *An economic miracle is needed if Bangladesh is to feed its huge and growing population.* | *Zena is one of a small but rapidly growing number of motorists choosing to buy a car over the Web.* | *Garbage collection is a growth industry, thanks to growing volumes of garbage – up 2-3% a year.*

mounting /ˈmaʊntɪŋ/ [adj only before noun] a **mounting** price or number is increasing and causes problems: *He struggled on in the face of mounting debts,* | *What are the reasons for mounting unemployment in the Arab countries?* | *Another year of mounting losses proved too much for Pepperdine's basketball coach.*

escalating /ˈeskəleɪtɪŋ/ [adj only before noun] **escalating** prices, problems etc are increasing quickly and making a situation worse than it was before: *Investors in the Sports Stadium project are worried by escalating construction costs.* | *rapidly escalating house prices* | *Twenty percent of the workforce are experiencing escalating stress levels.*

3 to increase a lot

- multiply
- double
- triple
- quadruple
- proliferate
- snowball

multiply /ˈmʌltɪplaɪ/ [v I] to increase greatly in number: *Since they started borrowing money, their problems have multiplied.* | *The number of settlements multiplied enormously.* | *The insects multiply rapidly during hot, dry summers.*

double /ˈdʌbəl/ [v I] to become twice as much or twice as many: *Welfare spending will nearly double by the year 2002.* | **+ to** *The number of female bank managers doubled from 104 to 208.* | **double in size/value** *In those thirty years, San Francisco doubled in size.*

triple ALSO **treble** British /ˈtrɪpəl, ˈtrebəl/ [v I] to become three times as much or three times as many: *The number of senior citizens living in poverty has trebled in the last three years.* | *The party's majority in Congress tripled as a result of the election.* | **triple in size/value** *The shares have trebled in value since trading resumed on Wednesday.*

quadruple /ˈkwɒdrʊpəl, kwɒˈdruː-‖kwɑːˈdruː-/ [v I] to become four times as much or four times as many: *In ten years, homicide rates tripled and suicide rates quadrupled.* | **+ to** *By the end of 1973, the price of oil had quadrupled to $11.65 a gallon.*

proliferate /prəˈlɪfəreɪt/ [v I] formal if something **proliferates**, it increases very quickly, and becomes more common: *The HIV virus is able to proliferate at an astonishing rate.* | *Child pornography is proliferating due to the increased use of computer chat rooms.* —**proliferation** /prəˌlɪfəˈreɪʃən/ [n U] **+ of** *the rapid proliferation of on-line catalogues*

snowball /ˈsnəʊbɔːl/ [v I] to increase in number, at first slowly and then faster and faster: *Unemployment snowballed at the beginning of the 1980s.* | *Things hadn't exactly been going our way, but after the first defeat, everything sort of snowballed.*

4 to increase quickly or suddenly

- shoot up
- soar
- rocket
- go through the roof
- spiral
- take off

shoot up /ˌʃuːt ˈʌp/ [phr v I] if something such as a price, number, or temperature **shoots up**, it increases quickly and suddenly: *As long as mortgage rates do not shoot up, property should remain a good investment.* | **+ to** *US exports to Mexico have already shot up to 130% since 1985.* | *A year ago the magazine had a circulation of 150,000, but since then that figure has shot up to an astonishing 2 million.*

soar /sɔːʳ/ [v I] to increase quickly to a high level **+ into** *Temperatures soared into the nineties.* | *The cost of a business Website can soar into millions of dollars.* | **+ to** *Last year, the drugs haul soared to 130,00 tablets.* | *The death toll soars to 376 in Chicago from last week's heat wave.* | **soar by 40%/£300/1 million etc** *In the first year of peace, Lebanon's GDP soared by almost 40%.* —**soaring** [adj only before noun] *a plan to tackle soaring crime rates* | *Industrial growth has brought power cuts, clogged roads and soaring property prices.*

rocket ALSO **skyrocket** /ˈrɒkɪt‖ˈrɑː-, ˈskaɪˌrɒkɪt‖-ˌrɑː-/ [v I] if costs, prices, profits, sales etc **rocket**, they increase very quickly to a very high level: *Interest rates have skyrocketed as credit has become scarce.* | *Why has the dollar rocketed against the yen in particular?* | **+ to** *Gold prices rocketed to their highest level since 1983.* —**rocketing/skyrocketing** [adj only before noun] *the skyrocketing cost of land*

go through the roof /ˌgəʊ θruː ðə ˈruːf/ [v phrase] informal if prices **go through the roof**, they increase to an extremely high level: *Following news of increased profits, the company's share price went through the roof.* | *Sales of Ray-Ban sunglasses went through the roof after Tom Cruise wore them in 'Risky Business'.*

spiral /ˈspaɪərəl/ [v I] if a debt or the cost of something **spirals**, it increases very quickly and uncontrollably: *Since the project started five years ago, costs have spiralled.* | *With inflation spiralling out of control, the country was close to economic collapse.* —**spiralling** [adj only before noun] *The government has asked the World Bank for help with its spiralling national debt.*

take off /ˌteɪk ˈɒf/ [phr v I] if numbers or prices **take off**, they begin to increase quickly after a long period when they did not increase: *With the introduction of user-friendly software, home computer sales suddenly took off.* | *Internet shopping will really take off when people become convinced that it is secure.*

5 to increase by gradually adding more

- accumulate
- build up
- pile up
- mount up
- collect
- gather

accumulate /əˈkjuːmjʊleɪt/ [v I] to increase gradually in number or amount until there is a large quantity in one place: *An army of 1650 plows and 2000 workers will be out this afternoon as snow begins to accumulate.* | *Sand had accumulated at the mouth of the river and formed a bank which boats could not pass.* | *Over a period of years, the drug will accumulate in the body and damage the nervous system.*

build up /ˌbɪld ˈʌp/ [phr v I] if something such as a

substance or a force **builds up** somewhere, it increases gradually as more of it is added or more of it appears: *Deposits of lime will stick to the surface and build up over the years.* | *As the temperature rises, the pressure builds up inside the chamber.* | *Fertilizers can contain salts that build up in the soil.*

pile up /ˌpaɪl ˈʌp/ [phr v I] informal if something such as work or debt **piles up**, it increases as more is added to it until there is a large quantity of it: *The work just keeps on piling up and makes me want to scream.* | *As her debts piled up, she came close to a nervous breakdown.*

mount up /ˌmaʊnt ˈʌp/ [phr v I] if prices, costs, debts etc **mount up**, they increase as more is added over a period of time, and cause more and more problems: *She finally had to go back to work to pay the bills that were mounting up.* | *The national debt has mounted up, growing to $1 trillion since Clinton took office.*

collect /kəˈlekt/ [v I] if something such as a liquid **collects** somewhere, it goes to that place and the amount there gradually increases: *As the tide came in, water collected to form small pools among the rocks.* | **+ on/inside/behind etc** *Rain collecting at the tip of the rock has formed huge icicles.* | *If condensation collects on the inside of the window, wipe it off with a clean cloth.*

gather /ˈgæðəʳ/ [v I] if a substance such as dirt, snow etc **gathers** somewhere, more and more of it appears in that place and stays there: *There were gaps between the floorboards where dust and bits of grime had gathered.* | **+ on/around/behind etc** *Snow gathered thickly in the folds of their clothes.* | *Harry was afraid. Sweat gathered on his upper lip.*

6 to make a number or amount increase

- increase
- raise
- put up
- jack up
- push up/drive up/force up
- boost
- double/triple/quadruple
- maximize

increase /ɪnˈkriːs/ [v T] *High alcohol consumption increases the risk of liver disease.* | *The Clean Air Act would increase the cost of electric power in the Midwest.* | *The party aims to increase the number of women elected to Congress.* | *We reduced the size of the magazine because we didn't want to increase the price.* | **increase sth to** *The company has increased its workforce to 1,500 employees* | **increase sth by 20%/$400/1 million etc** *a program to increase output by 14%*

raise /reɪz/ [v T] if someone raises **raises** a tax, price, temperature etc, they increase it: *The president should take the necessary steps of raising taxes and cutting public spending.* | *All the major airlines have raised their fares.* | **raise sth to $300/40C/200 etc** *The retirement age has been raised to 65 for both men and women.*

put up /ˌpʊt ˈʌp/ [phr v T] informal if someone **puts up** the cost or price of something, they increase it **put up sth** *They've put up the price of petrol again.* | **put sth up** *A solicitor can advise whether the landlord has a right to put the rent up.* | *This used to be quite a cheap restaurant but they've put their prices up since the last time I came here.*

jack up /ˌdʒæk ˈʌp/ [phr v T] informal to increase prices or amounts by a large amount, especially when this seems unreasonable **jack sth up** *I guess they must jack the price up in the summer, then mark it down in the winter.* | **jack up sth** *a proposal that would have jacked up taxi fares by as much as 30%*

push up/drive up/force up /ˌpʊʃ ˈʌp, ˌdraɪv ˈʌp, ˌfɔːʳs ˈʌp/ [phr v T] to make something increase – use this about things you would prefer to keep low, such as costs and prices **push/drive/force up sth** *An expansion of the weapons research program is sure to drive up defence costs.* | *In recent years, increased demand has forced up the price of copper on world markets.* | **push/ force/drive sth up** *Office vacancy rates have reached a low, pushing rents up sharply for office and industrial space.*

boost /buːst/ [v T] to increase something such as production, sales, or wages because they are not as high as you want them to be: *The plan was meant to boost agricultural production.* | *The multi-million dollar ad campaign has failed to boost sales.* | *Greater consumer access to the Internet has boosted electronic retailing.*

double/triple/quadruple /ˈdʌbəl, ˈtrɪpəl, ˈkwɒdrʊpəl, kwɒˈdruː-‖kwɑːˈdruː-/ [v T] to increase a number or amount by two, three, or four times: *The company has quadrupled Sonia's salary in just three years in recognition of her achievements.* | *The government doubled the sales tax on cigarettes from 20% to 40%.*

maximize ALSO **maximise** British /ˈmæksɪmaɪz/ [v T] to make something such as profit, power, or productivity increase to the highest level that you can achieve: *The bank's function is to maximize profits, and that requires some risk-taking.* | *To maximise power output, solar panels are placed on the highest part of the building.*

7 to increase by adding another number or amount

- add to
- augment
- put 10p/20p etc on

▸ *see also* **add**

add to /ˈæd tuː/ [v phrase] if a change to something, especially an improvement, **adds to** its cost, price, value, or amount, it causes the cost, price, value, or amount to increase: *Gardens that have been substantially improved will add to the value of your property.* | *New high-quality printing technology added $1,000 to the retail price of the computer.* | *The diversion added another hour to our journey.*

augment /ɔːgˈment/ [v T] formal to increase and improve the strength, value, effectiveness etc of something: *The cream contains ingredients that augment the skin's natural healing processes.* | *We pay performance bonuses that augment your annual salary.*

put 10p/20p etc on /ˌpʊt ten ˈpiː ɒn/ [phr v T] British if something such as a new tax or increased production cost **puts 10p/20p etc on** the price of something, it causes the price to increase by that much: *The new tax puts 20 pence on the price of a pack of cigarettes.* | *The increased cost of imported wheat will put 5p on the price of a loaf of bread.*

8 to increase the amount of something you do

- increase
- step up
- expand
- broaden
- extend
- intensify

increase /ɪnˈkriːs/ [v T] *We must increase public awareness of the health risks associated with sun-*

bathing. | *The government is increasing pressure on drug-traffickers.* | *The imposition of martial law will only increase violence and repression.*

step up /ˌstep ˈʌp/ [phr v T] to increase your efforts or activities, especially in order to improve a situation that is not as good as you want it to be **step up sth** *The US government stepped up its war against terrorism.* | *The police presence is to be stepped up at this year's carnival.* | **step it up** (=make a greater effort to achieve something) *It's good we were able to step it up at the end of the game.*

expand /ɪkˈspænd/ [v T] to increase something so that it covers a wider area or range of activities: *Dr. Martin also helped expand housing opportunities for people with AIDs.* | *The agency hopes to expand coverage of new musical talent on its Internet site.* | **expand sth to sth** *They fund programs that expand health benefits to wider segments of the community.*

broaden /ˈbrɔːdn/ [v T] to increase something such as knowledge, experience, or your range of activities: *At Missouri, Wright broadened his experience by working on a local newspaper.* | *The library is installing new technology to broaden access to its huge store of information.* | *The company has broadened its product range in the US.*

extend /ɪkˈstend/ [v T] to increase something such as your influence or control over something: *The US government is still trying to extend its influence over European politics.* | *We can extend our effectiveness enormously by the use of up-to-date technology.* | *Time Warner recently extended its reach to the world's biggest music business.*

intensify /ɪnˈtensəfaɪ/ [v T] to increase activities or efforts, especially against an enemy or someone who opposes you: *In the run-up to the election, terrorists have intensified their activities.* | *China is intensifying efforts to fight crime.* | *We have no choice but to intensify the strike campaign.* | *The latest merger will intensify competition among defense companies.* —**intensification** /ɪnˌtensəfɪˈkeɪʃən/ [n U] **+ of** *The statement signals an intensification of the bloody feud between opposing guerrilla factions.*

9 to turn or push a button to increase something

- turn up

turn up /ˌtɜːʳn ˈʌp/ [phr v T] **turn up the radio/television/heat etc** to increase the amount of sound coming out of a radio, television etc or the amount of heat coming from a heater, by turning or pushing a button **turn sth up** *Hey, turn this up for a second, I like this song.* | *Would you mind turning the heat up?* | **turn up sth** *We hooked up my stereo and turned up the volume as loud as it would go.* | *Is the sound turned up too loud for you?*

10 an increase in a number or amount

- increase
- growth
- rise
- build-up
- upturn

increase /ˈɪŋkriːs/ [n C] **+ in** *There will be no increase in student enrolments this year.* | *an increase in consumer spending* | **increase of 10/20/50% etc** *There was an increase of about 17% in the urban population between 1910 and 1920.* | **a 10%/12% etc increase** *Improved airline service led to an 18.7% increase in tourists to Africa last year.*

growth /grəʊθ/ [n U] an increase in amount, quantity, population etc **economic/population etc growth** *There is a great deal of uncertainty about the world's population growth.* | *favorable signs of economic growth* | *DIY outlets reported sales growth of 1.8%.* | **+ in** *The US portion of the Internet is experiencing rapid growth in the number of networks connected to it.* | **+ of** *the astonishing growth of on-line trading*

rise /raɪz/ [n singular] especially British an increase in numbers, level, population, or temperature **+ in** *The committee will investigate the rise in the number of hospital admissions.* | *This year a disappointingly small rise in pass rates.* | **+ of** *Global warming is responsible for a rise of 7 degrees Celsius in just over 50 years.*

build-up /ˈbɪld ʌp/ [n singular] a gradual increase in something harmful or bad: *This could signal the biggest military build-up since the Cold War.* | **+ of** *The changing world climate is probably due to a build-up of harmful gases such as carbon dioxide.*

upturn /ˈʌptɜːʳn/ [n singular] an increase in the amount of trade done by a country, company etc after a period of time when it was not increasing: *Only in the last two years have we seen signs of an economic upturn.* | **+ in** *The upturn in aviation traffic will help lift demand for commercial aircraft.*

11 an increase in an amount of money

- increase
- gain
- rise
- rise/raise
- hike
- increment

increase /ˈɪŋkriːs/ [n C] **tax/fare/price etc increase** *There could be fare increases of up to 10%.* | *A spokesman for the airline said that much of the cost increase was caused by tightening of security.* | **+ in** *a 12% increase in phone charges* | **a 50%/30% etc increase** *a 50% increase in the city's health budget*

gain /geɪn/ [n C] an increase in an amount of money, that brings an advantage to someone: *The share price ended the year with a 60% gain.* | **+ in** *The morning's gains in US stocks fell sharply.* | **+ of** *The Nikkei average experienced a gain of 140.19 points on Friday.*

rise /raɪz/ [n C] especially British an increase in costs, prices, taxes, or rent **rent/price/tax etc rise** *Tenants face a 60% rent rise.* | *The prime minister is considering substantial tax rises.* | **+ in** *The pension will increase in line with the rise in prices.*

rise British **/raise** American /raɪz, reɪz/ [n C usually singular] an increase in the amount of money you are paid for your work: *He received loud applause when he told the crowd that low wage-earners deserve a raise.* | *IT specialists rang up an average pay rise of 312% last year.* | **give sb a rise** *The State Government simply can't afford to give all teachers a raise.*

hike /haɪk/ [n C] a sudden increase in something such as prices, wages, or taxes: *Big gasoline hikes are expected in April.* | **tax/price/wage etc hike** *Pilots will get an 11% pay hike over four years.* | *Opponents argued the sales-tax hike was unfair.* | **+ in** *Trade Unions are proposing a hike in the minimum wage.*

increment /ˈɪŋkrəmənt/ [n C] formal an amount that is added regularly to someone's pay every year, every six months etc: *The contract includes a salary increment every six months.* | *Automatic pay increments based on length of service will be abolished.*

12 a sudden large increase

- leap
- explosion
- boom
- surge

leap /liːp/ [n C] a sudden large increase in the amount or number of something – use this especially about business costs, prices, activities etc: *Coffee and orange juice prices made their biggest leaps on Friday.* | **+ in** *Borrowers have been warned to expect another leap in bank interest rates.* | *Gold shares gained following a leap in the price of gold.* | **by leaps and bounds** (=use this to emphasize how quickly something is increasing) *I can see the Internet business growing by leaps and bounds.* —**leap** [v I] *Shares leapt about 5% to $32.375.*

explosion /ɪk'spləʊʒən/ [n C usually singular] a very sudden and very large increase in population, in an activity, or in the numbers of something: *We live in the century of population explosion, with the world's population doubling at least every 25 years.* | *These people are full of hope. An economic explosion is underway in their country.* | **+ of** *The company cannot meet demand, and has seen an explosion of customer complaints.* | *No-one can say where the amazing explosion of digital services will take us.* | **+ in** *Officials insist the case is unrelated to the explosion in homicide rates among teenagers.*

boom /buːm/ [n singular] a sudden large increase in something such as trade, economic success, or a particular area of activity: *The IT market is growing, thanks to the Internet boom.* | **+ in** *the boom in cellular phone ownership* | *a record-breaking boom in tourism* | **economic boom** (=a period of economic and financial success) *Canada enjoyed a real economic boom in the postwar years.* | **property/productivity spending etc boom** *Motorola is one of the leaders in the global technology boom.* | *The impact of the property boom was first felt in the financial markets.* | **baby boom** (=a period of time when many more babies are born) *A more pressing problem is Mexico's dramatic baby boom.* —**boom** [v I] *Cellnet has 800,000 subscribers, and business is booming.* | *Tourism boomed here in the late 1990s.*

surge /sɜːʳdʒ/ [n C] a sudden increase in something such as demand, profit, interest etc **+ in** *Last year there was a surge in the company's profits to $122m.* | *a 31% surge in divorce rates* | *Stores are expecting a surge in demand as Christmas approaches.* | *Her books enjoyed a huge surge in popularity in the mid-1980s.* | **+ of** *The unexpected surge of voters to the polls has surprised even opposition parties.* —**surge** [v T] *Orders from customers in the Far East have surged.* | **+ to** *By 2006, the liver transplant figure is likely to surge to at least 4.3 million.*

feelings increase

RELATED WORDS

see also **feel**

13 when a feeling becomes stronger

- grow
- increase
- intensify
- build up
- deepen
- mount

grow /grəʊ/ [v I] if a feeling **grows** it gradually becomes stronger: *Her confidence grew, and soon she was able to go out driving on her own.* | *The more I studied, the more my anxiety about the exam grew.* | *Fears are growing for the safety of the missing children.*

increase /ɪn'kriːs/ [v I] to become stronger – use this especially about a feeling that a lot of people have: *The excitement is increasing inside the stadium as we wait for the teams to come out onto the field.* | *The President's popularity has increased enormously in recent months.* —**increased** [adj only before noun] *Since going on the program, her 4-year-old son has shown an increased willingness to eat properly.*

intensify /ɪn'tensɪ̇faɪ/ [v I] written if a bad or unpleasant feeling such as fear or pain **intensifies**, it increases: *Their panic intensified, as they heard the gunshots getting closer.* | *The dizzy feeling in her head intensified, and she knew she was about to black out.* | *Throughout the 1920s and 1930s, racism and bigotry intensified.*

build up /ˌbɪld 'ʌp/ [phr v I] if a bad feeling such as anger **builds up**, it gradually increases until you feel you have to do something: *The pressure built up over the year, and eventually I had to leave my job.* | *I could feel the anger building up inside me.*

deepen /'diːpən/ [v I] if a strong feeling such as love, respect, or sadness **deepens**, it increases gradually: *With every new day, her despair only seemed to deepen.* | *As she watched the nuns working among the sick and dying, her respect for them deepened.* —**deepening** [adj] *Liza's deepening depression put a strain on the whole family.*

mount /maʊnt/ [v I] if a feeling, especially of worry or activity **mounts**, it becomes stronger: *As the dispute continues, tension is mounting on the border between the two countries.* | *Anxiety about job security mounted at the plant after profits fell by 68%.*

14 to make feelings become stronger

- increase
- strengthen
- heighten
- add to
- raise
- fuel

increase /ɪn'kriːs/ [v T] *Vague explanations of her illness only increased her fear and anxiety.* | *Some analysts say the new law could increase expectations of an economic recovery.* | *The cut in interest rates will help to increase confidence in the housing market.*

strengthen /'streŋθən, 'strenθən/ [v T] to make something such as someone's determination or belief increase so that it is even stronger than it was before: *The quarrel only served to strengthen my resolve to start out on my own.* | *A poor harvest in 1842, and the imminence of winter, strengthened their determination.* | *Woolley felt certain that he had made an important discovery and his conviction was strengthened as more evidence came to light.*

heighten /'haɪtn/ [v T] if something **heightens** knowledge, fears, the effect of something etc, it makes it increase so that it is felt more strongly: *Publicity has heightened awareness of the threats to the environment.* | *The divorce heightened speculation about a possible second marriage.* | *Fears of an invasion were heightened by long-range bomb attacks.*

add to /'æd tuː/ [phr v T] to increase a feeling or problem, so that it becomes worse: *I didn't want to add to the confusion, so I stayed quiet.* | *Adding to the burden are the continuing costs of German reunification.* | *Natural catastrophes like droughts have also added to the problems of the continent.* | **add insult to injury** informal (=to make a bad situation that you have caused much worse than it was before) *She runs off with another man, and to add insult to injury demands huge sums in alimony.*

raise /reɪz/ [v T] if something raises people's hopes, consciousness etc, it makes them more hopeful, conscious etc: *It's the first school in Scotland to become self-governing, and has raised deep concerns in the local community.* | *The human rights campaign has raised public awareness of the torture going on in the country.*

fuel /fjʊəl‖'fju:əl/ [v T] to make feelings of doubt, worry, hope etc grow stronger: *The President's absence from the May Day parade has fuelled speculation that he is seriously ill.* | *There are growing fears for the safety of the kidnap victims – fears that have been fuelled by rumours of new terrorist threats.*

15 becoming stronger

- increasing
- growing
- mounting

increasing /ɪn'kri:sɪŋ/ [adj only before noun] *She clenched her teeth against the steadily increasing pain.* | *The growth of extremist right-wing groups is an increasing concern.* | *Whatever you think of the fashion for 'boy bands', there's no denying their increasing popularity.*

growing /'grəʊɪŋ/ [adj only before noun] gradually increasing to a high level: *He spoke of his daughter's growing alienation from the Church.* | *There is growing opposition to the new tax proposals.* | *The incident added to growing concern about the extent of terrorist influence in the region.*

mounting /'maʊntɪŋ/ [adj only before noun] increasing to such a high level that something is likely to happen or be done: *There are reports of mounting violence in the village tribes.* | *The decision has been the cause of mounting tension in the capital.* | *Amid mounting excitement, an official came forward to announce the result of the election.*

16 an increase in the strength of feelings

- increase
- build-up
- surge

increase /'ɪŋkri:s/ [n C] **+ in** *There has been a marked increase in opposition to military action.* | *What is the reason for the increase in gang hostility in small towns?*

build-up /'bɪld ʌp/ [n C usually singular] a gradual increase in a particular feeling, especially a negative one **+ of** *The players always feel a huge build-up of tension and nerves before an important game.* | *Deal with any problems when necessary, so preventing a build-up of strain.*

surge /sɜːʳdʒ/ [n singular] a sudden and large increase in a feeling **+ of** *Sophie felt a surge of anger, but with an effort she suppressed it.* | *A surge of elation rushed through his body as he read the note for the third time.* | *There has been a tremendous surge of interest in Chinese medicine.*

independent

WHAT'S HERE

- **independent person** see **1 to 6**
- **independent country or organization** see **7 to 8**

independent person

RELATED WORDS

- *see also* **alone, need**

1 able to make your own decisions or do things by yourself

- independent
- self-reliant
- self-sufficient

independent /ˌɪndə̇'pendənt◂/ [adj] able to make your own decisions, organize your own life, and do things in your own way, without wanting help or advice from other people: *I quite like living alone. It's made me more independent.* | *I've always been attracted to strong, independent women.* | *Joe's still not very independent, and he tends to follow me around.* | **independent of sb** (=not dependent on them) *I suddenly realised that my precious son was a full-grown man, quite independent of his father and me.*

self-reliant /ˌself rɪ'laɪənt◂/ [adj] able to do things for yourself and solve problems by yourself, and able to live without depending on anyone else: *My parents raised me to be self-reliant, and not to depend on anyone.*

self-sufficient /ˌself sə'fɪʃənt◂/ [adj] able to live happily on your own, without needing a lot of friends or spending a lot of time with other people: *We grew up in a close-knit, self-sufficient family with few outside friends.* | *His father died when he was seven, and consequently Joe learned to be self-sufficient from an early age.*

2 not needing money, food etc from other people

- independent
- self-sufficient

independent /ˌɪndə̇'pendənt◂/ [adj] having your own money and not needing financial help from other people: *My mom was in fact quite independent. She had always had a job and her own bank account.* | *Changes in the rural economy turned many independent farmers to hired labourers.* | **financially independent** *Dad left me all his money when he died, which made me financially independent.*

self-sufficient /ˌself sə'fɪʃənt◂/ [adj] producing all the food and goods that you need, and not having to buy it from other people: *The Amish belong to a self-sufficient community that has existed for over 200 years.* | **+ in** *Britain used to be fully self-sufficient in coal.*

3 to live in an independent way

- be independent/lead an independent life
- take care of yourself
- stand on your own two feet
- go it alone
- do your own thing
- fend for yourself

be independent/lead an independent life /biː ˌɪndɪ̆ˈpendənt, liːd ən ˌɪndɪ̆pendənt ˈlaɪf/ [v phrase] to live in an independent way, without other people helping you or telling you what to do: *Alice was glad to be independent and making a life of her own at last.* | *What strategies does a growing child use to become independent?* | *Our main objective is to help disabled people lead independent lives within the community.*

take care of yourself ALSO **look after yourself** /teɪk ˌkeər əv jɔːʳˈself, lʊk ˌɑːftəʳ jɔːʳˈself‖-ˌæf-/ [v phrase] especially British to cook your own food, wash your own clothes, and do other basic things that are necessary to live: *Grandpa can't take care of himself any more so he's coming to live with us.* | *Many youngsters who've been brought up in care are often incapable of looking after themselves when they leave.*

stand on your own two feet /ˌstænd ɒn jɔːr ˌəʊn tuː ˈfiːt/ [v phrase] informal to live your life independently without any help from your family or the government: *She'll never learn to stand on her own feet if you keep giving her whatever she wants.* | *A year abroad gives students the chance to stand on their own two feet.*

go it alone /ˌgəʊ ɪt əˈləʊn/ [v phrase] informal to start working or living on your own, especially after working or living with other people in a family, organization etc: *The response to our proposal was lukewarm, so we felt we had to go it alone.* | *After years of working for a big company, she decided to go it alone and set up her own business.* | *When it comes to parenthood, more and more women are deciding to go it alone.*

do your own thing /ˌduː jɔːr əʊn ˈθɪŋ/ [v phrase] spoken to live in an independent way and do what you want to do, without being influenced by what other people think: *He has a couple of roommates but they kind of all do their own thing.* | *He's given up his job and is living in northern California, just doing his own thing.*

fend for yourself /ˌfend fəʳ jɔːʳˈself/ [v phrase] written to look after yourself, when you are used to being taken care of by someone else, or when being independent is very difficult: *The mother died before the cubs were old enough to fend for themselves.* | *Dad always wanted me to be able to fend for myself from a very early age.* | *The children were left to fend for themselves on the streets.*

4 by yourself without help or advice

- on your own/by yourself
- independently
- on your own initiative
- under your own steam

on your own/by yourself /ɒn jɔːr ˈəʊn, baɪ jɔːʳˈself/ [adv] *Bringing up a child on your own is hard work.* | *We can't have Jamie walk to school by himself.* | *You're not walking home at night on your own.* | *I didn't want to make a decision about it by myself, so I called Judy.* | **all on your own/all by yourself** (=use this to emphasize that someone does something on their own) *He went to China all on his own.* | *Did you do that all by yourself then?*

independently /ˌɪndɪ̆ˈpendəntli/ [adv] if you work or make decisions **independently**, you do not need help and advice from other people: *With a few exceptions, the students work well independently.* | *Margaret wanted to live independently, but would she ever manage it?* | *Once my child is writing independently, how can I help her become a more skillful speller?*

on your own initiative /ɒn jɔːr ˌəʊn ɪˈnɪʃətɪv/ [adv] using your own ideas about what needs to be done, instead of waiting for someone in authority to tell you what to do: *She was always happy to work on her own initiative, and set her own goals and deadlines.* | *When he was only fourteen, he wrote, on his own initiative, to every airline, asking to join the company.* | *We think the bomb was placed by an extremist, acting on his own initiative.*

under your own steam /ˌʌndəʳ jɔːr ˌəʊn ˈstiːm/ [adv] if you go somewhere **under your own steam**, you go there without help from anyone else: *Can you manage to get up to the house under your own steam while I bring up the food?* | *I never thought Sal and Thomas would make it here under their own steam!*

5 to be independent in the way you think

- think for yourself
- have a mind of your own
- know your own mind
- be your own man/woman

think for yourself /ˌθɪŋk fəʳ jɔːʳˈself/ [v phrase usually in infinitive or progressive] to make decisions or form opinions without expecting other people to help or approve of you: *Parents should encourage their children to think for themselves.* | *The purpose of this question is to force students to think for themselves.* | *'You're going to have to start thinking for yourself,' said David sternly.*

have a mind of your own /hæv ə ˌmaɪnd əv jɔːr ˈəʊn/ [v phrase not in progressive] to have a strong character and strong opinions that are not influenced by other people's: *She's a woman with a mind of her own, who says what she thinks.* | *But Mansell has a mind of his own, and he was adamant he would make racing his career.*

know your own mind /ˌnəʊ jɔːr əʊn ˈmaɪnd/ [v phrase not in progressive] to have a strong character and be confident about what you want to do: *Though not yet 15, Sara knows her own mind, and has already decided on a career.* | *I'm in my mid-thirties and ought to know my own mind by now, but I'm scared of getting married.*

be your own man/woman /biː jɔːr ˌəʊn ˈmæn, ˈwʊmən/ [v phrase] to be confident of your opinions, without letting other people influence you – use this when you approve of someone like this: *Stan was intellectual, confident and above all, his own man.* | *She didn't want to quarrel with him, but made it plain that she was her own woman now, with her own life to lead.* | *Sheila is very much her own woman. She'll listen to everyone and then make up her mind for herself.*

6 when you are independent

- independence
- self-sufficiency
- self-reliance

independence /ˌɪndɪ̆ˈpendəns/ [n U] *He was des-*

perate to get a job and regain his independence. | *Roz said she'd never marry because she valued her independence too much.* | *Though they want to exert their independence, these kids are not quite ready for it.* | *Your first pay cheque gives you a terrific sense of independence.* | **gain/win/achieve etc independence** *She no longer had that feeling of independence she had fought so hard to win.* | **financial/economic independence** *She worked hard to gain financial independence.*

self-sufficiency /ˌself səˈfɪʃənsi/ [n U] when you are independent, either because you can live happily without needing a lot of friends, or because you do not need to buy food or other products from other places: *I admired his air of self-sufficiency.* | *He promised to do more to help welfare recipients achieve self-sufficiency.* | *The Administration of Native Americans (ANA) promotes the goal of social and economic self-sufficiency for Indian tribes.*

self-reliance /ˌself rɪˈlaɪəns/ [n U] when you are independent, because you can solve your own problems and are able to do things by yourself, and do not need the help or support of anyone else: *The older children are beginning to develop self-reliance.* | *Both men display the fiery self-reliance that natives of Oregon tend to possess.*

independent country or organization

RELATED WORDS

▸ *see also* **country, government, control**

7 not controlled by or depending on another country or organization

- independent
- independence
- sovereign
- autonomous
- self-governing
- self-sufficient

independent /ˌɪndəˈpendənt◂/ [adj] *We must encourage independent governments, not economic satellites.* | **+ from** *The country became independent from France in 1964.* | *The country has three major network television stations, plus one independent station.* —**independently** [adv] *an independently run newspaper*

independence /ˌɪndəˈpendəns/ [n U] political freedom from control by the government of another country: *the American war of independence* | *the Vietnamese struggle for independence* | *There is a move to increase the independence of the judiciary.* | **+ from** *Gradually schools gained a certain amount of independence from the Church.* | **grant independence (to sb)** *The British granted independence to Ceylon in 1948.*

sovereign /ˈsɒvrən‖ˈsɑːv-/ [adj only before noun] not controlled by any other country – used especially in an official or political contexts: *It was a number of years before Canada was accepted by the world as a sovereign state.* | *The Hopi tribe asserted their rights as a sovereign nation.* | **sovereign rights/power/status** *We fully recognize France's sovereign power in that area.* —**sovereignty** [n U] *Britain was concerned that its sovereignty and cultural identity would be harmed by the treaty.*

autonomous /ɔːˈtɒnəməs‖ɔːˈtɑː-/ [adj] part of a country or organization that is **autonomous** is partly independent and has the right to organize most of its own activities, business etc: *Andorra is autonomous, with its external affairs managed by both France and Spain.* | *The councils, which are locally autonomous, act as courts for the whole area.* —**autonomously** [adv] *Local radio stations are supported by national radio, but operate autonomously.* —**autonomy** [n U] *There is a lot of popular support for some form of autonomy in the Basque area of France and Spain.*

self-governing /self ˈgʌvəʳnɪŋ/ [adj] a part of a country or organization that is **self-governing** is controlled by the people who live or work there, as opposed to the larger country or organization that it belongs to: *The farmers are members of a small self-governing co-operative group.* | *The Orthodox Church is composed of 23 self-governing churches.* | *Many of the larger communities felt they would be better off if they were self-governing.*

self-sufficient /ˌself səˈfɪʃənt◂/ [adj] a country or part of a country that is **self-sufficient** produces all the food and other products that it needs: *The new technologies have made India agriculturally self-sufficient.* | *Many areas of the world still have self-sufficient rural economies.* | **+ in** *France was self-sufficient in cereals, and exported its surplus.*

8 to no longer be controlled by another country

- become independent
- gain/win/get independence

become independent /bɪˌkʌm ɪndəˈpendənt/ [v phrase] *The Republic of Namibia became independent on 21 March 1990, ending 74 years of South African rule.* | **+ from** *The Solomon Islands became independent from Britain about 15 years ago.*

gain/win/get independence /ˌgeɪn, ˌwɪn, ˌget ɪndəˈpendəns/ [v phrase] to become independent after a war or a long struggle: *Political unity was the surest way to achieve independence.* | **+ from** *Since gaining independence from Britain in 1961, Sierra Leone has been attempting to unify and modernize the country.*

information

RELATED WORDS

▸ *see also* **know/not know, detail, find out, summarize, spread (2)**

1 information

- information
- fact
- details
- info
- material
- data

information /ˌɪnfəʳˈmeɪʃən/ [n U] facts or details about a situation, event, person, place etc: *We need more information before we make a decision.* | **+ about/on** *The book contains information on how to find a job abroad.* | *I'm looking for some information about breast cancer research.* | **give/provide information** *The tourist office will be able to give you the information you need.* | *The Web site provides the latest information on Medicare and Medicaid.* | **further information** written (=more information) *For further information, please write to the following address.* | **piece of information** *Ray just told me an interesting piece of information.* | **detailed information** (=containing a lot of facts) *The guidebook has detailed information about the hotels in the area.*

fact /fækt/ [n C usually plural] a piece of information that can be proved to be true: *I'm not interested in your opinions – I just want to know the facts.* | **+ about** *It's important that young people learn the facts about drugs.* | *The book is full of interesting facts about plant life.* | **+ that** *He's never tried to hide the fact that he spent time in jail.*

details /ˈdiːteɪlz‖dɪˈteɪlz/ [n plural] all the smaller pieces of information that you need to know about something that you already know about in a general way: *There's a big jazz festival in May. I'll give you the details if you want.* | **+ of/about** *The details of specific cases cannot be made public.* | *The doctor asked me for details about my eating and exercise habits.* | **provide/give details** *He said the meeting was next month, but he didn't give any specific details.* | **further details** written (=more details) *For further details, contact the conference organizer.* | **full details** (=all the details) *Full details about the company's plans will be announced in several months.*

info /ˈɪnfəʊ/ [n U] especially spoken information: *Sandra will give you all the info you need.* | **+ on/about** *For more info on the show, call this number.* | *The dinosaur exhibit is pretty neat with lots of info about each period.*

material /məˈtɪəriəl/ [n U] information that is used when you write a story, article, speech etc: *There wasn't enough material to write a whole book.* | *I've been unable to find any reference material on the subject of interracial adoptions.* | *The stories he collected became material for the biography he is now writing.*

data /ˈdeɪtə, ˈdɑːtə/ [n U] facts, numbers, and other information that have been collected and stored, especially on a computer: *This computer can store as much data as many larger models.* | *He has to trawl through vast amounts of economic data.* | **+ on/about** *The spacecraft has sent back new data about Jupiter's atmosphere.*

2 a collection of information

- file
- database
- record

file /faɪl/ [n C] a collection of information, about a person, subject etc that is kept by an organization such as a school, a company, or the police: *Only a few people are allowed to see these files.* | **+ on** *Could you bring me the file on the West murder, please?* | **keep a file on sb/sth** *The FBI keeps files on all suspected terrorists.* | **keep sth on file** (=store it in a file) *We keep copies of all applications on file.*

record /ˈrekɔːd‖-ərd/ [n C usually plural] information that is collected gradually over a long period of time, so that it can be looked at when necessary: *Our records are continually updated.* | **medical/personnel/criminal etc record** *According to your medical records, you had an operation five years ago.* | *I've checked the student records, and I can't find any mention of her name.* | **+ of** *The records of births, marriages, and deaths were all destroyed in the fire.* | **keep a record** (=write down details of things as they happen) *Keep a record of all your expenses during the trip.*

database /ˈdeɪtəˌbeɪs/ [n C] a very large collection of information kept on a computer: *We can check the database to see whether the book is in stock.* | **+ of** *The company has a database of over 23,000 hotels that allow pets.*

3 to write down information

- write down
- record

▸ *see also* **record, write**

write down /ˌraɪt ˈdaʊn/ [phr v T] **write sth down** *If I don't write his phone number down now, I'll forget it.* | **write down sth** *Make a chart and write down the results of the experiment.* | *He wrote down all the prices in a little notebook.*

record /rɪˈkɔːʳd/ [v T] to write down information or store it on a computer, so that it can be looked at later, especially official information about numbers or amounts: *Only 13 cases of this disease have ever been recorded.* | *The meteorological office recorded the lowest rainfall in 10 years.*

4 providing a lot of information

- informative
- enlightening

informative /ɪnˈfɔːʳmətɪv/ [adj] providing a lot of new or useful information: *The lecture was very informative and helpful.* | *Jim found the library staff friendly and informative.* | *The informative newsletter is published once every two months.*

enlightening /ɪnˈlaɪtənɪŋ/ [adj] formal providing a lot of new or useful information: *The President described his conversation with the Russian leader as enlightening.* | *She has given us some truly enlightening insights into the subject of personality disorders.*

in general

RELATED WORDS

▸ *see also* **most, usually, summarize**

1 when something is true about most situations, people, or events

- in general/generally/in most cases
- generally speaking/as a rule
- mostly
- most of the time
- on the whole/by and large
- for the most part
- tend

in general/generally/in most cases /ɪn ˈdʒenərəl, ˈdʒenərəli, ɪn ˈməʊst ˌkeɪsɪ̈z/ [adv] use this to say that something is usually true: *Women generally live longer than men.* | *In general, jobs for temporary workers are low-paid.* | *In general, students who get regular exercise do better in school.* | *Inner-city schools generally achieved lower exam grades than other schools.* | *Car theft is an increasingly common crime, and in most cases the offender is under 18.*

generally speaking/as a rule /ˌdʒenərəli ˈspiːkɪŋ, əz ə ˈruːl/ [adv] especially spoken use this to introduce a statement about what usually happens or is true: *Generally speaking, bright colors make people feel happier.* | *As a rule, French wines are more expensive than those from Eastern Europe.*

mostly /ˈməʊstli/ [adv] use this to say that something is true about most people, things, or occasions: *I drink sugar-free colas, mostly.* | *The students here are mostly Swiss and German, but sometimes we get a few Japanese, too.* | *He mostly writes novels, but he's published a book of poetry too.*

most of the time /ˈməʊst əv ðə ˌtaɪm/ [adv] especially spoken use this to say that something usually happens: *Our two-year-old is happy most of the time, but he wakes up from his naps in an awful mood.* | *Most of the time people vote for the party that offers them financial advantages.*

on the whole/by and large /ɒn ðə ˈhəʊl, ˌbaɪ ənd ˈlɑːʳdʒ/ [adv] use this to say that something is true most of the time but not every time: *By and large, print is easier to read than handwriting.* | *The candidates that the party selected tended, on the whole, to be middle-aged, male, and white.* | *Despite their age, the paintings are, on the whole, in very good condition.*

for the most part /fəʳ ðə ˈməʊst ˌpɑːʳt/ [adv] especially written use this to say that something is true in most cases: *The cell chemistry of these insects is, for the most part, poorly understood.* | *Ethnic minorities have struggled to retain their cultural identity, and have for the most part succeeded.*

tend /tend/ [v I] if something **tends** to happen, it usually happens or is true, but not always **tend to happen/do sth** *Young children tend to get sick more often than adults.* | *What tends to happen is that the poorest families end up in the worst housing.* | **tend to be sb who/that** *It tends to be the brighter kids who get all the teacher's attention.*

2 ways of expressing a general opinion

- in general/generally speaking/generally
- on the whole/all in all/all things considered
- on balance

in general/generally speaking/generally /ɪn ˈdʒenərəl, ˌdʒenərəli ˈspiːkɪŋ, ˈdʒenərəli/ [adv] spoken use this to give your opinion about what is true, what is best, or what people should do, in most cases: *In general I like cats better than dogs.* | *Generally, t-shirts are the best things for kids to wear almost anywhere.* | *I think generally speaking that the rural schools provide a better environment for the students.*

on the whole/all in all/all things considered /ɒn ðə ˈhəʊl, ˌɔːl ɪn ˈɔːl, ˌɔːl θɪŋz kənˈsɪdəʳd/ [adv] spoken use this when you have considered the whole of a situation, including the bad parts, and you are saying what you think or feel about it in general: *It's been a hard year, but on the whole I've learned a lot.* | *On the whole we're glad we came to live in Vancouver.* | *All in all, I think the conference was a great success.* | *All things considered, I'm sure we made the right decision.*

on balance /ɒn ˈbæləns/ [adv] formal spoken use this to give an opinion after considering all the arguments for and against that opinion: *On balance I think it would be better to cancel the arrangements.* | *Students have been very responsible, on balance, when choosing courses to provide a broad education.*

in/inside

RELATED WORDS

opposite: —— **out/outside**

▸ *see also* **contain, enter**

1 in a container or other enclosed space

- in
- inside
- contents

in /ɪn/ [prep] *There's some pizza in the refrigerator.* | *I think I have some tissues in my purse.* | *Perhaps I left my wallet in my other jacket pocket.* | *Valuables should be kept in the hotel safe.* | *She stayed in the car while I went to the bank.*

inside /ɪnˈsaɪd/ [prep/adv] in a container or other enclosed space and therefore completely covered or surrounded: *There's a key inside the envelope.* | *She opened the package to find another, smaller package inside.* | *Jem opened the box. Inside, surrounded by cotton wool, was a little brooch.*

contents /ˈkɒntents‖ˈkɑːn-/ [n plural] the things that are inside a box, room, bag etc: *The ship and its contents are at the bottom of the lake.* | *The customs officer opened my suitcase and examined the contents.* | **+ of** *Add the contents of the saucepan to the bean mixture.*

2 in a building or room

- in
- inside
- indoors
- indoor

in /ɪn/ [prep] *Francis and his friend were drinking tea in his room.* | *The movie was bad, but at least it was cool in the theater.* | *There isn't a comfortable chair in the house.* | *She had to spend a week in the hospital.*

inside /ɪnˈsaɪd/ [prep/adv] use this especially when you are comparing what is happening in a building or room with what is happening outside: *The lights were on inside the house.* | *Inside it was lovely and warm.* | *I sat outside the interview room and wondered what was going on inside.*

indoors /ɪnˈdɔːʳz/ [adv] inside a building, especially someone's home: *It was too sunny to think of staying indoors.* | *Some arts and crafts projects are too messy to be done indoors.*

indoor /ˈɪndɔːʳ/ [adj only before noun] use this about things or activities that are used or that happen inside buildings, not outdoors: *The hotel has a heated indoor swimming pool.* | *This year, the world indoor tennis championship will take place in Paris.* | *Traditionally, markets were held outdoors, but many cities in Britain now have indoor markets.*

3 the part of something that is inside

- the inside
- interior

the inside /ði ˈɪnsaɪd/ [n singular] **+ of** *All I've seen of Australia is the inside of a hotel room at Sydney airport.* | *The inside of a camera is painted black to prevent light reflecting onto the film.* | **from the inside** *The door had been locked from the inside and the police had to break it down in order to get in.*

interior /ɪnˈtɪəriəʳ/ [n C] written the inside of a building or car: *the car's leather interior* | *My eyes gradually became accustomed to the gloomy interior of the store.*

4 in a town, country, or area

- in
- inside
- within
- internal

in /ɪn/ [prep] *My husband hates driving in London.* | *Everyone in town knew Archie.* | *The company's Spanish subsidiary is based in Madrid.* | *There are many different species of wild cat in Africa and Asia.*

inside /ɪnˈsaɪd/ [prep] use this to emphasize that something is happening in a country or area, or is only known about by people in a country or area: *Enemy troops are now three miles inside their territory.* | *We in the West knew little about events inside Northern Korea.* | *The guerrillas were said to be operating from bases inside the country.*

within /wɪðˈɪn‖wɪðˈɪn, wɪθˈɪn/ [prep] inside the borders or limits of an area: *Children must remain within the school grounds during the lunch break.* | *If the ball lands within the white lines it counts as a fair serve.*

internal /ɪnˈtɜːʳnl/ [adj usually before noun] happening inside a country – use this especially to say that other countries should not become involved: *Russia faces many internal problems, for example inflation.* | *The US was accused of interfering in the internal affairs of the country.*

5 in a company, organization, or group

- in
- inside
- within
- internal
- in-house
- insider

in /ɪn/ [prep] *Homelessness is a major problem in society today.* | *The mood in the Republican Party is one of optimism.* | *Some analysts in Wall Street are predicting that the company will merge with a rival firm.*

inside /ɪnˈsaɪd/ [adv/prep] in an organization or company – use this to emphasize that something is happening or is known about only in that organization and not outside it: *From inside, the company seems less successful.* | *A struggle is going on inside the party between the moderates and the right wing.* —**inside** /ˈɪnsaɪd/ [adj only before noun] *According to inside information, many members of the security forces are concerned about this problem.* | *Police are saying it was an inside job* (=a crime committed by someone inside an organization).

within /wɪðˈɪn‖wɪðˈɪn, wɪθˈɪn/ [prep] existing or happening in a group, organization etc, not outside it: *The landowners have always regarded themselves as an elite group within society.* | *Different factions within the party are fighting for overall control.* | *Violence within the family is often alcohol-related.*

internal /ɪnˈtɜːʳnl/ [adj usually before noun] an **internal** activity, problem, plan etc is one that concerns only those people who are inside a company or organization but not anyone outside it: *Many companies use the program for internal accounting purposes.* | *After the accident, NASA conducted an internal investigation.* | *In November the directors wrote an internal memorandum suggesting that the company should close down three of its factories.* —**internally** [adv] *The job will only be advertised internally* (=inside the organization).

in-house /ˌɪn ˈhaʊs◂/ [adj only before noun] **in-house** training etc is carried out within a company; **in-house** employees work for one employer on a permanent basis: *Many companies run in-house management courses for their staff.* | *All our artwork is done by in-house designers; we don't normally use freelance people.* —**in-house** [adv] *This magazine is produced in-house.*

insider /ɪnˈsaɪdəʳ/ [n C] someone who has special knowledge about a company, organization, or group, because they belong to it or have close connections with it: *Insiders have been predicting that the company would be involved in a takeover bid for some time.* | *Political insiders believe Republicans won't gain control of the Senate.* | **insider trading** (=using special knowledge about what is happening inside a company) *Several people went to prison after the investigation into insider trading.*

6 in a person's body or mind

- in
- internal
- inside
- inner

in /ɪn/ [prep] *I have a pain in my stomach.* | *Paul felt a terrible cramp in his left leg.* | *We shall be studying the effects of these bacteria in the intestine.* | *All these memories of Judith are still fresh in my mind.*

internal /ɪnˈtɜːʳnl/ [adj usually before noun] use this about injuries, examinations, or organs inside your body: *Mrs Jones suffered serious internal injuries as a result of the accident.* | *The doctor said they found some signs of internal bleeding.* —**internally** [adv] *He was bleeding internally and had to be operated on immediately.*

inside /ɪnˈsaɪd/ [adv] if you feel angry, sad, excited etc **inside**, you have that feeling although you do not show it in the way you behave: *Kate tried to make jokes but inside she was furious.* | *I desperately needed some way to vent all the anger and frustration I felt inside.*

inner /ˈɪnəʳ/ [adj only before noun] use this about a feeling that you have in your mind but do not always show: *If he has any inner doubts, he doesn't show them.* | *Terri has an inner confidence that her sister lacks.*

7 in a book, newspaper, speech, or piece of writing etc

- in
- inside
- contents
- content

in /ɪn/ [prep] *Did you read that article in 'Newsweek'?* | *Romance! Adventure! Passion! They're all in this week's 'Woman' magazine.* | *There are some wonderful descriptive passages in the novel.*

inside /ɪnˈsaɪd/ [adv] on the inner pages of a newspaper or magazine – use this especially when you are advertising the newspaper etc and telling people what is in it: *Inside there are lots of handy hints to help you take better pictures.* | *Free inside! A monthly horoscope guide!*

contents /ˈkɒntents‖ˈkɑːn-/ [n plural] everything that is contained in a book, magazine, letter etc: *The letter was burned and its contents will never be known.* | **+ of** *A computer disk can store the entire contents of a set of encyclopedias.* | *The contents of the report are expected to show that the government acted wrongly.* | **table of contents** (=a list of what a book contains) *She glanced at the table of contents to see what stories were included.*

content /ˈkɒntent‖ˈkɑːn-/ [n singular/U] the ideas, facts, or opinions that are contained in a speech or piece of writing: *Many of the essays are political in content.* | *The software, designed for children, has good graphics and animation that doesn't overwhelm the content.* | **+ of** *People pay as much attention to your voice as to the content of your speech.*

8 from the outside towards the inside

- into
- in
- inside
- inwards/inward

into /ˈɪntə, (*before vowels*) ˈɪntʊ, (*strong*) ˈɪntuː/ [prep] from the outside towards the inside: *Jane went into the living-room and sat down on the sofa.* | *Pour half a pint of milk into a small pan and warm it gently.* | *Rachel jumped into her car and sped off in the direction of the hospital.* | *Edwards is charged with trying to smuggle 20 kg of cannabis into the country.*

in /ɪn/ [prep/adv] into a room, building, container, car etc: *Come in! The door's not locked.* | *A big car pulled up and the driver told me to get in.* | *Maureen stood at the door, looking in.* | *Do you want me to put it in a bag for you?* | *She went in the bathroom and turned on the tap.*

inside /ɪnˈsaɪd/ [prep/adv] into a building, room, container etc until completely in it and enclosed by it: *Tom ran back inside and called the police.* | *I put my hand inside my bag, searching for my passport.*

inwards/inward /ˈɪnwəʳdz, ˈɪnwəʳd/ [adv] towards the inside of a building, room, community etc: *The main door opens inwards.* | *All the windows faced inward across the courtyard.*

innocent

not guilty of a crime

RELATED WORDS

opposite: **guilty**

- *see also* **crime, judge, accuse, court/trial (12-19), honest, good**

1 innocent

- innocent
- not guilty
- blameless
- in the clear

innocent /ˈɪnəsənt/ [adj] if someone is **innocent** of a crime, they did not do it – use this especially about someone that other people think is guilty: *'I didn't kill him – I'm innocent!' Davies shouted.* | *Bates allowed an innocent man to go to jail for his crime.* | **+ of** *Jett maintains that he is completely innocent of the charges against him.* | **be presumed innocent** (=legally treated as being innocent) *Under criminal law people are presumed innocent until proved guilty.* —**innocence** [n U] when you are not guilty of a crime: *Her parents were convinced of her innocence.*

not guilty /nɒt ˈgɪlti/ [adj] if someone is **not guilty** of a crime, they did not do it – use this especially when a court has officially decided that someone did not do a crime: *You don't have anything to be afraid of if you are not guilty.* | *The evidence will show that my client is absolutely not guilty, Your Honour.* | **+ of** *She was convinced he wasn't guilty of the crime, no matter what anyone said.* | **verdict of not guilty** (=official judgement) *Within just a few minutes the jury of ranchers returned a verdict of not guilty.*

blameless /ˈbleɪmləs/ [adj] not having done anything wrong, or not responsible for something bad that has happened: *None of us is completely blameless – we all knew something like this could happen.* | *The women had made every effort to lead blameless lives.* | *Last week a special prosecutor ruled that the three officials were blameless.*

in the clear /ɪn ðə ˈklɪəʳ/ [adv] informal if you are **in the clear**, it cannot be officially proved that you have done something illegal or criminal: *If we all stick to the same story we'll be in the clear.* | **stay/keep in the clear** *By keeping his name off all the documents, he'd managed to stay in the clear.* | **put sb in the clear** *The testimony of the two witnesses seemed to put Richardson in the clear.*

2 to say publicly that you are innocent

- plead not guilty
- protest your innocence

plead not guilty /ˌpliːd ˌnɒt ˈgɪlti/ [v phrase] to say publicly and officially in a court of law, that you are innocent of a crime: *According to Maloney's lawyer, she will plead not guilty.* | **+ to** *Barkin pleaded not guilty to the rape charges in municipal court Thursday.* | *After pleading not guilty to the charges of conspiracy, Davis was released on bail.*

protest your innocence /prəˌtest jɔːr ˈɪnəsəns/ [v phrase] to say repeatedly that you are innocent, especially when other people think that you are guilty: *The men have protested their innocence for 25 years.* | *Schultz appeared in public again on Wednesday to protest her innocence and deny any wrong-doing.*

3 when a law court decides that someone is innocent

- find sb not guilty
- acquit
- clear

find sb not guilty /ˌfaɪnd (sb) ˌnɒt ˈgɪlti/ [v phrase] *We find the defendant not guilty, Your Honor.* | *Despite the large amount of evidence against him, the jury found Gibson not guilty.* | **+ of** *The two women were found not guilty of drug-trafficking.* | *It took the jurors less than three hours to find Gessler not guilty of murder.*

acquit /əˈkwɪt/ [v T usually in passive] if someone **is acquitted** by a law court, they are officially told they are not guilty of a crime: *Few observers expect the jury to acquit Mr Hoskins.* | *His lawyer thought he had a good chance of being acquitted at the trial, if no further evidence was found.* | **acquit sb of sth** *To her relief she was acquitted of all the charges laid against her.*

clear /klɪəʳ/ [v T usually in passive] if you **are cleared** of a crime, a court of law says that you are innocent, because it is impossible to legally prove that you are guilty: *After Pagones was cleared in court, he sued his accusers.* | **clear sb of sth** *A jury cleared the company of all criminal charges in connection with the accident.* | *Marshall was given his job back after being cleared of accusations that he abused drugs.*

in order to

in order to get something, achieve something, or make something happen

RELATED WORDS

- *see also* **purpose, reason**

- to do sth
- in order to do sth
- so (that)
- for
- with the aim of doing sth
- with a view to doing sth

to do sth /tə 'du: (sth)/ [adv] *She went to the bank to get some money.* | *Salt is spread on roads in cold weather to prevent the formation of ice.* | *To lose weight, you must eat sensibly.* | *You didn't come all that way just to see me, did you?* | **so as not to do sth** *When I get home late I sleep in the spare room, so as not to disturb my wife.*

in order to do sth /ɪn ˌɔːʳdəʳ tə 'du: (sth)/ [adv] done so that something else happens as a result, or necessary if something else is to be possible: *Many drug users get involved in crime simply in order to pay for their supplies of cocaine and heroin.* | *In order to be a doctor, you have to study for six years.* | **in order not to do sth** *In order not to offend anyone, I did not tell them the real reason for my visit.*

so (that) /'səʊ (ðət)/ [conjunction] if you do something **so that** you or another person can do something else, you do it in order to make the other thing possible: *She's studying English at night school so that she can go to university.* | *I'll move my car so you can get into the garage.* | *Steps must be taken so that this kind of disaster never happens again.*

for /fəʳ, (*strong*) fɔːʳ/ [prep] if you do something **for** something, you do it **for** a particular purpose: *She's gone into hospital for a check-up.* | *I went into the store for some tomatoes and came out with two bags of groceries.* | *We climbed up here for the view, and also because we wanted to get some exercise.*

with the aim of doing sth /wɪð ði ˌeɪm əv 'du:ɪŋ (sth)/ [adv] if you do something **with the aim of doing something** else, you do it in order to try and achieve this: *The Green Party was started with the aim of protecting the environment.* | *I originally went out to the Far East with the aim of setting up my own import-export business.*

with a view to doing sth /wɪð ə ˌvju: tə 'du:ɪŋ (sth)/ [adv] if you do something **with a view to doing something** else, you do it because you are planning to do something else later and this will help you to achieve it: *We bought the cottage with a view to settling down there after retirement.* | *The idea was to pool resources with a view to lowering operating costs.*

insist

to say firmly that someone must do something or that something must happen

RELATED WORDS

▸ *see also* **say, tell, must/don't have to**

- **insist**
- **demand**
- **put your foot down**
- **be adamant**
- **won't/wouldn't take no for an answer**
- **be insistent**
- **at sb's insistence**
- **won't/wouldn't hear of**

insist /ɪn'sɪst/ [v I/T] *'I really need to speak to you now.' 'Oh, all right if you insist.'* | *We hadn't intended to stay for another drink, but our host insisted.* | **+ (that)** *Mom always insists that we keep our rooms neat.* | *He was a religious man who insisted his children went to church every Sunday.* | **+ on** *Many workers now insist on a smoke-free environment.* | **+ on doing sth** *The man insisted on helping me find a taxi even though I told him I didn't need any help.*

demand /dɪ'mɑːnd‖dɪ'mænd/ [v T] to say very strongly and often angrily that something should be done or given to you: *Parents are demanding greater control over their children's education.* | *I caught Alice going through my letters and demanded an immediate explanation.* | **+ that** *State health inspectors have demanded that the city act immediately to clean the water supply.* | **+ to do sth** *The guards demanded to see her I.D. before they allowed her in the building.* | *Daley demanded to know why the police had not been called in to stop the rioting.*

put your foot down /ˌpʊt jɔːʳ 'fʊt ˌdaʊn/ [v phrase] to say firmly that someone must not do something or behave in a particular way: *You'd better put your foot down before those kids get completely out of control.* | *Ed was talking about dropping out of school, but Mom and Dad put their foot down.*

be adamant /bi: 'ædəmənt/ [v phrase] if someone **is adamant** about something, they say strongly that it must be done or that it is right and no one can persuade them to change their mind: *I didn't want to go to the party, but he was adamant and we ended up going.* | **+ about** *The protesters were adamant about staying and making sure their voices were heard.* | **+ that** *The company's managing director is adamant that there will be no compromise with the unions.* | **be adamant in your opposition/refusal/desire etc** *The district attorney has been adamant in her refusal to pursue the case.*

won't/wouldn't take no for an answer /ˌwəʊnt, ˌwʊdnt teɪk ˌnəʊ fər ən 'ɑːnsəʳ‖-'æn-/ [v phrase] informal if someone **won't take no for an answer,** they insist that you must do something, even though you have told them that you do not want to do it: *You simply must come to dinner on Saturday – I won't take no for an answer!* | *I told him that I didn't want to go out with him, but he wouldn't take no for an answer.*

be insistent /bi: ɪn'sɪstənt/ [v phrase] to say repeatedly and strongly that someone should do something, even though they disagree: *My boss finally got me to take the course – he's very insistent.* | **+ that** *Eric's parents have been insistent that he and his girlfriend get married.* | **+ on** *The principal would be less insistent on kids wearing school uniforms if the school had to pay for them.*

at sb's insistence /ət (sb's) ɪn'sɪstəns/ [adv] if you do something **at someone's insistence**, you do it because they say you must do it: *Byrd claims he was carrying the gun at his wife's insistence.* | *At Stevenson's insistence, Reynold's name was kept on the list.* | **at the insistence of sb** *U.S. troops were finally removed from the country at the insistence of Congress.*

won't/wouldn't hear of /wəʊnt, wʊdnt 'hɪər ɒv/ [v phrase] informal to insist that someone should not do something, especially because you want to help them in some way: *I've offered to pay Simon for fixing my car, but he won't hear of it.* | *Jack wouldn't hear of Debbie going back to work so soon after the baby was born.*

instead

RELATED WORDS

▸ *see also* **replace**

1 instead of another thing, place, time etc

- **instead**
- **rather than**
- **in place of**
- **in favour of**
- **in preference to**
- **in lieu**

instead /ɪn'sted/ [adv] *We didn't have enough money to go to a movie, so we went to the park instead.* | *I can't manage Thursday. Can we meet on Friday instead?* | **+ of** *Can I have soup instead of salad?* | **+ of doing sth** *You should talk to your teacher instead of just complaining to me about it.*

rather than /'rɑːðəʳ ðən‖'ræ-/ [prep] if you do or choose one thing **rather than** another, you do or choose the first thing because it seems better: *She uses lemon rather than vinegar in her salad dressings.* | *Rather than driving around all day looking for somewhere to park, why don't you take a bus into town?*

in place of /ɪn 'pleɪs ɒv/ [prep] if one thing is used **in place of** another, it is used instead of it or put in the place where the other thing was: *A Walt Disney film is being shown in place of the advertised programme.* | *For this recipe you can always use olive oil in place of butter.* | **in sth's place** *The newspaper has stopped having a crossword puzzle and in its place they now have a weekly wordsearch competition.*

in favour of British **/in favor of** American /ɪn 'feɪvər ɒv/ [prep] if you decide not to do, have, or accept one thing **in favour of** another, you choose the other because you think it is much better: *The original plan was abandoned in favour of a new proposal.* | *Communist theory and practice has been rejected in favour of American-style capitalism.*

in preference to /ɪn 'prefərəns tuː/ [prep] if you choose one thing **in preference to** another thing, you choose it instead of the other thing because you think it is better or more suitable: *In Languedoc, local wines are drunk in preference to wines from other parts of France.* | *Children often choose high-fat fast foods in preference to fresh, healthy ones.*

in lieu /ɪn 'ljuː‖-'luː/ [adv] something that is given **in lieu** of something else is given instead of that thing, especially in a work or business situation **a day/time off in lieu** *Because you worked on Sunday, you can have a day off in lieu.* | *Occasionally, he makes his staff work overtime and gives them time off in lieu.* | **+ of** *They used to give the landlord poultry and eggs in lieu of rent.*

2 instead of another person

- instead
- in sb's place/in place of sb
- for
- on behalf of sb/on sb's behalf

▸ *see also* **represent**

instead /ɪn'sted/ [adv] *Jo couldn't go to the meeting, so I said I'd go instead.* | **+ of** *Gillespie will play in midfield instead of Cochrane.* | *I can't understand why they chose him instead of you – you're much better qualified for the job.*

in sb's place/in place of sb /ɪn (sb's) 'pleɪs, ɪn 'pleɪs əv (sb)/ [adv] if you do something or go somewhere **in someone's place**, you do it or go there instead of them because they are not able to go: *Mr Lloyd resigned and asked Mr Graham to serve in his place.* | *I'm not playing in next week's game and I'm not sure who will be playing in my place.* | **in place of sb** *A new manager was appointed in place of Hoddle.*

for /fəʳ; (*strong*) fɔːʳ/ [prep] if you do something **for** someone, you do it instead of them, especially in order to help them: *The old man downstairs was ill, so Linda said she'd go shopping for him.* | *You shouldn't be carrying those heavy cases – let me do it for you.*

on behalf of sb/on sb's behalf /ɒn bɪ'hɑːf əv (sb), ɒn (sb's) bɪ'hɑːf‖-bɪ'hæf/ [adv] if you do something **on behalf of** someone, such as give a speech or making an official decision, you do it instead of them because they have asked you to represent them: *On behalf of everyone here, I'd like to wish you a long and happy retirement.* | *Richardson's lawyer agreed to speak to journalists on his behalf.*

instinct

1 a natural ability to know what to do

- instinct
- intuition
- feel
- feeling
- sixth sense

instinct /'ɪnstɪŋkt/ [n C/U] a natural ability to know what you should do without having to learn it or be told it: *He has tremendous business instincts.* | **first instinct** (=the first thing you want to do, before you think carefully) *My first instinct was to lie about it.* | **+ for** *Even a very young animal has a strong instinct for self-preservation.* | **on instinct** *I was terrified. I was just working on instinct and trying to survive.* | **by instinct** (=because of instinct) *Guys who have grown up on a ranch know almost by instinct what needs to be done to keep it running.* | **natural instinct** *A cat's natural instinct is to chase birds.* | **maternal instinct** (=instincts about wanting a baby and knowing how to care for it) *I don't know if it was maternal instinct or what, but I just knew my baby would be okay.*

intuition /ˌɪntju'ɪʃən‖-tu-, -tju-/ [n U] the ability to understand or know things by using your feelings instead of considering the facts: *Sometimes doctors have to base a diagnosis on intuition as much as on scientific tests.* | *She thought the baby would be a girl, and her intuition was correct.* | **trust your intuition** (=do what your intuition makes you want to do) *If you think there's something wrong about the situation, you should trust your intuition.*

feel /fiːl/ [v T] to **feel** that you know something, without understanding why you **feel** this **+ (that)** *She felt that something else was going to happen and that it wouldn't be good.* | *I felt someone was following me, but when I turned around, there was nobody there.* | **+ like** *I felt like if I didn't speak up then, I would never do it.*

feeling /'fiːlɪŋ/ [n C] if you have a **feeling** that something is true or that something will happen, you feel sure about it, even though you do not know why **have a feeling (that)** *I had a funny feeling that we would meet again* | *My fiancé's friends are planning a bachelor party for him, and I have a feeling something awful is going to happen.* | **gut feeling** informal (=a strong feeling that you are sure is right) *Her gut feeling was that he was lying.*

sixth sense /ˌsɪksθ 'sens/ [n singular] a mysterious ability to know about something without seeing it, hearing about it, being told about it etc **have a sixth sense** *Parents have a sixth sense when it comes to their children. They know when something's wrong.* | **+ about** *He told me he had a sixth sense about how his mother was doing.*

2 using instinct rather than knowledge

- instinctive
- intuitive

instinctive /ɪnˈstɪŋktɪv/ [adj] based on instinct rather than on knowledge or thought: *He's considered a smart, instinctive politician.* | *His instinctive reaction was to duck when he heard the shot, even though he knew it was pointless.* | *White jazz seemed old and intellectual, whereas black jazz was vital, swinging, instinctive.* —**instinctively** [adv] *Instinctively, I knew that something was wrong.*

intuitive /ɪnˈtjuːɪ̥tɪv‖-ˈtuː-, -ˈtjuː-/ [adj] an **intuitive** understanding, judgement, or idea is completely based on feelings, not on facts or reasons, but is still correct: *Great novelists have an intuitive understanding of the workings of human emotions.* | *She had an intuitive ability to size up people and their capabilities.* | *Women are supposed to be more intuitive than men, but I don't know if that's true.* —**intuitively** [adv] *Some managers seem to intuitively recognize the need to balance work life with home life.*

instructions

information about how to do something or about what to do

RELATED WORDS

- tell or order someone to do something *see* **tell (17-24)**
- *see also* **explain, tell**

- **instructions**
- **directions**
- **guidelines**
- **brief**
- **recipe**
- **manual**
- **guide**
- **handbook**
- **cookbook**

instructions /ɪnˈstrʌkʃənz/ [n plural] written or spoken information telling someone what to do or how something should be done: *I can't get the computer to work and I've lost the instructions.* | **give/leave (sb) instructions** *As the teacher, it's your job to give clear instructions to the children.* | **+ for** *Mum was going to work, so she left me some instructions for supper.* | *The President issued instructions for the continuance of the attack.* | **follow/carry out (sb's) instructions** (=do what the instructions tell you) *I've followed the instructions, but the machine still isn't working.* | *Mr Evans claimed that the solicitor had failed to carry out his mother's instructions.* | **read the instructions** *Before you take any medicine, always read the instructions on the bottle.* | **+ about/on** *It's extraordinary that the equipment doesn't come with instructions on how to use it.* | *His grandfather had left no instructions about what to do with his paintings.*

directions /dɪ̥ˈrekʃənz, daɪ-/ [n plural] a set of instructions, especially written ones, on how to do or use something **+ on** *For detailed directions on installing the software, see page 18.* | **give (sb) directions/give directions to sb** *The judge has the power to give appropriate directions to the jury before they consider their verdict.* | **follow directions** *These worksheets are designed to teach children how to solve problems and follow directions.*

guidelines /ˈgaɪdlaɪnz/ [n plural] official instructions about the best way to do something, especially something that could be difficult or dangerous: *Lauder urged the company to develop a set of guidelines that address sexual harassment in the workplace.* | **follow guidelines** *Air travelers can have stress-free trips if they follow a few simple guidelines.* | **issue/publish/lay down etc guidelines** *Medical staff have been issued with new guidelines for working with HIV patients.* | *The Ministry of Education has laid down strict guidelines as to the administration of the tests.* | **+ on** *New guidelines on how to move dangerous chemicals by road have just been published.*

brief /briːf/ [n singular] instructions that are given to someone about what their duties and responsibilities are in a job: *The brief given to the students was quite straightforward.* | **sb's brief is to do sth** *The committee's brief is to investigate and report on domestic violence in the region.* | *The architect's brief was to design an extension which would harmonize as much as possible with the existing building.* | **be part of sb's brief** *Dealing with financial matters is not part of my brief.*

recipe /ˈresɪ̥pi/ [n C] instructions on how to make a particular kind of food: *This soup is really good – you must give me the recipe.* | **+ for** *I've found a really great recipe for barbecue sauce.* | **have the recipe** *My Mum has the recipe for a really delicious prawn curry.*

manual /ˈmænjuəl/ [n C] a book that contains detailed instructions on how to operate a piece of equipment or machinery, or on how to do a job or activity: *Before you try to use the camera, read the manual carefully.* | *a computer manual* | **instruction manual** *The instruction manuals that accompany new computer software are often difficult to understand.* | **training manual** *a training manual for teachers* | **+ on** *Leach has written many popular manuals on childcare.* | **owner's manual/user's manual** (=one which shows you how to use your car, piece of equipment etc) *Consult your owner's manual for information on what oil to use and how often it should be changed.*

guide /gaɪd/ [n C] a book containing instructions and advice, that helps you do an activity or job properly, or to make the right choice about something: *This simple guide is essential if you are thinking of taking up hill walking.* | *the Good Schools Guide* | **+ to (doing) sth** *The book is an extremely useful guide to starting your own business.* | *a free guide to financial planning* | **+ for** *A guide for hospital staff will be published shortly, covering everything from simple hygiene to security regulations.*

handbook /ˈhændbʊk/ [n C] a book containing information and advice on a subject or product, produced by someone who knows a lot about it: *There are all kinds of health and fitness handbooks on the market these days.* | *The students' handbook gives information on how to find accommodation.* | **+ for** *a useful handbook for managers* | **+ on** *a handbook on basic psychology*

cookbook ALSO **recipe book** British /ˈkʊkbʊk, ˈresɪ̥pi bʊk/ [n C] a book that has instructions about how to cook different kinds of food: *There are an increasing number of recipe books with ideas for healthy meals that can be prepared quickly and easily.* | *an Indian recipe book* | **+ of** *an illustrated cookbook of Mexican recipes*

insult

RELATED WORDS

- *see also* **offend, rude**

1 to be very rude to someone

- **insult**
- **be rude to**
- **abuse**
- **shout/scream/hurl abuse at**
- **call sb names**
- **be an insult**

insult /ɪn'sʌlt/ [v T] to be very rude and unpleasant to someone, either by saying rude things to them or by making them feel stupid or unimportant: *Jarvis was fired for insulting a customer.* | *They offered me $20 for a whole day's work – I felt really insulted.*

be rude to /biː 'ruːd tuː/ [v phrase] to speak or behave towards someone in a way that offends them: *My mother doesn't like my boyfriend because he was rude to her once.* | *You shouldn't let her be so rude to you.*

abuse /ə'bjuːz/ [v T] to say a lot of rude, offensive, unpleasant things to someone, especially when you are angry with them: *The men were getting drunk on cheap beer and some had started abusing passers-by.* | **verbally abuse** (=to say something very rude to someone) *The player was reported to the tournament director for verbally abusing match officials.*

shout/scream/hurl abuse at /ˌʃaʊt, ˌskriːm, ˌhɜːʳl ə'bjuːs æt/ [v phrase] to shout a lot of rude and offensive things at someone: *The crowd screamed abuse as the two men accused of the murder left the court in police vans.* | *Strikers outside the factory gate were shouting abuse at anybody who tried to get past them.*

call sb names /ˌkɔːl (sb) 'neɪmz/ [v phrase] to try to offend someone by calling them rude names in the way that children do: *He tried to make Oliver cry by hitting him, pulling his hair, and calling him names.* | *'She said I was a fat pig.' 'Oh, I've been called far worse names than that.'*

be an insult /biː ən 'ɪnsʌlt/ [v phrase] if an action or someone's behaviour **is an insult**, it offends you because it shows no respect: *The pay offer of 2% was an insult.* | **+ to** *The girl's father claimed the portrait revealing his daughter's face was an insult to Islam.*

2 language or behaviour that insults someone

- insulting
- abusive

insulting /ɪn'sʌltɪŋ/ [adj] **insulting** remarks or behaviour are very rude and you feel offended by them: *She started making insulting comments about the size of my stomach.* | *I wasn't being deliberately insulting. I simply meant that more exercise would be good for you.* | *He was accused of using threatening or insulting behaviour and of assaulting a police officer.* | *I find his behaviour towards me extremely insulting.* | *Sexist language is very insulting to women.*

abusive /ə'bjuːsɪv/ [adj] very rude and using offensive language: *The woman became angry and abusive when she was not allowed into the hotel.* | *Smith was fined £500 for making foul and abusive comments to match officials.* | *Drunken football fans began directing a stream of abusive language at the policemen.* | *The way pupils use sexually abusive language to insult each other presents particular problems for teachers.*

3 words or actions that insult someone

- insult
- affront
- abuse

insult /'ɪnsʌlt/ [n C] something rude that someone says or does to someone else, that offends their intelligence, character, or appearance etc: *Outside the pub, a drunk was shouting insults at everyone who came past.* | *You mustn't wear your shoes inside the temple – it is a great insult.* | **hurl insults (at sb)** *People were hurling insults at the players as they walked off the pitch.* | **take sth as an insult** (=be insulted by it) *I said something about her new hairstyle and she took it as an insult.*

abuse /ə'bjuːs/ [n U] rude, offensive, or unpleasant things that someone says to someone else, especially when they are angry **shout/scream/hurl abuse** *People were shouting abuse at the Prime Minister as he sped away in a large car.* | *An angry mob screamed abuse and hurled missiles during clashes with police yesterday.* | *Demonstrators hurled abuse at councillors as they entered the council building in Glasgow.* | **term of abuse** (=a word used to insult someone) *By the late 1970s, the word 'hippie' had become a term of abuse.* | **torrent/stream of abuse** (=a lot of abuse) *Leaning out of the window, he let loose a stream of abuse.*

affront /ə'frʌnt/ [n C usually singular] formal a remark or action that offends someone because it treats them without any respect **+ to** *She felt that his behaviour was an affront to her dignity as a human being.* | *Lucy was so shocked by these affronts that she remained speechless for the rest of the evening.* | **personal affront** *Though I only intended it as a joke, he took it as a personal affront.*

intelligent

RELATED WORDS

opposite: **stupid/silly**

see also **idea, learn, study, know/not know, sensible, logical, invent**

1 good at learning, thinking, and understanding ideas

- intelligent
- clever
- bright
- have a good mind
- have a high IQ
- gifted
- brainy

intelligent /ɪn'telɨdʒənt/ [adj] having a high level of natural mental ability, so that you are good at thinking, learning, and understanding ideas: *Mark was an intelligent, ambitious young man, with a great future in front of him.* | *Some scientists claim that dolphins are more intelligent than humans.* | **highly intelligent** *'We're looking for highly intelligent young people, with a genuine interest in their subject,' a university spokesman said.*

clever especially British **/smart** especially American /'klevəʳ, smɑːʳt/ [adj] good at learning and understanding things quickly, and at thinking how to solve problems: *He's a smart kid who works hard and is focused on what he wants to do.* | *My sister was always much cleverer than me at school.* | **it is clever/smart of sb** *That was very clever of you, How did you do that?* | **it is clever/smart of sb to do sth** *Dick's had a bad injury, and it's probably smart of him not to play sports for a while.*

bright /braɪt/ [adj] intelligent and likely to be successful – use this especially about children and young people: *Even as a small child, it was obvious that Bobby was very bright.* | *When I first met her she was a bright young lawyer fresh out of law school.* | **best and brightest** *Companies want to prevent their best and brightest employees from being headhunted by rival organizations.*

have a good mind /hæv ə ˌgʊd ˈmaɪnd/ [v phrase] to be intelligent and able to think about things clearly, understand things quickly, and solve problems well: *Sean's teachers told him that he had a good mind and the ability to be an excellent student.*

have a high IQ /hæv ə ˌhaɪ aɪ ˈkjuː/ [v phrase] to be intelligent according to what you score on a special test: *Both the twins have a high IQ of around 150.* | *MENSA is an organization for people with high IQs.*

gifted /ˈgɪftɪ̇d/ [adj usually before noun] a child who is **gifted** is much more intelligent and quicker at learning than most other children: *In the past, gifted children have not always been given appropriate educational support.* | *Bloomsury House is a special school for girls and boys who are exceptionally gifted.*

brainy /ˈbreɪni/ [adj] informal very intelligent and especially good at studying: *At school Karen was always one of the brainy ones.* | *Why don't you ask Tom to help you with your homework – he's incredibly brainy.*

2 extremely intelligent

- brilliant
- genius

brilliant /ˈbrɪljənt/ [adj] a **brilliant** scientist, student, lawyer etc is one who is extremely intelligent and extremely successful at what they do: *The brilliant physicist Paul Dirac first put forward this theory back in 1990.* | *a brilliant historian*

genius /ˈdʒiːniəs/ [n C] someone with a very high level of intelligence, which only a few people have, especially someone who has original and important ideas: *Perot was a wonderful businessman and a genius in his own way.* | **mathematical/musical/artistic etc genius** *Einstein was probably the greatest mathematical genius of all time.*

3 quick to understand or make decisions

- quick
- sharp
- quick-witted
- wise
- be quick on the uptake

quick /kwɪk/ [adj not usually before noun] intelligent and able to understand things quickly: *Some children in the class are quicker than others.* | *She's very quick and able – seems to pick things up in no time.* | **quick at (doing) sth** *Craig was always quick at maths, but he had trouble with reading and writing.*

sharp /ʃɑːʳp/ [adj] someone who is **sharp** understands things very quickly, especially so that it is difficult to deceive or confuse them: *There's no point lying to her – she's much too sharp.* | **razor sharp** (=extremely sharp) *Those lawyers are razor sharp, and you've got to be careful about every single word you say.*

quick-witted /ˌkwɪk ˈwɪtɪ̇d◂/ [adj] able to understand things quickly and to answer people in an intelligent way: *John was always so quick-witted that I used to think he would have made a good secret agent.* | *Throughout a lifetime of public service, he proved himself a quick-witted negotiator.*

wise /waɪz/ [adj] a **wise** person makes good decisions and gives good advice, because they have a lot of experience of life – use this especially about older people: *She was a wise old woman, and we all valued her advice.* | *Burton didn't like what he was hearing, but he was wise enough to keep his thoughts to himself.* — **wisely** [adv] *The Queen ruled her people wisely for more than 60 years.*

be quick on the uptake /biː ˌkwɪk ɒn ðiː ˈʌpteɪk/ [v phrase] spoken informal someone who **is quick on the uptake** learns new things and understands a situation very quickly: *You're very quick on the uptake! How did you guess?* | *We're looking for new staff – people who are neat, enthusiastic and quick on the uptake.*

4 intelligent and well-educated

- educated
- intellectual
- learned
- academic
- brains
- intelligentsia

educated /ˈedjʊ̈keɪtɪ̇d‖ˈedʒə-/ [adj] someone who is **educated** is intelligent and knows a lot because they have had a good education, have read a lot etc: *You're smart, you're educated, you shouldn't have any trouble finding a job.* | *In general, children of educated parents tend to get better grades.* | **well educated** *The boy came from a good home, was well educated and had every advantage.* | **highly educated** *Nadia is a highly-educated, very motivated individual who will go far.*

intellectual /ˌɪntɪ̇ˈlektʃuəl◂/ [n C] an intelligent, well-educated person who spends a lot of their time thinking about, writing about, and discussing ideas, literature etc: *It's an organization of writers, artists and intellectuals, who come together to discuss their ideas.* | *The restaurant was once the meeting place for leading French left-wing intellectuals such as Sartre and de Beauvoir.*

learned /ˈlɜːʳnɪ̇d/ [adj] formal a **learned** person has read many books and knows a lot about many things, and is greatly respected because of their knowledge: *The old professor was obviously a very learned man.* | *It's true that art critics aren't as learned as art-historians in these matters.*

academic /ˌækəˈdemɪk◂/ [adj] someone who is **academic** is very good at studying and does well at school, university etc: *I wasn't very academic, and I left school at sixteen.* | *If you're academic, you can take some of your exams a year or two early.* | *Teachers must provide challenging activities for their more academic pupils.*

brains /breɪnz/ [n plural] the most intelligent person or people in a country, organization etc **the brains** *You'd better ask Toby. He's the brains around here.* | **best brains** *Many of Britain's best brains have left the country to go and work in America.*

intelligentsia /ɪnˌtelɪ̇ˈdʒentsiə/ [n singular] formal the most intelligent and highly educated people in a society such as the writers, thinkers, and artists: *The demonstrators belong to the middle classes and the intelligentsia, which have suffered most as a result of the government's economic policies.*

5 someone who is clever at dealing with people or situations

- clever
- shrewd
- astute
- canny
- resourceful
- streetwise
- be nobody's fool

clever especially British **/smart** especially American /ˈklevəʳ, smɑːʳt/ [adj] intelligent in a practical way, and able to use your intelligence to get advantages for yourself: *Ben Gurion was a cool, calculating and clever politician.* | *They won the case by being clever and hiring influential lawyers to help them.* | *She was smart and knew how to get men to give her what-*

ever she wanted. | **+ at doing sth** *Doug's always been clever at finding the best deals available.* —**cleverly** [adv] *Mum cleverly pretended that she hadn't heard what he'd said.*

shrewd /ʃruːd/ [adj] a **shrewd** person is good at deciding what people, situations etc are really like, so that it is difficult to deceive them – use this especially about people who are successful in business: *As a manager, Watson is both shrewd and tough.* | *Are you a shrewd businessman, quick to see an opportunity or a bargain?* | *Sachs was a shrewd judge of character, and chose his staff well.* —**shrewdly** [adv] *They shrewdly invested in copper just as the price started to rise.*

astute /əˈstjuːt‖əˈstuːt/ [adj] someone who is **astute** easily understands why people behave in a particular way, why a situation is happening etc, without anyone having to tell them: *Morgan was surprised at how astute she was. 'How did you know that?' he asked.* | *The scale of the riots seemed to surprise even the most astute commentators.* | **financially/politically etc astute** *The President's wife is often politically astute, ambitious and very influential in White House policy decisions.* —**astutely** [adv] *As one observer astutely pointed out, 'A week is a long time in politics.'*

canny /ˈkæni/ [adj] someone who is **canny** is very clever, especially in business, so that it is difficult to deceive them and they are able to take advantage of other people: *Pete Chambers is a canny fellow. Not one to miss an opportunity.* | *She's far too canny to keep her money in this country. She's got it safely hidden away in Switzerland, I expect.*

resourceful /rɪˈzɔːʳsfəl, -ˈsɔːʳs-/ [adj] clever at finding ways to deal with problems or difficult situations, using whatever material, information etc that is available to you: *We can influence our children's development by encouraging them to be resourceful when they play.* | *Keen competition in the arts, crafts and trade made the Greeks an inventive and resourceful people.*

streetwise /ˈstriːtwaɪz/ [adj] someone who is **streetwise** has a lot of experience of life in big cities, so they know what to do in difficult or dangerous situations: *He seemed very streetwise for a kid who had just left school.* | *Zachar is a streetwise guy from New York, a gambler who grew up playing the horses at Belmont Park.*

be nobody's fool /biː ˌnəʊbədiz ˈfuːl/ [v phrase] informal to be very difficult to trick or deceive because you have a lot of experience or knowledge of people: *Katherine could look after herself and she was nobody's fool when it came to money.*

6 clever in a dishonest or secret way

- cunning
- sly
- crafty
- wily

cunning /ˈkʌnɪŋ/ [adj] a **cunning** person gets what they want by thinking carefully about it, making secret plans, and deceiving people: *Hawkeye was very cunning – he always waited until his enemy was alone and unarmed before making his attack.* | *She's a cunning little devil! She left for school as usual, and then went into town instead with her friends.* —**cunningly** [adv] *A video camera had been cunningly hidden behind the mirror.*

sly /slaɪ/ [adj] a **sly** person secretly deceives people and is always thinking of ways to get advantages for themselves: *Eliot looked sly and deceitful, as though he wasn't telling us the whole truth.* | *He's a sly old devil isn't he! Nobody knew he had as much money as that!* | **on the sly** (=secretly and in a way that deceives people) *My parents didn't approve, but we continued to meet on the sly.* —**slyly** [adv] *Tom grinned slyly at Fiona, but deliberately said nothing.*

crafty /ˈkrɑːfti‖ˈkræf-/ [adj] a **crafty** person is good at getting what they want by planning carefully and secretly deceiving people, often in a way that other people admire: *Jerry was crafty – he got into the match free by crawling under the fence.* | *Crafty cyber-thieves have found that they can steal a lot of money in electronic bank thefts with very little risk.* —**craftily** [adv] *'Let's not tell him he's already paid us once,' she said craftily.*

wily /ˈwaɪli/ [adj usually before noun] a **wily** person has had a lot of experience of getting what they want by tricking people, so that it is very difficult to trick them: *Breen had a reputation for being a tough and wily negotiator.* | *The Fawcett brothers were too wily to be caught, and the local residents could get no help from the law.*

7 an annoying person who thinks they are clever

- know-it-all
- smart aleck
- smart-ass/wise guy
- be too clever by half

know-it-all ALSO **know-all** British /ˈnəʊ ɪt ɔːl, ˈnəʊ ɔːl/ [n C] spoken someone who annoys you because they always think they know the correct answers, know a lot about something etc: *OK, if you're such a know-it-all, you try and do it, then.* | *I just wish he'd stop being such a know-all all the time.*

smart aleck /ˈsmɑːʳt ˌælɪ̥k/ [n C] informal someone, especially a young person, who annoys you because they say funny or intelligent things in a rude way: *Glover was different to the rest of us. The son of university people. A smart aleck.* | *Some smart aleck at the back of the room kept standing up and asking awkward questions.* —**smart-aleck** [adj] *I'm not going to let some smart-aleck kid make a fool out of me.*

smart-ass/wise guy /ˈsmɑːʳt æs, ˈwaɪz gaɪ/ [n C] American informal someone who annoys you because they make jokes or give answers in a rude but funny way: *OK, smart-ass! If I want an answer from you I'll ask for it.* —**smart-ass** [adj only before noun] *Some smart-ass college kid started making fun of her accent.*

be too clever by half /biː tuː ˌklevəʳ baɪ ˈhɑːf‖-ˈhæf/ [v phrase] British informal use this about someone who uses their intelligence in a way that annoys other people, and will probably get into trouble at some time in the future: *Phil's good at thinking up excuses for his behaviour – he's too clever by half.*

8 a clever plan, idea, or way of doing something

- clever
- intelligent
- ingenious
- neat
- smart
- cunning
- crafty
- inspired
- bright idea

clever /ˈklevəʳ/ [adj] especially British a **clever** idea, plan, or way of doing something is good and works well: *It sounds like a clever idea. Do you think it'll work?* | *Virtual Listening Systems have introduced one of the year's most unusual and clever new* *products. | I've thought of a really clever way of making money.*

intelligent /ɪnˈtelɨdʒənt/ [adj] an **intelligent** idea, question etc is thought of or asked by someone who is intelligent: *Have you got any intelligent suggestions to make? | Anne was surprised to hear such an intelligent question coming from a very small child.*

ingenious /ɪnˈdʒiːniəs/ [adj] an **ingenious** method, idea, or piece of equipment is cleverly designed to do a job or solve a problem in a very original way: *A scanner is an ingenious device which enables you to feed pictures, photos or documents into a computer system. | American scientists have come up with an ingenious way of getting rid of cockroaches. | The catalogue is full of ingenious ideas for transforming your house into a dream home. | In the end it was Pete who thought of a really ingenious solution to the problem.*

neat /niːt/ [adj] an idea etc that is clever, simple, and effective: *One of our designers has come up with a neat idea for storing computer disks. | Taking up a sport is a neat way of meeting new people, and it's good for you too. | It's a complicated problem, and there's no neat solution.*

smart /smɑːʳt/ [adj] a system or machine such as a computer that is **smart** is cleverly designed and does something effectively: *The new software system is really smart and it's much quicker to use too.*

cunning /ˈkʌnɪŋ/ [adj] carefully planned, clever, and intended to deceive people: *They use all kinds of cunning tricks to make people give them money. | His leadership style was to maintain power through a combination of force and cunning strategy. | a cunning marketing ploy*

crafty /ˈkrɑːfti‖ˈkræf-/ [adj] a **crafty** plan or way of doing something etc is one that is cleverly planned and involves deceiving other people, in a way that people admire: *It was a crafty question. 'Why are you trying to catch me out?' he replied. | Jerry and Tony had worked out a crafty way of avoiding paying tax.*

inspired /ɪnˈspaɪəʳd/ [adj] an **inspired** idea, plan etc is extremely clever and impressive and is one that someone suddenly thinks of, without knowing how or why: *'How did you know the answer to that?' 'I didn't, it was just an inspired guess.' | Even the most inspired forecasts of how prices are going to move can't be right all the time. | The band represents some of the best young talent that's around, resulting in a sound that's both innovative and inspired.*

bright idea /ˌbraɪt aɪˈdɪə/ [n C] a clever idea about how to do something: *I like it! It sounds like a really bright idea. | I don't know what kind of present she'd like – if you have any bright ideas let me know.* | **have/come up with the bright idea of doing sth** (=often used humorously) *George came up with the bright idea of visiting every pub we passed.*

9 serious books, ideas etc that are intended for intelligent people

- intellectual
- scholarly
- highbrow
- profound
- serious

intellectual /ˌɪntɨˈlektʃuəl◂/ [adj] *She likes reading those trendy intellectual magazines about politics and society. | There seemed to be remarkably few cultural or intellectual events for the undergraduates at the university.*

scholarly /ˈskɒləʳli‖ˈskɑː-/ [adj only before noun] a book, article, or other piece of writing that is **scholarly** deals with a serious subject and is written in a very detailed way after a lot of study: *The organization is dedicated to scholarly research on life in the next millennium. | Fullington discovered 11 new species of land snails and wrote more than 90 scholarly articles and books.*

highbrow /ˈhaɪbraʊ/ [adj] intended for very intelligent and educated people and therefore not interesting for a lot of people: *He picked up a book that was lying on the floor. It was something highbrow – Kafka, I think. | Readers of tabloid newspapers are less interested in politics and less likely to tune into highbrow news programmes.*

profound /prəˈfaʊnd/ [adj] something such as an idea or statement that is **profound** shows a lot of knowledge and understanding of a serious subject: *The book contains a great many profound insights into human behaviour. | Further research has resulted in a more profound appreciation of the problem. | Burton's lecture was amusing as well as being profound.*

serious /ˈsɪəriəs/ [adj] dealing with a subject in an intelligent and sincere way rather than in an amusing way: *I must admit I find the serious newspapers rather boring. | At school we had to read works by serious writers like Shakespeare and Milton.*

10 the ability to learn well

- intelligence
- brains
- brilliance
- intellect
- genius
- wisdom

intelligence /ɪnˈtelɨdʒəns/ [n U] the ability to learn quickly, think clearly, and understand ideas well: *A child's intelligence develops rapidly between the ages of four and five. | Intelligence cannot be measured just by exam results. | In order to be a pilot you need to be of above average intelligence. | The department bases its selection process on a series of intelligence tests.*

brains /breɪnz/ [n plural] the ability to think quickly and well, remember a lot of facts, and be good at studying **sb's brains** *He has his mother's brains and his father's good looks. | With your brains, you should easily get into college.* | **have the brains (to do sth)** *Chloe had always been the one with the brains to really make something of herself.*

brilliance /ˈbrɪljəns/ [n U] a very high level of intelligence and ability: *Eddie's brilliance brought him top marks in the Harvard entrance exam. | His reputation was founded on his organizational abilities and his acknowledged brilliance as a leader of men.*

intellect /ˈɪntɨlekt/ [n U] the ability to think about and understand and express complicated ideas: *Our physical strength declines with age, but not necessarily our intellect.* | **the intellect** *Joyce's books seem designed to appeal to the intellect rather than the emotions.* | **a great/formidable etc intellect** *Rehnquist was a great scholar who possessed a formidable intellect.*

genius /ˈdʒiːniəs/ [n U] an extremely high level of intelligence, ability, and skill which only a few people have: *Could a computer ever achieve the genius of men like Newton and Einstein. | Maurice was always entertaining, but there was a touch of genius in the way he talked that night.* | **have a genius for (doing) sth** *Sandra will deal with it. That woman has a genius for organization.*

wisdom /ˈwɪzdəm/ [n U] knowledge and good judgement based on experience of life: *Paul learned to value his father's wisdom and advice.* | **the wisdom of**

sth *Some people were beginning to doubt the wisdom of their leader's decisions.* | **conventional wisdom** (=what is usually considered to be true and right) *Conventional wisdom says that the health of the economy is one of the most important factors that determines a president's chances of winning re-election.*

intend/ not intend

RELATED WORDS

▸ *see also* **no matter what/how much etc, deliberately, plan, accidentally, chance, organize**

1 to intend to do something

▸ intend to do sth
▸ mean to do sth
▸ be going to do sth
▸ plan to do sth
▸ be looking to do sth
▸ set out to do sth
▸ be out to do sth
▸ it is sb's intention to do sth
▸ with intent to do sth

intend to do sth /ɪnˌtend tə ˈduː (sth)/ [v phrase] if you **intend to do** something, you have decided that you want to do it at some time in the future: *I wasn't sure why he'd done it, but I intended to find out.* | *Most of these students intend to continue their education at university.* | *Her lawyers stated that they intended to call at least five witnesses.*

mean to do sth /ˌmiːn tə ˈduː (sth)/ [v phrase] especially spoken to intend to do something – use this especially when you forget to do something or did not have the chance to do it: *I've been meaning to phone Anne for ages.* | *I meant to tell you, but I forgot.* | *Sorry, I didn't mean to scare you.*

be going to do sth /biː ˌgəʊɪŋ tə ˈduː (sth)/ [v phrase] especially spoken if you **are going to do** something, you have arranged to do it at a particular time – use this to talk about definite arrangements: *Ruth and Al are going to move to Seattle.* | *I'm going to go to the hospital tomorrow.* | *The committee is going to have several meetings to get student input.*

plan to do sth /ˌplæn tə ˈduː (sth)/ [v phrase] to intend to do something – use this especially when you have thought carefully about when and how you will do something: *Josie's planning to return to work after she's had the baby.* | *We're planning to go on vacation in October.* | *The Board plans to release the report to the press on Sept. 11.*

be looking to do sth /biː ˌlʊkɪŋ tə ˈduː (sth)/ [v phrase] informal to intend to achieve something that you are sure you can achieve: *The company is looking to increase its sales in Europe during the next two years.* | *The Redskins will be looking to repeat their Super Bowl victory next season.*

set out to do sth /ˌset aʊt tə ˈduː (sth)/ [v phrase] to decide to do something and make plans for how you will achieve it, especially in a very determined way: *He set out to make Newcastle the best football team in the country.* | *The new administration set out to develop a better immigration policy.*

be out to do sth /biː ˌaʊt tə ˈduː (sth)/ [v phrase] informal to intend to do something and be determined to succeed: *A young man from Norway is out to be the youngest person ever to finish the race.* | *Manchester United are out to win the European Cup this year.* | **be out to get sb** (=to intend to do something that harms someone else) *Brock believes that Aaronson is out to ruin his reputation.*

it is sb's intention to do sth /ɪt ɪz (sb's) ɪnˌtenʃən tə ˈduː (sth)/ formal use this in public statements, news reports, meetings etc in order to tell people what someone intends to do: *It is our intention to become the number one distributor of health products in the UK.* | *It was never the department's intention to prevent teachers from trying out new ideas.*

with intent to do sth /wɪð ɪnˌtent tə ˈduː (sth)/ [adv] use this especially in legal contexts about someone who deliberately intends to do something bad **do sth with intent to do sth** *Kelly was accused of carrying a deadly weapon with intent to endanger life.* | *He is charged with using a false name with intent to commit fraud.*

2 to not intend to do something

▸ not intend to do sth
▸ not mean to do sth
▸ have no intention of doing sth
▸ have no plans to do sth/not have any plans to do sth
▸ not be serious

not intend to do sth /nɒt ɪnˌtend tə ˈduː (sth)/ [v phrase] if you **do not intend to do** something, you have decided that you will not do it: *She had not intended to speak at the meeting, but felt she had to.* | *I haven't seen the film, and I don't intend to.*

not mean to do sth /nɒt ˌmiːn tə ˈduː (sth)/ [v phrase] especially spoken use this to say that, although you did something, you did not do it deliberately: *They hadn't meant to stay out so late.* | *Look, I'm sorry. I didn't mean to upset you.*

have no intention of doing sth /hæv ˌnəʊ ɪnˌtenʃən əv ˈduːɪŋ (sth)/ [v phrase not in progressive] formal if you **have no intention of doing** something, you have firmly decided that you will definitely not do it: *Mr Brown announced that he had no intention of resigning.* | *The deadline is unreasonable, and they have no intention of trying to meet it.*

have no plans to do sth/not have any plans to do sth /hæv nəʊ ˌplænz tə ˈduː (sth), nɒt hæv eni ˌplænz tə ˈduː (sth)/ [v phrase not in progressive] if you **have no plans to do** something, you have not made a decision to do it, although you may decide to do it at a later time: *She has no plans to retire.* | *He has lived in Thailand for five years, and does not have any plans to go back to the States.*

not be serious /nɒt biː ˈsɪəriəs/ [v phrase] especially spoken to not really intend to do something that you have said that you will do: *He keeps saying he's going to quit, but I don't think he's serious.* | **+ about** *Critics said the government wasn't serious about the environment.* | **you can't be serious** spoken (=say this when you are surprised about what someone has said they intend to do) *You can't be serious about moving to New Orleans.*

3 something that you intend to do

▸ intention
▸ intent

intention ALSO **intent** /ɪnˈtenʃən, ɪnˈtent/ [n C] formal *Army leaders could not guess at the enemy's movements or intentions.* | **+ to do sth** *The government announced its intention to create 50,000 jobs by the end of the year.* | **with the intention of doing sth** *Bouvier returned to Europe with the intention of gathering further support for his cause.* | **have every intention of doing sth** (=use this to emphasize that someone intends to do something) *The lawyers had every intention of calling Smythe to the witness stand.*

intent /ɪnˈtent/ [n singular/U] formal what you intend to do: *The intent of the change was to give local officials more power to make decisions.* | **+ to do sth** *It is not my intent to deny the value of university education.* | **with intent** (=having the intention to do something – used in legal contexts) *He was convicted of possession of cocaine with intent to sell.*

4 when something is intended to do something

- be intended to do sth
- be meant to do sth/ be supposed to do sth

be intended to do sth /biː ɪnˌtendəd tə ˈduː (sth)/ [v phrase] to be done or made for a particular purpose: *The dress I was given was intended to fit someone much smaller.* | *The tests are intended to help teachers improve their teaching.*

be meant to do sth/be supposed to do sth /biː ˌment tə ˈduː (sth), biː səˌpəʊzd tə ˈduː (sth)/ [v phrase] to be intended to have a particular result or effect – use this especially when the result or effect is not achieved: *The new laws are supposed to prevent tax fraud.* | *'There's a Nightmare in My Closet' is a sweet book meant to help children confront their fears.*

5 to tell someone what you intend to do

- make your intentions clear/known
- put/lay your cards on the table

make your intentions clear/known /meɪk jɔːr ɪnˌtenʃənz ˈklɪəʳ, ˈnəʊn/ [v phrase] to let someone know what you intend to do, especially when you think that they do not expect it or will not like it: *The Senator has decided to run for president, and made his intentions known in a public statement Tuesday.* | *People who want to donate their organs after their deaths should make their intentions clear.*

put/lay your cards on the table /ˌpʊt, ˌleɪ jɔːʳ ˌkɑːʳdz ɒn ðə ˈteɪbəl/ [v phrase] informal to tell someone exactly what you intend to do, especially when you have kept it a secret before: *If they're willing to put all their cards on the table and negotiate, that's good.* | *If we want to reach an agreement, we'll have to lay all our cards on the table.*

6 intending to be helpful or kind, but causing problems

- mean well
- well-meaning
- good intentions
- well-meant/ well-intentioned

mean well /ˌmiːn ˈwel/ [v phrase not in progressive] to try to be helpful or kind, but really only cause problems for someone or annoy them: *The doctor meant well, but he was not really listening to me.* | *She means well, but she's a bit tactless.*

well-meaning /ˌwel ˈmiːnɪŋ◂/ [adj] intending to be helpful, but not able to achieve anything useful: *Well-meaning relatives gave me all kinds of advice.* | *Even well-meaning parents cannot protect their children from everything.*

good intentions /ˌgʊd ɪnˈtenʃənz/ [n plural] if you have **good intentions**, you think of doing something helpful or kind, but often never do it: *Good intentions are not enough. Make an exercise programme for yourself and keep to it.* | *The department's good intentions have been buried under a mountain of rules and paperwork.*

well-meant/well-intentioned /ˌwel ˈment◂, ˌwel ɪnˈtenʃənd◂/ [adj] an action or a statement that is **well-meant** or **well-intentioned** is intended to be kind or helpful, but either does not help at all, insults someone, or causes harm: *Recent changes in housing policy, though well-meant, have done more harm than good.* | *Well-intentioned grandparents sometimes interfere with a mother's way of bringing up her children.*

interested

RELATED WORDS

opposite: **boring/bored**

see also **interesting, excited/exciting, obsession**

1 feeling interested in something

- interested
- find sth interesting
- with interest
- interest in sth
- show/express (an) interest
- curious
- fascinated
- have a fascination with/for
- intrigued
- be into

interested /ˈɪntrəstəd/ [adj not usually before noun] if you are **interested** in something, you give it your attention because you want to know more about it: *The children seemed very interested when I showed them my photographs.* | *I can't remember the name of the book, but if you're interested I can find out.* | **+ in** *I've never really been interested in politics.* | *Bob first got interested in motor cycles when he was about sixteen.* | **+ to know/hear/see/learn etc sth** *You're an expert on legal problems – I'd be interested to know what you think.* | *We'd be very interested to hear your opinion about this.*

find sth interesting /ˌfaɪnd (sth) ˈɪntrəstɪŋ/ [v phrase] to feel interested in something because it is the type of thing that you usually like to know more about: *It's a book about travelling round India. I thought you'd find it interesting.* | **+ to read/watch/hear about etc** *I always find wildlife programmes interesting to watch.*

with interest /wɪð ˈɪntrəst/ [adv] especially written if you do something **with interest**, you do it in a way that shows you are interested: *Richard listened with interest to the conversation at the next table.* | **with great interest** *I read with great interest your article concerning the history of the university.*

interest in sth /ˈɪntrəst ɪn (sth)/ [n phrase] if there is **interest in** something, several or a lot of people are interested in it and want to find out more about it: *There has always been a lot of interest in the question of life on other planets.* | *The Head of Geography said the project was an example of the school's continuing interest in environmental issues.* | **take an interest in sth** *I was a teenager when I first took a serious interest in films.* | *Children with parents who take an interest in their education generally do better at school.*

show/express (an) interest /ˌʃəʊ, ɪkˌspres (ən) ˈɪntrəst/ [v phrase] to say or do something to show that you are interested in something: *If you think you'd like the job, you should at least express an interest.* | **+ in** *Several companies have already expressed interest in our research.* | *At a few weeks old, most babies are showing an interest in what is going on around them.*

curious /ˈkjʊəriəs/ [adj] eager to find out more about something because you are interested but do not know much about it: *The visitors were soon surrounded by a crowd of curious children.* | *I'm not being nosy, I'm just curious.* | **+ about** *People have always been curious about exactly how life on earth began.* | **curious to know/find out/discover etc sth** *He was curious to find out why she had left her job so suddenly.* —**curiously** [adv] *Everyone stared at us curiously, wondering who we were.* —**curiosity** /ˌkjʊəriˈɒsə̇ti‖-ˈɑːs-/ [n U] *She seems to have no curiosity as to who her natural parents are.* | *Out of curiosity, I started to read the record he's made.*

fascinated /ˈfæsə̇neɪtə̇d/ [adj not usually before noun] extremely interested in something that you are watching or listening to, especially because it is unusual: *She watched, fascinated, as the bird came closer until she could almost touch it.* | *The more I heard about him, the more fascinated I became.* | **+ by** *I was fascinated by her stories of her childhood in Africa.* | **+ to discover/find out/learn etc** *He was fascinated to discover that they had both been born in the same town on the same day.*

have a fascination with/for /hæv ə ˌfæsə̇ˈneɪʃən wɪð, fɔːʳ/ [v phrase] to have a very strong and often unusual interest in something: *I've always had this strange fascination with the circus.* | *Her writing shows a fascination for the darker side of life.*

intrigued /ɪnˈtriːgd/ [adj not before noun] interested by something and eager to know more about it, because it seems mysterious or strange: *'Stop me if I'm boring you.' 'No, please carry on – I'm intrigued!'* | *Scientists became intrigued by the rock, which appeared to have come from outer space.* | **+ by** *Diana was intrigued by Sue's cryptic message on the answerphone.* | **+ to find out/ learn/know etc** *I was intrigued to find that she spoke Aramaic.*

be into /biː ˈɪntuː/ [phr v T] British spoken informal to be very interested in a subject or activity, and to spend a lot of time on it because you enjoy it: *Both the kids are into computer games at the moment, and nothing else!* | **be into doing sth** *Luke's really into keeping fit – he goes running at 6 o'clock every day.*

2 so interested that you give all your attention to something

- absorbed
- gripped/riveted
- engrossed
- obsessed
- enthralled
- mesmerized
- spellbound
- be all ears

absorbed /əbˈsɔːʳbd, əbˈzɔːʳbd/ [adj not before noun] so interested in something that you give it all your attention and do not notice or pay attention to other things **+ in** *Penny and Sam were so absorbed in their game, that they didn't hear me call.* | *Dad was obviously far too absorbed in his own difficulties to be interested in mine.* | *I saw Bill walking across the park, absorbed in his own thoughts.*

gripped/riveted /grɪpt, ˈrɪvə̇tə̇d/ [adj not before noun] extremely interested by a book, film, event etc or by what someone is saying, so that you cannot stop reading, watching, listening etc: *It was a brilliant documentary. I sat absolutely riveted from beginning to end.* | *I was completely gripped as soon as I opened the book.* | **+ by** *We stopped the car, riveted by the sight of a village wedding in progress.*

engrossed /ɪnˈgrəʊst/ [adj not before noun] extremely interested in something such as a book or your work, so that you do not notice anything that is happening around you: *As she worked, she became so engrossed that she lost all sense of time.* | **+ in** *Jane was sitting in bed, engrossed in a novel.* | *They appeared to be engrossed in their conversation and I didn't want to disturb them.*

obsessed /əbˈsest/ [adj not before noun] to be too interested in something, so that you cannot stop thinking about it or spending your time on it: *He spends all his time fiddling about with cars – he's completely obsessed.* | **+ by/with** *As an artist, he was obsessed with sex and death.* | *People seem to be obsessed by health issues these days.* | **become obsessed** *She became obsessed with the idea of making money.* —**obsession** /əbˈseʃən/ [n C] *His interest in the Internet was rapidly becoming an obsession.*

enthralled /ɪnˈθrɔːld/ [adj] very interested and excited by a story or by something that you see or hear, so that you give all your attention to it: *From the opening line of the play, the audience was completely enthralled.* | **listen/watch etc enthralled** *We listened enthralled as she told us the story of her life.* | **+ by** *I was completely enthralled by the world of the theatre, and knew that I wanted to act.*

mesmerized ALSO **mesmerised** British /ˈmezməraɪzd/ [adj not before noun] unable to stop looking at something or listening to someone because they completely keep your attention: *She stood there mesmerized as he picked up the gun and turned it slowly towards her.* | **+ by** *It was as if the audience was completely mesmerized by the small figure on the stage.*

spellbound /ˈspelbaʊnd/ [adj] so interested by something, especially something strange or wonderful, that you are unable to move or think of anything else **listen/watch/wait etc spellbound** *Millions of Japanese listened spellbound as they heard the Emperor speak in public for the first time.* | **+ by** *On clear nights we were spellbound by the strange flickering of the Northern lights in the sky.* | **held sb spellbound** *The Firebird is a magical ballet that still holds audiences spellbound.*

be all ears /biː ˌɔːl ˈɪəʳz/ [v phrase] spoken to be extremely interested in what someone is telling you, and listen very carefully to it: *Tell me exactly what happened. I'm all ears.* | *Everyone was all ears as soon as I mentioned a cash prize.*

3 to make someone interested

- interest
- get sb interested
- fascinate
- intrigue
- rekindle/revive interest

interest /ˈɪntrə̇st/ [v T not in progressive] if something **interests** you, it makes you feel interested: *There was an article in yesterday's paper that might interest you.* | *It's always best to choose the subject that interests you, not the one your parents want you to do.* | *What interests me most is where he got all that money in the first place.*

get sb interested /ˌget (sb) ˈɪntrə̇stə̇d/ [v phrase] to make someone interested in a subject or activity, especially by trying to make it seem attractive or enjoyable: *If we can get enough people interested, we could start a reading group.* | **+ in** *I've tried to get Sam interested in sport, but all he wants to do is watch TV.*

fascinate /ˈfæsəneɪt/ [v T not in progressive] if something **fascinates** you, it makes you very interested, so that you want to spend a lot of time thinking about it, watching it etc: *Anything to do with computers fascinates him.* | *Cats fascinate me – I don't know why.* | **what fascinates me is** *What fascinates me about his poems is their apparent simplicity.*

intrigue /ɪnˈtriːg/ [v T] if something **intrigues** you, it makes you want to know more about it because there is something about it that you do not understand or cannot explain: *The final part of the letter intrigued him greatly.* | *One question has particularly intrigued those working on this study.*

rekindle/revive interest /riːˌkɪndl, rɪˌvaɪv ˈɪntrəst/ [v phrase] to make people interested in a particular subject again: *The discovery of the Titanic, twenty miles below the ocean surface, rekindled interest in the ship.* | *His book did much to revive interest in long-forgotten natural remedies.*

4 to become interested

- get/become interested
- get into
- get the bug

get/become interested /ˌget, bɪˌkʌm ˈɪntrəstəd/ [v phrase] *'Really?' he said. He was obviously getting interested.* | **+ in** *When did you first get really interested in baseball?* | *Early in his career, Piaget became interested in children's development.*

get into /get ˈɪntuː/ [phr v T] especially spoken, informal to start to become interested in something: *I never used to like jazz but I've been getting into it recently.* | *A lot of teenage boys suddenly get into fitness and weight-training.*

get the bug /ˌget ðə ˈbʌg/ [v phrase] informal to become interested in something, so that you want to do it a lot **get the gardening/travel/golf etc bug** *Since my college days I've always had the travel bug.* | *As soon as the kids got out on the slopes, they were bitten by the skiing bug.*

5 to stop being interested

- lose interest

lose interest /ˌluːz ˈɪntrəst/ [v phrase] to stop being interested in something that you were interested in before: *Dan used to play football every Sunday, but then he just lost interest.* | **+ in** *Recently she seems to have lost all interest in her work.*

6 not interested

- not be interested
- uninterested
- not interest
- show/express no interest
- lack of interest
- apathetic
- leave sb cold

▸ *see also* **boring/bored**

not be interested /nɒt biː ˈɪnstrəstəd/ [v phrase] *I started telling them about my vacation, but they weren't very interested.* | *Helen tried to persuade her sister to come with us, but she just wasn't interested.* | **+ in** *I'm sure you're not interested in hearing me talk about my ex-boyfriends.*

uninterested /ʌnˈɪntrəstəd/ [adj] not interested and not wanting to know about something: *Morris appeared to be completely uninterested in any of the suggestions I made.* | *'Oh is that all?' she said in an uninterested tone of voice.* | **+ in** *It's a pity that so many people are uninterested in science at school.*

not interest /nɒt ˈɪntrəst/ [v phrase] if a subject or activity **does not interest** you, you do not want to know about it or learn about it: *To be honest, politics doesn't interest me at all.* | *Everyone's always talking about the World Cup, but it just doesn't interest me.*

show/express no interest /ˌʃəʊ, ɪkˌspres nəʊ ˈɪntrəst/ [v phrase] to not be interested in something, and to not do or say anything that shows you are interested: *I try to talk to her about my work, but she shows no interest.* | *When we suggested going camping, no one expressed any interest.* | **+ in** *A lot of people have been to look at the house, but they've shown no interest in buying it.*

lack of interest /ˌlæk əv ˈɪntrəst/ [n phrase] if there is a **lack of interest** in something, people are not interested in it, especially when you would expect them to be interested: *The boy replied with a complete lack of interest.* | **+ in** *A depressed person often shows self-pity and a lack of interest in the outside world.*

apathetic /ˌæpəˈθetɪk◂/ [adj] someone who is **apathetic** about a particular activity or problem is not interested in it and does not care about it enough to try and change it: *Of course it matters whether you vote or not! Don't be so apathetic!* | **+ about** *People must realize that we can't afford to be apathetic about environmental issues any longer.* —**apathy** /ˈæpəθi/ [n U] *Sometimes the apathy of the electorate is quite depressing.* | *political apathy*

leave sb cold /ˌliːv (sb) ˈkəʊld/ [v phrase] informal if something **leaves you cold**, you do not feel at all interested in it, even though many other people are: *Why are people so crazy about opera? It leaves me completely cold.* | *All this talk about counselling and therapy left me cold.*

7 something you are interested in

- hobby
- interest
- pastime

hobby /ˈhɒbi‖ˈhɑː-/ [n C] an activity that you enjoy and think is interesting, and that you like to spend time doing when you are not working: *What are your hobbies?* | *Stamp collecting has been a hobby of mine ever since I was a child.* | **take up a hobby** *When people retire, they often take up new hobbies and start to make new friends.*

interest /ˈɪntrəst/ [n C] something you like to spend time doing or studying when you are not working, because you think it is interesting or entertaining: *Her interests were the same as most young girls – pop music, boys and clothes.* | *Golf is also one of his interests.* | *Josie isn't really an archaeologist, it's just an interest of hers.*

pastime /ˈpɑːstaɪm‖ˈpæs-/ [n C] something that you enjoy doing and think is interesting, that you do in the time when you are not working: *As a pastime, keeping and riding horses has always been very expensive.* | *Gardening is my mother's favourite pastime.* | *In southern Europe, shooting birds is a popular pastime.*

interesting

RELATED WORDS

opposite: —————————— **boring/bored**

▸ *see also* **interested, excited/exciting**

1 something that makes you feel interested

- ▸ **interesting**
- ▸ **fascinating**
- ▸ **intriguing**
- ▸ **be of interest**
- ▸ **stimulating**
- ▸ **hold your attention**
- ▸ **absorbing**

interesting /ˈɪntrɪstɪŋ/ [adj] if something is **interesting**, you give it your attention, because it is unusual or exciting or because it is something that you want to know about: *We saw an interesting film about African wildlife.* | *The most interesting thing about dinosaurs is the fact that they all died out so suddenly.* | *Michael's new job sounds really interesting.* | *There's a course in English business law at King's College that looks interesting.* | **find sth interesting** (=think something is interesting) *I found the book quite interesting even though it's not the sort of thing I'd normally read.* | **find it interesting (that)** *I find it interesting that no one has yet mentioned the President's appalling record on the economy.* | **it is interesting (that)** *It is interesting that the present recession is much deeper in the south than in the north.* | **it is interesting to do sth** *It would be interesting to know how much he earns.*

fascinating /ˈfæsɪneɪtɪŋ/ [adj] extremely interesting: *Singapore's exotic mix of cultures – mostly Chinese, Indian, and Malay – makes it a fascinating holiday destination.* | *The programme focuses on the fascinating story of Mary Shelley, the woman who, at just 18, wrote the horror masterpiece Frankenstein.* | **find sth fascinating** (=think something is fascinating) *We went round Chesmore Zoo the other day and found it fascinating.* | **it is fascinating to do sth** *It's fascinating to imagine what might have happened if the US had stayed out of World War II.*

intriguing /ɪnˈtriːɡɪŋ/ [adj] if something is **intriguing**, you want to know more about it because it is unusual or difficult to understand: *Taylor's latest CD presents the listener with an intriguing mixture of musical styles.* | **it is intriguing to do sth** *It is intriguing to note that only one of his books was published during his own lifetime.*

be of interest /biː əv ˈɪntrɪst/ [v phrase] if something **is of interest** to someone, they want to know more about it because it is related to a subject or activity that they are interested in: *Finally, in the last section of the talk I will cover a few miscellaneous topics which I think may be of interest.* | **+ to** *Pull your chair over. I heard something today that might be of interest to you.* | *It is expected that the results of the research programme will be of interest not only to academics, but also to the government.*

stimulating /ˈstɪmjʊleɪtɪŋ/ [adj] something that is **stimulating** is interesting and enjoyable because it gives you new ideas to think about: *Her lectures were always stimulating and covered a variety of subjects.* | *The Faculty is a large but welcoming and intellectually stimulating community.* | *The department is very well equipped and provides a stimulating environment for postgraduate research.* | *New York has always been an exciting and stimulating place to be.*

hold your attention /ˌhəʊld jɔːr əˈtenʃən/ [v phrase] if something such as a book, play, or speech **holds your attention**, it makes you keep reading, watching, or listening to it and stops you from thinking about other things: *The book holds the reader's attention completely throughout its 600 pages.* | *At large conferences speakers have to work harder to hold people's attention than at smaller ones.*

absorbing /əbˈsɔːʳbɪŋ, -ˈzɔːʳ-/ [adj] something that is **absorbing** holds your attention for a long time because it is very interesting and enjoyable: *Developing your own photographs can be an absorbing hobby.* | *In an absorbing book about how she learned to fly, Diane Ackerman tells why she chooses to risk her life.*

2 so interesting that you cannot stop watching, reading etc

- ▸ **riveting/gripping**
- ▸ **I couldn't put it down**
- ▸ **compelling**
- ▸ **engrossing**
- ▸ **mesmerizing/enthralling**
- ▸ **spellbinding**
- ▸ **page-turner**

riveting/gripping /ˈrɪvɪtɪŋ, ˈɡrɪpɪŋ/ [adj] a film, book etc that is **riveting** or **gripping** is so interesting or exciting that you do not want to stop watching it, reading it etc: *The novel is absolutely riveting from start to finish.* | *The story is a riveting one about two children who find an adventure game which becomes real as they are playing it.* | *Hitchcock's film 'The Birds' is a brilliant psychological thriller with a gripping climax.* | *The play is never quite interesting or gripping enough in the right places despite the considerable efforts of the actors.*

I couldn't put it down /aɪ ˌkʊdnt pʊt ɪt ˈdaʊn/ spoken say this about a book that was so enjoyable that you did not want to stop reading it: *What an amazing book! I just couldn't put it down.*

compelling /kəmˈpelɪŋ/ [adj] written a film, book etc that is **compelling** is so interesting that you feel you must keep watching or reading it: *The film was so compelling I could scarcely take my eyes off the screen for a second.* | *Orwell's 'Burmese Days' is a compelling account of life under British Colonial rule.*

engrossing /ɪŋˈɡrəʊsɪŋ/ [adj] something that is **engrossing**, such as a book or your work, is so interesting that you do not notice anything that is happening around you: *In his latest novel, Martin Amis gives us an engrossing tale of human trauma.* | *The daydream was so engrossing that she almost failed to notice Peter waving to her from the other side of the road.*

mesmerizing/enthralling /ˈmezməraɪzɪŋ, ɪnˈθrɔːlɪŋ/ [adj] a story, film, game etc that is **mesmerizing** or **enthralling** is very interesting and exciting, so that you give all your attention to it: *The band incorporates Spanish, Latin American and Middle Eastern influences into a powerful, mesmerizing mix.* | *Visitors to the show will find it an enthralling experience.* | *Sergei Rebrov scored the goal that finally ended an enthralling match.*

spellbinding /ˈspelbaɪndɪŋ/ [adj] a story, film, piece of music etc that is **spellbinding** is so original or interesting that you are unable to think about anything else while you are reading it, watching it etc: *One of the President's most spellbinding TV performances came on 27 July.* | *What she reveals in this novel is a spellbinding tale of her life in China.*

page-turner /ˈpeɪdʒ ˌtɜːʳnəʳ/ [n C] a book whose story is so interesting that you do not want to stop reading it and are very eager to find out what happens next: *Stephen King's latest novel promises to be another page-turner.*

3 an interesting period of time

- interesting
- eventful
- colourful
- there's never a dull moment

interesting /ˈɪntrǝ̇stɪŋ/ [adj] an **interesting** period of time has a lot of **interesting**, unusual, or exciting things happening during it: *Today's been really interesting, I enjoyed it very much.* | *At the age of 80 she still leads a very busy and interesting life.* | *The Renaissance must have been a very interesting time to have been alive.*

eventful /ɪˈventfəl/ [adj] full of interesting or important events: *The poet Arthur Rimbaud led a short but extremely eventful life.* | *It has been an eventful day in politics – two ministers have resigned and the Prime Minister has called an election.*

colourful British **/colorful** American /ˈkʌləʳfəl/ [adj usually before noun] containing a lot of unusual, exciting, and sometimes immoral events or behaviour: *There are many chapters in Wilkins' long, colorful life, including the time he spent in prison.* | *Coleman's colourful life is recorded in his autobiography, Reflections of a Racing Driver.* | *Riva is a welcoming town with a colourful history.*

there's never a dull moment /ðeəʳz ˌnevər ə ˌdʌl ˈməʊmənt/ spoken say this about a situation, film, story etc in which a lot of things happen, and you do not have time to be bored: *When you have three young children to look after there's never a dull moment.* | *There's never a dull moment in our house, especially as there are ten of us living here.* | *There's never a dull moment in the entire film, and Pierce Brosnan is superb in the James Bond role.*

4 an interesting city, building, work of art etc

- interesting
- fascinating
- unusual
- have character

interesting /ˈɪntrǝ̇stɪŋ/ [adj] a building, work of art, object etc that is **interesting** is unusual or special in some way: *The exhibition includes some interesting old musical instruments.* | *What makes San Francisco so interesting is its architecture, which is completely different from that of other American cities.*

fascinating /ˈfæsǝ̇neɪtɪŋ/ [adj] extremely interesting: *London is one of the most exciting and fascinating cities in the world.* | *It was a fascinating painting, with clever use of colour and light.* | *The Scottish Craft Centre has a fascinating range of pottery, jewellery and textiles for sale.* | *Alice Thornton's autobiography provides a fascinating account of family life in seventeenth-century England.*

unusual /ʌnˈjuːʒuəl, -ʒəl/ [adj] different in style from other buildings, cities, or works of art, and therefore interesting: *Louise makes hats that are eye-catching and unusual.* | *Yuri invited me to sample some of Osaka's more unusual restaurants.*

have character /hæv ˈkærǝ̇ktəʳ/ [v phrase not in progressive] if a place or a building **has character**, it is old and has a lot of unusual features which make it interesting and special: *The hotel has character and charm, and is ideal as a base for exploring the city.*

5 words for describing an interesting person

- interesting
- fascinating
- colourful
- a character

interesting /ˈɪntrǝ̇stɪŋ/ [adj] *The party was full of artists, actors, and other interesting people.* | *Lawyers get to represent lots of clients in their careers, but few as interesting as a president.* | **find sb interesting** (=think someone is interesting) *She found him interesting, attractive even.*

fascinating /ˈfæsǝ̇neɪtɪŋ/ [adj] extremely interesting and often attractive: *Nathan Bryce was the most handsome, fascinating, and ruthless man she had ever met.* | *It was easy to understand why Denise found Chris so fascinating.*

colourful British **/colorful** American /ˈkʌləʳfəl/ [adj usually before noun] a **colourful** person is interesting and often amusing because they are very unusual, especially because they behave in a way that does not follow society's usual rules: *The late Bob Johnston was one of the city's most colorful, beloved characters.* | *Throughout his life, O'Connor was a colourful and controversial character.*

a character /ə ˈkærǝ̇ktəʳ/ [n singular] someone who other people like and think is interesting, because they behave in an unusual and amusing way: *She's quite a character – people find her rather shocking, but I like her.* | *James is a real character, completely unpredictable but very funny.*

6 to make something more interesting

- make sth more interesting
- make sth come to life
- liven up
- jazz up
- add variety

make sth more interesting /ˌmeɪk (sth) mɔːr ˈɪntrǝ̇stɪŋ/ [v phrase] *Teachers are always trying to find new ways of making their lessons more interesting.* | *Sharing a house makes life much more interesting.*

make sth come to life ALSO **make sth come alive** /meɪk (sth) ˌkʌm tə ˈlaɪf, meɪk (sth) ˌkʌm əˈlaɪv/ [v phrase] to make something much more interesting, especially by making it seem more lively or real: *Campbell made the match come to life when he scored with a header in the 67th minute.* | *Cagney makes the character come alive through a combination of his looks and his skills as an actor.*

liven up ALSO **enliven** formal /ˌlaɪvən ˈʌp, ɪnˈlaɪvən/ [phr v T] to make something that is a little boring or ordinary become more interesting or exciting **liven sth up** *I wish Leo would come – he would liven the party up.* | *Bob tried to liven things up by telling some of his jokes.* | **liven up sth** *Tropical fruit such as mangoes and kiwis can help to liven up salad.*

jazz up /ˌdʒæz ˈʌp/ [phr v T] to make something seem more interesting and exciting by adding things to it that are colourful, modern etc **jazz up sth** *You can easily jazz up a plain outfit with some bright, colourful accessories.* | *The company's first product, WebSuite, allowed anyone with basic computer skills to jazz up a Web site.* | **jazz sth up** *They've really jazzed it up in here but I bet the food's still the same.*

add variety /ˌæd vəˈraɪəti/ [v phrase] to make something more interesting by adding something different or unusual: *Evergreen plants with interesting leaves, berries or flowers add variety to a window box* *throughout the year.* | **+ to** *Make sure you add variety to your child's diet with plenty of fresh fruit and vegetables.*

interfere

to try to influence a situation that you should not be involved in

RELATED WORDS

▸ *see also* **take part/be involved**

1 to interfere

- ▸ interfere
- ▸ meddle
- ▸ poke/stick your nose into
- ▸ put/shove/stick your oar in
- ▸ intrude

interfere /ˌɪntəʳˈfɪəʳ/ [v I] to try to influence a situation that you should not be involved in, for example by telling someone what to do or giving them advice that they do not want: *I'm sorry. I didn't mean to interfere, but I didn't want Glenda to be upset.* | *The protestors were peaceful, and the police decided not to interfere.* | **+ in** *She has no right to interfere in her son's marriage.* | *The US was accused of interfering in China's internal affairs.* —**interference** [n U] when someone interferes in a situation: **+ from** *The Internet should be allowed to develop without any interference from the government.*

meddle /ˈmedl/ [v I] to interfere in a situation that you do not understand or know enough about, and that someone else is responsible for dealing with **+ in** *Church leaders shouldn't meddle in politics.* | **+ with** *Most of us don't know our neighbors well enough to meddle with their lives.*

poke/stick your nose into /ˌpəʊk, ˌstɪk jɔːʳ ˈnəʊz ɪntuː/ [v phrase] informal to ask questions about someone else's private life and give them advice they do not want, in a way that annoys them: *No one wants the government sticking its nose into the personal affairs of citizens.* | *She's one of these people who is always poking her nose into other people's business.*

put/shove/stick your oar in British informal **/butt in** American informal /ˌpʊt, ˌʃʌv, ˌstɪk jɔːr ˈɔːr ɪn, ˌbʌt ˈɪn/ [v phrase] to give your opinion or advice to someone when they do not want it, because it is a private situation: *I don't want your dad over here sticking his oar in.*

intrude /ɪnˈtruːd/ [v I] to become involved in someone's private affairs when you know you have no right to be involved – use this especially when saying that you want to avoid doing this: *I don't want to intrude, but are you all right?* | *Sorry, I didn't mean to intrude. I didn't realize you were on the phone.* | **+ on** *It's very important not to intrude on the family's grief, whilst still helping with the funeral arrangements.* | **+ into** *Companies should not have the right to intrude into employees' personal lives by giving them psychological tests.* —**intrusion** /ɪnˈtruːʒən/ [n C/U] **+ in/into** *The magazine has apologised for any intrusion into the actor's private life.* —**intrusive** /ɪnˈtruːsɪv/ [adj] *I found the reporter's questions very intrusive.*

2 someone who interferes too much in other people's affairs

- ▸ busybody
- ▸ do-gooder
- ▸ interfering
- ▸ meddling/meddlesome

busybody /ˈbɪziˌbɒdi‖-ˌbɑːdi/ [n C] someone who likes interfering in other people's affairs, giving advice, and trying to influence what people do: *I can't believe the number of busybodies who ask me when I'm going to have another baby.*

do-gooder /ˌduː ˈgʊdəʳ‖ˈduː ˌgʊdər/ [n C] someone who tries to help other people and thinks that they are being helpful – use this about someone you think is in fact causing problems and when it would be better if they did not get involved: *Pearson isn't just a do-gooder – he's been in prison and wants to help others stay out.*

interfering /ˌɪntəʳˈfɪərɪŋ◂/ [adj] someone who is **interfering** often tries to influence situations they should not be involved in, and annoys people by doing this: *I wish that interfering brother of yours would keep out of my affairs.*

meddling/meddlesome /ˈmedlɪŋ, ˈmedlsəm/ [adj only before noun] a **meddling** or **meddlesome** person interferes in situations that they should not be involved in and do not always fully understand or know enough about: *He's skilled at dealing with meddlesome reporters.* | *Because of the new laws, food companies are complaining about meddling government.*

3 to not interfere

- ▸ mind your own business/it's none of your business
- ▸ stay/keep out of it
- ▸ be/have nothing to do with
- ▸ leave/let well alone

mind your own business/it's none of your business /ˌmaɪnd jɔːr əʊn ˈbɪznɪ̈s, ɪts ˌnʌn əv jɔːʳ ˈbɪznɪ̈s/ [v phrase] spoken say this when you want someone to stop interfering or asking questions about something that is private: *Whitney, you just mind your own business. He can do what he wants.* | *He wanted a copy of the will but I told him it was none of his business.* | *I didn't ask, because it's none of my business really, but I was sure curious.*

stay/keep out of it /ˌsteɪ, ˌkiːp ˈaʊt əv ɪt/ [v phrase] spoken informal to not get involved in a fight or an argument between other people: *It isn't your business, you stay out of it and let her handle it.* | *I know what I'm doing – you keep out of it.* | **stay/keep well out of it** (=not interfere at all) British *They're always arguing about money, but I try to stay well out of it.*

be/have nothing to do with ALSO **not have anything to do with sb** /biː, hæv ˌnʌθɪŋ tə ˈduː wɪð, nɒt hæv ˌeniθɪŋ tə ˈduː wɪð (sb)/ [v phrase] if a situation **has nothing to do with** someone, it is very personal and private, and that person has no right to interfere in it: *I really shouldn't have told her about it – it had nothing to do with her, really.* | *Back off and let me handle it. It's nothing to do with you.*

leave/let well alone British **/leave/let well enough alone** American /liːv, let ˌwel əˈləʊn, liːv, let ˌwel ɪnʌf əˈləʊn / [v phrase] spoken to not interfere or try to change a situation, because you might make it worse than before: *I should have left well enough alone, and never told my parents what had happened at all.* | *Once you've finished a project, leave well alone and go on to the next one.*

interrupt

RELATED WORDS

- to stop someone when they are doing something *see* **disturb**
- to stop someone doing something *see* **stop (25-33)**
- *see also* **talk**

1 to stop someone when they are speaking

- interrupt
- butt in
- cut in
- cut sb off/cut sb short
- break in

interrupt /ˌɪntəˈrʌpt/ [v I/T] to start speaking when someone else is already speaking: *I wish you wouldn't interrupt all the time.* | *I'm sorry I interrupted you.* | *He apologised for interrupting her speech.* —**interruption** [n C] *If there are any further interruptions, the whole class will stay behind.*

butt in /ˌbʌt ˈɪn/ [phr v I] spoken to interrupt someone rudely: *Will you please stop butting in!* | *Mom, Joe keeps butting in and he won't let me finish my story.*

cut in /ˌkʌt ˈɪn/ [phr v I] written to interrupt someone before they have finished talking, so that you can say something: *'There's this nice guy ...' 'I'm not interested,' Roz cut in, laughing.* | *Lila cut in again, answering before he could even open his mouth.*

cut sb off/cut sb short /ˌkʌt (sb) ˈɒf, ˌkʌt (sb) ˈʃɔːʳt/ [phr v T/v phrase] to interrupt someone before they have finished what they were going to say: *Her elder brother cut her off sharply – 'I won't have you speaking to your mother like that!'* | *I'm sorry to cut you short, Mrs Shaw, but I'm afraid we've run out of time.*

break in /ˌbreɪk ˈɪn/ [phr v I] to join a conversation by interrupting someone or by saying something suddenly: *'Sam, what on earth are you talking about?' she broke in at last.* | *'That's enough,' the guard broke in impatiently. 'Hurry up and say goodbye.'* | **+ on** *The tutor finally broke in on Sam's monologue, much to the relief of the rest of the class.*

2 to deliberately keep interrupting someone in public

- heckle
- barrack

heckle /ˈhekəl/ [v I/T] to deliberately interrupt a speaker or performer by shouting, especially to show that you do not agree with what they are saying: *Comedians usually have a few ready comments for members of the audience that come to heckle.* | *The speaker was heckled by a group of protestors.* —**heckling** [n U] *The speech was interrupted by endless heckling from a group of young men.* —**heckler** [n C] *The hecklers were thrown out of the conference hall.*

barrack /ˈbærək/ [v T] British to interrupt a speaker at a public meeting by shouting or making a noise so that no one can hear them, especially because you disapprove of what they are saying: *The politician was barracked by students at the back of the hall.* —**barracking** [n U] *The barracking always comes from a small minority who want to disrupt the meeting.*

introduce

RELATED WORDS

- to introduce yourself when you meet someone for the first time *see* **meet (3)**
- *see also* **start, first**

1 to talk or write about a subject for the first time

- introduce
- lead into
- preface

introduce /ˌɪntrəˈdjuːs‖-ˈduːs/ [v T] *The first chapter introduces the terms and ideas which will be studied.* | *Einstein introduced his theory of relativity in 1915, in a scientific paper.*

lead into /ˈliːd ɪntuː/ [v T not in passive] to begin to talk or write about a subject by talking about a similar subject first: *Her lecture began with a talk about her own experience, leading into a more general discussion.* | *Each Olympic event will be led into by sports experts explaining the format.*

preface /ˈprefəs/ [phr v T] written to say or write something about your subject before you talk about the main part of it: *He prefaced his criticisms by saying there was much to admire in the work.* | **+ with** *There are 45 tours, each prefaced with a historical overview of the area.*

2 speech or writing that introduces something

- introduction
- intro
- lead-in
- introductory
- preface/foreword
- prologue

introduction /ˌɪntrəˈdʌkʃən/ [n C] *After a brief introduction by the Chairman, the meeting began.* | *Powell wrote in the introduction that all the armed forces must work together as a team.*

intro /ˈɪntrəʊ/ [n C] spoken the introduction to a speech: *I'll start off with a brief intro.* | *In his intro he said he didn't know much about language teaching.*

lead-in /ˈliːd ɪn/ [n C] a short statement that comes before the main part of a speech or piece of writing to tell you what it is about: *The lead-in to a news item should only take a few seconds.* | *The last sentence in a paragraph should form a lead-in to what is to be discussed in the next paragraph.*

introductory /ˌɪntrəˈdʌktəri◂/ [adj only before noun] giving a short introduction to a subject before it is discussed or studied in more detail: *Wilson will give the introductory speech at the education conference.* | *an introductory course on American literature*

preface/foreword /ˈprefəs, ˈfɔːʳwɜːʳd/ [n C] a short piece of writing at the beginning of a book, before the main part, that tells what the book is about or the reason for writing it: *In his preface, the author sums up what he has learned from two years of observing political life.* | *According to the foreword, the cookbook aims to celebrate the rich variety of Chinese food.*

prologue /ˈprəʊlɒg‖-lɔːg, -lɑːg/ [n C] an introduction to a piece of writing, for example a play or a long poem: *The play begins with a brief prologue.* | **+ to** *the prologue to Shakespeare's Henry V*

invent

RELATED WORDS

▸ *see also* **idea, new, design, make**

1 to think of a new idea, design, or name for something

- ▸ **invent**
- ▸ **create**
- ▸ **come up with/think up**
- ▸ **devise**
- ▸ **make up**
- ▸ **conceive**
- ▸ **dream up**
- ▸ **coin**

invent /ɪnˈvent/ [v T] to think of an idea for a new product, machine etc for the first time, and design it and make it: *Alexander Graham Bell invented the telephone.* | *Television was invented in the 1920s.* | *Theremin invented the weird electronic instrument that provided soundtracks to 1950s science-fiction movies.* —**invention** [n U] when someone has invented a new product **+ of** *This discovery was to lead to the invention of the nuclear bomb.*

create /kriˈeɪt/ [v T] to make something new in art, literature, fashion etc: *Agatha Christie created the character Hercule Poirot.* | *Mary Quant created a whole new look for women's clothes in the 1960s.*

come up with/think up /ˌkʌm ˈʌp wɪð, ˌθɪŋk ˈʌp/ [phr v T] informal to produce a new idea, name, method etc by thinking carefully about it **think up/ come up with sth** *See if you can come up with a better name for it.* | *We need to think up some new ideas for the Christmas show.* | **think sth up** *We don't just think this stuff up. It's the way good lawyers always operate.*

devise /dɪˈvaɪz/ [v T] to invent a way of doing something, especially one that is clever and complicated: *The exercise programme was devised by a leading health expert.* | *Scientists have devised a test that shows who is most likely to get the disease.*

make up /ˌmeɪk ˈʌp/ [phr v T] to invent something such as a story or song, usually without writing it down **make up sth** *For Halloween, the children made up stories about wolves and witches.* | *When my mother was in a good mood, she would make up songs about us.* | **make sth up** *That's a good riddle. Did you make it up yourself?*

conceive /kənˈsiːv/ [v I/T] formal to think of a new idea, plan, or piece of work and develop it in your mind, until it is ready to be used, made etc: *'We wanted to make something new and original,' said Colin Smith, the man who conceived the show.* | *The painting is beautifully conceived in every way – composition, colour and texture.* | **+ of** *The young Edvard Munch conceived of a radically new approach to his art.*

dream up /ˌdriːm ˈʌp/ [phr v T] to think of a plan, idea, method etc, especially one that other people think is strange or unlikely to succeed **dream up sth** *Banks seem to spend a lot of time dreaming up ways to get more money from their customers.* | *The machine looked like it had been dreamed up by a surrealist painter.* | **dream sth up** *'It's too complicated for me,' Polly whispered; 'how do they dream these things up?'*

coin /kɔɪn/ [v T] to invent a word or phrase: *The term 'black hole' was coined in 1969 by the American scientist John Wheeler.* | *A Polish refugee coined the term 'genocide' to describe attempts to kill an entire group of people.* —**coinage** /ˈkɔɪnɪdʒ/ [n C] *The word 'yuppie' is a coinage of the 1960s which found a new fame in the 1980s.*

2 someone who invents something

- ▸ **inventor**
- ▸ **creator**
- ▸ **originator**
- ▸ **the father of sth**

inventor /ɪnˈventəʳ/ [n C] someone who has invented something, or whose job is to invent things, especially machines: *Franklin was a scientist, an inventor, and a statesman.* | *Marconi was the inventor of radio.* | *The patent lists six inventors who worked on the system.*

creator /kriˈeɪtəʳ/ [n C] the writer, artist, or designer who first produced a well-known story, character, fashion etc **+ of** *Walt Disney, the creator of Mickey Mouse* | *Diaghilev is considered by many to be the creator of the first modern dance company.*

originator /əˈrɪdʒəneɪtəʳ/ [n phrase] the person who first invented something, especially an idea **+ of** *Stokely Carmichael was probably the originator of the term 'black power.'* | *Alberti was the originator of the violin's design even though Stradivari made it famous.*

the father of sth /ðə ˈfɑːðər əv (sth)/ [n phrase] the man who first invented a new way of thinking or a new area of study, or who first tried new methods, practices etc: *Sigmund Freud, the father of psychoanalysis, was born in 1856.* | *Lowe was the real father of modern computing and a very important figure in IBM's ranks.*

3 something that someone has invented

- ▸ **invention**
- ▸ **creation**
- ▸ **innovation**
- ▸ **brainchild**

invention /ɪnˈvenʃən/ [n C] *The Hydro-Ram is an invention which makes it easier for firemen to get people out of crashed cars.* | *The wedge is an important early mechanical invention.* | *More than any other single invention, writing has transformed human consciousness.*

creation /kriˈeɪʃən/ [n C] something such as a completely new fashion, a character in a book etc, that someone has invented using their imagination: *Agatha Christie's greatest fictional creation was the Belgian detective, Hercule Poirot.* | *Chef Michael Almay's creations will make you want to come back again and again.*

innovation /ˌɪnəˈveɪʃən/ [n C] something new that is being used for the first time, or a new way of doing something: *In those days, the automobile was a recent innovation.* | *Electric lighting was still considered a daring innovation when it was installed in my grandfather's house.* | **+ in** *Innovations in information technology have completely transformed the way students work.*

brainchild /ˈbreɪntʃaɪld/ [n singular] something that a particular person invented, especially something such as an idea, method, or system **+ of** *The new computer system is the brainchild of our systems manager.* | *A new game, the brainchild of Andrew Wilson, was launched in 1999.*

invite

RELATED WORDS

▸ *see also* **visit, party**

1 to invite someone

▸ invite/ask
▸ invitation
▸ ask sb out
▸ have sb over
▸ invite/ask sb along
▸ entertain

invite/ask /ɪnˈvaɪt, ɑːsk‖æsk/ [v T] to ask someone to come to a party, wedding, meal etc. **Ask** is more informal than **invite**: *It's going to be a big wedding – they've invited over a hundred people.* | *'Are you going to Emma's party?' 'No, I haven't been asked.'* | *I'd love to come – thanks for asking me.* | *It is a great honour to have been invited here tonight.* | **invite/ask sb to a party/wedding/meal etc** *I was invited to a couple of his dinner parties last year.* | *Do you think we should ask Carol and Helen to the party?* | **invite/ask sb for lunch/dinner** *Madeleine has invited us for dinner on Saturday.* | **invite/ask sb to do sth** *Hane's parents have asked me to come and stay with them for a couple of weeks.* | **invite sb over** (=invite someone to your house for a meal, party etc) *It won't be a big do, we're just inviting a few close friends over.* | **invite/ask sb in** (=invite a visitor into your home) *He invited me in for a coffee.*

invitation /ˌɪnvəˈteɪʃən/ [n singular] when someone is invited to a party, wedding, meal etc **at sb's invitation** *They had come aboard at Charles's invitation.* | **turn down an invitation** (=not accept it) *I'm afraid I have to turn down your invitation to dinner.* | **accept an/sb's invitation** *Winston gratefully accepted the invitation.*

ask sb out /ˌɑːsk (sb) ˈaʊt‖ˌæsk-/ [phr v T] to ask someone to go to a restaurant, a film etc with you because you want to start a romantic relationship with them: *Why don't you ask her out? Or are you too shy?* | *You asked her out? What did she say?*

have sb over /ˌhæv (sb) ˈəʊvəʳ/ [phr v T not in passive] if you **have someone over**, they come to your home to have a meal or to spend time with you because you have invited them: *My father is having some colleagues over from the University tonight.* | *I want to have Danielle over to play with me.* | **have sb over for drinks/dinner etc** *We had Nick's parents over for dinner on Saturday.*

invite/ask sb along /ɪnˌvaɪt, ˌɑːsk (sb) əˈlɒŋ‖ˌæsk (sb) əˈlɔːŋ/ [phr v T] to invite someone to go somewhere with you and a group of other people: *Do you mind if I invite one of my friends along?* | *Whose idea was it to ask Danni along?*

entertain /ˌentəʳˈteɪn/ [v I/T] to provide a meal or social activity for someone in your home, either because they are your friends, or because they are people you work with: *This is an easy but impressive dish if you are entertaining at home.* | *About a fifth of their income is spent on entertaining clients.*

2 a message inviting someone

▸ invitation

invitation ALSO **invite** especially American /ˌɪnvəˈteɪʃən, ˈɪnvaɪt/ [n C] a message inviting someone to a party, wedding etc: *Thanks for your invitation. I'd love to come.* | *How many invitations did you send out?* | *a wedding invitation* | **+ to** *Did you get an invite to Paul's wedding?*

3 someone who you invite

▸ guest

guest /gest/ [n C] someone who is staying at your home, or who has come to your party, wedding etc because you invited them: *We have guests staying with us this week.* | *a wedding guest* | *Are we allowed to bring a guest?* | **guest list** (=a list of the people who have been invited to a party) *All three of you are on the guest list, of course.* | **guest room** (=a room in your house where guests can sleep) *Just put the presents in the guest room for now.*

4 someone who comes without being invited

▸ uninvited
▸ gatecrasher

uninvited /ˌʌnɪnˈvaɪtədˌ/ [adj/adv] **show up/turn up etc uninvited** *A few people showed up uninvited.* | **uninvited guest/visitor** *Fielding had come to the party, bringing several uninvited guests.*

gatecrasher British ALSO **crasher** American /ˈgeɪtˌkræʃəʳ, ˈkræʃəʳ/ [n C] someone who goes to a party but was not invited, especially someone who causes trouble: *The police want to trace everyone who was at the party, including about forty gatecrashers.* —**gatecrash** [v I/T] *Apparently, Roger and he tried to gatecrash a private party taking place at the hotel.*

Jj

jealous

RELATED WORDS

▸ *see also* **love, relationship, want/not want**

1 because someone loves another person

▸ jealous
▸ possessive
▸ jealousy

jealous /ˈdʒeləs/ [adj] angry and unhappy because you think your husband, girlfriend etc loves someone else more than they love you: *Some parents feel jealous if their child loves the nanny or babysitter.* | *Corwin has several female friends, and says his wife has never been jealous.* | *Police believe the shootings may have been the work of a jealous boyfriend.* | **get jealous** (=become jealous) *My girlfriend gets jealous if I even look at another woman.* | **make sb jealous** *Trying to make your boyfriend or girlfriend jealous isn't a good idea.* | **+ of** *Some fathers are jealous of the attention a new baby receives, even if they won't admit it.* —**jealously** [adv] *He watched jealously as Rose danced with his brother.*

possessive /pəˈzesɪv/ [adj] someone who is **possessive** wants their husband or wife, children, friends etc to love only them, and does not like them spending time with other people: *She was too possessive, always wanting to know where I was, who I was with.* | **+ of/about** *She is extremely possessive about* *her university friends, and doesn't like them mixing independently with her workmates.*

jealousy /'dʒeləsi/ [n U] the angry, unhappy feeling you have when you think your husband, girlfriend etc loves someone else more than they love you: *The police believe Morgan strangled his girlfriend in a fit of jealousy.* | *For a moment, she was overcome by jealousy.* | **+ of** *How should a single mother deal with her son's jealousy of her new boyfriend?*

2 because you want something that someone else has

- jealous
- envious
- envy
- jealousy
- envy
- sour grapes

jealous /'dʒeləs/ [adj not usually before noun] you feel **jealous** when someone has something that you want, and you are annoyed that they have it and you do not: *Maybe he's jealous because I got the job and he didn't.* | **+ of** *I guess some of the other kids are jealous of her talent.* | *Rasputin was killed by men who were jealous of his influence with the Russian royal family.*

envious /'enviəs/ [adj] especially written you feel **envious** when someone has something nice or special, and you wish that you had it too: *I see people who have opportunities I don't have, and I get envious.* | *She looks good, and enjoys the envious stares of other women.* | **+ of** *Lewis was envious of Forney's success.* —**enviously** [adv] *She glanced enviously at Emma's slim figure.*

envy /'envi/ [v T] to wish that you had the same abilities, possessions etc as someone else: *I envied her. She looked so calm and capable.* | **envy sb for sth** *He always envied his brother for the way he made friends so easily.* | **envy sb sth** *I envied him his freedom to do or say what he wanted.*

jealousy /'dʒeləsi/ [n U] a feeling of wanting something that someone else has, especially when this makes you angry or unhappy: *Professional jealousy can cause huge problems in the office.* | **+ of** *On one level, the story of Snow White is about a mother's jealousy of her daughter's beauty and sexuality.*

envy /'envi/ [n U] the feeling you have when you want something that someone else has: *It was difficult to hide her envy as Jim described his new job.* | **green with envy** (=very envious) *Before you get green with envy, I had to do a lot of stuff that wasn't so glamorous, too.* | **be the envy of sb** (=be something that someone else would like to have) *The country has a low crime rate that is the envy of most other countries.*

sour grapes /ˌsaʊəʳ 'greɪps/ [n plural] spoken say this when you think that someone's bad or angry behaviour is caused by jealousy: *Brown said his rival's comments were just sour grapes..*

job

RELATED WORDS

- leave your job *see* **leave (22-23)**
- not accept someone for a job *see* **reject (6)**
- when someone does someone else's job *see* **replace (1-4)**
- you are responsible for something as part of your job *see* **responsible**
- *see also* **work, company, business, earn, position/rank, in charge of**

1 a job

- job
- work
- profession
- occupation
- business
- what sb does
- trade
- career
- vocation
- livelihood
- line of work/business
- employment

job /dʒɒb‖dʒɑːb/ [n C] the work that you do regularly in order to earn money, especially when you work for an employer: *My first job was in a record store.* | *Daniel starts his new job on Monday.* | *She has a well-paid job in the tax department.* | **get a job** *Ted got a job as a bartender.* | **find a job** (=get a job after trying to get a lot of different jobs) *Her son still hasn't been able to find a job.* | **look for a job** (=try to get one) *She's looking for a job in the music business.* | **hold a job** (=have a job) *If a woman is qualified, she should hold any job in government she wants.* | **part-time job** (=when you work less than the usual number of hours each week) *I had a part-time job while I was in college.* | **job losses/job cuts** (=when a lot of people lose their jobs) *The company announced 74,000 job cuts and 21 factory closures.*

work /wɜːʳk/ [n U] **work** that someone does regularly to earn money, either by working for an employer or working for themselves: *My father started work when he was 14.* | *Most people stop work when they are 65.* | *I usually start work each day around 9 am and finish about 6 pm.* | *The work's really interesting but the pay's lousy.* | **look for work** (=to try to get work) *Lena graduated from college six months ago and she's still looking for work.* | **find work** (=to get work) *He eventually found work as a labourer on a construction site.* | **return to work/go back to work** (=to start work again after several weeks, months, or years) *Women often return to work after they have had children.* | *His injuries have made it impossible for him to go back to work.* | **at work** (=at the place where you work) *Her mother tried to call her at home and then at work.* | **to work** (=to the place where you work) *Alexander commutes 30 miles to work each day.* | **after/before work** (=before you start or after you finish your work each day) *They sometimes play tennis after work.*

profession /prə'feʃən/ [n C] work such as law, medicine, or teaching, for which you need special training and education: *Many teachers are thinking about leaving the profession for more highly paid careers.* | **the teaching/medical/legal etc profession** *There are now a lot more women in the legal profession.* | **go into/enter a profession** *There was a big demand for accountants in the 1980s, and many graduates entered the profession at this time.*

occupation /ˌɒkjᵿ'peɪʃən‖ˌɑːk-/ [n C] the type of work that someone usually does – used especially on official forms: *Please write your name, address, and occupation in the spaces below.* | *Part-time workers often work in low-paid occupations.*

business /'bɪznᵻs/ [n C/U] the general type of work that you do, such as buying and selling a particular type of thing: *In our business the first rule is that the customer is always right.* | *'What type of business are you in?' 'I run a catering company.'* | **the newspaper/used-car/movie etc business** *The used-car business has a pretty bad reputation.*

what sb does /ˌwɒt (sb) 'dʌz/ spoken use this to ask what someone's job is: *What does your husband do?* | *She used to work for an accounting firm, but I'm not sure what she does now.*

trade /treɪd/ [n C] a skilled job in which you use your hands to do things, such as building houses, making furniture, or repairing cars: *Most of the men had worked in skilled trades such as carpentry or printing.* | *Young men and women can learn a trade in the military.* | **be a bricklayer/carpenter etc by trade** *His father had been a bricklayer by trade.*

career /kəˈrɪəʳ/ [n C] the type of work that you do for most of your working life, which involves several similar jobs over a long period of time: *Like his father, Tommy chose a career in the Army.* | *Later on in his career he became first secretary at the British Embassy in Washington.* | *The scandal destroyed his career as a politician.* | **+ in** *I wanted to find out more about careers in publishing.*

vocation /vəʊˈkeɪʃən/ [n C] a job such as being a nurse, priest, or teacher that you do because you have a strong feeling that you want to do it, especially because you want to help people: *Nursing is hard work and often low paid, but for many people it is a vocation.* | *He was quite young when he decided he had a religious vocation.*

livelihood /ˈlaɪvlihʊd/ [n C] the work that you do in order to earn enough money to live on or the thing that provides the work for you to do: *Most of the people here depend on tourism for their livelihood.* | *Fishermen are angry about the new EC fishing regulations because they feel that their livelihood is being threatened.*

line of work/business /ˌlaɪn əv ˈwɜːʳk, ˈbɪznɪ̈s/ [n phrase] the type of work or job that you do: *I meet some interesting people in my line of work.* | *Henson had to leave real-estate, which had been his line of business since 1969.*

employment /ɪmˈplɔɪmənt/ [n U] when people work or have jobs – used especially in official documents, news reports etc: *I have not yet signed a contract of employment.* | *A Japanese company plans to set up a factory in the area, so this should provide some employment for local people.* | **be in employment** (=have a job) *Are you in full-time employment, Mr Edwards?*

2 a job in a company or organization

- post
- position
- capacity

post /pəʊst/ [n C] an important job in a company or organization, especially in an organization that moves its workers to different jobs **+ of** *She has been offered the post of director of UNICEF.* | **take up a post** (=start doing a particular job) *When he took up his present post at the BBC he was only 23.* | **teaching/government/director's etc post** *Environmentalists supported Murphy as the best candidate for the director's post.*

position /pəˈzɪʃən/ [n C] a job at a particular level in a company or organization **+ of** *We have decided to offer you the position of sales assistant starting next Monday.* | **hold a position** (=have a particular job) *What position did you hold at your previous company?* | **fill a position** (=to give someone a particular job) *Always look for the best person to fill any position, regardless of age, race, or gender.*

capacity /kəˈpæsɪ̈ti/ [n singular] formal if someone does something in a particular **capacity**, they do it because they have a particular job and it is part of that job **in sb's capacity as sth** *I'm here in my capacity as Union Representative.* | *In her capacity as war correspondent for ABC News, she has traveled all over the world.* | **in an advisory legal/financial etc capacity** *He works for this firm in a legal capacity, giving advice on international law.*

3 relating to a job

- job
- professional
- occupational
- vocational

job /dʒɒb‖dʒɑːb/ [adj only before noun] *The salary's not very good, but there's a lot of job satisfaction.* | *It says in the job description that we're only supposed to work 35 hours a week.* | *The bad thing about working at holiday resorts is that there's no job security.*

professional /prəˈfeʃənəl/ [adj only before noun] relating to a job such as teaching, medicine, or law, for which you need special training and have to pass special examinations: *The RSA course in teaching is a recognized professional qualification.* | *Lawyers have their own professional association, which operates a strict code of conduct.* | *You are advised to seek professional legal advice if in any doubt about the contract details.*

occupational /ˌɒkjʊ̈ˈpeɪʃənəl◂‖ˌɑːk-/ [adj only before noun] relating to the particular type of job that you do: *Occupational injuries and even deaths are quite common in the coal mining industry.* | *The survey studied the incidence of cancer among different occupational groups.*

vocational /vəʊˈkeɪʃənəl/ [adj usually before noun] **vocational** training or schools teach you the skills to do a particular job: *Not all the courses are purely vocational.* | *The Job Corps is a vocational training program for low-income youths.*

4 to have a job

- have a job
- be employed
- self-employed
- hold (down) a job
- be in work

have a job /hæv ə ˈdʒɒb‖-ˈdʒɑːb/ [v phrase not in progressive] *I've had a job since the day I left high school.* | *George had a well-paid job in a computer firm.* | **have a steady job** (=one that seems certain to last) *If you have a decent salary and a steady job, you can usually get a loan.*

be employed /biː ɪmˈplɔɪd/ [v phrase] to have a job – used especially in official contexts or in writing: *To qualify for the program, at least one parent must be employed.* | **+ by** *Curtis was employed by a car rental agency.* | **+ at** *A graduate of Stanford, she is employed at Jackson, Cole, Roberts & Green, a respected law firm.*

self-employed /ˌself ɪmˈplɔɪd◂/ [adj] someone who is **self-employed** works for a business that they own or gets paid for work by various companies or people, and is not directly employed by a single company or organization: *He is a self-employed music teacher.* | *I've been self-employed for over 10 years.*

hold (down) a job /ˌhəʊld (daʊn) ə ˈdʒɒb‖-ˈdʒɑːb/ [v phrase] to have a job, especially one that is for a particular period of time, or when it is difficult to keep working: *She was the first woman to hold the job of mayor.* | *Even men who had always been able to hold down a job found themselves unemployed.*

be in work /biː ɪn ˈwɜːʳk/ [v phrase] British to have a job – use this when you are comparing someone who has a job with other people who do not have jobs: *She was the only one in the family to be in work.* | *It's often difficult for people who are in work to appreciate the problems of the unemployed.*

5 to not have a job

- not have a job/be without a job
- be out of work
- unemployed
- jobless
- be on the dole

not have a job/be without a job /nɒt hæv ə 'dʒɒb, biː wɪð,aʊt ə 'dʒɒb‖-'dʒɑːb/ [v phrase not in progressive] *I don't have a job yet, but I'm going for an interview tomorrow.* | *She's been without a job now for three months.* | *Many of the students who leave the course this summer won't have a job to go to.*

be out of work /biː ˌaʊt əv 'wɜːʳk/ [v phrase] to not have a job, especially for a long period of time: *I've been out of work for two years.* | *At the age of 33, he suddenly found himself out of work and without much hope of finding any.* | **be thrown out of work** (=to suddenly lose your job) *The company's bankruptcy meant that 5,000 people were thrown out of work.* — **out-of-work** [adj phrase] *She is an out-of-work actress.*

unemployed /ˌʌnɪm'plɔɪd◂/ [adj] an **unemployed** person does not have a job: *Fifty per cent of the men in this town are unemployed.* | **unemployed teacher/clerk/factory worker etc** (=some one who usually works as a teacher etc) *The accused man is an unemployed labourer from South London.* | **the unemployed** (=people who are unemployed) *The government is not doing enough to help the unemployed.* — **unemployment** [n U] *There has been a sharp rise in unemployment.*

jobless /'dʒɒbləs‖'dʒɑːb-/ [adj] people who are **jobless** do not have jobs – used especially in news reports: *The factory closure will leave 3,000 workers jobless.* | *Jobless youths are a major cause of concern.* | **the jobless** (=people who do not have jobs) *The bill would allow the jobless to collect 4 to 20 weeks of additional benefits.*

be on the dole British **/be on welfare/on unemployment** American /biː ɒn ðə 'dəʊl, biː ɒn 'welfeəʳ, ɒn ˌʌnɪm'plɔɪmənt/ [v phrase] to be receiving money from the government because you do not have a job: *Many people on welfare don't have anyone to take care of the kids while they train for a job.* | *Just about everyone on the estate is one the dole. Jobs are scarce.* | *He spent five months on unemployment before finding a job that paid much less than his previous job.* | **go on the dole/go on welfare** (=start getting money from the government because you do not have a job) *Students used to be allowed to go on the dole in the summer holidays, but the government has stopped that.* | *Rivera lost his job, and the family had to go on welfare.*

6 a job that is available

- vacancy
- opening
- opportunity

vacancy /'veɪkənsi/ [n C] a job that is available, and that someone could start doing immediately: *There might be some vacancies at the hospital.* | **+ for** *A vacancy exists for an import/export sales manager at our Paris office.* | **fill a vacancy** (=find someone to do the job) *Skilled workers are few, and employers are having trouble filling vacancies.*

opening /'əʊpənɪŋ/ [n C] a job that is available – used especially by managers or by people asking about jobs: *Of the fourteen openings, only one went to a minority candidate.* | **+ for** *I was wondering if you had any openings for sales staff?* | **job openings** *The journal has been a good way to publicize job openings.*

opportunity /ˌɒpə'tjuːnɪ̇ti‖ˌɑːpər'tuː-/ [n C usually plural] the chance to do a job that you want to do, which could lead to a good permanent job **+ for** *There are several opportunities for experienced designers and researchers.* | **career opportunities** *Career opportunities for nurses have improved in the last 10 years.*

7 to give someone a job

- give sb a job
- employ
- take on
- engage
- appoint
- recruit
- sign up

give sb a job /ˌgɪv (sb) ə 'dʒɒb‖-'dʒɑːb/ [v phrase] *If I give you the job, how soon can you begin?* | *After law school, he was given a job in the city's legal department.* | **+ as** *Goldman gave her a job as his assistant.*

employ ALSO **hire** especially American /ɪm'plɔɪ, haɪəʳ/ [v T] to give someone a job and pay them for the work they do for you: *Since he came out of prison no one will employ him.* | *The company has been accused of not hiring enough women.* | **+ as** *I was employed as a night-watchman by the local hospital.* | *She was hired as marketing director for a biotechnology firm.* — **employment** [n U] *This letter outlines the terms and conditions of employment* (=the conditions of your job).

take on /ˌteɪk 'ɒn / [phr v T] if a company **takes on** someone, it gives them a job – use this especially about a job that might not be permanent or when a lot of people are given jobs at the same time **take on sb** *We're not taking on any more staff at the moment.* | **take sb etc on** *Franklin needed an assistant, and he got funding from the department to take one on.* | **take sb on as sth** *The director took me on as a messenger while they were filming in my village.*

engage /ɪn'geɪdʒ/ [v T] British formal to give someone a job: *The vet was increasingly busy and had to engage two new assistants.* | **engage sb as sth** *Paul was engaged as a junior clerk at a very low wage.*

appoint /ə'pɔɪnt/ [v T] to choose someone for a job, especially an important job: *The French president has appointed a new Minister for Culture.* | *The committee was appointed to make recommendations on housing development in the area.* | **appoint sb as director/manager etc** *When he was governor, Brown appointed Rose Bird as chief justice of the California Supreme Court.* | **appoint sb director/manager etc** *Schreiber was appointed director of human resources.* | **appoint sb to a job/post/ position etc** *This is the first time that a woman has been appointed to the post.* — **appointment** [n C] *His appointment to the position of Senior Surgeon was unexpected.*

recruit /rɪ'kruːt/ [v I/T] to find new people to work for a company or organization such as the army: *The police department is trying to recruit more black officers.* | *It's getting more and more difficult to recruit experienced staff.* — **recruit** [n C] someone who has been recruited: *At many banks, young recruits first work as tellers.*

sign up ALSO **sign** American /ˌsaɪn 'ʌp, saɪn/ [phr v T] if a football team, record company, film company etc **signs up** or **signs** someone, they agree to give them a job and make them sign an official contract: *Allegre was signed by the New York Jets.* | *Six episodes of the show have been taped, and the actors have been signed for six more.* | **sign up sb** *England soccer star Paul Gascoigne was signed up by a top Italian club.* | **sign sb up** *The band have just completed a highly* *successful US tour, and several record companies have offered to sign them up.*

8 to move to a more important job

- **promote**
- **make sb sth**
- **promotion**
- **advancement**
- **move/go/climb up the ladder**
- **upgrade**

promote /prəˈməʊt/ [v T usually in passive] to give someone who works in an organization a more important job than the one they had before: *The company promotes women and minorities whenever possible.* | **be promoted** *Did you hear that David's been promoted?* | **promote sb to sth** *Shula was promoted to head coach of the Cincinnati Bengals in 1991.*

make sb sth /meɪk (sb) (sth)/ [v phrase] to move someone to another job, usually a better, more important one within the same organization: *No-one thought they would make him manager so soon after joining the company.* | *He's been made Head of Security at the Chicago National Bank.*

promotion /prəˈməʊʃən/ [n C/U] when someone is given a more important job in an organization: *Civil service tests determine promotion in government jobs.* | *What are my chances of promotion if I stay here?* | **get a promotion** *She got a promotion last year.*

advancement /ədˈvɑːnsmənt‖ədˈvæn-/ [n U] formal when someone moves up to a better, more important job: *Many people are forced to move from one city to another in search of better jobs or career advancement.*

move/go/climb up the ladder ALSO **work your way up the ladder** /ˌmuːv, ˌgəʊ, ˌklaɪm ʌp ðə ˈlædəʳ, ˌwɜːʳk jɔːʳ weɪ ʌp ðə ˈlædəʳ/ [v phrase] to gradually become more and more successful, and get better, more important jobs: *Feldman started working for the company at age 18, and slowly worked his way up the ladder.* | *Education is vital to help these children to move up the career ladder.*

upgrade /ˌʌpˈgreɪd/ [v T] to move someone up in a job, especially by making the job they are already doing more important, and by paying them more for it: *The women demanded that their work be upgraded.* | **upgrade sb to sth** *After the inspector's visit all temporary workers were upgraded to permanent status.*

9 doing something for a job, rather than for enjoyment

- **for a living**
- **professional**

for a living /fər ə ˈlɪvɪŋ/ [adv] if someone does something **for a living**, they do it as a job in order to get money to live – use this especially about something that other people do only for fun: *She actually tastes wine for a living!* | *No one in the show acts or sings for a living.*

professional ALSO **pro** informal /prəˈfeʃənəl, prəʊ/ [adj] a **professional** musician, tennis player, photographer etc is one who plays music etc as their job and earns money from it: *Professional basketball players can earn huge sums of money.* | **turn professional** (=become a professional musician, player etc) *He was a keen amateur photographer for many years before he turned professional.* — **professional** [n C] *Most athletes these days are highly-trained professionals, who spend their whole time practising or competing.*

10 a job that you have in addition to your main job

- **sideline**
- **on the side**
- **moonlight**

sideline /ˈsaɪdlaɪn/ [n C usually singular] a job that you do in addition to your main job, especially because it is something that you enjoy or are interested in: *I sometimes take wedding photographs on Saturdays – it's a nice little sideline and it gives me a bit of extra cash.* | **as a sideline** *Tracy intended to run the seed business as a sideline, but it soon became her full-time job.*

on the side /ɒn ðə ˈsaɪd/ [adv] if you do a job **on the side**, you do it secretly or unofficially, in addition to your main job: *It is difficult to estimate the number of people doing part-time jobs on the side.* | *He sometimes does a bit of gardening on the side when he is short of money.*

moonlight /ˈmuːnlaɪt/ [v I] to do another job, usually in the evenings or at night, in addition to your main job: *Carlos is an auto mechanic who moonlights fixing the cars of friends.* | *Sarton has been moonlighting for five years to supplement his income.* | **+ as** *Some police officers moonlight as security guards.*

join

RELATED WORDS

- to join in *see* **take part/be involved**
- *see also* **with/together, unite**

WHAT'S HERE

● **to join sth together**	see **1 to 6**
● **to join an organization**	see **7 to 10**

to join sth together

RELATED WORDS

- *see also* **attach, stick, fasten/unfasten, tie/untie**

1 to join two things together with wire, glue etc

- **join**
- **attach**
- **fix**
- **fasten**
- **connect**
- **link**

join /dʒɔɪn / [v T] to **join** two things together, for example by using glue or a piece of wood or metal: *Join the two pieces of wood using a strong glue.* | **join sth together** *Doctors had to use a metal rod to join the two pieces of bone together.* | *Join the sleeve and the shoulder parts together.*

attach /əˈtætʃ/ [v T] to join one thing to another, so that it stays in position but can be removed later **attach sth to sth** *It took a couple of minutes to attach the trailer to the back of the truck.* | *The doctor attached a tiny monitor to the baby's head.* | **be attached to sth** *The references and diagrams were attached to the document.*

fix /fɪks/ [v T] especially British to join one thing firmly to another, using screws, nails, or glue, so that it stays there permanently **be fixed to sth** *The chairs and* *tables were fixed to the floor.* | **fix sth to sth** *They disconnected the gas, and fixed the water heater to an outside wall.*

fasten /ˈfɑːsən‖ˈfæ-/ [v T] to fix one thing firmly to another, using string, wire, or tape, in a way that makes it easy to remove later **fasten sth to sth** *Claire carefully fastened the brooch to her dress.* | **be fastened to sth** *Snowflake ornaments and tiny red ribbons were fastened to the Christmas tree.*

connect /kəˈnekt/ [v T] to join two pieces of equipment together with a wire or a pipe, so that electricity, water, gas etc can pass from one to the other **connect sth to sth** *Have you connected the speakers to the amplifier?* | **be connected to sth** *The scanner is connected to a computer that prints the name and price of each grocery item at the checkout.*

link /lɪŋk/ [v T] to connect two computers, machines, or systems so that electronic signals can pass from one to the other: *The two TV stations are linked by satellite.* | **link sth to sth** *The college provides technology to all faculty members and students to link them to the Internet.* | **be linked to sth** *All the PCs in the office are linked to a main server.*

2 when a wire, pipe etc goes between two things so that they are joined

- connect
- link
- connection

connect /kəˈnekt/ [v T] if something such as a wire or pipe **connects** two things, it goes between them, especially so that something can get from one to the other **connect sth to sth** *The hoses which connect the radiator to the engine are leaking.* | *The umbilical cord connects the baby to the placenta.* | **connect sth with sth** *Home workers are connected with the office by the Internet.* | **connect sth and sth** *Jennings has twisted the ligaments which connect the knee-cap and the lower part of the leg.*

link /lɪŋk/ [v T] if a wire **links** two machines or places, it connects them: *There is an underwater telephone cable linking the two islands.* | **link sth with sth** *There's a fault in the wire that links the printer with the computer.*

connection /kəˈnekʃən/ [n C] a wire or piece of metal that joins two parts of a machine or electrical system: *Carefully check all the electrical connections.* | **loose connection** (=one that is not joined properly) *There must be a loose connection somewhere – the phone isn't working.*

3 when something joins one place with another

- connect
- link
- link

connect /kəˈnekt/ [v T] **connect sth with sth** *The Golden Gate Bridge connects San Francisco with Marin County.* | **connect sth and sth** *The government was planning a new railway connecting Marseille and Paris.* | **be connected by sth** *The two lakes are connected by a narrow canal.*

link /lɪŋk/ [v T] if a bridge, road, railway or an air service **links** one place with another, it joins them together so that people can travel easily from one place to another: *They are planning a new high-speed railway to link the two capitals.* | *Batangas and Puerto Galera are linked by a ferry service which runs twice daily.* | **link sth with sth** *The Channel Tunnel has linked Britain with mainland Europe for the first time.* | **link sth and sth** *Interstate 5 links San Diego and Los Angeles.*

link /lɪŋk/ [n C] something that joins two places that are far apart, so that people can travel between them or communicate between them: *The two TV stations are joined by a satellite link.* | **+ between** *Rebels bombed the Beira railroad, a vital link between the capital and the port.* | *a telephone link between the two presidents*

4 when lines, roads, rivers etc come together and join

- join/meet
- converge
- merge

join/meet /dʒɔɪn, miːt/ [v I/T not in progressive] if two or more lines, roads, rivers etc **join** or **meet**, or if one **joins** or **meets** the other, they come together at a particular place: *The Monongahela River joins the Allegheny River in Pittsburgh.* | *The M11 meets the M25 near Epping.* | *Accidents are frequent where the two roads join.* | *The point where the two lines meet is called the apex of a triangle.*

converge /kənˈvɜːʳdʒ/ [v I not in progressive] formal if two or more roads, rivers, lines etc **converge**, they gradually become closer to each other and join together at a particular point: *The borders of Thailand, Laos and Burma all converge at this point.* | *Traffic is heavy where the two roads converge.* | **+ with** *The River Rhine converges with the Mosel at the city of Koblenz.*

merge /mɜːʳdʒ/ [v I not in progressive] if two roads or paths **merge**, they join together and become a single road or path: *When you get into London the two roads merge.* | **+ with** *The store is just near where South Street merges with Washburn Street.* | *After a while, the trail we were on merged with another, bigger trail.*

5 when things are joined together

- be joined/be joined together

be joined/be joined together /biː ˈdʒɔɪnd, biː ˌdʒɔɪnd təˈgeðəʳ/ [v phrase] *About 100 million years ago South America was joined to Africa.* | *The twins were joined together at birth and had to be separated in a very delicate operation.*

6 the place or part where two things join

- joint
- the join
- connection
- junction
- intersection

joint /dʒɔɪnt/ [n C] the place where two pieces of wood, metal, plastic etc are joined, especially so that they make one continuous piece: *One of the joints in the pipe was cracked and gas was escaping.* | *Duvall had just glued the joints of the chair and was tightening a vise to hold them in place.*

the join /ðə ˈdʒɔɪn/ [n singular] British the place where two or more pieces of something have been joined together, especially where it has been repaired: *It's been glued back together so well you can hardly see the join.* | *Years ago, someone had resealed the tank,* *and now water was beginning to leak from the rusty join.*

connection /kəˈnekʃən/ [n C] the place where something is joined to something else, through which electricity or information flows: *Check the connections to make sure all the wires are in the correct places.* | *By the end of the decade, direct satellite connections for the Internet may be available.* | *Intelligent people tend to have strong connections between the neurons in their brains.* | **loose connection** *There must be a loose connection somewhere that's stopping it from working.*

junction /ˈdʒʌŋkʃən/ [n C] British the place where two large roads, railway lines, rivers etc join or cross: *I live in a block of flats at the junction of Cambridge Road and Kilburn High Street.* | *One of Britain's worst rail accidents happened at Clapham Junction.*

intersection /ˌɪntərˈsekʃən, ˈɪntərsekʃən/ [n C] especially American the place where two roads cross each other: *The intersection is one of the busiest in the city.* | **+ of** *We waited at the intersection of Fulton Street and Gough Avenue for the lights to change.*

to join an organization

RELATED WORDS

opposite: —— **leave**

▸ *see also* **organization, army, member**

7 to join a club or organization

▸ **join**
▸ **become a member**
▸ **enrol**
▸ **enter**

join /dʒɔɪn/ [v I/T] to become a member of an organization such as a club, company, or political party: *2000 people joined the library last year.* | *Any child wanting to join the after-school club should see Mrs Williams.* | *A lot of people want to join, so there's a long waiting list.*

become a member /bɪˌkʌm ə ˈmembər/ [v phrase] to join an organization or club: *You have to be eighteen before you can become a member.* | **+ of** *Palmerton became a member of the church in 1984, when he was still in the Navy.* | *Several other countries had applied to become members of NATO.*

enrol British **/enroll** American /ɪnˈrəʊl/ [v I] to join an educational course, a class, a university etc, by officially adding your name to the list of people who attend: *Classes began soon after we enrolled.* | **+ in** *Two hundred and eighty women enrolled in the Argus club this year.* | *Most students who enroll in geology courses do not intend to become geologists.* | **+ at** *In 1966 he enrolled at the University of London to study history.* —**enrolment/enrollment** [n U] *Once we have received a cheque for the course fees, your enrolment will be complete.*

enter /ˈentər/ [v T] written to start working in a particular profession or company, or to start attending a particular educational institution: *Eighty percent of the children in the program had entered university with good grades.* | *When she first entered the teaching profession, children were much better behaved in the classroom.*

8 to join a military force

▸ **join**
▸ **join up**
▸ **enlist**

join /dʒɔɪn/ [v T] *He joined the navy when he was 16.* | *The advertising campaign is trying to persuade people to join the armed forces*

join up /ˌdʒɔɪn ˈʌp/ [phr v I] to join the armed forces, especially when there is a war: *Most of the boys went to town to join up.* | *When her brothers joined up in 1914, she took over the running of the business.*

enlist /ɪnˈlɪst/ [v I] to join the armed forces, because you want either to fight in a war of because you want a job as a soldier, sailor etc when there is not a war: *In the first year of the war a million men enlisted voluntarily.* | **+ in** *He enlisted in the air force and eventually became a pilot.*

9 to join an organization after being a member of a different one

▸ **go over to**

go over to /gəʊ ˈəʊvər tuː/ [phr v T not in passive] British to join a group or organization that opposes the one that you have left, especially because you disagree with something they have done: *They both went over to the Socialists because they disagreed with reforms to the health service.* | *There is a clause in the contract that prevents executives going over to the competition.*

10 to get someone to join a club or organization

▸ **recruit**

recruit /rɪˈkruːt/ [v I/T] to find people to work for, or become members of, an organization or group: *The Young Adventurers are trying to recruit more girls.* | *We're not recruiting at the moment.* | *For the controlled study on drinking habits, we recruited men between 35 and 45.* —**recruit** [n C] someone who has been recruited recently: *Peter is one of our new recruits.*

joke

▸ to make someone seem stupid by making jokes
see **make fun of(3-9)**

▸ *see also* **funny, serious, laugh**

1 something you say or write in order to be funny

▸ **joke**
▸ **funny story**
▸ **wisecrack**
▸ **one-liner**
▸ **gag**
▸ **punch line**
▸ **the one about ...**
▸ **pun**
▸ **double meaning/entendre**

joke /dʒəʊk/ [n C] *Have you heard any good jokes lately?* | *Wilson spoke for about 15 minutes, peppering his mainly serious message with jokes.* | **+ about** *Leno opened the show with a joke about the election.* | **get the joke** ALSO **see a joke** British (=understand a joke) *It wasn't that I didn't get the joke – I just didn't think it was funny.* | *Everyone laughed except Mr Broadbent, who didn't see the joke.* | **tell a joke** *It's a good idea to start a speech by telling a joke.* | **dirty joke** (=one about sex) *In some situations, a dirty joke can be considered sexual harassment.* | **private joke** (=a secret joke) *The two girls were whispering in the corner and giggling over some private joke.*

funny story /ˌfʌni ˈstɔːri/ [n C] a short story you tell to make people laugh: *It reminded her of a funny story she'd heard at work.* | **tell a funny story** *He began telling funny stories about the time he worked as a barman on a cruise ship.*

wisecrack /ˈwaɪzkræk/ [n C] informal something funny that someone says to try to make people laugh – use this especially when what they say annoys you: *Bob Hope would keep his audience laughing with an endless stream of jokes and wisecracks.* | *Amy responded with a wisecrack that got her in big trouble with the teacher.*

one-liner /ˌwʌn ˈlaɪnəʳ/ [n C] a short remark that is funny and clever: *There are some memorable one-liners in every Woody Allen film.* | *It's a hilarious scene with a succession of brilliant one-liners from Groucho Marx.*

gag /gæg/ [n C] a short joke, especially one told by a professional entertainer as part of a show: *His first job was writing gags for a famous comedian.* | **+ about** *He started the show with a few old gags about mothers-in-law.*

punch line /ˈpʌntʃ laɪn/ [n C] the sentence or phrase that comes at the end of a joke, and makes it funny: *He got to the end of the joke and couldn't remember the punch line.* | *I waited for the punch line, but it never came.*

the one about ... /ðə ˈwʌn əbaʊt .../ [n phrase] spoken say this when you are going to tell someone a joke about a particular subject: *Have you heard the one about the brown cow who goes into a bar?*

pun /pʌn/ [n C] a joke made by deliberately mixing up or mistaking two different meanings of the same word or two words with the same sound: *'Seven days without food makes one weak' is a pun on the words 'week' and 'weak', and also on the different meanings of 'one'.* | *The audience groaned at his pun.* | **(if you'll) pardon the pun** (=used to say that you know what you are going to say has two meanings) *'Pardon the pun, but we were all in the same boat,' said Navy Lieutenant Green.*

double meaning/entendre /ˌdʌbəl ˈmiːnɪŋ, ˌduːblɒnˈtɒndrə‖-blɑːnˈtɑːn-/ [n C] a joke made by deliberately using a word or phrase that has two possible meanings, one of which is about sex or sexual parts of the body: *Dirty jokes and double meanings are what makes the show funny.* | *The song's lyrics are full of double entendres.*

2 something that you do to make people laugh

- joke
- practical joke
- prank
- play a trick/joke
- as a joke
- for a laugh

joke /dʒəʊk/ [n C] *We didn't mean to frighten you. It was only a joke.* | *Inside the parcel there was an empty bottle. 'Is this some kind of joke?' he asked.* | **take a joke** (=accept a joke that is against you) *I can take a joke as well as anyone, but this isn't funny, it's embarrassing.*

practical joke /ˌpræktɪkəl ˈdʒəʊk/ [n C] a trick, especially one that is carefully planned that is intended to confuse and surprise someone and to make other people laugh at them: *The phone call was the sort of practical joke that radio stations often play on celebrities.* | **play a practical joke** *Police believe the circles in the crops are made by someone playing an elaborate practical joke.*

prank /præŋk/ [n C] a silly action that is intended as a harmless joke – use this especially when something serious happens as a result of it: *The fire was started as a prank.* | *Pushing her in the river seemed like a harmless prank, but it ended in tragedy.* | **pull/play a prank (on sb)** *Every year, the older kids pull pranks on new students.*

play a trick/joke /ˌpleɪ ə ˈtrɪk, ˈdʒəʊk / [v phrase] to surprise or deceive someone with a trick so that you and other people can laugh at them: *He didn't seem the type of boy to play jokes.* | **+ on** *When she didn't come, I thought she was playing a trick on me.*

as a joke ALSO **for a joke** British /əz ə ˈdʒəʊk, fər ə ˈdʒəʊk/ [adv] if you do something **as a joke** or **for a joke**, you do it because you think it will have amusing results or make people laugh: *You shouldn't spread rumours like that, even as a joke.* | *Once, for a joke, they changed round all the numbers on the doors.*

for a laugh /fər ə ˈlɑːf‖-ˈlæf/ [adv] British informal if you do something **for a laugh**, you do it for fun or to make people laugh: *Just for a laugh we hung all the pictures upside down.* | *Kevin set off the fire alarm for a laugh.*

3 to say something to make people laugh

- make a joke/crack a joke
- tell a joke
- joke
- wisecrack

make a joke/crack a joke /ˌmeɪk ə ˈdʒəʊk, ˌkræk ə ˈdʒəʊk/ [v phrase] *Nick cracked a joke to try to ease the tension.* | *My mother makes a joke of just about everything.* | **+ about** *This is a serious matter. I wish you wouldn't make jokes about it.*

tell a joke /ˌtel ə ˈdʒəʊk/ [v phrase] to tell someone a joke that you have heard or read somewhere else: *I tried to cheer him up by telling a joke.* | *I'm afraid I'm not very good at telling jokes.* | **tell sb a joke** *Pat told them a joke about two flies walking on the ceiling.*

joke /dʒəʊk/ [v I] to say funny things and talk in a way that is not serious: *A group of teenagers were standing at the corner, laughing and joking.* | *They're a good class to teach. You can joke and have a laugh with them.* | **+ about** *When he was a kid he was embarrassed about his height, but now he can joke about it.*

wisecrack /ˈwaɪzkræk/ [v I] to make funny remarks, especially ones that could annoy some people: *Grable made him mad by wisecracking about his weight.* | *The president appeared totally relaxed, chatting and wisecracking with reporters.*

4 someone who tells jokes or does things to make people laugh

- comedian/comic
- wit
- practical joker

comedian/comic /kəˈmiːdiən, ˈkɒmɪk‖ˈkɑː-/ [n C] a professional entertainer who makes people laugh: *Lenny Henry, the famous British comedian, will appear in a show in London next week.* | *Before becoming a film actor, he'd been a comic appearing regularly in cabaret.* | **stand-up comedian/comic** (=one who stands alone in front of the public and tells jokes) *Robin Williams first made his name as a stand-up comedian.*

wit /wɪt/ [n C] an intelligent person who is good at being funny in clever or original ways: *Rochester* *was well known as a wit in society circles.* | *A dozen writers and wits used to gather at the Algonquin Hotel for lunch.*

practical joker /ˌpræktɪkəl ˈdʒəʊkəʳ/ [n C] someone who does something in order to confuse or trick someone else, to make other people laugh: *The shop sold toys and gadgets for practical jokers.*

5 to pretend that something is true as a joke

- be joking/be kidding
- jokingly
- you're having me on
- be pulling sb's leg
- wind sb up

be joking/be kidding /biː ˈdʒəʊkɪŋ, biː ˈkɪdɪŋ/ [v phrase] informal to say something that is not true as a joke: *When he asked me to marry him I wasn't sure whether he was joking or being serious.* | **just/only kidding** *'You're just kidding, right Mom?' Joe asked anxiously.* | *Don't get mad – I was only joking!* | **are you kidding?/you're kidding!** (=say this when you think someone is joking) *You're kidding. You mean it only rains once a year there?* | *'They wanted $425 just for the room.' 'Are you kidding?'* | **no kidding** (=say this to show you are serious) *It was the best pizza I've ever eaten, no kidding.* | **no kidding?** (=say this when you think someone could be joking) *She's only sixteen? No kidding? She looks twenty-five.*

jokingly /ˈdʒəʊkɪŋli/ [adv] if you say something **jokingly** you say it to amuse people, and do not really mean it seriously: *Braden jokingly refers to her daughter as 'the demon.'*

you're having me on British **/you're putting me on** American /jɔːʳ ˌhævɪŋ miː ˈɒn, jɔːʳ ˌpʌtɪŋ miː ˈɒn/ [v phrase] spoken say this when you think someone is trying to make you believe something that is not true: *Come on, you guys, you're putting me on, right?* | *He makes £80,000 a year? You're having me on.*

be pulling sb's leg /biː ˌpʊlɪŋ (sb's) ˈleg/ [v phrase] informal to try to make someone believe something that is not true, as a friendly joke: *Is all this really true, or are you pulling my leg?* | *You don't really have to buy tickets. I was just pulling your leg.*

wind sb up /ˌwaɪnd (sb) ˈʌp/ [phr v T] British to say something that is untrue, or do or say something to deliberately annoy someone, as a joke: *I was only winding you up – don't take it so seriously!* —**wind-up** /ˈwaɪnd ʌp/ [n C] *What was meant to be a harmless wind-up ended up with the sacking of three men yesterday.*

6 not behaving or speaking seriously

- flippant
- playful
- facetious
- tongue-in-cheek

flippant /ˈflɪpənt/ [adj] not being serious about something that should be taken seriously, so that people think you do not care: *People ask me if I'm related to him, and my answer is usually a flippant 'No, but I wish I were.'* | *When asked what is wrong with the economy, analysts reply 'Not enough money.' This answer is not as flippant as it sounds.* | *Sorry if that sounded flippant or heartless – it wasn't meant to be.* —**flippantly** [adv] *'It's only money,' said Gabriella flippantly. 'Here today and gone tomorrow!'*

playful /ˈpleɪfəl/ [adj] actions or behaviour that are **playful** are not serious, but they are fun and friendly: *He gave me a playful slap on the shoulder.* | *She tried to sound playful but somehow the words came out the wrong way.* —**playfully** [adv] *Toby laughed, playfully telling her off.*

facetious /fəˈsiːʃəs/ [adj] making jokes or trying to be funny in a clever or unkind way that people think is annoying: *At the risk of sounding facetious, who really cares about what happens?* | *The speech saying drug users should be shot was clearly facetious, but it contained a serious point.* —**facetiously** [adv] *'What would we do without him?' said Chuck facetiously.*

tongue-in-cheek /ˌtʌŋ ɪn ˈtʃiːk/ [adj/adv] a remark, statement etc that is **tongue-in-cheek** is intended as a joke but is said or written in a serious or sincere way: *His tongue-in-cheek articles are brilliantly funny and very political.* | *'This just shows you what a great coach I am,' said Braden, tongue-in-cheek.*

judge

RELATED WORDS

- be judged in a court of law *see* **court/trial**
- *see also* **criticize, opinion, decide, accuse, crime**

1 to decide how good, bad etc someone or something is

- judge
- assess
- evaluate
- critique

judge /dʒʌdʒ/ [v T] to form an opinion about a person or situation, using your knowledge, experience, and intelligence: *The changes should be judged by their results.* | **+ when/whether/what etc** *How do you judge when a house needs a new roof?* | *2,000 foreign and local monitors were watching to judge whether the elections were free and fair.* | **judge sb/sth to be sth** *Women judged to be at high risk for breast cancer should be examined every year.* | **judging from/by sth** (=when you form an opinion based on a particular fact) *Judging from Monday night's game, the team still has a lot of work to do.* | **+ (that)** *Some students may judge that the benefits they receive from further education are less than the costs of that education.* | **judge it wise/proper/dangerous etc to do sth** formal *Dwight judged it dangerous to navigate in darkness in these waters.*

assess /əˈses/ [v T] to consider someone's work, ideas, or products, or to consider a situation or event, in order to judge how good they are, what standard they have reached, or how useful they might be to you: *This test provides an excellent way of assessing students' progress.* | *He has written a guidebook that assesses the quality of Californian hotels.* | *The booklet aims to help parents assess recent educational changes.* | **+ how/whether/what etc** *The committee will continue to assess how we can improve.* —**assessment** [n C] *The final chapter gives an assessment of various ideas and theories.*

evaluate /ɪˈvæljueɪt/ [v T] to carefully consider how useful or valuable an activity, plan, or suggestion is, especially in order to decide whether or not to start doing it or continue doing it: *There was not enough time to evaluate the information before the meeting.* | *The new drug is being evaluated in clinical trials.* | *The police force should not evaluate officers' performance in terms of the number of arrests they make.* —**evaluation** /ɪˌvæljuˈeɪʃən/ [n C/U] *Students provide the college with an evaluation of the courses they took at the end of each semester.*

critique /krɪˈtiːk/ [n C] an article, book, speech etc that carefully examines a subject and says what is good or bad about it: *The speech was a devastating critique of Reagan's economic policy.* | *Marx's critique of capitalism in the 19th century*

2 to decide who is the winner in a game, competition etc

- judge
- judge
- referee
- umpire

judge /dʒʌdʒ/ [v T] *Dillon and two other writers judged the poetry contest.* | *Pupils were judged in two categories: age 6 to 8, and age 9 to 12.* | *The annual flower show was judged by a TV celebrity and a professional horticulturist.* | **be judged the best/the winner etc** *A photograph of a stormy beach was judged 'best in show' by the panel.*

judge /dʒʌdʒ/ [n C] someone whose job is to **judge** a game, competition etc: *There are normally three judges for the national essay competition.*

referee ALSO **ref** informal /ˌrefəˈriː, ref/ [n C] someone whose job is to judge a sports game and make sure that the players obey the rules – for example in football: *The referee should never have allowed the first goal.* | *One of the players was sent off for arguing with the referee.*

umpire /ˈʌmpaɪəʳ/ [n C] someone whose job is to judge a sports game and make sure that the players obey the rules – for example in football and tennis: *I thought he was out, but the umpire called him safe.* | *Mack was thrown out of the game for hitting an umpire.*

3 to decide whether someone is wrong to do something

- judge
- pass judgment
- sit in judgement
- judgemental

judge /dʒʌdʒ/ [v I/T] to decide whether someone is wrong to do something – use this when you think someone has no right to do this: *What right does she have to judge me?* | *Don't judge other people unless you want to be judged yourself.* | *She should do what seems right to her. It isn't for me to judge.*

pass judgment ALSO **judgement** British /ˌpɑːs ˈdʒʌdʒmənt‖ˌpæs-/ [v phrase] to judge something or someone in a negative and often unreasonable way: *He refused to pass judgement until all the evidence was presented.* | **+ upon/on** *Society badly needs to learn not to pass judgment on people because of their background.*

sit in judgement /ˌsɪt ɪn ˈdʒʌdʒmənt/ [v phrase] British to judge whether someone's behaviour is good or bad – use this especially when you think someone should not be doing this: *I don't care how annoyed she is – she's got no absolutely no right to sit in judgement.* | **+ on/upon/over** *It seems wrong that 12 white men could sit in judgment on one black woman.*

judgemental British **/judgmental** American /dʒʌdʒˈmentl/ [adj] too ready to judge and criticize other people: *I try not to be judgmental, but if I think someone's being stupid, I'll say so.* | *The parenting class is run in an open, non-judgmental manner that lets people speak freely.* | **+ about** *The public is often judgmental about people's sexuality.*

4 to decide who is right in a quarrel

- adjudicate
- arbitrate
- arbitration

adjudicate /əˈdʒuːdɪkeɪt/ [v I] formal if someone, especially a lawyer, **adjudicates**, they officially form a judgement about who is legally right in an argument or disagreement: *The World Court adjudicates boundary disputes and commercial claims.* —**adjudicator** [n C] *Legal advisors and adjudicators were present at the trial.* —**adjudication** /əˌdʒuːdɪˈkeɪʃən/ [n U] *The situation has now become so serious that any form of adjudication would be impossible.*

arbitrate /ˈɑːʳbɪ̇treɪt/ [v I/T] to officially judge how an argument between two opposing groups or organizations can be settled: *As president of the European Council he arbitrated in an argument over cereal prices.* | *Most brokerage firms require customers to arbitrate disputes rather than file lawsuits.* | **+ between** *A local magistrate has been asked to arbitrate between farmers and conservationist groups.* —**arbitrator** [n C] *She works as an arbitrator between representatives of various competing businesses.*

arbitration /ˌɑːʳbɪ̇ˈtreɪʃən/ [n U] the process of judging officially who is right in an argument or disagreement, by someone who has been chosen by the opposing groups: *The case has been submitted for international arbitration.* | **go to arbitration** (=ask someone to arbitrate) *Both parties agreed to go to arbitration in order to avoid more strikes by the workers.*

5 to write your opinion of a new film, book etc

- review
- review
- write-up
- critic

review /rɪˈvjuː/ [v T] to write an article in a newspaper or magazine judging how good or bad a film, play, television programme, or book is: *Doig's new book is reviewed on page 4.* | *As well as being an author, she reviews books for the Sunday papers.* | *Eliot wrote to him after he reviewed 'The Use of Poetry.'* —**reviewer** [n C] *Reviewers praised Tisler's performance.*

review /rɪˈvjuː/ [n C] an article in a newspaper or magazine that judges a book, television programme, film etc: *Our first English assignment was to write a book review.* | *The movie got good reviews.* | **+ of** *Wilberforce had just written a long review of Darwin's book.*

write-up /ˈraɪt ʌp/ [n C] informal an article in a newspaper or magazine, that says how good or bad a new film, book, product etc is: *Did you see Martin Amis' write-up of the book in the Observer?* | *After a write-up in Yankee magazine, orders started pouring in.* | *The film didn't get a very good write-up in Time Out.*

critic /ˈkrɪtɪk/ [n C] someone who writes in newspapers or magazines or on television or radio, giving their judgement about books, films etc: *I didn't think the book was as bad as the critics said it was.* | **theatre/film/art etc critic** *For five years she was theater critic for the New Yorker.* | *Film critic Roger Ebert has a new partner for his movie-review television program.*

6 someone's ability to judge people or things

- judgment
- be a good/bad etc judge of

judgment ALSO **judgement** British /ˈdʒʌdʒmənt/ [n U] *The break-up of a serious relationship can often make us lose confidence in our own judgement.* | *Teachers need to have good judgement of pupils' needs and abilities.* | **sound judgement** (=good judgement) *Environmental rules are developed using good information and sound judgment.*

be a good/bad etc judge of /biː ə ˌgʊd ˈdʒʌdʒ ɒv/ [v phrase] be able to judge people or situations well, badly etc: *She'd always thought Mr Cunningham was a good judge of character.* | *Professional people are sometimes bad judges of their colleagues' conduct.*

7 a standard by which something is judged

- standard
- scale
- criterion
- benchmark
- yardstick

standard /ˈstændəʳd/ [n C] a level of quality, skill, achievement etc by which something is judged: *Shakespeare is the standard against which all playwrights must be measured.* | *Many Europeans who consider themselves to be poor are rich by the standards of some Third World countries.*

scale /skeɪl/ [n C] a set of standards, levels, or degrees against which you can compare and judge things: *On a scale of one to ten, ten being best, his new movie is a two.* | *The researchers devised a scale to measure people's attitudes toward certain types of behavior.*

criterion /kraɪˈtɪəriən/ [n C] a standard you use in order to judge people or things, especially one that may be different from the standard used by other people or organizations: *The company's criterion for success is high sales.* | *Changing the college admissions criteria will have a serious effect.* | **set of criteria** (=group of standards) *The group ranks cities according to its own set of criteria.* ▸ **USAGE** The plural of ***criterion*** is ***criteria***.

benchmark /ˈbentʃmɑːrk/ [n C usually singular] a very high standard of quality, achievement, or excellence, against which all other things have to be compared and judged: *Under Coach Wooden, UCLA men's basketball was so successful it was the benchmark other teams measured themselves against.* | **+ for** *In the 1960s and 1970s the Swedish political system was regarded as a benchmark for other European countries.*

yardstick /ˈjɑːʳdˌstɪk/ [n C usually singular] a person or thing that you compare another person or thing with, in order to judge how good or successful they are: *Many teachers say the primary school tests are not a useful educational yardstick.* | **+ for** *The hospital has developed a treatment for cancer which has become the yardstick for all other treatments.*

jump

RELATED WORDS

▸ *see also* **up, run, fail**

1 to jump in the air

- jump
- jump up and down
- hop
- skip
- leap
- dive

jump /dʒʌmp/ [v I] to push yourself off the ground or away from something, using your legs: *How high can you jump?* | *The driver jumped clear as his vehicle fell into the river below.* | **+ into/onto/up etc** *My cat always jumps up onto the table when I'm trying to work.* | *She jumped down from the wall.* —**jump** [n C] *Aziz won the event with a jump of 2 metres.*

jump up and down /ˌdʒʌmp ʌp ən ˈdaʊn/ [v phrase] to jump several times, always landing in the same place: *At the back of the stand, Redsox fans were jumping up and down with excitement.* | *Stop jumping up and down – keep still!*

hop /hɒp‖hɑːp/ [v I] to jump or move forward on one leg rather than two: *Mary was hopping anxiously from one foot to another.* | **+ along/around/over etc** *It's a game in which you hop around trying to knock the other players over.*

skip /skɪp/ [v I] if someone, especially a child, **skips** along, they move along with a little jump between their steps: *Can you skip to the other end of the playground.* | **+ along/around etc** *The children went skipping along the path.*

leap /liːp/ [v I] especially written to jump as far or high as you can **+ onto/through etc** *He leaped through the window and was gone.* | *Tessa leaped onto the boat just as it was moving away from the bank.* | *The fish leaped out of the water.* —**leap** [n C] *With a tremendous leap, James managed to catch the ball.*

dive /daɪv/ [v I] to jump into water with your head and arms first: *Roger was standing at the edge of the pool ready to dive.* | **+ into/in/off** *Evan dived off the rock into the sea.* | *The pool was deserted, and Lindsey wasted no time before diving in head-first.* —**dive** [n C] *That was a perfect dive.*

2 to go over something by jumping

- jump
- leap
- vault
- clear

jump /dʒʌmp/ [v I/T] **+ over/across** *The dog jumped the gate and ran away howling.* | *Ricky jumped across the stream and ran all the way home.* | *He raced down the garden and jumped over the wall.*

leap /liːp/ [v I/T] especially written to go over something with a long or high jump: *I leapt the fence to safety, leaving the dog snarling behind me.* | **+ over/across** *The bartender leapt over the bar and tried to stop the fight.*

vault /vɔːlt/ [v I/T] to jump over something, using your hands to help you: *He makes vaulting a five foot wall look easy.* | **+ over** *Jack vaulted over the railings.*

clear /klɪəʳ/ [v T] to jump over something easily without touching it, especially in a race: *He cleared the first two obstacles, but hit the top of the third.* | *There was a sprinkling of applause as the horses cleared the last fence.*

just

RELATED WORDS

- almost, but not quite *see* **almost**
- just one or just a small number or amount *see* **only**
- not important, special or interesting *see* **only**

WHAT'S HERE

- **just/a short time ago** see **1 to 2**
- **just/almost not** see **3 to 6**

just/a short time ago

1 when something happened a short time ago

- just
- only just
- a minute/second ago
- just now
- barely

just /dʒʌst/ [adv] *Sorry, she just left for home. Can I take a message? | The war had just ended, and the country's economy was in ruins. | You've had your hair cut, haven't you? I've just noticed. | I just heard the news! Congratulations!*

only just /ˌəʊnli ˈdʒʌst◂/ [adv] especially British a very short time ago: *It's noon, and she's only just got up. | I've only just passed my driving test, so I'm still a little nervous.*

a minute/second ago ALSO **a moment ago** especially British /ə ˈmɪnət, ˈsekənd əˌgəʊ, ə ˈməʊmənt əˌgəʊ/ [adv] spoken a very short time ago – use this especially when a situation has changed: *She was here a minute ago. | There was a phone call for you a second ago, but I didn't know where you were. | What did I do with my glasses? I had them in my hand a moment ago.*

just now ALSO **just this minute** British /ˌdʒʌst ˈnaʊ, ˌdʒʌst ðɪs ˈmɪnət/ [adv] spoken a very short time ago – use this especially when you are answering someone who is looking for someone else: *'Have you seen Carl?' 'I just this minute hung up on him.' | She just now left, so she should be home by six. | Didn't I just this minute tell you to tidy your room! | Sandy was on the Internet just now, that's why the phone was busy.*

barely ALSO **hardly/scarcely** British /ˈbeəʳli, ˈhɑːʳdli, ˈskeəʳsli/ [adv] spoken use this to say that something had just happened when something else happened: *I had scarcely opened the door when the dog came running in. | She had barely slept 10 minutes before she was woken up again. | The class had barely started when the fire bell rang. | Hardly had King finished speaking when a shot was fired by someone in the crowd.*

2 when someone has become a particular age a short time ago

- just turned 10/30/60 etc
- be barely 10/18/21 etc

- *see also* **age**

just turned 10/30/60 etc /ˌdʒʌst tɜːʳnd ˈten/ [adv] if someone has **just turned** a particular age, they have very recently had their birthday: *She just turned five in August. | When he retired, he'd just turned 65.*

be barely 10/18/21 etc /biː ˌbeəʳli ˈten/ [v phrase] if someone, usually a young person, is **barely** a particular age, they have only very recently had their birthday: *He's 35, and he's going out with a girl who's barely 18.*

just/almost not

RELATED WORDS

- *see also* **happen, almost**

3 when something happens, although it almost did not happen

- just
- barely
- almost didn't
- only just
- narrowly
- be a near/close thing
- by the skin of your teeth

just /dʒʌst/ [adv] *'Can I speak to Tony please?' 'Sorry, you've just missed him.' | If you hurry you'll just catch the 9.30 bus. | I just made it to class on time. | At the moment we're just making enough money to cover our costs. |* **just in time** (=with very little time to spare) *We got to the station just in time.*

barely /ˈbeəʳli/ [adv] if you **barely** do something, you succeed, although you almost fail: *The fog was so bad that we could barely see the road in front of us. | The staff here are barely coping with all the work.*

almost didn't ALSO **nearly didn't** British /ˌɔːlməʊst ˈdɪdnt, ˌnɪəʳli ˈdɪdnt/ *I saw him a week ago and I almost didn't recognize him, he'd lost so much weight. | My alarm clock is broken and I nearly didn't wake up in time this morning.*

only just British **/just barely** American /ˌəʊnli ˈdʒʌst◂, dʒʌst ˈbeəʳli/ [adv] use this when you succeed in doing something, but you want to emphasize how close you were to failing: *It was a close game. Beverly beat me, but only just. | I could just barely hear him. | The paperwork was only just completed in time for the conference. | The train was late, and I just barely made it to the meeting on time.*

narrowly /ˈnærəʊli/ [adv] **narrowly win/defeat/fail etc** if you **narrowly** win, lose etc, you win or lose by a very small number of points, votes etc: *The bill was narrowly defeated in the Senate. | She narrowly failed to beat the world record in the 100 metres sprint.*

be a near/close thing /biː ə ˌnɪəʳ, ˌkləʊs ˈθɪŋ/ [v phrase] British use this to say that something good happened, but it almost did not: *The Labour party won the election, but it was a very near thing. | He nearly died – it was a very close thing.*

by the skin of your teeth /baɪ ðə ˌskɪn əv jɔːʳ ˈtiːθ/ [adv] if you do something **by the skin of your teeth**, you succeed in doing it, but only by a very small amount of time, space etc: *The business is surviving, but only by the skin of its teeth. | The car broke down on the way to the airport and they just caught the plane by the skin of their teeth.*

4 when something bad almost happened, but did not

- narrowly
- close shave
- that was close!
- near miss

narrowly /ˈnærəʊli/ [adv] **narrowly avoid/miss/escape etc** to avoid something unpleasant or dangerous, although you almost do not avoid it: *A black BMW swerved, narrowly missing another car.* | *He narrowly escaped arrest when the police raided his house.* —**narrow** [adj only before noun] *Markov had a very narrow escape when his helicopter crashed.*

close shave British ALSO **close call** American /ˌkləʊs ˈʃeɪv, ˌkləʊs ˈkɔːl/ [n C] a situation in which something bad almost happens but does not: *A sniper's bullet went through the sleeve of his coat. It was a close shave but didn't even scratch him.* | *Joe breathed a sigh of relief as the guard passed on to the next cell: 'That was a close call!'*

that was close! /ˌðæt wəz ˈkləʊs/ spoken say this when you have managed to avoid something dangerous or unpleasant, but you almost did not: *Geez, that was close! Did you see that red car?*

near miss /ˌnɪəʳ ˈmɪs/ [n C] a situation in which something, especially a car or plane, almost hits something, but does not: *There were two near misses on the airport's runways between 1998 and 1999.* | *The asteroid flew within 106,000 miles of Earth, which astronomers considered a near miss.*

5 when you do something, but only with difficulty

- can hardly/barely
- can just about

can hardly/barely ALSO **can scarcely** British /kən ˈhɑːʳdli, ˈbeəʳli, kən ˈskeəʳsli/ [modal verb] if you **can hardly**, **can barely**, or **can scarcely** do something, you are able to do it but only with a lot of difficulty: *I was so tired I could hardly keep my eyes open.* | *She's not strong. She can barely walk without holding on to something.* | *He lay flat on his back, scarcely able to breathe, waiting for the ambulance.*

can just about /kən ˈdʒʌst əbaʊt/ [v phrase] if you **can just about** do something, you are able to do it but only with a lot of difficulty: *I could just about reach it.* | *I think I can just about manage to get there on time.* | *He's just about able to walk on his own again.*

6 when something is a particular size, amount etc, but no more

- just
- barely
- only just

just /dʒʌst/ [adv] *The house is just big enough for the whole family.* | *Pick the fruit when it's just ripe.*

barely /ˈbeəʳli/ [adv] if someone or something is **barely** a particular size, level, amount, distance etc, it is that size, level etc, but no bigger or more than that: *There was barely a gallon of gas in the tank.* | *He had barely a mile to go before finishing the race.* | *His voice was barely loud enough to be heard at the back of the theatre.* | *5000 gallons of water is barely enough to supply a fire truck for five minutes.*

only just British **/just barely** American /ˌəʊnli ˈdʒʌst◂, dʒʌst ˈbeəʳli/ [adv] use this when something is a particular size, level, amount, distance etc, but you want to emphasize that it is not any bigger or any more than that: *The cable's only just long enough to reach my desk.* | *We can walk. Her house is just barely around the corner.*

Kk

keep

RELATED WORDS

- to keep doing something *see* **continue**

WHAT'S HERE

- **to keep/continue to have** see **1 to 4**
- **to keep/store** see **5 to 7**
- **to keep sb in a place** see **8 to 11**

to keep/continue to have

RELATED WORDS

opposite: **get rid of**

- *see also* **save**

1 to keep something and not sell it or give or throw it away

- keep
- save
- hold on to sth/hang on to
- not part with
- retain

keep /kiːp/ [v T] *My mother kept all the letters my father ever wrote her.* | *I've decided to keep my car even though it's getting old.* | *I keep all my tickets and boarding passes as souvenirs.* | *Why do you want to keep all these old magazines?*

save /seɪv/ [v T] to keep something that you could throw away, because you might want to use it in the future: *When mom died we found a box full of old newspaper clippings she had saved.* | *Don't throw the wrapping paper away – I'm going to save it and use it again.*

hold on to/hang on to /ˌhəʊld ˈɒn tuː, ˌhæŋ ˈɒn tuː/ [phr v T] informal to keep something, especially because you might need it or it might become valuable at a later time: *Hold on to your ticket – you'll need it to get out of the station.* | *You should hang on to that painting. It might be worth something one day.* | *There's no point in hanging on to the baby clothes if you're not going to have more kids.*

not part with /nɒt ˈpɑːʳt wɪð/ [v phrase] if someone will **not part with** something, they refuse to sell it or give it to anyone else because they like it so much: *We offered her $200 for the lamp, but she didn't want to part with it.* | *Over the years he'd become very attached to his old car and wouldn't part with it for the world.*

retain /rɪˈteɪn/ [v T] formal to keep something, and not sell it, give it away, or get rid of it: *It is suggested that you retain copies of the documents for at least three years.* | *The treaty would not allow any country to produce, acquire, or retain chemical weapons.*

2 to keep something so that someone else can use it later

- keep/save sth for
- put sth by
- hold
- put/set sth aside for

keep/save sth for /'ki:p, 'seɪv (sth) fɔ:ʳ/ [v phrase] to not sell or give something to anyone else, so that someone can have it or use it later: *Let's save some of this pizza for Jill.* | *I haven't got enough money with me right now. Can you keep the vase for me while I go to the bank?* | *If you get any foreign stamps, could you save them for me? My nephew collects them.*

put sth by /ˌpʊt (sth) 'baɪ/ [phr v T] British informal to keep something for someone until they are able to collect it, pay for it etc: *If I pay you for the chairs now, could you put them by and I'll collect them tomorrow?*

hold /həʊld/ [v T] if a shop or a company **holds** something for someone, they keep it until the person can come to buy or get it: *Your tickets will be held at the box office until one hour before the performance.* | *I got the post office to hold our mail while we were away.*

put/set sth aside for /ˌpʊt, ˌset (sth) ə'saɪd fɔ:ʳ/ [v phrase] to keep something separate and not use it because someone is going to buy it or use it later: *One of the rooms was set aside for a yoga class.* | *They didn't have the dress I wanted but said they would put one aside for me when they had a delivery.*

3 to let someone keep their job

▸ keep on ▸ retain

keep on /ˌki:p 'ɒn / [phr v T] to continue to employ someone after they have been working in the same job for a period of time, especially because they have proved that they are good at it **keep sb on** *We cannot guarantee that we will be able to keep you on at the end of your contract.* | **keep on sb** *It seems a lot of these companies want to get rid of the old ones and keep on the young ones.*

retain /rɪ'teɪn/ [v T] formal to continue to employ someone, especially when you are getting rid of other people: *Only four members of the original marketing team will be retained next year.*

4 to keep the same character, feelings, qualities etc

▸ keep ▸ retain
▸ hold on to/hang on to

keep /ki:p/ [v T] *She's almost 60, but she has kept her good looks.* | *These cars are a good investment. They keep their value for many years.* | *I don't know how he managed to keep his sense of humour with all he's been through.*

hold on to/hang on to /ˌhəʊld 'ɒn tu:, ˌhæŋ 'ɒn tu:/ [phr v T] to keep the same character, feelings, qualities etc in spite of difficulties: *She held on to her dreams of stardom throughout her unsuccessful career.* | *I tried desperately to hang on to my sanity as events became more and more confused.* | *It's hard to hang on to your dignity when everyone treats you as if you're old and senile.*

retain /rɪ'teɪn/ [v T] formal to keep the same character, feelings, qualities etc in spite of other changes: *The new design will be more modern, while retaining the graceful shape of the original.* | *It's important that you retain a sense of proportion when you're feeling depressed.*

to keep/store

5 to keep something in a particular place

▸ keep ▸ preserve
▸ store ▸ hoard
▸ keep sth in storage

keep /ki:p/ [v T not in progressive] *Where do you keep the scissors?* | **keep sth in/on/under etc sth** *We always keep the car in the garage.* | *My grandfather kept his teeth in a glass next to his bed.* | *Visitors are advised to keep their valuables with them at all times.*

store /stɔ:ʳ/ [v T] to keep something for a long period of time so that it is ready for you to use when you need it: *Store the medicine in a cool place.* | *The warehouse is being used to store food and clothes for the refugees.* | *The government plans to store the nuclear waste at a site in Nevada.*

keep sth in storage /ˌki:p (sth) ɪn 'stɔ:rɪdʒ/ [v phrase] to store something, especially a large object or a large quantity of something, until the time when you are able to use it: *All our furniture is being kept in storage until we can find a new apartment.* | *The meat is kept in cold storage before being sent out to supermarkets.*

preserve /prɪ'zɜ:ʳv/ [v T] to store something such as food for a long time, especially after treating it in a special way so that it does not decay: *Early settlers preserved meat by drying and salting it.* | *Human organs, preserved in jars, lined the shelves of the laboratory.*

hoard /hɔ:ʳd/ [v T] to collect and keep a large quantity of something secretly, because you think it might be useful at some time in the future – use this when you think the person who does this worries too much about keeping things for the future: *My grandmother hoards everything – jam jars, plastic bags, pieces of string – her house is a mess.* | *They've been hoarding food and water, convinced that some kind of catastrophe is coming.*

6 to keep information

▸ keep ▸ file
▸ store ▸ keep a record/keep records
▸ keep sth on file

▸ *see also* **record**

keep /ki:p/ [v T] to **keep** a lot of different pieces of information together in one place, so that you can find them when you need them: *The police keep detailed information about everyone who has committed a crime.* | *Records of all births and deaths are kept in the county offices.*

store /stɔ:ʳ/ [v T] to keep large quantities of information, especially in a computer: *Huge amounts of information can be stored on a single CD-ROM.* | *The cards can be stored alphabetically.* | *Data regarding employees' salaries are stored on the computer at the main office.*

keep sth on file /ˌki:p (sth) ɒn 'faɪl/ [v phrase] to keep information in a computer or written down so that you can use it at a later time: *We have no job openings at the moment but we will keep your details on file.* | *Employees' records are kept on file for one year after they have left the company.*

file /faɪl/ [v T] to keep information in written form and in a special order, so that it is easy to find when you need it: *Barb, could you file these papers for me?* | *All the students' records are filed alphabetically.* | **file sth away** *Once a complaint is received it is usually filed away and forgotten.*

keep a record/keep records /ˌkiːp ə ˈrekɔːd‖-ərd, ˌkiːp ˈrekɔːdz‖-ərdz/ [v phrase] to keep information on a particular subject, especially so that you can see how it changes or develops **+ of** *You should keep written records of all business expenses.* | *The scientists are keeping a record of radioactive levels in the area.* | **+ on** *Schools keep records on all their students.*

7 things of the same type that you store

- supply
- stock
- reserve
- cache
- hoard

supply /səˈplaɪ/ [n C] a large quantity of something that you keep, and that you replace regularly because you use it often: *Food supplies in the camp were already running out.* | **+ of** *The hospital keeps a large supply of blood for use in emergencies.* | *First prize was a year's supply of baby food.*

stock /stɒk‖stɑːk/ [n C] the amount of a particular product that a shop keeps to be sold: *Buy now while stocks last!* | **+ of** *Someone came in half an hour ago and bought up our entire stock of Italian wine.* | *The new video store has a huge stock of movies to rent.*

reserve /rɪˈzɜːʳv/ [n C] something such as money, food, or water that you keep because you might need it in the future: *The country has foreign currency reserves of $83 billion.* | **+ of** *We had to rely on our emergency reserve of food while we were snowed in.* | **keep/hold sth in reserve** *They sold half the wood and kept the rest in reserve for winter.*

cache /kæʃ/ [n C] things, especially illegal drugs or weapons, that are kept hidden because they are illegal or secret: *The drug cache that the men were found in possession of was worth roughly $1 million.* | **+ of** *Police have found a cache of automatic weapons in a house in the city centre.*

hoard /hɔːʳd/ [n C] a large number of things of the same type that someone keeps secretly, so that they can use them if they need them – use this when you think the person who keeps these things worries too much about keeping things for the future **+ of** *I kept my own secret hoard of chocolate cookies in a big tin under the sink.*

to keep sb in a place

RELATED WORDS

- prison

opposite: —— **free**

8 to make someone stay in a place

- keep

keep /kiːp/ [v T] to make someone stay in a place: *They kept us there for over an hour while they checked our passports.* | *Don't let me keep you if you have other things to do.* | *I'd hate to have a job that kept me in the office all the time.* | **keep sb in** (=make a child stay at school as a punishment) British *The teacher kept us in after school because she said we'd been causing trouble.* | **keep sb after school** (=make a child stay at school as a punishment) American *I was always getting kept after school for something when I was a kid.* | **keep sb in** (=make someone stay in a hospital) British *They say they're going to keep her in overnight for observation, then do some tests on her tomorrow.*

9 to keep someone in a place as a prisoner

- keep
- hold
- hold sb prisoner/captive/hostage
- lock sb up/away
- confine
- detain
- hold/keep sb in custody

keep /kiːp/ [v T] to make someone stay in a place and not let them leave, especially as a prisoner: *You can't keep me here against my will – get out of my way.* | **keep sb in/at etc sth** *The guerrillas were keeping the hostages in a camp somewhere in the jungle.* | *Prisoners were kept in cells with no beds and no running water.*

hold /həʊld/ [v T] to keep someone somewhere, especially for a short period of time, before deciding what to do with them: *Police are holding two men for questioning in connection with the robbery.* | *No one knows where the kidnapped woman is being held.* | **hold sb in/at etc sth** *The prisoners were held at Andersonville until more suitable places were found.*

hold sb prisoner/captive/hostage /ˌhəʊld (sb) ˈprɪzənəʳ, ˈkæptɪv, ˈhɒstɪdʒ‖-ˈhɑː-/ [v phrase] to illegally keep someone in a place where they do not want to be, especially as a way of forcing someone to give you money or do what you want: *Police raided the building where rebels were holding 73 government employees captive.* | **+ in/at etc sth** *Four other US citizens are being held hostage by guerrillas in Colombia.* | *The woman had been held prisoner in Larkin's basement for 3 months.*

lock sb up/away /ˌlɒk (sb) ˈʌp, əˈweɪ‖ˌlɑːk-/ [phr v T] informal to put someone in a place, especially a prison, and lock it so that they cannot escape **lock sb up/away** *Didn't they lock his brother away for murder?* | **lock up/away sb** *The governor argues that locking up criminals has reduced the crime rate.* | *Prisoners are locked up in their cells for twenty three hours a day.*

confine /kənˈfaɪn/ [v T usually in passive] to keep someone in a room or small place, so that they cannot go where they want to **confine sb in sth** *The boy had been confined in a dark narrow room from early childhood by his parents.* | **confine sb to sth** *The judge is confining the jury to their hotel until after the verdict.*

detain /dɪˈteɪn/ [v T usually in passive] if the police **detain** someone who they think has done something illegal, they keep them somewhere, usually in order to ask them questions: *Three men from the ship have been detained for questioning by the Harbour Authorities.* | *The police are now allowed to detain terrorist suspects for as long as a week.*

hold/keep sb in custody /ˌhəʊld, ˌkiːp (sb) ɪn ˈkʌstədi/ [v phrase] if the police **hold** or **keep someone in custody** they keep them in prison until it is time for them to be judged in a court: *McCullough will be kept in custody until her trial on May 3rd.* | **hold/keep sb in police custody** (=in a police station) *A man has been arrested in connection with the murder and is being held in police custody.*

10 someone who is forced to stay in a place

- prisoner
- captive
- hostage

prisoner /ˈprɪzənəʳ/ [n C] someone who is kept in a place, especially a prison, as punishment for a crime: *The state now has 152,000 prisoners in 32 prisons.* | **prisoner of war** (=someone who is kept prisoner by the enemy during a war) *Her father spent three years as a prisoner of war in Korea.* | **political prisoner** (=someone who is in prison because of their political beliefs) *There have been reports of the systematic torture of political prisoners.* | **take sb prisoner** (=make someone your prisoner) *All the soldiers were either killed or taken prisoner.*

captive /ˈkæptɪv/ [n C] someone who is kept in a place illegally: *All the captives were kept in a darkened room with their hands tied.* | *The rebels promise to release their captives unharmed if their demands are met.* | **take sb captive** (=make someone your captive) *Armed gunmen broke into the church and took the priest captive.*

hostage /ˈhɒstɪdʒǁˈhɑː-/ [n C] someone who is illegally kept in a place by someone who threatens to harm or kill them as a way of making someone else pay money or do what they want: *The group has threatened to kill the hostages unless the government frees 15 political prisoners.* | *An attempt to rescue the American hostages ended in disaster.* | **take sb hostage** (=make someone your hostage) *The medical team were captured and taken hostage.*

11 when you are forced to stay somewhere

- be in custody
- be under arrest
- captivity
- imprisonment
- detention
- confinement

be in custody /biː ɪn ˈkʌstədi/ [v phrase] if someone who the police think is guilty of a crime **is in custody**, they are kept in prison until it is time for them to be judged in a court: *Parry was in custody for a month before being released.* | **be in police custody** (=in a police station) *The activist died under suspicious circumstances while he was in police custody.* | **be remanded in custody** (=be sent back to prison from a court until your trial) *Three men and a woman have been remanded in custody on fraud charges.*

be under arrest /biː ˌʌndər əˈrest/ [v phrase] if someone **is under arrest**, the police are keeping them guarded because they think they are guilty of a crime: *He's under arrest and may only be seen by his lawyer.* | **be under house arrest** (=not be allowed to leave your home) *The opposition leader has been under house arrest for the past few months.*

captivity /kæpˈtɪvəti/ [n U] when someone is being forced to stay in a place where they do not want to be – use this when this situation is illegal or wrong: *In his autobiography, Mandela describes his life during captivity.* | **in captivity** *The hostages are now entering their fourth week in captivity.*

imprisonment /ɪmˈprɪzənmənt/ [n U] when someone is being kept as a prisoner, especially as a punishment for a crime: *Johnson was sentenced to three years' imprisonment for causing a riot.* | *The offence is punishable by either a fine or imprisonment.* | **life imprisonment** (=for the rest of someone's life) *Garrison faces life imprisonment for his role in the killings.*

detention /dɪˈtenʃən/ [n U] when someone is being kept somewhere by the police, usually because they think that person has done something illegal and they want to ask them questions: *By the 1920s the average period of detention for new immigrants lasted two weeks.* | *A dissident, recently released from detention, gave a press conference in the capital today.* | **in detention** *About a dozen people remain in detention without trial.* | **take sb into detention** *They were taken into detention two weeks ago and still are not allowed visitors.* | **detention center** (=a place where someone is kept by the police) *There was another riot at the men's detention center yesterday.* | **juvenile detention** (=a place that is like a prison for young people) American *He was in and out of juvenile detention for drugs charges as a teenager.*

confinement /kənˈfaɪnmənt/ [n U] when someone is being kept in a room, prison etc: *He was sentenced to 5 months of home confinement for the crime.* | **solitary confinement** (=the state of being kept completely alone) *Prisoners are punished by being put in solitary confinement.*

kick

RELATED WORDS

- *see also* **hit, attack, hurt/injure, sport/game, score**

- kick
- give sb/sth a kick
- knee
- boot

kick /kɪk/ [v I/T] *The boy behind me kept kicking my chair.* | *He was dragged kicking and screaming into a waiting police car.* | *I could feel the baby kicking inside me.* | *One of the gang kicked him in the stomach.* | **kick sth along/over/around etc** *Who kicked the ball over the fence?* —**kick** [n C] a kicking action or movement: *One karate kick can kill someone.* | *And what a tremendous kick that was – straight into the goal from 200 yards.*

give sb/sth a kick /ˌɡɪv (sb/sth) ə ˈkɪk/ [v phrase] to kick someone or something once: *He gave the bundle a gentle kick, but still it didn't move.* | **give sth a good kick** (=kick it hard) *If the door won't open, just give it a good hard kick.*

knee /niː/ [v T] to hit someone using one of your knees: *She struggled free and kneed her attacker in the groin.*

boot /buːt/ [v T] to kick something hard, especially a ball: *He booted the ball up to the other end of the playing field.* | *Suddenly this big heavy guy came up and booted me in the stomach.*

kill

RELATED WORDS

- *see also* **die, dead, war, shoot, hit, accident, hurt/injure, illness/disease, violent, crime, explode, revenge**

1 to kill someone

- kill
- murder
- assassinate
- beat/kick/stab etc sb to death
- poison
- drown
- strangle
- bump off
- do away with

kill /kɪl/ [v I/T] to make someone die, especially deliberately or violently: *He claims that he didn't mean to kill his wife.* | *The police believe the man may kill again.* | *What the hell were you doing! You could have killed me!* | *Official sources say that 20 people were killed in last night's air raids.* | *My sixteen-year-old son Louis was killed by a drunk driver two years ago.*

murder /ˈmɜːʳdəʳ/ [v T] to deliberately kill someone, especially after planning to do it: *Wilson is accused of murdering his daughter and her boyfriend.* | *One of the country's top judges has been murdered by the Mafia.*

assassinate /əˈsæsəneɪt‖-səneɪt/ [v T] to murder an important or famous person, especially for political reasons: *President Lincoln was assassinated by John Wilkes Booth.* | *an attempt to assassinate the Pope* —**assassination** /əˌsæsəˈneɪʃən‖-sənˈeɪ-/ [n C/U] **+ of** *The assassination of Indira Gandhi caused a crisis in India.*

beat/kick/stab etc sb to death /ˌbiːt (sb) tə ˈdeθ/ [v phrase] to kill someone by beating them, kicking them, or attacking them with a knife: *The court heard how the man was beaten to death by racist thugs.* | *A social worker was found stabbed to death in her office last night.* | *Smith had apparently been kicked to death.*

poison /ˈpɔɪzən/ [v T] to kill someone by putting a very harmful substance in their food or drink: *He believed that somebody was trying to poison him.* | *She had already poisoned three members of her own family with arsenic.*

drown /draʊn/ [v T] to kill someone by holding their face under water for a long time: *He accused his brother of trying to drown him.*

strangle /ˈstræŋgəl/ [v T] to kill someone by pressing on their throat with both hands or with something such as a piece of string so that they cannot breathe: *Police said that the victim had been strangled.* | *He slid his hands around her neck and tried to strangle her.*

bump off /ˌbʌmp ˈɒf/ [phr v T] informal to kill someone – often used humorously **bump off sb/bump sb off** *He kept marrying rich women and then bumping them off.* | **have sb bumped off** (=arrange for someone to be killed) *His uncle decided to have him bumped off.*

do away with /ˌduː əˈweɪ wɪð/ [phr v T] informal to kill someone, especially because they are a threat or their death would be convenient: *Perhaps his wife had taken the opportunity to do away with her rival.*

2 the act or crime of killing someone

- murder
- homicide
- manslaughter
- killing
- assassination
- foul play

murder /ˈmɜːʳdəʳ/ [n C/U] the act or crime of deliberately killing someone: *New York paid tribute to the thousands of innocent people murdered on September 11th.* | *a series of brutal murders* | *The incidence of violent crimes – murder, rape, and assault – has increased in inner city areas.* | **+ of** *Ronny Jones was found guilty of the murder of a 15 year old girl.* | **commit murder** (=to murder someone) *The gun was found five miles from where the murder was committed.* | **attempted murder** (=the crime of unsuccessfully trying to kill someone) *He was charged with attempted murder and found guilty.* | **murder victim** *The murder victim has not yet been identified.*

homicide /ˈhɒməsaɪd‖ˈhɑː-/ [n C/U] the crime of killing someone, especially deliberately – used especially in American legal contexts: *70 per cent of homicides take place within the family.* | *As yet no evidence has been found to suggest that this death was homicide.* | **homicide case/charge/detective** *A newspaper article criticized his handling of a homicide case*

manslaughter /ˈmænˌslɔːtəʳ/ [n U] the crime of killing someone by accident, or while you are trying to defend yourself: *She denied murdering her husband, but pleaded guilty to manslaughter.* | *The court decided there was insufficient evidence for a manslaughter charge.* | **+ of** *The driver of the train was charged with the manslaughter of 13 people.*

killing /ˈkɪlɪŋ/ [n C/U] when someone is deliberately killed – used especially in news reports: *A terrorist group has claimed responsibility for the killing.* | **+ of** *The defendant claimed that he was only avenging the killing of his brother.* | **contract killing** (=when someone has been paid to kill someone else) *Perry said Taylor approached him and asked him to carry out a contract killing on Johnson.*

assassination /əˌsæsəˈneɪʃən‖-sənˈeɪ-/ [n C/U] when someone deliberately kills a famous or important person, especially for political reasons: *Three foreign diplomats have been killed in a series of assassinations.* | **+ of** *The assassination of Franz Ferdinand of Austria in Sarajevo led to the First World War.* | *Flowers were laid to commemorate the anniversary of the assassination of John Lennon.*

foul play /ˌfaʊl ˈpleɪ/ [n U] formal if the police think that **foul play** is involved in a person's death, they think that the person has been murdered: *There was no question of foul play – a suicide note was found near the body.* | *The medical report showed no signs of poison in the body but the police still suspect foul play.*

3 to kill a large number of people

- kill
- massacre
- slaughter
- exterminate

kill /kɪl/ [v T] *Thousands of the rebels were killed in a gun battle with government troops.* | *The gunman killed 22 people and wounded 15, before turning his gun on himself.*

massacre /ˈmæsəkəʳ/ [v T] to kill a large number of people easily, because they are not able to defend themselves well enough: *They have massacred hundreds of innocent people.* | *Claims by refugees that 1000 people had been massacred were denied by the local authorities.*

slaughter /ˈslɔːtəʳ/ [v T] to kill a large number of people in a very cruel or violent way: *Men ran through the village burning houses and slaughtering the inhabitants.* | *Men, women and children were slaughtered in groups by their captors.*

exterminate /ɪkˈstɜːʳməneɪt/ [v T] to kill large numbers of a particular group or race of people so that it no longer exists: *There was an attempt to exterminate ethnic groups in the north of the country.* —**extermination** /ɪkˌstɜːʳməˈneɪʃən/ [n U] **+ of** *In Tasmania there was total extermination of the aboriginal population.*

4 when a large number of people are killed

- massacre
- slaughter
- carnage
- mass murder
- genocide

massacre /ˈmæsəkəʳ/ [n C/U] when a large number of people are easily killed, because they are not able to defend themselves: *The soldiers who carried out the massacre have not been identified.* | **+ of** *The students claimed the two men had ordered the massacre of 200 people in Kwangju.*

slaughter /ˈslɔːtəʳ/ [n U] when a large number of people are killed in a very cruel or violent way: *The slaughter was terrible – the whole field was covered with bodies.* | *Many are determined to avenge the slaughter in the World Trade Center and the Pentagon.* | **+ of** *His war crimes included the deliberate slaughter of 250,000 individuals.*

carnage /ˈkɑːʳnɪdʒ/ [n U] when a large number of people are violently killed, especially in a war – used especially in newspapers: *The war was over. The carnage had ceased.* | *The foreign minister has asked ambassadors from several states to help end the carnage.*

mass murder /ˌmæs ˈmɜːʳdəʳ/ [n C/U] when one or more people kill a large number of people violently at about the same time: *Details are still emerging of this, the biggest mass murder in Canadian history.* | **+ of** *the mass murder of innocent people*

genocide /ˈdʒenəsaɪd/ [n U] when a whole group or race of people are killed in a planned and organized way: *What is going on is not just war, it is genocide.* | *In recent history, the existence of prejudice has led to violence and genocide.*

5 to kill yourself

- kill yourself
- suicide
- take your own life
- suicidal
- end it all

kill yourself /ˈkɪl jɔːʳself/ [v phrase] *He killed himself by jumping under a train.* | *She tried to kill herself when news of the scandal leaked out.* | *You'll kill yourself if you go on drinking like that.*

suicide /ˈsuːɪ̈saɪd, ˈsjuː-‖ˈsuː-/ [n C/U] when someone deliberately kills himself or herself: *Police are treating the man's death as suicide.* | *There is grave concern about the number of teenage suicides recorded last year.* | **commit suicide** *Barry threatened to commit suicide if she refused to marry him.* | **suicide attempt** *Stephen required hospital treatment after his suicide attempt.*

take your own life /ˌteɪk jɔːr əʊn ˈlaɪf/ [v phrase] formal to kill yourself: *Many religions consider that it is a sin to take your own life.* | *Desperately frustrated and alone, she could see no way out except to take her own life.*

suicidal /ˌsuːɪ̈ˈsaɪdl◂, ˌsjuː-‖ˌsuː-/ [adj] someone who is **suicidal** is likely to kill themselves because they are extremely unhappy: *The thought of having to stay in the house all day made me feel almost suicidal.* | **suicidal tendencies** (=behaviour that shows you may try to kill yourself) *Had the prisoner previously displayed suicidal tendencies?*

end it all /ˈend ɪt ɔːl/ [v phrase] informal if you want to **end it all**, you want to kill yourself because you are extremely unhappy, lonely etc – used especially in stories: *Sometimes I feel so low I just feel like ending it all.*

6 someone who kills another person

- murderer
- killer
- assassin
- hitman/contract killer
- psychopath

murderer /ˈmɜːʳdərəʳ/ [n C] someone who has deliberately killed another person: *Do you think the police will ever catch her murderer?* | *A convicted murderer was on the run last night after escaping from Lewes prison.* | **mass murderer** (=someone who has murdered a lot of people) *In prison he enjoyed reading biographies of other mass murderers.*

killer /ˈkɪləʳ/ [n C] someone who deliberately kills someone else – used especially in newspapers: *The victim's best friend, Joanne, is convinced the killer is local.* | *The judge described him as 'a cold-blooded killer'.* | **+ of** *Police are searching for the killer of a 9 year old boy.* | **serial killer** (=someone who has killed a number of people, one after the other) *Dr Shipman is the biggest serial killer of all time.*

assassin /əˈsæsɪ̈n/ [n C] someone who kills a famous or important person, sometimes because someone else has paid them to do it: *Although the assassins were never caught, it is commonly believed that they were working for the government.* | *His assassins must have been aware of his security arrangements.*

hitman/contract killer /ˈhɪtmæn, ˈkɒntrækt ˌkɪləʳ‖ˈkɑːn-/ [n C] someone who is paid to kill people illegally: *The hitman used the top floor room of a hotel opposite the square.* | *The police believe the murder could be the work of a contract killer.*

psychopath ALSO **psycho** informal /ˈsaɪkəpæθ, ˈsaɪkəʊ/ [n C] someone who has a mental illness that makes them kill people: *Dr Green said that, in his opinion, Perry was a dangerous psychopath who might kill again.*

7 when someone is killed as a punishment

- execute
- put sb to death
- capital punishment
- the death penalty
- death sentence
- capital offence
- be on death row
- condemned

execute /ˈeksɪ̈kjuːt/ [v T usually in passive] to kill someone as a punishment for a serious crime: *King Charles I was executed on 30th January 1649.* | *The two young men spent 6 months in jail waiting to be executed.* | **execute sb for sth** (=because of a particular crime) *This is a backward and cruel society, in which people are executed for homosexuality and adultery.* — **execution** /ˌeksɪ̈ˈkjuːʃən/ [n C/U] *No date has been set for her execution.* | *If his appeal fails, his last hope to avoid execution is the US Supreme Court.*

put sb to death /ˌpʊt (sb) tə ˈdeθ/ [v phrase] written to officially arrange for someone that you have power over to be killed – used especially in historical descriptions: *The chief priests wanted to arrest Jesus and put him to death.* | *No woman had been put to death in the state since the American Revolution.* | **have sb put to death** *The queen would have people put to death for her own amusement.*

capital punishment /ˌkæpɪ̈tl ˈpʌnɪʃmənt/ [n U] the system of killing criminals as a legal punishment: *I don't believe bringing back capital punishment would reduce crime.* | *Most people that we questioned were against capital punishment.*

the death penalty /ðə 'deθ ˌpenlti/ [n phrase] the legal punishment of being killed for a serious crime: *The death penalty does not exist in Britain.* | *Do you think they should bring back the death penalty?* | **carry the death penalty** (=to be a crime for which the punishment is death) *Murder is one of the few offences that carries the death penalty.*

death sentence /'deθ ˌsentəns/ [n C/U] the punishment of death that a judge decides to give to someone who is guilty of a serious crime **receive/be given a death sentence** *He is the youngest person ever to be given a death sentence in San Diego County.*

capital offence British **/capital offense** American ALSO **capital crime** /ˌkæpɪtl ə'fens, ˌkæpɪtl 'kraɪm/ [n C] an offence or crime that will be punished by death: *Drug-smuggling is a capital offence in many countries.*

be on death row /biː ɒn ˌdeθ 'rəʊ/ [v phrase] if a criminal **is on death row**, they are in prison before being killed as punishment for a crime, especially in the US: *Larson has been on death row since 1995 for murdering a taxi driver.*

condemned /kə'demd/ [adj only before noun] a **condemned** man, prisoner etc is in prison before he or she is killed as punishment for a crime: *The state allows no communication with a condemned man.* | *Here are the kitchens where the condemned prisoner's last meal was prepared.*

8 when someone is killed to stop them from suffering

- euthanasia
- mercy killing

euthanasia /ˌjuːθə'neɪziə‖-'neɪʒə/ [n U] when someone who is very old or very ill is killed in a painless way in order to stop them suffering any longer – use this to talk about this practice in general: *In the Netherlands euthanasia has already been legalized.* | *Most doctors are opposed to euthanasia on ethical grounds.*

mercy killing /'mɜːʳsi ˌkɪlɪŋ/ [n C/U] when someone who is very ill is killed in a painless way in order to stop them suffering any longer: *Some doctors carry out mercy killings by giving large quantities of pain-killing drugs.*

9 to cause death

- kill
- cause death
- kill off
- destroy
- be a killer
- wipe out
- decimate

kill /kɪl/ [v I/T] to cause someone's death – use this especially about accidents, diseases, or substances: *A car drove onto the pavement, killing three of Mrs Maguire's children.* | *The explosion killed 32 people.* | *The disease has already killed more than 2000 in Latin America.* | *Many people do not realize that these drugs are dangerous and can kill.* | **be killed in a crash/accident etc** *James Dean was killed in a car crash in 1955.*

cause death /ˌkɔːz 'deθ/ [v phrase] to make someone die: *Rhubarb leaves, either raw or cooked, can cause violent stomach pains or even death.* | *Research is being done into the virus that caused the death of 15,000 seals last summer.* | *The injuries sustained by the victim were not sufficient to have caused death in a healthy person.* —**cause of death** [n phrase] *The cause of death was a broken neck.*

kill off /ˌkɪl 'ɒf/ [phr v T] to cause the death of a group of plants or animals **kill off sth** *It was the cold winter of 1992 that finally killed off the last of the roses.* | *Pollution in the lakes and streams has been killing off many species of fish.* | **kill sth off** *If you plant your seedlings out too soon, a late frost might kill them off.*

destroy /dɪ'strɔɪ/ [v T] to kill things, especially plants and trees, so that they can never start to grow again: *A vast amount of the Amazonian rainforest is being destroyed every day.* | *Milk is heat treated for a few seconds to destroy bacteria.* —**destruction** /dɪ'strʌkʃən/ [n U] + **of** *We should be discouraging the unnecessary destruction of any wild species.*

be a killer /biː ə 'kɪləʳ/ [v phrase] if an illness **is a killer**, it kills a lot of people, especially because there is no cure: *In those days measles was a major killer.* | *Diphtheria is still a killer in many developing countries.*

wipe out /ˌwaɪp 'aʊt/ [phr v T] to kill a complete group or race of people, or all of a type of animal or plant, so that it no longer exists **wipe out sb/sth** *The entire village was wiped out.* | *Archaeologists think that massive floods could have wiped out the dinosaurs.* | **wipe sb/sth out** *The fur trade has wiped leopards out in some areas.*

decimate /'desəmeɪt/ [v T] to kill large numbers of the people, animals, or plants in a particular place: *Cambodia's 21-year war decimated the wildlife population.* | *His prize herd of cows has been decimated by an unknown disease.* —**decimation** /ˌdesə'meɪʃən/ [n U] + **of** *After the decimation of the rainforests, life on earth will be very different.*

10 able to kill you

- fatal
- lethal
- deadly
- killer
- mortal

fatal /'feɪtl/ [adj] a **fatal** accident, illness, or injury is one that causes death: *He suffered a fatal injury to the neck.* | + **to** *A sudden shock could be fatal to anyone with a weak heart.* —**fatally** [adv] **fatally injured/wounded** *The bank manager was fatally wounded during the robbery.*

lethal /'liːθəl/ [adj] something that is **lethal** can cause death – use this especially about weapons or substances: *The poison produced by the frog's skin is so lethal that it can paralyze a bird or a monkey immediately.* | *A lethal cocktail of pollutants is being poured into Scotland's coastal waters, according to Greenpeace.* | **lethal weapon** *Almost any sharp or pointed object can potentially be a lethal weapon.* | + **to** *Most pesticides are lethal to earthworms on or near the surface.*

deadly /'dedli/ [adj] something such as a disease or poison that is **deadly** can cause death: *In the First World War pneumonia was as deadly as bullets and shells.* | *Some mushrooms are edible while others, which look almost identical, contain deadly poisons.*

killer /'kɪləʳ/ [adj only before noun] a **killer** disease or thing could kill or has killed a lot of people – used especially in newspapers: *A swarm of killer bees has attacked 70 children in a village in northern Mexico.* | *Killer floods and hurricanes in Asia have destroyed whole towns.*

mortal /'mɔːʳtl/ [adj only before noun] a **mortal** injury, wound, or disease is one that causes death – used especially in literature: *He killed Leonardo and received a mortal wound himself.* | *He gathered all his strength to deliver his opponent the final mortal* *blow.* —**mortally** [adv] **mortally wounded/ill** *Wolfe and his opponent Montcalm were both mortally wounded in the battle.*

11 to kill an animal

- kill
- slaughter
- destroy
- put down/put to sleep
- cull

kill /kɪl/ [v T] *Is it morally acceptable to kill animals for food? | You shouldn't really kill spiders, even if you're frightened of them. | They were so hungry they killed the rest of their livestock that winter.*

slaughter /ˈslɔːtəʳ/ [v T usually in passive] to kill farm animals, either for their meat or skins, or because they are ill: *The only way to stop the virus spreading is by slaughtering all infected animals. | As part of the ceremony a cow was slaughtered and placed on the stone altar.* —**slaughter** [n U] *Most of the cattle will be sent for slaughter.*

destroy /dɪˈstrɔɪ/ [v T usually in passive] to kill an animal in a painless way, especially using drugs, because it is dangerous or in pain: *The Animal Disease Authority decided to destroy the cattle that were infected with the disease.* | **have sth destroyed** *The court ordered the owner of the rottweilers to have the dogs destroyed.*

put down/put to sleep British /ˌpʊt ˈdaʊn, ˌpʊt tə ˈsliːp/ [phr v T/v phrase usually in passive] to kill an animal, especially a pet, in a painless way, because it is very old or very ill, or is not wanted: *When our old cat became very sick we had to ask the vet to put her down. | She rescued Sandy from the Animal Shelter the day before he was due to be put to sleep.* | **have sth put down/put to sleep** *A blind dog is no use to a shepherd. I'm afraid I'm going to have to have him put down.*

cull /kʌl/ [v T] to kill a large number of animals, for example in order to stop a disease spreading or to keep the numbers of a particular animal population down: *Over two million sheep have been culled to prevent the spread of foot and mouth disease.* —**cull** [n C] *The cull is thought to have cost many farmers their livelihoods. | a seal cull*

kind

RELATED WORDS

- a kind of person or thing *see* **type**
- kind and generous *see* **generous/not generous**
- be kind to someone to make them feel better *see* **comfort/make sb feel better**
- *see also* **nice, friendly, selfish/not selfish**

1 kind

- kind
- kindness
- nice
- considerate/thoughtful
- good
- gentle
- sb's heart is in the right place

kind /kaɪnd/ [adj] someone who is **kind** tries to help people and make them happy or comfortable, and shows that they care about them: *Everyone loved Mary. She was the kindest, most generous person in the world.* | **+ to** *He's a good brother. He's always been kind to me.* | **it is kind of sb (to do sth)** *'Karen gave me a lift to the station.' 'That was kind of her.'* —**kindly** [adv] *Joan very kindly offered to wash the dishes.*

kindness /ˈkaɪndnəs/ [n U] kind behaviour: *What this child needs is a little love and kindness. | She was touched by this simple act of kindness.* | **+ to** *I shall never forget her kindness to me.*

nice /naɪs/ [adj] especially spoken someone who is **nice** is kind and friendly, and often helpful: *I've got a nice boss, and the pay's good. | 'She offered to pay for everything.' 'That was a nice gesture.'* | **+ to** *Why can't they just be nice to each other?* | **it is nice of sb (to do sth)** *It was nice of them to invite us.*

considerate/thoughtful /kənˈsɪdərət, ˈθɔːtfəl/ [adj] someone who is **considerate** or **thoughtful** thinks about other people's feelings and tries to do things that will make them happy or comfortable: *Louis was always considerate towards other people.* | **it is considerate/thoughtful of sb (to do sth)** *It was considerate of them to warn us that they might be late. | 'I didn't phone this afternoon. I thought you might be resting.' 'That was very thoughtful of you.'* —**consideration** /kənˌsɪdəˈreɪʃən/ [n U] *I could not believe that he could show such little consideration for others.*

good /gʊd/ [adj not before noun] if you are **good** to someone, especially someone who is old, young, sick etc, you are kind to them and give them what they need **+ to** *My stepfather's always been very good to me and treated me like one of his own children.* | **it is good of sb (to do sth)** *It's good of you to see me at such short notice.*

gentle /ˈdʒentl/ [adj] someone who is **gentle** is nice and kind, and is never angry or violent: *My father was a professional boxer, but at home with the family he was always quiet and gentle. | a sweet, gentle girl who wouldn't hurt a fly*

sb's heart is in the right place / (sb's) ˌhɑːʳt ɪz ɪn ðə ˌraɪt ˈpleɪs/ if you say that **someone's heart is in the right place,** you mean that they do not always do the right thing, but they are basically a good, kind person: *He can be rude and bad-tempered sometimes, but his heart's in the right place.*

2 kind to people who have problems or difficulties

- sympathetic
- understanding
- compassionate
- caring
- kind-hearted
- a shoulder to cry on

sympathetic /ˌsɪmpəˈθetɪk◂/ [adj] if someone is **sympathetic** when you are having problems, they say kind things to you and show that they feel sad about your situation: *Why don't you talk to Elizabeth? She's always sympathetic. | My friends were extremely sympathetic when they heard I'd lost my job. | Noticing my embarrassment, the teacher gave me a sympathetic smile.* —**sympathetically** [adv] *She listened sympathetically to all our complaints.*

understanding /ˌʌndəʳˈstændɪŋ/ [adj] an **understanding** person is kind and patient when someone has a problem, and does not get angry with them or criticize them: *I'm sorry I've been so bad-tempered lately. Anyway, thank you for being so understanding. | Irene often has to take time off work. Fortunately she has a very understanding boss.*

compassionate /kəmˈpæʃənət/ [adj] someone who is **compassionate** wants to help people who are suffering or having problems: *Alice was a compassionate woman who wanted to save children from violence and poverty. | We must try to create a more caring, more compassionate society.* —**compassion-**

ately [adv] *Political refugees need our protection and we urge the government to view their plight more compassionately.*

caring /ˈkeərɪŋ/ [adj] loving and sympathetic, especially so that you want to help people close to you when they are in trouble: *Sharon was lucky to have such caring parents at a time when she needed help.* | *It is possible for men to be tough and, at the same time, caring and sensitive.*

kind-hearted /ˌkaɪnd ˈhɑːʳtɪ̣d◂/ [adj] someone who is **kind-hearted** has a kind and sympathetic character: *Being a kind-hearted woman, she felt sorry for the poor child.* | *I wouldn't have helped him at all, but then I'm not as kind-hearted as you.*

a shoulder to cry on /ə ˌʃəʊldəʳ tə ˈkraɪ ɒn/ [n phrase] informal someone who will listen sympathetically when you tell them about your problems: *Remember, I'm always here if you need a shoulder to cry on.*

3 to treat someone very kindly or too kindly

- spoil
- pamper
- make a fuss of/fuss over

spoil /spɔɪl/ [v T] to treat someone, especially a child, too kindly and give them everything they want whether they should have it or not, so that they behave badly: *You're spoiling that kid. He's getting cheeky and selfish.* | **spoil sb rotten** (=spoil someone very much) *Danny was her favourite grandson and she spoiled him rotten.*

pamper /ˈpæmpəʳ/ [v T] to look after a person or animal very kindly, and spend a lot of time trying to make them happy and comfortable, sometimes in a way that is not good for their health or character: *She really pampers that dog – it's even got its own little bed next to hers.* | **pamper yourself** *Take some time out to pamper yourself with an aromatherapy massage.* —**pampered** [adj only before noun] *Pam was raised as the pampered daughter of a prosperous businessman.*

make a fuss of/fuss over /ˌmeɪk ə ˈfʌs ɒv, ˈfʌs əʊvəʳ/ [v phrase/phr v T] British to look after someone very well and pay a lot of attention to them: *When I came out of hospital and got back home, everyone made a great fuss of me and I loved it.* | *My sister was jealous because Dad made such a fuss of me.* | *I enjoyed having people fussing over me – it made me feel important.*

kiss

RELATED WORDS

- *see also* **love, sex, girlfriend/boyfriend, touch**

1 to kiss someone

- kiss
- give sb a kiss
- give sb a peck

kiss /kɪs/ [v T] to touch someone with your lips, usually on their lips or cheek, as a sign of love or as a greeting: *He wanted to kiss Liz, but he didn't dare.* | *When I was a child, I used to hate being kissed by visiting relatives.* | *Do you remember the first time you kissed a boy?* | *Timothy bent to kiss his aunt's cheek.* | **kiss sb on the lips/cheek/mouth etc** *His mother hugged him and kissed him on both cheeks.* | **kiss sb goodbye/goodnight** *Mrs Thomson kissed Maria goodbye, and handed her her suitcase.*

give sb a kiss /ˌgɪv (sb) ə ˈkɪs/ [v phrase] to kiss someone once, as a sign of love or as a greeting: *Come on, honey, give me a kiss.* | *Neil put his arm around me and gave me a quick kiss to reassure me.* | **give sb a kiss on the cheek/lips etc** *Karen flung her arms around his neck and gave him a big kiss on the lips.*

give sb a peck /ˌgɪv (sb) ə ˈpek/ [v phrase] to give someone a small, quick kiss on their cheek, often in a way that is slightly formal: *My grandmother gave me a quick peck, and went to bed.* | **give sb a peck on the mouth/cheek etc** *She gave him a peck on the cheek and told him not to worry.*

2 when two people kiss each other

- kiss
- snog
- neck
- smooch

kiss /kɪs/ [v I] *They kissed briefly, then he left the house.* | *They were on the sofa, curled up together, kissing.* —**kissing** [n U] *In my mother's day, kissing in public was severely frowned upon.*

snog /snɒg‖snɑːg/ [v I/T] British informal if two people, especially young people, **snog**, they kiss each other for a long time in a sexual way – used especially humorously: *Frances left the two of them snogging in a dark corner and went back to the dance floor.* | *Who's that guy snogging Fiona?* —**snogging** [n U] *Fifteen-year-old boys are often more interested in snogging than in football.*

neck /nek/ [v I usually in progressive] informal if two people, especially young people, are **necking**, they are kissing and touching each other in a sexual way: *Jemma found her friends necking in the back of the car.*

smooch /smuːtʃ/ [v I usually in progressive] informal if two people **are smooching**, they are kissing and holding each other in a romantic way: *In the semi-darkness, couples were smooching to sentimental love-songs.* | *The sales manager and the boss's wife were smooching in full view of everyone.*

3 an act of kissing

- kiss
- snog
- peck

kiss /kɪs/ [n C] *In the morning he woke her with gentle kisses.* | *'Have you got a kiss for your old Dad?' he asked.* | **give sb a kiss** *She gave him a quick kiss and said goodbye.*

snog /snɒg‖snɑːg/ [n singular] British informal if you have a **snog** with someone, you kiss them for a long time in a sexual way – used especially humorously: *Barry thought this might be an opportunity for a quick snog.*

peck /pek/ [n C] a small quick kiss, often one that is slightly formal **a peck on the cheek** *He gave her a really big kiss. Not just a peck on the cheek.*

know/not know

RELATED WORDS

- know how to do something *see* **can/can't**
- *see also* **instinct, realize, understand/not understand, predict**

WHAT'S HERE

● **to know sth**	see **1 to 11**
● **to not know sth**	see **12 to 21**
● **to know a person**	see **22 to 25**

to know sth

RELATED WORDS

- *see also* **intelligent, good at, find out**

1 to know a fact or piece of information

- **know**
- **realize**
- **be/become aware**
- **can tell**
- **appreciate**
- **be conscious**
- **know perfectly well**
- **know/learn from experience**

know /nəʊ/ [v I/T] to **know** a fact or piece of information: *I love this painting – do you know the name of the artist?* | *Jack's leaving. Didn't you know?* | **+ (that)** *I knew he was ill, but I didn't realize he had cancer.* | **+ how/what/where etc** *Do you know where Andy is?* | **+ about** *How much do you know about the Moore case?* | **+ of** *I know of one company where members of staff get their meals free.* | **know a lot about** *He knew a lot about baseball, and about how to pick great players.*

realize ALSO **realise** British /ˈrɪəlaɪz/ [v I/T] to know that a situation exists, and especially to know how important or serious it is: *None of us realized the danger we were in.* | *'She's been promoted to chief executive.' 'Oh, really? I didn't realize.'* | **+ (that)** *I realize that you are very busy, but could I talk to you for a few minutes?* | **+ how/what/why** *Even Horton's family hadn't realized how sick he was, both physically and emotionally.*

be/become aware /biː, bɪˌkʌm əˈweəʳ/ [v phrase] formal to know or begin to realize that a situation exists, often a serious one **+ of** *I am aware of the risks involved in the project, but I am willing to take them.* | *Children become aware of rules during this stage of development.* | **+ (that)** *The question is, was the Chief of Police aware that so much corruption existed within the police department?* | **well/acutely/keenly aware** (=used to emphasize that someone definitely knows something) *There were signs everywhere – the two men must have been well aware that they were hunting out of season.* | **painfully aware** (=aware of something that upsets you) *Abbey was always painfully aware that she was not as pretty as her sister.*

can tell /kən ˈtel/ [v phrase] especially spoken to know that something is true because you can see signs that show this: *She's going to have a baby – couldn't you tell?* | **+ (that)** *I could tell he worked outdoors, because he had a deep tan.* | **+ by/from** *You can tell by the look on her face that she's hiding something.* | **+ whether/what/how etc** *You can tell when kids aren't feeling well.* | *I couldn't tell exactly how old he was.* | **from what I can tell ...** *Don't worry. From what I can tell, you'll make a great father.*

appreciate /əˈpriːʃieɪt/ [v T not in progressive] to understand how serious a situation or problem is: *I wonder if he really appreciates the seriousness of the situation.* | **+ how/what/why** *Changes were taking place, though at the time no one fully appreciated how far-reaching these changes were to be.* | **+ (that)** *I appreciate that some of you have had to wait all night, and I thank you for your patience.*

be conscious /biː ˈkɒnʃəs‖-ˈkɑːn-/ [v phrase] to know that a particular situation exists and to have it in your mind continuously **+ of** *I was very conscious of the fact that this was an important meeting and that I had to make a good impression.* | *As oil prices rose, countries in the West suddenly became conscious of fuel efficiency.* | **+ (that)** *He was conscious that she was staring at him as he spoke.*

know perfectly well /nəʊ ˌpɜːʳfɪktli ˈwel/ [v phrase not in progressive] spoken use this to say that someone knows something, although they behave as if they do not **+ (that)** *He knows perfectly well, he's not allowed to park outside the main door.* | *I knew perfectly well that I had anorexia, but I wouldn't admit that it was a problem.* | **+ what/why/who etc** *You know perfectly well what I mean, so stop pretending you don't.*

know/learn from experience /ˌnəʊ, ˌlɜːʳn frəm ɪkˈspɪəriəns/ [v phrase not in progressive] to know what is likely to happen in a particular situation, because you have learned from your own experiences **+ (that)** *He knew from experience that most ship's captains were not adequately covered with life insurance.* | **know from past/personal/first-hand etc experience** *Kelly knew from personal experience that education is a ticket out of minimum-wage work.* | **know from bitter experience** (=know something because of a bad experience of something similar) *Sue learned from bitter experience not to rely on Martin in times of crisis.*

2 to know a place, a film, a book etc

- **know**
- **be familiar with**
- **be acquainted with**

know /nəʊ/ [v T not in progressive] if you **know** a place, you have been there before and spent time there; if you **know** a book, song, film etc, you have read it or seen it or heard it before: *'Do you know Boston at all?' 'Yes, I went to college there.'* | *I didn't know any of the songs they were singing.* | *Do you know that Hitchcock movie about a man who is being chased?* | **know sth by heart** (=know every word of a song, poem etc without having to read it) *The congregation seemed to know all the hymns by heart.* | **know somewhere like the back of your hand** informal (=know a place very well) *Tony had spent a lot of time in Tokyo and knew the place like the back of his hand.*

be familiar with /biː fəˈmɪliəʳ wɪð/ [v phrase] to know a thing or place well because you have seen it, read it, used it, or been there: *Are you familiar with this type of software?* | *I grew up near Lake George, so I'm very familiar with the towns around there.* | *Are you familiar with the works of George Eliot?*

be acquainted with /biː əˈkweɪntɪ̈d wɪð/ [v phrase] formal to know something: *I was not acquainted with the north-western part of the island.* | *Through art, children become acquainted with cultures other than their own.* | **be fully**

acquainted with *All our employees are fully acquainted with the safety procedures.*

3 to know a lot about something

- know (all) about
- knowledgeable
- be well versed in
- know sth inside (and) out
- be clued up
- specialize in
- know what you are talking about
- know your stuff

▸ *see also* **good at**

know (all) about /ˌnəʊ (ɔːl) əˈbaʊt/ [v T not in progressive] *My brother knows about cars. I'm sure he could fix it for you.* | *You can't become an architect unless you know all about building regulations.* | **know a lot about sth** *The old man knew a lot about the history of the village.* | **know all there is to know about sth** (=to know everything about a particular subject) *I thought I knew all there was to know about men, until I met Jason.*

knowledgeable /ˈnɒlɪdʒəbəl‖ˈnɑː-/ [adj] knowing a lot of facts about a particular subject, especially about something that not many people know about: *The sales staff are all knowledgeable, helpful, and cheerful.* | **+ about/in** *We are looking for people who are knowledgeable about the oil and banking industries.* | *Earley is a diligent reporter, knowledgeable in the field of espionage.*

be well versed in /biː ˌwel ˈvɜːʳst ɪn/ [v phrase] to know a lot about a particular subject because you have had a lot of experience of it: *The new prime minister is well versed in economic policy.* | *Victor Amadeus was reputed to be well versed in poisons and their antidotes.*

know sth inside (and) out /ˌnəʊ (sth) ˌɪnsaɪd (ənd) ˈaʊt/ [v phrase not in progressive] informal to know a particular subject very thoroughly: *She's very experienced – she knows the advertising business inside out.* | *You need to know your specialized subject inside and out.*

be clued up /biː ˌkluːd ˈʌp/ [v phrase] British informal to know all the facts that you need to know about a subject, especially because you have found it out before you start doing something **+ on** *Are you clued up on what points to look for when buying a used car?* | **+ about** *We'd better get clued up about this new computer system before we start using it.*

specialize in ALSO **specialise** British /ˈspeʃəlaɪz ɪn/ [v T] to know a lot about one particular subject or activity because you study it or do it more than any other: *My history professor specialized in Russian history.* | *The chef specializes in Hunan and Szechuan cuisine, but all the dishes we tried were delicious.*

know what you are talking about /ˌnəʊ wɒt juː ɑːʳ ˈtɔːkɪŋ əbaʊt/ [v phrase not in progressive] informal to know a lot about a particular subject so that your judgement can be trusted, especially because you have had a lot of experience: *Pilger knows what he is talking about, having spent several years as a reporter in Vietnam.* | *Rolim seemed to know what he was talking about, but his theories raised some questions for me.*

know your stuff /ˌnəʊ jɔːʳ ˈstʌf/ [v phrase not in progressive or passive] informal to know a lot about something, especially about how to do your job, in a way that other people think is impressive: *To pass that test the kids really have to know their stuff.* | *The doctor who came in looked very young. I was just hoping she knew her stuff.*

4 someone who knows a lot about something

- expert
- specialist
- authority
- pundit
- buff
- connoisseur
- boffin

expert /ˈekspɜːʳt/ [n C] someone who know a lot about a subject: *The team of experts includes psychiatrists, psychologists and social workers.* | **+ in/on** *an expert in French history* | *A draft of the document was reviewed by experts on hospital infection control.* | **medical/legal/financial etc expert** *Legal experts are saying that the man's conviction was unlawful.*

specialist /ˈspeʃəl̩ɪst/ [n C] someone who has studied a particular subject for a long time and knows much more about it than other people: *You really need a specialist for this job.* | **+ in** *Professor Williams teaches English Literature and is a specialist in the novels of George Orwell.* | **computer/marketing/engine etc specialist** *The Health Department is seeking the advice of a team of tropical disease specialists.*

authority /ɔːˈθɒrɪ̩ti, ə-‖əˈθɑː-, əˈθɔː-/ [n C usually singular] someone whose knowledge and opinions on a particular subject are greatly respected **+ on** *Reischauer became an authority on Japanese–American relations.* | *She was widely regarded as the country's leading authority on plant diseases.*

pundit /ˈpʌndɪ̩t/ [n C] someone who knows a lot about a subject, especially politics or economics, and who is asked to give their opinion about it on television, in newspapers etc: *If the pundits are right, the economic situation may become worse before the end of the year.* | *Hollywood pundits predicted the movie would grab the top spot in the ratings, but they were wrong.*

buff /bʌf/ [n C] someone who knows a lot about a particular activity or subject because they are very interested in it **film/jazz/computer etc buff** *'How many films did Hitchcock make?' 'Ask Paul, – he's a great film buff.'* | *The market for magazines for computer buffs is growing all the time.*

connoisseur /ˌkɒnəˈsɜːʳ‖ˌkɑː-/ [n C] someone who has great knowledge and experience of something such as art, furniture, food, or wine so that they can recognize what is the best: *The golden chanterelle, as it is commonly known, is a favorite among mushroom connoisseurs.* | **+ of** *Lord Burlington was a great collector and connoisseur of paintings.*

boffin /ˈbɒfɪ̩n‖ˈbɑː-/ [n C] informal British someone who knows a lot about a particular subject, especially a scientific or technical subject: *A few science boffins were asked for their opinions, but otherwise the article gave very little information.*

5 knowing a lot about something

- knowledgeable
- well-informed
- be a mine of information
- be well up on
- have your finger on the pulse
- keep abreast of/keep up to date with

knowledgeable /ˈnɒlɪdʒəbəl‖ˈnɑː-/ [adj] someone who is **knowledgeable** knows a lot of different facts, especially about a particular subject or activity: *Visitors should use reputable travel firms with knowledgeable guides, and avoid camping alone.* | **+ about/in** *Gradually the band became more* *knowledgeable about the business dealings in the music industry.*

well-informed /ˌwel ɪnˈfɔːʳmd◂/ [adj] knowing a lot about what is happening, especially about what is happening in the world: *'Le Monde' is a newspaper designed for well-informed readers.* | *According to one well-informed source, the two sides are very near to reaching an agreement.* | **+ about** *Abdul Karim was particularly well- informed about American politics.*

be a mine of information /biː ə ˌmaɪn əv ɪnfəʳˈmeɪʃən/ [v phrase] to know a lot about a particular subject or about various subjects, so that you are usually able to answer anything that people ask you: *The British Ambassador proved to be a mine of information on the subject of the Royal Family.*

be well up on British **/be up on** American /biː ˌwel ˈʌp ɒn, biː ˈʌp ɒn/ [v phrase] spoken to know a lot about something, including the most recent information: *How well up are you on men's fashion?* | *Don't ask me – I'm not really up on current events in that part of the world.*

have your finger on the pulse /hæv jɔːʳ ˌfɪŋgər ɒn ðə ˈpʌls/ [v phrase not in progressive or passive] to always know what changes and developments are happening in a particular situation or organization **+ of** *As a manager of a bookshop, I have to have my finger on the pulse of the publishing industry.*

keep abreast of/keep up to date with /kiːp əˈbrest ɒv, ˌkiːp ʌp tə ˈdeɪt wɪð/ [v phrase] to make sure that you know all the most recent news about what is happening somewhere or about new developments in a particular subject: *When we lived abroad, we always kept abreast of what was happening at home.* | *It's very important for students to keep up to date with developments in their own field of study.*

6 to know something so well you can repeat it from memory

- know sth by heart
- have sth off pat
- word perfect

know sth by heart ALSO **know sth off by heart** British /ˌnəʊ (sth) baɪ ˈhɑːʳt, ˌnəʊ (sth) ɒf baɪ ˈhɑːʳt/ [v phrase not in progressive] to know every word of a poem, story, song etc, that you have learned so that you can say it or sing it without making any mistakes: *Eleanor had heard the story so many times that she knew every word of it by heart.* | *I studied the poem until I knew it off by heart.*

have sth off pat British **/have sth down pat** American /ˌhæv (sth) ɒf ˈpæt, ˌhæv (sth) daʊn ˈpæt/ [v phrase not in progressive or passive] to be able to give a speech or an answer immediately and easily because you have learned it thoroughly or because you have said the same thing a lot of times before: *She only had to repeat the lines once or twice, and she'd have them down pat.* | *Like most politicians he had all his answers off pat, but he didn't have anything particularly new or interesting to say.*

word perfect /ˌwɜːʳd ˈpɜːʳfɪkt/ [adj] able to repeat something from memory in exactly the same way as it was said or written: *Each Monday the teacher made us recite a poem which had to be word perfect.*

7 to know a little about something

- know a little (bit) about
- have a smattering of
- have a working knowledge of
- can get by/be able to get by

know a little (bit) about ALSO **know a bit about** especially British /ˌnəʊ ə ˈlɪtl (bɪt) əbaʊt, ˌnəʊ ə ˈbɪt əbaʊt/ [v phrase not in progressive] *This excellent book can be understood by anyone who knows a little about social anthropology.* | *I know a bit about how psychiatry works, having been in therapy for years.*

have a smattering of /ˌhæv ə ˈsmætərɪŋ ɒv/ [v phrase not in progressive] to have only a small amount of knowledge about a subject, especially of a foreign language: *He only has a smattering of English, so it can be quite difficult trying to communicate with him.* | *I left school with no more than a smattering of scientific knowledge.*

have a working knowledge of /hæv ə ˌwɜːʳkɪŋ ˈnɒlɪdʒ ɒv‖-ˈnɑː-/ [v phrase not in progressive] to have enough knowledge of something such as a system or a foreign language to be able to use it, although your knowledge is limited: *You don't need to be an expert, but we do expect you to have a good working knowledge of computers.* | *For the system to work, mediators must have a working knowledge of the law.*

can get by/be able to get by /kən ˌget ˈbaɪ, biː ˌeɪbəl tə get ˈbaɪ/ [v phrase] spoken to know just enough about something, for example a foreign language, to be able to make yourself understood or do something successfully: *My Spanish isn't great, but I can get by as a tourist.* | **+ on/with** *'Can I still pass the course?' 'You may be able to get by on what you've already read.'*

8 to know something that most people do not know

- be in the know
- be in on
- be privy to
- knowing

be in the know /biː ɪn ðə ˈnəʊ/ [v phrase] to know secret information about something, for example a government plan or someone's private life, that only a small group of people know: *I heard it from someone who's in the know, so it must be true.* | *Those who were in the know bought land where the railway was to be built, and made enormous profits.* | *The people in the know are saying that the team doesn't have enough money to keep Wojek for another season.*

be in on /biː ˈɪn ɒn / [v phrase] informal to know about a secret plan or activity that only a small group of people know about, especially when you are involved in it: *The children are planning a surprise for Grandma. Are you in on this?* | *It turned out that some of the local cops were in on the deal too.* | **let sb in on sth** (=tell them about a secret) *We made the mistake of letting my sister in on the plan, and she, of course, told my parents.*

be privy to /bi ˈprɪvi tuː/ [v phrase] especially written to know about something that is kept a secret from most people, especially because someone trusts you enough to tell you about it: *She became a confidante of Churchill, and thus was privy to some of his thinking.* | *The Division was not privy to all the information being collected in Saigon.*

knowing /ˈnəʊɪŋ/ [adj only before noun] **knowing look/smile/wink etc** a look, smile etc that shows that you know something that other people do not know or that you share a secret with someone: *I saw him give her a knowing smile as she left the room.* | *Her questions and knowing looks unnerved him, almost as if she had figured him out.*

9 when most people know something

- everyone knows
- well known
- be common knowledge
- be no secret
- be an open secret
- freedom of information

everyone knows /ˌevriwʌn ˈnəʊz/ especially spoken say this when you think most people know something and you would be surprised if someone did not know it: *Haven't you heard Anja's pregnant? I thought everyone knew.* | **+ (that)** *Everyone knows that for a democracy to truly work, everyone has to get involved in some way.* | **+ how/what/why etc** *Surely everyone knows how to change a light bulb!*

well known /ˌwel ˈnəʊn/ [adv] use this about facts and ideas that most people know about, or that all the people in a particular group know about: *Her views on the single European currency were well known.* | **it is well known that** *It is well known that people who smoke are more likely to get lung diseases.* | *It was well known that Mr. Walters was interested in our mother.*

be common knowledge /biː ˌkɒmən ˈnɒlɪdʒ‖-ˌkɑːmən ˈnɑː-/ [v phrase] if information about someone **is common knowledge**, a lot of people know about it, even when that person would prefer to keep it a secret: *It's common knowledge here in Miami that this whole operation was paid for with cocaine money.* | **+ that** *It's already common knowledge that their marriage is breaking up.*

be no secret /biː nəʊ ˈsiːkrɪ̈t/ [v phrase] if an unpleasant fact is **no secret**, everyone knows about it: *Everyone knows they hate each other, it's no secret.* | **+ that** *It was no secret that Morrison was with the CIA, but nobody knew exactly what he did.*

be an open secret /biː ən ˌəʊpən ˈsiːkrɪ̈t/ [v phrase] if something **is an open secret**, it is supposed to be secret but most people know about it: *Her relationship with a French millionaire is pretty much an open secret around here.* | **+ that** *It's an open secret that organized crime has been financing films here for years.*

freedom of information /ˌfriːdəm əv ˌɪnfəʳˈmeɪʃən/ [n U] when a government allows people to know what is in official government records, documents etc: *Freedom of information should be a basic right in a democracy.*

10 facts and information that you know

- knowledge
- expertise
- know-how

▸ *see* **area (9)**

knowledge /ˈnɒlɪdʒ‖ˈnɑː-/ [n singular/U] facts and information that you know: *He doesn't have the skills or knowledge needed to do the job.* | **+ of** *My knowledge of Japanese is limited to a few phrases.* | **scientific/medical/technical etc knowledge** *Our assumptions are based on current scientific knowledge.*

expertise /ˌekspɜːʳˈtiːz/ [n U] special knowledge about how to do something, gained through study or practical experience: *The technical expertise was provided by a Japanese company.* | *His expertise will be invaluable to understanding technological challenges the BBC is facing.* | **+ in** *The organisation has employees with expertise in both medical and counselling services.*

know-how /ˈnəʊ haʊ/ [n U] practical knowledge about how to do something: *There was a lack of managerial and technical know-how in the steel industry.* | *The US supplied the machinery, the know-how, and most of the capital.*

11 to feel sure something is true even though you have no proof

- feel
- sense
- know
- have a feeling/get the feeling
- be aware/conscious

feel /fiːl/ [v T not in progressive] *I felt a definite sense of danger and impending disaster.* | **+ (that)** *I always felt I had the ability to become a reasonable actor.* | *It is a common experience to feel that an author writes well without being able to say exactly why.*

sense /sens/ [v T not in progressive] to feel that something is present or is happening where you are although you cannot see or hear anything to prove it: *We could sense an unwelcoming atmosphere.* | *I wasn't that thrilled with her performance, and I'm sure she sensed it.* | **+ (that)** *After a while, I sensed that he was no longer listening.*

know /nəʊ/ [v I/T not in progressive] to feel very strongly that something is true: *Everyone knew immediately how serious the situation was.* | **+ (that)** *I knew that this was going to happen.* | *I know damn well she won't keep her promise.* | **just know** *I knew it was a huge gamble, buying the stuff without seeing it, but I just knew it would be good quality.*

have a feeling/get the feeling /ˌhæv ə ˈfiːlɪŋ, ˌget ðə ˈfiːlɪŋ/ [v phrase not in progressive] to feel almost sure that something is true, although you have no proof **+ (that)** *As we walked along together, I had a feeling that we were both thinking the same thing.* | *Maybe we should leave him alone. I have a feeling he doesn't want us here.*

be aware/conscious /biː əˈweəʳ, ˈkɒnʃəs‖-ˈkɑːn-/ [v phrase] to know how someone is feeling or how a situation is changing although there are no clear signs to prove it, especially in a way that worries you **+ of** *Charles was uncomfortably aware of the woman's silent contempt for him.* | **+ that** *Slowly, she became conscious that there was some connection between the man and the girl.*

to not know sth

RELATED WORDS

▸ *see also* **secret**

12 to not know a fact or piece of information

- not know
- have no idea/not have a clue
- not have the faintest/slightest/foggiest idea
- (it) beats me
- don't ask me/how should I know?
- who knows?
- I give up

not know /nɒt ˈnəʊ/ [v phrase not in progressive] *'What time's the next train to Paris?' 'I'm sorry, I don't know.'* | *I wish I could tell you the name of the restaurant but I honestly don't know it.* | **not know anything about** *These days, record companies are* *usually owned by people who don't know anything about music.* | **+ how/what/why etc** *I don't know why it is so difficult to explain the concept to people.* | *No one knows if there really is a Loch Ness monster, or if it's just a myth.* | **+ (that)** *My mother never knew that they'd called the police out that night.*

have no idea/not have a clue /hæv ˌnəʊ aɪˈdɪə, nɒt hæv ə ˈkluː/ [v phrase not in progressive] especially spoken say this when you know nothing at all about the answer to a question, so that you cannot even guess what it might be: *'How much is this painting worth?' 'I'm sorry, I've no idea.'* | *When I asked where Louise had gone, he said he didn't have a clue.* | **+ what/how/who etc** *That guy obviously doesn't have a clue how to put a Web page together.* | *I fell asleep half way through the film, and I have absolutely no idea how it ended.*

not have the faintest/slightest/foggiest idea ALSO **not have the least idea** British /nɒt hæv ðə ˌfeɪntɪ̆st, ˌslaɪtɪ̆st, ˌfɒgiɪ̆st aɪˈdɪə‖-ˌfɑːg-, nɒt hæv ðə ˌliːst aɪˈdɪə/ [v phrase not in progressive] spoken say this when you want to say very strongly that you know nothing at all: *'Do you know where he was going after he left here?' 'I don't have the slightest idea.'* | **+ what/how/where etc** *I don't have the faintest idea what you're talking about – can you explain please?* | *Nobody at that time had the slightest idea about how caffeine affected the body.* | **+ about** *They didn't have the least idea about how to put up a tent.*

(it) beats me /(ɪt) ˌbiːts ˈmiː/ spoken say this when you do not know and cannot understand why something happens: *'What I can't understand is why they make you wait three months just to give you a stamp on your passport.' 'Beats me too.'* | **+ how/why etc** *It beats me how these kids can afford to spend so much money on clothes and CDs.*

don't ask me/how should I know? /ˌdəʊnt ɑːsk ˈmiː‖-æsk-, ˌhaʊ ʃʊd ˈaɪ nəʊ/ spoken informal say this when it is impossible for you to know the answer to a question, especially when you are annoyed or surprised that someone has asked you: *'Why is Sharon in such a bad mood?' 'How should I know – she never tells me anything.'* | *'We figured we could pay about $200 a week, right?' 'Don't ask me! I wasn't in on the conversation.'*

who knows? /ˌhuː ˈnəʊz/ spoken say this when you think it is impossible for anyone to know the answer to a question: *The world might end tomorrow. Who knows?*

I give up /aɪ ˌgɪv ˈʌp/ spoken say this when you do not know the answer to a difficult question or a joke, and you want someone to tell you: *'Guess who's coming to dinner tonight?' 'I give up. Tell me.'* | *'Why did the chicken cross the road?' 'I give up, why did the chicken cross the road?'*

13 to not know a place, film or book etc

- not know
- not be familiar with/ be unfamiliar with
- unfamiliar

not know /nɒt ˈnəʊ/ [v T not in progressive]

not be familiar with/be unfamiliar with /nɒt biː fəˈmɪliəʳ wɪð, biː ˌʌnfəˈmɪliəʳ wɪð/ [v phrase] to know little or nothing about a subject, book, play etc because you have not studied it, read it, or seen it: *I'm afraid I'm not familiar with Professor Vaughan's work.* | *For those of you who may not be familiar with the play I'll give a brief summary of the plot.* | *It is difficult for anyone unfamiliar with astronomy to grasp the concept of the Black Hole.*

unfamiliar /ˌʌnfəˈmɪliəʳ◂/ [adj] if someone or something is **unfamiliar** to you, you do not know them because you have never seen, heard, or experienced them before: *The voice on the phone sounded unfamiliar.* | *It took Steven some time to get used to his unfamiliar surroundings.* | **+ to** *The song is in Russian, a language unfamiliar to many singers.*

14 to not realize what is happening

- not know/not realize/have no idea
- be unaware/not be aware
- have no knowledge of
- unbeknown to sb
- little did I/she/he etc know
- for all I/you/ they etc know
- be unconscious of
- oblivious

not know/not realize/have no idea /nɒt ˈnəʊ, nɒt ˈrɪəlaɪz, hæv ˌnəʊ aɪˈdɪə/ [v phrase] *'It's my birthday today.' 'Oh, I didn't realize. I should have bought you a card.'* | **+ (that)** *I wish I'd brought my coat. I didn't know it would be so cold.* | *We didn't realize that he had quit, until he didn't show up at work that day.* | **+ what/how/where etc** *My wife and I had no idea how much we would depend upon Social Security in the future.*

be unaware/not be aware /biː ˌʌnəˈweəʳ, nɒt biː əˈweəʳ/ [v phrase] formal to not know about a situation or about something that is happening, especially when you should know about it **+ of** *The child was clearly unaware of the danger.* | *If any bad feelings existed between the two of them, I was not aware of it.* | **+ that** *His parents weren't even aware that he smoked.*

have no knowledge of /hæv ˌnəʊ ˈnɒlɪdʒ ɒv‖-ˈnɑː-/ [v phrase not in progressive] formal to know nothing about a subject or situation because you have not experienced it, read about it, or heard about it: *The general public has little or no knowledge of what is happening inside prisons.* | *The State Department said it had no knowledge of any threats to U.S. security.*

unbeknown to sb ALSO **unbeknownst to sb** /ˌʌnbɪˈnəʊn tə (sb), ˌʌnbɪˈnəʊnst tə (sb)/ [adv] use this about something that was happening without you knowing about it at the time: *Unbeknown to me, Denise had her own plan.* | *Unbeknownst to the public, he was involved in covering up the scandal that was to rock the nation.*

little did I/she/he etc know /ˌlɪtl dɪd aɪ ˈnəʊ/ [adv] use this when you did not know or imagine that something was true or would happen **+ that** *Little did she know that this picture would one day be worth more than a million dollars.* | *Little did I know then that I would be working in Los Angeles 35 years later.*

for all I/you/they etc know /fər ɔːl ˈaɪ ˌnəʊ/ spoken say this when you know almost nothing about a situation and to suggest something that might have happened or be true, especially something unlikely: *They may have gone to South America, for all we know.* | *You shouldn't have accepted a ride from him. For all you knew he might have been a mass murderer.*

be unconscious of /biː ʌnˈkɒnʃəs ɒv‖-ˈkɑːn-/ [v phrase] if you **are unconscious of** the effect of something that you have said or done, you do not realize how it affects other people: *She appeared to be unconscious of the amusement she had caused by her remarks.* | *Like many tourists they were unconscious of the fact that they had deeply offended their hosts.*

oblivious /əˈblɪviəs/ [adj] someone who is **oblivious** to what is happening around them does not notice it and continues to do other things without being affected by it **+ of** *They soon fell asleep, oblivious of the danger.* | **+ to** *The walkers in front crossed the ledge easily, seemingly oblivious to the fact that there was a 3000 foot drop on either side.* | *In the sitcom she plays a New York executive who's totally oblivious to the feelings of others.*

15 to not know anything about a subject

- not know anything/know nothing
- have no idea/not have a clue
- be a closed book

not know anything/know nothing /nɒt nəʊ ˈeniθɪŋ, nəʊ ˈnʌθɪŋ/ [v phrase not in progressive] *Don't ask me. I know nothing at all about fixing cars.* | *No one else at school knew anything about jazz.* | **know nothing of** formal *When he arrived in Venice he knew almost nothing of its history or culture.*

have no idea/not have a clue /hæv ˌnəʊ aɪˈdɪə, nɒt hæv ə ˈkluː/ [v phrase not in progressive] informal to know nothing at all about how to do something: *I'm amazed how he puts all the bits of the computer back together. I wouldn't have a clue.* | **+ about** *After nine years of marriage, he still didn't have a clue about what she really wanted.* | **+ how/what/where etc** *It became clear that the sales people didn't have any idea how to sell the new products.*

be a closed book /biː ə ˌkləʊzd ˈbʊk/ [v phrase] British a subject that **is a closed book** to someone is one that they know nothing about, and that they believe they will never understand: *For many people, science is something of a closed book.*

16 to not know about something that other people know

- be in the dark
- not be in on

be in the dark /biː ɪn ðə ˈdɑːʳk/ [v phrase] if you **are in the dark** about something, especially something important, you have not been told about it because other people want to keep it secret: *We have no idea why he's been arrested. We're still completely in the dark.* | **+ about** *Most board members were kept in the dark about this important financial information.* | *We're being kept in the dark about the dangers of food additives by the big food manufacturers.*

not be in on /nɒt biː ˈɪn ɒn/ [v phrase] informal if you **are not in on** a secret plan, you have not been told about it and are not involved in it: *They weren't in on the robbery – only me and my brother knew about it.*

17 to not know the most recent information about something

- be out of touch
- lose touch
- lose track of
- not be up on

be out of touch /biː ˌaʊt əv ˈtʌtʃ/ [v phrase] someone who **is out of touch** with something used to know about it but does not now know the most recent information about it, because they have not read about it or been involved in it for a long time: *I don't know what kind of music kids listen to these days – I'm really out of touch.* | **+ with** *The press accused MacGregor of being out of touch with the campaign he was supposed to be running.*

lose touch /ˌluːz ˈtʌtʃ/ [v phrase] if you **lose touch** with a situation or a subject, you no longer know the latest information about it and are unable to understand what is happening in it: *I must do some teaching again – I'm worried about losing touch.* | **+ with** *The French President has lost touch with the reality of the political situation in France.* | *When you're living abroad, it's easy to lose touch with what's going on back home.*

lose track of /ˌluːz ˈtræk ɒv/ [v phrase] if you **lose track of** something or someone, you no longer know where they are or what has happened to them: *I had the file on my desk a minute ago, but I seem to have lost track of it.* | *After the war they lost track of each other.* | *They fed us every twelve hours, but when you can't see the sun, you lose track of time.*

not be up on /nɒt biː ˈʌp ɒn/ [v phrase] informal if you **are not up on** the latest fashions, music, or news, you do not know about them: *I spend most of my time in the woods of Wyoming these days, so I'm not really up on all the latest fashions and movies.* | *My dad's not really up on what kids think these days.*

18 ways of saying that no one knows something

- who knows/who can say
- God knows/heaven knows
- it's anybody's guess
- there's no telling/knowing
- your guess is as good as mine

who knows/who can say /huː ˈnəʊz, ˌhuː kən ˈseɪ/ *Maybe the world will end tomorrow. Who can say?* | *He might come back and say he still loves me, who knows? Who cares?* | **+ what/where/why etc** *Who knows whether Mimi ever made it to Paris.*

God knows/heaven knows /ˌgɒd ˈnəʊz‖ˌgɑːd-, ˌhevən ˈnəʊz/ spoken say this when you mean that it is impossible to know something: *'Where'd she go?' 'God knows.'* | **+ what/who/why etc** *I've just missed my train, so God knows what time I'll get home now.* | *Heaven knows why she feels she can't trust her own parents.*

it's anybody's guess /ɪts ˈenibɒdiz ˌges‖-bɑː-/ spoken say this when neither you, nor anyone else knows the answer to a question or the truth about something, and any answer could be correct: *How he'd lived through it all is anybody's guess.* | **+ who/what/why etc** *It's anybody's guess who will come out on top when the winners are announced at the Grammy Awards this year.*

there's no telling/knowing /ðeəʳz ˌnəʊ ˈtelɪŋ, ˈnəʊɪŋ/ spoken say this when it is impossible to know what will happen, especially when you are worried that something bad might happen **+ who/what/why etc** *'He's a desperate man. There's no telling what he'll do next,' said Holmes.* | *There was no knowing when the flood waters might recede with so much rain in the forecast.*

your guess is as good as mine /ˌjɔːʳ ges ɪz əz ˌgʊd əz ˈmaɪn/ spoken say this when someone asks you a question and you do not know the answer, so that they are just as likely to guess the right answer as you are: *'Who do you think will win the World Cup?' 'Your guess is as good as mine.'*

19 not knowing about something

- ignorant
- ignorance
- uninformed
- ill-informed
- layman/lay person

ignorant /ˈɪgnərənt/ [adj] someone who is **ignorant** does not know facts or information that they should know: *I didn't like to ask him to explain more clearly because I didn't want to appear ignorant.* | **+ of** *There are still doctors who are ignorant of patients' rights, or who try to deny them.* | **+ about** *I'm very ignorant about politics.*

ignorance /ˈɪgnərəns/ [n U] when someone does not know facts or information that they should know: *I haven't read your latest book, so I hope you'll forgive my ignorance.* | **+ of** *He showed complete ignorance of the most basic historical facts.*

uninformed /ˌʌnɪnˈfɔːʳmd◂/ [adj] people or opinions that are **uninformed** show a lack of knowledge and information about the subject that they are discussing: *Careless or uninformed decisions during these huge storms can lead to loss of life and property.* | **+ about** *The Vice-President gave the impression of being remarkably uninformed about South American affairs.*

ill-informed /ˌɪl ɪnˈfɔːʳmd◂/ [adj] not knowing much about something or making mistakes about it because you have been given incorrect or not enough information: *He's either a liar or he's incredibly ill-informed.* | *Writers such as Oscar Wilde were the target of ill-informed and often hostile criticism simply because they were gay.* | **+ about** *For someone who wants to be a journalist, she's remarkably ill-informed about current affairs.*

layman/lay person /ˈleɪmən, ˈleɪ pɜːʳsən/ [n C] someone who has no special knowledge about a subject such as science or medicine, as opposed to people who have special knowledge or training: *Professor Hawking's book is intended for the lay person who has an interest in the field of nuclear physics and astronomy.* | **in layman's terms** (=using words a layman can understand) *Many superb doctors are incapable of communicating in layman's terms.*

20 something that people know nothing or very little about

- unknown
- the unknown
- uncharted
- unidentified
- little known

unknown /ˌʌnˈnəʊn◂/ [adj] *After they left Kathmandu they would be travelling through unknown territory.* | *There are still a great many unknown insect species in the world.* | *Yesterday the village was quite unknown, but today it's on the front page of all the newspapers.*

the unknown /ði ˌʌnˈnəʊn/ [n singular] a place or an experience that people have not been in before and that they are therefore often nervous about: *In 1492 Columbus and his group of tiny ships set off into the unknown.* | *Starting a new relationship with someone is always a journey into the unknown.* | **fear of the unknown** *The fear of the unknown prevents many people from making significant changes in their lives.*

uncharted /ʌnˈtʃɑːʳtɪ̈d/ [adj usually before noun] relating to places that have not been put on a map yet, or to situations that have not yet been experienced: *Space is filled with unknown stars and uncharted galaxies.* | **uncharted territory** *When Indian politicians established mass democracy in 1947, they knew they were entering uncharted territory.*

unidentified /ˌʌnaɪˈdentɪ̈faɪd◂/ [adj] if something is **unidentified**, people do not know what it is, what its name is, or who it belongs to – used especially in newspapers or in official reports: *A large unidentified object was spotted floating in the sea near our ship.* | *Two unidentified gunmen opened fire on the Consulate van.* | *The body remained unidentified until the police checked dental records.*

little known /ˌlɪtl ˈnəʊn◂/ [adj usually before noun] a **little known** place or thing is one that not many people know about: *He was born on a little known island off the south coast of Spain.* | *The kakapo is a little known species of parrot that lives in New Zealand.*

21 a person or place that not many people know or know about

- unknown
- little known/little-known
- obscure
- shadowy figure
- an unknown quantity

unknown /ˌʌnˈnəʊn◂/ [adj] *The picture was painted in the 15th Century by an unknown Italian artist.* | *Until their first single, the Beatles were virtually unknown outside Hamburg and Liverpool.* | **+ to** *The Internet has opened up a marketplace where sellers and buyers are virtually unknown to each other.*

little known/little-known /ˌlɪtl ˈnəʊn◂/ [adj usually before noun] a **little known** artist, film etc is one that very few people know about: *A little-known separatist group claimed responsibility for the explosion.* | *Bernardo Vittone is little known outside his native Italy.*

obscure /əbˈskjʊəʳ/ [adj] not at all well-known and usually not very important: *Picasso's first exhibition received only a short mention in an obscure Parisian newspaper.* | *The Silver Apples are one of those obscure bands that you might hear about, but never actually hear.* —**obscurity** [n U] *An American publishing company rescued him from obscurity and offered him $100,000 for his first novel.*

shadowy figure /ˌʃædəʊi ˈfɪgəʳ‖-ˈfɪgjər/ [n C] written a mysterious person that people know very little about, especially someone who seems dangerous: *Vogel, a high-ranking official in East Berlin, was one of the Cold War's most shadowy figures.*

an unknown quantity /ən ˌʌn-nəʊn ˈkwɒntɪ̈ti‖-ˈkwɑːn-/ [n phrase] someone that very little is known about, especially in relation to their abilities, so that you do not know if they will be successful: *The team's new pitcher has never played pro baseball before and is something of an unknown quantity.*

to know a person

RELATED WORDS

- *see also* **friend, meet**

22 to know someone

- know
- know sb by sight
- be acquainted with

know /nəʊ/ [v T not in progressive] if you **know** someone, you have met them before, can remember their face or name, and **know** something about them, such as where they live, what their job is etc: *Do you two know each other?* | *Everyone who knew her described her as a kind, generous person.* | *Do you know anyone who can repair a boiler?* | *Although we worked for him for years, Cathy was the only one who knew him well.*

know sb by sight /ˌnəʊ (sb) baɪ 'saɪt/ [v phrase] to be able to recognize someone but not know their name or anything else about them: *Bentson knew all the women by sight, but he'd never exchanged more than a few words with any of them.* | *Two or three of the salespeople knew me by sight.*

be acquainted with /bi: ə'kweɪntɪ̣d wɪð/ [v phrase] formal to know someone because you have met once or twice before but to not know much about them: *'Have you met Lee Davidson?' 'No, I don't think we're acquainted.'* | *He lived in Great Russell Street and became acquainted with Keynes and other famous British thinkers of the time.*

23 to start to know someone

- get to know
- get acquainted
- meet

get to know /ˌget tə 'nəʊ/ [v phrase] to start to become friends with someone by spending a lot of time with them and talking to them: *The volunteers had a lot of trouble getting to know the local people.* | *Being stuck on a small boat, you get to know someone pretty well.* | *Steve's alright once you get to know him.*

get acquainted /ˌget ə'kweɪntɪ̣d/ [v phrase] to start to know someone who you have only just met: *I'll leave you two alone so you can get acquainted.* | **+ with** *I had no problems getting acquainted with the girls, but the guys were a little harder.* | **get better acquainted** *Maybe we should invite Sam round for dinner so we can get better acquainted.*

meet /mi:t/ [v T] to see and talk to someone for the first time: *Where did you meet Michael?* | *Carol and I first met at university.* | *Branford took us to meet a few of his colleagues.*

24 someone you know, but not very well

- acquaintance
- have met/met

acquaintance /ə'kweɪntəns/ [n C] *She's just an acquaintance – I see her sometimes at night school.* | **business/childhood/musical etc acquaintance** (=one you know from business, childhood etc) *I first heard of the idea from a business acquaintance in Montpelier.* | **mutual acquaintance** (=one that you and someone else both know) *Jane and I met through a mutual acquaintance at a party.*

have met/met /həv 'met, met/ [v T] if you **have met** someone, you have seen and talked to them, although you do not know them very well: *'Do you know Chris?' 'Yes, we've met.'* | *We met once before at Jo's house.*

25 someone you do not know

- stranger

stranger /'streɪndʒə^r/ [n C] *The room was full of strangers.* | **be a stranger to sb** *After assuming office, he was reluctant to use the existing speech writers because they were strangers to him.* | **perfect/complete stranger** (=use this to emphasize that you do not know someone at all) *The boy was a complete stranger to me.*

Ll

land/ground

RELATED WORDS

see also **country, area, environment, beautiful (6)**

1 land that is owned by someone or is used for something

- land
- territory
- territorial
- field
- the grounds

land /lænd/ [n U] **land** that is owned by someone or that can be used for farming or building houses: *They moved to the country and bought some land.* | *Get off my land!* | **piece/plot of land** *Each family was given a small piece of land where they could grow food for themselves.* | **farmland** (=land that can be used for farming) *There is a shortage of suitable farmland in the south of the country.*

territory /'terɪ̣təri‖-tɔ:ri/ [n U] land that belongs to a country or that is controlled by a country during a war: *Miller had accidentally crossed into Iraqi territory and was arrested for spying.* | **enemy territory** (=land controlled by an enemy) *His plane was shot down over enemy territory.*

territorial /ˌterɪ̣'tɔ:riəl◂/ [adj only before noun] relating to land that is owned or controlled by a particular country or government: *A committee has been set up to deal with territorial disputes in the area.* | *The country has suffered substantial territorial losses in this war.*

field /fi:ld/ [n C] an area of land that is part of a farm, or that is used for playing sports: *We passed cows grazing in the fields.* | *a football field* | **+ of** *a field of wheat* | **playing field** British (=a field where sports are played) *We went out onto the school playing fields to watch a game of football.* | **open fields** *birds such as skylarks whose habitat is open fields and farmland*

the grounds /ðə 'graʊndz/ [n plural] the gardens and land around a big building such as a castle, school, or hospital: *Have you ever been to Penryn Castle? The grounds are beautiful.* | **the palace/school/hospital grounds** *The nurse said I could go for a short walk around the hospital grounds.*

2 what you see in an area of land

- landscape
- scenery

landscape /'lændskeɪp/ [n C usually singular] the land and features that you see around you in the countryside, or in the city: *The construction of dams has changed the character of the landscape.* | *an urban landscape of glittering modern buildings*

scenery /'si:nəri/ [n U] all the mountains, fields, forests etc that you see around you in the countryside, especially when these are beautiful: *We stayed in a peaceful Alpine village surrounded by magnificent scenery.*

3 the surface of the land

- ground
- terrain

ground /graʊnd/ [n U] *The ground was covered with snow.* | *He kicked Cook as he lay on the ground.* | *In the middle of the forest was a bare patch of marshy ground.* | *The ground sloped down from where we stood to the lake shore.*

terrain /teˈreɪn, tə-/ [n U] used when you are talking about how easy or difficult an area of land is to cross, for example because it is flat, has a lot of mountains etc: *The terrain on the island varies quite a bit.* | **difficult/rough/mountainous etc terrain** *They had to drive very slowly over the difficult terrain.* | *Boots are the best footwear on rough terrain.*

4 the land compared with the sea or air

- land
- the ground
- ashore

land /lænd/ [n U] the **land**, not the sea **on land** *They had defeated the enemy on land and at sea.* | *Reptiles reproduce by laying eggs on land or giving birth to live young.* | **dry land** (=the land when compared with being at sea) *Some repairs to the boat will have to wait until we're back on dry land.*

the ground /ðə ˈgraʊnd/ [n singular] the land, not the air – use this to talk about planes and birds: *Our plane was flying only 100 feet above the ground.* | *Spectators watched in horror as the aircraft plunged to the ground.*

ashore /əˈʃɔːʳ/ [adv] if you go **ashore**, you go on to the land from a boat or the sea. If you spend time **ashore**, you spend time on land before returning to your boat: *Most of the other passengers had gone ashore.* | *People were returning to their cabins after a day ashore.* | **be washed ashore** (=be pushed onto the land by the sea) *Two bodies were washed ashore last night.*

5 the substance that forms the surface of the land

- earth
- soil
- dirt

earth /ɜːʳθ/ [n U] the brown substance that the ground is made up of: *Outside, the sun beat down on the red baked earth of Provence.* | *Thousands of tons of earth were moved to build the dam.*

soil /sɔɪl/ [n U] the earth that plants grow in: *Roses do best in well-drained, slightly acid soil.* | **fertile soil** (=soil that plants grow well in) *Parsley should have a deep, moist, fertile soil for ideal growth.*

dirt /dɜːʳt/ [n U] American loose dry earth: *The kids were playing in the yard, digging in the dirt.*

6 land at the edge of water

- the coast
- the shore
- beach
- the seaside
- by the sea
- coastline

the coast /ðə ˈkəʊst/ [n singular] the part of a country that is close to the sea – use this when you are talking about a country or a large part of a country: *driving along the Californian coast, from San Francisco to LA* | **on the coast** (=on land that is close to the sea) *a little house on the coast of Brittany* | **off the coast** (=in the sea but close to the land) *They discovered oil off the northern coast of Scotland.* | **+ of** *The ship slowly made its way along the west coast of Africa.*

the shore /ðə ˈʃɔːʳ/ [n singular] the land along the edge of the sea or along the edge of a lake: *We could see a boat about a mile from the shore.* | **the shore of/the shores of** *a small town on the shores of Lake Ontario*

beach /biːtʃ/ [n C] an area of sand at the edge of the sea – use this especially to talk about a place where you go to relax and enjoy yourself: *The area has miles of unspoiled sandy beaches..* | **the beach** *By nine o'clock the beach was already crowded with people.* | *Let's go to the beach tomorrow.*

the seaside /ðə ˈsiːsaɪd/ [n singular] British a place at the edge of the sea – use this especially to talk about somewhere where you go for a holiday or to enjoy yourself: *When I was little we used to go to the seaside most weekends.*

by the sea British **/by the ocean** American /baɪ ðə ˈsiː, baɪ ði ˈəʊʃən/ on land next to the sea: *We bought a small cottage by the sea.* | *walking by the ocean in the early morning*

coastline /ˈkəʊstlaɪn/ [n C] the edge of the land next to the sea – use this especially to talk about a long length of this land or the shape it makes, for example as seen from the air: *The road follows the rugged coastline of northern France for nearly 100 miles.* | *Environmentalists are concerned about possible damage to some of the most beautiful stretches of Welsh coastline.* | *Far below us, we could just see the coastline of Argentina dimly outlined.*

language

RELATED WORDS

- *see also* **speak, translate, word, phrase, or sentence, meaning**

1 the words used by the people in a particular country or area

- language
- lingo
- dialect
- slang
- colloquial

language /ˈlæŋgwɪdʒ/ [n C] a system of words, phrases, and grammar that is used by the people who live in a particular country **speak a language** *'What language do they speak in Brazil?' 'Portuguese.'* | *She can speak four different languages – French, German, English, and Dutch.* | **foreign language** *Every pupil has to learn at least one foreign language.* | **official language** (=the language used by the government) *English is the island's official language, but people also speak French and Creole.* | **speak the language** (=be able to speak the language of the country you are in) *It's difficult living in a country where you don't speak the language.*

lingo /ˈlɪŋgəʊ/ [n singular] informal a foreign language **speak/know the lingo** *Travelling in Spain is much easier if you can speak the lingo.* | **learn/pick up the lingo** *He picked up the local lingo straight away.*

dialect /ˈdaɪəlekt/ [n C/U] a form of a language which is spoken by the people who live in one area of a country, and which has different words, grammar, or pronunciation from other forms of that language: *In this region, the dialect sounds a lot like German.* | *At home, they speak in dialect.* | **York-**

shire/German/Cantonese etc dialect *In some Yorkshire dialects, people say 'spice' instead of 'sweets' or 'candy'.* | **dialect word** *'Nowt' is a northern dialect word meaning 'nothing'.* | **+ of** *He spoke a dialect of French that I found hard to understand.*

slang /slæŋ/ [n U] very informal words used in a particular country or place: *I was totally confused by the slang that the other kids were using.* | **+ for** *'Bladdered' is slang for 'drunk'.* | **slang word/term/expression** *'Shepherd' was a slang term for a spy.* | **US/British/Southern etc slang** *'Baloney' is US slang for nonsense.*

colloquial /kəˈləʊkwiəl/ [adj] language that is **colloquial** is only used in conversation, not in formal situations: *It's a useful little phrase book, full of colloquial expressions.* | *The best way of improving your colloquial English is by listening to native speakers.* | *You shouldn't use phrases like 'sort of' in essays – they're too colloquial.*

2 the use of words to communicate

- language
- linguistic

language /ˈlæŋgwɪdʒ/ [n U] the use of words, grammar etc to communicate with other people: *Every child develops the natural ability to use language.* | *There are ways of communicating without language.*

linguistic /lɪŋˈgwɪstɪk/ [adj usually before noun] connected with people's ability to use language **linguistic ability/skills/development etc** *Hearing difficulties can slow down a child's linguistic development.* | *It is difficult to obtain accurate information on which to base an assessment of a child's linguistic abilities.*

3 the first language that you learn as a child

- sb's first language
- sb's mother tongue
- native speaker

sb's first language / (sb's) ˌfɜːʳst ˈlæŋgwɪdʒ/ [n C] the first language you learn as a child – use this when you are comparing someone's first language with other languages that they learn later: *My first language is Dutch.* | *My daughter has several classmates whose first language is Bengali.*

sb's mother tongue / (sb's) ˈmʌðəʳ ˌtʌŋ/ [n C] the first language you learn as a child – use this especially to talk about someone who now lives in a country where a different language is spoken: *We run classes for students whose mother tongue is not English.*

native speaker /ˌneɪtɪv ˈspiːkəʳ/ [n C] a **native speaker** of a language is someone who learned that language first as a child: *The book is aimed at learners of English rather than native speakers.* | **+ of** *There has been an assumption in the past that anyone who is a native speaker of English is equipped to teach English.*

4 when someone can speak more than one language

- bilingual
- sb's second language

bilingual /baɪˈlɪŋgwəl/ [adj] someone who is **bilingual** can speak two languages perfectly: *I'm bilingual – my mother was French.* | *Many of the pupils are bilingual in Welsh and English.*

sb's second language / (sb's) ˌsekənd ˈlæŋgwɪdʒ/ [n C] your **second language** is a language that you speak well and often use, but not the first language that you learned as a child: *Halima was born in Kenya. Her first language is Swahili, and her second language is English.*

5 the language used by a particular group of people

- language
- terminology
- jargon
- slang
- in layman's terms
- -speak

language /ˈlæŋgwɪdʒ/ [n U] the kind of words used by people in a particular job or activity **legal/medical/business etc language** *Books about physics are usually written in highly technical language.* | *People often find the medical language used by doctors confusing.* | **the language of sth** *a fascinating article about the language of baseball*

terminology /ˌtɜːʳmɪ̈ˈnɒlədʒi‖-ˈnɑː-/ [n U] the special words that people working in science, medicine, the law etc use to describe things: *It is important that lawyers use the correct terminology when they prepare contracts.* | **scientific/linguistic/computer etc terminology** *It was an interesting programme, which gave the facts without using too much scientific terminology.*

jargon /ˈdʒɑːʳgən‖-gən, -gɑːn/ [n U] words used by people who do a particular job or who are interested in a particular subject, which are difficult for ordinary people to understand: *When you first learn about computers, there is a whole lot of jargon to understand.* | **management/legal/medical/computer jargon** *I hate all this management jargon about 'upskilling' and 'downsizing'.*

slang /slæŋ/ [n U] informal words that are used by specific groups of people, for example soldiers or prisoners **army/soldiers'/prison etc slang** *'Doolally', meaning 'crazy', is 19th century soldiers' slang, and comes from the name of an Indian town.*

in layman's terms /ɪn ˈleɪmənz tɜːʳmz/ [adv] not using special, technical words that are hard to understand: *I want a book that will explain to me in layman's terms how my computer works.*

-speak /spiːk/ [suffix] **management/boardroom/PR etc -speak** a type of language and the words used by managers etc – use this especially to talk about a way of speaking that you think is silly or unnecessarily different from normal language: *'What on earth does he mean, "window"?' 'Oh, that's management-speak for "opportunity".'* | *Her email was so full of corporate-speak, you hardly realized that what she was saying was that we were all fired.*

last

RELATED WORDS

- last week/year etc *see* **before**

WHAT'S HERE

- **coming at the end** see **1 to 4**
- **last for a period of time** see **5 to 7**

coming at the end

RELATED WORDS

opposite: — **first**

1 coming at the end after all others

- last
- final
- closing
- concluding
- the latter

last /lɑːst‖læst/ [adj only before noun] happening or coming at the end, with no others after: *What time does the last train leave?* | *Could you repeat the last number for me please?* | *I really struggled on that last question.* | *Don't miss the last episode tonight at 8.00 p.m.* | *I may as well eat that last little piece.* | **very last** (=use this to emphasize that something is last) *The very last train leaves at 1.00 a.m.* | **the last time** *That was the last time I ever saw her.* (=I never saw her again) | **last chance** *Today is your last chance to visit the fashion show, which ends this evening.* | **the last** *That lecture was the last in the series.* —**last** [adv] *The teacher called out my name last.* | **leave sth till last** (=do sth after you have done everything else) *I do all our dishes, and leave the dog's dish till last.* | **keep/save sth for last** (=use, eat etc something after you have used, eaten etc everything else) *I'm saving that chocolate for last.*

final /ˈfaɪnl/ [adj only before noun] last in a series of actions, events, parts of a story etc: *Are you going to watch the final episode of 'The X-Files' tomorrow night?* | *He got as far as the final interviews, but he didn't get the job unfortunately.* | *I'd like to make one final point before we move on to another subject.* | **final stages/moments/minutes** (=at or near the end of a period or process) *The president appears tired but hopeful as the final stages of the negotiations begin today.* | *Whitney made both free throws in the final minute of the game.* | **final game/round/match etc** *A victory over Fresno State in the final game Saturday would produce a record run of wins.* | *The two men were tied for the lead going into today's final round of the Dunlop Phoenix golf tournament.* —**finally** [adv] *The ulcer continued to spread, and the doctors finally had to amputate.* | **and finally** *The cruise took them to Spain, Italy, Greece and finally Morocco, where they caught their flight home.*

closing /ˈkləʊzɪŋ/ [adj only before noun] the **closing** part of an event or period of time is the last part of it – use this especially when something important or exciting happens **the closing stages/chapter/sentence etc** *Marcos is expected to address the closing session of the conference later Monday.* | *The rider from the Netherlands is still in the lead as the Tour de France enters its closing stage today.* | *The closing scene of 'Casablanca' is one of the great moments of film history.* | **closing seconds/minutes/years etc** *Barnes scored the winning goal in the closing seconds of the game.* | *the closing years of the 20th century* | **closing argument** (=the final speech made by a lawyer in a court) *After the defense finishes its closing argument, the prosecution will have the opportunity to reply.*

concluding /kənˈkluːdɪŋ/ [adj] the **concluding** part of a piece of writing, a speech, or an organized event is the last part of it, which finishes it in the way that was planned **concluding stages/chapter/remarks etc** *We will return to these points in the concluding chapter.* | *In his concluding remarks, Santos drew attention to the issues facing developing countries.* | *The Appeal court will, at the concluding stage, test its own opinions against those of the judges in the original hearing.*

the latter /ðə ˈlætəʳ/ [n singular] formal the second of two things or people that are being compared with each other: *Opportunities for men and women, though especially the latter, are limited to employment in agriculture or domestic service.* | *There were two candidates for the presidency, Lyndon B Johnson and Senator Barry Goldwater. The latter was known to hold extreme right-wing views.* —**latter** [adj only before noun] *The classes consist of immigrants, and students who will return to their home countries at the end of the course. The latter group are preparing for the Cambridge Proficiency Certificate.*

2 to be the last one in a line, group, race etc

- be last
- come in last/finish last
- bring up the rear
- straggler

be last /biː ˈlɑːst‖-ˈlæst/ [v phrase] *There's no point in trying, because I know I'm going to be last.* | *We were last in a very long queue, so I knew we'd have a long wait.* | **be (the) last to do sth** *Sally was last to arrive.* | *His plane was always the first to take off, and the last to land.* | **be last in line** (=be the last person to have something, especially when this seems unfair) *I was the youngest in a family of four, so I was always last in line for clothes and toys.* | *Let's just say I don't want to be last in line for promotion.*

come in last/finish last ALSO **come last** British /ˌkʌm ɪn ˈlɑːst, ˌfɪnɪʃ ˈlɑːst, ˌkʌm ˈlɑːst‖-ˈlæst/ [v phrase not in progressive] to finish a race or competition in the last position: *Our school always comes in last in the regional competition.* | *Bakatin came last with just 3.4% of the vote.* | *Despite finishing last of six, he was only beaten by two lengths.*

bring up the rear /ˌbrɪŋ ʌp ðə ˈrɪəʳ/ [v phrase] to be last in a line or group of people, cars, ships etc that is moving forward: *We all followed our guide up the path, Marcus and I bringing up the rear.* | *The funeral hearse was followed by cars full of friends, and a company of Life Guards brought up the rear.*

straggler /ˈstræɡələʳ/ [n C] a person who is too slow to keep the same speed as the rest of the group they are with, so that they move along some distance behind: *A few stragglers got lost in the fog.* | *After three and a half hours, the stragglers were still coming through.*

3 the one just before the last one

- next to last/second to last
- the last but one
- penultimate

next to last/second to last /ˌnekst tə ˈlɑːst, ˌsekənd tə ˈlɑːst‖-ˈlæst/ [adj phrase only before noun] coming just before the last one in a series, list, line etc: *I've nearly finished this test. I'm on the next to last question.* | *'How much have you read?' 'I'm on the second to last chapter.'* | *It wasn't until the next to last day of the vacation that she dared to go to the beach.*

the last but one /ðə ˌlɑːst bət ˈwʌn‖-ˌlæst-/ [n/adj phrase] British the one just before the last one: *She had several husbands. Garry Burton, the last but one, was a real alcoholic.* | *He and his family escaped on the last but one ship to leave Hamburg.* | *There's a long row of houses and I live in the last but one.*

penultimate /pɪˈnʌltɪ̇mɪ̇t/ [adj only before noun] especially British, formal coming just before the last one: *We* *booked a moped for the penultimate day of the holiday.* | *Particularly impressive is the horn section on the penultimate track, 'Just Jivin' Around'.* | **penultimate stage/step** *These trials are actually the penultimate step toward choosing the Olympic team for this summer's games.* | **penultimate game/round/lap etc** *Eric scored a timely win in the penultimate round of the Formula 1 championship.* | *His horse slipped and fell at the penultimate fence.*

4 what you say to introduce the last thing in a speech etc

- finally
- lastly
- last but not least

finally /ˈfaɪnəl-i/ [adv] use this when something is the last thing you want to say, especially at the end of a long speech or piece of writing: *Finally, I'd like to thank all those people who helped make the conference such a success.* | *And finally, don't miss Albuquerque's amazing punk band, playing tonight at the Lunar Club.*

lastly /ˈlɑːstli‖ˈlæst-/ [adv] use this to say that something is the last of a list of things, or when something is the last thing you want to say: *Now lastly, before you all leave, I want to mention some tips for the interview stage.* | *And lastly, Delia, do you see the movement towards more and more computerization continuing in the future?* | *Firstly it's too big, secondly we can't afford it, and lastly we don't really need it.*

last but not least /ˌlɑːst bət nɒt ˈliːst‖ˌlæst-/ [adv] use this when you are mentioning the last person or thing in a list, to emphasize that they are just as important as all the others: *Last but not least, let me introduce Jane, our new accountant.* | *And last but not least, I thank Begona Canup for her interest in the book.* | **last but certainly not/by no means least** *Social Security has reduced poverty, and last, but by no means least, it has been a good deal for participants.*

last for a period of time

5 to continue for a particular period of time

- last
- take
- go on for
- drag on
- run
- extend over

last /lɑːst‖læst/ [v I] use this to say how long something continues: *Mexico achieved a remarkable 8% annual growth rate, but the new prosperity did not last.* | *Ours was a happy marriage, but I always feared it wouldn't last.* | **last 2 hours/6 months/a long time etc** *The whole opera lasts about four hours.* | *The earthquake lasted 30 seconds and caused 12,000 casualties.* | *The silence in the room seemed to last a very long time before she spoke.* | *rainstorms lasting all night long* | *Each consultation can last between 10 minutes and half an hour.* | **last for 2 hours/a long time/years etc** *The performance is expected to last for approximately 3 hours.* | *The effects of Josie's experience could last for years, doctors say.* | **last from/until etc** *The talks lasted until the early hours of the morning.* | *The drug produces a powerful cocaine-type high that lasts for days.* | *The Sung dynasty lasted from 960 to 1278.* | **last into the 19th century/1980s/next decade etc** *This phase of the educational campaign lasted into the 1960s.* | **last long** *Analysts are confident the downturn in share prices will not last long.* | *It's the worst cold I've ever had, but luckily it didn't last very long.* | **last forever** *I wanted the weekend to last forever.* | **last as long as** *The pilots say the walkout could last as long as two months.* —**long-lasting** /ˌlɒŋ ˈlɑːstɪŋ◂‖ˌlɔːŋ ˈlæs-/ [adj] *the profound and long-lasting consequences of the war*

take /teɪk/ [v T] use this when you want to say how much time is needed to do something or for something to happen **take 2 hours/6 months etc** *The bridge was closed, so the journey took much longer than usual.* | *Can you give me an idea how long this is going to take?* | *It took two years for Eddie to learn how to walk again.* | **take 2 hours/6 months etc to do** *The software will take a few minutes to load.* | *They're just fun books, they don't take very long to read.* | **take sb 2 hours/6 months etc to do** *Doing the painting alone will take him all day.* | **it takes (sb) 2 hours/six months etc to do sth** *It takes me about half an hour to get ready in the mornings.* | *It didn't take Susie long to find out what was going on between us.* | *It took three and a half hours to come back from Swansea.*

go on for /ˌgəʊ ˈɒn fɔːʳ/ [phr v T] if something, especially something boring or unpleasant, **goes on for** a particular period of time, that is how long it lasts: *The chairman's speech went on for what seemed like hours.* | *It sounds like the sort of meeting that could go on forever.* | *It starts at seven, but I don't know how long it goes on for.* | *It was a big lawsuit, and it went on for quite a while.*

drag on /ˌdræg ˈɒn/ [phr v I] use this about something that seems to continue for a long time: *The siege dragged on into its second month.* | **+ for** *I can't afford to let the case drag on for months.*

run /rʌn/ [v I] if a play, show, event etc runs for a particular period of time, it continues to be shown or performed for that period of time: *The Ideal Homes exhibition will run until 6 p.m. each day over the weekend.* | **+ for** *The play ran for two months on Broadway.* | *The media campaign features four commercials that will run for eight weeks.* | *One of the top sit-coms was 'On the Buses', which ran for sixty episodes* | **run and run** British (=used in newspapers, magazines etc to say that a play, show etc will be very successful and will be performed for a long time) *This is one that will, I believe, run and run.* —**run** [n C usually singular] *The show moves to London's West End after a month's run in Leicester's Gala Theatre.* —**longest-running** /ˌlɒŋgɪst ˈrʌnɪŋ◂‖ˌlɔːŋ-/ [adj only before noun] *Britain's longest-running chart show, Top of the Pops, looks set to close.*

extend over /ɪkˈstend əʊvəʳ/ [v phrase] if a process, activity, event etc **extends over** a long period of time, it continues for that period of time: *We had a marathon recording session extending over eighteen hours.* | *If the investigation is a sustained piece of work extending over a period of weeks, a diary will help to track events.*

6 to stay in good condition for a particular period of time

- last
- keep
- stay fresh

last /lɑːst‖læst/ [v I] use this about clothes, equipment, furniture etc to say how long they will remain in good condition: *Cheap saucepans can't really be expected to last.* | *It's amazing how long this car has lasted, really.* | *You can get washable plastic lace by the yard, which lasts much better than the real* *thing.* | **last (for) 7 years/2 months/a long time etc** *Some wine-makers will tell you that a cask lasts only for four years.* | *When the houses were put up in 1946, they really weren't meant to last more than ten years.* | **last (sb) a lifetime** (=last a very long time) *With care, a mahogany dining table will last you a lifetime.* | *Well-made golf clubs ought to last a lifetime, so it's worth paying the extra.*

keep /kiːp/ [v I not in progressive] use this about food or drink to say how long it will remain fresh: *You'd better eat these cakes today – they won't keep.* | **keep for 2 days/24 hours etc** *The yoghurt will keep for about a week in a refrigerator.* | **+ until/till** *Do you think this bacon will keep till tomorrow?* | **keep well** *Eat celery as soon as possible – it does not keep well for long periods.*

stay fresh /ˌsteɪ ˈfreʃ/ [v phrase] use this about food or about flowers that have been cut: *Homemade bread never stays as fresh as the stuff you buy in the supermarket.* | **stay fresh for 2 weeks/2 days/a long time etc** *Strain the stock and put in a sealed container. It should stay fresh for up to three days.* | *Bend the stems, as this will make the blooms stay fresh for longer.*

7 when a supply of something continues to be enough

- last
- make sth last
- eke out

last /lɑːst‖læst/ [v I] if a supply of something **lasts** for a particular period of time, there continues to be enough of it for someone to use until the end of that period **last (sb) two weeks/three days etc** *He knew they only had enough food to last another three days.* | *$400 won't last you long in Chicago.*

make sth last /ˌmeɪk (sth) ˈlɑːst‖-ˈlæst/ [v phrase] to use a supply of something carefully so that it is not all used quickly: *I sent my sister $500, with some advice on how to make it last.* | **make sth last longer/a long time etc** *You can add ice or additional mixer to alcoholic drinks make them last longer.* | *One group delayed spending the grant in order to make its funds last as long as possible.* | *She only had a small amount of food left, and knew she'd have to make it last the week.*

eke out /ˌiːk ˈaʊt/ [phr v T] to make a small amount of something such as food or money last longer, by carefully using only very small amounts of it – used especially in literature **eke out sth** *Dealers are mixing the drug with heroin and cocaine to eke out their supplies.* | *She lived on a shoestring during these years, eking out the pennies as best she could.* | **eke sth out** *I'm not ashamed to eke food out.*

late

RELATED WORDS

opposite: **early**

- make someone or something late *see* **delay**
- at the right time *see* **on time**
- when someone or something is almost too late *see* **on time (3)**
- *see also* **later, after, time**

1 arriving or leaving late

- late
- not on time
- latecomer

late /leɪt/ [adj/adv] arriving or leaving after the time that was arranged: *Andrew arrived late, as usual.* | **be late** *Sorry I'm late – my car wouldn't start.* | **+ for** *She often arrives late for work.* | **5 minutes/2 days etc late** *As usual, the bus was half an hour late.* | **late arrival/departure** *We apologize for the late arrival of Flight AZ709.*

not on time /nɒt ɒn ˈtaɪm/ [adv] not arriving or leaving at the time that was arranged: *The buses are never on time.* | *She knew if she wasn't on time that day she'd lose her job.* | *If we don't leave on time, we'll miss the flight!*

latecomer /ˈleɪtˌkʌməʳ/ [n C] someone who arrives after the time that something such as a meeting, play, or concert is supposed to start: *Latecomers will not be allowed into the concert hall until the interval.*

2 what you say when someone or something is late

- where have you been?
- what kept you?
- about time too
- what time do you call this?
- better late than never
- is that the time?

where have you been? /ˌweəʳ həv juː ˈbiːn‖-ˈbɪn/ spoken say this when someone arrives very late and you want to know why, because you are worried or annoyed: *Where have you been? You said you'd be here at three!*

what kept you? /wɒt ˈkept juː/ spoken say this when someone arrives late and you are a little annoyed: *'What kept you?' 'I couldn't find my glasses.'*

about time too British **/it's about time** American /əˌbaʊt ˌtaɪm ˈtuː, ɪts əˌbaʊt ˈtaɪm/ spoken say this when someone or something arrives or does something late, and you are annoyed because you have been waiting a long time: *'Look, here's the bus.' 'It's about time!'*

what time do you call this? /wɒt ˌtaɪm duː juː ˌkɔːl ˈðɪs/ British spoken say this when you are annoyed with someone because they have arrived very late: *What time do you call this, Martin? You were supposed to be here half an hour ago.*

better late than never /ˌbetəʳ ˌleɪt ðən ˈnevəʳ/ spoken say this when someone or something arrives or does something late but it does not matter very much: *'The pictures have finally arrived.' 'Well, better late than never.'*

is that the time? /ɪz ˌðæt ðə ˈtaɪm/ British say this when you suddenly realize that it is later than you thought it was: *Oh my god, is that the time? I've got to go!*

3 later than usual

- late
- late in life

late /leɪt/ [adv/adj] *The library stays open late on Fridays.* | **be late** *The harvest was late this year because of the bad weather.* | **work late** (=stay at work till later than usual) *I'm afraid I'll have to work late again tomorrow.* | **get up late** *It's really nice to get up late on Saturday mornings.* | **a late breakfast/lunch etc** *'Where's Bill?' 'He's having a late lunch.'*

late in life /ˌleɪt ɪn ˈlaɪf/ [adv] if you do something **late in life**, you do it when you are older than the age at which people usually do it: *Greg got married late in life.* | *Carter and Reagan had come into politics relatively late in life.*

4 what you say when someone or something is late

- late
- overdue
- be behind with
- be in arrears
- belated
- you're late

late /leɪt/ [adv/adj] *The meeting started late.* | *There are severe penalties for late payment of bills.* | **15 minutes/3 days etc late** *Tony handed in his homework a day late.*

overdue /ˌəʊvəʳˈdjuː◂‖-ˈduː◂/ [adj] use this about payments that should have been made or library books that should have been returned before now: *I must take these books back to the library – they're overdue.* | **three weeks/two months etc overdue** *The rent's three weeks overdue.*

be behind with /biː bɪˈhaɪnd wɪð/ [v phrase] to have not made one or more regular payments at the time when you should: *Jim's worried because he's behind with his loan repayments.* | **be two months etc behind with sth** *You're two months behind with the rent.* | **get/fall behind with sth** (=start to make payments late) *I'm getting behind with the mortgage and I don't know how I'm going to pay it.* | *Even when people fall behind with their payments, they continue to take on financial commitments.*

be in arrears /biː ɪn əˈrɪəʳz/ [v phrase] to have not made one or more regular payments at the time when you should: *In some areas, two out of three tenants are in arrears.* | **+ with** *Many countries are in arrears with their contributions.* | **be two months etc in arrears** *Over 60,000 Londoners are more than three months in arrears with their mortgage repayments.* | **get/fall into arrears** *The tax bills are sent out annually, so it's very easy for small employers to fall into arrears.*

belated /bɪˈleɪtɪ̈d/ [adj only before noun] done or given later than it should have been, usually with the result that it does not have the effect that it should have: *John made a belated attempt to apologize.* | *I got a belated birthday card from my cousin yesterday.* | *her belated realisation that he was in love with someone else*

you're late /jɔːʳ ˈleɪt/ spoken use this when someone arrives somewhere late: *You're late! Hurry up and get your books out and get on with your work.* | *You're late again, Chris! You'll be in trouble if you don't get your act together soon.*

5 to have done less than you planned to do

- be behind
- be behind schedule
- be running late

be behind /biː bɪˈhaɪnd/ [v phrase] informal to have done less of your work than you planned to do or should have done: *If you're so far behind that you can't finish it on time, give me a call and I'll come and help.* | **+ with** *I've got to stay late tonight because I'm a bit behind with my work.* | **get behind** *If you don't do your homework every week, you'll get behind in your studies.* | **way behind** (=very much behind) *We were way behind on the budget planning already when the new project came in.*

be behind schedule /biː bɪˌhaɪnd ˈʃedʒuːl‖-ˈskedʒʊl/ [v phrase] to be doing each part of a planned series of activities later than you planned to do it: *Sorry, I can't talk now – I'm behind schedule as it is.* | **be six months etc behind schedule** *The tunnel project is now 18 months behind schedule and £300 million over budget.*

be running late /biː ˌrʌnɪŋ ˈleɪt/ [v phrase] to have spent longer than planned doing the first part of something or the first of a series of activities: *We're running late – we'll have to hurry if we want to catch the 5 o'clock train.* | *The Queen's visit to the factory was running late, so she did not come to see the production department.*

6 too late

- too late
- miss
- it's a little late
- leave it too late/a bit late

too late /tuː ˈleɪt/ [adj/adv] so late that you cannot do or achieve what you had planned: *I'm afraid you're too late – I've just sold the last ticket.* | **arrive/finish etc too late** *We rushed to the store as soon as we left work but arrived too late.* | **+ to do sth** *They got to the airport too late to catch the plane.* | **it is too late (to do sth)** *By the time the doctor arrived, it was too late; he was already dead.* | *It's never too late to learn a new language.*

miss /mɪs/ [v T] to arrive too late to see an event, film etc, or too late to get on a plane, train etc: *You'd better hurry or you'll miss the start of the show.* | **miss the flight/train/bus/ferry** *I missed the bus and had to wait half an hour for the next one.*

it's a little late ALSO **a bit late in the day** British /ɪts ə ˌlɪtl ˈleɪt, ə bɪt ˌleɪt ɪn ðə ˈdeɪ/ spoken you say **it's a little late** when someone decides to do something but harm has already been done or there is no time left to do it **+ for** *Perhaps it's a bit late in the day for apologies.* | **+ to do sth** *It's a little late to start worrying about that now.*

leave it too late/a bit late British ALSO **let it go too long** American /ˌliːv ɪt tuː ˈleɪt, ə ˌbɪt ˈleɪt, let ɪt ˌgəʊ tuː ˈlɒŋ‖-ˈlɔːŋ/ [v phrase] to wait too long before doing something so that you are not likely to achieve what you hoped to achieve: *At last the government has decided to lower interest rates, but I think they've let it go too long.* | **+ to do sth** *You might have left it a bit too late to apply for a place at university for this academic year.*

7 late at night

- late
- the middle of the night
- late-night
- last thing at night
- the early hours
- till all hours

late /leɪt/ [adv/adj] **it's late** *Look, it's late and I'm tired – let's talk about this tomorrow.* | **it's getting late** *I must go home now, it's getting late.* | **late at night** *I don't like coming home late at night to an empty house.* | **stay up late** (=not go to bed until late) *They stayed up late to watch the end of the match.* | **have a late night** (=when you go to bed very late) *You look as if you've been having too many late nights recently.*

the middle of the night /ɪn ðə ˌmɪdl əv ðə ˈnaɪt/ [n phrase] late at night when most people are asleep: *In the middle of the night, I was woken by a loud noise downstairs.* | *Helen opened the door. 'Dave? What's wrong? It's the middle of the night!'*

late-night /ˈleɪt naɪt/ [adj only before noun] happening or shown late at night: *They kept us awake with their late-night parties.* | *late-night television* | *They stopped off for a late-night drink.*

last thing at night /ˌlɑːst θɪŋ ət ˈnaɪt‖ˌlæst-/ [adv] informal just before you go to bed: *The soldiers are supposed to polish their shoes last thing at night.*

the early hours /ði ˈɜːʳli ˌaʊəʳz/ [n phrase] a time which is very late at night, between about 1 o'clock and 4 o'clock in the morning: *The club didn't close till the early hours.* | **the early hours of the morning** *They reached San Francisco in the early hours of the morning.*

till all hours /tɪl ˌɔːl ˈaʊəʳz/ [adv] informal until very late at night – use this when you are annoyed by someone doing something too late at night: *She and her friends used to stay out till all hours, going from club to club.* | *Better not wake her – she was up till all hours last night, working.*

later

RELATED WORDS

opposite: **immediately**

▸ *see also* **after, future, early, soon**

1 at a later time

- later
- later on
- in
- from now
- after
- subsequently

later /ˈleɪtəʳ/ [adv] not now, or not at the time you are talking about, but some time after this: *Sorry, I'm busy right now – I'll speak to you later.* | *We heard later that he had gone back to Japan.* | **a month/two weeks/three years etc later** *She became ill in 1993, and died two years later.* | **much later** (=a long time after that time) *I didn't find out the truth until much later.* | **later that day/month/year etc** *Later that afternoon, Anna came to see me.* | **later in the day/month/year etc** *We are developing a training course to run later in the year.* —**later** [adj only before noun] *Dixon pleaded guilty to all the charges and will be sentenced at a later date.* | *In a later speech, the minister admitted he had been wrong.*

later on /ˌleɪtər ˈɒn/ [adv] at a later time during the same period or activity: *Label the pipes you will be working on to avoid confusion later on.* | *Later on, I'll be interviewing the Prime Minister, but first here is a summary of the news.*

in /ɪn/ [prep] use this to say how far ahead **in** the future something will happen **in a minute/24 hours/a week etc** *I'll be back in a couple of days.* | *The doctor would like to see you again in two weeks.* | **in an hour's time/a few minutes' time etc** *Just think, in a few hours' time we'll be in Seattle.*

from now /frəm ˈnaʊ/ [adv] **24 hours/a week/100 years etc from now** 24 hours, a week etc after this time: *Three weeks from now the exams will be over.* | *A hundred years from now there may be no rainforest left.*

after /ˈɑːftəʳ‖ˈæf-/ [prep] use this to talk about something that happened in the past, and to say how much later than a particular time or point it happened **after two days/a week etc** *After a few minutes, she fell asleep.* | *After ten days, their supplies of water were running low.* | **after a while/a bit** (=after some time) *After a while, we got tired of waiting and went home.*

subsequently /ˈsʌbsə̇kwəntli/ [adv] formal after the time or event that you are talking about: *The decision was subsequently reversed on appeal.* | *He was savagely attacked and sustained severe injuries from which he subsequently died.*

2 to arrange to do something at a later time

- postpone
- put off
- delay
- be pushed/moved/put back
- put sth on ice/put sth on the back burner
- procrastinate

postpone /pəʊsˈpəʊn/ [v T] to change the time when something was planned to happen, and arrange for it to happen later: *Several of today's football games have been postponed because of heavy snow.* | **postpone sth until/till sth** *They decided to postpone the wedding until Pam's mother was out of the hospital.* | **postpone sth for two days/three weeks etc** *In 1968, the Oscar ceremony was postponed for two days, following the assassination of Martin Luther King.*

put off /ˌpʊt ˈɒf/ [phr v T] to decide to do something later than you planned to do it or should do it, for example because there is a problem or because you do not want to do it now **put sth off/put off sth** *I really should go to the dentist, but I keep putting it off.* | **put sth off until/till sth** *The concert's been put off till next week.* | **put off doing sth** *The committee decided to put off making any decision until the new year.*

delay /dɪˈleɪ/ [v T] to not do something until something else has happened or until a more suitable time **delay sth until sth** *He decided to delay his departure until after he'd seen the Director.* | **delay doing sth** *The police delayed making any announcement until the girl's relatives had been contacted.*

be pushed/moved/put back /biː ˌpʊʃt, ˌmuːvd, pʊt ˈbæk/ [v phrase] if an event **is pushed back**, someone arranges for it to be held at a later time or date than originally planned **+ to** *The meeting has been put back to next Thursday.*

put sth on ice/put sth on the back burner /ˌpʊt (sth) ɒn ˈaɪs, ˌpʊt (sth) ɒn ðə ˌbæk ˈbɜːʳnəʳ/ [v phrase] to decide to do or deal with something at a later time, especially because there is a problem or because you have more important things to deal with immediately: *We're going to have to put our plans on ice until we can raise some more money.* | *I've put my acting career on the back burner for a while, while I concentrate on my writing.*

procrastinate /prəˈkræstə̇neɪt/ [v I] to delay doing something that you ought to do, usually because you do not want to do it – used especially to show disapproval: *He hesitated and procrastinated for weeks before he finally told her he wanted their relationship to end.* | **+ about/over** *Certain players are procrastinating over their contracts in order to see how much money they can squeeze out of their clubs.* —**procrastination** /prəˌkræstə̇ˈneɪʃən/ [n U] *She finally agreed to take the job after months of procrastination.*

3 in a later place in a book, list etc

- later
- later/further on

later /ˈleɪtəʳ/ [adv] in a part of a book, list, or document that comes after the point where you are now: *Later in the poem there is a reference to the poet's unhappy childhood.* —**later** [adj only before noun] *The author returns to the same subject in a later section of the book.* | *I will explain how to deal with this problem in a later chapter.*

later/further on /ˌleɪtər, ˌfɜːʳðər ˈɒn/ [adv] in a later part of a book, list, or document: *Later on in the article he repeats this statement.* | *Further on in the book we find a full description of the system.*

laugh

RELATED WORDS

▸ *see also* **funny, joke, smile, happy, enjoy**

1 to laugh because something is funny

▸ laugh ▸ laughter ▸ have a laugh ▸ chuckle ▸ giggle ▸ titter

laugh /lɑːf‖læf/ [v I] to **laugh** because something is funny or because you are enjoying yourself: *I laughed all the way through the film.* | *I thought Dad would be angry, but he just laughed.* | **+ about** *I couldn't understand what they were all laughing about.* | **+ at** *No-one laughed at his jokes.* | **burst out laughing** (=suddenly laugh loudly) *We just looked at each other and burst out laughing.* —**laugh** [n C] **give a laugh** *She gave a little nervous laugh and glanced towards Robyn.*

laughter /ˈlɑːftəʳ‖ˈlæf-/ [n U] the sound you make when you laugh: *We could hear laughter coming from the next room.* | **roar with laughter** (=laugh very loudly) *The show was a great success, and had the audience roaring with laughter.* | **burst/gurgle/ snort etc of laughter** *There was a burst of laughter when he appeared.* | *Thelma gave a gurgle of laughter.*

have a laugh /ˌhæv ə ˈlɑːf‖-ˈlæf/ [v phrase] especially British if people **have a laugh** about something, they all laugh about it together **+ about/at** *When I realised my mistake, we had a laugh about it.* | **have a good laugh** *It was a bit scary at the time, but afterwards we all had a good laugh.*

chuckle /ˈtʃʌkəl/ [v I/T] to laugh quietly, especially because you are thinking about something funny: *'Do you remember when Michelle fell in the river?' Morgan chuckled.* | **+ at/about** *'We used to get up to all kinds of mischief.' She chuckled at the memory.* | **chuckle to yourself** *Simon sat reading a magazine, chuckling to himself.* —**chuckle** [n C] **give a chuckle** *He gave a low, knowing chuckle.*

giggle /ˈgɪgəl/ [v I] to laugh quietly and repeatedly like a child because of something funny or because you are nervous or embarrassed: *She giggled nervously and went bright pink.* | **+ at/over** *Linda and Christina were giggling at some private joke.* —**giggle** [n C] *There were a few smothered giggles from the girls sitting by the pool.* | **fit of giggles** *She collapsed in a fit of giggles.*

titter /ˈtɪtəʳ/ [v I] to laugh quietly in a high voice, because you are nervous, embarrassed, or slightly amused: *As the teacher read the poem someone tittered.* —**titter** [n C] *'That could be dangerous!' said someone, and a titter ran round the room.*

2 to laugh in a cruel or nasty way

▸ laugh at ▸ snigger ▸ make fun of ▸ jeer

laugh at /ˈlɑːf æt‖ˈlæf-/ [phr v T] to laugh or make unkind jokes about someone, because you think they are stupid or silly: *The other children laughed at Lisa because her clothes were old-fashioned.* | *At first I was terrified of being laughed at.*

snigger British **/snicker** American /ˈsnɪgəʳ, ˈsnɪkəʳ/ [v I] to laugh quietly at something that is not supposed to be funny, for example when someone is hurt or embarrassed: *Ruth tripped and fell as she walked up the steps. The boys behind her sniggered.* | *As he walked across the stage, Billy could hear people snickering and whispering.*

make fun of /meɪk ˈfʌn ɒv/ [v phrase] to make someone or something seem stupid by laughing at them, or by saying things that make other people laugh at them: *Stop making fun of me!* | *The other girls used to make fun of the way she spoke.*

jeer /dʒɪəʳ/ [v I/T] if a group of people **jeer** at someone in a public place, they laugh unkindly at that person and shout rude things at them: *The boys jeered as she ran away.* | *He was booed and jeered by the spectators when he argued with the umpire.* | **+ at** *After the match the crowd were all jeering at him.*

3 to laugh loudly

▸ roar/howl/shriek etc with laughter ▸ laugh out loud ▸ cackle ▸ roar/howl/peal etc of laughter

roar/howl/shriek etc with laughter /ˌrɔːʳ wɪð ˈlɑːftəʳ‖-ˈlæf-/ [v phrase] to laugh very loudly because you think something is very funny: *Patsy chased him down the stairs, shrieking with laughter.* | **+ at** *Dad was roaring with laughter at something on TV and didn't hear me come in.* | *They howled with laughter at their own jokes.*

laugh out loud /ˌlɑːf aʊt ˈlaʊd‖ˌlæf-/ [v phrase] to suddenly laugh loudly because you think a situation, someone's words, something you are reading etc is very funny: *John threw back his head and laughed out loud.* | *Wodehouse is one of the few writers who can make me laugh out loud.*

cackle /ˈkækəl/ [v I/T] to laugh loudly and unpleasantly in a high voice, like someone who is mad: *When I said this, he started cackling like a madman.* | *'Oh we've got him now!' I cackled, dancing round the room.* —**cackle** [n C] *There was a cackle from the old lady. 'I know what you're after.'*

roar/howl/peal etc of laughter /ˌrɔːr əv ˈlɑːftəʳ‖-ˈlæf-/ [n phrase] a very loud laugh: *With a roar of laughter, he lifted her off her feet and swung her round.* | *Everyone burst into peals of laughter.*

4 to laugh a lot or for a long time

▸ can't stop laughing ▸ laugh helplessly/uncontrollably/hysterically ▸ have/get the giggles ▸ laugh your head off ▸ have hysterics ▸ fall about ▸ I nearly/almost died ▸ gales/fits of laughter

can't stop laughing /ˌkɑːnt stɒp ˈlɑːfɪŋ‖ˌkænt stɑːp ˈlæfɪŋ/ [v phrase] to be unable to stop yourself from laughing: *Jonathan kept making funny faces at me and I just couldn't stop laughing.* | *It's so embarrassing when everyone else is being serious and you can't stop laughing.*

laugh helplessly/uncontrollably/hysterically /ˌlɑːf ˈhelpləsli, ʌnkənˈtrəʊləbli, hɪˈsterɪkli‖ˌlæf-/ [v phrase] to laugh so much that you cannot control yourself and could not stop laughing if you wanted to: *They both leant against the wall, laughing helplessly.* | *She was laughing hysterically at the thought of Mr Taylor stepping out of his caravan with no clothes on.*

have/get the giggles ALSO **have/get a fit of the giggles** /ˌhæv, ˌget ðə ˈgɪgəlz, hæv, get ə ˌfɪt əv ðə ˈgɪgəlz/ [v phrase not in progressive] British informal to be unable to stop yourself laughing, especially in a situation when you should not laugh: *It's very difficult to be angry with somebody when you've got the giggles.* | *I got a dreadful fit of the giggles – I couldn't help myself!*

laugh your head off /ˌlɑːf jɔːʳ ˈhed ɒf‖ˌlæf-/ [v phrase] informal to laugh a lot and very loudly because of what someone says or does: *When I told him what had happened, he laughed his head off.* | *I can't believe we were so stupid. Our competitors must be laughing their heads off.*

have hysterics /ˌhæv hɪˈsterɪks/ [v phrase] to laugh a lot continuously and uncontrollably because someone says or does something extremely funny or stupid: *Everybody who heard this had hysterics.*

fall about /ˌfɔːl əˈbaʊt/ [phr v I] British to laugh a lot in a very happy and cheerful way, especially because something has happened that you did not expect: *When we heard the news, we just fell about!* | **fall about laughing** *When they saw what their father had done, they both fell about laughing.*

I nearly/almost died /aɪ ˌnɪəʳli, ˌɔːlməʊst ˈdaɪd/ informal if you say **I nearly** or **almost died**, you mean that something made you laugh so much that you almost couldn't stop laughing: *Did you see the look on his face? I nearly died.* | **nearly/almost die laughing** *He said this very solemnly, and they nearly died laughing.*

gales/fits of laughter /ˌgeɪlz, ˌfɪts əv ˈlɑːftəʳ‖-ˈlæf-/ [n phrase] written a lot of laughter: *Jack put the phone down, and the children collapsed in gales of laughter.* | *There was a brief stunned silence, and then the entire family went into fits of laughter.*

5 to make someone laugh

- make sb laugh
- crack sb up
- raise a laugh
- have sb in hysterics/stitches
- amuse

make sb laugh /ˌmeɪk (sb) ˈlɑːf‖-ˈlæf/ [v phrase] *Rachel used to make us all laugh by imitating the teacher.* | *Thanks for your letter. It really made me laugh.*

crack sb up /ˌkræk (sb) ˈʌp/ [phr v T] informal to be very funny and to make people laugh a lot: *Mr Bean really cracks me up. He's so funny.*

raise a laugh /ˌreɪz ə ˈlɑːf‖-ˈlæf/ [v phrase] to succeed in making people laugh, especially when they do not really feel like laughing: *None of my carefully-prepared jokes managed to raise a laugh.*

have sb in hysterics/stitches ALSO **have sb in fits** British /ˌhæv (sb) ɪn hɪˈsterɪks, ˈstɪtʃɪ̈z, ˌhæv (sb) ɪn ˈfɪts/ [v phrase] to make someone laugh uncontrollably: *Roger had us in hysterics with his account of his disastrous trip to Italy.* | *The cast included Paul Shane, whose quick wit had the audience in stitches.*

amuse /əˈmjuːz/ [v T] if something **amuses** someone, it makes them laugh or smile because it is fairly funny: *Something in the report had obviously amused him.* | **it amuses sb to see/think sth** *It amuses me to see politicians so eager to please at election time.*

6 to stop yourself laughing

- keep a straight face

keep a straight face /kiːp ə ˌstreɪt ˈfeɪs/ [v phrase] if you try to **keep a straight face**, you try not to laugh or smile, because it would be rude to laugh, or you do not want someone to know you are joking: *When reading some of the competition entries, it was hard to keep a straight face.* | *'I think I've lost that camera you lent me,' I said, trying to keep a straight face.* | **with a straight face** *With a completely straight face, Thomas announced he was joining the Girl Guides.*

law

RELATED WORDS

- *see also* **rule/regulation, legal, illegal, crime, obey, punish, limit, forbid, court/trial, strict/not strict**

1 an official rule that everyone must obey

- law
- legislation
- act
- bill
- statute
- bylaw

law /lɔː/ [n C] an official rule that everyone in a country or place must obey: *This law makes it illegal to smoke in public places.* | *The law defines drunkenness as a certain percentage of alcohol in the blood.* | **+ against** *Japan has very strict laws against guns and drugs.* | **under the law/according to the law** *Under the new law, anyone who assists in a suicide faces 10 years in prison.* | **+ on** *tough new laws on immigration* | *Both specific and general laws on child prostitution exist.* | **tax/gun/immigration etc law** *The current gun laws vary from state to state.*

legislation /ˌledʒɪ̈sˈleɪʃən/ [n U] a set of laws, especially ones that are made to control a new problem: *Legislation is needed to stop the spread of computer pornography.* | *The legislation requires motorcyclists to wear helmets.* | **+ on** *new legislation on the sale of alcohol*

act /ækt/ [n C] a law made by parliament or Congress – used in the official name of a law: *the 1991 Prevention of Terrorism Act* | *The Wagner Act prohibited employers from firing workers for joining a union.*

bill /bɪl/ [n C] a new law that has to be approved by members of the government before it can officially become a law: *Monday's debate on the defense bill lasted all night.* | **sign a bill** (=to approve a bill so that it becomes a law) *The president signed a bill that will help more families move from welfare to work.*

statute /ˈstætʃuːt/ [n C] a law that has been officially established by the government so that it is written down as the law: *In New Mexico, a state statute permits one minute of silent prayer at the beginning of school.* | *Unfortunately his lawyer could find no statute or point of law preventing his client's imprisonment.*

bylaw British **/ordinance** American /ˈbaɪlɔː, ˈɔːʳdɪ̈nəns‖-dənəns/ [n C] a law made by local government that people in a particular area or place must obey: *Fishing on this river is forbidden under a local bylaw.* | *a city ordinance prohibiting smoking in government buildings*

2 the whole system of laws of a country or place

- law
- legal system

law /lɔː/ [n U] the whole system of laws that everyone in a country or place must obey: *Andrew is studying* *law at Harvard University.* | *In 1873 French law was imposed in Vietnam.* | **break the law** (=disobey the law) *I didn't realize I was breaking the law.* | **federal law** American (=a law that everyone in the nation must obey) **state law** American (=a law that everyone in a state must obey) **international law** (=laws that govern how nations behave toward each other) *Refugees are accorded special protection under international law* | **by law** (=according to the system of laws) *By law, an advertiser can't use a person's name for commercial purposes without permission.* | **against the law** (=illegal because it is not part of the system of laws) *It's against the law to be drunk in public.* | **law and order** (=respect for the system of laws) *The soldiers were brought in to restore law and order after the riots.*

legal system /ˈliːgəl ˌsɪstɪ̆m/ [n C] the laws and the way that they work in a particular country: *Many people here have no faith in the legal system and do not expect to receive justice from it.* | *The American legal system says that you are innocent until proven guilty.*

3 part of a law or legal agreement

- article
- clause
- loophole

article /ˈɑːʳtɪkəl/ [n C] one of the parts, usually numbered, of a written law or legal agreement: *Article 1 of the constitution guarantees freedom of religion.* | *The country signed the treaty but then violated each of its 143 articles.*

clause /klɔːz/ [n C] a part of a written law or legal document, concerning a particular point or idea: *I was told that this clause would be removed from the contract.* | *Courts ruled that prayer in school violates a clause of the First Amendment.*

loophole /ˈluːphəʊl/ [n C] a detail that is missing from a law or legal document that makes it possible to avoid something in that law: *He pays very little tax because of some loophole in income tax legislation.* | **close a loophole** (=to add details to a law so that there is no way for people to avoid following it) *The new rules will close loopholes in British immigration law.*

4 to make a new law

- pass
- legislate

pass /pɑːs‖pæs/ [v T] to accept a new law in a government or parliament, so that it officially becomes a law: *Congress has passed an education-reform law.* | *The law was passed with only a few MPs voting against.*

legislate /ˈledʒɪ̆sleɪt/ [v I/T] to officially make laws that are intended to control a particular activity or situation **+ against** *Should parliament legislate against experiments on animals?* | **+ on** *The government was under a lot of public pressure to legislate on equal pay.* | **+ for** *Thomas Jefferson said that Britain had no right to legislate for its American colonies.* | **legislate sth** American *States are legislating stricter automobile safety measures for young children.*

5 ways of saying that a law is officially accepted

- become law
- get onto/reach the statute book

become law /bɪˌkʌm ˈlɔː/ [v phrase] if a new or suggested law **becomes law**, it is officially accepted and starts to exist: *The Education Bill finally became law last month.* | *Until the Food Protection Bill became law, the ministry had no power to ban dangerous pesticides.*

get onto/reach the statute book British ALSO **be on the books** American /ˌget ɒntə, ˌriːtʃ ðə ˈstætʃuːt bʊk, biː ɒn ðə ˈbʊks/ [v phrase] if a law **gets onto the statute book**, it officially becomes a law: *The Employment Bill was passed in 1982 but did not reach the statute book until 1984.* | *The laws have been on the books for decades, but city officials failed to enforce them.*

6 relating to the law

- legal
- legislative

legal /ˈliːgəl/ [adj only before noun] connected with laws and courts **legal advice** *People on low salaries can get free legal advice.* | **legal battle/dispute** (=when two people or organizations disagree about something, and this is judged in a court of law) *Neither side wanted a long and expensive legal battle.* | **legal fees** (=money you have to pay lawyers) *The American government does not pay the legal fees of Americans who are arrested abroad.*

legislative /ˈledʒɪ̆slətɪv‖-leɪtɪv/ [adj only before noun] connected with making laws **legislative assembly/council/body** *The Liberal Party has won control of the legislative assembly.* | **legislative power/authority/control** *Legislative authority rests with parliament.* | *The U.S. president has no legislative power, but he can make recommendations.*

lazy

RELATED WORDS

opposite: —— **work hard**

▸ *see also* **careless**

1 lazy

- lazy
- idle
- can't be bothered/couldn't be bothered

lazy /ˈleɪzi/ [adj] someone who is **lazy** does not like work or physical activity, and tries to avoid it: *Marian didn't do well at school. She was intelligent, but very lazy.* | *Get up, you lazy thing! It's nearly lunchtime.* | **a lazy day/week etc** (=a time when you relax and do not work hard) *We spent a lazy afternoon at the beach.* | *The lazy days of summer are finally here.* —**laziness** [n U] being lazy: *His bad exam results were due to laziness and nothing else.* | *Mark thinks that the welfare system encourages laziness.* —**lazily** [adv] *It was great to spend my day off lying lazily by the swimming pool.*

idle /ˈaɪdl/ [adj] someone who is **idle** is lazy and does not do enough work – used to show strong disapproval: *Wake up that idle young brother of yours and tell him it's time for school!* | **the idle rich** (=rich people who do not have to work to earn money) *Painting is a favorite hobby of the idle rich.* | **bone idle** British (=very lazy) *That husband of hers is bone idle. No wonder the house is such a mess.* —**idleness** [n U] *Her third son chose to live at home in idleness rather than follow a profession.*

can't be bothered/couldn't be bothered /ˌkɑːnt biː ˈbɒðəʳd, ˌkʊdnt biː ˈbɒðəʳd‖ˌkænt biː ˈbɑː-/

[v phrase] British spoken if you say that you **can't be bothered** to do something, you mean that you have decided not to do it because it is not interesting to you and you are feeling too lazy: *When I asked her to help me she said that she couldn't be bothered.* | **can't be bothered to do sth** *My hairdresser says I should use a hairdryer to dry my hair, but I can't be bothered to do it every day.* | *They complain so much about the government, but they can't be bothered to vote.*

2 a lazy person

- lazybones
- couch potato
- layabout
- skiver

lazybones /ˈleɪzibəʊnz/ [n singular] spoken informal a lazy person – use this especially when talking to someone that you like: *Hey, lazybones, how long are you planning on staying in bed?*

couch potato /ˈkaʊtʃ pəˌteɪtəʊ/ [n C] informal someone who spends a lot of time sitting and watching television: *'I was a complete couch potato,' Lewis said, 'I didn't even like walking to the store.'* | *Mitchell is a self-described 'couch potato'.*

layabout /ˈleɪəbaʊt/ [n C] British informal a lazy person who avoids work or responsibility: *How did you get mixed up with that layabout?* | *a bunch of hopeless layabouts*

skiver /ˈskaɪvəʳ/ [n C] British informal someone who is lazy and does not go to school, work etc: *I always thought Clive was a bit of a skiver.*

3 to behave in a lazy way

- sit/lounge/laze around
- shirk
- not lift a finger

sit/lounge/laze around /ˌsɪt, ˌlaʊndʒ, ˌleɪz əˈraʊnd/ [phr v I] informal to spend time sitting and relaxing and not doing any work: *We lazed around on the beach most of the day.* | *Why not finish your homework, instead of just sitting around doing nothing?* | *It's a perfect place to lounge around – hot sunshine and free drinks.*

shirk /ʃɜːʳk/ [v I/T] to deliberately avoid your work or your responsibilities because you are lazy, in a way that makes people not have respect for you: *We don't want anyone shirking round here – everyone is expected to earn their pay.* | **shirk your duties/responsibilities** *Our father never shirked his responsibilities.* | *John doesn't want to go to war, but he won't shirk his duty.* —**shirker** [n C] *It's amazing he hasn't been fired – everyone knows what a shirker he is.*

not lift a finger /nɒt ˌlɪft ə ˈfɪŋgəʳ/ [v phrase] informal to not help someone at all with work that must be done, such as cooking and cleaning, with the result that they have to do it all on their own: *Tim doesn't lift a finger when it comes to housework.* | **not lift a finger to help** *We spent the day moving furniture, but Sara didn't lift a finger to help.*

leader

RELATED WORDS

▸ *see also* **manager, position/rank, in charge of, power, government**

1 the leader of a group or country

- leader
- leadership
- president
- head of state
- prime minister
- ruler
- king
- queen
- figurehead

leader /ˈliːdəʳ/ [n C] someone who is in charge of a group of people, or someone who they have chosen to represent them: *The report has raised strong opposition from radical black leaders.* | *12,000 party members will vote next week to elect a new leader.* | **+ of** *the leader of the Communist party* | *The leaders of the rebel movement have been arrested.* | **world leader** (=the leader of a major country) *World leaders are meeting in Geneva today to consider the peace plan.* | **union/party/community etc leader** *To function effectively, a party leader has to be attentive to people's needs.* | *So far, business leaders have been encouraged by the government's economic policy.* | **gang leader** *Three members of the 'Hells Angels' group were convicted of the murder of a rival gang leader.* | **born leader** (=someone who is naturally very good at being a leader) *Peter was a born leader, and his chairmanship of the WWF could not have been more effective.* | **leader of the opposition** (=the leader of the group of people in a parliament who are not part of the government, and who argue against it) *The leader of the opposition has demanded an early election.*

leadership /ˈliːdəʳʃɪp/ [n singular with singular or plural verb in British English] the people in charge of a political party or country: *Party members had lost confidence in the leadership.* | *Turkey has lacked any clear leadership since the collapse of the coalition government four months ago.* | **+ of** *The leadership of the Association was criticized for not making its plans more easily accessible.*

president /ˈprezɪ̈dənt/ [n C] the official leader of a country that does not have a king or queen: *President Chirac visited Japan this week.* | *It was Dever's job to advise the president on his public image.* | **+ of** *the President of Egypt* —**presidential** /ˌprezɪ̈ˈdenʃəl◂/ [adj only before noun] *a presidential election* | *the 2004 presidential campaign*

head of state /ˌhed əv ˈsteɪt/ [n C] someone who leads a country or state: *President Clinton was the first head of state to sign the Comprehensive Test Ban Treaty.* | *Twenty-one heads of state will meet at the annual World Trade summit.*

prime minister /praɪm ˈmɪnɪ̈stəʳ/ [n C] the elected leader of the government in a country that has a parliament: *The British Prime Minister lives at 10 Downing Street.* | *Hashimoto was elected prime minister in 1998.* | **+ of** *the Prime Minister of India*

ruler /ˈruːləʳ/ [n C] someone, such as a king or queen or a military leader, who has the power to run the government of a country: *Several countries have condemned Nigeria's military rulers for human rights abuses.* | *King Priam was a firm, but just ruler.* | **+ of** *Ramses II, ruler of Egypt in 13,000 BC* | **hereditary ruler** (=the son or daughter of a ruler, who becomes the new ruler when that parent dies) *Some regimes are governed by hereditary rulers.*

king /kɪŋ/ [n C] a man who is the official leader of a country because he is a member of a royal family: *a portrait of King George VI* | **+ of** *King Juan Carlos of Spain* | *the King of Morocco*

queen /kwiːn/ [n C] a woman who is the official leader of a country because she is a member of a royal family, or a woman who is the wife of a king: *a* *new biography of Queen Elizabeth* | **+ of** *the Queen of Sweden* | *the King and Queen of Belgium*

figurehead /ˈfɪgəhed‖ˈfɪgjər-/ [n C usually singular] use this to describe someone who is recognized as the leader of a country or organization, although he or she does not have any real power: *The president is essentially a figurehead: the real power lies with the prime minister.* | *He was never more than a mere figurehead in the negotiations.*

2 to be the leader

- be the leader (of sth)
- lead
- leadership
- be fronted by
- rule

be the leader (of sth) /biː ðə ˈliːdər (əv (sth))/ [v phrase] *Margaret Haley was the leader of the Chicago Teachers' Federation.* | *Dang was born, raised and schooled to be a future leader of his country.* | *Ken, who was two years older than I, was our leader.* | *Karekin is the spiritual leader of more than 6 million Armenians worldwide.*

lead /liːd/ [v T not usually in progressive] to be in charge of an organization, especially a political party, or to be in charge of a country: *For many years, India's Congress Party was led by Mrs Indira Gandhi.* | *Jaruzelski led the country's Communist regime for nine years.* | *67% of voters said they would not trust him to lead the country.*

leadership /ˈliːdərʃɪp/ [n U] someone's **leadership** is their ability to lead people: *His forceful personality concealed his weak leadership and poor political acumen.* | *We want to identify employees who have leadership potential.* | **under sb's leadership/under the leadership of** *The marketing department was much more focused under his leadership.* | *Harvard has a formidable team of black academics, working under the leadership of Henry Louis Gates.* | **leadership style** (=the way that someone behaves as a leader) *He took office in January and quickly established his leadership style.*

be fronted by /biː ˈfrʌntɪd baɪ/ [v phrase] if an organization **is fronted by** a particular person, they are the leader of that organization and often appear in public to represent that organization: *The organization is fronted by Keith Flynn, who has been associated with other political groups in the past.*

rule /ruːl/ [v I/T] to be the leader of a country – use this about kings, queens, and other leaders who are not elected: *Henry VIII ruled England from 1509 to 1547.* | *Mary, Queen of Scots, only ruled for six years.* | *At that time, Persia was divided into several provinces, ruled by local khans.*

learn

RELATED WORDS

▸ *see also* **teach, study, subject, can/can't**

1 to learn how to do something, or learn about something

- learn
- study
- train
- pick up
- get the hang of
- master
- familiarize yourself with

learn /lɜːrn/ [v I/T] to **learn** how to do something, or to **learn** about a subject, especially by being taught or trained: *How long have you been learning German?* | *The CD is specially designed to let children learn at their own pace.* | **+ to do sth** *His daughter's learning to drive.* | *William learned to read when he was four.* | **learn how to do sth** (=learn a method or skill) *On this course, you will learn how to deal with communication problems.* | *How long did it take you to learn how to do this?* | **+ about** *Before you sail, you need to learn about basic boat controls.* | *Our children attend the group twice a week to learn about Sikhism.*

study /ˈstʌdi/ [v I/T] to learn about a subject by reading books and going to classes at a school or university **study English/Biology/Music etc** *Less than 10% of girls choose to study Science at school.* | *She's studying Music at Berkeley College in Boston.* | *My parents first met when dad was studying in England.* | **study to be a doctor/lawyer/accountant etc** *He's studying to be a lawyer.* | *Dad thinks I should study to be a doctor, but I'm not interested in medicine.* | **study for a test/diploma/an examination** *'Is Ian coming with us?' 'He can't – he's studying for his exams.'* | *Alan hardly studied for the test, but he still passed.*

train /treɪn/ [v I] to learn the skills and get the experience that you need in order to do a job: *Chris trained at an airbase in Honduras.* | **train to be a hairdresser/teacher/pilot/nurse etc** *Julie is training to be a nurse.* | *Her husband trained to be an auto mechanic, but he can't find a job.* | **train for a job/career/occupation** *Melanie trained for a career in music, but switched to photography in her early thirties.* | *We want to encourage people who left school early to train for better jobs.*

pick up /ˌpɪk ˈʌp/ [phr v T] informal to learn something easily, without making much effort or having lessons **pick up sth** *I picked up a few words of Turkish when I was in Istanbul.* | **pick sth up** *The rules are really easy – you'll pick them up.* | *Roy's a bright little boy, and he picks things up really quickly.*

get the hang of /ˌget ðə ˈhæŋ ɒv/ [v phrase] spoken to learn how to do something that is fairly complicated: *Using the software isn't difficult once you get the hang of it.* | *It took me ages to get the hang of using chopsticks.* | *That's it. You're getting the hang of it now.*

master /ˈmɑːstər‖ˈmæ-/ [v T] to learn a skill or a language completely so that you have no difficulty with it: *It takes years to master the art of weaving.* | *She soon got to know the local customs and eventually mastered the language.* | *Children have usually mastered the concepts of weight and length by the age of 8.*

familiarize yourself with ALSO **familiarise** British /fəˈmɪliəraɪz jɔːrself wɪð/ [v phrase] to learn about a subject, or how to do something, especially by reading books, notices, instructions etc, because you know you are going to need this knowledge in the future: *She prepared for the interview by familiarizing herself with all aspects of the company's work.* | *You must familiarize yourself with the evacuation procedure in case of a fire.*

2 to learn something so that you can remember it exactly

- learn
- memorize
- commit sth to memory

learn /lɜːrn/ [v T] to **learn** facts, words, or numbers, especially at school, so that you can remember them exactly: *What songs have you learnt at school,* *then?* | *I'm going to try to learn 12 new words each week.* | *Do you think you can learn this tune for Friday's performance?* | **learn sth (off) by heart** (=learn something so that you can repeat it exactly without reading it) *We had to learn a lot of poetry by heart when we were children.* | *Dad taught us a Sanskrit prayer, and we had to learn it off by heart and say it every day.* | **learn your lines** (=learn the words that you have to say in a play) *I've been trying to learn my lines, but I haven't gotten very far.* | **learn sth by rote** (=to learn something by repeating it without having to understand it, especially in a class) *The guide sounded as if he had learnt his speech by rote.* | *If you have a good memory you can learn things by rote, but can you apply it in practice?*

memorize ALSO **memorise** British /ˈmeməraɪz/ [v T] to learn numbers or words so well that you can remember them exactly: *Don't write your password down, memorize it.* | *He was only four when he memorized Martin Luther King's 'I have a dream' speech.* | *I recited the poem she had asked me to memorize.*

commit sth to memory /kəˌmɪt (sth) tə ˈmeməri/ [v phrase] formal to learn something, especially something long, so that you remember every word or detail of it: *Some really dedicated fans have committed entire passages of the movie to memory.* | *Sometimes, conductors have to commit complete scores to memory.*

3 someone who is learning something

- student
- trainee
- beginner
- apprentice
- learner

student /ˈstjuːdənt‖ˈstuː-/ [n C] someone who is studying at a school, college, or university: *She's a student at Cornell University.* | *extra help for disabled students* | *He was accused of attacking a fellow student.* | *a farewell party for the overseas students* | **law/medical/engineering etc student** *Law students always have a lot of work to do.* | **student nurse/teacher** (=someone who is studying to be a nurse or a teacher) *What was the social life like when you were a student nurse?* | **mature student** British (=a student who is over the age of 25, and who has worked before coming to university or college) *We have a large number of mature students here, some with small children.*

trainee /ˌtreɪˈniː◂/ [n C] someone who is learning a skill while working in a company or organization: *The new class of trainees was highly motivated.* | *I started out as a trainee on the trading floor, earning around $25,000 a year.* | **trainee accountant/reporter/salesman etc** *I got a job as a trainee reporter on the 'Daily Star'.* | *He spent three years as a trainee manager before getting his present position.*

beginner /bɪˈɡɪnəʳ/ [n C] someone who has recently started to learn something: *Japanese classes for beginners* | *The tennis club welcomes beginners as well as more advanced players.* | *As a beginner, she needs quite a lot of encouragement.*

apprentice /əˈprentɪ̈s/ [n C] someone who is learning all the skills that they need in order to do a job, especially a job that they do with their hands: *When I finish classes, I'm hoping to land a summer job as a chef's apprentice.* | **apprentice electrician/bricklayer/hairdresser etc** *I worked as an apprentice electrician for 18 months.* —**apprenticeship** [n] the period of time when you are an apprentice **serve an apprenticeship** *A 'Meister' in Germany serves a nine-year apprenticeship before he can run his own shop.* | **+ to** *John recalled his apprenticeship to a blacksmith in the early years of the Second World War.*

learner /ˈlɜːnəʳ/ [n C] someone who is learning a particular subject or skill, especially a foreign language and usually in a school: *A good teacher holds the learner's interest and stimulates them to find out more.* | **slow/fast/quick learner** *James was a fast learner, and was soon better at tennis than his coach.* | *You're a quick learner! It took me ages to get the hang of it.*

4 to learn about things by experiencing them in your life

- learn

learn /lɜːʳn/ [v I/T] to **learn** how you should behave or how to deal with situations, because of experiences you have had in your life **+ (that)** *I soon learned that it was best to keep quiet.* | *I had learnt that as a woman, if your talents are ignored at work, you must be assertive.* | **+ to do sth** *Gradually, I learned to trust her.* | *By sharing their problems, sufferers of the disease learn to cope with the symptoms.* | **learn sth from sth** *Have you learned anything from the experience?* | **learn from your mistakes** (=remember mistakes you have made, and be careful not to make them again) *What is important is to learn from our mistakes, so that we don't repeat them.* | **learn your lesson** (=to learn from a bad experience not to do the same thing again) *She'd been stupid, but she'd learned her lesson.* | *He felt that his son needed to learn some hard lessons about life.* | *There are important lessons to be learned from this election defeat.* | **learn sth the hard way** (=learn something by having an unpleasant experience) *Never lend money to your friends – that's something I learnt the hard way.* | *There are no shortcuts in this industry. I learned that the hard way this week.*

least

RELATED WORDS

opposite: **most**

- *see also* **less**

1 less than any other

- least

least /liːst/ [adv] *We were the least successful team in the competition.* | *Portugal would be my least favourite choice.* | *The people who are least able to afford healthcare are often the ones who need it most.* | *Air-conditioning is standard except on the least expensive model.* | *Which job would you least like to do?*

2 the smallest amount or number of something

- the least
- minimum
- the fewest
- the lowest

the least /ðə ˈliːst/ [quantifier] the smallest amount of something **the least** *We decided to buy the one that cost the least.* | *Those who have been in the most danger have the least to say about it.* | *Of all the EU countries, Britain spends the least on higher education.* | *The least I would expect would be an apology* (=I'd like more than just an apology). | **the least**

water/money/time etc *After trials, we chose the engine that used the least fuel.* | *I was the youngest, so I always got the least pocket money.* | *We've selected recipes that take the least time to prepare.* | *Find a route that is likely to have the least traffic.* | *We thought this decision would produce the least harm and disruption to residents.*

minimum /ˈmɪnɪ̈məm/ [adj/quantifier] the smallest possible number or amount of something or the smallest number or amount that is allowed: *The minimum salary for this post is $25,000.* | *We need a minimum number of two staff members on duty at lunchtime.* | *Frank was moved to a minimum-security prison for good behaviour.* | **minimum height/length/age/wage etc** *These workers are being paid less than the minimum wage.* | *The minimum age at which you can legally buy tobacco is 18.* | *The Police Department has reduced the minimum height requirement to encourage more women to join the force.* | **reduce/keep sth to a minimum** (=make the amount or number of something as small as possible) *Interruptions should be kept to a minimum.* | *The library book stock has already been reduced to a minimum.* | *We want to keep the number of mistakes to a minimum.* | **+ of** *This will enable the patient to move with a minimum of discomfort.* | *The course takes a minimum of three years.* | *Even for local games, you have to pay a minimum of $45 per game.* | **the minimum** *Five people in a group should be the minimum.* | **bare minimum** (=use this to emphasize how small the amount is) *A tiny crack in the tent allowed the bare minimum of light in.*

the fewest /ðə ˈfjuːɪ̈st/ [quantifier] the smallest number of something: *We plan to do the repairs in winter, when we have the fewest visitors.* | *Single men make the fewest complaints about women bosses.* | *Towns with the fewest amenities are usually the ones with the highest crime rates.* | *Young drivers under 25 have the highest number of accidents while those over 50 have the fewest.* | *In 1998, there were 71 homicides, the fewest since the 1950s.*

the lowest /ðə ˈləʊɪ̈st/ [adj] use this about numbers, prices, wages, temperatures, or levels: *In the last election, he was the candidate who got the lowest number of votes.* | *People who drank the least coffee had the lowest level of blood pressure.* | *The lowest charge for a rented car is $30 a day.* | *Does the company offering the lowest price really offer the best value?* | **the lowest for 6 months/in 15 years/since 2000 etc** *Interest rates are only 4%, the lowest for 25 years.* | *The infant mortality rate in Vietnam is now the lowest since 1997.* | *Overseas demand for corn is the lowest in 20 years.*

3 to be at the lowest level

- an all-time low
- low/lowest ebb

an all-time low /ən ˌɔːl taɪm ˈləʊ/ [n phrase] the lowest level ever reached **be at an all-time low** *Exports of manufactured goods are now at an all-time low.* | *Morale at the company is at an all-time low, and staff are leaving in droves.* | **sink to/fall to/reach an all-time low** *Ratings for the once-popular game show seem to have reached an all-time low.* | *The president's popularity has fallen to an all-time low.*

low/lowest ebb /ˌləʊ, ˌləʊɪ̈st ˈeb/ [n singular] the lowest level of success, hope, health etc **be at its/their lowest ebb** *Consumer confidence is at its lowest ebb since January.* | *With the company's fortunes at their lowest ebb for 25 years, lay-offs seem inevitable.* | **sth sinks/falls to its lowest ebb** *In the late 1980s, her career sank to its lowest ebb.* | *Relations with Washington have fallen to their lowest ebb.*

leave

RELATED WORDS

- to leave something somewhere *see* **put**
- to stay somewhere and not leave *see* **stay**

WHAT'S HERE

to leave a place

1 to go away from a place

- leave
- go
- go out
- go away
- go off

leave /liːv/ [v I/T not in passive] *Just as I was leaving, the phone rang.* | *I want to see you before I leave.* | *The police wanted to know what time he had left the office.* | *Hand back the identity card when you leave the building.*

go /gəʊ/ [v I] especially spoken to leave: *Let's go.* | *When does the next bus go?* | *We stayed another ten minutes and then we went.* | *I'll have to go soon – was there anything else you wanted to talk about?* | *Don't go just yet – it's not that late!*

go out /ˌgəʊ ˈaʊt/ [phr v I] to leave a room, house, or building, especially when you intend to return very soon: *I'm just going out for a minute, I won't be long.* | **+ of** *As she went out of the room she slammed the door.* | **+ to do sth** *He's just gone out to buy some bread.*

go away /ˌgəʊ əˈweɪ/ [phr v I] to leave a place, often for a long time or permanently: *I'm going away next week. Would you mind feeding the cat for me?* | *'Are you going away this summer?' 'Yes, we're going to Greece in August.'* | *He's been really unhappy since she went away.*

go off /ˌgəʊ ˈɒf / [phr v I] to leave a place suddenly or for a particular purpose, especially if you do not explain why you are going: *They just went off, without even saying goodbye.* | *Many trainees don't finish the course and go off and work in other areas.* | **+ to do sth** *When we could not find out what was wrong with the car, Billy went off to find a phone.*

2 what you say when you are going to leave

- I'm off
- I must go
- I must dash/fly
- I'd better make tracks
- I'm getting out of here

I'm off British **/I'm outta here** American informal /aɪm ˈɒf, aɪm ˈaʊtə hɪəʳ/ *Okay, I'm off now.* | *Right. I'm off to bed.* | *That's it. I'm outta here!*

I must go British **/I gotta go** American /aɪ ˌmʌst ˈgəʊ, aɪ ˌgɒtə ˈgəʊ‖-ˌgɑːtə-/ said when you have to go somewhere: *Anyway, I gotta go. Catch up with you later.* | **I must be going** *I must be going. I've got to pick the kids up at four.*

I must dash/fly /aɪ ˌmʌst ˈdæʃ, ˈflaɪ/ British said when you have to hurry: *I'll have another coffee,and then I must dash.*

I'd better make tracks ALSO **I'd better make a move** British /aɪd ˌbetəʳ meɪk ˈtræks, aɪd ˌbetəʳ meɪk ə ˈmuːv/ said when you want to start getting ready to leave soon: *We'd better make tracks, or we'll miss our train.* | *I think we'd better make a move before it gets dark.*

I'm getting out of here /aɪm ˌgetɪŋ ˈaʊt əv hɪəʳ/ said when you want to leave quickly to avoid danger or something unpleasant: *Oh no. It's him again. I'm getting out of here!*

3 ways of telling someone to leave

- go away
- get out
- get lost
- beat it/take a hike/bug off

go away /ˌgəʊ əˈweɪ/ *I wish you'd all just go away and leave me alone!* | *Major Ferguson opened a window, and shouted to the waiting reporters: 'You're wasting your time. Go away!'*

get out /ˌget ˈaʊt/ said when you want someone to leave the room, house etc immediately because you are angry with them or because there is some danger: *Get out! Just get out will you? I never want to see you again!* | **get out of here!** *Get out of here and leave me alone!*

get lost ALSO **push off/clear off** British /ˌget ˈlɒst‖-ˈlɔːst, ˌpʊʃ ˈɒf, ˌklɪər ˈɒf/ said when you want someone to go away because they are annoying you: *I've told you before that we don't need our windows cleaning, so just clear off and don't come back!* | *Look, just push off will you. You're getting on my nerves.* | *Get lost you creep! Stop following me.*

beat it/take a hike/bug off /ˈbiːt ɪt, ˌteɪk ə ˈhaɪk, ˌbʌg ˈɒf/ American informal said when you want someone to go away because they are annoying you: *Beat it, you two. I've had enough of you for one day.*

4 to leave at the start of a journey

- leave
- go
- set off
- be off
- depart
- take off
- drive off
- pull out
- (set) sail

leave /liːv/ [v I/T] *I have to leave early tomorrow morning to fly to Detroit.* | *Her plane leaves Hong Kong at 10.00.* | *When are you leaving to go on holiday?* | *When we arrived at the bus station, the bus had just left.* | **+ for** *I'm leaving for Paris on Tuesday.* | **+ from** *Coaches leave from Victoria every hour.*

go /gəʊ/ [v I] especially spoken to leave: *Let's go!* | *The trip is all planned – we're going in September.* | *Do you know what time the next bus goes?* | *I've packed all my bags, and I'm ready to go.*

set off /ˌset ˈɒf/ [phr v I] especially British to leave somewhere and begin a journey: *If we set off early in the morning we should reach the coast before dark.* | **+ for** *We set off for Brighton in good spirits.*

be off /biː ˈɒf/ [v phrase] British informal to leave and begin a journey: *I think we'd better be off now – it'll take at least an hour to get to the airport.* | **+ to** *When are you off to Canada?*

depart /dɪˈpɑːʳt/ [v I] to leave – used especially in official information about times when trains, planes, buses etc leave: *The bus was due to depart at any moment.* | **+ from** *The 12.15 shuttle service to Atlanta will depart from platform 16.* | **+ for** *The 06:33 Pullman will depart from London Euston from platform 4.* | *The train departs Waterloo at 09:00 hours on Saturday.* —**departure** /dɪˈpɑːʳtʃəʳ/ [n C/U] *The departure of flight BA 121 to Milan has been delayed by fog.* | *There are hourly departures to Washington during the week.*

take off /ˌteɪk ˈɒf/ [phr v I] if a plane **takes off**, it leaves the ground at the beginning of a flight: *Children spent hours watching the planes take off and land.* | *This is your Captain speaking. We are due to take off in five minutes.* | **+ from** *Planes were unable to take off from Gatwick owing to high winds.* —**takeoff** /ˈteɪkɒf‖-ɔːf/ [n C/U] *Seat-belts must remain fastened until after takeoff.*

drive off /ˌdraɪv ˈɒf/ [phr v I] to quickly start driving a car away from somewhere: *Eddie ran out of the house, jumped into his car, and drove off.* | *Someone had smashed into her car, and then just driven off.* | *Adrian just had time to see his father jump into the truck and drive off in a cloud of dust.*

pull out /ˌpʊl ˈaʊt/ [phr v I] if a train **pulls out**, it slowly gains speed as it leaves the station at the start of a journey: *We got there just as the train was pulling out.*

(set) sail /(ˌset) ˈseɪl/ [v I] to leave the port at the start of a journey by sea: *Thousands of people stood waving on the quay as the Titanic set sail.* | **+ for** *In November 1928, she set sail for India and arrived in Calcutta seven weeks later.* | **+ from** *It was a bitterly cold morning when we sailed from Dover.*

5 to leave a room or building for a short time

- nip/pop out

nip/pop out British informal **/step out** especially American /ˌnɪp, ˌpɒp ˈaʊt‖ˌpɑːp-, ˌstep ˈaʊt/ [phr v I] to leave a room or building for a short time: *I'm just nipping out to get some milk. Does anyone want anything?* | *She just stepped out for a breath of fresh air.*

6 to leave quickly in order to avoid trouble, danger etc

- run off/away
- shoot off
- not see someone for dust
- make yourself scarce

run off/away /ˌrʌn ˈɒf, əˈweɪ/ [phr v I] *They ran off as soon as they heard the police car coming.* | **+ to** *My brother ran away to South America to escape his debts.* | *Zimmerman was so scared, he just ran off.* | *Why did you run off like that? Was Joey nasty to you?*

shoot off /ˌʃuːt ˈɒf/ [phr v I] British informal to leave a place very quickly, often in order to avoid a difficult situation: *Arthur shot off before anyone could say anything.* | *I've really got to shoot off – I said I'd be home ten minutes ago.*

not see sb for dust /nɒt ˌsiː (sb) fəʳ ˈdʌst/ [v phrase not in progressive] British informal if you **do not see someone for dust**, they leave somewhere very quickly in order to avoid something, especially something that they should stay for: *If you tell him it's his turn to buy the drinks, you won't see him for dust!*

make yourself scarce /ˌmeɪk jɔːʳself 'skeəʳs/ [v phrase] informal to quickly leave a place when something embarrassing or awkward is likely to happen: *You'd better make yourselves scarce before the manager gets here.* | *When Gary and Clare began to argue, Reg decided to make himself scarce.*

7 to leave after doing something wrong or illegal

- escape
- get away
- make your getaway

escape /ɪ'skeɪp/ [v I] to leave after doing something wrong or illegal without being caught: *Police surrounded the building, but somehow the gunman managed to escape.* | **+ from** *He was one of nine men who escaped from prison in July.* | **+ through/by etc** *Four prisoners escaped through a hole in the fence.* | **+ with** *Thieves escaped with jewelry and $130,000 in cash.* —**escape** [n C] *The gang had planned their escape thoroughly.*

get away /ˌget ə'weɪ/ [phr v I] to succeed in leaving after doing something wrong or illegal, especially after being chased: *We ran after the mugger as fast as we could, but he got away.* | *He got away down a back alley.* | **+ with** *Thieves got away with silver and several valuable paintings, including one by Picasso.*

make your getaway /ˌmeɪk jɔːʳ 'getəweɪ/ [v phrase] to leave quickly after a crime, especially in a way that you have arranged: *The robbers made their getaway in a stolen car, which was waiting for them outside the bank.*

8 to leave quietly or secretly

- sneak off/away/out
- slip out/away
- slope off
- slink off/away

sneak off/away/out /ˌsniːk 'ɒf, ə'weɪ, 'aʊt / [phr v I] to leave quietly taking care not to be seen, usually when you want to do something else: *Occasionally she and a friend would sneak off during their free study hour.* | **+ from** *I don't know what he's up to, but he sneaks away from work early every Tuesday.* | **+ to** *Annie had sneaked out to the bar, hoping that her parents wouldn't notice she was gone.*

slip out/away /ˌslɪp 'aʊt, ə'weɪ/ [phr v I] to leave quietly and without being noticed: *Harriet glanced around, wondering if she could slip out unnoticed.* | **+ to do sth** *When everyone was busy talking I slipped away to join Beth for a quiet drink.*

slope off /ˌsləʊp 'ɒf / [phr v I] British informal to leave somewhere quietly and secretly, especially when you are avoiding work: *While the manager was away, Brian took the opportunity to slope off home an hour early every day.* | **+ to** *'Where's Sam?' 'I saw him sloping off to the pub half an hour ago.'*

slink off/away /ˌslɪŋk 'ɒf, ə'weɪ / [phr v I] to leave somewhere quietly, without being seen, especially because you are ashamed or afraid: *Alyssia had dumped her fiancé just two weeks before the wedding, and then slunk off to the south of France.*

9 to leave somewhere angrily

- walk out
- storm out
- flounce out

walk out /ˌwɔːk 'aʊt/ [phr v I] *Furious by now, I walked out, leaving him sitting there shocked and white-faced.*

storm out /ˌstɔːʳm 'aʊt/ [phr v I] to leave a room after a quarrel in a very noisy and angry way: *She yelled at me and stormed out, slamming the door behind her.* | **+ of** *He has been known to storm out of meetings on several occasions.*

flounce out /ˌflaʊns 'aʊt/ [phr v I] if someone, especially a woman, **flounces out** of a room, meeting, restaurant etc, she leaves in a way which shows that she is angry or thinks she has been treated unfairly: *'I'm not putting up with your sexist comments any more,' said Gilly, flouncing out.* | **+ of** *She flounced out of the restaurant, got into her car, and drove off into the night.*

10 to leave unwillingly

- tear/force yourself away
- can't bear to leave/go

tear/force yourself away /ˌteəʳ, ˌfɔːʳs jɔːʳself ə'weɪ/ [v phrase] to leave a place or person very unwillingly because you have to: *The view was so magnificent that it was difficult to tear ourselves away.* | **+ from** *Jake watched as police officers examined the body. It was a horrible sight, but he couldn't tear himself away from it.*

can't bear to leave/go ALSO **find it difficult to leave** /kɑːnt ˌbeəʳ tə 'liːv, 'gəʊ‖kænt-, faɪnd ɪt ˌdɪfɪkəlt tə 'liːv / [v phrase] to feel it is extremely difficult to leave a person or place that you like very much: *Kim couldn't bear to leave Danny, and cried all the way to the airport.* | *Ballesteros has always found it difficult to leave his home in Pedrena.* | **can hardly bear to leave** *We'd had such a great vacation, we could hardly bear to leave.*

11 to make someone leave a room or building

- throw/kick sb out
- show sb the door
- eject

throw/kick sb out ALSO **chuck sb out** British /ˌθrəʊ, ˌkɪk (sb) 'aʊt, ˌtʃʌk (sb) 'aʊt/ [phr v T] informal to make someone leave a room, building etc, especially because they have been behaving badly: *If you don't stop shouting, they'll throw us all out.* | *They got kicked out of the bar for starting a fight.*

show sb the door /ˌʃəʊ (sb) ðə 'dɔːʳ/ [v phrase] to tell someone to leave a building because they have done something that they should not have done or because they are not allowed in there: *A couple of security guards showed me the door after they saw my camera.* | *She lost her temper, started screaming, and was immediately shown the door.*

eject /ɪ'dʒekt/ [v T] British to make someone leave a public place by using force: *The manager threatened to have them ejected if there was any more trouble.* | **+ from** *Several demonstrators were ejected from the hall.*

12 when an army leaves a place, for example after a battle

- retreat
- withdraw
- pull out

retreat /rɪ'triːt/ [v I] if an army or group of soldiers **retreats**, it leaves an area because it is being defeated: *Lieutenant Peterson shouted the order to retreat.* | *In 1443, the Hungarian army advanced into Serbia, and the Turks were forced to retreat.*

—**retreat** [n C] *Napoleon's retreat from Moscow* | **be in retreat** (=be retreating) *An army in retreat can be even more dangerous than one that is advancing.*

withdraw /wɪð'drɔː, wɪθ-/ [v I] to leave an area, either to avoid being defeated or because the fighting has stopped: *As a result of the Paris peace negotiations, most American forces withdrew from Vietnam in 1973.* —**withdrawal** [n C/U] *There are proposals for the immediate withdrawal of federal troops from the province.*

pull out /ˌpʊl 'aʊt/ [phr v I] if an army or group of soldiers **pulls out**, it leaves a place, especially because it might be defeated **+ of** *Troops began pulling out of the region as soon as the order was given.*

13 when a crowd of people leave a place

- disperse
- scatter

disperse /dɪ'spɜːʳs/ [v I] if police or soldiers **disperse** a crowd, or if a crowd **disperses**, all the people in the crowd leave in different directions: *Twenty five officers were injured when police moved in to disperse a crowd of 200-300 youths.* | *The crowd began dispersing as soon as the ambulance had driven away.* | *The arrival of armed police made the students disperse.*

scatter /'skætəʳ/ [v I] if a crowd **scatters**,the people in the crowd leave quickly in different directions, especially because they are frightened: *There was a sudden crack of gunfire, and the crowd scattered.* | *The demonstrators suddenly turned and scattered in all directions.*

to leave your home/country

RELATED WORDS

▸ *see also* **home, country, come from**

14 to permanently leave the house where you live

- leave
- move out
- leave home
- run away
- vacate

leave /liːv/ [v I/T not in passive] to **leave** your home or the area where you live: *This has been such a lovely home – I'll be sorry to leave.* | *He left his hometown when he was 16, and he hasn't been back there since.* | *Thousands of people have already left the capital in order to get away from the fighting.*

move out /ˌmuːv 'aʊt/ [phr v I] to permanently leave your home, usually one you rent or share with someone else, taking all your possessions with you: *If the landlord raises the rent again, we'll just have to move out.* | *Diana and I aren't together any more. I've moved out.* | **+ of** *Tom moved out of his apartment in Toronto last month.*

leave home /ˌliːv 'həʊm/ [v phrase] if a young person **leaves home**, they leave their parents' house because they think they are old enough to live on their own: *Gwen had left home at 18 to find a job in New York.* | *The house is getting too big for us now that both the children have left home.* | *Jane was sure that her decision to leave home and marry Joe was the right one.*

run away /ˌrʌn ə'weɪ/ [phr v I] if a young person **runs away**, they secretly leave their parents' home or the place where they are living because they are very unhappy there: *I ran away at the age of twelve, but my Dad came and found me at the bus station before I could leave town.* | **+ to** *At the age of fifteen, Malcolm ran away to California.* | **run away from home** *Thousands of children run away from home each year.* —**runaway** /'rʌnəweɪ/ [n C] *This hostel helps runaways who don't want to go back to their families.*

vacate /və'keɪt, veɪ-‖'veɪkeɪt/ [v T] a word used especially in hotels, on notices etc meaning to leave the room or house you have been staying in, taking all your possessions with you: *Guests are requested to vacate their rooms before 12 o'clock on the day of departure.*

15 to leave your house and go to live in another one

- move
- move house

move /muːv/ [v I] *We're moving tomorrow, so I won't be at work for a couple of days.* | **+ to** *We're hoping to move to a bigger house by the end of the year.* | *In her early years her family had moved from one town to another, and she had never felt settled anywhere.* —**move** [n C] *Some of our furniture got broken in the move* (=while we were moving).

move house /ˌmuːv 'haʊs/ [v phrase] British to leave your house and go to live in another one: *I'm not looking forward to moving house – it'll be a lot of work.* | *'When are you moving house?' 'Next week, if everything goes to plan.'*

16 to make someone leave the house where they live

- throw/kick sb out
- evict
- give sb notice

throw/kick sb out ALSO **chuck sb out** British /ˌθrəʊ, kɪk (sb) 'aʊt, ˌtʃʌk (sb) 'aʊt/ [phr v T] to force someone to leave the place where they live: *Why were you thrown out of your apartment?* | *Their landlord's threatening to chuck them out.* | **throw sb out on the street** (=make someone leave their home immediately, even if they have nowhere else to go) *She was thrown out on the street when her family discovered she was pregnant.*

evict /ɪ'vɪkt/ [v T] to legally force someone to leave the house where they are living, especially because they should not be there or they have not paid their rent: *If we are evicted, we'll have nowhere to go.* | *They had been evicted for non-payment of rent.* | *Her mother, who has now been evicted from her home too, is staying with friends.* —**eviction** /ɪ'vɪkʃən/ [n C/U] *He faces eviction because he has not paid his rent.*

give sb notice /ˌgɪv (sb) 'nəʊtəs/ [v phrase] to tell someone officially that they must leave the place they are renting by a particular date: *How many weeks' notice does your landlord have to give you?* | **give sb notice to leave/quit** *It came as a complete surprise to them when they were given notice to quit their premises within six days.*

17 to leave your country or the area where you live

- emigrate
- migrate
- exodus

emigrate /ˈemɪgreɪt/ [v I] to leave your own country to live permanently in another country, especially one which is far away: *Millie's brother Dennis, and his wife Joan, decided to emigrate the following year.* | **+ to** *They later got married and emigrated to Australia in 1936.* | **+ from** *My parents emigrated from Britain to New Zealand just before I was born.* —**emigration** /ˌemɪˈgreɪʃən/ [n C/U] *A major reason for emigration was the higher salaries that could be earned in some other countries.*

migrate /maɪˈgreɪt‖ˈmaɪgreɪt/ [v I] if people, birds, or animals **migrate**, they leave their country or area in large numbers, but usually only for a limited period, in order to find food, warmer weather etc: *How do birds know when to migrate, and how do they find their way back home?* | **+ to** *Where there are areas of high unemployment, workers tend to migrate to other, wealthier parts of the country.* —**migration** /maɪˈgreɪʃən/ [n C/U] *Dr Baker has made detailed studies of the migration patterns of many birds.* —**migrant** /ˈmaɪgrənt/ [n C] someone who migrates: *The migrants travelled many miles before finally finding a suitable place to settle.*

exodus /ˈeksədəs/ [n singular] the movement of a large number of people who leave their country, city etc because they do not want to live there any longer, or because it is not safe for them to stay: *The exodus of refugees continued throughout the autumn.* | **mass exodus** (=when almost everyone leaves) *The island is facing a mass exodus of its young people.*

18 to make someone leave a country

- expel
- deport
- extradite
- repatriate
- exile/send into exile
- banish

expel /ɪkˈspel/ [v T] to make a foreigner leave a country because they have broken the law, or for political reasons: *The new government banned books, seized passports, expelled foreigners, and legalized detention without trial.* | **+ from** *Two foreign diplomats were expelled form Ethiopia on March 31.* —**expulsion** /ɪkˈspʌlʃən/ [n C/U] *When war was announced the government called for the immediate expulsion of all foreign journalists from the country.*

deport /dɪˈpɔːʳt/ [v T] if the authorities in a country **deport** a foreign person or a member of a particular race who is living in that country, they force them to leave **+ to** *The man has been deported back to the Irish Republic where he will face terrorism charges.* | **+ from** *Several football supporters were deported from Italy during the World Cup.* —**deportation** /ˌdiːpɔːʳˈteɪʃən/ [n C/U] *The US government has ordered his deportation.*

extradite /ˈekstrədaɪt/ [v T] to officially send someone back to another country where they are believed to have committed a crime, in order to be tried in a court of law: *The drug baron was extradited to the United States from Colombia.* | *Spanish authorities are seeking to have the couple extradited to answer further charges.* —**extradition** /ˌekstrəˈdɪʃən/ [n C/U] *The US government is seeking the extradition of the two men to face charges in the 2001 hijacking attacks.*

repatriate /riːˈpætrieɪt‖riːˈpeɪ-/ [v T] to officially send someone back to their home country, often by force and against their will: *Italy is using military helicopters to repatriate 292 Albanian refugees.* | *There was to be a cease-fire, and all prisoners of war were to be repatriated.* —**repatriation** /ˌriːpætriˈeɪʃən‖-peɪ-/ [n U] *A spokesman said that forced repatriation was unlikely to start before November.*

exile/send into exile /ˈeksaɪl, ˌsend ɪntʊ ˈeksaɪl/ [v T] to make someone leave their country for political reasons, for example because they oppose the government and are fighting against it: *The leader of the coup was exiled and the others imprisoned.* | *The Prince and his family were sent into exile after the revolution.* —**exile** [n C] *a radio station run by Cuban exiles in the United States* —**live/be in exile** [v phrase] *For many years she lived in exile in France.*

banish /ˈbænɪʃ/ [v T] to send someone away permanently from their country or from the area where they live, as an official punishment **+ to** *Napoleon was banished to the island of St Helena in 1815.*

to leave a school or college

RELATED WORDS

▸ *see also* **school/university**

19 to permanently leave your school, college etc

- leave
- graduate
- drop out

leave /liːv/ [v I/T not in passive] *I hated school and couldn't wait to leave.* | *I worked in an office when I first left school.* | *In the past, girls tended to leave full-time education earlier than boys.*

graduate /ˈgrædʒueɪt/ [v I] to successfully finish your studies at a university or at an American high school or college: *What are you going to do after you graduate?* | *When I graduate I want to study law at the Northeastern university.* | **+ from** *We both graduated from the same high school in Queens.*

drop out /ˌdrɒp ˈaʊt‖ˌdrɑːp-/ [phr v I] to leave school, college, or university before your course of study has finished and have no intention of returning **college/high-school dropout** *One third of the city's students drop out before graduation.* | **+ of** *He dropped out of art college and joined a band.*

20 someone who leaves school or college

- school-leaver
- dropout

school-leaver /ˈskuːl ˌliːvəʳ/ [n C] British someone who has left or who is going to leave school, college, or university, especially someone who is looking for a job: *Most towns have a careers service to help school-leavers find suitable jobs.* | *Fashion retailer seeks Sales Assistant – would suit enthusiastic school-leaver.*

dropout /ˈdrɒpaʊt‖ˈdrɑːp-/ [n C] someone who has left school, college or university before their course of study has finished and who has no intention of returning **high-school/college dropout** *His mother is a high-school dropout, trying to raise four children on less than $500 a month.*

21 to make someone leave school or college

- expel
- throw/kick out
- exclude

expel /ɪkˈspel/ [v T] to make someone leave school or college permanently because they have behaved badly **expel sb for sth** *The principal expelled John for stealing.* | **get/be expelled** *If they catch you dealing drugs, you'll get expelled.* —**expulsion** /ɪk'spʌlʃən/ [n C/U] *The threat of expulsion was enough to frighten the girls into improving their behaviour.* | *There have been five expulsions in this academic year alone.*

throw/kick out ALSO **chuck out** British /ˌθrəʊ, ˌkɪk 'aʊt, ˌtʃʊk 'aʊt/ [phr v T] informal to make someone leave school, college, or university permanently because of bad behaviour or for failing examinations: *She said she'd kick us out if she caught us doing it again.* | **+ of** *Do your parents know you've been kicked out of school yet?* | *He got chucked out of the LSE.*

exclude /ɪk'skluːd/ [v T] to officially say that a student can no longer attend his or her school, either for a short time or permanently, as a punishment for bad behaviour: *The report concluded that far more boys were excluded each year than girls.* | *The governing body decided to exclude Declan for two weeks.* | **+ from** *Kids who are excluded from school often end up getting into trouble with the police.* —**exclusion** [n C/U] *There is concern about the growing number of school exclusions in the area.* | *Exclusion – especially permanent exclusion – should only be used as a very last resort.*

to leave a job or organization

RELATED WORDS

opposite: —— **join**

▸ *see also* **job, organization, army, member**

22 to leave a job or organization

- leave
- quit
- resign
- retire
- hand in your notice/resignation
- pack/jack it in

leave /liːv/ [v I/T] *'Where's Marcia?' 'Oh, she left last week to have her baby.'* | *The directors did not want Daniel to leave, but they knew he could earn much more somewhere else.* | *I left my last job because I couldn't get along with my boss.* | *Chamberlain was a Cabinet Minister until he left the Liberal party in 1886.* | *After leaving the Navy, he started a new career in journalism.*

quit /kwɪt/ [v I/T] to leave a job or organization especially because you are not happy with it, or because you think you could do better somewhere else: *I've had enough of the way I'm treated here – I quit!* | *She quite her job and went traveling in South America.* | **+ as** *Harkness quit as director of the Olympic Regional Development Authority soon afterwards.*

resign /rɪ'zaɪn/ [v I/T] to officially and permanently leave a job, for example because you are no longer happy with it, or because the people you work with do not think you are doing it properly: *Nixon was the first US President to resign before the end of his term of office.* | *I wanted to resign, but my boss persuaded me to stay.* | **+ from** *She resigned from the board after profits fell by a further 3%.* | *Roberts replaces Jacob Winters, who resigned from the firm last month.* | **+ as** *The following years, he resigned as chairman of the committee.* | **resign your post/position** *The manager was forced to resign his post after allegations of corruption.* —**resignation** /ˌrezɪg'neɪʃən/ [n C/U] *There have been several calls for the Chancellor's resignation.*

retire /rɪ'taɪəʳ/ [v I] to permanently leave your job, usually because you have reached the age when most people stop working: *In the UK, men usually retire in their late 50s or early 60s.* | *If you retire at 50, you won't get your full pension.* | **+ from** *When Jean retired from modelling, she moved to Cornwall.* | *Jim Rutland retired from the Navy last year.* | **+ as** *He retired as Principal ten years ago, but still does a lot of fund-raising for the school.* —**retirement** [n U] *The people who cope best with retirement are those who have a number of hobbies and interests to occupy their time.* | **on (sb's) retirement** (=when someone retires) *On his retirement Mr Willis received a gold watch from his colleagues.* | **take early retirement** (=retire at a younger age than usual, especially when your company offers to pay for you to do this) *The number of teachers taking early retirement rose from 7,574 to 12,343 during the same period.*

hand in your notice/resignation /ˌhænd ɪn jɔːʳ 'nəʊtɪ̆s, ˌrezɪg'neɪʃən/ [v phrase] to write an official letter to your employer saying that you are going to leave your job on a particular date: *You have to hand in your notice at least four weeks before you leave.* | *The Foreign Minister officially handed in his resignation on December 11th.*

pack/jack it in /ˌpæk, ˌdʒæk ɪt 'ɪn/ [v phrase] British informal to leave your job, especially because you are bored with it: *Look if it's such a boring job, why don't you just jack it in?* | *Sometimes I feel like packing it all in and going off on a round-the-world trip.*

23 when someone is forced to leave their job

- lose your job
- fire
- sack/give sb the sack
- lay off
- make sb redundant
- redundancy
- suspend
- give sb (their) notice
- relieve sb of their duties/post

lose your job /ˌluːz jɔːʳ 'dʒɒb‖-'dʒɑːb/ [v phrase] *After she lost her job, she got more and more depressed and started drinking heavily.* | *Many people won't complain about pay and conditions because they're terrified of losing their jobs.* —**job losses** [n plural] when people are made to leave their jobs because their company can no longer afford to employ them – used especially in newspapers, on television etc: *The company announced 22,000 job losses over the next two years.* | *They're meeting to decide how to prevent further job losses.*

fire ALSO **dismiss** formal /faɪəʳ, dɪs'mɪs/ [v T] to make someone leave their job, especially because they have done something wrong: *He was just impossible to work with, and in the end they fired him.* | *Harris was caught stealing, and was dismissed immediately.* | *You're fired!* | **fire/dismiss sb for sth** *She was fired for serious professional misconduct.* | **+ from** *When Max was fired from his job the whole family had to pack up and leave town.* | *A New York art teacher who refused to take part in the daily flag ceremony was dismissed from her post.* —**dismissal** [n C/U] *She is claiming it is a case of unfair dismissal.*

sack sb/give sb the sack /'sæk (sb), ˌgɪv (sb) ðə 'sæk/ [v T/v phrase] British to make someone leave their job, for example, because they are not good enough at it, they are no longer needed, or they have done something wrong: *We can't really give him the sack just because he's unpopular.* | **sack sb for sth** *He was sacked for being drunk in the office.* | **get the sack** (=be sacked) *He had the good luck to work in an* *old family firm when nobody ever got the sack.* —**sacking** [n C] *Thompson told how his sacking had been a terrible shock that had left him feeling completely devastated.*

lay off /ˌleɪ ˈɒf / [phr v T] to make workers, especially workers in a large factory or organization, leave their jobs, because there is not enough work for them to do, or not enough money to pay their wages **lay off sb/lay sb off** *3000 car workers have been laid off at the factory in Cleveland.*

make sb redundant /ˌmeɪk (sb) rɪˈdʌndənt/ [v phrase] British to make someone leave their job, and usually pay them some money to do so, because they are no longer needed: *At least 2,000 computer programmers have been made redundant in the past year.* | *We lost our home when my husband was made redundant five years ago.*

redundancy /rɪˈdʌndənsi/ [n C/U] British a situation in which someone has to leave their job, and is usually paid some money to do so, because they are no longer needed by their company: *These redundancies are necessary for the company to be able to survive.* | *The board are planning a restructuring which could mean hundreds of redundancies.* | **voluntary redundancy** (=when a company asks workers if they want to leave their jobs, and offers to pay them money to do so) *We hope to achieve staffing cuts through voluntary redundancy and a freeze on recruitment.*

suspend /səˈspend/ [v T] to make someone leave a job or organization temporarily, either as a punishment for doing something wrong, or while the organization tries to find out whether they have done something wrong or not: *Two senior officials have been suspended on full pay pending a second internal inquiry.* | **+ from** *The Police Department has suspended six officers from duty while they investigate claims of fraud and corruption.*

give sb (their) notice /ˌgɪv (sb) (ðeəʳ) ˈnəʊtɪ̆s/ [v phrase] to tell someone that they must leave their job, either immediately or in a week, a month etc: *The company are planning to close down, and we've all been given two weeks' notice.* | *In the course of restructuring, over half the workforce were given their notice.*

relieve sb of their duties/post /rɪˌliːv (sb) əv ðeəʳ ˈdjuːtiz, ˈpəʊst‖-ˈduː-/ [v phrase] if someone with an important official job **is relieved of their duties** or **post**, their job is taken away from them, especially for a short time because people think they have done something very bad and this is being checked: *The Chief Inspector has been relieved of his duties pending another investigation by fellow officers.* | *The authorities have decided to relieve the professor of his post at the university until further notice, after complaints were made by one of his female students.*

24 to make someone leave a political party etc

- expel
- throw/kick out

expel /ɪkˈspel/ [v T] to officially make someone leave an organization, especially because they have done something wrong or harmful to the organization: *They threatened to expel him if he didn't follow the party line.* | **+ from** *In May the Nationalists were expelled from the government.*

throw/kick out ALSO **chuck out** British /ˌθrəʊ, ˌkɪk ˈaʊt, ˌtʃʌk ˈaʊt/ [phr v T] informal to officially make someone leave an organization, especially because they have done something wrong or harmful to the organization: *At the age of fourteen she was kicked out of the Young Communist League.* | *They are relying on the fact that Britain cannot be thrown out of the European Union.*

25 something that is given when someone leaves

- leaving
- farewell

leaving ALSO **farewell** American /ˈliːvɪŋ, feəʳˈwel/ [adj only before noun] **leaving party/present/gift/card etc** a party etc that is arranged for or given to someone who is **leaving** their job: *Are you going to Katie's leaving party on Friday?* | *She received a beautiful Waterford Crystal clock as a farewell present from all her colleagues.*

farewell /ˌfeəʳˈwel◂/ [adj only before noun] **farewell speech/dinner etc** a speech, dinner etc that happens because someone is leaving somewhere, especially when this is a formal or officially organized event: *A farewell dinner was given in her honour.* | *Eisenhower's farewell address to the American people*

26 when someone leaves the army, air force, or navy

- desert
- discharge
- go AWOL

desert /dɪˈzɜːʳt/ [v I] to leave the army, air force, or navy without permission: *The three men had tried to desert, but were brought back to camp and shot.* | **+ from** *He obtained the grenades from a friend who had deserted from the army.* —**desertion** /dɪˈzɜːʳʃən/ [n U] *The punishment for desertion* (=leaving the army etc without permission) *was death.* —**deserter** [n C] *a US Army deserter*

go AWOL /gəʊ ˌeɪ ˌdʌbəljuː əʊ ˈel, ˈeɪwɒl‖-ˈeɪwɔːl/ [v phrase] informal to leave your army unit without permission, often for a short period of time: *He went AWOL while on duty in Northern Ireland.*

discharge /dɪsˈtʃɑːʳdʒ/ [v T] to allow or force someone to leave the army, air force, or navy: *When Danny was discharged in 1961, he went to Los Angeles, looking for work.* | **+ from** *He lost both his legs in an explosion and was discharged from the navy.* —**discharge** /ˈdɪstʃɑːʳdʒ/ [n C] official permission to leave: *Tony wanted to get married as soon as he got his discharge from the army.*

to leave a relationship

RELATED WORDS

- *see also* **relationship**

27 to leave your husband, wife, girlfriend etc

- leave
- desert
- walk out
- abandon
- run/go off with

leave /liːv/ [v I/T] *She promised faithfully that she would never leave him.* | **leave sb for sb else** *Simon has left me for his secretary, after fifteen years of marriage.*

walk out /ˌwɔːk ˈaʊt/ [phr v I] to suddenly leave your husband, wife, girlfriend etc in a way that they think is unfair: *I was three months pregnant when Peter walked out.* | **+ on** *She remembered the day her* *father had walked out on them and how her mother had just sat on the stairs and cried.*

run/go off with /ˌrʌn, ˌgəʊ 'ɒf wɪð/ [phr v T] to suddenly leave your husband or wife in order to live with someone else and have a sexual relationship with them: *His wife ran off with one of the doctors at the hospital.*

desert /dɪ'zɜːʳt/ [v T] to leave your family, husband, children etc to avoid the responsibility of looking after them: *Mrs Hasan was deserted by her husband and had to support four children on her own.* | *His father had deserted the family when Graham was three years old.* —**deserted** [adj only before noun] *a deserted wife with two children, living on income support*

abandon /ə'bændən/ [v T] to leave someone who depends on you for support, especially a child or animal: *The baby was found abandoned outside a local mosque.* | *My sister abandoned her husband and three children and went to live in Holland.* | *a home for abandoned kittens and puppies*

28 to make a husband, wife, girlfriend etc leave

- **throw/kick out**

throw/kick out ALSO **chuck out** British /ˌθrəʊ, ˌkɪk 'aʊt, ˌtʃʌk 'aʊt/ [phr v T] informal to make someone such as your husband, wife etc leave because they have hurt you, made you angry etc: *He threw her out when he heard she was seeing other guys.*

legal

RELATED WORDS

opposite: **illegal**

- *see also* **law, crime, let/allow, official**

1 allowed by law

- **legal**
- **lawful**
- **legitimate**
- **above board**
- **within the law**
- **legality**

legal /'liːgəl/ [adj] something that is **legal** is allowed by law: *This trade in foreign currency is perfectly legal.* | **become legal** *Divorce finally became legal in 1992.* | *Over 3,000 gay couples have married since it became legal for them to do so last year.* | **legal tender** (=forms of money that are legally accepted) *In Maastricht, Dutch Guilders, Deutschmarks and Belgian Francs are all considered legal tender.* —**legally** [adv] *Fuchs had entered the country legally on a tourist visa.* | *The committee will investigate whether the funds were obtained legally.*

lawful /'lɔːfəl/ [adj] formal actions or methods that are **lawful** are allowed by law, especially as compared with actions or methods that are not legal: *Protesters must only use lawful methods of opposing the government.* | **it is lawful to do sth** *It is lawful to employ someone under the age of sixteen if their parents agree.* | *The FBI will use all reasonable and lawful means to gather intelligence information.* | *'Do you take this woman to be your lawful wedded wife?' intoned the priest. 'I do,' murmured Carlos.* —**lawfully** [adv] *When you claim Social Security benefits, you must prove that you are lawfully resident in this country.*

legitimate /lɪ̆'dʒɪtɪ̆mɪ̆t/ [adj] **legitimate** activities, organizations, or claims are done or work according to, normal laws and rules: *He is a criminal who runs a legitimate business as well.* | *Tobacco smuggling into the UK is seriously affecting the profits of legitimate importers.* | *How can I be sure that an online business is legitimate?* | *At least three of the dead woman's relatives have a legitimate claim to her house.* | *The government has refused to recognise the far-right group as a legitimate political party.*

above board /əˌbʌv 'bɔːʳd/ [adj phrase not before noun] an activity or a way of doing business that is **above board** is done legally, even if it may seem slightly dishonest: *He assured us that the insurance claim was honest and above board, but I'm not so sure.* | *I'm sure Peggy wouldn't let anything happen that wasn't perfectly open and above board.*

within the law /wɪðˌɪn ðə 'lɔː/ [adv] **act/keep/stay/remain/operate within the law** to make sure that what you do is legal: *He makes tough business deals, but he makes sure he always stays within the law.* | *Security forces must not only act within the law, but must be seen to do so.* | *Building contractors must operate within the law by ensuring that an acceptable standard of work is carried out.*

legality /lɪ'gælɪ̆ti/ [n U] formal whether something is legal or not **the legality of sth** *The European Court will decide on the legality of his claim.* | *The union immediately challenged the legality of the decision.* | **be of dubious/questionable/uncertain legality** (=when it is not clear whether something is legal or not) *The Appeal Court judge said that his conviction was of dubious legality.* | *This was the first of several actions that were of questionable legality, and which eventually led to his resignation.*

2 when the law says you must do something or have the right to do it

- **legal**
- **statutory**
- **constitutional**
- **according to the law**
- **by law**

legal /'liːgəl/ [adj only before noun] your **legal** rights, duties etc are the ones that the law says you have: *Consumers have the legal right to demand their money back if a product is faulty.* | *the legal duties of a parent* | *The alcohol content of his blood was three times over the legal limit.* | *The clerk to the court will reject any document that does not meet the legal requirements.* | **the legal owner** (=the owner according to the law) *She now become the legal owner of the land.* —**legally** [adv] according to the law: *If there is an accident, the owner of the vehicle will be legally responsible.* | *When does the contract become legally binding?* | **legally authorized/obliged/able etc** *Is my live-in girlfriend legally entitled to a share of the proceeds from the sale of the house?* | *Employers are legally obliged to consult trade unions about any redundancy proposals.*

statutory /'stætʃə̆təri‖-tɔːri/ [adj only before noun] **statutory right/duty/payment etc** a right, duty etc that the law says you have: *When you buy something, you have certain statutory rights as a consumer.* | *Local authorities have a statutory duty to house homeless families.* | *Officers have a statutory obligation to report any crime committed by a government employee.* | *The statutory fine for this offence is $250.*

constitutional /ˌkɒnstɪ̆'tjuːʃənəl◂‖ˌkɑːnstɪ̆'tuː-/ [adj] legal, according to the system of rules of a country: *Nobody seemed to know whether the President's action was constitutional or not.* | *A court decision in 1954 ruled that segregated education was not constitutional.* | **constitutional rights** *The court will rule on whether the prisoner's constitutional* *rights were violated.* —**constitutionally** [adv] *Although unusual, the Governor's action was constitutionally quite correct.*

according to the law /ə,kɔːʳdɪŋ tə ðə 'lɔː/ [adv] if something is done **according to the law**, it is done as the law says it should be: *The police must ensure that all interviews and interrogations are carried out according to the law.* | *Islamic court officials said the men would be tried according to Sharia Muslim law.* | *According to Singapore law, the immigration officers were within their rights to refuse me admission.*

by law /baɪ 'lɔː/ [adv] if something must be done **by law**, it must legally be done: *By law, the purchase must be completed within a month after the contracts are signed.* | **be required/allowed by law** *The wearing of seat belts in cars is required by law.* | *Donations must not exceed the limits that are allowed by law.* | *The government is required by law to provide education for all minors.*

3 to make something legal

- legalize
- make sth legal
- decriminalize
- legitimize

legalize ALSO **legalise** British /'liːgəlaɪz/ [v T] to change the law so that something becomes legal: *a campaign to legalise cannabis* | *Denmark recently legalized marriage between gay couples.* —**legalization** /,liːgəlaɪ'zeɪʃən‖-gələ-/ [n U] *calls for the legalization of voluntary euthanasia*

make sth legal /,meɪk (sth) 'liːgəl/ [v phrase] *57% of people wanted abortion to be made legal.* | *In November, marijuana was made legal for people with a recognized medical condition.* | **make it legal to do sth** *Texas law makes it legal to carry a concealed weapon.*

decriminalize ALSO **decriminalise** British /,diː'krɪmɪ̇nəlaɪz/ [v T] to make an illegal activity no longer a crime, so that the people who do it can no longer be punished by law: *Plenty of men and women think prostitution should be decriminalized.* | *He has openly said that he favours decriminalizing soft drugs.* —**decriminalization** /diː,krɪmɪ̇nəlaɪ'zeɪʃən‖-nələ-/ [n U] *the decriminalization of so-called 'recreational' drugs*

legitimize ALSO **legitimise** British /lɪ'dʒɪtɪ̇maɪz/ [v T] to change the law so that something someone is already doing, especially something morally wrong, is made legal: *He played a brief part in legitimizing black slavery.* | *Uganda's constitution still legitimized discrimination on the grounds of sex.* | *The National Salvation Front took power, later trying to legitimize its position with elections.*

lend

to let someone use something that they will give back to you later

RELATED WORDS

opposite: **borrow**
- *see also* **money, give, owe**

1 to lend something to someone

- lend
- let sb use/let sb have
- be on loan
- give sb a loan
- give sb the use/loan of
- loan a painting/work of art etc

lend ALSO **loan** especially American, spoken /lend, ləʊn/ [v T] to let someone have money which they will pay back later, or let them use something that is yours, which they will give back to you later **lend/loan sb sth** *Can you lend me $20?* | *I wish I'd never lent him my car.* | *We loaned him ten bucks, but he never paid it back.* | **lend/loan sth to sb** *Did you lend that book to Mike?* | *I lent my penknife to someone, but I can't remember who it was now.* | *The camera had been loaned to him by his cousin.*

let sb use/let sb have /,let (sb) 'juːz, ,let (sb) 'hæv/ [v phrase] to let someone use something that belongs to you, for a short time, especially something such as a room, a house, or something large or expensive: *Some friends are letting us use their house while they are on vacation.* | *I asked whether she'd let me use her skis, and she said no.* | *Jim was going to let me have his car while he's away, but he's changed his mind.*

be on loan /biː ɒn 'ləʊn/ [v phrase] something that **is on loan**, especially a library book or a painting, has been lent to a person or organization: *Is this your video or is it on loan?* | **+ from** *The museum has an exhibition of paintings on loan from the Louvre.* | **+ to** *It's a digital tape recorder, and it's on loan to me.* | **be out on loan** *If you type in the title, the computer tells you how many copies the library has, and whether they're out on loan.*

give sb a loan /,gɪv (sb) ə 'ləʊn/ [v phrase] to lend someone some money: *I thought Dad might give me a loan to set me up in business again.* | *'I can't afford it, it's too expensive.' 'Do you want me to give you a loan?'* | *The bank wouldn't give me a loan because they said I had a bad credit rating.*

give sb the use/loan of /,gɪv (sb) ðə 'juːs, 'ləʊn ɒv/ [v phrase] to allow someone to use something large such as a house or car, especially for a fixed period of time: *Mohammed's giving me the use of his office until I can find a place of my own.* | *We persuaded the manager to give us free loan of the room and equipment for rehearsals.* | *She was given the use of the church hall to hold the event.*

loan a painting/work of art etc /,ləʊn ə 'peɪntɪŋ / [v phrase] to lend a painting, work of art etc to a place where it can be shown to the public: *The gallery is currently exhibiting nine bronze statues loaned by the Victoria and Albert Museum.* | **loan sth to sb** *The Museum of Modern Art has agreed to loan its entire Warhol collection to the exhibition.* | *According to the agreement, the Monet painting is to be retained in France and loaned to the Musée d'Orsay for a limited period.* | **loaned from sb** *Visitors will be able to examine original documents loaned from the British Museum.*

2 to lend houses, land, machines etc for money

- rent out
- lease
- let
- hire out

rent out ALSO **rent** [v T] American /,rent 'aʊt, rent/ [phr v T] to allow someone to use a house, piece of land, vehicle etc that belongs to you, in exchange for money: *We rent cars by the hour, to save you money.* | *Some caterers will rent equipment and supplies for parties at a reasonable cost.* | **rent sth (out) to sb** *I'm thinking of renting the upstairs rooms to students.* | *The field at the back of the house is rented out to a local farmer.* | **rent sb sth** *We can rent you a luxury apartment for the duration of your stay.* | *I'm sorry, I've had an accident in the car you rented me this morning.* | **rent (out) sth (to sb)** *Mike raised some* *cash by renting out the two small workshops to local craftsmen.*

lease /liːs/ [v T] to allow a company, organization etc to use buildings, land, or equipment for a fixed period of time, in exchange for money **lease sth to sb** *The company plans to sell or lease its remaining stores to other supermarkets.* | *The aircraft had been leased to a Nigerian airline.* | **lease sb sth** *Internet start-ups are being helped by companies willing to lease them Web servers and space.*

let British **/rent** American /let, rent/ [v T] to allow someone to use a room, house, or office in exchange for money **let/rent sth to sb** *We usually rent our house to someone over the long vacation.* | *200,00 sq ft of land was let to a local firm.* | **let/rent out sth** British *We even had to rent out the garage to make ends meet.* | *The company owns about 170 cottages in Britain, which it lets out to tourists.* | **let/rent sth out** *Many residents hoped to rent their houses out during the Games.* | **To Let** British **/For Rent** American (=written on a sign to show that a room, house, or office is empty and can be rented) *Nellie's house had a 'To Let' sign in the window.*

hire out /ˌhaɪər ˈaʊt/ [phr v T] British to allow someone to use something such as a vehicle or clothes for a short period of time, in exchange for money **hire out sth** *They were partners in a business which hired out photocopiers.* | *Do you hire out golf clubs here?* | **hire sth/it/them out** *Brooke bought a Rolls Royce and started hiring it out for special occasions.*

3 a person or organization that lends money

- lender
- creditor
- loan-shark

lender /ˈlendəʳ/ [n C] a person or organization that lends money: *Despite competition from the building societies, banks are still the biggest lenders in Britain.* | *Mexico has borrowed heavily from private banks, the World Bank, and other international lenders.* | *Newspaper ads can be helpful in finding the lender with the most favourable interest rates.* | **mortgage/housing lender** (=an organization that lends people money to buy a house, flat etc) *Prudential is the fourth largest mortgage lender in the US.*

creditor /ˈkredɪ̇təʳ/ [n C] a person or business that is owed money by another person or business: *The failed company is currently in talks with its creditors.* | *He died owing his creditors over $20 million.*

loan-shark /ˈləʊn ʃɑːʳk/ [n C] informal a person or small business that lends money, at extremely high interest rates – use this when you disapprove of people who make money in this way: *His father killed himself after getting deeply in debt to a loan-shark.* | *These loan-sharks target the vulnerable, the people who are least able to pay the money back.*

4 money that is lent to someone

- loan

loan /ləʊn/ [n C] an amount of money that someone borrows: *The bank offered him a loan of £15,000 to set up a business.* | *He received hundreds of dollars in loans from the financial institutions.* | **bank loan** (=a loan from a bank) *a long-term bank loan* | **personal loan** (=a loan given to a person for their own use, rather than to a business) *Take out a Midland personal loan now and pay the money back in easy stages.* | **business loan** (=a loan to help someone start a business) *We have a full range of business loans to suit your needs.* | **student loan** (=a loan that the government gives to a student while they are at college or university) *Failure to repay a student loan can ruin that person's credit rating.* | **take out a loan** *She survived by taking out a bank loan and working extra hours.* | **repay a loan** *Mexico repaid its US loans through a successful program of economic reform.* | **+ to** *attempts to increase the safety of loans to foreign countries*

less

RELATED WORDS

opposite: **more**

▸ *see also* **reduce, least**

1 a smaller amount or number

- less
- fewer
- not as much/not so much
- not as many/not so many
- lower
- be in the/a minority

less /les/ [quantifier] a smaller amount of something. **Less** is used with uncountable nouns: *I earn less money now than I did then.* | *Surgery patients now spend much less time in the hospital.* | *Statistics show that nowadays people drink less beer and smoke fewer cigarettes than they used to.* | **+ than** *He always travels by bus because it costs less than travelling by train.* | *Clive knows even less than I do about this business.* | *It's a bit less than a mile from here to the station.* | **far less/a lot less** *As a result of these improvements, the car uses far less fuel.* | **+ of** *Studies show that people who receive medication when their pain first starts need less of it than people who wait longer.* | **less and less** (=when an amount keeps getting smaller as time passes) *As the drought became worse, there was less and less food available.*

fewer /ˈfjuːəʳ/ [quantifier] a smaller number of people or things. **Fewer** is used with countable nouns: *Schools in the suburbs have fewer discipline problems and better student attitudes.* | *Spending cuts will mean fewer social workers.* | **+ than** *No reservations are needed for groups of fewer than 15.* | **far fewer/a lot fewer** *There were far fewer women at the conference this year than last.* | **fewer and fewer** *Since 1985, fewer and fewer people have been drinking decaffeinated coffee, and the trend shows no signs of halting.*

not as much/not so much /nɒt əz ˈmʌtʃ, nɒt səʊ ˈmʌtʃ/ [quantifier] less than an amount. **Not as much** and **not so much** are used with uncountable nouns.: *There's a lot of snow on the upper slopes of the mountain, but there's not so much down here.* | **+ as** *The Chinese don't eat as much meat as Americans do.* | *Jim worked hard, but didn't earn as much money as he wanted.* | **+ of** *I didn't eat as much of the fish as Al, but I still got sick.*

not as many/not so many /nɒt əz ˈmeni, nɒt səʊ ˈmeni/ [quantifier] fewer than a number of people or things. **Not as many** and **not so many** are used with countable nouns: *'Last year our gift shop did very well,' said Amy. 'But this year we haven't had as many customers coming through the door.'* | *Law firms aren't hiring as many associates this year.* | *I don't own nearly as many clothes as my sister.* | *If I get milk and orange juice from the milkman, I don't need to make as many trips to the grocery store.*

lower /ˈləʊəʳ/ [adj] less than another number or level – use this about prices, wages, temperatures, grades, and other things that can be measured on a scale from high to low: *Foreign workers have fewer rights and get lower wages.* | *The program is broadcast in the morning, a time when advertising rates are much lower.* | **+ than** *I got lower grades than the other students in my class.*

be in the/a minority /biː ɪn ðə, ə maɪˈnɒrɨti ‖-məˈnɔː-/ [v phrase] if people of a particular type **are in the minority** in a particular group, they form less than half of the total group: *In the boardrooms of most big corporations, women are in the minority.* | *Quentin's supporters were clearly in a minority as the City Council heard arguments for his dismissal.*

2 less than a number or amount

- less than
- under
- below
- lower
- within
- minus

less than /ˈles ðən/ [prep] *Some of the miners were earning less than $2 an hour.* | *There she was, less than ten feet away from me, walking past with the other guests of honour.* | **for less than** *The average income here is far less than the national average.*

under /ˈʌndəʳ/ [prep] less than a particular age, price, amount, or number: *Children under 16 will not be admitted without an adult.* | *Where can you get a meal for under $5?* | **well under** *The stock market's highest point this week was well under what was predicted.*

below /bɪˈləʊ/ [prep] less than a particular temperature, speed, limit, or level: *At night, the temperature is often below freezing.* | **fall below sth** (=become less than) *The inflation rate has fallen below 6%.* | **far/well below** *The school's test scores are far below average.*

lower /ˈləʊəʳ/ [adj] a **lower** figure, amount, rate, level etc is less than the one you have already mentioned: *They rejected our estimate and suggested a lower figure.* | *There's no doubt that lower energy prices are having some short-term impact on the stock market.* | **+ than** *The divorce rate in Japan is much lower than in the U.S.*

within /wɪðˈɪn‖wɪðˈɪn, wɪθˈɪn/ [prep] at some point that is less than a particular period of time, distance, or limit: *The top prize is a trip to Hawaii, which must be taken within a year of the prize drawing.* | *Pupils living within two miles of the school are expected to pay their own bus fares.*

minus /ˈmaɪnəs/ [prep] **minus five/ten/twenty etc** use this about numbers that are less than zero or temperatures that are below zero degrees: *When we take away points for hitting obstacles, you get a final score of minus seven.* | *Tonight's low temperatures could reach minus twenty degrees in some areas.*

3 less interesting, expensive, difficult, exciting etc

- not as
- less

not as /ˈnɒt əz/ [adv] *Their first album sold over a million copies, but the second one wasn't as popular.* | **not as ... as** *It's not as cold as it was yesterday.* | *The beef was good, but it wasn't as tender as the chicken.* | *'How was the test?' 'Not as bad as I expected.'*

less /les/ [adv] *Of course, it would be less expensive to use frozen fish.* | **less ... than** *I want something less formal than a traditional wedding dress.* | **less and less** (=becoming less interesting, expensive etc all the time) *With the growth of telecommunications, the location of a company's headquarters is becoming less and less important.*

4 when something happens less than before

- less
- not as much

less /les/ [adv] **+ than** *This type of problem still occurs, but less than it did in the past.* | **a lot less** *Since we got the car, we walk a lot less than we used to.* | **less and less** (=when something keeps getting less as time passes) *He seemed to care less and less about the band, and eventually decided to leave.*

not as much /nɒt əz ˈmʌtʃ/ *Stan probably won't need to travel as much in his new job.* | **+ as** *'Do you still go swimming?' 'Not as much as I used to.'*

5 when prices, numbers etc become less

- go down/come down
- fall/drop
- decrease
- decline
- reduction
- cut
- plummet/plunge
- taper off
- dwindle
- slide
- take a nosedive

go down/come down /ˌgəʊ ˈdaʊn, ˌkʌm ˈdaʊn/ [phr v I] to become less: *Attendance at the school's basketball games has gone down significantly in the last few years.* | *I'm hoping the price will come down if I wait a while.*

fall/drop /fɔːl, drɒp‖drɑːp/ [v I] to become less, especially by a large amount: *Sales have fallen dramatically in Houston and Toronto.* | **+ to** *At night, the temperature drops to -20°C.* | **fall/drop from sth to sth** *Profits fell from £98.5 million to £76 million.* —**fall/drop** [n singular] **+ in** *The airline may be forced to make cutbacks because of a 15 percent fall in revenue* (=revenue has gone down by 15%). | *a sudden drop in the number of student nurses* | **a sharp fall/drop** (=when an amount goes down a lot and very suddenly) *a sharp fall in profits*

decrease /dɪˈkriːs/ [v I] to become less – used especially in writing about business or technical subjects: *Experts say that the time parents spend with their children is decreasing.* | **+ to** *The speed of rotation gradually decreases to zero.* —**decrease** /ˈdiːkriːs/ [n C] **+ in** *a 5 percent decrease in the value of the dollar* (=it goes down by 5%) **a significant/marked decrease** (=when something happens much less than it used to) *a significant decrease in the number of deaths from heart disease* —**decreasing** [adj only before noun] *decreasing levels of carbon dioxide in the air*

decline /dɪˈklaɪn/ [n C usually singular] a gradual decrease in the number or amount of something good or important so that the situation becomes worse: *Firms with large debts may not have the financial strength to survive a prolonged sales decline or a recession.* | **+ in** *We can expect a further decline in job vacancies.*

reduction /rɪˈdʌkʃən/ [n C] when a price, level etc is reduced – use this when something is reduced deliberately: *New production methods led to a cost reduction of about 50 percent.* | **+ in** *Cleaner fuel has contributed to a reduction in air pollution.* | *a reduction in working hours*

cut /kʌt/ [n C] a reduction in the amount or size of something made by a government or large organization – use this especially when talking about politics or business **+ in** *Cuts in the education budget have led to fewer teachers and larger classes.* | **pay/job/tax cuts** (=cuts in wages, number of jobs, or taxes) *The whole team agreed to take pay cuts, rather than see their colleagues lose their jobs.* | *Some senators have called for huge tax cuts to stimulate the economy.*

plummet/plunge /ˈplʌmɪ̇t, plʌndʒ/ [v I] to drop very rapidly and by a large amount: *As soon as the sun went down, the temperature plummeted.* | *The drought has caused the price of hay to soar, and the price of cattle has plummeted.* | **plummet/plunge 20 degrees/thirty points etc** *The stock market plunged 30 points when the news was announced.*

taper off /ˌteɪpər ˈɒf/ [phr v I] if a number or the amount of activity happening **tapers off**, it gradually decreases: *Towards sunset, the rain began to taper off.*

dwindle /ˈdwɪndl/ [v I] if supplies or numbers of something **dwindle**, they gradually decrease: *The country's foreign currency reserves have dwindled over the past few years.* | **+ to** *The original platoon of 30 men had dwindled to 12.* —**dwindling** [adj only before noun] *What can be done to preserve the world's dwindling natural resources?*

slide /slaɪd/ [v I] if a price or value **slides** it gradually decreases in a way that causes problems – used especially in news reports: *Prices will continue to slide unless production is reduced.* | *The dollar fell in late trading in New York yesterday and slid further this morning.*

take a nosedive ALSO **nosedive** /ˌteɪk ə ˈnəʊzdaɪv, ˈnəʊzdaɪv/ [v I] informal if the price or value of something **takes a nosedive**, it becomes lower very quickly and causes problems. If an economy **takes a nosedive** it become worse very quickly: *Since January, sales of cars and trucks, including minivans, have nosedived.* | *Shares on the stock exchange took another nosedive Friday.*

6 when feelings, qualities etc become less strong

- lessen
- subside
- wane
- recede

lessen /ˈlesən/ [v I] *Over time, the pain usually lessens, but this may take several months.* | *My love for the countryside has never lessened.*

subside /səbˈsaɪd/ [v I] if something such as fear, anxiety, trouble or laughter **subsides**, it gradually decreases: *After the rebel leaders were captured or killed, the trouble subsided.* | *The speaker puffed on his cigar while he waited for the laughter to subside.*

wane /weɪn/ [v I] if something such as people's liking or support for something or someone **wanes**, that feeling gradually becomes slightly less and will probably continue to decrease: *His popularity in the state began to wane almost immediately after the election.* | *Some countries' taste for purely American pop culture has waned.*

recede /rɪˈsiːd/ [v I] if a possibility or chance **recedes**, it gradually becomes less and less likely: *Since Donald lost his job, the hopes of our buying a house have receded even further.* | *As the threat of nuclear war receded, other things began to worry us.*

let/allow

RELATED WORDS

opposite: **forbid**

▸ *see also* **legal, illegal, limit, rule, regulation**

1 to let someone do something

- let
- allow
- say sb can do sth
- agree to
- permit
- authorize
- have no objection
- give your consent
- give sb/sth the go-ahead

let /let/ [v T not in passive] *We wanted to go camping, but our parents wouldn't let us.* | **let sb do sth** *Sue doesn't let her kids eat candy.* | *Thanks for letting me spend the night at your place.* | **let sb in/out** (=let someone go in or out of a place) *You'd better let the dog out.*

allow /əˈlaʊ/ [v T] if someone such as a teacher, official, or parent **allows** someone to do something, they let them do it **allow sb to do sth** *We do not allow people to smoke anywhere in the building.* | *Under federal law, Indian nations are allowed to operate casinos on their reservations, with the state's permission.* | **allow sb sth** formal (=allow them to have it) *Paul's bank now allows him £35 a week, and Geoff can withdraw no more than £40.* | **allow sb in/out etc** (=allow someone to go into or out of a place) *The manager doesn't allow children in the bar.*

say sb can do sth /ˌseɪ (sb) kən ˈduː (sth)/ [v phrase] especially spoken to tell someone that you will allow them to do something: *Mom says we can each have two cookies.* | *I thought you said we could use this room.*

agree to /əˈgriː tuː/ [phr v T] to decide to allow someone to do something because you have been persuaded to allow it: *The rebels finally agreed to a ban on terrorist activity.* | *McCaskill left the California Angels on Saturday and agreed to a three-year contract with the Chicago White Sox worth over $6 million.*

permit /pərˈmɪt/ [v T] if a law or a rule **permits** someone to do something, it allows them to do it: *Photography will not be permitted inside the courtroom.* | **permit sb to do sth** *The law permits foreign investors to own up to 25% of British companies.* —**permitted** [adj] officially allowed: *The water contained six times the permitted level of chlorine.*

authorize ALSO **authorise** British /ˈɔːθəraɪz/ [v T] to officially or legally allow someone to do something, especially by signing an official document: *Who authorized the decision to close the factory?* | *Among other matters, the city council authorized more funds for additional police officers.* | **authorize sb to do sth** *Only Congress can authorize the President to declare war.*

have no objection /hæv ˌnəʊ əbˈdʒekʃən/ [v phrase not in progressive] to not care whether someone does something or not, especially when they have asked for your permission or approval: *As long as your parents have no objection, you're very welcome to come on vacation with us.* | **have no objection to sb doing sth** *They said they had no objection to us leaving a little early.*

give your consent /ˌgɪv jɔːʳ kənˈsent/ [v phrase] to give final permission to allow something important to happen, which will affect yourself, your family, or your property: *Parents are required to give their* *written consent* (=give permission in writing) *before a child can be asked to participate in an interview.* | **give your consent to sth** *In September, he gave Dr. Arning his consent to conduct the experiment.*

give sb/sth the go-ahead ALSO **give sb/sth the green light** /ˌɡɪv (sb/sth) ðə ˈɡəʊ əhed, ˌɡɪv (sb/sth) ðə ˌɡriːn ˈlaɪt/ [v phrase] to give official permission for a planned activity to begin: *We're still waiting for the finance committee to give us the green light.* | *Councillors in Darlington gave the hotel development project the go-ahead in September.* | **give the go-ahead for sth** *We believe the nuclear programme should be given the go-ahead for further development.*

2 what you say to ask permission

- can I
- may I
- do you mind if/would you mind if/is it all right if

can I /ˈkæn aɪ/ *Can I borrow your pen for a minute?* | *Hey Dad, can I stay at Sara's house tonight?* | *Can I go to the bathroom?*

may I /ˈmeɪ aɪ/ use this to ask someone politely if you can do something: *May I ask you a question, Mr Simmonds?* | *May I see your ticket, please?*

do you mind if/would you mind if/is it all right if /ˌduː juː ˈmaɪnd ɪf, ˌwʊd juː ˈmaɪnd ɪf, ˌɪz ɪt ɔːl ˈraɪt ɪf/ use this when you are worried that what you want to do will annoy or interrupt someone else: *Is it all right if I smoke?* | *Do you mind if I open the window?* | *Would you mind if I made a call?*

3 what you say to give permission

- go ahead
- be my guest
- feel free
- help yourself
- of course/of course you can

go ahead /ˌɡəʊ əˈhed/ *'Can I watch TV?' 'Sure, go ahead.'* | **go right ahead** *'Is it OK if I eat the last apple?' 'Go right ahead.'* | **go ahead and do sth** *If you want to take a shower, just go ahead and take one.*

be my guest /ˌbiː maɪ ˈɡest/ when someone asks you if they can use something, especially something that belongs to you: *'Is it all right if I call my parents?' 'Be my guest.'* | *'Do you mind if I sit here?' 'Be my guest.'*

feel free /ˌfiːl ˈfriː/ when you want someone to do what they want without feeling that they need to ask you first: *'I hope you don't mind if I use your phone.' 'Of course not. Feel free.'* | **feel free to do sth** *Please feel free to stop me and ask questions whenever you like.*

help yourself /ˌhelp jɔːʳˈself/ when you want someone to take what they want, especially food or drink: *'Is there any beer left?' 'Sure, help yourself.'* | **help yourself to sth** *Help yourself to coffee and cake.*

of course/of course you can /əv ˈkɔːʳs, əv ˈkɔːʳs juː kæn/ spoken use this as a friendly way of telling someone they can do something: *'Can I take some more casserole?' 'Of course!'* | *'Do you mind of I sit here?' 'Of course you can.'*

4 to be allowed to do something

- can
- be allowed
- be permitted
- may
- be free to do sth

can /kən, (*strong*) kæn/ [modal verb] *Now that you're seventeen, you can learn to drive.* | *You can't park here.* | *Ask Jan if you can borrow a cup or two of milk.*

be allowed /biː əˈlaʊd/ [v phrase] to **be allowed** to do something, especially because a rule or law says you can do it **be allowed to do sth** *Are we allowed to use calculators on the test?* | **sth is allowed** *Lanterns and heaters are allowed on Forest Service lands if they are fueled by propane.* | **be allowed in/out/off/on etc** (=be allowed to go in, out, off etc) *Several international relief organizations had been allowed into the area to determine what help was needed.*

be permitted /biː pəʳˈmɪtᵻd / [v phrase] formal to be allowed to do something by an official order, rule, or law **be permitted to do sth** *Residents were not even permitted to fish in the reservoir.* | **sth is permitted** *Smoking is only permitted in the public lounge.*

may /meɪ/ [modal verb] formal to be allowed to do something: *Educational institutions may videotape copyrighted television programs, but the tape must be destroyed after 45 days.*

be free to do sth /biː ˌfriː tə ˈduː (sth)/ [v phrase] to be allowed to do something when you want or in the way that you want: *Workers are free to choose from a wide variety of insurance plans.* | *The winners of the competition are free to spend their prize money in any way they choose.*

5 to let something happen, without trying to stop it

- let/allow
- not stand in sb's way
- unchecked
- charter

let/allow /let, əˈlaʊ/ [v T] to let someone do something, or let something happen, especially something bad that you should try to stop. **Allow** is more formal than **let** **let sb/sth do sth** *You shouldn't let your husband treat you like that.* | *Don't let the dog get into the flowerbed.* | *It took all my willpower to remain cool and tell him not to let it happen again.* | **allow sth to do sth** *The government has allowed the present economic crisis to get completely out of control.* | *The hedge should not be allowed to grow higher than six feet.*

not stand in sb's way /nɒt ˌstænd ɪn (sb's) ˈweɪ/ [v phrase] to let someone do something that they have chosen to do, although you could stop them, especially because they want to do it very much: *If you really want to become a lawyer, I'm not going to stand in your way.* | *Sally knew that modelling would be her career, and she was going to make sure that nothing stood in her way.*

unchecked /ˌʌnˈtʃekt◂/ [adv] if something bad or unpleasant happens **unchecked**, it is allowed to continue to happen because no one is controlling it when they should be: *A fire broke out in the warehouse and raged unchecked for over two hours.* | *Over the last decade, the government has allowed the spread of poverty and unemployment to continue completely unchecked.*

charter /ˈtʃɑːʳtəʳ/ [n C] especially British, informal a law or official decision which seems to give someone the right to do something that most people think is morally wrong and should not be allowed **charter for sb to do sth** *This housing law would be a charter for dishonest landlords to cheat their tenants.* | **thieves'/tax dodgers' etc charter** *The police decision to reduce their burglary squad has been described as 'a thieves' charter'.*

6 to let someone do whatever they want

- give sb the freedom to do sth
- give sb free rein/give sb a free hand
- give sb carte blanche
- give sb a blank cheque
- give sb the run of

give sb the freedom to do sth /ˌgɪv (sb) ðə ˌfriːdəm tə 'duː (sth)/ [v phrase] *The children at the school are given complete freedom to study whatever subjects they want.* | *The major argument for capitalism is that it gives people freedom to make their own choices about what they do.*

give sb free rein/give sb a free hand /ˌgɪv (sb) ˌfriː 'reɪn, ˌgɪv (sb) ə ˌfriː 'hænd/ [v phrase] if someone who employs you **gives you free rein** to plan, make, or operate something, they let you decide what to do and how to do it: *We're giving the medical center a free hand as to how it spends the money.* | *The new chairman has been given a completely free hand to make whatever changes he thinks necessary.*

give sb carte blanche /ˌgɪv (sb) ˌkɑːʳt 'blɑːnʃ/ [v phrase] if someone in authority **gives** someone **carte blanche**, they give them complete power over what is done and how it is done – use this especially when you do not approve of the power they are given or the decisions they make: *The General seems to have been given carte blanche to attack whatever civilian targets he wants.* | *The Supreme Court's decision practically gives the police carte blanche to order everyone out when they stop a car.*

give sb a blank cheque British **/give sb a blank check** American /ˌgɪv (sb) ə ˌblæŋk 'tʃek/ [v phrase] to let someone have as much money as they need to do something – use this especially about government or business activity: *It no longer makes sense to give the Pentagon a blank check when funding for domestic programs is being reduced.* | *We cannot let our democracy become a matter of simply giving a bunch of politicians a blank cheque to govern us every five years.*

give sb the run of /ˌgɪv (sb) ðə 'rʌn ɒv/ [v phrase] to allow someone to stay in or use a place and do what they want there: *Gary and Kaye were often out at work till late evening, but gave us the run of the house.* | *He was given the run of Shaw's library while writing his biography.*

7 to let someone do something that is not usually allowed

- bend the rules
- make an exception
- concession
- excuse
- exempt
- waive

bend the rules /ˌbend ðə 'ruːlz/ [v phrase] to let someone do something that is slightly different from what the rules allow, especially when you do not officially tell anyone about it: *The state government was willing to bend the rules where necessary in order to create more jobs.* | *I'll try and get the housing department to bend the rules for us.*

make an exception /ˌmeɪk ən ɪk'sepʃən/ [v phrase] to allow someone to do something that is not usually allowed: *I'll make an exception this time, but next time you hand in an essay late I won't accept it.*

concession /kən'seʃən/ [n C] British a special right that a particular group of people are allowed to have, for example, by the government or by their employer: *Under the previous administration, rich landowners were given generous tax concessions.* | *Pensioners and disabled people get special concessions on buses and trains.*

excuse /ɪk'skjuːz/ [v T] to allow someone not to have to go to school, work etc, for example because they are ill **be excused from sth** *Can I be excused from swimming today? I've got a cold.* | *Kinney asked to be excused from his duties on the board.* | **excuse sb from sth** *I'll try to get them to excuse me from the meeting.*

exempt /ɪg'zempt/ [v T] if you **exempt** someone, you give them special permission not to have to do something that they and other people are normally expected to do **exempt sb from sth** *The new law exempts people who earn less than $8000 a year from paying any taxes.* | *My father was exempted from military service on the grounds of ill health.*

waive /weɪv/ [v T] to officially say that a rule or a legal punishment can be ignored, especially because in this particular situation it is not important or useful to keep to it: *The court decided to waive her fine as it was her first offence.* | *The industry asked the Federal Communications Commission to waive a rule that limits the amount of power used to send a data transmission over a telephone line.*

8 official permission to do something

- permission
- authorization
- consent
- clearance
- sb's say-so
- licence

permission /pəʳ'mɪʃən/ [n U] when someone officially allows you to do something **permission to do sth** *I had to get official permission to visit the prison.* | **with/without sb's permission** *We're not allowed to camp here without the farmer's permission.* | *The changes to the book were all made with the author's permission.*

authorization /ˌɔːθəraɪ'zeɪʃən‖ˌɔːθərə-/ [n U] official permission to do something, especially written permission, from someone in a position of authority: *I must get authorization from your bank before I can accept a cheque for over fifty pounds.* | **authorization to do sth** *As a result of growing world tensions, the army requested authorization to establish another base at Battery Cove.*

consent /kən'sent/ [n U] formal permission you give for something important that will affect you, your family, or your property **without sb's consent** *The young couple were married without their parents' consent.* | **give your consent** *The city authorities have given their consent to leases on two buildings in the centre of Moscow.* | **written consent** *Before a woman can have an abortion, she needs to have written consent from two doctors.*

clearance /'klɪərəns/ [n U] official permission given by someone in a position of authority, after checking that what someone wants to do is legal, safe, or likely to be successful: *We expect that we'll have clearance from the Justice Department for the buyout in the first quarter of the year.* | **clearance to do sth** *The pilot requested clearance to land at Narita Airport.*

sb's say-so / (sb's) 'seɪ-səʊ/ [n phrase] informal permission from someone, especially someone important **without sb's say-so** *Kathleen evidently ran things around the office and nothing could be done without her say-so.* | **on sb's say-so** *Tell him he can use the car, but only on my say-so.*

licence British **/license** American /'laɪsəns/ [n singular/U] official permission to do something, which is often used as a reason to do something wrong, especially something that will harm other people **license to do sth** *The Secret Service seems to think they have a license to tap anyone's phone in the interests of 'national security.'* | *Some manufacturers see the current labelling regulations as licence to mislead shoppers.*

9 an official document that gives permission

- permit
- licence
- warrant

permit /ˈpɜːmɪt‖ˈpɜːrmɪt, pərˈmɪt/ [n C] an official document that gives you permission to do something, for example permission to work somewhere or visit somewhere: *You can't park here unless you have a permit.* | **work permit** (=a permit to work in a particular country) *Many spouses of diplomats are unable to pursue their careers because they lack U.S. work permits.*

licence British **/license** American /ˈlaɪsəns/ [n C/U] an official document that allows you to do something, for example to drive a car or own a gun: *Do you have a licence for that gun?* | **driving licence** British /**driver's license** American *Rebecca's disability prevented her from getting a driver's license.*

warrant /ˈwɒrənt‖ˈwɔː-, ˈwɑː-/ [n C] a document giving the police permission to take someone in order to ask them questions, or to search inside a building: *A warrant has been issued for the arrest of a suspected terrorist.* | **search warrant** *You don't have to let the police in unless they have a search warrant.*

letter

RELATED WORDS

- to post or mail a letter *see* **send**
- *see also* **message, write, read, computers/internet/email, contact**

1 letters etc

- letter
- post
- note
- memo
- correspondence
- e-mail/email

letter /ˈletəʳ/ [n C] a written or printed message that is usually put in an envelope and sent by mail: *In a letter dated May 10th, the US government protested about the use of force in the republics.* | **letter from sb** *I got a letter from Anna today.* | **letter to sb** *Hamlin wrote a letter to the council, complaining about the incident.* | **write sb a letter** *Write me a letter and tell me all your news!* | **get/receive a letter** *David, who won first prize in the lottery, has received more than 100 letters from charities asking for money.*

post British **/mail** especially American /pəʊst, meɪl/ [n U] letters, papers, parcels etc that are sent and delivered using the postal system: *I picked up the mail – no letters, only bills today.* | *Paul was opening his post when Margot phoned.* | *There was a pile of mail and a number of telephone messages waiting for Victor.* | *When the post came, she searched anxiously for his scrawled handwriting.* | *Was there any post for me this morning?* | **by post** *You will receive the application form by post.* | **by mail** *You can apply for a passport by mail.* | **junk mail** (=advertisements and other mail that you do not want) *So much junk mail ends up in my mailbox nowadays; I just throw it all away!*

note /nəʊt/ [n C] a short informal letter written from one person to another: *Just a quick note to say Helen had a baby boy yesterday – 8lbs 6oz.* | **leave (sb) a note** *I forgot to leave them a note to tell them we won't be home by dinnertime.* | **suicide note** (=a note written just before someone kills themselves) *Police are puzzled about the man's death. There was no sign of a struggle and no suicide note.*

memo /ˈmeməʊ/ [n C] a short letter written from one person to another within a company or organization: *Mr. Fitchel said he made the suggestion in a memo to his superiors.* | **send (out) a memo** *The Managing Director sent out a memo to all employees saying there would be a meeting at 10 o'clock.*

correspondence /ˌkɒrɪ̇ˈspɒndəns‖ˌkɔːrɪ̇ˈspɑːn-, ˌkɑː-/ [n U] letters or e-mails that people write to each other regularly or over a long period of time: *Your fax should include copies of any correspondence you have received from our office.* | **+ with** *The biography is based on Marx's correspondence with Engels over 40 years.*

e-mail/email /ˈiː meɪl/ [n C/U] an electronic message sent using the Internet: *I came back from vacation to find 130 e-mails waiting for me.* | **send sb (an) e-mail** *Several people sent us e-mail asking for help with the software.* | **get an e-mail** *I got an e-mail from Emma the other day.* | **by email** *The reports are sent out weekly by email.* | **e-mail address** (=the letters or numbers that people use to send you e-mail) *The e-mail address for the dictionaries department is dict.edit@pearsoned-ema.com.*

2 ways of beginning a letter

- Dear Sir/Sirs/Sir or Madam
- Dear Mr Wiggins/ Ms Harper
- Dear Jim/Sarah etc
- Hi

Dear Sir/Sirs/Sir or Madam /ˌdɪəʳ ˈsɜːʳ, ˈsɜːʳz, ˌsɜːr ɔːʳ ˈmædəm/ use this in formal letters when you do not know the person's name: *Dear Sir or Madam, I am writing to ask for your help ....*

Dear Mr Wiggins/Ms Harper /ˌdɪəʳ mɪstəʳ ˈwɪgɪnz, mɪz ˈhɑːʳpəʳ/ use this in formal letters: *Dear Mr Bartholomew, Thank you for your quick response.*

Dear Jim/Sarah etc /ˌdɪəʳ ˈdʒɪm/ use this when you know the person well enough to use his or her first name: *Dear Jackie, How are you?*

Hi/Hey especially American /haɪ, heɪ/ use this in e-mails and letters to friends: *Hi, how's it going?* | *Hey Jenny – good to hear from you again.*

3 ways of ending a letter

- Yours faithfully
- Yours sincerely
- Yours truly,/Sincerely,/ Yours sincerely,
- love (from)
- All the best/Best wishes/With best wishes
- take care
- xxx
- regards
- PS

Yours faithfully /ˌjɔːʳz ˈfeɪθfəli/ British use this at the end of formal letters, which began with 'Dear Sir', 'Dear Madam' etc: *Yours faithfully, Adam Browning*

Yours sincerely /ˌjɔːʳz sɪnˈsɪəʳli/ British use this at the end of formal letters which begin with 'Dear Mr ... ', 'Dear Ms ... ' etc: *Yours sincerely, Mary Whitford*

Yours truly,/Sincerely,/Yours sincerely, /ˌjɔːʳz ˈtruːli, sɪnˈsɪəʳli/ American use this at the end of formal letters: *Yours truly, Donna Deavers*

love (from) /ˈlʌv (frəm)/ use this at the end of letter to members of your family, close friends etc: *I'll give you a call soon. Love, Brad*

All the best/Best wishes/With best wishes /ˌɔːl ðə ˈbest, ˌbest ˈwɪʃɪz, wɪð ˌbest ˈwɪʃɪz/ use this especially in letters or e-mails to friends and family: *All the best, Dad*

take care /ˌteɪk ˈkeəʳ/ use this at the end of letters to friends, to show that you will be thinking about them: *Take care, Martin and Sophie*

xxx ALSO **xoxo** American use this at the end of letters and notes to people you love. The X's represent kisses and the O's represent hugs: *xxx Moira*

regards /rɪˈgɑːʳdz/ use this especially in letters or e-mails to people you know or work with, especially people who are not family or close friends: *Regards, Jonathan Pryor*

PS British **/P.S.** American /ˌpiː ˈes/ use this when you want to add something after the end of a letter: *PS I love you.* | *PS Send my regards to Pauline.*

level

RELATED WORDS

- someone's position in an organization, society etc *see* **position/rank**
- *see also* **amount, number**

1 a point on a scale that measures quantity or quality

- **level**
- **point**
- **the 1000/two million etc mark**

level /ˈlevəl/ [n C] *When the temperature reaches a certain level the machine will switch off automatically.* | **noise levels** *Background noise levels at New York's J. F. Kennedy international airport are between 51-98 decibels.* | **+ of** *The water is treated to reduce the levels of pollution in it.*

point /pɔɪnt/ [n C] **boiling/freezing/melting etc point** the exact level at which something boils/freezes/melts etc: *The boiling point of water is 100 degrees Celsius.* | *By mixing metals it is possible to make alloys which are tougher and have a lower melting point than the individual metals.*

the 1000/two million etc mark /ðə ˌwʌn ˈθaʊzənd mɑːʳk/ [n phrase] if the number of something reaches **the 1000/two million etc mark** it reaches a particular level, especially a high level: *The average salary of players in the NHL is steadily climbing to the $1 million mark.* | **hit the 1000/two million etc mark** *Unemployment hit the three million mark in the UK in 1981.*

2 a level of ability or skill

- **level**
- **standard**

level /ˈlevəl/ [n C] how good someone is at doing something, for example a subject at school, a sport or game, or their work: *Students at this level tend to have a lot of problems with basic grammar.* | **+ of** *Employers always want their employees to maintain or increase their level of performance.* | **high/low level** *Each trainee is expected to show a high level of expertise before they graduate.*

standard /ˈstændəʳd/ [n C] the level of ability or skill that is needed for a particular job, sport, or activity: *If the pilot has not been trained to normal airline standards, he will not be employed by us.* | **reach/attain a standard** *I'm afraid you haven't quite reached the standard required for the job.* | **high/low standard** *Judges remarked on the high standard of this year's entries.*

lie

WHAT'S HERE

- **to lie down** see **1 to 2**
- **to tell a lie** see **3 to 6**

to lie down

RELATED WORDS

- *see also* **stand, sit, bend 2, rest, sleep, relax/relaxed**

1 to lie down after you have been standing or sitting

- **lie down**
- **lie**
- **stretch out**
- **sprawl/sprawl out**

lie down /ˌlaɪ ˈdaʊn/ [phr v I] to put yourself in a flat position on a surface such as a bed, especially in order to relax or to go to sleep: *You look really tired. Why don't you go and lie down for a while?* | *For this exercise, it is best to lie down, or sit with both feet on the floor.* | **+ on** *I didn't feel very well, so I lay down on the bed and tried to rest.*

lie /laɪ/ [v I] to put yourself in a flat position on a surface **+ on** *Libby switched off the light and lay on the couch, staring into the darkness.* | *Lie on the floor and put your legs in the air.* | **lie on your back/stomach** *The baby was lying on his back in his crib, perfectly content.*

stretch out /ˌstretʃ ˈaʊt/ [phr v I] to lie with your body and legs straight so that you can relax: *I think I'll go upstairs and stretch out for a little while.* | **+ on** *'I'm pooped,' said Homer, stretching out on his bunk.*

sprawl/sprawl out /sprɔːl, ˌsprɔːl ˈaʊt/ [phr v I] to lie or sit with your arms or legs stretched out in a lazy or careless way **+ on** *'What a beautiful day,' said Olly, sprawling out on the sand.* | *Kerry came into the room, obviously drunk, and sprawled on the bed.*

2 to be in a lying position

- **lie**
- **recline**
- **stretched out**
- **sprawled/sprawled out**
- **spreadeagled**

lie /laɪ/ [v I] to be in a flat position, for example on a bed or the floor **+ in/on etc** *I spent most of the morning lying in bed.* | **lie face down** *When they found him, he was lying face down in a pool of blood.* | **lie on your back/stomach** *Frank was lying there flat on his back, snoring away.*

recline /rɪˈklaɪn/ [v I] formal to lie or lean back in a very relaxed way **+ on** *Many of Roche's earlier paintings are of young men reclining on sofas.* | **+ in**

Reclining in a comfortable chair, David idly flipped through a magazine. —**reclining** [adj] *She later did a series of photographic studies of reclining nudes.*

stretched out /ˌstretʃt 'aʊt/ [adj phrase] lying with your body and legs straight in order to relax because your body is tired: *Sean was stretched out on the carpet, listening to music.* | *As she let herself in the front door, she caught sight of Stafford, stretched out on the sofa, a book in hand.* | **lie stretched out** *The dog lay stretched out in front of the fire.*

sprawled/sprawled out /sprɔːld, ˌsprɔːld 'aʊt/ [adj] lying or sitting with your arms or legs stretched out in a lazy or careless way: *There was Quinn, sprawled out on the grass, sound asleep.* | **lie sprawled/sprawled out** *The children were lying sprawled out in front of the television.*

spreadeagled /ˌspred'iːgəld‖'sprediːgəld/ [adj] especially British lying flat with your arms and legs spread as wide apart as possible: *Ellen lost her balance and ended up spreadeagled on her back on the pavement.* | *The court heard how he confronted the couple, forced them to lie spreadeagled on the ground, and pointed a gun at their heads.*

to tell a lie

RELATED WORDS

▸ *see also* **untrue, dishonest, cheat, rumour/rumor, trick/deceive, true**

3 to say or write something that is not true

- lie
- tell a lie
- tell tales
- tell fibs
- fib
- be economical with the truth
- perjury

lie /laɪ/ [v I] to deliberately tell someone something that is not true: *I looked at her face and just knew that she was lying.* | **+ to** *Don't lie to me! I know where you were last night.* | **+ about** *Movie stars always lie about their age.* | **lie through your teeth** (=to deliberately say something that is completely untrue, in a way that makes other people angry or upset) *'The witness was lying through his teeth,' said Davis, 'and should be charged with perjury.'*

tell a lie /ˌtel ə 'laɪ/ [v phrase] to deliberately tell someone something that is not true: *The guy's always telling lies.* | *Are you accusing me of telling lies?* | *The boys tell lies to get each other into trouble.* | **tell sb a lie** *Of course it's true. I wouldn't tell you a lie.*

tell tales /ˌtel 'teɪlz/ [v phrase] British if someone, especially a child, **tells tales**, they tell lies about someone else, in order to make you believe that the other person has behaved badly: *Daisy Venables, you naughty girl, have you been telling tales again?* | **+ on** *According to the children, telling tales on each other was as bad as cheating.*

tell fibs ALSO **tell porkies** British informal /ˌtel 'fɪbz, ˌtel 'pɔːʳkis/ [v phrase] to tell lies, especially ones that are not very important – used especially by children: *Now, Martin, you mustn't tell fibs.* | *His mother says that he sometimes tells fibs.*

fib /fɪb/ [v I] to tell a lie – especially one that is not very important: *When she asked if they wanted to stay for tea, Larry fibbed and said they had a few errands to run.* | **+ about** *He fibbed about his age.*

be economical with the truth /biː ekəˌnɒmɪkəl wɪð ðə 'truːθ‖-ˌnɑː-/ [v phrase usually in progressive] especially British to not tell the whole truth about something – use this in a humorous way to say indirectly that someone is lying: *Don't you feel like you're being a bit economical with the truth here?* | *Leonard had, as he put it, been 'economical with the truth' at times.*

perjury /'pɜːʳdʒəri/ [n U] the crime of telling a lie in a court of law when you have promised to tell the truth **commit perjury** *Do you realise that by lying to the court you have committed perjury?* | **charge sb with perjury** *Both witnesses are accused of giving false evidence and will likely be charged with perjury.* | **find sb guilty of perjury** *Hall was found guilty of perjury and obstruction of justice.*

4 something untrue that is said or written

- lie
- white lie
- fib
- falsehood
- half-truth
- misinformation
- disinformation
- propaganda
- smear campaign

lie /laɪ/ [n C] something that you say which you know is not true: *Jim said that he was planning to stay home and watch TV, but I knew it was a lie.* | **+ about** *How can the newspapers print all these lies about her?* | **a pack of lies** (=so many lies that you feel shocked or angry) *He called the report 'a pack of lies'.* | **a bald-faced/an outright/a downright lie** (=a clear and shocking lie) *Davenport said the congressman's allegations were nothing more than 'downright lies'.*

white lie /ˌwaɪt 'laɪ/ [n C] a lie that does not harm anyone, especially one that is told in order to avoid hurting someone's feelings: *It's just a little white lie. No real harm done.* | *I told him his suit looked wonderful, which was a white lie.* | *'I'm sorry I couldn't come. I had a really bad headache,' she explained, resorting to a white lie.*

fib /fɪb/ [n C] informal a lie, especially one that is not very important: *You're not telling me a fib, are you?* | **+ about** *I had to make up some fib about why I was late.*

falsehood /'fɔːlshʊd/ [n C] formal an untrue statement or story, especially one that has been carefully and deliberately invented to give people the wrong idea about someone or something: *Mudge, in a written statement Wednesday, said the article was a collection of 'falsehoods and misinformation'.* | **spread a falsehood** *Why Campbell had chosen to spread such a falsehood is a mystery.*

half-truth /'hɑːf truːθ‖'hæf-/ [n C] a statement that is almost a lie because it does not tell the whole truth about something: *McCarthy's blend of half-truths and lies ruined many careers in government and the professions.* | *Forbes' book on Bonham is littered with half-truths, and, in some cases, outright lies.*

misinformation /ˌmɪsɪnfəʳ'meɪʃən/ [n U] incorrect information, especially information that is deliberately intended to deceive people: *According to Kramer, the Internet is a storehouse of lies and misinformation.* | **+ about** *'For months, the Democrats have run television commercials filled with misinformation about the Republican Party,' said Dawson.*

disinformation /ˌdɪsɪnfəʳ'meɪʃən / [n U] false information which is given deliberately in order to hide the truth or confuse people, especially in political situations: *The Russian Foreign Ministry denounced the report as 'disinformation'.* | **+ about**

Logan said government agents are still spreading disinformation about leaders of the political reform movement.

propaganda /ˌprɒpəˈgændə‖ˌprɑː-/ [n U] false or partly false information that is spread by a government or political organization, in order to make people support and agree with their political aims and beliefs: *Propaganda is a tool of war.* | **Communist/US etc propaganda** *Radio Marti is still there, spewing its US propaganda across the waters toward Cuba.* | **propaganda campaign** (=an organized plan to spread propaganda) *In Najaf, Khomeini had begun a propaganda campaign against the Shah.* | **anti-Western/anti-Communist/anti-Labour etc propaganda** *a piece of anti-Communist propaganda*

smear campaign /ˈsmɪəʳ kæmˌpeɪn/ [n C] when people tell lies about someone in the newspapers, on television etc, in order to make people have a bad opinion of that person **mount a smear campaign against sb** *The Labour Party mounted a smear campaign against Livingstone before the election.*

5 to invent a false story, excuse, name etc

- make up
- invent
- fabricate
- cook up

make up /ˌmeɪk ˈʌp/ [phr v T] to think of a story, excuse, explanation etc that is not true, especially in order to deceive people or to protect yourself **make up sth** *I gave her the wrong name, and made up a telephone number with a Los Angeles area code.* | **make sth/it up** *You don't have to tell him why, just make something up.*

invent /ɪnˈvent/ [v T] to think of a story, excuse, name etc that is not true in order to deceive people: *I invented reasons for never seeing him again.* | *He began inventing excuses for why he had done nothing to help.* | *He invented fictional ancestors and a family history to impress the girls.*

fabricate /ˈfæbrɪkeɪt/ [v T] formal to think of a false story, piece of information etc in order to deceive people or prevent them from discovering the truth: *Officials were accused of fabricating the evidence that was given at the trial.* | *The woman said she fabricated her testimony because she thought she was going to get a $10,000 reward.* —**fabrication** /ˌfæbrɪˈkeɪʃən/ [n C/U] **pure fabrication** *Police now believe that the whole story was pure fabrication.*

cook up informal **/concoct** formal /ˌkʊk ˈʌp, kənˈkɒkt‖-ˈkɑːkt/ [phr v T] to spend time thinking of a false story, excuse, plant etc, especially with other people: *I cooked up an excuse so I could leave early.* | *His lawyers concocted a theory that the police had planted the evidence against him.* | **cook up a scheme** *He cooked up some crazy scheme for making money, and ended up being arrested.*

6 someone who lies

- liar
- fibber

liar /ˈlaɪəʳ/ [n C] *She may be stupid, but she's not a liar.* | **call sb a liar** *Are you calling me a liar?* | **compulsive/habitual/pathological liar** (=someone who cannot stop telling lies) *Coleman described the president as a 'pathological liar' and 'a criminal in the White House.'*

fibber /ˈfɪbəʳ/ [n C] someone who tells lies, especially ones that are not very important: *You are such a fibber!*

life

RELATED WORDS

▸ *see also* **alive, live, exist, dead, die**

1 the time when someone is alive

- life
- lifetime
- days
- lifespan
- life expectancy
- life cycle

life /laɪf/ [n C] the time when someone is alive **the happiest/saddest/worst etc day of your life** *The day our daughter was born was the happiest day of my life.* | **the rest of sb's life** *Sutcliffe was sent to jail for the rest of his life.* | **spend your life** *Dad spent his life building up this business.* | *How would you like to spend your life? What kind of work would you like to do?* | **for life** (=for the rest of your life) *The accident left him crippled for life.* | **sb's early life** (=when someone was young) *He knew very little about his mother's early life in Africa.* | **sb's adult life** *The first half of my adult life was spent in jail.* | **in later life** (=when you are old) *Lack of calcium can lead to bone disease in later life.*

lifetime /ˈlaɪftaɪm/ [n C usually singular] the time when someone is alive – use this when you are talking about how long someone lived and what happened in their life **in/during sb's lifetime** *He suffered a lot of pain in his short lifetime.* | *During Dickinson's lifetime, only a few of her works were actually published.* | **+ of** *The National Medal of Arts award is meant to honor a lifetime of achievement.* | **last a lifetime** (=last as long as someone lives) *A good tool should last a lifetime.* | **once-in-a-lifetime chance/opportunity** (=a chance or opportunity that will only happen once in a person's lifetime) *The visit to Tibet was a once-in-a-lifetime opportunity.*

days /deɪz/ [n plural] someone's life, especially a particular period of their life **sb's student days/school days** *I asked Debbie about her student days and she just laughed. 'I dropped out of school the day I turned 16,' she said.* | **sb's younger days** *In her younger days, she was quite a fancy dresser.* | **sb's early days** (=the time when someone has just started something, especially a job) *The play is based on the early days of cabaret singer Rosie Kincaid.* | **the rest of your days** (=the rest of your life) *Evelyn spent the rest of her days quietly in the country until her death in 1963.* | **end your days** (=spend the last part of your life doing something) *She ended her days in poverty.* | **sb's days as/with sth** (=a period of time in someone's life when they were doing a particular job or activity) *Michael knew Annette during her days as an off-Broadway actress.* | *I first became a fan of guitarist Cory Weldon during his days with the Leeds band, Sinister Minister.*

lifespan /ˈlaɪfspæn/ [n singular] the length of time that a person or animal usually lives **normal/natural/average lifespan** *The natural lifespan of a pig is 10-12 years.* | **short/long lifespan** *Saltwater fish have a shorter lifespan in the aquarium.* | **sb's lifespan** *Authorities estimate that smoking trims between 12 and 15 years off a person's lifespan.*

life expectancy /ˌlaɪf ɪkˈspektənsi/ [n C] the length of time that a person or animal is expected to live: *Women have a longer life expectancy than men.* | **low/high life expectancy** (=a short or long life) *Life expectancy was much lower then than it is now.* | **average life expectancy** *At the beginning of the century, the average life expectancy for Ameri-*

cans was less than 50 years. | **have a life expectancy of 64/78 etc years** (=be expected to live until you are 64/78 etc) *British males now have a life expectancy of around 77 years.*

life cycle /ˈlaɪf ˌsaɪkəl/ [n C] all the different stages in development that an animal or plant has in the time that it is alive: *Despite decades of study, the life cycle of the tiny shellfish, krill, is still something of a mystery.*

2 the kind of life that someone has

- life
- existence
- lifestyle
- way of life
- live well/happily/carefully etc

life /laɪf/ [n C] the kind of **life** that someone has: *Having a baby completely changes your life.* | **a happy/busy/exciting etc life** *Debbie has a really busy life, doesn't she?* | *They enjoyed a full and happy life together until his death in June 1999.* | **lead a happy/quiet/exciting etc life** *We've led a very quiet life since Ralph retired.* | **quality of life** (=the level of health, comfort and pleasure in someone's life) *By our actions today, we can improve the quality of life for future generations.* | **a better life** *Emigrating to the UK was their only chance for a better life.* | **a life of crime** (=when you make money by committing crimes instead of having a normal job) *He left school at 15, quickly turning to a life of crime.*

existence /ɪɡˈzɪstəns/ [n singular] the life that someone has, especially when they have difficult or bad experiences **a lonely/miserable/unhappy etc existence** *Elena faced a lonely existence in the big city.* | **lead a miserable/lonely etc existence** (=have a particular existence) *The workers lived a miserable existence and were treated like serfs.*

lifestyle /ˈlaɪfstaɪl/ [n C] the way someone lives and behaves, and the type of things they buy, eat etc **a healthy lifestyle** *You really need to think about leading a healthier lifestyle.* | **lavish/luxurious lifestyle** (=the lifestyle of someone who is very rich) *Hurst's lavish lifestyle is the stuff of legend.* | **extravagant lifestyle** (=a lifestyle that shows people how rich you are) *Even when in debt, he continued to enjoy an extravagant lifestyle.*

way of life /ˌweɪ əv ˈlaɪf/ [n phrase] the way in which a person or group of people lives, and the type of things they usually do **sb's way of life** *'How can we abandon our way of life?' asked the old sheep herder. 'It's all we know.'* | **become a way of life** *Casual dress has become a way of life in corporate Britain.* | **the British/German/American etc way of life** *Shopping is an important part of the American way of life.*

live well/happily/carefully etc /ˌlɪv ˈwel/ [v phrase] to live your life in a particular way: *Tom and Linda both earn good salaries – they live well and have a nice home.* | *One can live cheaply in London, although it's not easy.*

3 continuing for all of someone's life

- all your life
- for life
- lifelong

all your life /ˌɔːl jɔːʳ ˈlaɪf/ [adv] for the whole of your life: *I've known Jenny all my life.* | *Despite having worked hard all his life, Jimmy had saved very little for retirement.*

for life /fəʳ ˈlaɪf/ [adv] if something is **for life**, it will continue and not change for the rest of your life: *There's no such thing as a job for life these days.* | *As far as I'm concerned, when you get married it's for life.*

lifelong /ˈlaɪflɒŋ‖-lɔːŋ/ [adj only before noun] continuing for all of your life – use this about beliefs, feelings, or relationships that last for the whole of your life **lifelong supporter** *My father was a lifelong supporter of the Democrats.* | **lifelong ambition** (=something that you have always wanted to do) *It was her lifelong ambition to write a best-selling novel.* | **lifelong friends** (=friends for life) *The two remained lifelong friends.*

lift

RELATED WORDS

opposite: down (6)

- *see also* **carry, hold, put up**

1 to lift a person or thing

- lift
- lift up
- pick up
- raise
- scoop up/out
- hoist
- jack up

lift /lɪft/ [v T] to move something upwards to a higher position, especially something heavy, either by using your hands or a machine: *His doctor has told him that he must not lift anything heavy.* | *She lifted the lid from a huge pot and took a sniff.* | **+ onto/out of/over etc** *They lifted me onto a stretcher and took me to the ambulance.* | *Firemen had to use a mobile crane to lift the carriages back onto the rails.* | **lift sb bodily** (=lift someone's whole body up, using a lot of strength) *The massive bull lifted him bodily into the air and shook him repeatedly.*

lift up /ˌlɪft ˈʌp/ [phr v T] to move something upwards to a higher position and hold it there – use this especially about something fairly heavy that you use your hands to move **lift sb/sth up** *He lifted her up in his arms.* | **lift up sb/sth** *Can you help me lift up this table so we can get the carpet under it?* | *Six men lifted up the coffin and carried it out of the church.* | **lift sth up onto/out of/over etc** *I couldn't see the game so I asked my dad to lift me up onto his shoulders.*

pick up /ˌpɪk ˈʌp/ [phr v T] to lift something up from the ground, from a table etc, especially something small or light **pick up sb/sth** *She picked up her bag and left the room.* | *Maurin picked up the gun and put it in his pocket.* | *The lioness picked her cub up by its neck.* | **pick sb/sth up** *There are papers all over the floor – could you pick them up and put them away?* | *The little girl's mother laughed and bent down to pick her up.* | *The vacuum cleaner won't pick this stuff up.* | **pick up the phone** (=pick up the part of the telephone that you speak into, so that you can use it) *The phone rang and Hutton picked it up, frowning.*

raise /reɪz/ [v T] to move something to a higher position for a short time before lowering it again: *The bridge can be raised to allow ships to pass under it.* | *'Cheers, everyone!' said Larry, raising his glass.*

scoop up/out /ˌskuːp ˈʌp, ˈaʊt/ [v phrase] to dig or pick something up with a scoop (=a round deep spoon), a spoon, or with your curved hand **scoop sth up/out/off etc** *He scooped up a handful of sand and dropped it in the bucket.* | *Slice the eggs in half, then scoop out the yolks into a bowl.*

hoist /hɔɪst/ [v T] to lift up something which is heavy and difficult to carry **hoist sth on/onto/over** *Joe* *picked up the sack and hoisted it onto the truck.* | *The crowd hoisted him onto their shoulders and carried him triumphantly down the main street.*

jack up /ˌdʒæk ˈʌp/ [phr v T] to lift up the corner of a car using a special tool, in order to change the wheel or look under the car **jack up sth** *Fred jacked up the car and started to unscrew the wheel nuts.* | **jack sth up** *Why don't you jack it up and we'll have a look at the suspension?*

2 to lift a part of your body to a higher position

- raise
- lift
- put your hand up

raise /reɪz/ [v T] **raise your eyes/eyebrows/hand/arm etc** to move or turn your eyes, head etc upwards for a short time: *She raised her eyes from the newspaper when he came in.* | *If you have any questions, please raise your hand.* | *Lori raised her arms over her head.* | **+ to do sth** *Mum raised her hand to hit me and then stopped.*

lift ALSO **lift up** /lɪft, lɪft ʌp/ [v T] **lift your arm/leg/head** to move your arm, leg etc upwards, especially when this is difficult to do: *I was feeling so weak that I could hardly lift my head from the pillow.* | *The child lifted up her arms, asking to be picked up.* | *Lie on your side, use your hand for support, and lift your leg to the level of your shoulder.*

put your hand up /ˌpʊt jɔːʳ ˈhænd ʌp/ [v phrase] to move your arm upwards and keep it in the air, for example because you want to speak in a class or meeting, or because you are being counted: *Put your hand up if you know the answer.* | *If you are not able to take part, please put your hand up.*

light

RELATED WORDS

- light a fire *see* **fire, burn**

WHAT'S HERE

- **not dark** see **1 to 3**
- **not heavy** see **4 to 5**

not dark

RELATED WORDS

opposite: **dark**

- light colour *see* **colour/color**
- *see also* **bright, shine/shiny, reflect**

1 light from the sun, a fire, an electric light etc

- light
- it's light
- daylight
- sunlight
- moonlight
- glare
- glow
- beam
- ray

light /laɪt/ [n U] *Light was coming into the room through a crack in the door.* | *a gas lamp that gives as much light as a 100 watt bulb* | **the light** (=the amount of natural light in a place) *The light was fading, and I was afraid we wouldn't be home before dark.* | **good/strong/bright light** *The light isn't good enough to take a photograph.* | **poor/dim/fading light** *In the fading light she could just make out the shape of a tractor.* | **soft/warm light** *The valley was bathed in the soft light of dawn.* | **cold/harsh light** *the cold blue light of the Arctic* | **blinding/dazzling light** (=very strong light that hurts your eyes) *a sudden flash of blinding light* | **by the light of the moon/the fire/a candle** (=with only the moon etc to give light) *She sat reading by the light of the fire.*

it's light /ɪts ˈlaɪt/ spoken use this to say that there is natural daylight, so that you can see easily enough to do something: *Let's go now while it's still light.* | *It's not light enough to play outside.*

daylight /ˈdeɪlaɪt/ [n U] the natural light of day **in daylight** *I'd like to look at the house again in daylight.* | **daylight hours** (=the time when it is light) *The park is open during daylight hours.*

sunlight /ˈsʌnlaɪt/ [n U] the light from the sun: *Her long blonde hair was shining in the sunlight.* | *We emerged from the dark forest into the sunlight.* | **direct sunlight** *Keep the plant out of direct sunlight.*

moonlight /ˈmuːnlaɪt/ [n U] the light from the moon: *The trees looked strangely white in the moonlight.* | *Moonlight came in through the curtains, lighting up the children's sleeping faces.*

glare /gleəʳ/ [n singular] a very bright and unpleasant light that makes you want to close your eyes or turn your head away **+ of** *the glare of the car's headlights* | *The heat and glare of the furnace is immense.*

glow /gləʊ/ [n singular] a soft pleasant light, especially from something that is burning: *Candles give a warm glow to the room.* | **+ of** *the orange glow of the sunset*

beam /biːm/ [n C] a line of light shining from something such as a lamp: *We could see the beams of searchlights scanning the sky.* | **beam of light** *Maggie stumbled across the field with only a narrow beam of light from her flashlight to help her.*

ray /reɪ/ [n C] a line of light, especially one shining from the sun: *Use a sunscreen to protect your skin against the sun's harmful rays.* | *The first rays of the sun pierced the canopy of leaves above us, and the forest began to wake up.*

2 to make a place light

- light up
- light
- switch/turn/put on the light(s)
- illuminate

light up /ˌlaɪt ˈʌp/ [phr v T] to shine lights on a place so that people can see it well, or so that it looks attractive **light up sth/light sth up** *Fireworks lit up the night sky.* | *Their garden was lit up by dozens of coloured lamps.*

light /laɪt/ [v T] to put lights in a place so that people can see what is happening there: *What are you going to use to light the stage?* | **be lit by/with sth** *The room was lit by dozens of candles.*

switch/turn/put on the light(s) /ˌswɪtʃ, ˌtɜːʳn, ˌpʊt ɒn ðə ˈlaɪt(s)/ [v phrase] to turn or press a control to make an electric light produce light: *Can you put the light on? I can't see anything!* | *When I turned on the light, I realized the room was in chaos.*

illuminate /ɪˈluːmɪ̥neɪt, ɪˈljuː-‖ɪˈluː-/ [v T] to make a place light or shine light on something so that you can see it, especially in order to draw attention to something **illuminate sth** *Small lights illuminate different points on the map.* | *The blazing fire illuminated the china ornaments above the hearth.* | **be illuminated by/with sth** *A small path was* *illuminated by low orange lamps concealed in the flower beds.*

3 when the lights in a place are on

- the lights are on
- be lit up
- ablaze

the lights are on /ðə ˌlaɪts ɑːr ˈɒn/ *Although the lights were on, nobody answered the door.* | *The lights are still on in a couple of the offices.*

be lit up /biː ˌlɪt ˈʌp/ [v phrase] if a room, house, building etc **is lit up**, the lights are on inside or outside: *People were getting ready for dinner, and the house was all lit up.* | *In the town centre, the streets are all lit up for Christmas.* | **+ by/with** *The mosque is lit up by floodlights at night.*

ablaze /əˈbleɪz/ [adj not before noun] if a place or set of lights is **ablaze**, there is a lot of bright light because all the lights are turned on – used especially in literature: *The yacht passed us, its cabin lights ablaze.* | **+ with** *Every shop window is ablaze with bright Christmas lights.*

not heavy

RELATED WORDS

opposite: —— **heavy**

- *see also* **weigh**

4 not heavy

- light
- lightweight
- weightless

light /laɪt/ [adj] *You can carry this bag – it's fairly light.* | *Modern tennis rackets are much lighter than old-fashioned wooden ones.* | *Heat rises because hot air is lighter than cold air.* | **light as a feather** (=extremely light) *She was light as a feather to carry, and her hands were cold as ice.*

lightweight /ˈlaɪtweɪt/ [adj] **lightweight** clothes, materials, or equipment are specially made so that they weigh very little: *a lightweight summer suit* | *a strong, lightweight material such as titanium* | *Today's baby buggies are lightweight, compact, and easy to fold.*

weightless /ˈweɪtləs/ [adj] if someone or something is **weightless**, they seem to weigh much less than usual, especially because they are floating in space or water: *Astronauts have problems moving around in the spacecraft because they are virtually weightless.* — **weightlessness** [n U] *It takes a shuttle crew around a day to get used to the weightlessness of space.*

5 to make something lighter

- make sth lighter
- lighten

make sth lighter /ˌmeɪk (sth) ˈlaɪtəʳ/ [v phrase] *They had taken out all the drawers to make it lighter, before carrying it down the stairs.* | *Many parts are now made from plastic instead of steel, making cars lighter and more fuel-efficient.*

lighten /ˈlaɪtn/ [v T] to make something lighter, especially in order to make it easier to move or carry: *I'm sure you could lighten that suitcase a little if you only packed what you need.* | **lighten the load** *As weather conditions got worse, Watts and Peters abandoned their photographic equipment in order to lighten the load.*

like

RELATED WORDS

opposite: —— **dislike, hate**

- similar to someone or something else *see* **like/similar**
- the kind of music, clothes etc someone likes *see* **taste in music/clothes etc**
- *see also* **love, enjoy, admire, satisfied/not satisfied, prefer, favourite/favorite, enthusiastic/not enthusiastic, popular, attract/attraction, obsession, excited/exciting**

WHAT'S HERE

- **things** see **1 to 6**
- **people** see **7 to 9**

things

1 to like something

- like
- be into
- be fond of
- be keen on
- appeal to
- go down well
- be to your liking

like /laɪk/ [v T] to think that something is nice, attractive, enjoyable etc: *I like your dress – it's a beautiful colour.* | *Do you like spaghetti?* | **like sth about sth** *What did you like about the movie?* | **like doing sth/like to do sth** *I think Roy likes living alone.* | *I like to see the children enjoying themselves.*

be into /biː ˈɪntuː/ [v phrase] spoken to like doing a particular activity or be interested in a particular subject: *I know she's really into sports, so I thought I'd ask her to come skiing with us.* | *A lot of his relatives are into very weird New Age stuff.*

be fond of /biː ˈfɒnd ɒv‖-ˈfɑːnd-/ [v phrase] especially British to like something, especially something that you have liked for a long time: *Connie had always been fond of animals.* | *He had always been fond of drinking at lunchtime, perhaps too fond.*

be keen on /biː ˈkiːn ɒn/ [v phrase] especially British to like or be very interested in an activity or idea: *I know he's keen on opera. Let's take him to see 'La Traviata'.* | *I'm quite keen on the idea of having a fancy dress party.*

appeal to /əˈpiːl tuː/ [phr v T] if something **appeals to** you, you like it because it involves things that interest you or ideas that you agree with: *I'm sure this delightful book will appeal to children of all ages.* | *Does either suggestion appeal to you?*

go down well ALSO **go over well** American /ˌgəʊ daʊn ˈwel, ˌgəʊ əʊvəʳ ˈwel/ [v phrase] if something you do, or a book, film, performance etc **goes down well** with a group of people, they like it: *Her style of comedy is very British, but it goes down well in the States too.* | **+ with** *At the present time, military action would not go over well with the international community*

be to your liking /biː tə jɔːʳ ˈlaɪkɪŋ/ [v phrase] formal if something is **to your liking** it has the qualities that you like, or it is made in the way that you like: *Was the meal to your liking, Madam?* | *The surrounding countryside was very much to our liking.*

2 to like something very much

- love/adore
- be crazy about
- be attached to
- have a passion for
- be addicted to

love/adore /lʌv, əˈdɔːʳ/ [v T not in progressive] especially spoken to like something very much. **Adore** is stronger but less common than **love**: *We had a great time at Disneyland. The kids loved it.* | *I adore chocolate – I could live on it.* | **love/adore doing sth** *The older men loved hearing about Russ's success on the football field.* | *Jessie adored being the centre of attention.*

be crazy about ALSO **be mad about sth** British /biː ˈkreɪzi əbaʊt, biː ˈmæd əbaʊt (sth)/ [v phrase] informal to be extremely interested in an activity and spend a lot of time doing it or watching it: *Jonah's crazy about basketball.* | *She's always been mad about horses.*

be attached to /biː əˈtætʃt tuː/ [v phrase] to like something very much, especially something that you own or use, so that you would be upset if you lost it: *Mom gets very attached to her pets.* | *Casey had become quite attached to the comforts of his London home.*

have a passion for /ˌhæv ə ˈpæʃən fɔːʳ/ [v phrase not in progressive] to like an activity very much, because it gives you a lot of pleasure or excitement: *From a very early age he had a passion for fast cars.* | *To be a great performer, you have to work very hard and have a passion for the music you play.*

be addicted to /bi əˈdɪktɪ̈d tuː/ [v phrase] to enjoy doing something so much that you do it, watch it etc as often as you can and feel that you cannot stop doing it: *My son's addicted to computer games – he hardly ever comes out of his room.* | **be addicted** *I started watching the show out of curiosity, but now I'm addicted!*

3 to like something that could be bad for you

- can't resist
- have a weakness for
- be partial to
- not be averse to

can't resist /ˌkɑːnt rɪˈzɪst‖ˌkænt-/ [v phrase] to like something so much that you cannot refuse it when it is offered to you: *My mother could never resist expensive perfumes.* | **can't resist doing sth** *I couldn't resist stopping by the bakery on the way home.*

have a weakness for /ˌhæv ə ˈwiːknɪ̈s fɔːʳ/ [v phrase not in progressive] informal to like a particular kind of food, drink, or activity, even though you know it is not good for you or that other people might not approve of it: *Too many of the men in our family have a weakness for alcohol.* | *I have to admit I have a weakness for daytime soap operas.*

be partial to /biː ˈpɑːʳʃəl tuː/ [v phrase] to like something such as a particular food or drink, especially when you eat or drink it more than you should: *He was particularly partial to my mother's home-made wine.*

not be averse to /nɒt biː əˈvɜːʳs tuː/ [v phrase] to like something or like doing something, especially something that could be bad or dangerous. This is often used humorously about something that is not really very bad: *She's not averse to the occasional glass of wine.* | **not be averse to doing sth** *The company is highly competitive and not averse to taking risks.*

4 to begin to like something

- get to like
- grow on
- develop/acquire/get a taste for
- be an acquired taste

get to like /ˌget tə ˈlaɪk/ [v phrase] to begin to like something, especially something that you did not like at first: *The more the two women talked, the more they got to like each other.* | *I don't think I could ever get to like hip-hop.*

grow on /ˈgrəʊ ɒn/ [phr v T] if something **grows on you**, you gradually start to like it after a period of time: *I didn't like his accent much at first, but it kind of grows on you.* | *'The furniture in this place is a little weird.' 'Yeah, but it grows on you after a while.'*

develop/acquire/get a taste for ALSO **develop a liking for sth** /dɪˌveləp, əˌkwaɪər, ˌget ə ˈteɪst fəʳ, dɪˌveləp ə ˈlaɪkɪŋ fəʳ (sth)/ [v phrase] to begin to like something that you did not like or had not experienced before: *While Bev was married, she acquired a taste for luxurious living.* | *When her family moved to Hollywood, she developed a liking for movie magazines and film culture.* | *Sam soon got a taste for Thai green curry and sticky rice.*

be an acquired taste /biː ən əˌkwaɪəʳd ˈteɪst/ [v phrase] if something **is an acquired taste**, people tend not to like when they first try it, but begin to like it when they have tried it a few more times: *Dark beers and ales are an acquired taste, but there's nothing better on a cold winter night.* | *Like most modern jazz players, his music's a bit of an acquired taste.*

5 someone who likes something very much

- fan
- lover
- enthusiast
- freak
- junkie/addict
- devotee

fan /fæn/ [n C] someone who likes a particular sport, team, or famous entertainer very much: *Thousands of fans came to hear Oasis play.* | *a football fan* | **+ of** *Fans of Sylvester Stallone will enjoy this movie.*

lover /ˈlʌvəʳ/ [n C] someone who likes a particular activity very much **music/car/wine/animal etc lover** *We are a nation of animal lovers.* | *Every jazz lover dreams of visiting New Orleans.* | **+ of** *Lovers of night life won't be able to resist the many nightclubs in the area.*

enthusiast /ɪnˈθjuːziæst‖-ˈθuː-/ [n C] someone who likes a subject, activity, performer etc very much, is very interested in them and knows a lot about them: *Enthusiasts are willing to pay up to $12,000 for an original copy of the book.* | **football/film/jazz etc enthusiast** *Golf enthusiasts will be able to see the tournament live on TV.* | *The exhibition will be of interest to classic car owners and other motoring enthusiasts.*

freak /friːk/ [n C] informal someone who is extremely interested in a particular activity, especially when other people think they are a little strange for liking it so much **health/tv/sports etc freak** *Raw vegetables and nuts have always been a favourite with health-food freaks.* | *One Beatle's freak is reported to have paid $18,000 for Paul McCartney's birth certificate.*

junkie/addict /ˈdʒʌŋki, ˈædɪkt/ [n C] informal someone who does, eats, watches etc something a lot because they enjoy it so much that they cannot stop doing it – use this especially when you do not think someone should be spending so much time doing or being involved in a particular thing **TV/news/fast food etc junkie** *If you're a shopping junkie, then this is the channel for you!* | *You'd have to be a real political junkie to remember that Tsongas won the New Hampshire Primary in 1992.* | **TV/news/fast food etc addict** *My sons and my husband are all football addicts.*

devotee /ˌdevəˈtiː/ [n C] formal someone who likes something such as art or literature very much and spends a lot of their time and money on it: *He's a devotee of old Hollywood movies.* | *Urquhart, a rich devotee of the arts, made generous donations to the museum.*

6 something that you like

- likes and dislikes
- sb's passion/sb's love

likes and dislikes /ˌlaɪks ənd ˈdɪslaɪks/ [n phrase] all the things you like and do not like: *She never lets her personal likes and dislikes affect the way she treats people.* | *Employees were asked about their likes and dislikes, and also about how they felt about their working conditions.*

sb's passion/sb's love / (sb's) ˈpæʃən, (sb's) ˈlʌv/ [n C] something that you are deeply interested in and which you like so much that you are always excited about it: *Donna's latest passion is cooking and eating Mexican food.* | **sb's great/first love** *My father's great love was fishing.*

people

7 to like someone

- like
- be fond of
- be attached to
- have a soft spot for
- see sth in
- a man/woman after your own heart
- hit it off

like /laɪk/ [v T not in progressive] to think someone has good qualities so that you feel friendly towards them: *I've always liked Sally – she's a lot of fun.* | *Everybody liked Mr. Schofield, but he wasn't a very good teacher.* | *I never really liked her – she was always a bit stuck-up and condescending.*

be fond of /biː ˈfɒnd ɒv‖-ˈfɑːnd-/ [v phrase] to like someone very much, especially when you have known them for a long time: *You're very fond of Tyler, aren't you?* | *Over the years, the old man grew very fond of his nurse.*

be attached to /biː əˈtætʃt tuː/ [v phrase] to like someone that you have known for a long time, so that you would be upset if they left you: *We've grown quite attached to you, Annie, and we'll be very sorry to see you leave.* | *Nurses can easily get too attached to their patients.*

have a soft spot for /hæv ə ˌsɒft ˈspɒt fɔːʳ‖-ˌsɔːft ˈspɑːt-/ [v phrase not in progressive] informal to like one person in particular more than the other people in a group: *She's always had a soft spot for her youngest grandson.* | *I've had a soft spot for Janet ever since she took my side in the argument I had with Jimmy.*

see sth in /ˈsiː (sth) ɪn/ [v phrase not in progressive] to like someone because of a particular quality that they have, especially when other people do not notice that quality in them: *Tom's so innocent. He only sees the good in everyone he meets.* | *I can't figure out what Doug sees in her.*

a man/woman after your own heart /ə ˌmæn, ˌwʊmən ɑːftəʳ jɔːr ˌəʊn ˈhɑːʳt‖-æf-/ [n phrase] spoken someone that you like because they have the same attitudes that you have, or like the same things that you like: *I like the way she runs her business – a woman after my own heart.*

hit it off /ˌhɪt ɪt ˈɒf/ [v phrase] if two people **hit it off**, they like each other, especially as soon as they meet: *Art Howe asked him to come for an interview for the coaching job, and the two men hit it off immediately.* | *Those two didn't really hit it off at first, did they?* | **+ with** *You can't expect to hit it off with everyone you meet.*

8 to begin to like someone

- get/grow/come to like
- warm to
- take to sb/take a liking to

get/grow/come to like /ˌget, ˌgrəʊ, ˌkʌm tə ˈlaɪk/ [v phrase] to begin to like someone, especially someone that you did not like at first: *At first I thought she was a bit weird, but now I'm getting to like her.* | *Over the years, we grew to like each other, despite our differences.* | *I've gradually come to like Larry and his eccentric habits.*

warm to /ˈwɔːʳm tuː/ [phr v T not in passive] to begin to like someone and feel friendly towards them: *Her heart warmed to Amos. He was obviously a man who loved animals.* | *She was very nervous about introducing James to her children, but they warmed to him immediately.*

take to/take a liking to /ˈteɪk tuː, ˌteɪk ə ˈlaɪkɪŋ tuː/ [v T not in passive] to begin to like someone, especially when you have only known them for a very short time: *I introduced Anders to my brother and they took to each other immediately.* | *When Nicky takes to someone the way he's taken to you, he's your friend for life.* | *They only met yesterday, but I can tell Jim's taken a great liking to the girl.*

9 to make someone like you

- endear yourself to
- get on the right side of
- win the hearts of

endear yourself to /ɪnˈdɪəʳ jɔːʳˌself tuː/ [v phrase] to make someone like you by behaving in a way that pleases them: *'Can I help you Mrs Killigarew' he said, hoping to endear himself to her by remembering her name.* | *She was witty and charming and quickly managed to endear herself to her future mother-in-law.*

get on the right side of sb British informal ALSO **get on sb's good side** American informal /ˌget ɒn ðə ˌraɪt ˈsaɪd əv (sb), ˌget ɒn (sb's) ˌgʊd ˈsaɪd/ [v phrase] to do nice things for someone and avoid making them angry, in order to be sure they like you: *He's only sent me flowers because he's trying to get on the right side of me.* | *Chris doesn't care what he has to say to get on Miller's good side.*

win the hearts of /ˌwɪn ðə ˈhɑːʳts ɒv/ [v phrase] to make a lot of people like you very much, especially by doing something that they admire or approve of: *With the words, 'Ich bin ein Berliner,' J.F. Kennedy won the hearts of millions of Germans.* | *The slight, nervous-looking young gymnast won the hearts of a whole nation.*

like/similar

RELATED WORDS

opposite: —— **different**

- to like someone or something *see* **like**
- *see also* **same, equal/not equal, copy, artificial**

1 like something or someone else

- like
- similar
- alike
- much the same
- resemble/bear a resemblance to
- comparable
- akin to

like /laɪk/ [prep] similar to something or someone: *The houses here are like the ones in northern France.* | *My mother has a car like yours.* | **look/feel/sound/smell/taste like** *She laughed like a child and played with her hair.* | *This is such beautiful material – it feels like silk.* | *It looks a bit like a cactus.* | **something like** (=fairly similar) *This superb almost-flourless chocolate cake is something like a brownie for grownups.* | **nothing like** (=not at all similar) *Life at college was nothing like I expected.*

similar /ˈsɪmələʳ, ˈsɪmɪləʳ/ [adj] if one thing is **similar** to another, or if two or more things are **similar**, they are like each other: *I know how you feel, because I have a similar problem.* | *It's bigger than Jim's room, but it's very similar.* | *When you look at these two carpets, you can see that the patterns are very similar.* | **+ to** *Do you have anything similar to this material but cheaper?* | *The Marines also experimented with fast-attack vehicles, similar to dune buggies.*

alike /əˈlaɪk/ [adj not before noun] if two or more things or people are **alike**, they are very similar in some way: *You lawyers are all alike. You just talk a lot, tell a few lies, and send the bill.* | *I think my mother and I are very much alike in some ways.* | *As the personal computer market matured, computer makers have realized that not all PC buyers are alike.* | **look/think/sound etc alike** *The album is boring – all of their songs sound alike.*

much the same /ˌmʌtʃ ðə ˈseɪm/ [adj phrase] very similar: *Soldiers are much the same throughout the world.* | **+ as** *Bodie looks much the same as the day the mines closed down.* | **much the same .... .as/that** *The glass is still made in much the same way as it was 100 years ago.* | *The warranty would cover the electric car's battery pack in much the same way that gasoline engines are protected.* | **look/feel/smell/ taste much the same** *All these wines taste much the same.*

resemble/bear a resemblance to /rɪˈzembəl, ˌbeər ə rɪˈzembləns tuː/ [v T not in progressive or passive] to be similar in appearance or character: *Geraldine resembled her mother in every way.* | *Addis Ababa soon resembled an armed camp.* | **closely resemble** *We have produced a cloth made of pineapple fibre, closely resembling cotton but stronger.* | **bear a strong/close/striking resemblance to** *She's seventy-six, short, round and fair, and bears a strong resemblance to my own grandmother.* | **bear some/little/no resemblance to** *The London of the new millennium bears little resemblance to the London of my youth.*

comparable /ˈkɒmpərəbəl‖ˈkɑːm-/ [adj] similar in size, number, quality etc so that a comparison is possible: *Climatic conditions in the two countries are roughly comparable.* | **+ with/to** *The size of a dolphin's brain is comparable to a human's.* | **comparable in size/importance etc** *The planet Pluto is comparable in size to our Moon.*

akin to /əˈkɪn tuː/ [adj phrase] if something is **akin to** something else, it is very similar to it in character – used especially in literature: *It's a language closely akin to Arabic, and most Syrians would understand it.* | *It was with a feeling akin to despair that I realized the car was not going to start.*

2 in a similar way

- like
- similarly

like /laɪk/ [prep] in a similar way to someone or something: *I'd love to be able to sing like Ella Fitzgerald.* | *You're treating him like a child.* | *Huge trees had snapped like matchsticks in the hurricane-force winds.* | *Like many women her age, she struggled to find a balance between her career and her children.* | **just/exactly like sth** *She moves and talks exactly like her mother.*

similarly /ˈsɪmɪləʳli/ [adv] formal *The son followed his father's example and, similarly, the daughter modelled herself on her mother.* | **similarly situated/ expressed/inclined etc** *San Francisco and Rio de Janeiro are similarly situated, both standing at the entrance to great natural harbours.* | *This idea of creation is similarly expressed in a poem by Dylan Thomas.*

3 to make you think of another similar person or thing

- remind sb of
- be reminiscent of
- echo

remind sb of /rɪˈmaɪnd (sb) ɒv / [phr v T] to make you think of another thing or person because they are similar: *Sometimes, when you're angry, you remind me of your father.* | *The way he tells jokes reminds me of Jonathan.* | *What an ugly little building! It reminds me of a public lavatory.*

be reminiscent of /biː ˌreməˈnɪsənt ɒv/ [v phrase] formal if something or someone **is reminiscent of** another thing or person, they make you think of that other thing or person because they have a similar style, appearance, sound etc: *His singing is reminiscent of Bob Marley.* | *The Senator spoke of the drama of the situation in tones reminiscent of an evangelical preacher.* | *Her style of writing is somewhat reminiscent of Virginia Woolf.*

echo /ˈekəʊ/ [v T not in progressive] formal if something, especially a performance or a work of art **echoes** something that existed in the past, it makes you think of it because it is similar: *This new musical with its expensive costumes and scenery echoes the Hollywood glamour of the 1950s.* | *Her designs were informed by vintage Halston, 'Love Story' and the leisure suit, all echoing 1970s' style.*

4 to look very much like another person or thing

- look/be just like
- be the spitting image of
- could pass for/could be mistaken for

look/be just like ALSO **look/be exactly like** /lʊk, biː ˌdʒʌst ˈlaɪk, lʊk, biː ɪɡˌzæktli ˈlaɪk/ [v phrase] *That vase is just like one that I used to have.* | *He looks exactly like Clint Eastwood, except he's slightly taller.*

be the spitting image of ALSO **be the (living) image of** British /biː ðə ˌspɪtɪŋ ˈɪmɪdʒ ɒv, biː ðə (ˌlɪvɪŋ) ˈɪmɪdʒ ɒv/ [v phrase] informal to look almost exactly the same as someone else: *Everyone always said my aunt was the spitting image of Ingrid Bergman.* | *With that beautiful black hair, she is the living image of her mother.*

could pass for/could be mistaken for /kʊd ˈpɑːs fɔːʳ‖-ˈpæs-, kʊd biː mɪˈsteɪkən fɔːʳ/ [v phrase] if you **could pass for** or **be mistaken for** another person, you look so much like them that people might think you were the other person: *You could easily pass for your sister – you look just like her.* | *With her hair cut short, she could easily have been mistaken for a boy.*

5 someone who looks very much like someone else

- look-alike
- sb's double

look-alike /ˈlʊk əˌlaɪk/ [n C] a person who looks very much like another person, especially a famous person **Madonna/Elvis Presley etc look-alike** *Have you seen that new commercial with the Mel Gibson look-alike?* | *There were hundreds of Madonna look-alikes waiting outside Wembley Stadium for the concert.*

sb's double /(sb's) ˈdʌbəl/ [n C] especially British a person who looks exactly like another person: *I met your double at a party last night. I really thought it was you.*

6 to be like your mother, father, grandfather etc

- be like
- look like
- take after
- be a chip off the old block

be like /biː ˈlaɪk/ [v phrase] to have a very similar character to your mother, father, grandfather etc: *You're like your grandmother – obstinate and determined.* | **just/exactly like sb** *You and your dad – you're exactly like each other in temperament.*

look like /ˈlʊk laɪk/ [v phrase] to have a very similar appearance to your mother, father, grandfather etc: *My sister looks like my dad, but I look more like my mother.* | *Who does the baby look like?* | **just/exactly like** *You look just like your sister – I would've known you anywhere.*

take after /ˈteɪk ɑːftəʳ‖-æf-/ [phr v T not in progressive or passive] to be like your mother, father, grandfather etc, especially in character: *Aunt Arabella is very stubborn. Kim takes after her in that respect.* | *He spends a lot of time trying to dispel the myth that he takes after his famous, alcoholic father.*

be a chip off the old block /biː ə ˌtʃɪp ɒf ði ˌəʊld ˈblɒk‖-ˈblɑːk/ [v phrase] informal to be like your mother, father, grandfather etc in character or behaviour, used especially when talking about a good characteristic: *'That daughter of yours has a great sense of humour.' 'Yes, I like to think she's a chip off the old block!'*

7 to have similar characters or interests

- be two of a kind
- have a lot in common/have so much in common

be two of a kind /biː ˌtuː əv ə ˈkaɪnd/ [v phrase] if two people **are two of a kind**, they are very similar to each other in character or behaviour: *You're two of a kind, you and Doug – you can never be serious for even one minute!* | *They were two of a kind, both proud and stubborn, both hated by the community.*

have a lot in common/have so much in common /hæv ə ˌlɒt ɪn ˈkɒmən‖-ˌlɑːt ɪn ˈkɑː-, hæv ˌsəʊ mʌtʃ ɪn ˈkɒmən/ [v phrase not in progressive] two or more people who **have a lot in common** share similar interests, attitudes, tastes etc: *We like the same things and the same people. I think we have a lot in common.* | *You two have so much in common. You should be able to find a way to talk about things without fighting.*

8 to understand someone because you are like them

- relate to
- identify with

relate to /rɪˈleɪt tuː/ [v T not in passive] to be able to understand and be sympathetic to someone, because you have the same problems, situation etc as them: *Group work helps children learn to share things and relate to each other.* | *He seems to have difficulty relating to others and expressing his feelings.* | *She's a great teacher because she really relates to the kids.*

identify with /aɪˈdentəfaɪ wɪð/ [phr v T not in passive] to like someone because you feel that they are similar to you: *Which of the characters do you most identify with?* | *Winters believes she has been successful because people identify with her and trust her.* | *We can all identify with these people in their desire for freedom and independence.*

9 similar and equally good or bad

- there is little to choose between/there is not much to choose between
- be much of a muchness

there is little to choose between/there is not much to choose between /ðeər ɪz ˌlɪtl tə ˈtʃuːz bɪtwiːn, ðeər ɪz ˌnɒt mʌtʃ tə ˈtʃuːz bɪtwiːn/ if **there is little to choose between** two or more people or things, they are almost equally good or bad, especially so that you would not know which one to choose: *There's very little to choose between the two apartments in terms of space, so I think we should take the cheaper one.* | *When you look at the two candidates, there really isn't much to choose between them.*

be much of a muchness /biː ˌmʌtʃ əv ə ˈmʌtʃnəs/ [v phrase] British informal to be very similar and almost equally good or bad: *I can't really recommend any particular hotel. They're all much of a muchness.*

10 the quality of being similar

- similarity
- resemblance

similarity /ˌsɪməˈlærəti/ [n U] **+ between** *The author notes the similarity between Western and Chinese principles and sees them as having a common basis in science.* | **+ with/to** *We were able to tell the date of the statue because of its similarity with other statues of that period.* | **the similarity of sth (to sth)** *For generations, scientists and science-fiction writers talked about the similarity of Mars to Earth.*

resemblance /rɪˈzembləns/ [n singular/U] a similarity in appearance: *When you look at this painting and the one by Rembrandt, there is certainly a resemblance.* | **+ to** *Although the fish have little external resemblance to each other, skeletally they are quite similar.* | **family resemblance** (=a resemblance between members of the same family) *When he met Francesca's aunt he was instantly struck by the family resemblance.* | **striking resemblance** (=extremely strong resemblance) *The Japanese maple leaf bears a striking resemblance to a marijuana leaf.*

11 a particular way in which things or people are similar

- similarity
- parallel

similarity /ˌsɪmɪ̈ˈlærɪ̈ti/ [n C usually plural] *When comparing cultures, we often pay attention only to the differences without noticing the many similarities.* | **+ in** *The book classifies cheeses by similarities in flavour, rather than by ingredients.* | **+ between** *There is one important similarity between the two political systems.*

parallel /ˈpærəlel/ [n C usually plural] a particular way in which two things are similar, especially when it is possible to make an interesting comparison between them **+ between** *There are certain parallels between the situation in Europe today and that which existed 90 years ago.* | *Kakar finds parallels between the Hindi film and popular myths.*

limit

RELATED WORDS

- when there is not enough of something *see* **enough/not enough**
- *see also* **control, rule/regulation, law**

1 the largest amount that is allowed or possible

- limit
- maximum
- the most
- upper limit
- ceiling
- cut-off point

limit /ˈlɪmɪ̈t/ [n C usually singular] the highest number, speed, temperature etc that is allowed by a law or rule: *He borrowed money up to the limit that the bank allowed.* | **+ on** *There's no limit on the amount of money that may be brought into the US.* | **time/age/speed limit** *The Interstate speed limit is 65 m.p.h.* | **over/above the limit** *Pollution levels in the water were found to be over the official limit.* | **set a limit** (=decide what a limit will be) *Some families set limits on how much they spend on each other's Christmas present.*

maximum /ˈmæksɪ̈məm/ [adj only before noun] the **maximum** number or amount is the largest number or amount that is possible, normal, or allowed: *After leaving Calais, the train soon reaches its maximum speed of 300 kph.* | *Forty is the maximum number of passengers this bus is allowed to carry.* | *Ditikins faces a maximum sentence of 15 years in prison.* —**maximum** [n singular] **the maximum** *You don't have to wait long for a new passport – 3 weeks is about the maximum.* | **a maximum of £10/50%/30 degrees etc** *Individuals may donate a maximum of $1000 to the campaign.*

the most /ðə ˈməʊst/ [quantifier] the largest amount or number of something **+ (that)** *He likes to gamble, but the most he ever won was $1000.* | *Two cakes is the most that I can bake in my oven at one time.* | **at most/at the most** (=as the largest amount possible or allowed) *A new tyre would cost £70 at the very most.*

upper limit /ˌʌpəʳ ˈlɪmɪ̈t/ [n C usually singular] the largest amount of something that is allowed within a range: *The explosion had a force that was close to the upper limit allowed by nuclear arms treaties.* | **+ on** *The Pentagon did not set an upper limit on troop deployments during the war.*

ceiling /ˈsiːlɪŋ/ [n singular] the largest number or amount of something that is officially allowed – use this especially in business: *Import quotas may rise from the present ceiling of 18.5 million to 20 million.* | **+ on** *There is a ceiling on the amount of foreign investment allowed in any company in the country.* | **debt ceiling** (=the largest amount that a country is allowed to owe) *Congress was once again considering raising the federal debt ceiling.*

cut-off point /ˈkʌt ɒf ˌpɔɪnt/ [n C usually singular] the largest amount or number that is allowed before something stops happening, has an effect etc: *The machine's cut-off point is 1000 volts, which is the safety maximum.* | *Science has pushed back the cut-off point at which a woman can no longer bear children.*

2 the smallest amount that is allowed or possible

- the least
- minimum
- lower limit
- threshold

the least /ðə ˈliːst/ [quantifier] the smallest amount or number of something **+ (that)** *£20,000 is the least we could accept for a car of this type.* | *The least anyone around here works is about 50 hours per week.*

minimum /ˈmɪnɪ̈məm/ [adj] the **minimum** number or amount is the smallest number or amount that is possible or allowed: *What is the minimum wage these days?* | *The minimum age to buy cigarettes is 18.* —**minimum** [n singular] **the minimum** *He usually just pays the minimum each month on his credit cards.* | **a minimum of £10/50%/30 degrees etc** *You have to stay for a minimum of 7 days.* | **absolute/bare minimum** (=the very least number or amount) *The hospital has reduced staffing to an absolute minimum.* | **keep sth to a minimum** *Let's try to keep irrelevant comments to a minimum.*

lower limit /ˌləʊəʳ ˈlɪmɪ̈t/ [n C usually singular] the least amount of something that is allowed within a range: *Age 3 is really the lower limit for teaching children to swim.* | **+ of** *Deposits are subject to a lower limit of $400.*

threshold /ˈθreʃhəʊld, -ʃəʊld/ [n C] a number or level at which something begins to happen or to have an effect, especially the lowest number or level: *If the temperature falls below a particular threshold, a warning light comes on.* | *Under the proposal, those whose earnings were less than a $36,000 threshold would not have to pay taxes.*

3 when there are limits on what you can do

- limits
- limitations
- restrictions
- constraints
- be limited
- be restricted
- be constrained
- scope
- confines
- parameters

limits /ˈlɪmɪts/ [n plural] the rules or facts that control someone's freedom or their ability to do what they want **+ to** *There are practical limits to the number of cases we can deal with each day.* | **+ of** *He's well aware of the limits of his knowledge.* | **within limits** *We want our employees to enjoy themselves, within certain limits.*

limitations /ˌlɪmɪˈteɪʃənz/ [n plural] limits on what someone or something is able to do **+ of** *The limitations of the computer system make some operations very difficult.* | **+ on** *The president was unwilling to accept limitations on his power.* | **physical limitations** *Hikers should know their physical limitations and not take unnecessary risks.*

restrictions /rɪˈstrɪkʃənz/ [n plural] rules or laws that strictly control what you are allowed to do: *There are certain travel restrictions in effect in certain areas along the border.* | **+ on** *Unions are pressing for restrictions on steel imports from Japan.* | *Because of restrictions on reporting, newspapers were not allowed to cover the story.* | **impose restrictions** (=officially order that something must be limited) *New restrictions have been imposed on immigration.*

constraints /kənˈstreɪnts/ [n plural] facts or conditions that limit what you can do, for example not having enough time, money etc: *Because of time constraints two acts had to be cut from the show.* | **+ of** *The constraints of prison life are sometimes too much for people to bear.*

be limited /biː ˈlɪmɪtɪd/ [v phrase] to not be able to do everything that you want because things are not available, there are rules or laws about it etc: *Our choice of shops is somewhat limited because we don't have a car.* | **+ to** *We're limited to two weeks of vacation a year, so a three-week safari isn't possible.* | **+ by** *Many Hong Kong performers are limited by their lack of English skills in making the transition to Hollywood.*

be restricted /biː rɪˈstrɪktɪd/ [v phrase] if something **is restricted** to a particular amount, time, group etc, there are rules or other conditions limiting it to that amount, time, group etc: *Access to the President is restricted.* | **+ to** *In those days, visiting in the hospital was restricted to specific weekend hours only.* | **+ by** *Because Forbes was using his own money, he was not restricted by federal limits on campaign spending.*

be constrained /biː kənˈstreɪnd/ [v phrase] to be unable to do what you want to do because of facts or conditions, for example, because you do not have enough time or money: *Sharon's options were severely constrained because of the foolish choices she made as a teenager.* | **+ by** *Research is often constrained by lack of sufficient data.*

scope /skəʊp/ [n U] the range of things that a particular activity is allowed to include or have an effect on **+ of** *A clear statement of the goal and scope of a research project is a useful reference point.* | **within the scope** *It was determined that the Commissioner had been acting within the scope of his official duties.* | **beyond/outside the scope** *I'm afraid the matter falls outside the scope of this enquiry.* | **in scope** *Regulations are important in markets that are increasingly international in scope.* | **of enormous/historic/wide etc scope** *The ruling party has granted concessions of considerable scope.*

confines /ˈkɒnfaɪnz‖ˈkɑːn-/ [n plural] the limits on a situation, organization, activity etc that control what people are allowed to do **+ of** *She felt trapped by the narrow confines of the convent.* | **within the confines** *We must operate within the confines of the law.* | **beyond/outside the confines** *Hypothetical thinking goes beyond the confines of everyday experience.*

parameters /pəˈræmɪtəʳz/ [n plural] a set of limits within which an activity can be done – use this in business, education, or technical contexts: *In the private sector there are clear parameters which surround labour relations.* | **within/outside the parameters of sth** *It is only within the parameters of a clear set of goals that a national science program can be successful.*

4 to put a limit on something

- limit
- restrict
- set/impose/put a limit
- keep to/keep within
- confine
- fix

limit /ˈlɪmɪt/ [v T] to stop a number or amount from becoming too large, or stop someone from doing whatever they want: *The new law limits the number of foreign cars that can be imported.* | *Men hold most of the top jobs, and this limits women's opportunities for promotion.* | **limit sb/sth to sth** *Let's limit our discussion to the facts in the report.* | **limit yourself to sth** *As you look for material to write about, don't limit yourself to other people's ideas.*

restrict /rɪˈstrɪkt/ [v T] to strictly control and limit the size, amount, or range of something: *The law would restrict the sale of handguns.* | **restrict sb/sth to sth** *This year's AIDS conference is restricted in size to fewer than 3,000 participants.* | **restrict yourself to sth** *McGregor has said he will voluntarily restrict himself to $2.2 million in campaign spending.*

set/impose/put a limit /ˌset, ɪmˌpəʊz, ˌpʊt ə ˈlɪmɪt/ [v phrase] to control the size or amount of something, or to control an activity, by deciding what the limits of it will be **+ on** *Governments should put strict limits on tobacco advertising.* | *The courts have imposed limits on school officials' power to dismiss teachers.* | **set/impose a limit of sth** *The president set a time limit of 6 months for the negotiations to produce an agreement.* | **set/impose a limit** *Parents need to know when to set limits for their children's behavior.*

keep to/keep within /ˈkiːp tuː, ˈkiːp wɪðɪn/ [phr v T] if you **keep to** or **keep within** the limits of something, you make yourself stay within those limits: *We need to keep to the schedule if we're going to finish on time.* | *Keep within the speed limit and you should have no problems.*

confine /kənˈfaɪn/ [v T] to keep something within the limits of a particular activity or subject, especially when it is difficult for you to do this **confine sb/sth to sth** *Rebel troops have confined their attacks mainly to the southern part of the country.* | **confine yourself to sth** *The report confines itself to known and verifiable facts.*

fix /fɪks/ [v T] to decide on the limit of something, especially something that often changes, and make it stay the same for a long time: *Interest rates for savings accounts have been fixed at 7% for the rest of the year.* | *The project has finally been approved and the budget has been fixed.*

5 when there is a limit on the size or amount of something

- limited
- there are limits/there is a limit
- fixed
- finite

limited /ˈlɪmɪtɪd/ [adj] if something is **limited**, only a fixed amount is allowed or available: *We only have a limited amount of time in which to finish the work.* | *Call now – this offer is good for a limited time only.* | **+ to** *The class is limited to 20 students.*

there are limits/there is a limit /ˌðeər ɑːʳ ˈlɪmɪts, ˌðeər ɪz ə ˈlɪmɪt/ if **there are limits** or **there is a limit** to something, only a particular amount or number is possible or allowed, and not any more than that: *Of course, we'd like to have as many children as possible attend, but there are limits.* | **+ on** *According to the director, there's a limit on the number of computers we can buy.* | **+ to** *There are limits to what the human body can tolerate.*

fixed /fɪkst/ [adj] **fixed number/amount/price etc** one which has already been decided and which cannot be made higher or lower: *Our health insurance pays a fixed amount for each type of treatment, regardless of what it actually costs.* | *fixed interest rates* | *Fixed costs should be separated from variable costs when working out the annual accounts.*

finite /ˈfaɪnaɪt/ [adj] something that is **finite** has a limit and an end – use this especially in scientific contexts: *The speed at which light travels is finite.* | *The earth has a finite number of resources which we must protect.*

6 when there is no limit

- unlimited
- there is no limit
- boundless
- infinite
- the sky's the limit

unlimited /ʌnˈlɪmɪtɪd/ [adj] something that is **unlimited** has no fixed limit: *We pay $20 a month for unlimited Internet access.* | *The ticket is good for unlimited travel on the city's transportation system for 3 days.* | *At the time of the purchase, the extent of Alaska and its resources must have seemed unlimited.*

there is no limit /ðeər ɪz ˌnəʊ ˈlɪmɪt/ use this to say that someone can have or do as much of something as they want **+ to/on** *If we work together, there's no limit to what we can achieve.* | *There's no limit to the number of times you can register to win.*

boundless /ˈbaʊndləs/ [adj] having no limit – used especially in literature: *Taking care of small children is a job that requires boundless energy.* | *They felt lost and alone on the vast, boundless sea.*

infinite /ˈɪnfɪnɪt/ [adj] something that is **infinite** has no limit and no end, or does not have one that you can easily see – used especially in scientific contexts: *The variations of color that a human eye can see are infinite.* | *infinite space* | *A natural language contains an infinite number of grammatical sentences.*

the sky's the limit /ðə ˌskaɪz ðə ˈlɪmɪt/ if you say **the sky's the limit**, you mean that there is no upper limit on something such as the amount of money you can spend or on the success that you can have: *Pick out whatever you want – the sky's the limit.* | *We try to make our engineers feel that the sky's the limit when it comes to what they can design.*

line

1 a line on paper

- line
- dotted line

line /laɪn/ [n C] a long, thin, continuous mark on a surface: *The teacher had put a red line through the first sentence.* | *Mike drew a line along the wall to show where the tiles would come up to.* | **straight line** *Use your ruler to draw a straight line.* —**lined** [adj] paper that is lined has lines printed across it: *a letter written on pale blue lined paper*

dotted line /ˌdɒtɪd ˈlaɪn‖ˌdɑː-/ [n C] a line made up of dots that is marked on paper, especially to show the place where someone must write their name: *Sign on the dotted line, please.* | *The dotted line on the map shows the path that goes from the church down to the river.* | *Fold the paper along the dotted line.*

2 a line of colour

- stripe
- striped
- band
- streak

stripe /straɪp/ [n C] a straight line of colour on cloth, paper etc, usually part of a pattern where the line is repeated many times: *The American flag has red and white stripes.* | *He was wearing a grey suit with narrow blue stripes.* | *My horse had a big white stripe down the middle of his nose.*

striped ALSO **stripy** British spoken /straɪpt, ˈstraɪpi/ [adj] something which is **striped** or **stripy** has a pattern on it which is made of many narrow coloured lines which are close together: *He was wearing a navy blue suit and a striped shirt.* | *stripey socks* | **red and black striped/pink and blue striped etc** *My aunt knitted me a blue and white striped sweater for Christmas.*

band /bænd/ [n C] a thick coloured line: *a black snake with orange bands around its back* | **+ of** *There was a band of yellow in the rock.* | *How many bands of colour are there in a rainbow?*

streak /striːk/ [n C] a coloured line, especially one that is not straight or that has been made without any plan or pattern: *Her hair was brown, with streaks of gold.* | *Karen's dress had a big streak of red wine down the front.* | *'What have you been doing?' asked his mother, pointing at the streaks of dried mud on his arms and legs.*

3 a line on the ground or on the surface of something

- line
- rut
- tracks
- groove
- furrow

line /laɪn/ [n C] *If the ball goes over this line, it's out of play.* | **yellow line** (=a yellow line painted on the street which means that you cannot park there) *Monica got a fine yesterday for parking on a yellow line.*

rut /rʌt/ [n C] a deep line made in a dirt track by the wheels of vehicles: *The road to the farm had deep ruts in it.* | *The carriage became stuck in a rut, and we all had to get out and push.* —**rutted** [adj] having many deep ruts: *Gradually the road became more rutted and muddy.*

tracks /træks/ [n plural] lines on the ground that are left by the wheels of a vehicle: *The police were busy examining the tyre tracks of the two vehicles which were involved in the accident.* | *We followed the tracks down a lane and arrived at an abandoned farmhouse.*

groove /gruːv/ [n C] a thin line that has been cut into a surface, for example on a record: *The record player needle kept jumping out of the grooves.* | *Then you cut a groove into the wood, so that the two pieces can be slotted together.*

furrow /ˈfʌrəʊ‖ˈfɜːr-/ [n C] one of many long lines which have been dug in a field in order to plant crops: *All around the furrows in the fields were filled with snow.*

4 a line on cloth where it has been folded or crushed

- crease
- wrinkle
- wrinkled

crease /kriːs/ [n C] especially British a line on a piece of clothing or material where it has been folded or crushed: *When I unpacked my suitcase, all my shirts had creases in them.*

wrinkle /ˈrɪŋkəl/ [n C] especially American a line in a piece of clothing that is caused when it has not been folded or hung properly, but instead has been left somewhere untidily: *If you hang that dress over the bath, the steam will get the wrinkles out.* | *It's made from a special fabric that doesn't leave any wrinkles after you wash it.*

wrinkled especially American **/creased** especially British /ˈrɪŋkəld, kriːst/ [adj] clothes that are **wrinkled** or **creased** have a lot of wrinkles or creases in them: *Your tie's creased, you'll have to iron it.* | *Chris, as usual, came in wearing old jeans and a wrinkled T-shirt.*

5 a line on someone's face or skin

- line
- wrinkle
- wrinkled
- crease

line /laɪn/ [n C] *When she laughed, little lines formed at the corners of her eyes and mouth.* | *The deep lines on his forehead showed that he was a worried man.*

wrinkle /ˈrɪŋkəl/ [n C usually plural] a deep line on someone's face or skin, which is caused by growing old: *Her face was old and covered in wrinkles.* | *Delay the effects of ageing with a revolutionary new anti-wrinkle cream.*

wrinkled /ˈrɪŋkəld/ [adj] if someone's face or skin is **wrinkled**, it has a lot of wrinkles on it: *a small man with a balding head and a very wrinkled face* | *Mrs Franz sat on the step, shelling peas with her wrinkled old hands.*

crease /kriːs/ [n C] a deep line on someone's face or skin, which lasts for a short time because they are smiling, bending part of their body etc: *When he smiles, you can see the creases around his mouth and his eyes.* —**creased** [adj] *The baby howled, its face creased and pink.*

6 a line of things

- line
- row
- bank
- tier

line /laɪn/ [n C] several things that are standing next to each other or one behind the other **in a line** *Maisie had arranged her teddy bears in a line on the bed.* | **+ of** *In front of the house there is a line of tall trees.*

row /rəʊ/ [n C] a line of things that have been deliberately put next to each other, especially one of several lines that are arranged one behind the other: *The tiny cottages had been built in long rows.* | *They put a row of chairs out for the visitors.* | *Julie arranged her perfumes and creams in neat rows on the dressing table.* | **row upon row** (=many rows) *The back wall was covered with row upon row of files.*

bank /bæŋk/ [n C] a line of computers, televisions, or other electrical equipment **+ of** *Fans who couldn't get into the stadium watched the match on banks of TV monitors outside.* | *The scientists sit behind banks of computers, giving instructions to the crew of the spaceship.*

tier /tɪəʳ/ [n C] one of many rows of seats in a theatre, concert hall etc, which are at different levels **+ of** *We always sat in the top tier of seats.* | *Mason occupied two spaces on a tier of seats normally reserved for the board of directors and important visitors.*

7 a line of writing or numbers

- line
- column

line /laɪn/ [n C] a **line** of writing that goes across a page: *Martin opened the letter and read the first few lines – it was bad news.* | *Start reading at line 12.* | **+ of** *a few lines of poetry*

column /ˈkɒləm‖ˈkɑː-/ [n C] a line of numbers written under each other, that goes down a page: *Sales totals are shown in this column.* | *Add up the numbers in the column on the right.*

8 a line that separates two areas or countries

- border
- boundary

border /ˈbɔːʳdəʳ/ [n C] the official line that separates two countries, or the area close to this line: *They escaped across the border into Thailand.* | **+ with** *Iraq had put thousands of troops along its border with Kuwait.* | **+ between** *The town lies on the border between Chile and Argentina.* | **the German/Mexican/Swiss etc border** *Strasbourg is very close to the German border.* | **cross the border** *As soon as we crossed the border we began to see signs of poverty.* | **on the border** *Jeumont is a small town on the French-Belgian border.* | **border town/area/region** *The army's main task was to patrol the border regions.* | **border dispute** (=when two countries disagree about where the border should be) *The two presidents met for the first time to discuss their longstanding border dispute.*

boundary /ˈbaʊndəri/ [n C] the official line that marks the edge of an area of land, for example a farm or one of the parts of a country: *More and more people are moving outside the city boundaries.* | **+ between sth and sth** *The Mississippi River forms the boundary between Tennessee and Arkansas.* | **draw a boundary** (=(=decide where a boundary will be) *Politicians drew strangely shaped boundaries, in order to give themselves an advantage in the next election.*

9 to draw or mark a line on something

- draw a line
- underline
- rule

draw a line /ˌdrɔː ə ˈlaɪn/ [v phrase] *The teacher drew a line on the blackboard.* | *Someone's drawn a line through my name and written in theirs.*

underline /ˌʌndəʳˈlaɪn/ [v T] to draw a line under a word in order to make people notice it: *Don't forget to underline the title of the essay.* | *All the mistakes had been underlined in red ink.*

rule /ruːl/ [v T] formal to draw a straight line using a ruler or other straight edge: *He ruled three lines* *under the title of his essay.* | *She divided the page into four by ruling two diagonal lines across it.*

10 a line of people

- line
- row
- queue
- in single file
- procession
- parade
- column

line /laɪn/ [n C] a **line** of people who are standing behind each other or next to each other: *The Queen is walking slowly along the lines of soldiers, occasionally stopping to ask a question.* | **in a line** (=forming a line) *The photographer asked us to stand in a line.* | **form a line** (=make a line) *The teacher got the children to form a line before they went into the hall.*

row /rəʊ/ [n C] a line of people who have been arranged to stand or sit next to each other, especially when there are several lines of people arranged one behind another: *Can you see me in the photo? I'm in the back row on the left.* | **in a row** *The hotel staff stood in a row to greet their important guests.*

queue British **/line** American /kjuː, laɪn/ [n C] a number of people who are standing one behind another, waiting to do something: *There was a queue of about fifteen people at the bus stop.* | **+ for** *The line for the movie went right around the block.* | **form a queue/line** (=make a queue/line) *The women who were waiting outside the toilets began to form a queue.* | **in the queue** (=part of the queue) *Excuse me, are you in the queue?*

in single file /ɪn ˌsɪŋgəl ˈfaɪl/ [adv] if a group of people walk **in single file**, they walk one behind another in a line: *The path was so narrow that we had to walk in single file.*

procession /prəˈseʃən/ [n C] a group of people or vehicles that move slowly along in a line, especially as part of a public ceremony: *We were held up by a long funeral procession.* | *The children were eager to take part in the carnival procession.*

parade /pəˈreɪd/ [n C] an event in which a line of people such as musicians, dancers etc, or a line of decorated vehicles, go down the street while other people watch them in order to celebrate something: *A lot of soldiers were missing from the Victory parade.* | *When Johnson arrived home after the championships a big parade was held in his honour.*

column /ˈkɒləm‖ˈkɑː-/ [n C] a long moving line of people, especially soldiers: *The column of French soldiers passed us on their way to the battlefront.* | *Columns of men and women were making their way towards the central square.*

11 to stand in a line of people

- stand/wait/be in line
- queue
- queue up
- line

stand/wait/be in line ALSO **stand/wait on line** American /ˌstænd, ˌweɪt, biː ɪn ˈlaɪn, ˌstænd, ˌweɪt ɒn ˈlaɪn/ [v phrase] to stand in a line of people who are waiting to do something: *Jerry joined the crowd of people who were waiting in line outside the stadium.* | *Standing in line for hours at some government office was not exactly my idea of fun.* | **to do sth** *Are you in line to get tickets?*

queue /kjuː/ [v I] British to stand in a line of people who are waiting to do something: *We had to queue for hours in the rain.* | **+ to do sth** *One of the other passengers who was queueing to get on the train suddenly had a heart attack.* | **+ for** *Thousands queued for tickets to see the final.*

queue up British **/line up** American /ˌkjuː ˈʌp, ˌlaɪn ˈʌp/ [phr v I] to form a line or join a line of people who are standing one behind another in order to wait to do something, for example buy a ticket: *We queued up outside the stadium and had to wait over an hour for our tickets.* | **+ to do sth** *People began lining up to get into the movie theater.* | **+ for** *We used to have to queue up for bread every morning.*

line /laɪn/ [v T] if many people **line** a street, they stand next to each other in lines along the sides of it, especially in order to see an important person or event: *Hundreds of people lined the streets to see the football team go by.* | *The route taken by the Queen was lined with crowds of people waving flags.*

12 to arrange things or people in a line

- line up

line up /ˌlaɪn ˈʌp/ [phr v T] **line up sb/sth** *He lined up the plates on the table in front of them.* | **line sb/sth up** *They lined the prisoners up and shot them.* | *The horses were being lined up for the start of the race.*

liquid

RELATED WORDS

- *see also* **pour, flow, water, wet**

1 a liquid

- liquid
- fluid

liquid /ˈlɪkwɪ̈d/ [n C/U] a substance, such as water or milk, that is not a solid and not a gas: *Add most of the flour to the liquid and stir the mixture.* | *She screamed as the boiling liquid burned her skin.* —**liquid** [adj usually before noun] use this about something which is liquid, but which is usually a solid or a gas: *Treat your plants once a week with liquid fertiliser.* | *liquid soap* | *liquid nitrogen*

fluid /ˈfluːɪ̈d/ [n C/U] a liquid – used especially in technical contexts: *In extreme heat your body will lose fluid and salt.* | *Brake fluid was leaking out from under my car.* | **body/bodily fluids** *The HIV virus is transmitted though body fluids, during sexual intercourse.*

2 an amount of liquid

- drop
- blob
- pool

drop /drɒp‖drɑːp/ [n C] a very small amount of liquid in a round shape, that falls from somewhere **+ of** *Big drops of rain slid down the window pane.* | *Add a few drops of vanilla essence, the egg white and half the butter.* | *She applied a few drops of perfume behind her ears and smiled at her reflection in the mirror.*

blob /blɒb‖blɑːb/ [n C] a drop or small amount of thick liquid **blob of paint/glue/wax/grease etc** *Rita dropped a blob of paint on the new carpet.* | *Blobs of wax had dripped from the candle onto the table cloth.* | *Put a blob of glue on each surface and carefully press together.*

pool /puːl/ [n C] an area of liquid lying on a surface **+ of** *Trautman was lying in a pool of blood.* | *A pool of oil had collected under the car.*

3 a liquid that flows easily

- thin
- runny
- watery

thin /θɪn/ [adj] a **thin** liquid flows very easily – use this about liquids that are often thick: *The paint was too thin, and was dripping everywhere.* | *For these crepes you will need a fairly thin batter, so do not add too much flour.*

runny /ˈrʌni/ [adj] informal food that is **runny** is liquid but should be thicker than it is: *a boiled egg with a runny yolk* | *runny custard*

watery /ˈwɔːtəri‖ˈwɔː-, ˈwɑː-/ [adj] food or drink that is **watery** contains too much water, so that it does not taste or look good: *The coffee is horrible – really weak and watery.* | *All they had to eat for weeks was bread and watery cabbage soup.*

4 a liquid that is almost solid

- thick
- lumpy
- creamy
- smooth
- paste

thick /θɪk/ [adj] a **thick** liquid flows slowly because it is almost solid: *If you want to make the sauce thicker, add flour.* | *thick vegetable soup*

lumpy /ˈlʌmpi/ [adj] a liquid that is **lumpy** contains small solid pieces, so it is not as smooth as it should be: *This gravy is lumpy.* | *I hate lumpy porridge.*

creamy /ˈkriːmi/ [adj] thick and smooth like cream: *The tomato soup was hot, creamy and delicious.* | *Add the chocolate to the butter and eggs, stirring the mixture until it is thick and creamy.*

smooth /smuːð/ [adj] if a liquid is **smooth**, it is thick and has no lumps in it, especially because it has been mixed very well: *Beat the eggs and flour until they are smooth.* | *Blend the strawberries with a little icing sugar in a food processor until it forms a smooth purée.*

paste /peɪst/ [n C] a soft and usually sticky mixture of liquid and another substance, which you can spread easily: *Mix the flour in just enough milk to make a smooth paste.* | *Tahini is a paste made from ground sesame seeds.* | *He made a paste of mud and water.*

5 when something becomes a liquid

- melt
- dissolve
- thaw
- melt down
- molten
- condense
- soluble

melt /melt/ [v I] if something solid **melts** or if heat melts it, it becomes liquid: *The chocolate had melted and was all over the inside of her pocket.* | *Melt the butter in a saucepan and stir in the sugar.* —**melted** [adj only before noun] *a pasta dish topped with melted cheese*

dissolve /dɪˈzɒlv‖dɪˈzɑːlv/ [v I] if something solid **dissolves** or if you **dissolve** it, it is added to a liquid and mixed with it, so that it become liquid itself: *The crystals dissolve in water to create a purple liquid.* | *Dissolve the salt in 125 ml of hot water.*

thaw /θɔː/ [v I] if ice, snow, or a frozen lake or river **thaws**, it becomes a liquid because the temperature has become warmer: *The lake is frozen all winter, but it usually thaws in March.* | *The snow had started to thaw, and there was a faint scent of spring in the air.*

melt down /ˌmelt ˈdaʊn/ [phr v T] to melt something such as a metal object, especially so that you can make it into something different **melt down sth** *He melts down coins to make into earrings and ornaments.* | *Most of the brass in the church has been melted down and sold.* | **melt sth down** *We collected all the old candles and melted them down to make one big candle.*

molten /ˈməʊltən/ [adj only before noun] **molten** rock, metal, glass etc has been made into a liquid by being heated to a very high temperature: *You can watch craftsmen make beautiful vases out of molten glass.* | *The town was buried under a river of molten lava.* | *Castings are made by pouring molten metal into a mould and allowing it to solidify.*

condense /kənˈdens/ [v I] if gas or steam **condenses**, it becomes liquid by becoming colder: *Steam from the shower condensed on the cold bathroom mirror.* | *During cold nights, air condenses on the grass to form dew.* | **+ into** *The gaseous metal is put in a closed container and cooled so that it condenses into liquid zinc.*

soluble /ˈsɒljᵒbəl‖ˈsɑː-/ [adj] a solid substance that is **soluble** can be mixed into a liquid so that it becomes part of it: *soluble aspirin* | *The use of soluble chemical fertilizers is banned, as they seep into rivers and pollute the water supply.* | **be soluble in sth** *There are two sorts of vitamins: some are soluble in fat, and some soluble in water.* | **water-soluble/fat-soluble etc** (=soluble in water, fat etc) *Plants take up water-soluble minerals through their roots.*

6 when a liquid gets thicker

- thicken/get thicker
- set
- clot
- congeal

thicken/get thicker /ˈθɪkən, get ˈθɪkəʳ/ [v I/v phrase] if a liquid **thickens** or you thicken it, it becomes more solid and does not flow very easily: *When the sauce is just starting to thicken, pour it over the meat.* | *Now boil the mixture until it thickens.* | *As the temperature goes down, the oil in the engine gets thicker.*

set /set/ [v I] if a liquid **sets**, for example some types of food or plastics, it becomes solid or almost solid after a period of time: *Leave the jam in a cool place to set.* | *It's best to pour your yoghurt into small containers before it sets.* | *Has the glue set yet?*

clot /klɒt‖klɑːt/ [v I] if blood **clots**, it becomes thicker and more solid: *Blood had clotted on the cuts on his back and on his arms.* | *Some types of snake venom prevent blood from clotting.*

congeal /kənˈdʒiːl/ [v I] if a liquid **congeals**, it thickens and becomes unpleasantly sticky and almost solid as it becomes cooler: *Josie picked up a plate of congealed egg and beans, and scraped it into the bin.*

list

RELATED WORDS

▸ *see also* **record**

1 a list of things, places etc

▸ **list**
▸ **checklist**
▸ **inventory**
▸ **catalogue**

list /lɪst/ [n C] a set of names of things, places, jobs you need to do etc, which are written one below the other **+ of** *Could I have a list of hotels in Bournemouth and the surrounding area?* | **make a list** *I made a list of all the things I had to do that day.* | **on a list** *Henry's name wasn't on the list.* | **shopping list** (=a list of all the things you need to buy) *I forgot to bring my shopping list with me.*

checklist /ˈtʃekˌlɪst/ [n C] a list of things you need or things you have to do which you keep in order to help you remember them: *Use a checklist when visiting properties to buy, so that you keep a record of which features you liked and didn't like.* | **+ of** *Here is a checklist of things you need to buy before travelling to India.*

inventory /ˈɪnvəntri‖-tɔːri/ [n C] an official list of all the objects in a house, factory, or shop, written so that you can know exactly what is there **in/on an inventory** *Some of the things in the shop were not listed in the inventory.* | **+ of** *The company keeps a full inventory of its equipment.* | **make an inventory** *She made an inventory of everything in the apartment.*

catalogue especially British **/catalog** American /ˈkætəlɒg‖-lɔːg, -lɑːg/ [n C] a list that gives some information about each thing in a library, art collection etc so that people can find what they want: *There is a new catalogue of all the books in the library.* | *You will find information about all the sale items in our catalog.*

2 a list of people

▸ **list**
▸ **short list/shortlist**
▸ **register**
▸ **roll**
▸ **roster**

list /lɪst/ [n C] a set of the names of people in a particular place, on a course etc, written one below the other and kept as a record **+ of** *A list of competitors will be posted on the main notice board.* | **waiting list** (=a list of people who are waiting to do something) *I'm afraid the English course is already full, and there is a waiting list.* | **guest list** *This is the guest list for the wedding.* | **draw up a list** *I drew up a list of all the jobs I had to do in the house.* | **cross sb off the list** (=remove someone's name from a list) *Sarah's name had been crossed off the list of candidates.*

short list/shortlist /ˈʃɔːʳtlɪst/ [n C] British a list of a small group of people, chosen from a larger group, from which you choose one person for a job **on/onto a shortlist** *You were lucky to even get onto the shortlist.* | **draw up a shortlist (of people)** *After the first set of interviews, we will draw up a shortlist of candidates we wish to interview a second time.*

register /ˈredʒɪ̈stəʳ/ [n C] an official list containing the names of all the people, organizations, or things of a particular type **+ of** *a register of qualified translators* | *a civil register of births, deaths, and marriages* | **electoral register** (=an official list of people who can vote in an election) *Make sure your name is on the electoral register in good time.*

roll /rəʊl/ [n C] an official list of the names of people at a meeting, in a class etc: *The school now has a roll of over 2,000 children.* | **on a roll** *His name was not on the voters' roll.*

roster /ˈrɒstəʳ‖ˈrɑː-/ [n C] a list of people and the jobs they each have to do **+ for** *We organized a roster for cleaning the house.* | **on a roster** *I noticed that my name was not on the night duty roster.*

3 a list in a book

▸ **index**
▸ **contents**
▸ **bibliography**

index /ˈɪndeks/ [n C] an alphabetically arranged list of all the names and subjects in a book: *It's a lot quicker if you use the index.* | *Look under B in the index to see if biology is covered in the book.*

contents /ˈkɒntents‖ˈkɑːn-/ [n plural] a list, usually printed at the front of a book, which shows the main parts that the book is divided into: *I could tell the book was not what I wanted by looking at the contents.* | **contents page** *Sue opened the book and looked at the contents page.* | **table of contents** *There's no table of contents, so it's quite difficult to find the information you're looking for.*

bibliography /ˌbɪbliˈɒgrəfi‖-ˈɑːg-/ [n C] a list of all the books and articles on a particular subject, or all the books and articles that are used when you write something: *There is a short bibliography at the back of the book.* | **in a bibliography** *Details of suggested further reading are given in the bibliography.*

4 a list of events or activities

▸ **programme**
▸ **schedule**
▸ **agenda**

programme British **/program** American /ˈprəʊgræm/ [n C] a list of all the activities or events that have been planned, especially one that shows when each event will happen **on a programme** *First on the programme is a speech by the organizer, Mrs Jenkins.* | **+ of** *A spectacular program of exhibitions, displays and competitions has been planned.* | *Because of bad weather, our programme of events has had to be changed slightly.*

schedule /ˈʃedjuːl‖ˈskedʒʊl, -dʒəl/ [n C] a list of events or activities that shows when each one will happen: *According to the schedule, the first lecture begins at 9.00 am.* | *The President's schedule included a visit to a children's hospital.*

agenda /əˈdʒendə/ [n C] a list of the subjects that will be discussed at a meeting: *Have you got a copy of the agenda for tomorrow's meeting?* | **on an agenda** *What do you do if you want to discuss something that's not on the agenda?* | **(at the) top of an agenda** *The fuel crisis will be at the top of the agenda for today's board meeting.*

5 to make a list, or include something on a list

▸ **make a list**
▸ **catalogue**
▸ **itemize**
▸ **list**
▸ **shortlist**

make a list /ˌmeɪk ə ˈlɪst/ [v phrase] **+ of** *She made a list of all the things she would need on her trip.* | *A* *list has been made of all students who failed to attend lectures regularly.*

catalogue especially British **/catalog** American /ˈkætəlɒg‖-lɔːg, -lɑːg/ [v T] to make a well-arranged list of a large group of things so that people can find what they want: *We are still waiting for all the paintings to be identified and catalogued.*

itemize /ˈaɪtəmaɪz/ [v T] to write down all the separate parts or details of something in a list: *Donleavy carefully itemized the equipment.* | *Make sure the bill you receive is itemized and shows the individual price of each job that has been done.*

list /lɪst/ [v T] to give a **list** of names, places etc, or to include someone or something on a list: *a useful booklet, listing all the colleges that take part-time students* | *The books are listed alphabetically, according to the name of the author.* | **+ as** *Chapman lists rugby as one of his hobbies.*

shortlist /ˈʃɔːʳtlɪst/ [v T] British to include someone on a small list of people, chosen from a larger group, from which you choose one person for a job: *Three candidates have been shortlisted for the job.*

listen

RELATED WORDS

- listen carefully and pay attention *see* **attention**
- *see also* **hear, attention**

1 to listen to someone or something

- listen
- pay attention
- listen for/listen out for
- hear sb out

listen /ˈlɪsən/ [v I] to pay attention to what someone is saying or to a sound that you hear: *I didn't hear the answer, because I wasn't listening when she read it out.* | *If you listened in class you might get better grades.* | **+ to** *He listened carefully to every word I said.* | *I could listen to Placido Domingo all day – he has such a beautiful voice!* | **listen hard** (=try hard to hear something that is very quiet) *If you listen hard, you can hear the sound of the sea in the distance.* | **listen carefully** *The company has begun to listen more carefully to its customers, in a determined attempt to improve customer service.* | **listen intently** (=listen very carefully to hear what someone is saying) *Mrs Singh leaned forward, listening intently as they explained the procedure to her.*

pay attention /peɪ əˈtenʃən/ [v phrase] to listen carefully to what someone is saying: *I have some important information about travel arrangements, so please pay attention.* | *Billy's a smart kid, but he doesn't pay attention in class.* | **+ to** *She went on talking, but I wasn't really paying attention to what she was saying.* | *According to the survey, two-thirds of young people do not follow politics and pay no attention to election campaigns.*

listen for/listen out for /ˈlɪsən fɔːʳ, ˌlɪsən ˈaʊt fɔːʳ/ [phr v T] to listen carefully for a sound that you are expecting to hear, although you do not know when it will happen: *We hid behind the door, listening for the sound of the guard's footsteps.* | *The flight had been delayed, and so I waited in the departure lounge listening for announcements.* | *She lay in bed, listening out for the sound of his feet on the stairs.*

hear sb out /ˌhɪəʳ (sb) ˈaʊt/ [phr v T] to listen to all of what someone wants to tell you without interrupting them, especially when you disagree with them or do not believe them: *Hear me out first, Jane, and then you can say what you think.* | *Knapp heard him out patiently but still refused to change his mind.*

2 to secretly listen to someone

- listen in
- eavesdrop
- bug
- tap
- monitor

listen in /ˌlɪsən ˈɪn/ [phr v I] to listen to someone else's conversation when they do not know that you are listening, either on the telephone or when you are near them: *Whenever her boss had one of his 'private meetings', she always used to listen in.* | **+ on** *We tried to listen in on their conversation, but they were talking too quietly.* | *They used to have hours of fun listening in on what people were doing in their hotel rooms.*

eavesdrop /ˈiːvzdrɒp‖-drɑːp/ [v I] to secretly listen to someone else's conversation by standing near them, hiding behind a door etc: *How did you know I was going? You've been eavesdropping, haven't you!* | **+ on** *I caught him eavesdropping on our conversation.* | *Sue was able to eavesdrop on them through the open window.*

bug /bʌg/ [v T] to hide a small piece of electronic recording equipment in someone's room, car, office etc in order to listen secretly to what is said there: *Security agents bugged their offices and managed to get some evidence against them.* | *Wells was convinced the house was bugged and insisted on playing loud music while we talked.*

tap /tæp/ [v T] to connect a piece of electronic recording equipment to a telephone system so that you can listen to people's telephone conversations: *Later we realized our phones had been tapped and the police knew everything.* | *The President had to resign over an illegal phone-tapping operation.*

monitor /ˈmɒnətəʳ‖ˈmɑː-/ [v T] to listen to another country's radio or television broadcasts or radio messages in order to get information about that country: *Satellite technology means that enemy airwaves can be monitored more closely than ever before.*

3 what you say when telling someone to listen

- listen
- listen up

listen /ˈlɪsən/ spoken say this when you want someone to **listen** and pay attention to what you are saying: *Listen! There's someone coming upstairs!* | *Listen, I've just had a really good idea.*

listen up /ˌlɪsən ˈʌp/ spoken say this when you want someone, especially a group of people, to pay close attention to what you are saying, especially when you are giving them instructions: *Okay, class. Listen up. Open your books at page 33.* | *The directions are complicated so listen up.*

4 to listen to the radio

- listen to
- tune in

- *see also* **television/radio**

listen to /ˈlɪsən tuː/ [v phrase] to **listen to** a radio programme or a particular radio station: *Lucy sat in her car, listening to the radio.* | *I always listen to the* *news while I have my breakfast.* | *What station are you listening to?*

tune in /ˌtjuːn ˈɪn‖ˌtuːn-/ [phr v I] to turn on your radio and listen to a particular programme, especially if you do this at the same time each week: *Be sure to tune in next week at the same time for another exciting episode of 'Death Ray'.* | **+ to** *Tune in to the Breakfast Show tomorrow to win VIP tickets to the Lollapalooza festival on Long Island.*

5 someone who listens

- listener
- audience
- be a good listener

listener /ˈlɪsənəʳ/ [n C] someone who is listening to a speech, piece of music etc, or who regularly listens to a particular radio programme or station: *He paused momentarily to check that his listeners had fully appreciated the humour of his remark.* | *The programme already has more than two million listeners across the country.*

audience /ˈɔːdiəns‖ˈɔː-, ˈɑː-/ [n C with singular or plural verb in British English] a group of people who watch and listen to someone speaking or performing in public, or who listen to a radio or television programme or station: *The second comedian really made the audience laugh.* | *The audience consisted mainly of young girls under sixteen.* | *WMLD's audience is mainly young and black.* | *These two programs are both news and current affairs, but they cater for very different audiences.*

be a good listener /biː ə ˌgʊd ˈlɪsənəʳ/ [v phrase] if someone **is a good listener**, they always listen carefully and sympathetically when someone else is talking: *Cara's a really good listener, so she always has someone telling her their problems.*

little

WHAT'S HERE

- **a small amount** see **1 to 8**
- **a little/not very** see **9**

a small amount

RELATED WORDS

opposite: **lot**

- a little time *see* **short (9-10)**
- small in size *see* **small**
- *see also* **few/not many, amount/number**

1 a small amount of a substance

- a little
- a little bit
- not much
- a small amount
- trickle
- dab
- low

a little /ə ˈlɪtl/ [quantifier] *This glue's really strong – you only need to use a little.* | **a little water/money/time etc** *A little make-up would make her look so much more attractive.* | *The garden could do with a little rain.* | *Try putting a little oil on the hinge and see if it stops squeaking.* | **a little more/less** *If we all used a little less paper, we'd probably save a forest or two.* | **+ of** (=a small amount of a specific substance) *A little of the grease got on my skirt.*

a little bit ALSO **a bit** especially British /ə ˌlɪtl ˈbɪt, ə ˈbɪt/ [quantifier] informal a small amount of something: *You shouldn't have given me so much toothpaste – I only needed a little bit.* | **+ of** *A bit of detergent should get that stain out of your collar.* | *Save a little bit of the paint to do the trim.*

not much /nɒt ˈmʌtʃ/ [quantifier] only a small amount of something – use this especially when you expect or need more: *'How much paper is there in the printer?' 'Not much.'* | **not much water/ money/time etc** *There's not much light in this room, is there?* | *It was very cold, but there wasn't much snow on the ground.* | **not very much** *That's not very much paint if you're planning to paint the whole bedroom.* | **+ of** (=a small part of a specific substance) *You can use my shampoo but there's not much of it left.*

a small amount /ə ˌsmɔːl əˈmaʊnt / [quantifier] use this especially when it is a measured amount: *Squeeze a small amount onto the palm of your hand and spread the gel evenly through your hair.* | **+ of** *Stir-fry the vegetables in a small amount of oil.* | *Even a small amount of the drug can be detected in the test.* | *Small amounts of radiation were found on their clothing.* | **in small amounts** *Fluorine is present in small amounts on Mars.*

trickle /ˈtrɪkəl/ [quantifier] a small amount of a liquid, flowing out of something: *Because of the drought, the river has become little more than a trickle.* | **+ of** *There was a trickle of blood coming from the corner of his mouth.*

dab /dæb/ [quantifier] a small amount of a liquid, cream, or powder which has been put onto a surface with something such as a brush or with the fingers: *Can I use some of your perfume? I just want to put a dab on my wrist.* | **+ of** *She put a dab of ointment on the cut.* | *The car just needs a couple of dabs of paint here and there, and it'll be fine.*

low /ləʊ/ [adj] if something is **low** in fat, sugar, salt etc, it contains very little fat, sugar etc **+ in** *The casserole is low in calories and fat.* | *These new industrial cleaners are much lower in ammonia and other dangerous chemicals than before.* | **low-fat/-sugar/-cholesterol etc** *He's been on a low-cholesterol diet since his heart attack.* | **low fat/sugar/cholesterol etc content** *Non-dairy toppings tend to have lower fat content than whipping cream.*

2 a very small amount of a substance

- very little
- hardly/barely any
- almost no
- no ... to speak of
- trace

very little /ˌveri ˈlɪtl/ [quantifier] a very small amount, usually so that there is not enough to be useful, to be important etc: *There was no ink in the bottle and very little left in the pen.* | **very little water/money/time etc** *Fish contains very little fat.* | *The area has a lot of deer, but very little water and not much open space.*

hardly/barely any /scarcely any especially British /ˌhɑːʳdli, ˌbeəʳli ˈeni, ˌskeəʳsli ˈeni/ [quantifier] almost none at all: *Don't forget to order some more paper for the copy machine – there's barely any left.* | **hardly any water/money/time etc** *The ferns manage to grow with scarcely any sunlight.* | *He was fifty years old and his hair still had hardly any gray in it.*

almost no /ˌɔːlməʊst ˈnəʊ/ [quantifier] such a small amount that you can hardly see it, use it etc **almost no water/money/time** *Potatoes have almost no fat, but they're very filling.* | *He had a longish, plain face with a straight nose and almost no hair.* | **almost**

none *'How much glue is left?' 'Almost none.'* | **almost none of sth** *By the time the dentist had finished almost none of the existing tooth remained.*

no ... to speak of /nəʊ ... tə ˈspiːk ɒv/ [adv] if there is no rain, food, oil, etc **to speak of**, there is almost none and not enough to have any effect: *There had been no rain to speak of for ten weeks and the garden was dying.* | **none to speak of** *There's no fuel oil left – none to speak of, anyway.*

trace /treɪs/ [quantifier] an amount so small that it is very difficult to see: *She had very little grey hair, with just a trace near the temples.* | **+ of** *Police found traces of blood on the killer's shoes.* | *Tests have revealed traces of poison in his food.*

3 a small amount of food or drink

- a little
- a little bit
- not much
- very little
- hardly/barely any
- drop
- pinch
- dash

a little /ə ˈlɪtl/ [quantifier] *'Would you like some more coffee?' 'Just a little.'* | **a little water/meat/cake etc** *The next day Mark felt well enough to eat a little solid food.* | *Would you like a little ice cream with your pie?* | **+ of** (=a small amount of a specific food, drink etc) *I think I'll try a little of the casserole.* | **a little more/less** *If I were you I'd use a little less salt next time.*

a little bit ALSO **a bit** especially British /ə ˌlɪtl ˈbɪt, ə ˈbɪt/ [quantifier] informal a small amount: *'Can I serve you some soup?' 'Alright, but just a little bit.'* | **+ of** *He only ate a little bit of dinner and then went straight to bed.* | *Would you like a bit of bacon with your eggs?* | *We still have a little bit of cheese left, if you want it.* | **a (little) bit more/less** *Can I have a bit more red wine, please?*

not much /nɒt ˈmʌtʃ/ [quantifier] only a little – use this especially when you expect or need more: *'How much cake do you want?' 'Not much, I'm on a diet.'* | **not much water/meat/cake etc** *There's not much wine left, but I think we can each have a glass.* | **+ to eat/drink** *We need to do some shopping – there isn't much to eat at home.* | **not very much** *You haven't eaten very much. Do you feel okay?*

very little /ˌveri ˈlɪtl/ [quantifier] a very small amount, usually so small that there is not enough to have an effect, be useful etc: *We drink only occasionally, and even then very little.* | **very little water/meat/cake etc** *The soup is made with lots of vegetables but very little chicken.* | **+ of** *He ate very little of the food we had given him.*

hardly/barely any ALSO **scarcely any** especially British /ˌhɑːʳdli, ˌbeəʳli ˈeni, ˌskeəʳsli ˈeni/ [quantifier] almost none at all: *I thought you liked my lasagne, but you've eaten hardly any.* | **hardly any water/meat/cake etc** *There's barely any sugar in these cookies at all.* | *Since his heart attack he's eaten scarcely any red meat.*

drop /drɒp‖drɑːp/ [quantifier] informal a small amount of something that you drink: *'Do you take cream in your coffee?' 'Yes, just a drop, please.'* | **+ of** *Would you like a drop of soda in your whisky?* | *He hasn't had a drop of alcohol in 20 years.*

pinch /pɪntʃ/ [quantifier] a small amount of a powder such as salt, flour etc which you can hold between your thumb and first finger **+ of** *Add a pinch of salt and half a cup of breadcrumbs.* | *The stew normally tastes better with a pinch or two of dried herbs.*

dash /dæʃ/ [quantifier] a very small amount of a liquid which is added to a drink or to food, usually in order to give it a stronger taste **+ of** *It's just vodka with orange juice and a dash of lime juice.* | *The secret of this sauce is a couple of dashes of brandy added just at the end.*

4 a small amount of money

- a little
- not much
- very little
- next to nothing
- nominal
- negligible
- a drop in the ocean

a little /ə ˈlɪtl/ [quantifier] *Most people will give a little to charity if they are asked.* | **a little money/cash** *I have a little cash with me, but not enough to pay for both of us.* | **a little extra** *He earns a little extra by working on weekends.* | **a little over/under** (=a little more or less than an amount of money) *The car costs a little over $20,000.* | **a little more/less** *A private room costs a little more, but it's worth it.*

not much /nɒt ˈmʌtʃ/ [quantifier] there is only a small amount of money, especially when you expect or need more: *After paying rent he doesn't have much left to buy food and pay bills.* | **not much money/cash** *Pete didn't get much money when he sold his car.* | **not very much** *I don't think he earns very much working at the bank.*

very little /ˌveri ˈlɪtl/ [quantifier] a very small amount of money, so that there is not enough to have an effect: *He spends very little on food.* | *Considering they work so hard they're paid very little.* | **very little money/cash** *When Maria lost her job she had very little money in savings.*

next to nothing /ˌnekst tə ˈnʌθɪŋ/ [adv] if the amount that something costs is **next to nothing**, it is extremely cheap: *It costs next to nothing to go to an afternoon movie.* | *The company's profits climbed from next to nothing to $6 million in just two years.*

nominal /ˈnɒmɪ̈nəl‖ˈnɑː-/ [adj] a **nominal** sum, charge, or payment is very small, because what is important is that something is paid, even if it is much less than would usually be paid: *We are allowed to use the tennis courts for a nominal fee.* | **a nominal £1/$5 etc** *Tickets for the concert are a nominal $3 for students.*

negligible /ˈneglɪdʒɪ̈bəl/ [adj] an amount of money that is **negligible** is so small that it has no effect or is so small that it is not worth worrying about: *The cost of maintaining the machine is negligible.* | *Expenses for maintaining the investment fund are negligible – just half a percentage point of profit.*

a drop in the ocean British **/a drop in the bucket** American /ə ˌdrɒp ɪn ði ˈəʊʃən, ə ˌdrɒp ɪn ðə ˈbʌkɪ̈t‖-ˌdrɑːp-/ [n phrase] informal an amount is **a drop in the ocean** or **a drop in the bucket** when it seems very small compared with what is really needed: *The United States pledge of $100 million to the rainforest fund is a drop in the ocean.* | *Third World debt is so massive that recent pledges to reduce it are just a drop in the bucket.*

5 too little money

- paltry
- derisory
- pittance
- peanuts

paltry /ˈpɔːltri/ [adj only before noun] **paltry sum/amount/pay/value etc** such a small amount, sum etc that it is insulting to the people it is paid to: *Club owners in Kansas City paid paltry wages to jazz* *musicians but gave them steady work.* | *Last year workers were offered a paltry raise of only one percent.* | **a paltry £1/$5 etc** *Many of the workers in the factory received a paltry $2 a day.*

derisory /dɪˈraɪsəri/ [adj] formal, especially written a **derisory** amount of money that you are offered or paid is so small that it is not worth considering seriously: *Government increases in health expenditure are derisory.* | **a derisory £10/$100/10% etc** *The company's profits increased 35%, but they've only offered a derisory 2.5% pay increase.*

pittance /ˈpɪtəns/ [n singular] an extremely small amount of money, especially when you think the people who are being paid it are being treated unfairly: *They expect their staff to work hard, but the wages they pay are a pittance.* | **a mere/absolute pittance** *In the poorest parts of the country, children work 12-hour days for a mere pittance.*

peanuts /ˈpiːnʌts/ [n plural] informal a surprisingly small amount of money – use this when you are comparing two prices or amounts: *The workers get paid peanuts.* | *He's got so much money, $500 is just peanuts to him.*

6 a small amount of something such as a feeling etc

- a little
- a little bit
- not much
- a small amount of sth
- an element of sth
- taste

a little /ə ˈlɪtl/ [quantifier] *'Do you speak French?' 'Just a little.'* | **a little trouble/patience/help etc** *We had a little difficulty finding the place but we got there in the end.* | *You might need a little help getting started, but after that you should be fine.* | **+ of** *I can understand a little of the frustration he must be feeling.* | **a little more/less** *With a little more creativity they could have made the house look really nice.*

a little bit ALSO **a bit** especially British /ə ˌlɪtl ˈbɪt, ə ˈbɪt/ [quantifier] informal a little: *By now she was resisting him only a little bit.* | **+ of** *We had a little bit of trouble reading his handwriting.* | *He brings a bit of experience and a lot of enthusiasm to the job.* | **a (little) bit more/less** *I think a bit more discipline is needed with these children.*

not much /nɒt ˈmʌtʃ/ [quantifier] only a little: *Not much is known about her childhood.* | **not much trouble/patience/help etc** *He doesn't have much experience of running a business.* | *It was clear that not much thought had been put into the plan.* | **not very much** *We didn't have very much understanding of the problem then.*

a small amount of sth /ə ˌsmɔːl əˈmaʊnt əv (sth)/ [n phrase] a little of something: *There is a small amount of truth to what he says.* | *Big improvements can be made with only a small amount of training and effort.*

an element of sth /ən ˈeləmənt əv (sth)/ [n phrase] if there is **an element of** some quality such as truth, danger, or violence in something, there is a small amount of it, but enough to be noticed: *There is always an element of risk in mountain climbing.* | *She tried to maintain an element of mystery in her relationships.* | *Despite the agreement between the two countries, an element of uncertainty about the future remains.*

taste /teɪst/ [n singular] **a taste of power/happiness/fame etc** a short experience that shows you what it is like to have power, fame, happiness etc: *Alvin had had a brief taste of freedom and didn't want to live with his parents again.* | *She decided to become an actress after getting her first taste of fame in a local theatre production.*

7 a very small amount of something such as a feeling, quality etc

- very little
- almost no
- hardly/barely any
- a touch/hint/trace of sth
- little
- minimal
- negligible
- next to nothing

very little /ˌveri ˈlɪtl/ [quantifier] a very small amount, so that there is not enough to have an effect, be useful, important etc: *'How much do you know about computers?' 'Very little, I'm afraid.'* | **very little trouble/patience/help etc** *I had very little energy left.* | *Changing the law will make very little difference.* | *It makes very little sense for companies to maintain large inventories these days.*

almost no /ˌɔːlməʊst ˈnəʊ/ [quantifier] such a small amount that you can hardly notice it **almost no trouble/patience/help etc** *Scientists have paid almost no attention to the new theory.* | *She supports the bill although she admits it has almost no chance of being passed.* | *The birth control campaign was begun 10 years ago but has had almost no impact in the rural areas.* | **almost none** *'What progress have you made on your research project?' 'Almost none.'*

hardly/barely any ALSO **scarcely any** especially British /ˌhɑːʳdli, ˌbeəʳli ˈeni, ˌskeəʳsli ˈeni/ [quantifier] almost none at all: *She said she felt a lot of regret about leaving, but I felt hardly any at all.* | **hardly any trouble/patience/help etc** *They closed down the whole department with barely any notice to the staff.* | *Mark is so lazy, he makes scarcely any effort to improve his work.*

a touch/hint/trace of sth /ə ˈtʌtʃ, ˈhɪnt, ˈtreɪs əv (sth)/ [quantifier] a very small amount of something, that you almost do not notice: *'Are you ready yet?' asked Hazel, with a touch of irritation in her voice.* | *For the first time a hint of tension had crept into their relationship.* | *After speaking to her for a while, he began to detect a trace of a Southern accent.*

little /ˈlɪtl/ [quantifier] formal a small amount, especially when you expect more **little trouble/patience/help etc** *Little progress was made during the negotiations.* | *The report offers little hope that the economy will improve any time soon.* | *There seems to be little chance of him coming home for Christmas.*

minimal /ˈmɪnəməl/ [adj] a **minimal** amount of something is the smallest that is possible, so that it is not worth thinking or worrying about: *The new operating technique involves minimal risk to patients.* | *The impact of the sale on current employees should be minimal.* | *The crew had very little experience and were given minimal safety training.*

negligible /ˈneglɪdʒəbəl/ [adj] a **negligible** amount of something is so small that it has almost no effect at all: *The damage done to his property was negligible.* | *Economists say raising the minimum wage would have a negligible effect on employment rates.* | *The chances of a healthy adult contracting the disease are negligible.*

next to nothing /ˌnekst tə ˈnʌθɪŋ/ [adv] if you know, learn, say, hear etc **next to nothing** about something, then you know, learn etc very little about it: *I learned next to nothing at school – the teachers were awful.* | *My parents know next to nothing about the men I date.*

8 when something or someone moves or changes a little

- a little
- a little bit
- slightly
- not much

a little /ə ˈlɪtl/ [adv] *His work has improved a little since he began the special classes.* | *Gas prices have fallen a little, but they are still much higher than last year.* | *I could see that Mrs Ewing's hand was trembling a little.*

a little bit ALSO **a bit** British /ə ˌlɪtl ˈbɪt, ə ˈbɪt/ [adv] informal a little: *Do you mind if I open the window a little bit.* | *The centre of the town had changed a bit, but everything else was just as I remember it.* | *Isn't that house leaning a little bit to the right?*

slightly /ˈslaɪtli/ [adv] a little, but not enough to be important or easy to notice: *The temperature had risen slightly, but it was still very cold.* | *He stood for a moment, his body swaying slightly.*

not much /nɒt ˈmʌtʃ/ [adv] only a little and not as much as you might have expected: *Things haven't changed much over the past few years.* | *I added more memory to my computer, but its performance didn't improve much.*

a little/not very

9 a little tired/sad/older/bigger etc

- a little
- a little bit
- slightly
- not much
- not very

a little /ə ˈlɪtl/ [adv] *I'm feeling a little tired, I think I'll go upstairs and have a rest.* | *When you're a little older, you'll understand why I'm doing this.* | *'Do you feel sad that you're leaving?' 'Just a little.'*

a little bit ALSO **a (tiny) bit** British /ə ˌlɪtl ˈbɪt, ə (ˌtaɪni) ˈbɪt/ [adv] informal a little: *I think David was a bit disappointed I forgot his birthday.* | *I'm a little bit cold. Do you mind if I turn up the heat?* | *Aren't you a bit young to be going to nightclubs?* | *I tried on the dress but it was just a tiny bit small.*

slightly /ˈslaɪtli/ [adv] a little, but not enough to be important or to notice: *Florida has a slightly larger population than Illinois.* | *Sean's car is a slightly different colour.* | *Lynn's daughter is only slightly older than mine.*

not much /nɒt ˈmʌtʃ/ [adv] only a little and not as much as you might have expected: *We should be there soon. It's not much further.* | *His son's not much younger than I am.* | **not much good** *I'm not much good at explaining things.*

not very /nɒt ˈveri/ [adv] only a little or not at all: *The house isn't very old. It was built in the 1990s.* | *I still go running, but not very often.* | *'Was the bike expensive?' 'Not very.'* | *The President was not very happy that the information had been leaked to the press.*

live

RELATED WORDS

- period of time when someone or something is alive *see* **life**
- to live *see* **alive**
- to be alive after an accident, illness, or war *see* **survive**
- *see also* **home, place, country, come from**

1 to live in a place

- live
- be from
- reside
- grow up
- inhabit
- be populated by

live /lɪv/ [v I] to have your home in a particular place: *Where do you live?* | **+ in** *Do you like living in Tokyo?* | *Judy lives in that nice house on the corner.* | *How do you like living in the city again after so many years away from it?* | **+ at** *In 1905 Russell was living at 4 Ralston Street.* | **live at home** (=to live in your parents' house) *Donald is 30 years old, but he still lives at home.* | **live abroad** (=live in a foreign country) *They lived abroad for several years but moved back when the children were school age.* | **live in** (=live at the place where you work or study) British *Many students prefer to live in during their first year of study.*

be from /biː ˈfrɒm/ [v phrase] especially spoken use this to talk about the place where you live: *My name's Sharon and I'm from Harlow.* | *The man is believed to be from somewhere in the north of England.* | *Where are you from?*

reside /rɪˈzaɪd/ [v I] formal to live in a country, city, or area – used in official contexts **+ in** *Miss Badu grew up in Dallas but now resides in Brooklyn.* | *At that time there were many American writers residing in Paris.* | **+ at** *Miss Tonelli, how exactly did you come to reside at your current address?* | **reside abroad** (=live in a foreign country) *The government bureau has prepared a booklet for U.S. citizens residing abroad.*

grow up /ˌgrəʊ ˈʌp/ [phr v I] to live in a place during the time when you are a child: *This is the neighborhood where my father grew up.* | **+ in** *Margaret Hallworth was born in Manchester but grew up in North Wales.* | **+ on** *I grew up on a farm in eastern Pennsylvania.*

inhabit /ɪnˈhæbɪ̈t/ [v T usually in passive] if a group of people or animals **inhabit** an area of land, they live there, especially over a long period of time or permanently – used especially in reports and written contexts: *The island is mainly inhabited by sheep.* | *Some tribes still inhabit the more remote mountains and jungles of the country.*

be populated by /biː ˈpɒpjɪ̈leɪtɪ̈d baɪ‖-ˈpɑːp-/ [v phrase] if an area of land **is populated by** a particular type of people or animals, they are the people or animals who live there: *This area of Antarctica is populated only by seals and penguins.* | **be heavily populated by** (=to have a large number of a particular group) *Mindanao is an island in the southern Philippines heavily populated by Muslims.*

2 to start to live in a place

- settle
- set up house
- take up residence

settle /ˈsetl/ [v I] to start to live permanently in a country or city, after you have lived in several different places **+ in** *We lived in Thailand, then Singapore, and finally settled in Hong Kong.* | *The family settled in a small Nevada town where they opened a store.*

set up house /ˌset ʌp ˈhaʊs/ [v phrase] to start to live in your own home for the first time, for example after getting married or leaving your parents' home: *They first set up house together in Atlanta and moved to Miami three years later.* | *He rarely left the Brooklyn apartment where he had set up house.* | **+ with** *Her parents were very upset when she set up house with her boyfriend.*

take up residence /ˌteɪk ʌp ˈrezɪdəns/ [v phrase] formal to start to live in a country, city, or a building, especially in order to start working at a job **+ in** *He left the country in December to take up residence in Panama.* | **+ at** *In 1953 Diem took up residence at a monastery in Belgium.*

3 when you live in the same house as someone else

- live with
- share a house/apartment/room/flat with
- room with
- flatmate

live with /ˈlɪv wɪð/ [v phrase] *For two months I lived with a French family in Paris to improve my French.* | *What's the name of the guy you live with?* | *We've been trying to persuade Jack's elderly mother to come and live with us.*

share a house/apartment/room/flat with /ˌʃeər ə ˈhaʊs, əˈpɑːʳtmənt, ˈruːm, ˈflæt wɪð/ [v phrase] to live with someone who is not a member of your family and not your sexual partner: *My brother shares a house with four other students.* | *Kim and I shared an apartment when I first moved to L.A.*

room with /ˈruːm wɪð/ [v phrase] American to live in the same room as someone at college: *Do you remember Diane? I roomed with her at college.* | *Have you decided who you're going to room with next year?*

flatmate British **/roommate** American /ˈflætmeɪt, ˈruːm-meɪt/ [n C] someone that you share an apartment with, who is not a member of your family and not your sexual partner: *This is Rosalind, my flatmate.* | *You can't have a party without asking your flatmate first.* | *My roommate and I aren't getting along very well – I think I'm going to have to move.*

4 to live with someone who you have a sexual relationship with

- live with
- live together
- cohabit
- shack up

live with /ˈlɪv wɪð/ [phr v T] *I lived with Stuart for three years before we broke up.* | *Have you ever met the woman that Glen is living with?*

live together /ˈlɪv təˌgeðəʳ/ [phr v I] if two people **live together**, they live in the same house and have a sexual relationship: *These days people often live together before getting married.* | *Al really wants us to live together, but I'm not sure I'm ready.*

cohabit /ˌkəʊˈhæbɪt/ [v I] formal to live with someone as if you were married to them: *Only about one in three couples who cohabit end up getting married.* | **+ with** *Most divorcees either remarry or cohabit with another partner.* —**cohabitation** /kəʊˌhæbɪˈteɪʃən/ [n U] *In the past, cohabitation was strongly disapproved of.*

shack up /ˌʃæk ˈʌp/ [phr v I] informal to start to live with someone who you have a sexual relationship with – often used humorously **+ with** *He's shacking up with some girl he met at the beach.* | **be shacked up** (=be living together) *Once they were shacked up, all they did was fight.*

5 someone who lives in a place

- population
- resident
- inhabitant
- citizen
- local
- tenant
- occupant
- occupier
- squatter
- settler

population /ˌpɒpjʊˈleɪʃən‖ˌpɑːp-/ [n singular] all the people in a country or town or area, or the number of people who live in it: *In Ghana 46% of the population is under 16 years of age.* | *The patients have been isolated to keep the disease from spreading to the rest of the population.* | **+ of** *The population of Singapore is almost 3 million.* | **the adult/Muslim/black etc population** (=all the people in a place who are adult, Muslim etc) *Ninety percent of the adult population is literate.* | **population growth** *The U.S. has a rate of population growth that is five times that of Europe.*

resident /ˈrezɪdənt/ [n C] someone who lives in a particular area of a town, a particular street or building etc: *Local residents are protesting about the new road.* | *Parking spaces are for residents only.* | **+ of** *Residents of Glacier Bay are complaining about the pollution caused by cruise ships.*

inhabitant /ɪnˈhæbɪtənt/ [n C usually plural] written one of the people who live in a place, especially in a town or city or in an area of a country: *Copenhagen has about 1.4 million inhabitants.* | *This is a poor rural area, with only one doctor per 10,000 inhabitants.* | **+ of** *Nearly 36% of the inhabitants of Saudi Arabia are resident foreigners.*

citizen /ˈsɪtɪzən/ [n C] someone who lives in a particular country or city and who has the right to be protected by its laws: *The police asked if we were both British citizens.* | **+ of** *The court's ruling should be of interest to every citizen of Texas.*

local /ˈləʊkəl/ [n C usually plural] informal someone who lives in a particular area, especially in a village or small town: *If you get lost just ask one of the locals for directions.* | *Denver International Airport was built in an area that locals call 'Tornado Alley.'*

tenant /ˈtenənt/ [n C] someone who lives in a house, flat, or room and regularly pays money to the person who owns it: *Tenants are not allowed to keep pets.* | *Have you found any tenants for your house yet?* | **+ of** *Twelve tenants of the Lockwood housing complex are taking part in the lawsuit against their landlord.*

occupant /ˈɒkjʊpənt‖ˈɑːk-/ [n C] formal someone who lives in a particular house, room etc: *They have left all the furniture and carpets in the house for the next occupant.* | **+ of** *Occupants of the building are understandably upset about the high-rise going up next door.*

occupier /ˈɒkjʊpaɪəʳ‖ˈɑːk-/ [n C] especially British formal the person who lives in a particular house, flat etc – used especially in official documents: *The document has to be signed by the occupier of every household.* | **owner-occupier** (=someone who lives in a house that they own) *The new law affects everyone from tenants to owner-occupiers.*

squatter /ˈskwɒtəʳ‖ˈskwɑː-/ [n C] someone who lives in an empty building without paying rent and without having permission to live there: *Police have removed over 50 squatters from the housing estate.* | *Squatters insist that without their work, the buildings would have deteriorated to the point of being unusable.*

settler /ˈsetləʳ/ [n C] someone who goes to live in a place that people have never lived in before: *Many of the earliest settlers here dies from disease and hunger.* | *Settlers found a plentiful supply of fruit and game in the nearby forests.*

6 when a place has people living in it

- inhabited
- occupied
- populated
- residential area
- human habitation

inhabited /ɪnˈhæbᵻtᵻd/ [adj] an area of land or a building that is **inhabited** has people living in it: *Only two of the islands are inhabited.* | *This tiny town has been an inhabited area for over 3,000 years.*

occupied /ˈɒkjᵛpaɪd‖ˈɑːk-/ [adj not before noun] a building or room that is **occupied** has people living in it: *None of the flats is occupied – they've only just been built.*

populated /ˈpɒpjᵛleɪtᵻd‖ˈpɑːp-/ [adj] with people living there: *Bears are appearing more and more frequently in populated areas* | **densely/heavily populated** (=having many people) *The north-east has always been more densely populated than the rest of the country.* | **thinly/sparsely populated** (=having few people) *French Guiana is a sparsely populated wilderness.*

residential area /ˌrezᵻdenʃəl ˈeəriə/ [n C] an area where there are houses where people live: *The museum is about 6 blocks from downtown in a quiet residential area.* | *London's main airport is surrounded by densely populated residential areas.*

human habitation /ˌhjuːmən hæbᵻˈteɪʃən/ [n phrase] formal use this about a place that humans live in or have lived in in the past: *The only sign of human habitation was a charred area where there had once been a fire.*

7 suitable/not suitable for people to live in

- habitable
- be fit to live in
- uninhabitable
- unfit for human habitation

habitable /ˈhæbᵻtəbəl/ [adj] a building or area of land that is **habitable** is suitable for people to live in, for example because it is clean enough, warm enough, safe enough etc: *There are already plans to renovate the buildings and make them habitable.* | *Japan is mostly mountainous and has a only a relatively narrow strip of habitable land along the coasts.*

be fit to live in /biː ˌfɪt tə ˈlɪv ɪn/ [v phrase] if a building **is fit to live in**, it is in a suitable condition for people to live in it: *As soon as the farm was fit to live in, we moved all our things there.* | **not be fit to live in** (=not in a suitable condition for people to live in) *The first apartment we looked at just wasn't fit to live in.*

uninhabitable /ˌʌnɪnˈhæbᵻtəbəl/ [adj] not suitable for living in or on: *A nuclear accident would make the whole region uninhabitable.* | *Twenty of the houses damaged by the storm were declared uninhabitable.*

unfit for human habitation /ʌnˌfɪt fəʳ ˌhjuːmən hæbᵻˈteɪʃən/ [adj phrase] not suitable for people to live in, especially because of being dirty, cold, or wet – used especially in official contexts: *The court was told that Blake had charged hundreds of dollars in rent for rooms that were unfit for human habitation.* | *In the 1960s, the flats were declared unfit for human habitation and demolished.*

logical

when ideas, plans, decisions etc are reasonable and based on clear thinking

RELATED WORDS

- *see also* **sensible, stupid/silly, idea, plan**

1 ideas that are logical

- logical
- sound
- make sense
- rational
- reasonable
- reasoned
- well-thought-out
- coherent
- hang together
- add up

logical /ˈlɒdʒɪkəl‖ˈlɑː-/ [adj] ideas, decisions etc that are **logical** are based on a series of facts or ideas connected in a correct and intelligent way: *Your essay ought to take the form of a logical argument.* | *There is no logical reason for teaching boys and girls separately.* | **take sth to its logical conclusion** *If you took the anti-war arguments to their logical conclusion, you would destroy all weapons.* | **it is logical to do sth** *If they did not leave until yesterday, then it is logical to assume that they will arrive some time tomorrow.* —**logically** [adv] *He explained his reasons clearly and logically.*

sound /saʊnd/ [adj] reasons, ideas, advice etc that are **sound** are logical and sensible, and it is easy to agree with them or believe that they are right: *The company offers sound financial advice to individuals and businesses.* | *Is recycling glass a sound idea?* | *There is no sound reason for the closure of this factory.*

make sense /ˌmeɪk ˈsens/ [v phrase] an idea, decision or plan that **makes sense** is logical and easy to understand: *His arguments seem to make sense.* | **it makes sense for sth to happen** *It would make sense for the parents to be involved in this discussion.*

rational /ˈræʃənəl/ [adj] a way of thinking, explanation, idea etc that is **rational** is very logical and is based on clear practical or scientific reasons, rather than on your feelings or wishes: *We're looking for someone with a rational approach to dealing with problems.* | *There must be some rational explanation for this apparently bizarre phenomenon.* | *There appears to be no rational motive for the attack.* —**rationally** [adv] *He was so frightened that it was impossible for him to think rationally.*

reasonable /ˈriːzənəbəl/ [adj] something that is **reasonable** seems to be logical and likely to be true because of what you know of the situation: *It is a reasonable assumption that she knew him well, as she had the keys to his house.* | *Given that the patient smokes 50 cigarettes a day, it would be reasonable to assume there is some lung damage.*

reasoned /ˈriːzənd/ [adj usually before noun] a **reasoned** way of thinking about something is logical and has been thought about very carefully: *We must have an informed and reasoned debate of the moral issues involved.* | *It became clear that calm, reasoned arguments were not working in this volatile situation.*

well-thought-out /ˌwel θɔːt ˈaʊt◂/ [adj] a **well-thought-out** plan or way of doing something is carefully and logically planned: *Before we can apply for funding, we must have strong, well-thought-out proposals.* | *a well-thought-out strategy*

coherent /kəʊˈhɪərənt/ [adj] words, thoughts or ideas that are **coherent** are arranged in an order that makes them easy to understand: *He couldn't give a coherent account of what he'd been doing that night.* | *His book contains a coherent argument in favour of economic change.*

hang together /ˌhæŋ təˈgeðəʳ/ [phr v I] informal if a piece of writing or an explanation **hangs together**, it is easy to understand because its parts are connected in a way that seems natural and logical: *Her story doesn't hang together very well.*

add up /ˌæd ˈʌp/ [phr v I not in progressive] informal if a set of facts **add up**, they are logically connected so they provide a reasonable explanation of a situation: *I can see now that George was planning this all along – it all adds up.*

2 able to think in a logical way

- logical
- rational

logical /ˈlɒdʒɪkəl‖ˈlɑː-/ [adj] someone who is **logical** is good at thinking in a very careful, clear, and organized way: *Joe's very sharp and logical when it comes to money matters.* | *She's a clear and logical thinker.* | *Men often accuse women of not being logical.*

rational /ˈræʃənəl/ [adj] someone who is **rational** is able to think clearly and logically without letting their emotions influence their decision or opinions: *How can a rational man be taken in by these arguments?* | *Let's try and discuss this like two rational human beings.*

3 a logical way of thinking

- logic
- reasoning

logic /ˈlɒdʒɪk‖ˈlɑː-/ [n U] a way of thinking that is clear and sensible because it is based on a series of facts or ideas connected in a correct and intelligent way: *Sophie questioned the logic of his arguments.* | **+ behind** *I couldn't see the logic behind the decision to close the school.*

reasoning /ˈriːzənɪŋ/ [n U] a logical way of thinking, used especially to make decisions or to explain why something happened: *Although I understood her reasoning, I did not agree with her decision.* | **line of reasoning** (=the reasoning someone has used to find an answer, explanation etc for a particular problem) *I found it hard to follow his line of reasoning.* | **+ behind** *The architect was asked to explain the reasoning behind his new design.*

4 not logical

- illogical
- irrational
- not make sense/make no sense
- not hold water
- not stand up
- not add up

illogical /ɪˈlɒdʒɪkəl‖ɪˈlɑː-/ [adj] *Listen to your child's worries and fears, however illogical they may seem.* | *I found some of his arguments totally illogical.* | **it is illogical to do sth** *It is illogical to sell stocks and shares when their value is low.* | *Because we do not know what death is, it is illogical to fear it.*

irrational /ɪˈræʃənəl/ [adj] something someone says or does that is **irrational** is not logical and often seems slightly crazy, especially because it is based only on emotions: *His behaviour can be somewhat irrational at times.* | *She struggled to overcome her irrational fear of the dark.*

not make sense/make no sense /ˌnɒt meɪk ˈsens, ˌmeɪk nəʊ ˈsens/ [v phrase] something that **does not make sense**, especially someone's behaviour, is very difficult to understand because there seems to be no logical reason for it: *I can't understand why she's so annoyed – it doesn't make sense.* | *Increasing interest rates now would make no sense at all.* | **it makes no sense to do sth** *It makes no sense to invest more money in a project that is so obviously a failure.*

not hold water /ˌnɒt həʊld ˈwɔːtəʳ/ [v phrase not in progressive] informal an explanation that **does not hold water** does not seem logical and can be easily criticized or proved to be incorrect: *His account of events simply doesn't hold water.*

not stand up /ˌnɒt stænd ˈʌp/ [phr v I not in progressive] an explanation that **does not stand up** does not seem logical and can be easily criticized or proved to be incorrect: *He might be able to convince his lawyer that he's telling the truth, but his story won't stand up in court.* | **not stand up to criticism/analysis etc** *It's an interesting theory, but I don't think it will stand up to close examination.*

not add up /ˌnɒt æd ˈʌp/ [phr v I not in progressive] informal if a set of facts or statements do **not add up**, they do not seem to be logically connected, even though it is difficult to say why: *Why had she left the note? It just didn't add up.* | *There were a few things in his story that didn't add up.*

long

RELATED WORDS

opposite: **short**

WHAT'S HERE

- **long in length** — see **1 to 5**
- **long time** — see **6 to 13**

long in length

RELATED WORDS

- *see also* **measure**

1 long object/line/road etc

- long
- elongated

long /lɒŋ‖lɔːŋ/ [adj] something that is **long** has a great length or distance between its two ends: *Her hair was long, honey-blonde, and tied back in a ponytail.* | *She led them down a long corridor, through countless swinging doors.* | *a woman in a long black gown* | *Rome has the longest shopping street in Europe.*

elongated /ˈiːlɒŋgeɪtɪ̈d‖ɪˈlɔːŋ-/ [adj] much longer and narrower than usual: *Eucalyptus trees grow very tall and have elongated leaves.* | *The lizard's body is thin and elongated, enabling it to squeeze into cracks and crevices.* | *The candle cast its elongated shadow across the wall.*

2 long book/name/list etc

- long
- lengthy

long /lɒŋ‖lɔːŋ/ [adj] a **long** book, name etc has a lot of pages, words, letters, details etc in it: *The place has a long Welsh name that I can't pronounce.* | *I like the book, but the chapters are really long.* | *Oh dear, this is going to be a long list of things I was supposed to do but didn't.* | *I don't want to make a long speech, but I hope you'll bear with me while I mention a few people who have helped.*

lengthy /ˈleŋθi/ [adj] formal a **lengthy** book, document, or explanation has a lot of words and details in it, and is often quite boring: *a lengthy, two-volume book on conditions in modern China* | *The President gave a lengthy address to the nation on CBS last night.* | *a lengthy financial report* | *He later completed a lengthy study of Figurative Art.*

3 to make something longer

- make sth longer
- lengthen
- extend
- stretch

make sth longer /ˌmeɪk (sth) ˈlɒŋgəʳ‖-ˈlɔːŋ-/ [v phrase] *The sleeves on this jacket are too short; do you think you could make them just a little longer?* | *Mr Watson said my essay was OK, but maybe I should have made it longer.* | *If you want to make the story longer, embellish it and ask your child questions about the characters.*

lengthen /ˈleŋθən/ [v T] to make something longer especially in order to make it more suitable or useful: *He wore blue jeans, which had been lengthened with strips of denim.* | *This particular operation involves lengthening the Achilles tendon.*

extend /ɪkˈstend/ [v T] to make something such as a line, road, or passage longer so that it reaches further: *Miners have extended the tunnel in order to get a new supply of coal.* | **extend sth to sth** *They will extend the subway from central Buffalo to the smaller towns around the city.*

stretch /stretʃ/ [v T] to make a piece of string, elastic, cloth etc longer by pulling it: *Norma picked up a stocking, stretched it and then pulled it onto her foot.* | *Careful, don't stretch it, it'll snap!*

4 to become longer

- get longer
- lengthen
- stretch

get longer /ˌget ˈlɒŋgəʳ‖-ˈlɔːŋ-/ [v phrase] *You've lost weight, and your hair's got longer.* | *The traffic tailback seems to be getting longer, not shorter!* | **get longer and longer** (=become continuously longer) *The Internet may be booming, but the list of failed dotcom companies is getting longer and longer.* | *These forms seem to get longer and longer.*

lengthen /ˈleŋθən/ [v I] to gradually become longer: *As afternoon drew on and the shadows lengthened, her fears increased.* | *The crack seemed to open wider and lengthen before her eyes.* | *He smiled and the creases at the corners of his eyes lengthened.*

stretch /stretʃ/ [v I] if a piece of string, elastic, cloth etc **stretches**, it gets longer, especially because it is being pulled: *Uncle John pulled hard on the bell-rope, which stretched and then broke.* | *elasticated straps designed to stretch easily*

5 ways of saying how long something is

- long
- length

long /lɒŋ‖lɔːŋ/ [adj] **six feet/two metres etc long** *The room is about 10 metres long and 5 metres wide.* | *Some snakes can grow up to 30 feet long.* | *To read a report that's over 40 pages long? It would take me most of the day.* | **how long** *How long is the trailer? I don't think it will fit in the garage.* | *Look how long Ayesha's hair is getting.* | *Get me a measuring tape – I'll show you how long I want the skirt.*

length /leŋθ/ [n C/U] how long something is: *Do you want your hair at the back to be the same length as the sides?* | *Try these trousers, they look about the right length.* | **+ of** *Measure the length of all three sides of the triangle.* | *The windows stretch across the whole length of the wall.* | **a length of 4 feet/three inches etc** *These fish can grow to a length of four feet.* | **5 miles/12 inches etc in length** *The leaves reach 20-25 cm in length.* | **in length** *The two pieces of rope were unequal in length.* | **of equal length** (=when two things are of the same length) *Actually, no-one has legs of exactly equal length.* —**full-length** /ˌfʊl ˈleŋθ◂/ [adj] as long as it is possible for something to be: *There were even full-length mirrors in all the lifts.* | *a full-length fur coat*

long time

RELATED WORDS

▸ *see also* **continue, last (5-7), boring/bored**

6 a long time

- a long time
- a while
- long
- for long
- hours/months/years etc
- all day/week etc long
- ages
- forever
- for the longest time
- donkey's years
- in living memory

a long time /ə ˌlɒŋ ˈtaɪm‖-ˌlɔːŋ-/ [n phrase] *It's good to see you again, Ben – it's been a really long time.* | **(for) a long time** *He's lived here a long time.* | *The house has been empty for a long time.* | **in a long time** *I haven't heard from Chuck in a long time.* | *It's about the worst cold I've had in a long time.* | **a long time ago** *We met in August 1947, a long time ago.* | *I've been to California, but it was a very long time ago.* | **a very long time/a long, long time** *We've been friends for a very long time.* | *A long, long time ago, a king had three daughters.* | **it's a long time since** *It's a long time since I heard from Clive.* | **take (sb) a long time (to do sth)** *It's a big file, so it'll take a long time to print out.* | *It's taking you a long time to finish that assignment, isn't it?* | **last a long time** *That's a big notepad you have there, it should last a long time.*

a while /ə ˈwaɪl/ [n phrase] a fairly long time **for a while** *How's Lynne? I haven't seen her for a while.* | *So you guys were in Brazil for a while, huh?* | **in a while** *I haven't worn that jacket in a while.* | **after a while** *After a while, I realised he was serious.* | **a while ago/back** *He fought for the title a while ago.* | *'Is that a photo of him?' 'Yeah, that was taken a while back – his hair's longer now.'* | **it's (been) a while since** *It's been a while since I read the book, and I can't remember much about it, to be honest.* | **quite a while** (=a long time) *He's been going out with her quite a while now, hasn't he?* | **a long while** *I haven't played chess in a really long while.* | **a little while** *Can I hold her for a little while?* | *A little while later, Rick returned with the drinks.* | **take (sb) a while** *It took me a while before I could understand him.* | *Your leg will take a while to get better, Mary.*

long /lɒŋ‖lɔːŋ/ [adv] a **long** time, or for a **long** time: *Have you been waiting long?* | *I won't be long.* | *It* *has long been recognized that a high fat diet can cause heart problems.* | **long before/after** *Long after the war, the wreckage of his plane was discovered.* | *They ran out of things to talk about long before they arrived.* | *75 percent of the battered women in our survey stayed with their husbands long after most people would have left.* | **so long** *They've been together so long, I can't figure out why they don't get married.* | **long ago** *I guess it didn't happen very long ago.* | **take (sb) so long** *I don't visit very often because it takes so long to get over there.* | *I'm sorry this is taking so long.*

for long /fəʳ ˈlɒŋ‖-ˈlɔːŋ/ [adv usually in questions or negative sentences] for a long time: *Have you been working here for long?* | *I hope his speech doesn't go on for long.* | *He'll have to stay in hospital, but not for long.* | **for very long** *I haven't known them for very long.*

hours/months/years etc /ˈaʊəʳz/ [n plural] many hours, months, or years, and a lot longer than you expected: *It was years before we found out the truth.* | *Sorry I'm late. Had to wait hours for a bus.* | *Justin spends hours and hours just playing this one game.* | **for hours/months/years etc** *I must get the car serviced – I've been putting it off for months.* | *Henry seemed to be on the phone for hours last night.* | **months/years/hours etc ago** *I bought this pen years ago. Two pounds it cost me!* | *Rob went out hours ago, and he's not back yet.* | **be weeks/months/hours etc since** *It's been years since I was there, the place must have changed.*

all day/week etc long /ˌɔːl deɪ ˈlɒŋ‖-ˈlɔːŋ/ [adv] for the whole of one day, the whole of one week etc: *It's been snowing almost all day long.* | *I've been thinking about you all night long.*

ages /ˈeɪdʒ½z/ [n plural] especially British, spoken a very long time **(for) ages** *I've had that jar of coffee ages, you'd better throw it out.* | *Derek's been telling her for ages to get another job.* | **it's ages since** *It's ages since we played this game – I'd forgotten how good you are.* | *It seems like ages since we saw Ron and Eileen.* | **ages ago** (=a long time ago) *'When did you sell the car?' 'Ages ago!'* | *I emailed you ages ago – hasn't it arrived?* | **wait/spend ages** *I spent ages in town trying to find something to wear for the wedding.* | *We had to wait ages till the doctor could see us.* | **ages and ages** (=use this to emphasize how long something takes or lasts) *Oh come on, we haven't had chips for ages and ages.*

forever /fərˈevəʳ/ [adv] spoken a very long time, or too long: *Let me see the map, or we'll be driving round here forever.* | *God's love endures forever.* | **go on forever** *Well, I don't suppose the police will let the situation go on forever!* | *We had a game of Scrabble that seemed to go on forever.* | **last forever** *You go into marriage thinking it's going to last forever.* | *These wool blankets pretty much last forever, don't they?* | **forever and a day** (=use this to emphasize that something continues for a very long time) *I'm staying here. If I go with you, it'll take forever and a day.*

for the longest time /fəʳ ðə ˌlɒŋg½st ˈtaɪm‖-ˌlɔːŋ-/ [adv] American spoken if you wait, walk, stand etc **for the longest time**, you do it for a very long time: *We sat in the bar drinking for the longest time.* | *For the longest time, we didn't even realize he was gone.*

donkey's years /ˈdɒŋkiz ˌjɪəʳz‖ˈdɑːŋ-/ [n phrase] British informal a long time, used especially to say that something happened a very long time ago **for donkey's years** *She worked in the shop for donkey's years, although the pay was awful.* | **donkey's years ago** *We used to play golf together, but that was donkey's years ago.* | **donkey's years since** *It's donkey's years since I went to the movies.*

in living memory /ɪn ˌlɪvɪŋ ˈmeməri/ [adv] for as long as people who are still alive can remember: *It was the hottest summer in living memory.* | *For the first time in living memory, old Jack had left the island.* | **within living memory** *The site had only flooded once within living memory.*

7 continuing for a long time

- long
- lengthy
- long-running
- long-standing
- lasting
- lifelong
- prolonged
- lingering
- enduring
- abiding
- chronic

long /lɒŋ‖lɔːŋ/ [adj] continuing for a **long** time: *The play was good, but it was a little too long.* | *He died after a long illness.* | *It's a long flight – 15 hours.*

lengthy /ˈleŋθi/ [adj] a **lengthy** process or delay takes a long time so that you have to wait before you can do something: *She died of natural causes after a lengthy illness.* | *The runways have reopened, but travelers have been warned to expect lengthy delays.* | **lengthy process/procedure etc** *He was indicted on drug charges after a lengthy investigation by the US Drug Enforcement Administration.* | *The procedures for bringing a body back for burial are lengthy and complex.* | *Creating a new network system is a lengthy process.*

long-running /ˌlɒŋ ˈrʌnɪŋ◂‖ˌlɔːŋ-/ [adj only before noun] a **long-running** event or performance is one that continues for a very long time: *The action is the latest in a long-running battle between the US and Canada relating to Cuban relations.* | *The proposal would end a long-running dispute between the Internal Revenue and the petroleum producers.* | *The long-running musical 'Jesus Christ Superstar' is to close after more than 3,000 performances.*

long-standing /ˌlɒŋ ˈstændɪŋ◂‖ˌlɔːŋ-/ [adj only before noun] a **long-standing** situation, agreement, or arrangement has continued for a long time and is likely to continue for a long time in the future: *Motorola has a long-standing agreement to provide at least one week's training to all new employees.* | *The area is populated by Kurdish rebels who have long-standing grievances against Hussein.* | *GM maintains a long-standing policy of not commenting on market speculation and rumour.*

lasting /ˈlɑːstɪŋ‖ˈlæs-/ [adj only before noun] strong enough or great enough to continue for a long time: *The speech could do lasting damage to US–German relations.* | *Japan's creation of a Western-style economy has been the country's lasting achievement.* | **lasting effect/impact etc** *His next book is about the lasting effects of the Vietnam war.* | **lasting peace/friendship/agreement etc** *Until we all give up violence, there cannot possibly be lasting peace in the world.* | **leave/make a lasting impression** *The incident left a lasting impression on the young girl.*

lifelong /ˈlaɪflɒŋ‖-lɔːŋ/ [adj] continuing for all of someone's life – use this about relationships, interests and feelings etc: *She first visited Ireland when she was ten, and developed a lifelong interest in the country.* | *Depression has been a lifelong struggle for me.* | **lifelong ambition/dream etc** *According to his biographers, he had a lifelong ambition to make money.* | *For many people, owning their own business is a lifelong goal.* | **lifelong member/resident/friend etc** *Virginia Maples, a lifelong resident, praised the town for its neighborliness.* | *Alvin met the poet Hughes, who became a lifelong friend and confidante.*

prolonged /prəˈlɒŋd‖-ˈlɔːŋd/ [adj] continuing for a long time, or longer than you expected: *How are you going to explain your prolonged absence?* | *a prolonged and bloody battle for independence* | *Studies show that prolonged exposure to maternal depression can result in childhood mood disorders.*

lingering /ˈlɪŋgərɪŋ/ [adj only before noun] **lingering** doubts, hopes, or other feelings continue for a long time, especially long after a particular event: *She had a lingering sense of guilt for some time after breaking off her relationship with Henry.* | *For years, Mexico's primary feeling toward the US was one of lingering resentment.* | *What will be the lingering images of the Sydney Olympic Games?* | *If he had any lingering doubts about the marriage, he did not show it.*

enduring /ɪnˈdjʊərɪŋ‖-ˈdʊə-/ [adj] an **enduring** feeling, memory, influence, quality or relationship continues for a long time: *His childhood experiences had an enduring influence on his work.* | *My most enduring memory of my father is watching him clean his rifle.* | *The friendships formed in her schooldays proved to be the most enduring.* | *Cartoons have a universal and enduring appeal.*

abiding /əˈbaɪdɪŋ/ [adj] formal an **abiding** feeling, belief, or interest continues for a long time and is not likely to change: *She had a basic and abiding belief in democratic systems.* | *As a boy he had had an abiding curiosity about how things worked.* | *The internal security of his country was the President's other abiding concern.* | *His father had an abiding interest in nature.*

chronic /ˈkrɒnɪk‖ˈkrɑː-/ [adj usually before noun] a **chronic** illness or bad situation continues for a very long time or is permanent: *China has a chronic shortage of capital, so it must encourage saving.* | *the chronic decay of the inner city areas* | *We need to take steps to counter the chronic decline in our export market.* | *He suffers from chronic asthma.* —**chronically** [adv] *care of the chronically ill*

8 continuing for too long

- long-drawn-out
- long-winded
- protracted
- interminable
- drag on
- take ages/years/forever etc

long-drawn-out /ˌlɒŋ drɔːn ˈaʊt◂‖ˌlɔːŋ-/ [adj] a **long-drawn-out** process continues for a long time, is very tiring, and probably continues for longer than it needs to: *The long-drawn-out campaigns that precede every election in the US have already begun.* | *This war is too one-sided to be very long-drawn-out.* | *Netscape faces a long-drawn-out battle with software giant Microsoft.* | *Building up a successful herd is a long-drawn out process of careful buying and breeding.*

long-winded /ˌlɒŋ ˈwɪndɪd◂‖ˌlɔːŋ-/ [adj] a speech or piece of writing that is **long-winded** is too long and therefore boring or difficult to understand: *Jacques launched into a long-winded explanation that left us just as confused as before.* | *Her letters do tend to be a bit long-winded.* | *I'm sick of reading badly-written and long-winded scripts by candidates who should know better.*

protracted /prəˈtræktɪd/ [adj] something unpleasant that is **protracted** continues for a long time, which makes it worse than usual: *After a bloody and protracted struggle, the 'Mau-Mau' fighters forced Britain to grant independence.* | *This marks the first day of what is likely to be a protracted and bitter courtroom battle.* | *There was a protracted silence, after which Lydia said quietly, 'I'm to inherit all the money – you'll get nothing.'*

interminable /ɪnˈtɜːʳmɪnəbəl/ [adj] formal continuing for a very long time so that it becomes boring and you become impatient: *The ride back to the city seemed interminable.* | *What's the reason for all these interminable delays?* | *She wasn't looking forward to the interminable winter nights, alone in the cabin.* | *He launched into an interminable monologue about his last therapy session.* —**interminably** [adv] *The first course took an interminably long time to arrive.* | *He paused interminably after each question we asked him.*

drag on /ˌdræg ˈɒn / [phr v I] to continue for too long and so become boring or annoying: *Despair grew as the war dragged on.* | *Presidential campaigns seem to drag on forever.* | *If the stalemate drags on, there could be serious consequences for the town's population.* | **drag on for weeks/years etc** *Lawsuits about titles to land often drag on for years without settlement.* | *The fighting dragged on for another two years before a settlement was finally reached.* | **drag on into October/2002/next year etc** *Analysts fear the downturn will drag on into next year.* | **drag on until 1945/2.00 a.m. etc** *The meeting dragged on until late afternoon.*

take ages/years/forever etc /ˌteɪk ˈeɪdʒɪz/ [v phrase] to take much longer than seems reasonable: *Getting visas to visit America seemed to take ages.* | *The problem with letters is that they always get lost or take forever to arrive.* | *It'll take days to sort this mess out.* | **take sb ages/years/forever etc** *It took me ages to get all that washing done.* | *It took Josephine months to finish writing her dissertation.*

9 to continue for longer than was planned or expected

- overrun/run over
- run on

overrun/run over /ˌəʊvəˈrʌn, ˌrʌn ˈəʊvəʳ/ [v I/phr v I] if an activity such as a meeting or game **overruns** or **runs over**, it continues longer than it is supposed to do: *The meeting is going to overrun so we'd better find out what time they close the building.* | *If the ceremony runs over, I'll switch to Channel 17.* | **overrun by 10 minutes/an hour/two days etc** *The scenes were cut because the preceding programme overran by 10 minutes.* | **run over time** *Well, what do you know? We've run over time, and there's no time for questions.*

run on /ˌrʌn ˈɒn / [phr v I] informal to last for a long time, especially longer than expected or planned: *Don't allow meetings to run on; set an agenda and stick to it.* | *Business lunches do tend to run on sometimes.* | *Sorry, I'm running on a bit. What did you want to say?*

10 when you need a lot of time in order to do something

- take a long time
- time-consuming

take a long time /ˌteɪk ə ˌlɒŋ ˈtaɪm‖-ˌlɔːŋ-/ [v phrase] *Our visit took a long time, and we returned home late for lunch.* | *Downloading audio files via a modem takes a long time.* | **it takes (sb) a long time (to do sth)** *It took a long time to get to know him, but we became good friends in the end.* | *I've never done one of these tests before – it took me a long time.* | *It takes a long time for people in this community to accept you.*

time-consuming /ˈtaɪm kənˌsjuːmɪŋ‖-ˌsuː-/ [adj] a method, activity or process that is **time-consuming** takes a long time especially because it contains a lot of stages or separate pieces of work: *Repairs can be time-consuming and expensive.* | *Caring for a disabled child is a time-consuming, but ultimately rewarding, job.* | *We wanted to avoid costly, time-consuming legislation.*

11 art, writing, ideas etc that last for a long time

- timeless
- immortal
- classic

timeless /ˈtaɪmləs/ [adj] music, literature, art etc, that is **timeless** still seems important and interesting even though it was written or made a long time ago: *Crosby's 'It Ain't Necessarily So' remains a timeless classic.* | *In the south-west of England, the scenery is timeless and unmistakably agricultural.* | **timeless appeal/quality** *Shakespeare's plays have a timeless appeal to all audiences.* | *If a song is good enough, it has a timeless quality.*

immortal /ɪˈmɔːʳtl/ [adj only before noun] **immortal** words, lines etc are famous and are remembered for a long time after they are written or spoken: *In the immortal words of Henry Ford, 'History is bunk.'* | *J.M. Barrie's immortal tale of Peter Pan*

classic /ˈklæsɪk/ [adj only before noun] a **classic** book, film, design etc is one that is important or special and remains popular for a long time: *The Coca-Cola bottle is one of the classic designs of our century.* | *the classic Bogart version of 'The Maltese Falcon'* | *'Jane Eyre' is Bronte's classic novel of courage in the face of despair.* | *Professor Carey wrote the classic account of early explorations in Africa and Asia.*

12 to make something last longer

- prolong
- extend
- drag out
- spin out
- eke out

prolong /prəˈlɒŋ‖-ˈlɔːŋ/ [v T] to make something such as a feeling, process or activity last longer: *He asked her another question just to prolong the conversation.* | *Users turn to the drug in the belief that it prolongs and enhances sex.* | *It seems he's eager to prolong his trial for as long as possible.* | *A heart transplant might prolong his life for a few years.*

extend /ɪkˈstend/ [v T] to add extra time to something that had a limit on the amount of time it could last: *I'll have to ask the bank to extend the repayment time on my loan.* | *TV coverage of the match had to be extended when it went into extra time.* | *These cleaning devices are meant to extend the life of your cassettes.* | **extend sth to February/next year etc** *The current contract expires in December, but will be extended to February 2004.*

drag out /ˌdræg ˈaʊt/ [phr v T] to make a boring or unpleasant activity or piece of work last much longer than necessary, especially because you gain some advantage by doing this **drag sth out** *There was really no need to drag the meeting out that long.* | **drag out sth** *The protests could actually drag out the proceedings.*

spin out /ˌspɪn ˈaʊt/ [phr v T] British informal to deliberately make an activity last longer than necessary especially so that it fills the time available **spin sth out** *Well, the lawyers always spin it out, don't they – that's how they make their money!* | **spin out sth** *We were paid by the hour, so I spun out the work for as long as I could.*

eke out /ˌiːk ˈaʊt/ [phr v T] to make your money or food last as long as possible by spending or using it carefully **eke out sth** *I pictured her trying to eke out her money to last to the end of the month.* | **eke sth out** *We watered down the wine so as to eke it out for the remainder of the evening.* | **eke out a living/existence** *She eked out a miserable living as a washer woman.*

13 when someone lives for a very long time

- longevity

longevity /lɒnˈdʒevɪ̈ti‖lɑːn-, lɔːn-/ [n U] formal *The more successful we are at prolonging longevity, the more it will cost us in elderly care costs.* | *the disparity in the longevity of the sexes* | **health and longevity** *The people of this village enjoy good health and longevity.* | **sb's longevity** *He attributes his longevity to 'a simple diet and a glass of wine every day'.*

look

RELATED WORDS

- *see also* **see, watch, examine, look for**

WHAT'S HERE

- **to look at sth** — see **1 to 8**
- **what sb or sth looks like** — see **9 to 10**

to look at sth

1 to look at someone or something

- look
- take a look/have a look
- look over
- examine
- view
- admire

look /lʊk/ [v I] to turn your eyes towards something so that you can see it: *Look, there are some swans on the river.* | **+ at** *'Come on, it's time to go,' he said, looking at his watch.* | *Look at me when I'm talking to you.* | **+ into/out of/through/down etc** *Tom looked out the window over the dry, barren landscape.* | *I always look through the peephole before I open the door for anyone.* | *The teacher stopped and looked around to see if there were any questions.* | **look at sb/sth in amazement/disbelief/surprise etc** (=in a way that shows you are surprised or shocked) *'You were a hippie?' she asked, looking at her father in disbelief.* — **look** [n C] when you turn your eyes to look at someone or something: *Sarah needed only one look at her daughter's face to know something was wrong.* | *I was getting disapproving looks from the people around me.*

take a look/have a look /ˌteɪk ə ˈlʊk, ˌhæv ə ˈlʊk/ [v phrase] especially spoken to look at something, especially something interesting or unusual: *'I think there's something wrong with the car.' 'Do you want me to have a look?'* | **+ at** *We climbed to the top of the tower to have a look at the view.* | *'You'd better take a look at this,' she said, passing me a letter.* |

take/have a good look (=look very carefully) *Take a good look at the pictures and tell me if anyone looks familiar.* | **take/have a close look** (=look at something very closely) *He moved to the front of the crowd to have a closer look at the animal.*

look over /ˌlʊk ˈəʊvəʳ/ [phr v T] to quickly look at the details of someone or something, especially before you officially agree to buy it, use it etc **look over sb/sth** *We looked over several apartments before finally choosing this one.* | *If you want, I can look over your English homework for you.* | **look sb/sth etc over** *Would you care to look the document over before you sign?* | *Jessica hated the way the men in the bar looked her over.*

examine /ɪɡˈzæmɪ̇n/ [v T] to look at someone or something extremely carefully, especially because you want to find its faults or mistakes: *When the police examined the gun, they found Wright's fingerprints on it.* | *A team of investigators is examining the crash site.* | **examine sth closely** (=to examine very carefully) *Before buying an antique, examine it closely to avoid buying a fake.* | **examine sb/sth for sth** *The video shows women how to examine their breasts for cancer.* —**examination** /ɪɡˌzæmɪ̇ˈneɪʃən/ [n U] *After careful examination, Lloyd estimated the tree was 500 years old.* | **+ of** *Authorities still have not released findings from their examination of the dead sheep.* | **on closer examination** (=when you look at something more carefully) *On closer examination she realized that the bag was made of plastic, not leather.*

view /vjuː/ [v T] walk around a place in order to look at it, especially so that you can decide what your opinion about it is **view a house/garden/exhibition etc** *A few journalists were allowed to view the art exhibition the day before it opened.* | *I'd like to make an appointment to view the house on Clement Street that's for sale.*

admire /ədˈmaɪəʳ/ [v T] to look at something and think how beautiful or impressive it is: *I was just admiring your lovely garden.* | *We stopped at the top of the mountain to admire the view.*

2 to look for a long time

- stare
- gaze
- gape
- gawk
- eye
- look sb up and down

stare /steəʳ/ [v I] to look directly at someone or something for a long time, without moving your eyes: *It's not polite to stare, you know.* | **+ at** *Why are you staring at me like that?* | *She stared at the page for several minutes, trying to understand.* | *Ron kept silent and stared down at his food.* | **+ into/out of etc** *When he's depressed, he just sits there, staring off into space.* | **stare back (at sb)** (=stare at someone who is staring at you) *Everyone turned to look at him, and he stared stonily back.* | **stare (at sb/sth) in amazement/horror/disbelief etc** (=in a way that shows you are surprised or shocked) *Donna stared in horror as the man fell to the floor.* | **stare sb down** (=stare at someone until they stop staring at you) *Fenton stood tall and stared down the gunmen.* —**stare** [n C] a long direct look: *Charles didn't reply. He just gave his daughter an icy stare.* | **a blank/vacant stare** (=a long look that does not show any thought or emotion) *The suspect was described as having a blank stare after the shooting spree.*

gaze /ɡeɪz/ [v I] to look at something or someone for a long time, especially with a feeling of love or great pleasure – used especially in stories and literature **+ at** *I lay back on the sand and gazed at the stars above.* | *Ruth gazed down at the sleeping child.* | **+ out/into/through etc** *He stopped talking suddenly and gazed into the distance.* | *She sat gazing out the windows at the people walking by.* —**gaze** [n singular] **turn your gaze** *Toni turned her gaze back to the fireplace.*

gape /ɡeɪp/ [v I] to look at someone or something for a long time, especially with your mouth open, because you are very surprised or shocked: *People stopped to gape as she walked down the street in a see-through mini-dress.* | **+ at** *She stood there gaping at me, too shocked to speak.* | **gape in amazement/horror etc** *I could only gape in astonishment as I saw the man take the bottle from the shelf and put it under his coat.*

gawk ALSO **gawp** British /ɡɔːk, ɡɔːp/ [v I] to look at someone in a rude or annoying way, for example because they look unusual or are doing something unusual: *Tourists walked around gawking at the people in traditional costumes.* | *I wanted to kill the morons who had gathered around me, gawping and pointing.*

eye /aɪ/ [v T] to look at someone or something with interest or because you do not trust them: *Mavis eyed the old sewing machine. 'Does this still work?' she asked.* | *The two teams eyed each other warily, waiting for the game to begin.*

look sb up and down /ˌlʊk (sb) ʌp ən ˈdaʊn/ [v phrase] to look very carefully at someone's body and the clothes they are wearing, especially because you do not know them and you are trying to form an opinion of them: *The hotel manager slowly looked the old man up and down and then asked him to leave.* | *'Don't be silly – you don't need to lose weight,' he said, looking her up and down.*

3 to look quickly

- glance
- take a quick look/have a quick look
- peek/take a peek
- peep
- take one look

glance /ɡlɑːns‖ɡlæns/ [v I] to look quickly at someone or something and then look away again **+ at** *Dr Morse kept glancing nervously at his watch.* | *'Some of you may not be happy about what I have to say,' he began, glancing at Janey.* | **+ into/down/ through etc** *Glancing into Neil's room, she noticed that his suitcase was packed.* —**glance** [n C] **+ at** *A quick glance at the map showed that we were on the right road.* | **a backward glance** (=a quick look back at the place you have left) *I walked away without a wave or a backward glance.* | **a sidelong glance** (=a quick look to one side) *Tammy gave her sister a sidelong glance and the two started to giggle.*

take a quick look/have a quick look /ˌteɪk ə kwɪk ˈlʊk, ˌhæv ə kwɪk ˈlʊk/ [v phrase] to look at something quickly in order to check that everything is satisfactory **+ at/around/through etc** *He took a quick look in the mirror, and went out of the house.* | *She had a quick look around the room before letting the guests in.*

peek/take a peek /piːk, ˌteɪk ə ˈpiːk/ [v I/v phrase] to look at something quickly and secretly, especially from a place where you cannot be seen: *When I heard the noise in the next room, I couldn't resist having a peek.* | **+ at** *The little girl peeked at me from behind her grandmother's skirt.* | **+ in/into/through/over etc** *We tip-toed into the room and peeked in the crib without waking the baby.* | *She opened the door and took a quick peek inside.*

peep /piːp/ [v I] especially British to look at something quickly and secretly, especially from a place where you cannot be seen **+ through/into/round** *Bobby peeped around the corner to see if anyone was coming.* | *We peeped through a crack in the fence and saw Mrs Finley talking to a strange-looking man.*

take one look /teɪk ˌwʌn ˈlʊk/ [v phrase] to look quickly at someone or something that you have not seen before, and immediately decide what your opinion of them is: *They opened the door to the room, took one look, and decided to go to another hotel.* | **+ at** *She took one look at me and said she would not work with me.* | *The teacher took one look at his homework and told him he would have to redo it.*

4 to look angrily

- glare
- look daggers at
- give sb a dirty look
- scowl
- frown at
- if looks could kill

glare /gleəʳ/ [v I] to look angrily at someone: *He sat there in silence, glaring angrily.* | **+ at** *'You can go if you want, but I'm staying,' Denise said glaring at him.* | **+ toward/across/around etc** *Claude put down his fork and glared across the table.* —**glare** [n C] *He looked me straight in the eye with a stern glare.*

look daggers at /ˌlʊk ˈdægəʳz æt/ [v phrase] especially British to look at someone very angrily, as if you would like to hurt them: *When I asked him what he'd done with the money he just looked daggers at me and refused to speak.* | *Julie must have heard you talking about her, because she was looking daggers at you from the next table.*

give sb a dirty look ALSO **give sb a black/filthy look** British /ˌgɪv (sb) ə ˌdɜːʳti ˈlʊk, ˌgɪv (sb) ə ˌblæk, ˌfɪlθi ˈlʊk/ [v phrase] to quickly look at someone angrily to show that you are angry with them, especially in a situation when you cannot tell them that you are angry: *I don't know what I did to upset her, but she gave me a really filthy look when I walked into the meeting.* | *My aunt's friends always used to give me dirty looks when I brought my kids over, because they knew I wasn't married.*

scowl /skaʊl/ [v I] to look at someone in an angry way, or make an angry, unhappy expression with your face: *Jane scowled and told them to get out.* | *'What do you want?' said the old man, scowling.* | **+ at** *What are you scowling at me for? You asked me to wake you up.* —**scowl** [n C] *A teenage girl was sitting alone in a corner with a scowl on her face.*

frown at /ˈfraʊn æt/ [v phrase] to look at someone or something with an annoyed, confused, or disapproving expression on your face: *The teacher frowned at him and asked him to sit down.* | *When I got back to the table, Carolyn was frowning at the check.* | *'Sibling rivalry?' she asked, frowning at his use of psychological terms.* —**frown** [n C] **give sb a frown** *He walked past her, giving her a judgmental frown.*

if looks could kill /ɪf ˌlʊks kʊd ˈkɪl/ use this when you are telling someone how another person looked at you in a very angry way, and you found this funny or frightening: *You should've seen her face when she realized what I'd done – if looks could kill!*

5 to look hard and with difficulty

- squint
- peer
- screw up your eyes

squint /skwɪnt/ [v I] to look hard at something that you find difficult to see, and make your eyes narrower to try and see better: *Bring your glasses or you'll have to squint through the whole movie.* | **+ at** *She squinted at the sign but couldn't read what it said.* | **+ through/over/into etc** *Driving down the narrow country road, Blackthorne squinted into the darkness.*

peer /pɪəʳ/ [v I] to look with difficulty at someone or something, especially because you cannot see very well or there is not enough light **+ through/into/out etc** *Roger peered into the dark corridor to see what was making the noise.* | **+ at** *She adjusted her glasses and peered at the man.*

screw up your eyes /ˌskruː ʌp jɔːr ˈaɪz/ [v phrase] informal to try to make it easier to see something by almost closing your eyes, especially because the light is too bright or because what you are looking at is very small: *You have to screw up your eyes to see the figure in the bottom left of the picture.*

6 to look at a lot of things you might buy, read, etc

- look around/take a look around/have a look around
- browse
- window-shopping
- I'm just looking

look around/take a look around/have a look around /ˌlʊk əˈraʊnd, teɪk ə ˌlʊk əˈraʊnd, hæv ə ˌlʊk əˈraʊnd/ [phr v I/T/v phrase/v phrase] to walk around a shop or market or a place where tourists go, looking at a lot of different things: *I just want to take a quick look around and see if there's anything I want.* | *He makes a list of what he needs and then walks into the store and buys it, without looking around at all.* | *You're welcome to have a look around. We have a wide range of sportswear.*

browse /braʊz/ [v I] to spend time looking at things in a shop, especially books or records, without intending to buy anything: *Armando spent the afternoon browsing in Camden market.* | **+ through** *He found Jill in the gallery shop silently browsing through some books.*

window-shopping /ˈwɪndəʊ ˌʃɒpɪŋ‖-ˌʃɑː-/ [n U] the activity of looking at goods in shop windows without intending to buy anything: *We didn't have any money but we enjoyed window-shopping in Fifth Avenue.* | **go window-shopping** *Sometimes I go window-shopping after work.*

I'm just looking /aɪm ˌdʒʌst ˈlʊkɪŋ/ spoken say this to tell someone who works in a shop that you are only looking at things, and you do not intend to buy anything just now: *'Can I help you?' 'No thanks, I'm just looking.'*

7 to look at someone in a way that shows you are sexually interested in them

- leer
- ogle
- eye up
- make eyes at

leer /lɪəʳ/ [v I] to look and smile at someone in a way that shows a strong sexual interest, especially so that people feel a little frightened, embarrassed, or offended: *'Hey, baby. Do you like what you see?' he said, leering.* | **+ at** *The old man leered suggestively at the waitress.* | *Stopping his work for a second, the garage attendant leered at the girls in the car.* —**leer** [n singular] *He stood in the doorway, with a leer on his face, refusing to let her past.*

ogle /ˈəʊgəl/ [v T] to look at someone in an offensive way that shows you are sexually attracted to their body: *A group of men were ogling her from a bench across the street.* | *The beach was full of teenage boys who had come to ogle the girls in bikinis.*

eye up /ˌaɪ ˈʌp/ [phr v T] British informal to look at someone in a way that shows that you are sexually interested in them **eye sb up/eye up sb** *I'm not sure if he's eyeing me up or just staring at me.* | *Those two have been eyeing each other up all evening.*

make eyes at /ˌmeɪk ˈaɪz æt/ [v phrase] to make it clear to someone that you are sexually attracted to them by looking at them in a way that gets their attention: *Did you see those two making eyes at each other across the table?*

8 to stop looking at someone or something

- look away
- look up
- look around
- turn your face away
- avert your eyes/gaze

look away /ˌlʊk əˈweɪ/ [phr v I] to turn your eyes away from something that you were looking at: *The accident scene was so horrible that I had to look away.* | *The minute he looked away, I crumpled the piece of paper and shoved it in my coat pocket.* | **+ from** *She looked away from him, unable to tell him the truth*

look up /ˌlʊk ˈʌp/ [phr v I] to stop looking at something and turn your face upwards, in order to see someone or talk to them: *There was a loud bang outside the classroom, and we all looked up.* | **+ from** *'Goodbye, then,' she said, without even looking up from her book.*

look around ALSO **look round** British /ˌlʊk əˈraʊnd, ˌlʊk ˈraʊnd/ [phr v I] to turn your eyes away from what you were looking at and start to look at what is around you: *Alan put down his newspaper and looked around, 'What was that noise?'* | *The speaker finished her speech and looked round to see if there were any questions.*

turn your face away /ˌtɜːʳn jɔːʳ ˈfeɪs əweɪ/ [v phrase] to stop looking at someone or something by turning your face in another direction, especially because you are embarrassed or upset: *He burped loudly, and she turned her face away in disgust.* | **+ from** *Turning his face away from her, Glen began to cry.*

avert your eyes/gaze /əˌvɜːʳt jɔːr ˈaɪz, ˈgeɪz/ [v phrase] formal to deliberately turn your eyes away from what you are looking at, because you do not want to look at it any longer: *The two averted their eyes as they passed each other in the hall.* | *When Celia dropped her robe, Richard averted his gaze and stepped back awkwardly.*

what sb or sth looks like

RELATED WORDS

- *see also* **seem**

9 the way someone or something looks

- appearance
- looks
- look
- image

appearance /əˈpɪərəns/ [n C/U] *A layer of sand will give a natural appearance to the bottom of the aquarium.* | **sb's/sth's appearance** *I wish she'd do something about her appearance – she's always such a mess.* | *Concentrate on the content of your essay, not its appearance.* | **+ of** *The military activity was in stark contrast to the peaceful appearance of the islands.* | **have the appearance of sb/sth** (=look similar to someone or something) *The waitress, although she was only about 40, had the appearance of a very old woman.* | **in appearance** *The mushrooms are similar in appearance to poisonous ones, so you have to be careful.* | **judge by appearances** (=make decisions based on how someone or something looks) *Judging by appearances, things are back to normal.*

looks /lʊks/ [n plural] someone's appearance, especially when considering how good-looking they are. **Looks** is less formal than **appearance sb's looks** *Girls of that age are always worried about their looks.* | *Emily had refused to marry him on account of his looks.* | **good looks** (=a good-looking appearance) *People generally describe him as having boyish good looks.* | **keep/lose your (good) looks** (=remain or stop being good-looking) *She was 20 years older now, but had managed to keep her looks.*

look /lʊk/ [n C usually singular] the appearance of something, especially an appearance that has been deliberately planned or made **+ of** *The text is fine but the look of the page is all wrong.* | **have the look of** (=look similar to someone or something) *Sapporo, Japan, has the look of a Wisconsin city in winter.* | **by/from the look of sth** (=judging by its appearance) *From the look of it, I'd say the chair was about 100 years old, maybe 150.* | **the Bohemian/Versace/1960s etc look** *Her long straight hair and dark eye make-up give her a sort of late-'60s look.*

image /ˈɪmɪdʒ/ [n C usually singular] the appearance and character that someone deliberately tries to produce by dressing or behaving in a particular way: *I like her new image – it's a lot more dignified.* | *He doesn't really need those glasses – they're just part of his 'intellectual' image.* | **+ of** *Since I started working in this company, I have tried to maintain the image of a winner.* | **+ as** *The scandal has badly hurt her image as an honest politician.*

10 to have a particular appearance

- look
- look like

look /lʊk/ [v not usually in progressive] *Doesn't she look beautiful!* | *That coat looks nice and warm. Where did you get it?* | *The cake didn't look very good, but it tasted all right.* | *With his dark hair and dark eyes he looked Italian.* | *I'm glad you've shaved off that beard. It makes you look ten years younger!*

look like /ˈlʊk laɪk/ [v phrase] to have an appearance that is similar to someone or something else: *She looks a bit like my sister.* | *They just look like ordinary people to me.* | *In the moonlight the plane looked like a huge eagle soaring across the sky.*

look after

RELATED WORDS

- *see also* **child, baby, defend, protect, safe**

1 to look after someone

- look after/take care of
- care for sb
- mind
- babysit
- keep an eye on
- nurse
- carer

look after/take care of especially British /ˌlʊk ˈɑːftəʳ‖-ˈæf-, ˌteɪk ˈkeər ɒv/ [phr v T/v phrase] to spend time with a child or with someone who is old or sick, and make sure they are safe and have the things they need: *Can you look after the kids for me this afternoon?* | *I've told you, I can't come. There's no one to look after Frieda.* | *Jonathon has no idea what it means to take care of a baby all day long.* | *We specialize in helping caregivers who take care of relatives in their own homes.*

care for sb /ˈkeəʳ fəʳ (sb)/ [v T] to look after someone who is very ill or very old by doing everything for them: *Elsie had to leave her job to care for her sick father.* | *St Helen's Hospice, which cares for the terminally ill, is holding a special fund-raising week.* | *It is one of the only charities to care for Aids patients and ex-prisoners.*

mind /maɪnd/ [v T] British to look after children for a short time while their parents are out doing something else: *The woman who minds Pip and Emma collects them from school and gives them an evening meal.* | *Mothers who work part-time are able to mind other people's children when they are not working.*

babysit ALSO **sit** American /ˈbeɪbisɪt, sɪt/ [v I] to look after children in the evening while their parents go out somewhere, especially when they pay you a small amount of money for doing this: *I'll ask Jane to babysit on Wednesday night.* | *Ask Alex and Joan next time you're babysitting.* | **+ for** *He used to babysit for Mary when she worked nights.* | *Jenny sat for us last Friday evening when we went to the movies.*

keep an eye on /ˌkiːp ən ˈaɪ ɒn/ [v phrase] to stay with a child and watch them to see that they are safe, especially for a short time: *Benjy, I want you to stay in the yard where I can keep an eye on you.* | *Would you mind keeping an eye on Stacey while I go for a cigarette?* | **keep a close/careful/watchful eye on sb** *He warned parents to continue to keep a close eye on their children.*

nurse /nɜːʳs/ [v T] to look after someone who is ill and to make them well again or to make them comfortable: *Tony nursed his wife through her long illness without ever complaining.* | *Irina had wanted to nurse him, but the doctors had sent her away.* | **nurse sb back to health** (=look after a sick person until they are well again) *The monks tended his wounds and nursed him back to health.*

carer British **/caregiver** American /ˈkeərəʳ, ˈkeəʳˌgɪvəʳ/ [n C] someone who looks after another person who is too young or ill to look after himself or herself – used especially on official forms, in official letters, in newspapers etc: *Hospital staff can provide additional home support for carers.* | *We have a high number of volunteer carers at the day centre.* | *Like many caregivers, Marian gave up her job to provide 24-hour care for an elderly relative.*

2 to look after a child until he or she has grown up

- bring up/raise
- child-rearing
- custody
- residency

bring up/raise /ˌbrɪŋ ˈʌp, reɪz/ [phr v T/v T] to look after children until they have grown up and to teach them to develop particular beliefs and ways of behaving **bring sb up/raise sb** *She had brought him up as if he were her own son.* | **bring up sb/raise sb** *I don't need you to tell me how to bring up my son.* | *For five years we were neighbors, and we raised our kids together.* | **be brought up (by sb)/be raised (by sb)** *His father died when he was seven, and he was brought up by his mother.* | *I was born and raised in Alabama.* | **brought up to do sth** (=taught to believe, think, or act in a particular way) *I was brought up to trust people.* | *My parents brought me up to be truthful.* | **brought up a Catholic/Christian etc** (=brought up to believe in the Catholic/Christian religion) *I was raised a Catholic, but I don't go to church anymore.* | **raise a family/children etc** *Grandpa raised a family of ten on seven dollars a week.* | *We should raise our daughters to be as confident as our menfolk.* —**well-brought-up** /ˌwel brɔːt ˈʌp◂/ [adj] *I was a very well-brought up young lady.* —**upbringing** /ˈʌpbrɪŋɪŋ/ [n singular] *Your accent depends on where you live, your upbringing, that kind of thing.* | **have a strict/conventional/literary etc upbringing** *I had a strict religious upbringing.*

child-rearing /ˈtʃaɪld rɪərɪŋ/ [n U] the care of children while they are growing and developing – used especially in medical or educational contexts: *Men, in general, are as good at child-rearing as women.* | *Have you discussed child-rearing methods with your future husband?*

custody /ˈkʌstədi/ [n U] the legal right to have your child living with you after your marriage has officially ended **have/get/gain custody (of sb)** *The father has custody in only 10% of cases.* | *Fearing her uncle would gain custody of the child, she went into hiding.* | *If you leave me, I'll get custody of the kids, because everyone knows you're sick.* | **award/grant sb custody (of sb)** *Waltman's wife had been granted temporary custody of their child after her husband's arrest.* | **lose custody (of sb)** *I loved my three girls, and losing custody was the most traumatic thing that has ever happened to me.* | **joint custody** (=where both parents have equal rights to see and look after their child) *Tony insists he will seek joint custody of Joshua.*

residency /ˈrezədənsi/ [n U] the legal right and responsibility to look after a child in your own home after you are divorced: *The courts awarded residency to Trisha's father.* | *The parent who has residency often loses touch with the other partner's parents, meaning that the children lose one set of grandparents.*

3 to look after a child who is not your own for a long time

- adopt
- foster
- guardian
- in care

adopt /əˈdɒpt‖əˈdɑːpt/ [v I/T] to legally and permanently take someone else's child into your family and treat them as one of your own children: *Chinese babies are the favorite choice of Americans adopting children from abroad.* | *She had hoped to get pregnant, but when she failed, she and her husband decided to adopt.* | *He discovered that his guardian, Aunt Mimi, had not legally adopted him.* | *Teenagers who discover they were adopted often search for their biological parents when they are old enough.* —**adopted** [adj] *Their two adopted daughters were the only Asians in the town.*

foster /ˈfɒstəʳ‖ˈfɔː-, ˈfɑː-/ [v T] to take another person's child into your own family and look after them for a period of several weeks, months, or years, but without becoming their legal parent: *Fostering a teenager is obviously different from fostering a small child.* | *During my mother's long illness I was fostered by a middle-aged couple on the other side of town.* —**foster** [adj only before noun] **foster care** *Half a million American children are in foster care at any* *given time.* | **foster home** *Steve went to live in a series of foster homes.* | **foster-parents** (=a husband and wife who foster children) *It is sometimes difficult to find suitable foster-parents for a lively ten-year-old.* | **foster mother/father** *He ran away after his foster-mother accused him of stealing.* | **foster-child** (=children who are fostered) *She added to her regular income by taking in foster-children.* | *She finally adopted her foster-child, six-year old Shania.* | **foster-brother/foster-sister** (=a child who has been fostered by people who also have other children) *two New York subway cops who are also foster brothers*

guardian /ˈɡɑːʳdiən/ [n C] a person who has been legally appointed to look after a child whose parents are away or dead, or to look after someone who is too ill to be responsible for themselves: *The court must obtain the consent of the child's parent or guardian.* | *Children under 17 will only be admitted in the company of a parent or adult guardian.* | *Could you contact Mrs Smith's guardians and tell them she's been admitted to hospital?* | **legal guardian** *When Sara was 7, Aunt Maggie became her legal guardian.*

in care /ɪn ˈkeəʳ/ [adv] British a child who is **in care** does not live with his or her parents but is looked after in a special home paid for by the local council, for example because their own parents are dead or could not look after them properly: *Many youngsters who've been brought up in care are often incapable of looking after themselves.* | *The number of children in care in Oxfordshire is falling.*

4 someone who is paid to look after children

- babysitter
- childminder
- nanny
- au pair
- childcare/child care

babysitter ALSO **sitter** American /ˈbeɪbisɪtəʳ, ˈsɪtəʳ/ [n C] someone who is paid to look after children when their parents go out for the evening: *I'll come with you if I can get a babysitter for Friday.* | *I guess we should have some snacks around for the sitter.*

childminder British **/babysitter** OR **sitter** American /ˈtʃaɪldmaɪndəʳ, ˈbeɪbisɪtəʳ, ˈsɪtəʳ/ [n C] someone who is paid to look after children while their parents are at work: *Sheila's setting up in business as a registered childminder* (=on a special list of childminders that have been approved by the authorities). | *I asked my childminder to do what I do when Laura is naughty.*

nanny /ˈnæni/ [n C] a woman who is paid to look after someone else's children, and who sometimes lives in the house with the family: *He turned and flung himself into his nanny's arms.* | *I can't afford a nanny.*

au pair /əʊ ˈpeəʳ/ [n C] someone, usually a young person from a foreign country, who lives with a family and helps with work around the house and with looking after the children. **Au pairs** often do this kind of work in order to learn about another country and its language: *Working as an au pair, I spend most of my time with young children, so I dress casually.* | *Don't worry, the au pair will clean it up.*

childcare/child care ALSO **day care** American /ˈtʃaɪldkeəʳ, ˈdeɪ keəʳ/ [n U] an arrangement in which young children are looked after during the day while their parents are at work: *Even women in well-paid jobs, who can afford childcare, are faced with managing the home and a career.* | *After-school childcare is an area of particular importance to many working mothers.* | *How much does it cost an employer to provide daycare facilities?* | **childcare/daycare center** *She works in a daycare center.* | **in daycare** *Jordan's been in daycare since he was six months old.*

5 to look after someone by helping them

- look after
- attend to
- take sb under your wing

look after especially British ALSO **take care of** /ˌlʊk ˈɑːftəʳ‖-ˈæf-, ˌteɪk ˈkeər ɒv/ [phr v T] to make sure someone has everything they need and is safe and happy: *We had a lovely time in Dorset. Susan looked after us very nicely. She's a wonderful cook.* | *Paul's old enough to look after himself.* | *Don't worry about me. I can take care of myself.* | **be well looked after** (=always given everything you need) *Alex could see the horse had been well looked after.* | *Don't look so worried – she's being well looked after by the nurses.* | **take good care of sb** (=be very careful in order to keep sb healthy, happy, or safe) *Take good care of yourself while you're away.* | *They took very good care of me.* | *The firm is getting a reputation for taking better care of its customers than in the past.*

attend to /əˈtend tuː/ [phr v T] to give someone the care and help that you regularly give them, especially as part of your job: *Dr Gresham is busy at the moment attending to one of his patients.* | *The cabin crew will attend to the passengers' needs.* | *They worked happily together, feeding and attending to the livestock.*

take sb under your wing /ˌteɪk (sb) ʌndəʳ jɔːʳ ˈwɪŋ/ [v phrase] to start to look after a younger or less experienced person in a friendly way with the intention of helping them or protecting them while they gain experience: *Adrienne, eleven years older, had taken the 19-year-old singer under her wing.* | *He had sized me up, he said, and had decided to take me under his wing.*

6 to not look after someone properly

- neglect

neglect /nɪˈɡlekt/ [v T] to not look after someone properly, especially a child, although it is your responsibility to look after them: *He was neglected by his parents when he was very young.* | *Staff at the hostel were accused of neglecting and abusing children in their care.* | *Some teachers devote too much time to helping their slower students and neglect the brighter ones.* —**neglect** [n] *increases in homelessness, child abuse and neglect* | *He alleges that the orphanages have allowed children to die from medical neglect.*

7 to look after something

- look after
- keep an eye on
- maintain
- maintenance
- care
- upkeep

▸ *see also* **repair, condition (1-6)**

look after /ˌlʊk ˈɑːftəʳ‖-ˈæf-/ [phr v T] to keep something in good condition and make sure that it does not get broken, damaged, or stolen: *You can have a new bike for Christmas if you promise to look after it.* | *You could see someone had been looking after the* *garden, even though the house had been empty for years.* | *The miniature railway is looked after by local volunteers.* | **look after sth for sb** *You don't mind looking after the place for me while I'm away, do you?*

keep an eye on /ˌkiːp ən ˈaɪ ɒn/ [v phrase] especially spoken to look after something that belongs to someone else for a short time, by watching it to make sure that it does not get stolen or damaged: *Tom went into the library while I kept an eye on the bikes.* | *Does a neighbor keep an eye on your house while you are away?* | *Can you keep an eye on my bags while I go to the toilet?*

maintain /meɪnˈteɪn, mən-/ [v T] to make sure that a car, machine, place, or building is in good condition by checking it and repairing it when necessary: *Residents work in the downstairs shop, and also help to maintain the building.* | *His role is to maintain the society's fleet of vans, ready to respond in any emergency.* | *An attempt was being made to maintain the grounds, but weeds were starting to grow in the driveway.*

maintenance /ˈmeɪntənəns/ [n U] the job of maintaining a car, building, place, or machine: *A car is quite a big expense, especially when you consider maintenance.* | *Because there had been no maintenance, the college buildings were in a poor state.* | *the maintenance of public roads* | **routine maintenance** (=simple maintenance that must be done regularly) *Most gas appliances require routine maintenance once a year to ensure safety.* | **maintenance costs** (=the amount of money it costs to maintain something) *The city is paying $30,000 in annual maintenance costs.*

care /keəʳ/ [n U] the work or process of looking after something in order to keep it in good condition **+ of** *She has become a leading expert on the care and maintenance of Renaissance paintings.* | *Care of the environment has become a priority in government thinking.* | *These photocopiers require a little extra care to keep them running right.* | **hair-care/skin-care etc** *hair-care products* | *I'd advise you to follow a new skin care routine.*

upkeep /ˈʌpkiːp/ [n U] the continuous process and cost involved in keeping something in good condition, especially a building or garden **the upkeep of sth** *The trustees are responsible for the upkeep of the bridge.* | *The Council's contribution towards the upkeep of the church is very much appreciated.* | *You get more for your money if you buy an old house, but upkeep costs will be higher*

look for

RELATED WORDS

▸ *see also* **find out, lose, lost, find**

1 to look for someone or something when you do not know where they are

- look for
- try to find
- have a look
- search for
- in search of
- hunt

look for /ˈlʊk fɔːʳ/ [phr v T] to try to find something that you have lost, or someone who is not in the place where you expected them to be: *I'm looking for Simon – have you seen him?* | *I've been looking everywhere for that key! Where did you find it?*

try to find /ˌtraɪ tə ˈfaɪnd/ [v phrase] to look for someone or something, especially when it is difficult to find them: *Jill was up in the attic trying to find her old school books.* | *I tried to find Jack to tell him the news, but he wasn't anywhere around.*

have a look /ˌhæv ə ˈlʊk/ [v phrase] especially spoken to look for someone or something, especially when you do it quickly or when you only look in one place: *'I can't find my shoes.' 'Have a look in your bedroom.'* | **+ for** *I had a look for Clive but he wasn't in his office.* | **have a quick look** *I'll just have a quick look for that book before we go.* | **have a good look** (=look carefully and thoroughly) *We don't have time to find it now – we'll have a good look in the morning.*

search for /ˈsɜːʳtʃ fɔːʳ/ [v phrase] to look carefully and thoroughly for someone or something, especially when it is very important that you find them: *Coastguards are still searching for survivors from the ship.* | *Friends and neighbours joined police officers to search for clues.*

in search of /ɪn ˈsɜːʳtʃ ɒv/ [prep] especially spoken if you go **in search of** someone or something, you go somewhere in order to find them **go/set off in search of** *She stayed and talked for a while, then went off in search of Flynn.*

hunt /hʌnt/ [v I] to look urgently and thoroughly for someone or something in every possible place: *Friends and neighbors hunted everywhere, but no-one could find the child.* | **+ for** *I hunted all morning for the book of photos, but couldn't find it.*

2 to look for something or someone that you need or want

- look for
- try to find
- in search of
- search for
- look around for
- seek
- be on the lookout for
- hunting
- leave no stone unturned

look for /ˈlʊk fɔːʳ/ [phr v T] to try to find something or someone that you need: *Can you help me? I'm looking for a place to stay.* | *The company is looking for young, enthusiastic graduates to work in its sales department.* | *I spent months looking for a job, with no luck.*

try to find /ˌtraɪ tə ˈfaɪnd/ [v phrase] to look for something or someone that you need, especially when it is difficult and takes a long time: *I spent half an hour trying to find a parking space.* | *Drug companies are trying to find an alternative drug, which will not have such serious side-effects.*

in search of /ɪn ˈsɜːʳtʃ ɒv/ [prep] especially written if you go **in search of** something that you need, you go somewhere to try to find it: *Many young people move to the cities in search of a better future.*

search for /ˈsɜːʳtʃ fɔːʳ/ [v phrase] to spend time trying to find something or someone that you need: *I searched everywhere for a birthday present for Kim, but I found nothing I liked.* | *I was made redundant last year, and am still searching for a new job.* | *The school is currently searching for ways to save money.*

look around for /ˌlʊk əˈraʊnd fɔːʳ/ [v phrase] to look in different places or directions, in order to find a suitable person or thing that you need: *He looked around for somewhere to hang the wet towel.* | *We're always looking around for new products to add to our list.* | *They're looking around for a decent apartment, not too far from the city.*

seek /siːk/ [v T] formal to try to get or find something you need, for example advice, friendship, or a job: *Economics graduate, aged 25, with business experience, seeks interesting part-time work in the West London area.* | *If you are at all worried about your symptoms, you should seek medical advice.* | *The government is seeking support from teachers for its latest education reforms.*

be on the lookout for /biː ɒn ðə ˈlʊkaʊt fɔːʳ/ [v phrase] informal to be eagerly and continuously looking for something or someone that might be useful to you: *My mother's always on the lookout for a good bargain.* | *The club is always on the lookout for new young players.* | *The design department is constantly on the lookout for original ideas.*

hunting /ˈhʌntɪŋ/ [n U] **job/house/bargain etc hunting** when you are trying to find or get a job, house etc: *We rented a car and went house-hunting as soon as we arrived.* | *Job hunting takes a lot of effort and can be a long, depressing process.*

leave no stone unturned /ˌliːv nəʊ ˌstəʊn ʌnˈtɜːʳnd/ [v phrase] to do everything that you can to find something such as the answer to a problem – used especially in literature: *If a solution can be found, Mr Danby, I shall leave no stone unturned until I have found it.* | *Union leaders have promised to leave no stone unturned in their search for a way to keep the factory open.*

3 to look for information in a book, on a computer etc

- search
- surf
- look up
- go through
- trawl/trawl through
- scour
- browse

search /sɜːʳtʃ/ [v I/T] to look for information, a document, an Internet page etc on a computer: *You can search on the Internet for the names of dealers in your area.* | *I searched a few websites, but couldn't find the information I was looking for.* — **search** [n C] *I did a quick search on the Internet and found three airlines with tickets available on that date.*

surf /sɜːʳf/ [v T] **surf the net/Internet** to look at a lot of pages on the Internet, looking for something that interests you: *Many youngsters spend hours surfing the net.*

look up /ˌlʊk ˈʌp/ [phr v T] to try to find information by looking in a book, on a list, in computer records **look up sth** *If you look up the title of the book, you should then find the author.* | **look sth up** *If you don't know what it means, look it up in the dictionary.*

go through /ˈgəʊ θruː/ [phr v T] to carefully examine a piece of writing, a set of documents, an official record etc in order to find a piece of information or check that there are no mistakes: *He went through the contract quite carefully, checking all the details.* | *I've finished my essay, but I just need to go through it to check for spelling mistakes.*

trawl/trawl through /trɔːl, ˈtrɔːl θruː/ [v T/v phrase] to look through a large number of records, documents etc for a particular thing or piece of information: *She spent hours trawling through patients' medical records looking for evidence of negligence by doctors.* — **trawl** [n C] British *A trawl through the jobs pages of his local paper produced only one job that he wanted to apply for.*

scour /skaʊəʳ/ [v T] to read a piece of writing or document very carefully in order to find a piece of information that you need: *He spent half an hour scouring the newspaper for any mention of the fire.*

browse /braʊz/ [v I/T] to look for information on the Internet using a computer, especially when you do not know exactly what information you need or where to find it: *Browsing the net one afternoon, I came across Tom's homepage.* | *One company said that up to half of their employees spend over an hour's work time a day browsing the web.*

4 when the police are looking for a criminal

- look for/search for
- be after
- hunt

look for/search for /ˈlʊk fɔːʳ, ˈsɜːʳtʃ fɔːʳ/ [phr v T] to look for someone who has been involved in a crime or who has escaped from prison: *Police are still looking for three men who stole £55,000 from a post office in York.* | *Police searching for the killer of a nine-year-old girl have appealed to the public for help.*

be after /biː ˈɑːftəʳ‖-ˈæf-/ [phr v T] informal to be trying to find and catch someone who has done something wrong: *She said she was frightened because the police were after her.* | *The man we're after is one of the biggest drug-dealers in South America.*

hunt /hʌnt/ [v I/T] to search for a criminal – use this when a large number of police are making an organized search over a wide area **+ for** *Police are still hunting for the girl's killer.* | **hunt sb down** (=search for a criminal until you find them) *Many opponents of the regime who escaped abroad were later hunted down and killed.*

5 to search a place to try to find someone or something

- search
- scour
- comb
- drag a river/pond etc
- ransack
- raid
- turn somewhere inside out/upside down

search /sɜːʳtʃ/ [v I/T] *At the site, rescue workers have been searching systematically in the hope of finding more survivors.* | **search a place/area etc** *Police have searched the area near his home, but have so far found nothing.* | **search (a place) for** *Local people are still searching woods near the victim's home for any clues to help find her killer.*

scour /skaʊəʳ/ [v T] to search an area very carefully and thoroughly, looking for something that is very important **scour a place for** *A team of detectives is scouring the area for the murder weapon.* | *Developers are scouring the country for possible sites for these new superstores.*

comb /kəʊm/ [v T] to thoroughly examine a large area in great detail, especially by moving across it, looking for something or someone that is difficult to find: *Police and volunteers are combing the countryside in the hope of finding the missing boy.* | *Rescuers combed the hillsides but found no trace of the missing climbers.* | **comb a place for** *The children combed the shoreline for shells.*

drag a river/pond etc /ˌdræg ə ˈrɪvəʳ/ [v phrase] to search for something in a river, lake etc by pulling a heavy net along the bottom: *The murder weapon, a kitchen knife, was found when police dragged a nearby pond.*

ransack /ˈrænsæk/ [v T] to search a room, house, cupboard etc very thoroughly and roughly in order to find things or steal things, usually causing a lot of untidiness or damage: *Thieves broke in and ransacked the house.* | *The newspaper's offices were ransacked by members of the secret police.*

raid /reɪd/ [v T] if the police **raid** a place, they arrive there suddenly to look for criminals, drugs, or stolen goods: *The Casino nightclub has been closed since it was raided last month.* | *Police officers raided a house in North London last night, and found substantial quantities of illegal drugs.*

turn somewhere inside out/upside down /ˌtɜːʳn sʌmweəʳ ˌɪnsaɪd 'aʊt, ˌʌpsaɪd 'daʊn/ [v phrase] to search a house, a room etc very thoroughly, often making it very untidy: *We turned all the cupboards inside out but couldn't find the letters.* | *I turned the house upside down looking for my birth certificate.*

6 to look for something in a bag, box, pocket etc

- rummage/ rummage about
- fish around
- feel around
- fumble around/about
- go through
- search
- frisk

rummage/rummage about /'rʌmɪdʒ, ˌrʌmɪdʒ ə'baʊt/ [v I/v phrase] to look for something among a lot of other things that are all together by moving them around with your hands **+ in** *Louise rummaged in her bag and pulled out a small envelope.* | **+ for** *He unzipped his school bag and rummaged about for a pencil.*

fish around /ˌfɪʃ ə'raʊnd/ ALSO **fish about** /ˌfɪʃ ə'baʊt/ British [phr v I] to look for a small object in a large or deep container, especially using just your hands **+ in** *Sam fished about in his pockets and produced a few coins.* | **+ for** *He fished around in his bag for the letter.*

feel around /ˌfiːl ə'raʊnd/ ALSO **feel about** /ˌfiːl ə'baʊt/ British [phr v I] to search for something by touch without using your eyes: *She put her hand under the seat and felt around, but couldn't find anything.* | **+ for** *She felt around for the light switch.*

fumble around/about /ˌfʌmbəl ə'raʊnd, ə'baʊt/ [phr v I] to use your hands to look for something in an awkward way, especially because it is dark or you are nervous or in a hurry: *The phone rang and, half-asleep, Winston fumbled about to find the receiver.* | **+ in** *He fumbled around in the cupboard, desperately searching for his tablets.* | **+ for** *He fumbled around on the ground for his glasses.*

go through /'gəʊ θruː/ [phr v T] to search someone's clothes, bags, or possessions very thoroughly: *Customs officials went through his luggage but found nothing.* | *You have no right to go through my personal possessions!*

search /sɜːʳtʃ/ [v T] to **search** a person or their clothes to try to find drugs, weapons etc **be searched** *All visitors to the prison are thoroughly searched.* | **+ for** *The men were all searched for weapons and then allowed to enter.*

frisk /frɪsk/ [v T] if the police, airport officials etc **frisk** someone, they feel the person's clothes and body, looking for hidden weapons or drugs: *A guard frisked him expertly, then led him into a large room.* | **be frisked** *We were stopped by the police and frisked before being allowed into the building.* | **frisk sb for sth** *They pulled me aside and frisked me for weapons.*

7 an attempt to find something or someone

- search
- hunt
- raid
- wild goose chase

search /sɜːʳtʃ/ [n C] an attempt to find someone or something, especially when this is well organized and a lot of people are doing it **+ for** *Rescuers are continuing their search for survivors of the crash.* | *Their search for gold took them west to Washington State.* | **carry out a search** (=do a search) *FBI agents carried out a search of all the nightclubs in the area.* | **search party** (=an organized group of people searching for someone who is lost) *When the men did not return, the commanding officer sent out a search party.* | **house-to-house search** (=when every house in an area is searched) *Police are carrying out house-to-house searches in villages near the scene of the murder.*

hunt /hʌnt/ [n singular] an organized search by a lot of people, especially to find a criminal: *Police have launched a nationwide hunt for the killer.*

raid /reɪd/ [n C] a sudden visit by the police to a building in order to look for criminals, drugs, stolen goods etc: *Raids are almost a nightly occurrence at this club.* | **+ on** *Seven people were injured in last night's police raid on a house in Brixton, South London.*

wild goose chase /ˌwaɪld 'guːs ˌtʃeɪs/ [n singular] a search that is a waste of time and effort, either because the thing you are looking for does not exist or you have been given wrong information: *I had a feeling that the trip up to Edinburgh might turn out to be a wild goose chase.* | **send/take sb on a wild goose chase** *He lied and took us on a wild goose chase to North Yorkshire.*

loose

not fitting tightly or not firmly fixed

RELATED WORDS

opposite: **tight**

▸ *see also* **fasten/unfasten, clothes**

1 loose clothes

- loose
- baggy
- loose-fitting
- shapeless

loose /luːs/ [adj] **loose** clothes do not fit your body tightly: *She wore a long, loose linen jacket.* | *In hot weather, loose cotton clothes are more comfortable.* | *The top fitted me, but the shorts were a little loose round the waist.*

baggy /'bægi/ [adj] **baggy** clothes are designed to be big and loose and hide the real shape of your body: *Bill was wearing a polo shirt and baggy blue pants.* | *I like T-shirts as long as they're really baggy.*

loose-fitting /ˌluːs 'fɪtɪŋ◂/ [adj] loose, especially in order to be comfortable: *I wore loose-fitting clothes to protect me from the heat of the sun.* | *A kung fu suit should be loose-fitting, with buttons and a high collar.*

shapeless /'ʃeɪpləs/ [adj] large and loose, and having no shape or style: *He looked dirty and was wearing an ugly, shapeless suit.* | *Helen's hat was limp and shapeless from the rain.*

2 ways of saying that clothes become looser

▸ stretch ▸ give

stretch /stretʃ/ [v I/T] if clothes **stretch** or if you **stretch** them, they become looser and do not fit you properly any more: *I think this sweater must have stretched when I washed it.* | *'Can I borrow your boots?' 'No, you'll stretch them.'*

give /gɪv/ [v I] if tight clothes or shoes **give**, they become looser after you have been wearing them: *Don't worry if swimsuits are tight – they always give a little.* | *These shoes should start to give after you've worn them for a few weeks.*

3 to make clothes looser

▸ loosen ▸ let out

loosen /ˈluːsən/ [v T] to make a piece of clothing looser, especially by unfastening it: *Bill loosened his tie and lit a cigarette.* | *Loosen any tight clothing, and lay the patient on his side.* | *Eric leaned back in his chair and loosened his belt.*

let out /ˌlet ˈaʊt/ [phr v T] to make a piece of clothing looser by undoing the stitches and sewing it up again, so that it is a little bigger **let out sth/let sth out** *You'll either have to let that skirt out or lose some weight.*

4 a loose rope/knot/chain

▸ loose ▸ slack

loose /luːs/ [adj] a rope, knot, chain etc that is **loose** is not tied or stretched tightly, and is not a tight as it should be: *The guitar strings were loose, but none were broken.* | *There must be a wire loose, because this light isn't working.* —**loosely** [adv] *Charlie was holding the horse's reins loosely in one hand.*

slack /slæk/ [adj] a rope or chain that is **slack** is not stretched as tightly as it should be: *If the rope between climbers is slack, one slip can be fatal.* | **go slack** (=become less tight suddenly) *I let the rope go slack as the boat came closer.*

5 to make a rope/knot/chain looser

▸ loosen ▸ slacken

loosen /ˈluːsən/ [v T] to make something loose that has been pulled tight or fastened tightly: *He grasped one of the mules and began to loosen the hitch that held its load.*

slacken /ˈslækən/ [v I/T] to reduce the pressure on something such as a rope, so that it is no longer pulled as tightly as before – used especially in written contexts: *The boat surged forwards as he slackened the rope.* | *Don't allow the reins to slacken, keep them taut.* | **slacken off sth/slacken sth off** *Slacken off the line, and pull the fishing rod towards you.*

6 something that is not fixed firmly enough

▸ loose ▸ wobbly

loose /luːs/ [adj] something that is **loose** is not firmly fixed in the place where it should be: *Some of the floorboards are loose and they creak when you walk on them.* | *a loose tooth* | **come loose** (=gradually become looser) *One of the hinges on the box was coming loose.* | **work loose** (=become loose gradually after a long time, or after a lot of use) *Three bolts worked loose and caused the train to derail.* | **a loose connection** (=when electrical wires are not firmly connected) *The garage claimed it was just a loose connection.*

wobbly /ˈwɒbli‖ˈwɑː-/ [adj] something that is **wobbly** shakes or moves from side to side because it is not fixed as firmly as it should be: *Don't sit on that chair – it's got a wobbly leg.* | *The front wheels on the car seem wobbly.*

7 to make something loose that has been firmly or tightly fixed

▸ loosen

loosen /ˈluːsən/ [v T] to make something loose in order to remove it, for example a screw or lid that has been tightly fixed: *Could you loosen this lid for me?* | *He took a screwdriver from his pocket and began loosening the screws that secured the steel bars to the window frame.*

lose

RELATED WORDS

▸ when you do not know where you are *see* **lost**

WHAT'S HERE

- **lose/can't find** see **1 to 2**
- **lose/not win** see **3 to 6**

lose/can't find

1 to be unable to find someone or something

▸ lose ▸ mislay
▸ can't find ▸ loss

opposite — **find**

▸ *see also* **look for**

lose /luːz/ [v T] to be unable to find something, especially because you cannot remember where you put it: *If you lose your credit card, phone this number immediately.* | *'What are you looking for?' 'My purse. I think I might have lost it.'* | *Neil put the certificate in a drawer so he wouldn't lose it.*

can't find /ˌkɑːnt ˈfaɪnd‖ˌkænt-/ [v phrase] to be unable to find something or someone, especially after you have spent a long time looking for them: *She searched her pockets, but she couldn't find the tickets.* | *What's happened to Eric? I can't find him anywhere.*

mislay /mɪsˈleɪ/ [v T] formal to lose something for a short time, especially because you put it somewhere and then forgot where you put it: *I seem to have temporarily mislaid my keys. Have you seen them anywhere?* | *If your bank card is lost, mislaid or stolen, call our Card Hotline number.*

loss /lɒs‖lɔːs/ [n U] formal the fact that you have lost something: *The company cannot accept liability for loss or damage to a passenger's property.* | **the loss of sth** *You should report the loss of your passport to the consulate.*

2 someone or something that you cannot find

- missing
- lost
- disappear
- be nowhere to be seen/found

missing /ˈmɪsɪŋ/ [adj] a **missing** object is lost and may have been stolen; a **missing** person cannot be found and may be in danger: *She's been missing for three days now, and we're very worried.* | *The painting, which has been missing for almost half a century, only turned up when the owner of the house died.* | **+ from** *Police are 'very concerned' for the safety of a teenager who's been missing from home for three days.* | *Two pages were missing from my copy of the report.* | **go missing (from)** British (=become lost or be stolen) *A small sum of money went missing from the office last night.* | **report sb/sth missing (from)** (=tell someone in authority that someone or something is lost or stolen) *The man had reported his girlfriend missing three days after she disappeared.*

lost /lɒst‖lɔːst/ [adj] if something is **lost**, no-one knows where it is: *I've looked everywhere for the car keys. I think they must be lost.* | *Divers are searching for the plane's lost flight recorder.* | **get lost** *You haven't gotten my letter yet? It must have gotten lost in the mail.*

disappear /ˌdɪsəˈpɪəʳ/ [v I] if something or someone **disappears**, they cannot be found and you think they may have been stolen or may be in danger: *I thought I had a copy of the notes, but they seem to have disappeared somewhere.* | *The parents of an art student who disappeared in the middle of his exams have made an emotional plea for him to come home.* | **+ from** *The letter had mysteriously disappeared from the file overnight.* —**disappearance** [n C/U] *It's now three months since his disappearance.*

be nowhere to be seen/found /biː ˌnəʊweəʳ tə biː ˈsiːn, ˈfaʊnd/ [v phrase] if someone or something **is nowhere to be seen** or **nowhere to be found**, you have looked everywhere for them but still cannot find them: *Our tour guide was nowhere to be seen, so we set off to explore the city alone.* | *She'd looked everywhere for her glasses, but they were nowhere to be found.*

lose/not win

3 to lose a game, argument, election, war etc

- lose
- be beaten
- be defeated
- defeat
- meet your match
- take a beating

opposite ——— **win, beat/defeat**

▸ *see also* **compete with, sport/game, competition, gambling**

lose /luːz/ [v I/T] to **lose** a game, competition, fight, or war: *I always lose when I play tennis with my sister.* | **lose a game/fight/election etc** *Everyone expected the Democrats to lose the election.* | *The Chicago Bears lost their eighth game in a row* (=they lost eight games, one after the other). | **+ to** *England lost to Brazil in the final.* | *He lost his title unexpectedly to a man who is virtually unknown outside boxing circles.* | **lose 3-2/by 1 goal/by 10 votes/by 20 points etc** *The Springboks lost by only three points to the All Blacks.* | *The match was lost 3 to 1.* | **lose sb the game/competition/election etc** (=be the reason that someone lost) *Many people think that the Democrats' tax policies lost them the election.*

be beaten /biː ˈbiːtn/ [v phrase] to lose a game, competition, or race, often by a large amount or when you were expecting to win: *In 37 fights, Lewis has only been beaten once.* | *Jake sure doesn't like being beaten.* | **+ by** *The Barbarians were beaten in the quarter-finals by the Korean side.* | **get beaten** *We always seems to get beaten when we play in Europe.*

be defeated /biː dɪˈfiːtɪ̈d/ [v phrase] to lose an important or difficult battle, election, or game: *Government forces took control of the town after the rebel forces were defeated.* | **+ by** *Last night, the Raiders were defeated by a superior team.* | **be badly/heavily/decisively defeated** (=be very badly defeated) *He ran for Congress last year, but was decisively defeated.* | **be narrowly defeated** (=to lose but be very close to winning) *The Democratic Party was narrowly defeated in the general election, and will form a coalition with the Congress party.*

defeat /dɪˈfiːt/ [n C/U] when a person, team, or army is defeated in a game, competition, election, battle etc: *It was the Christian Democratic Party's fourth successive electoral defeat.* | **+ of** *the defeat of Napoleon at the battle of Waterloo* | **sb's defeat of sb** (=the fact that one person or team defeats another) *Scotland's defeat of Spain* | **sb's defeat by sb** (=the fact that one person or team is defeated by another) *Mr Taylor blamed bad publicity for his defeat by Mr Jones.* | **a crushing/humiliating/resounding defeat** *The captain offered no excuses for his team's humiliating defeat.* | *The New York Times described the withdrawal of troops as a resounding defeat for the government.* | **suffer a defeat** *She retired from the sport after suffering a series of humiliating defeats.*

meet your match /ˌmiːt jɔːʳ ˈmætʃ/ [v phrase not in progressive] if a very good player, team etc **meets their match**, they are beaten by an even better player, team etc, especially after a long period during which they were never beaten: *She's a good player but she'll meet her match when she plays Sara.* | **+ in** *I slowly started to realize I had met my match in Nigel.*

take a beating /ˌteɪk ə ˈbiːtɪŋ/ [v phrase] to lose very badly in a game of football, tennis etc: *'I hear you took a bit of a beating last night.' 'Yeah, we lost 12-2.'*

4 to stop trying to win

- admit/accept defeat
- give in
- surrender
- concede

admit/accept defeat /ədˌmɪt, əkˌsept dɪˈfiːt/ [v phrase] to stop playing, fighting, or trying to succeed because you know you will lose, especially after you have struggled to succeed for a long time: *The four climbers were eventually forced to admit defeat when weather conditions made it impossible to continue.* | *She simply refuses to accept defeat, no matter how bad things seem.*

give in /ˌgɪv ˈɪn/ [phr v I] to stop playing, fighting, arguing etc because you know that you are not good enough to win: *Marie's stubborn, and she doesn't give in easily.* | **+ to** *I figured if we gave in to them this time, they'd be back for another fight.* | *In the end, I had to give in to dad – he's usually right anyway.*

surrender /səˈrendəʳ/ [v I] to officially say that you want to stop fighting in a war because you realize that you cannot win: *Finally, on April 16th, the* *enemy surrendered.* | **+ to** *19 rebels hiding in the Czech embassy surrendered to the authorities.* —**surrender** [n singular/U] *The Milanese were starving, and forced into surrender.* | *Colonel Casado was anxious to negotiate a surrender.* | **unconditional surrender** (=complete acceptance of defeat) *General Haig would accept nothing less than unconditional surrender.*

concede /kən'siːd/ [v I/T] to admit that you are not going to win a battle, argument, or game because you are not strong enough or good enough to win: *Eventually, the chairman was forced to concede and announce his resignation.* | *'Sam, you have to apologise to her' – 'I know,' Sam conceded grudgingly.* | **concede defeat** (=admit you are defeated) *Matthew kept on arguing his point, unwilling to concede defeat.* | **+ that** *Environmentalists concede that it will not be easy to persuade car drivers to use their vehicles less often.* | **+ to** *We both had a point, but neither of us would concede to the other.*

5 when you are likely to lose a game etc

- be losing
- be behind
- trail
- outsider

be losing /biː 'luːzɪŋ/ [v phrase] to be in a position where you are likely to lose a game, competition, election or war because you are not doing as well as your opponent: *'Is Joachim winning?' 'No, he's losing.'* | **be losing the game/war etc** *It can be difficult not to show your frustration when you're losing the match.* | **be losing 3–1/by 15 points/by 2 goals etc** *'What's the score?' 'We're losing 3 – nil.'*

be behind /biː bɪ'haɪnd/ [v phrase] to be losing a game, competition, or election **be behind by two goals/by10 points etc** *The opinion polls show that the Republicans are behind by 3%.* | **be 10 points/a goal etc behind** *'How are we doing?' 'We're 10 points behind, I'm afraid.'* | **be a long way behind/be way behind** (=be losing by a large amount) *Although we only had a short break, we were a long way behind the front runners.* | *The Eagles are way behind. We'll never win at this rate.*

trail ALSO **trail behind** /treɪl, ˌtreɪl bɪ'haɪnd/ [v I/T] to be losing a game or competition, or election – used especially in news reports: *Penn State trail West Virginia by only 1 point.* | **trail 3–0/by 10 points/by 8 votes etc** *Sweden was trailing by 2 games to 1.* | *With his team trailing 72–78, the manager was forced to bring back his star player.* | **trail behind** *These two top drivers have left the others trailing behind.* | *Labour trailed third, behind the Conservative and Liberal parties.*

outsider /aʊt'saɪdəʳ/ [n C] a person or team that is not expected to win: *The defending champion was beaten by an outsider in the first round.* | *Smith, a little-known outsider with limited political experience, came from behind to score a surprise victory.* | **rank outsider** (=someone with a very small chance of winning) British *He started as a no-hoper – a rank outsider for the title.*

6 someone who has lost

- loser
- losing
- runner-up
- defeated

loser /'luːzəʳ/ [n C] the person or group that has lost a game, competition, or election: *The losers walked slowly off the field.* | *I'd like to congratulate all our entrants, the winners and the losers.* | **bad loser** (=someone who behaves badly when they lose) *You're just a bad loser Phil, that's your problem.*

losing /'luːzɪŋ/ [adj only before noun] **losing side/team etc** one that has lost: *Nobody wants to be on the losing side.* | *The quiz show gives losing contestants the chance to see what they would have won.*

runner-up /ˌrʌnər 'ʌp/ [n C] the person or team that comes second or third in a game, race, or competition: *100 lucky runners-up will receive a boxed set of CDs.* | *Gordon was also presented with a cheque as runner-up of the closely fought contest.*

defeated /dɪ'fiːtɨd/ [adj only before noun] **defeated army/finalist/opponent etc** one that lost the battle, war, game etc: *Let's have a quick word with the two defeated finalists.* | *The rebels hope to weaken the regime further by attacking its defeated and demoralised forces.*

lost

when you do not know where you are

RELATED WORDS

- when you can't find something *see* **lose**

1 to be lost

- be lost
- not know where you are

be lost /biː 'lɒst‖-'lɔːst/ [v phrase] to not know where you are, or not know the way to the place that you want to go to: *Excuse me, I'm lost. Could you tell me where the station is, please?* | *Eventually the three children realized they were lost.*

not know where you are /nɒt nəʊ ˌweəʳ juː 'ɑːʳ/ [v phrase not in progressive] if you do **not know where you are**, you do not recognize the place that you are in: *I really don't know where we are – can I take a look at the map.* | *By this time she no longer knew where she was, and was beginning to panic.*

2 to become lost

- get lost
- lose your way
- lose your bearings

get lost /ˌget 'lɒst‖-'lɔːst/ [v phrase] *I'll give you a map so that you don't get lost.* | *Sorry we're so late. We got lost.*

lose your way /ˌluːz jɔːʳ 'weɪ/ [v phrase] if you **lose your way**, you go in the wrong direction or take the wrong road when you are trying to go somewhere: *The climbers had lost their way in the dark.* | *If you lose your way, just stop and ask someone.*

lose your bearings /ˌluːz jɔːʳ 'beərɪŋz/ [v phrase] to become confused about which direction you should be going in, in a place that you do not know well: *She soon lost her bearings in the dense forest.* | *I was trying to get to the A22 and lost my bearings a bit in all the country lanes.*

3 a place where it is easy to get lost

- maze/labyrinth

maze/labyrinth /meɪz, 'læbərɪnθ/ [n C] a place where it is very easy to become lost, because it has a large number of paths, passages, or narrow streets that cross each other **+ of** *The old town is a labyrinth* *of narrow streets, with shops selling everything you could imagine.* | *The complex is a maze of car-ramps and driveways with signs pointing in all directions.*

lot

WHAT'S HERE

- **large amount or number** see **1 to 13**
- **very much** see **14**

large amount or number

RELATED WORDS

opposite: **few/not many, little**

- on many occasions *see* **often**
- *see also* **amount/number, enough/not enough, too/too much, some, big**

1 a large amount of something

- **a lot**
- **lots**
- **much**
- **a great/a good deal**
- **quite a bit/a fair amount**
- **tons**
- **piles/heaps/stacks**
- **a mountain of**
- **heavy**
- **a bundle**

a lot /ə ˈlɒt‖-ˈlɑːt/ [quantifier] *If you plan carefully, a trip to Europe doesn't have to cost a lot.* | **+ of** *We spent a lot of time just lying on the beach.* | *The book contains a lot of useful advice about setting up your own business.* | **a whole lot/an awful lot** (=a very large amount) *To most Americans, $150,000 sounds like a whole lot of money.* | **quite a lot** (=a fairly large amount of something) *Helen looks as if she's lost quite a lot of weight recently – is she on a diet?* | **a lot more/less** *Ask Susan – she knows a lot more about computers than I do.* | **a lot to do/see/learn etc** *We've painted the kitchen and the living room, but there's a lot to do in the other rooms.*

lots /lɒts‖lɑːts/ [quantifier] informal a large amount of something: *'How much money did you bring with you?' 'Lots.'* | **+ of** *It's a big house, so we've got lots of room for company.* | *There was lots of blood, but I don't think anyone got killed.* | **lots and lots** *You can't afford to stay there unless you've got lots and lots of money.* | **lots to see/do/learn etc** *You won't be bored – there's lots to do here.* | **lots more/less** *There's lots more beer in the cooler if you want some.*

much /mʌtʃ/ [quantifier] use this especially in questions and negatives. **Much** is also used in positive sentences in written English and in formal spoken English: *Do you know much about cars?* | **much pleasure/hope/sense etc** *It gives us much pleasure to announce the names of the winners.* | *Her answer didn't make much sense to me.* | **so much** *There was so much noise outside, I could hardly hear what she was saying.* | **too much** *I think Perry's had a little too much wine.* | **much to do/see/learn etc** *She never seems to have much to say.* | *He's very young and still has much to learn about how to deal with employees.* | **+ more/less** *We've had much less rain this year than last year.* | **+ of** (=a large part of something) *Much of Bangladesh remains flooded after last week's torrential rains.*

a great/a good deal /ə ˌgreɪt, ə ˌgʊd ˈdiːl/ [quantifier] a large amount of something such as time, money, effort, or knowledge: *We already know a great deal about the planet Jupiter.* | **+ of** *The job requires a great deal of patience and skill.* | *It sounds like a simple experiment, but it required a great deal of effort.* | *There's a good deal of evidence to show that eating red meat can cause heart disease.* | **+ more/less** *Audiences have responded to his latest show with a great deal more enthusiasm.*

quite a bit/a fair amount ALSO **a fair bit** British /ˌkwaɪt ə ˈbɪt, ə ˌfeər əˈmaʊnt, ə ˌfeəʳ ˈbɪt/ [quantifier] a large amount of something compared with the total amount that you have: *Don knows a fair bit about managing a company.* | **+ of** *I wasted a fair amount of time before I figured out what was wrong with the car.* | *There's been quite a bit of conflict between the new director and his staff.* | **+ more/less** *The tickets will cost quite a bit less money if you stay over the weekend.*

tons ALSO **loads** especially British **/masses** British /tʌnz, ləʊdz, ˈmæsɪ̈z/ [quantifier] informal a very large amount of something: *'How much space is there in the back of your car?' 'Masses.'* | *It was a fantastic meal – there was loads to eat.* | **+ of** *He made tons of money at some computer company.* | *She's a great athlete with loads of talent.* | *I've got tons of homework to do this weekend.* | **tons and tons/loads and loads etc** *There's tons and tons of information on the Internet if you're willing to look for it.*

piles/heaps/stacks /paɪlz, hiːps, stæks/ [quantifier] British informal a large amount of something, especially work or money: *'How much money have you saved?' 'Oh, stacks!'* | *I have piles to do when I get home tonight.* | **+ of** *Her family is very rich – they have heaps of money.*

a mountain of /ə ˈmaʊntɪ̈n ɒv/ [quantifier] a large amount of something such as work, debt, or information: *We had to complete a mountain of paperwork to get the loan.* | *The economies of Third World countries are often crippled by huge mountains of debt which they will never be able to repay.*

heavy /ˈhevi/ [adj] a lot or in very large amounts, especially when this is worse than expected **heavy rain/snow/traffic/fighting/losses/taxation** *The match went ahead despite the heavy rain.* | *It was a fierce battle, and losses on both sides were heavy.* | *Traffic was really heavy this morning – it took me over an hour to get here.*

a bundle /ə ˈbʌndl/ [quantifier] informal a large amount of money: *He lost a bundle in the stock market.* | **+ of** *If you end up hiring a lawyer, it could cost you a bundle of money.*

2 a large number of things or people

- **a lot**
- **lots**
- **many**
- **a large number of/large numbers of**
- **tons**
- **a bunch**
- **dozens**
- **numerous**
- **a host of**
- **quite a few**
- **a raft of**
- **multi**
- **multiple**

a lot /ə ˈlɒt‖-ˈlɑːt/ [quantifier] *I was surprised so few people were at the concert – I thought there'd be a lot there.* | **+ of** *A lot of tourists visit Venice in the summer.* | *John has lived in a lot of different places.* | **+ more/fewer/less** *I'm sure she has a lot more problems than I have.* | **quite a lot** *There were quite a lot of words that I couldn't understand.* | **a whole lot/an awful lot** *An awful lot of his customers are unhappy with his work.*

lots /lɒts‖lɑːts/ [quantifier] informal a lot of people or things: *'Have you gotten any responses to your ad?'*

'Yeah – lots.' | **+ of** *I've invited lots of people.* | *She asked lots of questions during the interview.* | **lots and lots of** *They've planted lots and lots of flowers in the back yard.* | **lots more/fewer/less** *We get lots more people in the bar on Fridays.*

many /'meni/ [quantifier] use this especially in questions and negative sentences. **Many** is also used in positive sentences in written English and in formal spoken English. **many questions/people/cars/thoughts etc** *Did you get many Christmas cards this year?* | *I don't know many people here, do you?* | **not many** *Not many people survived the crash.* | **so many** *There were so many people at the party, I never even saw Will.* | **too many** *They've got too many rules for me to remember them all.* | **+ of** (=many among a large number of people or things) *Many of the paintings burned, but the most valuable ones were saved.* | **for many years** *She worked as a reporter with CBS news for many years.* | **in many ways/places/cases etc** *There will be rain in many parts of the country tonight.* | **+ more/fewer/less** *We've had many fewer complaints since Doug took over the department.* | **the many** *The report hardly mentions the many patients who have benefited from the treatment.* | **a good many** *A good many scientists were opposed to the use of the bomb.* | **many a person/place/thing** *I've spent many a happy morning fishing from this spot.*

a large number of/large numbers of /ə ˌlɑːʳdʒ 'nʌmbər ɒv, ˌlɑːʳdʒ 'nʌmbəʳz ɒv/ [quantifier] a lot of a particular type of person or thing – used especially in newspapers and official reports: *Police seized a large number of weapons.* | *Large numbers of demonstrators were arrested during today's protest march.*

tons ALSO **loads** especially British **/masses** British /tʌnz, ləʊdz, 'mæsᵻz / [quantifier] informal a lot of people or things: *'How many strawberries did you pick?' 'Masses!'* | **+ of** *You can borrow one of my books if you want – I have tons of them.* | *The beach was really crowded – there were loads of people from all over Europe.* | **loads and loads/tons and tons etc** *There were loads and loads of empty seats at the game – I was kind of surprised.*

a bunch /ə 'bʌntʃ / [quantifier] American informal a lot of people or things: *'Do you have any markers I could borrow?' 'I've got a bunch – what colors do you need?'* | **+ of** *Rita finally showed up with a bunch of her friends.* | *I went to a bunch of different stores but I couldn't find a coat I liked.* | **a whole bunch** *A whole bunch of us are going to the beach – you want to come along?*

dozens /'dʌzənz / [quantifier] a large number of people, things etc but not usually more than a hundred: *At least five people died and dozens more were injured in a gas explosion just outside Paris.* | **+ of** *Since we put the advertisement in the paper we've had dozens of phone calls.* | *Baldwin was the author of six novels, four plays and dozens of essays and poems.* | **dozens and dozens** *The women see dozens and dozens of movies a year.*

numerous /'njuːmərəs‖'nuː-/ [adj] formal many: *The same problem has occurred before on numerous occasions.* | *Numerous books and movies have dealt with the issue of wife abuse.* | **too numerous to list/mention/name etc** (=so many that you cannot say all of them) *I want to thank all the people, too numerous to mention, who've helped me win this election.*

a host of /ə 'həʊst ɒv/ [quantifier] a large number of things or people, especially when this is impressive or surprising: *AIDS can indirectly result in a host of other illnesses.* | *Since he was elected, the president has been faced with a host of difficult problems.* | **a whole host of** *Their newest compact model has a whole host of exciting new features.*

quite a few /ˌkwaɪt ə 'fjuː/ [quantifier] a fairly large number of people, things etc: *He's been working at the company for quite a few years.* | *There have been quite a few accidents on this stretch of road.* | *'How many people are coming to the party?' 'Oh, quite a few.'* | **+ of** *She knows quite a few of the people who work at the hospital.*

a raft of /ə 'rɑːft ɒv‖-'ræft-/ [quantifier] especially American a large number of ideas, opinions, suggestions etc: *The President has a raft of new proposals for dealing with inner city decay.* | **a whole raft of** *By the end of the meeting we had a whole raft of new ideas for expansion.*

multi /'mʌlti/ [prefix] **multi-coloured/multi-national/multi-storey/multi-racial/multi-purpose/multi-million dollar etc** having or involving many colours, countries etc: *My new office is in a multi-storey building.* | *The company is a multi-national corporation, which has branches all over the world.* | *Russia has moved from a one-party dictatorship to a multi-party system of government.*

multiple /'mʌltᵻpəl/ [adj only before noun] **multiple injuries/wounds/burns/fractures** in many parts of the body: *She suffered multiple injuries after jumping out of a fifth floor window.* | *Lauda was pulled from his blazing car with multiple burns.*

3 a very large number of people or things

- hundreds/thousands
- a great many
- countless/innumerable
- everything but the kitchen sink

hundreds/thousands /'hʌndrᵻdz, 'θaʊzəndz / [quantifier] a lot of things or people – use this when you want to emphasize that you are talking about a very large number. You can use this informally when the number is actually less than a hundred: *Hundreds were left homeless by the flood.* | **+ of** *I've seen that movie hundreds of times.* | *It will cost thousands of dollars to repair the house.* | *From the 1880s to the early 1900s thousands of workers came to Hawaii from Japan.* | **hundreds and hundreds/thousands and thousands** ALSO **hundreds upon hundreds/thousands upon thousands** *The temple was filled with hundreds and hundreds of lanterns.* | **by the hundreds/thousands** *Starving animals in the region are dying by the thousands.*

a great many /ə ˌgreɪt 'meni/ [quantifier] use this when you want to emphasize that you are talking about something important: *We have seen a great many changes in the last twenty years.* | *There are still a great many questions that remain unanswered.* | **+ of** *The fire had destroyed a great many of the family's possessions.*

countless/innumerable /'kaʊntləs, ɪ'njuːmərəbəl‖ɪ'njuː-, ɪ'nuː-/ [adj only before noun] an extremely large number of things or people, that cannot be counted or imagined: *The mountains around the lake are filled with countless hiking trails.* | *There are innumerable variations on the folktale, but the basic story is the same throughout Europe.* | **countless millions** (=an extremely large group of people) *His music has brought joy to countless millions.*

everything but the kitchen sink /ˌevriθɪŋ bət ðə ˌkɪtʃᵻn sɪŋk/ [n phrase] informal an extremely large number of things of different types – use this especially when you think there are too many things: *When my parents come to stay with us, they bring everything but the kitchen sink!* | *Chatham refused to participate in what he called 'everything but the kitchen sink' art shows.*

4 more than enough of something that people need or want

- plenty
- more than enough
- bags of
- ample
- plentiful
- an abundance of
- abundant
- galore

plenty /ˈplenti / [quantifier] a lot of something or a lot of things or people, especially more than enough: *No thanks. I couldn't eat any more. I've had plenty.* | **+ of** *There's plenty of room in the hall closet.* | *We have plenty of glasses, but not enough plates.* | **plenty to do/eat/talk about etc** *The two men had plenty to talk about.* | **plenty of sth to do sth** *There's still plenty of time to take a walk or a bike ride before dinner.*

more than enough /ˈmɔːʳ ðən ɪˌnʌf/ [quantifier] more than you need – sometimes used to mean there is too much: *Here's some money for the ticket – $25 should be more than enough.* | **more than enough sth for sb** *There's more than enough food for everyone.* | **more than enough to do/think about etc** *I can't help with the planning. I've more than enough to do already.* | **more than enough to do sth** *He makes more than enough to live comfortably on.* | **more than enough sth to do sth** *Supporters have gathered more than enough signatures to put Fordham on the ballot.*

bags of /ˈbægz ɒv/ [quantifier] British informal a lot or more than enough of something that you need or want: *Don't rush; we've got bags of time.* | *The new manager is tremendously enthusiastic, and he's got bags of new ideas.*

ample /ˈæmpəl/ [adj usually before noun] more than enough: *These documents provide ample evidence of their guilt.* | *The program would ensure that Arizona has an ample supply of water for the next 20 years.* | **ample time/opportunity etc to do sth** *You will have ample opportunity to express your opinions during the debate.* —**amply** [adv] *The men have been amply rewarded for their services.*

plentiful /ˈplentɪfəl/ [adj] if something such as food or water is **plentiful**, there is more than enough of it available: *During the summer tomatoes are plentiful and cheap.* | *The river provides a plentiful supply of clean water to nearby villages.*

an abundance of /ən əˈbʌndəns ɒv/ [quantifier] formal a large quantity of something, usually more than is needed: *This book contains an abundance of valuable information.* | *An abundance of fruits and vegetables grow in Kenya's temperate climate.*

abundant /əˈbʌndənt/ [adj] formal existing in large quantities so that there is more than enough: *Latin America has an abundant labor force and natural resources.* | *During the 18th century land was cheap, grain was plentiful, and meat was abundant.* | **+ in** *Plant fossils are abundant in some types of rock.*

galore /gəˈlɔːʳ/ [adj only after noun] available in large quantities – used especially in advertisements about something that people may want: *There are bargains galore in our summer sale.* | *Lots of fun for the kids! Rides and games galore!*

5 a lot of unpleasant events in a short period of time

- spate of sth
- epidemic
- rash of sth
- wave

spate of sth /ˈspeɪt əv (sth)/ [n singular] *An alarming spate of bombings has caused widespread panic.* | *The company has yet to respond to the recent spate of lawsuits filed against it.* | *The party lost power three years ago after a spate of political scandals.*

epidemic /ˌepəˈdemɪk◂/ [n C] a lot of unpleasant activity of one particular kind which spreads quickly during a short period of time and which seems to be difficult to stop or control **+ of** *The recent epidemic of car thefts has been blamed on bored teenagers.* | **reach epidemic proportions** (=become like an epidemic) *Alcohol abuse has reached epidemic proportions in this country.*

rash of sth /ˈræʃ əv (sth)/ [n singular] a large number of unpleasant events or a particular kind that happen in a short period of time in many different places: *Emergency officials worry that the region may again be hit by a rash of wildfires this fall.* | *Experts are not sure what is causing the recent rash of mountain lion sightings.*

wave /weɪv/ [n C] a lot of unpleasant activity or actions suddenly becoming worse and increasing in a short period of time **+ of** *Security chiefs fear a new wave of terrorist bombings.* | *The country has been brought to a standstill by the latest wave of strikes.* | **crime wave** *The mayor has promised tough action in response to the city's rising crime wave.*

6 a lot of people or things all arriving at the same time

- flood of
- wave of
- deluge/avalanche of

flood of /ˈflʌd ɒv/ [n C] a very large amount of something or a very large number of things or people arriving in a short period of time: *Many fear that the flood of imports could weaken Britain's economy.* | *The town has been hit by a flood of visitors since it was featured in the movie.* | *The company was launched amid a flood of publicity a year ago.*

wave of /ˈweɪv ɒv/ [n C] a sudden increase in the number of people or things all arriving at the same time: *There was a great wave of immigrants to the U.S. at the beginning of the 20th century.* | *Students are responsible for sparking the latest wave of demonstrations.*

deluge/avalanche of /ˈdeljuːdʒ, ˈævəlɑːnʃ ɒv‖ -læntʃ-/ [n singular] a very large number of messages, letters etc all arriving suddenly at the same time, especially when there are too many: *He received a deluge of telegrams and messages of support from around the world.* | *Insurance companies are bracing themselves for an avalanche of claims following the hurricane.*

7 when a lot of people or things do something at the same time

- in large numbers
- in droves
- in force/strength
- by the hundreds/thousands
- thick and fast
- be dying/dropping like flies

in large numbers /ɪn ˌlɑːʳdʒ ˈnʌmbəʳz/ [adv] use this to say that a lot of people or things do something, or go or appear somewhere all at the same time: *During the dry season animals gather in large numbers around the water holes.* | *Young people are leaving the countryside and moving to the city in large numbers.*

in droves /ɪn ˈdrəʊvz/ [adv] if people go somewhere **in droves**, they go in large numbers especially when this surprises you: *Nurses are leaving the profession in droves.* | *People came in droves to watch the fireworks display.*

in force/strength /ɪn ˈfɔːʳs, ˈstreŋθ/ [adv] if people go somewhere **in force** or **in strength** a lot of them go together so that there is a large number of them in a particular place: *The police arrived in force to break up the crowd of demonstrators.* | *If Latino voters turn out in strength for the next election, results could be very different.*

by the hundreds/thousands /baɪ ðə ˈhʌndrɨdz, ˈθaʊzəndz/ [adv] if people do something **by the hundreds** or **by the thousands** very large groups of them are doing it at the same time: *People in the drought-stricken region are dying by the hundreds.* | *From all over the country, people came by the thousands to pay respect to their dead leader.*

thick and fast /ˌθɪk ən ˈfɑːst‖-ˈfæst/ [adv] if messages, events etc come **thick and fast**, a lot of them suddenly come or happen in a short time: *At first no one was interested in the job but now applications are coming in thick and fast.* | *Rumours flew thick and fast that the company was going to be sold.*

be dying/dropping like flies /biː ˌdaɪ-ɪŋ, ˌdrɒpɪŋ laɪk ˈflaɪz‖-ˌdrɑːp-/ [v phrase] to be dying or suddenly becoming ill in large numbers: *In the middle of the cholera epidemic, people were dropping like flies.* | *When Sam reached 70, it seemed his friends started dying like flies.*

8 when there is a lot of something in many areas

- common
- widespread
- extensive

common /ˈkɒmən‖ˈkɑː-/ [adj] if an object, animal, disease etc is **common**, there is a very large number or amount of objects, animals etc of this type in many different places: *Jones is a very common name in Britain.* | *Flatheads are a common type of fish and good to eat.* | *Malaria is particularly common near swamps where mosquitoes can breed.* —**commonly** [adv] *The pregnancy test is commonly available in supermarkets and drugstores.*

widespread /ˈwaɪdspred/ [adj] having an effect on a lot of people over a wide area: *Poverty in the region is widespread.* | **widespread damage/flooding/poverty etc** *Heavy rains have led to the most widespread flooding in a decade.* | *Ethiopia was suffering widespread famine and disease.*

extensive /ɪkˈstensɪv/ [adj] covering a large area or a large range of information, ideas etc: *Damage to the forests from the wildfires was extensive.* | *The ancient Greeks had an extensive knowledge of the stars.* | *Abortion has been the subject of extensive debate in the US.* —**extensively** [adv] *The band has toured extensively in the U.S. and Europe.*

9 done or believed by a lot of people

- common
- popular
- widespread
- widely

common /ˈkɒmən‖ˈkɑː-/ [adj] *Using 'lay' instead of 'lie' is a very common mistake.* | *It's becoming more and more common for women to keep their family name when they marry.* | *My daughter says politics is boring, which is a common attitude among teenagers.* —**commonly** [adv] *Aspirin is commonly used to relieve pain.* | **commonly known/understood/referred to as sth** (=known by a lot of people or most people in a particular way) *He leads the Student Environmental Action Coalition, more commonly known as SEAC.*

popular /ˈpɒpjɡləʳ‖ˈpɑːp-/ [adj only before noun] done, believed, or felt by a lot of ordinary people have: *There is still a lot of popular support for the ex-president.* | *I don't accept the popular view that all criminals should be put in prison.* | **contrary to popular belief** (=the opposite of what most ordinary people believe) *Contrary to popular belief, the Australian desert is often full of wildlife.* —**popularly** [adv] known, understood etc by a lot of ordinary people in a particular way: **popularly known/understood/referred to etc as sth** *The law seeks to regulate smokeless tobacco, popularly known as 'snuff.'*

widespread /ˈwaɪdspred/ [adj usually before noun] done, believed or felt by a lot of people in many different places: *There was now widespread public support for healthcare reform.* | *The airlines' failures were in part caused by widespread concern about air safety.* | *The practice of adding preservatives to basic foods is widespread.*

widely /ˈwaɪdli/ [adv] **widely accepted/believed/known/practised/used etc** done, believed or felt by a lot of people in many different places: *Silicon Valley is widely known as California's high-tech center.* | *A hundred years ago it was widely believed that there was life on Mars.* | *Asbestos was once widely used in the building industry.*

10 when someone does something a lot

- a lot
- much
- a good/great deal
- quite a bit/a fair amount
- heavy

a lot /ə ˈlɒt‖-ˈlɑːt/ [adv not before verb] *I'm really glad to meet you. Betty's talked a lot about you.* | *He really sweats a lot in hot weather like this.* | **a whole lot/an awful lot** *We didn't do an awful lot while Geraldine was here.* | **quite a lot** *He laughed quite a lot as he spoke.*

much /mʌtʃ/ [adv] use this in questions and negatives: *I haven't thought much about it.* | *Do you talk to Leslie much anymore?*

a good/great deal /ə ˌgʊd, ˌgreɪt ˈdiːl/ [adv not before verb] formal a lot: *I've thought a good deal about what you said.* | *Her knee makes it impossible to run, but she still walks a great deal.*

quite a bit/a fair amount ALSO **a fair bit** British /ˌkwaɪt ə ˈbɪt, ə ˌfeər əˈmaʊnt, ə ˌfeəʳ ˈbɪt/ [adv] fairly often or in fairly large amounts: *You've been travelling quite a bit lately, haven't you?* | *I exercise a fair amount – especially on weekends.* | *You have to stand around a fair bit in this job.*

heavy /ˈhevi/ [adj only before noun] **heavy smoking/drinking** smoking or drinking a lot, especially when this is bad for your health: *She has a bad cough, caused by heavy smoking.* | *The three soldiers are accused of killing the woman after a night of heavy drinking.* | **be a heavy smoker/drinker** (=smoke or drink a lot) *His first wife Joy was a heavy smoker who died of lung cancer.*

11 containing a lot of something

- be full of
- high
- rich

be full of /biː ˈfʊl ɒv/ [v phrase] if something **is full of** people or things, there are a lot of them in it: *In summer the town is full of tourists.* | *Her essay was full of mistakes.* | **be chock full of sth** (=be completely full of something) *The pamphlet is chock full of advice for people travelling abroad.*

high /haɪ/ [adj] something that is **high** in fat, sugar, salt etc contains a lot of fat, sugar etc **+ in** *The cereal is high in fiber and contains plenty of vitamin B.* | **high-fat/-sugar/-cholesterol etc** *I try to eat a low-fat, high-protein diet.* | **high metal/calcium/oxygen etc content** *The high oxygen content of Earth's atmosphere makes life here possible.*

rich /rɪtʃ/ [adj] something that is **rich** in a useful or valuable substance such as oil or iron, contains a lot of oil, iron etc **+ in** *Spinach is rich in iron and very good for you.* | *The land in this area is rich in minerals and ideal for growing crops.* | **oil-rich/copper-rich/diamond-rich etc** *Numerous companies sprang up employing thousands to work the oil-rich fields of Texas.*

12 producing a lot

- productive
- prolific

productive /prəˈdʌktɪv/ [adj] doing a job efficiently with good results, especially by producing a large quantity of something: *We should do something to reward our most productive employees.* | *The local paper factory has been forced to become more productive or face closure.*

prolific /prəˈlɪfɪk/ [adj] a writer or artist who is **prolific** produces a large number of works: *Ansle is a prolific writer of more than 200 romances.* | *As an artist, Benton was prolific – more than 1,900 drawings were found in his studio after his death.*

13 when there is a lot of unpleasant activity

- be rife
- be a hotbed of

be rife /biː ˈraɪf/ [v phrase] if something bad or unpleasant **is rife**, it is very common. If a place, situation, or activity **is rife with** something bad or unpleasant, the bad or unpleasant thing is very common there: *Foreigners doing business in the city say that corruption is rife there.* | **+ with** *The neighborhood is rife with illegal drug activity and violence.*

be a hotbed of /biː ə ˈhɒtbed ɒv‖-ˈhɑːt-/ [v phrase] use this about a place where there is a lot of an activity, especially a bad or violent one: *The political party has become a hotbed of nationalism and racial bigotry.* | *The exhibition's use of religious symbols has made it a hotbed of controversy.*

very much

RELATED WORDS

opposite: —— **little**

- *see also* **very, too/too much**

14 very much

- a lot
- very much
- a good/great deal
- quite a bit
- really
- greatly
- so much
- much
- enormously/ tremendously
- significantly

a lot /ə ˈlɒt‖-ˈlɑːt/ [adv not before verb] very much: *She's changed a lot since she's been here.* | *'How does your arm feel?' 'It still hurts a lot.'* | *I like her a lot, but I don't think I'm in love with her.* | **a lot better/worse/bigger/more etc** *Their new house is a lot bigger than their old one.* | *The tickets were a lot more expensive than we expected.* | **a whole lot/an awful lot** *I like the people a whole lot, but the pay isn't very good.*

very much /ˌveri ˈmʌtʃ/ [adv] use this especially to talk about people's feelings: *'Do you like living in Rome?' 'Yes, very much.'* | **like/admire/miss etc sb very much** *Lara liked being at college, but she missed her family very much.* | **like/enjoy sth very much** *We enjoyed the play very much – it was really well done.* | **very much wish/hope/doubt etc** formal *I doubt very much that he'll still be here in November.*

a good/great deal /ə ˌgʊd, ˌgreɪt ˈdiːl/ [adv not before verb] formal very much – use this especially to talk about changes, improvements, or differences: *Her work has improved a good deal over the past year.* | *By the next morning the swelling had already gone down a great deal.* | **+ better/worse/bigger/more etc** *The situation was a good deal worse than we had first thought.*

quite a bit /a fair bit British /ˌkwaɪt ə ˈbɪt, ə ˌfeəʳ ˈbɪt/ [adv] by a fairly large degree: *She's quite a bit shorter than I remembered.* | *Jim has improved quite a bit since he came home from the hospital.* | *The estimates were a fair bit higher than what the final figure was.*

really /ˈrɪəli/ [adv only before verb] especially spoken a lot – use this especially to talk about your feelings: *I really like your new haircut.* | *We really enjoy having a few friends over for dinner every once in a while.* | *What really annoys me is the way he never apologizes when he's late.*

greatly /ˈgreɪtli/ [adv usually before verb] formal a lot: *We greatly regret having caused you so much trouble and inconvenience.* | *The recent talks have greatly improved relations between North and South Korea.* | *I think we have all benefited greatly from Helen's knowledge and experience.* | **be greatly affected/amused/influenced etc** *The students were greatly amused by Professor Unwin's remark.* | *Critics say that the report's figures are greatly exaggerated.*

so much /səʊ ˈmʌtʃ/ [adv not usually before verb] use this especially when you are saying how much you love, want, or admire something or someone: *It's two years since Tony died. I miss him so much.* | *I wanted so much to go with him, but he wouldn't let me come.* | *Wordsworth returned to the lakes and hills that he loved so much.* | **+ better/worse/more etc** *I really like the living room arranged this way so much better than the way we used to have it.*

much /mʌtʃ/ [adv] use this in questions and negatives and in comparisons and before phrases with 'too': *Has he changed much?* | *'Did you enjoy the show?' 'Not much.'* | **much better/worse/bigger/more etc** *You get a much better view if you stand on a chair.* | *His family is much more important to him than his career.* | **much too big/old/tall etc** *The test was much too difficult for most of the students.* | *You're working much too hard, and you're letting the boss take advantage of you.*

enormously/tremendously /ɪ'nɔːʳməsli, trɪ'mendəsli/ [adv] use this to emphasize that you mean 'very much': *His English has improved tremendously.* | *I admire your mother enormously.* | *Prices can vary enormously from state to state.* | *Since the law was changed, the number of credit unions has grown tremendously.*

significantly /sɪg'nɪfɪkəntli/ [adv] use this when you are talking about a change or difference that is big enough to be important: *In New York and Los Angeles violent crime decreased significantly.* | *All ovens are different, and cooking times can vary significantly.* | **+ higher/lower/more etc** *Students who had completed the program scored significantly higher on standardized tests.*

loud

RELATED WORDS

opposite: — **quiet**

▸ *see also* **sound, voice**

1 loud

▸ loud
▸ noisy
▸ rowdy
▸ raucous
▸ booming

loud /laʊd/ [adj] something that is **loud** makes a lot of noise: *The music's too loud. Can you turn it down?* | *Three seconds later there was a loud bang and the hall was filled with smoke.* | *The boy gave a loud cry of pain.* —**loudly** [adv] *Bill had dozed off in his chair, and was snoring loudly.*

noisy /'nɔɪzi/ [adj] use this about places where there is a lot of noise, or about people and machines that make a lot of noise, especially when this annoys you: *The nightclub was crowded and noisy.* | *Their lives are being ruined by noisy neighbours.* | *People started to complain about his noisy motorbike.*

rowdy /'raʊdi/ [adj] a crowd that is **rowdy** makes too much noise and behaves badly: *They were thrown out of the bar for rowdy behaviour.* | *People living near the football stadium complain about litter and rowdy fans.* | *The meeting was a somewhat rowdy affair.* —**rowdiness** [n U] *There was a lot of shouting, swearing, and general rowdiness.* —**rowdily** [adv] *The children streamed out of the classrooms and rushed rowdily down the corridor.*

raucous /'rɔːkəs/ [adj] **raucous voice/laugh etc** a voice, laugh etc that is loud, rough and uncontrolled: *A howl of raucous laughter came from the kitchen.* | *He sat and finished his drink, ignoring the raucous voices from the other end of the bar.* —**raucously** [adv] *At midnight people poured out into the street shouting and laughing raucously.*

booming /'buːmɪŋ/ [adj usually before noun] **booming voice/laugh etc** a voice, laugh etc that is very loud and deep: *The speaker's booming voice easily reached the back of the theatre.* | *His booming laugh echoed around the room.*

2 extremely loud

▸ deafening
▸ at full blast/at full volume
▸ at the top of your voice
▸ thunderous
▸ piercing
▸ ear-splitting

deafening /'defənɪŋ/ [adj] a noise that is **deafening** is so loud that you cannot hear anything else: *Outside there was a deafening crash of thunder.* | *When she finished speaking, the applause was deafening.*

at full blast/at full volume /ət ˌfʊl 'blɑːst‖-'blæst, ət ˌfʊl 'vɒljuːm‖-'vɑːljəm/ [adv] if you play music or have the radio or television on **at full volume** or **at full blast**, it is as loud as it can be: *Joey was in his bedroom playing his CDs at full volume.* | *The radio was on at full blast, and everyone was dancing wildly.*

at the top of your voice British **/at the top of your lungs** American /ət ðə ˌtɒp əv jɔːʳ 'vɔɪs, ət ðə ˌtɒp əv jɔːʳ 'lʌŋz‖-ˌtɑːp-/ [adv] shouting as loudly as you can: *George ran after her, shouting, 'Stop!' at the top of his lungs.*

thunderous /'θʌndərəs/ [adj] extremely loud: | **thunderous applause** *The announcement was greeted with thunderous applause.*

piercing /'pɪəʳsɪŋ/ [adj] very high and loud, in a way that is painful or unpleasant to listen to: *Sammy put his fingers in his mouth and gave a piercing whistle.* | **piercing shriek/scream/cry etc** *Maggie let out a piercing scream.*

ear-splitting /'ɪəʳ splɪtɪŋ/ [adj] extremely loud, unpleasant, and almost painful to hear: *There was an ear-splitting roar as the jets took off.* | *The noise was ear-splitting as grenades landed all around us.*

3 a loud noise

▸ noise
▸ racket
▸ din
▸ commotion
▸ hubbub
▸ roar
▸ clamour

noise /nɔɪz/ [n C/U] a loud sound, especially an unpleasant one: *Traffic noise is a problem in inner-city areas.* | *The noise of the machines made it hard to talk.* | **make (a) noise** *Do you have to make so much noise?*

racket /'rækɪt/ [n singular] informal a loud, unpleasant noise: *It's impossible to work with that racket going on.* | **make a racket** *I wish those kids would stop making such a racket upstairs.*

din /dɪn/ [n singular] a loud, unpleasant noise, especially one made by a large number of people talking loudly, working etc: *The hall resounded with the din of thirty children scraping violins, banging drums and singing loudly.* | **above the din** *I shouted to make myself heard above the din.*

commotion /kə'məʊʃən/ [n singular/U] a sudden noisy activity, especially the noise of people arguing or fighting: *We heard a commotion downstairs and ran down to see what was happening.* | *Suddenly there was a commotion by the front door, and two police officers marched in.* | **in commotion** (=full of noisy activity) *Suddenly the whole street was in commotion.*

hubbub /'hʌbʌb/ [n singular] a loud, confused, unclear noise, made by many people talking at the same time: *It's a wonderful place to escape from the hubbub of London's busy streets.* | **over/above the hubbub** *His voice rose above the hubbub.*

roar /rɔːʳ/ [n C] a continuous loud noise, especially if made by a machine or a strong wind: *Inside, the gale was no more than a distant, muffled roar.* | *She heard the roar of a motorbike behind her.*

clamour British **/clamor** American /ˈklæməʳ/ [n singular] a loud noise, especially the noise made by an excited or confused crowd – used especially in literature: *The station was filled with the clamour of shouting voices and movement.* | *The noise in the auditorium had risen to a clamor.*

4 to make a loud noise

- boom/boom out
- roar
- thunder
- blare/blare out
- blast/blast out

boom/boom out /buːm, ˌbuːm ˈaʊt/ [v I] to make a loud, deep, hollow sound like the sound of a big gun: *Thunder boomed loudly overhead.* | *Rock music boomed from speakers above the stage.* | *Occasional volleys of shellfire boomed out from beyond the walls of the city.*

roar /rɔːʳ/ [v I] if something **roars**, especially a machine or a strong wind, it makes a continuous loud noise: *I stood by the waterfall, almost hypnotised by the roaring water.* | **roar through/past etc** *The wind roared through the forest.* | *Traffic roared along the highway.*

thunder /ˈθʌndəʳ/ [v I] if a machine, vehicle, etc **thunders**, it makes a loud, deep, powerful sound, especially when it is moving fast **thunder past/through/overhead etc** *The train thundered through the station.*

blare/blare out /bleəʳ, ˌbleər ˈaʊt/ [v I/T] if music or someone's voice **blares** or **blares out**, it comes from a radio, TV etc very loudly: *It was a horrible disco with lights flashing and music blaring.* | *A siren blared out somewhere behind us.* | **blare out sth** *A radio was blaring out pop music.*

blast/blast out /blɑːst, ˌblɑːst ˈaʊt‖ˌblæst-/ [v I/T] to produce a lot of loud noise, especially music: *The neighbors blasted religious music from their windows at all hours of the night.* | *Pop music blasted out from her radio.*

5 to make music, a radio, or a television louder

- turn up

turn up /ˌtɜːʳn ˈʌp/ [phr v T] to make music, a radio etc louder by turning a control **turn sth up** *Can you turn the television up? I can't hear it.* | **turn up sth** *Someone turned up the music, and people started dancing.*

6 how loud something is

- volume

volume /ˈvɒljuːm‖ˈvɑːljəm/ [n U] how loud a television, radio etc is: *This button here controls the volume.* | **turn the volume up/down** (=make it louder or quieter) *You can use the remote control to turn the volume up or down.* | *Turn the volume down – I can't hear myself think!*

love

RELATED WORDS

opposite: **hate**

▸ *see also* **like, sex, sexy, relationship, marry, girlfriend/boyfriend, gay, obsession**

1 to love someone especially in a sexual or romantic way

- love
- be in love
- be crazy about
- fancy
- have a crush on
- be infatuated
- be besotted

love /lʌv/ [v T not in progressive] to have a strong feeling of liking someone, caring about them, and being sexually attracted to them: *He stroked her hair and murmured, 'I love you.'* | *He was the only man she had ever loved.* | **love sb very much** *We still love each other very much.*

be in love /biː ɪn ˈlʌv/ [v phrase] to love someone very much, so that you think about them all the time and want to be with them all the time: *I think I'm in love!* | **+ with** *How can you marry Adam when you're in love with someone else?* | **be madly in love/very much in love** (=very strongly in love) *We were both seventeen and madly in love.*

be crazy about /biː ˈkreɪzi əbaʊt/ [v phrase] informal to love someone very much, especially in a way that you cannot control: *Jo's crazy about you.*

fancy /ˈfænsi/ [v T] British spoken to be sexually attracted to someone, especially someone that you do not know very well: *All the girls fancy Bob.* | *I think Stevie fancies you.*

have a crush on /ˌhæv ə ˈkrʌʃ ɒn/ [v phrase not in progressive] if someone, especially a young person, **has a crush on** someone they have an uncontrollable feeling of love for them, especially when there is no chance of having a relationship with them: *It is quite normal for adolescents to have crushes on pop stars.* | *The only reason I went to church every Sunday was that I had a crush on the minister.*

be infatuated /biː ɪnˈfætʃueɪtɪ̣d/ [adj] to have a strong and uncontrollable feeling of love for someone you do not know very well, which does not last for a long time: *Ever since she met Rod at a party she's been totally infatuated.* | **+ with** *Teenage girls sometimes become infatuated with their teachers.* —**infatuation** /ɪnˌfætʃuˈeɪʃən/ [n U] *I thought I was in love with Darren, but it was just infatuation.*

be besotted /biː bɪˈsɒtɪ̣d‖-ˈsɑː-/ [v phrase] to be so much in love with someone that you do not behave sensibly or think clearly: *She was too besotted to see what he was really like.* | **+ with** *He was obviously besotted with Julia.*

2 to start to love someone

- fall in love
- fall/be head-over-heels (in love)
- fall for
- love at first sight
- sweep sb off their feet

fall in love /ˌfɔːl ɪn ˈlʌv/ [v phrase] to begin to be in love with someone: *I suddenly realized that I'd fallen in love.* | **+ with** *I think I fell in love with Ralph the first time I met him.*

fall/be head-over-heels (in love) /fɔːl, biː ˌhed əʊvəʳ ˌhiːlz (ɪn ˈlʌv)/ [v phrase] to suddenly start to love someone a lot: *I met Sam at college, and immediately fell head-over-heels in love with him.* | *I was head-over-heels in love with someone who barely even noticed me.*

fall for /ˈfɔːl fɔːʳ/ [phr v T] informal to start to love someone: *She always seems to fall for the wrong type of man.* | *I fell for Dan almost immediately.*

love at first sight /ˌlʌv ət fɜːʳst ˈsaɪt/ [n phrase] a situation in which you start to love someone the first time you see them: *When I met Tracy it was love at first sight.* | *I don't believe in love at first sight.*

sweep sb off their feet /ˌswiːp (sb) ɒf ðeəʳ ˈfiːt/ [v phrase] if someone sweeps you off your feet, you start to love them very quickly, especially when you do not expect it to happen: *Then Peter came into my life and swept me off my feet.* | *She's just waiting to be swept off her feet by a handsome stranger.*

3 to like someone a lot and care about them

- love
- close
- be fond of
- care
- adore
- worship
- be devoted to
- dote on
- think the world of

love /lʌv/ [v T not in progressive] to **love** someone in your family, so that you care a lot about what happens to them, and you want them to be happy: *I really believed that my parents didn't love me.* | *He loved his stepdaughter as if she were his own child.*

close /kləʊs/ [adj not usually before noun] if people are **close**, they enjoy being together and they know and understand each other's feelings and thoughts: *My sister and I used to argue a lot, but now we're very close.* | *We have always been a close family.* | **+ to** *I'm still very close to my parents.*

be fond of /biː ˈfɒnd ɒv‖-ˈfɑːnd-/ [v phrase] to like someone very much, especially after spending a long time with them and getting to know them: *I'm very fond of my sister's children.* | *All teachers have children that they are particularly fond of.* | *We were all very fond of Mr Edwards.*

care /keəʳ/ [v I not in progressive] to feel love and concern for someone: *She thinks we're interfering but we're only doing it because we care.* | *Buy her some flowers to show her you really care.* | **+ about** *I'm very lucky to have a husband, family and friends who care about me.* | *Of course I care about Kirsty – that's why I want to help her.*

adore /əˈdɔːʳ/ [v T not in progressive] to love someone very much and feel proud of them: *Branwell Bronte adored his sister Anne.* | *She adores her grandchildren and is always buying them presents.*

worship /ˈwɜːʳʃɪp/ [v T not in progressive] to love and admire someone very much: *He worshipped his elder brother.* | **worship the ground sb walks on** (=love someone very much, even if they behave badly) *In Susie's eyes he can do no wrong – she worships the ground he walks on.*

be devoted to /biː dɪˈvəʊtɪ̈d tuː/ [v phrase] to love someone very much and be very loyal to them or spend all your time with them: *He is a good man, devoted to his wife and children.*

dote on /ˈdəʊt ɒn / [phr v T] to love someone, especially someone younger than you, very much and show this by your actions: *He'd do anything for his children – he really dotes on them.* | *She obviously dotes on her grandson.* | *You should visit your aunt more often, you know how she dotes on you all.*

think the world of /ˌθɪŋk ðə ˈwɜːʳld ɒv/ [v T not in progressive] to love and respect someone so much that they are very important in your life: *We all thought the world of Isaac and were devastated when he died.* | *He thinks the world of his uncle.*

4 a feeling of love

- love
- affection
- devotion
- passion
- infatuation

love /lʌv/ [n U] a feeling of **love**, either for someone that you are sexually attracted to, or for a member of your family: *All children need love, attention, and encouragement.* | **+ for** *She was never able to express her love for Henry.* | **unrequited love** (=romantic love that you feel for someone, but that they do not feel for you) *She nourishes a secret, unrequited love for Harry.*

affection /əˈfekʃən/ [n U] a gentle feeling of love for a friend or member of your family, which makes you want to be kind to them and show them that you love them: *She never seemed to show us any affection.* | *children who have been starved of affection* | **+ for** *Alison and I had been at school together, and I felt great affection for her.*

devotion /dɪˈvəʊʃən/ [n U] a strong feeling of loving and being loyal to someone, especially over a long period of time: *She had given her husband years of devotion and support.* | *Mary expected complete devotion from her lovers.*

passion /ˈpæʃən/ [n U] a strong and exciting feeling of love for someone you are extremely sexually attracted to: *All the passion in their marriage has died.* | *He loved her still, with just the same passion as he always had.*

infatuation /ɪnˌfætʃuˈeɪʃən/ [n C/U] unreasonably strong feelings of love that you have for only a short time, especially for someone that you do not know very well: *She hoped that his ridiculous infatuation would soon wear off.* | **+ with/for** *His infatuation with Diane seemed to be growing.*

5 showing that you love someone

- affectionate
- romantic
- loving
- passionate
- tender
- lovesick
- devoted
- doting
- lovey-dovey/gooey

affectionate /əˈfekʃənɪ̈t/ [adj] someone who is **affectionate** shows that they are very fond of another person by the way they behave towards them, for example by holding or kissing them: *She's a very affectionate child.* | *He gave me an affectionate hug and then left.*

romantic /rəʊˈmæntɪk, rə-/ [adj] something that is **romantic** gives you a feeling of love for your boyfriend, girlfriend, husband, wife etc – use this about places, or things people do or say: *We went for a lovely romantic walk by the lake.* | *Paris is such a romantic city.* | *I've always thought it would be so romantic to be serenaded.*

loving /ˈlʌvɪŋ/ [adj] behaving in a way that shows that you love someone, especially a member of your family: *Her husband was loving and supportive throughout her long illness.* | *She was a devoted wife and a very loving mother.*

passionate /ˈpæʃənɪ̈t/ [adj] involving strong feelings of sexual love: *She longed to have a mad, passionate affair with him.* | *As they got to know each other better, their love grew deeper and more passionate.*

tender /ˈtendəʳ/ [adj] loving and gentle, especially because you are concerned about someone: *When she spoke, her voice was full of tender concern.* | *Fleury saw an expression of tender devotion come over his father's face.* | **tender loving care** *I was feeling rather fragile, and in need of tender loving care.* —**tenderness** [n U] *He looked after his wife with infinite care and tenderness.*

lovesick /ˈlʌvˌsɪk/ [adj] spending all your time thinking about someone you love, especially someone who does not love you: *He knew he was behaving like a lovesick teenager.*

devoted /dɪˈvəʊtɪ̈d/ [adj only before noun] very loving and loyal towards someone: *With the support of his devoted wife, he carried on writing until the age of 73.* | *They remained devoted friends for many years.*

doting /ˈdəʊtɪŋ/ [adj only before noun] **doting mother/grandparent/husband etc** a mother, grandparent etc that shows that they love someone, especially someone younger, by paying them a lot of attention: *The doting grandmother smiled and chatted about how well the boy was doing at school.* | *She managed to find a rich and doting husband for herself.*

lovey-dovey/gooey /ˌlʌvi ˈdʌvi◂, ˈguːi/ [adj] informal expressing your love for someone in a way that other people think is silly: *It is possible to love someone without going all gooey over them.* | *We ended up sitting next to a lovey-dovey couple.*

6 someone you love

- sb's loved ones
- the one you love
- the love of your life
- old flame

▸ *see also* **girlfriend/boyfriend**

sb's loved ones / (sb's) ˈlʌvd wʌnz/ [n plural] the people you love, especially the members of your family: *Many prisoners find it difficult being separated from their loved ones.* | *They are fighting to protect their loved ones from oppression and violence.*

the one you love /ðə ˌwʌn juː ˈlʌv/ [n phrase] your boyfriend, girlfriend, husband, or wife – used especially in advertisements or sayings: *Flowers are the perfect gift for the one you love.* | *You know what they say: you always hurt the one you love.*

the love of your life /ðə ˌlʌv əv jɔːʳ ˈlaɪf/ [n phrase] the person who you have loved the most in your life: *Claude has always been the love of her life.* | *He knew as soon as he met her that Sumana would be the love of his life.*

old flame /ˌəʊld ˈfleɪm/ [n C] someone who was your girlfriend or boyfriend in the past, especially someone that you still like: *I met up with an old flame, and we sat and chatted for a while.*

7 stories, films etc about love

- romance/love story
- romantic

romance/love story /rəʊˈmæns, ˈrəʊmæns, ˈlʌv ˌstɔːri/ [n C] a story about two people who are in love with each other: *The book is very exciting, as well as being a wonderful love story.* | *a well-known writer of popular romances*

romantic /rəʊˈmæntɪk, rə-/ [adj] a **romantic** story or film is about people who are in love: *a romantic comedy in which Meg Ryan plays a single mother looking for love*

8 not loved

- unloved

unloved /ˌʌnˈlʌvd◂/ [adj] not loved by someone or anyone: *As a child I felt very unloved.* | *He was the unloved son of an unhappy marriage.*

low

RELATED WORDS

opposite: **high**

▸ low position or rank *see* **position/rank**

▸ *see also* **deep/not deep**

1 not high or not far off the ground

- low
- low-lying
- low-rise

low /ləʊ/ [adj] *The garden was surrounded by a low wall.* | *Some of the lowest branches were touching the ground.* | *In the middle of the room was a low table.* —**low** [adv] in a low position: *The plane flew low over the fields.* | *We had to bend down low to get through the opening.*

low-lying /ˌləʊ ˈlaɪ-ɪŋ◂/ [adj] **low-lying land/region/area etc** not very high above the level of the sea: *Low-lying land in river valleys is often subject to flooding.* | *Experts are predicting that the sea level will rise, flooding many low-lying areas.*

low-rise /ˌləʊ ˈraɪz◂/ [adj usually before noun] **low-rise** buildings are only one or two floors (=levels) high: *There are many advantages to low-rise buildings.* | *traditional, low-rise housing*

2 a low sound/voice etc

- low
- deep
- husky
- bass
- rich

low /ləʊ/ [adj] a **low** voice or musical note is not high on the scale of musical sound: *I can't sing the low notes.* | *He's got quite a low singing voice.*

deep /diːp/ [adj] a **deep** voice is low, strong, and pleasant: *David's familiar deep voice called out to her as she walked past.*

husky /ˈhʌski/ [adj] a **husky** voice is deep, quiet, and rough-sounding, especially in a way that is attractive: *She heard a husky voice call her name.* | *His voice dropped to a husky whisper.*

bass /beɪs/ [adj usually before noun] in the lowest part of the musical scale – used especially in music and singing: *Jim was asked to sing the bass solos.* | *You need to play the bass notes slightly louder.* | *He sang popular songs for us in his deep bass voice.*

rich /rɪtʃ/ [adj] a **rich** voice is low, strong, and pleasant to listen to: *He spoke in a strong, rich voice.* | *She had a wonderful deep, rich singing voice.*

3 a low temperature/level/rate/cost

- low

low /ləʊ/ [adj/adv] smaller than usual in level or number: *the lowest temperature ever recorded* | *Japan has a much lower crime rate than other countries.* | *the recent low level of unemployment*

loyal/not loyal

always giving support or love to someone so that you can be trusted by them

RELATED WORDS

- faithful to someone you have a sexual relationship with *see* **sex (5)**
- not faithful to someone you have a sexual relationship with *see* **sex (4)**
- *see also* **trust/not trust, betray**

1 loyal

- **loyal**
- **faithful**
- **devoted**
- **staunch**
- **stand by/stick by**
- **be true to**

loyal /ˈlɔɪəl/ [adj] someone who is **loyal** can be trusted to always give help or support to their friends, their country, their political party etc: *Many of the party's loyal supporters have begun to question his leadership.* | *She has been a good and loyal friend to me.* | **+ to** *The army remained loyal to the president.*

faithful /ˈfeɪθfəl/ [adj] someone who is **faithful** continues to support or serve someone for a long time: *The band still has a large number of faithful followers.* | *The majority of Mark's supporters remained faithful throughout the crisis.* | *His faithful dog Hachiko waited for him.* | **+ to** *Many older people still remain faithful to the party.*

devoted /dɪˈvəʊtɨd/ [adj] **devoted follower/friend/husband etc** a follower, friend etc who is very loyal to a person because they care deeply about them or because they enjoy or support what they do: *He described Mr Edwards as 'a good man and a devoted husband.'* | *Thousands of devoted fans waited in the rain for the group to arrive.*

staunch /stɔːntʃ‖stɔːntʃ, stɑːntʃ/ [adj usually before noun] **staunch supporter/ally/friend etc** someone who continues to be a strong supporter or a good friend in spite of problems or difficulties: *The US has been a staunch ally of ours for many years now.* | *He has been a staunch supporter of the Liberal Party for over thirty years.*

stand by/stick by /ˈstænd baɪ, ˈstɪk baɪ/ [phr v T] to give support to a friend or country that is in difficulty: *I was lucky that my family all stuck by me when I was in prison.* | *She said she would stand by him whatever happened.* | *They were supposed to be our allies but they didn't stand by us when war broke out.*

be true to /biː ˈtruː tuː/ [v phrase] to be loyal to someone, especially a close friend or someone you love – used especially in stories: *You've been true to me all these years. How can I reward you?* | *They would remain true to their old friend no matter what happened.*

2 loyal behaviour

- **loyalty**
- **devotion**
- **allegiance**
- **solidarity**

loyalty /ˈlɔɪəlti/ [n C/U] loyal behaviour: *I would like to thank you all for your loyalty.* | **+ to** *He acted out of loyalty to his friends.* | **your loyalty lies with sb** (=you should show loyalty to them) *Your loyalty lies first and foremost with your family.* | **unswerving loyalty** (=unchanging loyalty) *Dalton showed unswerving loyalty to his employer throughout the trial.* | **divided loyalties** (=feelings of loyalty to two different groups) *The war has created divided loyalties in many families, setting brother against brother and father against son.*

devotion /dɪˈvəʊʃən/ [n U] loyalty to someone you have strong feelings of admiration, respect etc for **+ to** *Her life was one of hard work and devotion to her family.* | **unfailing/unswerving devotion** (=unchanging devotion) *She cared for her stepmother with unfailing devotion throughout her long illness.*

allegiance /əˈliːdʒəns/ [n U] formal loyalty to a leader, organization, or country, especially when someone says publicly that they will be loyal: *Their allegiance is still to the Queen.* | **proclaim/pledge your allegiance to** *Opposition leaders have proclaimed their allegiance to the new government.*

solidarity /ˌsɒlɨˈdærɨti‖ˌsɑː-/ [n U] loyalty between different social or political groups or between all the people in a group, because they all have a shared purpose and need to work together to succeed **show/express solidarity** *Women all over the world have been demonstrating to show their solidarity.* | **+ among** *Solidarity among black people in South Africa is essential if progress is to be made.* | **+ with** *Other health professionals were quick to express their solidarity with nurses.*

3 not loyal

- **disloyal**
- **treacherous**

disloyal /dɪsˈlɔɪəl/ [adj] not loyal to your friends, your country, or the group you belong to: *Government MPs who voted against the bill were accused of being disloyal.* | *She felt disloyal and ashamed of herself.* | **+ to** *He didn't want to be disloyal to his employer.*

treacherous /ˈtretʃərəs/ [adj] someone who is **treacherous** is extremely disloyal and cannot be trusted because they secretly intend to harm other people in order to get advantages for themselves: *He knew he had been betrayed by a scheming and treacherous woman.*

4 disloyal behaviour

- **disloyalty**

disloyalty /dɪsˈlɔɪəlti/ [n U] when someone behaves in a way that is not loyal to their friends, country, or the group they belong to: *Other party members accused Simpson of disloyalty.* | **+ to** *I knew they all hated me for my disloyalty to the family.*

lucky

RELATED WORDS

opposite: —— **unlucky**

- *see also* **chance, risk, gambling**

1 a lucky person

- lucky
- fortunate
- jammy
- be in luck
- some people have all the luck
- lead a charmed life
- it's all right for some
- be lucky enough to do sth/have the good fortune to do sth
- fall on your feet
- be in the right place at the right time
- luck out

lucky /ˈlʌki/ [adj] if you are **lucky**, good things happen to you and things go well for you, because you have good luck and not because of hard work, careful planning etc: *Isn't she lucky – she can eat what she wants and she never gets fat.* | *There are monkeys and zebra, and if you're lucky you might see a lion.* | **+ to do sth** *I'm lucky to live in a nice house and be married to such a nice man.* | **+ (that)** *Arthur left the front door unlocked – we're lucky that nothing was stolen.* | **+ with** *Apart from the sprained ankle, I've been very lucky with injuries* (=I haven't had many). | **think/count yourself lucky** (=used to say that someone should consider themselves lucky) *He should count himself lucky not to have been blamed for the whole fiasco.*

fortunate /ˈfɔːʳtʃənət/ [adj] lucky, especially when you are luckier than other people. **Fortunate** is more formal than **lucky**: *David managed to escape, but the others were not so fortunate.* | **+ to do sth** *I am fortunate to work in a school where all the children are extremely motivated.*

jammy /ˈdʒæmi/ [adj] British informal use this about someone who is lucky to be able to do something, when you are jealous because you would like to do it: *That jammy devil Steve has got out of the washing up again.*

be in luck /biː ɪn ˈlʌk/ [v phrase] to be lucky, especially because you get the thing that you wanted although you did not really expect to get it: *You're in luck, there are still a few tickets left.* | *If you like Californian wine you could be in luck – we are giving away 100 bottles of Cabernet Sauvignon.*

some people have all the luck /ˌsʌm piːpəl hæv ˈɔːl ðə ˌlʌk/ you say **some people have all the luck** when you are talking about someone who is always very lucky, especially when you are jealous of their good luck: *It costs a fortune to buy a Porsche – some people have all the luck.*

lead a charmed life /liːd ə ˌtʃɑːʳmd ˈlaɪf/ [v phrase] to be lucky all the time, so that although you are often in dangerous situations, it seems that nothing can harm you: *By his own admission he had led a charmed life. He had survived a train crash when he was seventeen.*

it's all right for some /ɪts ˌɔːl raɪt fəʳ ˈsʌm/ British you say **it's all right for some** when you think someone else is lucky because they are enjoying themselves, having an easy life etc and you are jealous of them: *You're going to Hawaii? It's all right for some!* | *It's all right for some. I've got to stay in and work this evening.*

be lucky enough to do sth/have the good fortune to do sth /biː ˌlʌki ɪnʌf tə ˈduː (sth), ˌhæv ðə gʊd ˌfɔːʳtʃən tə ˈduː (sth) / [v phrase not in progressive] to be lucky because you have the chance to do something you wanted to do or something that most other people do not have the chance to do: *I went along to the audition with everyone else, and was lucky enough to get the part.* | *In 1957 I had the good fortune to be invited on a lecture tour of Switzerland.*

fall on your feet /ˌfɔːl ɒn jɔːʳ ˈfiːt/ [v phrase not in progressive] to be successful or get into a good situation as a result of good luck, especially after you have been experiencing difficulty: *Nathan had a series of jobs where he wasn't happy, but this time he's really fallen on his feet.* | *Don't worry about Nina – she always falls on her feet.*

be in the right place at the right time /biː ɪn ðə ˌraɪt ˌpleɪs ət ðə ˌraɪt ˈtaɪm/ [v phrase] to be lucky because you are in a particular place when something good is offered or becomes available: *'You did well to get that contract.' 'Not really, I just happened to be in the right place at the right time.'* | *Being a successful news photographer is all about being in the right place at the right time.*

luck out /ˌlʌk ˈaʊt/ [phr v I] American informal an expression meaning to be very lucky on a particular occasion: *I didn't have any idea what I was doing, but I lucked out and wound up with a good job.*

2 a lucky thing that happens

- lucky
- fortunate
- luckily/fortunately
- it's a good thing
- a stroke of luck
- be your lucky day/night etc
- miraculous
- fluke

lucky /ˈlʌki/ [adj] a **lucky** event happens because of good luck, and not because of hard work, careful planning etc **lucky guess/win/escape etc** *'How did you know he'd be there?' 'It was a lucky guess.'* | *Italy got a lucky goal in the last five minutes of the game.* | **it is lucky (that)** *'It's lucky that you remembered about the passports', said Barry as they drove away.*

fortunate /ˈfɔːʳtʃənət/ [adj] lucky – use this especially about something that happens which saves you from danger or serious trouble. **Fortunate** is more formal than **lucky** **it is fortunate (that)** *It is extremely fortunate that there was no-one in the building when the bomb went off.* | **+ for** *Some plants actually prefer a lot of shade, which is fortunate for gardeners choosing plants for gloomy corners.*

luckily/fortunately /ˈlʌkɪ̈li, ˈfɔːʳtʃənətli/ [adv] because of good luck – use this when something dangerous or unpleasant is avoided as a result of good luck: *I had forgotten my key, but luckily Ahmed was there and let me in.* | *Fortunately, there was no-one in the office when the fire started.* | **+ for** *Luckily for us it didn't rain till the evening.*

it's a good thing ALSO **it's a good job** British /ɪts ə ˌgʊd ˈθɪŋ, ɪts ə ˌgʊd ˈdʒɒb‖-ˈdʒɑːb/ spoken say this when something lucky happens that saves you from experiencing problems or danger **+ (that)** *It's a good thing I brought my camera.* | *It's a good job you didn't scream.*

a stroke of luck /ə ˌstrəʊk əv ˈlʌk/ [n C] something lucky that happens to you very unexpectedly and saves you from a difficult or inconvenient situation: *My car had broken down opposite a garage, which was a real stroke of luck.* | *Here's a letter from my father with a cheque inside – isn't that a stroke of luck!* | **it is a stroke of luck (that)** *It was a stroke of luck that they'd just substituted their usual penalty taker.*

be your lucky day/night etc /biː jɔːʳ ˌlʌki ˈdeɪ/ [v phrase] if it **is your lucky day, night etc**, you are lucky and something good happens then: *I have a feeling today's going to be my lucky day.* | *He kissed her again and then started up the car. Tonight was his lucky night.*

miraculous /mɪ'rækjᵿləs/ [adj] use this when something very dangerous or unpleasant is avoided as a result of good luck, in a way that is almost unbelievable: *A teenager had a miraculous escape last night when the car she was travelling in overturned.* | *The doctor gave her a month to live but she made a miraculous recovery.* | **it is miraculous (that)** *The emergency services said it was miraculous that no-one was seriously injured.* —**miraculously** [adv] *I suppose you thought that everything would miraculously work itself out.*

fluke /flu:k/ [n singular] informal something very surprising that only happens because of luck, not because of your skill or planning: *I'll have to win more than once, otherwise people will think it was a fluke.*

3 the way good things happen by chance

- luck

luck /lʌk/ [n U] the way that good things happen to someone by chance, not because of hard work, careful planning etc: *You'll need plenty of luck if you're hoping to succeed in the music business.* | **have luck (with sth)** *Did you have any luck with the job application?* | *You're not having much luck today, are you?* | **luck is on your side** (=you are lucky) *If luck was on our side, the garage would have delivered our car by now.* | **for (good) luck** (=as a way of bringing good luck) *'Please let it be him,' said Sara, keeping her fingers crossed for luck.* | **with (any) luck** (=if you are lucky) *With any luck we should reach the coast before it gets dark.* | **by luck** (=as a result of luck) *I found the place purely by luck.* | **sb's luck holds** (=they continue to be lucky) *If his luck held, no one would notice he had escaped for at least two hours.* | **sheer luck** (=only luck, and nothing else) *I got the right answer, but it was sheer luck.* | **a run of good luck** (=a period of time when you continually have good luck) *The company knew that their run of good luck would not last forever.*

4 telling someone you hope they will be lucky and successful

- good luck/best of luck
- wish sb luck

good luck/best of luck /ˌgʊd 'lʌk, ˌbest əv 'lʌk/ spoken say this to tell someone that you hope they will be lucky and successful: *Good luck Archie! Enjoy your new job.* | **+ with/in** *Best of luck with your driving test.*

wish sb luck /ˌwɪʃ (sb) 'lʌk/ [v phrase] to tell someone that you hope they will be lucky or successful, when they are about to do something difficult: *Wish me luck – I'll need it for this French exam.* | **+ in/with** *Brian asked me to wish you luck in your interview.*

5 when something brings you good luck

- lucky

lucky /'lʌki/ [adj] something that is **lucky** seems to help you to have good luck or be successful: *My lucky number is seven.* | **lucky charm** (=a small object, piece of jewellery etc that someone carries with them to bring them good luck) *She wears his wedding ring on a chain around her neck, as a lucky charm.*

6 things you say when hoping for good luck

- touch wood
- keep your fingers crossed

touch wood British **/knock on wood** American /ˌtʌtʃ 'wʊd, ˌnɒk ɒn 'wʊd‖ˌnɑ:k-/ [v phrase] spoken say this when you have been lucky up to now and you hope that you will not have any bad luck in the future: *I've never been in trouble with the police, touch wood.* | *We haven't missed a deadline yet, knock on wood.*

keep your fingers crossed /ˌki:p jɔ:ʳ 'fɪŋgəʳz ˌkrɒst‖-ˌkrɔ:st/ [v phrase] spoken say this when you are hoping for good luck for yourself or for other people: *We're hoping Bill will be well enough to play in the next game – we're keeping our fingers crossed, anyway.* | **+ for** *She's having her operation tomorrow, so keep your fingers crossed for her.*

Mm

machine

RELATED WORDS

- *see also* **computers/Internet/email, tool, equipment, repair, working, broken, condition, invent, switch on or off**

1 a machine

- machine
- device
- robot
- appliance
- machinery
- mechanism
- contraption

machine /mə'ʃi:n/ [n C] a piece of equipment that does a particular type of work, either in your home or in a factory, office etc, using power from an engine or from electricity: *a machine that fills beer bottles* | *One cable was damaged, which was causing the machine to shut down frequently.* | **sewing/washing/fax machine** (=a machine for sewing, washing clothes etc) *There is a washing machine in the basement of the building.* | **operate a machine** (=make it work) *It's possible to operate the machines by remote control.* | **by machine** *Ice could be made in huge quantities by machine.*

device /dɪ'vaɪs/ [n C] a piece of equipment that has been cleverly designed to do a particular job, for example one that makes measurements, records sounds or movements, or controls the operation of a machine: *An EEG is a device that records electrical activity in the brain.* | **+ for** *a device for controlling temperature* | *The farmers there still use the 'Archimedes Screw', an ancient device for raising water from a lake or well.* | **listening/measuring device** *They were both aware that there might be listening devices hidden in the room.* | **safety device** *The National Association for Elevator Safety says that most elevators have safety devices that prevent free-falls.*

robot /'rəʊbɒt‖-bɑ:t, -bət/ [n C] a machine that is controlled by a computer and can do some of the complicated jobs that humans do, such as making things in a factory: *With the flick of a switch, the robot picks up the bomb, carries it away from buildings, and blows it up.* | *One astronaut used the space shuttle's robot arm to pick up an 1800-pound satellite from space.*

appliance /ə'plaɪəns/ [n C] formal a piece of electrical equipment used in your home, such as a washing machine: *People are spending more of their income on goods such as cars and appliances.* | **domestic/household/home appliance** *To make it easier to return any unwanted purchases, save the original packaging, especially for electronics and household appliances.*

machinery /mə'ʃiːnəri/ [n U] machines in general, especially the large machines used in factories or on farms **heavy machinery** *The package says you shouldn't drive or operate heavy machinery after taking these pills.* | **industrial/farm machinery** *Industrial machinery and electronic equipment lead the nation's export list.* | *a company that manufactures farm machinery*

mechanism /'mekənɪzəm/ [n C] a piece of equipment that is designed to do a particular job inside a machine or larger piece of equipment: *The mechanism that raises the bridge was not working correctly.* | *Unfortunately, the water had damaged the firing mechanism inside the rocket.* | *The garlic press uses a screw mechanism to squeeze out juice and pulp.*

contraption /kən'træpʃən/ [n C] a machine that seems strange and awkward-looking and has lots of pieces joined together in a strange way: *Early cameras were large and expensive contraptions.* | *By demonstrating his floating contraption – part surfboard, part kayak and part sailboard – Halfon hopes to create a tide of attention.*

2 a thing that produces power for a machine or vehicle

- engine
- motor

engine /'endʒən/ [n C] the part of a car, aircraft etc that produces the power that makes it move: *Every time I try to start the engine, there's a strange knocking sound.* | *She left the car in the drive with the engine still running.* | *The SVT is available only with a six-cylinder engine.* | **automobile/jet etc engine** *Some residents fear the crops would attract birds that might be sucked into jet engines.* | **diesel engine** *For next year, the company will offer three cars with turbocharged diesel engines in the United States.*

motor /'məʊtər/ [n C] the part of a machine that makes it work or move, especially by using electrical power: *Just then, the motor failed and the boat began drifting out of control.* | **electric motor** *The ceiling fan is powered by an electric motor.*

3 relating to or done by machines

- mechanical
- automatic

mechanical /mɪ'kænɪkəl/ [adj] using machines, or getting power from an engine: *In a bakery, the bread is rarely kneaded by hand but by large mechanical mixers.* | **mechanical problem/fault/failure** (=when a machine is not working properly) *A mechanical problem may be to blame for the crash.* | **mechanical device** *Flemma said that a reliable mechanical device was needed for the thousands of patients who die while awaiting human heart transplants.* —**mechanically** [adv] *The bones can be removed mechanically before the birds are packaged for sale.*

automatic /ˌɔːtə'mætɪk◂/ [adj] **automatic** washing machines, weapons etc are designed to operate by themselves, without much human control or attention: *Automatic lights had come on in various parts of the house.* | *The camera has a 32mm glass lens, and its automatic shutter allows you to take photos in near-darkness without a flash.* | **automatic weapon/rifle** (=one that can fire many bullets quickly) *The soldiers lay on the highway with their automatic rifles beside them.* —**automatically** [adv] *The doors open automatically when you go near them.*

magic

RELATED WORDS

▸ *see also* **strange, mysterious, ghost**

1 magic

- magic
- witchcraft
- black magic
- spell
- the occult
- voodoo

magic /'mædʒɪk/ [n U] a secret power to make things happen or to do things that are normally impossible, by saying special words or doing special actions: *Do you believe in magic?* | *We only have limited knowledge about the practice of magic in the Middle Ages.* | **by magic** *Angela clapped her hands and the cats disappeared as if by magic.* —**magic** [adj only before noun] **magic words/number/powers** *Medea said the magic words that would bring her lover back to her.* | *The branch grew into a tree that had magic powers.*

witchcraft /'wɪtʃkrɑːft‖-kræft/ [n U] the use of magic to harm people and make bad things happen: *At that time, hundreds of women were burned at the stake for witchcraft.* | *People who were accused of practicing witchcraft were thrown into the lake.*

black magic /ˌblæk 'mædʒɪk/ [n U] the use of magic to make bad and evil things happen, often by groups of people who believe in it as a religion: *The papers were full of sensational reports on black magic, child killings, and drug raids by police.* | *Members of the group say they are not involved in devil worship or black magic.*

spell /spel/ [n C] words or actions that are used to make something magic happen **cast a spell** (=to say words that will make something magic happen) *The Lilac Fairy cast a spell that sent Aurora to sleep.* | **put a spell on sb** *When the old man was angry, he threatened to put a spell on the whole tribe.* | **under a spell** (=affected by a spell) *Carmelina knew that the bird was really the handsome prince under a spell from the wicked witch.*

the occult /ðə 'ɒkʌlt, ə'kʌlt‖-ə'kʌlt, 'ɑːkʌlt/ [n singular] spirits and magic, especially magic that involves communicating with evil spirits: *Throughout his life he maintained an interest in the occult.* | *By the late 1880s, the spreading fascination with the occult sparked a new direction among several young artists.*

voodoo /'vuːduː/ [n U] magical beliefs and practices that are used as a form of religion, especially in the Caribbean: *Jonnie said he was going to a voodoo ceremony that night.* | *a voodoo priest*

2 someone with magic powers

- witch
- fairy
- magician/wizard
- magician

witch /wɪtʃ/ [n C] a woman who is believed to have magic power, which she uses especially to harm people or make bad things happen; in stories, witches are usually shown dressed in black with a tall, pointed hat: *The old woman had only pretended to be so kind; she was in reality a wicked witch.*

fairy /'feəri/ [n C] an imaginary creature like a small person with wings, who has magic powers: *A beautiful fairy danced near him, and he reached out to catch her, but caught only her handkerchief.*

magician/wizard /mə'dʒɪʃən, 'wɪzəʳd/ [n C] a man who is believed to have magic power; in stories, magicians and wizards are usually shown as having a long beard and a pointed hat with stars and moons on it: *The wizard's ring had the power to make him invisible.* | *The magician knew that behind the door lay an enchanted garden.*

magician ALSO **conjuror** especially British /mə'dʒɪʃən, 'kʌndʒərəʳ‖'kɑːn-, 'kʌn-/ [n C] someone who does magic tricks in order to entertain people: *We watched in amazement as the magician made all the rings disappear.* | *The conjuror's tricks delighted the children.*

3 magic done as entertainment

- magic
- trick

magic /'mædʒɪk/ [n U] the skill of doing tricks that seem like **magic**, as a way of entertaining people: *The club features juggling and magic acts in addition to stand-up comedy.* | *an evening of magic and comedy*

trick /trɪk/ [n C] a skilful action that makes something happen which seems impossible, performed as entertainment **do/perform a trick** *It's hard to do a trick like this in front of so many people.* | **magic trick** ALSO **conjuring trick** British *Helen sat on the bed, clapping while her brother did magic tricks.* | **card trick** (=a trick done with playing cards) *John would sometimes perform card tricks for his buddies.*

main

RELATED WORDS

- see also **basic, important, in general**

1 more important than anything else

- main
- chief/principal
- major
- key
- primary
- prime
- predominant
- core

main /meɪn/ [adj only before noun] more important than anything else: *Ben's main problem was lack of money.* | *You should clearly state your main idea at the beginning of the essay.* | *We walked up the stairs to the main entrance of the building.* | *The main reason kids don't get vaccinated is that parents don't realize how important it is.*

chief/principal /tʃiːf, 'prɪnsɪpəl/ [adj only before noun] more important than anything else. **Chief** and **principal** mean the same as **main**, but they are used especially in written or formal English: *Coffee is the country's principal export.* | *Kendall's chief complaint about the opera is that the characters are not historically accurate.* | *The chief purpose of the march was to draw attention to the poor condition of schools.*

major /'meɪdʒəʳ/ [adj only before noun] one of the most important or serious things – use this especially when there is a small number of really important things, but a larger number of less important things: *Smoking is a major cause of heart disease.* | *I thought we agreed to talk to each other before making any major decisions.* | **major city** (=large and important city) *Gang activity that was limited to major cities has now spilled over to towns and rural areas.*

key /kiː/ [adj usually before noun] a **key** person or thing is one that is the most important because everything depends on them: *We don't have much time, so let's concentrate on the key issues.* | *Transport and communications are key areas of the economy.* | **be key to (doing) sth** *Laws are key to maintaining an orderly society.*

primary /'praɪməri‖-meri/ [adj only before noun] **primary concern/responsibility/reason/role etc** the most important one: *As always, security is our primary concern.* | *Financial reward is the primary reason most people work.*

prime /praɪm/ [adj only before noun] **prime suspect/target/candidate** the one most likely to be chosen: *Tourists are prime targets for theft and robbery.* | *The FBI regarded him as its prime suspect in the case.* | *Cheryl is a prime candidate for the new managerial position.*

predominant /prɪ'dɒmɪnənt‖-'dɑː-/ [adj] more noticeable, more powerful, or more common than others: *Yellow is the predominant color in most of his paintings.* | *When we visited the country, our predominant impression was one of poverty and hardship.*

core /kɔːʳ/ [adj usually before noun] use this about the main and most important parts of a subject, activity, plan etc: *We concentrate most on teaching the core skills of reading, writing, and mathematics.* | *The government will discuss what they say are the core issues of education and health care.*

2 the main part of a problem, idea, or belief

- crux
- essence
- heart
- core
- the bottom line

crux /krʌks/ [n singular] the most important part of a difficult problem, a question, or an argument etc that must be dealt with or understood before any further progress can be made: *Whether we can get funding or not is the crux.* | **the crux of the matter/problem/question etc** *Finding a cheap source of energy is really the crux of the matter.* | *The crux of the court case is whether consumers deserve a refund.*

essence /'esəns/ [n singular] the main feature or quality that gives something its own special character **the essence of sth** *Equality is the essence of democracy.* | *The essence of his teachings can be summed up in the phrase 'Know yourself.'*

heart /hɑːʳt/ [n singular] the most important part of a problem, consideration, question etc **the heart of the matter/problem/question etc** *Let's stop talking about irrelevant issues, and get to the heart of the matter.* | **lie at the heart of sth** *Money always lies at the heart of our fights.* | **go/get to the heart of sth** *This new book gets to the heart of the controversy over nuclear power.*

core /kɔːʳ/ [n singular] the main part of an idea, belief, way of thinking etc, that everything else depends on **the core of sth** *The core of the play's appeal is that the good guys win in the end.* | **to the core of sth** *She had the ability to cut through to the core of a problem.* | **at the core of sth** *The profit motive is at the core of the capitalist system.*

the bottom line /ðə ˌbɒtəm ˈlaɪn‖-ˌbɑː-/ [n phrase] the main fact about a situation, that must be accepted and cannot be changed or avoided: *Most people want to work in a place where they feel valued. That's the bottom line.* | **the bottom line is** *The bottom line is, he's gone and he's not coming back.*

3 the main ideas in a speech, piece of writing etc

- the main/key points
- the gist
- the thrust of sth
- essentials

the main/key points /ðə ˌmeɪn, ˌkiː ˈpɔɪnts/ [n phrase] the main ideas or the basic meaning of a speech, piece of writing etc: *I made a few notes of the main points I wanted to cover in the speech.* | *The following article explains four key points that all new investors should understand.*

the gist /ðə ˈdʒɪst/ [n singular] the general meaning of a speech, argument, piece of writing etc, without all the details **+ of** *The gist of the article is that children should have more rights in deciding their own futures.* | **get the gist** (=understand the general meaning) *I couldn't hear everything they said but I got the gist.*

the thrust of sth /ðə ˈθrʌst əv (sth)/ [n phrase] the main aim or purpose of an argument, speech, or political action: *The whole thrust of the US policy was to isolate Cuba.* | *The thrust of the case is whether the federal law overrides the state ban.*

essentials /ɪˈsenʃəlz/ [n plural] the most important facts or ideas in a statement, for example in a description of events or a set of arguments or opinions: *When reduced to their essentials, most religions are not so different.* | **+ of** *She was always very quick to grasp the essentials of an opponent's argument.*

4 ways of stating the main reason for something or the main part of something

- mainly
- largely/chiefly
- primarily/principally
- above all
- first and foremost

mainly /ˈmeɪnli/ [adv] use this to say what the main reason for something or the main part of something is: *I was asked to lead the meeting mainly because Kristin is out of town.* | *My new job's fairly boring – it's mainly typing.* | *The company sells its batteries mainly through electronics stores.*

largely/chiefly /ˈlɑːʳdʒli, ˈtʃiːfli/ [adv] **largely** and **chiefly** mean the same as **mainly**, but they are used especially in written or formal English: *The bird lives chiefly on mice and other small animals.* | *The report says that drug use is largely responsible for the 40% rise in the city's homicide rate.* | *Money raised by the new tax is to be used chiefly for road construction.*

primarily/principally /ˈpraɪmərəli‖praɪˈmerəli, ˈprɪnsəpli/ [adv] firstly and most importantly: *Foreign aid is intended principally for the south of the region.* | *The agency is primarily concerned with making sure the nation's food supplies are safe.* | *She has a degree in anthropology, but she's primarily a writer.*

above all /əˌbʌv ˈɔːl/ [adv] most importantly compared to other things, especially ones you have just mentioned: *Above all, she will be remembered for all the work she did in the community.* | *Teaching history means above all knowing how to tell a story.*

first and foremost /ˌfɜːʳst ənd ˈfɔːʳməʊst/ [adv] use this to say that something is the most important thing, and needs to be dealt with before anything else and given attention before anything else: *First and foremost, they are looking for ways to save money.* | *What children need first and foremost from their parents is a sense of security.*

make

RELATED WORDS

- to make someone do something *see* **force sb to do sth**
- to make a meal *see* **cook**
- to be made up of something *see* **consist of**
- *see also* **do/not do, invent, design, build/building**

1 to make something

- make
- produce
- manufacture
- mass-produce
- churn out/turn out
- create
- fashion
- build
- construct
- assemble

make /meɪk/ [v T] to produce something which did not exist before: *Diane makes all her own clothes.* | *The furniture was made by a Swedish firm.* | *They've just finished making a movie about life during the Civil War.* | *My camera was made in Taiwan.* | **make sb sth** *I'll make you a coffee, shall I?* | **be made of sth** (=to be made using a particular substance) *a bag made of leather* | **be made from sth** (=to be made by putting together different materials, substances, or parts) *People were living in huts made from mud, stones, and straw.* | **make sth out of/from sth** *You could make some cushion covers out of those curtains.*

produce /prəˈdjuːs‖-ˈduːs/ [v T] to make large quantities of food, equipment, or other goods by means of industrial processes: *The dairy produced over 1500 tonnes of butter per year.* | *They produce cheap goods for export to the United States.* | *a factory that produces high-quality steel*

manufacture /ˌmænjəˈfæktʃəʳ/ [v T] to make machines, equipment, cars etc in factories: *He works for a small company manufacturing aluminium products.* | *The car was designed, developed, and manufactured in collaboration with Honda.*

mass-produce /ˌmæs prəˈdjuːs‖-ˈduːs/ [v T] to make goods in very large quantities using special industrial processes: *Henry Ford made his fortune mass-producing the Model T.* | *The bike is the first mass-produced bicycle to have full front and rear suspension.*

churn out/turn out /ˌtʃɜːʳn ˈaʊt, ˌtɜːʳn ˈaʊt/ [phr v T] to make large quantities of things, especially without caring about quality **churn/turn out sth** *They turn out cheap souvenirs for tourists.* | *Churn-*

ing out pamphlets and booklets is ineffective if consumers cannot understand the messages. | **churn/turn sth out** *As long as people keep buying these products, the company will keep turning them out.*

create /kri'eɪt/ [v T] to invent something new and original in art, music, fashion etc: *Picasso created a completely new style of painting.* | *She wanted to create a garden to complement her beautiful home.* | *This dish was created by master chef Marco Pierre White.*

fashion /'fæʃən/ [v T] formal to make something using your hands or simple tools: *Two million years ago our ancestors began to fashion stone tools.* | **fashion sth from sth** *The man had fashioned a turban from a strip of torn cloth.*

build /bɪld/ [v T] to make something complicated, especially a building, machine, or vehicle, by putting parts together: *One of Jim's hobbies is building model airplanes.* | *John and his father built the cabin themselves.* | **build sth by hand** (=build something without using machines) *Every single car is built by hand at the company's headquarters near Turin.*

construct /kən'strʌkt/ [v T] to make something, especially something large, solid, and strong, by putting parts together: *It is easy to construct a wooden framework for plants to grow against.* | *Developers want to construct a replica of the 19th century steam yacht.* | **construct sth from sth** *The roof frames were constructed from thick, heavy timbers.*

assemble /ə'sembəl/ [v T] to make something such as a machine or a piece of furniture by putting together parts that have been made somewhere else: *It's one of those beds that you have to assemble yourself.* | *Our kits are very easy to assemble.* | *The apprentices worked in the shed where the new locomotives were assembled and the old ones repaired.* —**assembly** [n U] *Production had shifted completely to the assembly of wheelbarrows and other gardening equipment.*

2 to make something quickly using whatever materials you have

- knock off/knock up
- throw together
- rig up
- cobble together
- run up
- improvise
- makeshift

knock off/knock up informal /ˌnɒk 'ɒf, ˌnɒk 'ʌp‖ˌnɑːk-/ [phr v T] to make something quickly and without using much effort **knock off/up sth** *She was always good on the sewing machine. She could knock off an outfit in two hours.* | **knock sb up sth** British *I could knock you up a couple of poached eggs.*

throw together /'θrəʊ təˌgeðəʳ/ [phr v T] to make something quickly and not very carefully, especially because you are in a hurry **throw together sth** *Sheryl had thrown together his costume somewhat haphazardly.* | **throw sth together** *We had 15 minutes to throw lunch together, eat, and get changed.*

rig up /ˌrɪg 'ʌp/ [phr v T] to quickly make something such as a piece of equipment that you only need for a short time, using various materials that you have available **rig up sth** *You don't have blinds or curtains so you'll need to rig up something to shut out the sunlight.* | **rig sth up** *Can you rig a gate up to stop the dog getting into my room?* | *There's a shower rigged up at the back of the cabin.*

cobble together /ˌkɒbəl tə'geðəʳ‖ˌkɑː-/ [phr v T] to quickly and roughly make something by hand, using a few simple materials **cobble together sth** *She cobbled together a tent from a few pieces of string and a sheet.* | **cobble sth together into sth** *We were always searching for bits of junk we could cobble together into something artistic.*

run up /ˌrʌn 'ʌp/ [phr v T] British to quickly make a piece of clothing or some curtains, especially using a sewing machine: *There's a woman at the end of our street who will run up some curtains for me.* | *'I like your dress.' 'Oh, thank you. It's just something I ran up last night.'*

improvise /'ɪmprəvaɪz/ [v T] to make something using whatever you have available, when you do not have the correct materials: *They had improvised an alarm, using string and empty cans.* | **improvise sth out of sth** *I improvised a sling for his arm out of a strip of cloth.* —**improvised** [adj only before noun] *He was standing on an improvised stage.* | *an improvised shelter*

makeshift /'meɪkʃɪft/ [adj usually before noun] made using any materials or objects that are available at the time in order to be used only for a short time: *Using an old tree-trunk as a makeshift table, we ate our picnic.* | *When we reached the river we found that the makeshift bridge had been swept away.* | *They rigged up the canvas boat-cover as a makeshift sail.*

3 when a natural process makes something

- form
- produce
- create
- generate

form /fɔːʳm/ [v T] if a natural process or chemical reaction **forms** something, it makes it, especially over a period of time: *Hydrogen and oxygen combine to form water.* | *Coal is formed naturally from decomposed organic matter.*

produce /prə'djuːs‖-'duːs/ [v T] if a natural process or part of your body **produces** a substance, it makes it, usually for a particular purpose: *The stomach produces acids which help to digest food.* | *Carbon dioxide is produced during respiration.*

create /kri'eɪt/ [v T] if a natural process **creates** something, it makes something that was not there before: *Land movement created the Alps.* | *A bullet exceeding the speed of sound creates two shock waves.* | *We found that this chemical process created hydrogen chloride as a by-product.*

generate /'dʒenəreɪt/ [v T] **generate electricity/heat/power** to produce a lot of electricity, heat etc: *The friction between the satellite and the atmosphere generates great heat.* | *France generates a large part of its electricity from nuclear power.*

4 to make something into a particular shape

- form
- mould
- shape

form /fɔːʳm/ [v T] to make something into a particular shape, especially with your hands: *She cut away the corners to form a circle.* | **form sth into sth** *With a few clever twists, he had formed the balloon into the shape of a dog.*

mould British **/mold** American /məʊld/ [v T] to make clay or some other soft material into a particular shape by pressing it or putting it into a special hollow object: *Her movements were quick and graceful, like those of a potter moulding clay.* | **mould sth into**

sth *Mould the sausage meat into little balls.* —**moulded/molded** [adj] *a tool with a moulded rubber handle*

shape /ʃeɪp/ [v T] to make a soft material into a particular **shape**, especially by using your hands: *Gel is great for holding and shaping shorter hairstyles.* | **shape sth into sth** *She had soaked the leather to bend and shape it into the form of a small shoe.*

5 made by a person, not a machine

- handmade
- homemade

handmade /ˌhænd'meɪd◂/ [adj] use this about furniture, clothes etc that are made by skilled workers, not by machines in a factory: *All our goods are handmade, and we use only natural materials.* | *a beautiful handmade rug*

homemade /ˌhəʊm'meɪd◂/ [adj] use this about food and drinks that are made at home, not in a factory: *Try one of these homemade cookies. They're delicious.* | *a bowl of homemade soup*

6 a person, organization or country that makes something

- maker
- producer
- manufacturer

maker /'meɪkəʳ/ [n C] a company or person whose business is to make things to be sold, either by hand or using machines **+ of** *Makers of cars often think more about speed than about safety.* | **car/film/wine etc maker** *The wine maker has to decide when the crop is ready for picking.* | *Personal computer makers are likely to face continued pressure to keep prices low.*

producer /prə'dju:səʳ‖-'du:-/ [n C] a company or country that makes large quantities of something to be sold: *Many producers are being forced to cut costs and use cheaper materials.* | **+ of** *Japan is the biggest producer of stereo equipment.* | **oil/car/champagne etc producer** *OPEC is an organization of 13 major oil producers.*

manufacturer /ˌmænjᵿ'fæktʃərəʳ/ [n C] a company that makes things in large quantities, especially in a factory: *Complaints should be sent to the manufacturer.* | **+ of** *Alubend is one of the country's biggest manufacturers of aluminium tubes.* | **clothing/bicycle/TV etc manufacturer** *Clothing manufacturers have also felt the effects of the recession, as people spend less on clothes.*

7 when something is made

- production
- output
- manufacturing/manufacturing industry
- manufacture
- the creation of sth
- industry

production /prə'dʌkʃən/ [n U] when something is produced – use this especially about the number of things produced in a factory or in a particular industry: *As demand for the drug has grown, cocaine production has skyrocketed.* | *Bulmers will be making around 40 million gallons of cider this year – half Britain's total production.* | **+ of** *Most caustic soda is used in the production of aluminium.*

output /'aʊtpʊt/ [n C] the number of things made in a particular factory, industry, or country: *Output is up 30% on last year.* | *In manufacturing alone, smaller firms account for one in three jobs and a quarter of the total output.* | **+ of** *There has been a huge increase in the output of children's books.*

manufacturing/manufacturing industry /ˌmænjᵿ'fæktʃərɪŋ, ˌmænjᵿ'fæktʃərɪŋ ˌɪndəstri/ [n U] the part of industry that produces goods in factories: *We now have fewer factories and fewer workers in manufacturing than a decade ago.* | *In recent years, Botswana's manufacturing industry has grown and the country produces soap and dairy produce.*

manufacture /ˌmænjᵿ'fæktʃəʳ/ [n U] when goods are produced in factories: *Systems of this type have been used in car manufacture.* | **the manufacture of sth** *The firm now employs 640 people in the manufacture of frozen foods.*

the creation of sth /ðə kri'eɪʃən əv (sth)/ [n phrase] when something such as a new system, organization, or way of doing something is started: *The report proposed the creation of an independent Scottish parliament.* | *the creation of an information system for senior managers*

industry /'ɪndəstri/ [n C/U] when things are made in factories in order to be sold, or a company that does this: *Government money was poured into the economy in order to encourage industry.* | **manufacturing industry** *Manufacturing industry was virtually wiped out in the UK during the 1980s.* | **the steel/clothing/electronics etc industry** *Wages in the clothing industry were found to be lower than in any other sector.*

8 something that is made

- product

product /'prɒdʌkt‖'prɑ:-/ [n C] something that a company makes in large quantities in order to sell it: *a new range of skin-care products* | *There was a ban on meat pies, gelatine, and other British beef products.* | **product development** (=the work of developing good new products) *We spend a lot of money on product development.*

make fun of

RELATED WORDS

- *see also* **laugh, joke, criticize, unkind, stupid/silly**

1 to make fun of someone or something

- make fun of
- poke fun at
- tease
- pull sb's leg
- taunt
- send up
- sneer
- mock
- take the mickey
- take the piss

make fun of /ˌmeɪk 'fʌn ɒv/ [v phrase] to make someone or something seem stupid by making jokes about them: *They made fun of the girls and their new outfits.* | *You shouldn't make fun of other people's beliefs.* | *Peter didn't seem to realize that they were making fun of him.*

poke fun at /ˌpəʊk 'fʌn æt/ [v phrase] to make fun of someone or something, especially in an unkind way: *The other kids poked fun at him, saying his mother dressed him like a girl.* | *His plays ingeniously poked fun at the way the Communist Party corrupted language.*

tease /tiːz/ [v I/T] to make jokes about someone when you talk to them, either in an unkind way, or in a friendly way that shows you like them: *Sam's sisters used to tease him because he was overweight.* | *Don't get upset, Stuart, she's only teasing.* | **tease sb about sth** *Kevin's always teasing me about my cooking.*

pull sb's leg /ˌpʊl (sb's) ˈleg/ [v phrase] informal to make fun of someone in a friendly way by telling something that is not true: *Did Ronnie really call or are you just pulling my leg?* | **+ about** *Don't worry. I was just pulling your leg about moving – I'm not going anywhere.*

taunt /tɔːnt/ [v T] to repeatedly say unpleasant things to someone that show you do not respect them, in order to make them angry or upset: *She went on taunting him until he lost his temper.* | *When I didn't want to fight he would taunt me repeatedly. 'Coward,' he would say, 'coward, coward, coward ....'* | **taunt sb about sth** *He couldn't forget how they had taunted him about his appearance.* —**taunt** [n C] *Black players have to endure endless taunts.*

send up /ˌsend ˈʌp/ [phr v T] a book, film, or performance that **sends up** a group or person makes fun of them by copying them in a very funny way **send up sb** *Gibson's new play brilliantly sends up the upper classes and their attitudes.* | **send sb up** *Half the time, he uses his act to send himself up.*

sneer /snɪəʳ/ [v I] to show by your unpleasant attitude or remarks that you do not have a high opinion of someone or what they do: *Instead of helping, they just sat and sneered.* | **+ at** *He wanted to prove something to the critics who had sneered at his paintings.* —**sneer** [n C] *'And who might you be?' he said with a sneer.*

mock /mɒk‖mɑːk/ [v I/T] to make fun of a person, institution, belief etc, and show that you do not have a high opinion of them, sometimes in a friendly way: *Liz mocked him, saying that he was a coward.* | *The press mocked his attempts to appeal to young voters.* | *'Ooh, aren't you clever!' she mocked.* | *You mustn't mock – it's not their fault they don't know much about art.* —**mocking** /ˈmɒkɪŋ‖ˈmɑː-/ [adj usually before noun] *Their mocking laughter followed me out of the room, and echoed down the hall.* | *'He won't do it – he hasn't got the guts!' said a mocking voice from behind.*

take the mickey /ˌteɪk ðə ˈmɪki/ [v phrase] British informal to make someone look stupid, in either a friendly or unfriendly way, for example by saying something you do not mean or by copying their behaviour: *Just ignore him – he's just taking the mickey.* | *'You're a genius – you should go on one of those quiz shows!' 'Are you taking the mickey?'* | **+ out of** *They're always taking the mickey out of each other, but they're good friends really.*

take the piss /ˌteɪk ðə ˈpɪs/ [v phrase] informal to make fun of someone – some people consider this expression to be rude: *I didn't mean it – I was only taking the piss.* | **+ out of** *The show takes the piss out of virtually everyone, from politicians to eco-warriors.*

2 to make fun of someone by saying the opposite of what you mean

- sarcastic
- sarcasm

sarcastic /sɑːʳˈkæstɪk/ [adj] a **sarcastic** remark is one that makes fun of someone or something, because you say the opposite of what you really mean: *The children kept coming out with sarcastic remarks like 'Delicious!' and 'This is the best meal we've had in ages!'* | *The funny thing was, she had no idea that I was being sarcastic.* | **sarcastic voice/tone** *'Oh yes, that would be really easy,' she said in a sarcastic voice.* —**sarcastically** [adv] *'Don't work too hard, will you,' said Kris sarcastically.*

sarcasm /ˈsɑːʳkæzəm/ [n U] remarks that make fun of someone, because you say the opposite of what you really mean: *Susie found his sarcasm very hurtful, but she didn't reply.* | *'Oh, please don't apologize,' said Molly, her voice dripping with sarcasm* (=in a very sarcastic voice). | **heavy sarcasm** *'How generous of you,' he drawled with heavy sarcasm.* | **a note of sarcasm** *Do I detect a note of sarcasm in your voice?*

3 something that makes fun of someone or something

- spoof
- send-up
- parody
- satire

spoof /spuːf/ [n C] a film, book etc that makes fun of a serious type of film, book etc by copying it in a funny way **+ on/of** *'A Five Minute Hamlet' is a very funny spoof of Shakespeare's most famous play.* | *The film was a spoof on Hollywood cop movies.* —**spoof** [adj only before noun] *a mildly amusing spoof Western*

send-up /ˈsend ʌp/ [n C] a performance, film, article etc that makes fun of a situation or the behaviour of a group of people by copying it in a funny way **+ of** *His most famous movie is a hilarious send-up of life in ancient Rome.*

parody /ˈpærədi/ [n C] a piece of writing or music that is amusing because it makes fun of a famous piece of writing or music by clearly copying its style: *She writes enjoyable parodies in the style of 19th century romantic novels.* | **+ of** *Tallis has written a cruel parody of Hartman's prose.*

satire /ˈsætaɪəʳ/ [n C] a book, film, or play that criticizes something such as the government or people's behaviour by making fun of it in a clever way: *This is her first serious novel; up till now she has only written political satires.* | **+ on** *The film is a stinging satire on American politics.* —**satirical** /səˈtɪrɪkəl/ [adj] *Jonathan Swift's famous satirical novel, 'Gulliver's Travels'*

4 someone that people make fun of

- the butt of sth/sb
- laughing stock

the butt of sth/sb /ðə ˈbʌt əv (sth/sb)/ [n phrase] the person that someone often makes fun of or makes jokes about: *New Jersey used to be the butt of TV comics.* | **the butt of jokes/humour** *His name has already made him the butt of many jokes.*

laughing stock /ˈlɑːfɪŋ ˌstɒk‖ˈlæfɪŋ ˌstɑːk/ [n singular] if you are a **laughing stock**, a lot of people laugh at you because you have done something stupid or are very bad at something: *We can't do that – we'd be a laughing stock!* | **+ of** *When they crashed to defeat, they were the laughing stock of the tennis world.*

man

RELATED WORDS

- a young man *see* **young (4)**
- men and women in general *see* **person/people**
- father, girlfriend/boyfriend, woman, adult, child, sex, character

1 a man

- man
- guy
- gentleman
- the boys
- male
- male
- new man

man /mæn/ [n C] an adult male person: *There were two men and a woman in the car. | He had a very successful business and died a rich man. | You wouldn't understand how she feels – you're a man!*

guy informal ALSO **bloke** British informal /gaɪ, bləʊk/ [n C] a man: *Dave's a really nice guy. | Is he the guy who used to live next door to you? | That Simon seems like a decent bloke. | He bought the car from a bloke at his office.*

gentleman /ˈdʒentlmən/ [n C] a man – use this as a polite way of talking about a man: *Can you serve this gentleman please, Sarah? | Mr Marks, an elderly gentleman, was travelling with his daughter.* | **ladies and gentlemen** (=used in speeches) *Ladies and gentlemen, may I present Dr Nelson Mandela.*

the boys informal ALSO **the lads** British informal /ðə ˈbɔɪz, ðə ˈlædz/ [n plural] a group of men who are very friendly with each other or who work together or play in a team together: *I won't be home until late – I'm going out for a drink with the boys. | The lads played really well – we were unlucky not to win the game.*

male /meɪl/ [n C] a man – use this especially when talking about characteristics that are typical of men and not of women: *The film is a brilliant analysis of the typical American male. | Haemophilia is a condition found only in males.*

male /meɪl/ [adj] a **male** person is a man or a boy – use this especially when talking about jobs and work: *Most of the science teachers are male. | Salaries have increased for both male and female graduates. | The Health Service needs more male nurses.*

new man /ˌnjuː ˈmæn‖ˌnuː-/ [n C] a man who does not behave in a traditional male way or have traditionally male attitudes towards women, for example one who stays at home to look after the children or is happy to show his feelings: *I wouldn't say Tom was exactly a new man – he just enjoys looking after kids more than I do. | He considered himself to be a New Man, sensitive about things such as PMS and bad hair days.*

2 for men

- man's
- male

man's /mænz/ designed for men **a man's watch/suit/shirt etc** *She was barefoot and wearing a man's shirt over her jeans.* | **men's shoes/clothes/ magazines etc** *a shop selling handmade men's shoes*

male /meɪl/ [adj] for men – use this about jobs or activities that men usually do or places that are for men only: *More women are entering traditionally male jobs like engineering. | male pursuits such as football and golf* | **all-male** *For the first time women are being allowed into this previously all-male school.* | **male-only** *the male-only setting of the St Andrews Sporting Club*

3 typical of men

- masculine
- virile
- manly
- macho
- man
- laddish

masculine /ˈmæskjələn/ [adj] **masculine** behaviour or attitudes are considered to be more typical of a man than of a woman: *He wanted to say he was sorry but his masculine pride wouldn't let him. | Violence is an extreme form of traditionally masculine behaviour.*

virile /ˈvɪraɪl‖ˈvɪrəl/ [adj] looking or behaving in a way that is typical of a man, by being strong, full of energy etc, and therefore sexually attractive: *The girls were all gazing adoringly at his muscular, virile young body. | Craig was a younger and more virile version of his father.* —**virility** /vəˈrɪləti/ [n U] *Reports have shown that the older a man gets, the more obsessed he is with his virility.*

manly /ˈmænli/ [adj] having the qualities that people expect and admire in a man, such as being brave and strong: *In the portrait, the King looked manly and in control. | He was bronzed and athletic, with manly features and a steady gaze.* —**manliness** [n U] *In the past, manliness was equated with silence about personal feelings.*

macho /ˈmætʃəʊ‖ˈmɑː-/ [adj] a man who is **macho** behaves in a way that he thinks a man is expected to behave, for example by being brave, treating women badly, or not showing emotion: *On the outside he may seem to be very macho but inside he's very sensitive. | He's far too macho to drink mineral water.*

man /mæn/ [n C] a **man** who is brave and strong – use this especially when you are criticizing someone for not being like this: *Any other soldier would have told him to pull himself together and be a man.* | **a real man** *A real man wouldn't be scared of commitment.* | **he-man** (=a very brave, strong man) *a he-man like Arnold Schwarzenegger* | **be man enough to do sth** (=be brave and strong enough to do something) *Are you man enough to admit that you've been lying?* —**manhood** /ˈmænhʊd/ [n U] *In an effort to prove his manhood he had taken to stealing cars and drinking alcohol.*

laddish /ˈlædɪʃ/ [adj] relating to young men who behave in a typically male way, for example men who drink a lot of alcohol and spend a lot of time thinking or talking about sex: *The amount of laddish humour on TV these days can get a bit tedious. | He most famously played the part of Gary, the laddish flatmate in 'Men Behaving Badly'.*

4 what you call a man when you speak to him

- sir
- Mr
- mate
- mister

sir /səʳ, (strong) sɜːʳ/ formal used especially in formal letters or when speaking to customers, when you do not know a man's name: *I'm sorry sir, we're not serving chicken tonight. Can I recommend the fish?* | **Dear Sir** *Dear Sir, I am writing to apply for the position of Sales Executive advertised in yesterday's 'Times'.*

Mr British **/Mr.** American /ˈmɪstəʳ/ used before a man's family name when you are speaking or writing to him and want to be polite: *Mr Elstone, please may I borrow your pen? | Dear Mr. Pritchard, I am writing to remind you that your rent is now two months overdue.*

mate British informal **/buddy** American informal /meɪt, ˈbʌdi/ use this to talk to a man in a friendly way. **Mate** and **buddy** are also often used when talking to a man you do not know, when you are annoyed with him: *You look like you need a drink, mate. | 'Can I borrow your car' – 'No chance, mate.' | It's* *good to see you, buddy! How've you been?* | *Hey, buddy! That's my parking space you took.*

mister /ˈmɪstəʳ/ American spoken use this when you call out to a man and you do not know his name: *Hey, Mister! Look out!*

manager

RELATED WORDS

▸ *see also* **in charge of, position/rank, work, job, work for sb, tell (17-24)**

1 a manager

- ▸ **manager**
- ▸ **boss**
- ▸ **executive**
- ▸ **foreman**
- ▸ **supervisor**
- ▸ **line manager**
- ▸ **report to**

manager /ˈmænɪdʒəʳ/ [n C] someone whose job is to be in charge of a group of people, a project, a department, or a bank, shop, hotel etc: *I'd like to speak to the manager.* | **+ of** *the advertising manager of a mail-order company* | **bank/hotel/restaurant etc manager** *All new loans must be approved by the bank manager.* | **marketing/sales/accounts etc manager** *She's one of our regional sales managers.*

boss /bɒs‖bɔːs/ [n C] informal the person who is in charge of you at work: *Does your boss know you're looking for another job?* | *There's a new guy at work who's always trying to impress the boss.* | *The front page of the paper announced 'Company bosses get record pay increases'.*

executive /ɪgˈzekjᵊtɪv/ [n C] a manager, especially an important one: *We were visited by a young, dynamic executive from a small computer company.* | **+ for** *Clifford, a former congressman, is now an executive for a large charity.* | **executive stress** (=an illness suffered by managers who are under a lot of pressure in their jobs) *a psychiatrist who specializes in executive stress*

foreman /ˈfɔːʳmən/ [n C] someone who is in charge of a group of factory workers or builders, whose job is to make sure that the workers do what the manager wants: *Anton hated the foreman, who was never satisfied with anyone's work.* | **+ of** *He spoke as though he were a rich landowner instead of just the foreman of a modest building firm.*

supervisor /ˈsuːpəʳvaɪzəʳ, ˈsjuː-‖ˈsuː-/ [n C] someone who is in charge of a group of workers, such as cleaners or secretaries, in an office, factory, airport etc, whose job is to make sure that the workers do what the manager wants: *We still need to replace the office supervisor.* | **+ of** *She has worked her way up the company and is now supervisor of 50 staff members.*

line manager /ˈlaɪn ˌmænɪdʒəʳ/ [n C] the manager who is directly in charge of you in a company, rather than a more senior manager: *If you want to take a holiday, first ask your line manager.*

report to /rɪˈpɔːʳt tuː/ [phr v T] if you report to someone in a company, they are your line manager: *Jan is based in Birmingham and reports to the Head of Marketing.*

2 a manager in a high position

- ▸ **director**
- ▸ **chief executive**
- ▸ **president**
- ▸ **vice president**
- ▸ **chairman/chairwoman**
- ▸ **managing director**
- ▸ **head**

director /dᵊˈrektəʳ, daɪ-/ [n C] an important manager who is in charge of a company or a department in a company: *The directors are meeting today to discuss the company's future.* | **finance/sales/personnel etc director** *Have you met the new finance director?* | **+ of** *Dr Jane Wilde, director of the Health Promotion Agency*

chief executive ALSO **chief executive officer/CEO** American /ˌtʃiːf ɪgˈzekjᵊtɪv, ˌtʃiːf ɪgˈzekjᵊtɪv ˌɒfᵊsəʳ‖-ˌɔːf-, ˌsiː iː ˈəʊ/ [n C] the manager with most authority in the normal, everyday management of a company. This job is often combined with other jobs, such as that of president: *Universal Studios is looking for a new chief executive.* | **+ of** *the CEO of General Motors*

president /ˈprezᵊdənt/ [n C] the person in charge of a large company or organization, especially in the US: *Angry shareholders called for the resignation of the company president.* | **+ of** *the president of CBS news*

vice president /ˌvaɪs ˈprezᵊdənt/ American ABBREVIATION **VP** [n C] the person in a company or organization who is directly below the president in rank, and who is usually responsible for a particular part of the company: *Meyer hopes to become the company's first female vice president.* | **+ of/for** *the vice president for sales and marketing* | *the VP of corporate affairs*

chairman/chairwoman /ˈtʃeəʳmən, ˈtʃeəʳˌwʊmən/ [n C] the person who is in charge of a large company or organization, especially the most powerful member of its board: *Doreen's leaving party looked more like a board meeting, with the chairman and directors there to say goodbye.* | **+ of** *Manley gradually worked her way up, and within ten years became chairwoman of the board.* | *The Chairman of British Airways visited Downing Street last week.*

managing director /ˌmænɪdʒɪŋ dᵊˈrektəʳ/ [n C] British the person in charge of the daily management of a company or organization. This job is often combined with that of chairman **+ of** *Silva has been appointed managing director of the sales division.* | *He's the managing director of a small printing firm.*

head /hed/ [n C] the person in charge of an organization or department **+ of** *the former head of MI5, the British Intelligence Service* | *She's the head of research and development.*

3 a manager who is in a lower position

- ▸ **deputy**
- ▸ **second-in-command**

deputy /ˈdepjᵊti/ [n C] someone who is immediately below the rank of another manager, and who is officially in charge when that other person is away or ill **deputy director/manager/principal etc** *The deputy director is authorized to act in the director's absence.* | *He became the deputy head of the FBI at the age of only 36.*

second-in-command /ˌsekənd ɪn kəˈmɑːnd‖-ˈmænd/ [n C] a manager who is in charge of an organization or department when a more senior manager is not there: *I left the planning to my second-in-command while I was away.* | *She had been second-*

in-command at the nursing home and was now a senior manager in one of the big Boston hospitals.

4 a group of managers

- management
- the board/the board of directors
- head office
- the powers that be

management /ˈmænɪdʒmənt/ [n U/singular with singular or plural verb in British English] the people who are in charge of an organization, not the ordinary workers: *Talks between the workers and the management broke down today.* | **senior management** *Senior management seem to be completely out of touch with their staff's needs.*

the board/the board of directors /ðə ˈbɔːʳd, ðə ˌbɔːʳd əv dəˈrektəʳz/ [n singular with singular or plural verb in British English] the group of people who have been chosen to manage a company, and who meet regularly to make important decisions: *There are only two women on the company's board of directors.* | *Last year the board approved use of funds to improve staff training.* | **be appointed to the board (of directors)** *Carmichael was appointed to the board in July.* | **board meeting** *An emergency board meeting was hastily arranged.*

head office British **/the head office** American /(ðə) ˌhed ˈɒfəs‖-ˈɔːf-/ [n singular] the group of top managers of a company who work in it's central office and control the rest of the company's offices from there: *Head office must approve any order for new equipment.* | *In the past, strategy was dictated by the head office.*

the powers that be /ðə ˌpaʊəʳz ðət ˈbiː/ [n phrase] an expression meaning the management of an organization, used especially when the organization is so large that you do not know who the management is: *The powers that be have decided that our lunch breaks should be reduced to 45 minutes.*

5 the job of being a manager

- management
- managerial

management /ˈmænɪdʒmənt/ [n U] the job or skill of being a manager: *Val has finished college and is looking for a job in management.* | *a course aimed at improving management skills* | **good/bad management** *The failure of many small businesses is caused by bad management.*

managerial /ˌmænəˈdʒɪəriəl◂/ [adj only before noun] connected with being a manager – use this about the jobs that managers do or the skills that they need: *This is her first managerial job.* | *This is the biggest crisis of his managerial career.* | *Managerial skills and technical expertise are often in short supply.*

mark

RELATED WORDS

- a mark in a test or exam *see* **grade**
- *see also* **dirty, clean, spoil, wash**

1 a mark on something that spoils its appearance

- mark
- stain
- spot
- patch
- smudge

mark /mɑːʳk/ [n C] a spot or line on clothes, furniture, a wall, or floor etc, for example where it has been damaged, made dirty, or where someone has dropped liquid on it: *There are marks on the door where the cat has scratched it.* | **make a mark** *Hot cups of tea can make marks on polished tables.* | **dirty/greasy/sticky mark** *How did you get that dirty mark on your T-shirt?* | **dirt/grease/pencil mark** *His shoes had left dirt marks across the carpet.*

stain /steɪn/ [n C] a large mark that is difficult to remove, made when a liquid such as coffee or wine falls onto something: *I can't get this stain out of the carpet.* | **grass/coffee/wine/blood stain** *Salt is the best cure for a red wine stain.* —**stained** [adj] with a stain on it: *She pushed the crumpled, stained sheets into the washing-machine.* | **+ with** *His clothes were torn and stained with blood.*

spot /spɒt‖spɑːt/ [n C] a small round area on a surface, which is of a different colour from the rest of the surface and is made especially by drops of liquid **+ of** *Detectives found a few spots of blood on the carpet.* | **ink/paint/oil spots** *The letter was covered in small ink spots, as though his hand had been shaking as he wrote it.*

patch /pætʃ/ [n C] especially British an area where dirt, water, oil etc has made a mark on a floor, wall, or ceiling **greasy/dirty/damp patch** *There's a damp patch under the window.* | **patch of dirt/damp/grease** *Patches of grease covered the kitchen walls.*

smudge /smʌdʒ/ [n C] a dirty mark made when ink or paint is accidentally rubbed on a surface: *You can't hand your homework in with those smudges all over it.* | **+ of** *Ella had a smudge of green paint on her cheek.*

2 to make a mark

- stain
- mark
- leave a mark/leave a stain

stain /steɪn/ [v T] to make a large mark on something, which is difficult to remove: *The blackberry juice had stained their clothes and fingers.* | *She hoped the blood from the cut on her arm would not stain her blouse.*

mark /mɑːʳk/ [v T] to damage the surface of something by making a mark on it: *Put the lid on your pen so it doesn't mark the tablecloth.*

leave a mark/leave a stain /ˌliːv ə ˈmɑːʳk, ˌliːv ə ˈsteɪn/ [v phrase] to make a mark or stain on something, often without realizing you have done this **+ on** *The children walked through the kitchen in their boots, leaving muddy marks on the floor.* | *Builders' sand leaves an orange stain on paths.*

3 a mark on someone's skin

- mark
- pimple
- freckle
- scar
- bruise
- blotch
- blemish
- birthmark

mark /mɑːʳk/ [n C] a small area of skin that is a different colour from the rest of someone's skin: *He had two little marks on his face where his glasses had been.* | *She squeezed me so hard, she left a mark on my arm.*

pimple ALSO **spot** British **/zit** informal /ˈpɪmpəl, spɒt‖spɑːt, zɪt/ [n C] a small raised red mark, especially on someone's face, that appears suddenly and remains for a short time, often on young people: *He had a large red pimple on his nose.* | *When she was younger* *she had lovely skin, except for the occasional spot.* | *I can't go out tonight with this zit on my face!* | **come out in spots** *Call the doctor if you come out in spots or rashes.* —**pimply** American **spotty** British [adj] covered in pimples: *a youth with a pale pimply face* | *She came up in a spotty irritating rash.*

freckle /'frekəl/ [n C] a very small, light-brown mark, usually on the face and arms, which some light-skinned people have from birth or get when they spend time in the sun: *Sarah had freckles and red hair.* —**freckled** [adj] covered in freckles: *The little boys were freckled and fair-haired.* | *Her sleeves were rolled up, showing her strong, freckled arms.*

scar /skɑːʳ/ [n C] a permanent mark left after a cut or wound has become healthy again: *He had a scar across his forehead from hitting his head on the bottom of a swimming pool.* | **leave a scar** *They say the wound's quite deep, and will probably leave a scar.* —**scarred** [adj] skin that is scarred has a scar or scars on it: *He had black hair and a scarred face.* | *He was scarred from a bullet during the war.*

bruise /bruːz/ [n C] a purple or brown mark on your skin that you get because you have fallen, been hit etc: *How did you get that bruise on your shoulder?* | *I banged into the shelf so hard that I got an ugly purple bruise on my hip.* —**bruised** [adj] covered by a bruise: *a bruised wrist*

blotch /blɒtʃ‖blɑːtʃ/ [n C] a large coloured mark caused by illness: *He had no idea what was causing the red blotches on his skin.* | *I first noticed the purple blotches on my neck on Thursday.* —**blotchy** [adj] *Her face was all blotchy and her hair was a mess.*

blemish /'blemɪʃ/ [n C] a small mark that spoils the appearance of someone's skin: *Her skin was perfect – not a blemish on it.*

birthmark /'bɜːʳθmɑːʳk / [n C] a mark, usually red or brown, which is on someone's skin when they are born and remains there all their life: *The police identified the girl from a birthmark on her leg.*

4 a mark made by a particular person, thing, or animal

- mark
- footprint
- paw print
- tracks
- fingerprints/prints

mark /mɑːʳk/ [n C] *There are marks on the tarmac where the car left the road.* | **finger/tyre/claw marks** *I don't think the tractor came this way – there are no tyre marks in the mud.* | *You could see the claw marks on his body where the animal had attacked.*

footprint /'fʊtprɪnt/ [n C usually plural] a mark left on the ground by the foot of a person or animal: *He ran into the hallway, leaving wet footprints behind him.* | *The footprints in the yard were too big to be a dog's.*

paw print /'pɔː prɪnt/ [n C] a mark left by the foot of an animal such as a cat or dog: *The dog had left muddy paw prints all across the kitchen floor.*

tracks /træks/ [n plural] a line of marks left on the ground by a moving animal, person or vehicle: *We followed the wheel tracks across the field.* | *The tracks, which looked like a fox's, led directly into the forest.*

fingerprints/prints /'fɪŋgəʳprɪnts, prɪnts/ [n plural] the marks of a person's fingers, which cannot usually be seen without using a special powder, used by police to catch criminals: *The police were examining the doors and windows, looking for fingerprints.* | *Her prints were identified on one of the glasses.* | **have your fingerprints taken** *I had my fingerprints taken when I applied for a work permit.*

marry

RELATED WORDS

see also **divorce, relationship, love, family, girlfriend/boyfriend, sex**

1 to get married

- get married
- marry
- remarry
- elope
- marry into

get married /get 'mærid/ [v phrase] to officially become husband and wife: *Jenny and Tom were very young when they got married.* | *My daughter's getting married in July.* | **+ to** *Is he getting married to Sophie at last?*

marry /'mæri/ [v I/T] to get married to someone: *Will you marry me?* | *The only reason Carla married Henry was because she was pregnant.* | *Do you think your sister will ever marry?* | **marry young** *I married young – it was a mistake.*

remarry /ˌriː'mæri/ [v I/T] to marry another person after a previous marriage has finished, or to marry the same person again: *It was a pity our father never remarried after our mother's death.* | *Elizabeth Taylor remarried Richard Burton after they had divorced years earlier.*

elope /ɪ'ləʊp/ [v I] to secretly leave your parents' home in order to get married, especially without your parents' approval or permission: *If my father won't agree to the marriage, we'll just have to elope.* | **+ with** *Mary fell in love with Shelley and eloped with him to the Continent in 1814.*

marry into /'mæri ɪntuː/ [phr v T] if you **marry into** a family or a social class, you marry someone who belongs to it, and become part of it yourself: *Stefan would like to marry into a family just like his own.* | *the story of a poor Irish girl who marries into New York society* | **marry into money** (=marry someone who is rich or whose family is rich) *The only way Steven will ever be successful is if he marries into money.*

2 a relationship in which people are married

- marriage
- matrimony
- be married

marriage /'mærɪdʒ/ [n U] the relationship between two people who are married: *She already has two children from a previous marriage.* | *Do you think marriage is still important to young people?* | *Over a third of all marriages now end in divorce.* | *What's the secret of a successful marriage?* | **first/second etc marriage** *After a disastrous first marriage to a young soldier, Kylie didn't feel like rushing into another relationship.*

matrimony /'mætrɪ̈məni‖-məʊni/ [n U] formal the state of being married: *a couple bound in the state of holy matrimony*

be married /biː 'mærid/ [v phrase] to be someone's husband or wife: *My uncle and his wife were married for 65 years.* | *Is she married?*

3 to ask someone to marry you

- ask sb to marry you
- pop the question
- propose

ask sb to marry you /ˌɑːsk (sb) tə ˈmæri juː‖ˌæsk-/ [v phrase] *Don't tell anyone, but Timothy has asked me to marry him.* | *Are you asking me to marry you?*

propose /prəˈpəʊz/ [v I] formal to ask someone to marry you: *Did he get down on one knee to propose?* | **+ to** *I thought he was going to propose to me, but in fact he just wanted to borrow some money.* —**proposal** [n C] *Two days after their first meeting, Tom made Anna an official proposal of marriage.* (=he formally proposed)

pop the question /ˌpɒp ðə ˈkwestʃən‖ˌpɑːp-/ [v phrase] informal to ask someone to marry you: *Jane was delighted when Matt eventually popped the question.*

4 when you agree to get married

- engaged
- set a date
- engagement

engaged /ɪnˈgeɪdʒd/ [adj] if two people are **engaged**, they have agreed to get married to each other at some time in the future: *Todd and Ellen have been engaged for about 3 months now.* | **+ to** *He's engaged to Paul's sister.* | **get engaged** (=become engaged) *We got engaged at Christmas.* | **engaged to be married** *You'll be glad to hear that Ralph and I, with my father's consent, are engaged to be married.*

engagement /ɪnˈgeɪdʒmənt/ [n C usually singular] an agreement by two people to get married at some time in the future **announce your engagement** (=tell everyone that you are going to get married) *Glennis and John announced their engagement yesterday.* | **break off your engagement** (=say that you do not want to be engaged any more) *Anita broke off her engagement when she found out that Paulo had been seeing another woman.* | **engagement ring** *Has he bought you an engagement ring yet?*

set a date ALSO **fix/name the day** /ˌset ə ˈdeɪt, ˌfɪks, ˌneɪm ðə ˈdeɪ/ [v phrase] to decide on the exact day for the official marriage ceremony: *Lizzie and George have finally fixed a day for their marriage.* | *Have the two of you set a date yet?*

5 to find a husband or wife for someone

- marry off
- arranged marriage

marry off /ˌmæri ˈɒf / [phr v T] to find a husband or wife for your child, especially your daughter, because this is convenient for you **marry sb off** *If they couldn't marry Ellen off before her 21st birthday, nobody would marry her.* | **marry off sb** *My uncle married off my cousin when she was 16.* | **marry sb off to sb** *Because of the scandal Roberta was married off to a stranger and sent away from Rome.*

arranged marriage /əˌreɪndʒd ˈmærɪdʒ/ [n C] a marriage in which the parents choose a husband or wife for their child, especially because this is the custom in their society: *Vikram's parents have organized an arranged marriage for him in India but he already has a girlfriend here.* | *In an arranged marriage the husband often insists that the wife brings a dowry.*

6 the person you are going to marry

- fiancé/fiancée
- bride-to-be/husband-to-be

fiancé/fiancée /fiˈɒnseɪ‖ˌfiɑːnˈseɪ/ [n C] the man (**fiancé**) or woman (**fiancée**) that you are going to get married to: *I'd like you to meet Janice, my fiancée.* | *She didn't know Henry was Marie's fiancé.*

bride-to-be/husband-to-be /ˌbraɪd tə ˈbiː, ˌhʌzbənd tə ˈbiː/ [n C] a woman or man who is soon going to be married, used especially when you are talking about the plans for the wedding ceremony: *The magazine is aimed mainly at brides-to-be.* | *It's understandable if the husband-to-be feels nervous before the ceremony.*

7 ceremonies, celebrations etc when people get married

- wedding
- stag night
- marriage
- shower/bridal shower
- reception
- honeymoon
- hen night/hen party

wedding /ˈwedɪŋ/ [n C] an official ceremony at which two people get married, especially a religious ceremony: *Mom always cries at weddings.* | *After the wedding the bride and groom went straight to the airport for their flight to Fiji.* | **white wedding** British (=a marriage ceremony in a church in which the woman wears a white dress) *Are you going to have a traditional white wedding?* | **wedding ring/ceremony/invitation etc** *Have you sent out the wedding invitations yet?*

marriage /ˈmærɪdʒ/ [n C] the ceremony at which two people are legally married, whether it involves religion or not: *City Hall keeps a record of all the births, deaths and marriages in the county.* | *The marriage took place without the bride's parents' consent.* | **marriage certificate/licence** *We had to bring our marriage certificate to prove that we are married.*

reception /rɪˈsepʃən/ [n C] an event that follows a wedding ceremony in which there is a meal, speeches, and sometimes dancing: *We had our wedding reception in a local hotel.* | *I went to the church service, but not to the reception.*

honeymoon /ˈhʌnimuːn/ [n C] a holiday that two people go on when they have just got married: *We're thinking of going to Barbados for our honeymoon.* | **on (your) honeymoon** *We came to Paris on our honeymoon, and fell in love with the place.* | **honeymoon couple** *The Maldives is a popular destination for honeymoon couples.*

stag night British **/bachelor party** ALSO **stag party** American /ˈstæg naɪt, ˈbætʃələʳ ˌpɑːʳti, ˈstæg ˌpɑːʳti/ [n C] a party for a man and his male friends just before he gets married: *It's the best man's job to arrange the groom's stag night.* | *This is the club where John F. Kennedy had his bachelor party.*

shower/bridal shower /ˈʃaʊəʳ, ˈbraɪdl ˌʃaʊəʳ/ [n C] American a party for a woman and her female friends just before she gets married, when her friends give her gifts: *Melissa ended up getting three blenders at her bridal shower.*

hen night/hen party /ˈhen naɪt, ˈhen ˌpɑːʳti/ [n C] British a party for a woman and her female friends just before she gets married: *It's traditional to wear a silly hat on your hen night.*

8 to perform a marriage ceremony

- marry

marry /'mæri/ [v T] *The priest who married us forgot his lines during the ceremony.* | *Mum and Dad fell in love on the cruise and were married by the ship's captain.*

9 the people in a wedding

- bride
- groom/bridegroom
- the happy couple
- bridesmaid
- best man
- matron of honour
- maid of honour
- groomsman

bride /braɪd/ [n C] the woman who is getting married: *Everyone turned around as the bride entered the church.* | *Teenage brides are twice as likely to end up being divorced as women who marry later.* | *He took his young bride to live on the ranch in Wyoming.*

groom/bridegroom /gru:m, 'braɪdgru:m/ [n C] the man who is getting married: *It is traditional for the groom to buy presents for the bridesmaids.* | *Can I take a photograph of the bride and groom?*

the happy couple /ðə ˌhæpi 'kʌpəl/ [n phrase] informal a man and a woman who have just got married: *I'd like to propose a toast to the happy couple.* | *Everyone waved goodbye as the happy couple drove away.*

bridesmaid /'braɪdzmeɪd/ [n C] one of the women who help the bride on her wedding day, and who stand with her during the ceremony: *My three sisters were bridesmaids for me.*

best man /ˌbest 'mæn/ [n singular] the chief man who helps the groom on his wedding day, and who stands with him during the ceremony: *I was honoured that he asked me to be his best man.*

matron of honour British **/matron of honor** American /ˌmeɪtrən əv 'ɒnəʳ‖-'ɑ:n-/ [n C] the chief married woman who helps the bride on the day of her wedding, and who stands with her during the ceremony: *I asked my older sister, Louise, to be my matron of honor.*

maid of honour British **/maid of honor** American /ˌmeɪd əv 'ɒnəʳ‖-'ɑ:n-/ [n C] the chief unmarried woman who helps the bride on the day of her wedding and who stands with her during the ceremony: *Leslie couldn't decide which of her college friends she wanted for her maid of honor.*

groomsman /'gru:mzmən, 'grʊmz-/ [n C] American one of the men who help the groom on his wedding day, and who stand with him during the ceremony: *We need one groomsman for each bridesmaid.*

10 the people who are married

- couple
- newlyweds
- man and wife
- married
- wife
- husband
- spouse
- partner

couple /'kʌpəl/ [n C] two people who are married to each other, or who are having a romantic relationship: *An elderly couple live next door.* | *They're a nice couple, aren't they?* | **married couple** *Shirley and Bob are a young married couple with two small children.*

newlyweds /'nju:liwedz‖'nu:-/ [n plural] a man and woman who have recently married: *Everyone left at about midnight, leaving the newlyweds alone at last.* | *The hotel seemed to be full of newlyweds.*

man and wife /ˌmæn ənd 'waɪf/ [n phrase] formal a married couple **as man and wife** *Terry and Meena aren't married but they live together as man and wife.* | **pronounce sb man and wife** (=say that two people are officially married) *Mom burst into tears as the minister pronounced us man and wife.*

married /'mærid/ [adj] *Are you married or single?* | *We've been married for 25 years.* | **+ to** *Geraldine was married to the richest man in France and still pretended she couldn't afford a new outfit.* | **happily married** *Richard is happily married with two young children.*

wife /waɪf/ [n C] the woman that a man is married to: *My wife's career is very important to her.* | *Have you met the Ambassador's wife?* | **first/second etc wife** *He remarried after his first wife died of cancer.*

husband /'hʌzbənd/ [n C] the man that a woman is married to: *I don't like Francesca's husband very much.* | *How many husbands would stay at home and take care of the children while their wife goes out to work?* | **first/second etc husband** *Gary's her second husband.*

spouse /spaʊs, spaʊz/ [n C] formal the man or woman that someone is married to – use this in legal or official contexts: *You may choose to pay income tax jointly or separately from your spouse.*

partner /'pɑ:ʳtnəʳ/ [n C] the person that someone lives with in a romantic relationship – use this whether they are married or not: *Have you met my partner, Ray?* | *The office party is on Friday, but partners aren't invited.*

11 relating to people who are married

- married
- marital
- matrimonial

married /'mærid/ [adj only before noun] **married name** (=the name a woman uses after she is married, if she has changed her name to her husband's name) *Is Robertson your married name?* | **married life** (=your life as a married person) *After thirty-two years of married life Barbara had no illusions left.*

marital /'mærɪ̇tl/ [adj only before noun] **marital problems/violence/difficulties/breakdown** (=problems etc between people who are married) *The police have the power to stop people holding their marital disputes in public.* | **marital bliss** (=an extremely happy marriage) *It wasn't what you would call marital bliss, but it was a good, solid marriage.* | *Many wives do not report acts of marital violence to the police.* | **marital status** formal (=whether or not someone is married – used on official forms) *Age, sex and marital status all affect earnings and income.*

matrimonial /ˌmætrɪ̇'məʊniəl◂/ [adj usually before noun] formal belonging to or concerning a man and a woman who are married – used in legal or official contexts **the matrimonial home** *In the divorce proceedings, Marianne agreed to give up all rights to the matrimonial home.* | **a matrimonial conflict/dispute** *In any matrimonial conflict, it is always the children who suffer most.*

12 not married

- not married
- single
- unmarried
- bachelor
- spinster
- eligible

not married /nɒt 'mærid/ [adj] *He told her he wasn't married, but he was lying.* | *Jeff and Paula have two children, but they're not actually married.*

single /ˈsɪŋgəl/ [adj] someone who is **single** is not married or is not in a permanent romantic relationship with anyone: *Please fill in the section on the form that asks if you're single, married or divorced.* | *At my age it's difficult to meet single women.* | **single parent** *Many of the children at the school come from single parent families.* | **single mother** *I'm a single mother, so I don't have much money.* —**singles** [n plural] (=people who are single) *They met at a singles' bar.*

unmarried /ˌʌnˈmærid◂/ [adj] an **unmarried** person is someone who has never been married: *Mrs Travis has three unmarried sons.* | **unmarried mother** *Unmarried mothers can usually receive help from the State or Federal governments.*

bachelor /ˈbætʃələʳ/ [n C] a man who has never been married: *Ben was the only bachelor among all the married couples and felt quite out of place.* | **sb's bachelor days** *Now that Derek's bachelor days were over he'd have to start behaving in a more responsible manner.* | **bachelor flat** *His home had the look of a bachelor flat – clean but empty.*

spinster /ˈspɪnstəʳ/ [n C] a word meaning a woman who has never married, especially a woman who is no longer young, which some people now think is offensive: *Both my father's sisters were spinsters.* | **spinster aunt/sister/lady etc** *Sally lives with her mother and her spinster aunt.*

eligible /ˈelɪ̈dʒɪ̈bəl/ [adj] rich, attractive, and not married, and therefore very desirable as a husband or wife: *His father had suggested several eligible middle class girls to him.* | **eligible bachelor** *The world saw Jack as a rich eligible bachelor, but really he was very shy.*

13 not married any more

- divorced
- ex-husband/ex-wife
- be separated
- widow
- widower
- widowed

divorced /dɪ̈ˈvɔːʳst/ [adj] someone who is **divorced** has officially ended their marriage: *He's living with a divorced woman and her two children.* | *Yes, she used to be married, but she's been divorced since last year.* | **get divorced** (=officially end your marriage) *They got divorced only three years after they got married.*

ex-husband/ex-wife /ˌeks ˈhʌzbənd, ˌeks ˈwaɪf/ [n C] the man or woman that you used to be married to before getting divorced: *His ex-wife never lets him see the children.*

be separated /biː ˈsepəreɪtɪ̈d/ [v phrase] if a husband and wife **are separated**, they do not live with each other, because they are not happy together any more, but they are not divorced: *We're not divorced, but we've been separated for six months.*

widow /ˈwɪdəʊ/ [n C] a woman whose husband has died and who has not married again: *Mr Jarvis died yesterday, leaving a widow and four children.* | *Mourners at the funeral included Paul's widow, Sarah Jones.*

widower /ˈwɪdəʊəʳ/ [n C] a man whose wife has died and who has not married again: *Mr Wright, a widower with one son and two grandchildren, made his first parachute jump yesterday.*

widowed /ˈwɪdəʊd/ [adj] if someone is **widowed**, their wife or husband has died and they have not married again: *Joyce had come to Tucson to live with a recently widowed aunt.*

material

RELATED WORDS

▸ *see also* **soft, hard, strong (4-5)**

1 a solid or liquid substance

- substance
- material
- stuff
- matter

substance /ˈsʌbstəns/ [n C] a type of solid or liquid, such as a chemical, a mineral, or something produced by a plant: *Poisonous substances, such as garden chemicals, should be clearly labelled.* | *Resin is a dark, sticky substance.* | *the problem of disposing of radioactive substances* | *The green colour of the leaf is due to a substance called chlorophyll.*

material /məˈtɪəriəl/ [n C/U] any solid substance that can be used for making things: *Steel is a stronger material than iron.* | *The company supplies building materials such as bricks and cement.* | *A layer of insulating material should be placed between the panels and the solid wall.*

stuff /stʌf/ [n U] especially spoken, informal a substance: *What's that sticky stuff on the floor?* | *Do you have any of that clear plastic stuff to cover food with?*

matter /ˈmætəʳ/ [n U] formal any physical substance – used especially in science: *They are investigating an area of space that contains more than the usual amount of matter.* | *the forces exerted between particles of matter* | **vegetable/organic matter** *In order to decompose, all vegetable matter needs supplies of nitrogen.* | **waste matter** *Dietary fibre makes waste matter from the food we eat pass through our bodies quickly.*

2 material for making clothes, curtains etc

- material
- fabric
- cloth
- textiles

▸ *see also* **clothes**

material /məˈtɪəriəl/ [n C/U] a **material** woven from threads, which is used for making clothes or curtains, covering furniture etc: *She was wearing a long black dress made of some silky material.* | *Some materials are easier to dye than others.* | **dress/curtain material** *Could I have six metres of that curtain material?*

fabric /ˈfæbrɪk/ [n C/U] woven material: *I want to buy some fabric to make a skirt.* | *Man-made fabrics such as polyester are easy to wash and iron.* | *Rayon is used extensively to make furnishing fabrics.*

cloth /klɒθ‖klɔːθ/ [n U] woven material, especially made from natural substances such as cotton and wool: *The main trade was the production of woollen cloth.* | *She ran her eye over the rolls of brightly-coloured cloth displayed on the stall.* —**cloth** [adj] *The diamonds were contained in cloth bags* (=bags made of cloth).

textiles /ˈtekstaɪlz/ [n plural] formal woven material – use this especially to talk about the business of producing and selling material: *Textiles are one of Mexico's main exports.* | *Modern textiles can look too bright in an old building.* | **textile industry** *The textile industry is booming, with profits up 15% on last year.*

maybe

when you think something may happen or may be true, but you are not sure

RELATED WORDS

opposite: —————— **certainly/definitely**

▸ *see also* **probably, sure/not sure, possible**

- ▸ **maybe/perhaps**
- ▸ **may/might/could**
- ▸ **it is possible (that)/there's a chance (that)**
- ▸ **possibly**
- ▸ **conceivably**
- ▸ **you never know**
- ▸ **who knows?**

maybe/perhaps /ˈmeɪbi, pəʳˈhæps/ [adv] use this when you think that something may happen or may be true, but you are not sure. **Perhaps** is more formal than **maybe**.: *'Will you be there tomorrow?' 'I don't know, maybe.'* | *I wonder why she's late – maybe she missed the train.* | *The footprints belonged to a large cat, a tiger, perhaps.* | *I'm not sure why I couldn't sleep. Perhaps it was the coffee.* | **maybe not/perhaps not** *'It's not her fault that she can't get a job.' 'Well, maybe not, but she should make a little more effort.'* | *Housing prices will continue to rise, though perhaps not as much as was predicted last year.*

may/might/could /meɪ, maɪt, kʊd/ [modal verb] use this with other verbs, to show that something is possible, or likely, but you are not sure about it. **May** and **might** are more formal than **could**: *Take your umbrella – it might rain.* | *Hundreds of workers may lose their jobs if the strike continues.* | *We could be home before midnight if the traffic isn't too bad.* | **may/might/could have done sth** *'Bruce isn't here yet.' 'He may have decided not to come.'* | *It's a good thing we got her to the hospital right away – the doctor said she could have died if we'd waited.*

it is possible (that)/there's a chance (that) /ɪt ɪz ˈpɒsəbəl (ðət)‖-ˈpɑː-, ðeəʳz ə ˈtʃɑːns (ðət)‖-ˈtʃæns-/ use this when you think that something may happen or may be done, but that it is not very likely: *I might have to work on Saturday, so it's possible I won't be able to come to your party.* | *There's a chance that I'll be in California in October, so I might be able to visit you for a few days.* | **it is just possible (that)/there is just a chance (that)** (=when something is possible, but very unlikely) *Tomorrow should be sunny but there's just a chance of showers in the afternoon.* | *It's just possible we'll finish the job by tonight, but it'll probably be tomorrow.* | **outside chance/possibility** *Martinez will need surgery, but there's an outside chance he'll be playing again before the end of the season.* | **slim chance/possibility** *Sims has some numbness and weakness in her legs, and surgeons say there is a slim possibility of paralysis.*

possibly /ˈpɒsəbli‖ˈpɑː-/ [adv] use this when you think that something may be true, but you do not have enough information to be sure: *'Do you think she was murdered, inspector?' 'Possibly.'* | *He's playing in the US Open Golf Championships – possibly for the last time.* | *Stone is possibly America's finest film director.* | *The cancer was possibly caused by exposure to asbestos.* | *Trade between the two countries began in the 11th century, possibly even earlier.* | *Many analysts believe interest rates will rise, possibly as early as next spring.* | **quite possibly** (=very possibly) *The examination hall was vast, with at least 700 or 800 students and quite possibly as many as 1000.*

conceivably /kənˈsiːvəbli/ [adv] if you think something may **conceivably** happen or be true, it seems unlikely but you can imagine that it is possible: *Reservations are advised but you might conceivably find a hotel the day you arrive.* | *It is still unlikely, but unemployment could conceivably begin to fall by the end of the year.*

you never know /juː ˌnevəʳ ˈnəʊ/ spoken say this when you are not sure whether something will happen, because no one knows what will happen in the future: *I don't think I'll ever get married, but you never know.* | *Why don't you ask for a raise? You never know, they could say yes.*

who knows? /ˌhuː ˈnəʊz/ spoken say this when you have no way of knowing whether something is true or not true: *'Will you still be working here next year?' 'Who knows? Maybe I will, maybe I won't.'* | *Maybe he wasn't telling the truth. Who knows?*

meal

RELATED WORDS

▸ *see also* **cook, food, eat, delicious, horrible, taste, hungry/not hungry, greedy**

1 a meal

- ▸ **meal**
- ▸ **something to eat**
- ▸ **feed**

meal /miːl/ [n C] the food that you eat in the morning, in the middle of the day, or in the evening, either at home or in a restaurant: *The hotel was nice, and the meals were really good.* | *Miriam was silent all through the meal.* | *You shouldn't exercise after a big meal.* | **have a meal** *We had an excellent meal in a Chinese restaurant.* | **cook sb a meal** *Jeff cooked us a delicious meal last night.* | **go out for a meal** (=go to a restaurant) *Would you like to go out for a meal sometime, Emma?* | **take sb out for a meal** (=take someone to a restaurant and pay for their meal) *It was Lisa's birthday so we took her out for a meal.* | **main meal** (=the biggest meal of the day) *We usually have our main meal in the middle of the day.*

something to eat /ˌsʌmθɪŋ tʊ ˈiːt/ [n phrase] a meal, especially a small or quick meal: *Can I get you something to eat?* | **have something to eat** *We'll have something to eat, and then go out.*

feed British **/feeding** American /fiːd, ˈfiːdɪŋ/ [n C] a meal, consisting only of milk, that a baby has: *A young baby needs small feeds at frequent intervals.* | *Lois has gotten tired of the late night feedings.* | **have a feed** British *Her baby has its lunchtime feed, then goes to sleep.*

2 a meal in the morning

- ▸ **breakfast**
- ▸ **brunch**

breakfast /ˈbrekfəst/ [n C/U] the meal you eat when you get up in the morning: *What do you want for breakfast – cereal or toast?* | *After breakfast we went for a walk on the beach.* | **eat/have (your) breakfast** *George was having his breakfast when the phone rang.*

brunch /brʌntʃ/ [n C/U] especially American a meal eaten late in the morning, as a combination of breakfast and lunch: *On the first day of the vacation we all slept late, then had a huge brunch.* | *They served smoked salmon, cream cheese and bagels for brunch.*

3 a meal in the middle of the day

- lunch
- dinner
- midday meal

lunch /lʌntʃ/ [n C/U] the meal you eat in the middle of the day: *At work we are allowed one hour for lunch.* | *See you after lunch.* | **eat/have lunch** *Shall we have lunch before we go out?* | **a late/an early lunch** *We had an early lunch and spent the afternoon shopping.* | **Sunday lunch** British *We always have roast beef for Sunday lunch.*

dinner /ˈdɪnəʳ/ [n C/U] especially British the meal eaten in the middle of the day. This word is also used for large meals eaten in the middle of the day on Sundays or holidays.: *He comes home for his dinner, then goes back to the factory.* | **school dinner** (=a dinner which is provided for children at school) *She used to hate school dinners.* | **Sunday/Christmas/Thanksgiving dinner** *We had some friends round for Sunday dinner.* | *In one of my less lucid moments, I had volunteered to host Thanksgiving dinner.*

midday meal British **/noon meal** American /ˌmɪd-deɪ ˈmiːl, ˌnuːn ˈmiːl/ [n C] the meal eaten in the middle of the day – use this especially when describing what happens in other countries: *In Spain, the midday meal almost always starts with tomato salad.* | *The noon meal was carried out to the fields where the harvesters were working.*

4 a meal in the evening

- dinner
- supper
- tea
- evening meal

dinner /ˈdɪnəʳ/ [n C/U] the meal you eat in the evening: *What shall we have for dinner?* | *Sarah cooked us a really nice dinner.* | *At dinner, he announced that he was leaving home.* | *Shall we discuss this over dinner?* | **go out for dinner** (=go to a restaurant or to someone else's house) *We went out for dinner at the Ritz.* | **eat/have dinner** *Why don't you come and have dinner with us?*

supper /ˈsʌpəʳ/ [n C/U] especially British the meal you eat in the evening: *After supper we watched a video.* | **eat/have (your) supper** *I had my supper and went to bed.*

tea /tiː/ [n C/U] British a meal you eat at home early in the evening: *What's for tea?* | **have (your) tea** *The children came home from school, had tea and did their homework.*

evening meal /ˌiːvnɪŋ ˈmiːl/ [n C] the meal eaten in the evening: *After the evening meal they sat around the cooking-fire and talked.* | *Preparing the evening meal can take up to three hours.*

5 a formal meal

- dinner party
- dinner
- banquet
- luncheon

dinner party /ˈdɪnəʳ ˌpɑːʳti/ [n C] a formal meal in your home when you invite friends or guests: *He is a charming man, the kind of person you would want to sit next to at a dinner party.* | **have a dinner party** *We're having a dinner party on Tuesday. Would you like to come?*

dinner /ˈdɪnəʳ/ [n C] a formal evening meal for a large number of people, especially in a public place such as a hotel: *She had a ticket for a dinner and fashion show at the Castle Hotel.* | *Ann and I attended a dinner at the City Chamber of Commerce.*

banquet /ˈbæŋkwɪ̱t/ [n C] a special formal meal with a lot of very good food and a large number of people, especially important people, which usually takes place on a special public occasion: *A huge banquet was planned to celebrate the city's millennium.* | *a state banquet hosted by the French Prime Minister*

luncheon /ˈlʌntʃən/ [n C] a formal meal in the middle of the day for a large number of people, especially in a public place such as a hotel: *Over 200 attended the Women in Journalism luncheon last Tuesday.*

6 a meal outside

- picnic
- barbecue
- al fresco

picnic /ˈpɪknɪk/ [n C] a cold meal that you take to a park or the countryside to eat outside: *We took a picnic down to the beach.* | **have a picnic** *It was a beautiful day – we had a picnic by the river.* | **go on/for a picnic** *In summer, we sometimes go on picnics together.* | **a picnic area/table/basket** *Some campgrounds provide a picnic table right outside your door.* | **a picnic lunch** *Pack a picnic lunch and head for the country.*

barbecue /ˈbɑːʳbɪkjuː/ [n C] a party when you cook and eat food outside: *I'll get some burgers and ribs for the barbecue.* | **have a barbecue** *If the weather's nice we'll have a barbecue.*

al fresco /æl ˈfreskəʊ/ [adv] if you eat **al fresco**, you have a meal outdoors: *Guests can dine al fresco on a terrace with stunning views of the valley below.* | *I'd enjoy al fresco eating much more if it wasn't for all the wasps!*

7 a meal you buy in a restaurant and eat at home

- takeaway
- to take away

takeaway British [n C] **/takeout** American [n U] /ˈteɪkəweɪ, ˈteɪkaʊt/ a meal that you buy from a restaurant and then eat at home: *Dave just lives on beer and takeaways.* | *I don't feel like cooking tonight – can we get some takeout?* | *a takeout pizza*

to take away British **/to go** American /tə ˌteɪk əˈweɪ, tə ˈgəʊ/ [adv] food or drink **to take away** or **to go** is intended to be taken away from the restaurant where you have bought it so that you can eat it somewhere else: *Joe ordered a slice of pizza and a Coke to go.* | *Do you want that hamburger to eat here or to take away?*

8 a very large meal

- three-course meal
- feast
- heavy
- slap-up meal
- spread

three-course meal /ˌθriː kɔːʳs ˈmiːl/ [n C] a large meal with three separate parts, of the type that is usually served in restaurants: *I can't eat a three-course meal at lunch time – it's just too much.* | *You can get a three-course meal for $25 in the barbecue grill.*

feast /fiːst/ [n C] a very large meal for a large number of people, to celebrate a special occasion: *There were over sixty guests at the wedding feast.* | *The Christmas celebrations in Fiji are rounded off by a huge feast on Christmas Day.*

heavy /ˈhevi/ [adj usually before noun] a **heavy** meal, lunch, dinner etc is one in which you eat a lot of food, and that makes you feel tired and your stomach feel full: *You shouldn't eat a heavy meal before going swimming.* | *After a heavy lunch my father fell asleep almost immediately.*

slap-up meal /ˌslæp ʌp ˈmiːl/ [n C] British informal a large meal with a lot of good food: *If they give me the job I'll take you out for a slap-up meal.*

spread /spred/ [n C] informal a large meal for several people: *They were looking forward to the spread that Judith had prepared.*

9 a meal in which you choose and serve your own food

- buffet

buffet /ˈbʊfeɪ‖bəˈfeɪ/ [n C] a meal in which food is put on a table and you serve yourself from the things that are there: *We're not having a big formal meal at the wedding – just a buffet.* | *Try out all-you-can-eat buffet – only £5 per person* | **buffet lunch** *We'll have a buffet lunch at about one o'clock and a sit-down meal in the evening.*

10 a small meal

- light
- snack
- bite
- refreshments

light /laɪt/ [adj usually before noun] a **light** meal, lunch, etc is one in which you do not eat much food, especially food that contains a lot of fat, so that it does not make your stomach feel too full: *She prepared a light lunch of salad and cheese.* | *You can have a light meal four hours before the game but only have drinks after that.*

snack /snæk/ [n C] something such as an apple, some bread, or a bar of chocolate which you eat between meals: *Just before bedtime he had a snack of bread and cheese.* | *The children have mid-morning snacks at about 11 o'clock – usually fruit and a drink.*

bite /baɪt/ [n singular] informal a very small meal that you eat quickly: *We'll have a bite then go into town.* | **a bite to eat** *There's just time for a quick bite to eat before the film begins.*

refreshments /rɪˈfreʃmənts/ [n plural] small amounts of food and drink that are provided for people at a party, meeting etc: *The children walked around at the party offering refreshments.* | *Meetings are open to the public, and refreshments are provided.* | **light refreshments** *Catering tents provide coffee, snacks, and other light refreshments.*

11 part of a meal

- course
- dish
- starter
- dessert
- for afters

course /kɔːʳs/ [n C] one of the parts of a meal that are served one after the other: *The waiter brought the first course, a simple leek and potato soup.* | *a five-course banquet* | **main course** (=the biggest course in a meal) *For the main course we had roast turkey with vegetables.*

dish /dɪʃ/ [n C] a particular kind of food cooked in a particular way and served at a meal: *My favourite Italian dish is lasagne.* | *In addition to the extensive Tandoori menu, there is a wide selection of vegetarian dishes.*

starter British **/appetizer** American /ˈstɑːʳtəʳ, ˈæpɪ̈taɪzəʳ/ [n C] the first part of a meal in a restaurant: *What would you like for a starter – soup or garlic mushrooms?* | *a delightful appetizer of small clams*

dessert ALSO **pudding** British /dɪˈzɜːʳt, ˈpʊdɪŋ/ [n C/U] the sweet part of a meal that you have at the end: *'Would you like a dessert, Madam?' 'Yes please, I'll have the cheesecake.'* | **have sth for dessert/pudding** *I had fruit salad for dessert.* | *At children's parties, it's traditional to have jelly and ice-cream for pudding.*

for afters /fər ˈɑːftəʳz‖-ˈæf-/ [prep] British spoken if you have something **for afters**, you have it as your dessert: *We're having roast beef, with apple pie for afters.* | *For afters, it's rice pudding.*

meaning

RELATED WORDS

- *see also* **understand, word, phrase, or sentence, language, translate**

1 the meaning of something

- meaning
- sense
- significance
- definition
- connotation
- define

meaning /ˈmiːnɪŋ/ [n C/U] what a word, sign, or statement means: *This word 'spring' has several different meanings.* | *We convey meaning not only by our words but also by our actions.* | **+ of** *There is a chart that explains the meaning of all the symbols on the map.* | **hidden meaning** (=a meaning that is not directly stated) *Was there a hidden meaning behind his words?*

sense /sens/ [n C] one of the meanings of a word that has several meanings **+ of** *In the dictionary the different senses of each word are marked by numbers.* | **in its broadest/fullest sense** (=in the most general meaning of the word) *I'm using the word 'education' in its broadest sense here.*

significance /sɪgˈnɪfɪkəns/ [n U] the important meaning that something has, especially if the meaning is not immediately clear **+ of** *Freud explained the significance of some of the objects and situations in Anna's dream.* | **special significance** *Nothing can be more exciting than the first time you receive red roses. They have special significance.*

definition /ˌdefɪ̈ˈnɪʃən/ [n C] the way that you explain the meaning of a word **+ of** *Could one of the class give me a definition of the word 'equilibrium'?* | **sb's definition of sth** *Obviously your definition of 'rich' is very different from mine.*

connotation /ˌkɒnəˈteɪʃən‖ˌkɑː-/ [n C] a feeling or an idea that a word makes you think of that is not its actual meaning: *'Bermuda' with its connotations of fun and sun* | **positive/negative connotation** *For most people 'motherhood' has a very positive connotation.*

define /dɪˈfaɪn/ [v T] to explain the meaning of a word or phrase: *Each of us might define the concept of freedom in a slightly different way.* | **define sth as sth** *The dictionary defines it as 'a narrow passage'.* | **define sth loosely/broadly** (=define something in a way that is not very exact) *Dietary fibre can be loosely defined as the cell-wall material of plants.*

2 the main meaning of something

- point
- gist
- essence
- drift
- thrust
- substance

point /pɔɪnt/ [n singular] the main idea of an argument, discussion, statement etc that shows its general or most important meaning **the point of sth** *The point of the story did not emerge until the end of the film.* | **sb's point** *What's your point? Do you think I'm not good enough for your daughter?* | **miss the point** (=not understand the main idea) *The talk was about symbolism in art – Len missed the point and thought it was about painting techniques.* | **the point is ... .** (=used for mentioning the most important thing) *The point is, you should have told me where you were going.* | **come/get to the point** (=to reach the most important part of what you want to say) *'I'll come straight to the point,' said the doctor. 'I think you are suffering from depression.'*

gist /dʒɪst/ [n singular] the main idea and meaning of something such as an article or a speech **the gist of sth** *I don't know the whole story but this is the gist of it.* | **get the gist (of sth)** (=understand the gist of something) *Read the article once through to get the gist of it.* | *Students are encouraged to read the text, getting the gist, then go deeper into the meaning.*

essence /'esəns/ [n singular] the most important meaning of something such as an argument or piece of writing **the essence of sth** *The essence of his argument is that human character is formed by society.*

drift /drɪft/ [n singular] the main set of ideas involved in something such as an explanation, argument, or account of something **the drift of sth** *The drift of his letter is that he wants to come back.* | **catch/get/follow sb's drift** (=understand the basic idea of what someone is saying) *It was a complicated argument but I think I caught his drift.* | *I follow your drift, but I just don't believe it.*

thrust /θrʌst/ [n singular] the most important message of an argument, explanation etc, especially when it consists of a set of connected ideas leading to a final answer or idea **the thrust of sth** *It is difficult to argue with the thrust of Davidson's analysis of the situation.* | *The overall thrust of her argument was that women are still oppressed in all areas of life.*

substance /'sʌbstəns/ [n singular] formal the most important ideas contained in an argument or piece of writing **the substance of sth** *The substance of Marx's views is the same in both of these books.*

3 to have a particular meaning

- mean
- stand for
- represent
- symbolize
- denote
- connote

mean /miːn/ [v T not in progressive] to have a particular meaning – use this about words, signs, or statements: *What does 'abandon' mean?* | *'Poultry' means chickens, ducks, turkeys, and geese.* | *It says 'not suitable for children', which means anyone under 16.* | **+ (that)** *The flashing light means we're running out of gas.* | *'Downsizing' simply means that firms are tending to buy smaller computers to do jobs which used to require big ones.* | **what is meant by sth** *What is meant by the term 'random access'?*

stand for /'stænd fɔːʳ/ [phr v T] if a letter or group of letters **stands for** a word, name, or number, it is a short way of saying or writing it: *NATO stands for North Atlantic Treaty Organization.* | *What does the F in John F. Kennedy stand for?*

represent /ˌreprɪ'zent/ [v T not in progressive] if a shape, letter, object etc **represents** something, it is used as a sign for that thing in a map, plan, calculation etc: *The red lines on the map represent railways.* | *Single letters or combinations of letters represent different phonetic sounds.*

symbolize ALSO **symbolise** British /'sɪmbəlaɪz/ [v T not in progressive] if something such as an object or animal **symbolizes** an idea or quality, it is used as a sign to mean that idea or quality, especially in a story, a ceremony, or a particular society: *The lion symbolizes strength, the lamb symbolizes gentleness.* | *In Europe, the colour white symbolizes purity but in Asia it is often the symbol of deep mourning.* | *Cowardice is symbolized in the painting by the white feathers on the soldier's coat.*

denote /dɪ'nəʊt/ [v T not in progressive] if a word or number **denotes** something, it means it in a very exact sense – used especially in technical contexts: *The dotted line on the graph denotes profits.* | *The English word 'family' used to denote all the people in the house, including servants.* | *The quantity denoted by the letter E varies from experiment to experiment.*

connote /kə'nəʊt/ [v T not in progressive] if a word connotes something, it makes you think of feelings and ideas that are not its actual meaning: *The word 'jolly' often connotes that someone is fat.*

4 to intend a particular meaning

- mean

mean /miːn/ [v T not in progressive] to intend a particular meaning when you say something: *When you said 'the editor', did you mean me?* | *He said Sarah was a very close friend, but I'm not sure what he meant.* | **+ (that)** *I meant that we would have to leave early, that's all.* | **if you know what I mean** (=used to show that you are saying something in a less extreme way than you really mean) *She's kind of irritable, if you know what I mean.* | **what sb means is that ...** *So what he means is that we'll have to start the whole thing again.* | *What I meant was that I wouldn't have time to help, not that I didn't want to.*

5 when something has a meaning that is not directly stated

- suggest
- imply
- say
- implication
- undertone

suggest /sə'dʒest‖səg-/ [v T not in progressive] if a statement, fact, event etc **suggests** that something is true, it seems to mean that it is true or could be true, but this is not directly stated: *It is still not clear what these facts suggest – perhaps a new strain of the virus, or a completely new virus.* | **+ (that)** *All the evidence suggests that the problem has improved in recent years.* | *The victim had marks on his neck which seemed to suggest he had been strangled.*

imply /ɪm'plaɪ/ [v T not in progressive] if a statement, fact, event etc **implies** that something is true, it suggests very strongly that it is true: *His criticisms implied a lack of confidence in my work.* | **+ (that)** *The way he greeted the boys seemed to imply that he knew them quite well.* | *Just the fact that he's written to you implies he likes you.*

say /seɪ/ [v T] to **say** something in an indirect way – use this especially when you are saying what the real meaning of a statement is: *What do you think the writer is saying in this story?* | **+ (that)** *Are you saying I'm fat?* | *So what you're saying, Mr President, is that you don't have a policy on this issue.*

implication /ˌɪmplɪ̇ˈkeɪʃən/ [n C/U] a meaning that is not directly stated, but which seems to be intended: *He didn't actually accuse me of stealing, but that was the implication.* | **+ that** *Staff members were asked to work on Sundays, with the implication that they would lose their jobs if they refused.* | **by implication** (=the intended meaning is that) *The law bans organized protests and, by implication, any form of opposition.*

undertone /ˈʌndəʳtəʊn/ [n C] a feeling or attitude that seems to be part of a statement, even though it is not directly stated: *a story with racist undertones* | **+ of** *There was an unmistakable undertone of nationalist resentment in many of their remarks.*

6 to believe that something has a particular meaning

- interpret
- understand sth to mean
- read into
- take sth as
- infer
- read between the lines

interpret /ɪnˈtɜːʳprɪ̇t/ [v T] to choose to believe that what someone says or does has a particular meaning, especially if it is not easy to understand or is not completely clear: *How would you interpret her letter? Is she really hostile or just being ironic?* | *This dream can be interpreted in several different ways.* | **interpret sth as sth** *I interpreted her silence as anger.* | *They are worried that the workers might interpret the new law as a restriction of their rights.*

understand sth to mean /ʌndəʳˌstænd (sth) tə ˈmiːn/ [v phrase] to think that something has a particular meaning even though you cannot be completely sure that this is what it means: *Democracy was originally understood to mean the people governing themselves.* | *The Victorians understood 'The environment' to mean the background to human activity, in particular, industrial activity.*

read into /ˈriːd ɪntuː/ [phr v T] to think that something has a meaning that it does not in fact have, especially by thinking that it is more important than it really is **read sth into sth** *Be careful not to read your own modern opinions into this story.* | *The statement criticized journalists for reading too much into what he had said about the war.* | **read into sth sth** *Some critics have read into the more macabre scenes a subconscious hatred of his parents.*

take sth as /ˈteɪk (sth) æz/ [phr v T] to believe that what someone does or says has a particular meaning, especially if you think it shows their attitude towards you **take sth as an insult/compliment/ criticism etc** *Had he spoken like this to anyone else, it would have been taken as an insult.* | *I take it as a compliment when my students ask questions after class.* | **take sth as a sign/signal etc** *The investors took this interest rate cut as a sign that the Government was desperate.*

infer /ɪnˈfɜːʳ/ [v T] formal to think that something is true because another fact makes it seem likely, even though it does not prove it completely: *From this, astronomers can infer the presence of many more 'black holes'.* | **infer (from sth) that** *It seems reasonable to infer that the cause was not sabotage but a simple accident.* | *We can infer from the archaeological evidence that there was slavery in Carthage.*

read between the lines /ˌriːd bɪtwiːn ðə ˈlaɪnz/ [v phrase] to guess the real meaning of something by thinking very carefully and noticing that the meaning is different from what it at first seems to be: *Perseverance is required to understand the story and you have to read between the lines to find the book's full meaning.* | **reading between the lines** (=used to say what you think the real situation is) *Reading between the lines, I don't think they want to train people who might soon leave the company.*

7 someone's opinion about the meaning of something

- interpretation
- understanding
- reading

interpretation /ɪnˌtɜːʳprɪ̇ˈteɪʃən/ [n C/U] someone's opinion about the probable meaning of a statement, result, someone's actions etc: *One possible interpretation is that they want you to resign.* | **+ of** *the traditional interpretation of Marx's opinions* | **be open to interpretation** (=to be able to be interpreted in more than one way) *The word 'reasonable' is vague and open to interpretation.*

understanding /ˌʌndəʳˈstændɪŋ/ [n singular] someone's opinion about the meaning of a piece of writing or an action, used especially when they realize that there are other possible meanings **sb's understanding (of sth)** *According to my understanding of the letter, it means something quite different.* | *That was not my understanding of the regulations, and I resent your accusation that I failed to follow them correctly.*

reading /ˈriːdɪŋ/ [n singular] someone's opinion about the meaning of a statement, an event, or a situation after considering all the available information **sb's reading of sth** *What's your reading of the latest trade figures?* | *My reading of the situation is that this conflict is likely to get worse over the next few months.*

8 to be the most basic meaning of a statement

- basically/ essentially
- boil down to/come down to
- amount to
- in other words
- to that effect

basically/essentially /ˈbeɪsɪkli, ɪˈsenʃəli/ [adv] you say **basically** or **essentially** as a way of introducing the general meaning of a longer or more complicated statement: *I won't read it all to you, but basically they want us to leave the house.* | *Basically, the author is in favour of disarmament but with a few reservations.* | *This is essentially the same argument that Arnold used in 'Culture and Anarchy'.*

boil down to/come down to /ˌbɔɪl ˈdaʊn tuː, ˌkʌm ˈdaʊn tuː/ [phr v T not in progressive] if a long statement, argument, discussion etc **boils down to** or **comes down to** a simple fact, that is its simplest and most important meaning: *The argument boiled down to him saying I did and me saying I didn't.* | *That's what it boils down to then: he's not prepared to help us.* | *They make a variety of points, but what their complaints come down to is, no one seems to care.*

amount to /əˈmaʊnt tuː/ [phr v T not in progressive] if a statement **amounts to** something, that is what it means or that is the effect it has, especially if this is something that the person making the statement was deliberately trying to avoid: *The fact that he said he was sorry after the accident amounts to a con-*

fession of guilt. | *Their request for better working conditions amounted to a criticism of the management.*

in other words /ɪn ˌʌðəʳ ˈwɜːʳdz/ [adv] you say **in other words** when you are going to make clear the meaning of something you have just said, using simpler words: *He prides himself on his powers of persuasion – or, in other words, his salesmanship.* | *The books and materials are kept on closed access, in other words available only to the library staff.*

to that effect /tə ˌðæt ɪˈfekt/ [adv] you say that someone said something **to that effect**, when you are giving the general meaning of what they said, even if you do not use the same words: *I thought he was wrong and I said something to that effect at dinner.* | **words to that effect** *James said he was unhappy in his work or words to that effect.*

9 when it is not clear which meaning is intended

▸ **ambiguous**

▸ *see also* **clear/not clear (1-6)**

ambiguous /æmˈbɪgjuəs/ [adj] having more than one possible meaning, so that it is not clear which meaning is intended: *Unfortunately the instructions were ambiguous and we didn't know which part of the program to run.* | *She left a very ambiguous message on the answerphone last night.* | *The results of the experiments were ambiguous and they will have to be done again.* —**ambiguously** [adv] *The declaration was ambiguously worded.*

10 having no meaning

▸ **meaningless** ▸ **gobbledygook**
▸ **nonsense**

meaningless /ˈmiːnɪŋləs/ [adj] something that is **meaningless** has no meaning, and is therefore useless, wrong, or stupid: *I wish politicians would tell us the truth, instead of repeating their meaningless prepared answers.* | *The statement issued by the authorities was meaningless.* | *It is meaningless to ask what is 'real' or 'imaginary' in a story.*

nonsense /ˈnɒnsənsǁˈnɑːnsens/ [n U] speech or writing that has no meaning: *He described her comments as confused nonsense.* | **talk nonsense** *I don't intend to waste any more time listening to you talk nonsense.*

gobbledygook /ˈgɒbəldiguːkǁˈgɑːbəldigʊk, -guːk/ [n U] informal complicated language, especially in an official document, that seems to have no meaning: *I can't understand all this legal gobbledygook.*

measure

RELATED WORDS

▸ *see also* **count/calculate, weigh, distance, amount/number, long, short, heavy, light (4-5)**

1 to measure something

▸ **measure** ▸ **take a reading**
▸ **weigh** ▸ **meter**
▸ **time** ▸ **gauge**
▸ **take** ▸ **record**
▸ **read** ▸ **quantify**

measure /ˈmeʒəʳ/ [v T] to find out the size or amount of something, by using a special tool, machine, or system: *Can you measure the desk to see if it'll fit into that corner?* | *The GNP figures measure the rate of growth in the economy.* | *Electrodes were attached to his chest in order to measure his heart rate.* | **measure sth at sth** *Seismologists in Japan measured the earthquake at 7.7 on the Richter scale.* | *Some species of python have been measured at over 28 feet long.*

weigh /weɪ/ [v T] to find out how heavy something is by measuring its weight with special equipment: *Weigh all the ingredients carefully before mixing them together.* | **weigh yourself** *Every time I weigh myself I seem to have got heavier!*

time /taɪm/ [v T] to measure how long it takes for someone to do something or for something to happen: *We timed how long it took us to get there.* | *The swimming teacher always times us over 100 metres.* | **be timed at 20 miles per hour/3 minutes etc** *The fastest big cat, the cheetah, has been timed at over 60 mph.*

take /teɪk/ [v T] to measure how hot someone is, how fast their heart is beating etc, as part of a medical examination **take sb's pulse/temperature/blood pressure** *My mother took my temperature and sent me back to bed.* | *The doctor will take your blood pressure and check your weight.*

read /riːd/ [v T] to look at the number or result that a piece of equipment is showing when you are using it to measure something: *Someone came to read the electricity meter this morning.* | *The nurse read the thermometer and told me that my temperature was normal.*

take a reading /ˌteɪk ə ˈriːdɪŋ/ [v phrase] use this when a number or result often changes: *Scientists took readings over several weeks and found that there was no unusual volcanic activity.*

meter /ˈmiːtəʳ/ [v T] to measure how much of something such as gas, water, or electricity is used, so that the companies supplying the gas etc know how much their customers should pay: *The gas is metered and they send you a bill every three months.* | *They've introduced a system of metering the amount of water used in a household.*

gauge /geɪdʒ/ [v T] to guess or judge in advance how much something will measure, use, cost etc, according to all the things that affect it: *Recent polls have gauged the president's support at 85% or more.* | **gauge how many/how much etc** *When all the figures are available, it should be possible to gauge how much we'll need to spend.*

record /rɪˈkɔːʳd/ [v T] to measure the size, speed etc of something and keep the information so that it can be used later: *Police recorded his speed at 99.04 miles per hour.* | *Last year the company recorded a profit of £1.4 million.*

quantify /ˈkwɒntɪ̌faɪǁˈkwɑːn-/ [v T] formal to measure something and express it as a number or amount, so that it can be counted and compared to other amounts: *Just quantifying your financial goals will make you feel more in control of your future.* | *In the UK, the operation will not be performed until the risks are better understood and quantified.* | **difficult/hard/impossible etc to quantify** *It's difficult to quantify how long it will take to finish the project.*

2 the number or amount that you get when you measure something

▸ **measurement** ▸ **reading**

measurement /ˈmeʒəʳmənt/ [n C] a number or

amount that you get when you measure something: *What are the measurements of the bedroom?* | **take a measurement** *I'll just take a few measurements, then I can tell you how much paint you will need.* | **waist/chest/hip etc measurement** (=how much you measure around your waist, chest etc) *I think his chest measurement is 40, or maybe 42.* | **sb's measurements** (=someone's height, waist size etc) *I can easily alter the dress for you, but I'll need your exact measurements.*

reading /ˈriːdɪŋ/ [n C] a number or result that a piece of equipment shows when you are measuring something: *The electricity meter reading was much higher than I'd expected.* | *We use atmospheric pressure readings from barometers to forecast the weather.*

3 an amount or quantity used for measuring something

- unit
- measure

unit /ˈjuːnɪ̈t/ [n C] a fixed quantity, length, or weight that is used for measuring something, for example a metre or a pint are units: *What's the unit of currency in India?* | *It takes your body about an hour to burn up one unit of alcohol, such as half a pint of beer.* | *The asteroids all lie between 2.2 and 3.3 astronomical units from the sun.* | **unit of measurement** *A fathom is the unit of measurement used in calculating sea depth.*

measure /ˈmeʒəʳ/ [n singular] **+ of** a certain amount of liquid, especially alcohol, that you measure in any small container: *To make the drink, you will need one measure of red wine to two measures of lemonade.* | *a measure of brandy*

4 to be a particular size, length etc

- be
- weigh
- measure

be /bi, (*strong*) biː/ [v] to **be** a particular size, length, height, weight etc: *He's going on a diet. He's over two hundred pounds.* | *Our present altitude is 30,000 feet, and our speed is 500 miles per hour.* | **be 10 cms long/wide/deep/high/tall** *The room's about six metres long and four metres wide.* | **be 10 cms in length/ in depth/in width etc** *At the shallow end, the pool's less than one metre in depth.*

measure /ˈmeʒəʳ/ [v] to have a particular length, height, width, or depth, especially when it is known exactly: *The yacht measures eighty-four feet and is fitted out to the highest standards.* | *Surgeons use a laser with a beam measuring less than the width of a human hair.*

weigh /weɪ/ [v] to have a particular weight: *The blue whale is a vast creature, weighing up to 30 tons.* | *Our portable computer weighs 7 pounds and costs about $4000.* | *Allen is a fast runner, despite weighing 325 pounds and having a chest like a barrel.* | *How much do you weigh?*

5 able to be measured

- measurable
- quantifiable

measurable /ˈmeʒərəbəl/ [adj] if something is **measurable**, it is possible to measure it: *Pain and suffering are not measurable.* | **measurable benefits/improvements/results etc** *While the technique had little impact on infants, it produced measurable benefits with 7 to 9 year olds.*

quantifiable /ˈkwɒntɪ̈faɪəbəl‖ˈkwɑːn-/ [adj] formal if something is **quantifiable**, it is possible to measure it and show it as a number or amount, so that it can be compared to other numbers or amounts: *More complete and quantifiable data has come from the laboratory recently.* | *Managers should have clear goals and their performance should be quantifiable.*

medical treatment

RELATED WORDS

- to make someone unconscious by giving them a drug *see* **unconscious (3)**
- *see also* **drug, hospital, doctor, illness/disease, cure, recover, ill/sick, mentally ill, hurt/injure, pain**

1 treatment for an injury or illness

- treatment
- therapy
- medicine
- operation
- surgery
- injection
- jab

treatment /ˈtriːtmənt/ [n C/U] a medical method of curing someone who is ill or injured, for example by means of drugs or an operation **+ for** *Doctors are trying out a new treatment for depression.* | **+ of** *Natural poisons such as snake venom are now being used in the treatment of human nervous disorders.* | **receive treatment** *He's receiving treatment for cancer.* | **medical treatment** *They received medical treatment at the hospital after the assault.* | **course of treatment** *a course of treatment which should lead to an improvement in the patient's condition*

therapy /ˈθerəpi/ [n U] a series of treatments for a problem, especially a mental one, usually without drugs or operations: *The therapy involves getting the patient to tell the doctor about their early childhood.* | *This child is clearly very disturbed emotionally and may require long-term therapy.* | **be in therapy** *He's been in therapy for years, but he's still got a big self-esteem problem.* | **speech therapy** (=medical help to improve speech) *Will she need to have speech therapy?* | **physical therapy** *Don underwent months of physical therapy after the accident.*

medicine /ˈmedsən‖ˈmedɪ̈sən/ [n U] the science of understanding illness and injury, and the methods used for treating them: *Jane is studying medicine.* | *The discovery of penicillin revolutionized Western medicine.* | **alternative medicine** ALSO **complementary medicine** British (=medical treatments based on ideas that are different from the ideas of Western scientific medicine) *So why is complementary medicine gaining popularity?* | **conventional medicine** (=the usual form of medicine used in most Western countries, involving the use of drugs and operations) *Many of these people have been failed by conventional medicine or have rejected it.*

operation /ˌɒpəˈreɪʃən‖ˌɑː-/ [n C] if you have an **operation**, a doctor cuts into your body to remove or repair a part that is damaged **have an operation** *The doctor says I must have an operation.* | **+ on** *I had an operation on my knee last year.* | **carry out/ perform an operation** *Ask the surgeon how many times he has performed the operation before, and with what success.*

surgery /ˈsɜːʳdʒəri/ [n U] treatment by doctors in which they cut into someone's body to remove or repair a part that is damaged: *She needed emergency surgery after the accident.* | **+ on** *He's currently recovering from surgery on his right knee.* | **+ for** *Last year, she underwent surgery for breast cancer.* | **have/undergo surgery** *Before undergoing surgery, patients should discuss the various options with their doctor.* | **major/minor surgery** (=a serious/not very serious operation) *an injury requiring major surgery* | **knee/abdominal/heart etc surgery** *patients on the waiting list for heart surgery*

injection /ɪnˈdʒekʃən/ [n C] when a doctor or nurse gives someone a drug using a special needle **have an injection** *I hate having injections.* | **give sb an injection** *Mrs. Wilson, I'm going to give you an injection to help you relax.*

jab British **/shot** American /dʒæb, ʃɒt‖ʃɑːt/ [n C] informal an injection: *a typhoid jab* | **get a jab/shot** *The kids have to get their shots before they go to school.*

2 to give someone medical treatment

- treat
- operate

treat /triːt/ [v T] to try to make someone better when they are ill or injured, for example by giving them drugs or hospital care **treat sb for sth** *Doctors are treating him for cancer.* | **treat sth with sth** *Many common infections can be treated with antibiotics.*

operate /ˈɒpəreɪt‖ˈɑː-/ [v I] if a doctor **operates** on someone, he or she cuts them open in order to remove or repair a part of their body that is damaged: *The doctor says they'll have to operate straightaway, before the cancer spreads.* | **+ on** *It can be risky to operate on very old people.* | *They had to operate on my arm because it was broken in two places.*

meet

RELATED WORDS

- arrange to meet someone *see* **arrange**
- what you say when you meet someone *see* **hello**
- *see also* **visit, talk, contact**

1 to meet someone who you have arranged to meet

- meet
- meet with
- meet up/get together
- see
- hook up

meet /miːt/ [v I/T not in passive] to be in the same place as someone else because you have arranged to see them: *I'll meet you outside the theatre at 7 o'clock.* | *The two leaders are scheduled to meet again next month to continue the peace talks.* | *I used to meet her every week to discuss my work.* | *Meet me back here in half an hour – I just need to finish up a couple of things.* | **meet for lunch/coffee/a drink etc** *Let's meet for lunch one day next week.*

meet with /ˈmiːt wɪð/ [phr v T] especially American to meet someone in order to discuss something: *She's flying to New York tomorrow to meet with her agent.* | *The board of directors is meeting with representatives of the union tomorrow.* | *Supervisors should meet with their employees at least every other week to share information.*

meet up/get together /ˌmiːt ˈʌp, ˌget təˈgeðəʳ/ [phr v I] informal if friends **meet up** or **get together**, they meet in order to do something together, for example to have a meal or a drink: *Let's meet up after work.* | *The past few years, our family has only gotten together at Christmas.* | **+ with** *I usually meet up with my friends on a Friday night and go for a drink.* | **+ for lunch/coffee/a drink** *We must get together for lunch some time.*

see /siː/ [v T] to have an arranged meeting with someone: *Dr Thomas is seeing a client at 2:30.* | *I don't think I can see you this afternoon. How about tomorrow?* | **see sb about sth** (=see someone to discuss something) *'I've come to see Mr. Greene about a job,' he said nervously.*

hook up /ˌhʊk ˈʌp/ [phr v I] informal to meet someone in order to do something together socially, for example have a drink, go to a party etc: *We hooked up for lunch at Toscana in Brentwood.* | **+ with** *Matt and I went out for a drink and hooked up with Janet later on.*

2 to meet someone by chance

- meet
- bump into/run into
- see
- encounter
- network

meet /miːt/ [v T not in passive] to see someone by chance and talk to them: *I met Jill at the bus stop this morning.* | *You'll never guess who I met yesterday!* | *Ron's changed so much, you probably wouldn't recognize him if you met him on the street.*

bump into/run into /ˌbʌmp ˈɪntuː, ˌrʌn ˈɪntuː/ [phr v T] informal to meet someone that you know, by chance: *I'm glad I bumped into you. I wanted to ask you about tomorrow's history test.* | *I'm sorry I'm late – I ran into an old colleague I hadn't seen for ages.* | *She's always running into friends that she knows from school.*

see /siː/ [v T not in progressive] especially spoken, informal to meet someone by chance: *I saw Penny in town today.* | *If you see Ted, could you tell him I want to talk to him?*

encounter /ɪnˈkaʊntəʳ/ [v T] formal to meet someone by chance, especially someone you do not already know: *It was rare that she encountered interesting people through her work.* | *He encountered the young woman as she was leaving a coffee shop.*

network /ˈnetwɜːʳk/ [v I] to meet other people, especially other people who do the same work as you do, in order to share information, help each other etc: *The conference provided some excellent opportunities for networking and she made some useful business contacts.*

3 when you meet someone for the first time

- meet
- introduce
- this is
- make sb's acquaintance

meet /miːt/ [v T not in passive] to **meet** someone you have not met before: *Have you ever met his wife?* | *I was 15 years old when I met Andrew.* | *Dave, meet my brother Tom.* | *'How did you two meet?' 'We were on the same exchange program in Madrid.'* | *I'd like you all to meet my girlfriend, Claudia.* | **first meet** *Where did you first meet Dr Steiner?* | *Janet and Pete first met at a mutual friend's cocktail party.* | **nice/pleased/glad to meet you** (=use this to politely say 'hello' to someone you have just met) *'Hello, my name is Alan.' 'Hi, Alan. My name's Cindy. Nice to meet you.'* | *'Doug, I'd like you to meet my mother.' 'Oh, pleased to meet you, Mrs Haggerty.'*

introduce /ˌɪntrə'dju:s‖-'du:s/ [v T] if you **introduce** someone to a person they have never met before, you tell them each other's names: *Have you two been introduced?* | *Yes, we were introduced last year at your party.* | **introduce sb to sb** *That's a friend of mine from college. Do you want me to introduce you to him?* | **let me introduce** *Oh, Bob, let me introduce Rosie Webb, our new marketing manager.* | **allow me to introduce** formal *Please allow me to introduce myself. I'm John Fetty, the head of business development.*

this is /'ðɪs ɪz/ spoken say this when you are introducing someone to a person they have never met before: *'Sam, this is Julia – she's in college with me.' 'Hi, Julia, nice to meet you!'* | *'Mom, Dad, this is my friend Matt.' 'Hello, Matt, we've heard a lot about you.'*

make sb's acquaintance /ˌmeɪk (sb's) ə'kweɪntəns/ [v phrase] formal to meet someone for the first time: *I'm pleased to make your acquaintance.* | *After seeing the way Mr. Wyatt behaved at the party, I had little desire to make his acquaintance.*

4 when a large group comes together in one place

- meet
- gather
- assemble
- come together

meet /mi:t/ [v I] use this when a large group of people comes together in one place: *The book club meets on the first Thursday of every month.* | *The bus trip leaves at 9 am – everyone should meet in front of the station at 8.30.*

gather /'gæðər/ [v I] if a crowd or group of people **gathers**, they come together somewhere in order to do something or see something: *A small crowd gathered to watch the fight.* | *The family gathered on the porch to say goodbye.* | *Eager fans are already gathering outside the stadium.*

assemble /ə'sembəl/ [v I] if a group of people **assembles**, they all come together in the same place, especially as part of an organized plan: *Prisoners must assemble in the courtyard every morning for exercise.* | *Foreign diplomats and their wives had assembled in the Great Hall to meet the President.*

come together /ˌkʌm tə'geðər/ [phr v I] if people or groups who do not usually meet each other **come together**, they meet in order to discuss things, exchange ideas etc: *People came together from all over the country to attend the funeral.* | *Seminars provide an opportunity for students to come together and discuss a particular topic.*

5 to meet someone in order to take them somewhere

- meet
- pick up
- collect

meet /mi:t/ [v T] *We'll meet you at the airport and take you to your hotel.* | *The company is sending a car to meet Mr Hill at the station.* | *Our guide met us in the hotel lobby and spent the entire day with us.*

pick up /ˌpɪk 'ʌp/ [phr v T] to meet someone at a particular place in order to take them somewhere in a car, bus etc **pick sb up** *She picks her daughter up from school every day at four.* | *I told Virginia I'd pick her up about 8:00.* | **pick up sb** *I arranged to pick up Mr Clarke and take him to his accommodation.*

collect /kə'lekt/ [v T] British to meet someone at a particular place in order to take them somewhere: *Her father sent a taxi to collect her from the hotel.* | *If the last bus has left, I'll collect you.*

6 a meeting in order to discuss something

- meeting
- conference
- convention
- summit
- gathering

meeting /'mi:tɪŋ/ [n C] an occasion when people meet in order to discuss something: *Sorry I can't come – I have to go to a meeting.* | *Peter's in London for a business meeting.* | *I was in meetings all morning and didn't get a chance to look at your proposal.* | **have/hold a meeting** *I'm having a meeting with my client tomorrow to go over the case.* | *The committee will hold another meeting Wednesday to discuss the funding crisis.* | **attend a meeting** formal *According to people who attended the meeting, Ms. Robins refused to answer any questions about the deal.* | **call/arrange/organize a meeting** *The principal has called a meeting for 4.00.*

conference /'kɒnfərəns‖'kɑ:n-/ [n C] an organized event, especially one that continues for several days, at which a lot of people meet to discuss a particular subject and hear speeches about it: *Didn't you give a talk at the conference last year?* | **+ on** *She's an organizer of the International Conference on AIDS that the university has every year.* | **+ of** *Lewis recently spoke at a conference of women business leaders.* | **attend a conference** formal *Baxter was in Boston attending a conference on the environment.* | **hold a conference** *The Institute of Accountants is holding its conference in Edinburgh this year.*

convention /kən'venʃən/ [n C] a large meeting of members of a political organization or professional group for a particular purpose: *The Senator's speech at the Democratic Convention was well received.* | *Several hundred people are expected at the hotel next month for a huge sales convention.* | **+ of** *Lofgren told a convention of church activists that she wanted the money to be spent on local childrens' facilities.* | *an annual convention of the world bank* | **hold a convention** *The Reform Party will hold a national convention in August.*

summit /'sʌmɪ̣t/ [n C] a meeting between government leaders from important and powerful countries, to discuss international politics: *A U.S.–Russia summit is expected to take place in late March.* | **summit meeting/conference** *A summit meeting of OPEC leaders was called to find a solution to the oil crisis.* | *NATO leaders are preparing for a summit conference to decide the future of the alliance.* | **economic/anti-drug/AIDS etc summit** *The President will meet other Pacific Rim leaders at next week's economic summit.*

gathering /'gæðərɪŋ/ [n C] a crowd of people who have come together for a particular purpose, for example to listen to someone speak, to pray, or to discuss something: *It was quite a small gathering but the speeches were excellent.* | *They announced their engagement at a family gathering in Vermont.*

7 an occasion when you meet someone, especially by chance

- meeting
- encounter

meeting /'mi:tɪŋ/ [n C] *Our first meeting was in January, and I didn't see Martin again till May or June.* | **chance meeting** (=one that happens completely by chance) *Her affair with Harmon started with a chance meeting followed by a few casual phone calls.*

encounter /ɪn'kaʊntəʳ/ [n C] an unexpected meeting, which is often unpleasant: *He did not appear to remember our encounter last summer and just nodded when we were introduced.* | **chance encounter** (=one that happens completely by chance) *A chance encounter in a restaurant led to her first movie role.*

8 to not meet someone even though you have arranged to

- stand up
- not turn up/not show up

stand up /ˌstænd 'ʌp/ [phr v T] informal to deliberately not go to meet someone that you have arranged to meet, especially a friend, or a boyfriend or girlfriend **stand sb up** *She spent the whole evening wondering why her date had stood her up.* | **stand up sb** *If he continues to stand up his friends, he's not going to have any left.*

not turn up/not show up ALSO **not show** [v phrase] American /nɒt tɜːʳn 'ʌp, ˌnɒt ʃəʊ 'ʌp, nɒt 'ʃəʊ/ [phr v I] informal to not meet someone at the place you have arranged to meet them: *A few of us had arranged to meet in town, but Jenny didn't turn up.* | *Peter always says he'll come, and then he just doesn't show up.* | *I waited for an hour but she didn't show.*

member

RELATED WORDS

- to become a member of a club or organization *see* **join (7-10)**
- to stop being a member *see* **leave (22-25)**
- *see also* **organization**

1 a member of an organization or formal group

- member
- membership

member /'membəʳ/ [n C] a person, organization, country etc that belongs to a club, a political party, or a group: *The club is hoping to attract more members.* | **+ of** *She's a member of the local drama society.* | *Brooks is a very valuable member of the team.* | *Is Switzerland a member of the European Union?* | **club/union/party member** *80% of union members are opposed to going on strike over this issue.*

membership /'membəʳʃɪp/ [n singular with singular or plural verb in British English] all the members of a club or a similar organization: *The membership was totally against admitting women to the club.* | *Obviously the veterans' association has a rather old and declining membership.* | **have a membership of 50/100/1000 etc** *The Bishop's Stortford Photographic Society now has a membership of over 50.*

2 to be a member of an organization or formal group

- be a member of/belong to
- be in
- be on

be a member of/belong to /bi: ə 'membəʳ ɒv, bɪ'lɒŋ tu:‖-'lɔːŋ-/ [v phrase] *My sister's a member of the All Saints Fan Club.* | *Do you belong to a political party?*

be in /bi: 'ɪn/ [v phrase] to be a member of an organization or formal group, especially a large one: *Nina's son is in the army.* | *I used to really enjoy camping when I was in the Boy Scouts.* | **be in a team** British *It's great to have him back in the team.*

be on /bi: 'ɒn/ [v phrase] to be a member of a group such as a committee or team **be on a committee/council/board/panel** *Kathryn is on the school board for the district.* | **be on a team** *I wish he was on our team.*

3 when someone is a member

- membership
- affiliation

membership /'membəʳʃɪp/ [n U] when someone is a member of an organization or formal group: *What is the cost of membership?* | *Membership is limited to the under-40s.* | **+ of** British *Canada's membership of NATO* | **+ in** American *Did you renew your membership in the sailing club?* | **membership card** *When you join the society, you will be issued a membership card.*

affiliation /əˌfɪli'eɪʃən/ [n U] formal when someone is connected with a political party, religious organization etc – used in official contexts **political/religious affiliation** *They asked about his religious beliefs and political affiliation.* | **+ to/with** *Throughout his long life, he retained his affiliation to the Labour Party.*

mentally ill

RELATED WORDS

- a doctor who treats people who are mentally ill *see* **doctor**
- a hospital for people who are mentally ill *see* **hospital**
- *see also* **crazy, mind, illness/disease, cure, recover, medical treatment, drug**

1 mentally ill

- mentally ill
- mental
- insane
- mad
- unstable
- confused

mentally ill /ˌmentəli 'ɪl/ [adj phrase] someone who is **mentally ill** has an illness of the mind which affects the way that they behave: *Many of these homeless people have been mentally ill at some time.* | **the mentally ill** (=people who are mentally ill) *He works in a hostel for the mentally ill.*

mental /'mentl/ [adj only before noun] connected with **mental** illness or people who are mentally ill **mental hospital/patient/institution** *a hospital ward for non-violent mental patients* | **mental problem/disorder/breakdown** *We knew she had been having mental problems.*

insane /ɪn'seɪn/ [adj] formal permanently and seriously mentally ill, so that you cannot have a normal life – use this in legal contexts or in descriptions of people who lived in the past: *The man, who has attacked 13 women, was judged to be insane.* | **go insane** (=become seriously mentally ill) *Sometimes I thought I was going insane.*

mad British **crazy** especially American /mæd, 'kreɪzi/ [adj] mentally ill – use this in conversations or stories, but not in formal, medical, or legal English: *We soon realized that the old man was completely mad.* | *There's this crazy woman in our town who eats glass.* | **go mad/crazy** *They say she went mad after her family were killed in a fire.*

unstable /ʌnˈsteɪbəl/ [adj] if someone is **unstable**, their emotional state often changes very suddenly, and they are likely to become angry, violent etc: *Working with Clare every day, I began to realize how unstable she was.* | **emotionally/mentally unstable** *He is emotionally unstable, and his aggressive attitude often culminates in violence.*

confused /kənˈfjuːzd/ [adj] an old person who is **confused** has become mentally ill so that they cannot remember things or think clearly: *Aunt Clara had been so sharp, so witty, but now she is just a sad, confused old woman.*

2 mental illness

- mental illness
- madness
- insanity
- disorder
- depression
- senility

mental illness /ˌmentl ˈɪlnəs/ [n C/U] an illness of the mind: *Depression is a mental illness and can often be treated with drugs.* | *He had a history of mental illness and alcoholism.* | **suffer from (a) mental illness** *SANELINE is the first helpline for people suffering from mental illness.*

madness /ˈmædnəs/ [n U] especially British serious and permanent mental illness – used especially in literature, but not used in official or medical contexts: *By the end of the book, Peter's addiction has led him to madness and suicide.* | **feign madness** (=pretend to be mad) *Some prisoners feigned madness so that they would be released.*

insanity /ɪnˈsænəti/ [n U] formal serious and permanent mental illness – use this especially in legal contexts or in descriptions of people who lived in the past: *Hearing voices inside your head is a common symptom of insanity.* | *Hodge was found not guilty by reason of insanity.*

disorder /dɪsˈɔːʳdəʳ/ [n C] formal a mental illness – used especially by doctors **personality/ mood disorder** *Children who suffer from personality disorders often receive little or no treatment until it's too late.* | **psychiatric/mental disorder** *There was no evidence of her having a psychiatric disorder, although it was clear that she had become withdrawn since the breakup of her relationship.*

depression /dɪˈpreʃən/ [n U] a mental illness which makes you so anxious and unhappy that you cannot live a normal life **suffer from depression** *He has been suffering from depression since his wife died last year.* | **deep/severe depression** *She suffers from periods of deep depression, when she locks herself away and will speak to no one for weeks.*

senility /sɪˈnɪləti/ [n U] a mental illness that affects old people and makes them unable to think clearly and become confused very easily: *Of all the associated problems to do with getting old, senility is the one she dreads most.*

3 to become mentally ill

- have a (nervous) breakdown
- crack up
- go insane

have a (nervous) breakdown /hæv ə (ˌnɜːʳvəs) ˈbreɪkdaʊn/ [v phrase] to become mentally ill, usually as a result of working too hard or difficult emotional problems, and be temporarily unable to deal with ordinary things such as working or looking after your family: *After her divorce, Dora had a nervous breakdown and was off work for three months.* | *She sounds really bad. I think she's heading for a nervous breakdown.*

crack up /ˌkræk ˈʌp/ [phr v I] informal to suddenly become unable to continue your normal life, especially because you have been working too hard or doing something that is very frightening, dangerous etc: *I think Paul's cracking up under the strain of work.* | *Some people can't cope with the death of a loved one, and simply crack up.*

go insane ALSO **go mad** British **/go crazy** especially American /gəʊ ɪnˈseɪn, gəʊ ˈmæd, gəʊ ˈkreɪzi/ [v phrase] to become seriously and permanently mentally ill – used in ordinary English, but not official or medical contexts: *Eventually, rejected by Hamlet, Ophelia goes mad and drowns herself.* | *I wondered if I was going crazy. Everyone seemed to be against me.* | *Conditions on the oil rig are very unpleasant. You'd go insane if you had to stay more than a month or so.*

4 not mentally ill

- sane
- sanity
- of sound mind

sane /seɪn/ [adj] not mentally ill, so that you are able to make sensible decisions and lead your life in a normal way: *Of course he isn't mad. He's as sane as you or I.* | *No sane person would believe such garbage!* | **perfectly sane** (=completely sane) *To his neighbours, Peter appeared perfectly sane.*

sanity /ˈsænəti/ [n U] when you are mentally healthy: *If you have your health and your sanity, money isn't really important.* | *I began to doubt Donald's sanity as his story got stranger and stranger.*

of sound mind /əv ˌsaʊnd ˈmaɪnd/ [adj phrase] a legal expression meaning not mentally ill and able to be responsible for your decisions and actions: *You are allowed to vote only if you are over 18 and of sound mind.*

mention

RELATED WORDS

▸ *see also* **say, tell**

1 to mention someone or something

- mention
- refer to
- allude to
- touch on
- throw in
- namedropping

mention /ˈmenʃən/ [v T] to say something about a person, plan, event etc, especially during a conversation, without giving any details or saying very much: *When you were talking to Barbara, did she mention her mother at all?* | *We didn't really discuss the price, but somebody mentioned a figure of £300.* | **+ (that)** *Eve mentioned that you might be looking for a temporary job.* | **mention sth to sb** *She had started having nose bleeds, but when she mentioned this to her doctor, he told her not to worry.* | **worth mentioning** *'Why didn't you tell me?' 'It didn't seem worth mentioning.'* | **now (that) you mention it** (=used to agree when someone has introduced a new subject) *Now that you mention it, I did think she was behaving a little strangely last night.* | **mention sth in passing** (=mention something quickly, without spending much time on it) *Then he remembered that Liz had mentioned in passing that her father was a lawyer.*

refer to /rɪ'fɜːʳ tuː/ [phr v T] to say something about a person, plan, event etc in a conversation, speech, or piece of writing: *Although she didn't mention any names, everyone knew who she was referring to.* | *I apologized, and the matter was never referred to again.* | *I think what Mary was referring to earlier was her manager's inability to make the right decision.*

allude to /ə'luːd tuː/ [phr v T] formal to mention someone or something in a deliberately indirect way: *She has often alluded to a secret tragedy in her past.* | *When the director spoke of 'major problems', I assumed that he was alluding to mechanical failures in the computer system.*

touch on /'tʌtʃ ɒn/ [phr v T] to mention a subject or a fact during a speech, a lesson, a piece of writing etc, but without spending much time on it: *In my last lecture I touched on a number of important issues which I am now going to examine in some detail.*

throw in /ˌθrəʊ 'ɪn/ [phr v T] informal to mention something that is not closely connected with what you are saying, or that it is not necessary to mention **throw in sth/throw sth in** *He likes to throw in references to his days in the army.*

namedropping /'neɪmˌdrɒpɪŋ‖-ˌdrɑːp-/ [n U] the practice of mentioning the names of famous or important people that you know or meet, in order to impress other people: *I hate the namedropping that is a feature of most autobiographies.*

2 to start talking about something that you want to say more about

- bring up
- raise
- broach
- introduce

bring up /ˌbrɪŋ 'ʌp/ [phr v T] to start to talk about a subject during a conversation or meeting **bring up sth** *She wished she'd never brought up the subject of money.* | **bring sth up** *If you think safety is a problem, I suggest you bring it up at the next meeting.*

raise /reɪz/ [v T] to mention a subject that people should start to discuss or think about **raise an issue/matter/question etc** *A number of important issues were raised at the conference.* | *The matter of whether or not the Royal Family should pay taxes was first raised in an article in the Times.*

broach /brəʊtʃ/ [v T] to mention a subject that may be embarrassing or upsetting, or may cause an argument **broach a subject/matter/question etc** *He decided not to broach the subject of divorce until his wife had recovered from her illness.* | **broach sth with sb** *I think Susan is being bullied at school, but every time I try to broach the matter with her she refuses to talk about it.*

introduce /ˌɪntrə'djuːs‖-'duːs/ [v T] to mention a new subject or idea before talking or writing about it in more detail **introduce a subject/idea/topic etc** *She introduced the subject of sex without any embarrassment.* | *Then Meredith discovered that the way to get Harriet relaxed and talking was to introduce the topic of animals.*

3 when someone or something is mentioned

- mention
- reference

mention /'menʃən/ [n singular] when someone or something is mentioned – use this in the following phrases **there was no mention of sth** (=it was not mentioned) *There was no mention of a pay rise.* | **make no mention of sth** (=not mention something) *Mr Franks made no mention of any changes at the top of the company.* | **get a mention** (=be mentioned) *The case even got a mention in some of the national newspapers.*

reference /'refərəns/ [n C/U] when someone or something is mentioned, especially in a piece of formal writing, a speech, or an interview **+ to** *The poem contains references to places where the poet spent his childhood.* | **make no/any reference to sth** (=not mention something, or mention something) *The Queen made no reference to the incident in her speech.* | *Did he make any reference to his forthcoming trial?*

message

RELATED WORDS

- send a message *see* **send**
- *see also* **contact, letter, telephone, computers/Internet/email**

1 a message

- message
- note
- memo
- dispatch/despatch
- email/email message

message /'mesɪdʒ/ [n C] a spoken or written piece of information, request etc that you send to someone, especially by giving it to another person or leaving it somewhere: *When I got home, there were two messages on my answering machine.* | **+ from** *'What is it?' 'A message from the hospital. Harry's worse.'* | **+ for** *Where's Dick? I've got a message for him.* | **+ of** *He says he has received many messages of support from the public.* | **+ that** *I hope Frank got my message that I was going to be late.* | **leave a message** *I'm sorry, Mr Banks isn't here right now. Would you like to leave a message?*

note /nəʊt/ [n C] a short written message **leave a note** *He left a note on his desk saying he would be back in 5 minutes.* | **+ from** *He was devastated when he arrived home to find a note from his wife, telling him their marriage was over.* | **+ to** *She wrote a polite little note to Miss Henry, thanking her for her kindness.*

memo /'meməʊ/ [n C] a short official message to other people in a company or organization: *The meeting's been cancelled. Didn't you get my memo?* | **+ to** *I have sent out a memo to all staff, reminding them of the procedure for taking sick leave.* | **+ from** *He noticed a memo from the chairman on Wilson's desk.*

dispatch/despatch /dɪ'spætʃ/ [n C] a message sent between government or military officials, especially one containing important information: *This office has seen every State Department dispatch issued over the past 35 years.* | *As a courier for the Canadian Government, bearing important dispatches, Hayes was anxious to travel immediately.*

email/email message /'iː meɪl, 'iː meɪl ˌmesɪdʒ/ [n C] a message or document sent from one computer to another: *I sent him an e-mail yesterday, but I haven't got a reply yet.* | *Some companies automatically delete all e-mail messages more than three months old.* | **+ from** *I got an e-mail from her a couple of weeks ago – she sounded OK.*

2 someone who takes a message to someone

- messenger
- courier
- go-between

messenger /ˈmesɪndʒəʳ, -sən-/ [n C] someone who takes a message or whose job it is to take messages: *In the late afternoon a messenger arrived to inform me that the chief was on his way.* | *Captain Anderson did not come himself, but sent a messenger instead.* | *The king's messenger stayed in Rome for further talks.* | **messenger boy** *When he was sixteen Alan got a job as a messenger boy in an advertising agency.*

courier /ˈkʊriəʳ/ [n C] someone whose job it is to carry urgent messages, letters, parcels etc, especially for a company: *A courier arrived with the documents just before the meeting.* | **send sth by courier** *He said he'd be sending the report over by courier.*

go-between /ˈgəʊ bɪˌtwiːn/ [n C] someone who takes messages between two people or groups because they are not able to meet or do not want to meet: *Barnes isn't involved in the deal – he's just the go-between.* | **act as (a) go-between** *Simon was not a member of either group so he seemed a good candidate to act as a go-between.*

middle

RELATED WORDS

- between two or more people or things *see* **between**
- *see also* **edge, side, end**

1 the middle

- middle
- centre
- the heart of
- core

middle /ˈmɪdl/ [n singular] the part of something, such as a space or area, a piece of writing, or a period of time, which is half way between one side and the other, or halfway between the beginning and the end: *'Did you enjoy the movie?' 'It was OK but I got a little bored towards the middle.'* | **+ of** *Gary rowed out towards the middle of the lake.* | *It was the middle of summer.* | *Going through the middle of Tokyo in the rush hour can be a nightmare.*

centre British **/center** American /ˈsentəʳ/ [n C usually singular] the middle of a space, area, or object, especially the exact middle: *The flower has white petals, and is deep pink at the centre.* | *I love chocolates with soft centers.* | **the centre of sth** *Draw a line through the center of the circle.* | **at the centre/in the centre (of sth)** (=exactly in the middle of something) *A bomb has exploded in the crowded business district in the centre of the old city.* | **right in the centre** (=exactly in the centre) *The women all wore a red dot right in the centre of their foreheads.*

the heart of /ðə ˈhɑːʳt ɒv/ [n phrase] the middle of an area, town, or city: *The hotel is located in the heart of Moscow.* | *a quiet village in the heart of the English countryside*

core /kɔːʳ/ [n C] the central part of a large object such as a very large rock or the Earth: *The Earth has a solid inner core 2500 km in diameter.* | *Only the core of the volcano remained.*

2 in the middle

- in the middle
- middle
- central
- centre
- at/in the centre
- halfway
- mid-
- midway
- midpoint

in the middle /ɪn ðə ˈmɪdl/ [adv] *At the back there was a small garden with a fishpond in the middle.* | *I was never at the top of my class. I was somewhere in the middle, I suppose.* | **+ of** *Lizzie woke up in the middle of the night with a toothache.* | *At the time, the country was in the middle of an economic recession.*

middle /ˈmɪdl/ [adj only before noun] **the middle drawer/shelf/finger etc** the one in the middle: *You'll find the scissors in the middle drawer of my desk.* | *Jane was wearing a gold ring on her middle finger.* | *There were three children in my family, and I was the middle one.*

central /ˈsentrəl/ [adj only before noun] in the middle of an area, country, or town: *The houses face onto a central courtyard.* | *the tropical rainforest in central Africa* | *central London*

centre British **/center** American /ˈsentəʳ/ [adj only before noun] **centre door/panel/page etc** the door etc that is in the middle with others on either side: *On the center panel of the screen there is a painting of a Greek goddess.* | *There's usually a picture of some glamorous girl on the centre page.*

at/in the centre British **/at/in the center** American /æt, ɪn ðə ˈsentəʳ/ [adv] exactly in the middle of something: *It was a huge room with a high ceiling and an oak table in the centre.* | **+ of** *At the center of the atom is the nucleus.* | *The city of Turin stands at the centre of the Piedmontese plain.*

halfway /ˌhɑːfˈweɪ◂‖ˌhæf-/ [adv/adj] at the middle point between two places or of a period of time or event **+ across/between/down/up etc** *Our car broke down halfway across the bridge.* | *We were halfway down the mountain when it started snowing.* | *Joe was pretty unhappy and left the college halfway through the year.* | **the halfway mark** (=the middle point of sth) *The Scots opened up a 29–17 lead, and at the halfway mark they were still in front.*

mid- /mɪd-/ [prefix] in or near the middle of a period of time: *The house was built in the mid-18th century.* | *As the value of the US dollar fell in the mid-1980s, so did the value of UK reserves.* | *Let's meet again mid-week.*

midway /ˌmɪdˈweɪ◂‖ˈmɪdweɪ/ [adv] at the middle point of a distance, a period of time, or a set of numbers **+ between/through** *The islands lie in the Indian Ocean midway between Madagascar and Tanzania.* | *United took the lead midway through the first half.* | *At a guess, I'd say he was midway between 50 and 60.*

midpoint /ˈmɪdpɔɪnt/ [n C] the point that is an equal distance from either end of a process or scale: *The Redskins and the Giants were the leaders as the midpoint in the season drew near.* | **+ of** *By the midpoint of the twentieth century, the economy had begun to improve.*

mind

RELATED WORDS

- I don't mind *see* **don't care**
- *see also* **think, mental illness, intelligent, opinion, mentally ill, imagine**

1 your mind

- mind
- brain
- head
- subconscious
- psyche

mind /maɪnd/ [n C] what you use to think and imagine things: *His mind was full of big ideas for developing the company.* | *Dave struggled hard to push these worries out of his mind.* (=try not to think about them) | **in your mind** *She had a picture of him in her mind – tall, blond and handsome.* | **at the back of your mind** (=when an idea is not very clear or certain) *At the back of my mind I had the funny feeling that I'd met her somewhere before.* | **go/run through your mind** (=) *The same thoughts kept going through my mind and I couldn't get to sleep.* | **turn sth over in your mind** (=think about sth carefully) *It was an interesting idea. Jeff turned it over in his mind on the way to work.* | **what's going on in sb's mind** (=what sb is thinking) *I never know what's going on in her mind.* | **your mind wanders** (=you cannot make yourself concentrate on a particular subject, and you start thinking about other things) *The teacher talked on and on and my mind began to wander.*

brain /breɪn/ [n C] your ability to think and the way that you think: *My brain worked fast as I tried to decide what to do.* | *Branson has an excellent business brain.*

head /hed/ [n C] someone's mind – use this especially when talking about the thoughts that are in someone's mind: *Dan's head was full of big ideas.* | **what's going on in sb's head** (=what sb is thinking) *She's so quiet – you never quite know what's going on inside her head.*

subconscious /sʌbˈkɒnʃəs‖-ˈkɑːn-/ [n singular] the part of your mind that influences the way you think or behave, even though you may not realize this is happening, and which makes you have dreams **the subconscious** *When you go to sleep it is only the conscious mind that shuts down. The subconscious cannot do so.* | **sb's subconscious** *Our subconscious plays tricks with us sometimes and we may imagine that we are seeing things such as ghosts.* —**subconscious** [adj] *the subconscious mind* | *our subconscious desires*

psyche /ˈsaɪki/ [n singular] formal someone's mind, especially their feelings and attitudes, and the way these influence their character: *The need for love is deeply buried in our psyche.* | *the fragile psyche of a teenager* | **the human/female/American etc psyche** (=the typical psyche of a human, female etc) *Freud has provided an account of the human psyche's different stages of development.*

2 affecting your mind

- mental
- psychological
- subconscious
- subliminal

mental /ˈmentl/ [adj usually before noun] affecting your mind or happening in your mind: *After months of overworking, Briggs was suffering from mental and physical exhaustion.* | *It takes a lot of mental effort to understand these ideas.* | **mental picture/image** (=a picture that you have in your mind) *I'd never met Jane's boyfriend, but I had a clear mental picture of what he looked like.* | **mental illness/problem/breakdown** (=an illness, problem etc of your mind, not your body) *Rick had a complete mental breakdown after his family died in a car crash.* —**mentally** [adv] *By the end of the day we were mentally and physically worn out.*

psychological /ˌsaɪkəˈlɒdʒɪkəl◂‖-ˈlɑː-/ [adj] affecting the mind – use this especially about mental problems that influence the way someone behaves: *The cause of a physical illness can often be psychological.* | **a psychological problem** *She works with children who have psychological problems.* —**psychologically** [adv] *psychologically disturbed children*

subconscious ALSO **unconscious** /sʌbˈkɒnʃəs‖-ˈkɑːn-, ʌnˈkɒnʃəs‖-ˈkɑːn-/ [adj] **subconscious** feelings, desires, worries etc are hidden in your mind and you do not realize that you have them: *People who come to me for counselling are very often suffering from unconscious feelings of guilt.* | *a subconscious fear of failure* —**subconsciously** [adv] *Fathers are often subconsciously jealous of their sons.*

subliminal /sʌbˈlɪmɨnəl/ [adj] **subliminal** messages and images are hidden in advertisements, pictures etc and can influence your mind without you realizing it: *Any kind of subliminal advertising is illegal on British TV.* | *Young people are receiving constant subliminal messages glorifying pop stars, their cars, their girlfriends.*

mistake

RELATED WORDS

- by accident *see* **accidentally**
- *see also* **wrong, careless, confused**

1 mistake

- mistake
- error
- slip
- slip-up
- mix-up
- oversight
- slip of the tongue
- boob
- howler

mistake /mɨˈsteɪk/ [n C] something incorrect that you do, say, or write without intending to: *Your essay is full of mistakes.* | *Celia corrected the mistakes with a pen.* | **+ in** *a tiny mistake in their calculations* | **make a mistake** *Sampras was playing badly, making a lot of mistakes.* | **there's a mistake** *There must be some mistake – I definitely paid the bill last week.*

error /ˈerəʳ/ [n C/U] a mistake – use this especially to talk about mistakes in calculating or in using a language, system, or computer: *An error occurred in the processing of your application.* | **+ in** *There seems to be an error in the data.* | **human error** (=when a mistake is caused by people, not by a machine) *The report concluded that the accident was caused by human error.* | **computer error** (=a mistake caused by a computer) *Over 50 people were denied a vote through a computer error.*

slip /slɪp/ [n C] a small unimportant mistake that is easy to make **make a slip** *Don't worry – we all make slips from time to time.* | *People doing this kind of precision work can't afford to make the slightest slip.*

slip-up /ˈslɪp ʌp/ [n C] a careless mistake that may spoil a plan or process: *This whole situation only happened because of a slip-up by the bank.* | *If we are going to win the contract, we can't afford any more slip-ups.*

mix-up /ˈmɪks ʌp/ [n C] a careless mistake that causes confusion about details, for example someone's name, the time of a meeting etc: *The police have now returned Mr Sullivan's car and apologized for the mix-up.* | **+ over** *There was a mix-up over the* *train times and I arrived two hours late.* | **+ in** *I'm afraid there's been a mix-up in the booking – we were expecting you tomorrow.*

oversight /'əʊvəʳsaɪt/ [n C] a mistake that you make by not noticing something or by forgetting to do something: *I'm sure it was just an oversight that your name wasn't on the list.* | *The bank apologized for the oversight.* | *Due to an administrative oversight, several members of staff did not receive pay checks this month.*

slip of the tongue /ˌslɪp əv ðə 'tʌŋ/ [n phrase] when you accidentally say a different word from the word you intended to say, sometimes with embarrassing results: *He quickly corrected his unfortunate slip of the tongue.* | *Did I say 'Harlow'? Sorry, I meant 'Harrow'. It was just a slip of the tongue.*

boob British **/booboo** American /bu:b, 'bu:bu:/ [n singular] informal a silly mistake, especially one that amuses people: *We labelled the pictures with the wrong names, but the boob was spotted by one of our readers.* | **make a boob/booboo** *Whoops! I think I've made a booboo.*

howler /'haʊləʳ/ [n C] a very bad mistake, especially one that shows you do not know something: *He read out a selection of howlers from students' exam answers.*

2 a mistake in words that are written or printed

- mistake
- error
- misprint
- typo

mistake /mɪ̆'steɪk/ [n C] a **mistake** in words that are written, typed, or printed: *If you make a mistake, just cross it out.* | **+ in** *There's a mistake in the address.* | **spelling mistake** *Check your work carefully for any spelling mistakes.*

error /'erəʳ/ [n C] a mistake in words that are typed or printed: *'It says in this advertisement that the exhibition opens at 10.' 'That's an error.'* | **typing error** *She made very few typing errors.*

misprint /'mɪs-prɪnt/ [n C] a word or number that has been printed wrongly: *It can't really cost £20 – it must be a misprint.* | *In the last sentence, 'unclear' is a misprint for 'nuclear'.*

typo /'taɪpəʊ/ [n C] a small mistake in a piece of writing which someone has typed or printed: *The article was badly written and full of typos.*

3 a bad decision that causes problems for you

- mistake
- miscalculation
- error of judgment
- be a bad move
- blunder
- indiscretion

mistake /mɪ̆'steɪk/ [n C] something you do or decide that is not at all sensible and causes you a lot of problems **make a mistake** *My first marriage was a terrible failure. I don't want to make the same mistake again.* | *Don't make the mistake of underestimating your opponent.* | **it is a mistake to do sth** *It was a mistake to think that we could go on living on borrowed money.* | **big/serious/terrible mistake** *Buying the farm was the biggest mistake of her life.* | **learn from your mistakes** (=do things better after realizing you have made mistakes) *All I can say is, I think I've learnt from my mistakes.*

miscalculation /ˌmɪskælkjə̆'leɪʃən/ [n C] a mistake caused by planning something badly, and being wrong about the expected result: *The President's election defeat was the result of his own miscalculations.* | *I thought if I told Mark everything, it would be OK. That was a bad miscalculation.*

error of judgment /ˌerər əv 'dʒʌdʒmənt/ [n phrase] formal a mistake caused by judging a situation or person wrongly: *In my opinion, appointing his son as chief executive was a serious error of judgment.* | **make an error of judgment** *New, inexperienced members of staff are more liable to make errors of judgment.*

be a bad move /bi: ə ˌbæd 'mu:v/ [v phrase] informal if something you do **is a bad move**, it is a mistake because it puts you in a bad or dangerous situation: *He tried arguing with her. This was a bad move.* | *Perhaps her resignation wasn't such a bad move after all.* | **it is a bad move doing sth** *It was a bad move letting him come here in the first place.*

blunder /'blʌndəʳ/ [n C] a stupid mistake caused by not thinking carefully enough about what you are saying or doing, which could have very serious results: *It seems to be another public relations blunder by the government.* | *a series of management blunders* | **make a blunder** *She stopped, finally aware of the terrible blunder she had made.*

indiscretion /ˌɪndɪ'skreʃən/ [n C] a rather bad, silly, or immoral action by someone, especially someone in a public position – often used to make the action seem less bad **youthful indiscretion** *He dismissed his past association with racist groups as a youthful indiscretion.* | **commit an indiscretion** *She confessed that she had committed a minor sexual indiscretion.*

4 a silly mistake that causes social embarrassment

- put your foot in it
- faux pas
- gaffe

put your foot in it especially British **/put your foot in your mouth** especially American /ˌpʊt jɔːʳ 'fʊt ɪn ɪt, pʊt jɔːʳ ˌfʊt ɪn jɔːʳ 'maʊθ/ [v phrase] informal to make a stupid mistake by saying something that you should not say, for example because it upsets someone or because it is a secret: *She's a little weird isn't she? Oh no, have I put my foot in my mouth? Is she a friend of yours?* | *Simon wanted to finish the conversation before he put his foot in it any further.*

faux pas /ˌfəʊ 'pɑ:, 'fəʊ pɑ:/ [n C] a mistake made by saying or doing something in a social situation that embarrasses other people: *I asked her how Greg was, which was a bit of a faux pas considering they'd just split up.* | **commit/make a faux pas** *It was at that party that I committed the faux pas of spilling wine all over the host's wife.*

gaffe /gæf/ [n C] an embarrassing and stupid mistake made in a social situation or in public: *When she realized she had mistaken him for his brother, she was horrified at her gaffe.* | **make a gaffe** *The minister is well known for making gaffes in his speeches.*

5 to make a mistake

- make a mistake
- get sth wrong
- go wrong
- slip up
- blunder
- goof/goof up
- misjudge
- fall into the trap of doing sth

make a mistake /ˌmeɪk ə mɪ'steɪk/ [v phrase] *My spoken Spanish was okay, but I kept making mis-*

takes in my written work. | *Don't worry – everyone makes mistakes.*

get sth wrong /ˌget (sth) ˈrɒŋ‖-ˈrɔːŋ/ [v phrase] especially spoken to make a mistake in something that you do, say, or write, especially when this has bad or annoying results: *I've been here a year now, and my boss still gets my name wrong!* | *You've got your facts wrong, mate – he doesn't work here any more.* | **get it wrong** (=deal with something in the wrong way) *Once again, the government has got it wrong.*

go wrong /ˌgəʊ ˈrɒŋ‖-ˈrɔːŋ/ [v phrase] to make a mistake at a particular stage in a process, for example, with the result that the whole thing is spoiled: *Check your work again and see if you can spot where you went wrong.* | *If you follow the easy step-by-step instructions, you really can't go wrong.*

slip up /ˌslɪp ˈʌp/ [phr v I] to make a careless mistake, especially so that you lose some advantage, or spoil a chance that you had: *We'll just have to hope that the other teams slip up.* | **+ on** *He slipped up on just one detail.*

blunder /ˈblʌndəʳ/ [v I] to make a stupid mistake, usually with very serious results: *The government later admitted it had blundered in its handling of the affair.* | *He realized he had blundered by picking such an experienced player for the team.*

goof/goof up /guːf, ˌguːf ˈʌp/ [v I] American informal to make a silly mistake: *You really goofed up this time!* | *Some drivers admit they goofed. Others blame anyone except themselves.*

misjudge /mɪsˈdʒʌdʒ/ [v T] to make a mistake about a person, situation, or amount by wrongly thinking that they are one thing when in fact they are another: *I'm sorry – it seems I've misjudged you.* | *It's easy to misjudge the speed of a car heading toward you.* | *In fact, the US generals had seriously misjudged the determination and endurance of the North Vietnamese.*

fall into the trap of doing sth /ˌfɔːl ɪntə ðə ˌtræp əv ˈduːɪŋ (sth)/ [v phrase] to do something that seems good at the time but is not sensible: *Don't fall into the trap of trying to be too clever.* | *It is very easy for the mother to fall into the trap of offering the child only food that she knows the child likes.*

mix

RELATED WORDS

- to make a mistake and think that one thing or person is another *see* **confused**
- consisting of people or things of different kinds *see* **various/of different kinds**
- *see also* **pure**

1 to mix substances or liquids together

- mix
- combine
- stir
- beat
- blend
- whisk
- dilute

mix /mɪks/ [v T] to **mix** different liquids or substances together so that they can no longer be separated **mix sth and sth** *You can make green by mixing blue and yellow paint.* | **mix sth together** *Mix all the ingredients together in a large bowl.* | *If these two chemicals are mixed together, they will explode.* | **mix sth with sth** *Concrete is made by mixing gravel with sand, cement, and water.*

combine /kəmˈbaɪn/ [v T] to mix different substances or liquids together thoroughly in order to produce a new substance or liquid **combine sth and sth** *Combine the egg yolks and the cream, and cook over a low heat.* | **combine sth with sth** *Steel is produced by combining iron with carbon.* | *To maintain a constant standard, some wine producers combine this year's wine with stocks from the previous year.*

stir /stɜːʳ/ [v T] to mix things by moving them around in a container with a spoon or a stick: *Stir the paint to make sure that the colours are thoroughly mixed.* | **stir sth into sth** *I watched him as he stirred sugar into his coffee.* | **stir in sth/stir sth in** *When the butter has melted, stir in the soy sauce and ginger.* | *Add the grated cheese to the sauce and stir it in.*

beat /biːt/ [v T] to mix liquids or soft substances together when you are preparing food, with quick, strong movements of a fork, spoon, or special machine: *Carry on beating the eggs with a fork until they're light and fluffy.* | **beat sth together** *In a separate bowl, beat together the oil and flour.* | **beat sth into sth** *Beat the cream into the fruit puree, pour into bowls, and chill.*

blend /blend/ [v T] to mix liquids or soft substances when you are preparing food, in order to make one smooth substance, using something such as a fork or special machine: *Blend the sugar, eggs, and flour.* | **blend sth together** *The ingredients should be blended together until they are smooth.* | **blend sth into sth** *Beat the egg yolks with 2 tablespoons of water and blend them into the white sauce.*

whisk /wɪsk/ [v T] to mix foods that are soft or liquid very quickly so that air is mixed in, especially using a fork or special tool: *Whisk the eggs and sugar in a bowl over a pan of hot water.* | **whisk sth together** *He whisked the butter and eggs together, wondering if this was the right way to make an omelette.*

dilute /daɪˈluːt/ [v T] to mix a liquid with water in order to make it weaker: *For babies, dilute the fruit juice with at least the same amount of water.* | **dilute sth with sth** *Concentrated bleach can be diluted with water.*

2 to become mixed

- mix
- combine
- mingle

mix /mɪks/ [v I] *Oil and water do not mix.* | *After a short time the oxygen and the nitrogen molecules will start to mix.* | **+ with** *A heater introduces warm air to mix with incoming cold air.*

combine /kəmˈbaɪn/ [v I] if two or more substances or liquids **combine**, they mix to produce a new substance: *When the two chemicals combine, they form an explosive compound.* | **+ with** *Greenhouse gases combine with hydrocarbons to form smog.*

mingle /ˈmɪŋgəl/ [v I] if two or more liquids, smells, sounds etc **mingle**, they mix but can still be recognized separately: *The noise was tremendous; bombs, guns, and engines mingled in discordant sound.* | **+ with** *The smell of the sea mingled with the faint scent of the grass.* | *Water spread across the floor in a greasy stream, mingling with the pile of filthy rubbish.*

3 substances that have been mixed together

- mixture
- combination
- compound
- solution

mixture /ˈmɪkstʃəʳ/ [n C] several different liquids or substances that have been mixed together: *Place all the ingredients in a bowl and beat them until the mixture is smooth.* | *The car runs on a special ether-alcohol mixture that won't work in an ordinary engine.* | **+ of** *A special mixture of peat and soil is used for growing bonsai trees.*

combination /ˌkɒmbəˈneɪʃən‖ˌkɑːm-/ [n C] a mixture of different substances, colours etc that are used together: *Banana, orange juice, and cream may seem an odd combination, but together they make a delicious drink.* | **+ of** *The sweater is made of a combination of natural and synthetic fibres.*

compound /ˈkɒmpaʊnd‖ˈkɑːm-/ [n C] a mixture of two or more chemical substances that combine to produce a single substance with qualities that are different from the original substances – use this in scientific or technical contexts: *The soil was tested to make sure that it was free from ammonia or any other nitrogen compound.* | **chemical compound** *Sulphur dioxide and carbon dioxide are two common chemical compounds.*

solution /səˈluːʃən/ [n C] a liquid that has something mixed in with it – use this in scientific contexts: *Make a salt solution by dissolving 9 tablespoonfuls of cooking salt in a pint of water.* | *We are now going to measure the boiling points of the different solutions.*

4 mixed untidily together

- mixed up
- jumbled/jumbled up/jumbled together
- tangled

mixed up /ˌmɪkst ˈʌp◂/ [adj] things such as papers, clothes, or objects that are **mixed up** are put together untidily when they do not belong together, or are in the wrong order: *The drawer was full of mixed up bits of paper, old letters, and photographs.* | *The tapes are a bit mixed up, but it shouldn't take too long to sort them out.*

jumbled/jumbled up/jumbled together /ˈdʒʌmbəld, ˌdʒʌmbəld ˈʌp, ˌdʒʌmbəld təˈgeðəʳ/ [adj] things such as papers, books, clothes etc that are **jumbled** are mixed together very untidily, especially in a pile, so that it is difficult to find anything: *A jumbled collection of clothes lay on the floor.* | *The rucksack contains several pockets to prevent odds and ends getting jumbled up.* | *a drawer full of letters all jumbled together*

tangled /ˈtæŋgəld/ [adj] hair, grass, string etc that is **tangled** is mixed up and difficult to separate: *He ran a hand through his tangled hair.* | *The concrete highway was edged with tangled dry grass.*

5 to mix ideas, feelings, styles etc

- combine
- be a mixture of sth and sth
- bring together
- blend
- mingle
- merge

combine /kəmˈbaɪn/ [v T] to have different qualities or feelings at the same time, or to do very different activities at the same time **combine sth with sth** *This is a computer system that combines maximum flexibility with absolute accuracy.* | **combine sth and sth** *He designed the first great suspension bridge, an idea that combines beauty and function perfectly.*

be a mixture of sth and sth /biː ə ˈmɪkstʃər əv (sth) ən (sth)/ [v phrase] to contain different features or ideas, mixed together: *Her work is a mixture of classical and modern styles.* | *Billy's voice was a mixture of apprehension and indignation.*

bring together /ˌbrɪŋ təˈgeðəʳ/ [phr v T] if you **bring together** two or more elements, ideas, or characteristics, you mix them so that they can be seen at the same time: *It is a marvellous book, which brings together all the necessary elements of romance and adventure.* | *These opposing views should be brought together in a single paragraph, to form the conclusion to your essay.*

blend /blend/ [v T] if a piece of work, a film, a book etc **blends** two or more features or characteristics, it mixes them successfully **blend sth and sth** *The ballet company's repertoire blends tradition and creative innovation.* | **blend sth with sth** *Her first novel successfully blends a sense of innocence with overwhelming bitterness.*

mingle /ˈmɪŋgəl/ [v T] to show two very different characteristics or feelings at the same time, mixing them together: *Heraklion mingles traditional charm with a bustling centre of pavement cafes and shops.* | **mingle sth with sth** *Mingling genuine news with gossip, she made a lively companion.*

merge /mɜːʳdʒ/ [v T] to combine or join two things together to form one thing **merge sth with sth** *The library profession is merging new techniques with old to produce an unbeatable combination of management skills.*

6 a mixture of different people, qualities, ideas etc

- mixture
- combination
- mix
- blend
- a cross between sth and sth
- fusion
- hybrid

mixture /ˈmɪkstʃəʳ/ [n singular] *The house behind us was a strange architectural mixture.* | **+ of** *He looked at her with a mixture of admiration and curiosity.* | *A long French liner slipped majestically by with a mixture of European and Asian faces staring curiously from the decks.*

combination /ˌkɒmbəˈneɪʃən‖ˌkɑːm-/ [n C] a mixture of different ideas, problems etc happening together, or different people working together, which has a particular effect **+ of** *Our problems were due to a combination of bad management and lack of experience.* | *Their music is an odd combination of jazz and opera.* | **a good/bad/successful/disastrous etc combination** *They were a perfect combination – Anton as chef and Guy as restaurant manager.* | **a winning combination** (=a very successful combination) *If all the team are playing well, then don't change a winning combination.*

mix /mɪks/ [n singular] a mixture of different qualities or of different types of people **+ of** *The market square is a fascinating mix of ancient and modern.* | *She went to New York, where she began to meet a different mix of people – artists, designers, and art collectors.*

blend /blend/ [n singular] a mixture of different qualities or characteristics that combine successfully **+ of** *The England team is a good side, with a nice blend of experience and youthful energy.* | *Sometimes he seems to be an extraordinary blend of artist, poet and businessman.*

a cross between sth and sth /ə ˈkrɒs bɪtwiːn (sth) ən (sth) ‖-ˈkrɔːs-/ [n phrase] something that is **a cross between** one thing and another is a mixture of the two different things: *The expression on Paul's face was a cross between amusement and disbelief.* | *It's difficult to describe my job. I suppose I'm a cross between a secretary and a translator.* | *The use of chemical fertilizers has turned the farmer into a cross between an industrial chemist and a mechanic.*

fusion /ˈfjuːʒən/ [n singular] something such as a style of art or writing that is produced by combining different ideas, styles, qualities etc **+ of** *The film is a fusion of history and contemporary events.* | *His philosophy is a fusion of intellect and spiritual belief.*

hybrid /ˈhaɪbrɪ̣d/ [n C] something that is a mixture of two or more things, especially a plant that is produced from different types of plants **+ of** *a foodcrop that is a hybrid of wheat and rye* | *The new constitution was a hybrid of presidential and parliamentary systems.* | **a hybrid system/approach/method etc** *a hybrid approach combining the merits of both methods*

7 different emotions that are mixed together

- mixed
- combined
- mingled

mixed /mɪkst/ [adj] *Reactions to the announcement were somewhat mixed.* | **have mixed feelings/emotions** *The other girls had mixed feelings, some of them were happy for me but some were jealous.* | *Many new step-parents will admit to having mixed emotions about their new family.*

combined /kəmˈbaɪnd/ [adj] showing two very different feelings or emotions at the same time: *He had an air of combined gloom and relief.* | **+ with** *Their relief that war had been avoided was combined with sadness at what they had lost.*

mingled /ˈmɪŋgəld/ [adj] mixed, but still felt or shown as separate emotions: *The mingled emotions that haunted his mind were reflected in his eyes.* | **+ with** *As I spoke his expression was one of amazement mingled with fury.*

8 when different things do not mix well

- do not mix
- incompatible
- do not go well together

do not mix /ˌduː nɒt ˈmɪks/ [v phrase] if two different kinds of behaviour or activity **do not mix**, you cannot successfully continue with both of them at the same time: *People having affairs at work often find that business and romance don't mix.* | **+ with** *Heavy drinking does not mix with a successful family life.*

incompatible /ˌɪnkəmˈpætɪ̣bəl/ [adj] if two things or people are **incompatible**, they cannot easily exist together, work together, or live together: *The centre gives advice to women who find the demands of marriage and work incompatible.* | *After we got married, we realized we were completely incompatible.* | **+ with** *These computers are incompatible with our present system.*

do not go well together /ˌduː nɒt gəʊ ˈwel təˌgeðəʳ/ [v phrase] if two ideas, characteristics etc **do not go well together**, they do not mix easily or well: *In the experience of many European countries, socialism and religion do not go well together.*

moderate

RELATED WORDS

opposite: ———— **extreme**

1 moderate beliefs, opinions etc

- moderate
- middle-of-the-road
- middle ground
- the centre

moderate /ˈmɒdərɪ̣t‖ˈmɑː-/ [adj] having opinions or beliefs, especially about politics, that are not extreme and that most people consider reasonable or sensible: *The new church leaders are more moderate in their plans for reform.* | *The party's moderate leadership wants open relations with the West.* | *Moderate socialists believe in democratic reform rather than revolution.*

middle-of-the-road /ˌmɪdl əv ðə ˈrəʊd◂/ [adj] not including any extreme or important changes, and keeping to ordinary, safe political aims, especially in order to avoid criticism, opposition, or risk: *He made a direct appeal to middle-of-the-road voters.* | *Lee described her politics as 'middle-of-the-road.'*

middle ground /ˌmɪdl ˈgraʊnd/ [n singular] the area of political opinion that most people agree about, even if they support different political parties: *The health care proposal holds the middle ground, and reformers hope it will gain support.* | **find a middle ground** *This issue is so important the two parties are going to have to find a middle ground.* | **occupy the middle ground** (=support the opinions of the middle ground) *The Social Democrats wanted to occupy the middle ground between the Conservative and Labor parties in Britain.*

the centre British **/the center** American /ðə ˈsentəʳ/ [n singular] the area of political opinion between the opinions of the more extreme political parties: *The party has moved towards the centre in recent years.* | **centre-right/centre-left** (=having qualities of both the center and the right or left in politics) *He will require the backing of the center-left in order to advance his center-right agenda.*

2 a person who has moderate beliefs, opinions etc

- moderate

moderate /ˈmɒdərɪ̣t‖ˈmɑː-/ [n C] someone who has **moderate** opinions or beliefs, especially political ones: *A moderate was chosen as the new leader of the right-of-center party.* | *The government's new reforms have been generally well received by the moderates.*

modern

RELATED WORDS

opposite: ———— **old-fashioned**

- using the newest technology or methods *see* **advanced**
- *see also* **new, fashionable/not fashionable**

1 modern machines/buildings/methods

- modern
- the latest
- up-to-date
- futuristic
- state of the art

modern /ˈmɒdn‖ˈmɑːdərn/ [adj] using new methods, designs, or equipment: *Seattle has a very modern public transportation system.* | *The company occupies a bright, modern office building in the heart of the city.* | *Many criticisms have been made of modern farming methods.* | *the horrors of modern warfare*

the latest /ðə ˈleɪtɪst/ [adj only before noun] **the latest** machines, computers, and methods are the newest and best ones that are available: *The car is equipped with all the latest gadgets.* | *The latest model can print 15 pages every minute.* | **the latest in sth** (=the newest type of something) *You'll have a chance to try out the latest in kitchen equipment.* | **the very latest** *The operation will be performed using the very latest microsurgery techniques.*

up-to-date /ˌʌp tə ˈdeɪt◂/ [adj] **up-to-date** equipment, machines, or methods are very modern, and much better than the ones that many other people or organizations are still using: *The hospital has the most up-to-date equipment in Europe.* | *up-to-date training methods*

futuristic /ˌfjuːtʃəˈrɪstɪk◂/ [adj] something that is **futuristic** seems typical of things that will exist in the future, and often seems very exciting and unusual: *The futuristic sports stadium is the pride of the city.* | *The car, with its sleek futuristic styling, certainly looks impressive.*

state of the art /ˌsteɪt əv ði ˈɑːʳt◂/ [adj only before noun] use this about machines, buildings etc that use the most modern designs, methods, technology etc: *The company recently moved to their new state-of-the-art building in central London.* | *Using state-of-the-art technology, scientists are able to pinpoint the exact age of archaeological finds.* | *Her latest indulgence is a luxury state-of-the-art yacht that she keeps at St Tropez.*

2 modern art/literature/music/fashion

- modern
- contemporary
- the latest
- avant-garde

modern /ˈmɒdn‖ˈmɑːdərn/ [adj] **modern** art, literature, music etc uses styles that have been developed very recently and are deliberately different from traditional ones: *I like both modern dance and classical ballet.* | *Your work was my first route into an understanding of modern art.*

contemporary /kənˈtempərəri, -pəri‖-pəreri/ [adj only before noun] **contemporary** art, music, literature etc was produced or written recently: *Composers like Philip Glass have made contemporary music more popular.* | *I'm not very impressed by the works of many contemporary artists.*

the latest /ðə ˈleɪtɪst/ [adj only before noun] **the latest** fashion, style, design etc is the one that is the most modern and the most fashionable **the latest fashion** *She assured me that big sweaters were the latest fashion.* | **the latest in sth** (=the most fashionable type of something) *They stock the latest in designer footwear.*

avant-garde /ˌævɔːŋˈgɑːʳd◂‖ ˌævɑːŋ-/ [adj] **avant-garde** art, music, literature etc is extremely modern and often strange or hard to understand because it is very different from previous styles: *Although she likes avant-garde music, Lydia also plays classical guitar and piano.* | *His paintings are rather too avant-garde for my tastes.* | *an exhibition of work by avant-garde artists and sculptors*

3 modern ideas/ways of thinking

- modern
- progressive
- forward-looking
- go-ahead
- move/change with the times

modern /ˈmɒdn‖ˈmɑːdərn/ [adj] having new ideas or attitudes, rather than traditional or old-fashioned ones: *They're a very modern couple – he stays at home with the kids and she goes out to work.* | *The school is very modern in its approach to sex education.*

progressive /prəˈgresɪv/ [adj] using new methods to educate or bring up children, deal with social problems etc, especially when these methods are less strict than traditional ones: *She went to a progressive private school where the pupils could choose which lessons to attend.* | *the government's progressive policies for dealing with inner city problems*

forward-looking /ˈfɔːʳwəʳd lʊkɪŋ/ [adj] willing to use new and recently developed methods and ideas: *We like to think we're a forward-looking company that isn't afraid to use new ideas.* | *We need more forward-looking political thinking.*

go-ahead /ˈgəʊ əˌhed/ [adj only before noun] British always keen to use modern ideas and methods because you want to be successful: *Fortuna is a young, go-ahead computer company based in Düsseldorf.*

move/change with the times /ˌmuːv, ˌtʃeɪndʒ wɪð ðə ˈtaɪmz/ [v phrase] to change your way of living or working so that you are using modern ideas, methods etc, even though you may not want to: *I'm not keen on having a mobile phone, but I suppose we must all move with the times.* | *This is a town that has changed with the times and now provides every vacation facility you could wish for.*

4 to make something more modern

- update
- modernize
- bring sth up to date

update /ˌʌpˈdeɪt/ [v T] to improve something, so that it includes the most modern equipment, methods, or information: *The school has just updated all its computer equipment.* | *Nursing staff were sent on training courses to update their skills.*

modernize ALSO **modernise** British /ˈmɒdənaɪz‖ˈmɑːdər-/ [v T] to make big changes to a place or organization, by putting in modern equipment or modern systems, and getting rid of old ones: *It was an old farmhouse that had been modernized by the previous owner.* | *Our aim was to modernize the health service, and we succeeded.*

bring sth up to date /ˌbrɪŋ (sth) ʌp tə ˈdeɪt/ [v phrase] to get rid of any old-fashioned details or features that something has and add the newest ones that are available: *The system needs bringing up to date.* | *All the history textbooks we use have been revised and brought up to date.*

modest

RELATED WORDS

opposite: ——— **proud, boast, show off**

▸ *see also* **shy**

1 a modest person

▸ **modest** ▸ **humble**
▸ **self-effacing** ▸ **unpretentious**
▸ **unassuming**

modest /ˈmɒdɪ̈st‖ˈmɑː-/ [adj] unwilling to talk about your abilities or achievements and to say that you are good at something, even when you are: *Luke was too modest to talk about his past achievements.* | *She was a shy, modest person, never one to push herself forward.* —**modestly** [adv] *'I couldn't have done it without your help,' Alec replied modestly.*

self-effacing /ˌself ɪˈfeɪsɪŋ/ [adj] formal not wanting to talk about yourself or to attract attention: *Her husband was a quiet, self-effacing man who spent much of his time in his study.* | *In those days women were expected to be quiet, passive and self-effacing.*

unassuming /ˌʌnəˈsjuːmɪŋ◂, -ˈsuː-‖-ˈsuː-/ [adj] not wanting to be noticed and not expecting to be treated in a special way, because you do not think you are important: *I often see her in the library. She's such a nice, unassuming person.* | *By now Chapman was famous, but on a social level he remained as unassuming as ever.*

humble /ˈhʌmbəl/ [adj] thinking that you are unimportant and not as good or clever as other people, and therefore not expecting to be treated in a special way: *Their father was a genuinely humble man, who had worked hard for his family all his life.* | *Stephanie was humble enough to admit that others could probably do the job better than she could.* —**humbly** [adv] *'What do you think I should do?' Lydia asked humbly.*

unpretentious /ˌʌnprɪˈtenʃəs◂/ [adj] not trying to seem better than other people, even if you are rich, famous, clever etc: *Umbria is a wonderful region, where life is simple and the people are unpretentious country folk.* | *Jilly was surprised by how pleasant and unpretentious he was. Not like a big star at all.*

2 to be too modest

▸ **put/run yourself down** ▸ **underestimate yourself**
▸ **sell yourself short**

put/run yourself down /ˌpʊt, ˌrʌn jɔːʳself ˈdaʊn/ [v phrase] to tell people that you are less good, skilful etc than you really are: *He puts himself down, but he's really very gifted.* | *You know you're a good teacher. Don't run yourself down all the time.*

sell yourself short /ˌsel jɔːʳself ˈʃɔːʳt/ [v phrase] informal to not tell people enough about your skills, ability etc, especially in a situation where other people are deciding whether to offer you a job or choose you for something: *If you sell yourself short at the interview, you'll never get the job. Let them know how good you are.* | *You're brilliant at tennis – don't sell yourself short.*

underestimate yourself /ˌʌndərˈestɪ̈meɪt jɔːʳself/ [v phrase] to believe that you are less clever, good, skilful etc than you really are: *Don't underestimate yourself – you can easily win.* | *I think you underestimate yourself when you say you couldn't cope with a job like this.*

3 modest behaviour

▸ **modesty** ▸ **humility**

modesty /ˈmɒdɪ̈sti‖ˈmɑː-/ [n U] a modest way of behaving or talking: *His honesty and modesty endeared him to many people who valued his wise advice.* | *'I'm a bank manager,' she said, then added with typical modesty, 'of a very small bank.'* | **false modesty** (=when sb only pretends to be modest) *Miranda was not one for false modesty. She enjoyed being told that she was beautiful.*

humility /hjuːˈmɪlɪ̈ti/ [n U] when someone is not proud, and does not think that they are more important, clever etc than other people: *As I listened to him speak, I was filled with a sense of humility.* | *Mother Theresa remained a woman of great humility, despite all the attention and praise her work received.*

money

RELATED WORDS

▸ someone who wants a lot of money *see* **greedy**
▸ to have just enough money to live *see* **survive**
▸ *see also* **rich, poor, profit, earn, owe, cost, spend money/time, pay, sell, buy, expensive, cheap, free**

1 money

▸ **money** ▸ **dosh**
▸ **cash** ▸ **dough**

money /ˈmʌni/ [n U] what you use to buy things, what you earn by working etc: *We don't have enough money for a vacation this year.* | *I haven't got any money, if that's what you're after.* | *Do you think these trainers are worth the extra money?* | **money to do sth/money for sth** (=money you can use to pay for something) *Dad, can I have some money to buy some new jeans?* | *If she's got money to run a car, how come she gets the bus every day?* | *Shall I give you some money for petrol?* | **spend (your) money (on sth)** *I spend far too much money on Christmas presents.* | *Don't spend all your money on sweets.* | **save money** (=not spend much money) *'Are you coming out with us on Saturday?' 'No, I'm trying to save money.'* | **waste (your) money (on sth)** (=spend money on things you do not really need) *She wastes an awful lot of money on expensive clothes.* | *We're wasting public money, which would be better spent on improving the service we offer.* | **a waste of money** *Critics have described the project as 'a complete waste of money'.* | *Gillian said not to get any flowers – she thinks it's a waste of money.* | **good money** informal (=when the amount of money you earn or pay for something is quite large) *I enjoy the work, and I make good money.* | *You have to pay good money for a pedigree dog.*

cash /kæʃ/ [n U] money, especially money that is available for you to spend: *I don't have much cash at the moment. Could I pay you next week?* | *She earns extra cash by working as a waitress.* | *The Health Authority says that it simply has no extra cash from its £136 million budget.*

dosh /dɒʃ‖dɑːʃ/ [n U] British informal money: *He gave us loads of dosh, just for handing out leaflets.* | *He says* *if we don't come up with the dosh by Sunday, he's selling the car to someone else.*

dough /dəʊ/ [n U] informal money, especially a lot of money: *He only married her for her dough.* | *I'd go on vacation three times a year too, if I had his dough!*

2 money in the form of coins or notes

- money
- change
- cash

money /ˈmʌni/ [n U] *Whose money is this on the table?* | *I've left some money in the pot for your bus fare.* | *The thieves repeatedly demanded money and jewellery.* | **the right money** British (=the exact amount of money something costs) *This machine does not give change. Please have the right money ready.*

cash /kæʃ/ [n U] money – use this to emphasize that you mean coins and notes, and not cheques, bank cards etc: *Thieves stole a large amount of cash, and jewellery worth £50,000.* | **in cash** *Do you have a couple of dollars in cash?* | *I'll write you a cheque, and you can pay me back in cash later.* | **pay cash** (=to pay someone using notes and coins, rather than a cheque, credit card etc) *Are you paying cash for these items?* | *I heard she paid cash for her house back in the sixties.*

change /tʃeɪndʒ/ [n U] money in the form of coins, or the money you get back when you pay for something with more money than it cost: *I hope you've got some change for the bus, because I haven't.* | *Check your change* (=make sure you have been given the right amount) *before leaving the shop.* | **loose change** *I've got £20 and a bit of loose change as well.* | **small change** (=coins of low value) *You'll need some small change for the telephone.* | **the wrong change** (=when the amount of money you are given in change is incorrect) *Excuse me, I think you've given me the wrong change.* | **change for sth** (=lower value coins or notes in exchange for a coin or note of a higher value) *Does anyone have change for a five dollar bill?* | **$4/£2 etc in change** (=in the form of coins) *I've got a £10 note and about £5 in change.* | **exact change** (=the exact amount of money something costs) *This toll booth is for drivers with exact change only.*

3 the money that is used in a country

- currency
- money

currency /ˈkʌrənsi‖ˈkɜːr-/ [n C/U] the particular type of money that is used in a country: *Investors continued to swap yen for the currencies of nations that offer higher interest rates.* | *The dollar is now the overwhelming world currency.* | **French/Italian/US etc currency** *We soon got used to using Italian currency.* | **foreign currency** *Local banks give better rates for converting your traveler's checks into foreign currency.* | **local currency** *What's the local currency in Malta?* | **hard currency** (=a currency that keeps its value in relation to other currencies, and is used for international payments) *A lot of the food grown in Mexico is exported to earn hard currency.* | **single currency** (=the common currency used in many European Union countries) *You can argue about the single currency but you can't opt out of the European Single Market.*

money /ˈmʌni/ [n U] **French/Japanese etc money** *He put the Italian money in a separate billfold.* | *You can get a good exchange rate for German money at the moment.*

4 an amount of money

- amount
- figure
- sum

amount /əˈmaʊnt/ [n C/U] the money that something costs, is paid etc: *Work out the amount you spend each month on food and clothes.* | *He expects to spend a similar amount on getting his daughter through college.* | *He was fined $300,000, an amount that would ruin the average householder.* | **amount of money** *We spent an astonishing amount of money in town today.* | *The judge reduced the amount of money awarded to the victim.* | **small/large/considerable amount** *She has a pension, and receives a small amount from her ex-husband.* | **the full amount** (=all the money that someone owes, must pay etc) *You must pay the full amount in advance.* | **undisclosed amount** (=when someone does not say what the amount was) *Heinz Co. acquired the ailing food company for an undisclosed amount.*

sum /sʌm/ [n C] an amount of money – use this to say how large or small an amount is: *They are asking $40 for the new software, almost twice the sum it costs when bought via the Internet.* | **sum of money** *My uncle left me a small sum of money when he died.* | **sum of $100,000/£400 etc** *He offered to purchase the estate for the sum of $80,000.* | **large/small/considerable/enormous etc sum** *Stars like Chaplin earned $2000 a week, which was an enormous sum in those days.* | *Apple has spent huge sums in its drive to penetrate new markets.* | *She puts away small sums of money when she can afford to.* | *The store chain has been forced to pay hefty sums* (=a very large amount) *to female employees after it was sued for discrimination.* | **lump sum** (=an amount of money given in a single payment) *You can receive your bonus in monthly instalments, or as a lump sum.* | *a lump-sum payment* | **undisclosed sum** (=when someone does not say what the amount was) *The case was settled for an undisclosed sum last year.* | **princely sum** (=used to emphasize how small an amount is, when you think it should be bigger) *She and the other workers received the princely sum of $14 for the evening's work.*

figure /ˈfɪgəʳ‖ˈfɪgjər/ [n C] a particular amount of money that is stated or written down: *'We need $30,000 to get the project started.' 'How close are you to that figure?'* | *A comparison of the two figures shows the estimated profit on investment.* | **row/column of figures** (=a list of figures written one below the other) *Add up that row of figures, and transfer the full amount to the top of the next page.* | **a four-/five-/six-etc figure number** (=a number in the thousands, ten thousands, hundred thousands etc) *What's the point of a six-figure salary and no time to enjoy it?* | **final figure** (=the amount of money after everything has been added up) *The event raised $400,000 for charity, but that is not the final figure as donations are still coming in.*

5 a large amount of money

- a lot of money
- a bomb
- a fortune
- big money

a lot of money /ə ˌlɒt əv ˈmʌni‖-ˌlɑːt-/ [n phrase] a large amount of money: *The painting was sold for £20,000 in 1926, which was a lot of money in those days.* | **spend/pay/make a lot of money** *I don't want to spend a lot of money on holiday.* | *I'd pay her a lot of money to organize my life for me.* | *Do you make a lot of money doing this?* | **cost a lot of money** (=to be expensive) *That hi-fi looks as though it cost a lot of money.* | *It'll cost a lot of money to have the roof fixed.* | **be worth a lot of money** *These will be worth a lot of money in 50 years' time or so.* | **have a lot of money** *They don't have a lot of money, but they live comfortably.* | **be a lot of money for sth** (=used to emphasize how expensive something is) *Two hundred and fifty dollars is a lot of money just for a new carpet.* | **a whole lot of money** American spoken (=used to emphasize how large an amount is) *They wanted to charge me a whole lot of money just to change my car insurance.*

a fortune /ə 'fɔːʳtʃən/ [n singular] informal a lot of money: *I thought you were going to tell me you'd won a fortune!* | **cost (sb) a fortune** *The lighting effects alone must have cost a fortune.* | *It costs an absolute fortune to park in town these days, you know.* | *You're costing me a fortune in coffee!* | **make/spend/pay a fortune** *I paid a fortune for this car, and I've had nothing but trouble with it.* | *Walter made a fortune with his first book.* | **be worth a fortune** *That house must be worth a fortune!* | **a small fortune** (=used to emphasize that the amount of money was surprising or unexpected) *She earned a small fortune selling antique furniture, and retired when she was 45.*

a bomb /ə 'bɒm‖-'bɑːm/ [n singular] British informal a very large amount of money **cost (sb) a bomb** *It was lovely and I wanted it – the only problem was, it cost a bomb.* | **make/earn etc a bomb** *He's been earning a bomb repairing computers at home for people.* | *You won't make a bomb, but it's worth doing.* | **be worth a bomb** *The house is worth a bomb at today's prices.*

big money /ˌbɪg 'mʌni/ [n U] informal a large amount of money, especially money that is earned or paid in business: *He's hoping there's big money in this new business.* | *I'm making big money these days.* | *The investors are talking big money. At least $100,000.*

6 all the money that a person, company etc has

- money
- means
- assets
- finances
- savings
- resources

money /'mʌni/ [n U] *My grandmother left me all her money when she died.* | *The committee is meeting to discuss how the money should be spent this year.* | **make your money** (=earn all your money doing a particular type of business) *He had made his money as a butcher in Kingstown.*

means /miːnz/ [n plural] formal all the money that you have – especially when you are talking about whether you are able to pay for everything you need **have the means to do sth** *He had the means to pay, but he refused on principle.* | **beyond your means** (=costing more than you can afford) *I think private schooling would be well beyond our means.* | *She's been living beyond her means* (=spending more than she can really afford to), *and now the debts have caught her up.* | **within your means** (=not costing more than you can afford) *She was required to pay a $500 fee, which appeared to be within her means.* | *Money isn't a problem. We simply live within our means* (=do not spend more than we can afford to). | **private/independent means** (=money that someone has from property, investments etc rather than earning it by working) *He's given up his lecturing job, but he does have private means.* | *Many tropical countries welcome people of independent means as long-term residents.* | **limited/modest means** (=used to say that someone only has a small amount of money) *The best choice for elderly people with limited means is index-linked certificates.* | *A university professor who used his modest means to collect over 300 valuable artworks has donated them to the National Gallery.* | **means test** (=an official check to find out whether someone is poor enough to need money from the state) *The Council is introducing means tests for housing tenants.*

assets /'æsets/ [n plural] all of the money and property that a company or person owns, and which they may sell or use if necessary: *On her death, she wants all her assets to go to her husband.* | **assets of $1 billion/£300,000,000 etc** *With assets of just under $1 million, the business is still relatively small.* | **$1billion/£300,000,000 etc in assets** *Massachusetts Financial Services manages $43 billion in assets.* | **financial assets** *Tomorrow, the court will hear evidence relating to Simpson's financial assets.* | **personal assets** (=owned by an individual, rather than a company) *The directors' personal assets will not be at risk if the company does fold.*

finances /'faɪnænsɪ̈z, fɪ̈'nænsɪ̈z‖fɪ̈'nænsɪ̈z, 'faɪnænsɪ̈z/ [n plural] all the money that a person, company, organization etc has, especially when this is regularly checked so they know about any changes in it: *An accountant handles the school's finances.* | *She wondered if they'd ever get all their bills paid and their finances in order.* | **family/personal finances** *An investigation into his personal finances produced no evidence of fraud* | *To help the family finances, she went back to work at a retail store after William was born.* | **public/government finances** *Indeed, Lebanon's public finances and yawning trade deficit, do look depressing.* | *Government finances are strained to the hilt, dealing with essential services.* | **drain sb's finances/be a drain on sb's finances** (=to reduce someone's finances over a period of time, usually by an amount they cannot afford to lose) *Legal expenses had drained his finances, and he could no longer afford to pursue the case.* | *Many of the housing agencies represent a severe drain on the state's finances.*

savings /'seɪvɪŋz/ [n plural] the money which you have saved, which is usually kept in a bank or some other financial institution: *Your savings are safe with the Bank of America.* | *I should just take the money out of my savings and pay off my credit card.* | *Since we retired we've been living on our savings and a small pension.* | **life savings** (=all of the money you have saved) *He had invested his life savings in the new business.* | **retirement savings** (=the money you have saved so that you have something to live on when you retire) *Break yourself of the habit of borrowing from your retirement savings.* | **lose your savings** *Investors lost their savings, and some businessmen went bankrupt.* | **sink your savings into something** (=to spend all the money you have saved on a particular investment, plan etc) *He and his wife July sank their life savings into an unsuccessful attempt to build a marina on a reservoir in Colorado.*

resources /rɪ'zɔːsɪz, -'sɔːs-‖'riːsɔːrsɪ̈z/ [n plural] all the money, property, or goods that a company, organization, or country owns and that can be used to make more money or to provide services: *We have to make the best use of the resources we've got.* | **financial/economic resources** *The government must make more human and financial resources available for AIDS research.* | **limited/scarce resources** (=used to say that the amount of money available is small) *With limited resources, the club cannot continue to function without donations from members.* | **allocate resources (to sth)** (=decide how much money will be spent on particular things) *The process for allocating resources to military intelligence is severely flawed.* | **devote resources (to sth)** (=to spend money on a particular thing) *Few firms devote significant resources to research and development.* | **pool your resources** (=share your money with other people, so that you can all use it) *She and I pooled our resources – not much – and hired a car for the weekend.*

7 money that you receive regularly

- income
- pension
- Social Security
- benefit
- welfare
- allowance
- pocket money

income /ˈɪŋkʌm, ˈɪn-/ [n C/U] all the money that someone receives regularly, for example from their job, from their savings or from the government: *I'd love to know what his income is. He has so many new clothes and such an expensive car.* | *We knew we'd need another source of income if we were planning to have a big family.* | *Couples with joint incomes over $50,000 are the fastest growing segment of the housing market.* | **income of $200/£400 etc** *The whole family survives on the mother's monthly income of less than £500.* | **low income** *If you are on a low income, you may be entitled to free dental treatment.* | **regular income** *She receives a regular income from the investments she made twenty years ago.* | **monthly/annual/weekly/yearly income** *The average annual income in Hong Kong is now much higher than it was in 1994.*

pension ALSO **retirement plan** American /ˈpenʃən, rɪˈtaɪəʳmənt plæn/ [n C] an amount of money that old people receive regularly from the government, their former employer, or from an insurance company, because they have paid in money to the government etc over many years: *I don't know how you manage on your pension, Lil, I really don't.* | *He gets a pretty good pension from his old firm.* | *The company has a very generous retirement plan.* | **state pension** (=a pension from the government) *If a man retires at 58, he's actually got seven years to go before he draws his state pension.* | **old-age pension** British (=a pension that people receive from the government when they reach a particular age) *The government is considering linking the old-age pension to earnings.* | **disability/invalidity pension** British (=a pension given to someone who cannot work because they are ill or injured) *He retired from the force with a disability pension.* | *Martin still hasn't got his invalidity pension sorted out.* | **pension plan** ALSO **pension scheme** British (=an arrangement to pay people a pension) *Is there a pension scheme where you work?* | **draw a pension** (=receive a pension, especially one from the government) *How long have you been drawing a pension?* | **live on a pension** (=when your pension is the only money you receive) *Living on a pension isn't easy you know. You really have to scrimp and save.*

Social Security /ˌsəʊʃəl sɪˈkjʊərɪ̈ti/ [n U] in the UK, money that the government gives to people who are ill, old, or unemployed. In the US, money from a government programme that workers pay into, which provides them with money when they are old or unable to work, or the programme itself: *Once I've paid for my rent and food, most of my Social Security is used up.* | *an increase in spending on Social Security and Medicare* | **Social Security benefits/payments** *The government faces strong opposition to its proposals to cut Social Security payments.* | **be/live on Social Security** *How'd you find it, living on Social Security?* | **Social Security number** *Can you write your Social Security number in the box please?*

benefit USUALLY **benefits** American /ˈbenɪ̈fɪt(s)/ [n C/U] money that people receive from the government if they have no job, do not earn a lot, or are sick: *There are several benefits you can claim if you are unemployed.* | *You should find out about any benefits you're entitled to.* | **housing benefit** (=regular payments towards your rent) *Surely she'll be eligible for housing benefit?* | **unemployment benefit** (=regular payments to people who do not have a job) *If you were fired from your previous job, you may not be able to claim unemployment benefit.* | **child benefit** British (=regular payments made to mothers of children under 16) *Child benefit has been frozen for the last three or four years.* | **be/live on benefit** British *Two-thirds of lone parents are on benefit.*

welfare /ˈwelfeəʳ/ [n U] American the money that is paid by the government to people without jobs: *The amount of money that the government spends on welfare has halved in the past decade.* | *Getting people off welfare and into paying jobs is a major national priority.* | **welfare benefits/payments** *Annabelle stopped getting welfare benefits when her husband landed a minimum-wage job.* | **be/live on welfare** (=to be receiving money from the government) *Raising the minimum wage might make it more difficult for people on welfare to get a job.*

allowance /əˈlaʊəns/ [n C] money that someone receives regularly for a special reason, and that they do not earn by working: *Some students have an allowance from their parents.* | **clothing allowance** (=money for buying clothes) *Does your mom give you a clothing allowance?* | **monthly/weekly/yearly allowance** *In exchange for looking after the children, Annie has all her meals paid for and receives a small monthly allowance.* | *I think my yearly allowance is about three hundred, you know, so I'm rapidly running out.*

pocket money British **/allowance** American /ˈpɒkɪ̈t ˌmʌni‖ˈpɑː-, əˈlaʊəns/ [n U] a small amount of money that children receive from their parents every week: *What do you spend your allowance on, Jimmy?* | *You'll pay for that vase out of your pocket money.*

8 money given to a student to pay for his or her education

- grant
- scholarship

grant /grɑːnt‖grænt/ [n C] money that the government gives to someone to help them pay for their education: *Will I get a grant, even though both my parents are earning?* | **student grant** *Without a student grant, I'd never even have gone into higher education.*

scholarship /ˈskɒləʳʃɪp‖ˈskɑː-/ [n C] money that a student received from their school, college etc to pay for their education, especially because they have passed a special examination: *The Foundation's goals include providing scholarships for gifted young students.* | *Admitted to Mills College on a full scholarship, she graduated Phi Beta Kappa without a penny of help from her parents.* | **college scholarship** *The company has a small number of college scholarships to offer to employees' children.* | **athletic/drama/music etc scholarship** (=a scholarship given to someone who is very good at sport, acting, music etc) *I attended the University of Houston on an athletic scholarship.* | *At 9, he became a boy soprano, beginning a six-year music scholarship in a* *cathedral choir.* | **win/be awarded a scholarship** *When she was 18, she won a scholarship to study at the Conservatoire in Paris.* | *We're very proud of the five students from this school who were awarded scholarships.*

9 money for starting a new business or other activity

- finance
- capital
- funding
- investment
- sponsorship
- grant
- subsidy

finance British **/financing** American /'faɪnæns‖fə̇'næns, 'faɪnænsɪŋ‖fə̇'nænsɪŋ/ [n U] British money that you borrow or receive in order to pay for something important and expensive, for example for starting a business: *We can't continue our research unless we get more finance.* | *The business plan is strong, but without financing, it will never work.* | **+ for** *Scottish Homes is the nation's biggest source of finance for house building.* | **obtain/raise finance** *The next step was to obtain finance to develop the project.* | *You'll have to explain to them how you intend to raise the financing you need.* | **provide finance** *The European Investment Bank will provide finance for a variety of regional initiatives.*

capital /'kæpə̇tl/ [n U] a large amount of money that you can use to start a business or to pay for something that will later produce more money: *There is a shortage of capital for building new aircraft.* | *Our return on capital has more than doubled since 1980.* | **investment capital** *The plan is expected to create vast amounts of investment capital.* | **raise capital** *Since the stockmarket crash, companies have been trying to raise capital by selling new stock.*

funding /'fʌndɪŋ/ [n U] money that a government provides to pay for education, theatre, music etc, not for business activities: *The President has yet to approve the additional funding needed to implement the program.* | *If the funding were increased by just 12%, we could be close to a cure for the disease in five years.* | **+ of** *A special body advises the government on the funding of research.* | **+ for** *Cuts in funding for the arts has lead to the closure of several theatres.* | **government/federal/state/public funding** (=funding provided by the government) *Congress banned federal funding of embryo research in 1995.* | *The church is seeking an extra $300,000 in government funding.* | **lack of funding** (=not enough funding) *School facilities have deteriorated over the past six years because of a lack of funding.* | **provide funding** *The Center will also provide funding to improve data collection and research.*

investment /ɪn'vestmənt/ [n C/U] the money that people or organizations give to a company, business, or bank, because they expect that they will get back more money than they gave: *In ten years' time, your investment should be worth four times what it is now.* | *Once we have seen an improvement in the company's performance, we will think about further investment.* | *exciting investment opportunities* | **+ in** *We have the largest investment in microelectronics technology of any company in the world.* | **make an investment** *The Postal Service has made an extremely large investment in automated technology.* | **foreign investment** (=investment in a country that is not your own country) *Foreign investment peaked in November, when overseas investors took advantage of low prices.* | **sound investment** (=an investment that is not likely to lose money) *Buying shares in blue-chip companies is always a sound investment.*

sponsorship /'spɒnsəʳʃɪp‖'spɑːn-/ [n U] money that is provided by a company or by the government to pay for someone to do something or pay for something such as a sports event, art show etc: *We are looking for sponsorship from local businesses.* | *Companies can help projects by providing financial sponsorship, office space, or printing facilities.* | **+ of** *a ban on tobacco company sponsorship of sports events* | **government/state sponsorship** *The exhibition received £50,000 in government sponsorship.* | **corporate sponsorship** (=sponsorship from a private company) *Corporate sponsorship ensures that far more money finds its way into sport than would otherwise be the case.*

grant /grɑːnt‖grænt/ [n C] an amount of money that a government or other organization gives to someone to help pay for something good or useful, such as their education: *These grants will help communities address the problems faced by young people.* | **+ from** *You can get a grant from the council to pay for the repairs.* | **a grant of $400/£30 etc** *She received a grant of £20,000 from the Arts Council to set up the Centre.* | **government/state/federal grant** *Researchers at the University of San Francisco will receive a $6.7 million federal grant for research on ovarian cancer.* | **block grant** (=money that the central government gives to local government to help pay for roads, police, schools etc) *Our role is to decide how the block grant should be allocated.* | **development grant** (=money that a government gives to a country or a city to help pay for economic development in a particular area) *The building was converted into flats with the aid of an urban development grant.* | *Most regions in Spain and Portugal qualify for sizeable development grants from the EU.* | **research grant** (=a grant given to someone to do research in a particular subject) *Research grants are plentiful in science and engineering subjects, but much harder to get in the humanities.* | **award/give sb a grant** *He was awarded a $25,000 grant by the Rockefeller Foundation, which enabled him to finish the work.* | **apply for a grant** *To apply for a loan or grant, call 1-800-323-4140.* | *We're applying for a grant of £500 for equipment.* | **grant proposal** (=a special form that you fill in when you ask for a grant) *Jen was up all night writing her grant proposal.*

subsidy /'sʌbsə̇di/ [n C] money that the government provides to help a business or industry which might not be able to operate without this additional money: *The taskforce has recommended some kind of subsidy to help businesses get their Internet start-ups off the ground.* | *Lacking the generous subsidies that European orchestras receive, modern American groups are under increasing pressure to play popular pieces.* | **state/federal/government/public subsidy** *Without state subsidies, the railways couldn't survive.* | *Federal subsidies would be available to help employers pay the insurance premiums.* | *They built and financed a whole new suburb, and they did it without a public subsidy.* | **agricultural/farm subsidy** *US farmers are having trouble coping with the reductions in agricultural subsidies.* | *Farm subsidies totaled $53 billion last year.*

10 money that you pay to the government

- tax
- duty
- tariff
- taxpayer

tax /tæks/ [n C/U] money that you have to pay to the government, especially from the money you earn or as an additional payment when you buy something: *Although the tax on cigarettes has doubled in the* *past two years, sales are still going up.* | *proposals for an increase in taxes to pay for medical care* | **+ on** *Consumers are angry that the tax on petrol has gone up yet again.* | **cut/reduce tax** *The Republicans promised to reduce taxes before the last election.* | *The Chancellor said he would cut income tax by 2 pence in the pound.* | **income tax** (=tax that you pay according to how much money you earn) *He failed to report and pay income tax on a portion of his income.* | **sales tax** (=tax you pay on things that you buy) *Sales tax in the state is 8%.* | **after tax** (=after you have paid income tax) *I made over $600 a week, which was around $450 after tax.* | **tax avoidance/evasion** (=when someone tries to avoid paying tax, especially income tax) *He pleaded guilty to charges of fraud and tax evasion.*

duty /ˈdjuːti‖ˈduː-/ [n C/U] a tax you pay on something you buy, especially goods you have bought in another country: *You have to pay a duty on the value of goods worth over $500 that you bring into the country.* | **customs duty** *The customs duty on luxury cars went up last month.*

tariff /ˈtærɨ̥f/ [n C/U] a tax on goods coming into a country or going out of a country: *The aim of the organization is to reduce tariffs and promote free trade.*

taxpayer /ˈtæksˌpeɪəʳ/ [n C] someone who pays tax: *Are you a higher rate taxpayer, or do you pay the basic rate?* | **taxpayers' money** (=money the government gets from taxes) *This defence project is simply a waste of taxpayers' money.* | **the taxpayer** (=all the people in a country who pay tax) *Bonus payments to top officials cost the taxpayer millions of pounds each year.* | *Unemployment is up, and the poor old taxpayer has to foot the bill, as usual.* | *I think these bureaucrats have a jolly good time at the taxpayer's expense.*

11 money paid to someone to make them do something dishonest

- bribe
- kickback
- backhander

bribe /braɪb/ [n C] money that someone gives to a person in an official position, in order to persuade them to do something that they should not do: *The two brothers regularly used bribes and threats to further their business.* | **$400/£30,000/millions etc in bribes** *A customs official pocketed up to $500,000 in bribes for permitting cocaine to pass through the port.* | **offer (sb) a bribe** *In all his years of public service, he has only been offered a bribe once.* | *Foreign firms willing to offer bribes typically win 80% of international deals.* | **pay a bribe (to sb)** (=give someone a bribe) *Some companies in Belgium and France had paid bribes for the award of contracts.* | *They paid millions in bribes to tax officials in order to avoid investigation.* | **take/accept a bribe** *The judge admitted that he had accepted bribes.* | *During his term in office, he took bribes ranging from 22 million to 220 million yen.* | **cash bribe** (=in the form of notes, rather than a cheque) *He offered me a cash bribe to help him secure the contract.* — **bribery** [n U] when people give and accept bribes: *The inquiry showed that bribery was widespread.* | **bribery and corruption** *He was arrested on charges of bribery and corruption.* — **bribe** [v T] to offer someone a bribe: *He alleged that the manager had tried to bribe him during a business lunch in 1993.* | *The defence are arguing that he was bribed to withdraw his testimony.*

kickback /ˈkɪkbæk/ [n C] a large amount of money that someone pays to a person in an important position in a company or government, in exchange for dishonestly arranging a business deal **$300/£400,000/millions etc in kickbacks** *Top executives received millions of dollars in kickbacks.* | **accept/take a kickback** *He is on trial for allegedly accepting kickbacks from business.* | *He and his partner were charged with taking $300,000 in kickbacks in exchange for their political influence.* | **pay/offer a kickback** *The company paid kickbacks to local officials to win contracts worth millions of dollars.* | *A cardiologist was offered kickbacks by a pacemaker manufacturer.*

backhander /ˈbækhændəʳ/ [n C] British informal a small amount of money paid to someone to persuade them to do something that is dishonest but usually not very serious: *There's some suggestion that a backhander was involved.* | *Perhaps the landlord's getting a backhander from the estate agent.* | **£300/£10 etc in backhanders** *Fifty pounds has already gone in backhanders to the guys in the security office.*

12 money that you pay to your former husband or wife

- maintenance
- alimony

maintenance British **/child support** American /ˈmeɪntənəns, ˈtʃaɪld səˌpɔːʳt/ [n U] money that is paid regularly by someone to their former wife or husband in order to support their children: *Failure to pay child support is a growing problem.* | *I have no job and receive no maintenance from my children's father.* | *The judge set her child support at ten dollars a week.* | *He gives no money for the care of his son, and Aurora has abandoned plans to pursue child support.* | **maintenance/child support payments** *The court will now force him to meet maintenance payments.*

alimony /ˈælɨ̥məni‖-məʊni/ [n U] an amount of money that a court orders someone to pay regularly to their former husband or wife after their marriage has ended: *Because Jean had given up a career to support her husband's career, the court ordered him to pay alimony.* | *His alimony amounts to around one thousand dollars a month.*

13 money that is collected for a purpose

- fund
- kitty/pot

fund /fʌnd/ [n C] a large sum of money that is collected and kept, especially so that it can be used by a particular group of people who need it: *There's a special fund you can apply to, that pays for blind students to go to university.* | *If I'm successful in raising over £500, those funds will go to the Bible School.* | **£400/$30,000 etc in funds** *A total of $5,800 in church funds has been used to provide assistance to local people.* | **set up a fund** *They used this money to set up a fund for the refugees.* | **raise funds** *The event was held to raise funds to promote AIDS awareness among young gays.* | *The hand-sewn quilts will be sold at a Christmas Craft Fair to raise funds for the arts project.* | **appeal fund** (=a special fund that is set up to help someone who is ill, needs special help etc) *Supporters have set up an appeal fund to help Peter fight the case.* | *Tell us, Gillian, how much do you have in the appeal fund now?* | **slush fund** (=money that has been obtained secretly and illegally, and that is used for illegal purposes) *He is on trial for accepting kickbacks from business moguls to build his slush fund.*

kitty/pot /'kɪti, pɒt‖pɑːt/ [n C] informal a small sum of money that is collected from all the people in a group and used to buy their food or drinks, pay their bills etc: *'Are we having takeout tonight?' 'Depends how much is in the pot.'* | *Do you all just put a bit in the kitty each week for basics?* | *There's nothing in the kitty, so if anyone wants another drink they'll have to get it themselves.*

14 relating to money and the way it is used

- ▸ financial
- ▸ finance
- ▸ monetary
- ▸ fiscal
- ▸ economic
- ▸ economics

financial /fə'nænʃəl, faɪ-/ [adj only before noun] connected with money – use this about the way that people and organizations use and control their money: *Wall Street is the financial center of the US.* | *There is a possibility of a full-scale financial crisis, like the great crash of 1929.* | *Many libraries have found that their financial resources are stretched to the limit.* | *The accounts show that the school's financial position is very healthy.* | **financial support/backing/assistance etc** *He failed to get financial support from his employers.* | *The amount of financial aid offered has become more central to students' decisions about which school to attend.* | **financial dealings/transactions** *Revelations about his financial dealings could change his election prospects dramatically.* | *He developed computer software to handle complicated financial transactions.* | **financial difficulties/problems** *Joan has a lot of financial problems at the moment.* | *Mexico's financial difficulties increased rather than diminished.* | **financial year** British (=the 12-month period used by companies to calculate their accounts) *Norton have announced profits of £3.5 million for the financial year 2000-01.* —**financially** [adv] *She wanted to go out to work and be financially independent* | *Who would benefit financially from Bobby's death?* | *His parents support him financially.*

finance /'faɪnæns, fə'næns‖fə'næns, 'faɪnæns/ [n U] all the activities that are related to how a company or country uses or organizes its money: *He was an expert in finance and advised people where to invest their money.* | *The use of IT in areas such as accounting and finance has grown at an astonishing rate.* | *She works as a director of finance for an oil company.* | **finance minister/officer etc** *Kubo is slated to become Japan's next finance minister.* | **high finance** (=financial activities involving countries or big companies – used especially to show that you do not know very much about those activities) *The other guys in the office were ten to fifteen years my senior, and old hands in high finance.*

monetary /'mʌnətəri‖'mɑːnəteri/ [adj only before noun] relating to or involving money, especially the money that is available to the government of a country, and how it decides to spend it: *There's only one conclusion to make about this data on monetary growth.* | **monetary policy/control etc** *The IMF should not dictate how Mexico should run its monetary policies.* | *a plan to introduce monetary reform* | *Some economists question the effectiveness of monetary control as a means of regulating the economy.* | *European monetary union*

fiscal /'fɪskəl/ [adj only before noun] formal connected with money, taxes, debts, etc that are owned and managed by the government: *Perez stated that the current fiscal crisis was the result of the collapse of the oil industry.* | *It was thought that skillful monetary and fiscal intervention could rescue the economy.* | **fiscal policy** *The Council of Finances determined fiscal policy within the region.* | **fiscal deficit** *Columbia's fiscal deficit could soar to 1.6 percent of GDP.* | **fiscal year** especially American (=the 12-month period used by companies to calculate their accounts) *Over the past fiscal year, the school has received $250 million in federal dollars for 1,600 projects.* —**fiscally** [adv] *countries with fiscally sound* (=well-managed) *economies* | *The President is pro-business and fiscally conservative.*

economic /ˌekə'nɒmɪk◂, ˌiː-‖-'nɑː-/ [adj only before noun] connected with the way money is earned, spent, and controlled within a country or society: *The tax breaks will stimulate economic activity.* | *Florida will benefit from a number of economic trends that play to its strengths.* | **economic climate** (=general state of the economy) *In this kind of economic climate, employees prefer a lower salary in a job that is secure.* | **economic crisis** *Cuba is emerging from five years of economic crisis.* | *Investors took their money elsewhere, prompting a far-reaching economic crisis.* | **economic growth/development etc** *Slow economic growth and low consumer spending affected sales last year.* | *a wide variety of economic development strategies* | **economic recovery** *Investors are holding out from Mexican stocks until they see clear signs of an economic recovery.* | **economic sanctions** (=official laws that stop trade with another country, for political reasons) *The US has maintained tough economic sanctions on Cuba.* | **economic summit** (=an important meeting for the leaders of countries to discuss the world's economy) *World leaders gathered in the Miyako Hotel to map out the agenda for next month's economic summit.*

economics /ˌekə'nɒmɪks, ˌiː-‖-'nɑː-/ [n U] the study of how money is earned, spent, and controlled within a country or society: *He studied economics at Harvard University.* | *He knows very little about economics or international finance.* | *Keynes's theories have had an important influence on modern economics.*

15 to put money into a business, in order to make money

- ▸ invest
- ▸ put money into
- ▸ investor
- ▸ backer

invest /ɪn'vest/ [v I/T] to let a company, business, or bank use your money for a period of time, especially because you expect that you will get back more money than you gave: *I want to invest the money my aunt left me.* | *The Singapore government is interested in investing abroad.* | **+ in** *Investing in property is no longer as safe as it used to be.* | *Shares in CMG Information, which invests in Internet-related businesses, declined sharply in the spring.* | **invest £300,000/$400/money etc in sth** *I invested £5000 in my brother's printing business.* | **invest heavily** (=give a lot of money) *He had invested heavily in risky assets like junk bonds.*

put money into /ˌpʊt 'mʌni ɪntuː/ [v phrase] to give money to a company or business in order to help that company develop and be successful, especially because you expect that you will make a profit: *Home-owners who put their money into building society accounts could be losing thousands each year.* | *The biggest bonus is that KPBS didn't have to put any capital into the project.* | *The plan calls for each company to put in $100 million toward the new car plant.*

investor /ɪnˈvestəʳ/ [n C] someone who puts money into a business, company, or bank in order to make a profit in the future: *Having made the initial payment, the investor need make no further effort.* | **foreign investor** *Foreign investors have shown considerable interest in the venture.* | *Most of the venture funds have come from foreign investors.* | **small investor** (=someone with a small amount to invest) *Our financial consultants can advise the small investor.* | *The British Gas sale attracted 4.5 million applications from small investors.*

backer /ˈbækəʳ/ [n C] someone who supports a business plan by giving or lending money: *Things became even more difficult when one of his principal backers went bankrupt.* | **financial backer** *The directors closed the company after the financial backers pulled out of the operation.*

16 the financial system in a country or area

- economy

economy /ɪˈkɒnəmi‖ɪˈkɑː-/ [n C] *The government's management of the economy has been severely criticized.* | *Inflation is a major problem in many South American economies.* | **black/shadow economy** (=business activities that take place illegally, especially in order to avoid paying tax) *It is impossible to quantify the exact value of the black economy.* | *shadow economies that escape accurate analysis* | **global economy** (=the economy of the world, seen as whole) *In a global economy, the only way to maintain a competitive edge is to lead the world in innovation.* | **market/free-market economy** (=a system in which companies, rather than the government, decide what to produce and sell) *Poland is trying to move from a centrally planned socialist economy to a free-market capitalist economy.*

17 when a person or company has no money

- bankrupt
- insolvent
- go bust
- ruin

bankrupt /ˈbæŋkrʌpt/ [adj] a company or person that is **bankrupt** does not have enough money to pay their debts, and so they have to stop doing business: *Five years ago she was a successful actress, but now she is bankrupt.* | *He lent him several thousand dollars to help rescue his bankrupt textile business.* | **go bankrupt** (=become bankrupt) *Many small businesses will go bankrupt unless interest rates fall.* | **declare sb bankrupt** (=say officially that they are bankrupt) *He was declared bankrupt in the High Court yesterday.* —**bankrupt** [v T] *He realized that it would bankrupt the company if he continued the expansion.* —**bankruptcy** [n U] *It was no surprise when the Internet Startup firm declared bankruptcy.*

insolvent /ɪnˈsɒlvənt‖ɪnˈsɑːl-/ [adj] a company or business person that is **insolvent** has lost all their money: *A spokesman denied the bank was insolvent, but depositors are rushing to withdraw their money.* | *The court ordered the dissolution of seven insolvent housing loan companies.* | **become insolvent** *The company auditor has filed a warning that Eurotunnel is in danger of becoming insolvent.* | **declare sb insolvent** (=say officially that they are insolvent) *He withdrew savings from a major bank just two days before it was declared insolvent.* | **render sb insolvent** (=make someone insolvent) *The bank could even be rendered insolvent by such a large payment.* —**insolvency** [n U] *Accountants have been called in to save the firm from insolvency.* | *If they cannot repay the loan, they face insolvency.*

go bust /ˌgəʊ ˈbʌst/ [v phrase] informal to no longer have enough money to pay your debts, so that you have to stop doing business: *The supermarket isn't there any more. They went bust ages ago.* | *About 60,000 business go bust each year in the United States.*

ruin /ˈruːən/ [v T] if something **ruins** someone, it makes them lose all their money and property after working very hard for it, and they have to stop doing business: *Many firms have been ruined by hasty decisions.* | *The incident has all but ruined her financially.* | *She is still angry with the suppliers, who she says ruined her by failing to deliver on time.*

18 having no money to spend at the present time

- broke
- skint
- strapped for cash

broke /brəʊk/ [adj not before noun] informal having no money or very little money to spend at the moment: *'Can you lend me some money?' 'Sorry, I'm broke.'* | *She's just come back off holiday and she's completely broke.*

skint /skɪnt/ [adj not before noun] British informal having no money at the moment: *I sold my record collection when I was skint one time.* | *Can you lend me some money to tide me over? I'm a bit skint at the moment.*

strapped for cash /ˌstræpt fəʳ ˈkæʃ/ [adj phrase] not having enough money at the moment: *I'm warning you, we're really strapped for cash right now.* | *I'm a bit strapped for cash myself at the moment, but I'll see what I can do.*

more

RELATED WORDS

opposite: ———— **less**

- *see also* **increase, add, most**

WHAT'S HERE

- **more/another** see **1**
- **more than a number or amount** see **2 to 3**
- **more than before** see **4 to 5**
- **more than sb/sth else** see **6**

more/another

1 more of the same thing, or another one of the same things

- more
- another
- extra
- additional
- further
- added
- spare
- supplementary

more /mɔːʳ/ [quantifier] **more** of the same thing: *I gave him $200 last week, and he's already asking for more.* | *There were more riots in the capital last night when protestors clashed with police.* | **+ of** *Those interested in seeing more of the sculptor's work can visit the Sacre Monte museum.* | **three more/100**

more etc *Some of the students arrived today, and about 20 more will be here tomorrow.* | *I might buy a couple more of those scarves.* | **some more/any more/no more** *Is there any more beer in the fridge?* | *Why don't you go upstairs and do some more homework?* | *Officials are satisfied that no more bodies are buried in the ruins.* | **a few more** *Can you give me a few more minutes?* | **one more** (=the last of several) *I'll just have one more drink before I go.* | **a bit more** British **/a little (bit) more** American *Sally read a bit more of her book to keep her mind off things.*

another /əˈnʌðəʳ/ [determiner/pron] one more thing, person, or amount of the same kind: *Would you like another drink?* | *Look, your glass is cracked. I'll get you another.* | **+ of** *Still to come on Channel West, another of our special reports from Florida.* | **another ten minutes/five miles/two gallons etc** *Add the pasta and heat the soup for another ten minutes.* | *For another 80 bucks, you could have a wide-screen TV with Internet access.* | **another one** *Pass me another one of those folders.*

extra /ˈekstrə/ [adj/adv] more of something, in addition to the usual or standard amount or number: *Residents may use the hotel swimming pool at no extra charge.* | **extra ten minutes/three pounds/four gallons etc** *You get an extra 5% discount if you buy your software on-line.* | *The voting booths stayed open for an extra two hours in some states.* | **be/cost/charge etc extra** (=to be, cost, charge etc extra money) *Dinner costs $15, but wine is extra.* | *Most small providers offer their customers free Web space, but larger providers often charge extra.*

additional /əˈdɪʃənəl/ [adj only before noun] more than the amount or number that was agreed or expected at the beginning of something: *Our own car broke down, so we had the additional expense of renting a car.* | **an additional £10/10 miles/10 minutes etc** *Judge Mathes sentenced her first to a year and later to an additional three months in jail for contempt.*

further /ˈfɜːʳðəʳ/ [adj only before noun] formal more, in addition to what there is already or what has happened already: *The doctors are keeping her in hospital to do further tests.* | *For further information, contact the help line.* | **a further £10/10 miles/10 minutes etc** *Strike action will continue for a further 24 hours.*

added /ˈædɪ̵d/ [adj only before noun] **added advantage/benefit/protection etc** another advantage or more of something that makes something better or more effective: *The new computer is as good as the old one, with the added advantage of being smaller.* | *Buy a high-factor sun lotion, and wear a hat for added protection.*

spare /speəʳ/ [adj only before noun] a **spare** tyre, key, room etc is one that you have in addition to the ones you normally use, so that it is available if another one is needed: *We carried Ros upstairs and laid her on the spare bed.* | *Pauline keeps a spare key hanging in the closet upstairs.*

supplementary /ˌsʌplɪ̵ˈmentəri◂/ [adj] provided in addition to what already exists, in order to help people or improve something: *Some supplementary finance is available in the form of grants or loans.* | *The Investment Business Gazettes offer very useful supplementary information.*

more than a number or amount

2 more than a number, amount, age etc

- more
- over
- above
- greater than
- beyond
- in excess of
- upwards of
- plus

more /mɔːʳ/ [quantifier] **more** than a number or amount **+ than** *I've been working here for more than fifteen years.* | *More than 50,000 people attended the concert, which was held in Central Park.* | **much more/far more/a lot more/even more** *Rented accommodation costs much more in New York.* | *Sales executives earn about $200,000 a year, and those higher up the ladder can earn a lot more.* | **no more than/not more than** *The discussion lasted no more than 30 minutes.* | **10/100/$50 etc more** *It's a better hotel, but it costs about £50 more than the other one.* | **or more** *He could receive a prison sentence of five years or more.*

over /ˈəʊvəʳ/ [prep/adv] more than that number or amount – use this especially when it is not important to say exactly how much more: *I had to wait over half an hour for the train this morning.* | *We receive over 2,000 applications a year.* | *It's hot out there – I'd say it's over 90.* | **just over** (=slightly over) *She weighs just over 180 pounds.* | **well over/way over** (=a lot more) informal *Well over 30 schools took part in the fund-raising walk.* | *She was driving way over the speed limit.* | **3/10/12 etc and over** (=including and over a particular age) *NCI recommends that women aged 40 years and over are checked every two years.*

above /əˈbʌv/ [prep/adv] more than a number or level on a scale that can be exactly measured: *The temperature is about 2 degrees above zero.* | **just above** (=slightly above) *High speed trains average just above 150 mph.* | **well/way above** (=a lot more) informal *The government promised to increase teachers' pay well above the rate of inflation.* | **above average** (=more than usual) *All the students in the group were found to have above average IQ scores.* | **3/10/12 etc and above** (=including and above a particular figure) *A score of 70 and above indicates good spatial and map-reading skills.*

greater than /ˈgreɪtəʳ ðən/ [prep] formal more than a particular number or amount, especially a number: *Scientists have discovered eight craters on Venus with diameters greater than 100 km.* | *Imagine a device that could send a signal at a speed greater than the speed of light.* | **be greater than** *Economic growth this year is predicted to be greater than 1.5%.* | **be much/far/even greater than** *By the 1940s, the volume of domestic trade was much greater than trade with other countries.*

beyond /bɪˈjɒnd‖bɪˈjɑːnd/ [prep/adv] more than another number, amount, age etc – use this especially when the other number etc is a particular level or limit: *Inflation has now risen beyond the acceptable level of 5%.* | *In a number of professions, it is possible to continue working beyond retirement age.*

in excess of /ɪn ɪkˈses ɒv/ [prep] formal more than an amount or number – used especially in official documents, instructions, or reports: *The cyclone was travelling at speeds in excess of 21 mph.* | **be in excess of** *The population is now estimated to be in excess of 40 million.* | **well in excess of** (=a lot more) informal *The fire has caused well in excess of $500,000 worth of damage.*

upwards of ALSO **upward of** American /ˈʌpwəʳd(z) ɒv/ [prep] use this when the number or amount you mention is the lower limit, and there is possibly even more than that: *The Reynolds collection is valued at upward of $20 million.* | **10/$300/5 years etc and upwards** *The performance is suitable for children of 7 years and upwards.*

plus /plʌs/ [adj only after number] **10/100/1,500 etc plus** at least 10, 100 etc and more than that: *The drugs have a street value of $30,000 plus.* | *It took me three hours to back up the computer's 400-plus megabyte memory.*

3 to be more than a particular number or amount

- be more than
- exceed
- outnumber
- be up
- pass

be more than /biː ˈmɔːʳ ðən/ [v phrase] *The annual revenue is more than $15 billion.* | *New Haven's school drop-out rate is more than double the statewide average.* | **much/many more than** *a young woman who didn't look to be much more than 20* | *Many cases still go undetected – many more than are treated.*

exceed /ɪkˈsiːd/ [v T] formal to be more than a number or amount, especially a fixed number or limit – used especially in official reports or documents: *Legal requirements state that working hours must not exceed 42 hours a week.* | *In the Far East, home computer ownership is expected to exceed that of the US and Europe combined.* | **exceed sth by sth** *Births exceeded deaths by a ratio of 3 to 1.* | **far exceed** *Metcalf has achieved 49 touchdowns, far exceeding even those of his famous father.*

outnumber /aʊtˈnʌmbəʳ/ [v T] if one type of person or thing **outnumbers** another, there are more of the first type than of the second: *Women teachers outnumber their male colleagues by two to one.* (=there are twice as many women) | **greatly/far outnumber** *a city where bicycles greatly outnumber cars*

be up /biː ˈʌp/ [v phrase] if profits, sales, income etc **are up** they are larger than at a time in the past: *Most retailers expect sales to be up slightly compared with last year.* | *The American Stock Exchange was up 0.6% at 551.63.* | **+ by** *Support for the president was up by an astonishing 15% in the South.* | **be 10%/12 points etc up** *Germany's steel output was 3% up at 11.7 million tons.*

pass /pɑːs‖pæs/ [v T] if a number or total **passes** an amount, especially one that you have been trying to reach, it is more than that amount and will probably continue to increase: *If he stays injury-free, Stumpel should pass his personal best of 76 points.* | **pass the £100/1million etc mark** *Visits to our website passed the 100,000 mark in April.*

more than before

4 more than before

- more
- more
- a growing number/an increasing number
- increasingly
- greater
- higher
- increased
- gain ground

more /mɔːʳ/ [quantifier] *The new airport will just mean more noise, more traffic problems and higher land prices.* | **+ than** *I'm sure I weigh more than last year.* | **more sth than** *There are far more game shows on TV than there used to be.* | **much more/a lot more/a little more etc** *Derek earns a lot more now than he did in his previous job.* | **more and more** (=in a number or degree that steadily increases) *More and more people are retiring early.* | *It became more and more obvious that the boy was using drugs.*

more /mɔːʳ/ [adv] *People are using mobile phones more because they are cheaper.* | **+ than** *Visitors to the centre complained about the service more than last year.* | **more than ever before** *Our future competitiveness and prosperity depend more than ever before on technology and industry.* | **more and more** (=continuously increasing) *More and more, we are finding that students lack basic skills when they enter college.*

a growing number/an increasing number /ə ˌgrəʊɪŋ ˈnʌmbəʳ, ən ɪnˌkriːsɪŋ ˈnʌmbəʳ/ [quantifier] use this when the number of people that are doing something is not yet very large, but is increasing all the time **+ of** *Hong Kong was having to provide for a growing number of refugees.* | *Milo is one of a growing number of politicians who have become dissatisfied with the current government.* | **an ever-increasing/ever-growing number of** (=a number that is increasing all the time) *The islanders are trying to protect their environment from the ever-increasing number of Australian tourists.* | **in growing/increasing numbers** *'Suite' hotels – with full kitchens and sitting rooms – are dotting the roadside in increasing numbers.*

increasingly /ɪnˈkriːsɪŋli/ [adv] continuing to happen more often than before – use this when something is becoming more common but still does not happen all the time: *As the years passed, Celia became increasingly lonely and withdrawn.* | *Increasingly, people are relying on interactive media for a variety of services.*

greater /ˈgreɪtəʳ/ [adj] formal use this about a feeling or condition that is stronger or more noticeable than it was before: *After the war, the country began to enjoy greater prosperity.* | *The new legislation gave girls greater access to sports in schools.* | **+ than** *The need for people with computing skills is greater than ever before.*

higher /ˈhaɪəʳ/ [adj] use this about prices, speeds, or amounts that are bigger than they were before: *There is now a higher proportion of women in management jobs.* | *By focusing on quality rather than price, Bangalore's firms hope to secure higher profit margins.* | **+ than** *The cost of student accommodation is higher than it was a year ago.*

increased /ɪnˈkriːst/ [adj only before noun] greater than in the past: *After childbirth there is always an increased risk of back trouble.* | *Increased interest in healthy foods and the environment has led to greater consumer influence.*

gain ground /ˌgeɪn ˈgraʊnd/ [v phrase] if a belief, idea etc is **gaining ground**, more and more people believe it, do it etc: *an approach which is gaining ground in schools* | *Evangelical Christianity has been gaining ground since the Second World War.* | *Laurent died in 1853, but his ideas slowly gained ground over the next ten years.*

5 to become stronger, angrier etc than before

- get/become
- grow in/gain in
- more
- increasingly
- heightened

get/become /get, bɪ'kʌm/ [v] *As the days passed, Martha became more worried.* | *As you get older, your joints and muscles tend to get weaker.* | *I knew that if I resisted, he would get even angrier.* | *The mysterious phone calls were becoming more frequent.*

grow in/gain in /'grəʊ ɪn, 'geɪn ɪn/ [v phrase] to gradually get more of a useful or valuable quality: *The festival has been growing in popularity.* | *The business has continued to grow in productivity and profitability.* | *She gradually gained in self-confidence and ability.*

more /mɔːʳ/ [adv] use this to show that there is more of a quality or feeling than at another time: *It will gradually become more cloudy later in the day.* | **more ... than** *I guess Marlene is more neurotic than she used to be.* | **a lot/much/far more** *Everything was much more difficult than it is these days.* | **more and more** *The train went more and more slowly, and finally stopped completely.* | *We became more and more determined to succeed.*

increasingly /ɪn'kriːsɪŋli/ [adv] if someone or something is becoming **increasingly** difficult, important etc, they are continuing to become more difficult, more important etc as time passes: *As she watched him, Jody felt increasingly sure that she had made the right choice.* | **become/get increasingly** *It is getting increasingly difficult for the US to remain competitive in consumer products.*

heightened /'haɪtnd/ [adj only before noun] **heightened** feelings are felt more strongly: *heightened concerns about crime and violence in schools* | *A heightened awareness of healthy eating may lead to considerable benefits.*

more than sb/sth else

6 more than someone or something else

- more
- more
- greater
- higher
- to a greater extent/degree

more /mɔːʳ/ [adv] having a particular quality or characteristic to a greater degree than someone or something else: *You can see the buildings from the ground, of course, but they look more dramatic from the air.* | **+ than** *Anthony needs to practise more than the other students, but he gets it right in the end.* | **more ... than** *She's more intelligent than her brothers.* | *Most women felt that female bosses were 'more involved' than their male counterparts.* | **much/far/a little/a lot more** *People here are far more friendly than they are in England.* | *The old version of Tomb Raider was a lot more limited in scope than this one.* | **more like** *I think you look more like your aunt Margaret than your sister does.*

more /mɔːʳ/ [quantifier] **more** than another person, thing, or place: *The students with more experience help the newcomers get to grips with the course.* | **+ than** *So Claire earns more than you?* | *In the study, men showed more concern than the women who took part.*

greater /'greɪtəʳ/ [adj] use this about a feeling, quality, or amount that is larger than someone or something else's **+ than** *His understanding of Chinese philosophy is greater than any Westerner's I've met.* | **greater sth than** *We enjoy greater freedom than women in many other countries.*

higher /'haɪəʳ/ [adj] use this about prices, speeds, or amounts that are bigger than someone else's: *We tried to calculate the effect of a higher minimum wage on employment and hours worked.* | *Janette's SAT scores were higher than anyone elses.* | **higher sth than** *In the 1960s, Japan achieved a higher rate of economic growth than most other countries.*

to a greater extent/degree /tʊ ə ˌgreɪtər ɪk'stent, dɪ'griː/ [adv] happening more in one situation than in another – used in literary and scientific contexts: *This theme is developed in the novels of D.H. Lawrence, and to a greater extent E.M. Forster.* | **+ than** *Women, to a greater degree than men, tend to start abusing alcohol when they are under pressure at work.*

most

RELATED WORDS

opposite: —— **least**

▸ *see also* **more, main, in general**

1 most of an amount, group, or thing

- most
- almost all/nearly all
- the/a majority
- the bulk of
- the better part of/best part of
- the lion's share

most /məʊst/ [quantifier] the largest number of people or things, or the largest part of something: *What most people want is a peaceful life.* | *Most restaurants open at 7.* | *Most evenings we just stay in and watch TV.* | *Most research suggests that health is related to social class.* | **+ of** *Most of the people I spoke to were very worried.* | *Alex spent most of his allowance on books.* | *I've lived here most of my life, so I know the area pretty well.*

almost all/nearly all /ˌɔːlməʊst 'ɔːl, ˌnɪəʳli 'ɔːl/ [quantifier] *He likes almost all kinds of popular music.* | *We got nearly all our food from the farm.* | *The bed occupied nearly all the space in the room.* | **+ of** *Nearly all of my clothes are too small now.* | *Almost all of the world's tropical forests are in developing countries.*

the/a majority /ðə, ə mə'dʒɒrɪ̈ti‖-mə'dʒɔː-/ [quantifier] more than half of the people or things in a large group: *A poll of Democrats shows that a majority support the President.* | **+ of** *In June the majority of our students will be taking examinations.* | *They claim their campaign is supported by a majority of residents.* | **the vast/great/overwhelming majority** (=far more than half) *The great majority of accidents in the Alps occur while climbers are coming down.* | *an education policy that will please the vast majority of parents*

the bulk of /ðə 'bʌlk ɒv/ [quantifier] most of a large amount or number of something: *Throughout the Middle Ages, the bulk of the population lived in the country rather than in towns.* | *The bulk of the charity's income comes from private donations.*

the better part of/best part of /ðə ˌbetəʳ 'pɑːʳt ɒv, ˌbest 'pɑːʳt ɒv/ [quantifier] most of a period of time or of a distance, especially when the time or distance is too long: *It was the best part of a mile to the farm.* | *It'll probably take the best part of a week to sort it out.* | *I expect the whole procedure to take the better part of a morning.*

the lion's share /ðə 'laɪənz ˌʃeəʳ/ [n phrase] the biggest part of something valuable or good that is taken by one person, group, or organization, so that others get less: *Sarah only ate a few bites of the dessert, so I got the lion's share.* | **+ of** *Why should the* *state get the lion's share of people's money?* | *His company currently has the lion's share of the market.*

2 more than anyone or anything else

▸ **most** ▸ **the most**

most /məʊst/ [adv] more than anything else – use this especially to talk about something that you like, want, need, or worry about more than anything else: *The part we enjoyed most was the trip to the Grand Canyon.* | *What worries me most is the effect the divorce is having on the children.* | **most of all** (=much more than anything else) *What the people here need most of all is food and clean water.*

the most /ðə ˈməʊst/ [quantifier] a larger amount or number than anyone or anything else: *In a fair tax system those who earn the most should pay the most.* | *The player who scores the most points wins.* | *Which machine uses the most electricity?*

3 the largest amount possible

▸ **maximum** ▸ **top**
▸ **the most**

maximum /ˈmæksɪ̈məm/ [adj] the **maximum** amount of something is the largest amount that is possible or allowed: *Travelling at its maximum speed of 186 mph, the train reached Paris in less than two hours.* | *We want our message to reach the maximum number of people.* | *Both men are facing a maximum penalty of a year in jail.* | *We'll show you how to arrange the furniture in your office to make maximum use of the space available.* —**maximum** [n singular] *Thirty students per class is the maximum.* | **+ of** *Tourists can stay up to a maximum of 90 days.*

the most /ðə ˈməʊst/ [n singular] the largest amount that is possible: *I'm afraid £500 is the most I can offer you.* | *The most you can hope to achieve is a 10% increase in production.*

top /tɒp‖tɑːp/ [adj only before noun] a top speed, price, salary etc is the highest speed, price etc that is possible or is paid: *It's Hyundai's fastest car yet, with a top speed of 121 mph.* | *The top price paid was $1,200,000 for a print by Degas.*

4 when most people share a particular opinion

▸ **generally** ▸ **broad**

generally /ˈdʒenərəli/ [adv] something that is **generally** believed is believed by most people: *His first year as President was generally regarded as a success.* | *It is now generally accepted that the so-called 'Hitler Diaries' were forgeries.* —**general** [adj] *There is a general feeling* (=most people feel) *that the country lacks moral leadership.*

broad /brɔːd/ [adj only before noun] **broad agreement/consensus/acceptance** agreement among most people about something: *There was broad agreement on the issue of equal pay for women.* | *He had created a broad consensus among different groups of Americans.*

5 when there is much more of one type than of other types

▸ **mostly/mainly/largely** ▸ **predominate**
▸ **predominantly** ▸ **be in the majority**
▸ **a preponderance of**

mostly/mainly/largely /ˈməʊstli, ˈmeɪnli, ˈlɑːʳdʒli/ [adv] *Apart from the Nile valley, Egypt is mostly desert.* | *I used to read a lot of poetry, mainly love poetry.* | *The new immigrants were mainly from Southern Europe.* | *The surface of Mercury seems to consist largely of dust.*

predominantly /prɪˈdɒmɪ̈nəntli‖-ˈdɑː-/ [adv] if something, especially a group of people, is **predominantly** of a particular type, most of it is of that type: *The character Shylock is a Jew living in a predominantly Christian society.* | *As a civil engineer, Susan will be competing in a predominantly male profession.* | *Our economy is predominantly capitalist.*

predominate /prɪˈdɒmɪ̈neɪt‖-ˈdɑː-/ [v I] formal if people or things of a particular type **predominate** in a place or situation, they are present in greater numbers than other types of people or things: *Dairy farms predominate in Sussex.* | *In the summer, blue and pink flowers predominate, but there are white flowers, too, for contrast.*

be in the majority /biː ɪn ðə məˈdʒɒrɪ̈ti‖-məˈdʒɔː-/ [v phrase] if people of a particular kind **are in the majority** in an organization or group, they form the largest part of it: *The number of women on the committee has grown steadily and now they are in the majority.*

a preponderance of /ə prɪˈpɒndərəns ɒv‖-ˈpɑːn-/ [quantifier] formal if there is **a preponderance of** people or things of a particular type in a group, most of the people or things in the group are of that type – used especially when the group is being studied: *At some universities, there is a preponderance of older lecturers.* | *They chose to investigate reasons for the preponderance of large families among the poor and ill-educated.*

6 most often

▸ **mostly/mainly** ▸ **in most cases**
▸ **most of the time**

mostly/mainly /ˈməʊstli, ˈmeɪnli/ [adv] use this to say what someone does most, or who does something most: *We eat mostly Italian food.* | *She has to travel abroad a lot, mostly to Spain and France.* | *a singer whose records are bought mainly by teenage girls*

most of the time /ˈməʊst əv ðə ˌtaɪm/ [adv] for almost all of the time: *Most of the time at work I just answer the phone and type letters.* | *This place is really busy most of the time.*

in most cases /ɪn ˈməʊst ˌkeɪsɪ̈z/ [adv] used when something happens more than anything else: *In most cases the system that we have works very well.* | *The airline received about 500 complaints last year. In most cases these concerned delays and cancellations.*

mother

RELATED WORDS

▸ father, family, baby, child, woman, relationship

1 a mother

▸ **mother** ▸ **mum**

mother /ˈmʌðəʳ/ [n C] *My mother and father are both teachers.* | *Like most mothers, I always feel anxious* *when my children come home late.* | *The 29-year-old mother of two was attacked while walking her dog in woods near her home.* | **a single mother** (=a mother who looks after her children on her own, without a husband or partner) *As a single mother, Linda relies on state benefits which are nowhere near enough.*

mum British **/mom** American /mʌm, mɒm‖mɑːm/ [n C] informal someone's mother: *My mum and dad won't mind if you want to stay the night.* | *Alex's mom does all his cooking, washing, and ironing for him!* | *Sometimes it's difficult to get back into the job market after being a full-time mom.* | **a single mum/mom** (=a mother who looks after her children on her own, without a husband or partner) *Being a single mum is never easy.* | **a stay-at-home-mom** American (=a mother who stays at home to take care of her children rather than working elsewhere)

2 what you call your mother

- Mum
- Mummy
- Mother

Mum British **/Mom** American /mʌm, mɒm‖mɑːm/ [n] spoken a name you use to talk to your mother: *Mum, where can we play?* | *Happy birthday, Mom!* | *I told Mum that I wasn't going to be home for dinner tonight.*

Mummy British **/Mommy** American /ˈmʌmi, ˈmɒmi‖ˈmɑːmi/ [n] informal a name for your mother – used especially by young children or when you are talking to young children: *'Good night Mummy,' said Ben.* | *Don't cry – Mommy'll be back soon.*

Mother /ˈmʌðəʳ/ [n] a formal way of talking to your mother: *I think I can make my own decisions, Mother – I'm forty now you know!*

3 the time when a woman is a mother

- motherhood

motherhood /ˈmʌðəʳhʊd/ [n U] *It is not easy trying to combine motherhood and a job.* | *Women weren't expected to work in those days. The accepted pattern was marriage and motherhood.*

4 typical of a mother's feelings or behaviour

- maternal

maternal /məˈtɜːʳnl/ [adj only before noun] *My oldest sister, Roberta, used to fuss over me in a rather maternal manner.* | *Lack of maternal love can have a profound effect on a child's psychological development.*

5 behaving in a kind and caring way like a mother

- maternal
- motherly

maternal /məˈtɜːʳnl/ [adj] *Aunt Mary was a large, maternal woman who worked as a nurse in a children's hospital.* | **+ towards** *The older girls seemed to feel quite maternal towards the younger ones.*

motherly /ˈmʌðəʳli/ [adj] behaving like a mother, especially by being very kind and looking after people: *'Don't worry,' Laura said in a gentle motherly way.* | *Miss Gilbert was motherly but firm, an excellent teacher for the lower forms.*

move/not move

RELATED WORDS

- to move up or move something up *see* **up**
- *see also* **go, stop, send, travel, turn**

1 to move

- move
- movement
- stir
- make a move
- move over
- shift

move /muːv/ [v I/T] to go to a different place or to change the position of your body: *Every time I move I get a pain in my left shoulder.* | *Don't move, there's a spider on your back.* | **+ away/forward/towards etc** *Sarah moved away from the window.* | *My mother moved forward and grabbed my wrist.* | **move around** (=to different parts of an area) *I can hear someone moving around downstairs!*

movement /ˈmuːvmənt/ [n C/U] when someone or something moves: *Any movement will set off the alarm.* | *He watched her graceful movements as she came towards him.* | *The doctor thinks she'll recover quite a lot of movement, though maybe not all.* | **+ of** *the movement of the human heart* | **+ towards/across/through etc** *Make gentle sweeping movements across the hedge so that the blade can cut on both sides.* | **sudden movement** *I crept to the door, and with a sudden movement, opened it wide.*

stir /stɜːʳ/ [v I] especially written to make a slight movement, for example just before you wake up or start to speak: *The sleeping child stirred and opened her eyes.* | *The crowd began to stir as the band walked on stage.*

make a move /ˌmeɪk ə ˈmuːv/ [v phrase] to make a movement, especially as you start to do something or try to do something: *'The dog won't touch you,' she said, 'unless you make a move towards me.'* | *He made a move to kiss me, but I turned away.*

move over /ˌmuːv ˈəʊvəʳ/ [phr v I] to move to a different position in a bed, on a chair etc: *Move over a bit, I'm falling out of bed.* | *Penelope moved over and took the driver's seat.*

shift /ʃɪft/ [v I/T] British informal to move from one place or position to another, or to make something do this: *Jonas stood and listened, shifting uncomfortably from one foot to the other.* | *The sun had shifted to the west.* | *She shifted her gaze from me to Bobby with a look of suspicion.* | *The building's foundation has shifted, which is why there are cracks in the plaster.* | **shift your legs/arm/foot etc** *Tell Alan to shift his feet so Maggie can sit down.* | *The leather armchair creaked as Roberts shifted his bulk.*

2 moving

- moving
- be in motion

moving /ˈmuːvɪŋ/ [adj only before noun] not staying still, but changing position or going from one place to another **moving car/truck/vehicle etc** *The authorities believe the body was thrown from a moving vehicle.* | **moving part** *All the moving parts of the engine must be kept well-oiled.*

be in motion /biː ɪn ˈməʊʃən/ [v phrase] especially written if something, especially a vehicle or machine, **is in motion**, it is moving from one place or position to another: *Do not distract the driver while the vehicle is in motion.*

3 able to move

- mobile
- mobile
- mobility

mobile /ˈməʊbaɪl‖-bəl, -biːl/ [adj not before noun] especially British someone who is **mobile** can move and walk around normally: *He won't be mobile for some time. It's a bad knee sprain.* | *Ethel needed help on the stairs, but was otherwise mobile.*

mobile /ˈməʊbaɪl‖-bəl, -biːl/ [adj only before noun] **mobile library/shop/clinic etc** a library, shop etc that is in a vehicle and which moves around from place to place: *Remote areas are served by a number of weekly mobile clinics.* | *Neuman revealed that she nearly quit showbusiness to run a mobile massage parlour.* | *The community currently receives service from a rural mobile library.*

mobility /məʊˈbɪləti/ [n U] especially written someone's ability to move – use this especially about people who are very old, injured etc: *You'll experience some loss of mobility for a few weeks after the operation.* | *The weakening of bone tissue has a considerable effect on an elderly person's mobility.*

4 to keep moving your body or part of your body

- fidget
- can't keep still
- squirm
- wriggle
- writhe
- twitch

fidget /ˈfɪdʒət/ [v I] to keep moving or playing with your fingers, hands, feet etc, because you are bored or nervous: *Stop fidgeting, Sally, and pay attention.* | **fidget in your seat/chair** *She glared at the little boy, who had started fidgeting in his chair.* | **+ with** *Diana fidgeted nervously with her pencil.*

can't keep still /ˌkɑːnt kiːp ˈstɪl‖ˌkænt-/ [v phrase] spoken if you **can't keep still**, you keep moving your body because you are excited or nervous and you cannot relax: *I was so excited that I couldn't keep still.* | *Frankie has a lot of energy; he can hardly keep still for more than a few minutes.*

squirm /skwɜːʳm/ [v I] to make very small movements from side to side with your body, especially because you are in pain or uncomfortable: *The cat was squirming and he put it down.* | *Diane squirmed wildly as Gavin tickled her.* | **squirm in your seat/chair** *The little boy squirmed in his seat, anxious to get up and leave the table.* | **squirm with embarrassment/discomfort etc** *Laura's face reddened and she squirmed with embarrassment.*

wriggle /ˈrɪgəl/ [v I] to make small movements from side to side, especially in order to get into a particular position or to get through an opening **wriggle into/out/through etc** *The dog wriggled under the fence and escaped into the street.* | **wriggle free** *Shelly tried to wriggle free from him, but he held her firmly.*

writhe /raɪð/ [v I] to twist your body from side to side violently, especially because you are suffering pain: *As he received each blow, he writhed on the floor and cried out.* | **writhe in pain/agony** *Sarah was writhing in agony, clutching her leg.*

twitch /twɪtʃ/ [v I] if part of your body **twitches**, it makes small movements that you cannot control: *A muscle on Yang's face twitched.* | *My right eyelid wouldn't stop twitching.* —**twitch** [n C] *It's just a nervous twitch.* | *There was a twitch in my left cheek which I couldn't control.*

5 to move from side to side

- sway
- rock
- swing

sway /sweɪ/ [v I] to move slowly from one side to the other, especially in an irregular or uncontrolled way: *A light wind was making the branches sway.* | *Donny swayed drunkenly as he walked back to his car.* | **sway from side to side** *The ski lifts were swaying alarmingly from side to side.*

rock /rɒk‖rɑːk/ [v I/T] to move repeatedly from one side to another, with small gentle movements, or to make something do this: *Waves from a passing freighter rocked their boat.* | **rock back and forth** *The chair squeaked as I rocked back and forth.* | *Uncle Maury laughed until he was rocking back and forth.* | **rock from side to side** *Glenda sat beside the cradle, gently rocking it from side to side.*

swing /swɪŋ/ [v I] to move from side to side with long, usually regular movements: *We began the workout by swinging our arms.* | *The only sound was the creak of a sign swinging in the wind.* | **swing shut/open** *Doors swung open and then shut as hospital porters pushed a patient down the corridor.* | **swing from side to side** *The wooden bridge swung from side to side in a terrifying fashion.*

6 to move something from one place or position to another

- move
- transfer
- shift
- swing
- jerk

move /muːv/ [v T] to take something to a different place or change the position of something: *Will you move your car, please? It's blocking the road.* | *It took three men to move the piano.* | **move sth to/into sth** *We'll have to move the table into the hall.*

transfer /trænsˈfɜːʳ/ [v T] to move something and put it in a different place or container: *Transfer the mixture to a heavy cooking pan and add all remaining ingredients.* | **transfer sth (from sth) to sth** *Could I transfer $500 from my savings to my checking account?*

shift /ʃɪft/ [v T] British informal to move something from where it is: *When are you going to shift all this rubbish? It's making the place look a real mess.* | *Come on Des, give me a hand to shift these and then we can go home.*

swing /swɪŋ/ [v T] to move something quickly through the air with a long circular movement: *She swung the ax, hitting the log squarely in the middle.* | **swing sth back/over/across etc** *As you swing the golf club back, try to keep your eye on the ball.* —**swing** [n C] *With a heavy swing of the mallet, he drove the post into the ground.*

jerk /dʒɜːʳk/ [v T] to move something with a short, very sudden movement **jerk sth away/towards/up etc** *Mark jerked the phone away from the girl.* | *Graham had to jerk the steering wheel to the left to avoid a crash.* —**jerk** [n C] *The train moved off with a jerk.*

7 to move a company or its people to another place

- move
- transfer
- relocate
- shunt

move /muːv/ [v T] **move sb (from sth) to sth** *The Education Department is considering moving 500 full-*

time staff to Runcorn. | **move sth (from sth) to sth** *The company says it will move its distribution center to Chicago early next year.*

transfer /træns'fɜːʳ/ [v I/T] to move someone from one place to another, especially to another job, department, or office within the same organization **+ to** *Davidson transferred to another department last October.* | **transfer sb (from sth) to sth** *One option would be to transfer Struthers from London to New York.* | *Harding has been transferred to Albany prison, where he will complete his sentence.* —**transfer** /'trænsfɜːʳ/ [n C] *She's put in for a transfer* (=asked to be transferred) *to the Los Angeles office.*

relocate /ˌriːləʊ'keɪt‖riː'ləʊkeɪt/ [v I/T] to permanently move part or all of a company to another place, especially when this brings financial advantages: *If rents continue to rise, many local businesses may decide to relocate.* | **+ to/in** *The federal government is offering attractive tax breaks to corporations that relocate in areas of high unemployment.* | **relocate sth to/in sth** *We're relocating our educational software division to North Carolina.* —**relocation** /ˌriːləʊ'keɪʃən/ [n U] *Salary and other benefits are excellent and include a company car and help with relocation.* | **relocation expenses** *Does the company pay relocation expenses?*

shunt /ʃʌnt/ [v T] informal to move someone from one job to another, especially a less important one **shunt sb from/to/into sth** *I'm sick of being shunted from one department to another.* | *The company's solution to dealing with incompetent staff seems to be to shunt them into clerical jobs.*

8 to move to a new home

- move

move /muːv/ [v I] to go to live in a new place: *'Do they still live on Reighton Road?' 'No, they've moved.'* | **move house** (=go to live in a new house) British *The Chandlers are planning to move house in the next year or so.* | *Moving house can be extremely stressful.* | **+ to/from** *Did you know that Karen's moving to the US in August?* | *They moved from Burlington to Stowe about three months ago.* | **+ into** *She moved into the new house as soon as the papers were signed.*

9 to move something or someone that is difficult to move

- move
- shift
- free
- release

move /muːv/ [v T] *I tried to open the door, but I couldn't move it an inch.* | *The sculpture is heavy and very difficult to move.*

shift /ʃɪft/ [v T] British informal to move something, especially something large or heavy, from a position in which it is stuck: *The sofa is stuck in the doorway and I can't shift it.* | *There's no point trying to shift the car by ourselves – we'll have to get a truck to pull us out.*

free /friː/ [v T] to move something or someone from a position in which they are stuck or being held, especially with a sudden forceful movement: *We're going to need some rope to help free the girl.* | **free sb/sth from sth** *Kirk battled for eight hours to free himself from the wreckage.* | *Susan managed to free her right hand from her attacker with a violent twisting movement.* | **struggle to free yourself** *The horse's eyes were filled with terror as it struggled to free itself from the deep, sucking mud.*

release /rɪ'liːs/ [v T] to move something such as part of a machine from a position in which it is stuck or tightly fastened: *The bolts can only be released with a wrench.* | *Try to release the clamp gently.*

10 when it is difficult to move something

- can't move
- stuck
- jammed
- stiff
- paralysed
- stranded
- entangled
- won't budge/can't budge sth

can't move /ˌkɑːnt 'muːv‖ˌkænt-/ [v phrase] especially spoken if you **can't move**, you are unable to move, for example because you are injured: *Elsie was so frightened that she couldn't move.* | **can't move sth** *I can't move my leg – I think it's broken.*

stuck /stʌk/ [adj not before noun] someone or something that is **stuck** is fixed or trapped in a particular position or place and cannot move or be moved: *I can't open the window – it's stuck.* | **+ in/at/between etc** *The elevator was stuck between two floors.* | **get stuck** (=become stuck) *They tried to drive through the snow, but the car got stuck.* | **stuck in traffic** *Sorry I'm late. I got stuck in traffic.*

jammed /dʒæmd/ [adj not before noun] something that is **jammed** cannot be moved because it is trapped between two surfaces or trapped between parts of a machine: *The drawer's jammed – I can't get it open.* | **+ in/under/between etc** *The paper has got jammed in the printer again.*

stiff /stɪf/ [adj not usually before noun] if your fingers, back, neck, legs etc are **stiff**, it is difficult and usually painful for you to move them: *I woke up with a stiff neck this morning.* | *After a twelve hour plane ride, my back was stiff and sore.* | **feel stiff** *I felt really stiff after playing basketball last week.*

paralysed British **/paralyzed** American /'pærəlaɪzd/ [adj not before noun] when it is difficult or impossible to move your body **completely/partially paralyzed** *A car crash in 1997 left him completely paralysed.* | **+ with** *Deborah stood at the side of the stage, paralyzed with fear.*

stranded /'strændɪ̇d/ [adj] unable to move or be moved from a place: *After the flood, hundreds of stranded vehicles lined the roads.* | **+ on/in/at etc** *Whales occasionally swim too close to shore and become stranded in the shallow water.* | **leave sb stranded** *My car broke down, and I was left stranded by the side of the road.*

entangled ALSO **caught up** British /ɪn'tæŋgəld, ˌkɔːt 'ʌp/ [adj not before noun] if two or more things are **entangled** or **caught up**, they are completely twisted together so that they cannot move or separate **+ in** *His hands were entangled in the ropes.* | *My glasses were caught up in my hair and I couldn't take them off.* | **become/get entangled/caught up (in)** *A child swimming in the river had become entangled in the weeds and been drowned.* | *Our umbrellas got caught up as we tried to squeeze past each other.*

won't budge/can't budge sth /ˌwəʊnt 'bʌdʒ, ˌkɑːnt 'bʌdʒ (sth) ‖ˌkænt-/ [v phrase] if something **won't budge**, or you **can't budge** it, you cannot move it even though you try very hard: *Could you give me a hand with this box? It won't budge.* | *The dresser was so heavy that I couldn't even budge it.* | **not budge (sth) an inch** *I tried to raise the window, but it wouldn't budge an inch.*

11 not moving

- still
- stationary
- be at a standstill
- calm
- motionless
- immobile
- be glued/rooted to
- not move a muscle

still /stɪl/ [adj not before noun] not moving – use this especially about people who are not moving, or about places where there is no wind: *There was no wind and the trees were completely still.* | **still water** *Anna looked out across the still waters of the lake.* | **keep/stand/sit still** *Keep still while I tie your shoes.* | *Percy was so thrilled he could hardly sit still.*

stationary /ˈsteɪʃənəri‖-neri/ [adj] **stationary car/vehicle/truck/traffic** a car, vehicle etc that is not moving: *The truck swerved and hit a stationary vehicle.* | *a four-mile queue of stationary traffic*

be at a standstill /bi: ət ə ˈstændˌstɪl/ [v phrase] if traffic **is at a standstill** it is not moving. If rail or bus services **are at a standstill** they have stopped operating: *Traffic was at a standstill on the motorway.* | **bring sth to a standstill** (=make it stop moving or operating) *A severe storm brought rail services to a standstill yesterday.*

calm /kɑːm‖kɑːm, kɑːlm/ [adj] not moving because there is no wind **dead calm** (=completely calm) *The sea was dead calm.* | **calm night/evening etc** *The night was calm and warm.* | *It was a calm, clear, beautiful day.*

motionless /ˈməʊʃənləs/ [adj] completely still – used especially in literature: *Four motionless figures stood on the pier.* | **stand/sit/remain motionless** *I could see my father standing motionless in the doorway.* | *Kemp sat motionless as the verdict was read.*

immobile /ɪˈməʊbaɪl‖-bəl/ [adj] not moving or not able to move, especially because of fear or tiredness: *Brigg was immobile, his eyes fixed on the horizon.* | **+ with** *I stood there, immobile with terror.*

be glued/rooted to /bi: ˈgluːd, ˈruːtɪ̣d tuː/ [v phrase] to be unable to move from the place where you are standing or sitting because you are very frightened, surprised, or interested by something that is happening **be glued to the TV/your chair etc** *Dad was glued to the TV all day long.* | *We were glued to our chairs and listening intently to every word.* | **be glued/rooted to the spot** *I was rooted to the spot, unable to take my eyes off the strange creature.*

not move a muscle /nɒt ˌmuːv ə ˈmʌsəl/ [v phrase] to be completely still, especially because you are frightened or because you do not want someone to see you: *She hid behind the door, not moving a muscle.* | *I didn't dare move a muscle. He would have shot me.*

12 what you say to tell someone not to move

- don't move
- keep/stay still
- freeze
- stay (right) where you are

don't move /ˌdəʊnt ˈmuːv/ [v phrase] *Don't move or they'll see us.* | *Don't move. I'll be back in five minutes.*

keep/stay still /ˌkiːp, ˌsteɪ ˈstɪl/ [v phrase] used to tell someone not to change position or not to move any part of their body: *If you can't keep still, how can I cut your hair?* | *Can you keep still for a minute, Kim?* | *Be quiet and stay still.*

freeze /friːz/ [v I] used especially by police officers to tell someone to stop moving and stand completely still: *'Freeze! Drop your weapons!' shouted the policeman.*

stay (right) where you are /steɪ (ˌraɪt) weəʳ jʊ ˈɑːʳ/ [v phrase] used to tell someone not to go anywhere: *Stay where you are! Don't come any closer.* | *I'm going to look for a telephone. You stay right where you are until I come back.*

music

RELATED WORDS

- *see also* **sing, dance, sound, television/radio, perform/performance**

1 music

- music
- musical
- note
- tune
- melody
- harmony
- rhythm
- beat

music /ˈmjuːzɪk/ [n U] the sounds made by people singing or playing musical instruments, or the art and skill of writing, playing, or singing these sounds: *What kinds of music do you like?* | *The music was so loud you couldn't carry on a conversation.* | *Would you like to listen to some music?* | *The Royal College of Music* | *Did you study music at school?* | **live music** (=music that is not recorded) *The club has live music every Saturday night.* | **rock/pop/country/classical etc music** *I've never been a big fan of country music.*

musical /ˈmjuːzɪkəl/ [adj usually before noun] relating to music: *Do you play a musical instrument?* | *Her teachers told her she had no musical ability whatsoever.* | *O'Connor uses a wide variety of musical styles in his performances.*

note /nəʊt/ [n C] a single musical sound: *It is amazing how expressive she makes each note sound.* | *Some of the singers had a little trouble with the high notes.*

tune /tjuːn‖tuːn/ [n C] the main series of notes in a piece of music – use this especially when you think it is nice to listen to: *The music box plays the tune 'Send in the Clowns.'* | *I've heard that tune before, but I don't know the words to the song.*

melody /ˈmelədi/ [n C/U] the main series of notes in a piece of music that has many lines being played at the same time: *The song has a simple melody and beautiful lyrics.* | *Melody is not the central element in Martino's compositions – rhythm is more important.*

harmony /ˈhɑːʳməni/ [n C/U] the chords or lines of music that accompany (=support) the melody: *The harmonies in her symphonies are wonderfully rich.* | *All first year music students are required to take a class in harmony.*

rhythm /ˈrɪðəm/ [n C/U] a pattern of beats in music, that comes from the arrangement of the notes, the time between them, and the emphasis each note is given: *You need to feel the rhythm of the music in order to dance properly.* | *The band's music is known for its fiery Latin rhythms.*

beat /biːt/ [n singular] the main rhythm that a piece of music has: *Jessica moved her hips to the beat of the music.* | *Their new song has a good beat that you can dance to.*

2 a piece of music

- piece/piece of music
- song
- composition
- work
- number

piece/piece of music /piːs, ˌpiːs əv ˈmjuːzɪk/ [n C] an arrangement of musical notes that has been written by someone – use this about music without words: *The CD contains two pieces performed by the Tokyo String Quartet.* | *It's difficult to know ahead of time whether an audience will like a new piece of music.*

song /sɒŋ‖sɔːŋ/ [n C] a short piece of music with words for singing: *That's a pretty song – where did you learn it?* | *The song 'Yesterday' is one of the most often recorded songs in the world.* | *In the evenings we'd sit around the campfire and sing songs.*

composition /ˌkɒmpəˈzɪʃən‖ˌkɑːm-/ [n C] a piece of music – use this when you are considering the way the music is written: *Stone's composition 'Idaho' became a national hit when Benny Goodman recorded it for Columbia.* | *Zwilich's flute concerto was nominated for Best Contemporary Classical Composition.*

work /wɜːʳk/ [n C] a piece of music, especially a long classical one – use this in written or formal contexts: *The performance began with two of Mozart's early works.* | *Handel's 'Messiah' is one of the most majestic musical works ever written.*

number /ˈnʌmbəʳ/ [n C] a piece of popular music that forms part of a longer performance: *'The show's not very good.' 'We can leave after this number if you want.'* | *Nell Carter also appeared and performed a couple of upbeat numbers.*

3 to play music

- play
- perform
- on (the) drums/guitar/keyboards etc
- improvise
- jam
- play by ear

play /pleɪ/ [v I/T] to make music on a musical instrument: *Do you play in an orchestra?* | *Charles likes to play Celtic music on his flute.* | **play the piano/trumpet/drums etc** *I didn't know you could play the violin.*

perform /pəʳˈfɔːʳm/ [v I/T] formal to sing or play music in front of people who have come to listen: *She still gets very nervous about performing in public.* | *The orchestra will be at the Festival Hall tonight, performing a selection of works by Russian composers.*

on (the) drums/guitar/keyboards etc /ɒn (ðə) ˈdrʌmz/ [adv] playing a particular instrument in a band: *When they perform, Barbara sings and her older sister Suzie is on drums.* | *The recording features Norman Simmons on piano and Henry Johnson on guitar.*

improvise /ˈɪmprəvaɪz/ [v I/T] to perform music by creating it from your imagination while you play or sing: *You can't play jazz unless you can improvise.* | *Mike improvised a little farewell song at the end of the evening.*

jam /dʒæm/ [v I usually in progressive] to play jazz or rock music with other people in an informal way, without planning what you are going to play: *Some guys are getting together tonight at Scott's to jam.* | **+ with** *Matthews used to jam with drummer Carter Beauford and saxophonist LeRoi Moore.* | **jam session** (=an occasion when a group of musicians jam) *All-night jam sessions were common in Kansas City jazz clubs of the 1930s.*

play by ear /ˌpleɪ baɪ ˈɪəʳ/ [v phrase] to play a song or piece of music from memory without reading the written music: *He never took piano lessons – he just plays by ear.* | *With the Suzuki method, a child is trained to play by ear at an early age without any written music.*

4 someone who plays music

- musician
- performer
- player
- accompanist
- soloist
- street musician

musician /mjuːˈzɪʃən‖mjʊ-/ [n C] someone who plays a musical instrument very well or someone who does this as their job: *Ellen is one of our most talented young musicians.* | *The group is made up of local musicians who have been performing together for several years.*

performer /pəʳˈfɔːʳməʳ/ [n C] someone who sings or plays a musical instrument in order to entertain people: *Most performers feel nervous before they go on stage.* | *The festival provides an opportunity to hear some fine blues performers at reasonable prices.*

player /ˈpleɪəʳ/ [n C] **guitar/piano/trumpet etc player** (=someone who plays a particular musical instrument) *Simpson is a talented singer and piano player.* | *She sang 'I'll Fly Away,' accompanied by two guitar players.*

accompanist /əˈkʌmpənɪst/ [n C] someone who plays a musical instrument while someone else sings or plays the main tune: *I'd be happy to sing, but I'll need an accompanist.* | *Pianist Tommy Flanagan is among the finest accompanists in jazz history.*

soloist /ˈsəʊləʊɪst/ [n C] someone who plays or sings the main part of a piece of music alone, or with a musical group supporting them: *There will be four soloists in tonight's performance.* | *Violin soloist Jessica Solano will perform Mozart's Concerto No. 4.*

street musician ALSO **busker** British /ˈstriːt mjuːˌzɪʃən‖-mjʊ-, ˈbʌskəʳ/ [n C] someone who plays music in a public place such as a street or railway station, so that people will give them money: *A street musician sat on the other side of the courtyard, banging a drum.* | *In the summer, buskers fill the town's streets and public squares.*

5 to write music

- write
- compose
- set/put sth to music

write /raɪt/ [v I/T] to **write** a song or a piece of music: *I wrote the next song for my wife.* | *an opera written by Verdi* | *I sit at the piano when I write.*

compose /kəmˈpəʊz/ [v I/T] to write a piece of music, especially classical music: *Glass composed the music for Cocteau's movie.* | *a song composed by Schubert* | *The children will now play some pieces that they composed themselves.* | *Dario composes for a living.*

set/put sth to music /ˌset, ˌpʊt (sth) tə ˈmjuːzɪk/ [v phrase] to write music so that the words of a play, poem etc can be sung: *The Greek tragedy 'Elektra' was set to music by Richard Strauss.* | *She sat at the piano for hours, putting one of her poems to music.*

6 someone who writes music

- composer
- songwriter

composer /kəmˈpəʊzəʳ/ [n C] someone who writes music, especially classical music: *Henry Purcell was one of the greatest English composers.* | *Amelia likes German composers, particularly Wagner.*

songwriter /ˈsɒŋˌraɪtəʳ‖ˈsɔːŋ-/ [n C] someone who writes songs: *Most of Elton John's early hits were written by songwriter Bernie Taupin.* | **singer-songwriter** (=someone who writes songs and sings them) *Music on the show is performed by singer-songwriter Vonda Shepard.*

7 a public performance of music

- concert
- go to see
- performance
- gig
- festival

concert /ˈkɒnsəʳt‖ˈkɑːn-/ [n C] a performance given by musicians: *There's a free band concert in Reid Park this afternoon.* | *Amanda has a solo in the school chorus concert this year.* | **+ of** *Various performers will present a concert of Broadway music to benefit AIDS charities.* | **go to a concert** *On Friday we're going to a concert of modern African music.*

go to see /ˌgəʊ tə ˈsiː/ [v phrase] to **go to see** a particular singer or band perform – use this especially about going to see modern popular musicians: *Are you going to see Britney Spears this weekend?*

performance /pəʳˈfɔːʳməns/ [n C] when a musician or group of musicians performs a piece of music: *There are no tickets left for this evening's performance.* | **+ of** *It is the first performance of Berlioz's Requiem in this city in over 20 years.* | **live performance** (=a performance that is not recorded) *Have you ever heard a live performance of Beethoven's Seventh Symphony?*

gig /gɪg/ [n C] informal a performance by a musician or group of musicians playing modern popular music or jazz: *We have a gig in L.A. on Thursday.* | **do/play a gig** (=perform at a concert) *They are doing about 30 gigs on their European tour.*

festival /ˈfestɨvəl/ [n C] an event lasting for a few days or weeks each year, in which many different musical groups or singers perform. It takes place in the same place every year: *I first heard them play at the Pittsburgh Jazz Festival.* | *Are you going to the Glastonbury festival this year?*

must/ don't have to

RELATED WORDS

- *see also* **force sb to do sth, should/ought to, insist, forbid**
- **USAGE** Only use ***must*** in the present tense. The past tense of ***must*** is ***had to***, and the future tense is ***will have to***.

1 when a situation forces you to do something

- must do sth/have to do sth
- need to do sth
- be forced to do sth
- have no alternative

must do sth/have to do sth /ˌmʌst ˈduː (sth), ˌhæv tə ˈduː (sth)/ [v phrase] *We must get this work finished today.* | *Must you leave so soon?* | *Before we go and see Ian there's something I have to do.* | *Do we have to stay for the whole show?* | **have got to do sth** *I've got to go to London tomorrow for a meeting.* | **must/have to** *I didn't really want to go by train, but I had to because my car was still being repaired.* | *I hate to make the trip this time of year, but I really must.*

need to do sth /ˌniːd tə ˈduː (sth)/ [v phrase not in progressive] to have to do something because you think it is necessary or someone else thinks it is necessary: *We need to buy some more potatoes.* | *Simon knew that he needed to raise the money quickly.* | *Do I really need to go to this meeting?*

be forced to do sth /be compelled to do sth/be obliged to do sth /biː ˌfɔːʳst tə ˈduː (sth), biː kəmˌpeld tə ˈduː (sth), biː əˌblaɪdʒd tə ˈduː (sth)/ [v phrase] to have to do something that you do not want to do because you are in a situation that makes it impossible to avoid: *She was forced to retire early due to ill health.* | *We may be obliged to scrap the project if we don't get more funding.* | *Organizers were compelled to cancel the event after the sponsors pulled out.*

have no alternative /hæv ˌnəʊ ɔːlˈtɜːʳnətɪv/ [v phrase not in progressive] to have to do something, even though you do not want to, because there is nothing else you can possibly do in the situation: *The authorities say that they had to close the hospital – they had no alternative.* | **have no alternative but to do sth** *He had no alternative but to resign.*

2 when a rule or law forces you to do something

- must do sth/have to do sth
- be obliged to do sth
- be required to do sth
- have an obligation to do sth/be under an obligation to do sth
- compulsory
- mandatory
- obligatory

must do sth/have to do sth /ˌmʌst ˈduː (sth), ˌhæv tə ˈduː (sth)/ [v phrase] *All competitors must arrive by 10:00 a.m.* | *All visitors have to sign in at the main reception desk.* | *I'm not sure what the procedure is – you might have to make a written complaint.* | **must/have to** *I don't want to get rid of the animals, but we have to.*

be obliged to do sth /biː əˌblaɪdʒd tə ˈduː (sth)/ [v phrase] formal to have to do something, because of a legal or professional rule: *Doctors are obliged by law to try to keep their patients alive.* | *Members of parliament are obliged to declare all their financial interests.*

be required to do sth /biː rɪˌkwaɪəʳd tə ˈduː (sth)/ [v phrase] formal to have to do something – used especially in written notices and official documents: *Visitors are required to register their names on arrival.* | *Under the law the President is required* *to notify Congress when US troops are likely to be involved in hostilities.* | *Companies are legally required to keep records of all their financial transactions.*

have an obligation to do sth/be under an obligation to do sth /hæv ən ɒblɪˌgeɪʃən tə ˈduː (sth), biː ʌndər ən ɒblɪˌgeɪʃən tə ˈduː- (sth) ‖-ɑːb-/ [v phrase] to have to do something because it is the duty of someone in your position to do it, or because you have officially agreed to do it: *Anyone who rents a house is under an obligation to keep it clean and tidy.* | *Having promised to cut taxes, the government now has an obligation to do so.*

compulsory /kəmˈpʌlsəri/ [adj] something that is **compulsory** must be done, used, or provided because of a rule or law: *Smoke detectors are compulsory in all new buildings.* | *Compulsory education* (=when all children have to go to school) *was introduced in 1870.* | **+ for** *Maths and English are compulsory for all students.* | **it is compulsory (for sb) to do sth** *It is now compulsory for anyone claiming state benefit to register with a job centre.*

mandatory /ˈmændətəri‖-tɔːri/ [adj] something that is **mandatory** must be done because of the law: *Drug smuggling carries a mandatory death sentence.* | **+ for** *In some countries, wearing helmets is mandatory for all cyclists.*

obligatory /əˈblɪgətəri‖-tɔːri/ [adj] something that is **obligatory** must be done because of a rule or law, or because it is expected that you will do it: *Evening dress is usual, but not obligatory.* | **+ for** *Military service is obligatory for all men between 18 and 27.* | **it is obligatory (for sb) to do sth** *It is now obligatory for all competitors to wear face protectors.*

3 when you feel that you should do something because it would be right

- must do sth/have to do sth
- feel obliged to do sth
- feel compelled to do sth
- feel impelled to do sth

must do sth/have to do sth /ˌmʌst ˈduː (sth), ˌhæv tə ˈduː (sth)/ [v phrase] *Everyone will be expecting me so I have to go.* | *I must write and thank her for the lovely flowers she sent me.* | **must/have to** *I don't really want to spend Christmas with my family, but I suppose I have to.*

feel obliged to do sth /fiːl əˌblaɪdʒd tə ˈduː (sth)/ [v phrase] to feel that you should do something because other people expect you to do it and will be disappointed or upset if you do not: *I felt obliged to invite all my family, although I didn't really want to.*

feel compelled to do sth /fiːl kəmˌpeld tə ˈduː (sth)/ [v phrase] formal to feel very strongly that you must do something, because it is the right thing to do and people expect you to do it: *No one should feel compelled to take part. It should be voluntary.* | *I felt compelled to say something in Henry's defence.*

feel impelled to do sth /fiːl ɪmˌpeld tə ˈduː (sth)/ [v phrase] formal to feel that it is your moral duty to do something: *I feel impelled to write and tell you how disappointed I am with your newspaper.* | *Sarah felt impelled to stay at home and look after her parents.*

4 when a job, plan etc includes something that you must do

- entail
- involve

entail /ɪnˈteɪl/ [v T not in progressive] if a job, plan, piece of work etc **entails** something, you have to do it because this is part of the job, plan etc: *I didn't want to take on a job that would entail a lot of travelling.* | **entail doing sth** *The job entailed being on call twenty-four hours a day.*

involve /ɪnˈvɒlv‖ɪnˈvɑːlv/ [v T not in progressive] if something such as a job, plan, decision etc **involves** something, you have to do it because it is part of the job, plan etc: *Community service can involve anything from gardening to helping in old people's homes.* | **involve doing sth** *The plan involves converting the old canteen into a sports hall.*

5 when you do not have to do something

- not have to do sth
- there is no need to do sth
- unnecessary/not necessary
- not need to do sth/needn't do sth
- be under no obligation to do sth
- optional
- voluntary

not have to do sth /nɒt ˌhæv tə ˈduː (sth)/ [v phrase not in progressive] if you do **not have to do** something, you can do it if you want, but you are not forced to do it, either by a rule or by another person, or by the situation you are in: *Paola was fortunate in that she came from a wealthy family and didn't have to work.* | *You don't have to go if you don't want to.*

there is no need to do sth /ðeər ɪz ˌnəʊ niːd tə ˈduː (sth)/ spoken say this to tell someone that it is not necessary for them to do something: *There's no need to do the dishes – I'll do them in the morning.* | **there's no need for sb to do sth** *There's no need for you to bring any food – it's all being provided.*

unnecessary/not necessary /ʌnˈnesəsəri‖-seri, nɒt ˈnesəsəri‖-seri/ [adj] if something is **unnecessary** or **not necessary**, it is not needed or there is no good reason for you to do it: *They want to build another shopping mall here, but we think it's completely unnecessary.* | **it is unnecessary/not necessary to do sth** *It's not necessary to wash your hair every day.*

not need to do sth/needn't do sth /nɒt ˌniːd tə ˈduː (sth), ˌniːdnt ˈduː (sth)/ [v phrase not in progressive] to not have to do something, because it is not necessary: *You don't need to tell Sandy – she already knows.* | *You needn't come with me – I can find my own way to the station.* | *Marian was one of those lucky students who didn't need to work hard to do well.*

be under no obligation to do sth /biː ʌndəʳ nəʊ ɒblɪˌgeɪʃən tə ˈduː (sth) ‖-ɑːb-/ [v phrase] to not have to do something if you do not want to, especially in a situation where you might feel that you have to because other people will be upset or disappointed if you do not: *The firm is under no obligation to offer you a job.* | **not be under any obligation to do sth** *You are not under any obligation to buy anything.*

optional /ˈɒpʃənəl‖ˈɑːp-/ [adj] if something is **optional**, you do not have to do it or use it but you can if you want to: *You don't have to do French – it's optional.* | *The holiday price includes entertainment in the evenings, and there are optional excursions on offer every day.* | **+ for** *General Studies is optional for sixth-form students.*

voluntary /ˈvɒləntəri‖ˈvɑːlənteri/ [adj] a **voluntary** activity is one that you do because you want to do it, especially because you believe it is useful or will help other people, and not because you have to: *The council is trying to get more young people involved in doing voluntary work.* | *We get all our money from voluntary contributions.*

6 when you must not do something

- must not/mustn't
- can't

must not/mustn't /ˈmʌst nɒt, ˈmʌsənt/ [v] use this to tell or order someone not to do something: *This book must not be removed from the library.* | **must not/mustn't do sth** *Remember, you mustn't tell anyone about this.*

can't /kɑːnt‖kænt/ [v] spoken use this to say that someone is not allowed to do something: *'Ben wants to borrow the car.' 'Well tell him he can't.'* | **can't do sth** *I'm sorry, you know I can't discuss my work – it's confidential.*

mysterious

RELATED WORDS

- see also **strange, unusual, solve, understand, magic, ghost**

1 strange and difficult to explain or understand

- mysterious
- strange
- be a mystery
- be shrouded/veiled in mystery

mysterious /mɪˈstɪəriəs/ [adj] events, behaviour, or situations that are **mysterious** are difficult to explain or understand: *Police are investigating the mysterious disappearance of a young schoolteacher.* | *He was seen leaving the building at midnight with two men – it was all very mysterious.* | *She had been suffering from mysterious fits for five years before the doctors diagnosed epilepsy.* | **in mysterious circumstances** *The ship vanished in mysterious circumstances, never to be seen again.*

strange /streɪndʒ/ [adj] very different from what you expect or from what usually happens, in a way that makes you feel a little frightened or surprised: *You say she's at home? That's strange because she told me she was going abroad for two weeks.* | *His strange behaviour made Teresa suspicious.* | **it is strange that** *It was strange that she had had this baby with red hair when both she and her husband were very dark.*

be a mystery /biː ə ˈmɪstəri/ [v phrase] if something **is a mystery**, you cannot understand how or why it happens: *How had he escaped from prison without anyone's help? It was a mystery.* | **it's a mystery (to me) why/what etc** *It is a mystery to me why people decide to get married.* | **be a complete mystery** *Four years after the event, the scientist's suicide remains a complete mystery.*

be shrouded/veiled in mystery /biː ˌʃraʊdəd, ˌveɪld ɪn ˈmɪstəri/ [v phrase] if an event or a situation, especially one that happened a long time ago, **is shrouded in mystery**, it is mysterious because no one knows exactly what happened: *The exact circumstances of Marilyn Monroe's death are shrouded in mystery.* | *Stone age civilization, veiled in mystery as it is, has provided the greatest challenge to historians.*

2 happening in a mysterious way

- mysteriously
- strangely
- as if by magic

mysteriously /mɪˈstɪəriəsli/ [adv] *The letter had mysteriously appeared on my desk that morning.* | *Joseph was mysteriously absent from work that morning.* | *The aircraft had disappeared mysteriously from radar screens.*

strangely /ˈstreɪndʒli/ [adj] in a way that is very different from what you expect or from what usually happens, so that you feel a little frightened or surprised: *He looked at me strangely and said that he would come back later.* | *When we returned to the hotel we found the place strangely silent.*

as if by magic /əz ˌɪf baɪ ˈmædʒɪk/ [adv] if something happens **as if by magic**, it happens in a sudden and surprising way that seems impossible to explain: *The mysterious circles appeared in the fields overnight, as if by magic.* | *I was just wondering how I could get home, when suddenly, as if by magic, a taxi pulled up.*

3 a mysterious situation

- mystery
- enigma
- riddle
- puzzle

mystery /ˈmɪstəri/ [n C] an event or situation that no one can understand or explain **+ of** *No one has ever been able to explain the mystery of the Bermuda Triangle.* | **be a mystery to sb** *It's a mystery to me how Gayle managed to get here before us.* | **mystery illness/crash/phonecall etc** *Ten firemen were in hospital with a mystery illness last night.* | **unravel/solve a mystery** (=find an explanation for a mystery) *Police are still trying to unravel the mystery of how the prisoner managed to escape.* | **the mystery deepens** (=something becomes more difficult to explain) *The mystery deepens as more witnesses come forward to tell different stories.*

enigma /ɪˈnɪgmə/ [n C] a situation that is difficult to understand or explain, and that is interesting because of this: *As I studied more about their past, I became more puzzled, and the enigma expanded.* | **be something of an enigma** *It is something of an enigma how a man who could not bear to hurt a living thing could serve as defence secretary.*

riddle /ˈrɪdl/ [n C] something such as a question or a problem that people do not understand and cannot explain **+ of** *Doctors have found a new clue to the riddle of cot death.* | **solve a riddle** *Other interviewers who have met Geri have tried to solve the riddle of her success.* | **be a riddle to sb** *Why would Ian want to claim his inheritance and then give all his money away? It was a riddle to me.*

puzzle /ˈpʌzəl/ [n C] something that is very difficult to understand or explain but which can sometimes be explained by putting pieces of information together: *The police have almost solved the case but one important piece of the puzzle is still missing: the murder weapon.* | **solve a puzzle** *In 1953 the intricate puzzle of DNA's structure was solved in a Cambridge laboratory.*

4 people that are mysterious

- mysterious
- enigmatic
- be a mystery
- enigma

mysterious /mɪˈstɪəriəs/ [adj] if someone is **mysterious**, other people do not know much about them and do not understand their reasons for doing things: *You are a mysterious girl – why won't you tell me your name?* | *There was something mysterious about him, and she wanted to ask him a lot of questions.* | *He was an impostor – dark, frightening and mysterious.*

enigmatic /ˌenɪgˈmætɪk◂/ [adj] if someone is **enigmatic** it is difficult to understand their character or behaviour, especially because they keep information about themselves secret: *He was fascinated by the enigmatic actress.* | *Freud remains today an enigmatic figure.* | *Ever since the start of the journey Ahamado had remained enigmatic, silent and unforthcoming.* —**enigmatically** [adv] *Angela smiled enigmatically, as if she knew something that we didn't.*

be a mystery /biː ə ˈmɪstəri/ [v phrase] if someone **is a mystery**, you cannot explain or understand their behaviour **+ to** *Women are a complete mystery to me.*

enigma /ɪˈnɪgmə/ [n C] someone who is difficult to understand, and is therefore interesting: *Madeleine was still very much an enigma to him.*

Nn

name

RELATED WORDS

- *see also* **sign your name**

1 a person's name

- name
- first name
- Christian name
- middle name
- last name/surname
- maiden name
- family name
- initials
- title

name /neɪm/ [n C] *What's your name?* | *I'm not very good at remembering people's names.* | *His name is Raymond Ford.* | **full name** (=all your names) *Ayrton Senna's full name was Ayrton Senna da Silva.* | **sign your name** *She must have written to Laura without signing her name.* | **call sb's name** *The doctor will call your name when he is ready to see you.* | **mention sb by name** *She didn't mention you by name, but I'm sure it was you she was talking about.*

first name ALSO **given name** American /ˈfɜːʳst ˌneɪm, ˈgɪvən ˌneɪm/ [n C] the name that your parents choose for you when you are born, which in Western countries comes at the beginning of your full name: *Her first name is Liz. I don't know her surname.* | *Fill out the form with your last name, followed by your given name.*

Christian name /ˈkrɪstʃən ˌneɪm/ [n C] someone's first name, or the name that Christian parents choose for a baby when they christen it: *My mother's Christian name was Mary.*

middle name ALSO **second name** British /ˈmɪdl ˌneɪm, ˈsekənd ˌneɪm/ [n C] the name that comes between your first and last names: *John F. Kennedy's middle name was Fitzgerald.* | *Vicki won't tell anyone her second name.*

last name/surname /ˈlɑːst ˌneɪm‖ˈlæst-, ˈsɜːʳneɪm, / [n C] your last name, which is the same as your parents' name: *I know his first name, but I can't remember his last name.* | *Smith is the most common English surname.*

maiden name /ˈmeɪdn ˌneɪm/ [n C] the surname that a woman had before she was married: *My mother kept her maiden name when she got married.* (=did not change her name to her husband's name)

family name /ˈfæməli ˌneɪm/ [n C] the name that is shared by all the members of the same family: *Joseph Conrad's original family name was Korzeniowski.* | **carry on the family name** (=to pass on your family name to your children) *He died leaving no children to carry on the family name.*

initials /ɪˈnɪʃəlz/ [n plural] the first letters of each of your names: *There's no need to write out your full name. Just your initials will do.* | *a suitcase marked with the initials JR*

title /ˈtaɪtl/ [n C] a word such as Mrs, Miss, Ms, Mr, Dr, or Professor that you put before your name: *The title 'Ms' became much more popular in the 1980s.*

2 a name used by your friends and family that is not your real name

- nickname
- pet name

nickname /ˈnɪkneɪm/ [n C] a name given to someone by their friends or family, which is not their real name and is often chosen because of something about their appearance or behaviour: *At school, her nickname was Carrots because of her red hair.* | **earn sb a nickname** (=cause someone to have a particular nickname) *His black cloak earned him the nickname 'Dracula'.*

pet name /ˈpet ˌneɪm/ [n C] a name you call someone who you like very much, for example your boyfriend or a young child in your family: *Her pet name for him is Tiger.* | *She had pet names for all her grandchildren – Curly, Longlegs, and Coco.*

3 a name that someone uses that is not their real name

- false name
- stage name
- pseudonym
- pen name
- alias
- aka/a.k.a.
- under an assumed name
- go by the name of
- under the name of sth

false name /ˌfɔːls ˈneɪm/ [n C] a name that someone uses instead of their real name, so that people will not find out who they really are: *None of them had ever heard of Giles Williams, which was clearly a false name.* | **give/use a false name** *It is illegal to give a false name to your employer.* | **under a false name** (=using a false name) *The woman was a foreigner travelling under a false name.*

stage name /ˈsteɪdʒ ˌneɪm/ [n C] the name used by an actor, singer etc instead of their real name: *Greta Garbo was the stage name of Greta Gustavson, born in Stockholm in 1905.*

pseudonym /ˈsjuːdənɪm‖ˈsuːdn-ɪm/ [n C] a name used by someone, especially a writer, instead of their real name: *'Saki' was the pseudonym of the writer H.H.Monroe.* | **under the pseudonym** (=using the pseudonym) *Morton wrote a weekly column in 'The Daily Telegraph' under the pseudonym 'Beachcomber'.*

pen name /ˈpen neɪm/ [n C] a name used by a writer instead of their real name: *The name Voltaire was in fact a pen name – his real name was Francois Marie Arouet.* | **under the pen name** (=using the pen name) *She wrote her novels under the pen name George Eliot, because the publishers would not accept a manuscript written by a woman.*

alias /ˈeɪliəs/ [prep] a word meaning 'also known as', used when giving someone's real name, together with a different name they also use or are known by, especially because they are a criminal: *Carlos, alias 'The Jackal', is wanted by police in several countries.* | *We were introduced to Mrs Taylor, alias Meg Dods, author of the Housewife's Manual.* —**alias** [n C] *Roberts is known to use a number of aliases, including Bill Smith, Paul Williams, and even Count Von Blixenburg.*

aka/a.k.a. /ˌeɪ keɪ ˈeɪ/ an abbreviation meaning 'also known as', used when giving someone's real name together with a different name that they use or are known by, especially because they are a criminal: *Standing there in front of me was Peter Downs, a.k.a. 'The Leithgate Strangler'.*

under an assumed name /ʌndər ən əˌsjuːmd ˈneɪm‖-əˌsuːmd-/ [adv] if you do something **under an assumed name**, you do it using a name that is not your real name, especially in order to do it dishonestly or secretly: *He had rented a car under an assumed name.* | *She entered the private clinic under an assumed name, but the press still managed to find out.*

go by the name of /ˌgəʊ baɪ ðə ˈneɪm ɒv/ [v phrase] if someone **goes by the name of** something, they tell people that this is their name, when in fact it is not: *Herbert always hated his original name, so he went by the name of David.* | *The photographs resembled a man who lived in New York and went by the name of Ivan Denisovich.*

under the name of sth /ˌʌndəʳ ðə ˈneɪm əv (sth)/ [adv] using a different name from your real name: *They registered at the hotel under the name of Smith.* | *Bollard set up a company under the name of Mr M. Roberts.*

4 the name of a place, thing, product etc

- name
- title
- place name
- code name
- brand name
- proper noun

name /neɪm/ [n C] *I've forgotten the name of the street where she lives.* | **get its name from sth** *The village of Furnace got its name from the local industries of silver and iron smelting.* | **the Chinese/French etc name for sth** *The Chinese name for this plant means 'cat's ears'.*

title /ˈtaɪtl/ [n C] the name of a book, film, play, painting etc: *I've read one of her books, but I can't remember the title.* | *What's the title of this week's assignment?* | **under the title** *The film was released in the UK under the title 'Maybe Baby'.*

place name /ˈpleɪs ˌneɪm/ [n C] the name of a place such as a town or an area of a country: *In this part of the US many of the place names are of French origin.*

code name /ˈkəʊd ˌneɪm/ [n C] a secret name for something such as a military plan that you do not want other people to know about: *Operation Overlord was the code name of the Normandy landing which took place in June 1944.*

brand name /ˈbrænd ˌneɪm/ [n C] the name given to a product by the company that makes it, often including the name of the company itself: *Our customers prefer goods with brand names, such as Levis or Adidas.*

proper noun ALSO **proper name** /ˈprɒpəʳ ˌnaʊn, ˈprɒpəʳ ˌneɪm‖ˈprɑː-/ [n C] the name of a person, place, or organization, usually written with a capital letter at the beginning – used when talking about grammar: *Dictionaries don't usually list proper names.* | *Chicago, Stephen and Mount Everest are all proper nouns.*

5 to have a particular name

- sb's name is sth
- be called
- be named
- be known as
- be entitled
- go by the name of
- be termed

sb's name is sth / (sb's) ˈneɪm ɪz (sth) / *Hi! My name's Ted. I'm from Florida.* | *'Who's that man over there?' 'His name is Lucio Mannonetti and he owns the company.'*

be called /biː ˈkɔːld/ [v phrase] to have a particular name – use this about a person, thing, or place: *There's someone called Russell on the phone for you.* | *What's the new teacher called?* | *They are in favour of what is called 'sustainable development'.* | *It was scarcely big enough to be called a school – it was more like a garage.*

be named /biː ˈneɪmd/ [v phrase] someone who **is named** Paul, Jane etc has the name Paul, Jane etc: *Their new baby is named Caroline.* | *She went to the movies with some guy named Rudi.*

be known as /biː ˈnəʊn æz/ [v phrase] if someone or something **is known as** a particular name, that is the name that people call them, although it is not their real name: *This area is known as Little Odessa because there are a lot of Russians living there.* | **be known to sb as sth** *He was known to his friends as Rambo.* | **be better known as sth** *William Shatner is better known as Captain Kirk.*

be entitled /biː ɪnˈtaɪtld/ [v phrase] if a book, play, film, painting etc **is entitled** something, that is its name: *Her first published novel was entitled 'Rivers of Passion'.* | *Biko contributed a column to the student newspaper which was entitled 'I Write What I Like'.*

go by the name of /ˌgəʊ baɪ ðə ˈneɪm ɒv/ [v phrase] to be called something, use this especially when you are giving another better-known name for something: *This kind of chilli powder sometimes goes by the name of cayenne pepper.* | *The mixture of fish, rice and eggs goes by the name of kedgeree in most restaurants.*

be termed /biː ˈtɜːʳmd/ [v phrase] to be called by a particular name – used especially in scientific or technical contexts: *This process, in which liquid metal is poured into moulds, is usually termed die-casting.*

6 to give a name to someone or something

- call
- name
- christen
- rename

call /kɔːl/ [v T] **call sb Paul/Jane etc** *My mother wanted to call me Yuri.* | *Guidebooks call Chicago 'The Windy City'.* | *This is what psychologists call 'body language'.*

name /neɪm/ [v T] to officially give someone or something a name: *Have they named the baby yet?* | **name sb Paul/Jane etc** *We named our daughter Sarah.* | **name sb/sth after sb** ALSO **name sb/sth for sb** American *Bill was named after his father.* | *The new building is going to be named for Ronald Reagan.*

christen /ˈkrɪsən/ [v phrase] to give a baby its name at a Christian religious ceremony **christen sb Paul/Jane etc** *They christened him Patrick John.* | *She was christened Jessica, but everyone calls her Jess.*

rename /riːˈneɪm/ [v T] to give something a new and different name: *You can rename, delete, or copy files very easily.* | **rename sth sth** *New Amsterdam was renamed New York in the 17th Century.*

7 to publicly announce the name of someone

- name
- identify

name /neɪm/ [v T] to publicly say who someone is, by telling people his or her name: *She refused to name the father of her child.* | **name sb as sb** *Police have named the dead woman as Annabel Thomas.*

identify /aɪˈdentɪ̈faɪ/ [v T] to officially recognize someone and say that you know who they are, for example in order to help the police: *The victim identified her attacker in court.* | *Greg had to identify the body of his wife.*

8 when you cannot remember or do not use the exact name

- what's-his-name/what's-her-name
- so-and-so
- what's-its-name
- thingamijig
- doodad/doohickey
- such and such

what's-his-name/what's-her-name /ˈwɒts ɪz ˌneɪm, ˈwɒts ɜːʳ ˌneɪm/ [n phrase] spoken informal say this when you cannot remember someone's name: *She was with what's-his-name – you know, the one who wears orange jeans.* | *Send the report to what's-her-name in Accounting.*

so-and-so /ˈsəʊ ənd səʊ/ [n phrase] an expression meaning a particular person, used especially when you are mentioning someone that another person often talks about, and their actual name is not important: *Whenever you ask her about anything it's always 'so-and-so says this', or 'so-and-so says that' – she never gives her own honest opinion.* | *They're always gossiping about so-and-so having an affair with so-and-so.*

what's-its-name ALSO **whatsit** especially British **/whatchamacallit** American /ˈwɒts ɪts ˌneɪm, ˈwɒtsɪt, ˈwɒtʃəməˌkɔːlɪt‖ˈwɑːt-/ [n phrase] spoken informal say this when you cannot remember the name of something: *What you need is a what's-its-name ... a torque wrench.* | *Did you see that boy with the whatsit round his head?* | *'I'm going to have a whatchamacallit when I have a baby' – 'What, you mean an epidural?'.*

thingamijig ALSO **thingy** British /ˈθɪŋəmɪ̈dʒɪg, ˈθɪŋi/ [n C] informal a small object that does a particular job, whose name you have forgotten or do not know: *They have to use a special thingamijig to undo the nuts.* | *What's that plastic thingy called?*

doodad/doohickey /ˈduːdæd, ˈduːˌhɪki/ [n C] American a small object whose name you have forgotten or do not know: *She kept pressing the buttons on the remote control doodad.* | *What's this little doohickey for?*

such and such /ˈsʌtʃ ən ˌsʌtʃ/ [n phrase] an expression meaning a particular thing, used instead of giving examples of what you are talking about: *Americans are very proud of their country – they're always saying that such and such is the biggest in the whole world.* | **such and such a person/place etc** *You can say to me, I want such and such a photographer, and I'll try to get them for you.*

9 someone whose name is not known

- anonymous
- unnamed
- unidentified
- incognito
- unknown
- nameless

anonymous /əˈnɒnɪ̈məs‖əˈnɑː-/ [adj] someone who is **anonymous** does something without saying what their name is, or their name is not known: *The writer of the poem is anonymous.* | **an anonymous donor** (=someone who gives something but does not say publicly who they are) *$50,000 has been given to the charity by an anonymous donor from Utah.* | **anonymous letter/phone call** (=from someone who does not say their name) *I received anonymous phone calls warning me not to go to the police about what I'd seen.* | **sb wishes to remain anonymous** *One source, who wished to remain anonymous, said that he had seen the woman go into his room.* —**anonymously** [adv] *He sent the documents anonymously to a local newspaper.* —**anonymity** /ˌænəˈnɪmɪ̈ti/ [n U] *If you are needed as a witness, your anonymity will be guaranteed* (=we will promise that your name will not be made known to other people).

unnamed /ˌʌnˈneɪmd◂/ [adj] an **unnamed** person is someone whose name has not been made known publicly: *An unnamed bidder paid $23 million for the painting.* | *The newspaper received the information from an unnamed source.*

unidentified /ˌʌnaɪˈdentɪ̈faɪd◂/ [adj] an **unidentified** person is someone whose name is not known because police or government officials have been unable to find out who they are, or have not said who they are: *Five men were wounded by an unidentified gunman in Belfast city centre yesterday.* | *The three bodies found in the river remain unidentified.* | *An unidentified caller contacted the police and gave the names of the men involved in the robbery.*

incognito /ˌɪnkɒgˈniːtəʊ‖ˌɪnkɑːg-/ [adv] if a famous person goes somewhere **incognito**, they go there without telling people who they are: *He tried to go incognito but his bizarre disguise made him stand out even more.*

unknown /ˌʌnˈnəʊn◂/ [adj] an **unknown** person is someone whose name is not known because you do not know them or because they are not famous: *She said the flowers were from an unknown admirer.* | *We met near the Tomb of the Unknown Soldier.* | **+ to** *Most of the stars in the movie are unknown to US audiences.*

nameless /ˈneɪmləs/ [adj] a **nameless** person is one of many people who are not famous and whose names are not generally known: *No one gives much thought to the nameless millions who work in our factories.* | *the nameless victims of the nation's civil war*

10 when the name of someone or something is not suitable

- so-called
- misnomer
- nominal
- in name only
- self-styled

so-called /ˌsəʊ ˈkɔːld◂/ [adj only before noun] a word used to describe someone or something that has been given a name that you think is wrong: *I went to see the playwright's so-called masterpiece and was very disappointed by it.* | *A lot has been written in recent years about the so-called 'male menopause'.*

misnomer /mɪsˈnəʊməʳ/ [n C] formal a name that is not correct or does not seem suitable: *The Palace of Justice – a terrible misnomer – was set on fire by the workers.* | **be something of a misnomer** *The term 'black-headed gull' is something of a misnomer, since the bird's head is actually brown.*

nominal /ˈnɒmɪ̈nəl‖ˈnɑː-/ [adj] having the name of a job or position in society, but not actually doing that job or having the responsibilities that go with it: *It's fairly clear that he is only the nominal head of the local party – in fact he's got no authority at all.* | *The daughter had all the brains and did all the accounts – the son was just the nominal boss of the business.*

in name only /ɪn ˌneɪm ˈəʊnli/ [adv] having a name or title, but not having the qualities or character that go with that name: *It's a revolutionary party in name only – in fact it's quite conservative.* | *He will be my husband in name only – he knows I'm really in love with you.*

self-styled /ˈself staɪld/ [adj] use this about someone who gives himself or herself a particular title that you think they do not deserve and do not have a right to: *The self-styled Leader of the New Republic refused all attempts at negotiation by the former government.* | *These self-styled complementary therapists make a fortune out of preying on the gullibility of often very sick people.*

narrow

RELATED WORDS

opposite: — **wide**

- *see also* **thin**

1 not wide

- narrow

narrow /ˈnærəʊ/ [adj] a **narrow** road, river, bed, space etc is not wide when measured from one side to the other: *A steep, narrow path led down through the woods to the beach.* | *She climbed through a narrow gap in the fence.* | *The road was too narrow for me to overtake the car in front.* | *Nordic skis are longer, narrower and lighter than Alpine skis.*

2 to become narrower

- get narrower
- taper

get narrower ALSO **narrow** /get ˈnærəʊəʳ, ˈnærəʊ/ [v phrase] if something such as a road, river, path, or passage **gets narrower** or **narrows**, it becomes narrow: *At that point the path got narrower and more overgrown with weeds.* | *The streets were getting narrower, the houses taller as we approached the oldest part of the town.* | **+ to** *Having narrowed to about 50 feet in the canyon, the river was now moving with speed and fury.* | **narrow from sth to sth** *Up ahead the road was narrowing from three lanes to two.*

taper /ˈteɪpəʳ/ [v I] if something **tapers**, it is narrower at one end than the other **+ to** *In the north the island is six miles across, but it tapers to two in the south.* | **taper to a point** *The leaves are bright green and taper to a point at the tip.* | *The girl's forehead was broad, tapering to a delicate chin.* —**tapering** [adj only before noun] *She had beautiful hands with long tapering fingers.* —**tapered** [adj] *The columns supporting the arch are tapered and beautifully carved.*

natural

not made by humans or changed by humans

RELATED WORDS

opposite: — **artificial**

- land where there are trees and fields and not many buildings *see* **country (13-14)**
- feelings that are natural and normal *see* **normal/ordinary**
- *see also* **false, normal/ordinary**

1 plants/animals/places/substances

- natural
- wild
- in the wild
- raw
- virgin
- untamed
- unspoiled

natural /ˈnætʃərəl/ [adj usually before noun] not made, caused, or changed by humans: *It was fascinating to see the elephants in their natural environment.* | *The river had worn away the rock to form a natural bridge.* | *A pipeline carries natural gas from under the sea to the refinery inland.* | **natural resources** (=useful or valuable substances such as oil, coal etc that exist naturally in a particular country) *Zaire is a country with substantial natural resources.* —**naturally** [adv] *Is your hair naturally curly* (=do you do anything to it to make it curly?)

wild /waɪld/ [adj usually before noun] **wild** flowers, plants, and animals are in their natural state and have not been changed or controlled by humans: *There were lots of wild flowers growing by the roadside.* | *Wild strawberries are much smaller than the kind you get in shops.* | *In my opinion, wild animals should not be kept in zoos.* | **wildlife** (=wild animals, plants etc) *The island has an abundance of wildlife – animals, birds and fish.* | **grow wild** *Banana trees were growing wild on the edge of the forest.*

in the wild /ɪn ðə ˈwaɪld/ [adv] if animals live **in the wild**, they live in their natural state, not in a place such as a farm: *There are only about 5000 white rhino left living in the wild.*

raw /rɔː/ [adj usually before noun] **raw** sugar, silk, tobacco etc is in its natural state before or without being changed by a chemical process: *Ghana still imports both raw and processed tobacco.* | *The Princess was wearing a dark green dress made of raw silk.* | **raw materials** (=basic natural materials that are needed to produce things) *Japan depends* *on the outside world for virtually all of its raw materials, including oil.*

virgin /ˈvɜːʳdʒ̍n/ [adj only before noun] **virgin** forest, land etc is still in its natural state and has not been spoiled or changed by human beings: *Here we find immense virgin forests, similar to those of the Amazon and Indonesia.* | *In front of them were 500 miles of virgin plains almost uninhabited by white people.*

untamed /ˌʌnˈteɪmd◂/ [adj] an animal or place that is **untamed** has not been trained, controlled, or changed in any way by people, so that it is still completely wild: *Untamed horses roamed free in the wilds of the American plains.* | *These were the first railways, the first means of crossing wide open spaces that are still vast and untamed, even today.*

unspoiled ALSO **unspoilt** /ˌʌnˈspɔɪld◂, ˌʌnˈspɔɪlt◂/ British [adj] a place that is **unspoiled** is still in its beautiful natural state because no-one has built roads, buildings etc on it – use this especially about a place that has not been developed for tourists: *With its largely unspoiled natural beauty, Vietnam is rapidly becoming a destination for more and more foreign visitors.* | *The path leads eventually to a vast expanse of unspoilt woodland.* | *If you go further into the countryside, you will come across a number of unspoilt medieval walled villages.*

2 food/drink

- natural
- organic
- pure

natural /ˈnætʃərəl/ [adj usually before noun] produced without using chemicals: *The manufacturers claim that only natural ingredients are used in their products.* | *Today's consumers prefer drinks that contain natural flavourings.*

organic /ɔːʳˈgænɪk/ [adj usually before noun] **organic** fruit, vegetables etc have been grown without using chemicals to help them grow: *Most supermarkets now sell organic produce.* | *Organic fruit is generally more expensive.* | *Nowadays I only buy meat that is organic.*

pure /pjʊəʳ/ [adj only before noun] **pure** food or drink has not had anything added to it: *pure orange juice* | *Our burgers are made of 100% pure beef.*

near

RELATED WORDS

opposite: —— **far**

- *see also* **convenient**

1 not far away

- near
- close
- a short distance
- not far
- nearby
- neighbouring
- in the vicinity

near /nɪəʳ/ [prep/adv/adj] only a short distance from a person, place, or thing: *We camped in a forest near a large lake.* | *Don't go near the fire.* | *Have you ever been to Versailles? It's near Paris.* | *The place where we were going was much nearer than I thought.* | **near enough to do sth** *Bob was standing near enough to hear what they were saying.* | **nearer to sth/nearest to sth** *If we moved to Dallas we'd be nearer to my parents.* | *Only the people who were nearest to the speaker could actually hear what he said.* | **near here** *The accident happened somewhere near here.*

close /kləʊs/ [adv/adj] very near to something or someone, or almost touching them: *As we approached Abbeville, the gunfire sounded very close.* | **+ to** *Don't drive so close to the edge of the road.* | **+ behind/beside** *Suddenly we heard footsteps close behind us.* | **+ together** *The houses were built very close together, and the gardens were rather small.* | *Nancy came over and sat close beside me on the bed.* | **close by** (=near where you are) *Is there a gas station close by?*

a short distance /ə ˌʃɔːʳt ˈdɪstəns/ [n phrase] used to say that something is quite near something or someone **+ away** *I'd parked my car a short distance away, just around the corner.* | **+ from** *Harvard University is only a short distance from the center of Boston.* | **a short distance to the south/north etc** *The source of the river is a short distance to the south of here.*

not far /nɒt ˈfɑːʳ/ [adv] not a very long distance away – use this about somewhere that is near enough to be easy to get to: *'How far's the station?' 'Oh, not far – about ten minutes by car.'* | **+ from** *Asti is not far from the French border.* | **+ away** *Our hotel was in the centre of town but the beach wasn't far away.*

nearby /ˌnɪəʳˈbaɪ◂/ [adv] near the place where you are or the place you are talking about: *Dave, who was sitting nearby, laughed when he heard this.* | *The house is really nice, and a lot of my friends live nearby.* | *It was very convenient having the garage nearby.* —**nearby** [adj only before noun] *Lucy was staying with her aunt in the nearby town of Hamilton.*

neighbouring British **/neighboring** American /ˈneɪbərɪŋ/ [adj only before noun] a **neighbouring** country, town, area etc is near the place where you are or the place you are talking about: *The fair attracted thousands of people from neighbouring areas.* | *Soldiers and firemen from 13 neighboring towns wrestled with the blaze for hours.*

in the vicinity /ɪn ðə vɪˈsɪnɪ̍ti/ [adv] formal in the area around and near a particular place: *A white van was seen in the vicinity at about the time when the murder took place.* | **+ of** *In the past ten years there have been more cases of cancer in the vicinity of nuclear installations.*

2 near where you live

- local
- on your doorstep
- in your own backyard

local /ˈləʊkəl/ [adj only before noun] a **local** store, hospital etc is in the area where you live and that you are most likely to use: *Volunteers like Joyce go round local schools helping children with their reading problems.* | **sb's local school/cinema etc** *You can find all these books in your local library.* | *Polzeath is our local beach, but there are better surfing beaches further away.* —**locally** [adv] in the area near where you live or work: *We prefer to do all our shopping locally.* | *Do you work locally?*

on your doorstep /ɒn jɔːʳ ˈdɔːʳstep/ [adv] informal very near the place where you live: *We're very lucky to have the park right on our doorstep.* | *Homelessness is a problem that too many people ignore. Yet it's happening on our own doorstep.*

in your own backyard /ɪn jɔːr ˌəʊn bækˈjɑːʳd/ [adv] informal near the place where you live – use this especially when talking about something that you do not want there: *Most people want the new airport so long as it isn't in their own backyard.*

3 easy to get to

- within walking/driving etc distance
- within reach
- convenient/handy for sth
- around the corner
- be close at hand
- it's no distance
- be a stone's throw from

within walking/driving etc distance /wɪðɪn 'wɔːkɪŋ ˌdɪstəns/ [adv] if a place is **within walking distance**, it is not far away, and you can walk there easily: *There are several good restaurants within walking distance.* | **+ of** *Dr Goldthorpe lived within walking distance of the University.* | **within easy walking etc distance (of sth)** *Fortunately the house that we were renting was within easy driving distance of the shops.*

within reach /wɪðɪn 'riːtʃ/ [adv] near enough to a town or place for you to get there without too much difficulty **+ of** *It was just lucky that we were within reach of a hospital.* | **within easy reach** (=near enough to get to easily) *Around Salzburg there are literally dozens of exciting places to visit – all within easy reach.*

convenient/handy for sth British ALSO **convenient to sth** American /kən'viːniənt, 'hændi fəʳ (sth), kən'viːniənt tə (sth)/ [adj] if your home, office etc is **convenient for** or **handy for** a particular place, that place is near it and easy to reach: *The place where we live now is very convenient for the school – it's only a couple of minutes on foot.* | *My husband works in London so we're looking for a house that's handy for the station.* | *We found an apartment convenient to campus and public transportation.* —**conveniently** [adv] *The campsite was conveniently situated, close to the beach.*

around the corner ALSO **round the corner** British /əˌraʊnd ðə 'kɔːʳnəʳ, ˌraʊnd ðə 'kɔːʳnəʳ/ [adv] not far away, especially in the streets of a town: *'Is there a bank near here?' 'Sure, it's just around the corner.'* | *She won't be long, she's only gone round the corner.* | **+ from** *We met in a bar just around the corner from my apartment.*

be close at hand /biː ˌkləʊs ət 'hænd/ [v phrase] if a building or person **is close at hand**, they are very near and therefore available in case you need them: *The Exhibition Centre is a great day out, with plenty of parking and all the attractions of Manchester close at hand.* | *I'm very glad that, when my children were small, my mother was always close at hand.*

it's no distance /ɪts 'nəʊ ˌdɪstəns/ if you say **it's no distance**, you mean that a place is not far away and is therefore easy to get to: *We come up here regularly from London; it's no distance.* | **+ from** *It's no distance from here to Fifth Avenue. We can easily walk it.*

be a stone's throw from /biː ə 'stəʊnz θrəʊ frɒm/ [v phrase] if one place **is a stone's throw from** another place, it is only a very short distance from it, so that it is easy to get to: *I was born in Wembley, a stone's throw from the football stadium!* | **only a stone's throw from sth** *Stanford Hospital is only a stone's throw from where I live.* | **within a stone's throw of sth** *The river's within a stone's throw of our apartment – we can see it from the window.*

4 the nearest house/shop/station etc

- nearest
- the next

nearest /'nɪərɪ̈st/ [adj] the **nearest** shop, station etc that is closest to where you are: *Excuse me, where's the nearest subway station?*

the next /ðə 'nekst/ [determiner] the **next** house, street etc that is closest to the one you are in or the one you are talking about: *The people in the next apartment were making a lot of noise.* | *I had to move the car. It's just around the corner in the next street.*

5 the fact of being near

- nearness/closeness
- proximity

nearness/closeness /'nɪəʳnɪ̈s, 'kləʊsnɪ̈s/ [n U] **+ to** *The price of villas varies considerably, according to their facilities and their nearness to the sea.* | *Some of the people took advantage of their village's closeness to the border and made profits from smuggling.*

proximity /prɒk'sɪmɪ̈ti‖prɑːk-/ [n U] formal nearness **+ to** *San Francisco has a significant immigrant population because of its proximity to Asia.* | **+ of** *The proximity of schools, stores, hospitals, and so on is an important factor when purchasing a house.*

6 near enough to pick up/touch/hit

- handy
- within reach
- within range
- point-blank

handy /'hændi/ [adj not before noun] if something is **handy**, it is near enough for you to pick up and use quickly and easily **keep/have sth handy** *Make sure you keep your passport and ticket handy.* | *A lot of people in the States have a gun handy at night and when they travel.*

within reach /wɪðɪn 'riːtʃ/ [adv] if something is **within reach**, it is near enough for you to take hold of or touch when you stretch out your hand: *As soon as she was within reach he grabbed her wrist.* | **within easy reach** *Roy pulled the ashtray towards him so that it was within easy reach.* | **within sb's reach** *At this exploratory stage, small children will want to touch anything you leave within their reach.*

within range /wɪðɪn 'reɪndʒ/ [adv] if something is **within range**, it is near enough for you to attack it or for a weapon to reach it: *Once its prey is within range, the snake's head shoots forward to attack.* | **+ of** *The village is well within range of the rockets which are being fired.* | **come within range of sth** *A day later, the 'Tiger' convoy came within range of air attack.*

point-blank /ˌpɔɪnt 'blæŋk◂/ [adv] a gun fired **point-blank** is fired very close to the person or thing it is aimed at: *The men broke into the building at the dead of night, and shot their victims point-blank as they slept.* | —**point-blank** [adj] **at point-blank range** *Police say that she died as a result of a single bullet fired at point-blank range.*

7 near enough to see or hear clearly

- close up
- at close quarters
- up close
- close-up

close up /ˌkləʊs 'ʌp/ [adv] very near, especially so that you can see something clearly: *If you look at the painting close up you can see that it's a fake.* | **+ to** *Dragging a chair close up to the television screen, she sat down to watch the film.*

at close quarters /ət ˌkləʊs 'kwɔːʳtəʳz/ [adv] if you see or experience something **at close quarters**, often something dangerous or frightening, you are closer to it than usual, especially so that you can see it clearly: *From our hiding place we were able to observe the animals at close quarters.* | *This was the first time I had seen such poverty at close quarters.*

up close /ʌp 'kləʊs/ [adv] very near someone or something, especially after you have only seen them from a distance **come/get/go/move etc up close** *Brigit looked great from a distance, but when she came up close you could see that she wore a lot of make-up.* | *'All you have to do is to get up close,' Woolley said, 'and shoot straight.'*

close-up /'kləʊs ʌp/ [n C] a photograph taken from very near: *She brought the camera forward to get a close-up of the actor's face.* | **in close-up** (=from very near) *Each butterfly had been photographed in close-up so that you could see every detail.*

8 to get nearer to someone or something

- get near/close
- approach
- close in on
- near
- draw near

get near/close /ˌget 'nɪəʳ, 'kləʊs/ [v phrase] to go or come nearer to a person, place, or thing: *As Kay got near the house she began to feel nervous.* | **+ to** *We had been traveling for two hours and I knew that we must be getting close to Vancouver.* | **get near/close enough to do sth** *I couldn't get close enough to see what was happening.* | **get nearer/closer (to sth)** *People were running for shelter. The hurricane was getting closer and closer.* | *Every day the Russian tanks were getting nearer to Berlin.*

approach /ə'prəʊtʃ/ [v I/T not in passive] to move gradually closer to a person, place, or thing. **Approach** is more formal than **get near** and **get close**.: *The train slowed down as it started to approach the station.* | *We could hear footsteps approaching down the corridor.* —**approaching** [adj] *The speed of the approaching car was close to 80 mph.*

close in on /ˌkləʊz 'ɪn ɒn / [phr v not in passive] if a group of people **close in on** someone or something, they gradually move closer to them from all sides so that they surround them in a threatening way: *Well-organized bands of rebels began to close in on the capital.* | *The divers were surrounded by three sharks which were rapidly closing in on them.* | *TV crews closed in on Geldof as soon as he stepped out of his car.*

near /nɪəʳ/ [v T not in passive] to gradually get nearer to a place – used especially in stories or descriptions of events: *As she neared her home she could see a light in the window.*

draw near /ˌdrɔː 'nɪəʳ/ [v phrase] written to move closer to something or someone: *The two men were talking, but as we drew near they turned and stared at us.* | *Madge drew a little nearer so that she could hear what he was saying.* | **+ to** *The rebels hoped that many of the government troops would join them when they drew near to the city.*

9 to be getting nearer to a person or vehicle in front of you

- be catching up
- be gaining on/be closing on

be catching up /biː ˌkætʃɪŋ 'ʌp/ [v phrase] *On the last lap of the race, Gemma started to catch up, and it looked as though she could still win.* | **+ with** *Looking back I could see that the rest of the group were catching up with us.*

be gaining on/be closing on /biː 'geɪnɪŋ ɒn, biː 'kləʊzɪŋ ɒn/ [v phrase] to be steadily getting nearer to a person or vehicle in front of you that you are chasing or racing against, by going faster than them: *Donna looked in her rear-view mirror and saw with alarm that the Audi was still gaining on her.* | *Now 'Australia II' is closing on the American yacht and it could still win this race.*

10 to stay very near to someone or something

- stay close/keep close
- cling to
- hug

stay close/keep close /ˌsteɪ 'kləʊs, ˌkiːp 'kləʊs/ [v phrase] **+ to** *While the eggs are hatching the mother bird stays close to the nest.* | **+ together** *Once we're inside the cave, we must all keep close together. We don't want anyone to get lost.*

cling to /'klɪŋ tuː/ [v T not in passive] if someone, especially a child, **clings to** you, they stay close to you all the time, especially because they lack confidence and depend on you too much: *It's quite common for a child to cling to his or her mother on the first day at school.* | *One of the girls was clinging to me all night at the disco. I just couldn't get rid of her.*

hug /hʌg/ [v T not in passive] to stay very close to the edge or surface of something, especially while moving along it: *The new road will stretch from Barcelona to the Adriatic, hugging the Mediterranean coast.* | *A row of tiny feeding fish were hugging the rock surface where I stood.* | *After Dunseverik, the path hugs the clifftop near Brebane Head.*

11 to not go near to a person or place

- not go near/not come near
- stay away from/keep away from
- keep your distance
- keep back/stay back

not go near/not come near /nɒt gəʊ 'nɪəʳ, nɒt kʌm 'nɪəʳ/ [v phrase] *You'd better not come near me. I've got a bad cold.* | *People didn't go anywhere near the place at night. They were frightened of ghosts.* | *Don't go too near the fire!*

stay away from/keep away from /ˌsteɪ ə'weɪ frɒm, ˌkiːp ə'weɪ frɒm/ [v T] to never go near something or someone or to not go near them during a period of time, especially in order to avoid danger or trouble: *Stay away from the edge of the cliff.* | **stay/keep well away from sth/sb** *If I were you I'd keep well away from him. He doesn't have a good reputation.*

keep your distance /ˌkiːp jɔːʳ 'dɪstəns/ [v phrase] to not go too close to someone or something, especially because it might be dangerous or harmful to go near: *Police warned the public to keep their distance if they saw a man fitting this description.* | **+ from** *Stick to the paths, and make sure you keep your distance from nesting birds.*

keep back/stay back /ˌkiːp 'bæk, ˌsteɪ 'bæk/ [phr v I] if you tell someone to **keep back** or **stay back**, you mean that they should not come nearer, especially because of possible danger: *Keep back, everyone! The tree may come down at any moment.* | **keep/stay well back** *She lit the bonfire and told the children to stay well back.*

need/necessary

RELATED WORDS

- be addicted to drugs, drink etc *see* **addicted**
- *see also* **must/don't have to, important/not important**

1 to need something

- need
- need
- require
- could do with/could use
- be in need of
- there is a need for

need /niːd/ [v T not in progressive] if you **need** something, you must have it, because you cannot live, succeed, or do something without it: *It's cold outside – you'll need a coat.* | *I think she might need a doctor.* | *Do you need some help?* | **need sth for sth** *He needs the information for an article he's writing.* | **need to do sth** (=when it is necessary for someone to do something) *We need to take the cat to the vet.* | **need sb to do sth** *Do you still need volunteers to help clean up after the party?* | **badly need sth** (=need something very much) *The team badly needs a victory.*

need /niːd/ [v T not in progressive] to **need** to be cleaned, repaired, or given attention in some way **need cleaning/washing/mending etc** *My hair needs washing.* | *Don't forget, the plants need watering once a week.* | **need a wash/clean etc** *You don't have to paint UPVC windows, and they need only an occasional wash down with detergent.*

require /rɪˈkwaɪəʳ/ [v T not in progressive] formal to need something: *Guests who require special diets should inform the catering manager in advance.* | *Is there anything further you require, sir?*

could do with/could use /kʊd ˈduː wɪð, kʊd ˈjuːz/ [v phrase] spoken informal say that you **could do with** something or **could use** something when you feel that you need it and that it would improve things for you: *'Let's stop for a minute.' 'Sure, I could do with a rest.'* | *I could use a hand with this if you have a minute.* | *Boy, I sure could use a drink.*

be in need of /biː ɪn ˈniːd ɒv/ [v phrase] if someone **is in need of** help, advice, money etc, they need it because they are in a difficult situation: *Several people were in need of medical treatment.* | **badly in need of sth** *The country is badly in need of foreign investment.*

there is a need for /ðeər ɪz ə ˈniːd fɔːʳ/ [v phrase] if there **is a need for** something, it is needed by a group of people because it is useful or necessary in order to make a situation better: *There's always a need for blood donors.* | *There's no need for you to know my full name. Reggie will do.* | **there is an urgent need for sth** *There is an urgent need for a review of current immigration law.* | **there is a growing need for sth** *There's a growing need for computer programmers and IT people in many parts of Latin America.*

2 to need someone or something very much

- be desperate for
- be crying out for
- can't do without
- depend on/rely on
- be dependent on/be reliant on

be desperate for /biː ˈdespərɪ̈t fɔːʳ/ [v phrase] to urgently need something and want it very much: *Wendell was desperate for a girlfriend, yet crippled by his fear of rejection.* | *A cordon of police struggled to keep back onlookers and relatives desperate for news.*

be crying out for /biː ˌkraɪ-ɪŋ ˈaʊt fɔːʳ/ [v phrase] if a group of people are **crying out for** something such as help, food, or medicine, they need it very urgently because they are facing great difficulties without it: *The country is crying out for strong leadership.* | *As we all know, Birmingham has been crying out for a venue for local bands for several years.*

can't do without /ˌkɑːnt duː wɪðˈaʊt‖ˌkænt-/ [v phrase] to be unable to do the things that you have to do without someone who usually helps you or without something that you usually use: *I absolutely can't do without my mobile phone.* | *Patrick is an excellent assistant – I couldn't do without him.*

depend on/rely on /dɪˈpend ɒn, rɪˈlaɪ ɒn/ [phr v T] if you **depend on** or **rely on** someone or something, you need them because they provide you with something that you need **depend/rely on sb/sth** *He was growing to depend on her, he knew that.* | *Not surprisingly, businesses that rely on government contracts are being hit badly by the spending cuts.* | **depend/rely on sb to do sth** *Elvin depended on her to dress him, feed him and do many other tasks.* | *Many plants rely on birds to distribute their seeds.* | **depend/rely on sb for sth** *Having to depend on her father for financial support was just not worth it, Sylvia decided.* | **depend/rely heavily on/upon** (=depend/rely a lot on) *State and local governments rely heavily on sales and property taxes.* —**dependence** [n U] *Clearly, the US must reduce its dependence on foreign oil.* | *He is undergoing treatment for drug dependence.*

be dependent on/be reliant on /biː dɪˈpendənt ɒn, biː rɪˈlaɪənt ɒn/ [v phrase] if you **are dependent on** or **are reliant on** someone or something, you need them so much that you cannot exist or continue successfully without them, because they provide you with all the most important things you need: *In those days, he was very dependent on Connie and wouldn't do anything without first consulting her.* | **be dependent/reliant on sb/sth for sth** *Many old people are dependent on government benefits for their basic survival.* | **be heavily dependent/reliant on** (=be very reliant on) *Small companies are heavily reliant on the goodwill of the banks in order to keep going.*

3 necessary

- necessary
- essential
- vital
- indispensable
- be a necessity
- be a must
- required

necessary /ˈnesɪ̈səri‖-seri/ [adj] if something is **necessary**, you need to have it or do it: *He produced the necessary documents and handed them to her.* | **+ for** *Fats in our diet are necessary for both heat and energy.* | **if necessary** (=if it is necessary) *If necessary, we will have to employ some outside people to finish the job.* | **it is necessary (for sb) to do sth** formal *It will be necessary to close the pool while the repairs take place.* | *The doctor says it may be necessary for me to have an operation.*

essential /ɪˈsenʃəl/ [adj] if something is **essential**, you need it because you cannot be successful, healthy, safe etc without it: *If you're going hiking in the mountains, a decent pair of boots is essential.* | *The tourist industry is now acknowledged as an essential part of the Spanish economy.* | **+ for** *Cal-*

cium is essential for the development of healthy teeth and bones. | **it is essential to do sth** *It is essential to read any document carefully before you sign it.* | **it is essential that** *It is essential that the oil is checked every 10,000 km.*

vital /ˈvaɪtl/ [adj] if something is **vital**, it is extremely important and you will have serious problems if you do not have it or do it: *In this job, the ability to remain calm is vital.* | *The European Space Agency said that a vital piece of equipment on the craft had stopped functioning.* | **+ for** *Regular exercise is vital for your health.* | **it is vital that** *It is vital that you keep accurate tax records.*

indispensable /ˌɪndɪˈspensəbəl/ [adj] someone or something that is **indispensable** is extremely useful and it is almost impossible to do something without them: *If you're planning on going sightseeing around the old city, a guide is indispensable.* | **+ to** *The book will be indispensable to anyone who wishes to learn more about the British Royal Family.*

be a necessity /biː ə nɪˈsesɪti/ [v phrase] if something **is a necessity**, you must have it for your job or for your life, and it is not something that you only have for pleasure: *For most people, a good guidebook is a necessity when travelling.* | *If you live in a place like London, a car alarm is an absolute necessity.*

be a must /biː ə ˈmʌst/ [v phrase] informal if you say that something such as a book, film, or type of clothes **is a must**, you mean that people must read, see, or wear it, because it is very fashionable, enjoyable, interesting etc – used especially in advertisements and magazines: *If you're interested in the early history of aviation, this book is a must.* | **be a must for sb** *Ankle boots are a must for anyone who wants to keep up with the latest fashions this autumn.*

required ALSO **requisite** formal /rɪˈkwaɪəʳd, ˈrekwɪzɪt/ [adj only before noun] necessary for a particular purpose, especially according to a law or rule: *They failed to submit their plans in the required time limit.* | *If the proposed piece of legislation fails to get the requisite two-thirds majority in Parliament, it cannot become law.* | **+ for** *In my opinion, she does not have the qualifications required for the job.* | *Research and writing have become requisite for career advancement in academia.*

4 make it necessary to do something

- make it necessary
- necessitate

make it necessary /ˌmeɪk ɪt ˈnesɪsəri‖-seri/ [v phrase] **+ to do sth** *The heavy rain made it necessary to close several roads.* | *By 1870, larger ships and cargoes made it necessary to create a new port at Avonmouth.* | **make it necessary for sb to do sth** *Recent violence has made it necessary for security forces to take drastic measures.*

necessitate /nɪˈsesɪteɪt/ [v T not in progressive] formal to make it necessary for you to do something, especially something that is difficult or that you would prefer not to do: *Sales have dropped dramatically, necessitating cuts in production and employment.* | **necessitate doing sth** *The proposed festival would necessitate closing University Avenue between 14th and 24th Streets Northwest.*

5 something that is needed

- need
- necessity
- requirement

need /niːd/ [n singular] if there is a **need** for something, that thing is needed **+ for** *Carlton acknowledged that there was a need for stricter safety regulations at some of the sites.* | **+ to do sth** *The need to improve teaching standards is recognized; however, it is not something that is going to happen overnight.* | **feel the need to do sth** (=feel that you need to do something) *Don't you ever feel the need to take a vacation?*

necessity /nɪˈsesɪti/ [n C] something that you must have for your job or for your life, not something that you only have for pleasure: *I would say that TV has become more a necessity than a luxury, wouldn't you?* | **the bare necessities** (=the most important and necessary things such as clothes and food) *For several years, the family was forced to make do with just the bare necessities.*

requirement /rɪˈkwaɪəʳmənt/ [n C] the amount or level of something that it is necessary to have, especially one that has been officially decided or is officially advised: *The average daily food requirement for an adult is between 2000 and 3000 calories.* | **come up to/meet/satisfy a requirement** (=reach the necessary level or amount) *For the second year in a row, the city's water supply has failed to meet minimum purity requirements.*

6 when a job or activity needs a particular quality

- need
- take
- require
- call for

need /niːd/ [v T not in progressive] British if a job or activity **needs** a particular quality, you must have that quality in order to do it well: *Teaching children to read needs a lot of patience and skill.* | *It must have needed a great deal of self-discipline for you to lose so much weight in such a short time.* | *What are the qualities that are needed for the job?*

take /teɪk/ [v T not in progressive or passive] if a job or activity **takes** a particular quality, or a lot of time, money, effort etc, you must have that quality or spend a lot of time etc in order to do it: *Don't get discouraged. Learning a new language takes a lot of effort.* | **it takes sth to do sth** *It took us about five months to sell our house.* | *It takes strength and stamina to be a long-distance runner.*

require /rɪˈkwaɪəʳ/ [v T not in progressive] formal if a job or activity **requires** a particular quality, you have to have that quality in order to do it well: *A lot of patience is required to look after a disabled child.* | *As any couple will tell you, marriage requires commitment and sacrifice from both partners.*

call for /ˈkɔːl fɔːʳ/ [phr v T not in progressive] if doing something difficult **calls for** a particular quality or a particular type of behaviour, you must have that quality or behave in that way in order to succeed in doing it: *The Times crossword calls for a certain amount of literary knowledge.* | *Launching a new product is a highly complicated business, and careful planning is called for.*

7 to provide something that is needed or wanted

- meet/satisfy a need
- meet requirements
- meet demand
- fill a need

meet/satisfy a need /ˌmiːt, ˌsætɪsfaɪ ə ˈniːd/ [v phrase] if someone or something **meets** or **satisfies a need**, they give people what they need or want: *Public transportation here has failed to meet the com-*

munity's needs. | **+ of** *It's extremely difficult for one teacher to meet the needs of 16 students in a class when each is working at a different level.* | **satisfy a basic human need** *Belief in God or a supreme being seems to satisfy some basic human need.*

meet requirements ALSO **fulfil requirements** British **/fulfill requirements** American /ˌmiːt rɪˈkwaɪəʳmənts, fʊlˌfɪl rɪˈkwaɪəʳmənts/ [v phrase] if someone or something **meets** or **fulfils the requirements** that have been set for them, they reach the standards that are necessary, especially standards that have been officially decided: *Beginning in April, street vendors will be required to meet a tough new set of requirements.* | **+ for** *The group has been notified by school officials that it no longer meets the requirements for a voluntary student organization.*

meet demand /ˌmiːt ðə dɪˈmɑːnd‖-ˈmænd/ [v phrase] to provide enough quantities of a product so that everyone who wants one can have one: *Record stores are finding it difficult to meet the demand for the group's latest CD, Greasy Pole.* | **+ for** *Ford announced that it has increased production to meet demand for its new range of sports utility vehicle.*

fill a need /ˌfɪl ə ˈniːd/ [v phrase] if something **fills a need**, for example a new product or service, it gives people something that they have wanted but which they have not been able to have until now **+ for** *The restaurant fills a need for good healthful food and for a good place to meet.* | *This handsome book fills a need for a clear children's guide to the African-American tradition of Kwanzaa.*

8 when you do not need something

- don't need
- spare
- can do without
- have no use for
- have no need of
- can dispense with

don't need /ˌdəʊnt ˈniːd/ [v phrase] to not need something or someone: *Do you want these text books? I don't need them any more.* | *Listen, people with disabilities do not need or want your pity.* | *According to Mahoney, the company did not need the cash, but was selling the division in an effort to streamline its operations.*

spare /speəʳ/ [adj usually before noun] use this about something which you do not need now, but which is available so that you can use it later or let someone else use it: *We have two spare tickets for the game – do you want to come?* | *Some couples will start married life in a spare room at the home of one set of parents – usually the bride's.* | **spare change** *It seemed like every time I turned around, some bum was hitting me up for spare change.*

can do without ALSO **can manage without** /kən ˌduː wɪðˈaʊt, kən ˌmænɪdʒ wɪðˈaʊt/ [v phrase] to not need someone or something, because you can live normally or do what you need to do without them: *We should be able to manage without you for a few days.* | *'I can do without alcohol, but I can't do without the cigs,' O'Hare wheezed.*

have no use for /ˌhæv nəʊ ˈjuːs fɔːʳ/ [v phrase not in progressive] to not need someone or something because you no longer use them or cannot think of a way of using them: *The fish spend their lives in darkness, and, having no use for eyes, are totally blind.* | *If society has no use for old people, is it any wonder that older people feel that their lives are without meaning?*

have no need of /ˌhæv nəʊ ˈniːd ɒv/ [v phrase not in progressive] formal to not need something: *Japan has its own space program and has no need of American technology.*

can dispense with /kən dɪˈspens wɪð/ [v phrase] formal to not need to use or do something that you usually use or do, because it is no longer necessary: *The company decided that it could dispense with the middle management level altogether.* | **dispense with the formalities** (=to not use formal or very polite behaviour, such as introducing people to each other) *We all know each other here, so I think we can dispense with the formalities.*

9 not necessary

- unnecessary/not necessary
- hardly necessary
- needless
- gratuitous

unnecessary/not necessary /ʌnˈnesəsəri‖-seri, nɒt ˈnesəsəri‖-seri/ [adj] if something is **unnecessary** or **not necessary**, you do not need to have it or do it: *Don't fill your report with unnecessary information.* | *A lot of the expenses that he's claiming seem totally unnecessary.* | **it is unnecessary/not necessary to do sth** *It's not necessary to spend a lot of money on clothes to look good.* —**unnecessarily** [adv] *I think you're worrying unnecessarily. Just relax.*

hardly necessary /ˌhɑːʳdli ˈnesᵻsəri‖-seri/ [adj phrase] British not necessary at all – use this when you are surprised that someone thinks something is necessary: *They asked to see my passport, my driver's license, and my bank card, which was hardly necessary.* | *At first glance, it seems hardly necessary to make another film about Van Gogh.*

needless /ˈniːdləs/ [adj usually before noun] use this to describe bad things that are unnecessary because they could easily have been prevented or avoided: *'I am very saddened by this needless loss of life,' the President said at a news conference Tuesday.* | *He accused the local council of allowing a needless tragedy, through a policy of not fitting smoke detectors to council houses.* —**needlessly** [adv] *Each week, over 250,000 children die needlessly from starvation and disease.*

gratuitous /grəˈtjuːᵻtəs‖-ˈtuː-/ [adj usually before noun] done for no reason, and seeming shocking or offensive **gratuitous violence/insults/cruelty etc** *The network refused to televise the film because it contained too much gratuitous violence.* | *It was a completely gratuitous insult – I hadn't said anything to offend her.*

nervous

unable to relax, especially because you are worried or frightened

RELATED WORDS

- *see also* **worried/worrying, frightened/frightening, shy, clumsy, confident/not confident, embarrassed/embarrassing**

1 nervous

- nervous
- tense
- jumpy/jittery
- on edge
- uneasy
- panicky

nervous /ˈnɜːʳvəs/ [adj] *Bill looked nervous, and I could see his hands were shaking.* | **+ about** *Kelli was* *so nervous about her exam that she couldn't sleep.* | *I'm a little nervous about leaving the kids at home all alone.* | *Many investors are nervous about their investments after the recent drop in the stock market.* | **make sb nervous** *It makes me nervous when you drive that fast.* —**nervously** [adv] *He was pacing nervously up and down the room.* —**nervousness** [n U] *She tried to hide her nervousness, but it was clear she wasn't comfortable making the speech.*

tense /tens/ [adj] so worried about something that you cannot relax, and you easily get angry or upset: *I always feel tense after driving all day.* | *Mary's problems at work were making her tense and irritable.* | *You seem awfully tense – why don't you have a drink and try to relax?* —**tensely** [adv] *Everyone waited tensely for the winner's name to be announced.*

jumpy/jittery /ˈdʒʌmpi, ˈdʒɪtəri/ [adj] very nervous so that you are unable to relax and are easily surprised by sudden sounds or movements: *The dogs are jumpy tonight – I wonder if there's something outside.* | *She was getting jumpy thinking about the trip.* | *I was feeling extremely jittery – all I wanted was to leave the bar as quickly as possible.* | *Investors are jittery due to uncertainty about interest rates.*

on edge /ɒn ˈedʒ/ [adj phrase] if someone is **on edge** or if their nerves are **on edge**, they are nervous and likely to become angry or upset very easily: *Jerry had had a hard day and his nerves were on edge.* | *As reports of robberies continued to appear in the press, the whole community was increasingly on edge.*

uneasy /ʌnˈiːzi/ [adj] nervous that something bad might happen, so that you feel anxious and unable to relax until the danger has passed: *There's something I don't trust about him. He makes me feel very uneasy.* | *It was the same uneasy feeling he'd experienced that morning when he saw the police car outside.* | **+ about** *Rebecca was already beginning to feel uneasy about accepting the stranger's offer of a ride.* —**uneasily** [adv] *Boyd glanced around uneasily. 'Do you think anyone is watching us?'* —**uneasiness** [n U] *She looked at the clock with growing uneasiness – he was already two hours late.*

panicky /ˈpænɪki/ [adj] very nervous and anxious about something, especially when you are in a dangerous situation that you cannot control or change: *I began to feel panicky, sure that I was going to miss the train.* | *'Is he really dead?' Abe asked in a panicky voice.* | *After waiting for him for two hours, Lorna got panicky and called the police.*

2 to be nervous

- have butterflies
- be a nervous wreck
- be a bundle of nerves

have butterflies /hæv ˈbʌtəʳflaɪz/ [v phrase not in progressive] informal to feel nervous about doing something that you are going to do very soon because it is important and you want to do it well: *Some actors never have butterflies before going on stage.* | **have butterflies in your stomach** *It was the morning of the World Cup Final and most of the players had butterflies in their stomachs.*

be a nervous wreck /biː ə ˌnɜːʳvəs ˈrek/ [n C] if someone **is a nervous wreck**, they have been made so nervous that they have completely lost all their confidence and their ability to remain calm or think sensibly: *Before the plane took off she was a nervous wreck – she had to be strapped into her seat.* | *Even though I'd been practicing for months, by the day of the competition I was a nervous wreck.*

be a bundle of nerves /biː ə ˌbʌndl əv ˈnɜːʳvz/ [v phrase] informal to be so nervous that you are shaking and you find it impossible to behave calmly, especially for a long time: *Since she lost her job Rosie's been a bundle of nerves.* | *Harry was a bundle of nerves the whole time his wife was in the hospital.*

3 someone who is often or always nervous

- nervous
- highly-strung
- uptight

nervous /ˈnɜːʳvəs/ [adj only before noun] someone who is often or always worried and frightened that something unpleasant may happen: *She's such a nervous child we don't like to leave her on her own.* | *Mr Darby was a mild, nervous man who seemed to expect people to ignore him.*

highly-strung British **/high-strung** American /ˌhaɪli ˈstrʌŋ◂, ˌhaɪ ˈstrʌŋ◂/ [adj] always nervous and unable to relax, especially so that you react in a very extreme way to ordinary situations: *Mark's a little high-strung, so go easy on him.* | *Her main problem is that she is very highly-strung which tends to make other people feel nervous too.*

uptight /ʌpˈtaɪt/ [adj] informal unable to be relaxed about life in general, so that this makes you seem unfriendly and unhappy: *He tries to be kind, but he always seems a little uptight.* | *She's one of those narrow-minded, uptight people who think that for a work of art to be great it can't be pleasurable.*

4 a feeling of being nervous

- nerves
- tension

nerves /nɜːʳvz/ [n plural] the feeling of being nervous because you are worried or a little frightened about something, especially if this feeling is likely to affect your behaviour or performance: *Normally she's very relaxed and amusing. It must be nerves.* | **a case/attack of nerves** *She had a sudden attack of nerves and refused to go to see the dentist.* | **calm/steady etc your nerves** (=try to relax) *Arnie had a drink before the meeting to steady his nerves.* | **suffer from nerves** British *Although a competent teacher, he suffers from nerves when the students behave badly.*

tension /ˈtenʃən/ [n U] a feeling of being nervous and unable to relax, especially before something is about to happen: *Her voice trembled with tension.* | **tension is high** (=people feel very nervous) *The tension was high in Mexico as the day of the decision approached.* | **tension mounts** (=people feel more and more nervous) *A crowd gathered and tension mounted till the riot broke out.*

5 a situation in which people feel nervous

- tense
- strained
- uneasy
- unsettling
- nailbiting
- nerve-wracking
- charged

tense /tens/ [adj] a **tense** situation makes people feel nervous and anxious, especially because they are worried about what might happen next or what someone might do: *There was a tense silence, and then everyone began to laugh.* | *The negotiations became increasingly tense as the weeks went by.* | *The journey through the mountains went well even* *though there were a few tense moments when the car skidded.* | *When someone mentioned Andy's time in prison, the atmosphere grew tense.*

strained /streɪnd/ [adj] a situation that is **strained** makes people feel nervous, embarrassed, and uncomfortable, and unable to behave naturally: *After the argument there was a strained silence.* | *Since my father's affair things have been very strained between him and my mother.* | *The strained atmosphere at the dinner made it difficult to chat with people.*

uneasy /ʌn'iːzi/ [adj only before noun] a situation that is **uneasy** makes people feel a little nervous because they are uncertain about what will happen next or what someone might do: *After the speech there was an uneasy silence and nobody clapped.* | *Since the two sides declared a ceasefire, there has been an uneasy calm throughout the region.*

unsettling /ʌn'setlɪŋ/ [adj] an **unsettling** situation makes you feel slightly nervous and unable to relax or concentrate completely: *The weather forecast was unsettling – we had nowhere to go if a really big storm hit.* | *Greenspan delivered more unsettling news about the economy the next day.*

nailbiting /'neɪlbaɪtɪŋ/ [adj only before noun] a **nailbiting** situation is so exciting that it makes you nervous, especially because you are waiting for a result or decision: *Waiting to become a father is one of the most nailbiting situations a man can face.* | **nailbiting finish** *With three minutes left, the World Cup Final is set for a nailbiting finish.*

nerve-wracking /'nɜːʳv ˌrækɪŋ/ [adj] a **nerve-wracking** situation makes you feel very nervous because it is difficult or frightening: *Your first appearance on stage is always a nerve-wracking experience* | *Trying to keep track of all those little kids at the same time must be pretty nerve-wracking.*

charged /tʃɑːʳdʒd/ [adj usually before noun] a **charged** situation or subject makes people feel very nervous and is likely to cause arguments or violence: *Abortion is still a very emotionally charged issue in the U.S.* | **highly charged** *In a highly charged press conference, Armstrong defended his attack on the children.* | **charged atmosphere** *The already charged atmosphere erupted into violence when police told the crowd to disperse.*

6 to make someone feel nervous

- make sb nervous
- unsettle
- unnerve
- psych out
- put sb on edge

make sb nervous /ˌmeɪk (sb) 'nɜːʳvəs/ [v phrase] *Have you seen the way he looks at people? He makes me nervous.* | *Don't watch me while I'm typing – it makes me really nervous.* | *Thunder and lightning always make the horses nervous.*

unsettle /ʌn'setl/ [v T] if something **unsettles** you, it makes you feel slightly nervous and unable to relax or concentrate completely: *Ted's angry outbursts unsettled the whole family.* | *The threat of war has been enough to unsettle international oil traders.* | *She was still recovering from the accident so he avoided any subjects which might unsettle her.*

unnerve /ˌʌn'nɜːʳv/ [v T] to make someone very nervous, especially by shocking or surprising them: *Moore had been extremely unnerved by the FBI's visit.* | *The daily news stories of the worsening economy unnerved the nation.* —**unnerving** [adj] *a bizarre and unnerving crime*

psych out /ˌsaɪk 'aʊt/ [phr v T] to try to make someone, especially someone you are competing against in a game, lose their confidence and their ability to remain calm **psych out sb** *McEnroe often used his bad behaviour in difficult tennis matches to psych out his opponent.* | **psych sb out** *Whenever we play chess Bill tries to psych me out by smirking every time I make a move.*

put sb on edge /ˌpʊt (sb) ɒn 'edʒ/ [v phrase] to make someone feel very nervous so that they cannot relax: *Trying to keep the plan a secret put us all on edge.* | *Layoffs and work upheavals have put many employees on edge, both at work and at home.*

never

RELATED WORDS

opposite: — **always**

- almost never *see* **rare/rarely**
- *see also* **not, forbid, impossible**

- never
- not ever
- never ever/never, never
- never/not in a million years
- not once
- never for a moment/not for a moment
- at no time
- have never been known to do sth

never /'nevəʳ/ [adv] not once, or not at any time: *'Have you ever been to Paris?' 'No, never.'* | *Ali had never seen snow before.* | *The view was spectacular – I'll never forget it.* | *He walks right past me and never even says 'hello'.* | **never do/say etc sth** (=used to tell someone not to do something) *Never go there alone at night.* | **never have I/did he etc** (=used for emphasis) formal *Never in my whole life have I felt so angry.*

not ever /nɒt 'evəʳ/ [adv] not at any time: *I haven't ever had champagne before.* | *Don't ever do that again.* | *'I won't leave you,' she said, 'not ever.'*

never ever/never, never /ˌnevər 'evəʳ, ˌnevəʳ 'nevəʳ/ [adv] spoken say this when you want to emphasize strongly that something has never happened or will never happen: *You must never ever tell anyone what you heard tonight.* | *I'll never, never stop loving you.*

never/not in a million years /ˌnevəʳ, nɒt ɪn ə ˌmɪljən 'jɪəʳz/ [adv] spoken informal say this when you think it is completely impossible that something could ever happen: *You won't get Kieran to agree – not in a million years!*

not once /nɒt 'wʌns/ [adv] say this when you are surprised or annoyed because someone never did something, although they often had the opportunity to do it: *After all the help I've given her, she's never said thank you – not once!* | *My father hasn't once come here to see us, even though he lives quite nearby.* | **not once have I/did they etc** (=used for emphasis) formal *Not once did she think of giving up, despite all the problems involved.*

never for a moment/not for a moment /ˌnevəʳ fər ə 'məʊmənt, ˌnɒt fər ə 'məʊmənt/ [adv] if you say you **never for a moment** thought something, you are emphasizing that this idea never came into your mind: *I always knew that I would be famous one day. I never for a moment doubted it at all.* | *'Did you ever suspect that he was cheating on you?' 'No, not for one moment.'* | **never for a moment have I/did they etc** (=used for emphasis) formal *Never for a moment did it enter my mind that something was wrong.*

at no time /ət ˌnəʊ ˈtaɪm/ [adv] formal never in the past **at no time have I/did they etc** *At no time did anyone suggest that the drug was dangerous.* | *Despite what I'd been told about the local people's attitude to strangers, at no time did I encounter any rudeness.*

have never been known to do sth /həv ˌnevəʳ biːn nəʊn tə ˈduː (sth) ǁ-bɪn-/ [v phrase] you say that someone or something **has never been known to do something** when you mean that this has never happened before, so it is strange if it happens now: *We were very worried – Peter had never been known to disappear from home before.* | *Killer whales have never been known to attack humans without the provocation of a bullet or harpoon.*

new

RELATED WORDS

opposite: ——— **old**

- using the newest ideas, equipment etc *see* **advanced**
- *see also* **modern, fresh/not fresh, fashionable/not fashionable, recently**

1 recently made or produced

- **new**
- **latest**
- **be just out**
- **recent**
- **be hot off the press**

new /njuːǁnuː/ [adj] recently made, built, produced, or invented: *They pulled down the movie theater and built a new health club on the site.* | *the new issue of 'Time' magazine* | *Porsche's newest sports car will be unveiled at next week's Motor Show.* | **brand new** (=completely new) *Apparently there's going to be a brand new 'James Bond' movie out in the spring.* | **as good as new** *By the time we'd finished painting the boat, it looked as good as new.*

latest /ˈleɪtɪ̆st/ [adj] **the latest film/book/model/fashion etc** the film, book etc that has been produced or made most recently: *Have you seen Spielberg's latest movie?* | *the latest fashions from the Paris catwalks*

be just out /biː ˌdʒʌst ˈaʊt/ [v phrase] if a book, record, or film **is just out**, it has only recently arrived in the shops, cinemas etc: *REM's new album is just out.*

recent /ˈriːsənt/ [adj] a **recent** film, book etc is one that was made or produced only a short time ago: *The recent movie version of the book was not a big success.* | *There will be an exhibition of his most recent work at the Tate Gallery, starting this Saturday.* | *A recent study of Open University graduates found that students aged 60 – 65 had better results than any other age group.*

be hot off the press /biː ˌhɒt ɒf ðə ˈpresǁ-ˌhɑːt-/ [v phrase] if a book **is hot off the press**, it has only just become available to the public, so that anyone who has it is one of the first people to read it: *People were queuing up for the new Harry Potter book to arrive – hot off the press.*

2 recently bought, or not used before

- **new**
- **brand new**
- **fresh**

new /njuːǁnuː/ [adj] recently bought, or not used or owned by anyone before: *New and second-hand books for sale.* | *Do you like my new dress?* | *That's a nice jacket – is it new?* | **buy sth new** *I'd like to get a video camera but I can't afford to buy one new.*

brand new /ˌbrænd ˈnjuː◂ǁ-ˈnuː◂/ [adj] use this when you want to make it very clear that something has not been used or owned by anyone before: *My brother's just bought a brand new BMW.* | *When did you buy this sofa? It looks completely brand new.*

fresh /freʃ/ [adj usually before noun] clean or new and not used before **fresh sheet** *You'll have to start again on a fresh sheet of paper.* | **fresh page** *Please start each new question on a fresh page.* | **fresh towel** *The service at the hotel was amazing. We even had fresh towels every morning.* | **fresh clothes** *I'm just going to have a shower and put on some fresh clothes.*

3 food and drink that is new and still tastes good

- **fresh**
- **okay/OK/all right**

opposite ——— **decay**

fresh /freʃ/ [adj] **fresh** food has been recently made, killed, or picked, and it still tastes good: *Fresh fish tastes completely different to fish that has been frozen.* | *Do you think this meat smells fresh?* | **fresh from the oven/sea/garden** *The restaurant claims that all the vegetables used in its recipes are picked fresh from the garden every day.* —**freshly** [adv] *freshly baked bread*

okay/OK/all right /əʊˈkeɪ, ɔːl ˈraɪt/ [adj not before noun] spoken fresh enough to eat: *I'm not sure that these eggs are still okay.* | *The milk looked all right, but when I tasted it, it was horrible.* | **okay etc to eat/drink** *It's been kept in the refrigerator, so it should still be okay to eat.*

4 instead of the one that you had before

- **new**
- **another**
- **replace**
- **fresh**

new /njuːǁnuː/ [adj only before noun] your **new** job, home etc is the one you got most recently, and is different from the one you had before: *Don't forget to give me your new address.* | *Have you met Keith's new girlfriend?* | *After the divorce, she went off to Canada to start a new life.*

another /əˈnʌðəʳ/ [determiner/pron] if you want **another** job, **another** house etc, you want it instead of the one that you have now: *After ten years with the same firm I decided it was time to look for another job.* | *If you don't like one doctor, you can ask to see another.*

replace /rɪˈpleɪs/ [v T] if you **replace** something that is old or damaged, you put a new one in its place to be used instead of it: *I'll have to replace my car soon – this one's done 130,000 miles.* | *The roof was in such bad condition that it needed to be completely replaced.* | **replace sth with sth** *They're replacing the old windows with modern ones.*

fresh /freʃ/ [adj only before noun] new and recently made, added, brought etc in order to replace or add to the one before: *Shall I make a fresh pot of coffee? This one's cold.* | *It's surprising how a fresh coat of paint can improve the appearance of a room.* | *The camp had almost run out of food when helicopters arrived with fresh supplies.*

5 new ideas or ways of doing things

- new
- original
- revolutionary
- innovative
- innovation
- fresh
- novel
- novelty
- pioneering
- be in its infancy

new /nju:‖nu:/ [adj] **new** ideas or ways of doing things that did not exist before or had not been thought of before: *Does anyone have any new ideas?* | **new ways/methods of doing sth** *The hospital is doing a lot of research into new ways of treating asthma.* | *It's vital that we find new methods of producing and conserving energy.*

original /əˈrɪdʒənəl, -dʒənəl/ [adj] completely different from anything that has been thought of before **original idea/design/style** *My job is to think up creative and original advertising ideas* | **completely original** *Woolf's writing was completely original – nothing like it had ever been done before.* | *a jazz musician with a completely original style* | **highly original** *I was impressed by the highly original design of the house.*

revolutionary /ˌrevəˈlu:ʃənəri‖-ʃəneri/ [adj] a **revolutionary** idea, method, or invention is completely different from anything that existed before, and is likely to bring important changes or improvements: *Einstein's revolutionary theories made people look at the universe in a completely new way.* | *revolutionary technology for producing cheap, pollution-free energy* | *The new treatment for cancer is considered revolutionary.*

innovative /ˈɪnəˌveɪtɪv/ [adj] an **innovative** design, idea, plan etc is new, different and better than those that existed before, and shows a lot of imagination: *The city has introduced an innovative system of traffic control.* | *When it was first introduced, the electric car was described as one of the ten most innovative products of the year.* | **highly innovative** *The idea for the programme 'Big Brother' was highly innovative.*

innovation /ˌɪnəˈveɪʃən/ [n C] something such as a new idea, method, or system that has never been thought of before, especially one that is better than previous ones: *The kids-only Internet service is a great innovation which will help parents control their children's access to the Internet.* | **technological innovations** *All the latest technological innovations of cinema were used to create the special effects.* | **communication/software etc innovations** *What exactly will the impact of all these communication innovations be?*

fresh /freʃ/ [adj only before noun] a **fresh** idea, approach etc is new and different from previous ones, and may help to deal with a problem: *We need a fresh approach to this problem.* | *The negotiations won't make any progress unless one of the sides puts forward fresh proposals.* | *Toy manufacturers are always on the lookout for fresh ideas.*

novel /ˈnɒvəl‖ˈnɑ:-/ [adj usually before noun] a **novel** idea, method etc is new and interesting because it is unexpected and different from what has existed before: *Scientists have come up with a novel way of catching fish.* | *Tonight's TV news will be presented in a novel format.* | *I spent six months living in a monastery in northern India, which was a novel experience.*

novelty /ˈnɒvəlti‖ˈnɑ:-/ [n C] something that is interesting because it is new and unusual, especially when this makes people think it is not very serious: *Retail analysts say that electronic shopping remains a novelty for most people* | **it is a novelty for sb to do sth** *It was a novelty for people at college to see a student with two kids.* | **be something of a novelty** (=seem new and unusual) *Fast-food restaurants like McDonald's are still something of a novelty in Moscow.* —**novelty** [n U] the quality that makes something interesting because it is new and unusual **the novelty of sth** *I was still enjoying the novelty of being married, and referring to Jenny as 'my wife'.* | **the novelty wears off** (=it stops seeming new and unusual) *I loved driving to work at first, but the novelty soon wore off.*

pioneering /ˌpaɪəˈnɪərɪŋ◂/ [adj only before noun] **pioneering** work, research, efforts etc introduce completely new ways of doing things, which are later followed and developed by other people: *Moore's pioneering work on semiconductors has made him perhaps the most famous figure in Silicon Valley.* | *Pioneering research shows that the experiences of childhood help form the brain's circuits for music and maths, language and emotion.*

be in its infancy /bi: ɪn ɪts ˈɪnfənsi/ [v phrase] if a science or a new area of knowledge or study **is in its infancy**, people have just begun to find out more about it, to work with it etc: *The science of cybernetics is still in its infancy.* | *These rockets were built at a time when space technology was in its infancy.*

6 something that has just been discovered

- new
- newly discovered
- fresh

new /nju:‖nu:/ [adj usually before noun] *Scientists have found a new oilfield off the coast of Norway.* | *Her lawyers have come up with new evidence that may prove her innocence.* | *Important new discoveries in the field of radiology may lead to a breakthrough in the treatment of cancer.*

newly discovered /ˌnju:li dɪˈskʌvəʳd◂‖ˌnu:li-/ [adj phrase only before noun] a **newly discovered** object, place, piece of information etc has been discovered very recently: *The newly discovered planets around distant stars are similar to Jupiter in size.* | *Howard was working on the translation of a newly discovered novel by Jules Verne.* | *Newly discovered evidence showed that there had been a miscarriage of justice.*

fresh /freʃ/ [adj usually before noun] **fresh evidence/information** evidence or information that is new and adds to or changes what is already known about the situation: *Police say they are still hoping for fresh information about the missing girl.* | *The judge told the court that the fresh evidence could be of considerable significance.*

7 someone who has just started a new job, school etc

- new
- newcomer
- new arrival
- stranger
- fresh
- rookie
- fresher
- newbie
- new blood

new /nju:‖nu:/ [adj] someone who is **new** has only recently arrived in a place, started working in a particular job, or joined an organization: *You're new here, aren't you?* | *All new employees are given training.* | **+ to** *Children who are new to the school may need extra help.* | *We don't expect you to work as fast as everyone else, while you're still new to the job.* |

new recruit *Our club membership is flourishing – we've had a huge number of new recruits this year.*

newcomer /ˈnjuːkʌməʳ‖ˈnuː-/ [n C] someone who has only recently arrived in a place or only recently started a job, sport, or other activity: *The inhabitants of these remote mountain villages tend to be very suspicious of newcomers.* | *Our team will include some familiar faces as well as a few newcomers.* | **+ to** *Although she's a newcomer to the sport, she's already very successful.* | **comparative/relative newcomer** (=someone who has arrived or started doing something recently, compared to other people) *I was fifty and a comparative newcomer to computers.*

new arrival /ˌnjuː əˈraɪvəl‖ˌnuː-/ [n C] someone who has just arrived in a place, especially in order to live or work there: *Jim, this is our new arrival, Lyndsay. She'll be taking over from Bob.* | *1200 new arrivals, including small children and babies, were left sitting on the pavement outside the embassy.* | **the new arrival** (=a newly-born baby) *Gwyn's children, Craig and Laura, are thrilled with the new arrival.*

stranger /ˈstreɪndʒəʳ/ [n C] someone who has just arrived in a place which they have never been to before, and which they do not know much about: *The people I stayed with were very kind, so I didn't feel like a stranger for long.* | *Many of the farming families have lived here for hundreds of years, and tend to treat everyone else as strangers.*

fresh /freʃ/ [adj] someone who is **fresh** from a place of education has only just finished training and is not experienced when they arrive at a new job **+ from** *You can't expect teachers fresh from college to deal with large classes of difficult children.* | **+ out of** *We were under the command of a young lieutenant who was fresh out of officer training school.*

rookie /ˈrʊki/ [n C] American someone who has just started doing a job or playing a professional sport, and has little experience: *It was rookie coach, Ray Rhodes, who got the most credit for keeping the team in check.* | *a rookie cop*

fresher British **/freshman** American /ˈfreʃəʳ, ˈfreʃmən/ [n C] a student who has just started at a university or college: *I was eighteen years old and a freshman at Harvard.* | *a freshers' party* | *freshers' week*

newbie /ˈnjuːbi‖ˈnuː-/ [n C] informal someone who is a new user of a technology, especially the Internet: *The program is simple to use, even for newbies.*

new blood /ˌnjuː ˈblʌd‖ˌnuː-/ [n U] someone who starts a new job or joins an organization and is likely to make improvements, for example by introducing more modern ideas and methods: *They seem to be expecting everyone over 50 to step aside and make way for new blood.* | *After its membership halved in the past year, leaving mainly diehard right-wingers behind, the party now desperately needs new blood.*

8 experiences and feelings that you have never had before

- new
- newfound

new /njuː‖nuː/ [adj] *When I first left home, I enjoyed the new feeling of independence.* | **a whole new experience** *Living in the city was a whole new experience for Philip.*

newfound /ˈnjuːfaʊnd‖ˈnuː-/ [adj only before noun] **newfound** confidence, interest etc are feelings or qualities that you have gained very recently: *Encouraged by their success, the rebel forces advanced with newfound confidence.* | *She went back to her work full of newfound enthusiasm.* | *When I retired, it took me a while to enjoy my newfound freedom.*

9 a new government/company/country

- new
- young
- start-up

new /njuː‖nuː/ [adj] a **new** organization, government etc has only existed for a short time: *Within weeks of the election, the new government announced big tax cuts.* | *Thousands of new businesses are set up each year.* | *one of Europe's newest TV stations*

young /jʌŋ/ [adj] a **young** company or country is one which has not existed for very long and has not yet fully developed: *Most banks are keen to loan money to promising young businesses.* | *'Impact' is a lively young company which specializes in public relations.* | *As a country, Zimbabwe is still quite young.*

start-up /ˈstɑːʳt ʌp/ [adj only before noun] a **start-up** company is a new company that has recently been started, especially one that uses computers and the Internet: *Several start-up Net companies saw their share prices rocket in the first few years, only to see them plunge as the recession hit.* —**start-up** [n C] a start-up company: *There were 4000 start-ups in Silicon Valley in 1998.*

news

RELATED WORDS

- *see also* **information, television/radio, newspapers, government, politics**

1 news that people tell each other

- news
- the latest
- developments
- scandal

news /njuːz‖nuːz/ [n U] things that people tell each other about something that happened recently: *I've got some news for you.* | *That's great news!* | **+ of** *There hasn't been any news of him since he left home.* | **+ about** *Have you heard the news about Carole?* | **+ that** *He brought the news that their father was seriously ill.* | **sb's news** (=what someone has been doing recently) *Sit down and tell me all your news.* | **good/bad news** *Good news! Ian passed his driving test!* | *Well, the bad news is that the train is delayed by an hour.* | **have good/bad news for sb** *I'm afraid I have some bad news for you.* | **hear (the/my etc) news** *Have you heard the news? Sara's going to have a baby.* | **spread the news** (=tell a lot of people about it) *They're going to appoint a new chairman – spread the news!* | **break the news to sb** (=tell someone something that they did not know, especially something bad) *I just don't know how to break the news to Sherri. She'll be so disappointed.* | **the news breaks** (=when people hear some news) *Since the news broke, hundreds of people have called with messages of support.*

the latest /ðə ˈleɪtɪ̸st/ [n U] spoken the most recent news: *Have you heard the latest? Phil's going out with Judy!* | **+ about** *Oh, I haven't told you the latest about my car!* | **+ on** *What's the latest on the election?*

developments /dɪˈveləpmənts/ [n plural] the most recent changes in an important situation – used especially in news programmes on television or radio: *The President said today that he was watching developments in Asia with great interest.* | *There are no new developments to report at this stage.* | **further developments** (=more developments) *We'll be keeping you informed of any further developments throughout the day.*

scandal /'skændl/ [n C/U] shocking facts that are made public about someone's behaviour: *The newspapers only seem interested in gossip and scandal.* | **a scandal breaks** (=becomes known) *He resigned a few days after the scandal broke.* | **sex/drug/financial etc scandal** *a sex scandal involving senior politicians* | *the worst spy scandal in US history*

2 news on television or in a newspaper

- the news
- news
- news bulletin
- newsflash
- update/news update
- the headlines
- top story/lead story

the news /ðə 'nju:z‖-'nu:z/ [n singular] reports about recent events, reported in newspapers or on television, radio or the Internet: *He always reads the sports news first.* | *Welcome to the early evening news.* | *I was listening to the news this morning, but I didn't catch what they said about it.* | **on the news** (=on television or radio) *They said on the news that the visit has been cancelled.* | *Did you hear anything on the news about the bomb?* | **in the news** (=reported about on television, radio, in newspapers etc) *She's been in the news a lot recently.* | **follow the news** (=listen, read or watch the news regularly) *I don't know if you've been following the news, but I heard that three American servicemen were killed there.*

news /nju:z‖nu:z/ [n U] events that are reported in newspapers or in **news** programmes: *News is coming in about an oil spill in the South Atlantic.* | **+ about** *The paper was full of news about the peace negotiations.* | **local/national/regional news** *We deal mainly with local news.*

news bulletin /'nju:z ˌbʊlətɪn‖'nu:z-/ [n C] especially British a short news programme, in which only the most important pieces of news are read: *It was reported in news bulletins throughout the day that the astronauts were in trouble.* | *a weekly news bulletin*

newsflash especially British **/special report/ news bulletin** American /'nju:zflæʃ‖'nu:z-, ˌspeʃəl rɪ'pɔ:ʳt, 'nju:z ˌbʊlətɪn‖'nu:z-/ [n C] a piece of news that is so important that it is broadcast immediately, often in the middle of another programme: *We interrupt this programme to bring you a newsflash.* | *There were special reports about the accident on all the networks.* | *All the shows started late because of the news bulletin about the bombing.*

update/news update /'ʌpdeɪt, ˌnju:z ʌp'deɪt‖ˌnu:z-/ [n C] a broadcast report of the most recent news about something: *We will continue to bring you news updates throughout the day.* | **+ on** *the latest update on the rescue effort*

the headlines /ðə 'hedlaɪnz/ [n plural] the important points of the news, printed in big letters on the front page of a newspaper or read at the beginning of a news broadcast: *I just have time to glance at the headlines before I leave for work.* | *This is the six o'clock news. First, the headlines ...*

top story/lead story /ˌtɒp 'stɔ:ri‖ˌtɑ:p-, ˌli:d 'stɔ:ri/ [n C] American the most important piece of news that is reported at the beginning of a news broadcast: *Tonight's top story: unemployment is at a 20 year low.*

3 a news report

- report
- story
- item
- scoop
- exclusive
- coverage

report /rɪ'pɔ:ʳt/ [n C] *During the war, most reports were compiled under government restrictions.* | *As more reports emerge about his business affairs, his re-election looks increasingly unlikely.* | **news/weather/newspaper etc report** *We'll be giving you further news and weather reports every hour throughout the day.* | *Newspaper reports say Woods is 'delighted' with his success.* | **+ about/on** *A recent report on child abuse in The Guardian suggests that as many as one in ten children are at risk.* | **+ from** *We're getting reports from the scene of the fighting that 12 hostages have been killed.*

story /'stɔ:ri/ [n C] a report in a newspaper or news programme about a recent event or something that is interesting to the public: *The main story tonight is the earthquake in Albania.* | *a headline-grabbing story* | *The story I read in the newspaper said they intend to close the theatre down.* | **+ about/on** *There have been a lot of stories in the papers recently about contaminated food.* | **cover/front page story** (=the main story in a magazine or newspaper that is on its front cover) *the front page story in The Wall Street Journal* | **a story breaks** (=when something is reported in the news) *When the story broke, the police initially refused to release any further details.*

item /'aɪtəm/ [n C] a short report that is part of a news programme or newspaper, magazine etc: *The next item will be of special interest to viewers who are dog-owners.* | **+ on/about** *There's an item about the robbery on page seven.* | *I turned the page, and saw a small item about Muhammad Ali.* | **news item** *The news item announcing the verdict was much smaller than the item that announced his arrest.*

scoop /sku:p/ [n C usually singular] an important or exciting piece of news that is printed in one newspaper before it appears in any other: *It was his first major scoop and he promised not to reveal the source of his information.* | *CNN quickly recognised the opportunity for a scoop.*

exclusive /ɪk'sklu:sɪv/ [n C usually singular] an important or surprising piece of news that is printed in only one newspaper or broadcast by only one news programme, especially because someone has let them use the information before anyone else: *Michael Jackson has promised the network an exclusive.* | *We have exclusives that you won't find on other networks.* | **world exclusive** (=something that has never been reported anywhere before) *The newspaper has a reputation for good reporting and world exclusives.* —**exclusive** [adj only before noun] *At the end of the programme we have an exclusive interview with Senator Goldwater.*

coverage /'kʌvərɪdʒ/ [n U] the way an event or subject is reported in the news, especially how much space or time is given to reporting it: *Too much coverage is given to sport on TV and not enough to political issues.* | **+ of** *coverage of the Greek elections* | **media/television/press etc coverage** *The AIDS conference received extensive media coverage.* | *Leach had no difficulty getting press coverage for his stunts.*

4 to report the news

- report
- cover
- run a story

report /rɪˈpɔːʳt/ [v I/T] *We aim to report the news as fairly and fully as possible.* | *This is Gavin Williams, reporting from the United Nations in New York.* | *His victory was not widely reported in the Western media.* | **+ on** *The Post sent her to Bangladesh to report on the cholera epidemic.* | **+ that** *The newspaper reported that he had supplemented his income with thousands of dollars from the federal budget.* | **be reported to be/have done sth** (=reported in a newspaper or news programme) *He was reliably reported to be drunk at the White House reception.* | *She is reported to have thrown a glass of wine at her former boss.*

cover /ˈkʌvəʳ/ [v T] to report the details of an event or a series of events for a newspaper or news programme: *He was sent to Northern Ireland to cover the peace talks.* | *a magazine covering women's issues*

run a story /ˌrʌn ə ˈstɔːri/ [v phrase] if a newspaper or news programme **runs a story**, it reports a particular event, especially something that people did not previously know about: *The Editor decided not to run the story until all the facts were known.* | *USA Today did not run the story until Ashe had made his announcement.*

5 when something is reported in the news

- be in the news
- make the news/make news
- hit/make/grab the headlines

be in the news /biː ɪn ðə ˈnjuːz‖-ˈnuːz/ [v phrase] something or someone that **is in the news** is being written about in newspapers or talked about on television, radio etc: *Football teams like to make sure their star players are constantly in the news.* | *At that time, events in Chile were very much in the news.*

make the news/make news /ˌmeɪk ðə ˈnjuːz, ˌmeɪk ˈnjuːz‖-ˈnuːz/ [v phrase] to be considered important enough to be reported in a newspaper or news programme: *Twenty years ago, environmental issues rarely made the news.* | *The hoax made national news, and people were talking about it for weeks afterwards.* | *You made the news recently when you rescued a young boy from drowning – can you tell us a bit about that?*

hit/make/grab the headlines /ˌhɪt, ˌmeɪk, ˌgræb ðə ˈhedlaɪnz/ [v phrase] if something **hits**, **makes**, or **grabs the headlines**, it suddenly starts to be reported in all the main stories in newspapers or on television or radio: *He grabbed the headlines last year when he became the first man to win three Grand Prix races in a row.* | *Phil Andrews again hit the headlines by scoring three goals in last night's game.* | *Larson's handling of the case made national headlines last year.*

6 someone whose job is to report the news

- reporter
- journalist
- correspondent
- newsreader
- hack
- the press
- the media

reporter /rɪˈpɔːʳtəʳ/ [n C] someone who finds out about events and writes about them in newspapers or tells people about them on television or radio: *She works as a junior reporter for the Today programme.* | *a crowd of reporters* | *'We've reached a critical stage in the negotiations,' he told waiting reporters.* | **TV/newspaper/Washington Post etc reporter** *He used to work as a TV reporter in LA.*

journalist /ˈdʒɜːʳnəl-ɪ̇st/ [n C] someone who reports the news, especially for a newspaper, as their profession: *All foreign journalists have been told to leave the war zone as soon as possible.* | *An experienced journalist has a sense of what is likely to be relevant about a story.* | **sports/media/finance etc journalist** *After he retired from football he became a sports journalist for the Gazette.* | *Lee is one of the highest-paid finance journalists in the country.* —**journalism** [n U] the work of being a journalist: *After 10 years I left politics and went into journalism.*

correspondent /ˌkɒrɪ̇ˈspɒndənt‖ˌkɔːrɪ̇ˈspɑːn-, ˌkɑː-/ [n C] someone who reports the news about one particular subject or place, for a newspaper or news programme: *We now go over to our correspondent in Lisbon for a report on the election.* | **foreign/war/Washington etc correspondent** *He left his local paper to become the Daily Telegraph's defence correspondent.* | *He joined ABC as its chief foreign correspondent in 2000.*

newsreader British **/newscaster** American /ˈnjuːzˌriːdəʳ‖ˈnuːz-, ˈnjuːzˌkɑːstəʳ‖ˈnuːzˌkæs-/ [n C] someone whose job is to read the news on the television, radio etc: *I've always thought you have the right voice to be a newsreader.* | *She became well-known as a newscaster before getting her own talk show in Chicago.*

hack /hæk/ [n C] informal someone who writes for a newspaper, especially one whose writing is not good or interesting: *The latest scandal was quickly picked up by the hacks at The Post.* | *A group of hacks were huddled around the gates, waiting for her to emerge.*

the press /ðə ˈpres/ [n singular with singular or plural verb in British English] all newspapers and reporters, considered as a single group: *I never give interviews to the press.* | *The press have blown the story out of all proportion.* | **local/national/English etc press** *Make sure the local press are there to hear my speech.* | **in the press** (=in the newspapers) *There was a lot of speculation in the press that the Prime Minister was about to resign.* | **notify the press** *Palace staff waited several hours before notifying the press about the King's condition.*

the media /ðə ˈmiːdiə/ [n singular with singular or plural verb in British English] newspapers, radio, and television, considered as a single group: *The story received a huge amount of media attention.* | *A White House aide told the media everything he knew about the President's private life.* | **local/national/German etc media** *The Japanese media quoted Murayama as being 'very pleased' with the breakthrough.* | *local media reports* | **mass media** (=the media considered as something that reaches a very large number of people) *a case of mass media manipulation* | **in the media** (=in newspapers, on television, or on radio) *There wasn't much about the event in the media.*

newspapers

RELATED WORDS

▸ *see also* **news, write, read, rumour/rumor**

1 newspapers and magazines

- newspaper/paper
- magazine
- glossy magazine
- the press
- the media
- broadsheet
- tabloid

newspaper/paper /ˈnjuːsˌpeɪpəʳ‖ˈnuːz-, ˈpeɪpəʳ/ [n C] a set of large folded sheets of paper containing news, articles, pictures etc, which is printed and sold every day or every week: *Can I have a look at your newspaper, please?* | *It says in the paper that they're getting divorced.* | **Sunday paper** (=a paper that is sold every Sunday, and has more pages than papers sold on other days) *I like to sit in bed and read the Sunday papers.* | **local paper** (=a newspaper that gives news mainly about the town or area where it is printed) *Did you see Dave's picture in the local paper?* | **national newspaper** *'Asian Week' is a national newspaper printed in San Francisco.* | **daily/weekly newspaper** *She works as a sportswriter for the town's major daily newspaper, The Arizona Daily Star.*

magazine /ˌmægəˈziːn‖ˈmægəziːn/ [n C] a large, thin book with a paper cover, often printed on shiny paper, which contains stories, articles, photographs, and sometimes also news: *I bought some magazines for the trip – Cosmopolitan and Vanity Fair.* | *a photography magazine* | *Hillary Clinton is featured on the cover of this week's Time magazine.* | **women's/men's magazine** (=a magazine intended especially for women/men) *a model turned TV presenter, who has been on the cover of all the men's magazines*

glossy magazine ALSO **glossies** British /ˌglɒsi ˌmægəˈziːn‖ˌglɔːsi ˈmægəziːn, ˈglɒsiz‖ˈglɔː-/ [n C] a magazine for women printed on shiny paper, that has lots of photographs of fashionable clothes, and advertisements for beauty products: *Cosmopolitan, the original glossy for young women* | **the glossies** British (=these magazines considered as a group) *We've seen her golden smile and her figure in the glossies again and again.*

the press /ðə ˈpres/ [n singular] newspapers and the people who write for them: *Do you think the press has too much influence on politics?* | *Princess Diana was followed by the press wherever she went.* | **the popular press** (=newspapers that are read by a lot of people, usually for entertainment rather than for serious news) *Smith strongly denies reports in the popular press that he is addicted to cocaine.* | **the gutter press** British (=newspapers that have an extremely low standard of reporting – used to show strong disapproval) *His wife walked out, selling her story to the gutter press, and accusing him of being an alcoholic.* | **the quality press** British (=serious newspapers with a high standard of reporting) *The issue was debated by academics, and some sections of the quality press.*

the media /ðə ˈmiːdiə/ [n singular] all the organizations that are involved in providing information to the public, especially newspapers, television, and radio: *The letter must have been leaked to the media by a White House official.* | *The judge is worried that comments in the media might affect the result of the trial.*

broadsheet /ˈbrɔːdʃiːt/ [n plural] British newspapers printed on large sheets of paper, especially serious newspapers that people respect: *broadsheets such as The Times and The Telegraph* | *Broadsheets are aimed at an educated middle and upper-class readership.*

tabloid /ˈtæblɔɪd/ [n C] a newspaper that does not contain much serious news, but has stories about famous people, sport, sex etc – use this especially about newspapers that you think are not serious enough: *She claimed that she had had an affair with the President, and sold her story to the tabloids.*

2 parts of newspapers

- the front page
- the TV page/the sports pages etc
- headline
- article
- editorial
- column

the front page /ðə ˌfrʌnt ˈpeɪdʒ/ [n C] the first page of a newspaper, where all the most important news stories are shown: *His face was all over the front page of the News of the World.*

the TV page/the sports pages etc /ðə ˌtiː ˈviː peɪdʒ, ðə ˈspɔːʳts ˌpeɪdʒɪz / [n C/plural] a page or set of pages in a newspaper that tells you about television, sport etc: *Could you give me the sports page if you're finished with it?* | *I don't know why you buy a paper – you only read the television pages.*

headline /ˈhedlaɪn/ [n C] the words in big letters at the top of a newspaper report that tell you what the report is about: *I just saw the headline. I didn't have time to read the article.* | *The headline read: 'Pope to Visit Kazakhstan.'*

article /ˈɑːʳtɪkəl/ [n C] a piece of writing in a newspaper or magazine about a particular subject: *He began his career writing articles for the college magazine.* | **+ on/about** *Did you read that article on the Middle Eastern peace process?* | *There was an interesting article in the LA Times about bullying at work.* | **newspaper/magazine article** *He had once read a magazine article about it in the dentist's office.*

editorial /ˌedɪˈtɔːriəl◂/ [n C] a piece of writing in a newspaper that gives the personal opinion of the editor about something that is in the news: *Their editorials always criticize the government, whatever it does.*

column /ˈkɒləm‖ˈkɑː-/ [n C] an article by a particular writer that appears regularly in a newspaper or magazine: *a weekly column* | *Did you read Julie Burchill's column in the Guardian this week?*

3 people who work for newspapers

- reporter
- journalist
- correspondent
- editor
- hack
- columnist

reporter /rɪˈpɔːʳtəʳ/ [n C] someone whose job is to find out about news stories and write about them: *She works as a junior reporter on a local paper.* | *A crowd of reporters were waiting outside the house all night.*

journalist /ˈdʒɜːʳnəl-ɪst/ [n C] someone who writes for a newspaper or magazine: *She worked as a journalist on the New York Times.* | *My father hated journalists – he didn't trust any of them.* —**journalism** [n U] the work of being a journalist: *a career in journalism*

correspondent /ˌkɒrəˈspɒndənt‖ˌkɔːrəˈspɑːn-, ˌkɑː-/ [n C] someone who writes news articles about a particular subject, especially a serious one, for a newspaper **political/foreign/education etc correspondent** *'Schools in Crisis', by our education correspondent Nick Bacon.* | *Martin Bell worked for many years as the BBC's war correspondent, covering conflicts all over the world.*

editor /ˈedətəʳ/ [n C] the person in charge of a newspaper or magazine, whose job is to decide what should be written about **+ of** *Cummings is the editor of a local newspaper.* | **newspaper/magazine editor** *Berendt, a magazine editor and columnist (he was once editor of New York magazine), first visited Savannah in 1982.* | **business/sports etc editor** *Arch Ward became sports editor of the Chicago Tribune.*

hack /hæk/ [n C] informal a news reporter or journalist – use this about people you disapprove of or who you think produce bad quality writing: *The editor sent one of his hacks to interview the murderer's girlfriend.*

columnist /ˈkɒləmnəst, -ləməst‖ˈkɑː-/ [n C] someone who writes articles, especially about a particular subject, that appear regularly in a newspaper or magazine: *Tony Kornheiser is a columnist for the Washington Post, and a talk-show host on WTEM.* | **gossip/political/sports etc columnist** *Dan Dorfman, the influential financial columnist, was fired by Money magazine, the magazine's managing editor said Wednesday.* | *The ambitious couple threw large parties, inviting celebrities and gossip columnists.*

next to

RELATED WORDS

▸ *see also* **near**

1 next to someone or something

- next to
- by
- beside
- next door
- by/at sb's side
- at the side of sth/on the side of sth
- along
- side by side
- alongside
- two/three/four etc abreast

next to /ˈnekst tuː/ [prep] *Roy had the seat next to the window.* | *I parked my car next to yours.* | *'Have you and Chris met?' 'Yes, we were sitting next to each other at dinner.'* | *'Where's the French dictionary?' 'On the bottom shelf, next to the encyclopaedia.'* | **right next to** (=next to and very close to) *I couldn't believe it. There was Tom Cruise, right next to me!* | *The hotel was right next to the airport.*

by /baɪ/ [prep] next to or very close to something: *I saw him standing by the window.* | *Weymouth is a pretty little town by the sea.* | **by the side of sth** (=next to a river, road, path etc) *Several soldiers were sitting on the grass by the side of the road.* | **wait by the phone** *Relatives are anxiously waiting by the phone for more news about the plane crash.*

beside /bɪˈsaɪd/ [prep] next to or very close to someone or something: *Ella came and sat down beside me.* | *On the table beside the bed were several medicine bottles.* | *They were sitting beside the pool, eating breakfast.*

next door /nekst ˈdɔːʳ/ [adv] next to another building, room etc or living in the next house: *'Is this Maria's office?' 'No, hers is next door.'* | *Have you met the people who've just moved in next door?* | **+ to** *Why don't we meet at that little French bistro next door to the theater?* | **live next door to sb** *'How do you know Marsha?' 'I used to live next door to her.'*

by/at sb's side /baɪ, ət (sb's) ˈsaɪd/ [adv] standing, sitting, or placed next to someone, especially when they are doing something: *I like to have a Thesaurus at my side whenever I do any writing.* | *Dirk went and stood by her side, his arm around her slender waist.*

at the side of sth/on the side of sth /ət ðə ˈsaɪd əv (sth), ɒn ðə ˈsaɪd əv (sth)/ [prep] next to a road or path: *Richard left his motorcycle on the side of the road and started to walk.* | *Tests in April showed that police cars parked at the side of motorways reduce speeds by ten miles per hour on average.*

along /əˈlɒŋ‖əˈlɔːŋ/ [prep] in a line close to the side of a river, coast, border etc: *We followed the path along the shore for several miles.* | *Walk along the canal as far as the bridge.* | *The Rif Mountains were visible as we sailed along the African coast.* | **all along** (=from one end to another) *Troops were stationed all along the border.*

side by side /ˌsaɪd baɪ ˈsaɪd/ [adv] if two people are walking, sitting or lying **side by side**, they are next to each other: *We walked along slowly, side by side.* | *Sabina and Mel sat side by side in the back seat.*

alongside /əˌlɒŋˈsaɪd‖əˌlɔːŋ-/ [prep/adv] next to or along the side of something: *The two boats were moored alongside each other in the harbor.* | *I decided to take the path alongside the railway track.* | *The driver was just getting out of his car when a police car pulled up alongside.*

two/three/four etc abreast /ˌtuː əˈbrest/ [adv] if people walk **two/three/four etc abreast**, that number of them walk at the same speed next to each other: *The sidewalk was wide enough for us to walk three abreast.*

2 when something is next to something else

- the next
- adjacent
- adjoining

the next /ðə ˈnekst/ [determiner] **the next** room, house, street etc is the one immediately next to the one you are in: *I could hear a furious argument going on in the next room.* | *There's a bakery just around the corner in the next street.*

adjacent /əˈdʒeɪsənt/ [adj] formal a building or piece of land that is **adjacent** to another one is immediately next to it: *The blaze spread to two adjacent buildings before firefighters were able to contain it.* | **+ to** *Fields adjacent to the nuclear facility were found to have high levels of radioactivity.*

adjoining /əˈdʒɔɪnɪŋ/ [adj only before noun] formal an **adjoining** room, building, or piece of land is one that is next to another one and is actually joined to it: *We had adjoining rooms at the hotel, so we could just go backwards and forwards between them.* | *Three planes were waiting to take off on an adjoining runway.*

3 to be in a position next to something

- be next to
- adjoin
- border

be next to /bi: 'nekst tu:/ [v phrase] *Cindy's house was next to ours.* | *The primary school is next to the town hall.*

adjoin /ə'dʒɔɪn/ [v T] if a room, building, or piece of land **adjoins** another one, it is next to it and is actually joined to it – use this especially in written descriptions of buildings and property: *The kitchen adjoins the sitting room, which is spacious, high and airy.* | *The 100-acre parcel of land adjoins Seagal's ranch, about 30 miles north of Santa Barbara.*

border /'bɔːʳdəʳ/ [v T] to have a border with another country or area: *The Black Sea borders a half-dozen countries.* | *France borders Spain along the length of the Pyrenees.*

nice

1 nice person

- nice
- pleasant
- likeable
- lovely
- good-natured
- sweet
- charming
- lovable
- endearing
- engaging
- adorable

opposite ——— **horrible, unkind, cruel**

▸ *see also* **friendly, good**

nice /naɪs/ [adj] especially spoken friendly and kind: *Claire's really nice, isn't she?* | *He's one of the nicest people I know.* | **+ to** *I sometimes think she's only nice to me when she wants something.* | **it's nice of sb to do sth** *It was nice of them to offer to help.*

pleasant /'plezənt/ [adj] friendly, polite, and easy to talk to – use this especially about someone you do not know well: *I only met her once or twice but she seemed a very pleasant girl.* | *Most of the students we get here are extremely pleasant and keen to learn.* —**pleasantly** [adv] *'Nice to meet you,' he said pleasantly.*

likeable /'laɪkəbəl/ [adj] nice, and easy to like: *Ian is very likeable and has always had lots of friends.* | *The only likeable character in the whole movie is Judge White.*

lovely /'lʌvli/ [adj] especially British, informal very nice, kind, and friendly: *Old Dr Macintosh was a lovely man.* | *The staff at the hotel were lovely – so helpful and polite.*

good-natured ALSO **good-humoured** British **/good-humored** American /ˌgʊd 'neɪtʃəʳd◂, ˌgʊd 'hjuːməʳd◂/ [adj] someone who is **good-natured** is kind, helpful, and does not get angry easily: *Neil was a gentle good-natured chap, the type of man you instantly trust and feel comfortable around.* | *Ann's always good-humored, no matter what happens.* | *It was a difficult situation, but he managed to remain remarkably good-humoured.* —**good-naturedly/good humouredly** British **good humoredly** American [adv] *Tom admitted good-naturedly that he had been wrong.*

sweet /swiːt/ [adj] informal someone who is **sweet** is kind and gentle, and tries to make other people happy: *He's a really sweet guy but I couldn't date him.* | *Oh, thank you so much – you are sweet!* | **it is sweet of sb to do sth** *It was very sweet of you to buy me those flowers.*

charming /'tʃɑːʳmɪŋ/ [adj] able to make people like you or do things for you because you are attractive and have good manners: *He was charming, good-looking and in his early forties.* | *The Vice Chairman has a very charming wife and four children.* | *a charming smile* —**charmingly** [adv] *'You look lovely,' Naylor said charmingly.*

lovable ALSO **loveable** /'lʌvəbəl/ [adj] a **lovable** person is friendly and gentle in a way that is very attractive: *Matthew can be a difficult child, but most of the time he's very loveable.* | **a lovable idiot** *Crawford is best known to television audiences as a lovable idiot.*

endearing /ɪn'dɪərɪŋ/ [adj] an **endearing** quality, habit etc is one that makes you like the person who has it: *Louise's complete honesty was one of her most endearing qualities.* | *He had a boyish, slightly dreamy look that was very endearing.*

engaging /ɪn'geɪdʒɪŋ/ [adj] formal interesting or amusing in a way that makes people like you: *Komansky, the new chairman of the company, is a smart, straightforward, engaging fellow.* | *Wyatt described her as 'a lovely woman – sophisticated and engaging'.* | *an engaging personality* —**engagingly** [adv] *The main character is engagingly good-hearted and innocent.*

adorable /ə'dɔːrəbəl/ [adj] someone, especially a child or an animal, that is **adorable** is very attractive and makes you feel a lot of love towards them: *We eventually found the cat in the wardrobe, surrounded by six adorable kittens.* | **absolutely/simply/quite etc adorable** (=very adorable) *Have you seen their new baby – she's simply adorable!*

2 something you like or enjoy

- nice
- lovely
- pleasant
- delightful
- appealing
- great

opposite ——— **horrible**

▸ *see also* **enjoy, good**

nice /naɪs/ [adj] especially spoken *That's a nice jacket. Is it new?* | *Have a nice day.* | **+ to do sth** *It's so nice to see you again.* | **look/taste/smell nice** *You look really nice in that dress.* | **nice big/quite/long etc sth** *I got a nice long letter from Andreas this morning.* | *Why don't you go and have a nice hot bath?* | **nice and easy/quiet/smooth etc** *Feel this material. It's so nice and soft.*

lovely /'lʌvli/ [adj] especially British, informal very nice: *We had a lovely time at the beach.* | *Thank you for the lovely birthday present.* | **it is lovely to do sth** *It would be lovely to see you again.* | **look/taste/smell lovely** *Anna's perfume smells lovely.* | **lovely big/long etc sth** *They've got a lovely big house in the country.*

pleasant /'plezənt/ [adj] a **pleasant** place, occasion, or activity is one that you like, especially because it is peaceful, attractive, or relaxing: *We spent a pleasant evening chatting in the bar.* | *Relax in the peaceful and pleasant surroundings of our hotel.* | *My office was large and pleasant with a good view of the city.* —**pleasantly** [adv] *The party was out in the garden and was pleasantly informal.*

delightful /dɪ'laɪtfəl/ [adj] extremely nice, enjoyable, and pleasant: *Their new house is delightful, very spacious and light.* | *A simple salad and fresh bread can make a delightful meal.* | *There's a delightful moment towards the end of the film, when they see each other briefly again.* —**delightfully** [adv] *Hiroko's a cheerful person, with a delightfully wicked sense of humour.*

appealing /ə'piːlɪŋ/ [adj] something that is **appealing** has unusual and interesting qualities that make people like or enjoy it: *It's extremely difficult to create a really appealing advertisement.* | *The idea of a whole week at a health farm isn't very appealing.* | *Both cities have a wealth of attractions that make them appealing.* | **+ to** *According to Life magazine, cars with soft smooth shapes are supposed to be appealing to females.*

great ALSO **neat** especially American /greɪt, niːt/ [adj] spoken say this when you see something or something happens that you think is very good, enjoyable etc: *'Hey, this place is neat!' said Chris, looking out at the stunning view from the balcony.* | *You got the job? That's great!*

no

RELATED WORDS

- say no to an offer, suggestion, or request *see* **reject**
- say that you will not do something *see* **refuse**
- *see also* **not, none/nothing, refuse**

1 ways of saying no to a question, request, or suggestion

- **no**
- **not at all**
- **I'm afraid not**
- **of course not**
- **not really**
- **certainly not**
- **no way**
- **you must be joking/kidding**

no /nəʊ/ use this when someone asks you a question or makes a request or suggestion: *'Are you Italian?' 'No, I'm Spanish.'* | *'Shall I help you?' 'No, no – I can do it on my own, thanks.'* | **the answer's no** *If she asks to borrow any more money, the answer's no!*

not at all /ˌnɒt ət ˈɔːl/ use this when what someone has suggested is **not at all** true, or when saying you do not mind at all if someone does something: *'Your boys are keen on sport, aren't they?' 'Not at all – just the opposite in fact.'* | *'Is my radio bothering you?' 'Not at all – I'm quite enjoying it.'* | *'I'd like to be on my own for a while. Do you mind?' 'Not at all,' she said kindly.*

I'm afraid not /aɪm əˌfreɪd ˈnɒt/ use this when saying that you are sorry that you cannot do something that someone has asked you to do, do not have something someone has asked you for etc: *'Are you coming to the barbecue tomorrow?' 'No, I'm afraid not. I've promised to go and see my Mum.'* | *'Have you got change for £20?' 'No, I'm afraid not.'*

of course not /əv ˈkɔːʳs nɒt/ use this to say no very strongly, when you think what someone has suggested or asked is clearly unlikely or stupid: *'Are you serious about Sam?' 'Of course not, we're just good friends.'* | *'Don't tell anyone else, will you?' 'Of course not.'*

not really /nɒt ˈrɪəli/ use this when someone asks if you want to do something, if you like something etc, and although you say no you do not have very strong feelings about it: *'Do you want to come to the movie with us?' 'Not really. I think I'll just stay in and read.'* | *'But you quite enjoy your job, don't you?' 'Not really, no. I feel I could do with a change.'*

certainly not /ˌsɜːʳtnli ˈnɒt/ use this especially when forbidding someone to do something or when you are annoyed or shocked that they have suggested something: *'Can I have some wine?' 'Certainly not – you're far too young!'* | *'Are you thinking of resigning?' 'Certainly not.'*

no way /ˌnəʊ ˈweɪ/ informal use this when you are saying very strongly that you refuse to do something or when you are sure that something cannot possibly be true: *I'm not going to work late on Friday night! No way!* | *'Do you think we can make the trip in two hours?' 'No way! It'll take more like four.'* | *I don't believe he stole the money – no way!*

you must be joking/kidding /juː ˌmʌst biː ˈdʒəʊkɪŋ, ˈkɪdɪŋ/ informal use this when you think that what someone has asked or suggested seems stupid or dangerous and you would definitely not consider doing it: *'Want a ride on the back of my motorcycle?' 'You must be kidding.'* | *'Are you going out with Jake?' 'You must be joking! I wouldn't go out with him if he was the last person on earth.'*

2 to say no to a question, request or suggestion

- **say no**
- **answer/reply in the negative**

say no /seɪ ˈnəʊ/ [v phrase] *I asked him to come along to the restaurant with us, but he said no.* | *She's not likely to say no if you tell her the real reason you need the money.* | *I'm really busy at the moment, so I'm afraid I'll have to say no.*

answer/reply in the negative /ˌɑːnsəʳ, rɪˌplaɪ ɪn ðə ˈnegətɪv‖ˌæn-/ [v phrase] written to say no when you are asked something: *When asked to confirm whether all the missing soldiers were accounted for, the Lieutenant answered in the negative.* | *Workers were asked if they had reached their weekly targets, and if they replied in the negative, they were fired.*

3 ways of politely saying no when someone offers you something

- **no thanks/no thank you**
- **thanks all the same**

no thanks/no thank you /nəʊ ˈθæŋks, nəʊ ˈθæŋk juː/ use this as a polite way of saying no when someone offers you something: *'More coffee?' 'No thanks.'* | *If someone offers you a cigarette, just say no thanks.*

thanks all the same /ˌθæŋks ɔːl ðə ˈseɪm/ use this when you do not want something which someone has offered you, but you are grateful that they asked: *'Do you want to come in our car?' 'I've already got a lift, thanks all the same.'* | *'Can you come for dinner on Saturday?' 'Thanks all the same, but I'm afraid I'm busy on Saturday.'*

4 to shake your head as a way of saying no

- **shake your head**

shake your head /ˌʃeɪk jɔːʳ ˈhed/ [v phrase] *'Shall I give him a message from you?' Rosalie shook her head. 'No, I expect he'll be telephoning me.'* | *Even before I'd finished my sentence, Dad was already shaking his head.* | *She shook her head. 'I'm afraid I don't agree,' she said.*

no matter what/ how much etc

RELATED WORDS

▸ *see also* **intend/not intend**

- **no matter**
- **however**
- **whatever/ whichever/ whoever**
- **regardless**
- **irrespective of sth**
- **never mind**
- **come what may**

no matter /nəʊ ˈmætəʳ/ [adv] use this when you want to make it clear that nothing will change a situation, your intention etc **+ how much/many** *I'm determined to go to New York, no matter how much it costs.* | **+ what/who/when etc** *Paul always calls me every day, no matter where he is.* | *No matter what position he plays, he'll be a great asset to the team.* | **+ how good/small/hot etc** *I never win, no matter how hard I try.* | *Dad was determined to get to the truth, no matter how long it took.*

however /haʊˈevəʳ/ [adv] use this when the fact that something is very big, good etc does not change a situation **+ much/many** *However much I try, I just don't understand him at all.* | **however + adj/adv** *I could never watch any movie more than once, however good it is.* | *Each one of us, however old or however young, is a valuable member of society.*

whatever/whichever/whoever /wɒtˈevəʳ ‖wɑːt-, wɪtʃˈevəʳ, huːˈevəʳ/ [pron/determiner] used when it is not important what happens, who does something etc, because it does not change the situation or your intention: *'I don't care,' Carrie cried, 'whatever anyone says!'* | *We can take a taxi or the bus, whichever comes first.* | *He's a capable man. I'm sure he can deal with whatever problems arise.* | *Don't forget, it's your job to support your leader, whoever it is.* | **whichever of sb/sth** *Whichever of the cars you choose, I'm sure you'll be very pleased.*

regardless /rɪˈgɑːʳdləs/ [adv] use this when what is done is not affected by different situations, problems etc **+ of** *The rate of contribution to the pension plan is the same for all employees, regardless of age.* | **regardless of whether/what/who etc** *Many people stick with their banks regardless of whether they offer the best deal.* | **carry on/continue regardless** *It may rain by the end of the day, but we plan to carry on regardless.*

irrespective of sth /ˌɪrɪˈspektɪv əv (sth)/ [prep] use this when the same thing happens in every case without being affected by facts such as age, size, time, or position: *The job is open to anyone with the right qualifications, irrespective of their age.* | *Justice for all, irrespective of race or class, is everyone's right.* | **+ what/where/who etc** *All children should have access to the latest technology, irrespective of where they live or how much their parents earn.*

never mind /ˌnevəʳ ˈmaɪnd/ use this to say that something should be ignored because it does not affect the situation or your intention **never mind that!** *'How do you know so much about Jake anyway?' 'Never mind that!'* | **never mind sth** *I want this wedding to be perfect, never mind the cost.* | **+ what/why/when etc** *Never mind what Jalal says, Peter is a trusted member of our community.* | **+ that** *Never mind that it's late. I need to talk to you now.*

come what may /ˌkʌm wɒt ˈmeɪ/ use this when you are determined to do something whatever happens: *I'll be there come what may. I promise.* | *Some people are getting out of the country fast, but my cousin's family has decided to stay, come what may.*

none/nothing

RELATED WORDS

opposite: —— **lot**

▸ *see also* **not, never, amount/number, few/not many**

1 when there is not any of something

- **none**
- **not any**
- **no**
- **nothing/not anything**
- **zilch**
- **not one**
- **not a**
- **be nil**
- **bugger all**

none /nʌn/ [pron] not any of something, or not any people or things: *I was going to offer you some cake, but there's none left.* | *'Coffee?' 'None for me, thanks.'* | **+ of** *None of her friends live in London.* | *None of my clothes fit anymore.* | *Parents complain that none of the money set aside for the school has been spent on textbooks.* | **none at all/none whatsoever/absolutely none** especially spoken *'Do you have any objections to the plan, John?' 'None at all.'* | *'The mayor has no tolerance for violent criminals, absolutely none,' said a spokesperson.* | *Under the Constitution, the President has no legal authority – none whatsoever – to commit the United States to war.*

not any /nɒt ˈeni/ [determiner/pron] none: *You won't find any, I'm afraid I haven't been shopping yet.* | *There aren't any good book stores in town.* | *We won't be getting any extra-large shirts until tomorrow.* | *The clerk said he didn't have any change.* | *There won't be any time for questions after the lecture.* | **+ of** *I haven't read any of Henry Miller's novels.* | **not any more/not any left** spoken *She asked for a copy of the 'Boston Globe' but there weren't any left.*

no /nəʊ/ [determiner] not any or not one: *There are no buses on Sundays.* | *a very plain room, with no pictures on the wall* | *Do you mind having black coffee? There's no milk.* | *We've had no rain for three months.* | *There was no room in the car for anyone else.* | *I knocked on the door, but there was no reply.* | *He just started hitting her for no reason.* | *Some athletes have no intention of getting an education while they're at college.* | **no more** *There are no more classes until Monday.*

nothing/not anything /ˈnʌθɪŋ, nɒt ˈeniθɪŋ/ [pron] *There's nothing in this box.* | *Many older people don't know anything about computers.* | *I switched the TV on, but nothing happened.* | *'What are you doing?' 'Nothing.'* | **nothing new/serious/exciting etc** *Nothing exciting ever happens in this place!* | **nothing to eat/say/do etc** *There was nothing to do, so we just watched TV.* | *She hasn't had anything to eat all day.* | **nothing at all** *'Do you know anything about fixing cars?' 'No, nothing at all.'* | **nothing else** (=nothing more) *As he listened, he understood the word 'shimai', which means 'sister', but nothing else.* | **nothing else to say/do etc** *I had nothing else to do so I cleaned the kitchen.* | *We will make an announcement next week; we have nothing else to say until then.*

zilch /zɪltʃ/ [n U] especially American, spoken nothing: *She knows absolutely zilch about marketing.* | *The federal government does zilch to help struggling farmers.*

not one /nɒt 'wʌn/ [pron] none – use this when the situation is very unusual or unexpected: *'Do you have any batteries?' 'Not one. We've completely sold out.'* | *According to the report, of the 10 best cities in which to do business, not one is in California.* | **+ of** *We examined over a hundred machines and not one of them was working properly.*

not a /'nɒt ə/ [determiner] **not even one** *It all happened so fast, I didn't see a thing.* | *Usually there were voices to be heard coming from the living room, but tonight there was not a sound.* | *There wasn't a scrap of food in the house.* | **not a dickybird** British informal (=nothing at all) *I haven't heard a dickybird from him all morning.*

be nil /bi: 'nɪl/ [v phrase] if the amount of something **is nil**, there is none of it and you feel disappointed about it: *With their best player injured, England's chances of winning the game were just about nil.* | *Refreshment facilities for long-distance bus passengers are virtually nil.*

bugger all /ˌbʌgər 'ɔ:l/ [pron/determiner] British informal nothing or not any of something – this is an impolite expression which people use especially when they are angry: *I hope she does some work at home. She does bugger all in the office.* | *You'll get bugger all thanks for helping them.*

2 the number that means none

- zero
- nil
- nought
- o

zero /'zɪərəʊ‖'zi:rəʊ/ [n U] the number 0: *The zip code for Annandale is zero eight eight zero one.* | *The ZR1 can go from zero to sixty miles per hour in 4.3 seconds.* | **zero unemployment/growth/inflation etc** (=when there is none at all) *In the long run, zero inflation will bring lower interest rates.* | *The government aims to hold the country's population at zero-growth.*

nil British ALSO **zip** American informal /nɪl, zɪp/ [n U] zero – use this especially in sports results: *At the end of the first half it's Spurs two, Arsenal nil.* | *'Who won?' 'The Yankees, five-zip.'* | *By a seven-nil vote, the Council passed a resolution protecting the land from development.*

nought /nɔ:t/ [n U] British zero – used especially before or after a decimal point: *Interest rates rose by nought point three percent today.* | *'What did you score?' 'Nought out of ten.'*

o /əʊ/ zero – use this especially when saying a telephone number or the number after a decimal point. Pronounce this as the letter 'o': *I'll be in room four-o-nine.* | *It's an inner London phone number, so you dial o-two-o-seven.* | *One hundredth has the same value as point o one.*

3 less than none

- negative
- minus

- *see also* **less**

negative /'negətɪv/ [adj] **negative** numbers, figures etc are less than one: *My bank statement shows a negative balance.* | *Do you know how to multiply negative numbers?*

minus /'maɪnəs/ [adj only before noun] **minus 4 degrees/3%/10°F etc** four degrees, three per cent etc less than nothing: *The temperature dropped to almost minus 40.* | *a trade deficit of minus £4bn*

normal/ordinary

RELATED WORDS

opposite: **unusual, strange**

- ordinary and not interesting or exciting *see* **boring**
- *see also* **usually, common, used to/accustomed to, conventional, typical, special, crazy**

1 not special or unusual

- ordinary
- normal
- average
- standard
- routine
- conventional
- day-to-day
- regular
- mainstream
- everyday

ordinary /'ɔ:ʳdənri‖-dəneri/ [adj usually before noun] **ordinary** things are not special or unusual: *It's just an ordinary house in an ordinary street.* | *He wore an ordinary business suit with a white shirt and tie.* | *Can you get connected to the Internet through an ordinary telephone line?* | *Gillman's known for her photographs of ordinary household items.*

normal /'nɔ:ʳməl/ [adj] something that is **normal** is just as you would expect it to be, because it is not special or different: *The new Ford looks like any normal car, but it has a special advanced engine.* | *January 2nd is a public holiday in Scotland, but in England it is a normal working day.* | *Once the pain has gone away, you can resume your normal activities.* | **perfectly normal** *It was a perfectly normal flight until the plane suddenly started to shake.* | **it's normal** *It may have seemed unusually cold recently but experts say it's normal for this time of year.* | **above/below normal** *Tides will be six feet above normal this afternoon.* —**normally** [adv] *Now the strike is over, and trains are running normally.*

average /'ævərɪdʒ/ [adj only before noun] an **average** thing is a typical example of a particular type of thing: *The average bagel has 190 calories.* | *In an average week I watch about 20 hours of TV.*

standard /'stændəʳd/ [adj usually before noun] normal – use this especially about products or methods that are the most usual type, without any special features **standard model/size/shape/pattern** (=not special) *We make shoes in all standard sizes.* | *Prices start at $15,489 for the standard model.* | **standard practice/procedure** (=the way a job is usually done) *All hand-baggage was X-rayed – this is now standard practice at most airports.* | *Drug tests are a standard procedure following train accidents.* | **standard English/pronunciation/spelling** (=normally accepted as correct) *Students are encouraged to learn standard English because this is what they will need to know in the business world.*

routine /ru:'ti:n/ [adj usually before noun] use this about something that is done regularly as part of the normal system and not because of any special problem **routine check/inspection/examination etc** *The fault was discovered during a routine check of the plane.* | *Police found the heroin during a routine inspection of a ship.* | *It was on a Saturday 15 years ago that, during a routine visit to the doctor, I learned I had cancer.*

conventional /kən'venʃənəl/ [adj only before noun] a **conventional** method, piece of equipment, weapon etc is of the normal type that has been used for a long time – use this especially when you are comparing one thing with something else that is new or different: *A microwave cooks food much faster than a conventional oven.* | *The hospital provides both conventional and alternative medical treatments.* | **conventional weapons/arms/bombs etc** (=not nuclear weapons) *a new proposal to limit conventional weapons in Europe*

day-to-day /ˌdeɪ tə ˈdeɪ/ [adj only before noun] use this about the ordinary work, activities, and problems that happen every day: *As Managing Director, I am responsible for the day-to-day management of the company.* | *Reeve decided to immerse himself in the day-to-day affairs of his company until business improved.*

regular /ˈregjələʳ/ [adj only before noun] especially American ordinary but good enough for a particular purpose: *If they don't have Tylenol, just get me regular aspirin.* | *Even though the dye is quite strong, a regular shampoo will remove it.*

mainstream /ˈmeɪnstriːm/ [adj only before noun] **mainstream** books, ideas, organizations etc are not strange or extreme in any way, and are therefore popular with or suitable for most ordinary people: *After starting out as a romance novelist, she decided to try writing mainstream fiction.* | *Most disabled students are integrated into the mainstream educational system.* | *The mainstream political parties are losing support to smaller, more radical organizations.*

everyday /ˈevrideɪ/ [adj only before noun] ordinary, usual, or happening every day: *Noland makes sculptures out of everyday objects.* | *Arthritis made it difficult for him to do everyday things like take out the garbage or mow the lawn.* | *The first week of the course is spent teaching students English phrases needed for everyday life.*

2 very ordinary, and without any interesting or unusual features

- ordinary
- nondescript
- bland
- unremarkable

ordinary /ˈɔːʳdənri‖-dəneri/ [adj] *The house was clean and well kept, but very ordinary.* | *It's surprising that a girl as attractive as Sarah is going out with someone so ordinary looking.*

nondescript /ˈnɒndəˌskrɪpt‖ˌnɑːndəˈskrɪpt/ [adj] a person or object that is **nondescript** is not at all interesting to look at because they have no special or unusual features: *The only people in the waiting room were a couple of rather nondescript elderly ladies.* | *The detective drives a nondescript blue Ford, perfect for observing people unnoticed.* | *They were an average family living a boring life in a nondescript little house in the suburbs.*

bland /blænd/ [adj] very ordinary and not containing anything interesting, shocking etc, often in order to avoid offending or upsetting anyone: *The language in her speech was deliberately bland.* | *Most job descriptions are bland, boring and totally lacking in colour.* | *The college's bland appearance made it seem a little unfriendly.*

unremarkable /ˌʌnrɪˈmɑːʳkəbəl◂/ [adj] someone or something that is **unremarkable** is very ordinary and not especially different from most other people or things: *She had had just one adventure in her otherwise unremarkable life.* | *Josh was, I thought, a pleasant but unremarkable young man.*

3 ordinary people

- ordinary
- average
- the man/woman in the street
- the general public
- the rank and file
- the grass roots

ordinary /ˈɔːʳdənri‖-dəneri-/ [n plural] **ordinary** people are people who are not rich, famous, or powerful **ordinary people/folk** *Politicians don't care about ordinary people.* | *In the eighteenth century ordinary people had no access whatsoever to education.* | **ordinary guy/man/woman etc** *In the film 'Phenomenon', John Travolta plays an ordinary guy who becomes a genius overnight.*

average /ˈævərɪdʒ/ [adj only before noun] an **average** person is a typical example of a person: *The average family spends about £50 a week on food.* | *Foreign affairs do not usually interest the average voter.* | *There is concern that twenty years from now, the average American won't be able to afford to send his or her children to college.*

the man/woman in the street /ðə ˌmæn, ˌwʊmən ɪn ðə ˈstriːt/ [n phrase] a typical person who has ordinary opinions, likes the same things as most other people etc – used especially by journalists: *The advertising industry has to know exactly what the man in the street is thinking.* | *This latest legislation will not really affect the man or woman in the street.*

the general public /ðə ˌdʒenərəl ˈpʌblɪk/ [n phrase] all the ordinary people in a society or country, especially those without special knowledge of a subject: *Very little official information is given to the general public.* | *She is a poet who is admired by other poets but not well-known to the general public.* | *Organizers of the President's funeral plan a large ceremony for the general public, and a small, private affair for his family.*

the rank and file /ðə ˌræŋk ən ˈfaɪl/ [n phrase] the ordinary members of an organization, especially a political organization, when compared with its leaders: *The rank and file has lost confidence in the party leadership.* | *conflict between union leaders and the rank and file at an Alfa Romeo factory* —**rank-and-file** [adj only before noun] *rank-and-file members*

the grass roots /ðə ˌgrɑːs ˈruːts‖-ˌgræs-/ [n singular] the ordinary members at the bottom of a political or religious organization: *The decisions were taken by the party leadership without consulting the grass roots.* —**grassroots** /ˈgrɑːsruːts‖ˈgræs-/ [adj only before noun] *a grassroots campaign* | *The party is in some difficulty, but still has grassroots support.*

4 normal behaviour or feelings

- normal
- natural
- conventional
- it's human nature (to do sth)

normal /ˈnɔːʳməl/ [adj] if a person is **normal**, there is nothing strange about them, and they are mentally and physically healthy: *Any normal boy of his age would be interested in football.* | *Her breathing was normal, but she had a very high temperature.* | **it is normal (for sb) to do sth** *It is quite normal for children to be afraid of the dark.* | *When you start a new job, it's normal to feel somewhat overwhelmed.* | **perfectly normal** (=completely normal) *They seemed like a perfectly normal family.* —**normally** [adv] *Even a few hours before he committed suicide, he seemed to be behaving perfectly normally.*

natural /ˈnætʃərəl/ [adj] feelings that are **natural** are what you would normally expect in a particular situation, so there is no need to feel worried or embarrassed about them: *Anger is a natural reaction when you lose someone you love.* | **it is natural (for sb) to do sth** *I suppose it's natural for a mother to feel sad when her children leave home.* | *It isn't natural for a child to be so quiet.* | **perfectly/quite natural** (=completely natural) *It's perfectly natural to grieve for the loss of a pet.* | **it's only natural** spoken *Of course Jean misses her boyfriend – it's only natural.* | **it's only natural that** *It's only natural that people who spend a lot of time around computers either love them or hate them.*

conventional /kənˈvenʃənəl/ [adj] **conventional** people, behaviour, and opinions are the kind that most people in society think are normal and socially acceptable, although some people think they are boring and old-fashioned: *My mother was very conventional – she didn't approve of my hippie lifestyle.* | *a young man with conventional tastes in clothes and music* | **conventional wisdom** (=the opinion that most people consider to be normal and right) *Conventional wisdom holds that more money for education means better schools for children.* —**conventionally** [adv] *She was dressed very conventionally in a rather dull grey suit.*

it's human nature (to do sth) /ɪts ˌhjuːmən ˈneɪtʃəʳ (tə duː (sth))/ spoken use this to say that is it normal for people to want to do something: *It's human nature to want what we don't have.*

5 the normal situation

- get back to normal/return to normal
- normality

get back to normal/return to normal /get ˌbæk tə ˈnɔːʳməl, rɪˌtɜːʳn tə ˈnɔʳːməl/ [v phrase] if a situation **gets back to normal** or **returns to normal**, it becomes normal again after a period when it was not normal: *After the war it took a long time for things to get back to normal.* | *The strike has caused serious problems, but we hope bus services will quickly return to normal.*

normality ALSO **normalcy** American /nɔːʳˈmælə̇ti, ˈnɔːʳməlsi/ [n U] written a situation in which everything is normal and exactly how you would expect it to be: *The children soon settled down once normality was re-established.* | *Both leaders say they hope the relationship between their two countries will be restored to normality.* | *The town had a cheerful air of normalcy despite the extra policemen everywhere.*

6 not ordinary/not normal

- special
- no ordinary

special /ˈspeʃəl/ [adj] not ordinary, but more important, interesting, or impressive than usual: *Tomorrow is a very special day for us – it's our first wedding anniversary.* | *Is there any special reason why I should let you borrow my car?* | *Lianne's doctor put her on a special diet and told her to exercise regularly.* | *She had a special talent for learning languages.* | **something/anything/nothing special** *'Are you doing anything this weekend?' 'No, nothing special.'* | **special occasion** (=an important social event or celebration) *I only wear this suit on special occasions, like weddings.*

no ordinary /nəʊ ˈɔːʳdənri‖-dəneri/ [determiner] not at all ordinary, but very unusual, very impressive etc: *As soon as I got there, I realized that this was no ordinary family gathering.* | *The hundreds of reporters gathered outside the courtroom were a reminder that this was no ordinary trial.*

7 not ordinary/not normal in a very bad way

- abnormal
- unnatural
- deviant

abnormal /æbˈnɔːʳməl/ [adj usually before noun] very different from what is normal, in a way that is strange, worrying, or dangerous: *abnormal behaviour that may be a sign of mental illness* | *an abnormal chest x-ray* | *El Nino is caused by abnormal amounts of warm water in the Pacific Ocean.* | **it is abnormal (for sb) to do sth** *My parents thought it was abnormal for a boy to be interested in ballet.* —**abnormally** [adv] *abnormally low blood pressure* | *She became abnormally fascinated by death.* | *Snow this early in the season could mean we'll have an abnormally cold winter.* —**abnormality** /ˌæbnɔːˈmælə̇ti‖-nər-/ [n C/U] *The drug was found to cause genetic abnormalities in unborn children.* | *The tests will show if there is any abnormality in your nervous system.*

unnatural /ʌnˈnætʃərəl/ [adj] different from normal human behaviour in a way that seems morally wrong: *unnatural acts* | *In some countries, it's considered unnatural for women with families to want to work outside the home.* | *Brown spoke out against what he considered the unnatural lifestyles of unmarried couples who live together.* —**unnaturally** [adv] *Police allege that Ellis cruelly and unnaturally treated the two women in her care.*

deviant /ˈdiːviənt/ [adj] formal **deviant** behaviour or actions are considered to be very strange and morally unacceptable – often used about sexual or criminal behaviour: *The magazine shows people engaging in deviant sexual acts.* | *Certain practices that once were condemned as deviant are now considered fairly normal.*

not

RELATED WORDS

▸ *see also* **never, no, none/nothing, opposite**

1 not

- not
- not very
- not particularly
- not quite
- not exactly
- neither

not /nɒt / [adv] *It's not boring – it's really interesting.* | *David's not stupid. He knows what's going on.* | *This period of history is not well documented.* | *We're not going on holiday this year.* | *Buying a yacht isn't as expensive as you might imagine.* | *'Are you worried about your exams?' 'No, I'm not.'* | *It's not a computer – it's a word processor.*

not very /nɒt ˈveri/ [adv] not – use this especially when you do not want to state a negative quality directly: *I wouldn't recommend the fish – it's not very nice.* | *He isn't very clever, is he?* | *The figures were different, but at the time we thought it wasn't very important.*

not particularly /nɒt pəʳˈtɪkjə̇ləʳli/ [adv] not very, or not very much: *It was a good film, not particularly exciting, but enjoyable.* | *Birmingham isn't a* *particularly beautiful city.* | *I didn't particularly want to go out.*

not quite /nɒt 'kwaɪt/ [adv] not completely, but almost: *The paint's not quite dry yet.* | *We haven't quite finished yet.*

not exactly /nɒt ɪg'zæktli/ [adv] not very or completely: *She's not exactly fat, but she is slightly overweight.* | *What they're doing is not exactly dishonest, but it's not completely honest either.*

neither /'naɪðəʳ‖'ni:-/ [adv] use this to say that a negative statement that has just been made about someone is also true about someone else **neither am I/neither does she/neither have we etc** *'I've never been to Australia.' 'No, neither have I.'* | *Tom didn't believe a word she said, and neither did the police.*

2 stronger expressions meaning not

- not at all
- by no means/not by any means
- not in the least
- in no way
- not remotely
- hardly
- not be the world's best/greatest
- be no expert/genius/Einstein etc
- simply/just not

not at all /ˌnɒt ət 'ɔ:l/ [adv] use this to emphasize that something is definitely not true: *She's not at all happy about the situation.* | *The children didn't seem to be at all frightened.* | *No, no, no, that's wrong. That's not what I meant at all.*

by no means/not by any means /baɪ 'nəʊ mi:nz, nɒt baɪ 'eni mi:nz/ [adv] formal use this when you want to say strongly that something is not true: *It is by no means certain that you'll get your money back.* | *It's difficult, but by no means impossible.* | *It's not clear by any means where the money is going to come from to fund this project.*

not in the least ALSO **not a bit** especially British /ˌnɒt ɪn ðə 'li:st, ˌnɒt ə 'bɪt/ [adv] use this to say strongly that something is not true, especially when you would expect it to be true: *You're not in the least sorry, are you?* | *My essay wasn't a bit like yours.* | *'Was she annoyed?' 'Not a bit! She was delighted.'* | **not the least (bit)** *Henry wasn't the least bit worried.*

in no way /ɪn ˌnəʊ 'weɪ/ [adv] if something is **in no way** affected by something else, it is definitely not affected by it in any way: *This will in no way influence our original decision.* | *The damage is very slight and in no way reduces the value of the painting.*

not remotely /nɒt rɪ'məʊtli/ [adv] use this when something is completely untrue, impossible, different etc: *His arguments are not remotely convincing.* | *It was a stupid remark, and not remotely funny.* | *She didn't seem remotely interested in anything I had to say.*

hardly /'hɑ:ʳdli/ [adv] use this to emphasize that something is definitely not true, and if someone thinks it is true they are being a little stupid: *They only won 1-0 – hardly a great victory!* | *It's hardly surprising he's upset, considering the way you've treated him!* | *He's hardly a world chess champion – you should be able to beat him.* | *All these similarities could hardly be due to chance.*

not be the world's best/greatest /nɒt bi: ðə ˌwɜ:ʳldz 'best, 'greɪtɪ̇st/ [v phrase] use this to say that someone is not good at something: *I occasionally put up a few shelves, but I'm not exactly the world's greatest handyman.*

be no expert/genius/Einstein etc /bi: ˌnəʊ 'ekspɜ:ʳt/ [v phrase] an informal expression meaning to not have the skills, qualities etc of the person or type of person that you have mentioned: *Of course, I'm no expert but that wall really looks like it's leaning over.* | *Stephanie knows what she's doing. She's no fool.* | *He's quite a bright boy I suppose, but he's no Albert Einstein.*

simply/just not /'sɪmpli, 'dʒʌst nɒt/ [adj phrase] use this to emphasize strongly that something is not possible, likely, true etc: *I can't see any use in us talking about that idea at all – it's simply not practical.* | *For as long as she could remember she'd just never been interested in marriage and children.*

3 not one thing and not the other

- neither
- neither ... nor
- neither one thing nor the other

neither /'naɪðəʳ‖'ni:-/ [determiner/pron] use this to emphasize that you are talking about both of two people or things when you make a negative statement about them: *Neither side in the dispute seems willing to make any compromise.* | **+ of** *Neither of their children had shown any particular talent for music.*

neither ... nor /'naɪðəʳ... nɔ:ʳ‖'ni:-/ use this when you want to make a negative statement about two people, things, actions etc: *The company's chairman described the criticisms as 'neither accurate nor fair'.* | *Neither France nor Britain will be represented at the conference.* | *She neither accepted nor rejected his offer immediately.*

neither one thing nor the other /naɪðəʳ ˌwʌn θɪŋ nɔ:ʳ ði 'ʌðəʳ‖ni:-/ [adj phrase] use this about something that does not have enough of the qualities of either of two things, so that is not satisfactory or definite in either way: *Having had one Protestant parent and one Catholic parent, I was really neither one thing nor the other.* | *The play attempts to blend high tragedy with comedy, but just ends up being neither one thing nor the other.*

notice/ not notice

RELATED WORDS

- pay or get attention *see* **attention**
- not pay any attention to someone or something *see* **ignore**
- *see also* **realize, see**

1 to notice someone or something

- notice
- can see/can tell
- I see
- spot
- become aware/conscious
- catch sb's eye
- detect
- note
- observe
- perceive

notice /'nəʊtɪ̇s/ [v I/T not in progressive] to realize that something is there or that something is happening, when you see it, hear it, or feel it: *'Julie's home.' 'Yes, I noticed her bicycle outside.'* | *Do you notice anything different about my hair?* | **+ (that)** *As she was about to leave, she noticed that the kitchen window was open.* | *Dominic took a huge slice of cake, hoping no one would notice.* | *I noticed that he was rather quiet during dinner.* | **+ how/when/where etc** *Did you notice what he was wearing?* | *She was* *worried that her boss would notice how long she had been gone.* | **notice sb doing sth** *I was about to leave when I noticed someone coming up the driveway.*

can see/can tell /kən 'siː, kən 'tel/ [v phrase] to know that something is true, because you notice signs that show you this **+ (that)** *We could tell that she had been crying.* | *I can see you're not really enjoying this.*

I see /aɪ 'siː/ [v phrase] spoken say this to mention something that you have noticed **+ (that)** *I see that the new De Niro movie is playing this weekend.* | *I see you've been working out.*

spot /spɒt‖spɑːt/ [v T not in progressive] to see something or someone that is difficult to notice, or something or someone that no one else notices: *I'm glad you spotted the mistake before it was too late.* | *If you spot Mom and Dad coming, warn me.* | *I dropped my keys in the grass, but luckily Jim spotted them.* | **spot sb doing sth** *Police finally caught up with Serrano when he was spotted eating in an Upper East Side restaurant.* | **difficult/easy to spot** *She won't be difficult to spot – she's got pink hair and weighs about 300 pounds.*

become aware/conscious /bɪˌkʌm ə'weəʳ, 'kɒnʃəs‖-'kɑːn-/ [v phrase] to gradually begin to notice something **+ (that)** *I slowly became aware that I was the only woman in the bar.* | *He became conscious that everyone in the room had suddenly gotten quiet.* | **+ of** *It wasn't until after the game that he became aware of the bruises on his legs.* | *She became conscious of a growing amount of hostility between them.*

catch sb's eye /ˌkætʃ (sb's) 'aɪ/ [v phrase] if something or someone **catches your eye**, you notice them and like them because they are interesting, attractive, or unusual: *I was walking through the market when a beautiful dress caught my eye.* | *Wright caught the eye of filmmaker Spike Lee, who featured him in a jeans commercial.*

detect /dɪ'tekt/ [v T] to notice something that is difficult to see, hear etc, especially because it is very small, faint, or unclear: *Marlowe detected a faint smell of perfume as he entered the room.* | *She wasn't moving or responding, but he detected a slow heartbeat.* | *Do I detect a note of sarcasm in your voice?* | *The system is so sensitive that it can detect changes in temperature as small as 0.003 of a degree.* —**detection** /dɪ'tekʃən/ [n U] *A Geiger counter is designed for the detection of minute differences in radio activity.*

note /nəʊt/ [v T not in progressive] to notice a fact or detail and remember it, because it tells you something about a person or because it might be useful to you in the future: *I noted her habit of looking at the floor whenever I asked her a question.* | **+ how/when etc** *He chatted to her, noting how her face reddened every time Ian's name was mentioned.* | **+ that** *Note that the compound is more stable at high temperatures.* | **could/can not help but note that** *I couldn't help but note that Jenny doesn't phone or call around to see you anymore.* | **it should be noted that** *It should be noted that the witness did not recognize the defendant.*

observe /əb'zɜːʳv/ [v T not in progressive] formal to notice something as a result of watching or studying it closely: *I didn't observe anything out of the ordinary about her behaviour that day.* | **+ that** *Psychologists observed that the mice became more aggressive when they were put in smaller cages.* —**observation** /ˌɒbzəʳ'veɪʃən‖ˌɑːb-/ [n U] *I have learned much about child psychology from the observation of* (=by observing) *my own children.*

perceive /pəʳ'siːv/ [v T not in progressive] formal to notice something, especially something that is difficult to notice: *Although Jane thought her father seemed anxious and uneasy, Susan did not perceive any change in his looks or ways.* | **+ (that)** *The prime minister will only resign if he perceives there is no other way out of the crisis.* | *If they perceive that a military challenge threatens their country's interests, they will not hesitate to fight.*

2 to not notice something

- not notice
- miss
- overlook
- fail to notice
- escape sb's notice
- unnoticed
- unseen

not notice /nɒt 'nəʊtɪ̈s/ [v phrase not in progressive] *'Does Alex like your new hairstyle?' 'He didn't even notice.'* | *I saw Mike in town but he didn't notice me.* | **+ (that)** *He was so wrapped up in his studying that he didn't notice that the phone was ringing.* | *She didn't notice her jewelry box was missing until after the police had left.* | **+ how/who/what etc** *We were so busy we didn't notice how late it was.*

miss /mɪs/ [v T not in progressive] to not notice something because it is difficult to see: *She missed the exit and had to turn around.* | *Jo spotted a mistake that everyone else had missed.* | *It's easy to miss the entrance – the sign is hidden behind a tree.*

overlook /ˌəʊvəʳ'lʊk/ [v T not in progressive] to not notice something because you have not been careful enough: *They found some important evidence that the police had overlooked.* | *Make a list of what you need to bring so you don't overlook anything.* | **it's easy to overlook sb/sth** *The Hotel les Tipaniers, practically hidden between two much larger hotels, is easy to overlook but worth finding.*

fail to notice /ˌfeɪl tə 'nəʊtɪ̈s/ [v phrase not in progressive] written to not notice something, especially when this could have a serious result: *Atkinson failed to notice the car ahead of him was parked and drove straight into the back of it.* | *They were not prepared for his second heart attack, having failed to notice the warning signs.* | *There was a growing resentment among inmates which the prison authorities had either failed to notice or just ignored.*

escape sb's notice /ɪˌskeɪp (sb's) 'nəʊtɪ̈s/ [v phrase not in progressive] if a fact **escapes sb's notice**, they do not notice it, especially when they should have noticed it: *This problem has completely escaped his notice.* | *I'm amazed that there are so many restaurants in Tucson that have completely escaped my notice over the years.*

unnoticed /ʌn'nəʊtɪ̈st/ [adv] **go/pass/escape etc unnoticed** happen without anyone noticing: *The death of the former movie star passed unnoticed.* | *There were a lot of people at the party, which made it easy for Gary to slip away unnoticed.* | *Gradual hearing loss often goes unnoticed until substantial damage is done.*

unseen /ˌʌn'siːn◂/ [adv] secretly, without being seen: *The royal couple arrived unseen in an unmarked car.* | *He managed to creep out of the house unseen and slip out through the garden.*

3 good at noticing things

- observant
- perceptive
- not miss much
- eagle-eyed
- have eyes in the back of your head
- powers of observation

observant /əb'zɜːʳvənt/ [adj] good at noticing

things: *Men aren't very observant about things like hair or clothes.* | *An observant reader has pointed out an error on page 26.* | *She was insightful and observant, constantly surprising her parents by what she noticed.*

perceptive /pəʳˈseptɪv/ [adj] good at noticing and understanding situations or people's feelings: *I like her novels – she's so perceptive about people's relationships.* | *He was a perceptive and sophisticated man who was sensitive to other people's weaknesses.*

not miss much ALSO **not miss a trick** British **/not miss a thing** American /nɒt mɪs ˈmʌtʃ, nɒt mɪs ə ˈtrɪk, nɒt mɪs ə ˈθɪŋ / [v phrase] spoken if you do **not miss much** or do **not miss a trick** or **a thing**, you notice a lot about what is happening and what other people are doing or feeling: *'I think Alison and Peter are getting pretty friendly with each other.' 'You don't miss much, do you?'* | *He's still pretty sharp for an old man – he doesn't miss a thing.* | *We tried to keep it secret from Mum, but you know she doesn't miss a trick.*

eagle-eyed /ˌiːgəl ˈaɪd◂/ [adj only before noun] an **eagle-eyed** person is very good at noticing everything that people do or how they behave: *The hotel was run by an eagle-eyed old man who knew everything about all the guests.* | *Two eagle-eyed reporters noticed the politician leaving a prostitute's house.*

have eyes in the back of your head /hæv ˌaɪz ɪn ðə bæk əv jɔːʳ ˈhed/ [v phrase] if someone **has eyes in the back of their head**, they notice everything that is happening around them, even when they do not seem to be paying attention: *When you're looking after a two year old, you need to have eyes in the back of your head.*

powers of observation /ˌpaʊəʳz əv ɒbzəʳˈveɪʃən ‖-ɑːb-/ [n phrase] how good someone is at noticing things: *Keith would make a good detective – he has excellent powers of observation.* | *Her drawings displayed astonishing powers of observation.*

4 something that is easy to notice

- obvious
- noticeable
- conspicuous
- eye-catching
- stand out
- you can't miss it

obvious /ˈɒbviəs‖ˈɑːb-/ [adj] a fact that is **obvious** is easy to see or realize: *She tried to look grateful, but her disappointment was obvious.* | **it is obvious (to sb) that** *It's obvious that Paul is in love with Liz.* | *It was obvious to everyone that Gina was lying.* —**obviously** [adv] *The doctor said he wants Ann to come back for further tests and she's obviously very worried.*

noticeable /ˈnəʊtɪ̮səbəl/ [adj] easy to notice: *After two days there was a noticeable improvement in his health.* | *The new supermarket has had a noticeable effect on people's shopping habits.* | **it is noticeable that** *It was noticeable that no one at the party was under 40.* —**noticeably** [adv] *The upper branches of the tree are noticeably lighter in color.*

conspicuous /kənˈspɪkjuəs/ [adj] formal someone or something that is **conspicuous** is very easy to notice, especially because they look very different from everyone or everything around them: *It was a small country town, and Lauren looked very conspicuous in her fashionable New York clothes.* —**conspicuously** [adv] *Richmond was conspicuously absent from the NBA All-Star Game on Sunday.*

eye-catching /ˈaɪ ˌkætʃɪŋ/ [adj] **eye-catching** colours, designs, patterns etc are bright, attractive, and unusual, so everyone notices them: *an eye-catching ad* | *The posters come in several eye-catching designs.*

stand out /ˌstænd ˈaʊt/ [phr v I] if something **stands out**, it is easy to notice because it looks very different from everything around it: *A yellow background will make the black lettering stand out.* | *Joanna, a six-foot-three redhead, stood out in her small Iowa farm community like a palm tree in a cornfield.* | **+ against** *The dark shapes of the trees stood out against the evening sky.*

you can't miss it /juː ˌkɑːnt ˈmɪs ɪt‖-ˌkænt-/ spoken say this when you are telling someone how to get to a place that is very easy to find or to notice: *Their house has a pink door. You can't miss it.*

5 to make people notice you

- get attention/ attract attention

get attention/attract attention /ˌget əˈtenʃən, əˌtrækt əˈtenʃən/ [v phrase] to try to make someone notice you, by doing something that they will notice: *Young children sometimes behave badly simply in order to get attention.* | **get/attract sb's attention** *Phil was trying to attract the waiter's attention.*

now

RELATED WORDS

opposite: —— **then (2)**

▸ *see also* **modern, during, time, future, past**

1 now, at this time

- now
- already
- currently
- at the moment/presently
- at present/at the present time
- right now
- just now
- at this time

now /naʊ/ [adv] at this moment or at this time: *If we leave now we'll be there before dark.* | *It's not raining now, but they said it might rain later.* | *He used to coach high school basketball but now he's a realtor.* | **from now on** (=starting from now) *Students are to be in their seats by 8:00 from now on.* | *From now on, the U.S. government will rely on a new method to measure economic growth.*

already /ɔːlˈredi/ [adv] if something is **already** happening or **already** true, it began to happen or be true before now: *He's only three and he's already reading.* | *'Should I tell Kay?' 'She already knows.'* | *The show has already started.* | *Don't buy any more toys for the kids – they've got plenty already.* | *Was the apartment empty when you moved in or was it already furnished?*

currently /ˈkʌrəntli‖ˈkɜːr-/ [adv] now – use this when you are describing what the situation is at this time: *The firm currently employs 113 people.* | *Currently, the most a senior nurse can earn is £16,000.* | *Ms. Kelly is currently assisting another customer. May I help you?*

at the moment/presently /ət ðə ˈməʊmənt, ˈprezəntli/ [adv] now – use this especially to say that something is happening now but you do not expect it to continue for a long time: *I'm working in a restaurant at the moment.* | *Miss Hellman is away* *from her desk at the moment – can I have her call you back?* | *The official currency is the crown, presently about 30 to the dollar.*

at present/at the present time /ət ˈprezənt, ət ðə ˌprezənt ˈtaɪm/ [adv] formal if something is true **at present** or **at the present time**, it is true now but you do not expect it to be permanent: *The money available for public libraries will be less in future than at present.* | *We do not envisage any changes in the tax structure at the present time.*

right now /ˌraɪt ˈnaʊ/ [adv] spoken at this moment or at this time: *I need a new car but right now I can't afford one.* | *She's in Amsterdam right now but she should be in Paris by tomorrow night.*

just now /ˌdʒʌst ˈnaʊ/ [adv] British spoken at this exact moment – use this especially to say that you cannot do something immediately: *Sorry, I'm busy just now – can I call you later?*

at this time /ət ˌðɪs ˈtaɪm/ [adv] American at this particular time: *I have no further questions at this time, your honor.* | *'Do you have any health insurance?' 'Not at this time.'* | **at this time of day/night/ year etc** *What are you doing out at this time of night?* | *Gas prices always go up at this time of year.*

2 now, not in the past

- now
- nowadays/these days
- today
- in this day and age

now /naʊ/ [adv] use this when you are comparing the present situation with what happened in the past: *We used to be good friends but I don't see very much of her now.* | *Julie has moved to a new school and she's much happier now.*

nowadays/these days /ˈnaʊədeɪz, ˈðiːz ˌdeɪz/ [adv] use this when you are describing how life is different now from the way it was in the past. **These days** is more common in spoken English: *It seems you're not allowed to smoke anywhere nowadays.* | *Children can't play in the street these days – the traffic's too bad.* | *Nowadays, you hardly ever seen anyone wearing a tie to work.*

today /təˈdeɪ/ [adv] at the present time, especially when compared with the past: *Today, only a few of these beautiful animals survive.* | *Couples today are much more likely to marry in their 30s.* | *The cost to install solar panels has dropped from $20 a watt in 1980 to as little as $5 today.*

in this day and age /ɪn ˈðɪs deɪ ənd ˌeɪdʒ/ [adv] use this to show that you are surprised and shocked that something still happens now: *It's not right, in this day and age, that people all over the world are still starving.* | *It's amazing that you can still find a house for under $100,000 in this day and age.*

3 until now

- so far
- still
- yet
- up to now/until now
- up to the present day/until the present day

so far /ˌsəʊ ˈfɑːʳ/ [adv] until now – use this when you are talking about a situation that will continue or develop after this time: *There haven't been any problems so far.* | *This is the hottest day we've had so far this summer.* | *We've raised twelve thousand dollars so far, and we expect to reach our goal by the end of next week.*

still /stɪl/ [adv] use this to say that a situation which started in the past continues to exist now, especially when this is surprising: *He's been studying French for five years, and still can't speak the language.* | *Are you still going out with that guy you met at Heather's party?*

yet /jet/ [adv] use this in questions or negative statements, to talk or ask about things that you expected to happen before now: *Has the new washing machine arrived yet?* | *I haven't been to the new exhibit yet, but I hope to this weekend.* | *'Have you finished your homework?' 'Not yet.'*

up to now/until now /ˌʌp tə ˈnaʊ, ənˌtɪl ˈnaʊ/ [adv] use this about a situation which has existed until now, but which has started to change or will change in the future: *He hasn't gotten much time off from work up to now, so he's really looking forward to his vacation.* | *Until now, there has been no effective treatment for this disease.*

up to the present day/until the present day /ˌʌp tə ðə ˌprezənt ˈdeɪ, ənˌtɪl ðə ˌprezənt ˈdeɪ/ [adv] from a time in the past until modern times: *These two companies have dominated the industry from the end of World War II until the present day.* | *The beauty of Yosemite has inspired artists from Bierstadt's time right up to the present day.*

4 existing, happening, or relating to now

- present
- existing
- current
- today's/of today
- modern-day/present-day
- modern
- contemporary
- topical
- latter-day

present /ˈprezənt/ [adj only before noun] the **present** situation is the one that exists now; your **present** job, address etc is the one that you have now: *Arnaud lived in Los Angeles before moving to his present home in New York.* | *He warned that the present situation could get much worse.*

existing /ɪgˈzɪstɪŋ/ [adj only before noun] use this about things or situations that exist now, when you think they may be changed in the future: *The existing building is too small, and there are plans to replace it within the next five years.* | *Many people feel that the existing law discriminates against women.*

current /ˈkʌrənt‖ˈkɜːr-/ [adj only before noun] use this about a situation or activity which is happening now, but which is not expected to continue for a long time: *In the current economic situation, switching careers may not be such a good idea.* | *Coca-Cola's current advertising campaign* | **current level/rate/ price** *The aim is to reduce current pollution levels in the Black Sea.* | *According to one economist, at the current growth rate, China will have the largest economy in the world by 2030.*

today's/of today /təˈdeɪz, əv təˈdeɪ/ [adj] use this about social, economic, or political conditions and attitudes that exist now, when you are comparing them with those that existed in the past: *The first computers were extremely slow by today's standards.* | *The teenagers of today have a different attitude to sex.*

modern-day/present-day /ˈmɒdn deɪ‖ˈmɑː-dərn-, ˈprezənt deɪ/ [adj only before noun] a **present-day** situation, fact, idea etc is one that exists now rather than in the past: *Modern-day equipment has made mining much safer than it was.* | *There is no modern-day racing driver who could be compared with Fan-*

gio. | Prussia reached its zenith in 1795, encompassing most of northern Germany and present-day Poland.

modern /ˈmɒdn‖ˈmɑːdərn/ [adj only before noun] belonging to the present time or most recent time and not to the past: *I don't like modern architecture at all. | The pyramids are a remarkable piece of engineering, even judged by modern standards. | The most compelling work in the modern British theater is being created in the smaller and non-profit theaters.*

contemporary /kənˈtempərəri, -pəri‖-pəreri/ [adj only before noun] **contemporary** art, writing, thought, society etc is the type that exists, is accepted, or belongs to, the present time: *Contemporary Indian cinema has its roots in folk culture. | the declining importance of religion in contemporary societies*

topical /ˈtɒpɪkəl‖ˈtɑː-/ [adj] a story, subject, problem etc that is **topical** is interesting because it deals with something that is important at the moment: *It's an old story but it has a topical message. | In the 1970s, he recorded topical songs about Watergate and the Vietnam War. | The editor thinks that if an article isn't topical it isn't worth publishing.*

latter-day /ˈlætəʳ deɪ/ [adj only before noun] someone who exists now and is a very similar type of person as someone who existed in the past: *Romer portrayed himself as a latter-day Robin Hood who took money and gave it to the underprivileged.*

5 happening now, but likely to change

- for now/for the time being
- for the moment
- as of now
- for the present
- in the meanwhile/in the meantime

for now/for the time being /fəʳ ˈnaʊ, fəʳ ðə ˌtaɪm ˈbiːɪŋ/ [adv] for a short time, but not permanently – use this about a temporary arrangement or way of dealing with a situation: *Leave the groceries there for now – I'll put them away later. | For the time being he can stay here, but I want that dog out of here by the end of the week.*

for the moment /fəʳ ðə ˈməʊmənt/ [adv] especially spoken use this to say that something is true or happening now, but may change soon: *For the moment the city seems quiet, but the fighting could start again at any time. | 'How's your apartment?' 'It's fine for the moment, but I'd rather live nearer town.' | Assuming for the moment that you did get the job, where would you live?*

as of now /ˌæz əv ˈnaʊ/ [adv] American use this to say that something is true or happening now, but will probably change in the future: *As of now, there is no cure for multiple sclerosis. | My plan, as of now, is to graduate in May then start looking for a job in the fall.*

for the present /fəʳ ðə ˈprezənt/ [adv] formal *It is assumed, for the present, that the meeting will go ahead. | A reduction in interest rates seems highly unlikely for the present.*

in the meanwhile/in the meantime /ɪn ðə ˈmiːnwaɪl, ɪn ðə ˈmiːntaɪm/ [adv] between now and some time in the future, for example until a situation changes: *Payday is not until next week, but if you need any money in the meanwhile, let me know. | You probably won't receive the contract until Thursday but I can fax you a copy in the meantime.* | **meanwhile** *The flight will be announced soon. Meanwhile, please remain seated.*

6 when something does not happen now

- no longer
- not any more
- not now

no longer /nəʊ ˈlɒŋgəʳ‖-ˈlɔːŋ-/ [adv] use this to say that a situation that existed until recently does not exist now: *He no longer felt sure that he was right.* | **no longer + adj** *The bridge had collapsed, and it was no longer possible to cross the river.*

not any more /ˌnɒt eni ˈmɔːʳ/ [adv] used when something has changed, especially suddenly: *Alex doesn't work here any more. | Do what you like. I don't care any more! | At one time doctors recommended red meat as part of a healthy diet but not any more.*

not now /nɒt ˈnaʊ/ [adv] use this to say that something happened in the past, but it does not happen now: *When I was younger I spent hours lying out in the sun but not now. | People used to respect teachers, but they don't now.*

number

RELATED WORDS

- when a number reaches a particular level *see* **reach (2)**
- *see also* **count/calculate, amount, level, total, increase, reduce**

1 a written number

- number
- figure
- digit
- numeral

number /ˈnʌmbəʳ/ [n C] a word or sign that is used to talk about an exact quantity or to show the position of something in a series: *Each player has a number on the back of their shirt.* | **number 12/20/4 etc** *I live at number 12 Liverpool Road. | Raffle ticket number 241 wins the dinner for two at La Fiorentina.* | **even number** (=2,4,6,8,10 etc) *The game works best with an even number of children.* | **odd number** (=1,3,5,7,9 etc) *All the doors on this side of the street have odd numbers.* | **phone/passport/registration/licence etc number** *What's your phone number? | Write your social security number in the appropriate box of the tax form.*

figure /ˈfɪgəʳ‖ˈfɪgjər/ [n C] a number written as a sign, not as a word: *On a cheque, write the amount in words and in figures.* | **double figures** (=more than 9 and less than 100) British *Temperatures reached double figures for the first time this spring, going as high as 14 degrees.* | **single figures** (=less than 10) British *The inflation rate was still in single figures.* (=less than 10%) | **five-figure/six-figure etc** (=a number that has five, six etc figures in it) *The managing director earns a six-figure salary.* | **figure 8** (=a shape like the number 8) *The pond is shaped like a figure eight with a bridge across the middle.*

digit /ˈdɪdʒ$_{\text{ɪ}}^{\text{ə}}$t/ [n C] a single number between 0 and 9, for example 1, 5, or 8 – used especially in formal or technical contexts: *French telephone numbers have six digits. | This calculator can display only nine digits at a time. | To unlock the gate you must know the four-digit security code.* | **double-digit** (=more than 9 and less than 100)) American *The nation has not experienced double-digit inflation for many years.*

numeral /'nju:mərəl‖'nu:-/ [n C] a sign that represents a number in a particular number system, especially a system that is no longer generally used **Arabic/Roman/European etc numerals** *The European numbers 1, 2, 3 and so on, are based on Arabic numerals.* | *The date was written in Roman numerals – MCMLXXXII.*

2 a number used in representing a quantity

- number
- figure
- statistics
- toll

number /'nʌmbəʳ/ [n singular] a **number** of people, things etc, especially a **number** that has been counted for official purposes: *There have been several cases of tuberculosis, and the number is rising.* | **+ of** *The number of cars on the roads increased by 22% last year.* | *The regulations limit the number of students in each class.* | **a large/small etc number of people/things etc** *An enormous number of people wrote to complain about last night's show.*

figure /'fɪgəʳ‖'fɪgjər/ [n C] a number, especially an officially supplied number, showing an amount, how much something has increased, how much it has decreased etc: *Government figures published today show that unemployment is rising again.* | *The total value of all drugs seized by the police reached a record figure of $116,000,000.* | *Inflation in Japan is around 3%, while the German figure is now over 4%.* | **sales figures** *Retailers are reporting their November sales figures today.*

statistics /stə'tɪstɪks/ [n plural] information about financial matters, social changes etc, which is shown in the form of numbers: *Statistics show that the number of women managers has risen continuously for the last 25 years.* | *According to the latest government statistics, 2 million people retired last year.*

toll /təʊl/ [n C usually singular] the number of people killed or injured in accidents, by illness etc: *The final toll was 83 dead and more than 100 injured.* | **death toll** *The death toll from the earthquake has risen still further in the worst disaster since 1952.*

3 to write or put numbers on a set of things

- number
- numbered

number /'nʌmbəʳ/ [v T] to write or put numbers on a set of things: *We finished numbering the seats just as the audience began to arrive.* | *The program will automatically number the pages of your reports.* | *If you don't number your answers, how will I know which questions they refer to?*

numbered /'nʌmbəʳd/ [adj] something such as a seat, a ticket, or a page that is **numbered** has a number written on it: *The tickets are numbered, so you can find your seat quite easily.* | *A series of numbered diagrams illustrate the results of the experiment.* | **numbered from one/five etc to ten/fifteen etc** *The squares are numbered from one to ten.*

Oo

obey

RELATED WORDS

opposite: **disobey**

▸ *see also* **law, tell sb off, illegal, rule/regulation, behave**

1 to obey someone

- obey
- follow
- do what/as sb says
- do as you're told
- on-message

obey /əʊ'beɪ, ə-/ [v I/T] to do what someone in authority tells you to do: *Soldiers must always obey their commanding officer.* | *I knew that if I didn't obey, I would be shot.* | **obey an order/command/instruction** *You can teach most dogs to obey simple commands.* | *War criminals tried to justify their actions by saying that they were only obeying orders.*

follow /'fɒləʊ‖'fɑ:-/ [v T] to do what someone tells you to do, wants you to do, or thinks you should do **follow orders/instructions** *He was a military man, and therefore used to following orders.* | *I have followed your instructions exactly.* | **follow sb's advice** *Visitors to the city should follow police advice and not resist muggers.* | **follow sb's orders/instructions etc to the letter** (=do exactly what someone tells you) *You will not make a mistake if you follow these instructions to the letter.*

do what/as sb says /ˌdu: wɒt, əz (sb) 'sez/ [v phrase] especially spoken to do what someone has advised or ordered you to do: *I did what you said and took half a pill instead of a whole one.* | *'Sit down and listen,' Matt said. I did as he said.* | **do as I say** (=used by adults to tell children to do something) *I'm your father, and you'll do as I say.*

do as you're told /ˌdu: əz jɔ:ʳ 'təʊld/ [v phrase] especially spoken to obey someone and not do anything different – used by parents or teachers to tell children to do something: *If she doesn't do as she's told, send her to her room.*

on-message /ɒn 'mesɪdʒ/ [adj/adv] if a politician is **on-message** he or she is always publicly willing to support the ideas and aims of their party and to do what their leaders want them to do – used especially in newspapers: *The party leadership is desperately trying to get several senior members of the government back on-message.* | *Those who were firmly on-message dutifully defended the prime minister's actions to the media.*

2 to obey a law, rule, or custom

- obey
- comply with
- abide by
- keep to
- stick to the rules
- conform to
- observe
- respect
- toe the line
- go by the book/do sth by the book

obey /əʊ'beɪ, ə-/ [v T] to do what a law or rule says you must do: *Drivers obey speed laws only when they think the police are near.* | **obey the law** *All citizens* *must obey the law and be loyal to the Constitution.* | **obey the rules** *She was one of those people who obeyed the rules and was never irresponsible.*

comply with /kəm'plaɪ wɪð/ [v T] formal if you **comply with** a law or a decision, you do what it says you must do: *Companies must comply with European employment laws.* | *Failure to comply with these conditions could result in prosecution.*

abide by /ə'baɪd baɪ/ [v T] to accept and obey a decision, rule, agreement etc, even though you may not agree with it: *Those are the rules and regulations – we don't make them but we have to abide by them.* | *Players have to abide by the referee's decision.* | *Generally, journalists abide by an agreed code of practice.*

keep to /'ki:p tu:/ [v T] to always obey the law or rules closely and not ignore them: *If you keep to the rules nothing can go wrong.* | *Keep to the law, but apart from that, do whatever you have to do to find this man.* | *Do you always keep to the speed limit when you're driving?*

stick to the rules /ˌstɪk tə ðə 'ru:lz/ [v phrase] informal to do something exactly as it should be done, especially so that there is no chance of anything going wrong: *Everyone in the party has a responsibility to stick to the rules agreed by the party conference.* | *Failure to stick to the safety rules could result in disaster.*

conform to /kən'fɔ:ʳm tu:/ [v T] to be correct according to a rule or regulation: *British meat products now have to conform to strict hygiene regulations.* | *Many classroom interactions do not conform to the rules of normal conversation.*

observe /əb'zɜ:ʳv/ [v T] formal to take notice of and obey rules, laws, customs etc: *You can avoid danger by observing these simple rules.* | *Too many accidents are occurring at work because employers are not observing safety regulations.* | *We try to observe the local customs so that we don't offend people.* —**observance** [n U] *The police ensure strict observance of the law.*

respect /rɪ'spekt/ [v T] formal to obey the law or customs of a place, especially because you believe it is important to obey them: *The President is expected to respect the constitution.* | *He's an honest, responsible citizen who respects the law and is dedicated to his family.*

toe the line /ˌtəʊ ðə 'laɪn/ [v phrase] to obey the rules and behave in an acceptable way in your job or in an organization, even if you do not want to, do not agree etc: *They didn't agree, but as government employees they had to toe the line.* | *Gail realized that she had to toe the line if she wanted to keep her job.*

go by the book/do sth by the book /ˌgəʊ baɪ ðə 'bʊk, du: (sth) baɪ ðə 'bʊk/ [v phrase] to do something exactly according to the rules or instructions, rather than in your own way: *Police must always go completely by the book when making arrests.* | *My financial advisor is very straight – he does everything by the book.*

3 always doing what you are told to do

- obedient
- obedience
- law-abiding
- dutiful
- disciplined

obedient /ə'bi:diənt/ [adj] someone who is **obedient** always does what their parents, teachers, or people in authority tell them to do – use this especially about children: *Bruno was a quiet and obedient little boy.* | *Research shows that pupils who are good at maths tend to be more conformist and obedient than other pupils.* | **+ to** *The majority of people were obedient to the King, not questioning his government.*

obedience /ə'bi:diəns/ [n U] obedient behaviour **+ to** *Young children are expected to show obedience to their parents.* | **absolute/complete/total obedience** *The General demanded absolute obedience from his men.*

law-abiding /'lɔ: əˌbaɪdɪŋ/ [adj] always obeying the law because you think this is the right thing to do: *These men are all decent, tax-paying, law-abiding people.* | *There is a tendency to look back at a time when people were more peaceful and law-abiding.*

dutiful /'dju:tɪfəl‖'du:-/ [adj usually before noun] always doing what you are expected to do and always behaving in a loyal and obedient way: *Tom Campbell has been a loyal and dutiful employee of this firm for 25 years.* | *She rejected the traditional female roles of docile daughter and dutiful wife.*

disciplined /'dɪsəplənd/ [adj] a group of people that is **disciplined** has developed obedience or has been trained to be obedient: *They are a well-trained, disciplined and efficient fighting force.* | **well-disciplined** *The workforce is well-disciplined and eager to work.*

4 too willing to do what you are told to do

- submissive
- yes-man
- servile
- subservient
- slavish
- compliant
- blind obedience
- lackey

submissive /səb'mɪsɪv/ [adj] always willing to do what someone tells you to do even if it is unpleasant or they ask you in an unpleasant way: *My father was a violent, demanding man, who expected my mother to be completely submissive.* | *If you constantly try to make someone happy, you end up becoming submissive, saying yes when you don't really mean it.* —**submissively** [adv] *Carrigan smiled submissively and did what he was told.*

yes-man /'jes mæn/ [n C] informal someone who always agrees with and obeys their employer or leader etc: *It's no good applying for a job with him unless you're happy being a yes-man.* | *She packed the committees with yes-men and then did just what she liked.*

servile /'sɜ:ʳvaɪl‖-vəl, -vaɪl/ [adj] obeying someone too eagerly and showing them too much respect: *The driver asked in a servile tone for more instructions.* | *He was young and hard-working, though annoyingly servile.*

subservient /səb'sɜ:ʳviənt/ [adj] someone who is **subservient** is always willing to do what people tell them to do and behaves as if they expect to be told what to do: *The waiter had an excessively subservient manner that made us very uncomfortable.* | **+ to** *What she hated about being a nurse was having to be so subservient to doctors.*

slavish /'sleɪvɪʃ/ [adj] **slavish obedience/compliance/conformity etc** obeying much too easily without thinking or asking questions: *The women's slavish obedience disgusted me.* | *He was able to manipulate their slavish willingness to serve in the name of patriotism.* —**slavishly** [adv] *She made all the decisions, gave all the orders, and Ramón slavishly complied.*

compliant /kəm'plaɪənt/ [adj] too obedient because you are used to obeying people or because you are afraid not to obey: *It's depressing to see an intelligent, spirited young woman like her turning into a meek and compliant wife.* | *Patients who are less compliant may be forced to take medication against their will.*

blind obedience /ˌblaɪnd ə'biːdiəns/ [n U] when someone does whatever someone else tells them to do, without thinking for themselves about whether it is right or wrong: *With blind obedience, I allowed Victor to organize my life.*

lackey /'læki/ [n C] someone who is always too willing to do what someone else, especially someone in authority, tells them to do, even when this is wrong: *Many employees regarded Human Resources staff as little more than management lackeys.* | *Some poeple in the UK were worried that their country might be regarded as simply being a lackey of the US.*

5 when you have to do whatever someone tells you to do

- you're the boss/she's the boss etc
- be under sb's/the thumb
- be at sb's beck and call

you're the boss/she's the boss etc /ˌjɔːʳ ðə 'bɒs‖-'bɔːs/ spoken say this when you feel you have to do whatever someone says, even if you disagree: *Personally, I don't like dark-coloured wallpaper, but you're the boss.* | *If he tells you to do something, you do it, no questions, because he's the boss.*

be under sb's/the thumb /biː ˌʌndəʳ (sb's), ðə 'θʌm/ [v phrase] to be so strongly influenced by someone so that they control you completely and you do anything that they want you to do: *The President, senators, and deputies are all under the thumb of the military.* | **have sb under your thumb** *It was widely known that the mafia had the union under their thumb.*

be at sb's beck and call /biː ət (sb's) ˌbek ən 'kɔːl/ [v phrase] if you **are at someone's beck and call**, they are always telling you to do things for them, and you always have to be ready to do things for them: *I have never liked to be at anybody's beck and call.* | *She was always rushing around at her mother's beck and call.*

obsession

an unreasonably strong and continuous interest in someone or something

RELATED WORDS

- *see also* **interested, think, addicted, love**

1 an obsession about someone or something

- obsession
- mania
- fixation
- fascination
- fetish
- preoccupation

obsession /əb'seʃən/ [n C/U] an unreasonably strong and continuous interest in someone or something, so that you cannot stop thinking about them and your behaviour is seriously affected **become an obsession/turn into an obsession** *Julia's desire to stay slim has become an obsession.* | **+ with/for** *Picasso's obsession with death and sickness greatly influenced his work.* | *I knew that if I wasn't careful, my obsession for her could destroy me.* | **have an obsession** *Bowman has a dangerous obsession with speed.*

mania /'meɪniə/ [n C/U] a very strong desire for something or interest in something, especially one that affects a lot of people at the same time **+ for** *A mania for a game called Nibs ran through the school.* | *I had a mania for cleanliness, and once made him stay in all day while I washed all his clothes.* | **religious/gambling etc mania** *Aunt Edna was scathing about her cousin's religious mania.*

fixation /fɪk'seɪʃən/ [n C] an unnaturally strong interest in or love for someone or something **+ with/on** *our fixation with diet and fitness* | *The killing was the result of Dougherty's four year fixation with a co-worker who would not date him.*

fascination /ˌfæsǝ̇'neɪʃən/ [n singular] a very strong and unusual interest in a particular person, subject, or type of thing **+ with/for** *What's your sudden fascination with my boyfriend?* | *Mark has a fascination for all things electrical.*

fetish /'fetɪʃ, 'fiː-/ [n C] an extremely strong and unreasonable interest in something **+ for** *Americans seem to have a fetish for watering their golf courses.* | **a foot/hair/animal etc fetish** *She told stories about the band's alcoholic binges, their arrests on drug charges, and even about one member's foot fetish.*

preoccupation /priːˌɒkjǝ̈'peɪʃən‖-ˌɑːk-/ [n singular] a strong interest in one thing, usually because you are worried about it, which means that you cannot pay attention to other things **+ with** *Georgina's preoccupation with her appearance takes up most of her time.* | *Writing a will is not evidence of a morbid preoccupation with death.*

2 to have an obsession

- have an obsession with/for
- obsessed
- obsessive
- can't get sb/sth out of your mind
- have a thing about
- obsess
- have a one-track mind
- have an unhealthy interest in

have an obsession with/for /hæv ən əb'seʃən wɪð, fɔːʳ/ [v phrase] *My father always said I had an unhealthy obsession for spotty pop bands.* | *Our French teacher had a neurotic obsession with correct punctuation.*

obsessed /əb'sest/ [adj] someone who is **obsessed**, has an obsession about someone or something: *Madonna was being stalked by an obsessed fan.* | **+ by/with/about** *She was obsessed by Giles* | *He became obsessed in his old age with what to do with his immense wealth.* | *People are generally less obsessed about getting a tan than they used to be.*

obsessive /əb'sesɪv/ [adj] having an unreasonably strong and continuous interest in someone or something, so that you cannot stop thinking about them and your behaviour is seriously affected: *She's got this obsessive fear of losing control, so she never shows her emotions.* | *Deep anxiety can cause obsessive behaviour.* | **+ about** *I try to look after my body as best I can, but I'm not obsessive about it.*

can't get sb/sth out of your mind /ˌkɑːnt get (sb/sth) aʊt əv jɔːʳ 'maɪnd‖ˌkænt-/ [v phrase] to be unable to stop thinking about someone or something, even when you do not want to think about them: *Since the divorce, he hadn't been able to get*

Bonniet out of his mind. | *She knew the story wasn't true, but she couldn't get it out of her mind.*

have a thing about /hæv ə ˈθɪŋ əbaʊt/ [v phrase not in progressive] informal to have an unreasonably strong interest in, liking for, or fear of something: *Joanne's got a thing about her hair. She's always changing the style.* | *The Captain had a thing about neat handwriting; in fact he couldn't bear to look at anything that wasn't beautifully written.*

obsess /əbˈses/ [v I/T] if something **obsesses** someone, or they **obsess** about it, they think about it all the time and cannot think about anything else: *The idea that she was being punished began to obsess her.* | **+ about** *Some women obsess about their thighs and stomachs.*

have a one-track mind /hæv ə ˌwʌn træk ˈmaɪnd/ [v phrase not in progressive] to be continuously thinking about one subject so that you often talk about it when there is no reason to: *Boys of that age have a one track mind. All they think about is sex.*

have an unhealthy interest in /hæv ən ʌnˌhelθi ˈɪntrɪst ɪn/ [v phrase not in progressive] to have a strong and unnatural interest in something, so that you think about it a lot: *As a child, Quinlan had an unhealthy interest in death.*

obvious

RELATED WORDS

▸ *see also* **clear/not clear, notice/not notice, certainly/definitely**

1 very easy to notice or understand

- ▸ obvious
- ▸ clear
- ▸ obviously/clearly
- ▸ can tell
- ▸ it is easy to see
- ▸ noticeable
- ▸ perceptible
- ▸ distinct/definite
- ▸ apparent/evident
- ▸ conspicuous

obvious /ˈɒbviəs‖ˈɑːb-/ [adj] something that is **obvious** is very easy to notice or understand: *There is an obvious connection between the two murders.* | *'Why is she leaving?' 'Well, it's obvious, isn't it?'* | **it is obvious that** *It's obvious that something is wrong.* | *It was obvious from the start that my parents disliked Nancy.* | **it is obvious to sb** *It should be obvious to everyone that we need to make some changes.* | **for obvious reasons** (=when the reasons are so obvious that you do not need to say what they are) *For obvious reasons, we've had to cancel tonight's performance.*

clear /klɪəʳ/ [adj] if it is **clear** that something is true, it is easy to notice that it is true and you feel sure about it and have no doubts **it is clear that** *It was clear that Lesley was very upset by what had happened.* | **it is clear to sb** *It was clear to me that my father was dying.* | **it becomes clear** *It soon became clear that there were not enough police officers to deal with the situation.* | *It became clear after talking to him that Andrew wasn't going to cooperate.* | **clear evidence/example/sign etc** *There is clear evidence that certain diets reduce your chances of getting cancer.* | *clear signs of an economic recovery*

obviously/clearly /ˈɒbviəsli‖ˈɑːb-, ˈklɪəʳli/ [adv] use this to emphasize that it is easy to see that something is true: *We're obviously going to need more help.* | *Clearly, the situation is more complicated than we first thought.* | *The children were clearly upset.* | *Obviously, this guy's a complete fraud.* | *The language of the article clearly reveals the author's bias.*

can tell /kən ˈtel/ [v phrase] to know that something must be true because you can see signs that show this **+ (that)** *I can tell that Mark isn't happy here.* | *Even though it was dark, she could tell it was him.* | **+ if** *I can't tell if this is dirty or not. Can you?* | **+ by** *I could tell by the way she walked that her knee was still bothering her.*

it is easy to see /ɪt ɪz ˌiːzi tə ˈsiː/ if **it is easy to see** that something is true, it is very easy for anyone to notice or understand that fact **+ (that)** *It's easy to see that he isn't well.* | *It was easy to see that Minna was embarrassed by her father's behaviour.* | **+ how/why/what** *It's easy to see why this place is so popular.*

noticeable /ˈnəʊtɪsəbəl/ [adj] a **noticeable** difference, change, improvement etc is easy to notice **noticeable change** *The most noticeable change was in my younger brother, who had grown quite a bit and was now a third-grader.* | **noticeable improvement** *There has been a noticeable improvement in Jeremy's behaviour lately.* | **barely/hardly/scarcely noticeable** (=almost not noticeable) *Stop worrying about your pimples; they're barely noticeable.* | **it is noticeable that** *It was quite noticeable that everyone had been invited except for Gail.* —**noticeably** [adv] *The performance was noticeably better during the second half of the concert.*

perceptible /pəʳˈseptɪbəl/ [adj] formal a **perceptible** difference, change, improvement etc can be noticed even though it is small: *The influence of Sartre is perceptible in Hogan's novel.* | **perceptible change** *According to Reynolds, there has been a slight but perceptible change in public attitude lately.* | **barely/scarcely/hardly perceptible** (=almost not perceptible) *His lips curved in a barely perceptible smile.* | *When he asked if she wanted something to eat, she gave a barely perceptible nod.* —**perceptibly** [adv] *Outdoors, it was perceptibly colder.*

distinct/definite /dɪˈstɪŋkt, ˈdefənɪt/ [adj only before noun] a **distinct** or **definite** possibility, feeling, quality etc is noticeable and cannot be ignored **distinct/definite possibility** *A civil war is a distinct possibility.* | *Food shortages are so severe that mass starvation is a definite possibility.* | **distinct advantage** *Trigg's height should give him a distinct advantage in his match against Robinson.* | **distinct impression** *I had the distinct impression that Rachel was displeased.* —**distinctly/definitely** [adv] *I distinctly heard the noise again, this time coming from the cellar.*

apparent/evident /əˈpærənt, ˈevɪdənt/ [adj not usually before noun] obvious – used formally or in literature: *Even at the age of eight his musical talent was apparent.* | **for no apparent reason** (=without a clear reason) *Suddenly, and for no apparent reason, he turned his back and walked away.* | **it is evident (from sth) that** *From the look on Jill's face, it was evident that the news came as a complete shock.* | **it became apparent/evident that** *It became evident that Lena wasn't going to be able to handle the project on her own.* | *After a few months, it became apparent that Vicky did not have a genuine interest in her job.*

conspicuous /kənˈspɪkjuəs/ [adj] something or someone that is **conspicuous** is very easy to notice, because they are different from everything or everyone else around them: *Cuzco's few tourists are conspicuous as they explore the old cobbled streets.* | *Downtown business owners say they want the city's homeless shelter moved to a less conspicuous location.* —**conspicuously** [adv] *Airport officials became* *suspicious when the man tried to check what they describe as a conspicuously heavy bag.*

2 extremely obvious and impossible not to notice

- unmistakable
- blindingly/perfectly/quite obvious
- speaks for itself
- self-evident
- it sticks/stands out a mile
- it sticks/stands out like a sore thumb
- you just/only have to ...
- be written all over sb's face
- you can't miss it
- be staring sb in the face

unmistakable /ˌʌnmɪ̈ˈsteɪkəbəl/ [adj] **unmistakable sight/sound/smell etc** *The secretary of state said the measures are designed to send the regime a clear and unmistakable signal.* | *the unmistakable sounds of mariachi music* —**unmistakably** [adv] *The woman's accent was unmistakably French.*

blindingly/perfectly/quite obvious /ˌblaɪndɪŋli, ˌpɜːʳfɪktli, kwaɪt ˈɒbviəs‖-ˈɑːb-/ [adj] informal so obvious that it is impossible not to notice: *The reason she stopped smoking is perfectly obvious: she's pregnant.* | *a blindingly obvious mistake*

speaks for itself /ˌspiːks fər ɪtˈself/ [v phrase not in progressive] if you say that a fact **speaks for itself**, you mean it shows that something is so obviously good or obviously bad that you do not need to tell people how good or bad it is: *The quality of our products speaks for itself.* | *The fact that so many parents refuse to send their children to the school speaks for itself.*

self-evident /self ˈevɪ̈dənt/ [adj] formal facts, ideas etc that are **self-evident** are obvious and true, although some people may not accept them or know about them: *The facts in this case are self-evident and cannot be denied.* | *self-evident truths* | **it is self-evident that** *It is self-evident to most people that the government is under no obligation to finance the arts.*

it sticks/stands out a mile /ɪt ˌstɪks, ˌstændz aʊt ə ˈmaɪl/ British informal you say **it sticks** or **stands out a mile** when you think that someone's character, feelings, or background are obvious: *I'm absolutely sure he's a retired army officer. It sticks out a mile.* | *You can see he's desperately jealous. It stands out a mile.*

it sticks/stands out like a sore thumb /ɪt ˌstɪks, ˌstændz aʊt laɪk ə ˌsɔːʳ ˈθʌm/ you say **it sticks** or **stands out like a sore thumb** when something looks very different from everything around it: *I'm not going to the party dressed like this – I'd stick out like a sore thumb.*

you just/only have to ... /juː ˈdʒʌst, ˈəʊnli hæv tuː/ you say that **you only have to** look at something, read something etc when you think something is so obvious that anybody will notice it: *You only have to look at Turner's later oil paintings to see what a genius he was.* | *You just have to look at family photos from that time to see that there was a lot of sadness and bitterness over my parents' divorce.*

be written all over sb's face /biː ˌrɪtn ɔːl əʊvəʳ (sb's) ˈfeɪs/ [v phrase] if you say that a fact or feeling **is written all over someone's face** you mean that you can see, just by looking at the expression on their face, that it is true: *You're in love with him. It's written all over your face.* | *When Joey opened the package and saw that it wasn't a fire engine, the disappointment was written all over his face.*

you can't miss it /juː ˌkɑːnt ˈmɪs ɪt‖-ˌkænt-/ you say **you can't miss it** when you are giving someone directions to a place that is very easy to find or notice: *Their house is on the left. It has a pink door. You can't miss it.*

be staring sb in the face /biː ˌsteərɪŋ (sb) ɪn ðə ˈfeɪs/ [v phrase] if something such as a solution to a problem is **staring you in the face**, it is very obvious – use this especially when someone does not notice or realize something even though it is very obvious: *The solution was staring me in the face.* | *The answer had been staring him in the face for months.*

3 when something wrong, bad, or dishonest is very obvious

- blatant
- flagrant
- glaring
- patently

blatant /ˈbleɪtənt/ [adj usually before noun] use this about something that someone does which is clearly bad, but which they do not seem to be ashamed of: *a blatant lie* | *The company's refusal to hire him was a blatant act of discrimination.* | *a blatant disregard for public safety* —**blatantly** [adv] *blatantly racist comments*

flagrant /ˈfleɪgrənt/ [adj usually before noun] done in a very obvious way and showing no respect for laws, rules, or the truth etc: *The regime has often been criticized for its flagrant abuses of human rights.* | *Poison gas was used, in flagrant disregard of the Geneva Convention.* —**flagrantly** [adv] *For over six years, the mayor and his cronies have flagrantly misused public funds.*

glaring /ˈgleərɪŋ/ [adj only before noun] use this about mistakes or problems that are obviously bad or wrong: *It was a glaring error, which cost the company over $2 million in lost business.* | *'It was a glaring example of bad judgment,' said one official who asked not to be named.*

patently /ˈpeɪtntli‖ˈpæ-/ [adv] formal **patently false/absurd/ridiculous/impossible etc** obviously false, absurd etc, in a way that no reasonable person could disagree with: *Jenkins' explanation of the situation is patently absurd.* | *The statement is patently false and an embarrassing public demonstration of his weakness as university leader.*

4 not obvious

- subtle
- unobtrusive
- inconspicuous

subtle /ˈsʌtl/ [adj] a **subtle** change or difference is difficult to notice unless you look closely or think about it carefully: *The patterns look very similar, but there are subtle differences between them.* | *We noticed some deterioration in her speech, but it was very subtle.* | *It was around this time that I started to notice subtle changes in Clive's character.*

unobtrusive /ˌʌnəbˈtruːsɪv◂/ [adj] something, especially an object, that is **unobtrusive** is not very noticeable, especially because it is small or ordinary compared to other things: *The aerial is small and unobtrusive, fitting closely to the chimney stack.* | *The researchers will make their observations in the most unobtrusive way possible.* | *Hart, who attended law school with Danforth, remembers him as 'quiet and unobtrusive.'* —**unobtrusively** [adv] *The new hearing aid fits unobtrusively into the outer ear.*

inconspicuous /ˌɪnkənˈspɪkjuəs◂/ [adj] things or people that are **inconspicuous** are not noticeable because they look the same as the people or things around them: *Carpet cleaner should always be tested in an inconspicuous spot first.* | *The two bank robbers got in line at a nearby fast-food restaurant, hoping to be inconspicuous as police flooded the area.* —**inconspicuously** [adv] *Throughout the meal she was inconspicuously passing food to the dog under the table.* | *Arriving late, we tried to take our seats as inconspicuously as possible.*

offend

RELATED WORDS

▸ *see also* **insult, rude, angry, upset, criticize, revenge**

1 to offend someone

- offend
- insult
- get/put sb's back up
- cause offence

offend /əˈfend/ [v I/T] to make someone angry or upset by doing something that they think is socially or morally unacceptable or by being rude to them: *The programme contains scenes that may offend older viewers.* | *She stopped mid-sentence, anxious not to offend him.* | *He didn't speak during the meeting for fear of saying something that might offend.* | **offend (sb's) sensibilities** *He is a sensitive man, and it is not difficult to offend his sensibilities.*

insult /ɪnˈsʌlt/ [v T] to make someone very angry and upset, for example by doing something that shows you have little respect for them or do not think that they are very good at something: *In some cultures, you insult your host if you do not accept their offer of food.* | **insult sb by doing sth** *I won't insult you by explaining the rules of the game.* | **insult sb's intelligence** (=treat someone as if they are stupid) *questions that insult the intelligence of the interviewee* —**insult** /ˈɪnsʌlt/ [n C] *She took it as a personal insult that you did not ask her opinion about your book.*

get/put sb's back up /ˌget, ˌpʊt (sb's) ˈbæk ʌp/ [v phrase not in passive] British informal to make someone annoyed, especially without intending to: *It really gets my back up when salesmen call round to the house.* | *He treats everyone like children, and that's why he puts people's backs up.*

cause offence /ˌkɔːz əˈfens/ [v phrase] to offend someone – use this about words or actions that were not intended to offend anyone: *He later appeared on television to apologize for causing offence.* | **+ to** *I hope I didn't cause offence to anyone when I left early.* | **cause great offence** *A remark that is considered humorous in one culture can cause great offence in another.*

2 to feel offended

- offended
- insulted
- slighted
- put out
- take offence
- take sth personally
- take sth the wrong way
- take exception to

offended /əˈfendɪ̈d/ [adj not before noun] *She'll be offended if you don't say thank you for her help.* | **+ by** *He's always offended by jokes aimed at Irish people.* | **+ that** *He felt offended that she didn't want to go out with him.* | **deeply offended** *Some people may find rude jokes funny, but others may be deeply offended.*

insulted /ɪnˈsʌltɪ̈d/ [adj not before noun] very angry and upset, for example because someone has done something that shows they have little respect for you or your abilities: *Molly would be insulted if we didn't go and see her while we were in town.* | **+ by** *Please don't be insulted by anything I say.* | **+ that** *He felt insulted that they had not told him about the party.* | **deeply insulted** *We must eat as much as possible, or she will be deeply insulted.*

slighted /ˈslaɪtɪ̈d/ [adj not before noun] offended, especially because someone has not included you in their plans: *The guest list was very short, so no-one felt slighted because they hadn't been invited.*

put out /ˌpʊt ˈaʊt/ [adj not before noun] offended and surprised, especially because you feel that you have not been treated fairly: *When she said I was interfering, I was a bit put out.* | **+ about** *She was rather put out about being described as plain.* | **+ by** *The minister was not put out by the note of impatience in Cohen's voice.*

take offence /ˌteɪk əˈfens/ [v phrase] to feel offended by something someone says or does, especially something that does not seem serious to other people: *Don't mention her hairstyle. She'll probably take offence.* | *Please don't take offence, but I would prefer you not to swear in front of the children.* | **+ at** *He didn't seem to take offence at my lack of enthusiasm for his idea.* | **be quick to take offence** *He described her as a woman who is temperamental and quick to take offence.*

take sth personally /ˌteɪk (sth) ˈpɜːʳsənəli/ [v phrase] to feel offended by something, especially a criticism, even though it was not aimed at one particular person: *Anna took it personally when the boss said some people were not working hard enough.* | *This is a general criticism, so I hope none of you will take it personally.* | *I didn't take his rebuff too personally, since I was used to his habit of being rude to his juniors.*

take sth the wrong way /ˌteɪk (sth) ðə ˌrɒŋ ˈweɪ‖-ˌrɔːŋ- / [v phrase] to be offended by something someone says or does when it was not intended to offend you and you have understood it in the wrong way: *Daniel sat in silence, afraid whatever he said would be taken the wrong way.* | *Don't take this the wrong way, but your driving has really improved.*

take exception to /ˌteɪk ɪkˈsepʃən tuː/ [v phrase] formal to feel offended by something someone says, and to make it clear that you feel this way: *I took exception to what he said about my family.* | *Paul took exception to her advice, which he said undermined his self-esteem.* | **take great exception to sth** *I take great exception to the suggestion that I neglected my responsibilities.*

3 easily offended

- be/get easily offended
- touchy
- sensitive
- prude
- over-sensitive

be/get easily offended /biː, get ˌiːzɪ̈li əˈfendɪ̈d/ [v phrase] *Be careful what you say to Jenny; she's over-sensitive and easily offended.* | **+ by** *Barry gets easily offended by comments about his parents' divorce.*

touchy /ˈtʌtʃi/ [adj] too easily offended, especially so that people are afraid to talk to you, or offer advice: *Some authors get very touchy if you make even the slightest alteration to their work.* | *Why are* *you so touchy today?* | **+ about** *He's a great manager, but he is very touchy about his lack of qualifications.*

sensitive /ˈsensətɪv/ [adj] very easily offended by a particular thing: *Paul is too sensitive for this job. He can't take even the smallest criticism.* | **+ about** *He's sensitive about his bad teeth, so try not to look at them.* | *My children are very sensitive about being treated in a patronising way.*

prude /pruːd/ [n C] someone who is easily offended by anything that is rude or connected with sex, especially in a way that other people think is unnecessary: *Sarah's no prude, but she thought some of the sex scenes were quite shocking.* —**prudish** [adj] *Her mother was very prudish about sexual matters.*

over-sensitive /ˌəʊvəʳ ˈsensətɪv/ [adj] someone who is **over-sensitive** gets offended and upset very easily, because they always think other people are criticizing them, making fun of them etc: *It's not unusual for artists to be over-sensitive about their work.* | *Of course he wasn't saying you were overweight – you're just being over-sensitive.*

4 words for describing behaviour, remarks etc that offend people

- offensive
- insulting
- be an insult to
- objectionable

offensive /əˈfensɪv/ [adj] *Throughout the football game a small section of the crowd was chanting offensive slogans.* | *The BBC received a number of complaints about the offensive remarks made during the interview.* | **deeply offensive** (=very offensive) *These pornographic magazines are deeply offensive to women.* | **+ to** *Your comments are offensive to all Jews.* —**offensively** [adv] *As usual, he got drunk and behaved offensively towards the guests.*

insulting /ɪnˈsʌltɪŋ/ [adj] behaviour, remarks etc that are **insulting** offend someone a lot because they show a lack of respect for them or for their ability, honesty etc: *It's insulting when people assume I must be a racist because I'm from the South.* | **deeply insulting** (=very insulting) *I find your criticism deeply insulting.* | **+ to** *advice that is extremely insulting to unemployed people*

be an insult to /biː ən ˈɪnsʌlt tuː/ [v phrase] to offend a particular person or group of people by showing little respect for their intelligence, ability, beliefs etc: *Leaders described the mosque's destruction as an insult to Muslims.* | **be an insult to sb's intelligence/ability etc** *The lesson was awful. It was an insult to our intelligence.* | *If I didn't finish this meal it would be an insult to your superb cooking.*

objectionable /əbˈdʒekʃənəbəl/ [adj] something that is **objectionable** is likely to offend people because it is morally unacceptable or very unpleasant: *I thought the bedroom scenes were pretty objectionable and unnecessary.* | *Our goal is to get rid of many of the objectionable features of capitalism.* | **highly/deeply objectionable** *I find it highly objectionable to have to sit near people who are smoking.*

offer

RELATED WORDS

▸ *see also* **give, help, buy**

1 when you offer something to someone

- offer
- would you like ... ?
- can I get you ... ?
- help yourself
- have

offer /ˈɒfəʳ‖ˈɔː-, ˈɑː-/ [v T] to say that someone can have something if they want it **offer sb sth** *She didn't even offer me a cup of tea.* | *I've been offered the job!* | *Can I offer you a ride?* | *Why don't you offer them a drink while I finish getting dinner ready?* | **offer sth to sb** *Unfortunately, they offered the contract to someone else.*

would you like ... ? /wʊd juː ˈlaɪk / spoken say this as a polite way of offering something to someone: *We have some maps of the city – would you like one?* | *Would you like fries with that?*

can I get you ... ? /kən aɪ ˈget juː/ spoken say this when you are offering someone a drink or food, for example at a party: *Can I get you some coffee?* | *What can I get you? There's beer or wine.*

help yourself /ˌhelp jɔːʳˈself/ spoken say this to tell someone they can take anything they want from the food and drink that is available: *There's plenty of food, so help yourself.* | **+ to** *Help yourself to some salad.*

have /hæv/ spoken say this to persuade someone to take some food or drink that you are offering: *Have some of the pie – my Mom made it.* | *Go on, have another beer.*

2 when you offer to help

- offer
- volunteer
- come forward
- let me
- can I do sth/would you like me to do sth

offer /ˈɒfəʳ‖ˈɔː-, ˈɑː-/ [v I/T] to say that you will do something in order to help someone: *She was the kind of teacher who was always ready to offer advice and encouragement.* | **offer to do sth** *I offered to help her with the dishes.* | **thanks for offering** *'Do you want me to look after the children next week?' 'No, but thanks for offering.'*

volunteer /ˌvɒlənˈtɪəʳ‖ˌvɑː-/ [v I/T] to offer to do something, especially something difficult or unpleasant **volunteer to do sth** *Jill volunteered to go with me to the hospital.* | *Will anyone volunteer to help me clean up this mess?* | **+ for** *No one volunteered for night duty.*

come forward /ˌkʌm ˈfɔːʳwəʳd/ [v phrase] British to offer to give help, information, money etc, especially after someone has publicly requested something: *The number of operations may have to be limited unless more blood donors come forward.* | **come forward to do sth** *None of the parents came forward to help with the school party.* | **+ with** *The negotiations will come to an end unless someone comes forward with a new proposal.*

let me /ˈlet miː/ spoken say this when you are offering to help someone, especially when you want to be kind or friendly to them: *Let me drive you to the sta-*

tion. | *Let me give you a hand with that, mate.* | *Why don't you let me cook dinner tonight?*

can I do sth/would you like me to do sth ALSO **shall I do sth** British /ˌkæn aɪ 'duː (sth), wʊd juː ˌlaɪk miː tə 'duː (sth), ˌʃæl aɪ 'duː (sth)/ [v phrase] say this when you are offering to do something for someone: *Can I take your bag – it looks heavy.* | *Would you like me to mail that letter for you? I'm going into town.* | *Shall I make a copy for you?* | *'Can I get you anything else?' the waiter asked.*

3 to offer money for something

- offer
- make an offer
- bid

offer /'ɒfəʳ‖'ɔː-, 'ɑː-/ [v T] to say that you will pay someone a particular amount of money in exchange for something **offer sb sth** *Chaldon was offered a huge salary to become team manager.* | **offer (sb) sth for sth** *Police are offering a reward for information about the shooting.* | *Some guy offered me £2,000 for the car. I just laughed and hung up the phone.*

make an offer /ˌmeɪk ən 'ɒfəʳ‖-'ɔː-/ [v phrase] to offer a particular amount of money in order to buy a house, car etc **+ for/on** *Has anyone made an offer yet for the house?* | **+ of** *Immediately after they were shown the property, they made an offer of $165,000.* | **make sb a generous offer** *I'm prepared to make you a very generous offer.*

bid /bɪd/ [v I/T] to offer to pay a particular amount of money for something you want to buy, in competition with other people **bid $10/£20 etc for sth** *At the auction, I bid £50 for a small antique mirror, but it ended up selling for over £200.* | *Baxley International said on Friday that it bid $11 million in cash and stock to acquire the Los Angeles-based company.* | **bid for sth** *Competition between the two companies bidding for the contract is fierce.* | **bid against sb** *San Diego is asking private companies to bid against city workers to run one of the city's three water treatment plants.* —**bidder** [n C] *The equipment will be auctioned off to the highest bidder* (=the person who bids the highest amount).

4 something that you offer

- offer
- bid

offer /'ɒfəʳ‖'ɔː-, 'ɑː-/ [n C] something that someone has offered to give you or do for you, such as money, help, or advice **a good offer** *I'll sell the car if I get a good offer.* | **+ of** *Since the story ran in local papers, the family has received several offers of help.* | **accept an offer** (=say yes to it) *Pan Am accepted an offer to sell its African and Asian routes.* | **turn down/refuse/reject an offer** (=say no to it) *How could you refuse such a fantastic offer?*

bid /bɪd/ [n C] an offer to pay a particular amount of money for something, when other people are also offering different amounts of money, and hoping to buy it **+ for** *The highest bid for the painting was £400.* | **put in/submit/make a bid** (=say how much you will pay) *A number of companies have submitted bids to buy the supermarket chain.*

official

RELATED WORDS

▸ *see also* **legal, government, rule/regulation**

1 official

- official
- formal
- authorized
- on (the) record

official /ə'fɪʃəl/ [adj usually before noun] *What's the government's official policy on drugs education in schools?* | *You have to get official permission for building in a conservation area.* | **official report/document/data etc** *Most of the official records of the case were destroyed in a fire in 1965.* | **official procedure/guidelines/process etc** *The official procedure for obtaining a visa can turn into a bureaucratic nightmare.* | **official visit/duties/engagement etc** (=officially organized by a government etc) *The newspaper claims she spent over £50,000 on an official trip to Australia.* | **official explanation/line/reason etc** *The official explanation for the man's death was suicide.* —**officially** [adv] *In July 2001 it was officially announced that the factory was to close.* | *Plans for the new shopping mall are yet to be officially approved.* | *The need for greater protection for wildlife habitats is not always officially recognized.*

formal /'fɔːʳməl/ [adj] done officially and publicly, according to established rules and processes: *A formal agreement between the two countries was signed in 1999.* | *Fifteen formal complaints have been made about the hospital in the past year.* | *Her lawyers have made a formal request that she be allowed to stay in the country until her husband's trial.* —**formally** [adv] *A man has been arrested, but has not yet been formally charged.* | *The policy was formally abandoned by the government last year.* | *The regime is not formally recognized by the UN.*

authorized ALSO **authorised** British /'ɔːθəraɪzd/ [adj] officially approved, or having official permission from a government or other organization: *Check that you have the authorized version of the software.* | *We will send round one of our authorized representatives to discuss the purchase with you.* | *Access is only given to authorized personnel.*

on (the) record /ɒn (ðə) 'rekɔːd‖-ərd/ [adv] if a politician, government official etc says something **on (the) record**, they say it publicly and officially: *Mr Senator, will you now confirm on the record that none of these rumors are true?* | **be on record as saying/stating etc** *She's on record as saying that she would resign if the vote went against her.* | **go on (the) record** (=agree to say something officially) *Privately, many MPs are critical of the policy, but none is willing to go on the record.*

2 to make something official

- formalize

formalize ALSO **formalise** British /'fɔːʳməlaɪz/ [v T] to make something such as a plan, process, or agreement official, for example by signing a formal contract: *The new law is intended to further formalize the process of adopting children from overseas.* | *a charter to formalize patients' rights in public health services* | *Most measures to formalize wage negotiations have so far been very successful.*

3 not official

- unofficial
- informal
- off the record

unofficial /ˌʌnəˈfɪʃəl◂/ [adj] not done according to official rules or processes, or not officially approved by a government or other organization: *She seems to have become the unofficial spokesman for the group.* | *The Prime Minister discussed the matter with his German counterpart on an unofficial visit to his home last month.* | *Unofficial sources say that over 100 people were shot dead in the rioting.* —**unofficially** [adv] *The cost of the project is unofficially said to be around $2.5m.* | *Though the organization is now banned, its members still meet unofficially in each others' houses.*

informal /ɪnˈfɔːʳməl/ [adj] **informal** discussions, agreements, offers etc are not official and have not been officially approved: *The two companies have an informal arrangement to share each other's sports and leisure facilities.* | *The report was based on informal discussions with women MPs and their families.* | *I was offered the job after an informal interview in the staff canteen.* —**informally** [adv] *Until recently, holiday entitlement was informally agreed between individuals and their employer.* | *The group meets informally each month to discuss the progress of new students.*

off the record /ˌɒf ðə ˈrekɔːd‖-ərd/ [adv] if someone tells you something **off the record**, they are not giving you the official opinion of their organization and do not want what they say to be made public: *Strictly off the record, my feeling is that we are going to lose the election.* | *Off the record, police officers are saying they are more and more unwilling to arrest those found in possession of small amounts of cannabis.* —**off-the-record** [adj] *The party leader has appealed to her colleagues to end their damaging off-the-record remarks to the media.*

often

RELATED WORDS

opposite: —————— **never**

- *see also* **always, regular, continue, sometimes, usually**

1 when something happens many times

- often
- a lot
- frequently
- repeatedly
- again and again
- hundreds/thousands of times
- many times

often /ˈɒfən, ˈɒftən‖ˈɔːf-/ [adv] *I often see her walking past with the children on the way to school.* | *Dad wasn't often angry so I knew something terrible must have happened.* | **quite often** *'Have you ever been to the China Moon Café?' 'Yes – we go there quite often.'* | **not very often** *I have a cell phone, but I don't use it very often.* | **it's not often (that) sb does sth** *It's not often that you see a grass snake these days – they've become quite rare.* | *It's not often I get the chance to go to the movies.*

a lot /ə ˈlɒt‖-ˈlɑːt/ [adv] spoken if you do something **a lot**, you often do it: *It's nice to meet you. Wendy's talked about you a lot.* | *I used to walk a lot, but I've been very lazy recently.* | **quite a lot** British *She goes abroad on business quite a lot.*

frequently /ˈfriːkwəntli/ [adv] often – used especially in writing or more formal speech: *Passengers complain that trains are frequently cancelled.* | *You have to be willing to change jobs frequently if you want to get to the top in business.* | *Frequently, she would find herself gazing out of the window lost in thought.*

repeatedly /rɪˈpiːtɪ̈dli/ [adv] use this to emphasize that someone did something many times: *Graham's doctor had repeatedly warned him not to work so hard.* | *Max was punched and kicked repeatedly as he lay on the ground.* | *Al Gore has stated repeatedly, that the American economy is dependent upon a healthy environment.*

again and again /əˌgen ənd əˈgen/ [adv] use this to emphasize that the same thing has happened many times: *She kept asking the same question again and again.* | *Again and again I was thrown upwards from my bunk as the ship battled through the storm.*

hundreds/thousands of times /ˈhʌndrɪ̈dz, ˈθaʊzəndz əv ˌtaɪmz/ [adv] spoken say this when you are emphasizing that someone has done something many times in the past: *It was a sound he'd heard thousands of times before.* | *My grandmother must have spoken to him hundreds of times but, surprisingly, she didn't know his name.* | *I've been rejected hundreds of times, but if you don't try you never will get a job, will you?*

many times /ˈmeni taɪmz/ [adv] if someone has done something **many times**, they have done it often **sb has/had done sth many times (before)** *I had walked down this road many times before, but somehow today it seemed different.* | **as sb has/had done many times (before)** *The woman upstairs shouted down at us and threatened to call the police, as she had done many times before.* | *I looked down at the town, as I had done so many times as a young man, and remembered the people I had known there.*

2 too often, in a way that is annoying

- keep (on) doing sth
- always/all the time
- constantly/continually
- be forever doing sth
- half the time
- time and time again
- with great regularity
- ad nauseam

keep (on) doing sth /ˌkiːp (ɒn) ˈduːɪŋ (sth)/ [v phrase not in progressive] especially spoken to do something many times, in a way that is annoying: *Dad, Bobby keeps hitting me!* | *How can I explain if you keep on interrupting me?* | *I keep forgetting to mail this letter.*

always/all the time /ˈɔːlwɪ̈z, ˌɔːl ðə ˈtaɪm/ [adv] if someone or something is **always** doing something, or someone or something does something **all the time**, it annoys you because they do it too often: *I'm sick of Harold, he's always telling me what to do.* | *What do you mean you never see me? You're at my house all the time.* | *I don't know about you, but I'm always having arguments with people!* | *He was always trying to persuade me to go out drinking with him.*

constantly/continually /ˈkɒnstəntli‖ˈkɑːn-, kənˈtɪnjuəli/ [adv] use this when you are very annoyed because something happens repeatedly over a long period of time: *They seemed to be continually arguing.* | *I wish you'd clean up your room without having to be constantly reminded.*

be forever doing sth /biː fərˌevəʳ ˈduːɪŋ (sth)/ [v phrase] spoken if someone or something is **forever doing** something, they annoy you by doing it very often over a long period of time: *He never does his* *homework on time and is forever getting into trouble at school.* | *We bought a new washing machine. The old one was forever breaking down.*

half the time /ˈhɑːf ðə ˌtaɪm‖ˈhæf- / [adv] spoken say this when you are describing something annoying or bad that someone does very often: *Half the time the managers don't know what's going on.* | *I never know where he is – half the time he doesn't return my phone calls.*

time and time again /ˌtaɪm ən taɪm əˈgen/ [adv] use this to say that something has been done many times, especially when this is annoying or does not have any effect: *I've told you time and time again not to play with matches – it's dangerous.* | *I see people making the same mistakes, time and time again.*

with great regularity /wɪð ˌgreɪt regjᵿˈlærɪ̈ti/ [adv] if something happens **with great regularity**, it keeps happening, often in an annoying way: *Yes, the bank keep piling these outrageous charges on my bank account with great regularity.* | *With great regularity, wasps would fly in through the open window and get trapped behind the glass.*

ad nauseam /ˌædˈnɔːziəm, -iæm/ [adv] if someone talks about something **ad nauseam**, they talk about it for so long that it becomes very annoying or boring: *We've discussed this ad nauseam, and I don't see the point of going over the same ground again.* | *He goes on ad nauseam about how much better everything was in the old days.*

3 ways of saying what someone or something often does

- tend to do sth
- have a tendency to do sth
- be inclined to do sth
- have a habit of doing sth
- be apt to do sth

tend to do sth /ˌtend tə ˈduː (sth)/ [v phrase not in progressive] to often do a particular thing, and be likely to do it: *Dave tends to arrive late, so don't worry yet.* | *The problem with this model of car is that the gearbox tends to seize up.* | *My father tends to interfere too much in other people's business.* | *Recent studies show that girls tend to be better at languages than boys.*

have a tendency to do sth /hæv ə ˌtendənsi tə ˈduː (sth)/ [v phrase not in progressive] to often do something and be more likely to do it than other people or things are: *Divorced people have a tendency to live with new partners rather than marry again.* | *It's poor quality cloth, with a tendency to shrink.* | *Eliott's family has a tendency to put on weight, and so his parents enrolled him in a special gym for kids.*

be inclined to do sth /biː ɪnˌklaɪnd tə ˈduː (sth)/ [v phrase] if someone is **inclined to do** something, they do it fairly often or are fairly likely to do it, especially because they have a particular type of character: *Victor is inclined to be somewhat domineering.* | *Middle-class victims of crime are more inclined to contact the police.*

have a habit of doing sth /hæv ə ˌhæbɪ̈t əv ˈduːɪŋ (sth)/ [v phrase not in progressive] use this when you are warning someone that something has happened before and is likely to happen again: *Be careful not to annoy the boss. He has a habit of losing his temper.* | *We shouldn't rule out a Democrat victory yet. These things have a habit of changing just when you least expect it.*

be apt to do sth /biː ˌæpt tə ˈduː (sth)/ [v phrase] formal to often do something or be likely to do something, especially at a particular time or in a particular situation: *He was apt to get very upset when things went wrong.* | *The pond was apt to dry up during summer.*

4 often happening or often done

- frequent
- repeated
- habitual
- continual/constant

frequent /ˈfriːkwənt/ [adj] *His job involved making frequent trips to Saudi Arabia.* | *The doctor recommended frequent salt baths to help the wound heal.* | *My duties brought me into frequent contact with Captain Nagumo.* | *As the treatment began to take effect, her headaches became less frequent.* | **frequent visitor/traveller/flier etc** (=someone who visits, uses something etc frequently) *As a frequent business traveler, I have spent many nights in bland hotel rooms.* | *Simmons is a frequent guest on daytime TV talk shows.*

repeated /rɪˈpiːtɪ̈d/ [adj only before noun] **repeated** actions are done on several occasions, especially because they do not have any effect at first: *The torture involved repeated beatings and electric shock treatment.* | *There have been repeated requests for the United Nations to send peace-keeping forces to the area.* | *Massieu remains a free man, despite repeated attempts to arrest him on murder and drug charges.*

habitual /həˈbɪtʃuəl/ [adj] done often as a habit, especially when this is annoying to other people: *Ingrained attitudes and habitual ways of thinking are very difficult to change.* | *Tony's habitual laziness became even more extreme in winter, and he would sometimes stay in bed until mid afternoon.* | **habitual drinker/gambler/drug user/offender/felon etc** (=someone who does something bad or illegal) *My father was a habitual gambler, until my mother packed her bags and threatened to leave.* | *It is estimated that as many as half the young men in the community are habitual drug users.* —**habitually** [adv] *Bernstein habitually arrived at airports just moments before departure.*

continual/constant /kənˈtɪnjuəl, ˈkɒnstənt‖ˈkɑːn-/ [adj only before noun] use this about things that annoy you because they happen repeatedly over a long time: *It's impossible to work with these constant interruptions.* | *We've had continual problems with the computer system ever since it was installed.*

5 how often something happens

- how often
- how many times
- the number of times
- frequency

how often /haʊ ˈɒfən‖-ˈɔːf-/ [adv] *How often do you see your parents?* | *What should you feed a puppy and how often?* | *When Peter said I was heartless it made me wonder how often I'd shown my lack of sympathy.* | *It's amazing how often this kind of thing happens.*

how many times /ˌhaʊ meni ˈtaɪmz/ [adv] *How many times has she been married?* | *I can't remember how many times I've been to New York.* | **how many times a day/week/year etc** *How many times a week do you go swimming?* | *The doctor wanted to know how many times I went to the toilet in a day.*

the number of times /ðə ˌnʌmbər əv ˈtaɪmz/ [n phrase] exactly how often something happens: *The computer can tell you the number of times a word occurs in a piece of writing such as a book.* | *The rate of respiration is the number of times the patient* *breathes in and out during a given period.* | *Try to increase the number of times you exercise per week.*

frequency /ˈfriːkwənsi/ [n U] the number of times that something happens during a particular period of time **+ of** *The frequency of mining accidents has steadily decreased over the past 20 years.* | **high frequency** (=happening very often) *The high frequency of cases of diarrhoea is attributable to poor food hygiene.* | **with increasing frequency** (=more and more frequently) *Crimes of this type are happening with increasing frequency.*

old

WHAT'S HERE

- **not young** see **1 to 7**
- **not new** see **8 to 10**

not young

RELATED WORDS

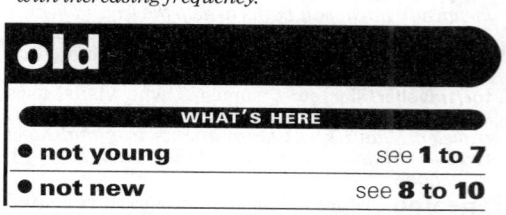

opposite: —— **young**

- how old someone is *see* **age**
- old and mentally ill *see* **mentally ill**

1 not young

- old
- elderly
- ageing/aging
- ancient
- be getting on
- not be as young as you were
- wrinkled
- wizened
- middle-aged

old /əʊld/ [adj] *She wanted to have a baby before she was too old.* | *For the first time in my life, I feel old.* | *An old man was in the park feeding the pigeons.* | **too old for sb** (=too old to have a romantic relationship with someone) *She shouldn't marry him – he's much too old for her.*

elderly /ˈeldəʳli/ [adj] old – use this as a polite way of talking about old people: *A group of elderly ladies sat drinking coffee in the cafeteria.* | *An elderly Englishwoman was seated next to me on the plane.* | *A few decades ago, the average cruise ship passenger was elderly, affluent, and retired. Not anymore.*

ageing/aging /ˈeɪdʒɪŋ/ [adj only before noun] **ageing rock star/movie star/hippy/romeo etc** one who is becoming old, especially in an unattractive way, and seems too old to be a rock star, film star etc: *The bar was fill with ageing hippies.* | *These days, most of the houses in the Hollywood Hills are owned by aging movie stars and rich businessmen.*

ancient /ˈeɪnʃənt/ [adj] especially British a humorous but slightly unkind word meaning very old: *He's not just old, he's ancient.* | **absolutely/completely/really etc ancient** *Mum looks absolutely ancient in this picture.*

be getting on /biː ˌgetɪŋ ˈɒn/ [v phrase] informal to be fairly old: *Cal is getting on a bit and doesn't play much golf anymore.* | **getting on in years** *Ethel's getting on in years now – she must be in her late 60s.*

not be as young as you were /nɒt biː əz ˌjʌŋ əz juː ˈwɜːʳ/ [v phrase] if you say you **are not as young as you were**, you mean you are getting old, especially so that you are not strong enough or healthy enough to do things that you used to do: *We do go out sometimes, but not very often. I guess we're not as young as we used to be.* | *'I'm not as young as I once was,' concedes the cigar-chomping, 48-year-old Mr. Tiant.*

wrinkled /ˈrɪŋkəld/ [adj] skin that is **wrinkled** has lines on it that are caused by old age: *Her face looked old and wrinkled in the morning light.* | **wrinkled old man/woman** *At the far end of the market, a wrinkled old woman sat smoking a pipe.*

wizened /ˈwɪzənd/ [adj] a **wizened** old man or woman has a small, bent body and lines on their skin because they are very old: *He barely recognized her wizened face and haggard features.* | **wizened old man/woman** *The door was opened by a wizened old man clutching a walking stick.*

middle-aged /ˌmɪdl ˈeɪdʒd◂/ [adj] not young anymore but not yet old, usually between the ages of around 40 to 65: *The condition predominantly affects middle-aged or elderly females.* | *a middle-aged businessman*

2 older than someone else

- older
- elder
- eldest
- oldest
- elders

older /ˈəʊldəʳ/ [adj] *I have one older brother and two younger brothers.* | *People say that older people need less sleep.* | **+ than** *Donna's husband's a lot older than she is.*

elder /ˈeldəʳ/ [adj only before noun] **elder brother/sister** someone's older brother or sister: *Wright's elder sister is also an actor.* | *John's elder brother died in a boating accident.*

eldest /ˈeldɪ̣st/ [adj] **eldest brother/sister/son/daughter** someone's oldest brother, sister, son, or daughter: *I shared a bedroom with my eldest sister.* | *Their eldest son, Howard, is an administrator at Castle Park High School.* | **the eldest** (=the oldest) *Rosie was the eldest of our four daughters.*

oldest /ˈəʊldɪ̣st/ [adj] *Did you know that the oldest woman in America is 110 years old?* | *Tonya, our oldest daughter, got married in April.*

elders /ˈeldəʳz/ [n plural] your **elders** are people who are older than you, such as your parents or teachers, and who you should therefore respect and be polite to **your elders** *Respect your elders.* | *You shouldn't talk to your elders like that!*

3 too old to do something

- be past it
- be over the hill
- be a bit long in the tooth

be past it /biː ˈpɑːst ɪt‖-ˈpæst-/ [v phrase] British informal *Talbot's past it – he should have given up playing basketball long ago.* | *I'm starting to think I'm past it – I'm not nearly as quick as I used to be.*

be over the hill /biː ˌəʊvəʳ ðə ˈhɪl/ [v phrase] if you **are over the hill**, you are no longer young or attractive, and your mental and physical abilities are getting weaker: *By that time, many in government viewed De Gaulle as over the hill.* | *According to the survey, many employers regard staff over the age of 45 as over the hill.*

be a bit long in the tooth /biː ə bɪt ˌlɒŋ ɪn ðə ˈtuːθ‖-ˌlɔːŋ-/ British **/be a little long in the tooth** /biː ə lɪtl ˌlɒŋ ɪn ðə ˈtuːθ‖-ˌlɔːŋ-/ American [v phrase] old, especially too old to do something: *A lot of the top English players are getting a bit long in the tooth.*

4 to become or start to look old

- get/grow old
- age
- ageing/aging
- show your age

get/grow old /ˌget, ˌgrəʊ ˈəʊld/ [v phrase] *Aunt Bertha's getting old now, and she needs someone to take care of her.* | **grow old gracefully** (=accept old age easily) *She wanted to grow old gracefully, and retire to a cottage in the country.*

age /eɪdʒ/ [v I] if someone **ages**, they change so that they look older, because they have lived a long time or because they have suffered a lot over a particular period: *I couldn't believe how much she had aged.* | *She noticed for the first time how Frederick had aged.* | *Western men tend to age more quickly than Japanese men.*

ageing/aging /ˈeɪdʒɪŋ/ [n U] the process of becoming old: *Our society is full of negative attitudes towards ageing and old people.* | **the ageing/aging process** *Some memory loss is a normal part of the aging process.* | **premature ageing/aging** (=ageing earlier than usual) *His hair was white and he showed other signs of premature ageing.*

show your age /ˌʃəʊ jɔːr ˈeɪdʒ/ [v phrase] if someone **shows their age**, they look older, or they talk or behave in a way that makes other people realize they are old: *She's still very beautiful, but she's starting to show her age now.* | *This is probably showing my age, but I remember when popcorn cost 25 cents and came in those little white paper bags.*

5 an old person

- old man/woman/lady etc
- the elderly
- senior citizen
- pensioner/old age pensioner
- retired
- old timer

old man/woman/lady etc /ˌəʊld ˈmæn/ [n C] *The old lady was rather deaf.* | *When the militia was called up, old men and boys were drafted as well.* | **dirty old man** (=an older man who is too sexually interested in younger women) *Charles wondered if he was becoming a dirty old man.* | **grumpy old man** (=an old man who is easily annoyed and complains a lot) *My grandfather was an old-fashioned, bigoted, grumpy old man.* —**the old** /ði ˈəʊld/ [n plural] old people: *The old and the sick were the first to be evacuated.*

the elderly /ði ˈeldəʳli/ [n plural] old people – used especially to talk about the needs of old people or services for them: *Right now, only 6 percent of the elderly in the United States receive public assistance.* | *The programs have been highly successful at reducing poverty rates among the elderly.*

senior citizen ALSO **senior** American /ˌsiːniəʳ ˈsɪtɪzən, ˈsiːniəʳ/ [n C] someone who is above the age of 60 – use this to talk about older people as a group, and their particular interests, rights etc: *Admission prices are £6 for adults, £5 for senior citizens and £3 for children.* | *Many seniors have very active lives.*

pensioner/old age pensioner /ˈpenʃənəʳ, ˌəʊld eɪdʒ ˈpenʃənəʳ/ [n C] British an old person who has stopped working and receives money from the government: *Many pensioners cannot afford to heat their homes in winter.* | *Old age pensioners can travel free on the buses.*

retired /rɪˈtaɪəʳd/ [adj] a **retired** person is someone who is old and has stopped working: *The company specializes in holidays for retired people.* | *Our neighbours were an old retired couple.* | **retired judge/engineer/police officer etc** *Among those attending was a retired federal judge from Philadelphia named Bennett Mayall.* —**retiree** /rɪˌtaɪəˈriː/ [n C] a retired person: *Florida is the perfect place for retirees.*

old timer /ˌəʊld ˈtaɪməʳ/ [n C] American informal an old man – often used humorously: *What can I do for you, old timer?* | *The three-day event is a chance for old timers to get together and swap war stories.*

6 relating to old people

- geriatric
- grey

geriatric /ˌdʒeriˈætrɪk◂/ [adj only before noun] **geriatric hospital/medicine/patient etc** *Geriatric hospitals are often severely under-staffed.* | *The clinic specializes in geriatric medicine.*

grey /greɪ/ [adj only before noun] British used about the political or economic power of old people as a group: *the grey power movement in Britain* | *Conservatives have started to realize that they cannot take the grey vote for granted.*

7 the time when someone is old

- old age
- dotage

old age /ˌəʊld ˈeɪdʒ◂/ [n U] the time in someone's life when they are old: *She's a little forgetful, but that comes with old age.* | *the problems of old age* | **in old age** British *By now, both were in extreme old age.*

dotage /ˈdəʊtɪdʒ/ [n] the time in someone's life when they are old, especially when their mind becomes weak – used especially in written English **in your dotage** *Thurmond is as mean in his dotage as he was in his younger days.*

not new

RELATED WORDS

opposite: —— **new**

- *see also* **old-fashioned**

8 not new

- old
- ancient
- age-old
- ancient
- be years old
- be as old as the hills

old /əʊld/ [adj] *Sue was wearing jeans and an old blue jacket.* | *What she loved most about the old house was its privacy and spaciousness.* | *The Luna Baglioni is one of the oldest hotels in Venice.*

ancient /ˈeɪnʃənt/ [adj] very old – use this about buildings, cities, countries, languages, or customs that existed many hundreds of years ago: *Rome is famous for its ancient monuments.* | *an ancient Greek vase* | **ancient Egypt/Rome/Babylon etc** *the pyramids of ancient Egypt* | **the ancient Egyptians/Chinese/Greeks etc** (=the people who lived in Egypt etc many hundreds of years ago) *The ancient Chinese believed that we are born with a finite amount of energy in our bodies called chi.*

age-old /ˈeɪdʒ əʊld/ [adj only before noun] **age-old symbol/custom/tradition etc** one that has existed for a very long time: *The vine is an age-old symbol of peace and prosperity.* | *man's age-old fear of snakes*

ancient /ˈeɪnʃənt/ [adj] informal very old, used especially for describing machines, equipment etc: *This refrigerator is ancient – it's time we bought a new one.* | *Doc drives an ancient Ford convertible.*

be years old /biː ˈjɪəʳz ˌəʊld/ [v phrase] British informal if you say that something **is years old**, you mean it is very old: *'I like your sweater.' 'Oh, thanks. It's years old – I've had it since I was a teenager.'*

be as old as the hills /biː əz ˌəʊld əz ðə ˈhɪlz/ [v phrase] stories, jokes, customs etc that **are as old as the hills** are so old that no one remembers when they were first invented: *That story is as old as the hills!*

9 when something has been used before

- old
- second-hand
- used

old /əʊld/ [adj only before noun] **old** clothes, books, chairs etc have already been worn or used a lot by someone else: *My parents are giving us their old sofa.* | *Do you have any old magazines the kids can cut up?* | *I was the youngest one in the family, so I had to wear my sisters' old clothes.*

second-hand /ˌsekənd ˈhænd◂/ [adj] **second-hand** books, clothes, cars etc have already been owned by someone else and are then sold: *Max spent the whole afternoon looking around a second-hand book store.* | *Do you know where I can buy a second-hand bicycle?* | *second-hand clothing* | **buy/get sth second-hand** *'Is that table new?' 'No, we got it second-hand.'*

used /juːzd/ [adj only before noun] a **used** car, book, musical instrument etc is one that someone else has already owned: *He made his money buying and selling used cars.* | *This huge Portland bookshop is crammed with more than 1 million new and used books organized into 122 subject areas.*

10 old and valuable

- antique
- vintage
- antique

antique /ænˈtiːk/ [adj] **antique** furniture, jewellery, clocks etc are old and valuable, and often beautiful to look at: *a lovely antique desk* | *Jacobs collects antique fountain pens.*

vintage /ˈvɪntɪdʒ/ [adj only before noun] use this about a car or a wine that is old and one of the best of its type: *'A lot of people have never been in an open car,' says Mike Jacobsen, a computer programmer, who has four vintage convertibles.* | *They lunched on lobster and strawberries, accompanied by a fine vintage champagne.*

antique /ænˈtiːk/ [n C usually plural] something such as a piece of furniture or a beautiful object that is old and valuable: *The house is full of valuable antiques.* | **antique shop/dealer/market** (=one that sells antiques) *While some of the people attending were looking to decorate their own houses, most appeared to be antique dealers.*

old-fashioned

RELATED WORDS

opposite: **modern**

▸ *see also* **old, fashionable/not fashionable, conventional/unconventional**

1 clothes/styles/words

- old-fashioned
- dated
- be on the way out

old-fashioned /ˌəʊld ˈfæʃənd◂/ [adj] **old-fashioned** clothes, styles, words etc are no longer considered modern or fashionable, although some people still wear them or still use them: *I don't wear that skirt now – it looks so old-fashioned.* | *'Wireless' is an old-fashioned word for radio.* | *Albert was a tall, gangling man with long blond hair, like an old-fashioned rock star's.*

dated /ˈdeɪtɪ̈d/ [adj not usually before noun] use this about clothes or styles that used to be fashionable, especially until recently, but now seem old-fashioned: *Just look at the hairstyles in this photo – they're so dated!* | *The song was a big hit last year, but it's already starting to sound dated.*

be on the way out /biː ɒn ðə ˌweɪ ˈaʊt/ [v phrase] to be gradually becoming less popular or common after having been very popular or fashionable: *It was said that coal was on the way out and would be replaced by nuclear energy.* | *When I was in high-school disco was already on the way out.*

2 machines/equipment

- old-fashioned
- outdated
- obsolete
- antiquated

old-fashioned /ˌəʊld ˈfæʃənd◂/ [adj] **old-fashioned** machines and equipment have a design that is no longer modern: *He rides one of those old-fashioned bikes with high handlebars.* | *A lot of the machines at the factory are very old-fashioned.* | *Old-fashioned ceiling fans have been making a comeback as a cheap and reliable alternative to air conditioning.*

outdated /ˌaʊtˈdeɪtɪ̈d◂/ [adj] use this about machines or equipment that use old-fashioned designs, and should be replaced with more modern ones: *It is hard to run a business with outdated equipment.* | *a rebel army, equipped only with outdated Russian weapons*

obsolete /ˈɒbsəliːt‖ˌɑːbsəˈliːt/ [adj] use this about machines and equipment that are no longer being produced, and that seem old-fashioned because newer machines have been invented which can do the job much better: *The old $5^1/_4$ inch floppy disks are now obsolete.* | **make sth obsolete** *a new type of 'Network Computer', which could make existing PCs obsolete within five years*

antiquated /ˈæntɪ̈kweɪtɪ̈d/ [adj] very old and old-fashioned and no longer suitable for modern needs: *My mother's antiquated vacuum cleaner still works, believe it or not.* | *Hospitals suffer from inadequate facilities, antiquated equipment and shortages of medical supplies.*

3 opinions/methods/systems

- old-fashioned
- outdated
- outmoded
- traditional
- unfashionable

old-fashioned /ˌəʊld ˈfæʃənd◂/ [adj] **old-fashioned** opinions and ways of living were common in the past, but are not the way most people think and behave now: *In those days, people believed that divorce was morally wrong, but this now seems very old-fashioned.* | *He has some very old-fashioned ideas about women.*

outdated /ˌaʊtˈdeɪtɪ̈d◂/ [adj] **outdated** opinions, methods, or systems are not suitable for modern times and need to be changed and made more modern: *Outdated laws and regulations are failing to keep crime on the Internet in check.* | *Outdated textbooks, decrepit buildings, overcrowded classrooms – the list of problems is long and growing.* | *The image of the civil service as a male, middle class bastion is now outdated.*

outmoded /aʊtˈməʊdɪ̈d/ [adj usually before noun] **outmoded belief/attitude/way of thinking etc** a way of thinking that was once popular but is not useful or suitable anymore: *The views of many of the senior professors reflect outmoded concepts and ideas.* | *The government's outmoded attitudes are dragging the whole country back into the nineteenth century.*

traditional /trəˈdɪʃənəl/ [adj] **traditional** opinions, methods, or customs have existed for a long time, and have not been changed or affected by modern ideas: *The local people still use traditional farming methods which have been used for hundreds of years.* | *the traditional idea that a woman's place is in the home* | *Tom went to a very traditional boys' school.*

unfashionable /ʌnˈfæʃənəbəl/ [adj] a belief or attitude that is **unfashionable** is no longer fashionable or popular: *Smoking has become very unfashionable in the last ten years.* | **it is unfashionable to do sth** *It's unfashionable these days to say you want to get married and give up your job, isn't it?*

4 books/information

- out-of-date/out of date

out-of-date/out of date /ˌaʊt əv ˈdeɪt◂/ [adj] use this about books, maps etc that do not contain the most recent information, or about information that is no longer right because the facts have changed: *The map we had with us was completely out of date.* | *an out-of-date guidebook*

5 places

- old-fashioned
- olde worlde
- be stuck/caught in a time-warp

old-fashioned /ˌəʊld ˈfæʃənd◂/ [adj] *In many ways the village is a very old-fashioned sort of place.* | *Cromer is a charmingly old-fashioned resort that has changed little over the years.*

olde worlde /ˌəʊldi ˈwɜːʳldi◂/ [adj phrase] British describing something, especially a shop or room, that has deliberately been made to look old-fashioned so that people will think it is more attractive: *I like your kitchen – it's very olde worlde.* | *a picturesque village with an ancient church, and plenty of olde worlde tea rooms*

be stuck/caught in a time-warp /biː ˌstʌk, ˌkɔːt ɪn ə ˈtaɪm wɔːʳp/ [v phrase] if a place is **stuck in a time-warp**, it has not changed and seems the same as it was many years ago: *That restaurant is still stuck in some kind of late-seventies time-warp.* | *The country had little contact with the outside world, and remained caught in something of a time-warp.*

6 people

- old-fashioned
- be living in the past
- behind the times
- straitlaced/straightlaced
- fuddy duddy
- old fogey
- old guard
- traditionalist

old-fashioned /ˌəʊld ˈfæʃənd◂/ [adj] *Mr Griffiths is a real old-fashioned teacher who still believes that learning lessons by heart is the best method.* | *My Dad was very old-fashioned and didn't approve of me going to nightclubs with my friends.*

be living in the past /biː ˌlɪvɪŋ ɪn ðə ˈpɑːst‖-ˈpæst/ [v phrase] to think and behave as if life is still like it was when you were young, especially because you do not like the modern world: *You've got to get over it, honey – you've got to stop living in the past.* | *Critics say Buchanan is living in the past, and remind him that the 1950s was a time when women were shackled to the kitchen, and African-Americans held back by discrimination.*

behind the times /bɪˌhaɪnd ðə ˈtaɪmz/ [adj phrase] a person or organization who is **behind the times**, is old-fashioned because they have not changed while the world around them has changed: *People in these parts tend to be way behind the times when it comes to issues such as women's rights.* | *Once the giants of British retailing, they are now seen as being behind the times.*

straitlaced/straightlaced /ˌstreɪtˈleɪst◂/ [adj] having a very strong, old-fashioned attitude to moral behaviour: *My aunt's very straitlaced – she'd be shocked if you mentioned sex.* | *They lost touch with Hermione after she married a very straightlaced Lutheran minister, and disappeared from the social scene.*

fuddy duddy /ˈfʌdi ˌdʌdi/ [n C] informal someone who you think is old-fashioned and boring because they disapprove of new ideas and are unwilling to change their attitudes: *Don't be such a fuddy duddy!* | *The election broadcast made the President look like a fuddy duddy with ridiculously old-fashioned ideas.* —**fuddy-duddy** [adj] *She has some rather fuddy-duddy ideas about what is proper music.*

old fogey /ˌəʊld ˈfəʊgi/ [n C] informal someone, usually an old person, who you disapprove of because they prefer old-fashioned ideas and ways of doing things to modern ones: *The old fogies all sit together and talk about the old days.* | *This country is being run by a bunch of old fogies – we need some fresh blood, people with initiative.*

old guard /ˈəʊld ˌgɑːʳd/ [n singular with singular or plural verb in British English] a group of people with old-fashioned opinions, who have been in an organization or society for a long time and oppose anyone who wants to change things: *Inevitably, the revolution is affecting the old guard much more than the rest of us.* | *The party's old guard have their own candidate for leader.*

traditionalist /trəˈdɪʃənəlɪ̈st/ [n C] a person who believes that the old ways of doing things are the best, and who does not like modern methods or ideas: *I'm something of a traditionalist myself, I'd much rather use pen and paper than a word-processor.* | *There are still many traditionalists in the church who strongly oppose the idea of women priests.*

7 extremely old-fashioned

- medieval
- out of the ark
- dinosaur
- anachronism
- archaic
- Dickensian
- the dark ages

medieval /ˌmediˈiːvəl◂‖ˌmiː-/ [adj] extremely old-fashioned and therefore annoying: *The plumbing in this house is medieval!* | **positively medieval** (=very medieval) *This so-called accounting system is positively medieval.*

out of the ark /ˌaʊt əv ði ˈɑːʳk/ [adj phrase] British informal extremely old-fashioned: *Their washing machine looks like it came out of the ark.* | *Her views on social policy are embarrassing – really out of the ark.*

dinosaur /ˈdaɪnəsɔːʳ/ [n C usually singular] a system, organization etc that is very old-fashioned and large and cannot continue to exist in the modern world: *The Health Service has become a dinosaur. It needs radical reform if it is to survive.* | *The line-up includes a number of rock-n-roll dinosaurs who should have hung up their guitars long ago.*

anachronism /əˈnækrənɪzəm/ [n C usually singular] something such as an organization or custom that belongs to a time in the past, and therefore appears very strange in the modern world: *The harvest festival celebrations in the town are an anachronism since almost everyone who lives there nowadays works in an office.* —**anachronistic** /əˌnækrəˈnɪstɪk◂/ [adj] *Many people believe that the role of the Royal Family in Britain is anachronistic.*

archaic /ɑːʳˈkeɪ-ɪk/ [adj] use this about something that was used a long time ago but which is now considered too old-fashioned and needs replacing: *The text was full of archaic spellings.* | *The laws that decide who owns items discovered on an archeological exploration are ridiculously archaic.*

Dickensian /dɪˈkenziən/ [adj] buildings, conditions etc that are **Dickensian** are extremely old-fashioned and below acceptable standards, for example because they are dangerous or unhealthy: *They were living in a Dickensian apartment block without proper heating or running water.* | **positively Dickensian** *The working conditions in the factory were positively Dickensian.*

the dark ages /ðə ˈdɑːʳk ˌeɪdʒ̬z/ [n phrase] use this to talk about a society, system, or way of thinking that is extremely old-fashioned, especially in its social attitudes: *Huge amounts of aid will be needed if this society is ever to drag itself out of the dark ages.* | *My brother still doesn't like the idea of having a woman boss – he's stuck in the dark ages!*

8 old-fashioned in a pleasant way

- old-fashioned
- quaint

old-fashioned /ˌəʊld ˈfæʃənd◂/ [adj] **old-fashioned** in a way that reminds you of nice things in the past: *The town has a lovely old-fashioned charm about it.* | *He was a nice, old-fashioned gentleman who would hold open the door for you or offer to carry your bags.* | **good old-fashioned** *good old-fashioned home cooking*

quaint /kweɪnt/ [adj] old-fashioned and unusual, but attractive and interesting – use this about small buildings or places, or about customs and beliefs: *We stayed in a quaint little fishing village in Cornwall.* | *quaint country cottages* | *Stigler scoffed at the quaint idea of university as a place where a professor and a small group of students can sit in a study and discuss great thoughts.*

once

on one occasion in the past

RELATED WORDS

- at once *see* **immediately**
- at once, at the same time *see* **time (19)**
- once again/once more *see* **again**
- *see also* **past**

- once
- one time
- on one occasion
- at one stage
- at one point
- one day

once /wʌns/ [adv] *They had met once on holiday, so they knew each other slightly.* | *She once called me a liar and I've never forgiven her.* | *I remember once it snowed on my birthday, and I was so excited.*

one time /ˌwʌn ˌtaɪm/ [adv] spoken once: *I remember coming home from school one time and finding we'd been burgled.* | *One time we went out fishing on the lake at night.*

on one occasion /ɒn ˈwʌn əˌkeɪʒən/ [adv] use this to give an example of when something you are talking about happened, especially when it is a particularly interesting or extreme example: *On one occasion, she rang his home and a strange woman answered.* | *She had some pretty frightening experiences. On one occasion her jeep was hijacked by a group of armed soldiers.*

at one stage /ət ˈwʌn ˌsteɪdʒ/ [adv] at one time during a period of time, process, or event in the past: *I dieted for many years, and at one stage I weighed only 71 kg.* | *It was a terrible winter. At one stage all the roads to the village were blocked by snow.* | *At one stage in the match, he was trailing by three games, but he managed to fight back.*

at one point /ət ˈwʌn ˌpɔɪnt/ [adv] at one time during an activity or period of time in the past: *At one point in the interview, he seemed close to tears.* | *'You play the piano very well,' I remember Mrs Saito remarking at one point.* | *I had several narrow escapes during the war, at one point just missing death when my plane was shot down.*

one day /ˌwʌn ˈdeɪ/ [adv] on a day in the past – use this especially when the exact day does not matter and you are telling the story of what happened: *I was sitting eating my breakfast one day when the telephone rang.* | *One day when we had nothing else to do, we went down to the river for a swim.* | *He used to come and go, then one day he went away and never came back.*

only

RELATED WORDS

- *see also* **few/not many, limit**

1 only one, or only a small number

- only
- just
- all
- nothing but
- one
- lone
- solitary
- sole
- exclusively

only /ˈəʊnli/ [adj/adv] **only** one person or thing, or **only** a small number of people or things, and not anyone or anything else: *There was only one dress that she really liked.* | *Only rich people were able to travel abroad in those days.* | *You can only take one piece of hand baggage onto the plane.* | *You get only two chances – if you fail the exam twice you can't take it again.* | **the only person/thing/place etc** *She's the only woman I've ever loved.* | **be only for sb** (=only one person or group can use something) *These seats are only for first class passengers.*

just /dʒʌst/ [adv] **especially spoken** only one person, thing, type, or group, or only a small number of them, especially when this is surprising: *'Were there a lot of people there?' 'No, just me and David.'* | *He started his own small shop – at first just selling newspapers, then books and magazines.* | *'Does everyone have to wear uniform?' 'No, just the first year students.'*

all /ɔːl/ [pron] the only thing or things, especially when this is disappointing, annoying, or surprising: *All Kevin ever talks about is football.* | *We were really hungry, but all we could find was some stale bread.* | *All I wanted was a bit of sympathy.*

nothing but /ˈnʌθɪŋ bət/ use this especially when you feel disappointed, annoyed, or surprised that something is the only thing there is or the only thing someone does: *There was nothing but salad to eat.* | *They did nothing but argue for the whole journey.*

one /wʌn/ [determiner] **one thing/person/time/ problem etc** the only person, thing etc and no others – use this to emphasize that there really is only **one** person or thing of this type **the one thing/person/ time/problem etc** *She was the one friend that I could trust.* | *The one thing I don't like about my car is the colour.* | *The one time I forgot my umbrella was the day it rained.* | **sb's one regret/friend/mistake etc** *My one regret is that I never told Brad how I felt.*

lone /ləʊn/ [adj only before noun] being the only one, when usually you would expect there to be more – used in newspapers and literature: *A lone gunman burst into his house and shot him dead.* | *Out of the stillness, a lone bird began to sing.*

solitary /ˈsɒlɪ̈təri‖ˈsɑːlɪ̈teri/ [adj only before noun] a **solitary** person, tree, building etc is the only one you can see in a place, and may therefore seem a little lonely or sad: *A solitary light shone in the street.* | *There was one solitary hotel left standing after the earthquake.* | *I could see a solitary figure outlined against the horizon.*

sole /səʊl/ [adj only before noun] **formal** the only person, thing etc, especially when you would expect there to be more or expect it to be different: *Everyone ignored my sole contribution to the conversation.* | **the sole person/thing etc** *In many households, the woman is the sole breadwinner* (=the only person who has a job). | **with the sole intention/objective/aim of doing sth** *I think he came here with the sole intention of causing trouble.* | **sb's sole concern/objective etc** *NASA's sole concern was the safety of the astronauts.*

exclusively /ɪkˈskluːsɪvli/ [adv] made of, including, or involving only one thing or group, especially something special or something that is of good quality: *This shop sells clothes made exclusively of Indian materials.* | *The office staff are almost exclusively female.*

2 a surprisingly small price/number/amount.

- only
- just
- is that all?
- a mere
- no more than

only /ˈəʊnli/ [adv] use this to say that a number, amount, price, size etc is surprisingly small: *I got these four chairs for only $99.* | *We only have a very small garden.* | *'Is it far?' 'No, it's only a mile away.'* | *She was only 17 when she got married.*

just /dʒʌst/ [adv] only a small amount, number, period of time etc, especially when this is surprising and good: *There is a beautiful park just 300 metres from the busiest shopping street.* | *It took the firefighters just three minutes to arrive.* | *His car hit a wall, but he escaped with just cuts and bruises.* | **just a little** ALSO **just a bit British spoken** (=only a small amount, number etc) *'Do you take milk?' 'Just a little, please.'*

is that all? /ɪz ˌðæt ˈɔːl/ **spoken** say this when you are surprised because you expected a number, price etc to be higher: *'The tickets are $10.' 'Is that all?'* | *Is that all the money you've got?*

a mere /ə ˈmɪəʳ/ [adv] use this to talk about something that is only a small amount or figure, or is lower than you would expect **a mere £50/three days/16% etc** *You can now buy computers from a mere £300.* | *The crossword took him a mere six and a half minutes.*

no more than /nəʊ ˈmɔːʳ ðən/ use this to emphasize that something is small, unimportant, difficult to notice etc: *We were standing no more than 10 yards away from the scene of the crime and we didn't realize it.* | *David watched the car drive slowly away, until it was no more than a speck in the distance.*

3 for one reason only and no other

- only
- just
- merely
- purely

only /ˈəʊnli/ [adv] for **only** one reason or purpose, and not for any others – use this especially when explaining why someone does something: *She only married him for his money.* | *Ms Walker said she only started stealing because her children were hungry.*

just /dʒʌst/ [adv] **especially spoken** only – use this when explaining why someone does something: *I think she just wanted someone to talk to.* | *I didn't mean to interfere – I was just trying to help.* | **just because** *Just because he looked at them in the wrong way, they beat him up and stole his money.*

merely /ˈmɪəʳli/ [adv] **formal** use this to emphasize that you are doing something only for the reason you say, and not for any other reason, especially when someone seems annoyed or upset: *The committee does not blame any individual; we are merely trying to find out how the accident happened.* | *You are not there to teach, but merely to supervise the children.*

purely /ˈpjʊəʳli/ [adv] for one reason or purpose only, and not involving anything else: *What we have is a purely business arrangement.* | *Most plants are planted purely for decoration.*

4 not particularly important, special, or interesting

- only/just
- merely
- nothing else
- mere
- nothing but/no more than

only/just /ˈəʊnli, dʒʌst/ [adv] use this to emphasize that someone or something is not particularly important, special, or interesting: *Don't ask me – I'm only the cleaner.* | *'What's for dinner?' 'Just pasta – nothing exciting.'* | **only/just another** *It's just another one of those daytime talk shows.*

merely /ˈmɪəʳli/ [adv] formal use this to emphasize that someone or something is not really important or special, although they may seem to be: *The President's position is merely ceremonial; it is the Chancellor who holds real power.* | *I wondered if the girl had meant more to him than being merely a casual friend.*

nothing else /ˌnʌθɪŋ ˈels/ [pron] only that, and not anything more important, more valuable, or more useful: *She sees him as a friend and nothing else.* | **if nothing else** *If nothing else the meeting serves as a useful way of getting everyone's ideas together.*

mere /mɪəʳ/ [adj only before noun] only – used especially when you do not expect very much from the thing you are describing, or you think it is unimportant: *How can you expect him to understand? He's a mere child.* | *There have been reports that she is going to resign, but it's mere speculation at the moment.* | *The mere mention of Ronan's name made her heart beat faster.*

nothing but/no more than /ˈnʌθɪŋ bʌt, nəʊ ˈmɔːʳ ðən/ use this about someone or something that is not nearly as good, special, interesting etc as they seem to be or pretend to be: *They say they're a moral, religious regime, but in fact they're nothing but a bunch of bullies and thugs.* | *As far as I can see, this proposal is no more than an attempt to disguise many of the mistakes management have made in the past.*

5 belonging or relating to only one thing, person, or group

- only
- just
- be limited/restricted to
- be confined to
- be unique to
- be peculiar to
- exclusive

only /ˈəʊnli/ [adv] *The bee orchid is a rare plant normally only found in Mediterranean climates.* | **women/men/ staff etc only** *Women only swimming sessions are held every Thursday.* | **only for** *High impact aerobics is only for people who are extremely fit.*

just /dʒʌst/ [adv] only affecting a particular group, place, time etc: *It is a disease which affects just male children.* | *Sam Mendes is highly regarded, not just in the UK.* | **+ for** *This class is just for beginners. Why don't you try the class next door?*

be limited/restricted to /biː ˈlɪmɪ̍tɪ̍d, rɪˈstrɪktɪ̍d tuː/ [v phrase] if something **is limited to** or **is restricted to** someone or something, it has been officially decided that only particular groups can do it or use it, or that it can only happen in particular places or situations: *Access to the files is limited to management.* | *The cultivation of rice has to be restricted to areas of high rainfall.*

be confined to /biː kənˈfaɪnd tuː/ [v phrase] to affect or happen to only one group of people, or in only one place or time: *So far, fighting has been confined to the capital city.* | *ME or 'Yuppie Flu', is not just confined to people in high-powered, well-paid jobs.*

be unique to /biː juːˈniːk tuː/ [v phrase] if an unusual or rare quality or characteristic **is unique to** a particular thing, person, place etc, only that thing, person, or place has it: *This type of tapestry work is unique to the region.* | *Each set of genes is unique to the individual.* —**uniquely** [adv] *There's something uniquely English about the scene.*

be peculiar to /biː pɪˈkjuːliəʳ tuː/ [v phrase] to belong very definitely to one particular person, place, period of time etc and not to any other: *This way of grinding corn is peculiar to North American Indians.* | *a gesture peculiar to himself* —**peculiarly** [adv] *a peculiarly South African phenomenon* (=it is only found in South Africa)

exclusive /ɪkˈskluːsɪv/ [adj only before noun] use this to describe something that only particular people have the advantage of having, doing, or using: *There will be exclusive coverage of the championship on Channel 5.* | *The recent takeover gave Rafferty exclusive control of the company.* | *Your password gives you exclusive access to your personal computer files.* —**exclusively** [adv] *Certain areas of the club are reserved exclusively for members.*

on/on top of

RELATED WORDS

- switch on *see* **switch on or off**
- on a particular subject *see* **about**
- on a particular day *see* **time (2)**
- *see also* **top, above, up, under/below**

1 on or on top of something

- on
- on top of
- onto
- over

on /ɒn‖ɑːn, ɔːn/ [prep] **on** the surface of something: *Richard put the letter down on the table.* | *Neil Armstrong was the first person ever to set foot on the Moon.* | *There weren't enough chairs so I had to sit on the floor.* | *Four bottles of wine were standing on the shelf.*

on top of /ɒn ˈtɒp ɒv‖-ˈtɑːp-/ [prep] on the highest part of something tall: *On top of the church was a large illuminated cross.* | *The plane crashed on top of Sugarbush Mountain, in Vermont.* | **one on top of the other** (=in a pile) *Joey stacked the crates one on top of the other.*

onto /ˈɒntuː/ [prep] into a position on the surface of something: *Nancy walked onto the stage and took the microphone in her hand.* | *Spoon the mixture onto the top of the cake and spread it evenly.*

over /ˈəʊvəʳ/ [prep] on something and covering it: *There was a white sheet over the victim's body.* | *She wore a coat over her sweater.* | **put/lay/throw sth over sth** *She put a blanket over the child's legs to keep him warm.* | **all over** (=on all parts of something) *He spilled beer all over my feet.* | *There were toys all over the floor.*

2 to be on the surface of water

- float
- afloat

float /fləʊt/ [v I] to be supported on the surface of water by the water itself: *Ice is less dense than water,* *which is why it floats.* | **float in the water** *Annie was floating on her back in the water.* | *They could see something pale and white floating in the water.* | **float on water/the surface/the river etc** *a cup of coffee with black bits floating on the surface* | **+ along/down etc** *The empty boat floated off down the river.* —**floating** [adj only before noun] *Floating plants are useful because they shade the surface of the water.* | *a massive floating platform*

afloat /əˈfləʊt/ [adj not before noun/adv] **be/stay/keep afloat** to stay on the surface of water without sinking: *I moved my hands and feet slightly to stay afloat.* | *Those in the water tried to hold on to the boats that were still afloat.*

on time

RELATED WORDS

opposite: late

▸ *see also* **time, late, early**

1 happening or arriving at the arranged time

- on time
- right on time
- bang/dead on time
- promptly/punctually
- on cue
- on the dot

on time /ɒn ˈtaɪm/ [adv] *The trains don't always arrive on time.* | *The company will lose money if the work isn't completed on time.* | *Did Philip pay up on time?* | **+ for** *I hate not being on time for class.*

right on time /ˌraɪt ɒn ˈtaɪm/ [adv] exactly on time: *Gary turned up right on time, holding a big bouquet of flowers.* | *Ah, Mrs Shields, you're right on time!*

bang/dead on time /ˌbæŋ, ˌded ɒn ˈtaɪm/ [adv] British informal exactly on time: *The baby arrived on the 16th – bang on time!* | *He looked at his watch. He was dead on time.*

promptly/punctually /ˈprɒmptli‖ˈprɑː-, ˈpʌŋktʃuəli/ [adv] if you do something **punctually** or **promptly**, you do it at the time that you arranged to do it: *Linda always pays her rent promptly on the 1st of the month.* | *Loretta arrived punctually at her office the next day at ten o'clock.*

on cue /ɒn ˈkjuː/ [adv] if you do something **on cue**, you do it exactly at the moment when other people expect you to do it: *Jim told one of his terrible jokes and everyone laughed on cue.* | **as if on cue** *'Ashley should be here soon', said Jo, and as if on cue, there was a knock at the door.* | **right/bang on cue** *We were looking out over the sea when, right on cue, the dolphins appeared.*

on the dot /ɒn ðə ˈdɒt‖-ˈdɑːt/ [adv] **at 6.30/ten o'clock/ seven etc on the dot** at 6.30, ten o'clock etc exactly: *He gets annoyed if his lunch isn't ready at one o'clock on the dot.* | *I expect you to arrive at 7:30 on the dot.*

2 someone who is always on time

- punctual

punctual /ˈpʌŋktʃuəl/ [adj] someone who is **punctual** always arrives or does things when they are supposed to: *Dinner is served at seven: please try to be punctual.* | *Our clients are usually punctual – you would be too if you were paying $10 a minute.* —**punctuality** /ˌpʌŋktʃuˈæləti/ [n U] *Punctuality is not one of my strong points, I must admit.* | *Cadets are taught discipline, neatness and punctuality.*

3 when something happens before it is too late

- in time
- just in time
- in the nick of time
- not a moment too soon
- at the last minute
- at the eleventh hour
- catch
- cut it fine
- before it's too late

in time /ɪn ˈtaɪm/ [adv] *David said he'd take me to the concert, if he's home in time.* | *If you don't leave enough space between your car and the car in front, you may not be able to stop in time.* | **+ to do sth** *Don't worry, I'll be back in time to cook dinner.* | *She's hoping to be out of hospital in time to celebrate her birthday at home.* | **+ for** *Do you think you'll be fit in time for Saturday's race?*

just in time /ˌdʒʌst ɪn ˈtaɪm/ [adv] happening or done in time, but almost too late: *She put her foot on the brakes just in time.* | **+ to do sth** *He got to the airport just in time to catch the flight to Madrid.* | **+ for** *Come in. You're just in time for a cup of coffee.* | **only just in time** British *We were only just in time. A few more minutes and the bank would have been closed.*

in the nick of time /ɪn ðə ˌnɪk əv ˈtaɪm/ [adv] informal just in time to prevent something bad from happening – often used in stories: *Radio contact was established in the nick of time and we managed to transmit a message to the ship.* | **just in the nick of time** *She escaped from her smoke-filled home just in the nick of time.*

not a moment too soon /nɒt ə ˌməʊmənt tuː ˈsuːn/ [adv] just in time to prevent something very bad from happening: *The ambulance finally arrived, not a moment too soon.*

at the last minute /ət ðə ˌlɑːst ˈmɪnət‖-ˌlæst-/ [adv] if something happens **at the last minute**, it happens at the latest possible time, just before it is too late: *An American businessman stepped in at the last minute to rescue the company.* | *Realizing its error at the last minute, the magazine just managed to correct the offending headline.*

at the eleventh hour /ət ði ɪˌlevənθ ˈaʊəʳ/ [adv] if something happens **at the eleventh hour**, it happens at the latest possible time, just before it is too late – use this when you had almost given up hoping that something would happen: *War was averted at the eleventh hour when both sides agreed to talks.* —**eleventh-hour** [adj only before noun] *Fernandez waits on Death Row, hoping for an eleventh-hour reprieve.*

catch /kætʃ/ [v T] to manage to do something, talk to someone, see something etc just before it is too late: *I managed to catch her just as she was leaving the office.* | **catch the post** British (=post letters etc in time for them to be collected that day) *The letters were all addressed and stamped, and there was still plenty of time to catch the post.* | **catch the news/a TV programme etc** *She was rushing to catch her favorite show on TV.*

cut it fine British **/cut it close** American /ˌkʌt ɪt ˈfaɪn, ˌkʌt ɪt ˈkləʊs/ [v phrase] to have very little time left before you have to be somewhere or do something, so that you are almost late: *Kelly had 10 minutes to reach the studio – even in normal traffic that was cutting it close.* | **cut it a bit fine** *You're cutting it a bit fine aren't you? The show starts in 2 minutes.* | **cut it pretty close** *We cut it pretty close – we only had 30 minutes to get to the airport.*

before it's too late /bɪˌfɔːr ɪts tuː ˈleɪt/ use this to tell or warn someone to do something now in order to prevent something bad from happening that they will not be able to change later: *You'd better get that letter back from her somehow, before it's too late.* | *We are urging the government to stop the bombing now, before it's too late.*

4 to finish a piece of work within the time that is allowed for it

- meet a deadline
- on schedule

meet a deadline /ˌmiːt ə ˈdedlaɪn/ [v phrase] to finish some work within the time that you have been allowed to do it, especially when it is very important that it is done by that time: *Journalists have to work very quickly in order to meet their deadlines.* | *Without extra help, it's going to be very difficult to meet the Friday deadline.*

on schedule /ɒn ˈʃedʒuːl‖-ˈskedʒʊl/ [adj/adv] if a piece of work, especially a piece of work that continues for a long time, is finished **on schedule**, it is done within the time that has been allowed for it to be done: *The builders were lazy and failed to finish the boat on schedule.* | **be on schedule** *So far we are on schedule and the project should come to an end in two months, as planned.*

open

RELATED WORDS

opposite: —— **shut**

- *see also* **fasten/unfasten, tie/untie**

1 to open a door, window, box etc

- open
- unlock
- force open
- break open
- prise open
- try
- break down
- wind down/roll down
- open up

open /ˈəʊpən/ [v T] *It's very hot in here. Do you mind if I open the window?* | *The drawer's locked – you need a key to open it.* | **open sth wide** *He opened the door wide, and gestured for me to come in.*

unlock /ʌnˈlɒk‖-ˈlɑːk/ [v T] to turn the a key in the lock on a door, drawer, cupboard etc so that you can open it: *Unlock the door! We can't get out!* | *Which of these keys unlocks the safe?* | *'Come and see', Jo said, unlocking a huge iron gate.*

force open /ˌfɔːʳs ˈəʊpən/ [v phrase] to open a drawer, window, cupboard etc by using force, often with a tool **force sth/it open** *The door's stuck – we'll have to force it open.* | **force open sth** *The burglars had forced open the window with an iron bar.* | *It looked as though the shed had been forced open.*

break open /ˌbreɪk ˈəʊpən/ [v phrase] to open a container by using force, so that it is damaged **break open sth** *We managed to break open the crate with an axe.* | **break sth/it/them open** *There's no key for the suitcase – we'll have to break it open.* | *Gulls carry shellfish into the air, then drop them onto hard surfaces to break them open.*

prise open British **/pry open** American /ˌpraɪz ˈəʊpən, ˌpraɪ ˈəʊpən/ [v phrase] to open something by forcing one part of it away from the other part, using a tool **prise sth/it/them open** *All the flats were boarded up, but we managed to prise a few boards open.* | **prise open sth** *Laura leaned forward to pry open the crate.* | **prise the lid off** (=remove the lid to open it) *I picked up the coffee tin and, using a knife, prised the lid off.*

try /traɪ/ [v T not in passive] to **try** to open a door or window in order to see if it is locked: *I knocked, then tried the door. It was open, but the room was empty.* | *I went around the back to try the windows, but they were all locked.*

break down /ˌbreɪk ˈdaʊn/ [phr v T] to completely break a locked door in order to get into a room or building **break down sth** *Firemen had to break the door down.* | **break sth/it down** *Open the door now or we'll break it down!*

wind down/roll down British /ˌwaɪnd ˈdaʊn, ˌrəʊl ˈdaʊn/ [phr v T] to open a car window, especially by turning a handle **wind/roll down sth** *The driver wound down his window and asked us the way to the stadium.* | **wind/roll sth down** *Mom, will you roll your window down a little please?*

open up /ˌəʊpən ˈʌp/ spoken use this to tell someone to open a door: *Open up – it's the police!*

2 when a door or window opens

- open
- burst/fly open

open /ˈəʊpən/ [v I] *The train doors open and close automatically.* | *The door slowly opened and a small boy entered the room.* | *After a short discussion with the customs officers, the gates opened and the truck moved off.*

burst/fly open /ˌbɜːʳst, ˌflaɪ ˈəʊpən/ [v phrase] to open very suddenly – used especially in stories or descriptions: *Before Mr Carey could speak, the door burst open and Mr Watson rushed into the room.* | *Every time we go round a corner, the passenger door flies open.*

3 an open door or window

- open
- ajar

open /ˈəʊpən/ [adj] *Carrie stood in front of the open window.* | *The office door was open, and I could hear everything they said.* | **push/slide/kick etc sth open** *In the mirror, she saw him slide open one of his drawers.* | **wide open** *Do you know you left the window wide open all night?*

ajar /əˈdʒɑːʳ/ [adj not before noun] a door that is **ajar** is slightly open – used in written English: *She had left her bedroom door ajar and could hear her parents talking downstairs.* | **slightly ajar** *To his right was a large walk-in cupboard, its door slightly ajar.*

4 to open a bottle, can, jar

- open
- unscrew
- crack open
- uncork

open /ˈəʊpən/ [v T] to **open** a bottle, box, or other container by removing or lifting its top or lid: *Ask the waiter to open another bottle of champagne.* | *a little gadget that helps you to open jars*

unscrew /ʌnˈskruː/ [v T] to remove the top or lid of a bottle or container by turning it: *Robyn unscrewed a jar of moisturiser and smoothed it over her face.* | *Pills are stored in containers with tops that are difficult for children to unscrew.*

crack open /ˌkræk ˈəʊpən/ [phr v T] to open a bottle of alcohol **crack open sth** *Let's crack open a bottle of* *champagne.* | **crack sth/it open** *We cracked a few cans of beer open and sat down to watch the game.*

uncork /ʌn'kɔːʳk/ [v T] to open a bottle of wine by removing the cork. The cork is a piece of wood which is put in the top of the bottle: *Ray uncorked the bottle and offered me a glass of wine.*

5 to open a packet or something that is folded or rolled

- open
- unwrap
- unfold
- unroll

open /'əʊpən/ [v T] *Aren't you going to open your letter?* | *Judy opened another pack of cigarettes.* | *When I received the parcel, it had already been opened.*

unwrap /ʌn'ræp/ [v T] to open a package by removing the paper that is wrapped around it: *I just love unwrapping Christmas presents!* | *Sarah sat down and unwrapped her sandwiches.*

unfold /ʌn'fəʊld/ [v T] to open something that was folded, such as a piece of paper or cloth: *They unfolded the tablecloth and set out the picnic.* | *The receipt had been folded and unfolded so many times that it was almost in pieces.*

unroll /ʌn'rəʊl/ [v T] to spread out something that was rolled up, so that it lies flat: *He unrolled the map and spread it on the table.* | *While we were admiring the rugs, the shopkeeper started to unroll a splendid carpet.*

6 to open your eyes or mouth

- open your eyes/mouth
- open
- gaping

open your eyes/mouth /ˌəʊpən jɔːr 'aɪz, 'maʊθ/ [v phrase] *She opened her eyes and sat up in bed.* | **open (your mouth) wide** *The dentist told me to open my mouth a little wider.* | *Open wide. I need to look at the back of your throat.*

open /'əʊpən/ [adj not usually before noun] when your mouth or eyes are open: *She sleeps with her eyes half open.* | **can hardly keep your eyes open** *I was so tired I could hardly keep my eyes open.* | **wide open** (=open as much as possible) *Ben was staring at her with his mouth wide open.*

gaping /'geɪpɪŋ/ [adj] if someone's mouth is **gaping**, it is wide open, especially because they are very shocked or surprised: *Flies crawled over the gaping mouth of the injured man.*

7 when a shop, bank, restaurant etc opens

- open
- open

open /'əʊpən/ [v I] if a shop, bank, restaurant etc **opens** at a particular time in the day, people can use it from that time: *'What times do the banks open?' 'Normally at around 9.30.'* | *On Saturdays, the restaurant opens at 7 p.m.* | **open early/late** *Unknown to me, the office had opened early, and all the tickets had been sold.*

open /'əʊpən/ [adj not before noun] if a shop, bank, restaurant etc is **open**, it is available for people to use: *The World Café is open from 10 a.m. till 11 p.m.*

opinion

RELATED WORDS

- stop people from expressing their opinions *see* **stop (27)**
- the opinion that people have of a person, organization etc *see* **reputation, accept, reject, against/oppose**
- have a particular opinion *see* **think (9-11)**
- *see also* **agree, support, in general, disagree, idea, moderate, extreme**

1 what you think about something

- opinion
- what you think of/about sth
- view
- attitude
- thoughts
- feelings
- ideas
- sentiment

opinion /ə'pɪnjən/ [n C] *Please phone in with your comments and opinions.* | *Opinions vary widely on this matter.* | **+ of** *The rating a film gets reflects the opinions of our reviewers.* | **my/your/her etc opinion** *Do you really want my opinion?* | *He acknowledged that he had no evidence to support his opinion.* | **+ on/about** *They have very different opinions about religion.* | *Many board members said they had no opinion on Goldman's proposal.* | **in my/our etc opinion** *In my opinion, most lawyers are overpaid.* | *This is, in the opinion of the critics, their best record for years.* | **have a high/low opinion of sth/sb** (=think something or someone is good or bad) *Politicians generally have a low opinion of the press.* | **give/express an opinion** *About 100 people showed up to express their opinions about the project.* | **ask sb's opinion** *In 10 years of teaching, I have never been asked my opinion on any matter of policy.* | **sb is entitled to their opinion** (=say this when you disagree with someone else's opinion) *He's entitled to his opinion, of course, but it does not give him the right to be offensive.* | **be of the opinion that** (=have a particular opinion) formal *The coroner was of the opinion that the man had been dead for only 24 hours.*

what you think of/about sth /ˌwɒt juː 'θɪŋk əv, əbaʊt (sth)/ [n phrase] especially spoken your opinion about something, especially whether you think it is good or bad: *What do you think of her new CD?* | *Tell me what you think about the design.* | *No one ever really stops and asks kids what they think about things.* | *Well, I know what I think, but you might not agree.*

view /vjuː/ [n C] your opinion about something, especially about a serious or important subject: *It is natural for children to have different views from their parents.* | **+ that** *I don't agree with the view that longer prison sentences stop people from committing crime.* | **in my/his/John's etc view** *In Freud's view, people's dreams often reveal their unconscious fears.* | **+ about/on** *Malthus will always be known mainly for his views on population.* | *The survey reflected a very conservative view about what the ideal family structure should be.* | **express a view** *Stein was expressing the view of many fellow war veterans.* | **take a view that** *Most nineteenth century scientists took the view that the universe had no purpose or meaning.*

attitude /'ætɪ̥tjuːd‖-tuːd/ [n C] what you think and feel about something or someone, especially when this is shown in the way you behave towards them: *I* *don't understand your attitude. Why don't you like her?* | *The book explains some of the attitudes and values of the Victorians.* | **+ to/towards** *Since the 1960s, there has been a big change in people's attitudes to sex before marriage.* | **take the attitude that** *Officials took the attitude that the problem was not their responsibility.*

thoughts /θɔ:ts/ [n plural] your opinion about something, especially about what should be done about it, after you have thought about it carefully **+ about/on** *Does anyone have any thoughts or suggestions about how we should spend the money?* | *I was anxious to hear his thoughts on the scenes I had written.* | **have thoughts** *Please get back to me with any thoughts you might have on this.*

feelings /'fi:lɪŋz/ [n plural] what you think about something, especially when you have very strong or angry **feelings** about it: *He makes decisions without ever taking my feelings into account.* | **+ about** *Kids' feelings about everything from reading to exercise are influenced by their parents.* | **strong feelings** *She has very strong feelings about this election.*

ideas /aɪ'dɪəz/ [n plural] what you think about something, especially about the best way to deal with something: *I'm not sure his ideas will be very popular with the voters.* | **+ about/on** *His ideas about marriage and divorce were very old-fashioned.* | *I'd like your ideas on how we can improve our working relationship.*

sentiment /'sentəmənt/ [n C/U] especially written an opinion, especially one that is based on emotion: *The speeches were full of nationalist sentiments.* | *Most people were outraged by the bombing, and their letters of sympathy reflected this sentiment.* | **public/popular sentiment** (=what most people think) *Several meetings were held to determine what public sentiment was on the issue.*

2 an opinion that is influenced by the situation you are in

- point of view
- viewpoint
- standpoint
- angle
- perspective

point of view /ˌpɔɪnt əv 'vju:/ [n C] what you think about something, especially when this is influenced by the situation you are in: *People seemed afraid to express a point of view that was different from the government's.* | *If Allen had ever been the victim of a crime, he might have a slightly different point of view.* | **from sb's point of view** *The story is told from the daughter's point of view.* | *From a farmer's point of view, foxes are a nuisance.* | **listen to sb's point of view** *She's always ready to listen to other people's point of view.*

viewpoint /'vju:pɔɪnt/ [n C] a particular way of thinking about a problem or subject: *We need to seriously consider all the different viewpoints on the issue.* | **from a historical/feminist/democratic etc viewpoint** *The book looks at the Royal family from a sociological and historical viewpoint.* | **from the viewpoint of sb** *The TV series examines childhood from the viewpoints of twelve different families.*

standpoint /'stændpɔɪnt/ [n C] a particular way of thinking about something, especially of someone who is involved in a situation or who has to make a professional judgment about it **from sb's standpoint** *From the teacher's standpoint, the new tests just mean more work.* | **from a financial/political/literary etc standpoint** *His books have sold in the millions, but from a literary standpoint they aren't really very good.*

angle /'æŋgəl/ [n C] one of a number of ways of thinking about something that should be considered when dealing with a particular problem or subject: *Advertisers need to find the right angle to make their product appeal to consumers.* | *The article gives the reader a fresh angle on pop culture.* | **look at/view/examine etc sth from an angle** *Thompson says his committee has looked at the problem from every possible angle.* | **+ on** *They wanted an ordinary worker's angle on the new system.*

perspective /pər'spektɪv/ [n C] a way of thinking about something which is influenced by the kind of person you are or by things that have happened to you: *You believe him, but you've only heard his perspective.* | *Different people bring different perspectives and values to the workplace.* | **from sb's perspective** *Feminists say that the book was written from a male perspective.* | **+ on** *A prisoner has a different perspective on prison life than a guard.*

3 what a particular group think about something

- opinion
- thinking
- school of thought
- body of opinion

opinion /ə'pɪnjən/ [n U] an **opinion** shared by a group of people, especially a particular profession or group of people who can influence what is decided **government/professional/medical etc opinion** *Medical opinion is divided as to the effectiveness of the new drug.* | **world opinion** *Their refusal to obey UN regulations had a major effect on world opinion.*

thinking /'θɪŋkɪŋ/ [n U] an opinion that a group has at a particular time, especially about the best way of doing something: *His statements closely reflect government thinking.* | *There has been a change in thinking in terms of the influence of diet on the disease.* | **+ on** *The report goes against current thinking on what is best for working parents.*

school of thought /ˌsku:l əv 'θɔ:t/ [n phrase] an opinion shared by a group of people who have a very different way of looking at a problem or subject from that of another group of people: *There are two schools of thought. One wants to control inflation, while the other is more interested in boosting employment.* | *According to one school of thought, the disease is caused by a genetic defect.*

body of opinion /ˌbɒdi əv ə'pɪnjən‖ˌbɑ:di-/ [n C] an opinion shared by a large group of people, that is considered to be important or that should be listened to: *A significant body of opinion is strongly opposed to the new proposals.* | *There is a growing body of opinion that says we should put the environment first.*

4 what most people think about something

- public opinion/popular opinion
- consensus
- majority view

public opinion/popular opinion /ˌpʌblɪk ə'pɪnjən, ˌpɒpjələr ə'pɪnjən‖ˌpɑ:-/ [n U] what most of the people of a country think about a particular subject, idea, or problem: *Responding to public opinion, the government introduced new controls on guns.* | *Popular opinion is quite easily swayed by the* *media. | Public opinion should not influence every policy decision. | The shooting of an intruder by a farmer has sharply divided popular opinion.*

consensus /kən'sensəs/ [n C/U] a basic opinion with which most of the people in a particular group agree in a general way: *Events in Eastern Europe shifted popular consensus against a new generation of nuclear weapons.* | **+ that** *There was a growing consensus that the Prime Minister should resign.* | **consensus of opinion** *There appears to be a consensus of opinion that the pilot was not at fault.*

majority view /mə'dʒɒrɨti ˌvjuː‖-'dʒɔːr-/ [n singular] what most of the people in a group or a society think about something: *The majority view seems to be that we need more police officers on local streets. | The mayor was quick to point out that the racist group did not represent a majority view in the community.*

5 the official opinion of a person or group

- position
- line
- stance
- where sb stands

position /pə'zɪʃən/ [n C usually singular] what a government, political party, or a person has decided to be their official or public opinion: *It's important that the Socialists clarify their position before the conference.* | **+ on** *We have made our position on disarmament perfectly clear.* | **take a position** *She takes the position that all asylum seekers should be made welcome.*

line /laɪn/ [n C usually singular] the publicly stated opinion of a political party, government etc, which all their members are supposed to agree with **party/government/official etc line** *The whip's job is to persuade members of his party to support the party line on issues that come before Congress.* | **+ on** *What's his line on abortion?* | **take a line on sth** *There was pressure for the President to take a tough line on welfare issues.*

stance /stɑːns‖stæns/ [n C] the publicly stated opinion of a person, group, newspaper etc towards something, especially a political matter: *The political stance of the paper means it is unlikely to report the affair in a balanced way. | The official stance is that the lottery money should be used for the arts and education.* | **+ on** *His tough stance on crime appeals to voters.* | **take a stance on sth** *The council has taken a pro-growth, pro-business stance on development issues.*

where sb stands /weəʳ (sb) 'stændz/ the publicly stated opinion of a person or group, especially when previously this may not have been clear: *Voters need to know where each candidate stands.* | **+ on** *Where do the Democrats stand on the issue of sanctions?*

opposite

WHAT'S HERE

- **opposite/different** see **1 to 4**
- **opposite direction** see **5**
- **opposite/facing each other** see **6**

opposite/different

opposite ———————— **same**
see also **different**

1 when two things or people are completely different

- opposite
- be opposites
- reverse
- be the antithesis of

opposite /'ɒpəzɨt‖'ɑː-/ [adj] as different as possible from something else: *We have opposite viewpoints on almost everything. | During the summer there wasn't enough rain, but now we have the opposite problem. | Getting angry with him didn't work, so I tried the opposite approach.* | **the opposite result/effect/ conclusion etc** *The medicine was supposed to make him sleepy, but it had the opposite effect.*

be opposites /biː 'ɒpəzɪts‖-'ɑːp-/ [v phrase] if two people or things **are opposites**, they are as different as possible from each other: *Although the sweet and sour flavours are opposites, they combine very well in this oriental dish.* | **be complete opposites** *In both looks and personality the girls were complete opposites.* | **+ in** *We were alike in interests and tastes, but we were opposites in temperament.*

reverse /rɪ'vɜːʳs/ [adj only before noun] opposite to what is usual or to what has just been stated: *In some families the father goes out to work and the mother stays at home. In others, the reverse situation is true. | His advice had the reverse effect to that intended.*

be the antithesis of /biː ði æn'tɪθɨsɨs ɒv/ [v phrase] formal to be completely opposite in quality or character to something: *Love is the antithesis of selfishness. | His policies are the antitheses of all that makes us a decent, tolerant society.*

2 someone or something that is completely different from someone or something else

- the opposite
- the reverse
- the other way around
- vice versa
- go to the opposite extreme/go from one extreme to the other

the opposite /ði 'ɒpəzɨt‖-'ɑːp-/ [n singular] *Our first baby hardly ever cried in the night, but our second is the opposite – we never get any sleep.* | **+ of** *'Light' is the opposite of both 'dark' and 'heavy'.* | **do the opposite** *They asked for our advice and then did the opposite!* | **exactly/just the opposite** *I thought she'd be upset by the news, but her reaction was exactly the opposite.*

the reverse /ðə rɪ'vɜːʳs/ [n singular] formal the exact opposite of the situation, idea, process that has just been mentioned: *The acid must be added to the water – doing the reverse can be highly dangerous. | The economic situation is certainly improving, although widespread unemployment suggests the reverse.* | **+ of** *He said that the rioters had been killed accidentally, the reverse of what had actually happened.*

the other way around /round British /ðiː ˌʌðəʳ weɪ ə'raʊnd, 'raʊnd/ [n phrase] the opposite of what you thought or of what someone has just said: *No, the street was named after the college, not the other way around* (=the college was not named after the street). | *I thought he was the boss and she was his secretary, but in fact it was the other way around.*

vice versa /ˌvaɪs ˈvɜːʳsə, ˌvaɪsi-/ [adv] used to talk about the opposite of a situation that you have just mentioned: *Whenever I'm at home, my husband seems to be out, and vice versa* (=when I am out, he's at home)*!* | *Astronomers were still uncertain whether the Earth travelled around the Sun or vice-versa.* | *Dutch speakers can usually understand German quite well, but not vice versa.*

go to the opposite extreme/go from one extreme to the other /gəʊ tə ði ˌɒpəzɪt ɪkˈstriːm‖-ˌɑːp-, gəʊ frəm ˌwʌn ɪkˌstriːm tə ði ˈʌðəʳ/ [v phrase] to stop doing one thing far too much, but then start doing the opposite far too much: *She used to eat too much, but now she's gone to the opposite extreme and is practically starving herself.* | *Doug's gone from one extreme to the other – it used to be impossible to drag him away from the TV. Now we can't get him to stay home.*

3 opposite opinions, statements etc

- opposite
- opposing
- diametrically opposed
- on the contrary
- just the opposite/reverse

opposite /ˈɒpəzɪ̈t‖ˈɑːp-/ [adj] *We're good friends, but we have opposite views when it comes to politics.* | *It is strange how two scientists studying the same problem can come to completely opposite conclusions.* | *Margaret has very strong opinions, but she always tries to understand the opposite point of view.*

opposing /əˈpəʊzɪŋ/ [adj only before noun] **opposing** opinions, beliefs, statements etc are the opposite of each other: *Bobbie and Jo have opposing views on marriage.* | *Brad was prepared to accept that opposing beliefs could be held equally strongly and passionately.* | *The Party seems to be unsure which of two opposing political philosophies to follow.*

diametrically opposed /daɪəˌmetrɪkli əˈpəʊzd/ [adj] completely opposite to and completely disagreeing with each other: *He feels that his Christian beliefs and the principles of capitalism are diametrically opposed.*

on the contrary /ɒn ðe ˈkɒntrəri‖-ˈkɑːntreri/ [adv] formal spoken use this to tell someone that the opposite of what they say is true: *'Do you think the divorce will upset her family?' 'On the contrary. It will probably come as a relief.'* | *'You probably aren't interested in my opinion.' 'On the contrary, any ideas you have to add would be very welcome.'*

just the opposite/reverse ALSO **quite the opposite/reverse** especially British, spoken /ˌdʒʌst ði ˈɒpəzɪ̈t, rɪˈvɜːʳs, ˌkwaɪt ði ˈɒpəzɪ̈t, rɪˈvɜːʳs‖-ˈɑːp-/ [adv] use this to tell someone that the opposite of a situation or statement is true: *My friends say I spend too much time studying, but my parents say just the opposite.* | *We were not in love at the time – quite the opposite in fact.*

4 a statement or situation that contains two opposite ideas

- paradox

paradox /ˈpærədɒks‖-dɑːks/ [n C] a statement or situation that contains two opposite ideas or parts, so that it seems strange that they could both be true at the same time: *There's a paradox in the fact that although we're living longer than ever before, people are more obsessed with health issues than they ever were.* —**paradoxical** /ˌpærəˈdɒksɪ̈kəl‖-ˈdɑːks-/ [adj] *Raising interest rates seems a paradoxical way of bringing down inflation.* —**paradoxically** [adv] *Paradoxically, it's the parents who try to protect their children most who can make them unable to cope with risky situations on their own.*

opposite direction

opposite —— same
see also direction

5 in or from the opposite direction

- the other way
- the opposite direction/ the other direction
- in opposite directions

the other way /ði ˌʌðəʳ ˈweɪ/ [adv] in or from the opposite direction: *Turn around and face the other way.* | *I waved to her but she didn't see – she was looking the other way.* | *When you're overtaking, make sure there's nothing coming the other way.*

the opposite direction/the other direction /ði ˌɒpəzɪ̈t dɪ̈ˈrekʃən‖-ˌɑːp-, ði ˌʌðəʳ dɪ̈ˈrekʃən/ [n phrase] **in the opposite/other direction** *The driver sped off in the opposite direction.* | *Gloria and Mae set off one way while Ruth and Sarah went in the other direction.* | **from the opposite direction** *While everyone was watching the action on the left of the stage, the dancers entered from the opposite direction*

in opposite directions /ɪn ˌɒpəzɪ̈t dɪ̈ˈrekʃənz‖-ˌɑːp-/ [adv] moving or facing in the opposite direction from each other: *There were two paths going in opposite directions.* | *Two trains travelling in opposite directions crashed, killing twenty passengers.*

opposite/facing each other

6 to be opposite something or someone

- opposite
- face
- across
- face to face
- on the other side

opposite /ˈɒpəzɪ̈t‖ˈɑːp-/ [adv/prep/adj] something that is **opposite** something else is facing it, for example on the other side of the street or on the other side of a table. In American English this is not used as an adverb: *The bathroom is opposite the bedroom.* | *When you get off the bus, you'll see a grocery store on the opposite side of the street.* | **directly opposite** (=exactly opposite) *The entrance to the park is directly opposite our house.* | **diagonally opposite** (=opposite and to one side) *Diagonally opposite the stove is a large stone sink.* | **the house/chair/man etc opposite** *Pointing to the chair opposite, he said 'Come and talk to me for a while'.* | **sit/stand etc opposite** *There was a thin dark woman sitting opposite me.* | **live opposite** (=to live in the opposite house) *The only contact she has is with the woman who lives opposite.*

face /feɪs/ [v T] if one person, building, seat etc **faces** another, they are opposite each other, and each has their front towards the other: *Courtney's apartment faces the harbour.* | *The seat facing mine was empty.* | *They stood facing each other for a few minutes.*

across /əˈkrɒs‖əˈkrɔːs/ [prep] **across the street/road/river/table etc** opposite from where you are, and on the other side of the street, road etc: *She lives across the road.* | *The prisoners' cells faced each other across an aisle.* | **across the street/road etc from sb/sth** *Bill sat down across the desk from him.* | *Across the street from where we were standing was a little park.* | **+ from** (=across the road from a place) *There's a hotel across from the station where we can go.*

face to face /ˌfeɪs tə ˈfeɪs/ [adv] if two people are **face to face**, they are very close to and facing each other **sit/stand face to face** *We sat face to face across a narrow table.* | *They stood face to face, each struggling to control his temper.* | **come face to face with sb** (=suddenly and unexpectedly face someone) *Turning the corner I came face to face with a security guard.*

on the other side /ɒn ði ˌʌðəʳ ˈsaɪd/ [adv] on the opposite side of something: *If you look across the lake, you can see Donald's house on the other side.* | **+ of** *You can park on the other side of the road.* | *There was a little boat moored on the other side of the river.*

order

the order in which things are arranged or the order in which things happen

RELATED WORDS

- order someone to do something *see* **tell (17-24)**
- order a meal, drink etc *see* **ask (9)**
- put things in order *see* **arrange**
- when everything is properly organized *see* **organize**
- in order to do sth *see* **in order to**
- *see also* **after, before, last, first**

1 order

- **order**
- **sequence**
- **pattern**

order /ˈɔːʳdəʳ/ [n C/U] the way that events happen or that information is arranged, showing which is first, which is second, and so on **in this/that/what/any order** *It doesn't matter which order you answer the questions in.* | *Movie scenes are not shot in the order in which they are shown.* | **+ of** *We were given a printed sheet showing the order of events for the day.* | **in order of importance/difficulty/size etc** (=when the most important thing is first, then the next most important etc) *List three choices in order of preference.* | *The subjects that students enjoyed most were, in order of popularity, music, history, and art.* | **in alphabetical order** (=with 'a' first, then 'b', then 'c' etc) *The games were displayed on a long wall, in alphabetical order, from Acrobats to Wheel of Fortune.*

sequence /ˈsiːkwəns/ [n C] the specific order in which a number of events, actions, or pieces of information follow one another: *White, who is doing research on the disease, was able to determine its DNA sequence.* | **+ of** *The dance is basically a sequence of steps that you repeat over and over again.* | *Basic computer code consists of sequences of ones and zeros.* | **in sequence** *X-rays are taken in rapid sequence to get an image of the arteries leading to the heart.*

pattern /ˈpætən‖ˈpætərn/ [n C] the order in which things usually happen or someone usually does something, which you notice because it seems to be regular: *Women's lives used to follow a predictable pattern: school, then marriage and children.* | **+ of** *Critics of the police say they see a pattern of racism and abuse by officers.* | **follow a pattern** (=happen in the same way) *Police say that each of the murders follows the same pattern.*

2 in the correct order

- **in the right order**
- **the right way round**

in the right order /ɪn ðə ˌraɪt ˈɔːʳdəʳ/ [adv] *Are all the pages in the right order?* | *It is important to add each ingredient in the right order.*

the right way round /ðə ˌraɪt weɪ ˈraʊnd/ [adv] British in the order that people expect or consider to be correct, especially after being in the wrong order: *Mark the pieces so that you put them back the right way round.*

3 in the wrong order

- **in the wrong order/out of order**
- **mixed up**
- **the wrong way round**
- **backwards**

in the wrong order/out of order /ɪn ðə ˌrɒŋ ˈɔːʳdəʳ‖-ˌrɔːŋ-, ˌaʊt əv ˈɔːʳdəʳ/ [adv] *A cake can be ruined by adding ingredients in the wrong order.* | *The files were completely out of order.*

mixed up /ˌmɪkst ˈʌp/ [adj not before noun] in the wrong order: *The letters are all mixed up and you have to put them in the right order.* | *The pages were all mixed up, and I only have five minutes before the deadline.*

the wrong way round /ðə ˌrɒŋ weɪ ˈraʊnd‖-ˌrɔːŋ- / [adv] British in the wrong order, especially when there is only one order that people expect or consider to be correct: *The printer made an error and the pages were bound the wrong way round.*

backwards ALSO **backward** American /ˈbækwəʳd(z)/ [adv] starting at the end and finishing at the beginning: *Can you say the alphabet backwards?* | *Count backward from 10.*

4 doing things one after the other

- **in order**
- **one by one/one after another**
- **in turn**
- **take turns**

in order /ɪn ˈɔːʳdəʳ/ [adv] *It's easier if you count things up in order, so that you don't get confused.* | *A route is given to the postman, and he makes deliveries in order.*

one by one/one after another /ˌwʌn baɪ ˈwʌn, ˌwʌn ɑːftər əˈnʌðəʳ‖-æf-/ [adv] doing things separately and in a particular order, rather than all together: *One by one, the students were called in to be interviewed.* | *The toy is made so that when you hold the top square, the rest fall down one after another, making a clacking noise.*

in turn /ɪn ˈtɜːʳn/ [adv] one person, then the next, then the next etc: *I was hard on my eldest son, and he, in turn, was mean to his little brother.* | *We distribute the book to charities, and those organizations in turn give the books to needy children.*

take turns ALSO **take it in turns** British /ˌteɪk ˈtɜːʳnz, ˌteɪk ɪt ɪn ˈtɜːʳnz/ [v phrase] if two or more people **take turns** or **take it in turns** to do something, they decide to do it in order, one person after another, so that it is shared equally and fairly:

Small children find it almost impossible to take turns. | **take turns doing sth** *We take turns doing the dishes.* | **take turns to do sth** *Mandy and Debbie took it in turns to look after the baby.*

organization

RELATED WORDS

- part of an organization *see* **part (4)**
- *see also* **group, company (7-10), member, join, leave (22-26)**

1 a large well organized group of people who work together

- **organization**
- **institute**
- **institution**

organization ALSO **organisation** British /ˌɔːʳgənaɪˈzeɪʃən‖ -gənə-/ [n C] a large group of people who work together in business, politics, education, sport etc: *Greenpeace is an international organization that works to protect the environment.* | *one of Europe's leading human rights organizations* | *Most big organizations employ their own legal experts.* | *the World Health Organization*

institution /ˌɪnstɪ̇ˈtjuːʃən‖-ˈtuː-/ [n C] an organization that does educational, scientific, or financial work, especially a large and important organization that has existed for a long time **financial/educational/medical institution** *The change in the law has been welcomed by banks, insurance companies, and other financial institutions.* | *A major study of women and heart disease is being carried out by the Johns Hopkins Medical Institution.*

institute /ˈɪnstɪ̇tjuːt‖-tuːt/ [n C] an educational, scientific, or professional organization: *My colleague is a scientist at the Massachusetts Institute of Technology.* | *the National Cancer Institute* | *The work was carried out by the Silsoe Research Institute in Bedfordshire.*

2 an official organization that has political aims or responsibilities

- **party**
- **bureau**
- **authority**
- **body**
- **council**

party /ˈpɑːʳti/ [n C with singular or plural verb in British English] an organization of people who all have the same political ideas, which you can vote for in elections: *The Republican Party now has a majority in Congress.* | **political party** *All the major political parties have given their support to this initiative.* | **join a party** *He first joined the Communist party when he was a student.* | **party member** *All party members will have the right to vote for the new leader.*

authority /ɔːˈθɒrɪ̇ti, ə-‖əˈθɑː-, əˈθɔː-/ [n C with singular or plural verb in British English] an official organization, or a local government department, which has power in public affairs, provides public services etc: *The number of complaints received by the Police Complaints Authority has risen sharply in recent years.* | **health authority** British *Contact your local health authority for details of the scheme in your area.*

council /ˈkaʊnsəl/ [n C with singular or plural verb in British English] an official organization responsible for the public services in a town or area, or a large organization which represents particular people: *A complaints system is being set up to make it easier for residents to complain about the service that the council offers.* | *The club got a grant from the Sports Council to help pay for new changing rooms.* | **town/city/county council** *She's been elected onto the city council.* | *The plan for the new housing development is now being considered by Essex County Council.*

bureau /ˈbjʊərəʊ/ [n C] American a government department with particular responsibilities: *the Federal Bureau of Investigations* | *He is now Director of the Maritime Transport Bureau.*

body /ˈbɒdi‖ˈbɑːdi/ [n C with singular or plural verb in British English] any organization made up of people working together, especially in government, making laws or advising people **governing body** *UEFA is the governing body for European football.* | **advisory body** *Belfast City Airport Forum is a new advisory body set up to discuss environmental issues affecting the airport and the surrounding area.*

3 an organization that gives help or advice

- **charity**
- **trust**
- **fund**

charity /ˈtʃærɪ̇ti/ [n C with singular or plural verb in British English] an organization which raises money in order to help people who are poor, ill etc, and does not make any profit for itself: *All the major charities are appealing for funds to help the victims of the disaster.* | *My mother does a lot of fund raising for local charities.*

fund /fʌnd/ [n C] an organization that collects money and uses it to help people or do some other good work: *New York's Inner City Scholarship Fund pays the college fees of students from poorer families.* | *All the money raised will be donated to the Cancer Research Fund.*

trust /trʌst/ [n C with singular or plural verb in British English] British an organization that receives money which it then uses to help people or do some other good work: *A new trust has been set up to promote the arts in inner city areas.* | *The Mental Health Trust works to raise awareness of mental illness and help people suffering from mental problems.*

4 an organization for people who have the same interests or aims

- **club**
- **union**
- **society**
- **league**
- **association**
- **federation**

club /klʌb/ [n C with singular or plural verb in British English] a group of people who meet regularly to do something that they are all interested in, for example a particular activity or sport: *They've set up a chess club at school.* | *the North Manchester Judo Club* | **join a club** *Why don't you join your local swimming club if you're keen on swimming?* | **belong to a club** (=be a member of a club) *They both belong to the local tennis club.*

society /səˈsaɪɪ̇ti/ [n C] an organization for people who have the same interest or aim, especially a large official organization: *He joined the university film society as a way of making friends.* | *the Royal Society for the Protection of Birds* | *the president of the American Historical Society*

association /əˌsəʊsiˈeɪʃən, əˌsəʊʃi-/ [n C] an important organization for people in a particular profession, activity, sport etc, which officially represents its members and has the power to make rules: *The new health care proposals have been criticized by the British Medical Association.* | *The National Basketball Association negotiates TV rights for important games.* | **+ of** *the National Association of Head Teachers*

union /ˈjuːnjən/ [n C] an organization formed by workers to protect their rights and improve their pay and working conditions: *The largest teachers' union supports the education reforms.* | **+ of** *the National Union of Mineworkers.* | **trade union** British **labor union** American *The President could not rely on the support of the labor unions.* | **join a union** *Some workers refused to join the union.*

league /liːg/ [n C with singular or plural verb in British English] an organization consisting of people, countries, or groups that have joined together because they have the same aim: *The League of Nations was formed to promote international peace and security.* | *Morocco is a member of the Arab League.* | *Leaders of the Football League met to discuss the problems of violence at football games.*

federation /ˌfedəˈreɪʃən/ [n C with singular or plural verb in British English] a group of separate organizations or clubs which have joined together to help and support each other: *He is now chairman of the British Olympic Federation.* | *Her case was supported by the Chicago Teachers Federation.* | **+ of** *the National Federation of Master Builders*

organize

- to put things or people in a particular order *see* **arrange**
- to do something or arrange for something to happen *see* **arrange**
- *see also* **order, plan, system, efficient/not efficient, effective/not effective, tidy, untidy**

1 to arrange something in a particular way

- organize
- sort out
- structure

organize ALSO **organise** British /ˈɔːʳgənaɪz/ [v T] to arrange something so that it is clear, effective, or tidy: *I like the way you've organized the information in the report.* | *You need to organize your financial records and figure out exactly how much money you owe.* | **organize sth into groups/piles/sections etc** *The paintings in the exhibition are organized into five sections.* —**organization** also **organisation** British /ˌɔːʳgənaɪˈzeɪʃən‖-gənə-/ [n U] the way something is organized: *Getting the project finished on time required careful organization and a lot of teamwork.*

sort out /ˌsɔːʳt ˈaʊt/ [phr v T] to organize a group of things that is mixed up or untidy, or organize a lot of information that is confusing or unclear **sort out sth** *After class we needed time to sort out the enormous amount of information we had been given.* | *First let's sort out all the pieces before we try putting them together.* | **sort sth out** *When are you going to sort all these files out?*

structure /ˈstrʌktʃəʳ/ [v T] to carefully organize a piece of writing or a system so that it is easy to understand or use: *I have structured the book so that the main points are revisited several times.* | *If we structure the meeting effectively, I think we should be able to cover everything.* —**structure** [n U] *The structure of the U.S. education system lacks centralization.*

2 when something is organized so that it works well

- organized
- well-organized
- structured
- well-run
- well-ordered
- order

organized ALSO **organised** British /ˈɔːʳgənaɪzd/ [adj] arranged in a way that is effective and likely to be successful: *Tonight after supper we want to have a more organized discussion.* | *Bernstein was convinced that an organized effort had been made to conceal the facts of the case.* | *Anti-war dissent erupted into organized demonstrations several times in the Johnson administration.*

well-organized ALSO **well-organised** British /ˌwel ˈɔːʳgənaɪzd/ [adj] organized in a careful and thorough way, so that everything works very well: *The exhibition was very well organized.* | *Both candidates ran effective well-organized campaigns.* | *A well-organized network of women's groups has led the call for equal rights.*

structured /ˈstrʌktʃəʳd/ [adj] information, methods, or systems that are **structured** are organized so that they have a clear and carefully organized structure that is easy to use or understand: *a structured learning plan* | *The situation has made us aware of the need for a more structured approach to dealing with prisoners' problems.* | **well-structured** *Here are some steps for creating a well-structured document.* | **highly structured** *The social workers' home visits are highly structured, with specific goals and learning objectives.*

well-run /ˌwel ˈrʌn/ [adj] a business or organization that is **well-run** is efficient because of good management and organization: *The Klausner is a comfortable well-run hotel.* | *The city's transportation system is clean, safe, and well run.*

well-ordered /ˌwel ˈɔːʳdəʳd◂/ [adj] a **well-ordered** place, organization, way of life etc has been carefully organized so that nothing goes wrong, nothing unexpected happens, and everything is where it should be: *Mary has such a well-ordered household – it makes ours look like total chaos.* | *The town was a neat, well-ordered, red brick town dotted with trees.*

order /ˈɔːʳdəʳ/ [n U] a situation in which everything is controlled, well organized, and correctly arranged: *Can we have a bit of order here? Someone straighten those desks out to start with!* | **impose order** (=give something order) *He developed a filing system to try to impose order on the mass of information.*

3 when something is not organized well

- disorganized
- badly organized
- badly run
- chaotic
- be a mess/be a shambles
- in disarray

disorganized ALSO **disorganised** British /dɪsˈɔːʳgənaɪzd/ [adj] not arranged according to any kind of order or plan: *She gave a long disorganized speech that left everyone confused.* | **totally/completely disorganized** *Her files were completely disorganized – she could never find anything she wanted.* | *a totally disorganized rescue effort*

badly organized ALSO **badly organised** British /ˌbædli 'ɔːʳɡənaɪzd/ [adj] not well organized – use this about events or activities that are not successful, because they have not been planned well: *The festival was very badly organized – nobody seemed to know what they were doing.* | *There was widespread criticism that the relief operation was slow and badly organized.*

badly run /ˌbædli 'rʌn/ [adj] a business or organization that is **badly run** produces bad results because it is badly managed or organized: *The company is not badly run, but it still has not made a profit.* | *Critics say that the mayor's office is badly run and corrupt.*

chaotic /keɪ'ɒtɪk‖-'ɑːtɪk/ [adj] extremely disorganized: *The city is a sprawling chaotic metropolis of some eight million residents.* | *Newscasts continued to broadcast images of the chaotic minutes after the shooting.* | *We flew on the day after Christmas and the situation at the airport was completely chaotic.*

be a mess/be a shambles /biː ə 'mes, biː ə 'ʃæmbəlz/ [v phrase] informal if a situation or event **is a mess** or **a shambles**, it is very badly organized or badly controlled, and nothing good or useful is being achieved: *The social security system in this country is a mess.* | **a complete/hopeless etc mess** *The whole conference was a complete mess from start to finish.* | **in a mess/shambles** *The prolonged war has left the nation's economy in a shambles.*

in disarray /ɪn ˌdɪsə'reɪ/ [adv] if a group such as a political party is **in disarray**, it is disorganized and no longer effective, especially because the people who belong to it cannot agree with each other and cannot work together: *The defeated army retreated in disarray.* | **in complete/total etc disarray** *The Democrats were in complete disarray after last year's disastrous elections.* | **throw sth into disarray** (=make it become disorganized) *The chairman's resignation threw the organization into disarray.*

4 a disorganized situation

- chaos
- disorder
- confusion

chaos /'keɪ-ɒs‖-ɑːs/ [n U] a situation in which everything or everyone seems to be extremely disorganized or completely out of control: *The earthquake caused widespread chaos throughout the region.* | **in chaos** *When McNamara got the job, the department was in chaos.* | **complete/utter/total etc chaos** *Passengers spoke of complete chaos as the fire spread through the ship.* | **political/social/economic etc chaos** *Zbitski said the reform coalition must find a way to steer the country out of its political and economic chaos.*

disorder /dɪs'ɔːʳdəʳ/ [n U] formal a situation in which things are disorganized or untidy, or people are disorganized and out of control **in disorder** *After several hours of fierce fighting, the rebel troops retreated in disorder.* | *The entire apartment was in disorder, but nothing seemed to have been stolen.* | **civil/social/public disorder** *The country's civil war came at the end of a long period of social disorder.*

confusion /kən'fjuːʒən/ [n U] a situation in which no one is sure what is happening and there is a lot of noise and activity: *The bombers escaped in the confusion following the explosion.* | *We made our way through the noise and confusion of the marketplace to our hotel.*

5 someone who always organizes their work, life etc well

- organized
- businesslike
- together

organized ALSO **organised** British /'ɔːʳɡənaɪzd/ [adj] *In order to do this job well, you have to be very organized.* | **well-organized** *Well-organized troops have succeeded in recapturing the town.*

businesslike /'bɪznə̇s-laɪk/ [adj] someone who is **businesslike** deals with people effectively and does not waste time on things that are not important: *Ted was friendly but businesslike and very much in charge.* | *Gates gave a brief, businesslike explanation of his plans for the company.* | *The representatives were serious businesslike diplomats who disliked small talk.*

together /tə'geðəʳ/ [adj] informal use this about someone who always thinks clearly and does things in a sensible, organized way that you admire: *You'll have to be a bit more together when you have kids.* | *Rosie's a really together person – she'll be great as the coordinator.*

6 someone who organizes their work, life etc badly

- disorganized
- not very (well) organized
- sb hasn't got it together/sb doesn't have it together

disorganized /dɪs'ɔːʳɡənaɪzd/ [adj] *Graham's far too disorganized to be a good teacher.* | *I'm sorry I'm so disorganized – I just haven't had time to get everything ready.* | **completely/hopelessly disorganized** *It's no use asking her to do anything – she's completely disorganized.*

not very (well) organized /ˌnɒt veri (wel) 'ɔːʳɡənaɪzd/ [v phrase] especially spoken use this to say that someone does not organize their work, life etc very well. **Not very organized** is not as strong as **disorganized**.: *He's a nice guy, but he's not very organized and he forgets a lot of things.* | *I'm not a very organized person – maybe you should ask somebody else to make the arrangements.*

sb hasn't got it together/sb doesn't have it together / (sb) ˌhæzənt gɒt ɪt tə'geðəʳ‖-gɑːt-, (sb) ˌdʌzənt hæv ɪt tə'geðəʳ/ informal use this about someone who has not organized their work, life etc in a sensible way and therefore has been unable to be successful: *He hasn't got it together enough to go out and get a job.* | *Kim has to do all the wedding planning, because her fiancé just doesn't have it together.*

out/outside

RELATED WORDS

opposite: **in/inside**

▸ to not be at home *see* **home**

1 not inside a building

- outside
- out
- outdoors/out of doors
- in the open air

outside /aʊt'saɪd/ [adv] *When I woke up it was still dark outside.* | *It's such a nice day. Why don't you* *play outside? | Outside, joggers in shorts and t-shirts ran by.*

out /aʊt/ [adv] **out in/under/there etc** *Parents stood out in the rain waiting to collect their children from school. | We camped and slept out under the stars every night. | What's that dog doing out there in our yard?*

outdoors/out of doors /ˌaʊtˈdɔːʳz, ˌaʊt əv ˈdɔːʳz/ [adv] not inside any buildings – use this especially to talk about pleasant or healthy things that you do outside: *We often eat outdoors on summer evenings. | Kids should spend as much time out of doors as possible. | Move the pots outdoors as soon as there is no more danger of frost.*

in the open air /ɪn ði ˌəʊpən ˈeəʳ/ [adv] not inside a building, but outside where the air is fresh: *Mexicans traditionally dry chillies in the open air. |* **out in the open air** *It was nice to be out in the open air after being stuck in the office all day.*

2 outside a place, country, organization etc

- outside
- out of
- the outside world

outside ALSO **outside of** American /aʊtˈsaɪd, aʊtˈsaɪd ɒv/ [prep] *It was the Emperor's first journey outside Japan since 1921. | This is the only museum of its kind outside London. | He is well-regarded even outside of the company.*

out of /ˈaʊt ɒv/ [prep] not in the place where you usually are: *She'd been out of the country for three months, traveling in Europe. | The prisoners spend only four hours a day out of their cells.*

the outside world /ði ˌaʊtsaɪd ˈwɜːʳld/ [n phrase] the rest of the world, which you do not know about or do not have many connections with, because you only know a particular small place and small group of people: *At the time, the country prevented citizens from having any relations with the outside world. | Many of the prisoners have no contact at all with the outside world. | Telephone and cable lines link your home office to the outside world.*

3 close to a place, town etc, but not in it

- outside
- out of

outside ALSO **outside of** American /aʊtˈsaɪd, aʊtˈsaɪd ɒv/ [prep] *Most of the development is outside the city centre. | He first played hockey on frozen ponds outside of town. |* **just outside** (=very close to a place) *The university is situated on a hill just outside the city. |* **two miles/three kilometres etc outside** (=two miles etc away from a place) *The train stopped three miles outside Doncaster.*

out of /ˈaʊt ɒv/ [prep] **two miles/three kilometres etc out of** (=two miles etc away from a place) *The car broke down just a few miles out of town. |* **ten minutes/two hours etc out of** *Mason's farm is about ten minutes' drive out of the town of Taber.*

4 not in a room or building but close to it

- outside
- out

outside ALSO **outside of** American /aʊtˈsaɪd, aʊtˈsaɪd ɒv/ [adv/prep] *Could you wait outside, please? | Some people were collecting for charity outside of the supermarket. | A crowd of people were standing outside the theatre. |* **just outside** (=very close to a room or building) *The car was parked just outside the house, on the driveway.*

out /aʊt/ [adv] **out here/there/in etc** *You go on in. I'll wait out here. | Leave your coat out in the hallway.*

5 moving or looking away from the inside of something

- out
- out of
- outside
- out
- outwards

out /aʊt/ [adv] moving or looking away from the inside of a place, building, container etc: *Janice opened the door and looked out. | Two firemen carried his body out and laid it on the ground. | When I dropped my bag, some of my money must have fallen out. |* **out came/jumped/fell etc** *I heard meowing, opened the trunk of the car, and out jumped a thin black cat.*

out of /ˈaʊt ɒv/ [prep] moving or looking away from the inside of a place, building, container etc: *She's coming out of the office now. | Don't lean so far out of the window. It's dangerous. | Thousands of refugees are now streaming out of the city.*

outside /aʊtˈsaɪd, ˈaʊtsaɪd/ [adv/prep] out of a building or room: *Why don't you go outside and get some fresh air? | I walked outside to the car. | The police asked each person in turn to step outside the room for questioning.*

out ALSO **out of** /aʊt, ˈaʊt ɒv/ [prep] **out the door/window** moving or looking **out** of the door or window: *She ran out the door and down the street. | If you look out of the bedroom window, you can see the ocean. | Hey, look out the window! See the hot-air balloon?*

outwards British **/outward** American /ˈaʊtwəʳd(z)/ [adv] away from the inside or centre, towards the outside: *The windows open outward. | As the plane exploded, the metal of the fuselage was blown outwards. | London is expanding outwards at an alarming rate, swallowing up large areas of beautiful countryside.*

6 on or covering the outside of something

- external
- outer

external /ɪkˈstɜːʳnl/ [adj only before noun] *The external walls of the castle are beginning to crumble. | Most backpacks today have internal rather than external frames | There are no external signs of injury.*

outer /ˈaʊtəʳ/ [adj only before noun] **outer skin/layer/wall/shell etc** on the outside of something: *Boil the beans for ten minutes and then remove the tough outer skin. | the rocks that make up the outer layers of the Earth's surface | the outer wall of the temple*

7 the part of something that you see from the outside

- the outside
- the exterior

the outside /ði ˈaʊtsaɪd/ [n singular] *The outside is green, the inside is blue. |* **+ of** *The outside of the house needs painting. |* **on the outside** *The emergency blankets are lined with plastic on the outside* *and paper on the inside.* | **from the outside** *The door can only be locked from the outside.*

the exterior /ðiː ɪk'stɪəriəʳ/ [n singular] the outside part or surface of a building, vehicle etc – used especially in technical contexts: *The building has an attractive wood exterior.* | **+ of** *The exterior of Durham cathedral is one of the most magnificent in England.* | *Clean the exterior of the car thoroughly before applying paint.*

8 happening or existing outside a building rather than inside

- outside
- outdoor
- open-air

outside /'aʊtsaɪd/ [adj only before noun] **outside toilet/staircase/door etc** one that is **outside** or on the **outside** of a building: *When my dad was growing up, they only had an outside toilet.* | *You reach the apartment by going up an outside staircase at the back of the building.*

outdoor /ˌaʊt'dɔːʳ◂/ [adj only before noun] happening, existing, used outside etc: *The hotel has an outdoor swimming pool.* | *The program of outdoor activities includes skiing, climbing, and hiking.* | *Younger volunteers tend to prefer outdoor work.*

open-air /ˌəʊpən 'eəʳ/ [adj only before noun] **open-air cafe/restaurant/market/meeting/concert etc** one that is outside, especially because it is pleasant to be outside: *We had lunch at an open-air cafe in the city square.* | *There's a big open-air market there on Saturdays.* | *In summer there are open-air concerts and theatre performances in the park.*

9 coming from outside a country or organization

- outside
- external
- outsider

outside /'aʊtsaɪd/ [adj only before noun] **outside consultants/workers/observers etc** people who do not belong to a particular company or organization: *Outside observers believe that the election was conducted fairly.* | *There were seven applicants for the position, including three outside candidates.* | *The government uses outside contractors for some of the work.*

external /ɪk'stɜːʳnl/ [adj only before noun] **external interference/pressure/forces etc** from outside a particular country or organization: *Without external pressure, it is unlikely the civil rights abuses would have stopped.* | *An external auditor is brought in to examine the accounts.*

outsider /aʊt'saɪdəʳ/ [n C] a person who does not belong in a particular group or organization or who is not accepted by it: *An outsider, for example someone from another school district, should evaluate the teachers.* | *The university library is closed to outsiders.* | *We don't want outsiders getting involved in our local politics.*

owe

RELATED WORDS

▸ *see also* **borrow, lend, pay, money**

1 to owe money to someone

- owe
- be in debt
- be overdrawn
- be in the red
- be in arrears
- be behind with

owe /əʊ/ [v T] if you **owe** someone money, you have to pay them, either because you borrowed money from them or because you got something from them and have not yet paid for it: *The business collapsed, owing $50 million.* | *His job was to phone people who owed money and demand immediate payment.* | **owe sb sth** *You still owe me $5.* | **owe sth to sb** *We owe a lot of money to the bank.* | **owe sb sth for sth** *How much do we owe you for the milk?*

be in debt /biː ɪn 'det/ [v phrase] if you **are in debt**, you owe a lot of money and you have difficulty paying it: *The helpline offers financial advice to people who are in debt.* | **get into debt** (=start being in debt) *We got into debt when my wife lost her job.* | **be £1000/$2000 etc in debt** (=owe that amount) *The report showed that most students were over £1000 in debt on leaving college.* | **be heavily in debt** (=owe a very large amount of money) *Karen was forced to give up her job to look after her daughter, and the family is now heavily in debt.*

be overdrawn /biː ˌəʊvəʳ'drɔːn/ [v phrase] to owe money to your bank because you have spent more than you had in your bank account: *I'm always overdrawn at the end of the month.* | **be $100/£200 etc overdrawn** *The bank wrote to tell us we were $500 overdrawn.*

be in the red /biː ɪn ðə 'red/ [v phrase] to have spent more than you have earned: *My son's bank account is usually in the red.* | *After five quarters in the red, the business will soon be profitable.* | **be deep in the red** (=owe a lot more than you have) *Overseas payments could keep the country deep in the red for the next decade.*

be in arrears /biː ɪn ə'rɪəʳz/ [v phrase] to have not paid money, such as rent, that you should pay at a particular time every month, year etc – used especially in official or legal documents: *Two out of three tenants are in arrears.* | **be 6 months/3 weeks etc in arrears** *The number of mortgages over 12 months in arrears is rising.* | **be £1000/$200 etc in arrears** *The country is reported to be $6 billion in arrears on its $115 billion debt.* | **+ with/on** *The courts can obtain payments for those in arrears with consumer credit agreements.*

be behind with /biː bɪ'haɪnd wɪð/ [v phrase] to have not paid an amount that you should pay regularly at the right time: *I have no money in my bank account, and I'm behind with my rent.* | **fall behind with sth** *Unemployment is the major cause of people falling behind with their mortgage repayments.*

2 to owe a lot of money

- be deep/heavily in debt
- be up to your neck/ears in debt

be deep/heavily in debt /biː ˌdiːp, ˌhevɪli ɪn 'det/ [v phrase] to owe a lot more money than you can pay: *When my father died we discovered that he was* *heavily in debt.* | *A disastrous attempt to expand left the airline deep in debt.* | **+ to** *The country is already heavily in debt to foreign banks.*

be up to your neck/ears in debt /biː ˌʌp tə jɔːʳ ˌnek, ˌɪəʳz ɪn 'det/ [v phrase] informal to owe very large sums of money that you cannot pay: *Knowing that I was up to my ears in debt, Edwin offered to help me out.* | *When their business failed, they found themselves up to their necks in debt.*

3 to begin to owe money

- get into debt
- run up a debt
- default

get into debt /ˌget ɪntə 'det/ [v phrase] *The only way we could avoid getting into debt was to borrow money from our parents.* | **get heavily into debt** (=begin to owe a lot of money) *They got so heavily into debt that they couldn't even pay the interest on their loans.*

run up a debt /ˌrʌn ʌp ə 'det/ [v phrase] to allow your debts to increase quickly, especially by continuing to spend money that you do not really have: *The government has run up an unrepayable debt of $6 billion.* | **run up debts** *I'm not in the habit of running up debts.* | *His son was wild and irresponsible and had run up debts that he expected his father to pay.*

default /dɪ'fɔːlt/ [v I] to not pay back a debt that you should pay according to the law: *If the purchaser defaults, the house becomes the property of the savings and loan company.* | **+ on** *In those days, anyone who defaulted on a loan was put in prison.* — **default** [n C/U] *Loans are often refused to poorer borrowers because the risk of default is greater.*

4 money that someone owes

- debt
- overdraft
- liabilities
- borrowings
- IOU

debt /det/ [n C/U] money that you owe, especially a large amount: *Debt is one of the main social problems of our time.* | **+ of** *The government now has debts of $2.5 billion.* | **pay off/repay a debt** (=pay all the money that you owe) *It took us three years to pay off all our debts.* | **write off a debt** (=agree that it will not and does not need to be repaid) *He protected less profitable state farms by writing off their debts.* | **foreign debt** (=money owed by foreign countries) *To pay the interest on our foreign debt, we will have to import less.* | **a bad debt** (=a debt that will never be repaid) *Lenders must try and protect themselves against bad debts.*

overdraft /'əʊvəʳdrɑːft‖-dræft/ [n C] an amount of money that you owe to your bank when you have spent more money that you had in your bank account: *I've already got an enormous overdraft.* | **a £100/$1500 etc overdraft** *When he left college, he had a $3000 overdraft.*

liabilities /ˌlaɪə'bɪlɨtiz/ [n plural] the debts that a company, government etc is legally responsible to pay – used especially in legal and business contexts: *The chart shows the movements in the company's liabilities and assets during a particular trading period.* | *US external net liabilities rose throughout the 1980s.*

borrowings /'bɒrəʊɪŋz‖'bɑː-, 'bɔː-/ [n plural] the total amount of money that a company has borrowed and owes – used in business contexts: *Borrowings at the end of the year amounted to nearly $27 million.* | *The company was now so large it could increase its borrowings to almost any figure it chose.*

IOU /ˌaɪ əʊ 'juː/ [n C] a note that you write saying that you owe someone money or that you will pay for something later – often used by journalists as an informal word for a legal agreement in which one business or organization owes another money: *Essentially, a bond is an IOU.* | **give sb an IOU** *There was anger among farmers, who were being given IOUs instead of cash for their crops.*

5 when debts have not been paid

- unpaid
- due
- outstanding
- owing

unpaid /ˌʌn'peɪd◂/ [adj] *She left a number of unpaid bills when she went back home.* | *The card holder is liable for any unpaid debts.* | **go/remain unpaid** *Last month they owed £500. This went unpaid and the arrears will total £1000 by December.*

due /djuː‖duː/ [adj not before noun] an amount of money that is **due** should be paid now: *The computer printout shows the name and address of the buyer, the quantity ordered and the amount due.* | *Million dollar interest payments will be due in two years.*

outstanding /aʊt'stændɪŋ/ [adj] an amount of money that is **outstanding** is still owed to someone: *The government plans to reduce its outstanding debt, freeing capital for investment.* | *The amount outstanding on your house mortgage and any other loans will be counted as liabilities.*

owing /'əʊɪŋ/ [adj not before noun] an amount of money that is **owing** is still left to be paid: *The total amount owing at the end of ten years will be over $20,000.* | *Most of the money has been repaid but there is still £5 owing.*

6 someone who owes money

- debtor

debtor /'detəʳ/ [n C] *Some of the debtors cannot afford to pay these high interest rates.* | *Usually, both creditors and debtors are excluded from the sale.* | **a debtor company/country** *Debtor countries cannot develop to their full potential while continuing to pay off such massive foreign debts.*

7 someone that money is owed to

- creditor

creditor /'kredɨtəʳ/ [n C] *When George inherited some money, the first thing he did was to pay his creditors.* | *The UN warned creditors to ease Brazil's debt burden or see the country go bankrupt.*

8 to not owe any money

- be in credit
- be in the black
- keep your head above water
- solvent
- afloat

be in credit /biː ɪn 'kredɨt/ [v phrase] if your bank account **is in credit,** there is money in it and you do not owe the bank anything: *I can see from my monthly bank statements whether I'm in credit or not.* | **remain/stay in credit** *We offer free banking for customers whose accounts remain in credit.*

be in the black /biː ɪn ðə 'blæk/ [v phrase] if someone is **in the black**, they have earned more than they owe or have spent: *The newly reorganized company is now in the black.* | *Our oil and gas operations are comfortably in the black.* | **get sth into the black** *We have to get our account into the black otherwise the bank will never give us a mortgage.*

keep your head above water /kiːp jɔːʳ ˌhed əbʌv 'wɔːtəʳ/ [v phrase] informal to stay out of debt, although it is difficult to do this because you have very little money: *Although I've been out of a job for three months, I've managed to keep my head above water.* | *If I get this raise, we'll just about keep our heads above water until next year.*

solvent /'sɒlvənt‖'sɑːl-/ [adj] earning enough money to not have to borrow or get into debt: *We've been financially solvent for the last 5 years.* | *Companies need to know that those with whom they are trading are solvent and can pay for goods and services supplied to them*

afloat /ə'fləʊt/ [adv] if a company or organization stays or remains **afloat**, it manages to keep operating because its debts are not so bad that it has to close; if you keep a company or organization **afloat**, you stop it from getting into so much debt that it has to close: *It was the summer of 1991, and I was struggling hard to keep my business afloat.* | *David Henry lent the company $1bn out of his own personal fortune in order to help it stay afloat.* | *The organization remains afloat by renting out its skilled technicians to other companies.*

9 to agree that money that someone owes does not have to be paid

- write off

write off /ˌraɪt 'ɒf / [phr v T] to officially say that a company or country no longer has to pay a debt, especially because they will probably never be able to pay it **write off sth** *European governments were persuaded to write off the republic's largest debts.* | *A number of the company's debts were written off even before they went bankrupt.* | **write sth off** *We'll never see that money again so we might as well write it off.* —**write-off** /'raɪt ɒf/ [n C] *The corporation is still suffering from $350 million in losses and write-offs* (=amounts of money written off).

own

RELATED WORDS

- on your own *see* **alone**
- *see also* **have**

1 to own something

- own
- have
- possess
- control/have control of
- hold
- have a stake in
- interest

own /əʊn/ [v T not in progressive] if you **own** something, especially something big like a house, a car, or a company, it is your property and you have the legal right to have it: *We don't own the apartment, we're just renting it.* | *Clark owns about 40 companies in northern Europe.* | *They stayed in a villa once owned by the writer, Somerset Maugham.* | **privately owned** (=owned by an individual person, not by a company or government) *In National Parks, although the land is privately owned, there are strict controls on the use of the land.*

have ALSO **have got** especially British /hæv, həv 'gɒt‖-'gɑːt/ [v T not in progressive] to own something, especially something that ordinary people are likely to own: *We don't have a T.V.* | *How many of your students have a computer?* | *What kind of car has she got?* | *I've worked hard for everything I've got.*

possess /pə'zes/ [v T not in progressive] formal to own something – use this especially in negative sentences to say that someone does not own something that most people own: *Very few families in this area possess a telephone.* | *He never wore a suit – I don't think he possessed one.* | *Because of his gambling, he lost everything he possessed.*

control/have control of /kən'trəʊl, hæv kən-'trəʊl ɒv/ [v T/v phrase] to own a larger part of a company than other people so that you have power to make decisions about that company: *As well as owning Mirror Group Newspapers, the Maxwell Corporation also controlled several other businesses.* | *The Johnson family has effective control of the company, owning almost 60% of the shares.*

hold /həʊld/ [v T] to own part of a company because you own a number of the equal parts into which it is divided: *She works for Le Monde, where the staff hold a significant stake in the company.* | *a situation in which a husband and wife both hold shares in a family company* —**holding** [n C] *Mr Davis has a 30% holding in* (=owns 30% of) *Montague Enterprises.*

have a stake in /ˌhæv ə 'steɪk ɪn/ [v phrase not in progressive] to own part of a company and therefore be able to have a share in the money it makes: *Labatt beer has a 45% stake in the Blue Jays baseball team.* | *She has a stake in her husband's company, which she will have to give up if they divorce.*

interest /'ɪntrɪ̈st/ [n C] if a person, company, or government has an **interest** in a business, they own part of that business **+ in** *The bank has interests in several companies, including a 15% share of Morgan's Brewery.* | **controlling interest** (=a large enough part of the company or business to give you the power to make decisions about it) *Although the government has made some shares in National Oil Products available, it intends to maintain its controlling interest.*

2 when someone owns something

- belong to
- be the property of
- be mine/yours/John's etc
- my/your/his etc
- your own
- of your own
- personal

belong to /bɪ'lɒŋ tuː‖-'lɔːŋ-/ [v T not in progressive] if something **belongs to** someone, they own it: *This watch belonged to my grandfather.* | *Who does that Walkman belong to?* | *A car believed to belong to the bank robbers was found abandoned yesterday.*

be the property of /biː ðə 'prɒpəʳti ɒv‖-'prɑː-/ [v phrase] formal to belong to someone – often written on books, clothes etc to show who owns them: *This hymn book is the property of Pitt Street Methodist Church.* | *If he defaults on the loan, the land will become the property of the bank.*

be mine/yours/John's etc /biː 'maɪn/ [v phrase] if something **is mine/yours/John's etc**, it belongs to me, you, John etc: *'Hey, that's my pen!' – 'Sorry! I didn't know it was yours.'* | *'Whose bike is that?' 'It's Martin's.'* | *The money wasn't Sara's to lend you in the first place* (=Sara didn't have the right to lend it).

my/your/his etc /maɪ, jɔːʳ, hɪz/ [determiner] belonging to me, you, him etc: *Please can you move your car? It's blocking my driveway.* | *I've got a problem with my dishwasher.* | *My grandmother lives near your place – just around the corner in fact.*

your own /jɔːr 'əʊn/ [determiner/pron] belonging to you and not to anyone else: *You can rent skis or you can bring your own.* | *Joe left the company to set up his own business.*

of your own /əv jɔːr 'əʊn/ [adj phrase] **a room/car/computer etc of your own** one that belongs to you and no one else, especially when this is something you want to own: *Our neighbours let us use their garage, but we really need one of our own.* | *The charity provides accommodation for homeless people, and helps them find homes of their own.*

personal /'pɜːsənəl‖'pɜːr-/ [adj only before noun] belonging only to you – used especially in official contexts **sb's personal possessions/property/belongings** *The dead man's personal possessions were sent back to his family.* | **my/their etc own personal** *You can arm and disarm the alarm system using your own personal access code.*

3 the person who owns something

- owner
- landlord/landlady
- proprietor
- householder
- home-owner

owner /'əʊnəʳ/ [n C] the person who owns something: *The previous owner painted the outside of the house yellow.* | **+ of** *The owners of the company live abroad.* | **the proud owner of sth** *He is the proud owner of two Olympic gold medals.* | **car/dog/home etc owner** *Car owners are facing a 10% rise in the price of gasoline.*

landlord/landlady /'lændlɔːʳd, 'lændleɪdi/ [n C] someone who owns a building and is paid money by the people who live in it or use it: *Our landlord has promised to fix the heating by Tuesday.* | *College accommodation offices provide lists of private landlords and landladies.*

proprietor /prə'praɪətəʳ/ [n C] someone who owns and runs a business, especially a small business such as a shop or a restaurant: *Eddy Shah, the former national newspaper proprietor* | *My father had fallen victim to an unscrupulous garage proprietor.* | **+ of** *As proprietors of the general store, Mr and Mrs Stacey knew everything that went on in the town.*

householder /'haʊsˌhəʊldəʳ/ [n C] someone who owns or lives in a house – used especially in official or legal contexts: *The police are giving advice to householders on how to improve the security of their homes.* | *Householders and tradesmen both use the refuse dump to dispose of their garbage.*

home-owner /'həʊm ˌəʊnəʳ/ [n C] someone who owns their own home: *The latest rise in interest rates is bad news for home-owners.* | *The latest trend is for home-owners to carry out improvements before selling their properties.*

4 the things that someone owns

- property
- possessions
- things
- belongings
- assets
- worldly goods

property /'prɒpəʳti‖'prɑː-/ [n U] things someone owns, especially large expensive things such as houses, land, or cars: *Some of the stolen property was discovered in an empty warehouse.* | **school/church/army etc property** *The boys have been charged with damaging school property.* | **private property** *Many state documents were considered as the officer's private property.*

possessions /pə'zeʃənz/ [n plural] all the things that a person owns, which they keep in their home or carry with them: *They lost all their possessions in the floods.* | **personal possessions** *Prisoners are allowed no personal possessions such as photographs of their families.* | **sb's most treasured/cherished/prized possessions** *One of my most treasured possessions is a small book of prayers.*

things spoken ALSO **stuff** spoken informal /θɪŋz, stʌf/ [n plural] **things** such as clothes, records, books, furniture etc that you own **sb's things/stuff** *She always leaves her things all over the floor.* | *I don't how know I'm going to fit all my stuff into the new apartment.*

belongings /bɪ'lɒŋɪŋz‖bɪ'lɔːŋ-/ [n plural] things you own such as clothes, equipment, bags etc, especially things you take with you when you are travelling somewhere: *They packed all their belongings into the car and left the city that night.* | **personal belongings** *It doesn't cost much to insure your personal belongings.*

assets /'æsets/ [n plural] property that a person or a company owns and which they would be able to sell if they needed money – used especially in legal or business contexts: *The company has mining assets worth 8 billion Rand.* | **freeze sb's assets** (=not allow them to sell them) *The government announced that it had frozen the assets of three senior bank officials.*

worldly goods /ˌwɜːʳldli 'gʊdz/ [n plural] all the things that you own – use this especially as a joke when you do not own much: *Two old chairs, a broken jug, and half a candle: these were all his worldly goods.* | *All her worldly goods were contained in four cardboard boxes.*

5 to say you have a right to be the legal owner or something

- lay claim to
- stake your claim

lay claim to /ˌleɪ 'kleɪm tuː/ [v phrase] to say that you have a right to own something, especially something that is owned by someone else: *Both Britain and Argentina lay claim to the Falkland Islands.* | *A stranger who said he was my father's brother had arrived to lay claim to his fortune.*

stake your claim /ˌsteɪk jɔːʳ 'kleɪm/ [v phrase] to say publicly that you believe you have a right to own something, especially when other people also say they have a right to own it: *If you want some of the furniture, now's the time to stake your claim.*

Pp

pain

RELATED WORDS

- to reduce pain *see* **reduce (2)**
- *see also* **hurt/injure, ill/sick, illness/disease, suffer, medical treatment, doctor, drugs**

1 pain

- pain
- ache
- headache/toothache/backache/stomach ache
- aches and pains
- spasm
- twinge

pain /peɪn/ [n C/U] the feeling you have when part of your body hurts: *The pain is getting worse.* | *You won't feel any pain during the operation.* | *He told the doctor he was suffering from chest pains.* | **a pain in your chest/leg/back etc** *In college, Durban began to suffer from headaches and pain in his arms and legs* | **severe/excruciating pain** (=very bad pain) *A slipped disc can cause severe back pain.* | **ease the pain** (=make you feel less pain) *The drug is often used to ease the pain of dying cancer patients.* | **labor pains (American) / labour pains (British)** (=before giving birth) *Kerry had to drive herself to the hospital when the labor pains began.*

ache /eɪk/ [n C] a pain that continues for a long time but is not very sharp: *The ache in my leg muscles had almost gone.* | **dull ache** (=a continuous annoying ache) *Lisa felt a dull ache spreading up her arm.*

headache/toothache/backache/stomach ache /ˈhedeɪk, ˈtuːθ-eɪk, ˈbækeɪk, ˈstʌmək eɪk/ [n C/U] a continuous pain in a part of your body **have/get a headache** *I always get a headache when I've been using the computer.* | **have toothache/backache/stomach ache** British *I'm not surprised you have stomach ache – you eat too fast.* | **have a toothache/a backache/a stomach ache** American *I had a backache after fifteen minutes of shovelling snow.* | **a splitting headache** (=a very bad headache) *We were planning to go out last night, but Marcia had a splitting headache.*

aches and pains /ˌeɪks ən ˈpeɪnz/ [n phrase] many small pains which you feel at the same time, especially when you move, for example as the result of too much exercise or growing old: *Grandma said that apart from a few aches and pains she was feeling quite well.* | *Jenny ran slower and slower, complaining all the way of various aches and pains.*

spasm /ˈspæzəm/ [n C] a sudden sharp pain which makes your body or part of your body shake uncontrollably for a short time: *He lay on the ground, breathless and frightened, waiting for the next spasm.* | **spasm of pain** *A spasm of pain twisted Cheviot's face.* | **muscle spasm** *The muscle spasms started in his lower left leg and spread upwards.*

twinge /twɪndʒ/ [n C] a sudden but not severe pain that comes and then disappears quickly: *I'd had the odd twinge now and again, but my heart-attack was totally unexpected.* | **twinge of pain/rheumatism etc** *George felt a twinge of pain in his ankle from when he had slipped on the ice.*

2 when a part of your body feels painful

- painful
- sore
- tender
- hurt
- ache
- sting
- throb

painful /ˈpeɪnfəl/ [adj] a part of your body that feels **painful** makes you feel pain: *Jim's knee was still painful where he had fallen on it.* | *The child suffered painful stomach cramps and vomiting after drinking one of the contaminated drinks.*

sore /sɔːʳ/ [adj] a part of your body that is **sore** hurts when you touch or use it, and is often red: *His eyes looked red and sore, as if he had been rubbing them.* | *Martin was unable to score at all in the game, complaining of a sore knee.* | **sore throat** *She missed more than ten performances that year due to a persistent sore throat and cough.*

tender /ˈtendəʳ/ [adj] a part of the body that is **tender** is painful when it is touched: *My mouth was tender and swollen where he had hit me.* | *Now I'm going to press down on several places around your knee, and you tell me when it feels tender.*

hurt /hɜːʳt/ [v I] if a part of your body **hurts**, you feel pain in it, for example because you have hit it or cut it, or because you are ill: *My neck felt stiff and my shoulder hurt.* | *I fell and banged my knee, and it really hurts.*

ache /eɪk/ [v I] if a part of your body **aches**, you feel a pain in it that is continuous but not very strong – use this about pains in your arms, legs, or back, or in your head or stomach: *My arms ached from carrying all the groceries.* | *She felt hot and her head was beginning to ache.* | *I went to dance class last week, and I've been aching ever since.*

sting /stɪŋ/ [v I] to hurt with a sudden sharp pain for a short time – use this about your eyes or your skin: *The smoke made our eyes sting.* | *His cheek stung where his mother had slapped him.*

throb /θrɒb‖θrɑːb/ [v I] if a part of your body **throbs** you feel pain that seems to get stronger and weaker in a regular repeated pattern: *By late afternoon my head was throbbing, and I couldn't see straight.* | *He limped heavily, nursing his throbbing ankle.* | **a throbbing pain** *I felt a throbbing pain in my left shin, and pulled up my trouser leg to see what was causing it.*

3 to feel pain

- feel/have a pain in
- be in pain
- be in agony

feel/have a pain in /ˌfiːl, ˌhæv ə ˈpeɪn ɪn/ [v phrase not in progressive] to have a pain in a particular part of your body: *She came into casualty complaining that she had a pain in her side.* | *The next morning, after feeling a sharp pain in his fingers, Gonzalez was treated for frostbite at City Hospital.*

be in pain /biː ɪn ˈpeɪn/ [v phrase] to be experiencing a lot of pain: *Young children cry if they are in pain, if they are hungry or if they are left alone.* | *Someone was crying, as if they were in pain.* | **be in constant pain** (=be in pain all the time) *Some of these patients are very sick and in constant pain.* | **be in a lot of pain/be in great pain** *Caroline's been in a lot of pain since the operation.*

be in agony /biː ɪn ˈægəni/ [v phrase] to feel a lot of very severe pain: *He was in agony. We had to carry him up the stairs.* | *My mother lived for four more days, but she was in agony.*

4 when something makes someone feel pain

- hurt
- sting
- irritate
- agonizing/excruciating
- be agony

hurt /hɜːʳt/ [v I/T] if something or someone **hurts** you, they make you feel pain: *Did it hurt when they stuck the needle in?* | *Stop it – you're hurting me.*

sting /stɪŋ/ [v I/T] to cause a sudden sharp pain on your skin or in your eyes for a short time: *The antiseptic might sting a little.* | *The smoke stung my eyes.*

irritate /ˈɪrɪteɪt/ [v T] if a substance **irritates** a part of your body, especially your eyes or your skin, it makes it become sore: *The pollen irritated my eyes, which were red and streaming with tears.* | *Nineteen percent of women will still use a beauty product, even if it irritates their skin.* —**irritation** /ˌɪrɪˈteɪʃən/ [n U] *Stop using the cream immediately if it causes irritation.*

agonizing/excruciating /ˈægənaɪzɪŋ, ɪkˈskruːʃieɪtɪŋ/ [adj] if pain or a particular movement is **agonizing** or **excruciating**, it is extremely strong so that you are almost unable to move or do something: *The pain moved to my elbow, and it became agonizing to even lift my arm.* | *The excruciating pain in his kidneys made him gasp.*

be agony /biː ˈægəni/ [v phrase] especially British, informal if something you do or something someone does to you **is agony**, it hurts a lot: *It was agony having my tooth removed – I don't think the dentist knew what he was doing.* | *Climbing five flights of stairs with all those bags was absolute bloody agony.*

5 when there is no pain

- not hurt
- painless
- not feel a thing

not hurt /nɒt ˈhɜːʳt/ [v phrase] if something **does not hurt**, it is not painful: *I twisted my ankle a little, but it doesn't hurt.* | *Don't worry - it's a very quick procedure and it won't hurt.*

painless /ˈpeɪnləs/ [adj] something that is **painless** does not hurt – use this especially when someone is worried that it might hurt: *The operation is simple and painless.*

not feel a thing /nɒt ˌfiːl ə ˈθɪŋ/ [v phrase] spoken to not feel any pain at all: *Don't worry about the injection – you won't feel a thing.* | *The guys who were fighting were so drunk, I'm sure they didn't feel a thing.*

paint

RELATED WORDS

- *see also* **draw, picture, colour/color, pattern, decorate, art/culture**

1 to paint pictures

- paint

paint /peɪnt/ [v I/T] to make a picture of someone or something, by putting **paint** on a surface with a brush: *Geraint was sitting on the beach, painting the seagulls and the fishing boats.* | *The exhibition focuses on the urban pictures painted by Camille Pissarro in the last decade of his career.* | **paint a picture (of)** *I'm going to paint a picture of the church.* | **paint in oils/watercolours etc** *The pictures in Paul Gunn's exhibition were all landscapes, most beautifully painted in oils.* —**painting** [n U] the activity of painting pictures: *I'm not very good at painting.* | *a painting class*

2 someone who paints pictures

- painter
- artist

painter /ˈpeɪntəʳ/ [n C] someone who paints pictures: *This is by the great Spanish painter, Goya.* | *Michelangelo, sculptor, painter, architect, and poet, died in 1564.* | **portrait painter** (=someone who paints pictures of people) *Sir Henry Raeburn, the famous Scots portrait painter* | **landscape painter** (=someone who paints pictures of places, the countryside etc) *Turner was probably the greatest landscape painter that England has ever produced.*

artist /ˈɑːʳtɪst/ [n C] someone who produces works of art, especially paintings or drawings: *an exhibition of works by Italian artists* | *At that time Picasso was a struggling artist, little known outside Paris.* | *We asked a local artist to come and show her work to the students.*

3 to paint walls/doors/rooms etc

- paint
- decorate
- redecorate
- respray

paint /peɪnt/ [v I/T] to put **paint** on walls, doors, pieces of furniture etc: *I'm going to paint the bathroom tomorrow.* | **paint sth blue/red/white etc** *What colour did you paint the doors?* | *The walls were painted tomato red, with matching red drapes.*

decorate /ˈdekəreɪt/ [v I/T] especially British to paint the inside of a house or put paper on the walls: *They've just finished decorating the kitchen.* | *We spent all weekend decorating.* | **have sth decorated** (=pay someone to decorate it) *Mum had the whole house decorated before she moved in.*

redecorate /riːˈdekəreɪt/ [v T] to change the paint or paper on the walls of a house or room **redecorate sth** *When they first moved in, they completely redecorated the whole house.* | **have sth redecorated** (=pay someone to redecorate it) *We're thinking of having our house redecorated – can you recommend anyone?*

respray /riːˈspreɪ/ [v T] to change the colour of a car by putting new paint on it: *The thieves had resprayed the truck and changed the license plates.* | *After the accident I took the car to a garage to have it resprayed.*

4 someone who paints walls, houses etc as their job

- painter
- decorator

painter /ˈpeɪntəʳ/ [n C] someone who paints walls, houses etc as their job: *The painters are upstairs painting the offices at the moment.* | **house painter** *Adolf Hitler worked as a house painter in Austria before becoming involved in politics.*

decorator /ˈdekəreɪtəʳ/ [n C] someone whose job is to paint houses and put paper on the walls inside: *The decorators have left their ladders and paints all over the house – it a real mess.* | *We wanted the work to be done properly, so we decided to get the decorators in.*

5 words for describing something that has been painted

- painted

painted /ˈpeɪntɪd/ [adj] *On the shelf there was a painted statue of the Virgin Mary.* | *The temple was decorated with brightly painted figures and bits of colored glass.* | **hand-painted** (=painted by a person, not a machine) *a beautiful hand-painted vase* | **painted blue/green etc** *The front door was painted* *yellow.* | **be painted in sth** *beautiful jewel boxes painted in distinctive shades of red, yellow, blue, green* | *a row of humble fisherman's cottages, painted in pastel tones of pink, ochre, and yellow* | **+ with** *The vases were painted with pictures of flowers and butterflies.*

part

RELATED WORDS

▸ *see also* **piece, partly, consist of**

1 a part of an object/substance/area

- part
- bit
- piece
- component
- ingredient
- constituent
- portion
- section
- segment

part /pɑːʳt/ [n C] *When you have filled in the form, keep the top part and send the other part to the bank.* | *All our replacement parts are guaranteed, if you have your car serviced with us each year.* | **+ of** *What part of Russia are you from?* | *This is the widest part of the river.* | *Malaria is still common in many parts of Africa.*

bit /bɪt/ [n C] **especially British, spoken** a small part of an object or area: *'Would you like a slice of cake?' 'I'll just have a little bit, please.'* | **+ of** *the bit of the garden where the fruit trees are* | *I found some bits of glass in my sandwich.*

piece /piːs/ [n C] one of several different parts that must be joined together to make something: *a 1000-piece jigsaw puzzle* | **in pieces** (=as separate pieces) *The equipment had to be taken apart and transported in pieces.*

component /kəmˈpəʊnənt/ [n C] one of the separate parts of a machine or a system, that is necessary to make the machine or system work: *The factory makes aircraft engine components.* | *All the components should be tested before they are assembled.* | **+ of** *Gaining confidence is a major component of developing leadership skills.*

ingredient /ɪnˈgriːdiənt/ [n C] one of the types of food that are used to make a dish or a meal: *Weigh all the ingredients before you start.* | *a list of ingredients* | *The main ingredients can be prepared and frozen in advance.* | **+ for** *Coconut is a basic ingredient for many curries and other Asian dishes.*

constituent /kənˈstɪtʃuənt/ [n C] **formal** one of the chemical substances that something is made of: *Scientists have to break the compound down into its constituents in order to analyze it.* | **+ of** *Magnesium and sodium are the main constituents of salt.*

portion /ˈpɔːʳʃən/ [n C] a part of something larger, especially a part that is different from the other parts – used especially in a technical context: *Fuel is carried in the lower portion of the rocket.* | **+ of** *Surgeons have had to remove portions of his stomach and intestine.* | *The research suggests we only use a small portion of our brains at any one time.*

section /ˈsekʃən/ [n C] a part of something that is clearly different and separate from the other parts **+ of** *The final section of this chapter will deal with recent developments.* | *First class seats are in the front section of the plane.* | *The disease spread through the poorer sections of the city.*

segment /ˈsegmənt/ [n C] a part of something such as a fruit, insect etc that is naturally divided, or a part of something that has been divided into separate, roughly equal parts: *Decorate the cake with orange segments.* | *An ant's body is divided into three distinct segments.* | **+ of** *Each sales team targets its efforts at a particular segment of the general population.*

2 part of a total amount or number

- proportion
- fraction
- percentage

proportion /prəˈpɔːʳʃən/ [n C] a part of an amount or number – use this when you are comparing the part with the whole amount or number **+ of** *What proportion of your income do you spend on food?* | **high/large etc proportion** *The new jobs would largely be unskilled and a high proportion would be in inner city areas.* | *A significant proportion of the elderly are dependent on the basic state pension.* | **small/tiny proportion** *We get a small proportion of our funding from the government.*

fraction /ˈfrækʃən/ [n C] a small part of an amount or number, especially a very small part **+ of** *Employees' salaries are just a fraction of the total cost of the project.* | *Faxes are expensive, when you consider you can send emails at a fraction of the cost* (=for very much less money). | **small/tiny fraction** *a problem that affects only a small fraction of the total population*

percentage /pəʳˈsentɪdʒ/ [n C] a part of an amount or number that can be measured and shown exactly compared to the total **+ of** *What percentage of our students passed the exam?* | *The percentage of pensioners living below the poverty line has increased by 15% in the last four years.* | **high/large percentage** *A high percentage of the coffee they produce goes to the US.* | **small percentage** *Only a small percentage of African American employees were considered for promotion.*

3 part of a story/book/film/play etc

- part
- bit
- episode
- instalment
- chapter
- scene
- extract
- excerpt
- clip

part /pɑːʳt/ [n C] *Jane Austen's 'Pride and Prejudice', adapted for radio in six parts* | **+ of** *I've finished the first part of my thesis.* | **+ about** *Did you understand the part about switching the modem speed?* | **Part One/Part 2 etc** (=one of the main parts that a book, TV story etc is divided into) *Part One ends with the death of the hero's father.*

bit /bɪt/ [n C] **British spoken** a small part of a story or film: *My favourite bit is when they try to escape.* | **+ of** *Some bits of the book are actually quite funny.*

episode /ˈepɪsəʊd/ [n C] a part of a story on radio or television that is told in separate parts, usually weekly: *That was one of the best episodes – I wish I'd got it on tape.* | *Brad Pitt made a guest appearance on last week's episode.* | *Ernie directed all 12 of the half-hour episodes for television.* | **+ of** *I've never even seen an episode of Star Trek.*

instalment British **/installment** American /ɪnˈstɔːlmənt/ [n C] part of a story that is told in several parts printed regularly in a magazine or newspaper over a period of time: *Oliver Stone was in Thailand shooting the final instalment in his Vietnam trilogy, Heaven And Earth.* | **weekly/monthly instalments** *Dickens wrote his novels in weekly instalments for a magazine.* | **+ of** *We are proud to present the second* *instalment of our fantastic six-part competition to win a Renault Clio.*

chapter /'tʃæptəʳ/ [n C] one of the parts that a book is divided into: *These matters are dealt with in Chapters 8 & 9.* | *'Have you finished 'Lord of the Rings' yet?' 'I'm on the last chapter.'*

scene /siːn/ [n C] one of the smaller parts of a play or film in which the same characters appear or the events happen in the same place: *The sex scenes between Depardieu and Brochet are sensitively filmed.* | *The ghost appears in Act 2, Scene 1.* | **opening/closing scene** (=the first or the last scene) *The opening scene of the movie features the gangsters discussing their next heist.*

extract /'ekstrækt/ [n C] a part taken from something such as a book or a speech in order to show its most important points or to show what the whole of it is like: *In the following extract, Jones presents the arguments in favour of nuclear power.* | **+ from** *The book contains previously unpublished material, including extracts from diaries, letters and taped interviews.*

excerpt /'eksɜːʳpt/ [n C] a short part taken from a film, book, speech, piece of music etc **+ from** *I'd like to read out a short excerpt from the poem.* | *The following excerpt is from one of my students' essays.* | *He played some excerpts from Grieg's piano concerto.*

clip /klɪp/ [n C] a short part of a film or other recording that is taken and used in another film or in a television programme: *The police have released a video clip of the attack.* | *The new software makes it possible to cut and paste sound or video clips from one application to another.* | **+ from** *I saw a clip from the new Michael Douglas movie on TV last night.*

4 part of an organization

- branch
- department
- division
- section
- sector
- wing
- the ... side

branch /brɑːntʃ‖bræntʃ/ [n C] a shop, office, or bank in a particular area that is part of a larger organization: *Our store has branches all over the country.* | *I'm sorry, we can't change foreign currency. We're only a small branch, you see.* | **+ of** *You can deposit money at any branch of the Northwest Pacific Bank.*

department /dɪ'pɑːʳtmənt/ [n C] a **department** of a large organization, such as a company, school, or hospital, is a part of it that is responsible for a particular kind of work: *Our department deals mainly with exports.* | *Which department do you work in?* | **Sales/Accounts/Planning etc Department** (=in a company or large organization) *Melissa is in charge of the Marketing Department.* | **Art/History/Science etc Department** (=in a school or university) *She works in the Humanities department* | **the Department of Science/English/Trade etc** (=in a school or university, or other large organization, especially a government) *the Department of Trade and Industry* | *the Department of Experimental Psychology*

division /də̥'vɪʒən/ [n C] a large part of an organization, especially a company, which often includes several smaller parts: *The sales and advertising departments are both part of the marketing division.* | *I work in the administration division as a mail mover.* | **+ of** *the Japanese division of American Express*

section /'sekʃən/ [n C] a part of an organization, especially a part of a company or a political group, that is responsible for a special area of its work: *The party's Young Conservatives section is growing fast.* | *The tutor asked the brass section to play their piece again.* | **+ of** *We had to go to the 'late payments' section of the Financial Aid office.*

sector /'sektəʳ/ [n C] a part of an area of economic activity, such as industry or trade **manufacturing/business/retail etc sector** *The growth in the number of home computers has boosted the electronics sector.* | *The new sales tax caused problems for the retail sector* (=the shops and stores that sell goods to the public). | **public sector** (=organizations that the government owns) *The main source of work here is public sector employment.* | **private/independent sector** (=organizations that the government does not own) *Private sector pay increases were again above the rate of inflation.*

wing /wɪŋ/ [n C] a part of a political party or a similar organization that has different ideas from the rest of the party, or is involved in different activities **right/left wing** *The racist right wing staged their biggest demonstration yet in the main square.* | **political/military wing** *The Tamil Tigers have had a political wing since 1976, but never registered it as a legal party.* | **+ of** *They were members of the Marxist wing of the Socialist Party.*

the ... side /ðə ... saɪd/ [n singular] informal **the financial/business/marketing etc side** a particular part of an organization's activity: *I'm in charge of production, and Martha takes care of the financial side.*

5 one of the parts of a process

- part
- bit
- stage
- step
- phase

part /pɑːʳt/ [n C] *Organizing the party was easy, the hardest part was getting my parents to agree to it.* | **+ of** *Which part of your job do you enjoy most?* | *She spent the early part of her life in Barcelona.* | *Part of the research program involved interviewing teenagers in inner-city areas.*

bit /bɪt/ [n C] British spoken a part of an activity, plan, or job: *Alan did the easy bit – it was me who did all the hard work!* | **+ of** *I'll probably do a bit of gardening this weekend.*

stage /steɪdʒ/ [n C] one of several parts of a long process, which happen one after another: *Dan has never gone through a rebellious stage.* | **+ of** *Many women feel depressed during the early stages of pregnancy.* | **+ in** *We saw a video showing the second stage in the development of a human embryo.* | **at this stage** (=now) *At this stage of the election campaign, it is impossible to say who will win.* | **reach/be at/get to the stage** (=to be at a particular part of a process) *We reached the stage where we'd given up any hopes of seeing our daughter alive.* | *'How's your dissertation coming on?' 'I'm at the writing-up stage.'*

step /step/ [n C] one of the parts of a process that you have to do or deal with in order to go on to the next one: *The next step will be to make the pasta sauce.* | *The first step towards achieving peace in the region will be to elect a government that represents all the people.* | **one step at a time** (=used to say that you should deal with one part of a process thoroughly before worrying about the next one) *The doctors say I'll make a full recovery, but I'm going to have to take it one step at a time.*

phase /feɪz/ [n C] a separate part in the development or growth of something: *I'd like to discuss the production phase at this morning's meeting.* | **+ in** *There* *are three phases in the lifecycle of a butterfly.* | **initial/primary/first phase** (=the first part) *The initial phase of the project should take about three months.* | **final/last phase** (=the last part) *As the war enters its final phase, the UN will probably consider lifting sanctions.*

6 part of a situation/subject/someone's character

- aspect
- side
- dimension
- factor
- element
- feature

see also **character**

aspect /'æspekt/ [n C] one of the many parts of a situation or subject, which can each be considered separately: *The inspectors will examine health and safety aspects at the plant.* | **+ of** *Chris is dealing with the commercial aspects of this ambitious project.* | *The country was on the brink of war, and fear and uncertainty permeated every aspect of daily life.*

side /saɪd/ [n C] one part of a situation or someone's character – use this especially when you are comparing one part with another: *Weiskopf was a talented and successful man, but he did have a cruel side.* | **+ of** *I'd like to move away from the theory now, to concentrate on the practical side of engineering.* | **the negative/positive/lighter/funny side** *You are enthusiastic, but on the negative side, you can be impatient and critical.* | *Try to see the funny side of the situation.* | *the lighter side of the conference, as seen by our political cartoonist*

dimension /daɪ'menʃən, dɪ̵-/ [n C] a part of a situation that makes you look at the situation in a particular way: *The arrival of the South African team has brought a new dimension to the competition.* | **+ of** *The political dimensions of the incident are clear.* | *a revival of interest in the spiritual and moral dimensions of life* | **the human dimension** (=making you think of people's feelings, rather than things) *The new art gallery is impressive, but I felt the human dimension had been lost.*

factor /'fæktəʳ/ [n C] one of the parts or features of a situation, each of which has a different effect or importance: *There are one or two factors we haven't considered yet.* | *The issue of abortion rights is obviously not the only factor affecting the female vote.* | *Traders said several factors contributed to Nasdaq's weakness.* | **+ in** *The most important factor in professional sport is psychology.* | *His formal education was a less significant factor in his upbringing than practical experience.*

element /'elɪ̵mənt/ [n C] one of the separate parts of something such as a person's character, a system or process, or a piece of writing: *The planning proposals have three main elements.* | **+ of** *There's always been an element of competition between me and my brother.* | **+ in** *Instead of a single plot, there are several elements in the story.* | *We've reached the stage where public image is the most important element in the Presidency.* | **key element** (=most important element) *I see helping the community as one of the key elements of my work.*

feature /'fiːtʃəʳ/ [n C] a part of something that is different in some way from the rest of it: *Are there any special features about the way Ireland trains its teachers?* | **+ of** *Federalism remains a very important feature of American politics.* | *One of the features of auto-immune diseases is that they are often genetically similar.*

7 to be a part of something

- be part of
- form (a) part of
- inherent

be part of /biː 'pɑːʳt ɒv/ [v phrase] *Falling over is part of the process of learning to ski.* | *It is part of the doctor's job to give advice on emotional problems.* | *Restrictions on foreign trade are part of the state's economic and legal system.*

form (a) part of /ˌfɔːʳm (ə) 'pɑːʳt ɒv/ [v phrase] to be one of the things that together make up something larger or more important: *Group discussion forms a major part of classwork.* | *The company forms part of the United Holdings group.* | *These three books form part of a series on religion in the modern world.*

inherent /ɪn'hɪərənt, -'her-/ [adj] an **inherent** fact, problem, quality etc is one that is a natural part of an activity or situation and cannot be separated from it: *Money is unfortunately an inherent part of politics.* | **+ in** *Surgical procedures have many risks inherent in them.* | *the uncertainties that are inherent in the research and development process* —**inherently** [adv] *Is mankind an inherently violent species?*

partly

not completely

RELATED WORDS

opposite: **completely**

see also **part, some, several, almost**

- partly
- partially
- half
- not completely/entirely
- to some extent/to a certain extent/up to a point
- to a degree/to some degree
- in part

partly /'pɑːʳtli/ [adv] *The road was partly blocked by a fallen tree.* | *What he told us was only partly true.* | *He was educated partly in Glasgow and partly in London.* | **partly because** *The accident happened partly because we were having an argument in the car.*

partially /'pɑːʳʃəli/ [adv] if something **partially** happens, it does not happen completely or does not include all of something: *The house was partially destroyed by the explosion.* | *The ice had partially melted and there was a pool of water on the table.* | *The advertising campaign was only partially successful.* —**partial** [adj] *They have asked for a partial lifting of the ban on fur trading.*

half /hɑːf‖hæf/ [adv] **half-eaten/half-finished etc** if something is **half-eaten, half-finished** etc, **half** of it has been eaten, finished etc: *There was a half-smoked cigarette in the ashtray.* | *'That's good,' he said dully, putting down his half-eaten sandwich.* | *I found him sitting on his bed, half-dressed.* | *The houses were half-submerged by the flood water.*

not completely/entirely /ˌnɒt kəm'pliːtli, ɪn'taɪəʳli/ [adv] use this especially to say that you are only partly sure about something or that you only partly agree with or believe something: *'Who was he hiding from?' 'I'm not completely sure.'* | *I'm not entirely convinced that we have enough control over schools as it is.* | *'So, is everything clear?' 'Not entirely.'*

to some extent/to a certain extent/up to a point /tə ˈsʌm ɪkˌstent, tʊ ə ˈsɜːʳtn ɪkˌstent, ˌʌp tʊ ə ˈpɔɪnt/ [adv] use this to say that something is partly true but not completely true: *Doing well in exams is to some extent a matter of luck.* | *To a certain extent it was our own fault that we lost the contract.* | *His figures were correct – up to a point.*

to a degree/to some degree /tʊ ə dɪˈgriː, tə ˈsʌm dɪˌgriː/ [adv] formal partly or in a limited way – used especially in discussions and arguments: *The situation has been improved to a degree in recent months.* | *Golding's novel is to some degree experimental in style.*

in part /ɪn ˈpɑːʳt/ [adv] formal if something happens **in part** because of something, it is partly caused by it: *They developed their ideas in part from important work by Paykel.* | *Although bad management was the major factor, the firm's problems were due in part to a fall-off in demand.*

party

RELATED WORDS

- *see also* **celebrate, invite, drink, dance, meal**

1 a party

- party
- get-together
- do
- shower
- bash

party /ˈpɑːʳti/ [n C] a social event, especially in someone's house, when people talk, drink, eat, and dance: *We're having a party at my house. Do you want to come?* | *Did you go to Stella's party?* | **invite sb to a party** *How many people have they invited to the party?* | **surprise party** *We gave her a surprise party at a local bar.* | **a birthday/Halloween/Christmas/engagement etc party** (=to celebrate a birthday, Halloween etc) *Over a hundred children came to the annual Christmas party.* | **dinner party** (=a party at someone's house in the evening, when people have a meal) *I gave my first dinner party last weekend.* | **office party** (=a party for people who work together) *Office parties are fun if you're young, free, and single.* | **fancy dress party** British **/costume party** American (=a party where people wear strange, funny, or historical clothes) *You're invited to a fancy dress party.* | **cocktail party** (=a fairly formal party in the evening, at which alcoholic drinks are served) *I went to a cocktail party in the lobby of the Ritz once.*

get-together /ˈget təˌgeðəʳ/ [n C] an informal party, often to celebrate something: *Shana's picture won first prize, so we had a little get-together to celebrate.* | *a big family get-together*

do /duː/ [n C] British spoken a party **a bit of a do** *A friend of mine's having a bit of a do in town tomorrow night.* | **leaving do** (=for someone who is leaving the place where they work) *Are you going to Darren's leaving do?*

shower /ˈʃaʊəʳ/ [n C] American a party at which presents are given to a woman who is getting married or having a baby: *We're giving a shower for Beth next week.* | *I want to thank both of you again for your beautiful shower gifts.* | **bridal/wedding shower** (=for a woman who is getting married) *What did you give Chris for her wedding shower?* | **baby shower** (=for a woman who is going to have a baby) *We didn't play any of the usual games at the baby shower.*

bash /bæʃ/ [n C] informal a big party: *The band are flying out to Ibiza tonight for a huge four-day celebrity bash.*

2 a formal or official party

- function
- reception

function /ˈfʌŋkʃən/ [n C] a large formal or official party, usually for important people: *The Lavender Room can be booked for functions or parties.* | **corporate function** (=for a company) *His specialist service is in constant demand for big corporate functions.* | **state function** (=official government party) *Part of her duties is attending official state functions.*

reception /rɪˈsepʃən/ [n C] a large formal or official party, usually held to welcome someone or to celebrate something: *On the second night, the captain always holds a formal reception for the crew and passengers.* | *The pair were spotted together at a champagne reception at the Imperial Hotel.* | **attend a reception** *Two hundred guests attended an evening reception, held in honor of the Chancellor's visit.* | **wedding reception** (=a big party held after a wedding) *The wedding reception will take place at the Lennox Hotel, starting at 3.30 pm.*

3 to have a party

- have
- throw a party
- hold
- give
- host
- entertain

have /hæv/ [v T] **have a party/get-together/reception etc** *We used to have a big Christmas party every year.* | *The couple had their wedding reception at the Museum of Modern Art.* | *Mark, my boss, had a surprise party to welcome me home.*

throw a party /ˌθrəʊ ə ˈpɑːʳti/ [v phrase] to have a party at your home, often a big or expensive one, especially in order to celebrate something: *He threw a huge party to celebrate making his first million dollars.* | **+ for** *The staff and patients threw a going-away party for Dr Rogers.* | *The Krugers threw an impromptu cocktail party for him in the backyard.*

hold /həʊld/ [v T] **hold a party/dinner/reception/function etc** to have a formal or official party: *The anniversary dinner was held Wednesday night at the Washington Hilton.* | *They are holding a fund-raising reception on Friday in the City Hall.*

give /gɪv/ [v T] **give a party/dinner party/lunch party etc** to be the person who organizes a party: *I'm giving a dinner party on Thursday night. Would you like to come?* | *On Maggie's last night in the house, Jo gave a little farewell party.* | **give a party for sb** *The prospect of giving a dinner party for my boyfriend's snobbish parents filled me with gloom.* | *The last show of the tour was in Atlanta, and I decided to give a party for the singers and musicians.*

host /həʊst/ [v T] **host a party/dinner party/reception etc** to be the person who organizes a formal party and officially welcomes the guests: *Colette will be hosting a cocktail reception at 6.00 pm in the Grosvenor Suite.* | *Last year, the city hosted a three-day gay pride festival.*

entertain /ˌentəʳˈteɪn/ [v I/T] to give parties, especially fairly formal parties, for people who are not particularly close friends, for example business customers: *I meet a lot of people, but I don't entertain much myself.* | *Being a sociable person, Eva loved entertaining.* | *An important part of the job is entertaining business clients.*

4 to go to a party

- go to
- attend
- party
- partying

go to /ˈgəʊ tuː/ [phr v T] *Are you going to the Christmas party? | Over 150 people went to her 21st birthday party.*

attend /əˈtend/ [v I/T] especially written to go to a formal party: *The Duchess of York attended the charity reception, along with her two daughters. | Some of the most glittering celebrities in the country are expected to attend.*

party /ˈpɑːʳti/ [v I] informal to spend time enjoying yourself at a party or at parties, especially when this involves drinking a lot of alcohol, dancing etc: *They partied till 7 in the morning. | I could party all night long!*

partying /ˈpɑːʳtiŋ/ [n U] the activity of drinking, dancing, meeting people etc at parties: *My life was an endless round of photo shoots, interviews, and serious partying. | Partying and having a good time was all she seemed interested in. | Around about 2 am, the partying came to an abrupt halt.*

5 the people at a party

- host
- hostess
- guest
- gatecrasher

host /həʊst/ [n C] the person who invites people to a party and provides them with food and drink: *I was intrigued to learn that our Chinese host had spent many years in Chicago.*

hostess /ˈhəʊstɪ̈s/ [n C] a woman who invites people to a party and provides them with food and drink: *Pam, you've been a great hostess – thank you.*

guest /gest/ [n C] someone who goes to a party: *Lily poured her guest a glass of sherry. | After the wedding, the couple staged a huge reception for over 250 guests.* | **guest of honour** British **/guest of honor** American (=the most important guest at a party) *This year's guest of honour will be the novelist Margaret Attwood.*

gatecrasher ALSO **party crasher** American /ˈgeɪtˌkræʃəʳ, ˈpɑːʳti ˌkræʃəʳ/ [n C] someone who goes to a party that they have not been invited to: *Lee says the damage was caused by a couple of unknown gatecrashers.*

pass/go past

to go past a place, person, or thing

RELATED WORDS

- to pass an exam or test *see* **test**
- when time passes *see* **time (25-27)**
- *see also* **go, drive, walk, run**

- past
- by
- pass
- overtake

past /pɑːst‖pæst/ [adv/prep] if you go **past** someone or something, you go beside and then beyond them **walk/go/drive etc past (sb/sth)** *He walked straight past her without looking at her. | Will you be going past the library on your way home? | Drivers sped past, heading for Oxford.*

by /baɪ/ [adv] past a person **go/walk/float etc by** *I lay on the grass and watched the clouds floating by. | One woman reported seeing a man go by on a motorcycle.*

pass /pɑːs‖pæs/ [v I/T] to go past a place or person: *I'll get you some aspirin – I pass the drugstore on the way to work. | They kept quiet until the soldiers had passed. | A big Cadillac passed us as we walked up the hill.* — **passing** [adj only before noun] going past: *They could hardly hear themselves talk above the noise from the passing traffic | He hailed a passing taxi.*

overtake /ˌəʊvəʳˈteɪk/ [v I/T] British to pass a moving vehicle or person because you want to get in front of them: *Before you start to overtake, make sure the road is clear ahead of you. | On the way, we overtook a battered old Renault.*

past

RELATED WORDS

opposite: **future**

- *see also* **then, time, before, remember, tradition**

1 the past

- the past
- past

the past /ðə ˈpɑːst‖-ˈpæst/ [n singular] the time that existed before the present time: *My grandfather enjoys talking about the past. | There were several horse-drawn carriages, as a nostalgic reminder of the past.* | **in the past** (=during the time before now) *I decided to ask Anna, as she had always been very helpful in the past. | In the past, doctors seemed to have more time for their patients than they do today.* | **the distant past** (=a long time before the present) *The programme describes events which took place in the distant past, towards the end of the last ice-age.* | **the recent past** (=not a long time before the present) | *It's hard to see events from the very recent past in their proper historical perspective.* | **a thing of the past** (=something that used to happen or exist, but does not any more) *For many people, a relaxing weekend has become a thing of the past.* | **past mistakes** *Our goal was to learn from our past mistakes and to use the lessons on this project.* |

past /pɑːst‖pæst/ [adj only before noun] **past** events, experiences etc happened before now: *He's learned a lot from his past experience. | Judging by her past performance, I'd say Rowena will do very well. | Groups have put a lot into past projects, and have always seen an excellent result.* | **the past 10 years/2weeks etc** (=the 10 years, 2 weeks etc before now) *The past few months have been very difficult for Mary. | For the past two weeks, I've been doing my boss's job while she's away on business. | the enormous changes of the past 30 years*

2 all the things that have happened in the past

- sb's/sth's past
- history
- record

sb's/sth's past / (sb's/sth's) ˈpɑːst‖-ˈpæst/ [n singular] all the things that have happened to someone in the past: *Greg didn't like to talk about his past, | The newspapers had been investigating the President's past, hoping to find some scandal. | The elegant buildings on the sea front give us a glimpse of Brighton's more glorious past.*

history /ˈhɪstəri/ [n singular] all the things that have happened in the past, especially to a country, a town, or an organization **the history of sth/sth's his-**

tory *India has been invaded several times in its history.* | *a book about the history of the United Nations*

record /ˈrekɔːd‖-ərd/ [n singular] all the things that a person, organization, country etc has done in the past, especially when talking about how good or bad they are **a good/bad/poor etc record** *As an employee, his record is outstanding.* | *The US had serious concerns over the country's poor human rights record.* | **+ of** *The department has a long record of high achievement.* | **+ on** *The industry's record on conservation is not very impressive.* | **track record** (=a record that shows how experienced or skilful a person or organization is) *HMA has a great track record of managing hospitals.*

3 when something happened or was true in the past but not now

- used to
- once/at one time
- (back) then/at one time
- in the past
- in those days/in the old days
- in the olden days
- formerly

used to /ˈjuːst tuː/ [modal verb] if someone or something **used to** do something, they did it for a period of time in the past, or they did it regularly in the past, but they do not do it now: *'Do you smoke?' 'No, but I used to.'* | **used to do sth** *We used to live in Glasgow when I was young.* | **there used to be** *Thirty years ago, there used to be a market in the town.* | **never used to** *It never used to rain as much as this.* | **didn't use to do sth** spoken *I was surprised to see her driving – she didn't use to.* | **used not to do sth** formal *He used not to be so critical of other people's behaviour.*

once/at one time /wʌns, ət ˌwʌn ˈtaɪm/ [adv] during a period of time in the past but not now – use this when it is not important to say exactly when this period was: *Apparently he once worked for the FBI.* | *It is a big city now, but at one time the population was only 50,000.* | *a sports car once owned by Paul McCartney*

(back) then/at that time /(bæk) ˈðen, ət ˈðæt ˌtaɪm/ [adv] during a particular period of time in the past – use this when you are comparing that period with the present: *I was a student in the 1950s, and things were very different then.* | *At that time most married women stayed at home.*

in the past /ɪn ðə ˈpɑːst‖-ˈpæst/ [adv] use this to talk about a situation that existed before the present time but does not exist now: *In the past, most children didn't go to school at all.* | *Women were not allowed to vote or own property in the past.*

in those days/in the old days /ɪn ˈðəʊz ˌdeɪz, ɪn ði ˈəʊld ˌdeɪz/ [adv] use this to talk about a long time ago in your life, or in your parents' or grandparents' lives, when things were different: *My great grandfather earned £5 a week, which was a lot of money in those days.* | *In the old days there was no bridge over the river, and we crossed it by boat.* | **in the good old days** (=at a time when you think that things were better than now) *In the good old days people showed more respect to the older generation.*

in the olden days /ɪn ði ˈəʊldn ˌdeɪz/ [adv] at a time before you were born, especially hundreds of years ago: *The children all wanted to know what life was like in the olden days.*

formerly /ˈfɔːʳməʳli/ [adv] written in the past, before the present situation existed: *The local school was formerly a hospital.* | *Peru was formerly ruled by the Spanish.*

4 to try to do things as they were done in the past

- go back
- put/turn the clock back
- live in the past

go back /ˌgəʊ ˈbæk/ [phr v I] to return to an earlier time in your life, so that you can experience something again or change something that you did then – use this to say that you wish you could do this **+ to** *I wish I could go back to my school days.* | *Wouldn't it be nice if we could go back to the days when life was slower than it is today.* | **you can't go back** *It's no use having regrets. You can't go back!*

put/turn the clock back /ˌpʊt, ˌtɜːʳn ðə ˈklɒk ˌbæk‖-ˈklɑːk-/ [v phrase] to live part of your life again, so that you could do something in a different way, or experience something again: *If I could turn the clock back, I don't think I'd study law again.* | **+ to** *It would be nice to put the clock back to the years when Mum and Dad were still alive.*

live in the past /ˌlɪv ɪn ðə ˈpɑːst‖-ˈpæst/ [v phrase] to try to behave or live as you did at some time in the past, usually because you do not like your present situation or you are unhappy that things have changed: *It's no good living in the past. You have to get on with your life.* | *As people get older, they often tend to live in the past.*

5 on one occasion in the past

- once
- one time
- one day/morning/afternoon
- on one occasion
- at one stage
- at one point

once /wʌns/ [adv] *She once called me a liar – I've never forgiven her.* | *Once, when I was a little boy, I found a gold watch on the beach.*

one time /ˈwʌn ˌtaɪm/ [adv] informal on one occasion in the past: *One time we went out fishing on the lake at night.* | *Aileen came round to tea one time, and we did our homework together.*

one day/morning/afternoon /wʌn ˈdeɪ, ˈmɔːʳnɪŋ, ˌɑftəʳˈnuːn‖-ˌæf-/ [adv] on a day, morning, or afternoon in the past – use this when it is not important to say exactly which day it is: *Then, one day he went away and never came back.* | *I was having my breakfast one morning when the telephone rang.* | *One day, when we had nothing else to do, we went for a swim in the river.*

on one occasion /ɒn ˈwʌn əˌkeɪʒən/ [adv] something that happened **on one occasion** happened once in the past, but is often typical of what usually happens: *He drinks far too much. On one occasion I saw him drink a whole bottle of vodka.* | *On one occasion I made the mistake of arriving at work late and my boss has never let me forget it.*

at one stage /ət ˈwʌn ˌsteɪdʒ/ [adv] if a particular situation existed **at one stage** during a period in the past, it existed, but only at that time: *It was a terrible winter. At one stage, we had to dig our way out of the house.* | *At one stage during the competition, it looked as though our team might win.* | *I went on a diet and at one stage I weighed only 71 kg.*

at one point /ət ˈwʌn ˌpɔɪnt/ [adv] if something happened, especially something interesting or important, **at one point** during an activity or period of time in the past, it happened then: *At one point in the interview Gorbachev admitted he had* *made serious mistakes.* | *'You play the piano very well,' I remember Mrs Saito remarking at one point.*

pattern

RELATED WORDS

- *see also* **design, art/culture, paint, draw, colour/color, decorate, material, clothes**

- **pattern**
- **design**
- **markings**
- **motif**
- **patterning**

pattern /ˈpætən‖ˈpætərn/ [n C] a regular arrangement of shapes, colours, or lines, especially one that is used to decorate paper, cloth, plates etc: *I'm looking for a wallpaper with a nice bold pattern.* | *a navy blue silk blouse with a white flowery pattern* | **+ of** *patterns of sunlight and shadow on the ground*

design /dɪˈzaɪn/ [n C] a pattern or shape which is used to decorate something such as cloth or paper: *This design is very common on Turkish carpets.* | *brightly coloured curtains with an attractive floral design*

markings /ˈmɑːʳkɪŋz/ [n plural] the natural patterns on the skin, fur, or feathers of animals or birds: *The bird can be easily recognized by its unusual red and yellow markings.*

motif /məʊˈtiːf/ [n C] a single shape which is repeated to form a pattern which decorates something **a fish/flower/sun etc motif** *She was wearing a plain white T-shirt with a fish motif in blue and green.*

patterning /ˈpætənɪŋ‖ˈpætərnɪŋ/ [n U] the pattern that covers the surface of an object, animal, plant etc: *The zebra has very distinctive patterning.* | *Look at the beautiful delicate patterning around the base of the vase.*

pause

RELATED WORDS

- *see also* **stop, rest**

1 to stop doing something for a short time before continuing

- **pause**
- **stop**
- **hesitate**

pause /pɔːz/ [v I] written to stop speaking or stop doing something for a very short time before starting again: *Kim was reading her e-mail, but she paused and looked up when I came in.* | *Lawrence paused and turned to me: 'Look, if you don't think it's a good idea, don't go.'* | **pause for breath** (=use this when you need to rest for a moment, especially when you are talking) *She talked for about twenty minutes without even pausing for breath.* | **+ to do sth** *We waited while Graham paused to light a cigarette.*

stop /stɒp‖stɑːp/ [v I] to **stop** doing something for a short time, before continuing again: *Can we stop at the next services and get something to eat?* | **stop for coffee/lunch/a break etc** (=stop what you are doing, so you can have coffee, lunch etc) *We'll stop for lunch at 12:30.* | **stop to look/listen/watch/talk/rest etc** (=stop in order to look at something etc) *We stopped to listen to a group of boys who were playing guitars in the street.* | *I stopped to rest for a few minutes.* | **stop doing sth (for a moment/while etc)** *Could you stop making that noise for a moment?* | *The baby hadn't stopped crying for two whole hours.*

hesitate /ˈhezɪteɪt/ [v I] to stop for a moment and wait before doing something, because you feel unsure or nervous about it: *She hesitated for a moment before replying.* | *Barry stood at the door, hesitating. Should he walk straight in or knock?* —**hesitation** /ˌhezɪˈteɪʃən/ [n U] when someone hesitates: *'Definitely', he said, without any hesitation.*

2 to stop doing something in order to rest, eat etc

- **have/take a break**
- **take five**
- **take a breather**
- **break for lunch/coffee/Christmas etc**
- **take time out**
- **adjourn**

have/take a break /ˌhæv, ˌteɪk ə ˈbreɪk/ [v phrase] especially spoken to stop working for a while in order to rest, eat etc: *We're all getting tired. Let's take a break for ten minutes.* | *Is it all right if we have a break at about 10.30?* | **have a quick/short/five minute etc break** *If you're working at a computer, it's best if you have a quick break at least once an hour.*

take five /ˌteɪk ˈfaɪv/ [v phrase] American informal to stop for a while in order to rest: *Let's take five and get some coffee.*

take a breather /ˌteɪk ə ˈbriːðəʳ/ [v phrase] informal to stop for a while because you want a rest, especially because you have been doing something very difficult or tiring: *It's 12 o' clock. Why don't we take a breather?* | *I'd only been running for five minutes, but I had to stop and take a breather.*

break for lunch/coffee/Christmas etc /ˌbreɪk fəʳ ˈlʌntʃ/ [v phrase] to stop working and have lunch, a coffee break, a holiday etc: *At 12.30, the committee broke for lunch.* | *There's still an enormous amount of work to do before we break for Christmas.*

take time out /teɪk ˌtaɪm ˈaʊt/ [v phrase] to stop for a while and rest, either because you are tired or in order to do something else: *Try to take time out and get together with the kids.* | **+ to do sth** *Taking time out to relax each day is important during pregnancy.* | **+ from/of** *The President took time out from his busy schedule to speak to the crowds.*

adjourn ALSO **recess** American /əˈdʒɜːʳn, rɪˈses/ [v I/T] formal if a meeting or court **adjourns**, or if someone in authority **adjourns** it, the meeting or court stops for a short time, for example so that more information can be collected: *If there are no more questions, the committee will adjourn until tomorrow morning.* | *'The court will recess for twenty minutes,' Judge Bart said.* | *The trial was adjourned for two weeks until the psychiatrist's report was ready.*

3 a period of time when you stop doing something

- **break**
- **pause**
- **respite**
- **letup**
- **lull**
- **breathing space**

break /breɪk/ [n C] a long or short period when you stop your work or normal activities, before continuing them again later: *She returned to her job after a six-month break.* | **+ from** *After finishing school,*

Craig felt he needed a break from studying. | **lunch/coffee/tea break** (=when you stop work to have lunch, coffee etc) *You get a one hour lunch break, and fifteen minutes for a coffee break in the afternoon.*

pause /pɔːz/ [n C] written a short period during which you stop speaking or stop doing something before starting again: *After a long pause, Barney said: 'Yes, I suppose you're right.'* | **+ in** *There was a pause in the conversation as everyone turned to say hello to Paul.* | **a pregnant pause** (=a pause when someone is expected to say something, especially something awkward or embarrassing) *'Where's Matt?' There was a long and pregnant pause.*

respite /'respɪt, -paɪt‖-pɪt/ [n singular] a short time when something unpleasant stops happening so that the situation is temporarily better: *The noise went on all night, without a single moment's respite.* | **+ from** *The citizens had only a few days' respite from the conflict, before the shelling began again.* | **be no/little respite** *Weathermen yesterday warned that there would be no respite from the gales.* | **a brief/short-lived/temporary respite** *The drug can only provide a brief respite from the pain.* | **a welcome respite** *Some mothers regard work as a welcome respite from the stress of looking after a home and children.*

letup /'letʌp/ [n singular] a short time when something unpleasant stops happening so that the situation is temporarily better. **Letup** is more informal than **respite**: *There was a short letup in the downpour after lunch.* | **without (a) letup** *The fighting raged without a letup through the night,* | **+ in** *Kline warned against any letup in the pilot's concentration.*

lull /lʌl/ [n C] a temporary break in busy activity, noise, talking, fighting etc: *There was a lull, and then the thunder came again.* | **+ in** *Managers at Metrocentre have reported a lull in the recession, as takings continue to soar.* | *For two days there had been a lull in the fighting.* | *I waited for a lull in the conversation, before getting up to go.*

breathing space /'briːðɪŋ ˌspeɪs/ [n C/U] a short time when you stop doing something difficult, tiring etc, so that people have time to think more clearly about the situation: *At last a temporary agreement was reached, which gave both sides a breathing space.* | **+ to do sth** *After the divorce, I badly needed some breathing space to try and rebuild my life.*

4 a short period of time when schoolwork, a meeting, a game etc stops

- break
- intermission
- interlude
- adjournment
- recess

break /breɪk/ [n C/U] a short time between school classes when children can play, eat something etc: *The children have a fifteen-minute break at 11 o'clock.* | *Could you come and see me during afternoon break?*

intermission ALSO **interval** British /ˌɪntəʳ'mɪʃən, 'ɪntəʳvəl/ [n C] a planned pause during a play, concert, or film: *There will now be a short intermission.* | *Drinks will be on sale during the interval.*

interlude /'ɪntəʳluːd/ [n C] a planned pause during a play or concert, when music is often played **a musical/comic etc interlude** *Halfway through the performance there was a short musical interlude.* | *The dance provided a delightful comic interlude.*

adjournment [n C] especially British **/recess** [n C/U] especially American /ə'dʒɜːʳnmənt, rɪ'ses‖'riːses/ a pause when a court, formal meeting, talks etc stop for a short time, so that more information can be collected or so that people can discuss something: *Mr Robertson applied for an adjournment, to see if witnesses could be traced.* | *The heated debate continued after a ninety-minute adjournment.* | *Peace talks resumed on June 15th, after a month-long recess.* | **call a recess** *At four o'clock, the judge called a recess, and the jury was led out of the courtroom.* | **be in recess** *The court will be in recess for twenty minutes.*

recess /rɪ'ses‖'riːses/ [n C/U] when Parliament or Congress stops meeting for a period of time, in order to have a holiday **the summer/Easter/Christmas recess** *The Bill was brought before the House of Commons and passed before the summer recess.* | *Congress's two-week Easter recess* | **be in recess** *The House is in recess until January 22nd, when it will vote on the Bill.*

pay

RELATED WORDS

- money that someone is paid for their work *see* **earn**
- *see also* **buy, money, spend**

1 to pay for something

- pay
- meet the cost of
- foot the bill
- fork out/shell out
- cough up
- stump up

pay /peɪ/ [v I/T] to give money in exchange for goods or services: *Several fans tried to get in without paying.* | *Please pay at the desk.* | *I need £4.50 to pay the window cleaner.* | **+ for** *Have you paid for the tickets?* | **pay £20/$40 etc for sth** *She paid $5,000 for three nights in a hotel in New York City.* | **pay a bill/rent/tax etc** *Tom paid his bill at the cashier's desk.* | *There was no point in paying rent on an empty apartment for two months.* | **pay cash** (=pay using coins, notes etc) *They don't have health insurance, so they have to pay cash for doctor's visits.* | **pay by cheque/credit card etc** *Pay by credit card at least ten days before departure.*

meet the cost of /ˌmiːt ðə 'kɒst ɒv‖-'kɔːst-/ [v phrase] if a company or organization **meets the cost of** something, it pays for it for someone else, especially when they do not have a legal duty to do this: *We will meet the cost of any expenses you may incur when travelling to your interview.* | **+ of doing sth** *A local firm has agreed to meet the cost of sending ten lucky prize-winners on a dream holiday.*

foot the bill /ˌfʊt ðə 'bɪl/ [v phrase] to pay for something for someone else, especially when you do not want to or do not think that you should: *It will be, as usual, the taxpayer who will be footing the bill.* | **+ for** *The program asks businesses to foot the bill for daily newspapers in the classroom.*

fork out/shell out /ˌfɔːʳk 'aʊt, ˌʃel 'aʊt/ [phr v I/T] informal to pay a lot of money for something because you have to and not because you want to, especially for something you need: *The policy affects how much we will have to shell out at the petrol station.* | **fork out £100/$10,000/a lot of money etc** *He had to fork out £500 to get his car fixed.* | *Fans are having to shell out roughly $65 per seat for football games.* | **fork out**

£100/$20,000/a lot of money etc on sb/sth *From the time you enroll them in nursery school, you're forking out a fortune on the kids.* | **+ for** *$13 seems like a lot of money to shell out for a bottle of wine.*

cough up /ˌkɒf ˈʌp‖ˌkɔːf-/ [phr v I/T] informal to pay money for something, especially money that you owe or that someone has persuaded you to pay: *You owe me twenty pounds. Come on, cough up!* | **cough up £3/$100/a few pence etc** *You have to cough up $2 just to get into the park.*

stump up /ˌstʌmp ˈʌp/ [phr v I/T] British informal to pay for something, usually when someone else thinks you should: *His dad wouldn't stump up for a new bike.* | **stump up £50/$200/a lot of money etc** *Everybody in the office stumped up a few pounds for his leaving present.*

2 to pay for someone else's food, drink, ticket etc

- pay
- treat
- pick up the tab
- be on me
- buy a round
- it's my shout

pay /peɪ/ [v I] to **pay** for someone else, for example for their meal, drink, or ticket: *If I go out for a meal with my parents, they always pay.* | **+ for** *When we got to the ferry, Eddie took out a five-dollar bill and paid for Terry and me.* | *Who paid for your driving lessons?* | **pay for sb to do sth** *My company paid for me to go to evening classes.*

treat /triːt/ [v T] to buy something such as a meal or theatre ticket for someone, because you like them or want to celebrate something: *As it's your birthday, I thought I'd treat you.* | **treat sb to sth** *We treated Sally to lunch at the Savoy.* —**treat** [n C usually singular] *Let me take you to dinner. My treat.*

pick up the tab /ˌpɪk ʌp ðə ˈtæb/ [v phrase] to pay for something, especially when it is not necessarily your responsibility or duty to do this: *We all went out to dinner, and Adam picked up the tab.* | **+ for** *Usually the book publisher, not the author, picks up the tab for a publicity tour.*

be on me /biː ɒn ˈmiː/ [v phrase] spoken say **the drinks are on me, this meal's on me etc** when you are telling someone you will pay for their drinks, their meal etc: *Order whatever you like – this is on me!* | *Put your money away – the drinks are on us.*

buy a round /ˌbaɪ ə ˈraʊnd/ [v phrase] to buy drinks for the people you are with in a bar: *Joe bought a round of drinks for everyone.*

it's my shout /ɪts ˈmaɪ ʃaʊt/ British spoken say this when it is your turn to buy the drinks for the people you are with in a bar: *No, it's my shout. What are you drinking?*

3 to have enough money to pay for something

- can afford
- be able to pay

can afford /kən əˈfɔːʳd/ [v phrase] if you **can afford** something, you have enough money to pay for it: *I'd love to visit Australia, but I just can't afford it.* | *I had to move because I couldn't afford the rent any more.* | **+ to do sth** *How can you afford to eat in restaurants all the time?* | *He's finally earning more, so he can afford to have a holiday this year.*

be able to pay /biː ˌeɪbəl tə ˈpeɪ/ [v phrase] to have enough money to pay for something such as a tax or a bill: *They say they will have all the money on Friday, but I don't think they'll be able to pay.* | *Some people just aren't able to pay the tax.* | **+ for** *Many people use credit as a way of buying goods they are not able to pay for.*

4 to pay someone to do something

- pay
- tip
- make it worth sb's while
- buy off

pay /peɪ/ [v T] to **pay** someone for work: *How much do they pay you?* | **pay sb for (doing) sth** *They still haven't paid her for the work she did last year.* | *Did she pay you for taking care of her kids?* | **be/get paid** *We get paid at the end of every month.* | **pay sb £100/$200 etc** *Ziedler was ready to pay her $2000 a week.* | **pay sb to do sth** *If you pay someone to work in your house, you have to pay Social Security taxes on the wages.* | **pay well/badly** *Jobs in areas that use mathematical skills, such as computer programming, tend to pay well.* —**paid** [adj] *Many Britons receive four or five weeks of paid holiday a year.* | **well/highly paid** (=paid a lot) *He has a very well-paid job in finance.* | *a highly paid executive* | **badly paid** (=not paid much) *Most badly paid jobs are done by women.* | *The job is exhausting and badly paid.*

tip /tɪp/ [v T] to pay a waiter, taxi driver etc a little extra money: *Did you tip the waiter?* | *It's usual to tip about 15% in restaurants.* —**tipping** [n U] *A service charge is included on the bill, so tipping isn't necessary.*

make it worth sb's while /meɪk ɪt ˌwɜːʳθ (sb's) ˈwaɪl/ [v phrase] informal if you tell someone you will **make it worth their while**, you mean you will give them money if they agree to do something for you, especially something dishonest or not convenient: *I didn't want to lend Terry my car, but he said he'd make it worth my while.* | *The basketball federation in Kuwait offered him a coaching job, and made it worth his while.*

buy off /ˌbaɪ ˈɒf / [phr v T] to give someone money to stop them from causing trouble or doing something that they have threatened to do **buy sb off/buy off sb** *Do you really think the cops can't be bought off?* | **buy sb off with sth** *The management has been trying to buy off union activists with substantial pay offers.*

5 to pay someone to do something dishonest or illegal

- bribe
- kickback
- backhander/bung

bribe /braɪb/ [v T] to give money to someone in an official position, in order to persuade them to do something that they should not do: *Santo was convicted of bribing tax inspectors in Italy.* | **bribe sb to do sth** *He bribed a guard to smuggle a note out of the prison.* | **bribe sb into doing sth** *Judges are bribed or threatened into making decisions favorable to drug traffickers.* —**bribe** [n C] money that you use to bribe someone: *The judge was accused of accepting bribes.* —**bribery** [n U] when people are bribed: *There was widespread bribery and corruption in the police department.*

kickback /ˈkɪkbæk/ [n C] a large amount of money paid to someone in a high position in a company or government, for arranging a business deal for you: *Top executives received millions of dollars in kickbacks.* | *He offered me $20,000 as a kickback if I'd push through a $500,000 loan.*

backhander/bung /ˈbækhændəʳ, bʌŋ/ [n C] British informal a small amount of money paid to someone to persuade them to do something that is dishonest but usually not very serious: *He denies accepting backhanders, though he admits being offered them.* | *George gave the bouncer a bung, and we got into the nightclub.*

6 to pay back money that you owe someone

- pay back
- repay
- pay off
- pay up
- settle
- clear
- give sb their money back/give sb a refund
- reimburse
- rebate

pay back /ˌpeɪ ˈbæk/ [phr v T] to give someone back money that you have borrowed from them **pay sb back** *I'll pay you back tomorrow.* | **pay back sth** *How are you going to pay back all that money?* | *He's paid back about half of what he owes us.* | **pay back a loan/debt etc** *After graduation, the student must begin to pay back the loan.*

repay /rɪˈpeɪ/ [v T] to pay a large amount of money that you owe, especially to a bank: *The loan has to be repaid within two years.* | *There were doubts about the country's ability to repay the debt.* | *My parents lent me the money to buy a car, and I repaid them over the next year.*

pay off /ˌpeɪ ˈɒf / [phr v T] to finish paying back an amount of money that you have borrowed **pay off a debt/loan/mortgage etc** *The mortgage will be paid off over twenty-five years.* | *He paid off the loan six months early.* | **pay a debt/loan/mortgage etc off** *The country hopes to pay all its debts off within twenty years.*

pay up /ˌpeɪ ˈʌp/ [phr v I] to pay money that you owe, especially when you do not want to or when you are late paying it: *If they don't pay up we will take legal action.* | *The company paid up eventually, but only after repeated threats and reminders.*

settle /ˈsetl/ [v T] **settle an account/bill/loan etc** to pay money that you owe someone – used especially in business contexts: *Please settle this account within two weeks.* | *I settled the bill and left the restaurant.*

clear /klɪəʳ/ [v T] to finally pay all the money that you owe, after some time or with some difficulty: *This cheque should clear my overdraft.* | *We're hoping that we can clear all our debts by the end of the year.*

give sb their money back/give sb a refund /ˌgɪv (sb) ðeəʳ ˈmʌni ˌbæk, ˌgɪv (sb) ə ˈriːfʌnd/ [v phrase] to give back to someone the money that they paid for something, especially because they are not satisfied with what they bought or there is something wrong with it: *We'll give you a refund if you're not entirely satisfied.* | *It's the wrong size. Do you think they'll give me my money back?* —**refund** [n C] the money you get when someone gives you a refund: *You can't have a refund unless you bring us the receipt.* | **tax refund** American *I think I should get a pretty big tax refund this year.* —**refund** /rɪˈfʌnd/ [v T] formal *The fee will be refunded upon presentation of the receipt.*

reimburse /ˌriːɪmˈbɜːʳs/ [v T] formal to pay money to someone for something that they have had to pay for or have lost because of you: *Pay for the hotel room when you leave, and the company will reimburse you later.* | *He wouldn't let me reimburse him for the cost of his journey.* | *We pay for any repairs that need doing to the house, and are reimbursed by the landlord.*

rebate /ˈriːbeɪt/ [n C] an amount of money that is paid back to you, especially because you have paid too much in taxes, rent etc. In American English a tax **rebate** is called a **tax refund**: *The Ford Citibank credit card offers a 5 percent rebate on the purchase of a new Ford car or truck.* | **tax/rent rebate** British *We were delighted to hear that we were entitled to a tax rebate of over £1000.*

7 to pay for something before you receive it

- pay in advance
- up front
- make/put a down payment on
- put/make/pay a deposit on
- put $100/£100 etc down on
- put sth on layaway

pay in advance /ˌpeɪ ɪn ədˈvɑːns‖-ˈvæns/ [v phrase] to pay for something before you receive it: *Customs fees are paid in advance as part of your airline ticket.* | *Don't pay cash in advance for any service.*

up front /ʌp ˈfrʌnt/ [adv] if you pay for something **up front**, you pay or partly pay for it before you receive it, especially in order to show the person you are paying that they can trust you: *I paid the builders £100 up front and will give them the rest when the job's finished.* | *We've had so many unpaid bills that we've started to demand payment up front.*

make/put a down payment on /meɪk, pʊt ə ˌdaʊn ˈpeɪmənt ɒn/ [v phrase] to pay part of the cost of something expensive, especially a home or car, and agree to pay the rest at a later time: *We saved enough money to make a down payment on a house.* | *He borrowed money from his family to put a down payment on a truck.*

put/make/pay a deposit on /ˌpʊt, ˌmeɪk, ˌpeɪ ə dɪˈpɒzɪ̊t ɒn‖-ˈpɑː-/ [v phrase] to pay part of the cost of something before you buy it, especially so that no one else can buy it instead of you: *We've put a deposit on a round-the-world tour.* | *The Center has helped several poor families pay the deposit on a better apartment.*

put $100/£100 etc down on /pʊt ə ˌhʌndrɪ̊d dɒləʳz ˈdaʊn ɒn‖-dɑːl-/ [phr v T] to pay money towards the cost of something so that you can be sure it will be sold to you: *I've put £200 down on a new bedroom carpet.* | *Greg's parents are going to give us some money to put down on a car.*

put sth on layaway /ˌpʊt (sth) ɒn ˈleɪəweɪ/ [v phrase] American to pay part of the money for something you buy at a store, such as a piece of clothing or a gift, so that the store keeps it for you until you can pay the rest: *I'd like to put this sweater on layaway, please.*

8 to buy something and pay for it later

- get/buy sth on credit
- put sth on the slate

get/buy sth on credit /ˌget, ˌbaɪ (sth) ɒn ˈkredɪ̊t/ [v phrase] to buy something and pay for it later, usually by making small regular payments: *Most people have to make major purchases on credit.* | *In 2001, 56% of new cars were bought on credit.*

put sth on the slate /ˌpʊt (sth) ɒn ðə ˈsleɪt/ [v phrase] to receive goods or services, especially in small shops or places where you know the owner, and agree to pay for them at a later time: *Can I put it on the slate, and I'll pay at the end of the week?*

9 to pay money to someone because they have suffered an injury, loss, damage etc

- compensate
- damages
- compensation

compensate /ˈkɒmpənseɪt‖ˈkɑːm-/ [v I/T] *People are entitled to be compensated fully whenever they are injured by others' carelessness.* | **+ for** *No amount of money can compensate for my father's death.* | **compensate sb for sth** *The workers have still not been compensated for their loss of wages.*

damages /ˈdæmɪdʒɪ̈z/ [n plural] money that a law court orders someone to pay to you because they have caused you harm **pay sb damages** *Survivors of the air crash were paid $10000 each in damages.* | **award sb damages** (=agree that damages should be paid) *Damages of £2500 were awarded by the court.*

compensation /ˌkɒmpənˈseɪʃən‖ˌkɑːm-/ [n U] money that someone pays you because they have caused you harm, loss, or damage to your property: *The government cannot take private property for public use without compensation.* | **pay sb compensation** *His employers paid him $5000 compensation for his broken leg.* | **+ for** *See if you can get some compensation from the airline for your lost baggage.*

10 to provide money for someone else to live on

- provide for
- support
- pay maintenance
- pay child support
- pay alimony

provide for /prəˈvaɪd fɔːʳ/ [v T] to provide money for your family to live on: *When she was unemployed it was very difficult to provide for her children.* | *A life insurance policy enables you to provide for your family after your death.* | **well provided for** *He left his family well-provided for.*

support /səˈpɔːʳt/ [v T] to provide enough money for someone to pay for all the things they need, especially if you do this by working: *He has a wife and two children to support.* | *A lot of people can barely earn enough to support themselves, let alone their families.* | *My parents didn't have to support me when I was at college because I received a grant.*

pay maintenance /peɪ ˈmeɪntənəns/ [v phrase] British to pay a regular amount of money to the person you used to be married to, especially to support children of yours that you no longer live with: *Maintenance will be paid until the child reaches 18 or leaves full-time education.*

pay child support /peɪ ˈtʃaɪld səˌpɔːʳt/ [v phrase] to pay a regular amount of money to help support children of yours that you no longer live with: *He had been paying child support for his two children since 1985.*

pay alimony /peɪ ˈælɪ̈məni‖-məʊni/ [v phrase] to pay a regular amount of money to the person you used to be married to: *The judge ordered McFadden to pay alimony of $2,400 a month.*

11 to provide money to help someone do something

- subsidize
- sponsor
- fund
- bankroll
- underwrite
- put money into
- finance/back
- pour money into
- throw money at

subsidize ALSO **subsidise** British /ˈsʌbsɪ̈daɪz/ [v T] if a government or other organization **subsidizes** something, it pays part of the cost: *Many companies subsidize meals for their workers.* | *a government-subsidized health service* | *The city council subsidizes the local orchestra.*

sponsor /ˈspɒnsəʳ‖ˈspɑːn-/ [v T] if a company **sponsors** something such as sports event, a theatre, or an art show, it provides some of the money that is needed, often as a form of advertising: *The new league will be sponsored by Pepsi Cola.* | *The bank is sponsoring an art exhibition.* —**sponsor** [n C] *Sponsors' corporate logos are placed on the boards surrounding the field.*

fund /fʌnd/ [v T] to provide all the money needed to pay for something, especially an important or expensive plan: *Both schools and industry will be involved in funding the new training projects.* | *a charity funded by private donations* | *The state should fund the arts for the benefit of us all.*

bankroll /ˈbæŋkrəʊl/ [v T] informal to provide the money for something such as a business or a plan: *The competition is being bankrolled by a New York businessman and computer enthusiast.* | *Ed Bass, a millionaire from Texas, bankrolled the Biosphere project.*

underwrite /ˌʌndəˈraɪt/ [v T] to provide the money needed for something and agree to take responsibility and pay any debts if it fails: *The British government has agreed to underwrite the project with a grant of £5 million.* | *The venture was underwritten by several companies.*

put money into /ˌpʊt ˈmʌni ɪntuː/ [v phrase] to provide some of the money needed to start or continue in business, hoping that you will get more money back if the business is successful: *Small investors and large companies have both put money into the exhibition.* | *He put all his money into a dotcom company that later failed.*

finance/back /faɪˈnæns‖ˈfaɪnæns, bæk/ [v T] to provide the money needed to pay for something, especially by doing something to earn or collect that money: *The government uses money from taxes to finance higher education.* | *She gave swimming lessons to finance her stay in Australia.* | *It's a great show, but he can't find anyone to back it.* | *The bank is eager to back business ideas by local people.*

pour money into /ˌpɔːʳ ˈmʌni ɪntuː/ [v phrase] to provide a lot of money over a period of time to pay for something, especially something that will later be unsuccessful: *Many biotech companies are not yet profitable, as they continue to pour money into research and trials.*

throw money at /ˌθrəʊ ˈmʌni æt/ [v phrase] to provide a lot of money for something, especially government money – use this when you do not think that this is the best way of solving a problem or improving a situation: *The way to solve the education crisis is not necessarily to throw money at it.* | *The Republicans see him as a liberal whose only solution to the nation's problems was to throw money at them.*

12 an amount of money that is paid

- payment
- instalment
- deposit/down payment
- down payment
- tip

payment /ˈpeɪmənt/ [n C] an amount of money that you pay for something, especially when it is only one part of the total amount you have to pay: *Your first payment is due on July 16th.* | **mortgage/car/credit card etc payment** *The family spends about $1,800 a month on their mortgage payments.* | **make a payment** *He makes monthly payments into his ex-wife's bank account.* | **+ of** *They have a monthly car payment of £220.*

instalment British **/installment** American /ɪnˈstɔːlmənt/ [n C] a regular payment you make to pay back money that you have borrowed or to pay for things that you have already received: *To avoid penalties, pay the installments by the December 10 and April 10 dates.* | **instalment of £250/$1000 etc** *I borrowed $2000, which was to be paid back in monthly installments of $250.* | **in instalments** *You can pay me in instalments if you can't afford to give me all the money back in one go.*

deposit/down payment /dɪˈpɒzɪt‖dɪˈpɑː-, ˌdaʊn ˈpeɪmənt/ [n C] part of the cost of something that you pay before you get it, so that it will not be sold to anyone else and so that the seller is certain that you will buy it: *Most stores ask for a small deposit if they are to keep goods for you.* | **$20/£5 etc deposit** *Yes, we have plenty of rooms available, but you'll have to pay a $20 deposit.* | **+ on** *She's paid the deposit on a new bed.* | **leave a deposit** *Would you mind leaving a deposit? You can collect the picture when it's ready next week.*

down payment /ˌdaʊn ˈpeɪmənt/ [n C] the first amount of money that you pay for something expensive, which you will continue to pay for over a long period of time: *For a 40 percent down payment on a new car, the company will arrange a no-interest loan.* | **make a down payment on sth** *We almost have enough to make a down payment on the house.*

tip /tɪp/ [n C] a small amount of money that you give someone such as a waiter or taxi-driver in addition to the ordinary payment: *The boy carried my suitcases up to my room and then stood waiting for a tip.* | *A 15% tip is considered usual if the service was good.* | **leave a tip** *We finished our lunch and left a tip on the table for the waiter.*

13 money that you have to pay as a punishment

- fine
- fine

fine /faɪn/ [n C] *I got a fine for parking on a double yellow line.* | **heavy fine** *There are heavy fines for drink-driving. You might even go to prison.* | **£30/$100 fine** *He got a $75 fine for speeding.* | **library fine/parking fine etc** *If you're going into town, will you go and pay my library fines for me please?*

fine /faɪn/ [v T] to make someone pay money as a punishment **fine sb for sth** *Stores will be fined for selling cigarettes or tobacco to minors.* | **fine sb £5/$100 etc** *The company was fined $1.6 million for breaking environmental regulations.* | **be/get fined** *You will be fined for any lost library books.*

14 a piece of paper that shows how much you must pay

- bill
- check
- tab
- invoice

bill /bɪl/ [n C] a piece of paper that tells you how much you must pay for services you have received or for work that has been done for you: *Can I have the bill, please?* | **telephone/gas/electricity etc bill** *We've just had a huge telephone bill.* | **pay a bill** *They left the hotel without paying the bill.* | **a bill for £50/$100 etc** *The garage sent me a bill for £400.* | **the bill comes to** (=the amount on the bill adds up to) *The bill for the meal came to $75, including wine.*

check /tʃek/ [n singular] American a piece of paper that tells you how much you must pay in a restaurant: *A waiter came over and handed me the check.* | **pay the check** *Let me pay the check.*

tab /tæb/ [n singular] informal a bill that is added up at the end of a period of time, showing how much you owe for drinks, food etc: *The bride's father paid the tab for the party.* | **put sth on the tab** *He ordered dinner and asked for it to be put on his tab.* | **run up a tab** *In just two days, she'd run up a bar tab of $175.*

invoice /ˈɪnvɔɪs/ [n C] a bill given to you by a company or organization, which tells you how much you owe them for goods, services or work that they have provided: *You will find the invoice attached to the box.* | *They sent him an invoice at the end of the month.* | **invoice for £250/$300 etc** *We have received an invoice for $250.*

15 to tell someone in writing how much they should pay you

- bill
- invoice

bill /bɪl/ [v T] to send someone a document showing how much money they must pay you, for goods or services they have received: *Some lawyers bill clients up to $300 an hour.* | **bill sb for sth** *One lobbyist billed the environmental group $20,000 for nine-months' work.*

invoice /ˈɪnvɔɪs/ [v T] if a company or organization **invoices** you, they send you a bill showing how much you have to pay for goods and services they have provided: *You will be invoiced as soon as the work is completed.* | **invoice sb for sth** *The company invoiced us for the cost of using their conference hall.*

16 when you are paid or not paid for doing an activity or sport

- professional
- amateur
- voluntary
- unpaid

professional /prəˈfeʃənəl/ [adj only before noun] a **professional** sports player, musician, actor etc gets paid for playing, acting etc, and they do it as their job: *Professional basketball players can earn millions of dollars.* —**professional** [n C] someone who gets paid for doing a job, sport, or activity that most people do for enjoyment: *The play is performed by 50 local actors led by four professionals.*

amateur /ˈæmətəʳ, -tʃʊəʳ, -tʃəʳ, ˌæməˈtɜːʳ/ [adj only before noun] an **amateur** sports player, musician, actor etc does not get paid for playing, acting etc, but they do it for enjoyment: *A group of amateur actors performed 'Romeo and Juliet'.* | *an amateur photographer* — **amateur** [n C] someone who does an activity or sport for enjoyment, and not as their job: *The orchestra is made up entirely of amateurs.*

voluntary British **/volunteer** American /ˈvɒləntəri‖ˈvɑːlənteri, ˌvɒlənˈtɪəʳ‖ˌvɑː-/ [adj usually before noun] **voluntary** or **volunteer** work is done by people who do it because they believe it is useful, and do not expect to be paid: *When she retired, she did a lot of voluntary work for the Red Cross.*

unpaid /ˌʌnˈpeɪd◂/ [adj] not paid **unpaid worker/volunteer etc** *Perry stayed on with the Agency as an unpaid adviser.* | **unpaid work/service/overtime etc** *Employees were often required to work unpaid overtime.* | **unpaid leave/holiday/vacation** *The company allows its employees to take unpaid leave for various reasons.*

peace

RELATED WORDS

opposite: **war**

▸ *see also* **fight**

1 when there is no war

- ▸ **peace**
- ▸ **peacetime**
- ▸ **peaceful**
- ▸ **be at peace with**

peace /piːs/ [n U] when there is no war: *There has been peace in the region for six years now.* | **peace talks/negotiations** (=when enemies meet and talk, to try and achieve peace) *The United States urged Moscow and the rebels to resume peace talks.* | **a peace agreement/deal/settlement** *More than 250,000 people died before a peace agreement was reached.* | **the peace process** (=a continuing attempt, over a long period, to achieve peace between enemies.) *the Middle East peace process* | **world peace** *It was a dangerous situation that threatened world peace.* | **peace movement** (=an organization that works to try to prevent wars) *All her life she'd been an active member of the peace movement.*

peacetime /ˈpiːstaɪm/ [n U] a period of time when a country is not fighting a war – use this when comparing this period with a time when there is war: *A country's army may be quite small during peacetime.* | *In peacetime, the Hercules aircraft has been used for distributing food to famine areas.* | *The talks were aimed at establishing normal peacetime relations between the two countries.*

peaceful /ˈpiːsfəl/ [adj] use this about changes or events that happen without war or fighting: *There was a relatively peaceful transfer of power from the military government to the new democracy.* | *a peaceful solution to the troubles in the region* —**peacefully** [adv] *Can they achieve their independence peacefully?*

be at peace with /biː ət ˈpiːs wɪð/ [v phrase] if two or more countries **are at peace with** each other, they are not fighting each other and have a friendly relationship: *From 1564 until 1585, England was at peace with most of her neighbours.* | *For the next 25 years, Britain managd to remain at peace with France.*

2 when two countries agree to stop fighting

- ▸ **ceasefire**
- ▸ **truce**
- ▸ **peace treaty**
- ▸ **make peace**
- ▸ **lay down arms**

ceasefire /ˈsiːsfaɪəʳ/ [n C] an agreement to stop fighting for a limited period of time, especially in order to talk about making peace: *The ceasefire won't last unless both sides are prepared to compromise.* | **+ between** *a ceasefire between the warring forces in the south* | **ceasefire agreement** *Both leaders signed the ceasefire agreement.* | **agree to/achieve a ceasefire** *The government had failed in numerous attempts to achieve a ceasefire through negotiation.* | **violate the ceasefire** (=start fighting again during a ceasefire) *So far no one has violated the three-day ceasefire.*

truce /truːs/ [n C] an agreement to stop fighting for a short time, especially in order to discuss making peace: *The rebels have ended a 17-month-old truce, and could strike at any time.* | **+ between** *a truce between the rival Christian forces* | **call/negotiate/secure etc a truce** *The two sides have been unable to negotiate a truce.*

peace treaty /ˈpiːs ˌtriːti/ [n C] a written agreement between two enemies saying that they agree to end the war: *Both countries agreed to work towards a peace treaty.* | **+ between** *On July 12th, the South Korean President called for a peace treaty between the two states.* | **negotiate/draw up/sign/conclude a peace treaty** *The left-wing guerrilla movement finally signed a peace treaty with the government on March 9th.*

make peace /ˌmeɪk ˈpiːs/ [v phrase] if two countries **make peace**, they stop fighting and agree to end the war: *France and Spain made peace in 1659 after a war lasting 25 years.* | **+ with** *The two armies made peace with each other in 1918.*

lay down arms /ˌleɪ daʊn ˈɑːʳmz/ [v phrase] if soldiers **lay down** their **arms**, they stop fighting – used especially in literature and descriptions of historical events: *No sooner had they laid down their arms than the English broke their word and attacked.* | *In March, the Popular Liberation Army laid down arms and registered as a political party.*

3 to try to prevent or end a war

- ▸ **keep the peace**
- ▸ **peace-keeping**
- ▸ **peacekeepers**
- ▸ **mediate between**

keep the peace /ˌkiːp ðə ˈpiːs/ [v phrase] to prevent a war or fighting between two countries, or between two opposing armies within a country: *The President sent federal troops to Grenada to keep the peace.* | **+ between** *In the past, air support from the RAF base at Aden had been enough to keep the peace between the rival warring tribes.*

peace-keeping /ˈpiːs kiːpɪŋ/ [adj only before noun] **peace-keeping force/troops/mission etc** intended to prevent two opposing armies, especially within a country, from fighting: *A United Nations peacekeeping force has been sent to the area.* | *Panama called for the United States to withdraw its peacekeeping army.*

peacekeepers /ˈpiːsˌkiːpəʳz/ [n plural] soldiers who have been sent to a country where there is a war or fighting in order to keep the peace between the two sides: *American ground troops are to join the UN peacekeepers to try to stop the war from spreading.*

mediate between /ˈmiːdieɪt bɪˌtwiːn/ [v phrase] to help two or more countries or armies that have been at war to make peace with each other by discussing the situation: *An Iranian delegation visited northern Iraq to mediate between rival Kurdish groups.* —**mediation** /ˌmiːdiˈeɪʃən/ [n U] *They hoped that Russia's mediation would end the war.* —**mediator**

/ˈmiːdieɪtəʳ/ [n C] *He received the Nobel Prize for his work as a mediator in the Palestine conflict.*

4 someone who is against war

- pacifist
- anti-war
- peace-loving
- peace movement
- peace protester/demonstrator

pacifist /ˈpæsɪfɪst/ [n C] someone who believes that all war and violence is wrong: *Bergson was imprisoned as a pacifist during the World War I.*

anti-war /ˌænti ˈwɔːʳ◂/ [adj only before noun] strongly against war, especially a war that your country is fighting at the present time **anti-war protest/demonstration/campaigner** *During the Gulf War, there were several big anti-war demonstrations.* | *Anti-war feeling grew stronger in the US as the Vietnam conflict went on.*

peace-loving /ˈpiːs ˌlʌvɪŋ/ [adj] a group of people or countries that are **peace-loving** believe strongly in peace rather than war: *The Australian Aboriginals are a peace-loving race who live simply off the land.* | *As a nation, they are gentle and peace-loving.*

peace movement /ˈpiːs ˌmuːvmənt/ [n U] all the people who protest against wars in general or against a particular war: *He was a tireless campaigner for the peace movement during the cold war.* | *The peace movement held a massive rally in Hyde Park today.*

peace protester/demonstrator /ˈpiːs prəˌtestəʳ, ˈdemənstreɪtəʳ/ [n C] someone who joins in an organized protest against a war: *Peace protesters broke into the Administration building and occupied it for six days.* | *Some 40,000 peace demonstrators gathered in Bonn yesterday to protest agains the bombing.*

peaceful

RELATED WORDS

- when there is no war *see* **peace**
- *see also* **quiet, calm, busy/not busy**

1 peaceful

- peaceful
- calm
- quiet
- sleepy
- tranquil
- restful
- still

peaceful /ˈpiːsfəl/ [adj] if a place or situation is **peaceful,** it makes you feel calm and relaxed because there is no unpleasant noise or activity: *Langcliffe is a peaceful little village.* | *It's so nice and peaceful here.* | *After a career as a journalist, she was looking forward to a happy and peaceful retirement.*

calm /kɑːm‖kɑːm, kɑːlm/ [adj] if a place is **calm,** there is no violence or excited activity there, especially after a period when there has been violence or excitement: *After yesterday's fighting, the region is now calm again.* | *Once on board, you can relax in calm, comfortable surroundings.*

quiet /ˈkwaɪət/ [adj] a **quiet** place or time is one without much activity, noise, or excitement, or without many people: *Since the last big outbreak of fighting six days ago, the city has been strangely quiet.* | *The roads are usually pretty quiet at this time of day.* | **a quiet night/evening in** (=an evening at home, rather than going out) *Let's have a nice quiet evening in, for a change.* | **a quiet life** *While he liked to go out partying, she wanted a quiet life.*

sleepy /ˈsliːpi/ [adj only before noun] a **sleepy** town or village is a quiet, peaceful one, where there is very little to do and exciting things do not usually happen: *Ten years ago, this was a sleepy fishing village.* | *She headed for the High Street, the only lively spot in the sleepy little town.*

tranquil /ˈtræŋkwɪl/ [adj] a place that is **tranquil** is pleasantly quiet and makes you feel relaxed: *In summer, the normally calm, tranquil streets fill with crowds of tourists.* | *Efforts are being made to make life more tranquil in Japan's noisy and overcrowded cities.*

restful /ˈrestfəl/ [adj] a **restful** time or place is a quiet and relaxing one: *I'm looking forward to a quiet, restful summer vacation.* | *Her suite of rooms was cool and restful.* | *He woke after a long, restful sleep, feeling refreshed.*

still /stɪl/ [adj] without wind, movement, or noise: *It was a long, hot, still September afternoon.* | *Everything was very still inside the little chapel. Nothing broke the silence.*

2 a peaceful state or situation

- peace
- calm
- tranquillity

peace /piːs/ [n U] a peaceful situation with no unpleasant noise or interruptions: *Top footballer Bobby Mimms loves coming back to the peace of his home village in North Yorkshire.* | *Residents say that the new development would shatter the peace of their area.* | **peace and quiet** *They've gone to the countryside for some peace and quiet.* | **do sth in peace** (=do something without being interrupted) *Now go away and let me get on with my work in peace.*

calm /kɑːm‖kɑːm, kɑːlm/ [n U] a situation in which there is no noise, anxious activity, or violence: *What we need now is a period of calm and stability.* | **an atmosphere/sense of calm** *Inside the new gallery, there is an atmosphere of calm.* | **appeal/call for calm** *The Prime Minister visited the centre of the rioting and called for calm.* | **restore calm** *By October 17th, the police had managed to restore calm.*

tranquillity British **/tranquility** American /træŋˈkwɪlɪti/ [n U] a pleasantly peaceful situation, especially one in which nothing seems to change: *Nothing ever happens to disturb the tranquillity of this little town, hidden in the Tuscan hills.*

3 a peaceful place

- haven
- oasis

haven /ˈheɪvən/ [n C usually singular] a quiet, peaceful place where you can relax or be on your own: *More and more people are swapping their suburban house for a peaceful rural haven.* | **+ of** *The airport chapel offers a haven of peace only metres away from the bustle of the departure lounge.*

oasis /əʊˈeɪsɪs/ [n C usually singular] a peaceful place with busy places around it: *Masongill is a peaceful oasis undisturbed by tourists.* | **+ of** *The little resort is an oasis of calm on the lively island of Majorca.*

perfect

RELATED WORDS

- in perfect condition *see* **condition**
- containing only one substance, not mixed with anything else *see* **pure**
- *see also* **best, good, suitable, convenient, right**

1 very good, with nothing wrong

- perfect
- flawless/faultless
- model
- impeccable
- can't fault
- unblemished
- perfection

perfect /ˈpɜːʳfɪkt/ [adj] someone or something that is **perfect** is good in every way and could not be any better: *We had a wonderful vacation – the weather was perfect.* | **absolutely perfect** *The meal was absolutely perfect.* | **be in perfect health** (=use this especially about someone who is old) *My mother's in perfect health, even though she's nearly 80.* | **the perfect husband/secretary/couple etc** *Beth and Martin always seemed to be the perfect couple.* —**perfectly** [adv] *It's a beautiful dress, and it fits perfectly.*

flawless/faultless /ˈflɔːləs, ˈfɔːltləs/ [adj] formal completely perfect, with no mistakes or faults at all: *Hiroshi's English was flawless.* | *He gave a faultless performance as Macbeth.*

model /ˈmɒdl‖ˈmɑːdl/ [adj only before noun] **model husband/wife/student etc** someone who has all the qualities that a husband, wife, student etc should have: *Karen was a model student: hardworking, intelligent and enthusiastic.* | *Chris always got to work early and left late – the model employee.*

impeccable /ɪmˈpekəbəl/ [adj] formal behaviour that is **impeccable**, is so good that it is impossible to find anything wrong with it **impeccable manners/behaviour/taste etc** *Macdonald was an aristocratic character with impeccable manners.* | *As I expected, her house was decorated with impeccable taste.* | **impeccable qualifications/credentials** (=documents that show that your experience or skills are perfect for a particular job or situation) *On paper, her qualifications seemed to be impeccable.* —**impeccably** [adv] *Gary came in, impeccably dressed in a dark blue suit.* | *There was a long church service, but the kids managed to behave impeccably.*

can't fault /ˌkɑːnt ˈfɔːlt‖ˌkænt-/ [v phrase] say you **can't fault** something, when you cannot criticize it because it has no faults or mistakes: *I can't fault her driving, except that it's rather fast.* | *No one could fault the way he handled the crisis.*

unblemished /ˌʌnˈblemɪʃt/ [adj] perfect over a long period of time: *The report stated that Stewart's character had remained completely unblemished.* | **an unblemished reputation/record/past etc** *Mrs Falconer had an unblemished record of 27 years service with the company.* | *He has established an unblemished reputation for accuracy.*

perfection /pəʳˈfekʃən/ [n U] when something is so good that it could not be any better: *Don't expect perfection in your relationships.* | **to perfection** (=perfectly) *The pasta was cooked to perfection.*

2 the best and most suitable person or thing

- perfect
- ideal
- just right
- be just the thing
- tailor-made

perfect /ˈpɜːʳfɪkt/ [adj] completely suitable for a person or situation: *A dry white wine is perfect with any fish dish.* | **+ for** *This dress will be perfect for the summer.* | *perfect weather for a picnic* | **the perfect place/time/job etc** *That sounds like the perfect job for you.*

ideal /aɪˈdɪəl/ [adj] very suitable and exactly what you want: *The house was a little too small so it was not ideal.* | **+ for** *It's a very relaxed hotel, ideal for families with young children.* | **sb's ideal man/woman/job/house etc** (=one that has all the qualities you like best) *My ideal man would be someone like Mel Gibson.*

just right /ˌdʒʌst ˈraɪt/ [adj phrase] spoken suitable in every way: *'Do these new curtains look OK?' 'Yes, they're just right.'* | **+ for** *I'm glad they're getting married – they're just right for each other.*

be just the thing ALSO **be just the job** British /biː ˌdʒʌst ðə ˈθɪŋ, biː ˌdʒʌst ðə ˈdʒɒb‖-ˈdʒɑːb/ [v phrase] informal to be exactly what is needed: *Cold lemonade is just the thing on a hot day.* | **+ for** *A tall hedge would be just the job for that side of the garden.*

tailor-made /ˌteɪləʳ ˈmeɪd◂/ [adj] specially designed for you, so that it is exactly what you need or want: *If you are an independent traveller, we can arrange a tailor-made tour.* | **+ for** *Our company can provide you with an insurance policy that is tailor-made for you.* | **+ to do sth** *In the USA and Canada, a house is often tailor-made to fit the needs of the family that will live in it.*

3 to make something perfect

- perfect
- bring something to perfection
- perfectionist

perfect /pəʳˈfekt/ [v T] *The only way to perfect your accent is to go and live in France.* | *James was out on the ski slope, trying to perfect his short turns.* | *This technique was perfected by the Ancient Egyptians.* | **perfect the art/technique of (doing) sth** *After eighteen years of marriage to Gemma, Ronald had perfected the art of keeping the peace.*

bring something to perfection /ˌbrɪŋ (sth) tə pəʳˈfekʃən/ [v phrase] written to make something perfect over a long period of time, especially when this takes a lot of care, practice, or skill: *Keeping the wine in a cool place for five years will bring it to perfection.* | *It requires considerable practise to bring the skill of weaving to perfection.*

perfectionist /pəʳˈfekʃənɪ̥st/ [n C] someone who is not satisfied with anything unless it is completely perfect: *Mart Kenney was a perfectionist, and his high standards were an example to everyone else.* | *She worked carefully on her drawing, with all the attention to detail of the perfectionist.*

4 ways of saying what you would like to happen if everything was perfect

- ideally
- in an ideal world/in a perfect world

ideally /aɪˈdɪəli/ [adv] use this when saying what you would like to happen if everything was perfect: *Ideally, we'd like to provide regular training for everyone.* | *In order to win, you must throw your opponent, ideally onto his back.*

in an ideal world/in a perfect world /ɪn ən ˌaɪdɪəl ˈwɜːʳld, ɪn ə ˌpɜːʳfɪkt ˈwɜːʳld/ [adv] use this to say what would happen if the situation were perfect, even though you know that the situation can never be perfect: *In an ideal world we would be recycling and reusing everything.* | *Of course, in an ideal world there would be no war.*

5 not perfect

- imperfect
- flawed

imperfect /ɪmˈpɜːʳfɪkt/ [adj] formal not completely correct or perfect: *Imperfect goods are sold off cheaply.* | *In general, people have a very imperfect knowledge of the law.* | *You have to accept that most relationships are imperfect.* | *She has anxieties and fears, like anyone else in this imperfect world.*

flawed /flɔːd/ [adj] something such as a plan, idea, or system that is **flawed**, has a fault which prevents it from working as well as it should do: *Each party rejected the other's approach, saying it was flawed.* | *flawed logic* | *The results are based on flawed interpretations of the data.* | **deeply/seriously etc flawed** *Birch's analysis of the situation was deeply flawed.*

6 in a perfect way

- perfectly
- to perfection

perfectly /ˈpɜːʳfɪktli/ [adv] *The coffee machine seems to work perfectly now.* | *He was perfectly dressed in a dark suit and tie.* | *After two years in Spain, Kate spoke the language perfectly.*

to perfection /tə pəʳˈfekʃən/ [adv] if something happens, or has been done **to perfection**, it is perfect and you are very pleased with it: *Marge tried on the dress and it fitted to perfection.* | *By September the apples had ripened to perfection.*

7 perfect as an idea, but impossible in reality

- ideal
- utopian
- idealized

ideal /aɪˈdɪəl/ [adj] *Plato dreamed of an ideal society.* | *A completely new kitchen would be ideal, but I don't think that we can afford it.* —**ideal** [n C] **the ideal of sth** *the ideal of equality*

utopian /juːˈtəʊpiən/ [adj usually before noun] a **utopian** society is one in which you imagine there is a perfect social or political situation, although this is unlikely to ever really exist: *The debate was about the impossibility of a utopian society.* | **a utopian dream** (=when you think about and wish for utopian society) *Marxism was a Utopian dream.*

idealized ALSO **idealised** British /aɪˈdɪəlaɪzd/ [adj] an **idealized** view or description of something considers or shows it as perfect when really it is not: *I think you have an idealized idea of what a doctor does.* | *The film showed an idealized view of rural life in the nineteenth century.* | *an idealized image of motherhood*

8 to think that someone or something is perfect when they are not

- idealize
- put sb on a pedestal
- can do no wrong

idealize ALSO **idealise** British /aɪˈdɪəlaɪz/ [v T] to consider or show someone or something as perfect, without noticing their faults: *People often idealize the past.* | *She always idealized her father, who had died when she was five.*

put sb on a pedestal /ˌpʊt (sb) ɒn ə ˈpedɪstəl/ [v phrase] to wrongly think that someone is perfect so that you are unable to treat them as an ordinary person: *It's very common for men to put women they love on a pedestal.*

can do no wrong /kən ˌduː nəʊ ˈrɒŋ‖-ˈrɔːŋ/ [v phrase] if one person thinks that another person **can do no wrong**, they think they are perfect, even though they really do have faults: *Whatever trouble Eddy gets into, Mum still thinks he can do no wrong.* | *Of course, the fans believe that the players can do no wrong.*

perform/performance

RELATED WORDS

- to perform an operation, ceremony, duty etc *see* **do (1)**
- to practise performing something *see* **practise/practice**
- *see also* **actor/actress, clap, dance, music, sing, art/culture**

1 to take part in a show, concert, play etc

- perform
- appear
- be in sth

perform /pəʳˈfɔːʳm/ [v I/T] to **perform** in a play or show: *Before every concert, she worries about how well she will perform.* | **perform a play/show/song etc** *The children perform a Christmas pantomime every year.* | *Russell's one-woman show, Shirley Valentine, was first performed by Pauline Collins.* —**performance** /pəʳˈfɔːʳməns/ [n C] *Paltrow won an Oscar for her performance in 'Shakespeare in Love'* | *A packed arena with a receptive crowd lifts any singer's performance.*

appear /əˈpɪəʳ/ [v I] to be one of the actors, singers, dancers etc that can be seen performing in a film, play, or show **+ in** *Pavarotti will be appearing in a number of concerts over the summer.* | *The American actors' union threatened to prevent her from appearing in the New York version of the show.* | **appear as sb** (=play a particular character) *Hopkins will be appearing as Willie Lomax in next week's production.*

be in sth /biː ˈɪn (sth)/ [phr v T] especially spoken to act in a particular play, film, or television show: *Do you remember Larry Hagman? He used to be in 'Dallas'.* | *It's my ambition to be in a film.*

2 to perform without having planned or practised something

▸ improvise ▸ ad-lib

improvise /ˈɪmprəvaɪz/ [v I/T] to play music, give a speech, act on stage etc without having planned or practised what you are going to do: *Modern jazz players like to take a theme and improvise around it.* | *It was difficult to believe that the whole sketch was improvised.* —**improvisation** /ˌɪmprəvaɪˈzeɪʃən‖ɪmˌprɑːvə-/ [n C/U] *His new album is full of improvisations.* | *Rapping relies heavily on improvisation.*

ad-lib /ˌæd ˈlɪb/ [v I/T] to say or sing something as part of a public performance or speech without having planned or practised it: *No one could remember the song very well, so we had to ad-lib.* | *The other actors were thrown into confusion when she started ad-libbing her final speech.*

3 someone who performs in a show, concert, play etc

▸ performer ▸ artist

performer /pərˈfɔːrmər/ [n C] someone who performs in a show, concert etc: *Enrico is impressive both as a performer and a choreographer.* | *As a jazz performer she is astounding, capable of expressing a broad range of feeling and expression.* | **a seasoned performer** (=someone who has been performing for a long time) *Tara is a seasoned performer who started acting at the age of 10.*

artist /ˈɑːrtɪst/ [n C] a professional performer, especially in music, dance, or the theatre: *Many of the artists in the show donated their fees to charity.* | **a recording artist** *The band are not just successful recording artists – they are constantly touring and playing live to sell-out crowds.*

4 to arrange and perform a show, concert, play etc

▸ put on ▸ do
▸ stage ▸ present

put on /ˌpʊt ˈɒn/ [phr v T] to arrange and perform in a show, concert, play etc **put on sth** *The students are putting on an end of term concert.* | *A special show is being put on to raise money for famine victims in Africa.*

stage /steɪdʒ/ [v T] to arrange and perform a show, concert, play etc especially one that needs a lot of planning and organization and costs a lot of money: *It cost thousands of pounds to stage the concert, including performers' fees and the hire of equipment.* | *They staged a magnificent production of 'Aida' in the amphitheatre.*

do /duː/ [v T] informal to arrange and perform a show, concert, play etc: *We're doing 'The Merchant of Venice' at the local theater for two weeks.* | *I've done dozens of shows in the north of England, and the audiences were great!*

present /prɪˈzent/ [v T] if an organization such as a theatre **presents** a show, concert, play etc it provides the money and arranges for it to be performed: *The National Theatre is presenting 'King Lear' later this month.* | *This evening PBS presents the first part of a six-part historical drama about the Civil War.*

5 an occasion on which a play, piece of music etc is performed

▸ performance

performance /pərˈfɔːrməns/ [n C] *The evening performance will begin at 8:00 pm.* | **+ of** *There was a performance of 'Giselle' in the San Diego State Open Air Theatre.*

6 something that is performed in public to entertain people

▸ show ▸ act
▸ production

show /ʃəʊ/ [n C] something that is performed in public to entertain people, usually with music, songs, and dancing: *We went to see a show on Broadway when we were in New York.* | **put on a show** *Every year the theatre puts on a show that runs until the end of January.* | **a one-man show** *Cowan's one-man show opens on April 16th.*

production /prəˈdʌkʃən/ [n C] a play, film, television programme etc which has been prepared to be performed to the public: *Have you seen the new Shakespeare production at the Arts Center?* | **+ of** *He will star in the Los Angeles production of 'Phantom of the Opera' this year.* | **put on a production/stage a production** *The Riverside Theatre is used to staging major productions.*

act /ækt/ [n C] a short performance as part of a show which has several different performances in it: *We used to do a comedy act together.* | *Part of his act involves dressing up as a woman.* | **a circus/mime/juggling act** *He was injured in a circus act that went wrong.*

7 the business of entertaining people with shows, plays, films etc

▸ entertainment ▸ showbusiness

entertainment /ˌentərˈteɪnmənt/ [n U] the business of entertaining people with shows, plays, films etc: *Blackpool was where I got my first taste of the world of entertainment.* | *Frankie is known throughout the entertainment business as an energetic performer.*

showbusiness ALSO **showbiz** informal /ˈʃəʊˌbɪznɪs, ˈʃəʊbɪz/ [n U] the entertainment industry, for example film, television, and popular theatre: *Famous sportsmen and people from the world of showbusiness are among their clients.* | *Here's Sarah with the latest showbiz gossip.* | **in showbusiness/showbiz** *What made you decide on a career in showbusiness?*

personally/yourself

RELATED WORDS

▸ *see also* **alone**

1 when you do something yourself

▸ yourself/myself etc ▸ in person
▸ personally ▸ by hand

yourself/myself etc /jɔːʳˈself, maɪˈself/ [pron] if you do something **yourself**, no-one else does it for you: *I made these curtains myself.* | *Why can't your boyfriend cook lunch himself?* | *'Could you pass me that book?' 'Get it yourself!'*

personally /ˈpɜːʳsənəli/ [adv] if an important person does something **personally**, they do it, although you would normally expect someone else to do it for them: *The President wrote to us personally to thank us for our hard work.* | *The Commander in Chief visited the island personally, and took steps toward strengthening the defense facilities and fortification.*

in person /ɪn ˈpɜːʳsən/ [adv] if you do something **in person**, you do it by going somewhere yourself, rather than by asking someone else to do it: *My letters were all returned to me, so I decided to go around to her house in person.* | *The prince was renowned for his bravery, and chose to lead his troops in person.*

by hand /baɪ ˈhænd/ [adv] if you deliver a letter, parcel etc **by hand**, you deliver it yourself instead of posting it: *The letter had been delivered by hand, and was addressed to Mrs Zippie Isaacs.*

2 when you meet or talk to someone directly

- personally/in person
- face to face
- to sb's face
- in the flesh

personally/in person /ˈpɜːʳsənəli, ɪn ˈpɜːʳsən/ [adv] if you meet or talk to someone **personally** or **in person**, you do it by going somewhere yourself, instead of writing, telephoning, or asking someone else to do it: *We thought we'd pay you a visit, as we would like to thank you personally for all your help.* | *If this is your first passport, you must apply in person, bringing with you proof of U.S. citizenship.* | *The author of the book had not personally met with the publishers before its publication.*

face to face /ˌfeɪs tə ˈfeɪs/ [adv] if you meet or talk to someone **face to face**, you are in the same place as them and looking directly at them: *The senator cannot meet every voter face to face, but he is certainly doing his best.* | **come face to face with** (=meet someone personally, especially when you do not want to) *Victims who go to court dread coming face to face with their attacker again.* | *I stuck my head out of my tent, and came face to face with a cow.* —**face-to-face** [adj only before noun] *In a face-to-face confrontation angry demonstrators threw bricks and bottles at the police.*

to sb's face /tə (sb's) feɪs/ [adv] if you say something **to sb's face**, especially something unkind or critical, you say it directly to them, instead of to other people **say sth to sb's face** *If she doesn't like my work, I wish she'd say so to my face.* | **tell sb (sth) to their face** *I didn't love him anymore, but I couldn't bring myself to tell him to his face.*

in the flesh /ɪn ðə ˈfleʃ/ [adv] informal if you meet or see someone **in the flesh**, you are in the same place as them, rather than seeing them on television or in a film – use this especially about well-known people: *I saw her outside the TV studios – she looks much older in the flesh.* | *Michael Jordan was my hero, and meeting him in the flesh was a real thrill.*

3 something that you do or experience yourself

- personal
- direct
- first-hand

personal /ˈpɜːʳsənəl/ [adj only before noun] use this when describing something that you do, learn, or experience yourself: *The President made a personal appeal to the terrorists.* | *I intend to take personal responsibility for seeing that the documents reach you in time.* | **personal experience** *The novel is based on the author's own personal experience.* | **personal contact** (=when you meet and deal with people yourself directly) *I liked talking to people and solving problems, but as you get promoted within a firm you lose that personal contact.*

direct /d̥ɪˈrekt, daɪ-/ [adj only before noun] done or learned yourself, without help from anyone else, or information from anywhere else: *From 1914 to 1918 the British people had their first direct experience of war from the air.* | **direct contact** *We have had no direct contact with any government officials.* —**directly** [adv] *She's not directly involved in the selling side of the business.* —**direct** [adv] *I had to contact the suppliers direct* (=directly).

first-hand /ˌfɜːʳst ˈhænd◂/ [adj only before noun] **first-hand information/experience/account etc** information etc that is the result of actually seeing something or experiencing something, rather than the result of reading about it or hearing about it: *Our new chef worked in Paris for many years, so he has first- hand knowledge of French cooking.* | *Clara knew from first-hand experience that living in a foreign country would be difficult.* | *This letter remains the only first-hand account of life on the island in the 17th century.* —**at first hand** [adv] *Work placements are an opportunity for students to learn at first hand about the world of business.*

4 experienced or done through someone else, not personally

- second-hand
- indirect
- vicarious

second-hand /ˌsekənd ˈhænd◂/ [adv] if you hear about something **second-hand**, you hear about it from another person or by reading about it, for example in a newspaper: *I was abroad at the time, so I got the news second-hand.* | *We only learnt about their divorce second-hand from some mutual friends.*

indirect /ˌɪnd̥ɪˈrekt◂/ [adj] use this when describing something that you do not do, learn, or experience yourself, but through someone else: *Since he left his wife Rick has only had indirect contact with his children.* —**indirectly** [adv] *He saw his art as a way to communicate, indirectly, how it felt to be black in America at that time.*

vicarious /vɪˈkeəriəs‖vaɪ-/ [adj only before noun] **vicarious pleasure/satisfaction/excitement etc** pleasure etc experienced by watching or reading about someone else doing something, rather than by doing it yourself: *Mothers often get some vicarious pleasure from their children's success.* | *Many people enjoyed the vicarious thrill of military victory.*

person/people

RELATED WORDS

- ordinary people *see* **normal/ordinary**
- a group of people *see* **group**
- *see also* **man, woman, child, everyone, character, nice, horrible**

1 a person

- person
- someone/somebody
- human being/human
- individual
- character

person /ˈpɜːʳsən/ [n C] *I think Sue's a really nice person.* | *He's the only person I know who can speak Chinese.* | *There were over 200 people at the meeting.* | *The streets were suddenly full of people.*

someone/somebody /ˈsʌmwʌn, ˈsʌmbɒdi, -bədi‖-ˈbɑːdi, -bədi/ [pron] a person – use this when you do not know who the person is, or when it is not important to say who it is: *Someone phoned you but I didn't get their name.* | *What would you do if somebody tried to rob you in the street?* | **someone else/somebody else** (=another person) *Can't you get someone else to clean the kitchen for you?*

human being/human /ˌhjuːmən ˈbiːɪŋ, ˈhjuːmən/ [n C] a person – use this when you are comparing people with animals or machines: *The drug had never before been tested on a human being.* | *Computers have replaced humans in many factories.*

individual /ˌɪndɪˈvɪdʒuəl/ [n C] a person – use this especially when you are talking about responsibility or choice: *It is the responsibility of each individual within the class to make sure they have the correct books.* | *The decision to have an operation should be up to the individual involved.*

character /ˈkærɪktəʳ/ [n C] a person who seems strange, interesting etc: *A couple of suspicious-looking characters were standing outside the house.* | *Beneath his brash, noisy exterior was a much shrewder and lonelier character than he admitted.*

2 people in general

- people
- everyone/everybody
- folks
- the human race
- mankind/humankind
- man
- humanity
- the public
- society
- folk
- social

people /ˈpiːpəl/ [n plural] **people** in general: *People are getting very worried about rising crime.* | *I don't want people to feel sorry for me.* | **most/some people** *Most people hate writing essays, but I quite like it.*

everyone/everybody /ˈevriwʌn, ˈevriˌbɒdi‖-ˌbɑːdi/ [pron] all people – use this to make general statements about how people behave, what people like etc: *Don't you like ice-cream? I thought everyone liked it!* | *Everybody has the right to a good education.* | *Everyone knows that smoking is bad for you.*

folks /fəʊks/ [n plural] American spoken people: *Folks around here have been pretty angry about the governor's actions.* | **most/some folks** *Some folks think the schools are better now than they were twenty years ago.*

the human race /ðə ˌhjuːmən ˈreɪs/ [n phrase] all the people in the world, considered as one group: *Pollution is threatening the future of the human race.* | **the entire/whole human race** *The entire human race could be wiped out by nuclear war.* | **a member of the human race** *Until then, no member of the human race had ever been able to make a map of the whole world.*

mankind/humankind /mænˈkaɪnd, ˌhjuːmənˈkaɪnd/ [n U] people in general – used especially when talking about their history and development, or how something affects their continued existence: *The Americans exploded the first nuclear weapon in the history of mankind.* | *Travelling into space was a great advance for mankind.* | *In the interests of humankind we must stop destroying our planet.*

man /mæn/ [n U] people in general – use this when you are comparing humans with other living things. Some people do not use this word because it can seem offensive to women: *Jericho is the oldest continuously inhabited city known to man.* | *The grandeur of the mountains is a constant reminder of man's insignificance.* | *The Dutch reclamation of their land is a classic case of man's struggle against nature.*

humanity /hjuːˈmænɪti/ [n U] people in general – use this especially when you are talking about people's rights to be treated like all other humans and not suffer cruelty, hunger etc: *30% of humanity live in conditions of terrible poverty.* | **a crime against humanity** *The General was accused of committing crimes against humanity.*

the public /ðə ˈpʌblɪk/ [n singular with singular or plural verb in British English] ordinary people who do not belong to the government, the police etc, and do not have any special rights: *The castle is open to the public during the summer.* | *The public ought to know how the money from taxes is being spent.* | **a member of the public** *Some of these politicians never meet ordinary members of the public.* | **the general public** *Tickets will become available to the general public in June.* — **public** [adj only before noun] *Public attitudes to homosexuality are gradually changing.* | *The plan cannot succeed without public support.*

society /səˈsaɪɪti/ [n U] people in general – use this to talk about people as an organized group with a system of laws and accepted behaviour: *Islamic society* | *The judge described Smith as 'a danger to society'.* | **member of society** *We want our students to become useful and responsible members of society.*

folk /fəʊk/ [n plural] **young/old/ rich/country/city etc folk** people of a particular type or from a particular area, considered together as a group: *The young folk need to have a place where they can go in the evenings.* | *Stella's ambition is to get a job working with old folk.* | *His parents were hard-working country folk.*

social /ˈsəʊʃəl/ [adj only before noun] use this about conditions, problems, and changes that affect all the people in society: *Rising unemployment led to even more social problems.* | *social changes that brought women even greater freedom*

3 all the people in a particular area, city, country etc

- population
- the people
- the French/Germans/Japanese etc
- community
- Londoners/New Yorkers/Parisians etc

population /ˌpɒpjʊˈleɪʃən‖ˌpɑː-/ [n C with singular or

plural verb in British English] all the people who live in a town or country – use this when saying how many people live there, or giving some facts about them **the population of Tokyo/Greece etc** *In 1966 the population of Lima was about two million.* | **a population of five million/twenty million etc** *New Jersey has a population of around 7.6 million.* | **the black/Catholic/male population** (=all the black people, Catholic people etc in a place) *30% of the male population suffers from heart disease.* | **the general population** (=people in general compared with a particular group) *In our study, significantly more miners complained of weight loss than the general population.*

the people /ðə ˈpiːpəl/ **[n plural]** all **the people** who live in a particular place **the British/Korean/Nigerian etc people** *Reagan's views were shared by a majority of the American people.* | **the people of Paris/China etc** *the awful sufferings of the people of Sarajevo*

the French/Germans/Japanese etc /ðə ˈfrentʃ/ **[n plural]** all the people who live in France, Germany etc – use this when describing them in a general way or as a political force: *The French are famous for their love of good food.* | *The Chinese are trying to industrialize without changing the essential nature of their society.*

community /kəˈmjuːnəti/ **[n C]** a group of people who live in the same area, especially when they all belong to the same religious group or race: *The murder has shocked the local community.* | **the Jewish/Muslim/Greek etc community** *New York's Jewish community*

Londoners/New Yorkers/Parisians etc /ˈlʌndənəʳz/ people who live in London, New York, Paris etc: *For most New Yorkers, life will never be the same again.* | *The Milanese* (=people from Milan) *elected a new mayor yesterday.*

4 a person in a story

- character
- hero
- heroine

character /ˈkærəktəʳ/ **[n C]** a person in a story in a book, film, or play: *It was a wonderful story – the characters were so convincing.* | **the main/central character** *The interesting thing about the play is the conflict between the two main characters.*

hero /ˈhɪərəʊ/ **[n C]** the man or boy who is the main character in a book, play, film etc, who people admire because he is good, strong, brave, honest etc **+ of** *Indiana Jones is the hero of the film.* | **tragic hero** (=a hero who suffers a lot) *Hamlet is Shakespeare's most famous tragic hero.*

heroine /ˈherəʊən/ **[n C]** the woman or girl who is the main character in a book, play, film etc, who people admire because she is good, strong, brave, honest etc **+ of** *The heroine of her latest novel is a middle-class English woman.*

5 relating to people, not animals or machines

- human

human /ˈhjuːmən/ **[adj only before noun]** use this about people's abilities, character, or behaviour, when you are comparing people with animals or machines: *the effects of pollution on the human and animal population* | *Bacteria cannot be seen with the human eye.*

6 for each person

- per person
- a head
- per capita

per person /pəʳ ˈpɜːʳsən/ **[adv]** **$500/2 pieces etc per person** $500, two pieces etc for each person: *There were only two pieces of bread per person.* | *You can get a decent meal for less than £20 per person.*

a head /ə ˈhed/ **[adv]** **$10/£5 etc a head** use this to say how much something costs for each person: *We paid £5 a head for our Christmas dinner.* | *Guests were paying $800 a head for luxury hotel accommodation.*

per capita /pəʳ ˈkæpətə/ **[adv/adj]** if something costs a particular amount, or someone uses a particular amount etc **per capita**, that is how much each person pays, uses etc – used especially in business, politics, or economics: *Among the largest consumers of energy per capita is the United States.* | **per capita income/expenditure/consumption etc** *The average per capita income has decreased over the past five years.* | *In Europe the per capita supply of trained medical staff has increased dramatically.*

7 no people

- no one/nobody
- not a soul

no one/nobody /ˈnəʊ wʌn, ˈnəʊbədi/ **[pron]** no person or people: *No-one was home, so I left a note.* | *He explained what had happened but nobody believed him.* | **no one at all/nobody at all** *Nobody had supported him, nobody at all.*

not a soul /ˌnɒt ə ˈsəʊl/ **[n phrase]** no one – use this when it is unusual or surprising that there is no one somewhere: *It was strange. There wasn't a soul in the street.* | **not a soul to be seen/not a soul in sight** *Steve looked in every room, but there was no sound and not a soul to be seen.*

persuade

RELATED WORDS

- *see also* **suggest, advertising, insist, advise**

1 to persuade someone to do something

- persuade
- persuasion
- get sb to do sth
- influence
- encourage
- talk sb into
- put sb up to

persuade /pəʳˈsweɪd/ **[v T]** to make someone agree to do something, by giving them reasons why they should do it: *Neil didn't want to come at first, but we persuaded him.* | **persuade sb to do sth** *I tried to persuade his ex-girlfriend to talk to him, but she said no.* | *Teachers need ways to persuade more parents to attend parent-teacher evenings.* | **+ (that)** *He was convicted of the murder, but he is still trying to persuade the public that he's innocent.*

persuasion /pəʳˈsweɪʒən/ **[n U]** things that you say in order to persuade someone to do something: *They hope to end the conflict using persuasion rather than threats.* | **+ to** *The Republican leader used every means of persuasion to get senators to vote against the bill.* | **take persuasion** *It took a lot of persuasion to get Dad to agree to the idea.* | **gentle/friendly persuasion** (=persuading someone without using threats) *Until the law was passed, the agency could only use gentle persuasion to get industries to reduce waste.* | **powers of persuasion** (=skills used for persuading) *The fate of the bill in Congress will depend on Brady's powers of persuasion.*

get sb to do sth /ˌget (sb) tə ˈduː (sth)/ [v phrase] informal to make someone do what you want them to do, especially by trying to persuade them over a long time: *I'm sure I can get Eddie to do it.* | *My girlfriend is always trying to get me to stop smoking.* | *Parents learn ways to talk to and carry a baby to get it to stop crying.*

influence /ˈɪnfluəns/ [v T] to affect what someone decides to do, but without directly persuading them: *I hope you weren't influenced by anything that your brother said.* | *Do TV programs influence children's behaviour?* | *Judges should not be influenced by political motives.*

encourage /ɪnˈkʌrɪdʒ‖ɪnˈkɜːr-/ [v T] to try to persuade someone to do something, because you think it will be good for them **encourage sb to do sth** *Her parents encouraged her to cook and even paid her to make dinner twice a week.* | *Patricia encouraged me to apply for the job.* | *We want to encourage more children to use the library.*

talk sb into /ˌtɔːk (sb) ˈɪntuː/ [phr v T] informal to persuade someone to do something that they do not want to do **+ doing sth** *I managed to talk them into paying me more money.* | *Officers said they tried to talk Wilson into leaving the bar, but he started to struggle.* | **talk sb into it** *I didn't really want to go to the party, but Dave talked me into it.*

put sb up to /ˌpʊt (sb) ˈʌp tuː/ [phr v T] to persuade someone to do something wrong or stupid, especially when they would not have thought of doing it themselves: *We want to know why they did it and if anyone put them up to it.* | *Did someone put you up to this?*

2 to gently persuade someone to do something

- get round
- coax
- sweet-talk
- cajole

get round British **/get around** American /ˌget ˈraʊnd, ˌget əˈraʊnd/ [phr v T not in progressive or passive] to persuade someone to do something that you want them to do by being very nice to them, making them laugh etc: *I managed to get round him by saying he could borrow my car on Saturday.* | *She can always manage to get around her dad.*

coax /kəʊks/ [v T] to persuade someone to do something that they do not want to do by talking to them gently for a long time until they agree to do it: *'Oh come on, Vic,' she coaxed, 'We need you, don't let us down.'* | **coax sb to do sth** *The U.S. is trying to coax both sides to take part in talks.* | **coax sb into doing sth** *The children had to be coaxed into coming with us.*

sweet-talk /ˈswiːt tɔːk/ [v T] informal to say nice things to someone, especially things that are not true, in order to persuade them to do something for you: *You can sweet-talk me all night long, but I'm not going home with you!* | **sweet-talk sb into doing sth** *She sweet-talked him into lending her the money.*

cajole /kəˈdʒəʊl/ [v I/T] to persuade someone to do something that they do not want to do by being nice to them, praising them etc until they agree to do it: *Ed cajoled and pleaded, but couldn't get her to change her mind.* | **cajole sb into doing sth** *She cajoles the kids into doing their best.* | **cajole sb to do sth** *He managed to cajole Hayden to take part in the program.*

3 to try hard to persuade someone

- put pressure on
- lean on
- twist sb's arm

put pressure on ALSO **pressure** American /pʊt ˈpreʃər ɒn, ˈpreʃəʳ/ [v phrase/v T] to keep trying to persuade someone to do something by using threats or unfair influence: *Threats of dismissal were intended to put pressure on the strikers.* | *Some of the girls started having sex mainly because their boyfriends were pressuring them.* | **put pressure on sb to do sth** *Her parents put pressure on her and her boyfriend to get married.* | **pressure sb to do sth** *Residents are pressuring the mayor to let them manage their own housing association.*

lean on /ˈliːn ɒn/ [phr v T] informal to use threats or influence to persuade someone to do something: *If the US wants to get South American governments to lean on drug growers, it'll have to be prepared to offer something in return.* | **lean on sb to do sth** *New members have been leaning on Senate leaders to make some changes.*

twist sb's arm /ˌtwɪst (sb's) ˈɑːʳm/ [v phrase] informal to persuade someone to do something they have said they do not want to do – use this humorously when the person will really enjoy what you have persuaded them to do: *I'm sure he would never have come if I hadn't twisted his arm a little.* | *'Go on, have another drink.' 'Oh well, if you twist my arm.'*

4 to persuade someone that something is true, right, or good

- convince
- persuade
- satisfy
- win sb over
- bring/talk sb round
- convert
- win hearts and minds

convince /kənˈvɪns / [v T] to make someone feel completely sure that something is true or right, especially when they doubted it before: *I knew it would be hard to convince my father, because he wanted me to go to university.* | **convince sb (that)** *The government is trying to convince the public that it's getting tough on corruption.* | **convince sb of sth** *In the end she convinced the jury of her innocence.*

persuade /pəʳˈsweɪd/ [v T] to make someone believe that something is true or right, especially when they doubted it before **persuade sb (that)** *He eventually managed to persuade me that the documents were genuine.* | *After this accident, it will be difficult for the government to persuade people that nuclear power stations are safe.* | **persuade sb of sth** *We want to persuade them of the value of diplomacy and talks to resolve disputes.*

satisfy /ˈsætɪ̥sfaɪ/ [v T] to give enough information to make someone in authority believe that something is true: *Her explanation failed to satisfy the jury.* | **satisfy sb (that)** *Applicants will have to satisfy the committee that they are suitable for the job.* | **be satisfied with/that** (=accept something as true) *The police said that they were satisfied with his story and let him go free.*

win sb over /ˌwɪn (sb) ˈəʊvəʳ/ [phr v T] to persuade someone to support your ideas or opinions, by making them believe that you are right, or by being nice to them: *He could not be won over by bribes or promises.* | **win sb over/win over sb** *Cochran's arguments won over the jury.* | **+ to** *Doctors who saw her work were quickly won over to her methods.*

bring/talk sb round British **/bring sb around** American /ˌbrɪŋ, ˌtɔːk (sb) ˈraʊnd, ˌbrɪŋ (sb) əˈraʊnd/ [phr v T] to persuade someone to change their opinion so that they agree with you, especially by spending a long time talking to them and giving them reasons why you are right: *At first my parents didn't like the idea, but I think I've managed to bring them round.* | *I'll have to talk my mother round, but I'm sure she'll say yes.* | **+ to** *In the end I brought him around to my point of view.*

convert /kənˈvɜːʳt/ [v T] to change someone's opinion or beliefs about something, so that they begin to like it or believe it is right: *I didn't use to like Indian food, but Cathy's converted me.* | **convert sb to sth** *Concerns about cruel farming methods converted her to vegetarianism.*

win hearts and minds /wɪn ˌhɑːʳts ən ˈmaɪndz/ [v phrase] to persuade a lot of people or most people to support what you are doing and believe that it is right – used especially in political contexts: *It's no use giving people short term sweeteners – what we have to do is to go out there and win hearts and minds.* | *If they succeed in winning the hearts and minds of the ethnic minorities here, they should sweep into power at the next election.*

5 the use of film, newspapers etc to persuade people

- propaganda
- spin

propaganda /ˌprɒpəˈgændə‖ˌprɑː-/ [n U] the clever use of newspapers, film, television etc in order to persuade the public to accept particular political ideas, often by giving incomplete or false information: *I object when political propaganda is pushed through my letter box at election times.*

spin /spɪn/ [n U] when someone, especially a government, political party etc, gives information in a way that is intended to persuade people that they, their ideas, their plans etc are good: *What we would like to see is more realistic policies and less Labour Party spin.* | **put a spin on sth** *Whatever spin the government tries to put on it, this can be seen as nothing less than a massive defeat.* | *The senator was determined to put a positive spin on the affair.*

6 reasons, explanations etc that persuade you to believe something

- convincing
- compelling
- persuasive

convincing /kənˈvɪnsɪŋ/ [adj] a **convincing** reason, explanation, or excuse makes you believe that something is true or right: *Jurors thought the defence's arguments were very convincing.* | *There is convincing evidence that smoking causes heart disease.* | *Archeologists found convincing proof that the Vikings had landed in North America.*

persuasive /pəʳˈsweɪsɪv/ [adj] **persuasive** arguments, proof etc make people believe that something is true or right, by giving them good reasons: *Barratt's argument was persuasive, but the managers still turned down his proposal.* | *He made a persuasive case for making the changes.* | *We found no persuasive evidence of illegal activity.*

compelling /kəmˈpelɪŋ/ [adj] a **compelling** reason, argument etc is one that is so strong and powerful that it can persuade you that something is true or that something should be done: *Freud's approach to the analysis of dreams is highly compelling.* | *It is hard to find a more compelling reason to quit smoking than the fact that it affects your children's health.*

7 to persuade someone by making something seem very good

- tempt
- entice
- lure

tempt /tempt/ [v T] to make someone want to do something by making it seem enjoyable, exciting etc: *Travel companies tempt people with special offers.* | **tempt sb to do sth** *The club is giving away free T-shirts in order to tempt people to join.* | *The arrangement tempts employees to win contracts even by illegal means.* | **tempt sb into doing sth** *Don't be tempted into betting money on the horses.*

lure /lʊəʳ, ljʊəʳ‖lʊər/ [v T] to persuade someone to go somewhere or to do something, especially something which they should not do, or something that might harm them **lure sb into/to/away etc** *The boy apparently lured the girl into his bedroom and attacked her.* | **lure sb into doing sth** *Peasants were lured into joining the People's Army by the promises of large sums of money for their families.*

entice /ɪnˈtaɪs/ [v T] to offer someone something they want in order to persuade them to do something: *The banks are offering special low rates in an attempt to entice prospective customers.* | **entice sb to do sth** *The ads entice young people to smoke.* | **entice sb into doing sth** *The company hopes to entice shareholders into agreeing to a merger.*

8 something good that is used to persuade someone

- incentive
- carrot
- sweetener
- inducement

incentive /ɪnˈsentɪv/ [n C/U] something that encourages you to work harder, start new activities etc: *The school gives incentives such as more play time to kids who work hard.* | *The new plan will provide strong incentives for young people to improve their skills.* | **+ to do sth** *When prices are so low, farmers have little incentive to increase production.* | **tax/cash/financial incentives** (=offers to reduce taxes, give someone money etc) *The government is offering special tax incentives to people wanting to start up small businesses.*

sweetener /ˈswiːtnəʳ/ [n C] something that is offered to someone to make a deal or plan seem more attractive, so that they will accept it: *The new airport is an unpopular development but the government has promised £4 million in grants to the local community as a sweetener.*

carrot /ˈkærət/ [n C usually singular] informal a reward that is offered to someone to encourage them to do something: *The U.S. has held out the carrot of more aid and investment.* | **carrot and stick** (=a combination of rewards and punishments) *Governments were forced to adopt a carrot and stick approach to the trade unions.*

inducement /ɪnˈdjuːsmənt‖ɪnˈduːs-/ [n C/U] something such as a gift that you offer to someone in order to persuade them to do what you want: *The prices are the main inducement – everything is much cheaper here than at the mall.* | **+ to do sth** *I don't think the tax reduction will be an inducement to save more.* | **cash/financial inducement** *As a way of reducing the workforce, workers are being offered cash inducements to retire.* | **+ for sb to do sth** *The* *government want to use this as an inducement for developing countries to open up their markets.*

9 good at persuading people

- persuasive
- forceful
- pushy
- smooth-talking
- slick

persuasive /pəʳ'sweɪsɪv/ [adj] *Like most politicians, she can be very persuasive when she wants to be.* | *He is a very persuasive speaker.* —**persuasively** [adv] *She gave her evidence calmly and persuasively.*

forceful /'fɔːʳsfəl/ [adj] able to express your ideas and opinions in a strong, confident way so that you persuade people to agree with you: *a manager with a forceful personality* | *He can be arrogant and forceful.* | *Betty Friedan was a forceful advocate of women's rights.* —**forcefully** [adv] *For over an hour she spoke forcefully about the famine in Africa.*

pushy /'pʊʃi/ [adj] someone who is **pushy** annoys people by trying hard to make them do what they want, especially by repeatedly asking them or telling them to do something: *A good salesman is polite, enthusiastic, and not too pushy.* | *Pushy journalists shouted questions from the crowd.*

smooth-talking /'smuːð ˌtɔːkɪŋ/ [adj only before noun] a **smooth-talking** person is usually insincere or dishonest although they have a pleasant, confident way of talking which easily persuades people: *a smooth-talking car salesman* | *A smooth-talking young man was offering to buy her a drink.*

slick /slɪk/ [adj] good at persuading people by talking to them in a clever, confident way, but usually insincere or dishonest: *I don't trust her. She's too slick.* | *He's got a bunch of slick lawyers to get him out of paying the $11 million he owes us.*

10 too easily persuaded by other people

- be a pushover
- be a soft touch
- naïve
- gullible
- impressionable
- easily-led

be a pushover /biː ə 'pʊʃəʊvəʳ/ [v phrase] someone who **is a pushover** is very easy to persuade, and you can get them to do what you want them to do: *She's a kind and gentle person, but she's no pushover.*

be a soft touch /biː ə ˌsɒft 'tʌtʃ‖-ˌsɔːft-/ [v phrase] to be someone who can be easily persuaded to give someone what they want, especially because you are too kind and sympathetic: *It's important that the kids don't think the teacher is a soft touch.*

naïve /naɪ'iːv‖nɑː'iːv/ [adj] someone who is **naïve** is so young or inexperienced that they are likely to be easily persuaded to believe something: *I was so naïve – I believed everything the army told me about my husband's death.* | *She's either stupid or naïve if she thinks he really cares about her.*

gullible /'gʌlə̇bəl/ [adj] easily persuaded or tricked into believing that something is true: *It's easy to blame the public for being gullible enough to buy dieting products, but it's the companies who sell them who should take responsibility.* | *She was described by her neighbors as a sweet but gullible woman who allowed the man to live in her house as a source of extra money.*

impressionable /ɪm'preʃənəbəl/ [adj] someone who is **impressionable**, especially a young person, is easily influenced and can easily be persuaded to do things or to change their opinions: *Unfortunately, the show's message to millions of impressionable teens is that it's OK to take drugs.* | **at an impressionable age** (=when you are young and impressionable) *I've always wanted to do martial arts – maybe I saw too many Jackie Chan movies at an impressionable age.*

easily-led /ˌiːzə̇li 'led/ [adj not before noun] British someone who is **easily-led** does not have a strong character and can easily be persuaded to do things, even things that are wrong: *She's young and rather easily-led.* | *My son's rather easily-led and tends to get in with the wrong crowd at school.*

11 to persuade someone not to do something

- persuade sb not to do sth
- talk sb out of
- discourage
- put off
- deter

persuade sb not to do sth /pəʳˌsweɪd (sb) nɒt tə 'duː (sth)/ [v phrase] to make someone decide not to do something, by giving them reasons why they should not do it: *Catherine persuaded him not to resign.* | *The program hopes to persuade school children not to try smoking or drugs.*

talk sb out of /ˌtɔːk (sb) 'aʊt ɒv/ [phr v T] to talk to someone about something they are planning to do, and persuade them not to do it **talk sb out of sth** *I nearly cancelled the wedding, but my best friend talked me out of it.* | *Police officers talked a man out of a suicide jump off the bridge.* | **talk sb out of doing sth** *Her father talked her out of studying history because he thought she would hate it.*

discourage /dɪs'kʌrɪdʒ‖-'kɜːr-/ [v T] to stop someone wanting to do something, by making them think that it will be difficult or unpleasant: *We need to discourage the use of cars for short journeys.* | *Leave the lights on when you're out in order to discourage burglars.* | **discourage sb from doing sth** *Girls are sometimes discouraged from studying subjects like engineering and physics.*

put off /ˌpʊt 'ɒf / [phr v T] informal to make someone lose interest in something that they want or were thinking of doing, by making it seem difficult or unpleasant: *I'm not going to be put off by his threats.* | **put sb off doing sth** *A lot of people are put off becoming teachers by the long hours and the low pay.*

deter /dɪ'tɜːʳ/ [v T] written to make someone decide not to do something by making them realize that it will be difficult or dangerous or will have unpleasant results: *The new alarm system should deter car thieves.* | **deter sb from doing sth** *The unpleasant taste the drug produces is used to deter alcoholics from drinking.*

12 something that persuades someone not to do something

- deterrent
- disincentive

deterrent /dɪ'terənt‖-'tɜːr-/ [n C] something that makes people afraid to or less likely to do something: *Window locks are a cheap and effective deterrent.* | **+ to** *The special paint is meant to be a deterrent to graffiti artists.* | **+ against** *The fines are large enough to be an effective deterrent against speeding.* | **act/serve as a deterrent** *Experts do not agree about whether the death penalty acts as a deterrent.*

disincentive /ˌdɪsɪnˈsentɪv/ [n C] a disadvantage which makes people less willing to do something: *We're trying to attract more graduates into nursing, but the salary and hours are strong disincentives.* | **+ to** *Raising taxes on unearned income would be a major disincentive to saving and investment.*

picture

RELATED WORDS

▸ *see also* **draw, paint, colour/color, pattern, design, decorate, art/culture**

1 a picture that you paint or draw

- ▸ picture
- ▸ painting
- ▸ drawing
- ▸ sketch
- ▸ illustration
- ▸ poster
- ▸ portrait
- ▸ landscape
- ▸ study
- ▸ nude

picture /ˈpɪktʃəʳ/ [n C] a painting or drawing: *Van Gogh's 'Sunflowers' is one of the most famous pictures in the world.* | *an early picture by the French Impressionist painter Claude Monet* | **+ of** *There was a picture of a windmill on the bedroom wall.* | **sb's picture** (=a painting or drawing of someone) *The house belonged to the Duke of Wellington, and his picture hangs in the hall.* | **draw/paint a picture** *I didn't know the word in Japanese so I drew a little picture.* | **do a picture** spoken (=draw or paint a picture) *Daisy did a lovely picture of a cat at school today.*

painting /ˈpeɪntɪŋ/ [n C] a picture that someone has painted: *an exhibition of paintings by French artists* | *The museum has an impressive collection of early 20th century American paintings.* | **+ of** *a painting of the Grand Canal in Venice by Canaletto* | *Gaugin is famous for his paintings of native women on the Pacific island of Tahiti.* | **do a painting** *Dali did several paintings of his wife.*

drawing /ˈdrɔːɪŋ/ [n C] a picture that has been drawn using a pen or pencil: *The classroom was bright and cheerful, with childrens' drawings on the walls.* | **+ of** *On the wall was a drawing of a woman's head by Matisse.* | **do a drawing** *Degas did a series of drawings of dancers at the ballet school in Paris.*

sketch /sketʃ/ [n C] a picture consisting of a few lines drawn quickly with a pen or pencil **+ of** *I thought your sketches of the garden were very attractive.* | **do/make a sketch** *The architect did a sketch of how the building will look when it's finished.* | **quick/rough sketch** (=a sketch done very quickly) *Gabriella did a quick sketch of her baby daughter.*

illustration /ˌɪləˈstreɪʃən/ [n C] a picture in a book, which shows people or events that have been mentioned in the book: *The new encyclopedia is full of color illustrations and photographs.* | *Who did the illustrations for the book? They're lovely.*

poster /ˈpəʊstəʳ/ [n C] a very large picture or photograph printed on paper, which you put on a wall for decoration **+ of** *Anna's bedroom wall was covered in posters of James Dean and Marilyn Monroe.*

portrait /ˈpɔːʳtrɪt/ [n C] a painting, drawing, or photograph of a person **+ of** *A full-length portrait of the Queen hung on the wall.* | **paint a portrait** *The artist Hans Holbein was best known for painting portraits.* | **self-portrait** (=a picture of the artist done by the artist) *Rembrandt's 'Self-portrait with feather in cap'* | *A series of 43 self-portraits by Greek-born American Lucas Samaras (b. 1936) have been donated to the Museum of Modern Art, New York.*

landscape /ˈlændskeɪp/ [n C] a painting or photograph showing an area of countryside: *'What kind of photographs do you take?' 'Mostly landscapes, and some portraits.'* | **landscape painter/artist/photographer** *Constable is probably England's most famous landscape artist.*

study /ˈstʌdi/ [n C] a small detailed drawing, especially one which is done in order to prepare for a larger picture, or as part of a series of drawings of the same kind of subject **+ of** *Renoir did several studies of small plants and flowers.* | **+ for** *The exhibition includes a series of studies by Picasso for his painting Guernica.*

nude /njuːd‖nuːd/ [n C] a picture of someone without any clothes on: *To be honest, I prefer his flower pictures to his nudes.* | *a nude by Picasso*

2 a humorous drawing

- ▸ cartoon
- ▸ caricature

cartoon /kɑːʳˈtuːn/ [n C] a humorous drawing, especially in a newspaper or a magazine, often with a joke written under it: *The cartoon shows a group of elephants trying to get into a phone-box.* | *a satirical cartoon that appears in the Washington Post*

caricature /ˈkærɪkətʃʊəʳ/ [n C] a humorous drawing that makes certain parts of people's faces or bodies seem larger or stranger than they really are, in order to make them look funny: *We had our caricatures drawn by a street artist while we were on vacation in Turkey.* | **+ of** *Politicians are used to having caricatures of themselves printed in newspapers.*

3 a photograph

- ▸ photograph
- ▸ photo/picture
- ▸ snap
- ▸ shot
- ▸ mug shot
- ▸ photography

photograph /ˈfəʊtəgrɑːf‖-græf/ [n C] a picture made using a camera **+ of** *Ansel Adams' photographs of the American wilderness are now worth thousands of dollars.* | **take a photograph** *Visitors are not allowed to take photographs inside the Museum.* | *My camera's fully automatic and takes really good photographs.* | **sb's photograph** (=a photograph of someone) *I hate having my photograph taken.* | **wedding/passport/ graduation etc photograph** *The photographer asked all the guests to stand still and pose for the wedding photograph.*

photo/picture /ˈfəʊtəʊ, ˈpɪktʃəʳ/ [n C] a photograph – use this especially when you are talking about photographs of you, your friends, your family, places you have visited etc: *Karen showed me a picture of her new boyfriend – he's very good-looking!* | **take a photo/picture** *Did you take any good photos while you were in Paris?* | **sb's photo/picture** (=a photo or picture of someone) *Do you want me to take your photo?* | *I saw her picture in the paper the other day.*

snap especially British **/snapshot** especially American /snæp, ˈsnæpʃɒt‖-ʃɑːt/ [n C] informal a photograph which you take yourself, for example of your family or on holiday, not one that is taken by a professional photographer: *They're just snapshots, but some of them are really good.* | **take a snap/snapshot** *Did you take any snaps in Greece?* | **+ of** *She showed me a snapshot of her three children.* | **holiday snaps** British

Patrick was showing his holiday snaps to everyone in the office.

shot /ʃɒt‖ʃɑːt/ [n C] a photograph that you take for a specific purpose, often one that you have to go to a particular place in order to take: *I got some great shots of Mount Fuji with the sun setting behind it.* | **take a shot** *The cars went past so quickly that she only had time to take a couple of shots.*

mug shot /ˈmʌg ʃɒt‖-ʃɑːt/ [n C] informal a photograph of a criminal's face, taken by the police: *The police showed me some mug shots, and I had to say if any of them looked like the man who attacked me.*

photography /fəˈtɒgrəfi‖-ˈtɑː-/ [n U] the art or profession of taking photographs: *Chris is studying photography at night school.* | *an exhibition of Irwin Penn's renowned fashion photography for Vogue magazine*

4 what you see in a mirror, on a screen, or on water

- image
- reflection

image /ˈɪmɪdʒ/ [n C] a picture on the screen of a television, cinema, or computer: *The images on a computer screen are made up of thousands of tiny dots.* | *the flickering images of an old silent movie* | *The digitized images can be stored on a computer hard disk, or printed out on special photographic paper.*

reflection /rɪˈflekʃən/ [n C] what you see when you look in a mirror or at the surface of water: *Anna stood looking at her reflection in the mirror.* | *the reflection of the moon on the surface of the lake*

5 the front or back of a picture

- foreground
- background

foreground /ˈfɔːʳgraʊnd/ [n C usually singular] the nearest part of a scene in a picture or photograph **in the foreground** *In the foreground of the picture is a man with a black beard, dressed in rough workingman's clothes and a hat.*

background /ˈbækgraʊnd/ [n C usually singular] the area behind something or someone in a picture or photograph **in the background** *It was a photo of everyone in my class, with the school building in the background.*

piece

RELATED WORDS

- one of the parts that something is made of *see* **part**
- piece of work *see* **work (4, 10-11)**
- *see also* **separate, cut, break, tear**

1 a part of something that has been separated from the rest

- piece
- bit

piece /piːs/ [n C] an amount of something that has been broken, cut, or separated from something larger: *a pack of chicken pieces* | **+ of** *There were pieces of broken glass all over the road.* | *a simple boat made from a few pieces of wood* | **cut/break etc sth into pieces** *Tim cut the pie into eight pieces.* | **tear/break/smash etc sth to pieces** *The old wreck had been smashed to pieces on the island's rocks.* | **in pieces** (=broken into many pieces) *The vase lay in pieces on the floor.* | **fall to pieces** *The books were eagerly borrowed and well used, and they finally fell to pieces.*

bit /bɪt/ [n C] especially spoken a small piece of something: *I'd like to try that cake. Just give me a small bit please.* | **+ of** *Have you got a bit of paper I can write your address on?* | **little/small/tiny bits** *There were little bits of food all over the carpet.* | **break/smash/blow etc sth to bits** *There'll be a war, and we'll all be blown to bits!* | **fall to bits** British *The jumper was very cheap – it'll probably fall to bits the first time I wear it.*

2 a piece that has a regular shape

- block
- cube
- slab
- bar

block /blɒk‖blɑːk/ [n C] a large solid piece of wood, stone, or ice that has straight sides: *Concrete blocks were used by most builders in the 1960s when constructing office buildings.* | **+ of** *The fish were lying on huge blocks of ice to keep them cold.* | **cut sth into blocks** *The ice was cut into blocks and stored in a special shed.*

cube /kjuːb/ [n C] a solid object with six equal square sides **ice cube** *For a joke, he put an ice cube down the back of her dress.* | **+ of** *She dropped a cube of sugar into her tea and stirred it with a spoon.* | **cut/chop sth into cubes** *Cut the melon into 2cm cubes and leave to soak in some port or red wine.*

slab /slæb/ [n C] a thick, flat, heavy piece of something such as stone **stone/concrete/marble slab** *His grave is covered by a huge marble slab.* | **+ of** *Slabs of concrete had been used to build a pathway for people to walk on.* | *The butcher's counter was covered in huge slabs of red meat and the air smelled of blood.*

bar /bɑːʳ/ [n C] a fairly long, thick piece of something such as metal, soap, or chocolate: *We go through so much soap in our family that I buy about 10 bars a month.* | **bar of chocolate/soap/gold** *I used to buy a bar of chocolate every day and give half to my friend.* | **chocolate/candy/gold bar** *I helped him take the wrapper off his candy bar.* | *The gold bars were transported from the bank in an armored truck.*

3 a piece that does not have a regular shape

- chunk
- lump
- hunk
- dollop

chunk /tʃʌŋk/ [n C] a piece of something solid that does not have a regular shape: *a can of pineapple chunks* | **+ of** *A large chunk of plaster had fallen from the ceiling.* | *Peanut butter is best spread on chunks of crusty bread.* | **cut/break etc sth into chunks** *Cut the potatoes into chunks and boil them for 15 minutes.*

lump /lʌmp/ [n C] a small piece of something solid that does not have a regular shape: *There are a lot of lumps in this sauce.* | **+ of** *Throw a few more lumps of coal on the fire.* | *I was almost hit by a lump of rock that fell from the cliff.*

hunk /hʌŋk/ [n C] a large, irregularly-shaped piece of something, especially food, that has been cut or torn from a bigger piece **hunk of meat/bread/cheese etc** *For lunch I had cheese with a hunk of bread and a glass of red wine.* | *Jack cut off a hunk of meat and handed it to Simon.*

dollop /ˈdɒləp‖ˈdɑː-/ [n C] a piece of a thick liquid or soft substance, usually served from a spoon **+ of** *He put a dollop of honey on his bread and spread it around with a knife.* | *Louise watched as the dollop of mashed potato fell onto her plate.*

4 a thin flat piece

- sheet
- strip
- slip
- pane
- slice

sheet /ʃiːt/ [n C] a thin flat piece of something such as paper, glass, or metal, usually with four straight sides: *Wrapping paper is sold in sheets or rolls.* | **+ of** *She decorated a sheet of mirrored glass with a few pressed flowers.* | *Sinks can be pressed from a single sheet of steel.*

strip /strɪp/ [n C] a thin flat piece of something such as cloth or paper **+ of** *You will need a strip of stiff cardboard to make this hat.* | **cut/snip etc sth into strips** *She then snipped the satin into thin strips.*

slip /slɪp/ [n C] a small narrow piece of paper, usually with information written on it: *The bank clerk handed me an official blue slip to sign.* | **+ of** *Everyone who votes has to fill in a slip of paper in order to register.* | **wage slip** British **/pay slip** American (=a slip of paper that shows how much you have been paid) *I looked through my wallet for last month's wage slip.*

pane /peɪn/ [n C] a flat piece of glass which has been cut to the size of a window **+ of** *The bullet shattered two panes of glass.* | **window pane** *I watched the rain as it pounded against the window pane.*

slice /slaɪs/ [n C] a thin flat piece of food such as bread, meat, or cheese that has been cut from a bigger piece using a knife: *'Would you like some more toast?' 'Just one more slice, please.'* | **+ of** *I admired the thick slices of plum cake arranged on the plate.* | **cut/carve sth into slices** *The beef was carved into slices so thin you could almost see through them.*

5 a very small piece

- grain
- flake
- speck
- fleck
- crumb
- morsel

grain /greɪn/ [n C] a very small hard piece of something such as sand or salt: *If you drop any rice you'll have to pick up every single grain.* | **+ of** *You always end up with grains of sand in your food when you eat at the beach.* | *A few grains of the tablet are left at the bottom of the glass.*

flake /fleɪk/ [n C] a very small, flat piece of something such as snow or skin, that breaks easily: *Her sunburnt skin was beginning to peel off in big flakes.* | **+ of** *Large white flakes of snow fell upon the cold ground.* | *She brushed the flakes of dandruff from her shoulder.*

speck /spek/ [n C] a piece of dust, dirt etc that is so small you almost cannot see it: *She realized that the specks on his shirt were not dirt but blood.* | **+ of** *The room looked immaculate, not a speck of dust anywhere.*

fleck /flek/ [n C] a small piece of dirt, dust, mud etc, usually in the form of a small mark or spot, that can be seen on a surface **+ of** *There were flecks of mud on my trousers after the walk in the woods.* | *By the time he'd finished painting the ceiling the whole floor was covered with flecks of red paint.*

crumb /krʌm/ [n C] a very small piece of food such as bread or cake: *Put a plate under your chin to catch the crumbs.* | *Cameron quickly swallowed his coffee and bread, and wiped the crumbs from his mouth.* | **breadcrumbs** *Roll the fish in breadcrumbs and grill it for half an hour.*

morsel /ˈmɔːʳsəl/ [n C] a word meaning a very small piece of food, used especially in literature: *She had cleared her plate of every morsel.* | **+ of** *Two gulls were fighting over a morsel of food.*

6 a small piece of something bigger

- fragment
- scrap
- splinter
- chip

fragment /ˈfrægmənt/ [n C] a small piece of something bigger, such as cloth, dishes, or building materials, that has been broken or torn: *The bullet had pierced the bone, leaving behind fragments which the surgeon was unable to remove.* | **+ of** *He was piecing together torn fragments of a letter.* | *The excavation of a Roman town house revealed fragments of a mosaic floor.*

scrap /skræp/ [n C] a very small piece of something such as paper, cloth, or food that is no longer useful or needed: *The birds would eat any leftover food scraps.* | **+ of** *He scribbled a note on an old scrap of paper.* | *This quilt was lovingly made from scraps of material.*

splinter /ˈsplɪntəʳ/ [n C] an extremely small, thin, and sharp piece of something such as wood, glass, or metal that was formed when the wood, glass, or metal was broken: *The doctor removed the small steel splinters that had lodged themselves in my leg in the explosion.* | **+ of** *The window smashed and splinters of glass flew everywhere.* | *She sucked so hard that she drew the splinter of wood out of her finger.*

chip /tʃɪp/ [n C] a small, irregularly-shaped piece of something such as wood or stone that remains after someone has been cutting or working with the wood or stone: *Wood chips covered the floor in the carpenter's workshop.* | **+ of** *After the decorators had left there were chips of plaster all over the lobby.*

place

RELATED WORDS

- put sth somewhere *see* **put**
- *see also* **area, town, country, space, here/not here, there**

1 a place

- place
- location
- spot
- site
- venue
- whereabouts

place /pleɪs/ [n C] *Plant the daisies in a sunny place.* | *Keep your passport in a safe place.* | *a quiet, private place to read in* | *Britain is one of the most highly populated places in the world.* | **a place to sit/eat/sleep etc** *Sign your name on the list, and find yourself a place to sit.* | *I was looking for a place to park the car.* | **+ for** *This would be a great place for a party!* | **right/wrong place** *Are you sure this is the right place? I don't see Emma.*

location /ləʊˈkeɪʃən/ [n C] a place in which someone lives, something happens, or something is built – used especially in business, advertising, or in official contexts: *a new hotel in an attractive location* | *The time, date, and location of the conference have not yet been announced.* | *Authorities say they have pinpointed the location of the sunken ship.*

spot /spɒt‖spɑːt/ [n C] a place, especially a pleasant place, where you spend time or live: *We camped in a pleasant, shady spot beside the river.* | *There are bike trails to the highest spot on the island, which has magnificent views of San Francisco.* | *Put some of the hardier plants outdoors in a protected spot.* | **+ for** *It looked like a perfect spot for a picnic.* | **holiday spot** British **/vacation spot** American *Las Vegas has a growing reputation as an entertainment and vacation spot.*

site /saɪt/ [n C] a place where something such as a building exists now, is going to exist in the future, or where something existed in the past: *an important archaeological site* | *The town has purchased a site on Villa Avenue for the new library.* | **+ of** *A home for the elderly will be built on the site of the old hospital.* | **building site** British **/construction site** American (=place where a new building is being built) *Green fences were put up around the construction site.*

venue /ˈvenjuː/ [n C] a place for an arranged event or meeting, for example a sports or musical event: *The concert's still on Saturday but the venue has been changed.* | **+ for** *The restaurant is one of the few venues for jazz music in the area.* | *Ministers have not yet agreed on a venue for the next Conference on European Security.*

whereabouts /ˈweərəbaʊts/ [n U with singular or plural verb in British English] the place or area where someone or something is, especially when this is unknown or is being kept secret **sb's whereabouts** *The police received an anonymous tip about the suspect's whereabouts.* | *Despite numerous searches and enquiries, her whereabouts are still unknown.* | **+ of** *The police have appealed for information concerning the whereabouts of the stolen car used in the robbery.* | *They tried to torture him into revealing the whereabouts of the $90 million, but he didn't know anything.*

2 the exact place where something is or happens

- position
- point
- spot
- exact/precise location

position /pəˈzɪʃən/ [n C] the exact place where something or someone is, especially in relation to other things or people: *Jessica moved to a position where she could see the stage better.* | *Bombs were dropped on the enemy position.* | *You can tell roughly what time it is by the sun's position.*

point /pɔɪnt/ [n C] a particular place on a line or on a surface, especially a place that is used for measuring distances, heights etc: *The river at this point is half a mile wide.* | *Soon they came to a point where the road divided.* | *Ward Hill, at over 700 feet, is the island's highest point.*

spot /spɒt‖spɑːt/ [n C] the exact place where something is or happens: *People had left flowers at the spot where the police officer was killed.* | **the exact/very/same etc spot** *The museum sits on the exact spot where gold was first discovered.* | *She agreed to meet him at the same spot the next evening.*

exact/precise location /ɪɡˌzækt, prɪˌsaɪs ləʊˈkeɪʃən/ [n singular] written the exact place where something is or happens: *The exact location of the ship, which sank in 1857, is being kept secret.* | *A military spokesman would not reveal the exact location of the search area.* | *Molecular biologists have found the precise location of the gene.*

3 ways of talking about where someone or something is, where they are from etc

- where
- whereabouts
- where on earth/where in the world

where /weəʳ/ [adv/conjunction] *Where are you?* | *This is where we keep all our junk.* | *I can't remember where I last saw it.* | *Could you tell me where the nearest tourist information office is?* | *Where are you going?* | *Where did you buy those shoes?* | **where ... to** *Neighbours have no idea where the couple have moved to.* | **where to?** spoken (=used to ask someone where they are going) *'Would you like to come with us tonight?' 'Where to?'* | **where ... from** *Where did you get that magazine from?* | **where sb comes from** *In all that time Naomi never told me where she came from.*

whereabouts /ˈweərəbaʊts/ [adv/conjunction] especially spoken use this when you are asking in what general area something is: *Did he say whereabouts he hid it?* | *'I'm from Thailand.' 'Whereabouts?'* | *Whereabouts in Scotland is Perthshire?*

where on earth/where in the world /ˌweər ɒn ˈɜːʳθ, ˌweər ɪn ðə ˈwɜːʳld/ where – use this especially to show surprise or disapproval: *Where on earth are you going dressed like that?* | *We've been looking for you for hours. Where in the world have you been?* | *When he woke up, he could not remember where on earth he was.*

4 in a place

- in
- at
- on

in /ɪn/ [prep] **in Africa/the city/the mountains/Oxford Street etc in** a country, town, area etc: *'Where's Annie?' 'She's in the yard.'* | *I'm going to a conference in Tokyo.* | *The plane crashed in the Andes.* | *John spent several years teaching in Zimbabwe.* | *She lives in Fern Street.* | *In the park there were two football matches going on.* | *European manufacturers are facing ever increasing competition from companies in the Far East.*

at /ət, (*strong*) æt/ [prep] **at the bank/the doctor's/the theatre/the airport/school etc** in a place where you go for a particular purpose: *I'll meet you at the station at 6.30.* | *Joe's at the dentist.* | *'Where were you last night?' 'We were at a play.'* | *I get the shopping done when the kids are at school.*

on /ɒn‖ɑːn, ɔːn/ [prep] **on the island/the coast/the outskirts/Oxford Street etc on** a particular piece of land: *It's a beautiful little fishing village on the south coast.* | *We could go to that Chinese restaurant on 23rd street.* | *Most superstores are built on the edge of town.*

5 in or to a place, when you do not know which place

- somewhere
- someplace
- be around

somewhere /ˈsʌmweəʳ/ [adv] *She lives somewhere near Manchester.* | *I know I saw it somewhere, but I can't remember exactly where.* | *From somewhere along the corridor there came the sound of laughter.* | **somewhere to live/sleep/sit etc** *She needs to find somewhere to live before starting her new job.*

someplace /ˈsʌmpleɪs/ [adv] American informal somewhere: *I want to go someplace warm on vacation.* | *She lives someplace up near Portland, and I haven't seen her for years.* | **someplace to live/eat/sleep etc** *A lot of people who use the guide are looking for someplace to eat.*

be around /biː əˈraʊnd/ [v phrase] to be near the place where you are or where something you are talking about is – use this when you do not know exactly where someone or something is: *Is Bob around?* | *It's got to be around here somewhere.* | *There are some good restaurants around there.*

6 in another place, not here

- somewhere else
- elsewhere

somewhere else ALSO **someplace else** American /ˌsʌmweər ˈels, ˌsʌmpleɪs ˈels/ [adv] in or to another place: *Go and play somewhere else, I'm trying to work.* | *When the landfill is full, the city will have to find someplace else to dump the garbage.* | *If labor is cheaper somewhere else, that's where companies will go to build new factories.*

elsewhere /elsˈweəʳ, ˈelsweəʳ‖ˈelsweər/ [adv] in or to another place or other places: *He'll work as a freelance consultant, unless he finds a better job elsewhere.* | *Make your home difficult to get into, and burglars will go elsewhere.* | *In North America and Europe, cats are companions for many people. Elsewhere, they are not regarded as pets.* | **+ in** *Elsewhere in the region, conditions are significantly better.*

7 a place where someone usually is or often goes

- haunt
- hangout
- sb's place

haunt /hɔːnt/ [n C] a place such as a bar or park that someone likes to go to often, especially in order to meet people: *Cafes like 'Les Deux Magots' were once the favourite haunts of French artists and intellectuals.* | **old haunts** (=where someone used to go at another time in their life) *Johnson will be revisting all his old haunts in Washington.*

hangout /ˈhæŋaʊt/ [n C] informal a place where a particular group of people, especially young people, often go to meet, talk etc: *In New York, try one of the celebrity hangouts, such as the Russian Tea Room or Elaine's.* | *a teenage hangout on Fountain Street* | **+ for** *The bar is a favorite hangout for soldiers from the nearby base.*

sb's place / (sb's) ˈpleɪs/ [n phrase] the place where someone usually sits or stands, especially in a bar, at work, or in their home: *Gerard was in his usual place by the fire when I reached the pub.* | **take your place** (=sit or stand in a place where you usually sit or stand) *The children took their places, and the teacher began calling the roll.*

8 when an object is in a particular place

- be
- stand
- lie

be /bi, (*strong*) biː/ [v not in progressive] *Do you know where my keys are?* | **be in/on/near/there etc** *The television is in the living room.* | *Your supper's in the oven.* | *There's a letter for you on the table.*

stand /stænd/ [v I] to be in a particular place in an upright position: *The linoleum was dented where a washer and dryer once stood.* | **stand in/on/near/there etc** *A single tall candle stood in the middle of the table.* | *A Christmas tree stood near the fireplace.*

lie /laɪ/ [v I] to be in a flat position on a surface – use this about paper, clothes, books, or other things that can be placed flat **lie in/on/near/there etc** *Several letters were lying on the table.* | *The children's clothes were lying all over the bedroom floor.* | *Her packed suitcase was lying near the door.*

9 when a country, town, company etc is in a particular place

- be
- be located/situated
- stand
- be based

be /bi, (*strong*) biː/ [v not in progressive] **be in/on/near/there etc** *Egypt is in North Africa.* | *The bank is on the next corner.* | *Can you tell me where the station is?*

be located/situated /biː ləʊˈkeɪtɪ̵d‖-ˈləʊkeɪtɪ̵d, ˈsɪtʃueɪtɪ̵d/ [v phrase] if a building **is located/situated** in a particular street, town, or area, it is in that place. **Be located/situated** is more formal than **be**. **+ in/at/near/there etc** *The bookshop is located at 120 Charing Cross Road.* | *A U.S. Air Force Base is located nearby.* | *The Duke's home is situated in an attractive part of central London.* | **conveniently/ pleasantly/ ideally situated** *a new hotel, conveniently situated close to the airport* | **conveniently/pleasantly/ideally located** *The two fisheries are ideally located between major markets in New York and Boston.*

stand /stænd/ [v I] if a building or structure stands somewhere, it is in that place: *There is a parking lot now where the old school once stood.* | **+ in/near/on there etc** *The house stood next to a church.*

be based /biː ˈbeɪst/ [v phrase] if a company or organization **is based** in a place, its main offices are there **+ in/at** *The United Nations is based in New York.* | *More than 200 aircraft will be based at Miramar Air Force Base.* | **London-based/Tokyo-based etc** *a London-based insurance company*

10 when something is usually kept in a place

- go/belong
- its/their place

go/belong /gəʊ, bɪˈlɒŋ‖-ˈlɔːŋ/ [v I not in progressive] especially spoken if something **goes** or **belongs** in a place, it should always be put there when it is not being used: *Put everything back where it belongs when you're through.* | **+ in/on/under etc** *'Where do these plates go?' 'They go in the cupboard above the sink.'* | *The books belong in the shelves, not on the floor.*

its/their place /ɪts, ðeəʳ ˈpleɪs/ [n phrase] the place where something is normally kept or put: *The kids never put anything back in its place.* | **its/their usual place** *I can't find the coffee tin – it isn't in its usual place.*

11 not in any place

- nowhere/not anywhere
- no place

nowhere/not anywhere /ˈnəʊweəʳ, nɒt ˈeniweəʳ/ [adv] not in any place or to any place: *Where's Nick? I can't find him anywhere.* | *Yeah, I'll wait. I'm not going anywhere.* | *a path that seemed to lead nowhere* | **nowhere else/not anywhere else** (=no other place) *In the Sonoran Desert there are plants that grow nowhere else in the country.* | **nowhere to live/sit/stay** *The hall was already full, and there was nowhere to sit.*

no place /ˈnəʊ pleɪs/ [adv] American informal nowhere: *She had no place else to live, so I let her stay in my apartment.* | *I was lonely and broke with no place to go.* | *We had no place else to rehearse.*

plan

RELATED WORDS

see also **prepare, design, organize, arrange, intend/not intend**

1 a plan to do something

- plan
- plan of action/game plan
- strategy
- programme
- policy
- scheme
- budget
- blueprint

plan /plæn/ [n C] something that you have decided to do, and the methods you will use to do it: *Her plan is to finish her degree and then go and teach in Japan.* | **+ to do sth** *The school has plans to build a computer centre.* | **+ for** *NASA has announced plans for a new space mission to Mars.* | **business/career etc plan** *You can't get a loan to start a new company if you don't have a good business plan.* | **make plans** *By January, many people are already making plans for their summer holidays.* | **go according to plan** (=when things happen exactly as you intended) *Everything went according to plan, and we all crossed the river safely.* | **a plan falls through** (=when you cannot do what you intended to do, because something unexpected happens) *There was an airline strike in India, and all our plans fell through at the last minute.* | **plan A/plan B** (=use this when you are saying that you have two possible plans, in case the first one is not successful) *Plan A obviously wasn't going to work, so we had to resort to plan B.*

plan of action/game plan /ˌplæn əv ˈækʃən, ˈgeɪm plæn/ [n phrase] informal a detailed plan explaining exactly how to achieve something: *Here's my game plan, Roger. I want to make the magazine a monthly, and cut it down to sixty or seventy pages.* | **decide/devise/put forward etc a plan of action** *If the problem continues, discuss a plan of action with your colleagues.*

strategy /ˈstrætɪ̇dʒi/ [n C] a carefully designed plan for achieving something that is difficult and may take a long time **+ for doing sth** *We need a new strategy for increasing our sales in Europe.* | *Murdoch bought several TV stations, as part of his strategy for building a media empire.* | **+ of** *The rebels' strategy of guerrilla warfare has been remarkably successful.* | **a/an campaign/economic/military etc strategy** *the President's long-term economic strategy*

programme British **/program** American /ˈprəʊgræm/ [n C] a series of activities, organized by a government or other large organization, that is designed to achieve something important and will continue for a long time **+ of** *The irrigation project is part of a programme of aid to West Africa.* | **training/research/space etc programme** *It's a major research program, aimed at developing cheaper fuels.* | **launch a programme** *The government has launched a programme to help unemployed young people find work.*

policy /ˈpɒlɪ̇si‖ˈpɑː-/ [n C] a plan or set of principles agreed by the members of a government, a political group, a company etc, that says how they intend to deal with a particular subject or problem: *It is not our policy to reveal our clients' names.* | **environmental/monetary/economic etc policy** *Most large companies these days operate an equal opportunities policy.* | *US foreign policy* (=towards other countries) | **+ on** *the government's policy on Europe* | **+ towards** *The Cuban revolution resulted in a reassessment of Washington's policy towards the Third World generally.* | **+ of** *A new ruler might adopt a policy of drastically cutting back oil production in order to boost prices.*

scheme /skiːm/ [n C] British an official plan that is intended to help particular groups of people, for example people who are very poor, without jobs, or who need a better education **+ to do sth** *Several organizations run schemes to help women find work after their children have started school.* | **a training/literacy/resettlement etc scheme** *The government's Youth Training Scheme soon ran into difficulties.* | *Adult literacy schemes have been run with great success in the inner cities.*

budget /ˈbʌdʒɪ̇t/ [n C] a plan that shows exactly what things you will spend a particular amount of money on **household/food/advertising etc budget** *Mum always worked out the household budget according to what we could afford.* | *The company has had to cut £46,000 from its advertising budget.* | **over/under budget** (=having spent more or less than the amount planned) *Several of our recent projects have been wildly over budget.* | *The renovation work to St George's Hall was completed six months ahead of schedule and under budget.* | **budget deficit** (=a situation in which more money has been spent than is available) *Texas faces a budget deficit of over $4 billion.* | **balance the/your budget** (=make sure that only the money available is spent) *The council has said that jobs will have to be cut in order to balance the budget.*

blueprint /ˈbluːˌprɪnt/ [n C] a completely new plan for important changes or ways of dealing with a problem **+ for** *Conservation groups have suggested a blueprint for a 'Green World'.* | *A panel of advisors is urging The White House to adopt a blueprint for dealing with such emergencies.*

2 a plan to do something bad

- plot
- conspiracy
- scheme
- intrigue

plot /plɒt‖plɑːt/ [n C] a secret plan to do something bad, especially to the members of a government: *The plot was quickly discovered, and five men were arrested.* | **+ to do sth** *a plot to assassinate the President* | **+ against** *Janis was suspected of masterminding a plot against US airlines in East Asia.*

conspiracy /kənˈspɪrəsi/ [n C/U] a secret and usually complicated plan made by two or more people to do something bad or illegal together **+ to do sth** *There was a conspiracy to defraud the company of millions of dollars.* | **+ against** *Reynolds was charged with conspiracy against the government.*

scheme /skiːm/ [n C] a plan to do something bad or illegal, especially one that you consider to be stupid or unlikely to be successful: *He's always coming up with these dumb schemes for making money that just land us in trouble.*

intrigue /ˈɪntriːg/ [n U] secret planning and arrangements, agreed in order to gain advantages and power for yourself: *The world of politics is a world of deception and intrigue.*

3 a plan of the times when things will happen

- timetable
- schedule
- programme

timetable British **/schedule** American /ˈtaɪmˌteɪbəl, ˈʃedjuːl‖ˈskedʒʊl/ [n C] a written list that shows the exact times when something will happen, for example when planes or buses leave, or when classes at school take place: *The timetable said there was another train at 6.15.* | *According to my schedule, we've got Math first and then Biology.* | **bus/train/school timetable** *Have you got the new bus timetable for this year?* | **+ of** *I'd like a schedule of the flights from Boston to New York, please.*

schedule /ˈʃedjuːl‖ˈskedʒʊl, -dʒəl/ [n C] a detailed plan of what someone is going to do and when they will do it, especially someone important: *The President's schedule includes a two-day visit to St Petersburg.* | **busy/tight schedule** (=when you plan to do a lot of things in a short time) *She has a pretty tight schedule, but she may be able to meet you for lunch.* | **light schedule** (=one that is not very busy) *I make sure that I have a fairly light schedule in the summer when the kids are on vacation.* | **on schedule** (=at or according to the time planned) *Tom arrived on schedule at twenty to eight.* | **ahead of/behind schedule** (=before/later than the time planned) *For once, I managed to finish the book I was writing ahead of schedule.* | *Due to the bad weather, the building work was already behind schedule.*

programme British **/program** American /ˈprəʊgræm/ [n C] a plan that shows the order of activities at a ceremony, sports meeting, public event etc: *The next race on today's program is the women's 1000 meters.* | *Who is organizing the conference programme?*

4 someone who plans something

- planner
- architect
- mastermind

planner /ˈplænəʳ/ [n C] someone who works for a government or a company, and who plans how future situations and problems should be dealt with according to what they think is likely to happen: *The proposal will be carefully examined by a committee of executives, planners and consultants.* | **financial/military/environmental etc planners** *Economic planners fear that there will be a 5% fall in real incomes next year.* | *a financial planner* | *Military planners and diplomats worry that the North's increasing distress over food supplies could provoke it to invade the South.*

architect /ˈɑːʳkɪ̈tekt/ [n C] the person who originally thought of an important and successful plan, especially in politics or business **the architect of sth** *Beveridge is usually thought of as the architect of the British National Health Service.* | *the chief architect of the election victory*

mastermind /ˈmɑːstəʳmaɪnd‖ˈmæs-/ [n C] a person who cleverly plans a complicated operation, especially in order to carry out a crime: *The court heard that it was Mrs Thompson who was the mastermind, not her husband.* | **the mastermind behind/of sth** *Andres is the mastermind behind a huge drug-smuggling operation.* | **a criminal mastermind** *The film stars Morgan Freeman as a criminal mastermind.*

5 to make plans

- plan
- make plans
- make arrangements
- work out
- map out
- budget
- formulate
- mastermind

plan /plæn/ [v I/T] to think carefully about something you are going to do, and decide how you will do it: *Sue spent months planning her trip.* | *The burglary had obviously been very carefully planned.* | **+ how/what/where etc** *Have you planned how you're going to spend your prize money?* | **+ for** *I think we should plan for about 50 guests.* | *We're planning for rain because the forecast isn't good.* | **have sth planned** (=have planned something carefully already) *Don't worry, I have the whole evening planned.* —**planning** [n U] the activity of deciding how you will do something that you intend to do: *After weeks of planning, the big day finally arrived.* | **financial/town/military etc planning** *Increasing traffic congestion is a major influence on town planning.*

make plans /ˌmeɪk ˈplænz/ [v phrase] to think about and talk about something that you intend to do, especially something that needs to be carefully planned: *We sat around the table, talking, laughing, and making plans.* | **+ for** *I've already started to make plans for the wedding – there's so much to do.*

make arrangements /ˌmeɪk əˈreɪndʒmənts/ [v phrase] to organize the details of an event or trip, such as the times in which things will happen: *I'd booked the flight and made all the arrangements well in advance.* | **+ for** *John's brother kindly made the arrangements for the funeral.* | **+ to do sth** *Vivian and her boyfriend are making arrangements to join us in Australia.* | **+ with** *Please telephone and make arrangements with my secretary.*

work out especially British ALSO **figure out** American /ˌwɜːʳk ˈaʊt, ˌfɪgər ˈaʊt‖ˌfɪgjər-/ [phr v T] to think carefully about how you are going to do something, especially something complicated or difficult, and plan a good way of doing it: *Management consultant Peter Brant worked out the schedule in October 1983.* | *UN negotiators have figured out a plan which they hope will be acceptable to both sides.* | **work/figure out a way of doing sth** *The first thing you'll have to do is figure out a way of earning the money.* | **+ what/where/ how etc** *I'll certainly go back to my job once I've worked out who's going to look after the kids during the day.* | **have it all worked/figured out** (=have completely planned how you are going to do something) *The killer, whoever he was, had it all worked out.*

map out /ˌmæp ˈaʊt/ [phr v T] to plan all the details of how something is going to develop in the future, especially over a long period of time: *Representatives from several European countries met to map out details of the proposed aid program.* | **have your future/career/education etc mapped out** *Jodie has her career all mapped out.* | *By the time he was 15, his parents already had his future mapped out.*

budget /ˈbʌdʒɪ̈t/ [v I/T] to plan how you will spend your money during a certain period of time or for a particular activity: *Mark's capable of earning a lot, but he's no idea how to budget or save.* | *Our annual expenditure on training has been carefully budgeted.* | **+ for** *At university, young people have to budget for their living expenses, and organise their time.* —**budgeting** [n U] *The job will involve budgeting and decision-making, as well as managing the project.*

formulate /ˈfɔːʳmjʊ̈leɪt/ [v T] if members of a government, company, or other organization **formulate** a plan or proposal, they decide the details of what is going to be done: *Changes to the education system should be formulated by teachers not politicians.* | **formulate a plan/policy/proposal etc** *The government has set up a working party to formulate proposals for reducing environmental pollution.* —**formulation** /ˌfɔːʳmjʊ̈ˈleɪʃən/ [n U] **the formulation of sth** *A small group of advisers helps the President with the formulation of foreign policy.*

mastermind /ˈmɑːstəʳmaɪnd‖ˈmæs-/ [v T] to be the person who is in charge of planning a complicated or difficult operation, especially a crime: *The raid, one of the most daring crimes of the century, was masterminded by Italian playboy, Giovanni Cattani.* | *Well-known as a tough industrialist, he masterminded 50 company takeovers in one year.*

6 to plan something that will happen a long time in the future

- plan ahead
- look ahead
- forward planning

plan ahead /ˌplæn əˈhed/ [phr v I] *Once you have children, it's wise to plan ahead.* | *Fluctuations in oil prices on the world market make it impossible for developing countries to plan ahead.* | **+ for** *It's never too soon to start planning ahead for your retirement.*

look ahead /ˌlʊk əˈhed/ [phr v I] to think about what may happen in the future so that you are aware of it when you make plans: *By looking ahead, management are then in a good position to anticipate potential problems.* | **+ to** *All footballers have to look ahead to the time when they leave the game.*

forward planning British **/future planning** American /ˌfɔːʳwəʳd ˈplænɪŋ, ˌfjuːtʃəʳ ˈplænɪŋ/ [n U] the activity of thinking carefully about what will happen in the future, and including this in your present plans, especially in order to make possible problems easier to deal with when the time comes: *With a little more forward planning, we could have avoided these problems.* | *Expert advice is available for investors who wish to engage in future planning.*

7 to plan something bad

- plot
- scheme
- conspire

plot /plɒt‖plɑːt/ [v I/T] to make secret plans to do something wrong or illegal: *The court heard how Mrs Taylor and her lover had plotted the murder of her husband.* | **+ to do sth** *Three men were charged with plotting to plant the biggest bomb ever in Central London.* | **+ against** *Plotting against the government was punishable by death.*

scheme /skiːm/ [v I] to secretly make clever and dishonest plans to get or achieve something **+ to do sth** *Behind the scenes, a small group was scheming to remove the Chairman from office.* | *Against all the rules of the competition, Nick was scheming to win.* | **+ against** *As the King got older, he became convinced that his family were scheming against him.*

conspire /kənˈspaɪəʳ/ [v I] if two or more people **conspire** to do something illegal or harmful, they plan secretly to do it **+ to do sth** *Ten men were convicted of conspiring to bomb the UN and the FBI buildings in New York.* | *Kevin Maxwell faced two charges of conspiring to defraud pensioners.* | **+ against** *The President called a meeting and accused his aides of conspiring against him.* | **+ with** *There was no doubt that they were conspiring with other African guerrilla movements.* —**conspirator** /kənˈspɪrətəʳ/ [n C] *The conspirators* (=people who are conspiring) | *met in a disused warehouse to discuss their plans.*

8 ways of saying that something is being planned

- be in the pipeline
- be in the planning stages
- afoot

be in the pipeline /biː ɪn ðə ˈpaɪplaɪn/ [v phrase] if something such as a new product or a change **is in the pipeline**, it is being planned and prepared and it will be ready soon: *After considerable market research, several new products are now in the pipeline.* | *There are one or two important changes in the pipeline.*

be in the planning stages ALSO **be at the planning stage** British /biː ɪn ðə ˈplænɪŋ ˌsteɪdʒɪ̈z, biː ət ðə ˈplænɪŋ ˌsteɪdʒ/ [v phrase] if something such as a product **is in the planning stages**, it is being planned, but the final details have not yet been decided: *A new museum is currently at the planning stage at Bowness.* | *The programme is only in the planning stages, and is not likely to be broadcast until next year.*

afoot /əˈfʊt/ [adj not before noun] if something new, interesting, strange, or dishonest **is afoot**, someone is planning it, especially secretly: *From information received, it was thought that some illegal activity was afoot.* | *A quick look round the research and development facility in Versailles revealed a number of interesting software projects afoot.* | **plans/changes/moves etc are afoot** *Plans are now afoot for an important exhibition of Canaletto in England.* | *Apparently, moves are afoot to ban smoking in public places.*

9 words for describing something that has been planned

- planned
- scheduled
- strategic
- well/carefully thought out

planned /plænd/ [adj] *Some people prefer a vacation with a lot of planned activities.* | *The number of planned job cuts by major US businesses declined in October from a year ago.*

scheduled /ˈʃedjuːld‖ˈskedʒʊld, -dʒəld/ [adj] planned to happen at a particular time: *Heavy snow closed airports and forced the cancellation of scheduled budget talks at the White House.* | **+ to do sth** *A UN mission was scheduled to leave on February 29.* | **+ for** *The play was originally scheduled for October, but it had to be cancelled.*

strategic /strəˈtiːdʒɪk/ [adj only before noun] done as part of a plan, especially in a military, business, or political situation, in order to gain an advantage against your opponents: *The British army made a strategic withdrawal across the English Channel.* | *The two countries agreed to join together in a strategic alliance.* —**strategically** [adv] *Ammunition storage depots are strategically located throughout the country.*

well/carefully thought out /ˌwel, ˌkeəʳfəli θɔːt ˈaʊt/ [adj phrase] something that is **well thought out** has been carefully planned so that it will work well and achieve its desired results: *If you're planning to* *take a year out between school and university, it needs to be carefully thought out.* | *The average worker's long-term financial security will depend upon having a well-thought-out personal finance plan.*

10 not planned

- unplanned
- spontaneous
- impromptu
- not well thought out
- ad hoc

unplanned /ˌʌnˈplænd◂/ [adj] *As a surprise, we decided to make an unplanned visit to my mother's.* | *Very few burglaries are completely unplanned.* | *Unplanned pregnancies in the US each year are estimated at 3 million.*

spontaneous /spɒnˈteɪniəs‖spɑːn-/ [adj] something that is **spontaneous** is done because you suddenly feel you want to do it, not because you have arranged to do it or been asked to do it: *The crowd gave a spontaneous cheer when the news was announced.* | *The invitation was completely spontaneous.* | *an act of spontaneous generosity* —**spontaneously** [adv] *It's great when the children spontaneously show affection or appreciation.* —**spontaneity** /ˌspɒntəˈniːɪ̥ti, -ˈneɪɪ̥ti‖ˌspɑːn-/ [n U] *the beauty and spontaneity of African worship*

impromptu /ɪmˈprɒmptjuː‖ɪmˈprɑːmptuː/ [adj usually before noun] done or happening without any planning or preparation: *We finished the day with an impromptu game of football in a nearby field.* | *Jem's impromptu speech met with thunderous applause.*

not well thought out /nɒt ˌwel θɔːt ˈaʊt/ [adj phrase] something that is **not well thought out** has not been planned carefully enough and therefore is unlikely to work well: *Reagan's plan was a bold one, but it was not well thought out.* | *If your business proposal is not very well thought out, you will find it difficult to get financial backing.*

ad hoc /æd ˈhɒk‖-ˈhɑːk, -ˈhəʊk/ [adj phrase only before noun] not planned or organized in advance: *You never know when you might have to have an ad hoc meeting with a client.* | *Historical records have often been kept in an ad hoc way, so that our information is not complete.* | **on an ad hoc basis** (=when you need to do it, not in a planned way) *Most companies have some people working for them on an ad hoc basis.*

11 to not try to plan things, but deal with them as they happen

- take sth as it comes
- play it by ear
- live from day to day
- one day at a time

take sth as it comes /ˌteɪk (sth) əz ɪt ˈkʌmz/ [v phrase] to not worry about or plan for something that has not happened yet, but decide what to do when it happens: *I always think the best way of approaching an interview is to take it as it comes.* | **take things as they come** *The only way to manage when you have small kids is to take things as they come.* | **take life as it comes/take each day as it comes** *If I were you, I'd just enjoy each day and take life as it comes.*

play it by ear /ˌpleɪ ɪt baɪ ˈɪəʳ/ [v phrase] spoken to not make plans about how to deal with a particular situation, but decide to wait until it actually happens and hope that you will know what to do then: *'Shall we tell Dad what's happened?' 'Let's play it by ear and see what sort of mood he's in.'* | *We've booked the flight, but not the accommodation – we'll play it by ear when we get there.*

live from day to day /ˌlɪv frəm ˌdeɪ tə ˈdeɪ/ [v phrase] to not plan very far in the future because you have too many problems now to be able to think about what may happen later: *Since Jim got ill, we've just had to live from day to day.* | *There's nothing as depressing as living from day to day, as the unemployed are forced to do.*

one day at a time /wʌn ˌdeɪ ət ə ˈtaɪm/ [adv] if you deal with a problem or difficult situation **one day at a time**, you try to think about just what is happening in the present and do not try to plan what you will do in the future: *I've no idea where we'll live. Anyway, one day at a time.* | **take/live one day at a time** *In order to overcome their addiction, they have to learn to take one day at a time.*

play a game or sport

RELATED WORDS

▸ *see also* **take part/be involved, competition, score, game, sport/game, win, lose, beat/defeat, result**

1 to play a game or do a sport

- play
- do
- go

play /pleɪ/ [v I/T] to take part in a game or sport – use this especially about games in which you try to win against another person or team: *Karl loves basketball and plays almost every weekend.* | *Every Sunday we play Monopoly or some other board game.* | **+ in** *I'm playing in a tennis match this Sunday.* | **play football/tennis/golf/baseball etc** *It's been a long time since I played hockey.*

do /duː/ [v T] especially spoken use this especially when talking about sports that are not team sports: *I do aerobics twice a week.* | *He used to do karate when he was in college.*

go /gəʊ/ [v T] use this about sports whose names end in '-ing' **go climbing/swimming/running/riding etc** *John goes running every morning.* | *Make sure whoever you go climbing with is a safe and trustworthy partner.*

2 to play against someone else

- play (against)
- face
- give sb a game
- versus
- vs.

▸ *see also* **compete with**

play (against) /ˈpleɪ (əgenst)/ [v T not in passive] *Barcelona will play Milan in the final.* | *This was McDaniel's first game playing against his former teammates.* | **play tennis/golf/chess etc with sb** *Dad's out playing golf with Barry this morning.* | **play sb at tennis/golf etc** British *I'm playing Andy at tennis this afternoon.*

face ALSO **take on** /feɪs, ˌteɪk ˈɒn/ [v T/phr v T] to play against a person or team, especially one that will be difficult to beat – used in newspapers and broadcasts: *Tomorrow, Jane Wilkes, a first-round qualifier, takes on the world number one, Monica Seles.* | *UCLA will face North Carolina tonight at Pauley Pavilion.*

give sb a game /ˌgɪv (sb) ə ˈgeɪm/ [v phrase] British informal to play a game against another person, especially when it is not a serious or important game: *If you want to play chess ask Maria – she'll give you a game.*

versus /ˈvɜːʳsəs/ [prep] against another person or team: *Yesterday in the semi-final we saw Sampras versus Henman.* | *It's a friendly game – the women versus the men.*

vs. ALSO **v** British /ˈvɜːʳsəs, viː/ [prep] written abbreviation of versus: *Today's games include the Chicago Bulls vs. the Boston Celtics.* | *Gascoigne was back in the UK, to play in the England v France match.*

3 someone who plays a game or does a sport

- player
- competitor
- contestant
- sportsman/ sportswoman

player /ˈpleɪəʳ/ [n C] someone who takes part in a game or competition: *One of the players has been sent off the field.* | **baseball/tennis/chess etc player** *He is recognized as the world's greatest chess player.* | *The school has a reputation for producing top-class football players.*

competitor /kəmˈpetətəʳ/ [n C] someone who is competing, especially against a lot of people, in a particular game or competition: *The competitors tonight come from all over the world.* | *The competitors in the 100m sprint are being asked to take their places at the start.*

contestant /kənˈtestənt/ [n C] someone who takes part in a competition or game: *Contestants for the game show go through a tough selection process.* | *a beauty pageant contestant*

sportsman/sportswoman /ˈspɔːʳtsmən, ˈspɔːʳtsˌwʊmən/ [n C] someone who takes part in and is usually good at a sport, especially as a profession: *Tonight we remember one of the greatest sportsmen of our time.* | *The prizes are being presented by sportswoman Tessa Sanderson.* | *He won the magazine's 'Sportsman of the Year' award in 1999.*

4 a group of people who play together against another group

- team
- side
- squad

team /tiːm/ [n C with singular or plural verb in Brtiish English] a group of people who play together against another group: *Both teams are looking tired now.* | *Walsh coached the team to two Super Bowl championships.* | **play for a team** *Tim played for the national youth team but never became a professional.* | **in a team** British **/on a team** American *Peterson earned a place on the U.S. Olympic speedskating team.* | *They wouldn't let me play in the village under-12 team because I'm a girl.*

side /saɪd/ [n C] especially British a sports team: *They are playing today against one of the best sides in the country.* | *I don't know which side I want to win.*

squad /skwɒd‖skwɑːd/ [n C with singular or plural verb in British English] a group of players from which a team will be chosen: *Vivian McGrath was the star of the 1938 Davis Cup squad.* | *Only two starting players are returning from last year's women's basketball squad.*

5 a person or group of people you play against

- opponent
- opposition

opponent /əˈpəʊnənt/ [n C] someone you play against in a game or competition: *My opponent was the same age and height as myself.* | *Karpov defeated his 24-year-old opponent in 57 moves.* | *Manchester United will prove a formidable opponent this season.*

opposition /ˌɒpəˈzɪʃən‖ˌɑː-/ [n U] the person or team that you are playing against: *The team won all their games against local opposition, but lost in the international competition.* | *The opposition fought hard, but had no chance of winning.* | *Seles had reached the semi-finals without really facing any serious opposition.*

point at

to point at someone or something, to show which one you mean

RELATED WORDS

- *see also* **show**

- point
- indicate
- gesture at/towards
- point out

point /pɔɪnt/ [v I/T] to use your finger to show which person or thing you mean: *Children are taught that it's rude to point.* | **+ at** *'Look,' she said, pointing at a vase in a shop window.* | *The teacher pointed at Marcus and told him to come to the front of the class.* | **+ to/ towards** *'That's Margo's bouquet, on the table.' Mother pointed to a massive bunch of spring flowers.* | **point your finger at** *Don't point your finger at me.*

indicate /ˈɪndəkeɪt/ [v T] to show someone the person or thing you mean in a more polite way than pointing, for example by looking at them or moving your head slightly: *'Shall we go in here?' Calvin indicated the cafe.* | *'I'd like you to meet Todd,' he said, indicating a tall man standing next to him.*

gesture at/towards /ˈdʒestʃər æt, təˌwɔːʳdz/ [v phrase] to point towards a person or thing by holding out your hand towards them: *'I'm not going out in this weather,' said Lydia, gesturing at the heavy rain outside.* | *'Do you see all these people here?' She gestured towards the hospital corridor.*

point out /ˌpɔɪnt ˈaʊt/ [phr v T] to show someone a person or thing, especially one that they are interested to know about, by pointing **point out sb/sth** *John pointed out the building where he worked.* | **point sb/sth out** *She wanted to know which was my house, so I pointed it out to her as we drove past.* | **point out sb/sth to sb** *I asked him to point out the new headteacher to me at the party.*

polite

RELATED WORDS

opposite: **rude**

- *see also* **nice, kind, friendly, behave**

1 words for describing someone who is polite

- polite
- respectful
- civil
- courteous
- well-mannered

polite /pəˈlaɪt/ [adj] someone who is **polite** follows the rules of social behaviour and shows respect for other people and their feelings: *He seemed a very polite young man.* | *a polite request* | **it is polite to do sth** *I didn't really care what she thought about the book, but I thought it would be polite to ask her.* | *It's not considered polite to ask someone how much they earn.* | **+ to** *She's always extremely polite to me, but I never know what she's really thinking.* | **make polite conversation** (=talk politely about unimportant things, especially to someone you do not know very well) *The last thing I felt like doing was making polite conversation with my roommate's parents.* —**politely** [adv] *'I hope your mother is well?' he asked politely.*

respectful /rɪˈspektfəl/ [adj] showing proper respect for someone who is older than you, has a higher position than you etc: *They waited in respectful silence as the funeral procession went past.* | **+ to/towards** *If children were taught to be more respectful towards their elders, maybe these crimes wouldn't happen so often.*

civil /ˈsɪvəl/ [adj] polite in a rather formal way, without necessarily being friendly: *I expect a civil answer when I ask you a question.* | **+ to/towards** *I wish you'd be a little more civil towards our guests.* —**civilly** [adv] *She tried to speak to him civilly, in spite of the bitterness that she still felt towards him.* —**civility** /sɪ̇ˈvɪlɪ̇ti/ [n U] *Throughout my stay on the island I was treated with the utmost civility* (=extremely civilly) *by everyone there.*

courteous /ˈkɜːʳtiəs/ [adj] someone who is **courteous** is polite and considers the needs of other people, especially in formal situations when you do not know the other people well: *Airline staff must be courteous at all times, even when passengers are not.* | *I received a courteous letter from Jane's mother thanking me for my help.* | **+ to** *He was always kind and courteous to me, but we never really became friends.* —**courteously** [adv] *Customers are always treated courteously in our stores.*

well-mannered /ˌwel ˈmænəʳd◂/ [adj] someone who is **well-mannered** has good manners, and always knows the correct way to behave in social situations: *Henry was a typical Oxford man – well-mannered, easy-going, and very sure of himself.* | *The children were good little things, well-mannered, and beautifully dressed.*

2 careful not to upset or embarrass someone

- tactful
- diplomatic
- discreet
- polite

tactful /ˈtæktfəl/ [adj] careful not to mention something that may upset or embarrass someone: *Mandy thought her mother's outfit was a little too fancy, but was too tactful to say so.* | **it is tactful of sb to do sth** *It wasn't very tactful of you to ask whether he'd put on weight.* | **a tactful way of doing sth** *'Besides ... ' Melissa hesitated, trying to think of a tactful way of telling him the truth.* —**tactfully** [adv] *Clare tactfully changed the subject when someone started talking about weddings.*

diplomatic /ˌdɪpləˈmætɪk◂/ [adj] skilful in the way that you deal with other people, and carefully avoiding saying anything that might offend or annoy them: *A good secretary needs to be efficient, and above all diplomatic.* | *Robson was trying to be as diplomatic as possible – he didn't want to risk losing a promotion.* —**diplomatically** [adv] *My father suggested diplomatically that becoming an astronaut might not be as easy as I thought.*

discreet /dɪˈskriːt/ [adj] someone who is **discreet** is careful not to say anything that will embarrass another person, especially by making sure that secret or private information does not become generally known: *Andrew's very discreet – he won't tell anyone you're leaving.* | *We offer a discreet and personal service to our clients.* —**discreetly** [adv] *The lawyer murmured discreetly that he would like to speak to her alone.*

polite /pəˈlaɪt/ [adj] careful not to offend someone, especially by not being completely honest when telling them what you think about something: *Did you mean what you said about my dress, or were you just being polite?* | **+ about** *The guests were all very polite about the meal, but inside Joan just wanted to cry.* —**politely** [adv] *When she asked what I thought of the meal I lied politely, and said it was great.*

3 behaving in a very polite and formal way

- formal
- correct
- stiff

formal /ˈfɔːʳməl/ [adj] *Our boss is very formal – he doesn't call anyone by their first name.* | *A lot of people found my father rather formal and aloof, particularly when they first met him.* | *You shouldn't use 'Yours faithfully' – it's much too formal for this kind of letter.* —**formally** [adv] *He stood by the door to welcome the guests, bowing formally to each one in turn.*

correct /kəˈrekt/ [adj not usually before noun] strictly following all of the rules of polite and formal behaviour, even when this is not necessary: *Andrew's marriage proposal was very correct and proper.* | *One must be correct about these things, mustn't one?*

stiff /stɪf/ [adj not usually before noun] very formal and difficult to talk to, in a way that makes other people feel uncomfortable: *She gives the impression of being rather stiff and unfriendly, but I think that's because she's basically shy.* | *Their goodbyes were stiff and formal.* —**stiffly** [adv] *Dr Aziz replied stiffly, 'I do not consider Mrs Moore my friend.'*

4 polite behaviour

- politeness
- manners
- good manners
- courtesy
- tact
- formality

politeness /pəˈlaɪtnɪ̇s/ [n U] *During my stay in Japan, I was treated with great politeness by everyone I met.* | *American businessmen were surprised that their French colleagues wanted to shake hands each morning, a formal sign of politeness in the US.* | **out of politeness** (=simply in order to be polite) *I don't like cake, but I accepted a piece out of politeness.*

manners /ˈmænəʳz/ [n plural] polite ways of behaving that parents teach their children for situations such as eating, meeting people, or asking for something: *I wish she'd teach that boy of hers some manners!* | **table manners** (=behaviour when you eat)

Our kids' table manners are appalling – it's like living in the zoo.

good manners /ˌgʊd ˈmænəʳz/ [n plural] someone who has **good manners** knows how to behave politely in social situations, for example, when to say 'please' and 'thank you': *My mother was impressed with Tony's good manners.* | **have good manners** *We teach our children to speak correctly and to have good manners, and when they become teenagers they do exactly the opposite.* | **have the good manners to do sth** *At least she had the good manners to let us know she would be late.* | **it is good manners (to do sth)** (=it is polite to do something) *It wouldn't be good manners to leave so soon – the party has only just started.*

courtesy /ˈkɜːʳtəsi/ [n U] polite behaviour that pays attention to the needs of other people, especially people you do not know well: *Businessmen value the service and courtesy offered by traditional hotels.* | *When you contact a government office, you should receive efficient service and be treated with courtesy.* | **out of courtesy** (=simply in order to be polite) *I don't think she wanted us to come and stay with her, she just offered out of courtesy.* | **have the courtesy to do sth** (=used especially when you are annoyed with someone who has behaved impolitely) *I wish he'd had the courtesy to tell me when he was coming back.*

tact /tækt/ [n U] the quality of being polite and careful about what you say, in order to avoid making other people feel embarrassed or upset: *Helping people who have marriage problems requires a great deal of tact and patience.* | *The old woman thrust a picture of a plain-looking girl into Meryl's hand. 'Your granddaughter? She's lovely,' said Meryl with tact.*

formality /fɔːʳˈmæləti/ [n U] a polite and rather formal way of behaving, which avoids being too friendly: *The following morning, Mr Harrison greeted her with careful formality.* | *When I re-read my letter I saw that I had written it with a formality that I did not intend.*

5 words for describing children who behave politely and well

- well-behaved
- well-brought up
- good

well-behaved /ˌwel bɪˈheɪvd◂/ [adj] a **well-behaved** child is polite and does not cause trouble or make noise: *His older brother was quieter and far better-behaved.* | *She was a thoughtful, kind, and well-behaved girl.* | *Their children are so well-behaved it seems almost unnatural.*

good /gʊd/ [adj] a child who is **good** behaves in a polite, obedient and helpful way: *She's a good girl – I'm sure she won't give you any trouble.* | *What good children – they went to bed as soon as I told them to!* | *If you're good you can stay up till eight o'clock tonight.*

well-brought up /ˌwel brɔːt ˈʌp◂/ [adj phrase] a child or young adult who is **well-brought up** always behaves well because their parents have taught them to be polite: *They are well-brought-up children, and have a great respect for their teachers.* | *David is very well-brought up, but he does have a nasty temper sometimes.*

6 polite, confident, and relaxed, but in an insincere way

- smooth
- suave

smooth /smuːð/ [adj] someone who is **smooth**, especially a man, has good manners and a relaxed, confident way of talking to people, but in a way that you do not completely trust: *Smooth and charming, Francis was the kind of man your mother would love you to marry.* | *Don't let his smooth manner fool you – he's just after your money.*

suave /swɑːv/ [adj] very polite, pleasant and stylish, especially in a way that is intended to be attractive to women: *Reginald was suave, handsome and charming.* | *He was tall and suave, careful in dress, careful in behaviour.*

politics

RELATED WORDS

- having extreme political opinions *see* **extreme**
- having moderate political opinions *see* **moderate**
- *see also* **government, leader, vote, represent, opinion, against/oppose, protest, rebellion, public services**

1 activities and ideas relating to the government of a country or area

- politics
- political

politics /ˈpɒlətɪks‖ˈpɑː-/ [n U] *Maria is very interested in politics and current affairs.* | **be in politics/be involved in politics** *She's been in politics for over twenty years.* | **go into politics/enter politics** (=begin to work or be active in politics) *He made the decision to go into politics last year.* | **British/French/American etc politics** *The University runs a course in American politics and government.* | **party politics** (=politics involving official political organizations that compete against each other in order to gain power) *Most of the people questioned thought that unions should not get involved in party politics.* | **local politics** (=politics in one part of a country) *Thomson has always been deeply involved in local politics.* | **the world of politics** *an important figure in the world of politics*

political /pəˈlɪtɪkəl/ [adj usually before noun] connected with the government of a country or local area: *The people are demanding political change.* | *She began her political career as a city councillor.* | *He asked me to explain the British political system.* | **political party** (=an organization with particular opinions that tries to gain power in a country) *There are two main political parties in the US.* | **political animal** (=someone who enjoys being involved in politics) *McEnroe loves the atmosphere at Westminster – he's a real political animal.*

2 someone who works in politics

- politician
- statesman/stateswoman
- MP/member of parliament
- congressman/congresswoman
- senator
- spin doctor

politician /ˌpɒləˈtɪʃən‖ˌpɑː-/ [n C] someone who works in politics, especially a member of parliament: *Hargreaves is a clever and ambitious politician.* | *the wife of a leading British politician* | **left-wing/right-wing politician** *Many right-wing politicians opposed the treaty.*

statesman/stateswoman /ˈsteɪtsmən, ˈsteɪtsˌwʊmən/ [n C] an important and very experienced politician who is admired and respected both in their own country and in other countries: *European statesmen are meeting in Paris today to discuss the crisis in the Middle East.* | *She is now one of America's leading stateswomen.*

MP/member of parliament /ˌem ˈpiː, ˌmembər əv ˈpɑːrləmənt/ [n C] someone who has been elected to a parliament, especially in Britain or in a country that has a similar system of government, such as India, Australia, or South Africa: *There are still very few women members of parliament.* | *The conference will open with a speech by Barbara Morland, MP.* | **Labour/Conservative/Liberal MP (for)** *the Labour MP for Birmingham South*

congressman/congresswoman /ˈkɒŋgrəsmən‖ˈkɑːŋ-, ˈkɒŋgrəsˌwʊmən‖ˈkɑːŋ-/ [n C] someone who is a member of the US Congress, especially of the House of Representatives: *Many congressmen are keen to promote research into renewable energy sources.* | *The proposals were first put forward by Congresswoman Eleanor Baines.* | **+ from** *The Congressman from Iowa spoke for three hours.*

senator /ˈsenətər/ [n C] a member of the US Senate or a similar institution: *The President met with a group of senators and congressmen to discuss energy policy.* | *The debate was opened by Senator Robinson.* | **+ from** *The Democratic Senator from New York held a press conference yesterday.*

spin doctor /ˈspɪn ˌdɒktər‖-ˌdɑːk-/ [n C] someone who is used by a political party to influence people's opinions by cleverly controlling what is reported in the news: *The party spin doctors would like us to believe that the government is committed to improving the environment.*

3 different types of political opinions and parties

- right-wing
- left-wing
- the left
- the right
- the centre

right-wing /ˌraɪt ˈwɪŋ◂/ [adj] supporting the political aims of groups that strongly support conservative ideas and the capitalist economic system: *He is known for his extreme right-wing views.* | *a right-wing conservative MP* —**right-winger** [n C] *The policy is supported by right-wingers within the party.*

left-wing /ˌleft ˈwɪŋ◂/ [adj] supporting the political aims of groups such as Socialists and Communists: *A lot of colleagues were put off by her left-wing opinions.* | *a left-wing politician* —**left-winger** [n C] *He is popular with left-wingers in the party.*

the left ALSO **the Left** /ðə ˈleft/ [n singular] political parties such as the Socialists and Communists: *The new law has been severely criticized by politicians on the left.*

the right ALSO **the Right** /ðə ˈraɪt/ [n singular] political parties which strongly support conservative ideas and the capitalist economic system: *Politicians on the right have welcomed these new proposals.*

the centre British **/the center** American /ðə ˈsentər/ [n singular] a middle position in politics which does not support extreme ideas: *The party seems to be becoming less radical, and drifting more towards the centre.*

poor

RELATED WORDS

opposite: —— **rich**

▸ *see also* **money, owe, earn, borrow**

1 having very little money

- poor
- badly off
- needy/in need
- impoverished
- poverty-stricken
- destitute

poor /pʊər/ [adj] *They were so poor they couldn't afford to buy shoes for their children.* | *She was born in a poor district of Chicago in 1925.* | *People who live in poor countries have a much lower life expectancy.* | *These cuts will hit the poorest members of society.* | *Some Democrats believed they lost the election because many poor women didn't turn out to vote.* | **dirt poor** American (=extremely poor) *Her mother grew up dirt poor among migrant workers in Alabama.*

badly off /ˌbædli ˈɒf/ [adj not before noun] having less money than most other people: *She was quite badly off for a while after her husband died.* | *We were pretty poor, but most of our friends were even worse off.* | *No matter how badly off we were, we never went to bed hungry.*

needy/in need /ˈniːdi, ɪn ˈniːd/ [adj] **needy** people or people who are **in need** do not have enough money to buy food, clothes etc, and deserve help: *The fund was established to help needy widows whose husbands had died in the war.* | *More aid should be given to needy families.* | *All profits from the concert will go to help children in need.*

impoverished /ɪmˈpɒvərɪʃt‖-ˈpɑː-/ [adj] formal very poor – use this especially about people or places that were not poor in the past: *His family became so impoverished they were forced to sell the farm.* | *All there was in the region was dry soil and impoverished villages.*

poverty-stricken /ˈpɒvərti ˌstrɪkən‖ˈpɑː-/ [adj usually before noun] written extremely poor, and suffering as a result of this: *At the moment, many poverty-stricken communities are experiencing a shortage of teachers.* | *His photographs show vividly the lives of poverty-stricken families in the Gorbals area of Glasgow.*

destitute /ˈdestətjuːt‖-tuːt/ [adj] especially written having no money or possessions, and often nowhere to live, especially when there seems to be no possibility of improving the situation: *In 1860 Father Murphy set up a home for orphans and destitute children.* | *The rest of her family all died in a smallpox epidemic, leaving her destitute.*

2 having very little money at the present time

- hard up
- broke
- skint
- be down on your luck

hard up /ˌhɑːrd ˈʌp◂/ [adj phrase not before noun] informal having little money at the present time and being unable to buy the things that you need: *I'm a little hard up just now – can I pay you back next week?* | *She was so hard up that she couldn't afford to heat her apartment.*

broke /brəʊk/ [adj not before noun] informal having no money at the moment: *We're always broke at the end of the month.* | *Lawrence was so broke he had to wear the same suit to work every day.* | **flat broke** (=completely broke) *He turned up at my house yesterday, flat broke and hungry.*

skint /skɪnt/ [adj not before noun] British spoken having no money at all: *I'm really skint – you couldn't lend me a few quid could you?* | *At that time I was skint, and I would have taken any job I could get.*

be down on your luck /biː ˌdaʊn ɒn jɔːʳ ˈlʌk/ [v phrase] informal to have had bad luck over a long period of time so that you now have very little money: *We bought the necklace from an old man who was down on his luck and in need of a penny or two.* — **down-on-your-luck** [adj only before noun] *In the film, Williams plays a down-on-his luck salesman whose wife has left him.*

3 having fewer opportunities in life because of being poor

- disadvantaged
- deprived
- underprivileged

disadvantaged /ˌdɪsədˈvɑːntɪdʒd◂‖-ˈvæn-/ [adj] especially written **disadvantaged** people or groups have less chance of being successful in life because they are poor – used especially in social or political contexts: *The university has announced plans to increase the number of students from minority and disadvantaged groups.* | *Quinn argued that an increase in the minimum wage would help the most disadvantaged Americans.*

underprivileged /ˌʌndəʳˈprɪvɪ̈lɪdʒd◂/ [adj usually before noun] having less money and worse living conditions than other people in a society, and little chance of being successful in life: *Princess Anne has done much to help underprivileged children all over the world.*

deprived /dɪˈpraɪvd/ [adj usually before noun] **deprived** people are very poor and are not able to find good jobs or get a good education. A **deprived** area is one in which people are poor and do not have many advantages: *Most mass demonstrations of this type happen in places where people are enormously deprived.* | *Children growing up in deprived areas are far more likely to turn to crime and drug abuse.* | *Girls from deprived backgrounds often become pregnant at an early age.*

4 the people in a society who are poor

- poor people/the poor/the needy
- the have-nots

poor people/the poor/the needy /ˈpʊəʳ ˌpiːpəl, ðə ˈpʊəʳ, ðə ˈniːdi/ [n plural] the people in a society who are poor: *The poor always suffer worst in a recession.* | *It was fairly common in Victorian times for middle-class women to work among the needy in the big industrial cities.* | *Finding adequate housing for the poor has been one of the city council's priorities.* | *The technological revolution has failed to improve the lives of poor people in developing countries.*

the have-nots /ðə ˈhæv nɒts/ [n plural] the people in society who are poor and have very few possessions compared to people who have a high income and own property, cars etc **the haves and have-nots** *Society seems to be increasingly divided into the haves* (=rich people) *and have-nots.*

5 when people have very little money

- poverty
- hard times

poverty /ˈpɒvəʳti‖ˈpɑː-/ [n U] *Charles was shocked by the poverty he saw in India.* | *Poverty and unemployment are two of the biggest causes of crime* | **dire/abject/grinding etc poverty** (=extreme poverty) *Seven out of every 10 Guatemalans live in dire poverty and half cannot read or write.* | **live/grow up/be raised etc in poverty** *Old people should not have to live in poverty.* | **the poverty line/level** (=the income below which a person or family is officially considered to be very poor and in need of help) *In Louisiana, one person in four lives below the poverty level.*

hard times /hɑːʳd ˈtaɪmz/ [n plural] a period when life is difficult because you have little money – use this when you are comparing this to other, better, times: *There were hard times during my childhood when my parents didn't have work, but generally we were happy.* | **fall on hard times** (=begin to experience hard times) *Many of the girls were from middle class families who had fallen on hard times.* | *After the war my father fell on hard times and sank deeply into debt.*

6 an area where poor people live

- inner city
- ghetto
- slum

▸ see also **condition**

inner city /ˌɪnəʳ ˈsɪti◂/ [n C] the part near the middle of a city where the buildings are in bad condition and where a lot of poor people live: *the problems of Britain's inner cities* — **inner-city** [adj only before noun] *inner-city schools*

slum /slʌm/ [n C] an area of a city where the houses are in very bad condition and the people are very poor and live in dirty, crowded, and unhealthy conditions: *Maria lives with her eight children in a slum outside Montevideo.* | **the slums** *I grew up in the East London slums.*

ghetto /ˈgetəʊ/ [n C] a poor and crowded part of a city, where people live separately from the rest of the population, especially people of one race or from one country. **Inner city** is now more common than **ghetto**: *a novel about life in the ghettos of New York* | *Ottovina lived on the South Side, in the Italian ghetto, and barely spoke any English at all.*

7 a poor country

- developing country/nation
- Third World

developing country/nation /dɪˌveləpɪŋ ˈkʌntri, ˈneɪʃən/ [n phrase] a country that is not rich and does not have much industry or business activity: *Bellamy called on the United States to increase aid to developing nations.* | *Leaders of developing countries from around the world met in Indonesia to devise ways to improve their economies.*

Third World /ˌθɜːʳd ˈwɜːʳld◂/ [adj] a **Third World** country or nation is poor and does not have much industry. **Third World** is used especially in a negative sense when talking about the problems that these countries face **the Third World** (=these countries in general) *Most of the population in the Third World is concentrated in large cities.* | **Third World country/nation** *Sometimes I think that England is becoming a Third World country.*

popular

RELATED WORDS

- *see also* **fashionable/not fashionable**

1 people, places, activities etc that a lot of people like

- **popular**
- **be in favour**
- **well-liked**
- **be in demand**
- **be big**

popular /ˈpɒpjᵊləʳ‖ˈpɑː-/ [adj] if someone or something is **popular**, a lot of people like them: *Lisa's one of the most popular girls in class.* | *Benidorm soon became a popular holiday resort.* | *Old-fashioned names are getting popular again.* | **+ with** *Chatlines have proved very popular with young people.*

be in favour British **/be in favor** American /biː ɪn ˈfeɪvəʳ/ [v phrase] if someone **is in favour**, they are liked and approved of at the present time, although this may not last: *Suzannah and I are both in favour at work at the moment.* | **be back in favour** (=be in favour again) *It looks as if Joey, her old boyfriend, is back in favor again.* | **+ with** *Her fresh approach to environmental issues makes her very much in favor with young voters.*

well-liked /ˌwel ˈlaɪkt◂/ [adj] someone who is **well-liked** has a lot of friends and is liked by most people: *She's a cheerful, good-natured girl, well-liked by all the people she works with.* | *As a politician, he may lack experience, but he's very well-liked.*

be in demand /biː ɪn dɪˈmɑːnd‖-ˈmænd/ [v phrase] if something such as a product or skill or a person **is in demand**, it is considered to be very valuable and a lot of people want to have it or use it: *High quality furniture will always be in demand.* | **be in great/big demand** *Graduates in Chinese are in great demand in an exciting variety of occupations.* | **be much/heavily in demand** *Her dramatic Latin looks caused her to be much in demand as a model.*

be big /biː ˈbɪg/ [v phrase] informal if a product, activity, or performer **is big** in a particular place or at a particular time, they are very popular **+ in** *Oasis were big in the early 90's.* | *The single is already big in the clubs, and has been remixed by the band.*

2 a popular book, film, song etc

- **best-seller**
- **blockbuster**
- **hit**

best-seller /ˌbest ˈseləʳ/ [n C] a book that a lot of people buy: *J.K. Rowling's latest book is certain to be a bestseller.* —**bestselling** [adj] *bestselling novelist Celia Brayfield, author of 'Pearls'*

blockbuster /ˈblɒkˌbʌstəʳ‖ˈblɑːk-/ [n C] a film that a lot of people watch and that makes a lot of money, especially a film with a lot of exciting action: *Bruce Willis's new blockbuster took $10.6 million in its first weekend.* | *'Roots' became a blockbuster TV series.*

hit /hɪt/ [n C] a record, film, show etc that a lot of people buy or go to see: *When I first heard the song I knew it would be a hit.* | **hit song/single/musical etc** *a new hit single from Janet Jackson* | **big hit** *'Titanic' was a big hit all over the world.*

3 to make something popular

- **popularize**

popularize ALSO **popularise** British /ˈpɒpjᵊlə-raɪz‖ˈpɑː-/ [v T] *Most attempts to popularise science and technology have failed.* | *Self-service supermarkets were first popularized by businessman Clarence Saunders.*

4 when something becomes popular again

- **revival**

revival /rɪˈvaɪvəl/ [n C] when something or someone becomes popular and fashionable again, for example a kind of music, a style of clothes, a writer, or a singer: *Sixties pop music enjoyed a big revival in the mid-90s.* | *There's been something of an Abba revival recently.*

5 not popular

- **unpopular**
- **out of favour**
- **there is no demand/call for**

unpopular /ʌnˈpɒpjᵊləʳ‖-ˈpɑː-/ [adj] if someone or something is **unpopular**, a lot of people do not like them: *The government is more unpopular now than it has been for years.* | *Mr Venables must be the most unpopular teacher in school.* | **+ with** *The taxes proved extremely unpopular with the electorate.*

out of favour British **/out of favor** American /ˌaʊt əv ˈfeɪvəʳ/ [adv] if a person, idea, or other thing **is out of favour**, people no longer approve of them or use them, although they used to be popular: *Smacking children seems to be out of favour these days.* | **go/fall out of favour (with sb)** *The classic jigsaw puzzle never goes out of favour with kids.* | *Journalists and producers who fell out of favour were fired immediately.*

there is no demand/call for /ðeər ɪz ˌnəʊ dɪˈmɑːnd, ˈkɔːl fɔːʳ‖-ˈmænd-/ [v phrase] if **there is no demand for** a product or service people do not want to buy it: *There's no demand for heavy immovable furniture any more.* | *Where there is no call for a continued food market, market buildings have proved highly adaptable.*

position/rank

RELATED WORDS

- position in society *see* **class (3-9)**
- *see also* **manager, power/powerful, control/not control, in charge of, company, organization**

1 your position or rank in an organization, company etc

- **position**
- **level**
- **rank**
- **status**
- **standing**
- **hierarchy**

position /pəˈzɪʃən/ [n C] your job in an organization, company, or profession – use this to talk about how important someone is and how much responsibility they have: *Her position in the company means that she is responsible for major financial deci-*

sions. | *He eventually became Lord Chancellor, the most powerful position in the British legal system.* | **hold a position** (=have a position) *Thorn holds one of the most senior positions in the Federal Bank.*

level /ˈlevəl/ [n C] all the jobs in an organization that are similar in importance and that pay similar amounts of money: *The company provides training for staff at all levels.* | *There are not many part-time workers in the middle and higher levels of management.*

rank /ræŋk/ [n C] someone's position in an organization such as the army or police force: *Gang members wear clothes or decorations that show the member's rank.* | **+ of** *He joined the Los Angeles police department and was eventually promoted to the rank of lieutenant.* | *Four of the boys in Boy Scout Troop 611 reached the rank of Eagle Scout.* | **hold a rank** (=have a rank) *The position of Secretary of State holds Cabinet rank.*

status /ˈsteɪtəs‖ˈsteɪtəs, ˈstæ-/ [n U] someone's position within an organization or within society, based on how important they are considered to be: *The tribe buried their dead with ornaments or tools that showed the dead person's status.* | **low/high status** *In the Middle Ages, priests and other religious figures had a very high status.* | **gain/lose status** *She gained celebrity status with her publication of 'Mastering the Art of French Cooking.'*

standing /ˈstændɪŋ/ [n singular/U] someone's position within society or a particular area of activity, based on the respect and admiration that other people have for them: *Stefano's standing as an artist has improved over the past few years.* | *Graduates from certain colleges have a lower standing in the eyes of employers.* | *a man of standing and wealth*

hierarchy /ˈhaɪrɑːʳki/ [n C/U] a system in which people have different positions in an organization, society etc, based on their level of importance: *Genotti was thought to be number two in the Sicilian Mafia hierarchy.* | *The school district reorganized the administrative hierarchy, which helped to save money.*

2 to be in a high position in an organization, company, or list

- be high up
- be high in/on
- be at the top

be high up /biː ˌhaɪ ˈʌp/ [v phrase] to be in a high position in an organization, company or list: *He works for NASA, fairly high up.* | **+ in** *Her father's quite high up in the company.* | *The reporter's sources were apparently high up in the government.*

be high in/on /biː ˈhaɪ ɪn, ɒn/ [v phrase] to have a high position in a list or table of the most successful or best teams, records etc **+ on** *Pele is high on the list of the world's best footballers.* | **+ in** *U2's new record is high in the charts.*

be at the top /biː ət ðə ˈtɒp‖-ˈtɑːp/ [v phrase] to have the highest position in an organization, company, or list: *Women at the top often have to work harder than men.* | **+ of** *The prizes will be awarded to 600 students who graduate at the top of their class.* | *The issue is at the top of the agenda.*

3 to be in a higher position than someone else

- above
- be senior to
- superior
- outrank

above /əˈbʌv/ [prep] in a higher position than someone else in an organization or company: *It's not the staff that are the problem. It's the people above them.* | *The next person above him is the sales manager.*

be senior to /biː ˈsiːniəʳ tuː/ [v phrase] to be in a higher position than someone else in an organization or company: *Technically I'm senior to Smith, but we do more or less the same job.* | *The men said they had no problems taking orders from women senior to them in rank.*

superior /suːˈpɪəriəʳ‖sʊ-/ [n C] your **superior** in the organization you work for is the person who has a higher rank than you: *He failed to follow a direct order from his superior.* | *Women who have been harassed by male superiors often don't complain because they are afraid of losing their jobs.*

outrank ALSO **rank** American /aʊtˈræŋk, ræŋk/ [v T] to be in a higher position in an organization, especially the army: *Successful sales staff will outrank less successful workers, regardless of qualifications.* | *Because Barnett ranks him, they have to be discreet about their romance.*

4 someone who has a high position

- senior
- top
- high-ranking/top ranking
- head

▸ *see also* **leader**

senior /ˈsiːniəʳ/ [adj only before noun] a **senior** manager, official etc is one who has an important position in an organization or company: *He's a senior executive at Volkswagen.* | *a job in senior management* | *one of the country's most senior judges*

top /tɒp‖tɑːp/ [adj only before noun] **top manager/lawyer/executive etc** someone who has one of the most powerful jobs in business, or one of the most important jobs in a profession: *The President met with top Korean businessmen.* | *a top fashion designer*

high-ranking/top ranking /ˌhaɪ ˈræŋkɪŋ◂, ˌtɒp ˈræŋkɪŋ◂‖ˌtɑːp-/ [adj only before noun] **a high-ranking officer/official/member etc** someone who has a high position in an organization like the police or army, or in a government department, but not in business: *A high-ranking State Department official was accused of selling secret information.* | *a high-ranking officer in the air force*

head /hed/ [adj only before noun] **head waiter/chef/coach etc** the most important waiter etc, who is in charge of the others: *Don Shula became the youngest head coach in NFL history.* | *The head counsellor commented that substance abuse was pervasive at the school.*

5 to be in a low position in an organization, company, or list

- be low down
- low-ranking
- be at the bottom
- be at the bottom of the pile

be low down /biː ˌləʊ ˈdaʊn/ [v phrase] to be in a low position in an organization, company, or list: *He doesn't have any authority over you, he's fairly low down.* | **+ in** *At that time I was still fairly low down in the company.* | *Surprisingly, last year's champions are low down in the league table.*

low-ranking /ˌləʊ ˈræŋkɪŋ◂/ [adj usually before noun] having a low position in an organization: *The scan-*

dal involved a number of low-ranking officials in the government. | *None of the low-ranking members were allowed to vote at the society's meeting.*

be at the bottom /biː ət ðə 'bɒtəm‖-'bɑː-/ [v phrase] to be in the lowest position in an organization, company, or list: *Richard started out at the bottom of the firm and worked his way to the top.* | *The team is at the bottom of the league.* | *You will start at the bottom of the pay scale, but you can expect a raise after 12 months.* | *The band's single has been moving steadily towards the bottom of the charts this month.*

be at the bottom of the pile /biː ət ðə ˌbɒtəm əv ðə 'paɪl‖-ˌbɑː-/ [v phrase] informal if a person **is at the bottom of the pile**, they are in the lowest position in society, are badly treated, are given the worst jobs etc: *Immigrants have always been at the bottom of the pile for housing.* | *At the bottom of the pile are the runners, young boys who carry messages all day.*

6 someone who is in a lower position than someone else

- junior
- assistant
- subordinate
- under
- report to

junior /'dʒuːniəʳ/ [adj only before noun] a **junior** doctor, officer etc does not have as much power or responsibility as other doctors, officers etc, especially because he or she has not been in the job for very long: *She started work as a junior reporter on a local newspaper.* | *The most junior officers wore a red stripe on their sleeves.*

assistant /ə'sɪstənt/ [adj only before noun] **assistant manager/editor/principal etc** someone whose job is just below the position of a manager, editor etc: *My mother is assistant principal at a school in Washington, D.C.* | *Noll, an assistant coach with the Colts, was hired by the Steelers as head coach.* —**assistant** [n C] *Hughes, who was Mott's assistant, will now become head coach.*

subordinate /sə'bɔːʳdənət/ [n C] someone who has a lower position and less authority than someone else in an organization: *Costello will have five direct subordinates.* | *The idea of being evaluated by subordinates makes some managers uneasy.*

under /'ʌndəʳ/ [prep] if people are **under** someone in authority, they work for that person and have a lower position: *She has at least 40 people under her at Shell.* | *Several of the employees under him complained of his bullying behavior.*

report to /rɪ'pɔːʳt tuː/ [v phrase] to have someone as your manager: *McKellon will report to Alan Selles, the company's chairman.* | *Alan has five members of the production team reporting to him.*

7 someone's position in a competition, race, list etc

- position
- place
- ranking

position /pə'zɪʃən/ [n C] the numbered **position** of someone or something in a competition, race, list etc **+ in** *Pollock rose to the No. 2 position in the company, but found that the higher she rose, the less she liked her job.* | *The company has a strong position in most international markets.* | **first/fourth etc position** *Jonson is in third position after the first part of the competition.*

place /pleɪs/ [n C] the position that someone achieves, especially in a race or competition, based on how well they perform against the others taking part: *Manchester United go up two places after their win at Liverpool.* | **first/third/eighth etc place** *The horse I was betting on finished in second place.* | **take first/third etc place** British /**get first/third etc place** American (=win first etc place) *Victoria took first place in a national essay writing competition.*

ranking /'ræŋkɪŋ/ [n C] the numbered position of someone in a sport, especially based on their performance in the previous year: *The football team lost their No. 1 ranking as a result of the decision.* | **world ranking** *At the end of this event, Davies is sure to have moved up a place in the world rankings.*

8 to have a particular position in a competition, race, list etc

- rank
- be first/second etc

rank /ræŋk/ [v I not in progressive/T] to be in a particular position in a competition, race, list etc: *The name Michael always ranks high on the list of the most popular boys' names.* | **rank sb as first/fourth/eighth etc** *Volleyball Monthly ranked the team third in the nation.* | **rank first/fourth/eighth etc** *Connell, a Canadian ranked 73rd in the world, won the third set.* | *Second-ranked Stanford beat the University of San Diego 103-68.* | **+ among/as etc** *Sandoz ranks as one of the 10 largest drug companies in the world.* | **be ranked first/fifth etc** *She was beaten by someone who was ranked only 200th in the world.*

be first/second etc ALSO **come first/second** British /biː 'fɜːʳst, kʌm 'fɜːʳst/ [v phrase] to be first, second etc in a competition or race: *Sandoz won, and Anderson was second.* | **+ in** *Michael Johnson came first in the 400m final.*

possible

RELATED WORDS

opposite: **impossible**

▸ *see also* **maybe, probably, can/can't**

1 when something can be done

- possible
- can be done
- possibility
- feasible
- workable
- doable
- attainable
- viable

possible /'pɒsəbəl‖'pɑː-/ [adj] something that is **possible**, can be done: *Travel to other planets may soon be possible.* | *Detectives can now check every criminal's records, which wouldn't be possible without computers.* | *The only possible way a woman could rise in class was to marry into a family of higher social standing than her own.* | **it is possible to do sth** *Is it possible to find a room in a good hotel for less than $100?* | **if possible** *I want to get back by 5 o'clock if possible.* | **as soon/quickly/big etc as possible** *Please let me know your answer as soon as possible.* | *We must get her to the hospital as quickly as possible.* | **humanly possible** (=use this to emphasize that you will do something as fast, as well etc as possible) *We will deal with all complaints as soon as is humanly possible.* | **do/try everything possible** *The doctors did everything possible to save her life.* —**possibly** [adv] *It was the best vacation you could possibly imagine.*

can be done /kæn biː ˈdʌn/ [v phrase] if something **can be done**, it is possible to do it: *The job can be done by Friday if we all make an effort.* | *I'm sure that more could be done to help the homeless.* | *Val got her MA while she was working full-time, so it can be done.*

possibility /ˌpɒsəˈbɪlətiǁˌpɑː-/ [n C] one of the things that you could try to do: *One possibility is to offer him more money.* | *Computers have opened up many exciting possibilities.* | **the possibility of doing sth** *We are considering the possibility of providing a new class for advanced students.*

feasible /ˈfiːzəbəl/ [adj] a plan, idea, or method that is **feasible** is possible and is likely to work: *Barrington suggest transporting the supplies by air. This of course is perfectly feasible.* | *We agreed on a feasible plan and within a week we implemented it.* | **it is feasible to do sth** *It is not feasible to have security cameras in every part of the building.* | **it is feasible that** *Da Silva considered it feasible that uranium could be produced on an industrial scale.* —**feasibility** /ˌfiːzəˈbɪləti/ [n U] whether something is feasible: *Experts are studying the feasibility of a solar energy project.*

workable /ˈwɜːʳkəbəl/ [adj] a **workable** way of doing something is a possible way of doing it – use this when you have had a lot of problems finding a suitable way: *There is a dispute over land but we believe we have found a workable solution to this problem.* | *A new plan provides for loans to students, but to make the system workable more government funding will be needed.*

doable /ˈduːəbəl/ [adj not before noun] informal a job that is **doable** is one that can be done: *You did well to even start the project – at first we didn't think it was doable at all.*

attainable /əˈteɪnəbəl/ [adj] an aim or standard that is **attainable** is one that can be achieved and it is reasonable to try to achieve it: *Perfect democracy is not attainable, nor is perfect freedom or perfect justice.* | *Every child should be educated to the highest attainable level.*

viable /ˈvaɪəbəl/ [adj] a **viable** way of doing something is one that is possible and should work well: *Do you think this is a viable proposition?* | *Nuclear energy is the only viable alternative to coal or gas.* | *They are in favour of the program, but they want strong assurances that it is viable.* —**viability** /ˌvaɪəˈbɪləti/ [n U] whether or not something is viable: *We are currently investigating the viability of this proposal.*

2 when something could happen

- possible
- possibility
- can
- potential
- there is a chance/possibility
- you never know

possible /ˈpɒsəbəlǁˈpɑː-/ [adj] if something is **possible**, there is a chance that it may happen or it may be true: *Accidents are always possible in heavy industries like mining.* | *You can't be a Muslim and a Catholic at the same time – it's just not possible.* | *technological changes and their possible effects on our lives* | **it is possible for sb to do sth** *It is possible for more than one person to win the competition.* | **it is possible that** *It is possible that the children are still alive.* —**possibly** [adv] *He could possibly be released from prison within three years.*

possibility /ˌpɒsəˈbɪlətiǁˌpɑː-/ [n C/U] something that can happen or may happen **+ of** *We could not ignore the possibility of an enemy attack.* | **there is a possibility that** *Unless there is some change in the economy, there is a possibility that the plant may close.* | **a real/distinct/strong possibility** (=something that is quite likely to happen) *A Republican victory in next month's elections now seems to be a real possibility.* | *There's a distinct possibility that there will be another earthquake.* | **a faint/slight possibility** *There is still a faint possibility that Sarah will be found safe and well.*

can /kən, (*strong*) kæn/ [modal verb] if something **can** happen, it is possible for it to happen at some time: *Mistakes can occur, even in the most carefully controlled situations.* | *A lot can happen in two years.* | *It can be warm in England, even in March.*

potential /pəˈtenʃəl/ [adj only before noun] a **potential** problem, advantage, effect etc is not a problem, advantage etc now, but it may become one in the future: *For the first time she realized the potential danger of her situation.* | *It is important for manufacturers to identify potential problems at the design stage.* | **potential customer/buyer/student etc** (=someone who may become a customer, buyer etc in the future) *a way of making the college more attractive to potential students*

there is a chance/possibility /ðeər ɪz ə ˈtʃɑːns, ˌpɒsəˈbɪlətiǁ-ˈtʃæns, ˌpɑː-/ [v phrase] use this to say that it is possible that something will happen **+ of** *On the northern hills there is always the possibility of a snow shower, even in June.* | **+ that** *Is there any chance that he will recover from his injury in time for the race?*

you never know /juː ˌnevəʳ ˈnəʊ/ say this to show that you think there is some possibility that something might happen, even though it seems unlikely: *I'd love to be a doctor, but you have to be very clever for that. Still, you never know.*

3 to make something possible

- make sth possible
- allow/enable
- permit
- pave the way for
- clear the way for

make sth possible /ˌmeɪk (sth) ˈpɒsəbəlǁ-ˈpɑː-/ [v phrase] *We are grateful to everyone who made this event possible.* | **make it possible for sb to do sth** *Satellite broadcasting made it possible for people all over the world to watch the 1960 Olympic Games.*

allow/enable /əˈlaʊ, ɪˈneɪbəl/ [v T] especially written to make it possible for someone to do something that they want to do **allow/enable sb to do sth** *The Internet allows people to send messages all over the world.* | *The sports school has enabled 10,000 youngsters to receive free tuition in a wide range of sports.*

permit /pəʳˈmɪt/ [v I/T] formal to make it possible for something to happen or for someone to do something: *I would like to go into this argument in some detail, but time does not permit it.* | **permit sb to do sth** *Unit pricing is a system that permits the customer to compare the costs of products.* | **weather/ time etc permitting** (=if the weather, time etc makes it possible) *In summer, meals are eaten in the garden, weather permitting.*

pave the way for /ˌpeɪv ðə ˈweɪ fɔːʳ/ [v phrase] to make it possible for something to happen by producing the right conditions for it: *Galileo's achievements in physical science paved the way for Newton's discoveries.* | *In 1930's Germany, the depression helped Hitler rise to power, paving the way for the Second World War.*

clear the way for /ˌklɪəʳ ðə ˈweɪ fɔːʳ/ [v phrase] to

make it possible for something to happen by removing difficulties that existed before: *The removal of trade restrictions cleared the way for a rapid development of East-West relations.* | *a vote that cleared the way for the ordination of women priests*

pour

to make liquid or a substance come out of a container

RELATED WORDS

- when a liquid or a substance pours out of somewhere *see* **flow**
- *see also* **liquid, full, empty**

- **pour**
- **spill**
- **empty**
- **sprinkle**
- **tip**
- **drizzle**

pour /pɔːʳ/ [v T] to make liquid or a substance flow steadily out of a container, by making the container lean to one side **pour sth into/out of sth** *She poured some milk into a glass.* | *Dan picked up the bucket and poured the sand out of it.* | **pour sth on/over/into sth** *Pour the garlic sauce over the hot chicken pieces.* | **+ in/out** *Gradually pour in the sherry and the stock.* | *Would you pour out the tea?*

spill /spɪl/ [v T] to accidentally make a liquid or substance come out of a container: *Careful – you'll spill it!* | **spill sth on/over/into sth** *Someone had spilled red wine all over the carpet.* | *A tanker has run aground, spilling 60,000 gallons of oil into the sea.*

empty /ˈempti/ [v T] to make a container empty by pouring out everything inside it: *Paul emptied the glass and washed it.* | *Could you empty the wastebasket – it's getting pretty full.* | **empty sth into/onto/over sth** *She emptied the contents of the tin into a pan.* | *We crept up behind him and emptied the bucket of water over his head.*

sprinkle /ˈsprɪŋkəl/ [v T] to pour or put a liquid or substance in small amounts onto something, especially food, so that the surface is thinly covered **sprinkle sth on/over sth** *Sprinkle the cheese over the beans.* | **sprinkle sth with sth** *Sprinkle the fish with lemon juice and herbs.*

tip /tɪp/ [v T] to pour something out of a container by turning it upside down **tip sth into/out of/onto sth** *She weighed out the flour and tipped it into the bowl.*

drizzle /ˈdrɪzəl/ [v T] to pour a liquid in small amounts over something, especially food – used especially in cooking instructions **drizzle sth over sth** *Drizzle a little French dressing over the salad.* | **drizzle sth with sth** *Slice the strawberries and drizzle them with the liqueur.*

power/powerful

RELATED WORDS

- political, legal, or social rights *see* **right (9-12)**
- *see also* **control/not control, in charge of, position/rank, government**

1 the ability to control people and events

- **power**
- **influence**
- **authority**
- **have a say**
- **muscle**
- **clout**
- **jurisdiction**

power /ˈpaʊəʳ/ [n U] the ability or the right to control other people and make decisions that affect them: *Do you think the police have too much power?* | *He was motivated by greed, envy, and the lust for power.* | **great/enormous power** *the enormous economic power of the United States* | **+ over** *The big Hollywood studios have a lot of power over what kind of films get made.* | **have the power to do sth** *Only Parliament has the power to make new laws.* | **a power struggle** (=a situation in which groups or leaders try to defeat each other and get complete control) *A power struggle developed between the president and the generals.*

influence /ˈɪnfluəns/ [n U] if someone has **influence**, they can use their important social position or their wealth to persuade other people to do things **+ in** *The Catholic Church has always had a lot of influence in Polish politics.* | **+ over** *The banks had too much influence over government policy.* | **sb's influence with sb** (=someone's ability to persuade someone else to do things) *Using her influence with her husband, Evita Peron won women the right to vote.*

authority /ɔːˈθɒrɪ̱ti, ə-‖əˈθɑː-, əˈθɔː-/ [n U] the right to make decisions and control people, which a person has because of their job or official position: *No one dared to question the principal's authority.* | **+ over** *In the British system, the mayor has no authority over the local police.* | **have the authority to do sth** *The King had the authority to raise taxes without the permission of parliament.*

have a say /ˌhæv ə ˈseɪ/ [v phrase] the right to give your opinion about a decision, so that you have some power to influence it: *If we're going to undertake such a big project, the voters should have a say.* | **+ in** *By giving the workers a greater say in the running of the company, we hope to increase cooperation and job satisfaction.* | **have the final say** (=have the power to make the final decision) *The Prisoner Review Board can recommend that a prisoner is released, but Illinois Gov. Jim Edgar has the final say.*

muscle /ˈmʌsəl/ [n U] power that someone has because of their money, political position, or strength, and which makes it possible for them to do things that other people or organizations cannot do: *The government has for years been trying to destroy the muscle of the trade unions.* | **have the muscle to do sth** *Hanson Trust has the muscle to buy up some of America's biggest companies.* | **financial/political muscle** *The Republicans do not have the political muscle to prevent the treaty being rejected by Congress.*

clout /klaʊt/ [n U] informal the power that you have to influence other people's decisions, especially because you can use your position or your knowledge to persuade people in authority to do what you want **have/carry clout** *The banks do not carry quite as much clout as they used to.* | **political/financial etc clout** *Doctors have considerably more political clout than teachers.*

jurisdiction /ˌdʒʊərɪ̱sˈdɪkʃən/ [n U] the power that a government, court, or organization has to make laws or to decide whether people are breaking the law – use this especially when you talk about the limits of this power: *In general, the American courts have no jurisdiction to deal with crimes outside the USA.* | *The Air Transit Authority's jurisdiction extends beyond the airport itself to include warehouses and associated buildings.* | **+ over** *The council has no jurisdiction over these matters.* | **be within/under sb's jurisdiction** *It's not within our jurisdiction to tell people what to do in the privacy of their own homes.* | **be outside sb's jurisdiction** *The courts said the claim raised 'political questions' that were outside its jurisdiction.*

2 having a lot of power

- powerful
- influential
- strong
- dominant
- all-powerful
- have friends in high places

powerful /'paʊəʳfəl/ [adj] a **powerful** person, organization, or country has a lot of power, and can control people and influence events: *Parliament had become more powerful than the King.* | *one of the most powerful men in US politics* | *Berlusconi was the owner of a powerful media empire.*

influential /ˌɪnflu'enʃəl◂/ [adj] someone who is **influential** can influence events, because they are rich, and therefore people pay attention to what they say: *Her uncle is a rich and influential businessman.* | *She is probably the most influential member of the finance committee.* | *an influential film critic* | **highly influential** (=very influential) *Galbraith was a highly influential writer on economic affairs.*

strong /strɒŋ‖strɔːŋ/ [adj] powerful – use this about a political group that is supported by a lot of people: *The communists were particularly strong in the big industrial cities.* | *There has been a strong anti-nuclear movement in Japan for many years.*

dominant /'dɒmɪ̈nənt‖'dɑː-/ [adj] more powerful than other people, groups, countries etc: *Gradually, Microsoft became the dominant company in the software business* | *At the time Portugal was the dominant naval power in the Mediterranean.*

all-powerful /ˌɔːl 'paʊəʳfəl◂/ [adj] having more power than anyone else, especially when this is not fair: *The all-powerful central committee meets twice a year.* | *Catherine the Great, the all-powerful ruler of the Russian Empire* | *Hollywood stars of the 30s were in awe of the all-powerful studio bosses.*

have friends in high places /hæv ˌfrends ɪn haɪ 'pleɪsɪ̈z/ [v phrase not in progressive] to have power or influence because you know people who have very important jobs and positions and who will help you if necessary: *Bowen had friends in high places, and managed to raise large sums of money from the Carnegie and Rockefeller Foundations.* | *The Achym family had friends in high places, including the powerful Lord Burghley, and were allowed to return.*

3 a country that has a lot of power

- world power
- superpower

world power /ˌwɜːʳld 'paʊəʳ/ [n C] a country that has a lot of economic and military power, and can influence what happens in other parts of the world: *The United States had replaced Great Britain as the dominant world power.* | *China is regaining its place as a world power, a status it enjoyed for 3,000 years and lost only a few centuries ago.*

superpower /'suːpəʳˌpaʊəʳ, 'sjuː-‖'suː-/ [n C] one of the most powerful countries in the world: *The United States, as the world's only remaining superpower, must continue making arms control a central element of its foreign policy.* | *He hinted at a bigger presence for the U.S. military in the Asian Pacific region where China is emerging as a superpower.*

4 to have an official position of power

- in power
- in authority
- in office
- rule
- ruling
- reign

in power /ɪn 'paʊəʳ/ [adj phrase] a person or political group that is **in power** has political control of a country or government: *The Socialists have been in power since the 1965 revolution.* | *The Congress Party in India lost its legislative majority in the late 1970s after nearly thirty years in power.* | **remain/stay in power** *Gorbachev could not have remained in power without the support of the Red Army.*

in authority /ɪn ɔː'θɒrɪ̈ti‖-ə'θɑː-/ [adj phrase] someone who is **in authority** has a job or position that gives them the right to tell other people what to do: *My mother demanded to speak to someone in authority.* | *Problems arise when people in authority can't keep discipline.*

in office /ɪn 'ɒfɪ̈s‖-'ɔːf-/ [adj phrase] someone, usually a government official, who is **in office**, has an important job or position with power: *The decision was made to remove the President after 30 years in office.* | **remain/continue in office** *Hayward has expressed his willingness to continue in office.*

rule /ruːl/ [v I/T] if a king, queen, political party, or organization **rules**, they have an official position of power in a country, and over the people who live there: *In 1860, Italy was a collection of small states ruled by princes and dukes.* | *While they ruled, the country remained isolated from the rest of the world.* | **rule France/Spain etc** *The Pol Pot regime ruled Cambodia from 1974 to 1978.* | **+ over** *Spain ruled over Portugal from 1580 to 1640.* | *Motamid had died, leaving his son Mostain to rule over Saragossa.* —**rule** [n U] *British rule in India came to an end in 1947.*

ruling /'ruːlɪŋ/ [adj] the **ruling** group or political party in an area or country is the one that is controlling it at the present time **ruling party/class/authority** *The ruling party is confident of winning the election.* | *the struggle between the workers and the ruling classes* | *The crisis sparked after the ruling party rushed through revisions of the labor and national security laws in a semi-secret parliamentary session.*

reign /reɪn/ [v I] if a king or queen **reigns**, they have an official position of power, although they may not have any real power over the government of the country: *Robert II reigned for 19 years and died in Dundonald Castle on 13th May, 1390.* | *The last Moorish king reigned there until 1492.* | **+ over** *Penda was king from 633 to 655, but it is not known who had reigned over the Mercians in the period before.* —**reign** [n singular] time when someone reigns: *Important reforms were initiated during the reign of Nicholas II.*

5 to get power

- come to power
- take office
- take power
- seize power
- take over

come to power /ˌkʌm tə ˈpaʊəʳ/ [v phrase] to take political control of a country, especially by being elected: *When Mrs Thatcher came to power in 1979, no one expected her to stay there for 13 years.* | *After coming to power, President Clinton tried to resolve the conflict.*

take office /ˌteɪk ˈɒfəs‖-ˈɔːf-/ [v phrase] if a person or political party **takes office**, they start working in an official position of power or take political control of a country: *Less than three weeks after Labour took office, an economic crisis developed.* | *When Olson took office in January 1939, he was the state's first Democratic governor in forty years.*

take power /ˌteɪk ˈpaʊəʳ/ [v phrase] to get control of a country through violence: *The Bolsheviks took power in 1917.* | *General da Souza had the intention of taking power through a coup d'etat.*

seize power /ˌsiːz ˈpaʊəʳ/ [v phrase] to get control of a country suddenly or quickly, by using military force: *Communist forces had come out in an attempt to seize power.* | *The Czar was overthrown when the revolutionaries seized power.*

take over /ˌteɪk ˈəʊvəʳ/ [v I/T] to take power from an existing government or organization by using military force: *A revolutionary government took over, featuring a reorganized council.* | *The authorities began to make the necessary arrangements for taking over the garrisons, which were still in the hands of the enemy.*

6 having no power

- powerless
- weak
- have no say

powerless /ˈpaʊəʳləs/ [adj] someone who is **powerless** has no power to control or influence what happens: *Blocked by the Democrats in the Senate, Bush appeared powerless.* | **+ against** *The people of Hungary were powerless against the tanks of the Red Army.* | **powerless to do sth** *The UN was powerless to prevent the war spreading.*

weak /wiːk/ [adj] someone who is **weak** does not have much power because they cannot make other people respect them or obey them: *These policies failed because the government was weak and ineffective.* | *a weak, indecisive principal* — **weakness** [n U] *The King's mercy towards the rebels was regarded as a sign of weakness.*

have no say /hæv ˌnəʊ ˈseɪ/ [v phrase not in progressive] to have no power to influence what happens because your opinion is ignored or regarded as unimportant: *Whenever we have to make an important decision, I feel that I have no say.* | **have no say in sth** *The French government allows the Annamese almost no say at all in running their affairs.*

practise/ practice

RELATED WORDS

▸ *see also* **study, improve, learn, can/can't, perform/performance, sport/game**

1 to practise for a competition, test, or performance

- practise
- train
- be in training
- work on
- work at
- rehearse
- go/run through
- keep your hand in

practise British **/practice** American /ˈpræktəs/ [v I/T] to do an activity and repeat it a lot in order to get better at it: *I'm learning how to play the piano, and I try to practise every day.* | *Practicing karate twice a week might be enough, but you should try to do it a bit more.* | *We're going to Paris for a week in summer, so that Bill can practise his French.* | **practise doing sth** *Practise speaking slowly and clearly.* | **+ for** *When I was practicing for the competition, I spent eight hours a day in the conservatory practice rooms.* | **practise on sb/sth** *I always wanted to be a hairdresser, and used to practise on my friends.*

train /treɪn/ [v I] to prepare for a race or game by exercising and practising: *If you're really going to run in the marathon, you need to start training now.* | *In the winter months, she trains in Montana.* | **+ for** *Tyson is training for the big fight next week.*

be in training /biː ɪn ˈtreɪnɪŋ/ [v phrase] especially British to be in the period before a sports event or competition when you practise a particular sport or physical activity in a planned and controlled way: *When I'm in training I spend at least four hours a day at the swimming pool.* | **+ for** *He's currently in training for an important race.*

work on /ˈwɜːʳk ɒn/ [v T] to practise a particular skill that you need to play a sport, a musical instrument etc, so that your whole performance improves: *Your tennis playing is getting better, but you need to work on your serve.* | *Scales and finger exercises are the areas to work on if you want to improve your technique.*

work at /ˈwɜːʳk æt/ [v T] to practise something over a long period of time and with a lot of effort in order to achieve a high enough standard: *You'll have to really work at it if you want to be a professional dancer.* | *Learning another language is never easy, but if you work at it you'll soon get results.*

rehearse /rɪˈhɜːʳs/ [v I/T] to practise something such as a play or concert, so that it is ready to be performed for the public: *The director made us rehearse the opening scenes over and over.* | *The band has been rehearsing at the studio all day.* | **+ for** *He is currently in New York rehearsing for 'The Taming of the Shrew.'*

go/run through /ˈgəʊ, ˈrʌn θruː/ [phr v T] to practise something such as a play, speech, or piece of music by reading or playing it from start to finish: *I promised to hear her go through her speech.* | *Let's go through it just once more.* | *We went through the whole symphony four times, and he still wasn't satisfied.*

keep your hand in /ˌkiːp jɔːʳ ˈhænd ɪn/ [v phrase] to practise something just enough to still be good at it but not enough to improve, especially when you no longer do it regularly: *He still comes around the gym occasionally, just to keep his hand in.* | *Although she has retired now, she keeps her hand in by giving her grandchildren music lessons.*

2 activities people do in order to practise

- practice
- training
- rehearsal
- run-through
- dry run
- exercise

practice /ˈpræktɨs/ [n C/U] things you do regularly in order to get better at something, or an occasion when you do these things: *You're getting better – you just need a little more practice.* | *I try and get some practice in before classes.* | *There are only three more practices before the concert.* | **piano/football/choir etc practice** *I scored two goals at hockey practice tonight.* | *Are you going to choir practice?*

training /ˈtreɪnɪŋ/ [n U] time that you spend practising and doing exercise in order to get better at a sport: *The team captain got a knee injury during training.* | **a training course/session/programme etc** *Training sessions are on Saturdays at 10 a.m.*

rehearsal /rɪˈhɜːʳsəl/ [n C/U] an occasion when all the people in a play, concert etc practise it in order to prepare for it to be performed for the public: *Changes to the script are often made during rehearsal.* | **+ of** *We're having our first rehearsal of 'Hamlet' tonight.* | **dress rehearsal** (=when everyone wears the clothes they will be wearing in the actual play) *Wednesday's dress rehearsal went fairly smoothly.*

run-through /ˈrʌn θruː/ [n C] when you practise a play, speech, piece of music etc by reading or playing it from start to finish: *Let's have one more run-through and then finish for today.* | *The cast could all have done with an extra run-through of some of the songs.*

dry run /ˌdraɪ ˈrʌn/ [n C] an event in which you practise something by doing it from start to finish, especially in order to make sure that it will work or happen successfully: *One of the pilots made an error during the dry run of the mission.* | *The recording was intended to be a dry run, but Warfield sang the song flawlessly.*

exercise /ˈeksəʳsaɪz/ [n C] an activity that is designed to make you practise a particular skill within a larger subject or area of activity: *The exercises in Chapter 3 are helpful for students learning the future tense.* | *a book of guitar exercises to improve finger flexibility*

3 when you have not practised for a long time

- rusty
- be out of practice

rusty /ˈrʌsti/ [adj not before noun] if your skill at something is **rusty**, it is not as good as it used to be, because you have not used it for a long time: *My Spanish is pretty rusty.* | *I hadn't practiced for a long time, so I was really rusty.*

be out of practice /biː ˌaʊt əv ˈpræktɨs/ [v phrase] if you **are out of practice**, you cannot do something as well as you could in the past, because you have not done it for a long time: *Sam said he's a little out of practice, but he'll play if we need him.*

praise

RELATED WORDS

opposite: —————— **criticize**

- to hit your hands together to show how much you like a performance *see* **clap**
- *see also* **admire, enthusiastic/unenthusiastic**

1 to praise someone or something

- praise
- congratulate
- compliment
- be complimentary about
- say good things about
- speak highly of
- pay tribute to
- put in a good word for

praise /preɪz/ [v T] to say that you admire someone or approve of something good that they have done: *Fire chiefs praised a 10-year-old girl who saved her brother's life yesterday.* | **praise sb for sth** *Local people were praised for their calm response to the crisis.* | **highly praised** *His column was a regular and highly praised feature of the newspaper.*

congratulate /kənˈgrætʃɨleɪt/ [v T] to tell someone that you are pleased or impressed because they have achieved something special: *I would like to congratulate all the prizewinners.* | **congratulate sb on (doing) sth** *The President congratulated him on winning the title.* | *I wrote a letter congratulating him on his appointment.* | **congratulate sb for (doing) sth** *The committee is to be congratulated for presenting its findings in such an informative manner.*

compliment /ˈkɒmplɨment‖ˈkɑːm-/ [v T] to tell someone that you like the way they look or that you are pleased with something that they have done: *She blushed when men complimented her.* | **compliment sb on sth** *Everyone complimented me on my new hairstyle.*

be complimentary about /biː ˌkɒmplɨˈmentəri əbaʊt‖-ˌkɑːm- / [v phrase] to say good or approving things about a person or their achievements: *Peter is always very complimentary about your work.* | *She was actually highly complimentary about you.*

say good things about /ˌseɪ gʊd ˈθɪŋz əbaʊt/ [v phrase] if you **say good things about** someone, you praise their abilities, usually in their work: *People are saying really good things about you – that you are well-trained, are thorough, conscientious …*

speak highly of /ˌspiːk ˈhaɪli ɒv/ [v phrase] to praise someone or their work because you admire them: *I'm so pleased to meet you – my wife has always spoken very highly of you.* | *All her former clients speak highly of her legal skills.*

pay tribute to /ˌpeɪ ˈtrɪbjuːt tuː/ [v phrase] to praise someone publicly, especially to show respect for them and what they have achieved: *John Motum, presenting the trophy, paid tribute to the players and coaches.* | *Friends of the actor paid tribute to his talent and expressed shock as news of his death became public.*

put in a good word for /ˌpʊt ɪn ə ˌgʊd ˈwɜːʳd fɔːʳ/ [v phrase] if someone **puts in a good word for** you with someone in a position of authority, they praise you to them, especially in order to help you to get a job or to avoid punishment: *The producers told me later that I got the job because Paul put in a good word for me.* | **put in a good word for sb with sb** *Can* *you put in a good word for me with your colleagues on the council?*

2 to praise someone or something a lot

- be full of praise for
- sing sb's praises
- rave about
- glorify
- heap/lavish praise on

be full of praise for /biː ˌfʊl əv ˈpreɪz fɔːʳ/ [v phrase] *The press were full of praise for the whole production.* | *Ramsey, who hosts a Christian radio show, is full of praise for the two new congressmen.*

sing sb's praises /ˌsɪŋ (sb's) ˈpreɪzɪz/ [v phrase] to praise someone very highly and very frequently: *Craig adored Jane and would sing her praises to anyone who would listen.* | *Feminists have long sung the praises of writers such as Germaine Greer and Simone de Beauvoir.*

rave about /ˈreɪv əbaʊt/ [phr v T] informal to talk or write about something, saying how wonderful you think it is: *Critics are raving about the new show.* | *I bought some of that Colombian coffee you used to rave about.*

glorify /ˈglɔːrɪfaɪ/ [v T] to praise someone and their achievements very highly, in order to make them seem more important than they really are: *The emperor's achievements were glorified in numerous poems.* | *The book is a vain attempt to glorify the name of one of the worst dictators in modern history.*

heap/lavish praise on /ˌhiːp, ˌlævɪʃ ˈpreɪz ɒn/ [v phrase] to say things that show you admire someone or approve of what they have done: *It's nice to receive a letter heaping praise on someone for a job well done, for a change.* | *She is modest and generous, lavishing praise on the musicians she has worked with.*

3 to be praised in newspapers or by many people

- get a good press
- get rave reviews
- acclaimed
- much-praised
- be hailed as

get a good press /get ə ˌgʊd ˈpres/ [v phrase] if something **gets a good press**, it is praised in the newspapers, on television etc: *I haven't read it yet, but I know her latest novel got a very good press.* | *Eastern European cars have never really had a good press in this country.*

get rave reviews /get ˌreɪv rɪˈvjuːz/ [v phrase] informal if something such as a new book, film, or play **gets rave reviews**, it is praised a lot in newspapers and magazines: *Her roles in 'Miami Vice' and 'A Room with a View' got rave reviews.* | *Despite getting rave reviews, the film was not a box office hit.*

acclaimed /əˈkleɪmd/ [adj] if something such as a film, performance, or achievement is **acclaimed**, it is praised publicly by people who have a lot of knowledge about that subject **highly acclaimed** *Paul Simon's solo career has resulted in a string of highly acclaimed albums.* | **widely acclaimed** *Her work on finding a cure for cancer has been widely acclaimed by her colleagues in the medical profession.* | **critically acclaimed** (=praised by critics) *'The West Wing' is one of the most critically acclaimed TV series in the USA.*

much-praised /ˌmʌtʃ ˈpreɪzd◂/ [adj] praised a lot by many people: *They run a much-praised restaurant in Soho.* | *The Beatles' album 'Sergeant Pepper' was much praised when it first came out.*

be hailed as /biː ˈheɪld æz/ [v phrase] if something or someone new **is hailed as** something, they are praised a lot and are called something very good: *She is being hailed as the new Marilyn Monroe.* | *The new peace agreement is being hailed as a major breakthrough.* | *When it was first introduced, the birth control pill was hailed as a wonder drug.*

4 to praise someone in an insincere way

- flatter
- butter up

flatter /ˈflætəʳ/ [v T] to say nice things that you do not mean about someone, especially in order to get something from them: *Flatter her a little – tell her she's beautiful.* | *His flattering comments embarrassed her.*

butter up /ˌbʌtər ˈʌp/ [phr v T] informal to say nice things to someone in order to make them do something you want **butter sb up** *It's no use trying to butter me up – I'm not changing my mind.* | **butter up sb** *The bank has to butter up investors in this fiercely competitive market.*

5 praise that is given to someone or something

- praise
- compliment
- flattery
- recognition
- commendation

praise /preɪz/ [n U] things you say to someone to show that you admire them or approve of what they have done **+ for** *The police deserve a lot of praise for the way they handled the situation.* | **win/earn praise** (=be praised for something) *The charity has earned widespread praise for its work.* | **high praise** (=praise from someone important or respected) *She said you have talent, and that's high praise coming from a best-selling author like her.*

compliment /ˈkɒmplɪmənt‖ˈkɑːm-/ [n C] what you say when you tell someone they look nice or they have done something well: *'You have lovely hair', said Bob to Emma, who blushed at the compliment.* | **pay/give sb a compliment** *He's always paying her compliments and buying her flowers.* | **shower sb with compliments** (=give someone a lot of compliments) *Rob always showered me with compliments and made me feel special.*

flattery /ˈflætəri/ [n U] nice things that you say about someone, which may not be true, in order to get something that you want from them: *She used a mixture of persuasion and flattery to get what she wanted.* | **flattery will get you nowhere** (=use this to tell someone that flattery will not help them get what they want) *I'll choose the best person for the job, so flattery will get you nowhere.*

recognition /ˌrekəgˈnɪʃən/ [n U] if someone gets **recognition** for their work, they get praised publicly, often after a long time: *She had to spend 10 years as a struggling artist, before receiving any recognition for her work.* | *Although he was popular in Europe, Hendrix had yet to achieve recognition in his home country.*

commendation /ˌkɒmənˈdeɪʃən‖ˌkɑː-/ [n C/U] formal an official statement praising someone, especially someone who has been very brave or very successful: *Patroni received an official commendation after rescuing twelve people from a sinking* *ship.* | *After winning the world championship, he received a note of commendation from the President.*

6 what you say when you praise someone

- well done
- way to go
- congratulations

well done British **/good job** American /ˌwel ˈdʌn, ˌgʊd ˈdʒɒb‖-ˈdʒɑːb/ spoken say this to someone when they have done something well or succeeded in doing something difficult: *Well done! You got all the answers right.* | *Good job, John! That was a great shot.*

congratulations /kənˌgrætʃəˈleɪʃənz/ say or write this to someone when they have done something good or special: *Congratulations! Is it a girl or boy?* | **+ on** *Congratulations on your new job, Jenny.* | **congratulations on doing sth** *Congratulations on passing your driving test.*

way to go /ˌweɪ tə ˈgəʊ/ American spoken informal use this to praise someone who has just done something very good or impressive: *'I got accepted at Stanford.' 'Way to go!'* | *Way to go Sam! Nice hit!*

7 words for describing statements that praise someone or something

- glowing
- favourable
- complimentary

glowing /ˈgləʊɪŋ/ [adj usually before noun] full of praise: *Despite glowing reviews about the company's core businesses, its shares have fallen.* | *The young soldiers who returned home gave glowing accounts of Paul's bravery and devotion to duty.* | **in glowing terms** (=with words of high praise) *Stephen always talks in glowing terms of your work.* —**glowingly** [adv] *The reviewers spoke glowingly about a young actor named Jack Nicholson.*

complimentary /ˌkɒmplɪˈmentəri◂‖ˌkɑːm-/ [adj] **complimentary** remarks say good and approving things about someone or their achievements **highly complimentary** *Everything I've heard about your work has been highly complimentary.*

favourable British **/favorable** American /ˈfeɪvərəbəl/ [adj] **favourable** reports, remarks etc say good things about the person, film, event etc that they are about: *Responses to his latest movie have generally been favourable.* | *I don't want to hear your opinion – unless it's favourable of course.*

8 words for describing behaviour or actions that deserve praise

- commendable
- laudable
- praiseworthy

commendable /kəˈmendəbəl/ [adj] formal deserving praise: *The headteacher thanked the boys for their efforts, which he said were most commendable.* | **with commendable speed/patience etc** *The whole workforce has adapted to the new computing system with commendable speed.* | *The police acted with commendable restraint, considering the amount of pressure they were under.* —**commendably** [adv] *The investigation was commendably thorough.*

praiseworthy /ˈpreɪzwɜːʳði/ [adj] deserving praise for your actions, efforts, and intentions even if the final result is not always completely successful: *Giving blood is regarded by most people as something praiseworthy.* | *Negotiators have made a praiseworthy attempt to bring the two sides together.*

laudable /ˈlɔːdəbəl/ [adj] formal deserving praise: *Equal pay for equal work is a laudable principle.* | *Such honesty is laudable and rare.*

pray

RELATED WORDS

▸ *see also* **religion, believe (7)**

1 to say a prayer

- pray
- grace
- worship
- be at prayer
- prayer

pray /preɪ/ [v I] to speak to God or to a god, either silently or aloud, especially to ask for help or to express thanks: *He got down on his knees and began to pray.* | **pray to God/the gods/Allah etc** *In her time of distress she prayed to Allah to help her.* | **pray for sb** (=pray because someone needs help) *We pray for the sick and for their families.* | **pray for sth** (=pray that sth will happen) *As their crops wilted, the people prayed for rain.* | **+ (that)** *Carly's parents are praying that the operation will succeed.*

worship /ˈwɜːʳʃɪp/ [v I/T] to pray, sing, or take part in a religious ceremony, in order to show love and respect for God or a god: *The whole family worshipped together at the chapel.* | *the people worshipping in the mosque* | *The Ancient Egyptians worshipped many gods.*

prayer /preəʳ/ [n C] words that you say when you are praying **+ for** *Our prayers for peace have been answered.* | *a prayer for the dead* | **say a prayer** *She knelt to say a prayer of profound thankfulness.* | **say your prayers** (=say prayers, usually at a regular time) *We always used to say our prayers before going to bed.*

grace /greɪs/ [n U] a prayer thanking God for the food you are going to eat, said before a meal **say grace** *Before we eat, I'd just like to say grace.*

be at prayer /biː ət ˈpreəʳ/ [v phrase] formal if someone **is at prayer**, they are praying at this moment: *The saint appeared to him in a vision while he was at prayer.*

2 the activity of praying

- prayer
- worship

prayer /preəʳ/ [n U] *The synagogue is used for prayer and study.* | *The monks here believe strongly in the power of prayer and meditation.* | **in prayer** (=while praying) *Their heads were bowed in prayer.*

worship /ˈwɜːʳʃɪp/ [n U] the activity of praying, singing etc in a religious building, usually in a group, in order to show love and respect for God or a god: *The villagers gather for worship in the little church every Sunday.* | **act of worship** *Christians, Muslims and Jews came together for an act of communal worship.* | **place of worship** *This church has been a place of worship for a thousand years.*

3 an occasion when people pray together

- prayers
- service

prayers /preəʳz/ [n plural] *They were forbidden to talk during prayers.* | **morning/evening prayers** *Immediately after supper Mrs Carey rang the bell for evening prayers.*

service /'sɜːʳvɪ̈s/ [n C] a religious ceremony when people pray, sing etc together: *We always go to the service on Sunday morning.* | *There were usually most people at the evening service.* | **marriage/funeral/christening etc service** *The priest who performed the marriage service is a friend of the family.*

predict

to say what will happen in the future

RELATED WORDS

▸ *see also* **future**

1 to say what will happen in the future

- predict
- forecast
- prophesy
- foretell
- second-guess

predict /prɪ'dɪkt/ [v T] to say what you think will happen in the future: *Most of the papers are predicting an easy victory for the Dallas Cowboys.* | *a major earthquake that no-one had predicted* | **+ (that)** *Some scientists predict that the Earth's temperature will rise by as much as 5° over the next 20 years.*

forecast /'fɔːʳkɑːst‖-kæst/ [v T] to publicly say what will happen in the future with the weather or the economic or political situation, especially when you have special or technical knowledge: *Property analysts forecast a fall in house prices.* | **forecast rain/fine weather/snow etc** *Rain is forecast for all parts of southern England tomorrow.* | **+ that** *Hardly anyone had forecast that the drought would last so long.*

prophesy /'prɒfɪ̈saɪ‖'prɑː-/ [v I/T] to say that something will happen, especially because you have religious or magical powers: *It is claimed that Ebba prophesied her own death from the plague.* | **+ that** *Jesus prophesied that one of his disciples would betray him.* | **+ about** *Her ability to prophesy about the future made many people think she was a witch.*

foretell /fɔːʳ'tel/ [v T] to say what will happen in the future, especially by using magical powers – used in literature and stories: *Nostradamus is said to have foretold the rise of Hitler.* | *Everything happened as Merlin foretold.*

second-guess /ˌsekənd 'ges/ [v T] to try to predict what an opponent will do in order to gain an advantage over them: *I just couldn't get the ball past him; he second-guessed me every time.* | *Second-guessing the bank's next move in the takeover bid proved very difficult.*

2 to think you know what is going to happen in the future

- foresee
- envisage
- see sth coming
- feel sth in your bones
- have a premonition
- see into the future

foresee /fɔːʳ'siː/ [v T] to know that something is going to happen before it actually happens: *No one foresaw the Great Depression of the thirties.* | *Businesses are alarmed at the costs they foresee in complying with the new rules.* | **+ that** *Ten years ago she could not have foreseen that her marriage would end in divorce.*

envisage ALSO **envision** /ɪn'vɪzɪdʒ, ɪn'vɪʒən/ [v T] to have a clear idea of something that will happen in the future, especially important changes in a situation: *I cannot envisage what the circumstances will be in twenty years' time.* | *Most of those who voted for independence did not envision war as the eventual outcome.* | *We do not envisage a general election for at least another two years.*

see sth coming /ˌsiː (sth) 'kʌmɪŋ/ [v phrase] to know or think you know what is going to happen because there are signs that it will: *Jason saw the stock market crash coming and sold most of his shares.* | *Then one day she just walked out – I suppose I should have seen it coming really.*

feel sth in your bones /ˌfiːl (sth) ɪn jɔːʳ 'bəʊnz/ [v phrase] informal to think that something is going to happen, especially something bad, not for any clear or specific reason, but just because you have a feeling that it will: *The trip's going to be a disaster – I can feel it in my bones.*

have a premonition /hæv ə ˌpriːmə'nɪʃən/ [v phrase] to have a strange or unexplainable feeling that something is going to happen, especially something unpleasant **+ (that)** *When Paola failed to phone, John had a horrible premonition that she was in danger.* | **+ of** *She shivered suddenly, and I wondered whether she had had a premonition of her own death.*

see into the future /ˌsiː ɪntə ðə 'fjuːtʃəʳ/ [v phrase] someone who can **see into the future** has the ability to know what will happen before it happens: *If I could only see into the future and know how this would all end.* | *Nobody can see into the future, and all stock exchange investment is a gamble.*

3 something that someone predicts will happen

- prediction
- forecast
- prophecy
- prognosis
- predicted
- projected

prediction /prɪ'dɪkʃən/ [n C] a statement saying what you think will happen in the future: *Despite their confident predictions, sales of the new car have not been very good.* | **make a prediction** *It's too early to make any predictions about the election results.*

forecast /'fɔːʳkɑːst‖-kæst/ [n C] a public statement saying what is likely to happen with the weather or with the economic or political situation, based on special or technical knowledge **the weather forecast** (=a statement in a newspaper, or on the TV or radio, saying what the weather will be like during the next few days) *According to the weather forecast, it's going to stay hot for the rest of the week.* | **give/make a forecast** *It is impossible to give an accurate forecast of company sales 10 years from now.*

prophecy /'prɒfɪ̈si‖'prɑː-/ [n C] a statement that says something will happen, especially made by someone with religious or magical powers **+ of** *The old woman's prophecies of disaster were soon fulfilled.* | **+ that** *Lij Yasu was never crowned, possibly because he believed a prophecy that if he became king he would die.* | *Amazingly, the manager's prophecy that the team would get into the first division seems to be coming true.*

prognosis /prɒg'nəʊsɪ̈s‖prɑːg-/ [n C] formal the likely result of a process such as an illness or a series of events that has already started: *Well, doctor, what's the prognosis?* | *By the early 1990s the prognosis for Communism wasn't at all good.*

predicted /prɪ'dɪktɪ̣d/ [adj usually before noun] showing what someone thinks will happen in the future: *More than a century after Marx, the predicted dissolution of capitalism has still not taken place.* | *There were several arrests for disorderly behaviour, but for the most part the much-predicted violence did not materialize.*

projected /prə'dʒektɪ̣d/ [adj usually before noun] **projected figures/sales/profits/results** the profits, sales etc that a business expects to achieve considering past and present performance: *Next year's projected sales are 5% higher than this year's.* | *The company's losses look likely to wipe out the projected profits on the ECR90 project.*

4 able to be predicted

- predictable
- foreseeable

predictable /prɪ'dɪktəbəl/ [adj] *The drug is usually effective but unfortunately the side effects are not always predictable.* | *There are few predictable elements to this conflict – the only certainty is that the situation will worsen before it gets better.* | **it is predictable that** *In the current economic climate it is fairly predictable that unemployment will continue to rise.*

foreseeable /fɔːʳ'siːəbəl/ [adj] able to be predicted within a particular period of time in the future: *Due to rising costs and delays in the delivery of equipment, losses are already foreseeable on the new tunnel project.* | **in the foreseeable future** *There will not be any redundancies in the foreseeable future.* | **foreseeable circumstances** *Your insurance policy should take into account all foreseeable circumstances.*

5 not able to be predicted

- can't say/tell
- unpredictable
- unforeseeable
- it remains to be seen

can't say/tell /ˌkɑːnt 'seɪ, 'tel‖ˌkænt-/ [v phrase] informal to be unable to say or predict what will happen **+ how/what/whether** *The doctors can't say whether he will recover at this stage.* | *I don't know if we'll stay together or not. I can't tell how I'll be feeling in a month's time.*

unpredictable /ˌʌnprɪ'dɪktəbəl/ [adj] something that is **unpredictable** is impossible to predict because the situation changes a lot and has no regular pattern: *Britain is well known for its unpredictable weather.* | *Mayoral elections are usually unpredictable, highly dependent on the particular appeal of personalities and the ability to form coalitions.* | **highly unpredictable** *The situation in the region's poorest country remains volatile and highly unpredictable.*

unforeseeable /ˌʌnfɔːʳ'siːəbəl/ [adj] a situation or event, especially a bad one, that is **unforeseeable** could not have been predicted because it is the result of unusually bad luck: *What happened the following weekend was as unforeseeable as a plane falling on your house.* | *The circumstances which combined to cause this accident were unforeseeable.*

it remains to be seen /ɪt rɪˌmeɪnz tə biː 'siːn/ use this to show that you are unable or unwilling to say what will happen, and so people have to wait and see: *'What is your next film going to be about?' 'Well, that remains to be seen.'* | *What remains to be seen now is whether it is too late to save the rainforests.* | **+ how/when/if etc** *It remains to be seen how many senior citizens will actually benefit from this new plan.*

6 someone with special powers to predict

- fortune teller
- clairvoyant
- psychic

fortune teller /'fɔːʳtʃən ˌteləʳ/ [n C] someone who tells people what will happen to them in the future and is paid for doing this: *I went to see a fortune teller, and she told me that I would meet the man of my dreams and have three children.*

clairvoyant /kleəʳ'vɔɪənt/ [n C] someone who has the ability to know what will happen in the future: *A clairvoyant predicted that something terrible would happen to the President.* —**clairvoyance** [n C] the ability to know what will happen in the future: *Local legends told of a family in which the women were all cursed with clairvoyance.*

psychic /'saɪkɪk/ [adj] spoken someone who is **psychic** is able to know what will happen in the future – used especially when saying that you cannot know what will happen, or when you are surprised that someone knew that something would happen: *How was I supposed to know she'd react like that? I'm not psychic!* | *How did you know I'd be here? You must be psychic!*

prefer

RELATED WORDS

▸ *see also* **like, better, enjoy, choose**

1 to like someone or something better than others

- prefer
- like better
- have a preference
- favour
- give me sb/sth any day!

prefer /prɪ'fɜːʳ/ [v T not in progressive] *Which bread do you prefer, brown or white?* | *'Which restaurant shall we go to?' 'I really don't mind. Whichever one you prefer.'* | **much prefer sb/sth** (=like something much better) *She doesn't like romantic fiction – she much prefers detective stories.* | *Brad Pitt? Oh no, I much prefer Russell Crowe!* | **prefer sb/sth to sb/ sth** *I'm beginning to like Japanese food. I certainly prefer rice to potatoes.* | **I'd prefer sth** *Dave wants to go to New York again, but I'd prefer somewhere more exotic.*

like better /ˌlaɪk 'betəʳ/ [v phrase not in progressive] especially spoken to like one person or thing more than another one: *Which do you like better, the red tie or the green one?* | **+ than** *I like our new teacher much better than the one we had before.* | *There was nothing she liked better than being in the limelight in front of the press and TV cameras.*

have a preference /hæv ə 'prefərəns/ [v phrase not in progressive] formal to prefer something – use this especially when you are discussing which one of several things should be chosen: *We could eat Chinese, Indian, or Italian. Do you have any preference?* | **+ for** *The new leader has a preference for people who come from the same area of the country as he does.* | **have no strong/particular preference**

(=you don't prefer any of them more than the others) *I really have no particular preference – you choose.* | **express a preference** (=say that you prefer one rather than others) *When I asked her about where she wanted the meeting to be held she didn't express any particular preference.*

favour British **/favor** American /'feɪvəʳ/ [v T not in progressive] if a person or group in a position of authority or influence **favours** something such as a plan, idea, or system, they think it is better than the others: *President Bush was known to favor the use of military force.* | *In the 1930s the Bauhaus school tended to favour a technological approach to art.*

give me sb/sth any day! /ˌgɪv miː (sb/sth) 'eni deɪ/ spoken informal used when you want to say that you strongly prefer one type of thing: *I can't stand English men – they're so boring. Give me an Italian any day!* | *Forget all your salad and beans and organic food – give me a thick juicy steak any day!*

2 to prefer to do one thing rather than another

- prefer
- would rather do sth
- would prefer to do sth
- would sooner do sth

prefer /prɪ'fɜːʳ/ [v T not in progressive] if someone **prefers** to do something, they like doing it better than something else **prefer to do sth** *French people usually prefer to buy goods that are made in France.* | *Most of my friends take the bus to school, but I prefer to walk.* | **prefer doing sth** *Mark likes lying on the beach, but I prefer visiting museums.* | **prefer doing sth to doing sth** *She seems to prefer watching soap operas to talking to me.*

would rather do sth /wʊd ˌrɑːðəʳ 'duː (sth) ‖-ˌræ-/ [v phrase] especially spoken if you **would rather** do something, you want to do it more than another thing you could do instead, or more than what you are doing now: *I'd rather wear my Reeboks if we're going to be walking around all day.* | **would rather do sth than do sth** *A significant group of young men would rather go to jail than join the army.* | **would much rather do sth** *'Do you want to stay for supper?' 'I'd much rather go home, if you don't mind.'* | **would rather sb did sth** especially British *I'd rather we went skiing this year instead of hiking.*

would prefer to do sth /wʊd prɪˌfɜːʳ tə 'duː (sth)/ [v phrase] if you **would prefer to do** something, you want to do it more than another thing you could do instead, or more than what you are doing now: *Any smart employer would prefer to hire an experienced worker over an unknown.* | *We would both prefer to live in the north of England, but there aren't many jobs there.* | **would prefer sb to do sth** *I'd prefer them to come next weekend rather than the one after.*

would sooner do sth /wʊd ˌsuːnəʳ 'duː (sth)/ [v phrase] if you **would sooner** do something, you would very much prefer to do it especially instead of something else that you dislike or that is unpleasant: *Marry him? I'd sooner die!* | *He's the kind of person who'd sooner help people than make money out of them.*

3 when one thing is preferred to another

- preferably
- preferable
- preferred

preferably /'prefərəbli/ [adv] *Come early in the week – on Monday preferably.* | *We're looking for well-qualified young people, preferably with good computer skills.* | *'And you need to get a can of beans.' 'Black or red?' 'Whichever they have. Preferably black.'*

preferable /'prefərəbəl/ [adj] formal a choice, result, situation etc that is **preferable** is one that you would prefer: *So we're agreed. Our preferable course of action is to do nothing until the report is published.* | *The most preferable arrangement would be for us to pay very low interest over a long period of time.* | **+ to** *As far as I'm concerned anything would be preferable to staying here alone.*

preferred /prɪ'fɜːʳd/ [adj only before noun] formal **preferred method/option/course of action etc** the method, choice etc that you would prefer when there are several to choose from: *The preferred method was to cut the grass early in the morning when it was still wet.* | *Yes, that would be my preferred course of action.*

prejudiced

disliking people who belong to a different race, sex, religion etc in a way that seems unreasonable and unfair

RELATED WORDS

- *see also* **unfair, class (3-9), race, sex, gay**

1 prejudiced

- prejudiced
- racist
- sexist
- homophobic
- xenophobic
- bigoted
- intolerant

prejudiced /'predʒədəst/ [adj] someone who is **prejudiced** dislikes people of a different race, sex, social class etc. Laws, systems etc that are **prejudiced** have the effect of treating people of a particular race, sex, class etc unfairly: *Even today Southern states are seen as being more racially prejudiced than other states.* | *an outdated and prejudiced set of laws* | **+ against** *People around here are sometimes prejudiced against Catholics.* | *He denies that he is prejudiced against women.*

racist /'reɪsəst/ [adj] believing that people of your race are naturally better, more intelligent etc than people of other races and therefore treating people of other races unfairly: *Asian kids in mostly white schools are well aware of the racist attitudes they face.* | *Community leaders have protested at the police's refusal to believe the attacks are racist in nature.* | *racist propaganda*

sexist /'seksəst/ [adj] behaving in a way that is unfair to people who belong to a particular sex. **Sexist** is usually used about people being unfair to women, and treating them unequally: *He has been accused of being sexist and insensitive.* | *Several women officers have complained about sexist attitudes in the police force.* | *He denies sending sexist and offensive material over the Internet to female colleagues.* | *a sexist remark*

homophobic /ˌhəʊmə'fəʊbɪk◂, ˌhɒ-‖ˌhəʊ-/ [adj] someone who is **homophobic** hates gay people: *The band's lyrics have been criticized for being homophobic and racist.* | *Homophobic attitudes are still very common among teenagers.* | *homophobic legislation*

xenophobic /ˌzenə'fəʊbɪk◂/ [adj] someone who is **xenophobic** dislikes people from other countries and will not accept them in their own country or willingly work with them: *The party is right-wing and xenophobic.* | *There are warnings that the xenophobic practices of UK companies are costing business and jobs.*

bigoted /ˈbɪgətɪ̈d/ [adj] having a completely unreasonable hatred for people of a different race, religion etc, based on strong and fixed opinions: *Bigoted attitudes don't change very quickly.* | *Her speech included a bigoted attack on Hispanics* | *He believes the political right in America is becoming dangerously bigoted.*

intolerant /ɪnˈtɒlərənt‖-ˈtɑː-/ [adj] refusing to accept that other people have the right to have different beliefs, customs, or opinions from your own: *The police chief has been accused of being intolerant and ignorant.* | *Intolerant societies are often also among the most technologically backward.* | **+ of** *The argument led to charges that the national organization is intolerant of dissent.*

2 prejudiced attitudes or behaviour

- prejudice
- racism/racial prejudice
- sexism
- homophobia
- xenophobia
- intolerance
- bigotry
- hate crime

prejudice /ˈpredʒədɪ̈s/ [n C/U] when people do not like or trust someone who is different from them, for example because they belong to a different race, country, or religion: *Almost all immigrant groups have faced prejudice in their new countries.* | *Able young men and women are still held back from success by prejudice.* | *You should learn to identify your own prejudices and deal with them.* | **+ against** *There is still a lot of prejudice against gay men.* | **racial prejudice** *measures to tackle the problem of racial prejudice in the police force* | **class prejudice** (=because of someone's social class) British *Criticizing people's accents in this way is nothing less than class prejudice.*

racism/racial prejudice /ˈreɪsɪzəm, ˌreɪʃəl ˈpredʒədɪ̈s/ [n U] the belief that people of your race are naturally better, more intelligent etc than people of other races, especially when this leads to unfair treatment, hatred, and violence: *The ANC never dropped its commitment to the fight against racism.* | *A French company has been accused of racism after sacking three Algerian workers.* | *Jackie Robinson overcame racial prejudice to become the first black baseball player in the Major leagues.* | *Racism will not be tolerated anywhere within this organization.*

sexism /ˈseksɪzəm/ [n U] prejudiced attitudes and unfair behaviour towards people who belong to a particular sex. **Sexism** is usually used about unfair treatment of women, but can be used about treatment of and attitudes towards men: *There is still a lot of subtle sexism on television and in magazines.* | *Sexism in advertising is becoming less common thanks to the new complaints commission.* | *a government report into sexism in the workplace*

homophobia /ˌhəʊməˈfəʊbiə, ˌhɒ-‖ˌhəʊ-/ [n U] hatred of or prejudiced attitudes towards gay people: *There is probably less homophobia in the movie industry than in many others.* | *The lives of many young gay people are ruined by unthinking and widespread homophobia in society.*

xenophobia /ˌzenəˈfəʊbiə/ [n U] hatred of or completely negative attitudes towards people from other countries: *In an atmosphere of growing xenophobia many foreigners were deported or even imprisoned.*

intolerance /ɪnˈtɒlərəns‖-ˈtɑː-/ [n U] unreasonable refusal to accept that other people have the right to have different beliefs, customs, or opinions from yours: *Religious intolerance has always been a major cause of war.* | *Many of our friends' lives have been shattered by intolerance, persecution and torture.*

bigotry /ˈbɪgətri/ [n U] a completely unreasonable hatred for people of a different race, religion etc, based on strong and fixed opinions: *Gay people face a constant struggle against bigotry.* | *Teach your children to recognize bigotry and not be a part of it.*

hate crime /ˈheɪt kraɪm/ [n C/U] a crime that is committed against someone because they belong to a particular group, for example because they are of a different race: *The police are setting up a new hate crime unit in East London.* | *Gay activists say hate crimes are on the increase.*

3 someone who is prejudiced

- bigot
- racist
- sexist
- chauvinist
- misogynist

bigot /ˈbɪgət/ [n C] someone who has a completely unreasonable hatred for people of a different race, religion etc, based on strong and fixed opinions: *Critics say the mayor is a bigot who is inflaming racial tensions in his city.* | *a religious bigot*

racist /ˈreɪsɪ̈st/ [n C] someone who believes that people of their own race are naturally better, more intelligent etc than people of other races, and therefore treat them badly and unfairly: *There has been a rise in attacks on asylum seekers made by skinheads and other racists.* | *He is accused of being a racist after refusing to be interviewed by a black journalist.* | *She denies being a racist, claiming to be merely patriotic.*

sexist /ˈseksɪ̈st/ [n C] someone who believes that their own sex is naturally better and deserves better jobs, education etc than the other, usually a man who thinks men are better than women: *My ex-husband was a real sexist, who didn't think our daughters should have jobs at all.* | *She vows to continue her fight against those she calls 'the racists and sexists who dominate the church'.*

chauvinist /ˈʃəʊvɪ̈nɪ̈st/ [n C] someone who believes that the group they belong to is better than other groups, especially men who believe that they are better than women, or people who believe that their country is best: *Religious chauvinists have been the main cause of trouble in the province.* | **male chauvinist** *A self-confessed male chauvinist, he had no idea how to look after himself after his wife died.* —**chauvinist** [adj] *Women often have to work twice as hard to overcome the chauvinist attitudes of their male colleagues.*

misogynist /mɪ̈ˈsɒdʒɪ̈nɪ̈st‖mɪ̈ˈsɑː-/ [n C] a man who hates women: *The movie is a moral tale about a misogynist who dies and is reborn as a beautiful woman.* —**misogynist** [adj] *The rapper has been accused of being misogynist and homophobic.*

prepare

RELATED WORDS

- ready, prepared *see* **ready/not ready**
- prepare food *see* **cook**
- *see also* **arrange, organize, practise/practice**

1 to prepare for something that will happen in the future

- prepare
- get ready
- make preparations
- in preparation for
- gear up
- do the groundwork
- mobilize

prepare /prɪˈpeəʳ/ [v I] to make plans or arrangements for something that will happen in the future, so that you will be ready when it happens: *I've been so busy that I've had no time to prepare.* | **+ for** *He only had a few hours to prepare for the interview.* | *People on the island are preparing for another storm.* | **+ to do sth** *The company is preparing to expand its European network.* —**preparatory** /prɪˈpærətəri‖-tɔːri/ [adj only before noun] done to prepare for something: *a series of preparatory meetings*

get ready /get ˈredi/ [v phrase] to do all the things you need to do to prepare for a special occasion or event: *We're looking forward to the trip, but there's so much to do to get ready.* | **+ for** *We've spent the last few days getting ready for Christmas.* | **+ to do sth** *It seems the whole country is getting ready to welcome the visiting president.*

make preparations /meɪk ˌprepəˈreɪʃənz/ [v phrase] to do all the things you must do in order to prepare for an important event: *We set a date of January 8 and began to make preparations.* | **+ for** *We started to make preparations for the wedding about a year ago.* | **make your preparations** *I made my preparations with great care.*

in preparation for /ɪn ˌprepəˈreɪʃən fɔːʳ/ [prep] if you do something **in preparation for** a planned event, you do something to make it possible or more likely to be successful: *Japan National Railways was split up in preparation for sale to private investors.* | *In preparation for Passover, all 'unclean' items are removed from the house.*

gear up /ˌgɪər ˈʌp/ [phr v I] if a company or organization **gears up** to do something important or difficult, they prepare to do it by making changes, buying things that will be needed etc **+ to do sth** *Retailers are already gearing up to meet the Christmas rush.* | **+ for** *The company will shortly be gearing up for a major expansion.*

do the groundwork ALSO **do the spadework** British /ˌduː ðə ˈgraʊndwɜːʳk, ˌduː ðə ˈspeɪdwɜːʳk/ [v phrase] to do the work that has to be done before something else can happen: *All the necessary groundwork for the advertising campaign has already been done.* | *Although I did most of the spadework, I wasn't given any credit for it.*

mobilize ALSO **mobilise** British /ˈməʊbɪ̮laɪz/ [v I/T] if a country or its army **mobilizes**, it prepares to fight a war: *Britain mobilized its forces.* | *While the US mobilizes, top-level diplomats are making a last attempt to reach a negotiated settlement.*

2 to prepare something so that it is ready to be used

- prepare
- get sth ready
- set up

prepare /prɪˈpeəʳ/ [v T] to **prepare** something such as a place, a machine, or piece of equipment for an event or activity that has been planned: *Before you start painting, prepare the walls by cleaning them and filling any cracks.* | *When they are not in the classroom, teachers spend much of their time preparing lessons.* | **prepare sth for sth** *The Americans are preparing two new satellites for launch.* | *Maintenance staff are busy preparing the field for tomorrow's big game.*

get sth ready /ˌget (sth) ˈredi/ [v phrase] to make sure something is ready to be used: *I'll get the car ready.* | **+ for** *Try to get all your things ready for school the night before.* | *Her main job is to do general cleaning and get the rooms ready for guests.*

set up /ˌset ˈʌp/ [phr v T] to prepare the equipment that is needed for an activity, by putting them in the right places, putting different pieces together etc **set up sth** *We've set up a microphone in the corner.* | *It was 6:30 and traders were already setting up their market stalls.* | **set sth up** *It'll take a few minutes to set the camera up.*

3 to prepare yourself for something that you have to do

- prepare yourself
- be prepared
- get ready
- brace yourself
- steel yourself
- psych yourself up
- work up to
- gear yourself up

prepare yourself /prɪˈpeəʳ jɔːʳˈself/ [v phrase] to make yourself mentally and physically ready for something that you will have to do: *Before starting to write an answer in an exam, prepare yourself by thinking about what you want to say.* | **+ for** *They prepared themselves for a long wait.* | *She has spent the last year preparing herself for the race.*

be prepared /biː prɪˈpeəʳd/ [v phrase] if you **are prepared** for something unpleasant or difficult, you expect it and you have thought about it, so that you can deal with it more easily: *The children were seasick last time, so this time we're prepared.* | **+ for** *I just wasn't prepared for such a difficult interview.* | **be well prepared** *Clark's lawyers were well prepared and confident.*

get ready /get ˈredi/ [v phrase] to do all the things you need to do in order to be ready to do something, especially things such as washing or dressing before you go somewhere: *You'd better go get ready – it's almost 8 o'clock.* | **+ to do sth** *I was just getting ready to go out when Tim called.* | **get yourself ready for sth** *In the stadium, the sprinters are getting themselves ready for the 100-metre race.*

brace yourself /ˈbreɪs jɔːʳself/ [v phrase] to prepare yourself for something unpleasant that is about to happen: *Here comes the boss, and she's not looking happy! You'd better brace yourself!* | **+ for** *Socialist party leaders are bracing themselves for defeat.* | **+ to do sth** *I didn't really want to hear the rest, but I braced myself to listen.*

steel yourself /ˈstiːl jɔːʳself/ [v phrase] to prepare yourself to do something that you know will be upsetting, frightening, or unpleasant: *I had to steel myself before I could tell her about the accident.* |

+ to do sth *She steeled herself to look at the body again.* | **+ for** *Jim steeled himself for a fight.*

psych yourself up /ˌsaɪk jɔːʳself ˈʌp/ [v phrase] informal to prepare yourself mentally for something difficult by making yourself believe that you can do it and that you really want to do it: *I tried to psych myself up before the interview.* | **+ for** *A lot of athletes use music to psych themselves up for a game.*

work up to /ˌwɜːʳk ˈʌp tuː/ [phr v T] to prepare yourself to do something that you do not want to do, by gradually making yourself more and more determined to do it: *I haven't asked him yet, but I'm working up to it.* | **work up to doing sth** *She's been working up to telling her boyfriend it's over.*

gear yourself up /ˌgɪəʳ jɔːʳself ˈʌp/ [v phrase] especially British to prepare yourself mentally for something such as a test or important game, by gradually making yourself believe that you can do it successfully: *The game's on Friday, so we're starting to gear ourselves up during training.* | **+ for** *He's been gearing himself up for his exams over the past few weeks.*

4 to prepare someone for something that they will have to do

- prepare
- groom
- train
- equip

▸ *see also* **teach**

prepare /prɪˈpeəʳ/ [v T] to **prepare** someone for something that they will have to do, by providing them with the skills, training, or experience that they will need: *The programs are aimed at preparing people who want to start up their own business.* | **prepare sb for sth** *Schools should do more to prepare children for the world of work.* | *Nothing could have prepared him for what he saw during the war.*

train /treɪn/ [v I/T] to prepare someone for a job, activity, or sporting event by teaching them the skills they need and encouraging them to practise: *The team is currently training in Hampshire.* | **train sb to do sth** *The staff must be trained to use the software correctly.* | **train sb for sth** *The troops had been trained for an important role in the battle.* | **+ for** *She's been training for the marathon for six months.*

groom /gruːm, grʊm/ [v T] to carefully prepare someone for an important job or for a particular position in society by training them over a long period of time **groom sb as sth** *Jiang was groomed as Deng's replacement* | **groom sb to be sth** *Mrs Adams had groomed her only daughter to be a perfect wife and mother.* | **groom sb for sth** *Most people believe he is being groomed for the party leadership.*

equip /ɪˈkwɪp/ [v T] to give someone the skills they need to deal with problems or difficult situations, especially by training them **equip sb to do sth** *A good education will equip your children to get a good job.* | **equip sb with sth** *We do our best to equip refugees with the skills they need for survival in a foreign culture.*

5 to provide the necessary conditions for something to happen

- set the scene
- lay the foundations
- pave the way

set the scene /ˌset ðə ˈsiːn/ [v phrase] if an action or event **sets the scene** for another event, it provides the conditions in which that event can take place **+ for** *The negotiations in Geneva have set the scene for a possible agreement later in the year.* | *Recent events have set the scene for a potentially violent confrontation between the demonstrators and the army.*

pave the way /ˌpeɪv ðə ˈweɪ/ [v phrase] to provide the conditions that will make something much easier to achieve in the future **+ for** *These experiments may pave the way for a vaccine against some forms of cancer.* | *The Married Women's Property Act paved the way for further legislation on women's rights.*

lay the foundations /ˌleɪ ðə faʊnˈdeɪʃənz/ [v phrase] to provide the conditions that will make it possible for something successful to take place much later **+ for** *Long-term planning after the war laid the foundations for the nation's steady economic growth.* | **+ of** *The two sides met in an attempt to lay the foundations of a future peace settlement.*

6 when you prepare something

- preparation
- preparations

preparation /ˌprepəˈreɪʃən/ [n U] the time and work that is needed to prepare for something: *Months of preparation have gone into organizing the festival.* | *This dessert needs very little preparation, and you can serve it right away.* | **+ for** *This is all part of the preparation for next month's vital election.* | **+ of** *Correct preparation of the canvas for painting is extremely important.*

preparations /ˌprepəˈreɪʃənz/ [n plural] all the things you have to do so that you will be ready for an important event: *Despite their preparations, hospital officials worry that they could not cope with a major epidemic.* | **+ for** *She's busy with the final preparations for the wedding.* | *Preparations for the conference are well under way.*

press

RELATED WORDS

▸ *see also* **push, squash**

1 to push something firmly, especially with your fingers

- press
- touch
- squeeze
- knead
- pinch

press /pres/ [v I/T] to push something firmly with your fingers or with your feet. In American English **push** is usually used to describe what you do to buttons, bells etc: *The doctor gently pressed her stomach.* | *I pressed the brake pedal, but nothing happened.* | **press sth down** *She stuffed the papers back in the box and pressed the lid down.* | **press a button/bell/key** British (=in order to make a machine work, a bell ring etc) *Which key do I press to delete it?* | *To get coffee, put your money in the machine and press the green button.*

squeeze /skwiːz/ [v T] to push something firmly inwards by pressing on both sides of it, especially with your hands or fingers: *I squeezed the toothpaste tube, but nothing came out.* | *a horrible doll that cried when you squeezed it* | **squeeze sth out of sth** *I can't squeeze any more tomato paste out of this tube.* | **squeeze sb's arm/hand** (=as a sign of love or friendship) *Alice squeezed my arm affectionately, and said goodbye.*

pinch /pɪntʃ/ [v T] to press someone's skin tightly between your fingers and thumb, so that it hurts: *Dad! Katy just pinched me!*

touch /tʌtʃ/ [v T] **especially American** to press a button, for example on a telephone or a computer screen, in order to make a choice, get information, or make something work – used especially in instructions: *For room service, touch button 9.*

knead /niːd/ [v T] to press a soft substance such as clay or dough (=a mixture of flour and water used to make bread) repeatedly with your hands: *She kneaded the dough and shaped it into loaves.* | *The clay should be kneaded thoroughly to remove any bubbles of air.*

2 to press something so that it becomes flatter or smaller

- press
- flatten
- roll
- compress

press /pres/ [v T] *We pressed the flowers between the pages of a book.* | **press sth into sth** (=press something to make it a different shape) *The cookie dough is then pressed into small shapes and baked in a hot oven.*

flatten /ˈflætn/ [v T] to press something into a flat shape: *Place the balls of cookie dough on a baking sheet, and flatten each one with your hand.* | *She said that the crash-helmet would flatten her hair-do.*

roll ALSO **roll out** [v T/phr v T] /rəʊl, ˌrəʊl ˈaʊt/ to make something flat using a tool or machine shaped like a tube: *Roll the pastry as thin as you can.* | **roll out sth/roll sth out** *Roll the dough out to a thickness of four centimetres.*

compress /kəmˈpres/ [v T] to press something together, so that it takes up less space – used especially in technical contexts: *Behind the factory is a machine that compresses old cars into blocks of scrap metal.* —**compression** /kəmˈpreʃən/ [n U] *The engine's efficiency depends on the effective compression of gas in all its cylinders.*

3 to press something to remove the liquid from it

- squeeze
- wring out

squeeze /skwiːz/ [v T] *Squeeze the lemons and pour the juice into a jug.* | *Alice squeezed the wet sponge.* | **freshly squeezed orange/lemon etc juice** (=juice that has been pressed from a fruit, and that has not had any chemicals, sugar etc added) *I start the day with a glass of freshly squeezed orange juice.*

wring out /ˌrɪŋ ˈaʊt/ [phr v T] to press and twist wet cloth or wet clothes in order to remove water from them **wring out sth** *Would you wring out these towels and hang them up to dry?* | **wring sth/it/them out** *I had to take off my skirt and wring it out when I got home.*

pretend

RELATED WORDS

- to pretend not to notice sb/sth *see* **ignore (2)**
- made to look real or natural *see* **artificial**
- polite in an insincere way *see* **polite (6)**
- *see also* **false, dishonest, lie, cheat, trick/deceive**

1 to pretend that something is true

- pretend
- make out
- be putting it on
- be faking it
- live a lie
- keep up appearances

pretend /prɪˈtend/ [v I/T] to behave as though something is true when you know that it is not: *We thought that he was really hurt, but he was just pretending.* | **+ (that)** *Bill closed his eyes, and pretended that the war was over and that he was safe at home.* | **pretend to do sth** *I pretended not to see her, and carried on walking down the street.* | **pretend to be happy/ill/angry etc** *She pretended to be ill and took a day off work.*

make out /ˌmeɪk ˈaʊt/ [phr v T] **informal** to pretend that a situation exists in order to deceive someone **+ (that)** *We managed to fool the ticket collector by making out we couldn't speak English.* | *Two days later Joyce phoned to ask about the check, so I had to make out I'd already mailed it.* | **make sth out to be** *They made it out to be a really interesting job, but in fact it was ridiculously boring.*

be putting it on /biː ˌpʌtɪŋ ɪt ˈɒn/ [v phrase] **spoken** to pretend to be ill, upset, injured etc, because you want to avoid doing something or you want people to feel sorry for you: *I don't think she's really ill – she's just putting it on because she doesn't want to go to school.* | *I couldn't tell if Harvey was putting it on, or if he really was upset.*

be faking it /biː ˈfeɪkɪŋ ɪt/ [v phrase] **informal** to pretend to be interested, ill etc, when you are not: *The kid is always saying he's too sick to go to school, and his parents figure he's faking it.* | *I look at all the faces around me. Are these people really that happy? Or are they just faking it like I am?*

live a lie /ˌlɪv ə ˈlaɪ/ [v phrase] to pretend all the time that you feel or believe something that you do not feel or believe: *I had to leave him – I couldn't go on living a lie.*

keep up appearances /ˌkiːp ʌp əˈpɪərənsɪ̈z/ [v phrase] to pretend that everything in your life is still as happy and successful as it used to be, even though you have suffered some kind of trouble or loss: *Of course, he tries to keep up appearances, but he lives entirely off borrowed money.* | *She put Christmas decorations in the window just to keep up appearances.*

2 to pretend to be someone else

- pretend
- make yourself out to be
- impersonate
- do an impersonation/do an impression
- role play
- pose as
- masquerade as
- disguise as

pretend /prɪˈtend/ [v T] to behave as if you are someone else and try to make other people believe this **pretend to be sb** *We pretended to be students and got into the club for free.* | **+ (that)** *They got into the house by pretending they worked for the electricity company.*

make yourself out to be /ˌmeɪk jɔːʳself ˈaʊt tə biː/ [v phrase] to pretend that you are cleverer, richer, more important etc than you really are: *Richard led us around the art gallery, making himself out to be some kind of expert on modern art.* | *What I don't like about her is that she makes herself out to be something special.*

impersonate /ɪm'pɜːʳsəneɪt/ [v T] to behave as though you are someone with official power or someone famous, either for dishonest reasons or in order to entertain people: *I got home to find him impersonating Elvis Presley in front of the mirror.* | *It's illegal to impersonate a police officer.*

do an impersonation/do an impression /duː ən ɪm,pɜːʳsə'neɪʃən, duː ən ɪm'preʃən/ [v phrase] to speak, walk, or behave like someone else, in order to make people laugh **+ of** *Stuart did a brilliant impersonation of the boss.* | *a comedian with his own TV show, who does impressions of famous politicians*

role play /'rəʊl pleɪ/ [n C/U] when you pretend to be someone else and behave as they would behave, especially as a way of learning about a situation or developing a skill: *The course uses role play to teach you how to deal with difficult or aggressive customers.*

pose as /'pəʊz æz/ [v phrase not in passive] to pretend to be someone else, especially someone in an official position, in order to make it easier for you to do something bad or illegal: *He posed as a doctor to gain access to the hospital.* | *There have been cases of thieves posing as telephone engineers to trick people into letting them into their homes.*

masquerade as /mæskə'reɪd æz/ [v T not in passive] to pretend that you are someone else, especially by dressing or behaving in the way that they do – used especially in literature and stories: *He got into the stadium masquerading as a security guard.* | *A journalist masquerading as a businessman approached the politicians, and offered them bribes.*

disguise as /dɪs'gaɪz æz/ [v T] to change your appearance, especially your clothes, so that you look like someone else and people cannot recognize you: *He escaped across the border disguised as a priest.* | **disguise yourself as** *Maybe you could disguise yourself as a waiter and sneak in there.*

3 someone who pretends to be someone else

- impostor
- charlatan
- bogus

impostor /ɪm'pɒstəʳ‖ɪm'pɑːs-/ [n C] someone who pretends to be someone else in order to deceive people and gain something such as money or power: *It was not the real Dr Frazer but an impostor.* | *The man registered at a Las Vegas hotel as Dustin Hoffman, and it wasn't until he left without paying his bill that people realized he was an impostor.*

charlatan /'ʃɑːʳlətən/ [n C] someone who pretends to have special skills or knowledge, for example as a doctor or teacher, when in fact they do not: *No. She isn't a miracle worker. She isn't even a doctor. She's a complete charlatan.* | *Some people said that he was one of the greatest philosophers who ever lived; others claimed he was a charlatan.*

bogus /'bəʊgəs/ [adj only before noun] pretending to have a particular job or position that you do not have, in order to do something dishonest or illegal: *The government has announced tough new measures to deal with bogus asylum-seekers.* | **bogus official/social worker/policeman etc** *The child was taken away from her parents by a bogus social worker.* | *There has been a spate of incidents where bogus officials have called on the homes of elderly people.*

4 to pretend something as a game

- pretend
- make believe
- play

pretend /prɪ'tend/ [v T] to **pretend** something as a game, or because you enjoy it **pretend (that)** *I like to drive around in my brother's BMW and pretend I'm a rich businessman.* | **pretend to be** *He burst into the room with a toy gun in his hand, pretending to be a gangster.*

make believe /'meɪk bə̥l̥,liːv/ [v phrase not in progressive] to pretend that pleasant things are happening, that you are someone or somewhere you want to be, etc **make believe (that)** *The two little girls used to make believe that they were princesses.* | **make believe** *Right, kids. We don't have any proper cowboy hats so you'll have to make believe.* —**make-believe** [n U] *She's not really a queen – it's only make-believe.*

play ALSO **play at** British /pleɪ, 'pleɪ æt/ [v] if children **play** or **play at** something, they pretend to be a particular type of person or to do a particular thing, as a game: *When I was young we played at pirates whenever we were on the beach.* | *When my sister was little, she always wanted to play school.* | **play doctors and nurses** *Did you ever play doctors and nurses when you were small?* | **play happy families** British / **play house** American (=pretend to be a family) *Come on – let's go inside and play house!*

5 pretending to be friendly, sincere etc

- insincere
- hypocritical
- phoney/phony
- two-faced
- false
- mock

insincere /,ɪnsɪn'sɪəʳ◂/ [adj] someone who is **insincere** says things that they do not really mean, for example when they praise you or say something friendly: *'It's so good to see you again,' she said, with an insincere smile.* | *an insincere compliment* | *He always praised everyone, so it was difficult to tell if he was being insincere or not.*

hypocritical /,hɪpə'krɪtɪkəl◂/ [adj] pretending to be morally good or to have beliefs that you do not really have: *I think it's a little hypocritical to get married in a church when you don't believe in God.* | *Politicians are so hypocritical – they preach about 'family values' while they all seem to be having affairs.* —**hypocrite** /'hɪpəkrɪt/ [n] someone who pretends to have strong opinions about how people should behave, but who does not behave like this themselves.: *My dad is such a hypocrite – he says I shouldn't smoke, but he smokes 20 a day.*

phoney/phony /'fəʊni/ [n C] especially American, informal someone who pretends to be good, clever, kind etc when really they are not: *When I realized what a phoney he was I was devastated.* | *I can't stand her – she's such a phoney.*

two-faced /,tuː 'feɪst◂/ [adj] pretending that you like someone by behaving in a friendly way towards them when you are with them, but behaving in an unkind way when they are not there: *I've never met anyone so two-faced: she's sweet and charming to your face, and then goes and complains about you to the boss!*

false /fɔːls/ [adj] **false** emotions are not real and the person is only pretending to feel them: *'Merry Christmas,' she said with false heartiness.* | *Her face took on a look of false delight.*

mock /mɒk‖mɑːk/ [adj only before noun] **mock surprise/horror/indignation etc** surprise etc that you pretend to feel, especially as a joke: *Diana gave her cousin a look of mock horror and then disappeared through the door, smiling.* | **in mock surprise/horror etc** (=showing mock surprise, horror etc) *The grey eyes widened in mock surprise. 'How unusual to meet you here,' she said sarcastically.* | *'It's not fair,' he complained, pulling at his hair in mock distress. 'I really wanted to visit your parents!'*

6 to change your way of speaking or behaving in order to impress people

- put on
- affected
- assume
- artificial

put on /ˌpʊt ˈɒn/ [phr v T] to speak or behave in a way that is not your usual way of speaking or behaving. **be putting it on** *He wasn't really drunk. He was just putting it on.* | **put on sth** *Whenever the boss is around she puts on this sick little smile.* | **put on an accent** *Valerie put on a posh accent and asked to see the manager immediately.*

affected /əˈfektɪ̣d/ [adj] someone who is **affected** is not natural or sincere because they are trying to make people think they are better than they really are: *I can't bear him – he's so loud and affected.* | *That stupid affected laugh of hers really annoys me.* | *She treated her guests with an affected politeness.*

assume /əˈsjuːm‖əˈsuːm/ [v T] formal to behave or speak in a way in which you do not usually behave or speak, especially so that you look more confident or feel better: *When socializing with his co-workers he would assume a hearty, over-bearing manner.* | *Assuming a carefree air, Luke picked up his jacket and walked to the door.*

artificial /ˌɑːʳtɪ̣ˈfɪʃəl◂/ [adj] a person or their behaviour that is **artificial** is not natural or sincere, because they are pretending to be something that they are not: *Carter was saying all the right things, but his smile was artificial, and I knew I couldn't trust him.* | *On the surface she seems quite a pleasant woman, but there's something very artificial about her.*

7 an attempt to pretend that something is true

- pretence
- charade
- sham
- front

pretence British **/pretense** American /prɪˈtens‖ˈpriːtens/ [n C usually singular] an attempt to pretend that something is true, especially in order to deceive people **+ of** *After my mother left, my father gave up even the pretense of caring for anyone besides himself.* | **+ that** *The worst thing about liberal academics is the pretence that they are somehow more open-minded than their opponents.* | **on the pretence that/of** (=pretending that it is the reason for what you are doing) *Wilson asked Carly out to dinner, on the pretence that he wanted to talk to her about business.* | *The first time she had called was on the pretense of finding out how Letia was.* | **make a pretence of doing sth** (=pretend to do it) *Mr Tellwright made no pretence of concealing his satisfaction.* | **keep up the pretence** (=continue pretending) *After two weeks he could keep up the pretence no longer and decided to tell her the truth.*

charade /ʃəˈrɑːd‖ʃəˈreɪd/ [n C] a situation in which people pretend that something is true and behave as if it were true, especially when everyone really knows that it is not true: *The trial was just a charade – the verdict had already been decided.* | *Simon told Susan that his marriage was a charade, continued only for the sake of the children.*

sham /ʃæm/ [n singular] an attempt to deceive people by pretending that something is true, especially if it is easy for people to see that it is not true: *She believed Rodney's sudden change in attitude was only a sham.* | *The election was a sham. Officials intimidated peasants into voting for the government candidates, or simply stuffed the ballot boxes.*

front /frʌnt/ [n singular] an organization or activity that seems to be legal and ordinary but which is secretly being used for an illegal purpose: *The club was just a front – Luchese's real business was drug smuggling and gun running.* | **+ for** *The charity has been accused of being a front for anti-government activity.*

prison

RELATED WORDS

▸ *see also* **punish, crime, court/trial, catch (3-6), escape, free (8-9), law**

1 a place where people are kept as punishment

- prison
- jail
- penitentiary
- cell
- detention centre

prison /ˈprɪzən/ [n C/U] a large building where people are kept as a punishment for a crime: *Conditions in the prison were shocking.* | *a maximum security prison* | **in prison** *Johnson pleaded guilty and was sentenced to five years in prison.* | *The prosecuting lawyers say that Price may face life in prison.* | **be released from prison** *When he was released from prison, Mandela was interviewed in Zambia.* | **prison officials/conditions/regulations etc** *Clayton will be released on Tuesday after serving seven years, prison officials said.* | **prison sentence** (=how long someone has to spend in prison) *a fifteen-year prison sentence*

jail /dʒeɪl/ [n C] a prison, or similar smaller building where prisoners who are waiting for a trial are kept: *This old building is the jail that Butch Cassidy escaped from in 1887.* | *Alfassi was taken to a cell in the Los Angeles County jail.* | **in jail** *58% of prisoners are in jail for non-violent crimes.* | **be put/thrown in jail** *The strikers were harassed, beaten and put in jail for trespassing.* | **go to jail/be sent to jail** *Grover got caught for not paying his taxes and went to jail.* | **jail sentence/term** (=how long someone has to spend in jail) *The riots ended with long jail terms for 338 mobsters.*

penitentiary /ˌpenɪ̣ˈtenʃəri/ [n C] American a large prison for people who are guilty of serious crimes: *The murderer served 10 years at the penitentiary in Stillwater.* | *the Ohio State penitentiary* | *the abandoned federal penitentiary on Alcatraz Island*

cell /sel/ [n C] a small room in a prison or police station, where someone is kept as a punishment: *Conditions were poor, and there were several prisoners to one cell.* | **prison/jail cell** *The prison cells have doors of heavy steel.*

detention centre British /**detention center** American /dɪˈtenʃən ˌsentəʳ/ [n C] a place where young people who have done something illegal are kept, because they are too young to go to prison: *Kevin, who had been abandoned by his mother, had been in and out of detention centres all his life.* | *a juvenile detention center*

2 to put someone in prison as a punishment

- put sb in prison/jail
- lock up
- throw sb in jail
- jail
- imprison
- incarcerate
- intern

put sb in prison/jail ALSO **send sb to prison/jail** /ˌpʊt (sb) ɪn ˈprɪzən, ˈdʒeɪl, ˌsend (sb) tə ˈprɪzən, ˈdʒeɪl/ [v phrase] to officially order someone to be taken to prison and kept there: *Eventually, her attacker was caught and put in prison.* | *The judge sent him to jail for seven years.*

lock up /ˌlɒk ˈʌp‖ˌlɑːk-/ [phr v T] informal to put someone in prison – use this especially when you think that someone deserves to be in prison **lock sb up** *Rapists deserve to be locked up for the rest of their lives.* | **lock up sb** *It costs $23,000 a year to lock up an adult.* | *Locking up more criminals has helped to reduce the crime rate and produce safer streets.*

throw sb in jail /ˌθrəʊ (sb) ɪn ˈdʒeɪl/ [v phrase] to put someone in prison – use this especially when you think that someone does not deserve to be in prison: *The court's decision suggests that it is OK to throw pregnant women in jail just because they are addicted.* | *When they called for free elections, the government threw them all in jail.*

jail /dʒeɪl/ [v T usually in passive] to put someone in prison for a fixed period of time – used especially in newspaper reports: *Many of the group's leaders have now been jailed.* | **be jailed for (doing) sth** *About 5000 people have been jailed for crimes of terrorism or treason since 1992.* | *Marco was arrested and jailed for accepting bribes from drug dealers.*

imprison /ɪmˈprɪzən/ [v T usually in passive] formal to put someone in prison – use this especially when you think the punishment is wrong or unfair: *Thousands of civilians were arrested, imprisoned and killed* | **be imprisoned for (doing) sth** *Two of the boys have been imprisoned for theft.* | *The priest had been imprisoned for preaching the gospel.* —**imprisonment** [n U] *The maximum penalty is three years' imprisonment.* | *It was a very sad case of false imprisonment.*

incarcerate /ɪnˈkɑːʳsəreɪt/ [v T usually in passive] to put someone in prison – used in newspapers, television etc and in formal contexts: *Carter spent 19 years incarcerated in New Jersey on murder charges.* | *There are too many people on death row who are innocent of the crimes for which they are incarcerated.* —**incarceration** /ɪnˌkɑːʳsəˈreɪʃən/ [n U] *Anyone speaking out against the regime faced death or incarceration.*

intern /ɪnˈtɜːʳn/ [v T usually in passive] to put someone, especially someone from another country, in prison during a war, because they are thought to be dangerous: *The French soldiers, who had surrendered without fighting, were interned in Hanoi.* | *Thousands died. And thousands were interned in forced labour camps.* —**internment** [n U] *One of the subjects for debate was the government's power of internment without trial.*

3 to force someone to stay in a place as a prisoner

- keep
- take sb hostage
- hold
- confine
- shut up

keep /kiːp/ [v T] to force someone to stay in a place, as if they were a prisoner: *West had abducted the young girl and kept her in his basement for 10 days.* | **keep sb prisoner** *Police think that the woman may have been kept prisoner for the twenty four hours before she was murdered.*

take sb hostage /ˌteɪk (sb) ˈhɒstɪdʒ‖-ˈhɑː-/ [v phrase] if an enemy or group of criminals **takes** someone **hostage**, they keep that person as a prisoner, and threaten to kill or injure them unless they get what they want: *The government is concerned that British troops might be taken hostage by guerrillas.* | *A band of human rights activists stormed the embassy and took several people hostage.*

hold /həʊld/ [v T] to keep someone in a place and not allow them to leave – used especially in news reports: *Police are holding two men in connection with the robbery.* | **hold sb prisoner/hostage/captive** *Several tourists were being held captive by rebels in Kashmir.* | *Militant prisoners held 24 guards hostage on Friday, as jail unrest spread throughout the country.*

confine /kənˈfaɪn/ [v T usually in passive] to make someone stay in a very small place, with the result that their freedom or movements are restricted **confine sb to sth** *The judge has confined the jury to their hotel until after the verdict.* | *All the illegal immigrants were confined to a small island in the harbour.* | **be confined in** *Brett was eventually confined in a psychiatric hospital, where he committed suicide.* —**confinement** [n U] *Many women spent a lifetime of virtual confinement in the home.* | **solitary confinement** (=when a prisoner is kept completely alone for a period of time) *Pratt spent the first eight years of his prison sentence in solitary confinement.*

shut up /ˌʃʌt ˈʌp/ [phr v T usually in passive] informal to put or keep someone in a place so that they are no longer free **shut sb up** *According to the legend, Acrisius built an underground house for his daughter. Here he shut her up and guarded her.* | *The lawyer claimed that his client had been shut up in a prison cell for hours, when there was no legal reason to keep him.*

4 to be in prison as a punishment

- be in prison/jail
- be inside
- do time
- serve

be in prison/jail /biː ɪn ˈprɪzən, ˈdʒeɪl/ [v phrase] *Both her sons are now in jail.* | *The two Irishmen were in prison for five years before they were found to be innocent.*

be inside /biː ɪnˈsaɪd/ [v phrase] informal to be in prison – used especially by someone who has been in prison and is talking about their experience: *'When I was inside,' said Jimmy. 'I really learned how to look after myself.'*

do time /ˌduː ˈtaɪm/ [v phrase] informal to be in prison for a period of time as a punishment for a crime: *Sid's wife ran off with another man while he was doing time.* | **+ for** *None of us knew that Greg had done time for stealing cars.*

serve /sɜːʳv/ [v T] to spend a period of time in prison, especially the period that a judge has said you must spend there **serve 3 years/6 months etc (for sth)** *Holt is currently serving five years for child abduction.* | **serve time (for sth)** *Both the brothers had criminal records and had served time for robbery.* | **serve time in prison/jail** *She met Schmidt while serving time in prison for drug possession.* | **serve a sentence** *Fowler was released after serving two-thirds of his sentence.*

5 to be kept in a place by the police

- be in custody
- be under arrest
- be detained

be in custody /biː ɪn ˈkʌstədi/ [v phrase] if someone who the police think is guilty of a crime **is in custody**, they are kept in prison until it is time for them to be judged in a law court: *The twenty-seven militants now in custody were arrested in raids last month.* | **be in police custody** *An inquiry has been launched following the death of a man in police custody.* | **be held in custody** *A woman is being held in custody in connection with the murder.* | **be remanded in custody** British (=be sent back to prison from a court until your trial) *Naylor was remanded in custody by Huyton magistrates until June 17th.*

be under arrest /biː ˌʌndər əˈrest/ [v phrase] if someone **is under arrest**, the police are keeping them guarded because they think they are guilty of a crime: *Police confirmed last night that Mr Joshi is under arrest.* | **+ for** *I'm afraid your son is under arrest for theft.*

be detained /biː dɪˈteɪnd/ [v phrase] to be kept somewhere by the police or army so that you cannot leave, and especially so that they can ask you questions: *On Tuesday last week, Finnegan was detained and questioned by fraud squad officers.* | **+ for** *He was detained for questioning about the terrorist attacks.*

6 someone who is in prison as a punishment for a crime

- prisoner
- convict
- inmate

prisoner /ˈprɪzənəʳ/ [n C] someone who is kept in prison as a punishment: *The prisoners are allowed an hour's exercise every day.* | **political prisoner** (=someone who is a prisoner because of their political beliefs) *Thousands of political prisoners remain imprisoned, frequently as a result of unfair trials.*

convict /ˈkɒnvɪkt‖ˈkɑːn-/ [n C] someone who has been proved guilty of a crime and has been sent to prison: *Sakhalin was an island where convicts were sent, 700 miles from Khabarovsk.* | **ex-convict** (=someone who used to be in prison) *Stubbs was an ex-convict who got a job as a security guard.* | **an escaped convict** (=someone who has escaped from prison) *There was a report on the news about an escaped convict.*

inmate /ˈɪnmeɪt/ [n C] a prisoner in a particular prison: *More than half the inmates were there for some sort of violent crime.* | **prison inmate** *The number of prison inmates has been increasing in recent years.*

7 someone who is kept in a place when they do not want to be there

- prisoner
- prisoner of war/POW
- captive
- hostage
- detainee

prisoner /ˈprɪzənəʳ/ [n C] *My parents were very strict. Sometimes I felt like a prisoner in my own home.* | *It's a science fiction story about people being taken to another planet as prisoners.* | **hold/keep sb prisoner** *Mann was held prisoner in the back of the Chevrolet and told she was going to be killed.*

prisoner of war/POW /ˌprɪzənər əv ˈwɔːʳ, ˌpiː əʊ ˈdʌbəljuː/ [n C] a soldier etc who is caught by the enemy during a war and kept as a prisoner: *There were general codes covering such matters as the treatment of prisoners of war.* | *a POW camp*

captive /ˈkæptɪv/ [n C] someone who is kept in a place illegally, especially in a war – used especially in literature: *All the captives were kept in a darkened room with their hands tied.* | *The rebels promised to release their captives unharmed if the government did as they said.*

hostage /ˈhɒstɪdʒ‖ˈhɑː-/ [n C] someone who is kept as a prisoner by an enemy country or organization, and is threatened with death or injury if that person's government or organization does not do what the enemy wants: *The terrorists say that they will kill the hostages if we don't agree to their demands.* | *An attempt to rescue the American hostages ended in disaster when a helicopter crashed.* | **take sb hostage** (=make someone your hostage) *The medical team were captured and taken hostage.* | **hold sb hostage** (=keep someone in a place as your hostage) *A British journalist was held hostage for over four years.*

detainee /ˌdiːteɪˈniː/ [n C] someone who is being kept in a place by the police while they are waiting to go to court, or so that the police can ask them questions about something illegal they may have done: *The government has ordered the trial of all detainees within six months.* | *According to a recent report, many detainees claim that police have mistreated them.*

8 when someone is kept in a place they do not want to be in

- captivity
- imprisonment
- detention

captivity /kæpˈtɪvəti/ [n U] *In his book, he describes what life was like during his long captivity.* | **in captivity** *The industrialist, who was captured on November 24th, was freed after 84 days in captivity.* | **be held/kept in captivity** *Folkes says that he was held in captivity for over a year.*

imprisonment /ɪmˈprɪzənmənt/ [n U] the state of being kept as a prisoner, especially as punishment for a crime: *Johnson was sentenced to three years' imprisonment for causing a riot.* | **life imprisonment** *Many women believe that the punishment for rape should be life imprisonment.*

detention /dɪˈtenʃən/ [n U] especially British when someone is kept in a place such as a prison because they may have done something illegal: *Cases of detention without trial were common in the last century.* | *Ormerod, aged 19, was sentenced to nine months' detention for possessing and supplying cannabis.* | **be held/kept in detention** *Marik, who* *had been held in detention for over a year, was eventually found not guilty.* | **release sb from detention** *Mrs Davis was released from detention yesterday and all charges have been dropped.*

9 the period of time that someone must spend in prison

- sentence

sentence /ˈsentəns/ [n C] the period of time that a judge decides that someone should spend in prison: *Belfast Appeal Court increased his sentence from five to nine years.* | **serve a sentence (for sth)** *He was recently freed after serving a sentence for leading anti-government riots.* | **serve a 2-year/10-year etc sentence** *Perrault is serving a 15-year sentence for fraud and tax evasion.* | **prison/jail sentence** *Moore began an eighteen-month prison sentence in November.* | **life sentence** (=when someone is in prison for the rest of their life) *Hailey is serving a life sentence, and is reported to be in poor health.* | **death sentence** (=when a judge says that a criminal's punishment is death) *If found guilty of first-degree murder, Bangham could face the death sentence.* —**sentence** [v T] *The judge said that his was a very serious crime, and sentenced him to eight years in prison.* | *60 prisoners have been sentenced to death in political trials.*

private

WHAT'S HERE

- **private and personal** see **1 to 6**
- **private/non-government** see **7 to 8**

private and personal

RELATED WORDS

opposite: **public**

- *see also* **secret**

1 private thoughts and feelings

- private
- secret
- intimate
- personal
- innermost

private /ˈpraɪvɪ̈t/ [adj] not for other people to know about: *We all have our private dreams, fantasies and secrets.* | *Guy had to obey his superiors, no matter what his private thoughts on the matter.* | *Brian had an irritating habit of saying, 'It'll be fine!', whenever she mentioned any of her private fears.* | **keep sth private** *Clarence refused to comment on the state of his marriage, saying, it 'is a private matter which we'd like to keep private.'* —**privately** [adv] *Simon seemed confident, but privately he grew increasingly anxious.*

secret /ˈsiːkrɪ̈t/ [adj] your **secret** thoughts and feelings are ones that you never show and never tell anyone else about: *I had a secret ambition to return to politics.* | **secret hopes/fears/desires etc** *Psychologists say that dreams can reveal our secret desires.* | *Williams' diaries reveal all his secret hopes and fears.* —**secretly** [adv] *She said nothing, though she secretly admired his courage.*

intimate /ˈɪntɪ̈mɪ̈t/ [adj] very private, and usually concerned with your relationships, sexual feelings etc: *Some people see nothing wrong with appearing on a TV show, and revealing their most intimate thoughts.* | *They held hands, walked along the beach, and shared intimate secrets.* | **intimate details** *You do not expect to see the most intimate details of your marriage splashed across the pages of the newspapers.*

personal /ˈpɜːʳsənəl/ [adj] your **personal** thoughts and feelings are ones that you feel deeply, and do not usually tell other people about: *I'm not going to tell you that – it's personal!* | **personal feelings/thoughts/problems** *She felt her problems were too personal to talk about.* | *In those days it was socially unacceptable for men to cry in public, or to express their personal feelings.*

innermost /ˈɪnəʳməʊst/ [adj only before noun] **innermost feelings/thoughts/secrets/desires etc** feelings, thoughts etc that are very important to you, but that you do not like to talk to other people about: *He's not the kind of person to reveal his innermost secrets, even to his closest friends.* | *She works with emotionally disturbed people, teaching them to express their innermost feelings through poetry.*

2 private conversations and letters

- private
- personal
- intimate

private /ˈpraɪvɪ̈t/ [adj] between yourself and another person, and not to be listened to or seen by anyone else: *He keeps his private papers locked away in the top drawer of his desk.* | *You shouldn't be listening to a private conversation!* | *The book contains extracts from his diary and private letters.*

personal /ˈpɜːʳsənəl/ [adj] **personal** letters and papers concern only yourself and are not for other people to read: *I'm sorry but my diary is personal. I don't let anyone else read it.* | *There was a letter on Sarah's desk marked 'personal'.*

intimate /ˈɪntɪ̈mɪ̈t/ [adj] **intimate** conversations etc are very private and usually concerned with your relationships, sexual feelings etc: *Some of the author's intimate correspondence was published after her death.* | *I saw that Brian was having an intimate conversation with an attractive young woman, and so I left quietly.*

3 not connected with work or public life

- private/personal
- domestic

private/personal /ˈpraɪvɪ̈t, ˈpɜːʳsənəl/ [adj] use this about things that are not connected with your work, which only concern you, your family, or close friends: *The senator's relationship with her family is a private matter – why put it on the front page of The Post?* | **private/personal life** *The newspapers are full of stories about the private lives of famous people.* | *She had worked with Bill for 5 years, but she knew nothing of his personal life.* | **personal relationship** *Dave was very successful in business, but always had problems in his personal relationships.* | **personal call/phone call/letter** *If you must make personal phone calls at work, please keep them short.* | **personal problem** *There are counsellors at the college to help students with personal problems.*

domestic /dəˈmestɪk/ [adj] concerning your life at home, especially with your family, and not your business or work: *Domestic problems are affecting his work.* | *History books do not tell us much about the domestic lives of our ancestors.* | *It can be diffi-*

cult for people with domestic responsibilities to work late at night.

4 when you are alone and other people cannot hear or see you

- privacy
- private
- in private

privacy /ˈprɪvəsi, ˈpraɪ-‖ˈpraɪ-/ [n U] when you are able to be alone, and not be heard or seen by other people: *The problem with open plan offices is that you don't have any privacy.* | *The condo was beautiful, and they had plenty of privacy, with a hot tub in a little private garden.* | **respect sb's privacy** (=let someone have some privacy) *The press has been asked to respect the privacy of the Royal Family during this very difficult time.* | **invade sb's privacy** (=to upset or annoy someone by not allowing them to have privacy) *Her husband's colleagues kept coming to the house, invading her privacy, and expecting food and drinks.* | **in the privacy of your own room/home etc** (=in a place where you can have some privacy) *I waited until I was in the privacy of my own room before I opened the letter.*

private /ˈpraɪvᵻt/ [adj] a **private** place is one in which you can be alone without anyone hearing you or seeing what you are doing: *I've got something to tell you. Can we go somewhere private?* | *The garden's very private – it's not overlooked by anyone.*

in private /ɪn ˈpraɪvᵻt/ [adv] if you do something **in private**, you do it when other people are not present: *Can I speak to you in private for a minute?*

5 unwilling to talk to other people about yourself

- private
- keep yourself to yourself

private /ˈpraɪvᵻt/ [adj only before noun] a **private** person is one who likes being alone and does not talk much about their thoughts or feelings: *Lou's a very private person – I don't know anything about her family.* | *Brando is a private man who almost never gives interviews to the press.*

keep yourself to yourself British **/keep to yourself** American /kiːp jɔːʳˌself tə jɔːʳˈself, ˌkiːp tə jɔːʳˈself/ [v phrase not usually in progressive] to not spend much time with other people and not talk much with other people, especially about your personal feelings or opinions: *Mrs Jackson, a widow who kept herself to herself, lived in the flat above.* | *Until he got used to his new school, Davy kept to himself and almost never spoke to the other children.*

6 what you say to tell someone that something is private

- it's none of your business/that's my business
- mind your own business

it's none of your business/that's my business /ɪts ˌnʌn əv jɔːʳ ˈbɪznᵻs, ðæts ˈmaɪ ˌbɪznᵻs/ use this to tell someone, who has asked you about something private, that you think they have no right to ask you: *'I don't care what you think, and anyway it's none of your business,' she said rather rudely.* | *'Where did you get the money?' 'That's my business.'* | **it's none of your business what/where/how etc** *It's none of your business how much I earn.*

mind your own business /ˌmaɪnd jɔːr əʊn ˈbɪznᵻs/ say this when someone is asking questions about your private life that you do not want to answer: *'Where did you sleep last night?' 'Mind your own business.'* | *I wish you'd stop interfering and mind your own business.*

private/non-government

RELATED WORDS

opposite: — **public**

- *see also* **business**

7 not controlled by the government

- private
- commercial
- independent
- the private sector
- private enterprise/free enterprise

private /ˈpraɪvᵻt/ [adj usually before noun] a **private** school, hospital etc is one that is not owned by the government and that you must pay money to use: *Private hospitals can afford to pay much higher salaries than state-run hospitals.* | *The government plans to sell part of the railway network to private investors.* | *Do you think the teaching in private schools is better than in state schools?* —**privately** [adv] *privately educated* (=at a private school) *Journalists flew in on a privately chartered plane.*

commercial /kəˈmɜːʳʃəl/ [adj only before noun] **commercial TV/radio/channel** a television or radio company that gets its money from advertising: *Most European countries have a mixture of commercial and state-run television.* | *Denmark's first commercial channel went on air on June 1, 1987.* | *the most popular commercial radio station in London*

independent /ˌɪndᵻˈpendənt◂/ [adj] not owned or paid for by the government: *Robin worked for one of the largest independent television companies.* | *Local companies and industries have been helping independent schools by providing buildings and equipment.*

the private sector /ðə ˈpraɪvᵻt ˌsektəʳ/ [n phrase] all the industries and services that are not owned or paid for by the government: *The government is now turning to the private sector for alternative ways of dealing with the country's transportation problems.* | **private sector spending/housing/finance etc** *Private sector housing is just too expensive for low-income families in the city at the moment.*

private enterprise/free enterprise /ˌpraɪvᵻt ˈentəʳpraɪz, ˌfriː ˈentəʳpraɪz/ [n U] the economic system in which industries, factories etc are owned and controlled by private companies and not by the government: *Sweden has always had a mixture of private enterprise and state control in its economy.* | *Margaret Thatcher tried to encourage private enterprise by selling off Britain's nationalized industries.* | *Even in the United States, free enterprise is subject to government controls.*

8 to make a public company or organization private

- privatize

privatize /ˈpraɪvᵻtaɪz/ [v T] if a government **privatizes** a government-controlled industry, service, or company, it sells it to private owners, who then manage it for their own profit: *Hungary has been very* *keen to privatize its major industries, following the democratic reforms of 1988.* | *Employees of the Strathtay bus company, which has been privatized, are concerned that drivers are about to be made redundant.* —**privatized** [adj] *The government plans to introduce a privatized health system.* —**privatization** /ˌpraɪvᵊtaɪˈzeɪʃən‖-tə-/ [n U] *The recent privatization of bus services has led to escalating prices.*

probably

RELATED WORDS

- *see also* **maybe, possible, sure/not sure, expect**

1 when it is likely that something will happen or is true

- probably
- likely
- probable
- be a strong possibility
- it looks as if/it looks like
- may/could/might well
- be on the cards
- I suppose
- I should think
- I wouldn't be surprised

probably /ˈprɒbəbli‖ˈprɑː-/ [adv] when something will **probably** happen or is **probably** true: *'Where is she?' 'Probably in her room.'* | *We'll probably be shooting the movie on location in Europe.* | *Archaeologists think the temple was probably built in the 3rd century AD.* | *He wrote dozens of books, but this is probably his best-known novel.*

likely /ˈlaɪkli/ [adj] something that is **likely** will probably happen or is probably true: *The most likely result is a win for the Democrats.* | **+ to do sth** *The price of petrol is likely to rise again this year.* | **very likely** *The jury is very likely to believe he was in the apartment at the time of the crime.* | **sth seems likely** *A peace settlement now seems likely.* | **it is likely (that)** *It is likely that the girl knew her killer.*

probable /ˈprɒbəbəl‖ˈprɑː-/ [adj] formal likely to be true or likely to happen **it is/seems probable (that)** *It seems probable that the election will be held in May.* | **highly probable** (=when something will almost certainly happen) *Unless the government agrees to further talks, a strike seems highly probable.* | **probable cause** *The report states that the probable cause of death was a heart attack.* | **probable cost/result/outcome etc** *The project will go ahead, at a probable cost of $2.1 million.*

be a strong possibility /biː ə ˌstrɒŋ pɒsᵊˈbɪlᵊti‖-ˌstrɔːŋ pɑː-/ [v phrase] to be very likely: *The withdrawal of the allied forces is now a strong possibility.* | **+ (that)** *There is a strong possibility that both the murders were committed by one man.* | **+ of** *The weather forecast says that there's a strong possibility of snow.*

it looks as if/it looks like /ɪt ˈlʊks əz ɪf, ɪt ˈlʊks laɪk/ spoken say this when the present situation makes you think that something is likely to happen or likely to be true: *There aren't any taxis. It looks as if we'll have to walk.* | *Ted should be here by now. It looks like he's been delayed.* | **it looks like being** British *From the agenda, it looks like being a long meeting.*

may/could/might well /meɪ, kʊd, maɪt ˈwel/ [modal verb] if something **may well** happen or **may well** be true, it is fairly likely to happen or to be true: *Take an umbrella. It might well rain later on.* | *That's only my opinion. I could well be wrong.* | *The eruption of Santorini in 1470 BC may well have been heard as far away as Britain.* | **it may well be (that)** *It could well be that it is too late for us to reverse the effects of global warming.* | **sth may well be the case** *'Apparently, interest rates could rise again next month.' 'Yes, that might well be the case.'*

be on the cards British **/be in the cards** American /biː ɒn ðə ˈkɑːʳdz, biː ɪn ðə ˈkɑːʳdz/ [v phrase] use this to say that something is likely to happen because of the present situation: *They say that another recession is on the cards.* | *No one was surprised when they got a divorce. It had been on the cards for years.* | *I was hoping for a promotion, but it doesn't seem to be in the cards right now.*

I suppose ALSO **I guess** American /aɪ səˈpəʊz, aɪ ˈges/ spoken say this when you think something is likely to be true or likely to happen **+ (that)** *There was no reply when I phoned – I suppose she's still at work.* | *I suppose that they'll do some sightseeing while they're here.* | *I guess Kathy will want to bring her boyfriend.* | **I suppose so/I guess so** (=use this to answer a question) *'Is Bill coming too?' 'I suppose so.'* | *'If you don't pass the test, will you take it again?' 'I guess so.'*

I should think British **/I would think/guess** American /ˌaɪ ʃʌd ˈθɪŋk, ˌaɪ wʊd ˈθɪŋk, ˈges/ spoken say this when you know enough about a situation to think something is likely to be true or likely to happen: *The garden's about 100 metres long, I would guess.* | **+ (that)** *I should think she's about 24 or 25.* | *I would think that almost everyone could get here on a Saturday.* | **I should/would think so** *'Will the match still go ahead?' 'Yes, I should think so.'*

I wouldn't be surprised /aɪ ˌwʊdnt biː səʳˈpraɪzd/ spoken say this when you know enough about a situation to think that something is likely to happen or be true, especially something special or unusual **+ if** *You know, I wouldn't be surprised if they decided to get married.* | **+ to hear/see/find etc that** *I wouldn't be surprised to hear that she'd left that job by now.*

2 very likely to happen or be true

- very likely/more than likely
- very probably
- almost certain
- in all probability
- ten to one

very likely/more than likely /ˌveri ˈlaɪkli, ˌmɔːʳ ðən ˈlaɪkli/ [adj] *An early end to the dispute is now very likely.* | *'Do you think she's still in love with him?' 'More than likely.'* | *Victory for the German team now seems more than likely.* | **+ to do sth** *Snow is very likely to spread across the region by the afternoon.* | **it's very likely (that)** *It's very likely that he'll be late – he usually is.* —**very likely** [adv] *If you want a job done quickly, you'll very likely have to do it yourself.*

very probably /ˌveri ˈprɒbəbli‖-ˈprɑː-/ [adv] especially written *The number of dead will very probably reach 2,000 by the end of the day.* | *The disease is very probably transmitted in water.*

almost certain /ˌɔːlməʊst ˈsɜːʳtn/ [adj] extremely likely to happen or be true **it is almost certain (that)** *It is almost certain that the government will lose the next election.* | **+ to do sth** *Bartholomew's family is almost certain to appeal the court's decision.* —**almost certainly** [adv] *If you don't follow the instructions, it'll almost certainly go wrong.*

in all probability /ɪn ˌɔːl prɒbəˈbɪlᵊti‖-prɑː-/ [adv] very probably – use this when you have considered something and you are giving your opinion about it: *In all probability, parts of the church date from even* *earlier than the twelfth century.* | *She knew that, in all probability, he was seeing other women as well as herself.*

ten to one /ˌten tə ˈwʌn/ [adv] spoken say this when you think it is extremely likely that something will happen or has happened **(it's)ten to one (that)** *Stop worrying, Mum. Ten to one Liz has just gone round to a friend's house.* | *It's ten to one you'll get the job – you're perfect for it.*

3 when something will probably be good

- ought to be/should be
- promise to be

ought to be/should be /ˈɔːt tə biː, ˈʃʊd biː/ [v phrase] use this to say that you think something or someone will probably be good, because of what you know about them: *The party should be fun. There's going to be a group playing and there's lots of drink.* | *She has all the right experience, so she ought to make an excellent manager.*

promise to be /ˈprɒmɪ̈s tə biː‖ˈprɑː-/ [v phrase] especially written if something that has just started **promises to be** good, exciting etc, it is very likely to be good, exciting etc: *The day promised to be bright and warm.* | *For those lucky enough to have tickets to the sold-out event, it promises to be a great evening of music.*

4 when something bad is likely to happen

- be heading for
- be in for
- threaten
- threat

be heading for /biː ˈhedɪŋ fɔːʳ/ [v phrase] if someone **is heading for** an unpleasant situation, it is becoming more and more likely that this situation will actually happen: *I'm worried about Molly. She looks as if she's heading for a nervous breakdown.* | *There are fears that the company could be heading for closure, following a bad year.*

be in for /biː ˈɪn fɔːʳ/ [v phrase] if you say you **are in for** something unpleasant, it is almost certain to happen to you fairly soon: *It's pretty stormy! I think we're in for a rough flight.* | *If they think they're going to build a new motorway near here, they're in for a shock.*

threaten /ˈθretn/ [v T] if something **threatens** to cause an unpleasant situation, it seems likely that it will cause it **+ to do sth** *The dispute threatened to damage East–West relations.* | *Somalia was again crippled by a drought that threatened to kill hundreds of thousands more.* | **threaten sb/sth with sth** *Our rainforests are being threatened with destruction, and the consequences will be severe.*

threat /θret/ [n C] something that is a **threat** is likely to cause something unpleasant to happen **+ of** *The threat of inflation and high interest rates led to a wage freeze.* | *the threat of invasion* | **+ to** *After the floods, contaminated water was a serious threat to public health.* | **pose a threat (for)** *Global warming poses a serious threat for the future.*

5 to be likely to be successful

- have/stand a good chance
- be set to do sth
- be on course

have/stand a good chance /hæv, stænd ə ˌgʊd ˈtʃɑːns ‖-ˈtʃæns/ [v phrase not in progressive] *'Do you think he'll get the job?' 'Well, he certainly has a very good chance.'* | **have/stand a good chance of doing sth** *I think Bart's design stands a really good chance of winning the competition.*

be set to do sth /biː ˌset tə ˈduː (sth)/ [v phrase] to be very likely to be successful because of being well prepared or because the present situation is favourable: *The band's new album is set to become the biggest hit of the year.* | **look set to do sth** *Shares in the company look set to soar.*

be on course /biː ɒn ˈkɔːʳs/ [v phrase] to be likely to achieve something because there has already been some success **+ for** *The business is on course for record profits this year.* | **+ to do sth** *After three major victories, the Brazilian team seemed on course to win the cup.*

6 to be likely to do something surprising or bad

- be quite capable of
- I wouldn't put it past sb

be quite capable of /biː ˌkwaɪt ˈkeɪpəbəl ɒv/ [v phrase] use this when you think that someone is fairly likely to do something bad or surprising, because of what you know about their character: *She promised to come, but she's quite capable of forgetting.* | *Don't believe it! He's quite capable of lying!*

I wouldn't put it past sb /aɪ ˌwʊdnt pʊt ɪt ˈpɑːst (sb) ‖-ˈpæst-/ informal use this to say that you think a particular person is fairly likely to do the bad or stupid thing that you are mentioning: *'She wouldn't have read my e-mail, would she?' 'Well, I wouldn't put it past her.'* | **+ to do sth** *I wouldn't put it past Kevin to have borrowed the car without asking.*

7 how likely it is that something will happen

- likelihood
- probability
- prospect
- chances
- odds

likelihood /ˈlaɪklihʊd/ [n U] **+ of** *As you get older, the likelihood of illness increases.* | *Studies have shown that there is a greater likelihood of teenagers having car accidents.* | **+ (that)** *There is little likelihood that the number of college places will go up this year.*

probability /ˌprɒbəˈbɪlɪ̈ti‖ˌprɑː-/ [n U] how likely it is that something will happen – use this especially about situations where you can calculate fairly exactly how likely something is **+ of** *The probability of catching the disease from your partner is extremely low.* | *We must increase our efforts to reduce the probability of such an accident happening again.* | **+ (that)** *There is a 90% probability that the hurricane will hit the coast of Florida later today.* | **a strong probability** *There is a strong probability that the problem will recur if we do not deal with it now.*

prospect /ˈprɒspekt‖ˈprɑː-/ [n C/U] the chance that something you hope for will happen soon **+ for** *The prospects for peace are improving.* | **no/little prospect of (doing) sth** *He had no job and no prospect of getting one.* | **there is every prospect of sth** (=it is very likely) *There is every prospect of an economic recovery next year.*

chances /ˈtʃɑːnsɪ̈z‖ˈtʃæn-/ [n plural] how likely it is that something you hope for will actually happen **chances of (doing) sth** *The new treatment will increase her chances of survival.* | *For these men the* *chances of getting another job are not very high.* | **what are the chances ... ?** *What are the chances of that happening twice in one month?* | **chances are (that)** ... (=it is likely that) *If you eat a balanced, low-fat diet, chances are your arteries will be healthy.*

odds /ɒdz‖ɑːdz/ [n plural] how likely it is that something will happen, especially when this can be stated in numbers **odds in favour of** *The odds in favour of a win for the Russian team are around 10 to 1.* | **odds of** *If you are male, the odds are about 1 in 12 of being colourblind.* | **odds against** *The odds against being killed in a plane crash are very high.*

8 possible but not likely

- unlikely
- improbable
- doubtful
- remote

unlikely /ʌn'laɪkli/ [adj] something that is **unlikely** will probably not happen or is probably not true: *She might come with us, but it's fairly unlikely.* | **+ to do sth** *A small amount of the drug is unlikely to have any harmful effects.* | **it is unlikely (that)** *It is unlikely that anyone saw the attack.*

improbable /ɪm'prɒbəbəl‖-'prɑː-/ [adj not before noun] formal unlikely to happen or unlikely to be true **highly improbable** *Carter claims he paid $4000 for the papers, which seems highly improbable.* | *The new pay agreement makes further industrial action by the union highly improbable.* | **it is/seems improbable that** *It seems improbable that America's allies will oppose the proposed arms reduction.* —**improbability** /ɪm,prɒbə'bɪləti‖-,prɑː-/ [n U] *Because of the improbability of an attack, the army has pulled its forces back from the border..*

doubtful /'daʊtfəl/ [adj] very unlikely to be true or very unlikely to happen: *'Is Maddy coming tonight?' 'It's looking doubtful – she was really sick.'* | **it is doubtful that** *It's doubtful that we'll finish this tonight.*

remote /rɪ'məʊt/ [adj] extremely unlikely to happen: *The chances of such an accident happening again are very remote.* | *There is only a remote prospect of peace in the region.* | *There is a remote possibility the program could be halted, if funding were cut.*

9 when it is unlikely that there will be a good result

- little chance/hope/possibility/prospect
- not stand/have much chance of
- an outside chance

little chance/hope/possibility/prospect /,lɪtl 'tʃɑːns, 'həʊp, ,pɒsə'bɪləti, 'prɒspekt‖-'tʃæns, -,pɑːs-, -'prɑː-/ [n phrase] if there is **little chance/hope** etc of something happening, it is unlikely to happen, although you want it to happen: *There's little chance of the hostages being released.* | *There seemed little prospect of any great decrease in unemployment.* | *I see little hope of improvement in relations between our two countries.*

not stand/have much chance of /nɒt ,stænd, ,hæv mʌtʃ 'tʃɑːns ɒv‖-'tʃæns-/ [v phrase not in progressive] to be unlikely to succeed in doing something: *Students who cannot read by this point do not stand much chance of getting the help they need.* | *We weren't opposed to the plan, but we didn't think it had much chance of succeeding.*

an outside chance /,aʊtsaɪd 'tʃɑːns‖-'tʃæns/ [n singular] a very small possibility of being successful **have an outside chance of (doing) sth** *She lost the first two games of the tournament, but still has an outside chance of winning the cup.* | **there is an outside chance (that)** *There's still an outside chance that the FBI will find the man they are looking for.*

problem

RELATED WORDS

▸ *see also* **difficult, fault, solve**

1 something that causes difficulties

- problem
- difficulty
- trouble
- hassle
- complication
- hitch
- hiccup
- snag
- catch
- teething troubles/pains/problems

problem /'prɒbləm‖'prɑː-/ [n C] a bad situation that must be dealt with, because it is causing harm or inconvenience, or it is stopping you from doing what you want to do **have a problem** *If you have any problems, give me a call.* | **+ with** *Sue's had a lot of problems with her neighbours recently.* | **cause/create problems** *The new traffic system is causing problems for everyone.* | **solve a problem** (=find a way to deal with it) *Scientists still have not solved the problem of what to do with nuclear waste.* | **the drug/crime etc problem** *Federal laws have almost no effect on the crime problem that concerns most people – crime on the streets.* | **+ of** *The problem of substance abuse in high school is widespread.* | **big/serious problem** *Our biggest problem is lack of money.* | *Whiteflies can be a serious problem that affects produce grown in California and other states.*

difficulty /'dɪfɪkəlti/ [n C usually plural/U] a problem that makes it more difficult to do something that you are trying to do: *I don't expect major difficulties, although there are still differences to be worked out.* | **+ with** *The main difficulty with this method is that it takes twice as long.* | **have difficulty with (doing) sth** *Youngsters may have difficulty applying the paint because of its thin consistency.* | **get into difficulty/difficulties** (=start to have problems in a situation) *Credit cards make it extremely easy to get into difficulty with debt.* | **economic/financial difficulty** *The nation faces severe economic difficulties.* | **language/technical/legal etc difficulty** *Police officers in most Californian cities need to be able to cope with language difficulties and cultural differences.* | **face/experience difficulty** *Some parents experienced difficulty when they tried to move their children to other schools.* | **be in difficulty/difficulties** (=be in a situation that has problems) *Manchester United won easily, and never seemed to be in any difficulty.* | **+ of doing sth** *The difficulties of counting whales makes most population figures extremely unreliable.*

trouble /'trʌbəl/ [n C/U] a problem or several problems that make something difficult, spoil your plans etc: *The trouble was caused by a loose connection in the fuse box.* | *If you used the same tape later and had no sound trouble, the problem is in the video recorder, not the tape.* | **+ with** *The pilot reported trouble with both engines.* | **have trouble** *We have had a lot of trouble with the car this year.* | **have trouble doing sth** *Norris had trouble finding work and is still unemployed.* | **cause trouble** *Snow and freezing temperatures caused trouble at many airports.* | **the trouble with sth** (=the one feature of something that is a problem) *The trouble with lasagne is that it takes so long to make.*

hassle /ˈhæsəl/ [n C/U] informal a problem or a series of problems that are annoying because they involve a lot of work, arguing, inconvenience etc: *The airline doesn't make seat assignments, which can be a hassle for travelers, but it saves money.* | *Shopping by mail avoids the hassles of crowded stores at Christmastime.* | **legal/bureaucratic etc hassles** *Byrd says he settled the claim to avoid legal hassles.* | **it's too much hassle** *I don't want to organize a big party – it's too much hassle.*

complication /ˌkɒmpləˈkeɪʃən‖ˌkɑːm-/ [n C] an additional problem that makes a situation even harder to deal with than it already is: *One complication is that the meals also need to be suitable for children of Islamic or Jewish faiths.* | *Legal and financial complications have made it impossible for the two companies to complete the deal on time.*

hitch /hɪtʃ/ [n C] a small problem within a long process: *The plan has a hitch: drilling holes for the owls in the trees will kill the trees.* | **without a hitch** (=without any problems) *The parade went off without a hitch, despite concern about protestors.* | *The shuttle landed without a hitch at Edwards Air Force Base.* | **there's a hitch** *There was a hitch – about half the employees did not want to move to a different city.* | **+ in** *Nelson refused to comment on reports of a last-minute hitch in the negotiations.* | **technical hitch** *There's been a slight technical hitch, so we'll have to postpone the video until later.*

hiccup /ˈhɪkʌp, -kəp/ [n C] a small problem which is not very important compared to other things: *There was a slight hiccup when I couldn't find my car keys, but finally we set off.* | *The airline industry's troubles are a mere hiccup in an otherwise upward growth trend.*

snag /snæg/ [n C] a small problem or disadvantage in something which is mainly good and satisfactory: *The cleanup effort was delayed for a few days by some technical snags and equipment problems.* | **hit a snag/run into a snag** *The case hit a snag in October when the judge handling it had to be replaced.* | **last-minute snag** *The House worked out some last-minute snags in the legislation.*

catch /kætʃ/ [n singular] a hidden problem or disadvantage in an offer that seems very good – use this especially when you think the problem has been deliberately hidden to trick people **there's a catch** *You get free meals and accommodation, but there's a catch – you have to look after the children.* | **with a catch** *Many of the best deals come with a catch: they are only good through early summer.* | **the catch is (that)** *The catch is that you can't enter the contest unless you have spent $50 in the store.*

teething troubles/pains/problems /ˈtiːðɪŋ ˌtrʌbəlz, ˌpeɪns, ˌprɒbləmz‖-ˌprɑː-/ [n plural] British small problems that a new company, product, system etc has at the beginning: *After a few teething troubles, the new car worked perfectly.* | *The disagreement was just one of the teething problems of the partnership.*

2 something that makes you feel worried or unhappy

- problem
- troubles

problem /ˈprɒbləm‖ˈprɑː-/ [n C usually plural] something that happens in your life that makes you feel worried, unhappy, or ill **have a problem** *Bill isn't sleeping well – I think he's having problems at school.* | **personal problems** *She's had a lot of personal problems – her mother died when she was eight.* | **health problems** *Tannen retired early due to health problems.*

troubles /ˈtrʌbəlz/ [n plural] things that make you feel worried and unhappy, especially problems that have continued for a long time: *It's nice to talk to someone about your troubles.* | *Parents can get wrapped up in their own troubles, and not notice how it's affecting their children.*

3 a problem that stops you from making progress

- setback
- hurdle
- stumbling block
- hindrance
- obstacle

setback /ˈsetbæk/ [n C] something that happens which stops you making progress or which makes things worse than they were before: *Arafat has survived crises, setbacks, and challenges to his leadership.* | **have/suffer a setback** *The peace talks have suffered a series of setbacks.* | **+ for** *The court's decision was a major setback for Bradley.* | **+ in** *Manning suffered a setback in his battle against alcoholism.* | **serious/major/big setback** *The two losses are a serious setback for the team's playoff hopes.* | **political/economic/legal etc setback** *The decision is a legal setback for the steel company.* | **business/election etc setback** *He had been depressed over a number of business setbacks.*

hurdle /ˈhɜːʳdl/ [n C] a problem or difficulty that must be dealt with before you can do or achieve something else: *The main hurdle at present is getting the council's permission.* | **legal/bureaucratic/political etc hurdle** *Women face a lot of legal hurdles trying to prove sexual harassment.* | *There are lots of bureaucratic hurdles to deal with when adopting a child.* | **+ for** *Requiring school uniforms can be a financial hurdle for the poor.* | **clear/pass a hurdle** *The bill has cleared all the hurdles before it and will soon become law.*

stumbling block /ˈstʌmblɪŋ blɒk‖-blɑːk/ [n C] a fact or situation that will make it very difficult for something to be achieved: *Negotiations with management broke off Tuesday, with wage proposals the stumbling block.* | **+ to** *Each side has accused the others of creating stumbling blocks to peace.* | **+ for** *Mortgage interest rates have fallen, but large down payments remain a stumbling block for house buyers.*

hindrance /ˈhɪndrəns/ [n C/U] something that makes it very difficult for you to do what you are trying to do: *America's top golfers played well despite the hindrance of early morning mist.* | *I concentrated on my career, feeling that a family would be a hindrance.* | **be a hindrance to** *The country's poor infrastructure is a major hindrance to importers.* | *The biggest hindrance to economic reform has been the lack of access to U.S. markets.* | **without hindrance** *Travelers can move through the country without hindrance.* | **more of a hindrance than a help** (=causing more problems than there would be otherwise) *The girls wanted to set the table, but they were more of a hindrance than a help.*

obstacle /ˈɒbstəkəl‖ˈɑːb-/ [n C] a difficult problem that stops someone or something making progress or developing: *The deal should go through, but there are several legal obstacles to overcome first.* | *There are a number of obstacles in the way of a lasting peace settlement.* | **+ to** *There's no reason why the fact of being a parent should be an obstacle to women's career progression.*

4 an extremely difficult or complicated problem

- dilemma
- catch-22
- no-win situation
- a chicken-and-egg problem/situation/ dilemma
- vicious circle

dilemma /dǝ̇'lemə, daɪ-/ [n C] a situation in which it is very difficult to decide what to do, because all the choices seem equally good or equally bad: *It is a common dilemma: Should you stay where you have friends and family, or take that good job in a far-away city?* | **face a dilemma** *With a child on each opposing team, Dad was faced with a dilemma: which supporters should he sit with?* | **ethical dilemma** *Writers are debating the ethical dilemma raised by the parents who did not want their Siamese twins separated.*

catch-22 /ˌkætʃ twenti 'tu:/ [n U] a situation in which you cannot do one thing until you do another thing, but you cannot do that thing until you do the first thing, with the result that you can do neither: *It's catch-22 – she can't get a job unless she has experience, and she can't get experience unless she has a job.* | **a catch-22 situation** *It's a catch-22 situation: The project won't receive government money until it is shown to be successful, but it cannot be successful without adequate funds.*

no-win situation /ˌnəʊ 'wɪn sɪtʃuˌeɪʃən/ [n singular] a situation in which something bad will happen whatever you decide to do: *It's a no-win situation – if I tell him, he'll be upset, but if I don't he'll be mad at me for not telling him.* | *Hospitals are in a no-win situation, since protecting patients' privacy may conflict with protecting the health of doctors, nurses, and other hospital workers.*

a chicken-and-egg problem/situation/ dilemma /ə ˌtʃɪkǝ̇n ənd 'eg ˌprɒbləm, sɪtʃuˌeɪʃən, dǝ̇ˌleməǁ-ˌprɑ:-/ [n phrase] a difficult situation in which you do not know which of two things was the cause of the other and which was the result, because neither could exist if the other did not: *We all hate lawyers, but they're in business because so many people sue each other: it's a classic chicken-and-egg situation.* | *The airport faces a chicken-and-egg dilemma: Airlines won't add more flights unless there is more demand, and there won't be more demand until there are more flights.*

vicious circle /ˌvɪʃəs 'sɜ:ʳkəl/ [n singular] a situation in which one problem causes another problem, that then causes the first problem again, so that the whole process continues to be repeated: *Many people who diet put on even more weight when they stop, creating a vicious circle.* | *More and more teenagers are caught in a vicious circle of drug addiction and crime.*

5 full of problems

- problematic
- fraught with problems/ difficulties
- minefield
- can of worms

problematic /ˌprɒblə'mætɪk◂ǁˌprɑ:-/ [adj] full of problems and difficult to deal with: *It is important to understand the problematic nature of historical evidence.* | *The new salary scale remains a problematic area.* | **highly problematic** *The Foreign Minister said that relations between the two countries are 'highly problematic'.*

fraught with problems/difficulties /ˌfrɔ:t wɪð 'prɒbləms, 'dɪfɪkəltizǁ-'prɑ:-/ [adj phrase] use this about an activity or plan that is full of unexpected problems which make it very difficult: *The preparations for the wedding were fraught with difficulties, but finally everything went well.* | *Legalization of drugs would be fraught with problems, but the 'war on drugs' causes problems too.*

minefield /'maɪnfi:ld/ [n singular] an activity or subject where you have to be very careful, because it is full of hidden problems and risks, so that it is very easy to make mistakes or upset people: *House-buying can be a minefield – you need a good lawyer.* | *Mozart's music seems so danceable, but most choreographers regard it as a minefield.*

can of worms /ˌkæn əv 'wɜ:ʳmz/ [n phrase] informal a situation or subject which at first seems to be simple and easy to deal with, but is full of complicated problems for anyone who gets involved with it: *Census questions about race are a pretty big can of worms.* | **open up a can of worms** (=suddenly find that you have to deal with a lot of difficult and unexpected problems) *The government opened up a can of worms when it decided to reorganize the education system.*

6 to have a problem

- have a problem
- have trouble/difficulty
- be in trouble
- have a hard time
- be faced with
- be up against
- come up against
- encounter
- run into problems/ difficulties
- have a lot on your plate

have a problem /ˌhæv ə 'prɒbləmǁ-'prɑ:-/ [v phrase] *If you have any problems, just come and ask me.* | *I had a few problems getting the copier to work.* | **+ with** *I'm having a bit of a problem with my dishwasher.* | *One landowner says he has never had any problems with hikers crossing his property.* | *Jane can be quite difficult to get on with – I've had one or two problems with her in the past.*

have trouble/difficulty /hæv 'trʌbəl, 'dɪfɪkəlti/ [v phrase] to have problems that make it more difficult to do something: *You look as if you're having trouble – do you want any help?* | **+ with** *I had some trouble with the car this morning.* | *She's having a little difficulty with her spelling.* | **have trouble/difficulty doing sth** *He had a lot of trouble finding a job.* | *The child was having difficulty breathing.*

be in trouble /bi: ɪn 'trʌbəl/ [v phrase] to have serious problems: *It's clear from these figures that the company is in trouble.* | *When someone's in trouble it's natural to try and help them.* | **get into trouble** (=start having serious problems) *I took out a loan but got into trouble when I lost my job.* | **in deep/serious/big trouble** (=have very serious problems) *Consular officers can help and advise you if you are in any serious trouble while abroad.*

have a hard time /hæv ə ˌhɑ:ʳd 'taɪm/ [v phrase] to have a lot of problems or a lot of difficulty doing something: *Premature babies have a hard time even under the best of circumstances.* | **have a hard time doing sth** *A lot of people are having a hard time making ends meet.* | *Anyone calling the 202 area code this weekend had a hard time getting through.*

be faced with /bi: 'feɪst wɪð/ [v phrase] to have a problem, a difficult choice, or the possibility of something bad happening soon: *We are often faced with dilemmas or problems which have no easy* *answers.* | *Manufacturing industries are faced with decreasing productivity and increasing international competition.* | *When faced with an unfamiliar word, good readers are able to make guesses based on the meaning and structure of the sentence.*

be up against /biː 'ʌp əgenst/ [v phrase] to have a difficult problem or opponent that you must deal with or fight against: *The company is up against tough competition from abroad.* | *When you're surfing and get hit by a wave, it's a reminder of what you're up against.* | *In the semi-finals he will be up against one of the best players in the game.*

come up against /ˌkʌm 'ʌp əgenst/ [v phrase] to start having problems or difficulties that you have to deal with: *Older people applying for jobs come up against an age barrier.* | *The committee found itself coming up against the prejudices of many staff when it tried to introduce new working practices.*

encounter /ɪn'kaʊntəʳ/ [v T] to experience problems, difficulties, or opposition while you are trying to do something: *Drivers on the M25 are likely to encounter fog and black ice tonight.* | *Many of the children encountered some difficulty in learning the material.* | *The government has encountered strong opposition over its plans to build a new airport.*

run into problems/difficulties /ˌrʌn ɪntə 'prɒbləmz, 'dɪfɪkəltiz‖-'prɑː-/ [v phrase] to unexpectedly start having problems while you are doing something: *The corporation has run into serious financial problems.* | *Our staff will be happy to answer your questions should you run into difficulties installing the equipment yourself.*

have a lot on your plate /hæv ə ˌlɒt ɒn jɔːʳ 'pleɪt‖-ˌlɑːt-/ [v phrase not in progressive] informal to have a lot of difficult problems to deal with or a lot of things to worry about: *Don't bother your mother – she's got a lot on her plate at the moment.* | *Susan's had a lot on her plate recently, what with the car accident and everything.*

7 to be in a very difficult situation

- be in a fix
- be in a tight spot/corner
- be in a mess/be a mess
- be in a difficult/awkward position
- be in an impossible position
- be in a quandary
- be in dire straits
- it's one thing after another

be in a fix /biː ɪn ə 'fɪks/ [v phrase] informal to be in a difficult situation and not know what to do: *The team's owner is in a fix – he's spent a lot to improve the stadium, but ticket sales are still declining.* | *Wyck's business consists of helping, for a fee, computer owners who are in a technical fix.*

be in a tight spot/corner /biː ɪn ə ˌtaɪt 'spɒt, 'kɔːʳnəʳ‖-'spɑːt-/ [v phrase] to be in a very difficult or dangerous situation, when there is very little you can do to get out of it: *A mobile phone lets you reach help when you're in a tight spot.* | *O'Neill had been in tight corners before, but never as tight as this one.* | **put sb in a tight spot** (=give someone a difficult problem) *Losing his job put them in a tight spot financially.*

be in a mess/be a mess /biː ɪn ə 'mes, biː ə 'mes/ [v phrase] to have so many problems that there is not much hope that things will get better, especially as a result of past mistakes: *The previous manager had left the restaurant's affairs in a terrible mess.* | **get into a mess** *How did you manage to get into this mess in the first place?* | **sb's life is a mess** (=they have a lot of problems and seem unable to deal with them) *Her boyfriend left her and she lost her job – her life is just a mess at the moment.*

be in a difficult/awkward position /biː ɪn ə ˌdɪfɪkəlt, ˌɔːkwəʳd pə'zɪʃən/ [v phrase] to be in a difficult situation because whatever you do, you are likely to offend someone or make things worse: *I was in a difficult position, as I was being asked to confront a man who had much more power than I did.* | **put sb in a difficult/awkward position** *Clara was angry at Harry for putting her in such an awkward position.*

be in an impossible position /biː ɪn ən ɪmˌpɒsəbəl pə'zɪʃən‖-ˌpɑː-/ [v phrase] to be in an extremely difficult situation, because whatever you do there will certainly be serious trouble: *I'm in an impossible position – if I criticize him he may resign, but if I don't he'll end up ruining the whole project.* | **put sb in an impossible position** *By bringing his objections out into the open, the Chancellor has put the Prime Minister in an impossible position.*

be in a quandary /biː ɪn ə 'kwɒndəri‖-'kwɑːn-/ [v phrase] to be in a very difficult situation and not be able to decide what is the best thing for you to do: *I was in a quandary – I didn't know whether to tell the police or not.* | *The government has got itself into a quandary over the new tax – if they abandon it they will be seen as weak, if they keep it they will be very unpopular.*

be in dire straits /biː ɪn ˌdaɪəʳ 'streɪts/ [v phrase] to have very serious problems, especially financial ones, which could have very serious results: *The company is in dire financial straits.* | *The team is in such dire straits they've even considered selling their three best players.*

it's one thing after another /ɪts ˌwʌn θɪŋ ɑːftər ə'nʌðəʳ‖-æf-/ spoken say this when you have had a series of problems and you feel that these problems will never end: *It's been one thing after another since I started renting out the place to students.* | *It's one thing after another with that stupid photocopier! What's wrong with it now?*

8 when a fact or situation causes problems

- cause/create/pose a problem
- make life difficult
- present a problem/difficulty
- troublesome
- be a headache
- plague
- dog

cause/create/pose a problem /ˌkɔːz, kriˌeɪt, ˌpəʊz ə 'prɒbləm‖-'prɑː-/ [v phrase] to cause a problem that has to be dealt with: *You would be the only woman on a staff of over thirty men, which could create problems.* | *Both parents and teachers are worried about the problems posed by drugs.* | **+ for** *Rebecca was frequently late for work, which caused problems for her colleagues.* | *Rising inflation could pose a major problem for the government.*

make life difficult /ˌmeɪk laɪf 'dɪfɪkəlt/ [v phrase] to cause problems for someone and make it difficult or inconvenient for them to do what they want to do: *Petty arguments between staff have made the manager's life difficult.* | **+ for** *The rail strikes are making life increasingly difficult for people who have to travel into London every day.*

present a problem/difficulty /prɪˌzent ə 'prɒbləm, 'dɪfɪkəlti‖-'prɑː-/ [v phrase] if an activity or a plan **presents a problem**, there is a problem connected with it that has to be dealt with: *Constructing* *a highway in this area would present enormous difficulties.* | **+ for** *Live television programmes present special problems for the broadcaster.* | **present sb with a problem/difficulty** *Britain's relationship with other members of the European Union presents Blair with problems, just as it did for the Tories.*

troublesome /ˈtrʌbəlsəm/ [adj] something that is **troublesome** keeps causing problems over a period of time: *The infection can be particularly troublesome if it affects the lungs or throat.* | *The plant is regarded as a troublesome weed in rice fields.*

be a headache /biː ə ˈhedeɪk/ [v phrase] informal to cause problems over a period of time that are difficult to deal with: *Messy walkways and picnic tables are just some of the headaches caused by the hundreds of ducks that gather by the lake.* | **+ for** *Censorship is always a constant headache for newspapers in the republic.* | **give sb a headache** *The scandal has given the minister a very public headache.*

plague /pleɪg/ [v T] if difficulties, illnesses, doubts, problems etc **plague** someone, there are a lot of them and they keep causing trouble for a long time: *Social problems plague these low-income communities.* | *The area is plagued by soil erosion and flooding.*

dog /dɒg‖dɔːg/ [v T] if a problem or bad luck **dogs** someone or something, it keeps causing trouble for a long time and prevents them from succeeding: *The team has been dogged by injury all season.* | *Zambia had none of the heritage of war and violence that dogged, say, Kenya or Zimbabwe.*

9 to make progress difficult

- hamper
- hinder
- impede

hamper /ˈhæmpəʳ/ [v T] to make it very difficult for an activity or plan to continue successfully: *Search efforts were hampered by strong winds and fifteen foot waves.* | *The police's work is hampered by people who file false complaints.* | *Health care costs are severely hampering the nation's small businesses.*

hinder /ˈhɪndəʳ/ [v T] to cause problems and therefore delay the development or progress of something: *Higher interest rates could hinder economic growth.* | *Society's attitudes about women hinder any real progress toward equality.* | *Heavy rains had hindered the expedition's progress through the northwest of the country.*

impede /ɪmˈpiːd/ [v T] to make progress or the development of something slower or more difficult: *Progress has been impeded by a number of economic factors.* | *In fact, the use of these drugs may even impede the patient's recovery.*

10 when someone causes problems, especially deliberately

- cause/create problems
- cause/make trouble
- make life difficult
- give sb a hard time
- rock the boat

cause/create problems /ˌkɔːz, kriˌeɪt ˈprɒbləmz‖-ˈprɑː-/ [v phrase] to cause a problem, even if you do not intend to: *After a while, John started causing problems in class.* | *They have two good running backs who can cause problems for our team's defense.* | *A popular independent candidate could create problems for the Democrats by taking away votes.*

cause/make trouble /ˌkɔːz, ˌmeɪk ˈtrʌbəl/ [v phrase] to deliberately cause problems, especially by starting arguments or fights: *Don't give him another drink, or he'll start causing trouble.* | *Some of the demonstrators were determined to make trouble, whatever the police did.* | *It's not just gang members that cause trouble, it's middle- and upper-class kids too.*

make life difficult /ˌmeɪk laɪf ˈdɪfɪkəlt/ [v phrase] to deliberately cause problems and make it difficult for someone to do something, for example in order to punish them or persuade them to do something: *They can't actually stop us, but they could make life difficult.* | **+ for** *Some employers have made life difficult for employees who need time off for extended illnesses.*

give sb a hard time /ˌgɪv (sb) ə ˌhɑːʳd ˈtaɪm/ [v phrase] informal to deliberately treat someone badly and cause trouble for them, for example by criticizing them, complaining, or asking them a lot of difficult questions: *When I first came here everyone gave me a really hard time, because I was the first woman to run a department.* | **+ about** *My mother gave me a really hard time about Freddy. She couldn't stand him.*

rock the boat /ˌrɒk ðə ˈbəʊt‖ˌrɑːk-/ [v phrase] informal to cause problems by making changes in a situation that everyone else thinks is satisfactory: *We have a pretty good life here. Why rock the boat?* | *Judge Thurgood Marshall never hesitated to rock the boat, from the beginning of his long legal career.* | *A lot of people have a don't-rock-the boat mentality that stops them from complaining.*

11 someone who causes a lot of problems

- troublemaker
- difficult/awkward

troublemaker /ˈtrʌbəlˌmeɪkəʳ/ [n C] someone who deliberately causes problems, especially by complaining a lot or trying to make people fight or argue: *The violence was started by a small group of troublemakers.* | *Women who point out cases of harassment risk being labelled troublemakers.*

difficult/awkward /ˈdɪfɪkəlt, ˈɔːkwəʳd/ [adj] someone who is **difficult** or **awkward** causes a lot of problems, because they behave in an unreasonable or unhelpful way: *Darren's always been such a difficult child.* | **+ about** *She's being really awkward about the divorce.*

12 to cause extra work or inconvenience for someone

- inconvenience sb/cause (sb) inconvenience
- put sb out
- trouble
- put sb to a lot of trouble

inconvenience sb/cause (sb) inconvenience /ˌɪnkənˈviːniəns sb, ˌkɔːz (sb) ɪnkənˈviːniəns/ [v T/v phrase] to cause problems for someone by making them do something that is inconvenient for them: *Would I be inconveniencing you if I arrived about ten thirty?* | *The builders promised the Browns that they would not be inconvenienced for more than two days.* | **cause inconvenience for sb** *It was weeks before a decision was made, which caused inconvenience for everyone.* | **cause sb inconvenience** *If you don't remember your password, you'll cause yourself a lot of inconvenience.*

put sb out /ˌpʊt (sb) ˈaʊt/ [phr v T] to make someone have to do something that is inconvenient for them by asking them to do something for you: *Are you* *sure you don't mind picking the children up from school? I don't want to put you out.* | *I hope I'm not putting you out, but I need someone to stay in the office at lunchtime today.*

trouble /ˈtrʌbəl/ [v T] to cause someone problems or more work than usual: *I didn't want to trouble you – you have your own problems.* | *She doesn't want to trouble you by asking lots of questions.*

put sb to a lot of trouble /ˌpʊt (sb) tʊ ə ˌlɒt əv ˈtrʌbəl ‖-ˌlɑːt-/ [v phrase] to make someone spend a lot of time or use a lot of effort in doing something for you: *We've put her to a lot of trouble. Why don't we get her some flowers?* | *I don't want to put you to any trouble.*

13 what you say when you are explaining a problem

- the trouble/problem is
- the thing is

the trouble/problem is /ðə ˌtrʌbəl, ˌprɒbləm ˈɪz‖-ˌprɑː-/ spoken say this when you are explaining why something is difficult or what is causing problems: *The trouble is, there's no-one here who really understands computers.* | **+ (that)** *The problem is that we can't really afford the plane fare.* | **the trouble/problem with sth is** *The trouble with using credit cards is that it's so easy to get into debt.*

the thing is /ðə ˌθɪŋ ˈɪz/ spoken informal say this when you are explaining to a friend why you cannot do what they want: *The thing is, I have an important exam next week.* | *I'd love to come, but the thing is, I promised to see Jim tonight.*

14 what you say to ask someone about a problem

- what's wrong/what's the matter
- what's up
- what's the problem
- do you have a problem with that?

what's wrong/what's the matter /ˌwɒts ˈrɒŋ‖-ˈrɔːŋ, ˌwɒts ðə ˈmætəʳ/ spoken say this when you are asking someone what is causing a problem, for example why they are upset, or why a machine will not work: *What's the matter? You look as if you've been crying.* | **+ with** *What's wrong with the TV?* | *What was the matter with Daniella yesterday?*

what's up /ˌwɒts ˈʌp/ spoken informal say this when you are asking someone if there is a problem that they want to talk about: *'Karen, can I talk to you for a minute?' 'Sure, what's up?'* | **what's up with sb?** (=say this when someone seems to have a problem) *What's up with Larry today?*

what's the problem /ˌwɒts ðə ˈprɒbləm‖-ˈprɑː-/ spoken say this when you are asking why someone cannot do something or why something will not work: *'I can't finish the last question.' 'Why? What's the problem?'* | *What's the problem? Is there something I can do?* | **+ with** *'I can't get my computer to work.' 'What's the problem with it?'*

do you have a problem with that? /duː juː hæv ə ˈprɒbləm wɪð ðæt‖-ˈprɑː-/ especially American, spoken say this to ask someone if they are unhappy about something you just said or suggested – use this when you are annoyed and want to be slightly rude: *'Is he going to sleep in your room?' 'I think so. Do you have a problem with that?'* | *'Are you all by yourself?' I said, 'Yes.' And I wanted to say 'you got a problem with that?'*

profit

RELATED WORDS

▸ see also **money, earn, pay, sell, business**

1 money that you make by doing business

- profit
- proceeds
- surplus
- gain

profit /ˈprɒfɪ̈t‖ˈprɑː-/ [n C/U] money that you make by doing business, for example when you sell something for more that it cost you to buy it or to produce it: *We aim to increase our profits by at least 5% every year.* | *For the first time, the company's annual profits were over $1 million.* | *They don't care who they sell weapons to. All they are interested in is profit.* | **make a profit** *They made a huge profit when they sold the business.*

proceeds /ˈprəʊsiːdz/ [n plural] all the money that you get from selling something, or from something such as a show or a sports event: *His first year in business was so successful that John could afford to buy a delivery van with the proceeds.* | *The proceeds of the sale of the house went to an animal-welfare charity, as stated in the owner's will.*

surplus /ˈsɜːʳpləs/ [n C] the amount of money that remains after a company or organization has paid all its costs, charges, wages etc: *Our surplus on book publishing last year was $47 million.* | *For the first time in 20 years Congress was working with a budget surplus.*

gain /geɪn/ [n U] the profit that someone makes – use this especially when you think that the person or company making the profit is only interested in getting money or an advantage for themselves **for gain** (=in order to make a profit) *If private hospitals are operating purely for gain, how can we be sure they have the patients' best interests at heart?* | **short-term gain** (=a situation in which profits may be made for a short time, but which may cause losses and problems in the future) *Companies just don't invest enough – short-term gain is all they think about.*

2 a profit from leaving money in the bank or lending it to a company

- interest
- return
- yield

interest /ˈɪntrɪ̈st/ [n U] an amount of profit that you make at an agreed rate when you put money into a bank or similar institution: *If you had half a million dollars you could easily live off the interest.* | *John had put his grandfather's money in the bank, and was getting $400 a month in interest.* | **rate of interest** (=the agreed amount paid as interest) *The best rate of interest the banks can offer is around 14 per cent.* | **high/low interest** *a high interest savings account*

return /rɪˈtɜːʳn/ [n C] the total profit that you get as a result of putting money into a bank, company etc – used especially in business: *The company offers the hope of big returns for people who buy its shares.* | **return on an investment** *The return on the initial investment was huge.*

yield /jiːld/ [n C] the exact amount of profit that you get as a result of lending money to a company, government etc – used especially in business: *We have calculated the probable yield from this investment at around 17%.* | *If you invest the money now, the yield after only twelve months will be $3160.*

3 to get a profit

- make
- earn
- make a profit
- make a killing

make /meɪk/ [v T] to get a profit, especially from business deals **make £1 million/$10,000 etc** *British Telecom made over $3 billion last year.* | **make money** *The restaurant makes a lot of money in the summer.* | **make money doing sth** *You could make a lot of money selling your photographs, they're excellent.* | **make millions/make a fortune** *Mandon, our richest cousin, had made a fortune in the cable TV business.* | **+ out of** *The entrepreneur boasted that he could make money out of anything, even pebbles in the beach.*

make a profit /ˌmeɪk ə ˈprɒfɪt‖-ˈprɑː-/ [v phrase] to get a profit from a business or from selling something: *Harry made a good profit – he bought the house for £45,000 and sold it for £55,000 six months later.* | *When you consider how much this meal would cost to prepare at home, you realize that the restaurant must be making an enormous profit.* | **make a profit of $53m/£600 etc** *The drug company Sasco made a profit of $53 million last year.* | **+ on** *Even though the price has been reduced, the builders will still make a profit on the sale.*

earn /ɜːʳn/ [v T] to make a profit from business or from putting money in a bank, lending it to a company etc: *The Washington Post Company earned $187 million in 1987.* | *Our finances look better if we include the profit earned on the sale of our London offices.* | *She decided to put the money in a high-earning investment account.*

make a killing /ˌmeɪk ə ˈkɪlɪŋ/ [v phrase] informal to get a very large profit quickly from one successful business deal: *He had made a killing on the stock exchange that morning.* | *Vito's a debonair middle-aged New Yorker, who's made a killing in advertising.*

4 to not make a profit

- unprofitable
- uneconomic

unprofitable /ʌnˈprɒfɪtəbəl‖-ˈprɑː-/ [adj] an **unprofitable** business or activity does not make a profit and is likely to have debts: *The company says that the publishing side of its division is unprofitable and must be closed down.* | *Unprofitable flight routes have been axed as recession hits the aviation industry.* | *The bank isn't likely to lend money to an unprofitable business like yours.*

uneconomic /ˌʌniːkəˈnɒmɪk, ˌʌnekə-‖-ˈnɑː-/ [adj] not making enough profits to be successful or to successfully compete with other companies, industries etc – use this especially when this is a reason for closing the company, industry etc: *Most of the old nationalized industries were labelled 'uneconomic' and sold off to private companies.* | *Workers in uneconomic areas of the economy fought hard to keep their factories and mines open.*

5 when a business produces a profit

- profitable
- money-spinner
- lucrative
- goldmine

profitable /ˈprɒfɪtəbəl‖ˈprɑː-/ [adj] a **profitable** business or activity makes a profit: *We don't sell children's clothes any more – it wasn't profitable enough.* | *It's only in the last year that our business has become profitable. Before that we were just managing to cover our costs.*

lucrative /ˈluːkrətɪv/ [adj] a type of business or activity that is **lucrative** produces a very large profit: *Catering is a very lucrative business if you succeed in it.* | *Sam's journalistic work was much more lucrative than his painting had ever been.* | *There is still an illegal but lucrative trade in ivory between Africa and South-East Asia.*

money-spinner /ˈmʌni ˌspɪnəʳ/ [n C] British informal a business or product that produces a large profit: *The little bar turned out to be a real moneyspinner.* | *The toy companies are always trying to find another money-spinner like Monopoly or the Barbie doll.*

goldmine /ˈgəʊldmaɪn/ [n C usually singular] informal a small business, especially a shop or restaurant, that produces a very large profit: *It's just a scruffy little beach café, but in summer it's an absolute goldmine.* | *I bet that corner shop's a goldmine.*

6 to not make a profit

- break even
- non-profitmaking

break even /ˌbreɪk ˈiːvən/ [v phrase] *The company made a small loss last year but this year has managed to break even.* | *We'll be just breaking even if we can get an average audience of 300.*

non-profitmaking /nɒn ˈprɒfɪtˌmeɪkɪŋ‖nɑːn ˈprɑː-/ [adj] British a company or business that is **non-profitmaking** does business so that its profits are used to provide money for hospitals, poor people etc: *Traidcraft is a non-profitmaking organization that buys goods from Indian workers at fair prices.*

7 to make a profit in an unfair way

- cash in on
- profiteering
- profit from
- exploit

cash in on /ˌkæʃ ˈɪn ɒn / [phr v T] to make a profit from a situation in a way that is wrong or unfair: *He's just cashing in on the fact that his wife is famous.* | *Have you noticed how the record companies cash in on the death of famous pop stars by re-releasing all their old records?*

profit from /ˈprɒfɪt frɒm‖ˈprɑː-/ [v phrase] to make a **profit from** a bad situation, instead of trying to help people: *Nobody should be allowed to profit from war and human suffering.* | *Crafty entrepreneurs like Harper profited from the ignorance of the masses.*

profiteering /ˌprɒfɪˈtɪərɪŋ‖ˌprɑː-/ [n U] when someone makes large profits from a bad situation by charging extremely high prices for things that people need to buy: *The emergency government brought in a special law to prevent hoarding and profiteering.* | *As food supplies dwindled, complaints against profiteering became more vociferous.*

exploit /ɪkˈsplɔɪt/ [v T] to make an unfair profit out of someone who is in a weaker position than yourself or who seriously needs the things you can sell them, do for them etc: *Measure are being taken to stop employment agencies exploiting foreign workers desperate to find a job.* | *Many 'New Age' therapists simply exploit the hopes and fears of sick people who would be better off going to their own doctor.* | *loan sharks who exploit the poor by charging up to 1000% interest per year.*

progress/ make progress

RELATED WORDS

▸ *see also* **continue, happen, succeed/successful**

1 make progress when you are trying to do something

▸ make progress ▸ progress ▸ go ▸ be getting there ▸ advance ▸ make headway ▸ move ▸ come along

make progress /ˌmeɪk ˈprəʊgres‖-ˈprɑː-/ [v phrase] if you **make progress**, you gradually start to achieve what you want: *Far too many people are still unemployed, but we are making progress.* | **+ in/on** *At Yalta, Russia and Ukraine made progress in several aspects of their bilateral relations.* | *Rapid progress has been made on the development of drugs for the treatment of Aids.* | **+ towards** British **/toward** American *The talks were aimed at making progress towards greater European union.*

progress /prəˈgres/ [v T] if something progresses, it develops in the way that you want and you gradually start to achieve what you want **progress well/quickly/successfully etc** *Work on the ship progressed quickly.* | *Bob was a very good football coach, and the team progressed very well.* | **progress according to plan** *So far the building work has progressed according to plan.*

go /gəʊ/ [v I usually in progressive] if a particular activity or piece of work **goes** well, fine etc, it happens in a way that is good, so that you can gradually achieve what you want **+ well/fine/better etc** *Fiona says that her new teaching job is going really well.* | *Things went better after the new computer system was installed.* | **How's sth going?** *'How are your exams going, Luke?' 'Fine, thanks.'* | **the way sth's going** *I feel very happy about the way the project's going so far.*

be getting there /biː ˈgetɪŋ ðeəʳ/ [v phrase] informal if you **are getting there**, you are starting to achieve what you want, after difficulties or problems that have made progress slow: *The company had a lot of problems initially, but they're getting there now.* | *It's been a struggle paying off all our debts, but I think at last we're getting there.*

advance /ədˈvɑːns‖ədˈvæns/ [v I] if something, especially scientific and technical knowledge, **advances**, it develops and improves: *Computer technology is advancing very rapidly.* | *Our knowledge of the deepest parts of the ocean has advanced considerably over the last ten years.*

make headway /ˌmeɪk ˈhedweɪ/ [v phrase] to make progress in spite of problems or difficulties, because you are determined and have worked hard: *Sylvia's teachers all say that she has made great headway this term.* | *The new agreement indicated that the government was at last making headway against the terrorists.* | **+ in** *If either side is to make any headway in these negotiations, they must be prepared to compromise.*

move /muːv/ [v I] if an event or activity **moves** quickly, slowly or in the right direction, it progresses in that way: *Things moved quickly once we had agreed a price on the house.* | *I think that the trade agreement is moving in the right direction.* | *Police say that the investigation is moving slowly, and they are hoping that more witnesses will come forward.*

come along ALSO **come on** British /ˌkʌm əˈlɒŋ‖-əˈlɔːŋ, ˌkʌm ˈɒn/ [phr v I] if something such as a piece of work **comes along**, it progresses in a very satisfactory way: *Mary's reading and writing has really started to come along recently.* | **+ well/fine/better etc** *The work on the new school sports centre is coming on very well.* | **How's sth coming along?** *'How's your project coming along?' 'Oh, fine, thanks.'*

2 to make progress very rapidly

▸ make great strides ▸ forge ahead ▸ come on in leaps and bounds

make great strides /meɪk ˌgreɪt ˈstraɪdz/ [v phrase] if people **make great strides**, they make progress very rapidly towards improving knowledge or methods, especially in scientific, technical, or educational areas: *Science has made great strides since the 1970s.* | **+ in** *Great strides have been made in reducing air pollution in US cities.* | *The conference highlighted the great strides made in education in Third World countries.* | **+ towards** British **/toward** American *We have made great strides towards equality between the sexes in legal status and rights.*

forge ahead /ˌfɔːʳdʒ əˈhed/ [phr v I] to make progress very quickly towards achieving something, especially faster than other people: *Our export sales have continued to forge ahead this year.* | **+ in** *Growing environmental fears have made climate research all the more important, and Europe is forging ahead in this field.* | **+ with** *The Prime Minister promised that the government would forge ahead with the reforms.*

come on in leaps and bounds British **/ improve/develop etc by leaps and bounds** American /kʌm ˌɒn ɪn ˌliːps ən ˈbaʊndz, ɪmˌpruːv baɪ ˌliːps ən ˈbaʊndz/ [v phrase usually in progressive] if a person or the study, development etc of something **comes on in leaps and bounds**, they make progress very quickly, especially in knowledge or ability: *Jake was slow to learn to read, but now he's coming on in leaps and bounds.* | *We were very surprised to see the way this field of philosophical thought has grown by leaps and bounds.*

3 to make no progress at all

▸ make no progress ▸ get nowhere ▸ go badly/not go well ▸ go around in circles ▸ stagnate

make no progress /meɪk ˌnəʊ ˈprəʊgres‖-ˈprɑː-/ [v phrase] to not progress at all with a piece of work or activity: *The lawyers are trying to reach an agreement but so far no progress has been made.* | **+ on** *Because of bad weather we made no progress on the house for the next three days.* | **+ in** *Police were making no progress in their efforts to trace a man seen near the scene of the murder.* | **+ with** *The city council have made no progress with their plans to rebuild the town hall.*

get nowhere /ˌget ˈnəʊweəʳ/ [v phrase] informal to not progress at all, even though you have worked hard: *I feel as though I'm getting nowhere in this job.* | *Not surprisingly, the peace talks got nowhere.* | **+ with** *Don started to learn Arabic, but he was getting nowhere with it.* | **get nowhere fast** *The project was* *eating up time and money and seemed to be getting nowhere fast.*

go badly/not go well /gəʊ 'bædli, ˌnɒt gəʊ 'wel/ [v phrase usually in progressive] if a piece of work or activity **goes badly**, it does not make progress or develop in the way you would like it to: *My essay isn't going very well. It's difficult to find any useful books on the subject.* | *Despite all the government's efforts, the war on drugs is going badly.*

go around in circles ALSO **go round in circles** British /gəʊ əˌraʊnd ɪn 'sɜːʳkəlz, gəʊ ˌraʊnd ɪn 'sɜːʳkəlz/ [v phrase usually in progressive] to keep discussing the same problems without making any decisions or finding any answers: *This conversation's going around in circles again.* | *Every time we try to reach a decision, we end up going round in circles.*

stagnate /stæg'neɪt‖'stægneɪt/ [v I] to stop developing or improving and often become worse: *Business here has stagnated compared with other wine-producing regions.* | *Everyone needs new challenges. Otherwise you just stagnate.*

4 success when you are trying to achieve something

- progress
- advance
- breakthrough
- milestone
- step
- stepping stone

progress /'prəʊgres‖'prɑː-/ [n U] *The new national tests are intended to keep a closer check on children's progress.* | **+ in** *Any progress in cancer research may help to save lives.* | **+ on** *Bad weather has prevented progress on retrieving the plane from the sea.* | **economic/political/social etc progress** *Spencer insisted that free enterprise was the key to social progress.*

advance /əd'vɑːns‖əd'væns/ [n C] a new discovery or invention that brings progress: *The discovery marks a significant technological advance.* | **+ in** *Dr Martineau had written an article about advances in medicine over the last five years.*

breakthrough /'breɪkθruː/ [n C] an important discovery or achievement that makes it possible to progress, especially one that happens suddenly after a long period of trying **a big/dramatic/major etc breakthrough** *Egypt and Jordan welcomed news of the deal as a major breakthrough.* | **+ in** *There has been an important breakthrough in the search for safe nuclear energy.* | **+ on** *Scientists at Merck were nearing a breakthrough on a new drug to treat HIV.* | **make/achieve a breakthrough** *Negotiators have made a breakthrough on the most difficult issue of employment security.*

milestone /'maɪlstəʊn/ [n C] a very important event in the progress of development of something, especially the first time that something important is done **+ in** *For most people, the birth of their first child is a milestone in their lives.* | **an important/major/significant etc milestone** *His decision to accept the university's offer was an important milestone in his career.* | **a milestone in the development/history/life etc of sth** *The album 'Kind Of Blue' proved to be a milestone in the development of modern jazz.* | *This year has seen another milestone in the life of the Society, in that our assets passed the £3 billion mark.* | **a milestone on/along the road to sth** *We believe that what we have agreed today will be a milestone on the road to true peace and prosperity in our country.* | **mark a milestone in sth** *The expedition marked a milestone in the history of exploration.*

step /step/ [n C] an action or discovery that brings progress and that combines with other actions or discoveries to take you closer to the result you want to achieve **a big/important/major etc step** *Of course, starting the job-search is always a big step.* | **+ in** *The discovery of penicillin was a gigantic step in the treatment of infections.* | **+ forward** *The new law on drunk driving is being seen as a major step forward.* | **+ towards** British **/toward** American *Identifying the cause of a disease must always be the first step towards finding a cure.* | **step in the right direction** *Re-thinking our management techniques would be an important step in the right direction.*

stepping stone /'stepɪŋ stəʊn/ [n C] an event or action that is not always very important itself but helps you to progress towards achieving something: *For the unemployed, temporary jobs can be a useful stepping stone.* | **+ to/towards** *A teaching post is often only a stepping stone to a better paid profession.* | *The agreement was an important diplomatic stepping stone towards independence.*

5 a situation in which there is no progress

- stalemate
- deadlock
- dead end
- impasse
- a step backwards

stalemate /'steɪlmeɪt/ [n singular/U] a situation in which no further progress can be made because two groups or organizations disagree with each other about what to do, and cannot think of any way to end the disagreement **reach a stalemate/be at a stalemate** *At that point the strike appeared to have reached a stalemate.* | *Negotiations with the 200 army rebels are at a stalemate.* | **end in stalemate** *It looks like the long-running dispute could end in stalemate.* | **+ between** *The proposal was aimed at ending the stalemate between environmentalist and business groups.* | **+ in** *the stalemate in the three-month long pay dispute* | **break a stalemate** (=make it possible for discussions to continue) *an attempt to break a stalemate in the Middle East peace process*

deadlock /'dedlɒk‖-lɑːk/ [n singular/U] a situation in which no further progress can be made because two groups disagree strongly with each other and refuse to change their minds: *In the same year the issue came before Parliament, but there was complete deadlock.* | **+ between** *There are hopes that an agreement can be made to break the deadlock between the White House and Congress.* | **+ over** *The deadlock over the US budget had turned away some investors.* | **end in deadlock** *Their first trial ended in deadlock when the jury could not reach an agreement.* | **break a deadlock** (=to make it possible to agree so that you can progress) *Syria and Israel broke a six-month deadlock in their talks when they sent peace envoys to Maryland.*

dead end /ˌded 'end◂/ [n singular] a situation in which it is impossible to make any further progress in your work or in what you are trying to do: *My mother thought that I should be a model, but I knew that was a dead end.* | **be/feel you are at a dead end** *At 52, Martin felt he was at a dead end professionally.* | **come to/hit/reach etc a dead end** (=stop making any progress) *The development of this drug has come to a dead end because of doubts about its safety.* —**dead-end** [adj] *A large number of young people who leave school at 16 end up in dead-end jobs.* | *My sister, Jess, was in a dead-end relationship from which she could see no escape.*

impasse /æmˈpɑːs‖ˈɪmpæs/ [n singular] formal a situation in which progress has stopped completely, especially because people cannot agree on what to do next **+ in** *The continuing impasse in negotiations made military conflict seem likely.* | **+ between** *an impasse between the US and its European trading partners* | **+ over** *There seemed no way to end the impasse over the Lockerbie affair.* | **reach an impasse/be at an impasse** *It was clear that the Soviet economy was at an impasse.* | *On July 25, the situation seemed to have reached an impasse.*

a step backwards /ə ˌstep ˈbækwəʳdz/ [n phrase] an action or change that makes a situation worse, so that the progress that has been made is lost **+ for** *Accepting the job would be a step backwards for me.* | *Several opposition leaders described the programme as a major step backwards for democracy.* | **take a step backwards** *Any sort of stress such as upset in the family may cause a child to take a step backwards in behaviour.*

promise

RELATED WORDS

▸ *see also* **agree**

1 to promise something

- promise
- assure
- give sb your word
- swear
- vow
- guarantee
- commit to
- pledge

promise /ˈprɒmɪ̈s‖ˈprɑː-/ [v I/T not usually in progressive] to tell someone that you will definitely do something that they want you to do or expect you to do: *'I can't take you to the beach today, after all.' 'But you promised!'* | **+ (that)** *Hurry up, we promised we wouldn't be late this time.* | *Richardson apologized and promised that appropriate action would be taken to fix the problem.* | **+ to do sth** *The government had promised to investigate the cause of the accident.* | **promise sb (that)** *I promised the kids I'd take them to a movie.* | **promise sb sth** (=promise to give someone something) *I promised Jamie a ride to school this morning.*

assure /əˈʃʊəʳ/ [v T] to tell someone that something will definitely happen or is definitely true, so that they are less worried or more confident **assure sb (that)** *The doctor assured me that I wouldn't feel any pain.* | *The airline has assured travellers there will be no further delays.*

give sb your word /ˌɡɪv (sb) jɔːʳ ˈwɜːʳd/ [v phrase] to promise someone very seriously and sincerely that you will do something: *Campus officials had given her their word. There was to be a raise in salary each year.* | **+ (that)** *I've given him my word that we'll take care of the house like it was ours.* | **give sb your word of honour/honor** *He had given her his word of honor that he would respect her wishes.*

swear /sweəʳ/ [v T] to make a very serious promise, especially publicly or in a law court **+ (that)** *During the ceremony you swear that you will serve the country loyally.* | **swear to sb (that)** *I swore to myself that I'd never do anything like it again.* | **+ to do sth** *Do you swear to tell the truth?* | **swear allegiance** (=promise to be loyal to a country) *New citizens are asked to swear allegiance during the citizenship ceremony.*

vow /vaʊ/ [v T] to firmly promise something, especially to yourself – used especially in literature **+ to do sth** *Ben vowed to avenge his mother's death.* | **+ (that)** *Daley vowed that the Police Department would be reformed.*

guarantee /ˌɡærənˈtiː/ [v T] to promise that something will happen or be provided, because you are going to make sure of this: *The king had guaranteed our safety on our journey.* | **+ (that)** *We guarantee that you won't lose your jobs when the company is taken over.* | *I can't guarantee the plan will work, but I'll give it a try.* | **guarantee sb sth** (=guarantee to give someone something) *The first emigrants to Canada were guaranteed 200 acres of land each.* —**guaranteed** [adj] *same day delivery guaranteed* | *The fridge is guaranteed for one year.* (=the company that makes it promises to repair or replace it if it breaks within a year)

commit to /kəˈmɪt tuː/ [v phrase] to promise to do something that will take a long time or involve a lot of effort: *Young people still need to learn how to commit to a job and have goals for themselves.* | **+ to do sth** *The organization needs volunteers who can commit to work four hours a week.* —**committed** [adj] **be committed to doing sth** *The church is committed to changing the role it allows women.*

pledge /pledʒ/ [v T] to publicly or officially promise to give help, support, or money to an organization, group, or person **+ to do sth** *Many rock stars have pledged to support the campaign to save the rainforests.* | **pledge sth to sb** *The government has pledged £500,000 worth of aid to the drought-stricken area.* | **pledge support/money/help etc** *Britain has pledged £1.3 million to the UN for refugee work.* | *The U.S. has pledged aid to the country.* | **pledge allegiance** (=promise to be loyal to a country) *Should new citizens of Canada pledge allegiance to the queen of Great Britain?*

2 a promise

- promise
- assurance
- guarantee
- commitment
- pledge
- oath
- undertaking

promise /ˈprɒmɪ̈s‖ˈprɑː-/ [n C] a statement telling someone that you will definitely do something that they want you to do: *'I'll call you tomorrow.' 'Is that a promise?'* | **+ of** *The refugees are relying on promises of food and aid from the West.* | **make a promise** *Making promises is risky for a company, but it usually does result in improved customer relations.* | **+ to do sth** *Scott made a campaign promise not to raise taxes.* | **+ that** *He left with a promise that he would be back before six.*

assurance /əˈʃʊərəns/ [n C] a promise that something will definitely happen or is definitely true, which makes someone less worried or more confident: *Despite all their assurances, they broke the agreement and signed a deal with a rival company.* | **+ that** *I need an assurance that you will support me.* | **give sb an assurance** *The manager gave me his personal assurance that the parts would be here today.* | **give sb an assurance about/on** *His lawyer was unwilling to give him any kind of assurance about the outcome of the trial.*

guarantee /ˌɡærənˈtiː/ [n C] a promise that something will happen or be provided, because you are going to make sure of this. A **guarantee** is also a formal written promise by a company to repair or replace a product free if it has a fault within a fixed period of time **+ that** *The contract contains a guarantee that the building will be finished within 6 months.* | *After the Second World War, Belgium* *wanted a guarantee that it would not be invaded again.* | **under guarantee** (=within the period when a company promises to repair a product free of charge if something goes wrong) *Is the camera still under guarantee?*

commitment /kəˈmɪtmənt/ [n C] a promise to do something that will take a long time or involve a lot of effort: *The peace talks ended with smiles and handshakes, but no commitment.* | *Marriage, ideally, is a lifelong commitment.* | **make a commitment** *The organization has made a commitment to plant 5,000 trees in San Francisco.* | **+ to** *The American adviser expressed America's commitment to Africa's economic development.* | **commitment to doing sth** *The governor has a strong commitment to creating jobs in the state.*

pledge /pledʒ/ [n C] a public or official promise to give help, support, or money to an organization, group, or person: *The Government has fulfilled at least 50% of its election pledges.* | **+ of** *We have received pledges of help from various organizations.* | **+ to do sth** *The coup leaders have ignored their pledges to hold democratic elections.*

oath /əʊθ/ [n C] a formal and serious promise, especially one that someone makes in a court of law **take/swear an oath** (=make a promise) *Adams was elected to the British Parliament, but refused to swear an oath to the English Queen.* | **under oath** (=while you have made a promise to tell the truth in a court of law) *He admitted that he had lied under oath.* | **oath of office** (=the promises you make when you are elected to a government position) *The president takes the oath of office in a public ceremony.* | **+ to do sth** *Public officials must take an oath to support the U.S. Constitution.*

undertaking /ˌʌndəʳˈteɪkɪŋ/ [n C] a public or official promise to do something, especially something difficult, which needs a lot of effort or money, and that you will be responsible for making sure that it is done **+ to do sth** *Khrushchev demanded an American undertaking not to attack Cuba.* | **+ that** *Before we can release you, we need an undertaking that you will not leave town before the trial.*

3 what you say when you promise something

- I promise
- I give you my word/ you have my word
- cross my heart
- I swear

I promise /aɪ ˈprɒmɪ̈s‖-ˈprɑː-/ *'Promise me you'll write to me.' 'I promise.'* | **+ (that)** *I won't go. I promise I won't go.*

I give you my word/you have my word /aɪ ˌɡɪv juː maɪ ˈwɜːʳd, juː ˌhæv maɪ ˈwɜːʳd/ say this when you want to make a very serious and sincere promise: *You won't regret this – I give you my word.* | **+ (that)** *I give you my word that I'll do everything I can.* | *Do I have your word, Mr Bigelow, that this problem will be corrected?*

cross my heart /ˌkrɒs maɪ ˈhɑːʳt‖ˌkrɔːs-/ say this when you are making a promise to someone you know well – used especially by children: *'Do you promise?' 'Cross my heart.'*

I swear /aɪ ˈsweəʳ/ say this when you are making a very firm promise, that you will never break. **I swear** is used in court: *I swear that the evidence I give will be the truth, the whole truth, and nothing but the truth.*

4 to do what you promised to do

- keep your promise/word
- deliver
- fulfil
- stand by/stick to
- be as good as your word
- keep your side of the bargain
- hold sb to

keep your promise/word /ˌkiːp jɔːʳ ˈprɒmɪ̈s, ˈwɜːʳd‖-ˈprɑː-/ [v phrase] *She was crying because she thought he had not kept his promise.* | *Respect your teenager's privacy. If you promise not to tell her father, keep your word.* | **+ to do sth** *The government has kept its promise to cut taxes, but this has meant cuts in services, too.*

deliver /dɪˈlɪvəʳ/ [v I/T] to do or provide what you promised, especially in politics or business when people are uncertain whether you can do this: *Election candidates frequently promise a lot more than they can deliver.* | *The Prime Minister's economic development strategy has not delivered the promised benefits.* | **deliver on a promise** *Yet again the management has failed to deliver on its promise to provide extra staff training.* | **deliver the goods** (=do or provide what you have promised) *Do you think she will be able to deliver the goods?*

fulfil British **/fulfill** American /fʊlˈfɪl/ [v T] formal to do what you have promised to do or what you must do, especially in politics or business **fulfil a pledge/promise/commitment** *Eisenhower finally fulfilled his campaign pledge to end the war in Korea.* | *In the ROTC program, students fulfill a service commitment after college, in return for a scholarship from the Army or Navy.* | **fulfil a duty/mission** *The general did not have confidence that the Fourth Fleet would be able to fulfil its mission.*

stand by/stick to /ˈstænd baɪ, ˈstɪk tuː/ [phr v T] to faithfully keep an earlier promise or agreement although there may now be reasons for not keeping it: *Despite his family's opposition, Jake stood by his promise to marry her.* | *How could she stick to the agreement now that everything had changed so drastically?* | *I stand by what I said during the campaign.*

be as good as your word /biː əz ˌɡʊd əz jɔːʳ ˈwɜːʳd/ [v phrase] use this when you are impressed with someone for doing what they promised to do: *The President promised to lower income taxes, and he's been as good as his word.*

keep your side of the bargain /kiːp ˌjɔːʳ saɪd əv ðə ˈbɑːʳɡɪ̈n/ [v phrase] to do what you promised to do as part of an agreement in which both sides promised to do something: *The strike has ended. The employers must now keep their side of the bargain and increase overtime pay.*

hold sb to /ˈhəʊld (sb) tuː/ [phr v T] to make sure that someone does what they have promised to do: *Parents and teachers need to agree on goals for students, and hold them to it.* | *Government officials need to be held to their promises.*

5 to not do what you promised to do

- break a promise
- go back on
- renege on

break a promise /ˌbreɪk ə ˈprɒmɪ̈s‖-ˈprɑː-/ [v phrase] *I said I'd take the girls to the movie, and I don't like to break a promise.* | **+ to do sth** *The government has broken its promise to reduce the size of the army.* | **broken promise** *Despite Roosevelt's broken promise to balance the budget, he was elected president four times.*

go back on /gəʊ 'bæk ɒn/ [phr v T] to change your mind and not do something that you had earlier promised to do: *He had gone back on his promise to stop drinking too many times.* | *The rebels had agreed to a ceasefire, but they've gone back on their word.*

renege on /rɪ'ni:g ɒn‖rɪ'nɪg-/ [phr v T] formal to fail to keep to officially agreed promises or responsibilities: *The government has had to renege on its commitment to full employment.* | *Kenoco Inc has reneged on its agreement to finance the film.*

protect

RELATED WORDS

▸ defend, look after, safe

1 to prevent someone or something from being harmed or damaged

- ▸ protect
- ▸ guard
- ▸ safeguard
- ▸ shield

protect /prə'tekt/ [v T] to keep someone or something safe from harm, injury, damage or illness: *The painting is protected by thick glass.* | *laws to protect the environment* | *A series of meetings were held to discuss security issues and teach women employees how to protect themselves.* | **protect sb/sth from sth** *Use high-factor sun lotion to protect your child's skin from the sun.* | **protect sb/sth against sth** *Garlic was once thought to protect people against evil spirits.*

guard /gɑ:ʳd/ [v T] to stay close to a person, a valuable object etc and watch them carefully, in order to make sure that they do not escape, get stolen, or get attacked: *An army lieutenant and 14 soldiers were guarding the air strip.* | **guard sb/sth against sb/sth** *Soldiers have been called in to guard the embassy against further attacks.*

safeguard /'seɪfgɑ:ʳd/ [v T] to protect something important, for example people's rights, health, or safety – use this especially about organizations and laws that provide protection: *Unless we fight pollution now, we cannot safeguard our children's future.* | *The new legislation will safeguard the rights of low-paid workers.* | **safeguard sth against sth** *Effective programs are available to safeguard your data against computer viruses.*

shield /ʃi:ld/ [v T] to protect someone from something harmful or unpleasant, especially by putting yourself or something else between them and the cause of the harm: *The elderly woman shielded her wounded husband.* | **shield sb/sth from sth** *The treated glass shields your eyes from the sun's ultraviolet rays.* | *Fuel taxes were reduced, shielding industry from the effects of the rise in oil prices.*

2 to protect someone by providing a place where they are safe from danger

- ▸ shelter
- ▸ give sb shelter/refuge
- ▸ asylum

shelter /'ʃeltəʳ/ [v T] to provide a place where someone is protected, for example from danger or from the weather: *Police are appealing to anyone who may be sheltering the wanted man to come forward.* | **shelter sb from sth** *They risked their own lives sheltering Jews from the Nazis.* | *An umbrella sheltered them from the sun.* — **sheltered** [adj only before noun] *We found a sheltered spot under the trees and waited for the rain to stop.*

give sb shelter/refuge /ˌgɪv (sb) 'ʃeltəʳ, 'refju:dʒ/ [v phrase] to protect someone who is in danger or being hunted by someone who wants to harm them, by giving them a safe place to stay: *The British government has been accused of giving shelter to known war criminals.* | *During the war, she gave refuge and arms to local resistance groups.*

asylum /ə'saɪləm/ [n U] protection given to someone by a government because they have escaped from fighting or political trouble in their own country: *The government described them as economic refugees who have no legal claim to asylum.* | **seek asylum** (=ask for asylum) *Gypsies from Eastern Europe have sought asylum in Britain.* | **grant sb asylum** (=give it to them officially) *Cubans who reach the U.S. are usually granted asylum.* | **political asylum** *They have sought political asylum in the United States.*

3 someone whose job is to protect a person or place

- ▸ guard
- ▸ bodyguard
- ▸ defender/guardian
- ▸ minder

guard /gɑ:ʳd/ [n C] someone whose job is to watch a place, person, or valuable object, in order to protect them or stop them escaping: *Guards at the embassy refused to let journalists enter.* | **security guard** (=someone whose job is to guard a building) *Two men overpowered the security guard and stole $20,000.* | **armed guard** (=one with a gun) *The captain put armed guards all around the camp.*

bodyguard /'bɒdigɑ:ʳd‖'bɑ:-/ [n C/U] a person or group of people whose job is to protect someone important: *The President arrived, surrounded by bodyguards.* | *a member of the Emperor's bodyguard*

defender/guardian /dɪ'fendəʳ, 'gɑ:ʳdiən/ [n C] a person or organization that protects, or appears to protect, someone or something that people think is important or morally right: *The group, known as the Defenders of Wildlife, have sued to protect the Louisiana black bear.* | *The film was banned as a result of protests by the Viewers Association and other so-called guardians of public morality.*

minder /'maɪndəʳ/ [n C] British informal someone employed by a rich or famous person to protect him or her: *Kylie will often shop in Kensington without her minders, dressed in dark glasses for anonymity.*

4 something that protects someone or something

- ▸ protection
- ▸ protective
- ▸ shelter
- ▸ shield
- ▸ guard
- ▸ protector
- ▸ safeguard

protection /prə'tekʃən/ [n U] something that protects you against harm or damage **+ against** *Their light summer clothes were no protection against the bitter cold.* | **give/provide protection** (=protect someone) *Vitamin C provides some protection against minor illnesses.* | **+ from** *At the time, the law gave women very little protection from violent husbands.*

protective /prə'tektɪv/ [adj only before noun] **protective** clothes, covers, substances etc protect someone or something from being hurt or damaged: *Wear* *protective glasses when working with the saw.* | *Motorcyclists must wear protective helmets.* | *Remove the disk from its protective packaging.* | **protective gear/clothing** *Burke was not wearing protective gear when the accident happened.*

shelter /'ʃeltəʳ/ [n C/U] a place where you will be protected from danger or from bad weather: *It began to rain and we all ran for shelter.* | **+ of** *William hurried towards the shelter of the old cowshed.* | **take shelter** (=find a safe place) *People took shelter from the flooding in churches and schools on high ground.* | **bomb shelter** (=a place, usually underground, that is safe from bombs) *Underground stations in London were used as bomb shelters during the Second World War.*

shield /ʃiːld/ [n C] an object or material that protects someone or something from harm or damage: *Suncream acts as a kind of shield against the sun's harmful ultraviolet rays.* | *The spacecraft is covered in a material that acts as a heat shield.* | *Before operating this machine, make sure the safety shield is in place.*

guard /gɑːʳd/ [n C] something that is, for example, fixed to a machine or worn on a part of your body, in order to provide protection against damage or injury: *You can buy guards for electric sockets that make it impossible for little children to stick their fingers into the holes.* | *Football players are strongly advised to wear shin guards.*

protector /prə'tektəʳ/ [n C] a piece of clothing or equipment that you wear or hold to protect a part of your body: *Hockey goalies wear a chest protector that is similar to the one a catcher in baseball wears.* | *A pocket protector will prevent ink staining your shirt.*

safeguard /'seɪfgɑːʳd/ [n C] something, for example a law or rule, that provides protection against danger, problems, or failure: *There's a safeguard built into the tenancy agreement that says the landlord must give you three months' notice to quit.* | *Anti-virus software is a simple safeguard that many computer users have not bothered to install.* | **+ against** *As a safeguard against misuse, memorize your PIN number immediately and destroy this advice slip.*

5 wanting to protect people

- protective
- overprotective
- wrap sb in cotton wool

protective /prə'tektɪv/ [adj] wanting to protect someone from harm or danger, often in a way that stops them behaving freely: *Society's attitude towards children who live in the streets is not always protective.* | **+ of** *My dad is very protective of me and has never liked any of my boyfriends.* | **+ towards** *A dog may feel protective towards family members, and attack people who go near them.*

overprotective /ˌəʊvəʳprə'tektɪv/ [adj] too anxious about wanting to protect someone from harm, danger etc in a way that seriously restricts that person's freedom, or stops them developing the skills they need for dealing with normal life: *My wife says I'm being overprotective, and that our daughter has grown into a responsible young woman.* | **overprotective mother/father/parent** *a spoilt rich kid with an overprotective mother*

wrap sb in cotton wool /ˌræp (sb) ɪn ˌkɒtn 'wʊl‖-ˌkɑːtn-/ [v phrase] British to protect someone too much by not allowing them to experience difficult or unpleasant situations, so that they find it difficult to deal with such situations when they have to: *I'm getting better, and I have no intention of spending my life wrapped in cotton wool.*

protest

when people show publicly that they do not agree with something

RELATED WORDS

- disagree, complain, against/oppose, violent, support, government, rebellion/revolution, environment

1 to show publicly that you disagree with something

- protest
- demonstrate
- march
- boycott
- riot

protest /prə'test/ [v I/T] if people **protest** about something, they show that they think it is wrong or unfair, for example by holding public meetings or writing letters to politicians: *When the army took power, huge crowds gathered in the capital to protest.* | **+ about/against** *Prisoners had climbed onto the roof to protest about conditions in the jail.* | **protest sth** American *a huge crowd of students protesting the globalization of trade*

demonstrate /'demənstreɪt/ [v I] to protest about something in an organized way, by having a large outdoor meeting or by marching through the streets: *Thousands of people demonstrated outside the parliament building last night.* | **+ against** *Thousands of workers and students demonstrated against US involvement in the war.*

march /mɑːʳtʃ/ [v I] to walk with a large group of people from one place to another, in order to show that you do not agree with something **+ through/to etc** *Over ten thousand workers marched through the capital demanding higher wages.* | **+ on** *Several thousand people marched on the French embassy.*

boycott /'bɔɪkɒt‖-kɑːt/ [v T] to not buy something, not go somewhere, or not take part in an event, in order to protest about the actions of a country or company: *Students have threatened to boycott certain banks as a protest at their investment policies.* | *Several countries have said they may boycott next year's Olympic Games.*

riot /'raɪət/ [v I] if a large group of people **riot**, they protest about something by fighting the police, damaging public buildings, or setting fire to things: *Prisoners in several jails have rioted in protest at their appalling conditions.* | *Gangs of youths rioted for two nights on the streets of the capital.* —**rioting** [n U] *Five days of rioting followed the police shooting of student leaders.*

2 ways of protesting about something

- protest
- demonstration
- march
- boycott
- riot
- sit-in

protest /'prəʊtest/ [n C/U] *The school has received over 3,000 letters of protest.* | *The protest begun by Soweto children rapidly spread throughout the country.* | **mass protest** (=a protest by a lot of people) *Over fifteen thousand people held a mass protest against racism in the country's capital.* | **storm of protest** (=a lot of angry protest) *The shooting provoked a storm of protest.* | **in protest at/against** *Prisoners have been holding hunger strikes in protest against their living* *conditions.* | *Public employees have threatened mass resignations in protest at the plans.*

demonstration ALSO **demo** British /ˌdemənˈstreɪʃən, ˈdeməʊ/ [n C] when a large number of people come together to protest about something, by having an outdoor meeting or marching through the streets: *The police had to break up yesterday's animal rights demonstration.* | *Some of the marchers called to us to come and join the demo.* | **+ against** *Over 3,000 people took part in a demonstration against the dumping of nuclear waste at sea.*

march /mɑːʳtʃ/ [n C] when a large group of people walk in an organized way from one place to another in order to protest about something: *Thousands of students took part in the march.* | **protest march** *Local trade union leaders joined in the protest march against cuts in government spending.*

boycott /ˈbɔɪkɒt‖-kɑːt/ [n C] when people protest against the actions of a country or company, for example by not buying its products, not attending its events etc **+ of** *Farmers are calling for a boycott of all imported meat.* | *a boycott of the peace talks*

riot /ˈraɪət/ [n C] violent and illegal behaviour by a large group of people in order to protest against something that they think is unfair and that has made them very angry: *Altogether the riots cost 130 lives and well over $700 million in property damage.* | *Racial tension boiled over in the inner city riots which spread across the nation last week.*

sit-in /ˈsɪt ɪn/ [n C] when people refuse to leave the place where they work or study until they are given the things they are asking for: *Workers at the factory organized a sit-in to draw attention to their grievances.*

3 someone who takes part in a public protest

- protester
- demonstrator
- marcher

protester /prəˈtestəʳ/ [n C usually plural] someone who protests about something with other people: *Thousands of protesters took to the streets to show their anger at the government.*

demonstrator /ˈdemənstreɪtəʳ/ [n C usually plural] someone who takes part in an organized event, such as a march or an outdoor meeting, to protest about something: *Thirteen demonstrators were killed when soldiers opened fire on the crowd.*

marcher /ˈmɑːʳtʃəʳ/ [n C] someone who takes part in an organized walk through an area in order to protest against something: *The Rev. Jesse Jackson led 1000 marchers through downtown Detroit to protest state welfare cuts.*

proud

RELATED WORDS

- to talk too proudly about yourself, your achievements etc *see* **boast**
- not wanting to talk proudly about your achievements, abilities etc *see* **modest**
- *see also* **show off, confident/not confident**

1 proud

- proud
- take pride in
- pride yourself on
- sb's pride and joy
- the pride of sth

proud /praʊd/ [adj] someone who is **proud** of their achievements, their school, their family etc is very pleased with them and feels that they are very good or special: *I felt so proud when my son went up to collect his medal.* | *the proud parents with their new baby* | **+ of** *Jane's very proud of her new car.* | *My students have worked hard, and I'm proud of them.* | **+ to be/do sth** *Morris was proud to be part of such a brilliant team.* | *I'm proud to say that all my children had a good education.* | **+ that** *He's very proud that his work has finally been published.* —**proudly** [adv] *She turned to the crowd, proudly holding up the silver cup.*

take pride in /teɪk ˈpraɪd ɪn/ [v phrase] to feel proud of your work, your appearance etc, and always try to keep it at a high standard: *I've always taken pride in my appearance.* | *The people of the Basque country take great pride in their local cuisine.* | **take pride in doing sth** *Teachers should take pride in improving the display work in their classrooms.*

pride yourself on /ˈpraɪd jɔːʳself ɒn/ [v phrase] to be especially proud of something that you do well or of a particular quality that you have: *Archer prided himself on his knowledge of Italian art.* | **pride yourself on doing something** *She prides herself on getting things done quickly.* | *Our staff pride themselves on offering guests a warm welcome.*

sb's pride and joy / (sb's) ˌpraɪd ən ˈdʒɔɪ/ [n phrase] if something that you own, something that you have made etc **is your pride and joy**, you are especially proud of it and it is very important to you: *Todd's magnificent Rolls Royce had been his pride and joy for many years.* | *The garden was my father's pride and joy, the real expression of his creativity.* | *Christina was an only child, her parents' pride and joy.*

the pride of sth /ðə ˈpraɪd ɒv (sth)/ [n phrase] the one thing or person in a particular group or place that people are most proud of: *Bolton's famous football team was the pride of the town.* | *The Mary Rose, which was the pride of Henry VIII's fleet, sank on her maiden voyage.*

2 too proud

- conceited/big-headed
- arrogant
- vain
- smug
- self-satisfied
- be full of yourself
- pleased with yourself
- think you're it
- let sth go to your head
- get too big for your boots

conceited/big-headed /kənˈsiːtɪ̈d, ˌbɪg ˈhedɪ̈d◂/ [adj] someone who is **conceited** or **big-headed** is too proud of their own achievements or abilities, in a way that annoys other people: *You're the most conceited, selfish person I've ever met!* | *I know this sounds big-headed, but I've always been good at French.*

arrogant /ˈærəgənt/ [adj] someone who is **arrogant** behaves as if their opinions are more important than other people's, and thinks that they are always right: *You are a rude and arrogant young man.* | *his arrogant disregard for other people's opinions* —**arrogantly** [adv] *They arrogantly assumed that their form of democracy was better than anyone else's.*

vain /veɪn/ [adj] someone who is **vain** thinks they are very good-looking, special, or intelligent: *She's a vain girl who is always thinking about her figure.* | *I am vain enough to want to look good, but not to style my hair and paint my toenails.*

smug /smʌg/ [adj] quietly pleased with yourself in an unpleasant and annoying way, because you think you are in a better position than other people: *Lawson comes over as smug and arrogant, but in fact he's quite a decent man.* | *If you knew, which I'm sure you did judging from your smug expression, why didn't you tell me?* | **+ about** *I felt very smug about not wasting paper.* —**smugly** [adv] *'I'm getting a motorcycle soon,' he announced smugly. 'My dad's buying me one for my eighteenth birthday.'*

self-satisfied /self 'sætəsfaɪd/ [adj] someone who is **self-satisfied** thinks that they are very clever, very successful etc, often without good reason, and shows this in an annoying way: *Doyle's self-satisfied smile irritated Haworth.* | *He was in his early 40s and had the self-satisfied air of someone who has achieved fame and success.* | *What makes a second-rate actress like Jean so self-satisfied, so over-confident?*

be full of yourself /biː 'fʊl əv jɔːʳˌself/ [v phrase] spoken to be always talking about your abilities and achievements and never show any interest in those of other people: *She's a good-looking woman, but too full of herself for my liking.* | *He was too full of himself to care about anyone else.*

pleased with yourself /'pliːzd wɪð jɔːʳself/ [adj phrase] feeling unreasonably proud of yourself, especially because you think you have done something clever: *I had made a big profit on the deal and was feeling inordinately pleased with myself.* | *After deceiving us all like that, she went away, no doubt very pleased with herself.*

think you're it ALSO **fancy yourself** British /ˌθɪŋk jɔːr 'ɪt, 'fænsi jɔːʳself/ [v phrase] spoken informal use this when you think someone is too proud of their abilities or appearance: *You think you're it don't you? Well you're not!* | *Like most young professional footballers, he really fancied himself.*

let sth go to your head /let (sth) ˌgəʊ tə jɔːʳ 'hed/ [v phrase] to start behaving as if you are very important as a result of something, for example a success or being praised by someone: *It's not surprising that young rock bands let success go to their heads.* | *I know you did well, but don't let it go to your head – the hardest part's still to come.*

get too big for your boots British **/too big for your britches** American /get tuː ˌbɪg fəʳ jɔːʳ 'buːts, tuː ˌbɪg fəʳ jɔːʳ 'brɪtʃəz/ [v phrase] informal to start thinking you are more important than you really are, especially because you have been successful in something: *Bonaparte wasn't all that bad. He was just a soldier who got too big for his boots.*

3 someone who thinks they are better than other people

- snob
- snobbish
- stuck-up
- pompous
- self-important
- haughty
- snotty

snob /snɒb‖snɑːb/ [n C] someone who thinks that they are better than people from a lower social class: *Since going to university he'd become a snob, embarrassed by his family.* | *I don't want to sound like a snob, but I found the decor vulgar.*

snobbish /'snɒbɪʃ‖'snɑː-/ [adj] someone who is **snobbish** thinks that they are better than people from a lower class, so that they will not be friendly with them or do the things they do: *Some people find her snobbish, but she's really just shy.* | *his snobbish attitude to soap operas on TV* | **+ about** *She's very snobbish about people who live in the suburbs.* —**snobbery** [n U] *To say that working class people are all the same is sheer snobbery* (=is being very snobbish).

stuck-up /ˌstʌk 'ʌp◂/ [adj] informal someone who is **stuck-up** thinks that they are better than other people, and behaves in a proud, unfriendly way: *The children who go to that school are a bit stuck-up.* | *a pompous, stuck-up little man*

pompous /'pɒmpəs‖'pɑːm-/ [adj] someone who is **pompous** tries to sound important, especially by using very long or formal words: *She found him pompous and annoying.* | *The headteacher gave a pompous speech about 'the values of learning'.*

self-important /ˌself ɪm'pɔːʳtənt◂/ [adj] thinking you are much more important than you really are: *As a waiter, he had grown to despise self-important customers.* | *He was one of those self-important little officials who made everyone call him 'Sir'.* —**self-importance** [n U] *He strutted into the room, full of his own self-importance.*

haughty /'hɔːti/ [adj] someone who is **haughty** behaves in a proud and very unfriendly way, as if they think other people are completely unimportant: *People thought of him as being haughty and difficult to talk to.* | *Jessica turned away with a haughty look on her face.* —**haughtily** [adv] *She refused his request, haughtily explaining that such things were beneath her.*

snotty /'snɒti‖'snɑː-/ [adj] informal rude and unfriendly because you think you are better than other people: *The hotel receptionist was a bit snotty to me this morning.* | *a bunch of snotty rich kids*

4 to think you are better than other people

- look down on
- be beneath
- think you're too good for

look down on /lʊk 'daʊn ɒn/ [phr v T] if you **look down on** other people, you think you are better or more important then them: *He looks down on anyone who hasn't had a college education.*

be beneath /biː bɪ'niːθ/ [v T] if it **is beneath** you to do something or to talk to someone, you think you are much too important to do it: *Do you think you could make the tea for once – or is that beneath you!* | **+ to do sth** *She was surprised to learn that he didn't think it was beneath him to help around the house.*

think you're too good for /ˌθɪŋk jɔːr tuː 'gʊd fɔːʳ/ [v phrase] if you say that someone **thinks they are too good for** a particular kind of work or for a particular person, you mean they are too proud to do that kind of work or to spend time with that person: *I suppose you think you're too good for us now you've inherited a fortune.* | *So you think you're too good for training college?*

5 the feeling you have when you are proud of something

- pride

pride /praɪd/ [n U] the feeling of being proud because of something special you have achieved, someone special you are connected with etc: *Chinese students have a sense of national pride.* | **do sth with pride** *He talked with great pride about his father's work.* | **+ in** *Her pride in her daughter knew no bounds.* | **bursting with pride** (=feeling extremely proud) *Bursting with pride, she stood up to receive her prize.*

6 an unreasonable feeling of pride

- arrogance
- conceit
- vanity

arrogance /'ærəgəns/ [n U] an unreasonable pride in your own abilities or qualities, which makes you behave rudely, as if other people were of no importance or interest: *'I ought to be in charge here,' said Jack with simple arrogance.* | *His arrogance and unwillingness to learn from others prevent him from being an effective member of the team.*

conceit /kən'si:t/ [n U] too much pride in your own abilities, appearance, or qualities, especially following a success which has made you behave as if you are very important: *After scoring the winning goal he almost danced along the road in his satisfaction and conceit.* | *I got so sick of his conceit that I threw the damn trophy out.*

vanity /'vænəti/ [n U] great pride in yourself so that you are always thinking about yourself, especially about your appearance: *His life is driven by vanity. He has to drive around in the most expensive car and wear the best designer clothes.* | *Jo's vanity wouldn't let her walk past a mirror without looking in it.*

7 a feeling of respect for yourself

- self-respect
- self-esteem
- dignity
- pride
- dignified

self-respect /ˌself rɪ'spekt/ [n U] a feeling of respect and confidence in yourself and in your abilities: *It is difficult to keep your self-respect when you have been unemployed for a long time* | *Serious illness often results in a loss of confidence and self-respect.*

self-esteem /ˌself ɪ'sti:m/ [n U] the feeling that you are someone who deserves to be liked, respected, and admired: *The program is designed to help children from broken families build their self-esteem.* | **low/high self-esteem** (=a bad or good feeling about yourself) *When I started seeing my therapist, I was suffering from very low self-esteem.*

dignity /'dɪgnəti/ [n U] the ability to behave in a calm way that shows that you respect yourself, even in difficult situations **do sth with dignity** *Very sick people should be allowed to die with dignity.* | **lose your dignity** *She lost her home and all her money, but she never lost her dignity.*

pride /praɪd/ [n U] the feeling that you deserve to be respected by other people – use this especially when this feeling is so strong that someone finds it difficult to admit they need help or that they are wrong: *He has too much pride to say he's sorry.* | *Her pride would not allow her to ask for help.* | **hurt sb's pride** *We don't like failing – it hurts our pride.*

dignified /'dɪgnəfaɪd/ [adj] behaving in a calm way, even in a difficult situation, so that other people respect and admire you: *She was a quiet, dignified old lady.* | *Jo listened to their criticisms in dignified silence.*

prove

RELATED WORDS

- *see also* **true, untrue, right, wrong**

1 to show that something is correct or true

- prove
- show
- demonstrate
- confirm
- support
- back up
- bear out
- substantiate
- validate
- corroborate

prove /pru:v/ [v T] to show that something is definitely true, by providing facts or information: *We're sure Jason took the money, but we can't prove it.* | *Until there is evidence to prove any of these claims, we cannot pass judgement.* | **+ that** *Can you prove that you were at home at the time of the attack?* | *He wanted to prove that he was just as clever as his sister.* | **prove sb wrong/innocent/guilty** *I would love to prove him wrong.* | **prove sth to sb** *I'm telling the truth, and I can prove it to you.* | **+ where/how etc** *Don't trust anyone who turns up at your door, unless they can prove who they are.* | **prove sth conclusively/beyond doubt** *His guilt has never been conclusively proven.*

show /ʃəʊ/ [v T] if facts or actions **show** that something is true, they prove that it is true: *The Prime Minister's comments show his ignorance of people's feelings.* | **+ (that)** *Research shows that smiling increases the levels of hormones that promote good health.* | **+ where/how etc** *These figures show how serious the company's problems are.* | **show sth/sb to be sth** *A scientific theory is only 'true' until someone shows it to be false or inaccurate.*

demonstrate /'demənstreɪt/ [v T] to do something or provide information which makes it very clear to people that something is true: *The studies demonstrate a clear link between smoking and heart disease.* | **+ (that)** *The President is anxious to demonstrate that he has a strong foreign policy.* | **+ where/how etc** *Try to round off your answer by demonstrating how your old job has prepared you to do the job you are applying for.*

confirm /kən'fɜ:ʳm/ [v T] if a piece of new information **confirms** an idea or belief that people already have, it shows that it is definitely true: *Police have found new evidence that confirms his story.* | **+ that** *The discovery seems to confirm that people lived here over 10,000 years ago.* | **confirm sb's worst fears** (=prove that something is as bad as someone thought it was) *In July his worst fears were confirmed: he had cancer.*

support /sə'pɔ:ʳt/ [v T not in progressive] **support a theory/claim/notion/ view etc** to help to prove that a belief, idea etc is probably true: *Do you have any evidence to support these claims?* | *The notion that women are worse drivers than men is simply not supported by the facts.* | *For twenty-five years he painstakingly amassed evidence to support his hypothesis.*

back up /ˌbæk 'ʌp/ [phr v T not in progressive] to provide additional information to help prove that a statement, belief, or explanation is correct **back up sth** *When you write a history essay, you should back up all your points with facts.* | **back sth/it/them up** *They claim they can give us the best deal, but can they back this up with guarantees?* | *Wright was accused of pretending to be injured, and this was backed up by video evidence.*

bear out /ˌbeər 'aʊt/ [phr v T not usually in progressive] if facts or information **bear out** a claim or opinion, they support it and help to prove that it is probably true **bear out sth** *Most of the available evidence bears out the view that students learn better in small classes than in large classes.* | *My warnings about*

Jean-Paul were later borne out by his dishonesty. | **bear sb out** (=prove what someone has said is true) *Last summer I predicted an increase in terrorist violence, and recent events have borne me out.*

substantiate /səb'stænʃieɪt/ [v T not in progressive] formal to provide additional information that helps to prove that a statement is correct, especially if the statement is difficult to believe **substantiate a claim/an allegation** *The authorities claimed they were conspiring to overthrow the government, but offered no evidence to substantiate these claims.* | *Allegations made by prisoners are usually only considered when substantiated by the evidence of a prison officer.*

validate /'vælɪdeɪt/ [v T not in progressive] formal to prove that information or results are correct by using scientific tests or very careful checking – used in scientific or technical contexts: *All the information used in this report has been validated by an independent panel of experts.* | *This is an interesting hypothesis, but all attempts to validate it have so far failed.*

corroborate /kə'rɒbəreɪt‖kə'rɑː-/ [v T not in progressive] formal to provide additional information which supports or agrees with something that most people already accept as true – used in scientific and legal contexts: *Levine claims that a third car was involved in the accident and witnesses have corroborated this.* | *Professor Carling's findings have been corroborated by more recent research.* | **corroborate a story** *There was no one to corroborate her story about the disturbance in the lounge.* | **corroborating evidence** *No doctor would order surgery on the basis of a single test result, without corroborating clinical evidence.*

2 to prove that something is wrong, untrue, or does not exist

- disprove
- refute
- debunk
- invalidate
- demolish
- explode
- negative

disprove /dɪs'pruːv/ [v T] to prove that something is wrong or not true: *She was able to produce figures that disproved Smith's argument.* | *The existence of God is a question of faith, and therefore impossible to prove or disprove.*

refute /rɪ'fjuːt/ [v T] formal to prove that what someone has said is not true: *I knew that he was lying but I had no evidence with which to refute his story.* | *The accusation has been wholly refuted by an in-depth analysis of the evidence.*

debunk /ˌdiː'bʌŋk/ [v T] to prove that something is not true, especially something that people have believed for a long time, and make it seem silly or unimportant: *In her book she debunks a lot of the claims made by astrologers.* | *Payton wants to debunk the myth that economics is a science.*

invalidate /ɪn'vælɪdeɪt/ [v T not in progressive] formal if a fact or piece of information **invalidates** an explanation or idea, it proves that it contains mistakes which make it unlikely to be true – used in scientific contexts: *None of the more recent views invalidates Hahnemann's original discoveries or teachings.* | *If we look closely at Professor Thomson's argument, we see that his conclusion is invalidated by a number of factual errors.*

demolish /dɪ'mɒlɪʃ‖dɪ'mɑː-/ [v T] to prove that an argument or idea is completely wrong: *It would not be difficult to demolish a theory that was so obviously a load of rubbish.* | *There was a time when the response 'that's a value judgement' would have demolished any argument in the educational field.*

explode /ɪk'spləʊd/ [v T] **explode a myth/rumour** to prove that something that many people think or believe is wrong or not true: *The report explodes the myth that men are bed-hopping rogues.*

negative /'negətɪv/ [adj] a **negative** result of a medical or chemical test does not show any sign of the condition you are testing for and therefore proves it does not exist in this person or situation: *All the athletes' drugs tests were negative.* | *a negative pregnancy test* | *The first brain scan proved negative.*

3 something that proves something is true

- proof
- evidence
- documentation
- living proof
- the acid test

proof /pruːf/ [n U] information or facts that prove that something is true: *He was the only person in the room when the money disappeared – what more proof do you want?* | *The police knew she was guilty, but they had no proof.* | **+ of** *You can't drink in bars without some proof of your age.* | **+ (that)** *There is no proof that he did it.* | **conclusive proof** (=something that definitely proves something is true) *It was alleged that he was stealing money from the till, but we never had any conclusive proof.*

evidence /'evɪdəns/ [n U] information that helps to prove whether something is true or not: *The police did not have enough evidence to charge anybody with the murder.* | **+ that** *There is some evidence that a small amount of alcohol is good for you.* | **+ of/for** *evidence of life on other planets* | **medical/scientific/forensic etc evidence** *There is no scientific evidence to support this theory.* | **evidence to suggest/indicate/show etc sth** *There is strong evidence to suggest that the Great Barrier Reef will have disappeared in 20 years time.* | **not a shred of evidence** (=no evidence at all) *There is not a shred of evidence to support such a theory.*

documentation /ˌdɒkjʊmən'teɪʃən, -men-‖ˌdɑːk-/ [n U] official documents that are used to prove that a claim or statement is true or correct: *Can you produce documentation to support your claim?* | *As there is no formal documentation of your business partnership, it has no legal status.*

living proof /ˌlɪvɪŋ 'pruːf/ [n C] a person, group, or place that proves that something is true or possible **+ of** *The team is living proof of the old saying that it's not whom you play that counts, but when you play them.* | *We know that English and French speakers can live together in Canada – Montreal is living proof of that.* | **+ that** *Jordan is living proof that you don't have to conform to the music industry's standards in order to be accepted.*

the acid test /ði ˌæsɪd 'test/ [n singular] a way of finding out whether something is as good as people say it is, whether it works, or when it is true: *The acid test of a good leader is the extent to which they select a style to suit the circumstances.*

provide/supply

to make something available for someone who wants it or needs it

RELATED WORDS

▸ *see also* **give, available/not available**

1 to provide something that is needed

▸ **provide**
▸ **supply**
▸ **fund**
▸ **offer**
▸ **equip**
▸ **issue**
▸ **lay on**
▸ **fix sb up with**

provide /prəˈvaɪd/ [v T] if a person or organization **provides** something, they make it available for someone who needs it or wants it: *Your bank should be able to provide financial advice.* | **provide sth for sb** *Free parking is provided for hotel guests.* | *The university should provide more facilities for disabled students.* | **provide sb with sth** *The money will be used to provide the school with new computer equipment.*

supply /səˈplaɪ/ [v T] to provide things for people, especially regularly and over a long period of time **supply sth to sb** *The company supplies fish to local shops and restaurants.* | **supply sb with sth** *The US government was accused of supplying the rebels with arms and equipment.*

fund /fʌnd/ [v T] to provide money for a person or organization so that they can do something: *The museum is funded by the local authority.* | *They suspect that the rebels are being funded by Western governments.*

offer /ˈɒfəʳ‖ˈɔːf-/ [v T] make something available to people if they want or need it, especially something that will be good for them, such as help, advice, or a chance to do something **offer sth to sb** *The booklet offers practical advice to new parents.* | **offer sb sth** *The prison now offers inmates the chance to study and take exams.* | **offer sth** *The shelter offers some protection from the icy winds.* | *Sending goods by road offers greater speed and flexibility.*

equip /ɪˈkwɪp/ [v T] to provide a person, group, or organization with the things they need for a particular kind of activity or work **equip sb with sth** *Police officers have been equipped with batons and riot shields in preparation for tonight's match.* | *We try to equip our students with the skills they will need in the world of work.* —**equipped** [adj] *The ship is modern and very well equipped.* | *This is one of the best equipped hospitals in the country.*

issue /ˈɪʃuː, ˈɪsjuː‖ˈɪʃuː/ [v T usually in passive] if an organization or someone in an official position **issues** equipment, clothes, weapons etc, they provide these things because people need them **issue sb with sth** *Police in Britain are not usually issued with guns.* | *Visitors are issued with identity cards to wear inside the factory.* | **issue sth to sb** *Blankets and warm clothes will be issued to those who need them.*

lay on /ˌleɪ ˈɒn/ [phr v T] British to provide things such as food or entertainment, so that they are available when people want them **lay on sth** *I've asked the catering manager to lay on refreshments at the meeting.* | **be laid on** *Games and entertainment were laid on in the afternoon.*

fix sb up with /ˌfɪks (sb) ˈʌp wɪð/ [phr v T] informal to provide someone with something that they need, especially in an unexpected situation: *Can you fix me up with a bed for the night?* | *I took the car to a nearby garage, and they managed to fix me up with a new tyre.*

2 to provide a service for a particular group of people

▸ **cater for**
▸ **serve**
▸ **provide for**

cater for ALSO **cater to** /ˈkeɪtəʳ fɔːʳ, ˈkeɪtəʳ tuː/ [phr v T] to provide services to a group of people, especially a group that has particular problems or particular needs: *The hostel caters for single people who are unable to find affordable accommodation.* | *The market now caters mainly to tourists.* | **be well catered for** *Children are well catered for at the Hotel Paradiso.* | **cater to sb's every need** *Cabin staff will cater to your every need.*

serve /sɜːʳv/ [v T] to provide a service for a very large group of people, especially those living in a particular area: *He served the community for over thirty years as a head teacher.* | *The new bus route will serve the villages to the west of York.* | **serve the needs of sb** *The center was opened four months ago to serve the health needs of a low-income neighborhood.*

provide for /prəˈvaɪd fɔːʳ/ [phr v T] to provide a service for a particular group of people, especially one that they really need: *The nursing home provides for all the needs of the elderly.* | *Local authorities must provide for the education of all children with learning difficulties.*

3 something that is provided

▸ **supply**
▸ **flow**
▸ **service**

supply /səˈplaɪ/ [n singular] a system of supplying things that people need, such as food or medicine **+ of** *We need to improve the supply of food to the area affected by the floods.* | *The steel industry depends on a regular supply of raw materials.* | **water/blood/electricity etc supply** *The patient suffered a sudden decrease in the blood supply to part of her brain.* | *The drought is threatening the water supply in some areas.*

flow /fləʊ/ [n singular] a continuous supply of something, especially from one place to another: *the flow of oil from the Middle East* | *The civil war has severely disrupted the flow of humanitarian aid to the region.*

service /ˈsɜːʳvə̇s/ [n C] an organization or system that provides something for people, or the product or help it provides: *A private car service is available from the airport.* | *Electrical service was cut off for up to five hours in some parts of the country yesterday.* | **provide/perform a service** *The business, if properly regulated, performs a useful service for lottery winners.*

4 a company or country that supplies things to people

▸ **supplier**
▸ **provider**

supplier /səˈplaɪəʳ/ [n C] a company or country that supplies things to people **+ of** *one of the world's biggest suppliers of defense equipment* | **the main/major supplier** *The company is now the main supplier of educational software to schools.*

provider /prəˈvaɪdəʳ/ [n C] a company or organization that provides a service for customers **education/health/healthcare provider** *schools, colleges and other education providers* | **service provider** *The company is now one of the regions main Internet service providers.* | **+ of** *a leading provider of personal financial services*

public

RELATED WORDS

opposite: —— **private**

- people in general *see* **person/people**
- *see also* **government, politics, public services**

1 for everyone to use

- **public**

public /ˈpʌblɪk/ [adj only before noun] a **public** place or **public** service is one that anyone can use, not one that is only for a particular person or group: *Could you tell me where the public telephones are?* | *Is this a public beach?* | *proposals to ban smoking in public places* | *They're always telling people to use public transport because there are too many cars on the roads.* | *You now have to pay to use the public toilets at the station.*

2 owned or paid for by the government

- **public**
- **state**
- **government**
- **federal**
- **nationalize**

public /ˈpʌblɪk/ [adj only before noun] **public** libraries, hospitals etc are provided and paid for by the government, not by private companies: *You can get the information from your local public library* | *We need to raise taxes to pay for better public healthcare.* | **public services** *garbage collection and other public services* | **public spending/expenditure** (=money spent by the government to provide public services) *There's been a big increase in public spending over the past three years.* | **the public sector** (=all the industries and services that are owned or paid for by the government) *I've worked in the public sector all my life, mainly in local government.* | *public sector employees* —**publicly owned** [adj] *Thatcher privatized publicly owned industries like electricity and telecommunications.*

state /steɪt/ [adj only before noun] owned, controlled, or paid for by the government. In the US **state** usually refers to the government of a particular **state**, not the national government: *The government has promised increased spending on the the state education system.* | *China's state radio station* | *Britain's state aid for industry generally falls far short of the sums seen in other countries.*

government /ˈgʌvəmənt, ˈgʌvənmənt‖ˈgʌvərn-/ [adj only before noun] provided, paid for, or run by the government: *How much government money is to be poured into this program?* | *The camps have been attacked several times by government forces.* | *The industry secretary has just announced a government initiative to address the problem.*

federal /ˈfedərəl/ [adj only before noun] owned or paid for by the national government of the US or a country organized in a similar way: *Federal funding for the project was cut last year* | *federal agencies* | *the Federal Bureau of Investigation* —**federally** [adv] *federally funded programs*

nationalize ALSO **nationalise** British /ˈnæʃənəlaɪz/ [v T] if a government **nationalizes** an industry or service, it buys it or takes control of it: *The mines were nationalized by the Labour Party.* | *Castro speeded up his land reforms and began to nationalize foreign holdings in Cuba.* —**nationalized/nationalised** [adj only before noun] *The government is trying to sell off as many nationalized industries as it can.*

3 when a lot of people can see you or know about what is happening

- **in public**
- **publicly**
- **public**
- **openly**
- **officially**

in public /ɪn ˈpʌblɪk/ [adv] if you do something **in public**, you do it in a place where a lot of people can see or hear you: *Most people feel nervous about speaking in public.* | *Her husband was always nice to her in public, but treated her badly at home.* | **appear in public** (=use this to say that a famous person is seen in public by ordinary people) *The Prince has not appeared in public since the announcement of his divorce.*

publicly /ˈpʌblɪkli/ [adv] if you do or say something **publicly**, you do or say it so that everyone knows about it, and you do not try to keep it secret: *He was put in prison after publicly criticizing the military government.* | *They plan to announce their engagement publicly in the New Year.*

public /ˈpʌblɪk/ [adj] **public** actions or events happen in a place where everyone can see or hear them: *It is one of the few countries where they still hold public executions.* | *In a public statement, Jackson and his wife announced their intention to get divorced.* | **a public place** (=a place where people can see or hear what you are doing) *Jeff was obviously calling from a public place.* | *Can we go somewhere quieter? This place is a bit public.*

openly /ˈəʊpənli/ [adv] if you do something **openly**, you do it in a public place and without being embarrassed or trying to hide what you are doing: *He was the first person to talk openly on TV about having AIDS.* | *Drugs are sold openly on the city streets.*

officially /əˈfɪʃəli/ [adv] if something is done **officially**, it is done by someone in authority, and made known to the public: *The changes to borders were officially announced in the European Parliament.* | *The details of the reforms are to be released officially next month.* | *thirty square miles of woodland that has been officially designated an Area of Outstanding Natural Beauty*

public services

things that are provided for people to use

RELATED WORDS

- to provide a service *see* **provide/supply**
- *see also* **public, private, government**

- **services**
- **facilities**
- **amenities**
- **utilities**
- **supply**

services /ˈsɜːʳvɪ̥sɪ̥z/ [n plural] things or systems that are provided by the government or other organizations for people to use, for example hospitals, public transport, or banks: *The 1980s saw a decline in manufacturing but a growth in services such as banking and retailing.* | **public services** *Will the use of private contractors improve public services?* | **financial/health/support etc services** *Regulation of banking and financial services was in need of an overhaul.* | *A national strike paralyzed postal services everywhere.* | **essential services** *Over the last twenty years, industrial action has affected a whole range of essential services.* | **the service sector** (=the part of industry that provides services) *Many women get jobs in the service sector.*

facilities /fəˈsɪlətiz/ [n plural] things that are provided in a place in order to make particular services or activities available: *The facilities at the hotel were excellent – tennis courts, swimming pool, several bars and a good restaurant.* | **sports/ leisure/childcare etc facilities** *The company does not yet have childcare facilities on the premises.* | **+ for** *Facilities for washing and drying clothes are hopelessly inadequate in many hostels for the homeless.*

amenities /əˈmiːnətiz‖əˈmen-/ [n plural] things such as shops, parks, or restaurants that make living or working in a place more pleasant: *I prefer this part of the city because there are plenty of good amenities.* | *The town has grown, and offers many more amenities – a new shopping mall, play areas and a variety of restaurants.* | **basic amenities** *The main problems in the refugee camp are overcrowding and a lack of basic amenities.*

utilities /juːˈtɪlətiz/ [n plural] organizations that supply necessary things such as electricity, water, and gas: *Government ownership of utilities should mean that gas and electricity costs are kept to a minimum.* | **public utilities** (=ones owned by the government) *Public utilities almost always make huge profits.*

supply /səˈplaɪ/ [n C usually singular] **electricity/water/gas supply** the system by which electricity, water, or gas is supplied to houses, factories etc: *The electricity supply is less reliable in mountainous areas of the country.* | **cut off a supply** (=stop the supply) *During the drought some households had their water supply cut off.*

pull

RELATED WORDS

opposite: —— **push, press**

▸ *see also* **carry**

1 to pull something with your hands

▸ **pull** ▸ **draw**
▸ **tug**

pull /pʊl/ [v I/T] to hold something and make it move towards you by moving your arms: *You need to pull this lever to start the machine.* | **pull sth up/towards/away etc** *He pulled her towards him and kissed her.* | *Pull the chair nearer to the fire.* | **pull hard** (=pull using a lot of effort) *Everyone took hold of the rope and pulled hard.* — **pull** [n C] **give sth a pull** *She gave a gentle pull on the reins, and the horse stopped.* | *That door sticks a bit – give it a good pull.*

tug /tʌg/ [v T] to pull something using one or more short quick movements: *The little girl was tugging her mother's sleeve, trying to get her attention.* | **+ at** *We tugged at the door but it still wouldn't open.* — **tug** [n C] **give sth a tug** *Tony gave Simon's T-shirt a tug, and they both left the room.*

draw /drɔː/ [v T] to pull someone or something slowly and smoothly in a particular direction **draw sth in/up/back/near etc** *She took my hand and drew me closer.* | *He wound in the line, steadily drawing the fish towards the bank.* | *Paula drew back the sheet and looked at the sleeping child.* | **draw the curtains/drapes** (=pull them so that they cover the windows) *It was getting dark so I drew the curtains and switched on the light.*

2 to pull something suddenly

▸ **jerk** ▸ **yank**

jerk /dʒɜːʳk/ [v T] to pull something with a sudden quick movement: *He jerked the string and the light came on.* | **jerk sth away/back/down etc** *Isabel jerked her hand away from his and shoved it in her pocket.* —**jerk** [n C] *She pulled the dog back with a sharp jerk of his leash.*

yank /jæŋk/ [v T] to pull something or someone with one sudden, quick and forceful movement, especially out of somewhere or away from something: *The other girls surrounded her, calling her names and yanking her hair.* | *Buddy yanked the drawer open, and took out the gun.* | **yank sth away/out/back etc** *His friends grabbed him and yanked him to his feet.* | *The child's mother caught him just in time, and yanked him away from the kerb.* —**yank** [n C] *I gave the lever a yank, and the machine started up.*

3 to pull something heavy

▸ **pull** ▸ **tow**
▸ **drag** ▸ **heave**
▸ **haul**

pull /pʊl/ [v T] to make a vehicle or piece of machinery move along behind – use this especially about animals or heavy vehicles that are attached to something they are pulling: *The Queen's carriage was pulled by two white horses.* | *a tractor pulling a plough*

drag /dræg/ [v T] to pull something or someone along the ground, especially because they are too heavy to carry **drag sth along/over/away etc** *One of the firemen went back in and dragged my husband out through the flames.* | *Pick up your chairs, children. Don't drag them along the floor.*

haul /hɔːl/ [v T] to pull something heavy with a strong continuous movement, often using a rope **haul sth along/out/away etc** *Somehow we managed to haul the boat out of the water and onto the bank.* | **haul in a net/rope** (=pull it towards you) *At about five o'clock the beach was full of activity, with the fishermen hauling in their nets.*

tow /təʊ/ [v T] if a vehicle or boat **tows** something, it pulls it behind it: *What's the speed limit for cars towing trailers?* | **tow sth to/from/along etc** *The damaged ship was towed to the nearest port.* | **tow sth away** (=tow a vehicle to a place where it can be repaired, or where it is not causing a problem) *The police had towed his car away because it was blocking the road.*

heave /hiːv/ [v I/T] to pull something very heavy with one great effort: *Everyone pull together now. Are you ready? Heave!* | **heave sth onto/into/over etc** *Rod bent down and heaved the sack onto his shoulder.*

punish

RELATED WORDS

- kill someone as a punishment *see* **kill (7)**
- *see also* **tell sb off, prison, judge, court/trial, law, crime, strict/not strict, revenge**

1 to punish someone

- **punish**
- **fine**
- **give sb 6 years/10 months etc**
- **sentence**
- **teach sb a lesson**
- **make sb pay**
- **penalize**
- **discipline**
- **punitive**
- **disciplinary**

punish /ˈpʌnɪʃ/ [v T] to do something unpleasant to someone because they have done something wrong, for example by putting them in prison, or making them do something that they do not want to do: *She was suspended while the school decided how to punish her.* | **punish sb for (doing) sth** *His parents punished him for disobedience.* | *The U.S. threatened to take away trading privileges as a way to punish the country for human rights violations.* | *Two instructors were punished for harassing female students.*

fine /faɪn/ [v T] to make someone pay money as a punishment: *Inspectors have the power to fine any passenger travelling without a ticket.* | **be fined £10/$100 etc** *She was fined $300 for reckless driving.* | **fine sb for (doing) sth** *One player was fined for fighting during the game.* | *The state fined the company for safety violations.*

give sb 6 years/10 months etc /gɪv (sb) ˌsɪks ˈjɪəʳz/ [v phrase] to send someone to prison for a particular period of time: *Because of the serious nature of the crime, the judge gave him 20 years.* | **+ for** *After a long trial she was given a life sentence for the bombings.*

sentence /ˈsentəns/ [v T] if a judge sentences a criminal, he or she gives them an official punishment, usually sending them to prison for a period of time **sentence sb for sth** *Brown will be sentenced for a series of sexual assaults.* | **sentence sb to 20 years/life imprisonment etc** *The judge sentenced Margolis to a year in prison.* | **sentence sb to 20 years/life imprisonment etc for sth** *Some countries will sentence you to seven or more years in prison for drug offences.* | **sentence sb to death** *60 prisoners have been sentenced to death in political trials.*

teach sb a lesson /ˌtiːtʃ (sb) ə ˈlesən/ [v phrase] to punish someone because you want to make sure that they will not behave badly again: *I hope a night in the cells has taught you a lesson.* | *He was treating me badly, so I left – I just wanted to teach him a lesson.*

make sb pay /ˌmeɪk (sb) ˈpeɪ/ [v phrase] informal to do something unpleasant to someone as a way of punishing them for something bad they have done to you or someone you know: *If I ever find out who did this, I'll make them pay!* | **+ for** *I wanted to make my father pay for his betrayal.* | *The prosecution asked jurors to make Mr. Sanderson pay for what he did.*

penalize ALSO **penalise** British /ˈpiːnəl-aɪz‖ˈpiː-, ˈpe-/ [v T] to officially punish someone, especially by taking away their right to do something or by limiting their freedom in some way: *New laws will penalize firms that continue to pollute the environment.* | *It is unfair that the whole class should be penalized because of the bad behaviour of a few students.* | **penalize sb for (doing) sth** *A referee may penalise players for wasting time.* | *The House of Representatives voted to penalize him for ethics violations.*

discipline /ˈdɪsɪ̥plɪ̥n/ [v T usually in passive] to punish someone who has broken the rules of an organization that they belong to or work for: *Officers are expected to discipline soldiers who do not keep their uniforms in good condition.* | **be disciplined** *Anyone who is regularly late for work is likely to be disciplined or dismissed.* | *Even when Morton and Collins started fighting on the field, neither player was disciplined.*

punitive /ˈpjuːnɪ̥tɪv/ [adj usually before noun] intended as a punishment **punitive action/measure/sanctions etc** *Government forces immediately took punitive action against the rebels.* | *The sanctions were a punitive measure used to try to force South Africa to reject apartheid.* | **punitive damages** (=money that a person or company has to pay to someone they have harmed – used in legal contexts) *The company was ordered to pay punitive damages in a sex discrimination case.*

disciplinary /ˈdɪsɪ̥plɪnəri, ˌdɪsɪ̥ˈplɪ-‖ˈdɪsɪ̥plɪ̥neri/ [adj only before noun] **disciplinary action/measures/charges etc** actions etc that are intended to punish someone for breaking a rule or law or to force them to obey rules: *The committee members promised that appropriate disciplinary measures would be taken against the offenders.* | *So far, not a single person has faced prosecution or disciplinary action over the case.*

2 to punish someone severely

- **come down on**
- **throw the book at**

come down on /ˌkʌm ˈdaʊn ɒn/ [v T not in passive] to immediately punish someone for something they have just done, because you want to make it clear that their actions are completely unacceptable **+ for** *Mrs Green really came down on him for swearing.* | **come down heavily/hard on sb** (=punish someone very severely) *In the examinations we shall come down hard on any student who attempts to cheat.* | *The authorities are threatening to come down more heavily on drink-driving offences.*

throw the book at /ˌθrəʊ ðə ˈbʊk æt/ [v phrase] informal if someone in authority **throws the book at** someone, they give them the severest punishment that can be given: *Unless you plead guilty, the prosecutors will throw the book at you.* | *Superior Court Judge Stephen Rosen threw the book at Davidson, sentencing him to six years in prison and ordering him to pay $1.6 million in restitution.*

3 to not punish someone

- **let sb off**
- **reprieve**
- **amnesty**

let sb off /ˌlet (sb) ˈɒf / [phr v T] to not punish someone, or give them a less severe punishment than they deserve: *I'll let you off this time, but don't do it again.* | **let sb off with a warning/a fine etc** (=only give them a warning etc, although they deserve a worse punishment) *He was caught shoplifting, but the police let him off with a warning.*

reprieve /rɪˈpriːv/ [n C] an official order stopping or delaying someone's punishment, especially when the punishment is death: *The group protested against a possible reprieve for an inmate on death row in Texas.* | **grant/give sb a reprieve** *He was granted a reprieve only a few hours before his execution.*

amnesty /'æmnəsti/ [n C] an official order forgiving people who have done something illegal or freeing prisoners – used especially in political contexts **issue/declare/proclaim an amnesty** *The President issued a general amnesty to all the rebels, including their leader.* | *The government has been forced to declare an amnesty for anyone who has not paid their taxes, because there are now too many to collect.*

4 a punishment

- punishment
- fine
- penalty
- sentence
- retribution

punishment /'pʌnɪʃmənt/ [n C/U] something that is done to someone in order to punish them: *In cases of sheep-stealing, the usual punishment was hanging.* | **+ for** *Punishments for bad behavior can range from time-outs to withdrawing privileges, such as television* | **capital punishment** (=the system of punishing people by killing them) *Some people are demanding the return of capital punishment for murder.* | **corporal punishment** (=punishing people, especially children, by hitting them) *Corporal punishment was banned in Sweden in 1979.*

fine /faɪn/ [n C] an amount of money that you are ordered to pay as a punishment **get a fine** (=be told to pay a fine) *I got a £100 fine for speeding.* | **+ for (doing) sth** *A fine will be imposed for overstaying your visa.* | *The penalty is a $250 fine for the first offense.* | **a heavy fine** (=a large fine) *There are heavy fines for drink-driving.*

penalty /'penlti/ [n C] an official punishment for someone who breaks a law, a rule, or a legal agreement **+ for** *The penalty for treason was always death.* | **the death penalty** (=a law that says you can be killed as a punishment) *Drug smugglers face the death penalty if they are caught.* | **a heavy/severe/stiff penalty** *The contract includes stiff financial penalties for failure to complete the work on time.*

sentence /'sentəns/ [n C] a punishment given by a judge in a court **a prison sentence** *He got a 10-year prison sentence.* | **the death sentence** (=when someone is punished by being killed) *The victim's family are demanding the death sentence for his attacker.* | **a life sentence** (=the punishment of spending the rest of your life in prison) *Berger is serving a life sentence for the murders.* | **a heavy/light sentence** (=a long or short time in prison) *Evans was given a light sentence in return for giving information to the police.*

retribution /ˌretrɨ'bju:ʃən/ [n U] formal when someone is severely punished for what they have done: *Employees need to be able to express their feelings without fear of retribution.* | **+ for** *Some officials felt that the bombings were retribution for the killing of the hijackers.* | **divine retribution** (=retribution from God) *The earthquake was seen by some people as divine retribution.*

5 to get a particular punishment

- get/be given
- be condemned

get/be given /get, bi: 'gɪvən/ [v T/v phrase] to be officially given a punishment: *He deserves to get at least 10 years in prison.* | *You'll probably just get a fine.* | *McLean was given a life sentence for his part in the bombing.*

be condemned /bi: kən'demd/ [v phrase] formal to be given a particular punishment by a court, especially a severe punishment **be condemned to 20 years/life imprisonment etc** *Thomas McMahon was condemned to life imprisonment for killing Lord Mountbatten.* | **be condemned for murder/robbery/theft etc** *He was taken away after being condemned for robbery and armed assault.* | **be condemned to death** *Lewis was condemned to death after a trial lasting a year and a half.* | **condemned man/woman/prisoner** (=someone who is condemned to death) *The prison rules allow no communication with a condemned man.*

6 to be punished

- be punished
- pay for
- take the rap
- face the music

be punished /bi: 'pʌnɪʃt/ [v phrase] to **be punished** for something bad that you have done: *If you commit a crime you must expect to be punished.* | **+ for** *Ellen was punished for being rude to her teacher.* | **be severely punished** *Anyone who disobeyed his orders was severely punished.*

pay for /'peɪ fɔ:ʳ/ [phr v T] to suffer for having done something wrong, especially for breaking the law: *I've spent the last three years in jail. I tell you, I've paid for what I did.* | **pay dearly for sth** (=be severely punished for something) *People who sell drugs to our children should pay dearly for it.*

take the rap /ˌteɪk ðə 'ræp/ [v phrase] informal to be punished or held responsible for something bad, especially for something you did not do: *Until the cause of the accident was proven, the company made it clear that it was not willing to take the rap.* | **+ for (doing) sth** *The defense argued that Green was set up to take the rap for the murder of Roy Robinson.* | *I prefer driving; I don't want to take the rap for getting lost.*

face the music /ˌfeɪs ðə 'mju:zɪk/ [v phrase] informal to be ready to accept punishment for something you have done: *Rather than face the music at a trial, Abingdon chose to plea bargain.*

7 to not be punished

- get off
- get away with
- beat the rap
- with impunity
- go unpunished

get off /ˌget 'ɒf/ [phr v I] informal if a criminal **gets off**, they get little or no official punishment for their crime: *If he gets off, it's because he has a smart lawyer.* | **get off easy** *You got off easy; you should have been expelled.* | **get off scot-free** (=escape punishment completely) *Despite the evidence against him, Heston got off scot-free.*

get away with /ˌget ə'weɪ wɪð/ [phr v T not in passive] to do something wrong and not be caught or not be punished for it: *He probably got away with about a dozen crimes before he was finally arrested for one.* | **get away with it** *He was the only child in the class who could be rude to the teacher and get away with it.* | **get away with murder** informal (=to be allowed to do anything you want and not be punished for it) *Ronnoe lets his kids get away with murder.*

beat the rap /ˌbi:t ðə 'ræp/ [v phrase] American informal to avoid being punished after breaking the law, especially because you cannot be proved guilty: *Frye was arrested on state and federal charges, but he managed to beat the rap.*

with impunity /wɪð ɪm'pju:nɨti/ [adv] if someone is able to do something wrong or illegal **with**

impunity, they can do it without any risk of being punished: *If you see others breaking the law with impunity, you may be tempted to do the same.* | *The previous regime was corrupt, and government officials were able to flout the law with impunity.*

go unpunished /ˌgəʊ ʌnˈpʌnɪʃt/ [v phrase] if bad behaviour, crime etc **goes unpunished,** the person who behaved badly or did something wrong is not punished for it: *Guards involved in drug deals went unpunished.* | *Hate crimes will not be tolerated and will not go unpunished.*

8 to not be punished severely enough

- get off with
- a slap on the wrist

get off with /ˌget ˈɒf wɪð/ [v phrase] to only receive a small punishment, especially when you deserve a much more severe one: *If you're lucky you'll get off with a warning, if you're not you'll have to pay a fine.* | *It's appalling that rapists can get off with such short prison sentences.* | **get off lightly** (=only receive a small punishment) *Phil kept complaining that the $500 fine was unfair, but I think he got off lightly.*

a slap on the wrist /ə ˌslæp ɒn ðə ˈrɪst/ [n phrase] informal a much smaller punishment that you deserve: *The fine was so low, it was little more than a slap on the wrist.* | *In the past, officers who mistreated prisoners often received a mere slap on the wrist.*

9 when someone is likely to be punished

- be in trouble
- have it coming

be in trouble /biː ɪn ˈtrʌbəl/ [v phrase] especially spoken if you **are in trouble**, you are likely to be punished because you have done something bad: *You'll be in trouble if they catch you cheating.* | **+ with** *My sister's in trouble with the police again.* | **get into trouble** *I'll get into trouble if my parents see me smoking.*

have it coming /ˌhæv ɪt ˈkʌmɪŋ/ [v phrase] informal use this to say that someone deserves to be punished or deserves something bad that happens to them: *A lot of people think the murdered man had it coming.* | **+ to** *He had it coming to him, the jerk.*

pure

RELATED WORDS

- containing no dirt or bacteria *see* **clean (2)**
- food, products etc that are produced without using chemicals *see* **natural (2)**

1 not mixed with anything else

- pure
- solid
- 100%
- neat/straight
- unadulterated

pure /pjʊəʳ/ [adj] not mixed with anything else: *The bottle contained 4 litres of pure alcohol.* | *When it first comes out of the ground, the oil is not very pure.* | **pure silk/wool/cotton** *Clothes made of pure cotton are much cooler than those made of mixed fibers.* | **20%/50% etc pure** *Crude cocaine is only about 25 percent pure.* —**purity** [n U] *The gold is then tested to determine its purity* (=to determine how pure it is).

solid /ˈsɒlɪ̈d‖ˈsɑː-/ [adj only before noun] **solid gold/silver/pine etc** made of gold, silver, wood etc that has not been mixed with any other metal or wood: *a solid gold necklace* | *The antiques dealer guessed that the furniture was Victorian and solid mahogany.*

100% /ˌhʌndrɪ̈d pəʳˈsent/ [adv] if something is **100%** beef, **100%** cotton etc, it is made only from beef or cotton, and has no other food or material added to it: *The label said '100% wool'.* | *The hamburgers at this restaurant are 100% beef.* | *a 100% graphite tennis racket*

neat/straight /niːt, streɪt/ [adj] if you have a strong alcoholic drink neat or straight, you do not mix it with another drink or with water: *He always drinks his whisky neat.* | *I'll have a straight vodka please.*

unadulterated /ˌʌnəˈdʌltəreɪtɪ̈d/ [adj] not mixed with other less pure substances: *Nowadays more and more people are choosing to buy unadulterated organic food, which has been grown without pesticides and chemicals.*

2 to make a substance pure

- purify
- refine
- distil

purify /ˈpjʊərɪ̈faɪ/ [v T] *You can purify water by boiling and filtering it.* | *It has been found that houseplants help purify the air.* | *The solution is purified by passing it through a carbon filter.* | *a bottle of purified linseed oil*

refine /rɪˈfaɪn/ [v T] to make a substance such as oil or metal pure using an industrial process: *The oil is piped to the coast, where it is refined.* | *The dealers buy raw cocaine in the south, refine it here, and smuggle it into the north.* | *After the first refining process the metal is washed.* | *refined petroleum*

distil British **/distill** American /dɪˈstɪl/ [v T] to make a liquid, for example alcohol or water, purer by heating it so that it becomes a gas and then allowing it to go cold again: *My grandfather used to distil whisky on the farm.* | *The solution is distilled until it is 95% pure.* | *Only distilled water should be used for cleaning contact lenses.* —**distillation** /ˌdɪstɪˈleɪʃən/ [n U] *Steam distillation is used to purify liquids.*

3 not pure

- impure
- impurity

impure /ɪmˈpjʊəʳ/ [adj] a substance that is **impure** is not pure and contains other substances: *New laws restrict the sale of impure chemicals.* | *The last sample was impure and quite useless for manufacturing purposes.*

impurity /ɪmˈpjʊərɪ̈ti/ [n C usually plural] something in a substance which should not be in it and which makes it not pure: *Lime is added to the liquid metal to remove all the impurities.* | *There were impurities in the aluminum.*

purpose

RELATED WORDS

- on purpose *see* **deliberately**
- *see also* **reason, in order to**

1 what you want to achieve when you do something

- purpose
- aim
- point
- idea
- objective
- object
- goal
- target
- end

purpose /ˈpɜːʳpəs/ [n C] the reason you do or plan something, and the thing you want to achieve when you do it: *The games have an educational purpose.* | **+ of** *The purpose of the experiment is to find better ways of treating battlefield wounds.* | **the main purpose** (=the most important purpose) *The main purpose of the meeting is to discuss who will be in the team.* | **sb's purpose in doing sth** *My purpose in writing this book was to draw attention to the problem of global warming.* | **for the purpose of (doing) sth** *There is no penalty if the quarterback deliberately throws the ball out of bounds for the purpose of stopping play.* | **for this/that purpose** *Read up on starting a small business. Loans can be obtained for this purpose.*

aim /eɪm/ [n C] something you hope to achieve: *Increasing student awareness of the issue is one of our aims.* | **political/business/economic etc aim** *Membership of NATO is one of the country's long-term political aims.* | **the aim is to do sth** *The organization's aims are to provide food for homeless people and help them find somewhere to live.* | *The aim was to enroll all children in schools close to their homes.* | **+ of** *The aim of the bombers was to destroy public property and get maximum publicity.*

point /pɔɪnt/ [n singular] the purpose of something that you are doing or planning – use this especially when someone does not understand what the purpose is **+ of** *The point of the experiment is to show how this chemical reacts with water.* | **the whole point** (=exactly the purpose of doing something) *The whole point of this TV show is to get you to buy Simmons' exercise videos.* | **see the point of sth** (=understand why someone does something) *I can't see the point of travelling all that way and then only staying for one day.* | **miss the/sb's point** (=not understand why someone does something) *You're missing my point completely – I'm not talking about restructuring the department* | **what's the point?** (=use this when you think there is no good reason for something) *Too many of these kids think, 'What's the point of going to college?'*

idea /aɪˈdɪə/ [n singular] the effect or result that you hope to achieve by doing something – use this especially when you are doubtful whether that effect or result can be achieved: *We make toys that are both fun and educational – at least that's the idea.* | **the idea is to do sth** *The idea of the centre was to provide a place where old people could go during the day.* | **the idea behind sth** *The idea behind the commercials is that reading is as cool and entertaining as their favorite bands.*

objective /əbˈdʒektɪv/ [n C] formal the thing that someone is trying to achieve, especially in business or politics: *The report focused on three of the business's objectives.* | **business/military/political objective** *State your business objectives clearly.* | **the objective is to do sth** *The objective of this computer game is to design a city.* | **achieve an objective** *The President believes that all military objectives have been achieved.* | **main/primary objective** *The company's main objective is to keep recyclable material out of landfills.*

object /ˈɒbdʒɪkt‖ˈɑːb-/ [n singular] the intended result of a plan, action, or activity, especially when this may be difficult to achieve **the object is to do sth** *In this game the object is to score as many points as you can in the time given.* | **+ of** *The object of the search was to find a small plane that has been missing for two days.* | **the object of the exercise** (=the object of whatever you are doing) *The object of the exercise is to keep kids in school, rather than let them leave without graduating.*

goal /gəʊl/ [n C] what a person, organization, or country hopes to achieve in the future, even though this might take quite a long time: *School children have definite goals towards which they can work.* | **the goal is to do sth** *Her goal is to find a company willing to donate money for research.* | **+ of** *The goal of the partnership is to improve his company's profit margin.* | **reach/meet a goal** *The Red Cross has reached its goal of raising $1.6 million for relief.*

target /ˈtɑːʳgət/ [n C] the exact result that a person or organization intends to achieve by doing something, often the amount of money they want to get: *The target for the appeal is £20,000, all of which will go to children's charities.* | *Our target is the release of all political prisoners.* | **meet/reach/achieve a target** *The government is struggling to reach its original target of $23 billion in spending cuts.* —**target** [adj only before noun] *The magazine has a target readership of half a million people* (=its target is half a million readers).

end /end/ [n C] the result that a person or group is trying to achieve, especially when this is bad or dishonest **political/personal etc ends** *Racial tensions in Fiji were exaggerated for political ends by leaders of the opposition.* | **the end does not justify the means** (=the way that someone tries to achieve something is wrong, even if what they want to achieve is good) *The demonstrators' ends do not justify their means.*

2 what something is intended to be used for

- be for
- function
- use

be for /biː ˈfɔːʳ/ [v phrase] to be intended to be used for a particular purpose: *This machine is for cleaning the carpet.* | *What's this little button for?* | *These shoes are for running, and these are for sports such as basketball.*

function /ˈfʌŋkʃən/ [n C] the purpose that a machine, tool, or piece of equipment is made for: *Each basket is designed to perform a specific function, from carrying corn to holding babies.* | **+ of** *Several instructors could not answer questions about the function of a particular switch.* | *The function of this gene is to block the uncontrolled division of cells; it therefore prevents the development of cancer.*

use /juːs/ [n C] a purpose that a machine, tool, plant etc can have: *It's main use is as a cleaning agent for metals.* | *Technology developed for the space program has civilian uses as well.*

3 to be intended for a particular purpose

- to be meant/supposed to do sth
- be intended to do sth
- be designed to do sth
- with the aim of doing sth

to be meant/supposed to do sth /tə biː ˌment, səˌpəʊzd tə 'duː (sth)/ [v phrase] to be done or made for a particular purpose, especially when the purpose is not achieved: *His artworks are meant to cause debate.* | *The police opened the package and found not a bomb, but a wallet meant to be someone's gift.* | *Thirty percent of the lottery ticket sales was supposed to go to education.*

be intended to do sth /biː ɪnˌtendəd tə 'duː (sth)/ [v phrase] to be done or made for a particular purpose: *The concert is intended to raise money for charity.* | *I didn't think the movie was as dramatic as it was intended to be.*

be designed to do sth /biː dɪˌzaɪnd tə 'duː (sth)/ [v phrase] to be made in a specific way in order to achieve a particular result: *The menu was designed to appeal to both children and adults.* | *Democrats say the law is designed to help only wealthy taxpayers.*

with the aim of doing sth /wɪð ði ˌeɪm əv 'duːɪŋ (sth)/ [prep] if something is done **with the aim of** achieving something, it is done in order to try and achieve it: *The center does research with the aim of improving the lives of poor Americans.* | *The committee will reform the tests, with the aim of better evaluating student performance.* | **with the express/deliberate etc aim of doing sth** *We ask students to write essays under examination conditions, with the deliberate aim of familiarizing them with these conditions.*

4 to decide to use someone or something for a particular purpose

- designate
- earmark

designate /'dezɪgneɪt/ [v T] to officially choose someone or something for a particular purpose, often with the result that they cannot be used for anything else: *Designate a driver who won't be drinking before going to a party or club.* | **designate sb/sth as sth** *Mattos Elementary has been designated as this area's 'home' school.* | **designate sb/sth for sb/sth** *One of the queues was designated for people with an EC passport.* | **designate sb/sth to do sth** *$6 million has been designated to make road safety improvements on Pacheco Pass.*

earmark /'ɪəʳmɑːʳk/ [v T usually in passive] to choose someone or something from among a larger group so that they can be used for a particular purpose in the future **earmark sb/sth for sth** *20% of the budget has already been earmarked for a new computer system.* | **earmark sb/sth to do sth** *The funds are earmarked to help pay for the cathedral's renovation.* | **earmark sb/sth as sth** *Dawson was earmarked as Reiner's successor as District Attorney.*

5 without any purpose

- pointless
- aimless
- senseless
- meaningless
- lack direction

pointless /'pɔɪntləs/ [adj] something that is **pointless** has no purpose and makes you angry or sad: *a film full of pointless violence* | *Never give your students pointless exercises to do – always provide interesting, meaningful tasks.* | **be pointless to do sth** *It is pointless to argue about who is more to blame.*

aimless /'eɪmləs/ [adj] not having any purpose or plan and therefore boring or sad: *The novel seems aimless, and the characters are stereotypes.* | *She changed from an aimless, pregnant teenager into a purposeful young woman.* —**aimlessly** [adv] *John wandered aimlessly all day and returned to his gloomy room in the evening.*

senseless /'sensləs/ [adj] a crime or something bad that is **senseless** seems to have no meaning or purpose and you cannot understand why someone would do it: *It was a senseless and cruel murder.* | *Smashing up trains is such a senseless form of vandalism.* | *The suicide was described as a senseless waste of a young woman's life.* —**senselessly** [adv] *How could you jeopardize your career so senselessly?* —**senselessness** [n U] *The public was shocked by the senselessness of the crime.*

meaningless /'miːnɪŋləs/ [adj] without any meaning or purpose and therefore boring, sad, or having no effect: *a meaningless campaign pledge* | *So many of us spend our lives doing meaningless work in huge faceless companies.* | *Several companies dismissed the ruling as 'meaningless,' saying it would have no effect on their operations.*

lack direction [v phrase] ALSO **lack of direction** [n phrase] /ˌlæk dəˈrekʃən, ˌlæk əv dəˈrekʃən/ if something **lacks direction** or has a **lack of direction**, it does not have a clear purpose and is not well organized: *It could have been a good film, but I felt it lacked direction.* | *He quit over the company's lack of direction.*

push

RELATED WORDS

▸ *see also* **pull, press, squash**

1 to push something or someone

- push
- give sth/sb a push
- shove
- give sth/sb a shove
- hustle
- bundle
- manhandle

push /pʊʃ/ [v I/T] to **push** something or someone, especially with your hands, so that they move away from you: *We pushed as hard as we could, but we couldn't get the bus to move.* | *Mum, William pushed me!* | **push sth/sb to/into/from etc sth** *She pushed the table into a corner of the classroom.* | *Pushing his plate to one side he called for the waiter.* | *Witnesses had seen the man push Mrs Cooper off the bridge into the canal.*

give sth/sb a push /ˌgɪv (sth/sb) ə 'pʊʃ/ [v phrase] to push something or someone once, so that you force them to move: *'Go away!' she said, giving him a push.* | *He reached out and gave the door a gentle push.*

shove /ʃʌv/ [v T] informal to push something or someone, using your hands or shoulders, in a rough or careless way: *The children were all pushing and shoving each other.* | **shove sb/sth against/aside/under etc sth** *One of the soldiers shoved her roughly against the wall.* | *Tom shoved his suitcase under the bed.* | *Armed police shoved the protestors aside to make way for the president's car.*

give sth/sb a shove /ˌgɪv (sth/sb) ə 'ʃʌv/ [v phrase] to push something or someone suddenly and strongly to force them to move: *If the door won't open just give it a shove.* | *'Mind your own business!' said Graham, giving me a shove.*

hustle /'hʌsəl/ [v T] to push someone along roughly in order to make them move forward quickly **hustle sb out/into etc** *Two policemen quickly appeared and* *hustled him out.* | *Martin seized her arm and hustled her away.* | *The two men were hustled into a police van and driven away.*

bundle /ˈbʌndl/ [v T] to quickly push someone or something into something such as a car, a bag, or a cupboard, for example because you are in a hurry or you want to hide something: *Her friends managed to get her out of the pub and bundled her home.* | **bundle sb/sth into sth** *He had been bundled into the back of a Volkswagen by three masked men.* | *I collected up the dirty washing and bundled it into the washing machine.*

manhandle /ˈmænhændl/ [v T] to move someone who does not want to move or something that is difficult to move by holding on to them and pushing them roughly **manhandle sb/sth into/out/towards etc** *The soldiers were manhandling two men into the yard.* | *The gang manhandled the stolen trailer through a gap in the fence.*

2 to push something that has wheels or rolls easily

- push
- wheel
- roll
- trundle

push /pʊʃ/ [v T] *Paul held the door open for a woman pushing a trolley of heavy books.* | **push sth in/around etc sth** *Shoppers were pushing their carts around the supermarket.* | *The car had run out of gas so they pushed it into a side-street.*

wheel /wiːl/ [v T] to push something with wheels while holding it with your hands **wheel sb/sth out/into/down etc** *As I arrived she was just wheeling her bicycle out of the shed.* | *I collected a trolley and wheeled it towards the frozen food section.* | *She hated being wheeled round in a wheelchair.*

roll /rəʊl/ [v T] to push a round object along so that it turns over and over and moves forward **roll sth up/down etc sth** *We had so much fun rolling stones down into the river.*

trundle /ˈtrʌndl/ [v T] to push something heavy that has wheels, slowly and with difficulty **trundle sth in/along etc** *The porters were trundling barrows loaded with vegetables into the market.* | *The soldiers trundled the massive gun carriage along the road.*

3 to push someone or something with your finger, elbow, or with something pointed

- nudge
- poke
- prod
- dig sb in the ribs

nudge /nʌdʒ/ [v T] to gently push someone with your elbow to get their attention, especially when you do not want anyone else to notice: *Toby nudged my arm. 'That's the guy I told you about,' he whispered.* | *Christine nudged me and giggled.* —**nudge** [n C] *Mark gave me a nudge and indicated two men who had just walked in.*

poke /pəʊk/ [v T] to push someone or something with your finger or with something sharp: *The boys poked the fish with sticks to see if it was still alive* | **poke sb in the eye/side/ribs** *Careful with that stick! You nearly poked me in the eye.* —**poke** [n C] *I gave dad a poke to wake him up.*

prod /prɒd‖prɑːd/ [v T] to gently push someone or something, using your finger or something such as a stick: *Sergeant Thompson raised his stick and prodded the soldier in the chest.* | *They walked around him, prodding and pinching him.* —**prod** [n C] *He gave the dog a quick prod with his foot.*

dig sb in the ribs /ˌdɪg (sb) ɪn ðə ˈrɪbz/ [v phrase] to suddenly push your finger or elbow into someone's body, to get their attention or tell them something: *Jenny dug me sharply in the ribs and told me to be quiet.* | *Edward laughed loudly, digging me in the ribs, wanting me to share the joke.*

4 to push an object into an opening or into something soft

- stick
- force
- stuff/shove
- ram
- plunge
- thrust
- squeeze
- jam

stick /stɪk/ [v T] to push a sharp object into something soft, or push something into a small space **stick sth into/up/inside etc sth** *They stuck pins into a map to show where the enemy's camps were.* | *The doctor had to stick a tube down my throat in order to examine my stomach.*

force /fɔːʳs/ [v T] to push something into a small space using a lot of strength **force sth into/through/down sth** *She tried to force her feet into the shoes but they were too small.* | *I finally managed to force the package through the small letterbox.*

stuff/shove /stʌf, ʃʌv/ [v T] informal to push something quickly and carelessly into a small space **shove/stuff sth into/up/down etc** *She shoved two more sweaters into her bag.* | *He quickly stuffed the letter down the side of the sofa.*

ram /ræm/ [v T] to push something very hard or violently into something **ram sth into sth** *She rammed the papers into her briefcase.* | *Construction workers had to spend the night ramming iron girders into place to support the building.*

plunge /plʌndʒ/ [v T] to push something deep inside another thing, especially violently or suddenly **plunge sth into sth** *Plunging both hands deep into the sack she rummaged among the parcels.* | *Then he plunged the knife into his victim's chest.*

thrust /θrʌst/ [v T] to push something suddenly and hard into an opening or into something soft **thrust sth into sth** *He thrust the knife deep into the animal's chest.* | *Thrusting the gun back into its holster, the man grinned at the body lying on the floor.* | *He thrust some money into my hand and told me to drive him to the airport.*

squeeze /skwiːz/ [v T] to push something with difficulty into a space that is too small **squeeze sth into sth** *I don't think I can squeeze any more files into this drawer.* | *It's no use trying to squeeze yourself into clothes that are too small for you.*

jam /dʒæm/ [v T] to push something forcefully into a small space, so that it fits tightly and is difficult to pull out again **jam sth under/into etc sth** *Just hold the door open while I jam a wedge under it.* | *Kelly poured himself another glass of wine and jammed the cork back into the bottle.*

5 to push people in order to move forward

- push
- shove
- barge
- force your way
- jostle
- elbow
- press

push /pʊʃ/ [v I/T] to **push** people, especially in a

crowd, in order to move past them or in order to make them move: *Can you tell the people at the back of the queue to stop pushing!* | **push your way through/into etc** *He pushed his way through the crowd.* | **+ past** *She pushed past me to the front of the line.*

shove /ʃʌv/ [v I/T] to push people in a rough and careless way with your hands, arms, or shoulders in order to move forward or past people: *The people moved forward towards the food, pushing and shoving to get there first.* | **shove your way through/into etc** *Peter shoved his way through the dense crowd in search of his son.* | **+ past** *Robert shoved past the others and made his way to the front of the room.*

barge /bɑːʳdʒ/ [v I] to move forward so fast and forcefully that you push someone as you pass them **+ into** *She just barged into me, without even apologizing.* | **+ past** *A woman carrying a large basket barged past me to the front of the line.*

force your way /ˌfɔːʳs jɔːʳ ˈweɪ/ [v phrase] to push hard in order to go somewhere when your way is blocked **+ through** *He forced his way through the dense crowd.* | **+ into** *Police forced their way into the flat and arrested two men.*

jostle /ˈdʒɒsəl‖ˈdʒɑː-/ [v I/T] to push against one person or several people so that you knock them to one side, especially in order to reach a place or get something before they do **+ for** *Passengers were jostling each other at the news kiosk for the last remaining copies of the evening paper.* | **+ to do sth** *The children moved forward, jostling to get to the front and see the magician.*

elbow /ˈelbəʊ/ [v T] to push with your elbows in order to move past people **elbow your way through/into etc** *She elbowed her way through the crowd.* | **elbow sb aside/elbow sb to one side** *Craig elbowed me aside roughly.* | *Elbowing me to one side, he took hold of the microphone.*

press /pres/ [v I] to push in order to move forward with the rest of the crowd **+ forward/round etc** *As the race started the crowd pressed forward towards the track.* | *The security men tried to hold back crowds of reporters pressing round the President's car.*

6 to push something to operate a machine

- **push/press**

- *see also* **switchon/off**

push/press /pʊʃ, pres/ [v T] **push/press a button** to push something that makes a machine operate: *It's very simple – you put the paper in and push a button, and the computer does the rest for you.* | *She pressed the button and the machine started to whirr.*

put

RELATED WORDS

- to fasten one thing to another *see* **attach**
- put on clothes *see* **clothes**
- put seeds or plants in the ground *see* **grow**
- to put liquid, powder etc somewhere by pouring it out of a container *see* **pour**
- to put information into a computer *see* **computer/Internet/email (6)**
- to put something where people won't find it *see* **hide**
- *see also* **lift, move, spread**

1 to put something somewhere

- **put**
- **place**
- **leave**
- **abandon**
- **position**
- **plant a bomb/explosives etc**
- **plant**
- **lay**
- **set down**
- **deposit**

put /pʊt/ [v T] to move something to a place or position and leave it there **put sth in/on/there etc** *Just put the bags on the table.* | *I can't remember where I put my keys.* | **put sth back** (=put it in the place where it was before or where it should be) *I put the letter back in the envelope.* | **put sth away** (=put it where it is usually kept) *It's time to put everything away now.* | **put sth down/put down sth** (=put something you are holding onto a surface) *She picked up a porcelain figurine and put it down again.* | **put sth up/put up sth** (=fasten something to a wall, ceiling, or in a high position) *I'm not allowed to put up any posters in my bedroom.*

place /pleɪs/ [v T] to carefully put something somewhere **place sth on/in/over/there etc** *Every week someone comes and places fresh flowers on her grave.* | *Place some lemon slices on the fish before serving it.* | *Food is placed in a large cage, and when the animal enters, the door drops down.* | *Winters placed his hand on my arm, holding me back.*

leave /liːv/ [v T] to put something in a place and not take it with you when you go: *Now, where did I leave my gym shoes?* | **leave sth in/on/on top of etc** *Just leave your umbrellas and things behind the door.* | *She had left all her personal belongings in the London apartment.* | **leave sth somewhere** *I'm sure I left my bag somewhere around here.*

abandon /əˈbændən/ [v T] to put someone or something somewhere and never go back to get them, for example because you want to get rid of them or because you are unable to take them with you: *Retreating troops were told to abandon their weapons and run as fast as they could towards the beach.* | *A new-born baby was found abandoned on the steps of a hospital yesterday.*

position /pəˈzɪʃən/ [v T] to carefully move something into the right **position** for a particular purpose: *Make sure you position the wheel correctly before you tighten up the nuts.* | *Federal troops were positioned around the city.*

plant a bomb/explosives etc /ˌplɑːnt ə ˈbɒm‖ˌplænt ə ˈbɑːm/ [v phrase] to put a bomb in a public place **plant sth in/at/outside/nearby etc** *The two men planted the bomb outside Harrods department store in London.* | **plant sth in/on/there etc** *No rebel group has claimed responsibility for planting the explosives in the van.*

plant /plɑːnt‖plænt/ [v T] to put something in someone's pocket, room, car etc in order to make them seem guilty of a crime: *It turned out the security services had planted the documents in his luggage.* | *He accused the police of planting evidence.*

lay /leɪ/ [v T] to put something on a surface, especially so that it is flat **lay sth on/across sth** *She unfolded the map and laid it on the table.* | **lay sth out/lay out sth** (=arrange something carefully on a surface) *Before you start packing, lay out all the clothes on the bed.* | **lay sth down/lay down sth** (=put something you are holding onto a surface) *Farley laid the gun down and surrendered.*

set down /ˌset ˈdaʊn/ [phr v T] to put down something big and heavy which you have been carrying – used especially in literature or stories **set**

sth/it/them down *They set the coffin down in front of the altar.* | **set down sth** *The movers brought in the dresser, which they set down against the wall.*

deposit /dɪˈpɒzɪ̈t‖dɪˈpɑː-/ [v T] to put something down – used especially when describing events in a formal or humorous way: *Aunt Augusta deposited the contents of her bag on the kitchen table.* | *After the lessons on the environment, children deposited much more litter in trash cans, rather than dropping it.*

2 to put something in the place where it was before

- put back
- return

put back /ˌpʊt ˈbæk/ [phr v T] to put something back in the place it is usually kept or in the place it was in before **put sth back** *Put the cups back in the cupboard when you've finished with them.* | *She took a quick look at the contents of the book, and then put it back on the shelf.* | **put back sth** *He had tidied up the room and put back all my things where they belonged.*

return /rɪˈtɜːʳn/ [v T] written to put something back in the place it was before: *Johnson carefully returned the document to its hiding place.* | *Return the pan to the heat and simmer for a further 5-10 minutes.*

3 to put something somewhere quickly or carelessly

- shove
- stick
- dump
- slam down
- thrust
- pop
- bung
- plonk

shove /ʃʌv/ [v T] informal to push something quickly or carelessly into a space or container **shove sth in/into/under etc** *Shove anything you don't want in that sack.* | *He bundled the papers together and shoved them into a drawer.*

stick /stɪk/ [v T] spoken to put something somewhere, especially quickly or carelessly **stick sth on/in/over sth** *I stuck the pictures in a drawer and forgot all about them.* | *'What should I do with these?' 'Oh, just stick them anywhere.'*

dump /dʌmp/ [v T] to carelessly drop something somewhere in an untidy way, especially something heavy: *People dump rubbish in the lanes, and the council is slow to clean it up.* | **dump sth on/in/there etc** *Who dumped all these books on my desk?* | **dump sth down** *I dumped my heavy suitcase down on the doorstep.*

slam down /ˌslæm ˈdaʊn/ [phr v T] to put something down somewhere quickly and violently because you are angry **slam sth down** *She slammed the cup down, and coffee splashed all over him.* | **slam down sth** *'To hell with you,' he shouted, and slammed down the phone.*

thrust /θrʌst/ [v T] to put something forcefully and suddenly into a place **thrust sth in/on/under etc** *Clark thrust a paper sack across the counter and demanded money.* | *She thrust the bag into my hands. 'Hide it,' she hissed.* | *He nervously thrust his hands into his pockets.*

pop /pɒp‖pɑːp/ [v T] informal to put something somewhere quickly for a short time **pop sth in/into/under etc** *She took out a piece of chewing gum and popped it in her mouth.* | *Pop it in the microwave for a couple of minutes.*

bung /bʌŋ/ [v T] British informal to put something somewhere quickly and without thinking carefully **bung sth in/into/on etc** *Could you bung those clothes into the washing machine for me?* | *Just sign the card, bung it in an envelope and send it off.*

plonk especially British **/plunk** American /plɒŋk‖plɑːŋk, plʌŋk/ [v T] to put something down somewhere noisily and carelessly **plonk sth on/in/there etc** *She brought a bottle of beer and a glass and plonked them on the table in front of me.* | *Gamblers plunked nickels and quarters into the slot machines.* | **plonk sth down** *Are those things for me? Just plonk them down anywhere.* | *Gary plunked a dollar down on the counter to pay for his Coke.*

4 to put several things on top of each other

- pile
- stack
- heap

pile /paɪl/ [v T] to put a lot of things on top of each other, especially in an untidy way **pile sth on/onto/there etc** *Gifts were piled under the Christmas tree.* | *Has anyone else noticed that towels dry faster when you don't pile them in the middle of the floor?* | **pile sth up** (=put a lot of things on top of each other in a tall pile) *He piled his dirty laundry up just outside my door.* | **be piling up** (=use this to say a pile is growing quickly) *We called the police when we noticed her newspapers and mail were piling up.*

stack /stæk/ [v T] to put things neatly on top of each other: *I'll start stacking the chairs.* | **stack sth against/in/on sth** *Boxes were stacked in the corner.* | **stack sth up** (=put a lot of things on top of each other in a tall pile) *My kids leave dirty plates stacked up in the sink until I get home.*

heap /hiːp/ [v T] to put a lot of things on top of each other in an untidy way **heap sth on/onto** *Cheap clothes and shoes were heaped on tables.* | **heap sth with sth** *a plate heaped with salad* | **heap sth in/into a pile** *Eileen collected the leaves, heaping them into piles for burning.* | **lie heaped** *Her clothes lay heaped together in a corner of the room.*

5 to put something into a hole or small space

- put
- slide
- tuck
- insert

put /pʊt/ [v T] **put sth in/into/inside etc** *I put the coin in my pocket.* | *When did you last put oil in the car?* | *She put the sales slip in the plastic bag with the dress.*

slide /slaɪd/ [v T] to move something smoothly into a small narrow space **slide sth into** *Slide your card into the machine and then tap in your number.* | *The coffin was slid into the waiting hearse.*

tuck /tʌk/ [v T] to put something in a small space so that it is covered and is safe, comfortable, or warm **tuck sth into/under/in etc** *It was starting to get cold, and she tucked her hands into the pockets of her jeans.* | *He tucked the newspaper under his arm and walked on.* | **be tucked in/under etc** *The boys were tucked in bed, fast asleep.*

insert /ɪnˈsɜːʳt/ [v T] to carefully put something into a hole or space, especially one where it is designed to go, for example in a machine or piece of equipment: *Insert the correct coins, then select the drink you want and press the button.* | **insert sth in/into/between etc** *A nurse carefully inserted the needle into my left arm.* | *A very thin sheet of paper is* *then inserted between the metal plates.* —**insertion** /ɪnˈsɜːʳʃən/ [n U] *After insertion* (=being inserted) *the pipe is filled with gas.*

6 to put something in a liquid for a short time

- dip
- dunk

dip /dɪp/ [v T] to put something into a liquid for a short time and take it out again **dip sth in/into sth** *Emily dipped her toes in the water and squealed.* | *Dip stale bread in egg and milk and fry it in butter to make French Toast.*

dunk /dʌŋk/ [v T] to dip something such as a piece of bread or cake into a hot drink or soup before eating it **dunk sth in/into sth** *Bill dunked a piece of bread in the soup.* | *My daughter likes to dunk her biscuits in my tea.*

7 to put paint, glue, make-up etc onto a surface

- put on
- slap on
- apply

put on /ˌpʊt ˈɒn / [phr v T] to put something such a paint or glue onto a surface, or make-up (=powders and colours that women **put on** their faces) onto your face **put sth on** *The paint had been put on too thickly, and it had dripped.* | **put on sth** *When you put the glue on, be careful not to get any on your fingers.* | *Patricia went upstairs to put on some lipstick.*

apply /əˈplaɪ/ [v T] to put something such as paint or glue onto a surface, or make-up (=powders and colours that women put on their faces) onto your face – used especially in written instructions on how to use it: *Apply the cream in the morning and the evening.* | *Make sure the surface is completely dry before applying the final coat of paint.*

slap on /ˌslæp ˈɒn / [phr v T] informal to put something such as paint or glue onto a surface, or make-up (=powders and colours that women put on their faces) onto your face quickly and without much care, and usually in large amounts **slap sth on** *Mike was slapping jam on a slice of bread.* | **slap on sth** *Slap on a coat of paint and it will look good as new.*

8 to put something in a sloping position

- lean
- stand
- rest
- prop

lean /liːn/ [v T] to put something in a sloping position so that it is against a wall or other surface and is supported by it: *She leaned the ladder against the house and climbed up to the window.* | **lean sth (up) against sth** *Soldiers leaned their M-16 rifles up against their tables as they ate.*

rest /rest/ [v T] to put something against a surface so that it is supported by it **rest sth on/against sth** *She slid down in her chair and rested her head on the back of the seat.* | *Resting his spade against the wall, he went to help Michael light the fire.*

stand /stænd/ [v T] to lean something in an almost upright position against something such as a wall **stand sth against/in etc** *Maggie stood her bicycle against the wall of the shed.* | *Just stand it in the corner, so it doesn't fall.*

prop /prɒp‖prɑːp/ [v T] to lean something against a wall or other surface, especially quickly and for a short time **prop sth against sth** *He propped his bicycle against the fence and ran inside.* | **stand/lie propped against sth** *An old guitar lay propped against a wall.*

9 to put something somewhere while it is not being used

- store
- stow
- stash

store /stɔːʳ/ [v T] to put something somewhere and keep it there until it is needed **store sth in/under etc** *Store the vegetables in a cool dark place.* | *The computer stores the information in its memory automatically.* | **store sth away** (=store something where it cannot be seen) *Instead of being distributed, the food was unloaded and stored away in a warehouse.*

stash /stæʃ / [v I/T] to put something such as money, valuable things, or drugs in a secret place, especially when you have them illegally: *The two men were looking for a place to stash their weapons.* | **stash away sth/stash sth away** *He has illegally stashed away as much as $50 in foreign bank accounts.* | **stash sth in sth** *The stolen goods had been stashed in a storage unit in Burbank.* | **have sth stashed away** *He must have all that money stashed away somewhere.*

stow /stəʊ/ [v T] to put something such as equipment or a bag neatly in a space until you need it again **stow sth in/on/under etc** *She stowed her luggage on the rack above her head and then sat down.* | **stow sth away** (=stow it where it cannot be seen) *In the daytime the mattress is stowed away in that cupboard.*

10 to put things into a bag, box, car etc before taking them somewhere

- pack
- load
- get packed
- load up

pack /pæk/ [v I/T] to put things into cases, bags, boxes etc so that you can take them somewhere: *We're going to Greece tomorrow, and I haven't started packing yet!* | *Did you remember to pack the suntan lotion?* | **pack a bag/suitcase** (=put things into a bag etc) *She packed her suitcase and set off for the airport.* | **pack sth into sth** *We packed all our books into boxes.*

get packed /ˌget ˈpækt/ [v phrase] spoken to put all the clothes and other things you need for travelling into bags: *How long do you think it'll take you to get packed?* | *By the time we'd gotten packed it was almost midnight.*

load /ləʊd/ [v T] to put goods, furniture, or other large objects into a large vehicle so that they can be taken somewhere **load sth into/onto sth** *I started loading the boxes into the truck.* | **be loaded with sth** *Trucks loaded with food and medicine waited at the border.* | **fully loaded** *When the planes are fully loaded, they aren't able to take off from this runway, as it is too short.*

load up /ˌləʊd ˈʌp/ [phr v I/T] to put a lot of things into a vehicle or boat, especially so that it is full **load up a truck/car etc** *Do you have time to help us load up the car?* | **+ with** *The ship's lifeboat was taken into Lerwick to load up with fresh vegetables.*

11 to put equipment in a place and make it ready to be used

- put in
- install
- fit

put in /ˌpʊt 'ɪn/ [phr v T] to put a new piece of machinery or equipment into a room or building **put in sth** *The landlord has promised to put in a new heating system.* | **put sth in** *The workmen are coming to put the new windows in today.*

install /ɪn'stɔːl/ [v T] to put a new piece of machinery or equipment into a room or building, and connect it to the electricity supply, water supply etc: *Crime has dropped since the video cameras were installed in the town centre.* | *The company is installing a new computer system.*

fit /fɪt/ [v T] to put a new part or piece of equipment into or onto something such as a machine or car: *I had to fit new locks after the burglary.*

12 to put someone in a place

- put
- post
- position

put /pʊt/ [v T] **put sb in/on/at etc** *They put me in a room on my own and locked the door.* | *The photographer arranged the wedding guests, putting the smallest ones at the front.* | *Grandmother was getting too frail to live on her own, so we had to put her in an old people's home.*

post /pəʊst/ [v T] to put a soldier or police officer in a position where they will be able to guard a place or watch whoever is coming in or going out: *They have posted guards at every door to make sure no one enters the building.* | *Sentries are being posted outside all government buildings.*

position /pə'zɪʃən/ [v T] to put a group of soldiers or police officers in a particular place, especially so that they are ready to guard it: *The French generals had positioned thousands of troops along the border.* | *Army units are to be positioned at all major installations including factories and power stations.*

13 to put money in a bank

- put in
- deposit

put in /ˌpʊt 'ɪn/ [phr v T] *How much did you put in?* | **put sth in the bank/an account** *I put $50 in my bank every week.* | *Any money that you put in your account will immediately start earning interest.* | **put money/a cheque/£100/$200 etc in** *When did you put the money in?*

deposit /dɪ'pɒzɪ̣t‖dɪ'pɑː-/ [v T] to put money into a bank account – used especially by people who work in banks: *The money is deposited in my account every month.* | *Our records show that you deposited $200 in your account on January 17th.*

Qq

quiet

RELATED WORDS

opposite: **loud**

- someone who doesn't talk much *see* **talk (13)**
- when there are not many people or there is not much activity *see* **busy/not busy**
- *see also* **peaceful**

1 words for describing a place that is quiet

- quiet
- silent
- you could hear a pin drop

quiet /'kwaɪət/ [adj] if a place is **quiet**, there is not much noise there: *Inside the church it was quiet and peaceful.* | *David and I found a quiet corner where we could talk.* | *I usually work in the dining room because it's the quietest room in the house.*

silent /'saɪlənt/ [adj] if a place is **silent**, there is no noise at all – used especially in stories or descriptions of events: *The streets of the city were silent in the moonlight.* | *Apart from the humming of the bees, all was silent and still.*

you could hear a pin drop /juː kʊd ˌhɪər ə 'pɪn drɒp‖-drɑːp/ if you say **you could hear a pin drop**, you mean it is very quiet, especially because no one is talking, and even a very small sound would be heard clearly: *It was so quiet in the hall you could hear a pin drop.* | *After he finished telling the story you could have heard a pin drop.*

2 when there is little or no noise

- silence
- hush

silence /'saɪləns/ [n C/U] when there are no sounds at all: *Nothing disturbed the silence of the night.* | *There was a long silence before anyone answered.* | **deathly silence** (=a silence that makes people feel nervous and uncomfortable) *'What did you do during the war?' Rob asked. There was a deathly silence, and everyone looked down at the table.*

hush /hʌʃ/ [n singular/U] a state in which there is little or no noise, especially in a place where people have all suddenly stopped talking – used especially in stories or descriptions of events: *There was a sudden hush as the musicians came onto the stage.* | **a hush falls/descends** (=people stop making noise) *Two men walked in and went up to the bar. A hush fell over the room.*

3 words for describing music, sounds, or voices that are quiet

- quiet
- low
- soft
- muffled
- hushed
- faint
- inaudible

quiet /'kwaɪət/ [adj] **quiet** sounds, voices, or music are not loud: *He spoke in a quiet yet confident voice.* |

There was a quiet knock at the door. —**quietly** [adv] *We were talking quietly so as not to wake the baby.*

low /ləʊ/ [adj] a **low** voice or sound is quiet and deep: *A low humming noise was coming from the refrigerator.* | **in a low voice** (=speaking quietly) *'Take care,' he said in a low voice.*

soft /sɒft‖sɔːft/ [adj] **soft** sounds, voices, or music are quiet, gentle, and pleasant: *He spoke with a soft Irish accent.* | *a whisper so soft that I could scarcely hear it* | *With candlelight and soft music, you can create a romantic atmosphere in your own home.* —**softly** [adv] *Music was playing softly in the background.* | *Through the open doorway, he could hear someone singing softly.*

muffled /ˈmʌfəld/ [adj] **muffled** voices or sounds are quiet and unclear, especially because they come from behind a wall or door: *We heard muffled shouts and screams from the bar below.* | *His voice was muffled, 'I'm in the bathroom. I'm stuck.'*

hushed /hʌʃt/ [adj usually before noun] a **hushed** voice, conversation, crowd etc is intentionally quiet, for example because someone is afraid of being heard or because they are waiting for some important news: *Two men in dark suits were having a hushed conversation in the corner.* | *A hushed congress heard the official declaration of war.* | *She spoke in a hushed whisper, 'I think my husband knows about us.'*

faint /feɪnt/ [adj] a **faint** sound is quiet and difficult to hear, especially because it comes from a long way away: *Jean opened the window, and heard the faint sound of the bells drifting across the Old Town.* | *The men went away, and we could hear their voices get fainter and fainter.* | *There was silence for a moment as they held each other's eyes, broken only by the faint sound of dance music from down below.*

inaudible /ɪnˈɔːdəbəl/ [adj] formal **inaudible** sounds are so quiet that you cannot hear them: *Her voice was so faint, it was almost inaudible.* | *Michael went bright red, and muttering something inaudible, he walked out of the room.* | *Aunt Jessica let out an inaudible sigh.*

4 words for describing people or machines that are quiet

- quiet
- silent
- without a sound
- not make a sound
- in silence

quiet /ˈkwaɪət/ [adj] if someone or something is **quiet**, they make little or no noise: *I want you all to be very quiet and listen carefully.* | *Our new washing machine is much quieter than the old one.* —**quietly** [adv] *The children were reading quietly at their desks.*

silent /ˈsaɪlənt/ [adj] written not making any sound at all: *The children remained silent and watchful as the police questioned their parents.* | *The engine is almost silent, even at high speed, and goes like a dream.* | **fall silent** (=stop talking) *The crowd fell silent as he stood up to speak.* —**silently** [adv] *Silently, the mist crept closer.*

without a sound /wɪðˌaʊt ə ˈsaʊnd/ [adv] if you do something or something happens **without a sound**, you do it or it happens with no noise at all – used especially in stories and descriptions of events: *The animal remained perfectly still, watching us without a sound.* | *There was a final shudder, and then the ship sank without a sound.* | *Each man died where he stood; they fell in their tracks without a sound.*

not make a sound /nɒt ˌmeɪk ə ˈsaʊnd/ [v phrase] to not make any noise at all: *Sit still, and don't make a sound.* | **without making a sound** *She managed to get into the house without making a sound.*

in silence /ɪn ˈsaɪləns/ [adv] written if you do something **in silence**, you do it without speaking: *Thousands of protesters stood in silence outside the prison gates.* | *We drank our coffee in silence.* | **in total/complete silence** *The two of them walked all the way to Matilda's house in complete silence.*

5 to become quieter

- get quieter
- go quiet
- die down
- fade away
- fall silent
- lower your voice

get quieter /get ˈkwaɪətəʳ/ [v phrase] *That buzzing noise seems to be getting quieter now.* | **grow quieter** (=get quieter gradually) *As we walked into the woods the noise of the traffic grew quieter.*

go quiet /gəʊ ˈkwaɪət/ [v phrase] especially British to stop speaking or making any noise at all, for example because you are shocked or embarrassed: *Lawrence went very quiet after Jo told him how she felt.*

die down /ˌdaɪ ˈdaʊn/ [phr v I] if shouting, music, laughter etc **dies down**, it gradually becomes quieter after being very loud: *Forrester waited for the laughter to die down, then carried on with his speech.* | *The music was dying down. The show was over.* | **+ to** *Jessie's wails died down to a whimper and then stopped altogether.*

fade away /ˌfeɪd əˈweɪ/ [phr v I] if a sound **fades away**, it gradually becomes quieter until you cannot hear it any more: *The sound of a police siren was slowly fading away into the distance.* | *She listened to Zach's footsteps fade away, as he walked down the staircase.*

fall silent /ˌfɔːl ˈsaɪlənt/ [v phrase] to suddenly stop talking and become quiet – used in literature and stories: *Dixon fell silent again, deep in thought.* | *'I had hoped ....', he began, and then fell silent again.* | *The bar-room door crashed open and the voices at the tables fell silent.*

lower your voice /ˌləʊəʳ jɔːʳ ˈvɔɪs/ [v phrase] to speak more quietly because you do not want other people to hear what you are saying: *Kath lowered her voice as she spoke.*

6 to make someone or something quieter

- quieten sb down
- silence
- hush
- muffle
- turn down
- shut sb up

quieten sb down British **/quiet sb down** American /ˌkwaɪətn (sb) ˈdaʊn, ˌkwaɪət (sb) ˈdaʊn/ [phr v T] to make someone quieter and calmer, when they are making a lot of noise because they are angry, excited, or upset: *I spent half the lesson trying to quieten them down.* | *Sue managed to quiet them both down and eventually stopped the argument.*

silence /ˈsaɪləns/ [v T] especially written to make someone suddenly stop speaking: *I opened my mouth to speak but she silenced me with an angry look.* | *Jim was livid, but Jane squeezed his arm to silence him.*

hush /hʌʃ/ [v T] to make someone, especially a child, make less noise or make no noise at all, especially by telling them in a quiet voice to stop talking or crying: *I turned to Margaret but was hushed before I could open my mouth.* | *David hushed me. 'Sh-h-h. You're not allowed to speak in here.'* | *She gave up trying to hush the baby and took him outside.*

muffle /ˈmʌfəl/ [v T] if something **muffles** a sound it makes it quieter and less clear: *The snow muffled the sound of the traffic.* | *He dragged her into the car, putting his hand over her mouth to muffle her screams.* | *John's voice was muffled by the door, and I couldn't tell what he was saying.*

turn down /ˌtɜːʳn ˈdaʊn/ [phr v T] to make a television, radio etc quieter by moving or turning a button or control **turn sth/it/them down** *Do you mind turning the radio down?* | *Turn that music down, you'll wake the whole street!* | **turn down sth** *She turned down the volume on the TV and picked up the phone.* | **turn sth right down** British /**turn sth all the way down** American (=make it as quiet as possible) *No wonder you can't hear anything – you've turned your hearing aid right down.*

shut sb up /ˌʃʌt (sb) ˈʌp/ [phr v T] informal to make someone be quiet, especially by speaking to them rudely or angrily: *Can't you shut those kids up?* | *The only way to shut her up is to give her something to eat.*

7 what you say to someone to tell them to be quiet

- shh
- shut up
- be quiet
- keep it down

shh /ʃ/ spoken say **shh** when you want someone to speak more quietly or make less noise: *Shh, keep the noise down, Timmy's asleep.*

shut up /ˌʃʌt ˈʌp/ informal a rude way of telling someone to stop talking: *Just shut up, will you! You're giving me a headache!* | **+ about** *Don't tell Grandma or she'll never shut up about it.* | *'The war, the war, the bloody war!' said Comfort, banging her fist on the table.'Why can't you all shut up about it?'*

be quiet /biː ˈkwaɪət/ [v phrase] spoken say **be quiet** to tell someone to stop talking or to make less noise, especially when you are annoyed with them: *'Be quiet, James!' she snapped.* | *Boys! Can you be quiet please? I can hardly hear myself think.*

keep it down /ˌkiːp ɪt ˈdaʊn/ say this when you want someone to speak more quietly or make less noise, especially because you do not want other people to hear them: *Keep it down! I'm trying to talk on the phone!* | *Hey you guys – keep it down, or Mom'll hear!*

Rr

race

RELATED WORDS

- sports race *see* **sport/game**
- *see also* **country, prejudiced**

1 people of a particular race or nationality

- race
- colour
- ethnicity
- ethnic

race /reɪs/ [n C/U] one of the main groups of people in the world, who have the same colour of skin and physical appearance as each other: *People should be treated equally, regardless of their race, age, or sex.* | *people of all races and religions* | *Studies are under way to find out why men of some races are more prone to some forms of cancer than others.* | **race relations** (=the relationship between people of different races) *The group is working to improve race relations in our cities.*

colour British **/color** American /ˈkʌləʳ/ [n C] the **colour** of someone's skin, which shows which race they belong to, especially whether they are black or white: *People of all colors and nationalities were at the ceremony.* | *You can't judge people by the colour of their skin.*

ethnicity /eθˈnɪsəti/ [n C/U] one of the group of people of a particular race or nationality who live in a place where there are other races or nationalities: *I couldn't tell her ethnicity from her last name.* | *Ethnicity should not be a factor in hiring decisions.* | *The Bay Area is a place where people of many ethnicities live together in relative harmony.*

ethnic /ˈeθnɪk/ [adj only before noun] **ethnic group/ethnic minority** a group of people of a particular race or nationality living in a place where most other people are of a different race: *The Indonesians of the city form a distinct ethnic group.* | *In the large cities of Africa, where different ethnic groups with many different languages are thrown together, people communicate in English or Swahili.* | **ethnic origin/background** (=the ethnic group that someone belongs to) *fighting in Bosnia between people from different ethnic backgrounds* | *In California it is illegal to refuse to do business with someone because of their race or ethnic origin.* —**ethnically** [adv] *There is probably no major public university campus quite as racially and ethnically diverse as the University of California.*

2 relating to race

- racial
- ethnic
- multiracial/multicultural
- interracial
- cosmopolitan
- mixed marriage

racial /ˈreɪʃəl/ [adj only before noun] **racial discrimination/prejudice/violence/attack** when people are treated unfairly or attacked because of their race: *Some people complained of racial discrimination in the way housing was allocated.* | *Racial violence used to be commonplace on the streets of the city.* | **racial harmony** (=when people of different races live together peacefully, and without any problems) *In Jamaica black and white people have lived together in racial harmony for many years.* | **racial profiling** (=the practice of police stopping some people only because of their race) *Local police deny that have used racial profiling when stopping motorists.* —**racially** [adv] *Kolbe grew up a vibrant, racially integrated quarter of Cape Town.* | **racially motivated** *Police suspect that the attack could be racially motivated.*

ethnic /ˈeθnɪk/ [adj only before noun] **ethnic divisions/unrest/violence** divisions, problems etc between groups of people of different races, or with different customs, living in the same place, especially when one group is smaller than the other: *Hundreds of people have been killed in the recent ethnic violence.* | *Ethnic unrest is spreading throughout the south-western republics of the former Soviet Union.* | **ethnic cleansing** (=when people are forced to leave their homes because of their ethnic group) *Reports of ethnic cleansing in former Yugoslavia* *forced the European states and the US into taking action.*

multiracial/multicultural /ˌmʌltɪˈreɪʃəl◂, ˌmʌltiˈkʌltʃərəl◂/ [adj only before noun] a **multiracial** or **multicultural** society, school, community etc is one in which people from several different races live together or work together, especially in a friendly way: *Britain became a multiracial society in the 1960s and 70s, after large-scale immigration from the West Indies and the Indian subcontinent.* | *a vibrant, multicultural neighborhood*

interracial /ˌɪntəˈreɪʃəl◂/ [adj only before noun] between people of different races: *The danger of an interracial war in South Africa still exists.* | *There has to be fairness and justice for black people before you can achieve a spirit of interracial harmony.* | **interracial marriage** *Interracial marriages are common in England these days.*

cosmopolitan /ˌkɒzməˈpɒlɨtən◂‖ˌkɑːzməˈpɑː-/ [adj] a **cosmopolitan** city, district, society etc is one in which people of many different races and nationalities live or go, which is therefore lively and interesting: *Istanbul is a great cosmopolitan city, situated between East and West.* | *She grew up in an apartment in a cosmopolitan district of Chicago.* | *The thing I like most about living in London is that it's so cosmopolitan.*

mixed marriage /ˌmɪkst ˈmærɪdʒ/ [n C/U] marriage between people of different races: *Mixed marriages are becoming more and more commonplace.*

3 when people are treated badly because of their race

▸ racism ▸ racist

racism /ˈreɪsɪzəm/ [n U] unfair treatment of people because of their race: *The company has been accused of racism after firing three Algerian workers.* | *the struggle against racism in our society* | **institutionalized racism** (=racism that has happened for so long in a society or organization, that it has become accepted as normal) *Institutionalized racism pervaded British society, and immigrant workers found themselves in unskilled jobs and with low social status.*

racist /ˈreɪsɨst/ [adj] **racist** statements, jokes, behaviour, or opinions are based on a dislike of people from other races and a feeling that your race is better than others: *racist attitudes* | *a comedian well known for his racist and sexist jokes* | *An African-American friend told me that she is subjected to racist behavior every day – at work, in the mall, in the park.*

4 someone who believes that their race is better than other races

▸ racist ▸ white supremacist

racist /ˈreɪsɨst/ [n C] someone who believes that their race is much better than other races – use this to show disapproval: *The minister denied that he was a racist, but called for tougher controls on immigration.* —**racist** [adj] *racist organizations like the British National Party and Combat 18*

white supremacist /ˌwaɪt səˈpreməsɨst/ [n C] someone who believes that white people are better than other races and that other races should be kept at a lower level: *Many white supremacists have chosen to set up compounds in unpopulated areas of the American West.*

5 when people of different races come together or are kept apart

▸ integration ▸ segregation

integration /ˌɪntɨˈgreɪʃən/ [n U] the bringing or coming together of people of different races so that they live and work peacefully together: *In the 1960s the government passed a law to promote racial integration in schools.* | *Members of extreme right wing parties are completely opposed to the integration of blacks into white South African society.* —**integrated** /ˈɪntɨgreɪtɨd/ [adj] *Aru was a perfectly integrated society.* (=one in which all the different races lived and worked together peacefully).

segregation /ˌsegrɪˈgeɪʃən/ [n U] keeping people of different races apart and making them live, work, or study separately, especially because one race believes that it is better than the other: *The US Supreme Court ruled in 1954 that segregation in schools was unconstitutional.* | *Legal segregation may be gone, but the idea of segregation survives, as middle class black families shun white areas, preferring to live in suburbs of their own.* —**segregated** /ˈsegrɪgeɪtɨd/ [adj] *Segregated restaurants are no longer allowed.*

rare/rarely

RELATED WORDS

opposite: **common, often**

▸ *see also* **few/not many**

1 not common and existing only in small numbers

▸ rare ▸ be few and far between
▸ scarce ▸ be/become a rarity
▸ not common ▸ there aren't many around
▸ be thin on the ground

rare /reəʳ/ [adj] an animal, plant, object etc that is **rare** does not exist in large numbers or in large amounts: *A new law to prevent the export of rare birds is to be introduced.* | *They're pretty rare. Only about a hundred were made.* | *The palace library contains some of the rarest books in Europe.* | *In Cholon's narrow streets, Europeans were far rarer than on the boulevards of Saigon.*

scarce /skeəʳs/ [adj] something that is **scarce**, especially something that people need such as food, clothing, or water, is not available in large enough numbers or amounts at the moment: *After the war, food and clothing were scarce.* | *With the increase in trade, good timber for shipbuilding was becoming scarcer.* | **scarce resources** *Government departments often found themselves competing for scarce resources.*

not common /nɒt ˈkɒmən‖-ˈkɑː-/ [adj] fairly rare, especially in one particular area or group: *Silver coins of this period are not common, and could be very valuable.* | *Although tigers still exist, they're not very common.*

be thin on the ground /biː ˌθɪn ɒn ðə ˈgraʊnd/ [v phrase] British if you say that people or things of a particular type **are thin on the ground**, you mean that there are very few available and they are hard to find when you need them: *Our only problem is finding staff, because good programmers are really* *thin on the ground.* | *Magazines about home improvement were very thin on the ground at the time – not like now.*

be few and far between /biː ˌfjuː ən ˌfɑːʳ bɪˈtwiːn/ [v phrase] to not be as common as you expect or as you would like: *The schools are crowded, and good teachers are few and far between.* | *Toys were few and far between, but the children invented games and played together.*

be/become a rarity /biː, bɪˌkʌm ə ˈreərɪ̈ti/ [n phrase] if something or someone **is a rarity**, it is surprising to find one, because very few exist: *The traditional costume is becoming a rarity, even in remote villages.* | **be something of a rarity** (=be fairly rare) *Women are still something of a rarity in senior management positions.*

there aren't many around /ðeər ˌɑːnt meni əˈraʊnd‖-ˌɑːrənt-/ [v phrase] informal use this to say that something is rare, especially something that has been made such as a machine, car, or piece of furniture: *He drives an original Volkswagen, and there aren't many of those around these days.*

2 not happening often

- rare
- uncommon/not common
- you don't often do sth
- infrequent

rare /reəʳ/ [adj] something that is **rare** does not happen often: *Snow is a rare sight here, except on the mountains.* | *On the rare occasions when we had to work hard, we enjoyed it.* | *In a rare moment of vanity, Carl removed his glasses.* | **it is rare for sb/sth to do sth** *It is very rare for anyone to actually die from bee stings in this country.*

uncommon/not common /ʌnˈkɒmən, ˌnɒt ˈkɒmən‖-ˈkɑːmən/ [adj] fairly rare: *Crimes against elderly people are still uncommon.* | *Her time in hospital had given her an empathy with her patients not common among physicians.* | **it is uncommon to do sth** *When I was young it was uncommon to see a man pushing a baby buggy.*

you don't often do sth /juː ˌdəʊnt ɒfən ˈduː (sth) ‖-ɔːfən-/ spoken if you say **you don't often** see something, find something etc, you mean this happens only very rarely: *You don't often find really good tropical fruit in this country.* | *We had over 200 replies. You don't often get such a good response from an advert.*

infrequent /ɪnˈfriːkwənt/ [adj] formal not happening often: *As time went on, her visits became more and more infrequent.* | *Cases of typhoid are relatively infrequent in Northern Europe.* | *Roger's infrequent letters home did not reveal much about his personal life.*

3 rarely/not often

- rarely/seldom
- not often
- hardly/scarcely ever
- once in a blue moon

rarely/seldom /ˈreəʳli, ˈseldəm/ [adv] not at all often. **Seldom** is more formal than **rarely** and is used especially in written English: *The Queen rarely speaks to journalists.* | *Discipline is rarely a problem in this school.* | *They're a very nice young couple, although I very seldom see them.* | **rarely does/has sb** *Very rarely do we have a complaint from any of our customers.* | *Seldom have I seen such a miraculous recovery in one of my patients.* | **rarely/seldom, if ever** *Anti-government demonstrations do occur, but they are seldom, if ever, reported in the press.*

not often /nɒt ˈɒfən‖-ˈɔːfən/ [adv] *I don't often see my grandchildren.* | *Sometimes, but not very often, Pippa persuaded her father to lend her his car.* | *Tina didn't get to work until ten o'clock this morning, which is unusual because she's not often late.* | **it's not often (that)** *Of course I'm going to take the job, it's not often that you get a chance like this.*

hardly/scarcely ever /ˌhɑːʳdli, ˌskeəʳsli ˈevəʳ/ [adv] almost never: *My grandmother hardly ever goes out of the house.* | *She's hardly ever ill.* | *We scarcely ever walk through the town without meeting someone we know.* | *There used to be a lot of disputes over land boundaries but nowadays such problems scarcely ever arise.*

once in a blue moon /ˌwʌns ɪn ə ˌbluː ˈmuːn/ [adv] informal extremely rarely: *I used to spend a lot of time in London, but now I only go there once in a blue moon.* | *Once in a blue moon Eric will offer to help with the dishes, but usually he doesn't do any housework at all.*

reach

RELATED WORDS

- *see also* **travel**

1 when something is long or high enough to reach something

- go (out/up/over etc) to sth
- reach
- go up to
- go down to
- come up to
- come down to
- stretch
- extend

go (out/up/over etc) to sth ALSO **go as far as sth** /gəʊ ˈaʊt tə (sth), gəʊ əz ˈfɑːr əz (sth)/ [v phrase not in progressive] to be long enough to reach a particular point: *I want a rug that goes right to the edge of the room.* | *You'll have to move the television a little this way. The plug won't go as far as the wall from there.* | **go all the way to sth** ALSO **go right the way to sth** British *The fence went all the way over to the other side of the park.*

reach /riːtʃ/ [v I/T not in progressive] to be long enough, high enough, or deep enough to get to a particular place or point: *It won't work – the ladder won't reach.* | *The snow almost reached my knees.* | *You see, the paint doesn't quite reach the edge of the paper.* | **+ as far as/down to etc** *I don't think these curtains will reach down to the floor.*

go up to /ˌgəʊ ˈʌp tuː/ [v phrase not in progressive] to be high enough to reach as far as a particular point: *She was wearing grey socks that went right up to her knees.* | *After the flood, the water level in the river almost went up to the top of the dam.* | **go all the way up to sth** ALSO **go right the way up to sth** British (=reach the whole distance to sth) *The Christmas tree went all the way up to the ceiling.*

go down to /ˌgəʊ ˈdaʊn tuː/ [v phrase not in progressive] to be long enough to reach down as far as a particular point: *The rope went down to the bottom of the cliff.* | *She had long blonde hair that went down to her waist.* | **go all the way down to sth** ALSO **go right the way down to sth** British (=reach a long way down) *The scar on his face went from his eye all the way down to his chin.*

come up to /ˌkʌm ˈʌp tuː/ [v phrase not in progressive] to reach up to a part of the body such as the knee, neck, or shoulder: *In the shallow end of the pool, the water comes up to my waist.* | *Freddie's been growing so fast – he already comes up to my shoulder.*

come down to /ˌkʌm ˈdaʊn tuː/ [v phrase not in progressive] if a piece of clothing **comes down to** a part of your body such as your elbows, waist, or knees, it is long enough to reach that part: *I can't wear this sweater – it almost comes down to my knees!* | *If you go into a mosque, you should wear sleeves that at least come down to your elbows.*

stretch /stretʃ/ [v I not in progressive] if something such as a river, road, or area of land **stretches** to a particular place, it reaches that place **+ down to** *We followed a small track that stretched down to the sea.* | **+ as far as** *We could see the mountains stretching as far as Vermont.* | **stretch from sth to sth** *Today, just 5% remains of the original wooded land that stretched from the Atlantic to the Mississippi.* | **stretch all the way to sth** ALSO **stretch right the way to sth** British *The oil slick stretched all the way to the horizon.* | **stretch into the distance/stretch as far as the eye can see** (=continue as far as you can see into the distance) *There were poppy fields stretching as far as the eye could see.*

extend /ɪkˈstend/ [v I not in progressive] if something such as a river or area of land **extends** as far as a particular place, it reaches that place – use this especially in technical writing, descriptions etc: **+ as far as/to etc** *The River Nile extends as far as Lake Victoria.* | *Smith Point is a small piece of land extending a hundred yards or so into the water.* | **extend all the way from sth to sth** ALSO **extend right the way from sth to sth** British *The Soviet Union extended all the way from the Baltic Sea to the Pacific Ocean.*

2 when a number or amount reaches a particular level

- reach
- hit
- attain
- touch

reach /riːtʃ/ [v T] if a number or amount **reaches** a particular level, it increases or decreases until it gets to that level: *Gold prices have reached their lowest level in 15 years.* | **reach $500/100 mph etc** *Wind speeds reached over 100 mph in coastal districts.* | *The value of most houses in this area has reached over £200,000.* | **reach a peak** (=reach the highest level) *Inflation continued to rise, reaching a peak of 28%.*

hit /hɪt/ [v T] to reach a very high or a very low level: *The temperature hit 40°C in parts of the country yesterday.* | *If sales continue to increase, output may hit the 500,000 mark this year.* | **hit rock bottom** (=reach an extremely low level) *Analysts say that the value of the Euro could hit rock bottom in the next few months.* | **hit an all-time low/high** (=reach the lowest or highest level ever) *As oil production increased, prices hit an all-time low.*

attain /əˈteɪn/ [v T] to reach a high level – use this in formal or technical contexts **attain a height/speed etc of sth** *When migrating, birds may attain a height of three thousand metres or more.* | *The latest model is capable of attaining speeds in excess of 300 kph.* | **attain a high of sth** *Share prices attained a high of $3.27.*

touch /tʌtʃ/ [v T] to reach a high or a low level for a very short time: *The plane touched the speed of sound in a power dive.* | **touch a high of sth** *Yesterday, the dollar touched a seventeen-week high of 1.4748 marks.*

3 when someone can reach something

- reach
- get to

reach /riːtʃ/ [v I/T not in progressive] to be able to touch something or take hold of it, by stretching your arm or moving your body: *Can you get that book down for me? I can't reach.* | *There's no point in having a shelf so high that you can't reach it.*

get to /ˈget tuː/ [v phrase not in progressive] to be able to reach something that you need by stretching your arm, moving your body etc, especially after you have been hurt: *She had fallen and broken her ankle and couldn't get to the phone.* | *Can you get to your coffee, if I put it here?*

4 to reach a place that you are travelling to

- reach
- get
- make it
- make
- get through
- accessible

reach /riːtʃ/ [v T not in progressive] to arrive at a place, especially after a long or difficult journey: *We didn't reach the hotel until midnight.* | *Some letters are taking up to two weeks to reach their destination.* | *In winter, parts of Northern Canada can only be reached by plane.*

get /get/ [v I not in progressive] especially spoken if you **get** to a place, you reach it **+ to** *By the time we got to New York, it was snowing.* | **+ home/here/there** *What time did you get home last night?* | **+ as far as** *We only got as far as the end of the road, then the car broke down.*

make it /ˈmeɪk ɪt/ [v phrase not in progressive] especially spoken to arrive at a place, especially when you were not sure that you would be able to get there: *The roads were so bad that I wasn't sure we would make it.* | *If we run, we should be able to make it before the bus leaves.* | **+ to/across/home etc** *Even though he couldn't swim, he managed to make it to the riverbank.* | *Thousands of refugees made it across the border.*

make /meɪk/ [v T not in progressive] to succeed in reaching a place, especially by a particular time: *We'll be lucky if we make San Fernando by nightfall.* | *The team aimed to make the South Pole and back in a month.*

get through /ˌget ˈθruː/ [phr v I] to succeed in reaching a particular place, after much danger and difficulty: *Heavy rains have prevented food supplies from getting through.* | **+ to** *Rescue teams finally got through to the survivors by digging a tunnel.*

accessible /əkˈsesəbəl/ [adj] easily reached, especially by car, boat, plane etc **easily accessible** *We chose to live in this area because both New York and Boston are easily accessible from here.* | *The banks of the River Holbeck are easily accessible to walkers and anglers.* | **accessible by boat/plane etc** *Because of the snow, many parts of the countryside are only accessible by helicopter.*

5 a place that is difficult or impossible to reach

- inaccessible

- *see also* **far, convenient**

inaccessible /ˌɪnək'sesəbəl/ [adj] impossible to reach: *The country consists mainly of dense jungles and inaccessible mountain ranges.* | **+ to** *The bathroom is situated at the top of a flight of stairs, making it inaccessible to the disabled.*

react

to behave in a particular way as a result of something that has happened

RELATED WORDS

- *see also* **behave, answer/reply**

1 to react to something

- react
- respond
- greet
- meet with
- overreact

react /ri'ækt/ [v I not in progressive] to say or do something because of what another person has said or done, or because of something that has happened: *How did your parents react when you told them you were going to marry Jim?* | *It's hard not to react badly when your kids are playing up.* | **+ to** *People reacted to the speech in different ways.* | *The chairman reacted angrily to the report and said it would make it much harder to reach a deal.* | **+ against** *Emma is not behaving very reasonably nowadays. I think she's reacting against her teachers' strictness.* | **react by doing sth** *A shot was fired, and the police reacted by firing into the crowd.* | **react with disappointment/laughter/violence etc** *When children perform poorly at school, parents often react with anger.* | *Many gays reacted with outrage at the tactic of 'outing' senior public figures.*

respond /rɪ'spɒnd‖rɪ'spɑːnd/ [v I] to react to something that someone has said to you, or something that someone has done to you or for you: *The more attention you pay him, the better he responds.* | **+ with** *Rob's smile was irresistible, and she responded with a grin.* | **+ to** *The children responded well to the day's activities.* | *The theatre has been slow to respond to the challenges presented by progressive drama.* | **respond by doing sth** *The demonstrators attacked and burned buildings and cars; the soldiers responded by opening fire.*

greet /griːt/ [v T usually in passive] to react to something with a particular attitude or with a particular action: *The news has been greeted angrily within Egyptian government circles.* | **be greeted with sth** *Donaldson's remarks were greeted with cautious enthusiasm.* | *The proposals were greeted with a mixture of skepticism and distrust.*

meet with /'miːt wɪð/ [phr v T] to get a particular reaction, especially a negative one: *The proposals met with fierce opposition from women's groups and labour unions.* | *Any attempts to impose a solution would be quite likely to meet with even more violence.* | **to be met with** *The US says any further attacks will be met with the full force of the US military.*

overreact /ˌəʊvəri'ækt/ [v I] to react too strongly to something that has happened, especially by becoming extremely angry, worried, or afraid: *Don't you think you're overreacting? I only said 'hi'. It's not as if we're having an affair!* | **+ to** *Some residents overreact to the problem of crime by just not going out at all.* | *The state has dramatically overreacted to the use of soft drugs.* | **+ with** *Overreacting with shock when a child uses a swear word is likely to make him use it again.*

2 to react to someone in the same way as they treat you

- reciprocate
- back
- give as good as you get

reciprocate /rɪ'sɪprəkeɪt/ [v I/T] formal to react to someone's feelings or actions towards you by showing the same feelings towards them, doing the same thing for them etc –use this especially when the feelings or actions are good: *We asked them over for dinner, hoping they would reciprocate.* | **reciprocate feelings/an invitation etc** *Although Miss Warton did not reciprocate John's feelings, she did nothing to discourage them.* | *My classmates would ask me over, but I never felt I could reciprocate the invitation.*

back /bæk/ [adv] if you smile **back**, hit someone **back** etc, you smile at someone, hit them etc, after they have done the same thing to you: *Carol yelled back, 'If it's so easy, you come and have a go!'* | *If Jamie rings, tell him I'll call him back.* | *The man just sat there smiling back at me.*

give as good as you get /ˌgɪv əz ˌgʊd əz juː 'get/ [v phrase] informal if someone who is being attacked or criticized **gives as good as they get**, they are just as violent or rude as the person who is attacking them: *Don't you worry about Tim. He may be small but he gives as good as he gets!* | *It was a tough interview, but I thought the President gave as good as he got.* | *At 87, Juran is still able to give as good as he gets.*

3 what someone says or does when they react to something

- reaction
- response
- feedback
- backlash
- overreaction

reaction /ri'ækʃən/ [n C] what someone says or does when they react to something: *My father was so surprised by this violent reaction that he fell silent.* | **+ to/against** *Maria's reaction to the birth of her sister was to demand more attention from her mother.* | **initial/first reaction** *I was stunned by the news, and my initial reaction was anger.* | *Can you tell us about your first reactions to this news?* | **gut reaction** (=a strong reaction that you have, although you are not sure why) *I wanted to write something thoughtful, not just leap in with my gut reaction.* | **knee-jerk reaction** (=a reaction you have without thinking about it first) *Environmentalists have a knee-jerk reaction against any sort of development, however 'green' it might be.*

response /rɪ'spɒns‖rɪ'spɑːns/ [n C] your reaction to something that someone has said to you, done to you, or asked you for: *The story has provoked a strong response from the Chinese.* | *'You've persuaded me,' she laughed, amazed at her own response.* | **+ to** *Tina's outburst was a delayed response to her husband's behaviour the week before.* | **get a response** *We've tried to include Susan in our social activities, but we get no response.* | **in response to sth** (=as a way of responding) *In* *response to local demand, we will be opening this store from nine till seven on Sundays.*

feedback /ˈfiːdbæk/ [n U] advice, criticism, praise etc that you give to someone, telling them how well they are working: *We are very encouraged by the feedback we've had from our shareholders.* | **give sb feedback/give feedback (to sb)** *Every Friday, Mr James would hand out the students' essays and give them some feedback.* | **+ on** *It is important to give employees regular feedback on their performance.* | **positive/negative feedback** *I'm lucky to work for an employer who gives positive feedback on my work.* —**feed back** [v not in progressive] *Regular reports are fed back to senior managers.*

backlash /ˈbæklæʃ/ [n C usually singular] an angry or violent reaction by a group of people to the actions or decisions of others **+ against** *Members of the Rifle and Pistol Club fear a public backlash against their sport after a recent armed raid in the village.* | *The attacks have sparked a bitter backlash against the revolutionary forces.* | **+ from** *a growing backlash from angry voters*

overreaction /ˌəʊvəriˈækʃən/ [n C/U] when someone reacts much too strongly to something: *I'm not arguing in favor of cannabis. I'm just saying we should be careful of overreaction.* | *The appeal court judge described the sentence as a gross overreaction to the recent spate of bombing campaigns.*

4 the ability to react quickly

- reactions
- reflexes

reactions /riˈækʃənz/ [n plural] to be able to react quickly to moving objects, danger etc: *Alcohol slows a driver's reactions, making it harder to avoid an accident.* | *He was a natural boxer, with a cold temper, fast reactions and a killer instinct.*

reflexes /ˈriːfleksɨz/ [n plural] the natural ability to react quickly and well to dangers etc, without having to think about what you are doing: *Bernice moved to slap him, but with lightning reflexes, he grasped her arm.* | *City got only one goal, and owed everything to the extraordinarily quick reflexes of their goalkeeper.*

read

RELATED WORDS

- *see also* **write, books, newspapers**

1 to read something

- read
- read out
- read aloud/read out loud

read /riːd/ [v I/T] *Read the instructions carefully before you start.* | *Have you read Jean Martin's latest novel?* | *Don't believe everything you read in the newspapers.* | *She learnt to read when she was only three years old.* | **+ about** *Did you read about that terrible car crash?* | **+ that** *I was astonished to read that half of all sixteen year olds have experimented with drugs.* | **read to sb/read sb sth** (=read something aloud, so that people can listen) *Our mother used to read to us every evening.* | *Read me Aunt Evelyn's letter while I cook dinner.* —**reading** [n U] the skill or activity of reading: *Children are taught reading and writing in their first years at school.* | *I do a lot of reading when I'm on vacation.* —**reader** [n C] someone who reads something: *The newspaper is trying to attract more young readers.*

read out /ˌriːd ˈaʊt/ [phr v T] to read something and say the words so that people can hear it **read out sth** *He opened the envelope and read out the name of the winner.* | **read sth out** *Read the numbers out and I'll write them down.* | **read sth out to sb** *Sarah read the letter out to me.*

read aloud/read out loud /ˌriːd əˈlaʊd, ˌriːd aʊt ˈlaʊd/ [v phrase] to read something and say the words so everyone can hear it **+ to** *After he went blind, she would read out loud to him from his favorite books.* | **+ from** *Sam read aloud from the note pinned to his door.* | **read sth aloud** *He picked up the letter and began to read it aloud.* | *The poem is intended to be read aloud.*

2 to read something quickly

- skim
- scan
- have a look at

skim /skɪm/ [v I/T] to read something quickly so that you get a general idea of what it is about: *I skimmed the newspaper but didn't see any report on the demonstration.* | **+ through** *She didn't have much time so she just skimmed through the report before the meeting.*

scan /skæn/ [v T] to read something quickly in order to find a particular piece of information: *She scanned the menu outside the restaurant, but decided it looked too expensive.* | **scan sth for sth** *Robert scanned the lists for his name.*

have a look at British **/take a look at** American /ˌhæv ə ˈlʊk æt, ˌteɪk ə ˈlʊk æt/ [v phrase] to read something quickly to check that there are no mistakes or problems: *Would you mind having a look at this report for me?* | *I've had a quick look at the insurance contract and everything appears to be in order.* | *Take a look at these figures – our profits are not looking good.*

3 to read only parts of something

- leaf/flick/thumb through
- dip into
- browse through

leaf/flick/thumb through /ˈliːf, ˈflɪk, ˈθʌm θruː (sth)/ [phr v T] to turn the pages of a book, magazine etc without reading much of it, looking for something interesting or useful: *She flicked through the guidebook, looking for somewhere to visit in the afternoon.* | *I began leafing through a magazine.* | *Gloria lay on her bed and idly thumbed through the pages of a travel brochure.*

dip into /ˈdɪp ɪntuː/ [phr v T] to read short parts of a book, magazine etc because you do not want to read the whole thing or because you are looking for a particular piece of information: *He had some books by his bed which he would dip into when he couldn't sleep.* | *This is a wonderful reference book to dip into for all sorts of fascinating information.*

browse through /ˈbraʊz θruː/ [phr v T] to turn the pages of a magazine or book, stopping to read parts that interest you: *I was browsing through a magazine at the station bookstall when I noticed Susan.*

4 to read something carefully

- read through/over
- pore over

read through/over /ˈriːd θruː, əʊvəʳ/ [phr v T] to read something carefully especially in order to check every detail or find any mistakes **read through/over sth** *It's important to read through your essay before you finally hand it in.* | *My professor read over my dissertation and said that he was very impressed with it.* | **read sth through/over** *I've finished writing the report – I've just got to read it through now.*

pore over /ˈpɔːr əʊvəʳ/ [v T] to read something for a long time, very carefully, and with great interest: *He was sitting at his desk poring over old maps of the area.* | *Ian shook his head as he pored over the report.*

5 to read something long or boring

- plough through
- wade through

plough through British **/plow through** American /ˈplaʊ θruː/ [phr v T] to read all of something even though it takes a long time and is boring: *I ploughed through all the documents related to the case.* | *After plowing through so many huge textbooks it was a relief to pick up a novel again.*

wade through /ˈweɪd θruː/ [phr v T] to read something that is very long and boring, or to read a lot of different pieces of writing such as letters, reports etc which together are long and boring to read: *We waded through a huge pile of applications, and finally selected six people to interview.* | *It's much easier to find the information on the Internet, rather than wading through piles of documents.*

6 to read a lot about something

- read up on

read up on /ˌriːd ˈʌp ɒn/ [phr v T] to read a lot about something or someone in order to find out about them: *I'll need to read up on the rules of the game if I'm going to referee.* | *Karen spent the summer reading up on the subjects she would be studying at college.*

7 someone who reads a lot

- voracious/avid reader
- bookworm
- well-read

voracious/avid reader ALSO **great/keen reader** British /vəˌreɪʃəs, ˌævɪ̈d ˈriːdəʳ, ˌgreɪt, ˌkiːn, ˈriːdəʳ/ [n C] someone who enjoys reading and reads a lot: *I was an avid reader as a child.* | *My grandchildren are great readers, so I always give them books for their birthday.* | **+ of** *Along with being an expert in business law, Martin is a voracious reader of detective stories.*

bookworm /ˈbʊkwɜːʳm/ [n C] informal someone who spends a lot of time reading: *I was a real bookworm when I was a child.* | *an ideal gift for the bookworm in the family*

well-read /ˌwel ˈred◂/ [adj] someone who is **well-read** has read a lot of books, often the most important or famous books, and has learned a lot of information from them: *Charles was a well-read and highly educated man.* | **+ in** *Although Jack stopped his studies at 19, he was very well-read, especially in the classics.*

8 the people who read a particular newspaper, book etc

- reader
- readership
- circulation

reader /ˈriːdəʳ/ [n C] someone who reads a particular newspaper, magazine, or a type of book: *The magazine needs to attract more young readers.* | *Her books appeal especially to women readers.* | *All Ms Atwood's readers will be delighted with her latest book.* | *The average reader of science-fiction is young and male.*

readership /ˈriːdəʳʃɪp/ [n singular] all the people who read a particular book, magazine, or newspaper: *The newspaper now has a readership of more than 500,000.* | *These books are obviously written for a young readership.* | **a broad/wide readership** *The magazine now hopes to attract a wider readership.*

circulation /ˌsɜːʳkjʊ̈ˈleɪʃən/ [n singular] the number of people who buy and read a particular newspaper or magazine **a circulation of 500,000/1 million etc** *The local newspaper has a circulation of around 16,000.* | **a small/large circulation** *It is a specialist journal with a relatively small circulation.*

9 able to read

- can read
- literate
- good/competent reader
- literacy

can read /kən ˈriːd/ [v phrase] *Tom could read by the age of four.* | *Very few people in the rural areas can read or write.*

literate /ˈlɪtərɪ̈t/ [adj] someone who is **literate** can read and write – use this about adults or older children: *Over the last hundred years, people have become healthier, more literate, and better educated.* | *Every student should be literate by the time he or she leaves primary school.*

good/competent reader /ˌgʊd, ˌkɒmpɪ̈tənt ˈriːdəʳ‖-ˌkɑːm-/ [n C] someone, usually a child who can read well: *Children are expected to be competent readers by the time they leave this class.* | *Good readers tend to be better at spelling than other children.*

literacy /ˈlɪtərəsi/ [n U] the fact of being able to read – use this especially to talk about how many people in a society can read and in educational contexts: *Cuba has one of the highest literacy rates in the world* (=more people can read there than anywhere else in the world)). | *Literacy levels amongst girls very quickly overtook those of boys.* | *She runs a project called 'Forward to Literary'.* | *special classes in basic skills such as literacy and numeracy*

10 not able to read

- cannot/can't read
- illiterate
- slow reader
- illiteracy

cannot/can't read /ˌkænɒt, ˌkɑːnt ˈriːd‖ˌkænɑːt, ˌkænt-/ [v phrase] to be unable to read at all: *A new report says that 25% of all 7-year-olds cannot read.* | *Jim couldn't read at all until he was fifteen.* | *It was not until I had lived with her for a year that I realized she couldn't read.*

illiterate /ɪˈlɪtərɪ̈t/ [adj] someone who is **illiterate** cannot read or write – use this about adults or older children: *His father was an illiterate farm worker.* | *If 70% of the population is illiterate, how do people know who they are voting for?*

slow reader /ˌsləʊ ˈriːdəʳ/ [n C] someone, especially a child, who can read, but not very well: *At first Katy was a slow reader, but now she reads all the time.* | *At the end of the day the teacher does half an hour's extra work with the slow readers.*

illiteracy /ɪˈlɪtərəsi/ [n U] the fact of being not able to read – use this especially to talk about how many people in a society cannot read: *Illiteracy rates among women in many countries are a serious cause for concern.* | *a society struggling to overcome poverty and illiteracy* | *The government has given extra funding to help tackle illiteracy in the inner cities.*

11 easy to read

- legible

legible /ˈledʒəbəl/ [adj] written clearly enough for you to read: *Is the date on the coin still legible?* | *Her writing was so tiny that it was barely legible.*

12 difficult or impossible to read

- can't read sth
- can't make out
- illegible
- indecipherable
- unreadable
- scrawl

can't read sth /ˌkɑːnt ˈriːd (sth) ‖ˌkænt-/ [v phrase] especially spoken use this to say that you are unable to read someone's writing: *I can't read the next word.* | *She couldn't read the name on the envelope.*

can't make out /ˌkɑːnt meɪk ˈaʊt‖ˌkænt-/ [v phrase] informal use this to say that you are unable to read a particular word because it is not written clearly: *I couldn't make out the name at the bottom of the letter.*

illegible /ɪˈledʒəbəl/ [adj] writing that is **illegible** is impossible to read because it is not written clearly: *I don't know what this note says – Dad's handwriting is totally illegible!* | *The label had got wet and was now illegible.*

indecipherable /ˌɪndɪˈsaɪfərəbəl/ [adj] writing that is **indecipherable** is impossible to read because it is very untidy, very unclear, or is in a language you do not understand: *The painting had an indecipherable signature in the corner.* | *His writing was tiny and indecipherable.* | *I received a blurred, indecipherable fax that didn't help at all.*

unreadable /ʌnˈriːdəbəl/ [adj] writing that is **unreadable** is impossible to read because it is very untidy or unclear: *The photocopy was poorly produced and almost unreadable.*

scrawl /skrɔːl/ [n C/U] something that someone has written in a very untidy way which is very difficult to read: *I couldn't read the doctor's scrawl.* | *I kept a diary then – pages and pages of tiny scrawl.*

13 enjoyable or interesting to read

- readable
- well-written
- worth reading
- make interesting reading
- be a good read
- page-turner
- unputdownable

readable /ˈriːdəbəl/ [adj] easy and interesting or enjoyable to read: *This is a well-written and readable introduction to the subject of linguistics.* | *Her articles are always readable and informative.*

well-written /ˌwel ˈrɪtn◂/ [adj] something that is **well-written** has been written in a good, clear style that makes it enjoyable or interesting to read: *The article was well written, informative and enjoyable.* | *This is a clever and well-written play.* | *Well-written notes are as good as any textbook and easier to absorb.*

worth reading /ˌwɜːʳθ ˈriːdɪŋ/ [adj phrase] a book or piece of writing that is **worth reading** is good enough or interesting enough to make you want to read it: *Have you seen Amis' latest book? It's worth reading.* | **be well worth reading** *It's an interesting book, and well worth reading.*

make interesting reading /meɪk ˌɪntrəstɪŋ ˈriːdɪŋ/ [v phrase] if you say that something **makes interesting reading**, you mean that it is interesting to read because it contains new or surprising information: *The story of their journey makes interesting reading.* | *The latest report on educational standards in our schools makes very interesting reading.*

be a good read /biː ə ˌgʊd ˈriːd/ [v phrase] informal if a book **is a good read**, it is enjoyable – use this when giving your opinion about a novel etc: *Her latest book is clever, funny, and well-written – a very good read.*

page-turner /ˈpeɪdʒ ˌtɜːʳnəʳ/ [n C] spoken a book that has an interesting or exciting story that makes you want to continue reading it to find out what happens next: *Stephen King's latest novel is, as usual, a real page-turner.*

unputdownable /ˌʌnpʊtˈdaʊnəbəl/ [adj] informal use this to talk about a book that is so interesting and exciting that you do not want to stop reading it until you get to the end: *'Unputdownable', raved the literary critic Helen Jewson, 'I read it at one sitting'.* | *This book might be an unputdownable expose of London's underworld, but its moral message is highly dubious.*

14 not enjoyable to read

- unreadable
- badly written

unreadable /ʌnˈriːdəbəl/ [adj] something that is **unreadable** is not enjoyable to read because it is not written in an interesting way: *The text was dense and unreadable.* | *The inclusion of so many figures and statistics makes the article virtually unreadable.*

badly written /ˌbædli ˈrɪtn◂/ [adj] if something is **badly written** it is not enjoyable to read because the style of the writing is not good: *The book was so badly written that I didn't get further than the first chapter.* | *The report was inaccurate and badly written.*

ready/not ready

RELATED WORDS

- when you think something will happen *see* **expect**
- *see also* **prepare, hurry**

1 when you are ready to do something

- ready
- prepared
- be ready to go
- be all set
- be geared up
- in readiness
- do sth when you are good and ready
- be good to go
- be ripe for

ready /ˈredi/ [adj not before noun] if you are **ready** for something, you have done everything that needs to be done in order to prepare for it: *Are you ready? The taxi's here.* | *When everyone is ready, I'll give the signal to start.* | **+ for** *I don't feel that I'm ready for the test yet.* | **+ to do sth** *Everything is packed and we're ready to leave.* | **get ready** (=prepare yourself to do something) *That's settled then. I'll go and get ready.* | *My sister always spends hours getting ready to go out.* | *It was soon time for the actors to get ready for the evening performance.* | **ready and waiting** *The wedding guests were all ready and waiting long before the bride arrived.* | **ready when you are** (=I am ready to do sth as soon as you are) *'Shall we go then?' 'Yes, ready when you are.'*

prepared /prɪˈpeəʳd/ [adj not before noun] ready to deal with a situation, because you were expecting it or because you have made careful preparations **+ for** *The police were prepared for trouble.* | *I was not prepared for all the questions they asked.* | **well prepared** *The team was well prepared and focussed on the issues.*

be ready to go /biː ˌredi tə ˈgəʊ/ [v phrase] to be ready and eager to start doing something: *On Christmas Day, the kids are always up and ready to go at 6 o'clock.* | *If everyone's ready to go, let's get started.*

be all set /biː ˌɔːl ˈset/ [v phrase] to be ready to start doing something that you have planned to do and want to do: *Dad got on his bike. 'Are you all set?' he called.* | **+ for** *The team are all set for another comfortable victory.* | **+ to do sth** *We were all set to start the barbecue when it started to rain.*

be geared up /biː ˌgɪəʳd ˈʌp/ [v phrase] if an organization or group of people **are geared up** for something that is going to happen, they have made careful plans so that they can deal with it as soon as it happens **+ for** *There are clear signs that the governor is geared up for a second attempt at the White House.* | **+ to do sth** *Companies that survive are the ones that are geared up to meet the demands of the future.* | **get geared up** *The airport was getting geared up to deal with a heavier schedule of flights.*

in readiness /ɪn ˈredinɪ̈s/ [adv] if you do something **in readiness** for something that you expect will happen, you do it so that you will be ready: *As the conflict grew worse, troops waited in readiness at the borders.* | **+ for** *A new stage and seating area has been built in readiness for tonight's sell-out performance.*

do sth when you are good and ready /ˌduː (sth) wen juː əʳ ˌgʊd ən ˈredi/ [v phrase] spoken used to tell someone who is impatient for you to do something that you will not do it until your are ready: *Dad says he'll come when he's good and ready.* | *Leave me alone! I'll tell her when I'm good and ready.*

be good to go /biː ˌgʊd tə ˈgəʊ/ [v phrase] American spoken to have completed all the necessary preparations and be ready to start doing something: *We just need to get you a pair of skis and you're good to go.* | *'Do you have all the hiking gear?' 'Yeah, I'm good to go.'*

be ripe for /biː ˈraɪp fɔːʳ/ [v phrase] to be in a suitable condition to be ready for something, especially a positive change: *Economists regard the region as being ripe for development.* | *After the divorce I was thoroughly fed up and ripe for a new start, so I agreed to take the job.*

2 ready to be used or eaten

- ready
- be in place
- ripe
- at the ready
- in readiness

ready /ˈredi/ [adj not before noun] if something is **ready**, you can use it or eat it immediately: *Lunch is ready!* | *When the pasta's ready, add the sauce.* | *I'm sorry, your car isn't ready yet, sir.* | **ready to eat/collect/use etc** *Your suit will be ready to pick up on Wednesday.* | *In a year's time, the wine will be ready to drink.* | *I tend to buy a lot of meals that are ready to eat* (=they have already been cooked). | **+ for** *Is everything ready for the party?* | **get sth ready** (=prepare it) *It took several months to get the boat ready for the voyage.*

be in place /biː ɪn ˈpleɪs/ [v phrase] if equipment, a system, a rule, or a plan **is in place**, it is ready to start being used: *A new PA system should be in place in the next three to six months.* | *When everything is in place, the building work begins, even if it means running two massive projects at the same time.* | *The uncertain economy is forcing us to accelerate cost-cutting plans that are already in place.*

ripe /raɪp/ [adj] **ripe** fruit is soft, sweet, and ready to eat: *Don't pick the apples until they're really ripe.* | *Is this melon ripe enough to eat?*

at the ready /ət ðə ˈredi/ [adv] if something is **at the ready**, it is nearby or in your hands, so that you can use it immediately if something happens and you need it: *Several reporters were outside, microphones at the ready.* | **have/keep sth at the ready** *I kept my camera at the ready in case the bird reappeared.* | **with sth at the ready** *Two police officers advanced, with guns at the ready.*

in readiness /ɪn ˈredinɪ̈s/ [adv] written ready to be used when something that you are expecting happens: *The table was carefully laid in readiness.* | **+ for** *Everything was laid out on the bed, in readiness for the new baby.*

3 ready to take action if it is needed

- be standing by
- be on standby
- be on call
- be on full alert

be standing by /biː ˌstændɪŋ ˈbaɪ/ [v phrase] to be ready to take action or provide something when it is needed: *Officers in full riot gear were standing by outside the police station.* | *A plane was standing by to take the hostages from the airport.*

be on standby /biː ɒn ˈstændbaɪ/ [v phrase] if a group of people, especially soldiers or police **are on standby**, they are waiting, ready to go somewhere if they are needed when something happens that is expected to happen soon: *Extra troops have been brought in, and riot police are on standby.* | *Bomb squads are on 24-hour standby because of the threats.* | **+ to do sth** *RAF medical crews are on standby to fly out to the war zone.*

be on call /biː ɒn ˈkɔːl/ [v phrase] if someone such as a doctor or engineer **is on call**, they are ready to give advice on the phone or go and help where they are needed, as part of their job: *As a doctor, you will be on call regularly at weekends.* | *There are four physiotherapists on call at the sports injury clinic.*

be on full alert /biː ɒn ˌfʊl əˈlɜːʳt/ [v phrase] if soldiers, police officers etc **are on full alert**, they are completely ready to deal with a dangerous situation: *All ships were on full alert.* | **put/place sth on full alert** *By 7 pm the President had placed American military forces on full alert.* | **+ for** *The police were on full alert for further riots.*

4 when you are not ready to do something

- not ready
- unprepared

not ready /nɒt 'redi/ [adj not before noun] if you are **not ready** for something, you have not done everything that needs to be done in order to prepare for it: *Wait a minute! I'm not ready yet.* | **+ for** *The coaches felt Stark wasn't ready for major league baseball yet.* | **+ to do sth** *I felt that I wasn't ready to make a final decision.*

unprepared /ˌʌnprɪ'peəʳd/ [adj not before noun] written not ready to deal with something because you were not expecting it, and have not thought about it or made plans **+ for** *Mexico was unprepared for war.* | *When I told her the news, I was totally unprepared for her reaction.* | **+ to do sth** *The study showed that 50% of the students were unprepared for work or college.*

5 not ready to eat or use

- not ready
- unripe

not ready /nɒt 'redi/ [adj not before noun] if something is **not ready**, you cannot use it or eat it immediately: *I'm afraid dinner's not ready yet.* | *The blackberries won't be ready for another week or two.* | **+ for** *The zero-emission care is not ready for mass production.* | **not ready to eat/drink/use etc** *The paint's not ready to use when you buy it. You have to mix it with water.*

unripe /ˌʌn'raɪp◂/ [adj] fruit that is **unripe** is not soft, sweet, or ready to eat: *Don't use unripe apples for making cider.* | *The cherries on the tree were still unripe.*

6 to do something or to happen when someone is not ready

- be caught napping
- catch sb off guard
- catch sb with their pants down
- catch sb on the hop
- wing it

be caught napping /biː ˌkɔːt 'næpɪŋ/ [v phrase] informal if you **are caught napping** by something that happens, you are not expecting it and are not ready to deal with it, although you should expect it and be ready for it: *Stock traders who ignore these signs are in danger of being caught napping when a recession hits.* | **+ by** *Nowadays, no company can afford to be caught napping by a technological development.*

catch sb off guard /ˌkætʃ (sb) ɒf 'gɑːʳd/ [v phrase] to say or do something when someone is not expecting it so that they cannot deal with it as well as they would like to: *'Are you married?' Vick asked, catching her off guard.* | *The Prime Minister admitted to being caught off guard by news of the attack.*

catch sb with their pants down /ˌkætʃ (sb) wɪð ðeəʳ 'pænts daʊn/ [v phrase usually in passive] informal to arrive or to do something when someone is not ready, and make them feel stupid or embarrassed: *The city got caught with its financial pants down, and the scandal has led to 12 high-level officials losing their jobs.*

catch sb on the hop /ˌkætʃ (sb) ɒn ðə 'hɒp‖ -'hɑːp/ [v phrase] British informal to do something, or to happen, when someone is not expecting it and is not ready to deal with it: *The dramatic fall in share prices caught even the experts on the hop.* | *Many politicians have been caught on the hop by a good interviewer.*

wing it /'wɪŋ ɪt/ [v phrase] informal to try to do something even though you are not ready, especially when you have to pretend you know more about something that you do: *If you are asked a question that you're not ready for, it's better to say 'I hadn't considered that' than to wing it and get it wrong.* | *We have to wing it in the first game, but we'll be more prepared for the next one.*

real

RELATED WORDS

- not made with natural materials *see* **artificial**
- intended to appear real in order to deceive people *see* **false**
- *see also* **pretend, honest, dishonest, imagine**

- **not false or artificial** see **1 to 4**
- **not imagined or invented** see **5 to 6**
- **when pictures, films etc seem real/don't seem real** see **7 to 8**

not false or artificial

1 not false or artificial

- real
- genuine
- authentic
- bona fide
- natural
- the real thing
- the genuine article
- the real McCoy

real /rɪəl/ [adj] not false or artificial: *Is that a real diamond?* | *Are those flowers real or artificial?* | *People call him Baz, but his real name is Reginald.*

genuine /'dʒenjuɪ̥n/ [adj] real, not just seeming to be real or pretending to be real: *For years people thought the picture was a genuine Van Gogh, but in fact it's a fake.* | *We need a much faster system for dealing with genuine refugees.* | *If a student has genuine religious objections to a school activity, they do not have to participate.*

authentic /ɔː'θentɪk/ [adj] **authentic** food, music, clothes etc are correct for the place or the period in history that they are supposed to be from: *a friendly restaurant offering authentic Greek food* | *They play music on authentic medieval instruments.* | *The dancers wore authentic Native American designs.*

bona fide /ˌbəʊnə 'faɪdi‖'bəʊnə faɪd/ [adj] people or things that are **bona fide** are really what they say they are, especially when this can be checked by looking at official records, personal papers etc: *This club is only open to bona fide members.* | *We have to check that he holds a bona fide qualification.* | *The company can only reimburse bona fide business-related expenses.*

natural /'nætʃərəl/ [adj] not artificial and no made by people: *I prefer natural fibres such as wool and cotton.* | *His natural hair color is brown.* | *We only use natural products.*

the real thing /ðə ˌrɪəl 'θɪŋ/ [n phrase] something that is the thing it is meant to be, and not a cheaper or lower quality thing: *Recorded music will never be as good as listening to the real thing.* | *I'd seen pictures of the painting, but it was very different seeing the real thing.*

the genuine article /ðə ˌdʒenjuɪ̥n 'ɑːrtɪkəl/ [n phrase] something such as a car, painting, or piece of furniture or clothing, that really is made, produced, or designed by a famous and admired person or company: *He owns a 1947 Ferrari – the genuine article.* | *With paintings it is sometimes difficult to distinguish the genuine article from a good reproduction.*

the real McCoy /ðə ˌrɪəl məˈkɔɪ/ [n phrase] informal something that is real, and not a cheaper, lower quality product: *The moment I smelled the cigar, I knew it was the real McCoy.* | *The dress had a designer label, but I couldn't tell if it was the real McCoy or a cheap imitation.*

2 having the qualities that make a particular type of person or thing real

- real
- true
- proper

real /rɪəl/ [adj only before noun] use this to emphasize that someone or something has the qualities that a particular kind of person or thing should have: *Jane's been a real friend to me over the years.* | *She's a real tomboy!* | *What the country needs now is a real leader.*

true /truː/ [adj only before noun] someone who is a **true** friend, believer etc is not just pretending to be one and has all of the qualities that a friend, believer etc is supposed to have: *He was a good partner and a true friend to me.* | *Being a true Red Sox fan, he never missed a game.* | *She makes the dance look easy – the mark of a true professional.* | *True Christians believe that Jesus is the Son of God.*

proper /ˈprɒpəʳ‖ˈprɑː-/ [adj only before noun] British real and not something similar which is not as good: *When are you going to get a proper job?* | *We don't have a proper guest room, but you can have the sofa in the study.*

3 when someone really feels something

- really
- real
- sincere
- genuine
- heartfelt
- from the heart
- truly
- true

really /ˈrɪəli/ [adv] when you **really** feel something, **really** want something etc, and you are not just pretending to feel it: *Do you think she's really sorry?* | *Do you really want to come with us? It'll be very boring for you.* | *I don't think she really believes she can win.*

real /rɪəl/ [adj] use this to describe feelings, attitudes and beliefs that someone really feels and is not just pretending to feel: *She was clearly in real pain.* | *He didn't show any real regret for the suffering he had caused.* | *Real commitment is needed from everyone on the team if we're going to make this project work.*

sincere /sɪnˈsɪəʳ/ [adj] if you are **sincere**, or have **sincere** feelings, you really feel or believe something and are not just pretending: *It is my sincere belief that if we work together we can achieve peace in this country.* | **+ in** *They seemed to be sincere in their concern for the children's welfare.* | **sincere thanks/apologies** formal *I would like to express my sincere thanks to all those who helped us.* —**sincerely** [adv] *I believe they sincerely want to find a peaceful solution to the dispute.*

genuine /ˈdʒenjuɪ̨n/ [adj] **genuine** feelings are real and not pretended – use this especially when you are surprised that someone has these feelings: *I'm not sure if her sympathy was really genuine.* | *For the first time on the trip, I saw genuine fear in his eyes.* | *This is the first genuine attempt to reach a peaceful settlement to the dispute.* —**genuinely** [adv] *Fred seemed genuinely interested in our work.*

heartfelt /ˈhɑːʳtfelt/ [adj usually before noun] very real and strongly felt: *Christine breathed a heartfelt sigh of relief.* | *She expressed her heartfelt thanks to all those who had helped and supported her.* | *Please accept our heartfelt sympathy on your sad loss.* | *The family made a heartfelt plea to the kidnappers to release their son.*

from the heart /frəm ðə ˈhɑːʳt/ [adv] if you say or mean something **from the heart**, you really mean it and feel it very strongly: *He stood up and spoke simply but from the heart.* | **from the bottom of sb's heart** *I want to thank you from the bottom of my heart.* | **straight from the heart** *I'm speaking straight from the heart when I say that I believe Marguerite deserves to be chairman.*

truly /ˈtruːli/ [adv] if you **truly** believe, want, or feel something, you believe, want, or feel it very strongly and are not just pretending: *I truly believe he is innocent.* | *She seems truly sorry for what she did.* | *I truly am impressed with your work.*

true /truː/ [adj usually before noun] a feeling that is **true** is real and strongly felt, not just pretended: *At last he had found true happiness.* | *As far as Gabby was concerned this was true love.*

4 when someone thinks or feels something but hides it

- really
- deep down
- underneath it all
- inside

really /ˈrɪəli/ [adv] used to say what someone's real thoughts and feelings are when they are pretending to think or feel something else: *Neither of us really wanted to stay in Texas, but we couldn't leave his family at that time.* | *She didn't complain, but I knew that really she was quite fed up with us all.* | *Don't trust James – all he's really interested in is your money.*

deep down /ˌdiːp ˈdaʊn/ [adv] if you think or feel something **deep down**, that is what you really think or feel even though you may not say or show it: *He pretends he doesn't care, but deep down I know he's very upset.* | *I kept pushing the team, but deep down I think I knew we wouldn't win.*

underneath it all /ʌndəʳˈniːθ ɪt ˌɔːl/ [adv] if someone is a particular kind of person **underneath it all**, this is what they are really like: *He likes to show people his tough side, but underneath it all, he's a decent person.*

inside /ɪnˈsaɪd/ [adv] if you feel something **inside**, that is the way you really feel, even though you do not show it: *I wish I knew what he was feeling inside.* | *These kids seem so aggressive, but inside they're terrified.*

not imagined or invented

5 when things or people really exist

- real
- actual
- true
- real live

real /rɪəl/ [adj] used to describe people or things that really exist and have not been imagined: *You can dress up either as a fictional character or a real* *person.* | **very real** *His problems are very real. I don't think you should laugh at him.* | *There was a very real danger of being robbed during the night.* —**reality** /ri'æləti/ [n U] *A lot of people use computer games as an escape from reality.*

actual /'æktʃuəl/ [adj only before noun] real, especially as compared with what is intended, believed, or what is usually expected: *How does the actual cost compare with the budget?* | *Although buses are supposed to run every fifteen minutes, the actual waiting time can be up to an hour.* | *The actual amount of water needed by the crop depends on the weather conditions.*

true /tru:/ [adj only before noun] the **true** value, nature, importance etc of something is its real value etc rather than what seems at first to be correct: *It is difficult to measure the true value of these amenities to the local community.* | *The true significance of the General's offer has yet to be established.*

real live /'rɪəl laɪv/ [adj phrase only before noun] informal a **real live** person or animal is one that is actually alive and real: *Seeing real live animals in a zoo is much more exciting that just watching them on television.* | *I've never met a real live movie star before!*

6 when information, statements etc are based on real facts

- true
- solid/concrete
- tangible

true /tru:/ [adj] based on facts and not imagined: *No, honestly, It's a true story.* | *She says her parents arrived here as refugees, but I know that's not true.*

solid/concrete /'sɒləd‖'sɑ:-, 'kɒŋkri:t‖kɑ:ŋ'kri:t/ [adj only before noun] based on things that can be proved to be true or real: *The police cannot arrest him until they have some solid evidence.* | *We had our suspicions, but no solid facts.* | *No one seems to have any concrete information about her.*

tangible /'tændʒəbəl/ [adj] firmly based on facts, able to be proved by being seen or experienced **tangible evidence/proof/results etc** *The discussions produced no tangible results.* | *There is no tangible evidence of dishonesty among the company's directors.*

when pictures, films etc seem real/don't seem real

7 when pictures, films etc make things seem real

- realistic
- lifelike
- realism
- true to life
- vivid

realistic /rɪə'lɪstɪk/ [adj] use this about books, pictures, and films that show or describe things as they really are: *The book includes some very realistic descriptions of life during the war.* | *A lot of people like paintings to look realistic.* | *Planning your dream home? You can build a more realistic model with our new 3-D kit.*

lifelike /'laɪflaɪk/ [adj] use this about pictures and models that look very like the real person or thing: *Outside the museum is a huge, lifelike model of a dinosaur.* | *The directors wanted the computer-generated images to look as lifelike as possible.*

realism /'rɪəlɪzəm/ [n U] the quality in a painting, film, story etc that makes it seem real and believable: *The battle scenes are described with extraordinary realism.* | *His style combines plain language and gritty realism.*

true to life /ˌtru: tə 'laɪf◂/ [adj phrase] a film, play, story etc that is **true to life**, shows or describes things as they really are: *It's a great story, but not always true to life.* | *The film gives us a true to life picture of 1920s Chicago.*

vivid /'vɪvəd/ [adj] **vivid** descriptions, memories, dreams etc are so clear that they seem real: *The book gives a vivid account of the author's journey through northern Africa.* | *I loved listening to his vivid descriptions of life in Italy.* | *One of my most vivid memories is of my first day at school.* | *The drug can make people suffer hallucinations and vivid nightmares.*

8 when pictures, films etc do not make things seem real

- abstract
- unrealistic
- contrived

abstract /'æbstrækt/ [adj] **abstract** paintings, pictures, designs etc contain shapes and images that represent real things and people but do not look like them: *a new exhibition of abstract paintings* | *A lot of people don't like abstract art.* | *It's an abstract design that's supposed to represent freedom and strength.*

unrealistic /ˌʌnrɪə'lɪstɪk/ [adj] something that is **unrealistic** shows or describes things in a way that does not seem real, and is therefore not very good or cannot be believed: *I found the play boring and the characters unrealistic.* | *The film is ruined by all the unrealistic plot twists.*

contrived /kən'traɪvd/ [adj] a story, situation etc that is **contrived** has been written or arranged in a way that seems false and not natural: *There's something very contrived about the whole story.* | *One critic described the movie as 'a stale and hopelessly contrived comedy'.*

realize

to notice or understand something that you did not notice or understand before

RELATED WORDS

▸ *see also* **understand/not understand, notice/not notice, know/not know, recognize**

- realize
- occur to
- become aware
- sink in
- dawn on
- strike
- hit
- wake up to the fact that
- it clicked
- bring sth home to

realize ALSO **realise** British /'rɪəlaɪz/ [v I/T] *Tim only realized his mistake the next day.* | *Without realising it, we had gone the wrong way.* | *Oh, is that your chair? Sorry, I didn't realize.* | **+ (that)** *She woke up and realised that there was someone moving around downstairs.*

occur to /ə'kɜ:ʳ tu:/ [phr v T] if something **occurs to** you, you suddenly realize that it might be true, especially when you had been thinking something completely different before **it occurs to sb (that)** *It suddenly occurred to me that maybe she was lying.* | *Didn't it ever occur to you that they would probably like to be alone together?*

become aware /bɪˌkʌm əˈweəʳ / [v phrase] to slowly realize something, especially over a fairly long period of time **+ of** *I was slowly becoming aware of how much Melissa was suffering.* | **+ that** *He became aware that the man sitting opposite was staring at him intently.*

sink in /ˌsɪŋk ˈɪn/ [phr v I] if a fact or someone's words **sink in**, you gradually realize their full meaning: *The news of the President's assassination had only just begun to sink in.* | *Winning this tournament means so much to me. It hasn't really sunk in yet.*

dawn on /ˈdɔːn ɒn/ [phr v T] if a fact **dawns on** you, you slowly start to realize it, especially when you should have realized it before: *The awful truth only dawned on me later.* | **it dawns on sb that** *It slowly dawned on her that they were all making fun of her.* | **it dawns on sb how/why etc** *It didn't dawn on me how seriously injured I was until I got to the hospital.*

strike /straɪk/ [v T not in progressive] if an idea or thought **strikes** you, you suddenly realize something **it strikes sb (that)** *It struck her one day, when she was walking home from school, that she hadn't thought about her weight for over a month.* | *It just struck me – you must have been in the same class as my brother.*

hit /hɪt/ [v T not in progressive] if a fact **hits** you, you suddenly realize its importance or its full meaning and you feel shocked: *The full impact of what he'd said hit me a few hours later.* | **it hits sb** *Suddenly it hit me. He was trying to ask me to marry him.*

wake up to the fact that /ˌweɪk ʌp tə ðə ˈfækt ðət/ [v phrase] to begin to fully realize and understand something, especially after you have avoided thinking about it because it is unpleasant or it makes you feel uncomfortable: *How long will it be before people wake up to the fact that anyone can catch AIDS.* | *The speaker warned that we must 'wake up to the fact that we are in a tough competitive market'.*

it clicked /ɪt ˈklɪkt/ spoken say this when you suddenly realize something that makes a subject or situation easy to understand: *Then it clicked. The man at the station must have been her brother!* | **+ what/how/where etc** *Finally it clicked what all the fuss had been about.*

bring sth home to /ˌbrɪŋ (sth) ˈhəʊm tuː/ [v phrase] to make someone realize how serious, difficult, or dangerous something is: *This is the last place you would expect there to be a murder. It just brings it home to you that this kind of thing can happen anywhere.* | *It often takes something like a heart attack to bring home to people the danger of smoking.*

reason

RELATED WORDS

▸ *see also* **cause, because, purpose, explain, sensible, logical, so/therefore, in order to**

1 why something happens or why someone does something

- ▸ reason
- ▸ explanation
- ▸ motive
- ▸ motivation
- ▸ pretext

reason /ˈriːzən/ [n C] what makes something happen, or what makes someone do something: *Why did he poison his wife? There must be a reason.* | **+ for** *Dad went off to find out the reason for the delay.* | **+ for doing sth** *What was your reason for leaving your last job?* | **+ to do sth** *You don't need a reason to phone her. Just call her up and say hello.* | **+ why** *There's no reason why Jon can't come with us.* | **+ (that)** *One of the main reasons that she looks so good is that she has her own personal stylist.* | **for personal/health/business etc reasons** *For security reasons, there were video cameras at the school entrance.* | **for some reason** especially spoken (=for a reason that you do not know or understand) *No, he isn't here – he had to go back to Poland for some reason.* | **for reasons best known to himself/herself etc** (=for secret reasons that other people do not know or understand) *For reasons best known to themselves, my parents were vehemently opposed to the idea.*

explanation /ˌekspləˈneɪʃən/ [n C] a fact, statement, or idea that helps you to understand why something has happened: *I don't know why he tested positive for drugs. The only explanation I can think of is that the samples got mixed up.* | **+ for** *Scientists have offered various explanations for these changes in climate.* | **possible explanation** *There are several possible explanations for girls' superior high school performance.*

motive /ˈməʊtɪv/ [n C] the reason that makes someone decide to do something, especially something bad or dishonest: *It's hard to understand her motives.* | **+ for/behind** *Police believe the motive for the murder was jealousy* | *The motive behind the killing of Agnes Law was robbery.* | **+ for doing sth** *Whatever your motives for coming over, I'm glad you did.* | **an ulterior motive** (=a hidden reason for doing something) *She was suspicious. Was there an ulterior motive behind his request?*

motivation /ˌməʊtəˈveɪʃən/ [n U] the strong feeling that is your reason for wanting to do something or achieve something, especially something that may take a long time to achieve: *She enjoyed the excitement of her work. Money was not her only motivation.* | **+ for** *Fame was the main motivation for their efforts.* | **+ for doing sth** *His motivation for wanting to stay on as manager is to see England as the top team in the world.*

pretext /ˈpriːtekst/ [n C] the reason that someone gives to explain why they do or do not do something but which is only partly true: *His sore leg was a pretext. He just wanted a day off work.* | **+ for** *Minor offences were sometimes used as a pretext for an arrest.* | **+ to do sth** *She couldn't find a pretext to visit Derek at home.* | **on the pretext of/that** (=giving the reason that) *He used to spend hours at her house on the pretext of giving her Japanese lessons.*

2 why something is right or should be done

- ▸ reason
- ▸ argument
- ▸ justification
- ▸ grounds
- ▸ cause
- ▸ rationale

reason /ˈriːzən/ [n C/U] **+ (why/that)** *The reason why we need these laws is to protect children from violent adults.* | **+ to do sth** *I can think of lots of reasons to get married.* | *You may be dissatisfied, but is that sufficient reason to resign?* | **have every reason to do sth** (=to have very good reasons for doing something) *We have every reason to believe he is guilty.* | **with good reason** (=when it is right or fair that someone does something) *The school is proud of its record, and with good reason.*

argument /ˈɑːʳgjɡmənt/ [n C] one of the reasons that someone uses to try to persuade someone to agree with them **+ that** *Do you agree with the argument that violence on TV makes people behave violently?* | **+ for/against** (=a reason why something should or should not be done) *What are the arguments for the legalization of cannabis?* | *The main argument against smoking is that it's bad for your health.*

justification /ˌdʒʌstɪfɪˈkeɪʃən/ [n C/U] a good reason for doing something that seems wrong: *She had her residence permit taken away, without any justification* | **+ for** *There's no justification for cruelty.* | **+ for doing sth** *What justification can there be for paying women lower wages?*

grounds /graʊndz/ [n plural] the reason that makes it right or fair for someone to do something – use this especially in legal or official contexts **+ for** *Is mental cruelty sufficient grounds for divorce?* | **on the grounds of sth** (=for this reason) *He had been fired from his job on the grounds of incompetence.* | *On what grounds are you claiming compensation?* | **on the grounds that** *She was prohibited from speaking to the students on the grounds that it would stir up trouble.*

cause /kɔːz/ [n U] a strong reason that makes you think you are right to feel or behave in a particular way **+ to do sth** *I've never had any cause to complain about my doctor.* | **with good/just cause** formal *He no longer loved her, and with just cause, because she had betrayed him.* | **without good/just cause** formal *We have little sympathy for people who leave their jobs without just cause.* | **cause for complaint/alarm/concern etc** *The child's behaviour is giving us cause for concern.* | *There is no cause for alarm about the safety of drinking water.*

rationale /ˌræʃəˈnɑːl‖-ˈnæl/ [n singular] formal the reason or series of reasons that someone has used to support a plan, suggestion, change etc **+ for/behind** *In the document he explains the rationale for his plan to build a car for the African market.* | *If you do not understand the rationale behind any action you are asked to take, be sure to find out.*

3 a reason explaining why you did something wrong

- excuse
- explanation

excuse /ɪkˈskjuːs/ [n C] something that you say to try to explain why you did something bad, so that people will forgive you: *Oh shut up Bill, I'm tired of listening to your excuses.* | **+ for** *He said his car had broken down, but it was just an excuse for coming home late.* | **make excuses** (=invent excuses in order to try to escape punishment or blame) *He doesn't make excuses when he gets something wrong.* | **feeble/pathetic/weak excuse** *That is the most feeble excuse for failing a test that I have ever heard.*

explanation /ˌekspləˈneɪʃən/ [n C] something that you say which gives good reasons for something wrong which you have done: *This work should have been finished a week ago. What's your explanation?* | **+ for** *He offered no explanation for his absence at the previous day's meeting.*

4 to be the reason why something happened or why someone does something

- be the reason
- explain
- account for
- motivate
- lie behind

be the reason /biː ðə ˈriːzən/ [v phrase] to **be the reason** why something happened or why someone did something **+ for/behind** *Nick's teachers think that problems at home are the reason for his poor schoolwork.* | **+ why** *He borrowed too much money, and that's the reason why his business failed.* | **+ (that)** *I knew that I had my weaknesses. Perhaps that is the reason that I was not more successful.*

explain /ɪkˈspleɪn/ [v T] if a fact or situation **explains** something, it helps you to understand why it happened: *We were all puzzled: what could explain his sudden change of mind?* | **+ why/what/how** *She couldn't sleep last night, which explains why she was in such a bad mood this morning.*

account for /əˈkaʊnt fɔːʳ/ [phr v T] formal to be the reason that explains why something strange or surprising happened: *If it's true that he was taking drugs, that would account for his strange behaviour.*

motivate /ˈməʊtɪveɪt/ [v T] to be someone's personal reason for doing something: *Not all people are motivated by self-interest.* | **motivate sb to do sth** *It's frustration that motivates babies to learn to walk.*

lie behind /ˌlaɪ bɪˈhaɪnd/ [phr v T not in passive] to be the secret or hidden reason for someone's action or behaviour: *I wonder what lies behind Arthur's sudden interest in golf?* | *I think that behind Tania's aggression lay a deep insecurity about herself.*

5 to be a good reason why something should be done

- justify
- make it right
- call for
- warrant

▸ *see also* **right**

justify /ˈdʒʌstɪfaɪ/ [v T] to be the fact or situation that makes it seem right or suitable to do something that would usually be wrong or unfair: *There is not enough evidence to justify such accusations.* | *No matter what the circumstances, street violence cannot be justified.*

make it right /ˌmeɪk ɪt ˈraɪt/ [v phrase not in progressive] if you say that something that is wrong or bad **makes it right** for you to do something wrong or bad, you mean that it makes your action acceptable: *It's wrong to steal and nothing you can say will make it right.* | **+ (for sb) to do sth** *Just because you know she cheats, that doesn't make it right for you to do the same.*

call for /ˈkɔːl fɔːʳ/ [phr v T not in progressive] if a situation **calls for** a particular behaviour or action, it is a good reason to behave or act in that way: *I hear that you two are getting married. This calls for a celebration.* | *It was a tricky situation that called for a lot of diplomacy.*

warrant /ˈwɒrənt‖ˈwɔː-, ˈwɑː-/ [v T] formal if a situation **warrants** a particular behaviour or action, the situation is so bad that there is a good reason to behave or act in that way: *Patients will only be given morphine if their medical condition warrants it.* | *The offences he has committed are not serious enough to warrant a full investigation.*

6 to tell someone the reason for something

- say why/tell sb why
- explain
- give a reason
- account for
- provide an explanation/come up with an explanation
- justify
- explain away

say why/tell sb why /ˌseɪ ˈwaɪ, ˌtel (sb) ˈwaɪ/ [v phrase] to tell someone why something happened: *I knew she was annoyed, but she wouldn't say why.* | *Can anyone tell us why there are no buses today?*

explain /ɪkˈspleɪn/ [v I/T] to tell someone the reason for something, so that they understand the situation better: *She just doesn't like me. How else can you explain her behaviour?* | *I don't have time to explain now – just come with me quickly!* | **+ why/how/what etc** *Doctors are unable to explain why the disease spread so quickly.* | **+ that** *Sarah explained that she hadn't been feeling well recently.* | **+ to** *It was difficult explaining to the children why their father was leaving home.*

give a reason /ˌgɪv ə ˈriːzən/ [v phrase] to tell someone why you are doing something, especially something surprising: *'He says he's not coming.' 'Oh, did he give a reason?'* | **give sb a reason** *The landlord told us we had to go, but we were never given any reason.*

account for /əˈkaʊnt fɔːʳ/ [phr v T not in progressive] to tell someone the reason for something that has happened, especially when people are looking for a reason to explain it: *If you walked home, how do you account for the fact that a witness said he saw you driving your van?* | *It is difficult to account for the big differences in their scores.*

provide an explanation/come up with an explanation /prəˌvaɪd ən ekspləˈneɪʃən, kʌm ˌʌp wɪð ən ˌekspləˈneɪʃən/ [v phrase] to tell someone the reason why something happened when they have asked you to explain. **Provide an explanation** is more formal than **come up with an explanation**: *In an attempt to provide an explanation she said she thought I had given her permission to be absent.* | *After failing to come up with an adequate explanation, Jones was arrested for robbery.*

justify /ˈdʒʌstɪ̈faɪ/ [v T] to tell someone why something that seems wrong is in fact right: *How can you justify the expense?* | **justify doing sth** *How can you possibly justify charging four pounds for a glass of beer?*

explain away /ɪkˌspleɪn əˈweɪ/ [phr v T] to tell someone the reason why you did something or why something happened, with the intention of making them think you have not done anything wrong or bad **explain away sth** *George was trying to explain away his outburst, saying that he'd been under a lot of pressure.* | *The government tried to explain away the police's unexpected brutality, but this only led to rioting.* | **explain sth away** *But there's broken glass all over the floor – how are we going to explain that away?*

7 when you have a particular reason for doing something

- have reasons
- be sb's reasons
- have ulterior motives
- vested interest

have reasons /ˌhæv ˈriːzənz/ [v phrase not in progressive] to have a reason for doing something – used especially when you do not want to say what that reason is: *I know I don't always explain myself, but you must always do what I say. I have reasons.* | **+ for** *Each of us had reasons for wanting to leave.* | **+ to do sth** *I have reasons not to confide in you or anyone else.* | **have your reasons** *I know it sounds silly but I have my reasons, believe me.*

be sb's reasons /biː (sb's) ˈriːzənz/ [v phrase] to be the reasons why someone does something, especially when you know they have a reason but do not know what it is: *Do you think that your decision is fair? What are your reasons?* | **+ for doing sth** *What were his reasons for leaving the country so quickly?*

have ulterior motives /hæv ʌlˌtɪəriəʳ ˈməʊtɪvz/ [v phrase not in progressive] to do something for a secret reason when everyone thinks you are doing it for a different reason: *You're so suspicious. Whenever I buy you a present, you think I have ulterior motives.* | *It was difficult to accept that she had no ulterior motives. Why would she want to see the office records?*

vested interest /ˌvestɪ̈d ˈɪntrɪ̈st/ [n C/U] if you have a **vested interest** in something happening, you have a strong reason for wanting it to happen because you will get an advantage from it: *The committee should be independent of all vested interest.* | **have a vested interest in sth** *Both the newspaper and the advertising agency have a vested interest in encouraging advertising.*

8 when there is no reason for someone's behaviour

- be no reason
- be no excuse/justification
- groundless
- unfounded

be no reason /biː nəʊ ˈriːzən/ [v phrase] use this to say that there is no reason for someone to think or behave in a particular way **+ to do sth** *I know I'm late, but that's no reason to lose your temper.* | **there is no reason for sth** *Please remain calm everyone. There is no reason for panic.*

be no excuse/justification /biː nəʊ ɪkˈskjuːs, ˌdʒʌstɪ̈fɪ̈ˈkeɪʃən/ [v phrase] use this to say that there is no acceptable reason for someone to think or behave in a bad or unfair way. **Be no justification** is more formal than **be no excuse**: *'But she started it.' 'That's no excuse.'* | **+ to do sth** *Ron may not be the most pleasant person to work with, but that's no justification to fire him.* | **there's no excuse/justification for sth** *There's no excuse for such childish behaviour from a grown man.*

groundless /ˈgraʊndləs/ [adj] **groundless** fears, suspicions etc that are unnecessary because there are no facts to base them on: *Fleury dismissed our fears as groundless, though he was secretly alarmed.* | *A message from Interpol confirmed that our Inspector's suspicions were far from groundless.*

unfounded /ʌnˈfaʊndɪ̈d/ [adj] worries, fears, hopes etc that are **unfounded** are wrong because there are no reasons to have these feelings: *I am going to prove to you that your suspicions are entirely unfounded.* | *All the signs indicate that the general's optimism is unfounded.*

rebellion/ revolution

RELATED WORDS

- when there is a complete change in the way people do something *see* **change (16)**
- to stop a rebellion *see* **stop (21)**
- *see also* **government, disobey, fight, war**

1 an attempt to change the government or other authority, often using violence

- rebellion
- revolution
- revolt
- insurrection
- uprising
- mutiny

rebellion /rɪ'beljən/ [n C/U] an organized attempt to change the government or other authority, often by using violence: *In 1968, a student rebellion in Paris sparked off a nationwide general strike.* | *The rebellion started in Kilalla and spread quickly through the Western provinces.* | **+ against** *The citizens of Kwangju rose in rebellion against the oppressive regime.* | *The Duke of Ormond led a military rebellion against the new king.* | **crush/put down a rebellion** (=use force to stop it) *Troops were used to put down a rebellion and arrest hundreds of protestors.* | *The rebellion was crushed by an army assault in which over 200 people died.* | **mount/stage a rebellion** (=begin a rebellion) *an unsuccessful attempt to mount a rebellion against British rule* | *A rebel army of political dissidents had staged a rebellion in December 1989.*

revolution /ˌrevə'luːʃən/ [n C/U] a successful attempt by the people of a country to change or destroy the government, often by using violence: *The 1789 revolution marked the end of the French monarchy.* | *Trotsky was one of the leading figures in the Russian Revolution of 1917.* | *Just 12 days after the emperor's death, the country erupted into revolution.* | *an era of rural unrest and peasant revolution* —**revolutionary** [adj] *In Africa, Asia, and Latin America, there were revolutionary movements eager for change.* | *We fervently embraced the new revolutionary ideals.*

revolt /rɪ'vəʊlt/ [n C/U] an attempt, especially one that only continues for a short time, to change the government by using violence: *In 1880, a peasant revolt swept the country in protest at the tax on salt.* | *Louverture headed the revolt of the slaves in the French colony of San Domingo.* | **+ against** *At a word from Gandhi, India would have risen in revolt.* | *Mayhew's remarks represented the first American call for revolt against England.* | **crush/ suppress/put down a revolt** *Army forces crushed the revolt, forcing many to flee the country.* | *The Confederate government provided troops to suppress slave revolts.* | *Herrera knew that if his government failed to put down the revolt, it would spread to outlying areas.*

insurrection /ˌɪnsə'rekʃən/ [n C/U] formal an organized attempt to change the government, through violence, especially an attempt that involves a large number of people: *It was widely believed that the outlaws had been plotting an insurrection.* | *the ruthless suppression of slave insurrections* | *an outbreak of insurrection* | **armed insurrection** (=an insurrection in which weapons are used) *The reign of civil disorder and terrorism culminated in armed insurrection.*

uprising /'ʌpˌraɪzɪŋ/ [n C/U] a sudden unplanned, and often unsuccessful attempt to change the government or other authority, using violence: *Peasant uprisings were the first signs of discontent among the people.* | *The new law prompted a pro-democracy uprising in the south.* | *The short-lived uprising fizzled out in the face of strong opposition from government forces.* | **+ against** *a failed uprising against French colonial rule* | **quell/put down an uprising** (=stop it) *The President took immediate steps to quell the uprising.* | *The new leader put down the uprising by dispatching government troops to the area.*

mutiny /'mjuːtɪni, -təni/ [n C/U] an organized attempt by a group of people in the army or navy to take power from their officers by refusing to obey their orders and using violence: *The film tells the story of a mutiny aboard a slave ship.* | *Thirteen soldiers were sentenced to life imprisonment for mutiny.*

2 an attempt by the army to take control of the government

- coup/coup d'état
- military takeover

coup/coup d'état /kuː, ˌkuː deɪ'tɑː‖-de'tɑː/ [n C] an attempt by the army to take control of the government: *Tomorrow is the anniversary of the coup that brought a military dictatorship to power here nine years ago.* | **+ against** *He led a successful coup against the government of Iraq.* | **military coup** *In April 1974, a military coup took place in Lisbon.* | **coup attempt/attempted coup** *The coup attempt was followed by police brutality, executions, and torture.* | *They smashed an attempted coup by the communists, leaving hundreds dead.* | **abortive/failed coup** (=one that does not succeed) *Peru offered refuge to officers who had taken part in the abortive coup.* | *The government imposed a state of emergency after the failed coup d'état.* | **stage a coup** (=attempt a coup) *The chief of the armed forces intended to take power by staging a coup d'état.*

military takeover /ˌmɪlɪtəri 'teɪkəʊvəʳ‖-teri-/ [n C] a successful attempt by the army to take control of their own country by removing the legal government: *The election was the first since the military takeover in 1980.* | *The economic crisis and the threat from separatist guerrillas led to a military takeover.*

3 to take part in a rebellion

- rebel
- revolt
- rise up
- mutiny

rebel /rɪ'bel/ [v I] *The eastern provinces are likely to rebel if they are not given more freedom.* | **+ against** *The slaves were punished for rebelling against their owners.* | *When the federal government refused this request, the Southern States rebelled.*

revolt /rɪ'vəʊlt/ [v I] to take part in an attempt, especially one that continues only for a short time, to change the government using violence: *When Napoleon won control of the region and attached it to Bavaria, the Tiroleans revolted.* | **+ against** *Some of the Arab tribes were persuaded to revolt against Turkish rule.* | *News reached the capital that two garrisons in the south had revolted against the government.*

rise up /ˌraɪz 'ʌp əgenst/ [phr v I] if people **rise up**, large numbers of them begin violently to oppose their government or other authority, especially without planning to do this: *First, the autoworkers rose up, followed by the steelworkers.* | *He forecast that the people of Egypt would rise up and overthrow the government.* | **+ against** *The people of Damascus rose up against their governors.* | *a proclamation urging the people to rise up against their masters* | **rise up in revolt/in arms/in rebellion** *The Maya farmers rose up in arms to demand greater democracy and freedom.* | *The troops would rise up in open rebellion if we tried to make them march any further.*

mutiny /ˈmjuːtɪni, -təni/ [v I] if a group in the army or navy **mutiny**, they try to take power from their officers by refusing to obey their orders and using violence: *At Odessa, the sailors of the Imperial navy mutinied.* | **+ against** *Army factions mutinied against orders from Beijing.*

4 someone who takes part in a rebellion

- rebel
- revolutionary
- guerrilla
- freedom fighter

rebel /ˈrebəl/ [n C] *The rebels attacked an airfield, exchanging fire with Russian troops.* | *A large number of rebels escaped to the east as the army closed in on Jaffra.* —**rebel** [adj only before noun] *Rebel forces have attacked the town of Kandahar.* | *The rebel leader has repeated his demands for the release of political prisoners.*

revolutionary /ˌrevəˈluːʃənəri‖-ʃəneri/ [n C] someone who takes part in or supports an attempt to change the government by using violence: *Having taken control of the capital city, the revolutionaries proceeded to form a new government.* | *Garcia Gutierrez wrote two plays with revolutionaries as their heroes.* —**revolutionary** [adj only before noun] *When revolutionary forces marched into Havana, Castro and Che Guevara took control of the army.* | *My father taught me several revolutionary songs.*

guerrilla /gəˈrɪlə/ [n C] someone who fights in an unofficial military group, trying to remove their country's existing government, especially by making surprise military attacks: *The guerrillas began their assault on March 8th.* | *Red Cross officials condemned the treatment that imprisoned guerrillas have received.* | *Four Western tourists held by armed guerrillas in Kashmir began their seventh month in captivity today.* —**guerrilla** [adj only before noun] *Poor peasants were the first recruits to the guerrilla forces.* | *In Greece, guerrilla warfare* (=war between guerrillas and an army) *raged on.*

freedom fighter /ˈfriːdəm ˌfaɪtəʳ/ [n C] someone who is fighting to try to remove their country's existing government – use this if you think that this is the right thing to do: *Ralph Fiennes plays an idealistic freedom fighter.* | *Young enthusiasts drove across the border to join the freedom fighters who had appealed to the world for help.*

5 someone who encourages rebellion

- agitator
- activist
- subversive

agitator /ˈædʒɪ̇teɪtəʳ/ [n C] someone who encourages people to oppose the government by trying to make them angry enough to use violence: *The riots were the work of political agitators.* | *The genuine protestors were joined by outside agitators, intent on encouraging violence.*

activist /ˈæktɪ̇vɪ̇st/ [n C] someone who spends a lot of time trying to encourage people to oppose the government or to accept new and different political beliefs: *The Global Communications Group links ecological and other political activists via the Net.* | *Clinton's AIDS 'czar' resigned after being criticized by gay activists for being weak.*

subversive /səbˈvɜːʳsɪv/ [n C] someone who is secretly trying to make their own government weak by encouraging people to oppose the government or to take part in a rebellion: *Pablo Picasso was for a long time regarded as a dangerous subversive.* | **alleged/potential/suspected subversive** (=someone that the authorities think is a subversive, but who may not be) *the kidnap and torture of a suspected subversive* | *CIA agents infiltrated the group, looking for alleged subversives.* —**subversive** [adj] *The loyalty oath was intended to protect students from so-called subversive teachers.*

6 actions, speeches etc that encourage rebellion

- sedition
- subversion

sedition /sɪˈdɪʃən/ [n U] actions, speeches etc that are intended to encourage people to oppose the government or to take part in a rebellion: *Hu was arrested on charges of sedition.* | *The clubs were suspected of being centres of sedition.* —**seditious** [adj] *He was sentenced to three years in prison for possession of seditious literature* (=literature that encourages sedition).

subversion /səbˈvɜːʳʃən‖-ʒən/ [n U] secret activities that are intended to encourage people to oppose the government or to take part in a rebellion: *Seventeen people were convicted of subversion following a coup attempt.* | *Many defectors provided the McCarthy committees with evidence of political subversion.* —**subversive** /səbˈvɜːʳsɪv/ [adj] *The magazine was banned by the government for being subversive* (=encouraging subversion). | *subversive propaganda*

recently

RELATED WORDS

see also **past, before**

1 only a short time ago

- recently
- not long ago
- a short time ago
- newly
- freshly
- the other day
- a short/little while ago
- a little while back

recently /ˈriːsəntli/ [adv] if something happened **recently**, it happened a short time before now, especially a few days or weeks ago: *The President has recently returned from a five day tour of South America.* | **only recently** *a new species of plant that was only recently discovered in southern Brazil* | **until recently** *He lived in Boston until quite recently.* | *Until recently, commercial fishermen had been allowed to shoot sea lions if they tried to steal their catch.* | **very recently** *'When did she go back to Italy?' 'Oh, very recently – just a couple of days ago.'* | **as recently as** (=used when something happened surprisingly recently) *As recently as the mid sixties, Nelson Rockefeller was considered unsuitable for the* *presidency because he had once been divorced.* | **recently discovered/completed/built etc** *a recently published textbook* | *the recently industrialized countries of Southeast Asia*

not long ago /nɒt ˌlɒŋ əˈgəʊ‖-ˌlɔːŋ-/ [adv] in the recent past: *Not long ago, computers were crude, unreliable machines, used by only a few experts.* | *Not long ago I asked a friend what her children gave her for her birthday. 'Peace,' she said. 'They went out for the day.'* | **not so long ago** *There was a time not so long ago when everyone felt confident about investing in property.*

a short time ago /ə ˌʃɔːʳt ˈtaɪm əˌgəʊ/ [adv] very recently: *So what is the government's reaction to this news? A short time ago our political correspondent Jon Lander spoke to the Foreign Secretary, Robin Cook.* | *The red wolf survived until a short time ago in east Texas, but is now believed extinct in the wild.* | **only/just a short time ago** *Seeing the tramp, Thomas remembered how he himself had been poor only a short time ago.*

newly /ˈnjuːli‖ˈnuːli/ [adv] **newly formed/created/appointed/married etc** formed, married etc very recently, especially during the last few days or weeks: *A newly married couple have moved into the house next door.* | *The group meets regularly in the newly built Chinese community center.* | *Mr Chandler is now director of the company's newly formed publishing division.*

freshly /ˈfreʃli/ [adv] **freshly cut/cooked/made/painted etc** cut, cooked etc a very short time ago, especially during the last few minutes or hours: *There's a pot of freshly made coffee on the kitchen table.* | *Add one clove of freshly crushed garlic.* | *Someone had placed a bunch of freshly cut roses on her desk.* | *At the beginning of term the school looked bright and clean with its freshly painted walls and polished floors.*

the other day /ði ˌʌðəʳ ˈdeɪ/ [adv] spoken use this to say that something happened or you did something recently: *I met Lucy the other day outside Budgens.* | *Well, did my dad tell you what happened to me in the car the other day?* | **just the other day** *I can't believe this weather – it was freezing just the other day!*

a short/little while ago /ə ˌʃɔːʳt, ˌlɪtl ˈwaɪl əˌgəʊ/ [adv] a short time ago, usually not more than a few hours: *'Is there a Mrs Lambert staying at the hotel?' 'Yes, she checked in a short while ago.'* | **just a short/little while ago** *Bobby's attorney gave me a call just a little while ago, to talk about the terms of the will.*

a little while back /ə ˌlɪtl waɪl ˈbæk/ [adv] informal fairly recently, usually a few weeks or months ago: *I broke my leg a little while back when I fell off a horse.*

2 happening over a period of time up to the present

- recently
- lately
- in the last/past few weeks/months etc
- in recent weeks/months etc

recently /ˈriːsəntli/ [adv] use this to say that something has been happening for a few weeks or months, and it is still happening now: *Her school work has been much better recently.* | *I haven't been feeling well recently.* | **just recently** *Just recently I've been thinking about changing my job.* | **more recently** *More recently, banks have offered customers the opportunity to change to PC or telephone banking.*

lately /ˈleɪtli/ [adv] in the recent past until now, especially during the weeks or days closest to now: *The company went through a bad time last year, but lately things have been improving.* | *I've been really busy lately, so I haven't been out much.* | *I don't know what's come over Angela lately – she's so moody.*

in the last/past few weeks/months etc /ɪn ðə ˌlɑːst, ˌpɑːst fjuː ˈwiːks‖-ˌlæst, ˌpæst-/ [adv] during the weeks or months closest to now: *Things have changed quite dramatically in the past few months.* | *I've been thinking about Kevin a lot in the last few days. I wonder how he's getting on?* | *In the past few years, 30,000 of these high-rise housing units have been torn down.*

in recent weeks/months etc /ɪn ˌriːsənt ˈwiːks/ [adv] formal during the weeks or months closest to now – used especially in news reports: *In recent months there have been rumors of at least two attempted coups.* | *Illicit drug use – notably marijuana – has been increasing in recent years, especially among the young.*

3 words for describing an event that has happened recently

- recent
- latest

recent /ˈriːsənt/ [adj usually before noun] use this about something that happened recently, especially a few days or weeks ago.: *He hadn't completely recovered from his recent illness.* | *A recent report said that small amounts of alcohol are good for the health.* | *The team returned to a heroes' welcome after their recent success in the European Championships.*

latest /ˈleɪtɪ̈st/ [adj usually before noun] someone's **latest** book, record, film etc is the one produced most recently; someone's **latest** action is the one that happened most recently: *In her latest movie she plays an LA cop.* | *The latest attempt to reach a peace settlement ended in failure.* | **the latest** (=the latest one) *This is the latest in a series of Mafia killings.*

4 words for describing news or information that is recent

- latest
- up-to-date
- up-to-the-minute

latest /ˈleɪtɪ̈st/ [adj usually before noun] the **latest** news, information etc is the most recent news, information etc: *Tune into Radio 5 Live for the latest news and sport.* | *For the latest information visit the German National Tourist Office website at http://www.germany-tourism.de.* | *The girls spent the evening catching up on the latest gossip.* | **the latest** (=the latest news) *Have you heard the latest? Nicky's getting married.*

up-to-date /ˌʌp tə ˈdeɪt◂/ [adj] **up-to-date** information is the most recent and correct information: *Is this map up-to-date? It doesn't seem to show the new road.* | *Foreign embassies or consulates in the United States can provide up-to-date information on their countries.*

up-to-the-minute /ˌʌp tə ðə ˈmɪnɪ̈t◂/ [adj only before noun] **up-to-the-minute** news or information is the most recent news or information about something that is likely to change very quickly all the time: *Visit www.sportsfanatic.com for up-to-the-minute results and sports news.* | *A computer link with Wall Street gives traders up-to-the-minute market data worldwide.*

recognize

to know who someone is or what something is, especially because you have seen them before

RELATED WORDS

- *see also* **know/not know, notice/not notice, realize**

1 to recognize someone or something

- **recognize**
- **know**
- **identify**
- **pick out**
- **tell**

recognize ALSO **recognise** British /ˈrekəgnaɪz, ˈrekən-/ [v T not in progressive] to know who someone is or what something is, especially because you have seen them before: *Lisa! I'm sorry – I didn't recognize you – you've had your hair cut!* | *I can't remember how the tune goes but I'll recognize it when I hear it.* | *That security guy never recognizes me. I always have to show him my ID.* | *They recognised my Michigan accent right away.* | **recognize sb from sth** *I recognized her from the movies, but she was much taller than I expected.* | *I recognize you from somewhere – don't you work at the bank?* | **recognize sb/sth as sth** *The waiter recognized one of his customers as someone he went to school with.* | *She recognised the voice on the phone as Tim's, but he sounded strange.* —**recognition** /ˌrekəgˈnɪʃən/ [n U] *There was no look of recognition on her face. She obviously had no idea who I was.* | *He waved, and she smiled in recognition.*

know /nəʊ/ [v T not in progressive] to recognize someone or something, especially when you have not seen them for some time or when they have changed a lot: *Would you know him if you saw him again?* | *The town has changed so much you wouldn't know the place.* | *You'll know him when you see him. He has red curly hair and is very tall and thin.*

identify /aɪˈdentɪfaɪ/ [v T] to recognize and name someone who has done something illegal or someone who has died: *The airline says it will be difficult to identify all the bodies retrieved from the crash.* | *Police hope that a member of the public will be able to identify a man seen acting suspiciously a few hours before the murder took place.* | *Dubois was identified by immigration control, and arrested at Kennedy airport.* | *proposals to identify the fathers of children born to single mothers* | **identify sb as sth** *Sara identified the man as Kang, a notorious gang leader and drug baron.* | *The girl, identified as Shelly Barnes, fell from the window when her mother's back was turned.* —**identification** /aɪˌdentɪfɪˈkeɪʃən/ [n U] *Dental records are a very reliable aid in the identification of badly burned bodies.* | *The case against Kelly hinged on Mr Gardener's identification of him.*

pick out /ˌpɪk ˈaʊt/ [phr v T] to recognize someone or something out of a group of things or people **pick out sb/sth** *Both men were picked out from an identity parade by witnesses.* | *It was hard to pick out faces he knew in the crowd.* | *Are there any questions that can help pick out a drug addict?* | **pick sb/sth out** *I was listening for Steve's voice, but it wasn't easy to pick it out among all the others.*

tell /tel/ [v I/T not in progressive] to be able to recognize someone or something, especially when this is not easy: *'What colour was the car?' 'I couldn't tell in the dark.'* | **+ (that)** *You look different in the photograph, although I can tell it's you.* | **+ who/what etc** *There's someone on the phone for you. I can't tell who it is.* | *'Can you tell what this is with your eyes shut?' 'It tastes of strawberry, but I'm not sure.'* | **tell the difference between sb/sth** *I find it really difficult to tell the difference between Frank and his brother.* | *If we don't use labelling, how can consumers tell the difference between organic and non-organic foods?* | **tell sth from sth else** (=to be able to recognize the difference between them) *It's a very good fake. You couldn't tell it from the real thing.* | *My kids have plenty of friends, and to be honest I can't tell one from another.* | **tell two things apart** (=to be able to recognize that they are different in some way) *Male ducks are easy to tell apart in the breeding season.* | *At the moment, we can only tell the twins apart by looking at their name tags.*

2 easy to recognize

- **familiar**
- **recognizable**
- **unmistakable**
- **there's no mistaking sb/sth**

familiar /fəˈmɪliəʳ/ [adj] someone or something that is **familiar** is easy to recognize, because you have seen or heard them many times before: *Gibson's name is familiar – what else did he write?* | *He scanned the audience, searching for a familiar face.* | *Mimicking the President's familiar accent, DJ Rogers told his listeners that aliens had invaded.* | **+ to** *The first track on the album will be instantly familiar to Billie Holliday fans.* | *The giant cross has become a familiar landmark to generations of San Franciscans.* | **look/sound/feel etc familiar** *That girl looks familiar. I'm sure I've met her before.* | **a familiar figure** (=someone who is often seen in a particular place and therefore is familiar to the people there) *Kylie soon became a familiar figure at some of London's top fashion stores.* | **a familiar face** (=someone you have met before) *It's nice to see a familiar face – I was afraid I wouldn't know anyone here.* | *The local policeman is now a familiar figure in our school.* | **faintly/vaguely familiar** (=only slightly familiar, so that you are not quite sure whether you know them or not) *The man seated at the next table looked faintly familiar.* | *She was singing along to a tune on the radio that sounded vaguely familiar.*

recognizable ALSO **recognisable** British /ˈrekəgnaɪzəbəl/ [adj] if something is **recognizable**, it is easy to recognize, for example because it has a particular sound or appearance: *No recognizable remains of Minoan ships have ever been found until now.* | *Many mental illnesses are only recognizable after many careful weeks spent talking to the patient.* | *Muffled noises were coming from the room, the only recognizable sound being her daughter's laughter.* | **+ as** *an animal so thin and weak it was barely recognizable as a horse* | *The body was so badly burned it was no longer recognizable as a human being.* | **+ by** *The staff are easily recognisable by their pale green uniforms.* | **easily/instantly/immediately recognizable** *Macy has an instantly recognizable voice.* | *On the outskirts of the town, we saw a building that was immediately recognizable as a prison.*

unmistakable /ˌʌnmɪˈsteɪkəbəl/ [adj] impossible not to recognize: *Shots rang out, and we heard the unmistakable sound of a human scream.* | *When an envelope arrived bearing Dad's unmistakable handwriting, I knew something must be wrong.* | *Her accent was unmistakable – Southern Ireland, probably West coast.* | *He'd started burning incense to disguise the unmistakable odour of marijuana coming from his bedroom.*

there's no mistaking sb/sth /ðeəʳz ˌnəʊ mɪ'steɪkɪŋ (sb/sth)/ [v phrase] spoken use this to say that someone or something is easy to recognize: *I turned round – there was no mistaking that voice – it was Billie.* | *There's no mistaking this as anything but a Japanese car.*

3 difficult to recognize

- strange
- unrecognizable
- unfamiliar
- beyond recognition

strange /streɪndʒ/ [adj only before noun] a **strange** person, voice, smell etc one that is not recognizable because it is different from other, similar things that you know already: *I could hear strange voices outside the room.* | *It was hard for her, going to live in a strange city where she knew no-one.* | *Mum, come quick! There's a strange man coming up the path.* | *Can you check out that strange noise outside?*

unrecognizable ALSO **unrecognisable** British /ʌn'rekəgnaɪzəbəl/ [adj not before noun] difficult or impossible to recognize: *We've recovered two bodies from the wreckage, but they are unrecognizable.* | *The explosion left nothing but small, unrecognizable pieces of the aircraft scattered over the field.* | **+ to** *Completely shaved and wearing prison clothes, the two sisters were unrecognizable to each other.*

unfamiliar /ˌʌnfə'mɪliəʳ◂/ [adj] something that is **unfamiliar** is not recognizable because you have never seen it, heard it, done it etc before: *She spoke with an unfamiliar accent.* | *She noticed an unfamiliar truck parked across the street.* | **+ to** *His name may be unfamiliar to Western audiences.*

beyond recognition ALSO **out of all recognition** /bɪˌjɒnd rekəg'nɪʃən‖-ˌjɑːnd-, aʊt əv ˌɔːl rekəg'nɪʃən/ [adv] if something has changed **beyond recognition** or **out of all recognition**, it has changed completely – use this to emphasize that it is completely different now: *The business has changed beyond recognition since Cyril took over from his father.* | *The Internet has altered our understanding of the world beyond all recognition.* | *Susan's playing has improved out of all recognition.*

record

RELATED WORDS

- *see also* **information**

1 to keep information about something, so that it can be used or looked at later

- record
- chart
- keep a record
- document
- register
- put/place sth on record
- log

record /rɪ'kɔːʳd/ [v T] to write down information or store it on a computer, so that it can be looked at later, especially official information about numbers or amounts: *Make sure you record the date you bought the tickets.* | *Only 13 cases of this disease have ever been recorded.* | **+ that** *A final communiqué recorded that 'a thorough and candid discussion has taken place'.*

chart /tʃɑːʳt/ [v T] to record information about a situation or a set of events over a period of time in order to show how it changes or develops: *She aims to chart new cases of cancer in areas around nuclear power stations.* | *The computer will chart the spacecraft's progress as it approaches Saturn.* | **+ how** *The article charts how adverts, in the past and in the present, have succeeded in linking the cigarette with sophistication.*

keep a record /ˌkiːp ə 'rekɔːd‖-ərd/ [v phrase] to write down details of things you have done or things that have happened because it may be important to have this information available at a later time: *The hospital has only just started to keep a record, but so far they have treated six people for this type of injury.* | **+ of** *She always keeps a record of how much money she spends.* | *Employees were asked to keep a detailed record of any accidents that occurred in the workplace.*

document /'dɒkjᵍment‖'dɑːk-/ [v T] to write about important events, activities, and developments and record all the facts and details connected with them: *Many writers have documented the changes in feminist politics over the last decade.* | *Attempts to document social problems in some parts of the country had been difficult.*

register /'redʒᵍstəʳ/ [v I/T] to put something such as your name on an official list or record: *You had to register a baby's birth within a month.* | **+ as** *They claimed that the new rules would discourage people from registering as unemployed.* | **+ with** *The new students were told that they must register with the University before they could claim their grants.* | **+ for** *More than 4.3 million people registered for shares.*

put/place sth on record /ˌpʊt, ˌpleɪs (sth) ɒn 'rekɔːd‖-ərd/ [v phrase] to publicly say something that you want to be recorded, because you think it is important: *Yes, we do remember your initial objections, but unfortunately you didn't place them on record.* | **put/place on record that** *The lawyer asked the court to put on record that her client had always been co-operative.*

log /lɒg‖lɔːg, lɑːg/ [v T] to make an official record of events or facts, either in writing or on a computer: *All deliveries must be logged.* | *The system can log the date and length of calls made by company employees.*

2 information that is kept so that it can be used or looked at later

- record
- archives
- register
- log
- chronicle

record /'rekɔːd‖-ərd/ [n C] information that is collected gradually over a long period of time, so that it can be looked at when necessary: *I've checked the student records, and I can't find any mention of her name.* | *The results of the blood test will be noted in your medical records.* | **+ of** *The hotel should have a record of who stayed there last month.*

archives /'ɑːʳkaɪvz/ [n plural] a collection of records that provide information about the history of a country, organization, family etc: *New evidence has come to light from the 40-year-old United Nations archives.* | *The Public Record Office is a central repository for all government archives.*

register /'redʒᵍstəʳ/ [n C] an official list of names kept for legal purposes that records information such as who attends a particular school, who has been born or has died, or who is legally allowed to do something: *Teachers were reminded that school attendance registers were actually legal documents.* | **electoral register** (=a list of the names and addresses of all the people who are old enough to vote) *Why are there 1 million people missing from the electoral register?* | **+ of** *To find out about her family history, she looked through the register of births, marriages, and deaths.*

log /lɒg‖lɔːg, lɑːg/ [n C] an official written record of something, especially a journey in a ship or plane: *He complained to a senior officer, who made a note in the ship's log.* | **+ of** *Alice had to write up a detailed log of the trip, complete with scientific data.*

chronicle /ˈkrɒnɪkəl‖ˈkrɑː-/ [n C] a historical record in which events are recorded in the order in which they happened: *Chronicles written by Roman scholars can give us a good idea of how their political system worked.* | **+ of** *The report is a chronicle of the history of the Party since its formation.*

recover

to become healthy again after an illness or injury, or to become strong and happy again after problems or unhappiness

RELATED WORDS

- *see also* **ill/sick, cure, illness/disease, accident, injure, sad**

1 to become healthy again after an illness or accident

- recover
- get better
- make a complete/full/good/slow recovery
- get over
- get well
- feel better
- improve
- be on the mend
- shake off

recover /rɪˈkʌvəʳ/ [v I] to become healthy again after you have had an illness, injury, or operation: *My mother's been very ill, and is still in hospital recovering.* | *Sammy needed to recover a little before they could move him to a hospital nearer his home.* | **+ from** *He never really recovered from the operation.* | **fully recover** (=completely recover) *It was several months before John had fully recovered from his heart attack.* —**recovery** [n U] the process of recovering from an illness or injury: *The doctors were surprised at Phillip's quick recovery.*

get better /ˌget ˈbetəʳ/ [v phrase] **especially spoken** to become healthy again after you have had an illness, injury, or operation: *I hope you get better soon.* | *My back has been quite bad recently, but it's getting better slowly.* | *I didn't remember anything about the accident, but little by little, as I got better, memories started coming back to me.*

make a complete/full/good/slow recovery /meɪk ə kəmˌpliːt, ˌfʊl, ˌgʊd, ˌsləʊ rɪˈkʌvəri/ [v phrase] to recover completely, fully, well, or slowly: *The disease has been caught early, and the doctors say she should make a complete recovery.* | *Thomas is making a good recovery, although he is still quite weak.* | **make a remarkable/amazing recovery** *Joe has made a remarkable recovery from the injuries he sustained in the accident.*

get over /ˌget ˈəʊvəʳ/ [phr v T] to recover from an illness, especially one that is not very serious: *Mark hasn't got over the flu yet. He still feels pretty weak.* | *I've had a nasty cold, but I'm getting over it now.* | *The doctor told Mum it was only a stomach upset, not food poisoning, and she would get over it in a day or two.*

get well /ˌget ˈwel/ [v phrase] to recover from an illness – use this especially when you are encouraging someone to recover: *Get well soon – we all miss you!* | *I hope you get well quickly.*

feel better /ˌfiːl ˈbetəʳ/ [v phrase] to feel less ill than you did before: *I hope you feel better soon.* | *My father's been quite ill, but he's starting to feel a bit better now.*

improve /ɪmˈpruːv/ [v I] if you or your health improves, you become less ill than you were before but not completely well. **Improve** is more formal than **feel better**: *Susie's improving gradually with this new treatment.* | *My health finally began to improve when I changed to a less stressful job.* | *She was told to go back to the doctor in two weeks if she hadn't improved.* —**improvement** [n U] *I'm afraid there have been no signs of improvement yet; she is still extremely ill.* | **a big/huge/vast improvement** *There's been a big improvement in his health over the last three months.*

be on the mend /biː ɒn ðə ˈmend/ [v phrase] if someone **is on the mend**, they are definitely showing signs of getting better after an illness or injury: *I'm glad to see you're on the mend again.* | *Kathy's been quite ill with flu, but I think she's on the mend now.*

shake off /ˌʃeɪk ˈɒf / [phr v T] to manage to recover from an illness such as a cold or an infection, which you have had for a fairly long time **shake sth off** *Towards the end of the year he caught flu, and he couldn't shake it off.* | **shake off sth** *It seems to be taking me a long time to shake off this cold.*

2 to spend time resting in order to recover

- recuperate
- convalesce

recuperate /rɪˈkjuːpəreɪt, -ˈkuː-/ [v I] to spend time resting in order to recover from an illness or operation: *It was a very difficult birth, and Mary is now recuperating at home with the baby.* | **+ after** *She's going to need time to recuperate after the operation.* —**recuperation** /rɪˌkjuːpəˈreɪʃən, -ˌkuː-/ [n U] the process of resting in order to recover from an illness, operation etc: *We decided to take Dad on holiday to help his recuperation.* | *I think you're going to need quite a long period of recuperation.*

convalesce /ˌkɒnvəˈles‖ˌkɑːn-/ [v I] to spend a long period of time recovering from a serious illness, especially by resting: *They travelled to Bermuda for six weeks so that David could convalesce in the sun.* | **+ after** *Jason is now convalescing at home after a major operation.* —**convalescence** [n U] a process of resting for a long time in order to recover from a serious illness: *They suggested that I spend a period of convalescence in the mountains.* | *During the second week of her convalescence Wanda felt that she was beginning to recover.*

3 to be better again after an illness or injury

- be better
- be well
- be fully recovered
- be cured
- be over
- be back on your feet (again)
- be up and about (again)
- be fit

be better /biː ˈbetəʳ/ [v phrase] if someone **is better** after an illness or injury, they have recovered, or they are in the process of recovering: *How are you?*

Are you better? | I'll just rest today, and, hopefully, I'll be better tomorrow. | I hope Robert's better by Saturday, because we need him for the team.

be well /biː 'wel/ [v phrase] if someone **is well**, they are healthy again, and they no longer have an illness or injury: *As soon as you're well we'll go to Florida and have a few weeks in the sun. | They couldn't really make any firm plans until Luis was well again.*

be fully recovered /biː ˌfʊli rɪ'kʌvəʳd/ [v phrase] to be completely well again after an illness or injury: *We were relieved to find that Barnes was fully recovered and able to take part in the race.* | **+ from** *Keep the patient still and quiet until he is fully recovered from the attack.*

be cured /biː 'kjʊəʳd/ [v phrase] if someone **is cured**, they are completely better because their illness has been treated successfully: *She's still rather weak, but her bronchitis seems to be cured.* | **+ of** *It is only after two or three years that the doctors can say you are definitely cured of cancer.* | **be completely cured** *He was always confident that he would be completely cured.*

be over /biː 'əʊvəʳ/ [v phrase] to be well again after an illness: *You've had a bad attack of malaria, but I think you're over it now.* | **be over the worst** *Her temperature is going down again – she seems to be over the worst.*

be back on your feet (again) /biː ˌbæk ɒn jɔːʳ 'fiːt (əgen)/ [v phrase] informal to be well again and able to live life as usual after being ill: *After a day or two in bed I'll be back on my feet again. | Wait till you're back on your feet before you start worrying about your exams.*

be up and about (again) /biː ˌʌp ənd ə'baʊt (əgen)/ [v phrase] to be out of bed and well enough to walk around again, after an illness or injury has forced you to stay in bed: *She's up and about now, and should be back at work in a day or two. | It's good to see you up and about again.*

be fit /biː 'fɪt/ [v phrase] especially British to be well again after having been ill, so that you are now able to move around as usual, exercise etc: *Don't come back to work until you're completely fit. | He should be back at training next week if he's fit.* | **be fit as a fiddle** (=be extremely fit) *Don't worry – I'll be as fit as a fiddle again by next week.*

4 to become strong or happy again after a period of problems or unhappiness

- recover
- get over
- bounce back

recover /rɪ'kʌvəʳ/ [v I] to become strong or happy again after experiencing problems or unhappiness: *Losing my job was a terrible blow, and it took me quite a while to recover.* | **+ from** *Mark never really recovered from the shock of his father's death. | It took a long time for the British economy to recover from the effects of the war.* —**recovery** [n U] *American aid played a major part in the country's economic recovery.*

get over /ˌget 'əʊvəʳ/ [phr v T] to recover from a particular problem or from a difficult or unhappy time: *It took Joe quite a long time to get over the divorce. | Don't worry about Henry – he'll soon get over it. | Children seem to get over things very quickly.*

bounce back /ˌbaʊns 'bæk/ [phr v I] informal to recover quickly and easily after problems or an unhappy period of time **+ after** *Liverpool's footballers hope to bounce back after their defeat in Europe last week.* | **+ from** *We are confident the business will bounce back from the recession.*

5 to be strong or happy again after a period of problems or unhappiness

- be over
- be/feel yourself again
- be back to normal

be over /biː 'əʊvəʳ/ [v phrase] *Experts believe that Colombia is now over the worst of its troubles. | Sharon seems to be over her reading difficulties now. | It took Greg a long time to cope with his parents' divorce, but I think he's over it now.*

be/feel yourself again /biː, ˌfiːl jɔːʳ'self əgen/ [v phrase] to feel mentally and physically well again after a period when you experienced emotional problems and unhappiness: *It's good to see that Mandy's herself again. | It wasn't until six months after my husband's death that I started to feel myself again.*

be back to normal /biː ˌbæk tə 'nɔːʳməl/ [v phrase] if a person **is back to normal**, they are just as they were before their problems or troubles started: *I think Judith was quite badly affected by shock, but she seems to be back to normal now.*

reduce

to make something smaller or less

RELATED WORDS

opposite: **increase**

▸ *see also* **less, small, stop**

1 to reduce the number, amount, price, or size of something

- reduce
- lower
- cut
- turn down
- decrease
- slash
- knock down
- halve
- roll back

reduce /rɪ'djuːs‖rɪ'duːs/ [v T] to make something less in amount or level: *I was hoping they would reduce the price a little.* | **greatly/significantly/dramatically reduce** *You can greatly reduce your heating bills by using low-energy heaters.* | **dramatically/drastically reduce** *Their income has been drastically reduced.* | **reduce sth by half/10%/2 years etc** *The new road will reduce traffic through the town by 30%. | Benefits will be reduced by $50 for each child who fails to attend school.* —**reduced** [adj] *Most airlines offer reduced prices for children.*

lower /'ləʊəʳ/ [v T] to reduce an amount, limit, or level – use this especially in writing about business or technical subjects: *After 20 minutes, lower the temperature to 200 degrees. | The Bundesbank is under pressure to lower interest rates.*

cut /kʌt/ [v T] to reduce something by a lot, especially prices, time, or money: *The new system is aimed at cutting the average waiting time.* | **cut sth by half/several weeks/ten per cent etc** *Because of the recession, salaries in the advertising industry have been cut by a half. | The mortgage insurance agency has cut costs by $2000 over the last 3 years, making it easier for people to buy homes.* | **cut sth from/to sth** *His annual leave has been cut from six weeks to just three.*

turn down /ˌtɜːʳn ˈdaʊn/ [phr v T] to reduce the level of sound, heat, light etc, especially by turning a control **turn sth down** *Could you turn the lights down – it's too bright in here.* | **turn down sth** *The weather wasn't as cold, so we decided to turn down the central heating.* | **turn sth down slightly/a little/a bit** *Would you mind turning the volume down a little?*

decrease /dɪˈkriːs/ [v T] to reduce something, especially by a fairly small amount or number: *Various methods are being explored in order to decrease the volume of traffic on our roads.* | *Better health education should help to decrease the incidence of heart disease.* | *Use of the new nets has significantly decreased the number of dolphins killed accidentally each year.*

slash /slæʃ/ [v T] informal to reduce prices by a very large amount – used especially in advertisements and newspapers: *American car manufacturers have started slashing prices in an effort to stimulate sales.* | *Public spending has been slashed over the past two years.* | **slash sth by 10%/half/75% etc** *Come to our Summer Sale, where prices have been slashed by up to 75%.*

knock down /ˌnɒk ˈdaʊn‖ˌnɑːk-/ [phr v T] informal to reduce the price of something by a large amount, especially in order to make it easier to sell **knock down sth** *Shops are knocking down prices in an effort to increase sales.* | **knock sth down** *In the end he knocked the price down to £70.*

halve /hɑːv‖hæv/ [v T] to reduce something by half: *The overseas aid budget has been almost halved, from $18m to just over $10m.*

roll back /ˌrəʊl ˈbæk/ [phr v T] American to reduce prices **roll back sth** *Most of the big downtown stores have rolled back their prices to dispose of winter stock.* | **roll sth back** *Rather than roll prices back, the company negotiated pay increases that ranged between 10 and 15 percent.*

2 to reduce pain, worry, or unpleasant feelings

- reduce
- lessen
- lighten
- relieve
- ease
- alleviate
- deaden/dull
- take the edge off
- allay

reduce /rɪˈdjuːs‖rɪˈduːs/ [v T] *They gave him drugs to reduce the pain.* | *Prompt action can often reduce the severity of shock in road accident victims.* | *Miriam finds that yoga and meditation help her in reducing stress.* | **greatly/significantly/dramatically reduce** *Stopping smoking can significantly reduce your risk of suffering a heart attack.*

lessen /ˈlesən/ [v T] to slightly reduce pain or bad feelings: *He shifted his position a little, in order to lessen the pain in his leg.* | *Everyone has their own ideas about the best way to lessen jet lag.* | *Boys are more likely to smoke to relieve stress than girls are.*

lighten /ˈlaɪtn/ [v T] to reduce the amount of work or worry that someone has **lighten sb's load/workload** *Maybe we should hire another secretary to lighten Barbara's workload.*

relieve /rɪˈliːv/ [v T] to make pain or feelings less unpleasant: *Peppermint has long been regarded as a plant that can relieve indigestion.* | *Magnetic board games can help relieve the boredom of long car journeys for kids.* | *Harry attempted a couple of jokes to relieve the tension of the occasion.* —**relief** /rɪˈliːf/ [n U] *Massage is excellent for the relief of stress.* | *Various methods can be used for pain relief during childbirth.*

ease /iːz/ [v T] to reduce pain or unpleasant feelings and make someone feel happier or more comfortable: *Rod rubbed his jaw to ease the pain a little.* | *The arrival of the others eased her embarrassment slightly.*

alleviate /əˈliːvieɪt/ [v T] formal to reduce pain, make a problem less serious, or reduce feelings such as being bored or anxious: *You can't cure a common cold, but you can alleviate the symptoms.* | *Western aid has helped to alleviate the situation in northern India.* —**alleviation** /əˌliːviˈeɪʃən/ [n U] *the alleviation of pain*

deaden/dull /ˈdedn, dʌl/ [v T] to reduce physical pain or emotional problems, especially with the result that you feel nothing at all: *They gave me a local anaesthetic to deaden the pain.* | *It was impossible not to think about her baby, but the drugs dulled her panic.*

take the edge off /ˌteɪk ði ˈedʒ ɒf/ [v phrase] to make something such as pain, hunger, or a shock slightly less unpleasant or upsetting: *I took a couple of painkillers, which took the edge off the pain.* | *Knowing that Peter was close by took the edge off my anxiety for my grandson.*

allay /əˈleɪ/ [v T] **allay sb's fears/concern/suspicions etc** formal to make someone much less frightened, concerned etc: *The government is anxious to allay public fears over the safety of beef.* | *Showing her his identity card went some way towards allaying her suspicions.*

3 to reduce the amount of something that you eat, drink, or use

- cut down
- reduce

cut down /ˌkʌt ˈdaʊn/ [phr v I] if you **cut down** on food, alcoholic drink, or tobacco, you eat, drink, or smoke less of it, especially in order to lose weight or to improve your health: *If you can't give up smoking completely, at least try to cut down.* | **+ on** *I'm trying to cut down on meat.*

reduce /rɪˈdjuːs‖rɪˈduːs/ [v T] to **reduce** the amount of something that you eat, drink, or use. **Reduce** is more formal than **cut down**: *Doctors are urging people to reduce the amount of salt in their diet.* | *Supermarkets can help promote healthy eating habits by reducing the amount of sugar and fat in their products.*

4 when a company reduces its activities, the amount it spends etc

- scale down
- cut back
- downsize/rightsize
- pare down
- rationalize
- wind down
- run down
- trim
- streamline

scale down ALSO **scale back** American /ˌskeɪl ˈdaʊn, ˌskeɪl ˈbæk/ [phr v T] to reduce something, such as the size of an organization or a plan, so that it is still operating but on a smaller level **scale down/back sth** *European central banks have scaled down their operations in South Africa.* | **scale sth down/back** *The two companies have announced plans to scale back production next year.* | *Development projects were scaled down, and some proposals for new buildings were put on hold.*

cut back /ˌkʌt ˈbæk/ [phr v I/T] to reduce the numbers of something or the time or money spent on something, especially because you can no longer afford to continue at the previous level **+ on** *Her friends know that she is under stress and have warned her to cut back on her workload.* | **cut back sth** *Our budget has been cut back this year.* | *Farmers have agreed to cut back wheat production.* | **cut sth back** *We have had to cut expenditure back in an effort to increase profits.* — **cutback** /ˈkʌtbæk/ [n C] *Schools and hospitals could suffer as a result of government cutbacks.* | **+ in** *There has been a significant cutback in the defence budget this year.*

downsize/rightsize /ˌdaʊnˈsaɪz, ˌraɪtˈsaɪz/ [v T] especially American to reduce the number of people who work for a company, especially in order to save money: *They are downsizing the workforce in a desperate attempt to save the firm.* | *Advised to rightsize its operation, the company has shrunk to 2,000 employees.*

pare down /ˌpeəʳ ˈdaʊn/ [phr v T] to reduce something by small amounts over a period of time so that the effect is not very serious or noticeable while it is happening **pare down sth** *The company has pared down expenditure and hopes to recoup its losses this year.* | **pare sth down** *We have managed to pare our costs down to the absolute minimum.*

rationalize ALSO **rationalise** British /ˈræʃənəlaɪz/ [v I/T] to try to make a company more effective by getting rid of unnecessary workers etc: *We are a small company, and we need to rationalize if we want to compete in this market.* | *The company has done a lot to rationalize production.*

wind down /ˌwaɪnd ˈdaʊn/ [phr v T] to gradually reduce the work of a company or organization so that it can be closed down completely **wind sth down** *The old sickness benefit system is slowly being wound down.* | **wind sth down** *I want to return in a few years' time – I've already started to wind the business down.*

run down /ˌrʌn ˈdaʊn/ [phr v T] especially British to deliberately make something such as a company, an industry, or a public service weaker and weaker, by giving it less and less money **run down sth** *Opposition leaders are accusing the government of running down the Health Service.* | **run sth down** *They buy up rival companies then just run them down.*

trim /trɪm/ [v T] to reduce something by a small amount that will not harm or change it very much, especially in order to save money: *By trimming costs and improving service the hotel has now started to make a profit again.* | **trim sth by 10% etc** *The proposed bill would trim welfare spending by $5 billion.*

streamline /ˈstriːmlaɪn/ [v T] to reduce the costs of something such as a service or industry by employing fewer people, reducing the number of things you produce or provide etc – used especially in business contexts: *The government is once again attempting to streamline the health care service in order to pay for tax cuts.* | *The company announced it was to streamline its operations and close down three factories in the UK.*

5 to make a written or spoken statement less forceful

- tone down
- moderate
- dilute

tone down /ˌtəʊn ˈdaʊn/ [phr v T] to reduce the effect of a speech or piece of writing, especially by making the language you use less forceful **tone sth down** *I felt my letter was worded too strongly, so I toned it down a bit.* | **tone down sth** *Wagner was forced to tone down his remarks about his opponent when it became obvious that the attacks were costing him votes.*

moderate /ˈmɒdəreɪt‖ˈmɑː-/ [v T] to make your language more acceptable, especially by not swearing or being very rude: *We had to ask Joan to moderate her language in front of the kids.* | *She apologized at once, and moderated her voice.*

dilute /daɪˈluːt/ [v T] to reduce the effect or force of an argument or belief, by accepting additional people, things, or ideas that may make it bigger but also weaker: *Right wing groups are determined to dilute the influence of the trade unions.* | *They felt that their original aims and demands were being diluted.*

6 to reduce something gradually

- erode
- eat into
- deplete
- chip away at
- whittle away

erode /ɪˈrəʊd/ [v T] to gradually reduce the amount or value of something, especially money, wages, or profits over a period of time: *Over the years, the value of our savings and investments has been eroded by inflation.* | **gradually/steadily erode** *High interest rates can gradually erode profit margins.*

eat into /ˈiːt ɪntuː/ [phr v T] if costs, rising prices, etc **eat into** the amount of money you have, they reduce its value: *Rising rents and travel expenses simply eat into any pay rise that nurses might get.* | *Theft from offices and factories eats into company profits.*

deplete /dɪˈpliːt/ [v T] to reduce the amount of something to a level that is too low: *Over the last few years, rainforests have been steadily depleted.* | *He knew that the area's rich plant life had been severely depleted by the huge herds of cows grazing the land.* | *CFC is just one chemical that depletes the ozone layer.*

chip away at /ˌtʃɪp əˈweɪ æt/ [phr v T] to gradually reduce the strength of something by repeated small amounts: *High interest rates can chip away at your profits.* | *The group continues to campaign for the rights of disabled people, chipping away at old prejudices.*

whittle away /ˌwɪtl əˈweɪ/ [phr v I/T] to reduce something by small amounts over a period of time, so that the final effect is very serious **+ at** *Congress is whittling away at our civil liberties.* | **whittle away sth** *Inflation has been whittling away the value of state pensions for the last fifteen years.* | **whittle sth away** *Lawmakers have gradually whittled the program's funding away over the last few years.*

7 a reduction in number, prices, levels etc

- reduction
- decrease
- drop/fall
- cut

reduction /rɪˈdʌkʃən/ [n C] when a price, level etc is reduced – use this when something is reduced deliberately: *We offer a reduction for groups of 10 or more.* | **+ in** *Cleaner fuel has contributed to a reduction in air pollution.* | *a reduction in working hours* | **a reduction of £10/$5/5% etc** (=a reduction by a particular amount) *There were reductions of up to 50% in some stores.* | **a big/huge/massive reduction** *There has been a big reduction in the number of issues the president addresses in any given week.* | **price reduction** *Several holiday firms are offering huge price reductions on winter holidays.*

decrease /ˈdiːkriːs/ [n C] when something happens less than it used to **+ in** *There has been a 15% decrease in violent crime* (=it has gone down by 15%). | **a significant/marked decrease** *In the last five years there has been a significant decrease in the number of deaths from heart disease.*

drop/fall /drɒp‖drɑːp, fɔːl/ [n singular] when a number or amount goes down suddenly or by a large amount **+ in** *Charities have reported a 25% fall in donations during the past year.* | **a sudden fall/drop** *Universities are reporting a sudden drop in the number of students studying science subjects.* | **a sharp fall/drop** *This year we have seen a sharp fall in profits.*

cut /kʌt/ [n C] a reduction in the amount or size of something made by a government or large organization – use this especially for talking about politics or business **+ in** *Cuts in the education budget have led to fewer teachers and larger classes.* | **a big/drastic cut** *There are to be big cuts in the health budget next year.* | **pay/job/tax cuts** (=cuts in wages, number of jobs, or taxes) *Nurses are protesting about further pay cuts.* | *The new management has promised that there will be no job cuts.*

reflect

if a surface or object reflects light, heat, sound etc, it throws back the light etc that hits it

RELATED WORDS

- *see also* **light, shine/shiny, sound**

1 to reflect light, heat, sound etc

- **reflect**

reflect /rɪˈflekt/ [v T] *The white painted walls reflected the firelight.* | *In warm weather, wear light-coloured clothing to reflect the heat.* | **be reflected in sth** *From my hotel room, I saw the lights of Budapest reflected in the Danube.* | *Picasso's 'Le Miroir' is a rear-view of a model reflected in a mirror.*

2 ways of saying that light, heat, sound etc reflects off something

- **reflect**
- **bounce off**
- **echo**

reflect /rɪˈflekt/ [v I] **+ off/from/between etc** *I was dazzled by the sunlight reflecting off the wet road.* | *The radar signal that reflects back from the airplane is received by the radar dish and is electronically analysed.*

bounce off /ˌbaʊns ˈɒf/ [phr v T] if something such as sound or a radio wave **bounces off** an object or surface, it reflects off it: *Her naturally loud voice seemed to bounce off the walls.* | *When atmospheric conditions are right, radio waves bounce off the ionosphere and can be received many thousands of miles away.*

echo /ˈekəʊ/ [v I] if sound **echoes**, it is reflected from something such as a wall or mountain so you can hear it repeated as it comes back to you: *The room was vast and empty and every smallest noise we made echoed.* | **+ off/through/throughout etc** *The thunder of the guns echoed throughout the valley.*

3 an image that is reflected

- **reflection**

reflection /rɪˈflekʃən/ [n C] *Anna stood looking at her reflection in the mirror.* | **+ of** *a reflection of the moon on the surface of the lake*

4 something that reflects light

- **mirror**
- **reflective**

mirror /ˈmɪrəʳ/ [n C] a piece of glass or other shiny or polished surface that reflects images: *The telescope contains a large convex mirror to collect the light.* | **in the mirror** *I saw her in the long mirror behind the bar, staring at me.* | *She never left the house without having a quick look at herself in the hall mirror.*

reflective /rɪˈflektɪv/ [adj] especially made to reflect light or heat: *It's important to wear special reflective clothing when riding a bike.* | *Survival bags are made of reflective material to prevent heat loss.* | **highly reflective** *The alloy, when polished, is highly reflective.*

refuse

RELATED WORDS

- to refuse to accept an offer, suggestion etc *see* **reject**
- not accept someone for a job or course *see* **reject**
- *see also* **no, yes, accept, let/allow**

1 to say that you will not do something

- **refuse**
- **refusal**
- **say no**
- **will not/won't**
- **not be prepared to do sth**
- **draw the line**
- **decline**

refuse /rɪˈfjuːz/ [v I] to tell someone firmly that you will not do something they asked you to do: *I asked Stevie if she would help us, but she refused.* | **+ to do sth** *If they refuse to leave, call the police.* | *The church refused to give legitimacy to the new state.* | **flatly refuse** (=refuse without explanation in a way that seems unreasonable) *Mother flatly refused to see the doctor.*

refusal /rɪˈfjuːzəl/ [n C usually singular] when someone refuses to do something that they have been asked to do: *He was upset by her refusal.* | *His request for a bigger room met with a blunt refusal.* | **+ to do sth** *She must understand the consequences of her refusal to accept medical treatment.* | *Refusal to do military service was a criminal offence.*

say no /ˌseɪ ˈnəʊ/ [v phrase] especially spoken to tell someone that you will not do what they asked you to do: *I asked Dad to lend me some money, but he said no.* | **+ no** *They asked me so nicely, I couldn't really say no to them.*

will not/won't /ˌwɪl ˈnɒt, wəʊnt/ [modal verb] especially spoken if someone **will not** or **won't** do something that they have been asked to do or told to do, they are determined not to do it: *He won't do anything that I ask him to do.* | *I won't sign the contract unless they offer me more money.*

not be prepared to do sth /nɒt biː prɪˌpeəʳd tə ˈduː (sth)/ [v phrase] to refuse to do something – use this when you think it is wrong or unfair that anyone should expect you to do something: *I'm not prepared to wait any longer.* | *The landlord says that he is not prepared to pay for the repairs.*

draw the line /ˌdrɔː ðə ˈlaɪn / [v phrase] to allow certain things, but feel that you must refuse when a particular point is reached: *Our rules about timekeeping are fairly flexible, but we have to draw the line somewhere.* | **+ at** *I don't mind your brother coming to stay, but I draw the line at him moving in!*

decline /dɪˈklaɪn/ [v I] formal to politely refuse to do what someone has asked you to do, especially when they have asked for your opinion or asked for information: *When asked to comment on details of the agreement, the President declined.* | **+ to do sth** *A security officer at the factory, who declined to give his name, said he had seen two men leave the building.* | *I asked Mr Hughes if he was satisfied with the jury's verdict but he declined to comment.*

2 what you say when you refuse to do something

- no
- no way
- forget it
- not likely
- and that's flat

no /nəʊ/ *'Can you come and help move these boxes?' 'No, sorry, I'm busy.'* | *'You're sick – you need to stay in bed.' 'No, I have to be at this meeting.'*

no way /ˌnəʊ ˈweɪ/ spoken use this to firmly refuse to do something and say that nothing will change your mind: *'Why don't you phone him and apologize.' 'No way – I haven't done anything wrong!'* | *No way am I going to look after all three children on my own!* | *There's no way I'm going to put up with rudeness like that!*

forget it /fəʳˈget ɪt/ spoken use this to tell someone that there is no chance at all of you doing something: *'Maybe things will sort themselves out in time.' 'Forget it, the relationship's over.'* | *As for the idea of going on holiday together, forget it!*

not likely /nɒt ˈlaɪkli/ British spoken use this when you think that what someone has asked you to do is stupid or dangerous: *'Are you coming to that lecture this evening?' 'Not likely – there's free beer at the Queen's Arms tonight!'*

and that's flat British spoken **that's final** American spoken /ən ˌðæts ˈflæt, ˌðæts ˈfaɪnl/ used after you have refused to do something, in order to show that you will not change your mind or discuss your decision: *I'm not coming, and that's flat. Now stop bothering me.* | *There's no way I'm helping Ted move again, and that's final.*

3 to refuse to give someone something

- refuse
- deny
- withhold

refuse /rɪˈfjuːz/ [v T] **refuse sb sth** *He was unable to attend the meeting in Moscow, because the Russian authorities had refused him a visa.* | *You wouldn't refuse an old friend a favour, would you?* | **refuse sth to sb** *Some banks are threatening to refuse loans to anyone who cannot provide suitable guarantees.*

deny /dɪˈnaɪ/ [v T usually in passive] if someone in authority **denies** someone something that they want, for example money, a right, or the chance to do something, they refuse to give it to them **deny sb sth** *His parents denied him the opportunity to go to university.* | **be denied sth** *The scientists have been denied the necessary funds for their research program.* | *Up to 450 disaster victims were denied compensation by their insurers.* | *She has been denied the right to appeal to the Supreme Court.*

withhold /wɪðˈhəʊld, wɪθ-/ [v T] to refuse to give someone something that they want – use this especially in official or legal contexts: *The new law allows you to withhold payment if you think a bill is incorrect.* | **withhold sth from sb** *Doctors do not have the right to withhold necessary treatment from a patient.*

regret/not regret

to feel sorry about something you have done or something that has happened

RELATED WORDS

- to tell someone you are sorry *see* **sorry/apologize**
- *see also* **unfortunately**

1 to wish you had not done something

- be sorry/feel sorry
- regret
- wish (that) you had/hadn't done sth
- regret

be sorry/feel sorry /biː ˈsɒri, fiːl ˈsɒri‖-ˈsɑːri/ [v phrase] to feel sad, embarrassed, or annoyed about something bad or stupid that you have done, and wish you had not done it **+ that** *Aunt Jean always felt a little sorry that she had never had children.* | *I was sorry I ever agreed to go with them.* | **+ for** (=sorry for something bad that you have done) *I am sorry for any embarrassment I may have caused.* | **+ about** (=sorry about something that has happened) *Richardson said she was very sorry about the incident.*

regret /rɪˈgret/ [v T] to wish that you had not done something, especially because it has bad results that affect you for a long time: *It was a stupid thing to say, and I immediately regretted it.* | *The owners said they regretted the decision to close the store, but felt unable to do otherwise.* | **+ (that)** *I think she regrets now that she never went to college.* | **regret doing sth** *I have always regretted giving up my piano lessons.* | **deeply regret** (=regret very much) *The Public Health ministry said it deeply regretted the error.*

wish (that) you had/hadn't done sth /ˌwɪʃ (ðət) juː həd, hædnt ˈdʌn (sth)/ [v phrase] to feel that you have done the wrong thing, and wish that you had behaved differently: *I wish I had told him the truth.* | *I wish I'd realized earlier how much money I could save.* | *She wished now that she had not agreed to go to the party.*

regret /rɪˈgret/ [n U] a feeling of sadness that you have when you think you have done the wrong thing, especially because it has bad results that affect you for a long time: *My main regret is that I never finished my college degree.* | **sigh/expression/feeling of regret** *'I was too young to know what I was doing,' said Martha with a deep sigh of regret.* | **express regret** *Officers expressed regret about the boy's death.*

2 what you say when you wish that you had not done something

- why did/didn't I do sth
- I could've kicked myself/I've been kicking myself etc

why did/didn't I do sth /ˌwaɪ dɪd, dɪdnt aɪ ˈduː (sth)/ spoken say this when you feel you have done the wrong thing, because things would have been better if you had done something differently: *Why did I say I'd clean the car? It's going to take hours!* | *He's such an idiot! Why did I ever find him attractive?* | *I'm so stupid. Why didn't I just write it down?*

I could've kicked myself/I've been kicking myself etc /aɪ ˌkʊdəv ˈkɪkt maɪself, aɪv biːn ˈkɪkɪŋ maɪself‖-bɪn-/ spoken say this when you are very sorry about something you have said or done, for example something embarrassing or upsetting, or something you did not want people to know: *I could've kicked myself when I realized she was standing right behind me.* | *I have kicked myself every day since then for not checking again to see that the doors were locked.*

3 something that you wish you had not done

- regret

regret /rɪˈgret/ [n C] *My one regret is that I never visited the Taj Mahal when I was in India.* | *Her biggest regret is that she turned down a job with Gardner's in 1985.* | *I knew that if I didn't make a clean break with Victor I should be filled with regrets for the rest of my life.*

4 when you think someone else will wish they had not done something

- sb will be sorry
- sb will live to regret it
- sb will be laughing on the other side of their face/mouth

sb will be sorry / (sb) wɪl biː ˈsɒri‖-ˈsɑːri/ spoken use this to say that someone will later regret what they have done, because something bad will happen as a result of their actions: *Ed, you'll be sorry you ever said that.* | *If you don't start studying for your exams, you'll be sorry later.*

sb will live to regret it / (sb) wɪl ˌlɪv tə rɪˈgret ɪt/ spoken use this to say that someone will regret what they have done at a later time, especially a few years from now: *He may think leaving his wife for the other woman is a good idea, but he'll live to regret it.* | *If you put all your money in this real estate deal, I guarantee you'll live to regret it.*

sb will be laughing on the other side of their face/mouth / (sb) wɪl biː ˌlɑːfɪŋ ɒn ði ˌʌðər saɪd əv ðeər ˈfeɪs, ˈmaʊθ‖-ˌlæf-/ spoken use this to say that although someone is happy about what they have done now, they will wish they had not done it later: *You'll be laughing out of the other side of your face when I start making money with this.*

5 to not regret doing something

- not regret
- not be sorry
- have no regrets
- sb would do the same (thing) again/sb would do it again
- I wouldn't change a thing

not regret /nɒt rɪˈgret/ [v T] *Even though this year has been a difficult one, I have never regretted my decision.* | **not regret doing sth** *I still miss him sometimes, but I don't regret breaking up with him.* | **not regret it** *It's worth trying to save a little every month – you won't regret it.*

not be sorry /nɒt biː ˈsɒri‖-ˈsɑːri/ [v phrase] to not feel sorry that you did something, especially when other people think you should **+ (that)** *I'm not sorry I never got married – I'm only sorry I didn't have any children.* | **+ to do sth** *She wasn't sorry to leave her job.* | **+ about** *Richards says she still isn't sorry about making jokes about the president.* | **+ for** *I'm not sorry for what I said. Somebody had to tell the truth, even if people don't like it.*

have no regrets /hæv ˌnəʊ rɪˈgrets/ [v phrase] to be glad that you did a particular thing or that things happened in a particular way: *I'm glad I left Britain and came to live in the US. I have no regrets.* | *She had decided to have the baby and had no regrets about her decision.* | **have few regrets** *Even though it's hard work they have few regrets about setting up their own business.*

sb would do the same (thing) again/sb would do it again /(sb) wʊd duː ðə ˌseɪm θɪŋ əˈgen, (sb) wʊd ˌduː ɪt əˈgen/ spoken use this when you are not at all sorry that you did something, especially something important in your life: *'Are you sorry you left home so young?' 'Oh no, I'd do the same thing again.'* | *He insulted me, so I hit him. And I'd do it again.* | *Julia doesn't regret having Ben, and if she could turn the clock back she'd do the same again.* | *I wasn't always happy, but I'd do it again if I had the chance.*

I wouldn't change a thing /aɪ ˌwʊdnt tʃeɪndʒ ə ˈθɪŋ/ spoken say this when you do not regret a situation that happened in the past, even if it involved problems or if it upset you at that time: *Sure, I was devastated when Harry went back to his wife, but even so I wouldn't change a thing.*

6 what you say when you are sorry to have to tell someone some bad news

- I'm sorry
- regret

I'm sorry /aɪm ˈsɒri‖-ˈsɑːri/ *'Could you lend me a couple of pounds, Katy?' 'Sorry, I don't have any money.'* | *I'm sorry that I can't help.* | **+ to do sth** *I'm sorry to have to tell you that your grandmother is in hospital.*

regret /rɪˈgret/ [v T] used in formal letters and official announcements giving someone some bad news: *The airport announced that due to bad weather all flights were cancelled, and they regretted any inconvenience this would cause.* | **regret to inform/tell/say etc** *The management regrets to inform you that your contract will not be renewed next month.* | *I regret to say that a number of statements made by the department were incorrect.*

7 with a feeling of sadness because you wish a situation was different

- with regret
- regretfully

with regret /wɪð rɪˈgret/ [adv] *He spoke with regret of his decision to leave office.* | *People who've left the town and then returned notice the changes most, sometimes with regret.* | **with deep/great regret**

(=with a lot of regret) *We have accepted her resignation with deep regret.*

regretfully /rɪˈgretfəli/ [adv] if you say or do something **regretfully**, you say or do it sadly because you do not want to say or do it: *'We'd better go back,' she said regretfully, 'before it rains.'* | *A news release issued by the singer's publicist said he had 'regretfully' severed all ties to the band because of 'creative differences'.* —**regretful** [adj] *He sounds more regretful than angry when he talks of his divorce.*

regular/ regularly

RELATED WORDS

- have a regular shape *see* **shape (5)**
- usually, sometimes, often

1 when you do something regularly, or something happens regularly

- **regularly**
- **regular**
- **every day/every week/every year etc**
- **hourly/daily/ weekly/monthly etc**
- **every other day/week/year etc**
- **alternate days/ weeks/years etc**

regularly /ˈregjʊləʳli/ [adv] if you do something **regularly**, you do it on many different occasions, usually with the same amount of time in between: *I've been going jogging regularly for a couple of years now.* | *Both my sons phone me regularly, usually once a week.* | *Company reports are published regularly and sent out to all shareholders.*

regular /ˈregjʊləʳ/ [adj usually before noun] a **regular** event or activity happens every hour, every week, every month etc, usually with the same amount of time in between: *Do you do any regular exercise?* | *It's important to visit your dentist for regular check-ups.* | *The Parent-Teacher Association has regular meetings every month.* | **on a regular basis** (=regularly) *More than 60% of adults drink wine on a regular basis.* | **at regular intervals** (=with equal amounts of time between) *The prison is inspected at regular intervals by government health officers.* | **a regular feature (of sth)** (=a regular event that has become an important part of something) *The exhibitions by young artists formed a regular feature of the London arts scene.*

every day/every week/every year etc /ˌevri ˈdeɪ/ [adv] *She cycles to work every day.* | *Every Sunday we go to my mother's for lunch.* | *The series has been on TV every week for forty years.*

hourly/daily/weekly/monthly etc /ˈaʊəʳli, ˈdeɪli, ˈwiːkli, ˈmʌnθli / [adj usually before noun] happening or done every hour, every day etc: *There are daily flights to Frankfurt.* | *a weekly current affairs programme* | *a monthly magazine* —**hourly/daily etc** /ˈaʊəʳli, ˈdeɪli/ [adv] *The news is broadcast hourly on Network Five.* | *Do you get paid monthly or weekly?*

every other day/week/year etc /ˌevri ˌʌðəʳ ˈdeɪ/ [adv] happening one day, week etc, but not the next and continuing in this way: *Every other Thursday there's a farmers' market in the town.* | *How often do you go shopping? Oh, every other day.*

alternate days/weeks/years etc /ɔːlˌtɜːnɪ̈t ˈdeɪz‖ˌɔːltərnɪ̈t-/ [adj phrase] especially British happening one day, week etc, but not the next and continuing in this way. **Alternate days etc** is more formal than **every other day etc**: *I have to work a 37 hour week, including alternate weekends.* | *Indoor bowls nights are held at the hall on alternate Tuesdays at 7.30.*

2 not regularly

- **every now and then/every so often**
- **on and off/off and on**
- **by/in fits and starts**
- **intermittent**
- **sporadic**
- **in waves**

every now and then/every so often /ˌevri naʊ ən ˈðen, ˌevri səʊ ˈɒfən‖-ˈɔːf-/ [adv] sometimes, but not very often and not regularly: *I only smoke every now and then, at a party or when we go out to eat.* | *Every so often the silence was broken by the sound of gunfire.*

on and off/off and on /ˌɒn ənd ˈɒf, ˌɒf ənd ˈɒn/ [adv] if you do something **on and off** or **off and on** during a long period, you do it for short periods but not regularly: *I've been trying to learn Spanish on and off for the past five years.* | *'Are you still going out with Bill?' 'Off and on.'*

by/in fits and starts /baɪ, ɪn ˌfɪts ənd ˈstɑːʳts/ [adv] repeatedly starting and stopping, but not regularly and never for more than a short time: *Unfortunately our research has only continued in fits and starts.* | **advance/grow/progress etc in fits and starts** *The disease progressed in fits and starts for at least two decades.* | *American military technology has advanced by fits and starts.*

intermittent /ˌɪntəʳˈmɪtənt◂/ [adj] happening repeatedly but not continuously: *There will be intermittent thunderstorms throughout the day.* | *After two days of intermittent fighting, order was finally restored.* —**intermittently** [adv] *I slept intermittently through the night.*

sporadic /spəˈrædɪk/ [adj] happening repeatedly over a fairly long time but not regularly and only for short periods within that time: *Our advertising campaigns have been too sporadic to have had a lot of success.* | *Since then he has been on sporadic drinking binges.* | **sporadic fighting/violence/shots/outbreaks etc** *There was rioting and sporadic fighting in the city as rival gangs clashed.* | *sporadic outbreaks of disease*

in waves /ɪn ˈweɪvz/ [adv] if something happens **in waves**, a short period of activity is followed by a pause, and then there is another short period of activity and another pause, and it continues in this way: *The recruitment of new staff has been proceeding in waves.* | *Pain and nausea swept over him in waves.*

3 with equal spaces in between

- **at regular intervals**
- **every metre/mile/ 10 kilometres etc**
- **evenly spaced**

at regular intervals /ət ˌregjʊlər ˈɪntəʳvəlz/ [adv] if things are arranged **at regular intervals**, they are arranged, usually in a line, with equal distances between them: *There are stations where runners can get water at regular intervals throughout the marathon.* | *Small trees can be planted at regular intervals along a path to create an avenue.*

every metre/mile/10 kilometres etc /ˌevri ˈmiːtəʳ/ [adv] at regular points that are a metre, mile etc apart along a line, road etc: *It was so steep that we* *had to stop and rest about every twenty metres.* | *There are coastguard stations every ten miles along the coast.*

evenly spaced /ˌiːvənli ˈspeɪst◂/ [adj phrase] arranged with regular spaces: *Our tents are evenly spaced over a large area to give you maximum privacy.* | *The word processor will arrange your text in evenly spaced columns.*

reject

RELATED WORDS

opposite: —— **accept**

- to say that you will not do something *see* **refuse**
- *see also* **no**

1 to reject an offer or suggestion

- reject
- not accept
- say no
- refuse
- turn down
- decline
- I'll take a rain check

reject /rɪˈdʒekt/ [v T] to say no very firmly to an offer or suggestion. **Reject** is more formal than **not accept** and **say no**: *Lauren rejected her parents' offer of financial help.* | *She rejected the idea that she should sue him.* | *The Secretary of State offered his resignation, which the President promptly rejected.* —**rejection** /rɪˈdʒekʃən/ [n U] *the government's outright rejection of the proposals*

not accept /nɒt əkˈsept/ [v phrase] to say no to an offer or invitation, especially because you think it would not be right to accept it: *She's given us all this stuff and she won't accept any money for it.* | *I decided not to accept their invitation.* | *Laney wouldn't accept what he considered an insulting pay offer.*

say no /seɪ ˈnəʊ/ [v phrase] especially spoken not accept an offer or suggestion: *I asked him if he wanted a drink, but he said no.* | *I'll offer to buy it from her, but I expect she'll say no.* | **+ to** *Mrs. Hill, still mentally alert, said no to any suggestions of further operations.*

refuse /rɪˈfjuːz/ [v I/T] to say you do not want something that you have been offered: *The offer was so good how could I refuse?* | *He never refuses a drink, does he?* | **+ to do sth** *Ms. Knight refused to accept the manager's apology.* | **flatly refuse** *He flatly refuses any offers of financial help.*

turn down /ˌtɜːʳn ˈdaʊn/ [phr v T] to say no to an offer – use this especially when someone refuses a good offer or opportunity, and this is surprising **turn sb/sth down** *They offered her a really good job, but she turned it down.* | *He said he'd help her with her training, but she turned him down.* | **turn down sb/sth** *If you turn down the opportunity to go to college, you'll always regret it.*

decline /dɪˈklaɪn/ [v I/T] formal to say no politely when someone invites you to do something: *Mr Casey regrets that he will have to decline your kind invitation owing to a prior engagement.* | *The bishop was invited to attend the opening ceremony, but he declined.* | **+ to do sth** *The Prime Minister was asked for his opinion but declined to comment.*

I'll take a rain check /aɪl ˌteɪk ə ˈreɪn tʃek/ spoken use this to tell someone that you cannot accept their invitation at the time they have suggested, but would like to do it at some time in the future: *'How about dinner tonight?' 'Sorry – I'll have to take a rain check on that.'*

2 to officially reject a request or suggestion

- reject
- throw out
- turn down
- refuse
- say no
- vote against/vote no
- veto
- give sth the thumbs down

reject /rɪˈdʒekt/ [v T] to use your official authority to formally refuse a request or suggestion: *Judge Gifford rejected the defense's request.* | *The immigration authorities have rejected his application for refugee status.* | *It was predicted that the Senate would reject the bill by about 60 to 40.* —**rejection** /rɪˈdʒekʃən/ [n U] *the rejection of the Equal Rights Bill by a small majority*

throw out /ˌθrəʊ ˈaʊt/ [phr v T] if a parliament, a council, or other official political organization **throws out** a plan or suggestion, they refuse to accept it or make it legal, especially after voting on it **throw out sth** *Local councillors threw out proposals for the building of a new stadium.* | **throw sth out** *The House passed the bill, but the Senate threw it out.*

turn down /ˌtɜːʳn ˈdaʊn/ [phr v T] to refuse to accept a request or to give someone permission to do something, especially when the request is a reasonable one **turn down sth** *Their application to build a new extension has been turned down by the planning authority.* | **turn sth down** *We put in a request for a little extra time for us to finish the project, but the board turned it down.*

refuse /rɪˈfjuːz/ [v] to officially decide that someone cannot have something they have asked for, or cannot do something they want to do **refuse an application/request/demand etc** *Judge Eyck refused his request for bail.* | *Over 2,000 applications for political asylum were refused last year.* | **refuse sb sth** *Under the law, doctors cannot refuse patients access to their own medical records.* | **refuse sth to sb** *The city is refusing contracts to firms that do not practice an equal opportunities policy.*

say no /seɪ ˈnəʊ / [v phrase] to officially refuse to accept a request, suggestion, or bad situation: *Employees have repeatedly requested child care facilities, but the company has always said no.* | **+ to** *We're hoping the government will at last say no to low wages and poverty.*

vote against/vote no /ˌvəʊt əˈgenst, ˌvəʊt ˈnəʊ/ [v phrase] to refuse to accept a plan, proposal, or new law by voting: *The majority of union members voted against further industrial action.* | *Homeowners voted against new bonds and higher taxes.* | *Only Councilwoman Shirley Lanion voted no.* | **vote no on sth** *I urge you to vote no on Measure A.*

veto /ˈviːtəʊ/ [v T] to use your position of power to refuse to allow something to happen, especially something that other people, organizations, or countries have agreed: *European plans to deregulate air fares were vetoed by Spain.* | *Requests to take foster children abroad are often vetoed by the biological parent.* | *The governor vetoed a bill that would have given some much-needed money to public libraries.* —**veto** [n C/U] *As a result of the president's veto the inner-cities program will not now go ahead.*

give sth the thumbs down ALSO **turn thumbs down on sth** American /gɪv (sth) ðə ˌθʌmz ˈdaʊn, tɜːʳn ˌθʌmz ˈdaʊn ɒn (sth)/ [v phrase] informal to reject a plan or suggestion: *The commission wisely gave the golf course proposal the thumbs down.* | *The city council turned thumbs down on*

Marison's new proposal, citing potential parking problems.

3 to state very firmly that you do not agree with something

- reject
- not accept
- dismiss

reject /rɪˈdʒekt/ [v T not in progressive] *The belief that the children of working mothers suffer is rejected by most child psychologists.* | *The audience is free to accept or reject Stone's interpretation of the facts.* | **reject a suggestion/idea/notion etc that** *Bush rejected suggestions that his tax cuts favored the most wealthy.* | *The author rejected accusations that his novel is blasphemous, but apologized for any offense it had caused.*

not accept /nɒt əkˈsept/ [v phrase] to **not accept** a statement, explanation, or decision because you think it is wrong or untrue: *Our managers claim the new system will increase efficiency but I don't accept that.* | *He said he wouldn't accept any excuses for missing the deadline.*

dismiss /dɪsˈmɪs/ [v T not in progressive] to refuse to accept someone's opinions, suggestions, proof etc without even considering it: *The judge dismissed most of the police evidence, saying it was clearly fabricated.* | *One leader dismissed the conference's findings on the environment as unproven.* | **dismiss sth out of hand** (=dismiss completely without any consideration at all) *The argument for higher tariffs cannot be dismissed out of hand.*

4 to reject ideas, beliefs, or ways of living

- reject
- turn your back on
- scorn
- drop out

reject /rɪˈdʒekt/ [v T] to **reject** ideas, beliefs, or ways of living, especially when you used to accept them in the past: *As an adult, she rejected her Catholic upbringing.* | *Vegetarians reject the idea that you must eat meat to get all the nutrients you need.* | *Feminists rejected traditional notions of the role of women in society.* —**rejection** /rɪˈdʒekʃən/ [n U] **+ of** *Sometimes she began to question her outright rejection of her parents' values.*

turn your back on /ˌtɜːʳn jɔːʳ ˈbæk ɒn/ [v phrase] to completely change your former beliefs and way of life, especially because you now think that they were wrong: *I had a sense of relief as I turned my back on the disasters of my first marriage.* | *Some journalists accused him of turning his back on a lot of the party's major principles.*

scorn /skɔːʳn/ [v T] to reject ideas, values, or behaviour because you think they are stupid, wrong, or old-fashioned: *My kids used to scorn my politics as right-wing selfishness.* | **scorn sth as sth** *Many young people scorn polite behaviour as insincere.*

drop out /ˌdrɒp ˈaʊt‖ˌdrɑːp-/ [phr v I] to refuse to live the way that other people usually live in your society, for example by not working in a job or living in an ordinary house: *While kids in the affluent sixties could afford to drop out, things were very different ten years later.* | *A group of young people dropped out and set up a commune in the middle of the forest.*

5 to reject someone who wants to be friendly or help you

- reject
- rebuff
- give sb the brush-off
- snub
- ostracize
- shun

reject /rɪˈdʒekt/ [v T] to refuse to speak or listen to someone who wants to be friendly with you or wants to help you: *Samantha had consistently rejected all Bob's offers of help.* | *She's scared to try to talk to him about it in case he rejects her again.* | *As a child he was repeatedly rejected by both parents.* —**rejection** /rɪˈdʒekʃən/ [n U] *Of course, you always risk rejection when you first ask someone out.*

rebuff /rɪˈbʌf/ [v T] to reject someone's friendly invitation or offer in an unpleasant or rude way, so that they feel offended: *She rebuffed all my attempts to make things up between us, till eventually my patience snapped.* | *Despite being rebuffed again and again, he continued to phone her.*

give sb the brush-off /ˌgɪv (sb) ðə ˈbrʌʃ ɒf/ [v phrase] informal to refuse to accept someone's help, friendship, invitations etc in a rude and unfriendly way: *Russell tried to give me the brush-off, but I don't give up that easily.* | *The new director of the Urban League was given the brush-off by City Hall.*

snub /snʌb/ [v T] to deliberately behave in an unfriendly way to someone, for example by ignoring them or being rude to them, so that they feel hurt: *Rosanna felt snubbed when she wasn't invited to the wedding.* | *High-schoolers will often snub anyone they feel is different or strange.* | *When the college invited him to speak, he was snubbed by students who felt his policies were unfair to minorities.* —**snub** [n C] *The assistant director took it as a snub when he was not invited to the conference.*

ostracize ALSO **ostracise** British /ˈɒstrəsaɪz‖ˈɑː-/ [v T] if a group of people **ostracize** a person or another group, they refuse to talk to them and make them feel that they are strongly disliked: *Many young people are unwilling to admit that they are gay because they fear being ostracized.* | *He had committed crimes so appalling that even other prisoners ostracized him.*

shun /ʃʌn/ [v T] to refuse to accept or be friendly with someone, especially because they are different from you in some way or have done something that you disapprove of: *Some young women are shunned by their families when they become pregnant outside of marriage.* | *Recently bereaved widows often feel they are being shunned by people who don't know what to say to them.*

6 to refuse to give someone a job, a place at college etc

- reject
- turn down
- not accept

reject /rɪˈdʒekt/ [v T] to formally tell someone, usually in writing, that they have not got the job or chance to study that they have asked for: *Several hundred people applied, but we had to reject nearly all of them.* | *Ian was rejected by the army because of his bad eyesight.* | *Jim was rejected by every college he applied to.* —**rejection** /rɪˈdʒekʃən/ [n C/U] *I got a rejection from Harvard, but I'm still waiting to hear from UCLA.*

turn down /ˌtɜːʳn ˈdaʊn/ [phr v T] to tell someone that they cannot have the job or chance to study that they have asked for, especially when there is a particular reason for doing this **turn sb down** *When Uncle John tried to join the army, they turned him down because he was too old.* | *Marion applied for a job teaching in Minneapolis, but she was turned down.* | **turn down sb** *We automatically turn down any candidate who makes spelling mistakes in their job application.*

not accept /nɒt əkˈsept/ [phr v T] to not give someone the job or chance to study that they have asked for: *He applied for several jobs at the amusement park, but wasn't accepted.* | *Most universities will not accept anyone without an interview.*

7 to refuse very firmly to accept or become involved in something

- not have/want anything to do with
- turn your nose up at/turn up your nose at
- I wouldn't touch it with a barge pole

not have/want anything to do with /nɒt hæv, wɒnt ˌeniθɪŋ tə ˈduː wɪð (sth) ‖-wɔːnt-/ [v phrase] to refuse to take part in an activity or get involved in something because you disapprove of it or think it will not work: *She said the idea was stupid and wouldn't have anything to do with it.* | *Most activists don't want anything to do with violent protests.*

turn your nose up at/turn up your nose at /ˌtɜːʳn jɔːʳ ˈnəʊz ʌp æt, ˌtɜːʳn ʌp jɔːʳ ˈnəʊz æt/ [v phrase] informal to refuse to accept something that someone offers you because you think it is not good enough for you: *Many older academics turn their noses up at subjects such as Media and Film studies.* | *He turned up his nose at a job washing dishes.*

I wouldn't touch it with a barge pole British **/I wouldn't touch it with a ten-foot pole** American /aɪ wʊdnt ˌtʌtʃ ɪt wɪð ə ˈbɑːʳdʒ pəʊl, aɪ wʊdnt ˌtʌtʃ ɪt wɪð ə ˌten fʊt ˈpəʊl/ use this to say that you will definitely not accept something, buy something, or get involved in something: *My nephew wants me to invest in his business, but frankly I wouldn't touch it with a barge pole.* | *Millions of people buy those cars, but I wouldn't touch one with a ten-foot pole.*

relationship

RELATED WORDS

- be connected with something *see* **connected/related**
- to start to know someone *see* **know/not know (23)**
- to end a relationship *see* **separate (7)**
- to leave a relationship *see* **leave (27-28)**
- *see also* **friend, friendly, unfriendly, girlfriend/boyfriend, sex, gay, marry, divorce**

1 the relationship between two people or groups

- relationship
- relations
- ties
- rapport
- bond
- chemistry
- affinity

relationship /rɪˈleɪʃənʃɪp/ [n C] the way that two people or groups feel about each other and behave towards each other: *Women are usually more interested in discussing relationships than men.* | **+ with** *His relationship with his parents had never been very good.* | *Successful companies know the importance of establishing good relationships with their customers.* | **+ between** *There has been a fundamental shift in the relationship between the U.S. and Russia.* | **a close relationship** (=when you know someone very well and like them a lot) *They'd known each other for years and had a very close relationship.*

relations /rɪˈleɪʃənz/ [n plural] the public relationship between groups, organizations, or countries, especially when this affects how well they work together **+ between** *Relations between management and workers have improved.* | **+ with** *We all understand the importance of maintaining good relations with China.* | **race relations** (=between people of different races) *Since the riot, race relations in the city have not been good.* | **diplomatic relations** (=between the governments of two countries) *The U.S. has not had normal diplomatic relations with Cuba since the 1960s.* | **industrial relations** British **labor relations** American (=between workers and managers) *The new contract should improve labor relations in the school district.* | **trade relations** (=involving exchanging goods between companies) *Trade relations between eastern and western Europe continue to expand.*

ties /taɪz/ [n plural] a strong relationship between two people, organizations, or countries, especially when they have responsibilities towards each other or official agreements with each other: *The group has stayed together because of cultural, social, and other ties.* | **+ with** *The country wants its independence, and intends to loosen its ties with Britain.* | **+ between** *Since the accident, the ties between father and son have grown even stronger.* | **family ties** (=between members of a family) *As younger members of the family moved away, the family ties began to weaken.*

rapport /ræˈpɔːʳ/ [n singular] a good relationship between people who understand and agree with each others' opinions and ideas **+ with** *You are lucky to have such a good rapport with your boss.* | **+ between** *There seems to be a better rapport between players and officials now than in the past.* | **establish a rapport** *Before you do business with someone, it is important to establish a rapport.* | **easy rapport** (=good rapport) *Alison and Johnny had an easy rapport that was clear to everyone.*

bond /bɒnd‖bɑːnd/ [n C] a very strong relationship between two people or groups that makes it difficult for them to separate from each other: *The mountain community is held together by deep historical and religious bonds.* | **+ between** *The bond between mother and child is extremely strong.* | **+ with** *It's almost inevitable that the client will form a very close bond with the therapist.* | **bonds of friendship/affection/attachment** *Over the years the two men had developed deep bonds of friendship.*

chemistry /ˈkemɪstri/ [n U] a good and often exciting and romantic relationship between two people who naturally like, understand, and admire each other, even if they have very different characters and attitudes: *Chuck's a nice guy, but the chemistry isn't right.* | **+ between** *As soon as we met I could feel the chemistry between us.* | *The chemistry between the two stars makes the movie a pleasure to watch.*

affinity /əˈfɪnɪti/ [n singular/U] a feeling of liking and understanding someone because you have the same interests or beliefs as them, or because you are in the same situation as them: *We have a deep affinity formed through many years of friendship.* | **+ between** *They seemed so different, yet he sensed an affinity between them.* | **+ with** *Venetians feel more affinity with inhabitants of Vienna than with those of Rome.*

2 to have a good relationship

- have a good relationship
- get along
- be on good terms
- close

have a good relationship /hæv ə ˌgʊd rɪˈleɪʃənʃɪp/ [v phrase not in progressive] when two people or groups are friendly towards each other and work well together: *My boss and I have a very good relationship.* | **+ with** *It's important that the school have a good relationship with the students' parents.* | *The president has a good working relationship with this Congress.*

get along ALSO **get on** British /get əˈlɒŋ‖-əˈlɔːŋ, get ˈɒn/ [phr v I] if two or more people **get along** or **get on**, they have a friendly relationship with each other: *I don't understand why you two girls don't get along.* | **+ with** *He's very easy to get along with.* | *Martin was chosen because he is a good administrator who gets along with everyone.* | **get along/on well** *We all get on really well, so we're going to share a flat next year.* | **get along/on like a house on fire** (=extremely well) *I wasn't sure whether David and Ann would like each other, but they got on like a house on fire.*

be on good terms /ˌbiː ɒn gʊd ˈtɜːʳmz/ [v phrase] if people are **on good terms**, they have a polite relationship and they can work well together, but they are not close friends: *They divorced several years ago, but they're still on good terms.* | **+ with** *We're on good terms with all our neighbours except the couple upstairs.* | *Taylor has managed to remain on good terms with his former employers.*

close /kləʊs/ [adj] if two or more people are **close**, they like each other very much, and can talk to each other about their feelings, their problems etc: *Dad and I have always been very close.* | **+ to** *She was never very close to her stepmother.* | **close friend** *It turns out that Julie is a close friend of my cousin Kelly.*

3 to have a bad relationship

- not get along
- have a falling-out
- incompatible
- drive a wedge between sb

not get along ALSO **not get on** British /nɒt get əˈlɒŋ‖-əˈlɔːŋ, nɒt get ˈɒn / [v phrase] if people do **not get along** or do **not get on**, they have a bad relationship and they often argue and disagree with each other: *Barney and I just don't get along.* | **+ with** *Troy doesn't get along with the coach, so he's thinking of quitting the team.* | *She never got on with her father and she hates her new stepmother.*

have a falling-out ALSO **fall out** British /hæv ə ˌfɔːlɪŋ ˈaʊt, ˌfɔːl ˈaʊt/ [v phrase/phr v I] if friends or relatives **have a falling-out** or they **fall out**, they have an argument and stop being friendly with each other: *They fell out last year, and they won't even speak to each other now.* | *The three children had an enormous falling-out over their inheritance when their father died.* | **+ with** *He's fallen out with his girlfriend again.* | *Daly had a falling-out with her boss, which led to her being fired.*

incompatible /ˌɪnkəmˈpætəbəl/ [adj] people who are **incompatible** cannot have a good relationship with each other because they are completely different in their characters, interests etc: *We're completely incompatible – she's a neat freak, and I hate to clean.* | *They've always seemed so incompatible – no wonder they're getting a divorce.*

drive a wedge between sb /ˌdraɪv ə ˈwedʒ bɪˈtwiːn (sb)/ [v phrase] if something **drives a wedge** between two people or groups, it has a bad effect on their relationship: *The war had driven a wedge between the President and his liberal supporters.* | *Romley's lawsuit drove the wedge even farther between the two former friends.*

4 to have a romantic or sexual relationship with someone

- go out with
- be seeing
- have a relationship
- have an affair
- be involved with
- date

go out with ALSO **go with** American /gəʊ ˈaʊt wɪð, ˈgəʊ wɪð/ [phr v T] to have someone as your girlfriend or boyfriend: *How long have you been going out with Mindy?* | *Is she still going with that guy who works at the gas station?* | **be going (out) together** *Mark and I have been going out together for four years.*

be seeing /biː ˈsiːɪŋ/ [v phrase] to have a romantic or sexual relationship with someone, especially a relationship that is not very serious and does not last very long: *Do you know if Tanya's seeing anyone at the moment?* | *A couple of years after they got married, he started seeing other women.*

have a relationship /ˌhæv ə rɪˈleɪʃənʃɪp/ [v phrase] to have a romantic or sexual relationship with someone, especially one that continues for a long time: *I have had several relationships before, but this is special.* | *They'd been having a relationship for over a year when Julie found out she was pregnant.* | **+ with** *Would you even consider having a relationship with a man like Denny?*

have an affair /ˌhæv ən əˈfeəʳ/ [v phrase] to have a secret sexual relationship with someone who is not your husband or wife: *I'd kill my husband if I found out he'd been having an affair.* | **+ with** *The senator has been accused of having an affair with his publicity assistant.*

be involved with /biː ɪnˈvɒlvd wɪð‖-ˈvɑːlvd-/ [v phrase] to be having a serious relationship with someone, especially someone who is not suitable for you: *She's involved with a much older man.* | *The school has strict rules against teachers becoming involved with students.* | *Brad doesn't want to get involved with anyone right now. He's still upset about Suzanne.*

date /deɪt/ [v phrase usually in progressive] American to be having a relationship with someone, especially a relationship that is not very serious yet: *How long have Paul and Sue been dating?* | *What is a man his age doing dating a 17-year-old?* | *I thought we were just friends, but when I started dating other men, he suddenly got really jealous.*

5 a romantic or sexual relationship

- relationship
- affair
- fling
- romance

relationship /rɪˈleɪʃənʃɪp/ [n C] when two people spend time together or live together because they are romantically or sexually attracted to each other: *After her marriage broke up, she had a series of disastrous relationships.* | **+ with** *I don't want to start a relationship with her, because I'm going back to South Africa.* | **+ between** *Relationships between people of different cultures are often extremely difficult.* | **be in a relationship** *Why are all the interesting men I meet already in relationships?* | **sexual relationship** *Several of the psychiatrists admitted to having sexual relationships with patients.* | **romantic relationship** *Even at 35, Bobby seemed unable to commit to a romantic relationship.*

affair /əˈfeəʳ/ [n C] a secret sexual relationship between two people, when one or both of them is married to someone else: *The affair had been going on for years before her husband found out.* | **+ with** *I had no idea that Mike had an affair with Carolyn!* | **love affair** *Burton had been involved in a love affair with a woman who ended up taking most of his money.*

fling /flɪŋ/ [n C] a short and not very serious relationship: *Yes, I did go out with him, but it was just a fling.* | *She wasn't interested in anything more than a casual fling.* | **+ with** *She left her husband after she learned about his fling with an exotic dancer.* | **have a fling** *They had a fling years ago.*

romance /rəʊˈmæns, rə-, ˈrəʊmæns/ [n C] an exciting and often short relationship between two people who feel very much in love with each other: *It was a beautiful summer romance, but they knew it couldn't last.* | *Richard and Penny had made no great secret of their romance, even though they were both married.* | **+ with** *My romance with Lois did not survive our high school graduation.*

relax/relaxed

RELATED WORDS

opposite: ——— **nervous, worried/worrying**
▸ *see also* **calm, comfortable, rest**

1 to relax

- ▸ relax
- ▸ unwind
- ▸ take it easy
- ▸ loosen up
- ▸ chill out/chill
- ▸ let your hair down
- ▸ let yourself go

relax /rɪˈlæks/ [v I] to make yourself feel calmer, more comfortable, and less worried, by resting or doing something enjoyable: *Just wait! In two weeks' time I'll be relaxing on a beach in Greece.* | *Trained staff will look after your children, so that you can relax and enjoy yourself.* | *For heaven's sake Keith, will you just sit down and relax for five minutes!*

unwind /ʌnˈwaɪnd/ [v I] to gradually relax after you have been working hard or worrying a lot: *After a couple of drinks, Tom began to unwind.* | *Set in spectacular countryside, the Shiga Hotel is the perfect place to unwind.* | *The world motorcross champion likes nothing better than unwinding in front of the TV.*

take it easy /ˌteɪk ɪt ˈiːzi/ [v phrase] to do everything slowly and with less effort than usual so that you do not become worried or tired, especially because you are not feeling strong or healthy: *Now that you've finished your exams, you can take it easy.* | *I'm going to put my feet up and take it easy this afternoon.* | **take things easy** *Pete will still have to take things easy for while.* | *My training schedule was very demanding last year, so I'm taking things a bit easier this year.* | **take it easy on yourself** *Take it easy on yourself for a few days. We'll talk later.*

loosen up /ˌluːsən ˈʌp/ [phr v I] informal if you **loosen up**, you become more relaxed and stop worrying about things: *Hey, loosen up! It's not worth getting upset about something she said.* | *Our drama teacher would do crazy things, just to get us to loosen up some.*

chill out/chill /ˌtʃɪl ˈaʊt, tʃɪl/ [phr v I/v I] spoken informal to relax and calm down, especially after doing something exciting: *The main reason I'm going to Jamaica is so I can lie on the beach and chill out without being distracted.* | *Would you like to come back to my place and just chill?*

let your hair down /ˌlet jɔːʳ ˈheəʳ daʊn/ [v phrase] informal to relax completely and enjoy yourself, especially in social situations: *I spotted Juanita really letting her hair down on the dance floor.* | *Chat rooms on the Internet are a place we can let our hair down and say what we think.*

let yourself go /ˌlet jɔːʳself ˈgəʊ/ [v phrase] to allow yourself to completely relax in a social situation, and not worry about what is polite, or about what other people may think: *He's quite scholarly, but he can be really funny when he lets himself go.* | *Dick took me to the party and, for once, I let myself go completely.*

2 to make someone feel more relaxed

- ▸ relax
- ▸ put sb at ease/make sb feel at ease
- ▸ loosen up
- ▸ relaxing

relax /rɪˈlæks/ [v T] *Meditation relaxes you and makes you feel more healthy.* | *The drink relaxed him so much he fell asleep.*

put sb at ease/make sb feel at ease ALSO **put sb at their ease** British /ˌpʊt (sb) ət ˈiːz, ˌmeɪk (sb) fiːl ət ˈiːz, ˌpʊt (sb) ət ðeər ˈiːz/ [v phrase] to make someone feel more relaxed, especially by talking to them in a calm, friendly way when they are in a difficult or worrying situation: *I did my best to make him feel at ease before the interview began.* | *Ginsberg had a talent for putting people instantly at ease.* | *He had succeeded in putting her at her ease, despite her natural shyness.*

loosen up /ˌluːsən ˈʌp/ [phr v I] informal if someone or something **loosens** you **up**, they make you feel happier and more relaxed about the things that are worrying you **loosen up sb** *Uncle Billy was a great preacher – he sure could loosen a crowd up.* | **loosen sb up** *At first, I just started drinking at parties, to help loosen me up.*

relaxing /rɪˈlæksɪŋ/ [adj] making you feel calm, comfortable, and not worried: *a relaxing massage* | *Tuscany is a good choice for a relaxing holiday.* | *Do something relaxing before going to bed – read a book, or take a hot bath.*

3 feeling relaxed

- ▸ relaxed
- ▸ laid-back
- ▸ easy-going
- ▸ be/feel at ease
- ▸ be/feel comfortable
- ▸ feel at home
- ▸ uninhibited

relaxed /rɪˈlækst/ [adj] feeling calm, comfortable, and not worried or annoyed: *The people in Hawaii are so relaxed – I could have stayed another fortnight.* | *Looking relaxed and confident, the president* *answered a barrage of questions from the press.* | **feel relaxed** *I think people feel more relaxed wearing casual clothes.*

laid-back /ˌleɪd ˈbæk◂/ [adj] informal relaxed, and not easily worried or annoyed: *My parents are pretty laid-back and don't mind me staying out late.* | *He seems like a laid-back kind of a guy.* | *a laid-back lifestyle*

easy-going /ˌiːzi ˈgəʊɪŋ◂/ [adj] informal happy and relaxed, and not often annoyed or angry: *You were always so relaxed and easy-going. It was one of the things I liked about you.* | *William did his best to maintain an easy-going, friendly relationship with everyone at camp.*

be/feel at ease /biː, fiːl ət ˈiːz/ [v phrase] feeling relaxed in a situation in which most people might feel a little nervous, uncomfortable, or anxious: *I've always felt completely at ease among the Palestinians.* | **+ with** *He was surprised to find himself so at ease with her father.* | *After six months in the job, I was starting to feel more at ease with the kids.*

be/feel comfortable /biː, fiːl ˈkʌmftəbəl‖ -ˈkʌmfərt-/ [v phrase] happy and without worries, especially because you are with someone you like and trust or because you are in a situation you are used to **+ with** *A lot of our female patients are not comfortable with the idea of a male doctor.* | **be/feel comfortable doing sth** *When choosing a baby-sitter, look for someone both you and your child feel comfortable with.* | *Would you be comfortable using this type of machinery?* | *This is an emotional issue, which most people aren't comfortable talking about.*

feel at home /ˌfiːl ət ˈhəʊm/ [v phrase] to feel relaxed because you are in a place or situation similar to one that you know very well: *As in your previous job, we also use computers a lot – so you should feel right at home here.* | **+ with** *He was fond of using his hands and felt at home with machinery.* | **feel at home doing sth** *Right now, I feel more at home writing for the stage rather than film.*

uninhibited /ˌʌnɪnˈhɪbɪ̈tɪ̈d◂/ [adj] very relaxed in the company of other people, and not at all shy about showing your true feelings and opinions: *Her acting is completely spontaneous and uninhibited.* | *The Trobriand islanders are happy, sexually uninhibited people.* | **+ about** *The boys were quite uninhibited about performing in front of strangers.*

religion

RELATED WORDS

- pray, believe (7)

1 a religion

- religion
- faith
- creed

religion /rɪˈlɪdʒən/ [n C/U] a **religion** is a set of beliefs that a group of people have about a god, and the ceremonies, customs, and rules that go with these beliefs. Religions and religious beliefs in general when considered as a subject are known as **religion**: *We spent hours discussing politics, religion, and poetry.* | *the Catholic religion* | *My parents' religion is very important to them.* | *The Buddhist and Shinto religions coexist in Japan.* | *We respect all religions here.* | **be against sb's religion** (=be not allowed by their religion) *She can't eat pork. It's against her religion.*

faith /feɪθ/ [n C] a religion, especially one of the large important world religions: *People of all faiths are welcome in this building.* | *One of the things our faith teaches us is that God created us in His own image.* | *The tensions are growing between members of different faiths.* | **the Jewish/Christian/Islamic/Hindu etc faith** *Most of the island's population belong to the Islamic faith.* | *Godparents agree to educate their godchild in the practice of the Christian faith.*

creed /kriːd/ [n C] a religion – use this when you are referring to the range of different religions that exist: *The belief in Jesus as a prophet is a major part of several world creeds.* | *Give everybody an equal chance, regardless of race, color, creed, or gender.* | **people of all creeds/people of every creed** *Mother Teresa offered her service and love to people of every caste and creed.* | *Our church welcomes people of various races, colors, and creeds.*

2 a religious group

- sect
- church
- cult

sect /sekt/ [n C] a religious group that is part of a larger religious group, but has slightly different beliefs and ceremonies: *Islam has two main sects: the Sunnis and the Shias.* | *A monk named Kashyapa is regarded as the founder of the Zen sect of Buddhism.* | *She is a member of a religious sect that was formed from various aspects of Asian religions.* | *a fundamentalist sect*

church /tʃɜːʳtʃ/ [n C] a smaller group within the Christian religion: *The evangelical churches are particularly strong in the big cities.* | *He took us to a Pentecostal meeting in one of the city's many black churches.* | **the Catholic/Methodist/Mormon etc Church** *Even though I belong to the Catholic Church, I don't agree with everything it says.* | **the Church of England/Scotland** *The Church of England finally agreed to accept the ordination of women priests.*

cult /kʌlt/ [n C] an extreme religious group that is not part of an established religion, and that many people think is strange and possibly harmful to the people who get involved in it: *Dozens of religious cults have appeared in the US, most making a fortune for their leaders.* | *Members of the cult are not allowed to marry or own property without permission.* | *A spokesman denied the group is a cult and said members could leave whenever they wanted.*

3 things that you believe because of your religion

- beliefs
- faith

beliefs /bɪˈliːfs/ [n plural] all the ideas that someone believes because of their religion: *Martin Luther King was assassinated because of his beliefs.* | *The religious beliefs and practices of Americans have hardly changed since the 1940s.* | *She refused to change her strongly-held beliefs.* | *They are acting in a way that directly contradicts Christian beliefs.*

faith /feɪθ/ [n U] a strong belief in a particular god or religion: *In spite of all that has happened, somehow she has held onto her faith.* | *Instead of celebrating their religious faith, they are forced to conceal it for fear of reprisals.* | **+ in** *Nothing could shake his faith in God.* | *The only reason I stayed in my marriage was because my faith in religion sustained me.*

4 relating to religion

- religious
- holy
- spiritual
- sacred
- divine
- faith-based/faith

religious /rɪˈlɪdʒəs/ [adj only before noun] *Religious education is compulsory in all English schools.* | *All acts of religious worship were banned.* | *The tutor discussed her own religious beliefs openly with the students.* | *Record companies feared the album might cause offence to people on religious grounds.* | *The walls were decorated with religious symbols.* | *a religious festival*

holy /ˈhəʊli/ [adj] connected with God and religion, and therefore treated in a special way, or thought to have special qualities or powers: *Jerusalem is a holy city for Jews, Christians, and Muslims.* | *In Islam, only the Qur'an is considered holy.* | *the holy month of Ramadan* | *The priest sprinkled each member of the congregation with holy water.*

spiritual /ˈspɪrɪ̈tʃuəl/ [adj] connected with the soul, the spirit, and religion, and not with physical things or ordinary human activities: *She came seeking spiritual guidance.* | *the spiritual leader of the Tibetan people* | *Just as the emotional needs of the mentally disabled are overlooked, so too are their spiritual needs.* | *The last sacrament represents the final step in Christ's spiritual journey.* —**spiritually** [adv] *Do you feel you've gained anything spiritually from the experience?* | *Eliot considered modern society to be both culturally and spiritually empty.*

sacred /ˈseɪkrɪ̈d/ [adj] very holy and therefore treated with great respect: *a choir specialising in sacred music* | *the miraculous power of sacred relics* | **consider sth sacred/regard sth as sacred** *The Japanese regard Mount Fuji as a sacred mountain.* | *Certain animals were considered sacred by the Aztecs.* | *The olive tree was regarded as sacred to the goddess Athena.*

divine /dɪ̈ˈvaɪn/ [adj] connected with or coming from God: *He offered a brief prayer for divine guidance.* | *The death of a child is commonly seen by members of the tribe as divine punishment.*

faith-based/faith /ˈfeɪθ beɪst, feɪθ/ [adj only before noun] involving or run by people or a particular religion – use this especially about schools and official religious groups: *The vast majority of people in the UK are opposed to more faith-based schools, saying they would be socially divisive.* | *Community leaders and those involved in faith organizations met to discuss what could be done about the recent disturbances.*

5 having strong religious beliefs

- religious
- practising
- devout
- pious
- orthodox
- fundamentalist

religious /rɪˈlɪdʒəs/ [adj] *At one time, I was very religious and a regular church-goer.* | *He's always been a religious man, and I think that has helped him.* | **deeply religious** (=very religious) *Like many Victorians, Ruskin was deeply religious.* | *Hooker was born on a Mississippi farm, to a deeply religious mother who disapproved of almost all music.*

practising British **/practicing** American /ˈpræktɪ̈sɪŋ/ [adj only before noun] **practising** Catholic, Jew, Muslim etc is actively involved in a particular religion and keeps its rules, customs etc: *Harri was the only practising Muslim in the class.* | *Over 500 of the prisoners are practising Christians.*

devout /dɪˈvaʊt/ [adj usually before noun] believing very strongly in a particular religion and carefully obeying all its rules **devout Muslim/Catholic/Jew etc** *Bernard was the most devout of all her sons.* | *Rachel's parents are devout Mormons.* | *The shema is still repeated daily by devout Jews the world over.* —**devoutly** [adv] *a devoutly religious family* | *She approached the altar with her head bowed devoutly and her eyes closed.*

pious /ˈpaɪəs/ [adj] having strong religious beliefs and showing this in the way you behave: *She reminded Corbett of a sweet, pious young nun he once knew.* | *Ethelred was not the most pious of kings, and his clashes with the church were stormy and frequent.* | **pious Jew/Muslim/Catholic etc** *There are 613 commandments required of a pious Jew.*

orthodox /ˈɔːʳθədɒks‖-dɑːks/ [adj] believing in, and following very closely, all the ideas, rules, and customs of one of the main religions, even when other people within the same religion do not always think they are important: *Orthodox Christianity teaches that Jesus was raised to life three days after he was crucified.* | *The Almoravids attempted to bring Africa back to orthodox Islamic practice.* | **orthodox Jew/Muslim/Christian etc** *This interpretation of Karma is rejected by orthodox Hindus.*

fundamentalist /ˌfʌndəˈmentəlɪ̈st/ [n C] someone who believes strongly that the laws of their religion must be followed very strictly: *The president's announcement is bound to anger religious fundamentalists.* | *When it comes to gay sex, fundamentalists and Catholics are more than willing to co-operate with each other.* | **Islamic/Muslim/Christian/Hindu etc fundamentalist** *The protest was led by a small group of Christian fundamentalists.* —**fundamentalist** [adj] *He claimed to speak for traditional family values and found support from various fundamentalist groups.* | *He belongs to the fundamentalist wing of the Umma party.*

6 to do something because of your religious beliefs

- observe
- be/feel called to do sth

observe /əbˈzɜːʳv/ [v T] if you **observe** a religious custom, you do something on a particular day or in a special way because it is part of your religion: *More than 90% of Jews said they observed the Day of Atonement.* | *Hakeem is currently observing the Muslim holy month of Ramadan, and fasts between sunrise and sunset.* | *Thursday is Ascension Day, when the church observes the bodily ascension of Christ into heaven.*

be/feel called to do sth /biː, fiːl ˌkɔːld tə ˈduː (sth)/ [v phrase] to do something because you feel that God is telling you to do it: *Father really felt he was called to preach by God.* | *Paul and his helpers were called to be missionaries for Jesus Christ.* | *Back then, people believed they were called to the ministry.*

7 to start to follow a particular religion

- become a Christian/Muslim/Buddhist etc
- convert
- turn to Jesus/the Lord/God/Christ

become a Christian/Muslim/Buddhist etc /bɪˌkʌm ə ˈkrɪstʃən/ [v phrase] *Saying the shahada is* *the first act through which you become a Muslim.* | *Most surprising of all, she's become a Buddhist.*

convert /kən'vɜːʳt/ [v I/T] if you **convert** to a particular religion, or if someone **converts** you, you join that religion: *Alpha is a religious programme that aims to change your life, not just convert you.* | **+ to** *My grandmother converted to Hinduism while living in India.* | *Within five years, he had converted thousands of Calvinists back to Catholicism.*

turn to Jesus/the Lord/God/Christ /ˌtɜːʳn tə 'dʒiːzəs, ðə 'lɔːʳd, 'gɒd, 'kraɪst‖-'gɑːd/ [v phrase] to become a Christian – used especially by Christians: *Do you turn to Jesus Christ our Lord and accept him as your Saviour?* | *Our message is a simple one – if you turn to God, God will bless and receive you.*

remain

to still exist after everything else has gone

RELATED WORDS

- stay in a place, not leave *see* **stay**
- continue to be the same, not change *see* **same (4), continue (11-12)**

1 to remain

- **left**
- **be left over**
- **remain**
- **survive**
- **be still standing/be left standing**
- **to spare**
- **to go**

left /left/ [adj not before noun] something or someone that is **left** is still there after everything or everyone else has gone or has been used: *Jones scored with only two minutes left in the fourth quarter.* | *Is there any milk left?* | *By 5 o'clock there was no one left in the office.* | **have sth left** *How much time do we have left to finish this?* | **the only one/person/thing etc left** *If Tracey leaves, I'll be the only girl left in the class.*

be left over /biː ˌleft 'əʊvəʳ/ [v phrase] something that **is left over**, especially money or food, is still there after you have used everything that you need: *I pay all the bills and save any money that is left over.* | **+ from** *Was there any food left over from the party?* | *Toy bears left over from an ad campaign will be donated to the children's hospital.*

remain /rɪ'meɪn/ [v I] formal if something **remains**, it still exists or is still available after everything else has gone, been used, or been dealt with: *We have dealt with most things, but a few small problems remain.* | *Some elements of the old class system still remain.* | **+ of** *Not much remained of the house after the fire.* | **remain to be done** *A few problems remain to be discussed.*

survive /səʳ'vaɪv/ [v I/T] to remain in existence even after a very long time has passed or after something dangerous has happened: *Many Roman roads still survive today.* | *The English language contains many Saxon words that have survived for over 1000 years.* | *Very few government buildings survived the bombing in Hanoi.*

be still standing/be left standing /biː ˌstɪl 'stændɪŋ, biː ˌleft 'stændɪŋ/ [v phrase] if something such as a building or tree **is still standing** or **is left standing** after a fire, explosion, or a very long time, it is left after many others have gone or been destroyed: *After the earthquake only a few houses were still standing.* | *Many of the trees Mrs. Socci planted are still standing, a hundred years later.* | *A stone chimney was the only thing left standing.* | *The old barracks are still standing on the north side of the island.*

to spare /tə 'speəʳ/ [adj phrase only after noun] if you have something such as money, time, or material **to spare**, there is some left after you have used as much as you need: *If you have time to spare, consider volunteering at your local school.* | **with sth to spare** *We arrived at the station with only a few seconds to spare before the train left.* | *Russia is large enough that you could fit the United States inside it with room to spare.*

to go /tə 'gəʊ/ [adj phrase only after noun] if you still have four miles, six hours, two years etc **to go**, you have that distance or length of time left before a journey or period of time is over: *Only another mile to go!* | *We've got another couple of hours to go before finishing.* | **with sth to go** *Evans scored with only two minutes to go in the game.*

2 words for describing someone or something that remains

- **remaining**
- **last**
- **spare**
- **leftover**
- **outstanding**

remaining /rɪ'meɪnɪŋ/ [adj only before noun] especially written the **remaining** people or things are the ones that are left when all the others have gone, been used, or been dealt with: *Combine the remaining ingredients, mixing well.* | *The remaining black bears are at risk from development in the area.* | *the Navy's one remaining aircraft-carrier*

last /lɑːst‖læst/ [adj only before noun] the **last** thing is the only one that remains: *I need to get some more film; this is my last roll.* | *The last five winners will be named next Tuesday.*

spare /speəʳ/ [adj usually before noun] left after everything else has been used, and therefore available to be used: *Are there any spare chairs we can borrow?* | *You can stay with us, we have a spare bedroom.* | **spare change** *I put my spare change in a charity collection box.* | **spare time** *A lot of kids don't have enough to do in their spare time, and that's when they get into trouble.*

leftover /'leftəʊvəʳ/ [adj only before noun] not used, not eaten etc at the end of a meal or an activity: *Use leftover turkey in casseroles and sandwiches.* | *She used leftover scraps of fabric to make a patchwork apron.* | *Take all your leftover bottles to be recycled.*

outstanding /aʊt'stændɪŋ/ [adj] work or money that is **outstanding** still has to be done or paid, especially after the time when it should have been done or paid: *We need time to catch up with outstanding orders.* | *Any outstanding claims must be settled by the end of the year.* | *There are a few problems still outstanding.*

3 the part of something that remains

- **the rest**
- **what is left of sth/ what remains of sth**
- **the last of sth**
- **the remainder**
- **the remains of sth**
- **leftovers**
- **ruins**
- **remnants**

the rest /ðə 'rest/ [n singular or plural] what is left after everything or everyone else has gone, been used, or been dealt with: *You carry these two bags and I'll bring the rest.* | *Homes were found for about 5,000 of the animals, but the rest had to be killed.* | **+ of** *What* *will you do with the rest of the money? | He'll be in a wheelchair for the rest of his life.*

what is left of sth/what remains of sth /ˌwɒt ɪz ˈleft əv (sth), ˌwɒt rɪˈmeɪnz əv (sth)/ [n phrase] the small amount that remains after everything else has gone, or been eaten, used, destroyed etc. **What remains of** is more formal than **what is left of**: *Soldiers were firing on what remained of the church. | At last she went, and I settled down to enjoy what was left of the afternoon.*

the last of sth /ðə ˈlɑːst əv (sth) ‖ -ˈlæst-/ [n phrase] the very last part of something that is left after everything else has gone: *The last of the tickets were sold Thursday. | This is the last of the paint, and I don't think it's going to be enough. | The judge sentenced the last of the three defendants in the case to 10 years.*

the remainder /ðə rɪˈmeɪndəʳ/ [n singular] formal the part of something that remains after everything else has gone: *£100 of the purchase price must be paid now, and the remainder is to be paid off in monthly installments.* | **+ of** *Simmer the soup uncovered for the remainder of the cooking time. | The school board agreed to suspend Linda Cole for the remainder of the school year.*

the remains of sth /ðə rɪˈmeɪnz əv (sth)/ [n plural] the part of something that remains after everything else has gone or been eaten, used, destroyed etc **+ of** *Archaeologists have discovered the remains of an ancient Roman village. | Each pile of gray ash was the remains of a house.*

leftovers /ˈleftˌəʊvəʳz/ [n plural] informal food that has not been eaten at the end of a meal: *We used the leftovers to make soup the next day. | It's a great way to use up leftovers.*

ruins /ˈruːɪ̥nz/ [n plural] the parts that remain when the rest of a building has been destroyed: *In Greece we spent a lot of time exploring old churches and ruins. | the ancient Mayan ruins at Chichen Itza* | **+ of** *Lumber was salvaged from the ruins of burned-out houses.*

remnants /ˈremnənts/ [n plural] the few parts of something that remain after people have stopped using it or after it has been destroyed: *Archeologists are worried that the ancient steps, walls, and other remnants may be lost forever.* | **+ from** *Two stained glass windows were remnants from when the building had been used as a church.* | **+ of** *Rescuers dug through the remnants of 342 cities, towns, and villages demolished in the earthquake. | The two leaders promised to work to remove any remnants of Cold War hostility.*

4 a very old object, custom etc that still exists

- relic
- hangover

relic /ˈrelɪk/ [n C] an object, custom, idea etc that is left from long ago in the past and that most people think is very old-fashioned: *The treaty is now a Cold War relic.* | **+ from** *The town is a relic from California's gold rush.* | **+ of** *Voters passed a bill to remove a law that is a relic of the state's racist past.*

hangover /ˈhæŋəʊvəʳ/ [n C usually singular] especially British something that is left over from a time in the past **+ from** *She knew that her feeling of awkwardness in social situations was a hangover from her schooldays | The company's debt is a hangover from its attempts to expand too rapidly.*

remember

RELATED WORDS

opposite: **forget**

▸ *see also* **remind/make sb remember, past**

1 to remember someone or something from the past

- remember
- think back/look back
- recall
- recollect
- reminisce
- memory
- nostalgia

remember /rɪˈmembəʳ/ [v I/T] if you **remember** something that happened, something you did, or someone or something you used to know, the thought of them comes back into your mind: *Do you remember your first day at school? | Oh yes, I remember now. We met him at the last conference, didn't we? | You remember the way to the bathroom, don't you? | Yes, I remember Janine. She lived in that house on the corner, and she had a pet rabbit.* | **+ who/what/where/how** *Can you remember what the man looked like? | I can't remember how the film ends.* | **+ (that)** *He remembered that he had felt just the same way when he first started working.* | **remember doing sth** *He remembered meeting her at a party once. | Older citizens remember eating soya beans during the Depression.* | **remember sb doing sth** *I don't remember him being that good at athletics in school. | He remembers Leonard coming home late at night, covered in blood.*

think back/look back /ˌθɪŋk ˈbæk, ˌlʊk ˈbæk/ [phr v I] especially spoken to think about something that happened in the past because you want to remember it: *She tried to think back and remember exactly what Jim had said. | Thinking back, I should have been more assertive.* | **+ to** *Think back to last year. Look how bad things were then. | When I think back to how it all started, I'm amazed.* | **+ on** *When I look back on those days, it always makes me sad. | When I think back on it now, I realize I expected too much from her.* | **think back five years/two days etc** (=try to remember what happened five years, two days etc ago) *I tried to think three years back. Where was it we had met?*

recall /rɪˈkɔːl/ [v I/T not in progressive] to deliberately remember a particular fact, event, or situation from the past in order to tell someone about it, especially in a law court or other official situation: *David recalled an incident that took place in the family home some 12 years previously. | 'I didn't like him very much,' Kev recalled. 'He was arrogant.' | As a child, she recalled, her parents had seemed very happy together.* | **+ what/how/when etc** *He didn't like to recall what a disaster his business venture had been.* | **+ that** *I recall that on at least one occasion I saw him taking money from the office.* | **recall doing sth** *Howard sighed. He could not recall ever being this tired before.* | **as I recall** (=that is what I recall) *The meeting went very well, as I recall.*

recollect /ˌrekəˈlekt/ [v T not usually in progressive] to be able to remember something, especially by deliberately trying to remember: *I recognize his face but I can't seem to recollect much about him. | 'The lawyers distorted what I wanted to say,' recollects Hansen grimly. | I can still recollect every detail of that meeting.* | **+ who/why/how etc** *Only later did she recollect where she'd seem him before.* | **+ that** *We have nine children, and I don't recollect that I ever* *felt the need to hit any of them.* | **recollect doing sth** *I do not recollect ever having been to Ohio, although my mother says we went there when I was a child.* —**recollection** /ˌrekəˈlekʃən/ [n C/U] **+ of** *He had no recollection of ever having received the money.*

reminisce /ˌremɪ̈ˈnɪs/ [v I] to talk about pleasant events, people, experiences etc from the past, because you want to remember them or enjoy talking about them: *At club meetings, we like to reminisce, remembering old times.* | **+ about** *I used to spend hours listening to my grandfather reminisce about life in the army.* | *Lazlo enjoyed reminiscing about his life in Poland before he went to America.* —**reminiscences** /ˌremɪ̈ˈnɪsənsɪ̈z/ [n plural] stories about events, people, experiences etc from the past, that people tell when they want to remember them: *David became a writer and published his reminiscences many years later.* | **+ about/of** *It was a night of pleasant talk, the two of them exchanging reminiscences about the war.*

memory /ˈmeməri/ [n C usually plural] something that you remember from the past about a person, place, or experience: *This place holds lots of memories for us.* | *Now, his experiences were just a painful memory.* | *We had to write a story about our earliest memory* (=the first event you can remember in your life). | **+ of** *I have lots of happy memories of my time in Japan.* | **bring back memories** (=makes someone think of a happy time in the past) *We're playing the old songs that I'm sure will bring back memories for you.*

nostalgia /nɒˈstældʒə‖nɑː-/ [n U] the slightly sad feeling you have when you remember happy things from the past: *There's a mood of nostalgia throughout the whole book.* | *a bittersweet film of nostalgia and innocence* | **+ for** *Reagan appealed to the average American's sense of nostalgia for a golden age.* —**nostalgic** [adj] making you remember happy times in the past: *a nostalgic visit to my home town* | *This song always makes me feel nostalgic.*

2 to try very hard to remember something

- try to remember
- think
- come back to
- cast your mind back
- rack your brains

try to remember /ˌtraɪ tə rɪˈmembəʳ/ [v phrase] *You must try to remember what happened – it's very important.* | *His name? Wait a minute. I'm trying to remember.* | **+ who/what/how etc** *I'm trying to remember how the theme tune goes.*

think /θɪŋk/ [v I] to try to remember something by deliberately thinking about it a lot **+ of** *You used to go out with the man from the bank, didn't you? I just can't think of his name.* | **try to think** *'What did you do with the keys?' 'Hang on, I'm just trying to think.'* | **+ what/why/how etc** *I can't think where I put it.* | *Just let me think what the title was.* | **think hard** (=use this to emphasize that you try to remember something) *If she thought hard enough, she could just about remember what her mother looked like.* | **think and think** (=think for a long time) *He thought and thought but he couldn't remember.*

come back to /ˌkʌm ˈbæk tuː/ [phr v I] if something **comes back to** you, you gradually start to remember it again after a lot of effort: *I can't think of the title at the moment, but it'll come back to me.* | *If you can remember all that, I'm sure the rest will come back to you.*

cast your mind back /ˌkɑːst jɔːʳ ˈmaɪnd bæk‖ˌkæst-/ [v phrase not in passive] British to try to remember something that happened a long time in the past: *Lisa, if you cast your mind back, I think you'll recall that it was your idea.* | **+ to** *Henry cast his mind back to the fateful evening.* | **+ over** *He frowned, casting his mind back over the conversation they had held.* | **cast your mind back forty years/three days etc** *Cast your mind back a few weeks to the Athletics Championship in Armagh.*

rack your brains /ˌræk jɔːʳ ˈbreɪnz/ [v phrase not in passive] to try extremely hard to remember something that you find very difficult to remember: *Desperately, Irvin racked his brains, but there was nothing he could tell them.* | *She racked her brains, trying to remember what David had said.* | **+ for** *They sat in silence, racking their brains for the name of the road.*

3 to remember something with difficulty

- vaguely remember
- have a hazy/vague recollection
- be on the tip of your tongue
- ring a bell

vaguely remember /ˌveɪgli rɪˈmembəʳ/ [v phrase] if you **vaguely remember** something, you can remember it slightly but not all the details are clear: *She still vaguely remembered her father, a distant figure who was barely ever there.* | **+ that** *I do vaguely remember, now that Kerry mentions it, that Pete was at the party.* | **+ what/how/who etc** *Bob, who'd been a vet in the army, vaguely remembered how to use a tourniquet.* | **vaguely remember doing sth** *He vaguely remembered meeting her in a club the night of the concert.*

have a hazy/vague recollection /hæv ə ˌheɪzi, ˌveɪg rekəˈlekʃən/ [v phrase] to be able to remember that something happened but not be able to remember the details clearly, especially because you did not notice the details at the time: *I do sort of remember meeting him, but I have only a hazy recollection.* | **+ of** *Davis claims he has only a vague recollection of the rape.* | **have a hazy/vague recollection of doing sth** *The next day she had a hazy recollection of getting drunk and dancing in a fountain.*

be on the tip of your tongue /biː ɒn ðə ˌtɪp əv jɔːʳ ˈtʌŋ/ [v phrase] if a name or word **is on the tip of your tongue**, you usually know it but have difficulty remembering it at the present moment: *His name's on the tip of my tongue. I'll think of it in a minute.* | *What was that place where they'd had dinner? It was on the tip of her tongue.*

ring a bell /ˌrɪŋ ə ˈbel/ [v phrase] if something, especially a name, **rings a bell**, you remember that you have seen or heard it before but you are now not sure of the details: *The name rings a bell, but I can't place it at the moment.* | **+ with** *'Gentle Ben's Brewing Company' will ring a bell with anyone who has lived in Arizona.*

4 to remember something very clearly

- remember sth well/vividly
- distinctly remember
- be fresh in your mind
- I can still hear/see/feel etc
- I will never forget
- remember sth as if it were yesterday
- relive
- stay with
- stick in your mind
- be haunted by

remember sth well/vividly /rɪˌmembəʳ (sth) ˈwel, ˈvɪvɪ̇dli/ [v phrase] *'Do you remember a guy called Casey?' 'Sure, I remember him well.'* | *It was a long, long time ago, but I remember it vividly.* | *What she remembered most vividly was the hopelessly sad expression in his eyes.* | **remember sth all too well/vividly** (=remember something that you would prefer to forget) *These men remember all too well the horrors of the Korean War.*

distinctly remember /dɪˌstɪŋktli rɪˈmembəʳ/ [v phrase] to remember the details about something extremely clearly, especially when it is not something that would usually stay in someone's memory **distinctly remember sth** *I distinctly remember her dress. It was blue with a red belt.* | **distinctly remember doing sth** *I distinctly remember being told that my father was away on a long business trip.* | **distinctly remember sb doing sth** *I distinctly remember him leaving the room at about 8.00 p.m.*

be fresh in your mind /biː ˌfreʃ ɪn jɔːʳ ˈmaɪnd/ [v phrase] if something **is fresh in your mind**, you remember it very clearly because it happened very recently or because it had a great effect on you: *The day war was declared is still fresh in my mind.* | *She wrote down the details of their conversation while they were still fresh in her mind.* | **with sth fresh in your mind** *It was going to be difficult forming a new relationship with the memory of Marian still fresh in his mind.*

I can still hear/see/feel etc /aɪ kən ˌstɪl ˈhɪəʳ/ to remember clearly the sight, sound, feel etc of something: *I can still see his face when I told him I wanted a divorce.* | *I can still hear my mother even now, singing away in the kitchen.* | *The next morning, on his way to the office, he could still feel the touch of her lips on his.*

I will never forget /aɪ wɪl ˌnevəʳ fəʳˈget/ especially spoken use this to say that you will remember something for a long time because it was very shocking, very enjoyable, very frightening etc: *I'll never forget the sight of him lying there in the hospital.* | *'I'm going to teach you a lesson you'll never forget,' said father grimly.* | **I'll never forget the first time/the day/the night etc** *I'll never forget the first time I ate sushi.* | *I'll never forget the day Linda told us she was gay.* | **+ how/what/who etc** *I'll never forget how he comforted me after my son died.*

remember sth as if it were yesterday /rɪˌmembəʳ (sth) əz ɪf ɪt wəʳ ˈjestəʳdi/ [v phrase] to remember something that happened a long time in the past so clearly that it seems to have happened very recently, especially because it had a great effect on you: *I remember sitting at that table and listening to him speak as if it were yesterday.* | *She remembers her husband being shot as if it were yesterday.*

relive /ˌriːˈlɪv/ [v T] to clearly remember something, especially an experience from the past, by imagining that you are doing it again now: *In my dreams, I often relived my fears and thought I was being attacked.* | *It's about a woman who is forced to relive her past when she discovers her long-lost brother.* | *I have relived that game many times and I still don't know how I missed the goal.*

stay with /ˈsteɪ wɪð/ [v T not in passive] if something such as an experience or event **stays with** you, you remember it for a very long time because it has such a great effect on you: *When a loved one dies, it stays with you – it doesn't just go away.* | **stay with someone for a long time/for the rest of their life** *The memory of the incident stayed with him for a long time.* | *Growing up in the countryside, she developed a passion for horses that stayed with her for the rest of her life.*

stick in your mind /ˌstɪk ɪn jɔːʳ ˈmaɪnd/ [v phrase] if an experience or event etc **sticks in your mind**, it is very difficult to forget: *That reminds me of another incident that sticks in my mind.* | *One picture of a young child especially stuck in my mind.* | *A trivial incident, perhaps, but one that has stuck in my mind.*

be haunted by /biː ˈhɔːntɪ̇d baɪ/ [v phrase] if you **are haunted by** something, especially something that you are worried about or afraid of, you find it extremely difficult to forget it so you are always thinking about it: *She was still haunted by what happened in Barcelona, although she had left twenty years earlier.* | *All his life, Whitman was haunted by a sense of loss and loneliness.*

5 when you will remember something for a long time

▸ memorable ▸ unforgettable

memorable /ˈmemərəbəl/ [adj] something that is **memorable**, especially an event or occasion, is so enjoyable, beautiful, unusual etc that you remember it for a long time: *One memorable afternoon, we visited a Shinto shrine.* | *What's your most memorable moment from your years on the stage?* | *The story was memorable because, as far as I recall, it was the only book in the school library that even mentioned a black person.*

unforgettable /ˌʌnfəʳˈgetəbəl/ [adj] something such as an event or occasion that is **unforgettable** has such a powerful effect on you that you will never be able to forget it: *The trip had been an unforgettable experience for both of them.* | *a series of unforgettable characters* | *one of the movie's unforgettable moments* | *To everyone who has ever heard a fairy tale, the image of being lost in a deep, dark wood is unforgettable.*

6 to remember something that you must do or need to have

▸ remember ▸ be sure
▸ not forget

remember /rɪˈmembəʳ/ [v I/T] *Did you remember your dictionary?* | *Remember, the examiner will expect you to demonstrate a knowledge of motorway driving too.* | **remember to do sth** *Did you remember to lock the back door?* | *I hope Dean remembers to buy some stamps.* | **+ (that)** *Do you think Kim remembers that we're supposed to be there at 8?*

not forget /nɒt fəʳˈget/ [v phrase] to remember something you must do – use this especially when it seems likely that you will not remember something: *Don't worry, I won't forget.* | *Don't forget your keys.* | **+ to do sth** *I hope she doesn't forget to water the plants.* | *You mustn't forget to switch that off when you've finished.* | **+ (that)** *I might be home late, but I haven't forgotten that we're going out.* | **don't forget to do sth** *Don't forget to turn out the lights before you leave.*

be sure /biː ˈʃʊəʳ/ [v phrase] if you tell someone to **be sure** to do something, you want them to remember that it is important that they do it **+ to do sth** *Be sure to ring me when you get in.* | **be sure and do sth** *Be sure and let me know if you need anything.* | **+ (that)** *Be sure that you make the effort to vote this year.* | *Be sure you have your driver's license and insurance ready to show the officer.*

7 to try to remember something that you may need to know later

- memorize
- note
- make a mental note
- bear/keep in mind

memorize ALSO **memorise** British /ˈmeməraɪz/ [v T] to learn facts, numbers, lines etc from a piece of writing or music, so that you can remember them later: *Wesley would pray for hours and memorize large sections of the Bible.* | *Don't write down your PIN number, memorize it.*

note /nəʊt/ [v T] to remember something, such as a fact or information, especially by writing it down, because you may need to know it in the future: *Before leaving, she noted the times of the return trains.* | **note down** (=to write the things you have to remember) *He read the text carefully, noting down the queries to be resolved later.* —**note** [n C] *I have notes to myself all over the house.* | **make a note of sth** *If you have any complaints, let me know and I'll make a note of them.*

make a mental note /meɪk ə ˌmentl ˈnəʊt/ [v phrase] to make yourself remember something because you may need to know it or do it in the future: *I let the remark pass, but made a mental note for myself.* | **+ to do sth** *I said nothing to Liz, but made a mental note to ask her sister about it later.* | **+ of** *As he came in, I made a mental note of where he put the keys.*

bear/keep in mind /ˌbeəʳ, ˌkiːp ɪn ˈmaɪnd/ [v phrase] to remember a fact or some information because it will be useful to you in the future **+ that** *Keep in mind that the teacher's previous experience in preparing students for the Cambridge exam can influence the results.* | **bear/keep sth in mind** *'You're always welcome to stay here, you know.' 'Thanks, I'll bear it in mind.'* | *For users unfamiliar with the system, there are a few general points to keep in mind.* | **be worth keeping/bearing sth in mind** *It's worth keeping in mind that drinks are cheaper before eight o'clock.*

8 the ability to remember things

- memory
- recall

memory /ˈmeməri/ [n singular] a person's ability to remember facts or past events: *He's got a good memory, but I wouldn't call him intelligent.* | **+ for** *I've got a terrible memory for names.* | **do sth from memory** *These stories were told and retold, mainly from memory.* | **lose your memory** (=no longer have the ability to remember things) *Was she losing her memory as well as her teeth?* | **photographic memory** (=the ability to remember exactly every detail of something you have seen) *She is blessed with a photographic memory.*

recall /rɪˈkɔːl‖rɪˈkɔːl, ˈriːkɔːl/ [n U] the ability to take information from your memory in order to use it: *Even in old age, his powers of recall were astonishing.* | *In advanced cases of the disease, there is a very rapid loss of recall and a decay of memory.* | **total recall** (=the ability to remember everything you want to remember) *Dinali has a brilliant mind, with almost total recall of what she has read.*

9 when you do something so that a person or event will not be forgotten

- in memory of sb/in sb's memory
- memorial
- commemorate

in memory of sb/in sb's memory /ɪn ˈmeməri əv (sb), ɪn (sb's) ˈmeməri/ [prep] if something is done **in memory of** someone who has died, it is done so that the person is not forgotten, and to show respect for them: *The monument was built in memory of all the soldiers who died in the war.* | *The statue was erected in 1888 in memory of John Wesley.* | *The inscription on the gravestone said simply, 'In memory of David James Flower 1892-1917.'* | *When Alfred Nobel died, an annual peace prize was established in his memory.*

memorial /mɪ̈ˈmɔːriəl/ [adj only before noun] a **memorial** concert, fund, service etc is made or done to show respect for someone who has died, especially someone who was important, so that that person will not be forgotten: *The memorial service was attended by the greatest names in Hollywood.* | *Eliot was asked to give the first Yeats memorial lecture in Dublin in 1940.* | *He met Saleh after a memorial ceremony for former president François Mitterrand.*

commemorate /kəˈmeməreɪt/ [v T] if something **commemorates** someone's death or an event where people died, it is done in order to show respect for them and to remind other people of the person or event: *The Eid commemorates the prophet Abraham's willingness to sacrifice his son at God's command.* | *When a famous citizen died, he was commemorated by a statue or a plaque.* | **commemorate sth with sth** *Vienna commemorated the 200th anniversary of Schubert's birth with a series of exhibitions and concerts.*

remind/make sb remember

RELATED WORDS

- to make you think of another similar person or thing *see* **like/similar (3)**
- *see also* **remember, forget**

1 to make someone remember something that they must do

- remind
- reminder
- don't forget

remind /rɪˈmaɪnd/ [v T] to make someone remember something they must do or something they need to know: *I'd love to have lunch next Wednesday, but you'll have to remind me.* | **remind sb about sth** *Pauline phoned to remind you about the party.* | **remind sb to do sth** *Remind me to buy some batteries for my Walkman, OK?* | **remind sb (that)** *I just want to remind you that your assignments must be completed by Friday.* | **remind sb how/what/when** *Write down a few notes to remind yourself what you want to say.* | **that reminds me** (=say this when someone says or does something that makes you remember to do something) spoken *Oh that reminds me – I'm supposed to take Cheryl to the airport tomorrow.*

reminder /rɪˈmaɪndəʳ/ [n C] a written note or something that someone says that reminds you about something you have forgotten or ignored, especially something that you must do: *The dentist's office sent you a reminder about your appointment next week.* | *Finally, a reminder that the school concert will be on December 17.*

don't forget /ˌdəʊnt fəʳˈget/ **spoken** say this to tell someone to remember something that you think they might forget: *Don't forget your keys.* | **+ to do sth** *Don't forget to mail that letter, will you?* | **+ (that)** *Don't forget that my mother's coming to visit this weekend.*

2 to make someone remember something they have forgotten

- jog sb's memory
- refresh sb's memory
- prompt

jog sb's memory /ˌdʒɒg (sb's) ˈmeməri‖ˌdʒɑːg-/ [v phrase] if a particular detail about someone or something **jogs someone's memory**, it makes them remember someone or something that they have forgotten: *Police hope the sketch will jog someone's memory and help identify the gunman.* | **+ about** *Something about what he said jogged my memory about an article I had read the month before.*

refresh sb's memory /rɪˌfreʃ (sb's) ˈmeməri/ [v phrase] to look at photographs, written information etc in order to help you remember facts or details that you already know but may have forgotten: *Before the exam he read through his notes once more to refresh his memory.* | *If you can't remember where you were on June 15, Mr Ball, maybe these photos will refresh your memory.*

prompt /prɒmpt‖prɑːmpt/ [v I/T] to remind someone, especially an actor in a play, what words to say when they have forgotten what they should say: *His job is to prompt the actors when they forget their lines.* | *Most of the children knew their lines so the director didn't need to prompt very much.* —**prompt** [n C] *He managed to say the whole speech without a single prompt.*

3 when something makes you remember something from the past

- remind sb of
- make sb think of
- bring/call to mind
- be a reminder
- bring back memories/take sb back
- evoke
- evocative
- come flooding back

remind sb of /rɪˈmaɪnd (sb) ɒv/ [v phrase] to make someone remember a person, thing, or time from the past: *The perfume always reminded him of his mother.* | *Walking across the field reminded me of the happy summers I'd spent on my grandparents' farm.* | **that reminds me of sb/sth** (=say this when someone says or does something that makes you remember someone or something) **spoken** *That reminds me of a joke I heard last week.*

make sb think of /ˌmeɪk (sb) ˈθɪŋk ɒv/ [v phrase] to remind someone of a person, experience, or time in your life: *I hate that smell – it makes me think of when I was in the hospital.* | *All this stuff just makes me think of Dan – I should get rid of it.* | *Baked beans always made her think of that first camping trip.*

bring/call to mind /ˌbrɪŋ, ˌkɔːl tə ˈmaɪnd / [v phrase] if events or experiences **bring to mind** something or **call to mind** something, they remind you of past events or experiences because they are very similar to them: *The case calls to mind the 1997 killing of a ten-year-old girl in upstate New York.* | *His account vividly brings to mind the descriptions of battles in Homer.*

be a reminder /biː ə rɪˈmaɪndəʳ/ [v phrase] to remind you of someone or something from the past, especially in a way that makes you sad: *The town wanted to forget the war but the destroyed bridge was a painful reminder.* | **+ of** *She kept all his letters as a reminder of their time together.* | **be a constant reminder** *The scar across his forehead was a constant reminder of the accident.*

bring back memories/take sb back /ˌbrɪŋ bæk ˈmeməriz, ˌteɪk (sb) ˈbæk/ [v phrase] if something **brings back memories** or **takes you back**, it reminds you of a particular and often pleasant event or experience from your past that you thought you had forgotten: *These old pictures really bring back some memories.* | *It's years since I heard any Beatles' music – it really takes me back.* | **bring back memories of sth** *The order and discipline of the job brought back memories of his army days.* | **take sb back to sth** *Staying in my old bedroom again takes me back to my childhood.*

evoke /ɪˈvəʊk/ [v T] **formal** to remind someone of how they felt at a particular time in the past by producing a particular feeling, emotion, or memory in them: *The movie evokes a simpler time when life was less complicated.* | *David hardly needed any encouragement to visit the sea, since it still evoked for him the happiest memories.*

evocative /ɪˈvɒkətɪv‖ɪˈvɑː-/ [adj] if something such as a poem, a painting, or an image is **evocative**, it makes people remember a particular part of their past by producing a particular feeling, emotion, or memory in them: *The air was full of evocative smells of flowers and freshly cut grass.* | **+ of** *The painting was evocative of all the sun and bright colours of Provence.*

come flooding back /kʌm ˌflʌdɪŋ ˈbæk/ [v phrase] if memories **come flooding back**, you suddenly remember them in a detailed way because of something that has happened: *As I began my speech all my teenage insecurities came flooding back.* | *He hadn't expected to see her, but he was surprised at how quickly memories of Paris came flooding back.*

4 to make you remember unpleasant experiences from the past

- drag up/rake up
- open/reopen old wounds

drag up/rake up /ˌdræg ˈʌp, ˌreɪk ˈʌp/ [phr v T] if someone **drags up** or **rakes up** things from the past that you would prefer to forget, they start talking about them and make you remember them **drag/rake sth up** *I said I was sorry, so I don't want you to keep raking it up again.* | **drag/rake up sth** *I don't know why you insist on dragging the past up every time we get together.*

open/reopen old wounds /ˌəʊpən, riˌəʊpən əʊld ˈwuːnds/ [v phrase] if an event or course of action **opens old wounds**, it reminds someone of an unpleasant experience from the past: *I'd prefer not to see my ex-wife – it will just open old wounds.* | *The spy trial has reopened old wounds in the immigrant community.*

remove

RELATED WORDS

- to take off clothes *see* **clothes (10-11)**
- to take something away from a place *see* **take**
- to get rid of something or someone *see* **get rid of**

1 to remove something from inside something else

- take out
- remove
- get out
- extract
- cut out
- pull out

take out /ˌteɪk ˈaʊt/ [phr v T] to take something from inside a container or place **take out sth** *She opened her briefcase and took out a letter.* | *I need to get to a cash machine and take out some money.* | *We'll have to take out the engine to fix the gearbox.* | **take sth out** *Roland reached inside his jacket and took his passport out.* | **take sth out of sth** *She took a few coins out of her purse.*

remove /rɪˈmuːv/ [v T] to take something from inside something. **Remove** is more formal than **take out**, and is used especially in writing: *Cut the fruit in half and remove the seeds.* | *He opened the torch and removed the bulb.* | **+ from** *Someone had removed some papers from the file.*

get out /ˌget ˈaʊt/ [phr v T] to remove something from deep inside something else, often when this is difficult **get sth out** *The spare wheel was right at the back of the boot under a load of suitcases, so it took me ages to get it out.* | **get sth out of sth** *It's important to get all the dirt out of the wound.* | **get out sth** *If you want to get out the old photo albums, you're going to have to dig in the bottom of that trunk.*

extract /ɪkˈstrækt/ [v T] to remove a natural substance from the ground or from a plant, or to take out someone's tooth: *42 tons of gold were extracted at the mine in 1987.* | *She had to have three teeth extracted.* | **extract sth from sth** *The nuts are crushed in order to extract the oil from them.* | *The bird uses its long beak to extract nectar from the flowers.*

cut out /ˌkʌt ˈaʊt/ [phr v T] to remove something from the inside of something else, using a knife **cut out sth** *Make sure you cut out any tough, gristly parts before you cook the meat.* | **cut sth out** *I knew I would have to cut the bullet out before the wound became infected.*

pull out /ˌpʊl ˈaʊt/ [phr v T] to suddenly take something out from a place where it cannot be seen, for example from a pocket, bag etc **pull out sth** *The man pulled out a gun and fired three shots.* | **pull sth out** *She pulled a notebook out and scribbled a few notes.*

2 to remove something that is fixed or joined to something else

- take off
- remove
- detach
- break/tear/cut off
- pick

take off /ˌteɪk ˈɒf/ [phr v T] to remove something that is fixed to something else **take sth off** *I took the lid off and tasted the soup.* | **take off sth** *He took off the old handle and fixed a new one in its place.*

remove /rɪˈmuːv/ [v T] to take off something that forms a piece or part of something else or that covers something else. **Remove** is more formal than **take off**, and is used especially in writing: *Remove all the fat, then cut the meat into cubes.* | *Make sure that the engine has cooled down before removing the radiator cap.* | **+ from** *She was in the hospital, having a lump removed from her breast.*

detach /dɪˈtætʃ/ [v T] formal to remove a piece or part of something that is designed to be removed: *Please detach the last section of this form, fill it in, and return it to us.* | *The control unit can be detached from the base.* —**detachable** [adj] *The coat has a detachable hood* (=that can be detached).

break/tear/cut off /ˌbreɪk, ˌteər, ˌkʌt ˈɒf/ [phr v T] to remove a part of something by breaking, tearing, cutting etc it **break/tear/cut off sth** *A van bumped into us, damaging one of the headlights and breaking off the aerial.* | *Tear off the coupon and send it to this address.* | *Winds reached over 100 mph, tearing off roofs and flattening trees.* | *He used to catch spiders and cut off their legs.* | **break/tear/cut sth off** *Gerard broke the handle off accidentally when he was trying to open the door.* | *I'd like to keep this part – is it alright if I tear it off?* | *He cut the top off the coconut.* | *He cut all his hair off as a protest.*

pick /pɪk/ [v T] to remove fruit from trees or flowers from the ground: *Migrant workers come to the orchard each autumn to pick apples.* | *I'll pick a few flowers to take to mum's.*

3 to remove something such as paint, dirt etc from a surface

- take off
- get off
- remove
- wipe/rub off
- scrape/scratch off
- peel off
- strip

take off /ˌteɪk ˈɒf/ [phr v T] **take off sth** *She was told to go to the washroom and take off her lipstick.* | **take sth off sth** *A standard detergent should take most of the grease off the surface.* | **take sth off** *Paint stripper is the easiest way to take old paint off.*

get off /ˌget ˈɒf/ [phr v T] to remove something such as paint, dirt, or marks from a surface **get sth off** *I don't know how I'm going to get this old varnish off.* | **get sth off sth** *How do you get mold stains off the wall?*

remove /rɪˈmuːv/ [v T] to take something off a surface, especially dirt, marks, or something that should not be there: *You can use lemon juice to remove the grease.* | **remove sth from sth** *Remove any dirt from the negative before printing the photograph.*

wipe/rub off /ˌwaɪp, ˌrʌb ˈɒf/ [phr v T] to remove something from a surface by wiping it or rubbing it with a cloth **wipe/rub sth off** *I wiped the paint off with my handkerchief.* | **wipe/rub sth off sth** *Mitchell tried to rub the dirt off the nameplate with his gloved thumb.* | *He wiped the dust off the piano.* | **wipe/rub off sth** *She picked up one of the shoes and carefully wiped off the mud.*

scrape/scratch off /ˌskreɪp, ˌskrætʃ ˈɒf/ [phr v T] to remove something from a surface by rubbing it with something sharp such as your fingernail or a knife **scrape/scratch off sth** *We started by scraping off the old wallpaper.* | *It took a long time to scrape off all the dirt and bits of food from the top of the cooker.* | *Someone had scratched some of the paint off my car.* | **scrape sth/it/them off** *The car was covered in rust and Joey had to scrape it off with a knife.* | *Lottery cards have silver panels which you scratch off to see if you have won a prize.*

peel off /ˌpiːl ˈɒf/ [phr v T] to remove something such as the skin of a fruit or a piece of paper from a surface, by gently pulling it **peel off sth** *Slice each avocado in half, then peel off the skin.* | **peel sth off** *When I peeled the label off I discovered that the old price was $2 cheaper.*

strip /strɪp/ [v T] to remove something that is covering the whole of a surface: *We stripped the doors down to the bare wood.* | **strip sth off** *I think we should strip the old varnish off and see what the wood's like underneath.*

4 to remove dirt from a piece of clothing or material

- get out
- shift
- come out
- wash out

get out /ˌget ˈaʊt/ [phr v T] to remove a mark from a piece of clothing or material **get sth out of sth** *What can I use to get these wine stains our of the tablecloth?* | **get sth out** *It's a pity about the mark on your shirt. Dry cleaning will probably get it out.*

shift /ʃɪft/ [v T] British informal to remove a mark which is difficult to remove from a piece of clothing or material: *I've washed the tablecloth three times, but I can't seem to shift these stains.* | *Blood stains are very difficult to shift.*

come out /ˌkʌm ˈaʊt/ [phr v I] if dirt or a mark **comes out**, it is removed by washing or cleaning: *Use plenty of washing powder otherwise mud and grass stains won't come out.*

wash out /ˌwɒʃ ˈaʊt‖ˌwɔːʃ-/ [phr v I] if dirt or a mark **washes out**, it is removed by washing: *A lot of hair dyes are designed to wash out after three or four washes.*

5 to remove writing, film, or music from paper, a tape etc

- delete
- rub out
- cross out
- erase
- cut
- edit out

delete /dɪˈliːt/ [v T] to remove part or all of a document in a computer, so that it no longer exists: *I think you should delete the second paragraph.* | *The computer automatically deletes any files you have not saved.*

rub out British **/erase** American /ˌrʌb ˈaʊt, ɪˈreɪz‖ɪˈreɪs/ [v T] to remove writing or pictures from paper by rubbing with a piece of rubber, or to remove writing or pictures from a board by rubbing with a cloth: *Use a pencil so you can erase your mistakes.* | **rub sth out** *I had to rub the whole thing out and start again.* | **rub out sth** *Someone had rubbed out my name.*

cross out /ˌkrɒs ˈaʊt‖ˌkrɔːs-/ [phr v T] to draw a line through a word to show that it was a mistake or that you want to change what you have written **cross out sth** *She crossed out the names of people who had left.* | **cross sth out** *That's not right. Cross it out and start again.*

erase /ɪˈreɪz‖ɪˈreɪs/ [v T] to remove writing, film, or music that has been recorded on a machine: *Is there any way I can erase this videotape so no one will see what's on it?* | *Somehow the magnets had erased the entire cassette.*

cut /kʌt/ [v T] to remove a section from a computer document, piece of writing, or film: *Some of the descriptions are a bit long and should be cut.* | *A couple of the scenes had to be cut because they were too violent.*

edit out /ˌedɪt ˈaʊt/ [phr v T] to remove something when you are preparing a book, piece of film etc for printing or broadcasting. **edit sth out** *If you make a mistake, don't worry – we can edit it out before the interview is shown.* | **edit out sth** *They had edited out several of the most important points in the article.*

6 the process of removing something

- removal
- extraction

removal /rɪˈmuːvəl/ [n U] **+ of** *Treatment usually consists of removal of the tumour combined with drug treatment.* | *Removal of the brake pads is a simple operation which can be done with a few basic tools.*

extraction /ɪkˈstrækʃən/ [n U] the process of removing a natural substance from the ground or from a plant, or removing a tooth from someone's body **+ of** *The protesters are opposed to the extraction of minerals in the area.* | *Dentists will only resort to extraction of a tooth when all other treatments have failed.*

7 a substance that is used to remove something

- remover
- stripper

remover /rɪˈmuːvəʳ/ [n C] **stain/paint/make-up etc remover** a substance that is used to remove stains, marks, make-up etc: *You can usually get coffee stains out with a stain remover.*

stripper /ˈstrɪpəʳ/ [n C] **paint/wallpaper stripper** a substance that is used to remove paint or wallpaper: *Always wear gloves when working with paint stripper.*

repair

RELATED WORDS

- *see also* **broken, damage, look after (7), condition (1-6)**

1 to repair something that is broken or damaged

- repair
- fix
- mend
- patch up
- overhaul
- service

repair /rɪˈpeəʳ/ [v T] if you **repair** something that is broken or not working properly, you work on it so that it is in good condition again: *Builders spent several weeks repairing the roof.* | *The plane was too badly damaged to be repaired.* | **get/have sth repaired** (=pay someone else to repair it) *How much will it cost to have the TV repaired?*

fix /fɪks/ [v T] to repair a machine or piece of equipment that is broken or not working properly: *I'll need to fix the boat before we can go out in it.* | **get/have sth fixed** (=pay someone else to fix it) *I must get my camera fixed before we go to France.*

mend /mend/ [v T] to repair something that is broken or not working, or something that has a hole in it. In American English **mend** is usually used about clothing: *The children are taught to mend their own clothes.* | *I called a service engineer in to mend the lift.*

patch up /ˌpætʃ ˈʌp/ [phr v T] to repair something that has a hole in quickly and not very thoroughly so that it is good enough to be used again for a short period of time **patch up sth** *We managed to patch up the roof enough to stop it leaking.* | **patch sth up** *The boat's got a hole in the side, but I'm just going to try and patch it up for now.*

overhaul /ˌəʊvəʳˈhɔːl/ [v T] to thoroughly examine a machine, vehicle, or piece of equipment and repair it if necessary: *The engine has been overhauled and runs much more smoothly now.* | **completely overhaul** *All the electrical wiring in the house was being completely overhauled because of the risk of fire.*

service /ˈsɜːʳvəs/ [v T] to examine a vehicle or machine, especially at fixed regular times, and repair it if necessary: *All our machinery is serviced regularly.* | *When was the plane last serviced?* | **have sth serviced** (=pay someone else to service it) *You should have your car serviced every six months.*

2 to repair something old to make it look or work like a new one

- renovate
- restore
- do up
- reconditioned

renovate /ˈrenəveɪt/ [v T] to thoroughly repair something, especially an old building, so that it looks as it did when it was first made: *The old theatre has been completely renovated and re-fitted.* | *We decided to buy an old house and renovate it ourselves.* | *He bought six old bicycles and renovated them.* —**renovation** /ˌrenəˈveɪʃən/ [n U] *a charming old property, suitable for renovation*

restore /rɪˈstɔːʳ/ [v T] to repair and clean an old and valuable building, vehicle, or work of art: *The building has been carefully restored after the fire.* | *Experts are still working to restore the painting.* | *He spent almost three years restoring a 1922 Rolls Royce.* —**restoration** /ˌrestəˈreɪʃən/ [n U] *The church was closed for restoration* (=so that it could be restored).

do up British informal **/fix up** American informal /ˌduː ˈʌp, ˌfɪks ˈʌp/ [phr v T] to repair an old vehicle or building so that it looks like a new one, especially as a way of making money **do/fix up sth** *He does up old cars and sells them.* | **do/fix sth up** *A builder bought the house and fixed it up.*

reconditioned /ˌriːkənˈdɪʃənd◂/ [adj] a **reconditioned** engine, motor, washing machine etc is an old machine that has been thoroughly repaired so that it works like a new one: *I managed to buy a reconditioned engine quite cheaply.* | *a shop selling new and reconditioned washing machines*

3 work done to repair something

- repairs
- maintenance
- service
- overhaul
- tune-up

repairs /rɪˈpeəʳz/ [n plural] *Who will pay for the repairs?* | **+ to** *The insurance will cover the cost of all repairs to the vehicle.* | **make/do/carry out repairs** *Builders are carrying out repairs to the roof and walls.*

maintenance /ˈmeɪntənəns/ [n U] regular work done to check, clean, and repair something so that it keeps working properly or remains in good condition: *The Highways Department is responsible for the construction and maintenance of bridges and roads.* | **car/motorcycle etc maintenance** *I knew nothing about car maintenance when I first bought my car.* | **routine maintenance** (=simple and regular maintenance) *The fault was discovered during routine maintenance work.*

service /ˈsɜːʳvəs/ [n C/U] an examination of a vehicle or machine that is done regularly to check that it is working properly and see if any repairs are necessary: *We recommend an annual service for all central heating boilers.* | *My car's due for service – I'll book it into a garage next week.* | *Any major problems with the car should be picked up at the 5,000 mile service.*

overhaul /ˈəʊvəʳhɔːl/ [n C] a thorough examination of a machine, vehicle, or piece of equipment, making repairs if necessary: *The electrical system needs a complete overhaul.* | *Work on the overhaul of the boiler has just started.*

tune-up /ˈtjuːn ʌp‖ˈtuːn-/ [n C] a process of making small changes and repairs to an engine so that it works as well as possible: *It's about time to take the car in for a tune-up again.* | *If you give the engine regular tune-ups, it will last much longer.*

4 too badly damaged to be repaired

- be beyond repair
- irreparable

be beyond repair /biː bɪˌjɒnd rɪˈpeəʳ‖-ˌjɑːnd-/ [v phrase] too badly damaged to be repaired – use this about objects, buildings, and vehicles: *Unfortunately, the engine is beyond repair.* | **be damaged beyond repair** *A lot of the furniture had been damaged beyond repair.*

irreparable /ɪˈrepərəbəl/ [adj] **irreparable** damage or harm to objects, buildings, or vehicles cannot be repaired: *The explosion caused irreparable damage to several buildings.* | *The forest suffered irreparable damage as a result of last year's fire.*

repeat

RELATED WORDS

- *see also* **again, say**

1 to do something again

- repeat
- do sth again
- redo
- retake

repeat /rɪˈpiːt/ [v T] to do something again or do something many times: *Holmes repeated the experiment several times and got the same results.* | *Repeat this exercise ten times every day and you'll soon have a flatter stomach.* | *After the students have finished, have them exchange roles and repeat the procedure.* —**repetition** /ˌrepəˈtɪʃən/ [n U] *Through constant repetition, he was starting to show some improvement in his skills.* | **+ of** *Repetition of movements is an important part of African dance.*

do sth again ALSO **do sth over** American /duː (sth) əˈgen, duː (sth) ˈəʊvəʳ/ [v phrase] to do something again, for example in order to practise it or because it was not done well enough the first time: *I'd like you to do this exercise again.* | *I'm afraid you'll have to do it over in pen.* | *She spilled coffee on the application form and had to do it all again.* | **do sth again and again/do sth over and over** *The coach made us do it again and again till we got it right.*

redo /riːˈduː/ [v T] to do something again because it was not done well enough the first time: *I can't read a word of this – you'll have to redo it.* | *They don't have the money to redo the plumbing right now.*

retake /ˌriːˈteɪk/ [v T] to do a written examination or other kind of test again because you have failed it: *Julie's had to retake her driving test at least three times.* | *He decided to retake the course and try to get a higher grade.* —**retake** /ˈriːteɪk/ [n C] British *The exam is in June. Retakes will be held in September.*

2 to say something again

- repeat
- say sth again
- reiterate
- repeat yourself
- repetition

repeat /rɪˈpiːt/ [v T] to say something again, for example because someone did not hear you or understand you: *'I just can't believe it,' he repeated.* | *Could you repeat the question? I wasn't listening.* | *The kidnappers have repeated their demand for ransom.* | **+ (that)** *She repeated that there was no need for alarm.* | **sth is worth repeating/sth bears repeating** *The news is hardly worth repeating.*

say sth again /ˌseɪ (sth) əˈgen/ [v phrase] especially spoken to say something again, either because someone did not hear you or because you want to emphasize it: *I'm sorry – could you say that again* | *I've said it before and I'll say it again: I've never trusted that man.* | *'It's OK. You're safe now,' she said again and again.* | **say again (that)** *Let me say again that the government has no intention of raising taxes.*

reiterate /riːˈɪtəreɪt/ [v T] formal to repeat an opinion or statement in order to make your meaning very clear: *The President reiterated his support for the treaty.* | **+ (that)** *Earlier in the day, Jones reiterated that he had no intention of firing Swenson.*

repeat yourself /rɪˈpiːt jɔːʳˈself/ [v phrase] to unintentionally repeat something you have already said: *Have I told you this before? Please stop me if I'm repeating myself.* | *Elmer seems pretty alert, but if you spend much time with him he starts to repeat himself.*

repetition /ˌrepəˈtɪʃən/ [n U] when you repeat something several times: *Repetition is good for helping children learn language.* | **+ of** *He builds his speeches around the repetition of certain key phrases.*

3 to repeat what someone else has said

- repeat
- quote
- quotation

repeat /rɪˈpiːt/ [v T] *Why do you have to repeat everything I say?* | *'He's planning to move,' she said, repeating what Bobby had told her.* | **repeat sth to yourself** (=repeat something, usually silently) *Henry kept repeating her phone number to himself so he wouldn't forget it.* | **repeat after me** *Repeat after me: 'I'm not going to waste any more money on lottery tickets.'*

quote /kwəʊt/ [v I/T] to repeat exactly something that someone else has said or written, especially someone famous: *He was always quoting clever sayings from Oscar Wilde's plays.* | **+ from** *To quote from the report: '6000 children die each day from curable diseases.'* | **don't quote me on it/that** (=say this when you are not completely sure of the facts you are stating) *I don't think the company is doing very well, but don't quote me on that.*

quotation /kwəʊˈteɪʃən/ [n C] a sentence or phrase from a book, poem etc, that you repeat because it is interesting or funny, or because it supports what you are saying: *I couldn't remember where I'd heard the quotation before.* | **+ from** *Spencer began his speech with a quotation from Karl Marx.*

4 to repeat the important parts of something

- go over
- recap

go over /ˌgəʊ ˈəʊvəʳ/ [phr v T] to repeat the important parts of a speech or explanation so that people can understand it better: *OK, I'll go over the plan one more time, but pay attention this time.* | *Don't worry if you don't understand everything – she'll go over the main points again at the end.*

recap ALSO **recapitulate** formal /riːˈkæp, ˌriːkəˈpɪtʃəleɪt/ [v I/T] to repeat the important parts of what has been said or done before in order to remind people: *At this point, I'd like to take a few moments to recap.* | *Before we start the discussion we should first recapitulate a little of last week's lecture.* | **+ on** British *She paused to recap on the story so far.*

5 to keep saying the same thing in an annoying way

- keep saying/asking/telling etc
- go on about

keep saying/asking/telling etc /ˌkiːp ˈseɪ-ɪŋ/ [v phrase] *She kept saying how rich her father was.* | *Don't keep telling me what to do – I know how to bake a cake.* | *The kids keep asking what time it is.*

go on about /gəʊ ˈɒn əbaʊt/ [phr v T] to keep talking about something in an annoying way: *She was going on about what a genius her brother is.* | **go on and on about sth** *I don't think I can stand another evening of Ted going on and on about his health problems.*

6 ways of asking someone to repeat something

- sorry?/pardon?
- what?/what did you say?
- would you mind repeating that?

sorry?/pardon? ALSO **excuse me?** American /ˈsɒri,‖ˈsɑːri, ˈpɑːʳdn, ɪkˈskjuːz miː/ spoken say this when you want to ask someone politely to repeat what they just said because you did not hear it: *'It's hot today, isn't it?' 'Pardon?'* | *'Could you tell me what time it is?' 'Sorry?'* | *'Damn,' I muttered. 'Excuse me?' said the clerk.*

what?/what did you say? /wɒt, ˌwɒt dɪd juː ˈseɪ/ spoken informal say this when you did not hear what someone said, or when you are surprised by what they said: *'Are you going to the bar?' 'What? Oh, yes, I suppose so.'* | *'Oh, shut up!' 'What did you say?'*

would you mind repeating that? ALSO **could you repeat that/the question etc?** /ˌwʊd juː ˌmaɪnd rɪˈpiːtɪŋ ðæt, ˌkʊd juː rɪˈpiːt ðæt/ use this in formal situations to ask someone to repeat something: *'My name's Marsden.' 'Would you mind repeating that, please?'* | *'How long have you been here?' 'I'm sorry, could you repeat that?'*

replace

RELATED WORDS

- instead of someone or something else *see* **instead**
- to put something where it was before *see* **put (2)**

1 to start doing a job that someone else used to do

- replace
- succeed
- take sb's place/take the place of sb
- take over
- supplant

replace /rɪˈpleɪs/ [v T] *We're looking for someone to replace our managing director.* | *The lead singer was replaced by Ray Willis back in 1992.* | *It was Johnson's first season after replacing Tom Landry as coach of the Cowboys.*

succeed /səkˈsiːd/ [v T] to be the next person to have a job or position, especially an important or powerful position, after someone else has left it or died: *The President appointed Harold Brown to succeed Les Aspin as chairman of the Commission in 1995.* | *George VI died in 1952, leaving his elder daughter Elizabeth to succeed him.*

take sb's place/take the place of sb /ˌteɪk (sb's) ˈpleɪs, ˌteɪk ðə ˈpleɪs əv (sb)/ [v phrase] to replace someone in a job or position, especially because you have similar skills and experience to them: *There's no one suitable to take Simon's place when he leaves.* | *If Mark fails to qualify as a trainee, Margaret is designated to take his place.* | *Thielen will take the place of Ray Owens on the board following Owens's retirement.*

take over /ˌteɪk ˈəʊvəʳ/ [phr v I/T] to replace someone in a job or position, and to continue the work they started: *The new manager took over in July.* | **+ from/for** *Do you think you'd be able to take over me when I'm gone?* | *The attorney general of New Jersey took over from the local district attorney in the case.* | **+ as** *We're pleased to announce that Mr. Schmidt will be taking over as Executive Director.* | **take over sth (from sb)** *Glover's understudy took over the role on Broadway.* | **take sth over (from sb)** *Maria's been my partner since I took the business over from my father.*

supplant /səˈplɑːnt‖səˈplænt/ [v T] to replace a competitor or enemy in a position of authority or influence, especially by using unfair methods: *General Salan was supplanted soon after the invasion by General Henri Navarre.* | *Adams, an excellent new pitcher, may supplant Hayes as starting pitcher by the end of the year.*

2 to do someone's job or work for a temporary period

- stand in for
- take over
- deputize
- sub for
- relieve
- cover for

stand in for /ˌstænd ˈɪn fɔːʳ/ [phr v T] to replace someone at work for a short time or on a particular occasion, because they are unable to be there: *Can you stand in for me at the meeting next week?* | *The President was unavailable and had the Vice President stand in for him.* | *During the dangerous scenes, a stunt woman stood in for Goldie Hawn.*

take over /ˌteɪk ˈəʊvəʳ/ [phr v I/T] to replace someone and do the same job as they were doing, so that they are free to have a rest or to do something else: *Liz, could you take over in reception while I make a couple of phone calls?* | **+ from/for** *Can I see you in my office, Carl? I'm sure Dan can take over from you.* | **take over sth** *After we'd stopped for lunch Sheila took over the driving for a while.*

deputize ALSO **deputise** /ˈdepjᵊtaɪz/ [v I] British to replace someone in a higher position for a limited period or on a particular occasion, especially when they are busy doing something else: *My boss had to go to the Caribbean unexpectedly and asked me to deputize.* | **+ for** *The Foreign Minister will be deputizing for the Prime Minister while he recovers from his operation.* | *Paine, the second in command, deputized for the Colonel.*

sub for /ˈsʌb fɔːʳ/ [phr v T] American informal to replace someone at work on a particular occasion, especially as a teacher or a member of a sports team: *Could you sub for me Monday? I have a doctor's appointment.* | *Eisenreich subbed for the injured Alou in Wednesday's game.*

relieve /rɪˈliːv/ [v T] to replace someone, especially a soldier, when they need a rest or when they have completed their hours of work: *Can anyone relieve Tammy? She's been on duty for ten hours without a break.* | *He was sent to Cairo to relieve Captain Roberts for a few days.*

cover for /ˈkʌvəʳ fɔːʳ/ [phr v T] to do the work, or to be ready to do the work, of someone who is absent: *Go and get some lunch. I'll cover for you.* | *My name's Dr Brown. I'm covering for Dr Steele while he's on holiday.*

3 someone who replaces another person

- replacement
- successor
- stand-in
- substitute
- acting
- supply teacher

replacement /rɪˈpleɪsmənt/ [n C] someone who replaces another person in a job or in a team, especially permanently: *Steve just announced he was leaving, but the coach has already started looking around for a replacement.* | **+ for** *I'm just a temporary replacement for the receptionist.* | *They asked Barbara to stay on until they could find a suitable replacement for her.*

successor /səkˈsesəʳ/ [n C] the next person to have a permanent job or position after someone else has left it: *Mason is Case's chosen successor as committee chairman.* | *Smyth resigned as Chief Superintendent two months ago and they still haven't appointed his successor.* | **+ to** *The Orchestra is currently searching for a successor to music director James Sedares.*

stand-in /ˈstænd ɪn/ [n C] someone who temporarily takes another person's place in a job or performance when they are unable to do it themselves, especially when this happens unexpectedly: *Ms Green couldn't be here today, so I'm her stand-in.* | *Ann was Shirley MacLaine's stand-in in the movie.* | **+ for** *I'd like Tom to act as a stand-in for Julian until he returns to work.*

substitute ALSO **sub** informal /ˈsʌbstᵊtjuːt‖-tuːt, sʌb/ [n C] someone who takes someone else's place in a team for a limited period of time, especially because the other person is injured or tired: *If Marsh has not fully recovered, his likely substitute will be Robinson.* | *With key players out of energy, it* *was a sub who scored six points in the last two minutes and won the game.* | **bring sb on as a substitute for sb** *Ten minutes into the second half Davies was brought on as substitute for Ward.*

acting /'æktɪŋ/ [adj only before noun] an **acting** chairman, director, manager is someone who replaces someone in a position of authority for a limited period of time: *While Kershaw was in the hospital Saunders became acting chairman.* | *Mrs Hamilton has been appointed acting head of the school until a permanent replacement can be found.*

supply teacher British **/substitute teacher** American ALSO **sub** American informal /sə'plaɪ ˌtiːtʃəʳ, 'sʌbstɪtjuːt ˌtiːtʃəʳ‖ -tuːt-, sʌb/ [n C] informal a teacher who replaces another teacher for a limited period of time: *We'll need a sub for Dawn's class tomorrow.* | *The kids always misbehave when they have a substitute teacher.* | *Ray was working as a supply teacher to earn some extra money.*

4 to put someone into someone else's job

- replace

replace /rɪ'pleɪs/ [v T] *They still haven't replaced three of the managers who resigned.* | *I hate to see Gretchen go – we'll never be able to replace her.* | **replace sb with sb** *The firm has been dismissing experienced staff and replacing them with younger people on lower salaries.*

5 to replace an older type of machine, method etc

- replace/take the place of
- supersede
- give way to

replace/take the place of /rɪ'pleɪs, ˌteɪk ðə 'pleɪs ɒv/ [v T/v phrase] *In most offices, computers have replaced the old typewriters.* | *One 'smart card' can take the place of cash, cheques, and credit cards.* | *Gas and electricity have almost completely replaced coal for domestic cooking and heating in Britain.* | *Ugly new concrete buildings have taken the place of the old houses.*

supersede /ˌsuːpəʳ'siːd, ˌsjuː-‖ˌsuː-/ [v T] if a new invention, idea, or method **supersedes** another one, it replaces it because it is more modern or effective: *Iron began to supersede bronze for tool making about 3000 years ago.* | *The computers used to be top of the line, but they have been superseded by more recent models.* | *It is unlikely that scientific thinking will ever entirely supersede superstition and religion.*

give way to /ˌgɪv 'weɪ tuː/ [v phrase] to be gradually replaced by something better, more suitable, or more advanced: *Hunting and fishing settlements gave way to small towns as the population grew.* | *With the rise in oil prices, big American cars were forced to give way to smaller, more economical models.*

6 to put something new in the place of something old, damaged, or broken

- replace
- renew
- change

replace /rɪ'pleɪs/ [v T] *Your car's in good condition but you ought to replace the tires.* | *Before we move in, the place has to be redecorated and all the carpets replaced.* | **replace sth with sth** *They're going to replace the old wooden bridge with one made of concrete.*

renew /rɪ'njuː‖rɪ'nuː/ [v T] British to replace something, such as a piece of machinery or equipment, after it has been used for a certain length of time and is damaged or likely to be damaged: *You should check the engine carefully, renewing any parts that are worn or damaged.* | *It is wise to renew your water filter every month, even though it may seem to be working satisfactorily.*

change /tʃeɪndʒ/ [v T] to replace a piece of equipment when it is broken or not working: *Can you change this light bulb for me? I can't reach.* | *All drivers should really know how to change a flat tire.* | *You should change or clean your furnace filter once a month to improve performance.*

7 to use one thing instead of something else or change one thing for another

- substitute
- switch/swap

substitute /'sʌbstɪtjuːt‖-tuːt/ [v T] to use something new or different instead of something else, especially when cooking: *If plums are difficult to find, figs can be substituted.* | **substitute sth for sth** *You can substitute margarine for butter in this recipe.*

switch/swap /swɪtʃ, swɒp‖swɑːp/ [v T] to secretly replace two things without someone knowing: *Someone must have switched the suitcases at the airport when I wasn't paying attention.* | **switch/swap sth for sth** *Wait till he goes out, then we can swap your book for his.*

represent

to speak or do things for someone else because they have asked you to, for example in a meeting, competition, or law court

RELATED WORDS

- to have a particular meaning *see* **meaning**
- *see also* **government (3)**

1 to represent a person or group

- represent
- on behalf of sb/on sb's behalf
- speak for
- act for
- play/run/swim etc for

represent /ˌreprɪ'zent/ [v T] if you **represent** a person or group at a meeting or in a law court or parliament, you give their opinions and make decisions for them; if you **represent** a country, school etc in a competition, you have been chosen to compete for that country or school: *Each class will elect two students to represent them on the School Council.* | *Trade Unions representing ambulance workers yesterday agreed to accept a 5% pay increase.* | *The new law has been criticized by groups representing disabled people.* | *The athletes will represent China in this year's Olympic Games.* | *Wilson was represented in court by a top criminal lawyer.*

on behalf of sb/on sb's behalf /ɒn bɪ'hɑːf əv (sb), ɒn (sb's) bɪ'hɑːf‖-bɪ'hæf/ [prep] if you speak to people **on behalf of** someone, you express their ideas, opinions, or feelings for them: *On behalf of* *everyone here, I'd like to wish Ted a long and happy retirement.* | *I would like to thank you all on my mother's behalf for all your cards and good wishes.* | **act on behalf of sb** *The lawyer acting on behalf of Mrs Anderson said he would continue the fight to clear her name.*

speak for /'spiːk fɔːʳ/ [phr v T] to represent a group of people by expressing their feelings, thoughts, or beliefs: *David Blunkett, speaking for the Labour Party, said more money should be spent on higher education.* | *I can only speak for my own family, not for the other families involved in this case.*

act for /'ækt fɔːʳ/ [phr v T not in passive] to represent someone by making decisions for them, especially legal or financial decisions: *It's a good idea to have an estate agent to act for you when you are selling a house.* | *Lawyers acting for the defendant asked for her case to be adjourned while they examined new evidence.*

play/run/swim etc for / 'pleɪ fɔːʳ/ [phr v T not in passive] if you **play, run, swim etc for** a school, club, or country, you represent it in a sports competition against other schools, clubs, or countries: *Playing rugby for England had always been one of his dreams.* | *I used to swim for my school.* | *Simon Short, running for Scotland, is in the lead as they come round the final bend.*

2 someone who represents a person or a group

- representative
- spokesman/ spokeswoman
- spokesperson
- agent
- envoy
- delegate
- mouthpiece

representative /ˌreprɪ'zentətɪv/ [n C] someone who has been chosen to represent an organization or country: *Japan has refused to send a representative to the talks in Geneva.* | *John Kohorn is the company's representative in Prague.* | **+ from** *the representative from Belgium* | **+ of** *We discussed these issues with a senior representative of the company.*

spokesman/spokeswoman /'spəʊksmən, 'spəʊksˌwʊmən/ [n C] a person who officially gives the opinions of an organization, company, government etc **+ for** *A spokesman for the company denied reports that the new drug could cause heart attacks.* | **government/ministry/party etc spokesman/ spokeswoman** *A government spokeswoman said the new laws would protect vulnerable children.* | *Mr Simon Hughes, a company spokesman, spoke to reporters after the meeting.*

spokesperson /'spəʊksˌpɜːʳsən/ [n C] a word meaning **spokesman** or **spokeswoman**, used especially when you do not want to say whether the person is a man or a woman **+ for** *A spokesperson for the company read to waiting reporters from a prepared statement.* | **+ on** *the Labour Party spokesperson on education* | **government/party/union etc spokesperson** *A government spokesperson has denied the allegations of corruption.*

agent /'eɪdʒənt/ [n C] a person or company which represents another person or company in business, financial, or legal matters: *The firm has an agent in Sydney who deals with the Australian side of the business.* | *The licence application must be signed by the applicant or his agent.* | **+ for** *The company is the UK agent for a top Danish furniture maker.*

envoy /'envɔɪ/ [n C] a person who is sent to another country as an official representative, especially by a government to discuss important matters such as war with another government: *The President met yesterday with an envoy from Pakistan.* | **send an envoy** *Iran agreed to send an envoy to the United Nations for talks on ending the war.* | *A special envoy was sent to Manila to try and secure the release of the hostages.*

delegate /'deləgət/ [n C] someone who is sent to an important meeting by a country or organization in order to represent them by speaking for them and voting for them: *I sat next to the Canadian delegate.* | **+ to** *The US delegate to the committee announced a grant of $75 million to help third world countries.* | **send a delegate** *Some local branches have refused to send delegates to the national conference.*

mouthpiece /'maʊθpiːs/ [n C usually singular] a person, organization, or newspaper which only gives the opinions of one person or organization and which does not have anything original to say: *In 1917 Stalin became editor of Pravda, the official mouthpiece of the Communist Party.* | *The Chemical Manufacturers Association is the mouthpiece of the American chemicals industry.*

3 a group of people who go somewhere to represent a country or organization

- delegation
- deputation
- mission

delegation /ˌdelə'geɪʃən/ [n C with singular or plural verb in British English] a team of people who have been sent by an organization or a country to represent them at an important meeting **+ of** *The health ministers agreed to meet a delegation of heart patients.* | **+ from** *A delegation from Nigeria has arrived to have talks with the British foreign minister.* | **send a delegation** *Headteachers have sent a delegation to London to ask the government to put more money into education.* | **lead a delegation** *The Dutch Prime Minister led a 12 member economic delegation to Indonesia to discuss future investments in the country.*

deputation /ˌdepjʊ'teɪʃən/ [n C with singular or plural verb in British English] formal a group of people representing a larger group who are sent to talk to a person in authority in order to make a complaint or a request **+ of** *A deputation of church leaders has met with the government to discuss the teaching of religion in schools.* | **meet/receive a deputation** *In the morning the minister received a deputation from the National Union of Farmers protesting about the government's plans to cut agricultural subsidies.*

mission /'mɪʃən/ [n C with singular or plural verb in British English] a group of people who are sent by their government to another country in order to discuss something: *The French President has sent a mission to the region to try to find a peace formula.* | **trade mission** (=a mission to discuss trade) *A British trade mission has arrived in Moscow.*

4 someone who officially represents their government

- diplomat
- diplomatic
- ambassador
- embassy

diplomat /'dɪpləmæt/ [n C] *Ambassador Thompson is an experienced diplomat who has served in France, South America, and the Middle East.* | *British and Argentinian diplomats met to discuss peace.*

diplomatic /ˌdɪplə'mætɪk◂/ [adj only before noun] relating to the people who officially represent their government in a foreign country: *Most members of the European diplomatic community have already left the country as war now seems inevitable.* | **diplomatic service** (=the government department that employs diplomats) *He joined the diplomatic service and was posted to Ankara.* | **diplomatic relations** (=the relationship between governments that depends on having diplomats in each others' countries) *The governments of Britain and Syria are anxious to re-establish diplomatic relations.*

ambassador /æm'bæsədəʳ/ [n C] a diplomat of the highest rank who is the official representative of their government in a foreign country **a British/French/US etc ambassador** *Sir Auckland Geddes is the British ambassador to Washington,* | **+ to** *Ms Takahashi was the first Japanese woman ever to be appointed ambassador to a foreign country.*

embassy /'embəsi/ [n C] the group of people who are sent to live in a foreign country in order to officially represent their government in that country **the British/French/American etc embassy** *Travellers in Spain who are worried about the situation are advised to contact the British Embassy in Madrid.* | *The American Embassy employs 50 local people in administrative positions.*

reputation

the general opinion that people have about a person, organization, place etc

RELATED WORDS

▸ *see also* **opinion, position/rank**

1 the opinion that people have about a person, organization etc

- ▸ reputation
- ▸ image
- ▸ name
- ▸ standing
- ▸ prestige
- ▸ stature
- ▸ character

reputation /ˌrepjʊ'teɪʃən/ [n C usually singular] the general opinion that people have about a person, organization etc based on what they have heard, read, seen, or experienced **+ as** *Despite her reputation as a trouble-maker, she was promoted to department manager.* | **+ for** *a brilliant director with a reputation for thoroughness* | **excellent/good/bad etc reputation** *I am surprised that a company with your good reputation would produce such poor quality goods.* | *She found his terrible reputation one of his greatest attractions.* | **have a good/bad etc reputation** *The school had an excellent academic reputation.* | *The area has a really bad reputation but it isn't as bad as people think.* | **win/earn/gain a reputation as sth** *The town's Dolphin Centre had gained a reputation as one of the best leisure complexes in the country.* | **have a reputation of/for being** *The mill has the reputation of being one of the most energy-efficient in the world.* | **live up to your reputation** (=be as good, bad etc as people say) *The restaurant certainly lived up to its reputation; the food was delicious.*

image /'ɪmɪdʒ/ [n singular] the idea that people have about a well-known person, company, or product – use this especially about an idea that is deliberately created through newspaper stories, advertising etc **+ as** *Perth is proud of its image as a breeding ground for 'don't-take-no-for-an-answer' entrepreneurs.* | **be bad/good for sb's image** *The President's advisers said it would be bad for his image to be photographed with union leaders.* | **improve your image** *The party is seeking to improve its image with female voters.* | **project an image** (=make an image) *The princess tried to project an image of herself as serious and hardworking.*

name /neɪm/ [n singular] the reputation a person or an organization has because of something they do or because of the quality of what they produce, usually when this is good **good/bad name** *He's a determined man and he values his good name.* | **have a name for doing sth** *This man has a name for making tough business deals.* | **get a good/bad name** *Teenagers tend to get a bad name for being moody.* | **make a name for yourself** (=become known and admired by many people) *Marks and Spencer have made a name for themselves as a producer of high quality goods at reasonable prices.*

standing /'stændɪŋ/ [n U] someone's reputation and position in a group or society, based on other peoples' opinion of them **social/moral/professional etc standing** *The class system in Great Britain encourages people to be very aware of their social standing.* | *This legal case is very likely to damage the company's professional standing.* | **national/international etc standing** *Jacques Tati was a man of international standing in the world of screen comedy.*

prestige /pre'stiːʒ/ [n U] the respect and good reputation a person, organization, profession etc has because they have a high position in society, are admired by people etc: *The teaching profession has lost the prestige it had in former times.* | *Hosting the Olympic Games would add to our country's international prestige.* | *Becoming a film star confers status, power, prestige and wealth.*

stature /'stætʃəʳ/ [n U] a reputation for being very good at something, very important, or very influential that makes people respect you: *At that time there were no other universities in England equal in stature to Oxford and Cambridge.* | **+ as** *As he got older, Picasso's stature as an artist increased.* | **of world/international etc stature** *a British architect of international stature*

character /'kærɪ̥ktəʳ/ [n U] formal someone's reputation, especially whether or not other people think they are honest or morally good: *A person's character is very important to me when I decide who I want to work with.* | **be of (good/bad) etc character** *Her husband was a man of good character, well-liked and respected by his colleagues.*

2 having a good reputation

- ▸ reputable
- ▸ prestigious
- ▸ be well thought of
- ▸ prestige

reputable /'repjʊ̥təbəl/ [adj] a **reputable** company or business person has a good reputation and can be trusted: *If you are going to be out late, book a taxi from a reputable firm.* | *We chose that company because we thought they were reputable.* | *Most reputable suppliers advertise in Birds magazine.* | **a reputable source** *Only buy floppy disks that have come from a reputable source.*

prestigious /pre'stɪdʒəs‖-'stiː-, -'stɪ-/ [adj only before noun] a **prestigious** organization, event, or product has a reputation of being one of the best of its kind and is highly respected: *I am a partner in one of Cleveland's oldest and most prestigious law firms.* | *The anxiously awaited invitations to the prestigious end-of-year dance began to arrive.* | *Women are attaining powerful and prestigious managerial positions.*

be well thought of /biː ˌwel ˈθɔːt ɒv/ [v phrase] if a person or their work **is well thought of**, they have a good reputation for the quality of their work: *Richards is well thought of within his own firm.* | *Millet's work is less well thought of today than it was during his lifetime.*

prestige /preˈstiːʒ/ [adj only before noun] **prestige** goods, products, services etc cost a lot and have a very good reputation: *There are always prestige neighbourhoods where only the wealthy or successful can afford to live.* | *champagne, caviar, truffles and other prestige goods*

3 to damage the reputation of someone or something

- harm/damage sb's reputation
- give sb/sth a bad name
- bring sb/sth into disrepute
- discredit/bring discredit on
- character assassination
- slur/stain on sth
- smear campaign/ whispering campaign

harm/damage sb's reputation /ˌhɑːʳm, ˌdæmɪdʒ (sb's) repjᵘˈteɪʃən/ [v phrase] *If a representative gets drunk at a convention, it may harm their firm's reputation.* | *Sabine was completely loyal to you. She would never do anything to damage your reputation.*

give sb/sth a bad name /gɪv (sb/sth) ə ˌbæd ˈneɪm/ [v phrase] to give a group or place a bad reputation by behaving in an unacceptable way: *Students who are rude and scruffy give the school a bad name.* | *The regular brawling and violence in the bar had given it a bad name.* | *He was the type of person that gives insurance salesmen a bad name.*

bring sb/sth into disrepute /ˌbrɪŋ (sb/sth) ɪntə ˌdɪsrɪˈpjuːt/ [v phrase] formal to damage the reputation of the organization that you work for or the job that you do by doing something bad or illegal – use this especially in legal or official contexts: *This is exactly the kind of incident that brings international companies into disrepute.* | *The officers were charged with bringing the police force into disrepute.*

discredit/bring discredit on /dɪsˈkredᵻt, ˌbrɪŋ dɪsˈkredᵻt ɒn/ [v T/v phrase] to make people stop trusting or believing in someone or something: *There was a plot by certain members of the opposition to discredit the government.* | *The old leaders were discredited by the massive defeats at Verdun and Flanders.* | *Through your selfishness, you have brought discredit on yourself and your whole family.*

character assassination /ˈkærᵻktər əsæsᵻˌneɪʃən/ [n C/U] a cruel and unfair attack on someone's character: *All too often politicians discredit themselves by engaging in character assassination.*

slur/stain on sth /ˈslɜːʳ, ˈsteɪn ɒn (sth)/ [n C] something that harms someone's character, reputation etc in someone's opinion **a slur/stain on sb's character/reputation etc** *Baker accused the press of casting a slur on his reputation.* | *He was discharged from the army without a stain on his character.*

smear campaign/whispering campaign /ˈsmɪəʳ kæmˌpeɪn, ˈwɪspərɪŋ kæmˌpeɪn/ [n C] an attempt to damage the reputation of a political opponent by secretly spreading false ideas about them, for example by telling a newspaper that they have done bad or dishonest things: *Kingsley denies all the rumours, saying he's the victim of a vicious smear campaign.* | **+ against** *Allegations of instability, untrustworthiness and lack of political judgement – all these were part of the whispering campaign against her.*

responsible

RELATED WORDS

- when someone is responsible for sth bad happening *see* **fault (3)**
- to be in charge of a company or group of people *see* **in charge of**

1 when it is someone's job or duty to do something

- be responsible for/have responsibility for
- be up to
- be in charge of
- take care of/look after
- the onus is on sb

be responsible for/have responsibility for /biː rɪˈspɒnsᵻbəl fɔːʳ‖-ˈspɑːn, hæv rɪˌspɒnsᵻˈbɪlᵻti fɔːʳ‖-ˌspɑːn-/ [v phrase] if you **are responsible for** or **have responsibility for** doing something, it is your job or your moral or legal duty to do it: *The CEO is responsible for the day-to-day operation of the company.* | *Why is it in our society that women are primarily responsible for raising children?* | *The Navy has responsibility for the defense of the island.* | *The health minister has overall responsibility for Britain's hospitals.*

be up to /biː ˈʌp tuː/ [v phrase] if something **is up to** you, you are the person who is supposed to do it: *She's done her part of the job. The rest is up to Phillip.* | **it is up to sb to do sth** *It is up to the teacher to keep the class quiet and working hard.*

be in charge of /biː ɪn ˈtʃɑːʳdʒ ɒv/ [v phrase] to be the person who controls something and is responsible for it: *Who's in charge of the club's finances?* | *The UN officer is in charge of coordinating all refugee programs in the region.* | *The agency in charge of enforcing Mexico's gun laws declined requests for an interview.*

take care of /look after British /ˌteɪk ˈkeər ɒv, ˌlʊk ˈɑːftəʳ‖-ˈæf-/ [phr v T] to be responsible for a particular part or area of an organization, process, system etc: *My assistant takes care of all the travel arrangements – you'll have to ask him.* | *Sally looks after the accounts, and I'm in charge of the building itself.*

the onus is on sb /ði ˈəʊnəs ɪz ɒn (sb)/ if **the onus is on** someone to do something important or to make sure that something important is done, it is their responsibility to do it, without waiting to be helped or told to do it: *The onus of restarting the economy is on the government.* | **+ to do sth** *The onus is on the taxpayer to make sure they pay enough tax.* | *At university the onus is on you to work hard – no one is going to force you.*

2 something that is your job or your duty to do

- responsibility
- sb's job
- sb's duty
- burden

- *see also* **area (9)**

responsibility /rɪˌspɒnsᵻˈbɪlᵻti‖rɪˌspɑːn-/ [n C] something that you have to do because it is your job or your duty, for example dealing with something or looking after someone: *The house is my responsibility, and I can't just let it fall apart.* | *Having children is a big responsibility and I'm not sure I'm ready for that yet.* | **+ to do sth** *It is a manager's responsibility to set clear expectations for his or her employees.* | **take on a responsibility** (=accept a responsibility) *I have a bad habit of taking on more responsibilities than I can handle.*

sb's job / (sb's) 'dʒɒb‖-'dʒɑːb/ [n phrase] spoken something that someone is responsible for doing: *I'm not doing the shopping – that's your job.* | *Agency employees must enforce regulations once they're approved. That's their job.* | **it's sb's job to do sth** *It's my job to make sure all the guests are comfortable.*

sb's duty / (sb's) 'djuːti‖-'duː-/ [n phrase] something that someone is officially, morally, or legally responsible for doing: *I don't give out parking tickets because I like to – it's my duty.* | **it is sb's duty to do sth** *I think it's your duty to tell her what you know.* | *My duty as a police officer is to find out the facts and communicate them to the proper people.* | **do your duty** *As the families wept openly, the prosecutor urged the jury to do its duty and convict Ballenger.*

burden /'bɜːʳdn/ [n C] something difficult or worrying that you are responsible for: *Running the business on my own can be a burden at times.* | **+ of doing sth** *The minister has the burden of explaining why he must raise taxes.* | **heavy burden** (=a very difficult burden) *She has three children and heavy financial burdens at home.* | **carry a burden** (=have that responsibility) *Carrying the burdens of leadership is never an easy task.*

3 to agree to be responsible for something

- take on
- assume responsibility for
- shoulder

take on /ˌteɪk 'ɒn / [phr v T] to agree to be responsible for something, especially something that will make you have a lot of work or pressure **take sth on** *I'm very busy. I'm afraid I can't take anything else on at the moment.* | **take on sth** *Alice always seems willing to take on extra work without complaining.*

assume responsibility for /əˌsjuːm rɪˌspɒnsəˈbɪləti fɔːʳ‖əˌsuːm rɪˌspɑːn-/ [v phrase] formal to take responsibility for something that must be done: *The ship's owner has assumed responsibility for cleaning up the oil spill.* | *It was natural for Richard, as elder son, to assume responsibility for the family.*

shoulder /'ʃəʊldəʳ/ [v T] to agree to take responsibility for something that will be difficult to deal with **shoulder responsibility/debts/the cost/burdens** *The burden of supporting the poor is shouldered mainly by charities.* | *The company is unwilling to shoulder the cost of installing a daycare center.*

4 to give the responsibility for doing something to another person

- make sb responsible for
- put sb in charge
- delegate
- pass the buck
- leave sth with
- leave it to
- entrust

make sb responsible for /ˌmeɪk (sb) rɪ'spɒnsəbəl fɔːʳ‖-'spɑːn-/ [v phrase] *The law makes the government responsible for clean up of the waste at these sites.* | *Our department has been made responsible for all areas of training.* | *The best way of ensuring that the chores are done is by making each child responsible for a different one.*

put sb in charge /ˌpʊt (sb) ɪn 'tʃɑːʳdʒ/ [v phrase] to give someone the responsibility of doing something or of making sure that it is done: *The boss is going to be out of the office next week, and he's putting me in charge.* | **+ of** *Who have they put in charge of the investigation?* | *He had done rather well in the job and had been put in charge of a whole chain of stores.*

delegate /'deləgeɪt/ [v I/T] to make someone you work with, especially someone in a lower position than you, responsible for a job or duty, so that you do not have to do it yourself: *New managers often find it difficult to delegate.* | *If you're so busy, why don't you delegate some of your work?*

pass the buck /ˌpɑːs ðə 'bʌk‖ˌpæs-/ [v phrase] to try not to accept responsibility for a problem or a mistake that you have made, by saying that it was someone else's fault: *It's easy to pass the buck and blame someone else for your failure.* | *Diplomats say NATO is clearly at fault, and that officials there are trying to pass the buck.*

leave sth with /'liːv (sth) wɪð/ [phr v T] British to make someone responsible for something that you cannot do or do not have time to do: *I didn't have time to do the accounts so I left them with Sophie.* | *Can we leave all this with you? It's just too complicated for us to understand.*

leave it to /'liːv ɪt tuː/ [v phrase] to make someone responsible for doing something, especially something that has already been started: *Leave it to me. I'll find you a place to stay.* | **leave it to sb to do sth** *Can I leave it to you to sort out the details of the conference?* | *The proposal leaves it to local communities to enforce the law.*

entrust /ɪn'trʌst/ [v T] formal to give someone the responsibility of doing something important, especially because you believe they will do it well and honestly **entrust sb/sth to sb** *I foolishly entrusted the task of collecting the money to Ron.* | **entrust sb with sth** *Managers show respect for employees by entrusting them with important decisions.* | **entrust sb/sth to the care of sb** *As a child Bertrand was entrusted to the care of nuns at a local convent.*

rest

RELATED WORDS

- to stay in a place and not leave it *see* **stay**
- to remain after others have gone *see* **remain**
- *see also* **sleep, relax/relaxed**

1 to rest

- rest
- take a rest
- relax
- take a break
- lie down
- put your feet up
- laze
- take it easy
- chill/chill out

rest /rest/ [v I] to stop working or stop being active, and sit down or lie down so that you become less tired: *If you're tired, we'll stop and rest for a while.* | *The doctor told me to take some time off work and try to rest.*

take a rest ALSO **have a rest** especially British /ˌteɪk ə 'rest, ˌhæv ə 'rest/ [v phrase] to rest for a short time in the middle of a tiring activity: *Don't stay in front of the computer for long periods of time – take a rest occasionally.* | *There was a TV in the hotel room, and sometimes I escaped up there to have a rest.* | **take/have a rest from sth** *A spokesman said that the Senator needed to take a rest from the campaign activity.*

relax /rɪ'læks/ [v I] to do something that makes you feel calm and comfortable and helps you to forget about your work and problems: *Take a deep breath, and relax.* | *They had a lovely weekend, relaxing and lying by the pool.* | **help sb (to) relax** *Drink this. It will help you relax.* —**relaxed** [adj] *He sounded relaxed and confident.* | **feel relaxed** *Now that I feel more relaxed about my performance, I'm looking forward to the game.*

take a break ALSO **have a break** especially British /ˌteɪk ə 'breɪk, ˌhæv ə 'breɪk/ [v phrase] to stop what you are doing for a short time, so that you can rest: *Let's take a break now for coffee.* | **take/have a short/quick break** *Is it all right if we have a short break at about 10:30?* | **take/have a break from sth** *I spoke to the Secretary of State as he took a break from preparing his speech.*

lie down ALSO **have a lie down/go for a lie down** British /ˌlaɪ 'daʊn, hæv ə 'laɪ daʊn, ˌgəʊ fər ə 'laɪ daʊn/ [phr v I] to put yourself in a flat position, usually on a bed, in order to rest when you are tired, although not necessarily in order to sleep: *During the day, I get so tired I have to lie down on the bed for a couple of hours.* | *Towards evening she grew tired, and went to her room for a lie down.*

put your feet up /ˌpʊt jɔːʳ 'fiːt ʌp/ [v phrase] informal to rest for a short time after a tiring activity, especially by sitting with your feet resting on something: *Well, at least put your feet up for a few minutes. Would you like a drink?* | *When you're pregnant and doing a full-time job, you must find time to put your feet up.*

laze /leɪz/ [v I always + adv/prep] to rest, especially by lying in a pleasant place, often when you should be working or doing something **laze in/on/around etc** *I found him lazing around in bed with a cup of coffee and the paper.* | *On the porch, two large cats sat lazing in the sun.*

take it easy ALSO **take things easy** /ˌteɪk ɪt 'iːzi, ˌteɪk θɪŋz 'iːzi/ [v phrase] to do things gently and with less effort than usual in order to avoid becoming worried or tired, especially because you are not feeling strong or healthy: *After the operation, I was told to take things easy for a month or two.* | *Maybe we should just go home and take it easy tonight.*

chill/chill out /tʃɪl, ˌtʃɪl 'aʊt/ [v I/phr v I] spoken to spend time resting or doing something enjoyable which does not need much effort: *We chilled out in front of the TV with a couple of beers.* | *Yeah, my family left a few minutes ago, so I'm just chilling for a while.*

2 a period when you rest

- rest
- break
- break
- relaxation

rest /rest/ [n C/U] a period of time when you do not have to do anything tiring or active, and you can relax or sleep: *By the fourth day, we were all in need of a rest.* | **get some/enough etc rest** *He eats a lot of junk food, and he doesn't get enough rest.* | **a good rest** (=one that makes you feel completely relaxed) *Make sure you have a good rest this weekend.*

break /breɪk/ [n C] a short time when you stop what you are doing so that you can rest or eat: *OK, let's run through it again straight after the break.* | **take/have a break from sth** *She's had a two-year break from competitive running, but now she's staging a comeback.* | **+ in** *I spoke to him briefly during a break in rehearsals.* | **without a break** (=not stopping to rest or eat) *Harry had worked for eight hours without a break.* | **coffee/tea/lunch break** *I'll phone you in my lunch break.*

break British **/recess** American /breɪk, rɪ'ses‖'riːses/ [n U] a time between classes when the children in a school can go outside and play, in order to rest from studying and learning: *The children played kickball during recess.* | *Come and see me at break, Tom.*

relaxation /ˌriːlæk'seɪʃən/ [n U] activities that you do to help you rest and stop thinking or worrying about your work, study etc: *You should find time for some relaxation every day* | *relaxation techniques, such as meditation* | *What do you do for relaxation?*

3 helping you to rest or relax

- restful
- relaxing

restful /'restfəl/ [adj] quiet and calm in a way that helps you rest and feel relaxed: *Our three-day stop at lake Navasha was restful and picturesque.* | *restful music*

relaxing /rɪ'læksɪŋ/ [adj] **relaxing** activities or places help you to rest because they make you feel more comfortable and less worried about your work, study etc: *I go to my brother's house in the country at weekends. It's so calm and relaxing there.* | *At the club you can choose between a relaxing bath and a massage.* | *We can help you find relaxing beaches where you will discover the real Mexico.*

result

RELATED WORDS

- result of a test/exam *see* **grade**
- *see also* **so/therefore, because, cause, reason, sport/game, test, vote**

1 the result of a game, competition, election etc

- result
- score

result /rɪ'zʌlt/ [n C] the final number of points, votes etc at the end of a competition, election etc. In British English, **result** can also be used to talk about the end of a game or sports match: *It was a really exciting game, and the result was 2-1 to West Germany.* | *These are excellent results for the Christian Democratic Party.*

score /skɔːʳ/ [n C] the number of points that each team has at the end of a game or competition: *At the end of the game, the score was 32-15.* | **what's the score** *What was the score?* | **final score** *The final score was 2-1 to Juventus.*

2 something that happens or exists because of something else

- result
- effect
- consequence
- implications
- outcome
- upshot
- end result
- net result/effect
- aftereffect

result /rɪˈzʌlt/ [n C] something that happens because of someone's actions or because of something else that happened before **+ of** *Her constant cough is the result of many years of smoking.* | *The results of the attack included two helicopters burnt out, and three groundcrew wounded.* | **with the result that** *More and more people are using cars, with the result that towns are much more polluted.* | **as a result** *Jobs are hard to get and, as a result, more young people are continuing their education.* | **a direct result of sth** (=caused by only one thing even if people think there may be other causes) *Her parents believe that her death was a direct result of medical error.*

effect /ɪˈfekt/ [n C] when a person or situation is changed by something that happens or something that someone does **+ of** *The effects of the oil spill were devastating for wildlife.* | *the harmful effects of radiation* | **have an effect/have no effect** *All my efforts to persuade them were beginning to have an effect.* | *I've been taking these pills for three days, but so far they've had no effect.* | **+ on** *The death of a parent can have very serious and long-lasting effects on a child.* | **have a bad/good effect (on sth/sb)** *Any increase in fuel costs could have a bad effect on business.*

consequence /ˈkɒnsəkwəns‖ˈkɑːnsəkwens/ [n C usually plural] the **consequences** of an action, decision etc are the things that happen as a result of it, which are usually bad **+ of** *Pain and illness are sometimes thought to be the unavoidable consequences of growing old.* | **+ for** *If river levels continue to rise, it will have very serious consequences for many people's homes.* | **take/face the consequences** (=accept the bad results of something you do) *People who run up big debts eventually have to face the consequences.* | **damaging/dire/disastrous etc consequences** *Safety procedures had been ignored, with disastrous consequences.*

implications /ˌɪmplɪˈkeɪʃənz/ [n plural] formal all the possible results that a plan, action, or discovery could have, especially when they affect what you think or do or what happens in the future **+ of** *The legal implications of the case are extremely significant.* | **+ for** *Any change in interest rates has important implications for most people's financial situation.* | **important/significant/profound etc implications** *The discovery of planets orbiting other suns has profound implications.*

outcome /ˈaʊtkʌm/ [n singular] the situation that exists at the end of a meeting, activity, or series of events, especially when no one knows what this will be until it actually happens: *Whatever the outcome, I hope we remain friends.* | *The talks had a better outcome than we had originally hoped.* | **+ of** *It's impossible to say for sure what the outcome of the election will be.* | **affect/influence the outcome** *The patient's general health and fitness can also affect the outcome of the disease.* | **predict the outcome** *At this point, I wouldn't even try to predict the outcome, but we're hoping for the best.*

upshot /ˈʌpʃɒt‖-ʃɑːt/ [n singular] the result of something, especially when it is a little unusual or unexpected **+ of** *What was the upshot of the trial?* | **the upshot is that** *The upshot of that experience was that I decided I didn't want to study medicine after all.*

end result /ˌend rɪˈzʌlt/ [n singular] the final situation that exists after a long time, process, or series of events: *It was impossible for many small businesses to survive, and the end result was the loss of many jobs.* | **the end result is that** *If students constantly fail, the end result is that they switch off any interest in learning.*

net result/effect /ˌnet rɪˈzʌlt, ɪˈfekt/ [n singular] the final situation that exists when you consider all the details and facts – use this when this situation is not good: *The net result of global warming will be a rise in sea levels.* | **the net result/effect is that** *The new system is designed to spread payments over several months but the net effect is that people pay more in total.*

aftereffect /ˈɑːftərɪˌfekt‖ˈæf-/ [n C usually plural] a bad effect that exists for a long time after the activity or event that caused it: *The earthquake struck a week ago but the city is still feeling the aftereffects.* | **+ of** *A large number of working days are lost through the aftereffects of alcohol abuse.* | **psychological aftereffects** *The psychological aftereffects of a tragedy like the Zeebrugge disaster can stay with the survivors for years.*

3 a result that happens in addition to the intended result

- side effect
- indirect result
- by-product
- corollary
- spin-off
- ramifications
- repercussions

side effect /ˈsaɪd ɪˌfekt/ [n C] a result that happens in addition to the result that you intended – use this especially about the unintended bad effects of medical treatment or drugs: *The drug can have side effects such as headaches and sickness.* | *Transplanting genes from one plant to another may have unintended side effects for the environment and the food supply.* | **+ of** *One of the side effects of chemotherapy is hair loss.* | **dangerous/nasty/unpleasant etc side effects** *These pills don't normally have any unpleasant side-effects.*

indirect result /ˌɪndəˌrekt rɪˈzʌlt/ [n C usually singular] a result that is indirectly caused by something you do or that happens **+ of** *The job losses were an indirect result of lower cost imports.* | *The increase in greenhouse gases is the direct result of pollution, and the indirect result of a reduction in the atmosphere's ability to absorb them.*

by-product /ˈbaɪ ˌprɒdʌkt‖-ˌprɑː-/ [n C] an unexpected result of an event or something you do, which happens in addition to the result you intended **+ of** *One of the by-products of the peace treaty was the growth of trade between the two nations.* | *Another by-product of space exploration is a growing awareness of this planet's fragile environment.*

corollary /kəˈrɒləri‖ˈkɔːrəleri, ˈkɑː-/ [n C] formal something that is certain to happen in addition to the result you intend, so that you expect it but do not usually want it **+ of** *Huge increases in unemployment were the corollary of the government's economic policy.* | **a logical/natural/necessary etc corollary (of sth)** *A rapid increase in population would be a natural corollary of any such changes in the birth control program.* | **the corollary of this is that** *The government has promised tax cuts, but the corollary of this is that there will be a reduction in public services.*

spin-off /ˈspɪn ɒf/ [n C] an unexpected but useful result of something that you do, that happens in addition to the result that was intended **+ for** *One of the main spin-offs for countries that host the Olympic Games is increased business for hotels, restaurants, and theatres.* | **have a spin-off** *Research into lasers has had important spin-offs for eye-surgery.*

ramifications /ˌræməfəˈkeɪʃənz/ [n plural] all the results of something you do, which affect people in ways that were not intended and which you do not always expect when you first make the decision to do it **+ of** *The ramifications of the decision whether to build a new airport or not are enormous.* | **+ for** *The course that people choose to do at university can have ramifications for the rest of their lives.* | **economic/legal/political etc ramifications** *Whatever the judges decide, the legal ramifications of the case will be with us for many years to come.* | **wider ramifications** (=more complicated results) *The introduction of national testing in schools had wider ramifications than people realized.*

repercussions /ˌriːpəʳˈkʌʃənz/ [n plural] the additional and usually bad results of something that happens, which continue to affect people for a long time afterwards in a way that was not intended or expected **+ of** *The psychological repercussions of the accident might affect her for the rest of her life.* | **have repercussions (on sth)** *The transport strike had all sorts of repercussions on other industries.* | **important/profound/serious etc repercussions** *A scandal like this could have serious repercussions on his political career.* | **economic/legal/political etc repercussions** *Even the possibility of a war in the Middle East has important political repercussions.*

4 when one thing happens because of another

- because of
- be a result of/result from
- be the product of
- come of
- stem from
- arise from
- come out of
- as a result of
- resulting/consequent

because of /bɪˈkɒz ɒv‖bɪˈkɔːz-/ [prep] if something happens **because of** an earlier problem, event etc, it happens as a result of it: *Sampras seemed likely to miss the US Open because of a back injury.* | *Because of problems with the fuel system, the launch has been put back a week.* | *She was chosen for the Peace Prize because of her courageous fight for democracy.*

be a result of/result from /biː ə rɪˈzʌlt ɒv, rɪˈzʌlt frɒm/ [v phrase] to happen because of something else that happened or was done: *Our success is the result of a great deal of hard work.* | *The big population increase in the US was partly the result of immigration.* | *It is thought that the train crash resulted from a fault on the line.*

be the product of /biː ðə ˈprɒdʌkt ɒv‖-ˈprɑː-/ [v phrase] to be the result of actions, experiences or good or bad conditions: *The agreement was the product of 21 months of negotiations.* | *Saturday's goal was the product of some poor defending by the opposing team.*

come of /ˈkʌm ɒv/ [phr v T not in progressive or passive] if something **comes of** a situation or activity, it happens because of it: *The company is interested in the merger: many positive things could come of it.* | **nothing came/has come etc of sth** (=nothing happened because of sth) *I've applied for that job, but so far nothing's come of it.* | **no good comes etc of sth** (=sth does not have a good result) *My mother always said that no good would come of the relationship.*

stem from /ˈstem frɒm/ [phr v T not in progressive or passive] if something, especially a problem, **stems from** something else, it develops because of it and is directly connected with it **+ from (doing) sth** *Many of my patients' anxieties stem from experiences in their childhood.* | *The dog's aggression stemmed from being kept locked up all day.* | **stem from the fact that** *Part of the education problem stems from the fact that class sizes have increased dramatically in the last 5 years.*

arise from /əˈraɪz frɒm/ [phr v T not in progressive or passive] if something such as a problem or difficult situation **arises from** something, it starts to exist because of it: *The argument arose from a misunderstanding.* | *Lung cancer is just one of the many diseases that arise from smoking too many cigarettes.* | **arise from the fact that** *The difficulty arises from the fact that there has been insufficient time to train new staff.*

come out of /ˌkʌm ˈaʊt ɒv/ [phr v T not in progressive or passive] to happen or exist as a helpful or useful result of someone's actions, decisions or discussions: *We're waiting to see what comes out of the inquiry before we make a decision.* | *Much of what came out of the Rio Summit did not have an immediate effect.*

as a result of /əz ə rɪˈzʌlt ɒv/ [prep] happening because of something else: *He died as a result of cold and exhaustion.* | *Over 60 drugs have been removed from sale as a result of recent tests.*

resulting/consequent /rɪˈzʌltɪŋ, ˈkɒnsəkwənt‖ˈkɑːn-/ [adj only before noun] happening or existing because of something else that happened before: *Burrows took the resulting penalty kick.* | *Without government support the factory would be forced to close, with the consequent loss of thousands of jobs.* | *Britain's resulting debt burden was greater than that of the French.*

5 to think that something happens because of something else

- put sth down to
- attribute sth to

put sth down to /ˌpʊt (sth) ˈdaʊn tuː/ [phr v T] to say or believe that one thing happens because of something else, when you are not completely sure that this is true: *When Charlie became ill, I was inclined to put it down to the pressures of his job.* | *No one was injured, and US officials put the incident down to 'high spirits'.*

attribute sth to /əˈtrɪbjuːt (sth) tuː‖-bjət-/ [phr v T] formal to say that someone or something is responsible for a situation or event – use this in official contexts: *The management attributed the success of the company to the new Marketing Director.* | *1150 deaths a year can be attributed to drunk driving.*

6 a series of events and results

- chain reaction
- knock-on effect
- domino effect

chain reaction /ˌtʃeɪn riˈækʃən/ [n C] a series of events, each of which is the result of the one before, and which cannot be stopped: *When oil prices rise, prices of other goods all over the world rise in a chain reaction.* | **+ of** *A chain reaction of events eventually led to the Prime Minister's resignation.* | **start/set off a chain reaction** *The revolution set off a chain reaction of revolts in neighbouring states.*

knock-on effect /ˈnɒk ɒn ɪˌfekt‖ˈnɑːk-/ [n C] British something that happens as a result of something that has happened before, and that you do not want to happen **+ of** *The knock-on effect of the rise in electricity prices is likely to be higher prices generally.* | **+ on** *Any reduction in community care for the elderly will have a knock-on effect on hospitals.*

domino effect /ˈdɒmɪ̥nəʊ ɪˌfekt‖ˈdɑː-/ [n singular] a series of events or actions, each one of which is caused by the effects of the previous one – use this especially about a series of bad things that happen: *If schools were allowed to become more selective, there would be a domino effect.* | **have a domino effect (on sth)** *Opponents of the scheme claimed that if the museum moved from Golden Gate Park it would have a domino effect on the other facilities.*

return

RELATED WORDS

- to give something back *see* **give (11)**
- to take someone or something back to the place they came from *see* **take (4)**
- to put something back in the place where it was before *see* **put (2)**
- *see also* **home, travel**

1 to go to the place where you were before

- go back
- come back
- return
- go home
- get in/get home
- be back
- back

go back /ˌgəʊ ˈbæk/ [phr v I] *I left my hometown 12 years ago, and I have no desire to go back.* | **+ to** *When will you be going back to Japan?* | **+ for** *We'll have to go back for the tickets – I think I left them on the desk.* | **+ in/out/inside/downstairs etc** *It's cold out here – shall we go back inside?* | *The phone started ringing again as soon as I went back upstairs.* | **go back the way you came** *Part of the trail was flooded, so we had to go back the way we had come.* | **go back home** *Frank's gone back home to visit his parents and won't be back for a week.*

come back /ˌkʌm ˈbæk/ [phr v I] if someone **comes back**, they return to the place where you are: *Rachel's left me, and I don't think she'll ever come back.* | **+ to** *When will you be coming back to London?* | **+ from** *He's just come back from a vacation in Miami.* | **+ for** *Whoever left the gloves will probably come back for them tomorrow.*

return /rɪˈtɜːʳn/ [v I] to go back or come back to the place where you were before. **Return** is used more in written or formal contexts than **go back** or **come back**: *I left early, but promised to return the next day.* | **+ to** *He had to return to India to look after his mother.* | **+ from** *Alastair returned from the office late that night.* | **return home** *As the soldiers returned home, their wives had to readjust to living with them again.*

go home /ˌgəʊ ˈhəʊm/ [v phrase] to return to your home or to the country where you were born: *It's late – I should go home now.* | *John used to go home once a month when he was at college.* | **+ to** *I've enjoyed my time in Europe, but I'm really looking forward to going home to America.*

get in/get home /ˌget ˈɪn, ˌget ˈhəʊm/ [v phrase] to return to the house where you live: *What time did you get in last night?* | *I usually get home about 7:30 – you can try calling me after that.* | **+ from** *He hasn't had anything to eat yet. He just got home from work.*

be back /biː ˈbæk/ [v phrase] to be in the place where you were before you went away: *Jack! What a surprise! How long have you been back?* | *Carol is away on business, but she should be back next week.* | *We'll get together when you're back from vacation.*

back /bæk/ [adv] **run/drive/fly/walk etc back** go back to where you were before by running, driving etc: *We took the train to Paris, but flew back.* | **+ to/from etc** *We cycled back from the beach in the evening.* | *It was a beautiful day, so I decided to walk back to the office.*

2 to go back to a place that you have visited before

- return/go back
- revisit

return/go back /rɪˈtɜːʳn, ˌgəʊ ˈbæk/ [v I/phr v I] *China was fascinating – I hope I'll be able to return one day.* | **+ for** *The dentist says I have to go back again next week for a check up.* | **+ to do sth** *These birds return to the same place every year to build their nests.* | *He'll have to go back to Moscow in June to finalize the deal.*

revisit /riːˈvɪzɪ̥t/ [v T] to go back to a place that you have been to before, especially a place that you like and that you have not visited for a long time: *Maria was eager to revisit her first school.* | *They revisited many of the places they had gone to on their honeymoon.*

3 when you return somewhere

- sb's return
- homecoming

sb's return / (sb's) rɪˈtɜːʳn/ [n phrase] formal *We eagerly await your return.* | *Immediately after his return he was forced to do his military service.* | **on sb's return** (=when they return) *On her return, she found that someone had broken into her apartment.* | **+ from** *Albertson died within one year of his return from Africa.*

homecoming /ˈhəʊmˌkʌmɪŋ/ [n singular] your return to your home or to the country where you were born after you have been away for a long time, especially when this is celebrated in some way: *We arranged a party for my brother's homecoming, when he returned from five years in Australia.* | *Coming back for her uncle's funeral was not a happy homecoming for her.*

4 a journey back to the place where you started

- return
- there and back

return /rɪˈtɜːʳn/ [adj only before noun] **return journey/trip/flight etc** *The sea was much calmer on the return voyage.* | *The return trip took about an hour less than the trip there.*

there and back /ˌðeər ən ˈbæk/ [adv] to a place and back again to the place that you started from: *How long will it take to drive there and back?* | *'How far is it to Milwaukee?' 'It's about 30 miles there and back.'*

5 a ticket that allows you to go somewhere and to return to where you started

- return/return ticket
- round-trip ticket

return/return ticket /rɪˈtɜːʳn, rɪˌtɜːʳn ˈtɪkɪ̥t/ [n C] British a ticket that includes your return journey: *How much is a return ticket to Dublin?* | *Would you like singles or returns, Sir?* — **return** [adv] *It costs $475 return to Helsinki* (=for a return ticket to Helsinki).

round-trip ticket /ˈraʊnd ˌtrɪp tɪkɨt/ [n C] American a ticket that includes your return journey: *There's no point in buying a one-way ticket when a round-trip ticket is the same price.* —**round-trip** [adv] *The ferry costs only $5 round-trip per person.*

revenge

RELATED WORDS

▸ see also **attack, punish**

1 to punish someone because they have harmed or offended you

- ▸ take/get revenge
- ▸ in retaliation
- ▸ in revenge
- ▸ get back at
- ▸ get/pay sb back
- ▸ get even
- ▸ avenge
- ▸ I'll get sb for this

take/get revenge /ˌteɪk, ˌget rɪˈvendʒ/ [v phrase] to do something to punish someone who has harmed you, your family, or your friends **+ on** *Gayle took revenge on her husband by cutting up all his best clothes.* | **+ for** *He was determined to get revenge for the murder of his sister.* | **take/get your revenge** *During the riot inmates took their revenge on prison guards.*

in retaliation /ɪn rɪˌtæliˈeɪʃən/ [adv] if you do something **in retaliation** for something that someone has done to you, you do it to make them suffer even more than you did: *Ross said he feared that he might be fired in retaliation.* | **+ for** *The President ordered the bombings in retaliation for the attack.*

in revenge /ɪn rɪˈvendʒ/ [adv] if you do something **in revenge** for something that someone has done to you, you do it to get revenge: *When she learned of her husband's affairs, she turned to another man in revenge.* | **+ for** *They murdered Gillespi in revenge for the death of their brother.*

get back at ALSO **get your own back (on)** British /get ˈbæk æt, ˌget jɔːr ˈəʊn bæk (ɒn)/ [v phrase] informal to do something which causes problems for someone, because they have done something that causes problems for you: *Dad won't let me go to the concert, but I'll get back at him.* | *Even if it took me ten years, I was determined to get my own back.* | *He kept looking for a chance to get his own back on Freddie.* | **+ for** *He wanted to get back at his supervisor for criticizing him in front of the other workers.*

get/pay sb back /ˌget, ˌpeɪ (sb) ˈbæk/ [phr v T] if you do something unpleasant or unkind to someone in order **to get** or **pay them back**, you do it in order to punish them because they have done something unkind or unpleasant to you: *So then I told everyone one of her secrets to pay her back.* | **+ for** *Someday I'll get you back for this!* | *John's being difficult about the divorce just to pay me back for leaving him.*

get even /ˌget ˈiːvən / [v phrase] informal if you **get even** with someone, you get revenge by doing something equally bad to them, in order to make yourself feel satisfied: *He decided to get even by letting the air out of her tires.* | **+ with** *What can I do to get even with him?* | *Hamilton's supporters later tried to get even with Jefferson by calling him an adulterer.*

avenge /əˈvendʒ/ [v T] if you **avenge** an action that someone has done to you, you do something unpleasant or unkind in order to get revenge – used especially in literature: *It was an insult which only Cassio's death could avenge.* | *The soldiers wanted to avenge their humiliating defeat the previous year.*

I'll get sb for this /aɪl ˈget (sb) fəʳ ˌðɪs/ spoken say this when someone has done something unpleasant to you and you are saying that you will get revenge: *I'll get you for this, you little brat.* | *Did you hear what he just said to me? I'll get him for this!*

2 action that is taken in order to punish someone who has harmed or offended you

- ▸ revenge
- ▸ reprisal
- ▸ vengeance
- ▸ vendetta
- ▸ tit for tat

revenge /rɪˈvendʒ/ [n U] *The motive for the murder was clearly revenge.* | **seek revenge** *Members of the party are seeking revenge for the assassination of their leader.* | **revenge attack/killing/bombing** *Fearing revenge attacks, the government has sealed off the borders.*

reprisal /rɪˈpraɪzəl/ [n C usually plural] an action, especially a military or political one, that is a reaction to something that has been done by a country, government, organization etc: *Some people will not report attacks to the police for fear of reprisals.* | *Demonstrators surged through the capital city yesterday, ignoring threats of reprisals from the government.* | **+ for** *His murder was a reprisal for an injury to a rival gang member.*

vengeance /ˈvendʒəns/ [n U] revenge, especially in the form of violent actions or behaviour, for something very harmful or violent that someone has done: *Her desire for vengeance led her to shoot her daughter's murderer.* | *Nothing can justify the gunmens' senseless acts of vengeance.*

vendetta /venˈdetə/ [n C] a quarrel between two people or groups of people that has continued for a long time and during which the two sides keep trying to get revenge on each other: *The killing was the result of a long-standing vendetta over gambling profits.* | **+ between** *The recent bombings may be a sign of a renewed vendetta between rival separatists.* | **+ against** *One of the gang members began a vendetta against her after she testified.* | **family/tribal/private/personal vendetta** *Ellis claims he is the victim of a conspiracy with a personal vendetta against him.*

tit for tat /ˌtɪt fəʳ ˈtæt/ [n phrase] something unpleasant done because someone has done something unpleasant to you: *I didn't invite her to my party because she didn't invite me to hers. It was just tit for tat.* | **tit-for-tat killings/bombings/raids etc** *Eight people have died in this latest round of tit-for-tat killings.*

rich

RELATED WORDS

opposite: —————— **poor**

▸ to earn a lot of money see **earn**

1 having a lot of money or possessions

- ▸ rich
- ▸ wealthy
- ▸ well off
- ▸ well-to-do
- ▸ affluent
- ▸ prosperous
- ▸ be comfortably off
- ▸ comfortable

rich /rɪtʃ/ [adj] *Her new boyfriend is very good-looking and very rich.* | *You have to be rich to afford any-*

thing in this shop. | *The rich countries of the world have promised more aid for developing countries.* | *Every year 'Fortune' magazine publishes a list of the 100 richest people in America.*

wealthy /ˈwelθi/ [adj] rich, especially through owning land, property, or valuable possessions over a long period of time: *She comes from a wealthy family, who own houses in London and Paris.* | *The new taxes were aimed at the largest and wealthiest corporations.* | *You would never have guessed from meeting him how immensely wealthy he was.* —**wealth** [n U] *The discovery of oil brought great wealth to the area* (=made the people there very wealthy). | *a country where there are extremes of wealth and poverty*

well off /ˌwel ˈɒf◂ / [adj] having more money than most people, so that you have a comfortable and easy life: *They were sufficiently well off to buy their own apartment.* | **relatively/reasonably well off** *a relatively well off family* | **better off** *The government claim that people are better off now than they have ever been.*

well-to-do /ˌwel tə ˈduː◂/ [adj] rich and respected because you have a fairly high position in society **well-to-do family/background** *He wants to find a husband from a well-to-do background for his daughter.* | *Surprisingly, police statistics show that many of these thefts were carried out by people from well-to-do families.* | **well-to-do area/neighbourhood** *Educational facilities are best in the more well-to-do residential areas.*

affluent /ˈæfluənt/ [adj] having a lot of money, especially as a result of your own hard work – use this when talking about people in a particular country or group in society: *As people become more affluent, so their standard and style of living improves.* | **affluent suburb** *We drove through affluent suburbs with large houses and tree-lined streets.* | **affluent society** *Consumer goods are a symbol of prestige in an affluent society.* —**affluence** [n U] *Since the Second World War there has been an increasing level of affluence in the West.*

prosperous /ˈprɒspərəs‖ˈprɑː-/ [adj] having a lot of money and a high standard of living, especially as a result of being successful in business: *a prosperous American businessman* | *After the war, Germany became one of Europe's most prosperous countries.* —**prosperity** /prɒˈsperəti‖prɑː-/ [n U] *The town's prosperity comes from the textile industry.*

be comfortably off /biː ˌkʌmftəbli ˈɒf‖-ˌkʌmfərt-/ [v phrase] to have enough money to live comfortably without worrying about money: *When the children were small we never had much money, but now we seem to be comfortably off.*

comfortable /ˈkʌmftəbəl, ˈkʌmfət-‖ˈkʌmfərt-, ˈkʌmft-/ [adj] having enough money to live comfortably without worrying about money – use this about people or their financial situation: *My wife and I are very lucky, really, we're comfortable, even though we're both retired.* | **have a comfortable life** *They've had a much more comfortable life since she started her new job.* | **in comfortable circumstances** *He had supposed Mrs Mack to have been in comfortable circumstances, so he was surprised when he saw her tiny apartment.*

2 extremely rich

- be loaded/be rolling in it
- stinking/filthy rich
- be worth a fortune/be worth millions
- have money to burn

be loaded/be rolling in it /biː ˈləʊdəd, biː ˈrəʊlɪŋ ɪn ɪt/ [v phrase] informal to be extremely rich: *Did you know Peter has three houses? He must be loaded.* | *Some of her friends are absolutely rolling in it.*

stinking/filthy rich /ˌstɪŋkɪŋ, ˌfɪlθi ˈrɪtʃ/ [adj phrase] spoken informal extremely rich – use this especially when you think this is unfair: *Gregory is filthy rich but he never gives a penny to charity.* | *This gorgeous woman walked in, beautifully dressed and obviously stinking rich.*

be worth a fortune/be worth millions /biː ˌwɜːʳθ ə ˈfɔːʳtʃən, biː ˌwɜːʳθ ˈmɪljənz/ [v phrase] to be extremely rich, especially because you have earned a lot of money in business, or through sport, entertainment etc: *Michael Jackson must be worth a fortune.* | *The Chief Executive started her career as a secretary, and now she's worth millions.*

have money to burn /hæv ˌmʌni tə ˈbɜːʳn/ [v phrase not in progressive] to have so much money that you can buy anything you want, even things that you do not need: *Every time I see her she's wearing something new. She must have money to burn.* | *Unless you've got money to burn, these expensive guitars are not the instruments to get you started.*

3 having a lot of money now, but not always rich

- flush
- be in the money

flush /flʌʃ/ [adj not before noun] informal *I'll buy the drinks, I'm feeling flush just now.* | *Alan gives his wife fifty dollars a week, or a little more if he's flush*

be in the money /biː ɪn ðə ˈmʌni/ [v phrase] informal to have a lot of money now because you have received some money unexpectedly, for example by winning a prize: *He used to be always wanting a loan, and then all at once, he was in the money.*

4 a rich person

- man/woman/person of means
- millionaire
- multi-millionaire
- magnate
- fat cat
- moneybags
- the rich
- the wealthy
- the haves and the have nots

man/woman/person of means /ˌmæn, ˌwʊmən, ˌpɜːʳsən əv ˈmiːnz/ [n phrase] a person who is very rich, usually because they own land, property etc or because they have a family that has always been rich: *Taylor is a man of means. His family owns several apartment blocks in New York.* | *These were people of means who could afford to pay expensive legal fees.*

millionaire /ˌmɪljəˈneəʳ/ [n C] a person who has a million pounds or dollars, or more: *The money to keep the hospital open was provided by a London millionaire.* | *I can't afford a new car just now. I'm no millionaire, you know.*

multi-millionaire /ˌmʌlti mɪljəˈneəʳ/ [n C] a person who has many millions of pounds or dollars: *Louis Berg is a multi-millionaire who made his money in the newspaper business.*

magnate /ˈmægneɪt, -nət/ [n C] a rich and powerful person in a particular industry: *Foundations set up by magnates such as Carnegie and Rockefeller provided most of the funding for the arts in the US.* | **steel/oil/shipping etc magnate** *She married a Texan oil magnate.* | *the property magnate who owns the Empire State Building*

fat cat /ˌfæt ˈkæt/ [n C] someone who makes a lot of money from a particular industry or business – use this about people who you think do not deserve to earn so much because they do not run their industry well, do not provide a good service etc: *They do not resent the city fat cats, but believe top businessmen deserve success.* | *Why should those fat cats get rich through our efforts?*

moneybags /ˈmʌnibægz/ [n singular] informal use this when you are saying in a humorous way that someone has a lot of money: *Nowadays, if you're not a moneybags, some places don't want to have anything to do with you.*

the rich /ðə ˈrɪtʃ/ [n plural] all the people who are rich in a particular country, society etc – use this especially when you are comparing them with people who are poor: *Under this government the rich seem to have got richer and the poor poorer.* | *Democracy gave the poor, as well as the rich, a part to play in governing the city.* | **the rich and famous** *a tour around the Hollywood homes of the rich and famous*

the wealthy /ðə ˈwelθi/ [n plural] people who are rich, especially through owning land, property, or valuable possessions over a long period of time, who have a lot of power or influence in society: *Private health care should not be only for the wealthy.* | *The hotel stood by a lake, where the wealthy went to go fishing or pigeon shooting.*

the haves and the have nots /ðə ˌhævz ən ðə ˌhæv ˈnɒts/ [n phrase] rich people and poor people – use this expression when you are comparing both groups: *The widening gap between the haves and the have nots is becoming very noticeable in New York.*

5 to become rich

- get rich
- make a fortune/bundle
- make good
- marry into money
- go from rags to riches
- be made/set up for life

get rich /ˌget ˈrɪtʃ/ [v phrase] *I'm trying to think of a way to get rich.* | **get rich (by) doing sth** *Mr Askin got rich selling second hand cars.* | **get rich quick** *The company promised its sales team that, if they worked hard enough, they would get rich quick.*

make a fortune/bundle ALSO **make a bomb** British /ˌmeɪk ə ˈfɔːʳtʃən, ˈbʌndl, ˌmeɪk ə ˈbɒm‖-ˈbɑːm/ [v phrase] informal to become very rich by earning or winning a lot of money: *If you're a good salesman you can make a bomb, but you have to work hard.* | *You shouldn't have sold your shares. You could have made a bundle.* | **make a fortune etc (by) doing sth** *Richard made a fortune breeding racehorses.*

make good /ˌmeɪk ˈgʊd/ [v phrase not in progressive] to become rich, especially when you are from a poor family – used especially in newspapers: *He's just a poor country boy who made good in the city.* | *Ian thinks that just because he made good, everybody else can too.*

marry into money /ˈmæri ɪntə ˌmʌni/ [v phrase] to become rich by marrying a rich person: *If you don't have any yourself, it's a pretty smart move to marry into money!*

go from rags to riches /gəʊ frəm ˌrægz tə ˈrɪtʃ-ɪ̵z/ [v phrase not in progressive] to become very rich after being extremely poor: *Although he came from a poor family, he managed to go from rags to riches.* — **rags-to-riches** [adj phrase] *a classic rags-to-riches story*

be made/set up for life /biː ˌmeɪd, set ˌʌp fəʳ ˈlaɪf/ [v phrase] if you say that someone **is made for life** or **is set up for life**, you mean they are extremely successful and so rich that they do not need to work any more: *Now he's got a contract to advertise sports clothing he'll be made for life.* | *Sylvester Stallone need never make another movie. He's already set up for life.*

6 ways of telling someone that you are not rich

- I'm not made of money
- money doesn't grow on trees

I'm not made of money /aɪm ˌnɒt ˈmeɪd əv ˌmʌni/ say this when someone wants you to spend more money than you think you can afford: *'Why don't you move to a bigger house?' 'I'm not made of money, you know!'*

money doesn't grow on trees /ˌmʌni dʌzənt ˌgrəʊ ɒn ˈtriːz/ say this when someone, such as your child, husband, or wife, is spending more of your money than you think you can afford: *Look how much you've spent on clothes this month! Money doesn't grow on trees, you know!*

right

RELATED WORDS

- right or suitable for a particular person, job, purpose etc *see* **suitable**
- morally correct *see* **good (13)**
- *see also* **fair**

WHAT'S HERE

- **right/correct** see **1 to 5**
- **right/justified** see **6 to 8**
- **right/to have the right to do sth** see **9 to 12**

right/correct

1 answers, statements, calculations etc that are correct

- right
- correct
- accurate

right /raɪt/ [adj] if something that someone says or thinks is **right**, it is correct or true, especially because it contains the true facts or details: *Yes, that's the right answer.* | *Is that the right time?* | *Excuse me, but the bill isn't right – we didn't have a Caesar salad.* | **that's right** spoken *'Your mother's a teacher, isn't she?' 'Yes, that's right.'*

correct /kəˈrekt/ [adj] something such as an answer, fact, or calculation that is **correct** is true, has no mistakes etc, especially because it is the only answer or result that is possible: *The first ten correct answers will win a prize.* | *This information is no longer correct.* | *The correct results are on page 482.*

accurate /ˈækjɪ̵rət/ [adj] information, measurements, descriptions etc that are **accurate** are completely correct and all the details are true: *She was able to give the police an accurate description of her attacker.* | *It is vital that the measurements be accu-*

rate. | The authorities still do not have accurate information on the number of people killed or injured in the crash.

2 to be correct in what you say or think

- be right
- get sth right
- be correct in saying/thinking etc
- be on the right track
- hit the nail on the head/put your finger on it
- be spot on
- infallible

be right /biː ˈraɪt/ [v phrase] *You're right – there's not going to be enough food for everyone.* | **+ about** *Durrell is absolutely right about the importance of software to the local economy.* | **be right about one thing** (=say this when part of someone's opinion or what they say is right, but the rest is wrong) *It's not a great album, but Samuels was right about one thing: it's going to sell in the millions.* | **be right in saying/thinking etc** *Moore is right in saying that the present tax system is unfair.*

get sth right /ˌget (sth) ˈraɪt/ [v phrase] to say the correct facts or details when you are telling a story, describing an event etc: *Make sure you get people's names right when you're sending out the invitations.* | *'I learned,' he stopped, wanting to get the words right, 'I learned I was selfish.'*

be correct in saying/thinking etc /biː kəˌrekt ɪn ˈseɪ-ɪŋ / [v phrase] if someone **is correct in saying** or **thinking** a particular fact, the fact is correct, especially when they are not sure if it is correct or not: *Monroe was correct in saying that unemployment has dropped in the last five years.* | *I believe I am correct in saying that two of the original computer languages were Cobol and Prolog.* | *The jury was correct in thinking that the prosecution had not presented a strong case.*

be on the right track /biː ɒn ðə ˌraɪt ˈtræk/ [v phrase] to not yet know the complete answer to a question or problem, but be close to finding it because you are already partly correct: *No, that's not quite right, but you're on the right track.* | *Researchers are still a long way from finding a cure for the disease, but many seem confident they are on the right track.*

hit the nail on the head/put your finger on it /hɪt ðə ˌneɪl ɒn ðə ˈhed, pʊt jɔːʳ ˈfɪŋgər ɒn ɪt/ [v phrase] to say something that is exactly right and that is the answer to a problem which people have been thinking about for a long time: *Garson hits the nail on the head – at the heart of the abortion debate is a religious issue.* | *Wyman put his finger on it when he said the truth was complicated.*

be spot on /biː ˌspɒt ˈɒn‖-ˌspɑːt-/ [v phrase] British informal to be exactly right, especially by guessing correctly: *'Is the answer 42?' 'You're spot on! Well done, Mary.'*

infallible /ɪnˈfæləbəl/ [adj] someone or something that is **infallible** is always right and never makes mistakes – use this especially to say that this is not usually true or is extremely rare: *Computer spell checkers are useful but far from infallible.* | *Juries are not infallible. Innocent people are convicted, and guilty people go free.*

3 in the correct order, position etc

- right
- correct
- the right way up
- the right way round

right /raɪt/ [adj] in the order, position etc that is correct or that someone thinks is correct: *If you don't push the buttons in the right order, nothing will happen.* | *Put the words in the right order to make a sentence.* | *She pushed the hat further back on her head. 'Does this look right?'* | *No, that's not quite right. Lower the left hand corner of the painting just a little more.*

correct /kəˈrekt/ [adj] the **correct** order, sequence, position etc is the exact one that is correct: *When arranged in the correct order, the letters will spell a word which you fill in on this grid.* | *The correct sequence of numbers must be entered to open the lock.*

the right way up /ðə ˌraɪt weɪ ˈʌp/ [adv] if something is **the right way up**, the top of it is facing up, the way it is intended to: *Make sure the box is the right way up before you open it.* | *The picture isn't hung the right way up.*

the right way round /ðə ˌraɪt weɪ ˈraʊnd/ [adv] British if something is **the right way round,** the front is facing in the correct direction: *Maria turned the medallion the right way round on its chain.* | *Be careful to fit the part onto the board the right way round.*

4 in the correct way

- correctly
- right
- rightly
- properly

correctly /kəˈrektli/ [adv] done or said without making any mistakes or with the correct facts or details, especially when there is only one possible way, answer or result: *We are confident the tests were carried out correctly.* | *The drug is quite safe if taken correctly.* | *Egg whites are correctly whipped when they hold their peaks.*

right /raɪt/ [adv not before verb] especially spoken something that is done **right** is done correctly and well, especially according to someone's own ideas or opinions: *Have I spelled your name right?* | *Most people can't do it right the first time.* | *The government can't seem to do anything right.*

rightly /ˈraɪtli/ [adv] done or said in a way that is correct, because you have all the correct facts or details: *As he rightly pointed out, there is no real evidence that the president acted improperly.* | *Buller's actions have been rightly criticized as ineffective.* | **rightly or wrongly** (=use this to show that it is true that someone feels or thinks something, even though what they feel or think may be wrong) *Rightly or wrongly, many employees feel pushed to work longer hours.*

properly /ˈprɒpəʳli‖ˈprɑː-/ [adv] especially British if you do something **properly**, you do it in the way it should be done: *He accused me of not doing my job properly.* | *It will take time to properly investigate the matter.* | *He questions whether the experiments were conducted properly.*

5 to make something correct

- correct
- correction
- set sb straight
- set the record straight

correct /kəˈrekt/ [v T] *Teachers spend many hours correcting students' assignments.* | *It will take us some time to correct all the mistakes.* | *Is there any way of politely correcting someone's grammar?* | **correct me if I'm wrong** (=say this when you think what you are saying is right, but you are not sure) *Correct me if I'm wrong, but haven't we met before?*

correction /kəˈrekʃən/ [n C] a mark or note correcting something on a piece of written work: *My essay was covered in corrections in red ink.* | *Corrections should be pencilled into the margins.* | *My Spanish teacher will point out errors, but we have to make the corrections ourselves.*

set sb straight ALSO **put sb straight** British /ˌset (sb) ˈstreɪt, ˌpʊt (sb) ˈstreɪt/ [v phrase] to tell someone the true facts when they have made a mistake, especially if you are annoyed by their mistake: *She quickly set me straight, saying that while she enjoys her job, she works mainly for the money.* | *Your friends are always ready to put you straight when you do something stupid.* | **+ about** *It's time to set people straight about why he was fired – he didn't act in a professional manner.*

set the record straight ALSO **put the record straight** British /ˌset ðə ˈrekɔːd streɪt, ˌpʊt ðə ˈrekɔːd streɪt‖-kərd-/ [v phrase] to tell people the true facts about something, especially in public, because you want to make it very clear that what is believed is in fact not correct: *It's time we put the record straight. The newspapers are wrong – this factory will not be closing down.* | *Paulson, wanting to set the record straight, called a press conference.*

right/justified

6 when it is right or reasonable to do something

- right
- justified
- reasonable
- I don't blame sb
- justifiable
- legitimate

right /raɪt/ [adj] use this to talk about what someone has done or may do, to say that you agree with it because it seems fair or reasonable **+ to do sth** *You were right to complain – the food was cold.* | *The screenwriter was right to focus on just one aspect of a long and complicated novel.* | **the right thing to do** *I took a pay cut to come here, but I'm sure it was the right thing to do.* | **do the right thing** *Do the right thing – turn off the TV and get the kids playing outside.*

justified /ˈdʒʌstɪfaɪd/ [adj not usually before noun] if you say that someone is **justified** in doing something, or that something they do is **justified**, you believe what they do is reasonable in that situation: *I don't think Colin's criticisms were really justified.* | **be/feel justified in doing sth** *The government feels justified in using military force to protect its own citizens.* | *The landlord may be justified in charging for any additional work that needs to be done.*

reasonable /ˈriːzənəbəl/ [adj] if an action is **reasonable**, it is fair and sensible: *Campaigners say that there is no reasonable objection to women becoming priests.* | **it is reasonable to do sth** *It is reasonable to expect members to pay a small fee.* | *It is reasonable to assume watching a lot of television at an early age interferes with development.* | **it is reasonable that** *It is reasonable that a prospective employer should want to know if someone has a criminal record.* —**reasonably** [adv] *Alison can't reasonably be expected to do the work of two people.*

I don't blame sb /aɪ ˌdəʊnt ˈbleɪm (sb)/ spoken informal say this when you can understand why someone has behaved in a particular way, and you think they were right: *'Sheila's left her husband.' 'Well, I don't blame her!'* | **+ for (doing) sth** *I don't blame you for losing your temper with Ann.* | *It may have been a joke, but you can't blame the women in the department for being angry.*

justifiable /ˈdʒʌstɪfaɪəbəl/ [adj] a **justifiable** feeling, action, or reaction is acceptable because there is a good reason for it: *Can violence ever be a justifiable method of protest?* | *Reed said the tax increases were not only justifiable, but unavoidable.* | *Is football a justifiable expense when the college cannot afford enough English classes to meet students' needs?* —**justifiably** [adv] *The company can justifiably claim that it has met all its obligations.*

legitimate /lɪˈdʒɪtɪmɪt/ [adj] fair, correct, or reasonable according to accepted rules, facts, or standards of behaviour: *He had a legitimate reason for being late.* | *The way governments treat their people is a legitimate concern for the international community.* | **it is legitimate to do sth** *It is legitimate to suggest that taxes should affect people with higher incomes more than they affect poorer people.* —**legitimately** [adv] *You could legitimately argue that the best way to bring down pollution levels is to ban cars completely.*

7 to have a good reason for thinking or doing something

- have a right to be scared/proud/happy etc
- justly
- good cause/reason
- rightly

have a right to be scared/proud/happy etc /hæv ə ˈraɪt tə biː ˌskeəʳd / [v phrase not in progressive] to have a good reason to behave in a particular way, especially in a way that you would not normally behave, or in a way that other people would usually disapprove of: *She's just got her exam results; she has the right to be proud of herself.* | *The problems are genuine and people have the right to be concerned.* | **have every right to be sth** (=have a very good reason to feel something) *After what happened last time we bought a car, I think we have every right to be wary.*

justly /ˈdʒʌstli/ [adv] if you are **justly** proud, angry, critical etc, you have a good reason for feeling this way or reacting in this way: *The Chinese are justly proud of their ancient culture.* | *The press has been justly critical of the delays in paying compensation.* | *Bordeaux is an area of France justly famous for its red wine.*

good cause/reason /ˌgʊd ˈkɔːz, ˈriːzən/ [adv] if someone does something, feels something, or thinks something with **good cause** or **good reason**, they have a good reason for what they do or think or feel **have good cause/reason to do sth** *The coach, watching his team, feels he has good reason to expect them to win.* | **for good cause/reason** *The company has been held up as a model employer, and for good reason. They have a good training program and excellent benefits.* | **with good cause/reason** *She is a jealous wife, and with good cause.*

rightly /ˈraɪtli/ [adv] formal if someone says or does something **rightly**, they are right and have good reasons to say it or do it: *The U.S. is rightly cautious about becoming involved.* | *Taxpayers rightly expect the government to be careful about spending.* | **rightly so** *Residents are outraged, and rightly so.* | **quite rightly** *Investors have quite rightly avoided this stock.*

8 to show that something is right to do

- justify

justify /ˈdʒʌstɨfaɪ/ [v T] to explain or show that there are good reasons for doing something that seems wrong to most people: *How can you justify a 200% pay rise!* | *People try to justify the breakdown of their marriage by blaming their spouse.* | **justify doing sth** *I don't think anyone can justify spending so much money on weapons.*

right/to have the right to do sth

9 a legal or official right

- right
- freedom
- entitlement
- claim
- rights
- by right

right /raɪt/ [n singular] when you should be able to have or do something, according to the law or according to moral ideas: *Free speech is a basic right in a democratic society.* | **+ to** *I disagree, but I respect his right to his opinion.* | **the right to do sth** *Women all over the world fought long and hard for the right to vote.* | **have the right to sth** *Everyone the right to a good basic education.* | **the right of veto/action/self-determination/free speech etc** *The executive council has the right of veto over the management's policy.*

freedom /ˈfriːdəm/ [n U] the right to do, say, think, or write something without being controlled or stopped by anyone **+ of** *No democracy can exist without freedom of speech and freedom of the press.* | **+ to do sth** *This change in the law will give parents more freedom to influence their children's education.* | **political/religious etc freedom** *The leaders of the demonstration made speeches demanding greater political freedom.*

entitlement /ɪnˈtaɪtlmənt/ [n C/U] the official right to have or receive something, especially money, that you get from a government or an employer: *Many people are still not aware of the entitlements they may be able to receive.* | **+ to** *The amount of money you earn does not affect your entitlement to child benefit for your children.* | **holiday/pension etc entitlement** *Holiday entitlements for temporary workers are less than for permanent staff.*

claim /kleɪm/ [n C] the right to have or be given something because you were its original owner, or because you have a moral right to it **+ to** *No one can dispute the Mohawks' claim to this land.* | *His claim to the house was finally recognized by the court.*

rights /raɪts/ [n plural] the legal control or possession of something such as a product, a book, an idea etc: *Elliott liked the book and bought the rights, planning to make it into a miniseries.* | **+ to** *This is the publishing company which brought the rights to Somerset Maugham's short stories.* | *ABC has exclusive rights to television coverage of the Olympics.*

by right /baɪ ˈraɪt/ [adv] if something is yours **by right**, you have a moral right to have it or be given it: *He believes that he is entitled by right to inherit from his father, despite his father's will.* | *Developers were met by angry locals protesting that the land was theirs by right.*

10 the political and social rights that everyone should have

- rights
- civil rights
- human rights
- equal rights
- equal opportunities
- civil liberties

rights /raɪts/ [n plural] the political and social freedom that everyone in a country should have: *Every individual should have basic rights.* | **+ of** *Some motorcyclists saw the helmet law as an infringement on the rights of the individual.* | **women's/workers'/victims' etc rights** *Laws enacted in the past ten years have gradually taken away workers' rights.* | *Allred is an attorney who has gained a national reputation fighting for women's rights.*

civil rights /ˌsɪvəl ˈraɪts/ [n plural] the rights that every person should have, such as the right to vote or be treated equally and fairly by the law, whatever their sex, race, or religion: *She had been actively involved in the struggle for civil rights in the US in the '60s.* | *The President has agreed to talks with civil rights campaigners.* | *The civil rights movement illustrates how people can change the constitution of their country.*

human rights /ˌhjuːmən ˈraɪts/ [n plural] the basic right that all people should have, including freedom and the right to be treated fairly and without cruelty by their government: *The Court ruled that hitting children was an abuse of human rights.* | *A number of leading human rights activists were arrested yesterday.* | *The regime has a long record of human rights violations.*

equal rights /ˌiːkwəl ˈraɪts/ [n plural] the rights of every person to be treated fairly and equally by the law or by society, whatever their sex, race, religion, or social position: *The battle for equal rights for women is not yet over.* | *The Americans were the first to make law the principle of equal rights for every individual.* | *Homosexual men and women are campaigning for equal rights.*

equal opportunities /ˌiːkwəl ɒpəˈtjuːnɨtiz‖ -ɑːpərˈtuː-/ [n plural] the right of every person to have a chance to get a job, go to university etc, whatever their sex, race, or social position: *Only in a completely classless society can there be equal opportunities for everyone.* | **equal opportunities legislation/programs etc** *Certain jobs were dominated by men until the equal opportunities legislation of the 1970s.*

civil liberties /ˌsɪvəl ˈlɪbəʳtiz/ [n plural] the rights of any citizen to do whatever they want as long as they respect the rights of other people, without having to ask anyone's permission, and the right to keep their personal information private: *The banning of public meetings was held to be a denial of civil liberties.* | *The ability of this software to gather information about individuals through the Web is worrying to civil liberties groups.*

11 a special right belonging to one person or group

- privilege
- prerogative
- birthright

privilege /ˈprɪvɨlɪdʒ/ [n C] a special right or advantage given to a person or group, because of their high social position, because they are a member of a club etc: *A good education should not just be a privilege of the rich.* | **give sb a privilege** *Why should famous people be given special privileges?* | **lose a privilege** *If the chores aren't done by the time the* *timer goes off, the kids lose privileges such as TV time.* | **the privilege of doing sth** *If prisoners behave well they are allowed the privilege of visiting their families at the weekend.* — **privileged** [adj] *Only privileged club members* (=those who have privileges) *can sit in the Royal Pavilion to watch matches.*

prerogative /prɪˈrɒgətɪv‖-ˈrɑː-/ [n C] formal a special right that only a particular person or group has because of their importance or position: *In the old days, a university education was the prerogative of the rich.* | **+ to do sth** *The governor has the prerogative to free prisoners.*

birthright /ˈbɜːʳθraɪt/ [n singular] a right that you should have because you have been born into a particular family, country, class etc: *The President ended his speech by saying 'Dignity and self-respect are the birthright of every American citizen.'* | *She seemed to regard an easy, comfortable life as some kind of birthright.*

12 to have or give someone a legal right

- have the right
- be entitled to
- give sb the right
- entitle
- be within your rights

have the right /ˌhæv ðə ˈraɪt/ [v phrase not in progressive] to be legally or officially allowed to do or have something **+ to do sth** *People should have a right to know what is on their credit history.* | *We have a constitutional right to defend ourselves, our family, and our property.* | **+ to** *Olivia felt she had a right to information about her illness.*

be entitled to /biː ɪnˈtaɪtld tuː/ [v phrase] formal to be legally allowed to have something or do something: *The public is entitled to information about how public money is spent.* | **be entitled to do sth** *You are legally entitled to take faulty goods back to the store where you bought them.* | *Your landlord is not entitled to charge you for the remainder of the month's rent.*

give sb the right /ˌgɪv (sb) ðə ˈraɪt/ [v phrase] to legally or officially allow someone to do or have something **+ to** *This government programme gives families on low incomes the right to extra financial help.* | **+ to do sth** *The new regulations give dissatisfied customers the right to receive a full refund.*

entitle /ɪnˈtaɪtl/ [v T] formal to legally or officially allow someone to do or have something **entitle sb to sth** *Being a member entitles you to discounts on tickets.* | **entitle sb to do sth** *Ethiopian Jews were entitled to immigrate to Israel under the Law of Return.*

be within your rights /biː wɪðˌɪn jɔːʳ ˈraɪts/ [v phrase] to have a legal right to do something, although it may seem unfair or unreasonable: *If Mrs Cobb wanted to take the company to court for unfair dismissal, she'd be within her rights.* | **+ to do sth** *If your actions have disturbed other tenants, your landlady is within her rights to give you notice to stop the actions or leave.*

risk

RELATED WORDS

▸ *see also* **dangerous, gambling, chance**

1 a possibility that something bad might happen

- risk
- danger
- threat
- hazard

risk /rɪsk/ [n C/U] a possibility that something harmful or unpleasant will happen, especially as a result of something else: *There are a lot of risks involved when you start your own business.* | **+ of** *People continue to smoke, despite knowing the risks of heart disease or cancer.* | **+ of doing sth** *Drivers often break the speed limit, and there's little risk of getting caught.* | **+ that** *We can't ignore the risk that fighting could spread throughout the region.* | **reduce/increase the risk of sth** *Clean the wound thoroughly to reduce the risk of infection.*

danger /ˈdeɪndʒəʳ/ [n C/U] the possibility that something dangerous or very unpleasant will happen, for example if a particular situation continues or is not dealt with: *The river has not flooded yet, but that does not mean the danger has passed.* | *The gas leak was quickly fixed, but workers at the factory say the danger remains real.* | **+ of** *Is there any danger of Mike being arrested?* | *Wear a hat and drink plenty of fluids to reduce the danger of sunstroke.* | **+ that** *There's a real danger that the region's forests will disappear completely in the next 50 years.*

threat /θret/ [n C usually singular] a strong possibility that something very bad will happen, especially something that will affect a lot of people: *Tuberculosis is a common threat when people live in crowded conditions.* | *The nuclear threat, while not gone completely, is reduced.* | **+ of** *Once again the people of Sudan face the threat of famine.* | **+ to** *The latest outbreak of the disease can be seen as the greatest threat to UK farmers yet.* | **+ that** *There is a threat that the violence will break out again.* | **pose a threat** (=be a threat) *It's nonsense to say that the protesters pose any threat to democratic society.*

hazard /ˈhæzəʳd/ [n C] a risk that cannot be avoided, because it is always there in a particular activity or situation: *For international traders, changes in the exchange rate are an unavoidable hazard.* | **+ of doing sth** *a study into the potential hazards of playing computer games for long periods of time* | **+ of** *Malaria is a common hazard of life in the region.* | **occupational hazard** (=a hazard that always exists in a particular job) *Serious lung disease seems to be an occupational hazard of working in mines.*

2 involving risk

- risky
- dangerous
- foolhardy
- high-risk
- a gamble
- dicey
- precarious

risky /ˈrɪski/ [adj] involving a risk: *It's always risky leaving your car out on the street overnight.* | *Being self-employed is much more risky than being a wage earner.* | *Risky investments can offer high yields, but also the possibility of greater losses.* | **+ to do sth** *The experiments would be too risky to perform on humans.*

dangerous /ˈdeɪndʒərəs/ [adj] risks that are not necessary and that could cause harm or serious problems: *Using humor in a job interview is a dangerous thing – you never know how the interviewer will react.* | *Women felt that complaining about sexual harrassment was dangerous, as there was always the threat of losing their jobs.* | **it is danger-**

ous to do sth *It is dangerous to assume that share prices will continue to rise.*

foolhardy /'fu:lhɑ:ʳdi/ [adj] an action that is **foolhardy** involves so much risk that someone seems stupid for trying it: *It was foolhardy to take the plane up alone, with so little flying experience.* | *The country was in such huge debt that any spending proposals looked foolhardy.* | *I drove to the hospital at a foolhardy speed, arriving just after my wife.*

high-risk /ˌhaɪ 'rɪsk◂/ [adj only before noun] something that is **high-risk** involves a lot of risk, but if you choose to do it and it is successful, you will have very good results: *It was a high-risk strategy to attack with such a small number of planes, but it was brilliantly successful.* | *a high-risk investment*

a gamble /ə 'gæmbəl/ [n singular] something risky that you do because you hope that it will succeed and that you will gain something from it: *A gamble by the quarterback on the final play allowed them to score.* | *Changing jobs is always a gamble, but the opportunity looks good.* | **a gamble pays off** (=it is successful) *Despite the serious doubts of his advisors, the President's gamble paid off.*

dicey /'daɪsi/ [adj] informal involving a serious risk that things will go wrong: *It's too dicey to base this policy on what might happen in the coming year.* | *Taking the mountain road is always a bit dicey at this time of year.*

precarious /prɪ'keəriəs/ [adj] involving a serious possibility of failure or loss: *No one would lend money to a company in such a precarious position.* | *The typical peasant farmer has a precarious existence, at the mercy of flood, disease and famine.* | *His political position has become extremely precarious.*

3 to do something even though there is a risk

- take a risk
- take a chance
- risk
- stick your neck out
- take the plunge
- at your own risk
- at the risk of doing sth
- risk-taking

take a risk /ˌteɪk ə 'rɪsk/ [v phrase] to decide to do something, even though you know that something bad or harmful might happen as a result: *I knew we were taking a risk when we lent him the money.* | *Nobody is successful in business without taking a few risks.* | *Climbers like the thrill that taking risks gives them.* | **take a calculated risk** (=decide to do something after thinking very carefully about the risks) *Most investors study the market and take calculated risks.*

take a chance ALSO **chance it** informal /ˌteɪk ə 'tʃɑ:ns, 'tʃɑ:ns ɪt‖-'tʃæns/ [v phrase] to decide to do something even though there is a risk, because you think that you will succeed: *Victor took a chance and set up his own company, which has been very successful.* | *Isaacs chanced it with a long three-point shot at goal in the last minute of the game.* | **+ on** (=hope that something happens) *He persuaded the record company to take a chance on the band, and it became a huge hit.* | **take chances** (=always be ready to take a chance, especially in your work) *There are a lot of people in the movie industry who are afraid to take chances and do new things.*

risk /rɪsk/ [v T] to do something that you know might have a harmful or negative result: *He risked a cautious glance over the wall, and saw a group of guards standing by the gate.* | **risk doing sth** *I decided to risk looking for a place to stay when I got there, rather than booking in advance.* | **risk it** *Road conditions were supposed to be pretty bad, but we decided to risk it.*

stick your neck out /ˌstɪk jɔ:ʳ 'nek aʊt/ [v phrase] informal to do something or give your opinion about something, even though you know there is a risk that you are wrong or will be criticized: *The evidence is good, but I won't stick my neck out until all the data is in.* | *Look, I'll stick my neck out and say it'll be finished by tomorrow evening.*

take the plunge /ˌteɪk ðə 'plʌndʒ/ [v phrase] to finally decide to do something important but which involves some risk, after thinking about it very carefully: *Forsyth took the plunge into politics in 1996.* | *'Are you two getting married?' 'Yes. We've decided to take the plunge.'*

at your own risk /ət jɔ:r ˌəʊn 'rɪsk/ [adv] if you do something **at your own risk**, it will be your own fault if something bad happens – used especially on official signs and notices to warn people: *Visitors who park their cars in the corner lot do so at their own risk.* | *Journalists were allowed into the area, but only at their own risk.*

at the risk of doing sth /ət ðə ˌrɪsk əv 'du:ɪŋ (sth)/ [prep] spoken say this when what you are going to say or do might make someone angry, upset etc: *A school has to be able to make rules about students' dress, even at the risk of upsetting parents.* | *At the risk of sounding like your mother, you'd better dress up warm.* | *This is a point which – at the risk of being boring – I must emphasize once again.*

risk-taking /'rɪsk teɪkɪŋ/ [n U] when people deliberately take risks in order to achieve something – use this especially about actions in business or dangerous sports: *The culture in Silicon Valley values risk-taking and entrepreneurship.* | *Risk-taking has long been a feature of the theatre company's productions, which have tackled many difficult issues.*

4 to do something that involves unnecessary risks

- be asking for trouble
- invite
- push your luck
- tempt fate
- be playing with fire

be asking for trouble /bi: 'ɑ:skɪŋ fəʳ ˌtrʌbəl‖-'æsk-/ [v phrase] to stupidly do something that is almost certain to be dangerous or cause trouble: *Anyone who buys second-hand car tires is just asking for trouble.* | *You need to have a good knowledge of the industry before you buy stocks, or you're asking for trouble.*

invite /ɪn'vaɪt/ [v T] especially written if you **invite** trouble, criticism, attack etc, you do something that seems likely to cause you trouble or that encourages people to criticize you, attack you etc: *If you don't maintain your car regularly, you're just inviting trouble.* | *Not to provide aid will just invite further catastrophe in the area.*

push your luck /ˌpʊʃ jɔ:ʳ 'lʌk/ [v phrase] informal to do something that involves a risk of failure, because you have been successful when you have done it before: *I think I'd be pushing my luck if I asked him to babysit again on such short notice.* | *Twelve months later, the captain of Sea Rover pushed his luck once too often.*

tempt fate /ˌtempt 'feɪt/ [v phrase] to do something that involves unnecessary risk, because you are too confident that there will be no problems: *It would be tempting fate to travel without a spare wheel.* | *By* *building houses in the steep canyons, Californians are tempting fate in the form of mudslides and fires.*

be playing with fire /biː ˌpleɪ-ɪŋ wɪð ˈfaɪəʳ/ [v phrase] to stupidly take a risk, especially by doing something or getting involved in a situation that is likely to have a very unpleasant result: *The government was warned it was playing with fire by arresting so-called 'separatist' leaders.* | *Anyone who gets involved with a married man is playing with fire.*

5 to risk losing something

- risk
- gamble/take a gamble
- put sth on the line
- stake sth on
- speculate

risk /rɪsk/ [v T] to **risk** losing something, especially in order to gain something else: *Companies cannot risk losing customers through computer problems.* | *The university has already cut its budget as much as possible without risking its quality and reputation.* | **risk sth on sth** *You'd have to be crazy to risk your money on an investment like that.*

gamble/take a gamble /ˈgæmbəl, ˌteɪk ə ˈgæmbəl/ [v I/T/v phrase] to do something even though there is a risk of failure or loss, because you will gain a lot if it is successful: *They seem to be gambling the whole future of the company in return for a quick short-term profit.* | *If we gamble and succeed, no one will mind. But if we gamble and fail, we'll probably lose our jobs.* | *In 1972, NBC took a gamble and created a show featuring Redd Foxx, a black comic whose stage routines were somewhat off-color.* | **+ that** *During the drought, water companies used water from the emergency reservoirs, gambling that normal rainfall would soon fill them up again.* | **+ on** *The team took a gamble on Whitney, who is fast and an accurate player, but only five-foot-nine.*

put sth on the line /ˌpʊt (sth) ɒn ðə ˈlaɪn/ [v phrase] if you put your job, career, reputation etc on the line, you risk losing your job, reputation etc if something is not successful or if you make the wrong decision: *Whatever type of company you have, you put your reputation on the line when you handle complaint calls.* | *Many workers feel they may be putting their jobs on the line if they protest about safety abuses.*

stake sth on /ˈsteɪk (sth) ɒn / [phr v T] to risk losing something important if the result of a plan or action is not successful: *Lincoln staked his political career on opposition to slavery.* | *She had staked her academic reputation on the accuracy of her research.*

speculate /ˈspekjᵍleɪt/ [v I] to buy a large amount of shares, land, or foreign money because you hope to make a big profit when you sell it, even though you risk losing your money: *Her father made his money speculating on the New York Stock Exchange.* | **speculate in shares/land etc** *Terry speculated heavily in mining shares and lost a lot of money.* —**speculation** /ˌspekjᵍˈleɪʃən/ [n U] *Irresponsible speculation can cause serious distortions in the stock market.*

6 when you are in a situation where there are risks

- risk
- run a risk
- be at risk
- be in danger
- high-risk
- lay yourself open to
- be on dangerous ground/in dangerous territory

risk /rɪsk/ [v T] to get into a situation where something very unpleasant might happen to you as a result of something you do: *Many refugees risk death or arrest in their attempts to flee persecution.* | **risk doing sth** *I don't want to risk offending your parents.* | **risk your life** *The Carnegie Hero awards are given to those who risk their lives to save others.*

run a risk /ˌrʌn ə ˈrɪsk/ [v phrase] to be in a situation where something bad might happen to you, especially because of something you do: *The people who use these drugs are often unaware of the risks they are running.* | **+ of doing sth** *Men run a greater risk of dying from heart disease than women.* | *Rather than running the risks of using harmful pesticides in your garden, try using natural or organic methods of pest control.*

be at risk /biː ət ˈrɪsk/ [v phrase] to be in a situation in which you risk being harmed or losing something very important or valuable: *The children were removed from the family because their father was violent and they were believed to be at risk.* | **+ of** ALSO **+ for** American *Those with fair skin are more at risk of skin cancers than those with dark skin.* | *Some firms provide health checks for employees who are at risk of back injury.*

be in danger /biː ɪn ˈdeɪndʒər/ [v phrase] to be in a situation in which something harmful might happen, often caused by your own actions: *The test helps identify pregnant women who are in danger of miscarriage.* | **+ of doing sth** *The Democrats are in danger of alienating their traditional supporters.* | *If the team doesn't start winning, Coach Sanders could be in danger of losing his job.*

high-risk /ˌhaɪ ˈrɪsk◂/ [adj only before noun] likely to be in particular danger of something bad happening, or likely to involve greater risks than usual: *high-risk occupations such as construction work* | *The AIDS awareness campaign was targeted mainly at high-risk groups, especially drug users and prostitutes.*

lay yourself open to ALSO **leave yourself open to** American /ˌleɪ jɔːʳself ˈəʊpən tuː, ˌliːv jɔːʳself ˈəʊpən tuː/ [v phrase] to do or say something that makes it likely that people will blame you, criticize you etc: *He has left himself open to charges of racism.* | *Any journalist who writes a story without checking his facts is simply laying himself open to criticism.*

be on dangerous ground/in dangerous territory /biː ɒn ˌdeɪndʒərəs ˈgraʊnd, ɪn ˌdeɪndʒərəs ˈterᵍtəri‖-tɔːri/ [v phrase] to talk about a particular subject when there is a risk that you may offend, annoy, or or upset someone: *A boss who puts his arm around an employee is on dangerous ground and could risk charges of harassment.* | *I realized I was in dangerous territory, and steered the conversation away from his business interests.*

7 in a situation where there are risks

- be at risk
- be in danger
- be in jeopardy
- be at stake
- be under threat
- be on the line

be at risk /biː ət ˈrɪsk/ [v phrase] if something is at risk, it could be harmed, destroyed or lost: *Unless funding becomes available, the entire project is at risk.* | **+ of** *Wildlife along the coastline is at risk of serious pollution from the tankers.* | **+ from** *The future of the party is clearly at risk from internal divisions.* —**at-risk** [adj only before noun] *at-risk children* | *at-risk patients*

be in danger /biː ɪn ˈdeɪndʒəʳ/ [v phrase] if something **is in danger**, especially something very important, there is a serious risk that it will be harmed, destroyed, or lost: *With the rise of the fascist right, democracy itself was in danger.* | **+ of doing sth** *The whole building is in danger of collapsing.* | *The achievements of the 1917 Revolution are now in danger of being forgotten.*

be in jeopardy /biː ɪn ˈdʒepəʳdi/ [v phrase] if something, especially a plan, an agreement, or a relationship **is in jeopardy,** there is a serious risk that it will fail, be lost, or be harmed: *Negotiations have broken down, and the peace agreement is now in jeopardy.* | *Lessing's career in football was in jeopardy after his back surgery in July.*

be at stake /biː ət ˈsteɪk/ [v phrase] if something important or valuable **is at stake**, there is a risk that it will be lost if something that you are doing is unsuccessful: *With a place in the final at stake, there was everything to play for.* | *The peace process will not end; there is too much at stake.*

be under threat /biː ˌʌndəʳ ˈθret/ [v phrase] if something important and valuable **is under threat**, there is a risk that it will be lost or destroyed unless someone takes action to stop the situation that causes it: *With so many new offices being built in London, a lot of important archaeological remains are under threat.* | **+ from** *Sensitive environmental areas are under threat from urban developers.* | **+ of** *Demand for coal fell, and many of the mines were under threat of closure.*

be on the line /biː ɒn ðə ˈlaɪn/ [v phrase] if something such as your job or people's opinion of you is **on the line**, there is a risk that you will lose it if you do not succeed in something that you are trying to do: *A company's reputation is on the line in the way it handles complaints.* | *Your job's on the line in this case – you'd better make sure you're right.*

8 to cause risks

- put sb/sth at risk
- threaten
- endanger
- jeopardize

put sb/sth at risk /ˌpʊt (sb/sth) ət ˈrɪsk/ [v phrase] to do something that makes it more likely that someone or something will be harmed: *The pilot has been accused of putting his passengers' lives at risk.* | *Development in the wetlands will put the environment and wildlife habitats at risk.* | **+ of** *Some people carry a gene that puts them at greater risk of certain cancers.*

threaten /ˈθretn/ [v T] to make it likely that something bad will happen to someone or something: *A severe drought is threatening the rice crop.* | *According to some scientists, global warming threatens the survival of the whole human race.*

endanger /ɪnˈdeɪndʒəʳ/ [v T] to put someone or something in a dangerous or harmful situation: *The U.S. was unwilling to do anything that might endanger the alliance with Japan.* | *The pilot refused to endanger the lives of his passengers by making an unscheduled landing.* | *If unemployment continues to rise, social stability may be endangered.*

jeopardize ALSO **put/place sth in jeopardy** /ˈdʒepəʳdaɪz, ˌpʊt, ˌpleɪs (sth) ɪn ˈdʒepəʳdi/ [v T] to do something that increases the risk that something good will be harmed or lost: *A scandal like this might jeopardize his political career.* | *The breaking of the ceasefire has put the whole peace process in jeopardy.* | **seriously jeopardize** *The country's economic future is seriously jeopardized by the mass emigration of young people.*

road/path

RELATED WORDS

- when a road changes direction *see* **turn (9)**
- when a road, path etc bends *see* **bend (7)**

1 in a town

- road
- street
- high street
- back street
- side street
- alley
- avenue/boulevard
- cul-de-sac/dead end/dead end street
- drive
- close
- crescent

road /rəʊd/ [n C] a hard level surface made for cars and other vehicles to travel on: *They're building a new road around the city centre.* | *I live at 37 King's Road, Birmingham.* | **cross the road** *Before crossing the road, stop, look, and listen.* | **by the side/edge of the road** *Something was lying in the gutter by the side of the road.* | **across/over the road** (=on the other side of the road) *A widow lives in the house just across the road.* | **along/down/up the road** (=on the same road) *I went to the girls' school down the road.* | **main road** (=a large road where there is likely to be a lot of traffic) *They turned left at the gas station, into the busy main road.* | **busy road** (=a road where there is a lot of traffic) *It's amazing how many schools front busy roads.*

street /striːt/ [n C] a road in the main part of a town, with houses, shops, or offices and sometimes a path down each side for people to walk on: *There were stores on both sides of the street.* | *Wall Street is a famous financial center in New York.* | **the streets of London/Paris/Istanbul etc** *Pablo loved wandering through the streets of Barcelona.* | **in/on the streets** *We need more police on the streets.* | **along/down/up the street** *Victoria can't walk down the street without someone recognizing her.* | **live in a street** British **/on a street** American *She had lived in the same street in London all her life.* | **sb's street** (=the street where someone lives) *Our street was just a row of brick terraced houses.*

high street British **/main street** American /ˈhaɪ striːt, ˈmeɪn striːt/ [n C] the **main street** in the middle of a town where most of the shops and offices are: *Our bank used to have a branch in every high street.* | *The small town of Whitehorse, Alaska consists of a half-mile long main street and a few scattered houses.* | *Albert Road is just off the High Street.*

back street ALSO **back alley** American /ˈbæk striːt, ˈbæk æli/ [n C] a small street, away from the main streets of a town, where there are no large shops or important buildings: *They went exploring the dark, narrow back alleys of the old part of town.* | *It took us almost an hour to find her house in a narrow little back street.*

side street /ˈsaɪd striːt/ [n C] a small quiet road away from any main roads: *If the car park's full you might find a space in one of the side streets.*

alley /ˈæli/ [n C] a very narrow street or path between buildings in a town: *A narrow alley led up between the houses to the main street.* | *Women in white aprons gossiped in the alley between the apartment blocks.*

avenue/boulevard /ˈævɪ̈njuː‖-nuː, ˈbuːlvɑːʳd‖ ˈbuːlə-, ˈbʊ-/ [n C] a wide road often with trees along each side of it, especially one that is long and straight – often used in street names: *She lives in a large house on Acacia Avenue.* | *New York's 5th Avenue* | *The apartment is located on Jackson Boulevard.* | *New Delhi, with its elegant wide avenues and impressive government buildings, is a complete contrast with Old Delhi.* | *There are plans to replace the old highway with a braod tree-lined boulevard.*

cul-de-sac/dead end/dead end street /ˈkʌl də sæk, ˌded ˈend, ˈded end ˌstriːt/ [n C] a street that is closed at one end so there is only one way in and out: *We got to know the neighbors on our cul-de-sac quite well.* | *Archie lives on a dead end street, so it is very quiet.* | *Honey, this is a dead end – you'll have to turn around.*

drive /draɪv/ [n C] a road with houses on it, especially a beautiful one – used in street names: *She was found dead at her home in Maple Drive.*

close /kləʊs/ [n C] British a road with houses along each side of it and with only one way in or out – used in street names: *Fran lives at 37 Appian Close.*

crescent /ˈkresənt/ [n C] British a street with a curved shape – used in street names: *Turn left into Badgerly Crescent.*

2 outside a town

- road
- lane
- dirt road
- track

road /rəʊd/ [n C] a **road** that connects towns or cities: *Route 66 used to be one of the main roads across the States.* | *I like driving on the French roads – they're so straight, and there isn't much traffic.* | **+ to** *As you leave the city, turn right and take the road to Madrid.*

lane /leɪn/ [n C] a narrow road in the countryside, connecting villages or farms: *The last stretch of road is a narrow lane bordered by trees.* | **country lane** *We rode our bicycles along pretty country lanes.*

dirt road /ˈdɜːʳt ˌrəʊd/ [n C] a narrow road with a dirt or soil surface: *A dirt road ran from the highway past the dump and into some trees.* | *Rain fell continuously and turned the winding dirt road into a river of slippery mud.*

track /træk/ [n C] British a narrow road, usually without a hard surface, leading to a farm or field: *The track was only wide enough for one car.*

3 a wide road for travelling quickly

- motorway
- highway
- expressway
- route
- by-pass
- ring road

motorway British **/freeway** American /ˈməʊtəʳweɪ, ˈfriːweɪ/ [n C] a wide road connecting cities and towns, on which cars can travel fast for long distances: *The speed limit on motorways is 70 mph.* | *We headed east on the Pasadena freeway.* | **a motorway bridge/cafe/garage etc** *A new motorway service station has been opened to encourage drivers to take a break.*

highway /ˈhaɪweɪ/ [n C] American a wide fast road that connects cities and towns: *I got onto the highway and drove as fast as I could.* | **highway 61/70 etc** *There's a rest stop somewhere on Highway 61.*

expressway /ɪkˈspresweɪ/ [n C] American a wide fast road that takes traffic into and out of a big city: *They took the expressway to the airport.*

route /ruːt‖ruːt, raʊt/ [n] American used in the names of some roads connecting towns and cities: *Rockland is hard to miss. Route 1 runs right through it.* | *the westerly side of Route 128*

by-pass /ˈbaɪ pɑːs‖-pæs/ [n C] British a road that goes around a town, so that people can avoid driving through the town: *It will be much quicker if we take the by-pass rather than drive through the middle of town.* | *The village has become much quieter since the creation of the by-pass.*

ring road British **/beltway** American /ˈrɪŋ rəʊd, ˈbeltweɪ/ [n C] a circular road that goes around the edge of a large town, with roads leading off it into the centre of the town: *The property is ideally placed for access to the centre and the ring road.* | **inner ring road** (=a ring road that is inside another road that goes around a town) *a car park beside the inner ring road* | *We took the beltway around the city.*

4 a path for people to walk on

- path
- pavement
- footpath
- trail

path /pɑːθ‖pæθ/ [n C] a long, narrow piece of ground for people to walk along: *A narrow path took us down to the river.* | **down/along a path** *He lead me down a path to a farmhouse.* | **garden path** *Mrs Smith was singing as she came up the garden path.*

pavement British **/sidewalk** American /ˈpeɪvmənt, ˈsaɪdwɔːk/ [n C] a path built along the side of a street for people to walk on: *Christopher wandered along the sidewalk, looking into store windows.* | *What annoys me is that everyone parks on the pavement in front of our house.*

footpath /ˈfʊtpɑːθ‖-pæθ/ [n C] British a public path for people to walk on in the country: *They followed the coastal footpath into the village.* | **public footpath** (=a path that anyone can use, especially one on private land) *There are over 1,000 miles of public footpaths within the national park boundaries.*

trail /treɪl/ [n C] American a path in the mountains or in the forest: *The trail follows the river most of the way to Avalanche Lake.*

rough/ not smooth

RELATED WORDS

- rough behaviour *see* **violent**
- a rough guess or calculation *see* **about/approximately**
- a rough voice *see* **voice**
- *see also* **flat/not flat**

1 not smooth

- rough
- coarse
- abrasive
- scaly
- calloused

rough /rʌf/ [adj] a **rough** surface is not smooth because it has lumps or holes in it: *The car bumped up and down as we drove across the rough ground.* | *He fell, cutting his forehead on the rough edge of a rock.* | *Hessian cloth provides a rough homespun texture that was popular in the 1950s.* —**roughness** [n U] *friction caused by the roughness of the road surface*

coarse /kɔːʳs/ [adj] something such as material or hair that is **coarse** feels rough and hard, especially because it is made of thick thread, hairs etc: *All the hospital beds were covered with coarse cotton sheets. | Her straight hair, once dark brown, was becoming grey and coarse. | The fisherman's skin was dark and coarse, his hands big and strong.*

abrasive /əˈbreɪsɪv/ [adj] an **abrasive** object or material has a hard rough surface that can damage other surfaces when it rubs against them: *Rub the table down with a fine abrasive paper before painting it. | If your body skin looks dull, removing dead skin with an abrasive glove can make a big difference.*

scaly /ˈskeɪli/ [adj] **scaly** skin is dry and rough: *To relieve tight or scaly skin, add a teaspoon of fine oil to your bathwater. | Dandruff is characterized by a scaly and sometimes itchy scalp.*

calloused /ˈkæləst/ [adj] hands that are **calloused** are covered with thick hard areas of skin, especially because of hard physical work: *His was a big, strong hand, roughly calloused from fieldwork. | He ran a calloused finger around the rim of his glass.*

2 to make a surface rough

- roughen

roughen /ˈrʌfən/ [v T usually in passive] *Her hands had been roughened by years of labouring. | the roughened old stump of a tree*

round

RELATED WORDS

- around something or moving around something *see* **around/round**
- *see also* **circle, shape**

1 shaped like a ball

- round
- spherical

round /raʊnd/ [adj] *The recipe calls for large round tomatoes. | His bald round head reminded her of Sam. | European watermelons are much rounder than the American variety. | His stomach was big and round from drinking too much beer.*

spherical /ˈsferɪkəl/ [adj] shaped like a ball – use this in technical contexts: *Edam cheeses are small and spherical in shape. | The earth is not quite spherical, because it is slightly flat at the poles. | La Geode, in Paris, is a unique spherical building with a cinema inside.*

2 shaped like a circle

- round
- circular
- oval

round /raʊnd/ [adj] *Violet stared at him with huge round eyes. | In the kitchen there was a round table with a vase of flowers on it. | She drew a round yellow sun in the center of the picture.*

circular /ˈsɜːʳkjələʳ/ [adj] shaped exactly like a circle: *The cattle are kept in a large circular enclosure. | The planets follow almost circular orbits around the sun. | The Villa Madama has a circular courtyard with rooms leading off it in all directions.*

oval /ˈəʊvəl/ [adj] shaped like a circle with slightly flat sides: *The portrait hung in an oval frame on the wall. | Some of the tables are oval in shape and some are round.*

3 an object shaped like a ball

- ball
- sphere
- globe

ball /bɔːl/ [n C] *Shape the cookie dough into balls and put them in the refrigerator. | When hedgehogs are in danger, they curl their bodies into tight balls.* | **+ of** *The kitten was playing with a ball of yarn. | Comets are balls of ice and dirt that circle the sun.*

sphere /sfɪəʳ/ [n C] shaped like a ball – use this in technical contexts: *At the top of each column is a perfect sphere of white marble. | The volume of a sphere is equal to twice the square of its radius, multiplied by pi.*

globe /gləʊb/ [n C] a ball-shaped object, especially one that is used for decoration: *For the occasion the town square was lit up by coloured globes strung together. | The stuffed birds had been encased in glass globes.*

4 with curved or slightly round sides

- curved
- rounded

curved /kɜːʳvd/ [adj] neither straight nor completely round: *The entrance is formed by two curved rows of large stones. | The bird uses its long curved bill to dig out worms and small insects. | Shaving mirrors are slightly curved in order to magnify the image.*

rounded /ˈraʊndɪ̈d/ [adj] a **rounded** surface does not have any sharp edges or points: *The knife had a rounded wooden handle. | Her nails were perfectly rounded and painted with delicate pink nail-polish. | The blocks have rounded edges that are safer for small children.*

5 shaped like a tube

- tubular
- cylindrical

tubular /ˈtjuːbjələʳ‖ˈtuː-/ [adj] formal a **tubular** object is hollow and shaped like a tube: *Inside a bicycle tire is a long tubular piece of rubber. | It was a shaky little card table with legs of tubular metal. | The Renaissance Center is a huge tubular steel and glass shopping mall.*

cylindrical /sɪ̈ˈlɪndrɪkəl/ [adj] a **cylindrical** object has straight sides and flat round ends: *The cylindrical glass jars are used for keeping spaghetti in. | Roll the bread dough into a cylindrical shape. | a cylindrical marble column*

rub

RELATED WORDS

- to rub something off *see* **remove (3)**
- to rub something out *see* **remove (5)**
- to clean something by rubbing it *see* **clean (6)**

1 to move your hand or a cloth several times over something

- rub
- give sth a rub
- scratch

rub /rʌb/ [v I/T] *Alice yawned and rubbed her eyes. | Rub the bowl with garlic before adding the breadcrumbs. | If you rub hard the knives will become* *really shiny.* | **rub sth into sth** *About once a month I rub wax into the table to keep it in good condition.* | **rub sth in** *Tom spread sun cream onto the baby's back and began to rub it in.* | **rub sth off/from sth** *The teacher turned and rubbed what he had written off the board.* | **rub sth off** *She washed her hands and face, rubbing the lipstick away with a flannel.* | **rub sth clean/dry/smooth etc** *precious stones that have been rubbed smooth and set in gold*

give sth a rub /ˌgɪv (sth) ə ˈrʌb/ [v phrase] British to rub something for a short time: *I gave the mirror a quick rub with a cloth and it was clean again.* | *'If you meet a young man', she instructed 'bite on your lips and give your cheeks a rub to bring up the colour'.*

scratch /skrætʃ/ [v I/T] to rub something, especially a part of the body, with your fingernails: *He sat thinking, scratching his head.* | *I had several mosquito bites, and it was difficult not to scratch them.* | *Don't scratch – it will only make the itching worse.*

2 to make one thing rub against another

- **rub**
- **scrape**
- **rub sth together**

rub /rʌb/ [v T] **rub sth against/on sth** *When the cat rubs its back against my legs, I know it's hungry.* | *Rubbing a dock leaf on a nettle sting is said to get rid of the pain.*

scrape /skreɪp/ [v T] to make something hard rub roughly on a hard surface: *Stop scraping your chair!* | **scrape sth on/against/across etc sth** *We scraped our shoes on the doorstep to get the mud off them.* | **scrape sth off (sth)** *I'll have to scrape the ice off the windscreen before we set off.*

rub sth together /ˌrʌb (sth) təˈgeðəʳ/ [phr v T] to rub two things together: *Jan rubbed his hands together to keep them warm.* | *Male crickets make a noise by rubbing their wings together.*

3 to move over a surface while pressing against it

- **rub**
- **scrape**
- **chafe**

rub /ˈrʌb əgenst/ [v I/T] to **rub** against something, often causing pain or damage: *This seatbelt is rubbing my shoulder.* | *Badly fitting shoes will rub more painfully if you are not wearing socks.* | **+ against** *The teacher rubbed against the blackboard, getting chalk all over his back.* | *These days rucksacks are made with specially padded straps so that they do not rub against the shoulders.*

scrape /skreɪp/ [v I/T] to rub roughly against a hard surface, often making a noise: *Outside snow plows were scraping the street.* | **+ on/against/along** *Three workmen came into the store – I could hear their boots scraping on the floor.* | *The sound of knives and forks scraping against plates filled the canteen.* | *It was not until we felt the exhaust pipe scraping along the road that we realized there was something wrong with the car.*

chafe /tʃeɪf/ [v I/T] to rub against a part of the body, making it sore: *The handcuff chafed his left wrist.* | *My dress was too tight under the arms and had a collar that chafed.*

rubbish/ garbage

things that you throw away because you do not want them

RELATED WORDS

- to throw rubbish away *see* **get rid of**
- to be very bad *see* **bad (1)**

- **rubbish**
- **garbage/trash**
- **waste paper**
- **litter**
- **refuse**
- **waste**

rubbish /ˈrʌbɪʃ/ [n U] British all the paper, empty bottles, cans, pieces of food etc that you throw away: *The dustmen collect the rubbish on Wednesdays.* | *There was rubbish and broken glass all over the grass.* | **put/take out the rubbish** (=put it in a rubbish bin outside your house ready to be collected) *Don't forget to put the rubbish out before you go to bed.* | **a rubbish bin** (=a container for rubbish) *Two stolen paintings have been found dumped in a rubbish bin.* | **rubbish dump/tip** (=a large open area where people's rubbish is taken after it is collected) *I rescued this table from a rubbish dump.*

garbage/trash /ˈgɑːʳbɪdʒ, træʃ/ [n U] American all the paper, empty bottles, cans, pieces of food etc that you throw away: *There were piles of trash in the backyard.* | **take out the garbage/trash** (=put it in a garbage can outside your house ready to be collected) *I do all the chores, from picking up the groceries to taking out the garbage.* | **garbage/trash can** (=a container for garbage) *Will someone please empty this trash can!* | **garbage truck** (=a truck that takes away garbage) *Ken drives a garbage truck for a living.*

waste paper /weɪst ˈpeɪpəʳ/ [n U] paper that you throw away, especially because it has been used: *There are two bins. One is for glass and one is for waste paper.* | **waste paper bin** British /waste paper basket American *She crumpled the letter up and put it in the waste paper basket.*

litter /ˈlɪtəʳ/ [n U] empty bottles, packets, and pieces of paper that people have dropped on the street or in a park: *These streets are full of litter.* | **drop litter** *You can be fined £100 for dropping litter.* | **pick up litter** *I am tired of picking up litter thrown by other people.* | **litter bin** British /litter basket American (=a container for litter) *a picnic area with large wooden tables and litter bins*

refuse /ˈrefjuːs/ [n U] formal all the things that are regularly thrown away from the houses, shops etc in an area: *Heaps of decaying refuse littered every street.* | **refuse collection** *Refuse collection has been seriously affected by the strike.* | **refuse disposal** (=destroying or burying refuse) *We are gradually developing safer and more effective methods of refuse disposal.* | **household/domestic refuse** (=refuse from houses) *facilities for recycling household refuse*

waste /weɪst/ [n U] useless materials which are left over, especially after an industrial process, and which must be thrown away: *Too much waste has been dumped into the North Sea.* | **industrial/chemical/nuclear waste** *Industrial waste had leaked into the water supply.* | **radioactive/toxic/hazardous waste** *The government has announced a ban on all imports of toxic waste from abroad.* | **waste disposal** (=destroying or burying waste) *The costs of waste disposal are rising all the time.*

rude

RELATED WORDS

opposite: **polite**

- to answer someone rudely *see* **answer (4)**
- to rudely pretend not to notice someone *see* **ignore (2)**
- rude jokes *see* **sex (18)**
- *see also* **insult, offend, criticize, horrible**

1 rude/not polite

- **rude**
- **impolite/not polite**
- **tactless**
- **abrasive**
- **bad manners**
- **bad-mannered/ill-mannered**
- **discourteous**
- **be unpleasant**
- **loutish**

rude /ruːd/ [adj] someone who is **rude** upsets or offends people by not following the rules of good social behaviour and not considering other people's feelings: *What a rude man! He just ignored me when I said 'Good morning'.* | *I don't mean to be rude, but could you tell your children to keep quiet?* | *He's one of the rudest people I've ever met.* | **+ to** *I know you're upset, but there's no need to be rude to your mother.* | **+ about** *Are you being rude about my cooking?* | **it is rude to do sth** *It's rude to interrupt people when they are speaking.* | **it is rude of sb to do sth** *I thought it was very rude of her not to answer my letter.* —**rudely** [adv] *Blair rudely pushed his way to the front of the line.* —**rudeness** [n U] *Please forgive me for my rudeness the other day.*

impolite/not polite /ˌɪmpəˈlaɪt, nɒt pəˈlaɪt/ [adj] not following the rules of accepted social behaviour, especially when someone does this without realizing it – use this especially about the things that people do or say, rather than about people themselves: *In Senegal it is considered impolite if you do not share your food.* | *You weren't very polite to her.* | **it is impolite/not polite to do sth** *I was tired, but I thought it might not be polite to leave so early.* | *It is impolite and inconsiderate for people to drop in uninvited.*

tactless /ˈtæktləs/ [adj] someone who is **tactless** upsets or embarrasses someone else, without intending to, by mentioning something that it would be better not to talk about: *I wanted to know about her divorce, but I thought it would be tactless to ask.* | *She was often tactless and insensitive.* | *tactless remarks*

abrasive /əˈbreɪsɪv/ [adj] seeming rude or unkind because you say what you think very directly, so that people are annoyed or offended: *Harris was abrasive and arrogant.* | *Anson's abrasive personality has landed her in trouble many times in the past.*

bad manners /bæd ˈmænəʳz/ [n plural] someone who has **bad manners** does not behave politely in social situations, for example by not saying 'please' and 'thank you': *Marilyn apologized for her husband's bad manners.* | **it is bad manners to do sth** *It is bad manners to talk with your mouth full.*

bad-mannered/ill-mannered /ˌbæd ˈmænəʳd◂, ˌɪl ˈmænəʳd◂/ [adj] behaving in a rude and unpleasant way, especially because of never having been taught how to be polite: *Her children are incredibly bad-mannered – she should be more strict with them.* | *Ill-mannered movie-goers talked and took cell phone calls during the picture.* | *As soon as some English people go abroad, they seem to change into bad-mannered, insensitive oafs.*

discourteous /dɪsˈkɜːʳtiəs/ [adj] formal not behaving in a polite way – use this especially about people's remarks or behaviour: *It would have seemed discourteous to refuse his offer.* | **+ to** *He claimed that the officer had been discourteous to him.*

be unpleasant /biː ʌnˈplezənt/ [v phrase] to deliberately behave in a rude and unfriendly way towards someone: *He can be very unpleasant when he's in a bad mood.* | *It isn't necessary to be that unpleasant, Mike.* | **+ to** *She was shocked at how unpleasant the children were to their mother.*

loutish /ˈlaʊtɪʃ/ [adj] rude, loud, and unpleasant – use this especially about people's behaviour: *The behaviour of some politicians in debates is simply loutish and intimidating.* | *They considered my boyfriend to be loutish and a bit stupid.* | *loutish behaviour*

2 when someone is rude to teachers, parents etc

- **disrespectful**
- **cheeky**
- **impertinent**
- **impudent**
- **insolent**
- **sassy**
- **disrespect**
- **diss**

disrespectful /ˌdɪsrɪˈspektfəl/ [adj] rude, especially towards someone you should respect, for example your parents or someone in authority: *A letter from the school arrived, saying that Joey had been both disobedient and disrespectful.* | **+ to** *In Chinese culture, it is considered disrespectful to both the living and the dead to live near a burial ground.* | **+ about** British *He thought I was being disrespectful about his country.* | **it is disrespectful (for sb) to do sth** *Some older people think it disrespectful for strangers to call them by their first name.*

cheeky /ˈtʃiːki/ [adj] British making rude remarks to or asking personal questions of someone you should respect – use this especially about children: *I don't like teaching that class – the kids are all so cheeky.* | *What do you mean, I'm fat? You cheeky devil!*

impertinent /ɪmˈpɜːʳtɪnənt/ [adj] rude and showing no respect for someone in authority, especially by saying things or asking questions about something that it is not your right to know or discuss: *By now he had gotten used to reporters' impertinent questions about his private life.* | *Could I ask how old you are, or would that be impertinent?* —**impertinence** [n U] *He had the impertinence to suggest I was not raising my children properly.* | *We will not tolerate such impertinence.*

impudent /ˈɪmpjʊdənt/ [adj] formal someone who is **impudent**, especially a child or young person, is rude and has no respect for people who are older or more important: *She didn't think the child's questions were endearing – just impudent.* | *On the cover was a picture on an impudent boy sticking out his tongue.* —**impudence** [n U] *He looked at me with a mixture of impudence and hostility.*

insolent /ˈɪnsələnt/ [adj] formal very rude to someone in authority and appearing to have no respect for them, especially by not doing what they tell you to do: *Although she didn't actually say anything offensive, her expression was sulky, insolent, and hostile.* —**insolence** [n U] *When I was young, such insolence would not have been tolerated.*

sassy /ˈsæsi/ [adj] American if a young person is **sassy**, they are not polite to teachers, parents, or other people in authority, especially because they argue or try to be funny when someone tells them what to do: *She was sassy and smart, and all the kids liked her.* | *Becky was a sassy, rambunctious New York girl he'd met when visiting his aunt.* | *a sassy brat*

disrespect /ˌdɪsrɪˈspekt/ [v T] to offend or behave in a rude way towards someone: *The ambassador said it had not been his intention to disrespect the US government.* | *Some students do feel that teachers disrespect them.*

diss /dɪs/ [v T] spoken informal to criticize someone rudely: *Just don't diss my little brother, OK?* | *Politicians are always dissing football supporters.*

3 when someone speaks to you in a rude way, using very few words

- curt
- terse
- brusque
- dismissive
- be short with
- abrupt

curt /kɜːʳt/ [adj] replying in very few words in a way that seems rude: *She answered their questions with a curt 'No comment'.* | *Polly was curt and businesslike with her clients.* | *Her story was sent back with a curt rejection note.* —**curtly** [adv] *'That will be all, thank you,' said Mrs Rice curtly.*

terse /tɜːʳs/ [adj usually before noun] a **terse** message, reply, statement etc uses very few words and is deliberately intended to make people stop speaking to you or asking you questions: *The terse announcement gave no reason for Harris's resignation.* | *'We're in the process of negotiations,' Russo said in a terse statement to reporters.* —**tersely** [adv] *a tersely worded White House announcement*

brusque /bruːsk, brʊsk‖brʌsk/ [adj] using few words and saying directly what you think, because that is the way you usually speak, even though it often seems rude to other people: *Mathison's brusque style tends to irritate colleagues.* | *In public he appears brusque and dismissive, but he is in fact a very caring person.* —**brusquely** [adv] *'It doesn't matter much anyway,' he responded brusquely.*

dismissive /dɪsˈmɪsɪv/ [adj] treating someone's ideas, suggestions, or problems as if they are not at all important or serious, especially by dealing with them in very few words and then changing the subject: *She was very dismissive when I tried to tell her about my problems at work.* | **+ of** *Teenagers who have jobs can be quite dismissive of their peers who don't.* —**disimissively** [adv] *'Forget it,' Bill had said dismissively when I tried to apologize.*

be short with /biː ˈʃɔːʳt wɪð/ [v phrase] to speak to someone in a rude way, using very few words, especially because you are angry with them: *I'm sorry if I was short with you, but I was worried about my interview.* | *She was very short with me. I wonder if I've offended her in some way.*

abrupt /əˈbrʌpt/ [adj] seeming rude and unfriendly because you answer questions or talk to someone in a quick, direct way, especially because you do not want to waste time in friendly conversation: *'It won't work,' Mitchell says in his abrupt, no-nonsense style.* | *His new boss was abrupt and didn't seem interested in his proposals.*

4 someone who behaves rudely

- yob
- jerk
- lout

yob /jɒb‖jɑːb/ [n C] British a young man who is rude, noisy, and sometimes violent: *A dozen yobs stood outside the pub.* | *Residents complained that yobs had been vandalizing their gardens.* | **yob culture** (=TV programmes, films, and other forms of entertainment that involve rudeness and unintelligent behaviour) *Our TV screens have been taken over by so-called yob culture.*

jerk /dʒɜːʳk/ [n C] especially American an annoying person who behaves in a stupid way, for example by behaving in a rude and unpleasant way: *Ignore him. He's just a jerk.* | *He's an unprofessional jerk who's always pestering the women in the office.* | **real/total jerk** *Her husband was being a real jerk about the divorce.*

lout /laʊt/ [n C] a man or boy who behaves in a rude and violent way: *A few foul-mouthed louts in the crowd were shouting racist abuse.* | *Only a lout would treat a woman that way.* | **lager louts** British (=young men who drink too much beer and behave in rude or violent way) *We stood at the bar being jostled by some thick-necked lager louts.*

5 to do something rude without seeming ashamed or embarrassed

- have the nerve
- have the gall to do sth

have the nerve ALSO **have the cheek** British /ˌhæv ðə ˈnɜːʳv, ˌhæv ðə ˈtʃiːk/ [v phrase] if someone **has the nerve** to do something, they do something that you think is so rude that you are surprised they did it **+ to do sth** *He forgot our anniversary and then had the nerve to ask what I got him when I reminded him about it.* | **have a nerve/cheek** British /**have (some) nerve** American *He's got a cheek, coming back at midnight and then expecting me to cook his dinner.* | **what a nerve/cheek** British /**what a nerve** American *What a nerve! I hope you didn't give him the money!*

have the gall to do sth /hæv ðə ˌɡɔːl tə ˈduː (sth)/ [v phrase] if someone **has the gall to do something**, they do something that you think is very rude and unreasonable: *I can't believe he had the gall to ask you for money.* | *Ruth was always on the phone and yet she had the gall to tell me off for making one call.*

6 rude and offensive words

- bad/foul language
- strong language
- colourful language
- four-letter word
- swear word
- obscenity
- unprintable

bad/foul language /ˌbæd, ˌfaʊl ˈlæŋɡwɪdʒ/ [n U] formal language that most people think is offensive: *Even very young children are using foul language at school.* | *The computer chip allows parents to block programs containing violence, sex, or bad language.*

strong language /ˌstrɒŋ ˈlæŋɡwɪdʒ‖ˌstrɔːŋ-/ [n U] language that most people think is offensive – used especially to warn people that there may be offensive words used in a film or television programme: *The following programme contains strong language, and some viewers may find it offensive.* | *The film has lots of violence, scenes of drug-taking, and strong language.*

colourful language /ˌkʌləʳfəl ˈlæŋɡwɪdʒ/ [n U] language that uses a lot of swear words – use this in humorous contexts: *The colourful language of some of the characters may make it unsuitable for younger viewers.*

four-letter word /ˌfɔːʳ letəʳ ˈwɜːʳd/ [n C] a word that most people think is extremely offensive, especially one that is connected with sex or the sexual organs: *Rap songs are full of four-letter words.* | *It's a family show, with no four-letter words.*

swear word /ˈsweəʳ wɜːʳd/ [n C] a rude and offensive word that people use especially when they are angry: *He wasn't the type of man to use swear words.* | *We had to take all the swear words out of the play.*

obscenity /əbˈsenəti/ [n C usually plural] a word or expression, especially about sex, that most people think is extremely offensive: *Someone had written obscenities all over the classroom wall.* | *Rick burst into the apartment, drunk and shouting obscenities.*

unprintable /ʌnˈprɪntəbəl/ [adj] remarks, words etc that are **unprintable** are too offensive to appear in a newspaper, magazine, or book: *Most of what she said in the interview was unprintable.* | *Chief McNally admits he's been called many things, some of them unprintable.*

7 to use rude and offensive words

- swear
- cuss
- foul-mouthed

swear /sweəʳ/ [v I] *He swore angrily when he realized he'd missed the train.* | *Don't swear like that in front of the children!* | **+ at** *Officers say the suspect swore at them and threw a punch.* —**swearing** [n U] *It was great to see a movie that didn't rely on swearing for its dialogue.*

cuss /kʌs/ [v I/T] American informal to swear: *Unlike his teammates, Jones doesn't drink or cuss.* | **+ at** *He started cussing at the policeman who stopped him.* | **cuss sb out/cuss out sb** (=swear at someone angrily) *Jeez, what if I get mad and start cussing out the kids in my class!*

foul-mouthed /ˌfaʊl ˈmaʊθt◂/ [adj] someone who is **foul-mouthed** swears a lot: *If kids are foul-mouthed and rude, it's probably because they hear that kind of language at home.* | *Kinison was known for his screaming, foul-mouthed comic routines.*

rule/regulation

RELATED WORDS

- the law of a country or society *see* **law**
- *see also* **strict/not strict, punish**

1 a rule

- rule
- regulation
- restriction
- law
- code
- rules and regulations

rule /ruːl/ [n C] an instruction that says what people are allowed to do or not allowed to do, for example in a game, or in a school or organization: *No one's allowed to ride with the driver. That's a company rule.* | *It says in the rules that every child has to wear school uniform.* | **against the rules** (=not allowed by the rules) *It is strictly against the rules for athletes to take drugs.* | **break a rule** (=disobey it) *I have no sympathy for Jonson. He broke the rules and got caught, that's all.* | **rules govern sth** (=say how something should be done) *There have been some changes in the rules governing the use of safety equipment.* | **hard and fast rule** (=a definite fixed rule) *These are just guidelines, not hard and fast rules.*

regulation /ˌregjəˈleɪʃən/ [n C usually plural] an official rule made by a government or organization, which is part of a set of rules: *Under the new regulations, coach drivers must take a break every four hours.* | **building/planning/environmental regulations** *The building regulations are very strict about the materials you can use.* | **safety/fire regulations** *Safety regulations affecting dangerous fluids must be scrupulously observed.* | **comply with/conform to a regulation** (=be correct according to a regulation) *All cars sold in Germany must conform to the regulations laid down by the Federal Road Safety Board.* | **contravene/breach a regulation** formal (=do something that is forbidden by it) *Anyone who takes milk from an unhealthy cow will be contravening public health regulations.*

restriction /rɪˈstrɪkʃən/ [n C usually plural] an official rule that limits what people can do **+ on** *There are restrictions on what you can bring into the country. Alcohol, for example, is totally forbidden.* | **impose a restriction** (=bring it into operation) *The restrictions imposed by the censors make objective reporting of news impossible.* | **lift a restriction** (=stop it from operating) *Congress voted to lift trade restrictions against Iran.* | **travel/price/import restrictions** (=rules that limit the amount that someone can travel, how much something can cost etc) *For a while they tried using price restrictions as a way of controlling inflation.*

law /lɔː/ [n C usually plural] one of the rules that say how a sport should be played: *FIFA is the organization that runs world football and decides whether any of the laws should be changed.* | **+ of** *the laws of cricket*

code /kəʊd/ [n C] a set of rules that people or organizations agree to obey but are not forced to obey **+ of** *He will be dealt with under our code of discipline.* | **code of practice** (=rules saying what a particular type of organization should or should not do) *A new code of practice governing the advertising of tobacco products is being introduced.* | **code of conduct** (=rules saying how members of a profession should behave) *Hobbs had blatantly ignored the legal profession's code of conduct.* | **moral/religious code** *people who follow some strict religious code*

rules and regulations /ˌruːlz ən regjəˈleɪʃənz/ [n phrase] a set of rules – use this when you think the rules are too detailed or cause unnecessary inconvenience: *There were so many petty rules and regulations that some companies stopped trying to export their products.*

2 rules of acceptable behaviour

- convention
- protocol
- etiquette
- unwritten law
- netiquette

convention /kənˈvenʃən/ [n C/U] the rules and customs of acceptable behaviour, which are generally accepted by the members of a group or society: *He is a flamboyant millionaire who ignores social conventions.* | **+ of** *She shocked her neighbours by ignoring every convention of respectable society.* | **a matter of convention** *It is a matter of convention that male business people usually wear suits.* | **defy convention** (=do something unconventional) *For the next four years they defied convention by living as man and wife when they were not.*

protocol /ˈprəʊtəkɒl‖-kɔːl/ [n U] the system of rules for behaviour on official occasions: *According to* *protocol, he was to arrive at the meeting exactly five minutes early.* | **breach of protocol** (=behaviour not according to protocol) *Touching the Queen was a breach of royal protocol.*

etiquette /ˈetɪket‖-kət/ [n U] the rules of polite behaviour in society or in a particular group: *Etiquette is especially important on occasions such as weddings and funerals.* | **breach of etiquette** (=behaviour not according to etiquette) *It was considered a breach of etiquette to refuse an invitation.* | **professional etiquette** (=the etiquette followed by people working in a particular profession) *Professional etiquette dictates that judges should not express their opinions about a case in public.*

unwritten law /ˌʌnrɪtn ˈlɔː/ [n C] a rule or way of behaving that is not official but is accepted by most members of a society or group: *It was an unwritten law of the Mafia that nobody should talk to the police.* | *Jobs like this never go to women – it just seems to be one of those unwritten laws of business.*

netiquette /ˈnetɪket/ [n U] informal the commonly accepted rules for polite behaviour when you are communicating with other people on the Internet: *Sending an angry e-mail in capital letters breaks the rules of netiquette.*

rumour

things that people say, which may or may not be true

RELATED WORDS

▸ *see also* **say, true, untrue, lie**

- **rumour**
- **speculation**
- **gossip**
- **scandal**
- **reports**
- **talk**
- **hearsay**
- **hear sth on/ through the grapevine**
- **be rumoured/ rumored to be**

rumour British **/rumor** American /ˈruːməʳ/ [n C/U] information which is passed from one person to another and which may or may not be true, especially information about people's private lives or about something that a government, company etc has done or is planning to do: *The truth finally came out after months of rumour and gossip.* | **+ about/of** *What's this rumour about you and Vince Foster?* | *There were rumours of bombings in the northern part of the country.* | **+ that** *The band denied the rumours that they may be splitting up.* | **hear a rumour** *Have you heard the rumour about him and his secretary?* | **spread a rumour** (=tell other people a rumour) *Someone's been spreading nasty rumours about me.* | **it's only a rumour** *I don't think he's going to resign. It's only a rumour.* | **rumour has it that** (=there is a rumour that) *Rumour has it that there will be major job cuts in the new year.*

speculation /ˌspekjəˈleɪʃən/ [n U] if there is **speculation** about something, especially about something that is happening in politics or public life, a lot of people are talking about it and trying to guess what the truth is – used especially in news reports **+ about** *There was a great deal of speculation about a possible merger involving Belgium's largest banks.* | **+ that** *Washington was buzzing with speculation that the senator would resign.* | **amid speculation** *Share prices increased amid speculation that the Bank of England would cut interest rates.* | **prompt/fuel etc speculation** (=start or increase speculation) *The news fuelled speculation that the President's health had become significantly worse.* | **pure/wild/idle speculation** (=speculation that is very unlikely to be true) *Reports that the couple are getting a divorce have been dismissed as wild speculation.*

gossip /ˈgɒsəp‖ˈgɑː-/ [n U] information which people tell each other about other people's private lives, and which may or may not be true, especially when this is done in an unkind or disapproving way: *I got back from my vacation eager to hear all the latest gossip.* | **+ about** *The conversation began to drift towards gossip about their colleagues.* | **exchange gossip (with sb)** (=tell each other gossip) *Mrs Busby was always ready to exchange local gossip with the customers who came into her shop.* | **gossip column** (=part of a newspaper that contains gossip about famous people) *Recently her name has showed up a lot in gossip columns.* | **malicious gossip** (=unkind and untrue gossip that someone spreads deliberately) *I don't believe Liz had an affair with him. That's just malicious gossip.*

scandal /ˈskændl/ [n C/U] when something immoral or shocking happens, often involving important people, organizations, or events, and it becomes known by the general public: *Have you heard the latest scandal? Mick Green's been arrested for bribery and corruption.* | **+ over** *The scandal over the deal forced the corporation's president to resign in disgrace.* | **a scandal breaks/erupts** *A major scandal erupted in November 1989, with the discovery that cattle in the UK and Netherlands had been given food contaminated with lead.*

reports /rɪˈpɔːʳts/ [n plural] information or news that you think might be true, although you do not have any definite proof **+ of** *The government has promised to investigate reports of police corruption.* | **unconfirmed reports** (=reports that have not yet been proved to be true) *We are getting unconfirmed reports of a gas explosion in downtown Los Angeles.*

talk /tɔːk/ [n U] what people tell each other about other people's personal lives, especially about their sexual relationships: *In those days there was always talk if two people lived together without being married.* | **just talk** (=a rumour that is unlikely to be true) *'They say he's having an affair with a colleague at work.' 'That's just talk.'*

hearsay /ˈhɪəʳseɪ/ [n U] something that you have been told, or that you have heard only indirectly, but which you have no way of proving to be either true or untrue: *All the accounts were based on hearsay rather than eye-witness reports.* | *Judge Wagenbach ruled that the statement was inadmissible as evidence, after Mr. Lamb's attourney argued that it was hearsay.* | **rely on hearsay** *A factual book is a lot better than relying on hearsay from friends.* | **hearsay evidence** (=evidence given in a court of law by someone who did not directly see something happen) *The court is not allowed to admit hearsay evidence.*

hear sth on/through the grapevine /ˌhɪəʳ (sth) ɒn, θruː ðə ˈgreɪpvaɪn/ [v phrase] if you **hear** some news or information **on** or **through the grapevine**, someone else tells it to you unofficially, often in conversation: *'Who told you I was moving house?' 'Oh, I just heard it on the grapevine.'* | *Freddie was distressed when, through the grapevine, he heard of Liza's marriage.* | **the school/hospital/industry etc grapevine** *According to the high-school grapevine, Kelly wants me to ask her out on a date.*

be rumoured/rumored to be /bi: 'ru:mərd tə bi:/ [v phrase] if someone or something **is rumoured to** be doing something, be happening, be in a particular condition etc, that is what you have heard people saying: *It's a five star hotel and rumored to be the best in Europe.* | *The hospital is rumoured to be heading for closure, after the government's announcement on cuts.*

run

RELATED WORDS

- to be in charge of an organization *see* **in charge of**
- *see also* **walk, exercise, hurry, move/not move, sport/game, escape**

1 to run

- run
- dash
- make a run/dash/break for
- sprint
- trot
- tear
- charge
- break into a run
- bound

run /rʌn/ [v I] *You'll have to run or you'll miss the bus.* | *He kept on running until he was out in the open country.* | **+ across/through/along etc** *A dog ran straight out in front of my car.* | *Run to the bathroom and get a towel.* | **run for the bus/train etc** (=in order to catch it) *Just running for the bus leaves me out of breath.* | **run away/off** (=run fast in order to leave a place) *They grabbed her purse and then ran off towards the subway.* | *Neil tried to catch the frightened animal, but it ran away from him.* | **run around/round** (=run in several different directions over a fairly large area, for fun) *The kids were running around and being silly.* | **run after sb/sth** (=chase someone) *Her dog was running after a rabbit and did not hear her calling.*

dash /dæʃ/ [v I] to run very quickly for a short distance, especially because you have to do something urgently **+ around/into/across etc** *Gillian saw two men dash past, but they didn't notice her.* | *I eventually found the place, and dashed up the stairs.* | **dash off** (=leave a place very quickly, for example because you are late) *We only have a few moments, because Heidi's got to dash off soon.* —**dash** [n singular]

make a run/dash/break for /meɪk ə 'rʌn, 'dæʃ, 'breɪk fɔ:r/ [v phrase] informal to start running quickly towards a place or thing to try to reach it or escape something: *It was raining, and we made a run for the car.* | *When the lecture was finally ovr, the students made a break for the exit.* | **make a run/dash/ break for it** (=try to escape) *As soon as the guard turns around, we'll make a run for it.* | **make a made dash for sth** (=run very quickly) *She heard the whistle and made a mad dash for the departing train.*

sprint /sprɪnt/ [v I] to run as fast as you can, usually over a short distance **+ towards/out/across etc** *Margaret sprinted down the street, almost collapsing when she reached us.* | **sprint for the bus/train etc** (=in order to catch it.) *The bus driver must have seen me sprinting for the bus, but he drove off.* —**sprint** [n C] *I made a quick sprint to the local shop for some coffee.*

trot /trɒt‖trɑ:t/ [v I] to run fairly slowly, taking short steps **+ in/across/towards etc** *She trotted softly through the passageway to the gate.* | *I looked up, and saw a dog trotting along the sidewalk toward me.* | **+ along/back/off** *Dorothy arrived, with a little dog trotting along behind her.*

tear /teər/ [v I] to run very quickly and without really looking where you are going, because you are in a hurry **+ along/past/through etc** *Bobby tore past, shouting something about being late for work.* | *A masked man came tearing out of the bank and jumped into a waiting car.* | **tear off** (=leave somewhere running very quickly) *Mary tore off downstairs, determined to see the visitors for herself.*

charge /tʃɑ:rdʒ/ [v I] to run quickly and with a lot of energy, especially when you are going to attack someone or something **+ at/towards/into etc** *The doors flew open, and Pascoe charged across the foyer, scattering people in all directions.* | *Riot police with batons charged at soccer fans twice during last night's international with Spain.* | **charge off** (=leave somewhere in a hurry) *Don't charge off, I want a word with you.*

break into a run /ˌbreɪk ɪntʊ ə 'rʌn/ [v phrase] to suddenly start running, especially after you have been walking: *Suddenly two of the prisoners broke into a run, heading as fast as they could for the fence.* | *He walked swiftly, resisting the urge to break into a run.*

bound /baʊnd/ [v I] to move quickly forward with long high jumps **+ towards/across/up etc** *A big black Alsatian dog came bounding up to her.* | *There was a shout, and suddenly Adrian bounded into the room.*

2 to run as a sport or for exercise

- run
- jog
- go for a run/jog
- sprint

run /rʌn/ [v I/T] to **run** in a race or for exercise: *I think I'll probably run for about 40 minutes, then come back for a shower.* | **run 2 miles/400metres etc** *She runs a couple of miles twice a week.* | *I ran four miles Saturday, and I can tell you I was exhausted after it.* | **run a marathon/race/the 400 metres etc** *Omar's running the marathon this year.* —**run** [n C] *After his run, he took a long shower.* —**running** [n U] *After my first baby I took up running* (=the sport of running) *to try to lose some weight.* —**runner** [n C] *Long distance runners follow a different training programme from other athletes.*

jog /dʒɒg‖dʒɑ:g/ [v I] to run fairly slowly for a long distance, for exercise, and to keep healthy: *Have you been jogging this morning?* | **jog along/down/past etc** *When I lived in Washington, I jogged along the river every morning.* | *There was a lady jogging down by the water with her dog.* —**jog** [n C] *I always feel better after a jog around the park.* —**jogging** [n U] *Jogging is the only sport both Dave and I enjoy.* —**jogger** [n C] *It's surprising how many joggers you see in the park in the mornings.*

go for a run/jog ALSO **go running/jogging** /ˌgəʊ fər ə 'rʌn, 'dʒɒg‖-'dʒɑ:g, gəʊ 'rʌnɪŋ, 'dʒɒgɪŋ ‖-'dʒɑ:-/ [v phrase] to go out and run in order to get exercise: *Kari and I are going for a run – would you like to come?* | *Do you fancy coming jogging with me?*

sprint /sprɪnt/ [v I] to run as fast as you can over a short distance, usually in a race: *Athletes who have been trained to sprint aren't usually very good at running long distances.* —**sprinter** [n C] *They chose Alex for the last leg of the relay race because he was an excellent sprinter.* —**sprint** [n C] *I beat my personal best for the 25-metre sprint.*

3 to run with short quick steps

- scurry
- scamper
- scuttle

scurry /ˈskʌri‖ˈskɜːri/ [v I] to run with short quick steps, especially when you need to move quickly to escape from danger **+ away/about/along etc** *We used to hear rats and mice scrurrying around in the attic at night.* | *His aides scurried about, murmuring to each other in Russian.*

scamper /ˈskæmpəʳ/ [v I] to run with very short quick steps, especially when running in a group and often in a playful way **+ away/down/up etc** *The monkeys scampered down the tree, anxious to investigate what was happening on the ground.* | *Children were scampering and wrestling in the playground.* | *Jenny scampered off in excitement to set up the game.*

scuttle /ˈskʌtl/ [v I] to run with short quick steps, especially to escape from something – use this especially about small animals **+ across/out/past etc** *A loud bang sent all the crabs scuttling across the sand.* | *He spotted a cockroach as it scuttled out from under a bin bag.*

Ss

sad

RELATED WORDS

opposite: **happy**

- to become happy again after a period of problems or sadness *see* **recover (4-5)**
- to make someone less sad *see* **reduce**
- *see also* **disappointed, upset, fed up, cry, feel**

1 feeling sad or unhappy

- sad
- unhappy
- upset
- miserable
- homesick
- dejected
- downcast
- glum/gloomy
- wistful
- mournful

sad /sæd/ [adj not usually before noun] not happy, especially because a happy time has ended, or because you feel sorry about someone else's unhappiness: *She felt sad as she waved goodbye.* | *Don't look so sad! It won't be long until the next holidays.* | *There was such a sad look in her eyes.* | **sad to see/hear/learn etc** *We were very sad to hear about Mrs Humphrey's death.* | **+ to do sth** *I was glad to be going home, but sad to leave all my friends.* | **+ about** *It's natural to feel sad about it when your children finally leave home.* —**sadly** [adv] *She shook her head sadly and sighed.*

unhappy /ʌnˈhæpi/ [adj] not happy, because you are in a situation, job, or relationship that you do not enjoy at all, and it seems likely to continue: *Neil was very unhappy at school.* | *Her parents' divorce left her feeling confused and unhappy* | **desperately/deeply unhappy** (=very unhappy) *She was desperately unhappy after Sean left her.* | **+ about** *I felt so unhappy about what he had said that I just sat down and cried.* —**unhappily** [adv] *'I really don't know what to do' said James, unhappily.*

upset /ʌpˈset/ [adj not before noun] unhappy because something unpleasant or disappointing has happened, so that you feel shocked or you want to cry: *Don't be upset. I'm sure she didn't mean to be unkind.* | *The children were very upset when we told them that we wouldn't be going to Disneyland.* | **get upset** *We'd better not tell Mum about what's happened. She'll only get upset.* | **+ about** *Liz is very upset about her uncle's death.* | **+ that** *'What's the matter with Rod?' 'I think he's still upset that we forgot his birthday.'*

miserable /ˈmɪzərəbəl/ [adj] extremely unhappy, because of the situation you are in, especially because you are lonely, hungry, cold etc: *He sat all alone in his room, thoroughly miserable.* | *The poor miserable animals were starving, dirty and wet.* | *All the staff seemed to look miserable and the atmosphere was not at all pleasant.* —**miserably** [adv] *He shook his head miserably, the tears pouring down his cheeks.*

homesick /ˈhəʊmˌsɪk/ [adj] unhappy because you are away from your home, your family, and your friends, and you wish you were back there: *My sister was very homesick when she first went to college.* | *They were both gazing out of the window like a couple of homesick kids.* | *Most people get homesick the first time they leave home.* | **+ for** *Sampras confessed that he was homesick for America after five weeks in Europe.*

dejected /dɪˈdʒektɪ̈d/ [adj] sad and disappointed because something you hoped for did not happen – use this especially when this is shown in the way that someone looks, sounds etc: *He looked utterly dejected when she told him he'd failed again.* | *Greg sounded dejected. 'Anything wrong?' I said.* | *One glance at the doctor's dejected expression answered my question.* | *Kirkwood was a particularly dejected figure after their defeat.* —**dejectedly** [adv] *She read the letter and looked up dejectedly.*

downcast /ˈdaʊnkɑːst‖-kæst/ [adj] sad or disappointed because of a situation or because something you hoped for did not happen: *Jamie seems very downcast at the moment. He misses Jenny terribly.* | *'You mustn't be downcast' he said. 'You can always try again.'* | *The photograph of her sitting on her own made her look lonely and downcast.*

glum/gloomy /glʌm, ˈgluːmi/ [adj] informal sad because something slightly bad has happened or you do not have much hope for the future: *Don't look so glum! Things aren't as bad as all that.* | *Monday morning? Feeling glum?* | *Sorry to be gloomy. I've had a bit of a bad day.* | *The doctor was a tall gloomy Scotsman.* | *The glum expression on the England manager's face said it all.* | *Why are you in such a gloomy mood?* —**glumly/gloomily** [adv] *'Raining again,' she said glumly.*

wistful /ˈwɪstfəl/ [adj] someone who looks **wistful** has a slightly sad and thoughtful expression on their face, especially because they are thinking about the past or want something they cannot have: *Simon's face grew wistful as he thought about his happy student days.* | *She looked at them with a wistful smile. 'I wish I could go with you.'* —**wistfully** [adv] *'We used to have lovely family holidays all together,' she said wistfully.*

mournful /ˈmɔːʳnfəl/ [adj] looking or sounding very sad, as if something very bad has happened: *His voice sounded so mournful that tears came into her eyes.* | *I could hear the slow, mournful music of the bagpipes.* | *The dog lay at his feet, looking up from* *time to time with big mournful eyes.* —**mournfully** [adv] *In the distance, a wolf howled mournfully.*

2 feeling sad or unhappy for a long time

- depressed
- down/low
- down in the dumps
- feel blue
- morose

depressed /dɪˈprest/ [adj not usually before noun] very unhappy and without any hope for a long time, and feeling that your life will never get better, sometimes so that this becomes a mental illness: *My sister's been really depressed since she lost her job.* | *A lot of people get depressed in the winter, when the weather's bad and there's very little sunlight.* | **+ about** *Greta often gets depressed about her weight.*

down/low / daʊn, ləʊ/ [adj not before noun] informal unhappy, especially because something bad has happened to you and you cannot see how to make the situation better: *John's pretty low at the moment – his business is losing money.* | *He's been feeling down since he failed his driving test for the fifth time.*

down in the dumps /ˌdaʊn ɪn ðə ˈdʌmps/ [adj phrase not before noun] informal feeling unhappy and not having much interest in what is happening around you, but usually in a way that is not very serious: *Mom's kind of down in the dumps at the moment – why don't you buy her something to cheer her up?* | *If you're feeling down in the dumps, come over and have a chat.*

feel blue /ˌfiːl ˈbluː/ [v phrase] informal to feel slightly sad or unhappy, because something bad has happened to you or sometimes for no particular reason: *Feeling blue? Don't know who to talk to? Phone Depression Hotline, 24 hours a day.*

morose /məˈrəʊs/ [adj] someone who is **morose** behaves in an unhappy, bad-tempered way, and does not speak much to other people: *Since the accident she's been morose and moody.* | *Frank was sitting alone at the table, looking morose.* | *Some people become morose and depressed when they first retire.*

3 extremely sad

- heartbroken
- devastated
- inconsolable

heartbroken /ˈhɑːʳtˌbrəʊkən/ [adj] extremely sad and sorry because something very bad has happened, especially to someone or something that you love or care about very much: *When her parents separated, she was heartbroken.* | *Heartbroken fans camped outside his house in Beverly Hills.* | **+ at/about** *Mr and Mrs Dudley were heartbroken at having to leave the home where they had lived for thirty years.*

devastated /ˈdevəsteɪtɪ̈d/ [adj] extremely sad and shocked because something very bad has happened, and you feel that this has ruined your life or your plans: *The whole town was devastated by the tragedy, in which fourteen schoolchildren died.* | **devastated to hear/find etc sth** *When we got back, we were devastated to find that the house had been burgled, and everything of value taken.*

inconsolable /ˌɪnkənˈsəʊləbəl/ [adj not usually before noun] so sad that other people cannot make you feel happier, especially because someone has died or because something very bad has happened: *After the death of her baby she was inconsolable.* | *Doris was inconsolable. How could her husband walk out on her like that?*

4 making you feel sad

- sad
- unhappy
- depressing
- upsetting
- miserable
- heartbreaking/heart-rending
- dismal
- dreary
- bleak

sad /sæd/ [adj usually before noun] use this about a story, piece of music, period of time etc that makes you feel sad **sad time/day/moment/occasion etc** *The day her son left home was one of the saddest days of her life.* | **sad news/story/song etc** *Fairuz sang a sad song that made us all feel homesick.* | *I don't like movies with sad endings.* | **it is sad that** *It's very sad that she died before her children grew up.*

unhappy /ʌnˈhæpi/ [adj] **unhappy childhood/marriage/year etc** a time when you are **unhappy** because you are in a difficult or unpleasant situation: *Phil was married for three unhappy years.* | *Looking at that photo always bring back unhappy memories.* | *an unhappy love affair*

depressing /dɪˈpresɪŋ/ [adj] a **depressing** experience, story, piece of news etc makes you feel that there is nothing to be happy about and not much hope for the future: *The Deerhunter was a very depressing movie about Vietnam.* | *It's such a depressing town – it's full of ugly, disused factories.* | *Listening to the news can be really depressing, when all you ever hear about is violence and crime.*

upsetting /ʌpˈsetɪŋ/ [adj] an **upsetting** experience or event makes you feel very sad and often shocked: *Seeing her lying there in a hospital bed was a very upsetting experience.* | *She can't talk about her son's death – she finds it too upsetting.* | **it is upsetting to find/know/learn etc sth** *It's very upsetting to arrive home and find that your house has been burgled.*

miserable /ˈmɪzərəbəl/ [adj] a time that is **miserable** is one when you are extremely unhappy because you are in a very unpleasant situation: *Factory workers during the 18th century led miserable lives.* | *The journey home was miserable. Everyone was depressed about losing the game.*

heartbreaking/heart-rending /ˈhɑːʳtˌbreɪkɪŋ, ˈhɑːʳt ˌrendɪŋ/ [adj] a story, event, piece of news etc that is **heartbreaking** makes you feel extremely sad and sorry or extremely disappointed: *It's a heartbreaking moment when a great sportsman finally decides that it's time to quit.* | *The decision to kill the infected animals was a heart-rending one for farmers.* | **it is heartbreaking to see/learn etc sth** *Having worked so hard to start the business, it would be heartbreaking to see it all collapse.*

dismal /ˈdɪzməl/ [adj] a **dismal** place, situation, or time makes you feel unhappy and not at all hopeful: *It was a grey, dismal November afternoon.* | *Melinda joined her husband in Moscow, but soon found life there bleak and dismal.* | *The profit margin on hardware sales for the first quarter was a dismal 29%.* —**dismally** [adv] *At the time there was a dismally weak market in the rest of Europe.*

dreary /ˈdrɪəri/ [adj] a place, activity, or time that is **dreary** is not at all interesting or enjoyable and makes you feel unhappy: *This room is so dreary. How can we brighten it up?* | *a dreary winter's day* | *Cooking for one person can be a dreary business, as many elderly people find.*

bleak /bliːk/ [adj] a place or situation that is **bleak** is one in which there is nothing to make you feel cheerful or hopeful about the future: *The wild landscape was bleak and bare.* | *He gazed around the empty, bleak little room in despair.* | *Many people were facing a financially bleak Christmas.* | *The chief executive said that the company was looking at a bleak future.* | **the outlook/prospect/future etc is bleak** *Prospects of success looked bleak as the opposition scored the first two goals.*

5 to make someone feel sad

- make sb (feel) sad/unhappy
- upset
- sadden
- depress
- get sb down
- break sb's heart
- be a downer
- drive sb to despair

make sb (feel) sad/unhappy /ˌmeɪk (sb) (fiːl) ˈsæd, ʌnˈhæpi/ [v phrase] *Something at school was making her unhappy, but she didn't want to talk about it.* | **it makes sb sad/unhappy to do sth** *It made me sad to see her looking so old and ill.*

upset /ʌpˈset/ [v T] to make someone feel sad and want to cry: *I'm sorry if I upset you – I didn't mean to.* | *The idea of having to change school seemed to upset him more than we thought it would.* | **it upsets sb to do sth** *Her father died when she was ten, and it still upsets her to think about it.*

sadden /ˈsædn/ [v T] if a situation or event **saddens** someone, it makes them feel sad, especially because they think that this type of situation or event should not happen: *Everyone was saddened by the news that housing is to be built on the fields beside Cliff Lane.* | *Those of us who knew him are shocked and saddened by his death.* | **it saddens sb to do sth** *Sometimes it saddened him to think that he was no longer young.* | **it saddens sb that** *It saddens me that there are people who go around vandalizing public places like this.*

depress /dɪˈpres/ [v T] to make someone feel very sad or unhappy, especially so that they feel that only bad things happen and they cannot change the situation: *Listening to the news can really depress you, if you let it.* | *Shaun decided to leave. The way the others were behaving was beginning to depress him.* | **it depresses sb to do sth** *It depressed me to think that five years ago I was earning more than I do now.*

get sb down /ˌget (sb) ˈdaʊn/ [phr v T] informal to gradually make someone feel unhappy and tired over a period of time: *The endless rain was beginning to get him down.* | *You can tell me if there's anything that's worrying you or getting you down.*

break sb's heart /ˌbreɪk (sb's) ˈhɑːʳt/ [v phrase] to make someone very sad and upset, especially because a relationship has ended or because they are very disappointed: *When Annie left him, it broke his heart.* | **it breaks sb's heart (that)** *It breaks my heart that his career has been ruined.* | **it breaks sb's heart to do sth** *It would break her heart to leave the lovely old stone house where she'd lived for so long.*

be a downer /biː ə ˈdaʊnəʳ/ [v phrase] spoken if something **is a downer**, it makes you feel unhappy, especially because it is not good or successful: *I thought the movie was going to be a total downer, but it wasn't.* | **on a downer** *The home team concluded its season on a big downer with a 2- 0 defeat.*

drive sb to despair /ˌdraɪv (sb) tə dɪˈspeəʳ/ [v phrase] to make someone feel very unhappy and without hope – use this especially when a bad situation is continuing and they cannot see how to change it: *There were times when the endless arguments drove him to despair.* | *By the time I was 17, the atmosphere at the school was driving me to despair.*

6 to feel sad and pity yourself

- feel sorry for yourself
- mope
- wallow in
- self-pity

feel sorry for yourself /fiːl ˈsɒri fəʳ jɔːʳself‖-ˈsɑːri-/ [v phrase] especially spoken to spend a lot of time thinking about how unlucky you are or how unfairly you have been treated, in a way that annoys other people: *Stop blaming other people and feeling sorry for yourself.* | *Andy was drinking too much again, and feeling sorry for himself.*

mope /məʊp/ [v I] to feel unhappy because of something bad that has happened, and to not be interested in doing anything, in a way that other people think is not reasonable: *Don't just lie there moping, waiting for the phone to ring.* | **+ around/about** (=go around a place moping) *He's not even attempting to look for a job – he just mopes around the house all day.* | **+ over** *There's no point moping over Jane – she's not worth it.*

wallow in /ˈwɒləʊ ɪn‖ˈwɑː-/ [phr v T not in passive] **wallow in self-pity/despair/misery etc** to keep thinking about how unhappy you are, in a way that makes other people think that you are actually enjoying feeling sorry for yourself and do not want to feel happier: *She told herself that she must try and learn from his criticism, rather than wallowing in self-pity.* | *It's no good wallowing in misery. You just have to get out there and find another job.*

self-pity /ˌself ˈpɪti/ [n U] the feeling you have when you feel sorry for yourself, because you think that you have been very unlucky or that you have been treated unfairly: *If you feel a wave of self-pity coming on, go and talk about it with friends.* | *Jenny told her story without any of the self-pity that I thought I would feel after such an ordeal.*

7 to feel sad because someone has died

- grieve
- be in mourning
- mourn
- mourning

grieve /griːv/ [v I/T not in passive] to feel extremely sad because someone that you love has died: *It is a terrible tragedy for this small community. Everyone here is grieving.* | **+ for/over** *Millet continued to grieve for his wife for many years after her death.* | **grieve sb's death/loss** *People must be allowed to grieve the loss of a relative for as long as they need to.* —**grieving** [adj] *the grieving families of the dead*

be in mourning /biː ɪn ˈmɔːʳnɪŋ/ [v phrase] to feel sadness and respect for someone who has died, and to show this by the way you behave publicly, the clothes you wear etc: *The whole town is in mourning after two boys died on a school trip to the US.* | *In those days you were expected to wear black while you were in mourning.* | **+ for** *The sport was united in mourning for Maskell, as a player, coach and commentator for most of the century.*

mourn /mɔːʳn/ [v I/T] to feel very sad because someone has died, and to show this in the way you behave: *All the neighbours and relations who had come to mourn stood around the coffin.* | **+ for** *My mother never stopped mourning for my sister Frances, who died when she was four.* | **mourn sb's**

death/loss *His death was mourned by hundreds of former pupils and countless friends.*

mourning /ˈmɔːʳnɪŋ/ [n U] the things people do and they way they behave, dress etc to show their sadness and respect for someone who has died – use this especially about formal or traditional actions and ceremonies: *Mourning for the death of your husband used to last up to a year.* | **day of mourning** (=an official period of mourning) *Friday was declared an international day of mourning for the victims.*

8 a sad feeling

- sadness
- unhappiness
- grief
- depression
- the blues
- misery
- melancholy
- sorrow
- heartache
- despondency
- despair

sadness /ˈsædnɪ̈s/ [n U] a sad feeling, caused especially when a happy time is ending, or when you feel sorry about someone else's unhappiness: *Her eyes were full of sadness.* | **with (great) sadness** *I remembered with great sadness all the friends I had left behind.* | **sense of sadness** *After her death, Charles felt a great sense of sadness and loss.*

unhappiness /ʌnˈhæpinɪ̈s/ [n U] the unhappy feeling you have when you are in a very difficult or unpleasant situation: *After years of unhappiness, she finally decided to leave him.* | *There is no doubt that unhappiness contributes to ill health.* | *You've no idea what unhappiness you cause your parents when you say that you want to leave home.*

grief /griːf/ [n U] especially written great sadness that you feel when someone you love has died: *Thousands of people sent floral tributes as an expression of their grief.* | *He was overcome with grief when his wife died.*

depression /dɪˈpreʃən/ [n U] a mental illness that makes someone feel so unhappy that they have no energy or hope for the future, and they cannot live a normal life: *The family had a history of alcoholism and depression.* | *Mild symptoms of anxiety and depression are often associated with social difficulties.* | **deep/severe depression** *My father had suffered from severe depression for many years.*

the blues /ðə ˈbluːz/ [n plural] a feeling of sadness that is not very serious, that you get sometimes for no particular reason **get/have the blues** *I often get the blues in February, before the spring arrives.* | **a fit of the blues** *It's very common for new mothers to have a fit of the blues after giving birth.* | **the Monday/post-Christmas etc blues** *Most people know what it's like to have the Monday morning blues.*

misery /ˈmɪzəri/ [n U] great unhappiness, caused especially by living or working in very bad conditions: *The high interest rates caused misery for millions of people.* | **the misery of sth/sb** *He talked openly about the misery of his marriage.* | *We cannot ignore the misery of the people in this country who are forced to live on the streets.*

melancholy /ˈmelənkəli‖-kɑːli/ [n U] written a feeling of sadness, especially one that continues for a long time: *He was a strange man, prone to melancholy and bouts of drinking.* | *Jake was fourteen and suffering from adolescent melancholy.*

sorrow /ˈsɒrəʊ‖ˈsɑː-, ˈsɔː-/ [n U] written the feeling of being very sad, especially because someone has died or because terrible things have happened to you: | **deep/great sorrow** *The deep sorrow she felt was obvious in the expression of her face.* | **in sorrow** *He turned quickly away, more in sorrow than in anger.* | **to sb's sorrow** *Six weeks later we heard, to our great sorrow, that he had died.*

heartache /ˈhɑːʳteɪk/ [n U] a feeling of unhappiness and worry, that often continues for a long time and is usually caused by problems in your personal life and relationships: *Her relationship with Tyler had brought her a great deal of heartache.* | *Being unpopular at school can cause real heartache to children of any age.* | **save/spare (sb) a lot of heartache** (=stop someone worrying and feeling unhappy) *If she had simply called them, her parents would have been spared a lot of heartache.*

despondency /dɪˈspɒndənsi‖-ˈspɑːn-/ [n U] formal a feeling of unhappiness, especially because you have been very disappointed and feel that you cannot change a situation: *Robyn walked away from the hospital with a feeling of despondency.* | *The sense of well-being of the 1980s was replaced by a mood of despondency.* | **gloom/doom and despondency** *The atmosphere amongst the workers was one of gloom and despondency.*

despair /dɪˈspeəʳ/ [n U] a feeling of great unhappiness, because very bad things have happened and you have no hope that anything will change: *I could see hunger, exhaustion and despair in their eyes.* | *There was a mood of despair about the quality of urban and industrial life.* | **in despair** *Left all alone in her room, she was in despair.* | **the depths of despair** *It seems that he had reached the depths of despair, and he finally took his own life.*

9 to make sb feel less sad

- cheer sb up
- comfort
- cheer up
- it's all right/it's OK

▸ *see also* **comfort/make sb feel better**

cheer sb up /ˌtʃɪəʳ (sb) ˈʌp/ [phr v T] to make someone feel happier when they are disappointed or sad about something: *Is there anything we can do to cheer you up?* | *She failed her test, so I'm taking her out to cheer her up.*

comfort /ˈkʌmfəʳt/ [v T] to make someone feel less upset by being kind to them and telling them not to worry: *Bill stroked her hair gently, trying to comfort her.* | *We did our best to comfort him, but he was obviously very upset.*

cheer up /ˌtʃɪər ˈʌp/ [phr v] spoken say this to tell someone to stop feeling disappointed or sad and try to be more cheerful: *Cheer up, Phil! It's only a game, and you can't win every time.* | *Cheer up! It's not the end of the world.*

it's all right/it's OK /ɪts ˌɔːl ˈraɪt, ɪts ˌəʊ ˈkeɪ/ spoken say this to make someone feel calmer or make them stop crying, when they are very upset and worried about something: *It's all right, honey, I'm here now.*

safe

RELATED WORDS

opposite: —— **dangerous**

1 not in danger of being killed, harmed, or attacked

- safe
- safely
- safety
- be out of danger
- secure
- security
- be in good/safe hands

safe /seɪf/ [adj not before noun] *Do you think she'll be safe in the house all alone?* | *As long as we keep to the main road we should be safe.* | **+ from** *The turtles lay their eggs in the damp sand where they are safe from predators.* | **safe and sound** (=safe and unharmed, especially after being in danger) *The missing children were eventually found at a friend's house, safe and sound.*

safely /ˈseɪfli/ [adv] if you do something **safely**, you succeed in doing it without being killed, harmed, or attacked: *Once we were safely back on shore, we checked the boat for damage.* | *Most air travellers would be prepared to pay more to be sure of travelling safely.*

safety /ˈseɪfti/ [n U] when you are safe from danger or harm: *The boy has been missing for six days, and there are fears for his safety.* | **for sb's safety** (=so that someone is safe) *For your own safety, please do not smoke until you are outside the plane.* | *For the safety of the public, this man must be caught.* | **in safety** *Our planes are regularly serviced, so that passengers can be sure they are travelling in safety.*

be out of danger /biː ˌaʊt əv ˈdeɪndʒəʳ/ [v phrase] to be safe, after being in a dangerous situation: *Once out of danger, he relaxed. 'Phew, that could have been nasty'.* | *Mary raced on, thankful for her escape. Even now, however, she was not out of danger.*

secure /sɪˈkjʊəʳ/ [adj] feeling safe and free from danger: *The children all slept together in the same bed, snug and secure.* | *She felt much more secure now that she had put a bolt on the door.* | **safe and secure** *Children need to feel safe and secure about the world they grow up in.*

security /sɪˈkjʊərɪ̩ti/ [n U] freedom from harm or danger, especially from the danger of being robbed, killed, or attacked **for sb's security** *For the security of passengers, all hand baggage is carefully checked.* | **false sense of security** (=when you feel safe but in fact you are not) *His wide-eyed innocence had lulled me into a false sense of security.*

be in good/safe hands /biː ɪn ˌgʊd, ˌseɪf ˈhændz/ [v phrase] if someone such as a child or sick person **is in good hands**, they are safe because doctors or other responsible people are looking after them: *Don't worry about the children. They're in safe hands with Monica.* | *Although Grandad was very ill in hospital, it was a comfort for us to know he was in good hands.*

2 not in danger of being lost, stolen, or damaged

- safe
- secure
- be as safe as houses

safe /seɪf/ [adj not before noun] *Your money will be safer in the bank.* | **it is safe to do sth** (=something will be safe if you do it) *Would it be safer to park my car in the driveway?* | **keep sth safe** *I'm trusting you with these documents, so make sure you keep them safe.*

secure /sɪˈkjʊəʳ/ [adj] safe, especially from thieves or other criminals: *Make sure the building is completely secure before you leave.* | *If your password gets known by anyone else, your data may not be secure.* | **+ from** *He kept his savings under his bed, secure from the prying eyes of his roommate.* —**security** [n U] *The security of the information depends on how many people know the access code.*

be as safe as houses /biː əz ˌseɪf əz ˈhaʊzɪ̩z/ [v phrase] British if your money or savings **are as safe as houses**, they are completely safe: *There's no financial risk. Your money is as safe as houses with us.*

3 a safe place

- safe
- be out of harm's way
- safety
- refuge
- haven
- sanctuary

safe /seɪf/ [adj] *We want the streets to be safe for our children.* | **in a safe place** *Keep the receipt in a safe place.* | **from/at a safe distance** (=far enough away from something dangerous) *Mothers held on to their children tightly, letting them watch the fireworks from a safe distance.* | **(at) a safe distance from sth** *Hiding in the hedge a safe distance from the truck, she waited for the man to appear.*

be out of harm's way /biː ˌaʊt əv ˌhɑːʳmz ˈweɪ/ [v phrase] if someone or something is **out of harm's way**, they are in a place where they cannot be hurt or damaged: *She put the glass vases on the top shelf, out of harm's way.* | **well out of harm's way** *The device sends the fish to the bottom of the pond, well out of harm's way.*

safety /ˈseɪfti/ [n U] a place where you are safe from danger **reach safety** *By the time the men reached safety, they were exhausted and half starved.* | **the safety of sth** *She rushed back to the safety of her own house.* | **carry/lead/take sb to safety** *The firefighters carried the children to safety.* | *A film cameraman was airlifted to safety yesterday after being trapped inside a volcano for two days.*

refuge /ˈrefjuːdʒ/ [n C/U] a place where you can go in order to escape from a dangerous or unpleasant situation **+ from** *The basement provided us with a refuge from the fighting.* | **+ for** *The Allies are being asked to provide more refuges for those fleeing the fighting.* | **place of refuge** *Zurich's importance as a business centre grew, as did its reputation as a place of refuge.* | **take refuge** (=go somewhere that is safe) *During the flooding, people took refuge in the hills.* | **seek refuge from sth** (=try to find a safe place, to escape from a dangerous situation) *Thousands of families came here seeking refuge from the civil war.*

haven /ˈheɪvən/ [n C] a peaceful place where people go in order to escape from danger or suffering, and where they feel very safe **+ for** *She finally found a place to escape to, a small haven for herself and her daughter.* | *The church is a haven of peace in one of London's busiest areas.* | **safe haven** (=a safe place) *The massacre took place in what was supposed to be a UN safe haven.*

sanctuary /ˈsæŋktʃuəri, -tʃəri‖-tʃueri/ [n C] a peaceful place that is safe and provides protection, especially for people who are in danger: *I thought of my bedroom as a sanctuary.* | *The Church should be a sanctuary for the oppressed.*

4 when something is not likely to cause harm

- safe
- harmless

safe /seɪf/ [adj] a **safe** activity, journey, way of doing something etc does not involve any danger: *Flying is one of the safest forms of travel.* | *Bye Sarah, have a safe journey.* | *the safe disposal of radioactive waste* | *Dr Williams said the drug would continue to be used because it was safe for most patients.* | **it is safe to do sth** *Is it safe to swim in the water here?* | **safe sex** (=sex that avoids the risk of disease) *Do teenagers know enough about safe sex and contraception?* | **perfectly safe** (=used especially to emphasize to someone that something is safe) *Our buses have* *to pass a safety test each year and are perfectly safe.* —**safely** [adv] *The nuclear waste is safely buried in the deepest part of the ocean.*

harmless /ˈhɑːʳmləs/ [adj] an animal or chemical that is **harmless** will not harm or injure anyone, even though it may seem dangerous: *Our dog makes a lot of noise, but he's perfectly harmless.* | *We need to persuade parents that almost all vaccines are harmless.* | **+ to** *Essential oils are harmless to skin, provided they are used correctly.*

5 activities or people who make people and places safer

- security
- safety

security /sɪˈkjʊərɪ̈ti/ [n U] things that are done to make sure that someone does not get attacked or robbed: *They need to improve security here – anyone could just walk in.* | *Security has been increased at all airports in the wake of the attacks.* | **security measures/checks/procedures** *Strict security measures were in force during the President's visit.* | **security guard/man** *A uniformed security man met them at the gate.* | **tight security** (=very careful security) *There is tight security at the airport and all baggage is being searched.* | **high security** (=carefully protected or made safe) *a high security prison*

safety /ˈseɪfti/ [n U] ways of preventing dangerous accidents: *Safety needs to be improved on all our railways.* | **safety measures/checks/precautions** *We handle many chemicals that require special safety precautions.* | **road safety** (=rules and methods for using roads safely) *All children should be taught road safety from an early age.* | **health and safety** *All employees will be issued with a health and safety handbook.*

same

RELATED WORDS

opposite: **different**

▸ *see also* **like/similar, equal/not equal, copy**

1 the same one

- the same
- common
- the very (same)/the self-same

the same /ðə ˈseɪm/ [adj only before noun] **the same** place, person, or thing, not a different one: *My friend and I went to the same school.* | *They work in different offices, but they have the same boss.* | *He could hardly believe that the woman sitting in front of him was the same one he'd seen on TV so many times.* | **the same ... as** *She was born on the same day as me.* | *I was staying in the same hotel as Nelson Mandela. Can you believe it!*

common /ˈkɒmən‖ˈkɑː-/ [adj only before noun] two or more people who have **common** aims, interests, beliefs etc have the same interests, aims, or beliefs: *We have a common goal – the creation of a united Europe.* | *Dating agencies try to match people with similar personalities and common interests.* | **common ground** (=opinions, beliefs etc shared between people) *There was a great deal of common ground between all the different representatives.*

the very (same)/the self-same /ðə ˌveri (ˈseɪm), ðə ˈself seɪm/ [adj phrase only before noun] use this to emphasize that someone or something is the same person or thing, not a different one, when this is interesting or surprising: *This is the very same house where Shakespeare wrote most of his plays.* | *Television gets most of its stories from the very tabloid newspapers it is so fond of attacking.* | *The self-same people who complain about low-flying aircraft are the ones who will be jetting off to Florida on their holidays next year.*

2 exactly like someone or something

- the same
- just like/exactly like
- identical
- can't tell the difference/can't tell them apart
- indistinguishable
- be no different from
- match
- word for word

the same /ðə ˈseɪm/ [adj/pron] *They were both wearing the same shoes.* | *We've opened up stores in the UK and we hope to do the same in the rest of Europe.* | *'We always get up late on Saturdays.' 'It's the same in our house.'* | **look/sound/taste etc the same** *The houses on the street all look the same.* | **just the same/exactly the same** (=not different in any way) *I tried three different types of wine, but they all tasted exactly the same to me.* | **all the same** *Take whichever you like – they're all the same.* | **the same ... as** *They were doing the same jobs as the men, but being paid less.*

just like/exactly like /dʒʌst ˈlaɪk, ɪgˌzæktli ˈlaɪk/ [adj only before noun] if someone or something is **just like** or **exactly like** someone or something else, there is very little difference between them: *You're just like my teacher.* | *There are insects that look exactly like green leaves.* | *This song sounds exactly like that one by The Beatles.* | **be just/exactly like doing sth** *We had often talked about emigrating to Australia. Suzie came from Melbourne, so it would be just like going home for her.*

identical /aɪˈdentɪkəl/ [adj] **identical** things are exactly the same in every way: *To me the two patterns looked identical.* | **+ to** *The picture is identical to the one in the museum of Modern Art in New York.* | **identical in size/colour/shape etc** *The tablets were identical in size, shape, and colour.*

can't tell the difference/can't tell them apart /ˌkɑːnt tel ðə ˈdɪfərəns, ˌkɑːnt tel ðəm əˈpɑːʳt‖ˌkænt-/ [v phrase] if you **can't tell the difference** between two people or things, or if you **can't tell them apart**, they look, sound, or seem exactly the same to you: *Emma and Louise sound so alike on the phone, I can't tell the difference.* | *They are identical twins and it's impossible to tell them apart.* | *These rap bands all sound the same to me – I can't tell them apart.* | **can't tell the difference between** *Don't let her help you with the gardening – she can't tell the difference between a weed and a strawberry plant!*

indistinguishable /ˌɪndɪˈstɪŋgwɪʃəbəl/ [adj not usually before noun] two people or things that are **indistinguishable** are so similar that it is impossible to know which is which or to see any differences between them: *In the storm the sky and sea were indistinguishable.* | *It was claimed that Russian and American defence policies were indistinguishable.* | **+ from** *He tasted the cheaper wine and found it indistinguishable from a superior one.*

be no different from /biː nəʊ ˈdɪfərənt frɒm/ [v phrase] use this especially when you expect something or someone to be different from another thing or person, but in fact they are the same: *People often think that movie stars are special in some way, but really they're no different from anybody else.* | *Life* *on the island is no different from life on the mainland.*

match /mætʃ/ [v I/T] if one thing **matches** another or if two things **match**, they look the same or have the same qualities or characteristics: *You can't go out wearing socks that don't match.* | *Their performance in government didn't quite match their election promises.*

word for word /ˌwɜːʳd fəʳ ˈwɜːʳd/ [adv] if you repeat or copy something **word for word**, you do it using exactly the same words: *Janice repeated word for word what Harold had told her.* | *It appears that someone has copied your essay word for word.*

3 the same in amount or number

- the same
- be as old/long/strong etc as
- equal
- equally

the same /ðə ˈseɪm/ [adj only before noun] *Both stores are charging the same price for CD players.* | **the same height/age/price etc as** *Her sister is the same age as me.* | *For much the same price as a flat in London, you can buy a luxury home in Barnsley.* | **exactly the same height/age/price etc** *We're both exactly the same height.*

be as old/long/strong etc as /biː əzː ˈəʊld əz/ [v phrase] to be the same age, length etc as someone or something else: *At 14, Richard was already as tall as his father.* | **+ as** *The loss of a pet can be just as upsetting as the death of a member of the family.*

equal /ˈiːkwəl/ [adj] two or more amounts, totals, levels etc that are **equal** are the same as each other: *You should spend an equal amount of time on each question in the test.* | **+ to** *A pint is equal to about half a litre.* | **of equal power/strength/weight etc** *Choose two stones of roughly equal weight and size.*

equally /ˈiːkwəli/ [adv] to the same degree: *Both schools seem equally good.* | *Club bosses and doormen are equally concerned about the situation.*

4 the same as before

- the same
- hasn't changed
- unchanged
- unaffected

see also **continue (11-12)**

the same /ðə ˈseɪm/ [adj/pron] *Now that Sam's retired, things won't be the same around here.* | *The people may be different, but their music remains the same.* | **+ as** *We went to the office Christmas party, but it was just the same as last year's.* | **the same as ever** *School's the same as ever – too much work and not enough time to do what I really want!* | **just the same/exactly the same** (=not changed in any way) *I hadn't seen John for ages, but he was still just the same.*

hasn't changed /ˌhæznt ˈtʃeɪndʒd/ [v phrase] if someone or something **hasn't changed**, they are the same as they were before, even though you have not seen them for a long time: *I went back to my old school for a visit – it hadn't changed.* | *He hasn't changed at all – he's still crazy about football.*

unchanged /ˌʌnˈtʃeɪndʒd◂/ [adj not before noun] still the same, especially after a long period of time when there would usually have been a lot of changes: *She kept her son's bedroom unchanged for years after his death.* | *On going back to visit the village after almost twenty years, Mrs Simons was surprised to find it unchanged.* | **remain unchanged** *They speak an Indian language which has remained virtually unchanged for centuries.*

unaffected /ˌʌnəˈfektɨd/ [adj not before noun] the same as before, and not changed or affected by something that has happened **remain unaffected** *The rest of the world was in recession, but the Soviet economy remained unaffected.* | **+ by** *The Queen's role remains the same, apparently unaffected by the changes and upheavals of recent years.*

5 always the same

- stay the same
- constant
- consistent
- unchanging

stay the same /ˌsteɪ ðə ˈseɪm/ [v phrase] to continue to be the same and not change: *The word 'sheep' doesn't take 's' in the plural – the ending stays the same.* | *Tamara lived in a government apartment, and the rent stayed the same for five years.*

constant /ˈkɒnstənt‖ˈkɑːn-/ [adj] an amount, temperature, rate etc that is **constant** stays the same and does not change: *It is important to store wine at a constant temperature.* | **remain constant** *The number of deaths from road accidents has remained constant over the last five years.*

consistent /kənˈsɪstənt/ [adj] always staying the same in your beliefs, your behaviour, the quality of your work etc: *She is one of the most consistent players on the tennis circuit.* | *To secure our future, we need a consistent economic strategy.* | **+ in** *Judges must be firm, fair and consistent in their application of the law.* —**consistently** [adv] *The team has played consistently well since the start of the season.*

unchanging /ʌnˈtʃeɪndʒɪŋ/ [adj] not changing, even when conditions or situations change: *Unlike us, most animals have needs that are fixed and unchanging.* | *She always had the same unchanging expression on her face, whatever mood she was in.*

6 when something is the same in all its parts

- uniform
- homogeneous

uniform /ˈjuːnɨfɔːʳm/ [adj] a thing or group that is **uniform** has the same appearance or characteristics in all its parts: *The temperature must be uniform in every area of the reactor.* | *The postal system operates a uniform price structure, so it always costs the same to send a letter.* | **+ in** *Grade A vegetables have to be uniform in size and without marks or blemishes.* —**uniformly** [adv] *Throughout the industry the standard of product is uniformly high.* —**uniformity** /ˌjuːnɨˈfɔːʳmɨti/ [n U] *Most modern housing developments show a tedious uniformity of design.*

homogeneous /ˌhəʊməˈdʒiːniəs/ [adj] formal having the same characteristics in every part, so that every single person or thing in a group is the same: *Women are not a homogeneous group.* | *Computers check whether each text is stylistically homogeneous.*

7 to make things the same

- standardize
- bring sth into line with

standardize ALSO **standardise** British /ˈstændəʳdaɪz/ [v T] to make sure that a particular type of product, service, activity etc is always made or done in exactly the same way: *They are standardising all the equipment throughout the area and bringing it* *up to British Standards safety requirements.* | *At first there were several competing designs of electric plug-sockets, but these were standardized in the 1920s.*

bring sth into line with /ˌbrɪŋ (sth) ɪntə ˈlaɪn wɪð/ [v phrase] to change something such as a rule or system so that it is the same as another generally accepted rule or system: *Our wage levels should be brought into line with those of our competitors.* | *There have been calls for the total abolition of car tax, which would bring car prices into line with those in the rest of Europe.*

8 when facts, situations, or numbers are the same

- correspond
- be consistent with
- agree
- tally
- coincide
- match up

correspond /ˌkɒrɪ̈ˈspɒnd‖ˌkɔːrɪ̈ˈspɑːnd, ˌkɑː-/ [v I not in progressive] if facts or situations **correspond**, they are the same as each other or have the same effect: *The dates quoted in these two documents do not correspond.* | **+ with** *The witness's statements correspond with the available evidence.* | **+ to** *His own domestic situation did not correspond very closely to his ideal of a loving, equal partnership.*

be consistent with /biː kənˈsɪstənt wɪð/ [v phrase] if something that is said, written, or done **is consistent with** a particular idea or piece of information, it says the same thing or follows the same principles: *The figures in the accounts must be consistent with the information given in the annual report.* | *Charging these very high fines is hardly consistent with your policy of 'user-friendly banking'.* | *This sort of repression is not consistent with a democratic system.*

agree /əˈgriː/ [v I not in progressive] if two pieces of information **agree** with each other, they are the same, and so they are both likely to be correct: *I'll have to check these calculations again – the totals don't agree.* | **+ with** *Your story doesn't agree with what the police have told us.*

tally /ˈtæli/ [v I not in progressive] if a piece of information **tallies** with another, they are the same; if two sets of numbers **tally**, they add up to the same thing.: *Check both sets of results to see if they tally.* | **+ with** *His account of the discovery of the body tallied with the testimony of his wife.*

coincide /ˌkəʊɪ̈nˈsaɪd/ [v I not in progressive] if two people's ideas, opinions, or wishes **coincide**, they are the same, even though this may be completely by chance: *For once our wishes coincided. We both wanted a quick divorce.* | **+ with** *His views coincided perfectly with our thinking.* | *Even if her advice does not coincide with what you want, I advise you to follow it.*

match up /ˌmætʃ ˈʌp/ [v I/phr v I not in progressive] if information from one place **matches up** with information from another, both sets of information are the same, which shows that they are both correct: *I've questioned both suspects and so far their stories just don't match up. One of them must be lying.* | **+ with** *You must make sure that your sales figures match up with your receipts at the end of each week.*

9 having the same position, effect, value etc as something else

- corresponding
- equivalent

corresponding /ˌkɒrɪ̈ˈspɒndɪŋ◂‖ˌkɔːrɪ̈ˈspɑːn-, ˌkɑː-/ [adj only before noun] *Compared with the corresponding period last year, average temperatures have been low.* | *The removal of American nuclear forces brought a corresponding withdrawal of Russian troops.* | *A big fall in steel productivity caused a corresponding decrease in profits.*

equivalent /ɪˈkwɪvələnt/ [adj] having the same importance, purpose, or value as something else: *He was fined $50 but given the choice of doing the equivalent amount of community work.* | *The US Congress is roughly equivalent to the British Parliament.* | **+ to** *His monthly US salary is equivalent to a year's pay here in Mexico.*

10 someone who has the same position in another company, organization, or group

- counterpart
- opposite number

counterpart /ˈkaʊntəʳpɑːʳt/ [n C] *Belgian government officials are discussing the matter with their counterparts in France.* | *Eighteenth-century urban dwellers lived in much worse conditions than their modern counterparts.*

opposite number /ˌɒpəzɪ̈t ˈnʌmbəʳ‖ˌɑː-/ [n C] someone who has the same job as someone else in a different organization: *The project was run jointly by Morris and his opposite number in the New York office.* | *After years of communication by telephone she finally met her opposite number in the Spanish government.*

11 to have the same beliefs, ideas, or opinions as someone else

- like-minded
- be on the same wavelength
- speak the same language
- be in tune with

like-minded /ˌlaɪk ˈmaɪndɪ̈d◂/ [adj] having the same attitudes and beliefs and enjoying the same things as someone else: *Being with like-minded people makes my job much more enjoyable.* | *She convinced a group of like-minded friends to join her trekking in the Himalayas.*

be on the same wavelength /biː ɒn ðə ˌseɪm ˈweɪvleŋθ/ [v phrase] to have the same opinions, attitudes, and feelings as someone else, so that you understand each other very well: *My mother and I just aren't on the same wavelength – she just can't understand why I don't want to get married.*

speak the same language /ˌspiːk ðə seɪm ˈlæŋgwɪdʒ/ [v phrase] to have the same opinions as someone else and agree about most things, so that you can exchange ideas easily and easily understand: *Politically they are our enemies, but when it comes to trade I think we speak the same language.* | *When your sales, marketing, and production people are all speaking the same language, it pays real dividends.*

be in tune with /biː ɪn ˈtjuːn wɪð‖-ˈtuːn-/ [v phrase] to have the same ideas and attitudes as a group, society, country etc and be easily accepted by it: *I'm not sure you're quite in tune with the philosophy of the organization.* | *Sartre's novels and plays were in tune with the revolutionary spirit of post-war France.*

satisfied/ not satisfied

RELATED WORDS

- self-satisfied *see* **proud (2)**
- *see also* **good enough, happy, like, complain**

1 when you think something is good enough

- satisfied
- happy
- pleased
- find/consider sth satisfactory

satisfied /ˈsætɪ̈sfaɪd/ [adj] the way you feel when you think that something is as good as it should be, for example someone's work or something you buy: *I did the whole essay again, but she still wasn't satisfied.* | *Sussman puffed on his pipe, a satisfied grin on his face.* | **+ with** *His boss seems satisfied with his work.* | *95% of passengers say they are satisfied with the bus service.* | **+ that** *Patients seemed satisfied that the standard of care was adequate.* | **satisfied customer** *A good travel agent knows that a satisfied customer will always come back.*

happy /ˈhæpi/ [adj not before noun] informal satisfied with what you have achieved: *Pinker stated that he was perfectly happy with the arrangement.* | **+ with** *Doctors said they were happy with how the operation had gone.* | **+ about** *I'd gotten a lot done over the weekend and was happy about that.*

pleased /pliːzd/ [adj not before noun] especially British the way you feel when you think something is very good and you feel very satisfied with it: *Were you pleased when you saw the results?* | **+ with** *Tom's teacher was pleased with his progress.* | *'How's your new car?' 'It's great – I'm really pleased with it.'*

find/consider sth satisfactory /ˌfaɪnd, kənˌsɪdəʳ (sth) ˌsætɪ̈sˈfæktəri/ [v phrase] to think something is good enough because it is of a high enough standard or it gives you what you need: *A decision was made that both sides found satisfactory.* | *The new rules will not affect schools that parents consider satisfactory.*

2 when you have what you want in your life, your job etc

- satisfied
- content
- fulfilled

satisfied ALSO **happy** informal /ˈsætɪ̈sfaɪd, ˈhæpi/ [adj not usually before noun] happy because you have what you want: *Delia won't be happy until she's earning more than her husband.* | *Bowman said he had been perfectly happy in his role as director, before the change in job specifications.* | **+ with** *I don't really want a bigger house – I'm satisfied with what I've got.* | *I'd be happy with a part-time job, as long as the wages were ok.* | **+ to do sth** *My kids are perfectly happy to watch the same videos over and over again.*

content /kənˈtent/ [adj not before noun] satisfied with everything in a situation, so that you do not want to change anything or ask for anything more: *The baby sat on its mother's lap, perfectly content.* | **+ to do sth** *At the moment my mother seems content to take things slowly.* | *He rarely talked about his own work, and was content to listen to the experiences of others.* | **+ with** *He was a strong, vital man, successful and content with his life.*

fulfilled /fʊlˈfɪld/ [adj not usually before noun] satisfied because you feel that your life or your work is interesting, useful, and important: *I think if I could write a song that I knew was good, not necessarily a big hit, I would feel fulfilled.* | *A young married woman, supposedly fulfilled by husband and children, confessed the emptiness of her life.*

3 making you feel satisfied

- satisfying
- fulfilling
- rewarding

satisfying /ˈsætɪ̈sfaɪ-ɪŋ/ [adj] a job, activity, or experience that is **satisfying** makes you feel satisfied, because you enjoy doing it and the results are often very good: *There's something very satisfying about baking your own bread.* | *Working with children with special needs can be a satisfying and rewarding experience.*

fulfilling /fʊlˈfɪlɪŋ/ [adj] something that is **fulfilling**, such as a job or way of life, makes you feel satisfied and happy, because you are using your abilities in a useful way: *Pruitt says that for him, fatherhood is creative and fulfilling.* | *Many older people who have no fulfilling personal relationships lavish their affection on pets.*

rewarding /rɪˈwɔːʳdɪŋ/ [adj] a job or activity that is **rewarding** is satisfying, because you feel you are doing something useful for yourself or for other people: *Nursing is a very rewarding job.* | *The literature course has been hard work, but very rewarding.* | *By planning for retirement, you can make it a happy and rewarding time of your life.*

4 the feeling that you have when you are satisfied

- satisfaction
- fulfilment
- contentment

satisfaction /ˌsætɪ̈sˈfækʃən/ [n U] the feeling of being satisfied, especially because you have achieved something good or useful: *Most teachers take great pride and satisfaction in their work, and enjoy working with young people.* | **with satisfaction** *She finished her letter, and read it through with satisfaction.* | **get satisfaction from sth** *He enjoys coaching the hockey team, and gets a lot of satisfaction from it.* | **+ with** *Warner's pay increase reflected his boss's satisfaction with his work.* | **job satisfaction** (=satisfaction that you get from doing your job) *The pay is pretty good, but you don't get much job satisfaction.*

fulfilment British **/fulfillment** American /fʊlˈfɪlmənt/ [n U] a feeling of being satisfied and happy with your life: *For many kids, music can be a way toward self-expression and fulfillment.* | *Seeing my work come to fruition gives me a strong sense of fulfilment.* | **find fulfilment (in sth)** *Some women do find fulfillment in being a mother, but it is wrong to assume that this is so for all women.* | **seek fulfilment** (=try to find it) *Thomas sought fulfilment in the religious life.*

contentment /kənˈtentmənt/ [n U] the feeling of being happy and satisfied because you have what you want or need, and do not want anything more: *Mitchell gave up his job, and says he found peace and contentment in living close to the land.* | *I look for smiles and expressions of contentment in people's faces as I pass, but I don't see them very often.*

5 to make someone feel satisfied

- satisfy
- keep sb satisfied/happy
- fulfil
- do sth to sb's satisfaction

satisfy /ˈsætɪ̵sfaɪ/ [v T not in progressive] to make someone feel satisfied by being or giving them what they want or need: *I tried on dozens of wedding dresses before I found one that satisfied me.* | *A compromise was eventually reached, but even this failed to satisfy environmentalists.*

keep sb satisfied/happy /ˌkiːp (sb) ˈsætɪ̵sfaɪd, ˈhæpi/ [v phrase] to make someone continue to feel satisfied with a situation or arrangement: *A company can only be successful as long as it keeps its customers satisfied.* | *Part of your job is to keep our clients happy.* | *Politicians pass legislation to keep their constituents happy.*

fulfil British **/fulfill** American /fʊlˈfɪl/ [v T] to give someone what they want or need: *You must give more detailed answers if you are to fulfil the examiner's expectations.* | *Schools should fulfill the needs of poorer children, giving them a chance in society.*

do sth to sb's satisfaction /duː (sth) tə (sb's) ˌsætɪ̵sˈfækʃən/ [v phrase] formal if you do something **to someone's satisfaction**, you do it in a way that is good enough and is what they want or need: *Kang has made most of the repairs to our satisfaction.* | *I hope this will settle the matter to your satisfaction.*

6 not satisfied

- not satisfied
- not be happy/be unhappy
- be fed up
- displeased
- not content
- disgruntled

not satisfied ALSO **dissatisfied** formal /nɒt ˈsætɪ̵sfaɪd, dɪˈsætɪ̵sfaɪd/ [adj] the way you feel when something is not as good as you want or expect it to be: *We've offered to install brand new machines free of charge, but the company is still not satisfied.* | *The store issues refunds to dissatisfied customers.* | **+ with** *The teacher told James she wasn't satisfied with his work.* | *Employees of the company are increasingly dissatisfied with their jobs.* | **not fully satisfied** *If you are not fully satisfied with this product, your money will be refunded.* | **deeply dissatisfied** (=very dissatisfied) *Most rail-users were deeply dissatisfied with the sort of service they were getting.* —**dissatisfaction** /dɪˌsætɪ̵sˈfækjən, dɪsˌsæ-/ [n U] *Baker's increasing dissatisfaction with his role in the party led him to resign.*

not be happy/be unhappy /nɒt biː ˈhæpi, biː ʌnˈhæpi/ [adj not before noun] to feel annoyed and disappointed with something, because it has not been done well enough or you have not achieved what you wanted **+ about** *If you decide you're not happy about the way the dress fits, we'll alter it for you.* | *Wilkins was unhappy about being left off the U.S. Olympic team.* | **+ with** *Fans are not happy with the team's performance.* | *Employees were generally unhappy with their promotion prospects.*

be fed up /biː ˌfed ˈʌp/ [v phrase] British informal to be unhappy because you do not like the situation that you are in and you wish it would change: *It rained every day of our holiday. We were thoroughly fed up.* | **+ with** *I'm fed up with this job. It's so boring.* | *Tom's getting pretty fed up with married life. He never goes out any more.*

displeased /dɪsˈpliːzd/ [adj not before noun] formal not satisfied and a little annoyed about the way something has been done: *Sarah seemed displeased but did not say anything to me.* | *Bonner was displeased by Neeman's remarks.* | **+ about** *Several readers were displeased about the photos that accompanied the story.* | **+ with** *Singer was displeased with Barbra Streisand's adaptation of his story 'Yentl.'*

not content ALSO **discontented** formal /nɒt kənˈtent, ˌdɪskənˈtentɪ̵d/ [adj] not satisfied or happy because you want something better than what you have now: *Discontented workers joined the protests.* | **+ with** *Farmers were discontented with economic reforms that did not improve their businesses.* | *Marshall was not content with the draft of the contract.* —**discontent** [n U] *There have been demonstrations and other signs of discontent.*

disgruntled /dɪsˈgrʌntld/ [adj] not satisfied and slightly angry, especially because you feel you have been treated badly or unfairly: *It was the second pay cut in two years, and employees were becoming disgruntled.* | *After long delays, disgruntled passengers were taken to a nearby hotel.*

7 desires or needs that are never satisfied

- insatiable

insatiable /ɪnˈseɪʃəbəl/ [adj] an **insatiable** need, desire, demand etc is so strong that it never can be satisfied: *His curiosity about the natural world is insatiable.* | *She had an insatiable thirst for attention.* | *Humankind seems to have an insatiable urge to conquer and explore.*

save

WHAT'S HERE

• to save money	see **1 to 3**
• to save/rescue	see **4 to 7**
• to save for later	see **8**

to save money

RELATED WORDS

opposite: **spend money/time**

1 to save money

- save
- save up
- set aside
- scrimp and save

save /seɪv/ [v I/T] to gradually collect money by not spending all the money you have, especially when you regularly put some of it in a bank: *I find it very difficult to save – I just spend everything I get.* | *How long did it take you to save all that money?* | *It's a low-paid job, but she still manages to save a few dollars each week.* | *She planned to work until she had saved enough money to attend nursing school in Nashville.* | **+ for** (=save money in order to pay for something) *They've already started saving for their next vacation.*

save up /ˌseɪv ˈʌp/ [phr v I/T] to save money in order to buy something or to do something: *If you want a new bike you'll have to start saving up.* | *She's saved up enough money to take a course in computer sci-*

ence. | **+ to do sth** *Dave's been saving up for months to buy a new camera.* | **+ for** *It took me ages to save up for those trainers.*

set aside /ˌset əˈsaɪd/ [phr v T] to regularly save part of the money you earn, especially over a long period of time **set aside sth** *We've all been setting aside a little money each month for a trip to Disneyland.* | **set sth aside** *If you want to build up a good pension fund, you should start setting aside a small part of your earnings now.*

scrimp and save /ˌskrɪmp ən ˈseɪv/ [v phrase] to try to save money by spending less on the things you need and by saving what you can, especially when you do not earn very much: *After years of scrimping and saving, we've finally got enough money to go on a foreign holiday.* | **+ to do sth** *My parents had to scrimp and save for years to send me to college.*

2 to have money you have saved

- **have sth saved/have sth saved up**
- **have sth put by/put away**
- **have sth tucked away**

have sth saved/have sth saved up /hæv (sth) ˈseɪvd, hæv (sth) ˌseɪvd ˈʌp/ [v phrase] *It's a good thing I had some extra money saved – I didn't expect the car repairs to be so expensive.* | *Fortunately, we had enough saved up for a nice flat.*

have sth put by/put away /hæv (sth) ˌpʊt ˈbaɪ, ˌpʊt əˈweɪ/ [v phrase] if you **have** money **put by** or **put away**, you have saved it over a long period of time: *I think Philip has quite a lot of money put by.* | *I knew my aunt had a few thousand put away but I never realized she was practically a millionaire!*

have sth tucked away /hæv (sth) ˌtʌkt əˈweɪ/ [v phrase] if you **have** money **tucked away**, you have saved it, especially when other people do not know that you have it or where you keep it [v phrase] *It turned out that he had several million tucked away in a secret Swiss bank account.* | *I try to keep a little money tucked away for my retirement.*

3 the money you have saved

- **savings**
- **nest egg**

savings /ˈseɪvɪŋz/ [n plural] *The old woman kept her savings in a big jar under her bed.* | *I'm paying for the course out of my own savings.* | **+ of** *Do you have savings of £3000 or more?* | *You may qualify for state benefit if you have less than £8000 in savings.* | **sb's life savings** (=all the money you have saved in your life) *My parents spent their life savings on a retirement home in Florida.*

nest egg /ˈnest eg/ [n C usually singular] an amount of money that you have saved for the time when you stop working, get married etc: *This investment will be a nice little nest egg for you when you get married.* | *A long period of high inflation will eventually reduce the value of your nest egg.*

to save/rescue

RELATED WORDS

▸ *see also* **help**

4 to help someone in danger or a bad situation

- **save**
- **rescue**
- **come to the rescue**
- **pick up**

save /seɪv/ [v T] to stop someone from being killed or badly hurt, or help them out of a bad situation: *Ben would have died in the blaze if a fireman hadn't saved him.* | *The President had been shot from close range. It was only his bullet-proof vest that saved him.* | **save sb from sth** *Officer McCarthy had saved her from a savage attack in the park.* | *Environmentalists are campaigning to save the white rhinoceros from extinction.* | **save sb from doing sth** *Michael was saved from choking to death by Susie.* | **save sb's life** *Wearing a seat belt can help save your life.*

rescue /ˈreskjuː/ [v T] to save someone by removing them from a dangerous, difficult, or unpleasant situation, especially when this involves taking serious risks: *Firefighters worked for two hours to rescue people who were trapped in the bus.* | **rescue sb from sth** *We were rescued from the sinking ship by a passing fishing boat.* | *She was rescued from her underpaid factory job by a movie director searching for new talent.*

come to the rescue /ˌkʌm tə ðə ˈreskjuː/ [v phrase] to save someone from a dangerous, difficult, or unpleasant situation, when they urgently need help: *He attempted to rob another girl, but her friends came to the rescue.* | **come to sb's rescue** *The baby was destined to spend her life in an orphanage until a nurse came to her rescue.* | **+ of** *Agassi once again came to the rescue of his country in the quarter final of the Davis Cup.*

pick up /ˌpɪk ˈʌp/ [phr v T] to save someone from a dangerous place by taking them away in a boat or aircraft **pick up sb** *They spent the night near the top of the mountain, before being picked up by a helicopter.* | **pick sb up** *A lifeboat picked them up two miles from the coast.*

5 to help someone in a social situation

- **save/rescue**
- **come to the rescue**

save/rescue /seɪv, ˈreskjuː/ [v T] to do or say something that helps someone who is embarrassed or bored in a conversation or social situation: *I was stuck talking to Aunt Martha until Mom rescued me.* | *I felt embarrassed, not knowing how to answer his question, but Jane saved me by changing the subject.* | **+ from** *Excuse me a moment, I must go and rescue Mary from boring old Mr. Potter.*

come to the rescue /ˌkʌm tə ðə ˈreskjuː/ [v phrase] to do or say something that helps someone at exactly the right time when they are bored, embarrassed, or nervous in a conversation or social situation: *I was struggling to think of things to say until one of my colleagues came to the rescue.* | **come to sb's rescue** *I couldn't remember my doctor's name – fortunately Maria came to my rescue.*

6 to stop something from being damaged or lost

- save/rescue
- salvage

save/rescue /seɪv, 'reskjuː/ [v T] to save objects, buildings, places etc that are in danger of being damaged or destroyed: *We could only save some clothes and a few pieces of furniture before the house burned down.* | *The Landmark Trust is a charity which rescues buildings of architectural interest.* | **save/rescue sth from sth** *It is almost too late to save the rainforest from destruction.* | *A historic woollen mill has been rescued from the threat of demolition.*

salvage /'sælvɪdʒ/ [v T] to save something, especially something valuable, from a place where other things have already been damaged, destroyed, or lost: *Drivers hope to salvage some of the ship's cargo.* | *The fire had destroyed most of the building, but we managed to salvage a few valuable items.* | **salvage sth from sth** *The house was built of timber salvaged from an earlier building.*

7 to help an organization, business, relationship etc

- save
- rescue/come to the rescue
- bail out
- salvage
- throw sb a lifeline/throw a lifeline to sb

save /seɪv/ [v T] to do something to help a business, country, relationship etc that is having serious problems and will soon fail: *Bob and Martha worked hard to save their marriage, for the sake of the children.* | **save sth from sth** *Financial experts are trying to save one of Britain's biggest holiday companies from bankruptcy.*

rescue/come to the rescue /'reskjuː, ˌkʌm tə ðə 'reskjuː/ [v T/v phrase] to help an organization, business, or country that is having serious financial problems, for example by lending money or improving the way it is organized: *The World Bank hopes that these emergency measures will rescue the Zambian economy.* | *The city council had continued to overspend, assuming that the federal government would come to the rescue.* | **rescue sth from sth** *He reorganized the family business, rescuing it from severe debt.* —**rescue** [n U] *The rescue plan* | *involves a ten million dollar loan from the EU.*

bail out /ˌbeɪl 'aʊt/ [phr v T] to help a person, business, or organization that is having serious financial problems by lending or giving them money **bail out sb** *The government bailed out the ailing car company in order to protect jobs.* | **bail sb out** *He owed thousands of dollars, and his mother had to sell land to bail him out.* | **bail sb out of sth** *You can't expect your father to bail you out of trouble all the time.*

salvage /'sælvɪdʒ/ [v T] to do something to help a company or relationship when it is having serious problems, so that it does not fail completely: *The company is busy trying to salvage its core business.* | *Retailing and tourism can't salvage an ailing economy.* | **salvage sth from sth** *If you no longer care for your partner, it is time to ask what can be salvaged from your relationship.*

throw sb a lifeline/throw a lifeline to sb /ˌθrəʊ (sb) ə 'laɪflaɪn, ˌθrəʊ ə 'laɪflaɪn tə (sb)/ [v phrase] to save a person or company that is in serious financial difficulties and is soon going to fail, by giving them enough money to continue: *Just before my business went bankrupt, my father threw me a lifeline in the form of a $10,000 loan.* | *The Administration refuses to throw a lifeline to the troubled automobile industry.*

to save for later

RELATED WORDS

- keep

8 to save something to use later

- save/keep
- keep sth in reserve
- keep back
- conserve

save/keep /seɪv, kiːp/ [v T] to keep something and not use it now, so that you can use it later when you want it or need it: *Save some of the cheese to sprinkle on top of the sauce.* | *We can use half the wood now but we ought to keep the rest – we might need it.* | **save/keep sth for sth** *He took out his last cigarette, which he'd been saving for just this moment.* | **save/keep sth for sb** *We'd have kept some food for you if we'd known you were coming.* | **save/keep sth for later** *I'll keep some of these magazines for later, and read them on the plane.* | **save sth for a rainy day** (=save something to use at a time when you really need it) *Would you like some Scotch? I have a bottle somewhere that I've been saving for a rainy day.*

keep sth in reserve /ˌkiːp (sth) ɪn rɪ'zɜːʳv/ [v phrase] to save part of something, so that if the part that you are using is not good enough, large enough etc, you will have more to use: *Luckily I had kept some wine in reserve, in case the rest got finished quickly.* | **+ for** *It's a good idea to keep a little money in reserve for those unexpected emergencies.*

keep back /ˌkiːp 'bæk/ [phr v T] to not use or give away all of something, so that you still have some of it left for yourself or for another purpose **keep sth back** *Keep a small amount of icing back for the other cake.* | **keep back sth** *Most farmers are able to keep back enough of their crop for their own use.*

conserve /kən'sɜːʳv/ [v T] **conserve resources/energy/materials etc** to use something very carefully so that you will have enough for the future: *Recycling helps conserve natural and often limited resources.* | *As a way of conserving water, people were not allowed to use hosepipes or wash their cars.*

say

RELATED WORDS

- to say something again *see* **repeat**
- to say that someone has done something bad or illegal *see* **accuse**
- when people say something that may or may not be true *see* **rumour/rumor**
- *see also* **tell, speak, talk, shout, explain, criticize, mention, insist, thank**

1 to say something

- say
- pronounce
- mention
- point out
- express
- put it
- comment
- remark
- add

say /seɪ/ [v I/T] to **say** something using spoken or written words: *'I must be going,' she said.* | *'Where's Pam going?' 'I don't know. She didn't say.'* | *It says in* *today's paper that gas prices are going up again.* | **+ (that)** *James wrote to the bank and said we needed a loan.* | *Did Peter say that he would be late?* | **+ what/where/why etc** *Did they say how long the operation would take?* | **say hello/sorry/no etc (to sb)** *Lauren came over to say goodbye to us.* | *I asked Dad if he'd lend me some money, but he said no.* | **say sth to sb** *What did you say to her?* | **something/anything to say** *I couldn't think of anything to say.* | **say so** *If there's anything you're not happy about, please say so.*

pronounce /prəˈnaʊns/ [v T] to make the sound of a word or a part of a word in a particular way – use this also to ask or say what is the correct way to say something: *How do you pronounce your name?* | *Some students find it difficult to pronounce the word 'the'.* | *Words like 'chicken' and 'cheese' were once pronounced with a 'k'.* —**pronunciation** /prəˌnʌnsiˈeɪʃən/ [n C/U] *British and American pronunciation is often very different.*

mention /ˈmenʃən/ [v T] to talk about someone or something, but without giving details or saying very much about them: *He mentioned something about a party, but he didn't say when it was.* | *When I mentioned her name, he looked embarrassed.* | **+ (that)** *I forgot to mention that I won't be in tomorrow.* | **+ where/when/who etc** *Did he mention where he went to school?* | **it is worth mentioning that** *It is worth mentioning that young children are particularly vulnerable to accidents in the home.*

point out /ˌpɔɪnt ˈaʊt/ [phr v T] to tell someone something that they had not noticed or had not thought about: *As Sharon pointed out, the story was rather hard to believe.* | **point out sth** *He pointed out the dangers of setting off without the right equipment.* | **point out (that)** *It's worth pointing out that very few people ever die of this disease.* | **point sth out** *He never used to notice when people took advantage of him, so I started pointing it out.*

express /ɪkˈspres/ [v T] to let someone know your feelings, by putting them into words: *Ollie found it hard to express his feelings about the war.* | *Parents have expressed concern about the amount of violence in some children's shows.* | **express yourself** (=make people understand what you are thinking or feeling) *Young children often find it difficult to express themselves in words.*

put it /ˈpʊt ɪt/ [v phrase] to express an idea in a particular way, choosing your words carefully to explain what you mean simply or clearly **put it another way** *If you don't understand, I'll try and put it another way.* | **to put it bluntly/briefly/simply etc** *Their performance was, to put it bluntly, atrocious.* | **put it this way** spoken (=use this when you are trying to say something in the clearest possible way) *Put it this way: if we don't make a profit, we're out of a job.*

comment /ˈkɒment‖ˈkɑː-/ [v I/T] to say what your opinion is about someone or something that you have seen, heard, or read about: *'He only wears those clothes to prove that he's rich,' commented Harold.* | *Journalists asked General Curran how the campaign was going, but he refused to comment.* | **+ on/upon** *The prime minister was asked to comment on the crisis.* | **+ that** *Some critics have commented that the film lacks originality.*

remark /rɪˈmɑːʳk/ [v I/T not in passive] to say what you have noticed about a particular person, situation etc or to express an opinion about them: *'There's a strange smell in here,' she remarked.* | **+ that** *Kate remarked that it was amazing how much her kids knew about science.* | **+ on** (=notice something and then say something about it) *A lot of our customers remark on the quality of our workmanship.*

add /æd/ [v T] to say something more, after what has already been said or written: *Is there anything you'd like to add, Peter?* | *'Finally', she added, 'I would like to thank my family for their support'.* | **+ that** *I should add that I do not agree with Doctor Mitchell.*

2 to say something publicly or officially

- say
- announce
- state
- declare
- make/issue a statement
- lay down
- be worded

say /seɪ/ [v T] to **say** something publicly or officially, using spoken or written words **+ (that)** *The President said he had no intention of resigning.* | *The rules say that sports shoes must be worn in the gym at all times.* | **+ what/how/who etc** *The police are refusing to say where Davies is being held.*

announce /əˈnaʊns/ [v T] to officially tell people what has happened or what will happen, in a written or spoken public statement: *The Company announced profits of about $400 million.* | **+ (that)** *The Prime Minister has just announced there is to be a General Election next month.* | **announce your engagement** (=to officially tell people that you are going to get married) *They announced their engagement last year, but have still not set a date for their wedding.*

state /steɪt/ [v T] formal to say something publicly or officially, especially in clear, definite language: *The government needs to clearly state its policy on possible military action.* | **+ that** *The law states that you are innocent until proved guilty.* | *Justice Cohen stated clearly that no further action would be taken.*

declare /dɪˈkleəʳ/ [v T] to officially state that a particular situation exists or a person or thing is in a particular condition **declare sb insane/unfit/a traitor etc** *In the last century, mothers of illegitimate babies could be declared insane.* | *After nearly forty years' membership, the Communist party declared him a traitor.* | **+ (that)** *Finally, the doctor declared that the man was dead.* | **declare war/an amnesty/a state of emergency** *In 1941 the US declared war on the Axis powers.* | *A state of emergency has been declared in Bangladesh.*

make/issue a statement /ˌmeɪk, ˌɪʃuː ə ˈsteɪtmənt/ [v phrase] to say or write something publicly in order to tell people what you intend to do, what your opinion is etc – use this especially about politicians, business leaders, and other people in authority: *The party's environment spokesman intends to make a statement either today or tomorrow.* | *The president's press corps issued this statement today.*

lay down /ˌleɪ ˈdaʊn/ [phr v T] to officially state the rules that say what is allowed in a particular situation **lay down sth** *The new law lays down strict rules about the way guns may be bought and sold.* | **lay down that** *It is laid down in the club rules that guests are not allowed in unless they are accompanied by a club member.*

be worded /biː ˈwɜːʳdɪd/ [v phrase] if something such as an official statement or document **is worded** in a particular way, the speaker or writer has deliberately chosen their words in that way to get a particular effect: *His speech to the police officers about racial violence had to be very carefully worded.* | *The Defence Secretary made a public statement about the crisis, but it was worded in such a way as to give very little information.*

3 to say that something is definitely true

- claim
- maintain
- assert
- confirm
- testify
- swear
- certify
- insist
- protest
- deny

claim /kleɪm/ [v I/T] to say that something is true, even though it has not been proved and people may not believe it **+ (that)** *Martin claimed that he was with friends at the time of his wife's murder.* | *She claimed she was fired from her job for being pregnant.* | **+ to be sth** *She claims to be a descendent of Charles Dickens.* | **+ to have done sth** *Doctors claim to have discovered a cure for the disease.* | **+ responsibility/credit etc** *No one has yet claimed responsibility for planting the bomb.*

maintain /meɪn'teɪn, mən-/ [v T] to repeatedly say that something is true, especially when other people do not believe you **+ (that)** *My mother always maintains that I learned to talk at six months.* | *The authors of 'Superdiet' maintain you can lose pounds without eating less.*

assert /ə'sɜːʳt/ [v T] to state very firmly that something is true **+ (that)** *Professor Sykes has asserted that the skeleton, which was said to be man's first ancestor, is in fact a fake.* | *After 1947, Nehru began to assert his supremacy and sack party chiefs who opposed him.* | *If women are to have equal opportunity, they must loudly assert their ability to do all traditional 'male' jobs.*

confirm /kən'fɜːʳm/ [v T] if you **confirm** something that other people have already said is true, you say publicly that it is definitely true: *Mr Eastwood refused to confirm or deny the rumour.* | **+ (that)** *Police have confirmed that they are questioning a woman about the disappearance of baby Kelly Truman.*

testify /'testɨfaɪ/ [v I/T] to make a formal statement of what is true, especially in a court of law: *Police had to guard him in hospital until he was well enough to testify.* | **+ that** *I'm prepared to testify in court that I was in Carolyn's apartment that night.* | **+ against sb** (=say something intended to prove someone is guilty) *The witness who had testified against him withdrew her allegation.*

swear /sweəʳ/ [v T] informal to say very firmly that what you have said is the truth **+ (that)** *It was a mistake – she swears that she didn't mean to do it.* | *The plane flew so low that Geoff swears he saw one wing touch the top of a tree.* | **swear blind (that)** (=used for emphasizing that someone is telling the truth) *She swears blind that she never met the man.*

certify /'sɜːʳtɨfaɪ/ [v T] if someone such as a doctor or another professional person **certifies** something, they officially say that it is true **+ (that)** *Doctors have certified that the suspect was in a lot of pain at the time of the incident.* | **certify sb fit/dead/insane etc** *The doctor certified me unfit to go to work for the next month.*

insist /ɪn'sɪst/ [v T] to say and repeat that something is true, especially when a lot of people think that it might not be true **+ (that)** *Though there are no other witnesses, she insists she saw a man in the yard that night.* | *UFO spotters will always insist that their data is correct.*

protest /prə'test/ [v T] to firmly and repeatedly state that you have not done something wrong **+ (that)** *Marge protested that she had never had any kind of affair with Lawrence.* | **protest your innocence** (=say repeatedly that you did not commit a crime) *Throughout the trial Reilly protested his innocence.*

deny /dɪ'naɪ/ [v T] to say that you have not done something bad that people say you have done: *Bowlam denied all charges of selling drugs to children.* | **+ (that)** *The singer denies that he copied the tune from an old Beatles song.* | **+ doing sth** *Did he actually deny meeting Jenny that night?* | **flatly/categorically deny** (=deny very strongly) *The foreman had not informed us that the paraffin might explode. In fact he had categorically denied there was any danger.*

4 to say clearly what your opinion is

- say what you think
- speak your mind
- air your views
- have your say
- argue

say what you think /ˌseɪ wɒt juː 'θɪŋk/ [v phrase] *She usually says what she thinks even if it offends her political colleagues.* | **+ about/of** *I'll make a few suggestions, and the rest of you can say what you think about them.*

speak your mind /ˌspiːk jɔːʳ 'maɪnd/ [v phrase] to say what you think, even though what you say might upset or offend other people: *She's very direct and believes in speaking her mind.* | *We thought that the process of filming might stop people from speaking their minds.*

air your views /ˌeəʳ jɔːʳ 'vjuːz/ [v phrase] to say publicly what you think about something important, especially in a situation where it can be discussed: *Every Friday there is a meeting at the factory where the workers can air their views and discuss problems.* | *For a long time citizens were denied the right to air their views fully or to hold public debates.*

have your say /ˌhæv jɔːʳ 'seɪ/ [v phrase] to be allowed to say what you think about something, for example in a meeting or among a group of people: *You've had your say – now let someone else speak.* | **+ about** *At a public meeting yesterday, environmentalists were finally permitted to have their say about the future of the ancient forest.*

argue /'ɑːʳgjuː/ [v I/T] to state, giving clear reasons, that something is true, should be done etc, although other people are disagreeing with you **+ that** *She argued that taxes must be increased to pay for public services.* | *Film makers themselves would no doubt argue that their films do not influence people's behaviour.* | **+ for** (=argue that something should be done) *He argued for changes to the tax system so that it assisted people who undertook training.* | **+ against** (=argue that something should not be done) *Senator Harvey argued strongly against taking any form of military action.*

5 to say that something you previously said was true is not true

- take back
- withdraw
- retract

take back /ˌteɪk 'bæk/ [phr v T] to say that something you said previously is not true, especially because you now know it was unfair or wrong to say it **take back sth** *I want to take back some of the things I said yesterday.* | **take sth back** *If you don't take that back I'll never speak to you again.* | *Look, I'm sorry I accused you – I take it all back.*

withdraw /wɪð'drɔː, wɪθ-/ [v T] to publicly say that something you said earlier is not true, especially something offensive or unfair you have said about someone: *He has been asked to withdraw remarks he made in a national newspaper about the honesty of the president.* | *She withdrew her allegations of sex discrimination at work.* | **withdraw sth unreservedly** (=withdraw it completely) *Mary said that she was very sorry and that she withdrew the accusation unreservedly.*

retract /rɪ'trækt/ [v T] to formally or officially state that something you previously said is not true: *He confessed to the murder then later retracted his statement.* | *Galileo was not the first scientist to be forced to retract his theories.*

6 to say something in an indirect way

- imply
- suggest
- hint
- drop a hint
- in a roundabout way

imply /ɪm'plaɪ/ [v T] to say something that seems to mean that another thing is true, but without saying the other thing directly: *You seem to be implying something that is not quite true.* | **+ (that)** *Michael did imply that I could have the job if I wanted it.* | *The article implied that unemployed people are lazy and do not want to work.*

suggest /sə'dʒest‖səg-/ [v T] to say something in an indirect way, especially something bad that you prefer not to say directly: *What are you suggesting? Do you think I'm a thief?* | **+ (that)** *His letter seemed to suggest that he wasn't satisfied with my work.* | **I'm not suggesting** (=used for telling someone you are not criticizing them) *I'm not suggesting you deliberately tried to mislead us, just that you made a mistake.*

hint /hɪnt/ [v I/T] to say something in a very indirect way, but so that other people can guess what you mean **+ (that)** *Harry hinted that his friendship with Mona might have contributed to his marriage break-up.* | **+ at** *The President hinted at the possibility of military action.* —**hint** [n C] *His comments were a clear hint that tax rises might be necessary.*

drop a hint /ˌdrɒp ə 'hɪnt‖ˌdrɑːp-/ [v phrase] to say something that suggests that you want to do something or that you want someone to do something, but without saying it directly **+ about** *She kept dropping hints about her birthday, just to make sure none of us forgot about it.* | *My mother dropped several hints about us wallpapering her sitting room.*

in a roundabout way /ɪn ə ˌraʊndəbaʊt 'weɪ/ [adv] if you say something **in a roundabout way**, you say it in an indirect way, especially to avoid offending or embarrassing someone: *I told him, in a roundabout way, that he wasn't really good enough to join my English class.*

7 to say something suddenly or unexpectedly

- exclaim
- come out with
- blurt out

exclaim /ɪk'skleɪm/ [v T] to say something suddenly and loudly because you are angry, surprised, or excited: *'What a beautiful house!' she exclaimed.* | *'Aha'!', he exclaimed triumphantly. 'We knew you'd come'.*

come out with /ˌkʌm 'aʊt wɪð/ [phr v T] to suddenly say something, in an unplanned way, which other people find unusual or surprising: *It was strange to hear a little old lady come out with a swear word like that.* | *I don't want to make a speech – I'll only come out with something stupid that everyone will laugh at.* | *You never know what he'll come out with next.*

blurt out /ˌblɜːʳt 'aʊt/ [phr v T] to suddenly say something without thinking, especially something embarrassing or something that should be kept secret **blurt out sth** *She had blurted out my secret when she was upset, and now everyone knew about it.* | **blurt sth out** *He couldn't go through the agony of lying to them again, so he blurted everything out.* | **blurt out that** *She couldn't think of a good excuse, so blurted out that she was pregnant.*

8 to say something quietly or unclearly

- whisper
- mutter
- mumble
- murmur
- say sth under your breath
- grunt

whisper /'wɪspəʳ/ [v I/T] to say something very quietly, using your breath rather than your voice: *'Don't wake the baby,' whispered Jemima.* | *You don't have to whisper – there's no one around.* | **whisper sth in sb's ear** *Fran leant over and whispered something in her sister's ear.*

mutter /'mʌtəʳ/ [v I/T] to say something quietly, especially when you are annoyed but do not want someone to hear you complaining: *'Why do I have to do all the work?' she muttered.* | *Grant went out, muttering something about having to see a client.* | **mutter to yourself** *He was always muttering to himself about all the experiments he had to do that week.*

mumble /'mʌmbəl/ [v T] to say something quietly without pronouncing the words clearly, so that it is difficult to understand: *He mumbled something I didn't hear.* | **+ that** *All I could do was mumble that I regretted I hadn't taken my degree.* | **mumble a reply/an apology/your thanks etc** *Kaye could only mumble an apology.*

murmur /'mɜːʳməʳ/ [v T] to say something in a soft low voice, that is difficult to hear clearly: *He began stroking her hair and gently murmuring her name.* | *The child murmured something in its sleep.* | *She heard the priest murmuring a prayer at the front of the church.* —**murmur** [n C] *There were excited murmurs as the President entered the hall.*

say sth under your breath /ˌseɪ (sth) ʌndəʳ jɔːʳ 'breθ/ [v phrase] to say something extremely quietly, especially a criticism or something rude, so that no one will hear what you are saying: *'Stupid idiot,' he said under his breath as the old man walked away.*

grunt /grʌnt/ [v T] to say a few words in a low rough voice, especially when you are not really interested in what someone is saying to you: *'What about a stripy wallpaper for this room?' 'I dunno,' he grunted.* | *She grunted something I didn't catch.*

9 to say something angrily

- growl
- snarl

growl /graʊl/ [v T] to say something in a low angry voice, especially in order to make someone feel afraid: *'Come over here and say that,' he growled.* | *He walked into the house, growled a few words at my mother and then went upstairs to bed.*

snarl /snɑːʳl/ [v T] to say something in a nasty angry way: *'Keep your dirty hands off me,' he snarled.* | *Every time he asked her a question she snarled a bad-tempered answer.*

10 not saying anything

- silent
- be lost for words/be at a loss for words
- be struck dumb
- clam up
- speechless
- tongue-tied
- I don't know what to say
- words fail me
- bite your tongue

▸ *see also* **shy**

silent /ˈsaɪlənt/ [adj not before noun] especially written not speaking: *Phil was silent for a moment as he thought about his reply.* | **remain silent** *I wanted to say 'please don't go', but instead I remained silent, and she left.* | **fall silent** (=become silent) *The woman fell silent, though she kept darting angry glances at Jessica.*

be lost for words/be at a loss for words /biː ˌlɒst fəʳ ˈwɜːʳdz‖-ˌlɔːst, biː ət ə ˌlɒs fəʳ ˈwɜːʳdz ‖-ˌlɔːs-/ [v phrase] to be unable to say anything because you are very surprised or because you are not prepared for the situation that has suddenly happened: *No matter what happens he never seems lost for words.* | *She stared at his letter, clearly at a loss for words.*

be struck dumb /biː ˌstrʌk ˈdʌm/ [v phrase] to be suddenly unable to say anything because you are extremely surprised or shocked and cannot believe what has happened: *Amy was struck dumb. Was it possible that her own son had deceived her?* | **+ with** *When he arrived at the scene of the disaster, he was struck dumb with horror and amazement.*

clam up /ˌklæm ˈʌp/ [phr v I] informal to suddenly become unwilling to talk: *He always clams up when I ask him about his job – do you think he's doing something illegal?* | *The police took her in for questioning, but she clammed up when they asked about her boyfriend.*

speechless /ˈspiːtʃləs/ [adj not before noun] unable to say anything because you are very angry, surprised, or upset: *Anna was speechless. She had never seen such luxury before.* | **+ with** *Laura stared at him, absolutely speechless with rage.* | **leave/render sb speechless** (=make someone speechless) *His words dented her pride and left her speechless.*

tongue-tied /ˈtʌŋ taɪd/ [adj not before noun] unable or unwilling to say anything because you are nervous or embarrassed: *She became tongue-tied when she looked at the handsome man sitting beside her.* | *Nervousness affects people in different ways. While some people become tongue-tied, others cannot stop talking.*

I don't know what to say /aɪ ˌdəʊnt nəʊ wɒt tə ˈseɪ / spoken say this when someone gives you an unexpected present, or does something bad or shocking, and you cannot express how happy, angry etc you feel: *You're so kind! I don't know what to say.* | *Well, I don't know what to say. It's absolutely disgraceful!*

words fail me /ˌwɜːʳdz ˈfeɪl miː/ spoken say this when you are so shocked or angry that you cannot think of anything to say to express how you feel: *Just look at this mess. Look at it. It's ... Words fail me!*

bite your tongue /ˌbaɪt jɔːʳ ˈtʌŋ/ [v phrase] to not say anything even though you want very much to say what you think: *I had to bite my tongue to stop myself telling Neil exactly what I thought of his stupid plan.* | *She's so temperamental that even if you disagree with her it's better to bite your tongue and say nothing.*

11 something someone says

- remark
- comment
- thing to say
- point
- statement
- announcement
- declaration
- observation

remark /rɪˈmɑːʳk/ [n C] something that you say, for example about what you think or something that you have noticed: *What do you mean by that remark?* | *I'm fed up with your snide remarks.* | *Elliot had been accused of making racist remarks.* | **+ about** *I ignored his rude remark about my clothes.* | **+ on** *Some further remarks on this subject will be made in the next chapter.* | **make a remark** *Mr Hill sat down and made a few remarks about the weather.* | **casual/chance remark** (=something that you say for no particular reason) *It was just a casual remark – I didn't mean anything by it.*

comment /ˈkɒment‖ˈkɑː-/ [n C] something that you say or write, especially to give an opinion: *OK, that's what we are suggesting – does anyone have any comments?* | **+ on/about** *He made some comment about my dress, then carried on reading his book.* | *Her comments on interest rates had little impact on financial markets.* | **make a comment** *We were discussing her new movie, and Jill made some interesting comments about it.*

thing to say /ˌθɪŋ tə ˈseɪ/ [n phrase] **a strange/stupid/horrible etc thing to say** a remark that is strange, stupid etc: *What an awful thing to say about your mother!* | *I know it's a terrible thing to say, but sometimes I wish I'd never been born.*

point /pɔɪnt/ [n C] something you say, that people had not thought about or discussed until you mentioned it **+ about** *Michael's point about training is an interesting one.* | **good point** *That's a good point, and we should take it into consideration.* | **make a point** (=say something in a discussion, which people had not thought of before) *In his speech, Marks made the point that far more people died from smoking tobacco than from taking drugs.*

statement /ˈsteɪtmənt/ [n C] something that someone says or writes publicly in order to tell people what they intend to do, what their opinion is etc: *In a statement, the BBC admitted that it had given incorrect information.* | **make a statement** (=say something publicly) *The President will make a statement to the press this afternoon.*

announcement /əˈnaʊnsmənt/ [n C] a public or official statement telling people what has happened or what will happen: *The announcement was heard by millions of radio listeners this morning.* | **+ of/about** *I read the announcement of her death in today's paper.* | **make an announcement** *Silence, please. Mr Bennett is about to make an announcement.*

declaration /ˌdekləˈreɪʃən/ [n C] an important official statement, especially about what a government or organization intends to do **+ that** *They issued a declaration that it will be attempting to take over another three British companies.* | **declaration of war/independence/intent etc** *On the 19th of July a declaration of war was delivered in Berlin.*

observation /ˌɒbzəʳˈveɪʃən‖ˌɑːb-/ [n C] a remark in which you say what you think or have noticed about something **+ that** *The inspector began his report with the observation that the school was a happy place.* | **+ about** *I agree with your observations about the pricing of products.* | **make an observation** *A tour of Washington DC inspired one visitor to make some interesting observations about the gap between the rich and the poor.*

12 what people say about something

- according to
- rumour has it
- they say/people say
- apparently
- there is talk of
- supposedly

according to /əˈkɔːʳdɪŋ tuː/ [prep] use this to tell someone what someone else has said or written: *According to today's paper, 20 people died in the fire.* | *Rob's got a new girlfriend, according to Janine.*

rumour has it British /**rumor has it** American /ˌruːməʳ ˈhæz ɪt/ spoken say this when you are telling someone something that you heard from someone else, which may not actually be true: *To join the club, rumor had it, you had to be earning more than $100,000 a year.* | **+ (that)** *Rumour had it that she only married him for his money.*

they say/people say /ðeɪ ˈseɪ, ˌpiːpəl ˈseɪ/ spoken use this to say what a lot of people believe and say **+ (that)** *They say her husband's in prison.* | **so they say** (=use this when you are not sure whether something is true) *The test isn't difficult, or so they say.*

apparently /əˈpærəntli/ [adv] spoken use this to say what you have read or been told, although you do not directly know about it yourself: *It's going to be hot this weekend, apparently.* | *Apparently, Jim's a really good tennis player.*

there is talk of /ðeər ɪz ˈtɔːk ɒv/ spoken use this to tell someone about what may happen in the future, that you have heard other people talking about: *He was doing very well at college and there was talk of him being accepted for Harvard.* | *The company already does business with Germany and Japan and there's been some talk of a deal with the French.*

supposedly /səˈpəʊzɪ̈dli/ [adv] spoken say this when you have heard people saying that something is true but you do not believe it: *Richard was supposedly a tall, dark-eyed handsome man.* | *He was supposedly delivering some papers to her but I think it was just an excuse to see her.*

school/ university

RELATED WORDS

- leave school or college *see* **leave (19-21)**
- someone who studies at a school or university *see* **study**
- teach, study, learn, subject, class, grade

1 school

- school

school /skuːl/ [n C/U] a place where children go to learn and be taught, up to the age of 18: *My mother is a teacher at the local school.* | *The nearest school was 10 miles away.* | *I always liked school, but my sister hated it.* | *All the kids around here take the bus to school.* | **at school** (=attending school) especially British *She must be about 16 – she's still at school.* | **in school** especially American *Kyle is one of the most popular boys in school.* | **out of school** (=no longer at school) *I've only been out of school a couple of years, but I've forgotten all the math I learned.* | **go to school** (=attend school) *Jessica's still too young to go to school.* | **drop out of school** (=stop going to school before you finish) *Jake dropped out of school and started working at the bowling alley.* | **state school** British /**public school** American (=a school that is paid for by the government) *Teachers are complaining that the public schools do not receive adequate funding.* | **private school** ALSO **independent school** British (=a school that is paid for by parents) *Many parents want to send their children to private school because class sizes are smaller.* | **public school** British (=a school for rich people that their parents pay for) *He argued for the abolition of the public schools, which he says are elitist.* | **school uniform** *The children were all wearing school uniforms.*

2 schools for very young children

- nursery school
- preschool
- kindergarten

nursery school /ˈnɜːʳsəri ˈskul/ [n C/U] a school for children aged between about two and five where they play and do activities with other children: *Ian will soon be old enough to go to nursery school.*

preschool /ˈpriːskuːl/ [n C/U] American a school for children aged between about two and five: *Eastin is calling for a plan to provide free preschool for all 4-year-olds.* —**preschooler** [n C] *The educational program is aimed at preschoolers.*

kindergarten /ˈkɪndəʳgɑːʳtən/ [n C/U] American the first year of school for children aged 5: *Katie was one of the few children who could read when she started kindergarten.* | *Mrs. Marks was my kindergarten teacher.* —**kindergartner** /ˈkɪndəʳgɑːʳtnəʳ/ [n C] American *The kindergartners were making pictures with construction paper.*

3 schools for children between the ages of about 5 and 12

- primary school
- elementary school/grade school

primary school /ˈpraɪməri ˌskuːl/ [n C/U] in Britain, a school for children aged between five and eleven: *My father entered primary school in 1958.* | *Primary school children know more today than we did at that age.*

elementary school/grade school /elɪ̈ˈmentəri ˌskuːl, ˈgreɪd skuːl/ [n C/U] in the US, a school for children aged between five and twelve in some places, and five and ten in other places: *In grade school, Karen sang in the school chorus.* | *The senator met with a group of elementary school students learning about how government works.*

4 schools for older children

- secondary school
- middle school
- junior high school
- high school
- comprehensive school
- sixth form college

secondary school /ˈsekəndəri ˌskuːl‖-deri-/ [n C/U] in Britain, a school for children aged between 11 and 18; in the US, a name for **middle school, junior high school**, and **high school** considered together as a group: *Everyone in his family had at least completed secondary school.* | *As children enter secondary school, parents often do not have the necessary knowledge to help with homework.*

middle school /ˈmɪdl skuːl/ [n C/U] a school for children aged between 9 and 13 in Britain and 10 and 14 in some parts of the US: *Kim attends Byrd Middle School in Sun Valley.* | *The arts and crafts fair is geared toward middle school students.*

junior high school /ˌdʒuːniəʳ ˈhaɪ skuːl/ [n C/U] a school for children aged between 12 and 14 or 15, especially in some parts of the US: *I started taking French in junior high school.* | *Drug use among junior high school students has fallen.*

high school /ˈhaɪ skuːl/ [n C/U] in the US, a school for children aged between 15 or 16 and 18: *Brad was the captain of his high school football team.* | *The program requires high school students to take at least one college-level course.* | **go to high school** *Where do you go to high school?* | **graduate from high school** (=successfully complete high school) *He's been working full time since graduating from high school last June.*

comprehensive school /ˌkɒmprɪˈhensɪv skuːl ‖-ˌkɑːm-/ [n C/U] in Britain, a school for children aged 11-16 or 11-18 that most students attend because it accepts people of all abilities and is paid for by the government

sixth form college /ˈsɪksθ fɔːʳm ˌkɒlɪdʒ‖-ˌkɑː-/ [n C/U] in Britain, a college for students aged between 16 and 18

5 a place where people over 18 can study

- university
- college
- school
- law school/medical school/business school
- post-secondary
- postgraduate
- higher education
- adult education

university /ˌjuːnəˈvɜːʳsəti/ [n C/U] a place where students study one or two subjects at a high level, in order to get degrees: *the University of Chicago* | *In 1986 32% of Saudi Arabian university professors were women.* | **go to university** British *She wants to go to university to study biology.* | **be at university** British *Both my sisters are at university.*

college /ˈkɒlɪdʒ‖ˈkɑː-/ [n C/U] in the US a university; in Britain, a place where people can study academic subjects or practical skills after they leave secondary school, but which does not give degrees: *The grant money is for low-income college students.* | **go to college** *My brother never went to college, but he still has a very good job.* | **be at college** British **be in college** American *Our youngest daughter is in college now.* | **graduate from college** *We hadn't seen each other since we graduated from college.* | **college graduate** (=someone who has successfully completed college) *Many college graduates are unable to find work in their field.*

school /skuːl/ [n C/U] American informal a university or similar institution **go to school** (=study at a college or university) *Phil gave up his job, and he's going back to school next year.*

law school/medical school/business school /ˈlɔː skuːl, ˈmedɪkəl skuːl, ˈbɪznəs skuːl/ [n C] a university or part of a university where you study law, medicine, or business: *My father always wanted me to go to law school.* | *Harvard Business School* | *He's applied to all the best medical schools in the country.*

post-secondary /pəʊst ˈsekəndəri‖-deri/ [adj only before noun] American use this about education that takes place after a student has finished high school: *Eighty-five percent of high school students in the program go on to post-secondary education.* | *post-secondary institutions*

postgraduate especially British **/graduate** American /pəʊstˈgrædʒuət, ˈgrædʒuət/ [adj only before noun] use this about advanced education that takes place after a student has finished a university degree, or about students who study at this level: *She got a degree in history last year, and now she's doing a postgraduate course.* | *postgraduate research* | *We met when we were both graduate students at Berkeley.*

higher education /ˌhaɪər edjʊˈkeɪʃən‖-edʒə-/ [n U] education at a university or similar institution: *The U.S. community college system is the largest system of higher education in the world.* | *More women than ever are going on to higher education.*

adult education /ˌædʌlt edjʊˈkeɪʃən‖-edʒə-/ [n U] classes for adults, often in the evenings, either because they want to improve their skills or for interest and enjoyment: *The government needs to do more to fund adult education for the unemployed.*

6 one of the periods into which the year is divided at school, university etc

- term
- semester
- the school year/the academic year
- quarter

term /tɜːʳm/ [n C] one of the three periods that the year is divided into at British school and most British universities; in the US, a name for any of the main periods into which a school year is divided: *As a graduate student, he spent a term at Wichita State University.* | *The main exams are at the end of the summer term.*

semester /səˈmestəʳ/ [n C] one of the two or three periods that the year is divided into at American schools and most American universities: *He attended Bennington College for three semesters.* | **fall/spring semester** *Fall semester starts the 28th of August.*

the school year/the academic year /ðə ˌskuːl ˈjɪəʳ, ði ˌækədemɪk ˈjɪəʳ/ [n singular] the period of the year when there are school or university classes: *In Japan the school year starts in April and ends in February or March.* | *The end of the academic year with its final exams is very stressful for many students.*

quarter /ˈkwɔːʳtəʳ/ [n C] one of the four main periods that the year is divided into at some American schools and universities **fall/winter/spring/summer quarter** *She was back in Michigan in time to teach spring quarter.*

7 what you get when you finish a course successfully

- diploma
- qualification
- degree
- master's degree/master's
- doctorate/PhD

diploma /dəˈpləʊmə/ [n C] in Britain, a document that shows that someone has successfully completed a course of study or passed an examination; in the US, a document showing that a student has successfully completed their high school, college, or university education: *Everyone was given a diploma at the end of the course.* | **high school/college diploma** *Anyone with a high school diploma can enroll in the course.*

qualification /ˌkwɒlǝ̇fǝ̇ˈkeɪʃən‖ˌkwɑː-/ [n C usually plural] British you get a **qualification** when you finish a course and pass examinations at the end of it: *The two-year course leads to a teaching qualification.* | *List your qualifications in the space below.* | **academic qualification** *She left school at 16, with no academic qualifications.*

degree /dɪˈgriː/ [n C] the qualification that you get when you successfully finish a course at university: *Cohn has a degree in political science from the University of Chicago.* | *Her dream is to get a degree in computer science and then get a high-paying job.* | **do a degree/take a degree** British (=study in order to get one) *Maggie is doing a degree in psychology.*

master's degree/master's /ˈmɑːstəʳz dɪˌgriː, ˈmɑːstəʳz‖ˈmæs-/ [n C] an advanced degree that you get by studying for one or two years after getting your first degree: *Getting a master's should help you get a better job.* | **+ in** *Successful applicants will have a master's degree in social work.*

doctorate/PhD /ˈdɒktərǝ̇t‖ˈdɑːk-, ˌpiː eɪtʃ ˈdiː/ [n C] the most advanced type of degree, which you study for on your own for several years, doing work and writing a long report explaining what you have discovered: *Bedell later earned a doctorate from Columbia University.* | **+ in** *She had a PhD in industrial robotics.*

8 the process of studying and being taught

- education
- educational
- academic

education /ˌedjʊˈkeɪʃən‖ˌedʒə-/ [n U] the whole process by which people learn and develop their minds in schools, colleges, and universities: *The government should spend more on education.* | *My parents wanted me to have a good education.* | *Kerry hasn't decided if she'll continue her education or not.* | **public education** (=paid for by the government) especially American *All children in the state have a right to public education.* | **private education** (=paid for by parents, not provided by the government) *Many parents cannot afford private education for their children.*

educational /ˌedjʊˈkeɪʃənəl‖ˌedʒə-/ [adj usually before noun] relating to education: *Different children have different educational needs.* | *We offer a wide range of educational and sporting activities.* | **educational institution/establishment** (=a school, college, or university) *Many educational institutions have not been able make needed improvements because of funding cuts.* | **educational system** *The American educational system is in need of reform.* | **educational opportunity** *Low-income children do not have the same educational opportunities as children from wealthier families.*

academic /ˌækəˈdemɪk◂/ [adj usually before noun] relating to education, especially at college or university level: *Leon was unemployed, and had no academic qualifications.* | *Increased self-confidence can help improve academic achievement.* | *Her name is well known in academic circles.* | *The new law raises concerns about academic freedom.*

score

RELATED WORDS

- a letter or number that shows how well you have done in a test *see* **grade**
- *see also* **game, sport, result, test, throw (2)**

1 to get points in a game or sport

- score
- get
- make
- hit

score /skɔːʳ/ [v I/T] to get points in a game, competition, or sport: *San Francisco scored twice in the last ten minutes of the game.* | **score a point/goal** *Tottenham scored the first goal of the game.* | *In Scrabble you score points by making words on the board.*

get /get/ [v T] informal to score points in a game, competition, or sport: *When you get a total of 5 points it's your turn to throw the dice.* | *Stevens got only 10 goals in 41 games, and decided to leave the Boston Bruins.*

make /meɪk/ [v T] especially American to score points in a game, competition, or sport: *Jordan made 34 points to put his team into the lead.* | *He ran 30 yards to make his second touchdown of the quarter.*

hit /hɪt/ [v T] to get a point or points by hitting a ball etc: *The batter hit a home run.* | *Greg Davis didn't disappoint his teammates, hitting six field goals in six attempts.*

2 when two teams or players have the same score

- draw
- be two all/be four all etc
- equalize

draw especially British **/tie** especially American /drɔː, taɪ/ [n C] when both players or teams have the same number of points at the end of a game: *'What was the result of the Barcelona v Real Madrid game?' 'It was a draw.'* | *The game ended in a tie.*

be two all/be four all etc /biː ˌtuː ˈɔːl/ [v phrase] spoken say this when both players or teams have two points, four points etc in a game: *It's two all at the moment, but United seems the better team.* | *'What was the final score'? 'One all.'*

equalize ALSO **equalise** British /ˈiːkwəlaɪz/ [v I] to score a goal or point in a team game such as football, so that the number of points or goals that each team has is equal: *Liverpool equalized in the last minute.* | *Manchester United were a goal down against Real Madrid when Bobby Charlton equalized.*

3 the points scored in a game or sport

- point
- score
- goal
- result
- run

point /pɔɪnt/ [n C] a unit you get when you achieve something during a game or competition: *Steve Jones is 15 points ahead.* | *Damon Hill leads the Formula 1 Championship, with 58 points from 6 races.*

score /skɔːʳ/ [n C] the number of points that the two teams or players have in a game: *What's the score?* |

The score at half-time was 12-18. | **final score** (=the score at the end of the game) *The final score went up on the scoreboard, and the crowd let out a roar.*

goal /gəʊl/ [n C] the point you get when you make the ball go into the net in sports such as football or hockey: *Goal! Right in the last minute, England have scored.* | **get/score a goal** *Florin Raducioiu scored four goals, putting Romania in the lead.*

result /rɪˈzʌlt/ [n C] especially British the final number of points at the end of a competition: *Turn to BBC1 for the latest football results.* | *D'you know the result of the Arsenal game?*

run /rʌn/ [n C] the point you get in cricket or baseball: *The West Indies beat Australia by 273 runs.* | **score/get/hit a run** *Camilli scored 936 runs in 12 major-league seasons.*

scream

RELATED WORDS

- *see also* **shout, frightened/frightening, pain, angry**

1 to scream

- scream
- shriek
- screech
- squeal
- yelp
- let out a scream/shriek

scream /skriːm/ [v I/T] to make a loud, high noise, or say something in a loud, high voice, because you are excited, frightened, angry, or in pain: *Everyone panicked, and people started screaming.* | *'Go away!' she screamed* | **+ at** *Sammy screamed at me to stay back.* | **+ for** *The boy screamed for help.* | **scream with pain/delight/terror etc** *She woke up screaming with terror.*

shriek /ʃriːk/ [v I/T] to make a sudden short screaming sound or shout something because you are very frightened, excited etc: *Bella turned and shrieked his name.* | *'Keep away from me!' she shrieked.* | **shriek with excitement/laughter/fear etc** *The children began shrieking with hysterical laughter.* | **+ at** *The two women shrieked at one another over the noise of the machines.*

screech /skriːtʃ/ [v I/T] to make long, high unpleasant sounds or shout something in an unpleasantly loud, high voice, especially because you are angry: *Sue grabbed him, screeching, and started hitting him with her fists.* | *'Get out!' she screeched angrily. 'I hate you!'* | **+ at** *Maria suddenly started screeching at Bruno.*

squeal /skwiːl/ [v I/T] to make a sudden very high screaming sound, because you are excited, amused, frightened, or in pain: *The children squealed and fought among themselves.* | *'Don't you dare!' Bobby squealed.* | **squeal with excitement/laughter/delight/pain etc** *The boy squealed with pain and surprise.* | *They all tumbled into the water, squealing with delight.*

yelp /jelp/ [v I] to give a short cry because you have just been hurt: *The boy grinned, and then yelped as someone hit him in the back.* | *Sophie yelped with pain and dropped the pan.*

let out a scream/shriek /ˌlet aʊt ə ˈskriːm, ˈʃriːk/ [v phrase] to scream or shriek suddenly **+ of** *Karen let out a scream of terror, as if she had seen a ghost.* | *The children ran down the hill, letting out shrieks of delight.*

2 the sound of someone screaming

- scream
- shriek
- squeal
- yelp

scream /skriːm/ [n C] *We could hear screams coming from inside the blazing building.* | *The battlefield echoed with the screams of the wounded and the dying.*

shriek /ʃriːk/ [n C] a sudden short screaming sound made by someone who is very frightened, excited, or amused: *I was woken up by a loud shriek from the bathroom.* | **a shriek of delight/laughter** *With a shriek of delight, she threw herself into the water.* | *Almost before he started speaking they all burst into shrieks of laughter.*

squeal /skwiːl/ [n C] a sudden high screaming sound, when frightened or excited: *Suddenly there was a bump and an awful squeal.* | **squeals of delight/joy/laughter** *The sight of the food brought squeals of delight from the children.*

yelp /jelp/ [n C] a short cry of pain because you have just been hurt: *She jumped back from the fire with a sudden yelp of pain.*

secret

RELATED WORDS

- to tell someone a secret *see* **tell (11-16)**
- to take part in something secret *see* **take part/be involved (7)**
- thoughts and feelings you want to keep secret *see* **private**
- *see also* **spy, know/not know**

1 secret information/plans/places/activities

- secret
- confidential
- classified
- sensitive
- covert
- undercover
- be veiled in secrecy/shrouded in secrecy/cloaked in secrecy
- hush-hush
- cloak-and-dagger

secret /ˈsiːkrɪ̈t/ [adj] if something is **secret**, not many people know about it, and they agree not to tell anyone else about it: *The letter was written in a secret code.* | *Secret documents containing details of Britain's defence plans have been stolen.* | *The president's schedule is secret, but there is speculation that he will visit UN troops in the area.* | **remain/stay secret** *I hope you see how vital it is that our conversation remains secret.* | **top secret** (=when an official document, piece of information etc is very secret) *The experiments were top secret.* | **secret ballot** (=a secret vote) *The Leader of the House will be selected by secret ballot.*

confidential /ˌkɒnfɪ̈ˈdenʃəl◂‖ˌkɑːn-/ [adj] **confidential** information is known only by a few official people, and must not be told to anyone else, for example because it contains military secrets or private details about people: *We hold confidential records on each employee.* | *Always protect confidential files by locking them with a password.* | *An employee secretly gave confidential memos to the press.* | **highly confidential** (=very confidential) *The information we received is of a highly confidential nature and relates to national security.*

classified /ˈklæsɪ̈faɪd/ [adj] **classified** information or documents are ones that the government has ordered to be kept secret: *There is evidence that Huang had access to classified information.* | *Only licensed companies are eligible to receive, store, or send classified material.*

sensitive /ˈsensɪ̈tɪv/ [adj] information or documents that are **sensitive** are likely to cause problems or embarrassment if they are made public and therefore they are kept secret: *A teenager used his personal computer to break into sensitive US Air Force files.* | *Your competitors may have access to the company intranet, so never discuss commercially sensitive issues on-line.* | **highly sensitive** *The minister admitted that highly sensitive documents had been leaked to the press.*

covert /ˈkʌvəʳtˌ ˈkəʊvɜːʳt / [adj only before noun] done secretly, especially by a government or official organization, often involving breaking the law: *The chief investigator resigned, amid allegations of covert and probably illegal operations.* | *The abuse of residents in the home was confirmed by covert video surveillance.* —**covertly** [adv] *We're able to operate covertly to monitor the situation.*

undercover /ˌʌndəʳˈkʌvəʳ◂/ [adj usually before noun] working secretly – use this about the activities of the police, the army etc: *Six members of a drug-smuggling gang were arrested after an 18-month undercover police operation.* | *The unit is equipped to deal with a variety of situations, including undercover surveillance.* —**undercover** [adv] **work/go undercover** *Griffiths plays a New York police officer who goes undercover to investigate the murder of a young Jewish man.*

be veiled in secrecy/shrouded in secrecy/cloaked in secrecy /biː ˌveɪld ɪn ˈsiːkrəsi, ˌʃraʊdɪ̈d ɪn ˈsiːkrəsi, ˌkləʊkt ɪn ˈsiːkrəsi/ [v phrase] if something **is veiled**, **cloaked**, or **shrouded in secrecy**, very little is known about it and it seems very mysterious: *In Japan, the private lives of the Emperor and his family were once veiled in secrecy.* | *The President's exact itinerary was cloaked in secrecy for security reasons.* | *This ground-breaking work is shrouded in secrecy on the instruction of the company's lawyers.*

hush-hush /ˌhʌʃ ˈhʌʃ◂‖ˈhʌʃ hʌʃ/ [adj] informal kept officially secret: *His death was really hush-hush. It was so covered up that you wondered if it wasn't a suicide.* | *'The Manhattan Project' was the insiders' name for the hush-hush project.*

cloak-and-dagger /ˌkləʊk ən ˈdægəʳ/ [adj only before noun] use this about methods and activities that involve a lot of secrecy, especially when this seems unnecessary: *He was arrested after a cloak-and-dagger operation involving the CIA and MI6.*

2 something that is secret

- secret
- skeleton in your cupboard

secret /ˈsiːkrɪ̈t/ [n C] something that you do not want other people to know about: *I'm not supposed to be telling you this, it's a secret.* | *Only Jasper knew my secret.* | **tell sb a secret** *Come over here, Luke wants to tell you a secret.* | **remain/stay a secret** *We lived in a small village and I knew that the news wouldn't remain a secret for very long.* | **trade secret** (=information that a company keeps secret from other companies) *The task force will concentrate on stopping the theft of trade secrets.* | **state secret** (=information that a government keeps secret) *A scientist has been arrested for revealing state secrets concerning chemical weapons.* | **family secret** (=one that only some members of a family know about) *It's one of those family secrets that we don't talk about much.* | **a closely-guarded/well kept secret** (=one that is kept very secret) *His whereabouts are a closely-guarded secret.* | **the secret is out/the secret comes out** (=when people get to know something that was being kept secret) *Yes, the secret's out I'm afraid. I'm to be a grandmother.*

skeleton in your cupboard British **/skeleton in your closet** American /ˌskelɪ̈tən ɪn jɔːʳ ˈkʌbəʳd, ˌskelɪ̈tən ɪn jɔːʳ ˈklɒzɪ̈t‖-ˈklɑːzɪ̈t/ [n phrase] a secret about yourself that you have kept hidden for a long time because you are ashamed or embarrassed about it: *None of us is perfect – we all have a little skeleton somewhere in the closet that we'd rather other people didn't know about.*

3 secret organizations and people who do secret work

- secret
- underground
- clandestine
- undercover

secret /ˈsiːkrɪ̈t/ [adj] **secret police/agent/society etc** *She was kept under surveillance by the secret police for over three years.* | *The film tells the story of a Swiss secret agent who masquerades as a grocer in order to uncover a drugs ring.* | *a senior member of the secret service*

underground /ˌʌndəʳˈgraʊnd◂/ [adj/adv] **underground organization/newspaper/movement etc** one that is secret and opposes the government, especially when it is too dangerous to do this publicly: *Slowly, the underground resistance movement grew.* | *Nearly 2,000 defeated fighters joined the underground Communist forces concealed in the Mekong delta.* | *He was suspended from his job for writing an editorial in an underground paper.* | **go underground/be forced underground** (=become an underground organization) *In 1795, the United Irish Society went underground as a revolutionary movement.*

clandestine /klænˈdestɪ̈n/ [adj] **clandestine organization/force/operation etc** one that is secret, and usually illegal: *The doctor was arrested after she was named as a member of a clandestine socialist movement.* | *His clandestine meetings with PLO officials had been secretly recorded.*

undercover /ˌʌndəʳˈkʌvəʳ◂/ [adj usually before noun] **undercover agent/police officer/investigator etc** one who works secretly for the police or government in order to catch criminals: *He was arrested after trying to sell guns to an undercover FBI agent.* | *People dived aside as undercover cops ambushed a planned post office raid.*

4 to not tell other people about a secret

- not tell
- keep sth secret
- can keep a secret
- keep quiet
- keep sth from
- keep sth under wraps
- discretion
- secrecy
- confidentiality

not tell /nɒt ˈtel/ [v phrase] to **not tell** someone about something: *I told you not to tell anyone!* | *'Who's that letter from?' 'I'm not telling you.'* | **not tell sb what/how/why etc** *Henry wouldn't tell me what the surprise was.* | *Penny laughed, but she wouldn't tell me why.* | **+ about** *Vinny didn't tell the police about his visit to Mahoney's apartment.* | *You'd better not tell Elizabeth about this.* | **+ of** *Margaret had not yet told her sons of her planned engagement.* | **+ (that)**

Carl felt I'd been deceiving him all these years by not telling him I was gay. | **without telling sb** *I was annoyed that he'd left without telling me.*

keep sth secret /ˌkiːp (sth) ˈsiːkrɪ̈t/ [v phrase] to not tell other people something, because you want it to remain secret: *They wanted to keep their relationship secret for as long as possible.* | *The graves were covered up in a deliberate attempt to keep the killings secret.* | *So you've been keeping it secret all this time?* | **+ from** *Mary kept her illness secret, even from family members.*

can keep a secret /kən ˌkiːp ə ˈsiːkrɪ̈t/ [v phrase] someone who **can keep a secret** will not tell your secrets to other people, so you can trust them with secret information: *Can you keep a secret?* | *'Can I trust you?' 'I'm honest, and I can keep a secret'.*

keep quiet /kiːp ˈkwaɪət/ [v phrase] to deliberately not talk about something in public, especially something you are ashamed or embarrassed about: *Parotti had threatened to expose the illegal arrangements unless he was paid $50,000 to keep quiet.* | *Some people disagree with what the government is doing, but they keep quiet for fear of reprisals.* | **+ about** *We used to keep quiet about some of the things that went on in the prison.* | **+ over** *I think they should have kept quiet over that.* | **keep sth quiet** (=keep something secret) *The minister denied that the case had been kept quiet or hidden.* | **keep sb quiet** (=do something to stop someone telling a secret) *She'd been brutally murdered to keep her quiet.*

keep sth from /ˈkiːp (sth) frɒm/ [phr v T] to deliberately not tell someone about something, especially because you think they would be upset if they knew the truth: *Edward never told anyone about his illness. He even tried to keep it from his wife.* | *The president has a reputation for keeping key decisions from even his closest aides.* | *She tried in every way to keep the truth from her parents.*

keep sth under wraps /ˌkiːp (sth) ʌndəʳ ˈræps/ [v phrase] to not allow people to know about something that has been officially planned or decided **be kept under wraps** *It's been suggested the report was kept under wraps to avoid controversy.* | *Ford's new range of cars is being kept firmly under wraps until the Geneva auto show.*

discretion /dɪˈskreʃən/ [n U] the ability to judge when you should or should not tell people things that you know about someone or something: *Absolute discretion is required from everyone working for the Royal Family.* | **leave sth to sb's discretion** *I leave it to your discretion as to whether you should tell your colleagues.* | **show/exercise discretion** *TV commentators have shown great discretion, glossing over the problems in her personal life.* | *Can junior managers be trusted to exercise discretion when making decisions?* | **be the (very) soul of discretion** (=be the sort of person who will never tell something that should be kept secret) *You can tell Martin anything – he's the very soul of discretion.*

secrecy /ˈsiːkrɪ̈si/ [n U] when what someone does or says is kept very secret, so that only a few people know about it: *There is a great deal of secrecy within the organization.* | *Why all the secrecy? You've got nothing to be ashamed of.* | **utmost secrecy** *Our commanding officer emphasized the need to maintain the utmost secrecy about the operation at all times.* | **swear sb to secrecy** (=make someone promise that they will not tell other people a secret) *Anna swore me to secrecy on the subject of her family until her book came out.* | **a veil/shroud/cloak of secrecy** *The gunmen tracked down their target, despite the shroud of secrecy surrounding his whereabouts.*

confidentiality /ˌkɒnfɪ̈denʃiˈælɪ̈ti‖ˌkɑːn-/ [n U] the trust that exists between people who share secrets, especially between a professional person such as a doctor or lawyer and someone who gives them private advice: *Alexander declined to comment, citing attorney–client confidentiality.* | *Researchers should always be able to guarantee complete confidentiality for their subjects.* | *Data encryption ensures the privacy and confidentiality of email messages.* | **breach/violate confidentiality** (=to break confidentiality by telling someone a secret) *The health clinic has again been caught violating patient confidentiality.* | **breach of confidentiality** *You doctor should not have told your parents about the abortion – that was a blatant breach of confidentiality.*

5 done secretly

- secretly/in secret/in secrecy
- on the quiet
- behind closed doors
- in private/privately
- behind sb's back
- surreptitiously
- furtively

secretly/in secret/in secrecy /ˈsiːkrɪ̈tli, ɪn ˈsɪːkrɪ̈t, ɪn ˈsiːkrəsi/ [adv] done without anyone else knowing: *Many civilians were secretly killed and buried by soldiers.* | *My parents didn't approve of our relationship, and we had to meet in secret.* | *Operating in secrecy, intelligence agencies are often seen as mysterious and unaccountable for their actions.*

on the quiet /ɒn ðə ˈkwaɪət/ [adv] if you do something **on the quiet**, you do it secretly, especially because you think that people will disapprove of what you are doing: *His doctor has told him he mustn't drink, but he still has the occasional brandy on the quiet.* | *He used to flirt with the two girls, on the quiet, when his wife wasn't looking.*

behind closed doors /bɪˌhaɪnd kləʊzd ˈdɔːʳz/ [adv] if important official meetings, discussions, or decisions take place **behind closed doors**, they take place secretly without the public being allowed to see or hear them: *The board members met behind closed doors to discuss the deal.* | *Although America is a democracy, a lot of key decisions are made behind closed doors by unelected advisers.*

in private/privately /ɪn ˈpraɪvɪ̈t, ˈpraɪvɪ̈tli/ [adv] if you do something **in private** or **privately**, you do it where other people cannot see or hear you: *Can I have a word with you in private?* | *Although party officials give the President their public support, many are saying in private that he may have to resign.* | *Generations of Native American children in state schools were punished for speaking their own language, even privately.*

behind sb's back /bɪˌhaɪnd (sb's) ˈbæk/ [adv] if you do something or say something unpleasant about someone **behind their back**, you do or say it without telling them: *I thought you were my friend. Now I find you've been talking about me behind my back.* | *People laughed at him behind his back.* | *He agrees with his boss to his face, but then criticizes him behind his back.* | **go behind sb's back** *I'm not happy about you going behind my back like that. You should have told me.*

surreptitiously /ˌsʌrəpˈtɪʃəsli/ [adv] if you do something **surreptitiously**, you do it while other people are not looking because you do not want them to see you doing it: *She glanced surreptitiously up at the clock.* | *I found myself studying his face surreptitiously.* | *Greenpeace claim that toxic waste has been dumped surreptitiously on west coast beaches.*

furtively /ˈfɜːʳtɪvli/ [adv] if you do something **furtively**, you do it in a way which makes you look as if you are keeping something secret, especially something wrong that you have done: *She looked around furtively to make sure no one was watching.* | *The older boys hovered furtively outside the school gates, clutching thinly rolled cigarettes.*

6 behaving as if you have a secret

- secretive
- cagey
- play your cards close to your chest
- furtive
- secret
- closet

secretive /ˈsiːkrətɪv, sɪˈkriːtɪv/ [adj] unwilling to let other people know what you are doing, or to give them information about yourself: *Years of living alone had made her secretive and unwilling to trust anyone.* | *Why did Stephen always have to be so secretive in his business dealings?* | *Much of the discussion focused upon North Korea's highly secretive nuclear program.* | **+ about** *Kath's very secretive about her past, isn't she?*

cagey /ˈkeɪdʒi/ [adj] informal unwilling to tell people definitely what your plans, intentions, or opinions are – use this especially when you cannot think of a good reason for someone doing this: *He gets very cagey whenever I ask him about his job.* | **+ about** *She's very cagey about what she spends her money on, don't you think?* | **play it cagey** American *Coach Bob Dwyer is playing it cagey over his choice of a replacement skipper.*

play your cards close to your chest British **/play your cards close to your vest** American /pleɪ jɔːʳ ˌkɑːʳdz kləʊs tə jɔːʳ ˈtʃest, pleɪ jɔːʳ ˌkɑːʳdz kləʊs tə jɔːʳ ˈvest/ [v phrase] if someone **plays their cards close to their chest** or **vest**, they do not allow other people to know what they are planning to do next: *Roslin, known for playing his cards close to his vest, declined to comment.*

furtive /ˈfɜːʳtɪv/ [adj] someone who is **furtive** or behaves in a **furtive** way looks as though they are keeping something secret, especially something wrong that they have done: *His movements were quick and furtive, and he spoke in a whisper.* | *Miss Baggely appeared unconfident, almost furtive.* | *The two girls exchanged furtive glances across the dinner table and tried hard not to giggle.*

secret /ˈsiːkrət/ [adj only before noun] doing something only in **secret**, so that other people do not know you are doing it: *I actually think he's probably a secret Republican voter.* | *He hid the fact that he was a secret drinker from his employees for many years.*

closet /ˈklɒzət‖ˈklɑː-, ˈklɔː-/ [adj] **closet alcoholic/homosexual/communist etc** one who is secretly an alcoholic, homosexual etc: *He finally came out in 1998, after years as a closet homosexual.*

see

RELATED WORDS

- to understand something *see* **understand**
- *see also* **watch, look, notice/not notice, clear/not clear**

1 to see someone or something

- see
- catch sight of/catch a glimpse of
- spot
- set eyes on
- witness
- sight
- get a look (at)
- see first hand

see /siː/ [v T not in progressive] *I saw your brother in town this morning.* | *Have you seen my pen anywhere?* | *If you see either of these men, inform the police immediately.* | *Did you see a white van parked out here earlier today?* | *When did you last see your dog?* | **see sb doing sth** *I saw Matt coming out of the cinema with Jane.* | *I first saw her feeding the ducks in the park.* | **see sb do sth** *She saw him get into a Porsche driven by a dark-haired woman.* | *I didn't see her arrive because I had my back turned.* | **see who/what/where etc** *It was too dark for her to see who the woman was.* | *Have you seen what Jake's done to his bedroom?* | **can see sb/sth** *Shh! I can see someone moving in the bushes.* | **see sth with your own eyes** (=see something or someone yourself, especially something strange or surprising) *'How do you know it's true?' 'Because I saw it with my own eyes!'*

catch sight of/catch a glimpse of /ˌkætʃ ˈsaɪt ɒv, ˌkætʃ ə ˈglɪmps ɒv/ [v phrase] especially written to see someone or something for only a very short time, and not very clearly: *Rick caught sight of the driver's face as the car raced by.* | *Lynn caught a brief glimpse of herself in the mirror.*

spot /spɒt‖spɑːt/ [v T not in progressive] to suddenly see someone or something that you have been looking for, or something interesting or unusual: *A resident spotted a man sitting in his car watching the explosion and notified the police.* | *He was spotted in the Manhattan area in mid-May.* | *I spotted this article about it in the paper.*

set eyes on ALSO **clap eyes on** British /ˌset ˈaɪz ɒn, ˌklæp ˈaɪz ɒn/ [v phrase] to see someone or something – use this either when talking about the time when you first saw them, or when saying strongly that you have never seen them or never want to see them again: *This was the woman he was going to marry – he knew it the moment he set eyes on her.* | *I'd never clapped eyes on the guy before in my life.* | *I hoped we would never set eyes on one another again.*

witness /ˈwɪtnəs/ [v T] to see something happen, especially an accident, a crime, or an important event: *Police are appealing for information from anyone who witnessed the attack.* | *The crash was witnessed by millions of viewers who were watching the race on TV.* —**witness** [n C] *In court, a witness said he had seen O'Grady punch the woman in the face.* | **+ to** *Police are appealing for witnesses to an arson attack on an apartment block.*

sight /saɪt/ [v T not in progressive] especially written to suddenly see something or someone from a long distance, especially when you have been looking for a long time: *The missing boys were sighted by a rescue helicopter.* | *At least ten birds have been sighted feeding on the lake this year.* | *We sighted a fishing boat in the distance.* —**sighting** [n C] **+ of** *No further sightings of the fur seal were reported until the early 90s.* | **the first sighting** (=when something is seen for the first time) *the first sighting of Halley's Comet*

get a look (at) /ˌget ə ˈlʊk (æt)/ [v phrase] to be able to see someone or something clearly, even though you see them for only a very short time **get a good/proper look (at)** *Hold it up to the light so I can get a proper look at it.* | *I don't think I could identify him. I didn't really get a good look.* | **get a better look (at)** *She stood on her toes to get a better look.* | **get a close look (at)** *I didn't get a close look at the driver, but I think he was middle-aged.* | *We drove into the prohibited zone, to get a closer look.*

see first hand ALSO **see at first hand** British /ˌsiː fɜːʳst ˈhænd, ˌsiː ət fɜːʳst ˈhænd/ [v phrase] if you **see first hand** something that is happening, you see it yourself, rather than being told about it by someone else: *Travelling in rural Thailand, I saw first hand* *the devastating effects of economic reform.* | *Central News has been to South America to see at first hand the lives that Oxfam hopes to improve.*

2 to be able to see something, but with difficulty

▸ make out ▸ distinguish

make out /ˌmeɪk ˈaʊt/ [phr v T not in progressive] to see someone or something, but only with difficulty **make out sth** *Among the trees below, he could make out a yellow pick-up truck.* | *I could just make out Murphy in the bed next to mine.* | **make it out** *Some crystals are so small, a microscope is needed to make them out.* | **make out what/where/who** *It was difficult to make out where the rocks ended and the sea began.* | *At first, I couldn't make out what I was seeing.*

distinguish /dɪˈstɪŋgwɪʃ/ [v T not in progressive] formal to see the shape of someone or something with difficulty: *The room was too dimly lit for me to distinguish anything clearly.* | *It was just possible to distinguish the darkened village below.*

3 when something happens in a place where everyone can see

▸ in full view of ▸ in front of ▸ before your (very) eyes ▸ in broad daylight

in full view of /ɪn ˌfʊl ˈvjuː ɒv/ [prep] if someone does something, especially something unpleasant or shocking, **in full view of** a group of people, they do it in a place where people can see it clearly: *The muggers stole his mobile and wallet in full view of a crowd of shoppers.* | *He made an obscene gesture in full view of TV cameras.*

in front of /ɪn ˈfrʌnt ɒv/ [prep] if something happens **in front of** someone, it happens where they can see it, especially when it is shocking or unpleasant: *The man was shot in front of his wife and three children.* | *The waitress complained that her employer had humiliated her in front of customers.* | **right in front of sb** (=use this to emphasize how shocking something is) *Mom grabbed my arm and scolded me, right in front of all my friends.*

before your (very) eyes /bɪˌfɔːʳ jɔːʳ (veri) ˈaɪz/ [adv] if something surprising or shocking happens **before your eyes**, it happens very close to you, so that you can see it clearly: *Before our very eyes, he produced $50,000 out of his suitcase and offered to buy the house.* | **right before your eyes** *When you see someone murdered right before your eyes, you don't forget it easily.*

in broad daylight /ɪn ˌbrɔːd ˈdeɪlaɪt/ [prep] if a crime or something shocking happens **in broad daylight**, it happens during the day in a public place where people can see it: *He gunned down a man in broad daylight and got away.* | *A woman was attacked in broad daylight, right in front of our office.*

4 something that you see

▸ sight ▸ view ▸ scene ▸ panorama ▸ spectacle ▸ visual

sight /saɪt/ [n C/U] something that you see, or when you see something: *Sunrise over the Himalayas is a magnificent sight.* | *It was a sight so awe-inspiring we could have stayed for hours.* | **the sight of sth** (=when you see something) *I can't stand the sight of blood.* | **at the sight of sth** *Even Charles cheered up at the sight of the food.* | **(at) first sight** (=the first time you see someone or something) *When I met my husband, it was love at first sight.* | *It was our first sight of land after 15 months at sea.* | **on sight** (=as soon as you see someone or something) *The superintendent issued orders to shoot looters and arsonists on sight.* | **a familiar/common sight** (=something that you often see) *Homeless kids are now a familiar sight on London's streets.* | **a sorry sight** (=someone or something that makes you feel sad or sympathetic) *Gavin looked a sorry sight – his jaw was broken, and he had a black eye.* | **quite a sight** (=used to emphasize how impressive, beautiful, funny etc something looks) *We looked at the huge crowd gathering below us. 'It's quite a sight, isn't it?'*

view /vjuː/ [n C] the area you can see from a window or place, especially when it is beautiful or when you are able to see something from a place: *We lived in a town house, with a spectacular view of the East China Sea.* | *Is it the superb views that bring you back here each year?* | **+ of** *Edwina's office was south-facing, with a view of the lake.* | **get/have a good view (of sth)** (=be able to see all of it) *We had a good view of the firework display from Ron's balcony.* | **provide/afford/offer a view** (=to have very good views – used especially in advertisements) *The hotel is situated on a hill, providing panoramic views of the city.* | *The open-air terrace affords unparalleled views of the Big Apple.* | **a room/apartment/office etc with a view** *We were very, very lucky to get an apartment with a view.* | *Dan was delighted to get a room with breathtaking views of the Los Angeles basin.*

scene /siːn/ [n C] what you see in a place – used especially when you are describing a place where something unusual or shocking is happening: *The village is a scene of devastation after the heavy rains.* | *I had to laugh at the absurdity of the scene.* | *Reporters described the horrific scenes which followed the bombing.* | **+ of** *There are scenes of confusion here as refugees pour out of the city.*

panorama /ˌpænəˈrɑːmə‖-ˈræmə/ [n C] an impressive view of a very large area that stretches a long way across in front of you: *At sunrise, they surveyed the vast panorama of snow-covered hills and mountains.* | *The white limestone formed a dramatic panorama against the darkening sky.* — **panoramic** /ˌpænəˈræmɪk◂/ [adj] **panoramic view** *an apartment with panoramic views of the Hudson River*

spectacle /ˈspektəkəl/ [n C usually singular] something that you see that is very surprising, strange, or shocking **the spectacle of** *Visitors to London are often shocked by the spectacle of people begging in the streets.* | **a strange/bizarre/tragic etc spectacle** *The sight of European tourists dancing in grass skirts made a bizarre spectacle.* | **make a spectacle of yourself** (=to do something silly, surprising, or shocking when a lot of people can see you) *She knew she was making a spectacle of herself with her childish outburst, but she couldn't seem to help herself.*

visual /ˈvɪʒuəl/ [adj usually before noun] designed to be seen or having a particular effect when seen: *The movie is greatly enhanced by its stunning visual effects.* | *Teachers have been using visual aids in the classroom for decades.* | *Children learn to read by interpreting visual symbols.* — **visually** [adv] *As well as being nutritious, food needs to be visually attractive.* | *Use a variety of bright bold colors to make your design visually attractive.*

5 when something can be seen

- visible
- visibility
- in sight/within sight
- show
- in view
- appear
- come into sight/come into view

visible /ˈvɪzə̇bəl/ [adj] *Detectives found no visible signs of a struggle.* | **+ from/at/above etc** *The church tower is visible from the next village.* | *Only the top of his head was visible above the water.* | *A single headlight was suddenly visible far below them.* | *Trim any visible fat before frying the meat.* | **clearly visible** *The bullet holes are still clearly visible in the walls.* | **barely/hardly/scarcely visible** *The marks are in faint gold, and hardly visible.* | **visible to the naked eye** (=visible without using special instruments to help you) *These stars are barely visible to the naked eye.* —**visibly** [adv] **visibly upset/moved/shaken etc** (=when you can see that someone is upset etc) *The Kings were visibly shaken when the judge passed sentence.* | *The questions made her visibly nervous.*

visibility /ˌvɪzə̇ˈbɪlə̇ti/ [n U] how far it is possible to see, especially when this is affected by weather conditions – used especially in weather reports: *Fog has reduced visibility to under 20 metres.* | **good visibility** (=when the air is clear so you can see a long distance) *Conditions are perfect for the yacht race; there is a light wind and visibility is good.* | **poor/zero/low visibility** (=when it is difficult to see very far) *Poor visibility made skiing extremely hazardous.* | *Most modern planes can land in zero visibility.*

in sight/within sight /ɪn ˈsaɪt, wɪðɪn ˈsaɪt/ [adv] if something or someone is **in sight** or **within sight**, you can see them from where you are: *The only building in sight was a small wooden cabin.* | *The boat was stopped by the US coastguard within sight of shore.* | *It was a glorious summer day, with not a cloud in sight.* | *It was late afternoon, and there wasn't a soul in sight.* | *Meredith looked around – there was no-one in sight.* | *The taxi driver was still nowhere in sight.* | **come in/within sight of** (=to come close enough to a place to see it) *It was several hours before the three men came within sight of the city.*

show /ʃəʊ/ [v I] if something **shows**, people can see it, especially when you do not want them to: *Don't worry about that mark – it won't show.* | *Your slip is showing, did you know?*

in view /ɪn ˈvjuː/ [adv] if something or someone is **in view**, they can be seen from where you are and are not hidden by anything: *David pulled the blankets up so only the top of his head remained in view.* | *There were no buildings in view to suggest the presence of any humans.* | **keep sb in view** *Place the child's desk near the teacher's, so that the child can keep the teacher in view.*

appear /əˈpɪəʳ/ [v I] if someone or something **appears**, you begin to see them or you suddenly see them: *The stars appeared one by one in the sky.* | **+ at/in/on etc** *At that moment, Kenny appeared in the doorway.* | *I heard a tap, and Lila's face appeared at the window.* | *A drop-down menu appeared on the screen, and I clicked 'Format'.* | **+ from behind/under etc** *A man suddenly appeared from behind the bushes.* | **appear (as if) from nowhere** (=appear suddenly, without any warning) *Just then, Gillian appeared as if from nowhere.* | *A gray sedan appeared from nowhere in the fast lane.*

come into sight/come into view /ˌkʌm ɪntə ˈsaɪt, ˌkʌm ɪntə ˈvjuː/ [v phrase] if someone or something **comes into sight**, they move into a position where you can see them: *The crowd cheered as the President's motorcade came into sight.* | *I heard the splash of oars, and a rowing boat came into view.*

6 when something cannot be seen or is difficult to see

- invisible
- out of sight
- lose sight of
- dim
- indistinct
- blind spot

invisible /ɪnˈvɪzə̇bəl/ [adj] if something is **invisible**, it cannot be seen: *The gas is invisible but highly dangerous.* | *Word Perfect uses invisible codes for many different functions.* | *He nodded toward the distant ship, invisible in the darkness.* | **invisible to the naked eye** (=invisible without using special instruments to help you) *The space probe can photograph parts of the electronic spectrum that are invisible to the naked eye.*

out of sight /ˌaʊt əv ˈsaɪt/ [adv] if someone or something is **out of sight**, you cannot see them, for example because they are too far away or they are behind something else: *Jim waited until his parents' car was out of sight and then left the house.* | *It's best to keep your purse out of sight in this office.* | **drop/pass out of sight** (=move to a position where you cannot be seen) *We both quickly dropped out of sight behind the desk.* | *The car passed out of sight over the hill.* | **+ of** *He would punch and kick me as soon as we were out of sight of the teachers.*

lose sight of /ˌluːz ˈsaɪt ɒv/ [v phrase] to no longer be able to see someone or something because they have moved too far away from you, especially when you are chasing them: *Police lost sight of the man when he ran into a crowd of people.* | *They gave up the chase, losing sight of the car as it turned the corner.*

dim /dɪm/ [adj usually before noun] **dim shape/outline/figure etc** one that is difficult to see because it is too far away or because there is not enough light: *He saw the dim outline of the taxi-driver's head inside the cab.* | *There was enough starlight coming in the window to make out the dim shapes of bunkbeds and rucksacks.* —**dimly** [adv] *The distant coastline was dimly outlined against the evening sky.*

indistinct /ˌɪndɪˈstɪŋkt◂/ [adj] something that is **indistinct** is difficult to see because its edges are unclear or it is very small: *Even with the binoculars, I could barely make out the indistinct shapes gliding through the water.* | *All the police have to go on is a grainy, indistinct video clip.*

blind spot /ˈblaɪnd spɒt‖-spɑːt/ [n phrase] part of a place that is within the area that you can see, but that you cannot see properly or easily: *His son walked into his blind spot just as he was reversing the car.* | *The recent escapes have prompted prison officers to install video camera surveillance of the blind spot.*

7 something you think you see that is not really there

- hallucination
- illusion
- mirage
- vision
- be seeing things

▸ *see also* **imagine**

hallucination /həˌluːsə̇ˈneɪʃən/ [n C] an experience of seeing something which is not really there, for example because you have been taking drugs or because you are ill **suffer/have hallucinations** *I suffered horrendous hallucinations and flashbacks, and quit using LSD.* | *In tests, the drug caused patients to have hallucinations.*

illusion /ɪˈluːʒən/ [n C] something that you imagine you can see, that is either not there at all, or is actually something else: *The road appears to get narrower as you look into the distance, but it's just an illusion.* | **give/create an illusion of sth** *It's a small room, but the mirrors create an illusion of space.* | *She isn't particularly tall, but her upright posture gives an illusion of height.*

mirage /ˈmɪrɑːʒ‖məˈrɑːʒ/ [n C] something, especially an area of water in a desert, that you think you can see in the distance but which is not really there, caused by hot air conditions: *She thought at first it must be the edge of the sea, then realised it was a mirage.* | *an eerie no-man's land where travellers see mirages*

vision /ˈvɪʒən/ [n C] something that you imagine you can see, especially as part of a strong religious experience: *In her vision, Joan of Arc saw an angel telling her to go and fight for France.* | **+ of** *Three days before she died, Rita was blessed with a vision of Our Lord.* | **have visions** *Many people claim to have had visions while praying at Lourdes.*

be seeing things /biː ˈsiːɪŋ θɪŋz/ [v phrase] spoken to imagine that you are seeing something that is not there – use this especially to say that you are so surprised at something that you see that you almost cannot believe it: *I thought I saw Patty arrive. I must be seeing things today.*

8 something you can see through

- clear
- see-through
- transparent

clear /klɪəʳ/ [adj] if water, air, or glass is **clear**, you can easily see through it: *The lake was so clear you could see the plants on the bottom.* | *On a clear day, you can see Mount Fuji from Tokyo.* | *I only realised later that the clear liquid in the glass must have been vodka.* | **crystal-clear** (=use this to emphasize how clear something is) *The water was crystal-clear, edged by sparkling white sand.*

transparent /trænˈspærənt, -ˈspeər-/ [adj] use this about objects or materials that you can see through: *The box has a transparent plastic lid so you can see what's inside.* | *The boy's arms and hands were so thin they seemed almost transparent.*

see-through /ˈsiː θruː/ [adj usually before noun] **see-through** clothes are made of thin material that you can see through: *a see-through blouse* | *She posed for 'Vogue' in a see-through black teddy.*

9 something you cannot see through

- opaque
- frosted

opaque /əʊˈpeɪk/ [adj] *As the liquid cools it becomes cloudy and opaque.* | *Keep herbs and spices in opaque glass bottles to protect them from sunlight.*

frosted /ˈfrɒstəd‖ˈfrɔː-/ [adj] glass that is **frosted** is fairly thick and with an uneven surface that is difficult or impossible to see through: *Two frosted glass doors opened into an elegant lobby.* | *Alice took another long drink from the tall frosted glass.* | *The frosted windows let in a weak light.*

10 when something makes you unable to see

- blind
- dazzle

blind /blaɪnd/ [v T] if a light **blinds** you, it is so bright that you cannot look into it and it makes you unable to see for a few moments afterwards: *Onlookers were blinded by the flash of the explosion.* | *She adjusted the mirror to avoid being blinded by the glare.* | *The floodlight had blinded him and he couldn't see to reload his gun.* —**blinding** [adj] *The light was blinding, and she covered her face.* | *The first bomb exploded with a blinding flash.*

dazzle /ˈdæzəl/ [v T] if a very bright light **dazzles** you, it is so strong that you cannot see anything else, especially when this may have dangerous results: *If you are dazzled by oncoming traffic, slow down and look for a place to stop.* | *She slowly opened her eyes, only to be dazzled by a strong shaft of sunlight.* | *I moved aside so that the light no longer dazzled me.* —**dazzling** [adj] *The brightness of the sunlight was dazzling after so long in the gloom.*

11 unable to see

- blind
- can't see

blind /blaɪnd/ [adj] someone who is **blind** cannot see at all: *Blake is now over 90, and almost blind.* | *The operation left their son blind and brain-damaged.* | *There's a blind man who sells popcorn on the corner.* | **go blind** (=become blind) *Without treatment, the patient will go blind.* | **the blind** (=people who are blind) *a radio programme specially for the blind* —**blind** [v T often in passive] to make someone unable to see, either for a short time or permanently: *The crash happened after drivers were blinded by a mixture of fog and thick black smoke.* | *A riding accident left her blinded in one eye.* —**blindness** [n U] *This tiny black fly is the biggest cause of blindness in Central Africa.*

can't see /ˌkɑːnt ˈsiː‖ˌkænt-/ [v phrase] especially spoken if you **can't see**, you are unable to see things, either because there is something wrong with your sight, or because something is preventing you seeing clearly: *He makes fun of me because I can't see that well.* | *It was pitch black and I couldn't see.* | *You can't see from here, but they're out there.* | *That was the morning I got up, and I couldn't see.*

12 unable to see very well

- short-sighted
- visually impaired
- long-sighted
- as blind as a bat
- partially sighted

short-sighted /ˌʃɔːʳt ˈsaɪtəd◂/ [adj] unable to see things that are far away: *'Are you short-sighted then?' 'Yeah, can't see a thing without my lenses.'*

long-sighted British /**far-sighted** American /ˌlɒŋ ˈsaɪtəd◂‖ˌlɔːŋ-, ˌfɑːʳ ˈsaɪtəd◂/ [adj] only able to see things that are far away and unable to see things that are close to you such as the writing in a book: *My daughter's long-sighted and wears reading glasses.* | *Many people become far-sighted as they grow older.*

partially sighted /ˌpɑːʳʃəli ˈsaɪtəd◂/ [adj] not able to see things very well at all, although not completely blind: *Tape copies are available free of charge to blind and partially sighted people.* | *I am partially sighted, which makes me a lot more vulnerable.*

visually impaired /ˌvɪʒuəli ɪmˈpeəʳd/ [adj phrase] completely blind or unable to see much – use this especially to talk about special services or equipment for this group of people: *Instructions can also be obained in Braille for the visually impaired.* | *Visually impaired people have as much right to full access to educational courses as anyone else.*

as blind as a bat /əz ˌblaɪnd əz ə ˈbæt/ [adv] informal having great difficulty in seeing things: *Didn't you see me coming? You must be as blind as a bat!* | *She's as blind as a bat without her glasses.*

13 the ability to see

- sight
- eyesight
- vision
- can see

sight /saɪt/ [n U] the ability to see: *There are five senses: sight, smell, hearing, taste, and touch.* | **partial sight** (=when someone can only see a little) *'Has Peter got any sight at all now?' 'Only partial sight, in one eye.'* | **impaired sight** (=damaged) *Nicole has suffered since birth from impaired sight as a result of cerebral palsy.* | **lose your sight** (=become unable to see) *She lost her sight at the age of 12 following an illness.*

eyesight /ˈaɪsaɪt/ [n U] the ability to see – use this to talk about how well or badly someone can see: *My eyesight's got a lot worse over the last few years.* | *an eyesight test* | **good/bad eyesight** *You must have good eyesight. I can't even make it out from here.*

vision /ˈvɪʒən/ [n U] the ability to see – use this especially about damage to someone's sight or when someone's sight is affected by an injury, by alcohol etc: *When he woke up he had a splitting headache and his vision was blurred.* | *When I have a migraine, I can't stand up without vomiting and my vision is distorted.* | **have vision** (=be able to see) *My aunt still has some vision in her left eye – she can make out colours and shapes.* | **double vision** (=when you seem to see two of everything) *He complained that the new lenses gave him double vision and headaches.* | **20-20 vision** (=perfect vision) *Until she was eighteen she had 20-20 vision – now she has to wear glasses.*

can see /kən ˈsiː/ [v phrase] if you **can see**, you are able to see things, especially after you have been unable to: *Thanks to a new operation, Ann can see for the first time in her life.* | *Turn the light on so we can see!*

seem

1 to seem

- seem
- appear
- look
- sound
- come across as
- give the impression
- strike sb as
- show signs of
- have all the hallmarks of
- smack of

seem /siːm/ [v not in progressive] if someone or something **seems** happy, dishonest, true etc, that is what you think they are, even though you are not completely certain **seem nice/happy/strange etc (to sb)** *Katie seems happy at her new school.* | *The whole situation seems very strange to me.* | **+ to be/do sth** *Lack of money seems to be the main problem.* | *Ricky graduated, but didn't seem to know what to do with his life. He was drifting.* | **it seems (that)/it seems to sb (that)** (=use this to say what you think about a situation) *It seems that someone forgot to lock the door.* | *It seemed to Jim that Amy was worried about something.* | **seem like** especially spoken (=seem to be) *Kevin seems like a nice guy.* | *'Why did you move to New York?' 'It seemed like a good idea at the time.'* | **there seems to be** *There seems to be something wrong with the TV.* | **it seems as if** *There were so many delays – it seemed as if we would never get home.* | **it seems likely/possible/probable (that)** *It seems likely that they will release the hostages soon.*

appear /əˈpɪəʳ/ [v not in progressive] formal to seem **appear to be/do sth** *My father appeared to be in good health.* | *The archaeologists uncovered both domestic structures and what appear to have been commercial buildings.* | **appear calm/rude/angry etc** *It's difficult to ask someone their age without appearing rude.* | *The city appeared calm after the previous night's fighting.* | **it appears (that)** *Police said it appeared that John Seidler's death was an accident, but an investigation continues.*

look /lʊk/ [v] if someone or something **looks** good, bad, tired etc, that is how they seem to you when you **look** at them: *That book looks interesting.* | *Warren looked tired after his long drive.* | *We had run out of money, and the situation looked pretty hopeless.* | **look like sth** *She's really pretty – she looks like a model.* | *The burglar was holding what looked like a shotgun.* | **look as if** *You look as if you haven't slept all night.* | **it looks as if** (=use this to say how a situation seems to you) *It looks as if we are going to need more help.*

sound /saʊnd/ [v] if someone or something **sounds** good, bad, strange, angry etc, that is how they seem to you when you hear about them, read about them, or hear them: *Istanbul sounds really exciting.* | *He sounds a pretty strange person.* | *I called my dad and told him what has happened. He sounded really angry.* | **sound like** *'We're all going clubbing tomorrow night.' 'That sounds like fun.'* | **it sounds (to me) as if** (=use this to say how a situation seems to you when you hear about it) *It sounds to me as if he needs to see a doctor.*

come across as /ˌkʌm əˈkrɒs æz‖-əˈkrɔːs-/ [v phrase] to seem to have particular qualities or characteristics, especially because of the way you talk to or behave towards other people: *In the book, Strayhorn comes across as a sympathetic human being, while Stan Getz emerges as a volatile character with a violent temper.* | **come across as being sth** *He often comes across as being rather cold and arrogant.* | **come across well/badly** *She doesn't come across well in interviews, but she's very good at her job.*

give the impression /ˌgɪv ði ɪmˈpreʃən/ [v phrase] if someone or something **gives the impression** that something about them is true, they make other people think it is true, especially when it is not **+ (that)** *Paul liked to give everyone the impression that he knew a lot about cars.* | *We always leave the lights on when we go out at night, to give the impression there's someone in the house.* | **+ of** *Mirrors are used in the dining room in order to give the impression of space.*

strike sb as /ˈstraɪk (sb) æz/ [v phrase] if a person or situation **strikes** you **as** strange, interesting, unusual etc, this is your opinion of how they seem: *What strikes me as odd is the fact that she didn't report the burglary to the police.* | *She didn't strike me as the type who would want to become a teacher.* | **strike sb as being/having sth** *He never struck me as being very interested in politics.*

show signs of /ˌʃəʊ ˈsaɪnz ɒv/ [v phrase] if someone or something **shows signs of** age, improvement, tiredness etc, some features of their appearance or behaviour make them seem old, better, tired etc: *The economy is showing no signs of any improvement.* | *Doctors at the hospital say Mr Crowther is beginning to show signs of recovery, although he is still in intensive care.* | **show signs of doing sth** *If the soil shows signs of drying out, water it sparingly.*

have all the hallmarks of /hæv ˌɔːl ðə ˈhɔːlmɑːʳks ɒv/ [v phrase not in progressive] if a thing or event **has all the hallmarks of** something, it has all the typical features of someone's work or actions, and therefore seems to have been done or made by them: *The explosion has all the hallmarks of a terrorist attack.* | *The painting isn't signed by Matisse, but it has all the hallmarks of one of his later works.*

smack of /ˈsmæk ɒv/ [phr v T] to seem to involve or be caused by a particular attitude, feeling, or intention, especially a bad one: *The government's new asylum bill seems inhumane, and smacks of racism.* | *The chairman's decision is disturbing, and smacks of dishonesty.*

2 ways of saying what seems to be happening,

- on the surface
- outwardly
- to all appearances
- on the face of it
- seemingly
- apparent
- seeming
- superficial

on the surface /ɒn ðə ˈsɜːʳfɪ̈s/ [adv] if a person, place, or situation is pleasant, normal, calm etc **on the surface**, they seem that way until you know them better: *On the surface, life seemed normal in Beirut at that time.* | *Mike was very pleasant on the surface, but he had a nasty temper.*

outwardly /ˈaʊtwəʳdli/ [adv] if someone is **outwardly** calm, happy etc, that is how they seem to be, but in fact they are probably nervous, unhappy etc: *Outwardly she seemed contented and happy with life.* | **outwardly calm/unconcerned etc** *Henry remained calm and outwardly unaffected by the terrible events of the previous day.*

to all appearances /tʊ ˌɔːl əˈpɪərənsɪ̈z/ [adv] use this when something seems to be true about someone or something especially when it is not true: *To all appearances, they were a happily married couple.*

on the face of it /ɒn ðə ˈfeɪs əv ɪt/ [adv] use this to say that something seems true, you mean that it seems true, but you are not at all certain that it actually is, because you do not know all the facts: *On the face of it, this seems like a perfectly good idea – we must wait and see if it turns out well.* | *On the face of it, he appeared to be an ideal candidate for the position.*

seemingly /ˈsiːmɪŋli/ [adv] **seemingly impossible/endless/unimportant etc** seeming to be impossible, endless, unimportant etc, especially when this is not actually true: *Running a mile in under 4 minutes was a seemingly impossible task.* | *I looked down at the seemingly endless expanse of green of the Serengeti Plain.* | *The music was strange, seemingly without a melody.*

apparent /əˈpærənt/ [adj only before noun] **apparent** abilities, feelings, or attitudes seem to be real, but you cannot be sure if they are: *She was upset by her father-in-law's apparent dislike of her.* | *What shocked me was the parents' apparent lack of interest in their child.* —**apparently** [adv] *He walked away from the crash, apparently unhurt.*

seeming /ˈsiːmɪŋ/ [adj only before noun] formal **seeming** to be true about someone's feelings, attitudes, or abilities: *I wondered about Richard's seeming reluctance to talk about his family.* | *The professor became frustrated by his students' seeming inability to understand simple questions.*

superficial /ˌsuːpəʳˈfɪʃəl◂, ˌsjuː-‖ˌsuː-/ [adj] feelings, attitudes, or qualities that are **superficial** are not real or true, even though someone or something seems to have them: *The people are friendly, but only in a superficial way.* | *The landscape bore a superficial resemblance to England's green and pleasant land, and each house had a small suburban garden.*

3 when you think that something will happen or is true because of the way something seems

- judging by/judging from/going by
- from the way
- you'd think/anyone would think
- from

judging by/judging from/going by /ˈdʒʌdʒɪŋ baɪ, ˈdʒʌdʒɪŋ frɒm, ˈgəʊɪŋ baɪ/ [prep] *Judging by Michael's expression I'd say he wasn't in a very good mood today.* | *She looks like a student, judging from the number of books she's carrying under her arm.* | *Going by the quality of the runners, I think this week's 800 metres final could produce a new Olympic record.*

from the way /frəm ðə ˈweɪ/ [conjunction] use this to say that something seems to be true because of the way someone or something looks or the way they do something: *It was clear from the way Dorothy spoke that she was worried about something.* | *From the way the body was lying, I'd say it was suicide.*

you'd think/anyone would think /juːd ˈθɪŋk, ˌeniwʌn wʊd ˈθɪŋk/ use this when you want to say that someone is making a situation seem much more serious or important than it really is: *He's only cut his finger but you'd think he was bleeding to death, the amount of noise he's making.* | *Mary's spent at least three days cleaning up and preparing the meal – anyone would think she was expecting royalty!*

from /frəm, (*strong*) frɒm‖frəm, (*strong*) frʌm, frɑːm/ [prep] **from sb's face/voice/clothes etc** use this to say that because of the way someone's face etc looks or sounds, something seems to be true: *From his voice I'd say he was born somewhere in the North of England.* | *She looked from her clothes like some kind of high-powered executive.*

4 when something or someone is different from the way they seem

- there's more to sb/sth than meets the eye
- deceptive
- deceptively
- not be what you seem

there's more to sb/sth than meets the eye /ðeəʳz ˌmɔːʳ tə (sb/sth) ðən ˌmiːts ði ˈaɪ/ use this to say that someone or something is more interesting, important, intelligent etc than they seem to be: *'I didn't know he wrote poetry.' 'Yes – he also does painting. There's more to him than meets the eye.'* | *People think of Bradford as a dull industrial city, but there is more to it than meets the eye.* | *It looks like a simple case of burglary, but there may be more to it than meets the eye.*

deceptive /dɪˈseptɪv/ [adj] seeming to be good, friendly, safe etc, but in fact being very different:

The sea here is very deceptive – it looks calm but is in fact very dangerous. | *Federal organizations have been monitoring the Internet for deceptive advertisements, consumer fraud, and other unlawful activities.* | **appearances can be deceptive** (=what seems to be true may not be true) *I know appearances can be deceptive, but Jeffrey didn't seem like a wife-beater.*

deceptively /dɪ'septɪvli/ [adv] **deceptively simple/easy etc** seeming simple, easy etc, but actually very difficult: *The first question seemed deceptively simple.* | *The cycling route looks deceptively easy, especially when seen from a car.*

not be what you seem /ˌnɒt bi: wɒt ju: 'si:m/ [v phrase] use this to say that someone is not what they seem to be, especially because they are deliberately trying to trick you: *There's something odd about him – I don't think he's what he seems. He might be a cop.* | *I've been doing a little research – our Mr Malamute is not what he seems.*

5 the way something seems

- appearance
- impression
- semblance of

appearance /ə'pɪərəns/ [n C] if someone or something has the **appearance** of being a particular kind of person or thing, they seem to be like that, but in fact they may not be **give the appearance of** (=seem like) *Karen gives the appearance of being confident, but she isn't really.* | *The wall was painted with little squares to give the appearance of mosaic.* | **appearances can be deceptive** (=what seems to be true may not be true) *This mushroom looks harmless enough, but appearances can be deceptive and it is in fact very poisonous.*

impression /ɪm'preʃən/ [n C] your **impression** of someone or something is the way they seem to you **+ of** *What's your impression of Frank as a boss?* | **get the impression (that)** (=think something is a fact because it seems true) *We got the impression that Sally wasn't very pleased to see us.* | *For some reason she got the impression that you didn't like her.* | **give the impression (that)** (=make people believe something, by making it seem to be true) *In her book, she gives the impression that she was a close friend of the Prince, but in fact she only met him twice.* | **a good/a bad/the wrong impression** *In an interview don't say anything negative about your current employer – it gives a bad impression.* | *If she joked with him, he would think she was flirting, and she didn't want him to get the wrong impression.* | **first impression** (=how someone or something seems to you the first time you see them) *My first impression of England was of a grey and rainy place.*

semblance of /'sembləns ɒv/ [n singular] **semblance of truth/normality/stability etc** when something seems to be true, normal etc – use this especially in negative sentences when something seems only very slightly true, normal etc, or to say that it does not seem this at all: *Any semblance of democracy quickly disappeared when the military government announced it was taking over.* | *A novel needs to have some semblance of truth, or the reader will quickly lose interest in it.*

selfish/ not selfish

RELATED WORDS

see also **generous/not generous, proud**

1 selfish

- selfish
- self-centred
- egocentric
- think of nobody but yourself/only think about yourself
- look out for yourself/look after number one

selfish /'selfɪʃ/ [adj] someone who is **selfish** only thinks about what they need or want, and never thinks about how other people feel or what other people want: *Amy, don't be selfish. Let the others have a turn.* | *Carter has never been a selfish player.* | *It's not that I'm selfish. I just don't loan out my tools anymore.* | *Sometimes it's all right to be a little selfish, and forget about everyone else for a change.* —**selfishly** [adv] *Her husband behaved extremely selfishly.*

self-centred British **/self-centered** American /ˌself 'sentəʳd◂/ [adj] paying so much attention to yourself that you do not notice what is happening to other people: *He was too self-centered to notice how unhappy Ruth was.* | *Jill's attractive and pleasant to talk to, but she's extremely self-centred.* | *Our whole society has become selfish and self-centered.*

egocentric /ˌi:gəʊ'sentrɪk, ˌe-/ [adj] someone who is **egocentric** believes that what they do and think is much more important than what anyone else thinks or does: *Fox plays an egocentric movie star.* | *He was a man of undoubted genius, but bad-tempered, egocentric, and impossible to live with.* | *Older children are less egocentric than younger ones, and more willing to accept other people's ideas.*

think of nobody but yourself/only think about yourself /θɪŋk əv ˌnəʊbədi bət jɔ:ʳ'self, əʊnli ˌθɪŋk əbaʊt jɔ:ʳ'self/ [v phrase] informal to be selfish, especially when you are making plans or arrangements: *Before I had children, I only thought about myself and what I wanted.* | *You never think about anyone but yourself – we needed that money!*

look out for yourself/look after number one /lʊk ˌaʊt fəʳ jɔ:ʳ'self, lʊk ˌɑ:ftəʳ ˌnʌmbəʳ 'wʌn ‖-ˌæf-/ [v phrase] informal to behave selfishly, especially in a situation where this is necessary because everyone else is doing the same: *I don't blame anyone for looking out for themselves, that's human nature.* | *In the 1980s, the message was clear – look out for number one and give no thought to the rest of society.*

2 selfish behaviour or a selfish attitude

- selfishness
- self-interest
- I'm all right, Jack

selfishness /'selfɪʃnɪ̈s/ [n U] *At the time, I didn't see my decision as selfishness.* | *I was appalled by the greed and selfishness of some of the men I worked with.* | **pure selfishness** *Miller's crime, that of espionage, was a crime motivated by pure selfishness, said the trial judge.*

self-interest /self ˈɪntrɪ̇st/ [n U] a selfish attitude that makes you do things only for selfish reasons, especially in business or politics: *Advertising is most effective when it appeals directly to people's self-interest.* | *Our country's role in the world must be determined by economic self-interest.*

I'm all right, Jack /ˌaɪm ɔːl ˈraɪt ˌdʒæk/ British informal someone with an **I'm all right, Jack** attitude is only concerned that their own life is satisfactory, and does not care about other people – used especially in newspapers: *The Prime Minister criticized people for their 'I'm all right, Jack' approach to social policy.*

3 not selfish

- unselfish
- selfless
- altruistic

unselfish /ʌnˈselfɪʃ/ [adj] *She is an outgoing, unselfish, and loving person.* | *It's a good team – they listen to the coaching and they're unselfish with the ball.* | *Abernathy was a man of great courage and an unselfish dedication to a just cause.* —**unselfishly** [adv] *Throughout her career she unselfishly devoted herself to the cause of free, universal education.*

selfless /ˈselfləs/ [adj] caring only about other people's needs, not your own, and never behaving selfishly: *The idea of the selfless, self-sacrificing mother is not one that appeals to most women these days.* | **selfless devotion/sacrifice/concern etc** *We must remember the selfless sacrifice of our soldiers.* —**selflessly** [adv] *The medical staff here work selflessly and tirelessly, seven days a week.*

altruistic /ˌæltruˈɪstɪk◂/ [adj] sincerely concerned about other people and willing to help them or give money to them if they need it, without trying to get any advantage for yourself: *You can't expect a large corporation to be altruistic.* | *Companies that donate books or equipment to schools that collect their tokens are not being entirely altruistic – after all, you have to buy the products to get the tokens.* —**altruism** /ˈæltru-ɪzəm/ [n U] *Top politicians aren't usually motivated by altruism.*

sell

RELATED WORDS

- *see also* **buy, shop/store, cost, advertising, business, expensive, cheap**

1 to sell something

- sell
- sell off
- export
- sell up
- serve
- deal in
- the sale of sth
- flog
- peddle
- trading

sell /sel/ [v I/T] to give something to someone in exchange for money: *Tom's thinking of selling his motorcycle and buying a new one.* | *If you can, wait to sell until prices are high.* | *Postcards and souvenirs were being sold outside the cathedral.* | **sell sb sth** *The company sold Braugh $100,000 worth of computers at discounted rates.* | **sell sth to sb** *It is illegal to sell tobacco to anyone under the age of 18.* | *The painting was sold to an art gallery in Philadelphia.* | **sell sth for £250/$50 etc** *The antique buttons are very valuable, and we sell them for £100 and upwards.*

sell off /ˌsel ˈɒf/ [phr v T] to sell something, usually a group of things, at a reduced price in order to get rid of it quickly, because you need the money soon, or because it will not last a long time **sell sth off** *The bakery usually sells its cakes off at half price just before closing time.* | **sell off sth** *After the funeral the house contents were sold off quickly to pay all his debts.* | *The school district may be forced to close schools and sell off land in order to make much-needed repairs.*

export /ɪkˈspɔːʳt/ [v T] if a country or a company **exports** its products, it sends them to another country in order to sell them: *Japanese televisions and hi-fi systems are exported all over the world.* | *Ancient artefacts cannot be exported.* | **export sth to France/the UK/Japan etc** *In 1986 they exported 210,000 cases of wine to the UK.* —**exporter** [n C] *Saudi Arabia is one of the world's leading exporters of oil.* —**export** [adj only before noun] *Export earnings are lower than last year.*

sell up /ˌsel ˈʌp/ [phr v I/T] British to sell your house, your business, or other things you own in order to move to a different place or to do something different: *Why don't we sell up and move to Canada? Property is really cheap there!* | *My parents sold up the farm and went to live in Glasgow.*

serve /sɜːʳv/ [v T] if someone who works in a shop or a bar **serves** a customer, they help them to buy or choose the goods that they want: *There was a line of people in front of me who were all waiting to be served.* | *Estrada was serving a customer when the fire started.* | *It is illegal to serve alcoholic drinks to anyone under 18.*

deal in /ˈdiːl ɪn/ [v T] to buy and sell a particular kind of goods as part of your business: *The gallery deals mostly in paintings but they do sometimes sell photographs.* | *Tax agents are visiting more than 5,000 businesses that deal in expensive items such as cars, boats, and jewels.*

the sale of sth /ðə ˈseɪl əv (sth)/ [n phrase] when something is sold: *The rebels are using money from the sale of drugs to buy weapons.* | *The law prohibits the sale and consumption of alcohol on unlicensed premises.*

flog /flɒg‖flɑːg/ [v T] British informal to sell something, especially something that is of low quality or that has something wrong with it: *There was a man at the market who was flogging watches for £10 each.* | **flog sb sth** *Don't let him flog you his car – he's had endless trouble with it.*

peddle /ˈpedl/ [v T] to sell goods, usually things that are cheap, especially by going from place to place rather than selling them in a shop: *Street vendors peddled flowers and candles.* | *Belloni started her bakery business by peddling her homemade bread to local stores.*

trading /ˈtreɪdɪŋ/ [n U] the activity of selling goods or shares in companies: *Trading started briskly on the New York Stock Exchange this morning.* | **stop/cease trading** *The company ran out of money and was forced to cease trading.*

2 to sell illegal goods

- peddle
- deal in
- push
- trafficking
- black market

peddle /ˈpedl/ [v T] to sell illegal drugs to people: *The gang earned as much as $10 million a month peddling heroin and cocaine.* | **peddle sth to sb** *Stricter punishments will be given to those convicted of peddling drugs to children.*

deal in /ˈdiːl ɪn/ [v T] to buy and sell illegal goods such as drugs or weapons: *The police suspect him of dealing in stolen goods.* | *Police believe Fry was dealing in narcotics.* | *The article accuses Davis of dealing in arms.*

push /pʊʃ/ [v T] informal to sell illegal drugs, especially to people who are trying them for the first time, to make them want more: *Anyone caught pushing heroin or cocaine is given a long prison sentence.*

trafficking /ˈtræfɪkɪŋ/ [n U] selling large quantities of illegal drugs or taking them into another country in order to sell them: *In Thailand the penalty for drug trafficking is death.* | *Customs officials claim to have uncovered a major drug-trafficking ring.* | **+ in** *The two girls were arrested for trafficking in hard drugs.*

black market /ˌblæk ˈmɑːʳkɪ̣t/ [n C usually singular] the system by which people illegally buy and sell goods or foreign money, especially for high prices, often because these things are difficult to obtain legally: *Authorities are worried about the growing black market in the city.* | **on the black market** *You can get a much better rate for your dollar on the black market than in a bank.* | **+ in** *The immigration service is concerned about a thriving black market in phoney ID cards and working permits.* —**black market** [adj] *A man came up to me in the street and offered to sell me some black market cigarettes.* | *The people here are forced to pay exorbitant black market prices for everyday goods such as food and clothes.*

3 to sell something to the person who offers the most money

- auction
- auction
- put sth up for auction
- come/go under the hammer

auction ALSO **auction off** /ˈɔːkʃən, ˌɔːkʃən ˈɒf/ [v T] *One of the Beatles' guitars is being auctioned for charity.* | *The contents of the house were auctioned to pay off the family's debts.*

auction /ˈɔːkʃən/ [n C] a public meeting at which things are sold to the person who offers to pay the most money: *The buyer did not attend the auction, but sent a representative to place the bids.* | **hold an auction** *Sotheby's decided to hold auctions in Japan twice a year.* | **at (an) auction** *Bikes that have not been claimed by the owners will be sold at a public auction January 11.* | *How much do you think the painting would fetch at auction?*

put sth up for auction /ˌpʊt (sth) ˌʌp fər ˈɔːkʃən/ [v phrase] to arrange for something be sold at a public meeting to the person who offers to pay the most money: *After months trying to sell the farm, they decided to put it up for auction.* | *One of the world's finest collections of vintage cars is to be put up for auction.*

come/go under the hammer /ˌkʌm, ˌgəʊ ʌndəʳ ðə ˈhæməʳ/ [v phrase] informal if something **comes** or **goes under the hammer**, especially something valuable such as a famous painting, it is sold at an auction: *A collection of prints and paintings by Picasso came under the hammer at Sotheby's yesterday.*

4 someone who sells things in a shop

- shopkeeper
- proprietor
- merchant
- sales assistant
- salesman/saleswoman/salesperson
- sales staff
- vendor

shopkeeper /ˈʃɒpˌkiːpəʳ‖ˈʃɑːp-/ [n C] especially British someone who owns or is in charge of a small shop: *The shopkeeper chased the boys out of his shop, accusing them of stealing.* | *Many immigrants have been highly successful as shopkeepers.*

proprietor /prəˈpraɪətəʳ/ [n C] formal someone who owns a small shop: *Proprietor Ginny Gavin serves fresh croissants and fruit at breakfast to guests at her inn.* | **+ of** *Dan Conrad, the proprietor of Conrad's Bookstore, says that small stores such as his offer service and convenience.*

merchant /ˈmɜːʳtʃənt/ [n C] American written someone who owns or is in charge of a shop: *Local merchants have had trouble with vandals breaking windows.* | *Merchants say sales have not been affected by the road repairs.*

sales assistant ALSO **shop assistant** British **/sales clerk** American /ˈseɪlz əˌsɪstənt, ˈʃɒp əˌsɪstənt‖ˈʃɑːp-, ˈseɪlz ˌklɑːk‖-ˌklɜːrk/ [n C] someone who deals with customers in a shop and sells them things: *Rowan worked as a sales assistant in a Beverly Hills shopping mall.* | *She's a shop assistant in the shoe department.* | *Get advice from a knowledgeable sales clerk.*

salesman/saleswoman/salesperson /ˈseɪlzmən, ˈseɪlzˌwʊmən, ˈseɪlzˌpɜːʳsən/ [n C] someone whose job is to persuade people, shops, and companies to buy their company's products: *I worked for a while as a salesman for a big computer corporation.* | *Gail has been the firm's top saleswoman for the last two years.*

sales staff /ˈseɪlz ˌstɑːf‖-ˌstæf/ [n C with singular or plural verb in British English] the members of a company whose job is to persuade people to buy that company's products, or to sell goods to people in a shop: *The company has a sales staff of 600.* | *Customers liked the personal service the sales staff provided.*

vendor /ˈvendəʳ/ [n C] someone who sells things to people in the street: *Outside the theatre, there was a row of flower vendors.* | *Frank stopped to buy the evening paper from a news vendor.* | **street vendor** *Flags sold by street vendors fluttered in the crowd of about 5,000.*

5 a person or company that sells goods, shares etc

- retailer
- wholesaler
- merchant
- dealer
- trader
- seller

retailer /ˈriːteɪləʳ/ [n C] a company or person that sells goods to the public in a shop – used especially in business contexts: *Our products are sold through the Body Shop and other well-known retailers.* | *Retailers face their slowest business period in January and February.* | **clothing/furnishings/women's etc retailer** *Talbot's is a women's retailer with 20 stores in California.* | **high-street retailer** British (=a company that has shops in the main shopping area of several towns) *One high-street retailer has gone out of business.*

wholesaler /ˈhəʊlˌseɪləʳ/ [n C] a person or company that sells goods in large quantities and at low prices, especially to other companies that then sell the goods to the public: *The early morning market is for wholesalers only, the general public have to wait until later in the day.* | **fish/meat/clothing etc wholesaler** *Fisherman are involved in a price dispute with fish wholesalers.*

merchant /ˈmɜːʳtʃənt/ [n C] a person or company that buys and sells large quantities of goods such as wine, or basic materials such as coal and wood: *She was born in 1432, the daughter of a wealthy London merchant.* | **arms/wine/antiques etc merchant** *an international arms merchant*

dealer /ˈdiːləʳ/ [n C] a person or a company that buys and sells a particular type of goods, or that sells a particular company's products: *Make sure you buy your used car from an authorised dealer.* | *'The market has been strong,' said one dealer.* | **art/car/antique etc dealer** *She bought the painting from a Swiss art dealer.* | **bond/securities/currency etc dealer** *According to a senior currency dealer, the pound is likely to continue to rise against the dollar.*

trader /ˈtreɪdəʳ/ [n C] someone who buys and sells goods, especially in a very far away place, or who buys and sells shares on the financial market: *Traders enter the amount of stock they want to buy or sell, and the computer calculates a price.* | **fur/slave/arms etc trader** *Montreal was founded by French fur traders in the 17th century.* | **bond/currency/stock etc trader** *Bond traders worried about inflation have driven up interest rates on long-term bonds.*

seller /ˈseləʳ/ [n C] the person who sells something to another person or company in a business deal: *Both buyer and seller should agree on the terms before the contract is signed.*

6 someone who sells things illegally

- pusher/dealer
- tout

pusher/dealer /ˈpʊʃəʳ, ˈdiːləʳ/ [n C] someone who buys and sells illegal drugs: *Dealers were selling heroin outside the stadium.* | *Drug pushers have been warned to stay away from the club.* | *Residents complain of cocaine and heroin dealers selling on the streets outside their homes.*

tout British **/scalper** American /taʊt, ˈskælpəʳ/ [n C] someone who stands outside a sports event or concert and sells tickets for it at high prices: *Touts were selling tickets to the match for £50 or more.* | *Organisers of the concert were worried there would be trouble from ticket touts.* | *Scalpers wanted $150 for seats that normally sell for $40.*

7 something that is sold

- goods
- product
- merchandise
- export

goods /gʊdz/ [n plural] things that are produced in order to be sold: *The store sells a wide range of goods.* | *The cost of almost all goods and services soared when price controls were removed.* | *We import a lot of electrical goods from Japan.*

product /ˈprɒdʌkt‖ˈprɑː-/ [n C] something that is made, grown, or designed in order to be sold: *There is less demand now for products like coal and steel.* | *The new product took more than three years to develop before being put on the market.* | *The company manufactures and delivers paper and paper products.*

merchandise /ˈmɜːʳtʃəndaɪz, -daɪs/ [n U] things that are produced in order to be sold, especially when they are shown for sale in a shop – used especially in business contexts: *The merchandise is attractively displayed and the assistants are friendly and helpful.* | *The fire at the warehouse destroyed merchandise valued at over $2 million.*

export /ˈekspɔːʳt/ [n C usually plural] goods that are sent to a foreign country in order to be sold: *The value of China's exports to the US rose by over 50% last year.* | *Britain's total exports to the other EU member states now exceed imports.* | *The country's main export is coal.*

8 to make something available for people to buy

- put sth on the market
- put sth up for sale
- bring out
- launch
- publish
- release

put sth on the market ALSO **come/go on the market** /ˌpʊt (sth) ɒn ðə ˈmɑːʳkɪ̠t, ˌkʌm, ˌgəʊ ɒn ðə ˈmɑːʳkɪ̠t/ [v phrase] *We put our house on the market last September and we still haven't sold it.* | *The drug came on the market in the late 1990s and has been widely prescribed.* | *The car will probably sell for around $50,000 when it goes on the market.* | *Most wines are left to mature before they are put on the market.*

put sth up for sale /ˌpʊt (sth) ʌp fəʳ ˈseɪl/ [v phrase] to make something such as a house, business, or piece of land available for people to buy: *The historic property has been put up for sale.* | *After the merger, parts of the business are likely to be put up for sale.*

bring out /ˌbrɪŋ ˈaʊt/ [phr v T] if a company **brings out** a new product that they have made, they make it available for people to buy **bring out sth** *Kodak brought out a camera which stores up to 100 images on a computer disc.* | **bring sth out** *The two cookbooks have sold well, and Doubleday is bringing them out in new paperback editions.*

launch /lɔːntʃ/ [v T] if a company **launches** a new product, they publicly announce, especially with a lot of advertising, that it is available for people to buy: *Fiat launched a tiny 'city car' especially for Europe's narrow, crowded streets.* | *Fezza, the clothes designer, launched his first collection in 1980.*

publish /ˈpʌblɪʃ/ [v T] to print a book, magazine, or newspaper and make it available for people to buy: *Ladybird publish books for young children.* | *Amateur Photographer is published every Tuesday.* | *Rowling's latest Harry Potter novel sold millions of copies as soon as it was published.* —**publication** /ˌpʌblɪˈkeɪʃən/ [n U] when something is published: *Since the publication of her book, she's received thousands of letters from women who have had similar experiences.* —**publisher** [n C] a company that publishes books: *None of the big UK publishers wanted to do a paperback version of the book.*

release /rɪˈliːs/ [v T] if a company **releases** a record or film, it makes it available for people to buy or see: *Her new album will be released at the end of the month.* | *Carrey's new comedy is due to be released in the US very soon.* —**release** [n C] something that has been released: *The band's latest release* (=record that has been released) | *should be in the stores Friday.*

9 available for people to buy

- for sale
- be up for sale
- be on sale
- on the market

for sale /fəʳ 'seɪl/ [adj phrase] if something is **for sale**, the person who owns it wants to sell it: *There are several houses for sale in our street.* | *There was 'for sale' notice in the car's window.* | *The festival will have food and crafts for sale, games for children, and music.*

be up for sale /biː ˌʌp fəʳ 'seɪl/ [v phrase] if something such as a house, a shop, or a piece of land **is up for sale**, it has been publicly announced that it is available for people to buy: *The house has been up for sale for months.* | *Several subsidiary businesses are up for sale.*

be on sale /biː ɒn 'seɪl/ [v phrase] if a product **is on sale**, you can buy it in the shops: *These cameras are on sale in most electrical stores.* | **go on sale** (=begin to be available) *The new model Toyota goes on sale next month.*

on the market /ɒn ðə 'mɑːʳkɪ̥t/ [adj phrase] goods that are **on the market** are available for people to buy – use this especially when you are comparing products of the same general type: *It's one of the cheapest computers on the market.* | *There may be better shoes on the market, but this is the one the kids want.* | **+ for** *The house was on the market for $475,000.*

10 to stop selling something

- take sth off the market
- withdraw
- recall

take sth off the market /ˌteɪk (sth) ɒf ðə 'mɑːʳkɪ̥t/ [v phrase] if a company **takes** a product **off the market**, it stops producing it and shops stop selling it: *The mineral water was taken off the market while tests were being made.* | *Sales of the newspaper were so poor that it was taken off the market within a couple of months.* | *The Federal Drug Administration has said that all products containing the additive must be taken off the market immediately.*

withdraw /wɪð'drɔː, wɪθ-/ [v T] if a shop or a company **withdraws** a product, it makes it unavailable for people to buy by removing it from shops: *Newsagents across the country have withdrawn the magazine after numerous complaints from women's groups.* | *After two children had been hurt, the company was forced to withdraw the toy from store shelves.* | **withdraw sth from sale** *Christmas decorations were withdrawn from sale yesterday following a fire-risk warning.* —**withdrawal** [n U] *Stores have agreed to the withdrawal of the offending videos.*

recall /rɪ'kɔːl/ [v T] if a company **recalls** a product, they ask all the shops that sell it and the people that have bought it to send it back to them for checking, because there may be something wrong with it: *Thousands of car baby-seats have had to be recalled after a fault was discovered in the safety harness.* | *The company voluntarily recalled about 11,000 of the devices to check them for defects.* —**recall** /rɪ'kɔːl‖rɪ'kɔːl, 'riːkɔːl/ [n U] *They put a notice in the press ordering the recall of all the baby food that might have been contaminated.*

11 the amount of something that is sold

- sales
- turnover

sales /seɪlz/ [n plural] the number of products that a business sells, or the value of the products it sells: *A big price increase led to a fall in sales.* | **+ of** *Sales of the book have been astonishing.* | *Coupons for discounts on certain products have increased sales of those products.*

turnover /'tɜːʳnˌəʊvəʳ/ [n singular] the value of goods or services that a company sells over a particular period of time: *Turnover at the two restaurants was about $7.4 million this year.* | *Recently the company has been trying to increase its turnover by diversifying into other fields.*

12 when a lot of something is sold

- sell
- best-selling
- best-seller
- outsell
- be selling like hot cakes
- do a roaring trade

sell /sel/ [v I] *Books that don't sell are sent back to the publishers.* | *The handcrafted rocking horses have sold well across the United States.* | *The last model didn't sell as well as they'd expected.*

best-selling /ˌbest 'selɪŋ◂/ [adj only before noun] a **best-selling** product is one that is sold in large numbers, especially more than any other product of the same type: *Agatha Christie is said to be the world's best-selling author.* | *a list of the week's best-selling music and children's videos* | *Chanel Number 5 is the best-selling scent of all time.*

best-seller/bestseller/best seller /ˌbest 'seləʳ/ [n C] a book, game, video, record etc that has been bought by a very large number of people: *Several TV movies have been based on best sellers by Danielle Steel.* | *Every year there's a toy that becomes a hard-to-find best-seller.* | **bestseller list** (=an official list of what has sold most) *All four Harry Potter books are currently on the bestseller list.*

outsell /aʊt'sel/ [v T] if one product **outsells** another, more of it is sold than the other product: *His latest album has outsold all his other records put together.* | *Chardonnay continues to outsell other wines.*

be selling like hot cakes /biː ˌselɪŋ laɪk ˌhɒt 'keɪks‖-ˌhɑːt-/ [v phrase] informal if a product **is selling like hot cakes**, it is being sold very quickly and in large amounts because people very much want to buy it: *Grisham's new book is selling like hot cakes.*

do a roaring trade /duː ə ˌrɔːrɪŋ 'treɪd/ [v phrase] British if a shop or a person that sells a particular type of goods **is doing a roaring trade**, they are selling large quantities of goods because a lot of people suddenly want to buy them: *Since the heatwave started, ice cream vendors have been doing a roaring trade.* | **+ in** *The shops outside the station were doing a roaring trade in umbrellas.*

13 when all of something has been sold

- sell out
- be a sell-out
- be out of stock
- be booked up/fully booked

sell out /ˌsel 'aʊt/ [phr v I] if a shop, ticket office etc **sells out** of goods or tickets, or if goods or tickets

sell out, all of them are sold so there are no more available: *I went to the store to get some bread but they had sold out.* | *Sunday newspapers often sell out by 10 o'clock.* | **+ of** *They opened at 8 o'clock, and by 8.30 they had sold out of tickets for the big game.* | **be sold out** (=when all the tickets for a performance or sports event have been sold) *We couldn't get tickets anywhere – the show was completely sold out.*

be a sell-out /biː ə 'sel aʊt/ [v phrase] if a play, football game, concert etc **is a sell-out**, it is very popular and all the tickets for it have been sold: *The band's European tour was a sell-out.* | **sell-out crowd** *The Mariners beat the Angels in front of a sell-out crowd.*

be out of stock /biː ˌaʊt əv 'stɒk‖-'stɑːk/ [v phrase] if a product or the shop selling the product **is out of stock**, the shop does not have any of that product available now, because they have sold all of it: *The scooters are popular and are often out of stock.* | *We're out of stock, but we can put one on order for you.*

be booked up/fully booked /biː ˌbʊkt 'ʌp, ˌfʊli 'bʊkt/ [v phrase] if a hotel, restaurant, or organized trip somewhere **is booked up** or **fully booked**, all the places have been bought and there are no more available: *Flights to the US are all booked up this time of year.* | *Popular campsites are fully booked on weekends for most of the summer.* | *All the hotels in the area are booked up months in advance.*

send

RELATED WORDS

▸ *see also* **letter, message**

1 to send a letter, message, parcel etc

- send
- post
- fax
- email/e-mail
- send off
- send in
- send out
- circulate
- dispatch/despatch
- get sth off
- put sth in the post

send /send/ [v T] *Send a cheque for £50 with your order.* | *How many Christmas cards did you send?* | **send sb sth** *Perhaps I should send him a note of apology.* | *She sent him a furious email.* | **send sth to sth** *He sent a dozen red roses to his girlfriend on her birthday.* | *MI5 intercepted a message sent from a business firm in Paris to The Hague.* —**sender** [n C] *The sender of the first correct answer wins a trip to London.*

post British **/mail** especially American /pəʊst, meɪl/ [v T] to send a letter, package etc by putting it in a letter box or taking it to the **post** office: *I must remember to post Joey's birthday card.* | *You may choose not to mail the payment until the due date.* | **post/mail sth to sb** *Could you mail those photographs to me?* | *Tickets will be posted to you unless otherwise requested.* | **post/mail sb sth** *I mailed my dad a postcard from Alaska.*

fax /fæks/ [v T] to send someone a copy of a document or message electronically down a telephone line, using a fax machine: *Shall I fax the report or mail it?* | **fax sth to sb** *The order will be faxed directly to the manufacturer.* | **fax sb sth** *They've agreed to fax us their proposals tomorrow.* —**faxed** [adj] sent by fax: *In a faxed letter, he said he would not be returning to work.*

email/e-mail /'iːmeɪl/ [v T] to send a message directly from one computer to another computer, using the Internet: *You can email Richard in Sydney.* | **email sb sth** *I'll e-mail you his address when I get home.* | **email sth to sb** *She spent the next hour e-mailing her resume to prospective employers.*

send off /ˌsend 'ɒf/ [phr v T] to send something somewhere so that it can be dealt with **send sth off** *I must send this film off to be processed.* | **send off sth** *When did you send off your application form?*

send in /ˌsend 'ɪn/ [phr v T] to send something to an organization by mail, so that it can be dealt with **send sth in** *We've sent our passports in to get them renewed.* | **send in sth** *The final date for sending in completed application forms is July 3rd.* | *Almost 1000 questionnaires have already been sent in.*

send out /ˌsend 'aʊt/ [phr v T] to send something to a lot of people **send out sth** *The club sends out a monthly newsletter to all its members.* | *Officials are sending out information packs to 4000 firms in the area.* | **send sth out** *We posted the wedding invitations in batches, rather than sending them all out at the same time.*

circulate /'sɜːʳkjɡleɪt/ [v T] to send a letter or written message to each person in a group in order to make sure that everyone receives the information you want them to receive: *While Shelley was still at school, he circulated a pamphlet attacking religion.* | **circulate sth around/to/through etc** *Sneed had circulated a letter round the department explaining the new pay cuts.* | *A list of well-known fraudsters was circulated to all local police chiefs.* | **be widely circulated** (=circulated to a lot of people) *The results of the survey were widely circulated.*

dispatch/despatch /dɪ'spætʃ/ [v T] formal to send something to someone, especially something they have ordered or are expecting: *The seller had agreed to dispatch the goods free of charge.* | **dispatch sth to sth** *The proofs were then despatched to London for printing.*

get sth off /ˌget (sth) 'ɒf / [phr v T] informal to send something by mail, especially when it is urgent: *She managed to get all the letters off before five o'clock.* | **+ to** *I'll get this off to you first thing in the morning.*

put sth in the post /ˌpʊt (sth) ɪn ðə 'pəʊst/ [v phrase] British to put a letter, parcel etc into a post box or take it to a post office to be sent: *I'll put a cheque in the post for you tonight.*

2 to send something to someone after it has come to you

- forward
- send on
- send back/return
- redirect

forward /'fɔːʳwəʳd/ [v T] to send something to another person after it has come to you, so that they can deal with it: *I asked the landlord to forward all my mail, but he didn't.* | **forward sth to sb** *After the report had been translated, it was forwarded to Admiral Turner.* | **forward sb sth** *Could you forward me her email, and I'll get back to her.*

send on /ˌsend 'ɒn / [phr v T] to send someone's letters or possessions to them at their new address because they have moved house **send sth on (to sb)** *If any letters arrive, please send them on to me in Los Angeles.* | **send on sth** *I promised that I'd send on her final salary cheque.*

send back/return /ˌsend 'bæk, rɪ'tɜːʳn/ [v T] to send something back to the person who sent it. **Return** is more formal than **send back** and is used especially in writing. **send sth back** *She sent all Patrick's letters back without opening them.* | **send back sth** *Complete all the details, then send back the form.* | **return sth (to sb)** *I would be grateful if you would sign the attached copy of this letter and return it to me.*

redirect /ˌriːdaɪˈrekt, -də̇-/ [v T] to write someone's new address on a letter or parcel that has arrived for them, and send it to them: *I've asked the new owners to redirect all our letters.* | **redirect sth to sth** *I'm redirecting all his letters to his college.*

3 to send someone somewhere

- send
- pack off
- dispatch/despatch
- send in
- send out
- be posted
- be stationed

send /send/ [v T] to make someone or something go somewhere **send sb/sth out/to/back etc** *He sent the children out of the room so we could talk.* | *There are no plans to send British troops to the area.* | *He travelled all over the world, but decided to send his son to school in England.*

pack off /ˌpæk ˈɒf / [phr v T] to send someone to another place very quickly, especially so that you do not have to deal with them or they do not cause you any problems **pack sb off (to)** *They gave her her supper and then packed her off to bed.* | **be packed off (to)** *To prevent a scandal, John was rapidly packed off to another city.*

dispatch/despatch /dɪˈspætʃ/ [v T] formal to send someone or something to a place, especially so that they can help in a difficult or dangerous situation: *The government dispatched 150 police to restore order.* | *As soon as the news reached them, a second airplane was despatched.* | **dispatch sb/sth to** *A recovery vehicle was immediately dispatched to the area.*

send in /ˌsend ˈɪn/ [phr v T] to send a group of soldiers, police, medical workers etc somewhere to deal with a difficult or dangerous situation **send in sb** *After the earthquake, the Red Cross sent in medical teams from around the world.* | **send sb in** *Sending troops in would only make the situation worse.*

send out /ˌsend ˈaʊt/ [phr v T] to send someone somewhere to do a particular job, especially somewhere far away **send out sb** *The paper sent out several teams of reporters to follow the progress of the war.* | *Their top computer engineers were sent out to tackle the problem.* | **send sb out** *We'll send a mechanic out as soon as we can.*

be posted /biː ˈpəʊstə̇d/ [v phrase] if someone such as a soldier or government official **is posted** to a place, especially somewhere abroad, they are sent there to do their job **+ to** *My father was posted to Hong Kong when I was six.* | *He joined the company three years ago and is hoping to be posted to Asia soon.* | **+ as** *Terry's just heard he's been posted as liaison officer on the USS Nebraska.*

be stationed /biː ˈsteɪʃənd/ [v phrase] if a member of an army, navy, or air force **is stationed** somewhere, they are sent to that place for a period of military duty **+ in/at/there etc** *My uncle was stationed in Burma during the war.* | *At the weekend, all the local bars were full of soldiers stationed at Fort Bragg.*

4 when something sends out signals, light, heat etc

- send out
- give out
- give off
- emit
- radiate
- cast/throw

send out /ˌsend ˈaʊt/ [phr v T] *The beacon sends out a beam of light every thirty seconds.* | *He lit a fire, which sent out clouds of dense smoke.* | *The radar sends out radio waves and listens for echoes from enemy craft.*

give out /ˌgɪv ˈaʊt/ [phr v T] to send out light, sound, heat etc: *The oil lamp gave out a pleasant yellowish light.* | *The musical triangle gives out a clear, beautiful note when struck.* | *The stun gun, when applied to the body, gives out a sharp electric shock.*

give off /ˌgɪv ˈɒf / [phr v T] to send out heat, smells, gas etc as a result of a natural or chemical process: *The plant gives off a delicate smell of lemons.* | *Gas heaters should only be used in well-ventilated rooms as they give off carbon monoxide.*

emit /ɪˈmɪt/ [v T] formal to send out heat, light, smells, gas etc: *When minerals such as quartz are heated, they emit light.* | *The Earth emits natural radiation.*

radiate /ˈreɪdieɪt/ [v T] especially written to send out light or heat in all directions from a central point: *The sun radiates both warmth and light.* | *The old and faded lights radiated a feeble glow upon the walls.*

cast/throw /kɑːst‖kæst, θrəʊ/ [v T] to send out light onto a surface or onto a particular area – used especially in stories and descriptions: *The sun shining through the trees cast a pattern of light and shade on the footpath.* | *Candles in tarnished holders threw a warm light over the room.*

sensible

RELATED WORDS

opposite: **stupid/silly, crazy**

see also **logical, calm**

1 people

- sensible
- reasonable
- responsible
- mature
- rational
- practical/realistic/pragmatic
- no-nonsense
- down-to-earth
- talk sense
- have your head screwed on
- sane

sensible /ˈsensə̇bəl/ [adj] someone who is **sensible** is unlikely to do anything stupid, because they judge situations well and make good decisions: *Laura's a pretty sensible girl. I don't think she'd talk to strangers.* | *He's one of the few sensible people on the council.* | **be sensible** spoken *Be sensible – you can't go out without a coat in this weather.* | **+ about** *People are far more sensible about what and how much they drink these days.*

reasonable /ˈriːzənəbəl/ [adj] someone who is **reasonable** makes sensible decisions that are fair to everyone: *She's usually very reasonable as a boss, but now and again her temper flares up.* | *Let's try and discuss this in a calm and reasonable way.* | **be reasonable** spoken *Be reasonable, Paul – I'm only trying to help.*

responsible /rɪˈspɒnsəbəl‖rɪˈspɑːn-/ [adj] someone who is **responsible** can be trusted to do what they should do and to think about the results of their actions: *We aim to educate our children to become socially responsible citizens.* | *I'm a responsible adult. I can make my own choices.* —**responsibly** [adv] *People should have their driving licences taken away if they can't drive responsibly.*

mature /məˈtʃʊəʳ/ [adj] a child or young person who is **mature** behaves in a sensible way, as you would expect an older person to behave: *She's very mature for her age.* | *After two years of college, the students have a much more mature attitude.* —**maturity** [n U] *Ask yourself if you have the maturity and stability to raise a baby.*

rational /ˈræʃənəl/ [adj] if someone is **rational**, their actions are based on a clear understanding of the facts of a situation, and are not influenced by their feelings or imagination: *Taking action to defend yourself is a completely rational reaction if you're being attacked.* | *Many of the patients have long histories of drug abuse, and they're not always rational.* —**rationally** [adv] *Do people behave completely rationally when they vote in elections?*

practical/realistic/pragmatic /ˈpræktɪkəl, ˌrɪəˈlɪstɪk◂, prægˈmætɪk/ [adj] having the ability to understand situations and to know what is or is not possible: *She's a practical manager who realizes that a happy workforce is also a productive one.* | *The people of this country need to be more realistic – you can't have lower taxes as well as higher spending on health and pensions.* | *She is a tough, pragmatic, intuitive leader.*

no-nonsense /nəʊ ˈnɒnsəns‖-ˈnɑːnsens/ [adj only before noun] direct and dealing with things in a practical way, without wasting time on things that do not matter: *Mathews is a no-nonsense veteran of the police department.* | *Jason, with his no-nonsense approach, has been an asset to the project.*

down-to-earth /ˌdaʊn tʊ ˈɜːʳθ◂/ [adj] someone who is **down-to-earth** is practical and honest, and does not think they are more important, more intelligent etc than other people: *She's sophisticated, but also practical and down-to-earth.* | *People are surprised by what an unpretentious, down-to-earth guy he really is.*

talk sense /ˌtɔːk ˈsens/ [v phrase] especially spoken if someone **talks sense**, they express sensible ideas or opinions that you agree with: *Someone who could talk sense would get my vote, but most politicians don't.*

have your head screwed on British **/have your head screwed on right** American /hæv jɔːʳ ˈhed skruːd ɒn, hæv jɔːʳ ˈhed skruːd ɒn ˌraɪt/ [v phrase not in progressive] use this about someone who will always behave sensibly in a difficult or confusing situation: *Don't worry about Sheila. She's got her head screwed on.* | *Anyone who can raise three such normal kids in Hollywood must have their head screwed on right.*

sane /seɪn/ [adj] able to think clearly and likely to behave in a sensible way, especially when other people are not being sensible: *I don't think any sane person would take his threats seriously.* | *It was a relief to hear one sane voice among all the shouting and hysteria.* | **keep sb sane** *Exercise keeps me sane. If I didn't exercise, the stress would get to me.*

2 decisions/plans/ideas/actions

- sensible
- make sense
- be a good idea
- reasonable
- rational
- practical/realistic
- pragmatic
- logical
- wise
- within reason

sensible /ˈsensəbəl/ [adj] a **sensible** decision, idea, plan etc is likely to have good results because it is based on good, practical reasons: *He gave me some very sensible advice.* | *If anyone has any sensible suggestions as to how to deal with this, please let me know.* | **it is sensible to do sth** *It would have been more sensible to save the money than to spend it all on clothes.* | **the sensible thing to do** (=used to give advice) *The sensible thing to do would be to rest until you feel better.* —**sensibly** [adv] *She had sensibly decided to leave the car at home.*

make sense /ˌmeɪk ˈsens/ [v phrase] especially spoken if something **makes sense**, it seems a very sensible thing to do: *There are parts of the plan that simply don't make sense.* | **it makes sense (for sb) to do sth** *It made sense for Sam to live nearer the college.* | *It may not make sense to rebuild the houses damaged by the floods.*

be a good idea /biː ə ˌgʊd aɪˈdɪə/ [v phrase] especially spoken to seem to be the right and sensible thing to do: *Yes, I think a short meeting this afternoon would be a good idea.* | *'Should I phone him?' 'I don't think that's a good idea.'* | **it's a good idea to do sth** *It's a good idea to tell a friend if you are going on a date with someone you don't know well.*

reasonable /ˈriːzənəbəl/ [adj] a **reasonable** idea, request, action etc seems sensible and fair, and you can understand the reasons for it: *I thought her request for more information was reasonable, but it was refused.* | *I'll go along with any reasonable plan.* | **it is reasonable to assume/believe/suppose** *It's reasonable to assume that most prices will go up again.*

rational /ˈræʃənəl/ [adj] based on facts and intelligent thinking, and not influenced by feelings or the imagination: *Education helps us to make rational decisions.* | *People's behaviour isn't always purely rational.* —**rationally** [adv] *We must consider the problem rationally.*

practical/realistic /ˈpræktɪkəl, ˌrɪəˈlɪstɪk◂/ [adj] based on a good understanding of what is or is not possible: *The city authorities are trying to work out a practical solution to the problem of homelessness.* | *Starting my own business isn't a very realistic idea at the moment.* | *If you want to sell your home, be realistic about the price.*

pragmatic /prægˈmætɪk/ [adj] based on facts and what is likely to really succeed, but not always considering other things such as people's feelings, or attempting anything more exciting or risky: *Pragmatic considerations led the government to abandon pure Marxist policies.* | *We need a pragmatic approach to sex education in schools.*

logical /ˈlɒdʒɪkəl‖ˈlɑː-/ [adj] a **logical** action or decision seems to be clearly the right thing to do, because it is based on thinking intelligently about all the facts of a situation, and not based on feelings or emotions: *As I wanted to travel to other countries, studying languages was the logical choice.* | *This is the logical place to build a new airport.* | *It seemed logical to start by visiting the scene of the crime.*

wise /waɪz/ [adj] a **wise** decision or action is based on good judgement and on your experience of life: *'I've decided to apply for that job.' 'I think that's a* *very wise decision.'* | *a wise investment* | **it is wise (for sb) to do sth** *He thought it might be wise not to tell her what had happened.* | *Do you think it's wise for him to travel alone?*

within reason /wɪðɪn 'riːzən/ [adv] according to what is generally accepted as being sensible and reasonable and no more: *Children should, within reason, be able to experiment with many different activities.* | *Within reason, the city does what it can to prevent traffic accidents.*

3 to start behaving sensibly after not being sensible

- come to your senses
- see reason
- get real

come to your senses /ˌkʌm tə jɔːʳ 'sensɪ̈z/ [v phrase] *He'd be crazy to leave Liza – it's about time he came to his senses.* | *Her parents finally came to their senses and realized they couldn't force her to marry someone she didn't like.*

see reason /siː 'riːzən/ [v phrase] to start behaving sensibly after listening to advice or arguments from other people: *I wish he'd see reason and stop putting so much pressure on me.*

get real /get 'rɪəl/ [v phrase] spoken use this to tell someone that they are not being sensible or practical, for example if they think that a difficult problem will be easy to deal with: *Get real. It's pretty hard for a young woman on her first job to take a case of sexual harassment to court.* | *'We could always ask Dad for more money.' 'Get real! We'd be grounded for a month!'*

4 to try to persuade someone to behave sensibly

- talk some sense into
- get sb to see reason
- bring sb to their senses

talk some sense into /ˌtɔːk səm 'sens ɪntuː/ [v phrase] *It took some time to calm him down and talk some sense into him.* | *Will you try and talk some sense into him – he says he's going to drop out of school.*

get sb to see reason /ˌget (sb) tə ˌsiː 'riːzən/ [v phrase] to manage, with some difficulty, to persuade someone to behave sensibly by talking to them about the situation: *I just can't get her to see reason.* | *Eventually we managed to get the border guards to see reason.*

bring sb to their senses /ˌbrɪŋ (sb) tə ðeəʳ 'sensɪ̈z/ [v phrase] if something that has happened, especially an unpleasant surprise, **brings someone to their senses**, it makes them stop behaving in a stupid way and start behaving sensibly: *Seeing so many friends dying of drug-related illnesses was what brought me to my senses.* | *It took a lawsuit to bring them to their senses.*

5 the ability to make sensible decisions

- common sense
- sense/good sense

common sense /ˌkɒmən 'sens◂‖ˌkɑː-/ [n U] the ability to make intelligent, practical decision based on your experience or on what is generally accepted as being true – use this about something that is clearly true, so it is sensible to believe it: *Obviously people are going to respond better to praise than to criticism – that's just common sense.* | **common sense tells you ...** *Common sense tells you to keep candles away from small children and pets.* | **have common sense** *She's highly intelligent and intellectual, but she's got no practical common sense.* | **use your common sense** *It's not difficult to work out the answer – you just have to use your common sense.*
—**common-sense** [adj only before noun] *She has written a common-sense guide to diet and exercise.*

sense/good sense /sens, ˌgʊd 'sens/ [n U] the ability to behave in an intelligent and sensible way, and to avoid doing anything stupid: *I sometimes wish you'd show more sense.* | *No-one in the group seemed to have Charlie's good sense.* | **have the (good) sense to do sth** *Luckily, Sheena had the good sense to call the police before Baxter left the building.* | *I'm sure she has too much sense to give him her address.*

separate

RELATED WORDS

opposite: **together, join**

▸ *see also* **alone, independent, relationship**

1 not together

- separate
- apart
- separately

separate /'sepərɪ̈t/ [adj] not together: *All the children have separate bedrooms.* | *a university with three separate campuses* | *The cities of Long Beach and Los Angeles are completely separate.* | **+ from** *The nursery was separate from the main school.* | **keep sth separate** *He likes to keep his work and his family life separate.* | *Keep your bank card and your PIN number separate.*

apart /ə'pɑːʳt/ [adv] if people or things are **apart**, they are in different places and there is a distance between them: *I hate it when we're apart.* | **live apart** *Jo and Sam decided to try living apart for a while.* | **move/drift apart** *Since the universe began, the galaxies have gradually moved further apart.* | **+ from** *Helen noticed one little boy standing apart from the rest of the group.* | **50 miles/100 kilometres etc apart** *The two cities are less than 30 km apart.* | **keep sb apart** *The two sets of rival fans had to be kept apart by the police.*

separately /'sepərɪ̈tli/ [adv] not together, but at separate times or in separate places: *The couple arrived separately at London Airport yesterday.* | *Books for more advanced students are listed separately.* | *Each of the men talked to her separately after the meeting.*

2 to separate something into two or more parts

- separate
- divide
- split
- break up
- break down
- take apart
- dismantle
- take sth to pieces

separate /'sepəreɪt/ [v T] *This is a technique used to separate the components of a mixture.* | **separate sth into sth** *He sat at a desk, separating a pile of mail into 'urgent' and 'non-urgent'.*

divide /dǝ̇ˈvaɪd/ [v T] to separate something into a number of separate parts or things **divide sth into sth** *We divided the pizza into three and had a slice each.* | *Some of the big old houses have been divided into apartments.* | **divide up sth/divide sth up** *He said that dividing up the company would make the units more profitable.*

split /splɪt/ [v T] to separate something that used to be a single thing or a single group into two or more different parts: *Rutherford first split the atom on 3rd January 1919.* | **split sth in half/in two** (=so that it makes two equal parts) *He split the company in half, and then sold both new companies to different buyers.* | **split sth into sth** (=into two, three etc parts) *For this exercise, I'm going to split the class into three groups.*

break up /ˌbreɪk ˈʌp/ [phr v T] to separate something into several smaller parts **break up sth** *The police were attacked as they tried to break up the crowd.* | **break sth up** *If you have to give a long explanation, try to break it up.* | **break sth up into sth** *You can break a subject up into sections and guide your learners through it one section at a time.*

break down /ˌbreɪk ˈdaʊn/ [phr v T] to separate something such as a report or a job into parts, especially in order to make it easier to understand or easier to do **break down sth** *Try to break down the calculation and get the students to do it in stages.* | **break sth down** *If you find a piece of music hard to play, break it down into small sections and practise each one slowly.*

take apart /ˌteɪk əˈpɑːʳt/ [phr v T] to separate a machine, piece of equipment etc into parts **take sth apart** *He'd shown her how to take a gun apart and clean it.* | **take apart sth** *He spends his time taking apart old clocks and watches.*

dismantle /dɪsˈmæntl/ [v T] to separate a large or complicated machine into parts, for example so that it can no longer be used or in order to make it easier to move, repair etc: *Jimmy was in the garage, dismantling his bike.* | *The first thing the soldiers did was to dismantle the enemy's surveillance equipment.*

take sth to pieces /ˌteɪk (sth) tə ˈpiːsǝ̇z/ [v phrase] to separate something into pieces, especially in order to check for a fault or to clean it: *He took the toy to pieces to find out how it worked.* | *The parcel contained a gun that had been taken to pieces.*

3 to become separated into two different parts

- separate
- split
- break up
- be in pieces
- come to pieces

separate /ˈsepəreɪt/ [v I] to become separated into different parts, usually in a natural way: *Hair conditioner helps your curls to separate.* | **+ into** *The whole process separates quite naturally into three smaller stages.* | *As the milk turns sour, it separates into thick curds and watery liquid.* | **+ from** *At this point, the satellite separates from its launcher.*

split /splɪt/ [v I] to become separated into two or more parts or groups: *What happens when an atom splits?* | **+ into** *The class split into two. Half of us went to the museum and half to the cathedral.* | *When you electrolyse water it splits into hydrogen and oxygen.*

break up /ˌbreɪk ˈʌp/ [phr v I] to separate into several smaller parts: *In spring the icebergs begin to break up.* | *The crowd broke up slowly.* | **+ into** *Eventually, the old ruling group broke up into a number of political parties.*

be in pieces /biː ɪn ˈpiːsǝ̇z/ [v phrase] if something **is in pieces**, it has been separated into pieces: *The table Alan was supposed to have put together was still in pieces when I arrived home.* | *Within a few minutes he had the car engine in pieces on the garage floor.*

come to pieces /ˌkʌm tə ˈpiːsǝ̇z/ [v phrase] if something **comes to pieces**, it is designed so that it can be broken into its separate parts without being damaged: *The bed comes to pieces, so we can fit it in the car.*

4 when something keeps two things, places, or people separate

- separate
- divide

separate /ˈsepəreɪt/ [v T] *A tall fence separates the two houses.* | *Items in the list should be separated by commas.* | **separate sth from sth** *The diaphragm is the strong muscular wall that separates the chest from the stomach.*

divide /dǝ̇ˈvaɪd/ [v T] to keep two areas or two parts of an area separate from each other: *Only a thin partition divides the room.* | **divide sth from sth** *A busy highway divides one half of the town from the other.* | *The chapel is divided from the rest of the church by a screen.*

5 to separate things or people so that they are no longer close or touching

- separate
- part
- keep apart

separate /ˈsepəreɪt/ [v T] *If you two don't stop talking during class, I'll have to separate you.* | *Some of the pages had got stuck together and I couldn't separate them.* | **separate sth from sth** *Break an egg into a bowl and separate the white from the yolk.* | *Farmers separate calves from their mothers when they are only a few days old.*

part /pɑːʳt/ [v T] to separate two things or parts that are together, making a space in the middle of them: *Joe parted the curtains and the sunlight came flooding in.* | *She parted the branches with her hands as she moved further into the forest.*

keep apart /ˌkiːp əˈpɑːʳt/ [phr v T] to stop things from touching each other or coming together, especially in order to prevent something from happening: *The plastic casing keeps the wires apart.* | *After mating, male and female sheep are usually kept apart.*

6 to separate people from each other, the rest of society etc

- separate
- keep sb apart
- isolate
- cut sb off from
- segregate
- segregation
- apartheid
- in quarantine

separate /ˈsepəreɪt/ [v T] to keep two or more people apart, especially so that they cannot cause any trouble together: *Teachers thought it best to separate Paul and Fred and put them in different classes.* | **separate sb from sb** *Separating prisoners from each other is sometimes the only way of preventing riots.*

keep sb apart /ˌkiːp (sb) əˈpɑːʳt/ [phr v T] to separate two or more people so that they cannot talk to or harm each other: *At the party it seemed only sensible to keep her ex-husband and her new boyfriend apart.* | **+ from** *Sex offenders are often kept apart from other prisoners for their own safety.*

isolate /ˈaɪsəleɪt/ [v T] to keep someone away from other people, especially because they are suffering from an infectious disease: *We used to routinely isolate people who had measles.* | **isolate sb from** *The six other patients were immediately isolated from the infected four.* —**isolation** /ˌaɪsəˈleɪʃən/ [n U] *She could not bear the isolation of being at home alone all day.*

cut sb off from /ˌkʌt (sb) ˈɒf frɒm/ [v phrase] to separate someone from the people they are usually with: *She realized that he was trying to cut her off from her friends.* | *It's easy to get cut off from your family when you first go overseas.*

segregate /ˈsegrɪgeɪt/ [v T] to separate one group of people from others, especially because of their race, sex, religion etc: *Schools should not segregate children with disabilities.* | *Faith-based schools would only segregate society further.* | **be segregated from** *Male prisoners were strictly segregated from the females.* —**segregated** [adj] *At that time, the beaches in South Africa were segregated.*

segregation /ˌsegrɪˈgeɪʃən/ [n U] the practice of keeping people of different races apart and making them live, work, or study separately, especially because one race believes that members of the other race are not as good as they are: *Racial segregation in schools still exists in some southern states.* | *Civil rights protestors called for an end to all segregation.*

apartheid /əˈpɑːʳtheɪt, -teɪt, -taɪt, -taɪd/ [n U] the former South African political and social system in which black and white races had to go to separate schools, live in separate areas etc as a way of keeping white people in their position of power: *Mandela was in prison for over 25 years for opposing apartheid in South Africa.* | *an anti-apartheid organization*

in quarantine /ɪn ˈkwɒrəntiːn‖-ˈkwɑː-/ [adv] separated from other people because you have or may have an infectious illness that they could catch if they were with you: *One of the crew caught smallpox, and soon they were all in quarantine.* | **put sb in quarantine** *All animals entering the UK used to have to be put in quarantine.*

7 when two or more people stop having a relationship, friendship etc

- separate
- split up
- part
- break up
- drift apart
- go their separate ways
- estranged
- separation

▸ *see also* **divorce, leave (27-28)**

separate /ˈsepəreɪt/ [v I] to start to live apart from a sexual partner you used to live with or are married to: *They separated several years ago, but they're not divorced.* | *Kids are put under a tremendous emotional strain when their parents separate.*

split up /ˌsplɪt ˈʌp/ [phr v I] if two people **split up**, they stop having a relationship with each other, especially a sexual relationship: *They're always arguing, but I don't think they'll ever split up.* | **+ with** *He started drinking heavily after he split up with Debbie.*

part /pɑːʳt/ [v I] to separate from someone so that your relationship ends – used especially in literature: *They parted in a fairly amicable way.* | *She hoped that she and Jonathan would never part.*

break up /ˌbreɪk ˈʌp/ [phr v I] if two people **break up**, or if their relationship **breaks up**, they stop having a relationship with each other: *Tom and I broke up last year.* | *Newspaper stories often have a lot to do with showbusiness marriages breaking up.* | **+ with** *I can't imagine ever breaking up with my wife.* —**break-up** /ˈbreɪk ʌp/ [n C] *What finally caused the break-up of your marriage?*

drift apart /ˌdrɪft əˈpɑːʳt/ [v phrase] if people **drift apart**, they gradually become less friendly and see each other less, until their relationship finally ends: *Over the years my schoolfriends and I have drifted apart.* | *Teddy and Maria never really argued – they just drifted apart.*

go their separate ways /ˌgəʊ ðeəʳ ˌsepərə̇t ˈweɪz/ [v phrase] if a group of friends **go their separate ways**, they each go to different places and start doing different things: *After we left college we all went our separate ways and I never saw those friends again.*

estranged /ɪˈstreɪndʒd/ [adj] separated from a relation, especially a close one such as a husband or mother, so that you almost never see them, for example because you have had a serious argument **sb's estranged wife/husband/father etc** *He is hoping for a reconciliation with his estranged wife Hillary.* | *In 1975, he wrote a formal letter to his estranged father.* | **be estranged from sb** *We provide support to people who are estranged from their families.*

separation /ˌsepəˈreɪʃən/ [n C/U] a situation in which a husband and wife agree to live apart from each other even though they are still married: *In the case of separation or divorce, the children's needs should come first.* | *Since the separation they've each been seeing different people.* | **trial separation** (=to see if it is better or worse being separated) *He said he understood her doubts and perhaps a trial separation might be the answer.*

8 to deliberately separate yourself from another person, group etc

- split from
- cut yourself off
- sever links/connections/relations/ties
- detach/distance yourself from

split from /ˈsplɪt frɒm / [v phrase] to deliberately separate yourself from a larger group or organization, especially because you no longer want to work with them: *Last year, he split from the rock band, 'Hot City'.* | *The left wing of the party is likely to split from its parent organization.*

cut yourself off /ˌkʌt jɔːʳself ˈɒf/ [v phrase] to deliberately separate yourself from a group of people, usually permanently, because you want to be alone or independent: *She had cut herself off, and when David left her she had no one to turn to.* | **+ from** *Quite deliberately, she cut herself off from the rest of the family.*

sever links/connections/relations/ties /ˌsevəʳ ˈlɪŋks, kəˈnekʃənz, rɪˈleɪʃənz, ˈtaɪz / [v phrase] to formally and permanently end a relationship with another person, company, country etc: *Throughout the seventies, the government was urged* *to sever all links with South Africa.* | *Tobolewski, like many immigrants into America, severed all his ties with his Polish background.*

detach/distance yourself from /dɪˈtætʃ, ˈdɪstəns jɔːʳself frɒm/ [v phrase] to deliberately separate yourself from a person, organization etc, because you do not want people to think you are connected with it or are responsible for something that they are doing: *The government is seeking to detach itself from the latest financial scandal.* | *Diplomats saw his resignation as a way of distancing himself from an unpopular government.*

series

RELATED WORDS

▸ *see also* **list, order, after**

1 a series of events, things, numbers, people etc

- ▸ series
- ▸ sequence
- ▸ string of
- ▸ succession
- ▸ chain of events
- ▸ stream of
- ▸ catalogue of failures/disasters/errors etc
- ▸ course of drugs/treatment/injections

series /ˈsɪəriːz/ [n singular] several things that happen one after the other: *What is the next number in the series – 12, 24, 48, 96?* | **+ of** *There has been a series of accidents on the M25.* | *The orchestra is giving a series of concerts to raise money for charity.* | *Police smashed a major drugs ring after a series of dawn raids.*

sequence /ˈsiːkwəns/ [n C usually singular] the order in which events or actions follow one another, or the order in which they are supposed to follow one another: *The keys have to be turned in a particular sequence to open the safe.* | **+ of** *The sequence of movements for this particular dance is quite difficult to learn.* | **sequence of events** *The report detailed the sequence of events that led to the oil spill.* | **in sequence** *The chairs are numbered in sequence.*

string of /ˈstrɪŋ ɒv/ [n phrase] a series of similar events that happen very close together, or a group of similar things that exist or are found very close together: *O'Neill had a string of successes with his first four plays.* | *a string of tiny islands off the coast of Florida* | *Jackson was imprisoned in 1934 for a string of sensational crimes.*

succession /səkˈseʃən / [n singular] a number of events, relationships, people etc following closely after each other, especially when it is bad that there have been so many of them **+ of** *The project has had a succession of legal problems.* | *Like many rich kids, Georgie was raised by a succession of underpaid nannies.* | **in succession** *We lost four important games in succession.*

chain of events ALSO **train of events** British /ˌtʃeɪn əv ɪˈvents, ˌtreɪn əv ɪˈvents/ [n phrase] a series of events, especially a series in which each thing that happens causes the next one to happen: *The 6 month trial focused on the chain of events leading to the murder.* | *The book details the train of events that led to the outbreak of the First World War.*

stream of /ˈstriːm ɒv/ [n phrase] a long and almost continuous series of events, people, objects etc that follow closely after each other **+ of** *Guides take the non-stop stream of visitors around the castle.* | **in an endless stream** (=continuously, in large numbers) *Refugees were pouring across the border in an endless stream.*

catalogue of failures/disasters/errors etc ALSO **catalog** American /ˌkætəlɒg əv ˈfeɪljəʳz‖-lɔːg-/ [n phrase] a series of failures, disasters etc that happen one after the other and never seem to stop: *The bombing is the latest addition to the catalogue of terrorist crimes.* | *The official report into the disaster points up a whole catalog of errors and oversights.*

course of drugs/treatment/injections /ˌkɔːʳs əv ˈdrʌgz, ˈtriːtmənt, ɪnˈdʒekʃənz/ [n phrase] a planned process of medical treatment, consisting of a series of regular amounts of treatment, drugs etc over a fixed period: *Europeans usually need to have a course of injections before travelling to India.* | *The disease can be easily cured with a simple course of antibiotics.*

2 a series of television programmes, books etc

- ▸ series
- ▸ serial

▸ *see also* **television/radio, books**

series /ˈsɪəriːz/ [n C] a regular **series** of television programmes, books etc that tell the same story or are the same kind of programme, book etc: *A new TV series called 'The Hamilton Dynasty' will be starting next autumn.* | *Rowling's 'Harry Potter' series for children has been amazingly successful.* | **+ of** *a series of articles about the state of the economy*

serial /ˈsɪəriəl/ [n C] a story that is broadcast in several separate parts on television or radio, or printed in separate parts in a magazine or newspaper: *The BBC sells most of its successful serials to the US.* | *Don't miss the latest episode in our serial, 'David Copperfield.'* — **serialize** [v T] make a book etc into a serial: *Her novel 'The Awakening' was recently serialized on TV.*

3 happening or doing something in a series

- ▸ successive
- ▸ consecutive
- ▸ straight
- ▸ in succession
- ▸ one after the other/one after another
- ▸ in a row
- ▸ running
- ▸ alternate

successive /səkˈsesɪv/ [adj only before noun] happening one after the other: *Successive nights without sleep make any new parent feel ready to quit.* | *Jackson became the first batter since Babe Ruth to hit three successive home runs in a single game.* | *Successive governments have failed to tackle the problem of international debt.*

consecutive /kənˈsekjᵊtɪv/ [adj] **consecutive** days, years etc come after one another, with no breaks in between: *The company has made a profit for seven consecutive years.* | *You must get a doctor's certificate if you're off work sick for more than three consecutive days.*

straight /streɪt/ [adj/adv] happening immediately one after another in a series, especially in an unusually long series: *The temperatures was 40 degrees below zero for two weeks straight.* | *She is hoping to beat her personal record of 21 straight victories.*

in succession /ɪn səkˈseʃən/ [adv] if something happens on a number of occasions, days, years etc **in succession**, it happens on each of those occasions, days, years etc, without a break: *She's won the championship four times in succession.* | *It's not advisable to plant wheat in the same field for more than two years in succession.*

one after the other/one after another /ˌwʌn ɑːftəʳ ði ˈʌðəʳ, ˌwʌn ɑːftər əˈnʌðəʳ‖-æf-/ [adv] if a number of events happen **one after the other** or **one after another**, each one happens soon after the previous one: *One after another they got up and left the room.* | *He was so thirsty that he drank five glasses of water, one after the other.* | *She smoked nervously throughout the meeting, one cigarette after another.*

in a row /ɪn ə ˈrəʊ/ [adv] done two or more times, one after another, without a break: *Last week I overslept three days in a row.* | *The Blazers have won 11 games in a row.*

running /ˈrʌnɪŋ/ [adv] if you do something for the third time, fifth time etc **running**, you do it that number of times without a break: *This is the fourth time running you've been late.* | *Spender won the Cambridge Poetry Prize three years running.*

alternate /ɔːlˈtɜːnɪ̍t‖ˈɔːltɜːr-, ˈæl-/ [adj only before noun] two **alternate** actions, events, feelings etc are done in a fixed order, first one, then the other, then the first one again etc: *He worked alternate night and day shifts.* | *Italian cities have imposed alternate-day driving rules in an effort to reduce pollution.* | **alternate Sundays/weekends etc** (=first one Sunday or weekend, but not the next, then the next Sunday or weekend but not the next etc) *She visits her parents on alternate Sundays.* —**alternately** [adv] *The child lay there for three days, alternately sweating and shivering.*

serious

WHAT'S HERE

- **serious situation** see **1 to 2**
- **serious/not joking** see **3 to 9**

serious situation

RELATED WORDS

- *see also* **bad, important, accident, illness/disease, disease, crime, situation**

1 when a situation, problem accident etc is bad

- serious
- bad
- grave
- critical
- desperate
- acute
- grim
- be no laughing matter
- be a matter of life and death/be a matter of life or death
- be no joke

serious /ˈsɪəriəs/ [adj] very bad – use this about problems, accidents, illnesses, or crimes: *The recent storms have caused serious damage.* | *The climbers got into serious difficulties and had to be air-lifted to safety.* | *In the last two weeks, the situation has become more serious, with riots and strikes spreading across the country.* | *Violent crime is a serious problem in and around the capital.* | *The boy was taken to hospital with serious head injuries.* —**seriously** [adv] *The collapse in coffee prices has seriously affected the economies of Brazil and Colombia.* | **seriously ill/injured** *Her father is seriously ill in hospital.* —**seriousness** [n U] *The public are beginning to realize the seriousness of drunk driving.*

bad /bæd/ [adj] a problem, illness, or accident that is **bad** is severe, and makes you feel worried: *The pain was really bad.* | *Paul's off work – he's got a bad cold.* | *Judy had been in a bad car crash several years before, and was still too nervous to drive.* | **things are bad** (=a situation is bad) spoken *Things are bad in York – some people's houses have been flooded three times.* —**badly** [adv] **badly injured/damaged/affected etc** *Two of the passengers were killed, and the driver was badly injured.* | *The front of the shop had been blown away, and the roof was badly damaged.*

grave /greɪv/ [adj] formal a **grave** situation or mistake is very serious and worrying because people are in danger and because the situation seems likely to get worse: *The situation is grave – war now seems inevitable.* | *The ambassador declared that there would be grave consequences if the hostages were not released.* | **grave danger** *A thick fog descended on the mountain, and I knew that we were in grave danger.* | **grave risk** *There was a grave risk that the operation would leave him partly paralysed.* | **grave mistake/error** *'It would be a grave mistake,' said the president, 'to ignore the problem, and pretend that it will go away.'* —**gravely** [adv] **gravely ill** *Leopold's mother was gravely ill, and he returned to Vienna as quickly as he could.* —**gravity** /ˈgrævɪ̍ti/ [n U] when something is grave: *He didn't seem to realize the gravity of the situation.*

critical /ˈkrɪtɪkəl/ [adj] a **critical** situation is very serious and dangerous and might get worse very suddenly – use this especially when people will die if it does not improve: *The situation is said to be critical and the army has been brought in to disperse the mob.* | *Things are now critical. Hospitals have no medicine, and people are running out of food.* | **be in a critical condition** British /**be in critical condition** American (=so ill or badly injured that you could die) *Eight people were killed and four are still in a critical condition.* —**critically** [adv] **critically ill/injured** *A police officer is critically ill after being shot in the chest.*

desperate /ˈdespərɪ̍t/ [adj] a **desperate** situation or problem is very serious or dangerous, and it does not seem possible that it will improve – use this especially when people will die if it does not improve: *Refugees on the border are living in appalling conditions with desperate shortages of food, medicine and water.* | *The situation was desperate. The enemy were now only a mile away.* | **be in desperate need of sth** *The hospital is full of people in desperate need of medical attention.*

acute /əˈkjuːt/ [adj] an **acute** illness, problem, or situation is one that has become very serious or dangerous, and needs to be dealt with quickly: *She was taken to the hospital suffering from acute appendicitis.* | *Patients suffering from acute depression may well need medication.* | *Nowhere is the problem more acute than Los Angeles County, where gang-related homicide is on the increase.* | *In San Diego, the shortage of skilled workers is acute.*

grim /grɪm/ [adj] a situation or piece of news that is **grim** is serious and unpleasant, and people think it will not get better: *The situation is grim for the innocent people, caught up in this conflict.* | *Rescue workers are continuing the grim task of searching for bodies.* | **grim news** *The next few weeks brought more grim news, as the economic crisis began to deepen.* | **grim prospect** (=something bad that will probably happen) *Two thousand car workers face the grim prospect of redundancy.* | **things look grim**

(=the situation seems grim) *Things look pretty grim for farmers at the moment.*

be no laughing matter /biː nəʊ ˈlɑːfɪŋ ˌmætəʳ ‖-ˈlæf-/ [v phrase] **spoken** use this to say that something is serious and not something you should joke about: *Getting up for work at 5am every day is no laughing matter, especially in winter.* | *English teachers often joked that they could not pass the exam, but for the students it was no laughing matter.*

be a matter of life and death/be a matter of life or death /biː ə ˌmætər əv ˌlaɪf ən ˈdeθ, biː ə ˌmætər əv ˌlaɪf ɔːʳ ˈdeθ/ [v phrase] if a situation **is a matter of life and death**, it is very serious, and what you do will affect whether the situation ends well or not – use this especially when it is possible that someone will die: *People grow their own food, and the success of their harvest is literally a matter of life or death.* | *In this town football isn't just a game – it's a matter of life and death.*

be no joke /biː ˌnəʊ ˈdʒəʊk/ [v phrase] **informal** if you say that a situation or event **is no joke**, it is difficult or unpleasant: *It's no joke if you have an accident in the mountains – it's fifty miles to the nearest hospital.* | *Crossing the road was no joke with all the early morning traffic.*

2 a bad situation that might get worse

- crisis
- emergency

▸ *see also* **disaster**

crisis /ˈkraɪsɪ̇s/ [n C] a very bad situation in which there is a risk that serious problems will become suddenly worse – use this about political or economic affairs or personal or emotional problems: *Their marriage was going through a crisis which almost ended in divorce.* | *The Cuban missile crisis in 1960 was probably the closest we have been to nuclear war.* | *In recent years, the country has suffered a profound political and economic crisis, and deprivation is acute.* | **in crisis** *The Health Service is in crisis.* | *a charity set up to help families in crisis* | **in a crisis** *We need someone who can stay calm in a crisis.* | **spark a crisis** (=cause a crisis to start) *The President announced his resignation, sparking a crisis in the government.*

emergency /ɪˈmɜːʳdʒənsi/ [n C] a very serious situation, such as an accident, that happens suddenly and needs to be dealt with immediately: *Staff are trained to deal with any emergency.* | *A fire started in the cargo area, and the pilot was forced to make an emergency landing.* | *The victim was rushed to hospital for emergency surgery.* | **in an emergency** (=if there is an emergency) *In an emergency, dial 911 for police, the fire department or an ambulance.* | **the emergency services** British (=the organizations that come to help you if there is an emergency) *The emergency services in this area simply couldn't cope if there were a major accident or terrorist attack.*

serious/not joking

RELATED WORDS

▸ *see also* **joke**

3 to really mean what you say

- be serious
- mean
- not joking
- seriously
- mean business
- be in earnest

be serious /biː ˈsɪəriəs/ [v phrase] to really mean what you say or really intend to do something: *Do you think she was serious when she said she used to be an actress?* | *Listen! I'm serious! I'm not lending you any more money!* | **+ about** *Tina's quite intelligent, but she's not really serious about her schoolwork.* | **serious about doing sth** *I hope Jeff's serious about giving up smoking.* | **get serious about sth** (=start dealing with a problem in a determined way) *Car manufacturers should get serious about making security a design priority.* | **deadly serious** (=extremely serious) *Her voice suddenly sounded deadly serious.* | **be perfectly/absolutely serious** (=be serious in a situation where it is hard to believe that someone could be) *'Look!' he said, 'I am perfectly serious. I'm willing to give you $10,000 for your land.'*

mean /miːn/ [v phrase not in progressive] if someone **means** what they say, they are being serious when they say it, and they are not pretending or lying **mean it** **especially spoken** *I mean it – I'll scream if you don't let me go.* | *She told me she loved me – but I wasn't sure if she meant it.* | **mean what you say** *I meant what I said, I never want to see you again.*

not joking /nɒt ˈdʒəʊkɪŋ/ [v phrase] if you say you are **not joking**, you really mean what you say, even though it seems surprising or unlikely: *There must be about 10 of them in that car – I'm not joking.* | *She told him she'd call the police if he bothered her again, and she wasn't joking.*

seriously /ˈsɪəriəsli/ [adv] if you say or do something **seriously**, you really mean it, really intend to do it, or really think it is important: *Are you seriously suggesting that she should give up her job in order to look after her husband?* | **seriously intend/want/attempt etc to do sth** *Those who seriously attempt to kill themselves usually manage to do so.* | **seriously concerned/interested/worried etc** *She was talking about children's social education at a time when no one else was seriously concerned with it.*

mean business /ˌmiːn ˈbɪznɪ̇s/ [v phrase] **spoken** if someone **means business**, it is very clear that they will definitely do what they say or what they are threatening to do: *The man had a gun. It was obvious he meant business.*

be in earnest /biː ɪn ˈɜːʳnɪ̇st/ [v phrase] if someone **is in earnest**, they really mean what they say, especially when they are saying what they want or what they intend to do: *I'm sure he was in earnest when he said he wanted to marry her.* | **be very much in earnest** *She spoke lightly, but it was obvious that she was very much in earnest.*

4 to believe someone really means what they say

- take sb seriously

take sb seriously /ˌteɪk (sb) ˈsɪəriəsli/ [v phrase] to believe that what someone says or does is serious, and worth paying attention to: *Kevin paused for a moment, not sure if Ralph would take him seriously.* | *He said he was going to build a boat in his back yard, but I didn't take him seriously!*

5 used to tell someone that you are serious, or to ask if someone is serious

- really/seriously
- no kidding
- in all seriousness
- joking apart

really/seriously /ˈrɪəli, ˈsɪəriəsli/ [adv] **spoken** say this to emphasize that something surprising is really true, or to ask whether something surprising is really true **really?/seriously?** *'She's quit her job.' 'Seriously?'* | *'It took three hours to travel ten miles, the traffic was so bad.' 'Really? You must be exhausted.'*

no kidding /nəʊ 'kɪdɪŋ/ **especially American, spoken** say this when you think other people will not believe that you are telling the truth, or to ask if someone is joking because what they say does not seem true: *I'm telling you, this guy's as fast as Carl Lewis – no kidding!* | *'She's getting married again.' 'No kidding?'*

in all seriousness /ɪn ˌɔːl 'sɪəriəsnɪ̇s/ **[adv] spoken** say this when you are telling someone about something that will be hard for them to believe: *He asked me, in all seriousness, if I would marry him next week.* | *She had heard someone say, in all seriousness, that women would never make good golfers because of the shape of their bodies.*

joking apart /ˌdʒəʊkɪŋ ə'pɑːʳt/ **British spoken** say this to show that you are now being serious about something, after you and other people have been joking about it: *Joking apart, I do feel somebody should tell him what we think. It's for his own good.*

6 someone who is quiet and does not laugh or joke much

- serious
- earnest
- sober
- have no sense of humour
- stuffy
- humourless

serious /'sɪəriəs/ **[adj]** someone who is **serious** is quiet and sensible, and does not seem to enjoy laughing and joking: *Friends described him as a serious and thoughtful man.* | **+ about** *Laura was always very serious about her work.*

earnest /'ɜːʳnɪ̇st/ **[adj]** someone who is **earnest** is very serious or too serious, and believes that what they say or do is very important – use this especially about someone who is young or not very experienced: *One earnest young man asked De Mille about the philosophical meaning of his films.* | *a group of earnest musicians dressed completely in black* —**earnestly** **[adv]** *The men began to talk earnestly about protecting the Earth for future generations.*

sober /'səʊbəʳ/ **[adj]** someone who is **sober** is very serious and thinks carefully about things, and does not laugh or joke very often: *I went to see Professor Dandavate, a sober and respected academic.* | *a sober-looking man in a grey suit*

have no sense of humour British **/have no sense of humor** American /hæv ˌnəʊ sens əv 'hjuːməʳ/ **[v phrase not in progressive]** someone who **has no sense of humour** does not understand jokes, funny situations, etc – use this especially when you think someone like this is annoying or boring: *He didn't laugh at any of my jokes. Maybe taxi drivers just don't have a sense of humor.* | *My grandmother didn't have much of a sense of humour, and she could never understand what we were laughing about.*

stuffy /'stʌfi/ **[adj]** someone who is **stuffy** does not laugh or smile at things that other people think are funny, because they are a little formal and have old-fashioned attitudes: *Victor was as old-fashioned as his father, and equally stuffy.* | *Come on Dad. Don't be so stuffy!*

humourless British **/humorless** American /'hjuːməʳləs‖'hjuː-, 'juː-/ **[adj]** someone who is **humourless** never laughs at anything and never tries to be funny or tell jokes: *I knew Deaver at college, and remember him as cold, humorless, and aloof.* | *Since the death of his wife he has become isolated, defensive and humorless.*

7 behaving in a serious way

- serious
- take sth seriously
- grave
- solemn
- sombre
- grim

serious /'sɪəriəs/ **[adj]** if someone says or does something in a **serious** way, they think that what they are saying or doing is important and should not be joked about: *All the other people in the office seemed to have a very serious attitude towards their work.* | **+ about** *The band are only young, but they're very serious about their music.*

take sth seriously /ˌteɪk (sth) 'sɪəriəsli/ **[v phrase]** to think that something is important, and spend a lot of time and effort on it: *I wish Dan would take his work more seriously.* | *She certainly takes her politics seriously – she's always out at meetings.* | **take life seriously** (=think that everything in life is very important and serious) *He seemed much older than he was, and took life a little too seriously.*

grave /greɪv/ **[adj] written** quiet and very serious, especially because something important or worrying has happened: *Holmes looked grave, and stood deep in worried thought for a minute or two.* | *His expression became very grave when we told him what had happened.* —**gravely** *'We might be too late,' she said gravely.*

solemn /'sɒləm‖'sɑː-/ **[adj]** very serious because of an important or sad occasion or ceremony: *Everyone stood respectfully, and looked solemn throughout the funeral service.* | *The judge read the verdict in a clear and solemn voice.* —**solemnly** **[adv]** *They listened solemnly as the list of those missing at sea was read out.*

sombre British **/somber** American /'sɒmbəʳ‖'sɑːm-/ **[adj]** sad, quiet, and serious because something unpleasant or worrying has happened or is going to happen: *They sat in somber silence.* | *The sun was shining brightly, but the mood was sombre.*

grim /grɪm/ **[adj]** serious and not smiling, because you are angry, upset, or worried about something: *She looked grim and upset, standing silently in the corner.* | *A grim-faced diplomat read out the declaration of war.* —**grimly** **[adv]** *This is going to be an awful week, he thought grimly.*

8 to look serious when you are joking

- keep a straight face
- straightfaced
- deadpan

▸ *see also* **joke**

keep a straight face /kiːp ə ˌstreɪt 'feɪs/ **[v phrase]** to stop yourself from laughing or smiling when you are joking or when you think something is funny: *Barbara tried to keep a straight face, but in the end she just couldn't help laughing.* | *He looked so ridiculous – I don't know how I managed to keep a straight face.*

straightfaced /ˌstreɪt'feɪst◂/ **[adv]** if you say something **straightfaced**, you do not show by your expression that it is just a joke and is not really true: *Lea told him, completely straightfaced, that sunglasses are called moonglasses in Canada.*

deadpan /'dedpæn/ **[adj/adv]** if you do or say something funny in a **deadpan** way, you deliberately do or say it without smiling or laughing: *Laurel and*

Hardy played all their great comic roles completely deadpan. | *the deadpan humour of TV comic Paul Merton* | *His tone was completely deadpan, and it was difficult to tell if he was joking or not.*

9 to tell someone to stop being too serious

- lighten up

lighten up /ˌlaɪtn ˈʌp/ spoken use this to tell someone not to be so serious about something and to relax about it: *Hey, lighten up! It's only a game, you know!* | *'But we're not supposed to leave campus at lunchtime, we'll get into trouble.' 'Lighten up, it'll be fine.'*

sex

WHAT'S HERE

- **relating to being male or female** see **1 to 3**
- **sexual activities** see **4 to 13**
- **illegal sexual activities** see **14 to 15**
- **books, jokes, films, remarks etc about sex** see **16 to 19**

relating to being male or female

RELATED WORDS

- *see also* **man, woman, gay**

1 male or female

- sex
- gender
- sexual

sex /seks/ [n C/U] someone's **sex** is whether they are male or female: *You have to put your name, age, and sex on the form.* | *You can now find out your baby's sex before it is born.* | *Eating disorders affect people of both sexes, not just girls.* | **the same sex** *Are the twins the same sex?* | **the opposite sex** (=the sex which is not your own) *Rupert has never shown much interest in members of the opposite sex.* | **sex discrimination** (=unfair treatment of someone because of their sex) *Most women are confronted by sex discrimination at some time in their working lives.*

gender /ˈdʒendəʳ/ [n C/U] someone's **gender** is whether they are male or female – used especially in writing about politics and society, or in job advertisements: *The job is open to any suitably qualified person regardless of age, gender, or race.* | **gender distinction/difference/division** (=a difference between men and women) *Sociologists believe that gender differences in voting will gradually disappear.* | **gender bias/stereotyping** (=treating someone in a particular way because of their gender) *an interesting study on gender bias in the classroom*

sexual /ˈsekʃuəl/ [adj usually before noun] relating to the differences between male and female or the characteristics of men or women: *Birds have developed a sexual difference in the colours of their feathers.* | **sexual equality/inequality** (=equality or inequality between men and women) *Sexual inequality exists, to some degree, in every society.* | **sexual politics** (=social and political behaviour and ideas relating to men and women) *Men say that they are confused by today's sexual politics in the workplace.* —**sexually** [adv] *Male and female behaviour is partly sexually determined and partly learned.*

2 places for people of both sexes

- mixed
- coed
- unisex

mixed /mɪkst/ [adj] British a **mixed** school, class, group etc is for people of both sexes: *Brisbane High was a mixed school so we had plenty to distract us from our lessons.* | *One hall of residence is for men, one is for women and the third is mixed.*

coed /ˌkəʊˈed◂‖ˈkəʊed/ [adj] American a school, camp etc that is **coed** is for students or other people of both sexes: *Many coed schools provide excellent education.* | *Almost all college students live in coed dormitories or in houses shared with friends.*

unisex /ˈjuːnɪseks/ [adj] use this for describing places that are for both men and women, especially when these places are usually for either men or women: *He prefers having his hair cut in a unisex salon.* | *a unisex toilet*

3 for people of one sex

- single-sex

single-sex /ˌsɪŋgəl ˈseks◂/ [adj only before noun] *Single-sex schools often achieve better academic results because there is no rivalry between the sexes.* | *Churches rarely have single-sex choirs these days.*

sexual activities

RELATED WORDS

- *see also* **relationship, marry, love, kiss, sexy, girlfriend/boyfriend**

4 to have sex with someone

- have sex
- sex
- make love
- sleep with sb/sleep together
- go to bed
- have (sexual) intercourse
- shag
- bonk
- lose your virginity
- mate
- sexual relations

have sex /hæv ˈseks/ [v phrase] *Teenagers should be taught to think carefully before having sex.* | **+ with** *Would you have sex with someone on your first date?* | *He's never had sex with anyone but his wife.*

sex /seks/ [n U] the act of having **sex** with someone: *She had no interest in sex after the baby was born.* | **safe sex** (=methods of protecting yourself against sexual disease while you are having sex) *Some people ignore advice about safe sex and do not wear condoms.* | **sex education** (=teaching young people about sex) *a refreshing and unusual approach to sex education*

make love /meɪk ˈlʌv/ [v phrase] if two people **make love**, they have sex because they like or love each other: *All day they made love on the unmade bed.* | **+ with/to** *She thought about Tom Cruise every time she made love with her boyfriend.*

sleep with sb/sleep together /ˈsliːp wɪð (sb), ˈsliːp təgeðəʳ/ [phr v T not in passive/phr v I] to have sex with someone you are not married to, especially regularly and over a period of time: *She's been sleeping with this guy Mark since the summer.* | *When did you first find out that Betty and your husband were sleeping together?*

go to bed /ˌgəʊ tə ˈbed/ [v phrase not in progressive] to have sex with someone on one occasion, especially because they ask you or persuade you to do so: *I remember the first time we went to bed.* | **+ with** *He said he'd give me the job if I went to bed with him.*

have (sexual) intercourse /hæv (ˌsekʃuəl) ˈɪntəʳkɔːʳs/ [v phrase] formal to have sex with someone – used especially in medical or legal contexts: *The doctor asked him when he had last had intercourse.* | *You are strongly advised to wear a condom while having sexual intercourse.* | **+ with** *The victim later claimed that her attacker forced her to have sexual intercourse with him.* —**intercourse/sexual intercourse** [n U] *The AIDS virus can be passed on during sexual intercourse.*

shag /ʃæg/ [v I/T] especially British, informal to have sex with someone – used especially humorously: *To hear him talk, you'd think he's shagged every woman in town!* | *All she ever thinks about is shagging.* —**shag** [n C] *I don't know where they are – they've probably gone upstairs for a shag.*

bonk /bɒŋk‖bɑːŋk/ [v I/T] British informal to have sex with someone – used humorously: *They said she'd bonked every man in college.* | *My mother walked in and caught us bonking.* —**bonk** [n C] *A quick bonk in a lay-by is not my idea of romance.*

lose your virginity /ˌluːz jɔːʳ vɜːʳˈdʒɪnɪ̍ti/ [v phrase] to have sex for the first time in your life: *I lost my virginity at the age of seventeen.* | **+ to** *She had lost her virginity to a law student while at university.*

mate /meɪt/ [v I] if birds or animals **mate**, they have sex in order to produce babies: *The birds mate in April and the eggs are hatched by June.* | **a mating call/dance/ritual** (=something an animal does when it wants to mate) *Two pigeons performed an elaborate and very noisy mating dance.* | **the mating season/period** (=the time of year when animals mate) *During the mating season, foxes become much more vocal.*

sexual relations /ˌsekʃuəl rɪˈleɪʃənz/ [n plural] formal when you have sex with someone – used especially in legal contexts: *Love has nothing to do with sexual relations.* | **+ between** *In most cultures, sexual relations between adults and children are totally unacceptable.*

5 to persuade someone to have sex

- seduce
- get sb into bed

seduce /sɪˈdjuːs/ [v T] to persuade someone to have sex with you, especially someone who is younger than you or has less sexual experience: *He accused Paul of trying to seduce his daughter.* | *She had been seduced by a man who deserted her and went off to sea.* —**seduction** /sɪˈdʌkʃən/ [n U] *The seduction of rich men was a game that she loved to play.*

get sb into bed /ˌget (sb) ɪntə ˈbed/ [v phrase] informal to persuade someone to have sex with you: *Some men say they love you just to get you into bed.*

6 to have sex with a lot of people

- sleep around
- casual sex
- promiscuous
- orgy
- slut
- stud
- nymphomaniac

sleep around /ˌsliːp əˈraʊnd/ [phr v I] informal to have sex with many different people over a period of time, usually without having a serious relationship with any of them: *I don't sleep around any more, not since I met Jack.* | *If you sleep around, you increase your risk of getting AIDS.*

casual sex /ˌkæʒuəl ˈseks/ [n U] when someone has sex with someone without intending to have a serious relationship with them, especially when they do this many times: *I've only known you a few days Luke, and I don't go in for casual sex.* | *It wasn't difficult to pick up people for casual sex, but it was difficult to form any sort of relationship with someone.*

promiscuous /prəˈmɪskjuəs/ [adj] someone who is **promiscuous** has sex with many different people, usually without having a serious relationship with any of them: *Promiscuous men are rarely criticized as severely as promiscuous women.* | *The survey found that single men aged 18–35 were more promiscuous than any other social group.* —**promiscuity** /ˌprɒmɪ̍ˈskjuːɪ̍ti‖ˌprɑː-/ [n U] *The introduction of free contraceptives led to an increase in promiscuity.*

orgy /ˈɔːʳdʒi/ [n C] a wild party where people have sex with a lot of different people: *a wild drunken orgy* | *What do you think's going to happen? I'm not going to an orgy or anything.*

slut ALSO **slag** /slʌt, slæg/ [n C] informal an insulting word for a woman who has sex with a lot of different men over a period of time – used to show strong disapproval: *He made me take off the red lipstick, saying it made me look like a slut.* | *That little slag slept with my husband.*

stud /stʌd/ [n C] informal a man who has sex with a lot of different women over a period of time – use this especially when the man is proud of his sexual activities: *Josh had a reputation of being the college stud.* | *A woman who behaves promiscuously is called a slut, but a man who behaves the same way is admiringly called a stud.*

nymphomaniac /ˌnɪmfəˈmeɪniæk/ [n C] a woman who always wants to have sex or has sex with a lot of people, and is therefore considered morally bad: *Even these days, a woman who has a lot of boyfriends is labelled a 'nymphomaniac'.*

7 when someone has sex with someone who is not their husband, girlfriend etc

- unfaithful
- cheat on sb
- affair
- adultery
- infidelity

unfaithful /ʌnˈfeɪθfəl/ [adj] if someone is **unfaithful**, they have sex with someone who is not their husband, girlfriend etc: *Why do women stay with unfaithful partners?* | *Jeff promised he'd never be unfaithful again.* | **+ to** *He accused me of being unfaithful to him.*

cheat on sb /ˈtʃiːt ɒn (sb)/ [phr v T] informal if someone **cheats on** their husband, girlfriend etc, they secretly have sex with someone else: *What would you do if your boyfriend cheated on you?*

affair /ə'feəʳ/ [n C] a secret sexual relationship between two people when at least one of them is married to someone else: *Their affair lasted for six years.* | **love affair** *They finally confessed their secret love affair.* | **have an affair (with sb)** *He accused his wife of having an affair.* | *My wife thinks I'm having an affair with someone at work.*

adultery /ə'dʌltəri/ [n U] the act of having sex with someone who is not your husband or wife, when you are married: *She finally left her husband because of his adultery.* | **commit adultery** formal (=have sex with someone who is not your husband or wife) *60% of men admit to committing adultery at some time during their marriages.*

infidelity /ˌɪnfɪ'delɪti/ [n U] formal when someone who is married has sex with someone who is not their husband or wife: *Her husband never knew of her infidelity.* | **marital infidelity** *There had been rumours for a long time of Clinton's marital infidelity.*

8 when someone has sex only with their husband, girlfriend etc

- faithful

faithful /'feɪθfəl/ [adj] someone who is **faithful** only has sex with their husband, girlfriend etc: *I've always been faithful, I've never cheated on you, not once!* | **+ to** *The survey found that 39% of British women are faithful to one partner over a lifetime.*

9 someone's sexual feelings, needs, or behaviour

- sexual
- sexuality
- sex drive
- desire
- lust
- libido

sexual /'sekʃuəl/ [adj] relating to **sexual** feelings or behaviour: *Dr Ruth offers advice on sexual problems.* | *It's important to take your partner's sexual needs into consideration.* | *He had to admit that his feelings for her were mostly sexual.* —**sexually** [adv] *70% of all males are still sexually active* (=they still have sex) *at the age of seventy.*

sexuality /ˌsekʃu'ælɪti/ [n U] someone's sexual feelings or needs, that are part of their basic character: *Teenagers are often confused about their sexuality, for example whether they are gay or straight.* | **female/male sexuality** *She has written a fascinating book on female sexuality.* | **sb's sexuality** *Gradually he came to understand and accept his own sexuality.*

sex drive /'seks draɪv/ [n C usually singular] someone's desire to have sex – use this especially to talk about how strong or weak this is: *These drugs may affect your sex drive.* | *For many men, having a powerful sex drive is essential to their confidence.*

desire /dɪ'zaɪəʳ/ [n C/U] a very strong feeling of wanting to have sex with someone, because you think they are very beautiful or sexually attractive – used especially in literature: *As she held him close she was filled with desire.* | *When she was drunk she could hardly contain her sexual desires.* | **+ for** *The smell of her perfume was enough to awaken his desire for her.*

lust /lʌst/ [n U] a very strong feeling of wanting to have sex with someone – use this when you are showing that someone's feeling is only physical and does not involve love: *These were not feelings of love but of lust, pure and simple.* | *He was a man possessed by greed, jealousy and lust.*

libido /lɪ'biːdəʊ/ [n singular/U] someone's need to have sex – use this especially in medical contexts: *Drinking too much often results in a loss of libido.* | *Most doctors agree that a suppressed libido is often associated with emotional and psychological problems.*

10 wanting to have sex

- excited
- aroused
- horny/randy

excited /ɪk'saɪtɪd/ [adj] having strong physical feelings that you want to have sex with someone: *As she kissed him, he became more and more excited.* | **sexually excited** *He was getting sexually excited, and his breathing became short and fast.*

aroused /ə'raʊzd/ [adj] if you are **aroused**, you want to have sex with someone, usually because of the way they look or something they have done to make your body feel sexually excited: *She didn't have a lot of experience, but she knew when a man was aroused and when he wasn't.* | **sexually aroused** *You are more likely to have a useful conversation about safer sex if you don't leave it until you are sexually aroused.*

horny/randy British /'hɔːʳni, 'rændi/ [adj] feeling sexually excited and wanting to have sex with someone: *Thinking about her made me feel really randy.* | *I don't want a room-mate who acts like a horny teenager with every woman he meets.*

11 to be sexually attracted to someone

- be attracted to
- fancy
- be interested in
- want
- lust after

be attracted to /biː ə'træktɪd tuː/ [v phrase] to feel attracted to someone so that you would like to have a sexual relationship with them: *I've always been very attracted to blondes.* | *I don't know why I was ever attracted to him in the first place.* | **strongly attracted to** *She didn't really like him as a person, but she felt strongly attracted to him.*

fancy /'fænsi/ [v T] British informal to be sexually attracted to someone: *Everyone knows you fancy Sara. Why don't you ask her out?* | *Fenella really fancied the drummer and went over to chat to him after the concert.*

be interested in /biː 'ɪntrɪstɪd ɪn/ [v phrase] to feel sexually attracted to someone, used especially when you are being polite and do not want to say that you have sexual feelings for them: *She's not really been interested in anyone since the divorce.* |

want /wɒnt‖wɔːnt/ [v T] to feel very attracted to someone and to **want** to have sex with them: *'I want you,' she whispered, 'I want you now.'* | *He was obsessed with her and wanted her desperately.*

lust after /'lʌst ɑːftəʳ‖-æf-/ [phr v T] informal to be strongly sexually attracted to someone and think about having sex with them: *You must really enjoy it, having all those fans lusting after you!*

12 someone who thinks about sex all the time

- sex maniac
- dirty old man
- lecherous

sex maniac /'seks ˌmeɪniæk/ [n C] informal someone who always wants to have sex or thinks about sex all the time and is unable to control these feelings: *You can't go out with him – he's a sex maniac.*

dirty old man /ˌdɜːʳti əʊld ˈmæn/ [n C] informal a middle-aged or old man who is always looking at or touching young women or girls in a sexual way: *She was followed through the park by some dirty old man in a raincoat.* | *One of the school doctors was a dirty old man who always wanted to examine the girls.*

lecherous /ˈletʃərəs/ [adj] a man who is **lecherous** is always looking at, thinking about, or talking to women in a sexual way that is unpleasant and offensive: *He was as lecherous as always, telling rude jokes and trying to kiss all the girls.* | *Her driving instructor was a disgusting lecherous old devil – always touching her knee.*

13 when someone does not have sex

- virgin
- celibate
- platonic
- be just (good) friends

virgin /ˈvɜːʳdʒɪn/ [n C] someone who has never had sex: *Some men will not marry a woman who is no longer a virgin.* | *At 27 he was still a virgin and very shy about it.* —**virginity** /vɜːʳˈdʒɪnɪti/ [n U] *Women in some countries are expected to keep their virginity until marriage – the same rule doesn't apply to men.*

celibate /ˈselɪbɪt/ [adj] someone who is **celibate** has chosen not to have sex at all, especially for religious reasons: *He had remained celibate for three years before he met Hannah.* | *She was not prepared for a celibate life in the Church.* —**celibacy** [n U] *He had taken a vow of celibacy* (=promised to remain celibate) *at eighteen, when he became a priest.*

platonic /pləˈtɒnɪk‖-ˈtɑː-/ [adj] a **platonic** relationship is one between people who do not have sex with each other, but are just friends – use this especially when other people think they are having a sexual relationship: *Their relationship was strictly platonic, even though she was living in his apartment.* | *In the novel, Edward and Susannah present a perfect model of platonic love.*

be just (good) friends /biː ˌdʒʌst (gʊd) ˈfrendz/ [v phrase] use this to say that two people are not having a sexual relationship: *'Are you going out with Liam?' 'No, we're just good friends.'* | *I keep telling my mother that Peter and I are just friends but she doesn't seem to believe me.*

illegal sexual activities

14 someone who has sex with people for money

- prostitute
- hooker
- call-girl
- rent boy
- prostitution
- whore

prostitute /ˈprɒstɪtjuːt‖ˈprɑːstɪtuːt/ [n C] someone, usually a woman, who has sex with people for money: *She didn't look like a prostitute. She wasn't even wearing any make-up.* | *In the evenings the prostitutes would line the streets, calling out to passing men.* | **male prostitute** *Male prostitutes lined the street looking for customers.*

hooker /ˈhʊkəʳ/ [n C] American informal a woman who has sex with men for money: *Change those clothes – you look like a hooker.* | *Some of the hookers in Vegas are under 13 years old.*

call-girl /ˈkɔːl gɜːʳl/ [n C] a woman who has sex with men for money and arranges to meet them by telephone: *She was earning $5000 a night working as a high-class call-girl.*

rent boy /ˈrent bɔɪ/ [n C] British a boy or young man who has sex with other men in return for money: *There were rent boys as young as twelve or thirteen waiting outside the bars.*

prostitution /ˌprɒstɪˈtjuːʃən‖ˌprɑːstɪˈtuː-/ [n U] the activity or business of having sex with people for money: *Criminal gangs control all the drugs, gambling and prostitution in the city.* | *Most of these girls give up prostitution when they're about 30 and settle down and marry.* | **turn to prostitution** (=become a prostitute) *Women can become so desperate for money that they turn to prostitution.*

whore /hɔːʳ/ [n C] an offensive word for a woman who has sex with people for money – use this when you want to show that you strongly disapprove of someone who does this: *We're dealing with a professional escort, not some dumb whore.*

15 to attack or harm someone in a sexual way

- rape
- rape
- abuse/sexually abuse
- molest
- sexual harassment

rape /reɪp/ [v T] to force someone to have sex when they do not want to: *He was accused of raping his ex-girlfriend.* | *The woman was raped and then murdered by her kidnapper.* —**rapist** [n C] *Rapists and child sex offenders are kept separate from other prisoners.*

rape /reɪp/ [n C/U] the crime of forcing someone to have sex when they do not want to: *It was not the first time he had been accused of rape.* | *Rape victims receive special counselling and are treated very sensitively.* | *A woman's sexual history should not be introduced in a rape trial.*

abuse/sexually abuse /əˈbjuːz, ˌsekʃuəli əˈbjuːz/ [v T/v phrase] to harm a child by forcing them to have sex or touching them in a sexual way, especially over a long period of time: *He had been sexually abusing his daughter since she was eleven years old.* —**abuse** /əˈbjuːs/ [n U] *The police are investigating claims of child abuse.* —**sexual abuse** [n U] *None of the children showed signs of sexual abuse.*

molest /məˈlest/ [v T] to harm or upset someone by touching them in a sexual way: *Her father had molested her and her sisters when they were children.* —**child-molesting** [n U] *He has not seen his child since the allegations of child-molesting were made.*

sexual harassment /ˌsekʃuəl ˈhærəsmənt/ [n U] when someone, especially someone you work with, regularly makes sexual remarks, looks at you in a sexual way, or tries to touch you in a sexual way that you do not want. **Sexual harassment** can be punished by law: *Victims of sexual harassment are often afraid to report it in case they lose their jobs.* | *She successfully prosecuted her boss for sexual harassment.*

books, jokes, films, remarks etc about sex

16 books, films, or pictures that are about sex

- pornography
- pornographic
- erotic
- adult
- steamy
- raunchy

pornography ALSO **porn** informal /pɔːʳˈnɒgrəfi‖-ˈnɑː-, pɔːʳn/ [n U] films, magazines, or pictures that show sexual acts and are intended to make people feel sexually excited: *It is now clear that there is a link between pornography and sex crimes.* | **hard-core pornography** (=very pornographic materials, which may be illegal) *Two trucks full of hard-core pornography were seized by customs officials today.* | **hard porn** (=very pornographic) *a back-street movie theater showing hard-porn movies* | **soft porn** (=slightly pornographic material) *81 per cent of our readers said they regularly watched soft-porn movies.*

pornographic /ˌpɔːʳnəˈgræfɪk◂/ [adj] a **pornographic** film, magazine, or picture shows or describes sexual acts in order to make people sexually excited: *He admitted possessing nude photographs, but denied they were pornographic.* | *She was offered $50,000 to pose for a pornographic magazine.*

erotic /ɪˈrɒtɪk‖ɪˈrɑː-/ [adj] an **erotic** book, film, painting etc shows or describes sexual acts in a way that is deliberately sexually exciting but is also artistic: *He wrote both poetry and erotic literature.* | *A number of scenes in the film were very erotic.*

adult /ˈædʌlt, əˈdʌlt/ [adj only before noun] **adult film/magazine/entertainment etc** an **adult** film etc is not suitable for children or young people because it shows sexual acts or images: *Adult magazines in shops must be kept where children cannot see them.*

steamy /ˈstiːmi/ [adj] a **steamy** play, film etc shows sexual acts that people find exciting and slightly shocking: *The movie contains some pretty steamy scenes!* | *His latest production is a steamy thriller set in Hong Kong.*

raunchy /ˈrɔːntʃi/ [adj] a **raunchy** film, performance etc has a lot of parts in it that are about sex, and that are slightly exciting, amusing, or shocking: *Bette Midler came up with a typically raunchy performance that delighted the audience.*

17 books, jokes, remarks etc that are about sex and are offensive

- obscene
- dirty
- indecent
- lewd
- blue
- filthy
- off-color
- smut

obscene /əbˈsiːn/ [adj] **obscene** words or pictures are about sex and are very offensive: *'Lady Chatterley's Lover' was banned as an obscene book.* | *He was charged with smuggling obscene materials into the UK.*

dirty /ˈdɜːʳti/ [adj only before noun] informal **dirty** books, jokes, films etc are about sex – use this especially to show that you think these are unpleasant: *They just sit around telling dirty jokes – it's very boring.* | *He used to keep a collection of dirty books hidden under his bed.*

indecent /ɪnˈdiːsənt/ [adj] clothes that are **indecent** show parts of the body that are usually covered; actions or movements that are **indecent** are sexual, but in a way many people think is not pleasant or acceptable: *You can't wear that dress to the dinner party – it's positively indecent!* | *Models were forced into all sorts of indecent poses for the camera.*

lewd /luːd/ [adj] **lewd** remarks or behaviour show that the person saying them or doing something is thinking about sex, and they are usually offensive: *'Say no more!' he grinned, giving her a lewd wink.* | *Although his jokes were a little lewd, he always made us laugh.*

blue /bluː/ [adj] informal films, jokes etc that are **blue** are about sex and usually use offensive language: *I found the kids watching a blue movie on the video last night.* | *Her jokes are too blue for most audiences.*

filthy /ˈfɪlθi/ [adj] showing or describing sexual acts in a very offensive way: *The magazine printed filthy pictures that shocked everyone.*

off-color /ɒf ˈkʌləʳ/ [adj] American jokes, stories, remarks etc that are **off-color** talk about sex in a way that is not acceptable in a particular situation: *He occasionally tells an off-color joke, but his image is practically that of a saint.*

smut /smʌt/ [n U] informal books, stories, films etc that are about sex – use this when you strongly disapprove of this: *There's too much violence and smut on TV these days.*

18 books, jokes, remarks etc that are about sex in an amusing way

- risqué
- suggestive
- innuendo
- rude
- naughty

risqué ALSO **saucy** informal /ˈrɪskeɪ‖rɪˈskeɪ, ˈsɔːsi/ [adj] a joke, remark, song etc that is **risqué** or **saucy** is about sex and is slightly shocking and amusing: *Those jokes are a bit risqué – don't tell them in front of your grandparents.* | *Edgar kept us entertained with a stream of unusual and rather saucy stories.*

suggestive /səˈdʒestɪv‖səg-/ [adj] remarks, questions etc that are **suggestive** have a slightly hidden meaning that is about sex: *When she worked in the pub, men used to make suggestive remarks to her all the time.* | *The film 'Tom Jones' is famous for its sexually suggestive eating scene.*

innuendo /ˌɪnjuˈendəʊ/ [n C/U] remarks that are intended to make you think about sex even though they do not directly mention sex: *The programme consists of an hour of sexist banter and innuendo.* | *She found his relentless sexual innuendoes irritating.*

rude /ruːd/ [adj] British jokes, stories, songs etc that are **rude** deal with sex or parts of the body, especially in a slightly stupid way: *I don't want to hear any more of your rude jokes, Damien – shut up.* | *If you are going to tell the children some of your stories make sure they aren't too rude.*

naughty /ˈnɔːti‖ˈnɔːti, ˈnɑːti/ [adj] British spoken use this to describe magazines, pictures, songs etc that deal with sex in a rude, but not very serious, way: *Dennis sat on his bed reading a naughty magazine.* | *They were reading an American novel that seemed to have had all the naughty bits cut out.*

19 when someone talks about sex in an offensive way

- crude
- coarse
- vulgar

crude /kruːd/ [adj] someone who is **crude** talks about sex in a way that is direct and offensive, and is often deliberately trying to shock people: *The comedian wasn't funny at all; he was just crude and offensive.* | *She was worried that her husband's crude remarks might have upset some of the guests.*

coarse /kɔːʳs/ [adj] someone who is **coarse** is impolite and offensive in the way they talk about sex: *She tried to ignore his coarse jokes and crude innuendoes – he was obviously drunk.*

vulgar /ˈvʌlgəʳ/ [adj] someone who is **vulgar** or who makes **vulgar** jokes and remarks talks about sex in a very direct and offensive way: *He ruined the evening with his vulgar talk about women and about how much he could drink.*

sexy

RELATED WORDS

- to talk to someone in a way that shows you are attracted to them *see* **talk (9)**
- *see also* **sex, beautiful**

1 someone who is sexually attractive

- sexy
- attractive
- sex appeal
- desirable
- voluptuous
- alluring

sexy /ˈseksi/ [adj] sexually attractive to people, either because of your body, your good looks, or attractive personality: *Peter is strong, good looking, and very sexy.* | *The advertisement showed a sexy young woman in a short skirt standing beside a sports car.* | *Her flushed cheeks, wide eyes, and slightly opened mouth made her look sexy.* —**sexiness** [n U] *I think I was first attracted to her overt sexiness.*

attractive /əˈtræktɪv/ [adj] someone who is **attractive** has a personality or appearance that makes other people sexually attracted to them: *It's enough for me that my husband thinks I'm sexually attractive.* | **+ to** *I don't know what makes Jamie so attractive to women.* | **find sb attractive** (=think they are attractive) *She's very nice but I don't really find her attractive.*

sex appeal /ˈseks əˌpiːl/ [n U] someone's appearance, behaviour, or personality that makes them sexually attractive: *Tanya uses her sex appeal to get whatever she wants.* | **have sex appeal** *Barry's a really nice guy, but he has absolutely no sex appeal.*

desirable /dɪˈzaɪərəbəl/ [adj] formal someone who is **desirable** makes you feel sexually attracted to them: *Ray was still in good shape and far more desirable than most men his age.*

voluptuous /vəˈlʌptʃuəs/ [adj] a woman who is **voluptuous** has large breasts and an attractive, rounded body, so that men feel sexually attracted to her: *Everyone turned to look at Gordon and his voluptuous mistress as they entered the room.*

alluring /əˈljʊərɪŋ‖əˈlʊə-/ [adj] written a woman who is **alluring** attracts men in a sexual way, because she seems to be exciting and a little mysterious: *Helene was an alluring beauty whom few men could resist.* | *She was encouraged to use her feminine charms, to be coy and alluring.*

2 clothes, movements, remarks etc that are sexually attractive

- sexy
- sensual/sensuous
- provocative
- seductive
- suggestive
- be a turn-on

sexy /ˈseksi/ [adj] sexually attractive: *He's got a really deep sexy voice.* | *I think leather pants are really sexy.* | *Gabby dived into the pool leaving her sexy black dress draped over a chair.*

sensual/sensuous /ˈsenʃuəl, ˈsenʃuəs/ [adj] seeming to show strong sexual feelings and a desire for sexual pleasure: *Peter leaned forward and kissed the girl's sensual red lips.* | *The artist became obsessed by her strange, sensual beauty.* —**sensuality** /ˌsenʃuˈæləti/ [n U] *The sensuality of the woman's face was emphasized by her off-the-shoulder dress.*

provocative /prəˈvɒkətɪv‖-ˈvɑː-/ [adj] intended to make someone feel sexually excited: *The magazine is full of pictures of partially dressed women in provocative poses.* —**provocatively** [adv] *'Why don't you show me,' said Rhonda, parting her lips provocatively.*

seductive /sɪˈdʌktɪv/ [adj] very sexually attractive, and making you want to have sex, especially when you should not: *From across the room, I noticed that Philip was giving me a seductive stare.* —**seductively** [adv] *He sat down beside me and started whispering seductively in my ear.*

suggestive /səˈdʒestɪv‖səg-/ [adj] are intended to make you think about sex: *Several of the most sexually suggestive scenes have been cut from the film.* | *Victor winked at her, and his smile was so wickedly suggestive that Francesca blushed.* —**suggestively** [adv] *The young women were dancing suggestively to the music.*

be a turn-on /biː ə ˈtɜːʳn ɒn/ [v phrase] informal something that you think it is sexually exciting: *The sight of all those half-naked men may be a turn-on to some women, but I find it unappealing.*

3 not sexy

- be a turn-off
- sexless

be a turn-off /biː ə ˈtɜːʳn ɒf/ [v phrase] informal to be not at all sexually attractive: *I wish you wouldn't wear your socks in bed – it's such a turn-off.*

sexless /ˈseksləs/ [adj] British not sexually attractive, because of not having any strong male or female qualities: *I don't find him attractive at all, he's such a sexless lump.*

shake

1 when things shake

- shake
- rattle
- wobble
- vibrate
- shudder
- judder
- jolt

shake /ʃeɪk/ [v I] if something **shakes**, it makes very small quick movements from side to side or up and down: *Ed was playing his music so loud that the whole house shook.* | *Suddenly the ground beneath* *my feet began to shake.* | *The car slowed down, shook for a moment and then stopped.*

rattle /ˈrætl/ [v I] to shake and repeatedly hit against something else, making a continuous noise: *The windows were rattling in the wind.* | *I woke up to the sound of cups and plates rattling, and knew that Dad was already up.* —**rattle** [n singular] *Just then we heard the rattle of a key in the lock.*

wobble /ˈwɒbəl‖ˈwɑː-/ [v I] if something **wobbles**, it moves from side to side because it is not steady or not well balanced: *The chair wobbled under her weight and then fell over.* | *Jerry came in carrying a tray of glasses that were wobbling alarmingly.* —**wobbly** [adj] *Do you think this ladder's safe? It feels a bit wobbly.*

vibrate /vaɪˈbreɪt‖ˈvaɪbreɪt/ [v I] to shake continuously with very small, very fast movements, for example because of the effects of a very loud noise: *Some insects' wings vibrate so fast that the movement is invisible to the human eye.* | **+ to** *Everything in the room was vibrating to the beat of the drum.* —**vibration** /vaɪˈbreɪʃən/ [n C/U] *The movement and vibration of the car soon sent the children to sleep.*

shudder /ˈʃʌdəʳ/ [v I] if something such as a piece of machinery or a vehicle **shudders**, it shakes uncontrollably with very small movements: *Our house was so close to the railway that you could feel it shudder every time a train went by.* | **shudder to a halt** (=shake a lot and then stop) *The train shuddered to a halt at the station.* —**shudder** [n C] *A series of shudders went through the ship as the mine exploded.*

judder /ˈdʒʌdəʳ/ [v I] especially British if something **judders**, it shakes with small, quick movements, especially because something is stopping it moving freely or smoothly: *Jackson took his Land Rover off the track and it juddered over 15 metres of grass.* | *The elevator doors juddered open when we reached the fifth floor.* | **judder to a halt** (=shake a lot and then stop) *Something was obviously wrong with the car and eventually it just juddered to a halt.* —**judder** [n C] *With a final judder, the car stopped altogether.*

jolt /dʒəʊlt/ [v I] to move up and down or from side to side with sudden large movements – use this especially about a vehicle or machine that is not working well or moving smoothly: *Our coach jolted and stopped. Then it started again.* | **+ along/over/through etc** *He ran down the hill, the backpack jolting from side to side on his back.* | **jolt to a halt/stop** *Everyone was alarmed when the elevator jolted to a halt.* —**jolt** [n C] *The train stopped with a sudden jolt.*

2 when your body, hand etc shakes

- shake
- tremble
- shiver
- shudder
- twitch
- quiver
- convulsion

▸ *see also* **cold, frightened/frightening, nervous**

shake /ʃeɪk/ [v I] if you **shake**, your body makes small quick uncontrolled movements, for example because you are frightened, nervous, or angry: *My hands were shaking so much I could hardly write my name on the exam paper.* | **shake with fear/anger/laughter etc** (=shake because you are frightened, angry etc) *The others were all shaking with laughter.*

tremble /ˈtrembəl/ [v I] to shake very slightly, especially because you are frightened or upset: *Jane's lip began to tremble and I though she was going to cry.* | *The dog sat trembling in a corner.* | **tremble with anger/emotion/fear etc** *Polly hid behind the door, trembling with fear.*

shiver /ˈʃɪvəʳ/ [v I] to shake because you are cold, or because of an emotion such as fear: *Julia shivered and pulled her coat more tightly around her.* | *You're shivering! Do you want to go indoors?* | **shiver with excitement/fear/horror etc** *Lizzy looked out at the thick snow and shivered with excitement.* —**shiver** [n C] *'It's freezing!' Tom said with a shiver.* | **send a shiver down your spine** (=make you shiver because you are frightened) *The story he told me sent a shiver down my spine.*

shudder /ˈʃʌdəʳ/ [v I] to shake uncontrollably for a short moment, especially because the idea of something is very unpleasant or upsetting: *Dave tried to kiss Julia but she shuddered and turned away.* | *I shuddered to think of my son all alone in New York.* —**shudder** [n C] *'I can't even stand to be in the same room as him!' she said with a shudder.*

twitch /twɪtʃ/ [v I] if a part of your body **twitches**, it makes a very small, sudden movement, especially when you do not want this to happen but you cannot control it: *Mac was very nervous. A muscle on his face began to twitch.* | *Roberta's mouth twitched as she tried to stop herself laughing out loud.* —**twitch** [n C] *A twitch of anxiety crossed my father's face.*

quiver /ˈkwɪvəʳ/ [v I] to shake so slightly that it is difficult for other people to notice, especially because you are very excited, nervous, or angry: *John's hands were quivering as he put down his papers and started his speech.* | **quiver with anger/excitement/fear etc** *The children stood there quivering with excitement as I opened the package.*

convulsion /kənˈvʌlʃən/ [n C usually plural] when your body shakes violently and uncontrollably because you are very ill **have convulsions** *The baby was sweating and crying. She started to have convulsions again.* | **go into convulsions** *Andrew died after taking the drug, which had caused him to go into convulsions.*

3 to make something shake

- shake
- make sth shake
- give sth a shake
- agitate

shake /ʃeɪk/ [v T] to make something move up and down or from side to side with small quick movements: *Shake the bottle before you open it.* | *She shook the blanket to get rid of all the dust.* | *The huge explosion shook houses up to five miles away.*

make sth shake /ˌmeɪk (sth) ˈʃeɪk/ [v phrase] to make a place or object shake – use this especially about loud noises or strong movements or explosions: *The music was so loud that it made the floor shake.* | *Every time a train passed it made the whole house shake.*

give sth a shake /ˌɡɪv (sth) ə ˈʃeɪk/ [v phrase] especially British to hold something and shake it a few times: *I gave the box a shake to see if there was anything inside.* | *Martha took the tablecloth outside and gave it a good shake.*

agitate /ˈædʒəteɪt/ [v T] to shake a liquid quickly – use this especially in technical or scientific contexts: *Mix the two solutions together and agitate the bottle.*

4 to shake a part of your body

- shake
- wiggle
- waggle
- wag

shake /ʃeɪk/ [v T] *Brad got up and shook his legs to get all the grass off.* | *She shook her long blonde* *hair.* | **shake your head** (=move your head from side to side as a way of saying 'no') *Mom shook her head. 'You can't go out again at this time of night.'* | **shake your fist (at sb)** (=shake your closed hand in front of someone as a way of showing that you are angry) *'Women drivers!' the truck driver yelled, shaking his fist at me.*

wiggle /ˈwɪgəl/ [v T] to move your toes, fingers, bottom etc with a series of small movements: *Karen sat in front of the fire and wiggled her toes.* | *Marilyn Monroe was able to wiggle her hips in a way that drove men wild.*

waggle /ˈwægəl/ [v T] **British** to move part of your body, especially your bottom, legs, or toes, from side to side or up and down, with fairly large movements: *The children were told to lie on their backs and waggle their legs in the air.* | *I've always wanted to be able to waggle my ears.*

wag /wæg/ [v T] if a dog **wags** its tail, it moves its tail from side to side; if a person **wags** their finger or head, they shake it repeatedly, especially in order to show that they do not like something that someone has done: *A dog wags its tail in order to show friendliness and pleasure.* | *'You shouldn't have done that!' Mum said, wagging her finger at me.*

5 to shake hands as a greeting

- shake hands

▸ *see also* **meet, hello**

shake hands /ˌʃeɪk ˈhændz/ [v phrase] if two people **shake hands**, they each hold the other person's hand and move it up and down with their own, as a polite or formal greeting: *The two leaders shook hands and walked into the White House.* | **+ with** *The picture shows him shaking hands with the Prime Minister.*

shape

RELATED WORDS

▸ *see also* **circle**

1 the shape of something or someone

- shape
- form
- figure
- silhouette
- profile
- outline
- contour
- lines

shape /ʃeɪp/ [n C/U] the **shape** that something is, for example a square, a circle etc: *You can get pasta in lots of different shapes.* | *What shape is the swimming pool?* | *The fruits are similar in shape and size to plums.* | *The desks form a U-shape, so that the teacher can interact easily with the students.* | *The pool was custom built, it is an unusual shape.* | *If a mole changes color or shape, see a doctor.*

form /fɔːʳm/ [n C] the shape of something – use this especially to talk about art or when the shape is not very clear: *Sleeping forms lay in groups and rows on the earth floor.* | *The painting consists of a series of interlocking forms.*

figure /ˈfɪgəʳ‖ˈfɪgjər/ [n C] the shape of a person: *There were figures painted on the walls of the cave.* | *Dark figures emerged from the building, and disappeared into the night.* | **+ of** *I saw the figure of a woman below the bridge.*

silhouette /ˌsɪluˈet/ [n C] the dark shape of something or someone seen against a bright background: *The trees were silhouettes in the morning fog.* | **+ of** *I saw the silhouette of someone waiting under the streetlight.*

profile /ˈprəʊfaɪl/ [n C] the shape of someone's face when seen from the side: *an artist's sketch of McMillan's profile* | *He sat by the window, his handsome profile outlined against the sky.* | **in profile** *They showed her a photo of a young brunette, taken in profile.*

outline /ˈaʊtlaɪn/ [n C] a line around the edge of something that shows its shape **+ of** *The outline of a footprint was visible in the snow.* | *On the envelopes had been stamped the outlines of Santa Claus, holly, and a reindeer.*

contour /ˈkɒntʊəʳ‖ˈkɑːn-/ [n C] the outer shape of something, that has a lot of curves, especially an area of land or a person's body: *The seat is adjustable to fit the contours of your back.* | *A topographical map shows the contours of the earth's surface.*

lines /laɪnz/ [n plural] the outer shape of something long or tall, especially something that looks very graceful or attractive: *The dress's flowing lines are attractive on most women.* | **+ of** *He noticed the long, slim lines of her legs beneath the colorful cotton skirt.*

2 having a particular shape

- be round/square/rectangular etc
- shaped
- in the shape of sth

be round/square/rectangular etc /biː ˈraʊnd/ [v phrase] use this to say what shape something is: *The windows were round, like the windows on a ship.* | *'What shape is the table?' 'It's long and rectangular.'* | **be round/square etc in shape** *There was another building, octagonal in shape, close by.*

shaped /ʃeɪpt/ [adj] use this to say that something has the same shape as something else **star-shaped/heart-shaped/L-shaped etc** *He gave me a necklace with a heart-shaped locket.* | *Gus lived in an apartment in a U-shaped courtyard.* | **+ like** *On the table were salt and pepper shakers shaped like teddy bears.*

in the shape of sth /ɪn ðə ˈʃeɪp əv (sth)/ [prep] use this to say that something has the same shape as something else: *a beautiful blue bowl in the shape of a flower* | *There was a big chocolate cake in the shape of a heart on the main table.*

3 having a strange or wrong shape

- deformed
- distorted
- misshapen
- lopsided
- lose its shape

deformed /dɪˈfɔːʳmd/ [adj] something that is **deformed**, especially part of a living thing, has the wrong shape, usually because it has grown or developed wrongly: *She had survived polio, but her right leg was weak and deformed.* | *The desert plants were strange deformed bushes with bizarrely twisted branches.* —**deformity** [n C/U] *The drug was shown to cause deformity in a high proportion of babies born to mothers taking it.*

distorted /dɪˈstɔːʳtɪ̬d/ [adj] something that is **distorted** has been twisted out of its correct or original shape: *As a result of the crash, the remains of the vehicles were distorted out of all recognition.* | *After* *treatment, her distorted hip had straightened, so that her legs were the same length.*

misshapen /ˌmɪsˈʃeɪpən, mɪˈʃeɪ-/ [adj] having the wrong shape, usually because of growing that way over a long period of time: *The old woman's fingers were misshapen and useless.* | *Misshapen carrots and potatoes were fed to the pigs.*

lopsided /ˌlɒpˈsaɪdəd◂‖ˌlɑːp-/ [adj] something that is **lopsided** does not have the same shape on each side, for example because one side is higher than the other: *She gave me a lopsided smile.* | *a note written in a child's lopsided handwriting* | *His whole face was lopsided, one cheek badly scarred.*

lose its shape /ˌluːz ɪts ˈʃeɪp/ [v phrase] especially British if something such as a hat, coat, or skirt **loses its shape**, it becomes the wrong shape because it has been worn a lot: *His battered old hat had completely lost its shape.* | *She was wearing an old jumper that had lost its shape.*

4 having no clear or exact shape

- shapeless
- amorphous

shapeless /ˈʃeɪpləs/ [adj] something, especially a piece of clothing, that is **shapeless** has no clear or definite shape, and often looks unattractive: *He was wearing a shapeless grey coat which really did not fit him.* | *People trudged on, carrying shapeless bundles full of clothes or bedding.*

amorphous /əˈmɔːʳfəs/ [adj] formal having no definite shape that can be described or recognized because everything you can see is unclear or is mixed together: *The molten rock hardens into amorphous forms.* | *In her later works, large, amorphous shapes seem to float on the canvas.*

5 having a regular shape

- regular
- symmetrical

regular /ˈregjələʳ/ [adj] evenly shaped with parts or sides of equal size: *Draw a regular hexagon with 90 mm sides.* | *She was attractive rather than beautiful, with regular features and dark hair.*

symmetrical /sɪˈmetrɪkəl/ [adj] if something is **symmetrical**, its two halves, on either side of a central line, are exactly alike: *The leaves of most trees are symmetrical in shape.* | *Palladio built the Villa Rotunda following a symmetrical plan.* —**symmetry** /ˈsɪmətri/ [n U] *the delicate symmetry of a snowflake*

6 having a shape that is not regular

- irregular
- asymmetrical

irregular /ɪˈregjələʳ/ [adj] unevenly shaped with parts or sides of unequal size: *Lake Powell's irregular coastline has many unspoiled beaches and secluded inlets.* | *I recognized the doctor's messy, irregular handwriting.* —**irregularly** [adj] *a large, irregularly shaped room*

asymmetrical /ˌeɪsəˈmetrɪkəl/ [adj] if something is **asymmetrical**, one half of it is not the same as the other – used in formal and technical contexts: *The design of the house is consciously asymmetrical with a large tower at one end.*

share

1 to use something with another person

- share
- shared
- pool
- communal

share /ʃeəʳ/ [v I/T] if two or more people **share** something, they all use it together or all have the right to use it: *We don't have enough books, so some of you will have to share.* | *I have my own room, but we share the kitchen and bathroom.* | **share sth with sb** *You could share a taxi with me if you like.* | **+ with** *If two adults share with two children under 16* (=share a room), *the children stay free.*

pool /puːl/ [v T] **pool your ideas/money/resources etc** if people **pool** their ideas etc, they put them together so that everyone can use them and gain from them: *Why don't we get together and pool our ideas?* | *If we all pool our money I'm sure we'll have enough to buy her a present.*

shared /ʃeəʳd/ [adj usually before noun] used by two or more people: *Eventually, Tim, Laura, and Ann moved into a shared house.* | *Many drug addicts become infected with HIV by using shared needles.* | *The problem with having a shared telephone is that someone else always seems to be using it.*

communal /ˈkɒmjənəl, kəˈmjuː-‖ˈkɑː-/ [adj usually before noun] shared by a group of people who live together: *There are four bedrooms in the house, and a large communal kitchen.* | *The college has communal dining rooms, nurseries and clinics.*

2 to do something with another person

- share
- alternate
- take it in turns/take turns

share /ʃeəʳ/ [v T] if two people **share** a job or activity, they each do a part of it: *Judy and I shared the driving, so it wasn't too tiring.* | **share sth with sb** *She shares the job with another woman who also has a young child.*

take it in turns/take turns /ˌteɪk ɪt ɪn ˈtɜːʳnz, ˌteɪk ˈtɜːʳnz/ [v phrase] if two or more people **take it in turns** or **take turns** to do something, they do it one after the other, and each person does it several times: *If the housework is too much for one person, why don't you take it in turns?* | **+ to do sth** *Everyone took turns to patrol the streets at night.* | **+ (at/in) doing sth** *We took turns sitting in the front seat.* | *Reading need not be a solitary activity. Students can take turns in reading aloud.*

alternate /ˈɔːltɜːʳneɪt/ [v I] if two people **alternate**, one person does something one time and the other person does it the next time, changing regularly: *You'll have to alternate. One of you can use the room in the mornings, and the other in the evenings.* | *The class has two teachers who alternate on a weekly basis.*

3 to divide something so that two or more people get a part of it

- share/share out
- split
- divide/divide up
- distribute
- redistribute
- carve up

share/share out /ʃeəʳ, ˌʃeər ˈaʊt/ [v T/phr v T] to divide something so that several people have a part of it: *We agreed that we would share the prize money if we won.* | **share sth among/between sb** *She shared the cake between the children.* | **share out sth** *Profits from the sale of tickets were shared out among the members of the band.* | **share sth out** *We'll share what's left out between the three of us.*

split /splɪt/ [v T] if a small number of people **split** something, especially money, they divide it into equal parts and take a part each: *They planned to rob a bank, split the money, and leave the country.* | **split sth among/between sb** *He said that the land should be split between his four sons.* | **split sth two/three/four etc ways** (=to divide something between two, three etc people) *I think we should split whatever we get four ways.*

divide/divide up /dɪˈvaɪd, dɪˌvaɪd ˈʌp/ [v T/phr v T] to separate something into two or more parts **divide sth between sb** *Hitler and Stalin agreed to divide Poland between them.* | **divide up sth/divide sth up between sb** *We divided up the rest of the pie between us.* | **divide up sth/divide sth up** *Have you decided how you're going to divide up the money?*

distribute /dɪˈstrɪbjuːt/ [v T] to share something such as wealth or power among different people, groups, or organizations: *We must try to distribute the country's wealth so that we help those who need it most.* | *The party's aim is to distribute power more evenly among the people.*

redistribute /ˌriːdɪˈstrɪbjuːt/ [v T] to share something, especially money, in a different way from before, so that more people have a fair share of it: *The socialists are committed to redistributing wealth.* | *The tax will be collected nationally and the money raised will be redistributed to local authorities.*

carve up /ˌkɑːʳv ˈʌp/ [phr v T] if two or more people, organizations, or countries **carve** something **up**, especially land or a company belonging to someone else, they divide it into separate parts and share it between them **carve up sth** *The British and French carved up the Ottoman Empire at the end of World War I.* | **carve sth up** *The two companies wanted to acquire the business and carve it up.*

4 to share the cost of something

- share
- split
- go halves

share /ʃeəʳ/ [v T] *We pay rent separately, but we share the other bills.* | *It's only fair that they should share the running costs of the car.*

split /splɪt/ [v T] to share the cost of something between two people or groups **split sth between/with sb** *We decided to split the bill between us.* | *The US is hoping to split the cost of developing the new plane with Japan.* | **split sth down the middle** (=each person pays half) *At first, her earnings were split down the middle with her agent.*

go halves /gəʊ ˈhɑːvz‖-ˈhævz/ [v phrase] if two people **go halves**, they each pay half of the cost of something they are buying together: *If the wine is expensive, we can go halves.* | **go halves with sb (on sth)** *Why don't you go halves with him on the cost of the trip?*

5 the part of something that someone gets or owns

- share
- allocation
- cut
- portion
- slice of the cake
- stake

share /ʃeəʳ/ [n C] the part of something that one person gets or owns when something is shared between several people: *If your grandfather left any money, you will get your share.* | **+ of** *Wilson's share of the business is worth $500,000.* | **+ in** *An Australian businessman has bought a 10 percent share in the project.*

allocation /ˌæləˈkeɪʃən/ [n C] the share of something, especially money, that has been officially given to a person or an organization: *The allocation for atomic research has been doubled.* | *Schools will be given cash allocations per student.* | *Special ticket allocations were made for members of the company and their guests.*

cut /kʌt/ [n singular] informal someone's share of something, especially money: *How much is my cut going to be?* | *The distributors and the wholesalers all get their cut, and this is what pushes up the price.* | **+ of** *Investigators found that her cut of the profits amounted to more than 25%.*

portion /ˈpɔːʳʃən/ [n C] a part of something that is divided into different parts, especially equal parts: *The money should be shared out in equal portions between all members of the family.* | *Most of the profit goes to the retailer; some goes to the middleman, and the remaining portion goes to the producer.* | **+ of** *A major portion of the budget is spent on defence.*

slice of the cake /ˌslaɪs əv ðə ˈkeɪk/ [n phrase] a share of something such as a company's profits or the sales of a product that someone wants to get, or believes they have a right to: *Since the company's announcement of record profits, workers are demanding a bigger slice of the cake.* | *By building cars in Britain, Toyota aim to win an even larger slice of the cake.*

stake /steɪk/ [n C] a large or important part of something that you own or pay for, especially when this involves some risk **+ in** *China has a major stake in the project.* | *She went into business by acquiring a stake in a copper mine in Australia.* | *The American investor boosted his stake in the company to 15%.*

sharp

RELATED WORDS

▸ *see also* **cut, end (4)**

1 sharp

- sharp
- razor-sharp
- pointed
- jagged
- spiky
- prickly

sharp /ʃɑːʳp/ [adj] something that is **sharp** can easily cut things or make holes in them, because it has a very narrow blade or point: *Be careful. That knife's very sharp.* | *You'll need some sharp scissors.* | *Puppies mean to be playful, but their sharp teeth can give you a nasty bite.*

razor-sharp /ˈreɪzəʳ ʃɑːʳp/ [adj] extremely sharp and possibly dangerous: *His sword was a wicked weapon, three feet in length and razor-sharp.* | *Over millions of years, some of the reptiles developed razor-sharp teeth.*

pointed /ˈpɔɪntɪ̣d/ [adj] long, thin, and ending in a point: *He picked up a pointed stick and began drawing in the sand.* | *a plant with long pointed leaves*

jagged /ˈdʒægɪ̣d/ [adj] having an irregular edge with a lot of sharp points: *Many ships have been torn apart on the jagged rocks that ring the shoreline.* | *The window had gone, and the floor was covered with jagged pieces of glass.*

spiky /ˈspaɪki/ [adj] having a lot of points: *He had a leather jacket and short, spiky hair.* | *Some corals are quite smooth, others are sharp and spiky.* | *a spiky cactus plant*

prickly /ˈprɪkli/ [adj] something that is **prickly**, especially a plant, is covered in a lot of sharp points: *Keep prickly plants and bushes away from any paths and seats in the garden.* | *Sea urchins and starfish feel prickly to the touch.*

2 to make something sharp

- sharpen

sharpen /ˈʃɑːʳpən/ [v T] *Nick sat down at his desk, sharpened his pencil and began to draw.* | *My mother used a special stone to sharpen kitchen knives.*

3 not sharp

- blunt

blunt /blʌnt/ [adj] *I cut myself shaving with a blunt razor.* | *It's difficult to achieve a good result if you use blunt tools.* | *a blunt pencil* | **a blunt instrument** (=something not sharp used as a weapon) *Police say the victim was hit with a blunt instrument, possibly a hammer.*

shine/shiny

RELATED WORDS

- *see also* **bright, light, clean, reflect**

1 when light comes from the sun, a lamp, a surface etc

- shine
- glow
- gleam
- blaze
- flash
- flicker
- blink

shine /ʃaɪn/ [v I] if the sun, a lamp etc **shines**, it sends out bright light: *It wasn't very warm, but at least the sun was shining.* | *She could see the lights of Hong Kong shining in the distance.* | *A light shone in a window of one of the houses.* | **+ in/on** *Could you move that lamp? It's shining right in my eyes.* | **shine brightly** *The streetlights shone brightly and the sidewalks were filled with people.*

glow /gləʊ/ [v I] to make a warm soft light that is not very bright: *The evening sun glowed in the sky.* | *A few lumps of coal still glowed in the fire.* | *The windows were glowing with a warm, yellow light.* —**glow** [n singular] **+ of** *There faces were lit by the warm glow of the fire.*

gleam /gliːm/ [v I] to shine brightly, especially by throwing back light off a very smooth surface: *A Rolls Royce was parked outside, gleaming in the sunshine.* | *The floors gleamed, and the house smelled sweetly of soap and fresh air.* | *The old walnut dining table gleamed under the chandelier.* | **+ with** *On his left was the galley, a tiny kitchen gleaming with stainless steel.* —**gleaming** [adj] *In the candlelight, Nula's gleaming hair fell like silk on her shoulders.* —**gleam** [n singular] **+ of** *I heard the back door of the house open, and saw the gleam of a lantern.*

blaze /bleɪz/ [v I] to give off an extremely bright light: *The midday sun blazed down on us.* | *The windows of the cathedral were blazing with coloured light.* | *Lights blazed in every room in the house.* —**blazing** [adj only before noun] *A line of camels moved across the dunes under a blazing sky.* —**blaze** [n singular] **+ of** *The rabbit stopped, caught in the blaze of the car's headlights.*

flash /flæʃ/ [v I/T] to shine brightly for a very short time, or make something do this: *Lightning flashed across the sky.* | *A police car sped through the intersection, lights flashing.* | **flash sth at/toward/into sb/sth** *Why did that guy flash his headlights at me?* —**flash** [n C] *There was a bright flash of light as the bomb exploded.*

flicker /ˈflɪkəʳ/ [v I] use this about a weak flame or light that keeps becoming almost dark, so that it seems to be soon going to stop shining: *The candle flickered a few times and then went out.* | *The lights flickered; I wondered if we were about to lose our power.*

blink /blɪŋk/ [v I] if a light on a machine **blinks**, it goes on and off, especially in order to make you notice something: *When I got in, the message light on my answering machine was blinking.* | *The neon lights on the theater blinked red and blue.*

2 to shine with small bright points of light

- sparkle
- twinkle
- glitter
- shimmer
- glisten

sparkle /ˈspɑːʳkəl/ [v I] if something such as a jewel, water, or ice **sparkles**, it shines with many small, bright points of light, especially under the light: *She wore a diamond necklace, which sparkled in the light of the fire.* | *Dwayne's eyes sparkled as he laughed.* | *When the sun came up, the snow sparkled as if it were studded with millions of diamonds.* —**sparkling** [adj only before noun] *a pair of beautiful sparkling earrings*

twinkle /ˈtwɪŋkəl/ [v I] if something such as a light, or a star **twinkles**, it shines in the dark or under the light with small points of light: *The lights of the town twinkled faintly in the distance.* | *Over her shoulder, the stars twinkled in the black sky.*

glitter /ˈglɪtəʳ/ [v I] if something such as a jewel, a star, or ice **glitters**, it shines attractively, especially under the light, with very bright, small points of light: *The frost glittered on the ground.* | *Jewels glittered in the dim light of the cave.* | *The chandelier glittered, its crystal teardrops like small golden suns.*

shimmer /ˈʃɪməʳ/ [v I] especially written to shine with a soft light that seems to move very slightly and very quickly up and down or from side to side: *When he moved, his silk green shirt shimmered.* | *The lake shimmered in the moonlight.*

glisten /ˈglɪsən/ [v I] if something **glistens**, it shines because it is wet or oily and shines the light back from its surface: *The grey roofs glistened after the rain.* | **+ with** *When we finished the set, Katie's face was red and glistening with sweat.*

3 when something shines in the dark

- luminous
- fluorescent
- glow in the dark
- Day-Glo

luminous /ˈluːmɪ̇nəs/ [adj] something that is **luminous** shines in the dark, especially because it is made from or painted with a substance that shines: *It's a good idea to paint your bike with luminous paint so that you are more visible to motorists.* | *He couldn't tell what time it was since his watch didn't have a luminous dial.*

fluorescent /flʊəˈresənt‖flʊə-, flɔː-/ [adj] made from a very brightly coloured material which throws back light from its surface very strongly, and can easily be seen: *If you plan to jog along roadsides, it's a good idea to wear at least one article of fluorescent clothing.* | *I'm sorry, but fluorescent green socks are just not suitable for a job interview.*

glow in the dark /ˌgləʊ ɪn ðə ˈdɑːʳk/ [v phrase] something that **glows in the dark** gives off a continuous soft light and can be easily seen when it is dark, especially because it is covered in special paint: *One of the children was playing with a yo-yo which glowed in the dark.* | *Outside the cathedral, vendors were selling small statues of the Virgin which glowed in the dark.*

Day-Glo /ˈdeɪ gləʊ/ [adj] trademark having a very bright orange, green, yellow, or pink color: *Dickie was dressed in a Day-Glo orange vest, jeans and running shoes.* | *Outside the club, a woman was handing out day-glo green fliers.*

4 having a surface that shines

- shiny
- glossy
- sleek
- silky
- polished
- gleaming
- shimmering
- glistening

shiny /ˈʃaɪni/ [adj] *She wore a fashionable jacket and high shiny boots.* | *At 7:30 p.m. sharp, a shiny limousine pulled in front of the building.* | *To keep the surface shiny, apply a clear, high-gloss varnish.*

glossy /ˈglɒsi‖ˈglɔːsi, ˈglɑːsi/ [adj] **glossy** hair or fur looks shiny and healthy; **glossy** magazines and books use expensive shiny paper: *She stroked the horse's long glossy neck.* | *There was a stack of glossy magazines on the coffee table.*

sleek /sliːk/ [adj] hair or fur that is **sleek** is shiny and smooth, especially because it is in good condition: *The cat purred as Ben stroked its sleek fur.* | *Linda looked wonderful at the party; her hair was long and sleek, her make-up perfect.*

silky /ˈsɪlki/ [adj] hair, material etc that is **silky** is soft and smooth to touch and looks shiny: *You're so lucky to have such lovely, silky hair.* | *Her skirt and jacket were made of smooth, silky fabric.*

polished /ˈpɒlɪʃt‖ˈpɑː-/ [adj] something such as wood, metal, or stone that is **polished** has been made shiny by being rubbed: *Her nails were beautifully shaped and polished.* | *a polished oak floor*

gleaming /ˈgliːmɪŋ/ [adj] **gleaming** objects or vehicles are shiny because they are very new or clean: *Every surface in the kitchen was polished and gleaming.* | *A gleaming Harley Davidson motorcycle stood parked outside the bar.*

shimmering /ˈʃɪmərɪŋ/ [adj only before noun] shining with a soft, unsteady light: *They looked out across the shimmering water of the lagoon.* | *Gabby pulled a shimmering gold evening dress out of a box and held it in front of her.*

glistening /ˈglɪsənɪŋ/ [adj only before noun] shining like something that is wet: *His glistening bald head moved from side to side in time to the music.* | *The harpoon sank into the whale's glistening skin.*

5 having a surface that shines like metal

- metallic
- silvery

metallic /mɪ̇ˈtælɪk/ [adj usually before noun] **metallic** paint shines like metal **metallic blue/green/purple etc** *There was a metallic grey VW Golf parked outside cabin fifteen.*

silvery /ˈsɪlvəri/ [adj] shiny with a colour like silver: *Small silvery fish darted through the shallow water of the creek.* | *The hills looked silvery in the moonlight.*

6 the shiny appearance of something

- shine
- sheen
- gloss
- lustre

shine /ʃaɪn/ [n singular] *They polished their boots to a dazzling shine.* | *Linseed oil helps restore the shine to a dull surface.*

sheen /ʃiːn/ [n singular] a soft, smooth, shiny appearance: *Her elegant dress had a silver sheen.* | **+ of** *A light sheen of perspiration covered his upper lip.*

gloss /glɒs‖glɔːs, glɑːs/ [n singular] the shiny appearance of something that is of good quality or in good condition: *The gel is guaranteed to add gloss even to the dullest hair.* | *Stephanie did not look well. The gloss had gone from her blond hair and her skin was splotchy looking.* | **high gloss** (=a very shiny gloss) *The silverware had been polished to a high gloss.*

lustre British **/luster** American /ˈlʌstəʳ/ [n U] written a soft, attractive, shiny appearance: *Autumn had given the trees that extra golden lustre.* | *The herb can be used as a hair rinse to add luster.* | *Wax is sprayed on the apples to give them more luster.*

7 not shiny

- dull
- matt
- tarnished

dull /dʌl/ [adj] a colour or surface that is **dull** is not bright or shiny: *Her hair was a dull, darkish brown.* | *They chose a red clay pot decorated with patterns in dull white paint.*

matt ALSO **matte** American /mæt/ [adj only before noun] **matt surface/paint/finish etc** a **matt** surface is designed not to be shiny – use this about paint, skin, surfaces etc that you do not want to be shiny: *Do you want matt paint or gloss paint?* | *When you drop off the photos, be sure to request matte finish.*

tarnished /ˈtɑːʳnɪʃt/ [adj] no longer shiny – use this about bright metals such as silver: *He wore a tarnished watch chain across his waistcoat.* | *You shouldn't let the silverware get so tarnished.*

shocked/shocking

RELATED WORDS

- *see also* **surprised/surprising, frightened/frightening, suddenly, upset, horrible**

1 surprised and upset because something bad has happened

- shocked
- horrified
- appalled
- devastated/shattered
- traumatized
- be in a state of shock
- shaken/shaken up
- aghast

shocked /ʃɒkt‖ʃɑːkt/ [adj] *I was shocked when I saw the size of the telephone bill.* | *Everyone seemed really shocked when I told them I'd started smoking.* | **+ (that)** *I'm shocked that you've let things get this far.* | **+ at** *I was shocked at the change in his appearance.* | *Gabby was shocked by how unpleasant they were to their mother.* | **be shocked to hear/learn/find sth etc** *We were shocked to hear about Brian's heart attack – he's so young.* | *When I returned, I was shocked to discover that Rod had lost his job.* | **deeply shocked** (=very shocked) *We were deeply shocked to hear of the baby's death.*

horrified /ˈhɒrɪfaɪd‖ˈhɔː-, ˈhɑː-/ [adj] extremely shocked by something very unpleasant or frightening that has happened: *Horrified passengers saw the man fall under the train.* | *There was a horrified look on his face.* | **+ by** *The Prime Minister issued a statement saying he was 'shocked and horrified' by the massacre.*

appalled /əˈpɔːld/ [adj not before noun] very shocked by something that is very bad or unpleasant **+ by** *I knew everyone in the room was appalled by my behaviour, but I didn't care.* | *Appalled at the state of the kitchen, she set about scrubbing away the layers of grime and grease.* | **+ that** *We're absolutely appalled that the newspapers can freely make allegations about this company.* | **appalled to hear/see/ find out etc** *I was appalled to learn that a serial killer was running a drugs operation in a high-security prison.*

devastated/shattered /ˈdevəsteɪtɪd, ˈʃætəʳd/ [adj] so shocked and upset by something terrible that has happened that you cannot continue with your life: *Without warning, my husband moved out, leaving me so shattered I couldn't continue.* | **+ by** *I went back to my motel, devastated by the news of her death.*

traumatized ALSO **traumatised** British /ˈtrɔːmətaɪzd/ [adj] if someone is **traumatized** by a bad event or experience, it badly affects the way they behave or react to things for a long time afterwards: *The attack on her in August 1990 had left her traumatized and unable to leave the house.* | *a frightened, traumatized child* | **+ by** *Some students were traumatized by the anatomy classes, while others were unaffected.*

be in a state of shock /biː ɪn ə ˌsteɪt əv ˈʃɒk‖-ˈʃɑːk/ [v phrase] to feel very shocked by something, so that you cannot do things properly or talk about things clearly for a long time afterwards: *Two days after the earthquake, many people were still in a state of shock.* | *He arrived at my house in a state of shock, unable to tell me clearly what had happened.*

shaken/shaken up /ˈʃeɪkən, ˌʃeɪkən ˈʌp/ [adj not usually before noun] shocked and feeling weak and nervous, because something very unpleasant or frightening has happened: *He was pulled from the wreckage of the car, alive but very shaken.* | *The fire in the hotel was not very serious but everyone was shaken up by it.* | **+ by** *She was visibly shaken by the severity of her sentence, and left the court in tears.* | **badly shaken** *She was badly shaken by the attack and found it difficult to describe her ordeal to the police.*

aghast /əˈgɑːst‖əˈgæst/ [adj not before noun] written very shocked by something that you have just been told or have found out about: *'Ten thousand pounds!' she said, aghast.* | *Some of the Republican policies have left feminists dismayed and aghast.* | **+ at** *Mr Sullivan seemed aghast at the prospect of losing his only daughter to this arrogant young man.*

2 so shocked that you show it in your behaviour or appearance

- speechless
- stunned
- dazed
- gobsmacked

speechless /ˈspiːtʃləs/ [adj not before noun] so shocked, angry, upset etc that you cannot speak: *The chairman was speechless when he heard that he had been dismissed.* | *Almost speechless, her mother managed to gasp out, 'And how long has this been going on?'* | **leave sb speechless** *Her children's behaviour is sometimes so bad that it leaves her speechless.* | **speechless with rage/ horror/shock etc** *I didn't answer. I was speechless with rage.* | *The little girl seemed speechless with terror.* | **I'm speechless** spoken (=used to say how shocked or surprised you are) *Well, I'm speechless Anna. I really don't know what to say.*

stunned /stʌnd/ [adj] so shocked that you are unable to react immediately: *The news of his brother's death left him too stunned to speak.* | *Canada was completely stunned by the shooting, for it thinks of itself as a peaceful, gentle nation.* | *She looked pale and stunned – it was clear that something awful had happened.* | **+ by** *His brother seemed stunned by the verdict.* | **stunned silence** (=when people stop talking, because something shocking has happened) *After a stunned silence, Peggy added, 'And I'm not going to change my mind.'*

dazed /deɪzd/ [adj] very shocked and unable to think clearly or do anything to improve the situation: *I stumbled from the office, feeling dazed and confused, and not really knowing where I was.* | *He stood there with a dazed expression on his face watching her pack her bags.* | **+ by** *Daphne is in hospital, still dazed by the events of the last ten days.*

gobsmacked /ˈgɒbsmækt‖ˈgɑːb-/ [adj] British spoken so shocked that you cannot speak for a short time: *'Do you feel surprised by your win?' 'Gobsmacked would be closer to the truth.'*

3 to make someone feel shocked

- shock
- come as a shock (to sb)
- stun
- knock/throw sb for a loop
- shake sb up
- rock

shock /ʃɒk‖ʃɑːk/ [v I/T not in progressive] to make someone feel very surprised and upset: *What really shocked me was that no-one seemed to care about all the beggars.* | **it shocks sb to see/realize/hear etc** *It shocked us to see how ill she looked.* | **shock sb into**

doing sth *I just felt I had to shock her into taking some action.* | **shock sb into sth** *My father was shocked into silence.*

come as a shock (to sb) /ˌkʌm əz ə ˈʃɒk (tə (sb))‖-ˈʃɑːk-/ [v phrase not in progressive] if something unpleasant **comes as a shock**, it makes you feel surprised and upset because you were not expecting it at all: *I know this will come as a shock to you Ray, but try to understand how I feel.* | *The revelations of child abuse at the home have come as a profound shock to parents and social workers.*

stun /stʌn/ [v T not in progressive] if something **stuns** you, especially a piece of news, it makes you feel so surprised and upset that you cannot speak or do anything immediately afterwards: *Sasha was too stunned by what had happened to say a word.* | *His words stunned her, and she stared at him in disbelief.*

knock/throw sb for a loop /ˌnɒk, ˌθrəʊ (sb) fər ə ˈluːp‖ˌnɑːk-/ [v phrase not in progressive] American informal if something unexpected **knocks** someone **for a loop**, it shocks or upsets them: *Joanna's resignation really threw me for a loop.* | *His next question totally knocked me for a loop. He said, 'So what makes you think you're good enough to get into law school?'*

shake sb up /ˌʃeɪk (sb) ˈʌp/ [phr v T] if an unpleasant experience **shakes** someone **up**, they are shocked and upset by it: *Did that lightning shake you up, honey?* | *Katherine was one of the fairest people you could ever hope to meet, so her criticism really shook me up.*

rock /rɒk‖rɑːk/ [v T] if a piece of news **rocks** a large group of people or an organization, it shocks them – used especially in news reports: *The scandal has rocked the banking world.* | *The law firm was rocked by accusations of bribery and dishonesty.*

4 making you feel shocked

- **shocking**
- **devastating/shattering**

shocking /ˈʃɒkɪŋ‖ˈʃɑː-/ [adj] making you feel shocked and upset: *These shocking events horrified the entire world.* | *The report revealed some shocking new facts about the effect of drinking on health.* | *It can be quite shocking for a child to see the changes in his or her body as puberty approaches.*

devastating/shattering /ˈdevəsteɪtɪŋ, ˈʃætərɪŋ/ [adj usually before noun] extremely shocking and upsetting: *Losing your job can be a psychologically devastating experience.* | *a shattering personal crisis*

5 the feeling of being shocked

- **shock**
- **horror**

shock /ʃɒk‖ʃɑːk/ [n U] the unpleasant feeling of surprise that you have when something bad happens, especially when you do not expect it: *Fellow students expressed shock and dismay over the racist incidents.* | **with shock** *We listened to the announcer with shock and disbelief – another bomb had exploded in the city.*

horror /ˈhɒrəʳ‖ˈhɔː-, ˈhɑː-/ [n U] a very strong feeling of surprise and disbelief that you have when something very unpleasant or frightening happens: *It's hard for me even now to relate my feelings of horror and incredulity about what happened.* | **in horror** *She screamed again and stared in horror at what lay in the doorway.* | **with horror** *He was trembling with horror and disbelief.* | **to my/your/his etc horror** *To my horror, I saw James' car draw up outside the gate.*

6 something that shocks you

- **shock**
- **blow**
- **bombshell**
- **rude awakening**

shock /ʃɒk‖ʃɑːk/ [n C] something very bad or unpleasant that happens to you and that you did not expect: *'The bill came to almost £500.' 'That must have been a shock.'* | **get a shock** *Gary got a shock when his ex-girlfriend turned up on his doorstep.* | **give sb a shock** *It gave me a shock to realize that I had almost died.* | **with a shock** *He realised with a faint shock that it was Lulu, much older but still beautiful.* | **be in for a shock** (=used to say someone will be shocked when they discover something) *If the FBI thought they could outwit him, they were in for a shock.* | **a rude shock** British (=a big and very unpleasant shock) *Going on holiday with Ian had been a rude shock – he'd been argumentative, mean and not at all what she'd expected.*

blow /bləʊ/ [n C] an unpleasant event or piece of news that makes you shocked, upset, and disappointed: *Not being allowed to return to her own country was a blow from which she never really recovered.* | **+ to** *The Colorado river was closed, a bitter blow to rafters and kayakers who may have to wait seven years for a river use permit.* | **deal sb a blow** *His championship hopes were dealt a savage blow last night when he received a hamstring injury.*

bombshell /ˈbɒmʃel‖ˈbɑːm-/ [n C] a piece of news which is extremely shocking and bad **drop a bombshell** (=tell people something very shocking or surprising) *Then Vanessa dropped the bombshell that she was leaving – and leaving that night.* | **come as a bombshell** *For the board of directors, the news of the crash came as a bombshell.*

rude awakening /ˌruːd əˈweɪkənɪŋ/ [n C] a sudden shock that happens when you find out the unpleasant truth about a situation: *Moving to the city was a rude awakening for an innocent country girl like Eli.* | **be in for a rude awakening** (=used to say that someone will be unpleasantly shocked when they discover something) *I was expecting the oral exam to be easy, but I was in for a rude awakening.*

7 feeling shocked and offended

- **shocked**
- **outraged**
- **scandalized**
- **outrage**

shocked /ʃɒkt‖ʃɑːkt/ [adj] surprised, upset, and offended by an event or by someone's behaviour, when you think it is morally wrong or unfair: *Shocked viewers jammed the switchboard with complaints.* | **+ by** *I am truly shocked by the content of the program.* | **+ at** *She was shocked at her own depraved behavior.* —**shock** [v T] *The shows are designed deliberately to shock audiences.*

outraged /ˈaʊtreɪdʒd/ [adj] very shocked and angry about something you think is morally wrong or unfair: *We were outraged when we heard the rapist had only got a two year sentence.* | *His remarks, intended to calm the crisis, only served to alarm the already outraged Black community.* | **+ at/by** *My mother was outraged at the idea that she might be kept from seeing her grandchildren.* —**outrage** [v T not in progressive] *His remarks puzzled some people and outraged others.*

scandalized ALSO **scandalised** British /ˈskændl-aɪzd/ [adj] very shocked and offended by something that you disapprove of, especially because it is morally wrong – use this especially when a lot of people feel this way: *Their scandalized neighbours began a petition to remove them from the neighbourhood.* | **+ by** *At first, the public was scandalized by his nude paintings.* | **+ by** *The country was scandalized by the news of the President's alleged affair.* —**scandalize** also **scandalise** British [v T not in progressive] *She had scandalized her family and embarrassed her husband.*

outrage /'aʊtreɪdʒ/ [n U] the strong feeling of being shocked and angry about something such as a public statement or action that you think is morally wrong or unfair: *The sense of anger and outrage within the community seemed to grow by the hour.* | *Prominent Republicans have expressed outrage at the decision.* | *The anarchic music of punk caused public outrage when it first burst upon the scene.*

shoot

RELATED WORDS

▸ *see also* **kill, hurt/injure, weapon, army, war, crime, violent**

1 to fire a gun or other weapon

- shoot
- fire
- open fire
- take a shot at
- take a potshot at
- shell
- bombard

shoot /ʃuːt/ [v I] to point a gun towards someone or something, and make bullets come out of it in order to kill or injure them: *If you move, I'll shoot.* | *Make sure you hold the gun steady and shoot straight.* | **+ at** *Armed robbers who shot at a security guard are still being hunted by police.* | *We used to shoot at empty bottles for practice.* | **shoot to kill** (=in order to kill someone) *The Defence Minister had ordered troops to shoot to kill if attacked.*

fire /faɪəʳ/ [v I/T] to make bullets come out of a gun, or send an explosive object towards someone or something: *He regained his balance, took aim, and fired.* | **+ into** *The police fired into the air to make the crowd break up.* | **+ at** *As soon as we crossed the border, enemy troops started firing at us.* | **fire a shot/bullet/round** *Kendrick fired three shots at the President's car.* | **fire a gun/weapon/pistol etc** *Suddenly the car stopped, and the passenger got out and fired a Kalashnikov rifle at the police car.*

open fire /ˌəʊpən 'faɪəʳ/ [v phrase] to start shooting: *The colonel gave the order for the soldiers to open fire.* | **+ on** *Troops opened fire on a group of unarmed demonstrators in the city centre.*

take a shot at /ˌteɪk ə 'ʃɒt æt‖-'ʃɑːt-/ [v phrase] to shoot once at someone or something, hoping to hit them: *Agent Cooper stood back and took a shot at the lock on the door.* | *The police claim that someone took a shot at them, and they had to withdraw for their own safety.*

take a potshot at /ˌteɪk ə 'pɒtʃɒt æt‖-'pɑːtʃɑːt-/ [v phrase] to shoot at someone or something, especially from far away, without aiming carefully: *A bird flew out of the tree and Harry took a potshot at it.* | *Somebody was taking potshots at us from behind the bushes.*

shell /ʃel/ [v T] to shoot at enemy soldiers, cities etc in a war, using large guns that can shoot from long distances: *British warships began shelling German positions along the coast.* | *Border towns have been shelled by enemy aircraft for the past two months.*

bombard /bɒm'bɑːʳd‖bɑːm-/ [v T] to shoot at a place using a lot of large guns all firing at the same time: *The allied forces bombarded the enemy trenches for weeks.* | **bombard sb/sth with sth** *Cromwell's men had been bombarding the fort with their artillery for several days.*

2 to shoot someone or something

- shoot
- shoot down
- be hit
- gun down
- pick off

shoot /ʃuːt/ [v T] to kill or injure someone by firing bullets from a gun: *I was afraid they were going to shoot us.* | *Rico had been shot by a member of a rival gang.* | **shoot sb in the back/chest/leg etc** *He had been shot in the chest but managed to crawl to safety.* | **shoot sb dead** *A tourist was shot dead by muggers in New Orleans last night.*

shoot down /ˌʃuːt 'daʊn/ [phr v T] to shoot an aircraft so that it falls from the sky **shoot sth down** *Local militiamen shot down a federal army helicopter as it flew over the capital.* | **shoot down sth** *They said the plane had been on a spy mission and they were justified in shooting it down.*

be hit /biː 'hɪt/ [v phrase] to be injured or damaged by bullets: *I didn't realize he'd been hit until he fell to the ground.* | *One of our planes has been hit.* | **be hit in the chest/face etc** *He was hit in the arm by a sniper's bullet but carried on fighting.*

gun down /ˌɡʌn 'daʊn/ [phr v T] to shoot someone, especially someone who cannot defend themselves, so that they are killed or badly injured **gun down sb** *The bank robbers gunned down two employees who tried to stop them getting away.* | **gun sb down** *Two men dragged him out of his home, and gunned him down in the street.*

pick off /ˌpɪk 'ɒf/ [phr v T] to shoot people or animals one by one from a distance **pick off sb** *Jesse hid behind a rock and picked off the sheriff's men one by one as they rode past.* | **pick sb off** *Our rifles were much more powerful and we were able to pick the enemy off before they could even fire at us.*

3 to be shot at by someone

- be shot at
- under fire
- be caught in the crossfire

be shot at /biː 'ʃɒt æt‖-'ʃɑːt-/ [v phrase] *I heard a bullet whistle past my ear, and I realized we were being shot at.* | *The UN troops shouldn't be there just to be shot at – they should be allowed to defend themselves.*

under fire /ʌndəʳ 'faɪəʳ/ [adv] if someone is **under fire**, they are being shot at, especially by several people during a battle: *The men's faces were white with fear – none of them had ever been under fire before.* | **under heavy fire** (=being shot at repeatedly) *Although they were under heavy fire from all sides, they managed to get the wounded off the battlefield.* | **come under fire** (=start being shot at) *Troops sent to quell the fighting came under fire themselves.*

be caught in the crossfire /biː ˌkɔːt ɪn ðə 'krɒsfaɪəʳ‖-'krɔːs-/ [v phrase] if someone **is caught in the crossfire**, they are trapped between two groups of people who are shooting at each other, and may be shot accidentally themselves: *Two civilians were killed when they were caught in the crossfire between the police and the protestors.*

4 to point a gun or weapon carefully before shooting

- **aim**
- **take aim**

aim /eɪm/ [v I/T] to choose the place, person etc that you want to hit and point your gun or weapon at it carefully: *He picked up his shotgun, aimed, then fired.* | *The firing squad were already aiming their rifles and waiting for the order to shoot.* | **+ at** *Which part of the target were you aiming at?* | **aim for sb's head/chest etc** *You can tell he was a professional killer – they always aim for the chest.* | **aim sth at sth** *The rocket-launchers are aimed at Washington.*

take aim /ˌteɪk ˈeɪm/ [v phrase not in passive] to point a gun or weapon towards someone or something when preparing to shoot them: *For those few seconds when they are taking aim, the soldiers are exposed to enemy fire.*

5 when someone shoots a gun

- **shot**
- **shooting**
- **gunfire**
- **fire**
- **volley**
- **bombardment**
- **barrage**
- **shelling**
- **hail of bullets**

shot /ʃɒt‖ʃɑːt/ [n C] an attempt to shoot someone or something: *His first shot missed. The second hit its target.* | **fire a shot** *Police fired shots into the air and used water cannon to disperse the crowd.*

shooting /ˈʃuːtɪŋ/ [n C] when someone is shot at, and killed or injured: *Oswald was seen running away from the building just after the shooting.* | *There has been an alarming increase in the number of shootings on our streets.*

gunfire /ˈgʌnfaɪəʳ/ [n U] the repeated shooting of a gun or guns: *At least 4 people were killed by gunfire when police stormed the building.* | **a volley/hail of gunfire** *Joseph sprinted away to dodge the volley of gunfire.* | **an exchange of gunfire** (=when people shoot at each other) *A soldier was killed during an exchange of gunfire at the border station.*

fire /faɪəʳ/ [n U] the repeated shooting of a gun, guns, or other weapons: *The ship was hit by fire from a German plane.* | *There was a sudden burst of machine gun fire.* | **enemy fire** *We noticed that the enemy fire was now being directed at our part of the field.*

volley /ˈvɒli‖ˈvɑːli/ [n C] several shots fired together from several weapons at the same time: *Before it was lowered into the ground, a volley of shots was fired over the General's coffin.* | **fire a volley** *The soldiers fired a volley into the air as a warning to the crowd.*

bombardment /bɒmˈbɑːʳdmənt‖bɑːm-/ [n U] the continuous firing of a lot of large guns in order to attack an enemy town, city etc in a war: *The Germans began their bombardment of Paris in early 1870.* | *The devastating air bombardment of the last four weeks is only the latest of a series of assaults by foreign armies.*

barrage /ˈbærɑːʒ‖bəˈrɑːʒ/ [n C usually singular] the continuous firing of a lot of guns, especially in a war: *US warplanes continued their barrage again this morning.* | *a barrage of machine-gun fire*

shelling /ˈʃelɪŋ/ [n U] the shooting at enemy soldiers, cities etc in a war, using large guns that can shoot from long distances: *Soon after dawn there was another round of heavy shelling in the eastern part of the city.*

hail of bullets /ˌheɪl əv ˈbʊlɪ̇ts/ [n phrase] a lot of bullets that have been fired – used especially in written descriptions: *Wallace died in a hail of bullets in Los Angeles, the victim of a drive-by killing.*

6 the sound of shooting

- **shot/gunshot**
- **gunfire**

shot/gunshot /ʃɒt‖ʃɑːt, ˈgʌnʃɒt‖-ʃɑːt/ [n C] the noise made by a gun when it is fired: *One witness claimed she had heard eight shots.* | *An occasional gunshot can still be heard, but no-one knows who fires them.* | **a shot rings out** written *Shots rang out from across the street as someone tried to break up the fight.*

gunfire /ˈgʌnfaɪəʳ/ [n U] the sound made by several guns being fired, especially in a war: *Enemy gunfire could be heard from several kilometres away.* | *The earth shook with the sound of heavy gunfire.*

7 someone who uses a gun

- **gunman**
- **sniper**
- **marksman**
- **be a good/bad etc shot**

gunman /ˈgʌnmən/ [n C] someone who uses a gun to kill someone – use this especially about a criminal or someone who is using a gun illegally: *Two gunmen opened fire on a bus taking children to school.* | *Was President Kennedy killed by a lone gunman, or was there a conspiracy?* | *Hooded gunmen burst into a home in Lima on Sunday and shot to death at least 15 people.*

sniper /ˈsnaɪpəʳ/ [n C] someone who hides, especially in a high place, and shoots at enemy soldiers: *Weapons were found at three locations believed to be used by snipers.* | *A sniper's bullet pierced his windshield and hit him in the eye.*

marksman /ˈmɑːʳksmən/ [n C] someone who is very well trained and very skilful at using a gun, either for sport or for their job with the army or the police: *Police marksmen surrounded the building.* | *A marksman was called in to try and hit the enemy's machine gun post.*

be a good/bad etc shot /biː ə ˌgʊd ˈʃɒt‖-ˈʃɑːt/ [v phrase] someone who **is a good** or **bad shot** is good or bad at shooting: *You'd have to be a really good shot to get that bird from here.* | *I used to be the best shot in the whole school.*

shop/store

RELATED WORDS

- *see also* **buy, sell, cheap, expensive, cost, spend money/time, business**

1 a shop

- **shop**
- **chain store**
- **retail outlet**

shop especially British **/store** especially American /ʃɒp‖ʃɑːp, stɔːʳ/ [n C] a building or place where things are sold: *Could you run down to the shop and get me some cigarettes?* | *A lot of the stores on the main street had been boarded up.* | *I asked in my local record shop but they couldn't help me.* | *I saw Helen at the grocery store this morning.* | *I got it from the secondhand* *furniture shop.* | *a new health food shop* | *It's where the old jewelry store used to be.*

chain store /ˈtʃeɪn stɔːʳ/ [n C] one of a group of large shops that have the same name and are owned by the same company: *A lot of the old Victorian buildings are being pulled down to make way for chain stores.*

retail outlet /ˈriːteɪl ˌaʊtlet/ [n C] a shop where a company sells its goods – use this in business or legal contexts: *Benetton has retail outlets in every major European city.* | *The company has been forced to close hundreds of its retail outlets.*

2 different types of shop

- supermarket
- convenience store
- corner shop
- bakery
- butcher
- delicatessen
- off licence
- chemist
- pharmacy
- hardware store
- newsagent's/newsagent
- newstand/newsstand
- kiosk
- stall

supermarket ALSO **grocery store** American /ˈsuːpəʳˌmɑːʳkɪ̈t, ˈgrəʊsəri ˌstɔːʳ/ [n C] a large shop that sells a wide range of things, especially food, cleaning materials, and other things that people buy regularly: *Can you get pine nuts in the grocery store?* | *There are plans to open a new supermarket next year.*

convenience store /kənˈviːniəns ˌstɔːʳ/ [n C] especially American a shop in your local area that sells food, alcohol, magazines etc and is often open 24 hours a day: *Believe me, if his father wasn't so rich, that guy would be working in a convenience store.*

corner shop British **/corner store** American /ˈkɔːʳnəʳ ˌʃɒp‖-ˌʃɑːp, ˈkɔːʳnəʳ ˌstɔːʳ/ [n C] a small local shop, usually on the corner of a street, that sells food, newspapers, cigarettes etc: *The corner shop's started selling sandwiches now, and I'd rather go there than the supermarket.* | *His parents ran a little corner store in the Castro in San Francisco.*

bakery ALSO **baker's** British /ˈbeɪkəri, ˈbeɪkəʳz/ [n C] a shop that sells bread and cakes, especially one that also makes the bread and cakes: *She runs a French bakery in North London.*

butcher British **/butcher shop** American /ˈbʊtʃəʳ, ˈbʊtʃəʳ ˌʃɒp‖-ˌʃɑːp/ [n C] a shop that sells meat: *Many small independent butchers are closing down.*

delicatessen ALSO **deli** informal /ˌdelɪkəˈtesən, ˈdeli/ [n C] a shop, or part of a larger shop, that sells high quality food such as cheeses and cold meats, often from different countries: *There's an Italian deli here and their homemade ravioli is delicious.* | **deli counter** (=the part in a large shop where high-quality cheese, cold meat etc is sold) *I had to wait for fifteen minutes at the deli counter this morning.*

off licence British ALSO **offie** informal ALSO **liquor store** American /ˈɒf ˌlaɪsəns, ˈɒfi‖ˈɔː-, ˈlɪkəʳ stɔːʳ/ [n C] a shop that sells beer, wine, and other alcoholic drinks that you drink at home

chemist ALSO **chemist's** British **/drugstore** American /ˈkemɪ̈st, ˈkemɪ̈sts, ˈdrʌgstɔːʳ/ [n C] a shop that sells medicines, beauty and baby products etc

pharmacy /ˈfɑːʳməsi/ [n C] especially American a shop or part of a shop where medicines are made and sold

hardware store ALSO **hardware shop** British /ˈhɑːdweəʳ ˌstɔːʳ, ˈhɑːdweəʳ ˌʃɒp‖-ˌʃɑːp/ [n C] a shop that sells equipment and tools that you can use in your home or garden

newsagent's/newsagent /ˈnjuːzˌeɪdʒənts, ˈnjuːzˌeɪdʒənt‖ˈnuːz-/ [n C] British a shop that sells newspapers and magazines, cigarettes, chocolates etc: *Ruth waited for him outside the newsagent's.*

newstand/newsstand /ˈnjuːzstænd‖ˈnuːz-/ [n C] a small structure on a street, that sells newspapers and magazines: *He bought a paper at a newstand near the entrance to the park.*

kiosk /ˈkiːɒsk‖-ɑːsk/ [n C] a very small shop on a street, that has an open window where you can buy newspapers, cigarettes, chocolate etc: *There must be a kiosk selling phone cards around here somewhere.*

stall especially British **/stand** American /stɔːl, stænd/ [n C] a table, especially in a market, where goods are placed: *Justin used to mind the stall while his father was in the cafe, drinking.* | *I bought a few trinkets at the souvenir stand.* | **market stall** *The trouble is, you can't really try the clothes on at a market stall.*

3 big shops

- department store
- superstore
- DIY store
- garden centre

department store /dɪˈpɑːʳtmənt ˌstɔːʳ/ [n C] a very large shop that is divided into several big parts, each of which sells one type of thing, such as clothes, furniture, or kitchen equipment: *We couldn't find anything we wanted in the big department stores, and then we came across this little boutique.*

superstore /ˈsuːpəʳstɔːʳ, ˈsjuː-‖ˈsuː-/ [n C] British a very large modern shop, especially one that is built outside the centre of a city: *A new Tesco superstore is being planned for the site.*

DIY store British **/home improvement center** American /ˌdiː aɪ ˈwaɪ stɔːʳ, ˌhəʊm ɪmˈpruːvmənt ˌsentəʳ/ [n C] a very large shop that sells equipment and tools for repairing and decorating your home: *You'll find these at your local home improvement center.*

garden centre British **/nursery** especially American /ˈgɑːʳdn ˌsentəʳ, ˈnɜːʳsəri/ [n C] a place that sells a wide range of plants, seeds, and things for your garden: *It's the only good garden centre around here.*

4 a lot of shops together in one place

- shopping centre
- mall/shopping mall
- strip mall
- precinct
- market

shopping centre British **/shopping center** American /ˈʃɒpɪŋ ˌsentəʳ‖ˈʃɑːp-/ [n C] an area in a town where there are a lot of shops that have all been built together in the same place: *The boy was found dead two days after he disappeared from a shopping centre.* | *They had a big Santa exhibition on at the shopping center.*

mall/shopping mall /mɔːl, ˈʃɒpɪŋ mɔːl‖ˈʃɑːp-/ [n C] especially American a very large building with lots of shops inside it, and often also cinemas, restaurants etc: *We'll probably go to the mall and check out the beds there.* | *It's difficult to get a parking space at Shepherd's Mall.*

strip mall /ˈstrɪp mɔːl/ [n C] American a row of shops in one long building that has space to park cars around it: *Strip malls were springing up all over town, and the local residents were up in arms.*

precinct /ˈpriːsɪŋkt/ [n C] British an area of a town where there are a lot of shops, especially one where vehicles are not allowed: *They've got a lovely new*

Burton's open in the precinct now. | **shopping precinct** *They wandered around the shopping precinct for an hour while Suzie was having her hair cut.* | **pedestrian precinct** *I think they should make the whole area a pedestrian precinct.*

market /ˈmɑːʳkə̇t/ [n C] an area, usually outdoors, where people buy and sell many different types of things: *I bet you could have got that cheaper at the market.* | *You occasionally see eel in the fish market, but it's quite rare these days.* | **farmer's market** (=place where farmers can sell what they grow and other food) **flea market** (=place where old and used things are sold)

5 people who work in a shop

- sales assistant/shop assistant
- manager
- shopkeeper
- market trader

sales assistant/shop assistant British **/sales clerk** American /ˈseɪlz əˌsɪstənt, ˈʃɒp əˌsɪstənt‖ˈʃɑːp-, ˈseɪlz ˌklɑːk‖-ˌklɜːrk/ [n C] someone whose job is to serve customers and sell things in a shop, especially in a big shop such as a department store: *She was a bit rude, that shop assistant, don't you think?* | *I'm working weekends as a sales clerk.*

manager /ˈmænɪdʒəʳ/ [n C] someone who is in charge of a shop: *I'd like to see the manager please.* | **branch/area manager** (=someone who is manager of all the shops owned by one particular company in one area) *Ron was promoted to branch manager of the North West region.*

shopkeeper /ˈʃɒpˌkiːpəʳ‖ˈʃɑːp-/ [n C] British someone who owns or manages a small shop: *A lot of the smaller shopkeepers didn't have any insurance at all.* | *The money for the Christmas lights was raised by a group of local shopkeepers, who want to attract shoppers to the area.*

market trader /ˈmɑːʳkə̇t ˌtreɪdəʳ/ [n C] British someone who sells things in a market: *The market traders have started a petition to try and stop the development going ahead.*

short

WHAT'S HERE

- **short/not long** see **1 to 6**
- **short person** see **7 to 8**
- **short time** see **9 to 10**

short/not long

RELATED WORDS

opposite: **long**

- to make a short statement that describes the main points of a speech, plan etc *see* **summarize**
- *see also* **distance**

1 short in length or distance

- short
- stubby/stumpy

short /ʃɔːʳt/ [adj] if something is **short**, there is only a small length or distance from one end of it to the other: *These curtains are much too short.* | *She has short curly hair and wears glasses.* | *a short-sleeved T-shirt* | *You look different – your hair's shorter.* | *The hotel is just a short distance from the station.* | *Chris went for a short walk to clear his head.* | **short cut** (=a shorter, and therefore quicker, way of getting to a place) *Sandy took a short cut home.* | *Do you know any short cuts to the hospital?*

stubby/stumpy /ˈstʌbi, ˈstʌmpi/ [adj] body parts that are **stubby** or **stumpy** are short and thick: *Pheasants have short stubby wings which enable them to fly very fast and low.* | *a fat little boy with stumpy legs*

2 when something you say or write is short

- short
- brief
- concise
- succinct

see also **summarize**

short /ʃɔːʳt/ [adj] a **short** piece of writing or speech does not have many pages or words: *Graham made a short speech of thanks after the ceremony.* | *a book of short stories* | *The chapters are really short, so I read a couple every night.* | *We had a short pep talk from the coach before the game.* | *Please write a short paragraph explaining your reasons for applying to this college.*

brief /briːf/ [adj] a **brief** note, description, remark etc uses very few words and gives very few details: *The book begins with a brief outline of the history of modern China.* | *We just have to write a very brief piece on what we did in the vacation.* | *There was a brief note with the flowers.*

concise /kənˈsaɪs/ [adj] short and clear, and with no unnecessary words: *Saussure expressed his arguments in a concise and logical way.* | *Sergeant Hanks gave us concise, sensible instructions.* | **clear and concise** *Make sure that your answers are as clear and concise as possible.*

succinct /səkˈsɪŋkt/ [adj] formal expressing something well but with very few words: *The new labelling is more succinct and advises consumers simply that oat bran may help prevent heart disease.* —**succinctly** [adv] *Spell out your work objectives clearly and succinctly.* | **say/put sth succinctly** (=say something in a succinct way) *As Susan put it so succinctly 'No overtime pay, no work!'*

3 to make something shorter

- shorten
- make sth shorter
- cut
- cut down
- condense

shorten /ˈʃɔːʳtn/ [v T] to make something shorter, especially by removing part of it: *I heard she had an operation to shorten her nose.* | *You can improve your writing just by shortening some of these long sentences.* | *It costs £12 to get trousers shortened.* | *This essay's still too long, I'll have to shorten it by a couple of thousand words.* | **shorten sth to sth** *His name's Lawrence, but it's usually shortened to Larry.*

make sth shorter /ˌmeɪk (sth) ˈʃɔːʳtəʳ/ [v phrase] to make something shorter, especially by removing part of it: *You could make your speech shorter by taking out all the quotations.* | **make sth one metre/two centimetres etc shorter** *Engineers have removed a section of the pipeline, making it about a hundred metres shorter.*

cut /kʌt/ [v T] to make a film or piece of writing shorter by removing parts from it: *Even after it had* *been cut, the film was still over three hours long.* | *I had to cut huge chunks out to get this essay to the right length.* | **cut sth from sth** *It's so difficult to cut even a couple of scenes from a play without losing some of the story.*

cut down /ˌkʌt ˈdaʊn/ [phr v T] to make a piece of writing shorter by removing parts of it completely **cut sth down** *The introduction's too long. Can you try and cut it down?* | *Did you have to cut your dissertation down?* | **cut down sth** *They want me to cut down my article so that it'll all fit onto one page.*

condense /kənˈdens/ [v T] to shorten something spoken or written, by not giving as much detail, or by using fewer words to give the same information: *I'd like to condense that statement still further.* | **condense sth into sth** *Hawkins condensed all his writings into one volume for publication.* | *How could he condense all he had lived through into a sixty-minute speech?*

4 when a book or piece of writing has been made shorter

- shortened
- abridged

shortened /ˈʃɔːʳtnd/ [adj] **shortened version (of sth)** *This chapter is a shortened version of a paper that was written in 1977.* | *a shortened version of the Jewish creed* | **in (a) shortened form** *The book contains many of the most popular stories from the Bible in shortened form.*

abridged /əˈbrɪdʒd/ [adj] **abridged version/edition/account (of sth)** a shortened version of a piece of writing or speech, which keeps its basic structure and meaning: *The following article is an abridged version of a speech given by Porter in May 2000.* | *The book is an abridged account of his experiences in India before Independence.*

5 to say or write something using as few words as possible

- be brief
- keep it short

be brief /biː ˈbriːf/ [v phrase] to say something using as few words as possible, because you do not have much time: *Lieutenant, I'll be brief and I'll be candid – when do you plan to leave?* | *I'm sure you're all very busy, so I'll be brief.* | *I'll be as brief as possible so as not to waste your time.*

keep it short /ˌkiːp ɪt ˈʃɔːʳt/ [v phrase] informal to say or write something using as few words as possible: *I'll keep it short as I don't have much time.* | *Tell me, but keep it short, I'm in the middle of something.* | **keep it short and sweet/short and simple** *Mr Chairman, I think I've got five minutes, so I'll keep it fairly short and sweet.*

6 when a name or word is a shorter way of saying something

- be short for
- stand for
- for short
- abbreviate
- abbreviation

be short for /biː ˈʃɔːʳt fɔːʳ/ [v phrase] *VHF is short for Very High Frequency.* | *'Is 'Shelley' short for anything?' 'Yes, my real name's Michelle.'* | *What's 'ISP' short for?*

stand for /ˈstænd fɔːʳ/ [phr v T] if a letter **stands for** a name or word, it is the first letter of that name or word: *'What does 'NAC' stand for?' 'National Aerobics Championships'.* | *On a US ship, you see 'USS', standing for 'United States Ship'.* | *The 'F' in 'John F Kennedy' stood for 'Fitzgerald'.*

for short /fəʳ ˈʃɔːʳt/ [adv] if you call someone or something a particular name **for short**, you call them by a name that is a shorter way of saying their real name: *Hi, my name's Moses – Mo for short.* | *He's actually called Jeremy, but everyone who knows him calls him Jem for short.*

abbreviate /əˈbriːvieɪt/ [v T usually in passive] to make a long name or word shorter so that it is easier to say or write: *Is it correct to abbreviate 'Avenue', 'Street' and so on when writing an address on an envelope?* | **be abbreviated to sth** *The word 'kilogram' is usually abbreviated to 'kg'.*

abbreviation /əˌbriːviˈeɪʃən/ [n C] a shorter way of saying a word or the name of something such as an organization or someone's job, especially by using the first letters of words instead of the whole words: *Disk Operating Systems are usually known by the abbreviation DOS.* | *a Dictionary of Acronyms and Abbreviations* | *I never knew the abbreviation 'GI' stood for 'Government Issue'.* | **+ for** *BBC is an abbreviation for British Broadcasting Corporation.*

short person

RELATED WORDS

opposite: —————— **tall**

7 not tall

- short
- not very tall
- small
- little
- petite
- stocky
- squat

short /ʃɔːʳt/ [adj] not as tall as most people: *'What does she look like?' 'She's short and fat, with brown hair.'* | *a short, stocky man with powerful shoulders* | *Mr Haddad was several inches shorter than his wife.*

not very tall /nɒt veri ˈtɔːl/ [adj phrase] fairly short: *She's not very tall – about 1.4 metres, I'd say.* | *Well, I'm not very tall and my legs are short, so I always had trouble in the hurdle race.*

small /smɔːl/ [adj] not as big or as tall as most people: *a small man in a dark suit* | *How come I always seem to go out with small men?* | *My sister's quite a bit smaller and slimmer than me.* | **small for his/her age** (=smaller than other children of the same age) *Bobby's small for his age, but he's perfectly healthy.*

little /ˈlɪtl/ [adj only before noun] short and small, used especially to describe children or old people: *We saw a little old lady with a walking-stick.* | *Who's this little boy in the blue sweater?* | *I haven't seen one of those since I was a little girl.*

petite /pəˈtiːt/ [adj] a woman who is **petite** is attractively short and thin: *His wife was a petite dark-haired woman in her early thirties.*

stocky /ˈstɒki‖ˈstɑː-/ [adj] a man who is **stocky** is fairly short and looks heavy and often strong: *Brandon's quite stocky really, isn't he?* | *He's a big stocky bloke and he plays rugby.*

squat /skwɒt‖skwɑːt/ [adj] short and fat, especially in an unattractive way: *The cook was short and squat, with thick eyebrows and a slight moustache.* | *a shabby, squat, balding man in an old raincoat*

8 very short

- tiny
- diminutive

tiny /ˈtaɪni/ [adj] *A tiny old lady answered the door.* | *She's tiny, but she belts out these old blues songs like you wouldn't believe.* | *They look so funny together. She's really tiny and her husband's about six foot five.* | **tiny little** informal *She was holding a tiny little baby in her arms.*

diminutive /dəˈmɪnjətɪv/ [adj] written unusually small and thin: *Peter was a shy, diminutive man who seldom said anything to anyone.* | *A diminutive figure appeared in the doorway.*

short time

RELATED WORDS

opposite: —— **long**

- *see also* **time, temporary**

9 a short time

- a short time
- a little while/a short while
- a minute/a moment
- a second/an instant
- a bit

a short time /ə ˌʃɔːʳt ˈtaɪm/ [n singular] *Unfortunately, we could only spend a short time together.* | *The talk should only last a short time.* | **in/within a short time** *How did you manage to do all this in such a short time?* | *The police arrived within a very short time.* | **+ ago** *Your friends left a short time ago.* | **for a short time** *I think he went to prison for a short time.*

a little while/a short while /ə ˌlɪtl ˈwaɪl, ə ˌʃɔːʳt ˈwaɪl/ [n singular] a short period of time, during or after which something happens: *It always takes a little while to get used to the climate.* | **for a short/little while** *Bob's only worked here for a short while, about six months I think.* | **+ ago** *He died a little while ago.* | *She was in the papers a short while ago.* | **after/in a little/short while** *If you take the pills now, your headache will go after a short while.* | *Don't start that now, it'll be time to go in a little while.*

a minute/a moment /ə ˈmɪnət, ə ˈməʊmənt/ [n singular] a very short time, no more than a few minutes: *Just a moment Susie, can I have a quick word with you?* | *Can I borrow your pen a minute?* | *Wait a minute, I'm nearly ready.* | **a minute/moment ago** *Where's Charles gone? He was here a moment ago.* | **for/in a minute/moment** *Sit down for a minute and rest your legs.* | *Mark should be back in a moment.* | *I'll be with you in a minute.*

a second/an instant /ə ˈsekənd, ən ˈɪnstənt/ [n singular] an extremely short time, no more than a few seconds: *Do you mind switching the telly on a second?* | *An instant later, she let out a piercing scream.* | *'Yes,' she declared, without an instant's hesitation.* | *'Have you finished writing?' 'No, hang on a second.'* | **for a second/an instant** *Can I stop you there, just for a second?* | *Just hold that end for a second while I fix this to the wall.* | *Did her eyes flicker open for an instant?* | **in a second/an instant** *Mr Smart's on the other line, can he call you back in a second?* | *We both fell asleep in an instant.*

a bit /ə ˈbɪt/ [n singular] British spoken a short time, usually just a few minutes: *I waited, and a bit later the phone went again – it was Bill.* | *Oh, wait a bit, can't you?* | **after/for/in a bit** *I think I'll lie down for a bit.* | *'Are you coming?' 'Yes, in a bit.'* | *After a bit, Bill had started to tire of her company.*

10 continuing for only a short time

- short
- quick
- brief
- not take long
- temporary
- short-lived
- passing
- ephemeral

short /ʃɔːʳt/ [adj] continuing for only a **short** time: *The meeting was shorter than I'd expected.* | *the shortest day of the year* | *a short course in aromatherapy* | *It would have been better if they'd closed the road for a short period of time while the repairs were done.*

quick /kwɪk/ [adj only before noun] a **quick** action takes only a very short time, because you are in a hurry: *I took a quick look at the map.* | *Do I have time for a quick shower before we go out?* | *She's going to give me a quick lesson on Feng Shui this afternoon.* | *Can I ask just one quick question?*

brief /briːf/ [adj] a **brief** pause, visit etc is short, especially because there is not much time available: *It was impossible to see everything during our brief visit to Paris.* | *After a brief intermission, the performance continued.*

not take long /nɒt teɪk ˈlɒŋ‖-ˈlɔːŋ/ [v phrase] if something does **not take long**, you do it and finish it in a short time: *Let me show you how to use the program – it won't take long.* | **not take long to do** *We'll have the chicken drumsticks – they won't take long to thaw.* | **it doesn't take (sb) long to do sth** *It didn't take long to solve the problem.* | *It sure didn't take you long to smell the food!*

temporary /ˈtempərəri, -pəri‖-pəreri/ [adj] something that is **temporary** is expected to continue for only a short time and will not be permanent: *The doctor says the swelling is just temporary and should go down in a few days.* | *a temporary driver's license* | *They're living in temporary accommodation at the moment.* | **temporary workers/staff/job etc** *Demand for temporary workers continues to rise.* | *Ben's found a temporary job until November.* —**temporarily** [adv] for a limited period of time: *The library is temporarily closed for repairs.*

short-lived /ˌʃɔːʳt ˈlɪvd◂/ [adj] something that is **short-lived** ends sooner than you want it to – use this especially about a feeling or relationship: *They had a passionate but short-lived affair.* | *We were glad to be home, but our happiness was short-lived.* | *However, the President's popularity may prove to be short-lived.*

passing /ˈpɑːsɪŋ‖ˈpæ-/ [adj only before noun] **passing thought/interest/fashion/phase etc** one that continues for a short time and then quickly disappears: *At the time, I didn't give Alison so much as a passing thought – I had other things on my mind.* | *Most people take only a passing interest in their horoscope.* | *Whether this is just a passing fad or a lasting fashion trend, only time will tell.*

ephemeral /ɪˈfemərəl/ [adj] formal continuing for only a short time – used especially in literature: *No dictionary can really capture something as fleeting and ephemeral as slang.* | *Hopes of political unity in the region have proved ephemeral.*

should/ought to

RELATED WORDS

- *see also* **must, advise**

1 when you should do something because it is your duty or is right

- **should**
- **ought to**
- **had better (do sth)**
- **be supposed to (do sth)**
- **be expected to do sth**
- **it is sb's job (to do sth)**
- **it's up to sb (to do sth)**
- **be sb's duty (to do sth)/have a duty (to do sth)**

should /ʃʊd / [modal verb] if you **should** do something, it is your duty to do it, or it is the best thing to do because it is right, fair, or honest: *I don't feel like working late tonight but I suppose I should.* | **+ do sth** *I think you should tell her the truth.* | *You really should go see him while he's in the hospital.* | *Should we contact Joe's parents and tell them what's happened?* | **should not/shouldn't do sth** *You shouldn't talk to your father like that.* | **should have done sth** (=it was the right thing to do, but someone did not do it) *They should have given you your money back.* | **shouldn't have done sth** (=it was the wrong thing to do, but someone did it) *I'm sorry. I shouldn't have shouted at you.*

ought to /ˈɔːt tuː / [modal verb] use this to say that someone should do something because you think that it is right or that it is the best thing to do: *'Do you think we should tell him?' 'Well, we ought to really.'* | **+ to do sth** *You ought to go to church more often.* | *Do you think we ought to call the police?* | *The Government ought to spend more on education.* | **ought not to do sth** *I think animals have rights, and we ought not to use them for experiments.*

had better (do sth) /həd ˌbetəʳ (ˈduː (sth))/ [v phrase] especially spoken use this to say that you think someone should do something because it would be the correct, polite, or fair thing to do: *I had better phone Alan and tell him I'm going to be late.* | *You'd better apologize to your mother for forgetting her birthday.* | **had better not do sth** *We'd better not tell anyone about this just yet.* | **had better** *'Do you think we ought to tell Jane about the money?' 'Yes, I think we'd better.'*

be supposed to (do sth) /biː səˌpəʊzd tə (ˈduː (sth))/ [v phrase] use this to say that someone should do something because there is a rule that says they should, because they have been told to do it, or because it is part of their job: *You're supposed to knock before you come in.* | *Put that cigarette out! You're not supposed to smoke in here.* | *What time are we supposed to meet?* | *I don't know why they're blaming him – he only did what he was supposed to.*

be expected to do sth /biː ɪkˌspektɪ̣d tə ˈduː (sth)/ [v phrase] use this to say that people think someone should do something because of their position, age etc: *In many societies women are expected to stay at home.* | *The employees are well-paid but they're also expected to work long hours.*

it is sb's job (to do sth) /ɪt ɪz (sb's) ˌdʒɒb (tə ˈduː (sth) ‖-ˌdʒɑːb-/ spoken use this to say that someone is responsible for doing something, because it is officially part of their job, or because they have agreed to do it: *It's my job to check that the equipment is in good working order.* | *I thought we'd agreed it was Mike's job to send out all the invitations.*

it's up to sb (to do sth) /ɪts ˌʌp tə (sb) (tə ˈduː (sth))/ spoken say this to emphasize that a particular person is responsible for doing something: *It's up to parents to teach their children the difference between right and wrong.* | **it's up to sb** (=a particular person is responsible for making a decision) *I really don't think we should have to work on Saturday but it's not up to me.*

be sb's duty (to do sth)/have a duty (to do sth) /biː (sb's) ˌdjuːti (tə ˈduː (sth)), hæv ə ˌdjuːti tə ˈduː (sth) ‖-ˌduːti-/ [v phrase not in progressive] use this to say that someone should do something because it is their legal or moral duty: *It is the judge's duty to give a fair summary of both sides of the case.* | *The government has a duty to provide education for every child.*

2 when you should so something because it is sensible or healthy

- **should**
- **ought to (do sth)**
- **had better (do sth)**
- **it's/that's a good idea**
- **it's worth**
- **advisable**

should /ʃʊd/ [modal verb] if you **should** do something, it is the best thing to do because it is good for you or it will help you – use this especially in suggestions or to give advice: *'Do you think I should talk to a doctor about the pain in my back?' 'Yes, you should.'* | **+ do sth** *Everyone keeps telling me I should give up smoking.* | *Should I wear the red dress or the black one?* | **should not/shouldn't do sth** *They shouldn't worry so much. Everything will be all right.* | **should have done sth** (=it was the best thing to do, but someone did not do it) *I should have started saving for my retirement when I was younger.* | **shouldn't have done sth** (=it was not a sensible thing to do but someone did it) *We shouldn't have bought such a big car.*

ought to (do sth) /ˌɔːt tə (ˈduː (sth))/ [v phrase] use this to say that you think someone should do something because it is good for them or will help them: *The doctor told Dan he ought to exercise more.* | *You ought to ask Eric. I'm sure he'd be happy to help.*

had better (do sth) /həd ˌbetəʳ (ˈduː (sth))/ [v phrase not in progressive] especially spoken use this to say that you think someone should do something because it is sensible or it will help them avoid problems: *You'd better be careful with that knife.* | *It was starting to snow and we thought we had better go home.*

it's/that's a good idea /ɪts, ðæts ə ˌgʊd aɪˈdɪə/ spoken say this to emphasize that you think an idea or suggestion will help someone or prevent problems: *'I'll check the oil before we set off.' 'Yes, that's a good idea.'* | **+ to do sth** *It's a good idea to photocopy your passport in case it gets stolen.*

it's worth /ɪts ˈwɜːʳθ / especially spoken use this to say that someone should spend the time, money, or effort needed to do something, because they will gain something useful from it **+ doing** *It's worth comparing a range of models before deciding which one to buy.* | **it's worth the time/effort etc** *It's worth all the hard work and preparation to make the show a real success.* | **it's worth it** *Get the car thoroughly checked by a professional. It may cost a bit of money but it's worth it, believe me.* | **it's well worth it/doing sth etc** *The movie was a little difficult to follow at first but it's well worth seeing.*

advisable /ədˈvaɪzəbəl/ [adj not before noun] formal if something is **advisable**, someone should do it or use it in order to avoid problems and succeed in what they are trying to do: *Use of the drug is not con-*

sidered advisable when driving or using machinery. | **it is advisable to do sth** *It is advisable to take some warm clothing with you, as the weather can change quite suddenly.* —**advisability** /ədˌvaɪzəˈbɪlәti/ [n U] *She wondered about the advisability of exercising* (=whether or not it was advisable) *during pregnancy.*

shout

RELATED WORDS

▸ *see also* **scream, cry, tell sb off, angry, loud**

1 to say something very loudly

- ▸ shout
- ▸ yell
- ▸ scream
- ▸ raise your voice
- ▸ call out
- ▸ cry out
- ▸ cry
- ▸ cheer
- ▸ roar
- ▸ bawl
- ▸ bellow

shout /ʃaʊt/ [v I/T] to say something very loudly, because you want to make sure that someone hears you, or because you are angry or excited: *'Get out!' she shouted angrily.* | *There was so much noise from the engine that we had to shout to hear each other.* | *The protesters marched through the streets, shouting slogans.* | **+ at** *I wish you'd stop shouting at the children* | **shout sth out/shout out sth** *Linda leant out of the widow and shouted out my name.*

yell /jel/ [v I/T] to shout very loudly, for example because you are very angry or excited, or because you want to get someone's attention. **Yell** is more informal than **shout**: *'Don't touch me,' she yelled.* | *The music blaring in the bar was forcing us both to yell to be heard.* | **+ at** *The children were yelling at each other across the street.* | **yell out sth/yell sth out** *He opened the door and yelled out 'Anybody home?'*

scream /skriːm/ [v I/T] to shout in a very loud high voice, because you are so angry, afraid, excited etc that you cannot control your voice: *The man pulled a gun, and two of the women near me started screaming.* | *'Help me!' she screamed.* | **+ at** *Maria felt like screaming at her husband.* | **scream with pain/delight/terror etc** *As a child, I used to wake up screaming with terror in the middle of the night.*

raise your voice /ˌreɪz jɔːʳ ˈvɔɪs/ [v phrase] to speak more loudly than usual because you are angry about something: *I never heard my father raise his voice in his life.* | **+ at/to** *Don't you raise your voice at me!* | **raised voices** (=the sound of people talking loudly because they are angry) *We heard raised voices coming from the next room, and then a cry.*

call out ALSO **call** [v T] /ˌkɔːl ˈaʊt, kɔːl/ [phr v I/T] to shout loudly because you want to get someone's attention, to let someone know where you are etc: *'Is there anybody there?' he called out, but there was no reply.* | *She called out his name but he didn't look back.* | *Just call me if you need anything. I'm right here.* | **+ for** *I thought I heard someone calling for help.* | **+ to** *The prisoners used to call out to each other from their cells.*

cry out /ˌkraɪ ˈaʊt/ [phr v I] to make a sudden loud noise, for example when you are suddenly hurt or afraid: *'Careful!' she cried out. 'There's a snake!'* | **cry out in fear/pain/surprise etc** *Chris fell, crying out in pain.*

cry /kraɪ/ [v T] written to shout something loudly, especially because you are feeling strong emotions such as pain or excitement: *'I can't move,' Lesley cried. 'I think I've broken my leg.'* | *'Come and see what I've found!' Kurt cried.*

cheer /tʃɪəʳ/ [v I/T] to shout as a way of showing happiness, approval, or support of someone or something: *At the end, the whole audience stood up clapping and cheering.* | **+ for** *I saw the way the crowd cheered for him, and I thought, 'I want to be like that!'* | **cheer sb** British *The speaker was cheered loudly when he called for a total ban on nuclear weapons.* | **cheer sb on** (=encourage someone to do something by cheering them as they do it) *All the mums and dads come to cheer their kids on.*

roar /rɔːʳ/ [v I/T] to shout in a very loud voice because you are extremely angry or want to frighten someone: *Suddenly the teacher roared my name across the classroom.* | *'You idiot!' he roared.* | **+ at** *'Get down and don't move,' the man roared at her.*

bawl /bɔːl/ [v I/T] to shout very loudly and rudely in order to make sure that people hear what you are saying: *'Stop that thief!' he bawled at the top of his voice.* | *One of the prison guards was bawling orders across the yard.* | **+ at** *That couple next door are always shouting and bawling at each other.*

bellow /ˈbeləʊ/ [v I/T] to shout in a very loud deep voice, especially when you want a lot of people to hear you: *'Be quiet!' the teacher bellowed.* | *The officer in charge was bellowing instructions through a loudspeaker.* | **+ at** *Then the referee started to blow his whistle and bellow at me.*

2 something said very loudly

- ▸ shout
- ▸ scream
- ▸ yell
- ▸ roar
- ▸ cry
- ▸ cheer

shout /ʃaʊt/ [n C] a loud call that expresses anger, excitement etc, or is made in order to get someone's attention: *As we got near the stadium, we could hear the shouts of the crowd.* | **a shout of excitement/joy/pleasure etc** *Just then Angie burst in with a shout of excitement.* | **give a shout** *He gave a shout of joy as he realised he'd won the race.*

scream /skriːm/ [n C] a sudden loud shout or cry that expresses fear, excitement etc: *We could hear screams coming from the burning building.* | **a scream of fear/pain/delight etc** *A gun went off, and I heard a scream of fear from inside the room.* | **give a scream** *Charlie gave a scream of delight as he opened the present.*

yell /jel/ [n C] a very loud shout that expresses great anger, excitement etc or is made in order to get someone's attention: *A great yell went up from the crowd. Liverpool had scored.* | **a yell of alarm/fear/anger etc** *Steve could no longer prevent a yell of frustration.* | **give/let out a yell** *Christine gave a yell of alarm as blood spurted from the wound.*

roar /rɔːʳ/ [n C] a very loud deep shout, especially one that expresses anger, pain, amusement, or excitement: *I love to hear the roar of the crowd at a Blue Jays baseball game.* | **a roar of anger/pain/laughter etc** *There were roars of laughter coming from the living room.* | *I shall never forget his roar of anguish on hearing the terrible news.*

cry /kraɪ/ [n C] a loud shout: *As they left the stage there were cries of 'More! More!'* | **cry for help** *We heard a child's cries for help coming from the river.*

cheer /tʃɪəʳ/ [n C] a shout of happiness, praise, approval, or encouragement: *A deafening cheer rose from the crowd as the band walked onto the stage.* | **give a cheer** *Let's all give a big cheer for the newly married couple! Hip, hip, hooray!*

show

WHAT'S HERE

- **to show/let sb see sth** see **1 to 7**
- **to show/be a sign of sth** see **8 to 12**
- **to show your thoughts or feelings** see **13 to 17**

to show/let sb see sth

RELATED WORDS

opposite: **hide**

see also **point at, see, explain**

1 to let someone see something

- show
- let sb see
- let sb take a look
- present
- produce
- flash
- expose
- reveal

show /ʃəʊ/ [v T] to let someone see something, especially by holding it out in front of them: *Everyone has to show their identity cards at the entrance to the building.* | **show sb sth** *Stephanie showed us her engagement ring.* | *Show me what you're hiding under the desk, Johnny.* | **show sb sth** *You have to show the security guard your pass.* | **show sth to sb** *Neil showed his Pokemon card collection to Harry.*

let sb see /ˌlet (sb) ˈsiː/ [v phrase] especially spoken to show something to someone, especially because they have asked to see it: *Could you let me see the menu?* | *How would you feel if I wrote something about you, but I wouldn't let you see it?* | *Hold it up to the light and let me see what color it is.*

let sb take a look ALSO **let sb have a look** British /ˌlet (sb) teɪk ə ˈlʊk, ˌlet (sb) hæv ə ˈlʊk/ [v phrase] to show something to someone, especially so that they can look at it closely, for example in order to fix it: *At least let Mike take a look – he might be able to help.* | **+ at** *Let me have a look at your necklace. Perhaps I can fix it.* | *Take your shirt off, and let me take a look at that cut on your shoulder.*

present /prɪˈzent/ [v T] to show something such as an official document or ticket to someone in an official position: *Please present your boarding card at the gate.* | **present sth to sb** *All passports must be presented to the immigration officer.*

produce /prəˈdjuːs‖-ˈduːs/ [v T] formal to take something such as a ticket or official paper out of your pocket or bag and show it to someone in an official position: *The man fired from the car window when he was asked by a police officer to produce a license for the weapon.* | *Failure to produce a valid insurance certificate may result in criminal prosecution.*

flash /flæʃ/ [v T] to very quickly show something such as a ticket to someone when you are entering or leaving a place: *He flashed his membership card as passed through the door.* | **flash sth at sb** *Two police officers burst in, the latter hurriedly flashing his ID card at her as they made their way upstairs.*

expose /ɪkˈspəʊz/ [v T] formal to let someone see something that is usually covered or hidden: *The animal opened its mouth, exposing rows of sharp white teeth.* | *The receding tide had exposed huge expanses of sand.* —**exposed** [adj] *A freezing wind bit at her exposed legs, and she huddled closer to the fire.*

reveal /rɪˈviːl/ [v T] to let someone see something that is usually hidden or that they did not know was there: *She lifted the lid of the box to reveal a life-size porcelain baby doll.* | *A medical examination may reveal evidence of dietary deficiencies.*

2 to show someone where something is

- show
- point to
- point out
- mark
- indicate

show /ʃəʊ/ [v T] **show (sb) where** *The secretary showed him where to hang his coat.* | *Please find enclosed a map showing where our offices are* | **show sb sth** *Uncle Joe showed me the best place to go fishing.* | **show sb the way** *I'll show you the way to the station. It's not far.*

point to /ˈpɔɪnt tuː/ [v phrase not in passive] to show someone where someone or something is, by pointing towards it with your finger: *He took out a map and pointed to the island.* | *'The whiskey's over there,' Katie said, pointing to a bottle on the table.* | *Can you point to the one you want?*

point out /ˌpɔɪnt ˈaʊt/ [phr v T] to show someone a particular person or thing that you want them to notice, especially by pointing towards it with your finger **point out sb/sth** *As we drove through Baltimore, Mary pointed out the house where she was born.* | **point sb/sth out** *Which one's your boss? Can you point her out?* | **point out sth to sb** *'Aren't they beautiful?' said the guide, pointing out the paintings on the ceiling to us.* | **point out sth for sb** *Once they'd been pointed out for me, I had no trouble identifying the major stars and planets.*

mark /mɑːʳk/ [v T] to show where something is by putting an object there or making a mark: *Michael gave us a map of the city and marked some places of interest to visit.* | *He put a slip of paper in his book to mark his page.* | *A barbed wire fence marks the boundary between the two communities.* | **mark the spot** *The church marks the spot where St Peter died.*

indicate /ˈɪndɪ̇keɪt/ [v I/T] to show where something or someone is by pointing with part of your body: *The Director indicated a small table, where the items were on display.* | *'Shall we go in here?' He indicated the coffee bar.* | **indicate (sth) with sth** *'That's my boss,' he said, indicating with a nod of his head.*

3 to show information or measurements on a machine or sign

- show
- say
- display
- indicate
- register

show /ʃəʊ/ [v T] *The airline's passenger brochure shows air-routes, aircraft speeds and arrival and departure times.* | *A menu showing the options will appear on the computer screen.* | *I think that clock must be showing the wrong time.* | **+ that** *The graph shows that gas volume increases with temperature.*

say /seɪ/ [v T not in passive] especially spoken to show a particular distance, time, speed etc: *Although we must have done about 100 miles, the petrol gauge still said half-full.* | *What does your watch say? I think mine's stopped.*

display /dɪ'spleɪ/ [v T] if a computer or sign **displays** information, it shows the information in a way that makes it easy to see or notice: *Press 'Enter' to display the sorted mailing list.* | *The licence must be clearly displayed in the car windscreen.*

indicate /'ɪndəkeɪt/ [v T] if an instrument for measuring **indicates** information, it shows that information: *The temperature gauge indicated zero.* | *This dial indicates oil pressure in the engine.*

register /'redʒəstəʳ/ [v T] if a piece of equipment **registers** a particular speed, distance, time etc, that speed, distance etc has reached a particular point on the equipment's scale: *The jelly is ready for bottling when the thermometer registers 165 degrees.* | *Wind speeds registering between 70 and 100 mph have been recorded.* | *The biggest quake registered 5.2 on the Richter scale.*

4 to show art, paintings, products etc to a lot of people

- show
- display
- exhibit
- be on show/on display
- unveil

show /ʃəʊ/ [v I/T] to **show** something such as paintings or interesting objects, especially a collection of them, by putting them in a public place so that a lot of people can see them: *She hopes to show her paintings at the Institute of Contemporary Art.* | *His work-in-progress is currently showing at the Guildhall in Manchester.* | **be shown** *Some of Bresson's best photographs are being shown at the National Portrait Gallery this month.*

display /dɪ'spleɪ/ [v T] if a shop, museum etc **displays** things, it arranges them in a way that makes it possible for people to see them clearly: *The store windows were displaying the latest spring fashions.* | *Many stalls displayed the work of local artists and craftsmen.* | *In one room, late 19th and early 20th century paintings are displayed.*

exhibit /ɪg'zɪbət/ [v T] to show a special collection of paintings, photographs etc in a public place where people can look at them: *The gallery exhibits mainly contemporary sculpture and photography.* | *Picasso's paintings have been exhibited in galleries and museums all over the world.* | *The sculpture was first exhibited at the Canadian National Exhibition.* —**exhibit** [n C] something that is exhibited: *All exhibits are listed in the catalogue.*

be on show/on display /biː ɒn 'ʃəʊ, ɒn dɪ'spleɪ/ [v phrase] if works of art, new products, or interesting objects **are on display**, they have been put in a public place where people can look at them: *The Supermac Computer was on display at the Umax booth.* | *As expected, there were dozens of cellular phones on display.* | *Several famous paintings by Leonardo da Vinci are on show at the National Gallery.* | **go on display/show** (=start to be shown for the first time) *Schiele's watercolours go on show here for two months, starting August 24.*

unveil /ˌʌn'veɪl/ [v T] to show or officially tell people about a new product, plan etc for the first time: *GM's solar-powered car was unveiled at last month's Geneva auto show.* | *The government has unveiled its plans for the future of Britain's armed forces.*

5 when paintings, art, products etc are shown publicly

- exhibition/show
- display

exhibition/show ALSO **exhibit** American /ˌeksə'bɪʃən, ʃəʊ, ɪg'zɪbət/ [n C] an event at which a collection of paintings, interesting objects etc are shown to the public for a period of time: *All the photographs in the exhibition are for sale.* | **photographic/trade/Picasso etc exhibition** *Milan is hosting an international trade exhibition this month.* | *The exhibit, entitled 'Search and Destroy', proved to be very popular.* | **+ of** *Davis is organizing an exhibition of paintings by contemporary black artists.*

display /dɪ'spleɪ/ [n C] a group of things that are shown together for people to look at: *They held a spectacular firework display to mark the new millennium.* | **+ of** *The festival of Lucia is a dazzling display of the art, music and dance of an ancient culture.* | *a display of Shona sculpture from Zimbabwe*

6 to show someone a house, building, or place

- show sb sth
- show sb around
- conduct
- take sb on a tour

show sb sth /'ʃəʊ (sb sth)/ [v phrase] to show someone a house, building, or other place by walking with them around it and telling them about it: *Let me show you the garden.* | *It's worth asking a local guide to show you the sights.* | *The real estate agent showed them house after house, but they couldn't find one they liked.*

show sb around ALSO **show sb round** British /ˌʃəʊ (sb) ə'raʊnd, ˌʃəʊ (sb) 'raʊnd/ [phr v T] to show someone the interesting or important parts of a place or building when they first visit it: *She'd never been to Oxford before, so I offered to show her round.* | *Later, he showed Margaret all around his new house.* | *In the afternoon, we were shown around the Kennedy Space Center.*

conduct /kən'dʌkt/ [v T] to show someone a building or place on an official tour **+ around** *The visitors were conducted around the factory by senior managers.* | *An officer was sent to conduct the journalists around the shattered building.* —**conducted tour** [n C] an organized trip in which an official guide shows people a place: *We went on a conducted tour of the castle.*

take sb on a tour /ˌteɪk (sb) ɒn ə 'tʊəʳ/ [v phrase] to show someone a city, museum, house etc, and tell them about all the important or interesting parts of it: *Gregory took us on a riverboat tour down the Volga.* | *Officials were taken on a tour of the one-time maximum security prison.*

7 to show someone something because you are proud of it

- show off
- flaunt
- flourish
- parade

see also **show off, proud, boast**

show off /ˌʃəʊ 'ɒf/ [phr v T] to show someone or something that you are proud of to other people **show off sth/sb (to sb)** *She raised her wrist, showing off a sparkling diamond bracelet.* | *At last, this was a chance to show off her talents before a real audience.* | **show sth/sb off (to sb)** *He wanted to show his daughter off to everybody.*

flaunt /flɔːnt‖flɔːnt, flɑːnt/ [v T] to let people see your valuable possessions so that they know you are rich or successful, in a way that annoys people: *Others have called him arrogant, for flaunting his millionaire lifestyle.* | *He's very rich, but he doesn't like to flaunt his wealth or waste his money.* | *If you've got it, flaunt it!*

flourish /ˈflʌrɪʃ‖ˈflɜːrɪʃ/ [v T] to wave something in your hand in order to make people notice it: *She came in excitedly, flourishing a letter with her exam results.* | *The painting showed two gates guarded by imposing military figures flourishing swords.*

parade /pəˈreɪd/ [v T] if someone **parades** another person, they show that person in public for others to see, usually proudly or as if they own them **+ across/through/beside etc** *The captured soldiers were paraded through the streets of the city.* | *The senator loves parading his beautiful new wife before the nation.*

to show/be a sign of sth

RELATED WORDS

▸ *see also* **prove**

8 when something shows that something else is true

- ▸ **show**
- ▸ **be a sign**
- ▸ **demonstrate**
- ▸ **mean**
- ▸ **make clear**
- ▸ **reflect**
- ▸ **illustrate**
- ▸ **tell**
- ▸ **be evidence**
- ▸ **reveal**

show /ʃəʊ/ [v T not in progressive] to prove that something is true: *Her nervousness is shown by a tendency to laugh a lot in public.* | **show (sb) how/what/why etc** *It cost $5000 to repair the car – that shows how bad the damage was!* | *It shows you what they think of their customers, if they can't even be bothered to answer your letter!* | **show sth/sb to do sth** *Caffeine has been shown to have a good effect on mental performance.* | **+ (that)** *The evidence shows that this area was probably the site of a Roman settlement.* | *The polls clearly show that the voters are dissatisfied with the present government.* | **it (just) goes to show** (=use to emphasize that something proves that what you are saying is true) *It just goes to show that we can all learn from experience, whether we're 8 or 80.*

be a sign /biː ə ˈsaɪn/ [v phrase] if an event or action **is a sign** of something else, it is one of the things that shows that something is probably true **+ of** *The public opposition to the airport is a sign of how much people's attitudes have changed.* | *A cluttered desk is a sign of a creative mind.* | **+ that** *When a dog wags his tail, it's a sign that he's happy.* | **be a sure/clear sign** *My mother pursed her lips, a sure sign of displeasure.* | **take/view/see sth as a sign that** (=decide that it shows something) *When she didn't return my calls, I took it as a sign that she just wasn't interested.*

demonstrate /ˈdemənstreɪt/ [v T not in progressive] formal to show very clearly that something is true – use this especially in official or technical contexts: *His commitment to the company is demonstrated by his work on the project.* | **+ how/why/whether etc** *Here are some examples that demonstrate how badly some students write their resumés.* | *The assessment center gives each applicant the opportunity to demonstrate whether they are suited to the work.* | **+ that** *I'm afraid this whole episode demonstrates that we have become less compassionate as a society.* | **demonstrate (sth) to sb** *You've got to be able to demonstrate to people that the union can help in these cases.*

mean /miːn/ [v T not in progressive or passive] if an event or action **means** something, you can guess from it that something has happened or is true: *Cloudy water from the taps usually means problems with your storage tank.* | *A free economy does not mean the absence of any economic control.* | **+ (that)** *This sort of behaviour means that the child is definitely unhappy.* | *If A is false, does that also mean proposition B is false?* | **must mean** *Her car's not there, so that must mean she's gone to pick him up.*

make clear /ˌmeɪk ˈklɪəʳ/ [v phrase not in progressive] to show very clearly that something is true **make it clear (that)** *This new evidence makes it clear that Rourke was acting independently of the others.* | **make it clear what/why/how etc** *The look in her eyes made it clear what she meant.* | **make clear sth** *The Unabomber's diary makes clear his loathing and contempt for society.*

reflect /rɪˈflekt/ [v T not in progressive] if something **reflects** a situation or fact, it is a result of that situation or fact and shows clearly that the situation or fact exists: *The three-year guarantee reflects the company's confidence in the quality of its products.* | *His fair, freckled skin and blue eyes reflect his Irish heritage.* | *This poll reflects what the Republicans of California are sensing.* | **be reflected in** *The culture of a nation is always reflected in its language.*

illustrate /ˈɪləstreɪt/ [v T not in progressive] to be an example which shows that a fact is true or that a situation exists: *As this story illustrates, some stars have become as bored as audiences by Hollywood extravagance.* | *This point can be illustrated by two brief examples.* | **+ how/why/what** *The experiment illustrates how careful you have to be when interpreting results.*

tell /tel/ [v T not in progressive or passive] if a situation, detail etc **tells** you something, it helps you to know, understand, or guess more about something: *What does this tell us about the experience of young immigrants to this country?* | **tell sb how many/much etc** *Unfortunately, the photographs can tell us very little about the potential for life on Mars.* | **tell sb that** *The research told us that many drug addicts were returning to heroin up to three years after the treatment.*

be evidence /biː ˈevɪdəns/ [v phrase] if a situation, detail, fact **is evidence** of a general situation, attitude, type of behaviour etc, it shows that it exists **+ of** *Changes in sexual laws in recent years are evidence of a gradual movement towards greater tolerance.* | **+ that** *Journalists argue that being attacked by both sides is evidence that their coverage is fair.* | *This is clear evidence that the crime figures do not represent the true situation.*

reveal /rɪˈviːl/ [v T not in progressive] to show something that most people did not know or realize is true: *The way he spoke in the bar afterwards revealed prejudice and bitterness that I had never suspected.* | *Separate holidays and weekends apart reveal more clearly than any words the state of their marriage.* | **+ how/why/what etc** *The President's refusal to meet the press reveals just how serious the crisis is.* | *Positive tests have revealed why some athletes were so reluctant to co-operate.* | **+ that** *The fact that there are no black officers in the entire regiment reveals that the army is not serious about its anti-discrimination policies.* —**revealing** [adj] *a very revealing statement*

9 when something shows that something else is likely to be true

- suggest
- indicate
- give the impression
- point to
- imply
- implicate
- be indicative of

suggest /sə'dʒest‖səg-/ [v T not in progressive] to show that something is probably true, even though there is no definite proof: *In fact, the situation is far worse than these figures suggest.* | **+ (that)** *There was nothing in his letter to suggest that he might have been unhappy or depressed.* | *The drop in trading suggests the Asian economies may be headed for recession.* | **suggest sth to sb** *A child's behavior might suggest to others that there are problems at home.* | **strongly suggest** (=show that something is very likely) *The door had not been forced open, which strongly suggests that the victim was known to her killer.*

indicate /'ɪndɪ̣keɪt/ [v T not in progressive] if scientific facts, tests, official figures etc **indicate** something, they show that it is likely to be true: *How badly reform is needed was indicated recently by the rising youth crime figures.* | **+ (that)** *Research indicates that the drug can be harmful to pregnant women.* | *Campaign finance records indicate many of the guests were donors to his own party.*

give the impression /ˌgɪv ði ɪm'preʃən/ [v phrase not usually in progressive] to make people think that a particular situation exists, even though this may not actually be true: *She wasn't stupid, though at times she gave that impression.* | **+ (that)** *The luxurious offices gave the impression that the company had plenty of money to spare.* | **+ of** *All this splendour and ceremony may at first give the impression of high culture and sophistication.* | **give the impression that** *He gave me the impression that he didn't really rate my work.*

point to /'pɔɪnt tuː/ [phr v T not in progressive or passive] to show that a particular explanation for something is likely to be true or that something is likely to happen in the future: *All the evidence points to a fatty diet being the main cause of heart disease in the West.* | *The poor economic climate and the attitude of leading executives both point to a grim future.*

imply /ɪm'plaɪ/ [v T not in progressive] if a fact or piece of information, especially scientific information, **implies** something, it shows that it is likely to be true: *Among the ruins there are inscriptions, implying some degree of literacy even in the 9th century BC.* | *As the examples imply, some markets are local while others are national or international in scope.* | **+ (that)** *The results imply that the disease originated in West Africa.*

implicate /'ɪmplɪ̣keɪt/ [v T] to show that someone or something is likely to be involved in or connected to something, especially something bad or harmful: *According to the prosecution, DNA tests 'irrefutably' implicate Henson.* | **+ in** *Sexually transmitted diseases have long been implicated in infertility.* | **+ as** *Seafood is increasingly implicated as the source of the hepatitis A virus.* | **implicate himself/yourself etc** (=show, suggest, or prove that he etc has committed a crime) *Simon knew he couldn't possibly provide a blood sample without implicating himself.*

be indicative of /biː ɪn'dɪkətɪv ɒv/ [v phrase] formal if something **is indicative of** an event or situation, it shows that the event or situation is likely to exist or be true, but it is not definite that it does: *Persistent abdominal pain may be indicative of appendicitis.* | *The absence of any famous female composers is more indicative of male dominance than male genius.*

10 to show that someone or something is good

- show
- say a lot for/about
- be a tribute to
- reflect well on
- be a testament to

show /ʃəʊ/ [v T not in progressive] *His performance shows great talent.* | *Lieutenant Marche's actions showed great courage and leadership.* | **+ how/what/why etc** *This latest album certainly shows why Pine is rated a first-class jazz musician among his peers.*

say a lot for/about ALSO **say a great deal for/about** /ˌseɪ ə 'lɒt fɔːʳ, əbaʊt‖-'lɑːt-, ˌseɪ ə greɪt 'diːl fɔːʳ, əbaʊt/ [v phrase not in progressive] informal to show very clearly that someone has good qualities, though those qualities are not always named: *The decision says a great deal for Chang's courage and convictions.* | *To have those sort of setbacks and still keep everything together says a lot about Richard.* | **+ that** *It says a lot for Banks that he decided to finish the race even though he had no hope of winning.*

be a tribute to /biː ə 'trɪbjuːt tuː/ [v phrase] if a fact or achievement **is a tribute to** someone or something, it shows their good qualities because it is a result of those qualities: *It was a tribute to her teaching methods that most of the children passed the tests.* | *That the book was ever finished was a tribute to the patience and dedication of all concerned.*

reflect well on /rɪˌflekt 'wel ɒn/ [v phrase not usually in progressive] if an action or event **reflects well on** a person or organization, it shows that they have good qualities or abilities, and this makes people's opinion of them improve: *Military success always reflects well on the government in power at the time.* | *This win reflects well on the growing strength of our young players.* | *The television coverage of the trial reflected well on NBC.*

be a testament to /biː ə 'testɪ̣mənt tuː/ [v phrase] formal if something **is testament to** a particular quality or person, it shows how good, strong, skilled etc that quality or person really is: *The incredible precision of the equipment is testament to the mechanical skill of the engineers who built it.* | *It is a testament to the greatness of Rodgers & Hart that their music still sounds as fresh and vital as the day it was written.*

11 to show that someone or something is bad

- show
- not say much for
- be a reflection on
- reflect badly on
- be a comment on
- be symptomatic of
- be an indictment of
- make a mockery of

show /ʃəʊ/ [v T not in progressive] *His approach to the problem showed a complete lack of understanding.* | **+ how/what/why etc** *This just shows how the standard of reporting has declined over the past ten years.* | *Maddie's remarks showed why she is disliked and feared by her fellow workers.*

not say much for ALSO **not say a lot for sb/sth** /nɒt seɪ 'mʌtʃ fɔːʳ, nɒt seɪ ə 'lɒt fɔːʳ (sb/sth) ‖-'lɑːt-/ [v phrase not in progressive] if a fact or achievement does **not say much for** someone or something, it shows very clearly that they are not as good, skilful etc as they should be: *Only a quarter of the class passed the exam, which doesn't say much for the quality of the teaching.* | *It doesn't say much for the media that they are criticizing something they haven't even seen yet.*

be a reflection on /biː ə rɪˈflekʃən ɒn/ [v phrase] if a bad situation or a bad result **is a reflection on** someone or something, it shows their character, abilities, or qualities are not very good, because the bad situation or result is their fault: *'It's no reflection on you,' Fred explained kindly. 'My mum's always like that with my girlfriends.'* | *When children are criticized, mothers often see it as a reflection on themselves.*

reflect badly on ALSO **not reflect well on sb/sth** /rɪˌflekt ˈbædli ɒn, nɒt rɪˌflekt ˈwel ɒn (sb/sth)/ [v phrase not usually in progressive] if an action or event **reflects badly on** someone, it shows that they have bad qualities, and this makes people's opinion of them become worse: *The way that the refugees have been treated reflects very badly on the government.* | *Both women knew that squabbling in public would reflect badly on both of them.*

be a comment on /biː ə ˈkɒment ɒn‖-ˈkɑː-/ [v phrase] if a bad situation **is a comment on** problems or changes that affect all of society, it shows that these problems or changes exist and have a bad influence: *The increasing focus on sex and violence in most movies is a comment on the changing tastes of the movie-going public.* | **be a sad/damning comment on** *The food queues were a sad comment on the quality of life in the new republic.* | *To suggest that people are only honest when it can benefit them, is a damning comment on the human character.*

be symptomatic of ALSO **be a symptom of** /biː ˌsɪmptəˈmætɪk ɒv, biː ə ˈsɪmptəm ɒv/ [v phrase] formal if a small problem **is symptomatic of** a more serious or general problem, it shows that the more serious or general problem exists: *The whole episode was symptomatic of the US determination to avoid another Cuba.* | *Noisy classrooms are a symptom of a breakdown in authority.*

be an indictment of /biː ən ɪnˈdaɪtmənt ɒv/ [v phrase] to show very clearly that a system, plan etc is very bad, very wrong, or is not working in the way that it should: *The movie is neither an indictment nor an endorsement of capital punishment.* | **be a glaring/sad/serious etc indictment of sth** (=be a very clear sign of something bad) *Numbers of casualties among refugees represent an appalling indictment of Western policy.* | *It is a serious indictment of a medical profession so arrogant that it dismisses out of hand any 'alternative' forms of therapy.*

make a mockery of /ˌmeɪk ə ˈmɒkəri ɒv‖-ˈmɑːk-/ [v phrase] to show that something such as a system, principle, or idea is completely false, stupid, or ineffective – use this especially when you think it is wrong that something should be made to seem bad or wrong: *If that man gets released, it will make a mockery of our legal system.* | *Recent expenditure on defense has made a mockery of government promises to improve the lives of ordinary Russians.*

12 to show that something is going to happen

- mean
- spell
- bode well/ill
- herald

mean /miːn/ [v T not in progressive or passive] to be a sign that something is very likely to happen: *Dark clouds usually mean rain.* | **+ (that)** *High interest rates and high inflation mean a recession is not far away.* | *His new responsibilities at work mean Leroy will rarely see his children.* | **take sth to mean (that)** (=believe that something is a sign of something) *Stein took off his glasses and rested his head on the back of the chair. I took this to mean that he wasn't going to say any more.*

spell /spel/ [v T not in progressive or passive] if a situation or action **spells** trouble, problems etc, it makes you expect that something bad will happen, because there are clear signs that it will: *No one thinks this could spell the closure of the firm, but things could be better.* | *Out-of-town retail developments often spell the death of independent high street shops.*

bode well/ill /ˌbəʊd ˈwel, ˈɪl/ [v phrase not usually in progressive] formal to be a sign that something good or bad is likely to happen in the future: *Gandalf's late arrival did not bode well.* | **+ for** *The drop in profits bodes ill for Japan's semiconductor industry.* | *The high early viewing figures bode well for writers Lane and Harvey, who hope to achieve network success.*

herald /ˈherəld/ [v T not in progressive] to be a sign that something is going to happen soon, especially something important – used especially in literature or newspapers: *In February, the first storks arrive, heralding spring.* | *What changes do the attacks herald for everyday life in the US?* | *His prosecution perhaps heralds an end to the systematic corruption that has stained this government's reputation.* | **herald sth as** *Taxol has been heralded as a breakthrough in cancer treatment.*

to show your thoughts or feelings

RELATED WORDS

opposite: **hide**

▸ *see also* **feel**

13 to show your thoughts or feelings

- show
- display
- demonstrate
- exhibit
- register

show /ʃəʊ/ [v T] to behave in a way that shows people how you feel or what you character is like: *Paul didn't show much interest in the idea.* | *I just want you to show some respect, just for once.* | *If you're pleased, you've got a funny way of showing it.* | **show how angry/upset/happy etc you are** *The hostages showed great courage in a very frightening situation.* | *I was determined not to show how upset I felt.*

display /dɪˈspleɪ/ [v T] to behave in a way that shows people how you feel or what your character is like. **Display** is more formal than **show**: *I'm displaying my ignorance here, but could you just tell us exactly what your job as a geologist involves?* | *The previous government displayed a notable lack of enthusiasm for women's rights.* | *The contestants here today have displayed tremendous skill.* —**display** [n C] *a display of strength* | *Ian never did like public displays of affection.*

demonstrate /ˈdemənstreɪt/ [v T] to do something in order to deliberately and clearly show an attitude or feeling: *Brenda wanted to demonstrate her sympathy in a practical way.* | *The new law was intended to demonstrate the government's concern for the lowest paid workers.*

exhibit /ɪgˈzɪbɪ̣t/ [v T] formal to clearly show how you feel: *The prisoner exhibited no emotion when the sentence was read out.* | *Anyone who exhibits extreme anxiety in the face of potential danger is unlikely to become an effective military leader.*

register /ˈredʒɪ̣stəʳ/ [v T] especially written to show a feeling by the expression on your face, especially when you are reacting to something that happens or to what someone has said: *Caitlin watched his face, which registered a mixture of alarm and astonishment.* | *It was only when I mentioned the money that she registered a flicker of interest.*

14 to show your feelings, attitudes etc when you do not intend to

- can't hide
- reveal
- betray

can't hide /ˌkɑːnt ˈhaɪd‖ˌkænt-/ [v phrase] if you **can't hide** a feeling, you cannot stop yourself from showing it because the feeling is so strong: *Kris couldn't hide her delight at my situation.* | *'It'll be okay,' said Kang, unable to hide his disappointment.* | **+ from** *He couldn't hide his envy from her.*

reveal /rɪˈviːl/ [v T not usually in progressive] to show a feeling, quality, or attitude, especially without realizing that you are showing it: *The look on my face must have revealed my embarrassment.* | *Carter's face was a blank, revealing no emotion.* | *A slight trembling of his hands revealed his growing excitement.*

betray /bɪˈtreɪ/ [v T not in progressive or passive] to show a feeling, attitude, quality etc when you do not want or intend to: *His words were calm, but his voice betrayed his very real concern and anxiety.* | *Barker's comments on Germany betrayed a woeful ignorance of history and recent politics.*

15 someone who usually shows what they feel and think

- open
- demonstrative

open /ˈəʊpən/ [adj] someone who is **open** does not try to hide what they are feeling or thinking: *He had a very open nature.* | *My New Year resolution is to be more honest and open towards other people.* | **+ about** *Julia was quite open about her disappointment.* | *So I'll lose my job, just for being open about my beliefs.* —**openly** [adv] *She spoke openly about her fears.* | *You openly disobeyed your father.*

demonstrative /dɪˈmɒnstrətɪv‖dɪˈmɑːn-/ [adj] someone who is **demonstrative** shows feelings of friendliness or love clearly and without being embarrassed, for example by kissing or touching: *His parents were never very demonstrative towards him, so he finds it hard to show his own feelings.* | *She's not a very demonstrative person, but her friends are important to her.*

16 someone who does not usually show what they feel or think

- reserved
- introverted
- undemonstrative

▸ *see also* **shy**

reserved /rɪˈzɜːʳvd/ [adj] someone who is **reserved** is usually quiet and unwilling to talk about or show their feelings: *Are you cautious and reserved, or adventurous and uninhibited?* | *They are very reserved people, the English. It takes some time to get to know them.*

introverted /ˈɪntrəvɜːʳtɪ̣d/ [adj] someone who is **introverted** is quiet and prefers not to be with other people, and does not talk about their feelings or opinions: *He is described as an introverted teenager, with a love of horses.* | *I was probably more introverted than Arthur when we were children.* —**introvert** [n C] *I think everyone has a bit of the introvert in them.*

undemonstrative /ˌʌndɪˈmɒnstrətɪv‖-ˈmɑːn-/ [adj] someone who is **undemonstrative** does not show feelings of friendliness or love for other people, for example by kissing or touching them: *Neighbours say he was quiet, undemonstrative and always carefully dressed.*

17 to help someone or something show a particular feeling or quality

- bring out

bring out /ˌbrɪŋ ˈaʊt/ [phr v T] *Competitive games bring out my aggressive side.* | *Counsellors are specially trained to bring out people's innermost fears and emotions.* | **bring out the best/ worst in sb** (=make them show their best or worst qualities) *For some reason, Christmas always seemed to bring out the worst in Dad.*

show off

RELATED WORDS

opposite: **modest**

▸ *see also* **boast, proud, show**

1 to behave in a way that makes other people notice you

- show off
- strut your stuff

show off /ˌʃəʊ ˈɒf/ [phr v I] to keep doing things and saying things in order to show people how clever you are, how brave or strong you are etc – use this especially when you disapprove of this behaviour: *He doesn't usually drive as fast as this. He's just showing off because you're here.* | *Billy, please stop showing off and sit down quietly!* | **show off in front of sb** *I think he was trying to show off in front of the girls.* | **show off to sb** British *We used to wear as much make-up as we dared, in order to show off to our friends.*

strut your stuff /ˌstrʌt jɔːʳ ˈstʌf/ [v phrase] informal to do something that you do well, usually in a way that shows you are proud of yourself: *We watched the sixteen year olds strutting their stuff on the dance floor.* | *He likes to strut his stuff on the stage in the annual Shakespeare production.*

2 someone who shows off

- show-off
- exhibitionist
- poser

show-off /ˈʃəʊ ɒf/ [n C] someone who is always doing or saying things in order to make other people admire them – use this especially when you disapprove of this behaviour: *Dave can be a real* *show-off at times.* | *You have to be a bit of a show-off to be an actor.*

exhibitionist /ˌeksəˈbɪʃənəst/ [n C] someone who publicly behaves in a way in which most people would usually only behave in private, in order to attract attention: *I've always liked singing for an audience – I guess I'm just an exhibitionist.* | *Most of the dresses in the show are unwearable, unless you're an exhibitionist.*

poser /ˈpəʊzəʳ/ [n C] British spoken someone who behaves in a way that they think will make them seem clever, fashionable, or well-educated, even when they are not – used especially humorously: *Did you hear him going on about his Porsches? What a poser!*

3 behaving in a way that makes people notice you

- **flamboyant**
- **dramatic**
- **ostentatious**
- **flashy**
- **pretentious**

flamboyant /flæmˈbɔɪənt/ [adj] someone who is **flamboyant** behaves, performs, or dresses in an extremely confident, and often unusual way that makes other people notice them: *He is one of football's most flamboyant characters.* | *a flamboyant French businessman* | *a young woman in flamboyant clothes*

dramatic /drəˈmætɪk/ [adj only before noun] if you do something in a **dramatic** way, you do it in a loud or noticeable way that is intended to get people's attention: *She raised her hands in a dramatic gesture of despair.* | *Rumpole produced the evidence with a dramatic flourish.* | *Rosa made a dramatic entrance into the room, wearing a tiny red dress.*

ostentatious /ˌɒstənˈteɪʃəs‖ˌɑː-/ [adj] doing things or buying things only in order to show people that you have a lot of money or because you want them to admire you or be jealous of you: *I thought of framing the letter, but that would be ostentatious.* | *They built themselves huge, ostentatious houses.* —**ostentatiously** [adv] *The women were ostentatiously dressed in designer evening dresses.*

flashy /ˈflæʃi/ [adj] someone who is **flashy** likes to show off about how much money or how many expensive things they have – use this when you do not approve of someone who does this: *a flashy young businessman*

pretentious /prɪˈtenʃəs/ [adj] doing something in a way that is intended to show how artistic or well-educated you are, in order to make people admire you – used to show disapproval: *I found Susie unbearably pretentious.* | *He has a pretentious style of writing, using four very difficult words where one simple one would do.* —**pretentiousness** [n U] *I can't bear pretentiousness of any kind.* —**pretentiously** [adv] *I bought some cheese in a small shop which rather pretentiously called itself a delicatessen.*

shut

RELATED WORDS

opposite: —— **open**

▸ *see also* **fasten/unfasten**

1 to close a door, window, gate etc

- **shut**
- **close**
- **slam**
- **push/kick/slide etc sth shut**
- **pull/push the door to**
- **draw the curtains/close the curtains**

shut /ʃʌt/ [v T] to move a door, window, gate etc so that it is no longer open: *Come in and shut the door behind you.* | *Someone had shut the gate to stop the sheep getting out onto the road.* | *She heard Charlotte downstairs shutting the windows, and locking up for the night.*

close /kləʊz/ [v T] to shut something, especially in a careful way: *Do you mind if I close the window?* | *She took the necklace out of the box and closed the lid.*

slam /slæm/ [v T] to shut a door quickly so that it makes a loud noise, especially because you are angry: *Jane marched out of the room slamming the door behind her.* | *He slammed the door so hard that the glass cracked.*

push/kick/slide etc sth shut /ˌpʊʃ (sth) ˈʃʌt/ [v phrase] to push, kick, slide etc something so that it shuts: *The woman pushed the door shut with her foot.* | *It started raining, so I quickly pulled the window shut.* | *'Sorry, we're closed,' said the official, sliding the wooden panel shut.*

pull/push the door to /ˌpʊl, ˌpʊʃ ðə dɔːʳ ˈtuː/ [v phrase] to move a door so that it is almost shut: *'Tell me what's wrong,' I said, pulling the door to.* | *She pushed the door to against the blinding sunlight.*

draw the curtains/close the curtains /ˌdrɔː ðə ˈkɜːʳtnz, ˌkləʊz ðə ˈkɜːʳtnz/ [v phrase] to close curtains by pulling them across a window: *Let's draw the curtains. We don't want people looking in.* | *The curtains were closed and the room was in darkness.*

2 to close a container

- **shut/close**
- **put the lid on**
- **screw on**

shut/close /ʃʌt, kləʊz/ [v T] to close a container, such as a box, case, or bottle: *As the teacher appeared, Matt shut the box quickly.* | *Russell shut his briefcase with a snap, and the meeting was over.* | *Put lids on all the jars and close them tightly.*

put the lid on /ˌpʊt ðə ˈlɪd ɒn/ [v phrase] to shut a container such as a bottle or box by putting a lid onto it: *Put the lid on the cookie jar when you've finished with it!* | *If you leave cooked food in a pan, you should always put the lid on.*

screw on /ˌskruː ˈɒn/ [phr v T] to shut a container such as a bottle by putting the lid on and turning it round and round until it cannot be turned any more **screw on sth** *I screwed on the top of the bottle as tightly as I could.* | **screw sth back on** *The fuel tank cap hadn't been screwed back on properly, and it came off when I drove away.* | **screw sth on** *She screwed the lid of the jar on again.*

3 to close your eyes/mouth

- **close/shut**

close/shut /kləʊz, ʃʌt/ [v T] to close your eyes or mouth: *I lay down and closed my eyes.* | *He shut his eyes and listened to the music.* | *Lara opened her mouth to speak, then closed it again.*

4 to become shut

- close/shut
- slam
- slide/blow/swing etc shut

close/shut /kləʊz, ʃʌt/ [v I] to become shut: *He walked out and the door shut behind him.* | *There was a bang as the gates shut.* | *Her eyes closed, and she fell into a deep sleep.*

slam ALSO **slam shut** /slæm, ˌslæm ˈʃʌt/ [v I] if a door **slams** or **slams shut**, it shuts quickly and makes a loud noise: *Outside in the street, car doors slammed and people were shouting.* | *She heard a door slam shut and the sound of footsteps on the path.*

slide/blow/swing etc shut /ˌslaɪd ˈʃʌt/ [v phrase] if a door, window, gate etc **slides**, **blows**, **swings etc shut**, it shuts by sliding, being blown, swinging etc: *The window suddenly blew shut, with a loud bang.* | *The elevator doors silently slid shut.*

5 to shut something so that it cannot be opened

- lock
- lock up
- bolt
- bar
- lock sb out

lock /lɒk‖lɑːk/ [v T] to shut something such as a door, window, or box by turning a key in a lock: *As she left the house she locked the door.* | *Don't forget to lock the car.* | *He locked the safe and put the key in his pocket.*

lock up /ˌlɒk ˈʌp‖ˌlɑːk-/ [phr v T] to lock something such as a vehicle or a building **lock up sth** *I had locked up my office for the night and gone home.* | *He always keeps his desk locked up.* | **lock sth up** *You should take basic precautions like locking your car up.*

bolt /bəʊlt/ [v T] to shut a door by sliding a small metal bar across both the door and its frame so that it cannot be opened from the other side: *My husband always bolts all the doors before going to bed.*

bar /bɑːʳ/ [v T] to shut a door or window and put a **bar**, a piece of wood, etc across it so that people cannot get in or out: *The owner of the house had barred the back door.* | *Some of the survivors said that one of the fire exits had been barred.*

lock sb out /ˌlɒk (sb) ˈaʊt‖ˌlɑːk-/ [v phrase] to prevent someone from entering a room or building by locking the door: *If she wasn't home by midnight her father would lock her out.* | **lock yourself out** (=not be able to get back into a place you have locked) *We always leave a key with a neighbour in case we lock ourselves out.*

6 to close an entrance or opening

- block up
- plug/plug up
- seal

block up /ˌblɒk ˈʌp‖ˌblɑːk-/ [phr v T] to put something into a hole or entrance so that it is permanently closed **block sth up** *Martha tried to block the mouse holes up, but new ones kept appearing.* | **block up sth** *Some of the windows in the church had been blocked up.* | *He blocked up the entrance to the tunnel with stones.*

plug/plug up /plʌg, ˌplʌg ˈʌp/ [v T/phr v T] to put something into a hole in order to stop a liquid from getting through: *We tried to plug the hole in the bottom of the boat with a plastic bag.* | *They didn't have enough material to plug up the gaps around the pipe.*

seal /siːl/ [v T] to close an entrance or container with something that completely prevents air or water from getting in or out: *If you seal the jars well, the jam will keep for months or even years.* | *In this experiment, the chamber must be completely sealed.*

7 when a door, entrance, lid etc has been shut

- shut/closed
- locked
- bolted
- sealed

shut/closed /ʃʌt, kləʊzd/ [adj not before noun] not open: *Make sure all the windows are shut before you go out.* | *The gates were closed, and there was no other way in.* | **tight shut** *Keep your eyes tight shut.*

locked /lɒkt‖lɑːkt/ [adj] something that is **locked** has been shut using a key: *Jamie tried the door. 'It's locked,' he said.* | *All office workers should keep their personal belongings in a locked drawer.* | *I need my coat out of your car – is it locked?*

bolted /ˈbəʊltɨd/ [adj] a door that is **bolted** has been shut by using a metal bar that slides across and prevents the door from being opened from the other side: *The door's bolted, we'll have to break it down.* | *Burglars can always find a way in, in spite of bolted doors and windows.*

sealed /siːld/ [adj] shut with something that prevents air or water from getting in or out: *Plants cannot survive in a sealed jar.* | *Sealed nuclear waste containers are then enclosed in concrete.*

8 when a shop or office is closed

- close
- be closed

- unable to continue in business *see* **fail (8)**

close ALSO **shut** /kləʊz, ʃʌt/ [v I] British if a shop or office **shuts** or **closes**, it stops being open for business: *'What time does the bank shut?' 'Four o'clock.'* | *Most of the stores close at 6:30.*

be closed ALSO **be shut** /biː ˈkləʊzd, biː ˈʃʌt/ [v phrase] if a shop or office **is shut** or **is closed**, it is not open for business: *The ticket office was closed.* | *It was nine o'clock and all the stores were shut.*

shy

RELATED WORDS

- someone who doesn't talk much *see* **talk (13)**
- *see also* **confident/not confident, embarrassed/embarrassing, nervous, worried/worrying, modest**

1 not confident about talking to people

- shy
- timid
- bashful
- coy
- diffident

shy /ʃaɪ/ [adj] not confident about talking to people, especially people you do not know: *David was always rather quiet and shy at school.* | *Carrie looked up at him and gave him a shy smile.* | **painfully shy** (=extremely shy) *He was painfully shy in public, but completely different at home with his family.* | **too shy to do sth** *I was too shy to ask her out on a date.* | **go all shy** spoken (=suddenly become very shy) *Look, she's gone all shy – stop teasing her.* | **shy with girls/boys/adults etc** (=shy when you are talking to girls, boys etc) *Because little Danny spent all his time with his mother, he was rather shy with men.* —**shyly** [adv] *She looked shyly away when he said anything nice about her.*

timid /ˈtɪmɪ̈d/ [adj] frightened to talk to people or to give your opinion, because you have very little confidence: *Ralph's wife was a small, timid woman who hardly ever spoke.* | *'May I come in?' said a timid little voice.* —**timidly** [adv] *'Can I go home now?' Sue asked, timidly.*

bashful /ˈbæʃfəl/ [adj] someone who is **bashful** is unwilling to give their opinions or do something that they would enjoy, especially because they are embarrassed or afraid that they will look stupid: *Don't be bashful about telling your family how you feel.* | *Kirsty gave Willy a bashful grin.* —**bashfully** [adv] *Bashfully, he kissed the bride lightly on her cheek.*

coy /kɔɪ/ [adj] someone who is **coy** deliberately behaves in a shy way because they think it is attractive: *Teresa blushed when she saw me and turned very coy.* | *Her mother encouraged her to use her feminine charm, to be coy and alluring.* —**coyly** [adv] *'Oh I don't know if I could do that!' she said coyly.*

diffident /ˈdɪfɪ̈dənt/ [adj] formal someone who is **diffident** does not like talking about their achievements or is not confident of their abilities: *Shaun became noticeably diffident when the conversation turned to the subject of his promotion.* | **+ about** *Joe was humble and diffident about his own success.* —**diffidently** [adv] *'I couldn't possibly do an article for your magazine,' said Irene diffidently, 'I don't write any more.'*

2 not wanting to be too friendly or to show your feelings

- reserved
- withdrawn
- introverted
- inhibited

reserved /rɪˈzɜːʳvd/ [adj] someone who is **reserved** tries not to show their feelings to other people and does not talk a lot: *English people have a reputation for being very reserved.* | *That shy reserved young man had turned into a confident adult.*

withdrawn /wɪðˈdrɔːn, wɪθ-/ [adj] not wanting to talk to anyone, especially because you are upset or unhappy: *Mike was silent and withdrawn that evening.* | *After her husband died Priscilla became very withdrawn and seldom left her home.* | *He'd always been an unhappy, withdrawn little boy.*

introverted /ˈɪntrəvɜːʳtɪ̈d/ [adj] someone who is **introverted** thinks too much about their own interests or problems and it is difficult for them to talk to people: *Peters is just too introverted to be a good manager.* | *The young girl, once so lively, became introverted and developed a nervous stammer.* —**introvert** [n C] someone who is introverted: *Chris was a bit of an introvert and didn't have many friends.*

inhibited /ɪnˈhɪbɪ̈tɪ̈d/ [adj] shy and unwilling to express your feelings, especially feelings concerned with sex or with your own body: *I am far too inhibited to have rows with people.* | *He accused her of being snobbish and emotionally inhibited.* | **+ about** *Young people of the nineteenth century were, in general, extremely inhibited about sex.*

3 to stop being shy

- come out of your shell
- bring sb out of their shell
- open up

come out of your shell /kʌm ˌaʊt əv jɔːʳ ˈʃel/ [v phrase] to become less shy and more willing to talk to people, especially as the result of an experience that has made you more confident: *When he first joined the company he was very quiet but now he's come out of his shell a lot.* | *Her manner is a little diffident, but she'll soon come out of her shell with a little encouragement.*

bring sb out of their shell /ˌbrɪŋ (sb) aʊt əv ðeəʳ ˈʃel/ [v phrase] to make someone less shy and more willing to talk to other people: *Emma was always such a shy girl, but these drama classes have really brought her out of her shell.* | *If Nick stayed with you this vacation, perhaps it would bring him out of his shell a little.*

open up /ˌəʊpən ˈʌp/ [phr v I] to gradually stop being shy, and become more willing to talk about yourself: *On our third date Melissa began to open up and told me about her family and about the years she spent in Italy.* | **+ to** *Many people find it easier to open up to a trained professional, such as a counsellor.*

4 shy feelings or behaviour

- shyness
- inhibition

shyness /ˈʃaɪnɪ̈s/ [n U] *A course in assertiveness could help her overcome her shyness.* | *Greg wanted to ask Julie for a date, but shyness always held him back.*

inhibition /ˌɪnhɪˈbɪʃən/ [n C/U] an uncomfortable feeling of shyness that makes it difficult for you to behave naturally, show your feelings, or do things that may be embarrassing: *I was amazed at Sam's lack of inhibition about singing in public.* | **lose your inhibitions** (=stop having inhibitions) *Alcohol can make you lose all your inhibitions – but you may regret this the next morning!*

sick/vomit

when food comes up from your stomach

RELATED WORDS

- *see also* **ill/sick, horrible**

1 to vomit

- throw up
- vomit
- puke
- bring up
- regurgitate
- retch/heave
- gag

throw up ALSO **be sick** British /ˌθrəʊ ˈʌp, biː ˈsɪk/ [phr v I/T] bring food or drink up from your stomach out through your mouth because you are ill, drunk, shocked etc: *Keith's had a particularly nasty form of the illness – he's even been throwing up with it.* | *One of my worst memories is of being sick in school assembly.* | *Just thinking about it makes me want to throw up.* | *The dog's been sick all over the carpet.* | **throw sth up** *I tried giving him some cool, boiled water, but he even threw that up.*

vomit /ˈvɒmɪ̈t‖ˈvɑː-/ [v I] to bring food or drink up from your stomach out through your mouth – used especially in medical contexts: *If she starts vomiting, contact the doctor immediately.* —**vomit** [n U] *The car seat was covered with vomit.* | *Morrison died after choking on his own vomit.*

puke /barf American /pju:k, bɑ:ʳf/ [v I] informal to bring food or drink up from your stomach out through your mouth because you are ill, drunk etc: *It smells like someone puked in here.* | *I could barely stand up without barfing.*

bring up /ˌbrɪŋ ˈʌp/ [phr v T] to bring food or drink up from your stomach out through your mouth, especially just after eating or drinking **bring up sth** *It is quite normal for your baby to bring up some milk after feeding.* | **bring sth/it up** *'Did you try giving him steamed fish?' 'Yes, but he brought it all up again.'*

regurgitate /rɪˈgɜ:ʳdʒɪteɪt/ [v T] if birds or animals **regurgitate** something they have just eaten, they bring it up through their mouth, for example in order to feed it to their young: *The chicks will feed on the partially-digested food regurgitated by the parent.*

retch/heave /retʃ, hi:v/ [v I] if you **retch** or **heave**, your stomach muscles move in an uncontrollable way as though you are going to vomit: *He was doubled over in pain, gasping and retching as if his insides were on fire.* | *The stench from the bed was enough to make Detective Saunders heave.*

gag /gæg/ [v I] if you **gag**, your throat moves as though you are going to vomit, especially because you have tasted or smelled something very unpleasant: *I could hardly eat the fish without gagging.* | **+ at/on** *Janir took a sip of the medicine and gagged at the vile taste.* | *Joe gagged on his first cigarette, red-faced and choking.*

2 when you think you are going to vomit

- feel sick
- feel queasy/nauseous
- nausea
- be going to throw up

feel sick ALSO **feel sick to your stomach** American /ˌfi:l ˈsɪk, fi:l ˌsɪk tə jɔ:ʳ ˈstʌmək/ [v phrase] to have the feeling that you are going to vomit: *If you feel sick, there's the bowl, okay?* | *I had no urge to smoke when I was pregnant. It made me feel sick to my stomach.* | *He developed a severe headache and felt very sick by day three.*

feel queasy/nauseous /fi:l ˈkwi:zi, ˈnɔ:ziəs/ [adj] to have the sick feeling you get in your stomach and head when you think you are going to vomit: *He felt queasy as soon as the boat started to move.* | *Just the thought of all that food's made me feel quite queasy.*

nausea /ˈnɔ:ziə, -siə‖-ziə, -ʃə/ [n U] the feeling that you have when you think you are going to vomit – used especially in medical contexts: *Cancer drugs often have unpleasant side effects, such as nausea and loss of hair.* | *Nausea swept over me as I looked at the body of the dead boy.*

be going to throw up ALSO **be going to be sick** British /bi: ˌgəʊɪŋ tə θrəʊ ˈʌp, bi: ˌgəʊɪŋ tə bi: ˈsɪk/ [v phrase] if you feel that you **are going to throw up** or you **are going to be sick**, you feel that you are going to vomit very soon: *'I think I'm going to be sick,' said a small voice from the back of the classroom.* | *You look very pale – you're not going to throw up are you?*

3 the physical condition of being sick

- vomiting
- morning sickness

vomiting /ˈvɒmɪtɪŋ‖ˈvɑ:-/ [n U] *Symptoms include dizziness, vomiting and headache.* | *Persistent vomiting can lead to dehydration.*

morning sickness /ˌmɔ:ʳnɪŋ ˈsɪknɪs/ [n U] a feeling of sickness that some women have when they are expecting a baby: *Morning sickness usually disappears after the third month of pregnancy.*

side

RELATED WORDS

see also **edge, middle**

1 the part that is furthest from the middle

- side
- edge
- end
- margin

side /saɪd/ [n C] one of the parts of an area that is furthest from the middle and closest to the edge **+ of** *Two men were sitting at the side of the road.* | *Dancers came on from both sides of the stage.* | *People had formed a long queue that went around the sides of the room.* | **on the side (of sth)** *Just put your things over there on the side.* | *There were high walls on all four sides of the prison yard.*

edge /edʒ/ [n C] the part around an object or area that is furthest from its centre, or the part along its side where its surface ends: *A group of children were playing at the water's edge.* | **+ of** *The edges of the carpet were torn.* | *Keep away from the edge of the cliff – you might fall.* | **on the edge of sth** *He set the ashtray down on the edge of the table.* | **at the edge of sth** (=next to the edge) *We camped right at the edge of the desert.*

end /end/ [n C] one of the two parts of a long object or area that are furthest from each other **+ of** *He cut a thick slice from the end of the loaf.* | **at one end of sth** *Mrs Deacon sat at one end of the long table and I sat at the other.* | **at both ends** *There are scoreboards at both ends of the stadium.* | **at each end** *A boy was carrying a stick across his shoulders with a pail of water at each end.*

margin /ˈmɑ:ʳdʒɪn/ [n C] the empty space on the left or right side of a page of writing: *Someone had written a note in the left-hand margin.* | *She widened the margins so her essay would look longer.*

2 one of the two areas on either side of a line, wall, river etc

- side
- bank

side /saɪd/ [n C] *A small river cuts through the property with the house on one side and the gardens on the other.* | **+ of** *This side of the fence is private property.* | *From the other side of the wall came the sounds of children playing.*

bank /bæŋk/ [n C] the land along the side of a river: *The sun was setting behind the opposite bank.* | **on the bank/banks of sth** *They were building a new theatre on the south bank of the Thames.* | *Portland is a sprawling city on the banks of the Willamette River.*

3 one of two sides of something thin and flat

▸ side

side /saɪd/ [n C] one of two sides of something that is very thin and flat, for example a piece of paper, a leaf or a coin etc: *Instructions on how to get there are on the other side.* | **+ of** *Look at the beautiful decorations on this side of the coin.*

4 not the front, back, top, or bottom

▸ side

side /saɪd/ [n C] one of the two surfaces of a building, vehicle, or object that is not the front, back, top, or bottom: *One of its sides was covered with intricate patterns.* | **+ of** *A truck ran into the side of the car, killing the driver and two passengers.* | **on the side of sth** *Something had been inscribed on the side of the box.* | **at the side of sth** *There was another entrance at the side of the building.*

5 the left or right half of an object, area, or road

▸ side

side /saɪd/ [n C] *OK, let's have all the girls on this side and all the boys on that side.* | **+ of** *You stay on your side of the bed and I'll stay on mine.* | *The left side of the brain controls the right side of the body.* | **on the left-hand/right-hand/other side** *In Japan they drive on the left-hand side of the road.*

6 towards the side, or from side to side

▸ sideways
▸ to one side/to the side
▸ from side to side

▸ *see also* **move (5)**

sideways /ˈsaɪdweɪz/ [adv] moving, looking, or facing to the left or right instead of straight ahead: *The car skidded sideways off the road.* | *Tony swayed sideways but caught himself before he fell.* | *If we turn the chest sideways, I think we can get it through the door.*

to one side/to the side /tə ˌwʌn ˈsaɪd, tə ðə ˈsaɪd/ [adv] if someone or something moves **to one side** or **to the side**, they move from where they are to the left or to the right: *She pushed her plate to one side and leaned forward.* | *Could you move a little to the side so we can get past?*

from side to side /frəm ˌsaɪd tə ˈsaɪd/ [adv] moving continuously, first to one side then to the other: *The tractor swayed from side to side, almost throwing me out of my seat.* | *Ezra rocked impatiently from side to side as he waited.*

sign

WHAT'S HERE

● **sign/symbol**	see **1 to 2**
● **sign/gesture**	see **3 to 4**
● **sign/indication**	see **5**

sign/symbol

1 a written sign that gives instructions or information

▸ sign
▸ notice
▸ poster

sign /saɪn/ [n C] *There was a big sign above the entrance.* | *A neon sign flashed on and off in the window.* | *Didn't you see the 'No smoking' sign?* | *Turn left and then follow the signs till you get to the freeway.* | **traffic/road sign** (=a sign that gives information to drivers) *Out in the desert there are hardly any road signs along the highway.*

notice /ˈnəʊtɪ̣s/ [n C] especially British a piece of paper giving instructions or information, that is put in a place where people can see it: *The details of the trip are on that notice over there.* | **put up a notice** *I'll put up a notice about the meeting on the bulletin board.* | **take down a notice** *Now that the sale is over someone needs to take down the notices.*

poster /ˈpəʊstəʳ/ [n C] a large printed piece of paper that is put on a wall in a public place, and that gives information about something that is going to happen, for example a film or concert: *Sandra collects old movie posters.* | *Ernst's supporters have plastered his election posters over walls and cars.* | **+ for** *There are posters for the Van Gogh exhibition everywhere.*

2 a picture or shape that has a particular meaning

▸ sign
▸ symbol
▸ logo
▸ emblem
▸ insignia

▸ *see also* **meaning**

sign /saɪn/ [n C] a picture or shape that has a particular meaning, and that is well known and often used: *You've forgotten to put the dollar sign before the total amount.* | *Where's the percentage sign on this keyboard?*

symbol /ˈsɪmbəl/ [n C] a picture, shape, or design that has a particular meaning or represents an idea: *The walls were covered with magical symbols.* | *For several years Prince used a symbol instead of his name.* | **+ of** *The dove is a symbol of peace.* | **+ for** *The ancient Egyptians had no symbol for 'zero.'*

logo /ˈləʊgəʊ/ [n C] a sign that has been designed to represent an organization or product: *The baseball team has a new logo.* | *His costume had the Superman logo across the chest.* | *You can buy bags with the company logo on them in the gift shop.*

emblem /ˈembləm/ [n C] a picture of an object, flower, animal etc that is used to represent a country or organization: *Scotland's emblem is the this-*

tle. | *The jacket had a tiny Olympic emblem on the pocket.* | **+ of** *The hammer and sickle is the emblem of the Communist Party.*

insignia /ɪnˈsɪgniə/ [n plural] shapes, pictures, decorations etc that represent a powerful group, especially a military organization: *Someone had spray-painted gang insignia on his car.* | *They collect clothing with FBI insignia on it so they can pretend to be federal agents.*

sign/gesture

RELATED WORDS

▸ *see also* **say, tell, show**

3 a movement or sound that you make to tell someone something

- ▸ sign
- ▸ signal
- ▸ gesture
- ▸ nod

sign /saɪn/ [n C] a movement that you make in order to tell someone something: *He raised his hand in a sign of greeting.* | **+ (that)** *Mardas threw his hands in the air – a sign to his supporters that victory was theirs.* | **+ for sb to do sth** *When the teacher puts her finger to her lips, it's a sign for you all to be quiet.*

signal /ˈsɪgnəl/ [n C] a sound or movement that you make in order to tell someone to do something **give a signal** *Don't start yet – wait until I give the signal.* | **+ to do sth** *The soldiers were waiting for the signal to start firing.* | **+ for sb to do sth** *When I nod my head, that's the signal for you to start playing the music.* | **hand signals** *Stock brokers use roughly 300 hand signals on the trading floor.*

gesture /ˈdʒestʃəʳ/ [n C] a movement of your hands, arms, or head that shows how you feel, especially when you are very worried or angry **+ of** *Jim raised his hands in a gesture of despair.* | **make a gesture** *Someone in another car started making gestures and pointing at our tires.* | **make a rude gesture** *The fight started when one of the fans made a rude gesture at a player.*

nod /nɒd‖nɑːd/ [n C] a slight downward movement you make with your head to say 'yes' to something or to say that something can begin: *I asked if he was hungry, and he responded with a nod.* | **give (sb) a nod** *Daniels gave a slight nod, and Bill started to speak.*

4 to make a movement or sound to tell someone something

- ▸ make a sign
- ▸ signal
- ▸ give the signal
- ▸ wave
- ▸ wink
- ▸ nod/nod your head
- ▸ gesture
- ▸ motion
- ▸ beckon

make a sign /ˌmeɪk ə ˈsaɪn/ [v phrase] to make a movement, especially with your hand, in order to tell someone something: *I'll make a sign when I'm ready.* | *The President made a sign to indicate that he wanted to leave.* | **+ (that)** *From across the room Marla made a sign that she had seen me come in.*

signal /ˈsɪgnəl/ [v I/T] to make a movement or sound in order to give instructions or information: *A sailor began signalling with two flags.* | **+ to** *Graham finished his drink and signalled to the waiter.* | **+ that** *An official signalled that it was time for the race to begin.* | **+ sb to do sth** *Slowly he inched around the corner, signalling for the others to follow.*

give the signal /ˌgɪv ðə ˈsɪgnəl/ [v phrase] to make a previously agreed sign that tells someone that they should start doing something: *When I give the signal, I want you all to start clapping.* | **give (sb) the signal to do sth** *The dog waited patiently until his master gave him the signal to eat.*

wave /weɪv/ [v I/T] to move your hand or arm from one side to the other, for example in order to get someone's attention or to tell them something: *She continued to wave as the car drove out of sight.* | **+ at** *Who's that waving at you?* | **+ to** *The emperor waved to the crowd from the palace balcony.* | **+ for sb to do sth** *Yolanda waved for us to come over.* | **wave sb through/on** (=wave to show someone that they can go through or continue their journey) *The customs officer at the border waved us through.* | **wave goodbye** (=wave to someone who is leaving) *Her parents stood in the doorway and waved goodbye.* — **wave** [n C] **give sb a wave** (=wave at someone in order to say hello or goodbye) *I gave him a friendly wave.*

wink /wɪŋk/ [v I] to quickly close and open one eye, in order to show that you are joking or that you share a secret with someone: *Ben grinned at his father and winked.* | **+ at** *'The weather's so nice, I'm thinking of calling in sick tomorrow,' she said, winking at me.* — **wink** [n C] when you close and open one eye quickly: *'Don't worry,' he said with a wink. 'I won't tell anyone about this.'*

nod/nod your head /nɒd, ˌnɒd jɔːʳ ˈhed‖ˌnɑːd-/ [v phrase] to make a slight downward movement with your head to say 'yes' or 'hello' or to say that something can begin: *Rob nodded his head in agreement.* | *'Has he really left you?' I asked. Josie nodded miserably.* | **+ at/to** *The two men nodded to each other, as if they'd met before.* | **+ for sb to do sth** *She nodded for Mike to lead the way.*

gesture /ˈdʒestʃəʳ/ [v I] to use a movement of your hand, especially to tell someone to go to a place or to emphasize your meaning when you are saying something: *The man was gesturing wildly, but we couldn't understand what he wanted.* | **+ to/at** *'Please sit down,' said Winters, gesturing at the chair facing his own.* | **+ to** *Celia began listing their recent purchases and gestured proudly to the fountain.* | **+ for sb to do sth** *I turned to see a large policeman gesturing for us to move along.*

motion /ˈməʊʃən/ [v I/T] to use a short movement of your arm or hand to tell someone what to do or where to go **+ to** *Neil finished his meal, and then motioned to the waitress.* | **+ for sb to do sth** *Seeing Bert in the doorway, I motioned for him to come in.* | **motion sb to do sth** *Kemp started to object, but I motioned him to be quiet.*

beckon /ˈbekən/ [v I/T] to use a movement of your finger or head to tell someone to come towards you: *She beckoned and he came running immediately.* | *He was leaning over the wall, beckoning me.* | **+ to** *Jan beckoned to me, but I knew better than to sit next to her.* | **beckon sb in/over/to etc** *'Come and look at this,' he said, beckoning me over to the window.*

sign/indication

RELATED WORDS

▸ *see also* **show (8-12), prove**

5 something that shows what is true or what is happening

- ▸ sign
- ▸ indication
- ▸ evidence
- ▸ symptom
- ▸ trace
- ▸ manifestation
- ▸ omen
- ▸ telltale
- ▸ be a giveaway

sign /saɪn/ [n C] an event or fact that shows that something is true or that something is happening: *Therapy should begin when the first signs are noticed.* | **+ of** *Stan has some of the early signs of heart disease.* | *Police searched the house thoroughly but found no signs of a break-in.* | **+ (that)** *A score of 80 or more is a sign that you are doing very well.* | **be a sure sign (of/that)** (=show that something is definitely true) *When Emma offers to help you it's a sure sign that she wants something from you!* | **a good/hopeful/encouraging sign** (=a sign that things are improving) *The rise in consumer spending is an encouraging sign that the economy may be recovering.*

indication /ˌɪndɪ̇ˈkeɪʃən/ [n C/U] something, especially someone's behaviour or what they say, that makes you believe that something is probably happening or has probably happened **+ of** *There was no indication of forced entry to the building.* | **+ (that)** *There are indications that the Labour Party will win the next election.* | **give no/any/a good indication of sth** *If she knew what was going on outside, she gave no indication of it.* | *The daily pollen count can give a good indication of the amount of allergens in the air.* | **give/show every indication of (doing) sth** *The two parties have shown every indication of a willingness to compromise.*

evidence /ˈevɪ̇dəns/ [n U] facts, objects etc that show that something exists or is true: *Without any evidence we cannot prove that she was involved in murder.* | **+ of** *People have been looking for evidence of life on other planets for years.* | **+ that** *We can find no evidence that he ever worked for the company.* | **visible evidence** *There was no visible evidence that humans had ever lived in this valley.*

symptom /ˈsɪmptəm/ [n C] a sign that someone has an illness or that a serious problem exists: *First the doctor asked me to describe my symptoms.* | **+ of** *The first symptoms of hepatitis are tiredness, vomiting, and loss of weight.* | *In his speech the Bishop labelled these crimes as a symptom of society's moral decline.*

trace /treɪs/ [n C] a very small sign that a particular situation exists or is true **+ of** *The thief was careful not to leave any trace of his activities.* | *Many local people were very eager to get rid of the last traces of their town's shameful past.* | **with/without a trace of sth** *Hans speaks English beautifully, without a trace of a foreign accent.*

manifestation /ˌmænɪ̇feˈsteɪʃən‖-fə-/ [n C] *formal* a very clear sign that a particular situation or feeling exists **+ of** *This latest outbreak of violence is a clear manifestation of discontent in the city.* | *Some men feel that showing their emotions is a manifestation of weakness.*

omen /ˈəʊmən/ [n C] something that happens which you think is a sign that something good or bad is going to happen in the future: *Do you think the rain is some kind of omen?* | **bad omen** *George thought the car breaking down on the way to his wedding was a bad omen.* | **good omen** *'Maybe this is a good omen,' said Jill, seeing a blue sky for the first time in weeks.*

telltale /ˈtelteɪl/ [adj only before noun] **tell-tale signs/marks/symptoms etc** signs that something is happening that are not very easy to notice, unless you know exactly what to look for: *In his face you could see the first tell-tale signs of alcoholism.* | *Teachers are encouraged to look for telltale signs of abuse among their students.*

be a giveaway /biː ə ˈgɪvəweɪ/ [v phrase] if you say that something **is a giveaway**, you mean it clearly shows you the real truth about something, rather than what someone would like you to believe: *Those fake beams are a giveaway – it isn't really an old pub.* | **be a dead giveaway** (=show very clearly) *That nervous twitching was always a dead giveaway that he'd done something wrong.*

simple

WHAT'S HERE

- **simple/not complicated** see **1 to 4**
- **simple/plain** see **5**

simple/not complicated

RELATED WORDS

opposite: —— **complicated**

▸ *see also* **easy**

1 when methods, systems, explanations, or words are not complicated

- ▸ simple
- ▸ straightforward
- ▸ uncomplicated
- ▸ unsophisticated
- ▸ elementary
- ▸ plain English
- ▸ rough and ready

simple /ˈsɪmpəl/ [adj] not complicated, and therefore easy to understand: *Speak slowly and use simple words so that everyone understands.* | *His children find European numbering simpler than the Chinese system.* | *There must be a perfectly simple explanation.* | **be simple to do sth** *Many vegetarian meals are delicious and simple to prepare.* | **keep/make sth simple** *The secret of successful dinner parties? Keep it simple.* —**simply** [adv] *Try to express your ideas more simply.* —**simplicity** /sɪmˈplɪsɪ̇ti/ [n U] when something is easy to use or understand: *The simplicity of the system is its great advantage.* | *For simplicity, let's pretend for a moment that the Earth does not revolve.*

straightforward /ˌstreɪtˈfɔːʳwəʳd◂/ [adj] simple – use this especially about explanations, instructions, and methods which contain nothing difficult or unexpected: *The new networking system is fairly straightforward – you shouldn't have any problems.* | *There are two straightforward ways of achieving this result.*

uncomplicated /ʌnˈkɒmplɪ̇keɪtɪ̇d‖-ˈkɑːm-/ [adj] simple and without any unnecessary features that could cause problems or confuse you: *Tom can now carry out uncomplicated tasks without help.* | *There are several basic techniques to learn, but they are uncomplicated enough to be mastered in one session.*

unsophisticated /ˌʌnsəˈfɪstɪkeɪtɪd◂/ [adj] a method or process that is **unsophisticated** is very simple compared to the most modern ones: *It may be a pretty unsophisticated system, but it has worked well for over fifty years.* | *In comparison with modern methods, it seems an incredibly slow and unsophisticated way of making cars.*

elementary /ˌeləˈmentəri◂/ [adj] needing only simple skills or knowledge to do or understand: *She had difficulty with even the most elementary tasks.* | *an elementary course in word-processing*

plain English /pleɪn ˈɪŋglɪʃ/ [n U] English that people can easily understand, without any difficult or confusing words **in plain English** *I wish they'd write in plain English, instead of all this business jargon.* | *'The theory of informed consent'? What does that mean, in plain English?*

rough and ready /ˌrʌf ən ˈredi/ [adj phrase] a **rough and ready** system, calculation, way of doing something etc uses a quick, simple method but ignores small details and therefore does not produce a completely perfect result: *Here are my calculations. They're a little rough and ready as yet, but you'll get a general idea.* | *Justice was administered in a rough and ready fashion, without using courts or juries.*

2 when machines or tools are not complicated

- simple
- basic
- crude
- primitive
- rudimentary
- unsophisticated
- low-tech

simple /ˈsɪmpəl/ [adj] a **simple** machine, tool etc has only a few parts and is not made in a complicated way: *The tribes of Central New Guinea use very simple tools such as hammers and axes.* | *Very young children will be satisfied with the simplest of toys.*

basic /ˈbeɪsɪk/ [adj] **basic** machines, equipment, or tools only have the most necessary features and you cannot use them to do unusual, difficult, or complicated things: *The hospital lacked even the most basic medical equipment.* | *It's only six years old, but already my home PC is basic compared to today's models.*

crude /kruːd/ [adj] something that is **crude** has been made or done in a simple way, without paying much attention to unnecessary details or features: *The men started gathering wood to construct a crude shelter.* | *The earliest skis were crude, consisting of short boards covered in fur skins.* | **a crude form of sth** *Babbage's great calculating machine was a crude form of computer.* —**crudely** [adv] *They lived in crudely built huts.*

primitive /ˈprɪmɪtɪv/ [adj] a tool or machine that is **primitive** is very simple when compared to modern tools or machines that do the same job, and is not as good: *In those days, dental equipment was primitive and a visit to the dentist was a painful experience.* | *It is a primitive but effective device for raising water from a well.* | *a primitive design*

rudimentary /ˌruːdɪˈmentəri◂/ [adj] tools, machines etc that are **rudimentary** are very simple and are only able to do very simple jobs: *The tools that the ancient Egyptians used to build their temples were extremely rudimentary.* | *The system has a rudimentary Internet browser, but it's very slow.*

unsophisticated /ˌʌnsəˈfɪstɪkeɪtɪd◂/ [adj] tools or machines that are **unsophisticated** do not have many of the features that more modern or more advanced tools or machines have: *They still use some relatively unsophisticated machinery.* | *It may look unsophisticated compared to modern high-tech cameras, but it produces fantastic pictures.*

low-tech /ˌləʊ ˈtek◂/ [adj] equipment, vehicles, machines etc that are **low-tech** have a very simple design but this is often seen as an advantage because they are cheaper or more practical: *The company manufactures the low-tech parts in Mexico, and then assembles here.* | *He uses low-tech theatrical devices to great effect.*

3 to make something simpler

- simplify
- streamline

simplify /ˈsɪmplɪfaɪ/ [v T] to make something simpler and easier to use or understand: *The government is planning to simplify the tax laws.* | *These gadgets do simplify food preparation, but are they really worth the money?* —**simplified** [adj] something that is simplified has been made easier to understand: *The text uses simplified Chinese characters.* | *a simplified form of worship*

streamline /ˈstriːmlaɪn/ [v T] to make a method or system simpler, quicker, and usually cheaper – used especially in business contexts: *The new computer has made it possible to streamline our data processing operations.* | *The Cut and Paste command can be used to streamline the process of inserting information.* —**streamlined** [adj] *There will be no layoffs, thanks to streamlined administration and government subsidies.*

4 to make something seem simpler than it really is

- oversimplify
- simplistic
- generalize
- see things in black and white

oversimplify /ˌəʊvərˈsɪmplɪfaɪ/ [v I/T] *There's a tendency in news reports to oversimplify complex issues to make the news more entertaining.* | *I know I'm oversimplifying, but these are the values on which I try to base my decisions.* —**oversimplified** [adj] *We were presented with a vastly oversimplified version of events.* —**oversimplification** /ˌəʊvərˌsɪmplɪfɪˈkeɪʃən/ [n C/U] *This statement is an oversimplification, but it contains an element of truth.*

simplistic /sɪmˈplɪstɪk/ [adj] an opinion or way of thinking about something that is **simplistic** treats difficult things in too simple a way: *a simplistic 'more is better' philosophy* | **be simplistic to** *His critics say it may have been overly simplistic to use only two experimental methods.* | *It would be simplistic to suggest that the Bible promotes male domination.*

generalize ALSO **generalise** British /ˈdʒenərəlaɪz/ [v I] to say that something is true of all the people in a group simply because it is true of some of them: *I know I shouldn't generalize, but I do think men find it hard to show their feelings.* | **+ from** *The study group was very small, and it's hard to generalize from just a few cases.* | **+ about** *The polls show that it is difficult to generalize about which issues were most important to voters.* —**generalization** /ˌdʒenərəlaɪˈzeɪʃən‖-lə-/ [n C/U] *I know it's a generalization, but you must admit that bands these days have less originality than in the past.*

see things in black and white /ˌsiː θɪŋz ɪn ˌblæk ən ˈwaɪt/ [v phrase] if someone **sees things in**

black and white, they tend to judge people in a very simple way as being either completely bad or completely good, completely right or completely wrong etc: *My son sees life in black and white. To him, the world is full of greedy capitalists and underpaid workers.*

simple/plain

RELATED WORDS

▸ *see also* **decorate**

5 not having a lot of decoration or things added

- ▸ **simple**
- ▸ **plain**
- ▸ **basic**
- ▸ **austere**
- ▸ **spartan**
- ▸ **stark**
- ▸ **simplicity**
- ▸ **nothing fancy**
- ▸ **no-frills**

simple /ˈsɪmpəl/ [adj] **simple** food, clothes, or designs do not have a lot of decoration or unnecessary things added, but they are usually attractive or enjoyable: *She wore a simple black dress.* | *The meal was simple, but delicious.*

plain /pleɪn/ [adj] **plain** food, clothes, or designs do not have anything added or any decoration, and may be a little boring: *He put the letter in a plain brown envelope.* | *Do you have any plain white shirts?* | *The chapel was a small, plain, whitewashed building.*

basic /ˈbeɪsɪk/ [adj] **basic** food, rooms, or designs only have the necessary features, and do not include things that make them more comfortable, more attractive etc: *Some of the hotels in the mountains are pretty basic.* | *The basic model costs £30,000, which includes insurance and car tax.* | *basic cooking utensils*

austere /ɔːˈstɪəʳ, ɒ-‖ɔː-/ [adj] a room or building that is **austere** is not decorated, has very little and very plain furniture, and is usually uncomfortable: *Students ate in an austere hall built by New England Puritans.* | *The crematorium chapel was cold and austere.* —**austerity** /ɔːˈsterɪ̇ti, ɒ-‖ɔː-/ [n U] *Protestant churches often have an appearance of extreme simplicity and austerity.*

spartan /ˈspɑːʳtn/ [adj] **spartan** conditions or ways of living are simple and without any comfort: *The accommodation is pretty spartan, so take extra blankets and bedding.* | *It was a spartan existence, with no running water or electricity.*

stark /stɑːʳk/ [adj] something, especially a room, that has a **stark** appearance has no decorations and looks uncomfortable: *The waiting room was stark, with hard, stiff chairs and lit by a single lightbulb.* | *stark chrome furniture*

simplicity /sɪmˈplɪsɪ̇ti/ [n U] the attractive quality of being simple, and not having a lot of decoration or things added: *The jacket follows the lines of the body with graceful simplicity.* | *Van Gogh was attracted to the beauty and simplicity of a common table or kitchen chair.*

nothing fancy /ˌnʌθɪŋ ˈfænsi/ [adj phrase] informal plain or simple with nothing special or unnecessary added: *The Lodge is nothing fancy – just a row of cottages huddled on the side of a hill overlooking the sea.* | *This was his favourite meal. Nothing fancy, just steak and salad.*

no-frills /ˌnəʊ ˈfrɪlz◂/ [adj only before noun] a **no-frills** shop, restaurant, or service provides only the things that you really need and nothing else: *The meeting was held at a no-frills hotel 30 minutes from corporate headquarters.* | *Try the smaller, no-frills airlines for cheap late flights.*

since

since a particular time or event in the past

RELATED WORDS

▸ *see also* **after, during**

- ▸ **since**
- ▸ **ever since**
- ▸ **for**
- ▸ **from**
- ▸ **starting from**

since /sɪns/ [prep/adv/conjunction] all the time from a time, date, year or event in the past until now: *I've had this car since 1992.* | *She hasn't had a night out since she had the baby.* | *The turkey must be done by now – it's been in the oven since 11 o'clock.* | *I saw her early this morning, but I haven't seen her since.* | **since when** (=how long?) *Since when have you had a computer?* | **since doing sth** *Since leaving the army, he's spent most of his time looking for a job.* | **since then** *He arrived in Hollywood back in 1952. Since then he's appeared in over 100 movies.*

ever since /ˌevəʳ ˈsɪns/ [prep/adv/conjunction] since a time, date, or event a long time ago: *I've been getting these pains in my back ever since I fell down the stairs.* | *He's been acting different ever since his arrest.* | *Joan had been an early riser ever since she was a child.* | *Ever since I can remember, I've wanted to be a dancer.* | *Matt moved to San Francisco in 1984 to go to medical school, and he's been there ever since.* | **ever since then** *I started an exercise program five years ago, and ever since then I've felt a lot better.*

for /fəʳ, (*strong*) fɔːʳ/ [prep] during the whole of a period of time until now: *Omar's been studying English for two years now.* | *We've been waiting here for over two hours!* | *Daniel's been complaining of a stomach ache for a couple of days.* | **for a while** (=for a fairly long time) *I hadn't seen Tim for a while, and I was surprised by how much weight he'd gained.*

from /frəm, (*strong*) frɒm‖frəm, (*strong*) frʌm, frɑːm/ [prep] continuously after a particular time in the past: *From the first time we met, I knew we would be good friends.* | **right from** *Timmy Connell has been a problem in class right from the beginning of term.* | **from then on** (=from a time already mentioned) *We had a big fight that fall, and from then on he never treated me the same.*

starting from /ˈstɑːʳtɪŋ frɒm/ [prep] continuously after an exact time or important event in the past: *Benson became chairman of the company on October 12th, and starting from that day things have steadily improved.*

sing

RELATED WORDS

▸ *see also* **dance, music, perform/performance**

1 to sing

- ▸ **sing**
- ▸ **singing**
- ▸ **belt out**
- ▸ **burst into song**
- ▸ **croon**
- ▸ **on vocals**

sing /sɪŋ/ [v I/T] to make musical sounds with your voice, especially the words of a song: *Sophie sings in the church choir.* | *I could hear someone singing downstairs.* | **sing a song/tune/hymn etc** *They sat together and sang songs.* | *All the family sang 'Happy Birthday' as Dad came in.* | **sing sb sth** *Come on, David, sing us a song!* | **+ to** *She sat in a corner, singing softly to her baby.* | **sing along** (=sing with someone who is already singing) *Sing along if you know the words.* | **sing in tune/out of tune** (=sing the right or wrong notes) *Anyone who could play an instrument or sing in tune was enlisted to take part in the concert.*

singing /ˈsɪŋɪŋ/ [n U] the activity of singing: *I hear Frank's taken up singing again.* | *Everyone joined in with the singing.* | *He asked her why she didn't make use of her talent and give singing lessons.* | **singing career** *Danni decided to come to England to launch her singing career.*

belt out /ˌbelt ˈaʊt/ [phr v T] to sing a song loudly and powerfully **belt out sth** *The choir belted out songs from West End shows for over an hour.* | **belt it out** *This is a big theatre – you have to really belt it out.*

burst into song /ˌbɜːʳst ɪntə ˈsɒŋ‖-ˈsɔːŋ/ [v phrase] to suddenly start singing: *He felt so happy he wanted to burst into song.* | *The orchestra played a few notes and the choir burst into song.*

croon /kruːn/ [v I/T] to sing in a very soft, musical way: *A woman gently crooned the tune of a lullaby.* | *She wandered around the tables, while crooning 'Embraceable You'.*

on vocals /ɒn ˈvəʊkəlz/ [adv] if a member of a band is **on vocals**, they are singing the song's words: *The band was formed in 1999, with Stevie on vocals.* | **on backing vocals** (=singing the background tune, not the main one) *We went to see a band who had Julia Fordham on backing vocals.*

2 to make a musical sound without words

- hum
- whistle

hum /hʌm/ [v I/T] to make musical sounds with your voice, but with your mouth closed: *She hummed softly to herself as she worked.* | *Musicals are uplifting, and you are sure to leave the theatre humming a cheerful tune.*

whistle /ˈwɪsəl/ [v I/T] to make musical sounds by blowing air out between your lips: *He stacked crates one on top of the other, whistling as he did so.* | *You've been whistling that tune all day.*

3 someone who sings

- singer
- vocalist
- choir
- chorus

singer /ˈsɪŋəʳ/ [n C] someone who sings, especially as their job: *I wanted to have a career as a singer.* | **opera/jazz/blues/rock etc singer** *Jodie dreamed of being a rock singer.* | **a good/bad/terrible etc singer** *She's very pretty, and a good singer too.* | **lead singer** (=the main singer in a band) *Mick Jagger, the lead singer with the Rolling Stones* | **backing singer** (=someone who sings the background tune, not the main tune) *In those days we had a band with a brass section and a couple of female backing singers.*

vocalist /ˈvəʊkələ̇st/ [n C] a singer in a group that plays popular music: *The female vocalist came on in a long white gown.* | *He's a session musician, providing studio backing to well-known vocalists.* | **lead vocalist** (=main vocalist) *Tom, the lead vocalist, is also a talented guitarist.*

choir /kwaɪəʳ/ [n C] a large group of singers who regularly sing in a church or school or with a group of musicians: *I have always sung in choirs.* | *He's a member of a Welsh Male Voice Choir.* | *The school choir performed Vivaldi's Gloria.* | *Ray Charles and Aretha Franklin started singing in gospel choirs, not at music lessons.*

chorus /ˈkɔːrəs/ [n C] a large group of people who sing together, for example people from a particular town or school: *The chorus's singing was excellent, and so was the orchestral playing.*

4 relating to singing

- vocal
- choral

vocal /ˈvəʊkəl/ [adj] relating to singing or someone's singing voice: *The band's stunning vocal harmonies have earned them a big name in the States.* | *the Beach Boys and other early '60s teen vocal groups*

choral /ˈkɔːrəl/ [adj] relating to music or singing done by a choir: *traditional Welsh choral music* | *The programme includes choral works, and music for string orchestra.*

sit

RELATED WORDS

▸ *see also* **stand, lie, bend (2)**

1 to be sitting in a chair, on the floor etc

- sit
- sit up
- sit back
- be seated
- lounge
- slump/be slumped
- slouch/be slouched

sit /sɪt/ [v I] to be in a chair, on the floor etc, with the weight of your body resting on your bottom, not on your feet: *Is it okay if I sit here?* | *Do you want to sit next to Brian?* | *Let's go sit outside.* | *A woman in a huge hat came and sat right in front of us.* | *Billy sat on the edge of the desk, swinging his legs.* | *I saw a man with grey hair sitting in the car next to Jean.* | *Come and sit on Mommy's knee.* | **sit at a desk/table/bar/fire etc** *A grey-haired woman was sitting at the reception desk.* | **sit around a desk/table etc** *We all used to sit around the kitchen table, smoking and chatting.* | **sit still** (=sit quietly without moving) *I wish you children would sit still for 10 minutes.*

sit up /ˌsɪt ˈʌp/ [phr v I] to move your body so that you are sitting, after you have been lying down, or to sit so that your back is straight: *When I got home, Nigel was sitting up in bed.* | *Sit up like a big girl, and eat your dinner.* | **sit up straight** (=sit with your back very straight) *Cadets here are taught to always dress neatly and to sit up straight.*

sit back /ˌsɪt ˈbæk/ [phr v I] to lean your back against the back of the chair, after you have been sitting straight, especially because this is more comfortable: *Just sit back, relax, and enjoy the music.* | *Mel sat back on the couch and admired the view of the city.*

be seated /biː ˈsiːtə̇d/ [v phrase] **formal** to be sitting in a particular chair or place, especially because someone has asked or arranged for you to sit there: *The meal cannot start until everyone is seated.* | *John was seated on my left.* | *Helen was more than* *pleased to be seated beside Chris. She'd always wanted to meet him.*

lounge /laʊndʒ/ [v I] to sit so that you are very comfortable and relaxed, sometimes almost lying down **+ on** *I dried off, then lounged on a hammock at the poolside.* | **+ in** *Are you the sort of person who likes to lounge in bed at the weekend?*

slump /be slumped /slʌmp, biː ˈslʌmpt/ [v I] to be sitting with the top of your body leaning forwards or sideways and down, as if you are very tired or as if you are unconscious **+ forward/in/against etc** *He slumped further forward, his lips parted and his eyes closed.* | *She slumped back in her seat.* | **be slumped in/on/under etc** *Brad was slumped in front of the television watching the game.* | *Theresa found him slumped over the keyboard.* | **sit slumped** *A young man sat slumped behind the hotel desk, showing little interest in the new arrivals.*

slouch/be slouched /slaʊtʃ, biː ˈslaʊtʃt/ [v I/v phrase] to sit in a tired or lazy way, often with your head down and your shoulders sloping downwards: *Marie, don't slouch, sit up straight.* | **slouch back/against/in etc** *Cantor slouched back in his seat and lit a cigarette.* | *I slouched on a bench and watched the children feed the swans.* | **be slouched in/over/beside etc** *One boy was slouched down in his chair, with a baseball cap almost covering his eyes.*

2 to sit after you have been standing

- sit down
- sit
- take your seat
- sink into

sit down /ˌsɪt ˈdaʊn/ [phr v I] to sit on a chair, bed, floor etc, after you have been standing: *Come in and sit down.* | *Oh, it's nice to sit down after all that waiting.* | *Fay sat down on the edge of the bed.* | *Pull up a chair, and sit down right here.*

sit /sɪt/ [v I] to **sit** in a particular place or position after you have been standing **+ beside/against/next to etc** *It's so hot in here. Shall we go and sit by the window?* | *Come and sit next to me – I haven't seen you for ages.* | *He sat down right beside me.* | **sit up** (=sit after lying down) *After a few days, he was finally allowed to sit up in bed.*

take your seat /ˌteɪk jɔːʳ ˈsiːt/ [v phrase] to sit down in your chair in a public place such as a theatre or cinema, so that you can watch a play, film, ceremony etc: *Would the audience please take their seats – the show will begin in five minutes.* | *She waved before taking her seat at the back of the church.*

sink into /ˈsɪŋk ɪntuː/ [phr v T] to sit in a comfortable chair, by letting yourself fall back into it, especially because you are tired: *It had been an exhausting day. Christina gratefully sank into the armchair and kicked off her shoes.*

3 to sit with your legs in a particular position

- kneel
- sit cross-legged
- squat
- sit astride
- straddle

kneel ALSO **kneel down** /niːl, ˌniːl ˈdaʊn/ [v I] to be or move into a position in which your knees are on the floor and your body is upright: *He told them to kneel, then began to say a prayer.* | *Grandpa knelt down and lifted the little girl into his arms.* | *An old woman was kneeling at the altar, her hands clasping a rosary.* | *You'll need to bring a small mat to kneel on.*

sit cross-legged /sɪt ˌkrɒs ˈlegd‖-ˌkrɔːs ˈlegəd/ [v phrase] to sit on the ground or floor with your knees bent and your feet crossed in front of you: *Several children sat cross-legged on the floor in front of her.* | *They were sitting on the bed cross-legged and giggling.*

squat ALSO **squat down** /skwɒt, ˌskwɒt ˈdaʊn ‖skwɑːt/ [v I usually in progressive] to put your body into a position in which your feet are flat on the ground, your knees are bent up to your chest, and your bottom is off the ground, or to move into this position: *A little boy was squatting at the edge of the pool.* | *People squatted around the fire in small groups* | *He squatted down beside me and offered me a cigarette.*

sit astride /ˌsɪt əˈstraɪd/ [v phrase] to sit on something or someone, with one leg on each side: *He sat astride a motorcycle.* | *He pinned her to the ground by her shoulders, sitting astride her so that she couldn't move.*

straddle /ˈstrædl/ [v T] to sit on someone or something with one leg on each side, especially when you have to stretch a long way to do this: *He sat facing her, straddling the small wooden chair.* | *I looked up to see her straddling one of the huge branches of the oak tree.*

4 a place where you can sit

- seat
- place

seat /siːt/ [n C] something you can sit on, especially in a bus, plane, theatre etc: *Our seats were right at the front of the airplane.* | *He leaned back in his seat and lit a cigarette.* | *When we arrived, every seat was filled, so we stood at the back.* | *There was blood and broken glass all over the front seats.* | *'Slow down!' yelled Ben from the back seat.* | *comfortable padded theater seats*

place /pleɪs/ [n C] a particular seat where you sit for a formal meal or in a public **place** – use this especially to talk about whether seats are available: *We'd better hurry and get to our places before the show starts.* | *I don't think there are enough places for everyone.* | **take your place** (=sit in the seat that you are expected to sit in) *Jennifer quietly took her place at the table.*

5 what you say to tell someone to sit

- sit down
- have a seat/take a seat
- please be seated
- sit

sit down /ˌsɪt ˈdaʊn/ spoken *Sit down – I have some bad news for you.* | *Sit down and finish your breakfast.*

have a seat/take a seat /ˌhæv ə ˈsiːt, ˌteɪk ə ˈsiːt/ [v phrase] spoken say this to politely ask someone to sit down, especially someone you do not know well: *Take a seat. Mr Bennet will be available in a moment.* | *You'd better have a seat, Mr Hanks. This may take some time.*

please be seated /ˌpliːz biː ˈsiːtəd/ formal say this to a group of people to ask them politely to sit down, especially at a public occasion or ceremony: *Would the audience please be seated.* | *Please do be seated. This won't take a moment.*

sit /sɪt/ spoken say this to a dog when you want it to **sit** down: *Sit, Bowser, sit! Good dog!*

6 something that is done while sitting

- sedentary
- sit-down

sedentary /ˈsedəntəri‖-teri/ [adj] if someone is **sedentary** or they have a **sedentary** job, they spend most of their time sitting down: *The exercise program was aimed at men in their fifties and sixties who were previously sedentary.* | *People with sedentary jobs generally need to eat less than those in very active occupations.* | *health problems caused by a sedentary lifestyle*

sit-down /ˈsɪt daʊn/ [adj only before noun] **sit-down meal/dinner etc** a meal etc in which everyone in a group, usually a large group, sits at tables: *We usually organize a sit-down dinner, but we wanted to go for something less formal this year.* | *We offer a cafeteria and a sit-down service at very reasonable rates.*

situation

RELATED WORDS

▸ *see also* **happen**

1 what is happening in a particular place or at a particular time

- situation
- circumstances
- things
- case
- what's going on
- conditions
- state of affairs
- state of play
- scenario
- environment
- climate
- set-up

situation /ˌsɪtʃuˈeɪʃən/ [n C usually singular] the combination of all the things that are happening in a particular place and at a particular time, especially when this is causing problems: *I tried to explain the situation to my boss.* | *With no rain for six months, the situation in the region was becoming desperate.* | *The economic situation in the US is getting better.* | *The news of more stock market losses could make the difficult economic situation worse.* | **in a situation** *If you are ever in a situation where someone starts shooting, drop to the ground.* | *In the present situation, I don't think it would be a good idea to try to sell your house.*

circumstances /ˈsɜːʳkəmstænsɪ̇z/ [n plural] the situation at a particular time, which influences what people do, what they decide, and what can happen **the circumstances** *TV cameras are sometimes allowed in the courts, but it depends on the circumstances.* | **in the circumstances** (=because of the circumstances) *We don't normally allow people in after 8 pm, but in the circumstances we'll make an exception.* | **in some/certain/normal etc circumstances** *An applicant's age may be taken into consideration in some circumstances.* | **under some/the/certain etc circumstances** *Under normal circumstances I would never have left the children with a stranger.*

things /θɪŋz/ [n plural] especially spoken, informal the general situation that exists, especially the way it affects people's lives: *Don't worry! Things can't get any worse.* | *Things haven't changed much since I wrote to you last.* | *Now that we have kids, things are really different.*

case /keɪs/ [n C] a particular situation – use this especially when you are comparing one situation with others to show how they are similar or different: *In cases like this, the company has to be sold off to someone who can cope with the debt.* | **in cases of** *The law limits work in underground mines to eight hours per day, except in cases of emergency.* | **in this/that case** *'It's supposed to rain tomorrow.' 'Well, in that case, we won't go.'* | **in some/a few/many cases** *In some cases, mail carriers could not get to mailboxes surrounded by plowed snow.*

what's going on /ˌwɒts gəʊɪŋ ˈɒn/ [n phrase] use this especially to ask or say what is happening in a situation: *Nobody could tell her what was going on.* | *I've been waiting here for nearly two hours! Does anyone know what's going on?* | *What's going on? Why won't you talk to me?*

conditions /kənˈdɪʃənz/ [n plural] all the things that affect the way people live or work, such as a country's economic situation, whether people have enough food, the places they live in etc: *Conditions in the city are getting rapidly worse.* | *How can people live in such dreadful conditions?* | *Employees are demanding better working conditions and higher wages.* | *a study into the social conditions of the nineteenth century*

state of affairs /ˌsteɪt əv əˈfeəʳz/ [n phrase] an unsatisfactory, disappointing, or unusual situation that causes a lot of problems: *Crisis has always been the normal state of affairs in our country's politics.* | **sorry/sad state of affairs** (=bad state of affairs) *It's a sad state of affairs when a leader can't take the time to address the true problems facing his country.*

state of play /ˌsteɪt əv ˈpleɪ/ [n phrase] British what is happening now in a situation that is still developing and is likely to change – use this especially in business and political contexts: *Every four weeks we get a briefing from the managers, giving us the state of play.* | *The current state of play in Anglo-French relations is best characterized as 'cautious cooperation'.*

scenario /sɪ̇ˈnɑːriəʊ‖-ˈnæ-, -ˈne-/ [n C] a situation that could possibly happen but has not happened yet – use this especially when you are discussing what might happen: *Under the most hopeful scenario, it will take 20 years to clean up the mess.* | **worst-case/nightmare scenario** (=the worst possible situation) *In a worst-case scenario all life on the planet would be wiped out by a nuclear war.* | *This is every politician's nightmare scenario.*

environment /ɪnˈvaɪərənmənt/ [n C] all the things that influence the way you live, work, and develop, such as the physical conditions you live in and the people around you: *Do girls learn better in an all-female environment?* | *I didn't feel that the neighborhood was a very safe environment for kids.* | **working/home environment** *We have tried to create a working environment in which everyone can develop their skills.*

climate /ˈklaɪmɪ̇t/ [n C usually singular] the economic, social, and political situation that exists at a particular time – use this especially when you are discussing what can be done or what people believe at that time: *In today's political climate the return of communism seems impossible.* | *Hopefully, when the financial climate gets better we'll be able to take on more workers.* | **climate of hostility/distrust etc** *The revelations of corruption have led to a climate of distrust in the capital.* | **climate of opinion** (=what people generally think) *The climate of opinion on the sensitive topic of euthanasia is changing gradually.*

set-up /ˈset ʌp/ [n C] the way something such as a family, company, or country is arranged, especially a way that you do not understand or do not approve of: *They're divorced, but they're still living in the same house – it seems like a strange set-up to me.* | *It's* *an impressive set-up. The foundation brings in half a million dollars a day.*

2 your personal situation

- situation
- circumstances
- position
- case
- plight

situation /ˌsɪtʃuˈeɪʃən/ [n C usually singular] the **situation** you are in, for example how much money you earn, where you live, whether you are married or have children etc: *For most refugees, the situation is pretty hopeless.* | *In your situation, I would have done exactly the same thing.* | *The proper investment balance depends on each investor's situation.*

circumstances /ˈsɜːʳkəmstænsɪ̣z/ [n plural] your personal situation, for example how much money you earn, where you live, whether you are married or have children etc – used especially in official contexts: *The organization provides aid to people in desperate circumstances.* | *Please contact your Social Security office if there is any change in your circumstances.*

position /pəˈzɪʃən/ [n C usually singular] the situation that someone is in, especially a difficult or embarrassing situation that restricts what they can do: *In her position, I'm not sure what I'd do.* | **the position of sb** *Few rich people can really appreciate the position of the single mother living on welfare.* | **put sb in an awkward/difficult/embarrassing etc position** *Ed asked me to lie for him to help save his job, which put me in a very awkward position.*

case /keɪs/ [n C usually singular] a particular person's or group's situation – use this especially to compare one situation with others to show how they are similar or different **in sb's case** *In my case, when I started teaching I enjoyed it right away.* | **in the case of** *Doctors have often achieved amazing results, as in the case of 11-year-old Jason.* | **case-by-case** (=considering each person's situation separately) *72-hour airport visas can be extended, but decisions are made on a case-by-case basis.*

plight /plaɪt/ [n singular] especially written a very difficult, unpleasant, or dangerous situation that is difficult to escape from: *Roy was sympathetic to her plight and offered to help her look for her daughter.* | **the plight of** *His chief concern is the plight of kids growing up in the ghettoes.*

3 when a situation affects what happens or what you do

- under/in the circumstances
- given the situation/circumstances
- the way things are
- as it is
- as things stand/the way things stand
- force of circumstances

under/in the circumstances /ˌʌndəʳ, ɪn ðə ˈsɜːʳkəmstænsɪ̣z/ [adv] use this to say that you think something should happen because of the situation now: *Normally I would have gone straight home, but under the circumstances I thought I should check on my mother.* | *Under the circumstances, I think the only thing you can do is apologize.* | *In the circumstances, it might be better if I gave the lecture rather than you.*

given the situation/circumstances /ˌgɪvən ðə sɪtʃuˈeɪʃən, ˈsɜːʳkəmstænsɪ̣z/ [adv] use this when you think that something is not surprising if you consider the situation it happened in: *They tried to contact everyone and given the circumstances, I think they did very well.* | *Given the situation, the police officer's reaction is understandable.*

the way things are /ðə ˌweɪ θɪŋz ˈɑːʳ/ use this when you are saying that something is necessary, impossible, difficult etc because of the present situation, which is not very good: *The way things are, we hardly ever manage to go out together except at the weekend.* | *The way things are at work, I'm surprised more people haven't quit.*

as it is /ˌæz ɪt ˈɪz/ [adv] use this when the situation now is different from the situation you expected or needed: *We were hoping to finish by 5 o'clock, but as it is, we'll be lucky to finish by 8!* | *Why start an argument? You're in enough trouble as it is!*

as things stand/the way things stand /ˌæz θɪŋz ˈstænd, ðə ˌweɪ θɪŋz ˈstænd/ [adv] use this when something happens, is true, or must be done because of the way the situation is now, although the situation may change in the future: *People talk about the British constitution, but as things stand there is no real constitution.* | *We may get a few more applicants, but the way things stand Mr. Davis looks like the best candidate.*

force of circumstances /ˌfɔːʳs əv ˈsɜːʳkəmstænsɪ̣z/ [n phrase] especially British if something happens by **force of circumstances**, it happens differently from the way you expect or intend because the situation has changed: *By force of circumstances, I found myself having to share an office with my previous manager.* | *Force of circumstances compelled the senator to retire in 1934.*

size

RELATED WORDS

- see also **big, small, tall, high, wide, narrow, measure, fit/not fit**

1 how big or small something is

- size
- how big
- area
- dimensions
- extent

size /saɪz/ [n C/U] *What size is that shirt?* | *Your desk is exactly the same size as mine.* | **the size of** *The price will depend on the size and quality of the carpet.* | **(be) the size of** (=the same size as something else) *Fire has destroyed an area of forest the size of Luxembourg.* | **(be) twice/half/three times etc the size of** (=twice as big, half as big etc as something else) *The seeds are very small, about half the size of a grain of salt.* | **of different/various sizes** *There were several pieces of wood of different sizes.* | **double/triple etc in size** *Cover the dough and allow it to rise until it has doubled in size.* | **grow/increase/shrink etc in size** *The black spots on her skin seemed to be slowly increasing in size.* | **vary/differ/range etc in size** *The American states vary enormously in size, from very large to very small.* | **(of) this/that size** (=as big as this one or that one) *In a class this size, there will always be a few problems.*

how big /haʊ ˈbɪg/ [adj phrase] use this to ask or talk about the size of something: *How big is the table? Do you think it'll fit in the trunk?* | *How big is the Dead Sea?* | *We need to know how big the rooms are.*

area /ˈeəriə/ [n C/U] the amount of space that a flat surface such as a floor or field covers **+ of** *The boat's sail had an area of more than 50 square yards.* | *Cal-*

culate the area of the walls and ceiling before you buy the paint. | **surface area** *The rate at which an ice cube melts depends on its surface area.*

dimensions /daɪˈmenʃənz, dɪ̥-/ [n plural] the height, width, and length of an object, building etc – use this especially to give exact measurements: *The dimensions are printed on the side of the box.* | **+ of** *What are the dimensions of the dining-room table?*

extent /ɪkˈstent/ [n U] the size of a large area: *The extent of the Red Creek ranch is enormous.* | **in extent** *The principality measured about 16,500 kilometres in extent.*

2 the amount of something that something can contain

- capacity
- volume

- *see also* **contain**

capacity /kəˈpæsɪ̥ti/ [n singular] the amount that a container will hold **+ of** *The capacity of the tank should be 500 gallons or more.* | *The computer's memory has a capacity of over 200 megabytes.* | **be filled to capacity** *All the storage units were filled to capacity.*

volume /ˈvɒljuːm‖ˈvɑːljəm/ [n U] the amount of space that a substance fills or an object contains **+ of** *Help me figure out the volume of this fish tank.* | *The shifting of continents has an impact on the volume of water the oceans can contain.*

3 to be a particular size

- be 5 metres high/2 miles long/6 centimetres wide etc
- be 10 metres by 5 metres/be 10 inches by 8 inches etc
- measure
- cover
- extend over

be 5 metres high/2 miles long/6 centimetres wide etc /biː ˌfaɪv miːtəʳz ˈhaɪ/ [v phrase] use this to say how high, how long etc something is: *The river Nile is over 6,000 kilometres long.* | *In some places the path is only a couple of feet wide.*

be 10 metres by 5 metres/be 10 inches by 8 inches etc /biː ˌten miːtəʳz baɪ ˈfaɪv miːtəʳz/ use this to say what the size of an area, object, or room is, for example, **10 metres by 5 metres** means 10 metres long and 5 metres wide: *The kitchen is 4 metres by 2 metres.* | *The publicity photos are 8 by 10 inches.*

measure /ˈmeʒəʳ/ [v not in progressive] to be a particular size, length, or amount **measure 10 metres/6 feet etc** *The tree in the backyard measures 30 feet in height.* | *Put the soil into a sack measuring 50 centimetres across.* | **measure 10 m by 15 m/5 cm by 20 cm etc** *The foam seat pad measures 19 by 22 inches and is a quarter-inch thick.*

cover /ˈkʌvəʳ/ [v T not in progressive] if something such as a city or a forest **covers** a particular area, it is the same size as that area: *The building is nine stories high and covers three city blocks.* | *St Anne's Wood isn't very big – it only covers a few miles.*

extend over /ɪkˈstend əʊvəʳ/ [v phrase] if something such as a system or type of land **extends over** a large area, that is the size of the area in which it is used or exists: *Rice fields extend over two-thirds of the area.* | *The irrigation system extends over the whole country but is difficult to maintain.*

sleep

RELATED WORDS

- *see also* **tired/tiring, rest, wake up/get up, unconscious**

1 to sleep

- sleep
- sleep
- be asleep
- get some sleep
- have a kip/get some kip
- slumber

sleep /sliːp/ [v I] *Charlotte was sleeping and her mother didn't want to wake her.* | *If my snoring is that bad, I'll go down and sleep on the sofa.* | **sleep (for) 2 hours/ten minutes etc** *I had slept only a few hours, but I had to get up early.* | *I'm so tired, I could sleep for a week.* | *Is the baby sleeping all night now?* | **sleep well/badly** *I didn't sleep very well last night, so I couldn't concentrate on the exam.* —**sleeping** [adj only before noun] *I watched the sleeping child, the gentle rise and fall of her breast.*

sleep /sliːp/ [n singular/U] the time when you are sleeping: *Eight hours' sleep a night is enough for most people.* | *Depression can be caused simply by a lack of sleep.* | **get some/a lot/not much etc sleep** *I don't suppose you got much sleep last night.* | **in your sleep** (=while you are sleeping) *Katie sometimes talks in her sleep.* | *Grandad died peacefully in his sleep.* | **deep sleep** (=a sleep that is difficult to wake up from) *A sudden noise on the street woke Eileen from a deep sleep.*

be asleep /biː əˈsliːp/ [v phrase] to be sleeping: *It was nine o'clock and Nicky was still asleep.* | *We found mom asleep on the sofa.* | *Deborah, are you asleep?* | **be fast/sound asleep** (=sleeping very well) *By the time her father had carried her up to bed, the child was sound asleep.* | *The baby had been fast asleep ever since we arrived.* | **be half asleep** (=nearly asleep) *The old man was half asleep and barely able to respond to the policeman's questions.*

get some sleep ALSO **catch up on some sleep** /ˌget səm ˈsliːp, kætʃ ˌʌp ɒn səm ˈsliːp/ [v phrase] to sleep after a period of time when you have not been able to sleep because of illness, worry, work etc: *You must stop worrying and try to get some sleep.* | *I'll have to finish the job, but I can catch up on some sleep tomorrow night.*

have a kip/get some kip /ˌhæv ə ˈkɪp, ˌget səm ˈkɪp/ [v phrase] British informal to sleep, especially when you are very tired and you need to sleep: *You can have a kip in the car on the way.* | *There's nothing worse than other people around when you're trying to get some kip.*

slumber /ˈslʌmbəʳ/ [n singular] written sleep – used especially in literature: *He had fallen into a deep slumber by the fire.* | *The giants awoke from their enchanted slumber.* —**slumber** [v I] *Coleridge wrote the line 'My cradled infant slumbers peacefully' after the death of his son.*

2 to sleep for a short time

- have a nap
- doze
- snooze
- grab/snatch some sleep
- have a sleep

have a nap especially British **/take a nap** especially American /ˌhæv ə ˈnæp, ˌteɪk ə ˈnæp/ [v phrase] to sleep for a short time during the day: *I was having a nap by the fire one evening when I was woken up by the doorbell* | *Try to take a nap in the afternoons if you're feeling tired.* | *The director always takes a nap around this time.* —**nap** [n C] *A short nap can be enough to make you feel more energetic in the afternoon.*

doze /dəʊz/ [v I] to sleep lightly for a short time, so that you wake up and go back to sleep again, often while you are sitting in a chair or when you do not intend to: *He left his mother dozing by the fire.* | *Geoff lay dozing gently in a sunlounger.* | **doze fitfully** (=to sleep for very short periods) *Some people managed to sleep, but most of us just dozed fitfully.* —**doze** [n singular] *She lapsed into a doze.*

snooze /have/take a snooze /snuːz, ˌhæv, ˌteɪk ə ˈsnuːz/ [v I] to sleep for a short time, especially during the day when you do not usually sleep: *The baby was snoozing peacefully in her stroller, so we stopped to have a drink.* | *The study showed that if pilots on long-haul flights take a brief snooze in the cockpit, they're more alert for the landing.*

grab/snatch some sleep /ˌgræb, ˌsnætʃ səm ˈsliːp/ [v phrase] informal to sleep for a short time when you have a chance to, because you are very busy and cannot sleep at your usual time: *I'll go home, snatch a couple of hours' sleep and meet you at four.* | *I grabbed a little sleep on the train, but it wasn't enough.*

have a sleep /ˌhæv ə ˈsliːp/ [v phrase] British to sleep for a short time during the day because you are tired: *Are you tired? Why don't you have a sleep this afternoon?*

3 to start sleeping

- go to sleep
- fall asleep
- doze off
- drop off
- nod off
- drift off
- be off
- be out like a light
- crash out/flake out

go to sleep /ˌgəʊ tə ˈsliːp/ [v phrase] *Are you two going to stop talking and go to sleep?* | *I looked over at Dave, but he had gone to sleep.* | *He lay on the sofa and pretended to go to sleep.* | **go back to sleep** (=go to sleep again after waking up) *If I wake up in the night, it takes me ages to go back to sleep.*

fall asleep /ˌfɔːl əˈsliːp/ [v phrase] to go to sleep – use this especially when you do not intend to, when you go to sleep quickly, or when going to sleep has been difficult: *Dad always falls asleep in front of the TV after Sunday lunch.* | *Has Monica fallen asleep yet?* | *I must have fallen asleep with the light on last night.* | **fall asleep at the wheel** (=while you are driving) *One in seven road accidents is caused by drivers falling asleep at the wheel.*

doze off /ˌdəʊz ˈɒf/ [phr v I] to go to sleep when you do not intend to and sleep lightly for a short time: *Sorry, I must have dozed off for a few minutes.* | *I was just beginning to doze off when the telephone rang.*

drop off /ˌdrɒp ˈɒf‖ˌdrɑːp-/ [phr v I] to go to sleep easily and peacefully: *At around 12.30, she did eventually drop off for an hour or so.* | *She kept dropping off for a few minutes, before waking with a start.* | **drop off to sleep** *Janir had dropped off to sleep on the living room couch.*

nod off /ˌnɒd ˈɒf‖ˌnɑːd-/ [phr v I] to go to sleep when you are sitting down, especially when you are trying hard to stay awake: *Sarah had almost nodded off when Victor suddenly spoke.* | *As the speaker droned on, only the occasional nudge from my husband kept me from nodding off.*

drift off /ˌdrɪft ˈɒf/ [phr v I] to go to sleep gradually: *He must have drifted off again, for when he awoke, the train had come to a halt.* | *She was just starting to drift off, when she heard a scream downstairs.* | **drift off to sleep** *That night as he drifted off to sleep, Quincy tried to imagine what the day would have been like if Marta had been there.*

be off /biː ˈɒf/ [phr v I] British if someone, especially a baby, **is off**, they have started sleeping: *Is the baby off yet?* | *I always wait until he's off before I turn the light out.*

be out like a light /biː ˌaʊt laɪk ə ˈlaɪt/ [v phrase] informal to go to sleep very quickly and deeply because you are very tired: *I went back to bed, and was out like a light.* | *After a day on the ranch, you'll be out like a light, I can tell you.*

crash out/flake out /ˌkræʃ ˈaʊt, ˌfleɪk ˈaʊt/ [phr v I] informal to fall asleep very quickly, especially in a place where you do not normally sleep: *'Did you get any sleep last night?' 'Yeah, I crashed out as soon as my head hit the pillow.'* | *He'd flaked out on my bed.*

4 to get into your bed in order to sleep

- go to bed
- be in bed
- bedtime
- turn in
- hit the sack
- retire

go to bed /ˌgəʊ tə ˈbed/ [v phrase] *Do you want to go to bed, or watch the movie?* | *Mom, do I have to go to bed right now?* | *She had planned to go to bed early that night, but a friend stopped by to see her.* | **+ at** *I went to bed at nine last night, and I'm still tired.* | **go straight to bed** (=go to bed very shortly after doing something else) *Marianne took a shower and went straight to bed.*

be in bed /biː ɪn ˈbed/ [v phrase] to be lying in your bed in order to go to sleep: *Sorry, were you in bed? I thought it might be too late to call you.* | *I'm usually in bed by 10.30 on weekdays.* | *You were supposed to be in bed by now!*

bedtime /ˈbedtaɪm/ [n U] the time when you go to bed in order to sleep: *It's late – it must be nearly bedtime.* | *Lucy, 7.30 is bedtime, you know that.* | *This medicine should be taken at bedtime and first thing in the morning.* | **my/your/his etc bedtime** (=the time when you usually go to bed) *Isn't it your bedtime?* | **past (your/his etc) bedtime** (=after the time when you normally go to bed) *It's past my bedtime – I really must get some sleep.*

turn in /ˌtɜːʳn ˈɪn/ [phr v I] informal to go to bed after you have been doing something such as talking with other people or working for a long time: *Come on you guys, it's time to turn in.* | *I'm going to have to turn in. I'm not used to these late nights.*

hit the sack ALSO **hit the hay** /ˌhɪt ðə ˈsæk, hɪt ðə ˈheɪ/ [v phrase] informal to go to bed when it is very late or you are very tired: *Usually I come home, eat dinner, watch a little TV, and then hit the sack by 9:30 or 10:00.* | *I'm bushed. I think I'll hit the hay.*

retire /rɪˈtaɪəʳ/ [v I] formal or written to go to bed: *The captain retired at ten o'clock with a glass of whisky.* | **retire to bed** *Mary Ellen always had to set the fire for the next morning before retiring to bed.*

5 to sleep well and not wake up during the night

- sleep well/soundly
- have/get a good night's sleep
- have a good sleep
- sleep like a log
- sleep through
- be a heavy/good/sound sleeper
- be dead to the world

sleep well/soundly /ˌsliːp ˈwel, ˈsaʊndli/ [v phrase] to sleep without waking up, until the time when you are ready to wake up: *'Did the storm keep you awake?' 'No, I slept very well.'* | *I don't want you to worry. Sleep well.* | *The day had been long and difficult, but Gita slept soundly until morning.*

have/get a good night's sleep /hæv, get ə ˌgʊd naɪts ˈsliːp/ [v phrase] to sleep well for a whole night and get a good rest so that you do not feel tired in the morning: *After getting a good night's sleep, Pedro awoke refreshed and full of energy.* | *Unfortunately, fatigue cannot be cured just by having a good night's sleep.* | *I think we both need a good night's sleep. I'm too tired to talk about it now.*

have a good sleep /hæv ə ˌgʊd ˈsliːp/ [v phrase] informal to sleep very well: *You'll feel better after you've had a good sleep.* | *We both had a good sleep on the plane, so the jetlag wasn't too bad for either of us.*

sleep like a log /ˌsliːp laɪk ə ˈlɒg‖-ˈlɔːg/ [v phrase] to sleep very well and not wake up during the night, even if there is noise: *Cara slept like a log right through the storm.* | *It was deathly quiet, and I slept like a log all night.*

sleep through /ˈsliːp θruː/ [v T] to stay asleep while something noisy is happening around you: *His prison cellmate had slept through the tragedy.* | *Can you imagine paying all that money to see an opera, and then sleeping through the whole thing?* | *I sometimes think Dave could sleep through a world war.*

be a heavy/good/sound sleeper /biː ə ˌhevi, ˌgʊd, ˌsaʊnd ˈsliːpəʳ/ [v phrase] to always sleep very deeply and not wake up easily, even if there is a lot of noise: *The traffic won't bother me – I'm a heavy sleeper.* | *Normally, she was a good sleeper, but that night she lay awake, tossing and turning.*

be dead to the world /biː ˌded tə ðə ˈwɜːʳld/ [v phrase] informal to be sleeping so deeply that it is very difficult to wake you: *I'm sorry I didn't hear the phone – I must have been dead to the world this morning.*

6 to sleep badly or be unable to sleep

- sleep badly/not sleep well
- can't get to sleep
- not get much sleep
- be a light sleeper
- not sleep a wink
- lie awake
- toss and turn
- sleepless night
- restless night
- insomnia
- sleeplessness

sleep badly/not sleep well /ˌsliːp ˈbædli, nɒt sliːp ˈwel/ [v phrase] to wake up often during the night, and not feel rested or comfortable: *I'm sorry, I didn't sleep very well last night and it's put me in a bad mood.* | *They slept badly on the hard bamboo floor.*

can't get to sleep /ˌkɑːnt get tə ˈsliːp‖ˌkænt-/ [v phrase] to be unable to go to sleep especially because of noise, worries, pain etc: *If you can't get to sleep, don't get up or have a meal or snack; relax and read quietly instead.* | *I just couldn't get to sleep, what with all the traffic and people in the street.*

not get much sleep /nɒt ˌget mʌtʃ ˈsliːp/ [v phrase] to sleep badly and only for short periods, especially because of noise, worries, pain etc: *The people next door are having a party, so we probably won't get much sleep tonight.* | *She cried all last night and I didn't get much sleep either.*

be a light sleeper /biː ə ˌlaɪt ˈsliːpəʳ/ [v phrase] to be someone who is easily woken when there is any movement or noise: *I'm a light sleeper – so I woke up as soon as I heard him come in.* | *I just hope your dad isn't a light sleeper.*

not sleep a wink /nɒt ˌsliːp ə ˈwɪŋk/ [v phrase] informal to not sleep at all during the night, especially because you are worried, angry, upset etc: *I was so worried, I didn't sleep a wink last night.* | **hardly/barely sleep a wink** *He had hardly slept a wink all night, beside himself with jealousy and anger.*

lie awake /ˌlaɪ əˈweɪk/ [v phrase] to be in bed unable to sleep, especially because you are worried or excited about something: *I used to lie awake at night wondering what had happened to her.* | *I lay awake the whole night after I read the letter, thinking about what it could mean.* | *We'd lie awake, listening to our parents arguing in the room below.*

toss and turn /ˌtɒs ən ˈtɜːʳn‖ˌtɔːs-/ [v phrase] to keep changing your position in bed because you are unable to sleep and do not feel comfortable: *She had slept badly, tossing and turning before falling into a fitful doze.* | *Do you fall asleep as soon as your head hits the pillow, or do you toss and turn for hours before dropping off?*

sleepless night /ˌsliːpləs ˈnaɪt/ [n C] a night when you cannot sleep at all: *After a sleepless night, she looked almost as pale and exhausted as Elinor.* | **give sb a sleepless night** (=make someone worry so much that they cannot sleep) *He's given us a few sleepless nights over the years, but we love him.* | **spend a sleepless night** *Tom had spent a sleepless night on the sofa.*

restless night /ˌrestləs ˈnaɪt/ [n C] a night during which you sleep badly, keep changing your position in bed, and wake up often: *Another restless night followed, but she determinedly settled down to work again the next morning.* | *I'd had quite a restless night, and breakfast didn't look appetizing.*

insomnia /ɪnˈsɒmniə‖ɪnˈsɑːm-/ [n U] the inability to sleep at night: *Working outdoors all day certainly did wonders for my insomnia.* | *a cure for insomnia* | **suffer from insomnia** *He suffered from insomnia and was taking sleeping pills each night.* | **chronic insomnia** (=when this happens to you a lot over a long period of time) *My mother was alarmed by my fits of weeping and chronic insomnia.* —**insomniac** /ɪnˈsɒmniæk‖ɪnˈsɑːm-/ [n C] someone who does not sleep well: *I'm an incurable insomniac so I get a lot of my work done while the world sleeps.*

sleeplessness /ˈsliːpləsnɪs/ [n U] an inability to sleep that continues for several nights or more: *His eyes were still red-rimmed from tears and sleeplessness.* | *Sleeplessness and loss of appetite are common signs of stress.*

7 to sleep for longer than usual

- sleep in
- sleep off

sleep in ALSO **lie in/have a lie-in** British /ˌsliːp ˈɪn, ˌlaɪ ˈɪn, hæv ə ˈlaɪ ɪn/ [phr v I] to deliberately sleep until a later time than usual, and get up late: *Where are Diane and Mike? Sleeping in again, huh?* | *There's not much chance of a lie-in when you've got three kids.* | *We had a lie-in and breakfast in bed.*

sleep off /ˌsliːp ɪt ˈɒf/ [phr v T] to sleep for a long time, in order to stop feeling the effects of alcohol, drugs etc **sleep sth off** *In the end I decided the best thing was to put you to bed and let you sleep it off.* | **sleep off sth** *Martin's still in bed, sleeping off his hangover.* | *He was taken to the local hospital and kept in overnight to sleep off the effects of the drug.*

8 to sleep in a place where you do not usually sleep

- sleep over
- crash
- doss

sleep over /ˌsliːp ˈəʊvəʳ/ [phr v I] to sleep for one night at someone else's house: *Are your friends sleeping over tonight?* | **+ at** *Is it okay if I sleep over at Sam's house tomorrow night?*

crash ALSO **crash out** /kræʃ, ˌkræʃ ˈaʊt/ [v I/phr v I] informal to sleep the night in a place you do not normally sleep, for example at a friend's house or on the floor of someone's room: *You can crash out at my place if you like.* | *Would you mind if I crashed on your couch?*

doss /dɒs‖dɑːs/ British informal [v I] to sleep in a place where you do not usually sleep, especially not on a proper bed: *The party finished late, so I just dossed on the floor at Adele's.* | **doss down** *You can stay here, if you don't mind dossing down on the floor.*

9 to sleep outdoors

- sleep out
- sleep rough

sleep out /ˌsliːp ˈaʊt/ [phr v I] *What I like most about camping is sleeping out.* | *Over 100 people will be sleeping out in Glasgow tonight to highlight the plight of the homeless.* | *Bring a sleeping bag with you, because we're going to sleep out and walk back tomorrow.*

sleep rough /ˌsliːp ˈrʌf/ [v phrase] British to sleep outside or in an empty building because you have no home or nowhere to stay: *Hundreds of homeless people have to sleep rough every night in London.* | *The number of teenagers sleeping rough on the streets is on the increase.* | *I was forced to sleep rough that night in a disused warehouse.*

10 to make someone go to sleep

- put/send sb to sleep
- get sb off to sleep
- put sb to bed

put/send sb to sleep /ˌpʊt, ˌsend (sb) tə ˈsliːp/ [v phrase] if something such as music or a warm drink **sends you to sleep**, it relaxes you so much that you go to sleep easily: *Certain types of music always send me to sleep.* | *'Drink this,' mother said, 'It'll send you to sleep.'* | *The sound of her rhythmic breathing finally put me to sleep, and we both slept until the sun rose.*

get sb off to sleep /ˌget (sb) ɒf tə ˈsliːp/ [v phrase] especially British to make a baby or a young child go to sleep, for example by singing to them or reading them a story: *It's sometimes very difficult to get my young son off to sleep when he's excited.* | *She cried for a while but I finally got her off to sleep.*

put sb to bed /ˌpʊt (sb) tə ˈbed/ [v phrase] to get a baby or young child ready for the night and put them in their beds so that they will sleep: *Usually, I put the kids to bed at about 8:00.* | *In those days, many children were put to bed before dark in the summer months.*

11 to not go to bed and not sleep

- stay up
- wait up
- awake

stay up /ˌsteɪ ˈʌp/ [phr v I] to not go to bed at the usual time or when other people do, but to stay awake and do things: *You guys go ahead and go to bed. I think I'll stay up for a while.* | *Kate stayed up all night by his bedside.* | *Didn't you even stay up on election night?* | *We went to bed, but Julie and Kate stayed up talking and playing cards.* | **stay up till the small/wee hours** (=keep awake until very late or nearly morning) *That night Carl stayed up into the small hours, preparing work for the next day.*

wait up /ˌweɪt ˈʌp/ [phr v I] to keep awake and not go to bed at the usual time because you are waiting for someone to come home: *Julie's parents waited up all night but she never came home.* | *I'll be home late tonight, so don't wait up.* | **+ for** *I should go – Marie will be waiting up for me.*

awake /əˈweɪk/ [adj not before noun] not sleeping: *John, are you awake? I think I heard someone downstairs.* | *When she returned to the bedroom, Jamie was awake.* | **wide awake** (=awake and not tired at all) *I was still wide awake at 2:00 a.m. when Jody came home.* | **half awake** (=only partly awake) *Gretchen wandered into the kitchen, only half awake and looking for coffee.* | **stay awake** *Ellen was determined to stay awake, despite the late hour.* —**awake** [adv] *I was jolted awake by a blaring car horn outside.* | *The next morning, Benjamin shook me awake.*

12 to stop someone sleeping

- keep sb awake
- keep sb up

keep sb awake /ˌkiːp (sb) əˈweɪk/ [v phrase] *Molly kept Paula awake all night talking.* | *Angry neighbours say they are regularly kept awake by guests leaving the hotel late at night.* | *These terrifying thoughts sometimes kept me awake for hours.*

keep sb up /ˌkiːp (sb) ˈʌp/ [phr v T] to prevent someone from going to bed or from going to sleep when they want to go to sleep: *Arnold would keep us all up with his long, rambling stories.* | *I'm often kept up by the noise of laughter and music from next door.*

13 someone who likes to be awake at night

- night owl

night owl /ˈnaɪt aʊl/ [n C] someone who enjoys being awake or working late at night: *I've become a bit of a night owl since I started living alone.*

slide

RELATED WORDS

- *see also* **move, fall**

1 to move smoothly across a surface

- slide
- glide
- slither
- slip
- skid
- aquaplane

slide /slaɪd/ [v I/T] to move smoothly across a surface, or to make something do this: *We slipped and slid, losing our balance on the ice* | **+ around** *The children were having a great time, sliding around on the polished floor.* | **+ off/across/along etc** *Several glasses slid off the tray and crashed to the floor.* | *Harry slid across the bench so he was sitting next to me.* | **slide sth across/along/towards etc** *'Your money,' said White, as he slid a roll of banknotes across the table.* | *Fold the omelette over, slide it onto a plate, and serve immediately.*

glide /glaɪd/ [v I] to move smoothly and quietly across a surface, especially in a graceful way: *Your skis should glide naturally as you move across the snow.* | **+ across/along/around etc** *A swan glided across the surface of the lake.* | *The rattlesnake can see in the dark and makes no noise as it glides along.*

slither /'slɪðəʳ/ [v I] to slide across a slippery surface in a series of movements **+ away/off/across etc** *The snake slithered away through the grass.* | *Tom slithered down the muddy bank into the water.* | *As Katie fell asleep her book fell from her hands and slithered off the bed.*

slip /slɪp/ [v I] to accidentally slide a short distance, especially so that you fall down: *He slipped and fell. I think he's broken his arm.* | **+ on** *As the boys went down the path they slipped on the wet leaves.* | **+ down/across etc** *These glasses keep slipping down my nose.*

skid /skɪd/ [v I] if something **skids**, especially a car or a bicycle, it suddenly slides as it is moving along and is difficult to control: *The car in front of me skidded and I slammed the brakes on to avoid it.* | **+ across/along etc** *Nineteen people were injured today when a bus skidded off the road into a ditch.* | **+ on** *They set off down the road, the dogs skidding on the hard packed snow.* | **skid to a halt/stop** *She skidded to a halt, jumped off her scooter, and ran into the house.* —**skid** [n C] *Turn the steering wheel in the direction of, and not against, a skid.*

aquaplane British **/hydroplane** American /'ækwəpleɪn, 'haɪdrəʊˌpleɪn/ [v I] if a car **aquaplanes** or **hydroplanes**, it slides on a wet road: *In wet weather cars sometimes aquaplane when you brake heavily.* | *Porous asphalt tyres were developed to cut the risk of hydroplaning.*

2 a surface that makes you slide

- slippery
- slick

slippery ALSO **slippy** British spoken /'slɪpəri, 'slɪpi/ [adj] a **slippery** surface is so smooth or wet that it is difficult to stand or move safely on it: *Be careful – the floor is very slippery.* | *The pavements are a bit slippy so we have to walk carefully.* | *These boots give a good grip, even on slippery rocks.* | **+ with** *In places, the towpath is slippery with mud.*

slick /slɪk/ [adj] American a surface that is **slick** is smooth and slippery: *They couldn't climb up the slick lime walls of the pit.*

slow

RELATED WORDS

opposite: **fast**

- lasting or taking a long time *see* **long (6-13)**

1 moving slowly or doing something slowly

- slow
- slowly
- slow-moving
- leisurely
- in slow-motion
- at low speed
- at a snail's pace
- sluggish
- slowcoach

slow /sləʊ/ [adj] not moving quickly or not doing something quickly: *The train was slow, noisy, and uncomfortable.* | *I was always one of the slowest runners in my class.* | *My computer's really slow compared to the ones at school.* | **+ to do sth** *Farmers in the region have been slow to adopt modern agricultural methods.* | **+ in doing sth** *The CIA has been slow in turning over the documents that Congress requested.*

slowly /'sləʊli/ [adv] *He got up slowly out of his chair and came towards me.* | *Can you speak more slowly? I can't understand what you're saying.* | *Large white clouds drifted slowly across the deep blue sky.* | *Lynne slowly began to realize the job wasn't as easy as it seemed.*

slow-moving /ˌsləʊ 'muːvɪŋ◂/ [adj usually before noun] moving slowly, especially because of being prevented from moving faster: *In the evenings the roads out of town are clogged with slow-moving traffic.* | *Lubbers are slow-moving flightless insects native to the southeastern U.S.* | *The canal's water was muddy and slow-moving.*

leisurely /'leʒəʳli‖'liː-/ [adj usually before noun] moving or doing something slowly, especially because you are enjoying what you are doing and do not have to hurry: *Sunday mornings she gets up late and then has a leisurely breakfast with her family.* | *We spent a leisurely afternoon talking about old times.* | **at a leisurely pace** *The two set off walking down the beach at a leisurely pace.*

in slow-motion /ɪn ˌsləʊ 'məʊʃən/ [adv] showing images or movement at a slower speed than is normal – use this especially about pictures in a film: *The car crash seemed to take place in slow-motion.* | *The documentary showed the hawk's dive in slow-motion.* | *Fans who taped the show can replay it in slow-motion to read the messages that whizzed by on screen.*

at low speed /ət ˌləʊ 'spiːd/ [adv] if a vehicle travels **at low speed**, it moves more slowly than it usually does: *You'll save money on petrol if you drive your car at low speed.* | *The car came towards them at low speed, and then someone leaned out the back window and started shooting.* —**low-speed** /'ləʊ spiːd/ [adj only before noun] *Low-speed crashes can still prove deadly, especially to children.*

at a snail's pace /ət ə 'sneɪlz peɪs/ [adv] moving or doing something extremely slowly, especially when this is annoying: *Traffic was moving at a snail's pace.* | *The development project seems to be moving at a snail's pace.*

sluggish /'slʌgɪʃ/ [adj] moving more slowly than usual, especially because of a loss of power or energy: *The car felt sluggish as we drove up the hill.* | *The children were tired and sluggish and didn't seem interested in any of the games.* —**sluggishly** [adv] *'I should probably go,' Mike said, rising sluggishly from the sofa.*

slowcoach British **/slowpoke** American /'sləʊkəʊtʃ, 'sləʊpəʊk/ [n C] spoken someone who does something too slowly, works too slowly, walks too slowly, etc: *Come on, slowcoach! If you don't hurry up, we'll be late.* | *I hate getting stuck behind these slowpokes on the highway.*

2 happening or changing slowly

- slow
- slowly
- gradually
- gradual
- little by little/bit by bit
- slowly but surely
- by degrees

slow /sləʊ/ [adj] *She's making a slow recovery after her illness.* | *Rebuilding the country's economy is likely to be a long, slow process.* | *For the first few months that I was taking lessons, my progress was extremely slow.*

slowly /ˈsləʊli/ [adv] *The situation is slowly improving.* | *Slowly prices began to fall.* | *Their relationship has developed slowly, but they now consider each other close friends.*

gradually /ˈgrædʒuəli/ [adv] slowly over a period of time: *The climate is gradually becoming drier and warmer.* | *As the weeks passed, I gradually accepted the idea of him leaving.* | *Most patients gradually develop a resistance to the drug.*

gradual /ˈgrædʒuəl/ [adj] happening, developing, or changing slowly over a long period of time: *I had noticed a gradual improvement in her written work.* | *The chart showed a gradual rise in his temperature over the previous eight hours.* | *Because the cell destruction is gradual, a victim's pancreas can function normally for years.*

little by little/bit by bit /ˌlɪtl baɪ ˈlɪtl, ˌbɪt baɪ ˈbɪt/ [adv] happening or done slowly in a series of small amounts or stages – use this especially about something that is gradually improving: *Little by little, Greg's health improved.* | *Bit by bit, the dogs got used to their new surroundings.* | *Then add the olive oil, little by little, beating continuously until the sauce thickens.*

slowly but surely /ˌsləʊli bət ˈʃʊəʳli/ [adv] if something, especially an improvement in something, happens **slowly but surely**, it happens slowly and steadily until it is completed: *Slowly but surely, the company is becoming successful again.* | *She's getting better, slowly but surely.*

by degrees /baɪ dɪˈgriːz/ [adv] happening, developing, or changing very slowly, through a series of small changes that may be difficult to notice: *By degrees, little children grow less dependent on their parents.* | *The storm intensified by degrees until the rain was pouring down.*

3 to do something slowly

- take your time
- be in no hurry
- take it slowly/take things slowly
- dawdle

take your time /ˌteɪk jɔːʳ ˈtaɪm/ [v phrase] to do something slowly because you do not want to hurry, for example when you are making a decision or doing a difficult piece of work: *Just take your time. You don't have to decide immediately.* | **+ over/about** *Not wanting to seem too eager, Susan took her time about replying to the invitation.* | **+ doing sth** *Alice took her time telling the story, making sure to include every detail.*

be in no hurry /biː ɪn ˌnəʊ ˈhʌri‖-ˈhɜːri/ [v phrase] use this when someone is happy to do something slowly, usually because they are enjoying what they are doing and want to continue doing it: *'Do you mind if we look around a little more?' 'Not at all. I'm in no hurry.'* | **+ to do sth** *The sun was shining and I was in no hurry to get back to the office.*

take it slowly/take things slowly /ˌteɪk ɪt ˈsləʊli, ˌteɪk θɪŋz ˈsləʊli/ [v phrase] to deliberately do something slowly over a long period of time, because you will get better results if you do it that way: *Let's take it slowly, one step at a time, okay?* | *You've just had a serious operation – you'll have to take things slowly for the next few weeks.*

dawdle /ˈdɔːdl/ [v I] to move or work too slowly, especially because you are not really paying attention to what you are doing: *We'll never get all the shopping done today if you dawdle like this.* | **+ over** *I can't see why those guys in the office are dawdling over this.*

4 to move more slowly or do something more slowly

- slow down
- reduce speed

slow down /ˌsləʊ ˈdaʊn/ [phr v I/T] to move or do something more slowly, or make someone do this: *Slow down! You're driving too fast!* | *Everyone's always rushing around trying to get things done – we all need to slow down and take it easy.* | **slow sb down** *We could have been here hours ago, but the rain slowed us down.*

reduce speed /rɪˌdjuːs ˈspiːd‖-ˌduːs-/ [v phrase] to drive more slowly than before – used especially on road signs or in official instructions: *Reduce speed now – roadworks ahead.* | *There is heavy fog on all roads tonight so drivers are advised to reduce speed and drive with extra care.*

5 to move more slowly than the other people

- fall/drop behind
- lag behind

fall/drop behind /ˌfɔːl, ˌdrɒp- bɪˈhaɪnd‖ˌdrɑːp-/ [phr v I/T] to move more slowly than the other people you are with, so that you become separated from them: *A half an hour into the hike, two of the boys had already fallen behind.* | *The ship was so slow it dropped far behind the rest of the convoy.*

lag behind /ˌlæg bɪˈhaɪnd/ [phr v I/T] to walk or move more slowly than other people in the group you are with: *He deliberately lagged behind so he could have a cigarette.* | *We started walking faster, not wanting to lag behind the rest of the group.*

6 to move slowly towards or away from something or someone

- crawl
- inch
- edge
- creep

crawl /krɔːl/ [v I] if a vehicle **crawls**, it moves very slowly, because there is a lot of other traffic on the road, or because something is preventing it from moving at its usual speed **+ along/down/up etc** *The old Buick barely managed to crawl up the hill.* | *We sat in the car with the radio on, crawling along behind a long line of other cars.* —**at a crawl** /æt ə ˈkrɔːl/ [adv] very slowly: *Due to a major road accident, southbound traffic is moving at a crawl.*

inch /ɪntʃ/ [v I] to move very slowly and carefully, stopping regularly, for example because there is not much space or because you do not want to be noticed **+ towards/forward/across etc** *The car inched forward into the narrow parking space.* | *We watched the cat inching along the ground, not taking its eyes off the bird for a second.* | **inch your way**

along/towards/across etc *I inched my way across the crowded room to where Lou was standing.*

edge /edʒ/ [v I] to move very slowly and carefully, stopping regularly, for example because you do not want to be noticed or because it would be dangerous to move more quickly **edge along/towards/across etc** *I started edging towards the door, hoping to slip away unnoticed. | He kept an eye on me as he edged across the room. | Billy edged along the ledge, trying not to look down.*

creep /kriːp/ [v I] if light, a shadow, mist, water etc **creeps** somewhere, it moves so slowly that you almost do not notice it; if someone **creeps** somewhere, they move slowly and quietly so that they will not be noticed **+ across/towards/up etc** *Clouds crept across the horizon, just above the line of trees. | Armed men in ski masks crept up on the van and raked it with gunfire. | As the sun began to set, long shadows seemed to creep out of the corners. | We crept down to the deserted library at the other end of the hall, so that we could talk.*

small

RELATED WORDS

opposite: **big**

▸ *see also* **short, few/not many, less, narrow, thin**

1 small in size

- ▸ **small**
- ▸ **little**
- ▸ **compact**
- ▸ **pocket**
- ▸ **dainty**

small /smɔːl/ [adj] *His office was a small room at the top of the building. | Which is the smallest state in the US? | Mrs Newman was small and slightly plump, with a round face. | People are buying smaller cars because they are cheaper to run. | These shoes are too small for me.*

little /ˈlɪtl/ [adj only before noun] small – use this especially to show how you feel about someone or something, for example to show that you like them, dislike them, or feel sorry for them: *It's just a little souvenir I brought back from Italy | What an annoying little boy! | Oh, the poor little thing, he's hurt his paw. | What a lovely little dog! | They bought a nice little house near the beach.*

compact /kəmˈpækt, ˈkɒmpækt‖kəmˈpækt/ [adj] a house, room etc that is **compact** is small but comfortable and convenient, because the space has been used effectively; a **compact** camera, computer etc is designed to be small and easy to carry: *The apartment was ideal for the two of us – small but compact. | There is a compact dining area, which feels cozy rather than cramped. | The PowerShot is a compact unit that weighs less than 11 ounces and fits easily in your pocket.*

pocket /ˈpɒkət‖ˈpɑː-/ [adj only before noun] **pocket calculator/torch/camera etc** one that is small and that you can carry easily, for example in your **pocket** or bag: *Students are allowed to take pocket calculators into their exams. | She took a pocket mirror out of her handbag and put on some lipstick. | a pocket dictionary*

dainty /ˈdeɪnti/ [adj] an object that is **dainty** is small and delicate in an attractive way: *We drank Turkish coffee out of dainty china cups. | She was wearing a short black dress and dainty black sandals.*

2 extremely small in size

- ▸ **tiny**
- ▸ **minute**
- ▸ **minuscule**
- ▸ **microscopic**
- ▸ **miniature**

tiny /ˈtaɪni/ [adj] *Have you seen Vic's apartment? It's tiny. | Luke put out his hand and touched the tiny fingers of his baby daughter. | a tiny village in the mountains* | **tiny little** *The box was full of tiny little blue and white beads.*

minute /maɪˈnjuːt‖-ˈnuːt/ [adj] extremely small and difficult to see: *Police found minute traces of blood on the car seats. | Her writing's so minute that it's difficult to read. | The problem was caused by minute particles of dust getting in the disk drive.*

minuscule /ˈmɪnəskjuːl/ [adj] a lot smaller than usual, especially in a way that seems surprising: *Compared to its adult size, a new-born kangaroo is minuscule. | The pool was surrounded by bronzed girls wearing minuscule bikinis.*

microscopic /ˌmaɪkrəˈskɒpɪk◂‖-ˈskɑː-/ [adj] an object or living creature that is **microscopic** is so small that it is difficult or impossible to see without using special equipment: *The skin is covered with microscopic hairs, invisible to the naked eye. | A primitive form of microscopic life may have existed on Mars billions of years ago. | Many of these organisms are microscopic in size.*

miniature /ˈmɪnətʃəʳ‖ˈmɪniə-/ [adj usually before noun] very small, but made just like something of normal size: *Next to the beach there's a miniature railway. | The locket contained a miniature portrait of her late husband. | a miniature TV with a 2 inch screen*

3 small numbers/amounts

- ▸ **small**
- ▸ **low**
- ▸ **tiny**
- ▸ **minute**

small /smɔːl/ [adj] *There wasn't really much I could buy with such a small amount. | Only a small number of people eventually turned up. | The level of radiation in the atmosphere is really very small.*

low /ləʊ/ [adj] **low** prices, wages, levels etc are less than usual or less than they should be: *It's a good time to buy a computer, because prices are low. | Farm workers are complaining about long hours and low wages. | Low interest rates mean good news for home owners.*

tiny /ˈtaɪni/ [adj] a **tiny** number or amount is extremely small: *Only a tiny fraction of our profit comes from book sales. | You only need to use a tiny amount of salt. | The proportion of babies that suffer from the disease is tiny.* | **a tiny majority** (=a very small number of a much larger group) *Millions of people buy lottery tickets, but only a tiny majority ever win anything.*

minute /maɪˈnjuːt‖-ˈnuːt/ [adj] a **minute** amount is extremely small, and is often so small that it makes very little difference to something: *Only minute amounts of the chemical were found in the water supply. | The substance is so toxic that even a minute dose of it could be fatal.*

4 small and not making much difference to something

- ▸ **small**
- ▸ **slight**
- ▸ **minor**
- ▸ **infinitesimal**
- ▸ **tiny**
- ▸ **minute**

small /smɔːl/ [adj] *I want to make a few small changes to the design.* | *There is still one small problem that we haven't dealt with.* | *Government statistics showed a small drop in the annual rate of inflation.*

slight /slaɪt/ [adj usually before noun] small and not very important or not very noticeable: *There has been a slight change of plan.* | *The doctor says there has been a slight improvement in her condition.* | *He was a good friend – always available to help at the slightest sign of need.* | **not the slightest** (=none at all) *Tom? I haven't the slightest idea where he is.* | *US foreign policy at the time hadn't made the slightest difference in the situation.*

minor /ˈmaɪnə/ [adj only before noun] not important enough or serious enough to worry about: *She fell off her horse, but suffered only minor injuries.* | *The contract seems fine, except for a few minor details.* | *With one or two minor changes, the course is the same as last year.*

infinitesimal /ˌɪnfɪnəˈtesəməl◂/ [adj] an **infinitesimal** amount, risk etc is so small that it makes very little difference or is not worth worrying about: *Even an infinitesimal change in temperature will be recorded by the equipment.* | *I'd say the chances of your catching the disease are infinitesimal.* —**infinitesimally** [adv] *The eggs of the lice are infinitesimally small and very easy to miss.*

tiny /ˈtaɪni/ [adj] extremely small: *I've made one or two tiny alterations, but otherwise the house is the same as when I bought it.* | *There's been a tiny decrease in the number of people out of work.*

minute /maɪˈnjuːt‖-ˈnuːt/ [adj] a change or difference that is **minute** is so small that it is difficult to see it or notice any effects resulting from it: *The equipment records minute changes in air pressure.*

5 rooms, houses etc that are too small

- cramped
- poky/pokey

cramped /kræmpt/ [adj] a room, space, or vehicle that is **cramped** is uncomfortable because there is not enough space inside it for people to move around: *I hated working in that cramped little office.* | *Conditions on board the ship were extremely cramped.*

poky/pokey British ALSO **dinky** American /ˈpəʊki, ˈdɪŋki/ [adj] small, unattractive, and uncomfortable to be in: *The whole family lives in two pokey little rooms at the back of the building.* | *There was only one dinky store with a few cans of soup and some other useless junk for sale.*

6 to become smaller in size

- get smaller
- shrink
- shrivel/shrivel up

get smaller /ˌget ˈsmɔːləʳ/ [v phrase] *The dot got smaller and smaller and vanished from the screen.* | *Am I getting fatter or are these jeans getting smaller?*

shrink /ʃrɪŋk/ [v I] if something **shrinks**, especially clothes, it becomes smaller because of the effect of water or heat: *Don't wash that sweater in the machine – it'll shrink.* | *Oh no! My skirt has shrunk!*

shrivel/shrivel up /ˈʃrɪvəl, ˌʃrɪvəl ˈʌp/ [v I/phr v I] if something such as a plant or a fruit **shrivels** or **shrivels up**, it becomes smaller as water is removed from it, for example as a result of heat: *Eventually the grapes will shrivel and become raisins,* | *The crops were beginning to shrivel up in the heat.* —**shrivelled/shrivelled up** [adj] *I don't want this orange, it's all shrivelled up.*

smell

RELATED WORDS

see also **taste, horrible, delicious**

1 a smell

- smell
- odour
- scent

smell /smel/ [n C] something that you notice by using your nose: *What's that smell? Is something burning?* | *We had the carpet cleaned, but we couldn't get rid of the musty smell.* | *The wonderful smells from the kitchen made her mouth water.* | **+ of** *I really hate the smell of stale beer.*

odour British **/odor** American /ˈəʊdəʳ/ [n C] a strong smell that is easy to recognize: *Each ant's nest has its own odor that ants use to recognize it.* | **+ of** *Lingering in the air was the unmistakeable odor of barbecue smoke.* | *We immediately noticed the heavy odour of opium in the room.*

scent /sent/ [n C] the smell left by animals: *The dogs followed the fox's scent to the edge of the forest.* | **+ of** *The deer caught the scent of the man, and sprang off over the hill.*

2 a good smell

- scent/fragrance/perfume
- aroma

scent/fragrance/perfume /sent, ˈfreɪgrəns, ˈpɜːʳfjuːm/ [n C] a pleasant smell, especially from flowers, plants, or fruit: *The trees were so thick with flowers their scent was almost overpowering.* | *The flowers have been prized over the centuries for their heady perfume.* | **+ of** *The fragrance of lilacs always reminds me of spring.* | *A cool autumn breeze blew past, carrying with it the scent of pine.*

aroma /əˈrəʊmə/ [n C] a pleasant smell, especially from food or coffee: *Each of the cheeses has its own texture, flavour, and aroma.* | **+ of** *The aroma of coffee brought Christine into the small cafe.* | *The rich aroma of freshly baked bread filled the whole house.*

3 a bad smell

- smell
- odour
- stench
- stink
- pong

smell /smel/ [n C] *There's a smell in here – open the window.* | *The food looked good, but the smell was awful.* | **+ of** *The smells of dead fish and rotting garbage were more than he could stand.* | **bad smell** *There was a bad smell coming from the cupboard.*

odour British **/odor** American /ˈəʊdəʳ/ [n C] a strong, unpleasant smell that is easy to recognize: *The air freshener is supposed to get rid of unpleasant household odors.* | **+ of** *Around the camps there was always the pungent order of kerosene burning human waste.* | **body odour/odor** *The man sitting next to me had body odor and bad breath.*

stench /stentʃ/ [n singular] a very strong unpleasant smell, especially one that is so bad it makes it hard for you to breathe or makes you feel sick: *The dead body had begun to rot, and the stench was overpowering.* | **+ of** *I couldn't bear to go in the room with its stench of beer and vomit.*

stink /stɪŋk/ [n singular] a strong and very unpleasant smell, especially from something that is decaying: *The stink from the drains is almost unbearable in summer.* | **+ of** *The stink of burning rubber permeated the hot summer air.*

pong /pɒŋ ‖ pɑːŋ/ [n singular] British informal a bad smell: *What a pong! This place hasn't been cleaned for years!*

4 to have a good smell

- smell nice/good
- fragrant
- fresh
- aromatic
- sweet-smelling
- delicate
- perfumed

smell nice/good /ˌsmel ˈnaɪs, ˈgʊd/ [v phrase not in progressive] to have a pleasant smell: *Something smells good. What are you cooking?* | *You smell so good – is that a new perfume?* | *I put lavender in my cupboard to make my clothes smell nice.*

fragrant /ˈfreɪgrənt/ [adj] having a light, pleasant smell, especially of flowers: *The plant has fragrant red and white flowers.* | *The forest was cool and fragrant, and the walk through it calmed my spirits.* | *Choose from one of Chanel's new range of fragrant body lotions.*

fresh /freʃ/ [adj] having a clean, natural, pleasant smell: *If you eat garlic, have some parsley afterwards to keep your breath fresh.* | *The fields have such a clean, fresh smell after the rain.*

aromatic /ˌærəˈmætɪk◂/ [adj] having a pleasant smell – use this especially about plants and leaves that are used in cooking: *Thai basil is fast growing and wonderfully aromatic.* | *This kind of massage is a gentle treatment using aromatic oils.*

sweet-smelling /ˌswiːt ˈsmelɪŋ◂/ [adj] having a strong, sweet smell: *The room was warm, sweet-smelling, and luxurious.* | *The plant produces tiny, but sweet-smelling white flowers.* | *The old city lay among sweet-smelling pine woods and almond groves.*

delicate /ˈdelɪkɨt/ [adj] a **delicate** smell is pleasant but sometimes difficult to notice: *The delicate scent of roses hung in the air.* | *This soup has a marvellous, delicate fragrance and a slightly sweet taste.*

perfumed /ˈpɜːfjuːmd ‖ pərˈfjuːmd/ [adj] having a strong but pleasant smell – use this especially about something that has been given a smell by a particular product: *He stood so close to her that he could smell the perfumed soap on her skin.* | *perfumed lotions* | *The poodle came back from the groomers perfumed, with a tiny bow behind each ear.*

5 to have a bad smell

- smelly
- smell
- stink
- reek
- stinking
- stink the place out
- musty
- stale
- acrid

smelly /ˈsmeli/ [adj] *The hut was dark and smelly.* | *Don't leave your smelly sneakers lying around the living room.* | *The lake was rapidly turning brown and smelly from the factory wastes.*

smell /smel/ [v I] to have an unpleasant smell: *Does my breath smell?* | *We need to clean the cat's litter box – it's starting to smell.* | **smell bad/awful/terrible/disgusting** *Not only does he smell bad – he's mean and ugly too.* | *Many people like the taste of jackfruit, but it smells terrible.*

stink /stɪŋk/ [v I not in progressive] to have a strong and unpleasant smell: *Her room is filthy, and it stinks.* | *How can you eat that cheese? It stinks.* | **+ of** *His clothes stank of cigarette smoke.* | **stink to high heaven** *You boys stink to high heaven – go inside and take a shower.*

reek /riːk/ [v I not in progressive] to have a very strong smell of something unpleasant: *Get that dog out of here – he reeks.* | **+ of** *He came running into the house, reeking of sweat.* | *The tiny office reeked of onions and cigarette smoke.* | *Where have you been – you reek of alcohol?*

stinking /ˈstɪŋkɪŋ/ [adj only before noun] having a very strong unpleasant smell: *The yards were full of stinking garbage cans, and untidy lines of washing.* | *He pointed to the stinking hole that we were to use as a toilet.*

stink the place out British **/stink the place up** American /ˌstɪŋk ðə ˈpleɪs aʊt, ˌstɪŋk ðə ˈpleɪs ʌp/ [v phrase] informal to make a whole room smell bad: *You're not bringing that cat in here – it'll stink the place out.* | *She made fish for dinner and stunk the place up.*

musty /ˈmʌsti/ [adj] things such as books, clothes, or rooms that are **musty** have a smell that is old and not fresh, especially because they have not been used or been in fresh air for a long time: *The hotel room was dark and musty.* | *The library was full of musty old books which no one wanted to read.*

stale /steɪl/ [adj] having a smell that is not fresh, especially because you can still smell something such as old cigarette smoke or old cooking smells: *She noticed the stale smell of drink on his breath.* | *The air in the office was stale and heavy.* | *It was cold outside and the smell of stale tobacco clung to their winter coats.*

acrid /ˈækrɨd/ [adj] having a sharp, unpleasant smell, especially one that hurts your nose: *The chemical has an acrid smell.* | *When I opened the door, acrid white smoke came billowing out.* | *The air was stale and acrid, and a cluster of black flies hovered over the bed.*

6 having a strong smell

- strong
- pungent
- powerful
- heady

strong /strɒŋ‖strɔːŋ/ [adj] *There's a strong smell of gas in here.* | *Her perfume is so strong – it makes me gag.* | *Goat's cheese has a strong smell.* | **strong-smelling** *Pete had covered himself in strong-smelling aftershave.*

pungent /ˈpʌndʒənt/ [adj] having a very strong, sharp, and often unpleasant smell: *Garlic has a pungent aroma.* | *Pungent diesel fumes poured from the back of the truck.*

powerful /ˈpaʊəʳfəl/ [adj] very strong, and sometimes unpleasant: *Ammonia has a very powerful, distinctive smell.* | *The powerful smell of cabbage, sardines, and body odor filled the train.*

heady /ˈhedi/ [adj only before noun] **heady smell/scent/perfume** a smell etc that is very strong and sweet, like a powerful smell of flowers: *A heady scent of jasmine hung in the summer air.* | *Diane loved the blossoms and the heady aroma of the wild rose bush.*

7 to smell something

- smell
- sniff
- get/catch a whiff of sth
- scent
- sense of smell

smell /smel/ [v T not in passive] to notice the smell of something, especially by putting your nose near it: *Smell these roses – aren't they lovely?* | *If you smell gas in the apartment, call this number immediately.* | *I swear I haven't had anything to drink. Smell my breath.* | **can smell** (=notice a smell) *I can smell something burning – are you sure you turned the oven off?*

sniff /snɪf/ [v I/T not in passive] to take quick breaths through your nose in order to smell something: *He opened the milk and sniffed it.* | *Otto looked around quickly to make sure no one was looking and then sniffed his armpits.* | **+ at** *The dog was rushing around excitedly, sniffing at the ground.*

get/catch a whiff of sth /ˌget, ˌkætʃ ə ˈwɪf əv (sth)/ [v phrase] informal to notice a smell, just for a short time: *I caught a whiff of roast beef as I walked past the kitchen.* | *Lisa passed so close to Paul that he got a whiff of her perfume.*

scent /sent/ [v T not in progressive] if an animal **scents** something, especially another animal, it can smell that it is near: *The dog had scented something in the bushes.* | *Police dogs have a very keen sense of smell and can scent even the slightest traces of drugs.*

sense of smell /ˌsens əv ˈsmel/ [n phrase] *Blind people often have a much better sense of smell than other people.* | *Smoking can really ruin a person's sense of smell.* | **keen sense of smell** (=very good one) *Pigs have a keen sense of smell, which is why they are used to find truffles.*

8 to have a particular smell

- smell
- have a good/bad etc smell
- give off

smell /smel/ [v I not in progressive] **+ of** *She smelled of alcohol and was unsteady on her feet.* | *The whole house smells of garlic – what are you cooking?* | **+ like** *It smells like a hospital in here – has someone been using disinfectant?* | **smell nice/horrible/sweet etc** *This hand cream smells lovely, what's it called?* | *The meat smelled horrible, and I refused to eat it.*

have a good/bad etc smell /hæv ə ˌgʊd ˈsmel/ [v phrase not in progressive] *The wine has a light, lemony smell.* | *Clothes washed in some detergents have a chemical smell.* | *The house was empty, and the rooms had a stale, damp smell.*

give off /ˌgɪv ˈɒf/ [phr v T] to produce a particular type of smell that is fairly strong **give off sth** *The mixture gave off a strong odor of sulfur.* | *The covers were damp from humidity and gave off a mildewy smell.* | *When dried, the flowers will continue to give off their fragrance for months and even years.*

smile

RELATED WORDS

▸ *see also* **laugh, happy, funny, friendly**

1 to smile

- smile
- grin
- beam
- sb's face lights up
- break into a smile/grin
- be all smiles
- force a smile

smile /smaɪl/ [v I] to make your mouth curve upwards, as a sign that you are happy or amused or that you want to be friendly: *She smiled and said, 'Good morning.'* | *Kathy couldn't help smiling as the children came back into the room.* | *'Stop worrying, you look very nice,' she smiled reassuringly.* (=said with a smile) | *My father rarely smiled.* | **+ at** *The twins turned and smiled at each other, sharing a private joke.* | *He winked, and she smiled back at him.* | **smile broadly** (=smile with your mouth very wide) *She smiled broadly when her name was called.* | **make sb smile** *He can make people smile just by walking into a room.* —**smiling** [adj only before noun] *The road was lined with smiling school children.*

grin /grɪn/ [v I] to give a big happy smile: *Grinning shyly, he offered her a drink.* | *'I've been a complete idiot', grinned Ian.* (=said with a grin) | **grin broadly** (=grin with your mouth very wide) *She sat back down again, grinning broadly.* | **+ at** *She kept grinning at me as if we were old friends.* | **grin from ear to ear** informal (=to grin a lot because you are very happy) *She was holding the baby, and grinning from ear to ear.*

beam /biːm/ [v I] to smile for a long time, especially because you are very pleased about or proud of something or someone: *Her parents stood there beaming as she went up to receive the prize.* | **+ at** *After the song was over, Miss Timms beamed at the class.* | **beam with pleasure/pride etc** *Daddy sat in the first pew, beaming with pride.* | *Just a short time before, they had been beaming with optimism.*

sb's face lights up / (sb's) ˌfeɪs laɪts ˈʌp/ if **someone's face lights up**, they suddenly look happy, for example because they have received some good news: *He gave her the letter and watched as her face lit up.* | *The moment she walked into the room, Bob's face lit up.*

break into a smile/grin /ˌbreɪk ɪntʊ ə ˈsmaɪl, ˈgrɪn/ [v phrase] to suddenly start smiling: *All at once she broke into a smile as she remembered what had happened.* | *She broke into a grin, and started to run towards me.* | *'We're going to have a visitor,' said her mother, and Anna's face broke into a smile at the thought.*

be all smiles /biː ˌɔːl ˈsmaɪlz/ [v phrase] to be very happy, smile a lot, and be friendly toward other people, especially because a situation is the way you want it: *I don't understand it – he was all smiles this morning and now he won't talk to me.*

force a smile /ˌfɔːʳs ə ˈsmaɪl/ [v phrase] to try hard to smile when you do not feel happy: *'I'm getting married,' he said. Somehow I managed to force a smile.* | *Alice forced a smile, hoping it looked natural.*

2 to smile in an unpleasant way

- smirk
- leer
- sneer

smirk /smɜːʳk/ [v I] to smile in an unpleasant way, for example because you are pleased about someone else's bad luck or because you know something that they do not know: *She sits there smirking as if she's the only one who knows the answer.* | *'You realise you'll be stuck out here on your own, don't you?' he* *smirked.* (=said with a smirk) | **+ at** *What are you smirking at?*

leer /lɪəʳ/ [v I] to smile in a way that is unpleasant or threatening and that shows unwelcome sexual interest in someone: *The man with the gold tooth leered and slapped his hand on her knee.* | **+ at** *My boss was a disgusting man who used to leer at me whenever he passed by my desk.*

sneer /snɪəʳ/ [v I] to smile in an unpleasant and offensive way that shows you think someone is stupid or less good than you: *As she read the letter, she started to sneer.* | *Some clients would sneer or smile sarcastically when I showed them my old laptop – until they saw what it could do.* | **+ at** *She'd not forgotten how Gareth had laughed and sneered at them when they'd first tried to be friendly.*

3 a smile

- **smile**
- **grin**
- **smirk**
- **leer**
- **sneer**

smile /smaɪl/ [n C] the look on your face when you make your mouth curve upwards to show that you are happy, friendly, amused etc: *Helga has a lovely smile.* | *Johnny's broad smile changed slowly to a frown.* | *'Hi,' said Sophie, with the most radiant smile I have ever seen.* | **break into a smile** (=to suddenly start smiling) *She clapped her hands and broke into one of her huge smiles.* | **give sb a smile** (=smile at them) *Barry gave the old lady a warm smile.* | **with a smile on your face** *He fell asleep with a contented smile on his face.* | **have a smile on your face** *She's really happy for me; she has a big smile on her face.*

grin /grɪn/ [n C] a big happy smile: *Her face broke into a delighted grin.* | *Joel gave her a wicked grin.* | *The television camera captured his sheepish grin as he stepped from the train.* | **give sb a grin** (=grin at them) *William gave her a friendly grin as he walked past.*

smirk /smɜːʳk/ [n C] an unpleasant, satisfied smile, for example when you are pleased about someone else's bad luck or when you think you know something that they do not know: *Penny's lips curved in a superior smirk as he rushed from the room.*

leer /lɪəʳ/ [n C] an unpleasant or threatening smile, showing an unwelcome sexual interest in someone: *He leaned over the girl with a leer and she could smell the whisky on his breath.* | *The look on my cousin's face changed from its usual cocky leer to one of complete bewilderment.*

sneer /snɪəʳ/ [n C] an unpleasant, offensive smile, that shows that you think that someone is stupid or that you are better than them: *'And what's your name?' he demanded, his lip curling into a sneer.*

smoking

RELATED WORDS

▸ *see also* **fire, burn, addicted**

1 to smoke a cigarette, pipe etc

- **smoke**
- **smoking**
- **puff on**
- **draw on**

smoke /sməʊk/ [v I/T not in passive] to breathe in **smoke** from a cigarette, pipe etc, either from one cigarette etc or regularly: *How old were you when you started smoking?* | *Do you mind if I smoke?* | *He sat behind his desk, smoking a fat cigar.* | *Sue never smoked a cigarette in her life, yet she still got lung cancer.* | *Anyone who smokes 40 a day can expect to have a lot of health problems.*

smoking /ˈsməʊkɪŋ/ [n U] the habit or act of smoking: *Some teenage girls think that smoking helps keep their weight down.* | *Smoking is not allowed in any part of the building.* | *These days smoking is seen as an anti-social habit.* | **passive smoking** (=when you breathe in the smoke from other people's cigarettes) *Roy believed his illness was caused by passive smoking.*

puff on /ˈpʌf ɒn/ [v phrase] to take small amounts of smoke into your mouth from a cigarette, cigar, or pipe: *He lit a cigar and puffed on it thoughtfully.* | *They drove in silence, Charlie contentedly puffing on his pipe.*

draw on /ˈdrɔː ɒn/ [phr v T] to breathe in a lot of smoke from a cigarette, pipe etc in one long breath: *She lit her last cigarette, and drew on it slowly.*

2 to smoke a lot

- **smoke a lot/smoke heavily**
- **smoke like a chimney**
- **chain-smoke**

smoke a lot/smoke heavily /ˌsməʊk ə ˈlɒt‖-ˈlɑːt, ˌsməʊk ˈhevəli/ [v phrase] *When we were students, we all used to smoke a lot.* | *This disease is more common in people who smoke heavily.*

smoke like a chimney /ˌsməʊk laɪk ə ˈtʃɪmni/ [v phrase] British informal to smoke a lot, especially too much: *She's only thirteen and she already smokes like a chimney.*

chain-smoke /ˈtʃeɪn sməʊk/ [v I/T] to smoke one cigarette after another, without a break: *James sat silently through her speech, chain-smoking.* | *Although he chain-smoked cigarettes, his hands were unstained.*

3 someone who smokes

- **smoker**
- **heavy smoker**
- **chain-smoker**

smoker /ˈsməʊkəʳ/ [n C] someone who smokes regularly: *The survey shows that most smokers would like to stop smoking.* | *The average smoker spends about £35 a week on cigarettes.*

heavy smoker /ˌhevi ˈsməʊkəʳ/ [n C] someone who regularly smokes a lot: *He had been a heavy smoker all his life and only stopped when his doctor told him to.*

chain-smoker /ˈtʃeɪn ˌsməʊkəʳ/ [n C] someone who smokes a lot of cigarettes, and who lights another cigarette immediately after finishing one: *I noticed that the thin, nervous man was a chain-smoker.*

4 not smoking

- **don't smoke**
- **stop smoking**
- **non-smoker**
- **no-smoking**
- **non-smoking**
- **smoke-free**

don't smoke /ˌdəʊnt ˈsməʊk/ [v I] if you **don't smoke**, you never smoke cigarettes, pipes etc: *He doesn't smoke or drink.* | *'Cigarette?' 'No thanks, I don't smoke.'*

stop smoking ALSO **give up smoking** /ˌstɒp ˈsməʊkɪŋ‖ˌstɑːp-, ˌgɪv ʌp ˈsməʊkɪŋ/ especially British **/quit smoking** ALSO **quit** especially American /ˌkwɪt ˈsməʊkɪŋ, kwɪt/ to stop smoking, especially when you make a firm decision that you will not smoke again: *Make a list of all the benefits of stopping smoking, for example better health, fresher breath, and more money.* | *I'm trying to give up smoking, but it isn't easy.* | *I didn't gain any weight when I quit smoking.*

non-smoker ALSO **nonsmoker** American /nɒn ˈsməʊkəʳ‖nɑːn-/ [n C] someone who never smokes: *This part of the restaurant is reserved for non-smokers.* | *Non-smokers get cheaper health insurance.*

no-smoking /nəʊ ˈsməʊkɪŋ/ [adj only before noun] use this about rules or signs that say people must not smoke in a particular area: *There were big no-smoking signs on all the walls.* | *The company has a no-smoking policy in all its offices.* | *Most restaurants and cafes have set aside small no-smoking areas.*

non-smoking /nɒn ˈsməʊkɪŋ‖nɑːn-/ [adj] use this about places where you are not allowed to smoke: *I asked for a seat in the non-smoking section of the plane.*

smoke-free /ˌsməʊk ˈfriː◂/ [adj] a restaurant, room etc that is **smoke-free** does not have any areas where people can smoke: *Most workers prefer a smoke-free environment at the office.* | *We are calling for all airlines to be smoke-free.*

5 to light a cigarette, pipe etc

- light
- light up
- give sb a light
- have you got a light?

light /laɪt/ [v T] to make a cigarette, cigar, or pipe start burning: *The old man struck a match and lit his pipe.* | *I leaned forward to light her cigarette.*

light up /ˌlaɪt ˈʌp/ [phr v I/T] to light a cigarette, pipe etc for yourself: *They're not allowed to smoke at work, so they all light up as soon as they leave.* | *She lit up another cigarette.*

give sb a light /ˌgɪv (sb) ə ˈlaɪt/ [v phrase] to give someone a match or let them use your lighter so that they can light their cigarette: *Give us a light, will you?* | *Henry will give you a light.*

have you got a light? British **/do you have a light?** American /ˌhæv juː gɒt ə ˈlaɪt‖-gɑːt-, ˌduː juː hæv ə ˈlaɪt/ spoken say this to ask someone for a match or a lighter to light your cigarette: *Excuse me, do you have a light?*

6 to make a cigarette, pipe etc stop burning

- put out
- extinguish
- stub out

put out /ˌpʊt ˈaʊt/ [phr v T] to make a cigarette, cigar, or pipe stop burning **put out sth** *Bill put out his pipe and stood up to leave.* | **put sth out** *Put that cigarette out at once!*

extinguish /ɪkˈstɪŋgwɪʃ/ [v T] formal to put out a cigarette, cigar, or pipe – used especially in official notices or announcements: *Passengers are requested to extinguish all cigarettes when the red light goes on.*

stub out /ˌstʌb ˈaʊt/ [phr v T] to put out a cigarette by pressing the end of it against something **stub out sth** *She nervously stubbed out her cigarette, and immediately lit another one.* | **stub sth out** *He smoked three cigarettes and stubbed them out in his saucer.*

soft

RELATED WORDS

opposite: — **hard**

▸ *see also* **weak**

1 soft and easy to press or crush

- soft
- tender
- spongy
- springy

soft /sɒft‖sɔːft/ [adj] *She fell over several times, but came to no harm in the soft new snow.* | *a selection of hard and soft cheeses* | *I need a softer pillow.* —**softness** [n U] *It's the padding and type of springs used that give a mattress its softness.* | *The softness of gold makes it relatively easy to use for ornamental purposes.*

tender /ˈtendəʳ/ [adj] use this about meat and vegetables that are soft and easy to cut because they have been cooked well: *Cook the curry for another 40 minutes or until the meat is tender.* —**tenderness** [n U] *Methods of cooking such as braising and stewing are used to increase tenderness in tougher cuts of meat.*

spongy /ˈspʌndʒi/ [adj] soft and full of holes that contain air or liquid: *The ground was wet and spongy underfoot.* | *Protecting the edge of the bone is a layer of soft, spongy tissue.*

springy /ˈsprɪŋi/ [adj] use this about grass or ground that returns to its original shape after someone has walked on it: *Instinctively, I took off my shoes and felt the springy grass beneath my bare feet.* | *The stag was now at full gallop on the springy turf.*

2 soft and pleasant to touch

- soft
- fluffy
- velvety

soft /sɒft‖sɔːft/ [adj] *Her hair was soft and silky.* | *Apply the polish with a soft cloth.* | *an expensive pair of soft leather gloves* | *Use a good handcream to keep your hands soft.* —**softness** [n U] *He stroked the satin softness of her hair.*

fluffy /ˈflʌfi/ [adj] covered in soft, light threads, fur, or feathers: *She found a towel, huge and fluffy, and wrapped it around herself.* | *After a few days, there would be dozens of fluffy little chicks hatching out.*

velvety /ˈvelvəti/ [adj] soft, smooth, and shiny and pleasant to touch: *His skin felt soft and velvety, like a baby's.* | *She buried her nose in the fragrant, velvety petals.*

3 soft and wet

- squashy
- squishy

squashy British **/mushy** American /ˈskwɒʃi‖ˈskwɑːʃi, ˈmʌʃi/ [adj] use this about fruit or vegetables that are soft and wet, for example because they are not fresh or have been cooked for too long: *All I had left in the fridge was a lemon and a couple of squashy tomatoes.* | *mushy Brussels sprouts and lumpy gravy* | *Use firm, ripe pears, not ones that have gone mushy.*

squishy /ˈskwɪʃi/ [adj] use this about mud that is very soft and makes a wet sound when you walk in it: *The ground was soft and squishy, and she felt mud oozing over the top of her shoes.*

4 soft and not stiff or firm

- limp
- floppy

limp /lɪmp/ [adj] use this about something that is not as stiff or firm as it should be: *He held the boy's small, limp body in his arms, and wept.* | *By the time we got there, all that was left were some rather limp sandwiches.*

floppy /ˈflɒpi‖ˈflɑːpi/ [adj] use this about something that is soft and hangs loosely downwards: *He wore a large, floppy hat.* | *a toy rabbit with big, floppy ears* | *He is good-looking with floppy black hair, brown eyes and a lean muscular body.*

5 to become or make something soft

- get soft
- soften

get soft ALSO **go soft** British /get ˈsɒft, gəʊ ˈsɒft‖-ˈsɔːft/ [v phrase] *The wax will get softer as it is heated.* | *Put the butter in the fridge or it'll go soft.*

soften /ˈsɒfən‖ˈsɔː-/ [v I/T] to become soft or to make something soft: *Soak the raisins in warm water till they soften.* | *It's a disease that softens and then destroys the bones.* —**softened** [adj only before noun] *Beat the egg with the softened butter and warm milk.*

solve

WHAT'S HERE

- **to solve a problem** see **1 to 4**
- **to find the answer or explanation to sth** see **5 to 7**

to solve a problem

RELATED WORDS

- *see also* **deal with**

1 to successfully deal with a problem

- solve
- find/come up with a solution
- resolve
- put right
- cure
- remedy
- sort out
- sort
- iron out

solve /sɒlv‖sɑːlv, sɔːlv/ [v T] *They thought money would solve all their problems.* | *The roof used to leak but last week I fitted some new tiles and that seems to have solved the problem.* | *The government is to launch a new building programme in an attempt to solve the housing crisis.*

find/come up with a solution /ˌfaɪnd, kʌm ˌʌp wɪð ə səˈluːʃən/ [v phrase] to think of a way to solve a problem, especially a complicated political or social problem: *Crime is rapidly increasing in our inner cities. We must find a solution.* | *Civil war seems increasingly likely unless the government comes up with a solution.* | **+ to** *European governments are working together to find a solution to the problem of nuclear waste.*

resolve /rɪˈzɒlv‖rɪˈzɑːlv, rɪˈzɔːlv/ [v T] formal to successfully deal with a problem or unpleasant situation so that it no longer exists: *Talking is the only way to resolve your differences.* | *It is difficult to see how this conflict can be resolved without taking the matter to court.*

put right /ˌpʊt ˈraɪt/ [v phrase] to deal with an unsatisfactory situation, especially by making sure that any damage that has been caused is paid for, removed, stopped etc **put sth right** *There seems to be something wrong with the computer but we hope to put it right before too long.* | *If there is bullying in the classroom, it is the teacher who should put the problem right.* | **put right sth** *This government intends to put right everything that the last government did wrong.*

cure /kjʊəʳ/ [v T] to permanently solve a practical problem so that it does not happen again: *If your computer stops working, re-booting might cure the problem.* | *Beveridge believed that unemployment could be cured by state intervention.*

remedy /ˈremədi/ [v T] to deal with an unsatisfactory situation, especially an unfair one, so that the situation no longer exists or is greatly improved: *There have been several tragic rail accidents. The government must act quickly to remedy this situation.* | *Equal rights for women were necessary to remedy the injustices done to them over the centuries.*

sort out /ˌsɔːʳt ˈaʊt/ [phr v T] to remove any problems or difficulties from a situation, especially before doing something else **sort sth out** *I'm afraid I can't help you until I've sorted my own problems out.* | **sort things out** *There's been a serious misunderstanding; I'll try to sort things out and then I'll phone you back.* | **sort out sth** *You can't possibly start decorating yet. We haven't sorted out the roof yet.* | **get sth sorted out** *I want to get everything sorted out before I leave.*

sort /sɔːʳt/ [v T] British informal to successfully deal with a problem: *Don't worry about the money. I'll sort it, OK?* | *You should be able to sort this without my help.*

iron out /ˌaɪəʳn ˈaʊt/ [phr v T] to remove any small problems or difficulties before you start something, especially by discussing them, so that they do not cause problems later **iron sth out** *We need to iron a few things out before we move in together.* | **iron out sth** *We decided it was best to iron out our differences at an early stage in the production.*

2 a solution to a problem

- solution
- answer
- cure
- remedy
- panacea
- way out

solution /səˈluːʃən/ [n C] *One possible solution might be to borrow the money.* | *A dentist could put in a temporary filling, but that's not the perfect solution.* | **+ to/for** *Sleeping tablets are not the best solution to insomnia as they upset the natural rhythm of sleep.* | **find/come up with a solution** *We can help you find a solution to all your financial problems.*

answer /ˈɑːnsəʳ‖ˈæn-/ [n C] a way of dealing with a problem or unsatisfactory situation, especially one that has been worrying you for a long time: *The city council has to find a better way of dealing with domestic waste. One answer is to burn it.* | **+ to** *A bank loan seemed like the answer to all our problems.* | **there are no easy answers** *There are no easy answers to today's environmental problems.*

cure /kjʊəʳ/ [n C] a way of dealing with a problem, especially a practical problem, so that it does not happen again: *The experts believe they know the causes of the crime wave but they cannot agree on a* *cure.* | **+ for** *Adding a little oil into the mechanism is one of the best cures for a noisy engine.* | **miracle/wonder cure** (=a very effective cure) *It's not a miracle cure, but moisturiser can make your skin less dry.*

remedy /ˈremədi/ [n C] a way of dealing with a problem or unsatisfactory situation by improving it or getting rid of it completely: *If you find it hard to live on your present salary, the best remedy would be to change jobs.* | **+ for** *One remedy for racial attacks would be to educate our children more about social issues.*

panacea /ˌpænəˈsɪə/ [n C] formal something that people hope will solve all their problems: *Electoral reform is not a panacea. It causes almost as many problems as it solves.* | **+ for** *Librarians welcomed computerization as the panacea for all their cataloguing problems.*

way out /ˌweɪ ˈaʊt/ [n C] a way of dealing with an unpleasant situation so that it no longer exists: *We are faced with a very difficult situation, but there must be a way out.* | **+ of** *I don't see any way out of the present deadlock.*

3 when a problem or difficult situation is solved by itself

- sort itself out
- resolve itself
- work out

sort itself out /ˌsɔːʳt ɪtself ˈaʊt/ [v phrase] if a problem or unsatisfactory situation **sorts itself out**, it either stops happening or is solved without you having to do anything: *This situation is not going to sort itself out. We have to do something.* | *Childhood problems and anxieties have a habit of sorting themselves out.*

resolve itself /rɪˈzɒlv ɪtself‖-ˈzɑːlv-/ [v phrase] if a complicated problem **resolves itself**, it either stops being a problem or is solved without you having to do anything: *Fortunately, our employee problem resolved itself when two workers moved house and resigned voluntarily.* | *If we are patient the whole problem will resolve itself in due course.*

work out /ˌwɜːʳk ˈaʊt/ [phr v I/T] if a problem or bad situation **works out** or **works itself out**, it gradually gets solved without you having to do anything: *Try not to worry. I'm sure everything will work out in the end.* | *I've found that major problems tent to either go away or somehow work themselves out.*

4 not solved or difficult to solve

- unresolved
- insoluble
- intractable

unresolved /ˌʌnrɪˈzɒlvd◂‖-ˈzɑːlvd◂, -ˈzɔːlvd◂/ [adj] an **unresolved** problem still exists because it has not been dealt with successfully: *A number of problems are still unresolved.* | *The design of the new shopping mall is almost complete, although there are still some unresolved difficulties.*

insoluble /ɪnˈsɒljəbəl‖ɪnˈsɑːl-/ [adj] formal an **insoluble** problem is very difficult or impossible to solve: *The government has to deal with what seems like an insoluble political problem – racial harmony within the community.* | *The cleaning-up operation after the oil spill will be difficult but not insoluble.*

intractable /ɪnˈtræktəbəl/ [adj] formal an **intractable** problem is one that is so difficult and complicated that it is impossible to solve it however hard you try: *The disposal of toxic wastes is one of the most intractable problems facing industrialized societies.*

to find the answer or explanation to sth

RELATED WORDS

▸ *see also* **find out, understand/not understand, explain, mysterious**

5 to find the answer or explanation to something

- solve
- figure out/work out
- find an explanation
- clear up
- crack
- unravel

solve /sɒlv‖sɑːlv, sɔːlv/ [v T] to find the explanation to something that is difficult to understand, for example a crime or a mystery: *The role of the press is to sell newspapers, not to solve crime.* | *At last astronomers have solved the mystery of the rings encircling the planet Saturn.* | *These games encourage children's ability to solve puzzles using their mathematical skills.*

figure out/work out /ˌfɪgər ˈaʊt, ˌwɜːʳk ˈaʊt‖ˌfɪgjər-/ [phr v T] to find the explanation for something that is difficult to understand, by thinking carefully about it and using the information available to you **+ how/why/what etc** *My husband bought me a knitting machine for Christmas but I still haven't figured out how it works.* | *From the evidence gathered from witnesses we should be able to work out what happened that night.* | **figure/work out sth** *The police haven't even managed to figure out a motive.* | **figure/work sth out** *Don't tell him the answer – let him work it out for himself.*

find an explanation /ˌfaɪnd ən eksplәˈneɪʃən/ [v phrase] to find a way of explaining something, especially after trying for a fairly long time: *Sheena has had these stomach pains before, but the doctors think they have found an explanation this time.* | **+ for** *No one has been able to find a rational explanation for the ship's sudden disappearance.*

clear up /ˌklɪər ˈʌp/ [phr v T] to find the whole explanation for something that is strange and difficult to understand, so that it is completely solved **clear up sth** *I was hoping that your research would clear up a question that has been bothering me.* | **clear sth up** *Can you clear something up for us? How old are you?* | *The Dreyfus case was never completely cleared up. It remains a mystery.*

crack /kræk/ [v T] informal to find the explanation for something such as a crime or something that is difficult to understand, especially after trying for a long time: *It's a tough case but I'm determined to crack it.* | *Give Tom a mathematical puzzle and he'll just keep on trying till he cracks it.*

unravel /ʌnˈrævəl/ [v T] to gradually find the explanation for something that is difficult to understand because it is very complicated: *We are only just beginning to unravel the mysteries of the human brain.* | *Can scientists unravel the complex interactions of chemicals within foods?*

6 when something is difficult to solve

- puzzle
- mystify
- baffle
- perplex

puzzle /ˈpʌzəl/ [v T] to be difficult for someone to explain or understand: *There are things that still* *puzzle me about this new computer system.* | *What puzzles me about the robbery, is how they managed to enter the building unseen.* —**puzzling** [adj] *It's puzzling that no-one saw her leave.*

mystify /ˈmɪstɪ̇faɪ/ [v T] if something **mystifies** you, it is impossible for you to understand or explain: *Why you want to leave such a good job mystifies me.* | *Detective Oakley was mystified. He had never seen such a strange set of evidence in the whole of his career.* —**mystifying** [adj] *The way adults behave is sometimes mystifying to children.*

baffle /ˈbæfəl/ [v T] if something **baffles** you it is very confusing and impossible for you to understand: *What baffles me is how anyone could escape from the jail in broad daylight.* | *We've spent weeks investigating this case and it's got us completely baffled.* —**baffling** [adj] *I found the whole episode quite baffling.*

perplex /pərˈpleks/ [v T] formal if something **perplexes** you, it is confusing, worrying, and difficult for you to understand: *The question of how the murderer had gained entry to the house perplexed the police for several weeks.* —**perplexing** [adj] *The deterioration of the ozone layer is a perplexing phenomenon.*

7 something that has never been solved

- unsolved
- unexplained

unsolved /ˌʌnˈsɒlvd◂‖-ˈsɑːlvd◂, -ˈsɔːlvd◂/ [adj] *All too often, crimes of violence are left unsolved.* | *What happened to the men on the expedition will always be an unsolved mystery.*

unexplained /ˌʌnɪkˈspleɪnd◂/ [adj] an event or fact that is **unexplained** has never been explained so no one knows exactly what happened: *For years, Sukhbir's death remained unexplained.* | *There had been three unexplained fires at the school in the previous six months.*

some/several

RELATED WORDS

- see also **few/not many, lot**

1 some, but not a large number

- some
- a few
- several
- a number of
- a couple of

some /səm, (*strong*) sʌm/ [determiner/pron] a number of people or things, but not a large number – use this when you are not saying exactly what the number is: *There were some children playing in the street.* | *'Have we got any biscuits?' 'Yes, I've just bought some.'* | **+ of** *Come over here and meet some of my friends.* | **some more** *I've got some more photos of her upstairs.* | **some other** *There are some other reasons as well as those I have mentioned.*

a few /ə ˈfjuː/ [quantifier] a small number of people, things etc: *'Are there any chocolates left?' 'Only a few.'* | *They went to China a few years ago.* | *We know a few people who work in advertising.* | **+ of** *I'm going to the club with a few of my friends.*

several /ˈsevərəl/ [quantifier] more than a few people or things, but not a large number: *The President visited several states on his tour.* | *We've had several meetings, but nothing has been agreed.* | *She's been to Japan several times.* | **+ of** *I've read several of his books and they're really good.* | *Several of the islands have beautiful beaches.*

a number of /ə ˈnʌmbər ɒv/ [quantifier] several: *A number of people said they had seen the stolen van earlier in the day.* | *We have received a number of complaints about last night's programme.* | *A number of her ideas were very good indeed.*

a couple of /ə ˈkʌpəl ɒv/ [quantifier] informal a very small number but at least two: *I'd just like to ask you a couple of questions before you go.* | *Those baskets are nice, and they only cost a couple of quid.* | *There wasn't much mail this morning – just a couple of bills.*

2 some, but not a large amount

- some
- a certain amount of
- a measure of

some /səm, (*strong*) sʌm/ [determiner/pron] an amount of something, but not a large amount – use this when you are not saying exactly what the amount is: *Can I borrow some money, Dad?* | *I need some time to think about what you've said.* | *'We've run out of milk.' 'Do you want me to go and get some?'* | **+ of** (=not the whole thing) *Have some of this cake – it's delicious.* | **some more** *Would you like some more wine?*

a certain amount of /ə ˌsɜːrtn əˈmaʊnt ɒv/ [quantifier] a fairly large amount – use this to talk about people's feelings, abilities etc: *It's a job that requires a certain amount of intelligence and skill.* | *A certain amount of stress is unavoidable in daily life.*

a measure of /ə ˈmeʒər ɒv/ [quantifier] formal a fairly large amount of something, especially something good: *There is a measure of flexibility in the system.* | *Having a job gives me a measure of independence.*

3 some, but not all

- some

some /sʌm/ [quantifier] **some** but not all of a number or amount: *Some trees lose their leaves in the autumn.* | *Some students only come here because they want to have fun, not because they want to learn.* | **+ of** (=not all the people or things in a group) *'Have you met Jack's friends?' 'Some of them.'* | *I've only spent some of the money.*

sometimes

RELATED WORDS

- at some time in the future *see* **future (2)**
- *see also* **usually, always, often**

1 sometimes

- sometimes
- occasionally
- every so often
- once in a while
- at times
- now and again/now and then
- from time to time
- off and on/on and off

sometimes /ˈsʌmtaɪmz/ [adv] on some occasions, but not always: *Sometimes I drive to work and sometimes I walk.* | *Traffic noise is sometimes a problem.* | *The journey takes about an hour, sometimes* *even longer. | Injuries of this type sometimes take a long time to heal.*

occasionally /əˈkeɪʒənəli/ [adv] use this to talk about something that only happens a few times, and does not happen often: *Occasionally we go out to restaurants, but mostly we eat at home. | Kay's moods sometimes made life difficult, and occasionally impossible.* | **very occasionally** (=not at all often) *He lives in Australia now, so we only see him very occasionally.*

every so often /ˌevri səʊ ˈɒfən‖-ˈɔːfən/ [adv] at fairly regular periods but not often: *Every so often, Frank looked up at me and smiled. | The silence was broken every so often by the sound of guns in the distance.*

once in a while /ˌwʌns ɪn ə ˈwaɪl/ [adv] sometimes but not at all often: *It would be nice if we could see each other once in a while. | Teaching art can be fairly dull, but once in a while I come across a talent that really excites me.* | **every once in a while** (=fairly rarely) *Every once in a while he disappears for days on end.*

at times /ət ˈtaɪmz/ [adv] if something happens **at times**, it happens on particular occasions but it is not normal or typical of what usually happens: *In a job like this, you're bound to feel a little stressed at times. | At times even the most talented athletes lose their motivation.*

now and again/now and then /ˌnaʊ ənd əˈgen, ˌnaʊ ən ˈðen/ [adv] use this to talk about something that sometimes happens that is different from what happens most of the time: *I wear hats now and again, but they don't really suit me. | Now and then she would check on the baby sleeping in the next room.* | **every now and again/every now and then** *Every now and again a passenger would pass through the carriage on the way to the bathroom.*

from time to time /frəm ˌtaɪm tə ˈtaɪm/ [adv] sometimes, but not at all regularly and not very often: *This is the kind of problem that we all have from time to time. | From time to time a helicopter flew by, but mostly the sky remained clear.*

off and on/on and off /ˌɒf ənd ˈɒn, ˌɒn ənd ˈɒf/ [adv] **especially spoken** for short periods, but not continuously or regularly, over a long period of time: *We've been going out together for five years, off and on. | I worked in bars on and off for two years before I decided to go back to college.*

2 words for describing something that happens sometimes but not often

- occasional
- the odd
- intermittent
- periodic
- casual

occasional /əˈkeɪʒənəl/ [adj only before noun] *The prisoners are allowed occasional visits from their relatives.* | **the occasional/an occasional** *The street was silent except for the occasional burst of laughter from one of the workmen. | I didn't know Terry very well, but we went out for an occasional drink together.*

the odd /ði ˈɒd‖-ˈɑːd/ [adj phrase only before noun] **the odd drink/game/occasion etc** especially spoken a few drinks, games etc at various times, but not often and not regularly: *Jim and I have the odd game of cards together. | We get the odd complaint from customers, but mostly they're very satisfied.*

intermittent /ˌɪntəʳˈmɪtənt◂/ [adj usually before noun] happening for short irregular periods, often with long periods in between, not continuously: *She is the sort of person who works with intense but intermittent effort. | The afternoon will be warm but unsettled, with intermittent light rain.*

periodic /ˌpɪəriˈɒdɪk◂‖-ˈɑːd-/ [adj only before noun] happening sometimes, usually every few months, years etc: *She suffered periodic bouts of depression. | Periodic failures of the olive crop kept the country in constant debt. | The budget is subject to periodic review.* —**periodically** [adv] *Children's homes are periodically inspected by government inspectors.*

casual /ˈkæʒuəl/ [adj] **casual user/visitor etc** someone who does not often use something, visit somewhere etc: *Casual users of the library may not realize that they now need a computerized ticket. | Charging an entry fee for museums will not affect the casual visitor very much.*

soon

RELATED WORDS

- too soon *see* **early (2)**
- *see also* **immediately**

1 in a short time from now or from a particular time

- soon
- before long
- shortly
- in the near future/in the not too distant future
- won't be long
- it wasn't long before
- quickly

soon /suːn/ [adv] in a short time from now, or a short time after something else happens: *It'll soon be Christmas. | Driving in the city was hard at first, but she soon got used to it. | Why wasn't I told about this sooner?* | **as soon as possible** *Please reply as soon as possible.* | **as soon as you can** *I came as soon as I could.* | **the sooner the better** (=used to say that it is important that something is done very soon) *We need to get him to a hospital, and the sooner the better.* | **after/afterwards** *They set off soon after breakfast.*

before long /bɪˌfɔːʳ ˈlɒŋ‖-ˈlɔːŋ/ [adv] after a fairly short time: *Those two will be getting married before long. | Her eyelids began to droop and before long she was fast asleep.*

shortly /ˈʃɔːʳtli/ [adv] soon – use this especially about something that you know will happen soon: *We apologize for the delay – the train will be leaving shortly. | The President will shortly be on his way to Italy for a trade conference.* | **+ after** *Her last novel was published shortly after her death.*

in the near future/in the not too distant future /ɪn ðə ˌnɪəʳ ˈfjuːtʃəʳ, ɪn ðə ˌnɒt tuː ˌdɪstənt ˈfjuːtʃəʳ/ [adv] use this to talk about something that will happen in the next few weeks or months, although you do not know exactly when: *She doesn't have a driver's license, but is hoping to pass her test in the near future. | A new health club is to be built here in the not too distant future.*

won't be long /ˌwəʊnt biː ˈlɒŋ‖-ˈlɔːŋ/ [v phrase] spoken use this to say that something will happen soon or someone will arrive soon: *Dinner won't be long. | 'When's Dad coming home?' 'He won't be long.'* | **it won't be long before** *It won't be long before we're off on vacation.*

it wasn't long before /ɪt ˌwɒzənt ˈlɒŋ bɪfɔːʳ‖-ˌwɑːzənt ˈlɔːŋ-/ use this to talk about something that happened fairly soon after a particular event: *They started playing together in June 1961, and it wasn't long before they got a recording contract.*

quickly /'kwɪkli/ [adv] if you do something **quickly**, you do it very soon after something else happens: *Alex was knocked to the ground, but he quickly recovered.* | *Fortunately, India quickly returned to calm after Mrs Gandhi's death.*

2 very soon

- in no time/in no time at all
- in a minute/in a moment
- any minute/moment/time now
- any day/any day now
- at any moment/minute
- momentarily
- before you know it

in no time/in no time at all /ɪn 'nəʊ taɪm, ɪn ˌnəʊ taɪm ət 'ɔːl/ [adv] use this to talk about something good that will happen very soon or that happened a very short time after something else: *Don't worry – you'll be back to normal in no time.* | *In no time at all he had built up a big following among the local black community.*

in a minute/in a moment /ɪn ə 'mɪnɪ̈t, ɪn ə 'məʊmənt/ [adv] spoken use this to talk about something that will happen or that you will do within a few minutes: *The coffee will be ready in a minute.* | *Don't keep nagging me – I'll do it in a minute!* | *We will return to the subject of tax in a moment.*

any minute/moment/time now /ˌeni 'mɪnɪ̈t, 'məʊmənt, taɪm 'naʊ/ [adv] spoken use this to say that something will happen in a very short time from now, but you do not know exactly when: *My father's due to arrive any minute now.* | *Any moment now the final whistle will be blown.* | *If she hasn't had the baby already, she's going to have it any time now.*

any day/any day now /ˌeni 'deɪ, ˌeni deɪ 'naʊ/ [adv] spoken use this to say that something will happen at some time in the next few days, but you do not know exactly when: *The letter should be with you any day now.* | *His ship was due back from the Pacific any day now.*

at any moment/minute /ət ˌeni 'məʊmənt, 'mɪnɪ̈t/ [adv] use this to talk about something that may happen very soon, especially something dangerous or unpleasant: *He could have another heart attack at any moment.* | *We knew that war might break out at any moment.* | *The car looked as though it would fall apart at any minute.*

momentarily /'məʊməntərɪ̈li‖ˌməʊmən'terɪ̈li/ [adv] American use this to tell someone politely that something will happen very soon: *Mr Ewing will see you momentarily, sir.*

before you know it /bɪˌfɔːʳ juː 'nəʊ ɪt/ [adv] spoken use this to say that something will happen or be done very soon and before you really realize it is happening: *You'll be fully recovered before you know it.* | *You offer to iron his shirt and before you know it, he expects you to do all the housework.*

3 to be going to happen soon

- be coming up
- be in sight
- be around the corner
- be in the offing
- imminent
- forthcoming
- upcoming

be coming up /biː ˌkʌmɪŋ 'ʌp/ [v phrase] spoken *I'm pretty busy right now – I have exams coming up next week.* | *With Christmas coming up, we didn't have much spare money.*

be in sight /biː ɪn 'saɪt/ [v phrase] if something that you are hoping for is **in sight**, you think it will probably happen soon: *A solution to the problem now seems in sight.* | **be nowhere in sight** (=not likely to happen soon) *The end of the economic nightmare is still nowhere in sight.*

be around the corner ALSO **be round the corner** British /biː əˌraʊnd ðə 'kɔːʳnəʳ, biː ˌraʊnd ðə 'kɔːʳnəʳ/ [v phrase] if something **is around the corner**, it might happen very soon but you cannot be completely sure: *In life, you never quite know what's around the corner.* | *He continues to hint that the end of his playing career may be round the corner.* | **be just around the corner** *They keep telling us that better economic times are just around the corner.*

be in the offing /biː ɪn ði 'ɒfɪŋ‖-'ɔːf-/ [v phrase] to be likely to happen soon, although you do not know exactly when: *Appeals are common when a general election is in the offing.* | *According to the company, these deals had been in the offing for some time.*

imminent /'ɪmɪ̈nənt/ [adj] something that is **imminent**, especially something important, unpleasant, or dangerous, is likely to happen very soon: *Soon it became clear to everyone that war was imminent.* | *With the election imminent, Churchill returned to London.* | *Some of the buildings were in a state of imminent collapse.* | **imminent danger** *The child was in imminent danger of falling into the water.*

forthcoming /ˌfɔːʳθ'kʌmɪŋ◂/ [adj only before noun] a **forthcoming** event has been planned to happen soon: *Dixon was convinced he could win the forthcoming election.* | *The matter will be discussed at the forthcoming general meeting.* | *Forthcoming attractions include a magician and a quiz competition.*

upcoming /'ʌpˌkʌmɪŋ/ [adj only before noun] American an **upcoming** event, especially a political event, has been planned to happen: *The space program will be reviewed during the upcoming congressional session.* | *He was preparing the federal budget for the upcoming fiscal year.*

4 when something unpleasant is going to happen soon

- loom
- hang over
- be brewing
- impending

loom /luːm/ [v I] if a problem or difficulty **looms**, it is likely to happen soon: *As the day of my interview loomed, I became increasingly nervous.* | *With the prospect of bankruptcy looming, life is getting tough for small businesses.*

hang over /ˌhæŋ 'əʊvəʳ/ [phr v T not in passive] if something dangerous or unpleasant **hangs over** you, it is likely to happen soon and this makes you feel worried and nervous: *The threat of nuclear war hangs over mankind.* | *With the court case hanging over us, we couldn't enjoy our vacation.*

be brewing /biː 'bruːɪŋ/ [v phrase] if problems, difficulties, arguments etc **are brewing**, they are starting to develop and will probably happen soon: *Union bosses fear that a strike is brewing in the coal industry.* | *A major political row over the European question had been brewing for some time.*

impending /ɪm'pendɪŋ/ [adj only before noun] an **impending** event or situation, especially an unpleasant one, is going to happen very soon: *Extra troops were usually a sign of an impending attack.* | *We were sorry to hear about Arlene's impending divorce.* | *warnings of an impending ecological disaster*

sorry/apologize

RELATED WORDS

- to feel sorry for something you have done *see* **regret/not regret**
- to feel sorry for someone who has a problem *see* **sympathize**

1 to tell someone that you are sorry you did something

- say you are sorry
- say sorry
- apologize
- be apologetic
- apology

say you are sorry /ˌseɪ juː əʳ ˈsɒri‖-ˈsɑːri / [v phrase] to tell someone you are sorry that you have upset them or done something that causes problems for them: *Sometimes it's not easy to say you are sorry.* | **+ (that)** *She finally arrived, and said she was sorry we had been kept waiting.*

say sorry /ˌseɪ ˈsɒri‖-ˈsɑːri/ [v phrase] especially spoken to tell someone that you are sorry you have upset them or done something bad: *She says she won't see him again unless he says sorry.* | **+ to** *Go and say sorry to your mother, Andrew.* | **+ for (doing) sth** *I don't think I should say sorry for doing what at the time I believed to be right.*

apologize ALSO **apologise** British /əˈpɒlədʒaɪz‖əˈpɑː-/ [v I] to tell someone that you are sorry, especially in a formal situation or when you do not know the person well: *I don't know why I apologized, because I didn't do anything wrong.* | **+ for** *I must apologize for my son's behaviour – he isn't usually this moody.* | **+ for doing sth** *The bank wrote to apologise for overcharging me.* | **+ to** *The US has apologized to Britain for the accident that cost nine British lives.* | **apologize profusely** (=apologize very much) *She rushed into the hotel, apologizing profusely for being so late.*

be apologetic /biː əˌpɒləˈdʒetɪk◂‖-əˌpɑː-/ [v phrase] to keep saying you are sorry because you feel guilty or embarrassed about something you have done: *The manager was apologetic, but said that Sue would have to contact head office if she wanted a refund.* | **+ about** *He was most apologetic about not being able to come to the party.*

apology /əˈpɒlədʒi‖əˈpɑː-/ [n C/U] something that you say or write to tell someone that you are sorry: *The story was full of lies, and the paper had to print an apology.* | *In a written apology, the BBC admitted they had misled the public.* | **accept sb's apology/apologies** formal *Please accept our apologies for taking so long to deliver the materials you requested.* | **owe sb an apology** *I never thought she'd get the job. I guess I owe her an apology.* | **demand an apology** *Blake was wrongfully arrested and is now demanding an apology from the police.* | **letter of apology** *As he reflected on his appalling behaviour, he mentally composed a letter of apology to his host.*

2 what you say to tell someone that you are sorry

- sorry/I'm sorry
- excuse me
- I beg your pardon
- I apologize
- I owe you an apology
- forgive me
- please accept my apologies

sorry/I'm sorry /ˈsɒri, aɪm ˈsɒri‖-ˈsɑːri/ spoken say this to tell someone you are sorry that you upset them or caused problems for them; you can also say this as a polite way of excusing yourself for a small mistake: *I'm sorry, I didn't mean to be rude.* | *Sorry, did I step on your foot?* | **I'm very/really/terribly sorry** *I'm really sorry, Joanna. I've broken one of your glasses.* | **+ (that)** *I'm sorry that I shouted at you.* | *Sorry we're late, Shelley.* | **+ about** *Sorry about all the noise.* | **+ to do sth** *I'm sorry to bother you, but I need to discuss my essay.* | **+ for (doing sth)** *I'm sorry for barging in without ringing the bell.*

excuse me /ɪkˈskjuːz miː/ especially American, spoken say this to tell someone you are sorry because you accidentally touched them or made a small or embarrassing mistake: *Oh, excuse me, is that your bag I just stood on?* | *Excuse me – I didn't realize there was anyone in here.*

I beg your pardon /aɪ ˌbeg jɔːʳ ˈpɑːʳdn/ formal spoken say this when you make a small mistake and you want to say sorry politely: *'That's my pen.' 'Oh, I beg your pardon – I thought it was mine.'*

I apologize ALSO **I apologise** British /aɪ əˈpɒlədʒaɪz‖-əˈpɑː-/ say this to apologize in a fairly formal way, for example when you have upset someone or done something wrong or unfair: *You were right and I was wrong. I apologize.* | *I apologize in advance if anyone's offended by this.* | **+ for** *I apologise for writing to you like this, out of the blue.*

I owe you an apology /aɪ ˌəʊ juː ən əˈpɒlədʒi‖-əˈpɑː-/ say this when you have done something that you later find out to be wrong or unfair: *It seems I owe you an apology – I was supposed to phone you on Saturday night.* | **+ for (doing sth)** *I think I owe you an apology for my behaviour the other night.*

forgive me /fəʳˈgɪv miː/ say this when you have done something wrong or have upset someone, or when you are going to say or ask something that might seem rude or offensive: *Forgive me, I didn't mean to offend you.* | **+ for doing sth** *Forgive me for asking, but how old are you?* | *Forgive me for saying this, but you really don't look well at all.*

please accept my apologies /pliːz əkˌsept maɪ əˈpɒlədʒiz‖-əˈpɑː-/ used in formal letters: *Please accept my apologies. I will be taking steps to ensure this does not happen again.* | **+ for** *Please accept my apologies for any inconvenience this error has caused.*

so/therefore

ways of saying what the result of something is

RELATED WORDS

- *see also* **result, cause**

- so
- therefore
- so big/tall/old etc (that)
- such a bad day/an old car/a tall man etc (that)
- so that/with the result that
- as a result/consequently
- then

so /səʊ/ [conjunction/adv] use this to say that someone does something or something happens as a result of something else: *There was nothing on TV, so I decided to go to bed.* | *The rest of the week I'm busy, I'm afraid, so it'll have to be Monday.* | *The shop doesn't open until 11am and so it loses a lot of business.*

therefore /ˈðeəʳfɔːʳ/ [adv] so – use this in formal speech and writing: *The building work is taking quite a long time, and therefore costing us money.* | *Jewish weddings are both religious and civil. Therefore two official applications for marriage are necessary.*

so big/tall/old etc (that) /səʊ bɪɡ (ðət)/ [adv] use this to say that because someone or something is very big, tall etc, something happens as a result: *I was so busy today that I didn't have time for lunch.* | *He always thought he was so good looking that no woman would turn him down.*

such a bad day/an old car/a tall man etc (that) /ˌsʌtʃ ə bæd ˈdeɪ (ðət)/ use this to say that because it is a very bad day, a very old car etc something happens or someone does something as a result: *It was such a nice day that we decided to go for a picnic.* | *The dress was such a bargain, I had to buy it.* | *Paul remained silent for such a long time that we were beginning to wonder if he'd fallen asleep.*

so that/with the result that /ˈsəʊ ðət, wɪð ðə rɪˈzʌlt ðət/ [conjunction] use this to say that because of a particular situation, another situation exists or happens. **With the result that** is more formal than **so that**: *His hair was very long and covered his eyes, so that you could hardly see his face.* | *A car pulled out right in front of me, so that I had to slam on the brakes.* | *The company paid excellent salaries and provided good working conditions, with the result that its employees were of a very high standard.*

as a result/consequently /əz ə rɪˈzʌlt, ˈkɒnsə̇kwəntli‖ˈkɑːnsə̇ˌkwentli/ [adv] use this to say that because of a particular situation, something else happens or is true. **Consequently** is more formal than **as a result**: *I had made a lot of contacts, and had good job opportunities as a result.* | *The virus attacks the plant, the flower does not open, and consequently no seeds are produced.*

then /ðen/ [adv] use this to say what you would expect the result of an action or situation to be: *'My father's quite laid back.' 'Then he won't mind if you borrow his car, will he?'* | *'I'm full up.' 'Does that mean you don't want any dessert then?'*

sound

RELATED WORDS

- a high sound *see* **high (7)**
- a low sound *see* **low (2)**
- *see also* **loud, quiet, reflect, voice, music**

1 a sound

- sound
- noise

sound /saʊnd/ [n C/U] something that you hear: *The only sound in the house was the ticking of the clock.* | *Something's wrong with the TV – you can see the pictures, but there's no sound.* | **+ of** *From the next room came the sound of laughter.* | **a clicking/tapping/buzzing etc sound** *What's that funny rattling sound coming from the back of the car?* | **sights and sounds** (=things that you see and hear) *the fascinating sights and sounds of Marrakesh*

noise /nɔɪz/ [n C/U] a sound, especially a loud or unpleasant one: *Why are the children making so much noise out there?* | *Are you sure you locked the door? I thought I heard a noise downstairs.* | **+ of** *The noise of the traffic kept me awake all night.* | **a banging/cracking/scratching etc noise** *Can you hear that funny scratching noise?* | **a loud noise** *There was a loud cracking noise and then the chair collapsed.*

2 using sound or connected with sound

- sound
- acoustic

sound /saʊnd/ [adj only before noun] **sound waves** (=the form that sound takes when it travels) *The ear picks up sound waves and converts them into signals that it sends to the brain.* | **sound effects** (=sounds produced to make it seem that something is happening) *A tense atmosphere is easy to create on stage with some sinister music and creepy sound effects.*

acoustic /əˈkuːstɪk/ [adj only before noun] related to sound, especially the way in which people hear sounds – used especially in technical contexts: *Various pieces of recording equipment are used to produce interesting acoustic effects.* | *Deaf people get no acoustic feedback when they talk, so their speech is often impaired.*

3 to make a sound

- make a sound/ make a noise
- go
- with
- go off
- emit
- let out

make a sound/make a noise /ˌmeɪk ə ˈsaʊnd, ˌmeɪk ə ˈnɔɪz/ [v phrase] *I knew that if I made any sound, they would find me.* | *The engine made a very strange noise when I tried to start the car.* | **make a buzzing/creaking/tapping etc sound** *Every time someone opens that door, it makes a terrible creaking sound.* | **+ like** *The lamb was making a sound like a baby crying.*

go /ɡəʊ/ [v phrase not in progressive] **go bang/beep/pop etc** especially spoken to make a short loud sound: *I was using the hairdryer and suddenly it went bang and stopped working.* | *The microwave should go ping when it's finished.*

with /wɪð, wɪθ/ [prep] **with a bang/crash/thud etc** making a loud sound: *The picture fell to the floor with a loud crash.* | *Rockets flew into the air and then exploded with a terrific bang.*

go off /ˌɡəʊ ˈɒf/ [phr v I] if something **goes off**, it starts making a noise – use this about warning bells, clocks that tell you it is time to get up etc: *My neighbour's car alarm went off three times last night.* | *I get up as soon as the alarm clock goes off at 7:15.*

emit /ɪˈmɪt/ [v T] to make a particular kind of sound – use this especially in scientific and technical contexts: *The machine emits regular bleeps which indicate the heart rate.* | *Sounds emitted by the dolphins were recorded with an underwater microphone.*

let out /ˌlet ˈaʊt/ [v T] if someone **lets out** a particular kind of sound, they make it, especially when something surprises, frightens, or hurts them: *'It can't be true,' Maria said, letting out a sob.* | *A hand touched her shoulder. She let out a scream.*

4 to make a high sound

- creak
- squeak
- screech

creak /kriːk/ [v I] if something **creaks**, especially something wooden such as a door, bed, or stair, it makes a long, high noise when someone puts pressure on it: *In the hall the floorboards creaked and the walls were damp.* | **creak open** *The key clicked inside the lock and the door creaked open.* —**creak/creaking** [n singular] *Then I heard the creak of someone's footsteps on the stairs.* | *the creaking of the boats in the harbour*

squeak /skwiːk/ [v I] if something **squeaks**, it makes a very high noise as it is moved, pushed etc, especially because two parts of it cannot rub smoothly together: *His chair squeaked loudly as he swivelled round to face me.* | *The rubber soles of my shoes squeaked on the shiny floor.* —**squeak** [n singular] *The only sound was the soft squeak of the marker on the board.* —**squeaky** [adj] *an old desk with squeaky drawers*

screech /skriːtʃ/ [v I] to make a loud, long, unpleasant high sound, like the sound made by car tyres when the car stops suddenly: *The train screeched as it pulled into the station.* —**screech** [n singular] *There was the screech of brakes and then a tremendous bang.*

5 sounds made by something hitting or falling onto something

- bang
- thud
- crack
- crash
- clatter
- bump
- thump

bang /bæŋ/ [n C] a loud sound caused especially when something hard or heavy hits something else or falls on a surface: *I heard a loud bang – it sounded like something had fallen down upstairs.* | **make a bang** *Small children are often frightened of fireworks that make a bang.* | **close/land/collide etc with a bang** *The lid of the box fell shut with a bang.*

thud /θʌd/ [n C] the low dull sound produced when something heavy but soft hits something else or falls on a surface: *I heard a shot, followed by a thud as his body hit the floor.* | **hit/drop/land etc with a thud** *A snowball hit her on the back of the neck with a soft thud.* | **the thud of** *Suddenly we heard the thud of horses' hooves.*

crack /kræk/ [n C] a loud sudden very sharp sound like the sound of a stick being broken: *The branch broke with a sudden crack.* | *As I hit the floor, I heard a loud crack in my arm.*

crash /kræʃ/ [n C] the very loud sound produced when something hard such as metal or glass hits something else or falls on a surface, especially when damage is caused: *There was a loud crash in the bedroom and my dad started yelling.* | **fall/land/hit etc sth with a crash** *The whole tray of dishes fell to the floor with a crash.*

clatter /ˈklætəʳ/ [n singular] the loud sound produced when a lot of hard things hit against each other or hit a hard surface: *The clatter in the kitchen told me that Mum was already up.* | **fall/drop etc sth with a clatter** *Bert put down his tools with a clatter, and looked round the room.* | **the clatter of sth** *Just then there was the clatter of hooves on the road outside.*

bump /bʌmp/ [n C] the dull, fairly quiet sound produced when something such as part of your body hits something or falls against a surface: *At night, the old house seemed to be full of strange creaks and bumps.* | **fall/sit down/hit etc sth with a bump** *Martin sat down suddenly with a bump.*

thump /θʌmp/ [n C] the dull, fairly loud sound produced when something heavy suddenly hits something else or falls hard on a surface: *There was a loud thump as Eddie threw Luther back against the wall.* | **hit sth/fall etc with a thump** *A suitcase toppled off the top of the wardrobe and landed on the floor with a thump.*

6 sounds made by something repeatedly hitting something

- knocking
- rap/rapping
- patter
- rattle
- tap

knocking /ˈnɒkɪŋ‖ˈnɑː-/ [n singular] the sound produced when something hard keeps hitting another hard surface: *One of the machines started to make a strange knocking sound.* | *The builders' knocking and hammering made it difficult for me to concentrate on my work.*

rap/rapping /ræp, ˈræpɪŋ/ [n singular] the sound produced when someone keeps hitting a surface, especially a door or window, with their hand or with a hard object **+ at/on etc** *A violent rap at the door made me run downstairs.* | *I was kept awake by the rapping of a branch on my window.*

patter /ˈpætəʳ/ [v I] to make a quiet irregular sound, like the sound of rain falling or quick, light steps **+ on/in etc** *Raindrops were pattering on the car roof.* | **+ about/around** (=move around with a pattering sound) *I could hear feet shuffling and pattering about upstairs.* —**patter/pattering** [n singular] **the patter of sth** *the patter of mice in the attic*

rattle /ˈrætl/ [v I] if something **rattles**, it makes a hard, quickly repeated sound, especially because part of it is loose and keeps hitting against something: *There's something rattling inside the washing machine.* | **+ about/around** (=move around with a rattling sound) *Sometimes, the bolts work loose and start rattling around.* | **rattle along/past etc** (=move somewhere making a rattling sound) *A battered old Chevrolet rattled past.* —**rattle/rattling** [n singular] *I heard the rattle of a key in the door, and knew David was home.*

tap /tæp/ [v I] to produce a sound by lightly and repeatedly hitting a hard surface **+ on/against** *Is that someone tapping on the door?* | *It sounded as though something outside was tapping against the window.* —**tapping** [n singular] *What are they doing next door? I can't stand this constant tapping on the wall.*

7 sounds made by glass or metal hitting something

- clink
- clank
- clang
- jingle
- ring
- tinkle

clink /klɪŋk/ [v I] if something made of glass or metal **clinks**, it makes a short ringing sound as it hits another glass or metal object: *Their champagne glasses clinked. 'Happy Anniversary Darling,' Roger said.* | **+ against** *She wore at least twenty bracelets, which clinked against each other every time she moved her arm.* —**clink/clinking** [n singular] *The clink of dishes in the dining room told him that dinner would soon be ready.* —**clinking** [adj] *sounds of clinking cutlery and glass*

clank /klæŋk/ [v I] if something heavy made of metal **clanks**, it makes a short, loud noise as it hits another metal object: *The train's carriages clanked and rattled as it crept into the station.* | *In the harbor, the boats' rigging clanked noisily in the high wind.* —**clank/clanking** [n singular] *Then I heard the clank-*

ing of the metal gates outside, followed by footsteps on the path.

clang /klæŋ/ [v I] if something metal **clangs**, it makes a loud, long ringing noise when it hits another metal object: *Somewhere inside the courtyard a bell clanged.* | **clang shut** *The prison door clanged shut again.* —**clang** [n singular] *I dropped the metal bar and it hit the floor with a loud clang.* —**clanging** [adj] *The sound echoed in Matt's head like a clanging cymbal.*

jingle /ˈdʒɪŋgəl/ [v I] if a set of things **jingle**, especially things made of metal or glass, they make a continuous high musical sound as they hit each other: *The coins in his pocket jingled together noisily.* | *A herd of goats crossed the beach, the bells around their necks jingling cheerfully.* —**jingle** [n singular] *Just then there was the jingle of keys outside the door.*

ring /rɪŋ/ [v I] if something **rings**, it makes a high, loud, continuous sound after it hits another object: *If you tap something made of good glass, it should keep ringing for quite a long time.* —**ringing** [adj] *There was a ringing sound in my ears.*

tinkle /ˈtɪŋkəl/ [v I] to produce the pleasant, high, continuous sound that is made, for example, by light pieces of glass or metal hitting each other: *I rang the bell and heard it tinkle inside.* | *The ring fell from her hands and went tinkling across the floor.* —**tinkle/tinkling** [n singular] *the tinkle of glass and china*

8 sounds made by guns, bombs etc

- bang
- boom
- roar
- rumble

bang /bæŋ/ [n C] a short sudden loud noise made by a gun, bomb etc: *'I heard a bang and then I heard shots,' said Saxton, a tourist from Australia.* | **loud bang** *There was a loud bang as the bomb exploded.* | **go off/explode etc with a bang** *The firework went off with a loud bang.*

boom /buːm/ [n C] an extremely loud noise that can be heard for several seconds after it begins: *The boom of cannon continued for most of the day.* | *There was a loud boom. The chemical works was on fire.* | **sonic boom** (=the loud noise made when a plane, spacecraft etc passes the speed of sound) *A sonic boom was heard by observers on the shore as the meteorite fell to earth.*

roar /rɔːʳ/ [n C] an extremely loud noise that gets gradually louder and continues for a fairly long time: *With a great roar, the whole building was engulfed in flames.* | *We threw ourselves to the ground as the roar of an explosion thundered over us.*

rumble /ˈrʌmbəl/ [v I] to make a very low sound, like the sound of distant thunder, that gets quieter then louder continuously: *In the distance, thunder rumbled across the sky.* | *The sound of rebel gunfire rumbled in the hills.* —**rumble** [n singular] *What began as a rumble became a powerful roar as the volcano erupted.*

9 sounds made by something burning or cooking

- crackle
- sizzle

crackle /ˈkrækəl/ [v I] if a fire or something burning in a fire **crackles**, it makes a repeated sharp sound: *A log crackled on the fire.* | *In the living-room, a huge fire was crackling away.* —**crackle** [n singular] *the crackle of the bonfire*

sizzle /ˈsɪzəl/ [v I] to produce the continuous sound that is made, for example by food being cooked in very hot oil: *Bacon was sizzling in the frying pan.* | *It was so hot that the water just sizzled and evaporated.* —**sizzle** [n singular] *The sizzle and smell of hamburgers and sausages greeted us as we walked out the back door.*

10 quiet gentle sounds

- murmur
- rustle
- swish

murmur /ˈmɜːʳməʳ/ [n singular] the continuous, low, quiet sound of something that is a fairly long way away or that is continuously there as well as other noises: *Jan had the radio on in the room above, but it was no more than a murmur.* | **the murmur of sth** *The murmur of distant traffic reached us when the wind was in the east.*

rustle /ˈrʌsəl/ [v I] if things such as papers, leaves, or clothes **rustle**, they make a continuous quiet sound as they rub against each other: *Leaves rustled in the summer breeze.* | *The tissue paper rustled in the silence as she unwrapped the gift.* —**rustle** [n singular] *There was no sound in the library except for the occasional rustle of papers.*

swish /swɪʃ/ [n singular] the smooth quiet sound produced when something such as a skirt or curtains moves quickly through the air: *The magnificent red stage curtains opened with a swish.* | **the swish of sth** *Just then there was the swish of wings right above my head.* —**swish** [v T] *Horses try to keep flies off by swishing their tails from side to side.*

11 sounds made by gas or air

- hiss
- fizz

hiss /hɪs/ [v I] if something such as a tyre, ball, or part of a machine **hisses**, it makes a continuous high sound as air, water etc escapes from it: *Air hissed out of the tyre.* | *It sounded as though gas was hissing out of a pipe.* —**hiss** [n singular] *The train halted with a loud hiss of escaping steam.*

fizz /fɪz/ [v I] to produce the continuous high sound that is made for example by some kinds of drinks that produce bubbles when they are poured into a glass: *I dropped the tablet in the glass. It fizzed and dissolved.* | *The firework fizzed for a moment and then went off with a bang.*

12 sounds made by machines, engines, cars etc

- buzz
- hum
- whirr
- whine
- beep
- roar
- tick

buzz /bʌz/ [v I] to make a continuous sound, for example, like the sound made by bees: *Police helicopters buzzed backwards and forwards over the area all day.* | *The whole office seemed to be buzzing with the sound of machinery.* —**buzz** [n singular] *I could hear the buzz of a chainsaw far away among the trees.*

hum /hʌm/ [v I] to make a soft, low continuous sound like the sound made by some electric or electronic equipment: *The refrigerator hummed softly in the corner.* | *The computer was still on, humming away.* —**hum** [n singular] *the hum of the air conditioning*

whirr /wɜːʳ/ [v I] to make a fairly quiet, regular sound like something turning very quickly and beating against the air: *The video recorder whirred and rewound.* | *Already the plane's propellers were whirring into action.* —**whirr** [n singular] *At last the engine started up with a grinding whirr.*

whine /waɪn/ [n singular] an unpleasant long high sound, especially produced by an engine or vehicle running at very high speed: *The sky was filled with the whine and roar of bombers.*

beep ALSO **bleep** British /biːp, bliːp/ [n C] a high, sometimes repeated, electronic sound sent out by a machine, especially in order to attract someone's attention: *You'll hear a bleep when the photocopier's finished printing.* | *Someone's pager beeped in the middle of the best scene in the play.* —**beep/bleep** [v I] *The machine bleeps if you leave it switched on for more than 10 minutes.*

roar /rɔːʳ/ [v I] if a car, plane etc engine **roars**, it makes a very loud noise when it is near full power: *The Ferrari roared and shot off down the road.* | **+ past/along etc** (=move with a roaring sound) *There was the sound of a siren and several police cars roared past.* —**roar** [n singular] *The boat's motor made quite a roar.*

tick /tɪk/ [v I] if a clock or other machine **ticks**, it makes a quiet, regular, repeated sound: *I find it impossible to sleep if there's a clock ticking in the room.* | *As usual, there was a bomb ticking somewhere and James Bond had to find it.* —**tick/ticking** [n singular] *Jeremy waited anxiously, listening to the ticking of the clock on the wall.*

13 sounds made by bells or horns

- ring
- toll
- chime
- honk
- hoot

ring /rɪŋ/ [v I] to make a sound like that of a bell: *The phone's ringing.* | *A burglar alarm was ringing further along the road.* | *At that moment, the door bell rang.*

toll /təʊl/ [v I] written if a large bell **tolls**, it makes regular, separate ringing sounds, especially as a sign of someone's death: *The funeral procession left the church as the bells began to toll.*

chime /tʃaɪm/ [v I/T] if a bell or clock **chimes**, it makes a single ringing sound or a small number of ringing sounds, especially in order to tell you what time it is: *I heard a clock chime softly in the next door room.* | *Across the valley, church bells were chiming.* | **chime six/eight/twelve etc** (=ring six, eight, twelve etc times to show the time) *A clock chimed six.* —**chime** [n C] *The shop door opened with a chime.*

honk /hɒŋk‖hɔːŋk/ [v I/T] informal if you **honk** a vehicle's horn or if the horn **honks**, it makes a loud clear sound which continues for only a few seconds: *Several horns honked impatiently.* | *The truck driver honked his horn and waited.*

hoot /huːt/ [v I/T] British if you **hoot** a vehicle's horn, or if the horn **hoots**, it makes a loud clear sound which continues for only a few seconds and is like a single musical note: *A horn hooted behind me. It was Don in his little red car.* | *All the other drivers were tooting their horns and yelling at me to move my car.* —**hoot/hooting** [n C] *The hooting of a horn made me turn round.*

14 sounds made by liquids or something wet

- splash
- squelch
- gurgle
- plop
- bubble

splash /splæʃ/ [n C] the sound that a liquid makes when it falls from a height, hits something hard, or is moved rapidly around: *There was a splash behind the boat as a large silver fish jumped out of the water.* | *Judging from the shouts and splashes coming from the pool, everyone was having a lot of fun.* | **fall/land etc with a splash** *Ashlee fell into the river with a loud splash.* —**splash** [v I] *The waterfall cascaded over the rocks and splashed into a pool at the bottom.*

squelch /skweltʃ/ [v I] British to make a sound like someone walking in soft, wet mud, or to move somewhere making this sound: *It had been raining hard and my boots squelched as I walked across the park.* | **+ along/past/through etc** *Ankle deep in mud, we squelched across the meadow.* | **squelch around** *Melvin was squelching around in the yard outside the cowshed.*

gurgle /ˈgɜːʳgəl/ [v I] if something such as a stream **gurgles**, it makes a low irregular sound like water flowing through a pipe: *The pipes in the attic gurgle in the night and keep me awake.* | *The washing machine gurgled as it changed cycles.* —**gurgle** [n singular] *Somewhere nearby there was the gentle gurgle of a stream.*

plop /plɒp‖plɑːp/ [v I] to make a sound like something solid falling directly into water **+ into/onto etc** *Noah threw a stone high into the air and it plopped into the river.* | *Several letters plopped onto the doormat.* —**plop/plopping** [n singular] *The frog reached the stream and jumped in with a plop.*

bubble /ˈbʌbəl/ [v I] to make the continuous repeated sound that is made, for example, by water boiling: *A large saucepan of soup was bubbling on the stove.* —**bubbling** [adj] *Josh lay back in the bubbling jacuzzi.*

15 when a sound is repeated or continues for a long time

- echo
- reverberate
- resonate
- resound

echo /ˈekəʊ/ [v I] if a sound **echoes**, you hear the last part of it again because it was made in a large empty room, near a high wall etc: *I heard footsteps echoing down the corridor.* —**echo** [n C] *There was the sound of gunshot and then its echo in the mountains.*

reverberate /rɪˈvɜːʳbəreɪt/ [v I] if a loud sound **reverberates**, or a building **reverberates** with a sound, the sound is repeated or continues for a fairly long time, so that the building or room where it is seems to shake **+ around/along/through etc** *The sound of a train passing reverberated through the house.* | **+ with** *At four o'clock the school bell goes, and the whole school reverberates with the sound of running feet and slamming doors.* —**reverberation** /rɪˌvɜːʳbəˈreɪʃən/ [n C/U] *The last reverberations of the thunder were just dying down.*

resonate /ˈrezəneɪt/ [v I] if something such as music or a musical instrument **resonates**, it makes a continuous, rich, musical sound: *The sounds of Beethoven's 5th Symphony resonated through the house.* —**resonant** [adj] *His voice was deep, rich and resonant.*

resound /rɪˈzaʊnd/ [v I] if a very loud sound **resounds**, it continues for a fairly long time, filling a place with sound: *Raymond's huge laugh resounded everywhere we went.* | **+ around/in/ through etc** *As he fell, his scream resounded through the canyon.*

space

WHAT'S HERE

- **a space that is available to use** see **1 to 4**
- **a space between two things** see **5**

a space that is available to use

RELATED WORDS

▸ *see also* **area**

1 space

- ▸ **space**
- ▸ **room**
- ▸ **leg room**
- ▸ **elbow room**
- ▸ **floorspace**

space /speɪs/ [n C/U] an empty area that can be used or filled by things or people: *I wish we had more space in our office.* | *There's a space on the form where you write the name of your school.* | **+ for** *We don't have enough space for all our furniture.* | **+ to do sth** *Could you find me a space to store these boxes in?* | **storage/closet/disk etc space** *Our apartment is small, and doesn't have much storage space.* | **living/parking space** *Tens of thousands of acres of farmland are swallowed up each year by developers seeking living space for the city's fast-growing population.* | **office space** *We help corporations to relocate, and give them advice on how to maximize office space.* | **empty space** *Where Marion's photo had once been was now an empty space.* | **green** (=space where there are grass and trees) *The city would be unbearable in the summer without its green spaces.* | **open space** (=space where there are no buildings) *London's parks and open spaces* | *the wide open spaces of the American West*

room /ruːm, rʊm/ [n U] enough space available to put things in, or to use for a particular purpose: *We can't sit there, there's not enough room.* | **have room for** *Do you have room for this in your bag?* | **leave room for** (=make sure there is enough room for) *Leave room for people to get by.* | **+ to do sth** *He didn't think he had room to pass the car in front.* | **room to spare** (=some room available) *They had no room to spare in their car, so we had to take a taxi.*

leg room /ˈleg ruːm/ [n U] space for your legs, especially in a vehicle: *I enjoy flying Air Canada, because they give you plenty of leg room.*

elbow room /ˈelbəʊ ruːm/ [n U] informal space to move or work easily: *They stood in the crowd, fighting for elbow room.* | *In October the museums and art galleries are less crowded, and there's more elbow room in restaurants.*

floorspace ALSO **floor space** /ˈflɔːʳspeɪs/ [n U] the area of the floor of a room, especially the area that can be used: *The workshop is quite big but there's not much floorspace.* | *There was just enough floor space for a desk, a chair, and a filing cabinet.*

2 to provide space for something

- ▸ **make room**
- ▸ **clear a space**
- ▸ **make way**

make room /ˌmeɪk ˈruːm/ [v phrase] to remove or move someone or something in order to provide space for another person or thing **+ for** *The theater was torn down in the early '80s, to make room for the Horton Plaza Shopping Center.* | *The campers made room for us around the fire.* | *There are two more people coming – can you make room for them to sit down?*

clear a space /ˌklɪər ə ˈspeɪs/ [v phrase] to move things, especially things that were untidy, to provide a space for something: *She cleared a space on her desk to put her computer.* | *The gardener was clearing a space so he could plant the young seedlings.*

make way /ˌmeɪk ˈweɪ/ [phr v I] if a crowd **makes way** for someone or something, it divides to make a space for that person or thing to pass: *If you can all make way please, so we can get through.* | **+ for** *The onlookers stepped back to make way for the ambulance to pass.*

3 ways of saying how much space there is somewhere

- ▸ **hold**
- ▸ **take**
- ▸ **seat**
- ▸ **sleep**

▸ *see also* **contain**

hold /həʊld/ [v T] if a container or room **holds** a particular number or amount, there is space for that number or amount: *This jug holds about a pint.* | *The hotel dining room can hold up to 50 people.* | *The gas tank on a small car should hold at least six gallons.*

take /teɪk/ [v T not in progressive or passive] to only have enough space to contain a particular number of things, people etc or a particular amount of something: *My car can only take five people.* | *The freezer will take about 50 litres of ice cream.* | *I'll have to throw out some clothes – the closet can't take any more.*

seat /siːt/ [v T] if a vehicle, room, or table **seats** a particular number of people, there is enough space for that number of people to sit: *The auditorium seats 500 people.* | *The Boeing 747 seats 400-425 passengers.*

sleep /sliːp/ [v T] if a house or room **sleeps** a particular number of people, there is enough space for that number of people to **sleep** there: *You can rent a country cottage that sleeps six from as little as £300 a week.*

4 when there is not a lot of space

- ▸ **a tight squeeze**
- ▸ **tight**
- ▸ **cramped**

▸ *see also* **small**

a tight squeeze /ə ˌtaɪt ˈskwiːz/ [n phrase] when there is only just enough space for things or people to fit: *It was a tight squeeze, but everything eventually fitted into my suitcase.* | *Put the spare bed in here – it will be a tight squeeze but it's only temporary.*

tight /taɪt/ [adj] if space is **tight**, there is not a lot of it: *We sell furniture specially designed for homes where space is tight.* | *I've never been very good at reversing into tight parking spaces.*

cramped /kræmpt/ [adj] if a room or building is **cramped**, there is not enough space to be able to move around it comfortably: *Conditions on board ship were extremely cramped and uncomfortable.* | *I couldn't wait to move out of my cramped apartment.*

a space between two things

5 a space between two things

- space
- gap
- opening

space /speɪs/ [n C] *Plant cells contain liquid in spaces called vacuoles.* | **+ between** *The children hid in the space between the wall and the sofa.* | *The space between the old building and the Morgan mansion has been converted into a marble-paved court, with plantings and a fountain.*

gap /gæp/ [n C] a space between two objects or surfaces from which there is something missing **+ in** *Freddie managed to squeeze through a gap in the fence and run away.* | **+ between** *Melanie's dentist says that as she gets older the gap between her two front teeth will disappear.* | **fill/fill in a gap** *Melianthus is a good plant for filling in gaps in flower borders.*

opening /ˈəʊpənɪŋ/ [n C] a space through which something can pass or through which you can see: *Now there is just a gap where the buildings used to stand.* | **+ in** *'It's only Fred,' said Joyce, looking through an opening in the curtains.* | *The dog darted through an opening in the hedge, chasing a rabbit.*

speak

RELATED WORDS

- to make a speech *see* **talk (18-19)**
- *see also* **language, say, talk, tell, voice**

1 to speak

- speak
- talk
- whisper

speak /spiːk/ [v I] to produce words with your voice: *How old are babies when they learn to speak?* | *Sean didn't speak the whole time we were in the car.* | *Don't interrupt me when I'm speaking.* | **speak up** (=speak louder) *Can you speak up? – I can't hear you.*

talk /tɔːk/ [v I] to produce words with your voice in order to have a conversation, tell people what you think etc: *You're not supposed to talk in the library.* | *Please don't all talk at the same time.*

whisper /ˈwɪspəʳ/ [v I] to speak very quietly, using your breath rather than your voice: *We had to whisper because Jill's mother was in the next room.* | *Why are you two whispering?*

2 to speak unclearly

- stammer/stutter
- mumble
- slur
- lisp

stammer/stutter /ˈstæməʳ, ˈstʌtəʳ/ [v I/T] to speak with difficulty because you cannot stop yourself repeating the first sound in some words, usually several times: *Savio was a shy man who stuttered when he was nervous.* | *'I d-d-don't know,' he stammered.* | *Most kids who stammer eventually grow out of it.* —**stutter/stammer/have a stutter/stammer** [n singular] *I used to visit a speech therapist every week because I had a stammer.*

mumble /ˈmʌmbəl/ [v I/T] to speak quietly and not at all clearly, so that it is difficult for people to understand you: *Don't mumble – I can't hear what you're saying.* | *An old man sat on the curb, mumbling and laughing to himself.* | **+ about** *He looked embarrassed, and mumbled something about being sorry.*

slur /slɜːʳ/ [v I/T] to speak unclearly, without separating your words or sounds correctly, usually because you are tired or have been drinking alcohol: *After just a couple of drinks, she starts to slur.* | **slur your words** *When Lionel is tired he tends to slur his words.* —**slurred** [adj] *After many years of boxing, Garcia's speech is slow and slurred.*

lisp /lɪsp/ [v I/T] to speak unclearly because you have difficulty pronouncing 's' sounds: *As a child she used to lisp.* | *'What time ith it?' he lisped.* —**lisp** [n singular] *Bobbi speaks with a slight lisp.*

3 to speak a language

- speak
- know
- fluent
- bilingual
- multilingual
- speaker

speak /spiːk/ [v T not in progressive] *Nadia speaks six languages.* | **speak French/Japanese/Russian etc** *Is there anyone here who can speak Arabic?*

know /nəʊ/ [v T not in progressive] to be able to speak, read, and understand some of a particular foreign language: *I know enough Italian to travel around there.* | *Do you know any Polish?*

fluent /ˈfluːənt/ [adj] very good at speaking a foreign language, so that you can speak it quickly without stopping and you understand it very well **fluent in English/German/Thai etc** *Applicants should be fluent in Cantonese.* | **fluent French/Arabic/Japanese etc** *Ann speaks fluent Italian.* —**fluently** [adv] *Douglas speaks Hindi fluently.*

bilingual /baɪˈlɪŋgwəl/ [adj] able to speak two languages very well: *About 80 percent of the school's students are bilingual.*

multilingual /ˌmʌltɪˈlɪŋgwəl◂/ [adj] able to speak several languages very well: *Many people who work at the European Parliament are multilingual.* —**multilingualism** [n U] *Multilingualism is very common in several parts of Africa.*

speaker /ˈspiːkəʳ/ [n C] someone who can speak a particular language **speaker of English/Russian/Arabic etc** *Speakers of Cantonese often cannot understand speakers of Mandarin.* | **English/Spanish/Urdu etc speaker** *The hotel has two English speakers on its staff.* | **native speaker** (=learnt a particular language as their first language as a child) *All our English teachers are native speakers.*

4 to speak a little of a foreign language

- get by
- know a few words
- have a smattering of
- broken

get by /ˌget ˈbaɪ/ [phr v I] to speak enough of a language to be able to buy things, ask for help etc: *He went to Tokyo and within a few weeks knew enough*

Japanese to get by. | **+ in** *I've just bought a book called 'Get By In Portuguese'.*

know a few words /ˌnəʊ ə fjuː ˈwɜːʳdz/ [v phrase not in progressive] to be able to speak a few words of a language: *'Do you speak Korean?' 'I only know a few words.'* | **+ of** *I used to know a few words of German but I've forgotten them all.*

have a smattering of /hæv ə ˈsmætərɪŋ ɒv/ [v phrase not in progressive] to be able to speak a small but useful amount of a language: *Martin is fluent in French, and also has a smattering of Swedish.*

broken /ˈbrəʊkən/ [adj only before noun] **broken English/French etc** English, French etc that is spoken slowly and badly by someone who only knows a little of the language: *The two students, one Chinese, the other Greek, communicated in broken English.*

5 the way someone speaks

- pronunciation
- accent
- speech

pronunciation /prəˌnʌnsiˈeɪʃən/ [n singular] the way someone says the words and sounds of a language: *Gianni has problems with his grammar but his pronunciation is very good.*

accent /ˈæksənt‖ˈæksent/ [n C] the way someone speaks a language, which shows which country or which part of a country they come from, and that sometimes shows which social class they come from: *Maria speaks Spanish with a Mexican accent.* | *I knew from his accent that he was from the South.* | *She spoke with a distinctly upper class accent.* | **a strong/broad accent** (=an accent that is easy to notice) *Her companion had a broad Australian accent.* | *His accent was so strong that I couldn't understand a word he was saying.*

speech /spiːtʃ/ [n U] the way someone speaks – use this especially when this is affected by illness, drugs etc: *His speech was slurred and he was having trouble standing straight.* | **speech impediment** (=a permanent speech problem, which makes it difficult to pronounce particular sounds) *Natalie was born with a slight speech impediment.*

6 spoken, not written

- spoken
- oral
- verbal
- by word of mouth

opposite ——— **write (14)**

spoken /ˈspəʊkən/ [adj usually before noun] **spoken** language is produced with the voice, not written down: *This book will help you with both spoken and written English.* | *Idiomatic and spoken phrases tend to differ widely throughout the country.*

oral /ˈɔːrəl/ [adj usually before noun] using spoken rather than written language – use this especially about tests and exams: *We had a 15-minute oral exam in German.* | *Anglo-Saxon stories and poems were part of a largely oral culture.*

verbal /ˈvɜːʳbəl/ [adj usually before noun] spoken rather than written – use this especially about agreements, warnings, announcements etc that have never been written down and are therefore not always official: *We had a verbal agreement but no written contract.* | *Federal authorities gave Alascom verbal approval to begin the project.*

by word of mouth /baɪ ˌwɜːʳd əv ˈmaʊθ/ [adv] if you find something out **by word of mouth**, you find it out because someone tells you, not because you have seen it advertised, read about it in a newspaper etc: *He learned about the job by word of mouth.* | *The tribe's history was passed on by word of mouth.* — **word-of-mouth** [adj only before noun] *A word-of-mouth recommendation is probably the best form of advertising.*

7 the ability to speak

- speech

speech /spiːtʃ/ [n U] *Only humans are capable of speech.* | *The left side of the brain controls speech.*

8 not able to speak

- can't speak
- lose your voice
- mute
- dumb
- be at a loss for words/be lost for words

can't speak /ˌkɑːnt ˈspiːk‖ˌkænt-/ [v phrase] to be unable to speak because you are too ill, weak, frightened etc: *I was so terrified, I couldn't speak.* | *A lump welled up in his throat and he could not speak.*

lose your voice /ˌluːz jɔːʳ ˈvɔɪs/ [v phrase] to become unable to speak because of illness, or because you have been using your voice too much: *On the first night of the show, the star of the play lost his voice and couldn't perform.*

mute /mjuːt/ [adj] unable to speak, especially permanently – use this especially in medical contexts: *A stroke left her mute and unable to use her legs.*

dumb /dʌm/ [adj] permanently unable to speak because of a physical condition – many people now consider this word to be offensive: *According to the story, he was struck dumb* (=made dumb) *by the gods.* | *She was born deaf and dumb.*

be at a loss for words/be lost for words /biː ət ə ˌlɒs fəʳ ˈwɜːʳdz‖-ˌlɔːs-, biː ˌlɒst fəʳ ˈwɜːʳdz‖-ˌlɔːst-/ [v phrase] to be unable to say anything because you are very surprised, upset etc: *Rimes, who is rarely at a loss for words, was overcome with emotion as she received her award.*

special

special

RELATED WORDS

- *see also* **unusual, different**

- special
- specially
- particular
- unique

special /ˈspeʃəl/ [adj] something that is **special** is different from other things, for example because it is better, more important, or intended for a particular purpose: *United Airlines is offering a special deal on flights to London.* | *Let us know if you have any special dietary needs in advance.* | *Today is a very special day for us – it was 50 years ago that we first met.* | *Did you do anything special at the weekend?* | *I made a special effort to be nice to him.* | **special occasion** (=a wedding, birthday, or other time when people celebrate something) *He has a dark suit, which he only wears on special occasions.*

specially /ˈspeʃəli/ [adv] **specially designed/made/chosen etc** designed, made, built etc for a special purpose: *a new range of beauty products specially designed for teenagers* | *Customs officers use spe-*

cially trained dogs for drug searches. | *Did you get your ring specially made?*

particular /pərˈtɪkjələr/ [adj only before noun] use this to emphasize that something is different or separate from other things of the same kind, or that something is more important than other things: *Is there any particular reason why you want to go back to Japan?* | *Each class will focus on one particular aspect of American culture.* | **be of particular interest/importance (to sb)** *This discovery is of particular interest to scientists studying the origins of the universe.*

unique /juːˈniːk/ [adj] someone or something that is **unique** is so special and unusual that it is the only one of its kind – use this especially about things or people that you think are extremely good: *It was a unique achievement – no-one has ever won the championship five times before.* | *The exhibition provided a unique opportunity to see all of the artist's work.* | *Every child is unique, with their own needs, preferences and talents.*

speed

how fast something moves or is done

RELATED WORDS

▸ *see also* **fast, slow**

- ▸ **speed**
- ▸ **rate**
- ▸ **pace**
- ▸ **velocity**
- ▸ **momentum**
- ▸ **miles per hour/metres per second etc**

speed /spiːd/ [n C/U] *The train's designers claim it is capable of attaining speeds in excess of 350 kph.* | *sensors which monitor speed and body movement* | **+ of** *What was the speed of the car at the time of the accident?* | *the internal processing speed of a computer* | **at a speed of 50 mph/10 metres per second etc** *The Earth moves round the Sun at a speed of 30 km per second.* | **at a constant/steady speed** (=keeping the same speed all the time) *Keep driving at a constant speed until I tell you differently.* | **top speed** (=the fastest speed that a car, plane etc can reach) *The Ferrari Testarossa has a top speed of 188 mph.*

rate /reɪt/ [n C] how fast things happen, change, or develop **at a faster/slower/different etc rate** *Individual children develop physically and emotionally at different rates.* | **at an alarming rate** (=very fast) *Our money was running out at an alarming rate.* | **+ of** *The amount of light available will determine the plant's rate of growth.* | *equipment that can load ships at a rate of 5000 tonnes a day*

pace /peɪs/ [n C usually singular] how fast someone walks or runs, or how fast they work or do things **at a brisk/steady/gentle etc pace** *The soldiers were marching at a steady pace.* | **at a leisurely pace** (=at a slow comfortable speed) *We climbed at a leisurely pace, stopping occasionally to enjoy the view.* | **+ of** *The pace of political change has been rapid.* | **pace of work/life** *I'm enjoying the relaxed pace of life of Jamaica.* | **at your own pace** (=at a speed that is right for you) *The Kumon method involves students learning at their own pace.*

velocity /vəˈlɒsəti‖vəˈlɑː-/ [n C/U] the speed at which something moves in a particular direction – use this especially in technical contexts: *This instrument is used for measuring wind velocity.* | **+ of** *an experiment to try to predict the velocity of a moving object* | **high velocity** *a beam of high velocity electrons*

momentum /məʊˈmentəm, mə-/ [n U] the force that makes a moving object keep moving: *We are trying to measure the position and momentum of an electron as accurately as possible.* | **gain/gather momentum** (=move faster) *As the slope got steeper, the sled gathered momentum.* | **lose momentum** (=move slower) *The ball was moving along, slowly losing momentum on the bumpy ground.*

miles per hour/metres per second etc /ˌmaɪlz pər ˈaʊər/ [n phrase] use these expressions to say how fast something moves: *The maximum speed on British motorways is 70 miles per hour.* | *Sound travels through the air at about 340 metres per second.* | *a propeller that revolves at a rate of 150 revolutions per minute*

spend money/time

WHAT'S HERE

- **spend money** see **1 to 9**
- **spend time** see **10 to 13**

spend money

RELATED WORDS

▸ *see also* **pay, buy, cost, cheap, expensive, shop/store, money, generous/not generous**

1 to use money to buy things

- ▸ **spend**
- ▸ **pay**
- ▸ **pay out**
- ▸ **give**
- ▸ **break into**
- ▸ **pay good money for**

spend /spend/ [v I/T] to use money to buy things: *Everyone spends more at Christmas – it's an important time for business.* | *During the recession, even the tourists weren't spending.* | **spend £5/$10/a dollar etc** *I bought two skirts and a T-shirt and I only spent $50.* | **+ on** *We spend about £85 a week on food.* | *The government has promised to spend more money on education.* | *She spends most of her salary on clothes.* | **spend money on doing sth** *They spend quite a lot of money each week on eating out.*

pay /peɪ/ [v I/T] to spend £5, $10 etc on something because that is what it costs: *Of course you have to pay more if you want to travel in the summer.* | *What quality accommodation you get depends on how much you're prepared to pay.* | **+ for** *I like your new car – how much did you pay for it?* | **pay £5/$10/a dollar etc for** *They paid over $100 each for tickets.* | *The set meal costs £15 but you have to pay extra for wine.*

pay out /ˌpeɪ ˈaʊt/ [phr v I/T] to spend more money on something than you want to spend or more than you think is fair: *£65! I don't want to pay out that much!* | **+ for** *You have to pay out so much money for car repairs these days.* | **+ on** *The idea of paying out half my salary on rent didn't sound too good.* | **pay out £5/$10 etc** *Did you know that Eddy paid out nearly £2000 for his new computer?*

give /gɪv/ [v I/T] informal to pay a particular amount of money for something, especially when you are buying it from another person, so that the price is not fixed: *'I don't really want to spend that much.' 'OK, how much are you prepared to give?'* | **+ for** *Did they give you the asking price for the house?* | **give (sb) £5/$10 etc** *He said he'd give £40 for the painting, so I said yes.*

break into /ˈbreɪk ɪntuː/ [phr v T] to start spending an amount of money that you have saved or that you were keeping for a particular purpose before you really wanted to: *We had to break into our savings to pay the hospital fees.* | *I really want to avoid having to break into the money I was saving for college.*

pay good money for /ˌpeɪ gʊd ˈmʌni fɔːʳ/ [v phrase] spoken use this to talk about something you paid a reasonable price for, so you expect it to be of good quality or used properly so that your money has not been wasted: *I paid good money for that tennis racquet and it broke the first time I used it.* | *What's the point of paying good money for a wedding dress when I'm only going to wear it once?*

2 to spend a lot of money

- spend a lot
- go to great expense
- spare no expense
- shell out/fork out
- go on a spending spree
- money is no object
- live the high life

spend a lot /ˌspend ə ˈlɒt‖-ˈlɑːt/ [v phrase] *You don't have to spend a lot to be fashionable – you just need a sense of style.* | **+ on** *They must have spent a lot on their new kitchen. It's made of solid oak* | **spend a lot of money** *In recent years the company has spent a lot of money on new technology.*

go to great expense /gəʊ tə ˌgreɪt ɪkˈspens/ [v phrase] to spend very large amounts of money on something important, even if it costs you more than you can afford: *The wedding was wonderful. Your parents obviously went to great expense.* | **+ to do sth** *Please let us have your comments on the plans for the new offices – we're going to great expense to get everything just right.*

spare no expense /speəʳ ˌnəʊ ɪkˈspens/ [v phrase] to spend as much money as is necessary to get what you want or make something successful, without worrying about the cost: *The organizers were told to spare no expense – this was going to be the biggest show on Earth.* | **no expense spared** *'Go out and buy whatever you want,' he said, 'no expense spared!'*

shell out/fork out /ˌʃel ˈaʊt, ˌfɔːʳk ˈaʊt/ [phr v T] spoken informal to have to spend more money on something than you think is fair or reasonable: *No, we can't afford to go to the bowling alley – I've forked out enough already today.* | **shell out #50/$100 etc** *Insurance companies are having to shell out millions of pounds to the victims of the floods.* | **+ on** *I'm not shelling out any more money on this old car. It's not worth it!* | **+ for** *I failed my driving test and Dad said that he wasn't forking out for any more lessons for me.*

go on a spending spree /ˌgəʊ ɒn ə ˈspendɪŋ ˌspriː/ [v phrase] informal to spend a lot of money and buy a lot of things in a short time for enjoyment, especially when other people think this is stupid or a waste of money: *Jilly and I decided to cheer ourselves up and go on a spending spree.* | *You haven't been on another spending spree, have you? What did you buy this time?*

money is no object /ˌmʌni ɪz nəʊ ˈɒbdʒɪkt‖-ˈɑːb-/ use this to say that you do not care how much money you spend on something even if it is a lot: *Simon always ordered the best. It was obvious that money was no object.* | **money no object** *Choose whatever outfit you want – money no object!*

live the high life /ˌlɪv ðə ˈhaɪ laɪf/ [v phrase] to enjoy yourself by going out often and spending a lot of money, especially with rich or important people: *For several years they lived the high life with Hollywood stars and celebrities.* | *You've been living the high life recently, haven't you! You're always going out to clubs and fancy restaurants.*

3 to spend money quickly or carelessly

- squander
- blow
- go through
- spend money like water/like there's no tomorrow

squander /ˈskwɒndəʳ‖ˈskwɑːn-/ [v T] to spend all the money you have on unnecessary things instead of saving it or using it carefully: *In less than three years he had squandered the entire family fortune.* | *There was no money to pay the rent. They'd already squandered the little that they had.* | **+ on** *Here's £50 but don't just go and squander it on beer!*

blow /bləʊ/ [v T] informal to spend a lot of money on something expensive and enjoyable, especially something that you do not really need **blow £50/$100 etc on sth** *We blew $3000 on a trip to Barbados.* | **blow it all/blow the lot** British (=spend everything) *He won £500,000 in the National Lottery, but he's already blown the lot.*

go through ALSO **get through sth** British /ˌgəʊ ˈθruː, ˌget ˈθruː (sth)/ [phr v T not in passive] to spend the money that you have more quickly than expected, so that you have nothing left: *I got through all of my money in less than a month and had to get my parents to send me more.* | **go through £100/$2000 etc** *The hotel was really expensive. We went through $3000 in the first week.*

spend money like water/like there's no tomorrow /spend ˌmʌni laɪk ˈwɔːtəʳ, laɪk ðeəʳz ˌnəʊ təˈmɒrəʊ‖-ˈmɔː-/ [v phrase] informal to spend a lot of money very quickly and carelessly without worrying how much you are spending or how long your money will last: *Richard spends money like there's no tomorrow! Where does he get it all from?* | *I don't trust myself with a credit card – I spend money like water as it is.*

4 to spend less money

- cut down
- economize
- scrimp and save
- tighten your belt
- budget

cut down /ˌkʌt ˈdaʊn/ [phr v I/T] to reduce the amount of money that you regularly spend: *We've had to cut down a lot since Craig lost his job – it's been very hard for us.* | **+ on** *She's already cut down on going out and buying clothes, but she doesn't have enough money to start paying off her debts.* | **cut down sb's expenses/bills etc** *The department has overspent this year and we will have to cut down our expenses.*

economize ALSO **economise** British /ɪˈkɒnəmaɪz‖ɪˈkɑː-/ [v I] to spend less money by buying only the things that you really need, or by buying cheaper things: *Sorry, I can't come out tonight – I'm trying to economize.* | *We're economizing this year by having a cheaper vacation.* | **+ on** (=spend less money on something) *Families on low incomes are having to economize on food and heating costs.*

scrimp and save /ˌskrɪmp ən ˈseɪv/ [v phrase] to spend as little money as possible, only buying things you really need, because you have very little money and want to save it to use in the future: *Chris's parents scrimped and saved so that he could go to college.* | *I had hardly any money left and was scrimping and saving just to buy the bare necessities.*

tighten your belt /ˌtaɪtn jɔːʳ ˈbelt/ [v phrase] to spend less money than you usually do because there is less money available: *Most people have to tighten their belts a little when they retire.* | *Governments and companies are forced to tighten their belts during a recession.*

budget /ˈbʌdʒɪ̵t/ [v I] to carefully plan and control how much you spend: *We'll have to budget more carefully in the future. We've spent far more than we can afford.* | **+ for** *By the time I had budgeted for food and rent I only had a few pounds left.*

5 spending as little as possible

- on a shoestring
- on the cheap
- skimp on

on a shoestring /ɒn ə ˈʃuːstrɪŋ/ [adv] if you make a film, run a business etc **on a shoestring**, you spend very little money on it, but it is usually a success: *Nearly all of our research had to be conducted on a shoestring.* | *The paper started on a shoestring, but soon had a circulation of over 100,000 readers.* —**shoestring** [adj only before noun] using very little money: *a shoestring budget*

skimp on /ˈskɪmp ɒn / [phr v T not in passive] to not spend enough money on important materials, equipment etc, so that what you are doing or making is unsuccessful or of bad quality: *There's no point in skimping on essentials such as food and heating.* | *A company will never get anywhere by skimping on training and technology.*

on the cheap /ɒn ðə ˈtʃiːp/ [adv] British if you do or make something **on the cheap**, you spend as little money as possible on it, so that it is often unsuccessful or of bad quality: *You only had to look at the houses to see that they'd been built on the cheap.* | *It's impossible to provide good nursing care on the cheap.*

6 someone who spends a lot of money carelessly

- extravagant
- big spender
- spendthrift

extravagant /ɪkˈstrævəgənt/ [adj] spending more money than you can afford on expensive things that you do not really need: *$400 on a dress! That's a bit extravagant, isn't it?* | *Rich and extravagant parents are spending more and more money on their children's parties.* —**extravagantly** [adv] *She put the money in to a savings account so she wasn't tempted to spend it extravagantly.*

spendthrift /ˈspendˌθrɪft/ [n C] formal someone who spends money carelessly even when they know that they do cannot afford to: *I remember him as a charming but irresponsible spendthrift.* | *She was by no means a spendthrift, but somehow all the money disappeared anyway.*

big spender /ˌbɪg ˈspendəʳ/ [n C] a rich person who spends a lot of money, especially in order to impress other people: *I didn't trust him at all. He was a big spender, that's all.* | *This is the time of year when all the big spenders pour into Las Vegas hotels and casinos.*

7 someone who spends money carefully

- thrifty
- economical
- careful
- frugal

thrifty /ˈθrɪfti/ [adj] spending money carefully and cleverly so that nothing is wasted and you can manage with the money you have: *Mrs Jones was a very thrifty woman who never wasted anything.* | *By being thrifty and shopping wisely you can feed an entire family on as little as $100 a week.* —**thrift** [n U] *The old values of thrift* (=being thrifty) *and hard work seem to be things of the past.*

careful /ˈkeəʳfəl/ [adj not before noun] spending money only on things that are necessary or cheap because you want your money to last as long as possible: *I wouldn't say he was mean – he's just careful.* | **careful with money** *Once you've spent your allowance there won't be any more. You must learn to be more careful with money.*

economical /ˌekəˈnɒmɪkəl, ˌiː-‖-ˈnɑː-/ [adj] spending money carefully and sensibly so that you do not spend more than necessary: *I'm trying to be more economical when I go shopping, and only buying what I really need.* | *Tim's a very economical person,. He always looks around for the best buys.* —**economically** [adv] *By shopping economically, you can save a lot of money on your weekly bill.*

frugal /ˈfruːgəl/ [adj] spending as little money as possible, even on things that are necessary such as food and drink, especially because you are poor: *He was very frugal, and would often use a tea bag three or four times over.* | *The monks lead a frugal life, allowing themselves only the bare essentials.* —**frugally** [adv] *We moved to a little house in the country and tried to live as frugally as possible.*

8 someone who hates spending money

- stingy
- tight-fisted
- mean
- miser
- cheap

stingy /ˈstɪndʒi/ [adj] not generous with your money, even though you are not poor: *Don't be so stingy! It's your turn to buy me a drink.* | *It's no use asking him – he's too stingy to give money to charity.*

mean /miːn/ [adj] British someone who is **mean** does not like spending money or sharing what they have with other people: *Rick's so mean he never even buys his wife a birthday present.* | *My father was a mean old man who resented every penny he spent on us.*

cheap /tʃiːp/ [adj] American, especially spoken someone who is **cheap** does not like spending money, and always tries to avoid spending it: *Uncle Matt was really cheap – he used to stay with us for weeks, and he never paid for anything.*

tight-fisted /ˌtaɪt ˈfɪstɪ̵d◂/ [adj] informal not generous with money – use this about people who annoy you because they have money but do not like spending it: *He was known to have made a fortune on the stock market, but was nonetheless notoriously tight-fisted.*

miser /ˈmaɪzəʳ/ [n C] someone who hates spending money, and prefers to save as much as possible – use this especially about someone who has collected a lot of money by doing this: *Mr Henny was a miser who had thousands of pounds hidden away under his bed.*

9 the amount that you spend

- spending/expenditure
- costs
- outlay
- outgoings
- overheads
- expenses
- budget

spending/expenditure /ˈspendɪŋ, ɪkˈspendɪtʃəʳ/ [n U] the amount of money that is spent, especially by a government or other organization: *The government intends to cut its expenditure by 10% next year.* | **public spending/expenditure** (=by a government) *The answer to inadequate health care is to increase public spending, not reduce it.* | **+ on** *Company spending on staff benefits has been cut dramatically in recent years.*

costs /kɒsts‖kɔːsts/ [n plural] the money that a person or organization has to spend regularly on heating, rent, electricity etc: *What are your annual fuel costs?* | **cut costs** (=reduce costs) *Falling sales have forced companies to cut costs.* | **running costs** (=the cost of owning and using something) *I'm looking for a car with low running costs.*

outlay /ˈaʊtleɪ/ [n singular] the amount of money that someone must spend when they first start a new business or activity: *The best business is one with a small outlay and with no risk involved.* | **+ on** *When we built the factory the outlay on machinery was heavy but we were able to buy all the latest equipment.* | **initial outlay** (=outlay in the beginning) *T-shirts are easy to produce, requiring little initial outlay and a minimum of time and effort.*

outgoings /ˈaʊtˌgəʊɪŋz/ [n plural] the amount of money that someone has to spend regularly on rent, bills, food etc for their home or business: *The outgoings on a house this size are very high.* | *I wrote a check for $200 to cover various outgoings.*

overheads British **/overhead** American /ˈəʊvəʳhed(z)/ [n plural/n singular] the amount of money that a company or a business person has to spend on rent, their workers' pay, office furniture etc: *The cost of the movie was high because of the large production overhead.* | *The company's overheads were much lower this year owing to the closure of several offices nationwide.* | *Restaurant prices have been put up to cover the ever-increasing overheads.*

expenses /ɪkˈspensɨz/ [n plural] the money that you spend on things that you need, for example on food, rent, and travel: *John and Rachel have a new baby, so they have a lot of expenses right now.* | **travel/living/medical etc expenses** *Living expenses are much higher in London.* | *The company doesn't pay my travel expenses.*

budget /ˈbʌdʒɨt/ [n C usually singular] the amount of money that you have planned to spend or that is available to spend on a particular thing: *You can choose any type of wood for your furniture, according to your budget.* | *Government cuts in the defence budget have meant a loss of 2000 jobs.*

spend time

RELATED WORDS

see also **wait, stay, time, do**

10 to spend time

- spend
- pass the time
- kill
- busy yourself
- hang out

spend /spend/ [v T] to **spend** time somewhere, with someone, or doing something **spend time** *I never seem to have any time to spend with the children.* | **spend an hour/two days/a week etc** *Dani spends hours on the phone.* | **spend an hour/two days/a week etc doing sth** *Fay spent a year in Italy teaching English.* | *He spent the whole morning reading the report.*

pass the time /ˌpɑːs ðə ˈtaɪm‖ˌpæs-/ [v phrase] to spend time doing something unimportant, because you have nothing else to do: *I started doing a crossword to pass the time.* | **+ doing sth** *The security guards used to pass their time playing cards.*

kill /kɪl/ [v T] **kill time/a couple of hours etc** informal to do something in order to make time seem to pass more quickly while you are waiting for something: *I was early, so I sat in a café, killing time.* | *The train doesn't leave till two, so we have a couple of hours to kill.*

busy yourself /ˈbɪzi jɔːʳself/ [v phrase] to keep yourself busy doing things, especially because you cannot think of anything else to do or to stop yourself from getting bored **+ doing sth** *Martin sat down nervously and busied himself rearranging the papers on his desk.* | **+ with** *Mrs Smithers pottered about busying herself with light household tasks.*

hang out /ˌhæŋ ˈaʊt/ [phr v I] informal to often spend a lot of your time in a particular place or with a particular person or group: *You'll probably find Dave at the pool hall – he often hangs out there.* | **+ with** *I used to hang out with them when I was at college.*

11 to spend time working

- put in
- devote

put in /ˌpʊt ˈɪn/ [phr v T] *She usually ends up putting in several extra hours work at weekends.* | *When I'm preparing for a tournament I put in thirty or forty hours of training a week.*

devote /dɪˈvəʊt/ [v T] to spend a long time working hard at a particular thing, especially something important: *He's decided to give up racing and devote all his time to his farm in Ireland.* | *She intends to devote the next ten years to her charitable work.*

12 to spend a period of time in a particular job or in prison

- serve
- do

serve /sɜːʳv/ [v T] *Reagan was serving his second term as President at the time.* | *Smith has already served a ten-year sentence for armed robbery.*

do /duː/ [v T] informal to spend a long time doing a difficult job or doing something that you are forced to do: *As a young teacher she did two years in one of the city's toughest schools.* | **do time** *I did my time in the army like everyone else.*

13 to use your time badly

- waste
- lose

waste /weɪst/ [v T] to use your time badly, by doing nothing or by doing something that is not useful: *Stop wasting time. We have to finish this today.* | *I must have wasted two hours trying to fix this machine.* | *Sometimes she feels she's wasted her life.*

lose /luːz/ [v T] to not use your time for what you intended, for example because of delays, interruptions etc: *While you're talking, we're losing valuable time.* | *The work is already behind schedule. The firm's lost at least 45 days through staff illness.*

spoil

RELATED WORDS

- to spoil a child *see* **kind (2)**
- *see also* **damage, break, destroy, mark**

1 to make something look, taste, or seem much less good

- **spoil**
- **ruin**
- **mar**
- **detract from**

spoil /spɔɪl/ [v T not usually in progressive] *A badly positioned path can spoil the appearance of a garden.* | *The power station is extremely ugly, and it spoils the view of the sea.* | **spoil sth for sb** *New housing developments are spoiling the countryside for everyone.*

ruin /ˈruːɪ̇n/ [v T] to completely spoil something: *The rain had ruined her best velvet skirt.* | *Don't use harsh soap to wash your face. It will ruin your skin.* | *Protestors say that the proposed new airport will ruin this peaceful area.*

mar /mɑːʳ/ [v T] written to spoil the appearance or beauty of a person or place: *Electricity cables and oil pipelines mar many of the world's most beautiful landscapes.* | *He had handsome Arabic features, marred by a long scar across his face.*

detract from /dɪˈtrækt frɒm / [phr v T not usually in progressive] to slightly spoil something that is generally very good, beautiful, impressive etc: *Even a bruise on her cheekbone did not detract from her beauty.* | *The proposed building would detract from the character of the surrounding area.*

2 to spoil someone's work or plans

- **spoil**
- **ruin**
- **mess up**
- **undermine**
- **screw up**
- **sabotage**
- **throw a spanner in the works**
- **pour cold water on**

spoil /spɔɪl/ [v T] *Don't let me spoil your plans.* | *This scandal could spoil the Senator's chances of becoming President.* | *We were going to get married, but then war broke out and spoiled everything.* | **spoil sth for sb** *Starting a family so soon would definitely spoil her career prospects for her.*

ruin /ˈruːɪ̇n/ [v T] to completely spoil what someone has been trying to do: *Surely you don't want to ruin all our good work, do you?* | *Serious in-fighting ruined the Conservatives' chances of winning the election.*

mess up /ˌmes ˈʌp/ [phr v T] informal to spoil something important or something that has been carefully planned **mess up sth** *The travel agents messed up the arrangements and there was no room for us at the hotel.* | **mess sth up** *We secretly organized a party for her, but then Bill messed everything up by telling her about it.*

undermine /ˌʌndəʳˈmaɪn/ [v T] to spoil something that has taken a long time to develop: *The kidnappings undermined several months of delicate peace negotiations.* | *The US was accused of undermining international efforts to combat global warming.*

screw up /ˌskruː ˈʌp/ [phr v T] informal to completely spoil something such as a plan, especially by doing something stupid: *Someone screwed up and what was supposed to be a confidential email was copies to everyone in the company.* | **screw sth up** *I can't trust you to do anything right can I? You always manage to screw things up.* | **screw up sth** *There was no way he was going to allow her to screw up his plans.*

sabotage /ˈsæbətɑːʒ/ [v T] to deliberately spoil someone's plans or arrangements because you do not want them to succeed: *Her father sabotaged her acting ambitions by refusing to let her go to drama school.* | *The attack is being seen as a deliberate attempt to sabotage the peace talks.*

throw a spanner in the works British **/throw a monkey wrench in/into sth** American /ˌθrəʊ ə ˈspænər ɪn ðə ˌwɜːʳks, ˌθrəʊ ə ˈmʌŋki rentʃ ɪn, ɪntə (sth)/ [v phrase] informal to unexpectedly do something that prevents a plan or process from continuing or succeeding: *'He won't lend us the money after all.' 'Well, that's really thrown a spanner in the works, hasn't it?'* | *The President's veto threw a wrench into a program that had already been approved by a big majority of the Congress.*

pour cold water on /ˌpɔːʳ kəʊld ˈwɔːtər ɒn/ [v phrase] to spoil someone's plan, suggestion, or attitude towards something, by saying something that makes it seem less attractive or less likely to succeed: *Her mother had poured cold water on the whole idea of Eva going to Africa.* | *The committee's final report, just published, pours cold water on government proposals for helping the unemployed.*

3 to spoil a relationship or friendship

- **spoil**
- **sour**
- **poison**
- **destroy**

spoil /spɔɪl/ [v T] *His jealousy spoiled their relationship, and she left him after a few months.* | *The assassination attempt has definitely spoilt the previously positive atmosphere between the opposing parties.*

sour /saʊəʳ/ [v T] to spoil a friendly relationship between people, especially when this happens gradually: *The affair did not seem to have soured their friendship.* | *The global trend towards higher taxation on fuel consumption is souring relations with leading oil-producing states.* | *The incident was serious enough to sour the atmosphere for weeks.*

poison /ˈpɔɪzən/ [v T] to spoil a relationship, especially a close one, by causing a situation in which people can no longer trust each other: *Our marriage was poisoned by mistrust, deceit and jealousy.*

destroy /dɪˈstrɔɪ/ [v T] to completely spoil a relationship or friendship: *I don't want this to destroy our friendship.* | *Her feelings of self-doubt had destroyed every relationship that she had ever had.*

4 to make an event less enjoyable or successful

- **spoil**
- **ruin**
- **mar**
- **put a damper on**
- **cast a shadow over**

spoil /spɔɪl/ [v T] *The bad weather completely spoiled our holiday.* | *Why did you have to invite Jerry? You've spoiled the whole weekend.* | *This was her moment of glory, and she wasn't going to let anyone spoil it.* | **spoil sth for sb** *She wanted to do her own thing, but was afraid of spoiling Christmas for the rest of the family.* | **spoil things** *He got very drunk that evening, and seemed determined to spoil things for all of us.*

ruin /ˈruːɪ̇n/ [v T] to completely spoil an event or occasion, with the result that no-one enjoys it: *How can* *you prevent stomach upsets from ruining your holiday?* | **ruin sth for sb** *John and Sandy argued all the time, which completely ruined the evening for the rest of us.*

mar /mɑːʳ/ [v T usually in passive] if something unpleasant such as an argument or accident **mars** a big or important event, it makes it less enjoyable or less successful: *Outbreaks of fighting and lawlessness marred the New Year celebrations.* | *The race was marred by a horrific accident involving Niki Lauda.*

put a damper on /ˌpʊt ə ˈdæmpər ɒn/ [v phrase] if bad news, bad weather etc **puts a damper on** something, especially on a social event such as a party, it spoils people's enjoyment of it: *The bad news put a damper on the celebrations.* | *Torrential rain put a damper on the event, sending bedraggled guests squelching across lawns to seek shelter.*

cast a shadow over /ˌkɑːst ə ˈʃædəʊ əʊvəʳ ‖ˌkæst-/ [v phrase] if something **casts a shadow over** an event, period of time etc, it makes people feel less happy or hopeful because they are worrying about it: *The threat of war cast a shadow over the summer of 1939.* | *This argument with Kuroda did, I must admit, cast a shadow over my mood.*

5 to spoil the good opinion that people have of someone

- spoil sb's image
- damage sb's reputation
- damaging
- discredit
- smear campaign

spoil sb's image /ˌspɔɪl (sb's) ˈɪmɪdʒ/ [v phrase] to spoil the idea that people have about someone, especially a famous person who is often on television, in newspapers and magazines etc: *The star's cleancut image has been spoiled by accusations of gambling and drug-taking.*

damage sb's reputation /ˌdæmɪdʒ (sb's) repjʊˈteɪʃən/ [v T] to make people no longer have a good opinion about someone, especially a politician or someone with an important job: *My main concern was to prevent this incident from damaging my reputation.*

damaging /ˈdæmɪdʒɪŋ/ [adj] containing information about someone's dishonest or immoral behaviour, which damages the good opinion that people have of them: *We can't risk any damaging scandals just before a Presidential election.* | *His career had been ruined by the sensational and damaging stories that appeared in the popular press.* | **+ to** *The recent court cases have been very damaging to the public image of the medical profession.*

discredit /dɪsˈkredɪ̈t/ [v T] to damage the good opinion that people have of a person or organization, especially when this is done deliberately and in order to get an advantage: *It was a blatant attempt to discredit the Prime Minister.* | *There were reports that his campaign team had been trying to dig up information that might discredit his rival.*

smear campaign /ˈsmɪəʳ kæmˌpeɪn/ [n C] when an organization such as a political party or newspaper deliberately tries to find out and tell people about bad things someone in a public position has done, for example so that people are less likely to vote for them: *The magistrates who investigated his business empire have been made victims of a smear campaign.* | **+ against** *He called on people to ignore what he called a smear campaign against the government.*

6 someone who spoils things

- wet blanket
- spoiler
- spoilsport
- party pooper
- killjoy

wet blanket /ˌwet ˈblæŋkɪ̈t‖ˈwet ˌblæŋ-/ [n C] informal someone who spoils a happy event for other people, especially by refusing to join in with everyone else: *Stop being a wet blanket and come and dance.* | *Does he have to come on vacation with us? He's such a wet blanket!*

spoiler /ˈspɔɪləʳ/ [n C] someone who deliberately spoils someone else's enjoyment, happiness, or plans: *My ex-husband was a real spoiler who turned every happy event into a nightmare.*

spoilsport /ˈspɔɪlspɔːʳt/ [n C] informal someone who spoils other people's enjoyment, especially by trying to prevent them from doing something: *'I don't think we should go in there – someone might see us.' 'Oh, don't be such a spoilsport – come on!'*

party pooper /ˈpɑːʳti ˌpuːpəʳ/ [n C] spoken informal someone who spoils other people's fun, for example by saying that they should not be doing what they are doing: *When he said it was time to wind things up, the others accused him of being a party pooper.*

killjoy /ˈkɪldʒɔɪ/ [n C] informal someone who disapproves of things that other people enjoy and who tries to stop them enjoying themselves: *We wanted to do a sponsored dance after work but those killjoys in Head Office wouldn't let us.*

7 not spoiled

- unspoiled/unspoilt
- unblemished

unspoiled/unspoilt /ˌʌnˈspɔɪld◂, ˌʌnˈspɔɪlt◂/ [adj] a place or area that is **unspoiled** or **unspoilt** has not been spoiled by being changed: *This is one of Africa's oldest remaining areas of unspoilt rainforest.* | *an unspoiled fishing village on the Mediterranean coast* | *It was only by the grace of God that the village remained largely unspoiled.*

unblemished /ˌʌnˈblemɪʃt/ [adj] not spoiled in any way – use this about the opinion people have of someone or how well someone has done their job: *Lord Edwards is retiring after an unblemished career that has lasted thirty years.* | *an unblemished record of service to the community* | *She is a woman with an unblemished reputation of fairness and competence.*

sport/game

RELATED WORDS

- *see also* **game, exercise, competition, play a game or sport, win, lose, beat/defeat, compete with, score, result, practise/practice, fit/not fit**

1 physical activities in which people compete against each other

- sport
- games
- gym (class)

sport [n U] British **/sports** [n plural] American /spɔːʳt, spɔːʳts/ physical activities that need effort and skill and that are usually competitive: *She's interested in cinema, music and sport.* | *Sport has always been* *very important in this part of the country.* | **do sport** British *We don't do much sport at my school.* | **play sports** especially American *Today's kids need to spend less time watching television, and more time playing sports.*

games /geɪmz/ [n plural] British a period of time in school when you do organized sports activities such as football, tennis etc, usually outdoors: *The boys have games on Monday, Wednesday and Friday afternoons.* | *Hurry up or you'll be late for your games lesson.*

gym (class) ALSO **P.E.** ALSO **Phys. Ed.** American /'dʒɪm (klɑːs‖klæs), ˌpiː 'iː, ˌfɪz 'ed/ [n U] a period of time in school when you do organized physical activities: *Sometimes in Phys. Ed. we're allowed to go on the trampolines.* | *How many times a week do you have P.E.?*

2 a particular sport or game

- sport
- game

sport /spɔːʳt/ [n C] a physical activity in which people or teams play, race etc against each other and try to win: *His favourite sports are swimming and tennis.* | *Motorcycle racing can be a dangerous sport.* | **play a sport** *Which sports do you play at school?* | **do a sport** *I think everyone should do at least one sport, in order to keep fit.*

game /geɪm/ [n C] a sport that you play against another player or team, according to a set of rules: *Rugby is a very exciting, fast-moving game.* | **do/play games** *The girls at King Edward's play all sorts of games – basketball, hockey, tennis, to name just a few.*

3 used for sport or related to sport

- sports
- sporting

sports /spɔːʳts/ [adj only before noun] *Is there a shop that sells sports equipment near here?* | *Here is a list of the sports clubs in your area.* | *Heavy rain has flooded the sports field: all fixtures have been cancelled for a month.*

sporting /'spɔːʳtɪŋ/ [adj only before noun] **sporting activities/events/facilities etc** *The Italian Grand Prix is one of the great sporting events of the year.* | *The hotel has four restaurants, a bar and a disco, as well as an impressive range of sporting facilities.* | *Sponsorship is important for sporting activities such as golf, football, cricket and motor-racing.*

4 an occasion when people compete against each other in a sport

- game
- match
- race

game /geɪm/ [n C] an occasion when two people or two teams compete against each other in a sport: *Barcelona beat Real Madrid 3-2 in a thrilling game.* | *I got two tickets for the Bulls' game.* | *Who won last night's game?* | **game of tennis/squash etc** *How about a game of tennis this evening?* | **basketball/football etc game** *Do you want to come and watch the volleyball game this Saturday?*

match /mætʃ/ [n C] especially British an occasion when two people or two teams compete against each other in a sport: *Are you going to the match tomorrow?* | *If we win the next three matches, we could still go through to the semi-final.* | **a football/cricket/boxing etc match** *A cricket match was in progress on the school sports field.*

race /reɪs/ [n C] a competition in which several people try to run, drive, ride, swim etc faster than each other: *What time does the first race start?* | *Hill won the race, and Schumacher finished second.* | **boat/car/horse etc race** *Her husband spent all their money gambling on horse races.* | *the annual university boat race between Oxford and Cambridge*

5 someone who does a sport

- player
- sportsman/sportswoman
- athlete

player /'pleɪəʳ/ [n C] someone who belongs to a sports team or who regularly does a sport: *One of the players had been injured, and had to leave the field.* | **baseball/basketball etc player** *Kelleher was a star basketball player in high school and college.*

sportsman/sportswoman /'spɔːʳtsmən, 'spɔːʳtsˌwʊmən/ [n C] someone who is good at sport, especially someone who does it as their job: *Every top sportsman needs the motivation of a fresh challenge.* | *Today's professional sportsmen can expect to earn enormous sums of money.* | *Mrs Hashimoto described herself as a keen sportswoman, fond of golf, tennis and swimming.*

athlete /'æθliːt/ [n C] someone who is very good at sport, especially someone who does sports such as running, throwing things, or jumping over high bars: *The way he got to that ball shows what a superb athlete he is.* | *Over 150 athletes will compete in the Indoor Championships at Gateshead International Stadium.* | *It was discovered that three of our Olympic athletes had taken drugs.*

6 a group of people who play against another group

- team
- side
- captain

team /tiːm/ [n C with singular or plural verb in British English] a group of people who play together against another group in a sport: *The women's team were beaten 6-2.* | **football/baseball/cricket etc team** *I think the Yankees are one of the coolest baseball teams around.* | **support a team** (=like it best and want it to win) *Which football team do you support?* | **be in a team** British /**be on a team** American *If you want to be on the team, you have to turn up for regular training.*

side /saɪd/ [n C] British one of two teams who are playing against each other: *Supporters of both sides braved the cold wet weather to watch the match.* | *Our side only needed one more goal to win.*

captain /'kæptɨn/ [n C] the main player in a team, who tells the other players what to do: *The captain must have given his team quite a talking-to at half time.* | **+ of** *Who's the captain of England?* | **team captain** *Shelley's the girls' team captain this year.*

7 a place where you do a sport

- field
- pitch
- court
- leisure centre/complex
- gym
- pool/swimming pool
- stadium

field /fiːld/ [n C] a large area of ground, usually covered in grass, where team sports are played: *The crowd cheered as the players ran onto the field.* | **baseball/football/sports etc field** *The football field was too muddy to play on, so the game was cancelled* | *Some open spaces north of the city will be made into sports fields for leisure activities.* | **playing field** *Several school playing fields have been sold off to raise money.*

pitch /pɪtʃ/ [n C] British a sports field: *Some of the fans rushed onto the pitch at the end of the match* | **cricket/football etc pitch** *The village has attractive playing fields, with a football and cricket pitch.*

court /kɔːʳt/ [n C] an area with lines painted on the ground, where two people or teams play a game such as tennis or basketball: *The courts are floodlit at night so that you can play all the year round.* | **tennis/basketball/squash etc court** *The new leisure complex has a sauna, jacuzzi, swimming pool and tennis courts.*

leisure centre/complex /ˈleʒəʳ ˌsentəʳ, ˌkɒmpleks‖ˈliː-, ˌkɑːm-/ [n C] British a building where you can do various different sports: *The council is planning to build a multi-million pound leisure centre outside the town.*

gym /dʒɪm/ [n C] a building where there are machines that you can use to do exercises that make you fitter and stronger, or where you can do exercise classes etc. A **gym** is also a large room that is built especially for sports to be played in, for example in a school or university: *I've just signed up for an exercise class at the gym.* | *Ed goes to the gym to do weight training several times a week.* | *It was raining, so we had to play football in the gym this afternoon.*

pool/swimming pool /puːl, ˈswɪmɪŋ puːl/ [n C] a place where you can swim, consisting of a large hole in the ground that has been built and filled with water, either outdoors or inside a building: *The house, with its own tennis court and swimming-pool, is for sale at £700.000.* | *There's an open air pool at Woodstock that's great when it's really hot.* | *What we want is a hotel with a big heated pool, in case it rains.*

stadium /ˈsteɪdiəm/ [n C] a large sports field with seats all around it, where people go to watch sports: *The stadium has a capacity of at least 10,000.* | **football/baseball/sports stadium** *Denver has a new airport, a new baseball stadium, and a reputation as a good place to live.*

8 the person who makes sure that players obey the rules

- referee/umpire
- judges

referee/umpire /ˌrefəˈriː, ˈʌmpaɪəʳ/ [n C] the person who makes sure that the players obey the rules and decides if points have been won according to the rules. Use **referee** about football, basketball, hockey, and boxing. Use **umpire** about baseball, cricket, and tennis: *To United's disbelief, the referee failed to award the goal.* | *He made no attempt to hide his disgust at the umpire's decision, which cost him the match.* —**referee/umpire** [v I/T] *Who's refereeing the match?*

judges /ˈdʒʌdʒɪz/ [n plural] the people who decide which person is the best in a competition such as skating, horse-riding etc, where people do not compete in teams: *The judges awarded first prize to 14-year-old Amanda Colton, on her horse, Donna.*

9 the points you get when you play a sport

- point
- score
- goal

point /pɔɪnt/ [n C] a unit used to show what you have achieved in a sport or game: *Steve Jones is 15 points ahead.* | *Damon Hill led the Formula 1 Championship, with 58 points from 6 races.* | **get/score a point** *We lost the game when the Giants scored 14 points in the last quarter.* | *In darts, you get 50 points for hitting the bullseye.*

goal /gəʊl/ [n C] the point you get when you make the ball go into the net in sports such as football or hockey: *England's only goal came midway through the second half.* | **score a goal** *Venturini has scored the first goal in each of the two US victories in the Olympics.* | **get a goal** *Spurs got two goals in the last five minutes of the game.* | **an own goal** (=when a player sends the ball into the wrong net, and so scores a point for the other team) *We won, but only because of an 88th minute own goal from the other side.*

score /skɔːʳ/ [n C] the number of points that the two teams or players have in a game: *What's the score?* | *The score at half time was 12-18.* | **final score** (=the score at the end of the game) *After two hours and twenty minutes of play, the final score was 3-2.*

10 when two teams or players have the same score

- tie/draw
- be two all/be four all etc

tie /draw especially British /taɪ, drɔː/ [n C] when both players or teams have the same number of points at the end of a game: *'What was the result of the Barcelona v Real Madrid game?' 'It was a draw.'* | *The second game was very exciting, but it ended in a tie.*

be two all/be four all etc /biː ˌtuː ˈɔːl/ [v phrase] spoken say this when both players or teams have two points, four points etc in a game: *It's two all at the moment, but United seems to be the better team.* | *'What was the final score?' 'One all.'*

11 someone who watches a sport

- spectator
- supporter
- fan

spectator /spekˈteɪtəʳ‖ˈspekteɪ-/ [n C] someone who goes to a game and watches people playing a sport: *I'm not playing myself, I'm just a spectator.* | *Over 30,000 spectators turned out for the women's basketball match against Zaire.*

fan /fæn/ [n C] someone who likes a particular sport, or a particular team, and often goes to watch a game or watch a team play: *Thousands of fans queued to buy tickets.* | **football/cricket/hockey etc fan** *Over 200 British football fans were sent home after the violence in Rimini.* | **United/England/Yankee etc fans** *Leeds fans howled in anguish as Arsenal scored another goal.*

supporter /səˈpɔːʳtəʳ/ [n C] British someone who likes a particular sport or team and often goes to watch a game or watch a team play – use this especially about football: *Several supporters were arrested outside the stadium.* | *The town was full of football supporters, waiting for the big day.* | **Milan/Liverpool**

etc supporter *Milan supporters cheered as they scored their first goal in two games.* —**support** [v T] to like a particular team and want it to win: *'Which team do you support?' 'Oh, Manchester United, of course!'*

spread

to cover a larger area or affect a bigger group

1 fire/liquid/gas

- spread
- permeate
- run

spread /spred/ [v I] if fire, liquid, smoke etc **spreads**, it moves outwards in all directions to cover a larger area: *The forest fires in the Northwest are spreading out of control.* | **+ through/across/to etc** *By then, the flood water had spread across 80 square miles of farmland.* | *She knocked over her glass, and a dark pool of wine spread over the tablecloth.* | *The fire quickly spread to several nearby factories.*

permeate /ˈpɜːʳmieɪt/ [v T] if a gas, liquid, smoke etc **permeates** a space or substance, it gradually spreads through the whole of it: *Soon the gas had permeated the entire area.* | *The stench of smoke permeated the air.*

run /rʌn/ [v I] if a colour **runs**, it spreads beyond where it should be and begins to colour other things, especially because it has got wet: *I'm afraid the colors ran when I washed your shirt.* | *She had started crying and her make-up was running down her face.*

2 information/feelings/ideas/problems etc

- spread
- get around/go around
- circulate
- disseminate
- spill over

spread /spred/ [v I/T] if information, an idea, or a feeling **spreads**, or if you **spread** it, more and more people begin to know about it or be affected by it: *After she died at a San Jose hospital, word spread fast.* | *News of the disaster was spreading quickly.* | *Rumors about Amy spread through the school.* | *The lawsuit charged the magazine with spreading lies about the company and its products.* | **+ to/into/through etc** *Panic spread through downtown Port-au-Prince.* —**spread** [n U]

get around/go around ALSO **get round** British /ˌget əˈraʊnd, ˌgəʊ əˈraʊnd, ˌget ˈraʊnd/ [phr v I] if news or information **gets around** or **goes around**, people tell other people, so that soon a lot of people know about it: *News soon got around that Nick was back in Barnstable.* | *It's a small place, so news and gossip gets around pretty quickly.* | *It didn't take long for word to get around that Moore was leaving the company.*

circulate /ˈsɜːʳkjᵍleɪt/ [v I] if news, information, stories etc **circulate**, they spread through a large group of people, especially because each person tells it to someone else: *The organization's intranet system allows information to circulate rapidly.* | *Rumors began circulating that she was seriously ill.* | **+ among** *The letter was circulated among news organizations nationwide.*

disseminate /dɪˈsemᵻneɪt/ [v T] formal to spread information, ideas etc as widely as possible, especially in order to influence the way people think or behave: *Racist messages are being widely disseminated via the Internet.* | *The Health Education Council is the central agency for disseminating information about disease prevention.* —**dissemination** /dɪˌsemᵻˈneɪʃən/ [n U] *It is very dangerous for a government to have complete control over the dissemination of information within a country.*

spill over /ˌspɪl ˈəʊvəʳ/ [phr v I] if a problem or bad situation **spills over**, it spreads beyond the place or situation in which it starts, and begins to affect other places, people, or areas of activity **+ to/into/from etc** *It is easy to allow personal emotions to spill over into your work.* | *Government chiefs are worried that the refugee problem might spill over from neighboring countries.*

3 when a disease spreads

- spread
- go around
- infectious
- catch
- catching
- contagious

see also **illness/disease**

spread /spred/ [v I/T] if a disease **spreads** or **is spread**, it is passed from one person to another, and it affects more and more people: *Malaria, spread by mosquitoes, is one of the biggest public health problems in Africa.* | *AIDS is not spread by common everyday contact.* | **+ through/to/across/from** *Cholera is spreading through the refugee camps at an alarming rate.* | *Meyer and his team were the first to show how the disease spreads from animals to humans.* —**spread** [n U] **+ of** *The only way to prevent the spread of tuberculosis is to cure those infected by the disease.*

go around ALSO **go round** British /ˌgəʊ əˈraʊnd, ˌgəʊ ˈraʊnd/ [phr v I/T] if an illness **goes around**, it spreads from one person to another, especially in a school, office etc: *There's some type of throat infection going around at the moment.* | *If one child gets flu, it seems to go round the entire school within a week.*

infectious /ɪnˈfekʃəs/ [adj] an **infectious** disease is spread by being passed from one person to another: *Heavy drinkers are generally more susceptible to infectious diseases.* | *Doctors say that the disease is most infectious in the first twenty-four hours.* | **highly infectious** (=very infectious) *The vaccine protects against Hepatitis B, a highly infectious virus.*

catch /kætʃ/ [v T] to get an illness from another person – use this especially about illnesses that are not very serious: *Kristen has the flu, so I guess we'll all catch it.* | *Dion caught a cold on vacation.*

catching /ˈkætʃɪŋ/ [adj not before noun] informal an illness or condition that is **catching**, especially one that is not very serious, can spread from one person to another: *I hope Shelly's cold isn't catching.* | *I'm keeping Timmy home from school. He has measles and you know how catching it is.*

contagious /kənˈteɪdʒəs/ [adj] an illness that is **contagious** can spread easily from one person to another, especially by touch: *Most eye infections are contagious.* | **highly contagious** (=very contagious) *Chicken pox is highly contagious.*

4 to spread things over a wide area

- spread
- scatter

spread /spred/ [v T] *The wind spreads the seeds so that the plants can reproduce.* | **spread sth over/**

across/ through etc *A single tractor was slowly spreading fertilizer over a huge wheatfield.*

scatter /ˈskætəʳ/ [v T] to spread things over a wide area in an irregular and unplanned way: *The storm scattered tiles everywhere.* | **scatter sth over/ around/across etc** *Why don't you scatter a few cushions around the room?*

5 when people or things are spread over a wide area

- scattered
- spread out
- sprawling
- dotted
- strewn

scattered /ˈskætəʳd/ [adj not before noun] things that are **scattered** are spread over a large area in an irregular or untidy way **+ about/over/among etc** *There were books scattered all about their cottage.* | *Pieces of twisted metal and rusted pipe lay scattered around the yard.*

spread out /ˌspred ˈaʊt/ [adj phrase not before noun] things that are **spread out** are spread over a large area with a lot of space between them **+ on/among/across** *Diane had her newspaper spread out all over the floor.* | *Several small cabins were spread out across the property.*

sprawling /ˈsprɔːlɪŋ/ [adj only before noun] spread across a wide area – use this about towns, buildings, or groups of buildings that you think take up too much space and are ugly or unpleasant: *The sprawling conference and resort center even has its own transportation system.* | *a sprawling city of 2.6 million*

dotted /ˈdɒtɪ̵d‖ˈdɑːt-/ [adj not before noun] if a number of things of the same type are **dotted** around an area, they are spread over it irregularly and unevenly **+ around/along/here and there etc** *All we saw were a few workmen's cottages dotted here and there along the road.* | *Picnic tables were dotted among the trees.* | **+ with** *Their street was dotted with burned-out and boarded-up buildings.*

strewn /struːn/ [adj not before noun] spread unevenly in a way that looks very untidy **+ over/around etc** *Clothes were strewn all over the bedroom floor.* | **+ with** *Glover's yard was strewn with garbage and builders' debris.*

6 when people go in many directions

- spread
- scatter
- spread out
- fan out
- split up

spread /spred/ [v I] **+ northwards/eastwards etc** *Refugees have entered the south of the country and are spreading northwards.*

scatter /ˈskætəʳ/ [v I] if a group of people **scatters**, everyone suddenly moves in different directions, especially in order to escape from danger: *When a police van drove by, the boys scattered.* | *At the sound of gunfire, the crowd scattered in all directions.*

spread out /ˌspred ˈaʊt/ [phr v I/T] if a group of people **spreads out**, each person moves into a position where they are as far from the others as possible: *'Spread out!' the sergeant shouted. 'I want the whole area searched.'* | *I'm sure you'd be more comfortable if you spread yourselves out a little.* | **+ across/ through etc** *Members of the tribe are spread out over hundreds of square miles.*

fan out /ˌfæn ˈaʊt/ [phr v I] if a group of people who are searching for someone or something **fans out**, they spread themselves across an area in order to make sure that they search the whole area: *The men were told to fan out and begin the search.* | *Scores of FBI agents fanned out on Monday to interview potential witnesses.*

split up /ˌsplɪt ˈʌp/ [phr v I] if a group of people **split up**, they decide not to stay together as a group because they will be able to move faster, find something more easily etc if they are alone or in smaller groups: *The U.N. team split up to inspect several sites in the south of the country.* | **split up into groups/ teams/twos etc** *We'd have a much better chance of finding the child if we split up into groups.*

7 to spread butter, glue etc on a surface

- spread
- smear

spread /spred/ [v T] to put a thin layer of a soft substance, such as butter or glue, on a surface, so that it covers it **spread sth on/over sth** *Make sure that you spread the glue on both surfaces.* | *He spread plaster on the walls.* | *Spread the frosting over the warm pastries.* | **spread sth with sth** *She spread the toast with butter and jam.*

smear /smɪəʳ/ [v T] to spread a liquid or soft substance over a surface, especially carelessly or when you do not have to keep it within an exact area **smear sth on/smear on sth** *'What time did we say we'd meet them?' she asked, smearing on a bright red lipstick.* | **smear sth with** *Before setting out on their walk, they smeared themselves with sunblock.*

8 to open something out and arrange it on a surface

- spread/spread out
- lay out

spread/spread out /spred, ˌspred ˈaʊt/ [v T/phr v T] to open something such as a sheet, a map, or a newspaper, and arrange it so that it lies flat on a table, the floor, or another surface **spread out sth** *Jim spread out a blanket for her to sit on.* | **spread sth out/over/on etc** *Spread the map out and let's have a look.* | *I spread the towels over the radiator to dry.*

lay out /ˌleɪ ˈaʊt/ [phr v T] to spread something on a table, floor etc, especially so that it can be more easily seen or used later **lay sth out** *They spent over an hour laying the food out for the party.* | **lay out sth** *I laid all four bathing suits out on the counter and tried to picture myself in one of them.*

spy

to secretly collect information about an enemy government or competing organization

RELATED WORDS

- to secretly watch someone *see* **watch (5)**
- *see also* **secret, find out**

1 to spy

- spy
- espionage
- be in the pay of
- infiltrate
- counterespionage

spy /spaɪ/ [v I] to secretly collect information about an enemy government: *A former US diplomat has* *confessed to spying.* | **+ on** *For years the satellite spied on secret weapon bases.* | **+ for** *Philby had been spying for the Russians for several years.* —**spying** [n U] *The 11 men had allegedly been involved in spying.* | *He had been accused of spying and held without trial for ten years.*

espionage /ˈespiənɑːʒ/ [n U] the collecting of political, military, or industrial secrets from another country or organization: *Zakharov, a KGB agent, was charged with espionage.* | **industrial espionage** (=the collecting of secrets about a competing company) *The banks take precautions to prevent any attempts at industrial espionage while confidential documents are on the premises.*

be in the pay of /biː ɪn ðə ˈpeɪ ɒv/ [v phrase] if someone **is in the pay of** a country or organization, they are being paid by that country or organization to spy for them: *Before becoming President, the general was in the pay of the CIA.* | *There were persistent rumours that the former head of British Intelligence was in the pay of the Soviet Union.*

infiltrate /ˈɪnfɪltreɪt‖ɪnˈfɪltreɪt, ˈɪnfɪl-/ [v T] to secretly join a group or organization whose principles or activities you strongly oppose, in order to find out more about them, or to harm them in some way: *The Communists effectively infiltrated the government and the political parties.* | *Police attempts to infiltrate neo-Nazi groups have been largely unsuccessful.* | *Everyone knew the organization had been infiltrated by government agents, but could not prove it.* —**infiltrator** [n C] *There has always been a danger of enemy infiltrators in the organization.* —**infiltration** /ˌɪnfɪlˈtreɪʃən/ [n U] *Finally, weakened by infiltration and sabotage, Black Aid Action folded in 1967.*

counterespionage /ˌkaʊntərˈespiənɑːʒ/ [n U] the activity of trying to find out about and prevent an enemy from spying in your own country: *His novels deal with the world of spies, espionage and counterespionage.* | *the murder of two counterespionage officers*

2 someone who spies

- spy
- agent
- mole

spy /spaɪ/ [n C] *He was suspected of having been a spy during the war.* | *The job of the secret police was to hunt down spies and traitors.*

agent /ˈeɪdʒənt/ [n C] someone working for a government or police department who tries to get secret information about another country or organization: *Wray was filmed passing money to an enemy agent.* | *a book of memoirs written by a retired MI5 agent, Peter Wright* | **secret agent** *He had been a secret agent of the enemy all along.*

mole /məʊl/ [n C] someone who works inside an organization who gives secret information to someone on the outside, for example a newspaper: *The government suspects there is a mole who is leaking information to the press.* | *The mole was discovered to be the 25-year-old secretary of the minister.*

squash

RELATED WORDS

▸ *see also* **press, flat/not flat**

1 to press something so hard that it breaks, folds, or becomes flat

- squash
- crush
- flatten
- mash
- grind
- pound
- press
- screw up
- crumple/crumple up

squash /skwɒʃ‖skwɑːʃ, skwɔːʃ/ [v T] to damage something, especially something soft, by pressing it and making it flat: *Someone sat on my hat and squashed it.* | *He wouldn't even squash a fly, let alone murder someone.* | **squash sth flat** *He squashed the can flat between his hands.*

crush /krʌʃ/ [v T] to press something so hard that it gets damaged or broken into pieces: *His leg was crushed in the accident.* | *Coconuts have to be crushed in order to extract their oil.* | *He closed his fist over the flower, crushing it into a pulp.*

flatten /ˈflætn/ [v T] to squash something until it is completely flat: *He fell against me so heavily I thought he was going to flatten me.* | *Her little car was completely flattened in the accident.*

mash /mæʃ/ [v T] to press fruit or cooked vegetables with a fork or similar tool, until they are soft and smooth: *Mash the bananas and add them to the mixture.* | **mash sth up/mash up sth** *Boil the potatoes and then mash them up.*

grind /graɪnd/ [v T] to break something such as coffee beans or corn into powder, using a machine or special tool: *Grind some black pepper over the salad.* | **grind sth into sth** *These huge stones were once used for grinding wheat into flour.*

pound /paʊnd/ [v T] to press or hit something repeatedly, especially using a tool, so that it breaks into very small pieces or becomes soft or flat: *He pounded some garlic and ginger and put it in the pan.* | **pound sth flat** *Here the loose earth had been pounded flat by thousands of feet.*

press /pres/ [v T] to crush a fruit or vegetable using special equipment to remove the juice, oil etc: *Friends come to help us gather the crop and press the grapes.* | *Enough olives had been gathered and pressed to produce 1000 litres of cooking oil.*

screw up /ˌskruː ˈʌp/ [phr v T] to press a piece of paper or cloth into the shape of a ball **screw up sth** *Sally screwed up the letter she was writing and threw it into the wastebasket.* | **screw sth/it up** *He screwed his handkerchief up into a ball and put it in his pocket.*

crumple/crumple up /ˈkrʌmpəl, ˌkrʌmpəl ˈʌp/ [v T/phr v T] to press a piece of paper or cloth so that it becomes smaller or bent: *He crumpled the cheque and threw it across the room.* | *Crumple up the bedclothes so it looks as though you slept there.*

2 when something has been squashed

- squashed
- crushed
- flattened
- mashed
- ground

squashed /skwɒʃt‖skwɑːʃt, skwɔːʃt/ [adj] something soft that is **squashed** is damaged because it has been pressed and made flatter: *He held out a squashed packet of cigarettes and offered me one.* | *We can't give her those chocolates – they're all squashed.*

crushed /krʌʃt/ [adj] something that is **crushed** has been squashed and broken by something heavy:

Remove the butter from the heat and stir in the crushed biscuits. | *The dog hurtled through the garden, leaving a trail of crushed plants.*

flattened /ˈflætnd/ [adj] squashed until completely flat: *There was a flattened Coca-Cola can on the ground.* | *a mountain of flattened cardboard boxes*

mashed /mæʃt/ [adj] **mashed** food has been squashed with something such as a fork until it is soft and smooth: *He ate the mashed potatoes but not the meat.* | *a spoonful of mashed swede*

ground /graʊnd/ [adj] **ground** coffee, corn, or other food has been made into powder using a special machine or tool: *freshly ground black coffee* | *ground almonds*

stand

WHAT'S HERE

- **to stand upright on your feet** see **1 to 4**
- **to accept an unpleasant situation** see **5 to 7**

to stand upright on your feet

RELATED WORDS

- to get up after being asleep *see* **wake up/get up**
- *see also* **sit, lie, bend (2)**

1 to be in a standing position

- **stand**
- **stand up**
- **be on your feet**
- **on tiptoe/on tiptoes**
- **lean**

stand /stænd/ [v I] to be on your feet in an upright position: *There were no seats, so we had to stand.* | **+ next to/beside/in etc** *I was standing next to the entrance.* | *A young girl stood in the doorway, sheltering from the rain.* | *When we entered, he was standing by his desk.* | *A hundred policemen stood arm-in-arm in front of the cathedral.* | **stand doing sth** (=stand while you are doing something) *She stood watching him as he turned to go.* | **stand and do sth** *I stood and stared at him in amazement.* | **stand up straight** (=with your back and legs straight) *The ceilings were so low that Mark couldn't stand up straight.* | **stand still** (=stand without moving) *Stand still while I brush your hair.* | *He stood still, his feet rooted to the ground in fear.*

stand up /ˌstænd ˈʌp/ [phr v I] to stand rather than be sitting, lying down, or kneeling: *It's generally better to do this exercise standing up.* | *The seats were all taken and we had to stand up all the way from Tokyo to Nagoya.*

be on your feet /biː ɒn jɔːʳ ˈfiːt/ [v phrase] to be standing, especially for a long time, with the result that you feel tired – use this especially about people who have to stand and walk a lot in their jobs: *You go. I've been on my feet all day, and I need a rest.* | *She'd been on her feet all morning without once sitting down.*

on tiptoe/on tiptoes ALSO **on your tiptoes** /ɒn ˈtɪptəʊ(z), ɒn jɔːʳ ˈtɪptəʊz/ [adv] standing on your toes, especially when you stretch your body in order to see something or reach something: *She was up on her tiptoes, with her arm about his neck.* | **stand on tiptoe** *She stood on her tiptoes to open the high window.* | *People were standing on tiptoe to try and see what was happening.*

lean /liːn/ [v I] to stand while resting part of your body against a wall, a table etc **+ against/on** *Kay was leaning against the wall, smoking a cigarette.* | *Joe leaned on the gate and watched as they drove away.*

2 to stand after sitting or lying down

- **get up**
- **stand up**
- **get to your feet**
- **rise**
- **stand to do sth**

get up /ˌget ˈʌp/ [phr v I] to stand after you have been sitting, bending, or lying down: *She got up and turned off the TV.* | *I can't get up. Give me a hand, will you?* | *I watched how slowly he got up, how stiff he seemed.* | **get up from a chair/seat/sofa etc** *Max got up from his chair and shook her hand.* | *When Maura came in, he got up from the table and poured the coffee.* | **get up off the floor/ground/grass etc** *One of her friends helped her to get up off the floor.* | *I got up off the grass and strolled over to where Rob was sitting.* | **get up to do sth/get up and do sth** *I was left with Maria when the others got up to dance.*

stand up /ˌstænd ˈʌp/ [phr v I] to stand after you have been sitting: *'I have to go now,' she said, standing up.* | *Could you all stand up please.* | *He stood up to shake Mel's hand.* | *Abruptly she stood up, and got ready to leave.*

get to your feet /ˌget tə jɔːʳ ˈfiːt/ [v phrase] to stand up, especially slowly or when it is difficult for you: *He got to his feet, and we shook hands.* | *My attorney got slowly to his feet, breathing heavily.*

rise /raɪz/ [v I] formal to stand up – use this especially in descriptions of events and formal ceremonies: *The old woman rose stiffly and held out her hand.* | *The congregation rose as the bride entered the cathedral.* | **rise from your seat/the table/a chair etc** *The chairman had already risen from his seat and was beginning his speech.* | **rise to your feet** *Audience members rose to their feet, cheering and clapping.*

stand to do sth /ˌstænd tə ˈduː (sth)/ [v phrase] to stand up in order to do something, especially at a special event or formal occasion: *The Senate stood to welcome the new President.* | *Would you all please stand to sing hymn 106?*

3 to stand with your back straight

- **stand up straight**
- **stand to attention**
- **draw/pull yourself up to your full height**
- **straighten up**

stand up straight /ˌstænd ʌp ˈstreɪt/ [v phrase] *Stand up straight with your back against the wall.* | *The pain in his stomach was so severe that he could no longer stand up straight.*

stand to attention ALSO **stand at attention** /ˌstænd tʊ əˈtenʃən, ˌstænd ət əˈtenʃən/ [v phrase] if someone such as a soldier or a police officer **stands to attention**, they stand with their backs straight, their arms straight down by their sides, and their feet close together: *The colonel gave the order for the men to stand to attention.* | *We stood at attention until we were given permission to leave.*

draw/pull yourself up to your full height /ˌdrɔː, ˌpʊl jɔːʳself ˌʌp tə jɔːʳ ˌfʊl ˈhaɪt/ [v phrase] to stand up as straight as you can because you are angry with someone or are determined to make them listen to you: *I drew myself up to my full height and informed him that the President had sent me down here personally.* | *Trembling inside, I stepped out of the car and pulled myself up to my full height to face my adversary.*

straighten up /ˌstreɪtn ˈʌp/ [phr v I] to stand up after bending down low: *She bent over the body, and when she straightened up there were tears in her eyes.* | *If you're lifting something heavy, be careful not to hurt your back when you straighten up.*

4 to put your foot on something

- step on/in
- stamp on

step on/in ALSO **tread on/in** British /ˈstep ɒn, ɪn, ˈtred ɒn, ɪn/ [phr v T] to put your foot down on something while you are standing or walking, especially accidentally: *I think I must have stepped on some glass.* | *I trod in some mud in the park, and tracked it into the house.* | *Ow, you trod on my foot, you clumsy brute!*

stamp on /ˈstæmp ɒn / [phr v T] to deliberately put your foot down very hard on something: *There was a big cockroach in the kitchen and Barbara stamped on it.* | *In a recent incident, youths stamped on a police officer's head as she lay injured.*

to accept an unpleasant situation

RELATED WORDS

- *see also* **accept (5), bad**

5 to accept an unpleasant situation

- put up with
- can stand
- bear
- tolerate
- endure
- take/handle
- live with
- be hard to stomach
- grin and bear it

put up with /ˌpʊt ˈʌp wɪð/ [phr v T] to accept an annoying situation or someone's annoying behaviour, without trying to stop it or change it: *I don't know how you put up with all this noise day after day.* | *You see what I have to put up with – the kids never stop arguing.* | *Well, you put up with the danger and bad conditions, because you need to feed your family.*

can stand /kən ˈstænd/ [v phrase not in progressive or passive] to accept or be forced to accept an unpleasant situation: *Don't bring me your problems, I've already got as much trouble as I can stand.* | *There are cats in every room. I don't know how she can stand it.* | **+ doing sth** *I don't think I'll be able to stand sharing an office with Dana.* | **stand another hour/minute/ moment etc** *Can you stand another minute of this awful music? Shall I turn it off?*

bear /beəʳ/ [v T not usually in progressive or passive] to accept pain or an unpleasant situation that makes you angry, sad, or upset: *My leg really hurts – I'm not sure how much longer I can bear it.* | *Talking to a counsellor can help divorcees to bear the pain of separation.* | *The trial was a great scandal but she bore it all with courage and dignity.* | **be hard to bear** *Her loneliness was hard to bear, after her husband died.*

tolerate /ˈtɒləreɪt‖ˈtɑː-/ [v T] to accept an annoying situation or someone's annoying behaviour, without trying to stop it or change it. **Tolerate** is more formal than **put up with**: *She seems to be able to tolerate any kind of behaviour from the students.* | *For years, the workers have had to tolerate low wages and terrible working conditions.* | *If you can tolerate the side-effects, HRT can help the symptoms enormously.*

endure /ɪnˈdjʊəʳ‖ɪnˈdʊər/ [v T] written to accept or be forced to accept a very unpleasant or difficult situation for a long time: *She endured a barrage of open abuse and racism during her time at college.* | *The people in this country have endured almost a decade of economic hardship.*

take/handle /teɪk, ˈhændl/ [v T] informal to accept an unpleasant situation or someone's unpleasant behaviour without becoming upset: *I've tried to be understanding, but quite honestly, this is more than I can take.* | *Tell me what happened – I can handle it.* | *Are you going to argue with me, or are you just going to stand there and take it?*

live with /ˈlɪv wɪð/ [phr v T] to accept an unpleasant situation as a permanent part of your life that you cannot change: *You have to learn to live with stress.* | *I found the burden of guilt very difficult to live with.* | *None of us really like the new system, but we've got to learn to live with it.* | **live with yourself** (=accept something bad or wrong that you have done) *You should be careful before you do anything rash. Remember, you'll have to live with yourself afterwards.*

be hard to stomach /biː ˌhɑːʳd tə ˈstʌmək/ [v phrase] to be difficult for you to accept: *Every year the Christmas shopping season seems to start earlier, a fact which many people find hard to stomach.* | *I found this lecture from Chris of all people hard to stomach.*

grin and bear it /ˌgrɪn ən ˈbeər ɪt/ [v phrase] spoken to accept an unpleasant or difficult situation as happily as you can, because you cannot change it: *Well, I said to myself, I'll just have to grin and bear it.* | *The message was clear – no matter how insulting passengers became, we couldn't do anything but grin and bear it.*

6 something unpleasant that you can stand

- bearable
- tolerable

bearable /ˈbeərəbəl/ [adj not before noun] a situation or type of behaviour that is **bearable** is difficult or unpleasant, but you are just able to bear it: *The only things that made her life bearable were the occasional visits from her grandchildren.* | *His leg hasn't quite healed yet, but pain-killers make it bearable.*

tolerable /ˈtɒlərəbəl‖ˈtɑː-/ [adj] a situation that is **tolerable** is bad but you are able to accept it and deal with it: *It was a tolerable existence, but only just.* | *The new measures can only hope to keep fraud at tolerable levels.* | *An active social life may make the boredom of work more tolerable.*

7 when a situation is so bad that you cannot stand it

- can't stand
- can't take/handle
- can't stomach
- can't abide
- unbearable
- intolerable
- unacceptable

can't stand ALSO **can't bear** especially British /ˌkɑːnt ˈstænd, ˌkɑːnt ˈbeəʳ‖ˌkænt-/ [v phrase] to be unable to accept an unpleasant situation: *Europeans never stay there for long. They can't stand the heat.* | *I can't bear the smell of stale cigarette smoke in her hair.* | **can't stand/bear the thought of sth** *She couldn't stand the thought of losing her children.* | **can't stand/bear to do sth/can't stand/bear doing sth** *I couldn't bear to listen to her screams.*

can't take/handle /ˌkɑːnt ˈteɪk, ˈhændl‖ˌkænt-/ [v phrase] especially spoken to be unable to accept an unpleasant situation without becoming angry or upset, especially when someone's behaviour is not fair or reasonable: *Careful what you say – he can't take criticism.* | *She just keeps crying and throwing tantrums – I can't handle much more of it.* | **can't take/handle sth any more** *I just couldn't take it any more. I left the next day.*

can't stomach /ˌkɑːnt ˈstʌmək‖ˌkænt-/ [v phrase] to be unable to stand something because thinking about it makes you feel sick or angry: *He really can't stomach the sight of blood.*

can't abide /ˌkɑːnt əˈbaɪd‖ˌkænt-/ [v phrase] formal to be completely unable to stand someone or something that is very annoying: *If there's one thing I cannot abide, it's spoilt children.* | *Mary couldn't abide shopping on Saturdays because the stores were always so crowded.*

unbearable /ʌnˈbeərəbəl/ [adj] something that is **unbearable**, such as a pain or a bad situation, is too bad for you to deal with or live with: *Without him, my life would be unbearable.* | *The stench from the sink was almost unbearable.* | *The strain eventually became unbearable, and Adam started seeing a psychiatrist.*

intolerable /ɪnˈtɒlərəbəl‖-ˈtɑː-/ [adj] too difficult, unpleasant, or annoying to stand: *Living conditions at the camp were intolerable.* | *Passengers faced intolerable delays and disruption due to the bad weather conditions.* | *All the media attention during the trial had put the family under intolerable strain.* —**intolerably** [adv] *I'm sorry, I behaved intolerably.* | *an intolerably stupid question*

unacceptable /ˌʌnəkˈseptəbəl/ [adj] something that is **unacceptable** is wrong and cannot be accepted or allowed to continue: *Most women said they thought the ruling was unfair and unacceptable.* | *The plan was rejected because it involved an 'unacceptable risk to public safety'.* | *We regard the idea of being able to choose the sex of your baby as wholly unacceptable.* —**unacceptably** [adv] *The payroll tax is an unacceptably heavy burden on working Americans.* | *His work is unacceptably sloppy.*

start

WHAT'S HERE

● **to start doing sth**	see **1 to 9**
● **to start happening**	see **10 to 12**
● **to make sth start**	see **13 to 17**

to start doing sth

RELATED WORDS

opposite: **stop, finish**

▸ *see also* **beginning, first**

1 to start doing something

- ▸ **start**
- ▸ **begin**
- ▸ **get down to**
- ▸ **start on**
- ▸ **set about/set to work**
- ▸ **proceed to do sth**
- ▸ **settle down to**
- ▸ **launch into**
- ▸ **embark on/upon**
- ▸ **come to/grow to/get to**
- ▸ **get cracking**

start /stɑːʳt/ [v I/T] *We can't start until Carol gets here.* | *I'm starting a new job next week.* | *Have you started that book yet?* (=started reading it) | **+ doing sth** *I've just started learning German.* | *It was getting dark so we started looking for a place to stay the night.* | **+ to do sth** *Halfway through the performance, she started to feel a little faint.* | *Outside, it was starting to rain.*

begin /bɪˈgɪn/ [v I/T] to start doing something. **Begin** is more formal than **start** and is used especially in written English: *Once the children were quiet, the teacher began.* | *They began their holiday in Italy, and then went on to Greece.* | **+ to do sth** *More and more people are beginning to do their shopping on-line.* | *'What do you mean?' she said, beginning to laugh.* | **+ doing sth** *The audience suddenly began shouting and cheering.*

get down to /ˌget ˈdaʊn tuː/ [phr v T] to finally start doing something, especially work, after you have been avoiding doing it or after something has prevented you from doing it: *Come on Sam – it's time you got down to some homework.* | **+ to doing sth** *When the summer comes, we must get down to painting the outside of the house.* | **get down to business** *OK, can everyone take a seat now, and we'll get down to business.*

start on /ˈstɑːʳt ɒn / [phr v T] to start a piece of work that will take a fairly long time: *The exam was almost over and I hadn't even started on question 3.* | *It was time to start on all those little jobs around the house that he'd been putting off.* | *We can't start on the building work until planning permission comes through.*

set about/set to work /ˈset əbaʊt, ˌset tə ˈwɜːʳk/ [phr v T/v phrase] to start a long and fairly difficult piece of work, especially in an energetic and determined way: *Philip set about the task with a great deal of energy and enthusiasm.* | *Why don't we set to work really early, and try to get it finished in one day?* | **+ doing sth** *If there is a serious problem, it's far better to admit it and set about tackling it.* | **set to work to do sth** *Workmen had already set to work to clear the fallen trees.* | **set to work on sth** *Once in power, the government set to work on major reforms to the tax system.*

proceed to do sth /prəˌsiːd tə ˈduː (sth)/ [v phrase] to start doing something after you have finished doing something else: *Martin marched into the shop and proceeded to hurl abuse at the girl behind the counter.* | *After listening carefully to my advice, she proceeded to do the exact opposite!*

settle down to /ˌsetl ˈdaʊn tuː/ [v phrase] to start doing something after a delay or interruption that has stopped you giving it your full attention: *After lunch the children settled down to finish their science projects.* | **+ to doing sth** *It was two o'clock before I could finally settle down to writing the next chapter.*

launch into /ˈlɔːntʃ ɪntuː/ [phr v T] to suddenly start a long speech or story, especially if you are criticizing something or giving an entertaining description of something: *Annie arrived late and immediately launched into a lengthy description of the terrible traffic on the roads.* | *At that point the* *young man stood up and launched into a passionate party-political speech.*

embark on/upon /ɪm'bɑːʳk ɒn, əpɒn / [phr v T] to start a large piece of work or an important activity, especially one that will be difficult or will take a long time: *In the 1950s China embarked on a massive program of industrialization and mechanization.* | *After leaving his office job, he embarked upon a highly successful writing career.*

come to/grow to/get to /'kʌm tuː, 'grəʊ tuː, 'get tuː/ [phr v T] to gradually start to like, fear, expect etc something over a period of time: *Rowling's latest book is full of all the magic and excitement that her young readers have come to expect.* | *At first I thought he was a bit strange, but I grew to like and respect him over the years.* | *My teacher said that this wasn't the kind of work that she'd come to expect of me.*

get cracking /ˌget 'krækɪŋ/ [v phrase] spoken informal to start doing something immediately, because you are in a hurry or there is a lot to do: *Come on! – get cracking. I want this whole house clean by the time I get back.* | *You'd better get cracking if you want to get to the airport by ten.*

2 to start an activity, job, speech etc by doing the first part of it

- start by/begin by
- start with/begin with
- lead off
- kick off with

start by/begin by /'stɑːʳt baɪ, bɪ'gɪn baɪ/ [v phrase not in passive] to do something as the first part of an activity or job **+ doing sth** *There were two interviewers and they began by asking me questions about my last job.* | *When you're drawing a face, you should start by trying to imagine the bones underneath.*

start with/begin with /'stɑːʳt wɪð, bɪ'gɪn wɪð/ [phr v T not in passive] to think about, introduce, or deal with something as the first part of an activity: *If I were you, I'd start with the easy questions.* | *The lecturer began with a short account of the history of the UN.* | *Decorating the place was a huge job, and we started with the kitchen and the hall.*

lead off /ˌliːd 'ɒf/ [phr v I/T not in passive] to start something such as a meeting or discussion by introducing a subject or speaking first: *Is there anyone here who would like to lead off the debate?* | *The Chief Executive led off by pointing out that a merger was only one option.* | **+ with** *We asked the sales director to lead off with the latest sales figures.*

kick off with /ˌkɪk 'ɒf wɪð / [phr v T not in passive] informal to do something as the first part of an activity or an event such as a party or a concert: *Let's kick off with an Indian meal somewhere, and go on to a club after that.* | **kick off sth with sth** *Phelps kicked off an outstanding night's music with a beautifully played Mozart Symphony.*

3 to be the person who starts something

- make the first move
- take the initiative

make the first move /meɪk ðə ˌfɜːʳst 'muːv/ [v phrase] to be the first one to do something in a situation where both sides feel nervous, embarrassed, angry etc: *I'd always been attracted to her, but I was too shy to make the first move.* | **+ to do sth** *The employees made the first move to end the strike.*

take the initiative /ˌteɪk ði ɪ'nɪʃətɪv/ [v phrase] to be the first one to do something in a situation, especially when you think people are being silly because they are waiting for someone else to do it first: *Everyone was standing around in silence, so I took the initiative and tried to explain why we had come.* | *The disarmament talks failed because neither side was prepared to risk taking the initiative.*

4 to start a journey

- set off/set out
- start for
- start off
- hit the road
- get going

▸ *see also* **travel**

set off/set out /ˌset 'ɒf, ˌset 'aʊt/ [phr v I] to start a long journey or start going somewhere, especially if your journey has been planned or has a special purpose: *What time do you have to set off in the morning?* | *We had meant to set out before lunch but nobody was ready to leave.* | **+ towards/along/in the direction of etc** *Packing herself a couple of sandwiches, she set off along the cliff path.* | *The weather had been fine on the morning that the climbers set out up the last part of the mountain.* | **+ for** *My mother was only twenty when she married my father and set off for Addis Ababa.* | **+ from** *The Royal Navy set out from Portsmouth on July 13th.* | **+ to do** *Columbus set out to discover America in the fifteenth century.*

start for /'stɑːʳt fɔːʳ/ [phr v T] to start a journey to a particular place: *When are you starting for Seattle?* | *It was already dark by the time we started for home.*

start off /ˌstɑːʳt 'ɒf / [phr v I] to start moving away from a place where you have been, especially if you are driving a car, riding a bicycle etc: *Before starting off you should check that your seat and mirrors are properly adjusted.* | **+ along/towards/down etc** *The riders got back on their horses and started off along the track again.*

hit the road /ˌhɪt ðə 'rəʊd/ [v phrase] informal to start a journey: *It's time we hit the road.* | *The group will be hitting the road again in the new year, in order to promote their new album.*

get going /ˌget 'gəʊɪŋ/ [v phrase] informal to start a journey or start going somewhere, especially when you are late or when there has been a delay: *Let's get going now or we'll miss the train.* | *The coach was supposed to leave at 10:30 but we eventually got going at 3 o'clock.* | *Get going, you two! Didn't you hear the school bell?*

5 to start doing something regularly

- start/begin
- take up
- turn to
- take to doing sth
- get into the habit of

start/begin /stɑːʳt, bɪ'gɪn/ [v T] to start doing something that you then do regularly. **Begin** is more formal than **start** and is used especially in written English **+ doing sth** *I started going to the gym two years ago.* | *She was only 16 when she began seeing Alan.* | **+ to do sth** *His parents got divorced last year – that's when he started to take drugs.*

take up /ˌteɪk 'ʌp/ [phr v T] to become interested in a sport or activity, and start to spend time doing it: *When did Bryan take up golf?* | *Your pictures are so good – you could take up painting as a profession.*

turn to /'tɜːʳn tuː/ [phr v T] to start doing something dangerous or illegal: *Hal turned to drinking after his wife and kids were killed in a car crash.* |

Research shows that young people without jobs are most likely to turn to crime.

take to doing sth /ˌteɪk tə ˈduːɪŋ (sth)/ [v phrase not in passive] to start doing something frequently, especially something that is annoying or worrying: *There's a big ginger cat that's taken to coming in our house at night.* | *My daughter took to spending hours alone in her room, only coming downstairs for meals.*

get into the habit of /ˌget ɪntə ðə ˈhæbɪt ɒv/ [v phrase] to start to do something so often that it becomes a habit: *I only used to have one or two cigarettes, but then I got into the habit of it.* | **+ of doing sth** *Try to get into the habit of planning your work at the beginning of the day.*

6 to help or encourage someone to start doing something new

- introduce sb to
- start sb on
- initiate sb into

introduce sb to /ˌɪntrəˈdjuːs (sb) tuː‖-ˈduːs-/ [v phrase] to make someone start doing something or start enjoying something, by telling them about it or showing it to them: *Her father introduced her to rock 'n' roll when she was a little girl.* | **introduce sb to doing sth** *It was my sports teacher who first introduced me to skiing.*

initiate sb into /ɪˈnɪʃieɪt (sb) ɪntuː / [v phrase] to give someone the chance to do something for the first time, especially something unusual or complicated: *People come to me to be initiated into meditation, as a way of handling stress.* | *He tried to initiate her into the mysteries of Chinese cooking.*

start sb on /ˈstɑːʳt (sb) ɒn / [v phrase] to make someone start doing something regularly, especially because it will be good for them: *Most parents start their babies on solid foods when they are about 4 months old.* | *The doctor said that he wants to start Dad on a special low-cholesterol diet.*

7 to start doing something again in a better way

- start afresh/make a fresh start/make a new start
- start over

start afresh/make a fresh start/make a new start /ˌstɑːʳt əˈfreʃ, meɪk ə ˌfreʃ ˈstɑːʳt, meɪk ə ˌnjuː ˈstɑːʳt‖-ˌnuː-/ [v phrase] to start doing something again from the beginning, because you want to do it better or differently from before: *I see the new job as a chance to start afresh.* | *The money we won made it possible for us to pay off all our debts and make a new start.* | *He's determined to make a fresh start when he gets out of prison.*

start over /ˌstɑːʳt ˈəʊvəʳ/ [phr v I] American to go back to the beginning of something and start again: *If you make a keying error, just delete it and start over.* | *In 1960 the family fled the island of Cuba and, like many others, started over in Miami.*

8 to start doing something successfully

- make a good start/get off to a good start
- get off to a flying start

make a good start/get off to a good start /meɪk ə ˌgʊd ˈstɑːʳt, get ˌɒf tʊ ə ˌgʊd ˈstɑːʳt/ [v phrase] *I haven't finished all my Christmas shopping yet but I've made a good start.* | *Chelsea got off to a good start with a victory over Southampton on the first day of the season.*

get off to a flying start /get ˌɒf tʊ ə ˌflaɪ-ɪŋ ˈstɑːʳt/ [v phrase] to start doing something very successfully: *Kate's got off to a flying start. She was promoted twice in the first six months.*

9 to start doing something unsuccessfully

- get off to a bad start
- false start
- get/start off on the wrong foot

get off to a bad start /get ˌɒf tʊ ə ˌbæd ˈstɑːʳt/ [v phrase] *I got off to a bad start at the interview by spilling my coffee all over my notes.* | *The senator got off to a bad start, twice forgetting the name of the town he was in.*

get/start off on the wrong foot /get, stɑːʳt ˌɒf ɒn ðə ˌrɒŋ ˈfʊt‖ -ˌrɔːŋ-/ [v phrase] to start something such as a relationship or job and be unsuccessful at the beginning, for example by unintentionally making people upset or angry: *What should I wear on my first day? I don't want to start off on the wrong foot.* | *John seems to have got off on the wrong foot with Angela – she won't even speak to him.*

false start /ˌfɔːls ˈstɑːʳt/ [n C] an unsuccessful attempt to start doing something such as a piece of work or a plan: *After a number of false starts, the Channel Tunnel between England and France finally went ahead in the late 80s.*

to start happening

RELATED WORDS

opposite: **stop, finish**

▸ *see also* **beginning, happen**

10 to start happening

- start/begin
- kick off
- open

start/begin /stɑːʳt, bɪˈgɪn/ [v I] **begin** is more formal than **start**, and is used especially in written English: *Do you know what time our first class starts?* | *My day starts at 5 or 6 o'clock, when the baby wakes up.* | *The movie was just beginning when Richard and James arrived.* | *Work on the new bridge will begin next year.*

open /ˈəʊpən/ [v I] if a play or show **opens**, it starts being shown to the public: *Andrew Lloyd Webber's new musical will open later this year.* | *A permanent exhibition of Moore's work will open next year.*

kick off /ˌkɪk ˈɒf / [phr v I] informal if a planned event such as a game or a meeting **kicks off**, it starts: *If the meeting kicks off on time, we should be finished by 12 o'clock.* | **+ with** *The carnival kicked off with a wonderful firework display.*

11 to start to exist

- come into being/existence
- arise
- be born
- spring up
- the arrival of

come into being/existence /ˌkʌm ɪntə ˈbiːɪŋ, ɪgˈzɪstəns/ [v phrase] if something such as an organization or a country **comes into being** or **into existence**, it starts to exist: *Pakistan came into existence as an independent country in 1947.* | *Darwin's theory of evolution explains how different species came into being.*

spring up /ˌsprɪŋ ˈʌp/ [phr v I] to suddenly start to exist in a very short period of time: *Dozens of websites have sprung up to provide information for travelers.* | *New dot.com companies are springing up all the time.*

arise /əˈraɪz/ [v I] if something such as a problem, a difficulty, or an argument **arises**, it appears or starts, usually as a result of something else happening: *When a conflict arises in the workplace, you should aim to repair the relationship as quickly as possible.* | **+ from/out of** *Low achievement at school often arises from poverty and bad social conditions.* | **if/when/should etc the need arise** (=if etc it becomes necessary) *All staff are expected to do some overtime, if the need arises.*

be born /biː ˈbɔːʳn/ [v phrase] if an important idea, group, or organization **is born**, it starts to exist – use this especially when you are describing the history of something: *With the invention of the electric guitar, rock 'n' roll was born.* | *Picasso was painting pictures in a Cubist style long before the Cubist movement was born.*

the arrival of /ði əˈraɪvəl ɒv/ [n phrase] when something new starts to exist or be used: *The arrival of the railroads after the Civil War produced a huge building boom in California.* | *the arrival of gene technology*

12 when something bad starts to happen

- break out
- outbreak
- erupt
- set in

break out /ˌbreɪk ˈaʊt/ [phr v I] to start happening – use this about unpleasant things like fires, wars, or diseases: *A fire broke out on the top floor of the building.* | *Late last night, fighting broke out between gangs of rival football fans.*

outbreak /ˈaʊtbreɪk / [n C] when something unpleasant starts happening, such as a fire, war, or disease: *Thousands of people died as the result of this latest cholera outbreak.* | **+ of** *There's been an outbreak of food poisoning at the hotel.* | *The system started to operate in late 1914, a few months after the outbreak of war in Europe.*

erupt /ɪˈrʌpt/ [v I] if fighting, violence etc **erupts**, it starts very suddenly: *A fight over a game of cards had erupted in the corner of the bar.* | *Massive and often violent protests erupted across the country.* | *Gang violence can erupt for no apparent reason.*

set in /ˌset ˈɪn/ [phr v I] if something bad **sets in**, for example bad weather or an illness, it starts and seems likely to continue: *It looks as if the rain has set in for the day.* | *The doctors operated immediately to prevent any infection setting in.* | *Worldwide economic recession set in during the early 1980s.*

to make sth start

RELATED WORDS

opposite: **stop**

▸ *see also* **beginning, cause**

13 to make something start happening

- start
- launch
- open
- initiate
- spark off
- set in motion
- get/start/set the ball rolling
- get things moving
- (let's) get this show on the road

start /stɑːʳt/ [v T] to make something **start** happening: *The police have already started an investigation.* | *The referee couldn't start the game because there were fans on the field.* | *A 'safe neighbourhood' campaign has been started by local residents.*

launch /lɔːntʃ/ [v T] **launch an attack/appeal/inquiry etc** to start a public or military activity, when there is a clear aim that you want to achieve: *Rebel forces launched an attack on the capital.* | *Police are launching a major murder inquiry.* | *The local hospital has launched a campaign to raise money for new X-ray equipment.*

open /ˈəʊpən/ [v T] **open an investigation/inquiry** to start an official process of gathering information about a particular problem, in order to find out what caused it or to find a solution: *Police have opened an investigation into the girl's disappearance.* | *The Football Association are to open an inquiry into recent crowd trouble.*

initiate /ɪˈnɪʃieɪt/ [v T] formal to start something such as an official process or discussion about something important: *Peace talks have been initiated in an attempt to avert full scale war.* | *The couple plan to initiate legal proceedings against the police.*

spark off /ˌspɑːʳk ˈɒf/ [phr v T] to make something happen, especially something serious, difficult, or important: *The murder sparked off a wave of protests in the city.* | *Recent freak weather conditions have sparked off renewed fears about the effects of global warming.*

set in motion ALSO **set into motion** American /ˌset ɪn ˈməʊʃən, set ɪntə ˈməʊʃən/ [v phrase] to start a process or series of events that will continue for a long time even if you take no further action: *A few months later the divorce procedure was set in motion.* | *The government had already set into motion a series of reforms.* | *Wait's actions had set in motion a chain of events that would eventually result in his dismissal.*

get/start/set the ball rolling /ˌget, ˌstɑːʳt, ˌset ðə ˈbɔːl ˌrəʊlɪŋ/ [v phrase] informal to start a meeting, discussion, event etc by doing something in order to encourage other people to take part in it as well: *Mark stood up and asked the first question to get the ball rolling.* | *To start the ball rolling, the government was asked to contribute £50,000 to the new charity.*

get things moving /ˌget θɪŋz ˈmuːvɪŋ/ [v phrase] to make a process start by doing or arranging the first part of it, after which it will become easier: *Change is certainly needed and the new headteacher needs to get things moving quickly.* | *Once we got things moving, the deal went through very quickly.*

(let's) get this show on the road /(lets) get ðɪs ˌʃəʊ ɒn ðə ˈrəʊd/ [v phrase] spoken use this to say that you now want to start something that you have been planning: *Are you all packed and ready? Right, let's get this show on the road.* | *We're having another meeting next week, hopefully to really get this show on the road.*

14 to officially start a new system, method, rule etc

- introduce/bring in
- phase in
- come into effect/operation

introduce/bring in /ˌɪntrəˈdjuːs‖-ˈduːs, ˌbrɪŋ ˈɪn/ [v T/phr v T] to officially start a new system, method, or rule for the first time: *The company is thinking of introducing medical tests for all employees.* | *New safety measures will be introduced next month.* | *The city authorities are bringing in new parking regulations next month.*

phase in /ˌfeɪz ˈɪn/ [phr v T] to introduce a new law or rule gradually, over a fairly long period of time: *The new technology will be phased in over a five year period.* | *In an attempt to reduce opposition to its tax reforms, the government plans to phase them in gradually.*

come into effect/operation /ˌkʌm ɪntʊ ɪˈfekt, ˌɒpəˈreɪʃən‖-ˌɑːp-/ [v phrase] if a new law or system **comes into effect** or **comes into operation**, it starts to be used officially: *The new law came into effect in 1991.* | *Eventually a ban on the sale of fireworks to children came into operation.*

15 to start a new business or organization

- start/start up
- open
- set up
- establish
- found
- inception

start/start up /stɑːʳt, ˌstɑːʳt ˈʌp/ [v T/phr v T] to start a new business or organization: *Luigi's family came here in 1966 and started up a chain of restaurants.* | *John decided to start his own textile business shortly after the war.*

open /ˈəʊpən/ [v T] to start a business that provides services to the public, such as a shop, restaurant, or hotel: *They just opened a new supermarket on Van Nuys Boulevard.* | *The rail company plans to open several new lines over the next five years.*

set up /ˌset ˈʌp/ [phr v T] to start a new business by making all the necessary arrangements, buying equipment etc: *Kate and her partner are setting up their own printing business.* | **set up in business** (=to start to run your own business) *The Enterprise Center runs courses for people who want to set up in business on their own.* | **+ as** *Dad set up as a builder in 1990 and now he employs over twenty men.*

establish /ɪˈstæblɪʃ/ [v T] to start an important organization that is intended to be permanent, or that continues for a very long time: *The company was established in 1899.* | *Most of the money will be used to establish local industries and mobilize the work-force.* —**establishment** [n U] *The establishment of NATO in 1949 gave the US a leading role in the defence of Europe.*

found /faʊnd/ [v T usually in passive] to start an organization, school, hospital etc, especially by providing the money for it – use this especially about something that was started a long time ago: *Who originally founded the college?* | *The bank was founded 60 years ago in Munich.* —**foundation** /faʊnˈdeɪʃən/ [n U] *The hospital has served the needs of the local community since its foundation in 1863.*

inception /ɪnˈsepʃən/ [n singular] formal the start of an organization, institution, or programme: *Within a few years of its inception, the charity was involved in aid projects all around the world.* | *Not long after their inception, the welfare programs were under attack.*

16 when something starts a natural process

- start
- activate
- set off

start /stɑːʳt/ [v T] *Investigators still aren't sure what started the fire.* | *It is thought that the avalanche was started by a small rock-fall on the higher slopes.* | *Adding acid to the test tube starts a chemical process which leads to the formation of crystals.*

activate /ˈæktɨveɪt/ [v T] to start a natural process, especially one that will continue for a fairly long time – used especially in scientific contexts: *The process is activated by sunlight.* | *In certain rare circumstances, these vaccines could activate disease.*

set off /ˌset ˈɒf/ [phr v T] to start a natural process, usually accidentally and with the result that it is difficult to stop it: *In 1992, tidal waves set off by a strong earthquake killed around 2000 people.* | *The splitting of an atom sets off an explosive chain reaction.*

17 to start an old law, custom, system etc after a long time

- bring back
- reintroduce
- revive
- restore
- resurrect

bring back /ˌbrɪŋ ˈbæk/ [phr v T] to start using a custom, system, law etc again, that was used in the past but then stopped: *Do you think they should bring back the death penalty?* | *They're talking about bringing back formal grammar teaching.*

reintroduce /ˌriːɪntrəˈdjuːs‖-ˈduːs/ [v T] to start using a law or system again after you had previously stopped using it: *Many people think that student grants should be reintroduced.* | *They are reintroducing English as the official language in schools throughout the country.* —**reintroduction** /ˌriːɪntrəˈdʌkʃən/ [n U] *the reintroduction of compulsory military service*

revive /rɪˈvaɪv/ [v T] to start or strengthen something such as an old practice, custom, or idea after it had begun to disappear, so that it becomes popular again: *a campaign to revive the tradition of holding a two-minute silence on Armistice Day* | *They are planning to revive the old Saint's Day parades through town.* —**revival** [n C] *a revival of interest in sixties music and style*

restore /rɪˈstɔːʳ/ [v T] to introduce an old law, rule etc that had been completely stopped: *The earlier restrictions on currency exchange have now been restored.* —**restoration** /ˌrestəˈreɪʃən/ [n U] *Next week there will be a debate on the restoration of capital punishment.*

resurrect /ˌrezəˈrekt/ [v T] to start an old practice, custom, system etc again after it has not existed for a long time, especially because you think that a changed situation makes it necessary or useful again: *Old theories about the origin of the universe have recently been resurrected.* | *There's a growing drive to resurrect the ancient woodland tradition of charcoal burning.*

stay

RELATED WORDS

opposite: —— **leave**

- to be left after others have gone *see* **remain**
- *see also* **visit, travel**

1 to stay in a place and not leave it

- stay
- remain
- stay put
- sit tight
- stay in
- stick around
- stop

stay /steɪ/ [v I] *Stay where you are and don't move.* | *I'm coming too. I'm not staying here on my own.* | *Neighbors keep to themselves around here, they stay inside.* | **+ with** *He stayed with the baby until she fell asleep.* | **stay (for) 3 hours/two days/a while etc** *John only stayed at the party for a couple of hours.* | *Don't go so soon – can't you stay just a little longer?* | **stay for dinner/a drink/a game of cards etc** *You're welcome to stay for lunch, you know.* | *Are you staying for a drink, or do you have to go?* | **stay to dinner/tea etc** *Mom always seated me next to him whenever he stayed to supper.* | **+ to do something** *Are you staying to watch the game?* | **stay behind** (=stay in a place after other people have left) *He stayed behind after class to ask the teacher a few questions.*

remain /rɪˈmeɪn/ [v I not usually in progressive] formal to stay: *Some 2,000 students, lecturers and university workers remained inside, refusing to leave.* | *He was determined to remain out west until he had made his fortune.* | **+ at/in** *The judge ruled that Borkin should remain in jail until his case is heard.* | *He had finished, but he remained at the microphone for a few minutes, gazing at the audience.* | **+ with** *The children will remain with their mother.* | **remain behind** (=to stay in a place after other people have left) *The others were dismissed, but Harwood was asked to remain behind.*

stay put /ˌsteɪ ˈpʊt/ [v phrase] to stay in the same place and not try to move from there: *He won't stay put long enough for me to take his photo.* | *I've decided to stay put until after Christmas, but after that I want to start looking for a new apartment.*

sit tight /ˌsɪt ˈtaɪt/ [v phrase] to stay in the same place and wait until a difficult or dangerous situation has ended before moving: *You sit tight while I go and get some help.*

stay in ALSO **stop in** British /ˌsteɪ ˈɪn, ˌstɒp ˈɪn‖ˌstɑːp-/ [phr v I] informal to **stay in** your house and not go out, especially in the evening, instead of going out to enjoy yourself: *I've got to stay in and look after my sister on Friday night.* | *So, are you going out or stopping in tonight?*

stick around /ˌstɪk əˈraʊnd/ [phr v I] informal to stay in the same place for a short time, especially because you are waiting for someone, or expecting something to happen: *If you don't feel like sticking around here, we could find a place to get some coffee.* | **stick around for ten minutes/a while etc** *Do you guys want to stick around for a while?*

stop /stɒp‖stɑːp/ [v I] British informal to stay somewhere for a short time, especially at someone's house: *I'm not stopping, I've just popped in to pick up some books.* | **stop for tea/a chat/a cup of coffee etc** *Why don't you stop for lunch – there's loads of food.*

2 to stay in the same job, school etc and not leave it

- stay
- stay on
- remain
- stay put

stay /steɪ/ [v I] to continue to **stay** in the same job, school etc and not leave it: *Do you think she'd stay if we offered her a raise?* | **+ at/with** *I've stayed at the same company for seven years, and I'd like to stick around for a while longer.* | *I didn't want to stay with Jordan's all my life – I wanted a real career, one with a future.* | **stay (on) at school** (=continue to go to school) British *Most students stay at school until they are 16 or 17.* | **stay in school** American (=continue to go to school) *We're trying to persuade our daughter to stay in school for another year.* | **+ in** *Alice has never stayed in the same job for more than a year.*

stay on /ˌsteɪ ˈɒn/ [phr v I] to stay in a job, school etc for a longer time than you had planned, or after other people have left: *Alvin came here initially as a session musician, but he stayed on.* | *There was little encouragement for those over 65 to stay on after retirement.* | **stay on at school/university/college etc** *He stayed on at college for an extra year to do a Master's degree.* | *Forty-four per cent of fifth formers now choose to stay on at school.* | **+ to do sth** *He entered University College to study zoology and stayed on to work in genetics.*

remain /rɪˈmeɪn/ [v I not in progressive] formal to stay in the same job, school etc and not leave it **+ at/in/with** *He's decided to remain in his present job for the time being.* | *Williams was offered $200,000 to remain with the Defense Department.* | **+ as** *Sir Rocco Forte will remain as chief executive of the UK hotels company.*

stay put /ˌsteɪ ˈpʊt/ [v phrase] to stay in the same job, school etc, especially because you have to and not because you want to: *If you stay put, you'll be even more miserable in a year's time.*

3 to stay somewhere a little longer

- stay on
- stay late
- stay (in) after school
- linger

stay on /ˌsteɪ ˈɒn/ [phr v I] to stay somewhere after other people have gone, or after you expected to leave: *The others went back to the hotel, but I stayed on in the bar, chatting to Alan.* | *It's okay, I'll stay on until you're ready to leave.* | *About 40 members of the audience stayed on after the performance for a glass of wine.* | **+ to do sth** *I'll be late home – I'm staying on to help organize the exhibition.*

stay late /ˌsteɪ ˈleɪt/ [v phrase] to stay somewhere after other people have gone, often because you have work to do: *Employees regularly stay late to complete tasks, but they are not paid overtime.* | *In those days, teachers enjoyed running reading clubs, and stayed late after the bell to do so.*

stay (in) after school /ˌsteɪ (ɪn) ɑːftəʳ ˈskuːl‖-ˌæf-/ [v phrase] if a student has to **stay after school**, they have to stay at the school for a short period of time after the other students have left, usually as a punishment: *If Sean failed to complete any of his classwork assignments, he had to stay after school until they were finished.*

linger /ˈlɪŋgəʳ/ [v I] to stay in a place a little longer, either because you are hoping to see someone, or because you are enjoying yourself: *Jack lingered for a while in the hall, hoping to get the chance to talk with her.* | *She lingered for a moment, uncertain what* *to do, then turned on her heel and left abruptly.* | **+ over** *As she lingered over her coffee, the sky began to darken and heavy rain clouds swept in.* | **+ on** *A few fans lingered on after the concert was over.*

4 to stay somewhere too long

- outstay your welcome/overstay your welcome

outstay your welcome/overstay your welcome /aʊtˌsteɪ jɔːʳ ˈwelkəm, əʊvəʳˌsteɪ jɔːʳ ˈwelkəm/ [v phrase] to visit or stay with someone for too long, so that they wish you would go: *Isn't it time your friends left? They've outstayed their welcome a bit.* | *She was so worried about overstaying her welcome that she left after only one night.*

5 to stay in someone's house or at a hotel

- stay
- visit
- board
- lodge

stay /steɪ/ [v I] to spend a few days, weeks etc at someone else's house or at a hotel, but not live there permanently: *Where in New Hampshire were you staying?* | *How long are you staying?* | **stay (for) a few months/two weeks etc** *I was having such a good time in Paris that I phoned my mother to say I was staying another week.* | **+ at/in** *I stayed at my brother's house for a couple of weeks.* | *Which hotel are you staying at?* | **+ with** (=stay at someone's house) *You could stay with John and Anne while you're in London.* | **stay the night/stay over/stay overnight** British (=sleep at someone else's house) *Is it all right if I stay the night?* | *You can stay over, Gail, if it would help.* | **come to stay** *One of Sarah's friends is coming to stay with us this summer.*

visit ALSO **visit with** American /ˈvɪzə̇t, ˈvɪzə̇t wɪð/ [v I/T] to go to the house of a friend or relative and stay there for some time, because you want to see them: *I went to visit her last winter and I really had a great time.* | *How much do you visit with your Mom and Dad while you're here?* | *So are you just visiting friends out here or something?* | *She sent me some photographs of when she visited in December.*

board /bɔːʳd/ [v I] to stay in a room in a family house or in a house where other people have rooms, and where some or all of your meals are provided: *Phoebe boards here during the week and goes home at weekends.* | **+ with** *I boarded with the Jansens until I found a place of my own.*

lodge /lɒdʒ‖lɑːdʒ/ [v I] British if you **lodge** in someone's house or in a hotel, you pay money to stay there **+ in/at/with** *Mrs Gould and her niece are lodging in the Rising Sun.* | *His wife and kids were forced to lodge with friends until they found a place of their own.*

6 someone who is staying in a hotel or someone's house

- guest
- lodger

guest /gest/ [n C] someone who is staying with friends or relatives or at a hotel: *The hotel bar is for guests only.* | *I'm really busy – I'm expecting guests this weekend.* | *Police evacuated hotel guests after staff received a bomb threat.* | **have a guest** (=have someone staying with you at your home as a guest) *We had guests over Christmas – three of them stayed until the New Year.*

lodger /ˈlɒdʒəʳ‖ˈlɑː-/ [n C] British someone who pays rent to live in a room in someone else's house: *Are you still looking for a lodger?* | *This young lady's our new lodger.* | **have a lodger/have sb as a lodger** *We had lodgers all through the war, most of them evacuees.* | **take in a lodger** (=start having a lodger in your home) *If you're having trouble paying your mortgage, consider taking in a lodger or at least renting out a room.*

7 a place where you can stay for a short period of time

- a place to stay/somewhere to stay
- accommodation
- lodgings
- guest house
- boarding house
- bed and breakfast
- digs

a place to stay/somewhere to stay /ə ˌpleɪs tə ˈsteɪ, ˌsʌmweəʳ tə ˈsteɪ/ [n phrase] especially spoken a place where you can stay, for example a hotel or a room in someone's house: *She needs somewhere to stay while she's at college.* | *If I can't find a place to stay, maybe I could stay at your pad.*

accommodation ALSO **accommodations** American /əˌkɒməˈdeɪʃən(z) ‖ əˌkɑː-/ [n U/n plural] a place where you pay money to stay, for example a hotel or a room that you rent: *The price includes flights, accommodation and transport.* | *You won't find any really luxurious accommodations, but there are adequate hotels and guest houses.* | *The cost of the six-day trip includes meals and motel accommodations.* | *The cost of rented accommodation keeps going up.*

lodgings /ˈlɒdʒɪŋz‖ˈlɑː-/ [n plural] British a house where you pay rent to the people who own it so that you can live in one of their rooms: *The Henstocks were lucky enough to find lodgings in the village while they awaited a new home.* | *She's going to stay in lodgings until she finds a place of her own.* | **board and lodgings** (=when the price you pay includes some or all of your meals) *She was given free board and lodgings at the school where she worked.*

guest house /ˈgest haʊs/ [n C] a small hotel where it is fairly cheap to stay, or a small house close to a larger house, where visitors can stay: *They told me the old cinema had been turned into a guest house.* | *We pulled up at a little guest house, but there were no vacancies there.*

boarding house /ˈbɔːʳdɪŋ ˌhaʊs/ [n C] a private house where you pay to sleep and eat, and where you stay for a short time: *He took two rooms in a private boarding house.* | *Some of the boarding houses we stayed in were really run-down.*

bed and breakfast ALSO **B and B** /ˌbed ən ˈbrekfəst, ˌbiː ən ˈbiː/ [n U] a small hotel or house where you pay to sleep for the night and have breakfast the next morning: *We found a cheap bed and breakfast near the coast.* | *'Where will you stay when you get there?' 'Oh, a B and B or a little guest house I expect.'*

digs /dɪgz/ [n plural] British informal a room in a house that you pay rent for, especially temporarily, for example because you are a student: *In our third year at university, we moved into digs in Elm Street.*

8 to let someone stay in your home

- have sb to stay/have sb staying
- put sb up
- take sb in

have sb to stay/have sb staying /hæv (sb) tə ˈsteɪ, hæv (sb) ˈsteɪ-ɪŋ/ [v phrase] especially spoken if you **have someone to stay**, or **have someone staying**, they stay at your house for a few days, weeks etc: *I'm busy all next week – I've got people to stay.* | *Don't plan anything for next weekend because I might be having my sister to stay.* | *We often had overseas students staying with us over the summer.*

put sb up /ˌpʊt (sb) ˈʌp/ [phr v T] especially spoken to let a friend stay in your home for a short time, and provide them with a bed to sleep in: *'Where are you staying?' 'Carole's putting us up for a couple of days.'* | *They put me up in the spare room for a few days while I sorted things out.*

take sb in /ˌteɪk (sb) ˈɪn/ [phr v T] to offer someone a place to live, especially because they need your help **take in sb** *For every child we take in, thousands are left to look after themselves on the streets.* | **take sb in** *When Mary's parents threw her out, my mother took her in.*

9 the time when you stay somewhere

- stay
- visit

stay /steɪ/ [n singular] the time when you **stay** in a place, for example when you go somewhere on holiday or for business: *So how was the rest of your stay?* | **+ in** *I met her during my stay in Venice.*

visit /ˈvɪzɪ̣t/ [n C] the time when you go to stay somewhere, especially in order to see people or see a place: *It was my first visit to my wife's parents' house.* | *She took the whole class out there for a visit.*

steal

RELATED WORDS

- *see also* **take, dishonest, crime**

1 to steal something

- steal
- take
- nick/pinch
- rip off
- go off with/walk off with
- help yourself to
- pilfer
- swipe
- snitch

steal /stiːl/ [v I/T] to take something that does not belong to you without the owner's permission in a dishonest or illegal way: *Thousands of cars get stolen every year.* | *In the end he had to steal in order to survive.* | **+ from** *drug addicts who steal from their friends and families* | **steal sth from** *Thieves stole paintings worth $5 million from a Paris art gallery.* | **have sth stolen** *It's strange he should have had so many things stolen in just a week.* | **get stolen** *My grandfather refused to put his money in a bank because he was afraid it would get stolen.* —**stealing** [n U] *Many people don't regard cheating on their taxes as stealing.*

take /teɪk/ [v T] to steal something, especially money or things that can be carried away: *Someone has been taking money from the cash box.* | *The burglars took our TV and stereo, but they didn't find the jewellery.*

nick/pinch /nɪk, pɪntʃ/ [v T] British spoken to steal something: *I wonder where she got that coat – do you think she nicked it?* | *Jimmy was caught pinching money from his mum's purse.*

rip off /ˌrɪp ˈɒf / [phr v T] spoken to steal something, especially someone's personal possessions **rip off sth** *While I was out, someone went into my hotel room and ripped off the rest of my travelers' checks.*

go off with/walk off with /ˌgəʊ ˈɒf wɪð, ˌwɔːk ˈɒf wɪð/ [phr v T not in passive] to steal something very easily, by picking it up and walking away with it, usually without anyone noticing: *My bag's disappeared! That woman must have walked off with it!* | *Guards in the lobby prevent employees from going off with computers and sensitive documents.*

help yourself to /ˌhelp jɔːʳˈself tuː/ [v phrase] informal to steal something very easily without anyone trying to stop you: *While no one was looking Louise and Alice helped themselves to some apples and bananas.* | *Burglars cut through the ceiling and helped themselves to $3.6 million in jewels.*

pilfer /ˈpɪlfəʳ/ [v T] to steal things, especially small things or things you do not think are very valuable: *The farmer caught them pilfering apples from his orchard.* | *The villagers pilfered stones from ancient ruined cities to build their houses.* —**pilfering** [n U] *Losses from stores through shoplifting and pilfering amounted to over a billion dollars last year.*

swipe /swaɪp/ [v T] informal to steal something quickly when someone is not looking: *While I was swimming in the river, somebody swiped all my clothes!* | *I wish I knew who'd swiped my earrings.*

snitch /snɪtʃ/ [v T] American informal to steal something, especially something small and not very valuable: *The supermarket has a problem with kids snitching candy bars off the shelves.* | *He watched as Grover snitched two packets of sugar from behind the counter.*

2 to steal from a house, shop, or bank

- rob
- burgle
- shoplift
- hold up
- loot

rob /rɒb‖rɑːb/ [v T] to steal money or property from a bank, shop etc, especially by using threats or violence: *He got five years in jail for robbing a gas station.* | *Two men robbed the Central Bank yesterday, escaping with over $1 million.*

burgle /ˈbɜːʳgəl/ British /**burglarize** /ˈbɜːʳgləraɪz/ American [v T] to illegally enter a house or office and steal things: *He was caught burgling the house of a police officer.* | *Our apartment has been burglarized twice since we moved here.*

shoplift /ˈʃɒpˌlɪft‖ˈʃɑːp-/ [v I/T usually in progressive] to steal things from a shop, for example by hiding them under your clothes or in a bag: *The clerk spotted the girl shoplifting and stopped her from leaving the store.*

hold up /ˌhəʊld ˈʌp/ [phr v T] to go into a bank, shop etc with a gun and demand money: *The men who held up the store were wearing Halloween masks.* | *He was arrested and charged with holding up a cab driver.*

loot /luːt/ [v I/T] to steal things from shops or other buildings, especially during a war or at a time when the police or army have lost control of an area: *His* *store was broken into and looted during the riot.* | *As the army advanced toward Mantes it burned and looted everything that lay in its path.* —**looting** [n U] *Additional police officers were put on the street to prevent looting.* —**looter** [n C] *In full view of our cameras, looters calmly walked off with TVs, radios, and VCRs.*

3 to steal from someone in the street

- rob
- mug
- snatch

rob /rɒb‖rɑːb/ [v T] to steal money or possessions from someone, especially using threats or violence and in a public place such as a street: *Two men tried to rob him as he left the restaurant.* | *The woman had been robbed and was badly shaken.*

mug /mʌg/ [v T usually in passive] to violently attack someone in the street and rob them: *She decided to move from the city after she was mugged for the third time in less than a year.*

snatch /snætʃ/ [v T] to steal someone's bag from them in the street and then run away: *A young boy pushed her over and snatched her purse as she fell.*

4 to steal money that you have been trusted to look after

- embezzle
- misappropriate
- have your fingers in the till

embezzle /ɪmˈbezəl/ [v T] to steal money from the place where you work, especially over a long period of time: *The court was told that Julie had been embezzling funds for the last two years.* | *He embezzled large amounts of money to finance his gambling.*

misappropriate /ˌmɪsəˈprəʊprieɪt/ [v T] formal to steal money that you had been trusted to keep safe: *During the trial, Raabe admitted that he misappropriated $80,000 of church funds.*

have your fingers in the till /hæv jɔːʳ ˌfɪŋgəʳz ɪn ðə ˈtɪl/ [v phrase not in progressive] British informal to steal money from the place where you work, especially when your work involves handling money: *They knew that money was going missing and Davy was eventually caught with his fingers in the till.*

5 someone who steals

- thief
- robber
- burglar
- shoplifter
- pickpocket
- mugger
- joyrider
- kleptomaniac

thief /θiːf/ [n C] someone who steals things, usually secretly and without violence: *The thieves had been careful not to leave any fingerprints.* | *She accused me of being a thief and a liar.* | **car thief/jewel thief etc** (=someone who steals cars, jewels etc) *Warning! Car thieves are operating in this area.*

robber /ˈrɒbəʳ‖ˈrɑː-/ [n C] someone who steals from banks, offices, houses etc, especially by using threats or violence: *The robbers forced bank staff to give them £4000 in cash.* | **bank robber** (=someone who robs a bank) *A young teller was shot dead by bank robbers today.* | **armed robber** (=a robber with a gun)

burglar /ˈbɜːʳgləʳ/ [n C] someone who illegally gets into a house, office etc and steals things: *Police believe the burglar got in through the kitchen window.*

shoplifter /ˈʃɒpˌlɪftəʳ‖ˈʃɑːp-/ [n C] someone who takes things from shops without paying for them, especially by hiding them in their clothes or in a bag: *The store has installed hidden cameras to catch shoplifters.* | *They have a policy of prosecuting all shoplifters.*

pickpocket /ˈpɪkˌpɒkɪ̥t‖-ˌpɑː-/ [n C] someone who steals from people in a public place, by taking things from their pockets or bags without them noticing: *There are a lot of pickpockets in crowded tourist areas, so look after your belongings.*

mugger /ˈmʌgəʳ/ [n C] a thief who violently attacks someone in the street and robs them: *Harry suffered serious head injuries when he was attacked by a gang of muggers.*

joyrider /ˈdʒɔɪraɪdəʳ/ [n C] someone who steals a car and drives it very fast for fun: *Two joyriders died when their car crashed during a police chase.*

kleptomaniac /ˌkleptəˈmeɪniæk/ [n C] someone who has a mental illness that makes them want to steal things, especially small things: *She must be some kind of kleptomaniac – she can't go into a bar without coming out with a stack of glasses.*

6 the crime of stealing

- theft
- robbery
- burglary
- shoplifting
- embezzlement
- joyriding
- larceny

theft /θeft/ [n U] *This warehouse is not adequately protected against theft or vandalism.* | *The mayor is taking credit for decreases in theft since he took office.* | **car/luggage/bicycle etc theft** *The rate of bicycle theft in this area is very high.*

robbery /ˈrɒbəri‖ˈrɑː-/ [n U] the crime of stealing money or other things from a bank, shop etc, especially by using threats or violence: *Perkins was given five years in prison for robbery with violence.* | *Robbery was believed to be the motive for the killing.* | **armed robbery** (=when robbers carry weapons) *He made two escape attempts while serving a sentence for armed robbery.*

burglary /ˈbɜːʳgləri/ [n U] the crime of illegally entering a house, office etc and stealing things: *Foster had been in prison twice already for burglary.* | *Burglary, murder and rape are all on the increase.* | *If you live in an area where burglary is common, it may be worth investing in an alarm system.*

shoplifting /ˈʃɒpˌlɪftɪŋ‖ˈʃɑːp-/ [n U] the crime of taking things from shops without paying for them: *Shoplifting cost the major stores millions of dollars last year.*

embezzlement /ɪmˈbezəlmənt/ [n U] the crime of stealing money from the place where you work, especially over a long period of time: *Taylor left the country to escape charges of embezzlement.* | **+ of** *The judge sentenced Walker to five years in prison for embezzlement of state funds.*

joyriding /ˈdʒɔɪraɪdɪŋ/ [n U] the crime of stealing a car and driving it very fast for fun: *Anyone found guilty of joyriding can now be sentenced for up to five years in prison.*

larceny /ˈlɑːʳsəni/ [n U] the crime of stealing – used especially in the American legal system: *Brook now faces probable jail after an indictment for larceny and income tax evasion.*

7 when someone steals something

- burglary
- robbery
- break-in
- hold-up
- theft
- mugging
- raid
- job

burglary /ˈbɜːʳgləri/ [n C] when someone enters a house or other building illegally and steals things: *Call the police – there's been a burglary.* | *Most burglaries occur when a house or apartment is empty.*

robbery /ˈrɒbəri‖ˈrɑː-/ [n C] when someone steals money or other things from a bank, shop etc, especially by using threats or violence: *I took part in my first robbery when I was only thirteen years old.* | *In the first nine months of this year there were 9611 street robberies involving violence.* | **+ of** *Police claim to have found the gun used in this morning's robbery of a downtown convenience store.* | **bank robbery** *The police are investigating a series of bank robberies.*

break-in /ˈbreɪk ɪn/ [n C] when someone breaks a door or window in order to enter a place and steal things: *There was a break-in at the college last night – they took all the computers.*

hold-up ALSO **stick-up** American informal /ˈhəʊld ʌp, ˈstɪk ʌp/ [n C] when someone goes into a bank or shop with a gun and demands money: *A man was shot dead in a hold-up at a downtown bank.*

theft /θeft/ [n C] formal when something is stolen: *If your passport has been stolen, report the theft to your nearest embassy immediately.* | **+ of** *Security has been tightened since the theft of a $150,000 oil painting.* | **car/bicycle etc thefts** *Police believe they have found the man responsible for a series of car thefts in the past year.*

mugging /ˈmʌgɪŋ/ [n C] a violent attack on someone in the street in order to rob them: *There have been a number of muggings outside downtown hotels recently.*

raid /reɪd/ [n C] when someone goes into a bank or shop while it is open, and steals money or other things using threats or violence: *The police accused the woman of planning a huge armed bank raid in Scotland.* | **+ on** *Detectives managed to catch the gunman who had taken three hostages in a raid on a jeweller's shop.* | **carry out a raid** *Police have released a photo of a man they believe carried out a raid on a supermarket.*

job /dʒɒb‖dʒɑːb/ [n C] informal a crime that involves stealing: *Her boyfriend was put in prison after a bank job* (=theft from a bank). | **inside job** (=done by someone within the organization) *The police are convinced it was an inside job.*

8 something that has been stolen

- stolen
- loot
- haul

stolen /ˈstəʊlən/ [adj] *Thieves can sell stolen passports for a lot of money.* | *The antiques he was selling turned out to be stolen.* | **stolen goods** *Wilson was convicted of theft and handling stolen goods.*

loot /luːt/ [n U] informal the things that have been stolen during a particular robbery: *The gunman stuffed the loot into a paper bag and ran outside to a waiting car.* | *Two weeks later, police found the loot hidden in an abandoned warehouse.*

haul /hɔːl/ [n C] a large amount of things that have been stolen: *Trevino hid the haul in his mother's closet for over a year.* | *The police caught three men examining their haul in a house in north London.* | *a drugs haul*

stick

RELATED WORDS

- *see also* **join, attach, fasten/unfasten, tie/untie**

1 to join one thing to another, especially using glue

- stick
- stick down
- glue

stick /stɪk/ [v T] to join one thing to another thing, especially by using glue or tape with glue on it **stick sth on/in sth** *It took hours to stick all these photos in my album.* | *She stuck her chewing gum on the bottom of the chair.* | **stick sth to sth** *Stick this note to Chris's computer so he sees it when he gets back.* | **stick together** *Paul stuck two pieces of paper together.* | **stick sth back together** *The vase broke into several pieces, but I was able to stick them all back together.*

stick down /ˌstɪk ˈdaʊn/ [phr v T] to fix something to a surface, using glue and pushing down on it **stick sth down** *The label's coming off. Can you stick it down again?* | **stick down sth** *Make sure you stick down the envelope properly, the contents are confidential.*

glue /gluː/ [v T] to use **glue** to join things together, when you are making something or repairing something **glue sth to/onto sth** *I tried to glue the handle back onto the cup.* | **glue sth (back) together** *You make the model by cutting out these shapes and gluing them together.*

2 when one thing sticks to another

- stick
- stick together
- grip
- adhere

stick /stɪk/ [v I] if something **sticks** to something else, it becomes joined to it when it touches it, because it has glue or a sticky substance on it: *She pressed down the flap of the envelope, but it didn't stick.* | **+ to** *Peter was very hot, and his shirt was sticking to his back.*

stick together /ˌstɪk təˈgeðəʳ/ [phr v I] if two or more things **stick together**, they stick to each other because they have a sticky substance on them: *I spilled coffee on my book and some of the pages stuck together.* | *The chocolates are covered with powdered sugar to keep them from sticking together.*

grip /grɪp/ [v T] to stick to something firmly and without slipping, by pushing against it – used especially about tyres or shoes: *The car has wide tyres which grip the road really well.* —**grip** [n U] *If you're going rock-climbing, make sure you wear shoes that will give you a good grip.*

adhere /ədˈhɪəʳ/ [v I] formal to become stuck to a surface or to another object: *Peeling paint must be scraped away so that new paint will adhere.* | **+ to** *The machine is cleaned regularly to stop dirt adhering to the working parts.* | *Edam cheeses have waxed coatings which adhere tightly to the cheese.*

3 something that will stick to something else

- glue
- sticky
- adhesive

glue /gluː/ [n C/U] a liquid or soft substance that you use to stick things together: *Wait for the glue to dry before you sit on it.*

sticky /ˈstɪki/ [adj] something that is **sticky** sticks to other things: *Add flour to the mixture to prevent it from becoming sticky.* | *She wrote the address on a sticky label and stuck it to her computer.*

adhesive /ədˈhiːsɪv/ [adj usually before noun] **adhesive** material or paper is covered with a sticky substance such as glue, that makes it stick to surfaces: *The first aid box has adhesive dressings and antiseptic cream in it.* | *He attached the paper to the wall with special adhesive tape.* | **self-adhesive** (=sticky on one side and able stick to something without glue or liquid) *self-adhesive envelopes*

stick out

to come out further than the rest of something

1 to stick out

- stick out
- stick up
- protrude
- jut out
- poke out
- bulge
- project

stick out /ˌstɪk ˈaʊt/ [phr v I] to **stick out** from a surface or through an opening: *The fridge door won't shut because there's something sticking out.* | *His large ears stuck out almost at right angles.* | **+ of/from/through etc** *A neatly folded handkerchief was sticking out of his jacket pocket.* | *A pair of skis stuck out through the car window.*

stick up /ˌstɪk ˈʌp/ [phr v I] to stick out and point upwards: *His hair was white, and stuck up in tufts on his head.* | *Can you see that branch that's sticking up?* | **+ from/through/out of etc** *He saw a hand sticking up through the snow.* | *A church steeple stuck up above the roofs of the surrounding cottages.*

protrude /prəˈtruːd‖prəʊ-/ [v I] formal to stick out, especially to stick out further than is usual or expected **+ from/through/into etc** *I noticed a metal pipe protruding from the wall.* | *The largest stone can be seen protruding above the level of the river.* | *She injured herself on a screw that protruded 2 inches out of the bench.*

jut out /ˌdʒʌt ˈaʊt/ [phr v I] if something **juts out**, for example a piece of land or a part of a building, it sticks out sharply and in a way that is very noticeable **+ from/of/through etc** *Our guide led us to where a flat rock juts out from the side of the cliff.* | *a slim piece of land jutting out into the Gulf of Mexico* | **jut 2 feet/100 metres etc out** *Our rafts floated downstream towards the icebergs, which jutted 30 feet out of the water.*

poke out /ˌpəʊk ˈaʊt/ [phr v I] if part of something **pokes out**, it sticks out or sticks up and can be seen, while the rest of it is covered **+ of/from/through etc** *I looked across the street and saw Mike's head poking out above the fence.* | *The first snowdrops poked out through the frozen ground.*

bulge /bʌldʒ/ [v I] if something **bulges**, it sticks out more than usual in a rounded shape: *His cheeks bulged, and his face turned purple with rage.* | **+ out/from/through etc** *Father's face was flushed, and his eyes bulged out.* | **+ with** *Her purse bulged with keys, cigarettes, scraps of paper, and old receipts.*

project /prəˈdʒekt/ [v I] formal if part of a building, mountain, or other very large object **projects** somewhere, it sticks out in that direction **+ into/over/from/through etc** *Two walkways projected over the gorge on both sides of the river.* | *The pier would be 1000 metres long and project about 400 metres into the sea.*

2 words for describing something that sticks out

- prominent
- protruding
- bulging

prominent /ˈprɒmɪ̥nənt‖ˈprɑː-/ [adj] a part of someone's body that is **prominent** is larger than usual and sticks out in a way that people notice: *His face was tanned, the cheekbones high and prominent.* | *Her nose was quite prominent, and she had small, even teeth.* | *a heart-shaped face, slightly prominent teeth and small eyes*

protruding /prəˈtruːdɪŋ‖prəʊ-/ [adj only before noun] sticking out more than is normal, or in a dangerous way: *Dentists have developed a new device to correct protruding teeth.* | *Roy examined the letter carefully for protruding wires.*

bulging /ˈbʌldʒɪŋ/ [adj only before noun] sticking out in a rounded shape: *He had bulging blue eyes, a large nose and a long chin.* | *She pushed her bulging suitcase under the chair.*

3 something that sticks out

- bulge
- lump
- bump

bulge /bʌldʒ/ [n C] something, especially a part of the body, that sticks out in a rounded shape: *Her tailored suit fitted neatly, hiding the slight bulges of middle-age.* | *At five months pregnant, the bulge was beginning to show.*

lump /lʌmp/ [n C] something, especially something small, that sticks up in a rounded shape from your skin or from a surface: *She saw a lump under the bedclothes.* | *He put the gun in his pocket, where it made a slight lump.* | *He had a lump on his forehead the size of a golf ball.*

bump /bʌmp/ [n C] something that sticks up in a rounded shape, especially from the surface of something: *The car rattled every time it went over a bump.* | *A small bump had started to develop over Irene's eye.* | *I nearly stumbled over a bump in the ground.*

4 to make part of your body stick out

- stick out
- poke out
- put out

stick out /ˌstɪk ˈaʊt/ [phr v T] **stick sth out** *A woman stuck her head out of the window and told us to come upstairs.* | *He stuck his lower lip out and frowned.* | **stick out sth** *He stuck out a hand. 'Hi, I'm Melvyn.'* | *I stuck out my thumb and caught a ride to Tay Ninh.* | **stick your tongue out (at sb)** (=in order to be rude to someone) *Dan made a face and stuck his tongue out.*

poke out /ˌpəʊk ˈaʊt/ [phr v T] to stick part of your body out for a short time from something that it is inside or behind **poke sth out** *A young doctor poked his head out, and called me into the examination room.* | **poke out sth** *He poked out his tongue and looked at it carefully in the mirror.*

put out /ˌpʊt ˈaʊt/ [phr v T] to stick a part of your body out of something, especially slowly or carefully **put sth out** *He put his head out slowly and looked up the corridor.* | **put out sth** *He put out his hands and Officer Johnson clicked on the handcuffs.*

stop

WHAT'S HERE

- **to stop doing sth** — see **1 to 9**
- **to stop moving** — see **10 to 13**
- **to stop happening** — see **14 to 15**
- **to stop sth that is happening** — see **16 to 23**
- **to prevent sth from happening** — see **24 to 32**

to stop doing sth

RELATED WORDS

opposite: **start**
- to finish doing something *see* **finish**
- to stop for a short time *see* **pause**

1 to stop doing something

- stop
- finish
- quit
- cease

stop /stɒp‖stɑːp/ [v I/T] to no longer do something that you had been doing: *He wrote quickly, but from time to time he stopped and looked out of the window.* | **+ doing sth** *I stopped reading and turned out the light.* | *Please will you all stop making so much noise!* | **stop what you are doing** *Could you stop what you are doing and pay attention, please?* | **stop for lunch/coffee/a break etc** *What time do you want to stop for lunch?*

finish /ˈfɪnɪʃ/ [v I/T] to stop doing something because you have completed it: *She spoke for ten minutes, and when she had finished the audience cheered.* | *We should have finished the job by next week.* | **+ doing sth** *Have you finished reading the papers?* | *After you've finished painting the house you can start on the garage.*

quit /kwɪt/ [v I/T] especially American, spoken to stop doing something, especially something that annoys other people **+ doing sth** *I wish he'd quit bothering me.* | *They should quit complaining and just get on with their job!*

cease /siːs/ [v I/T] formal to stop doing something: *All conversation ceased as the two police officers entered.* | *The factory has now ceased production and will close next month.* | **+ doing sth** *The mill ceased operating commercially two years ago.* | **+ to do sth** *Many of these firms have now ceased to exist.*

2 what you say when you tell someone to stop doing something

- stop
- quit
- cut it out
- lay off

stop /stɒp‖stɑːp/ [v I/T] spoken *Stop what you're doing when the buzzer sounds.* | **+ doing sth** *Will you please stop talking and listen to me!* | **stop it/that** *Stop it! You're hurting me.*

quit /kwɪt/ [v I/T] American spoken say this to tell someone to stop doing something because it annoys you **quit it/that** *Quit that! You're driving me crazy.* | *I hated the way she was teasing me. 'Quit it!' I said.* | **+ doing sth** *Quit fooling around and pay attention.*

cut it out ALSO **pack it in** British /ˌkʌt ɪt ˈaʊt, ˌpæk ɪt ˈɪn/ [v phrase] use this to tell someone to stop doing something because it annoys you: *Come on, you two, cut it out!* | *Just cut it out, Jim. Stop acting like a kid.* | *Oh, pack it in you lot, or we're going straight home.*

lay off /ˌleɪ ˈɒf/ [phr v I/T] say this when you want someone to stop doing or saying something that is annoying you: *Look, I don't want to argue with you, so just lay off.* | *Lay off the swearing, if you don't mind.* | *Hey, lay off Vinnie, will you? He hasn't done you any harm.*

3 to stop doing something without successfully completing it

- give up
- quit
- abandon
- drop
- leave it at that

give up /ˌgɪv ˈʌp/ [phr v I/T] to stop trying to do something because it is too difficult or because you are not determined enough: *I made several attempts to repair the damage, but gave up in the end.* | *Come on, don't give up yet!* | **give up sth** *We will never give up our struggle.* | **give up doing sth** *I've given up trying to get her to change her mind.* | **give sth up** *We did start a protest, but gave it up when we realized we would never be successful.*

quit /kwɪt/ [v I/T] especially American to stop doing something before you have successfully completed it: *Bill was cold, hungry and tired and he wanted to quit.* | *She was having a lot of trouble finding a job, but she refused to quit.* | **+ doing sth** *I knew I'd never be any good at school, so I just quit trying.*

abandon /əˈbændən/ [v T] to stop doing something that you had planned or started, because there are too many other problems involved: *The government has now abandoned its plans to privatize parts of the health service.* | *All attempts to find a peaceful solution to the conflict have now been abandoned.* | *Owing to rough weather, the coast guard had been forced to abandon the search.*

drop /drɒp‖drɑːp/ [v T] to stop doing something that you have already started or that you intended to do: *Because of strong opposition, the government has dropped plans to increase taxes on fuel.* | **drop everything** *I'm too busy to just drop everything and go out for the day.*

leave it at that /ˌliːv ɪt ət ˈðæt/ [v phrase] informal to stop doing something because you are satisfied that you have done enough: *We've got most of the heavy work done, so I think we can leave it at that for today.*

4 to stop doing an activity that you used to do regularly

- stop
- give up
- drop

stop /stɒp‖stɑːp/ [v I/T] *I used to play a lot of tennis, but I had to stop when I injured my knee.* | **+ doing sth** *I stopped going to church after I left home.* | *There's not much demand for this type of car, so we stopped making them.*

give up /ˌgɪv ˈʌp/ [phr v T] to stop doing something that you used to do regularly, for example because you are no longer physically able to do it **+ doing sth** *As he grew older he gave up going for walks and seldom went out.* | *After the accident she had to give up riding and farming.* | **give up sth** *He gave up his job so that he could look after his wife.* | **give sth up** *I used to really enjoy dancing, but I had to give it up after I became ill.*

drop /drɒp‖drɑːp/ [v T] to stop studying a subject at school, college, or university: *I think I may drop French next year and concentrate on my other languages.* | *You can drop one subject at the end of this year if you're finding you've got too much work.*

5 to stop a bad or unhealthy habit

- stop
- quit
- give up
- break the habit/kick the habit
- come off
- grow out of

▸ *see also* **addicted, smoking, drug, drink (6), healthy/unhealthy**

stop /stɒp‖stɑːp/ [v I/T] *She had smoked for nearly twenty years before she finally managed to stop.* | **+ doing sth** *The health advice to people is simple – stop eating so much fat and eat more fruit and vegetables.*

quit /kwɪt/ [v I/T] informal to stop doing something that that has been an unhealthy or harmful habit: *If you've smoked for a long time it can be very difficult to quit.* | **+ doing sth** *They told me at the hospital to quit drinking for a while.* | *I quit taking the pills because they were making me put on weight.*

give up /ˌgɪv ˈʌp/ [phr v I/T] to stop doing something such as smoking, drinking alcohol, or taking drugs because it is harmful or unhealthy: *If you smoke, try to give up or at least cut down.* | *She gave up drinking over 10 years ago.*

break the habit/kick the habit /ˌbreɪk ðə ˈhæbɪ̆t, ˌkɪk ðə ˈhæbɪ̆t/ [v phrase] informal to stop doing something that has been a habit for a long time, especially a bad or dangerous habit: *The centre provides help for addicts who have kicked their habit and want to stay away from drugs.* | *Some smokers use hypnosis to help them kick the habit.*

come off /ˌkʌm ˈɒf/ [phr v T not in passive] to stop taking medicine or drugs that you have been taking regularly: *The doctor told me I could come off the drugs six months after the operation.* | *People need help to come off hard drugs like heroin and cocaine.*

grow out of /ˌgrəʊ ˈaʊt ɒv/ [phr v T] if a child **grows out of** a habit, he or she stops doing it as they get older **grow out of it** *Wetting the bed is a common problem, but children nearly always grow out of it.* | *He became obsessed with football at the age of four, and he's never grown out of it!*

6 to stop having a particular type of food or drink

- cut out
- lay off

▸ *see also* **drink (6), healthy/unhealthy**

cut out /ˌkʌt ˈaʊt/ [phr v T] to stop eating a particular type of food, especially for health reasons: *With this diet, I have to cut out bread, cookies, and cakes.* | *Try cutting out red meat and dairy produce, and see if your symptoms improve.*

lay off /ˌleɪ ˈɒf/ [phr v T] spoken to stop eating, drinking, or using a particular type of food, drink, or drug, especially for health reasons: *I'm trying to lay off rich food for a while to lose some weight.* | *If he really wants to write the book, he'll need to lay off the drink until he does it.*

7 to stop working at the end of the day or during the day

- stop work
- finish work
- knock off
- call it a day
- pack up

stop work /ˌstɒp ˈwɜːʳk‖ˌstɑːp-/ [v phrase] British *We stop work at half past three on Fridays.* | *They stopped work for a few minutes to consider his offer.*

finish work /ˌfɪnɪʃ ˈwɜːʳk/ [v phrase] especially British to stop work at the end of the day: *What time do you finish work?* | **finish** (=finish work) *I don't finish until seven tonight, so I'll be late home.*

knock off /ˌnɒk ˈɒf‖ˌnɑːk-/ [phr v I] spoken to stop work – use this especially to talk about a particular time that you stop work: *Is it OK if I knock off a little early tonight?* | *I usually knock off at about six.*

call it a day /ˌkɔːl ɪt ə ˈdeɪ/ [v phrase] informal to decide to stop working because you have done enough work, because you are very tired, or because it is late: *We realized we weren't going to get the job finished, so we decided to call it a day.* | *Look, we're all tired – let's call it a day.*

pack up /ˌpæk ˈʌp/ [phr v I] British to stop work, put away your work equipment, and go home: *Everyone packed up and went home.* | *OK, guys – it's time to pack up now.*

8 to stop working at the end of your working life

- retire

retire /rɪˈtaɪəʳ/ [v I] *Mrs Davies retired after 45 years with the company.* | *Everyone should have the right to a pension when they retire.* | *My father retired at 65.* —**retirement** [n U] *Since her retirement she's been spending more time with her grandchildren.* | *He was determined to enjoy his retirement.* | **early retirement** (=before the usual or official age) *More and more police officers are taking early retirement.*

9 words for describing something that you are unable to stop doing

- compulsive

▸ *see also* **gambling**

compulsive /kəmˈpʌlsɪv/ [adj] **compulsive behaviour/gambling/eating etc** something, especially something harmful, that you do because you cannot stop yourself: *Her problem is her compulsive eating.* | *Compulsive behaviour is often a symptom of deeper psychological problems.* | **a compulsive liar/eater/gambler etc** (=someone who is unable to stop lying, eating etc) *He's a compulsive liar – you can't believe a word he says.*

to stop moving

RELATED WORDS

▸ *see also* **move/not move**

10 to stop walking, running etc

- **stop**
- **come to a halt**
- **stop dead/stop dead in your tracks**
- **freeze**

stop /stɒp‖stɑːp/ [v I] *I was exhausted, and had to stop and rest.* | *Stop! Wait a minute!* | *I saw Maria and stopped to say hello.* | *We stopped at the next village to get supplies.*

come to a halt /ˌkʌm tʊ ə ˈhɔːlt/ [v phrase] to slow down and stop: *The group of tourists came to a halt outside the museum.* | *He walked back across the restaurant and came to a halt beside our table.*

stop dead/stop dead in your tracks /ˌstɒp ˈded, stɒp ˌded ɪn jɔːʳ ˈtræks‖ˌstɑːp-/ [v phrase] to suddenly stop, especially because something has surprised or frightened you or you suddenly notice it: *Katie stopped dead and stared at him.* | *Francesca stopped dead in her tracks. 'What did you just say?' she demanded.*

freeze /friːz/ [v I] to stop moving very suddenly and stay completely still and quiet: *I froze, and listened. Someone was in my apartment.* | *Captain O'Leary raised his gun and shouted 'Freeze!'*

11 when a vehicle stops moving

- **stop**
- **pull up**
- **pull in**
- **pull over**
- **come to a stop/come to a halt**
- **come to a standstill/grind to a halt**
- **brake**
- **slam on the brakes**

stop /stɒp‖stɑːp/ [v I] if a vehicle or its driver **stops**, the vehicle stops moving: *Could you stop just here on the left?* | *We'd better stop at the next gas station.* | *A yellow car stopped outside the house.*

pull up /ˌpʊl ˈʌp/ [phr v I] if a car or its driver **pulls up**, the car comes closer to something or someone and stops **+ at/outside/next to etc** *We pulled up at a small cafe just outside Bordeaux.* | *A blue van pulled up behind us.*

pull in /ˌpʊl ˈɪn/ [phr v I] if a car or its driver **pulls in**, the driver stops the car at the side of the road or in a parking space: *I rounded the corner, looking for a place to pull in.* | *Jeff parked in front of the house and I pulled in beside him.*

pull over /ˌpʊl ˈəʊvəʳ/ [phr v I] if a car or its driver **pulls over**, the driver drives to the side of the road and stops: *A policeman was standing by the side of the road, signalling to me to pull over.* | *I pulled over and looked at the map.* | *The truck pulled over and a man got out.*

come to a stop/come to a halt /ˌkʌm tʊ ə ˈstɒp‖-ˈstɑːp, ˌkʌm tʊ ə ˈhɔːlt/ [v phrase] especially written to gradually get slower and then stop: *The taxi came to a stop outside the hotel.* | *The bus slowed down and came to a halt at some traffic lights.* | **come to a sudden/abrupt halt/stop** *As Jamie spoke, the train came to an abrupt halt, nearly throwing us all on the floor.*

come to a standstill/grind to a halt /ˌkʌm tʊ ə ˈstændstɪl, ˌgraɪnd tʊ ə ˈhɔːlt/ [v phrase] especially written to gradually get slower and then stop completely – use this about traffic or about a vehicle: *The train came to a standstill about a mile outside Abbeville and didn't move for 20 minutes.* | *Traffic in the city ground to a halt as the streets filled with angry demonstrators.*

brake /breɪk/ [v I] if a vehicle or its driver **brakes**, the driver makes it slow down or stop by using the brakes: *I saw a roadblock ahead, and braked.* | **brake hard/sharply** *A bus came round the corner and braked sharply.*

slam on the brakes /ˌslæm ɒn ðə ˈbreɪks/ [v phrase] to make a car, bus etc stop very suddenly by pressing very hard on the brakes: *I slammed on the brakes, skidding to a stop.*

12 when a bus, train etc regularly stops at particular places

- **stop**
- **call at**

stop /stɒp‖stɑːp/ [v I] if a train or bus **stops** at a place, it regularly stops there to let people on and off: *Does this train stop at Lyon?* | *The bus stops at the top of the hill.* —**stop** [n C] a place where a bus or train stops: *Excuse me, could you tell me what the next stop is?* | *We need to get off at the next stop.*

call at /ˈkɔːl æt/ [phr v T] British if a train or bus **calls at** a particular place, it stops there as part of its regular journey to let people on and off: *This is the 14:30 to Bristol, calling at Reading and Bath.* | *Does this train call at York?*

13 to make someone stop moving

- **stop**
- **restrain**
- **hold back**
- **stop sb dead/stop sb dead in their tracks**
- **flag down**
- **pull over**
- **intercept**

stop /stɒp‖stɑːp/ [v T] *The police are stopping drivers to ask questions about the accident.* | *The truck was stopped by customs officers for a routine check.* | *A man stopped me in the street and asked if I knew where the theatre was.*

restrain /rɪˈstreɪn/ [v T] to hold someone so that they cannot move forward or attack someone: *It took three men to restrain him.* | *Mary got up to go after them, but I put out my arm to restrain her.*

hold back /ˌhəʊld ˈbæk/ [phr v T] to prevent someone from moving forward or into a place: *They put up huge barriers to hold back the crowd.* | *My father held me back, otherwise I would have rushed up onto the stage.*

stop sb dead/stop sb (dead) in their tracks /ˌstɒp (sb) ˈded, ˌstɒp (sb) (ˌded) ɪn ðeəʳ ˈtræks‖ˌstɑːp-/ [v phrase] to surprise or frighten you, so that you stop suddenly: *Seeing the policeman there stopped me dead. I didn't know what to do.* | *Jim was stopped in his tracks by the sound of a rifle behind him.*

flag down /ˌflæg ˈdaʊn/ [phr v T] to stop a car that is coming towards you by waving your arms **flag down sth** *I managed to flag down a passing car and ask for help.* | **flag sth/sb down** *The patrolman stepped out in front of the truck to flag it down.*

pull over /ˌpʊl ˈəʊvə/ [phr v T] if someone, especially a police officer **pulls you over**, they make you stop driving and park at the side of the road: *The police pulled me over and checked my licence.* | *He got pulled over on the way home and had to take a breath test.*

intercept /ˌɪntəʳˈsept/ [v T] to stop something such as a boat or plane, before it has finished its journey or achieved its purpose: *Two British ships were sent to intercept the convoy.* | *All three fighter planes were intercepted and destroyed.*

to stop happening

RELATED WORDS

opposite: —— **start**

- the end of a period, time, event, or story *see* **end**
- to stop happening before starting again *see* **pause**
- to stop burning *see* **burn**
- *see also* **finish**

14 to stop happening

- stop
- come to an end
- cease

stop /stɒp‖stɑːp/ [v I] *It seemed the fighting would never stop.* | *Catherine stood watching the rain, hoping it would stop soon.* | *Suddenly, the cheering stopped and there was a deathly silence.* | *This waste of the earth's resources must stop.*

come to an end /ˌkʌm tʊ ən ˈend/ [v phrase] if something that has been happening for a long time **comes to an end**, it stops happening: *When we had children, all our trips to theatres and cinemas came to an end.* | *Research at the college came to an end in 1870.* | *All good things must come to an end.*

cease /siːs/ [v I] formal to stop happening: *Hostilities between the two countries have now ceased.* | *Presently, the rain ceased and the sun came out.* | **cease altogether** (=stop completely) *The sound of gunfire gradually receded and then ceased altogether.*

15 to gradually stop happening

- fizzle out
- peter out
- wear off
- fade away

fizzle out /ˌfɪzəl ˈaʊt/ [phr v I] informal to gradually end in a disappointing way – use this about an activity, a relationship, or people's interest in something: *Their romance fizzled out after a few months.* | *The movie made a great start, but the action seemed to fizzle out halfway through.*

peter out /ˌpiːtər ˈaʊt/ [phr v I] to gradually become less and less and then stop happening completely: *By midday the rain had petered out.* | *The road petered out into a muddy track.* | *The protest campaign petered out after a few weeks.*

wear off /ˌweər ˈɒf/ [phr v I] if pain or the effect of something **wears off**, it gradually becomes less until it stops completely: *The effects of the anaesthetic will wear off within a few hours.* | *The shock has not worn off yet and he seems to be walking around in a daze.* | **the novelty wears off** (=when you stop feeling interested or excited about something because it is no longer new) *The kids spent hours on the computer at first, but the novelty soon wore off.*

fade away /ˌfeɪd əˈweɪ/ [phr v I] if a sound **fades away**, it gradually gets quieter and finally stops: *He waited until the sound of the engines had faded away.* | *As the music faded away the audience broke into enthusiastic applause.*

to stop sth that is happening

RELATED WORDS

- to make something stop burning *see* **burn**

16 to make something stop happening or continuing

- stop
- put an end to
- bring to an end
- halt
- call off
- cut short
- abort
- suspend
- pull the plug on
- freeze

stop /stɒp‖stɑːp/ [v T] to make someone **stop** doing something, or make something **stop** happening: *The referee stopped the fight when one of the boxers was badly injured.* | *It is now time to stop the war and begin negotiations for peace.* | *Officials are planning to take court action to stop publication of the book.* | **stop sb doing sth** *I gave my little brother some chocolate to stop him crying.*

put an end to /ˌpʊt ən ˈend tuː/ [v phrase] to stop something, especially so that it never starts again: *An injury like this could put an end to her dancing career.* | *The outbreak of war put an end to their romance.*

bring to an end /ˌbrɪŋ tʊ ən ˈend/ [v phrase] to finally and permanently end something that has continued for a long time **bring sth to an end** *A treaty was signed which finally brought the conflict to an end.* | **bring to an end sth** *There are calls for the Prime Minister to bring to an end the uncertainty about the election date.*

halt /hɔːlt/ [v T] to make something stop changing, developing, or progressing: *The government is determined to halt the trade in illegal animal furs.* | *All his efforts had failed to halt the increase in street crime.*

call off /ˌkɔːl ˈɒf/ [phr v T] to decide that a planned action or activity should be stopped after it has already started: *The union decided to call off the strike when they were offered a 10% pay rise.* | *The meeting was called off at the last minute.* | *The hunt for the missing boy had to be called off because of severe weather conditions.*

cut short /ˌkʌt ˈʃɔːʳt/ [phr v T] to stop an activity earlier than was planned, especially because of something unexpected such as illness or bad news: *She was forced to cut short her holiday and return to the UK.* | *His education was cut short when his father died of a sudden illness.*

abort /əˈbɔːʳt/ [v T] to stop an action that has been started, because it would be too dangerous to continue: *The mission was aborted after news came of the capture of the city.* | *The plane had already started its descent when the pilot received orders to abort his landing.*

suspend /səˈspend/ [v T] to officially order that something should be stopped, when you intend to let it start again at a later time: *We have decided to suspend all production at the factory until safety checks can be carried out.* | *All pay increases are to be* *suspended until further notice.* | *The trial was suspended after threats were made against witnesses.* —**suspension** /sə'spenʃən/ [n U] **+ of** *The President has announced the suspension of all military action in the region.*

pull the plug on /ˌpʊl ðə 'plʌg ɒn/ [v phrase] informal to stop giving money to a plan or planned business activity so that it cannot continue: *The city council has pulled the plug on the new housing development.* | *Over 1000 workers lost their jobs when the company pulled the plug on plans to open ten new stores.*

freeze /fri:z/ [v T] to keep prices or wages at the same level and not increase them: *The company has announced that it intends to freeze all salaries for a year.* | *All government employees have had their salaries frozen at last year's levels.* —**freeze** [n C usually singular] *The prime minister has announced a freeze on income tax for two years.*

17 to stop something quickly before it has time to develop

- nip sth in the bud
- squash
- kill

nip sth in the bud /ˌnɪp (sth) ɪn ðə 'bʌd/ [v phrase] to stop a bad situation or bad behaviour when it first starts, before it can develop further: *If I'd known about their plan I could have nipped it in the bud there and then.* | *It's important to nip this problem in the bud.*

squash /skwɒʃ‖skwɑ:ʃ, skwɔ:ʃ/ [v T] to quickly stop something such as opposition to your plans that is likely to cause you trouble: *Her lawyers acted quickly to squash any of her husband's claims on her property.* | **squash a rumour** *The chairman acted quickly to squash rumours of a takeover bid.*

kill /kɪl/ [v T] to stop something quickly and completely: *Losing funding now would kill the project.* | *Mr Howard released a statement in an effort to kill speculation in the press.*

18 to stop normal work or services from continuing

- paralyse
- bring sth to a standstill

paralyse British ALSO **paralyze** American /'pærəlaɪz/ [v T] to make it impossible for an industry, system, service etc to continue working normally: *Strike action has paralysed the region's public transport system.* | *Over Illinois, the storm broke, paralyzing the state with blizzards and freezing temperatures.*

bring sth to a standstill /ˌbrɪŋ (sth) tʊ ə 'stændstɪl/ [v phrase] to make it impossible for an industry, system, service etc to continue working normally: *Unexpected bad weather has brought London to a standstill.* | *Further interest rate rises may bring the manufacturing industry to a standstill.* | *Rail services have been brought to a standstill by severe flooding in many areas.* | **bring sth to a virtual standstill** *Traffic was brought to a virtual standstill as protestors drove in convoy along the motorways.*

19 to end the use of a system, service, or organization

- phase out
- discontinue

phase out /ˌfeɪz 'aʊt/ [phr v T] to gradually end the use of a system, product, or service **phase out sth** *Ministers agreed to phase out the old voting system within two years.* | *Older prisons will be phased out over the next few years.* | **phase sth out** *The committee acknowledged that these chemicals are highly dangerous, and agreed to phase them out gradually.*

discontinue /ˌdɪskən'tɪnju:/ [v T] to stop providing something that has been available or provided regularly over a period of time: *Doctors decided to discontinue the treatment when it became clear that the boy had no chance of recovering.* | *If fewer than ten students sign up, the course will be discontinued.*

20 to stop something bad or illegal that people are doing

- stop
- put a stop to
- stamp out
- crack down on
- call a halt to
- clamp down on
- curb

stop /stɒp‖stɑ:p/ [v T] *We must take action to stop this illegal trade in ivory.* | *All the staff are determined to stop bullying in the school.* | **stop sb from doing sth** *The new measures are intended to stop troublemakers from travelling abroad to football matches.*

put a stop to /ˌpʊt ə 'stɒp tu:‖-'stɑ:p-/ [v phrase] to stop an activity, especially one that you consider to be harmful or unacceptable: *Using children in this way is pure exploitation, and it's time we put a stop to it!* | *She knew that if she didn't put a stop to their squabbling now, it could go on for weeks.*

stamp out /ˌstæmp 'aʊt/ [phr v T] to completely stop an illegal or harmful activity: *The police have introduced new measures to help stamp out violence on the city's streets.* | *We are determined to stamp out prostitution in this neighborhood.*

crack down on /ˌkræk 'daʊn ɒn/ [phr v T] to take severe action to stop an illegal activity: *The authorities are determined to crack down on terrorism.* | *Teachers must crack down on bullying as soon as they become aware of it.* | *Only by cracking down on dealers, can we stop young people getting involved with drugs.* —**crack-down** /'kræk daʊn/ [n C] **+ on** *Davies was eventually caught during a government crack-down on tax evasion.*

call a halt to /ˌkɔ:l ə 'hɔ:lt tu:/ [v phrase] to officially order that an activity should be stopped, especially after it has continued for a long time: *The government has called a halt to the exporting of live animals.* | *Companies must call a halt to the dumping of toxic waste at sea.*

clamp down on /ˌklæmp 'daʊn ɒn/ [phr v T] if someone in authority **clamps down on** an activity or group of people, they take firm action to stop something that is illegal or against the rules: *The new, tougher laws are intended clamp down on the carrying of knives and other weapons.* | *If we don't clamp down on these troublemakers now, the situation could get out of control.* —**clampdown** /'klæmpdaʊn/ [n C usually singular] **+ on** *Police say the clampdown on drink-driving has been highly successful.* | *The new administration has promised a clampdown on corruption.*

curb /kɜ:ʳb/ [v T] to prevent something harmful from increasing and start to control and reduce it: *The only way to curb the spread of the disease is by immunizing the entire population.* | *The government is introducing new measures aimed at curbing inflation.*

21 to stop opposition to a government

- suppress
- put down
- break up
- subdue
- crush
- quell

suppress /sə'pres/ [v T] to stop people opposing or fighting against the government, by using military force or by making their activities illegal: *The army acted swiftly to suppress the uprising.* | *Any opposition to the regime is ruthlessly suppressed.* | *The authorities suppressed publication of the journal.*

put down /ˌpʊt 'daʊn/ [phr v T usually in passive] **put down a revolt/rebellion/uprising etc** to stop it by using military force against the people involved: *The uprising was quickly put down.* | *The rebellion was put down and its leaders were executed.*

break up /ˌbreɪk 'ʌp/ [phr v T] if the police or army **break up** something such as an organized protest, they use force to stop it **break up sth** *The police were instructed to break up the demonstration and arrest the ringleaders.* | **break sth up** *The protest continued peacefully until government troops moved in to break it up.*

subdue /səb'djuː‖-'duː/ [v T] to take action to stop people behaving in a violent, angry way, especially by using force: *The soldiers managed to subdue the angry crowd.* | *The army has been used to subdue unrest in the country's capital.*

crush /krʌʃ/ [v T] to use severe methods to stop people who are fighting or opposing you: *The rebellion was quickly crushed by forces loyal to the President.* | *The army is stationed near the capital, ready to crush any signs of a revolt.*

quell /kwel/ [v T] especially written to make violent opposition stop by using force when it first starts, before it becomes impossible to control: *Extra police were called in to quell the disturbance.* | *An anti-government riot was promptly quelled by soldiers using guns and teargas.*

22 to end a relationship

- end
- break off
- sever

▸ *see also* **leave (27-28)**

end /end/ [v T] *The affair ended after it was made public by the newspapers.* | *Our relationship just isn't working. I've decided to end it.* —**end** [n singular] *We had a huge row, which marked the end of our friendship.*

break off /ˌbreɪk 'ɒf/ [phr v T] to end a relationship or connection with someone, especially an official one: *The Senator has been urged to break off all links with arms companies.* | *In the wake of the bombing, the UK is threatening to break off diplomatic relations.* | *His girlfriend has just told him that she wants to break off their engagement.*

sever /'sevəʳ/ [v T] formal **sever ties/links/relations etc** to completely end your relationship or connection with someone or something: *Since the job required that he be politically neutral, he had to sever his links with the Socialist Party.* | *Britain immediately severed relations with the three countries involved.*

23 a process that cannot be stopped

- unstoppable
- remorseless
- inexorable
- irreversible

unstoppable /ʌn'stɒpəbəl‖-'stɑːp-/ [adj] a process or action that is **unstoppable** cannot be stopped: *Political change is now unstoppable, and the regime will eventually collapse.* | *The war could unleash unstoppable political and economic changes.* | *Her rise to fame seems to be unstoppable.*

remorseless /rɪ'mɔːʳsləs/ [adj] a process that is **remorseless** continues in an unpleasant and threatening way and it seems to be impossible to stop: *The remorseless spread of the virus has led to the deaths of thousands.* | *the remorseless advance of the invading army* —**remorselessly** [adv] *The destruction of the rainforests has gone on remorselessly for the past 30 years.*

inexorable /ɪn'eksərəbəl/ [adj] formal use this about a gradual process that cannot be stopped, especially one which leads to something very bad happening: *His jealousy sets him on an inexorable course towards murder.* | *the inexorable decline in Britain's manufacturing industry* —**inexorably** [adv] *The story moves inexorably towards its tragic climax.*

irreversible /ˌɪrɪ'vɜːʳsəbəl/ [adj] a process of change that is **irreversible** cannot be stopped, and the situation that existed before cannot return: *New technology has brought about irreversible changes in society.* | *Despite claims made by skin-care manufacturers, the effects of ageing are irreversible.*

to prevent something from happening

RELATED WORDS

opposite: **allow**

▸ *see also* **forbid, control**

24 to prevent someone from doing what they want to do

- prevent
- stop
- keep sb from doing sth
- restrain
- hold back
- get in the way of
- discourage

prevent /prɪ'vent/ [v T] to make it impossible for someone to do something that they want to do **prevent sb from doing sth** *A leg injury may prevent Shearer from playing in tomorrow's game.* | *There were reports that some people had been prevented from voting in the election.*

stop /stɒp‖stɑːp/ [v T] to **stop** someone from doing something that they want to do, especially by controlling them in an unreasonable way: *I've made up my mind to leave home, and you can't stop me.* | **stop sb (from) doing sth** *My parents tried to stop me seeing Anne.* | *The government has taken legal action to stop the BBC from broadcasting a documentary about the Secret Service.*

keep sb from doing sth /ˌkiːp (sb) frəm 'duːɪŋ (sth)/ [phr v T] to prevent someone from doing something, especially something that might be harmful or upsetting: *Staying busy kept her from thinking about her illness.* | *It was all I could do to keep myself from hitting him.*

restrain /rɪ'streɪn/ [v T] to prevent someone from doing something harmful or stupid, either by physically stopping them or by persuading them not to do it: *Roger stepped forward and Martin put out his arm to restrain him.* | **restrain yourself** *She wanted to ask him all about his private life, but wisely restrained herself.* | **restrain sb from doing sth** *His arm was hurting him and he had to be restrained from doing too much.*

hold back /ˌhəʊld 'bæk/ [phr v T] to prevent someone or something from moving forward or making progress **hold back sb/sth** *The police had already erected crash barriers to hold back the advancing crowds.* | *The poor economic situation has held back investment in new technology.* | **hold sb/sth back** *Bill leapt to his feet to go after the girl, but the others held him back.* | *She always felt that being a woman had held her back in her career.*

get in the way of /ˌget ɪn ðə 'weɪ ɒv/ [v phrase] to make someone too busy to do something else, especially something they should do: *Don't let your social life get in the way of your education.*

discourage /dɪs'kʌrɪdʒ‖-'kɜːr-/ [v T] to make it less likely that someone will do something, for example by showing them that it may have a bad or unwelcome result: *Higher taxes are likely to discourage investment.* | *It is a well known fact that a negative working environment discourages creativity.* | **discourage sb from doing sth** *Higher cigarette prices do not seem to discourage people from smoking.*

25 to make sure that something does not happen

- prevent/stop
- avoid
- avert
- head off
- guard against

prevent/stop /prɪ'vent, stɒp‖stɑːp/ [v T] to make sure that something will not happen or cannot happen, especially something bad. **Prevent** is more formal than **stop**: *Many people now believe that a good diet can help to prevent cancer.* | *The new laws are designed to stop discrimination in the workplace.* | **prevent/stop sth (from) happening** *A special valve prevents the waste gases from escaping.* | *Stretch the rope out to stop it getting twisted and tangled up.* —**prevention** /prɪ'venʃən/ [n U] *How does a healthy diet help in the prevention of heart attacks?* | **crime prevention** *The police are very happy to talk to local groups about crime prevention.*

avoid /ə'vɔɪd/ [v T] to do something to prevent something bad that may happen: *The company is anxious to avoid an expensive court case.* | *We take every precaution to avoid accidents.* | **avoid sth at all costs** (=do everything possible to avoid something happening) *Civilian casualties must be avoided at all costs.*

avert /ə'vɜːrt/ [v T] formal to do something to prevent something bad that will happen very soon if you do not do anything: *It may already be too late to avert another disaster.* | *Talks will be held today in a final attempt to avert strike action.*

head off /ˌhed 'ɒf/ [phr v T] to do something to stop a difficult or unpleasant situation from developing, when it seems very likely to happen soon: *They agreed to meet government ministers in an attempt to head off a major conflict.* | *We managed to head off a financial crisis last year, but we may not be so lucky this year.*

guard against /'gɑːrd əˌgenst/ [phr v T] to carefully plan and think about what you can do in order to prevent something bad from happening: *The city council is taking emergency measures to guard against flooding in the city centre.* | *Use sunscreen on your skin to help guard against skin cancer.*

26 to prevent a plan or action from succeeding

- block
- obstruct
- thwart
- foil

block /blɒk‖blɑːk/ [v T] to use something such as a law or an official order to prevent someone from doing something that they have been planning to do: *Britain has threatened to block new EU legislation on human rights.* | *The deal was blocked by the chairman, who was unwilling to commit so much company money to a risky investment.*

obstruct /əb'strʌkt/ [v T] to try to prevent someone from doing something by deliberately making it much more difficult for them: *The House of Lords has been accused of obstructing change and preventing scientific progress.* | *It is an offence to obstruct the police during the course of their duty.* —**obstruction** /əb'strʌkʃən/ [n C/U] *The counting of votes was delayed in some areas because of obstruction by local officials.* | **+ of** *He was arrested and charged with the obstruction of a police officer.*

thwart /θwɔːrt/ [v T] formal to prevent someone from doing something, especially something that they very much want to do because it is personally important to them: *Harry knew now that nothing could thwart his plans.* | *An attempt to smuggle heroin worth £30 million into the country has been thwarted by customs officials.*

foil /fɔɪl/ [v T] to prevent something bad or criminal that someone is planning to do, by being more clever than they are: *The government has foiled an attempted military coup.* | *The burglar was foiled by a passer-by who noticed the broken window and phoned the police.*

27 to stop people from expressing their opinions

- silence
- muzzle
- gag

silence /'saɪləns/ [v T] to prevent someone from expressing their opinions or telling people something that you want kept secret: *The Mafia uses threats of physical violence or death to silence any opposition.* | *Opponents of the regime are quickly silenced.*

muzzle /'mʌzəl/ [v T] to prevent someone such as a politician or news reporter from publicly expressing their opinions, information, or ideas: *Democracy activists have been effectively muzzled by these tough new laws.* | **muzzle the press/media** *Attempts to muzzle the country's media have failed.*

gag /gæg/ [v T] to use your authority unfairly to prevent someone from telling people something or expressing their opinions – used especially in newspapers: *The government has once again used concerns about 'National Security' as an excuse to gag the press.* | *The prime minister has been accused of attempting to gag members of his government who do not agree with his policies.*

28 to stop yourself from having or showing a feeling

- hold back
- stifle
- suppress
- overcome/conquer

hold back /ˌhəʊld ˈbæk/ [phr v T] to try hard to stop yourself laughing, crying, or showing anger **hold back sth** *Jack held back his tears and pretended not to be disappointed.* | *Sarah held back a sob of relief.* | **hold sth back** *I wanted to laugh, but I managed to hold it back.* | *She struggled to hold her feelings back.*

stifle /ˈstaɪfəl/ [v T] **stifle a yawn/a smile/laughter etc** to try to stop yourself showing that you are tired, amused etc especially because you do not want to seem rude: *She stifled a yawn as the boss read out the sales figures.* | *Maria looked away and stifled a giggle.*

suppress /səˈpres/ [v T] written to make a strong effort to stop yourself from showing feelings of anger, sadness etc: *I suppressed an urge to laugh.* | *He looked at me, waiting with suppressed anger.* | *It's not good to suppress your feelings.*

overcome/conquer /ˌəʊvəʳˈkʌm, ˈkɒŋkəʳ‖ˈkɑːŋ-/ [v T] to manage to stop feeling something that affects you very strongly, for example fear, pain etc: *She managed to overcome her shyness, and stepped forward to introduce herself.* | *Hilton stepped into the room, fighting to conquer his feelings of disgust.*

29 a problem that prevents you from achieving something

- obstacle
- a bar to sth
- limiting

obstacle /ˈɒbstəkəl‖ˈɑːb-/ [n C] a problem that makes it difficult but not impossible for you to achieve what you want to achieve: *The lack of money is a serious obstacle that could prevent the project from succeeding.* | **+ to** *The greatest obstacle to economic progress has been mass unemployment.* | **overcome an obstacle** (=deal with it successfully) *She had to overcome a lot of obstacles to finally make it to drama college.*

a bar to sth /ə ˈbɑːʳ tə (sth)/ [n phrase] something that prevents someone from achieving what they want: *His disability was no bar to his entry into the profession.* | *Differences in religious beliefs are not necessarily a bar to a good relationship.*

limiting /ˈlɪmɨtɪŋ/ [adj] preventing something from improving, developing, growing etc: *I found the lack of available reference books very limiting.* | *There is a lot of research that still needs to be done, but money is an important limiting factor.*

30 to prevent someone from going somewhere

- be in the way
- block
- obstruct
- barrier
- blockade

be in the way /biː ɪn ðə ˈweɪ/ [v phrase] if someone or something **is in the way**, they are in a position that stops you from going where you want: *There's a car in the way and I can't get out of the garage.* | **be in sb's way** *Could you move please Sonia. You're in my way.*

block /blɒk‖blɑːk/ [v T] if objects or people **block** a road, entrance etc, they lie or stand right across it, so that no-one can pass through: *A big truck had turned over on its side, and it was blocking the road.* | *Hundreds of protesters blocked the entrance to the President's palace.*

obstruct /əbˈstrʌkt/ [v T] to block or almost block a road, entrance etc: *A small aircraft now obstructed the runway.* | *The driveway was obstructed by piles of stones and gravel.* —**obstruction** [n C] *A truck was causing an obstruction on the road.* | *Construction workers building the tunnel have encountered a number of obstructions.*

barrier /ˈbæriəʳ/ [n C] something that has been deliberately put somewhere, especially across a road or entrance, to prevent people from entering a place: *The automatic barrier lifted as we drove up.* | *The driver slowed down as he approached the police barrier.* | *Only a flimsy barrier stops the crowd from spilling onto the field.*

blockade /blɒˈkeɪd‖blɑː-/ [v T] to use military force to prevent people or goods from entering or leaving an area: *In June 1948 the Russians blockaded the western sectors of Berlin.* | *A US fleet blockaded the port of Veracruz.* —**blockade** [n C] *Getting food supplies through the blockade is almost impossible.*

31 intended to prevent something happening

- preventive/preventative
- pre-emptive

preventive/preventative /prɪˈventɪv, prɪˈventətɪv/ [adj only before noun] intended to prevent something from happening or getting worse: *We should spend more money educating people about preventive medicine.* | *Schools must take preventative measures so that this type of tragedy never happens again.* | *Preventative action can easily be taken to avoid damp occurring in your house.*

pre-emptive /priˈemptɪv/ [adj] **pre-emptive strike/action/attack** an action that is done to harm someone before they can harm you – use this especially about official or military actions: *The US says it is prepared to launch a pre-emptive strike with nuclear weapons if it is threatened.*

32 something that can be prevented

- preventable
- avoidable

preventable /prɪˈventəbəl/ [adj] something bad that is **preventable**, can be prevented: *Whooping cough and measles are both preventable diseases.* | *Many of these deaths each year are preventable.*

avoidable /əˈvɔɪdəbəl/ [adj] difficulties or problems that are **avoidable** can be prevented, and therefore you should not have to deal with them: *Running out of gas is annoying and easily avoidable.* | *Too many children are still injured in avoidable accidents.*

story

RELATED WORDS

▸ *see also* **film/movie, books**

1 a story

▸ **story**
▸ **tale**
▸ **fiction**
▸ **myth**
▸ **legend**
▸ **anecdote**
▸ **saga**
▸ **epic**

story /ˈstɔːri/ [n C] a description of real or imaginary events, which is told or written to entertain people: *All children love stories.* | *The film was OK, but I didn't think the story was very realistic.* | *a book of short stories* | **tell/read sb a story** *Sally, will you read us a story?* | **+ about** *Grandpa's always telling us stories about when he was a boy* | **+ of** *The movie tells the story of a young girl brought up in the Deep South in the 1930s.* | **ghost/love story** *We sat around the fire telling ghost stories.* | **fairy story** (=a story about imaginary people, creatures, and events) *He looked like some giant from a fairy story.* | **true story** (=about events that really happened) *The film is based on a true story.*

tale /teɪl/ [n C] an exciting story about imaginary events **+ of** *'Treasure Island' – a tale of pirates and adventure* | **tell a tale** *She told us many tales about when our father was a child.* | **fairy tale** (=a story about imaginary creatures, people, and events) *Hans Christian Andersen's fairy tales*

fiction /ˈfɪkʃən/ [n U] writing that describes imaginary people and events: *So much modern fiction is full of sex and violence.* | **work of fiction** *Although it is a work of fiction, it is based on fact.* | **crime/romantic/historical etc fiction** *Adopting the style of romantic fiction, she said, 'I love him passionately'.* | **science fiction** (=stories about imaginary future times) *a science fiction novel* — **fictional** [adj] *I had to remind myself these were fictional characters, not real people.*

myth /mɪθ/ [n C/U] a very old story, about gods and magical creatures: *The myth tells of how the gods sent fire to the earth in flashes of lightning.* | *a ballet based on a Greek myth* | *The heroes of myth all had some point of weakness.*

legend /ˈledʒənd/ [n C/U] an old story, usually about strange events or people with magic powers: *According to legend, the whole castle was washed into the sea.* | **+ of** *the legend of Robin Hood* | **legend has it (that)** (=according to legend) *Legend has it that Sarah Heln, who died in 1913, was shut alive inside a lead coffin.*

anecdote /ˈænɪkdəʊt/ [n C] a short funny story about something that really happened: *Personal anecdotes have no place in an academic essay.* | **+ about** *The book is full of amusing anecdotes about his time in the police force.*

saga /ˈsɑːgə/ [n C] a story about a series of connected events or adventures that take place over a long period of time, especially events involving one family: *The novel is a historical saga, set in Tudor times.* | **+ of** *Her saga of the rise and fall of a powerful family dynasty was a great commercial success.*

epic /ˈepɪk/ [n C] a story told in a long book, film, or poem which is about great or exciting events, especially in history: *The film was billed as an epic – an adventure story that would take the world and the box-office by storm.* | *The history of a single event has been spun out to fill a 255 page epic.* | **epic poem/hero/style etc** *the epic poem 'Beowulf'*

2 stories that are intended to teach people something

▸ **allegory**
▸ **parable**
▸ **fable**

allegory /ˈælɪ̈gəri‖-gɔːri/ [n C] a story in which the events and characters represent something or someone else from the real world: *'Animal Farm' is an allegory in which the animals represent the Russian people and Farmer Jones the old Tsarist regime.* | **+ of** *The film was a dark, powerful allegory of life in post-war America.*

parable /ˈpærəbəl/ [n C] a short simple story that is used to teach something, especially what is morally right: *Christ used parables to explain moral questions in a way that people could understand.* | *It is a kind of parable for the eighties – a lesson about the destructiveness of greed.* | **+ of** *the parable of 'The Prodigal Son'*

fable /ˈfeɪbəl/ [n C] a story that has a moral message, especially a story in which animals are used to represent people's good and bad behaviour: *The best-known of Aesop's fables is 'The Tortoise and the Hare'.* | *The life of Howard Hughes cannot fail to remind us of the fable of Midas.*

3 someone in a story

▸ **character**
▸ **hero**
▸ **heroine**

character /ˈkærɪ̈ktəʳ/ [n C] one of the people in a story: *The two main characters in the book are a young boy and his teacher.* | *Each group is named after a fictional character like Mickey Mouse.*

hero /ˈhɪərəʊ/ [n C] the man or boy who is the main character in a story: *In cinema, the hero always got the girl and the bad guy was always punished.* | *Shakespeare's best-known tragic hero is probably Hamlet.* | **+ of** *Who was the hero of 'The Catcher in the Rye'?*

heroine /ˈherəʊɪn/ [n C] the woman or girl who is the main character in a story: *The story is narrated entirely by the heroine.* | *She seems to see herself as some kind of romantic heroine in a trashy novel.*

4 the events in a story

▸ **plot**
▸ **storyline**

plot /plɒt‖plɑːt/ [n C] the series of events that happen in a book, play, film etc, and the way they are all connected: *The plot was so complicated that I was totally confused by the time I was two chapters in.* | *The book doesn't have much of a plot, but its characters are fantastic.*

storyline /ˈstɔːrilaɪn/ [n C] the main story of a book, play, film etc: *Anna's marriage problems form the main storyline in Episode One.* | *The storyline was too far-fetched, and none of the actors were particularly good.*

5 the story of a real person's life

▸ **biography**
▸ **life**
▸ **life story**

biography /baɪˈɒgrəfi‖-ˈɑːg-/ [n C] a book that is the

story of a famous person's life: *She is the author of several books, including a biography of the artist Salvador Dali.* | *Isaac Deutscher's outstanding biographies of Stalin and Trotsky*

life /laɪf/ [n C usually singular] the story of a famous person's **life**, as described in a book, or shown in paintings or a film: *Boswell's Life of Samuel Johnson was published in 1791.* | *The lower series of frescoes describe the life of Saint Francis of Assisi.*

life story /ˈlaɪf ˌstɔːri/ [n C] an account, especially a spoken account, of the main events that have happened in someone's life: *When you meet someone for the first time, they don't want your entire life story in detail.* | *The newspaper has been running his life story for the past two weeks.*

6 the story of your own life

- autobiography
- memoirs
- story of your life

autobiography /ˌɔːtəbaɪˈɒgrəfi‖-ˈɑːg-/ [n C] the story of your own life, which you have written yourself: *In his autobiography he described his life as an explorer in some of the remotest parts of the earth.* | *Her autobiography will be published next month, and will be a guaranteed bestseller.*

memoirs /ˈmemwɑːʳz/ [n plural] the story of your own life which you have written yourself, especially your involvement in important political or military events: *In his memoirs he gives a new insight into several political scandals of the pre-war years.* | *The duke's memoirs will be serialised in the Sunday Times.*

story of your life /ˌstɔːri əv jɔːʳ ˈlaɪf/ [n phrase] a spoken account of the main events that have happened in your life, especially if they are boring or unpleasant **tell sb the story of your life** *He told me the story of his life right from the early days in a poor part of Washington.* | *She began to tell him the story of her life, a long catalogue of disappointment and gloom.*

straight

RELATED WORDS

opposite: **bent**

- *see also* **vertical**

1 straight lines or objects

- straight

straight /streɪt/ [adj] **straight** lines, roads, edges etc have no bends or curves: *First, draw two straight lines across the page using a ruler.* | *Her hair is blonde and very straight.* | *Anne loved Rome, with its open spaces and long straight avenues.* | **dead straight** especially British (=completely straight) *The road ran dead straight for 50 miles across the desert.*

2 travelling or moving in a straight line

- straight
- go straight on
- in a straight line
- direct
- as the crow flies

straight /streɪt/ [adv] *Terry was so drunk he couldn't walk straight.* | **+ ahead/down/towards etc** *If you look straight ahead, you'll see the church in the distance.* | *Jane was walking purposefully along the hall, straight towards us.*

go straight on British **/go straight** American /ˌgəʊ streɪt ˈɒn, gəʊ ˈstreɪt/ [v phrase] spoken to continue travelling ahead in the same direction as before, without turning left or right – use this when you are telling people which way to go: *When you get to the intersection, go straight.* | *Keep going straight on through the town and when you come to the school, turn left.*

in a straight line /ɪn ə ˌstreɪt ˈlaɪn/ [adv] if something moves **in a straight line**, it does not turn to the left or to the right: *Light always travels in a straight line.* | *It's difficult to walk in a straight line with your eyes closed.*

direct /dʒ̍ˈrekt, ˌdaɪˈrekt◂/ [adj] going straight from one place to another without changing direction: *Which is the most direct route to London from here?* | *The Chin tracks in India follow the most direct line between villages, regardless of gradient.*

as the crow flies /əz ðə ˈkrəʊ ˌflaɪz/ [adv] following a straight line between two places – use this to say what is the shortest possible distance between them: *The distance between the two towns is only 10 kilometres as the crow flies, but it can take up to 2 hours along the narrow coastal road.*

3 sitting or standing straight

- upright

upright /ˈʌp-raɪt/ [adv] sitting or standing with your back and neck straight, not bent: *The roof of the cave was so low he couldn't stand upright.* | *Pulling herself upright on her walking frame, she moved across the room to the stairs.* | **bolt upright** (=with your back very straight) *There was a sudden noise outside and she sat bolt upright in bed.* —**upright** [adj] *An upright posture in a chair or bed helps the patient to breathe more easily.*

4 to become straight or make something straight

- straighten out
- straighten
- straighten
- sit up

straighten out /ˌstreɪtn ˈaʊt/ [phr v I/T] to become straight or to make something straight: *The road twisted and turned for a few miles and then straightened out again.* | **straighten out sth** *He had straightened out all the paperclips on his desk, but had done no work.* | **straighten sth out** *Gemma needed surgery to straighten her crooked knee out.*

straighten /ˈstreɪtn/ [v T] to make something straight: *The car's in the garage having its front bumper straightened.* | *Gradually straighten your legs until you are standing upright.*

straighten ALSO **straighten up** /ˈstreɪtn, ˌstreɪtn ˈʌp/ [v I/phr v I] to make your back straight when sitting or standing: *Alan straightened in his chair.* | *She straightened up as Melissa approached, pulling off her gardening gloves.*

sit up /ˌsɪt ˈʌp/ [phr v I] to make your back straight when sitting: *He sat up in his chair when I started talking about Chris.* | **sit up straight** *Sit up straight and put a cushion behind your lower back.*

strange

unusual in a way that makes you feel surprised, frightened, worried etc

RELATED WORDS

▸ *see also* **unusual, crazy, mysterious, frightened/frightening, magic, ghost**

1 strange situations, experiences, smells, tastes etc

- ▸ **strange**
- ▸ **funny**
- ▸ **peculiar**
- ▸ **mysterious**
- ▸ **weird**
- ▸ **bizarre**
- ▸ **eerie**
- ▸ **surreal**
- ▸ **curious**
- ▸ **ironic**

strange /streɪndʒ/ [adj] very different from what you expect or from what usually happens, in a way that makes you feel a little frightened or surprised: *A strange noise woke her up.* | *I had a strange feeling that I'd been there before.* | *Amanda's eyes glowed in a strange way, like a cat's.* | *He seemed to know lots of things about me, but the strange thing is I didn't even tell him my name.* | **it is strange that** *It's strange that you've never met him – he lives in your street.* —**strangely** [adv] *The downtown streets were strangely empty and peaceful.*

funny ALSO **odd** especially British /ˈfʌni, ɒd‖ɑːd/ [adj] something **funny** or **odd** is a little strange and it makes you feel slightly worried or surprised because you cannot explain it or you do not know what it is: *There's a funny smell coming from the fridge.* | *Thumps and laughter and odd noises were coming out of the living room.* | **it is funny/odd that** *It seems odd that no one noticed him coming in.* | *It's funny that he managed to hit the ball because he never hits it in practice.* | **that's funny/that's odd** spoken *'Your keys aren't here.' 'That's funny – I'm sure I left them on the table.'* —**oddly** [adv] *The eggplant was limp and oddly pale.* | **oddly enough** *Oddly enough, I didn't feel at all nervous about visiting the prison.*

peculiar /pɪˈkjuːliəʳ/ [adj] strange and slightly unpleasant: *This meat tastes peculiar.* | *I've been having very peculiar dreams the past few weeks.* | *I heard a peculiar warbling from the living room.*

mysterious /mɪˈstɪəriəs/ [adj] use this about something that people know very little about and that is difficult to explain or understand: *No one could offer an explanation for his mysterious disappearance.* | *I kept getting mysterious phone calls where the caller would hang up as soon as I answered.* | **under mysterious circumstances** *Two weeks later, the shop burned to the ground under mysterious circumstances.* —**mysteriously** [adv] *Mysteriously, no one had noticed anyone leave or enter the room.*

weird /wɪəʳd/ [adj] a **weird** experience, feeling, sight, or sound is strange and very different from what you are used to: *She only had lipstick on her bottom lip which looked pretty weird.* | *It's a weird feeling to go back to a place that you lived in a long time ago.*

bizarre /bɪ̇ˈzɑːʳ/ [adj] extremely strange, and very different from what is generally considered to be normal, especially in a frightening or slightly worrying way: *Woods disappeared in very bizarre circumstances, and no trace of him has ever been found.* | *It was bizarre – if we took longer than five minutes in the bathroom, we had to explain why to our manager.*

eerie /ˈɪəri/ [adj] strange and frightening: *An eerie howl filled the cave.* | *I had the eerie feeling that somebody was watching me.* | *The pumps were shut off now. It was eerie, being in the factory without their sound.* —**eerily** [adv] *The forest around them remained eerily silent.*

surreal /səˈrɪəl/ [adj] extremely strange, because nothing seems connected with real life or normal experiences, and things happen or appear together that do not belong together: *Living on the commune turned out to be a surreal experience.* | *The whole trial and the media circus surrounding it was surreal.*

curious /ˈkjʊəriəs/ [adj usually before noun] strange and surprising but interesting, so that you want to know more about it: *Life in the village was a curious combination of the old and the very new.* | *He had come to some curious arrangement with his landlady.* —**curiously** [adv] *It was a curiously organized office.*

ironic /aɪˈrɒnɪk‖aɪˈrɑː-/ [adj] an **ironic** situation seems strange and amusing, because something happens that you would not expect at all: *Her car was stolen from outside the police station, which is pretty ironic.* | *One of the study's ironic discoveries is that TV trials educate the public about the justice system better than actual trials.* | **it is ironic that** *It's ironic that professional athletes are often such unhealthy people.* —**ironically** [adv] *Ironically, it was his very success which led to the media attention and his eventual downfall.*

2 strange people, behaviour, objects or ideas

- ▸ **strange**
- ▸ **eccentric**
- ▸ **weird**
- ▸ **bizarre**
- ▸ **outlandish**
- ▸ **funny/odd**
- ▸ **peculiar**
- ▸ **kinky**
- ▸ **warped**

strange /streɪndʒ/ [adj] *Pearl was a strange girl who never played with the other children.* | *He's very strange – you never really know what he's thinking.* | *Marla has some strange ideas about raising children.* —**strangely** [adv] *Witnesses said the man was carrying a gun and behaving strangely.*

eccentric /ɪkˈsentrɪk/ [adj] an **eccentric** person has strange and slightly crazy habits or ideas, which people think are amusing: *Our neighbour is an eccentric old lady who has about 25 cats.* | *Mr. Withers is a little eccentric, but he's basically harmless.*

weird /wɪəʳd/ [adj] strange and slightly frightening, and making you feel uncomfortable: *I don't really want to spend the evening with Helen – she's so weird.* | *She's dating a really weird guy who's into witchcraft and black magic.* | *The museum has a collection of the weirdest sculptures I've ever seen.*

bizarre /bɪ̇ˈzɑːʳ/ [adj] extremely strange, and very different from what is generally considered to be normal, especially in a frightening or slightly worrying way: *They tell the most bizarre stories about him.* | *The marriage between the two stars was as bizarre as it was short-lived.* | *Colin later took his own life in a bizarre suicide pact with his mother.* —**bizarrely** [adv] *Roland was dressed rather bizarrely in the robes of a priest.*

outlandish /aʊtˈlændɪʃ/ [adj] something that is **outlandish** is very strange, and not at all like anything you are used to: *Parts of Lisa's story sounded outlandish, and no one would believe her.* | *She came* *to the party wearing an outlandish costume and blond wig.*

funny/odd /ˈfʌni, ɒd‖ɑːd/ [adj] especially British slightly strange and difficult to understand: *Did Anna warn you that her aunt is rather ... well, rather odd?* | *He's a bit funny – sometimes he's very friendly, other times he just ignores you.*

peculiar /pɪˈkjuːliəʳ/ [adj] slightly strange, and different from what you would normally expect, especially in a way that is either amusing or a little worrying: *She's actually very friendly in her own peculiar way.* | *Glenn started acting peculiar after his wife's funeral.*

kinky /ˈkɪŋki/ [adj] someone who is **kinky**, or who does **kinky** things, has strange ways of getting sexual excitement: *kinky sex* | *I think he's a bit kinky – but I like him.*

warped /wɔːʳpt/ [adj] informal someone who is **warped** has ideas or thoughts that most people think are unpleasant and strange: *Some of my professors at college were pretty warped.* | *In his statement the chief of police said, 'We are dealing with a warped mind, and we have to take all precautions.'* | *Only someone with a warped sense of humor would think the accident is funny.*

3 a strange person

- weirdo
- oddball
- freak
- crank

weirdo /ˈwɪəʳdəʊ/ [n C] informal someone who is very strange in an unpleasant and sometimes threatening way: *There's a weirdo who stands in front of the store and talks to himself.* | *When I travel by underground I always seem to end up sitting next to some weirdo.*

oddball /ˈɒdbɔːl‖ˈɑːd-/ [n C] informal a strange person: *Most of my family's OK, but my brother's a bit of an oddball.* | *Growing up, most of the other kids considered me an oddball.*

freak /friːk/ [n C] informal a very strange person, especially one who behaves oddly and has strange ideas: *The guy is probably just some freak who saw her on TV and decided he loves her.* | **control/neat/fast food etc freak** *Her husband's a control freak – he won't let her leave the house without him.*

crank /kræŋk/ [n C] British someone who other people think is strange, especially because they have beliefs, aims, or habits that are thought to be very unusual or too extreme: *Vegetarians were once regarded as cranks.* | *Call me a crank, but I think the world was a lot better before mobile phones came along.*

strict/not strict

RELATED WORDS

▸ *see also* **rule/regulation, obey, disobey, punish, tell sb off**

1 people/organizations

- strict
- firm
- tough
- stern
- harsh
- authoritarian
- be a stickler for
- disciplinarian

strict /strɪkt/ [adj] someone who is **strict** makes people obey rules and refuses to let people disobey them – use this especially about parents, teachers, or organizations: *Teachers need to be strict, but also fair.* | **+ with** *I think you're too strict with your children.* | **+ about** *The manager is very strict about people getting to work on time.* | *Most schools are quite strict about the way students dress.* —**strictly** [adv] *They brought their children up very strictly.*

firm /fɜːʳm/ [adj] if you are **firm** with someone, you tell them that they must accept what you say because you are not going to change it: *Emily was polite but firm – her answer was 'no'.* | **+ with** *You'll just have to be firm with him and tell him he can't have any more money.* —**firmly** [adv] *'No,' she said firmly, 'you can't go.'* | *She told me quite firmly that she wasn't prepared to give any more time to the project.*

tough /tʌf/ [adj] informal determined that your orders or decisions will be obeyed, especially in order to make sure a situation or someone's progress improves – use this especially when you think that someone is right to be strict: *The chancellor has got to be tough and keep government spending down.* | **+ on** *We need a government that is tough on crime.* | **+ with** *She's quite tough with her students.*

stern /stɜːʳn/ [adj] written strict in a serious, disapproving, and unfriendly way: *Her grandfather was a stern man who rarely smiled.* | *Sheila walked into the museum, under the stern gaze of the curator.* —**sternly** [adv] *'What's all this nonsense about?' asked my uncle sternly.*

harsh /hɑːʳʃ/ [adj] cruel and not sympathetic in the way that you deal with bad behaviour or mistakes: *It may seem harsh to punish him, but he has to learn that this kind of behaviour is unacceptable.* | *Her reaction to the child's bad behaviour was unnecessarily harsh.* —**harshly** [adv] *He spoke firmly but not harshly.*

authoritarian /ɔːˌθɒrɪ̇ˈteəriən‖ɔːˌθɑː-, əˌθɔː-/ [adj] forcing people to obey rules or laws, and punishing them severely if they do not: *Their father was authoritarian in the home, insisting on total obedience.* | *Many people are now demanding a more democratic and less authoritarian form of government.* | **authoritarian regime** *an extreme right-wing, authoritarian regime*

be a stickler for /biː ə ˈstɪkləʳ fɔːʳ/ [v phrase] to demand that people keep strictly to rules, customs etc, especially in a way that people think is unnecessary and old-fashioned: *The caretaker is a real stickler for rules.* | *My mother was a stickler for cleanliness.*

disciplinarian /ˌdɪsɪ̇plɪ̇ˈneəriən/ [n C] a very strict person who believes that people should obey rules and orders, and who punishes those who do not: *The store manager was a disciplinarian, but was always fair to his staff.* | **strict disciplinarian** *She was a wonderful teacher, but a strict disciplinarian.*

2 rules/laws/systems

- strict
- tough
- harsh
- stringent
- rigid
- tight
- draconian

strict /strɪkt/ [adj usually before noun] **strict** rules, laws, etc are very clear and must always be obeyed: *There are strict rules about the use of dangerous chemicals.* | *He had strict instructions to return the key to me.* —**strictly** [adv] *Smoking is strictly forbidden in this area.*

tough /tʌf/ [adj] **tough** laws or rules are very strict and do not allow much freedom: *The federal government is introducing tough new rules to control immigration.* | *Opposition leaders are demanding tougher laws against drinking and driving.*

harsh /hɑːʳʃ/ [adj] a **harsh** law or system of government has strict rules and severe punishments – use this about something that you think is unfair and too strict: *The government has brought in harsh measures to combat the rioting taking place in many cities.* | *a harsh military regime* —**harshly** [adv] *Many of the prisoners were treated very harshly.*

stringent /ˈstrɪndʒənt/ [adj] controlled very strictly by rules that have very high standards **stringent controls/measures/regulations etc** *There are now stringent controls on pollution from all power stations.* | *stringent air safety regulations*

rigid /ˈrɪdʒ̇d/ [adj] **rigid** systems or rules are very strict and difficult to change: *He built the team through hard training and rigid discipline.* | *It is not possible to lay down rigid rules on sentencing – judges must be free to use their discretion.*

tight /taɪt/ [adj] **tight** controls or limits are very strict about what is allowed and what is not allowed: *The report recommends tighter controls on the advertising of cigarettes.* | *Laws controlling the emission of greenhouse gases are not nearly tight enough.*

draconian /drəˈkəʊniən/ [adj] formal **draconian laws/measures/penalties etc** laws or punishments that are extremely strict or cruel: *The government has imposed draconian penalties for anyone found in possession of illegal drugs.* | *Draconian measures have been implemented to control population growth.*

3 to treat someone strictly

- be hard on
- get tough with
- stand/take no nonsense
- rule with a rod of iron
- keep a tight rein on

be hard on /biː ˈhɑːʳd ɒn/ [v phrase] to treat someone very strictly and sometimes unfairly: *Sometimes I think you're too hard on that boy.* | *Don't be too hard on her. She didn't mean to break it.*

get tough with /get ˈtʌf wɪð/ [v phrase] to begin to treat someone strictly because they have been doing something that is wrong or illegal: *At last the government is starting to get tough with dealers who sell dangerous second-hard cars.* | *Football clubs have been told that they must get tough with violent fans.*

stand/take no nonsense /ˌstænd, ˌteɪk nəʊ ˈnɒnsəns‖-ˈnɑːnsens/ [v phrase] if you say that you **stand** or **take no nonsense**, you mean you treat other people strictly, but in a way that makes people respect you: *I won't stand any nonsense. I want you all in bed by nine o'clock.* | **+ from** *She was a very good teacher who would take no nonsense from her students.*

rule with a rod of iron /ˌruːl wɪð ə ˌrɒd əv ˈaɪəʳn‖-ˌrɑːd-/ [v phrase not in progressive] to control an organization or group of people very strictly, by always punishing people if they do not obey you: *Their mother ruled their life with a rod of iron.* | *The Secret police ruled the city with a rod of iron.*

keep a tight rein on /kiːp ə ˌtaɪt ˈreɪn ɒn/ [v phrase] to strictly control someone's behaviour, for example by not allowing them to do things without asking your permission: *They keep a very tight rein on their children.* | *The government has promised to keep a tight rein on public spending.*

4 to deal very strictly with bad behaviour or crime

- come down hard on
- crack down on
- clamp down on
- tighten up

come down hard on /ˌkʌm daʊn ˈhɑːʳd ɒn/ [v phrase] to deal very strictly with a bad behaviour or crime by punishing people severely for it: *You'll find that Mr Evans comes down very hard on people who don't do their job properly.* | *The authorities are really coming down hard on tax evasion.*

crack down on /ˌkræk ˈdaʊn ɒn / [phr v T] to start dealing with an illegal activity in a much stricter way than before: *The Athletics Federation plans to crack down on drug and steroid abuse by athletes.* | *The government has promised to crack down on crime.* | *City authorities were quick to crack down on the rioters.* —**crack-down** /ˈkræk daʊn/ [n C] *In the first week of the police crack-down, over 500 car thieves were arrested.* | **+ on** *a crack-down on drug dealers*

clamp down on /ˌklæmp ˈdaʊn ɒn / [phr v T] to treat a particular crime or activity much more strictly than before to stop it from becoming more common: *New laws will clamp down on the illegal smuggling of cigarettes and tobacco.* | *Recently the courts have clamped down on joy-riding.* —**clamp-down** /ˈklæmp daʊn/ [n C] **+ on** *Children's organizations are calling for a clamp-down on TV violence.*

tighten up /ˌtaɪtn ˈʌp/ [phr v T] to make rules, laws, or controls more strict so that it is harder for people to break them: *The prime minister has promised to tighten up the law on carbon dioxide emissions.* | **+ on** *The music industry is determined to tighten up on the illegal copying of CDs.*

5 punishments/criticism

- severe
- heavy
- stiff

severe /s̈ˈvɪəʳ/ [adj] use this to describe a punishment or criticism that is very strict: *There are very severe penalties for drug dealing.* | *Many people feel the punishment should have been more severe.* | *The organization has been the subject of severe criticism for the way it treated its staff.* —**severely** [adv] *Anyone caught breaking the rules will be severely punished.*

heavy /ˈhevi/ [adj] use this to describe a punishment that is strict **heavy fine** *Companies that continue to cause pollution will now face heavy fines.* | **heavy penalty** *There are heavy penalties for anyone caught in possession of counterfeit money.*

stiff /stɪf/ [adj] use this to describe an official punishment that is more strict than usual **stiff fine** *Motorists who do not obey the rules will face stiff fines of up to £3000.* | **stiff penalty** *Magistrates now have the power to impose stiff penalties on the parents of children who fail to turn up for school.* | **stiff sentence** *For crimes involving the use of guns, the sentences are particularly stiff.*

6 to make rules less strict

- relax

relax /rɪˈlæks/ [v T] to make rules, laws, or controls less strict: *The government proposes to relax the rules on bringing pets into the country.* | *Local residents are protesting against plans to relax laws controlling pub opening hours.*

7 to become less strict

- relent
- soften
- mellow
- go easy on
- ease up on
- let up on

relent /rɪˈlent/ [v I] to change your mind and decide to be less strict about something: *Marjorie finally relented and agreed to meet him.* | *Prison officials relented and allowed Wilson to receive visits from his family.* | *He begged and begged to be allowed to go to the game, and in the end I relented.*

soften /ˈsɒfən‖ˈsɔː-/ [v I/T] to become less strict and more sympathetic towards someone: *The inspector looked angry but then softened when he saw the boy's frightened expression.* | *The government seems to have softened its attitude towards single parents.*

mellow /ˈmeləʊ/ [v I] to change your attitude and become less strict, especially over a long period of time: *She's mellowed a lot since she retired.* | **mellow with age/time** *He hasn't always been so understanding. He's really mellowed with age.*

go easy on /ˌgəʊ ˈiːzi ɒn/ [v phrase] especially spoken to treat someone less strictly than usual, especially because they have special problems or difficulties: *Go easy on her. She's had a very difficult time since her parents died.* | *I think you should go easy on Jim.*

ease up on /ˌiːz ˈʌp ɒn/ [phr v T] to stop treating someone so strictly, especially because they do not deserve it or because they are affected badly by it: *I've decided we need to ease up on Sally and take the pressure off her for a while.*

let up on /ˌlet ˈʌp ɒn / [phr v T] to treat someone less strictly, especially temporarily after a period of strict treatment: *If you let up on him he'll have a chance to show that he can behave himself.* | *She never lets up on those poor kids!*

8 people/attitudes that are not strict

- lenient
- easy-going
- soft
- tolerant
- tolerance
- liberal
- broad-minded
- permissive
- lax
- over-indulgent

lenient /ˈliːniənt/ [adj] not strict in the way that you punish people or control their behaviour: *The younger teachers generally had a more lenient attitude towards their students.* | **+ with** *Some police officers have criticized judges for being too lenient with car thieves and burglars.* —**leniently** [adv] *The courts will often deal quite leniently with first-time offenders.* —**leniency** [n U] when someone is not strict: *This report shows that wealthy people are treated with more leniency when they break the law.*

easy-going /ˌiːzi ˈgəʊɪŋ◂/ [adj] someone who is **easy-going** does not care about being strict, and is usually calm and relaxed: *Our parents are pretty easy-going, and they don't mind if we stay out late.*

soft /sɒft‖sɔːft/ [adj] someone who is **soft** seems weak because they are not strict enough with other people: *He doesn't have the right personality to be an army officer, he's too soft.* | **+ on** *They accused the government of being too soft on crime.*

tolerant /ˈtɒlərənt‖ˈtɑː-/ [adj] allowing people to do, say, or believe what they like without fear of being punished or criticized: *I've tried to adopt a fairly tolerant attitude towards his behaviour.* | **+ of** *She's not very tolerant of other people's failings.* | **+ towards** *You should try to be more tolerant towards other people.*

tolerance /ˈtɒlərəns‖ˈtɑː-/ [n U] behaviour or an attitude that allows people to do, say, or believe what they like without fear of being punished or criticized: *Tolerance was not a quality you associated with my parents.* | **+ of** *The government is beginning to show more tolerance of opposition groups.* | **+ towards** *The school encourages an attitude of tolerance towards all people.*

liberal /ˈlɪbərəl/ [adj] willing to understand and respect other people's ideas, opinions, and behaviour, even if you do not approve of them: *I was fortunate enough to have very liberal parents.* | *He has quite liberal views for someone of his generation.*

broad-minded /ˌbrɔːd ˈmaɪndɪ̣d/ [adj] willing to accept and respect other people's beliefs or behaviour although they many be very different from your own: *My mother's quite broad-minded. She understands my decision to bring up my baby on my own.*

permissive /pərˈmɪsɪv/ [adj] a **permissive** society or person allows behaviour, especially sexual behaviour, that many other people disapprove of: *In the permissive society of the 1960s anything was possible.* | *It's not always true that young people have a more permissive attitude towards sex.* —**permissiveness** [n U] *Some parents are worried that their children might be corrupted by western permissiveness.*

lax /læks/ [adj] not strict enough, especially through laziness or carelessness: *The report criticizes the lax security at many prisons.* | **+ about** *I think the school has been too lax about bad behaviour in the past.* —**laxity** [n U] formal *She accused Henry of moral laxity.*

over-indulgent /ˌəʊvər ɪnˈdʌldʒənt◂/ [adj] allowing someone, especially a child, to behave in whatever way they want because you love them: *Parents can easily fall into the trap of being over-indulgent with their first child.* | *She was brought up by a succession of over-indulgent relations.*

9 criticism/punishment that is not strict

- light
- lenient
- mild

light /laɪt/ [adj] *The sentence was surprisingly light for such a serious offence.* | *Some ministers are suggesting that there should be much lighter penalties for first-time offenders.*

lenient /ˈliːniənt/ [adj] an official punishment that is **lenient** is not severe: *The prosecution lawyer challenged the sentence as being unduly lenient.* | *He was given a comparatively lenient fine.*

mild /maɪld/ [adj] criticism or a punishment that is **mild** is not strict, especially in a way that is surprising: *Many drug dealers are prepared to take the risk because they know that if they are caught the punishment will be mild.* | *Her proposals were welcomed by most people, with only mild criticism from a few of her opponents.*

strike

to stop working in order to demand higher wages, better conditions etc

RELATED WORDS

- to hit someone or something *see* **hit**
- *see also* **stop, work, protest, government, politics, rebellion/revolution**

1 to stop working in order to get higher wages etc

- go on strike
- strike
- come out on strike
- walk out
- down tools
- be on strike

go on strike /ˌgəʊ ɒn ˈstraɪk/ [v phrase] if workers **go on strike**, they stop working in order to demand better pay or working conditions, or to protest about something: *In 1926, all Britain's miners, railway workers, and transport workers went on strike.* | **+ for** *The engineers have gone on strike for better pay and shorter working hours.* | **go on indefinite strike** (=go on strike until something is done to change a situation) *From tomorrow, we're going on indefinite strike unless something's done to reduce the number of accidents in the factory.*

strike /straɪk/ [v I] if workers **strike**, they stop working in order to demand higher wages etc – used especially in news reports: *Female workers are often more reluctant than men to strike in order to get what they want.* | **+ for** *Teachers were not striking for higher pay, but for higher standards in education.* —**striking** [adj only before noun] *Outside the offices, standing in the rain, were 1400 striking clerical workers.*

come out on strike /ˌkʌm aʊt ɒn ˈstraɪk/ [v phrase] British if a group of workers **come out on strike**, they deliberately stop working as a protest, especially after discussions with their employers have failed to produce any agreement: *Union leaders are calling on their members to come out on strike from next Monday.* | **+ in support of sb/sth** *The government just didn't expect teachers to come out on strike in support of the miners.*

walk out /ˌwɔːk ˈaʊt/ [phr v I] if workers **walk out**, they stop working and leave the place where they are working, especially when this has not been planned but happens as a protest about something that has just happened: *This afternoon, three hundred car workers walked out as a protest over cuts in overtime.* | *Ambulance drivers have threatened to walk out if their pay claim is rejected.* —**walk-out** /ˈwɔːk aʊt/ [n C] *What started as a walk-out in a small factory in Manchester was to develop into a national and long-running strike.*

down tools /ˌdaʊn ˈtuːlz/ [v phrase] British if workers in a factory **down tools**, they stop working as a protest about something that has just happened: *After their workmate was sacked, the other machinists all downed tools until she was reinstated.*

be on strike /biː ɒn ˈstraɪk/ [v phrase] if workers **are on strike**, they have stopped working in order to demand higher wages etc: *Some two-thirds of the country's diamond miners are now on strike.* | **be out on strike** *There were frequent power cuts when the electricity workers were out on strike.*

2 when workers are on strike

- strike
- industrial action
- work-to-rule
- stoppage
- go-slow

strike /straɪk/ [n C] *The offices were closed by a strike that lasted two months.* | **miners'/teachers'/railworkers' etc strike** *Since the miners' strike, thirty of the mines in the area have been closed.* | **coal/rail/dock etc strike** *The roads were a nightmare as commuters were hit by a rail strike.* | **call a strike** (=ask workers to strike) *When union bosses called a strike in protest over low pay, the response was overwhelming.* | **call off a strike** (=stop striking) *The administration has officially asked transportation workers to call off their strike.* | **general strike** (=when most workers in a country strike) *Following a general strike and calls for his resignation, the President was arrested on 26 March.* | **strike action** *Shipbuilders and dockers were solidly in favour of strike action in support of their claim.*

industrial action /ɪnˌdʌstriəl ˈækʃən/ [n U] when a group of workers try to persuade their employer to improve pay or conditions, either by going on strike or by doing less work than they usually do: *Exactly what form the industrial action will take is not yet known.* | *Most of the workers are against industrial action, but are asking for talks with employers.* | **take industrial action** *A survey of 2,000 federation members had shown that 48% believed police should have the right to take industrial action.*

work-to-rule /ˌwɜːʳk tə ˈruːl/ [n singular] when workers do only the amount of work they legally have to do and no more, as a protests against something: *Because of their work-to-rule, teachers were no longer taking after-school clubs or supervising lunch hours.*

stoppage British ALSO **work stoppage** American /ˈstɒpɪdʒ, ˈwɜːʳk ˌstɒpɪdʒ‖ˈstɑː-/ [n C] when a group of workers stop working for a short time until their complaint, protest, or demand is dealt with: *Customs officers will return to work today after a twenty-four hour stoppage.* | *Railworkers in central Poland also joined the stoppage, cutting the link with the industrial south-west.* | *The plan is likely to be met with work stoppages and other labor disruptions.*

go-slow /ˌgəʊ ˈsləʊ/ [n C] British when a group of workers deliberately work more slowly than usual as a way of protesting about low wages, bad working conditions etc: *The hospital seemed to be treating as many patients as possible before the go-slow came into effect.*

strong

RELATED WORDS

opposite: —— **weak**

- strong taste *see* **taste**
- strong smell *see* **smell**
- *see also* **healthy/unhealthy, fit/not fit, power/powerful, brave/not brave, hard, feel, believe, determined**

1 having a strong body

- strong
- powerful
- muscular
- well-built
- strapping
- brawny

strong /strɒŋ‖strɔːŋ/ [adj] someone who is **strong** has big muscles and can lift heavy things, do a lot of physical work etc: *It took four strong men to lift the piano.* | *Unless you have very strong arms, get a workman to do the drilling for you.* | **big and strong** *Sarah's big and strong, just like the men she works with.* | **as strong as an ox** (=very strong) *Twenty years of working in the steel mill had made him as strong as an ox.*

powerful /ˈpaʊəʳfəl/ [adj] very strong – use this about someone's body, arms, muscles etc: *He was a tall man with a powerful physique.*

muscular /ˈmʌskjᵍləʳ/ [adj] someone who is **muscular** looks strong because you can see that they have big muscles: *She liked men who were tall and muscular.* | *He had broad shoulders and muscular arms.* | *He kept his firm muscular body in shape with an hour's run every morning.*

well-built /ˌwel 'bɪlt◂/ [adj] a **well-built** man is strong and tall in an attractive way: *A well-built young man in uniform came to our table and asked the time.* | *Witnesses have described the attacker as white, six feet tall and well-built.*

strapping /'stræpɪŋ/ [adj only before noun] a **strapping** young man or young woman is strong, tall, and looks healthy and active: *She remembered Martin as a strapping youth with a big appetite.* | *The farmer's daughters were a fine pair of strapping young girls.*

brawny /'brɔːni/ [adj] strong, with big muscles – use this especially to talk about someone who looks physically strong rather than intelligent: *The gardener's assistant arrived – a brawny youth who never said a word.* | *He had a football player's physique: big head, thick neck, brawny shoulders, and heavy legs.*

2 strong and healthy, and able to deal with illnesses, difficult conditions etc

- strong
- sturdy
- robust
- hardy
- tough
- resilient

strong /strɒŋ‖strɔːŋ/ [adj] *She had three young daughters, all strong and healthy.* | *After a week in bed I felt strong enough to try walking a few steps.* | **have a strong constitution** (=have a naturally strong and healthy body) *Despite his strong constitution, his health was beginning to suffer.*

sturdy /'stɜːʳdi/ [adj] strong and healthy-looking, and a little short: *Maria was small and sturdy, with dark hair and dark eyes.* | *Mrs Harding herself was thin and frail but her son was a sturdy sixteen-year-old.* | *The ponies used underground were sturdy little animals that came originally from Northern Spain.*

robust /rə'bʌst, 'rəʊbʌst/ [adj] someone who is **robust**, is strong and healthy and unlikely to become ill or get tired easily: *Though he was over seventy, he was still robust and active.* | *Less robust persons might need a siesta, but Eva worked right through from dawn till dusk.*

hardy /'hɑːʳdi/ [adj] people who are **hardy** are naturally strong and healthy and can live in very difficult or uncomfortable conditions: *The people who lived in the hills were a hardy and hard-working race.* | *Charolais cattle do not like rain or too much cold. They are not hardy animals.*

tough /tʌf/ [adj] physically and mentally strong, so that you can live through very difficult conditions: *When Aunt Agnes caught cholera out in India, we all expected her to die – but she's a tough old lady and she pulled through.* | *I know she's only a kid, but she's tough.*

resilient /rɪ'zɪliənt/ [adj] someone who is **resilient**, especially a young person, is strong and healthy, so that they are only affected for a short time by illness, difficulties, or sudden changes in their lives: *Amy will soon be out of hospital – children of her age are very resilient.* | *Being twenty-three years old and quite resilient, I got over the shock pretty quickly.*

3 physical strength

- strength
- power
- brawn
- force
- stamina
- staying power
- endurance

strength /streŋθ, strenθ/ [n U] the ability to lift or carry heavy things, to do a lot of physical work etc: *Men are better at some sports because of their greater physical strength.* | *Regular gym sessions will improve both your health and strength.* | *I didn't have the strength to climb any further.* | *Diana pulled on the rope with all her strength.* | **build up your strength** *Bill was doing a lot of exercise to build up his strength.*

power /'paʊəʳ/ [n U] a lot of physical strength in a particular part of your body: *Mike had tremendous power in his forearms.* | *A dynamometer is used to measure muscle power.*

brawn /brɔːn/ [n U] physical strength, use this especially to compare strength with intelligence or skill: *You can't be good at tennis if you rely on brawn alone – it takes skill as well.* | *The battle was won by brain rather than brawn.*

force /fɔːʳs/ [n U] physical strength that is needed to be able to push, pull, or lift something: *I had to use force to get the window open.* | **physical force** *The use of physical force by teachers tended to promote violent behaviour by pupils.*

stamina /'stæm̩ɪnə/ [n U] the ability to work hard, run, play sports etc for a long time without getting tired: *You need stamina to be a long-distance runner.* | *exercises to increase your strength and stamina*

staying power /'steɪ-ɪŋ ˌpaʊəʳ/ [n U] the ability to continue doing something difficult until it is finished: *You have to admire her staying power. No one else has managed to stick that job for more than a year!* | *Ahmedi's performances were world-class in the 1500 metres but he just didn't have the staying power for longer races.*

endurance /ɪn'djʊərəns‖ɪn'dʊər-/ [n U] the physical and mental strength you need to be able to continue in a very difficult, unpleasant, or uncomfortable situation for a long time: *The people showed great courage, patience, and endurance during the long years of the war.* | **endurance test** *The triathlon is the ultimate endurance test.* | **test of sb's endurance** (=a situation that needs great endurance) *The expeditions behind enemy lines were a tremendous test of one's endurance and nerves.*

4 strong thing/material

- strong
- solid
- tough
- durable
- heavy-duty
- hardwearing
- reinforced
- unbreakable
- indestructible

strong /strɒŋ‖strɔːŋ/ [adj] something that is **strong** cannot be broken or destroyed easily: *The bags are made of strong black plastic* | *You'll need a strong piece of rope for towing the car.* | *After full heat treatment, the alloy proved to be five times as strong as the pure aluminium.* —**strength** /streŋθ, strenθ/ [n U] *If internal timbers are removed, the strength of the roof will be seriously impaired.*

solid /'sɒl̩ɪd‖'sɑː-/ [adj] a building or piece of furniture that is **solid** is strong and well made: *The table seemed solid enough, so I climbed up onto it.* | *rows of* *solid little houses built of local stone* | **as solid as a rock** (=very solid) *He rapped his knuckles against the body of the sink unit. It was as solid as a rock.*

tough /tʌf/ [adj] not easily cut or damaged – use this about cloth, leather, plastic etc: *The sailors wore jackets made from tough waterproof cotton.* | *a pair of tough leather boots* | *Normal floor paint might not be tough enough for the garage.*

durable /ˈdjʊərəbəl‖ˈdʊər-/ [adj] substances or products that are **durable** are strong and will last a long time, even if they are used a lot: *Bronze is harder and more durable than tin.* | *What you need for Africa is a simple, durable and inexpensive vehicle.* | *The roofs are constructed from heavy and durable timbers, usually teak or mahogany.* —**durability** /ˌdjʊərəˈbɪlɪti‖ˌdʊər-/ [n U] *We tested several products for quality and durability.*

heavy-duty /ˌhevi ˈdjuːti◂‖-ˈduːti◂/ [adj only before noun] **heavy-duty** materials, tools, machines etc are specially made to be stronger than usual, often because they are going to be used a lot or used in difficult conditions: *If you are going to put an electric cable underground, you must use the special heavy-duty type.* | *The emergency equipment includes food, a first-aid kit, and a heavy-duty flashlight.*

hardwearing /ˌhɑːʳdˈweərɪŋ◂/ [adj] a **hardwearing** cloth or material is strong and will last a long time, even if it is used a lot: *Polyester is not particularly hardwearing but it is cheap.* | *It's best to lay a good quality, hardwearing carpet.*

reinforced /ˌriːɪnˈfɔːʳst◂/ [adj only before noun] a **reinforced** material or part has had other materials or parts added to make it stronger: *A reinforced concrete dome, two metres thick, protects the radioactive core of the nuclear reactor.* | *Like all the clothes in the range it has specially reinforced seams.*

unbreakable /ʌnˈbreɪkəbəl/ [adj] something that is **unbreakable** is difficult or impossible to break because it is made of a very strong substance: *Make sure your patio doors are made of unbreakable glass.* | *a virtually unbreakable vacuum flask*

indestructible /ˌɪndɪˈstrʌktɪbəl/ [adj] impossible to break, damage or destroy: *Until the accident, the ship was considered indestructible.* | *There is little point putting an indestructible door in a frame that will rot in 10 years.*

5 to make something stronger

- make sth stronger
- strengthen
- reinforce

make sth stronger /ˌmeɪk (sth) ˈstrɒŋgəʳ‖-ˈstrɔːŋ-/ [v phrase] to make something physically stronger: *I've put in some extra posts to make the fence stronger.* | *A final heat treatment makes the glass much stronger and improves its optical qualities.*

strengthen /ˈstreŋθən, ˈstrenθən/ [v T] to make something strong, especially by adding something else: *The ship's decks will have to be strengthened to carry the extra weight.* | *a set of exercises to strengthen the leg muscles* | *The walls were strengthened with steel rods.*

reinforce /ˌriːɪnˈfɔːʳs/ [v T] to make part of a building or structure stronger: *Huge beams have been added at the top of the walls to reinforce the carved medieval roof.* | *The sea wall at Southend is being reinforced with tons of cement.*

6 a strong feeling/belief

- strong
- intense
- passionate
- powerful
- deep
- fervent
- ardent

strong /strɒŋ‖strɔːŋ/ [adj] *The subject of abortion always arouses strong emotions.* | *Stapleton has very strong views on capital punishment.* | *She had a strong urge to sell everything she owned and travel abroad.* | *The new police have received strong support from local residents.* —**strongly** [adv] *I don't let people smoke in my house – it's something I feel very strongly about.* —**strength** /streŋθ, strenθ/ [n U] *The President could not ignore the strength of public opinion.*

intense /ɪnˈtens/ [adj] a feeling that is **intense** is extremely strong: *It would give me intense pleasure to beat him at tennis.* | *As we waited for the winner to be announced, the excitement was intense.* | *Every car was stopped and searched, which caused intense annoyance to the drivers.* —**intensely** [adv] *From the moment I first met him I disliked him intensely.*

passionate /ˈpæʃənɪt/ [adj] involving strong feelings, especially about what is right and wrong: *I remember many passionate arguments taking place around this table.* | **+ about** *He's passionate about the need to protect the environment.* | **passionate believer/opponent/supporter etc** *Thatcher has always been a passionate believer in the ideals of a free market economy.* —**passionately** [adv] *He was passionately against nuclear weapons.* —**passion** [n U] *He delivered his speech with passion and conviction.*

powerful /ˈpaʊəʳfəl/ [adj] having a great effect on someone: *Jealousy is a very powerful emotion.* | *Her desire to hit him was so powerful that she had to force herself to leave the room at once.*

deep /diːp/ [adj] a **deep** feeling is one that you feel very strongly, especially a feeling of love, disappointment, or sympathy: *I have always had a deep affection for your family.* | *The news came as a deep disappointment to us all.* | *Please accept our deepest sympathies.* (=used when someone has died) —**deeply** [adv] *He was deeply offended by their remarks.*

fervent /ˈfɜːʳvənt/ [adj usually before noun] very strong and sincere: *Despite her troubled life she has always had a fervent belief in God.* | **fervent admirer/supporter/believer etc** *Most of the people here are fervent supporters of self-determination.* —**fervently** [adv] *He will be remembered as a politician who fervently argued for what he believed in.*

ardent /ˈɑːʳdənt/ [adj usually before noun] formal very strong and sincere: *He was a man of strong beliefs and had always given ardent support to the Reform cause.* | *Even his most ardent supporters disagreed with this move.* —**ardently** [adv] *She ardently believed that women should have the same rights as men and was determined to fight for this.*

study

RELATED WORDS

- *see also* **learn, subject, school/university, teach, test, read**

1 to study something at school, university etc

- study
- take
- do
- major in
- minor in
- take lessons
- read
- place

study /'stʌdi/ [v I/T] to learn about a subject by reading books, going to classes etc: *It's difficult to study when the weather's so hot.* | *I've been studying English for six years now.* | *His parents sent him to Moscow to study physics, chemistry, and mathematics.* | *If you study hard, you'll be able to get into a good university.* | **+ to be sth** *She's at business school, studying to be an accountant.* | **+ under** (=receive lessons from a famous teacher) *Nicoll was himself a noted psychologist and studied under Jung in Zurich.*

take /teɪk/ [v T] to study a subject – use this to talk about subjects that you choose to study at school, college, university etc: *What classes are you taking next semester?* | *In my final year, I decided to take English, French, and economics.* | *All freshmen have to take at least one composition course.*

do /du:/ [v T] British informal to study a particular subject at school or university: *I can't decide whether to do German or Spanish next year.* | *Did you do computing at school?* | **do a course** *Why not do a language course at your local college?*

major in /'meɪdʒər ɪn/ [phr v T not in passive] American to study something as your main subject at a college or university: *What are you majoring in?* | *Diane majored in psychology at the University of Washington.*

minor in /'maɪnər ɪn/ [phr v T not in passive] American if you **minor** in a subject, it is the second most important subject you study at a college or university: *I'm planning to study computer science, but I still might minor in English.*

take lessons ALSO **have lessons** British /ˌteɪk 'lesənz, ˌhæv 'lesənz/ [v phrase] to pay for lessons from a teacher in order to study a subject or skill in your free time: *My mother wants me to take violin lessons.* | *I'm having Spanish lessons after work.* | **+ in** *Students at the school can even take lessons in golf.*

read /ri:d/ [v T not in passive] British formal to study a subject at university: *Oliver is reading philosophy at Oxford.* | *She went on to read medicine at Edinburgh.*

place /pleɪs/ [n C] British an offer or opportunity to study as a student at a particular school, college, or university: *Studies show that students from wealthier backgrounds are more likely to be offered places at high-achieving schools.* | **have/get a place (at)** *Jenny has a place to study law at Exeter this year.* | *If I get a place at Manchester, I'll take it.*

2 to study to prepare for an examination

- study
- revise
- cram
- swot
- bone up on

study /'stʌdi/ [v I/T] to learn the information you need to prepare yourself for a test or examination: *I'm going to spend the afternoon studying my notes.* | *The test is supposed to be hard – aren't you going to study at all?* | **+ for** *He studied for the bar exam all year, and he still didn't pass.* | *I can't go to the movie tonight – I have a big test to study for.*

revise /rɪ'vaɪz/ [v I/T] British to read books, notes etc in order to prepare for an examination that you are going to take: *Ahmed's upstairs, revising.* | *What are you revising tonight?* | **+ for** *The library was full of students revising for the final exams.*

cram /kræm/ [v I] informal to study very hard just before an examination, especially because you do not know enough: *You'll really have to cram if you want to pass the test.* | **+ for** *Everyone's cramming for their final exams.*

swot /swɒt‖swɑ:t/ [v I] British informal to study for an examination: *He's sure to pass – he's been swotting away for months.* | **+ for** *I was too busy swotting for my exams to be much interested in girls.*

bone up on /ˌbəʊn 'ʌp ɒn/ [phr v T] informal to study a particular subject to prepare for a test or examination: *I've been boning up on my Latin for the entrance exam.*

3 to study something in order to discover new facts

- study
- analyse
- do/conduct research
- research

study /'stʌdi/ [v T] to examine something carefully, do tests on it etc, in order to find out more about it and discover new facts: *She spent several years studying the behaviour of gorillas in Africa.* | *The discovery will be of great interest to scientists studying the origins of the universe.* | **+ how/why/when etc** *NASA has used the space shuttle to study how materials perform in a weightless environment.*

analyse British **/analyze** American /'ænəl-aɪz/ [v T] to carefully examine information, reports, the results of tests etc, in order to understand something better: *We use a special computer program to analyse all the sales figures.* | *We will have to analyze the results of the survey before making any decisions.* —**analysis** /ə'nælɪsɪs/ [n C/U] *He's written a careful analysis of the drug problem in America.*

do/conduct research ALSO **carry out research** /du:, kənˌdʌkt rɪ'sɜ:ʳtʃ, ˌkæri aʊt rɪ'sɜ:ʳtʃ/ [v phrase] to study a subject in a careful, detailed way, in order to discover new information or produce new ideas about it: *Dr. Cooper is a surgeon who does research at Harvard University.* | *The organization's laboratories conduct advanced research in areas such as electronics, biotechnology, and engineering.* | **+ into/on** *Baskin has made several trips to Nicaragua to carry out research on land distribution.*

research /rɪ'sɜ:ʳtʃ/ [v I/T] to study a subject in a careful, detailed way, in order to discover new information or produce new ideas about it: *Vargas began researching his family's history 12 years ago.* | *It is important to research the market fully before offering a new product for sale.* | **+ into** British *Doctors researching into the causes of the disease believe they may have found a cure.*

4 the work that you do when you study something

- sb's studies
- homework
- coursework
- revision
- study
- research

sb's studies / (sb's) 'stʌdiz/ [n plural] all the work that someone does when they are a student at school or university: *My uncle asked me how I was enjoying my studies.* | *James interrupted his studies to travel around Europe for a year.* | *She plans to continue her studies at Colgate in the fall.*

homework /'həʊmwɜːʳk/ [n U] work that a school student is given to do during free time, not during lessons: *Don't you kids have any homework?* | *Mrs Burgess gives more homework than the other teachers.* | **do your homework** *Go to your room and do your math homework before you start watching TV.*

coursework /'kɔːʳswɜːʳk/ [n U] all the work that a student has to do as part of a course of study, but not the examinations: *The diploma requires 30 hours of coursework.* | *Half of the marks are for the exam, and half are for coursework.*

revision /rɪ'vɪʒən/ [n U] British when you read books, notes etc in order to prepare for an examination that you are going to do: *How is your history revision going?* | **do revision** *I can't come out tonight – I've got a lot of revision to do.*

study /'stʌdi/ [n C] a piece of work, especially one that includes a written report, that involves studying a particular subject in order to find out more about it: *Recent studies have shown that women find it harder than men to give up smoking.* | **+ on** *Berne has published a review of studies on sex education programs in public schools.* | **+ of** *Our comparative study of political culture includes five democracies.* | **do/conduct/carry out a study** *We're doing a study into how much time people spend watching television each day.*

research /rɪ'sɜːʳtʃ, 'riːsɜːʳtʃ/ [n U] careful, detailed work that you do in order to discover new information or produce new ideas about a particular subject: *Recent research has shown that human language is much older than we previously thought.* | **+ into** *More research is needed into the ways in which this virus is spread.* | **+ on** *He hopes that his book will inspire more research on alcoholism.* | **scientific/historical/clinical etc research** *There is no scientific research to back up the company's claims.* | **do/conduct/carry out research** *She's doing research into the connection between crime and poverty.* | *Many of the questions can be answered without carrying out any new research.*

5 a student

- student
- pupil
- learner
- schoolboy/schoolgirl/schoolchild
- schoolkid
- undergraduate
- English/history etc major
- postgraduate

student /'stjuːdənt‖'stuː-/ [n C] someone who is studying at school, university etc: *We would welcome suggestions from both teachers and students.* | *Student leaders had organized a sit-in to protest against the war.* | **high school/college etc student** *The study found that drug use among high school students is rising.* | **English/engineering/business etc student** *Seventy percent of the university's business students have job offers by graduation.* | **+ of** *Wiggins was a student of theology for many years before leaving the seminary.* | **student days** (=the time when you were a student) *Mira hadn't seen Brad since their student days at the University of Wisconsin.*

pupil /'pjuːpəl/ [n C] especially British a child who studies at a school: *The school has over 700 pupils.* | *The new law reduces the number of pupils per class in the first four years of schooling.*

learner /'lɜːʳnəʳ/ [n C] someone who is learning about a particular subject – used especially by teachers and people talking about the needs of students: *A major aim of education is to improve learners' understanding of the world around them.* | *At the end of each chapter there is a series of exercises designed to help the learner.*

schoolboy/schoolgirl/schoolchild /'skuːlbɔɪ, 'skuːlgɜːʳl, 'skuːltʃaɪld/ [n C] especially British a child who studies at a school: *He was quickly surrounded by schoolgirls asking for his autograph.* | *Only 10% of British schoolchildren attend private schools.*

schoolkid /'skuːlkɪd/ [n C] informal a child who studies at a school: *I was just a schoolkid – I didn't know anything about poetry or literature.* | *They were standing outside giggling away like a couple of naughty schoolkids.*

undergraduate /ˌʌndəʳ'grædʒuɪ̈t/ [n C] someone who is studying at a university in order to get their first degree: *They met when they were undergraduates at Cambridge.* | *The loans, which are based on financial need, are limited to $3000 for undergraduates.* —**undergraduate** [adj] *This textbook is primarily intended for undergraduate students of history.*

English/history etc major /ˌɪŋglɪʃ 'meɪdʒəʳ/ [n C] American someone who is studying English, history etc as their main subject at a college or university: *Her boyfriend was a political science major at Berkeley.* | *I was a biology major in college, but I've forgotten almost everything I learned.*

postgraduate British **/graduate student** American /ˌpəʊst'grædʒuɪ̈t, 'grædʒuɪ̈t ˌstjuːdənt‖-ˌstuː-/ [n C] someone who is studying for a higher degree after their first degree: *About half the graduate students in the program come from overseas.* | *He has three postgraduates helping him with his research.* —**postgraduate** especially British **graduate** American [adj only before noun] *Most of the people in the department hold postgraduate degrees.*

stupid/silly

WHAT'S HERE

- **not sensible** see **1 to 4**
- **not intelligent** see **5 to 6**

not sensible

RELATED WORDS

opposite: **sensible**

▸ *see also* **crazy, risk**

1 stupid behaviour, actions, ideas etc

- stupid
- dumb
- silly
- daft
- foolish
- ill-advised
- unwise
- irrational

stupid /'stju:pɪ̣d‖'stu:-/ [adj] someone who is **stupid** or does **stupid** things does things that are not at all sensible and may have bad results: *You stupid boy! I've told you not to play with matches!* | *Withdraw the police from the area? I've never heard such a stupid idea!* | *Well, if you're stupid enough to skate on the lake, you deserve to fall in.* | *Don't you call me a stupid idiot!* | **+ to do sth** *You'd have to be stupid not to take advantage of a great offer like this!* | **do sth stupid** *I was very drunk last night – I hope I didn't do anything stupid.* | **it is stupid (of sb) to do sth** *It was stupid of me to believe her of course, but I did.* | **a stupid thing to say/do** *That was a stupid thing to say.* | *I didn't say you were stupid, I said it was a stupid thing to do.* —**stupidly** [adv] *Stupidly, I agreed to lend him some money.* | *I'm sorry I reacted so stupidly.*

dumb /dʌm/ [adj] especially American, spoken stupid: *She's always asking such dumb questions.* | *She told him Jeff was just a friend, and he was dumb enough to believe her.* | *Oh, I just did the dumbest thing back there, I forgot my briefcase.*

silly /'sɪli/ [adj] someone who is **silly** or who says **silly** things does or says things that are not sensible or serious, and that may make them feel embarrassed later: *Now don't be silly, get up off the floor.* | *You've made a lot of silly mistakes in this essay.* | *I have a question which might sound a bit silly.* | **it is silly to do sth** *I think you're silly to worry so much about your hair.* | **it is silly of sb** *That was silly of me – I just locked the trunk and the keys are inside.* | **silly little** *You're just a silly little boy.* | **a silly thing to do/say** *I had locked myself out, which was a silly thing to do.*

daft /dɑ:ft‖dæft/ [adj] British informal stupid in what you do or say, but often in a way that is also amusing: *Is this another of your daft ideas?* | *Don't be daft! Of course you're not too old to go clubbing.* | *Well, what's the daftest thing you've ever done at work?* | **daft thing to do/say** *What a daft thing to say!* | **daft as a brush** (=used to say that someone is very daft) *She's as daft as a brush, honestly she is.*

foolish /'fu:lɪʃ/ [adj] formal stupid and not thinking sensibly about the possible results of what you do: *Jan realised later that her behaviour had been very foolish.* | *I think the board of directors made a foolish choice that it will later regret.* | **it is foolish (of sb) to do sth** *It was a warning she would have been foolish to ignore.* —**foolishly** [adv] *I had just $7 left, and foolishly squandered $5 in the bar that night.*

ill-advised /ˌɪl əd'vaɪzd◂/ [adj] formal an action or plan that is **ill-advised** is stupid because it will probably cause problems in the future or be unsuccessful: *In an ill-advised effort to improve matters, they sent him to boarding school.* | *The bank claims that the company's losses are the result of an ill-advised decision to declare bankruptcy.*

unwise /ʌn'waɪz/ [adj] done without thinking carefully enough about the possible disadvantages that may result: *She knew the marriage was unwise, but she wanted a husband and a family.* | *A Defence Department spokesman described the comments as 'extraordinarily unwise'.* | *His appointment as chief executive proved to be a very unwise decision.* | *It's unwise to travel alone in certain parts of the city, so always take a cab.* —**unwisely** [adv] *Perhaps unwisely, the President apologised for the tax raise.*

irrational /ɪ'ræʃənəl/ [adj] **irrational** actions, feelings, or beliefs are not based on clear thinking or sensible reasons, so they are strange or hard to understand: *If Dane drinks even a couple of beers, he becomes irrational and even violent.* | *Jane's irrational hopes began to rise as she listened to him.* | **irrational fear of/about sth** *an irrational fear of flying* —**irrationally** [adv] *The man was causing a disturbance and acting irrationally.*

2 very stupid

- crazy
- ridiculous/absurd
- ludicrous
- laughable
- idiotic
- hare-brained
- inane

crazy /'kreɪzi/ [adj] not at all sensible or reasonable, especially in an annoying or shocking way: *I said I enjoyed doing exams, and she looked at me as if I was crazy!* | *Ian's got some crazy plan to drive all the way across Africa.* | *The farmers can make more money by not planting crops – it's crazy, isn't it?* | *You're crazy to think of hitch-hiking on your own.*

ridiculous/absurd /rɪ'dɪkjʊ̣ləs, əb'sɜ:ʳd/ [adj] something that is **ridiculous** or **absurd** is so stupid that you can hardly believe that it has been done, said etc: *I've never heard anything so ridiculous! Of course I haven't been trying to avoid you!* | *an absurd suggestion* | *This is ridiculous. You've only known him three days, and you're going on holiday with him!* | *It's absurd to think Porter flew into a murderous rage just because he had an argument with his girlfriend.* | **patently ridiculous/absurd** (=used to emphasize that something is very ridiculous indeed) *This patently absurd argument is often used by anti-gay groups.*

ludicrous /'lu:dɪ̣krəs/ [adj] completely unreasonable or unsuitable: *The telephone lines are only open during office hours, which is ludicrous in this day and age.* | *She wears short skirts and dyes her hair pink, which looks ludicrous on a woman her age.*

laughable /'lɑ:fəbəl‖'læf-/ [adj] so stupid and unbelievable that it makes you want to laugh: *The government's attempt to privatize the prison service has been simply laughable.* | *It would be laughable if it wasn't so serious.*

idiotic /ˌɪdi'ɒtɪk◂‖-'ɑ:tɪk◂/ [adj] very stupid and likely to involve unnecessary risks and dangers: *Wyatt was nearly killed as a result of that idiotic stunt.* | *If that wasn't idiotic enough, the company went on to sack fifty percent of its skilled workers, replacing them with untrained apprentices.*

hare-brained /'heəʳ breɪnd/ [adj usually before noun] **hare-brained scheme/plan etc** a plan that is very stupid and cannot possibly be successful: *Alice had to figure out how to pay the rent after Ralph spent the money on another of his hare-brained schemes.*

inane /ɪ'neɪn/ [adj] **inane remark/comment/conversation etc** stupid and completely meaningless: *Penny began an inane conversation about the book she was reading to fill the silence.* | *Bad acting, weak script and inane dialogue – this movie is truly awful.*

3 stupid and childish

- childish
- immature
- juvenile

childish /'tʃaɪldɪʃ/ [adj] someone who is **childish** annoys you by being unreasonable and unhelpful, or by complaining and being rude, as if they were a small child: *He said he wouldn't go out with us if Jerry was going too – he's so childish!* | *You know how childish he can be.* | *I'd like you to explain your childish behaviour.* —**childishly** [adv] *We both agreed we'd behaved childishly, and buried the hatchet by going to lunch together.*

immature /ˌɪməˈtʃʊəʳ‖-ˈtʊər/ [adj] someone who is **immature** behaves as if they were younger than they really are, so they are not as sensible or responsible as you expect them to be: *We were silly, immature teenagers, and we didn't know any better.* | *I was 19 when I went to college, but still very immature.* | *These kids are brilliant, but often socially immature.*

juvenile /ˈdʒuːvənaɪl‖-nəl, -naɪl/ [adj] someone who is **juvenile**, especially a young adult, behaves in a very silly way like a child, when they should be more sensible: *Some of the boys tried to involve me in their juvenile pranks, but I wasn't interested.* | *You wouldn't think that college students could be so juvenile.*

4 a stupid person

- idiot/fool
- wally
- jerk
- goof/goof ball
- dope
- dork

idiot/fool /ˈɪdiət, fuːl/ [n C] someone who does something very stupid or embarrassing: *You lost the tickets? How could you be such an idiot?* | *Anyone who tells you any different is either a fool or a liar.* | *Some idiot in a fast car is trying to overtake.* | *If you believe that, you're a bigger fool than I thought.* | *She was an idiot to drink so much on an empty stomach.* | **make a fool of yourself** (=do something that makes you seem very stupid) *It's increasingly common for the losers to go out kicking and screaming, and generally making fools of themselves.*

wally /ˈwɒli‖ˈwɑː-/ [n C] British informal someone who behaves in a stupid and annoying way: *Look at those wallies jumping around and pulling faces behind the TV reporter.* | *You look like a right wally in that hat.*

jerk /dʒɜːʳk/ [n C] especially American someone who is a little stupid and annoying, and who does not care if they upset or hurt other people: *Some jerk just drove right into the back of my car.* | *I liked the job, but the manager was a jerk.* | *Ow! You jerk, that hurt!* | **total/real jerk** *She seems to always end up in a relationship with some total jerk.*

goof/goof ball /guːf, ˈguːf bɔːl/ [n C] American informal someone who is stupid and embarrassing: *He's such a goof. I don't know what she sees in him.* | *He always acts like a real goof after a couple of glasses of wine.* | *Oh Mike's okay, he's just a bit of a goof ball.*

dope /dəʊp/ [n C] American informal someone who is stupid and does not think about what they say or do: *I'm sorry I was such a dope last night.* | *Oh you dope, you bought the wrong one.*

dork /dɔːʳk/ [n C] especially American, informal someone who you think is stupid and strange because they behave strangely or wear strange clothes: *I look like a real dork in this uniform.* | *Millions of listeners heard him call his production assistant a 'dork' live on air.*

not intelligent

RELATED WORDS

opposite: —— **intelligent**

- to talk to someone as if they were stupid *see* **talk 11**

5 not intelligent

- not very bright/intelligent/clever/smart
- stupid
- dumb
- thick
- dim
- brainless
- gormless
- unintelligent

not very bright/intelligent/clever/smart ALSO **not too bright/intelligent/clever/smart** /ˌnɒt veri ˈbraɪt, ɪnˈtelɪ̈dʒənt, ˈklevəʳ, ˈsmɑːʳt, ˌnɒt tuː ˈbraɪt, ɪnˈtelɪ̈dʒənt, ˈklevəʳ, ˈsmɑːʳt/ [adj] someone who is **not very bright/intelligent/clever/smart** is unable to learn and understand things quickly and easily: *Sometimes I think Sheila just isn't very bright.* | *Saja may be handsome, but he's not too smart.* | *Franco works hard but he isn't really very intelligent.* | *He treated me like a young and not very clever child.*

stupid /ˈstjuːpɪ̈d‖ˈstuː-/ [adj] not at all intelligent: *She talks to us as if we're completely stupid.* | *Poor Larry's too stupid to realize when you're making fun of him.* | *It's only stupid people who believe in all that astrology mumbo-jumbo.*

dumb /dʌm/ [adj] especially American, spoken not at all intelligent: *The athletic guys were seen as 'cute but dumb'.* | *You're so dumb, Clarissa!* | *If we look dumb enough, someone's bound to come and help us out.*

thick /θɪk/ [adj] British informal not at all intelligent: *He's a nice boy, but he's a bit thick, isn't he?* | *Not wishing to appear thick, but what exactly are you doing?* | **as thick as two short planks** (=very stupid) *Some of the students they let in these days are as thick as two short planks.*

dim /dɪm/ [adj] informal unintelligent and very slow to learn: *She's not the brightest kid in the class – in fact, she's quite dim.* | *I'm playing a guy who's well-meaning but kind of dim.*

brainless /ˈbreɪnləs/ [adj] informal completely stupid: *My sister's latest boyfriend is pretty brainless; it's impossible to have a conversation with him.* | *'You brainless scum!' he shouted after the departing boys.*

gormless /ˈgɔːʳmləs/ [adj] British informal very stupid – use this especially to describe someone who looks stupid or who never has their own ideas: *He just sat there with his mouth open looking really gormless.* | *a grinning, gormless boy*

unintelligent /ˌʌnɪnˈtelɪ̈dʒənt◂/ [adj] formal not as intelligent as most people: *It would be a mistake to assume that all football players are unintelligent.* | *He may not be as bright as his sister, but he's far from unintelligent.*

6 someone who is not intelligent

- idiot
- bimbo
- airhead
- moron

idiot /ˈɪdiət/ [n C] *Whenever I phone the bank I get through to some idiot who sounds about twelve years old.* | *Stop treating me like an idiot – I can count you know!*

bimbo /ˈbɪmbəʊ/ [n C] informal a young woman who is attractive but not very intelligent, especially one who spends time with rich and famous people: *Backstage, Paul was surrounded by bimbos in short skirts just waiting for him to notice them.* | *She plays an apparent bimbo who manages to outwit her boss.*

airhead /ˈeəʳhed/ [n C] informal a very stupid person: *He treats his women staff as if they're all airheads.* | *Then some overpaid TV airhead starts telling us how wonderful her producer is.*

moron /ˈmɔːrɒn‖-rɑːn/ [n C] an offensive word meaning a very stupid person: *What do you think I am, a complete moron?* | *Most media companies assume members of the general public are morons.* —**moronic** /məˈrɒnɪk‖-ˈrɑː-/ [adj] *There was one member of the newsgroup who kept emailing me with moronic questions.*

style/elegance

when something is attractive, skilful, fashionable etc

RELATED WORDS

- the way you do something *see* **way**
- *see also* **fashionable/not fashionable, beautiful, well-dressed, taste in clothes, music etc, suit/look good together**

1 style/elegance

- style
- elegance
- sophistication
- flair
- panache

style /staɪl/ [n U] *What she lacked in looks she made up for with her sensational style.* | *It does not really have the style and elegance of other luxury hotels.* | **with style** *If you want a cellphone with style, this is the one for you.* | **do sth in style** *The Thompsons always entertain in style.* | **go out in style** (=to finish something in a way that people admire) *Whitaker went out in style, beating Pernell comfortably.*

elegance /ˈeləgəns/ [n U] an attractive and graceful appearance or way of doing something, that is often simple but expensive: *Marlene Dietrich was once the symbol of glamour and elegance.* | *buildings that reflect the elegance of a bygone era*

sophistication /səˌfɪstəˈkeɪʃən/ [n U] a style that is based on confidence and wealth, and that shows an intelligent judgement about what is artistic and fashionable: *The capital city was once known as the centre of European culture and sophistication.* | *She was acutely aware of her own lack of sophistication.*

flair /fleəʳ/ [n singular/U] a natural ability to do things in interesting and original ways: *As a player he had a lot of flair, but it didn't help him win.* | *a combination of British practicality and French flair* | **with flair** *The room's interior was designed with taste and flair.*

panache /pəˈnæʃ, pæ-/ [n U] a confident artistic manner that makes even the simple things you do seem interesting or exciting **with panache** *She wore her clothes with typical Italian panache.* | **have panache** *The performance didn't have the panache you expect from a chart-topping rock band.*

2 having a lot of style or elegance

- stylish
- elegant
- sophisticated
- classy

stylish /ˈstaɪlɪʃ/ [adj] *The room was full of stylish furniture and expensive paintings.* | *She was a stylish woman, always dressed to suit the occasion.* —**stylishly** [adv] *The apartments are stylishly decorated and furnished, and all have sea views.*

elegant /ˈeləgənt/ [adj] having an attractive and graceful appearance or way of moving, dressing etc, often in a way that is expensive: *The house was elegant and well kept.* | *Vienna is a city of grand public buildings and elegant private ones.* | *The elegant figure of Mr Reed appeared in the doorway.* —**elegantly** [adv] *You can tell she used to be a dancer, she moves so elegantly.*

sophisticated /səˈfɪstəkeɪtəd/ [adj] having a confident and expensive appearance, and showing good judgement about what is artistic and fashionable: *She was glamorous and sophisticated, but seemed a little lonely.* | *Nothing beats black for the classic sophisticated look.* | **suave and sophisticated** *The suave, sophisticated 60-year-old singer is still performing and drawing crowds.*

classy /ˈklɑːsi‖ˈklæsi/ [adj] informal attractively and expensively dressed, decorated, or prepared: *Their wedding was a very classy affair.* | *a classy restaurant* | *She's smart, witty, and classy.*

subject

RELATED WORDS

- an area of knowledge *see* **area (9)**
- *see also* **discuss, study, teach, learn, school/university, about, test, grade**

1 something you talk about, write about etc

- subject
- subject matter
- topic
- thing
- issue
- question
- matter
- theme
- business
- any other business

subject /ˈsʌbdʒɪkt/ [n C] something that is talked about or written about, for example at a meeting, in an article, or in a conversation: *I read a lot of books about astronomy. It's a very interesting subject.* | *We talked about all sorts of subjects.* | *Bottle-collecting even has a website devoted to the subject.* | **the subject of crime/politics/animal rights etc** (=crime etc as a subject) *Until about 20 years ago, the subject of the environment was hardly discussed.* | **on the subject (of sth)** (=about a particular subject) *The first book on the subject was published in 1900.* | *He has very little to say on the subject of the accusations made against him.* | **change the subject** (=start talking about something different) *I could see John was embarrassed, so I changed the subject.* | **drop the subject** (=to stop talking about something) *This is getting us nowhere. Let's just drop the subject, okay?*

subject matter /ˈsʌbdʒɪkt ˌmætəʳ/ [n U] what is being talked about, or what a film, book, play etc is about: *There has been no attempt to arrange the books according to subject matter.* | *Sagan published a book relating to the subject matter in his TV show.* | *'The People versus Larry Flynt' was given an '18' certificate because it contains adult subject matter.*

topic /ˈtɒpɪk‖ˈtɑː-/ [n C] a subject that people often discuss or write about, in books, newspapers, at school etc: *The rise of Islam is a popular topic these days.* | *Type the topic into the search field, and let the browser search all relevant sites.* | *Dole's absence was the topic of radio talk shows.*

thing /θɪŋ/ [n C] especially spoken something that people talk about or think about: *The first thing we have to discuss is the price.* | *The only thing she ever talks about is her boyfriend.* | *We talked about the old days and other things.*

issue /ˈɪʃuː, ˈɪsjuː‖ˈɪʃuː/ [n C] an important subject that people discuss and argue about: *We'll be looking at a broad range of important issues in this chapter.* | *Genetic manipulation is a fairly topical issue these days.* | *a book dealing with environmental issues* | **+ of** *the issue of drugs in sports* | **major/big/key/main issue** (=a very important issue) *Global warming and youth crime are the key issues in the election campaign.*

question /ˈkwestʃən/ [n C] a difficult subject or problem that has often been discussed but still needs to be solved: *The real question here is how can we integrate asylum seekers into communities.* | *How can we best help less developed countries? That's the really important question.* | **+ of** *In the 1980s the question of whether photography was an art went to court.* | **raise a question** (=make people consider a problem) *These operations can save lives, but they raise difficult questions about animal rights.*

matter /ˈmætəʳ/ [n C] a subject that people disagree about or are concerned about, and that needs to be considered and discussed in order to deal with it: *The matter is being argued and discussed in families up and down the country.* | *Foreign affairs were not the only matters we discussed.* | *This meeting is being held to deal with the serious matter of possible racism in our hiring practices.* | **+ of** *The first item on the agenda today is the matter of public transportation.*

theme /θiːm/ [n C] an important idea that appears several times in a book, film etc, and slowly influences the way it develops: *One of the themes of the book is the relationship between people and nature.* | *George Eliot shows real concern for religious and moral themes.* | *The play's central theme is greed and its corrupting effects.*

business /ˈbɪznɪ̇s/ [n U] something that needs to be discussed at a **business** or political meeting: *Right, could we get started please? We've a lot of business to get through this morning.*

any other business /ˌeni ʌðəʳ ˈbɪznɪ̇s/ British in a meeting, subjects that are not on the list of things to discuss, but that people may want to talk about: *Is there any other business before we close the meeting?*

2 a part of a subject that is being discussed or written about

- point
- aspect

point /pɔɪnt/ [n C] a fact, suggestion, detail etc that is part of a subject being considered, discussed, or written about: *There are a number of other points to be discussed before we finish.* | *The final point in the President's speech was the most controversial.* | *Make a list of the main points in the article.* | **make a point** (=get someone to understand your suggestion, argument etc) *Exactly what point are you trying to make, Nick?*

aspect /ˈæspekt/ [n C] one part of a subject, problem, etc or one particular way of considering the subject: *Women are interested in the car's technological aspects just as much as men are.* | **+ of** *We're focused on the financial, rather than social, aspects of the problem.* | *This book deals with the economic, social, and religious aspects of Egyptian society.*

3 a subject that you study at school or university

- subject
- discipline
- major
- field

subject /ˈsʌbdʒɪkt/ [n C] one of the things that you study at school or university, for example English, history, or mathematics: *English was my favourite subject at school.* | *What subjects are you studying?*

major /ˈmeɪdʒəʳ/ [n C] American the main subject that you study at university: *'What was your major?' 'Political Science'.* —**major in math/humanities etc** /ˌmeɪdʒər ɪn ˈmæθ/ [phr v T] to study mathematics etc as your main subject: *I don't think he majored in maths, I think it was applied physics.*

discipline /ˈdɪsɪ̇plɪ̇n/ [n C] one of the areas of knowledge such as history, chemistry, economics etc that is studied and taught at a university: *The traditional academic disciplines are less popular among students, who now prefer subjects such as business studies.* | *a new artificial intelligence project involving researchers from a wide range of disciplines*

field /fiːld/ [n C] an area of knowledge that is studied by scientists or by people studying it at a very high level, for example in a university: *These fields boast among the highest professional wages in the nation.* | **in the/his/her etc field** *Cole is the most noted expert in the field.* | *Webster is a great success in his chosen field.* | **field of work/study/research etc** *What exactly is your field of study?*

4 all of the subjects that you study as part of your work at school or university

- course
- curriculum
- syllabus

course ALSO **class** American /kɔːʳs, klɑːs‖klæs/ [n C] a series of lessons on a subject, often with an examination at the end: *Are you enjoying the course?* | *a schedule of the classes for the fall semester* | *The college is offering three basic computer courses this year.* | **+ in/on** *She began a 12 week course on modern art.* | **take a course/class** ALSO **do a course** British *She's taking a class in art history.* | *I've decided to do a course in aromatherapy.*

syllabus /ˈsɪləbəs/ [n C] a plan that states exactly what should be taught to students who are studying a subject, especially a list of what they may be tested on in their examinations: *The summer term was very short and the teacher didn't manage to cover the whole syllabus.* | *the first-year syllabus* | **be on the syllabus** (=be part of the syllabus) *We have to study algebra – it's on the syllabus for the course.*

curriculum /kəˈrɪkjɪ̇ləm/ [n C] the range of subjects that has been officially chosen to be taught at a school or at all schools in a country: *Are politicians the best people to be developing the educational curriculum?* | *changes to the school curriculum* | *We cover the curriculum by choosing things the kids will be interested in.*

5 to start talking about a subject

- get onto

get onto /get ˈɒntu/ [phr v T] **get onto the subject/topic/question of** to start talking about a subject after talking about something else that is connected to it in some way: *How on earth did we get onto the subject of dogs?* | *Whenever Ma got onto that subject, my head would start to spin.*

6 to talk about the subject you are supposed to be talking about

- get/come to the point
- stick to the point
- to the point

get/come to the point /ˌget, ˌkʌm tə ðə ˈpɔɪnt/ [v phrase] to start talking about the subject you are supposed to be talking about or really want to talk about, especially after you have been talking about something else: *He chatted abut the weather for a while before coming to the point.* | *'We know that already,' interrupted Steve impatiently. 'Get to the point'.* | **get/come straight/right to the point** (=get immediately to the point) *She came straight to the point. 'When do you think you'll be able to pay me back?'* | *Well, gentlemen, let's get right to the point.*

stick to the point ALSO **keep to the point** British /ˌstɪk tə ðə ˈpɔɪnt, ˌkiːp tə ðə ˈpɔɪnt/ [v phrase] to continue talking only about the subject you are supposed to be talking about, and not talk about things that are not connected with it: *Can we try, please, to stick to the point – we don't have much time.* | *Mike seems to be quite incapable of keeping to the point.*

to the point /tə ðə ˈpɔɪnt/ [adj phrase] something that someone says or writes that is **to the point** is only about the subject they are supposed to be talking about, and not about anything else: *The chairman's speech was short and to the point.* | *Korean newspapers only have four pages, so stories have to be very much to the point.*

7 to stop talking about the subject you are supposed to be talking about

- get off the subject
- digress
- be/get sidetracked
- stray from
- ramble
- lose your train of thought
- where was I?

get off the subject ALSO **go off the subject** British /get ˌɒf ðə ˈsʌbdʒɪkt, gəʊ ˌɒf ðə ˈsʌbdʒɪkt/ [v phrase] *I think we're getting off the subject. Could we get back to the main point, please?* | *Well, going off the subject a minute, what about that Uri Geller chap?*

digress /daɪˈgres/ [v I] formal to move away from the main subject that you have been talking or writing about, especially for a short time during a speech or story: *Before we do that, I'd like to digress for a minute and say a word or two about the new books.* —**digression** /daɪˈgreʃən/ [n C] *This is a slight digression, but can I make a point here?*

be/get sidetracked /biː, get ˈsaɪdtrækt/ [v phrase] if you are talking about something and **are sidetracked** or **get sidetracked**, you allow yourself to start talking or thinking about something else, especially something less important: *I was going to ask him, but he got sidetracked by this guy and I never got a chance.* | *Don't be sidetracked by the way the interviewer asks the questions – just keep making the relevant points.*

stray from /ˈstreɪ frɒm/ [phr v T] if you **stray from** the subject you are talking about, you start talking about other things instead, for example, because you cannot keep your attention on the main subject: *Promise yourself that you'll try not to stray from the issue at hand.* | *Well, we've strayed quite a way from space exploration.*

ramble /ˈræmbəl/ [v I] to talk, especially for a long time, moving from one subject to another without any clear order, so that your listener becomes bored or confused: *In his diary, the Unabomber rambled at length about the evils of technology.* | **ramble on** (=ramble continuously and in an annoying way) *I sat down and let him ramble on for a few minutes.* —**rambling** [adj] *Without a teleprompter, his speeches are long and rambling.* | *a rambling, 20-minute monologue*

lose your train of thought ALSO **lose the thread** /ˌluːz jɔːʳ ˌtreɪn əv ˈθɔːt, ˌluːz ðə ˈθred/ [v phrase] to become confused about or forget the connection between the things you are saying, especially so that you have to stop talking and think about what you want to say next: *The audience's reaction surprised him, and he lost his train of thought for a moment.* | *I'm sorry, I seem to have lost my thread.* | **lose the thread of sth** *Arthur paused, feeling he was beginning to lose the thread of his argument.*

where was I? /weəʳ ˈwɒz aɪ‖-ˈwɑːz-/ spoken say this when you want to continue what you were saying before you were interrupted, but you cannot remember what you were saying: *Thanks for that, Gillian. Now, where was I?* | *So, where was I? Oh yes, the accession of Henry the Fifth.*

succeed/ successful

RELATED WORDS

opposite: —— **fail**

- to succeed in a test or examination *see* **test**
- *see also* **win, effective/not effective**

WHAT'S HERE

- **to succeed in doing sth** see **1 to 5**
- **to be successful in your work or in business** see **6 to 11**

to succeed in doing sth

1 to succeed in doing something

- succeed
- manage
- be successful
- have some success/have limited success
- make progress
- achieve
- accomplish
- get results

succeed /səkˈsiːd/ [v I not in progressive] to do something that you hoped to do, tried to do, or wanted to do: *She wanted to be the first woman to climb Mount Everest and she almost succeeded.* | *I tried to reassure Billy's mother that it was a passing phase, but I don't think I succeeded.* | *Muir succeeds where other designers have failed – her clothes are original, yet stylish.* | **+ in doing sth** *In one year, we've succeeded in increasing profits by 40%.* | **+ at** *I admired Goldie, because she had succeeded at a task that had even defeated my mother.*

manage /ˈmænɪdʒ/ [v I/T not in progressive] to succeed in doing something difficult after trying very hard, especially when you almost do not succeed: *Martin still hasn't got his invalidity pension sorted out, but he's managing all right at the moment.* | *If you hadn't have been here, I don't think I would have managed.* | *I don't know how he managed it, but the crisis is over.* | *Can you manage that door Mike? It looks awfully heavy.* | **+ to do sth** *He finally managed to find an apartment near his office.* | *At least three hostages managed to escape.* | **manage with/without sth** *Well, I suppose we could just about manage without electricity for the night.*

be successful /bi: sək'sesfəl/ [v phrase] to succeed in doing something, especially something that needs a lot of work or effort such as passing a test or getting a job: *Does Joey have a realistic chance of being successful at the audition?* | **+ in doing sth** *If I'm successful in raising over £500, those funds will go to the Bible School.* — **successfully** [adv] *Mr Malik has successfully completed the advanced course in Business Management.*

have some success/have limited success /hæv ˌsʌm sək'ses, hæv ˌlɪmɪtɪd sək'ses/ [v phrase] to be fairly successful in doing something, or to achieve part of what you wanted to achieve: *Our aim was to disrupt the enemy's transport network and we had some success.* | *If we only have some success in reducing the number infected with HIV, I feel it will have been worthwhile.* | **+ in doing sth** *The Santa Barbara seismic research team has had some success in predicting earthquakes.*

make progress /meɪk 'prəʊgres‖-'prɑː-/ [v phrase] to gradually start to achieve something that you want to achieve, by working hard: *I'm not very good at Japanese yet, but I feel I am making progress.* | *We have made very great progress in reducing the number of deaths on our roads.* | **+ with/towards/on** *At last I began to make some progress with my research.* | **+ in doing sth** *BEA has made good progress in implementing the new health and safety regulations.*

achieve /ə'tʃiːv/ [v T] to succeed in doing something important, especially something that other people will admire you for: *She's achieved a lot in the short time she's been with the company.* | *The reason I achieve good results is because I work hard – and so could you.* | *When you get your MA, you really feel that you've achieved something.* | *He had achieved all his goals for the organization, and felt there were no challenges left there for him.*

accomplish /ə'kʌmplɪʃ‖ə'kɑːm-, ə'kʌm-/ [v T] to succeed in doing or finishing something good that you have planned to do, after trying hard for a long time: *What exactly do you hope to accomplish this year?* | *She found the job frustrating, and felt she wasn't accomplishing anything there.*

get results /ˌget rɪ'zʌlts/ [v phrase] if you **get results**, you achieve what you are trying to do: *It was three or four years before we really started getting results.* | *This shows that if we devote sufficient energy and resources to a problem, we get results.* | *As I manager, I pride myself on getting results.*

2 to succeed in doing something difficult

- make it
- get there
- do it
- pull off/bring off/carry off
- turn up trumps/come up trumps

make it /'meɪk ɪt/ [v phrase not in progressive] especially spoken to succeed in doing something that is difficult or that seems impossible: *Gina has her driving test today. I hope she makes it.* | *He went out for it, he played hard, and he made it.* | *Jody thinks only three teams will make it to the final.* | *Did Margaret make it home the other night?* | *Will he make it out alive?*

get there /'get ðeəʳ/ [v phrase] especially spoken to succeed in doing something, especially after a lot of effort over a long period of time: *I aim to have my own company by the time I'm thirty, but sometimes I wonder if I'll ever get there.* | *Anna found the coursework hard, but knew she'd get there in the end.* | *I knew we'd get there eventually, it was just a question of when.*

do it /'duː ɪt/ [v phrase not in progressive] especially spoken to succeed in doing something, especially something difficult or something that needs a lot of effort: *We did it! We won the cup!* | *You did it! Congratulations!*

pull off/bring off/carry off /ˌpʊl 'ɒf, ˌbrɪŋ 'ɒf, ˌkæri 'ɒf/ [phr v T] to manage to do something difficult, when other people did not think that you could succeed **pull/bring/carry off sth** *In the opening game, Italy pulled off a sensational 1-0 victory over Germany.* | *I think you need a really good sense of humour to carry off something like this.* | *We had a hard time bringing off the last conference we held here.* | **pull/bring/carry sth off** *I'd hardly cooked a proper meal for years, and I was wondering if I could still pull it off.* | *I doubt if we could have carried it off without your help.*

turn up trumps/come up trumps /ˌtɜːʳn ʌp 'trʌmps, ˌkʌm ʌp 'trʌmps/ [v phrase not in progressive] informal if someone **comes** or **turns up trumps**, they succeed in doing something difficult or providing something that is needed, especially when this makes you feel pleased or grateful: *We were getting into serious difficulties, but Ron came up trumps again.* | *Well, I got three people interested in helping, so if they all turn up trumps, we should reach our target.*

3 when something has the result that you want it to have

- succeed
- successful
- work
- go well
- have some success
- come out right/turn out right
- come off
- pay off
- bear fruit
- fruitful

succeed /sək'siːd/ [v I not in progressive] if something that you plan to do or try to do **succeeds**, you get the result that you hoped for: *Both sides could make these talks succeed by seeking a real and lasting peace.* | *As long as the financial crisis continues, economic reform cannot possibly succeed.* | **+ in doing sth** *None of the measures taken by the government have succeeded in reducing the spread of violent crime.*

successful /sək'sesfəl/ [adj] if something that you plan to do or try to do is **successful** you get the result that you hoped for: *If the treatment is successful, she could be back at school next month.* | *a small but successful program to boost the number of African-Americans getting into college* | **highly successful** (=very successful) *It was a highly successful campaign.* | **the most successful** *This has been Baltimore's most successful art show ever.* | **so successful (... that)** *The case of Thailand illustrates why family planning programs have been so successful in many countries.* | **prove successful** (=be successful) *The scheme was started in January 2000, and has proved largely successful.* — **successfully** [adv] *The film successfully combines a good story line with a serious political message.*

work /wɜːʳk/ [v I] if a plan or method **works**, it produces the result that you want: *'I can't open this jar.' 'Try putting it under hot water. That sometimes works.'* | *I think your treatment worked Arnie, my headache's gone.* | *The recipe works just as well if you cook the fish in a microwave.*

go well /ˌgəʊ 'wel/ [v phrase] if something **goes well**, such as a meeting, party, or performance, everything happens in the way you wanted and there are no problems: *Ray met my parents for the first time this weekend, and it went really well.* | *The audition was OK, but it could have gone better I suppose.* | *Most people seem to think the party went well.* | **+ for** *Good luck with the project, and I hope everything goes well for you.*

have some success /hæv ˌsʌm səkˈses/ [v phrase] if a plan, method etc **has some success**, it is fairly successful: *The early warning system has had some success; for example Pacific coast residents get four hours notice of a potential earthquake.* | *Only in the late 1990s did efforts to reduce sectarian violence have some success.*

come out right/turn out right /ˌkʌm aʊt ˈraɪt, ˌtɜːʳn aʊt ˈraɪt/ [v phrase not usually in progressive] if something **comes out right** or **turns out right**, it succeeds in the end when it had seemed as though it would fail: *People enjoy romantic fiction because it offers a reassurance that things will always come out right.* | *Just when it looks as though everything will turn out right, tragedy strikes and Jenny dies of a fatal illness.* | **come out right in the end** *She's scared she'll fail her exams, but I think everything'll come out right in the end.*

come off /ˌkʌm ˈɒf / [phr v I not in progressive] if something that you arrange such as a party or trip **comes off**, it happens successfully even though there are problems in arranging it: *We had hoped to organize a trip to the theatre tonight, but it didn't come off.* | *Good try Tim. Shame it didn't quite come off.*

pay off /ˌpeɪ ˈɒf / [phr v I] if hard work, effort, a risk etc **pays off**, it has a successful result at a later time: *I think if you show a bit more consideration for other road users, you'll find it pays off.* | *We put a lot of hard work into local initiatives, and that's really starting to pay off now.*

bear fruit /ˌbeəʳ ˈfruːt/ [v phrase] if a plan, idea, or action **bears fruit**, it has the successful result that it was intended to have, especially after a long period of time: *The campaign for debt relief will not bear fruit for another two or three years.* | *I hope you feel your involvement has been worthwhile and has borne fruit.*

fruitful /ˈfruːtfəl/ [adj] a meeting, discussion etc that is **fruitful** is successful, useful, and produces good results: *So far, the investigation has not been very fruitful.* | *This was one of the most fruitful debates of the conference.* | *If the talks prove fruitful, the working groups will start bargaining in May.*

4 when something happens without any problems at all

- go like clockwork
- go smoothly
- without a hitch
- go according to plan

go like clockwork /ˌgəʊ laɪk ˈklɒkwɜːʳk‖-ˈklɑːk-/ [v phrase] if something you have arranged such as an event or journey **goes like clockwork**, it happens in exactly the way that was planned, with no problems at all: *After all that fuss, everything went like clockwork. You should have seen it.* | *'Everything go all right?' 'Like clockwork.'* | *All through that summer, work on the farm went like clockwork.*

go smoothly /ˌgəʊ ˈsmuːðli/ [v phrase] if a planned event, journey, piece of work etc **goes smoothly**, there are no problems to spoil it: *If all goes smoothly, elections are expected in May.* | *In rehearsal, everything went smoothly, even the difficult fight scenes.* | *My presentation went remarkably smoothly, until one student asked an awkward question right at the end.*

without a hitch /wɪðˌaʊt ə ˈhɪtʃ/ [adv] if a planned action or event happens **without a hitch**, it happens exactly as planned with no problems at all, even though some may have been expected: *The first phase of the operation was completed without a hitch.* | *TCI say they hope that approval will be granted for the takeover without a hitch.* | *Except for the priest forgetting the groom's middle name, the ceremony came off without a hitch.*

go according to plan /gəʊ əˌkɔːʳdɪŋ tə ˈplæn/ [v phrase] if something that has been carefully planned **goes according to plan**, it happens in exactly the way you planned it would: *Development of our new computer system is going according to plan and it should be in operation by October.*

5 something that you succeed in doing

- success
- achievement
- progress
- breakthrough
- accomplishment

success /səkˈses/ [n C/U] when someone or something is successful: *The president believed that his approach was the only one with any chance of success.* | *After her recent successes in Tokyo and New York, Bjork has returned to perform in England.* | *Auster was surprised at the success of his latest novel.* | *Critics have been astonished at the film's success.* | **be a success** *The concert was a great success.* | **+ in** *Success in business depends on hard work, determination, and good ideas.* | **(a) big/huge/outstanding etc success** *Many first-class students go on to have even greater success.*

achievement /əˈtʃiːvmənt/ [n C] something important that you succeed in doing by your own efforts and that other people admire: *Winning three gold medals is a remarkable achievement.* | *They read about his achievements in the press, and were filled with pride.* | *He didn't realize until much later what a spectacular achievement his father made in getting his commission as an officer.* | *Todd always downplayed his athletic achievements.*

progress /ˈprəʊgres‖ˈprɑː-/ [n U] when you gradually get closer to the result you want to achieve: *We are very pleased with your son's progress at school.* | *a progress report* | **+ in** *Progress in technology has changed people's lives dramatically.* | **+ towards** *We are making steady progress towards equal status for men and women.* | **make progress** *Yes, we've made progress. But there's so much more to do.* | *The two sides are making some progress toward a compromise.*

breakthrough /ˈbreɪkθruː/ [n C] an important discovery or achievement, especially one that happens suddenly after people have been trying for a long time: *This was an important breakthrough that had an enormous impact on the scientific community.* | **+ in** *Scientists are claiming a major breakthrough in the treatment of AIDS.* | *The technique is being described as a breakthrough in the field of telemedicine.* | **make a breakthrough** *Police say they have made a breakthrough in their search for the killer of Diane Sutton.*

accomplishment /əˈkʌmplɪʃmənt‖əˈkɑːm-, əˈkʌm-/ [n C] something good that someone has succeeded in doing and that they are proud of doing: *The Society is giving a dinner for top businesswomen, to reward and recognize their accomplish-*

ments. | *The team's undefeated run this year is an outstanding accomplishment.* | *The establishment of full diplomatic relations with China was a major accomplishment of the Carter administration.*

to be successful in your work or in business

6 to be successful in your work

- be successful
- do well
- get on/get ahead
- make it
- succeed
- rise to the top
- work your way up
- make your mark
- further/advance your career

▸ *see also* **ambitious**

be successful ALSO **be a success** /biː sək'sesfəl, biː ə sək'ses/ [v phrase] to earn a lot of money or to become well known and respected, because you do your job very well: *Five years ago he started his own business and now he's very successful.* | *I'm glad we appointed Cyril – he's proved to be a great success.* | *In order to be successful as a dancer, you need flair and stamina.* | *He's leaving the company, despite having been a big success as marketing manager.* | *People who are successful in their careers have found out what they like and do well.*

do well /ˌduː 'wel/ [v phrase] to be successful in your job, especially because you work hard: *Gail seemed so anxious to do well, and she worked really hard.* | *When the players do well, I praise them – but there are no rewards for coming second.* | *Neither of the kids was doing well in school.* | *Most of his tutors expected him to do well at Harvard.* | *My friend left college and went into law, and he's doing very well for himself.*

get on/get ahead /ˌget 'ɒn, ˌget ə'hed / [phr v I] to be successful in your job, especially because you have a very strong desire to succeed: *The people who get on are the ones who create their own opportunities.* | *My father's experience taught me a memorable lesson in how to get ahead.* | **get on in life/the world** *You may not like having to agree with everything the boss says, but often that's the way to get on in life.* | *If you want to get ahead in this world, kid, never take 'no' for an answer.*

make it /'meɪk ɪt/ [v phrase not in progressive] informal to become successful, especially in the sports or entertainment business: *He was a talented football player and I knew he'd make it.* | *We've fought long and hard to get where we are, and we deserve to make it.* | **make it big** (=become very successful) *Many actors move to America, hoping to make it big in Hollywood.* | **make it on your own** (=without any help from anyone) *Get as much advice from colleagues as you can – it can be difficult trying to make it on your own.*

succeed /sək'siːd/ [v I not usually in progressive] to become successful in your job by doing it well and continuing to work at it for a fairly long time: *People who have had setbacks are often the ones who are really driven to succeed.* | *a strong desire to succeed* | **succeed as a teacher/actor/musician etc** *If you don't change your attitude, you will never succeed as a manager in this firm.* | **+ at** *My parents always told me I'd succeed at anything I chose to do.* | **+ in** *A lot of people doubted that I could succeed in business for myself.*

rise to the top /ˌraɪz tə ðə 'tɒp‖-'tɑːp/ [v phrase] to get better and better jobs in a company, organization, or profession so that eventually you have one of the most important jobs in it: *Those who rise to the top in advertising can expect to earn in excess of $100,000.* | *I think we all like to believe that if someone is made of the right stuff, they will rise to the top.* | *A consummate professional, he rose to the top of the most competitive organization in the country.*

work your way up /ˌwɜːʳk jɔːʳ weɪ 'ʌp/ [v phrase] to work very hard in your job so that eventually you reach an important and high position: *While she was working her way up from dishwasher to chef, she was studying at night school to improve her grades.* | **work your way up to the top** *He started two years ago as an admin assistant, and worked his way up to the top.*

make your mark /ˌmeɪk jɔːʳ 'mɑːʳk/ [v phrase] to be successful in your job so that people notice you and respect your ability, especially because of a particular piece of work you have done: *In his early twenties, Terry was the typical ambitious graduate, full of ideas and eager to make his mark.* | *She instantly made her mark with a series of award-winning ad campaigns for high-profile clients.*

further/advance your career /ˌfɜːʳðəʳ, ədˌvɑːns jɔːʳ kə'rɪəʳ‖-ˌvæns-/ [v phrase] to gain more important and better paid jobs in your chosen area of work, especially by doing things that will get you noticed by more important people that you work with: *First, take a look at what you personally can do to advance your career.* | *In recent weeks, Janet has become aware that her colleague Alan has been using her to further his own career.*

7 when a company or product is successful

- be successful
- do well
- be a success
- succeed
- thrive
- prosper

be successful /biː sək'sesfəl/ [v phrase] *Unless we make a product that people want, we are not going to be successful.* | *To be successful, agencies must have in place a first-rate financial management system.* | *The new playstation has been less successful than the previous version.* | *The campaign was so successful that Harvard Business School adopted it as a case study.*

do well /ˌduː 'wel/ [v phrase] if a company or product **does well**, it is successful, especially in difficult conditions or when it has not existed for very long: *If the firm does well, your shares will be worth far more than you paid for them.* | *The producer would only say that sales of the video were 'doing very well indeed.'*

be a success /biː ə sək'ses/ [v phrase] if a company, product, film etc **is a success**, it makes a lot of money because a lot of people use it, buy it, or go to see it: *There was a lot of uncertainty about whether or not the picture would be a success.* | *We've started our own business. If it's a success we should be earning at least $3,000 per month.* | *The movie was, not surprisingly, a huge commercial success for Jordan.* | *The show was an even bigger success than he had dreamed.*

succeed /sək'siːd/ [v I not usually in progressive] if a company or product **succeeds**, it becomes successful and can continue to do business or be produced: *Even in remote areas people open restaurants, and surprisingly enough, they succeed.* | *Who'd think of designing a virtual rock-climbing game? Microsoft did, and it succeeded.*

thrive /θraɪv/ [v I] if a company, or industry **thrives**, it is very successful, especially because economic conditions are good or because a lot of people want to buy or use its products: *The IT explosion means that telecommunications companies are thriving.* | *It is still unclear whether dotcom companies will continue to thrive in the long-term future.* —**thriving** [adj] *a thriving organic supermarket*

prosper /ˈprɒspəʳ‖ˈprɑː-/ [v I] if a company, or industry **prospers**, it is successful and is able to make good profits because of good economic conditions or good management: *Over the next few years, our little bar prospered and grew in popularity.* | *India's software companies have prospered by keeping costs to a bare minimum.*

8 to start to be successful

- take off
- be on the way up
- up-and-coming
- be going places
- be on the up and up

take off /ˌteɪk ˈɒf/ [phr v I] if a product, company, your job etc **takes off**, it suddenly starts being successful: *Her singing career took off after an appearance on Johnny Carson's 'Tonight' show in America.* | *Before you knew it, 11 companies had settled here, and the place really took off.*

be on the way up /biː ɒn ðə ˌweɪ ˈʌp/ [v phrase] to be becoming richer, more successful etc: *He's not that famous a musician at the moment, but he's definitely on the way up.* | *starter homes for young couples on the way up*

up-and-coming /ˌʌp ən ˈkʌmɪŋ◂/ [adj phrase only before noun] **up-and-coming artist/player/executive etc** an artist, player etc, especially a young one, who is getting more and more successful and who will probably soon be famous: *Many up-and-coming young players have trials for the national football team.* | *an award for the best up-and-coming comic actress*

be going places /biː ˈgəʊɪŋ ˌpleɪsɪ̵z/ [v phrase] if you say that a person or company **is going places**, you mean that they are already achieving success and will probably be even more successful in the future: *Alvin was part of it all now. Only 24, and he was going places.* | *This company is clearly one that is going places.*

be on the up and up /biː ɒn ði ˌʌp ənd ˈʌp/ [v phrase] British to be getting more successful all the time: *A gliding club that started in a local farmer's barn says business is on the up and up.* | *We lost at Oxford, but since then we've been on the up and up and won our last four games.*

9 likely to be successful in the future

- have potential
- promising
- will go far/will go a long way
- have a great/bright future

have potential /hæv pəˈtenʃəl/ [v phrase not in progressive] if a person, company, or product **has potential**, they are likely to be successful in the future, especially if they develop in the right way: *Slater has enormous potential, and should soon be playing football for England.* | *She realized that cosmetics made from natural products had great commercial potential.* | **reach/fulfil/realize/achieve your (full) potential** (=be as successful as you have the ability to be) *Sadly, many students leave before they have the opportunity to achieve their potential.*

promising /ˈprɒmɪ̵sɪŋ‖ˈprɑː-/ [adj] likely, but not certain, to be very successful: *Jonathan is one of our most promising employees.* | *Matthew is a promising young dancer with lots of stage personality.* | *Peter gave up a promising career in chemical engineering to become a priest.*

will go far/will go a long way /wɪl ˌgəʊ ˈfɑːʳ, wɪl ˌgəʊ ə ˌlɒŋ ˈweɪ‖-ˌlɔːŋ-/ [v phrase] if someone **will go far** or **will go a long way**, they will be very successful, especially because they have shown natural ability in something or shown that they have the right sort of character to do something: *I remember watching her play, and thinking 'she'll go far.'* | *If this team keeps its mind on nothing but football, it will go a long, long way.*

have a great/bright future /hæv ə ˌgreɪt, ˌbraɪt ˈfjuːtʃəʳ/ [v phrase not in progressive] to be likely to be successful in whatever you choose to do as a job, especially because you are clever or have natural ability in something: *He is a successful student with a bright future.* | *Billy Joe has a great future in this team.* | *A man like you could have a great future here, but you've got to prove yourself.* | **have a great/bright future ahead of you** *She was an attractive girl with a bright future ahead of her when her life was cut short in a tragic car accident.*

10 a successful person

- successful
- high flyer
- achiever
- be a success story

successful /səkˈsesfəl/ [adj] use this about a **successful** person or a job in which someone is successful **successful businessman/star/lawyer etc** *Three years ago she married a successful businessman, and now she never sees her old friends.* | *a rich, successful entrepreneur* | *Eddie Murphy is one of Hollywood's most successful stars.* | *After a long run in the band Genesis, he had a successful solo career.*

high flyer /ˌhaɪ ˈflaɪəʳ/ [n C] someone who is extremely successful in their job, especially because they have an unusually high level of ability: *High flyers can expect promotion to Branch Manager by the time they're 30.* | *Jupe is an academic high-flyer and a gifted administrator.* | *The potential high flyers of the diplomatic service usually join as administrative trainees.* —**high-flying** [adj] *Veronica is a high-flying young solicitor who lives in one of the more exclusive suburbs of Paris.*

achiever /əˈtʃiːvəʳ/ [n C] someone who is determined, who works hard, and who is very successful at whatever they do: *Christopher came from a comfortable family of upper-middle-class achievers.* | *I guess it was clear to everyone that I was bright and an achiever.* | **high achiever** *The study shows that only-children tend to be high achievers in school.*

be a success story /biː ə səkˈses ˌstɔːri/ [v phrase] if someone's life or job **is a success story**, they have been very successful, especially when they start from a low position or from a situation that does not give them many advantages: *His life has been the classic American success story, from rags to riches.* | *Richard is one of our success stories – by accepting voluntary work, he was spared a prison sentence.* | *Hill represents a police success story, having risen up through the ranks to become chief inspector.*

11 a successful company or product

- successful
- thriving
- booming
- success story

▸ *see also* **sell**

successful /sək'sesfəl/ [adj] *What are the features that characterized the successful corporations of the past? | He returned to Merseyside after a successful tour with Johnny Gentle. | Our most successful product is based on a very simple idea. | Gradually, word spread, and we built up a very successful business indeed.*

thriving /'θraɪvɪŋ/ [adj] a company, organization, or industry that is **thriving** is very successful, especially because economic conditions are good or because a lot of people want to buy or use their products: *The nearby malls are thriving, and there's no need for another regional shopping centre. | He expanded the shipping trade and left a thriving business to his son. | the thriving fast-food and soft drinks industry*

booming /'buːmɪŋ/ [adj] a company or industry that is **booming** is extremely successful at a particular time, especially because economic conditions are good: *The need for personal protection has led to a booming private security industry here. | Every day, we hear that the IT industry is booming, but where's the real evidence of that?* | **business is booming** (=used to say that you are selling a lot of products and making a lot of money) *One company that specializes in fitting old computers with new parts says business is booming.*

success story /sək'ses ˌstɔːri/ [n singular] if a company or product is a **success story**, it has become extremely successful, especially suddenly: *Tonight, we're going to hear about another business success story from the North East. | Well, the success story might never have happened if the entrepreneur had taken the advice of his bank.*

suddenly

RELATED WORDS

▸ *see also* **surprised/surprising, fast**

1 suddenly

- suddenly
- all of a sudden
- out of the blue
- abruptly
- without warning
- on the spur of the moment
- from out of nowhere
- at short notice

suddenly /'sʌdnli/ [adv] if something happens **suddenly**, it happens quickly when you are not expecting it: *Suddenly there was a loud bang and all the lights went out. | I suddenly realized that there was someone following me.* | **die suddenly** (=die unexpectedly) *Several years ago her husband died suddenly at the age of 64.*

all of a sudden /ˌɔːl əv ə 'sʌdn/ [adv] suddenly – use this especially in stories or descriptions of past events: *We waited and waited, then all of a sudden we saw a sail on the horizon. | The way he decided to leave all of a sudden didn't make any sense.*

out of the blue /ˌaʊt əv ðə 'bluː/ [adv] if something happens **out of the blue**, you are not expecting it at all, and you are very surprised by it: *She told me, out of the blue, that she was going to live in New York.* | **completely out of the blue** *Do you remember Jane? Well, she phoned me yesterday, completely out of the blue.*

abruptly /ə'brʌptli/ [adv] if something ends or if someone moves or speaks **abruptly**, they do it suddenly and unexpectedly: *The party was stopped abruptly when the police turned up. | She turned abruptly and went back inside. | 'You may leave now,' he said, abruptly.*

without warning /wɪðˌaʊt 'wɔːʳnɪŋ/ [adv] if something bad or dangerous happens **without warning**, it happens suddenly and there were no signs that it was going to happen: *Without warning, tears began to roll down his cheeks. | At five to four Greg went into convulsions. It happened suddenly and without warning.*

on the spur of the moment /ɒn ðə ˌspɜːr əv ðə 'məʊmənt/ [adv] if you do something **on the spur of the moment**, you suddenly decide to do something that you had not planned to do: *I bought the car on the spur of the moment. | On the spur of the moment, we decided to head north that day instead of East.* —**spur-of-the-moment** [adj only before noun] *It was a spur-of-the-moment decision.*

from out of nowhere /frəm ˌaʊt əv 'nəʊweəʳ/ [adv] if you say that someone does something or something appears **from out of nowhere**, it happens suddenly so that you are surprised or shocked: *From out of nowhere he asked me to marry him. | I was doing 80 miles per hour when from out of nowhere this cop on a motorcycle pulled me over.*

at short notice /ət ˌʃɔːʳt 'nəʊtɪ̈s/ [adv] if something happens **at short notice**, it happens suddenly without you having time to prepare for it: *Both players pulled out of the competition yesterday at short notice. | Occasionally, tours may have to be cancelled at short notice.*

2 something that happens suddenly

- sudden
- dramatic
- abrupt
- snap

sudden /'sʌdn/ [adj] happening suddenly: *I felt a sudden sharp pain in my stomach. | Rebecca's decision to leave was very sudden. | Depression is sometimes brought on by a sudden change in your life.*

dramatic /drə'mætɪk/ [adj] happening suddenly, and making a situation either much better or much worse: *There has been a dramatic increase in homelessness over the past few years. | the dramatic changes that took place in Eastern Europe* —**dramatically** [adv] *Oil reserves have fallen dramatically since the war broke out.*

abrupt /ə'brʌpt/ [adj] sudden, unexpected, and often unwanted **abrupt end/departure/change etc** *The police brought the demonstration to an abrupt end. | His departure was abrupt and completely unexpected. | There has been an abrupt shift in the government thinking regarding these issues.*

snap /snæp/ [adj only before noun] **snap decision/judgement** a decision or judgement that is made very suddenly, often without thinking about it enough: *Snap decisions are not always the best decisions. | Usually she did not make snap judgements about people.*

suffer

when something painful or unpleasant happens to you

RELATED WORDS

- *see also* **pain, illness/disease, ill/sick**

1 to suffer

- suffer
- endure
- go through
- undergo
- be subjected to
- be in the grip of
- be in the throes of

suffer /ˈsʌfəʳ/ [v I/T] to experience physical or emotional pain when something bad happens to you: *Children always suffer when their parents get divorced.* | *In all wars, it's innocent civilians who suffer most.* | *Anne still suffers a lot of pain in her leg.* | **+ from** *Two hundred million people worldwide suffer from parasitic diseases.*

endure /ɪnˈdjʊəʳ‖ɪnˈdʊər/ [v T] **especially written** to experience pain or have difficult or unpleasant experiences over a long period – use this especially about people who are brave and patient: *She has endured ten years of painful back operations.* | *They were lost in the mountains for ten days, enduring hunger, thirst, and intense cold.*

go through /ˈgəʊ θruː/ [phr v T] to experience a lot of problems in your life over a long period of time: *Peter had lost his job, and the family was going through a very difficult time.* | *It's good to see Patrick looking so happy now, after all he's gone through in the last few years.*

undergo /ˌʌndəʳˈgəʊ/ [v T] to experience a very difficult or unpleasant situation that you have no control over and cannot stop: *The hostages were eventually released after undergoing a terrifying ordeal.* | *He underwent major heart surgery last year.* | *At that time she was undergoing tremendous emotional problems following the breakup of her marriage.*

be subjected to /biː səbˈdʒektɪ̈d tuː/ [v phrase] to be forced to experience something very unpleasant, such as unfair or violent treatment, especially over a long time: *Black people in the area are claiming they have been subjected to repeated racial attacks from police officers.* | *The charity helps children who have been subjected to domestic violence and sexual abuse.*

be in the grip of /biː ɪn ðə ˈgrɪp ɒv/ [v phrase] to be experiencing an extremely unpleasant or serious situation that you have no control over and cannot stop: *The Sudan was in the grip of its worst famine for 20 years.* | *Much of Europe was in the grip of postwar recession.*

be in the throes of /biː ɪn ðə ˈθrəʊz ɒv/ [v phrase] to be experiencing a difficult or unpleasant situation, especially one that continues a long time: *Kramer was in the throes of clinical depression and left the band for a while.* | *In the throes of the Great Depression, Franklin Roosevelt developed the economic plan called 'The New Deal'.*

2 to suffer because of bad things you have done or mistakes you have made

- suffer
- pay
- count the cost
- cost sb dearly/dear
- know/find out to your cost
- at a/some cost to

suffer /ˈsʌfəʳ/ [v I] *If you tell lies, it is you who will suffer in the end.* | **make sb suffer** *When his mother caught him cheating she really made him suffer.* | **+ for** *All over the world, people are suffering for their political or religious beliefs.* | *I shouldn't have drunk all that wine – I'll suffer for it tomorrow morning.*

pay /peɪ/ [v I/T] to have a bad experience as a way of being punished for something bad that you have done, mistakes you have made etc **+ for** *Miller refused to testify and paid for it by being labelled a communist.* | **make sb pay** *They think I've forgotten what they did to me, but I'll make them pay.* | **pay dearly** *She drank far too much at the party and paid dearly for it the next day.* | **pay the price/the penalty** *Tony didn't do any studying all year but paid the price when it came to the exams.*

count the cost /ˌkaʊnt ðə ˈkɒst‖-ˈkɔːst/ [v phrase] **British** to suffer or start having problems as a result of mistakes or decisions you made at an earlier time: *The school overspent on its budget last year, and now it's having to count the cost.* | **+ of** *We are now counting the cost of our earlier mistakes.*

cost sb dearly/dear /ˌkɒst (sb) ˈdɪəʳli, ˈdɪəʳ‖ˌkɔːst-/ [v phrase] if a mistake **costs someone dearly** or **costs someone dear**, they suffer a great deal because of it: *This scandal could cost the government dearly.* | *It was only a small mistake, but it cost us very dear.*

know/find out to your cost /ˌnəʊ, ˌfaɪnd aʊt tə jɔːʳ ˈkɒst‖-ˈkɔːst/ [v phrase] if you **know** or **find out** something **to your cost**, you realize that something that happened or something you did at an earlier time is now causing problems or is likely to cause problems in the future: *As we now know to our cost, the disease is highly contagious.* | *Many people have found out to their cost that insurance policies do not always cover damage from flooding.*

at a/some cost to /ət ə, sʌm ˈkɒst tuː‖-ˈkɔːst-/ [prep] if you do something **at a cost to** someone or something, that person suffers because you do it: *She's struggled to keep the family going on her own – at considerable cost to herself.* | *Ms Gideon has defended her cause at great cost to her personal and political reputation.*

3 something painful or unpleasant that you suffer

- suffering
- hardship
- plight
- agony
- torment
- adversity

suffering /ˈsʌfərɪŋ/ [n U] very unpleasant, painful, or upsetting conditions – use this especially about a situation that affects a lot of people: *The earthquake has caused massive damage and a great deal of human suffering.* | *Reporters described the suffering they had seen in the war zone.*

hardship /ˈhɑːʳdʃɪp/ [n C/U] when your life is difficult and uncomfortable, especially because you are very poor: *During the war we faced many hardships.* | *Rising food prices caused great hardship for* *most of the population.* | *Many students suffer financial hardship.*

plight /plaɪt/ [n singular] a difficult and unpleasant situation, in which people are suffering a lot and that makes you feel great sympathy for them: *The film deals with the nomadic desert people of the Sahel, whose plight has worsened in the recent years of drought.* | *A new report exposes the plight of skilled nurses, who work long hours for very low rates of pay.*

agony /ˈæɡəni/ [n U] a very sad, difficult, and unpleasant situation in which people suffer a lot, especially over a long time: *In the book she describes the agony of watching her child die.* | *With renewed fighting for control of the capital, there seems to be no end to the region's agony.*

torment /ˈtɔːʳment/ [n U] severe mental suffering, often continuing for a long time: *She suffered years of private torment over her decision to have her children adopted.* | *It's difficult for us to understand the torment the hostages are going through.*

adversity /ədˈvɜːʳsɪ̈ti/ [n U] written a situation in which you have continuing difficulties that seem to be caused by bad luck: *They have suffered more than their fair share of adversity and managed to overcome it every time.* | **in the face of adversity** (=when experiencing adversity) *She somehow manages to keep laughing in the face of adversity.*

4 someone who suffers

- victim
- casualty

victim /ˈvɪktɪ̈m/ [n C] someone who suffers because of an illness, accident, crime etc: *a murder victim* | *Heart attack victims stand a better chance if they are treated immediately.* | *They are launching a massive aid program to help the famine victims.* | **+ of** *Our aim is to help victims of crime.*

casualty /ˈkæʒuəlti/ [n C] someone who suffers as a result of an event or situation over which they have no control – used especially in news reports: *The corruption scandal has claimed yet another casualty: the Finance Minister, who was forced to resign last night.* | **+ of** *The company is the latest casualty of the worldwide recession.*

5 someone who seems to enjoy suffering

- masochist
- be a glutton for punishment
- martyr

masochist /ˈmæsəkɪst/ [n C] *He goes swimming in the sea in the middle of winter – he must be some kind of masochist.* —**masochistic** /ˌmæsəˈkɪstɪk◂/ [adj] *She seems to derive an almost masochistic pleasure from going out with men who treat her badly.*

be a glutton for punishment /biː ə ˌɡlʌtn fəʳ ˈpʌnɪʃmənt/ [v phrase] use this humorously about someone who seems to like being put in situations where they will suffer, when it could have been avoided: *Being a glutton for punishment, I agreed to organize yet another children's birthday party.*

martyr /ˈmɑːʳtəʳ/ [n C] someone who enjoys suffering because they make other people feel guilty about it, and therefore get sympathy and attention: *Don't be a martyr – ask for help if you need it.* | **play the martyr** (=behave like one) *We all like to play the martyr sometimes.*

suggest

RELATED WORDS

see also **advise, idea, warn, persuade**

1 to suggest something

- suggest
- make a suggestion
- recommend

suggest /səˈdʒest‖səɡ-/ [v T] to tell someone your idea about what they should do, where they should go etc, or about what you and they should do together: *'Why don't you come with us?' Alan suggested.* | *It was a sunny afternoon, and Jim suggested a trip to the beach.* | **+ (that)** *My Dad suggested that I should apply for the job.* | *I suggest we take a break and finish this later.* | **+ doing sth** *It was raining heavily, and she suggested calling a taxi.* | **+ where/how/when etc** *Can you suggest where we might be able to get a decent meal?*

make a suggestion /ˌmeɪk ə səˈdʒestʃən‖-səɡ-/ [v phrase] to suggest something that you think will help someone or will solve a problem: *Mr Chairman – may I make a suggestion?* | *One day her mother made a suggestion. 'Why don't you come back and live with your father and me?'* | *A professional consultant will make suggestions about the most suitable clients to approach for your particular type of work.*

recommend /ˌrekəˈmend/ [v T] to suggest something to someone because you know that it is good and you are sure that they will like it: *Can you recommend a good hotel near here?* | **recommend sth to sb** *Corfu was wonderful – I'd recommend it to anyone.* | **be highly recommended** (=people say that it is very good) *The hotel's restaurant comes highly recommended.*

2 to make a formal suggestion in a meeting, report etc

- propose
- recommend
- put forward
- put sth to/before
- float
- submit
- present
- be mooted

propose /prəˈpəʊz/ [v T] to formally suggest that something should be done, especially at a meeting: *The Russians proposed a treaty banning all nuclear tests.* | **+ (that)** *I propose that we discuss this at the next meeting.*

recommend /ˌrekəˈmend/ [v T] to officially suggest that something should be done, after you have considered the situation carefully: *The report recommends a number of changes in the existing law.* | **+ that** *The directors are recommending that shareholders accept Baldwin's offer.*

put forward /ˌpʊt ˈfɔːʳwəʳd/ [phr v T] to suggest plans, proposals etc, especially in order to start discussions about something that needs to be decided: *The United Nations has put forward a peace plan that it hopes will form the basis for discussions.* | *Management initially put forward a number of proposals which were wholly unacceptable to the union.*

put sth to/before /ˈpʊt (sth) tuː, bɪˌfɔːʳ/ [v phrase] to offer a group something such as a proposal or plan which they can accept or refuse: *The Government has spent £1 million on putting its case to the public.* | *We're going to put our plans before the com-*

mittee on Monday and we'll just have to hope that they are approved.

float /fləʊt/ [v T not usually in progressive] **float an idea/plan etc** to suggest an idea, plan etc in order to find out what other people think about it: *The administration had floated the idea of increased taxes on beer, spirits and tobacco.* | *The following month, David floated the possibility of launching a new TV company.*

submit /səbˈmɪt/ [v T] to offer a proposal, application etc so that an official person or group can consider it and decide whether to accept it: *Applications for planning permission must be submitted before noon tomorrow.* | **submit sth to sb** *We have submitted proposals for a new pay structure to the board of management.*

present /prɪˈzent/ [v T] to explain your ideas or plans to an official group so that they can decide whether to accept them: *We shall give you reasonable time to prepare and present your proposals.* | **present sth to sb** *Ms Rogers will present her ideas to the Board at next week's meeting.* | **present sb with sth** *We have been presented with a number of plans and will give careful consideration to all of them.*

be mooted /biː ˈmuːtɪ̵d/ [v phrase] if an idea or plan **is mooted**, it is suggested as something that could be done: *The scheme was first mooted two years ago.* | **+ for** *A 3,000 house development has been mooted for the disused airfield.*

3 to suggest someone as a suitable person for a job or official position

- suggest
- recommend
- put sb's name forward
- nominate
- propose

suggest /səˈdʒest‖səg-/ [v T] *All members are invited to suggest names.* | **suggest sb for sth** *Robert suggested his son for the vacant directorship.*

recommend /ˌrekəˈmend/ [v T] to suggest someone you know personally as suitable for a job or position, because you think they would do a good job: *Ask friends to recommend babysitters. That's the safest way.* | *The first applicant was recommended by a friend of the boss.* | **recommend sb for sth** *Who would you recommend for this job, Stuart?*

put sb's name forward /ˌpʊt (sb's) ˈneɪm fɔːʳwəʳd/ [v phrase] to formally suggest someone, usually in writing, to be elected to an official or political position: *The local Democratic party has put several names forward.* | **+ for** *The opposition leader announced that he would not be putting his name forward for re-election at the party's annual conference.*

nominate /ˈnɒmɪ̵neɪt‖ˈnɑː-/ [v T] to suggest someone for an important job or prize, especially when people will vote to make a decision: *We need a treasurer. Does anyone want to nominate somebody?* | **nominate sb for sth** *Jane Campion was one of the people nominated for the 'Best Director' award.* | **nominate sb as sth** *It was expected that he would nominate Bramwell as his successor.* | **nominate sb to sth** *The President has power to nominate people to certain key offices, including judge of the Supreme Court.* —**nomination** /ˌnɒmɪ̵ˈneɪʃən‖ˌnɑː-/ [n C/U] *His nomination as chief executive was approved by the board.* | *the Democratic nomination for President* (=the person nominated by the Democrats)

propose /prəˈpəʊz/ [v T] to formally suggest someone for an official position: *At the last meeting, Mrs Williams was proposed by several members.* | **+ for** *I would like to propose Mr Harrison for the position of Party Treasurer.*

4 something that someone suggests

- suggestion
- proposal
- recommendation
- proposition

suggestion /səˈdʒestʃən‖səg-/ [n C] something that someone suggests: *We welcome any suggestions from our viewers as to how to improve our service.* | **make a suggestion** *She made some useful suggestions about places we could visit.* | **have a suggestion** (=want to make a suggestion) *Does anyone have any other suggestions?* | **+ about** *We liked your suggestion about changing the timetable.* | **+ that** *Barry ignored my suggestion that he should try phoning her again.* | **open to suggestions** (=willing to listen to ideas) *You must be flexible and open to suggestions in this job.*

proposal /prəˈpəʊzəl/ [n C] a formal or official suggestion that something should be done: *They will consider our proposal at their next meeting.* | **put forward a proposal** (=make one) *Their role is to put forward proposals for change.* | **+ to do sth** *Their proposal to build a new airport has finally been rejected.* | **+ for** *They forwarded a list of proposals for the safe disposal of nuclear waste.*

recommendation /ˌrekəmenˈdeɪʃən/ [n C] a suggestion made, for example, by an official person or group, especially a suggestion that is contained in a report **make a recommendation** *The consultants have made several very good and valid recommendations.* | **accept a recommendation** *We accept that recommendation and will act on it as soon as possible.* | **on sb's recommendation** (=because someone has recommended it) *I bought the house on the realtor's recommendation and have regretted it ever since.*

proposition /ˌprɒpəˈzɪʃən‖ˌprɑː-/ [n C] a plan of action that is suggested, especially in business or politics: *I'll consider your proposition and let you know.* | *We are prepared to look at any reasonable proposition from the council.* | **make a proposition** *I have a proposition to make.*

5 what you say to suggest something

- can/may I make a suggestion
- I propose (that)
- why don't you/we/I etc
- how about/what about
- maybe/perhaps
- let's
- we may as well

can/may I make a suggestion /ˌkæn, ˌmeɪ aɪ ˌmeɪk ə səˈdʒestʃən‖-səg-/ use this to suggest something politely, especially when you think someone may be making a mistake: *Can I make a suggestion? Try adding a little more flour.* | *May I make a suggestion? I think we should stop and look at the map.*

I propose (that) /aɪ prəˈpəʊz (ðət)/ spoken use this for formally suggesting something that you think should be done, especially at a meeting: *I propose that we continue this meeting tomorrow.*

why don't you/we/I etc /ˈwaɪ dəʊnt juː/ informal say this when you think it would be a good idea to do something: *Why don't you wait for me downstairs? I won't be long.* | *If David wants someone to go with him, why doesn't he ask Jacky? I'm sure she'd enjoy it.* | *Why don't we go watch a movie tonight?*

how about/what about /ˈhaʊ əbaʊt, ˈwɒt əbaʊt/ informal use this to suggest something or offer something: *'How about a brandy?' said Tom.* | *What about going out for lunch one day next week? When are you free?*

maybe/perhaps /ˈmeɪbi, pəʳˈhæps/ [adv] spoken use this to suggest something in a gentle way: *Maybe we should try again tomorrow.* | *Perhaps you ought to introduce her to my son. They should get on well.*

let's /lets/ **let's go/have/do etc** use this when you want to suggest something that you and the people you are with should do: *Come on, let's dance.* | *We both need a break. Let's go away for the weekend.* | **let's not** *Let's not argue on our anniversary.* | **don't let's (British)** *Come on, don't let's waste any more time here.*

we may as well /wiː ˌmeɪ əz ˈwel/ use this to suggest something that is not very interesting or exciting, when you do not have any better ideas: *It's too late to go to the movies so we may as well watch TV.* | *I think we might as well buy this one. We're not going to find anything cheaper.*

suit/look good together

when clothes etc suit a person, or when things look good together

RELATED WORDS

▸ *see also* **clothes, style/elegance, suitable, fashionable/not fashionable**

1 to suit someone

- suit
- look good on
- flattering

suit /suːt, sjuːt‖suːt/ [v T not in progressive or passive] if something such as a piece of clothing or a colour **suits** someone, they look good when they wear it because it is the right colour, style etc: *Do you think this colour suits me?* | *Steve was wearing a red silk shirt that didn't suit him at all.* | *Your hair suits you like that.* | *That dress would really suit Annie.*

look good on /lʊk ˈgʊd ɒn/ [v phrase not in progressive] if a piece of clothing **looks good on** someone, it looks good when they are wearing it: *Why don't you wear that black dress? It looks really good on you.* | *Those trousers would look really good on you.*

flattering /ˈflætərɪŋ/ [adj] clothes or styles that are **flattering** help to make someone look more attractive, for example by making a fat person look thinner: *High-heeled shoes are flattering but not very comfortable.* | *She wore a plain black dress, quite simple but very flattering.*

2 to look good with something else

- go with
- go together
- match
- matching
- complement
- set off
- blend in

go with /ˈgəʊ wɪð/ [phr v T not in progressive or passive] *I'm not sure that those earrings will go with your dress.* | *That jacket will go really well with your blue skirt.* | *I love that pale blue wallpaper, but I don't think it would go with the carpet.*

go together /ˈgəʊ təˌgeðəʳ/ [phr v I not in progressive] if two things **go together**, they look good when they are worn or seen with each other: *That jacket and skirt don't really go together.* | *It's funny but the yellow walls and the black floor actually go together quite well.*

match /mætʃ/ [v I/T not in progressive] if something **matches** something else, or if two things **match**, they look good together because they are similar in colour or style: *She was wearing black high-heeled shoes that matched her skirt and jacket.* | *In the lounge everything matched; the curtains, the sofa, the carpet and the cushions.* | *I'm looking for a rug to match my bedroom curtains.* | **handbag/hat/shoes to match** (=that match) *For every outfit, Stephanie seemed to have a handbag and shoes to match.*

matching /ˈmætʃɪŋ/ [adj only before noun] **matching** pieces of clothing, furniture etc are similar to each other in colour or style and so look good together: *Emily was wearing a dark green skirt and matching blouse.* | *In the kitchen was a rustic oak table and six matching chairs.*

complement /ˈkɒmpl̩ment‖ˈkɑːm-/ [v T not in progressive] formal if a piece of clothing or a colour **complements** something, it makes it look more attractive: *A simple string of pearls will complement any outfit.* | *Soft, creamy bed linen adds a luxurious touch and complements any colour scheme.* | *She looked beautiful – the white silk of her blouse complemented her olive skin perfectly.*

set off /ˌset ˈɒf/ [phr v T] if one thing **sets off** another thing, it makes it look more attractive and noticeable, for example by being different in colour or style **set off sth** *The brass rail sets off the wooden panelling very nicely.* | **set sth off** *It's a lovely dress, and a brightly coloured silk scarf will set it off perfectly.*

blend in /ˌblend ˈɪn/ [phr v I] if something **blends in** with the things around it, it looks good with them because it has a similar colour or pattern to theirs and does not look very different from them: *The colour's perfect for our bedroom – it should blend in very nicely.* | **+ with** *I'm looking for some pale green curtains that will blend in with the walls.* | *Choose plants that will blend in with the existing garden scheme.*

3 to not look good with something else

- not match
- not go with/not go together
- clash

not match /nɒt ˈmætʃ/ [v I/T not in progressive] if two things do **not match**, they are not the same colour or style and so do not look attractive together: *That tie doesn't match your shirt.* | *I felt slightly out of place, and was conscious that my jacket and trousers didn't quite match.*

not go with/not go together /nɒt ˈgəʊ wɪð, nɒt ˈgəʊ təˌgeðəʳ/ [v phrase not in progressive] if one thing does **not go with** another, or if two things do **not go together**, they do not look attractive next to each other: *That shirt doesn't go with your blue trousers.* | *Pink and purple don't usually go very well together.*

clash /klæʃ/ [v I not in progressive] if two things **clash**, they look very bad when they are worn or seen together because they are completely different in style, colour etc: *Choose bright colors, but make sure they don't clash.* | **+ with** *That scarf clashes terribly with her green coat.* | *I can't wear red – it clashes with my hair.*

suitable

RELATED WORDS

opposite: —— **unsuitable**

▸ *see also* **convenient, best, perfect, suit/look good together**

1 suitable for a particular situation, job, purpose etc

- ▸ suitable
- ▸ right
- ▸ proper
- ▸ appropriate
- ▸ good
- ▸ suit
- ▸ be suited to
- ▸ be cut out for
- ▸ lends itself to

suitable /ˈsuːtəbəl, ˈsjuː-‖ˈsuː-/ [adj] something or someone that is **suitable** is the right type of thing or person for a purpose, job, or situation: *I still haven't found a suitable job.* | *You must wear something suitable – preferably black.* | **+ for** *The house would be suitable for a large family.* | *Plants of this type are suitable for use in an aquarium.* | **eminently suitable** (=very suitable) *The property is centrally located and eminently suitable for our purposes.* —**suitably** [adv] *Few of the young people were dressed suitably for the wedding.*

right /raɪt/ [adj] suitable. **Right** is used more in informal language than **suitable**: *I don't know the right word to describe it.* | *We've been thinking about selling the house, but I'm not sure the time is right.* | *We all agree that Carey is the right person for the job.* | **+ for** *It's a good school, but it wasn't really right for Melissa.*

proper /ˈprɒpəʳ‖ˈprɑː-/ [adj only before noun] suitable for a particular purpose or situation: *You can't climb a mountain without the proper equipment.* | *I can't make the repairs without the proper tools or materials.* | *With proper training, most people can learn leadership skills.* —**properly** [adv] *The machine operators had not been properly trained.*

appropriate /əˈprəʊpri-ɪ̈t/ [adj] suitable for a situation or purpose – use this especially about something that has been carefully chosen for a particular situation: *You will be given your orders at the appropriate time.* | *Considering what he did, I think the punishment was appropriate.* | **+ for** *Each member is given a special exercise routine that is appropriate for his or her needs* —**appropriately** [adv] *His manner at the funeral was appropriately solemn.*

good /gʊd/ [adj] especially spoken very suitable for a purpose or job – use this especially when there are several suitable people or things to choose from: *Bates would be a good person to have on the team.* | *Would now be a good time to discuss the plans for the conference?* | **+ for** *The big jars are good for storing rice or pasta.*

suit /suːt, sjuːt‖suːt/ [v T not in passive] something that **suits** a person, purpose, situation etc is suitable for them: *This is a job that would suit someone with a lot of experience abroad.* | *They found us a house close to the campus, which suited us very well.* | **suit sb's needs** *Make sure you choose a computer that suits your needs.* | **suit sb fine/well/perfectly** *The weather here suits me fine.*

be suited to /biː ˈsuːtɪ̈d tuː/ [v phrase] if someone or something **is suited to** a situation, purpose, or job they have the qualities that make them suitable for it: *Wearing a suit and tie just is not suited to a tropical climate.* | *Do you think his personality is suited to a career in teaching?* | **ideally/well/perfectly suited to sth** *The electric car is well suited to the needs of city drivers.*

be cut out for /biː ˌkʌt ˈaʊt fɔːʳ/ [v phrase] if someone **is cut out for** a particular job, they have personal qualities that are suitable for it and are therefore likely to succeed at it – use this especially in questions and negative sentences: *Maybe he's just not cut out for an acting career.* | *She knew she was cut out for more than scrubbing floors and doing laundry.*

lends itself to /ˈlendz ɪtself tuː/ [v phrase] if something **lends itself to** being used in a particular way, it has qualities that make it easy and suitable for using in that way: *Many of his poems lend themselves to songs very easily.* | *The marshy land at the mouth of the Neva River hardly lent itself to habitation.*

2 exactly suitable for a particular situation, job, purpose etc

- ▸ just right
- ▸ ideal
- ▸ be made for
- ▸ fit the bill

just right /ˌdʒʌst ˈraɪt/ [adj phrase] exactly suitable: *I moved into a small apartment close to the college – it was just right.* | **+ for** *Your new dress will be just right for the party.* | **just the right colour/size/age etc** *We found a cashmere scarf that was just the right color.* | *Setting the mood for romance means candlelight and just the right music.*

ideal /aɪˈdiəl/ [adj] the **ideal** thing or person is the most suitable one you can possibly choose, when there are many to choose from: *The trip is difficult, even under ideal conditions.* | *If you could complete the report by Friday, that would be ideal.* | **+ for** *With its tough suspension and 4-wheel drive, the truck is ideal for driving in the desert.*

be made for /biː ˈmeɪd fɔːʳ/ [v phrase] to be exactly right for a particular job or purpose: *The job is made for someone like you.* | *In the garden stood an old apple tree with low branches, just made for climbing.*

fit the bill /ˌfɪt ðə ˈbɪl/ [v phrase not in progressive or passive] to have exactly the qualities needed to be suitable for a particular job, situation etc: *We know what kind of house we want, but we haven't yet found one that fits the bill.* | *I need someone who can speak both French and Spanish. Do you know anyone who fits the bill?*

3 when two people are suitable for each other

- ▸ compatible
- ▸ be well-matched
- ▸ be made for each other
- ▸ be a perfect match/pair/couple
- ▸ be right for
- ▸ be ideally suited

compatible /kəmˈpætɪ̈bəl/ [adj] able to have a very good relationship with each other, because you have characters, interests, qualities etc that go well together: *Compatible couples generally share the same values and have similar lifestyles and goals.* | *The success of a relationship depends largely on how compatible two people are and how well they communicate.* —**compatibility** /kəmˌpætɪ̈ˈbɪlɪ̈ti/ [n U] *Compatibility is just as important as romantic love.*

be well-matched ALSO **be well-suited** British /biː ˌwel ˈmætʃt, biː ˌwel ˈsuːtɪ̈d/ [v phrase] if two people **are well-matched** or **well-suited**, they are suitable for each other because they agree about most things, like and dislike the same things etc: *They're a well-matched pair. He's ambitious, and she'll back him all the way.* | *Selina and I are very well-suited to each other. We seem to agree about most things.*

be made for each other /biː ˈmeɪd fər iːtʃ ˌʌðəʳ/ [v phrase] if two people **are made for each other**, they are naturally very suitable for each other: *Sam and Ellie are made for each other. I just can't think of either of them with anyone else.* | *When they met in Paris last fall, they fell immediately in love and knew they were made for each other.*

be a perfect match/pair/couple /biː ə ˌpɜːʳfɪkt ˈmætʃ, ˈpeəʳ, ˈkʌpəl/ [v phrase] to be exactly suitable for each other: *Isn't it great that Will and Sue are getting married? I really think they are a perfect match.* | *They're a perfect couple – Joe has charm and Delia has money.*

be right for ALSO **be the right one/person/man/woman etc for** /biː ˈraɪt fɔːʳ, biː ðə ˌraɪt ˈwʌn fɔːʳ/ [v phrase] if someone **is right for** someone else or **the right one for** them, they have the type of character, interests etc that make them likely to have a very good relationship with that person: *She's a nice girl, but I don't think she's right for my brother.* | *As soon as I met him, I knew he was the right one for me.*

be ideally suited /biː aɪˌdɪəli ˈsuːtɪ̈d/ [v phrase] British if two people **are ideally suited**, they are so suitable for each other that it would be very difficult to find a better relationship: *They are both as mad as each other. Ideally suited I would say.* | **+ for** *Malcom will be ideally suited for Angela. They have such a lot in common.*

4 when two things are good when done, eaten etc together

- go together/go with
- be just right with
- complement

go together/go with /ˈgəʊ təˌgeðəʳ, ˈgəʊ wɪð/ [v phrase not in progressive] if two things **go together**, or if one of them **goes with** the other, they are suitable for each other: *Lamb goes very well with herbs such as rosemary and thyme.* | *Do this skirt and blouse go together?* | *The company's old headquarters didn't go with their corporate image.*

be just right with /biː ˌdʒʌst ˈraɪt wɪð/ [v phrase] if one thing **is just right with** another, it goes with the other: *The wine is just right with a grilled steak.* | **be just the right thing with sth** *This jacket will be just the right thing with my blue skirt.*

complement /ˈkɒmplɪ̈ment‖ˈkɑːm-/ [v T not in progressive] if one type of food or drink **complements** another, it improves the taste because they taste good together: *The wine complemented the meal perfectly.* | *The chicken dish is complemented by wild rice or spiced couscous.*

summarize

to make a short statement that describes the main points of something

RELATED WORDS

▸ *see also* **short, write**

1 to summarize something

- summarize
- sum up
- recap/give (sb) a recap
- give (sb) a rundown

summarize ALSO **summarise** British /ˈsʌməraɪz/ [v I/T] to make a short statement giving only the main information, but not the details, of a report, plan, event etc: *Your final paragraph should summarize the main points of your essay.* | *The interview was summarized on the front page of the newspaper.* | *The report was detailed and thorough; it didn't just summarize.*

sum up /ˌsʌm ˈʌp/ [phr v I/T] to summarize something clearly and in very few words, especially at the end of a speech, report, or meeting: *The Chairman's job was to introduce the speakers and to sum up at the end of the debate.* | **sum up sth** *The last section of the report sums up the arguments on both sides.* | *In these few words the president summed up the feelings of the whole nation.* | **sum sth up** *I couldn't have summed it up better.*

recap/give (sb) a recap /riːˈkæp, ˌgɪv (sb) ə ˈriːkæp/ [v I/T/phr v I/T] to make a short spoken statement summarizing what has already been said in order to remind someone of it: *If you missed the previous episode, Alistair Cooke starts off each week by recapping the story so far.* | *To recap the legend: William Tell shot an apple off his son's head.* | **+ of** *At the end of the article, Kohn gives a recap of the proposals.*

give (sb) a rundown /ˌgɪv (sb) ə ˈrʌndaʊn/ [v phrase] to give someone a short, usually spoken report, especially about a series of events, including all the important facts: *Before we go to work on this, you'd better give us a complete rundown.* | **+ on** *Baseball cards give a rundown on each player's statistics.* | **+ of** *Can you give me a rundown of what was said at yesterday's meeting?*

2 a statement in which facts or ideas are summarized

- summary
- outline
- overview
- rundown
- precis
- synopsis

summary /ˈsʌməri/ [n C] a short statement that gives only the main ideas and facts of something that has been written or said: *'The progress we hoped for has clearly not developed,' the council said in the summary to its final report.* | *In its report on the speech, the radio carried a brief summary, but did not broadcast the whole thing.* | **+ of** *Write a two-page summary of the results of your research.* | *I've made a summary of the main points in the Secretary General's speech.* | **news summary** British (=a short programme reporting the main events in the news) *There will be a news summary at 9.05.*

outline /ˈaʊtlaɪn/ [n C usually singular] a short statement, especially a written one, that summarizes a statement or piece of writing and contains only the most important points: *Write a short outline covering the main points before you start on your essay.* | **+ of** *The book begins with an outline of the events that led to the First World War.* | **broad outline** (=a very general outline) *In this paper I will give a broad outline of the research we have been doing.* | **in outline** (=giving an outline) *This chapter shows, in outline, the way money circulates through the economy.*

overview /ˈəʊvəʳvjuː/ [n C usually singular] a short statement that summarizes a whole subject, situation, or problem in a general way: *Before we can consider the details we need to have an overview of the whole situation.* | **+ of** *The aim of the first chapter is to provide a general overview of the subjects that will be covered.*

rundown /ˈrʌndaʊn/ [n C usually singular] a report, especially a spoken one, that summarizes a set of events or a situation quickly and simply **+ of** *I want a complete rundown of what's been happening while I've been away.* | *What follows is a rundown of all the ways one company tries to market its products.* | **+ on** *Here is a rundown on the outdoor activities available in the resort.*

precis /ˈpreɪsiː‖preɪˈsiː/ [n C] a short piece of writing, especially one written by a student as a formal language exercise, intended to summarize the main points of a longer piece of writing **+ of** *I want you to write a precis of the whole passage in not more than 80 words.*

synopsis /sɪˈnɒpsəs‖-ˈnɑː-/ [n C] a short piece of writing that summarizes the story of a film, play, or book: *I read the synopsis and decided that it would make an interesting film.* | **+ of** *Please write a synopsis of the story, not more than 100 words long.*

3 what you say when you are going to summarize something

- to sum up/to summarize/in summary
- in a nutshell
- in short
- to cut a long story short

to sum up/to summarize/in summary /tə ˌsʌm ˈʌp, tə ˈsʌməraɪz, ɪn ˈsʌməri/ [phr v I/T/v I/T/adv] use this at the beginning of a sentence when you are going to summarize what has been said, especially at the end of a speech: *To sum up, the jury found the wrong person guilty.* | *To summarize, Bremer is saying 'you just have to trust me.'* | *In summary, don't waste your money on this book.*

in a nutshell /ɪn ə ˈnʌtʃel/ [adv] use this when you are summarizing a situation or idea in a few words: *In a nutshell, the state government is expected to be $2 million in debt by the end of the year.* | *A study of women at work says, in a nutshell, that opportunities have opened up dramatically.* | **put it in a nutshell** *Bob put it in a nutshell when he said the problems was essentially a lack of communication.*

in short /ɪn ˈʃɔːʳt/ [adv] use this to say the most important point about a situation in a few words: *In short, the report says that more money should be spent on education.* | *In short, the better a parent you are during the first 18 years, the better friends you'll be later.*

to cut a long story short especially British **/to make a long story short** American /tə kʌt ə ˌlɒŋ ˌstɔːri ˈʃɔːʳt, tə meɪk ə ˌlɒŋ ˌstɔːri ˈʃɔːʳt‖-ˌlɔːŋ-/ [adv] say this when you want to finish a story quickly and only tell people the most important parts: *To make a long story short, Stephen had a fight with Paul and ended up in the hospital.* | *I was a waitress in a bar and he was one of my customers, and that, to cut a long story short, is how we met.*

4 to describe something in a general way, giving only the main points

- outline
- sketch out

outline /ˈaʊtlaɪn/ [v T] to describe something such as an idea, plan, or report by giving the main points of it, especially in writing: *Each member of staff received a letter outlining their responsibilities and duties.* | *He declined to provide a copy of the report but agreed to outline its contents.*

sketch out /ˌsketʃ ˈaʊt/ [phr v T] to describe something such as a plan or an idea in a general way without giving any details or being very exact: *In his letter, Marx sketched out his ideas for a new work on the history of capitalism in Britain.* | *Could you sketch out for us exactly how you see this plan developing?*

support

RELATED WORDS

- to support a team or player *see* **sport/game (11)**
- *see also* **agree, help**

WHAT'S HERE

- **to agree with or help sb/sth** see **1 to 6**
- **to stop sb/sth from falling down** see **7 to 9**

to agree with or help sb/sth

RELATED WORDS

opposite: **against/oppose**

1 to agree with an idea/person/political party

- support
- be in favour of
- pro-
- be in sympathy with/sympathize with
- endorse
- advocate
- be with

support /səˈpɔːʳt/ [v T not in progressive] to agree with an idea, plan, political party etc, and want it to succeed: *I have always supported the Democrats.* | *She wrote a newspaper article supporting the idea of a minimum wage for workers.* | **strongly support** *Plans for a new school were strongly supported by local residents.* | **support sb in sth** *Public opinion in America supported Gandhi in his struggle for an independent India.* —**support** [n U] *The President could not get involved in the conflict without the support of the American people.* | **+ for** *There is growing support for environmental pressure groups such as Friends of the Earth and Greenpeace.*

be in favour of British **/be in favor of** American /biː ɪn ˈfeɪvər ɒv/ [v phrase] to support a plan or suggestion because you think it is a good idea: *Most UN delegates are in favour of the new peace plan.* | **+ doing sth** *Some teachers were in favour of retaining the existing system.* | **be all in favour of sth** especially spoken (=completely agree with) *I'm all in favour of people having smaller cars.*

pro- /prəʊ/ [prefix] **pro-democracy/pro-government/pro-independence etc** supporting democracy, the government etc: *The pro-independence group has been attacked and suppressed.* | *pro-western* *forces* | *The 'pro-choice' group believes in the right to abortion.*

be in sympathy with/sympathize with /biː ɪn 'sɪmpəθi wɪð, 'sɪmpəθaɪz wɪð/ [v phrase] to think that someone's aims or ideas, especially political ideas, are right and that you should support them: *Many Democrats were in sympathy with Reagan's policies on Nicaragua.* | *Soldiers were punished severely if they were suspected of sympathising with student agitators.*

endorse /ɪn'dɔːʳs/ [v T] to show publicly that you support a plan or action, especially by voting for it: *The convention endorsed the peace programme.* | *The President's position was endorsed by a large majority of the Senate.* | **fully endorse** *I fully endorse the measures taken to improve safety standards.* —**endorsement** [n U] *Before a bill can become law it has to have the full endorsement of both Houses of Parliament.*

advocate /'ædvəkeɪt/ [v T] formal to publicly support a plan or way of doing something, especially one that you have suggested yourself: *They advocated state control of all public services.* | *Some extremists are now openly advocating violence.*

be with /biː 'wɪð/ [v phrase] if you **are with** someone, you agree with what they are trying to do, and you are willing to help them: *We need people now for the anti-government march. Are you with us or against us?* | **be with sb all the way** (=support someone fully) *When you are fighting an election campaign, you need to feel that your party is with you all the way.*

2 someone who supports a person/political party/idea

- supporter
- support
- sympathizer
- follower
- following

supporter /sə'pɔːʳtəʳ/ [n C] someone who supports a person, political party, or idea: *She had always been one of the prime minister's strongest supporters.* | *a Labour Party supporter* | **+ of** *Supporters of women's rights are protesting against the court's decision.* | **staunch supporter (of)** (=very strong supporter) *Mill was a strong supporter of political reform.*

support /sə'pɔːʳt/ [n U] all the people who **support** a person, group, or plan: *The party's support has always been in the big cities.* | *Carter had seen his support dwindling in the southern states.*

sympathizer ALSO **sympathiser** British /'sɪmpəθaɪzəʳ/ [n C] someone who supports the ideas of a political organization but does not belong to it, especially an organization that is illegal: *His opponents accused him of being a Nazi sympathizer.* | *Money for the group's terrorist activities was supplied by sympathisers in the US.*

follower /'fɒləʊəʳ‖'fɑː-/ [n C] someone who supports the ideas of a political or religious leader: *Some of Biko's followers resented his friendship with a white journalist.* | **+ of** *the followers of Mahatma Gandhi*

following /'fɒləʊɪŋ‖'fɑː-/ [n C usually singular] all the people who support a person or organization: *The civil rights movement attracted a large following in the northern cities.* | *In both states, O'Reilly has a loyal following among hard-line conservatives.*

3 to give money or help to a person/group/plan

- support
- back
- in support of
- be behind
- back sb up
- throw your weight behind

support /sə'pɔːʳt/ [v T] to give help, encouragement, money etc to someone because you want them to succeed: *The rebels were supported by a number of foreign governments who provided arms and money.* | *Employers support the training program by offering places for young people.*

back /bæk/ [v T usually in passive] to support a person or plan by providing money or practical help – use this especially to talk about governments or other powerful groups that support something: *Several major insurance companies have agreed to back the healthcare reforms.* | *The plans for a new shopping mall are backed by the city council.*

in support of /ɪn sə'pɔːʳt ɒv/ [prep] if you do something **in support of** someone or something, you do it to show that you support them: *The miners came out on strike in support of the nurses.* | *a big demonstration in support of democratic reforms*

be behind /biː bɪ'haɪnd / [v phrase] to support and encourage someone in what they are trying to achieve: *My parents were behind me from the start, and bought me my first violin when I was just 3 years old.* | *Maisha struggled for years trying to make it as an artist, but her husband, Rudy, was always behind her.* | **be behind sb all the way** (=be ready to continue supporting them until they succeed) *Just do your best and remember that we are behind you all the way.*

back sb up /ˌbæk (sb) 'ʌp/ [phr v T] to support someone by saying that you agree with them or by giving information that shows they are right: *I was relying on you to back me up, why didn't you?* | *Eventually, after my impassioned pleas, backed up by my mother, Dad agreed to let me go to the concert.*

throw your weight behind /ˌθrəʊ jɔːʳ 'weɪt bɪˌhaɪnd/ [v phrase] to use all your influence and ability to make sure a person, group, or plan is successful: *Faced with a crisis, the Party united and threw its full weight behind the President.* | *Please throw your full weight behind us in our fund raising effort.*

4 the money or help that you give when you support someone

- support
- backing

support /sə'pɔːʳt/ [n U] the help and encouragement that you give to someone when you want them to succeed: *I couldn't have finished my degree without the support of my family.* | **financial support** (=money given to support something) *Private companies should not rely on financial support from the government.*

backing /'bækɪŋ/ [n U] money or practical help given to support a person or plan, especially by a government or other powerful group: *Does this policy have government backing?* | *The company failed to get sufficient financial backing, and never got off the ground.* | **+ of** *Chairman Robert Eaton said he has the backing of the vast majority of the company's major shareholders.*

5 to support someone against someone else

- **be on sb's side**
- **side with**
- **take sides**

be on sb's side /biː ɒn (sb's) ˈsaɪd/ [v phrase] to support one person or group against another in an argument, war etc: *Why did you keep agreeing with them? I thought you were on my side.* | *With most of the newspapers on their side, they have a good chance of winning the election.* | *Whose side are you on?*

side with /ˈsaɪd wɪð/ [phr v T not in passive] to support one person or group against another in an argument, especially in a way that seems unfair: *Why do you always side with Lucy?* | **side with sb against sb** *You wouldn't expect the union to side with the employers against their own members, would you?*

take sides /ˌteɪk ˈsaɪdz/ [v phrase] to support one of the two sides in an argument when it would be fairer not to support either of them: *I don't mind you two arguing, but don't ask me to take sides.* | *The chairwoman managed to stimulate a lively debate without taking sides herself.*

6 to persuade someone to support you

- **enlist support**
- **drum up support**

enlist support /ɪnˌlɪst səˈpɔːʳt/ [v phrase not in passive] formal to talk to people and persuade them to support you **enlist the support of** *Should you attempt to take your employer to court alone, or enlist the support of your trade union?* | **+ for** *He spent the whole month enlisting support for his reforms.* | **+ from** *The Labour Party hoped to enlist support from the middle classes by promising not to raise income tax.*

drum up support /ˌdrʌm ʌp səˈpɔːʳt/ [v phrase not in passive] to try to get a lot of people to support you: *Pop stars and TV personalities were brought in to publicize the campaign and drum up support.* | **+ for** *Drumming up support for a children's play group proved harder than she had expected.*

to stop sb/sth from falling down

7 to support something or someone so that they do not fall down

- **support**
- **hold up**
- **bear**
- **carry**
- **take sb's/sth's weight**
- **prop up**
- **shore up**

support /səˈpɔːʳt/ [v T] *Unfortunately, the branch was too weak to support his weight.* | *The ceiling was supported by huge stone columns.* | *Sitting at a table in the coffee shop, her chin supported by her hands, she was deep in thought.* | *Her body was so weak that she had to be supported by two nurses.* —**support** [n U] *The bridge fell down because it didn't have enough support.* —**supporting** [adj only before noun] *The roof was held up by supporting beams that ran right through my attic bedroom.*

hold up /ˌhəʊld ˈʌp/ [phr v T] to support the weight of something and prevent it from falling down. **Hold up** is more informal than **support** **hold up sth** *We can't knock that wall down. It's the one that holds up the house.* | *These poles hold up the outer part of the tent.* | **hold sth up** *Why don't we use some of these pieces of wood to hold it up?* | *The only thing holding the wall up was a frail-looking section of scaffolding.*

bear /beəʳ/ [v T] formal to support all the weight of something, especially something heavy: *The baby's narrow neck looked too fragile to bear the weight of its head.* | *The tunnel would have needed to be extremely strong to bear the full weight of the earth above.*

carry /ˈkæri/ [v T] if something **carries** a particular weight, it is able to support it, especially because it has been designed to: *The bridge could only carry up to two cars at a time.* | *The pillars have been specially strengthened in order to carry the weight of the new ceiling.* | *Front tyres tend to go down more quickly than back ones, because they carry more weight.*

take sb's/sth's weight /ˌteɪk (sb's/sth's) ˈweɪt/ [v phrase] to support the weight of someone or something – use this especially to say whether or not something is strong enough to do this: *I hope the ice is strong enough to take my weight.* | *I'm not sure if this table can take the weight of all these books.*

prop up /ˌprɒp ˈʌp‖ˌprɑːp-/ [phr v T] to stop something from falling by putting something else against it or under it **prop up sth** *The builders have propped up the walls with steel beams.* | **prop sth up** *I sat down and propped my feet up on the edge of the desk.*

shore up /ˌʃɔːr ˈʌp/ [phr v T] to support something such as a wall or a building that has been damaged or is in bad condition by putting big pieces of wood or metal against it **shore up sth** *The fence was shored up with sheets of old iron.* | **shore sth up** *Our huts were falling down, so we used branches to shore them up.*

8 to use something to support yourself

- **lean**
- **rest**
- **prop yourself up**
- **support yourself**
- **for support**

lean /liːn/ [v I/T] to support your body or part of your body by putting it on or against a surface such as a wall or a table **+ against** *Joe was leaning against the school wall, smoking a cigarette.* | **+ on** *She leaned on the railings and looked out at the sea.* | **lean your head/arms/elbows etc on** *It's sometimes considered bad manners to lean your elbows on the table when you're eating.* | **lean back on/against sth** *I leaned back on the pillows and closed my eyes.*

rest /rest/ [v I/T] to support your body or part of your body by putting it lightly on or against something **+ on** *Her head rested gently on his shoulder.* | *John rested his head on the back of the car-seat.* | **+ against** *I rested against a wall for a minute in order to tie up my shoe laces.*

prop yourself up /ˌprɒp jɔːʳself ˈʌp‖ˌprɑːp-/ [v phrase] to help yourself stand or sit straight by supporting your body against something, especially when you are ill or injured: *The soldier tried to prop himself up again using his crutches.* | **+ against/on** *I propped myself up against a wall and took a deep breath.*

support yourself /səˈpɔːʳt jɔːʳself/ [v phrase] to prevent yourself from falling by using a stick or by holding onto someone or something, especially because you are injured or weak: *They walked out together, the old man supporting himself with his stick.* | *Jessica managed to support herself by putting her arm around Gary's neck.*

for support /fəʳ səˈpɔːʳt/ [adv] if you use something such as a stick or another person **for support**, you use it or hold onto them in order to prevent yourself from falling: *As he fell over he grabbed at the table for support.* | *She moved towards Andrew, seeking his arm for support.* | *He's able to walk around on his own now, although he has to use a cane for support.*

9 something that is used to support something else

- support
- prop

support /səˈpɔːʳt/ [n C] an object or structure that is used to **support** the weight of something else: *Tall plants need supports to stop them being blown down.* | *The supports for the roof had fallen down, and the roof hung down on one side.*

prop /prɒp‖prɑːp/ [n C] a wooden stick or other object that is placed under something to support it: *The pit props were placed only a foot or two apart, to support a mile of rock above them.* | *The clothes prop had fallen down, and the washing was trailing in the mud.*

sure/not sure

RELATED WORDS

- make sure *see* **check**
- *see also* **know/not know, certainly/definitely**

WHAT'S HERE

- **sure** see **1 to 2**
- **not sure** see **3 to 5**

sure

1 when you feel sure about something

- sure
- certain
- positive
- convinced
- have no doubt
- know
- satisfied
- confident
- I bet
- must
- can't
- I'd put money on it

sure /ʃʊəʳ/ [adj not before noun] if you are **sure** about something, you believe that it is definitely true or correct: *'The car was a BMW' 'Are you sure?'* | **+ (that)** *I'm surprised she isn't here – I was sure she would come.* | *Are you quite sure that he understood your instructions?* | **+ about** *I think children are influenced by these films, but it's impossible to be sure about this.* | **+ of** *You need to be sure of your facts before making any accusations.* | **pretty sure** *I'm pretty sure Barbara still works here.* | **absolutely sure** *We do not believe this is the body of the missing girl, but we have to check to be absolutely sure.*

certain /ˈsɜːʳtn/ [adj not before noun] completely sure that something is true **+ (that)** *Are you certain you didn't leave your keys at home?* | **+ about** *He was certain about one thing – she would come back one day.* | **+ of** *She won't let you borrow the car – I'm certain of that.* | **absolutely certain** *Don't stop looking until you're absolutely certain you've found the place you want.*

positive /ˈpɒzətɪv‖ˈpɑː-/ [adj not before noun] especially spoken completely sure that something is true – use this especially when other people are saying it might not be true: *'Are you sure you locked the door?' 'Yes, I'm positive.'* | **+ (that)** *She said she was positive the exam was next Tuesday.* | **absolutely positive** *I'm absolutely positive I haven't made a mistake.*

convinced /kənˈvɪnst/ [adj not before noun] sure that something is true, even when you cannot prove it **+ (that)** *We've had no news of him, but we're convinced he's still alive.* | *She became convinced that her boyfriend was seeing someone else.* | **+ of** *Brown's wife was convinced of his innocence.*

have no doubt /hæv ˌnəʊ ˈdaʊt/ [v phrase not in progressive] to be so certain about something that there are no doubts in your mind **+ (that)** *I've no doubt that his story is true.* | **+ about/of** *My boss told me he had no doubt about my abilities as a salesman.*

know /nəʊ/ [v I/T not in progressive] to have a strong feeling that something is right or true, although there may be nothing to prove **+ (that)** *Sally knew that she and Carl would be the best of friends.* | *I just know your mother will love this necklace.* | *As soon as the phone rang, we knew something terrible must have happened.* | **know it** *She's going to pass – I just know it!*

satisfied /ˈsætəsfaɪd/ [adj not before noun] sure that you know the truth about something that has happened, because you have enough information **+ (that)** *Police are now satisfied that her death was an accident.*

confident /ˈkɒnfədənt‖ˈkɑːn-/ [adj not before noun] sure that something good will happen, or that you will be able to achieve what you want: *'Do you think you'll win tomorrow's game?' – 'Well, we're all feeling pretty confident'.* | **+ (that)** *Doctors are confident that he'll make a full recovery.* | **+ of** *A spokesman said the government was confident of winning the vote and would not discuss the possibility of defeat.*

I bet /aɪ ˈbet/ spoken informal say this when you feel sure that something is true **+ (that)** *I bet you're tired after such a long journey.* | *I bet she hasn't told her parents about this.*

must /məst, (*strong*) mʌst/ [modal verb] especially spoken if you say that something **must** be true or **must** have happened, you are sure about it, because of information you have or things you have noticed that make it seem very likely: *You must remember Sally Newton. She was in our French class.* | **must have** *Kim didn't answer when I called – she must have gone to bed.* | *She didn't get into movies just because her mother was a famous actress, but it must have helped.*

can't /kɑːnt‖kænt/ [modal verb] especially spoken if you say that something **can't** be true or **can't** have happened, you are sure that it is not true or has not happened: *He says he's 21 but he can't be older than 18.* | **can't have** *She can't have gone to bed yet – it's only 8 o'clock.* | *If you failed that exam you can't have worked very hard.*

I'd put money on it /aɪd pʊt ˈmʌni ɒn ɪt/ you say **I'd put money on it** when you are so sure of something that you would be willing to take the chance of losing money if you were wrong: *'Do you really think the president will win again?' 'I'd put money on it.'*

2 to make someone sure about something

- convince
- *see also* **persuade**

convince /kənˈvɪns/ [v T] to make someone sure about something, especially when this is difficult to do: *Our new policy on tax reform will certainly help the economy. The only problem will be convincing the voters.* | **convince sb (that)** *The discovery of a body finally convinced Mrs Hayes that her son was dead.* | *I had tried to convince my company's president that these ideas were viable.* | **convince sb of sth** *How many more deaths will it take to convince the authorities of the need to test drugs more thoroughly?*

not sure

RELATED WORDS

▸ *see also* **know/not know**

3 not sure if something is true or if something will happen

- not sure
- not certain
- not know
- unsure/uncertain
- doubt
- wonder

not sure /nɒt ˈʃʊəʳ/ [adj phrase not before noun] *'What time does the film start?' 'I think it's 8.30, but I'm not sure.'* | **+ how/whether/when etc** *I'm not sure where she lives.* | *I'm not sure how long it will take the bus to get there.* | **+ about** *If you're not sure about the meaning of a word, look it up in a dictionary.* | **+ of** *Use the 'Filesearch' function if you are not sure of the name of a file.* | **can't be sure** spoken (=when you think something is true, but you are not completely sure) *I can't be sure, but I think I saw Maggie coming out of the hospital this morning.*

not certain /nɒt ˈsɜːʳtn/ [adj phrase not before noun] not sure about something. **Not certain** is more formal than **not sure**: *The man you're looking for could be Keith, but I'm not certain.* | **+ about** *I'm not certain about what time the buses come – I usually cycle.* | **+ how/why/where etc** *I'm really not certain how much fuel we've got left.*

not know /nɒt ˈnəʊ/ [v phrase] to not be at all sure if something is true or if something will happen: *'How old is she?' 'Oh, I don't know – fifty, fifty-five?'* | **+ if/whether/how etc** *I phoned her but I don't know if she got my message.* | *We do not know whether the lake is safe for swimming in.* | **not know for sure** especially spoken *It could be this week but it might be much later. We don't know for sure.*

unsure/uncertain /ʌnˈʃʊəʳ, ʌnˈsɜːʳtn/ [adj not before noun] **Unsure** and **uncertain** are more formal than **not sure** and **not certain**. **+ about** *I'm still a bit unsure about how to use this software.* | **+ of** *Many workers are still unsure of their rights.* | **+ who/what/whether etc** *David decided to become a teacher but was uncertain which subject to specialize in.*

doubt /daʊt/ [n C/U] a feeling of not being sure whether something is true or correct **+ about** *There are still some doubts about her suitability for the job.* | **+ as to** *There seems to be some doubt as to what warnings were given.*

wonder /ˈwʌndəʳ/ [v I/T not in progressive] to think about something that you are not sure about, and try to guess what is true, what will happen, etc: *He says he's had no formal training but when you see how good his work is, you start to wonder.* | **+ if/how/whether etc** *I wonder if she'll recognize me after all these years.* | *He wondered whether he would be able to find the hotel again.*

4 not sure if you should do something or if something is good or right

- have doubts
- have reservations
- have misgivings
- have mixed feelings
- be dubious
- hesitant
- waver

have doubts /hæv ˈdaʊts/ [v phrase not in progressive] to not be sure whether you should do something or whether it is good or right: *Peter promised that it was all for the best, but I still had doubts.* | **+ about** *Any doubts Jo had about marrying him soon disappeared.* | **have your doubts** *We had our doubts about the car's reliability from the start.*

have reservations /hæv ˌrezəʳˈveɪʃənz/ [v phrase not in progressive] to feel that some things about a plan, idea etc are not good or right, so that you think there may be problems or difficulties: *I know you're very keen to move to the US, but I'm afraid I still have reservations.* | **+ about** *Many teachers are likely to have reservations about the new tests.*

have misgivings /hæv mɪsˈgɪvɪŋz/ [v phrase] to not be sure whether something is good or right, because you are worried about what will happen if it is done: *We didn't try to stop our son from joining the army, but we both had misgivings.* | **+ about** *Even the government's most loyal supporters have misgivings about changes to the education system.* | **have serious misgivings** (=be very unsure) *At the time, many doctors had serious misgivings about the new treatment.*

have mixed feelings /hæv ˌmɪkst ˈfiːlɪŋz/ [v phrase not in progressive] to be unable to say that something is definitely good or right, because there are both good and bad things about it: *I have very mixed feelings – I want to travel but I know I'll miss my family.* | **+ about** *She had mixed feelings about her daughter getting married so young.*

be dubious /biː ˈdjuːbiəs‖-ˈduː-/ [v phrase] to be not sure whether you should do something, because you can think of ways in which it could go wrong: *I was a bit dubious at first, but the water looked cool and inviting, so I dived in.* | **+ about** *Most universities are dubious about accepting students over the age of 30.*

hesitant /ˈhezətənt/ [adj not usually before noun] someone who is **hesitant** is nervous or unsure about doing something, and therefore pauses before doing it or does it slowly and without confidence: *He was a little hesitant at first, but soon he had told her everything.* | **+ about** *I was hesitant about approaching the boss directly.* | **+ to do sth** *It is not surprising that the government was hesitant to introduce such major reforms.* — **hesitantly** [adv] *The boy spoke slowly and hesitantly, unsure whether or not to trust us.*

waver /ˈweɪvəʳ/ [v I] to not make a definite decision because you have doubts **+ between** *Maya wavered between accepting and refusing his offer.* | **+ about** *If people have been wavering about giving the police information, this could be the thing to make them come forward.*

5 to make someone feel unsure about something

- make sb unsure/uncertain
- raise doubts
- it makes you wonder

make sb unsure/uncertain /meɪk (sb) ʌnˈʃʊəʳ, ʌnˈsɜːʳtn/ [v phrase] **+ about** *The news about* *the bomb made me uncertain about travelling to the area.* | **+ of** *Her previous experiences made her very unsure of the wisdom of marrying again.*

raise doubts /ˌreɪz 'daʊts/ [v phrase] to make people become unsure about something they were previously fairly sure about: *I don't want to raise too many doubts, but I wonder whether he's really fit for the job.* | **+ about/over** *Her report has raised doubts about the likely success of this project.* | **raise doubts in sb's mind** *The new evidence raised doubts in the minds of jury members.*

it makes you wonder /ɪt ˌmeɪks juː 'wʌndəʳ/ especially spoken use this to say that something makes you unsure about a previous belief: *They obviously know each other. It makes you wonder.* | **+ if/whether etc** *So many people believe in astrology, it makes you wonder if it's all true.* | *His behaviour after hearing my news made me wonder if he knew more than he had told me.*

surface

RELATED WORDS

- *see also* **out/outside, edge, side, middle, top**

1 the outside part of an object

- surface
- side
- face
- top

surface /'sɜːʳfɪ̇s/ [n C] *The plant has light green leaves with silver marks on their upper surfaces.* | *When using glue, make sure both surfaces are completely clean.* | *Half-empty glasses covered every flat surface in the room.* | **+ of** *Exfoliators remove dead cells from the surface of your skin.* | **work surface** (=a surface for preparing food etc) *In a kitchen all work surfaces should be kept spotlessly clean.*

side /saɪd/ [n C] one of the flat or upright surfaces of something such as a box, a piece of paper, or a shape with straight edges: *A cube has six sides.* | **+ of** *Please use both sides of the paper to write your answers.* | *The word FRAGILE was written on every side of the box in big, red letters.* | *I'll paint the other side of the fence after lunch.*

face /feɪs/ [n C] one of the large steep sides of something such as a mountain, or one of the outside surfaces of a cube, a diamond etc **+ of** *There were many unsuccessful attempts to climb the North Face of Mount Everest.* | *One of the faces of the cube has a line across it.* | **cliff/rock face** *The cliff face was starting to crumble into the sea.*

top /tɒp‖tɑːp/ [n C] the flat upper surface of an object: *This jewellery box would be worth a lot of money if the top wasn't chipped.* | *a dressing-table with a glass top* | **+ of** *The top of the piano was covered with a lace cloth.*

2 the top part of an area of water or land

- surface

surface /'sɜːʳfɪ̇s/ [n singular] *The moon's surface is covered with rocks and dust.* | *She watched as the bubbles rose to the surface and popped.* | **+ of** *Leaves floated on the surface of the pool.* | *The clay is about a metre below the surface of the soil.*

surprised/surprising

RELATED WORDS

- shocked by something bad that happens *see* **shocked/shocking**
- *see also* **expect/not expect**

1 surprised

- surprised
- amazed
- astonished/astounded
- be taken aback
- startled
- flabbergasted
- can't get over
- can't believe

surprised /səʳ'praɪzd/ [adj] if you are **surprised** by something that happens, you do not expect it, so it seems strange or unusual: *I was really surprised when I passed my driving test first time.* | *Carrie looked surprised. 'I didn't expect to see you here!'* | *We couldn't help laughing at the children's surprised faces.* | **+ to see/hear/learn etc** *We were surprised to see Drew's picture in the newspaper.* | **+ (that)** *I'm really surprised that he remembered my birthday.* | **+ at** *When I saw him again, I was surprised at how much older he looked.* | **+ by** *Julia seemed a little surprised by my question.* | **pleasantly surprised** (=surprised when something unexpectedly good happens) *His exam results were great – we were all very pleasantly surprised.*

amazed /ə'meɪzd/ [adj] use this about something that surprises you so much you almost cannot believe it: *Liz was amazed when she found out how much dinner had cost.* | **+ that** *I'm amazed that the bank keeps lending him money.* | **+ to see/learn/find out etc** *We were amazed to see John looking so well, so soon after his operation.* | **+ at/by** *She couldn't help feeling amazed at his stupidity.* | **+ by** *You'll be amazed by how much progress we've made.*

astonished/astounded /ə'stɒnɪʃt‖ə'stɑː-, ə'staʊndɪ̇d/ [adj] extremely surprised by something that happens, because it is very unusual or strange: *Mark was astonished when he read the message – what on earth could she mean?* | *We climbed out of the hole right in front of two astounded policemen.* | **+ (that)** *It was an extremely nasty accident and I was astonished that anyone had survived it.* | **+ at/by** *Everton admits to being astounded at the popularity of the book.* | **+ to hear/see/discover etc** *The whole town was astounded to hear of a plan to build an office building right next to the lake.*

be taken aback /biː ˌteɪkən ə'bæk/ [v phrase] to be so surprised or shocked by what someone has done or said that, for a moment, you do not know what to say: *I was taken aback to find an elderly woman sitting inside the door of the men's room.* | **+ by** *I was completely taken aback by his aggressive and unreasonable attitude.*

startled /'stɑːʳtld/ [adj] especially written surprised and a little frightened or worried because of something that has suddenly happened or something that someone said: *'Have we met somewhere before?' The man looked startled for a moment.* | **+ by** *They were startled by a sudden flash in the sky.*

flabbergasted /'flæbəʳgɑːstɪ̇d‖-gæs-/ [adj] informal so surprised by something that has happened that you do not know what to say: *The delivery men just left the furniture in my front yard. I was flabber-*

gasted. | **+ at/by** *Doctors said they were flabbergasted at the decision to close the hospital.*

can't get over /ˌkɑːnt get ˈəʊvəʳ‖ˌkænt-/ [v phrase] if you **can't get over** something that has happened, you are so surprised by it that you cannot believe it: *Madge couldn't get over how much Joe had grown since she'd last seen him.* | *I can't get over how much she eats – why doesn't she gain any weight?*

can't believe /ˌkɑːnt bəˈliːv‖ˌkænt-/ [v phrase] especially spoken say this when you are very surprised by something because it does not seem possible **can't believe it** *I can't believe it! Jane and Richard are getting married.* | **can't believe (that)** *She was a brilliant pianist – we couldn't believe she was only 15.* | **can't believe your eyes/ears** *The letter invited me to fly first class to New York for an interview on Monday – I could not believe my eyes!*

2 a feeling of being surprised

- surprise
- amazement
- astonishment

surprise /səʳˈpraɪz/ [n U] **sb's surprise** *You can imagine my surprise when I saw my sister's photograph on a magazine cover.* | **+ at** *I expressed some surprise at the elaborate welcome which had been prepared for me.* | **in/with surprise** *Sam stared at his girlfriend in surprise. 'What are you doing here?' he asked.* | **to sb's surprise/to the surprise of sb** *To everyone's complete surprise, the Labour Party lost the election.*

amazement /əˈmeɪzmənt/ [n U] a feeling of great surprise, especially because something has happened that you almost cannot believe **in/with amazement** *Fans looked on in amazement as Robbins missed a third goal for the team.* | *Nina looked at me with amazement. 'I don't believe you,' she said.* | **to sb's amazement/to the amazement of sb** *To our amazement, when we returned to China, the Moso tree had grown an impressive ninety feet.*

astonishment /əˈstɒnɪʃmənt‖əˈstɑː-/ [n U] a feeling of great surprise, especially at something you have seen or something someone has told you: *You should have seen the look of astonishment on his face!* | **in/with astonishment** *Everyone gasped in astonishment as the cars came around the last bend.* | **to sb's astonishment/to the astonishment of sb** *To everyone's astonishment, more than 100 people volunteered to help that day.*

3 so surprised that you cannot speak

- speechless
- be lost for words/be at a loss for words
- dumbfounded/dumbstruck
- gobsmacked

speechless /ˈspiːtʃləs/ [adj not before noun] so surprised, by something very good or very bad, that you do not know what to say: *When I told him I was pregnant, he was totally speechless.* | *Brian's remark left his boss speechless with anger.*

be lost for words/be at a loss for words /biː ˌlɒst fəʳ ˈwɜːʳdz‖-ˌlɔːst-, biː ət ə ˌlɒs fəʳ ˈwɜːʳdz‖-ˌlɔːs-/ [v phrase] to feel so surprised and full of emotion that you are unable to speak: *She rang me and told me that Tom had died. For once in my life I was lost for words.* | *When I saw the devastation from our window in the morning, I was at a loss for words.*

dumbfounded/dumbstruck /dʌmˈfaʊndəd, ˈdʌmstrʌk/ [adj] so surprised by something unexpected that has happened that you are confused and unable to speak: *I just remember feeling dumbstruck when I heard that John Lennon was dead.* | *Suddenly the stewardess started screaming while the passengers watched, dumbfounded.*

gobsmacked /ˈgɒbsmækt‖ˈgɑːb-/ [adj not before noun] British informal so surprised that you cannot speak: *'How did you feel when you heard that your wife was expecting triplets?' 'Gobsmacked – absolutely gobsmacked.'*

4 to make someone surprised

- surprise
- be a surprise/come as a surprise
- amaze
- astonish/astound
- take sb by surprise

surprise /səʳˈpraɪz/ [v T] *Diana's reaction surprised him – he hadn't realized that she was so upset.* | *The exam was actually quite easy, which surprised me.* | **what surprises sb is** *What surprised me most was how cheap everything was compared to at home.* | **it surprises sb that** *I have to say, it surprises me that they haven't gone bankrupt before now.* | **surprise yourself** (=do something that you thought you could not do, so that you are surprised) *Why don't you just have a go at skiing? You might surprise yourself.*

be a surprise/come as a surprise /biː ə səʳˈpraɪz, ˌkʌm əz ə səʳˈpraɪz/ [v phrase] if something **is a surprise**, or if it **comes as a surprise**, it surprises you: *'Bob and Linda are getting divorced.' 'That's a surprise – they seemed like the perfect couple.'* | *The firing of the team's star pitcher came as a surprise to fans and sports writers alike.* | **a complete surprise** (=a big surprise) *My brother's sudden visit home was a complete surprise.* | **+ to sb** *The announcement of his resignation was a complete surprise to everyone in the office.* | **it comes as a surprise to see/learn/find etc** *It comes as a surprise to learn what a high rate of illiteracy there is in this country.*

amaze /əˈmeɪz/ [v T not usually in progressive] to make someone feel extremely surprised, especially because something is very hard to believe: *Dave amazed his friends by leaving a well-paid job to travel around the world.* | **it amazes sb that** *It amazes me that no-one has thought of the idea sooner.*

astonish/astound /əˈstɒnɪʃ‖əˈstɑː-, əˈstaʊnd/ [v T not usually in progressive] to make someone feel extremely surprised: *My father's reaction astounded me. How could he be so calm!* | *Tammy astonished her doctors by learning to walk again within weeks of the accident.* | *They astounded audiences with their fanciful costumes and their fascinating tales.* | **what astonishes/astounds sb is** *What astonishes me is how incredibly inefficient so many companies seem to be.*

take sb by surprise ALSO **catch sb by surprise** American /ˌteɪk (sb) baɪ səʳˈpraɪz, ˌkætʃ (sb) baɪ səʳˈpraɪz/ [v phrase] if something **takes you by surprise**, it happens at a time when you are not expecting it: *The President's resignation took everyone by surprise.* | *The vehemence of her response took me by surprise.*

5 making you feel surprised

- surprising
- amazing
- astonishing/astounding
- unbelievable/incredible
- unexpected
- startling
- staggering
- mind-boggling

surprising /səʳˈpraɪzɪŋ/ [adj] *A surprising number of teenagers leave school without being able to read* *and write.* | *Some of the conclusions in the report were quite surprising.* | **it is surprising (that)** *Wasn't it surprising that so few people came to the party?* | **it is surprising to see/find/ learn etc** *In such a small town it was surprising to find so many really good restaurants.* | **it is surprising how/what etc** *Liddy really didn't want to change school, but it was surprising how quickly she got used to the new one.* —**surprisingly** [adv] *The hotel was surprisingly cheap.* | *Surprisingly, the roof is still in good condition since the storms.*

amazing /əˈmeɪzɪŋ/ [adj] very surprising – use this especially about something very good or impressive: *Hong Kong is an absolutely amazing city.* | *What an amazing achievement!* | **it is amazing how/what** *It's amazing how much work you can do in a day if you put your mind to it.* | **it is amazing that** *After 2000 years, it's amazing that the inscriptions are still clear enough to read.* | **it's amazing to see/find/think etc** *Isn't it amazing to think that men have actually stood on the moon?* —**amazingly** [adv] *Chris was amazingly lucky to pass the exam.* | *Five cars crashed into each other, but amazingly no-one was hurt.*

astonishing/astounding /əˈstɒnɪʃɪŋ‖əˈstɑː-, əˈstaʊndɪŋ/ [adj] something that is **astonishing** or **astounding** is so surprising that it is difficult to believe: *If you watch the way a spider makes its web, it's really astonishing.* | *The submarine was moving through the water at an astonishing speed.* | *The results of the tests were astounding.* | *In the area around London, house prices rose by an astounding 200 per cent in three years.* | **it is astonishing/ astounding that** *It was astounding that, as a mother, Sally also managed to do two jobs.* | **it is astonishing how/what** *It's astonishing how much things have changed since the arrival of computers.* | **it is astonishing to find/think/realize etc** *Isn't it astonishing to think that people may one day live for hundreds of years?*

unbelievable/incredible /ˌʌnbɪˈliːvəbəl, ɪnˈkredɪ̈bəl/ [adj] extremely surprising and difficult to believe: *He's so rude. It's unbelievable!* | *Over the next two weeks, we saw an incredible change in her character.* | **it is unbelievable/incredible that** *They were driving much too fast. It's incredible that no-one was hurt.* | **it is unbelievable how/what** *I think it was really unbelievable how he went on deceiving her for all those years.* | **it is unbelievable to see/think/ realize etc** *It's unbelievable to think how slow things were in the days before e-mail.* —**unbelievably/ incredibly** [adv] *Throughout the crisis, Bill remained incredibly calm.* | *It was a fantastic hotel, and unbelievably cheap.*

unexpected /ˌʌnɪkˈspektɪ̈d◂/ [adj] something that is **unexpected** makes you feel surprised because you did not expect it to happen or be true: *Her decision to leave was completely unexpected.* | *The new drug comes from an unexpected source – potatoes.* | *Ella's angry outburst was so unexpected that Mike really didn't know what to say.* —**unexpectedly** [adv] *Phil arrived unexpectedly early, while we were still having lunch.*

startling /ˈstɑːʳtlɪŋ/ [adj] a **startling** fact is one that you would never have expected to be true: *There has been a startling increase in the numbers of homeless people.* | *The programme documents startling new theories about the way the universe began.*

staggering /ˈstæɡərɪŋ/ [adj] a **staggering** number or amount is very surprising because it is so large: *Apparently, we spend a staggering £2.4 billion a year on food for our pets.* | *a staggering rise in crime* | *The results of the survey were staggering – over half the children said that they went to school without any breakfast.*

mind-boggling /ˈmaɪnd ˌbɒɡlɪŋ‖-ˌbɑː-/ [adj] informal something that is **mind-boggling** is so big, strange, or complicated that it is almost impossible to imagine or believe: *The amount of money that some countries spend on weapons is mind-boggling.* | *His salary is nothing compared to the mind-boggling figures earned by some sportsmen.* | **it is mind-boggling to think/realize etc** *It's mind-boggling to think that our solar system is only one among billions.*

6 something that happens which surprises you

- surprise
- shock
- surprise
- shock

surprise /səʳˈpraɪz/ [n C] something that you did not expect, especially something nice **it is a surprise** *It was a real surprise when Tony walked in. We thought he was still in America.* | *We've got Katie a bike for her birthday, but don't tell her – it's a surprise.* | **a complete surprise** (=one that you did not expect at all) *Anita didn't expect to get the job – it came as a complete surprise.* | **as a surprise** *Apparently her husband bought her the car as an anniversary surprise.* | **what a surprise!** spoken *Flowers? For me! What a lovely surprise!*

shock /ʃɒk‖ʃɑːk/ [n C] something bad or unpleasant that happens to you that you did not expect: *'The bill came to £500.' 'That must have been a shock.'* | **get a shock** *We got a terrible shock when the police rang to say that they had arrested our daughter.* | **give sb a shock** *It gave me a shock when I realized how close I had come to being killed.*

surprise /səʳˈpraɪz/ [adj only before noun] happening unexpectedly so that people are surprised: *Josh's friends gave him a surprise party to celebrate his 21st birthday.* | *The US were concerned about the possibility of a surprise attack by air or by sea.* | *Later, there was a surprise appearance by Schwazenneger himself.*

shock /ʃɒk‖ʃɑːk/ [adj only before noun] unpleasantly surprising because the result is different from what you expected: *Liverpool suffered a shock defeat at Halifax last night, beaten by five goals to nil.* | *The chairman made a shock announcement that 500 employees would lose their jobs.*

7 not surprising

- not surprising/ hardly surprising
- be no surprise/ come as no surprise
- I'm not surprised
- no wonder

not surprising/hardly surprising /ˌnɒt səʳˈpraɪzɪŋ, ˌhɑːʳdli səʳˈpraɪzɪŋ/ if something is **not surprising** or **hardly surprising**, you are not surprised by it because the situation makes it very likely to happen: *Now she's frightened to go out at night, which is hardly surprising after what happened to her.* | **it is not surprising/hardly surprising (that)** *It's not surprising that you're tired – you've been out every night this week.* —**not surprisingly** [adv] *Not surprisingly, she was very annoyed when he didn't turn up.*

be no surprise/come as no surprise /biː ˌnəʊ səʳˈpraɪz, ˌkʌm əz ˌnəʊ səʳˈpraɪz/ [v phrase] if something **is no surprise** or **comes as no surprise**, you are not surprised when it happens, because you expected it to happen **it is no surprise/it comes as no surprise** *It came as no surprise when President Santos announced his resignation.* | *Both Jade's parents are doctors so it was no surprise when she went to medical school.* | **+ that** *After years of struggle, it came as no surprise that the company went bankrupt.* | **+ to** *It was no surprise to anyone when they finally said that they were getting a divorce.*

I'm not surprised /aɪm ˌnɒt səʳˈpraɪzd/ **spoken** say this when you are not surprised about something bad that has happened because you can clearly see the reasons for it: *'I'm starving.' 'I'm not surprised, you haven't eaten all day.'* | **+ (that)** *I'm not surprised that she's fed up with him.*

no wonder /nəʊ ˈwʌndəʳ/ **spoken** say this when you realize the reason why something happened, so that it is not surprising any more: *No wonder my camera wasn't working – there's no battery in it!*

survive

to continue to live or exist in spite of accidents, illnesses, or serious difficulties

RELATED WORDS

▸ *see also* **alive, accident, illness/disease, war**

1 to not die in spite of an accident, illness, or war

- ▸ **survive**
- ▸ **survivor**
- ▸ **stay alive**
- ▸ **pull through**
- ▸ **escape**
- ▸ **live**
- ▸ **make it**
- ▸ **last**

survive /səʳˈvaɪv/ **[v I/T not in passive]** *Only 12 of the 140 passengers on the plane survived.* | *Doctors predicted that the baby would not survive with such severe disabilities.* | *My grandmother wouldn't survive another operation.* | *Not many of the insects survive the winter.* —**survival** **[n U]** *Chemical pollution is threatening the survival of many species of wildlife.*

survivor /səʳˈvaɪvəʳ/ **[n C]** someone who has survived an accident, war, illness etc: *So far rescue workers have found no sign of any survivors.* | *Survivors of the accident were rushed to the nearest hospital.* | **sole survivor** (=the only survivor) *An eight-month-old baby girl was the sole survivor of a car crash that killed both her parents.*

stay alive /ˌsteɪ əˈlaɪv/ **[v phrase]** to continue to live and not die when you are in a very dangerous situation, for example in a war or when you have very little food: *They managed to stay alive by eating roots and berries.* | *We had to ignore the terrible things going on around us, and just concentrate on staying alive.*

pull through /ˌpʊl ˈθruː/ **[phr v I]** to survive and get better after having a very serious illness or injury: *I was so ill that the doctors weren't sure if I was going to pull through.* | *The first few days after the accident were awful, and everyone was just praying he'd pull through.*

escape /ɪˈskeɪp/ **[v I/T]** to survive after being involved in a serious accident, especially because of good luck: *The driver was killed but his passenger escaped with only a few scratches.* | **escape injury/death etc** *The family escaped injury when a fire gutted their two-bedroom apartment.* | **narrowly escape** (=only just escape) *The prime minister narrowly escaped a terrorist bomb in 1999.* —**escape** **[n C]** *The fireman said they'd had a very lucky escape.*

live /lɪv/ **[v I not in progressive]** if you say that someone will **live**, you mean that they will survive, even though they have a very serious illness, injury etc: *One of the victims has severe burns and is not expected to live.* | **live or die** *Our baby was in the intensive care unit, and we didn't know whether she would live or die.* | **live to tell the tale/live to tell about it** (=survive a very dangerous experience, so that you are able to tell people about it afterwards) *There were ten in the lifeboat, but only three lived to tell the tale.*

make it /ˈmeɪk ɪt/ **[v phrase not in progressive] informal** to survive when you are in a very dangerous situation or when you have a very serious illness: *At one point I was so exhausted and weak that I didn't think I was going to make it.* | *I was surprised she had made it through the night.*

last /lɑːst‖læst/ **[v I/T]** if someone **lasts** a period of time, they continue to live during that period, even though they have a very serious illness or injury: *His breathing was getting worse and he was not expected to last the night.* | *It's amazing that she's managed to last this long, really.*

2 when something continues to exist in spite of difficulties

- ▸ **survive**
- ▸ **come through**
- ▸ **stay afloat**

survive /səʳˈvaɪv/ **[v I/T]** *Many of the small, independent businesses are struggling to survive.* | *Only a few of Leonardo's earlier paintings still survive.* | *Our friendship has survived the bad times and has grown stronger.* | *The Cathedral survived repeated bombings during the Second World War.* —**survival** **[n U]** *The survival of the president's plans to cut taxes remains in doubt.* —**surviving** **[adj only before noun]** *The museum possesses the only surviving manuscript of Cicero's letters.*

come through /ˌkʌm ˈθruː/ **[phr v I/T]** to survive a period of great difficulty: *If we can come through this crisis, the company's future looks bright.* | *The German team were in deep trouble at the beginning of the match but in the end they came through.*

stay afloat /ˌsteɪ əˈfləʊt/ **[v phrase]** if a company **stays afloat**, it continues to survive in spite of difficult financial problems that may force it to close: *Ever since we started the business two years ago, we've been struggling to stay afloat.*

3 to continue to live your normal life in spite of problems

- ▸ **survive**
- ▸ **survivor**
- ▸ **come through**
- ▸ **get through**

survive /səʳˈvaɪv/ **[v I/T]** *The program provides homeless kids with the basics they need to survive: food, shelter, and health care.* | *Liz Taylor has survived several broken marriages, as well as periods of drug and alcohol addiction.* | *I don't think I could survive another year as a teacher. It's just too stressful.*

survivor /səʳˈvaɪvəʳ/ **[n C]** someone who is used to dealing with great personal problems and difficulties and is able to survive them: *As more is revealed, the audience begins to see Wendy as a survivor rather than a victim.* | **a born survivor** (=someone who seems to have a natural ability to survive difficulties) *Although she's had an extremely hard life, Tina Turner is a born survivor.*

come through /ˌkʌm ˈθruː/ [phr v I/T] to successfully deal with a very difficult problem or experience and be able to continue with your normal life after it: *She's had problems before and she's always come through.* | *Some children come through their parents' divorcing better than others.*

get through /ˌget ˈθruː/ [phr v I/T] to succeed in reaching the end of a very difficult period or experience: *It was not an easy time for Tracy but her friends helped her get through.* | *'Oh Jane, how will I ever get through this?' she said, and the tears started flowing again.*

4 to continue to live a normal life even though you have very little money

- survive
- get by
- live on
- make ends meet
- keep your head above water
- subsist on
- eke out a living/an existence

survive /səʳˈvaɪv/ [v I] *When I look at how much we spend on food, I wonder how unemployed people are able to survive.* | **survive on £100 a week/a small income etc** *It's really difficult to survive on £120 a week in London.* | *I don't know how they expect me to survive on my salary.*

get by /ˌget ˈbaɪ/ [phr v I] to have enough money to buy the things you need to live: *We don't have a lot of money to spend on luxuries, but we get by.* | **get by on $5 a day/a small income etc** *When I was at college I used to be able to get by on $20 a week.*

live on /ˈlɪv ɒn/ [phr v I] if someone **lives on** a particular amount of money, this is all the money that they have to buy everything that they need: *How much do you need to live on?* | *$35,000 a year sounds like a lot of money, but it's scarcely enough to live on in New York.*

make ends meet /meɪk ˌendz ˈmiːt/ [v phrase] if it is difficult for you to **make ends meet**, it is difficult for you to pay for the things that you need in order to live: *Old people on pensions are finding it hard to make ends meet.* | *My mother had to work 12 hours a day in a factory just to make ends meet.*

keep your head above water /kiːp jɔːʳ ˌhed əbʌv ˈwɔːtəʳ/ [v phrase] to have just enough money to pay your debts or to avoid closing your business: *I'm just a pensioner, trying to keep my head above water.* | *Schools throughout the county are struggling to keep their heads above water.*

subsist on /səbˈsɪst ɒn/ [v T] formal if someone **subsists on** a very small amount of money or a very small amount of food, this is all they have to live on: *They subsist on eggs and beans most of the time.* | **subsist on a dollar a day/a small income etc** *The workers are expected to subsist on a dollar a day.* —**subsistence** [adj] *They live just above subsistence level* (=the lowest amount they need to live).

eke out a living/an existence /ˌiːk aʊt ə ˈlɪvɪŋ, ən ɪgˈzɪstəns/ [v phrase] to get just enough food or money to live on by doing a particular kind of work: *She eked out a living by selling firewood.* | *Farmers eked out a primitive existence on the dry, stony land.*

suspect

RELATED WORDS

- see also **accuse, crime**

1 to think that someone has done something wrong

- suspect
- suspicious
- suspicion
- have a sneaking suspicion
- have your suspicions
- smell a rat

suspect /səˈspekt/ [v T not in progressive] to think that someone is probably guilty of something illegal or dishonest: *Act naturally and no one will suspect you.* | **suspect sb of (doing) sth** *He had suspected her of lying for some time.* | *Both men had originally been suspected of Brown's murder.* | **suspect murder/foul play** (=suspect that there has been a murder) *A man has been found dead in his home and the police suspect foul play.* —**suspected** [adj only before noun] *The police or social services will investigate any suspected case of child abuse.* | *Six people were killed in a suspected arson attack on a hotel.*

suspicious /səˈspɪʃəs/ [adj] thinking that someone might be guilty of doing something wrong or dishonest, without being sure: *I started to get suspicious when I found a hotel bill in Sarah's pocket.* | **+ of** *The police were suspicious of Simpson because his story did not quite make sense.* | **+ about** *His employer became suspicious about the amount of money he was claiming for expenses.* | **suspicious mind** *You have a very suspicious mind, Mary. No, I had nothing to do with this.*

suspicion /səˈspɪʃən/ [n C/U] a feeling that someone is probably guilty of doing something wrong or dishonest: *I had no solid evidence, only vague suspicions.* | **+ of** *She had always had a deep suspicion of journalists and reporters.* | **deep suspicion** *'What's that behind your back?', Maria said with a look of deep suspicion.* | **arouse/cause suspicion** (=make people suspect you) *The money was taken out of the bank in small amounts so as not to arouse suspicion.* | **on suspicion of murder/theft etc** (=because the police suspect you are guilty of murder etc) *He's been arrested on suspicion of murder.*

have a sneaking suspicion /hæv ə ˌsniːkɪŋ səˈspɪʃən/ [v phrase not in progressive] to have a slight feeling that someone has done something wrong, without having any definite information **+ that** *I had a sneaking suspicion that my agent was not telling me the truth.*

have your suspicions /ˌhæv jɔːʳ səˈspɪʃənz/ [v phrase not in progressive] to think you probably know who did something wrong: *I don't know for definite who stole the money, but I have my suspicions.*

smell a rat /ˌsmel ə ˈræt/ [v phrase not in progressive] informal to guess that someone is doing something bad or dishonest, even though you do not know exactly what it is: *We started to smell a rat when they asked for an extra £500 deposit.*

2 when something makes you suspect someone

- suspicious
- fishy
- shady

suspicious /sə'spɪʃəs/ [adj] *We thought his behaviour was suspicious and called the police immediately.* | *There was a suspicious silence as I opened the door.* | *The public have been asked to report anything suspicious at once.* | **in suspicious circumstances** *A full murder inquiry was launched after the company chairman died in suspicious circumstances.* —**suspiciously** [adv] *A man was seen acting suspiciously just before the break-in.* | *Anyone offered suspiciously cheap goods should contact the police.*

fishy /'fɪʃi/ [adj not before noun] informal something that is **fishy** or sounds **fishy** makes you suspect that something bad or dishonest is being done: *Frank said there was nothing to worry about, but it all sounded very fishy to me.* | *There's something fishy about this business, if you ask me.*

shady ALSO **dodgy** British informal /'ʃeɪdi, 'dɒdʒi‖'dɑː-/ [adj] **shady** deals and other activities seem to have something dishonest or illegal about them. A **shady** person is someone who seems likely to be involved in dishonest or illegal activities: *We'd suspected for a while she was involved in something a bit shady.* | *He has been mixed up in a number of shady deals in the City.* | *His acceptance of a huge loan from a shady businessman looks suspicious to say the least.*

3 someone who is suspected of doing something wrong

- suspect
- suspected
- be under suspicion

suspect /'sʌspekt/ [n C] someone who the police believe may have done something illegal: *The police now have another name to add to their list of suspects.* | **prime/chief suspect** (=the person that the police suspect more than anyone else) *A 32-year-old man from London is the prime suspect in the murder investigation.* | **murder/rape etc suspect** (=a person suspected of a particular crime) *The murder suspect is in custody and will be charged soon.*

suspected /sə'spektɨd/ [adj only before noun] **suspected criminal/terrorist/ spy etc** someone who the police or government believe is a criminal: *He was attacked at his home after confronting a suspected burglar.* | *They have succeeded in bringing many suspected terrorists to justice.* | *All opponents or suspected opponents of the military government are being detained.*

be under suspicion /biː ˌʌndəʳ sə'spɪʃən/ [v phrase] if someone **is under suspicion**, people believe they may have done something illegal or dishonest: *Crates of whisky have been disappearing from the warehouse and a member of staff is under suspicion.*

sweat

RELATED WORDS

- *see also* **hot, wet, exercise, weather**

1 to sweat

- sweat
- perspire
- break out in a sweat/ break into a sweat
- be pouring/ dripping with sweat

sweat /swet/ [v I/T] when you **sweat** your skin becomes wet, because you are hot, nervous, ill etc: *You're sweating. Why don't you take your jacket off?* | *The heat from the lights was making her sweat and her make-up started to run.* | **sweat profusely** (=sweat a lot) *Sweating profusely and gripping the lectern, Anderson began his speech.* | **sweat like a pig/sweat buckets** spoken (=sweat a lot) *My God, it's hot in here – I'm sweating like a pig!* | *It was tough work. Within minutes we were all sweating buckets.*

perspire /pəʳ'spaɪəʳ/ [v I] formal to sweat: *She felt hot and awkward and started to perspire.* | *He was perspiring. It showed on his forehead.* | **perspire freely/profusely** (=perspire a lot) *James, who was perspiring profusely, took out a handkerchief and mopped his brow.*

break out in a sweat/break into a sweat /ˌbreɪk aʊt ɪn ə 'swet, ˌbreɪk ɪntʊ ə 'swet/ [v phrase] to start sweating, especially because you are nervous or afraid: *I was terrified. My hands were shaking, and I broke out in a sweat.* | *'It's got nothing to do with me,' she said, breaking into a sweat.* | **break out in a cold sweat/break into a cold sweat** *As the security guard approached, I broke into a cold sweat.*

be pouring/dripping with sweat /biː ˌpɔːrɪŋ, ˌdrɪpɪŋ wɪð 'swet/ [v phrase] to be sweating a lot: *What on earth have you been doing? You're dripping with sweat!* | *Melissa was pouring with sweat, and her hair was stuck to her face.*

2 the liquid that appears on your skin when you sweat

- sweat
- perspiration

sweat /swet/ [n U] *He stopped working for a moment to wipe the sweat off his face.* | *I got sweat in my eyes and couldn't see.* | **beads of sweat** (=drops of sweat) *Beads of sweat appeared on her forehead and she trembled visibly.*

perspiration /ˌpɜːʳspə'reɪʃən/ [n U] formal sweat: *a deodorant that protects against perspiration all day long* | *To keep your body cool, wear cotton clothing that absorbs perspiration.* | **beads of perspiration** (=drops of perspiration) *Beads of perspiration trickled down my back.*

3 covered in sweat

- sweaty
- be covered/ drenched/soaked in sweat

sweaty /'sweti/ [adj] *I'm all hot and sweaty. I think I'll take a shower.* | *He was a short fat guy with big sweaty hands.* | *The equipment manager collected the sweaty uniforms and took them down to the hotel laundry.*

be covered/drenched/soaked in sweat ALSO **be covered/drenched/soaked with sweat** /biː ˌkʌvəʳd, ˌdrentʃt, ˌsəʊkt ɪn 'swet, -wɪð 'swet/ [v phrase] to be very wet because you have been sweating a lot: *Ian came off the squash court covered in sweat.* | *I insist my cars have air conditioning – I hate arriving somewhere drenched with sweat.*

switch on or off

RELATED WORDS

- *see also* **television/radio, computers/internet/email, machine, start, stop**

1 to switch something on

- switch on
- turn on
- put on
- start
- get sth started/going
- set off
- activate
- set sth going
- push/press a button
- throw a switch

switch on /ˌswɪtʃ ˈɒn / [phr v T] to make something start working, for example by pressing a button – use this about things that use electricity, for example lights, televisions, or computers **switch on sth** *Will you switch on the television?* | *I switched on the radio to listen to the news.* | **switch sth on** *Do you mind if I switch the light on?* | *Exhaust fumes come into the car when I switch on the air conditioner.*

turn on /ˌtɜːʳn ˈɒn / [phr v T] to make something start working, for example by turning a tap or pressing a button – use this about things that use electricity, gas, or water **turn on sth** *He went into the bathroom and turned on the shower.* | *Use timers to turn on indoor lights while you are away.* | **turn sth on** *Do you want me to turn the lights on?*

put on /ˌpʊt ˈɒn/ [phr v T] to make a light, radio etc start working **put the light/radio/TV/kettle etc on** *Eva put the kettle on to make a cup of coffee.* | *Put the light on, then we can see what we're doing.* | *It was so cold I put the heating back on.*

start ALSO **start up** /stɑːʳt, ˌstɑːʳt ˈʌp/ [v T/phr v T] to make a car, engine, machine etc **start** working: *She started the car and backed slowly out of the garage.* | *Clean or replace the air filter before attempting to start the engine.*

get sth started/going /ˌget (sth) ˈstɑːʳtɨd, ˈgəʊɪŋ/ [v phrase] **get a car/engine/machine etc started/going** to succeed in making a car etc start after having some difficulty: *I couldn't get my car started this morning.* | *He rebuilt the engine and finally got it going.* | *It took the repairman an hour to get the washing machine going again.*

set off /ˌset ˈɒf/ [phr v T] to do something to make a piece of equipment that warns you about something start **set off sth** *Someone accidentally set off the fire alarm.* | *Smoke alarms can be set off by smoke from cigarettes, cooking, and fireplaces.* | **set sth off** *The alarm is so sensitive that the slightest movement will set it off.*

activate /ˈæktɨveɪt/ [v T] to make a system start operating – use this especially in technical contexts: *The bomb's firing mechanism is activated by a time-clock.* | *The smoke activated the sprinkler system.*

set sth going /ˌset (sth) ˈgəʊɪŋ/ [v phrase] to make a clock, toy, or other machine that does not have a power supply start moving: *Mr Carey wound up the old clock and gently set the pendulum going.* | *She pulled the lever that set the pump going and waited for the water.*

push/press a button /ˌpʊʃ, ˌpres ə ˈbʌtn/ [v phrase] to press a button which makes a machine start: *What happens when you press this button?* | *Somebody pushed the alarm button.*

throw a switch /ˌθrəʊ ə ˈswɪtʃ/ [v phrase] to pull a large control that switches on the electricity supply to something: *The Speaker of the House threw the switch for the Christmas tree lights in front of the Capitol building.*

2 to switch something off

- switch off
- turn off
- stop
- push/press a button
- put out
- turn out
- shut off/down
- unplug
- disconnect

switch off /ˌswɪtʃ ˈɒf / [phr v T] to make something stop working, for example by pressing a button – use this about things that use electricity, for example, lights, televisions, or computers **switch off sth** *Always switch off your computer when you've finished.* | **switch sth off** *It's OK – I switched the TV off before I went out.*

turn off /ˌtɜːʳn ˈɒf / [phr v T] to make something stop working, for example by pressing a button or turning a tap – use this about things that use electricity, gas, or water **turn off sth** *Would you turn off the heater before you go to bed?* | **turn sth off** *You forgot to turn the oven off!*

stop /stɒp‖stɑːp/ [v T] to make an engine or a machine **stop** working: *George stopped the engine and got out of the car.* | *We had to stop the pump and unblock it.*

push/press a button /ˌpʊʃ, ˌpres ə ˈbʌtn/ [v phrase] to press a button that makes a machine stop: *If you want it to stop, just press the red button.*

put out /ˌpʊt ˈaʊt/ [phr v T] to switch a light off **put out sth** *Norma put out the light and went to sleep.* | **put sth out** *Could you put the lamp out in the bedroom, please?*

turn out /ˌtɜːʳn ˈaʊt/ [phr v T] to make a light stop working by pressing a button: *Don't forget to turn out the lights when you go to bed, okay Annie?*

shut off/down /ˌʃʌt ˈɒf, ˈdaʊn/ [phr v T] if you **shut off** or **shut down** a machine, you make it stop operating: *The computer automatically shuts off the pump when no water is flowing.* | *The Department of Energy shut down the reactor because of safety considerations.*

unplug /ʌnˈplʌg/ [v T] to remove the thing that connects a piece of electrical equipment to the main electricity supply, so that it is no longer connected to it: *Did you remember to unplug the kettle?* | *I was getting a lot of crank calls, so I started unplugging my phone at night.*

disconnect /ˌdɪskəˈnekt/ [v T] formal to separate a piece of equipment from the main electricity or gas supply so that it is no longer connected to it: *Once a car has started, the engine would continue to run even if you disconnected the battery.*

3 when something is switched on

- on
- be switched on
- be turned on
- be running
- be going
- be working
- be ticking over

on /ɒn‖ɔːn, ɑːn/ [adv/adj not before noun] if something is **on**, it is working – use this about lights, machines, and other things that use electricity, gas, or water: *Is the heating on? I'm freezing.* | **leave sth on** *Did you leave the kitchen light on?* | **keep sth on** *In the winter, I keep the gas fire on all day.*

be switched on /biː ˌswɪtʃt ˈɒn/ [v phrase] use this about things that use electricity, for example, machines, computers, or heating equipment: *A green light shows that the computer is switched on.* | *I don't think he has his cell phone switched on.* | *Have you checked that the power is switched on?*

be turned on /biː ˌtɜːʳnd ˈɒn/ [v phrase] use this about machines or about the electricity, gas, or water supply: *If the boiler fails to light, first check that the gas is turned on.* | *Is the switch turned on?*

be running /biː ˈrʌnɪŋ/ [v phrase] if an engine or a machine **is running**, it is working and its parts are moving: *Do not touch the machine while it is running.* | **leave sth running** *Nick left the engine running to warm it up, while he buckled the children into their car seats.*

be going /biː ˈgəʊɪŋ/ [v phrase] especially spoken if a machine **is going**, it is working and its parts are moving: *The clock stopped during the night, but it's going again now.* | *The washing machine's going, I can hear it.*

be working /biː ˈwɜːʳkɪŋ/ [v phrase] if a machine or piece of equipment **is working**, it has been switched on and is doing what it is supposed to do: *You mustn't open the lid while the sterilizer is working.* | *You can hear the pump in the refrigerator when it's working.*

be ticking over /biː ˌtɪkɪŋ ˈəʊvəʳ/ [v phrase] British if an engine or a vehicle **is ticking over**, it is working just enough to be on, but at its lowest level: *The plane's engines were ticking over just enough to hold position in the air.* | *He left the car ticking over while he dashed into the house.*

4 when something is switched off

- off
- be switched off
- be turned off
- out
- disconnected
- off the hook

off /ɒf‖ɔːf/ [adv/adj not before noun] if something is **off**, someone has switched it **off** to make it stop working – use this about lights, machines, and other things that use electricity, gas, or water: *Is the cooker off? I can smell gas.* | *I don't think anyone's at home. All the lights are off.*

be switched off /biː ˌswɪtʃt ˈɒf/ [v phrase] use this about things that use electricity, for example, machines, computers, or heating equipment: *Do you mean the alarm was switched off all night?* | *He didn't realize the microphone was switched off.*

be turned off /biː ˌtɜːʳnd ˈɒf/ [v phrase] use this about lights or machines, or about the electricity, gas, or water supply: *Make sure everything's turned off before you leave the house.* | *The machine is only turned off for a few minutes at a time.*

out /aʊt/ [adv/adj not before noun] if a light is **out**, it is not shining because it has been switched off or because there is no electricity: *She must have left the office as her light is out.* | *All the lights in the house were out.*

disconnected /ˌdɪskəˈnektɪ̈d/ [adj not before noun] a machine, telephone, water supply etc that is **disconnected** has had its power supply, water supply, gas supply etc completely removed so that it cannot be used: *That washing machine doesn't work. It's been disconnected.* | *When the power was disconnected, he carefully removed the back of the computer.*

off the hook /ˌɒf ðə ˈhʊk/ [adj phrase] a telephone that is **off the hook** has not been put back correctly or has been arranged so you cannot receive any calls: *I've been trying to call her for about half an hour. I think her phone must be off the hook.* | **take the phone off the hook** *I locked the door and took the phone off the hook so no one could disturb me.*

5 when a machine, light etc switches on or off automatically

- come/go on
- switch/turn on
- go out
- go off
- shut off/down
- switch/turn off

come/go on /ˌkʌm, ˌgəʊ ˈɒn/ [phr v I] if a machine, light etc **comes** or **goes** on, it starts working, especially because you have set a time for it to start – use this about things that use electricity, gas, or water: *The heating comes on automatically.* | *Every so often, our TV just goes on by itself.*

switch/turn on /ˌswɪtʃ, ˌtɜːʳn ˈɒn/ [phr v I/T] if a machine, light etc **switches on**, it starts working – use this about things that use electricity: *Clap your hands twice, and the light switches on.* | **switch/turn itself on** *Water softening systems turn themselves on at night to clean the system.*

go out /ˌgəʊ ˈaʊt/ [phr v I] if a light **goes out**, it stops shining, for example because it is broken or because there is no electricity: *Suddenly all the lights went out.* | *The street lights have a light sensor that makes them automatically go out at dawn.*

go off /ˌgəʊ ˈɒf/ [phr v I] if a machine, light etc **goes off**, it stops working – use this about things that use electricity, water, or gas: *The heating goes off at 10:30.* | *After the 30-car train passed, the flashing red lights went off and the arms blocking traffic went up.*

shut off/down /ˌʃʌt ˈɒf, ˈdaʊn/ [phr v I/T] if a machine **shuts off** or **shuts down**, it stops operating: *The pump automatically shuts down when no water is flowing.* | **shut itself off/down** *Something caused the computer to switch itself off.*

switch/turn off /ˌswɪtʃ, ˌtɜːʳn ˈɒf/ [phr v I/T] if a machine, light etc **switches** or **turns off**, it stops working – use this about things that use electricity: *The bulb inside the refrigerator switches off when you close the door.* | **switch/turn itself off** *If an automatic can opener fails to turn itself off, food is probably jamming the cutter.*

sympathize

RELATED WORDS

- *see also* **comfort/make sb feel better, understand (2)**

1 to feel sorry because someone else is in a bad situation

- feel sorry for
- sympathize
- have/feel sympathy for
- feel for
- pity
- my heart goes out to
- take pity on
- understand

feel sorry for /ˌfiːl ˈsɒri fɔːʳ‖-ˈsɑːri-/ [v phrase] to feel sad for someone because they have had bad luck or they are in a bad situation: *I think he felt sorry for me because I'd just lost my wallet.* | *He'll probably go to jail for this. It's his wife I feel sorry for.* | *I feel sorry for the poor person who's going to have to sort this mess out.* | *I feel really sorry for young married couples these days. It's hard going for them.* | **can't help feeling sorry for sb** (=use this when you should not really feel sorry for someone, but you do) *I know he's being a jerk, but I can't help feeling a little sorry for him.*

sympathize ALSO **sympathise** British /ˈsɪmpəθaɪz/ [v I] to feel sad for someone who is having problems, because you understand how they feel: *My dear, I completely understand and sympathize, but there's not much I can do about it, really.* | **+ with** *She felt Mark should have sympathised with her and supported her, instead of criticizing.* | **sympathize with sb's plight/problems/dilemma** *It's hard not to sympathize with the plight of single parents in today's world.*

have/feel sympathy for /ˌhæv, ˌfiːl ˈsɪmpəθi fɔːʳ/ [v phrase] to feel sad for someone who is having problems, because you understand how they feel: *I have great sympathy for anyone who has lived through depression.* | *It wasn't possible not to feel sympathy for Anna – she'd lost her husband and her son in the space of only a few weeks.* | **have/feel deep sympathy for** *The judge said he had the deepest sympathy for Maria's situation, but that he had no option but to sentence her.*

feel for /ˈfiːl fɔːʳ/ [phr v T] to sympathize very strongly and sincerely with someone who has problems, is suffering etc: *Of course I feel for him – he's my brother. But he did bring it on himself.* | *You couldn't help but feel for Charles. He'd been so unlucky in life.*

pity /ˈpɪti/ [v T not in progressive] to feel very sorry for someone who is in a much worse situation than you: *I pity anyone who has to feed a family on such a low income.* | *I don't want you to pity me – I just want you to help me.* | *He felt pity for Marla out there all by herself in some little nowhere town.*

my heart goes out to /maɪ ˌhɑːʳt gəʊz ˈaʊt tuː/ spoken use this to say that you feel extremely sorry for someone, especially because something very sad has happened to them: *I know how awfully disappointed you must be, and my heart goes out to you.* | *My heart went out to all those poor little children standing shivering in the cold.*

take pity on /ˌteɪk ˈpɪti ɒn/ [v phrase] to feel sorry for someone and do something to help them: *The old couple, poor as they were, took pity on her and gave her food.* | *We walked on through the pouring rain until a kind driver took pity on us and offered us a ride.*

understand /ˌʌndəʳˈstænd/ [v I/T not in progressive] to realize that someone is unhappy or having problems, and behave kindly to them: *I'm sure if you talk to your boss, he'll understand.* | *You can only apologize, and hope that she'll understand.* | **+ why/what/how** *I completely understand how things are when money is tight.* | *We're trying very hard to understand what she's going through.*

2 to not feel sorry for someone in a bad situation

- have/feel no sympathy for
- my heart bleeds (for sb)

have/feel no sympathy for /hæv, fiːl ˌnəʊ ˈsɪmpəθi fɔːʳ/ [v phrase] to feel that someone's problems are their own fault: *I have no sympathy for him – he hasn't even tried to look for a job.* | *I'm afraid I don't have much sympathy for people who spend more than they can afford and then find themselves in debt.* | **have/feel little sympathy for sb** *The fact is that most Americans feel little sympathy for AIDS sufferers.*

my heart bleeds (for sb) /maɪ ˌhɑːʳt ˈbliːdz (fəʳ (sb))/ spoken use this humorously when you do not feel any sympathy at all for someone: *'He says he can't come out tonight because he has to look after the kids.' 'My heart bleeds! That must be the first time he's stayed in with them since they were born!'*

3 to tell someone that you sympathize with them

- offer your sympathy
- commiserate
- send/offer/express condolences

offer your sympathy /ˌɒfəʳ jɔːʳ ˈsɪmpəθi‖ˌɔːf-/ [v phrase] formal to tell someone that you feel sympathy for them, especially in a letter, after someone they love has died: *She wrote a short letter offering her sympathy.* | *Bouquets and hand-written cards offering sympathy surrounded the scene of the accident.* | **+ to** *My husband joins me in offering our sincere sympathy to you and to Susan at this sad time.*

commiserate /kəˈmɪzəreɪt/ [v I] formal to express your sympathy for someone when they are unhappy about something, especially something that is not really very serious: *'Poor Alistair!' she commiserated. 'Let me buy you lunch.'* | **+ with** *When he failed his driving test, I called him up and commiserated with him.* | **+ about** *In several of their letters, Hartley and Burns commiserated about the problems of old age.* —**commiseration** /kəˌmɪzəˈreɪʃən/ [n U] *'I'm afraid I didn't have any success,' I said, and my colleague shook his head in commiseration.*

send/offer/express condolences /ˌsend, ˌɒfəʳ, ɪkˌspres kənˈdəʊlənsɪ̈z‖-ˌɔːf-/ [v phrase] to express sympathy to someone whose close relative or friend has died – use this in formal or official situations **+ to** *We take this opportunity to send our condolences to the families of those who lost their lives in this disaster.* | *After the funeral, foreign ambassadors lined up to offer their condolences to the widow of the late president.* | **deep/heartfelt/sincere condolences** *In a statement read on television, Saleh expressed 'deepest condolences' to the families of the victims.*

4 what you say to tell someone that you sympathize

- I'm sorry
- I/we'll be thinking of you
- bad luck
- you have my deepest sympathy/with deepest sympathy

I'm sorry /aɪm ˈsɒri‖-ˈsɑːri/ spoken say this to tell someone you are sad that something bad has happened to them: *I heard about your father's death; I'm very sorry.* | *Jules, I am sorry. I had no idea.* | **+ about** *Mavis, I'm really sorry about your Ma. It must have been a terrible shock.*

I/we'll be thinking of you /aɪ, wiːl biː ˈθɪŋkɪŋ əv juː/ spoken say this to tell someone that you are worried about them and that you hope they will be all right: *Take care, Lucy. I'll be thinking of you.* | *Tell Harry I'll be thinking of him and I hope he'll be home soon.*

bad luck /ˌbæd ˈlʌk/ British spoken say this to show your sympathy for someone who has tried to do something and failed: *Bad luck, Paul. I'm sure you'll pass next time.* | *Oh what a shame. Bad luck Chris.*

you have my deepest sympathy/with deepest sympathy /juː ˌhæv maɪ ˌdiːpɪ̈st ˈsɪmpəθi, wɪð ˌdiːpɪ̈st ˈsɪmpəθi/ formal written use this in a letter to someone you do not know very well, whose close relative or friend has died: *We were so sorry to hear of your sister's death. You have our deepest sympathy.*

5 someone who is kind and shows sympathy

- sympathetic
- understanding
- compassionate
- caring
- a sympathetic ear/a shoulder to cry on

sympathetic /ˌsɪmpəˈθetɪk◂/ [adj] kind to people who are in an unpleasant situation, and ready to comfort them or share their problems: *My friends were all extremely sympathetic when they heard I'd lost my job.* | *Noticing my embarrassment, the teacher gave me a sympathetic smile.* | **+ to/towards** *Try being a bit more sympathetic towards her – you might get better results.* —**sympathetically** [adj] *She listened sympathetically to all our complaints.* | *Kramer nodded sympathetically.*

understanding /ˌʌndərˈstændɪŋ/ [adj] sympathetic and patient, even when someone behaves badly, because you understand their problems and feelings: *He's funny, energetic, understanding, and a great teacher.* | *Irene often has to take time off work. Fortunately she has a very understanding boss.* | *My parents were wonderfully understanding throughout my divorce.*

compassionate /kəmˈpæʃənɪt/ [adj] someone who is **compassionate** feels a lot of pity for people who are suffering and wants to help them: *The church has inspired countless compassionate men and women to help the needy in times of famine, war, and plague.* | **+ to/towards** *Our city has earned a reputation as a place where government is compassionate toward the poor and disadvantaged.* —**compassionately** [adv] *Political refugees need our protection and we urge the government to view their plight more compassionately.*

caring /ˈkeərɪŋ/ [adj] loving and sympathetic, especially so that you want to help people when they are in trouble: *Just because a family has money does not guarantee that the children have responsible and caring parents.* | *It is possible for men to be tough and, at the same time, caring and sensitive.*

a sympathetic ear/a shoulder to cry on /ə ˌsɪmpəθetɪk ˈɪər, ə ˌʃəʊldər tə ˈkraɪ ɒn/ [n phrase] someone who will listen sympathetically when you tell them about your troubles: *Remember your mother's always here if you need a shoulder to cry on.* | *Watt found a sympathetic ear when he described his family's situation to Captain Schiller.*

6 a feeling of sympathy

- sympathy
- pity
- compassion
- understanding

sympathy /ˈsɪmpəθi/ [n U] the feeling you have when you are sorry for someone who is having problems, and you understand how they feel: *Relatives of the aircrash victims were treated with great sympathy.* | *She looked at him with sympathy.* | *The trip also is intended to raise money and sympathy for the plight of the Tibetan people.* | **have/feel/express sympathy for sb** *The Prime Minister expressed outrage at the attack, and sympathy for the families of the victims.* | **deep sympathy** (=a very strong feeling of sympathy) *You have my deepest sympathy, and my thoughts are with you.*

pity /ˈpɪti/ [n U] a feeling that you have when you feel very sorry for someone, often when you are unable to help them: *It's a civil war. They don't want our pity, they need our help.* | *When I returned to school, my classmates looked at me with pity in their eyes.* | **feel/have pity** *I felt such pity for that young girl sitting alone in the bus station.* | **be full of pity/be filled with pity** *She was full of pity for the little boy with no one to love and care for him.*

compassion /kəmˈpæʃən/ [n U] a strong feeling of pity for someone who is suffering, and a desire to help them: *Of course we must insist on punishment, but the criminal must also be treated with compassion.* | **+ for/to/towards** *Russell's father had no compassion for his son's physical disabilities.* | *What are you doing now to show compassion toward the victims of torture?*

understanding /ˌʌndərˈstændɪŋ/ [n U] a sympathetic attitude to someone that is based on your understanding: *Demonstrate your empathy and understanding of your children's problems.* | *There seems to be a lack of understanding on the part of managers when it comes to employees' personal problems.* | *The book gave me an understanding of what it must be like to be addicted to drugs.*

7 relating to someone who is so unlucky, so unhappy etc that you feel sorry for them

- poor
- pitiful
- pathetic
- wretched

poor /pʊər/ [adj only before noun] especially spoken use this to talk to or about someone that you feel sorry for: *The poor girl gets blamed for everything that goes wrong.* | *Poor baby. Come here and let me give you a cuddle.* | **poor old** informal *I hear poor old Steve broke his ankle.*

pitiful /ˈpɪtɪfəl/ [adj] a **pitiful** person looks or sounds very sad and unlucky and you feel very sorry for them: *John looked pitiful, his whole body weak with exhaustion.* | *the pitiful cries of an injured puppy* | *The horses were in a pitiful condition, thin and covered with sores.* —**pitifully** [adv] *The woman sobbed pitifully, begging to be left alone.*

pathetic /pəˈθetɪk/ [adj] someone who is **pathetic** is someone that you feel sorry for even though you often also have no respect for them: *There is something pathetic about a 40-year-old man who still has his mother do his laundry.* | *Yang looked at me with a pathetic expression on his face.* | *We found a small dog sitting outside the back door, looking pathetic.* —**pathetically** [adv] *'No one ever listens to me,' she said pathetically.* | *Suddenly, he looks pathetically young and scared.*

wretched /ˈretʃɪd/ [adj] someone who is **wretched** is very unhappy or unlucky, so that you feel very sorry for them – used especially in literature: *With a violent drunkard for a husband, he thought, that wretched woman must lead a life of terror.* | *Billy lay on the bed, wretched and close to tears.*

8 to try to make someone feel sorry for you

- play on sb's sympathy
- hard-luck story/sob story

play on sb's sympathy ALSO **play for sympathy** /ˌpleɪ ɒn (sb's) ˈsɪmpəθi, ˌpleɪ fər ˈsɪmpəθi/ [v phrase] to unfairly try to make someone feel sorry for you, in order to gain an advantage for yourself: *She had lain in her bed for years, feigning illness and playing on the sympathy of her daughters.* | *He decided it was best to play for sympathy on this occasion, because she might know if he tried to lie.*

hard-luck story/sob story /ˌhɑːʳd ˈlʌk ˌstɔːri, ˈsɒb ˌstɔːri‖ˈsɑːb- / [n C] a story or explanation, especially one that is untrue, told by someone in order to make other people feel sorry for them: *A beggar approached me with some hard-luck story about an accident.* | **give sb a hard-luck/sob story** *The defendant gave us some sob story about a sick child.*

system

a system

RELATED WORDS

▸ *see also* **way (1-6), organize, arrange, order**

- ▸ **system**
- ▸ **set-up**
- ▸ **network**
- ▸ **framework**
- ▸ **structure**
- ▸ **mechanism**

system /ˈsɪstɪ̆m/ [n C] the way that something is organized, following fixed rules and methods, in order to provide a service or achieve an aim: *We're going to have to make some changes – this system just doesn't work.* | *Most teachers are opposed to recent changes in the education system.* | **+ of** *What we need is a cheap and reliable system of public transportation.* | *a democratic system of government* | **+ for (doing) sth** *They are introducing a system for dealing with enquiries from customers.*

set-up /ˈset ʌp/ [n C usually singular] informal the way in which things are organized or done within a company, school etc: *My last school was quite traditional, but it's a different set-up at the new one.* | *An efficient accounts set-up can not only save a company money: it can improve its relationship with its clients.*

network /ˈnetwɜːʳk/ [n C] a system of lines, tubes, wires, roads etc that are connected to each other: *A 24-hour strike brought the railway network to a standstill.* | *US companies have invested heavily in their telecommunications networks.* | **+ of** *A network of veins and arteries carries the blood around the body.*

framework /ˈfreɪmwɜːʳk/ [n C] a basic system of rules or ideas that people work within: *How do you feel you can develop your skills within the framework of the team?* | *We need a legal and political framework that is favourable to business.* | **+ for** *The aim of this legislation is to provide a framework for employers and trade unions to operate in.*

structure /ˈstrʌktʃəʳ/ [n C] a system, especially a complicated one with a lot of different levels: *Many visitors to the UK find the British class structure difficult to understand.* | **+ of** *She studied the organizational structure of the company to see whether it could be made more efficient.* | *The structure of the US banking system is changing.*

mechanism /ˈmekənɪzəm/ [n C] a system of rules that makes it possible for particular things to happen or for people to do something: *Many schools have a mechanism which allows parents to inspect classroom materials.* | **+ to do sth** *The peace plan includes a mechanism to share power between all four parties.* | **+ for (doing) sth** *The free market system is an imperfect mechanism for achieving full employment.*

Tt

take

WHAT'S HERE

to take sb or sth from one place to another

RELATED WORDS

▸ *see also* **carry, send, drive, travel**

1 to take someone or something from one place to another

- ▸ **take**
- ▸ **bring**
- ▸ **transport**
- ▸ **deliver**
- ▸ **escort**
- ▸ **whisk sb away**
- ▸ **drive**
- ▸ **fly**
- ▸ **ship**
- ▸ **carry**

take /teɪk/ [v T] to have someone or something with you when you go to another place: *Don't forget to take your keys.* | *I've started taking a packed lunch to work to save money.* | **take sb/sth to/out/into/home etc** *'Where's Dan?' 'He's taken the car to the garage.'* | *I can't stop, I've got to take the kids to school.* | *She was taken straight into the emergency room when we arrived.* | *Would you like me to take you home?* | *Are we allowed to take library books home with us?* | **take sb sth** *I took Alice a cup of tea.* | **take sb/sth with you** *Did he take the camera with him?* | *Take the dogs with you if you're going for a walk.*

bring /brɪŋ/ [v T] if someone **brings** a person or thing to the place where you are, they have that person or thing with them when they come: *I brought my Nikes – they're about the only decent shoes I have.* | *We've brought someone to see you!* | **bring sb to/into/out/home etc** *Everyone's bringing a bit of food and a bottle to the party.* | *When are you going to bring him in for his injections?* | *The only time we use the VCR is when they bring Joey to our house.* | *I brought some work home and tried to get it finished in the evening.* | **bring sb sth** *Robert asked the waiter to bring him the check.* | **bring sb/sth with you** *I hope he hasn't brought his brother with him.* | *Is it okay if I bring some clothes with me to wash?*

transport /trænˈspɔːʳt/ [v T] to move large quantities of goods or large numbers of people from one place to another, especially over a large distance: *The plane is used for transporting military personnel.* | **transport sb/sth to/from/across etc** *The company transports meat across the country in refrigerated containers.* | *Raw materials were transported to Phoenix from the reservations.* | *The inci-*

dent raised concerns about the safety and security of nuclear weapons being transported through Europe.

deliver /dɪˈlɪvəʳ/ [v I/T] to take letters, newspapers, goods etc to someone's home or office: *Your computer will be delivered between 9.00 a.m. and 2.00 p.m.* | *How soon can you deliver?* | **deliver sth to sb/sth** *If your order is ready, it will be delivered to you tomorrow.* | *Unfortunately the package was delivered to the wrong address.* —**delivery** [n C/U] when letters, newspapers, goods etc are taken to someone's house or office: *We offer free home delivery for every purchase over $150.* | *a newspaper delivery boy*

escort /ɪˈskɔːʳt/ [v T] to take someone to a place and make sure they cannot escape or that they arrive there safely **escort sb to/into/out etc** *The prisoner was escorted into the room by two police officers.* | *The guards escorted them to a waiting helicopter.* | *After he was sacked, he was escorted discreetly from the building by two senior managers.* —**escort** /ˈeskɔːʳt/ [n C/U] a person or group who escorts someone somewhere: *The agreement says weapons inspectors will be accompanied by Iraqi escorts.* | **armed/military/police escort** *They provided an armed escort for the journey back to Cairo.* | **under escort** *The three men left the court under police escort.*

whisk sb away /ˌwɪsk (sb) əˈweɪ/ [phr v T not in progressive] if the police, guards, or people who are looking after someone **whisk** someone **away** they take them away from a place very quickly, especially in a car: *He refused to talk to reporters and was whisked away by the authorities to an undisclosed location.* | *Two police officers stood outside, waiting to whisk her away as soon as she came out.*

drive /draɪv/ [v T] to take someone from one place to another in a car or other road vehicle **drive sb to/from/home etc** *The terrorists forced Mr Grey to drive them to the airport.* | *Tyson declined to give any comment to reporters and was driven away by a friend.* | *She didn't really want to drive herself to the doctor, so I said I'd take her.* | *Wayne usually drives Patti home from class because they live quite close to each other.*

fly /flaɪ/ [v T] to take people or goods from one place to another by plane **fly sb/sth to/from/back etc** *His company flew him to Rio to attend the conference.* | *I'm not allowed to fly visitors into the National Park area without permission.* | *Medical equipment and food are being flown into the areas worst hit by the disaster.*

ship /ʃɪp/ [v T] to take goods a long distance to another place in a **ship**, plane, truck or train, so that they can be used or sold **ship sth to/from/back etc** *About half of the whisky produced in Scotland is shipped to Japan and the US.* | *I'm a manufacturer, and I ship electronic goods across the Mexican border, so the new levies will definitely affect my business.* —**shipment** [n C/U] goods that are being shipped, or the process of shipping them: *a reduction in oil shipments* | *Hundreds of cars are lined up outside the factory, awaiting shipment to France and Holland.*

carry /ˈkæri/ [v T] if a ship, plane, train, or road vehicle **carries** people or goods, it takes them from one place to another: *Air India carried 1.66 million passengers last year.* | *The Jeep was carrying six men from the artillery brigade. Only one survived.* | **carry sb/sth to/from/across etc** *The ship was carrying a cargo of oil from Kuwait to Japan.* | *The train was carrying passengers from Moscow to St Petersburg.*

2 the process of taking goods or people from one place to another

- transport
- haulage
- in transit

transport British **/transportation** American /ˈtrænspɔːʳt, ˌtrænspɔːˈteɪʃən‖ˌtrænspər-/ [n U] *We need more investment in natural gas distribution and transportation.* | **+ to** *The price is $40, which includes transportation to the game and refreshments.* | **+ of** *The government is planning to tighten up regulations governing the transport of toxic waste.* | **transport costs/systems/companies etc** *Carrying goods by ship reduces transportation costs.* | *Critics have pointed to the lack of transport links to the new attraction.*

haulage British **/hauling** American /ˈhɔːlɪdʒ, ˈhɔːlɪŋ/ [n U] the business of taking large quantities of goods from one place to another: *Rail freight charges are high compared with the cost of road haulage.* | *The company also provides commercial hauling for the city of San Diego.* | **haulage company/costs/contractor etc** *Jean works for a road haulage company based in St Etienne.*

in transit /ɪn ˈtrænsə̇t, -zə̇t/ [adv] while being taken from one place to another: *A good insurance policy will cover the cost of goods lost or damaged in transit.* | *Cheese continues to ripen while in transit, so storage is important.*

3 to go to a place and take someone or something from there

- get
- pick up
- collect
- fetch

get /get/ [v T not in passive] to go to the place where someone or something is, and bring them back, or tell them to come back: *I'll get my coat and then we can go.* | *Dinner's ready. Can you get Jo?* | *I've got to get the kids in a few minutes.* | **get sb sth** (=get something for someone) *Could you get me my keys from the kitchen?* | *I'm going to get myself a beer, does anyone else want one?* | **go (and) get sb/sth** *Go and get your father. He's in the garden.* | *Forget the cooking, let's go get takeout.*

pick up /ˌpɪk ˈʌp/ [phr v T] to go to a place where someone or something is waiting for you or ready for you, and take them with you **pick sb/sth up** *Do you want me to come back and pick you guys up?* | *Nadia will pick you up at the airport.* | *Can you pick some milk up from the shop on your way home?* | **pick up sb/sth** *'Where's Diana?' 'She just left to pick up the kids from school.'* | *I'll pick up the tickets on my way home from work.* | *Hi, I've come to pick up a suit I left on Tuesday.*

collect /kəˈlekt/ [v T] British to go to the place where someone or something is waiting for you, and bring them back: *I'm at the station. Can you come and collect me?* | *We'll have to eat later, I'm collecting Grandma from the hospital this evening.* | *I've got a parcel to collect from the post office.*

fetch /fetʃ/ [v T] British to go to get someone or something that you need and bring them back: *Jim's gone to fetch the police.* | *Where's your mug? Go and fetch it.* | *Martha fetched a towel from the bathroom.* | **fetch sb sth** *Could you fetch me a screwdriver?*

4 to take someone or something back to the place where they came from

- take back
- bring back
- return

take back /ˌteɪk ˈbæk/ [phr v T] **take sb/sth back** *Paul asked the taxi driver to take him back to his hotel.* | *The dress was too big, so I took it back.* | *Would you like Daddy to take you back home?* | *You can take these CDs back with you.* | **take back sb/sth** *I have to take back the trailer I borrowed from Randy.* | *What would be a good present to take back for Anna?* | *Dee wanted a loaf to take back with her.*

bring back /ˌbrɪŋ ˈbæk/ [phr v T] to bring someone or something back to the place where you are now or to your home **bring sb/sth back** *Mrs Ali will bring you back from school today.* | *I was going to ask if you could bring that pair of jeans back with you.* | *Why don't you bring Barbara back here?* | *Thanks – I promise I'll bring it back tomorrow.* | **bring back sth** *When can you bring back those books I lent you?* | *They brought back some lovely cheese from France.* | *We're going to bring back some beer with us – do you want anything else?*

return /rɪˈtɜːʳn/ [v T] to bring or take something back to the place where you got it from: *Penny has still not returned the office keys.* | **return sth to sth** *Sign and keep the top sheet, and return the blue sheet to the office.* | *If there is a problem with the computer, you can return it to the store.*

5 to take something such as water, electricity, or gas from one place to another

- carry
- conduct
- convey

carry /ˈkæri/ [v T] *The electricity is carried by means of cables which are up to 30 cm thick.* | **carry sth to/from/across etc** *The pipelines, which carry oil across Alaska, are designed to withstand extremely low temperatures.* | *Rivers carry debris out to the sea, and it then settles on the bottom.*

conduct /kənˈdʌkt/ [v T] to take heat, electricity, or sound from one place to another through pipes or along wires: *Before Newton, people had great difficulty understanding how any metal could conduct electricity.* | **conduct sth from/to/away etc** *Water is used to conduct heat away from the reactor.* | *Specially treated copper wires conduct the signal from the amplifier to the speakers.*

convey /kənˈveɪ/ [v T] formal to take something such as water, electricity, or gas from one place to another: *A crack had developed in one of the main cooling pipes which are used to convey water.* | **convey sth to/from/across etc** *The blood is conveyed to the heart from the veins.*

6 to take someone somewhere and show them where to go, what to look at etc

- guide
- lead
- show
- usher
- shepherd

guide /gaɪd/ [v T] to take someone through or to a place that you know very well, showing them the way **guide sb to/through/along etc** *Sammler was a huge help, guiding me through the dangers of the city streets.* | *The travellers were guided around the Hindu Kush by local people who had lived there all their lives.*

lead /liːd/ [v T] to take a person or an animal to a place, especially by going in front of them **lead sb to/through/along etc** *Our guide seemed to be leading us towards a wooded area in the distance.* | *He led Julia through the house to his study.* | *The police officer took her arm and led her gently away.* | **lead the way** *In silence, Roland led the way back to the car.*

show /ʃəʊ/ [v T] to take someone to a place, such as a table in a restaurant or a hotel room, and leave them there **show sb to sth** *Could you show this gentleman to his table please.* | *I stood in the foyer, waiting to be shown to my apartment.*

usher /ˈʌʃəʳ/ [v T] to take someone to a place such as a room or building, especially as part of your job **usher sb into/to/towards etc** *At the front door stood two smart young men, who ushered the guests into the house.* | *Smiling, Smart ushered her to a waiting car outside.*

shepherd /ˈʃepəʳd/ [v T] to guide a large group of people in an orderly way **shepherd sb up/along/to etc** *The police officer shepherded everyone away and padlocked the church gates.* | *We expected to be asked to sit down, but instead we were shepherded out to an open patio at the back of the house.*

7 a person whose job is to take people somewhere, show them things etc

- guide
- usher
- docent

guide /gaɪd/ [n C] a person whose job is to take people to a place or show them around a place, especially because they know the area well: *You are advised not to enter the Kenyan game reserves without a guide.* | *That seems like a question for our experienced tour guide, Monika Koppel.* | *Our guide and interpreter said he enjoyed the work because he himself had learned much about the city.*

usher /ˈʌʃəʳ/ [n C] someone who guides people to their seats, for example at a wedding or in a cinema: *I worked as an usher at the local cinema during the holidays.* | *The usher handed us a songsheet and directed us to seats in the front row.*

docent /ˈdəʊsənt, dəʊˈsent/ [n C] American someone who guides you around a museum and tells you about what you are seeing: *She's a volunteer docent at the Smithsonian Institution.* | *At the J Paul Getty museum in Malibu, a docent was giving her usual tour.*

8 to take someone away using force

- take away
- abduct
- kidnap
- take sb hostage

take away /ˌteɪk əˈweɪ/ [phr v T] if soldiers, the police etc **take** someone **away**, they force that person to go with them **take sb away** *The soldiers took my son away and I never saw him again.* | *Luis told me how he'd been picked up by military police in the middle of the night, and taken away for questioning.* | **take away sb** *At that time police would often take away suspected revolutionaries and throw them in jail with a trial.*

abduct /əb'dʌkt, æb-/ [v T] to take someone away by force, especially a child or young person, often in order to kill them or sexually attack them – used especially in news reports: *The two high school girls were abducted at gunpoint on Tuesday.* | *Kurdish separatists have abducted a Japanese tourist and are demanding money for his safe return.* | **abduct sb from sth** *Several young women had been abducted from their villages and forced to work as prostitutes.* —**abduction** [n U] *The man is charged with the abduction and rape of a 12-year-old schoolgirl.*

kidnap /'kɪdnæp/ [v T] to take someone away by force and keep them as your prisoner, in order to make their family or their government give you money or other things you want: *Terrorists have kidnapped a French officer and are demanding $400,000 from the French government.* | *He was kidnapped by vigilantes in El Centro, beaten and robbed, and then set on fire.* —**kidnapping** [n C/U] when someone is kidnapped: *Most diplomats now travel with bodyguards, following a series of kidnappings.* | *He has been charged with the kidnapping of his ex-girlfriend.* | *victims of kidnapping*

take sb hostage /teɪk (sb) 'hɒstɪdʒ‖-'hɑː-/ [v phrase] to take someone and keep them as a prisoner, especially for political reasons, and threaten to kill them if their government does not do what you demand: *On January 6, six Italian nuns were taken hostage.* | *Guerrilla fighters seized the hospital yesterday, taking patients and staff hostage, although several dozen were later released.*

to take sth from sb

RELATED WORDS

opposite: **give**

▸ *see also* **steal, get, have/not have**

9 to take something from someone

- ▸ take
- ▸ grab/snatch
- ▸ take away
- ▸ seize
- ▸ impound
- ▸ confiscate
- ▸ commandeer
- ▸ deprive sb
- ▸ strip sb

take /teɪk/ [v T] to **take** something out of someone's hands: *Let me take your bags – you look exhausted.* | *Oh, mom, could you just take this for a second?* | *He took her coat, and hung it in the hall.* | **take sth from sb** *He walked slowly across the room and took the gun from her.* | **take sth off sb** informal *Can you take some of these books off me?*

grab/snatch /græb, snætʃ/ [v T] to take something from someone with a sudden violent movement: *He just grabbed my camera and ran off with it.* | **snatch/grab sth from sb/sth** *Gerry snatched her diary from the desk, and she lunged to grab it back.* | **snatch/grab sth off sb** informal *Paul grabbed the bag of sweets off his sister and ran away with it.*

take away /ˌteɪk ə'weɪ/ [phr v T] to take something important from someone, such as a possession or a right, either as a punishment or in a way that is wrong or unfair **take away sth** *Mom's threatened to take away my stereo if my schoolwork doesn't improve.* | *The new law would take away the rights of workers to go on strike.* | *That's stupid – it's like teaching someone to read, then taking away all their books!* | **take sth away** *No, Eli, I'm taking it away now!* | **take sth away from sb** *Even though Polly still needs it, the authorities have taken the wheelchair away from her.*

seize /siːz/ [v T] to take something such as drugs, guns, or documents from someone who is keeping them illegally or taking them from one place to another: *Police seized 53 weapons and made 42 arrests.* | *Over 52,000 E-tablets hidden in a car door were seized by customs officials.* | *Assets worth over $1 million were seized, along with documents relating to the company's financial dealings.*

impound /ɪm'paʊnd/ [v T] to take something such as a car or an animal away from someone and keep it in a special place until they are officially allowed to have it back: *The act will give the government new rights to impound untaxed cars and crush them.* | *The medical officer says that the animals will be impounded while tests are carried out.* | *Police recovered both items, and impounded a black BMW from the murder scene.*

confiscate /'kɒnfəskeɪt‖'kɑːn-/ [v T] to officially take something away from someone, either as a punishment or because they are not allowed to have it: *Your vehicle can be confiscated if you are transporting marijuana.* | *The authorities will confiscate firearms found on a boat or plane if the owner cannot show proof of US licensing.* | **confiscate sth from sb** *The group claims that billions of dollars in property and bank accounts was confiscated from Jewish businessmen in the Second World War.* —**confiscated** [adj] *The report concludes that no one knows what actually happened to the confiscated property.*

commandeer /ˌkɒmən'dɪəʳ‖ˌkɑː-/ [v T] if the army or other military organization **commandeers** something such as a vehicle or a building, they take it away from the owners in order to use it in a war: *Bud's truck had been commandeered by the regiment.* | *The officers had commandeered every house in the area.* | *A paramilitary group attempted to commandeer the bus and take it to Madrid.*

deprive sb /dɪ'praɪv (sb)/ [phr v T] to take away or not let someone have their rights, advantages etc, especially in a way that seems unfair: *Under Stalin, Soviet citizens were deprived of their most basic human rights.* | *The boy's parents claim the school's actions have effectively deprived their son of education.* | *Banning the carnival will deprive law-abiding citizens of a source of culturally valuable entertainment.*

strip sb /'strɪp (sb)/ [phr v T] to completely take away someone's rights, responsibilities, or a prize they have won, especially as a punishment for doing something wrong: *The captain was stripped of his licence after the collision.* | *He was formally stripped of his American citizenship.* | *The ruling authority stripped him of his boxing title after he was convicted of importing heroin.* | *The court ruled that Learer's conviction did not constitute grounds for stripping her of custody of her four children.*

to take sth from somewhere

RELATED WORDS

▸ *see also* **steal, carry**

10 to take something from the place where it is

- ▸ take
- ▸ take out
- ▸ pull out
- ▸ remove
- ▸ withdraw
- ▸ fish out

take /teɪk/ [v T] to **take** something from the place

where it is: *Have you taken my keys? I can't find them.* | **take sth from/off/down etc** *He took a dictionary down from the shelf.* | *Her camera was taken from the reception desk while no one was looking.* | *If anyone would like to take the uneaten food home, they're welcome to do so.*

take out /ˌteɪk ˈaʊt/ [phr v T] to take something from a place where it cannot be seen, for example from a pocket, drawer or container **take out sth** *He reached into his pocket and took out a handkerchief.* | *Today, I'm going to show you how to take out summer-flowering bulbs to store them for the winter.* | **take sth out** *Sally opened a pack of cigarettes, took one out and lit it.* | *I keep the forms in this folder here, so just take one out if you need one.* | **take sth out of sth** *Take that chewing gum out of your mouth!* | *Take the sachet out of the water after 3 minutes.*

pull out /ˌpʊl ˈaʊt/ [phr v T] to quickly take something from a place where it was hidden or could not be seen **pull out sth** *He pulled out a gun and fired three shots.* | **pull sth out** *I saw her pull a bag out from under the seat.* | **pull sth out of sth** *She pulled a pen out of her bag and began to scribble furiously.*

remove /rɪˈmuːv/ [v T] formal to take something away from the place where it is, especially something that you do not want or something that should not be there: *Please do not remove this notice.* | *The new technology will make it easier for surgeons to remove abnormal growths before they cause problems.* | **remove sth from sth** *Remove all the packaging from the pizza and place it in a preheated oven.* | *The relics were removed from the house and taken to a local museum for identification.*

withdraw /wɪðˈdrɔː, wɪθ-/ [v T] to take something out of something else, especially slowly or carefully – used especially in literature: *The ambassador frowned and withdrew the cigar from his mouth.* | *She withdrew her hand from his grasp, and turned to leave the room.*

fish out /ˌfɪʃ ˈaʊt/ [phr v T] informal to take something from a place where it is difficult to get things from **fish sth out** *The doctor fished his glasses out again and looked closely at Murphy's ear.* | **fish sth out from sth** *The young man fished a dirty bowl out from under the bed.* | **fish out sth** *Brody fished out a pack of cigarettes and lit one.* | **fish sth out of sth** *I fished it out of the trash – it's a perfectly good tea kettle.*

11 to take something from somewhere quickly and suddenly

- grab
- snatch
- whisk sth away

grab /græb/ [v T not usually in passive] to quickly and suddenly take something from the place where it is, especially because you are in a hurry: *Grab your coat, we're late.* | *I'm going to run downstairs and grab some books and stuff – I'll be right back.* | *It was chaos, everyone was just grabbing drinks from behind the bar.*

snatch /snætʃ/ [v T not usually in progressive] to take something quickly and violently from the place where it is: *When no one was looking, he snatched a tray of watches and ran out of the shop.* | *Someone's going to snatch your purse if you leave it sticking out of your bag like that.* | *Before I could say a word, he'd snatched the keys from the table and run out of the room.*

whisk sth away /ˌwɪsk (sth) əˈweɪ/ [phr v T not usually in progressive] to very quickly and suddenly take something from the place where it is, especially to prevent someone from seeing or touching it **whisk away sth** *The waiter whisked away my plate before I'd finished.* | **whisk away** *As soon as the baby was born he was whisked away and put in an incubator.*

12 to put out your hand to take something

- reach for
- grab/snatch at

reach for /ˈriːtʃ fɔːʳ/ [phr v T not in passive] *I reached for the salt, and knocked over a bottle of wine.* | *There was a noise outside, and Bill reached for his flashlight.*

grab/snatch at /ˈgræb, ˈsnætʃ æt/ [phr v T not in passive] to suddenly put out your hand in order to take something: *I grabbed at the boy's collar as he ran past.* | *I snatched at the reins and managed to haul him to a halt.*

13 to take money out of a bank

- take/get out
- withdraw

take/get out /ˌteɪk, ˌget ˈaʊt/ [phr v T] **take/get out sth** *I took out $50 yesterday, and I spent it already.* | *She took out all her savings and bought a one-way ticket to Rio.* | *How much did you get out?* | **take/get sth out** *Stop if you see a cashpoint, I have to get some money out.* | *You know if I take $50 out, I'll spend $50.* | **take/get sth out of sth** *Someone stole my cheque book and started using it to get money out of my account.* | *Dad wanted to lend me the money, so I wouldn't have to take it out of my savings.*

withdraw /wɪðˈdrɔː, wɪθ-/ [v T] to take money out of your bank – use this in official or business contexts: *This card allows the user to withdraw money at any time of day.* | **withdraw sth from sth** *I withdrew $200 from my savings account.* — **withdrawal** [n C/U] *Customers can only make three withdrawals in one day.*

take part/ be involved

RELATED WORDS

- to join a club, organization etc *see* **join (7-10)**
- to try and influence a situation that you should not be involved in *see* **interfere**
- *see also* **join, do/not do, include/not include**

1 to take part in an event, activity, discussion etc

- take part
- be involved
- participate
- play a part/role
- be active in
- contribute
- appear on
- be engaged in
- hands-on

take part /ˌteɪk ˈpɑːʳt/ [v phrase] *She wanted to take part but she was too ill.* | *The program teaches children about conservation, and about 30 schools are taking part.* | **+ in** *Nearly 500 teams took part in the competition.* | *Police have arrested a number of people who took part in the riot.* | *She was asked to take part in a TV debate on drugs.* | **take an active/leading part** *John has taken an active part in getting artists together for the festival.*

be involved /biː ɪnˈvɒlvd‖-ˈvɑːlvd/ [v phrase] to take part in an activity with a small number of other people, often something bad or illegal: *Choosing a school is an important decision, and both parents ought to be involved.* | **+ in** *At least three politicians are involved in the scandal.* | *The two men have denied being involved in Troy's kidnapping and murder.* | *Roughly two-thirds of high school students are involved in volunteer community work.*

participate /pɑːʳˈtɪsəpeɪt/ [v I] formal to take part in an activity, especially an organized activity: *There are regular class discussions, but some of the students never participate.* | *Being a spectator wasn't as enjoyable as participating.* | **+ in** *Over 300 local firms participated in the survey.* | *Members can participate in any of the trips organized by the club.* | *Our employees are encouraged to participate in the decision making process.* —**participation** /pɑːʳˌtɪsəˈpeɪʃən/ [n U] when people participate: *The play was produced for children and encourages audience participation.* | **+ in** *Our partners are demanding full participation in the decision-making process.*

play a part/role /ˌpleɪ ə ˈpɑːʳt, ˈrəʊl/ [v phrase] to take part in some way in an activity or piece of work, especially one which has a useful result or purpose: *Our goal is to make sure everyone plays a part and shares in the credit.* | *Although the budget committees guide Congress's actions on spending, every committee plays a role.* | **+ in** *Hart clearly played a role in the decision to change admission standards.* | *Together with the police everyone can play a part in improving the security of their neighborhood.* | **play an active/large/important etc part/role** *Men now play a larger part in looking after their children.* | *The most effective learning occurs when the child is allowed to play a more active role in the learning process.* | *The Secretary of State played a leading role in the government's successful foreign policy.* | *Schneider played a key role in getting the organization started.*

be active in /biː ˈæktɪv ɪn/ [v phrase] to actively take part in the work of an organization such as a political group or church: *He is very active in the church's work with homeless people.* | *In school I was very active in sports and student government.* | *Allen, who is still on the board, is no longer active in the day-to-day management of the company.*

contribute /kənˈtrɪbjuːt/ [v I/T] to actively take part in a group discussion or group activity, especially by giving your opinions and ideas: *When we have class debates we try and get all the kids to contribute.* | *During the discussions MacDonald seemed to be listening, but he had nothing to contribute.* | **contribute ideas/suggestions etc** *Readers are invited to contribute their opinions on any of the issues discussed here.*

appear on /əˈpɪər ɒn/ [v phrase] to take part in a TV or radio programme: *Forbes appeared on 'Meet the Press' to discuss recent political developments.* | *He has often appeared on the BBC sports programme 'A Question of Sport'.* —**appearance** [n C] *The six-year-old's talents earned him an appearance on the Oprah Winfrey show.*

be engaged in /biː ɪnˈgeɪdʒd ɪn/ [v phrase] formal to be taking part in an activity, a conversation etc, especially one that continues for a long period of time: *The Nationalists have been engaged in a bitter fifteen-year armed struggle for independence.* | *During dinner I found myself engaged in a long complicated discussion with the doctor's wife.*

hands-on /ˌhændz ˈɒn◂/ [adj usually before noun] involving doing or learning about something by taking part in it yourself, rather than just watching, reading about it, or hearing about it from someone else: *The training programs give students practical hands-on experience.* | *The exhibit includes numerous hands-on activities, including several archaeological dig stations.* | *Mr. Garvey is known as a hands-on manager with an in-depth knowledge of the whole company.*

2 to start taking part

- join in
- get involved
- get in on the act
- jump/climb/hop/get on the bandwagon
- muscle in on
- get/enter into the spirit

join in /ˌdʒɔɪn ˈɪn/ [phr v I/T] to start taking part in something that other people are already doing, especially something enjoyable such as a game, or a song: *When we get to the chorus I want everybody to join in!* | *James joined in the discussion to say that he agreed with what had been said.* | **join in sth** *We all wanted to join in the fun.* | **+ with** *As a child, I was too shy to join in with the other children's games.*

get involved /ˌget ɪnˈvɒlvd‖-ˈvɑːlvd/ [v phrase] to start to take part in something, often something that will cause you problems or take a lot of your time: *It's a private matter between the two of them, and I don't think we should get involved.* | **+ in** *When did Anderson first get involved in local politics?* | *I don't want to get involved in an argument with you on the phone.* | *The US seemed unwilling to get involved in another war.*

get in on the act /get ˌɪn ɒn ði ˈækt/ [v phrase] informal to start to take part in something that is already successful, especially a new type of business that other companies are already involved in: *Now that our exporting business to Eastern Europe has grown so successful, everyone wants to get in on the act.* | *Movie theater chains are expanding rapidly, and even small local theaters are getting in on the act.*

jump/climb/hop/get on the bandwagon /ˌdʒʌmp, ˌklaɪm, ˌhɒp, get ɒn ðə ˈbændwægən‖ˌhɑːp-/ [v phrase] informal to start to take part in an activity because a lot of other people are doing it and not necessarily because you believe in it: *More and more Republicans are hopping on the tax bandwagon to attract more voters.* | *Critics of the government's environmental policies say it has simply jumped on the bandwagon and has not done anything serious to fight pollution.*

muscle in on /ˌmʌsəl ˈɪn ɒn/ [v T] informal to deliberately interfere in a plan, activity etc that other people are organizing so that you can have some of the advantages of that situation: *I'm not going to let Jim muscle in on this deal – let him do his own negotiations.* | *Two men were killed when members of a rival gang tried to muscle in on their territory.*

get/enter into the spirit /ˌget, ˌentər ɪntə ðə ˈspɪrət/ [v phrase] to relax and take part in a party, celebration, or special occasion: *This year Pat decided to get into the spirit and decorate her house for Halloween.* | *Although Mark felt depressed he did his best to enter into the spirit for Julie's sake.* | **+ of** *You'll enjoy yourself much more if you just relax and try to get into the spirit of the occasion.*

3 to take part in a competition, exam, course etc

- compete/take part
- enter
- sign up
- enrol

compete/take part /kəm'piːt, ˌteɪk 'pɑːʳt/ [v I/v phrase] to take part in a competition or race: *Only cars over 50 years old are allowed to compete.* | *The competition was a great success. Nearly two hundred people took part.* | **+ in** *How many runners will be competing in the marathon?* | *Please contact Debbie if you would like to take part in the charity swim.*

enter ALSO **go in for sth** British /ˌentəʳ, ˌgəʊ 'ɪn fəʳ (sth)/ [v I/T/phr v T] to say that you will take part in a competition or race, for example by putting your name on a list: *Only students under 18 can enter.* | *Dad says he's going in for the talent contest.* | *Jay and Cindy entered the dance competition for fun – they had no idea they would win.* | *We went in for the crossword competition and won twenty-five pounds.*

sign up /ˌsaɪn 'ʌp/ [phr v I] to arrange to take part in a course of study by signing an agreement: *Did you sign up yet? The course starts in two weeks, you know.* | **+ for** *Gary can't find a job, so he's signed up for Unemployment Training.* | **+ to do sth** *I signed up to take an art class just to get out of the house in the evenings.*

enrol British **/enroll** American /ɪn'rəʊl/ [v I/T] to formally arrange to take part in a course of study: *The course is very popular, so it's best to enrol as soon as possible.* | **+ on** British /+ in American *I'd like to enrol on the German course, please.* | *Bill enrolled in a four-year teacher-training course in Albany.* | **+ for** British *That year Sam enroled for law studies in Cape Town.* —**enrolment** British/**enrollment** American [n U] *Enrollment will take place tomorrow in the main hall between 10:00 and 5:00.*

4 to arrange for someone to take part in a competition, exam etc

- enter
- put sb's name down/put sb down
- enrol

enter /'entəʳ/ [v T] to arrange for a person or animal to take part in a competition, race, or examination **enter sb/sth in sth** *Your cats are beautiful, have you ever entered them in a cat show?* | *As part of his training program, Lauck has been entered in Sunday's race.* | **enter sb/sth for sth** *Eight horses were entered for the first race.*

put sb's name down/put sb down /ˌpʊt (sb's) 'neɪm ˌdaʊn, ˌpʊt (sb) 'daʊn/ [v phrase/phr v T] to arrange for someone to take part in an organized activity by writing their name on a list: *If you think Stan would be willing to look after the kids, put his name down.* | **+ for** *Put Nancy and her husband down for the banquet – I know they're planning to come.* | **+ to do sth** *Can we put you down to help with refreshments, Carol?*

enrol British **/enroll** American /ɪn'rəʊl/ [v T] to formally arrange for someone to take part in a course of study **+ on** British /+ in American *His parents enrolled him in a military academy when he was only 8.* | *Anybody who has not yet been enrolled on the English course should contact the tutor.*

5 to get involved with something you did not want to get involved in

- get caught up in
- get drawn into
- get/become embroiled in

get caught up in /get ˌkɔːt 'ʌp ɪn/ [v phrase] to get involved in something dangerous, unpleasant, or illegal, without wanting to or intending to do this: *I don't want to get caught up in some petty argument with you.* | *It is easy for young people to get caught up in crime when there are so few jobs.* | *One unlucky group of American tourists got caught up in the country's civil war.*

get drawn into /get ˌdrɔːn 'ɪntuː/ [v phrase] to gradually be persuaded to get involved in something that you did not intend to get involved in: *U.N. peacekeepers have gotten drawn into the fighting they were trying to prevent.* | *Children who end up on the street are likely to get drawn into prostitution and petty crime.*

get/become embroiled in /ˌget, bɪˌkʌm ɪm'brɔɪld ɪn/ [v phrase] to get involved in a long and complicated discussion, argument, or struggle which you do not want to get involved in: *The airline became embroiled in a six-month battle with the pilots' union.* | *I don't want to get embroiled in some endless argument over money.*

6 to make someone take part in something

- involve
- drag sb into
- bring in

involve /ɪn'vɒlv‖ɪn'vɑːlv/ [v T] to ask or encourage someone to take part in something, especially by encouraging them to do this: *I always try to involve the whole class.* | **involve sb in sth** *A good manager will try to involve everyone in the decision-making process.* | *The school has gained improved exam results by involving parents more in their children's education.*

drag sb into /ˌdræg (sb) 'ɪntuː/ [phr v T] to make someone become involved in a situation that they do not want to become involved in, for example an argument or a problem: *Don't go dragging me into your silly family arguments – sort it out yourself.* | *UN troops run the risk of being dragged into local policing problems.*

bring in /ˌbrɪŋ 'ɪn/ [phr v T] to involve someone in an activity that they were not involved in before, especially so that they can provide help or advice **bring in sb** *The President brought in Ken Khachigian to write a speech for the occasion.* | *The Japanese technicians were brought in because of their expertise in electronics.* | **bring sb in** *I don't think there's any need to bring the police in until we're sure the money is missing.*

7 to know about something secret or dishonest and take part in it

- be in on
- be (a) party to
- have a hand in (doing) sth
- collude

be in on /biː 'ɪn ɒn (sth)/ [v T] informal to take part in or know all about an illegal or secret activity: *Is it true that the Chief of Police was in on the cover-up?* | *Jones denies being in on the plan to blow up the building.* | *He didn't have a clue about the surprise party, but everyone in the office was in on it.*

be (a) party to /biː (ə) 'pɑːʳti tuː/ [v phrase] formal to take part in something which is illegal or wrong: *My clients do not want to be party to tax evasion.* | *Prosecutors proved she was in the house and was a party to the murder.*

have a hand in (doing) sth /hæv ə ˌhænd ɪn ('duːɪŋ) (sth)/ [v phrase not in progressive] to be in some way secretly involved in something and be partly responsible for its results: *He is a member of one of the extremist groups that may have had a hand in the murder.* | *Do they suspect the government of having a hand in it?* | *My father may have had a hand in getting me the job.*

collude /kə'luːd/ [v I] to know about and encourage something wrong that someone else is doing **+ in** *How far can women be said to be colluding in their own lower employment status?* | **+ with** *There have been accusations that the prime minister secretly colluded with the leaders of the regime.*

8 someone who takes part in something

- participant
- competitor
- entrant
- contestant
- entry
- involved
- player

participant /pɑːʳ'tɪsəpənt/ [n C] formal someone who takes part in an organized event or activity: *This summer's children's art program had 14 participants.* | *At the end of the conference, all the participants were asked to fill out a questionnaire.* | **+ in** *Reyes is an active participant in the protest movement.*

competitor /kəm'petətəʳ/ [n C] someone who takes part in a race, game, or competition: *One of the competitors hurt her leg during the race.* | *Twenty-seven competitors from around the country will take part in Sunday's monster truck rally.*

entrant /'entrənt/ [n C] formal someone who takes part in a competition: *Davis was selected from 200,000 entrants to win the trip to the Super Bowl.* | *The winning entrant will receive a scholarship to the famous college of art and a year's supply of artist's materials.*

contestant /kən'testənt/ [n C] someone who takes part in a competition or game, especially one that is judged by a group of judges: *Suzanne was a beauty-queen contestant in college.* | *The questions that contestants must answer get more difficult as the game goes on.*

entry /'entri/ [n C] the piece of work or answer which someone has sent to be judged in a competition: *All entries for the contest must be received by August 1.* | *Her entry in the 'Funniest Photo Contest' won third prize.* | *Organizers of the Lawson short story competition have received over 100,000 entries.*

involved /ɪn'vɒlvd‖ɪn'vɑːlvd/ [adj only after noun] the people **involved** are the people who are taking part or who took part in an activity or event: *In court she gave evidence about her torture, naming the officers involved.* | *Most of the people involved have by now either died or moved away.* | *Following the riots, the university promised to discipline all those involved.*

player /'pleɪəʳ/ [n C] someone who takes part in a game: *Up to six players can play this game on-line.* | *It's now the turn of player number three.*

9 to not take part in something

- not take part/not participate
- take/have/play no part in
- withdraw
- pull/drop out
- opt out
- have nothing to do with
- take no further part in
- armchair
- on the sidelines

not take part/not participate /nɒt teɪk 'pɑːʳt, nɒt pɑːʳ'tɪsəpeɪt/ [v phrase] *The President was invited to appear on the program but decided not to take part.* | *We tried to include Reggie in the conversation, but he didn't participate.* | **+ in** *Party leaders have said they will not take part in the election.* | *She said that she didn't participate in the games because her shoulder was sore.*

take/have/play no part in /ˌteɪk, ˌhæv, ˌpleɪ nəʊ 'pɑːʳt ɪn/ [v phrase] formal to deliberately not take part in something, because you disagree with it or think it is wrong: *They were pacifists and would take no part in the war.* | *Jen would have no part in forcing Gwen out of her job.* | *I played no part in leaking the information to the press.*

withdraw /wɪð'drɔː, wɪθ-/ [v I] to decide not to take part in a competition, race, discussion etc, which you previously agreed to take part in: *Bower was leading in the polls, but he withdrew when the scandal hit the press.* | **+ from** *Clare had to withdraw from the race after injuring her knee.* | *It will be very sad if Jordan withdraws from politics altogether.*

pull/drop out /ˌpʊl, ˌdrɒp 'aʊt‖ˌdrɑːp-/ [phr v I] informal to suddenly decide not to take part in something, that has already started or is about to start, especially when this causes problems: *The show was cancelled when the star unexpectedly pulled out.* | *By the end of the semester about half of the students had dropped out.* | **+ of** *It's too late to pull out of the agreement now.* | *Most of the other Democratic candidates had already dropped out of the presidential race.*

opt out /ˌɒpt 'aʊt‖ˌɑːpt-/ [phr v I] to decide not to take part in an official system, especially one that has not started yet: *Employees who do not wish to be part of the company's healthcare program can opt out if they want to.* | **+ of** *The treaty gave Britain the right to opt out of the single European currency system.*

have nothing to do with /hæv ˌnʌθɪŋ tə 'duː wɪð/ [v phrase not in progressive] to not be involved in any way in something bad or illegal – use this especially when other people think that you were involved: *I'm sure that Tony had nothing to do with the robbery.* | *Connie had nothing to do with the break-up of my marriage.* | *The editor pointed out that he had nothing to do with the discredited advertising campaign.*

take no further part in /teɪk ˌnəʊ fɜːʳðəʳ 'pɑːʳt ɪn/ [v phrase] to stop taking part in something that you were actively involved in before: *Lineker was injured and took no further part in the game.* | *Schmidt's lawyer said that he would take no further part in the trial.*

armchair /'ɑːʳmtʃeəʳ, ˌɑːʳm'tʃeəʳ/ [adj only before noun] an **armchair** critic, sportsman, revolutionary etc is someone who does not take part in politics, sport etc but who reads a lot about it or watches it on television, especially someone who thinks they know better than the people doing it and is ready to give them advice: *It's very easy to be an armchair critic but much harder to come up with solutions that will work.* | *Armchair travellers can now visit the world's most exotic countries via the Internet.* | *Like most* *armchair sportsmen, Terry is sure he understands the game better than the referees.*

on the sidelines /ɒn ðə ˈsaɪdlaɪnz/ [adv] if you stay, sit, or wait **on the sidelines** when something is happening, you do not take part in it, even though you may want to or should do: *You can't just wait on the sidelines and hope things will improve.* | *How can we sit on the sidelines when thousands of innocent civilians are being killed.*

10 to not let someone take part

- leave out
- exclude
- drop

leave out /ˌliːv ˈaʊt/ [phr v T] to not include someone in an activity or in a group **leave sb out** *I can't believe she invited everyone else in the office and left me out.* | **leave out sb** *We meant to include everyone, but we accidentally left out three members.* | **leave sb out of sth** *Her husband was always leaving her out of his plans.*

exclude /ɪkˈskluːd/ [v T] to prevent someone from taking part in an activity, or from joining a group: *Joe felt sure the others were speaking Russian simply to exclude him.* | **exclude sb from sth** *The Catholic church continues to exclude women from the priesthood.* | *Stack belongs to a country club that once excluded blacks and Jews from membership.* —**exclusion** /ɪkˈskluːʒən/ [n U] **the exclusion of sb from sth** *The exclusion of minorities from the film industry is one of Hollywood's dirty little secrets.*

drop /drɒp‖drɑːp/ [v T] to decide that someone can no longer be in a team: *He couldn't run fast enough, so the coach dropped him.* | **drop sb from sth** *She was dropped from the badminton team because she missed practice too often.*

11 when you do not want to take part in something

- want no part in
- want nothing to do with
- count/leave me out

want no part in British **/want no part of sth** American /ˌwɒnt nəʊ ˈpɑːʳt ɪn, ˌwɒnt nəʊ ˈpɑːʳt əv (sth) ‖ˌwɑːnt-/ [v phrase not in progressive] to not want to take part at all in a plan or activity, especially because you disapprove of it: *I want no part in the deal if drugs are involved.* | *The Foundation's conservative leadership made it clear it wanted no part of anything controversial.*

want nothing to do with /wɒnt ˌnʌθɪŋ tə ˈduː wɪð‖wɑːnt-/ [v phrase not in progressive] to not want to take part in or be involved with something, especially because you disapprove of it: *'Is Robert going to help?' 'No, he wants nothing more to do with it.'* | *A large part of the membership wants nothing to do with the protests and demonstrations.*

count/leave me out /ˌkaʊnt, ˌliːv: miː ˈaʊt/ [v phrase] spoken say this when you do not want to take part in something which has been suggested: *If that's what you're going to do, you can count me out.* | *Leave me out. I'd be crazy to get involved in something like that.* | **leave me out of it** *You two have to settle it between yourselves – leave me out of it.*

talk

WHAT'S HERE

- **to talk to sb** see **1 to 17**
- **to make a speech** see **18 to 19**

to talk to sb

RELATED WORDS

- *see also* **say, speak, tell, discuss, mention, contact, interrupt**

1 to talk to someone

- talk
- speak
- say something
- chat
- have a conversation
- be in conversation
- make conversation/make small talk
- visit
- converse
- chat/live chat

talk /tɔːk/ [v I] to say something to someone, or have a conversation: *We sat around talking for hours.* | *two friends talking on the phone* | **+ about** *They talked about their favourite pop stars.* | **+ to** *Danny was talking to a girl he'd just met at the bar.* | *It's been nice talking to you.* | **talk with sb** American *I left Mario talking with my mother.*

speak /spiːk/ [v I] to talk to someone. **Speak** is more formal than **talk**: *The brothers haven't spoken since the funeral.* | **+ to** *There's a man from the Times on the phone who wants to speak to you.* | *I spoke to a few people at the party who knew him.*

say something /ˈseɪ sʌmθɪŋ/ [v phrase] *Did you say something? Sorry – I wasn't listening.* | *No one said anything.* | *The older woman said something in Spanish.* | **+ about** *I can remember him saying something about his mother being ill.* | **+ to** *Pradeep could hear her saying something to the nurse.*

chat /tʃæt/ [v I] especially British to talk in a friendly and informal way, especially about things that are not very important: *The girls were sitting on the steps, chatting.* | **+ about** *We drank our coffee and chatted about our experiences.* | **+ with/to** *Harry chatted to a couple of Australian tourists as we waited for the show to begin.*

have a conversation /hæv ə ˌkɒnvəʳˈseɪʃən‖-ˌkɑːn-/ [v phrase] to talk to someone for a period of time: *Could we just sit down and have a normal conversation without shouting?* | **+ about** *We were sitting around the kitchen table having a conversation about food and restaurants.*

be in conversation /biː ɪn ˌkɒnvəʳˈseɪʃən‖-ˌkɑːn-/ [v phrase] to be having a conversation, especially one that takes all your attention **+ with** *When I arrived, Diana was already in animated conversation with Mr Summers.* | **be deep in conversation** (=so that you do not notice what is happening around you) *The two men were deep in conversation as they walked up the path.*

make conversation/make small talk /ˌmeɪk kɒnvəʳˈseɪʃən‖-kɑːn-, meɪk ˈsmɔːl tɔːk/ [v phrase] to make an effort to have a conversation with someone, just in order to seem friendly or polite: *I tried to make small talk, but Darden wasn't interested.* | *'Why did you tell her that?' 'I was just making conversation.'* | **make polite conversation** *Sheila was* *sitting next to the boss's wife and felt obliged to make polite conversation.*

visit /ˈvɪzɪt/ [v I] American informal to talk in a relaxed way to someone you know well: *Mom and Aunt Jo were sitting drinking coffee and visiting.* | **+ with** *I don't see him that often, but I like to go and visit with him when I can.*

converse /kənˈvɜːʳs/ [v I] formal to have a conversation: *We met once and conversed briefly. That was the extent of our acquaintance.* | **+ with** *The conference gave me an opportunity to meet and converse with VIPs in relaxed surroundings.*

chat/live chat /tʃæt, ˌlaɪv ˈtʃæt/ [n U] when people talk to each other using the Internet by typing in what they want to say and having this sent immediately to someone using a computer in a different place: *On-line chat is becoming an increasingly popular way for young people to make new friends.* | *Log on to live chat this evening and put your questions to your favourite pop stars.*

2 to talk to someone about a problem, plan, or serious subject

- talk
- discuss
- speak to
- have a talk
- have a conversation
- talk over
- have a word with
- have a heart-to-heart talk/heart-to-heart
- talk shop
- talk turkey

talk /tɔːk/ [v I] *I think we need to talk.* | **+ about** *If you're having trouble at school, let's sit down and talk about it.* | **+ to** *Gerry wants to talk to his girlfriend before he makes a decision.* | **+ with** American *It's important to talk with your kids about drugs, alcohol, and sex.*

discuss /dɪˈskʌs/ [v T] if people **discuss** a subject or situation, they exchange ideas and opinions about it, so it is easier to make a decision or make plans: *The whole family got together to discuss funeral arrangements.* | *We never discuss our financial difficulties in front of the children.* | **+ what/how/where etc** *We need to discuss what kind of food we want at the party.* | **discuss sth with sb** *Don't make any plans yet – I want to discuss this with Jamie first.*

speak to ALSO **speak with** American /ˈspiːk tuː, ˈspiːk wɪð/ [phr v T] to talk to someone about something serious or official: *Maybe it's time for you to speak to a lawyer.* | *The woman had come all the way from Denver to speak with the President.* | **+ about** *I intend to speak to the manager about the way I have been treated.* | *Have you spoken with Michael about the scheduling conflict?*

have a talk /ˌhæv ə ˈtɔːk/ [v phrase] to talk to someone seriously about something you have planned to discuss, especially about a problem or future plans: *Don and I had a long talk, and I think we understand each other better now.* | **+ about** *I think it's time we had a talk about your future here in the company.* | **+ with** *If this behavior continues, I'm going to have to have a little talk with her.* | *Someone should have a serious talk with Lucy about the amount of alcohol she drinks.*

have a conversation /hæv ə ˌkɒnvəʳˈseɪʃən‖-ˌkɑːn-/ [v phrase] to talk to someone for a period of time about a serious subject: *The two leaders had a brief conversation yesterday.* | **+ with** *I've had conversations with several employers who say there are not enough qualified people to fill the jobs they have.* | **+ about** *We need to have a conversation with our lawyers about the will.*

talk over /ˌtɔːk ˈəʊvəʳ/ [phr v T] to talk to someone about all the details of a serious problem or difficult situation, in order to understand it better **talk sth over** *If you're worried about your work, come and see me and we'll talk it over.* | **talk over sth** *I took him out to dinner so we could talk over the problem.* | **talk sth over with sb** *It's often useful to talk things over with a trained counsellor.*

have a word with /ˌhæv ə ˈwɜːʳd wɪð/ [v phrase] to talk to someone quickly, and usually privately, about something serious: *His attitude got so bad his manager was forced to have a word with him.* | *Jim had a word with Mary, and she took the children out of the room.* | **I'd like (to have) a word with you** *I'd like a word with you in private.*

have a heart-to-heart talk/a heart-to-heart /ˌhæv ə ˌhɑːʳt tə hɑːʳt ˈtɔːk, ə ˌhɑːʳt tə ˈhɑːʳt/ [v phrase] to have a private conversation in which two people both say honestly and sincerely what they feel about something personal: *Don't go in there right now – I think Dean and Carlo are having a heart-to-heart.* | **+ with** *If you think your boss doesn't like you, have a heart-to-heart talk with her.*

talk shop /ˌtɔːk ˈʃɒp‖-ˈʃɑːp/ [v phrase] if two or more people who do the same work **talk shop**, they have a conversation about their work on a social occasion: *I don't want to go out to dinner with him and his lawyer friends – all they ever do is talk shop.*

talk turkey /ˌtɔːk ˈtɜːʳki/ [v phrase] American informal to talk seriously and honestly about matters that need to be agreed, especially business matters: *OK, enough joking around – let's talk turkey.*

3 to start a conversation

- get talking/chatting
- fall into conversation/strike up a conversation

get talking/chatting British **/get to talking** American /ˌget ˈtɔːkɪŋ, ˈtʃætɪŋ, ˌget tə ˈtɔːkɪŋ/ [v phrase] *The three of us sat down and after a while we got chatting.* | **+ to** *I hadn't been there long before someone got talking to me and invited me to a party.* | **+ about** *Somehow we got to talking about television shows from the '70s.*

fall into conversation/strike up a conversation ALSO **get into conversation** British /ˌfɔːl ɪntə kɒnvəʳˈseɪʃən, ˌstraɪk ʌp ə ˌkɒnvəʳˈseɪʃən, ˌget ɪntə kɒnvəʳˈseɪʃən‖-kɑːn-/ [v phrase] to start having a conversation with a stranger, often without intending or expecting to: *After a while the two travellers fell into conversation.* | **+ with** *She got into conversation with a woman at the baker's shop.* | *My Dad's always striking up conversations with other people in the park.*

4 to talk to someone for a long time about unimportant things

- gossip
- chatter
- natter
- pass the time of day
- shoot the breeze

gossip /ˈgɒsɪp‖ˈgɑː-/ [v I] to spend time talking to someone, especially someone you are friendly with, about things that are not particularly serious or important: *Cocteau's jazz club was the spot where artists gossiped and drank.* | **+ with** *I wasn't doing anything important – just gossiping with a neighbour.*

chatter /ˈtʃætəʳ/ [v I] to talk continuously for a long time about unimportant things – used especially in literature: *The tiny gray-haired woman chattered continuously as she demonstrated how to make a tortilla.* | **+ with** *They poured out of the school chattering with their friends.* | **+ about** *Michele sat there chattering about her minor ailments to anyone who would listen.* | **+ away/on** (=continuously) *I could hear the boys chattering away in the other room.*

natter /ˈnætəʳ/ [v I] British informal if two people **natter**, they talk continuously for a long time about unimportant things **+ with** *I can't stand about nattering all day with you* | **+ about** *Keith and Tom were nattering about cars and not doing a stroke of work.*

pass the time of day /ˌpɑːs ðə taɪm əv ˈdeɪ‖ˌpæs-/ [v phrase] to have a short, friendly conversation about unimportant things with someone you know, especially when you meet them by chance: *I just thought I'd stop by and pass the time of day.* | **+ with** *Whenever we met in the street, Mr. Kelly would stop and pass the time of day with me.*

shoot the breeze /ˌʃuːt ðə ˈbriːz/ [v phrase] American informal to have an informal conversation about unimportant things: *The men spent their evenings on the porch, shooting the breeze.* | **+ with** *Hemingway came into the bar almost every morning to read the papers, shoot the breeze with the regulars, and enjoy bracing double daiquiris.*

5 a conversation

- conversation
- chat
- small talk

conversation /ˌkɒnvəʳˈseɪʃən‖ˌkɑːn-/ [n C/U] when people talk to each other, especially in an informal situation: *Martha's a fascinating woman. I really enjoyed our conversation.* | *The noise of the traffic made conversation almost impossible.* | *They didn't realize someone was taping their telephone conversation.* | **+ with** *I was too shy to start a conversation with anyone there.* | **have a conversation** *Vicky was having a long conversation with the bartender.* | **topic of conversation** *Baker's resignation became a hot topic of conversation around the office.* | **come up in conversation** (=be mentioned as part of the conversation) *Every time his father's name came up in conversation, Tom became nervous.*

chat /tʃæt/ [n C] especially British an informal, friendly conversation: *He didn't want anything in particular. He just stopped for a chat.* | *Mary took Tina in the other room for a private chat.* | **have a chat** *I'm actually glad you're late – it gave Ken and me a chance to have a good chat.*

small talk /ˈsmɔːl tɔːk/ [n U] the kind of conversation in which people talk about unimportant things in order to be polite or to avoid serious subjects: *Most of what gets said at parties is just small talk.* | **make small talk** *Heath doesn't waste time making small talk – he comes straight to the point.*

6 to talk about other people's private lives

- gossip
- talk
- talk about sb behind their back
- tongues are wagging

▸ *see also* **rumour**

gossip /ˈgɒsəp‖ˈgɑː-/ [v I] to spend time talking without a serious purpose, usually about other people's private lives or behaviour: *It's best not to tell Frank anything. You know how he gossips.* | **+ about** *Those two old ladies sit there every day, gossiping about everyone in town.* —**gossip** [n U] *The public never seems to tire of Hollywood gossip.* | *I heard an interesting piece of gossip about Beth Ann.*

talk /tɔːk/ [v I] if you say that people **talk**, you mean that they **talk** about other people's private lives and behaviour, usually in a disapproving way: *We mustn't be seen together in public again. People are starting to talk.*

talk about sb behind their back /ˌtɔːk əbaʊt (sb) bɪˌhaɪnd ðeəʳ ˈbæk/ [v phrase] to talk about someone when they are not present: *I hate people who talk about you behind your back and then pretend to be nice to you when they meet you.*

tongues are wagging /ˌtʌŋz əʳ ˈwægɪŋ/ used for saying that many people are talking about someone's private life in an unkind or disapproving way: *Tongues are wagging about Hollywood's newest couple.* | **set tongues wagging** (=cause people to start talking about you) *Thurmond's marriage so soon after his wife died set tongues wagging.*

7 to talk too much about a particular thing

- go on
- harp on
- labour/belabour the point
- hold forth

go on ALSO **keep on** British /ˌgəʊ ˈɒn, ˌkiːp ˈɒn/ [phr v I] especially spoken to keep talking or complaining about something, in a way that is annoying or boring **+ about** *I wish you'd stop going on about how expensive everything is.* | *Lucy keeps on about little things that happened in the past until I want to scream.* | **go on and on** (=keep talking for a long time) *He went on and on until we were all practically asleep.*

harp on /ˈhɑːʳp ɒn/ [v I/T] to keep mentioning something in a way that other people find annoying: *Stop harping on the weather – we can't change it.* | **+ about** *If you harp on about their bad habits too long, the kids will just stop listening.*

labour/belabour the point British **/belabor the point** American /ˌleɪbəʳ, bɪˌleɪbəʳ ðə ˈpɔɪnt/ [v phrase] to express the same idea again and again with the intention of making it clear, but with the result that people get bored: *Everyone agrees with what you said – there's no need to belabor the point.* | *If the students aren't listening it may be because the teacher is labouring the point too much.*

hold forth /ˌhəʊld ˈfɔːʳθ/ [v phrase] to talk to a group of people you are with, giving your opinions or telling a story in a way that does not let other people have a chance to talk – use this when you think the situation is slightly humorous: *Grandma was holding forth as usual, retelling all the old family stories.* | **+ about/on** *Tom was in the corner, holding forth about the economic situation.* | *After a few drinks, he would hold forth for hours on government conspiracy theories.*

8 to talk for a long time in a confused or boring way

- ramble
- babble
- waffle
- witter on/rabbit on
- windbag/gasbag
- long-winded

ramble /ˈræmbəl/ [v I] to talk for too long in a confused way, changing the subject and forgetting what you have already said: *The trouble is once Dad gets started on a subject, he tends to ramble.* | **+ on** *Ida* *rambled on, but Anna wasn't listening to her.* | **+ about** *He was a little drunk and kept rambling on about the good old days.*

babble /'bæbəl/ [v I/T] to talk quickly and in a confused way so that you seem slightly silly, especially because you are nervous: *Don't pay any attention to her – she's just babbling.* | **+ on** *He babbled on and on until everyone had left the room.* | **+ about** *He was running around babbling about someone named Tulkeke.*

waffle /'wɒfəl‖'wɑː-/ [v I] British to talk for a long time without making your meaning clear and without really saying anything useful or important: *He didn't know what he was talking about – he was just waffling.* | *Interviewers dislike candidates who just sit there and waffle instead of answering the questions.* —**waffle** [n U] *There was a lot of polite waffle about how well the Princess and her family were looking before anyone got to the point.*

witter on/rabbit on /ˌwɪtər 'ɒn, ˌræbɨt 'ɒn / [phr v I] British informal to talk for a long time about something in a stupid and boring way: *It doesn't matter what she's talking about – she'll witter on for hours.* | *George just rabbited on, boring everyone to death with his silly nonsense.*

windbag/gasbag /'wɪndbæg, 'gæsbæg/ [n C usually singular] informal someone who talks too much, especially in a very boring way: *What a gasbag that Mrs Jenkins is! I've been stuck with her for over an hour.* | *There's a bunch of old windbags on the town council who don't know when to shut up.*

long-winded /ˌlɒŋ 'wɪndɨd◂‖ˌlɔːŋ-/ [adj] someone who is **long-winded** takes a long time to say something that they could say in a shorter time, which makes other people bored and impatient: *One long-winded speaker after another came to the podium.* | *Dad can be so long-winded sometimes, I cringe when he starts talking to someone new.*

9 to talk to someone in a way that shows you are attracted to them

- flirt
- chat up

flirt /flɜːʳt/ [v I] to talk to and behave towards someone as though you are sexually attracted to them, so that they will pay attention to you: *She was flirting and trying to get the waiter's attention.* | **+ with** *It embarrasses me when you flirt with other women in front of me.* | *No one had flirted with me in years, and I didn't really know how to respond.*

chat up /ˌtʃæt 'ʌp/ [phr v T] British to talk to someone in a way that shows you are sexually attracted to them, in order to try and make them interested in you **chat sb up** *I'm not in the mood to go to bars and wait for sad men to try to chat me up.* | **chat up sb** *When I left the party Kelly was still chatting up that tall guy in the kitchen.*

10 to talk to yourself

- talk to yourself
- think aloud/think out loud

talk to yourself /ˌtɔːk tə jɔːʳ'self/ [v phrase] *I think he's going crazy – he talks to himself all the time.* | *Betty was talking to herself under her breath as she worked.*

think aloud/think out loud /ˌθɪŋk ə'laʊd, ˌθɪŋk aʊt 'laʊd/ [v phrase] to say aloud what you are thinking, without meaning to talk to anyone else: *'I don't follow you.' 'That's OK. I'm just thinking out loud.'* | *She began to think aloud as she always did when she was faced with a difficult problem.*

11 to talk to someone as if they were stupid

- patronize
- talk down to

patronize ALSO **patronise** British /'pætrənaɪz‖'peɪ-, 'pæ-/ [v T] *Kids don't like to be patronized any more than adults do.* | *Just because you're older than me, it doesn't give you the right to patronize me.* —**patronizing** [adj] *a patronizing tone of voice* | *Don't be so patronizing with me.*

talk down to /ˌtɔːk 'daʊn tuː/ [phr v T] *I always get the feeling that repairmen are talking down to me, as if I don't know anything.* | *Krasny never talks down to his audience, assuming they can keep up with complex legal arguments.*

12 someone who talks a lot or too much

- talkative
- chatty
- chatterbox
- can talk the hind leg off a donkey
- gossip

talkative /'tɔːkətɪv/ [adj] someone who is **talkative** talks a lot: *The wine was making her more relaxed and talkative.* | *Somehow I always end up alone in a room with my talkative aunt.*

chatty /'tʃæti/ [adj] liking to talk a lot in a friendly way: *Nobles is a chatty, energetic 55-year-old.* | *The nurses at the hospital were pleasant and chatty, and they made me feel less nervous.*

chatterbox /'tʃætəʳbɒks‖-bɑːks/ [n C] informal someone, especially a child, who talks a lot in a friendly way: *Cathy's a real chatterbox – she's very friendly, but all that talking can wear you out.*

can talk the hind leg off a donkey British **/talks a blue streak** American /kən ˌtɔːk ðə ˌhaɪnd leg ɒf ə 'dɒŋki‖-'dɑːŋki, tɔːks ə ˌbluː 'striːk/ [v phrase] informal to talk a lot without stopping: *Once old Mulrooney got started there was no stopping him – that man could talk the hind leg off a donkey.* | *Annie had had too much to drink and was talking a blue streak.*

gossip /'gɒsɨp‖'gɑː-/ [n C] someone who likes talking about other people's private lives and behaviour: *Don't tell him anything private – he's a terrible gossip.* | *The town gossips had been spreading rumours about Bruce for months.*

13 someone who does not talk much

- quiet
- silent
- taciturn
- a man/woman of few words
- reticent

▸ *see also* **shy, quiet**

quiet /'kwaɪət/ [adj] someone who is **quiet** does not talk much. **Quiet** can be used generally about someone's character, or about a particular situation in which someone does not talk: *The new girl's quiet, but nice enough.* | *Steven's a very quiet boy who loves reading.* | *Tyrell was quiet early in the evening, but as he got to know us, he really opened up.*

silent /'saɪlənt/ [adj] written if someone is **silent**, they do not say anything. **Silent** is used before the noun if you are talking about someone's general character, and after the verb if you are talking about a particular situation: *Mrs. Welland was a mild silent woman with no strong opinions.* | **be/remain/stay silent** *Alice was laughing and joking, but her sister remained silent.*

taciturn /ˈtæsətɜːʳn/ [adj] formal someone who is **taciturn** usually does not talk much, so that they may seem a little unfriendly or bad-tempered: *The ship's captain was a taciturn man who spoke only to give orders.* | *It was unlike her to be so taciturn – she must have had something on her mind.*

a man/woman of few words /ə ˌmæn, ˌwʊmən əv ˌfjuː ˈwɜːʳdz/ [n phrase] someone who usually does not talk much, because they only speak when there is something important to say: *My father was a man of few words, but when he spoke everyone listened.* | *Neighbors remember her as a woman of few words whom everyone respected.*

reticent /ˈretəsənt/ [adj] unwilling to talk to other people or unwilling to talk about a particular subject: *Irma was a shy and reticent child.* | **+ about** *Auster was somewhat reticent about it at first, but finally admitted he was working on a new book.* —**reticence** [n U] *His reticence with strangers was sometimes interpreted as unfriendliness.*

14 to stop talking

- go quiet
- break off
- fall silent

go quiet /gəʊ ˈkwaɪət/ [v phrase] *She was happy to talk about her school and friends, but when I asked her about her parents, she went quiet.* | *Gerard suddenly realized that the people at the next table had gone quiet and were staring at them.*

break off /ˌbreɪk ˈɒf/ [phr v I/T] to suddenly stop talking without finishing what you were saying: *'It's not that I wanted to ...' he broke off and sighed.* | *Kathleen was just telling me about her new car when she suddenly broke off and ran to the window.* | **break off sth** *I was sorry to break off his conversation with Margaret, but I had to leave.*

fall silent /ˌfɔːl ˈsaɪlənt/ [v phrase] written to suddenly stop talking, especially because something has happened to make you feel afraid, sad etc: *'Explain yourself,' Mr O'Conner demanded. Paul fell silent, staring hard at the floor.* | *Everyone in the room fell silent, and Miss Rogers dozed peacefully her chair.*

15 what you say to someone to tell them to stop talking

- be quiet
- quiet down
- silence
- shut up

be quiet /biː ˈkwaɪət/ spoken say this when you want someone to stop talking: *Please be quiet for a moment.* | *Be quiet – I'm on the phone.* | *Just be quiet and let me finish the story.*

quiet down /ˌkwaɪət ˈdaʊn/ spoken say this when you want a group of people, especially a group you are in charge of, to stop talking: *All right, everybody, quiet down – we're about to stop.* | *Quiet down! I can't hear the TV.*

silence /ˈsaɪləns/ formal spoken used in formal situations, especially by someone in authority to tell people to be completely quiet: *Silence in court!* | *Silence! Will you please let the honourable Member finish what he is saying.*

shut up /ˌʃʌt ˈʌp/ spoken say this to rudely tell someone to stop talking: *Just shut up and listen to me.* | *Hey, shut up down there! We're trying to sleep.* | *No one wants to listen to you – why don't you shut up and sit down.*

16 to not talk about a particular subject

- not talk about
- not say anything about
- not mention
- keep off the subject/question of sth
- drop the subject/drop it
- steer clear of
- keep silent/quiet about
- gloss over

▸ *see also* **avoid**

not talk about /nɒt ˈtɔːk əbaʊt/ [v phrase] *It's been three months, but he won't talk about the accident.* | *She doesn't talk about her husband half as much as she did when he first died.* | *I don't know what my parents think about my living here – we never talk about it.*

not say anything about /nɒt seɪ ˈeniθɪŋ əˌbaʊt/ [v phrase] to not talk about something, because it could be embarrassing or difficult, or just because you did not think about talking about it: *Didn't she say anything about the party?* | *Don't say anything about the divorce – it will only upset her.* | *The company's policy is not to say anything about former employees other than to give their period of employment.*

not mention /nɒt ˈmenʃən/ [v T] to not talk about something, even for a short time or carelessly: *We were careful not to mention her son's legal problems.* | *He doesn't mention Cathy anymore when he writes – I wonder if they broke up?* | **+ (that)** *I didn't mention that we were going to the movies in front of John.*

keep off the subject/question of sth /ˌkiːp ɒf ðə ˈsʌbdʒɪkt, ˈkwestʃən əv (sth)/ [phr v T] to deliberately not talk about something, especially because the subject could be embarrassing or difficult: *I normally keep off the subject of ex-girlfriends on a first date.* | *Unless the interviewer asks you directly, keep off the question of why you left your last job.*

drop the subject/drop it /ˌdrɒp ðə ˈsʌbdʒɪkt, ˈdrɒp ɪt‖ˌdrɑːp-/ [v phrase] to deliberately stop talking about a particular subject, especially because it is embarrassing, upsetting, or annoying someone: *'You'll never get me to believe that!' she screeched, so I just nodded and dropped the subject.* | *Can we just drop the subject? I'm sick of hearing about it.* | *Look, just drop it, OK? I understood you the first time.*

steer clear of /ˌstɪəʳ ˈklɪər ɒv/ [v phrase] to deliberately not talk about something, especially because the subject could be embarrassing or difficult: *We try to steer clear of controversial issues in the workshops.* | *Her press agent asked the interviewer to steer clear of questions about her love life.*

keep silent/quiet about /ˌkiːp ˈsaɪlənt, ˈkwaɪət əbaʊt/ [v phrase] to not talk about an event or situation from the past for a long time, especially because it is very difficult to talk about: *He had kept silent about the murder for ten years before he went to the police.* | *They said they'd kill her if she didn't keep quiet about what she'd seen.*

gloss over /ˌglɒs ˈəʊvəʳ‖ˌglɔːs-/ [phr v T] if you **gloss over** unpleasant facts, you deliberately avoid talking about them or you only mention them quickly and without giving much detail: *It seems to me he was glossing over some major risks of the plan.* | *In a job interview you should highlight your strengths and gloss over your weaknesses.*

17 when people who have argued do not talk to each other

- not be talking/speaking
- not be on speaking terms
- send sb to Coventry
- the silent treatment

not be talking/speaking /nɒt biː ˈtɔːkɪŋ, ˈspiːkɪŋ/ [v phrase] *'Have you seen Tim lately?' 'No, we're not talking at the moment.'* | *When Claire and Andy aren't speaking, she usually calls me up to complain.*

not be on speaking terms /nɒt biː ɒn ˈspiːkɪŋ ˌtɜːʳmz/ [v phrase] if two people **are not on speaking terms**, their relationship has become so unfriendly that they refuse to talk to each other: *She wasn't on speaking terms with Rachel for several weeks afterwards.* | *By the end of the year, the two old friends were no longer on speaking terms.*

send sb to Coventry /ˌsend (sb) tə ˈkɒvəntri‖-ˈkɑːv-/ [v phrase] British if a group of people **send** someone **to Coventry**, they refuse to talk to that person as a way of punishing them for something: *I don't know why they won't talk to me. I didn't know I'd been sent to Coventry.* | *When he refused to join the strike, Joe's mates sent him to Coventry for three weeks.*

the silent treatment /ðə ˈsaɪlənt ˌtriːtmənt/ [v phrase] when one person does not talk to another person, usually to show that they are angry: *My sister tried the silent treatment on me, but I just ignored her.* | **give sb the silent treatment** *On the ride home, Vance's father gave him the silent treatment.*

to make a speech

18 when someone makes a speech

- speech
- talk
- speak
- talk
- address
- public speaking
- presentation

speech /spiːtʃ/ [n C] a formal situation, for example at a meeting or ceremony, in which you talk to a group of people about a particular subject, usually when you have planned and practised what you are going to say: *She left early to write her speech for the next day.* | *In her speech, Bauer proposed major changes in the welfare system.* | **+ about/on** *The senator's speech on farm subsidies did not attract a large audience.* | **make/give a speech** *To start with, the governor made a short speech welcoming the visiting dignitaries.*

talk /tɔːk/ [n C] a planned, but not very formal speech about a particular subject, for example at a meeting or on the radio: *There's an interesting series of talks by well-known writers on the radio this week.* | **+ on/about** *You should have heard Dr Cooper's talk on his trip to India – it was fascinating.* | **give a talk** *A researcher from our division gave a talk today about recent advances in cancer treatment.* | **give a talk to sb** *Alice Walker has been invited to give a talk to the literary group this evening.*

speak /spiːk/ [v I] to make a formal speech: *I've been invited to speak at the party's annual convention.* | *Who are they getting to speak at this year's graduation ceremony?* | **+ to** *Speaking to Congress, the President appealed for cooperation in dealing with the sagging economy.* | **+ on/about** *At the convention Ford spoke on immigration and social issues.*

talk /tɔːk/ [v I] to speak publicly to a group of people about a particular subject **+ about** *This evening Professor Welch will be talking about Shakespeare's historical plays.* | **+ to** *Powell talked to a group of industry leaders in Atlanta on Tuesday.*

address /əˈdres/ [v T] formal to make a speech to a large group of people **address a group/meeting/crowd/conference etc** *Rifkind addressed a news conference before leaving for Beijing yesterday.* | *Three Republican candidates addressed a group of 500 senior citizens concerning tax cuts.*

public speaking /ˌpʌblɪk ˈspiːkɪŋ/ [n U] the activity or art of making speeches in public: *The course I took in public speaking has really improved my self-confidence.* | *Executives in big companies need to have excellent public speaking skills.*

presentation /ˌprezənˈteɪʃən‖ˌpriːzen-, -zən-/ [n C] to give a talk for your company about something such as a new product or business idea: *The presentation went extremely well, with almost all of the audience requesting further information about our proposals.* | **give a presentation** *I was supposed to be giving a presentation that morning to some colleagues from the Japanese division.*

19 someone who makes a speech

- speaker
- orator

speaker /ˈspiːkəʳ/ [n C] someone who makes a speech in public: *Doug Williams is the first speaker in tonight's debate.* | *Everyone tells me I'm a good speaker, but I really hate doing it.* | **public speaker** *Kennedy was known as a brilliant public speaker.* | **guest speaker** (=someone who has been invited to come and give a speech or talk) *Each week the school has a different guest speaker come and talk to the students.* | **keynote speaker** (=someone who gives the most important speech at a big meeting) *Jennings was one of the keynote speakers at the conference's opening session Thursday.*

orator /ˈɒrətəʳ‖ˈɔː-, ˈɑː-/ [n C] someone who makes great public speeches and is good at persuading people to accept particular ideas, opinions, or principles: *Ogilvy had a reputation as a great orator.* | *Keyes is a fiery orator who built his campaign around his anti-abortion stand.*

tall

RELATED WORDS

opposite: **short**

- tall building, tree, mountain etc *see* **high (2)**

1 words for describing someone who is tall

- tall
- lanky
- gangling/gangly
- leggy
- a giant

tall /tɔːl/ [adj] *Martin was tall and thin, with curly blond hair.* | *At the age of fifteen he was already six foot three and the tallest boy in the school.* | *The photographer asked the taller people to stand at the back of the group.* | *Who is that tall bloke standing next to Diane?* | **grow tall/taller** *Sebastian was now fifteen, and had grown tall and strong.*

lanky /ˈlæŋki/ [adj] a man who is **lanky** is tall and thin, and has very long legs: *We were met by a tall,* *lanky youth called Yusef.* | *a lanky sixteen-year-old boy*

gangling/gangly /ˈgæŋglɪŋ, ˈgæŋgli/ [adj usually before noun] use this about a young person who is tall and thin with very long legs and arms, and moves in an awkward way: *Janet introduced me to her son, a shy, gangling teenager.* | *a tall, gangly youth*

leggy /ˈlegi/ [adj] a woman who is **leggy** is tall and attractive with long legs: *Robert arrived at the party with a leggy brunette.* | *a tall, leggy blonde*

a giant /ə ˈdʒaɪənt/ [n singular] use this about a man who is very tall, especially when you are surprised at how tall he is: *Bigger even than his father, who was a tall man, James was a giant.* | **a giant of a man** *The biggest of the three brothers was a sad-faced giant of a man.*

2 how tall someone is

- how tall
- 6 ft tall/2 m tall etc
- height
- stature

how tall /ˌhaʊ ˈtɔːl/ [adj phrase] use this to ask or talk about someone's height: *How tall are you?* | *I hadn't seen her for five years and I was amazed at how tall she was.*

6 ft tall/2 m tall etc /ˌsɪks fʊt ˈtɔːl/ [adj phrase] use this to say exactly how tall someone is: *John is 1.78 metres tall and weighs 95 kilos.* | *She was accompanied by her six foot tall boyfriend.*

height /haɪt/ [n C/U] how tall someone is **sb's height** *State your age, height, and weight.* | *Sally had always been self-conscious about her height.* | **be the same height** *She's about the same height as I am.*

stature /ˈstætʃəʳ/ [n U] formal someone's height, used especially when you are talking about their appearance: *The bank manager was a grey-haired man of imposing stature.* | **in stature** *I was by no means short in stature, but next to this man I felt like a dwarf.*

3 to be much taller than someone

- tower over/above
- dwarf

tower over/above /ˈtaʊər əʊvəʳ, əbʌv/ [phr v T] *When Howard stood up, he towered over his father.* | *A tall, broad-shouldered, striking figure, he towered above others around him.*

dwarf /dwɔːʳf/ [v T usually in passive] to be so much taller than someone else that you make them seem shorter than they really are: *Rachel was small and slight, and was dwarfed by the other competitors.*

taste

RELATED WORDS

- what kind of clothes, music etc someone likes *see* **taste in clothes, music etc**
- food that tastes very good *see* **delicious**
- food that tastes very bad *see* **horrible**
- food that no longer tastes fresh *see* **fresh/not fresh**
- *see also* **food, drink, eat, cook, smell, meal**

1 the taste of food or drink

- taste
- flavour
- hint
- aftertaste

taste /teɪst/ [n singular] the feeling that a particular food or drink produces in your mouth when you eat or drink it: *I never drink beer, I just don't like the taste.* | *a sour taste* | **+ of** *Have some water to take away the taste of the medicine.*

flavour British **/flavor** American /ˈfleɪvəʳ/ [n C/U] the pleasant, interesting, or strong taste that a particular kind of food or drink has: *This sauce has a really unusual flavour.* | *We have three flavors of ice cream – strawberry, chocolate, and vanilla.* | *The wine wasn't bad, but it didn't have much flavour.*

hint /hɪnt/ [n singular] a slight, pleasant taste of something that you can only just notice **+ of** *You might notice a hint of brandy in the sauce.* | *a wine that tastes of blackcurrants with just a hint of vanilla*

aftertaste /ˈɑːftəʳteɪst‖ˈæf-/ [n singular] the unpleasant taste that some kinds of food and drink leave in your mouth after you have swallowed them: *Some customers complained about the salty aftertaste.* | *The crab left too much of a fishy aftertaste.*

2 to have a particular taste

- taste
- have a sweet/strong/bitter etc taste
- flavoured

taste /teɪst/ [v I not in progressive] **taste + adjective** *This milk tastes strange – do you think it's OK to drink?* | **+ like** *It's a vegetarian pie, but it tastes just like meat!* | **+ of** (=have the taste of something) *I ordered chocolate ice cream but this tastes of coffee.*

have a sweet/strong/bitter etc taste /hæv ə ˌswiːt ˈteɪst/ [v phrase not in progressive] *The soup had a very strong, spicy taste.*

flavoured British **/flavored** American /ˈfleɪvəʳd/ [adj] use this to say what kind of taste something has: *We have a variety of flavored waters available.* | *The potato salad was flavored with onions, the way Mattie liked it.* | **lemon-flavoured/chocolate-flavoured etc** (=having the taste of lemon, chocolate etc added) *an orange-flavoured drink* | **highly flavoured/strongly flavoured etc** *The wines of Alsace are dry and delicately flavoured.*

3 with a sweet taste

- sweet
- sugary
- sickly
- sweeten

sweet /swiːt/ [adj] food or drink that is **sweet** has a taste like sugar: *Italian oranges are much sweeter than the ones we buy in Britain.* | *a cup of hot sweet tea*

sugary /ˈʃʊgəri/ [adj] very sweet or too sweet because a lot of sugar has been added: *Eat fruit between meals, and try to avoid sugary snacks.*

sickly /ˈsɪkli/ [adj] British tasting unpleasantly sweet: *The melons were overripe and had a sickly taste.*

sweeten /ˈswiːtn/ [v T] to make something taste sweet or sweeter: *Sprinkle sugar onto the cooked fruit to sweeten it.* | *a can of sweetened milk*

4 with a taste that is not sweet

- salty
- savoury
- bitter
- dry

salty /ˈsɔːlti/ [adj] **salty** foods taste of salt and are not sweet at all: *The french fries were too salty for me.* | *This wine would be excellent with a salty dish such as ham.*

savoury /ˈseɪvəri/ [adj] especially British **savoury** foods are not sweet but have the taste of meat, cheese, fish etc: *You can use this herb to flavour almost any savoury dish.* | *As a child I didn't like sweets, but I loved crisps, nuts, and anything savoury.*

bitter /ˈbɪtəʳ/ [adj] **bitter** foods, such as coffee without sugar or very dark chocolate, have a strong, sometimes unpleasant taste: *Try not to burn the oil, it will make the sauce taste bitter.* | *strong, bitter coffee* | *The herb rue has a bitter taste, which makes it unpopular for cooking.*

dry /draɪ/ [adj] a **dry** wine is not sweet at all: *We drank a dry white wine with our fish.* | *dry sherry*

5 with a sour taste

- sour
- tart
- sharp
- tangy

sour /saʊəʳ/ [adj] food that is **sour**, especially fruit, has a taste that stings your tongue slightly, like a lemon does: *The strawberries are a little sour – you may need to put sugar on them.* | *Kvass is a mild beer that is sometimes used in Russian cooking for its sour flavor.*

tart /tɑːʳt/ [adj] fruits that are **tart**, especially apples, sting your tongue and make water come into your mouth: *This tart citrus dressing is great on salads.* | *Red currants are quite tart and usually need sugar or honey.*

sharp /ʃɑːʳp/ [adj] having a strong but pleasant taste that stings your tongue: *The drink had a very sharp lemony taste.* | *I like this marmalade. It's very sharp.* | *The lemon juice gives the dressing its sharp flavour.*

tangy /ˈtæŋi/ [adj] having a fresh, pleasant taste that stings your tongue slightly: *The orange juice had a delicious tangy taste.* | *We made a tangy mayonnaise from yoghurt and honey.* —**tang** [n singular] the pleasantly sharp taste that some kinds of food or drink have: *The lime juice will give your sauce a delicious tang.* | *a unique cheese, smooth but leaving a salty tang behind on the tongue*

6 with a hot taste

- hot
- spicy
- fiery

hot /hɒt‖hɑːt/ [adj] food that has a **hot** taste seems to burn your mouth, and makes you want to drink a lot of water: *The curry was so hot I couldn't finish it.* | *The sauce had a hot, peppery taste.*

spicy /ˈspaɪsi/ [adj] **spicy** food tastes pleasantly hot and often seems to have a mix of different tastes: *Tina loves hot spicy food.* | *I added ginger and cumin to give the rice a spicy flavour.*

fiery /ˈfaɪəri/ [adj] food or drink that is **fiery** has an extremely hot taste that burns your throat: *Peter always makes really fiery chilli con carne.* | *Discard all the chilli seeds, unless you want an extremely fiery soup.*

7 with a strong taste

- strong
- rich
- full-flavoured
- full-bodied

strong /strɒŋ‖strɔːŋ/ [adj] food or drinks that are **strong** have a very noticeable and particular taste: *'How do you like your tea?' 'Strong please, with no sugar.'* | *I left the restaurant with rather a strong taste of onions in my mouth.* | *Stilton is a very strong English cheese, which has blue-green veins running through it.*

rich /rɪtʃ/ [adj] food that is **rich** contains a lot of cheese, cream, butter, or chocolate, and makes you feel full very quickly: *You mustn't eat too much rich food – it's bad for you.* | *The meat was browned to perfection and topped with a rich sauce.*

full-flavoured British **/full-flavored** American /ˌfʊl ˈfleɪvəʳd/ [adj] something such as cheese or coffee that is **full-flavoured** has a strong pleasant taste: *This coffee is strong and full-flavoured, excellent for after dinner.*

full-bodied /ˌfʊl ˈbɒdid◂‖-ˈbɑː-/ [adj] a **full-bodied** wine has a strong pleasant taste: *The beautiful color and full-bodied taste of these Australian wines make them an excellent accompaniment to meat dishes.*

8 with little or no taste

- tasteless
- bland
- have no taste/not have any taste
- not taste of anything
- mild
- delicate

tasteless /ˈteɪstləs/ [adj] food that is **tasteless** has little or no taste and is rather unpleasant: *Why is airplane food always so tasteless?* | *a plate of tasteless, overcooked vegetables*

bland /blænd/ [adj] food or drink that is **bland** has very little taste and is not interesting to eat or drink: *If the sauce is bland, add a little more vinegar.* | *At first, give the baby tiny portions of any bland food that has been sieved or pureed.*

have no taste/not have any taste /hæv ˌnəʊ ˈteɪst, nɒt hæv eni ˈteɪst/ [v phrase not in progressive] to have very little taste – use this especially when you think something should have more taste: *The most disappointing dish was the chicken-filled tortellini with a pesto sauce that had almost no taste.* | *You need to add salt or something – this doesn't have any taste at all.*

not taste of anything British informal **/not taste like anything** American informal /nɒt ˌteɪst əv ˈeniθɪŋ, nɒt ˌteɪst laɪk ˈeniθɪŋ/ [v phrase not in progressive] to have no particular taste: *I'm not sure what kind of soup this is supposed to be. It doesn't taste of anything to me.* | *The dessert wasn't awful, but it didn't taste like anything.*

mild /maɪld/ [adj] something such as cheese or coffee that is **mild** has a pleasant taste but is not hot or strong: *It's a smooth, mild coffee, excellent for finishing off a meal.* | *a mild cigar* | *a mild English cheese*

delicate /ˈdelɪkət/ [adj] a **delicate** taste or flavour is pleasant and not very strong: *The fish was served with a delicate mushroom sauce.* | *Salmon has quite a delicate flavour, and it should not be over-cooked.* —**delicately** [adv] *The vegetables had been cooked in a delicately flavoured marinade.*

9 to find out what something tastes like

- taste
- try
- have a taste

taste /teɪst/ [v T] to eat or drink something in order to find out what it tastes like: *You should taste my Dad's fried chicken, it's delicious.* | *'Go on then, taste it,' said my grandfather, pouring a little of his home-made wine into my glass.*

have a taste /ˌhæv ə 'teɪst/ [v phrase] to eat or drink a small amount of something, to find out what it tastes like – use this especially about something that someone has just cooked, made, or picked: *That cheese looks good. Can I have a taste?* | **+ of** *I know Clare is a good cook. I had a taste of her pumpkin pie.*

try /traɪ/ [v T not in passive] to eat or drink something in order to find out if you like it: *'Do you like goat's milk?' 'I don't know, I've never tried it.'* | *Have you tried Alison's carrot cake?*

10 when someone can recognize the taste that something has

- can taste
- sense of taste

can taste /kən 'teɪst/ [v phrase] if you **can taste** something, you can recognize its taste, especially when it is with other types of food or drink: *Can you taste the garlic in the sauce?* | *Don't pretend you haven't put vodka in my drink – I can taste it.*

sense of taste /ˌsens əv 'teɪst/ [n phrase] your natural ability to recognize differences between tastes: *Richard's cold has made him lose his sense of taste.* | *Our sense of taste is closely linked to our sense of smell.*

taste in clothes, music etc

RELATED WORDS

- *see also* **style/elegance**

1 a person's judgment in choosing things like clothes, music, furniture etc

- taste

taste /teɪst/ [n C/U] use this to talk about the kind of clothes, music, furniture etc that someone likes: *I don't think much of his taste.* | **+ in** *Tastes in fiction vary from person to person.* | *We have similar taste in music.* | **be a matter of taste** (=it depends on your taste) *It's not necessarily better or worse, it's just a matter of taste.* | **there's no accounting for taste** (=everyone has different taste in things) *I can't understand why she likes it, but as they say, there's no accounting for taste.*

2 good taste

- taste/good taste

taste/good taste /teɪst, ˌgʊd 'teɪst/ [n U] the ability to make good judgments about what kind of clothes, furniture etc is attractive or good: *The room was furnished with style and taste.* | *I admired their good taste in clothes.* | **a man/woman of taste** formal (=someone who has good taste) *Matisse said that a photograph by a man of taste could have the appearance of art.*

3 when someone has good taste

- have taste/have good taste
- discriminating
- discerning
- have a good eye for

have taste/have good taste /hæv 'teɪst, hæv ˌgʊd 'teɪst/ [v phrase not in progressive] to be able to make good judgments about which clothes, furniture etc are attractive or good and which are not: *Mrs Anderson has taste, and her home is lovely.* | *The Scotch was Johnnie Walker Black. 'This guy's got good taste,' I thought.* | **+ in** *Julie has really good taste in books.* | **have great/terrific/impeccable etc taste** *Robinson had impeccable taste.*

discerning /dɪ'sɜːʳnɪŋ/ [adj usually before noun] able to recognize things that are good or of high quality – use this especially when talking about buying things: *Discerning investors will find the guide useful.* | *You don't have to be wealthy to develop a discerning palate.* (=good taste in food)

discriminating /dɪ'skrɪmɪ̈neɪtɪŋ/ [adj] able to judge what is of good quality and what is not, especially because you have a lot of knowledge or experience: *As film audiences get older, they will become more discriminating.* | *Discriminating travelers return to St. Bartholomew's year after year.*

have a good eye for /hæv ə ˌgʊd 'aɪ fɔːʳ/ [v phrase not in progressive] to be good at noticing and recognizing what is attractive, of good quality etc, and which things look good together: *She has an incredibly good eye for fashion.* | *You need to have a good eye for colour and design if you are going to decorate your own house.*

4 something that has been made or chosen with good taste

- tasteful
- be in good taste

tasteful /'teɪstfəl/ [adj] made or chosen with good taste: *The room is filled with tasteful furnishings and original artworks.* | *My uncle wore a flannel suit, a spotless white shirt and a tasteful but sombre tie.* —**tastefully** [adv] *Griffiths sat behind a huge desk in a tastefully furnished office.* | *She was always tastefully dressed.*

be in good taste /biː ɪn ˌgʊd 'teɪst/ [v phrase] to be attractive and suitable in a way that shows good taste: *Whatever she wears, you can be sure it will be in good taste, and just right for the occasion.* | *The furniture and decor are all in the best possible taste.*

5 someone who does not have good taste

- have bad taste
- have no taste

have bad taste /hæv ˌbæd 'teɪst/ [v phrase not in progressive] to be unable to make good judgments about which clothes, furniture etc are attractive or good and which are not: *I know it's bad taste, but I like fluffy, lacy clothes.* | **+ in** *He has really bad taste in clothes.* | **have terrible/awful/appalling etc taste** *She* *just has such awful taste – I don't want her help picking out dresses.*

have no taste /hæv ˌnəʊ 'teɪst/ [v phrase not in progressive] to not have good taste: *It's unbelievable. The woman obviously has no taste at all.*

6 something that has not been made or chosen with good taste

- tasteless
- vulgar
- cheap
- naff
- tacky
- kitsch/kitschy

tasteless /'teɪstləs/ [adj] not made or chosen with good taste: *It was an ugly room with tasteless decorations and shabby furniture.* | *I think a lot of modern architecture is completely tasteless.*

vulgar /'vʌlgəʳ/ [adj] not chosen with taste – use this about things that cost a lot of money or are very brightly coloured, and are bought to impress people: *Vulgar fashions filled the store windows.* | *The article describes the vulgar excesses of the newly rich.* —**vulgarity** /vʌl'gærɪ̈ti/ [n U] *He was horrified by the vulgarity of his uncle's house.*

cheap /tʃiːp/ [adj] unattractive, of poor quality, and showing a lack of good taste: *The interior of the car is all plastic and has a cheap look about it.* | *The girls wore bright frilly dresses and were drenched in cheap perfume.*

naff /næf/ [adj] British informal use this about something that you think shows very bad taste: *Most people think taking a package holiday in Bognor is really naff.* | *Don't wear that shirt with those slacks – it looks naff.*

tacky /'tæki/ [adj] informal cheap-looking and showing very bad taste: *cheap, tacky furniture in bright colors* | *The room was decorated to look like a cartoon Swiss village, but managed to be cheerfully tacky.*

kitsch/kitschy /kɪtʃ, 'kɪtʃi/ [adj] cheap, unfashionable, and showing very bad taste, but often in an amusing way: *the kitschy decor of the Mexican restaurant* | *Tourists lined up to buy postcards and assorted kitsch souvenirs.*

teach

RELATED WORDS

- *see also* **learn, subject, explain, instructions, school/university**

1 to teach someone a skill or how to do something

- teach
- train
- coach
- instruct
- show sb the ropes

teach /tiːtʃ/ [v T] *I've always wanted to learn to ski – could you teach me?* | **teach sth to sb** *It took us several hours to teach all the dance moves to the girls.* | **teach sb sth** *Grandpa taught me a new card trick.* | **teach sb (how) to do sth** *Who taught you to drive?* | *My mother taught me how to cook.*

train /treɪn/ [v T] to teach someone the practical skills and knowledge that they need to do a job: *A lot of employers don't train their staff properly.* | **train sb to do sth** *All employees will be trained to use the new computer system.* | *The dog was trained to detect illegal drugs.* | **train sb in sth** *We train people in skills such as typing and business administration.* —**trained** [adj usually before noun] *The service is run by trained nurses.* | **fully trained** *All the staff are fully trained and willing to help in any way they can.*

coach /kəʊtʃ/ [v I/T] to teach a person or a team the skills they need for a sport: *He seems to enjoy coaching children.* | *We need someone to coach the school team.* | *As well as teaching French, Martin coached tennis in his spare time.*

instruct /ɪn'strʌkt/ [v T] to teach someone about something, especially a practical subject or skill, by explaining it and showing them what to do: *The person who instructed you obviously didn't know much about map-reading!* | **instruct sb in sth** *New recruits are instructed in marching and the handling of weapons.*

show sb the ropes /ˌʃəʊ (sb) ðə 'rəʊps/ [v phrase] informal to show someone how to do something such as a job that they are new to: *You'll need someone with you for the first few days to show you the ropes.* | *Susan will show you the ropes and answer any questions that you have.*

2 to teach in a school, college etc as your job

- teach
- lecture
- give

teach /tiːtʃ/ [v I/T] to **teach** in a school, college etc as your job: *I taught for a year in France.* | *She got a job teaching German at a local school.* | *I prefer teaching the older children.* | *Miss Himes teaches the youngest class, the four- and five-year-olds.* | **teach sth to sb** *She teaches English to Italian students.* | *Teaching literature to the fifth grade is no joke!* | **teach sb sth** *You must remember Mr Hughes – he used to teach us history.* | **teach school** American (=to teach in a school) *My Dad taught school in New York.*

lecture /'lektʃəʳ/ [v I] to teach in a university or college: *Before his retirement he lectured at the Institut Pasteur.* | **+ on** *She lectures on Shakespeare at Edinburgh University.* | **+ in** *For many years Dr Thornton lectured in Economics at University College.*

give /gɪv/ [v T] if someone **gives** a class, lecture, or course, they teach it: *Dr Hebden will be giving a lecture later this week on the role of women in the economy.* | *Who's giving the class this afternoon?*

3 to teach people how they should think or behave

- teach
- educate
- bring up
- instil
- brainwash
- condition
- indoctrinate

teach /tiːtʃ/ [v T] to **teach** someone, especially a child or young person, how to behave or what to believe **teach sb to do sth** *When I was young, children were taught to treat older people with respect.* | **teach sb (that)** *Joe's mother taught him that he could do anything, if only he tried hard enough.* | **teach sb sth** *Parents need to teach their children the difference between right and wrong.*

educate /'edjʊkeɪt‖'edʒə-/ [v T] to teach people, especially over a long period of time, about things that will be helpful to them in life: *We need to educate people so that they understand the importance of a good, healthy diet.* | **educate sb about sth** *Youngsters must be educated about the dangers of drugs.* |

educate sb to do sth *What we're trying to do is to educate young people to be responsible citizens.*

bring up /ˌbrɪŋ 'ʌp/ [phr v T] to teach your child or children how to behave or think as they grow up **bring sb up to do sth** *I was brought up to spend money carefully and save as much as I could.* | *Stan had been brought up to believe that a man should work to support his wife.* | **bring sb up in the belief/conviction/knowledge that** *Alison was brought up in the belief that she was in some way superior to other children.*

instil British **/instill** American /ɪn'stɪl/ [v T] formal to teach someone a way of thinking or behaving, especially relating to morals, good manners, over a long period of time: *We aim to teach the children discipline and instil a sense of duty.* | **instil sth in/into sb** *We have tried to instil good manners in our children from an early age.* | *She instilled tremendous enthusiasm into all her students.*

brainwash /'breɪnwɒʃ‖-wɔːʃ, -wɑːʃ/ [v T] to teach someone to believe something by continuously repeating it over a long period of time, especially when they are tired, weak, or confused, so that they accept it without questioning it: *Mrs Davis accused the cult of having brainwashed her daughter.* | **brainwash sb into doing sth** *For years we've been brainwashed by advertising into buying more and more things that we don't need.* —**brainwashing** [n U] *Brainwashing techniques include preventing the person from sleeping and depriving them of any human contact.*

condition /kən'dɪʃən/ [v T] to make someone think or react in a particular way by influencing their attitudes or reactions over a long period of time **condition sb to do sth** *He was conditioned to obey his father at all times.* | **condition sb into doing sth** *The people have been conditioned into thinking that anyone from outside their community represents a threat to them.* —**conditioning** [n U] *It can take years of therapy to undo early childhood conditioning.*

indoctrinate /ɪn'dɒktrɪ̈neɪt‖ɪn'dɑːk-/ [v T] to teach someone to accept a particular set of religious or political beliefs, without allowing them to discuss it, doubt it, or consider other possible beliefs: *Some politically active teachers were accused of trying to indoctrinate their students.* | **indoctrinate sb into doing sth** *Citizens were indoctrinated into believing that their leader was the source of all wisdom and goodness.* —**indoctrination** /ɪnˌdɒktrɪ̈'neɪʃən‖ɪnˌdɑːk-/ [n U] *She believes that all religious teaching in schools is indoctrination.*

4 the work of a teacher

- teaching
- training
- education
- instruction
- tuition

teaching /'tiːtʃɪŋ/ [n U] the work that a teacher does, or the job of being a teacher: *Andrea took some time off from teaching when her children were small.* | **go into teaching** (=become a teacher) *What made you go into teaching?* | **leave teaching** *He left teaching and took a job as a truck driver.*

training /'treɪnɪŋ/ [n U] when someone is taught the skills that they need for a job **have training** *Have you had any medical training?* | **give sb training** *All new staff should be given computer training.* | **training course** *We all had to go on a special training course to learn new sales techniques.*

education /ˌedjʊ'keɪʃən‖ˌedʒə-/ [n U] the work of teaching people in schools, colleges, universities etc: *The new policies have been welcomed by people working in education.* | *Jobs in education are not usually highly paid.* | *the Labour Party's spokeswoman on education*

instruction /ɪn'strʌkʃən/ [n U] teaching in a particular skill or subject: *Young drivers come to us for instruction in safe and skilful driving.* | *Half an hour's instruction from an experienced horse-rider is much better than anything you can learn from a book.* | **under instruction** (=being taught) *The trainees work at their machines under instruction from a supervisor.*

tuition /tjuː'ɪʃən‖tuː-/ [n U] teaching given privately to one person or a small group in a particular subject: *Nina's parents paid for extra tuition to help her with her maths.* | *Computerworld offers personal tuition on the latest equipment.*

5 someone who teaches

- teacher
- tutor
- instructor
- coach
- trainer
- professor
- lecturer
- academic
- educator
- faculty

teacher /'tiːtʃəʳ/ [n C] someone who teaches, especially someone whose job is to teach children in a school: *She's a teacher in the high school.* | *I remember having some pretty awful teachers when I was at school.* | **English/science/chemistry etc teacher** *The school doesn't have enough French teachers.* | **+ of** *a conference for teachers of English*

tutor /'tjuːtəʳ‖'tuː-/ [n C] someone who gives lessons to just one student or a small group of students: *When she was ill she studied at home with a private tutor.* | *They hired a private tutor to help Carlos with his English.*

instructor /ɪn'strʌktəʳ/ [n C] someone who teaches a sport or a practical skill **swimming/driving/riding etc instructor** *I managed to find a very good driving instructor.* | *a ski instructor*

coach /kəʊtʃ/ [n C] someone who trains a person or a team in a sport, and helps them to improve their skills **basketball/football/tennis etc coach** *We got a professional football coach to come and help us train the team.*

trainer /'treɪnəʳ/ [n C] someone who trains people in the skills they need to do a job: *Many companies now pay outside trainers to come in and teach management skills to their staff.* | *I work as a teacher trainer.*

professor /prə'fesəʳ/ [n C] a university teacher – used in Britain to mean a teacher of the highest rank, and in the US to mean any university teacher who has a higher degree such as a PhD: *The meeting will be chaired by Professor Andrew Jones.* | *Archie's father is a retired physics professor.* | **+ of** *She's a professor of history at Oxford University.*

lecturer /'lektʃərəʳ/ [n C] someone who teaches at a university or college: *Watson is now a lecturer at the University of Bradford.* | *a chemistry lecturer* | **+ in** *a lecturer in economics*

academic /ˌækə'demɪk/ [n C] someone who works, studies, and teaches in a university, and has a lot of knowledge about a particular subject: *Academics can usually get time off teaching to do their own research.*

educator /'edjʊkeɪtəʳ‖'edʒə-/ [n C] formal someone who teaches in a school, college, or university: *Most educators agree that intimidating children is not the best way to encourage them to learn.* | *Professor Tay-*

lor is generally recognized as one of the state's most respected educators.

faculty /'fækəlti/ [n C usually singular] American all the teachers in a college or university: *Norman White has been on the faculty at UCLA for over thirty years.* | *Nearly half the faculty turned out to show their support.*

6 designed or intended to teach something

- educational
- instructive
- learning

educational /ˌedjʊ'keɪʃənəl◂‖ˌedʒə-/ [adj] **educational** books, games, television programmes etc are designed to help you to learn something: *a shop selling educational toys for 7- to 11-year-olds* | *a leading publisher of educational books and software*

instructive /ɪn'strʌktɪv/ [adj] providing a lot of useful information, explanations, and knowledge about something: *Lectures must be interesting as well as instructive.* | *The books are designed to be both entertaining and instructive.*

learning /'lɜːʳnɪŋ/ [adj only before noun] use this about books, methods, activities etc that are intended to teach people something: *They stock a wide variety of learning materials for younger students.* | *How can we make the most of the Internet as a learning tool?*

tear

RELATED WORDS

- to cry because you are unhappy *see* **cry**
- *see also* **cut, break, damage, destroy, spoil**

1 to damage paper, cloth, or clothing

- tear
- rip
- ladder
- split

tear /teəʳ/ [v T] to damage paper, cloth, or clothing by pulling it too hard, or by letting it touch something sharp: *She unwrapped the present carefully, trying not to tear the paper.* | **tear sth on sth** *I had torn the knees of my jeans on the rough gravel.* | **tear sth out/tear out sth** *She tore a page out of her diary and wrote her phone number on it.* | **tear sth off/tear off sth** *The attendant tore off the parking ticket and handed it back.* | **tear sth open/tear open sth** *Peterson tore open the envelope.* | **tear a hole in sth** *I tore a hole in my jacket, climbing over the fence.* | **tear sth in half** *He took my ticket and tore it in half. 'Row J, seats 8 and 9.'*

rip /rɪp/ [v T] to tear something quickly or violently: *Stop pulling my dress! You'll rip it!* | **rip sth out/rip out sth** *You can see where the label has been ripped out.* | **rip sth on sth** *I ripped my skirt on a broken chair.* | **rip sth open/rip open sth** *Beth excitedly ripped open the package.*

ladder /'lædəʳ/ [v T] British if a woman **ladders** her tights or stockings, she accidentally tears them so that a line of stitches becomes loose: *Damn! I've laddered my tights!*

split /splɪt/ [v T] if you **split** your trousers, a long straight tear appears in them when you bend over or when you try to put on a pair that is too tight: *He bent down and split his trousers.*

2 to deliberately destroy something by tearing it into pieces

- tear up
- rip up
- shred
- tear/rip sth to shreds

tear up /ˌteər 'ʌp/ [phr v T] to tear a piece of paper or cloth into many pieces **tear up sth** *After Alan left, she tore up all his old letters.* | **tear sth up** *Pamela tore the note up and threw it in the wastebasket.* —**torn-up** /'tɔːʳn ʌp/ [adj] *Use torn-up newspaper to line the bottom of the rabbit's cage.*

rip up /ˌrɪp 'ʌp/ [phr v T] to tear something into pieces quickly or angrily **rip up sth** *Martine ripped up her essay and started again.* | **rip sth up** *He'd get frustrated and throw his pencil down and rip his paper up.*

shred /ʃred/ [v T] to deliberately destroy letters, secret documents etc by putting them through a special machine which cuts them into long thin pieces: *The superintendent gave his secretary some letters to shred.* | *Some photographs and important documents – the only evidence available – had been shredded.*

tear/rip sth to shreds /ˌteəʳ, ˌrɪp (sth) tə 'ʃredz/ [v phrase] to tear a piece of paper into very small pieces, especially because you are angry: *Karen tore his photograph to shreds.* | *He tore out the page and ripped it to shreds.*

3 to become torn accidentally

- tear
- rip
- split

tear /teəʳ/ [v I] *My jacket caught on a nail and tore.* | *Don't pull on the cloth, it will tear.* | **tear easily** *Be careful, the paper tears easily.*

rip /rɪp/ [v I] to become badly torn, especially as the result of a sudden movement: *Tom heard his shorts rip as he climbed over the gate.* | *My zipper was stuck, and the material around it ripped as I pulled on it.*

split /splɪt/ [v I] if material **splits**, a long straight tear appears in it: *Hudson's coat had split right up the back.* | *These shoes are so old the canvas had split.*

4 when something has been torn

- torn
- be in shreds
- frayed
- tattered
- ragged

torn /tɔːʳn/ [adj] when something made of cloth or paper has been torn: *He was wearing torn trousers and a ragged jacket.* | *The pages of the book were torn and faded.* | **get torn** *If the cover of a book gets torn, the library sends it to be repaired.*

be in shreds /biː ɪn 'ʃredz/ [v phrase] if a piece of cloth or paper **is in shreds**, it has been torn and damaged so much that it has almost fallen apart: *The curtains hung in shreds and the carpet was worn thin.* | *The clothes were handed down in the family, and by the time they reached the last child, they were in shreds.*

frayed /freɪd/ [adj] clothes or things made of cloth that are **frayed** are torn a little along the edges, usually because they have been used a lot: *He had on frayed jeans and an old white shirt.* | **frayed at the cuffs/collar/edges etc** *The jacket was a little frayed at the cuffs.*

tattered /ˈtætəʳd/ [adj] cloth, paper, or a piece of clothing that is **tattered** is torn in many places, especially because it has been used a lot: *A man in tattered blue dungarees was busy in the garage.* | *The old diary was yellowed and tattered.*

ragged /ˈrægɪ̈d/ [adj] clothes or things made of cloth that are **ragged** are torn and untidy, often because the people who own them are very poor: *The blanket she wore over her shoulders was ragged and filthy.* | *A man in ragged clothes was begging on the corner.*

5 a hole that is made when something is torn

- tear
- rip
- ladder

tear /teəʳ/ [n C] *How did you get that tear in your jacket?* | *There's a small tear near the corner of the painting.*

rip /rɪp/ [n C] a long hole that is made when something such as a piece of clothing is torn: *The rips in the boat's old sails had been patched again and again.* | *A rip in a repair worker's protective suit increases the risk of getting a shock as they work on the electricity lines.*

ladder British **/run** especially American /ˈlædəʳ, rʌn/ [n C] a line of torn stitches in a pair of tights etc: *There's a run in these pantyhose.* | **get a ladder/run** *I got a ladder in my tights.*

telephone

RELATED WORDS

- see also **contact, message, letter, computers/Internet/email**

1 to speak to someone by telephone

- call
- phone
- telephone
- ring/phone up
- give sb a call
- make a call/phone call/telephone call
- be on the phone
- give sb a buzz/ring
- get through

call /kɔːl/ [v I/T] *To find out more, call 555-1972.* | *Can you call Becky before six?* | *She called about twenty minutes ago.* | **+ for** *I'll call for a taxi now.* | **call round** British **/around** American (=call several people or organizations, especially to get information) *I called round to see if anyone knew where Tom was.* | *His secretary started calling around to find out where the commission was meeting.*

phone ALSO **ring** British /fəʊn, rɪŋ/ [v I/T] *I'll phone you if there's any news.* | *Shall I ring Sarah to see if she wants to come out with us?* | *Did anyone ring while I was out?* | *Jill phoned to tell you she'll see you tonight.* | **+ for** *Let's phone for a pizza tonight.* | **phone/ring round** British (=telephone several people or organizations, especially to get information) *You'd better ring round some travel agents to get some prices.*

telephone /ˈtelɪ̈fəʊn/ [v I/T] to speak to someone by telephone. **Telephone** is more formal than **phone** or **call**, and is used especially in writing: *About five o'clock, a woman telephoned Bernstein.* | *For details of your nearest tourist office telephone 4127.* | *Mr Dodd telephoned this morning.* | **+ for** *Write or telephone for more information.*

ring/phone up British **/call up** American /ˌrɪŋ, ˌfəʊn ˈʌp, ˌkɔːl ˈʌp/ [phr v I/T] to speak to someone by telephone, especially in order to have a friendly conversation with them or to ask for information: *Your uncle rang up about an hour ago.* | *'I don't know what time the last train is.' 'Well, phone up and find out.'* | **ring/call/phone up sb** *Why don't you call up Jackie and apologize?* | *She uses the office phone to phone up her friends in Sweden.* | **ring/call/phone sb up** *John called him up to make sure of the date of the graduation ceremony.* | *I might phone him up at home.*

give sb a call ALSO **give sb a ring** British /ˌgɪv (sb) ə ˈkɔːl, ˌgɪv (sb) ə ˈrɪŋ/ [v phrase] spoken to speak to someone by telephone – use this especially when you are telling someone that you will telephone them, or when you are asking them to telephone: *Just give me a call if you need anything.* | *Why don't I give you a ring later and find out when you'll be free?*

make a call/phone call/telephone call /ˌmeɪk ə ˈkɔːl, ˈfəʊn kɔːl, ˈtelɪ̈fəʊn ˌkɔːl/ [v phrase] to use the telephone to speak to someone: *Diana made a quick call to Munich before the meeting.* | *There's a pay phone in the lobby if you need to make a telephone call.* | *Limit the number of personal phone calls you make at work.*

be on the phone /biː ɒn ðə ˈfəʊn/ [v phrase] to be speaking to someone on the telephone: *Rosie's still on the phone.* | *There's someone on the phone for you.* | **+ to** *He was on the phone to a friend when he noticed the smoke.* | **+ with** *How long are workers on the phone with customers?* | **talk/speak on the phone** *Marie and I talk on the phone at least once a week.* | **have sb on the phone** (=to have someone calling you) *Mr Rogers, I have Anita Payne on the phone for you.*

give sb a buzz/ring informal ALSO **give sb a bell** British informal /ˌgɪv (sb) ə ˈbʌz, ˈrɪŋ, ˌgɪv (sb) ə ˈbel/ [v phrase] to telephone someone: *I'll give Larry a buzz. Maybe he'll want to go too.* | *Can you give Mary a bell? She rang earlier.* | *Give me a ring if you decide you can come.*

get through /ˌget ˈθruː/ [phr v I] to succeed in reaching someone by telephone: *I tried calling my parents, but I couldn't get through.* | **+ to** *Did you get through to Mr McWhirter?*

2 to make a telephone call that is paid for by the person you are telephoning

- reverse the charges

reverse the charges ALSO **call collect** American /rɪˌvɜːʳs ðə ˈtʃɑːʳdʒɪ̈z, ˌkɔːl kəˈlekt/ [v phrase] *Call collect if you need to.* | *If something goes wrong, call us and reverse the charges.* | **call sb collect** *Anyone with information may call Doug Howarth collect at 555-0976.*

3 to telephone someone again

- call back
- return a call/phone call/telephone call
- try again

call back ALSO **ring back** British /ˌkɔːl ˈbæk, ˌrɪŋ ˈbæk/ [phr v I/T] to telephone someone again, for example because they were not available when you telephoned them before: *'Would you like to leave a message?' 'No, that's okay. I'll call back later.'* | *I'm afraid Mr Jones is in a meeting. Could you ring back* *in about an hour?* | **call sb back** *'Does Jake want me to call him back?' 'No, he said to meet him at eight o'clock.'*

return a call/phone call/telephone call /rɪˌtɜːʳn ə 'kɔːl, 'fəʊn kɔːl, 'telɪ̈fəʊn ˌkɔːl/ [v phrase] to telephone someone because they telephoned you before when you were not available – use this especially in business contexts: *Gage did not return phone calls from reporters to his office Monday.* | *Dr Shapiro is busy right now, but I'll ask him to return your call when he's free.*

try again /ˌtraɪ ə'gen/ [v phrase] to telephone a number again because someone was already speaking on that line when you telephoned before: *I've already phoned him twice, but I suppose I'd better try again.* | **try sb/a number again** *It's engaged. I'll try her again later.*

4 a telephone call

- call/phone call/ telephone call

call/phone call/telephone call /kɔːl, 'fəʊn kɔːl, 'telɪ̈fəʊn ˌkɔːl/ [n C] *We keep getting calls from newspaper reporters.* | *One phone call to London got her a job interview.* | *After several telephone calls, detectives traced two witnesses to the accident.* | **+ for** *Mr Deckard, there's a call for you. Will you take it in your office?* | **long-distance call** (=to or from someone a long way away) *He made several long-distance calls to Hong Kong.* | **local call** (=to someone near you) *Local calls are free.*

5 someone who is making a telephone call

- caller

caller /'kɔːləʳ/ [n C] someone who is making a telephone call – used especially by people who work with telephones: *Did the caller leave a number?* | *Hold on please, I have an overseas call for you. Go ahead, caller.*

6 when you use the telephone in order to tell someone something

- on/over the phone
- by phone/ telephone

on/over the phone /ɒn, əʊvəʳ ðə 'fəʊn/ [adv] *You can buy them by credit card over the phone.* | *The ticket office told me on the phone that I'd have front-row seats in section D.* | *I didn't want to go into details on the phone, so we arranged a meeting in my office for the next day.* | *Maria started crying over the phone as she told me about it.*

by phone/telephone /baɪ 'fəʊn, 'telɪ̈fəʊn/ [adv] if you tell someone something **by phone** or **by telephone**, you make a telephone call to tell them it: *The survey questions 500 people a month by phone.* | *Reservations can be made by telephone, but must be confirmed in writing within seven days.*

7 to end a telephone call

- hang up
- put the phone down
- slam the phone down/slam down the phone
- get cut off/get disconnected
- ring off

hang up /ˌhæŋ 'ʌp/ [phr v I/T] to finish a telephone conversation or stop it before it has finished by putting down the receiver (=the part of a telephone you speak into): *If a caller is rude, just hang up.* | **hang up the phone/receiver** *I said I'd be right there. I hung up the phone and grabbed my purse and car keys.* | **hang up on sb** (=put the telephone down while someone is still talking) *Mitchell was furious and hung up on him.*

put the phone down /ˌpʊt ðə 'fəʊn daʊn/ [v phrase] especially British to put down the receiver (=the part of a telephone you speak into) after you have finished talking to someone: *There was a long pause, and she was about to put the phone down when the voice came back again.*

slam the phone down/slam down the phone /ˌslæm ðə 'fəʊn daʊn, ˌslæm daʊn ðə 'fəʊn/ [v phrase] to put the telephone down while someone is still speaking to you, because you are angry: *Call her. The worst thing she could do is slam down the phone.* | **+ on** *He tried to talk to her, but she slammed the phone down on him.*

get cut off/get disconnected /get ˌkʌt 'ɒf, get ˌdɪskə'nektɪ̈d/ [v phrase] if you **get cut off** or **get disconnected** when you are making a telephone call, the telephone suddenly stops working in the middle of your conversation and you cannot continue: *We got cut off in the middle of the conversation.* | *I don't know what happened, we just got disconnected.*

ring off /ˌrɪŋ 'ɒf / [phr v I] British to end a telephone call: *I suppose I'd better ring off now – we've been on the phone for over an hour.*

8 when a telephone line is busy

- busy
- on hold

busy ALSO **engaged** /'bɪzi, ɪn'geɪdʒd/ [adj] British a telephone line that is **busy** is already being used by the person that you want to telephone, so you cannot speak to them: *She tried to call Lisa, but the phone was busy.* | *I called Mom again, but it was still busy.* | *He tried Nick's suite again. This time the line was engaged.* | *Janice's number is still engaged. She's been on the phone all morning.* | **engaged tone** British/ **busy signal** American (=the sound a telephone makes when the person you are trying to call is already using the telephone) *I've been trying to call the customer helpline, but all I'm getting is a busy signal.*

on hold /ɒn 'həʊld/ [adv] waiting to speak to someone on the phone who cannot speak to you immediately because they are already speaking to someone else on the telephone: *You're always on hold for about 10 minutes before you get to talk to anyone.* | **put sb on hold** *I put Dana on hold while I tried to find Steve.*

9 when you want to leave a message for someone

- leave a message
- can/may I take a message?
- text
- voicemail

leave a message /ˌliːv ə 'mesɪdʒ/ [v phrase] *No, she didn't leave a message.* | **+ for** *Tom left a message for Mike on the answering machine.*

can/may I take a message? /ˌkæn, ˌmeɪ aɪ teɪk ə 'mesɪdʒ/ [v phrase] spoken say this on the telephone when you are offering to give a message to someone else: *I'm sorry, Mr. Perry isn't in yet. May I take a message?*

text /tekst/ [v T] to send a written message from your mobile phone to someone else's: *My daughter spends nearly all her time either on the phone or texting her friends.* | *Text me as soon as you get your exam results.*

voicemail /ˈvɔɪsmeɪl/ [n U] a system on the phone by which you can leave a spoken message for someone: *Hi Jen – I see I've reached your voicemail – I'll try and get back to you later.* | *I keep my voicemail on most mornings and deal with all my messages in the afternoon.*

television/radio

RELATED WORDS

- part of a television show *see* **part (3)**
- *see also* **actor/actress, news, switch on or off, advertising, film/movie**

1 television

- **television**
- **telly**
- **the box**
- **the small screen**

television ALSO **TV** informal /ˈteləvɪʒən, ˌteləˈvɪʒən, ˌtiː ˈviː/ [n U] the system of broadcasting pictures and sound, or the programmes that are broadcast in this way: *Television brings events like the Olympic games into millions of homes.* | *the educational uses of television* | **watch television/TV** *Nearly 80% of children watch TV after school.* | *People who watch a lot of television are more likely to be heavy.* | **on television/TV** *Kids have to learn that toys they see advertised on TV might not be as much fun as they look.* | **television/TV programme/show/series etc** *American television news programs are getting worse and worse.* | *a description of the fall season's new TV shows* —**television/TV** also **television/TV set** formal [n C] the box-shaped thing with a glass screen on which you watch programmes: *a wide-screen TV* | *He was sitting on the floor in front of the television.* | *We need to buy a new TV set.*

telly /ˈteli/ [n singular/U] British spoken the programmes that are broadcast on television or your television set: *It's true, I saw it on some show on the telly.* | **watch (the) telly** *You can watch telly after you've done your homework.* | **on telly** *Is there anything good on telly tonight?* —**telly** [n C] a television set: *We've just bought a new telly.*

the box British informal **/the tube** American informal /ðə ˈbɒks‖-ˈbɑːks, ðə ˈtjuːb‖-ˈtuːb/ [n singular] use this to talk about programmes on television or people's television sets: *The hours spent in front of the tube mean that children aren't participating in other forms of entertainment.* | **on the box/tube** *What's on the box?*

the small screen /ðə ˈsmɔːl ˌskriːn/ [n singular] television – use this especially when you are comparing television to films: *I had seen the movie before, but it didn't look as good on the small screen.* | *It's one of the best shows ever seen on the small screen.*

2 radio

- **radio**

radio /ˈreɪdiəʊ/ [n U] the system of broadcasting sound, or the programmes that are broadcast in this way: *The story was written specially for radio.* | **listen to the radio** *In the evening I usually watch TV or listen to the radio.* | **on the radio** *I've often heard that song on the radio, but I can't think what it's called.* | **radio programme/show/series etc** *Madden has a daily radio show on KSFO.* | **talk radio** (=radio programmes during which people call in to discuss a particular issue) *Rush Limbaugh is one of the biggest names in talk radio.* —**radio** [n C] the piece of electronic equipment that you listen to: *Do you have a radio in your car?*

3 when a programme is broadcast on television or radio

- **be on**
- **show**
- **broadcast**
- **televise**
- **screen**
- **be on the air**

be on /biː ˈɒn / [v phrase] if a programme **is on**, it is being broadcast and you can watch it on television or listen to it on the radio: *The Breakfast Show's on between 8 and 10 in the morning.* | *You shouldn't call him while the football's on.* | **be on television/TV/the radio** *There's a good concert on the radio this evening.* | *What's on TV tonight?*

show /ʃəʊ/ [v T] if a television company **shows** a particular programme, it makes the programme available for people to watch: *Highlights of the game will be shown on Channel 5.* | *They're showing 'Dangerous Liaisons' on Saturday night.* | *Should commercials be shown during children's programming?*

broadcast /ˈbrɔːdkɑːst‖-kæst/ [v I/T] if a television or radio company **broadcasts** a programme, they send it out so that people can watch it on television or listen to it on the radio: *The funeral was broadcast to the whole nation.* | *Radio WXLM broadcasts on 98.2 FM.* | **be broadcast live** (=when an event is shown at the same time that it is happening) *The whole race will be broadcast live from Monza.* —**broadcasting** [n U] *Meyer had no broadcasting experience when he created Midwest Television.*

televise /ˈteləvaɪz/ [v T] to show a particular event, speech, discussion etc on television: *This year's championships are not going to be televised at all.* | *The mayor plans to televise council meetings on cable channels.* | *a nationally televised speech*

screen /skriːn/ [v T usually in passive] to show a programme or film on television – used especially in newspapers or in the television industry: *'Border War' is to be screened by Channel Four later on in the week.* | *The film was under attack before it was even screened.*

be on the air /biː ɒn ði ˈeəʳ/ [v phrase] if a programme **is on the air**, it is being broadcast at that time, often at the same time that it is happening: *Someone called in while the programme was still on the air and identified the killer.* | *Winfrey revealed on the air that she had been sexually abused as a child.* | *The show was on the air for five years* (=it was broadcast at a regular time for five years).

4 a television or radio programme

- **programme**
- **show**
- **broadcast**
- **sitcom**
- **soap opera/soap**
- **documentary**

programme British **/program** American /ˈprəʊgræm/ [n C] a play, news report, performance etc that is broadcast on television or the radio at a particular time, often regularly: *It's one of my favourite programs.* | **+ about** *Did you see that programme about* *cricket on TV last night?* | **TV/television/radio programme** *When couples argue over which TV program to watch, the husband usually wins.* | **news/comedy/documentary etc programme** *a daily news programme aimed at teenagers*

show /ʃəʊ/ [n C] a television or radio programme, especially one that is entertaining or funny rather than a news or discussion programme: *I try and tape the shows I don't want to miss.* | **game/talk/quiz etc show** *'Who Wants to Be A Millionaire?' is one of the most successful game shows ever.* | **TV/television/radio show** *Spelling continues to produce hit television shows.*

broadcast /ˈbrɔːdkɑːst‖-kæst/ [n C] formal something that is **broadcast** on the radio or on television, especially a speech, discussion, or news programme: *The government has banned all broadcasts by opposition groups.* | **TV/television/radio broadcast** *In a nationwide TV broadcast, the prime minister explained why he was resigning.* | **live broadcast** (=a programme being broadcast at the same time as it is happening) *The exciting thing about the show is that it's a live broadcast and anything can happen.*

sitcom /ˈsɪtkɒm‖-kɑːm/ [n C] an amusing programme in which there is a different story each week about the same group of people: *Several family-oriented sitcoms are on in the early evening.* | *The popular British sitcom 'One Foot in the Grave' will finish this year.*

soap opera/soap /ˈsəʊp ˌɒpərə‖-ˌɑː-, səʊp/ [n C] a television or radio story about a group of people and their lives, which is broadcast regularly for many years: *American evening soap operas tend to be about the rich, while British soaps follow the lives of ordinary people.*

documentary /ˌdɒkjəˈmentəri◂‖ˌdɑːk-/ [n C] a programme that gives you facts and information about a serious subject, such as history, science, or social problems: *The documentary explores the success of a Jewish sect intent on keeping ancient traditions alive.* | **a TV/television documentary** *He made a TV documentary about the flower children of the sixties.* | **fly-on-the-wall documentary** (=one that shows the daily lives of people in detail, and that is made in a way that makes them forget they are being filmed) *a fly-on-the-wall documentary about teenage pregnancy*

5 a television or radio programme that is shown again

- rerun/repeat
- replay

rerun/repeat /ˈriːrʌn, rɪˈpiːt/ [n C] a television or radio programme that is shown again at a later time or date: *At this time of year, most of the primetime shows are reruns.* | *I'm not bothered about watching it tonight – it's a repeat of one I've already seen.*

replay ALSO **instant replay** American /ˈriːpleɪ, ˌɪnstənt ˈriːpleɪ/ [n C/U] a short part of a television programme, especially during a broadcast of a sporting event, that is shown again, often at a slower speed, so that people watching can see exactly what happened: *Television commentators often use the replays to criticize the officials.* | *The television cameras captured the violence and played it again in instant replay.*

6 an organization that broadcasts programmes

- station
- channel
- network
- the media/the mass media

station /ˈsteɪʃən/ [n C] a company or organization that broadcasts television or radio programmes: *What station are you listening to?* | **television/TV/radio station** *A reporter from a local television station was sent to interview Shaw.* | *Buck was sports director at radio station KMOX in St. Louis.*

channel /ˈtʃænl/ [n C] a particular set of programmes that is broadcast by one television company; there are usually several different channels, and you can choose which one you want to watch: *The final episode will be shown on Channel 4 tonight.* | **switch/change channels** *A lot of people switch channels during the commercials.* | **sports/nature/kids' etc channel** (=a channel that mainly shows sports, programmes about nature, programmes for children etc) *the sports channel on satellite TV*

network /ˈnetwɜːʳk/ [n C] a group of television or radio stations owned by the same company, which broadcasts the same programmes in different parts of a country: *The series is sponsored by Ford and will be shown over the ABC network.* | *The rankings list the programs and the network they are shown on.* | *Cable News Network shows 24 hours of news.*

the media/the mass media /ðə ˈmiːdiə, ðə ˌmæs ˈmiːdiə/ [n singular with singular or plural verb in British English] all the people and organizations that provide information for the public, including television, radio, and the newspapers: *Much of what children learn comes directly from the mass media.* | *The film has received enormous attention in the media.* | *There can be little doubt that in this country the media is very biased.*

7 to present a television or radio programme

- present
- host
- introduce

present /prɪˈzent/ [v T] especially British if someone **presents** a programme on television or the radio, they talk about what the programme will be about, tell you about what is happening, introduce the other people in it etc: *He was lucky enough to get a job presenting 'Blue Peter.'* | *Smiley presents 'Changing Rooms', the popular home decorating programme.*

host /həʊst/ [v T] if someone **hosts** a television or radio show, they introduce the other people in it, talk about what is happening etc – use this especially about shows in which people talk to each other and programmes in which there are a lot of short reports: *Smith hosts a sports show on a local radio station.* | *The show, hosted by journalist Robert Elms, features movie stars and singers.*

introduce /ˌɪntrəˈdjuːs‖-ˈduːs/ [v T] to speak at the beginning of a television or radio programme in order to tell people what it is about and who is in it: *And now here is Harvey Wolfsheim to introduce the show.* | *The concert will be introduced by Richard Baker, who will describe the music we are going to hear.*

8 someone who presents a television or radio programme

- presenter
- announcer
- host
- newsreader
- interviewer
- anchor
- commentator
- DJ/deejay
- VJ/veejay

presenter /prɪˈzentər/ [n C] British someone on a television or radio programme who tells you what the programme will be about, and introduces the other people in it: *The presenter read the news headlines.* | *Libby Purves, the radio presenter, has also written several novels.*

announcer /əˈnaʊnsər/ [n C] American someone on a television or radio programme who tells you what the programme will be about, or who tells you about a sports game as it is happening: *The announcer said that the contestants had been chosen at random.* | *Scully was the radio announcer for the Los Angeles Dodgers' games before moving to network television.*

host /həʊst/ [n C] someone who introduces the people on a show and who talks to people or about reports or scenes included in the programme – use this especially about talk shows, game shows, or quiz shows: *Minelli was the host for the two-hour awards program.* | *Jay Leno, the host of the 'Tonight' show*

newsreader British **/anchor/newscaster** American /ˈnjuːzˌriːdər‖ˈnuːz-, ˈæŋkər, ˈnjuːzˌkɑːstər‖ˈnuːzˌkæs-/ [n C] someone who reads the news on TV or radio, and introduces news reports: *Lehrer is the respected anchor of the News Hour.* | *John Humphrys became a top BBC foreign correspondent, newsreader, and co-presenter of Radio 4's Today programme.* | *Wilson is retiring after 20 years as a newscaster at Channel 7.*

interviewer /ˈɪntərvjuːər/ [n C] someone who asks a famous person questions on television, for example about their personal experiences, political opinions etc: *Paxman is seen as a tough interviewer who rarely lets politicians off the hook.* | *My most shocking moment as an interviewer was when a movie star came on drunk and threatened to hit my other guests.*

anchor /ˈæŋkər/ [n C] the main person who reads the news on a television news programme: *He was the anchor for the BBC's nine o'clock news for over 10 years.*

commentator /ˈkɒmənteɪtər‖ˈkɑː-/ [n C] someone on television or radio who describes an event as it is happening, especially a sports game: *Parcells, the former New York Giants coach, later became a sports commentator on television.*

DJ/deejay /ˌdiː ˈdʒeɪ◂/ [n C] someone who plays records and talks to people on a music programme on the radio: *Wolfman Jack was a famous deejay in the 1960s.* | *DJ Barry Scott hosts an oldies program on WZLX.*

VJ/veejay /ˌviː ˈdʒeɪ◂/ [n C] someone who introduces music videos on television: *Hunter is a former MTV veejay.*

9 someone who watches television or listens to the radio

- viewer
- listener
- audience
- couch potato

viewer /ˈvjuːər/ [n C] someone who watches television – used especially by people in the television business: *a programme that appeals to younger viewers* | *Some shows are cancelled before they get a chance to attract any viewers.* | *The networks have lost a substantial number of viewers to cable and video rentals.*

listener /ˈlɪsənər/ [n C] someone who listens to the radio – used especially by people in the radio business: *KCEA, a big-band radio station, relies on money from its listeners to keep running.* | *The station was flooded with calls from listeners after the show.*

audience /ˈɔːdiəns‖ˈɔː-, ˈɑː-/ [n C] all the people who watch or listen to a particular programme: *MTV's core audience is 18 to 24 year olds.* | *The program has an estimated audience of 5 million households.*

couch potato /ˈkaʊtʃ pəˌteɪtəʊ/ [n C] informal someone who watches too much television, and does not do other things: *Older adults who exercise are mentally sharper than their couch potato peers.* | *Use your free time creatively to show children there is more to life than being a couch potato.*

tell

RELATED WORDS

- to let people know your feelings or opinions *see* **express**
- to tell someone how to do something or how something works *see* **explain**
- to talk angrily to someone because they have done something wrong *see* **tell sb off**
- *see also* **say, speak, talk, insist, contact**

WHAT'S HERE

● **to tell sb sth**	see **1 to 10**
● **to tell sb a secret**	see **11 to 16**
● **to tell sb to do sth**	see **17 to 24**

to tell sb sth

1 to give someone information by speaking or writing to them

- tell
- let sb know
- inform
- notify
- bring sth to sb's attention/notice
- break the news (to sb)/break it to sb

tell /tel/ [v T] *If you'd told me earlier I might have been able to do something about it.* | **tell sb sth** *I want you to tell me all the details.* | *Who on earth told you that?* | *Can you tell me the quickest way to the centre of town?* | **tell sb (that)** *She wrote to tell me she was getting married.* | *We were told that the manager wanted to see us in his office immediately.* | **tell sb what/where/who etc** *Just tell me what happened.* | *Can you tell us where the nearest garage is?* | **tell sb about sth** *Have you told anyone about this?* | *One angry passenger claimed travellers were not told about the mechanical problems.*

let sb know /ˌlet (sb) ˈnəʊ/ [v phrase] especially spoken to tell someone something important that they need to know or want to know: *If you need any help, just let me know.* | *You mean she just left without letting anyone know?* | **+ about** *They said they'd let her know about the job by the end of the week.* | **let sb know sth** *I'll let you know our new address as soon as*

I have it. | **+ (that)** *When you get there, will you phone and let me know you arrived safely?* | **+ what/where/how etc** *Jean tried to get in touch with her husband to let him know what had happened.*

inform /ɪnˈfɔːʳm/ [v T] to officially or formally give someone information about something: *Do you think we ought to inform the police?* | **inform sb of/about sth** *You should inform your bank of any change of address.* | *Doctors should inform patients about the possible side effects of any drugs they prescribe.* | **inform sb (that)** *I am sorry to inform you that your application has been unsuccessful.*

notify /ˈnəʊtɪ̈faɪ/ [v T] formal to officially or formally give important information to someone, especially by telling them about something that has happened or that will happen: *Passengers are requested to notify a member of staff if they see suspicious packages.* | **notify sb of sth** *Police notified the boy's parents of his death immediately.* | **notify sb that** *Staff were notified several months in advance that they would be losing their jobs.* —**notification** /ˌnəʊtɪ̈fɪ̈ˈkeɪʃən/ [n U] *You can ask for notification in writing if you wish.*

bring sth to sb's attention/notice /ˌbrɪŋ (sth) tə (sb's) əˈtenʃən, ˈnəʊtɪ̈s/ [v phrase] to tell someone about something that they did not know but which they should know: *I am sure that your parents will want to know about this, and I will personally bring it to their attention.* | *The General Medical Council cannot investigate every controversial treatment brought to its attention.* | **it's been brought to my attention/notice that** *It's been brought to my notice that you've expressed your dislike of a certain member of the company.*

break the news (to sb)/break it to sb /ˌbreɪk ðə ˈnjuːz (tə (sb))‖-ˈnuːz-, ˈbreɪk ɪt tə (sb)/ [v phrase] to tell someone some bad news or something that might upset them: *Do you want to break the news or shall I?* | *She suspected that she had cancer, and that the doctors were trying to break it to her gradually.* | *After Jack's body was found, a policewoman had to break the news to his mother.* | **break it to sb that** *He was wondering how to break it to Celeste that their relationship was over.* | **break the news gently/break it to sb gently** (=tell someone something in a way that does not shock them too much) *Maybe I should speak to Connor first, so he can break the news gently to Patrick and Mary.*

2 ways of saying that a book, notice etc gives information

- tell
- give
- say

tell /tel/ [v T] **tell sb how/what/where etc** *This leaflet tells you how to apply for a driving licence.* | **tell sb sth** *The two dials in the middle tell you the airspeed and altitude.* | **tell sb (that)** *A sign told us it was the highest village in England.*

give /gɪv/ [v T] to provide information or details about something **give information/details/instructions etc** *The handbook gave full instructions on how to change the oil.* | *LA Weekly magazine gives information about what's on in Los Angeles every week.* | **give an account/description/report** *The article gave a vivid account of life after the earthquake.* | **give sb information/details etc** *The footprint could give police crucial details about the man's shoe size and probable weight and size.*

say /seɪ/ [v T] to give a particular piece of information about something **say sth about sth** *What does the guidebook say about the Opera House?* | **it says here (that)** (=it is written here that) *It says here that the police are closing in on the killer.*

3 to tell someone the most recent information

- keep sb informed
- keep sb up to date
- fill sb in
- brief
- give sb the low-down
- give sb an update on
- report

keep sb informed /ˌkiːp (sb) ɪnˈfɔːʳmd/ [v phrase] to give someone regular information about decisions, events etc, so that they know exactly what is happening: *I want to know what you decide, so keep me informed.* | **+ of/about** *We'll be keeping you informed of any new developments.* | *The doctor should be kept informed about any changes in your child's condition.* | **keep sb fully/well informed** *During the strike, the media kept the public fully informed about the situation.* | *Parents have complained that we are not keeping them very well informed of their children's progress.*

keep sb up to date /ˌkiːp (sb) ʌp tə ˈdeɪt/ [v phrase] to give someone regular information about what has been happening most recently: *We publish a weekly newsletter to keep everyone up to date.* | **+ with/on** *She reads the newspaper every day to keep herself up to date with financial affairs.* | *the magazine that keeps you up to date on all the latest in rock and pop*

fill sb in /ˌfɪl (sb) ˈɪn / [phr v T] to tell someone about things that have happened recently, which they do not know about because they have not talked to you for quite a long time or they have been somewhere else: *You didn't miss much – I'll fill you in later* | **+ on** *Marjorie filled us in on all the latest gossip.* | *Please can someone fill me in on anything I've missed?* | **fill sb in on what/where/when etc** *Bob filled me in on what he had been doing since we last met.*

brief /briːf/ [v T usually in passive] to give someone all the necessary information about a situation, so that they know exactly what is happening or so that they are prepared for something that they have to do: *Police officers were briefed before going out to arrest the suspects.* | **be fully/well briefed** *Make sure that the PR department are fully briefed on their role.* | *It was clear the witness had been well briefed.* | **brief sb on/about sth** *You'll be picked up from here tomorrow night and briefed on what you have to do.* | *DeGaulle flew back to England to be briefed about the invasion that was about to begin.* —**briefing** [n C] *The drug squad's briefing lasted twenty minutes.*

give sb the low-down /ˌgɪv (sb) ðə ˈləʊ daʊn/ [v phrase] informal to tell someone all the information they need to know about a situation: *'Have you heard about the deal with IBM?' 'Yes, John's just been giving me the low-down.'* | **+ on** *The travel reporter was giving the low-down on the evening's traffic chaos.*

give sb an update on /ˌgɪv (sb) ən ˈʌpdeɪt ɒn/ [v phrase] to tell someone the things that have happened concerning a particular piece of work, plan, or situation since they last saw you: *Let me give you an update on the trial.* | *Can you give me an update on any policy changes there've been since we last spoke?*

report /rɪˈpɔːʳt/ [v I/T] to officially tell someone about what has been happening in a particular area of work, especially because it is your job to do so: *Is there anything to report?* | **report to sb on sth** *Nicky reports to me on any new developments in the relevant technological fields.* | **report back (to sb)** *The* *delegation will report back to Congress on the situation inside China.*

4 to publicly tell a lot of people about something

▸ **announce** ▸ **publicize**
▸ **report**

announce /əˈnaʊns/ [v T] to tell the public about a decision that has been made, or about something that will happen: *The government has announced the date of the next election.* | *The winner of the award will be announced at a dinner at the Sheraton Hotel.* | **+ (that)** *The Spanish government announced that it would invest over $14,000 million in the Latin American region.* —**announcement** [n C/U] **+ that** *the announcement that Mr Reeves is to resign* | **make an announcement** *They are expected to make an announcement very soon.*

report /rɪˈpɔːʳt/ [v T] to give people news about what is happening, in newspapers, on television, or on the radio: *The local newspaper has reported several cases of meningitis in the area.* | **+ (that)** *Our foreign correspondent reports that conditions in the refugee camps are filthy and overcrowded.* | **+ on** *She was sent to Washington to report on the presidential elections.*

publicize ALSO **publicise** British /ˈpʌbl̩saɪz/ [v T] to use the newspapers, television etc to provide information about something such as a new product, a special event, or an important subject, because you want everyone to know about it: *She did a series of interviews to publicize her new book.* | *Orlov spent seven years in prison for publicizing human-rights violations.* | **well publicized** (=mentioned a lot in newspapers, on television etc) *The parade was well publicized, and thousands of people came to see it.* | *a well-publicized case*

5 to tell a story

▸ **tell (sb) a story** ▸ **storyteller**
▸ **narrate** ▸ **narrator**

tell (sb) a story /ˌtel (sb) ə ˈstɔːri/ [v phrase] *Some people are really good at telling stories.* | *You said you would tell me a story if I was good.* | **+ about** *He began by telling the children a story about a giant who was very unpopular with all the other giants because he wouldn't eat people.*

narrate /nəˈreɪt‖ˈnæreɪt, næˈreɪt, nə-/ [v T] to tell a story by describing all the events in order, especially at the same time as actors act them out: *'The Snowman', narrated by Bernard Cribbins* | *John Peace narrates his tale, taking us from his beginnings through university and professional training into his old age.*

storyteller /ˈstɔːriˌteləʳ/ [n C] a person who tells stories for entertainment: *He was a marvellous storyteller. The children would listen to him for hours.* | *In the old oral tradition, the storyteller was an important link with the past.*

narrator /nəˈreɪtəʳ‖ˈnæreɪ-, næˈreɪtəʳ, nə-/ [n C] the person in a story who seems to speak directly to the reader and who describes everything that happens – used especially when you write about literature: *Ishmael, the narrator of the story, tells the reader why he went to sea.* | *Flaubert's narrator enters Emma Bovary's consciousness from time to time, to describe events from her point of view.*

6 to let someone know something without telling them directly

▸ **make sth known** ▸ **not in so many words**
▸ **give sb to understand (that)**

make sth known /ˌmeɪk (sth) ˈnəʊn/ [v phrase] to let someone know something without telling them directly, for example by behaving in a particular way or by telling someone else who you know will then tell the person: *The Queen made her displeasure known by cancelling her visit.* | **make your feelings/views/wishes known** *People without the right to vote were often able to make their feelings known through demonstrations or riots.* | **make it known that** *The other boys in Steven's class took every opportunity to make it known that he was not accepted.*

give sb to understand (that) /ˌgɪv (sb) tʊ ˌʌndəʳˈstænd (ðət)/ [v phrase usually in passive] formal to make someone think that something is true, or that something will happen, but without actually saying this clearly: *A friend of your daughter's gave us to understand that you lived in Michigan.* | *Although I received no official indication, I was given to understand that I would be promoted within a year.*

not in so many words /nɒt ɪn ˌsəʊ meni ˈwɜːʳdz/ [prep] if someone lets you know something shocking, bad, or unkind, but **not in so many words**, they let you know that it is true without saying it directly: *'Did Sarah tell you she was leaving?' 'Not in so many words, no.'*

7 to tell someone something that someone else has told you

▸ **pass on** ▸ **relay**

pass on /ˌpɑːs ˈɒn‖ˌpæs-/ [phr v T] to give someone a message or some information that another person has asked you to give **pass on sth (to sb)** *Could you pass on my thanks for all these lovely gifts?* | *Please pass on my sympathy to Mr and Mrs Stanton.* | **pass sth on (to sb)** *She said she'd pass the message on to the other students.* | *I'm grateful for everything that has been said today, and I will be sure to pass it on.*

relay /ˈriːleɪ/ [v T] to send or give someone an official message, a piece of news, information etc which you have received from another person: *Mendoza relayed the news as soon as he returned to the base.* | **+ to** *The speaker opened the session by relaying some messages to the conference.*

8 to tell someone what you are feeling

▸ **get sth off your chest** ▸ **pour out your heart/soul**
▸ **confide in**

get sth off your chest /ˌget (sth) ɒf jɔːʳ ˈtʃest/ [v phrase] to tell someone about something that has been worrying you or annoying you for a long time so that you feel better afterwards: *I feel so much better now that I've got that off my chest.* | *Writing to you is a good way to get things off my chest.*

pour out your heart/soul /ˌpɔːr aʊt jɔːʳ ˈhɑːʳt, ˈsəʊl/ [v phrase] to tell someone everything about some strong emotions that you are feeling, especially feelings of unhappiness: *Suddenly, Jason burst into tears and poured out his heart, telling his* *mother all about everything.* | **+ to** *I had no idea Kay was so unhappy until she poured out her soul to me last night.*

confide in /kən'faɪd ɪn/ [phr v T] to tell someone about something very private or secret, especially a personal problem, because you feel that you can trust them: *He was a good listener and Elinor found it easy to confide in him.* | **+ about** *He wanted desperately to confide in someone about his feelings of failure.* | **+ that** *Harriet confided in me that she and Mark were considering divorce.*

9 to tell someone in authority about something wrong that someone has done

- tell on/tell
- rat on
- tell tales
- report
- inform on
- grass
- talk
- blow the whistle
- tip off
- name names
- nark

tell on/tell /'tel ɒn, tel/ [phr v T/v I] to tell someone in authority, especially a parent or teacher, about something wrong that someone has done – used by children: *I'm going to tell if you don't stop messing around.* | *Please don't tell on me – Mum thinks I've been staying at my friend's house.*

rat on ALSO **split on sb** British informal /'ræt ɒn, 'splɪt ɒn (sb)/ [phr v T] to tell someone in authority about something wrong that someone has done, especially when this seems disloyal: *Can you believe he ratted on his own brother?* | *Don't worry, Robert's reliable. He won't split on us.*

tell tales British **/tattle (on sb)** American /ˌtel 'teɪlz, 'tætl (ɒn (sb))/ [v phrase] if a child **tells tales** or **tattles on** someone, they tell a parent or teacher about something another child has done in order to cause trouble: *'Mum, Daniel's broken a plate.' 'Don't tell tales, dear.'* | *Sarah's teacher told her it was silly to keep tattling on her classmates.* | *You'll lose all your friends if you keep tattling.*

report /rɪ'pɔːʳt/ [v T] to give information about a crime, an accident etc to the police or to someone in authority: *I'd like to report a theft.* | **report sth to sb** *All accidents must be reported at once to the aviation authority.* | *Many rape victims are too scared to report the attack to the police.* | **report sb (for sth)** *A man has been reported for a number of alleged motoring offences.*

inform on /ɪn'fɔːʳm ɒn/ [phr v T] to secretly tell the police that someone you know has done something illegal: *Charlotte informed on her brother, who was then arrested for drug-dealing.* | *He categorically denied that he had ever informed on dissidents.*

grass British informal **/squeal** American informal /grɑːs‖græs, skwiːl/ [v I] to tell the police who is responsible for a crime or illegal activity when this seems disloyal: *When we got there the cops were waiting for us. Somebody must have squealed.* | **+ on** *If the others ever found out he'd squealed on them, they'd kill him.* | *You grassed on us to save your own life.* | **grass sb up** *I don't trust her – what if she grasses us up?*

talk /tɔːk/ [v I] to give the police information about a crime that you know about or are involved in, especially when they are questioning you officially about it: *The suspect was questioned for two hours, but refused to talk.* | *He said he'd come back and kill me if I talked.*

blow the whistle /ˌbləʊ ðə 'wɪsəl/ [v phrase] to let people know about an illegal activity which has been happening for a long time, especially when you have been helping to keep it secret: *He was shot because he knew too much and was about to blow the whistle.* | **+ about** *It was the factory manager who eventually blew the whistle about the pollution scandal.* | **+ on** *We'd better get her before she has a chance to blow the whistle on us.*

tip off /ˌtɪp 'ɒf/ [phr v T] to give the police or another authority information that will allow them to prevent a crime taking place **tip off sb** *Somebody must have tipped off the police. They were already waiting at the house.* | *The alert was started by another inmate who tipped off prison staff.* | **tip sb off** *I wonder who tipped them off.* | **tip sb off that** *His contact had not merely tipped him off that drugs were on the premises, he had told him where to look.*

name names /ˌneɪm 'neɪmz/ [v phrase] to make public the names of people who have done something wrong: *If you don't give me the money, I'm going to start naming names.* | *Someone – I won't name names – has been caught stealing from the stores.*

nark especially British, informal **/narc** especially American, informal /nɑːʳk/ [v I] to secretly tell the police or someone in authority about someone else's criminal activity, especially activities involving illegal drugs: *'How'd they get caught?' 'Somebody must've narked.'* | **+ on** *If things get too risky, Ken'll probably narc on you to the cops.*

10 someone who gives information to the police

- informer/informant
- grass
- nark
- stool pigeon
- source

informer/informant /ɪn'fɔːʳməʳ, ɪn'fɔːʳmənt/ [n C] someone who is part of or closely connected with a criminal organization but who secretly tells the police about its activities: *An informer had warned police about the bombing.* | **police informer/informant** *The three men were released on condition that they became police informants.*

grass /grɑːs‖græs/ [n C] British informal someone who secretly gives the police information about someone who is responsible for a crime, in return for money, when this seems disloyal: *I wouldn't inform on you – I'm no grass.*

nark especially British, informal **/narc** especially American, informal /nɑːʳk/ [n C] someone who is friendly with criminals and who secretly tells the police about their activities, especially activities involving illegal drugs: *I wouldn't trust that new guy – I think he's a narc.*

stool pigeon /'stuːl ˌpɪdʒɨn/ [n C] especially American a criminal who helps the police to trap other criminals by telling the police about a crime that is going to take place: *How could he ever live with himself after being a stool pigeon?*

source /sɔːʳs/ [n C] someone who gives information to the police, a newspaper etc, especially someone who does not want their name to be known: *It's the first duty of a journalist to protect his or her sources* (=not say who they are). | *Our source informed us that there was a possibility of another attack the following week, possibly in the central London area.*

to tell sb a secret

11 to tell someone something that was a secret

- tell
- reveal
- disclose
- make sth public
- divulge
- expose
- leak
- spill the beans
- let sb in on
- blab

tell /tel/ [v I/T] to **tell** someone something that should be kept secret: *What did she say? Tell me!* | *If someone asked me to keep a secret I would never tell.* | **tell sb where/what/who etc** *He didn't tell me where he got this information.* | **tell sb about sth** *Don't tell anyone about this just yet.* | **tell sb a secret** *Come here Eva – let me tell you a secret.* | **tell sb sth in the strictest confidence** (=tell someone something on the condition that they do not tell anyone) *I'm telling you this in the strictest confidence, so not a word to anyone.*

reveal /rɪ'viːl/ [v T] especially written to let people know about something that was previously kept secret: *The company has just revealed its plans for the coming year, including the opening of new offices in Paris.* | *What actually happened to the gold has never been revealed.* | **+ (that)** *Markov revealed that he had once worked for the CIA.* | *Ginsberg withdrew his application to become Attorney General after it was revealed that he had smoked marijuana at college.*

disclose /dɪs'kləʊz/ [v T] to publicly reveal something such as a fact or a name that has been kept secret or hidden: *The agent does not have to disclose the amount his client paid.* | **+ that** *In the report it was disclosed that neither pilot nor controller had any experience of the radar system in use at the time of the crash.* | **disclose information/details/evidence etc** *The Security Service is unlikely to disclose any information.* | **disclose sb's identity** (=say who someone is) *He refused to disclose the identity of the politician.* —**disclosure** /dɪs'kləʊʒəʳ/ [n C/U] *Investors were shocked by the disclosure* (=when it was disclosed) *that the company director had been spending millions on luxury yachts and villas.*

make sth public /ˌmeɪk (sth) 'pʌblɪk/ [v phrase] to make a piece of important information known to the public, especially after keeping it secret for some time: *The Senator will make his decision public on Friday.* | *Reporters learned the news on Friday but agreed not to make it public until the following day.* | **make it public that** *Freddie Mercury died only two days after making it public that he was suffering from AIDS.*

divulge /daɪ'vʌldʒ, dɨ-/ [v T] formal to give someone some very important and often personal information which was previously secret or unknown: *The other three companies refused to divulge their plans.* | **+ what/where/when etc** *I'm afraid I cannot divulge what Jameson said to me.* | **divulge sth to sb** *The contract forbids employees to divulge details of this work to anyone outside the company.*

expose /ɪk'spəʊz/ [v T] to tell the public about the secret activities of a person or organization, because you think that people ought to know about something morally wrong that is being done: *Her criminal activities were finally exposed in the Washington Post by political columnist Richard McCallum.* | **+ to** *They threatened to expose him to the media unless he changed his ways.*

leak /liːk/ [v T] to deliberately give secret government information to a newspaper or television company: *A man was charged today with leaking official secrets.* | *The Congressman was furious that the report had been leaked.* | **leak sth to sb** *The contents of the fax were leaked to the press* —**leak** [n C] *The scandal began with a leak to 'The Times'.*

spill the beans /ˌspɪl ðə 'biːnz/ [v phrase] informal to tell someone about something that has been planned and was supposed to be a secret: *'Does Phillip know about our plan?' 'Yes, someone must have spilled the beans.'* | *The class managed to keep the party a secret until Lorraine, unable to control herself any longer, spilled the beans.*

let sb in on /ˌlet (sb) 'ɪn ɒn/ [phr v T] informal to tell someone about a secret plan or idea so that they are involved in it, especially because you trust them: *We'll let you in on our plan if you promise to keep it a secret.* | *I know you're up to something so you might as well let me in on it.*

blab /blæb/ [v I] informal to tell someone a secret – use this when you disapprove of this: *OK I'll tell you, but you'd better not blab!* | **+ about** *She went and blabbed about Ernie's surprise party.* | **+ to** *Better not say anything about it to Mickey – he'll just end up blabbing to someone.*

12 to accidentally tell someone a secret

- let slip
- let the cat out of the bag
- give the game away

let slip /ˌlet 'slɪp/ [v phrase] **+ that** *Alex let slip that he had spoken to Julie on the phone and knew where she was.* | **let slip sth/let sth slip** *He inadvertently let slip the name of their new product.*

let the cat out of the bag /let ðə ˌkæt aʊt əv ðə 'bæg/ [v phrase] informal to accidentally tell someone something that allows them to guess a secret: *I'm sorry. Jim knows about last week's party. I'm afraid I let the cat out of the bag.* | *Some idiot's let the cat out of the bag – Mrs Simpson realizes there's something going on.*

give the game away British **/give the whole thing away** American informal /ˌgɪv ðə 'geɪm əˌweɪ, ˌgɪv ðə ˌhəʊl θɪŋ ə'weɪ/ [v phrase] to accidentally say something or do something that makes someone guess a secret: *Don't mention Dad's birthday or you'll give the game away.* | *If you don't want to give the whole thing away, take that stupid smile off your face!*

13 to deliberately not tell someone a secret

- not tell anyone
- keep sth (a) secret
- not breathe a word/not tell a soul
- keep quiet
- keep sth to yourself
- keep sth from
- keep back

not tell anyone /nɒt tel 'eniwʌn/ [v phrase] *I'm leaving next month to start another job, but don't tell anyone just yet.* | *She knew she had cancer, but she didn't tell anyone.*

keep sth (a) secret /ˌkiːp (sth) (ə) 'siːkrɨt/ [v phrase] to not tell other people about something or not let them find out about it: *He said it was vital to keep Operation Beehive secret.* | *It was impossible for the affair to be kept secret.* | **+ from** *At first I tried to keep my illness a secret from my wife.*

not breathe a word/not tell a soul /nɒt ˌbriːð ə 'wɜːʳd, nɒt ˌtel ə 'səʊl/ [v phrase] to not tell anyone anything at all about something, because it is very important that no one knows about it: *It's supposed to be a big surprise, so don't breathe a word.* | *Don't worry, I won't tell a soul about any of this.*

keep quiet /ˌkiːp 'kwaɪət/ [v phrase] to not tell anyone about something that you know is happening, especially something that other people would disapprove of because it is slightly illegal or unfair **+ about** *I wish I'd kept quiet about the money.* | *We'd better keep quiet about this for now.* | **keep it quiet** *We can give you a 10% raise, but not the others – so keep it quiet, won't you?*

keep sth to yourself /ˌkiːp (sth) tə jɔːʳ'self/ [v phrase] to not tell other people something that someone has told you, or something that you have found out about: *Don't tell Sam – he's incapable of keeping anything to himself.* | *Branson knew who the killer was, but had kept it to himself for twenty years.*

keep sth from /'kiːp (sth) frɒm/ [phr v T] to deliberately not tell someone something that you know, especially because you are worried about telling them, or because it might upset them: *If a patient is dying, I don't think doctors have a right to keep it from them.* | *I've tried to ask her what's worrying her, but she says it's nothing. I'm sure she's keeping something from me.*

keep back /ˌkiːp 'bæk/ [phr v T] to not tell someone certain facts about something when telling them everything else about it **keep sth back** *I got the feeling he was keeping something back.* | **keep back sth** *Although most of the facts were published the government kept back certain details that might prove embarrassing.* | **keep sth back from sb/keep back sth from sb** *I must now confess something which I kept back from you earlier.*

14 to not tell someone something they want to know

- withhold
- hold out on
- not give anything away
- not/never let on

withhold /wɪð'həʊld, wɪθ-/ [v T] to not give information, especially when you have been officially asked to do so **withhold information/evidence/facts etc** *Civil servants should be as helpful as possible, and withhold information only in the interests of national security.* | *When the article was published, I asked for my name to be withheld.* | **+ from** *He was accused of withholding vital evidence from the police.*

hold out on /ˌhəʊld 'aʊt ɒn/ [phr v T] informal to refuse to give someone the information that they want, even though they keep asking you: *We all feel that members of the Medical Research Council are holding out on us.* | *Why are you holding out on me like this? I'm your lawyer and I need to know what happened.*

not give anything away /nɒt gɪv ˌeniθɪŋ ə'weɪ/ [v phrase] to not tell anyone anything about something, especially about your plans or intentions, when they are asking about them or are very interested to know about them: *I asked Teresa if she thought she and Liam would get married, but she wouldn't give anything away.* | *Whatever the England manager's plans are for tonight, he's not giving anything away.*

not/never let on /nɒt, ˌnevəʳ let 'ɒn/ [v phrase] to not tell someone a secret, especially when they are asking you questions about a subject connected with that secret: *Don't worry – I won't let on.* | **+ about** *She never let on about her boyfriend's criminal past.*

15 ways of asking someone to tell you something

- tell me
- out with it/spit it out

tell me /'tel miː/ spoken *Tell me Caroline, do you trust me?* | **+ where/when/how etc** *Tell me where you left the money.* | *Come in and tell me what the problem is.* | **+ about** *Tell me about Thursday night. Did you visit Mrs Berry?* | **tell me sth** *Tell me a little about yourself.*

out with it/spit it out /'aʊt wɪð ɪt, ˌspɪt ɪt 'aʊt/ spoken say this when you are annoyed or angry because someone has not told you something: *I know there's something you're not telling us, so out with it!* | *His name, Cathy, his name! Out with it!* | *What have you done? Come on – spit it out!* | *Are you implying something? Spit it out then!*

16 to make someone not tell anyone about something

- swear sb to secrecy
- between you and me

swear sb to secrecy /ˌsweəʳ (sb) tə 'siːkrəsi/ [v phrase] to make someone seriously promise that they will not tell anyone about something you have told them or something that they know about: *'What's she doing here?' 'I'd better not say. She swore me to secrecy.'* | *Nobody knows much about the organization because its members are all sworn to secrecy.*

between you and me /bɪˌtwiːn ˌjuː ən 'miː/ [adv] spoken used when you are telling someone that what you are saying is a secret, and you do not want them to tell anyone else about it: *Between you and me, I think Elizabeth is a bit of a nightmare.*

to tell sb to do sth

17 to tell someone to do something

- tell
- order
- ask sb to do sth
- demand
- insist
- dictate

tell /tel/ [v T] *'Wait here!' he told the children.* | **tell sb to do sth** *The teacher told us to be quiet.* | *I thought I told you to be in bed by 10 o'clock!* | **tell sb not to do sth** *She told him not to phone her again.* | **tell sb (that)** *The doctors have told me that I should give up smoking.* | **tell sb how/what/where etc** *Don't tell me how to behave in public!* | *I'm in charge here, and I'm not going to have anyone telling me what to do.* | **do as you are told** (=used to tell children to obey) *Do as you're told and go and wash your hands.*

order /'ɔːʳdəʳ/ [v T] to tell someone to do something in a threatening way: *'Don't move', he ordered.* | **order sb to do sth** *A man with a gun ordered the woman to give him all her money.* | *He was ordered to pay £4000 towards the court costs of £10,000.* | **order sb out of/into/back etc** *She pointed her gun at him, ordering him out of the room.*

ask sb to do sth /ˌɑːsk (sb) tə 'duː (sth) ‖ˌæsk-/ [v phrase] to tell someone politely but firmly to do something or to stop doing something: *Mr Evans, I must ask you to come with me to the police station.* | **ask sb not to do sth** *Would you ask visitors not to park their cars in front of the entrance.*

demand /dɪ'mɑːnd‖dɪ'mænd/ [v T] to tell someone that they must do something, especially when you are angry or impatient and want them to do it immediately **+ (that)** *You should demand that they finish the job now, not some time in August.* | *Realizing that her husband had deceived her, she demanded that he tell her the whole truth.* | **demand an apology/a refund etc** (=tell someone that they must say they are sorry, give money back etc) *How dare you say that! I demand an apology.*

insist /ɪn'sɪst/ [v I/T] to tell someone firmly and repeatedly that they must do something, especially something that they do not want to do: *I didn't want to tell dad about the fight, but he insisted.* | **+ (that)** *I wanted to pay by cheque but the landlord insisted that I pay him in cash.* | *They're insisting we report the matter to the police right away.*

dictate /dɪk'teɪt‖'dɪkteɪt/ [v I] to tell someone exactly what they must do or how they must behave, as if you had power to make them obey you **+ to** *She refused to be dictated to by some stupid official in Washington.* | **+ how/what/where etc** *Your parents have no right to dictate how you should spend your money.*

18 to officially tell someone to do something

- order
- instruct
- give orders/ instructions
- issue orders/ instructions
- decree
- command
- direct sb to do sth
- subpoena

order /'ɔːʳdəʳ/ [v T] *Only the king has the power to order her release from prison.* | *After the accident the government ordered a full public enquiry.* | **order sb to do sth** *The colonel ordered his men to advance.* | *He was ordered to pay a total of £65 compensation.* | **+ that** *The court ordered that Gilmore should be executed.* | **order sb into/out of/back etc** *It wasn't until 1973 that Nixon finally ordered US troops out of Vietnam.*

instruct /ɪn'strʌkt/ [v T] to officially tell someone to do something, especially when you tell them exactly how it should be done **instruct sb to do sth** *It is a good idea to instruct a specialist company to inspect the property for damp.* | *One of the secretaries had been instructed to reserve me a seat on the next plane to London.* | **as instructed** (=in the way that you have been instructed) *She took the tablets three times every day, as instructed by her doctor.*

give orders/instructions /gɪv 'ɔːʳdəʳz, ɪn'strʌkʃənz/ [v phrase] if someone such as a leader or officer **gives orders** or **gives instructions**, they tell other people exactly what they must do **+ to do sth** *It was the police chief who had given orders to shoot.* | **+ that** *The doctor left after giving instructions that she should rest as much as possible.* | **give sb orders/instructions** *The General has given them orders to bomb the city.* | **give (sb) strict instructions** *We were given strict instructions that nobody should be allowed in the building without a security card.*

issue orders/instructions /ˌɪʃuː 'ɔːʳdəʳz, ɪn'strʌkʃənz/ [v phrase] if someone such as a leader or officer **issues orders** or **issues instructions**, they tell people exactly what they should do, especially by sending a written statement: *The EC plans to issue orders banning the sale of the drug.* | **+ that** *The Department of Defense has issued instructions that no one should enter the area without permission.*

decree /dɪ'kriː/ [v T] if a government, parliament, or court **decrees** that something should happen, they officially order it by making a law or by changing the existing law: *The government decreed a ban on all contact with the guerrillas by local and provincial government officials.* | **+ (that)** *In 1929 Parliament decreed that all women should have the right to vote.*

command /kə'mɑːnd‖kə'mænd/ [v T] if someone such as a king or a military officer **commands** someone to do something, they tell them officially that they must do it **command sb to do sth** *Admiral Boyle commanded the entire crew to assemble on deck.* | **+ that** *The King had the power to command that parliament be dissolved.*

direct sb to do sth /dʒ̊ˌrekt (sb) tə 'duː (sth)/ [v phrase] if someone in a position of legal authority such as a judge **directs** someone to do something, they order them to do it: *The judge directed the jury to find her not guilty.* | *He was jailed for refusing to answer questions when directed to do so in court.*

subpoena /sə'piːnə, səb-/ [n C] to officially order someone to appear in a court of law in order to answer questions – used in legal contexts: *If you refuse to attend the trial we can always get you subpoenaed.* | *Another three of the president's advisors were subpoenaed.*

19 to tell someone to come to you

- send for
- summon

send for /'send fɔːʳ/ [phr v T] to send someone a message ordering them to come to you: *We'd better send for a doctor – I think she's badly hurt.* | *She was sent for by the headteacher in her office.*

summon /'sʌmən/ [v T] to officially order someone to come to you: *President Clinton summoned his top White House aides to discuss the crisis.* | **+ to** *The Colonel had summoned him to Cancun for the meeting at the Rena Victoria Hotel.* | **summon sb to appear** (=summon them to a court of law) *I've been summoned to appear at Guildford Magistrates Court on June 1st.*

20 to change an order that someone has given

- override
- overrule

override /ˌəʊvə'raɪd/ [v T] to use your power to change an order or decision that was made by someone with less power than you: *Congress has the power to override the President's veto.* | *Churchill issued a new order overriding previous instructions.*

overrule /ˌəʊvə'ruːl/ [v T] to use your power to change an order or decision, especially one made by a court of law or by a military leader, because you think it is wrong: *After seeing new evidence the judge overruled the court's original decision.* | *A general commanding American troops on the battlefield found himself overruled by politicians back in Washington.*

21 ways of saying that you have been ordered to do something

- **on sb's orders/instructions**
- **under orders/instructions**
- **at sb's insistence**

on sb's orders/instructions /ɒn (sb's) ˈɔːʳdəʳz, ɪnˈstrʌkʃənz/ [adv] if you do something **on** someone's **orders**, or **on** someone's **instructions**, you do it because they have officially told you to do it: *On the instructions of the new military government, soldiers burned books and other documents.* | **acting on sb's orders/instructions** (=doing what someone has told you to do) *Sergeant Dean claims that he was acting on the orders of the police chief.*

under orders/instructions /ˌʌndər ˈɔːʳdəʳz, ɪnˈstrʌkʃənz/ [adv] if someone is **under orders** or **under instructions** to do something, they have been officially ordered to do it as part of their duty by the person they are working for **+ to do sth** *I am under instructions not to tell you the name of the person who has sent you the money.* | *The soldiers are under strict orders to abide by the ceasefire.* | **acting under orders/instructions** *State troopers acting under orders from the Mayor of Los Angeles have put down the riots.*

at sb's insistence /ət (sb's) ɪnˈsɪstəns/ [adv] if you do something **at** someone's **insistence**, you do it because they have firmly and repeatedly said that you must, even though you may not want to: *At Joanna's insistence we stayed the night at her house.* | *I took a local guide with me at the insistence of the government authorities.*

22 a statement telling someone to do something

- **order**
- **instructions**
- **command**
- **directive**
- **decree**

order /ˈɔːʳdəʳ/ [n C] an official statement ordering you to do something, given by someone with the power to do this, especially a military officer: *We are still waiting for orders from HQ.* | **obey/disobey an order** *The commander's orders must be obeyed at all times.* | *Anyone who disobeys this order will be punished.* | **that's an order** (=used to tell someone that they must definitely do something) *You will report to me at eight o'clock in the morning – and that's an order.* | **give (sb) an order** *I'm the one who gives the orders around here – just remember that.* | **+ to do sth** *General Bradley gave the order to advance.* | **sb's orders** (=the orders someone has been given) *My orders are to take you to the airport and put you on the first plane to Paris.* | **take orders from sb** (=obey someone) *I'm not taking orders from you!* | **on sb's orders** (=because of someone's order) *On Stalin's orders, the target for the 5 year plan was raised once again.*

instructions /ɪnˈstrʌkʃəns/ [n plural] a statement telling someone what they must do, usually giving them details of how they should do it: *Mr Patel's instructions are to phone him immediately if you get any news from the police.* | **+ to do sth** *Scott has just received instructions to return to Washington.* | **+ on** *We were given instructions on what to do in an emergency.* | **+ that** *Mrs Edwards left instructions that in the event of her death the money was to be shared between her sons.* | **follow/obey instructions** *If you'd followed my instructions carefully none of this would have happened.* | **detailed instructions** *The boss won't be here tomorrow, but she's left you detailed instructions so you'll know exactly what to do.* | **strict instructions** *Sometimes my mother visits me at work, although I have given her strict instructions not to do so.* | **sb's instructions** (=instructions someone has been given) *My instructions were to give the package to him personally.*

command /kəˈmɑːnd‖kəˈmænd/ [n C] an official order by someone such as a king or a military officer which must be obeyed: *An officer stood on one of the tanks and began shouting commands through a loudspeaker.* | **obey/disobey a command** *If any of the King's subjects refused to obey one of his commands, they were put to death.* | **give the command to do sth** *Admiral Collingwood gave the command to open fire.*

directive /dəˈrektɪv, daɪ-/ [n C] an official order which is made by a powerful organization and has the effect of a law: *Article 10 of the directive requires all food to be clearly labelled.* | **under a directive** (=as a result of a directive) *Under an EC directive unleaded petrol must be made available throughout Britain.*

decree /dɪˈkriː/ [n C/U] an official order which has the effect of a law and is made by someone such as a king, queen, or military government **issue a decree** (=send out a decree) *In 1637 the Emperor issued a decree ordering all foreigners to leave the country.* | **by decree** (=by making decrees) *The king dissolved parliament and ruled by decree.*

23 to give orders in a rude, unpleasant way

- **order sb around**
- **push sb around**
- **boss sb around**
- **lay down the law**
- **throw your weight around**

order sb around ALSO **order sb about** British /ˌɔːʳdəʳ (sb) əˈraʊnd, ˌɔːʳdəʳ (sb) əˈbaʊt/ [phr v T] if someone **orders you around** or **orders you about**, they keep telling you what to do in an annoying or unfair way, and they seem to enjoy it: *You won't get the best out of your staff by ordering them around like that.* | *I wish you'd stop ordering me about – I'm not your servant you know.*

push sb around /ˌpʊʃ (sb) əˈraʊnd/ [phr v T] to order someone to do things in a rude, impatient, and often threatening way: *I'm sick and tired of being pushed around by him.* | *You shouldn't let other people push you around – you've got to stand up for yourself.*

boss sb around ALSO **boss sb about** British /ˌbɒs (sb) əˈraʊnd, ˌbɒs (sb) əˈbaʊt‖ˌbɔːs- / [phr v T] to keep giving someone orders in an annoying way, even though you have no authority to do so: *My brother's always bossing me around and making me clean up after him.* | *She's a strong-minded woman – she doesn't let anyone boss her around.*

lay down the law /ˌleɪ daʊn ðə ˈlɔː/ [v phrase] to tell people what they should do in an annoying way because you enjoy giving orders and think that you are always right: *If Bob starts laying down the law, just tell him to shut up.*

throw your weight around /ˌθrəʊ jɔːʳ ˈweɪt əˌraʊnd/ [v phrase] to use your position of authority to tell other people what to do, in an unreasonable way: *She likes to throw her weight around – it makes her feel important.* | *Why is everyone so upset? Has George been throwing his weight around again?*

24 enjoying telling people what to do

- bossy
- dictatorial
- officious
- overbearing

bossy /ˈbɒsi‖ˈbɔːsi/ [adj] always telling people what to do, especially when you have no authority to do so: *She found Molly to be bossy and interfering.* | *'You can't wear that hat,' said Monica in her usual bossy voice.*

dictatorial /ˌdɪktəˈtɔːriəl◂/ [adj] someone who is **dictatorial** uses their power in an unreasonable way by always telling people what to do or what is correct, and ignoring their wishes or views: *His attitude has become increasingly dictatorial.* | *The Ministry of Trade was yesterday accused of being dictatorial in its plans for a new motorway in Kent.*

officious /əˈfɪʃəs/ [adj] someone who is **officious**, especially an unimportant official, is too eager to tell people what they must do and pays too much attention to unimportant rules: *The people at the tax department were very officious, and kept everyone waiting for hours while they checked their papers.* | *I got held up by an officious receptionist who wouldn't let me in until I'd answered all her questions.*

overbearing /ˌəʊvərˈbeərɪŋ/ [adj] someone who is **overbearing** has an unpleasant and threatening manner, as if they want to control you and expect to be obeyed, and refuses to listen to other people's opinions and arguments: *The manager can be very overbearing at times, and it's difficult to argue with him.* | *His wife felt stifled in the presence of her overbearing mother-in-law.*

tell sb off

to talk angrily to someone because they have done something wrong

RELATED WORDS

- *see also* **angry, criticize**

1 to tell someone off

- tell sb off
- give sb a talking-to
- lecture
- scold
- rebuke
- reprimand
- pull sb up
- have a bone to pick with

tell sb off /ˌtel (sb) ˈɒf/ [phr v T] *She's always telling her kids off and shouting at them.* | **+ for** *Did your Dad tell you off for getting home late?* | **+ about** *The manager said my work wasn't good enough. He really told me off about it.* | **get told off** *I was always getting told off for things I hadn't done when I was a kid.*

give sb a talking-to ALSO **give sb a telling-off** British /ˌgɪv (sb) ə ˈtɔːkɪŋ tuː, ˌgɪv (sb) ə ˌtelɪŋ ˈɒf/ [v phrase] to tell someone off, especially a child, to make it clear that you disapprove of something they have done: *Addicts don't stop what they're doing just because someone gives them a talking-to.* | *I remember being late for school and the teacher giving me such a telling-off.* | **give sb a good talking-to/telling-off** *You should give that child a good talking-to, if you want my opinion.*

lecture /ˈlektʃər/ [v T] spoken to talk angrily to someone for a long time, especially in a way that they think is not necessary or fair: *He was lectured by the headmaster in front of the whole school.* | **lecture sb on/about sth** *She's always lecturing me on bad manners.* | *After the violence on the field, the manager lectured the team about acceptable standards of behaviour.*

scold /skəʊld/ [v T] especially American if a parent, teacher, or other adult **scolds** a child, they tell them off: *I dreaded the thought of going home and being scolded by my father.* | **scold sb for sth** *Don't scold him for doing badly at school, he's doing his best.* | *Our parents were strict and we were frequently scolded for our bad behaviour.* —**scolding** [n C] *Betty got a severe scolding and had to apologize.*

rebuke /rɪˈbjuːk/ [v T] to talk severely to someone in order to criticize them for doing something which they knew was wrong: *When the extent of the pollution became known, the company was publicly rebuked by the Governor.* | **rebuke sb for (doing) sth** *Amnesty International rebuked the British government for its treatment of the refugees.* | *Welfare workers were sternly rebuked by the court for ignoring the woman's plea for help.* —**rebuke** [n C/U] *There was a hint of rebuke in his voice.* | *The magazine drew a stinging rebuke from the police, saying it would only encourage children to play with drugs.*

reprimand /ˈreprɪ̈mɑːnd‖-mænd/ [v T] to officially tell someone that they have done something wrong or illegal, especially by warning them that if they do it again they will be punished: *After the trial two police officers were suspended from duty; four others were reprimanded.* | **reprimand sb for (doing) sth** *The man was released after being officially reprimanded for illegal possession of a knife.* | **reprimand sb severely** *The foreman reprimanded the workers severely for not following safety procedures.*

pull sb up /ˌpʊl (sb) ˈʌp/ [phr v T] British to tell someone off for doing something that you do not approve of but that is not very bad **+ for** *Our teachers are always pulling us up for wearing the wrong uniform.* | **+ on** *I felt I had to pull her up on her lateness.*

have a bone to pick with /hæv ə ˈbəʊn tə ˌpɪk wɪð/ [v phrase] spoken use this to tell someone that they have done something to annoy you and that you are going to tell them off about it: *I've got a bone to pick with you – what are all these lies you've been spreading about me?*

2 to tell someone off very angrily or loudly

- give sb hell
- yell at
- chew out
- read sb the riot act
- give sb a dressing down
- bollock sb/give sb a bollocking

give sb hell /ˌgɪv (sb) ˈhel/ [v phrase] informal to shout at someone and make them suffer for doing something wrong: *I'd better go. My wife will give me hell if I'm late home again.* | *Caroline would give me hell for evermore if she thought I'd mistreated her best friend.*

yell at /ˈjel æt/ [phr v T] especially American to shout at or talk angrily to someone because they have done something wrong or annoying: *It was so embarrassing – he just started yelling at his wife.* | **get yelled at** spoken *I got yelled at at school because I was wearing the wrong shirt.*

chew out /ˌtʃuː ˈaʊt/ [phr v T] American informal to talk very angrily to someone for a long time about something wrong that they have done **chew sb out** *Even his mother used to chew him out in public.* | **chew out sb** *The Senate science and space subcommittee chewed out NASA for failing to conduct the necessary* *tests.* | **chew sb out for sth/chew out sb for sth** *The boss called Diane into his office and chewed her out for losing the Thurman account.*

read sb the riot act /ˌriːd (sb) ðə ˈraɪət ækt/ [v phrase] informal to tell someone off and warn them about what will happen if they continue with their bad behaviour: *They'll read him the riot act if he ever shows his face again.*

give sb a dressing down /ˌgɪv (sb) ə ˌdresɪŋ ˈdaʊn/ [v phrase] to tell someone off, especially in a way that makes them look stupid **+ for** *Elise was delighted I rang, but gave me a terrible dressing down for not ringing before or sending a postcard.*

bollock sb/give sb a bollocking /ˈbɒlək (sb), ˌgɪv (sb) ə ˈbɒləkɪŋ‖ˈbɑː-/ [v phrase] British informal to tell someone off by shouting at them. These are rude phrases: *Being bollocked by your daughter is a bit hard to take.* | **+ for** *My dad gave me a real bollocking for crashing his car.*

3 when you tell someone off

- talking-to
- reprimand
- lecture

talking-to informal ALSO **telling-off** British informal /ˈtɔːkɪŋ tuː, ˌtelɪŋ ˈɒf/ [n C] when someone, especially a child, is told off for being disobedient or for doing something wrong: *What Sarah needs is a good talking-to.* | *After a stern telling-off from the teacher, Billy left the room.*

reprimand /ˈreprɪmɑːnd‖-mænd/ [n C] when someone is officially told that they should not have done something, especially by warning them that they will be punished more severely if they do it again: *This time the police let him go with a reprimand as it was his first offence.* | **a severe reprimand** *David was fined £100, and Louis was given a severe reprimand for his behaviour.*

lecture /ˈlektʃəʳ/ [n C] when you talk to someone for a long time in order to tell them that they should not have done something, especially in a way that they find annoying **+ about** *She launched into another one of her lectures about why we should always do our homework.*

temporary

RELATED WORDS

opposite: —— **permanent**

▸ *see also* **short**

1 continuing or existing for only a limited period of time

- temporary
- short-term
- provisional
- interim
- stopgap

temporary /ˈtempərəri, -pəri‖-pəreri/ [adj] *I'm sure this is only a temporary problem.* | *These arrangements are only intended to be temporary until an alternative is found.* | *Temporary shelters were hastily constructed as the refugees started to pour in.* | **temporary job/employment** *I've got a temporary secretarial job, but I'm hoping to find something more permanent.* | **temporary staff/teacher/worker etc** (=who is temporary) *There are always plenty of temporary workers available during the summer months.* | **temporary accommodation** *Because of damage to their homes, many people had to stay in temporary accommodation for a few months.*

short-term /ˌʃɔːʳt ˈtɜːʳm◂/ [adj usually before noun] continuing, or intended to continue, for only a short time: *Quite a lot of our staff are employed on short-term contracts.* | *The development programme was established on a short-term basis, just over a year ago.* | *The Prime Minister emphasized the need to look to the future, rather than only considering the short-term results.* | **short-term memory** (=the ability to remember things that happened recently) *She can still remember things that happened fifty years ago, but her short-term memory is terrible!* —**short term** [n singular] **in the short term** (=in the near future, but perhaps not after that) *In the short term, interest rates are likely to remain the same.*

provisional /prəˈvɪʒənəl/ [adj] a **provisional** arrangement is temporary and can be changed or replaced in the future: *The management has made a provisional pay offer of 7%.* | *Following a series of provisional governments, the Dominican people elected Juan Bosch as their President.* | *I've made a booking at the hotel, but it's only provisional – I'll have to confirm it soon.* | **a provisional licence** British (=a driving licence that you have while you are learning to drive) *You have to get a provisional licence until you pass your test.* —**provisionally** [adv] *Two more series of the show are provisionally planned for next year.*

interim /ˈɪntərɪm/ [adj only before noun] an **interim** report, measure, arrangement etc is one that is used temporarily until a final or complete one is ready: *Eventually an interim agreement on arms control was reached.* | *The actual sales figures were 20% higher than those estimated in the interim report in July.* | *The government will announce interim measures to tackle fuel shortages.*

stopgap /ˈstɒpgæp‖ˈstɑːp-/ [n C] something that is done or used for a short time because there is an immediate need for it, but is replaced as soon as possible with something that is better – use this especially to show disapproval: *The first house we bought was only a stopgap, until we could afford something we really liked.* —**stopgap** [adj only before noun] **stopgap measures** *There is a trend towards favoring stopgap measures, instead of seeking long-term solutions to socioeconomic problems.*

2 for a limited time only

- temporarily
- for now/for the moment
- for the time being

temporarily /ˈtempərərɪli‖ˌtempəˈrerɪli/ [adv] *The library is temporarily closed for repairs.* | *Well, I suppose she can stay here temporarily, while she's looking for an apartment.*

for now/for the moment /fəʳ ˈnaʊ, fəʳ ðə ˈməʊmənt/ [adv] from now until a time in the future, especially when you do not know exactly when in the future: *For the moment, I'm quite happy in the job I'm doing.* | *Such popular programmes will go on being broadcast on Channel 3 – for now.* | *'The negotiations are continuing for the moment,' a spokesman said.*

for the time being /fəʳ ðə ˌtaɪm ˈbiːɪŋ/ [adv] for a short period of time from now, but not permanently: *For the time being, Mrs Gilman's classes will be taken by other teachers.* | *Although the government aims to encourage private enterprise, around one third of the economy will remain under state control, for the time being.*

test

WHAT'S HERE

- **test/exam** see **1 to 8**
- **test/experiment** see **9 to 12**

test/exam

RELATED WORDS

- answer a question *see* **answer (8-10)**
- the result of a test or exam *see* **grade**
- *see also* **learn, study, teach, subject, school/university**

1 a test of your knowledge or skill

- test
- exam
- quiz
- oral exam
- practical
- finals
- final/midterm
- assessment
- testing

test /test/ [n C] a set of spoken or written questions or practical activities, which are intended to find out how much someone knows about a subject or skill: *Several students were caught cheating on the test.* | *The committee is calling for national tests for American schoolchildren.* | **spelling/reading/biology etc test** *I have a chemistry test tomorrow.* | **driving/driver's test** *Did Lauren pass her driving test?* | **+ on** *Listen carefully, because there will be a test on this next week.*

exam ALSO **examination** formal /ɪɡˈzæm, ɪɡˌzæmɪ̇ˈneɪʃən/ [n C] an important test that you do at the end of a course of study or at the end of the school year: *Students are not allowed to talk during the examination.* | *He's upstairs, revising for an exam.* | **in an exam** British /**on an exam** American *How did you do in your exams?* | **entrance exam** (=an exam you must pass to enter a school or university) *In Japan, entrance exams are very important, and many children go to extra classes to prepare for them.* | **history/French/biology etc exam** *We have a biology exam tomorrow, and I haven't done any work for it yet.* | **final/midterm exam** American (=exams taken at the end or the middle of a particular class) *Final exams will be just before Christmas.*

quiz /kwɪz/ [n C] American a quick test that a teacher gives to a class, usually to check that students are learning the things they should be learning: *We have a history quiz every Monday.* | **pop quiz** (=a quiz that is not expected by the students) *He likes giving pop quizzes, to see if the kids are remembering anything.*

oral exam ALSO **oral** British /ˈɔːrəl ɪɡˌzæm, ˈɔːrəl/ [n C] an exam in which you answer questions by speaking, instead of writing, for example to test how good you are at speaking a foreign language: *You can either take an oral exam or do a 25 page essay.* | *Nicky got an A in her Spanish oral.*

practical /ˈpræktɪkəl/ [n C] British an exam that tests your ability to do or make things, rather than your ability to write about them, for example in subjects such as chemistry or cooking: *We've got our chemistry practical tomorrow morning.*

finals /ˈfaɪnlz/ [n plural] British the last exams that you take at the end of a British university course: *During my finals I was revising till 3 o'clock in the morning most days.*

final/midterm /ˈfaɪnl, ˌmɪdˈtɜːʳm◂/ [n C] American the test you take at the end of a particular class, or the test you take in the middle of that class: *This class will require two papers, a midterm, and a final.*

assessment /əˈsesmənt/ [n U] especially British a method used to find out how good a student is at a particular subject, for example by giving them written work, tests, or exams: *Assessment is by means of a written exam at the end of the course.* | **continuous assessment** (=assessment throughout a student's course of study, instead of only at the end) *Most schools nowadays prefer to use continuous assessment, because it gives a fairer picture of how the student has done during the whole year.*

testing /ˈtestɪŋ/ [n U] the system of using exams and tests to find out how good someone is at a particular subject: *The government plans to introduce compulsory testing in junior schools from the age of 7.* | *I believe that some sort of testing is always necessary in order to motivate students.*

2 to do a test or exam

- take
- do
- have
- sit

take /teɪk/ [v T] *Anna will be taking her music exam in the summer.* | *Most young people take the SAT exams in their last year of high school.* | *I took my driving test when I was 18.*

do /duː/ [v T] British **do** is more informal that **take**, and is used especially in conversation: *I'd better go home – I've got to do an exam in the morning.* | *The kids are doing a test this morning.*

have ALSO **have got** /hæv, həv ˈɡɒt‖-ˈɡɑːt/ [v T] if you **have** an exam tomorrow, next week etc, you are going to do it then: *We have a quiz every week on what we've been reading.* | *I have a written exam in the morning and an interview in the afternoon.* | *Lucy's got her driving test next week.*

sit /sɪt/ [v T] British to do a written school or college exam: *I sat my final exams last year.*

3 to do a test or exam again

- retake/take sth again
- resit

retake/take sth again /ˌriːˈteɪk, ˌteɪk (sth) əˈɡen/ [v T/v phrase] to do a test or exam again because you have previously failed it: *She wants to retake her French A-level exam.* | *Ralph retook his driver's test in June.* | *If you fail the test, you can always take it again* —**retake** /ˈriːteɪk/ [n C] British *Can you sit a retake?*

resit /ˌriːˈsɪt/ [v T] British to do a written school or college exam again because you have previously failed it: *It only makes sense to resit an exam if you strongly believe you will do better.* —**resit** /ˈriːsɪt/ [n C] *Is a resit possible?*

4 someone who does an exam

- candidate

candidate /ˈkændɪ̇dɪ̇t‖-deɪt, -dɪ̇t/ [n C] British someone who does an exam: *Candidates should be at their desks 5 minutes before the start of the examination.*

5 to give students a test or exam

- give sb a test
- test
- set sb a test/an exam
- examine

give sb a test /ˌɡɪv (sb) ə 'test/ [v phrase] to make someone do a test: *Schools are required to give students national standardized tests.* | **+ on** *The French teacher gave us a test on irregular verbs, and I got 100%.*

test /test/ [v T] to ask someone written or spoken questions to find out what they know about a subject: *New students are tested in math and reading, and placed in the appropriate class.* | **test sb on sth** *Tomorrow you'll be tested on the main events of the Civil War.*

set sb a test/an exam /ˌset (sb) ə 'test, ən ɪɡ'zæm/ [v phrase] British to choose the questions that are in a test or exam: *Next lesson I'm setting you all a test to see how much you've learned.* | *Whoever set the exam didn't seem to know the material very well.*

examine /ɪɡ'zæm$_{\partial}$n/ [v T] formal to ask someone questions in an exam in order to find out what they know about a particular subject: *To save time, students will be examined in groups of three.* | **examine sb on sth** *Students will be examined on all aspects of Russian literature and history.*

6 a person who judges a test or exam

- examiner

examiner /ɪɡ'zæm$_{\partial}$nəʳ/ [n C] British someone who judges exams or tests: *The examiner told him to relax and then asked him to turn on the engine.* | *Students who, in the opinion of the examiners, do not reach the required standard must take the exam again.*

7 to pass a test

- pass
- qualify
- graduate
- scrape through
- get through
- sail/breeze through
- pass/be given a pass

pass /pɑːs‖pæs/ [v I/T] to reach a high enough standard to succeed in an examination or test: *'I'm taking my driving test today.' 'Do you think you'll pass?'* | *New recruits have to pass a physical fitness test.* | **pass with flying colours** British **/colors** American (=pass a test or examination with very high marks) *She was so nervous about her examination results, but in fact she passed with flying colours.*

qualify /'kwɒl$_{\partial}$faɪ‖'kwɑː-/ [v I] especially British to pass all the examinations that you need in order to become a doctor, lawyer, engineer etc: *After qualifying, she joined the NatWest Bank as a corporate advisor.* | **+ as** *She wanted to improve her English so she could qualify as a translator.*

graduate /'ɡrædʒueɪt/ [v I] to pass all your final examinations at university or college, and get a degree. In the US, **graduate** also means to successfully complete your high school education: *What are you going to do after you graduate?* | **+ from** *Mitch graduated from Stanford in 1998 with a degree in biochemistry.* | **graduate in history/French/medicine etc** British *She graduated in modern languages and now works as an interpreter.*

scrape through /ˌskreɪp 'θruː/ [phr v I/T] especially British, informal to only just pass an examination, by getting only a few marks more than are necessary: *Daniel scraped through the entrance exam.* | *I scraped through my exams with marks just good enough to keep my place in the school of pharmacy.*

get through /ˌɡet 'θruː/ [phr v I/T] to pass a difficult test or examination: *The entrance exam is very difficult and only a small minority of candidates get through.* | **get sb through sth** *Reading that book at the last minute was the only thing that got me through the history exam.*

sail/breeze through /'seɪl, 'briːz θruː/ [phr v I/T] informal to pass a test or examination very easily: *'How'd his exams go?' 'He breezed through – no trouble at all.'* | **sail/breeze through sth** *She sailed through her driving test the first time.*

pass/be given a pass /pɑːs, biː ˌɡɪvən ə 'pɑːs‖-'pæs/ [v T/v phrase] *My teacher told me she passed me only because she knew I'd had a really hard year.* | *I didn't think the candidate deserved to be given a pass but the other examiners disagreed.*

8 to fail a test

- fail
- flunk
- bomb

fail /feɪl/ [v I/T] to not reach a high enough standard to succeed in a test or exam: *She failed her history class and has to take it again.* | *'How did Chris do in his driving test?' 'He failed.'* | *Many of the boys in the program had been failing at school.*

flunk /flʌŋk/ [v T] American informal to fail an exam: *He was cutting school and flunking classes.* | *She flunked the state bar exam four times before she finally passed.* | **flunk out** (=fail all your classes, so that you have to leave school) *Brant flunked out of college his first year.*

bomb /bɒm‖bɑːm/ [v I/T] American informal to fail a test or exam very badly: *I bombed on the quiz he gave us.* | *'How'd it go?' 'I bombed on the written section, but I think I did okay on the multiple choice part.'*

test/experiment

9 a test on something to check it or find out about it

- test
- experiment
- trial
- testing
- trial run
- pilot
- piloting

test /test/ [n C] a process that is used for finding out important information about something, for example whether a machine is working properly, whether a substance is safe, or whether someone has an illness: *a ban on nuclear tests* | **+ to determine/show/find etc** *Teachers can use the program to create tests to check children's progress.* | *A blood test can be done to determine who the baby's father is.* | **carry out a test/do a test** *Doctors did several tests to find out what was wrong.* | **+ on** *We carry out safety tests on all our products.* | **+ for** (=to find out if something exists) *There is a simple test for diabetes.* | **eye/blood/skin etc test** *A blood test will show if you are a possible bone marrow donor.* | **hearing/sight etc test** *Nine-month-old babies are given hearing tests by health visitors.*

experiment /ɪk'sper$_{\partial}$mənt/ [n C] a scientific test to find out how something is affected when you do something to it: *In one experiment, the men were not* *allowed to sleep and then were tested on how well they were able to concentrate.* | *The elderly people were taught meditation in the 12-week experiment.* | **do/carry out/perform an experiment** *They are doing experiments to learn more about the affects of alcohol on the brain.* | **+ on** (=an experiment using something) *The Institute plans to conduct no further experiments on monkeys.* —**experimental** /ɪkˌsperɨ-'mentl◂/ [adj] *an experimental medical treatment* —**experimentally** [adv] *The FDA has granted researchers permission to use the drug experimentally on humans.*

trial /'traɪəl/ [n C] a test in which a new product, such as a drug, a weapon, or a vehicle, is used by a small number of people in order to find out if it is safe and effective: *Results of the drug trial will be available soon.* | **+ of** *Probert is overseeing the trials of the new explosives.* | **clinical trial** (=a trial of a drug or treatment that is done carefully by doctors on humans) *Until now, the drug was only available to people taking part in clinical trials.*

testing /'testɪŋ/ [n U] formal when something such as a process, system, substance etc is being examined, in order to see whether it exists, is safe, or is working properly: *The U.S. conducted atomic weapons testing in Nevada during the 1950s.* | *The aircraft is still in the early stages of testing and production.* | **drug/genetic/AIDS etc testing** *Athletes will be subject to random drug testing.*

trial run /'traɪəl rʌn/ [n C] an occasion when you test a new method or system to see if it works well: *The national railroad is doing a few trial runs to test new equipment.*

pilot /'paɪlət/ [n C] a test in which a new idea or plan is used in a limited number of places or situations, in order to see if it is worth continuing or doing in a more general way: *The results of the pilot have been encouraging.* | **pilot study/project/program etc** *The government sponsored a pilot project to find out how the education reforms would work in schools.*

piloting /'paɪlətɪŋ/ [n U] a process in which a new system or product is tested using different groups of people in order to see how effective and popular it will be: *Extensive piloting has shown us our study book will be a useful aid to students.*

10 to do a test on something in order to check it or find out about it

- do a test/experiment
- test
- run a test
- carry out tests
- try out
- put sth to the test
- pilot

do a test/an experiment ALSO **conduct/perform an experiment/a test** formal /ˌduː ə 'test, ən ɪk'sperɨmənt, kənˌdʌkt, pərˌfɔːrm ən ɪk'sperɨmənt, ə 'test/ [v phrase] *He has a blood test done each week to see how effective the medication is.* | *Children can use the magnet to perform many simple experiments.* | *The company did not conduct adequate safety tests.* | **+ on** *The space shuttle crew conducted experiments on plants and cells in a special lab.*

test /test/ [v T] to do a **test** on something to find out whether it works or to get more information about it: *Test your brakes to check they are working correctly.* | *The devices were tested very carefully and are considered safe.* | **test sth on sb/sth** *These products have not been tested on animals.* | **test sth for sth** (=to find out whether it has a substance in it) *The water is being tested for signs of chemical pollution.*

run a test /ˌrʌn ə 'test/ [v phrase] to do a test, especially one that is often used, or one that has been prepared and is ready to be done: *Doctors ran tests to determine the cause of his irregular heartbeat.* | *We think the equipment is working fine, but we still need to run a few more tests.*

carry out tests /ˌkæri aʊt 'tests/ [v phrase] if someone such as a doctor or scientist **carries out tests**, they do a set of tests in order to find out what is wrong, what needs improving etc: *Police scientists are carrying out tests on the murder victim's clothes.* | *Results of tests carried out at this clinic are always strictly confidential.*

try out /ˌtraɪ 'aʊt/ [phr v T] to test an object such as a tool or piece of equipment by using it, or to test a plan or idea by doing it **try sth out** *Toy manufacturers use employees' children to try new products out.* | **try out sth** *He visited the center several times, trying out different computer software packages.*

put sth to the test /ˌpʊt (sth) tə ðə 'test/ [v phrase] to test something, such as an idea, a belief, or a product, to see if it works as well as someone says it does or as you think it will: *The system's effectiveness will soon be put to the test.* | *The soldiers worked out a strategy which was then put to the test in a training exercise.*

pilot /'paɪlət/ [v T] to test a new system or product using different groups of people in order to see how effective or popular it is: *The coursebook was piloted in schools all over Europe.*

11 to use a person or animal in a test

- experiment on
- test sth on
- screen
- vivisection

experiment on /ɪk'sperɨment ɒn/ [phr v T] to use someone or something in scientific tests in order to find out how they are affected when you do something to them: *For some disease research, experimenting on animals is very important.* | *Some of the government labs had experimented on humans without their consent.*

test sth on /'test (sth) ɒn/ [phr v T] to do tests in which a group of people or animals use a product, take a drug etc in order to see what their reaction is: *This face cream has not been tested on animals.* | *They've just received permission to begin testing the new drug on humans.*

screen /skriːn/ [v T] to test a person or a particular group of people to see if they have a particular illness or infection: *Because breast cancer is common in older women, we screen all women over 50.* | **screen sb/sth for** *If you receive blood in the United Kingdom it will already have been screened for HIV.* —**screening** [n U] *The company has recently introduced free health screening for all its employees.*

vivisection /ˌvɪvɨ'sekʃən/ [n U] the practice of doing tests on live animals, for example in order to increase medical knowledge or to test new products: *I'm not against vivisection, but obviously we all want to avoid animals suffering unnecessarily.* | *Without vivisection many of the recent anti-cancer advances simply would not have been made.*

12 a person or animal that is used in a test

- subject
- guinea pig

subject /ˈsʌbdʒɪkt/ [n C] formal a person or animal that is used in a test – use this especially in scientific contexts: *Subjects for this experiment represented a good cross-section of the American population.* | *All subjects were tested for perfect hearing before the experiment began.*

guinea pig /ˈgɪni pɪg/ [n C] informal a person or animal who takes part in a test to see how successful or useful a new idea, system, machine etc is, sometimes without being asked: *Would you both mind being the guinea pigs for a new recipe I want to try out?* | *Students are complaining that they are being used as guinea pigs for the new maths syllabus.*

thank

1 what you say when you thank someone

- thank you
- thanks
- ta/cheers
- that's very kind of you/good of you
- I appreciate it
- you shouldn't have
- you've saved my life
- I'd like to thank
- many thanks

thank you /ˈθæŋk juː/ say this when you want to thank someone politely: *'Would you like to come to dinner with us on Sunday?' 'Thank you, I'd love to.'* | **+ for** *Thank you for a splendid evening. I really enjoyed myself.* | *Thank you for letting me stay.* | **thank you very much** *It's lovely. Thank you very much.*

thanks /θæŋks/ spoken use this to thank someone for something they have just done or given you: *'Here's your coffee.' 'Thanks, Mom.'* | **+ for** *Thanks for coming. Hope we see you again next year.* | **thanks to sb** (=used in speeches) *Thanks to everyone for all the cards and flowers. They really cheered me up.* | **thanks a lot/a million** *'Here, let me help you.' 'Thanks a lot. That's great.'*

ta/cheers /tɑː, tʃɪəʳz/ British informal spoken say this when you want to thank someone for something they have just done or given you: *'Here's the book you wanted.' 'Ta.'* | *'I've made you a cup of tea.' 'Cheers.'*

that's very kind of you/good of you /ˌðæts veri ˈkaɪnd əv juː, ˈgʊd əv juː/ formal spoken say this when someone has generously offered to do something for you: *'Here, you can have my seat.' 'Thank you, that's very kind of you.'* | *'Would you like me to carry your shopping?' 'That's very good of you!'*

I appreciate it /aɪ əˈpriːʃieɪt ɪt/ spoken say this when you want to thank someone who has done a lot to help you: *Thanks for helping out on a Sunday – I appreciate it.* | **I really appreciate it** *I couldn't have managed without your support and encouragement. I really appreciate it.*

you shouldn't have /juː ˈʃʊdnt əv/ spoken say this when you want to thank someone who has given you something, especially something expensive: *What a beautiful ring! Oh Mike, you shouldn't have!*

you've saved my life /juːv ˌseɪvd maɪ ˈlaɪf/ spoken use this to thank someone who has got you out of a difficult situation, or solved a problem for you: *You've saved my life, Jim! Thank goodness you were here.*

I'd like to thank /aɪd ˌlaɪk tə ˈθæŋk/ spoken use this to thank someone in a formal speech: *I would like to thank everyone who helped at the school fair.* | **I'd like to thank sb for (doing) sth** *I'd like to thank Betty and Jim for organizing this wonderful party.*

many thanks /ˌmeni ˈθæŋks/ use this to thank someone, especially when writing a letter: *We received the pictures on Wednesday. Many thanks.* | **+ for** *Many thanks for your letter of the other day.*

2 to say thank you to someone

- thank
- say thank you
- show your appreciation
- express your thanks/gratitude
- acknowledge
- recognize
- in recognition of sth

thank /θæŋk/ [v T] to tell someone that you are pleased and grateful for something they have given you or done for you: *I spent three hours helping her and she didn't even thank me.* | **thank sb for (doing) sth** *We must write and thank Cathy for the present.* | *The Governor publicly thanked the people of Arizona for supporting him during his campaign.* | **thank sb profusely** (=thank someone a lot in a very obvious way) *A relieved Mr Maxwell thanked his lawyer profusely.*

say thank you /seɪ ˈθæŋk juː/ [v phrase] to thank someone for what they have done: *I wanted to come round and say thank you in person.* | **+ to** *This little gift is our way of saying thank you to everyone who worked so hard.* | **+ for** *Make sure you say thank you for your birthday presents.*

show your appreciation /ˌʃəʊ jɔːr əˌpriːʃiˈeɪʃən/ [v phrase] formal to show someone that you are grateful for something they have done, by giving them something or by doing something special for them: *He found a special way of showing his appreciation – dinner at the Ritz.* | **+ for** *We have decided to pay a special bonus to everyone on the staff to show our appreciation for their hard work during the year.*

express your thanks/gratitude /ɪkˌspres jɔːʳ ˈθæŋks, ˈgrætɪ̬tjuːd‖-tuːd/ [v phrase] formal to say how grateful you are to someone for something they have done – use this in a speech or in a letter **+ for** *I should like to express my thanks for all that you have done.* | **+ to** *He made a short speech expressing his gratitude to all those who had sent him letters of support.*

acknowledge /əkˈnɒlɪdʒ‖-ˈnɑː-/ [v T] to tell people publicly that someone has done something to help you and that you are grateful for it: *In his speech he acknowledged the help his parents gave him at the start of his career.* | *I did a lot of work on that book. It annoys me that the editor never acknowledged it.* —**acknowledgement** [n U] *She has received no official acknowledgement of her contribution to the fund.*

recognize ALSO **recognise** British /ˈrekəgnaɪz, ˈrekən-/ [v T] if a country or a large organization **recognizes** something important that someone has done for them, they officially and publicly thank them, by giving them something or doing something special for them: *The government recognized his bravery in the battle by awarding him the Military Cross.* | *Her contribution to horticulture was recognized when a new rose was named after her.*

in recognition of sth /ɪn ˌrekəgˈnɪʃən əv (sth)/ [prep] if you are given something **in recognition of** something you have done, it is publicly given to you as a way of thanking you: *He was awarded a knighthood in recognition of his work for charity.*

3 when you feel that you want to thank someone

- grateful
- thankful
- appreciate
- appreciative
- be indebted to
- owe
- gratitude
- appreciation

grateful /'greɪtfəl/ [adj] feeling that you want to thank someone, especially because they have done something for you and helped you a lot: *Dr Shah has received hundreds of letters from grateful patients.* | **+ for** *I'm really grateful for everything you've done for me.* | **+ to** *My daughter was rescued safely, and I am very grateful to the firemen.* —**gratefully** [adv] *We gratefully accepted her offer.*

thankful /'θæŋkfəl/ [adj not before noun] grateful that someone has done something, because if they had not done it the situation would have been much worse: *Take what they give you, and be thankful.* | **+ for** *I am always thankful for their enthusiasm and commitment.* | **+ that** *She was thankful that Louise had insisted she travel first class.*

appreciate /ə'priːʃieɪt/ [v T not in progressive] to be grateful to someone for something that they have done for you, because you realize that they did not have to do it or that they made a big effort to do it for you: *We really appreciate everything you've done for our daughter.* | *Alan asked me to tell you how much he appreciated your hospitality when he was in London.*

appreciative /ə'priːʃətɪv/ [adj] showing that you are pleased and grateful for someone's help or kindness: *He wrote a warm, appreciative letter, thanking her for everything she had done.* | *They weren't particularly appreciative the last time I helped them. I don't think I'll bother again.* | **+ of** *Our new boss is a real joy to work for. She's so appreciative of anything you do for her.*

be indebted to /biː ɪn'detɪ̇d tuː/ [v phrase] formal to feel very grateful to someone for something they have given you or done for you: *We are indebted to the National Archives for permission to print these photographs.* | **be greatly/deeply indebted to sb** *She said that she was greatly indebted to everyone who had supported her campaign.*

owe /əʊ/ [v T] if you say you **owe** someone something, you are grateful because they have helped you to succeed at something or to improve your life, and without their help this might not have been possible **owe a lot/a great deal to sb** *I owe a great deal to my publishers, who helped me to finish writing the book.* | **owe it all/everything to sb** *I owe it all to you. You were the only one who believed in me.* | **owe sb a lot/a great deal** *'I owe my parents a lot,' he admitted. 'They worked real hard to put me through college.'* | **owe a debt of gratitude to sb** *We all owe a debt of gratitude to Mrs Stevenson, who kindly donated the money for the project.*

gratitude /'grætɪ̇tjuːd‖-tuːd/ [n U] when you feel grateful, especially because someone has been kind to you **express/show gratitude (for sth)** *He wrote again, expressing gratitude for the help he had received.* | **a sense of gratitude** *She felt a deep sense of gratitude to the teacher who had encouraged her to go on to university.* | **in gratitude** (=because you are grateful) *'I'll take the van back, shall I?' he asked, and Elise nodded in gratitude.*

appreciation /əˌpriːʃi'eɪʃən/ [n U] a feeling that you want to thank someone for their help or service and to show them that you think it was important and valuable **show your appreciation** *To show his appreciation of her kindness he sent her some flowers.* | **in appreciation of sth** (=in order to show appreciation of) *In appreciation of Mr Mainwaring's years of service, the company presented him with a gold watch.* | **token of sb's appreciation** (=a sign of someone's appreciation) *We'd like you to accept this gift as a small token of our appreciation.*

4 something that you say or do to thank someone

- thanks
- thank-you letter/note
- acknowledgements

thanks /θæŋks/ [n plural] what you say or do to thank someone: *He won't get any thanks from them for being so honest.* | **+ for** *Please accept this bottle of champagne as our thanks for organizing the seminar.* | **letter/message etc of thanks** (=expressing thanks) *He wrote me a short letter of thanks.* | **without a word of thanks** (=without saying thank you) *She got up and left without a word of thanks.* | **a vote of thanks** (=a formal, public expression of thanks, especially at a meeting) *I'd like to propose a vote of thanks to Sandra for organizing the whole evening.*

thank-you letter/note /'θæŋk juː ˌletəʳ, ˌnəʊt/ [n C] a letter that you send to someone to thank them, for example when they have given you a present or when you have stayed at their house: *We spent three days after the wedding writing thank-you letters for all the presents we'd had.*

acknowledgements /ək'nɒlɪdʒmənts‖-'nɑː-/ [n plural] a note at the end or beginning of a book, article etc, in which the writer thanks all the people who helped him or her to produce it: *In the acknowledgements the authors thanked everyone who'd contributed to the book.* | *Her book was based on her ex-husband's letters and yet his name did not even appear in the acknowledgements.*

5 what you say to someone when they thank you

- don't mention it
- that's all right/that's OK
- you're welcome
- my pleasure/not at all
- think nothing of it/it was nothing
- no problem
- sure

don't mention it /ˌdəʊnt 'menʃən ɪt/ spoken *'Thanks for the lift!' 'Oh, don't mention it!'*

that's all right/that's OK /ˌðæts ɔːl 'raɪt, ˌðæts əʊ'keɪ/ informal spoken *'Thank you so much for looking after the children.' 'That's all right. I enjoyed having them.'*

you're welcome /jɔːʳ 'welkəm/ especially American, spoken *'Thanks a lot.' 'You're welcome!'*

my pleasure/not at all /ˌmaɪ 'pleʒəʳ, ˌnɒt ət 'ɔːl/ formal spoken *'It was very good of you to sing for us at such short notice.' 'My pleasure!'* | *'Thanks for dinner' 'Not at all – I enjoyed it'.*

think nothing of it/it was nothing /θɪŋk ˌnʌθɪŋ 'ɒv ɪt, ɪt wəz 'nʌθɪŋ/ spoken say this when someone has thanked you a lot for something you have done because they think it was very difficult for you to do: *'You shouldn't have gone to so much trouble, you know!' 'Oh, think nothing of it.'* | *'Thank you for all your help. I couldn't have done it without you.' 'Don't mention it. It was nothing.'*

no problem /ˌnəʊ ˈprɒbləm‖-ˈprɑːb-/ informal spoken say this to show that what someone has thanked you for was really a very easy thing for you to do: *'Thank you for coming all the way out here.' 'No problem, lady.'*

sure /ʃʊəʳ/ American spoken used as a reply to someone who has thanked you for something: *'Thanks for the ride.' 'Sure, no problem.'*

6 when someone does not thank you

- ungrateful
- ingratitude
- take sb for granted

ungrateful /ʌnˈgreɪtfəl/ [adj] someone who is **ungrateful** does not thank you when you do something for them, and this makes you annoyed or upset: *Our children are so ungrateful – they don't realize how much we do for them.* | *I am not prepared to go to jail for that ungrateful woman!*

ingratitude /ɪnˈgrætɪ̯tjuːd‖-tuːd/ [n U] a lack of any feeling of being grateful when someone has given you something or does something for you: *Such ingratitude! After all I've done for him, he treats me like dirt.* | *They were shocked by her ingratitude – she didn't seem to appreciate the trouble they had gone to.*

take sb for granted /ˌteɪk (sb) fəʳ ˈgrɑːntɪ̯d‖-ˈgræn-/ [v phrase] to expect someone to help you or do things for you because they always have done, and never thank them or show them that you are grateful: *Like many married couples, we had started to take each other for granted.* | *Kids usually take their mother for granted.*

then

RELATED WORDS

- *see also* **after, time, past, future**

1 ways of saying that one thing happens after another

- then
- next
- after that

then /ðen/ [adv] *We scraped all the old paint off the bike and then repainted it bright red.* | *Fry the onions gently, and then add the meat and cook for a few minutes.* | *First you need to collect all the information and make detailed notes. Then you can start to actually write your essay.*

next /nekst/ [adv] immediately after something – use this especially when the order in which things happen is important: *Everyone started fighting and someone threw a bottle. I forget what happened next.* | *Which of the candidates shall we interview next?* | *First you need to select the text you want to move. Next, click on the 'Move' command at the top of the screen.*

after that /ˌɑːftəʳ ˈðæt‖ˌæf-/ [adv] after something happens: *England had a man sent off in the first half, and after that the England team never really looked as though they could win the game.* | *The exhaust pipe fell off the car just as we were leaving, and after that it was just one disaster after another!*

2 at a particular time in the past

- then
- at that/the time
- in those days/back then
- at that point
- at that moment
- at that stage

then /ðen/ [adv] *She thought back over her early married life; everything had been so different then.* | *They were living in the country then, on a farm.* | *These days it's OK for women to smoke in public, but then it was unheard of.* | **then and only then** (=not until that time) *Bob sat down and read the letter again slowly. Then and only then did it begin to sink in that Stella was really dead.* | **just then** (=at that exact moment) *I sat down at my desk and got out a pile of reports to read. Just then, the phone rang.*

at that/the time /ət ˌðæt, ðə ˈtaɪm/ [adv] at a particular period of time in the past – use this especially when you are talking about what the situation was then as compared to the present time: *At that time, he was married to a woman called Jody.* | *I was offered a job in New York, but at the time I didn't want to move so far away from my family.* | *The accepted view at that time was that women should remain in the home and not go out to work.* | *I can't remember exactly what he said, but I do remember thinking it was very funny at the time.*

in those days/back then /ɪn ˈðəʊz ˌdeɪz, ˌbæk ˈðen/ [adv] at that time in the past – use this especially when you are comparing life in the past with life in the present: *We used to get paid £2 a week. That was a lot of money in those days.* | *In those days there was no proper road, just an old stony track through the woods.* | *Back then, most people left school at fourteen and started work.* | *I remember thinking, back then, that I would never get married.*

at that point /ət ˌðæt ˈpɔɪnt/ [adv] at that exact time during a past event or situation: *Miles got up to make his speech, and at that point several of the guests quietly slipped out of the room.* | *I thought he was dead. At that point, everything seemed hopeless.*

at that moment /ət ˌðæt ˈməʊmənt/ [adv] at the exact time when something happened or when someone did something – use this when describing past events or telling stories: *At that moment there was a knock on the door.* | *Fortunately, Jorge appeared at that moment and was able to help us load things into the van.* | **just at that moment** (=at that exact moment) *Just at that moment, the police arrived.*

at that stage /ət ˌðæt ˈsteɪdʒ/ [adv] during a particular period of time in the past, although things were going to change or develop later: *At that stage I lacked the experience to apply for a management post.* | *At that stage in the inquiry, the police still hoped that Maria might be alive.*

3 at a particular time in the future

- then
- at that point
- at that stage
- by that time

then /ðen/ [adv] *Wait until you've had your dinner, then you can go out to play.* | **by then** *Just wait until July – all the exams will be over by then.* | **until then** *We're not getting a new car until June, so this one will have to do us until then.* | *We'll probably see you again when we get to Budapest – until then goodbye and good luck!* | **then and only then** (=not until then) *Both sides must forget about the past. Then and only then can there be peace.*

at that point /ət ˌðæt ˈpɔɪnt/ [adv] at the exact moment during an event or process when something will happen: *At 7:45 the lights will go out in the hall, and at that point all the actors will move into their positions on the stage.*

at that stage /ət ˌðæt ˈsteɪdʒ/ [adv] at that particular time during a series of events: *The exams will be finished by the end of June. At that stage you can make a decision about which subjects to study next year.*

by that time /baɪ ˌðæt ˈtaɪm/ [adv] before a particular time actually arrives: *I have to go at 6 pm, but by that time we should have got through most of the work.* | **by which time** *The Connellys go to Africa in April, by which time they hope to have sold their house.*

there/not there

RELATED WORDS

opposite: —— **here**

- get there *see* **arrive (1)**
- there is/there are *see* **exist, happen**

1 a place that you are not in now

- **there**
- **over there**
- **that place**
- **around/near there**

there /ðeəʳ/ [adv] *I love Italy – I worked there for a year.* | *Jackie's arriving at the station at 3.15 and I said I'd meet her there.* | *When I came home Sean was just sitting there waiting for me.* | *We drove down to Baltimore, and on the way there we stopped for lunch.* | **right there** (=exactly there) *Where's my umbrella? I'm sure I left it right there, next to my bag.* | **from there** *We flew in to Munich and from there we took the train to Prague.* | **down/up/in etc there** *How did you get up there on the roof?*

over there /əʊvəʳ ˈðeəʳ/ [adv] in a place that you can see or point to but cannot touch: *My car's over there by that big tree.* | *See those rocks over there? Be careful to keep the boat away from them.*

that place /ˌðæt ˈpleɪs/ [n phrase] a place that you have mentioned or been in, especially a place that you feel strongly about: *You went to Camp Chippewa too? I hated that place.* | **in that place** *They'll never let us back in that place after the way you behaved.* | **to that place** *Do you remember we went down to that place along the river and had a barbecue?*

around/near there ALSO **round there** British /əˌraʊnd, ˌnɪəʳ ˈðeəʳ, ˌraʊnd ˈðeəʳ/ [adv] in the area near a place you have been talking about: *We usually go to Lake Como for our holidays – it's beautiful round there.* | *Judy's looking for an apartment in Greenwich Village. A lot of her friends live around there.* | *One of the largest tornadoes ever seen was photographed near there.*

2 to be in a place where you are not now

- **be there**
- **be around**
- **be in**
- **be present**

be there /biː ˈðeəʳ/ [v phrase] *'Have you seen the newspaper?' 'It's there, next to your chair.'* | *I want to be there when he comes out of surgery.* | *When I worked at the factory, I was there every day from nine till six.* | **be down/up/in etc there** *The bathroom's up there, on your right.*

be around /biː əˈraʊnd/ [v phrase] if someone or something **is around**, you know that they are there but you are not sure exactly where: *I tried to call you last night, but I guess you weren't around.* | *Go and look downstairs. There must be a coffee machine around somewhere.* | *It doesn't matter if no one is around – I'm still not going through a red light.*

be in /biː ˈɪn/ [v phrase] to **be in** your home, the place where you work etc, especially when you are expected to be: *Is Marsha in? I have a letter for her.* | *I'll phone back later when Mr Boswell is in.* | *I walked over to Sonia's house but when I got there only her brother was in.*

be present /biː ˈprezənt/ [v phrase] formal if a substance is present somewhere, it is there even though you cannot see it: *When acid is present, the chemical in the test tube turns red.* | **+ in** *The virus is present in tears and saliva, but in very small amounts.* | *Tests revealed that large quantities of alcohol were present in the driver's blood.*

3 to be at an event where you are not now

- **be there**
- **be at**
- **be present**
- **be on the scene**
- **be on the spot**
- **be in attendance**

be there /biː ˈðeəʳ/ [v phrase] *What was the game like? Were there many people there?* | *I went to a party last night and your sister was there too.* | *A lot of the people at the charity event were only there to look at other people.*

be at /biː æt/ [v phrase] if someone **is at** a particular event, they are there in order to see or hear it: *Most of the actors in the movie were at the New York preview.* | *I don't remember Uncle Bob. I don't think he was at the funeral.* | *Were you at the meeting when they announced the layoffs?*

be present /biː ˈprezənt/ [v phrase] formal if someone **is present** at a special or official event, they are there, especially because it is important that they should see what is happening: *The only people who were present for the ceremony were the bride and groom, the priest, and two witnesses.* | **+ at/for** *It was very important to Jim to be present for the birth of his first child.* | **those present** (=the people there) *Those present at the trial said that the accused looked cheerful.*

be on the scene /biː ɒn ðə ˈsiːn/ [v phrase] to be in the place where something such as an accident or crime has happened: *Journalists were on the scene within minutes of the plane crash.* | *A Safety Board team was on the scene Monday morning to try to determine the cause of the accident.*

be on the spot /biː ɒn ðə ˈspɒt‖-ˈspɑːt/ [v phrase] especially British to be in the place where something very interesting or exciting happens: *I'm going to the stadium. I want to be on the spot when they announce the international team.* | *Many reporters, in an attempt to be on the spot in war time, have ended up being killed.*

be in attendance /biː ɪn əˈtendəns/ [v phrase] formal to be at a special or important event, especially in order to take part in it: *Over 2000 police were in attendance at yesterday's demonstration.* | *The First Lady was in attendance for most of the conference sessions.* | *He always enjoyed going to Stewart's parties where famous people were sure to be in attendance.*

4 the number of people who are at an event

- attendance
- turnout
- bums on seats

attendance /ə'tendəns/ [n singular/U] the number of people who attend an event such as a game, a concert, or an important meeting: *The game had an attendance of over 50,000 people.* | **+ at** *Attendance at the national championships is already higher than expected.* | **good/high attendance** *We had pretty good attendance despite the bad weather.* | **poor/low attendance** *Considering the seriousness of the matter to be debated there was an unusually low attendance at the meeting.*

turnout /'tɜːʳnaʊt/ [n singular/U] the number of people who have decided to go to or take part in an event **+ for** *We had a much better turnout for the company picnic this year than last.* | **low/light/small turnout** *Turnout for the game was lighter than expected.* | **high/heavy/large turnout** *There was an unusually high turnout in the election, nearly twice the number predicted.*

bums on seats /ˌbʌmz ɒn 'siːts/ [n phrase] the number of people at an event, concert, play etc – use this especially when you think the people who organized the event are only interested in getting a lot of people there and do not really care about whether the event is good or not: *Inviting a soap star or two to your opening night is always a good way of getting bums on seats.*

5 to not be there

- not be there
- not be around
- be out/not be in
- be away/off
- absent
- missing

not be there /nɒt biː 'ðeəʳ/ [v phrase] *She says the bottle is in the cupboard, but it just isn't there.* | *He was supposed to wait for me by the fountain, but he wasn't there when I arrived.*

not be around /nɒt biː ə'raʊnd/ [phr v I] if someone or something **is not around**, they are not there, especially when you expect them to be somewhere nearby: *Maybe you should try talking to Michael when his wife isn't around.* | *According to Caroline, Larry isn't around much since he started traveling for work.*

be out/not be in /biː 'aʊt, nɒt biː 'ɪn/ [phr v I] to be out of your home, the place where you work etc usually for a short time: *He wasn't in, so I left a message.* | *She told me not to stop by today – she'll be out most of the day running errands.*

be away/off /biː ə'weɪ, 'ɒf/ [phr v I] informal to not be at work, for example, because you are ill or on holiday. In British English you can also use this when someone is not at school: *After I've been away for a few days, there's always so much work waiting when I get back.* | *Selina's off today? Then can you ask her to phone me when she's back in the office?* | **be off work/school** *He's been off work ever since he hurt his back in a riding accident.*

absent /'æbsənt/ [adj] formal if something is **absent**, it is not where it is expected to be. If someone is **absent** from school, work etc, they are not there, for example because they are ill: *The virus develops most quickly when antibodies are absent.* | *If you're absent more than five times, you fail the course.* | *While the boss was absent everyone started taking very long lunchbreaks.* | **+ from** *For some reason, Young's name was absent from the list.* | *The Adkinson children were absent from school about a dozen times last fall.*

missing /'mɪsɪŋ/ [adj] someone or something that is **missing** is not there, especially when you expect them to be there: *Some of the puzzle pieces are missing.* | *Can you spot the missing number in this series?* | *Suddenly he looked around and realized one of the children was missing.* | **+ from** *Three buttons were missing from his shirt.*

thick

RELATED WORDS

opposite: **thin**

- thick liquid *see* **liquid**
- *see also* **wide, narrow, big, fat**

1 thick

- thick
- chunky
- fat
- heavy

thick /θɪk/ [adj] if something such as a wall, a book, or a piece of glass is **thick**, there is a large distance between its two flat surfaces: *It's an old house with very thick stone walls.* | *The ground was covered in a thick layer of snow.* | *a thick slice of bread* | *shoes with thick rubber soles* | *Thicker curtains will give you more privacy.* —**thickness** [n U] **+ of** *The thickness of the old walls helped keep the rooms warm in winter and cool in summer.*

chunky /'tʃʌŋki/ [adj] especially British thick, solid, and heavy: *She wore a lot of chunky silver jewellery.* | *a sweater with chunky buttons* | *The books were small, chunky, and bright, specially designed for babies.*

fat /fæt/ [adj] a **fat** book, envelope, wallet etc is a book, envelope etc that is thick because there is a lot in it – use this especially as a humorous way of describing something that looks very thick: *He pulled out a fat wallet stuffed with banknotes.* | *A tall man was smoking a fat cigar.* | *a big fat book* | *The children's fat Christmas stockings bulged with surprises.*

heavy /'hevi/ [adj] **heavy** cloth or clothes are thick and usually warm: *He wore a heavy jacket and a wool ski hat.* | *The curtains were made of a heavy dark fabric which kept out all draughts and light.*

2 ways of talking about how thick something is

- how thick
- 2 cm/1 m etc thick
- thickness

how thick /haʊ 'θɪk/ [adj phrase] *The price of the glass will depend on how thick it is.* | *How thick is the ice on the lake now?* | *Check to see how thick the insulation is in your attic, and add more if necessary.*

2 cm/1 m etc thick /ˌtuː ˌsentɪmiːtəʳz θɪk/ [adj phrase] use this to say exactly how thick something is: *Cut the carrots into slices about half an inch thick.* | *In some places, the walls are over two metres thick.* | *Betts said the file on Mr Sorney was 10 inches thick.*

thickness /'θɪknɪ̈s/ [n C/U] the distance between the opposite surfaces of a solid object or material: *It's about the same thickness as a £1 coin.* | *The cheese slicer can be adjusted to cut slices of different thicknesses.*

thin

WHAT'S HERE

- **thin person** see **1 to 7**
- **thin object or material** see **8 to 11**

thin person

RELATED WORDS

opposite: —— **fat**

1 thin

- thin
- slight

thin /θɪn/ [adj] having very little fat on the body: *Larry was tall and thin with dark brown hair and bright blue eyes.* | *She looked pale, thin, and unhealthy.* | *I wish my legs were thinner.*

slight /slaɪt/ [adj] thin, delicate, often weak-looking, and usually not very tall: *Yoshida is a slight, quiet man with a grey beard.* | *a small, slight child with delicate-looking features*

2 thin in an attractive way

- slim
- slender
- willowy

slim /slɪm/ [adj] *She was tall, slim, blond, and really good-looking.* | *Mrs Ester was in her late thirties, about average height, with a slim figure.* | *You're looking slimmer – have you lost weight?* | **stay slim** *She looks great – how does she stay so slim?*

slender /ˈslendəʳ/ [adj] thin in an attractive and graceful way: *Gabriel was a tall slender young man with a light brown moustache.* | *Mandy was slender and very fair with long golden hair.* | *She had long, slender expressive hands, like a concert pianist.*

willowy /ˈwɪləʊi/ [adj] a woman or girl who is **willowy** is attractively tall and thin in a graceful way – used especially in romantic novels: *In contrast to Francesca, who was tall and willowy, Diana was small and curvy.* | *Anastasia was willowy and graceful, with grey eyes and long, straight red hair.*

3 thin and strong-looking

- lean
- wiry

lean /liːn/ [adj] thin and physically fit, especially because you do a lot of exercise or physical work: *He's a very handsome man: tall, lean and tanned with thick blond hair.* | *At seventy-two my grandfather was lean and strong and I expected him to live forever.* | *She had a runner's lean physique and an overall healthy glow.*

wiry /ˈwaɪəri/ [adj] a man or boy who is **wiry** is thin and strong, though often not very tall: *Father Vic was a wiry man in his late forties with a sharp nose and deep-set eyes.* | *a wiry little Broadway show dancer from Puerto Rico*

4 thin in a way that is not attractive

- skinny
- bony
- scrawny

skinny /ˈskɪni/ [adj] *a skinny kid with glasses* | *I was really skinny when I was a teenager.* | *Jacob placed his arm around her skinny shoulders.*

bony /ˈbəʊni/ [adj] a person or animal that is **bony** is extremely thin, so that the shape of their bones can be seen: *Now that she was older, Jean's bony fingers and wrists were too small for her jewelry.* | *When I picked up the cat it felt as bony as a skeleton.* | *Kinsit, a naturally small woman with a thin, bony face, found gaining weight difficult.*

scrawny /ˈskrɔːni/ [adj] small, thin, unattractive, and weak-looking, especially because your body has not grown enough: *Last time I saw him he was a scrawny kid in Levi's and a dirty T-shirt.* | *A few scrawny chickens were searching for scraps of food in the dry earth.*

5 too thin in a way that is unhealthy

- emaciated
- be skin and bone
- underweight

emaciated /ɪˈmeɪʃieɪtɨd/ [adj] someone who is **emaciated** is extremely thin because of hunger or serious illness and may die soon: *News came of the famine, and there were pictures of emaciated children on the TV.* | *Towards the end of his life he looked emaciated, his cheeks hollow and his eyes sunken.*

be skin and bone /biː ˌskɪn ən ˈbəʊn/ [v phrase] informal to be extremely thin in an unattractive and unhealthy way **be nothing but/no more than skin and bone** *When she died she was nothing but skin and bone.* | **be just/practically skin and bone** *The poor dog was practically skin and bone.*

underweight /ˌʌndəʳˈweɪt◂/ [adj] someone who is **underweight** weighs less than they should and is therefore unhealthy – used especially in a medical context: *The doctor says that I'm underweight and has put me on a special diet.* | *Women who consume large amounts of caffeine are more likely to give birth to underweight babies.*

6 having a thin face because you are very worried, tired etc

- drawn
- gaunt

drawn /drɔːn/ [adj] thin and unhappy-looking because of tiredness, illness, or worry: *Her face was pale and drawn, and she seemed to have been crying.* | *When Jack arrived he sat down slowly, his face drawn, with beads of sweat on his forehead.* | **look drawn** (=have a drawn expression on your face) *The doctor came out, looking drawn and exhausted.*

gaunt /gɔːnt/ [adj] extremely thin and pale, especially because you have been very ill or worried or because you have been working too hard: *When I visited him in hospital Albert looked terrible – his face was gaunt and his hair had turned grey.* | *The District Attorney at forty-four had the gaunt look of a man twenty years older.*

7 to become thinner

- lose weight
- be on a diet
- slim down
- shed
- waste away

lose weight /ˌluːz ˈweɪt/ [v phrase] to become thinner, either because you have been ill or because you want to look more attractive, be healthier etc: *The best way to lose weight is to eat less and do lots of exercise.* | *I'm really worried about my grandmother – she's lost a lot of weight recently.* | **lose three kilos/five pounds etc** *Alec lost seven pounds in a week and had to be re-admitted to the hospital.*

be on a diet /biː ɒn ə 'daɪət/ [v phrase] to eat less food than usual, or to eat only certain foods, because you want to become thinner and weigh less: *'Would you like some chocolate?' 'No thanks, I'm on a diet.'* | **go on a diet** (=start to be on a diet) *We're both going on a diet after Christmas.*

slim down /ˌslɪm 'daʊn/ [v I] especially British to become thinner, especially by eating less and doing more exercise: *She's really slimmed down a lot since I last saw her.* | **slim down to eight stone/100 pounds etc** *He's trying to slim down to eleven stone.*

shed /ʃed/ [v T] to lose a particular amount of weight quickly: *I'd like to shed a few pounds.* | *Stone's doctor ordered him to shed some weight and quit smoking.* | *Gascoigne has shed nearly 6 kilos in pre-season training and looks much fitter.*

waste away /ˌweɪst ə'weɪ/ [phr v I] to become dangerously thin and weak, usually as a result of illness: *There was nothing we could do – she just wasted away and within six weeks she was dead.* | *His muscles were slowly wasting away because of his illness.*

thin object or material

RELATED WORDS

opposite: —— **thick**

‣ *see also* **narrow**

8 flat and thin

- thin
- paper-thin
- slim

thin /θɪn/ [adj] *a thin slice of bread* | *In her pocket was a thin leather wallet containing six ten dollar bills.* | *The lake was covered with a thin layer of ice.* | *How do you get your sugar cookies so thin, Dagmar?*

paper-thin /ˌpeɪpəʳ 'θɪn◂/ [adj] extremely thin – use this about thin pieces of food or about walls that are very thin: *paper-thin slices of raw beef* | *The walls in this apartment are paper-thin; I can hear everything they're saying next door.*

slim /slɪm/ [adj] a book, box etc that is **slim** is thin in an attractive way and usually of good quality: *Claude gave me a slim gold box for holding my business cards.* | *a slim volume of poetry*

9 long and thin

- thin
- slender

thin /θɪn/ [adj] *The roof is supported by thin iron columns.* | *a thin blue line* | *a wire as thin as a human hair*

slender /'slendəʳ/ [adj] a stem, stick etc that is **slender** is long and thin in a graceful, attractive way: *The pictures are held in place by three slender brass rods.* | *slender white candles* | *A spider was hanging from a slender thread.*

10 words for describing thin material

- thin
- fine
- light/lightweight
- flimsy

thin /θɪn/ [adj] *Martin wore a thin cotton shirt under his sweater.* | *It was a chilly night, and he had only a thin blanket for warmth.*

fine /faɪn/ [adj] very thin, delicate, and usually of good quality: *fine china* | *a fine chiffon veil with embroidered edges*

light/lightweight /laɪt, 'laɪtweɪt/ [adj] clothes that are **light** or **lightweight** are thin and not very warm: *She took a light sweater, in case it was cool outside.* | *In a warm climate people wear loose, lightweight clothing.* | *I don't think it'll be that cold – do you have anything more lightweight?*

flimsy /'flɪmzi/ [adj] too thin and light, use this about clothes or material that you can easily see through or that do not protect your body: *It was impossible for me to sleep under a single flimsy blanket on such a cold night.* | *flimsy underwear*

11 to become thinner

- get/grow thinner
- taper

get/grow thinner /ˌget, ˌgrəʊ 'θɪnəʳ/ [v phrase] *Rubber gets thinner if you stretch it.* | *The line of smoke grew thinner and thinner as it drifted up into the sky.*

taper /'teɪpəʳ/ [v I] if something long and thin **tapers**, it gets gradually thinner at one end **+ to** *The walls are 7 feet thick at the base and taper to 28 inches at the top.* | **taper off** (=taper and come to an end) *The human spine tapers off at its base.* —**tapering** [adj] *long tapering fingers*

thing

RELATED WORDS

‣ *see also* **tool, equipment**

1 a thing

- thing
- something
- object
- item
- article
- artefact/artifact

thing /θɪŋ/ [n C] use this instead of the name of something when you do not need to say its name or when you do not know what it is called. You can use **thing** when you mean a physical object, or something such as an event, an idea, or something that someone says: *What's that thing on the kitchen table?* | *There were several things that I wanted to discuss.* | *I cried during the whole thing.* | *The first thing we need to do is call Becky.* | **adjective + thing** *We went to the aquarium, and they have this neat new thing where the tide goes in and out over a rock pool.*

something /'sʌmθɪŋ/ [pron] a thing – use this especially when you do not know what the thing is, or you have not decided yet what it will be: *I need to get something for Greg – it's his birthday tomorrow.* | *There's something on your shirt, on the back.* | *Something went wrong with the pumping system in the pool.* | **something + adjective** *Do you want to hear something really funny?* | *He wanted to get her something special, something expensive.* | **something else** (=another thing) *I've just remembered some-*

thing else I wanted to tell you. | **something to eat/wear/read etc** *I need to have something to eat before we go out.* | **or something** (=or something similar) *There's a stone or a nail or something stuck in my shoe.*

object /ˈɒbdʒɪkt‖ˈɑːb-/ [n C] a separate solid thing, especially one that you can touch or hold in your hand: *Children should be able to point to each object as they count it.* | *The sculpture is made from objects he found on beaches in Mexico.* | **inanimate object** (=a thing that is not alive) *After his stroke, he was able to name inanimate objects like saws and shovels, but unable to name most living things.*

item /ˈaɪtəm/ [n C] one particular thing, especially one that is being bought or sold: *The line at the checkout was for people with eight items or fewer.* | *A comfortable, adjustable chair is the single most important item for the health of a computer user.* | *The museum has over 5,000 items of historical interest.* | **item of clothing/furniture/jewellery etc** (=a single piece of clothing, furniture, jewellery etc) *The main item of jewellery worn by men, other than a watch, is cuff links.* | **household item** American (=an object used in the house) *Bring any old household items for the sale.* | **luxury item** (=an expensive item that is not really necessary) *Many of the things that people in the West take for granted are considered to be luxury items here.* | **collector's item** (=a rare item that some people would pay a lot of money to have) *My aunt discovered that her old doll was a collector's item and worth a lot of money.*

article /ˈɑːʳtɪkəl/ [n C] formal a thing, especially one of a group of things: *Each article has a written history printed on a card below the display.* | **article of clothing/furniture/jewellery etc** (=a single piece of clothing, furniture, jewellery etc) *She didn't take much with her, just a few articles of clothing and a towel.* | **household article** British (=an object used in the house) *Most of our wedding presents were household articles.*

artefact/artifact /ˈɑːʳtɪ̣fækt/ [n C] an object that someone has made, such as a tool or piece of jewellery, especially one that is interesting because it is very old, comes from a different country etc: *Many Bronze Age artifacts were discovered at Luddesdown.* | *Do not buy any artefacts unless they have an export permit.*

2 several things of different types

- things
- stuff
- junk
- odds and ends
- bits and pieces
- paraphernalia

things /θɪŋz/ [n plural] use this when you are talking about two or more **things** of different types and you do not need to say what they are: *I threw a few things into a bag and ran to the car.* | **sb's things** spoken (=the things that someone owns or that they are carrying with them) *She's coming back later to get her things.* | **all sorts/kinds of things** (=a lot of different types of things) *They sell furniture, toys, cards – all sorts of things.*

stuff /stʌf/ [n U] informal spoken objects or possessions of different types: *I don't know how we're going to get all this stuff into the car.* | **sb's stuff** *You're not going to have a lot of time to pack up your stuff before you move.*

junk /dʒʌŋk/ [n U] spoken things that are not useful and should be thrown away, for example because they are old or broken: *I must clean out this cupboard – it's absolutely full of junk.* | *They have so much junk in their yard. It makes the neighborhood look awful.*

odds and ends /ˌɒdz ənd ˈendz‖ˌɑːdz-/ [n phrase] several different things, especially small things that are not of much value: *In the drawer she found a photograph, an old hairbrush, and various other odds and ends.* | *Odds and ends that haven't sold have been drastically reduced in price.*

bits and pieces ALSO **bits and bobs** British /ˌbɪts ən ˈpiːsɪ̣z, ˌbɪts ən ˈbɒbz‖-ˈbɑːbz/ [n phrase] informal a number of small objects that are all different from each other: *There are all sorts of bits and pieces in this box.* | *Do any of these bits and bobs belong to you?*

paraphernalia /ˌpærəfəʳˈneɪliə/ [n U] a large number of different things which you need for a particular activity – you can often use this humorously: *The car is packed solid with all our camping paraphernalia.* | *She was charged with possessing drug paraphernalia.*

3 what you say when you do not know the name of something or cannot remember it

- what's its name/whatchamacallit
- thingy/thingamajig
- thing

what's its name/whatchamacallit ALSO **whatsit** British /ˈwɒts ɪts ˌneɪm, ˈwɒtʃəməˌkɔːlɪt‖ˈwɑː-, ˈwɒtsɪt‖ˈwɑːt-/ [n phrase] informal spoken say this when you do not know the name of something or cannot remember it exactly: *Do you have a what's its name – you know, one of those things for taking off wallpaper?* | *I've broken the whatchamacallit on my purse.* | *You need one of those whatsits to turn the bolt.*

thingy/thingamajig /ˈθɪŋi, ˈθɪŋəmɪ̣dʒɪg/ [n C] informal spoken say this especially when you do not want to try to think about the exact name of something: *You squeeze this little thingamajig, and it forces air into the pocket.* | *The towels are on the thingy at the top of the stairs.*

thing /θɪŋ/ [n C] spoken something whose name you do not know exactly but that has particular features or is a type of the **thing** you are mentioning: *He's got one of those electronic things, you know, that you can record all your addresses in.* | **noun + thing** *What's that box thing on the table?* | *She was wearing one of those Spanish type jacket things.*

think

WHAT'S HERE

- **to think about sth** see **1 to 6**
- **to have a thought** see **7**
- **to have a particular opinion** see **8 to 10**
- **to think that sth is true, but not be sure** see **11 to 12**

to think about sth

RELATED WORDS

- to try not to think about something *see* **forget**
- pay attention to what you are doing *see* **attention**
- *see also* **confused**

1 to think about something before making a decision

- think
- consider
- think over
- think through
- give sth some thought
- sleep on it
- mull over
- be under consideration

think /θɪŋk/ [v I] *Give me time to think.* | *It's a difficult question. Think carefully before you answer.* | **+ about** *I've been thinking about how to tell Marcia the bad news.* | *'What are you going to do with your day off?' 'I don't know – I haven't really thought about it yet.'* | **think hard** (=think carefully) *You have to think hard and ask yourself, 'Do I want to give up everything to do this?'* | **stop to think** *You never even stopped to think how this might be affecting your family!*

consider /kənˈsɪdəʳ/ [v T] to think about something carefully before deciding what to do: *Before buying a car you should consider the cost of insuring it.* | **consider doing sth** *Have you considered working as a journalist?*

think over /ˌθɪŋk ˈəʊvəʳ/ [phr v T] to think carefully about an idea, suggestion, or offer before deciding what to do **think sth over** *After thinking it over, I've decided to accept the offer.* | **think over sth** *Think over what I told you, and give me your answer when you're ready.*

think through /ˌθɪŋk ˈθruː/ [phr v T] to think carefully and thoroughly about all the possible results and effects of something you are doing or plan to do **think through sth** *The government is being criticized for not thinking through the consequences of further tax cuts.* | *It seems to me the whole plan was very badly thought through.* | **think sth through** *Before you commit yourself to this contract you should take a couple of hours to think it through.*

give sth some thought ALSO **have a think** British /ˌɡɪv (sth) səm ˈθɔːt, ˌhæv ə ˈθɪŋk/ [v phrase] to spend some time thinking carefully about a question or problem in order to decide what to do: *My agent really wanted me to do the movie, but after giving it some thought I decided not to.* | *I'm still not sure what's the best route to take. I'll have a think about it tonight.*

sleep on it /ˈsliːp ɒn ɪt/ [v phrase] to delay making a decision about a difficult problem until the next day in order to have more time to think about it: *There's no obligation to do anything at all. Sleep on it, and tell me what you think in the morning.*

mull over /ˌmʌl ˈəʊvəʳ/ [phr v T not in passive] to spend a long time thinking carefully about a plan or idea **mull over sth** *If you are mulling over the idea of starting a new business, remember that there are many things that can affect your decision.* | **mull sth over** *After almost two decades of mulling it over in his mind, Sayles finally made his Texas movie.*

be under consideration /biː ˌʌndəʳ kənˌsɪdəˈreɪʃən/ [v phrase] if a plan, request, suggestion etc **is under consideration**, it is being considered and discussed so that an official decision can be made: *A new pension plan for employees is now under consideration.* | *One of the amendments under consideration proposes that all European countries reduce pollution levels by 30%.*

2 to think about something a lot

- give sth a lot of thought
- have sth on your mind
- can't stop thinking about sb/sth
- dwell on
- brood
- be wrapped up in
- be preoccupied
- have sth on the brain
- turn sth over in your mind

give sth a lot of thought /ˌɡɪv (sth) ə ˌlɒt əv ˈθɔːt‖-ˌlɑːt- / [v phrase] *I've given this a lot of thought, because we all know that health care issues are very important today.* | **give a lot of thought to sth** *Tony has given a lot of thought to what made his father a legendary coach.* | *Many of the new West-Coast designers have obviously given a lot of thought to their furniture designs.*

have sth on your mind /hæv (sth) ɒn jɔːʳ ˈmaɪnd/ [v phrase not in progressive] to be thinking about something all the time, especially because you are worried about it: *She has something on her mind, but she won't tell us what it is.* | *'Should we tell Dad?' 'No, he's got a lot on his mind right now.'* | **be on sb's mind** *Come on, tell me what's on your mind.* | *I'm not looking forward to the interview. It's been on my mind all week.*

can't stop thinking about sb/sth ALSO **can't get sb/sth out of my mind** /ˌkɑːnt stɒp ˈθɪŋkɪŋ əbaʊt (sb/sth) ‖ˌkænt stɑːp-, ˌkɑːnt get (sb/sth) aʊt əv maɪ ˈmaɪnd / [v phrase] informal to be unable to stop thinking about someone or something, even when you do not want to think about them: *After the first three months of the pregnancy were over, I just couldn't stop thinking about food.* | *I just can't get that poor family out of my mind.*

dwell on /ˈdwel ɒn/ [phr v T not usually in passive] to spend too much time thinking about something sad or unpleasant – use this especially when telling someone not to do this: *Brian's still dwelling too much on the past, in my opinion.* | *There's no use in dwelling on problems that we can't do anything about.*

brood /bruːd/ [v I] to keep thinking for a long time about something that worries you or that makes you angry or upset: *Austin sat in the corner brooding and looking sorry for himself.* | **+ on/over/about** *You can't spend all your time at home brooding about the way he treated you.* | *The poetry spends a lot of time brooding over death.*

be wrapped up in /biː ˌræpt ˈʌp ɪn/ [v phrase] to spend all your time thinking about something that concerns you, for example your work, so that you have no time to think about other things or other people: *These days she's so wrapped up in her children she never sees anybody.* | *Sometimes the professors are so wrapped up in their graduate students, they ignore the undergraduates.*

be preoccupied /biː prɪˈɒkjʊpaɪd‖-ˈɑːk-/ [v phrase] to be thinking all the time about something that is worrying you or that is important to you, so that it is difficult to think about anything else: *What is being done to end the crisis which has preoccupied the country's political leadership?* | **+ with** *My mother was preoccupied with my brother and his illness, so I was allowed to do what I wanted.*

have sth on the brain /hæv (sth) ɒn ðə ˈbreɪn/ [v phrase] spoken to be always thinking about a particular thing – use this when you want to say that someone thinks about something far too much: *It's unbelievable – you have sex on the brain 24 hours a day!*

turn sth over in your mind /ˌtɜːʳn (sth) əʊvər ɪn jɔːʳ 'maɪnd/ [v phrase] to think about something carefully and repeatedly, especially something you do not fully understand or that you have not made a final decision about: *When Dan left, Mae stayed there, turning his invitation over in her mind.* | *As he studied the picture of the little boy, he began to turn an idea over in his mind.*

3 to think about something you might do in the future

- think about/of
- contemplate
- consider
- toy with the idea of

think about/of /'θɪŋk əbaʊt, ɒv/ [v T not in passive] *Have you ever thought about a cruise to the Bahamas?* | **think about/of doing sth** *I'm thinking of specializing in Russian and Chinese.* | *We thought about going away for a week or two, but neither of us have time.*

contemplate /'kɒntəmpleɪt‖'kɑːn-/ [v T] to think seriously about something important you intend to do in the future – use this especially in written and formal contexts: *Isn't 17 a little young to be contemplating marriage?* | **contemplate doing sth** *Many years ago he had contemplated writing a book about his childhood.* | *The government was contemplating fining anyone who was found within the island's danger zone.*

consider /kən'sɪdəʳ/ [v T] to think about something that you might possibly do in the future, but without definitely deciding whether you will do it or not: *We began to consider the possibility of moving to Japan permanently.* | *For any skin problem, it's worth considering a change of diet.* | **consider doing sth** *I considered driving out to Atlantic City to meet her.* | *Have you considered getting a new car?*

toy with the idea of /'tɔɪ wɪð ði aɪˌdɪər ɒv/ [v phrase] to think about doing something in the future, but not very seriously because you probably will not do it: *Lately I've been toying with the idea of a trip to South America.* | **toy with the idea of doing sth** *He began toying with the idea of writing a book about his years in the FBI.* | *As late as the age of forty, I toyed with the idea of going back to college.*

4 to think about the advantages and disadvantages of something

- take stock
- weigh/weigh up

take stock /ˌteɪk 'stɒk‖-'stɑːk/ [v phrase] to think carefully about the situation you are in, and about the way it has developed so far, in order to decide what to do next: *Between projects, Morrison tries to rest, take stock, and do some gardening for relaxation.* | **+ of** *Now that the crisis is over, it is time to take stock of the political situation in the region.* | *It's time to take stock of what our government does and weed out the wasteful and ineffective programs.*

weigh/weigh up /weɪ, ˌweɪ 'ʌp/ [v T] to carefully consider a plan or choice by comparing all the advantages and disadvantages involved, so that you can make a decision: *I've been weighing up all the pros and cons of moving to London.* | *Investors are weighing their next moves after the stock market climbed to record heights yesterday.* | **weigh sth against sth** *After weighing the cost of the new program against supposed benefits, the directors decided to cancel the project.*

5 when someone is thinking about something

- thoughtful
- pensive
- be lost/deep in thought

thoughtful /'θɔːtfəl/ [adj] someone who is **thoughtful** has a serious expression on their face and does not say anything, because they are thinking deeply about something: *Suddenly he became more thoughtful, and his eyes filmed over with sadness.* | *My mother sat and watched me eating my food with a thoughtful expression on her face – I could tell she had something to say.*

pensive /'pensɪv/ [adj] thinking deeply about something and seeming a little sad – use this especially in literary contexts: *He kept looking over at her sad, pensive face.* | *As he ended his trip, the usually upbeat Mr. Liebenow was in a pensive mood.* —**pensively** [adv] *Molly looked pensively out at the soft September day.*

be lost/deep in thought /biː ˌlɒst, ˌdiːp ɪn 'θɔːt‖-ˌlɔːst-/ [v phrase] to be thinking so deeply about something that you do not notice what is happening around you: *She'd been so deep in thought, she hadn't heard the man open the dining room door.* | *Her mother stood folding the wash, lost in thought.*

6 when you do or say something without thinking

- without thinking
- off the top of your head
- in the heat of the moment
- automatic
- automatically
- reflex
- knee-jerk reaction
- off-the-cuff

without thinking /wɪðˌaʊt 'θɪŋkɪŋ/ [adv] *Without thinking, Charlotte hugged the girl to try to comfort her.* | **+ about** *Most US companies are still spewing out carbon dioxide without thinking about its potential costs.*

off the top of your head /ɒf ðə ˌtɒp əv jɔːʳ 'hed‖-ˌtɑːp-/ [adv] spoken if you give an answer **off the top of your head**, you say it without thinking about it for very long and without being sure it is correct: *'How much is the house worth?' 'Off the top of my head, I'd say it's worth maybe $160,000.'*

in the heat of the moment /ɪn ðə ˌhiːt əv ðə 'məʊmənt/ [adv] if you say or do something **in the heat of the moment**, you do it very suddenly and without thinking when you are feeling angry or excited, so that you feel sorry about it afterwards: *'In the heat of the moment, my emotions took over and I hit him,' Harper admitted.* | *Our children need to know not only how to prevent pregnancies, but also the long-term effects of a decision they make in the heat of the moment.*

automatic /ˌɔːtə'mætɪk◂/ [adj] an **automatic** response, reaction, or answer is one that happens immediately and without you having to think, especially because you have done it many times before: *A teacher's automatic reaction is to correct mistakes in language.* | *Elizabeth immediately flew into a rage – her automatic response to any kind of criticism.*

automatically /ˌɔːtə'mætɪkli/ [adv] if you do something **automatically**, you do it as a natural reaction and without thinking, because it is what you always do: *His mother continued to talk angrily, and Tim's thoughts automatically switched to more pleasant subjects.* | *You cannot automatically assume that everything your teacher says is correct.*

reflex /ˈriːfleks/ [adj only before noun] a **reflex** action, response, or movement is a physical movement that you make as a natural reaction to something, without having to think about doing it: *a reflex eye movement* | *At birth, an infant can perform only simple reflex actions and behaviours.*

knee-jerk reaction /ˈniː dʒɜːʳk riˌækʃən/ [n C] a reaction that someone makes without thinking at all, because it is the way they always react – use this about a reaction that you expect and disapprove of: *Their knee-jerk reaction is to object to everything the management suggests.* | *If a journalist's judgement is questioned, the knee-jerk reaction is usually, 'I have a right to print whatever I want, so I will.'*

off-the-cuff /ˌɒf ðə ˈkʌf/ [adj] an **off-the-cuff** remark is one that you make without thinking carefully and without any preparation: *The press officer said that the president's statement was an off-the-cuff remark, not as an official statement of policy.* —**off the cuff** [adv] *Speaking off the cuff and with emotion, Pope John Paul II described his disappointment with the recent course of Western history.*

to have a thought

7 when a thought comes into your mind

- think
- have an idea
- have a thought
- occur to
- cross sb's mind
- enter sb's mind
- strike
- come to mind/spring to mind

think /θɪŋk/ [v I/T] to have an idea or thought in your mind, especially one that appears suddenly: *What are you thinking right now?* | **+ of** *I've just thought of a really good idea.* | *Has she thought of any names for the baby?* | *'Did you ask Rita?' 'No, I didn't think of that.'* | **think of doing sth** *There was water spraying everywhere, but nobody even thought of turning it off.* | **think (that)** *I think I'll go and see what's happening out there.*

have an idea /ˌhæv ən aɪˈdɪə/ [v phrase] to think of an idea: *I have an idea. Why don't I drive the kids to school and then you can stay here.* | *Let me know if you have any good ideas.* | *Theresa had another idea. We would hitchhike to her hometown, and live in her brother's garage* | **+ for** *Collings had an idea for a device that would block out TV programs that parents didn't want their children to watch.*

have a thought /ˌhæv ə ˈθɔːt/ [v phrase not in progressive] spoken to think something: *I've just had an awful thought. What if all the banks are closed?* | *I had an interesting thought today when I was talking to Anita. Do you realize that she's never asked us to her house in all the time we've known her?*

occur to /əˈkɜːʳ tuː/ [phr v T not in progressive or passive] if a new thought **occurs to** you, you suddenly think it **it occurs to sb that** *It suddenly occurred to Miranda that perhaps no one would believe her story.* | *Didn't it occur to you that I might be worried?* | **sth occurs to sb** *The possibility that he might be wrong never occurs to him.* | **it occurs to sb to do sth** *As I thought about Mel and David and how similar they were, it occurred to me to introduce them to each other.*

cross sb's mind /ˌkrɒs (sb's) ˈmaɪnd‖ˌkrɔːs- / [v phrase not in progressive] if a thought **crosses someone's mind** they think about it for a short time: *'Why didn't you call me?' 'The thought did cross my mind while I was shopping this afternoon, but then I forgot all about it.* | **it crossed sb's mind that** *It crossed my mind that I was the only female coach on the committee, but that made me more determined than ever.* | **it crossed sb's mind to do sth** *Several times it had crossed his mind to check on the car, but he never actually did it.* | **it never crossed sb's mind** *'It never crossed my mind to give up,' he said. 'It became an obsession.'*

enter sb's mind /ˌentəʳ (sb's) ˈmaɪnd/ [v phrase not in progressive] if a thought **enters** someone's **mind**, they begin to think about it **it entered sb's mind that** *At that moment it entered my mind that maybe someone was trying to kill him.* | **it entered sb's mind to do sth** *Did it ever enter your mind to take out the garbage?* | **it never entered sb's mind** *It never entered my mind that Philip might be jealous.*

strike /straɪk/ [v T not in progressive or passive] if a thought or idea **strikes** you, you suddenly think it, especially because of something you have just seen or heard **it strikes sb that** *I looked around the glittering room and it struck me that I was probably the poorest person there.* | **strike sb as + adjective** *My mother was always asking questions, and it struck me as odd that she didn't ask one on this occasion.*

come to mind/spring to mind /ˌkʌm tə ˈmaɪnd, ˌsprɪŋ tə ˈmaɪnd/ [v phrase not in progressive] if something **comes** or **springs to mind**, you suddenly think it, especially in relation to a particular subject that you are considering: *As I read the letter again, a number of thoughts came to mind.* | *Henry asked the first question that came to mind.* | *I love the circus life, but when people asked me what I wanted to be when I was older, 'circus performer' was not what sprang to mind.*

to have a particular opinion

RELATED WORDS

- *see also* **opinion**

8 to have a particular opinion

- think
- believe
- feel
- figure
- reckon
- consider
- regard/see
- think of sb/sth as/look on sb/sth as
- take the view that/be of the opinion that
- be recognized/acknowledged as

think /θɪŋk/ [v T not in progressive] **+ (that)** *We didn't think that the concert was very good.* | *She thinks I'm crazy to leave my job.* | *I thought we had a good meeting yesterday.* | **what do you think of sb/sth** (=what is your opinion about them?) *What did you think of the new car? Did you drive it?*

believe /bə̇ˈliːv/ [v T not in progressive] to have an opinion that you are sure is right, especially about something important such as life, religion, or politics **+ (that)** *The party believes strongly that health care should be provided for everyone.* | *We believe human rights are more important than economic considerations.*

feel /fiːl/ [v T not in progressive] to have a strong opinion, but one which is based on your feelings rather than on facts **+ (that)** *Liz's parents feel she isn't old enough to leave home.* | *I feel that we're just beginning to make progress, and that it would be wrong to stop now.*

figure /ˈfɪgəʳ‖ˈfɪgjər/ [v T not in progressive or passive] especially American, informal to develop a particular opinion about a situation after considering it carefully: *What do you figure his chances of winning are?* | **+ (that)** *The operation went fine, and they figure he'll be home next week.* | *I'm telling you because I figure you're the only one who can keep a secret.*

reckon /ˈrekən/ [v T not in progressive] especially British, informal to have a particular opinion about something or someone: *What do you reckon – would this make a good present for Donald's birthday?* | **+ (that)** *They reckon the French team's better than ours.* | **be reckoned to be sth** *This hotel is reckoned to be one of the best in the country.*

consider /kənˈsɪdəʳ/ [v T not in progressive] formal to have an opinion about someone or something after thinking carefully about them **consider sb/sth sth** *We do not consider this film suitable for young children.* | *I would consider it an honour to serve on the Executive Committee.* | **consider sb/sth to be sth** *She is considered to be one of the finest pianists of her generation.*

regard/see /rɪˈgɑːʳd, siː/ [v T not in progressive] to think that someone or something is a particular kind of person or thing **regard sb/sth as sth** *She regards herself more as an entertainer than a singer.* | *America was seen as the land of opportunity.* | *Several members of the government have said they regard the Minister's statement as ridiculous.*

think of sb/sth as/look on sb/sth as /ˈθɪŋk əv (sb/sth) æz, ˈlʊk ɒn (sb/sth) æz/ [v T not usually in progressive] to think that someone or something is a particular kind of person or thing, especially when your opinion is wrong, unusual, or unfair: *Most people think of Leonardo da Vinci as a great artist, but he was also a great scientist.* | *Learning a language should be thought of as a natural process.* | *Even doctors may look on these patients as drug addicts and treat them as social outcasts.*

take the view that/be of the opinion that /ˌteɪk ðə ˈvjuː ðət, biː əv ði əˈpɪnjən ðət/ [v phrase not in progressive] to decide to have a particular opinion about a situation or about life in general, especially when other people have different opinions – use this in formal or written contexts: *Nineteenth century scientists took the view that the Universe was meaningless.* | *Aristotle was of the opinion that there would always be rich and poor within society.* | *The committee is of the opinion that the contract is not legally binding.*

be recognized/acknowledged as /biː ˈrekəgnaɪzd, əkˈnɒlɪdʒd æz‖-ˈnɑː-/ [v phrase] to be thought of as being important or very good by a large number of people: *Von Braun was then acknowledged as the world's foremost expert on rocket engineering.* | *Lawrence's novel was rejected at first, but it later came to be recognized as a work of genius.*

9 the way you generally think about something

- attitude
- mentality
- way of thinking
- outlook
- world view
- mindset

attitude /ˈætɪtjuːd‖-tuːd/ [n C] *When I told them I was a doctor their whole attitude changed.* | *What I don't need is somebody with an attitude problem.* | **+ to/towards** *His attitude to his new job seemed to be very negative.* | *In order to change attitudes towards employing women, the government is bringing in new laws.* | **+ of** *They maintained an attitude of defiance to social conventions.*

mentality /menˈtæləti/ [n C usually singular] an attitude that a particular group of people has, which makes them behave in a way that you think is stupid or wrong: *I don't understand the mentality of these teenagers.* | *She despised the bourgeois mentality of the professional class.* | *You know, I wonder if this is a male kind of mentality.*

way of thinking /ˌweɪ əv ˈθɪnkɪŋ/ [n phrase] the attitude of a person or group, especially about what other people should or should not do: *You'll come to understand my way of thinking when you're my age and you have your own children to worry about.* | *I was glad to be with people who shared my way of thinking.*

outlook /ˈaʊtlʊk/ [n C] someone's general attitude to life: *After a good vacation, you'll have a completely different outlook.* | *The farmers were narrowly provincial in their outlook.* | **+ on** (=attitude to life etc) *His outlook on life is largely a result of his strict education.*

world view /ˌwɜːʳld ˈvjuː/ [n singular] the attitude that a person, group or nation has towards life or the world: *The traditional Indian world view is based on certain definite concepts.* | *the Communist world view* | *He believes the change in the world view has occurred because of the new developments in communications.*

mindset /ˈmaɪndset/ [n singular] the way a particular person or group tends to think, especially when this is difficult to change: *The residents of this city have an insular mindset, so strangers are not always made welcome.* | *The mindset of that generation was definitely more obedient than today's.* | *There does seem to have been a slight shift in the government's mindset in the light of recent events.*

10 what you say when giving your opinion

- I think/believe
- in my opinion
- as far as I'm/we're concerned
- if you ask me
- to me
- as I see it/the way I see it
- personally

I think/believe /aɪ ˈθɪŋk, bəˈliːv/ spoken say this when giving your opinion. **I believe** is more formal than **I think** **+ (that)** *I think it's a great idea.* | *I believe that we can do better than this.*

in my opinion /ɪn ˈmaɪ əˌpɪnjən/ [adv] use this especially in formal contexts: *In my opinion, most people learn best by doing, not by sitting in a classroom and reading about it.* | *She is, in my opinion, one of the foremost artists of our time.*

as far as I'm/we're concerned /əz ˌfɑːr əz ˈaɪm, ˈwɪəʳ kənˌsɜːʳnd/ [adv] especially spoken use this especially when you do not care if other people do not agree with your opinion: *He says he tried hard to make the relationship work, but it wasn't hard enough as far as I'm concerned.* | *I will not go on a plane. As far as I'm concerned, they're just accidents waiting to happen.*

if you ask me /ɪf juː ˌɑsk ˈmiː‖-ˌæsk-/ [adv] spoken say this especially when you are giving your opinion about a particular problem: *If you ask me, getting rid of the death tax is the best thing they could do.* | *All this stuff about poisons in the water supply is a load of hogwash, if you ask me.*

to me /tə ˈmiː/ [adv] spoken say this when giving your opinion: *To me, the system seemed too complicated for most people.* | *They call Ned Kelly a criminal, but to me he will always be a hero.*

as I see it/the way I see it /əz ˈaɪ ˌsiː ɪt, ðə ˌweɪ ˈaɪ ˌsiː ɪt/ [adv] say this when giving your opinion: *As I see it, there are two alternatives. We can either stay with your parents or rent a place.* | *The way I see it, if you don't borrow money now, you'll lose the opportunity to expand the business.*

personally /ˈpɜːʳsənəli/ [adv] spoken say this to emphasize that something is your opinion: *Personally, I think it's a crazy idea.* | *Personally, I don't care how it gets done, as long as it's done quickly.* | **personally speaking** *Personally speaking, I think it's a great name for a cigarette.*

to think that sth is true, but not be sure

RELATED WORDS

- see also **sure/not sure, doubt**

11 to think that something is true, but not be sure

- think/believe
- assume
- assumption
- be under the impression (that)
- suspect
- believe
- presume
- presumably
- suppose
- take it for granted

think/believe /θɪŋk, bəˈliːv/ [v T not in progressive] to think something is true, but you are not completely sure. **Believe** is more formal than **think** + (that) *I think Jill moved to the new house last week.* | *'Is it painted?' 'No, I think it's a mosaic.'* | **I think so/I believe so** (=say this to answer 'yes' to a question when you are fairly sure that something is true) *'Has James gone home?' 'Yes, I think so.'*

assume /əˈsjuːm‖əˈsuːm/ [v T] to think that something is true, although you have no proof: *You shouldn't just assume things without getting all the facts.* | + (that) *I just assumed that the woman standing next to Jack was his wife.* | *We assume that other industrialized nations are going to help with money for food and other supplies.* | **we can safely assume** (=it is reasonably certain) *I think we can safely assume that the practice is legal.*

assumption /əˈsʌmpʃən/ [n C] something that you think is true although you have no proof: *Yes the Socialists will probably win – that seems a fair assumption.* | **make the assumption that** *At that time we had to make the assumption that the disease was spreading and take action to stop it.* | **on the assumption that** *Eden acted on the assumption that his allies would support him.*

be under the impression (that) /biː ˌʌndəʳ ði ɪmˈpreʃən (ðət)/ [v phrase] to wrongly believe that something is true, because of something you have heard or seen: *I was under the impression that you couldn't get a parking ticket on private property.* | **be under the mistaken impression (that)** *The average American is under the mistaken impression that wildlife refuges have been set up to protect animals.*

suspect /səˈspekt/ [v T not in progressive] to think that something is probably true, especially something bad + (that) *I suspect that he never really loved her.* | *No one suspected anything was wrong.* | **as sb suspected** *As we suspected, there is a problem with the braking system, and it will be replaced.*

believe /bəˈliːv/ [v T not in progressive] to feel sure that something is true because of information that you have, although there is always some possibility that you are wrong + (that) *Police believe that the money was stolen by a gang of youths.* | **believe sb to be capable/honest/a fool etc** *I had always believed Catherine to be absolutely honest in money matters.* | **firmly believe** *Both sides firmly believe that a peace settlement is now possible.*

presume /prɪˈzjuːm‖-ˈzuːm/ [v T not in progressive] to be fairly sure of something, especially because you have a good reason to think so, although you have no proof + (that) *The committee presumed that its decisions would be carried out.* | **presume sb/sth to be sb/sth** *Many scientists presumed the new damage to the forests to be the result of higher levels of pollution.* | **be presumed innocent/dead/responsible etc** *The defendant is presumed innocent until proved guilty.*

presumably /prɪˈzjuːməbli‖-ˈzuː-/ [adv] if you say something **presumably** is a fact, you think it must be true because of the information you have: *Several of the villagers disappeared, presumably killed by enemy soldiers.* | *The audience hears the word so many times during the play that presumably they learn what it means if they didn't already know.*

suppose /səˈpəʊz/ [v T not in progressive] to think that something is probably true, especially because of some information you have – use this in written or formal contexts + (that) *We have no reason to suppose that the girl is dead.* | *There are many reasons to suppose that Shakespeare was familiar with the stories of medieval Italy.*

take it for granted /ˌteɪk ɪt fəʳ ˈgrɑːntəd‖-ˈgræn-/ [v phrase] to be sure that something is true without ever asking yourself whether you are right or not: *I never asked if she was single – I just took it for granted.* | + (that) *I took if for granted that Steven would still be working for us when the new project started.*

12 what you say when you think something is true, but you are not sure

- I think
- I suppose
- I guess
- get the impression/feeling/idea
- as far as I know
- I imagine
- as far as I'm aware
- to the best of my knowledge
- I take it

I think /aɪ ˈθɪŋk / spoken *She'll be here about 9, I think.* | + (that) *I think the dog must have eaten it.* | **I think so** *'Is Matthew still here?' 'I think so – I've just seen him.'* | **I would think so** *'Will Jenny be at the meeting?' 'I would think so.'*

I suppose /aɪ səˈpəʊz/ spoken say this when you think that something is probably true but you are not really sure: *Having a burglar alarm makes you feel safer, I suppose.* | + (that) *I suppose we can pay by credit card but we'd better check first.* | **I suppose so** (=say this to answer a question) *'Will the children be disappointed?' 'Yes, I suppose so.'*

I guess /aɪ ˈges/ especially American, spoken say this when you think that something is probably true but you are not really sure: *Rob just got tired of living with her, I guess.* | + (that) *I guess this is the best way to do it.* | **I guess so** *'Is the truck safe to drive now?' 'I guess so.'*

get the impression/feeling/idea /ˌget ði ɪmˈpreʃən, ˈfiːlɪŋ, aɪˈdɪə/ [v phrase not in progressive] to start to think something is a fact because of various things that happen, because of the way someone is behaving etc **+ (that)** *I got the impression she was actually quite nervous about it.* | *Walking down the main street, you get the feeling that nothing ever happens in this town.* | *I don't want you to get the idea that I don't like him.* | **get this/that idea** *'He thinks you're angry with them.' 'Where on earth did he get that idea?'*

as far as I know /əz ˌfɑːr əz ˈaɪ nəʊ/ **spoken** say this when you think that something is true, although you realize that you may not know all the facts: *As far as I know, Caroline's never been married.* | *Alaska doesn't have any drilling sites off the coast, as far as I know.*

I imagine /aɪ ɪˈmædʒɪn/ **spoken** say this when you think that something is likely to be true, although what you say is only based on your opinion **+ (that)** *I imagine she's stuck in a traffic jam or something.* | **I would imagine (that)** *I would imagine that Libby could help you – she knows a lot about legal things.*

as far as I'm aware /əz ˌfɑːr əz ˈaɪm əˌweəʳ/ **spoken** say this when you want to make it clear that there may be things you do not know about a situation: *As far as I am aware, Mr Cusner and his family are still living in Cleveland, Ohio.*

to the best of my knowledge /tə ðə ˌbest əv maɪ ˈnɒlɪdʒ‖-ˈnɑː-/ **formal spoken** say this when you want to make it clear that you are not completely sure about the statement you are making: *To the best of my knowledge, this is the first time that anyone has translated these poems into English.*

I take it /aɪ ˈteɪk ɪt/ **spoken** say this when you think that something is true and you are asking someone else to tell you that you are right **+ (that)** *I take it that you're Rob's sister?* | *So can we take it that you'll be at the meeting?* | *You've made plans for the future, I take it?*

thirsty

feeling that you want to drink something

RELATED WORDS

- *see also* **drink, hungry**

- **thirsty**
- **need a drink**
- **be dying for**
- **dry**
- **parched**
- **dehydrated**
- **thirst**

thirsty /ˈθɜːʳsti/ **[adj]** *Are you thirsty? Do you want some juice?* | *On a hot day, your dog can become very thirsty, so make sure they have plenty of water.* | *By the time you actually feel thirsty, your body is already slightly dehydrated.* | *Stands were set up to satisfy the thousands of thirsty people expected at the event.* | **thirsty work British** (=an activity that makes you thirsty, used especially humorously when you want an alcoholic drink) *I'll have a beer. Gardening is thirsty work, you know.*

need a drink /ˌniːd ə ˈdrɪŋk/ **[v phrase] especially spoken** to want to drink something, especially because you are very thirsty or because you want an alcoholic drink: *Jeez it's hot. I need a drink.* | *I need another drink if we're going to keep talking about this.*

be dying for ALSO **be gasping for British** /biː ˈdaɪ-ɪŋ fɔːʳ, biː ˈɡɑːspɪŋ fɔːʳ‖-ˈɡæs-/ **[v phrase] spoken** to want to drink something very much: *We were dying for a Coke, so we stopped at a fast-food place.* | *I'm gasping for a cup of tea.* | **be dying for a drink** (=to want to drink something, especially alcohol) *I'm dying for a drink. Want to go for a pint?*

dry /draɪ/ **[adj]** when your throat or mouth is **dry**, it has very little liquid in it, so that you feel that you want a drink: *My throat was so dry I could hardly speak.*

parched /pɑːʳtʃt/ **[adj]** if someone is **parched** they are very thirsty. You can also say that they have a **parched** throat or **parched** lips when they are very dry and they need a drink: *She put her water bottle to his parched lips.* | *Give me a sip of that, I'm parched.* | *They were dirty and parched, but in remarkably good condition after the rescue.*

dehydrated /ˌdiːhaɪˈdreɪtɪd‖diːˈhaɪdreɪtɪd/ **[adj]** someone who is **dehydrated** does not have enough liquid in their body and feels weak and ill: *When exercising, especially in the heat, drink often or you will become dehydrated.* | **severely dehydrated** *Children who have diarrhoea can quickly become severely dehydrated.*

thirst /θɜːʳst/ **[n singular]** the feeling of wanting to drink something: *The soldiers suffered constantly from hunger and thirst.* | **quench your thirst** (=get rid of your thirst by drinking something) *After a workout, juices are excellent because they quench your thirst and replace fluids and carbohydrates.* | **die of thirst** (=died from a lack of something to drink) *Seven people died of thirst after their truck broke down on an isolated desert road.* | **work up a thirst** (=do work or exercise that makes you thirsty) *The bars and cafes cater to tourists who have worked up a thirst sightseeing.*

threaten

to say that you will harm someone if they do not do what you want

RELATED WORDS

- likely to harm someone *see* **dangerous**
- *see also* **force sb to do sth, violent, attack, warn, frightened/frightening**

1 to threaten someone

- **threaten**
- **intimidate**
- **warn sb off**
- **hold sb to ransom**
- **make/issue threats**
- **get at/get to/nobble**
- **under duress**

threaten /ˈθretn/ **[v T]** to tell someone that you will hurt them or cause serious problems for them if they do not do what you want: *Then he started threatening me and saying that my family might get hurt.* | **+ to do sth** *When they found out he was an American, the soldiers threatened to kill him.* | *Every time we have a quarrel, she threatens to leave me.* | **threaten sb with a knife/gun etc** *After threatening the manager with a knife, he stole £300 and ran off.* | **threaten sb with violence/jail/legal action etc** (=say you will hurt someone, put them in prison etc) *I was threatened with jail if I published the story.*

intimidate /ɪnˈtɪmɪdeɪt/ **[v T]** to try to make someone do what you want by making them feel afraid: *He's being kept in jail until the trial so that he can't intimidate any of the witnesses.* | *The boss is quite tough, but don't let him intimidate you.* | **intimidate sb into doing sth** *Some workers are saying that they were intimidated into accepting the pay cuts, with threats of job losses.* — **intimidating** **[adj]** *He found the interviewers' manner aggressive and intimidating.*

warn sb off /ˌwɔːʳn (sb) ˈɒf/ **[phr v T]** to try to make someone stay away from somewhere or stop doing something by warning or threatening them: *Journalists trying to investigate the scandal were warned off by the FBI.* | **warn sb off sth** *The old man warned them off his land.* | **warn sb off doing sth** *Joanna's brothers had warned him off seeing her again.*

hold sb to ransom /ˌhəʊld (sb) tə ˈrænsəm/ [v phrase] British to force a group, organization, or government to give you what you want by threatening to cause political or financial difficulties if they do not: *What gives cheaper fuel campaigners the right to hold the country to ransom?* | *The president said that the company would not be held to ransom by strikes.*

make/issue threats /ˌmeɪk, ˌɪʃuː ˈθrets/ [v phrase] to repeatedly threaten to harm someone: *He wanted more money and over the next few weeks made further threats.* | **+ about** *It's a waste of time issuing vague threats about imposing sanctions – we should send in the army.* | **+ against** *Threats have been made against the judge who is investigating the case.*

get at/get to/nobble /ˈget æt, ˈget tuː, ˈnɒbəl ‖ˈnɑː-/ [phr v T/phr v T/v T usually in passive] informal to threaten witnesses, judges, or other people involved in a court case in order to influence the court's decision: *The trial had to be abandoned when it was discovered that jury members had been got at by the Mafia.* | *He didn't like the idea that he had been nobbled, especially by a woman.* | *When the police questioned Davis, it was clear someone else had gotten to him first.*

under duress /ˌʌndəʳ djʊˈres‖-dʊ-/ [adv] formal achieved by using unfair threats to force someone to admit something or give something to someone: *The confession had been obtained under duress, and therefore could not be allowed as evidence.* | *In her defence, the accused said that she had been acting under duress when she took the money.*

2 to threaten someone in order to get money from them

▸ blackmail ▸ extort

blackmail /ˈblækmeɪl/ [v T] to force someone to give you money or do what you want, by threatening to tell people about something that they want to keep secret: *You cannot blackmail a man who has nothing to hide.* | *The priest was being blackmailed by a woman who said he was the father of her child.* | **blackmail sb into (doing) sth** *She had tried to use the photographs to blackmail him into marrying her.* | *We will not be blackmailed into silence.* —**blackmail** [n U] *Bates got a 5-year jail sentence for blackmail.* | *'If you don't give me the money, I'm going to tell your wife.' 'This is blackmail!'*

extort /ɪkˈstɔːʳt/ [v T] to get money from someone by threatening them: *He sought to extort money by threatening to reveal secrets about his boss's private life.* | **extort sth from sb** *For years the gang extorted money from local storekeepers.* —**extortion** /ɪkˈstɔːʳʃən/ [n U] the crime of extorting money: *The defendant pleaded guilty to two counts of extortion.*

3 behaving in a threatening way

▸ threatening ▸ menacing

threatening /ˈθretnɪŋ/ [adj] **threatening** words or behaviour are intended to make someone feel afraid, so that they do what you want: *'You listen to me!' he said in a threatening voice.* | *He was arrested for threatening behaviour and using abusive language.* | **threatening letter/phone call** *Before the attack I'd received several threatening phone calls.*

menacing /ˈmenɪ̇sɪŋ/ [adj] making you feel frightened, especially in a quiet way and even though nothing violent is actually said or done: *One of the guards gave a low, menacing laugh.* | *There was something strange and rather menacing about the way she spoke.* —**menacingly** [adv] *The teacher towered menacingly above him.*

4 something you say or write in order to threaten someone

▸ threat ▸ ultimatum

threat /θret/ [n C] when you tell someone that you will hurt them or cause serious problems for them if they do not do what you want: *I'm prepared to listen to him, but I'm not going to respond to threats.* | **make threats** *He denied making threats to kill her.* | **receive a threat** *Immigrant families in the area have received threats from right-wing extremist groups.* | **death threat** (=when someone threatens to kill you) *She claims she received anonymous death threats after she gave evidence in the trial.* | **carry out a threat** (=do what you threatened to do) *He showed no sign of carrying out his threat of making them pay.*

ultimatum /ˌʌltɪ̇ˈmeɪtəm/ [n C] a final, often official, warning that unless someone does something you will punish or attack them **give sb an ultimatum** *She's ignored all my previous warnings about being late for work, so I've decided to give her an ultimatum.* | **issue an ultimatum** *The hijackers have issued an ultimatum – either the government releases the prisoners or the plane will be blown up.*

5 actions that threaten someone

▸ intimidation ▸ threatening behaviour
▸ menace

intimidation /ɪnˌtɪmɪ̇ˈdeɪʃən/ [n U] when you try to make someone do what you want by making them feel afraid: *Hoskins used intimidation and violence to get money from local restaurant owners.* | *The killings are part of a campaign of intimidation against opposition supporters.*

menace /ˈmenɪ̇s/ [n U] a way of behaving or speaking that makes people think that you are threatening them, even though you do not actually say or do anything violent: *His voice was soft but his tone and expression were full of menace.* | *Her manner suddenly changed from friendliness and warmth to one of faint menace.*

threatening behaviour /ˌθretnɪŋ bɪˈheɪvjəʳ/ [n U] British the criminal offence of behaving in a threatening way towards someone – use this in legal contexts: *He was charged with being drunk and disorderly and using threatening behaviour.*

throw

WHAT'S HERE

- **to throw sth through the air** — see **1 to 5**
- **to throw rubbish or unwanted things away** — see **6 to 7**

to throw sth through the air

1 to throw something

- throw
- chuck
- sling
- toss
- lob
- pitch
- hurl
- fling

throw /θrəʊ/ [v T] to make something such as a ball fly through the air by moving your arm quickly and letting it go: *The boys were throwing and catching a frisbee on the beach.* | **throw sth on/onto/across/down etc sth** *John stood on the beach, throwing stones into the waves.* | **throw sth at sb/sth** (=in order to try and hit them) *She was so angry that she threw the pan straight at my head.* | *A couple of kids started throwing stones at my window.* | **throw sb sth** (=when you want someone to catch something) *Carrie threw him a box of matches.* | **throw sth to sb** *The La Scala crowd cheered and threw flowers to the 57-year-old tenor.*

chuck /tʃʌk/ [v T] informal to throw something, especially in a careless way **chuck sth on/out of/into etc sth** *She took off her shoes and chucked them on the floor.* | **chuck sb sth** *Chuck me those cigarettes, would you?*

sling /slɪŋ/ [v T] to throw something carelessly, especially using a lot of force **sling sth into/down/over etc sth** *The baggage handlers just sling the cases in the back of the bus – they don't care if anything gets broken.* | *He watched horrified as they slung the body over the cliff.*

toss /tɒs‖tɔːs/ [v T] to throw something, especially in a careless, relaxed way **toss sth into/out of/down etc sth** *The fire was started when a passing motorist carelessly tossed a cigarette out of his car.* | **toss sb sth** *He tossed her last week's edition of the 'Herald'.* | **toss sth to sb** *'Catch!' said Sandra, tossing her bag to Andy.*

lob /lɒb‖lɑːb/ [v T] to throw something so that it goes high in the air before coming down **lob sth over/across etc sth** *Local kids keep lobbing empty beer cans over our fence.* | **lob sth at sb** (=when you want to hit them) *Someone lobbed a book at me, and it hit me in the face.*

pitch /pɪtʃ/ [v T] American to throw something quickly and carelessly **pitch sth across/over/onto etc sth** *Tod pitched his coat onto the sofa and ran toward the kitchen.* | **pitch sth to sb** (=when you want someone to catch something) *She pitched the ball to the little boy.*

hurl /hɜːʳl/ [v T] to throw a heavy object in a violent way, especially because you are angry **hurl sth at sb/sth** (=when you want to hit them) *Some demonstrators began hurling bricks at the police.* | **hurl sth into/out of/across etc sth** *He picked up the chair and hurled it across the room.*

fling /flɪŋ/ [v T] to throw something quickly and with a lot of force **fling sth out of/down/into etc sth** *He pulled the knife from her hand and flung it out of the window.* | **fling sth at sb** (=when you want to hit them) *When he gave her the tickets she ripped them up and flung them at him.* | **fling sb sth** (=when you want someone to catch something) *We flung him the safety rope.*

2 to throw a ball in a game

- throw
- pass
- pitch
- bowl

▸ *see also* **sport/game, score**

throw /θrəʊ/ [v T] *He threw the ball so hard it went over their heads.* | **throw sth at/into etc sth** *Julie threw the basketball straight into the net.* | **throw sth to sb** *Cromartie ran after the ball and threw it back to the pitcher in one smooth movement.* —**throw** [n C] *That was a very long throw – at least 80 yards.*

pass /pɑːs‖pæs/ [v I/T] to throw the ball to another player in your team: *You should have passed and let Joe take the shot.* | **+ to** *Johnson passes to White, White passes to Eliot, and Eliot scores!* | **pass sth to sb** *The quarterback passed the ball to Olson, who ran in for a touchdown.*

pitch /pɪtʃ/ [v I/T] to throw the ball in baseball so that someone from the other team can try to hit it with the bat: *Johnny learned to pitch by aiming at a target his Dad had painted on the side of the garage.* | *Ryan pitched a curve ball which easily beat the batter.* —**pitch** [n C] *The pitch went wide.*

bowl /bəʊl/ [v I/T] to throw the ball in cricket so that someone from the other team can try to hit it with the bat: *The batsman straightened up as Warne came in to bowl.* | *He's a very aggressive bowler – he always bowls the ball straight at the batsman's body.*

3 to throw something small and light with your fingers

- toss/flip
- flick

toss/flip /tɒs‖tɔːs, flɪp/ [v T] *Mum tried to toss the pancake but unfortunately it missed the pan and hit the floor.* | **toss/flip sth into/over etc sth** *Josh took a mint and flipped it into his mouth like a dime.* | **toss/flip a coin** (=make a coin go upwards and spin in the air, for example as a way of deciding something) *We couldn't decide which movie to go to, so in the end we just flipped a coin.*

flick /flɪk/ [v T] to make something small and light go forward through the air with a quick movement of your thumb and finger **flick sth off/into/over etc sth** *He paused and flicked a mosquito off his arm.* | **flick sth at sb** (=in order to try and hit someone) *Stop flicking water at me!*

4 to attack someone by throwing things at them

- pelt
- stone
- bombard

pelt /pelt/ [v T] **pelt sb with sth** *The boys sat in the back of the class, pelting each other with pieces of rolled up paper.* | *When the Vice-president toured the area in 1958 he was pelted with rotten eggs by angry farmers.* | **pelt sth at sb** *Demonstrators were pelting rocks and bottles at police.*

stone /stəʊn/ [v T] to throw stones at someone or something, in order to injure or damage them: *During the riot the mob started stoning the British embassy.* | **stone sb to death** (=throw stones at them until they are killed, especially as a punishment) *The thieves were caught and sentenced to be stoned to death.*

bombard /bɒmˈbɑːʳd‖bɑːm-/ [v T] to attack someone by throwing large numbers of things at them at the same time **bombard sb with sth** *My brothers bombarded me with snowballs as soon as I stepped out of the house.* | *When the police tried to advance they were bombarded with petrol bombs.*

5 when a sudden force throws someone or something through the air

- throw
- send sb/sth flying
- catapult/propel
- pitch

throw /θrəʊ/ [v T] **throw sb/sth into/off/out of etc sth** *The blast from the explosion threw debris high up into the air.* | *I was cycling home when I got hit by a car and thrown off my bike.* | *A small plane was lifted up and thrown across the tarmac by a freak gust of wind.*

send sb/sth flying /ˌsend (sb/sth) ˈflaɪ-ɪŋ/ [v phrase] to make someone or something suddenly move forward or through the air: *He swung round suddenly, sending the papers on his desk flying.* | *Her foot caught on something on the ground. Whatever it was, it sent her flying.*

catapult/propel /ˈkætəpʌlt, prəˈpel/ [v T] to suddenly push someone or something very hard so that they move extremely quickly through the air **catapult sb/sth into/over/out of etc sth** *The car crashed into a tree and the driver was catapulted through the windshield.* | *I felt myself being propelled into the air by the force of the explosion.*

pitch /pɪtʃ/ [v T] if something such as a strong wind or a sudden movement **pitches** someone off a boat or a high place, it makes them fall off it **pitch sb into/over/out of etc sth** *A sudden gust of wind pitched him off the ledge and he was left hanging by his safety rope.* | *Two of the crew were pitched overboard when a big wave hit their ship.*

to throw rubbish or other unwanted things away

RELATED WORDS

- *see also* **get rid of**

6 to throw something away

- throw away
- throw out
- get rid of
- toss/chuck
- dispose of sth
- discard
- dump

throw away ALSO **chuck away** British informal /ˌθrəʊ əˈweɪ, ˌtʃʌk əˈweɪ/ [phr v T] **throw/chuck sth away** *I've thrown his photograph away and I never want to see his face again.* | *It's a nice dress. It would be a shame to chuck it away.* | *To avoid the risk of infection, needles must be used once and then thrown away immediately.* | **throw/chuck away sth** *Some employers throw away all incorrectly hand-written applications without even reading them.* | *In the bin there were a few scraps of food his mum had chucked away.*

throw out ALSO **chuck out** especially British, informal / **toss out** American informal /ˌθrəʊ ˈaʊt, ˌtʃʌk ˈaʊt, ˌtɒs ˈaʊt‖ˌtɔːs-/ [phr v T] to get rid of something, especially when you are trying to make a place more tidy or to make space for new things **throw/chuck/toss sth out** *You haven't thrown those magazines out have you?* | *We chucked a lot of stuff out when we moved house.* | **throw/chuck/toss out sth** *She would do nothing for days then spring into action and spend a day throwing out all the garbage, cleaning the bathroom, and dusting.* | *Why don't you toss out all those old books. You'll never want to read them again.*

get rid of /get ˈrɪd ɒv/ [v phrase] to throw something away, especially something old or dirty: *I think it's time we got rid of all these old toys.* | *If you hate that furniture so much why don't you get rid of it and buy some new stuff.* | **get rid of sth for sb** *Give me the empty bottles – I'll get rid of them for you.*

toss/chuck /tɒs‖tɔːs, tʃʌk/ [v T] American informal to get rid of something, especially when you are trying to make a place more tidy or to make room for new things: *If you don't want any of these shoes, I'm going to toss them.* | *'What should I do with all your old text books?' 'Just chuck them out – I'm never going to need them.'*

dispose of sth /dɪsˈpəʊz əv (sth)/ [v T] formal to throw away something that you do not want or no longer need, by putting it in a suitable place: *Please dispose of this wrapper carefully.* | *Nuclear waste can cause serious damage to the environment if not disposed of properly.* —**disposal** [n U] *This is an incinerator for the disposal of hospital waste, such as used syringes.*

discard /dɪsˈkɑːʳd/ [v T] formal to throw away something that you no longer need, especially by dropping it on the ground or leaving it somewhere you should not: *People who discard their litter in the streets should have to pay heavy fines.* | *A child had become trapped in a refrigerator discarded in a vacant lot.* —**discarded** [adj only before noun] *The police believe that the fire was started by a discarded cigarette.*

dump /dʌmp/ [v T] to throw away something dangerous or something no one wants, especially by leaving it in an unsuitable place **dump sth in/into sth** *People who want to get rid of old cars sometimes dump them in the woods.* | *Toxic waste is being dumped into the ocean.* | *The half-burned bodies were dumped in mass graves.*

7 designed to be used once and then thrown away

- disposable

disposable /dɪˈspəʊzəbəl/ [adj] *Didn't you know you can buy disposable contact lenses now?* | *a disposable toothbrush* | *disposable nappies*

tidy

RELATED WORDS

opposite: **untidy**

- *see also* **clean, arrange, organize**

1 a tidy place/room/group of things

- tidy
- neat
- immaculate
- well-kept

tidy /ˈtaɪdi/ [adj] British a place, room etc that is **tidy** looks nice because everything has been arranged and put in the right place **tidy**: *Andrew's apartment is always so tidy.* | *That looks a bit tidier now, doesn't it?* | *a tidy desk* | **keep sth tidy** *I think the least you* *could do is keep your own bedroom tidy.* | *My job was to mow the grass and keep the garden looking generally tidy.* | **clean and tidy/neat and tidy/nice and tidy** *We spent the morning getting the whole house clean and tidy.* | *I want to leave the place nice and tidy before we go.*

neat /niːt/ [adj] use this about things that are carefully arranged or shaped in a way that is nice to look at: *Mrs Woodie cut the sandwiches in neat squares.* | *The room was neat, though a bit dusty.* | *Billy's cottage was set back off the road, behind a neat little hedge.* | **neat pile/row** *He put his clothes in a neat pile on the bed.* | *His jackets were arranged in a neat row in the closet.* | **neat and tidy** *I like to see everything looking neat and tidy.* —**neatly** [adv] *All the books were neatly arranged on the shelves.* | *He took off his jacket and folded it neatly on his lap.*

immaculate /ɪˈmækjələt/ [adj] a place or thing that is **immaculate** is perfectly clean and neat – use this to emphasize how clean something looks: *Our house was immaculate, and Mother taught us to be polite and deferential to visitors.* | *a tiny harbour ringed with immaculate white clapboard houses* | **immaculate suit/shirt/uniform etc** *He was dressed in an immaculate navy suit and a crisp white shirt.* | *tall, blond soldiers in immaculate uniforms* —**immaculately** [adv] *Like the house, the garden was neat and immaculately kept.*

well-kept /ˌwel ˈkept◂/ [adj] a **well-kept** building or garden is very well cared for and looks neat and clean: *Our old house, now covered with ivy, still looked pretty and well-kept.* | *Visitors should tour the palace, but don't forget the well-kept grounds – well worth a visit.*

2 to make a place tidy

- tidy/tidy up
- straighten/straighten up
- clean up
- clear up
- pick up
- get sth straight
- sort out

tidy/tidy up /ˈtaɪdi, ˌtaɪdi ˈʌp/ [v T/phr v I/T] to make a room, desk, or drawer tidy: *If you're not going to watch the football, you can tidy your room.* | *I haven't had time to tidy up yet.* | *I want this whole place tidied before I get back, ok?* | **tidy up sth** *You can start tidying up that mess you've made now.* | *She hung about after work, tidying up her desk.* | **tidy sth up** *Will you help me tidy the kitchen up a bit?* | **tidy sth away** (=put something in the place where you usually keep it) *Come on, let's have these toys tidied away now.* | **tidy up after sb** (=to have to clean a room and put things away after someone has been in there) *Both my sons think mothers are just here to tidy up after them.*

straighten/straighten up /ˈstreɪtn, ˌstreɪtn ˈʌp/ [v T/phr v I/T] American to make a place tidy and clean, by putting things in the right place or arranging them neatly: *Make the bed and straighten up in there.* | *Kelly, when you're through with your break, would you straighten the office?* | **straighten sth up** *The city's janitors went on strike, leaving thousands of workers to straighten their own offices up and empty their own trash.* | **straighten up sth** *After the kids have left for school, I straighten up the house.* | *You're not leaving till you get your room straightened up.*

clean up /ˌkliːn ˈʌp/ [phr v I/T] to make a place tidy and clean, by putting things away and removing dust or dirt: *Do you want me to help clean up?* | **clean sth up** *Thanks for cleaning the place up – I really appreciate it.* | *It took us two or three days to clean it all up.* | **clean up sth** *Every time Jasper cooked for me, he would carefully clean up all the pans and plates he'd used.*

clear up /ˌklɪər ˈʌp/ [phr v I/T] British to get rid of all the things that are making a place dirty or untidy: *Who's going to clear up after the party?* | *John's offered to clear up the churchyard this weekend.* | **clear sth up** *It'll take ages to clear this up.* | *It looked as if Marie had already cleared the place up.* | **clear up sth** *Someone's got to clear up this mess!* | *Wait for me, I just need to clear up my desk.* | **clear up after sb** (=tidy a place after someone else has made it untidy) *I spend my life clearing up after the children.*

pick up /ˌpɪk ˈʌp/ [phr v T] to put things away neatly in order to make a place tidy **pick up sth** *Could you pick up the newspapers and magazines for me?* | **pick sth up** *Help me pick these things up. We have company coming.* | **pick up after sb** (=put away things that someone else has used) especially American *I feel like I spend all my time picking up after the kids.*

get sth straight /ˌget (sth) ˈstreɪt/ [v phrase] British informal to tidy a place and put everything where it should be: *I like to get the house straight while the kids are at the youth club.* | *One of these days I'll get this garage straight.*

sort out /ˌsɔːʳt ˈaʊt/ [phr v T] especially British to organize something that is mixed up or untidy **sort sth out** *I'm going to sit down quietly one day and sort my CDs out.* | **sort out sth** *I need to sort out the food cupboard, and make a shopping list.* | *We've got to sort out all our stuff to take home tonight.*

3 words for describing someone who always likes to keep things tidy

- neat/tidy
- houseproud
- neat freak

neat/tidy /niːt, ˈtaɪdi/ [adj] someone who is **neat** or **tidy** always like to keep things in their right place: *I've never been very neat but my husband is just the opposite.* | *Malcolm's always been tidy, even as a kid.*

houseproud /ˈhaʊspraʊd/ [adj] British someone, especially a woman, who is **houseproud** wants their home to always look extremely clean and tidy, and spends a lot of time keeping it like this: *She has a reputation for being very houseproud.* | *Elaine's houseproud ways got on his nerves, but it was better than living alone.*

neat freak /ˈniːt friːk/ [n C] American spoken someone who always wants their things and their house to be very neat and clean, in a way that other people find annoying: *Melissa is a neat freak and Doug is kind of a slob, so the two of them are always fighting.*

4 someone who looks tidy

- neatly dressed
- immaculate
- clean-cut
- not have a hair out of place

neatly dressed /ˌniːtli ˈdrest◂/ [adj phrase] someone who has a neat appearance because of the type of clothes they are wearing: *I rang the bell, and a neatly dressed maid answered the door.* | *She was in her mid-forties, neatly dressed with a quiet air of authority.*

immaculate /ɪˈmækjələt/ [adj] looking perfectly neat and clean, because you take a lot of care about your clothes, your hair etc: *Leonardo appeared, immaculate as ever in a dark suit and tie.* | *She was always elegantly dressed and absolutely immacu-*

late. | *A small but immaculate figure stood in the doorway.* —**immaculately** [adv] **immaculately dressed/groomed** *Ten minutes later she reappeared, immaculately dressed in a red linen tunic with matching pumps.* | *Though she was still immaculately groomed, there seemed somehow less poise about her.*

clean-cut /ˈkliːn kʌt/ [adj] a man who is **clean-cut** looks neat and clean: *a handsome, clean-cut man* | *Where Clinton was rugged and earthy, Gore is clean-cut and preppy.*

not have a hair out of place /nɒt hæv ə ˌheər aʊt əv ˈpleɪs/ [v phrase] to have a very neat appearance: *He sat at his desk, not a hair out of place, and turning a pencil over in his hand.* | *He seemed stern and austere and never had a hair out of place.*

5 tidy work/writing

- neat

neat /niːt/ [adj] work or writing that is **neat** has been done very carefully: *Gina has very small neat handwriting.* | *Draw a rough diagram – it doesn't have to be very neat.*

tie/untie

RELATED WORDS

- to join together the two sides of something *see* **fasten/unfasten**

1 to fasten things together, using rope, string etc

- tie
- tie up
- do up
- lash
- rope sb together

tie /taɪ/ [v T] to fasten one thing to another using rope, string, wire etc **tie sth to/around/onto etc sth** *Don't forget to tie this label onto your suitcase.* | *The washing line was tied to a tree.* | *Saul tied one end of the rope around a large rock and lowered himself over the cliff.* | **tie a package/parcel** (=keep it closed by putting string around it) *The package had been tied with strong green string.* | **tie sth together** *If the rope is too short, tie two pieces together.* | *When the teacher stood up, he found that his shoes had been tied together.*

tie up /ˌtaɪ ˈʌp/ [phr v T] to tie things together so that they are held firmly together **tie sth up** *I put the coins in a piece of cloth, tied it up and put the package in my bag.* | **tie up sth** *Clara tied up all the books again and put the bundle under the desk.*

do up /ˌduː ˈʌp/ [phr v T] especially British, informal to tie or fasten something, especially a piece of clothing **do sth up** *Could you do up the back of this dress for me?* | **do up your shoes/laces** (=tie the strings on your shoes) *Do up your laces before you trip and fall.*

lash /læʃ/ [v T] to tie something very tightly to something else so that it will not move at all **lash sth to sth** *The bags were lashed tightly to the roof of the jeep.* | **lash sth together** *The sailors made a raft by lashing tree-trunks together.*

rope sb together /ˌrəʊp (sb) təˈgeðəʳ/ [phr v T usually in passive] to tie things or people to each other using a fairly long piece of rope, so that they are connected to each other at a distance: *The climbers were roped together for safety and proceeded cautiously.*

2 to prevent someone from escaping by tying rope around them

- tie up
- tie
- bind
- shackle
- tether

tie up /ˌtaɪ ˈʌp/ [phr v T] to tie someone's arms and legs with rope so that they cannot move **tie sb up/tie up sb** *The soldiers tied them up and beat them.* | *Mrs Bennett had been tied up and left in the back of the van.*

tie /taɪ/ [v T] to prevent a person or animal from escaping by tying them with rope etc **tie sb to sth** *The terrorists tied the hostages to their chairs.* | *Her horse was tied to a tree.* | **tie sb's hands/feet together** *The kidnappers had tied his hands together and blindfolded him.*

bind /baɪnd/ [v T usually in passive] to tie someone's arms, legs etc so that they cannot move at all – used in literature or in newspapers: *The hostages had been bound and gagged and left in a corner of the room.* | **bind sb hand and foot** *It was like being bound hand and foot to a torturer's chair.*

shackle /ˈʃækəl/ [v T] to tie someone's legs or arms with a thick chain: *The prisoners were shackled together and forced to walk 600 miles across country.*

tether /ˈteðəʳ/ [v T] to tie an animal such as a dog or horse to something, using a rope, so that it can move around but cannot walk away: *The farmer tethered a goat in the field and left it there for the day.* | **tether sth to sth** *My horse had been tethered to a post, but somehow it escaped.*

3 to tie a knot in something

- tie
- knot

tie /taɪ/ [v T] to **tie** a knot in a piece of string, rope, cloth etc **tie a knot in sth** *Quickly tying a knot in his tie, John finished dressing and went to work.* | **tie a knot/bow** *At school camp they taught us how to tie various knots.* | **tie the laces/tapes etc** *Pull both ends tight, tie the tapes, then inflate the life jacket.*

knot /nɒt‖nɑːt/ [v T] to tie a **knot** in something in order to fasten it: *He tied the rope to the tree, knotted it, and attached the other end to his car.* | **knot sth around sth** *Britt casually knotted a silk scarf around her neck.*

4 to untie something

- undo
- untie
- disentangle

undo /ʌnˈduː/ [v T] to remove the string or rope from something so that it is no longer held together: *I can't undo the string!* | *She undid the ribbon and let her hair fall over her shoulders.*

untie /ʌnˈtaɪ/ [v T] to remove or unfasten the string or rope that joins one thing to another: *Someone had untied the boat and it had floated away.* | *It was several hours before anyone found me and untied me.*

disentangle /ˌdɪsɪ̣nˈtæŋgəl/ [v T] to untie a group of wires, ropes etc that have all been mixed together: *The balls of wool were all mixed up, and I couldn't disentangle them.*

tight

RELATED WORDS

opposite: —————— **loose**

- to hold something tightly *see* **hold (2)**
- ways of saying that clothes do not fit *see* **fit/not fit**
- *see also* **attach, fasten/unfasten**

1 tight clothes

- **tight**
- **skintight**
- **tight-fitting/close-fitting**

tight /taɪt/ [adj] **tight** clothes or shoes are only just big enough for you to wear, and they are often uncomfortable: *This skirt is far too tight.* | *Tight shoes can cause corns and other foot problems.* | *I never wear tight clothes – I just don't feel comfortable in them.*

skintight /ˈskɪntaɪt/ [adj] **skintight** clothes are very tight and fit exactly to the shape of your body, especially in a way that looks sexually attractive: *Suzy was wearing a sleeveless skintight dress and sandals.* | *a pair of skintight jeans*

tight-fitting/close-fitting /ˌtaɪt ˈfɪtɪŋ◂, ˌkləʊs ˈfɪtɪŋ◂/ [adj] **tight-fitting** or **close-fitting** clothes are deliberately made to be tight when they are worn: *Standing next to him was a small, thin woman in a close-fitting black suit.* | *The diver's wet suit should be tight-fitting, yet allow reasonable freedom of movement.*

2 when a rope, wire etc has been pulled or stretched tight

- **tight**
- **taut**

tight /taɪt/ [adj] rope, wire, cloth etc that is **tight** has been pulled or stretched as far as possible so that it is straight or it cannot move: *If the straps aren't tight enough, the saddle can slip.* | *'Seat belt tight? Good, this could be a rough ride.'* —**tightly** [adv] **tightly wrapped** *Sylvia handed me a large parcel, tightly wrapped in brown paper.*

taut /tɔːt/ [adj] written stretched very tight: *The skin of his face felt dry and taut.* | *He massaged the taut muscles of her neck.* | *A single strand of taut barbed wire was strung along the top of the garden wall.*

3 fastened tight

- **tight**
- **firmly**
- **securely**
- **fast**

tight /taɪt/ [adj] a screw, lid, cover etc that is **tight** has been firmly fixed and is difficult to move: *Check that the screws are tight.* | *Cover with a tight lid and refrigerate.*

firmly /ˈfɜːʳmli/ [adv] if something is **firmly** closed or fixed, it has been closed or fixed so that it cannot move: *The posts must be fixed firmly in the ground.* | *When leaving the house, check that all doors and windows are firmly closed and locked.*

securely /sɪˈkjʊəʳli/ [adv] if something is **securely** fastened or fixed, it has been carefully fastened or fixed so that it will not move or open and cause an accident: *We made sure that our bags were securely fastened to the roof of the car.* | *A large safety screen, securely fixed to the wall, will prevent a child coming into contact with a fire.*

fast /fɑːst‖fæst/ [adv] if something is held, stuck, or tied **fast** it is held, stuck, or tied so tightly that it cannot be moved at all: *The front of the boat was stuck fast in the mud.* | *The spare tyre on the back of the Jeep was held fast by three strong bolts.*

4 to make something tight

- **tighten**
- **pull sth tight**
- **stretch**

tighten /ˈtaɪtn/ [v T] to make something tight, either by fastening it firmly so that it cannot move, or by pulling it until it is tight **tighten a screw/bolt** (=by turning it) *Tighten the screws gradually until the wheel is firmly in place.* | *He changed the spanner for one the correct size and tightened the nut.* | **tighten a rope/belt/string etc** *I think the fan belt needs to be tightened.*

pull sth tight /ˌpʊl (sth) ˈtaɪt/ [v phrase] to pull a string, rope etc hard, so that it becomes tight: *Brian wrapped some string round the parcel and pulled it tight.* | *She buttoned her jacket all the way up and pulled the collar tight around her neck.*

stretch /stretʃ/ [v T] to pull a piece of rope, cloth, rubber etc so that it becomes tight, making it slightly longer than it normally is: *Seth stretched the phone cord around the corner so that he could speak in private.* | **stretch sth over/between etc sth** *He stretched a large tarpaulin over the vehicle, tying it down at the corners.*

time

RELATED WORDS

- to continue for a period of time *see* **last**
- to spend time doing something *see* **spend money/time**
- free time *see* **time (10-11)**
- to happen or arrive on time *see* **on time**
- *see also* **future, past, now, free time, temporary**

WHAT'S HERE

what time is it?

1 when you ask what time it is

- **ask (sb) the time/ask (sb) what time it is**
- **what time is it?**
- **have you got the time?**
- **what time do you make it?**

ask (sb) the time/ask (sb) what time it is /ˌɑːsk (sb) ðə ˈtaɪm, ˌɑːsk (sb) wɒt ˈtaɪm ɪt ɪz‖ˌæsk-/ [v phrase] to ask someone to tell you the time: *She was walking home near Colbayns School when a man approached her and asked her the time.* | *She was distracted for a moment by someone asking the time.* | *Go and ask Dad what time it is.* | *If you've got a watch, why are you asking what time it is?*

what time is it? ALSO **what's the time?** British /wɒt ˈtaɪm ɪz ɪt, ˌwɒts ðə ˈtaɪm/ spoken say this to ask someone you are with to tell you the time: *'What time is it?' 'Just after four o'clock.'* | *What's the time? Is it after 10?*

have you got the time? British **/do you have the time?** American /ˌhæv juː gɒt ðə ˈtaɪm‖-gɑːt-, duː juː ˌhæv ðə ˈtaɪm/ spoken say this to ask someone the time, when you do not know whether they have a watch: *Sorry to trouble you, but do you have the time?* | **have the right time** *Does anyone have the right time here?* | **have the time on you** British *Excuse me! Have you got the right time on you please?*

what time do you make it? British **/what time do you have?** American /wɒt ˈtaɪm duː juː ˌmeɪk ɪt, wɒt ˈtaɪm duː juː ˌhæv/ spoken say this when you are asking someone who has a watch, especially because you think your own watch may be wrong: *What time do you make it, Emma? My watch has stopped.* | *What time do you have, Dave? I don't want to miss my plane.*

2 ways of saying what time it is

- o'clock
- just before/after
- to
- past
- it's getting on for
- bang/dead on

o'clock /əˈklɒk‖əˈklɑːk/ [adv] use this when the time is exactly a particular hour: *It's 5 o'clock.* | *It's exactly 10 o'clock.*

just before/after ALSO **just gone** British /ˈdʒʌst bɪfɔːʳ, ɑːftəʳ‖-æf-, ˈdʒʌst gɒn‖-gɔːn/ [prep] use this when the time is a little before or after a particular hour: *It's just before 6.* | *It's just after 10 o'clock.* | *It's just gone midnight.* (=just after)

to ALSO **of** American /tuː, ɒv/ [prep] use this **to** say that the time is a particular number of minutes before a particular hour: *It's ten to six.* | *It doesn't get dark until about twenty to ten.* | *It's a quarter of eleven.* | *Joe, by the ten of eight you're going upstairs and that's only about a half hour from now.*

past ALSO **after** American /pɑːst‖pæst, ˈɑːftəʳ‖ˈæf-/ use this to say that the time is a particular number of minutes after a particular hour: *It's quarter past four.* | *It's ten after five.* | *It's quarter after eight, and Laurie's showing up at nine.* | *It's half past two.*

it's getting on for /ɪts ˌgetɪŋ ˈɒn fɔːʳ/ British use this to say that it is almost a particular time, especially when you are guessing what time it might be: *It's getting on for five o'clock.* | *I should think it's getting on for ten by now.*

bang/dead on /ˈbæŋ, ˈded ɒn/ [adv] British informal use this to say that it is exactly a particular time: *'What time is it?' 'Bang on midnight.'* | *I make it dead on half past by my watch.* | *We finished bang on eight, and we were back home by nine.*

time when sth happens

3 a time when something happens

- time
- occasion
- moment/point

time /taɪm/ [n C] a **time** when someone does something or something happens – use this especially to talk about something that happens more than once: *Do you remember that time Tim got really drunk at Sarah's party?* | *Play it really loud this time.* | **the only/same/last etc time** *The last time we ate meat was at Thanksgiving.* | *The only time I've seen him with a girl was that party at Mike's place.* | *Give us a call next time you're in town.* | *That was around the same time that I met Linda.* | **the first/second/third etc time** *Is this the first time you've played pool?* | *Sandra, that's the third time I've asked you to keep quiet.* | *Alex won the 100 metres for the fifth time in a row* (=he won five times, and no one else won the race in between). | **four/six/several etc times** *This is my favourite film – I've seen it five times.* | *It's silly – I've met him several times, but I can never remember his name.* | **a number of times** formal (=use this to say something happened several times) *She's been to Greece a number of times.* | *I've heard Jessie play a number of times, and I think he's great.* | **every/each time** *Every time I met her, she asked me about the children.* | **time when** *Do you remember the time when Dad lost the car keys?*

occasion /əˈkeɪʒən/ [n C] formal a time when something happens **on one/that etc occasion** *The witness said that on both occasions he noticed Davis because of his heavily tattooed arms.* | *On one occasion, Anna fainted while out shopping with friends.* | *She had met Zahid on a previous occasion.* | **on numerous/several occasions** (=use this to emphasize that something happened many times) *I've suggested that she should move on numerous occasions, but she never takes any notice.* | *I remember Michael sleeping in your room on several occasions and mom not knowing about it.*

moment/point /ˈməʊmənt, pɔɪnt/ [n C] an exact time when something happens, during a longer process or series of events: *The play went well, apart from one embarrassing moment when I dropped a cup.* | *At several points during the meeting, Adler threatened to walk out.* | *My most special moment with dad was when I was announced as the winner of Junior Beauty Contest.* | **moment/point in time** *At that precise moment in time, Binh walked in.*

4 what hour, day etc something happens

- time
- date
- hours
- hour
- timing
- at
- on
- in
- ago
- on/at the stroke of

time /taɪm/ [n C] the particular minute or hour of the day when something is planned to happen, or the particular minute or hour that it happened in the past **the time of sth** *Could I have the times of the trains to Birmingham please?* | *This leaflet lists the dates and times of all the concerts.* | *The police are still trying to establish the exact time of her death.* | **what time?** *What time did you see the man leave the bus station?* | *What time do you usually start in the mornings?* | *What time is the news on?* | **depar-**

ture/arrival time (=the time when a train, plane, etc leaves or arrives) *The departure times are posted on our website.* | *The plane's estimated arrival time is 19:45.* | **opening/closing time** (=the time when a shop, office etc opens or closes) *We went into a cafe and sat there until closing time.* | *I've got to get this to the video store by closing time.* | **opening times** (=the normal times when a shop is open) *Check with the museum for opening times at www.musart.co.* | **lunchtime/dinnertime etc** (=the time when you have a meal) *Robbie! It's suppertime!* | **time of year/day etc** *The winds are pretty strong at this time of year.* | *There won't be much traffic on the roads at this time of night.* | **by that time** (=after a particular hour of the day or night has passed) *Well, most people had gone to bed by that time of night.* | *She apologized for being late, but by that time I was really annoyed with her.*

date /deɪt/ [n C] the day, month, or year when something is planned to happen, or happened: *Do you know the date when the house was built?* | *We still haven't received notification of the exam date.* | **the date(s) of sth** *Give me the dates of the American War of Independence.* | *June 9th is the date of the European elections.* | **+ for** *We need to arrange a date for the next meeting.* | *A date for his release has not yet been agreed.* | **set a date (for sth)** (=choose a particular date) *Have they set a date for the wedding yet?* | **birth date/date of birth** (=the date on which someone was born) *It helps if you provide your birth date and Social Security number.* | *Could I have your name and your date of birth please?* | **start date** (=the date when something begins, especially a job) *I later received confirmation of my new job in a letter indicating the start date.* | **closing date** (=the date when a competition, offer etc ends) *The closing date for entries is 3 March 2001.* | **expiry date** British **/expiration date** American (=the date on which something can no longer be used) *Key in your credit card details, including the expiration date of the card.* | *Are you sure these yoghurts are ok? Have you checked the expiry date?* | **launch/release date** (=the date when a new product, film, etc is shown to people) *'Snow White' had a December release date to capture the Christmas market.*

hours /aʊəʳz/ [n plural] a fixed period of time in the day when a particular activity, business etc happens: *I'd like to return something to your store – what are your hours?* | **office/opening/business hours** (=when an office, shop etc is open) *Our telephone hotline is open during regular business hours.* | **visiting hours** (=when you can visit someone in the hospital) *Visiting hours are from 2 to 5 every day.* | **after hours** (=after an office, shop etc is closed) *After hours callers can leave a voicemail message.* | **out of hours** British (=before or after the usual business hours) *What was Tom doing in the office out of hours?*

hour /aʊəʳ/ [n C] a particular period or point of time during the day or night **at this hour** (=very late at night or early in the morning) *Sir, I'm sorry to bother you at this hour.* | **at some ungodly hour** informal (=very late or very early) *We had to get up at some ungodly hour to catch our train.* | **at all hours** *There's something happening on our street at all hours of the day and night.* | **lunch/dinner hour** *I hate telemarketers who call during the dinner hour.*

timing /ˈtaɪmɪŋ/ [n U] a word meaning the time, day, or date that something is planned to happen, used especially when you are considering how suitable this is **+ of** *The voter survey is crucial to the timing of the election.*

at /ət, (*strong*) æt/ [prep] use this with hours and minutes of the day, special holidays, or the beginning or end of a period of time **at six o'clock/half-past four/midnight/lunchtime etc** *He starts work at 10, and finishes at 6:30.* | *Would you like to go to the sandwich bar at lunchtime?* | *I have a hospital appointment at 9.00 am.* | **at Christmas/Easter/New Year** *We get a week's holiday at Easter.* | *What are you doing at Christmas?* | **at the end/beginning/start (of sth)** *Frank joined the navy at the beginning of the war.* | *We get paid at the end of the week.* | *The students all do a short test at the start of term.*

on /ɒn‖ɑːn, ɔːn/ [prep] use this with particular days: *The team holds a meeting on the first Monday of every month.* | *I tried to catch him on the last day of term, but he'd already left.* | **on Monday/Tuesday night/Friday evening etc** *We're going out for dinner on Friday.* | *Are you doing anything special on Saturday night?* | **on August 12th/March 2nd etc** *She was born on May 12, 1913.* | *The course starts on 14 October.* | **on my birthday/their wedding day/Valentine's day etc** *Did you call dad on Father's Day?* | *Aren't you coming here on Christmas Day?* | **on Thursdays/Fridays etc** ALSO **on a Thursday/Friday etc** British (=every Thursday, Friday etc) *Her husband takes her shopping on a Saturday to Asda.* | *We always go to the pub on Fridays.*

in /ɪn/ [prep] use this with parts of the day, particular years, or particular months, and seasons of the year **in the morning/afternoon/evening** *I'm usually too tired to cook a meal in the evening.* | *We didn't get to bed until 3 o'clock in the morning.* | **first thing in the morning** (=very early in the morning) *I want to be ready to leave first thing in the morning.* | **in 1892/2001 etc** *In 2004, the Olympic Games will be held in Athens.* | **in the fifties/sixties/1990s etc** (=from 1950 to 1959, 1960 to 1969 etc) *He did a lot of abstract art in the sixties, but he's moved on since then.* | **in January/February/the autumn etc** *I came to England in the summer of 1995.* | *The series returns in the autumn.* | *'How old is Philip now?' 'He's four in December'.*

ago /əˈgəʊ/ [adv] use this to say how far back in the past something happened **5 minutes/an hour/100 years etc ago** *Michael left the office 20 minutes ago.* | *'When did you hurt your back?' 'About a fortnight ago'.* | *My daughter was married just over a year ago.* | **a long time ago** *I met your father once, a long time ago.* | **a short time ago/a little while ago** *Did you see that program about genetics that was on a little while ago?* | **a minute/moment ago** *I had my keys a minute ago, and now I can't find them.* | **not so long ago** (=used to say that something was quite a short time ago) *We went down to see a show in London not so long ago.* | **how long ago?** (=used to ask how far back in the past something happened) *How long ago was that, Dad?* | *How long ago did you buy the computer?*

on/at the stroke of /ɒn, ət ðə ˈstrəʊk ɒv/ [prep] at exactly a particular time and not any earlier or later: *On the stroke of midnight, the British flag was lowered for the last time over Delhi.* | *The judge entered the courtroom at the stroke of nine.*

5 a list of times of trains, classes, or activities

▸ timetable/schedule ▸ timetable
▸ schedule

timetable British **/schedule** American /ˈtaɪmˌteɪbəl, ˈʃedjuːl‖ˈskedʒʊl, -dʒəl/ [n C] a list that shows the times when something will happen, for example when planes or buses leave, or when classes at school take place: *Teachers will be giving out copies* *of the new timetable in the first class today.* | *Train services shown in this timetable are subject to alteration or cancellation at short notice.* | *After I'd found my room, I sat down to look carefully at my schedule.* | **bus/train etc timetable** *The train schedules are all on the website now.* | **TV/radio schedule** *The events have been arranged to match TV schedules.* | **+ of** *I'd like a schedule of flights from Boston to New York.*

schedule /ˈʃedjuːl‖ˈskedʒʊl, -dʒəl/ [n C] a detailed plan of activities that have been organized, showing for example the times when someone will do something, or the times when activities will start and finish: *The President's schedule includes a two-day visit to St Petersburg.* | *The flight was cancelled, and that really messed our schedule up.* | **+ for** *Do you have a schedule for the tour?* | *What's the schedule for today's meeting?* | **according to schedule** *The director was given a budget of $10 million and so far the film seems to be going according to schedule.* | **ahead of/behind schedule** (=earlier/later than the time that was planned) *I know, we're a week behind schedule already.* | **on schedule** (=at the time that was planned) *The building should be completed on schedule.* | **stick/keep to a schedule** *It's important that everyone on the project keeps to the schedule.* | **work/training etc schedule** *Do you have a work schedule for this week, Doreen?* | *Various minor ailments can interfere with your training schedule.* | **busy schedule** (=when there is a lot to do) *She took time out of a busy schedule to talk to us.* | **tight schedule** (=when there is not very much time to do things) *With this new project in the offing, I'm going to be working to a very tight schedule.*

timetable /ˈtaɪmˌteɪbəl/ [n C usually singular] a plan that shows when parts of an important and long process, especially a political one, will happen: *Party leaders met to discuss a new constitution and an electoral timetable.* | **+ for** *Their purpose would be to set a timetable for the conversion of British cars to low-octane fuel.* | *He gave no indication of a timetable for the approval of the changes.*

6 to arrange a time for something to happen

- schedule
- time
- pencil in

▸ *see also* **arrange (3-6)**

schedule /ˈʃedjuːl‖ˈskedʒʊl, -dʒəl/ [v T] to arrange for an activity or event to happen at a particular time: *Monday's performance of St Matthew's Passion is scheduled to start at 7.30 pm.* | *If you schedule your practice routine to include one exercise a week, you should learn the musical scale pretty quickly.* | **schedule sth for tomorrow/next week/Dec 4 etc** *I've scheduled a meeting for tomorrow. I hope everyone can attend.* | *The first game is provisionally scheduled for January 26.*

time /taɪm/ [v T] to arrange for an activity or event to happen at a particular **time**, especially because this is the most suitable or convenient time: *The meditation class will be timed so that it does not coincide with the noisier exercise classes.* | *The release of the document was shrewdly timed.* | **time sth for 12 noon/12.45 etc** *Stephen timed his arrival for exactly six o'clock.* | *The first track race is timed for 11.15.*

pencil in /ˌpensəl ˈɪn/ [phr v T] to arrange a time for something to happen, especially when you may want to change this later **pencil in sth** *Political commentators are pencilling in July 30th, August 6th or August 13th as possible election dates.* | **pencil sth in** *we'll pencil May 15 in as a reserve date.* | **pencil sth in for Dec 4/next week etc** *Greg's pencilled the sale in for December 15.* | *The band are pencilled in for a show in the King's Hall on January 18.*

how long

7 how long something continues

- how long
- for
- since
- until
- from ... until
- from ... to ...
- through
- Monday-Friday/ 6:00-8:00

how long /haʊ ˈlɒŋ‖-ˈlɔːŋ/ use this to ask about or talk about how many minutes, hours, days, or years something continues for: *How long have you been waiting?* | *I don't know how long the repair will last, but it should get you home.* | *How long are you going to be in the bathroom?* | *How long have you two known each other?* | *So how long did you live on Long Island?*

for /fəʳ, (*strong*) fɔːʳ/ [prep] use this to say how long something continues **for an hour/two days/a long time etc** *'How long did you live in Spain?' 'Oh, for about three years.'* | *We seem to have been waiting for ages.* | *We talked for a while.* | *Omar's been learning English for two years now.* | *I only worked there for three months.*

since /sɪns/ [prep/conjunction/adv] all the time from a time or event in the past until now: *I've had this car since 1992.* | *I've been smoking since I was 14.* | *Graham's become a lot more confident since he finished his training.* | *I saw her this morning, but I haven't seen her since.* | **ever since** *Jack has had a fascination with cars ever since he was four.* | *They bought the caravan last summer, and they've had trouble with it ever since.*

until ALSO **till** especially spoken /ʌnˈtɪl, tɪl/ [prep/conjunction] if something happens **until** or **till** a time or event, it continues and then stops at that time or event: *David worked as a teacher until 1989.* | *I'll be at home until 5:30 if you want to phone me.* | *She polished the car until it shone.* | *I didn't learn to drive until I was 31.* | *The library's only open till five on Saturdays.* | *Just wait till I've finished my coffee.*

from ... until ALSO **from ... till ...** especially spoken /frəm ... ʌnˈtɪl, frəm ... tɪl/ [prep/conjunction] use this to say that something starts happening at one time or event and continues until another time or event: *I have a class Monday from five o'clock till eight o'clock at night.* | *I lived there from the age of 14 until I went to college.* | *Max edited the paper from 1950 until he retired in 1989.*

from ... to ... /frəm ... tə .../ [prep] use this to say that something starts at a particular time and stops at a later time **from May to September/from 9 am to 5 pm etc** *Eisenhower was President from 1952 to 1956.* | *I'm going to use the computer lab from eight to ten Friday morning.* | *My plan is to train seriously from January to July.*

through /θruː/ [prep] American **May through September/Monday through Friday etc** starting in May and continuing until September, starting on Monday and continuing until and including Friday, etc: *The store is open Monday through Saturday.* | *'When will you be away?' 'The 17th through the 19th.'*

Monday-Friday/6:00-8:00 /ˌmʌndi tə ˈfraɪdi, ˌsɪks tʊ ˈeɪt/ written starting on Monday and continuing until and including Friday, starting at 6 o'clock and continuing until 8 o'clock etc – used on signs and notices: *Visit the exhibition of modern art, open every day, 9:30-6:00.* | *A special fishing licence is required for the season (May-September).*

8 the period of time that something lasts or takes

- length of time
- duration
- time scale

length of time /ˌleŋθ əv 'taɪm/ [n phrase] **a considerable/reasonable length of time** *The noise went on for a considerable length of time.* | *Make sure that the speakers only talk for a reasonable length of time, so that everyone gets a chance to take part.* | **+ (that)** *Dress the wound quickly, to reduce the length of time it is exposed to infection.* | **the length of time it takes to do sth** *Typically, the length of time it takes an adult to fall asleep is 10 to 15 minutes.*

duration /djʊ'reɪʃən‖dʊ-/ [n U] formal the length of time that something lasts for: *Zoe's temper tantrums had increased both in volume and duration.* | **two years'/a month's etc duration** *After a long voyage of two years' duration, he arrived in Canton in 1669.* | *These workshops, usually of one or two days' duration, bring teachers and industrial managers together.* | **+ of** *The doctor will ask you about the duration and frequency of your headaches.* | *He refused to comment on his salary or the duration of his contract.* | **for the duration (of sth)** *It was decided that we would stay with my cousins for the duration of the war.*

time scale /'taɪm skeɪl/ [n C] the period of time during which something develops or exists, especially as compared with another period that is much longer or shorter: *Compared to how long it took for the Universe to evolve, our human time scale is tiny.* | *Carbon dioxide is removed from the atmosphere by a number of processes that operate on different time scales.* | *In today's computer industry, the whole time scale of new product development is far shorter than it was 10 years ago.*

short time/long time

9 a short time

- a minute/moment
- a second
- not long
- a bit
- a little/short while
- a short/brief space of time

▸ *see also* **short (9-10)**

a minute/moment /ə 'mɪnɪ̆t, 'məʊmənt/ [n singular] a very short time: *Can I show you something? It'll only take a minute.* | *Luke thought for a moment and then said: 'Would you like to come too?'* | *Can you turn that off a minute* (=for a minute)*?* | **in a minute/moment** *Yes, I'm coming in a moment.* | **a minute/moment ago** *Helen was here a minute ago. You've just missed her.* | **for a minute/moment** *If you'd been quiet for a minute, I'd explain what happened.*

a second ALSO **a sec** informal /ə 'sekənd, ə 'sek/ [n singular] spoken a very short time – use this especially when asking someone to wait for a short time: *Just a second – I think it's on the desk upstairs.* | **for a second/sec** *For a second there, I forgot what it was called.* | **in a second/sec** *Hang on, I'll be with you in a sec.*

not long /nɒt 'lɒŋ‖-'lɔːŋ/ [n phrase] a short time: *'How long will it take?' 'Oh, not long – just a couple of hours.'* | *I saw her not long ago.* | **not long before/after** *His book was published not long after he died.* | *It wasn't long before Gemma lost all interest in the new puppy.* | **not long to go** (=used to say that something will happen in a short time) *'When's the baby due?' 'Three weeks, so there's not long to go.'* | **won't be long** (=use this to say that someone or something will come or return soon) *I'm popping to the shop, I won't be long.* | *Supper won't be long.*

a bit /ə 'bɪt/ [n singular] especially British, spoken a short time: *Wait a bit, I've nearly finished.* | *I sat down, and after a bit, the phone rang.* | *Do you mind looking after the kids for a bit while I go out?*

a little/short while /ə ˌlɪtl, ˌʃɔːʳt 'waɪl/ [n singular] a short period of time, during or after which something happens: *Bob's only worked here for a short while, about six months I think.* | *It always takes a little while to get used to the climate.* | **a little/short while ago** *He was on the telly a short while ago.*

a short/brief space of time /ə ˌʃɔːʳt, ˌbriːf speɪs əv 'taɪm/ [n phrase] a short period of time during which a lot of things happen **in/within a short space of time** *It's amazing how much you can learn in such a short space of time.* | *In the brief space of time since the war ended, citizens have managed to rebuild over half the city.* | *She had gained an awful lot of journalistic experience within a short space of time.*

10 a long time

- a long time
- long
- all day/night/year/week
- hours/weeks/years
- ages
- donkey's years/ages
- the longest time

▸ *see also* **long (6-13)**

a long time /ə ˌlɒŋ 'taɪm‖-ˌlɔːŋ-/ *They've been married for 30 years – that's a long time.* | *It takes me a long time to really trust people.* | **for a long time** *The house has been empty for a long time.* | *Have you been waiting here for a long time?* | **in a long time** *It's the worst cold I've had in a long time.* | *I haven't worn this dress in such a long time.* | **a long time ago** *He died a long time ago.* | *The accident happened such a long time ago that I can't remember much about it.* | **a very long time/a long, long time** *I've had those books for a long, long time.* | *It's very well built and should last a very long time.*

long /lɒŋ‖lɔːŋ/ [adv] *It has long been recognized that a high-fat diet can cause heart problems.* | *She's convinced that Grandmother is not going to live long.* | *The journey took longer than I thought it would.* | **long before/after** (=a long time before/after) *Long after the war, the wreckage of his plane was discovered.* | *She was wearing fake fur long before it became fashionable.* | **for long** (=for a long time) *Have you been working here for long?* | *The phone rang for so long, I hung up in the end.* | **long ago** *I guess it didn't happen very long ago.* | **take (sb) so long** *Why is it taking so long?* | *I bet it doesn't take your mom so long to make an apple pie.*

all day/night/year/week /ɔːl 'deɪ, 'naɪt, 'jɪəʳ, 'wiːk/ [adv] continuing for the whole day, night, year etc – use this especially to emphasize that it is a long time: *It's going to take us all night to finish marking these papers!* | *He's in London all week, and only comes home at the weekends.* | **all day/week etc long** *I've been working all day long.* | *Susie, you must have been on the phone all night long!*

hours/weeks/years /aʊəʳz, wi:ks, jɪəʳz/ many hours, weeks, or years – use this to emphasize the length of time, or to say that it is much longer than you think it should be: *It's years since I rode a bike.* | *My wife had to wait months for a hospital appointment.* | **for years/hours etc** *I lived there for years.* | **in years/hours etc** *That's one of the best films I've seen in years.*

ages /ˈeɪdʒɪ̈z/ [n plural] especially British, spoken a very long time: *It seems like ages since we had a holiday.* | **take (sb) ages** *This software takes ages to load.* | *It took him ages to guess who it was in the photo.* | **for ages** *I've been waiting here for ages.* | **ages ago** *'When did you last see Barbara?' 'Oh, ages ago.'* | **ages and ages** (=use this to emphasize how long something takes or lasts) *It's the first time for ages and ages he's taken me out.*

donkey's years/ages /ˈdɒŋkiz jiəʳz‖ˈdɑːŋ-, ˈeɪdʒɪ̈z/ [n phrase] British informal a long time, use this especially to say that something happened a very long time ago **for donkey's years/ages** *Some of these medicines have been in the stockroom for donkey's years.* | *That's been going on for donkey's ages – didn't you know?* | **donkey's years/ages ago** *We used to play golf together, but that was donkey's years ago.*

the longest time /ðə ˌlɒŋgɪ̈st ˈtaɪm‖-ˌlɔːŋ-/ [adv] American a very long time: *It took me the longest time to figure out how to work the sunroof in this car.* | *For the longest time, I thought Nathan was Asian.*

11 a fairly long time

- a while

a while ALSO **some time** formal /ə ˈwaɪl, sʌm ˈtaɪm/ a fairly long time: *He was furious, and it took him a while to calm down.* | *It may be some time before the company starts to make a profit.* | **for a while/for some time** *We hadn't seen him for a while, and he'd completely changed.* | *I've known Paul for some time, and I'm sure he wouldn't have said that.* | **after a while/after some time** *After a while, I realized what he meant.* | *Not a single vehicle passed, but after some time they heard the roar of planes taking off at the airfield.* | **quite a while/quite some time** *When she left school, it was quite a while before she found a job.* | *I stayed in the Stage Coach Inn, but it's been quite some time ago.* | **a while since/some time since** *It's been a while since we last heard from Jo.* | *The team has spent some time since their last defeat on new tactics.* | **a while ago/some time ago** *The cafe was taken over a while ago.* | *We arranged the meeting some time ago – were you not informed?*

period of time

12 a period of time

- period
- time
- term
- season
- stretch
- stint
- spell
- a bad patch

period /ˈpɪəriəd/ [n C] especially written a particular length of time with a beginning and an end **+ of** *These accounts are drawn up for a period of 52 weeks.* | *After a brief period of independence, Belorussia came under Soviet rule.* | **for a period** *You shouldn't sit in front of a computer screen for long periods without a break.* | *Anne had difficulty holding down a job for any period of time.* | **period of time** *The work had to be completed within a limited period of time.* | **long/short period** *The company expects a growth in profitability over a longer period.* | *Then, within a short period, his mother, father, and brother all died.* | **a ten-day/three-year etc period** *The money can be paid back over a five-year period.* | *The researchers observed mothers and their new infants for a three-day period.* | **over a period** *The restoration of the ceiling was completed over a period of two years.* | **during a period** *During this period, Tanya was making very little money.* | *black immigration into Britain during the post-war period*

time /taɪm/ [n singular] a period of **time** – use this especially to talk about a period in the past, or when you are not saying whether the period was long or short: *Bill had lost his job, and it was a difficult time for him.* | *I really enjoyed my time at university.* | **at one time** (=at a period of time in the past, but not now) *At one time, Hakami was ranked 32nd in the world.* | *Martin had been at one time a student at Leiden University in the Netherlands.* | **for the time being** (=for a short period of time, starting now) *You can stay in the spare room for the time being, until you find a place.* | *Entrance fees to the exhibit have been reduced for the time being.* | **during that/this time** *He played for Barcelona for four years, and during that time they won two major competitions.* | **for a time** *He chatted to us for a time, then left.* | *For a time, the 1,600 seater hall was home to a Saturday night film show, before being converted to a night club.* | **after a time** *After a time, I began to feel more relaxed.* | *All systems settle down after a time.*

term /tɜːʳm/ [n C] a length of time that is officially fixed for someone's period of responsibility or power, for someone's period in prison, or for a business contract: *Mr Toplak had just started his term as vice-president of the company.* | *The Socialists are hoping to secure another term in government.* | *The bank says that they can extend the term of our mortgage.* | **first/second etc term** *General Herrera was elected to a third term of office as President.* | *He hopes to visit China during his second term in office.* | **7-year/2-month etc term** *He recently completed a two-year term as chairman.* | **term of imprisonment** (=formal) *Political dissidents are sentenced to long terms of imprisonment.* | **prison/jail term** *She had her jail term cut for good behaviour.* | **term of/in office** (=term for holding an official position) *He is halfway into his term of office.* | *The Democrats are hoping to deny him a third term in office.* | **fixed term** (=when the term of a business or employment contract is set to a particular length) *The managers were all hired for a fixed term.* | **serve a term** *Malik is now serving a three-year term in prison.* | *Elected members of the House of Assembly serve a six-year term.*

season /ˈsiːzən/ [n C] a period of several weeks or months, at the same time every year, during which a particular activity takes place: *The Bulls would consider re-signing him next season.* | **the 2001/2001-02 etc season** *Smith should own the record outright by the third or fourth game of the 2001 season.* | **breeding/hunting/fishing/baseball etc season** *When does the baseball season start?* | *Foxes become very noisy at the height of the mating season.* | *The latest challenge is to promote the LSO's winter concert season.*

stretch /stretʃ/ [n C] a period of time between other periods, especially one during which there is not much activity or no interruptions: *During their worst stretch of 1996, the Padres lost 19 of their 23 games.* | *He spent several brief stretches in jail for minor offences.* | *This is the last game in a four-day stretch here at the Forum.* | **stretch of time** *Sometimes between battles, there were long stretches of time when nothing happened.*

stint /stɪnt/ [n C] informal a period of time doing a particular job or course, often quite a short period: *After a stint in the army, Bill worked in sales.* | *Krem began his career with the Victoria Symphony, followed by stints with orchestras in Winnipeg and Quebec.* | **+ of** *Dimascio was promoted after serving a stint of five years as a sergeant pilot.* | **a five-year/six-day etc stint** *He has changed his schedule to a three-day stint, which starts Friday.* | **short/brief stint** *Rick was fired in August after a brief stint with a Portland courier service.* | **do/serve a stint** *She served a two-year stint as an aide to Congressman Jim McNulty.* | *We should thank Mary for the long stint she's done as party treasurer.*

spell /spel/ [n C] a period of a particular type of activity, weather etc, usually a short period: *After a brief spell in the army, I returned to teaching.* | **+ of** *He's had a spell of bad luck recently.* | **a cold/wet/dry etc spell** *We had another cold spell last week.*

a bad patch /ə 'bæd ˌpætʃ/ [n phrase] British a short period of trouble, difficulty, or unhappiness, experienced by someone who is usually happy, successful etc **go through a bad patch** (=experience a period of trouble etc) *He went through a bad patch after his wife died, but now he seems to be back to normal.* | **hit a bad patch** (=start to experience a period of trouble etc) *The team aren't doing so well at the moment are they? They seem to have hit a bad patch.*

13 a period of time in history

- period
- era
- age

period /'pɪəriəd/ [n C] a particular **period** of time in history, especially a **period** that is studied as a historical subject: *Which period of history are you studying at the moment?* | *We will be examining some original documents from the period.* | **the Roman/Tudor etc period** *Many of Britain's roads were built originally in the Roman period.* | *This chapter will focus primarily on the Neolithic period in Europe.*

era /'ɪərə/ [n C] a period of time in history that is remembered because of important political, religious, or artistic events and achievements, that make it different from other periods **+ in/of** *an exciting era in technological sophistication* | *We live in an era of breathtaking change.* | **end of an era** *When Charles De Gaulle died, it seemed like the end of an era.* | **a new era** *The treaty marks the dawn of a new era in East–West relations.* | **the Roman/Christian/Stalin/McCarthy etc era** *archaeological remains dating from the late Roman era* | *During the McCarthy era, hundreds of innocent US citizens were persecuted for their beliefs.*

age /eɪdʒ/ [n C] a period of time in history that represents a particular stage in the development of civilization or machines and tools **+ of** *Newton lived in an age of exploration and discovery.* | *In this age of the Internet, finding a job can be much easier.* | **Stone Age/Nuclear Age etc** *These simple tools were used for hunting in the Stone Age.* | *the architecture of the industrial age* | **golden age** (=the period considered to be the best, the most successful etc) *Many consider the '30s and '40s to be the golden age of Hollywood movies.*

right time/wrong time

14 the right time or a good time to do something

- the right time
- a good time
- come at the right time/come at a good time
- be the time
- timing
- timely
- well-timed
- an opportune moment/time

the right time /ðə ˌraɪt 'taɪm/ [n phrase] the best time to do something, when you are most likely to get the result that you want: *Yes, I'm going to ask him – I'm just waiting for the right time.* | **+ to do sth** *It seemed like the right time to start planning something new.* | *I don't think it's the right time to tell Jeff.* | **the right time of day/year** *If you get here at the right time of day, you might get to see the birds feeding.* | *This really isn't the right time of the year to start working on the house.*

a good time /ə ˌgʊd 'taɪm/ [n phrase] a suitable or convenient time: *I'd like to come on Saturday – would that be a good time?* | **+ for** *11 o'clock would be quite a good time for me, if you can make it.* | **+ to do sth** *Now is a good time to start applying for jobs.* | *Right after the Easter break is a good time to visit Florida.* | *I'll be here all day Friday, so when would be a good time to meet?*

come at the right time/come at a good time /kʌm ət ðə ˌraɪt 'taɪm, kʌm ət ə ˌgʊd 'taɪm/ [n phrase] if something **comes at the right time** or **comes at a good time**, it happens when you need or want it to happen: *I lost my job last month, so this offer has come at just the right time.* | *Well, you're news comes at a good time, Helen.*

be the time /bi: ðə 'taɪm/ [v phrase] an expression meaning to be the right time to do something important, use this especially when you are advising someone what they should do **+ to do sth** *If you're going to buy a house, now's the time to do it.* | **+ for** *The reason I'm saying 'no' is because right now is not the time for making a mess in here.*

timing /'taɪmɪŋ/ [n U] the ability to choose the right time to do something, especially when this is a skill you have learned or practised: *When you're a comedian, timing is very important.* | *He eventually played in another 28 games, but his timing and rhythm never returned.* | **good/perfect etc timing** *'Well, life's just full of surprises,' she retorted, with a comic's perfect timing.* | *You guys have good timing, we just started to eat.* | **sense of timing** (=the ability to choose the right time to do something, especially when this is a natural ability that you have) *Even at the end, George Burns never lost his impeccable sense of timing.*

timely /'taɪmli/ [adj] actions, decisions etc that are **timely** happen at the right time, especially with the result that they prevent something bad from happening: *The Government's intervention was timely and may have prevented economic disaster.* | *The database will provide timely and accurate information on the current status of the business.* | *The fighting in the Ardennes came as a timely reminder that the West still needed the Russian army.*

well-timed /ˌwel 'taɪmd◂/ [adj] done at the right time so that it is likely to have a successful result: *She took a sip of water during a well-timed pause, and waited for my reply.* | *Wallace made a well-timed run through the midfield, collected the pass and* *scored with a low shot. | The conference is well timed since most companies will have their third-quarter profits in by now.*

an opportune moment/time /ən ˌɒpətjuːn ˈməʊmənt, ˈtaɪm‖-ˌɑːpərtuːn-/ [n phrase] formal a time when you are most likely to be successful, or a time which is convenient: *For those who are waiting for the most opportune time to invest in a home, this is an excellent time to do that. | This seemed like an opportune moment to ask the government to mount a tree-planting program.*

15 the wrong time or a bad time for something

- the wrong time
- a bad time/not a good time
- come at a bad time/come at the wrong time/not come at a good time
- be no time/not be the time
- badly timed/ill-timed
- an inopportune moment/time

the wrong time /ðə ˌrɒŋ ˈtaɪm‖-ˌrɔːŋ-/ [n phrase] a time when you should not do something, because you will probably not be successful: *It's a case of the right idea at the wrong time.* | **+ to do sth** *I think this is the wrong time to ask for a pay increase. | It seemed like the wrong time in my life to risk making yet another major change.*

a bad time/not a good time /ə ˌbæd ˈtaɪm, nɒt ə ˌgʊd ˈtaɪm/ [n phrase] a time when something is not convenient or likely to be successful or that will cause problems: *I really would like to come, but I'm afraid this is a bad time.* | **to do sth** *If it's not a good time to talk, I can call back.*

come at a bad time/come at the wrong time/not come at a good time /kʌm ət ə ˌbæd ˈtaɪm, kʌm ət ðə ˌrɒŋ ˈtaɪm‖-ˌrɔːŋ-, nɒt kʌm ət ə ˌgʊd ˈtaɪm/ [v phrase] to happen at a time when something it not likely to be successful or that will cause problems: *These economic problems have come at the wrong time for the Republican Party. | The widening trade gap is coming at a bad time for the president. | The COE's resignation has not come at a good time for the company.*

be no time/not be the time /biː ˌnəʊ ˈtaɪm, ˌnɒt biː ðə ˈtaɪm/ [v phrase] an expression meaning to be the wrong time to do something, use this especially when you are telling someone what they should do or how they should behave **+ for** *This is no time for that kind of talk. If you can't be decent, keep your mouth shut. | It's not the time for politeness and etiquette when there are lives at stake.* | **+ to do sth** *This was not the time to get angry, but Jodie couldn't help herself.*

badly timed/ill-timed /ˌbædli ˈtaɪmd, ˌɪl ˈtaɪmd◂/ [adj] done at the wrong time so that it is likely to have an unsuccessful result: *Wilkins' outburst could not have been more ill-timed. | Resentment over the chairman's badly timed remarks is growing. | The gesture was sincere, but ill-timed.*

an inopportune moment/time /ən ɪnˌɒpətjuːn ˈməʊmənt, ˈtaɪm‖-ˌɪnɑːpərtuːn-/ [n phrase] formal a bad time, especially because it is inconvenient: *He had wanted to visit the troops over Christmas, but the general said it would be an inopportune time. | He always seems to say exactly the wrong thing at the most inopportune moment.*

same time

16 at the same time

- at the same time
- together
- at once
- at one time
- simultaneously

at the same time /ət ðə ˌseɪm ˈtaɪm/ [adv] *Charlie and I arrived at the same time. | Are you supposed to press these two buttons at the same time? | We've launched an appeal, and at the same time we are sending out supplies, shelters, and blankets.* | **+ as** *His wife had a baby at the same time as Elaine. | You must have been at Harvard at the same time as I was.* | **all at the same time** (=when you do several things at the same time) *So you want to talk to them, identify that they are a candidate, and then give them the test all at the same time?*

together /təˈgeðəʳ/ [adv] if two or more people or things do the same thing **together**, they do it at the same time and usually in the same place: *The Baltimore and Boston trains came in together. | Three runners crossed the line together.*

at once /ət ˈwʌns/ [adv] if two or more things happen **at once**, they happen at the same time and this is annoying or causes problems: *I can't understand what you're saying when you both talk at once. | You're trying to do too many things at once. | Anyone know the answer? Don't all shout at once, put your hand up.* | **all at once** *You can't have three weeks' holiday all at once, you'll have to take them separately.*

at one time /ət ˌwʌn ˈtaɪm/ [adv] if someone does two or more things **at one time**, they do them at the same time, especially if this is difficult or impressive: *This word processor allows you to work with two documents at one time. | There aren't many places around here where you can cater for fifty or so people at one time. | You feel like you are going in twelve different directions at one time.* | **all at one time** *See, I can lock the doors all at one time.*

simultaneously /ˌsɪməlˈteɪniəsli‖ˌsaɪ-/ [adv] if two or more things happen **simultaneously**, they happen at exactly the same time: *The system can simultaneously search up to 16 databases. | People can't write and listen simultaneously. | Videoconferencing enables us to address audiences all over the nation simultaneously.*

17 while something else is happening

- while
- meanwhile
- as

while ALSO **whilst** British /waɪl, waɪlst/ [conjunction] during the same period of time that something is happening: *I bought a magazine while I was waiting for the train. | Did you get a lot of work done whilst the kids were out? | I'll just make a phone call while you finish the dishes. | He was afraid he'd have another fit whilst he was driving.*

meanwhile /ˈmiːnwaɪl/ [adv] while something else is happening: *Leave the vegetables to simmer, and meanwhile bring a large pot of water to a boil. | Three helicopters scanned the area; the soldiers meanwhile were looking into back gardens, dustbins, and under hedgerows.*

as /əz, (*strong*) æz/ [conjunction] if something happens **as** something else is happening, it happens at the same time: *As we were leaving, Carole and her friends arrived.* | *There was a shocked silence as he spoke.* | *The sensor uses an infrared beam to 'read' a vehicle's exhaust emissions as it drives past.* | **just as** (=at exactly the same time as) *He ran into the road just as a car was coming.* | *The phone rang just as he stepped out of the shower.* | **as soon as** *As soon as I pulled in, the engine went dead.* | *I fell asleep as soon as my head hit the pillow.*

18 to happen or do things at the same time

- coincide
- clash
- tie in with
- juggle

coincide /ˌkəʊɪ̥nˈsaɪd/ [v I] if something **coincides** with something else, or if two things **coincide**, they happen at the same time as each other, usually by chance: *When our vacations coincided, we often holidayed together.* | **+ with** *His speech coincided with the release of a report on the New England economy.* | *I had to cancel our lunch date, as it coincided with my hospital appointment.* | **timed/arranged to coincide** (=arranged so that something coincides) *The exhibition was timed to coincide with the anniversary celebrations.* | *They have arranged the launch to coincide with the start of the college term.*

clash /klæʃ/ [v I] if one event **clashes** with another, or if two events **clash**, they are arranged to happen at the same time, and this usually causes problems or is inconvenient: *We can go to both classes if they don't clash.* | **+ with** *We've rescheduled the next meeting – it clashed with a conference that most of us will be attending.* | *'Are you watching Family Fortunes tonight?' 'No, it clashes with the Tina Turner interview on Channel 3.'*

tie in with /ˌtaɪ ˈɪn wɪð/ [phr v T] to arrange an event so that it happens at the same time as something else, because this helps you in some way: *His publishers have tied the release in with his new television series.* | *AIDS education can be tied in with existing health education programs.*

juggle /ˈdʒʌgəl/ [v T] to try to do two or more things at the same time, even though this is difficult and you are very busy: *The film is about a maintenance man who juggles three jobs to provide for his family.* | *suburban working mothers who juggle careers, families, and after-school sports* | **juggle sth and sth** *I don't think any man can ever understand the difficulties of juggling motherhood and politics.* | **juggle sth with sth** *With school starting, Anna will have to juggle her love of swimming with her homework.*

to have enough time

19 to have enough time to do something

- have time/have the time
- there is time
- when you have a moment/minute
- it's not too late

have time/have the time /ˌhæv ˈtaɪm, ˌhæv ðə ˈtaɪm/ [v phrase not in progressive] *If you have time, I could show you around the rest of the house.* | *Do you think we have the time?* | **+ to do sth** *Few agencies have the time or the staff to train new employees.* | *She put the phone down before I had time to reply.* | *Just leave it on my desk till I have time to deal with it.* | **+ for** *Do you have time for a quick drink?* | *Perhaps next year I'll have more time for gardening.*

there is time /ðeər ɪz ˈtaɪm/ use this to say there is enough time for someone to do something: *We thought we'd go to the museum, and maybe have some lunch too, if there's time.* | *If you hurry there should be time for a little shopping.* | *I guess there's time for a bedtime story, Lauren.* | **there is time for sb to do sth** *There's still time for you to change your mind, you know.* | *Is there time for me to wash my hair before we leave?* | **+ to do sth** *I don't think there's time to paint the whole wall today.*

when you have a moment/minute /ˌwen juː hæv ə ˈməʊmənt, ˈmɪnɪ̥t/ [adv] use this to mean 'when you have a small amount of spare time during a period when you are very busy', especially when you are asking someone to do something: *When you have a minute, Josie, I'd like to talk to you.* | *Do you have a minute? I have a couple of questions to ask.* | *These letters are ready for you to sign when you have a moment.* | **have a spare moment/minute** *If you have a spare moment, could you read through my essay?* | *It's quite rare that I have a spare minute these days.*

it's not too late /ɪts ˌnɒt tuː ˈleɪt/ use this to say that there is still enough time for someone to do something **+ to do sth** *If you haven't got roses in your garden, it's not too late to plant now.* | *It's still not too late to get a flu vaccine.* | **it's not too late for sb to do sth** *He insists it's not too late for United to win the cup, though he admits it will be an uphill struggle.*

20 to have very little time to do something

- have (very) little time/not have much time
- be short of time
- be pressed/pushed for time

have (very) little time/not have much time /hæv (ˌveri) lɪtl ˈtaɪm, nɒt hæv ˌmʌtʃ ˈtaɪm/ [v phrase not in progressive] **+ for** *I don't have much time for visiting, parties and so on.* | **+ to do sth** *We had very little time to train for the big game.* | *I'm afraid I have had very little time to entertain you or introduce you to anyone.* | *'Have you decided yet?' 'I've not had much time to think about it.'*

be short of time /biː ˌʃɔːʳt əv ˈtaɪm/ [v phrase] to have very little time to do something, especially because you have a lot of things to do: *If you're short of time, I recommend seeing at least the museum and the cathedral.* | *She was puzzled, but too short of time to argue with him.* | **run short of time** *As we're running short of time, let me end with just one example of what I mean.*

be pressed/pushed for time /biː ˌprest, ˌpʊʃt fəʳ ˈtaɪm/ [v phrase] to have very little time to do something, especially with the result that you have to do it very quickly: *I was pressed for time in my few days in Sydney, and did not have the opportunity to explore the city.* | *It's probably best to avoid the main roads unless you're really pushed for time.*

21 to not have enough time to do something

- not have (the) time/have no time
- there is no time
- run out of time

not have (the) time/have no time /nɒt hæv (ðə) ˈtaɪm, hæv ˌnəʊ ˈtaɪm/ [v phrase not in progressive] *I'll look at it later. I haven't got time at the moment.* | *Harold was supposed to organize the trip, but he just didn't have the time.* | **+ to do sth** *I didn't have time to* *take a shower this morning.* | *I haven't had time to write those letters yet.* | *We won't have time to practice tonight.* | **+ for** *I don't have time for lunch.* | *She says she has no time for relaxation.*

there is no time /ðeər ɪz ˌnəʊ 'taɪm/ use this to say that there is not enough time for someone to do something **+ to do sth** *The train was about to leave, and there was no time to buy a ticket.* | *There's no time to go through all these applications this morning.* | **+ for** *Look, there's no time for that now. We have to get moving.*

run out of time /ˌrʌn aʊt əv 'taɪm/ [v phrase] to be unable to finish doing something within the time that you have to do it in: *I'm sorry, we seem to have run out of time. Thanks to everyone who took part.* | *I have to finish this by tomorrow, and I'm running out of time.*

time passes

22 when a period of time passes

- pass/go by
- elapse
- the passage/passing of time

pass/go by /pɑːs‖pæs, ˌgəʊ 'baɪ/ [v I/phr v I] *Three weeks passed, and Max had still not found a job.* | *Years passed before she could bring herself to call me 'Frank' without the 'Mister'.* | *Hardly a week goes by when I do not think of you.* | **time passes/goes by** *The side effects tend to subside as time passes.* | *I was trying to calculate how much time had gone by since I heard the scream.*

elapse /ɪ'læps/ [v I not in progressive] formal if a period of time elapses, it passes, especially between two events **+ before/since/between** *Nine years elapsed before he produced his eighth symphony.* | *It seems remarkable that nearly thirty years has elapsed since there was a major museum exhibition in the city.* | *A surprisingly long time had elapsed between the discovery of the body and the arrival of the police.*

the passage/passing of time /ðə ˌpæsɪdʒ, ˌpɑːsɪŋ əv 'taɪm/ [n phrase] the process of time passing over a long period, especially when people or things change during this time – used especially in stories or descriptions: *Two children, a successful marriage, and the passage of time had helped Maisie to forget her unhappy childhood.* | *The early recordings have hardly stood up well to the passage of time.* | *The passing of time did little to lessen his grief.* | **with the passage of time** *Behaviour and social attitudes change with the passing of time.* | *These ancient settlements have perished with the passage of time.*

23 time passes quickly

- go fast/quickly
- fly by
- time flies
- tick away

go fast/quickly /ˌgəʊ 'fɑːst, 'kwɪkli‖-'fæst/ [v phrase] *The rest of the weekend went too quickly – he wanted it to last forever.* | *Today can't go fast enough for me.* | *The summer seems to have come and gone so quickly.* | **make sth go faster/more quickly** (=to make work, a journey etc seem to take less time than it really does) *Reading on the train makes the journey go more quickly.* | *It's great having you to talk to. It makes the time go faster.*

fly by /'flaɪ baɪ/ [phr v I] if a period of time **flies by**, it seems to pass very quickly, especially when you have been very busy or enjoying yourself: *The afternoon flew by as they went through the next scene together.* | *Hours can fly by as I write, and I don't even notice.* | *Time is flying by quickly now and it seems impossible that there are only three months left.*

time flies /ˌtaɪm 'flaɪz/ use this when you are surprised at how quickly the time has passed, especially when you have been enjoying yourself: *Is Richard eight already? Doesn't time fly?* | *'Hasn't the afternoon passed quickly?' said Carol. 'Time flies when you're having fun.'*

tick away /ˌtɪk ə'weɪ/ [phr v I] if the minutes, the hours, time etc **tick away**, it passes, especially when you must do something before a particular time or when you are frightened or nervous: *He had to watch the minutes tick away while the emergency services tried to locate him.* | *Aware of how the minutes were ticking away, Julia desperately scribbled down the last few answers.*

24 time passes slowly

- go slowly
- drag

go slowly /ˌgəʊ 'sləʊli/ [v phrase] *The rest of the day went very slowly for Anne.* | *The lesson lasted all morning, and seemed to go even more slowly than usual.*

drag /dræg/ [v I] if time **drags**, it seems to pass very slowly, especially because you are bored: *Why do physics lessons always seem to drag?* | **+ by/on** *The day dragged on, and there was still no sign of Jake.* | *As time dragged on, I gradually got worse.* | *As the months drag by, you find out who your real friends are.*

tired/tiring

RELATED WORDS

- *see also* **sleep, wake up/get up**

1 tired after exercise or work

- tired
- exhausted
- tired out/worn out
- shattered
- weary
- drained
- knackered
- beat/pooped/bushed
- be dead on your feet/be ready to drop

tired /taɪəʳd/ [adj] *I usually feel too tired to cook dinner after a day at the office.* | *We sat down and stretched out our tired legs.* | *They came back from their long walk, tired but relaxed.* | *Overly tired drivers can be nearly as dangerous as drunk drivers.* | **get tired** (=start to feel tired) *Can we stop soon? I'm getting really tired.*

exhausted /ɪg'zɔːstɪ̈d/ [adj] very tired, especially because you have been doing a sport or other hard physical activity, and you have used all your energy: *I was exhausted every day when I first started teaching, but I'm used to it now.* | *The exhausted dancers collapsed as they stepped off the stage.* | **+ from/by** *The five of them were still exhausted from their 36-hour train ride.* | **completely/absolutely exhausted** *We had been walking for over 20 miles, and we were completely exhausted.*

tired out/worn out /ˌtaɪəʳd 'aʊt, ˌwɔːʳn 'aʊt/ [adj not before noun] very tired, especially after a lot of hard work, physical exercise, or travelling: *Come in and sit down. You look worn out.* | *The men had been working in the fields all day and they were tired out.* |

+ from/by *Susan and Lloyd were both tired out from feeding, bathing, and putting the children to bed.*

shattered /ˈʃætəʳd/ [adj not before noun] British very tired, especially as a result of mental effort or worry: *When he came out of the exam he felt shattered.* | *I've had a terrible day at the office and I'm absolutely shattered.*

weary /ˈwɪəri/ [adj] written so tired after a very long period of working, travelling, or great mental effort that you feel you can hardly continue with what you are doing: *After the hike the two were so weary they fell asleep immediately.* | *Snow in Boston closed down the airport, causing even more delays for weary travellers.* | **grow weary** *My head grew weary from trying to follow his arguments.* —**wearily** [adv] *A middle-aged waitress came wearily over to them to take their order.*

drained /dreɪnd/ [adj not before noun] very tired and feeling as if all your energy has gone, especially as a result of an unpleasant emotional experience, such as being worried, upset, or shocked: *By the end of the day I felt drained, with nothing to show for all my work.* | *After losing the game, Coach Saylor came to the press conference looking and sounding emotionally drained.*

knackered /ˈnækəʳd/ [adj not before noun] British very tired: *I've been up since four o'clock this morning – I'm absolutely knackered!* | *When you're training a team sometimes it's good to push them until they're knackered.*

beat/pooped/bushed /biːt, puːpt, bʊʃt/ [adj not before noun] American informal very tired: *Wow, I'm pooped. I don't feel like going to the gym tonight.* | *You look beat – what have you been doing?* | *Will you excuse me? I'm bushed – I think I'll go to bed.*

be dead on your feet/be ready to drop /biː ˌded ɒn jɔːʳ ˈfiːt, biː ˌredi tə ˈdrɒp‖-ˈdrɑːp/ [v phrase] informal to be so tired that you are almost unable to stay standing: *After fourteen hours of non-stop work I was dead on my feet.* | *For goodness' sake go home! You look ready to drop.*

2 wanting to sleep

- tired
- sleepy
- drowsy
- half-asleep
- can hardly/can barely/can't keep your eyes open

tired /taɪəʳd/ [adj] *The kids were really tired, so we sent them to bed.* | *I tried to watch the news on TV, but I was too tired to stay awake.*

sleepy /ˈsliːpi/ [adj] if you are **sleepy**, you want to sleep immediately and your eyes are starting to close: *'Aren't you sleepy?' 'No, I took a nap this afternoon.'* | *It's no easy task getting three sleepy children out of the car and into the house.* | *We arrived at the hotel late at night, and were too sleepy to notice how beautiful it was.* —**sleepily** [adv] *'What time is it?' she said sleepily.*

drowsy /ˈdraʊzi/ [adj] starting to sleep because you are in a warm place or because you have drunk alcohol or taken medicine: *You shouldn't drive after taking these pills – they can make you drowsy.* | *Len had drunk too much wine, and he felt cosy and drowsy in spite of the coffee.*

half-asleep /ˌhɑːf əˈsliːp◂‖ˌhæf-/ [adj not before noun] very nearly asleep because you are tired and sleepy: *'Wyatt, what is it?' Sue called, half-asleep, from the bedroom.* | *Moira was half-asleep when the phone rang and it took her a few seconds to realize what it was.*

can hardly/can barely/can't keep your eyes open /kən ˌhɑːʳdli, kən ˌbeəʳli, ˌkɑːnt kiːp jɔːʳ ˈaɪz ˌəʊpən‖ˌkænt-/ [v phrase] to feel so tired that you find it hard to stay awake: *I can't keep my eyes open – I've got to go to bed.* | *The kids were still full of energy, but Julie and I could hardly keep our eyes open.* | *By the time we finally got home, I could barely keep my eyes open.*

3 tired and having no interest in anything

- lethargic
- listless

lethargic /lɪ̈ˈθɑːʳdʒɪk/ [adj] feeling tired and lazy, as if you have no interest in doing anything: *All this hot weather is making me feel lethargic.* | *Patients with depression may be lethargic during the day and unable to sleep at night.* | *The spectacular play inspired his lethargic teammates to start playing harder.*

listless /ˈlɪstləs/ [adj] feeling tired and not interested in anything, especially because you are ill: *Tim is listless on the job and keeps making dumb mistakes.* | *The last few years of my mother's life she was tired and listless most of the time.* | *She had to keep thinking up new ways to hold the attention of her listless pupils.*

4 looking tired

- tired
- washed-out
- bleary-eyed
- drawn

tired /taɪəʳd/ [adj] *I've never seen him look so tired.* | **tired eyes/face etc** *Look at their tired little faces.* | *She had tired-looking bags under her eyes.*

washed-out /ˌwɒʃt ˈaʊt‖ˌwɑːʃt-/ [adj not before noun] especially British looking tired and unhealthy: *The last time I saw Helena she was looking pretty washed-out. Is she alright?*

bleary-eyed /ˌblɪəri ˈaɪd◂/ [adj] with red, half-open eyes, especially as a result of lack of sleep: *After twelve hours of driving Jean was bleary-eyed and stiff.* | *The bleary-eyed engineers were still hard at work when everyone else arrived the next day.*

drawn /drɔːn/ [adj] someone who looks **drawn** is tired from illness, worry, or working too hard, and their face looks thin and pale: *Terry's face was pale and drawn when she finally arrived.* | *The emergency meeting had lasted all night, and the President looked drawn as he read the statement.*

5 to become tired

- get tired
- flag
- tire yourself out/wear yourself out/exhaust yourself
- burn out/burn yourself out
- run out of steam
- tire yourself

get tired /ˌget ˈtaɪəʳd/ [v phrase] *If you get tired, just stop for a while.* | *We talked until we both got tired and decided to go to bed.* | *Since her illness, she finds that she gets tired really easily.*

flag /flæg/ [v I] to start to get tired, especially if you are doing something that needs a lot of energy: *Jenny taught for four hours straight without flagging.* | *By the fifth game, I could see that my opponent was beginning to flag.*

tire yourself out/wear yourself out/ exhaust yourself /ˌtaɪəʳ jɔːʳself ˈaʊt, ˌweəʳ jɔːʳself 'aʊt, ɪg'zɔːst jɔːʳself/ [v phrase] to become tired by doing things that take a lot of effort: *The baby's stopped crying. He must have tired himself out.* | *You're going to wear yourself out if you keep working so hard.* | *My poor mother had exhausted herself trying to get ready for company.*

burn out/burn yourself out /ˌbɜːʳn 'aʊt, ˌbɜːʳn jɔːʳself 'aʊt/ [phr v I/v phrase] to become tired, ill, and unable to continue, as a result of working too hard for too long, especially because you want very much to be successful: *If you don't stop working nights and weekends, you'll burn yourself out.* | *Most of these high-flying young executives burn out before they're 30.* —**burnt-out/burned out** /ˌbɜːʳnt 'aʊt◂, ˌbɜːʳnd 'aʊt◂/ [adj] *Most of the school's teachers have been there for years and are burnt out.*

run out of steam /ˌrʌn aʊt əv 'stiːm/ [v phrase] to become so tired that you do not have enough energy to finish what you are doing, especially when you have been working hard for a long time: *The home team seemed to run out of steam well before the game was over.* | *Gail started the project with a lot of energy and enthusiasm, but at some point she just ran out of steam.*

tire yourself /'taɪəʳ jɔːʳself/ [v phrase] to become tired because of things that you do: *Get plenty of rest and try not to tire yourself unnecessarily.*

6 to make someone feel tired

- tire/wear out
- exhaust
- tire
- take it out of/ do sb in
- it nearly killed me

tire/wear out /ˌtaɪər, ˌweər 'aʊt/ [phr v T] **tire/wear sb out** *Their constant quarrelling is wearing us out.* | **tire/wear out sb** *The thin air at high altitudes usually tires out people who are not used to the mountains.*

exhaust /ɪg'zɔːst/ [v T] to make someone feel very tired: *The effort of swimming against the current exhausted him.* | **it exhausts sb to do sth** *It exhausted him to talk for too long, but he loved hearing all the theater gossip.*

tire /taɪəʳ/ [v T] to make someone feel tired, especially someone who gets tired easily because they are old or ill: *I won't tire you with a long visit. I just wanted to stop in and see how you were doing.*

take it out of sb/do sb in /ˌteɪk ɪt 'aʊt əv (sb), ˌduː (sb) 'ɪn/ [v phrase/phr v T] informal to make you feel as if you have no energy left: *Dale's a construction worker. You know, that sort of work really takes it out of you.* | *It wasn't the cooking so much as all the cleaning up that did me in.*

it nearly killed me /ɪt ˌnɪəʳli 'kɪld miː/ spoken use this to say that doing a very hard job or activity made you feel extremely tired: *It nearly killed me carrying that fridge up the stairs!*

7 making you feel tired

- tiring
- exhausting
- hard
- wearing

tiring /'taɪərɪŋ/ [adj] something that is **tiring** makes you feel tired: *The journey was really tiring.* | *Sam couldn't wait for the whole tiring ordeal to be over.* | **a tiring day/week etc** *I've had such a tiring day. I just want to take a bath and go to bed.*

exhausting /ɪg'zɔːstɪŋ/ [adj] something that is **exhausting** makes you feel very weak and very tired: *She's just returned from another exhausting lecture tour.* | *I had to drive nine hours without a break – it was exhausting.* | *Starting a small business can be the most physically and mentally exhausting task you've ever done.*

hard /hɑːʳd/ [adj usually before noun] a **hard** day, journey etc is one that makes you feel very tired because you have to work very **hard**, travel a long distance, or deal with a lot of problems: *Taking care of a two-year-old is hard work.* | *It was a long hard walk back to the nearest town.* | *When I come home from a hard day at work, I don't feel like talking to anyone.*

wearing /'weərɪŋ/ [adj not before noun] a person, activity, or situation that is **wearing** is very tiring because it uses up a lot of your mental energy: *I find her constant questions and chatter rather wearing.* | *Kids of that age can be very wearing, can't they?*

8 the feeling of being tired

- tiredness
- exhaustion
- drowsiness
- fatigue
- lethargy
- jet-lag
- burnout

tiredness /'taɪəʳdnɪ̈s/ [n U] *Tiredness and headaches are common signs of stress.* | *Camomile tea soothes the nerves and relieves tiredness.* | *A terrible tiredness had overcome her, leaving her no energy for extra activities.*

exhaustion /ɪg'zɔːstʃən/ [n U] the feeling of being very tired: *The soldiers were suffering from exhaustion after long days and nights of marching.* | *The signs of chronic exhaustion showed in Martha's face.* | **from/with exhaustion** *One of the players collapsed with exhaustion and had to be carried off the field.*

drowsiness /'draʊzinɪ̈s/ [n U] the feeling of wanting to sleep that you sometimes get when you are in a warm place or when you have drunk alcohol or taken medicine: *The drug can cause drowsiness.* | *Robert stopped fighting the drowsiness and sank back in the soft chair.*

fatigue /fə'tiːg/ [n U] a feeling of being very tired and weak – used especially in medical contexts: *Symptoms of the illness include fever, fatigue, and loss of appetite.* | *Driving in stressful conditions can lead to muscle fatigue.* | *She seemed depressed and was beginning to show signs of fatigue.*

lethargy /'leθəʳdʒi/ [n U] formal extreme tiredness that makes you feel very lazy, so that you do not want to do anything and you are not interested in anything: *Another common symptom of a hangover is lethargy and muscular weakness.* | *It is not unusual for new mothers to go to the doctor complaining of tiredness, lethargy, and mild depression.*

jet-lag /'dʒet læg/ [n U] a feeling of tiredness and confusion which you sometimes get when you fly to a part of the world where the time is different from the place you have left: *I always get jet-lag when I fly from London to New York.* —**jet-lagged** [adj] suffering from jet-lag: *On the first morning of the conference, most of us were still jet-lagged.*

burnout /'bɜːʳnaʊt/ [n U] when you have worked so hard over a long period of time that you become too mentally and physically tired to continue: *Young boys recruited at an early age by soccer clubs often suffer from burnout before they're out of their teens.*

toilet

1 a toilet/rest room

- toilet
- bathroom
- loo/bog
- restroom/ washroom
- the gents
- the ladies
- lavatory
- WC

toilet /ˈtɔɪlət/ [n C] British a room containing a toilet: *'Where's the toilet?' 'Downstairs on the right.'* | **men's/women's/ladies' toilets** *There's a huge queue in the ladies' toilets.* | **public toilets** *Pat refuses to use the public toilets in this country because they are always so dirty.*

bathroom /ˈbɑːθrʊm -ruːm‖ˈbæθ-/ [n singular] a toilet, especially in someone's house: *The bathroom is next to Jack's room.* | *'Can I use your bathroom?' 'Sure, go ahead.'*

loo/bog British informal **/john** American informal /luː, bɒg‖bɑːg, dʒɒn‖dʒɑːn/ [n C] a toilet: *Where's the loo?* | *Tony's in the john. He'll be back in a minute.* | *It's a good pub, but the bogs are terrible!*

restroom/washroom /ˈrestruːm, ˈwɒʃruːm‖ˈwɑːʃ-/ [n C] American the toilets in a public place: *Do you have restrooms here?* | *There's no paper in the washroom.*

the gents British **/the men's room** American /ðə ˈdʒents, ðə ˈmenz ruːm/ [n singular] the men's toilets in a public place: *Can you tell me where the men's room is please?* | *'Where's Kevin?' 'He went to the gents.'*

the ladies British **/the ladies' room** American /ðə ˈleɪdiz, ðə ˈleɪdiz ruːm/ [n singular] the women's toilets in a public place: *Wait for me outside. I'm going to the ladies.* | *The ladies' room is just around the corner.*

lavatory /ˈlævətəri‖-tɔːri/ [n C] formal a toilet: *Even the lavatory was luxurious, with a marble interior and soft, white hand towels.* | **public lavatory** *The public lavatories are situated on the other side of the beach.*

WC /ˌdʌbəljuː ˈsiː/ [n C] especially British, written a toilet – used especially in written information about buildings: *All our holiday apartments have a double bedroom, small kitchen, bathroom, and WC.*

2 to use the toilet

- go to the toilet/ bathroom/loo etc
- powder your nose

go to the toilet/bathroom/loo etc /ˌgəʊ tə ðə ˈtɔɪlət/ [v phrase] *Mummy! I want to go to the toilet.* | *Hang on a minute – I'm just going to the loo.* | *I thought you went to the bathroom before we left.*

powder your nose /ˌpaʊdər jɔːr ˈnəʊz/ [v phrase] to go to the toilet – used humorously by women to avoid saying this directly: *You get the drinks in – I'll just go and powder my nose.*

tool

a tool

RELATED WORDS

- *see also* **equipment, machine, thing**

- tool
- instrument
- gadget
- device
- implement
- utensil

tool /tuːl/ [n C] a thing that you hold in your hand and use to repair, cut, or make something: *He couldn't finish repairing the engine because he didn't have the right tools.* | **+ for** *a tool for cutting metal* | **gardening/kitchen/mining tools** *All my gardening tools had been stolen from the shed.* | **tool box** (=a strong box that tools are kept in) *He took a spanner from his tool box and tightened up the bolts on the gate.* | **tool kit** (=a set of tools that are kept together) *A good tool kit should contain pliers, screwdrivers, and wire-cutters.*

instrument /ˈɪnstrəmənt/ [n C] a small tool or device used especially by doctors and scientists, for doing careful or delicate work: *I sat in the dentist's chair and looked at the row of instruments beside me.* | *The microscope is perhaps the most widely used scientific instrument.* | *The company specializes in the manufacture of high quality writing instruments.*

gadget /ˈgædʒət/ [n C] a small tool that has been cleverly designed to help you do something more easily: *He showed her several electronic gadgets, such as a watch that you can use as a phone.* | *It's a clever little gadget which you can use to cut vegetables into attractive shapes.* | *A sales assistant was demonstrating several kitchen gadgets to a crowd of shoppers.*

device /dɪˈvaɪs/ [n C] a piece of equipment that has been cleverly designed to do a particular job, for example one that makes measurements, records sounds, or controls the operation of a machine: *An EEG is a device that records electrical activity in the brain.* | **+ for doing sth** *a thermostatic device for controlling temperature* | *The farmers there still use the 'Archimedes Screw', an ancient device for raising water from a lake or well.*

implement /ˈɪmpləmənt/ [n C] formal a tool or simple machine used for a particular job, especially when working in the garden or on a farm: *The native women grind the wheat with heavy stone implements.* | *It is best to cut weeds off at the roots with an implement such as a hoe.* | **farming/cooking/writing etc implements** *Some children find it difficult to hold their writing implements.*

utensil /juːˈtensəl/ [n C] a piece of equipment, especially one used in the kitchen to prepare food: *Peter found the potato peeler in a drawer full of utensils.* | *We packed a few essential cooking utensils such as pots and a can opener for our camping trip.* | *You will find a wide range of kitchen utensils in our cookshop on the second floor.*

too/too much

1 too

- too

too /tuː/ [adv] more than is right or necessary, or more than you want: *They didn't give him the job.*

They said he was too old. | *Don't work too hard!* | *It's too hot in here.* | **too big/small/tired etc to do sth** *I was too tired to get up off the couch.* | *She's still too upset to talk about it.* | **far too small/way too big etc** *$200! That's way too expensive.* | *The temperature was well below zero – far too cold to spend more than a few minutes on deck.* | **too old/quick/big etc for** *My room's too narrow for a king-size bed.* | *Military officials believed that the harbor was too shallow for torpedo launches.*

2 too much or too many

- too much
- too many
- an excess of
- glut
- too much of a good thing
- excessive
- inordinate
- overkill

too much /ˌtuː ˈmʌtʃ◂/ [quantifier] use this about amounts or costs: *Jim drinks too much.* | *That kid talks too much.* | *You spend too much time worrying about things.* | **far/way too much** *I'm sure my parents paid way too much for the land.* | *The surveys took up far too much time, and they were difficult to understand.* | **+ for** *There was too much baggage for one person to carry.*

too many /ˌtuː ˈmeni◂/ [quantifier] use this about number of people or things: *I've brought some more chairs – I hope I didn't bring too many.* | *She can't come – she says she has too many things to do.* | **far/way too many** *Far too many postgraduate students never finish their projects once begun.* | **+ for** *There were too many bags for one person to carry.*

an excess of /ən ɪkˈses ɒv/ [quantifier] formal too much of something: *an excess of alcohol* | *An excess of fertilizer is harmful to trees and other garden plants.*

glut /glʌt/ [n C usually singular] a situation in which there is too much of a product available at a particular time, which often results in the price of the product being cut **+ of** *A glut of bonds on the market pushed prices down.* | *When there is a glut of milk more products like yoghurt are made.*

too much of a good thing /tuː ˌmʌtʃ əv ə ˌgʊd ˈθɪŋ/ [n phrase] if you say that something is **too much of a good thing**, you mean that it would be good in small amounts but you have too much of it: *Many Koreans believe that the rush of foreign products may be too much of a good thing.* | *Getting six boxes of chocolates for my birthday was really too much of a good thing.*

excessive /ɪkˈsesɪv/ [adj] use this about an amount, cost, or level which is much too high, especially when you think it is wrong or unfair that it is so high: *The campaign is trying to stop the excessive use of chemicals in farming.* | *$10 for two cups of coffee seems excessive.* | *As usual, the opposition claims the government is guilty of excessive spending.*

inordinate /ɪˈnɔːʳdənə̇t/ [adj only before noun] formal much more than is reasonable, especially when this is unfair to other people or means that other things are not given enough attention: *Scientists have been criticized for devoting an inordinate amount of time to research on animals.* | *a man of inordinate ambition*

overkill /ˈəʊvəʳkɪl/ [n U] a situation in which something is done so much that it is no longer interesting or effective: *Of course, it's a serious disaster, but some of these sensational newspaper reports are just overkill.* | *Many felt that the money spent amounted to overkill, and that a cheaper, less glossy advertising campaign would have been just as effective.*

3 to do something too much

- try/think/push etc too hard
- overdo it
- overreact
- go too far/take sth too far
- go to extremes
- to excess
- over the top
- overload
- overindulge/overindulge yourself
- flog sth to death

try/think/push etc too hard /ˌtraɪ tuː ˈhɑːʳd/ to do something with too much effort, so that you do not get the result you want: *You're hitting the ball too hard.* | *I think you've been working too hard – you need a rest* | *Many parents try too hard to engineer a safe environment for their child, with disastrous results.*

overdo it /ˌəʊvəʳˈduː ɪt/ especially spoken to do or say something too much, especially to do too much work or exercise: *You need more exercise, but be careful not to overdo it.* | *The tour guide managed to be funny and informative, without overdoing it.*

overreact /ˌəʊvəriˈækt/ [v I] to get too angry or too worried when something happens which is not in fact very serious: *Don't you think you're overreacting a little? I'm only ten minutes late.* | **+ to** *I think people have overreacted to the advertisement – we didn't intend of offend anyone.*

go too far/take sth too far /ˌgəʊ tuː ˈfɑːʳ, ˌteɪk (sth) tuː ˈfɑːʳ/ [v phrase] to do something so much or to such a great degree that you offend, upset, or annoy people, especially because you do not know when it is reasonable to stop: *Officials were worried that the Chairman's criticisms had gone too far.* | *John had taken the joke too far and now Betty was crying.* | **+ in doing sth** *We all agree there have to be some controls, but the government has gone too far in ordering all immigration to be stopped.*

go to extremes /ˌgəʊ tʊ ɪkˈstriːmz/ [v phrase] to do something so much, state something so strongly etc, that people consider your actions unacceptable and unreasonable: *Hunt went to such extremes to get his promotion that everyone at the office hates him now.* | *You don't have to go to extremes to become healthier – a little exercise and slight changes to your diet can work wonders.*

to excess /tʊ ɪkˈses/ [adv] if you do something **to excess**, you do it so much that it is wrong or harmful: *The government enthusiastically supports US foreign policy, sometimes to excess.* | *He drank to excess, occasionally causing scenes in front of CIA officials.*

over the top /ˌəʊvəʳ ðə ˈtɒp ‖-ˈtɑːp/ [adj/adv] something you say or do that is **over the top** is extreme, so that it is either very funny and entertaining, or very annoying or offensive: *Some of his remarks about women were really over the top.* | *The show was supposed to be a kind of over-the-top satire – it wasn't supposed to be taken seriously.* | **go over the top** *The movie's drawn-out finale goes over the top in its attempt to keep the audience in suspense.*

overload /ˌəʊvəʳˈləʊd/ [v T] to give someone too much work to do or try to make a system handle too much work: *We can't take money from a school system that is already overloaded.* | *They overloaded the computer system, and the whole thing just stopped.* | *Projects should stretch people and make them work hard, but not overload them.*

overindulge/overindulge yourself /ˌəʊvərɪnˈdʌldʒ, ˌəʊvərɪnˈdʌldʒ jɔːʳself/ [v I/T] use this humorously when you have eaten too much rich food or drunk too much alcohol: *Schneider told quite a funny* *story about how he had overindulged one night.* | *What's the point of a vacation, after all, if not to overindulge yourself?*

flog sth to death /ˌflɒg (sth) tə ˈdeθ‖ˌflɑːg-/ [v phrase] British informal to talk too much about a subject or repeat a joke or story too often, so that no one is interested in it any more: *It was a good story a month ago, but the newspapers have really flogged it to death.*

4 not needed because there is already enough

- excess
- surplus

excess /ˈekses/ [adj only before noun] an additional amount that is not wanted or needed because there is already enough of something: *Excess vitamin D can cause kidney damage in young children.* | *Cut off the excess fat from the meat before cooking.* | *The excess pounds had given him a double chin and a neck that made his shirt collar look too tight.*

surplus /ˈsɜːʳpləs/ [n C] the additional amount of something, especially something that you produce or grow, which is more than you need and which can therefore be given or sold to other people: *The Gulf States produce more oil than they need and sell the surplus to the rest of the world.* | *Government subsidies have resulted in huge grain surpluses.* | *The budget surplus could be used to hire and train more border guards.* —**surplus** [adj only before noun] *The State raised $130 million by selling off surplus land.*

5 not too much

- not too/very much
- not too/very many
- not too big/hard/loud etc
- moderate
- in moderation
- keep sth in proportion

not too/very much /nɒt tuː, veri ˈmʌtʃ/ [adv] *Not too much pizza for me please, I'm on a diet.* | *I won't give you very much homework tonight, so you have time to finish your essay.* | **not eat/drink/ talk etc too much** *Don't talk too much now – you need to rest.*

not too/very many /nɒt tuː, veri ˈmeni/ [adv] *You can have a few chips, but not too many.* | *Not very many people were interested in the project.*

not too big/hard/loud etc /nɒt tuː ˈbɪg/ [adv] *I wasn't too upset when they told me I hadn't got the job.* | *It was a beautiful sunny day and not too cold.* | *Don't hit it too hard – just nudge it over the net.*

moderate /ˈmɒdərɨ̇t‖ˈmɑː-/ [adj] not too much – use this about eating, drinking, and other things that could be unhealthy if you did them too much: *Moderate exercise, such as walking and swimming, can help to prevent heart disease.* | *New studies show that moderate drinking is good for you.*

in moderation /ɪn ˌmɒdəˈreɪʃən ‖ -ˌmɑː-/ [adv] if you eat or drink something **in moderation**, you do not eat or drink too much of it: *He only drinks wine in moderation.* | *Children should be taught not about 'bad foods' and 'good foods,' but rather to eat a wide variety of foods in moderation.*

keep sth in proportion /ˌkiːp (sth) ɪn prəˈpɔːʳʃən/ [v phrase] to not allow yourself to become so excited, annoyed etc by an event or situation that you lose a sense of what is reasonable, sensible, or possible: *My confidence was so low it was difficult to keep things in proportion – the smallest problem seemed like a major tragedy.* | *The Party's recent successes in the polls are encouraging but they need to be kept in proportion.*

top

RELATED WORDS

opposite: **bottom**

- on top of *see* **on/on top of**
- the best *see* **best**
- *see also* **up, high**

1 the top part of something

- top
- summit
- crest

top /tɒp‖tɑːp/ [n C] the **top** or highest part of something: *When you paint, you should start at the top and work your way down.* | **+ of** *The top of the mountain is covered with snow.* | *The tops of the trees swayed in the breeze.* | *There's a wonderful view from the top of the tower.* | **tree-top/roof-top/hill-top etc** *I looked out over the roof-tops towards the mountains beyond.*

summit /ˈsʌmɨ̇t/ [n C] the top of a mountain: *It took the climbers four hours to reach the summit.* | **+ of** *In the distance we could see the snow-covered summit of Mount Kilimanjaro.* | *We took a small train to the summit of Pike's Peak.*

crest /krest/ [n C] especially written the top of a hill or wave: *There's a trail up there that follows the length of the crest.* | **+ of** *When I reached the crest of the hill, I turned to look back.* | *In the distance we could see a small boat riding the crests of the waves.*

2 at the top of something

- on top
- at the top

on top /ɒn ˈtɒp‖-ˈtɑːp/ [adv] on the top surface or highest point of something: *She brought me an enormous dish of ice cream with a bright red cherry on top.* | **+ of** *The church stood on top of a hill.* | *On top of the cupboard was an old trunk, covered in dust.*

at the top /ət ðə ˈtɒp‖-ˈtɑːp/ [adv] on or near the top of something: *The vase has a small crack at the top.* | **+ of** *He was waiting for me at the top of the stairs.* | *Don't forget to write your name at the top of the test before you turn it in.*

3 when something is nearest the top

- top
- upper
- topmost/uppermost

top /tɒp‖tɑːp/ [adj only before noun] *The books are on the top shelf.* | *Put the papers in the top drawer of the filing cabinet.* | *We moved into an apartment on the top floor of the building.*

upper /ˈʌpəʳ/ [adj only before noun] at the top above the lower part of something: *Several of her upper teeth were missing.* | *He already had a light growth of hair on his upper lip.* | *Most meteorites do not make it through Earth's upper atmosphere.*

topmost/uppermost /ˈtɒpməʊst‖ˈtɑːp-, ˈʌpəʳməʊst/ [adj only before noun] formal the **topmost** or **uppermost** part of something is the highest of all its parts, right at the top: *Human bones were found in the uppermost level of rock.* | *Janey went to the back of the house, sat on the topmost step, and wept.*

total

RELATED WORDS

- affecting or including everything *see* **all/everything**
- totally impossible, ridiculous, refuse, ignore etc *see* **completely**
- *see also* **count/calculate, amount, number, add**

1 a total

- **total**
- **total**
- **altogether/in all**
- **grand total**
- **subtotal**
- **gross**

total /ˈtəʊtl/ [n C] the number or amount that there is, when everything has been counted or added together: *You had 29 points plus 33 points, so the total is 62.* | *A company spokesperson said 28,000 jobs or 70% of the total will be cut.* | **+ of** *The three defendants were jailed for a total of 30 years.* | *A total of $950 million was spent on the new transportation system.*

total /ˈtəʊtl/ [adj only before noun] the **total** number or amount is the number that there is when everything has been counted and added together: *The total cost was far higher than we had expected.* | *People of Chinese origin made up about 10% of the total population.* | *The Performing Arts Department's total budget for the year was $6.3 million.*

altogether/in all /ˌɔːltəˈgeðəʳ◂, ɪn ˈɔːl/ [adv] use this to say or ask what a total amount is, including everything that could be included: *Altogether 680 women took part in the conference.* | *On the wall are rows of stickers, 35 in all, each representing a team victory.*

grand total /ˌgrænd ˈtəʊtl/ [n singular] the total when everything has been included – use this especially in a humorous way when the final total is surprisingly small: *The grand total for both meals was $6.73.* | **+ of** *A grand total of six people showed up for the lecture.*

subtotal /ˈsʌbˌtəʊtl/ [n C] the total of a single set of figures, for example on a bill, which does not include other amounts that will be added later to make the final total: *The subtotal for parts was $23. With labor costs, the bill came to $36.*

gross /grəʊs/ [adj only before noun] a **gross** amount or figure is the total amount before anything such as tax is taken away: *My gross annual income, before tax, is just over £18,000.* | *The company's gross earnings were up $12 million over last year.* | *The gross weight of the package is 10 kilos, including the packaging.* —**gross** [adv] *She earns about $100,000 a year gross.*

2 when several numbers produce another number as a total

- **come to**
- **reach**
- **make**
- **add up to**
- **amount to**
- **total**
- **number**

come to /ˈkʌm tuː/ [phr v T] to be the total amount when everything is counted: *Including wine, the bill came to $70.* | *Total profits from all sources for the year came to about $15 million.*

reach /riːtʃ/ [v T] if a total **reaches** 10, 50, 100 etc, it increases until it is equal to that number: *Hurricane damage could reach billions of dollars.* | *China's economic output is likely to reach $13 trillion within the next few years.* | *The city's population is expected to reach 12 million by the year 2010.*

make /meɪk/ [v T not in passive] if numbers added together **make** 10, 50, 100 etc, that is the answer or the total: *Two plus two makes four.* | *If Jane comes, that will make six of us.* | *There are eight submarines as well as the ships, making a total fleet of 34.*

add up to /ˌæd ˈʌp tuː/ [phr v T] if a set of several figures **adds up to** 10, 50 etc, that is the total when you add them all together: *The three angles of a triangle add up to 180 degrees.* | *If you follow the diet exactly, it adds up to about 1,200 calories per day.* | *With the hotel, the flights, and the food, it all added up to much more than I had expected.*

amount to /əˈmaʊnt tuː/ [phr v T] to reach a total, especially a large total: *Credit card fraud amounts to about $17 million a year.* | *Nationally, deaths from smoking-related illnesses amount to about 30 people each day.* | *A thousand-word essay might amount to roughly 6,000 bytes on a computer disk.*

total /ˈtəʊtl/ [v T not in progressive] to reach a particular **total** – used especially in official contexts: *The company was forced to pay fines and penalties totalling $24.8.* | *The number of people included in the study totalled 170.*

number /ˈnʌmbəʳ/ [v T not in progressive] if a group of people or things **numbers** a particular figure, especially a large figure, that is the total when they are all included: *The crowd of students numbered at least 2000.* | *In the capital, unemployed workers now number 12% of the workforce.*

touch

RELATED WORDS

- *see also* **hold, feel (3)**

1 to put your hand on someone or something

- **touch**
- **feel**
- **run your hand over/along/across/through etc**
- **rub**
- **scratch**
- **fiddle with**

touch /tʌtʃ/ [v T] to put your fingers or hand onto someone or something: *Don't touch the plates – they're hot!* | *I cut my knee last week, and it still hurts if I touch it.* | *Barry never lets anyone touch the piano.* | *'What are you thinking?' she asked, touching his arm.*

feel /fiːl/ [v T not usually in passive] to touch something in order to find out how hard or soft, hot, cold etc it is: *Just feel this material – it's so soft!* | *The nurse felt his forehead to see if he had a fever.* | *'The flowers look so real – I can't believe they're silk,' she said, feeling the petals.*

run your hand over/along/across/through etc /ˌrʌn jɔːʳ ˈhænd əʊvəʳ/ [v phrase] to move your hand over something and feel the surface of it: *She ran her hand over the satiny black surface of the piano.* | *The man took off his cap and ran his hand through his thick brown hair.* | *I ran my hand along the wall, looking for a light switch.*

rub /rʌb/ [v T] to move your hands or fingers quickly backwards and forwards over part of your body, while pressing down, especially in order to make a pain less severe: *Colin yawned and rubbed his eyes.* | *Could you rub my neck? It's really stiff.* | *Bill had fallen on the path and was rubbing his knee.*

scratch /skrætʃ/ [v I/T] to rub your finger nails hard on part of your skin, for example because it itches: *Don't scratch – the rash will get infected.* | *He sat scratching his head, trying to think of the answer.* | *There's a spot in the middle of my back that itches – can you scratch it for me?*

fiddle with /ˈfɪdl wɪð/ [phr v T] to hold something small in your hands and keep moving it around, especially because you are nervous or bored: *She fiddled nervously with her watch strap.* | *Stop fiddling with your toys and pay attention.*

2 to touch someone or something in a gentle or loving way

- stroke
- pat
- tickle
- caress
- fondle

- see also **kiss**

stroke /strəʊk/ [v T] to move your hand or fingers over part of someone's body in a gentle, loving way: *Miss Poole calmed herself by stroking the cat's fur.* | *Her mother sat beside her and stroked her forehead until she fell asleep again.* | *The old priest stroked his white beard as he listened.*

pat /pæt/ [v T] to touch someone lightly several times with the flat part of your hand, in order to comfort them or to show them that you are pleased: *'Don't worry,' he said, patting her hand gently.* | *'The baby's due in March,' Caroline said grinning and patting her stomach.* | **pat sb on the shoulder/arm/head etc** *She bent down and patted the dog on the head.*

tickle /ˈtɪkəl/ [v T] to run your fingers quickly and gently over a sensitive part of someone's body, in order to make them laugh: *I hate being tickled.* | *When I was little my older brother would tickle me till tears ran down my face.*

caress /kəˈres/ [v T] to move your hand or fingers gently over part of someone's body in a gentle, loving, or sexual way: *Barbara held the tiny baby close and caressed his cheek.* | *He began caressing her with a surprising gentleness.*

fondle /ˈfɒndl‖ˈfɑːndl/ [v T] to move your hand or fingers over a part of someone's body in a loving or sexual way – use this especially about touching someone in a sexual way that is not wanted: *He sat fondling her feet as she lay back in the armchair.* | *The women allege that top male executives routinely fondled female employees.*

3 to touch someone or something accidentally

- touch
- come into contact
- brush
- skim
- graze

touch /tʌtʃ/ [v T] *I'm sorry – I didn't mean to touch your sore arm.* | *The plane came down so low that it's wings touched the trees.* —**touch** [n singular] *With the touch of a wrong button, she could ruin the whole program.*

come into contact /ˌkʌm ɪntə ˈkɒntækt‖-ˈkɑːn-/ [v phrase] to touch something, especially when something else happens immediately as a result: *When the two chemicals come into contact, they explode.* | **+ with** *If the cleaner comes into contact with your eyes, rinse well with warm water and contact a doctor.* | *As many as 25 workers at the laboratory may have come into contact with the infected monkeys.*

brush /brʌʃ/ [v I/T] to accidentally touch someone or something lightly when passing them: *The car brushed the hedges on both sides of the narrow lane.* | **+ against** *I felt something brush against the back of my head.* | *As she passed, her bare arm brushed against his arm, sending a shiver down his spine.*

skim /skɪm/ [v T] to touch something lightly when moving over it very quickly: *Seagulls skimmed the water, looking for fish.* | *He threw a flat stone and watched it skim the surface of the lake.* | *Planes skimmed the treetops as they flew in with tanks full of water to put out the fire.*

graze /greɪz/ [v T] to touch something lightly when passing it, sometimes causing damage: *The bullet grazed the corner of the building, just missing my arm.* | *I just barely grazed her bumper, but she's claiming I wrecked her car.*

4 when two things are so close that they touch each other

- touch

touch /tʌtʃ/ [v I] *He drew me closer until our bodies were touching.* | *Don't let the wires touch or you'll get a very bad shock.* | *Put the cards face down on the table so that the edges are touching.*

5 what something feels like when you touch it

- feel
- to the touch
- texture

feel /fiːl/ [linking verb] **feel + adjective** *The stones felt rough and warm under my feet.* | *My skin felt waxy and I wanted to bathe.* | **feel like sth** *Good imitation leather looks and feels like the real thing.* —**feel** [n singular] *There was nothing Lucy liked more than the feel of fur against her skin.*

to the touch /tə ðə ˈtʌtʃ/ [adv] if something is cold, hard, soft etc **to the touch**, it feels cold, hard etc: *Cotton sheets are cool and smooth to the touch.* | *Water the soil when it becomes dry to the touch.* | *The dog's luxurious golden coat was thick and oily to the touch.*

texture /ˈtekstʃəʳ/ [n C/U] the way the surface of something feels, especially how rough or smooth it feels: *The wood in the table had a lovely smooth texture.* | **coarse/smooth/gritty etc in texture** *Cotton is coarser in texture than silk.*

6 what you say to tell someone not to touch something

- don't touch
- leave sth alone
- hands off

don't touch /ˌdəʊnt ˈtʌtʃ/ [v phrase] spoken use this when you are telling someone, especially a child, not to touch something: *Don't touch! That's daddy's work.* | *Those glasses were very expensive. You can look but don't touch.* | *Don't touch the iron – it's hot.* | *How many times do I have to tell you – don't touch my things!*

leave sth alone /ˌliːv (sth) əˈləʊn/ [phr v T] use this when you are telling someone not to touch something they are already touching: *That's a very delicate piece of equipment – please leave it alone.* | *Our neighbor would have cut the tree down if I hadn't told him to leave it alone.*

hands off /ˌhændz ˈɒf/ [v phrase] spoken say this when you are angrily telling someone not to touch something, especially when they are trying to take it away: *Hands off my coat!* | **get/take/keep your hands off sth** *Get your hands off my car!*

towards

RELATED WORDS

▸ *see also* **go, direction, near**

1 towards

- towards
- in the direction of sth
- for
- bound
- at

towards ALSO **toward** American /təˈwɔːʳd(z)/ [prep] moving, looking, or pointing in a particular direction: *If you walk along the river bank towards Skipton you come to a bridge.* | *She stood with her back toward the window.* | *Glancing towards me, he started to laugh.* | *He looked toward the ceiling of his tiny apartment.* | *The plane banked and turned toward the mountains.* | **slide/push/throw etc sth towards sb/sth** *He slid the plate of cookies toward her.*

in the direction of sth /ɪn ðə dɪˈrekʃən əv (sth)/ [prep] towards a place or object, but not moving, looking, or pointing directly at it: *Tyler strode off in the direction of Foxwood.* | *People were making a move in the direction of the dining room.* | **in sb's direction** *I glanced in her direction and our eyes met.* | **in the general direction of sth** (=generally towards) *He waved a hand in the general direction of the bar. 'Another drink?'*

for /fəʳ, (*strong*) fɔːʳ/ [prep] **set off/make/head for** to start to go towards a particular place, especially in a determined way: *We set off for Boston at daybreak.* | *When it started to rain we headed for the trees as fast as we could.* | *It's getting dark – we'd better make for home.*

bound /baʊnd/ [adj] **London/Paris/north/east etc bound** towards a particular place or direction – use this especially about planes, trains, cars etc and the direction in which a road, railway track etc is going in: *The London bound train leaves at 22.00 hours.* | *There have been several delays to southbound rail services.* | *We were travelling westbound on Interstate 90.* | *All inward bound flights are being cancelled due to heavy fog.*

at /ət, (*strong*) æt/ [prep] if you look, smile, wave, throw something etc **at** someone, you look, smile etc in their direction: *The children stared at the eerie old house.* | *Nick looked back and grinned at her.* | *I threw the ball at Joe and hit him on the back of the neck.*

2 to go or come towards someone or something

- go towards
- come towards
- head towards
- make/head for
- make a beeline for
- advance on
- approach

go towards ALSO **go toward** American /ˌgəʊ təˈwɔːʳd(z)/ [v phrase not in passive] to go away from where you are towards a particular place: *Go towards the church and take the first turning on your left.* | *He watched her going toward West End Avenue.*

come towards ALSO **come toward** American /ˌkʌm təˈwɔːʳd(z)/ [v phrase not in passive] to come to where you are from a particular direction: *He looked up to see two policemen coming towards him.* | *As we came toward the house, the door flew open and out came Polly.*

head towards ALSO **head toward** American /ˌhed təˈwɔːd(z)/ [v phrase not in passive] to move in the direction of something or someone, especially directly or in a determined way: *The bus was heading towards the Friedrich-Strasse railway station.* | *They saw the patrol boat turn and head towards them.*

make/head for /ˈmeɪk, ˈhed fɔːʳ/ [phr v T] to move quickly towards somewhere, especially so that you can do something when you get there: *As he made for the door he tripped and fell heavily.* | *We headed for the nearest island to try and repair our boat.*

make a beeline for /ˌmeɪk ə ˈbiːlaɪn fɔːʳ/ [v phrase] to walk directly to a place or person as quickly as possible, especially because there is something you want there or someone you want to talk to: *I made a beeline for the bar and ordered myself a double whisky.* | *Jeff made a beeline for a table where two pretty Russian girls were sitting.*

advance on /ədˈvɑːns ɒn‖-ˈvæns- / [phr v T] written to move towards someone or something, especially in order to attack them: *In May 1681 a force of about 2500 troops advanced on Mondovi.* | *He moved towards her as though he was advancing on a dangerous animal.*

approach /əˈprəʊtʃ/ [v I/T] written to come towards a particular person or place: *As they approached the wood, a deer ran out of the trees.* | *We walked silently, so they would not hear us approach.*

3 to go towards someone because you want to speak to them

- come up to
- approach
- sidle up

come up to /ˌkʌm ˈʌp tuː/ [phr v T not in passive] to walk towards someone and stop next to them, especially because you want to say something: *An old guy come up to me in the street and asked for a dime for coffee.* | *Total strangers used to come up to me and tell me how much they'd enjoyed the show.*

approach /əˈprəʊtʃ/ [v T] to walk towards someone you do not know, especially so that you can ask them something: *A tourist approached us and asked us the way to the theatre.* | *Several people approached Fleming as he left the hall.* | *She was approached by a waiter.*

sidle up /ˌsaɪdl ˈʌp/ [phr v I] to move quietly towards someone, trying not to be noticed, so that they do not realize you are there until you are next to them: *I was sitting in the back row, when Harry sidled up and sat down next to me.* | **+ to** *He sidled up to me without a word and slipped a note in my pocket.*

town

RELATED WORDS

opposite: ———————— **country (13-14)**

▸ area of a town *see* **area (2)**

1 a town

- town
- city
- village
- settlement

town /taʊn/ [n C] a place where a lot of people live with houses, streets, shops etc: *More and more people were seeking work in the growing towns.* | *The town is situated some 23 miles north of London.* | *a small town in the Midwest* | **a seaside/industrial/market town** *La Coruna is a pretty seaside town on the north-western tip of Spain.* | **part of town** *Steyne Street was a narrow street in a shabby but respectable part of town.* | **the town of Warrington/Poitiers/Kimball etc** written *A large sign announced that we were entering the town of Knock.* | **town and country** (=people who live in towns and people who live in the country) *deep divisions in wealth between town and country*

city /ˈsɪti/ [n C] a big and important town that is often the centre of government for an area, has a lot of trade and industry, and is likely to contain important political, educational, or religious institutions: *You should visit San Francisco. It's a beautiful city.* | *The major industrial cities were getting increasingly overcrowded.* | **a big/crowded/medieval etc city** *I was alone in a big city in a new country.* | *Leeds is a thriving, vibrant, and prosperous city.* | **the city of Belfast/Jerusalem/Boston etc** written *The city of Barcelona is famous for its wonderful architecture.* | *the ancient city of Damascus*

village /ˈvɪlɪdʒ/ [n C] a very small town in the country: *There are some nice little pubs in the villages round here.* | *She left her village in the north of Thailand and went to live in Bangkok.*

settlement /ˈsetlmənt/ [n C] a place where people come to live for the first time and where they build a village or town: *She lived in a small settlement on the edge of the desert.* | *Settlements started to appear all along the river.* | *The tools were found in an early Iron Age settlement.*

2 the centre of a town or city

- centre
- downtown
- in/into town
- inner city

centre British **/center** American /ˈsentəʳ/ [n C] the part of a town or city where most of the shops, banks, theatres etc are: *a charming little town with an unspoiled medieval centre* | **+ of** *I work in the centre of London, so I can easily go shopping after work.* | **city centre** British **/city center** American *A bomb went off in the city center and 19 people were killed.* | **town centre** British *She's gone into the town centre to do some shopping.*

downtown /ˌdaʊnˈtaʊn◂/ [adv] American in or to the part of a city where most of the shops, banks, theatres etc are: *She lives in a really beautiful apartment downtown.* | **go downtown** *I have to go downtown later.* —**downtown** /ˈdaʊntaʊn/ [n singular] *The downtown was deserted that night.*

in/into town /ɪn, ɪntə ˈtaʊn/ [adv] British spoken in or into the centre of a town or city: *I suggest we meet somewhere in town and have lunch together.* | *He bought us tickets to the best show in town.* | *I'm going into town. Do you want anything?* | *Can you give me a lift into town?*

inner city /ˌɪnəʳ ˈsɪti◂/ [n C] the areas that are close to the centre of a big city, especially where many poorer people live and there are often social problems – use this especially in political and economic contexts: *policies aimed at revitalizing America's inner cities* | **the inner city** *Suburban styles of life are very different from those in the inner city.* —**inner-city** [adj only before noun] *Crime is a big problem in inner-city areas.* | *children from inner-city schools*

3 the areas at the edge of a town or city

- suburb
- outskirts
- out-of-town
- urban sprawl

suburb /ˈsʌbɜːʳb/ [n C] an area around the edges of a city, where many people live because it is quieter and there is more space than in the centre **+ of** *I was born and brought up in a suburb of New York City.* | **the suburbs** *More and more people are moving to the suburbs every year.* | *All the social workers come in from their comfortable homes in the suburbs.* | **a wealthy/middle-class/respectable etc suburb** *They have just bought a house in Pacific Palisades, a wealthy suburb of Los Angeles.* —**suburban** /səˈbɜːʳbən/ [adj] *a typical suburban house*

outskirts /ˈaʊtskɜːʳts/ [n plural] the area around the edge of a city or just outside it: *The Cité De Science is a futuristic complex in the Parisian outskirts.* | **on the outskirts** *His body was discovered on the city's outskirts three days later.* | **the outskirts of Tokyo/London etc** *By 9 o'clock we reached the outskirts of Berlin.* | **the outskirts of town** *There are plans to build a new shopping mall on the outskirts of town.*

out-of-town /ˌaʊt əv ˈtaʊn◂/ [adj only before noun] British **out-of-town** shops, cinemas etc are built outside a town, so that people from the town have to drive to them: *an out-of-town shopping centre* | *Town centre shops face a threat from large out-of-town developments which offer hundreds of shops under one roof.*

urban sprawl /ˌɜːʳbən ˈsprɔːl/ [n U] a large area of buildings, factories etc around the edges of a city that used to be countryside – use this to describe places that are ugly, noisy, or unpleasant: *At that time, little was done to control the urban sprawl.* | *The natural habitats of Britain's wildlife have been ravaged by urban sprawl and pollution.*

4 the town where you are from

- home town
- home

▸ *see also* **come from, home**

home town /ˌhəʊm ˈtaʊn/ [n C] the town where you were born, where you lived as a child, or where you live now: *Sarajevo is my home town and I did not want to leave.* | **+ of** *Johnson lived in Seattle for ten years before returning to his home town of Cody, Wyoming.*

home /həʊm/ [n C] the place where you were born or the place where you usually live, especially if this is where you feel happy and want to live: *Her home, she said, was in Hong Kong, but she hadn't been there since she was a child.* | **feel like home** *I've lived in Madrid for many years, and it feels like home to me now.*

5 the biggest or most important town in a country or area

- capital
- metropolis

capital /ˈkæpɪ̥tl/ [n C] the town or city where the government of a country or area is: *Rome is one of* *the world's most beautiful capitals.* | **+ of** *What's the capital of Canada?* | **capital city** *The tour includes a trip to Budapest, Hungary's capital city.* | **state/regional/provincial etc capital** *Sacramento is the state capital of California.*

metropolis /mɪ̥ˈtrɒpəlɪ̥s‖mɪ̥ˈtrɑː-/ [n C usually singular] the largest, most important city in a country or area – use this especially to emphasize that a city is busy and full of people and activity: *After 1850 Paris grew quickly into a busy metropolis.* | *They drove quickly, leaving the immense metropolis behind them.* | **+ of** *Our aim is to make Sydney the musical metropolis of the world.*

6 relating to or in a town

- town
- city
- village
- urban
- civic
- municipal
- downtown
- metropolitan

town /taʊn/ [adj only before noun] *The town council has proposed a new road building project.* | *With better town planning, traffic problems could be avoided.* | **town square** (=a square in the centre of a town) *A market is held daily in the town square.*

city /ˈsɪti/ [adj only before noun] relating to or in a city: *The city library cost over $15 million to build.* | *Residents blame city officials for poor housing conditions.* | *the city authorities* | **city streets** *Beneath the city streets is a network of sewers.* | **city life** *City life is becoming increasingly dangerous.*

village /ˈvɪlɪdʒ/ [adj only before noun] British relating to a village: *There is a village festival every year at the beginning of May.* | *Has village life changed significantly in the last few years?* | **village shop/school/hall etc** *We have a church, one pub and a village shop.*

urban /ˈɜːʳbən/ [adj only before noun] relating to towns and cities, the people who live in them, or the things that happen in them: *The problem of air pollution is especially serious in urban areas.* | *China's growing urban population* | *post-war urban planning* | *urban growth*

civic /ˈsɪvɪk/ [adj only before noun] relating to the government of a city or town: *Civic leaders cannot agree on what is best for the city.* | *An important civic function is taking place in the city hall this evening.* | *Harlow Council has always been generous with civic funding for music and the arts.* | *It is the civil duty of every citizen to vote.*

municipal /mjuːˈnɪsɪ̥pəl‖mjʊ-/ [adj only before noun] relating to the government of a town or city or to the public services it provides: *Municipal elections will be held on April 12th.* | *Not far from the town centre is the municipal park.* | *The museum and other municipal buildings are threatened.*

downtown /ˈdaʊntaʊn/ [adj only before noun] American in or belonging to the main business area in the centre of a town or city: *Taylor worked in a dingy little office in downtown Chicago.* | *Many downtown department stores are moving out into the wealthier suburbs.* | *a downtown hotel*

metropolitan /ˌmetrəˈpɒlɪ̥tən◂‖-ˈpɑː-/ [adj only before noun] relating to a large city: *Some workers can only afford homes outside metropolitan areas.* | *the metropolitan authorities*

tradition

a belief or custom that has existed among a group of people for a very long time

RELATED WORDS

▸ *see also* **conventional/unconventional, habit**

1 a tradition

- tradition
- traditional
- custom
- customary
- institution

tradition /trəˈdɪʃən/ [n C] a belief, custom, or way of doing something that has existed for a very long time in a particular country or among a particular group of people: *A lot of the old traditions are dying out.* | *Every village has its own traditions.* | **+ of** *The region has a tradition of winemaking which goes back to Roman times.* | **+ that** *It's still the tradition here that the eldest son inherits all the family's money and land.* | **family tradition** *We always go for a long walk on Christmas morning – it's a family tradition.*

traditional /trəˈdɪʃənəl/ [adj] belonging to the traditions of a country or group of people – use this about music, food, clothes, customs etc: *A group of children will perform traditional dances.* | **traditional African/French/English etc** *The dancers were wearing traditional African costume.* | *The restaurant offers a wide range of traditional French food.* | **it is traditional to do sth** *In the US it is traditional to dress up in costumes on Halloween.* —**traditionally** [adv] *a special dish that is traditionally eaten at New Year*

custom /ˈkʌstəm/ [n C] a way of behaving that has existed for a long time among a group of people, and is considered normal or polite – use this especially to talk about other countries or other times: *Sadly, a lot of the old customs are now dying out.* | **+ of** *The custom of sending birthday cards began in the 19th century.* | **it is the custom (for sb) to do sth** *It is the custom in Japan to take your shoes off when you go into someone's house.* | *In those days it was the custom for farmers to give part of their crop to the lord of the manor.*

customary /ˈkʌstəməri‖-meri/ [adj] something that is **customary** is considered normal or polite because it is the way it is usually done by a group of people: *The man at the hotel welcomed us with the customary greeting.* | **it is customary (for sb) to do sth** *It is customary for the man to propose to the woman.*

institution /ˌɪnstɪ̥ˈtjuːʃən‖-ˈtuː-/ [n C usually singular] a custom, belief or way of doing something that has become established and accepted as part of normal life among a particular group of people: *Trading in ivory had become an institution in this part of Africa.* | **+ of** *Church leaders are meeting this week to discuss ways of preserving the institution of marriage.*

2 all the customs and beliefs of a country or group

- tradition
- folklore
- heritage
- culture

tradition /trəˈdɪʃən/ [n U] all the beliefs and ways of behaving that have existed for a very long time in a particular country or among a particular group of people: *There is great respect for tradition among the older members of the community.* | **by tradition** (=according to a tradition) *By tradition, it is the bride's parents who pay for the wedding.*

folklore /ˈfəʊklɔːʳ/ [n U] old stories which the people in a country or area have told each other for a very long time, and which often contain historical or religious ideas **according to folklore** *According to folklore, King Arthur will one day return to become King of Britain.* | **in folklore** *In folklore the snake is often a symbol of evil.*

heritage /ˈherɪ̇tɪdʒ/ [n U] art, literature, and traditions that are considered to belong as a right to all the people in a society, especially because they form an important part of a country's history: *The town takes great pride in its architectural heritage.* | **national heritage** *These works of art are considered of great importance to Russia's national heritage.* | **+ of** *The castle is part of the heritage of Wales and should be preserved for the people of Wales.*

culture /ˈkʌltʃəʳ/ [n C/U] all the customs, beliefs, and practices of a particular society or among a particular group of people: *The trip offers you a unique opportunity to experience the culture of the remote hill tribes of the north.* | *In what ways do British and Australian culture differ?*

3 a special event that is part of a tradition

- ceremony
- ceremonial
- ritual
- rite

ceremony /ˈserɪ̇məni‖-məʊni/ [n C] a special formal event which is part of the religious or social tradition of a place, and in which there is a fixed set of words and actions **wedding/funeral etc ceremony** *After the wedding ceremony we went to a reception at the bride's parents' house.* | **hold a ceremony** (=have a ceremony) *A ceremony is held every year to remember those who died in the war.* | **attend a ceremony** *Over 2,000 people attended the official opening ceremony of the Olympic Games.*

ceremonial /ˌserɪ̇ˈməʊniəl◂/ [adj only before noun] **ceremonial** clothes, objects, and activities are used in important religious or social ceremonies: *The Queen was in full ceremonial dress for the state opening of Parliament.* | *His right hand rested on his ceremonial sword.* | *The full costume is only worn on important ceremonial occasions.*

ritual /ˈrɪtʃuəl/ [n C/U] a set of words and actions that are always done in the same way, for example as part of a religious ceremony: *The book examines rituals for childbirth from different parts of the world.* | *After an elaborate ritual, the boys are formally accepted into the tribe.* | **perform a ritual** *The ritual is performed in order to thank the Sun Goddess for the rice harvest.*

rite /raɪt/ [n C] a special action that is done as part of an important religious or social ceremony, especially one that only particular people, for example priests, are allowed to perform: *Buddhist rites* | **perform a rite** *The Batak chieftains perform the traditional initiation rite.* | **last rites** (=final prayers and ceremonies for someone who is dying) *A priest was called to perform last rites for the dying woman.* | **funeral rites** *The body cannot be buried until the funeral rites have been performed.*

4 to not do something in the usual or traditional way

- break with tradition/break with the past
- a break with tradition/a break with the past

break with tradition/break with the past /ˌbreɪk wɪð trəˈdɪʃən, ˌbreɪk wɪð ðə ˈpɑːst‖-ˈpæst/ [v phrase] to stop doing things the way they have always been done in the past: *The Church has finally broken with tradition and allowed women into the ministry.* | *I think it's time to break with the past and rewrite the constitution.*

a break with tradition/a break with the past /ə ˌbreɪk wɪð trəˈdɪʃən, ə ˌbreɪk wɪð ðə ˈpɑːst‖-ˈpæst/ [n phrase] when you stop doing things the way they have always been done in the past: *In a significant break with tradition, the Queen will not attend this year's ceremony.* | *Political leaders are calling for a break with the past and a new spirit of cooperation.*

translate

to change writing or speech into another language

RELATED WORDS

- *see also* **language, meaning, word, phrase or sentence, explain**

1 to translate something

- translate
- interpret
- put sth into English/French/Japanese etc

translate /trænsˈleɪt, trænz-/ [v I/T] to change one language, especially in a piece of writing, into another: *She has translated a number of his books.* | **translate sth from sth** *Michael Meyer translated the play from the original Norwegian.* | **translate sth into sth** *Can you translate this into French?* | *The book has been translated into 27 languages.* | **translate from sth into sth** *The best translators usually translate from a foreign language into their native language.* —**translation** [n U] *Most computer programs that do automatic translation do not do a very good job.* | **simultaneous translation** (=the process of translating what someone is saying while they say it) *Courtroom interpreters provided simultaneous translation.*

interpret /ɪnˈtɜːʳprɪ̇t/ [v I/T] to immediately translate what is being said to someone in a foreign language, so that it can be understood or replied to: *No one in our tour group spoke Spanish so we had to ask the guide to interpret.* | *We'll have to find someone who speaks Chinese to interpret the questions and answers for our guests.* | **+ for** *I had to interpret for my boss on the last trip to Japan.* | *During lunch, Ben interpreted for Sasha, who didn't speak a word of English.*

put sth into English/French/Japanese etc /ˌpʊt (sth) ɪntʊ ˈɪŋglɪʃ/ [v phrase] British to translate a short piece of writing into a foreign language: *I've written a birthday message for Fabio. Could you put it into Italian for me?* | *You lived in Berlin – help me put this into German.*

2 something which has been translated

- translation
- version
- in translation

translation /træns'leɪʃən, trænz-/ [n C] a piece of language, especially a piece of writing, that has been changed from one language into another: *Many of the poems are translations, but the sounds and rhythms are similar to the original language.* | **Spanish/English/Latin etc translation** *It is a Latin translation of a Greek manuscript.* | **+ of** *I've only read the English translation of the book, not the Japanese original.* | **direct translation** *'It goes without saying' is a direct translation of a French phrase.* | **be lost in (the) translation** (=when the real meaning of something cannot be translated in a completely satisfactory way) *Much of the humour of the book was unfortunately lost in translation.* | **lose sth in (the) translation** *His arguments are still powerful, but I think they lose some impact in translation.*

version /'vɜːʳʃən‖-ʒən/ [n C] **English/Japanese/French etc version** (=a translation of a book, poem etc in that language) *Most people would agree that the Italian version sounds better.* | **+ of** *I had trouble understanding the French, so I got the English version of the book from the library and read it.*

in translation /ɪn træns'leɪʃən/ [adv] if you read something **in translation**, you read it after it has been translated from another language: *I don't really like reading poetry in translation.* | *All of Brecht's plays are available in translation.*

3 someone who translates

- translator
- interpreter

translator /træns'leɪtəʳ, trænz-/ [n C] someone who translates from one language to another: *She worked in Geneva as a translator.* | *The publishers are looking for an American translator for his novels.* | **through a translator** (=using a translator) *Speaking through a translator, Li told of his early life.*

interpreter /ɪn'tɜːʳprətəʳ/ [n C] someone who immediately translates spoken language, for example when politicians from different countries are speaking to each other: *If I'm going to make the speech, I'll need an interpreter.* | *Both Presidents were accompanied by their interpreters.* | **through an interpreter** (=using an interpreter) *The only way we could figure out what they were saying was through an interpreter.*

travel

RELATED WORDS

- *see also* **go, holiday/vacation, drive, leave, arrive, stop, return, road/path, direction, way (9-10)**

1 to travel to a place

- go
- travel
- go on a trip/take a trip
- make a journey
- en route
- be on the move
- cross

go /gəʊ/ [v I] to **go** to a place that is away from where you live, especially for a holiday or for business: *My parents are in the Caribbean for Christmas, but I couldn't go this year.* | **+ (over/out/up/down) to** *We're going to Malta this summer.* | *We went up to Montreal for a long weekend.* | *She's been out to Africa several times on diplomatic visits.*

travel /'trævəl/ [v I] to make a journey from one place to another – use this to talk about going to a place that is a long way from your home or when you are going to many different places: *I love to travel.* | **+ from/to/across/through etc** *We travelled from China to Russia by train.* | *They had been travelling over the dry desert terrain for five days.*

go on a trip/take a trip /ˌgəʊ ɒn ə 'trɪp, ˌteɪk ə 'trɪp/ [v phrase] to go somewhere for a short time before returning home: *The geography class has taken a trip to Wales.* | *I'm going on a business trip to Japan next week.* | **+ to/through/up/around etc** *We decided to go on a trip through the Rocky Mountains in the spring.* | *Let's take a trip up the Rhine and stop at some of the castles along the way.*

make a journey /ˌmeɪk ə 'dʒɜːʳni/ [v phrase] especially British to travel to a place, especially when it is a long way away and the journey is difficult: *Every year he was supposed to go, and every year he could think of excuses for not making the journey.* | *When the tribe ran out of food, they had no choice but to make the journey north to more fertile ground.*

en route /ˌɒn 'ruːt‖ˌɑːn-/ [adv] on the way to somewhere: *We stopped en route to meet some friends in Brussels.* | **+ to/from/for** *The flight was en route from Tokyo to Sydney when it experienced engine trouble.*

be on the move /biː ɒn ðə 'muːv/ [v phrase] to travel from one place to another, especially because it is difficult or impossible for you to stay where you were: *He was always on the move, never staying in one town more than a few days.* | *The guerrillas stay on the move to avoid capture.* | *Thousands of refugees are on the move, fleeing heavy shelling in their home towns.*

cross /krɒs‖krɔːs/ [v T] to travel across a very large area such as a desert, an ocean, or an area of mountains: *It took a lot of courage to cross the Rocky Mountains in those days.* | *They crossed the Atlantic in a convoy of fifty ships.*

2 the activity of travelling

- travel

travel /'trævəl/ [n U] *Her interests are politics, music, and travel.* | *a travel programme* | **+ from/to/between etc** *In the 19th century, travel between the two countries was extremely difficult.* | **air/space/road/etc travel** *Future generations can possibly look forward to space travel as a holiday option.*

3 different ways of travelling

- drive
- fly
- sail
- by car/boat/plane/train
- on foot
- take
- by air/by sea/by land
- overland
- hitchhike/hitch
- backpacking

drive /draɪv/ [v I] to travel in a car: *'How are you going to get there?' 'I'm driving.'* | **+ to/from** *Jenny drove to the coast for the weekend.*

fly /flaɪ/ [v I] to travel by plane: *My mother never liked flying.* | **+ to/from etc** *We'll be flying from New York to Munich.*

sail /seɪl/ [v I] to travel by boat or ship: *We sail first thing in the morning* | **+ to/from** *He sailed from Southampton on May 6th.*

by car/boat/plane/train /baɪ 'kɑːʳ, 'bəʊt, 'pleɪn, 'treɪn/ [adv] travelling in a car, boat, plane, or train: *'Did you come by car?' 'No, by train.'* | *Some of the beaches can only be reached by boat.* | *We didn't have much time, so we decided to go by plane.*

on foot /ɒn 'fʊt/ [adv] if you go somewhere **on foot**, you walk there: *The two men had attempted to cross the mountains on foot.*

take /teɪk/ [v T] if you **take** a train, bus, or plane, you travel in it: *What's the best way to get downtown? Should I take a bus?* | *Take the subway to Montgomery Station and walk from there.*

by air/by sea/by land /baɪ 'eəʳ, baɪ 'siː, baɪ 'lænd/ [adv] if you travel **by air**, **by sea**, or **by land** you travel by plane, in a boat, or on land: *It's much quicker if you go by air, but it's also more expensive.* | *Troops entered the region by land and sea.*

overland /ˌəʊvəʳ'lænd◂/ [adv] by train, car, bus etc, especially over a long distance, when people would normally go by plane or ship: *It's certainly quicker to fly but we thought it would be more exciting to go overland.* —**overland** [adj only before noun] *The overland route is very difficult at times.*

hitchhike/hitch ALSO **hitch a ride** American /'hɪtʃ-haɪk, hɪtʃ, ˌhɪtʃ ə 'raɪd/ [v I/v I/T] to travel by standing by the side of the road asking people in cars to stop and take you to the place you want to go: *He lost all his money in a casino in Vegas and had to hitchhike back to San Francisco.* | *We hitched a ride with a trucker who took us all the way to the Virginia border.* | *It's a lot cheaper to hitch but it's also more dangerous.*

backpacking /'bækˌpækɪŋ/ [n U] the activity of travelling independently to a lot of different areas, carrying your clothes etc in a special bag on your back: *Backpacking is especially popular among students and young people.* | *a backpacking trip* | **go backpacking** *Last year, he went backpacking in the US.*

4 to travel a particular distance

- go
- do
- cover

go /gəʊ/ [v T] **go 40 miles/five kilometres etc** to travel a particular distance, especially as only part of a journey: *We had only gone about five miles when I started to feel sick.* | *How far have we gone today?*

do /duː/ [v T] especially British **do 20 miles/30 kilometres etc** to travel for 20 miles, 30 kilometres etc: *We were riding through the hills, but we still managed to do 30 miles each day.* | *I bought the car for £3500, and it's only done 30,000 miles!*

cover /'kʌvəʳ/ [v T] to travel a particular distance, especially a long distance, that is part of a longer journey you are making: *It took him three days to cover the distance from Laingsbury to Albertsville.* | *In one twenty-five day period, he covered 800 miles.*

5 when you travel somewhere without stopping

- non-stop
- direct

non-stop /ˌnɒn 'stɒp◂‖ˌnɑːn 'stɑːp◂/ [adj/adv] if you travel somewhere **non-stop**, especially on a plane, you do not stop until you get there: *You can fly non-stop to Hong Kong, but it's more expensive.* | **non-stop flight/trip/voyage etc** *Is there a non-stop flight to Delhi?*

direct /dɪ'rekt, ˌdaɪ'rekt◂/ [adj/adv] without stopping on a journey or without changing from one train, plane etc to another: *There isn't a direct flight – you'll have to change planes in Miami.* | *With this ticket you can travel direct from Paris to Berlin overnight.*

6 to travel to another country

- go abroad
- go overseas
- visit
- go out to

go abroad /ˌgəʊ ə'brɔːd/ [v phrase] to travel to another country, especially for pleasure and interest: *Here's a list of things to think about before you go abroad.* | *I'm the only person I know who's never been abroad or even on a plane.* | **be abroad** *When their mother died she was unable to contact her brother because he was abroad somewhere.*

go overseas /ˌgəʊ əʊvəʳ'siːz/ [v phrase] to travel to another country in order to stay there for a long time, for example because you have been sent to work there: *I wrote a letter to the interviewer, explaining that I was going overseas for six months.* | *The soldiers underwent training for three months before the unit went overseas.*

visit /'vɪzət/ [v T] to travel to another country for a short time, especially because you want to find out what it is like: *He was the first traveller from the British Isles to visit Abyssinia.* | *Thousands of Americans visit Thailand each year.*

go out to /ˌgəʊ 'aʊt tuː/ [phr v T not in passive] British to travel to another country that is a long way away: *He went out to West Africa in 1962 and has been there ever since.* | *The Chief Financial Officer went out to Korea to oversee the merger.*

7 to travel as part of your job

- travel
- commute
- tour
- be on tour

travel /'trævəl/ [v I] *Do you have to travel a lot in your new job?* | *The post will involve you travelling to Germany about three times a year.* —**travelling** British /**traveling** American [n U] *The job involves a certain amount of travelling.*

commute /kə'mjuːt/ [v I] to travel every day to get to work because you live in a different city or town from the one you work in: *I don't mind commuting on the train as long as I have a good book to read.* | *Kendall commutes into the city every day from Waltham.*

tour /tʊəʳ/ [v I/T] if a sports team, entertainer, politician etc **tours**, they travel to many different places in order to play, perform, or be seen: *Haynes recorded with Charlie Parker and toured with Sarah Vaughan in the 1950s.* | *The theatre company will tour later this year.* | **tour the country/the US/Russia etc** *The team is currently touring Australia in a series of friendly games.*

be on tour /biː ɒn 'tʊəʳ/ [v phrase] if a musician, actor, sportsman etc **is on tour**, he or she is travelling to many different places so that people can see them play or perform: *Jennings is currently on tour, promoting and reading from his new children's book.* | *At the moment the band is on tour in Europe.*

8 to travel to a lot of different places

- travel around
- tour
- do
- get around
- explore
- see the world
- on your travels

travel around ALSO **travel round** British /ˌtrævəl əˈraʊnd, ˌtrævəl ˈraʊnd/ [phr v I/T] to travel to a lot of different places, especially when you do not plan exactly where you are going: *David travelled around a lot in the '60s and '70s.* | **travel around Europe/the North/Canada etc** *I'd love to have a job that let me travel around the world.* | *She's been traveling around the country trying to get big companies interested in her ideas.*

tour /tʊəʳ/ [v T] British to travel to a lot of different places within a particular area or country, especially for pleasure and interest: *For our summer vacation this year we're touring Spain in a camper.* | *We shall tour the city for two hours and then meet back at the bus.*

do /duː/ [v T] spoken to travel to a lot of different places in a particular area, especially as part of a holiday: *Last year we did the Greek Islands but we were thinking of the USA this year.* | *There's not a whole lot to see, so you can do the city in two or three days.*

get around ALSO **get round** British /ˌget əˈraʊnd, ˌget ˈraʊnd/ [phr v I/T] to travel to a large number of places, usually in a short time: *The metro system in Mexico City is very good. It makes it really easy to get around.* | **get around London/Europe/the Midwest etc** *You can use free shuttle buses to get around the city.*

explore /ɪkˈsplɔːʳ/ [v I/T] to travel to many different places in a particular area, because you are interested to find out more about them: *We'll be in Istanbul for three days, so there will be plenty of time to explore.* | *Whenever possible, she and Flynn would go off and explore the countryside, taking a picnic with them.*

see the world /ˌsiː ðə ˈwɜːʳld/ [v phrase] to travel around to different places all over the world so that you get the experience of living in other countries: *After leaving college and earning some money he set off to see the world.*

on your travels /ɒn jɔːʳ ˈtrævəlz/ [adv] if you do something **on your travels**, you do it while you are travelling to different places: *I picked up a few words of Chinese on my travels, but I don't speak it fluently.* | **+ to** *Corbett met a number of his contacts on his travels to Taiwan.*

9 a journey

- journey
- trip
- tour
- flight
- ride
- drive
- crossing
- voyage
- expedition
- trek

journey /ˈdʒɜːʳni/ [n C] especially British the period you spend travelling from one place to another – use this especially about someone travelling for a long distance or when talking about someone regularly travelling somewhere, for example to school or work: *We had an awful journey – there was heavy snow and the car broke down* | **bus/train/car etc journey** *It was a long train journey to St Petersburg.* | **a two-hour/five-mile journey** *They arrived in Nice after an eight-hour journey by car.* | **make a journey** *These birds make an incredible 10,000-kilometre journey to Africa every winter.*

trip /trɪp/ [n C] a journey in which you go to a place, stay there for a short time, and then come back. In American English, **trip** can be used to mean any journey: *We had a fantastic trip – the flight was fine and the hotel was perfect.* | *The trip to the coast took longer than we expected.* | **take a trip/go on a trip** *They decided to take a trip to Paris.* | **on a trip** (=taking a trip) *My husband's away on a business trip in China.* | **business/school/skiing etc trip** *My dad and I used to go on a camping trip alone together every summer.* | **a two-hour/five-mile etc trip** American *It's only a three-hour trip by plane to Seattle.* | **boat/car/plane etc trip** *It's such a nice day – how about going on a boat trip?* | **road trip** American (=a long trip in a car) *My friend and I took several road trips to New York City.*

tour /tʊəʳ/ [n C] a journey for pleasure during which you visit several different towns, areas etc. A **tour** is also an organized journey made by an entertainer, sports team, or politician in order to perform, play, or speak in several places: *Did you see Bruce Springsteen on his last tour?* | **+ of** *We took a bicycle tour of Tuscany.* | *The prime minister has left for a three-week tour of South America.* | **on tour** *Norton is on tour promoting her new children's book.* | **a leg of a tour** (=part of a tour) *The last leg of the tour will take the team to Dallas.* | **package tour** (=planned holiday with all costs included) *They like to take package tours because they hate dealing with details.*

flight /flaɪt/ [n C] a journey in a plane: *All flights to Tokyo were delayed because of bad weather.* | **a 30-minute/3-hour etc flight** *It's a 7-hour flight to New York.*

ride /raɪd/ [n C] a short journey in a vehicle such as a car, or on a bicycle or a horse: *He pretended to be asleep for the entire two hour ride.* | **bike/car/horse etc ride** *On the car ride back from the airport he told her all about his trip.* | **go for a ride** (=ride somewhere just for enjoyment) *She took me to see the horse and asked if I wanted to go for a ride.*

drive /draɪv/ [n singular] a journey in a car: *It's a beautiful day for a drive in the country.* | **a 12-hour/15-minute etc drive** *It's about a 20-minute drive into the city from here.* | **take a drive/go for a drive** *Let's take a drive out to the farm.*

crossing /ˈkrɒsɪŋ‖ˈkrɔː-/ [n C] a short journey in a boat or ship from one side of a lake, river, or sea to the other: *The crossing from Dover to Calais is often very rough.*

voyage /ˈvɔɪ-ɪdʒ/ [n C] a long journey in a boat or ship: *In those days, the voyage to Australia was long and dangerous.*

expedition /ˌekspɪ̈ˈdɪʃən/ [n C] a long journey, especially one made by a group of people, to visit a dangerous place or a place that has never been visited before: *The purpose of the expedition was to explore the North American coastline.* | *an expedition to the North Pole*

trek /trek/ [n C] a long and difficult journey, for example over mountains or through forests, especially when you are walking. Some people also go on treks for interest and enjoyment: *The team is preparing for a two week trek across the Atlas Mountains.*

10 a short journey

- go out for the day
- day trip
- a commute
- outing
- excursion

go out for the day /gəʊ ˌaʊt fəʳ ðə ˈdeɪ/ [v phrase] to visit a beach, an area of countryside, a town etc for pleasure and come back home on the same day: *It's such a lovely day – let's go out for the day and visit the zoo.*

day trip /'deɪ trɪp/ [n C] a visit to a beach, an area of countryside, a town etc when you go there and come back the same day: *It would be nice to take a day trip to Chicago to do some shopping.*

a commute /ə kə'mjuːt/ [n C usually singular] a journey that someone makes each day to work, especially when they live a fairly long way away from their work: *The commute from Kent into London can be horrendous.* | **a 1-hour/20-minute etc commute** *I had no money, two small children, and a 90-minute commute to work each day.*

outing /'aʊtɪŋ/ [n C] a short journey on which a group of people go to visit a local place of interest, the theatre etc **+ to** *Mrs Pollack took her class on an outing to the local museum.* | **school/church etc outing** *a school outing to the ballet*

excursion /ɪk'skɜːʳʃən‖-ʒən/ [n C] a short journey arranged so that a group of people can visit a place of interest, especially while they are already on holiday: *The resort also offers daily excursions to nearby towns.* | **+ to** *One day he took an excursion to the other end of the island for a change of scene.*

11 someone who is travelling

- traveller
- passenger
- commuter
- tourist
- travelling
- well-travelled
- jet-setter
- backpacker

traveller British **/traveler** American /'trævələʳ/ [n C] *Many travellers find that facilities for young children are often inadequate.* | *Travelers going to malarial regions should see their doctor before they start.* | **air/rail/sea etc traveller** *80,000 air travellers pass through the terminal every day.* | **business travellers** (=people travelling as part of their job) *These days most airlines concentrate their advertising on business travelers.* | **seasoned traveller** (=someone who has travelled a lot) *As a seasoned traveller I know the value of being able to speak at least a few words of the local language.*

passenger /'pæsɪndʒəʳ, -sən-/ [n C] someone who is travelling in a vehicle, boat, or plane, but is not the driver: *The driver and all three passengers were killed in the crash.* | *The airport was jammed with thousands of passengers from delayed or cancelled flights.*

commuter /kə'mjuːtəʳ/ [n C] someone who lives in a different town, city etc from the one where they work, and who therefore travels a long distance every day to get to work: *It was a small shop that catered to commuters and local workers.* | **commuter train/plane etc** *Each region has one organization controlling buses and operating its commuter trains.*

tourist /'tʊərɪ̇st/ [n C] someone who travels around and visits places for pleasure, while they are on holiday: *A park ranger was answering the tourists' questions as they looked out over the canyon.* | *A tourist visa is required for most nationalities.*

travelling British **/traveling** American /'trævəlɪŋ/ [adj only before noun] moving from place to place in order to work, perform etc: *His father was a travelling salesman and was very rarely at home.* | *The traveling show includes historical films as well as 300 genuine artifacts that kids can handle.*

well-travelled British **/well-traveled** American /ˌwel 'trævəld◂/ [adj] someone who is **well-travelled** has visited a lot of different places around the world: *Sanders' parents were well-traveled, well-educated people.*

jet-setter /'dʒet ˌsetəʳ/ [n C] informal a rich and fashionable person who travels a lot: *Duke, heir to a tobacco fortune and an international jet-setter, died at the age of 80.* —**jet-setting** [adj] *He built the hotel to provide accommodation for jet-setting guests at his daughter's wedding.*

backpacker /'bækˌpækəʳ/ [n C] someone who travels independently to a lot of different areas, carrying their clothes etc in a special bag on their back: *The bar was full of young Australian backpackers.* | *She runs a downtown hostel for backpackers – the cost only $5 a night.* | *Fears are growing for the safety of a British backpacker who went missing in Vietnam last week.*

12 someone does not live in one particular place

- migrant
- drifter
- nomad
- vagrant

migrant /'maɪgrənt/ [n C] someone who has travelled from one place or country to another in order to find work: *Many of the city's poorest residents are migrants from rural areas.* | *400 migrants won the right to stay in the country yesterday, after a ten-year battle.* —**migrant** [adj] *Life for migrant workers is a constant struggle to survive.*

drifter /'drɪftəʳ/ [n C] someone who continually travels from one place to another without ever planning where to go next and without ever having a fixed job: *His grandfather was a drifter from New Mexico, who spent half his life brawling and drinking.*

nomad /'nəʊmæd/ [n C] a member of a tribe of people who do not live permanently in one place, but travel around looking for food for their animals, warmer weather etc: *The film follows the nomads as they cross the desert with their camels.* —**nomadic** /nəʊ'mædɪk/ [adj] *The Aborigines are a nomadic people indigenous to Australia.*

vagrant ALSO **transient** American /'veɪgrənt, 'trænziənt‖'trænʃənt/ [n C] someone who has no job, no home etc and who travels around and sleeps outdoors: *City authorities are planning a campaign to get an estimated 300,000 vagrants off the streets.* | *The town has never been particularly welcoming to transients.*

13 the place that you are travelling to

- destination
- be on the way to
- bound

destination /ˌdestɪ̇'neɪʃən/ [n C usually singular] *At the border you will be asked your destination and how long you plan to stay.* | *The glorious Inca ruins are the main tourist destination in Peru.* | **arrive at/reach your destination** *By the time he reached his destination, seven days later, he was half-starved and broke.*

be on the way to /biː ɒn ðə 'weɪ tuː/ [v phrase] if you **are on the way to** somewhere, you are travelling towards it: *We were already on the way to the airport when we realized we'd forgotten our passports.* | *I don't know where she is. She's probably on her way to London by now.*

bound /baʊnd/ [adj] travelling in a particular direction **+ for** *We passed a ferry full of people bound for* *one of the outer islands.* | **eastbound/westbound etc** *It was dark when the southbound international express finally passed by.* | **London-bound/Chicago-bound etc** *Take the London-bound train but get off two stations before the end of the line.*

14 a strong desire to travel

- wanderlust
- itchy feet

wanderlust /ˈwɒndəʳlʌst‖ˈwɑːn-/ [n U] written a strong desire to travel and to experience life in other countries: *It was not wanderlust alone that made him keen to visit Brazil. He thought he might hear news of his natural mother there.*

itchy feet /ˌɪtʃi ˈfiːt/ [n plural] British informal the desire to travel, which makes it difficult for you to stay in one place for very long: *I always get itchy feet at this time of year, in the spring.*

trick/deceive

RELATED WORDS

- to use someone for your own advantage *see* **use (20-21)**
- *see also* **dishonest, cheat, false, lie, trust/not trust, betray**

1 to trick someone and make them believe something that is not true

- trick
- con
- deceive
- fool
- mislead
- set sb up
- put one over on
- pull the wool over sb's eyes
- lead sb on
- take sb for a ride
- double-cross
- dupe

trick /trɪk/ [v T] to make someone believe something that is not true, in order to get something from them or make them do something: *I realized then that I had been tricked, but it was too late.* | *I'm not trying to trick you – just answer the question.* | **trick sb into doing sth** *The old man's sons had tricked him into signing the papers.* | **trick sb out of sth** (=take something from someone by tricking them) *A man posing as an insurance agent tricked her out of thousands of dollars.*

con /kɒn‖kɑːn/ [v T] informal to trick someone: *He was trying to con me, and I knew it.* | **con sb into doing sth** *They conned the school district into buying the property.* | **con sb out of sth** (=take something from someone by tricking them) *She conned me out of $50.*

deceive /dɪˈsiːv/ [v I/T] especially written to make someone who trusts you believe something that is not true because it is useful for you if they believe it: *This was a deliberate attempt to deceive the public.* | *Many children's lies are unplanned and not actually designed to deceive.* | *All through the summer Paula was deceiving her husband while she was seeing another man.* | **deceive sb into doing sth** *Thousands of home buyers were deceived into buying homes at inflated prices.* | **deceive yourself** *If you think that everyone is happy with the plan, you're deceiving yourself.*

fool /fuːl/ [v T] to make someone believe something that is not true by using a clever but simple trick: *His hairpiece doesn't fool anyone.* | **fool sb into doing sth** *They managed to fool the police into thinking they had left the country.* | **have sb fooled** *The brothers' act had us all fooled.* | **you can't fool me** spoken *You can't fool me – I know he's already given you the money.* | **fool yourself** *Maybe I was just fooling myself, but I really thought he liked me.*

mislead /mɪsˈliːd/ [v I/T] to make people believe something that is not true, by deliberately not giving them all the facts, or by saying something that is only partly true: *The report is a deliberate and obvious attempt to mislead.* | *They were accused of misleading customers about the nutritional value of their product.* | **mislead sb into doing sth** *Agents are accused of misleading clients into signing up for savings plans that were actually insurance policies.*

set sb up /ˌset (sb) ˈʌp/ [phr v T] to trick someone into doing something that they will be punished for or embarrassed by: *He said, following his arrest last fall, that the FBI had set him up.* | *Terry and Donald think I set them up, but it's all a big misunderstanding.*

put one over on /ˌpʊt wʌn ˈəʊvər ɒn/ [v phrase not in passive] informal to deceive someone, especially someone who is cleverer than you are, or someone who is not easily deceived: *That's the last time he puts one over on me!* | *Lawyers claim that the tobacco industry, by failing to tell everything it knew about smoking, was putting one over on its customers.*

pull the wool over sb's eyes /ˌpʊl ðə ˌwʊl əʊvəʳ (sb's) ˈaɪz/ [v phrase] informal to deceive someone, usually by hiding some facts or information: *Don't try and pull the wool over my eyes – I can tell you've been smoking.* | *The politicians are just trying to pull the wool over voters' eyes again.*

lead sb on /ˌliːd (sb) ˈɒn / [phr v T] to make someone believe you and trust you, especially by making them think you are romantically interested in them: *I can't tell if he really cares about me or if he's just leading me on?* | *I didn't mean to lead Cassie on, but I didn't want to hurt her feelings either.*

take sb for a ride /ˌteɪk (sb) fər ə ˈraɪd/ [v phrase] informal to deceive someone, especially so that you can get their money: *I'd already given him £50 when I realized he was taking me for a ride.* | *After the deal was signed, I felt like I'd been taken for a ride.*

double-cross /ˌdʌbəl ˈkrɒs‖-ˈkrɔːs/ [v T] to cheat someone you pretended to be helping or working with, especially by helping their enemies: *I'm warning you – if you double-cross me, I'll kill you.* | *Harry and Danny double-crossed the gang and escaped with all the money.*

dupe /djuːp‖duːp/ [v T] informal to trick or deceive someone, especially so that they become involved in someone else's dishonest activity without realizing it: *The spies duped government and military officials alike.* | **dupe sb into doing sth** *The perpetrators of the hoax managed to dupe respectable journalists into printing their story.*

2 to be tricked or deceived by someone

- be tricked/deceived
- be taken in
- fall for
- be fooled
- be set up
- be duped

be tricked/deceived /biː ˈtrɪkt, dɪˈsiːvd/ [v phrase] *He knew he'd been tricked, but it was too late to do anything.* | **+ by** *Don't feel bad – you weren't the only one who was deceived by his lies.*

be taken in /biː ˌteɪkən ˈɪn/ [v phrase] to be deceived by someone's words or behaviour, so that you believe something about them that is not true: *He seemed so confident, that I was completely taken in.* | **+ by** *We were all taken in by the scheme and invested far more money than we should have.*

fall for /ˈfɔːl fɔːʳ/ [v T not in passive] to stupidly believe something that is untrue and is intended to deceive you: *Doug is too clever to fall for a story like that!* | *She completely fell for his nonsense about being rich and famous.*

be fooled /biː ˈfuːld/ [v phrase] to be deceived by someone's behaviour, words, or appearance, especially when the result is not serious: *Don't let yourself be fooled – she's not as nice as she seems.* | **+ by** *A lot of people were fooled by what he said, but I was sure he was lying.*

be set up /biː ˌset ˈʌp/ [v phrase] to be tricked into doing something that results in you being punished or embarrassed: *I'm innocent! I was set up!* | **+ by** *The young man's claim that he had been set up by the police was eventually supported by several witnesses.*

be duped /biː ˈdjuːpt‖-ˈduːpt/ [v phrase] to be deceived by someone, especially so that you become involved in their dishonest activity without realizing it: *When the police arrived to arrest her, she realized she had been duped.* | **+ by** *Richie couldn't believe he had been set up and duped by his friends.*

3 a trick

- trick
- trap
- deception
- ruse
- hoax
- congame/con
- put-up job
- scam
- diversion
- decoy

trick /trɪk/ [n C] a clever plan designed to make someone believe something that you want them to believe, or do something that you want them to do: *He pretended to be sick as a trick to get her to visit him.* | *Don't send her any money – it might be a trick.* | **a trick question** (=a question that is cleverly designed to make someone give a wrong answer) *He refused to answer, suspecting they were asking him a trick question.*

trap /træp/ [n C] a clever plan designed to harm someone, for example by making them go somewhere where they will be caught or attacked, or making them say something they will be punished for: *I didn't take the money with me, because I was worried it might be a trap.* | *Sensing the lawyer's trap, Horvath refused to answer.*

deception /dɪˈsepʃən/ [n C] especially written something that is said or done with the deliberate intention of deceiving people: *Ann quickly saw through his lies and deceptions.* | *What began as a misunderstanding quickly became a deliberate deception on the part of the network.*

ruse /ruːz‖ruːs, ruːz/ [n C] a trick, especially one that is amusing and not very serious: *It was just a ruse to get what I wanted!* | *She asked to use the telephone as a ruse to enter the house.*

hoax /həʊks/ [n C] a false warning about something dangerous, given especially to someone in an official position, for example the police: *To everybody's great relief, the bomb scare turned out to be a hoax.* | *I got an email about another computer virus, but I'm pretty sure it's just a hoax.*

congame/con /ˈkɒngeɪm‖ˈkɑːn-, kɒn‖kɑːn/ [n C] informal a trick to get someone's money or make someone do something: *The two men were involved in an elaborate con to cheat investors out of their money.* | *Senior citizens are usually easy targets for con games.*

put-up job /ˈpʊt ʌp ˌdʒɒb‖-ˌdʒɑːb/ [n C] when something that happens is not what it seems to be, and is really an attempt to deceive people: *Journalists suspected that the kidnapping was a put-up job.* | *The demonstration was a put-up job, organized by the authorities so they could arrest the cult leaders.*

scam /skæm/ [n C] informal a clever and dishonest plan to get money: *The welfare scam was costing the federal government hundreds of thousands of dollars.* | *The offer of a 'free' vacation to Florida sounds like a scam to me.*

diversion /daɪˈvɜːʳʃən, də̇-‖-ʒən/ [n C] a trick that is intended to take someone's attention away from what someone else is trying to do: *Some of the prisoners started a fight as a diversion to give the others time to escape.* | **create a diversion** *Rioters created a diversion by setting fire to vehicles close to the police station.*

decoy /ˈdiːkɔɪ/ [n C] a person or thing that is used to trick someone by taking their attention away from an illegal or criminal act: *You act as a decoy and we'll sneak out the back.* | *The burglars started the fire as a decoy so that they could escape from police.*

4 someone who is deceived

- dupe
- sucker
- mug

dupe /djuːp‖duːp/ [n C] someone who is tricked by someone else, especially so that they become involved in the other person's dishonest plans without realizing it: *Investigators believe Dailey was a dupe for international drug smugglers.* | **unwitting dupe** *Some portray the family as unwitting dupes of conspiracy theorists.*

sucker /ˈsʌkəʳ/ [n C] informal someone who believes everything they are told, even when it is clearly not true: *I know I'm a sucker. I'll give $10 to anyone who tells me they're hungry or wants a cup of coffee.* | *Some poor suckers had paid more than three times what they should have for the tickets.*

mug /mʌg/ [n C] British informal someone who is easily deceived, especially so that they do much more or give much more than is fair or reasonable: *He's asked me to work over the weekend again – he must think I'm some kind of mug.* | *Don't be a mug! That picture's not worth as much as that!*

5 someone who tricks other people

- con man/con artist/scam artist
- crook
- charlatan
- quack
- shyster
- snake-oil salesman/peddler

con man/con artist/scam artist /ˈkɒn mæn, ˈkɒn ˌɑːʳtə̇st‖ˈkɑːn-, ˈskæm ˌɑːʳtə̇st/ [n C] someone who tries to get money from people by tricking them: *A pair of con men have been tricking older people in the community out of their life savings.* | *Don't be fooled by con artists who promise enormous returns on your investment with no risk.* | *Petty scam artists victimize tourists on the streets.*

crook /krʊk/ [n C] informal a dishonest person who steals things or tricks people: *I wouldn't do business with him – he's a crook.* | *People have accused me of being a crook, but I didn't take any money that wasn't mine.*

charlatan /ˈʃɑːʳlətən/ [n C] someone who pretends to have special skills and abilities and tricks people into believing them: *Some psychic charlatan con-*

vinced her she was going to die in six months. | *Charlatans advertise a variety of fat-reducing treatments in the back of magazines.*

quack /kwæk/ [n C] informal a dishonest person who pretends to be a doctor who can cure diseases: *Larry paid some quack over a thousand dollars to cure his insomnia.* | *That quack doesn't know anything about treating heart disease.*

shyster /ˈʃaɪstəʳ/ [n C] American informal a dishonest person, especially a lawyer: *Their lawyer is a shyster who would do anything to win a case.* | *Once the shysters get involved, you can be sure we'll end up in court.*

snake-oil salesman/peddler /ˈsneɪk ɔɪl ˌseɪlzmən, ˈpedləʳ/ [n C] American someone who deceives people by persuading them to accept false information, solutions etc that are not effective: *Critics have called the Senator a smooth-talking snake-oil peddler.* | *Latenight TV is full of snake-oil salesmen offering get-rich-quick schemes.*

6 when someone tricks or deceives someone

- deception
- deceit
- set up
- trickery

deception /dɪˈsepʃən/ [n U] the act of deceiving someone, especially by telling them lies: *I'm sure many businessmen use some form of deception, at times, to achieve their objectives.* | *She was stunned by the lies and deception her husband had used to hide his affairs.*

deceit /dɪˈsiːt/ [n U] the act of deceiving someone – use this to show strong disapproval: *His political opponents have accused him of corruption and deceit.* | *He now found himself in a world where deceit was accepted, even expected.*

set up /ˈset ʌp/ [n C] a situation in which someone is tricked into doing something that results in them being punished: *Is this some kind of a set up? Why should I believe you?* | *The whole thing was a set up to get Burley to confess.*

trickery /ˈtrɪkəri/ [n U] especially written the use of clever plans or actions to deceive someone: *It was a piece of political trickery that enraged the opposition.* | *He's managed to get as far as he has through slick talking and trickery.*

7 intended to deceive

- deceitful
- misleading
- under false pretences

deceitful /dɪˈsiːtfəl/ [adj] words or actions that are **deceitful** are intended to deceive someone: *He got the contract, but only by being deceitful.* | *I don't trust her. I think she has a deceitful smile.* | *The company has engaged in deceitful practices for years.*

misleading /mɪsˈliːdɪŋ/ [adj] **misleading** information or statements make people believe something that is not true, especially by not giving them all the facts: *The advertisements were deliberately misleading and false.* | *In court Robbins made misleading statements about his involvement.* | **it is misleading to say/treat/speak of etc** *It would be misleading to say that the recession will soon be over.* —**misleadingly** [adv] *Private schools in Britain are often misleadingly called public schools.*

under false pretences British **/under false pretenses** American /ʌndəʳ ˌfɔːls prɪˈtensɪ̈z‖ -ˈpriːtensɪ̈z/ [adv] if you do something **under false pretences**, you do it by pretending that the situation is different from what it really is: *He got a loan from the bank under false pretences.* | *Immigration officers attempt to catch people entering the country under false pretenses.*

true

RELATED WORDS

opposite: **untrue**

▸ *see also* **honest, right, believe, trust/not trust, rumour/rumor, doubt**

1 when something is true

- be true
- be the truth
- sth goes for
- it is a fact
- be the case
- truthful
- accurate
- valid

be true /biː ˈtruː/ [v phrase] something that **is true** is based on real facts and was not invented or imagined: *Everything I have told you is true.* | *At first I couldn't believe it was really true.* | *The movie is based on a true story.* | *If the rumours are true, we may all have a new boss by the end of the month.* | **it is true (that)** *It's true that our schools have suffered in the past from a lack of funding, but we are changing that.*

be the truth /biː ðə ˈtruːθ/ [v phrase] to be true: *There's no way I can do any more work than I do now, and that's the truth.* | *We think that what she says is the truth – she probably didn't intend to steal the money.*

sth goes for / (sth) ˈgəʊz fɔːʳ/ [v T not in progressive or passive] use this to say that something that is true about one person or group is also true about another one: *We encourage the kids in the program to work together, and the same thing goes for the adults too.* | *There are some bad teachers in state schools, but the same thing goes for private schools as well.*

it is a fact /ɪt ɪz ə ˈfækt/ use this to emphasize that something is definitely true **+ that** *It is a fact that more children in this country die in road accidents than from any other cause.*

be the case /biː ðə ˈkeɪs/ [v phrase] if a situation **is the case**, that is the way the situation truly is **it is the case that** *It used to be the case that British industry was plagued by strikes, but this is no longer true.* | **as is often/usually the case** *The doctor prescribed drugs for the child, as is often the case with this illness.* | *He thinks I'm complaining about nothing, but that's just not the case.*

truthful /ˈtruːθfəl/ [adj] a **truthful** answer or statement contains no lies: *Our citizens have a right to expect truthful reports from their government.* | *Justice Department officials who reviewed his statement found it to be truthful.*

accurate /ˈækjʊ̈rət/ [adj] descriptions, information, or numbers that are **accurate** are based on facts, do not contain mistakes, and tell you exactly what is happening: *Greene gives a remarkably accurate description of life in Saigon in the early '50s.* | *I think your assessment of the current economic situation is pretty accurate.*

valid /ˈvælɪ̈d/ [adj] ideas that are **valid** are based on what is true and reasonable, and should be accepted or considered seriously: *This may not be a valid conclusion – we haven't tested it thoroughly yet.* | *Many of Rousseau's ideas are just as valid today as they* *were in the 18th century.* | *The government still hasn't produced a valid argument in favour of its policies on immigration.* —**validity** /vəˈlɪdʒɪti/ [n U] *Lawyers are questioning the validity of the city's new telecom contract.*

2 when facts are shown to be true after being examined

- stand/hold up
- check out

stand/hold up /ˌstænd, ˌhəʊld ˈʌp/ [phr v I] if an idea, or an explanation **stands up** or **holds up**, it is shown to be true when carefully examined or questioned: *Although his argument is appealing, it doesn't really hold up.* | **stand up to examination/scrutiny** (=be shown to be true after being carefully checked) *None of her theories about language really stands up to close scrutiny.* | **stand/hold up in court** *My lawyer told me there was no point in starting the case, because it wouldn't stand up in a court of law.*

check out /ˌtʃek ˈaʊt/ [phr v I] if something that someone has told you **checks out**, it is proved to be true when you check it: *Everything she says checks out on our computer files.* | *If his alibi doesn't check out the police are going to charge him with murder.*

3 definitely true

- undeniable/indisputable
- be the gospel truth/be gospel

undeniable/indisputable /ˌʌndɪˈnaɪəbəl, ˌɪndɪˈspjuːtəbəl/ [adj] definitely true, so that no one could argue or disagree about it: *The fact that she was intelligent was undeniable.* | **it is undeniable that** *It is undeniable that Africa is a very different place to what it was fifty years ago.* | **indisputable evidence/proof etc** *The evidence against her appears indisputable.* | *Researchers were hoping that the rock samples would give them indisputable proof of life on Mars.*

be the gospel truth/be gospel /biː ðə ˌɡɒspəl ˈtruːθ, biː ˈɡɒspəl‖-ˌɡɑːs-/ [v phrase] use this to emphasize that something is definitely true: *When I was at school I thought that everything my teachers told me was the gospel truth.* | *Many myths about pregnancy are repeated as if they were gospel.*

4 only partly true, not completely true

- be partly true/partially true
- there's something in sth
- there's some truth in/to sth
- element/grain of truth

be partly true/partially true /biː ˌpɑːʳtli ˈtruː, ˌpɑːʳʃəli ˈtruː/ [v phrase] *This statement is partly true, but it leaves out some important facts.* | *The stories were easy to believe because they were partially true.*

there's some truth in/to sth /ðeəʳz ˌsʌm ˈtruːθ ɪn, tə (sth)/ spoken use this to say that something is partly true: *Do you think there's any truth to these rumours?* | *There's some truth in the old belief that carrots are good for the eyesight.*

there's something in sth British **/there's something to sth** American /ðeəʳz ˌsʌmθɪŋ ˈɪn (sth), ðeəʳz ˌsʌmθɪŋ ˈtuː (sth)/ spoken use this to say that there is some value or truth in an idea or statement, even if most of it seems unlikely or untrue: *The more I study astrology, the more I'm convinced that there could be something in it.* | *There might just be something to what she's been teaching.*

element/grain of truth /ˌeləmənt, ˌɡreɪn əv ˈtruːθ/ [n phrase] if you say there is an **element** or **grain of truth** in a story or an explanation, you mean that there is a little truth in it: *Most myths have a grain of truth in them.* | *There's an element of truth in what he says, but the conclusions he comes to are rubbish.*

5 to say what is true

- tell the truth
- to tell the truth
- truthful
- stick to the facts

tell the truth /ˌtel ðə ˈtruːθ/ [v phrase] to say what really happened or what the true situation is: *Nobody believes me, even though I'm the only one telling the truth!* | **tell sb the truth** *You should have told him the truth.* | *Just tell me the truth – did he give you the letter or not?*

truthful /ˈtruːθfəl/ [adj] someone who is **truthful** says what is true and does not tell lies: *Lucy's normally an extremely truthful little girl.* | **truthful (with sb) about** *I've always been truthful with him about my other boyfriends.* —**truthfully** [adv] *I want you to answer me truthfully.*

to tell the truth /tə ˌtel ðə ˈtruːθ/ [adv] spoken say this when you want to be honest about something, even if it is something unpleasant that other people may not like: *To tell the truth I'll be glad when the kids are back at school.* | **to tell you the truth** *I'm not really in the mood for going out. To tell you the truth, I'd rather stay in and watch TV.*

stick to the facts /ˌstɪk tə ðə ˈfækts/ [v phrase] to tell the truth about things that really happened and not invent things or give your opinions: *Witnesses were asked to stick to the facts and leave aside all emotion and sentiment.* | *'In my opinion, she was going to meet her lover.' 'Could you just stick to the facts, please.'*

6 ways of saying that something is really true

- really
- truly
- honestly

really /ˈrɪəli/ [adv] spoken *Is your cousin really a movie star?* | *It's all so long ago now, it's difficult to believe that any of it really happened.* | *'She's leaving her husband, you know.' 'Really?'*

honestly /ˈɒnəstli‖ˈɑːn-/ [adv] spoken say this to emphasize that someone should believe what you are saying: *I was going to give you it back, honestly.* | *I honestly don't think we'll be in court all day tomorrow.* | *Honestly, it makes no difference to me where we have the wedding.*

truly /ˈtruːli/ [adv] use this to emphasize that you are sincere about what you are saying and really mean it **truly sorry/happy/surprised etc** *I'm truly sorry. I didn't mean to upset you.* | *For the first time in her life she felt truly happy.* | **truly believe/think etc** *If we truly believe we can win, then we have a very good chance at doing it.*

7 the true information or facts about something

- the truth
- truth
- fact
- home truths

the truth /ðə 'truːθ/ [n singular] **+ about** *We may never know the truth about what really happened to Marilyn Monroe.* | *Scientists believe they are close to finding out the truth about the origins of the universe.* | **the truth is (that)** *The truth is that the idea of having kids terrifies him.* | **the simple/plain truth** (=the truth about something, especially when this is unpleasant) *The simple truth is that I just don't love him anymore.* | **the truth comes out** (=the truth becomes known) *Nixon tried to cover up the burglary, but the truth had to come out in the end.*

fact /fækt/ [n C] a true piece of information about something: *The most important thing is to find out what the facts are and put the scandal behind us.* | *Gentry still owed Mr Tilly $7,000, a fact he failed to mention when he was arrested.* | **+ that** *It is a fact that the world is round.* | **hard facts** (=definite facts that cannot be argued with) *You need to back up your theory with one or two hard facts.*

truth /truːθ/ [n C/U] important facts or principles about life, the world etc that are always true in all situations: *Science is based around the search for truth.* | *Ellis explains how truth and freedom are linked.* | *fundamental truths about human nature*

home truths /ˌhəʊm 'truːðs/ [n plural] British facts about someone which are unpleasant for them to know but are true: *It's about time someone told that woman a few home truths.*

trust/not trust

RELATED WORDS

▸ *see also* **honest, dishonest, lie, trick/deceive, cheat, betray**

1 when you think someone is honest

▸ trust
▸ trustworthy

trust /trʌst/ [v T not usually in progressive] to believe that someone is honest and will not tell lies, cheat you, or do anything that would harm you: *David's one of my oldest friends – I trust him completely.* | **can trust sb** (=feel sure that they are honest) *The hardest thing is finding a car dealer you can trust!* | **(can) trust sb to do sth** *'He's only fourteen.' 'I know, but I think we can trust him to look after the baby for an hour.'*

trustworthy /'trʌstˌwɜːʳði/ [adj] especially written if someone is **trustworthy**, you can trust them because they are honest: *We got the information from a trustworthy source.* | *Most of our employees are pretty trustworthy, I think.*

2 when you can be sure that someone will do what you want

▸ can depend/rely on sb
▸ reliable
▸ responsible
▸ loyal

can depend/rely on sb /kən dɪ'pend, rɪ'laɪ ɒn (sb)/ [v phrase] if you **can depend on** someone or **can rely on** them, you can be sure that they will do what you want or need them to do: *It's going to be a stressful time – you'll need to have someone with you who you can depend on.* | **+ to do sth** *We knew we could rely on Tom to bring some good music.*

reliable /rɪ'laɪəbəl/ [adj] someone who is **reliable** can be trusted to do what they say they will do and not make any mistakes: *It's strange Ben isn't here. He's usually so reliable.* | *In many offices the most reliable people with the longest service are the secretaries.*

responsible /rɪ'spɒnsɪ̈bəl‖rɪ'spɑːn-/ [adj] someone who is **responsible** can be trusted to behave in a sensible way, so you do not need to worry that they will do something careless or stupid: *We never worried about letting Sam babysit our kids – he'd always seemed very responsible and intelligent.* | *He treated me as if I wasn't responsible enough to be given the tools to do my job.* | **responsible behaviour/decisions etc** *Two new programs are being developed to help promote responsible sexual behavior.*

loyal /'lɔɪəl/ [adj] someone who is **loyal** can be trusted to always give help or support to their friends, their country, their political party etc: *a loyal supporter of the Green Party* | *She was described as a loyal friend of the Princess.* | **+ to** *Although they continue to argue, she remains fiercely loyal to her mother.* —**loyalty** [n C/U] loyal behaviour: *The attempted coup failed, thanks to the loyalty of the army.*

3 the feeling that you can trust someone

▸ trust
▸ confidence
▸ faith
▸ blind faith

trust /trʌst/ [n U] *After the scandal, the company lost the trust of many of its clients.* | *Establishing trust is the first thing a good teacher does with any student.* | **+ in** *Despite her many misfortunes, her trust in God was never shaken.* | **put/place (your) trust in someone** (=trust sb) *People put their trust in their elected officials and expect them to do the best job they can.* | **betray sb's trust** (=do something that shows they should not have trusted you) *She has betrayed the trust which we placed in her.* | **mutual trust** (=when two people or groups trust each other) *To be good leaders, managers must create a climate of mutual trust and respect.*

confidence /'kɒnfɪ̈dəns‖'kɑːn-/ [n U] a strong belief that you can trust a person, system, product etc, and that they will do what they say they will or do what they are supposed to do: *The new president has the confidence and backing of all of the leaders of the surrounding states.* | **+ in** *It's obviously very important to build up the consumer's confidence in our product.* | **lose confidence** *Opinion polls show that the voters have lost confidence in the administration.* | **public confidence** (=the confidence of the people) *The agency works hard to increase public confidence so that people are not afraid to report racist incidents.* | **crisis of confidence** (=when confidence in a person, system etc becomes very weak) *The country's highly respected Finance Ministry is facing a crisis of confidence that will be difficult to reverse.*

faith /feɪθ/ [n U] a strong belief that someone or something can always be depended on to do or say what is right or good **+ in** *My mother's total faith in God always amazed me.* | **have faith** *He had great faith in her judgement, and consulted her about everything.* | **lose faith** *After what she's been through, I can understand why she's lost faith in the legal system.*

blind faith /ˌblaɪnd 'feɪθ/ [n U] a very strong and unreasonable belief that someone can always be trusted, especially when it is wrong or dangerous to trust them: *There's a great difference between ordinary loyalty and blind faith.* | **+ in** *Many doctors are worried by the villagers' blind faith in traditional healing methods.*

4 words for describing someone who always trusts other people

- trusting
- naïve

trusting /'trʌstɪŋ/ [adj] always **trusting** other people, especially when this means you can be easily tricked: *Sometimes you're too trusting. You shouldn't lend money to anyone who says they need it.* | *She had an innocent, trusting nature, and I worried about how she'd cope in the big city.*

naïve /naɪ'i:v‖nɑ:'i:v/ [adj] always trusting other people, especially when this means you are easily tricked – use this especially about people who are young or do not have much experience: *At the time, I was very naïve and truly believed that our leaders were people of great ability and intellect.* | *Rogers isn't naïve enough to think that his film will rake in money, but he thinks it will be well-received.* —**naïvely** [adv] *I rather naïvely gave my address to a man I met in an Internet chat room.*

5 something you can trust

- reliable
- can rely/depend on sth

reliable /rɪ'laɪəbəl/ [adj] a **reliable** machine, system etc always works well; **reliable** information, books etc do not contain mistakes and are likely to be correct: *Do you have a reliable map of the area?* | *My car's quite old, but it's still pretty reliable.* | *In those days there was no reliable system of transportation between Alaska and the rest of the US.*

can rely/depend on sth /kən rɪ'laɪ, dɪ'pend ɒn (sth)/ [v phrase] if you **can depend on** something or **can rely on** it, you can be sure that it will always work well: *You can depend on the postal service here. It's very good.* | *If we can rely on the weather report, it's going to be hot tomorrow.* | *Of course people will use their cars if they cannot depend on buses and trains to get them to work.*

6 not trust

- not trust
- can't rely on
- unreliable
- be suspicious of
- distrust/mistrust

not trust /nɒt 'trʌst/ [v T] *I don't know what to do. I mean if I can't trust my best friend, who can I trust?* | *Don't trust him. He's lying.* | **not trust sb with sth** *I wouldn't trust him with my money.* | *It can be difficult to trust anyone with some of your innermost secrets.* | **not trust sb an inch** British (=not trust someone at all) *I thing you're mad giving him such an important job. I wouldn't trust him an inch.* | **not trust sb as far as you can throw them** (=not trust someone at all) *As for his 'advisors', he said he wouldn't trust them as far as he could throw them.*

can't rely on ALSO **can't trust sb/sth** /ˌkɑ:nt rɪ'laɪ ɒn, ˌkɑ:nt 'trʌst (sb/sth) ‖ˌkænt-/ [v phrase] to be unable to trust someone to do what they say they will do, or to be unable to trust a machine, system etc to work well: *You can't rely on the buses. I've stood here for twenty minutes waiting for one to come.* | **+ to do sth** *We need clearer regulations, but you can't trust the government to simplify anything.*

unreliable /ˌʌnrɪ'laɪəbəl◂/ [adj] if someone is **unreliable**, you cannot be sure that they will do what they say they will do; if a machine, car etc is **unreliable**, it often stops working and you cannot be sure it will work well: *We could ask our neighbours to feed the cat, but they're a little unreliable.* | *Telephone service in most of the country is unreliable.*

be suspicious of /bi: sə'spɪʃəs ɒv/ [v phrase] to have a feeling that you should not trust someone or something, although you are not sure why: *I'm always suspicious of people who offer me money.* | **deeply suspicious** (=very suspicious) *She had no proof at all, but nonetheless was deeply suspicious of her former friend's motives.*

distrust/mistrust /dɪs'trʌst, mɪs'trʌst/ [v T] to not trust someone: *'Was she seeing a doctor?' 'No, to my knowledge she mistrusted doctors.'* | *He distrusted people who were too friendly too quickly.*

7 the feeling that you cannot trust someone

- distrust/mistrust
- suspicion

distrust/mistrust /dɪs'trʌst, mɪs'trʌst/ [n U] *The talks took place in an atmosphere of hostility and distrust.* | *The city's school system has been hurt by low morale and public mistrust.* | **+ of** *Dylan's natural mistrust of reporters makes him a difficult man to interview.*

suspicion /sə'spɪʃən/ [n U] the feeling that you cannot trust someone, even though you may not know exactly why: *Terry's grandmother looked at me with suspicion and demanded, 'Who's this?'* | *When I asked about Gerald, Susan's usually kind face clouded with fear and suspicion.* | **arouse suspicion** (=make people feel suspicion) *The timing of his trip aroused suspicion among his government colleagues.*

8 words for describing someone who does not usually trust other people

- suspicious
- distrustful/mistrustful

suspicious /sə'spɪʃəs/ [adj] *The officials we met in the capital looked suspicious and tense, as if they were expecting us to declare war on them.* | **+ of** *The local people were suspicious of me because of my somewhat unusual lifestyle.*

distrustful/mistrustful /dɪs'trʌstfəl, mɪs'trʌstfəl/ [adj] *He was unsociable and distrustful, but also a fanatical worker.* | **+ of** *For nearly a whole century, Eastern and Western Europe remained deeply distrustful of each other.* | *Many people are still very mistrustful of computers.*

9 ways of describing someone who you do not trust

- sb can't be trusted
- sb looks/seems suspicious

sb can't be trusted / (sb) ˌkɑ:nt bi: 'trʌstɨd‖-ˌkænt-/ spoken say this about someone you do not trust: *Many people feel that lawyers can't be trusted, that they are just out for the money and nothing else.* | **+ to do sth** *Sharon can't be trusted to look after her own money, let alone deal with other people's.* | **+ with** *Don't say anything to Ed – he can't be trusted with confidential information.*

sb looks/seems suspicious / (sb) ˌlʊks, ˌsi:mz sə'spɪʃəs/ use this about someone whose appearance or behaviour makes you think that they may intend to do something dishonest or harmful: *The cop said we looked suspicious and that he was arresting us – just for standing on a corner! | The whole operation seemed very suspicious to me, so I thought I'd take a closer look.*

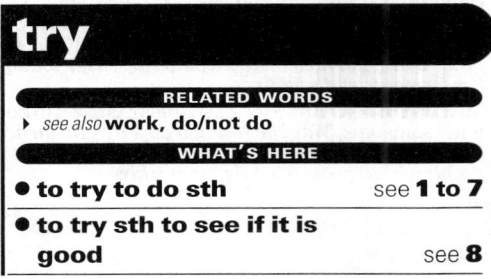

try

RELATED WORDS

▸ *see also* **work, do/not do**

WHAT'S HERE

to try to do sth

1 to try to do something

- try
- attempt
- have a try
- see if you can do sth
- make an attempt
- endeavour to do sth
- seek to do sth
- struggle to do sth

try /traɪ/ [v I/T] *Sorry I didn't phone you. I did try, but your line was busy. | I tried all the keys, but none of them would open the door.* | **+ to do sth** *I tried to get another job but I had no luck. | Try to relax and empty your mind. | He tried to walk past me down the stairs, but I stopped him.* | **try hard** (=try using a lot of effort) *I was trying hard to concentrate, but my mind kept wandering.* | **try doing sth** *You could try parking by the library – there's usually room in the car park there.* | **try and do sth** *I'll tell some jokes to try and cheer him up.* —**try** [n C] *Don't give up yet – have another try.*

attempt /əˈtempt/ [v T] to try to do something, especially something that is difficult, dangerous, or new: *No one has attempted this experiment before. | A rescue was attempted by Coast Guards, but it was not successful.* | **+ to do sth** *Any prisoner who attempts to escape will be shot. | Someone had attempted to open the car door. | They are attempting to become the first to climb Everest without oxygen tanks.*

have a try ALSO **have a go** especially British /ˌhæv ə ˈtraɪ, ˌhæv ə ˈgəʊ/ [v phrase] spoken to try to do something, especially when you think you may not succeed: *I can't get the lid off this jar. Do you want to have a try? | Have a go – you might be able to get the answer.* | **have a try/go at doing sth** *We had a go at trying to coax the cat indoors using scraps of food.*

see if you can do sth /ˌsiː ɪf juː kən ˈduː (sth)/ [v phrase not in past tense] spoken to try to do something – use this either to offer to do something for someone, or to ask someone to do something for you: *If you want to come to the show, I'll see if I can get you a ticket. | See if you can get him to change his mind.*

make an attempt /ˌmeɪk ən əˈtempt/ [v phrase] to try on one occasion to do something, especially something difficult, dangerous, or new **+ to do sth** *I made an attempt to apologize, but Brian wouldn't even talk to me. | Several attempts were made to negotiate with the gunmen.* | **make no attempt to do sth** *The protesters made no attempt to resist arrest.*

endeavour to do sth British **/endeavor to do sth** American /ɪnˌdevəʳ tə ˈduː (sth)/ [v phrase] formal to try to do something: *We always endeavour to provide our customers with the highest standards of service. | I remained for some time endeavouring to engage Mr Campbell in conversation.*

seek to do sth /ˌsiːk tə ˈduː (sth)/ [v phrase] formal to try to achieve something, especially something that may take a long time but which you think is important: *The Smiths are now seeking to take their case to the European Court. | For over two decades the USA sought to prevent the spread of communism in Southeast Asia. | Our economic policies seek to increase productivity, expand markets and create jobs.*

struggle to do sth /ˌstrʌgəl tə ˈduː (sth)/ [v phrase] to try to do something that is difficult: *There are too many families struggling to survive on low incomes. | I found my father struggling to lift one end of an enormous chest of drawers. | She struggled to express her feelings.* —**struggle** [n C] **+ to do sth** *Animals face a real struggle to survive in these harsh conditions.*

2 to try very hard to do something

- try hard
- make an effort
- strive
- be at pains to do sth
- go to great lengths to do sth

try hard /ˌtraɪ ˈhɑːʳd/ [v phrase] to make a lot of effort, because you want very much to do something: *No matter how hard I tried, I couldn't get the window to open.* | **+ to do sth** *I was trying hard not to laugh. | You must try harder to get your homework done on time.*

make an effort /ˌmeɪk ən ˈefəʳt/ [v phrase] to try hard to do something, especially something you do not want to do but you think you should do: *Can't you make more of an effort?* | **+ to do sth** *I made an effort to sound interested in what he was saying. | I wish you'd make an effort to get on with my friends.* | **make no effort to do sth** *She makes absolutely no effort to see the other person's point of view.*

strive /straɪv/ [v I] formal to try hard to achieve something, especially when this is difficult **+ to do sth** *Toni has been striving to achieve musical recognition for the past ten years.* | **+ for** *The company must constantly strive for greater efficiency.*

be at pains to do sth /biː ət ˌpeɪnz tə ˈduː (sth)/ [v phrase] to make a lot of effort to do something, especially to explain something people do not understand correctly: *Mrs Henessy was at pains to say that she was fighting for a principle, not just for financial compensation.*

go to great lengths to do sth /gəʊ tə ˌgreɪt ˌleŋθs tə ˈduː (sth)/ [v phrase] to be willing to use any method that is necessary in order to achieve something, even if this involves being dishonest, breaking the law etc: *Health professionals have gone to great lengths to reassure patients that the treatment is safe. | Some firms will go to great lengths, including spying, to obtain information about their competitors.*

3 to try as hard as you can

- try as hard as you can
- do/try your best
- do the best you can
- pull out all the stops
- give sth your best shot
- do your utmost
- do everything/all you can
- give your all
- as best you can
- to the best of your ability

try as hard as you can /traɪ əz ˌhɑːʳd əz juː ˈkæn/ [v phrase] *Come on, try as hard as you can!* | *I tried as hard as I could, but I still couldn't get everything into one suitcase.* | **+ to do sth** *She tried as hard as she could to look interested.*

do/try your best /ˌduː, ˌtraɪ jɔːʳ ˈbest/ [v phrase] to try as hard as you can, even when the situation is difficult and you are not sure if you will succeed: *I don't know if I'll manage to get everything finished by Friday, but I'll certainly do my best.* | **+ to do sth** *Harry did his best to sound calm, but it was obvious that he was really annoyed.* | *She tried her best not to laugh.*

do the best you can /duː ðə ˌbest juː ˈkæn/ [v phrase] to try as hard as you can to do something, even though it is difficult or you do not have enough time, money etc to do it really well: *It's a very tough exam but just do the best you can.* | *More medical supplies will be arriving next week – until then, doctors and nurses must do the best they can.* | **+ to do sth** *I did the best I could to make him change his mind, but he refused.*

pull out all the stops /ˌpʊl aʊt ˌɔːl ðə ˈstɒps‖-ˈstɑːps/ [v phrase] informal to do everything possible to make an event, celebration, competition etc successful: *They gave me a great leaving party – they really pulled out all the stops.* | *If we pull out all the stops we should still be able to meet our deadline.*

give sth your best shot /ˌgɪv (sth) jɔːʳ ˌbest ˈʃɒt‖-ˈʃɑːt/ [v phrase] informal to try to do something as well as you can, even though you do not have all the necessary skills or equipment: *I'm not promising I'll succeed, but I'll give it my best shot.*

do your utmost /ˌduː jɔːr ˈʌtməʊst/ [v phrase] to try as much as you possibly can, and for as long as possible, to achieve something very difficult: *We have done our utmost. There is no more we could possibly do.* | **+ to do sth** *The Secretary of State assured reporters that the Administration was doing its utmost to avoid war.*

do everything/all you can /duː ˌevriθɪŋ, ˌɔːl juː ˈkæn/ [v phrase] to use every possible method to try to do something: *I'm trying to help – I'm doing everything I possibly can.* | *I did everything I could to raise money, including selling my house.* | *Her mother did all she could to encourage Tracy to study medicine.*

give your all /ˌgɪv jɔːr ˈɔːl/ [v phrase] to use all your energy and determination to achieve something that is personally very important to you: *She gave her all in the last race, but it wasn't quite good enough to win.*

as best you can /əz ˌbest juː ˈkæn/ [adv] if you do something **as best you can**, especially something difficult or unpleasant, you try as hard as you can to do it because you cannot change the situation: *I cleaned the car up as best I could, but it still looked a mess.* | *We'll have to manage as best we can without you.*

to the best of your ability /tə ðə ˌbest əv jɔːr əˈbɪlɪ̍ti/ [adv] if you do something **to the best of your ability**, you do it as well as you can, even if you are not sure that you are doing it very well: *I have always done my work to the best of my ability.* | *All the children competed and performed to the best of their ability.*

4 to try to do something even though you might not succeed

- have a go
- give it a go/a try/a whirl

have a go /ˌhæv ə ˈgəʊ/ [v phrase] *I'm not sure I'll be able to persuade him, but I'll certainly have a go.* | **+ at** *I'll have a go at repairing the roof myself.*

give it a go/a try/a whirl /ˌgɪv ɪt ə ˈgəʊ, ə ˈtraɪ, ə ˈwɜːʳl/ [v phrase] spoken informal to try to do something you have not tried before and do not know if you will be successful at: *I've never done any acting before, but I'll give it a try.* | *It sounds like a great idea – let's give it a whirl.* | *You ought to give it a go at least.*

5 to try to get a job, position, prize etc

- try for
- go for
- try out for
- angle for
- make a bid for
- shoot for
- struggle for
- go all out
- audition

try for /ˈtraɪ fɔːʳ/ [phr v T] to try to get something you want very much, for example a job, a prize, or a chance to study somewhere: *Why don't you try for this job as an Assistant Scientific Officer?* | *I've decided to try for Harvard University.*

go for /ˈgəʊ fɔːʳ/ [phr v T] to try to get something you want very much, especially something that is difficult to achieve, such as a prize or a high position: *Why don't you go for a music scholarship?* | *Are you going to go for the senior manager's job?*

try out for /ˌtraɪ ˈaʊt fɔːʳ/ [phr v T] American to try to get chosen for a sports team or for a part in a play: *Joan tried out for the school basketball team.* | *I'm not going to bother trying out for the play – I know I'm not good enough!*

angle for /ˈæŋgəl fɔːʳ/ [phr v T not in passsive] to try to make someone give you something or say something good about you without asking them directly: *He was talking to Helen, angling for an invitation to her next party.* | *She asked us how she looked, obviously angling for a compliment.*

make a bid for /ˌmeɪk ə ˈbɪd fɔːʳ/ [v phrase] to try to get an important job or a position of power – used mainly in newspapers: *The party now feels the time is right to make a bid for power.* | **make a successful/unsuccessful bid for sth** *Mr Meaney made an unsuccessful bid for the presidency two years ago.*

shoot for /ˈʃuːt fɔːʳ/ [phr v T] American informal to try to get an important job or achieve something very difficult: *There are five Democrat candidates shooting for president this year.* | *Management is shooting for a 40% increase in productivity over six months.* | *I think you should go for it – shoot for the top!*

struggle for /ˈstrʌgəl fɔːʳ/ [v phrase] to make a lot of effort over a long period to get something that is very important to you, but that is very difficult to get: *The people are still struggling for liberation from a brutal, oppressive regime.* | *Many small businesses are struggling for survival in this difficult economic climate.* | *He struggled for the right words to say.* —**struggle** [n C] **+ for** *They are making some progress in their struggle for equal rights.*

go all out /gəʊ ˌɔːl ˈaʊt/ [v phrase] to put all your energy and determination into trying to get or win something **+ for** *The German team will be going all out for a win in next Saturday's game.* | **+ to do sth** *We're going all out to make our sales target this year.*

audition /ɔːˈdɪʃən/ [v I] to try to get a part in a play, concert, film etc by performing to a group of people who will judge whether or not you are suitable for it **+ for** *She met her husband when she auditioned for the part of Ophelia in an all-black production of 'Hamlet'.*

6 to try very hard to help someone

- bend over backwards to do sth
- go out of your way to do sth
- take the trouble to do sth

bend over backwards to do sth /ˌbend əʊvəʳ ˌbækwəʳdz tə 'du: (sth)/ [v phrase] to make every possible effort to be helpful or to please someone, even when this causes you difficulty or inconvenience: *I bend over backwards to help him, but I never get any thanks for it.* | *The school have bent over backwards to accommodate Jan's mobility difficulties.*

go out of your way to do sth /gəʊ ˌaʊt əv jɔ:ʳ ˌweɪ tə 'du: (sth)/ [v phrase] to make a special effort to help someone, especially someone who needs help and support: *When Annie arrived, Harriman went out of his way to make life pleasant for her.* | *Jennifer knew what a difficult time I was having, and went out of her way to be friendly.*

take the trouble to do sth /ˌteɪk ðə ˌtrʌbəl tə 'du: (sth)/ [v phrase] to make a special effort to do something you think will be useful or helpful: *Take the trouble to learn all of your students' names. They will appreciate it.* | *My bank manager took the trouble to write a very detailed letter answering my inquiry.* | *The head of department has been very helpful – he even took the trouble to show me round the premises during his lunch hour.*

7 when you try to do something

- attempt
- effort
- campaign
- drive

attempt /ə'tempt/ [n C] when you try to do something, especially something you have not tried before: *After four attempts, Mike finally passed his driving test.* | **+ an attempt to do sth** *All my attempts to get the machine working failed miserably.* | *It was a deliberate attempt to mislead the voters.* | **make an attempt** *The climbers will make another attempt to reach the summit today.* | **in an attempt to do sth** *The government has announced that it will fund an extra 10,000 doctors in an attempt to reduce waiting times for operations.*

effort /'efəʳt/ [n C/U] an attempt to do something, especially when this involves a lot of hard work or determination: *Cleaning up polluted rivers will take considerable time and effort.* | *Faster and faster he pulled on the rope, gasping with the effort.* | **+ to do sth** *All his efforts to convince Lucy failed.* | **+ at** *The workers went on strike after efforts at negotiation with management broke down.* | **in an effort to do sth** *The company has announced 500 job losses in an effort to cut costs.*

campaign /kæm'peɪn/ [n C] a planned series of activities that are intended to persuade people to do something or to bring social or political change **+ to do sth** *The government's campaign to recruit more black police officers has not been a success.* | **+ for** *the campaign for prison reform* | **election campaign** (=a campaign to win an election) *All kinds of extravagant promises were made during the election campaign.* | **advertising campaign** *The company has spent over £50 million on its latest advertising campaign.* | **launch/mount a campaign** (=start a campaign) *The company has launched an advertising campaign in the hope of attracting new customers.*

drive /draɪv/ [n C] a planned effort, especially by a company or a government, to achieve a particular kind of improvement within a short time **+ for** *We need a new drive for investment in Britain's inner cities.* | **+ to do sth** *The government must continue this drive to find new, cleaner forms of energy.* | **efficiency/economy/modernization etc drive** *As part of the bank's efficiency drive substantial cuts are being made in the workforce.*

to try sth to see if it is good

8 to try something to see if it is good

- try
- try out
- give sth a try
- sample
- have a go/bash
- try your hand at
- experiment with
- trial and error

try /traɪ/ [v T] to do or use something for a short time in order to find out if it is successful, if you enjoy it, or if it is suitable: *I tried aerobics once, but I didn't really enjoy it.* | *Have you tried those new barbecue-flavoured crisps?* | *His mother tried threats, bribery – everything, but Danny still refused to go to school.* | *There was no answer at his workplace, so Mandy tried his home number.* | **try doing sth** *I think you should try planning your essays in rough before you start writing.*

try out /ˌtraɪ 'aʊt/ [phr v T] to use a new method, a new product, or something that you have learned, in order to find out how good, how successful, or how suitable it is **try out sth** *They sell paint in very small cans so you can try out the different colours at home.* | *Dietmar enjoyed trying out his English on American troops stationed in Berlin.* | **try sth out** *It was six months before she had a chance to try her songs out in front of a live audience.*

give sth a try /ˌgɪv (sth) ə 'traɪ/ [v phrase] to try using or doing something, although you are not sure if it will succeed or if it is suitable or good: *I'm not sure that writing to complain will do much good, but we can give it a try.* | *Why don't we give that new wine bar a try?*

sample /'sɑ:mpl‖'sæm-/ [v T] to try an activity to see if you enjoy it and if you would like to do it some more: *The hotel provides an excellent base from which visitors can sample the delights of scuba diving and waterskiing.*

have a go/bash /ˌhæv ə 'gəʊ, 'bæʃ/ [v phrase] British informal to do something for the first time to see whether you can do it, whether you enjoy it etc: *She's never tried skiing before, but she's willing to have a go.* | *The competition's open to anyone, so why not have a bash?* | **have a go/bash at doing sth** *Most kids get the opportunity to have a bash at writing poetry when they're at school.* | **have a go on sth** (=try using a machine) *Can I have a go on your computer?*

try your hand at /ˌtraɪ jɔ:ʳ 'hænd æt/ [v phrase] to try an activity that is new to you and that interests you, especially something that you need to learn special skills for: *He first tried his hand at motor racing in 1963, but without much success.* | **try your hand at doing sth** *After she lost her job, she thought she'd try her hand at writing a novel.*

experiment with /ɪk'sperɪment wɪð/ [phr v T] to try something in order to see what it is like or what effect it has: *We're experimenting with a new filing system.* | *A new wave of rock bands experimented with different rhythms and beats.* | *A lot of fourteen and fifteen year olds experiment with drugs.*

trial and error /ˌtraɪəl ənd ˈerəʳ/ [n phrase] the process of trying a lot of different ways of doing something, in order to find out which one works best **by trial and error** (=using trial and error) *We found out by trial and error which plants could survive the dry conditions.* | **a process of trial and error** *We learn new skills through a process of trial and error.*

turn

to turn around, to change direction, or to turn upside down

1 to go around in circles

- turn
- go around
- spin
- rotate/revolve
- go/run/drive etc around in circles
- go/run/drive etc around and around
- whirl
- spiral
- swirl
- circle
- twirl

turn /tɜːʳn/ [v I] if something **turns**, it moves around a fixed central point: *Slowly the wheels of the train began to turn.* | *I heard the door knob turning, and then Frank opened the door and tiptoed in.* | *As the propeller stopped turning, Grady ran up to the plane.*

go around ALSO **go round** British /ˌgəʊ əˈraʊnd, ˌgəʊ ˈraʊnd/ [phr v I] to move in a continuous circular movement: *When the fan goes around it forces the warm air back down.* | *The gear was going round, but it didn't seem to be catching on anything.*

spin /spɪn/ [v I] to turn around many times very quickly: *The ice skater began to spin faster and faster.* | *The wheels were spinning in the mud, but the car wouldn't move.* | **+ around** ALSO **+ round** British *The boy was spinning around in his father's desk chair.*

rotate/revolve /rəʊˈteɪt‖ˈrəʊteɪt, rɪˈvɒlv‖rɪˈvɑːlv/ [v I] to turn around and around a fixed point: *The Earth rotates on its axis once every twenty-four hours.* | *A disco ball revolved slowly over the empty dance floor.* | *The stage rotates giving the audience a constantly changing view.*

go/run/drive etc around in circles ALSO **go/run/drive etc round in circles** especially British /gəʊ əˌraʊnd ɪn ˈsɜːʳkəlz, ˌgəʊ raʊnd ɪn ˈsɜːʳkəlz/ [v phrase] to go, run, drive etc continuously or repeatedly around in a circular way: *The children went round in circles till the music stopped.* | *We were driving around in circles, weaving through the parking lot.*

go/run/drive etc around and around ALSO **go/run/drive etc round and round** British /gəʊ əˌraʊnd ənd əˈraʊnd, gəʊ ˌraʊnd ənd ˈraʊnd/ [v phrase] to go around in circles many times: *Billy will sit and watch his train going round and round on its little track for hours.* | *The steers walked restlessly around and around their pen.*

whirl /wɜːʳl/ [v I] to spin around extremely quickly, often in an uncontrolled way: *The blades of the helicopter whirled powerfully overhead.* | **+ around** ALSO **+ round** British *Flies whirled round the piles of sticky sweets.* | *Dust and sand were whirling around in the air, as the desert wind began to get stronger.*

spiral /ˈspaɪərəl/ [v I] to move slowly upwards or downwards in a circular way around a central point, while also moving either in towards the centre or out from it: *Smoke spiralled upward from the chimney.* | *We watched the leaves spiral down from the trees in the cold autumn wind.*

swirl /swɜːʳl/ [v I] if water, dust, mist etc **swirls**, it keeps turning around quickly in a twisting, circular movement: *Dust swirled like smoke in the evening sunshine.* | **+ around** ALSO **round** British *Jessie's pale dress swirled round her slender ankles.* | *The wind swirling around the tree had blown all the snow away from its trunk.*

circle /ˈsɜːʳkəl/ [v I/T] if a bird or aircraft **circles**, it flies around above a particular place, waiting for something: *We all looked towards the sky where the vultures were circling.* | *The plane circled the runway several times before landing.* | **+ overhead/above etc** *Helicopters circled overhead, trying to get pictures of the crime scene.*

twirl /twɜːʳl/ [v I] if someone twirls, they spin around very quickly, especially as part of a dance: *Rachel took her father's hand and twirled in and out under his arm.* | **+ around/about** *Half a dozen couples were twirling about to a waltz.*

2 to make something turn around

- turn
- twist
- wind
- swivel
- twiddle

turn /tɜːʳn/ [v T] to make something **turn** by moving it with your hand: *Tim turned the handle slowly and pushed open the door.* | *She put the key in the ignition and turned it, but nothing happened.* | **turn sth around** (=so that it is facing the opposite direction) *If we turn the table around we can fit more chairs in the room.*

twist /twɪst/ [v T] to turn something with a quick firm circular movement: *'I can't get the top off.' 'Try twisting it the other way.'* | *We twisted and tugged to get the mussels loose from their shells.*

wind /waɪnd/ [v T] to turn something such as a handle or part of a machine around and around, especially in order to make something move or start working: *You wind the handle on the side to make the music play.* | *She wound the car window down to speak to the police officer.* | *My watch has stopped – I must have forgotten to wind it.*

swivel /ˈswɪvəl/ [v T] to turn something around on a central rod or point, usually so that it is facing a different direction: *He swivelled the camera on the tripod to follow her as she crossed the yard.* | **swivel sth around** ALSO **swivel sth round** British *She swivelled the computer screen around so that I could see it too.*

twiddle British **/twirl** American /ˈtwɪdl, twɜːʳl/ [v T] to turn something small backwards and forwards many times with your fingers, especially because you are bored, or are trying to make something work: *She sat in the bar twirling the stem of her wine glass, wishing she were somewhere else.* | *He kept twiddling the knobs on the radio trying to get a signal.*

3 to make something turn in circles very quickly

- spin
- twirl
- whirl

spin /spɪn/ [v T] to make something turn around and around extremely quickly: *Spin the wheel of the* *bicycle to make sure that it is fastened correctly.* | *He spun the dial on the padlock right, then left, then right again.*

twirl /twɜːʳl/ [v T] to repeatedly make something turn in circles or spin around, especially with your fingers: *I've never been able to twirl a baton.* | *He picked up a pen and twirled it between his fingers.* | *The man, without answering, began to twirl the ends of his moustache.*

whirl /wɜːʳl/ [v T] to make something spin around in the air extremely quickly: *Whirl the ingredients in a blender at high speed for a minute.* | *The warriors approached, whirling their swords and spears in the air.*

4 a turning movement

- **turn**
- **revolution**
- **spin**

turn /tɜːʳn/ [n C] the circular movement that a person or object makes when turning something or being turned: *She can do a 360-degree turn on water skis.* | *Loosen the screw one complete turn in order to release the valve.* | **+ of** *With three swift turns of the wheel, he steered the boat away from the rocks.*

revolution /ˌrevəˈluːʃən/ [n C] one complete circular movement around a fixed or central point – use this in technical contexts: *The shaft spins at 950 revolutions per minute.* | *The planet rotates in the same direction as its revolution around the sun.*

spin /spɪn/ [n C/U] a very fast turn that is repeated many times: *He made a quick spin to avoid the oncoming player.* | **+ of** *the spin of a propeller*

5 turning with a circular movement

- **revolving**
- **rotating**

revolving /rɪˈvɒlvɪŋ‖-ˈvɑːl-/ [adj only before noun] designed to turn with a circular movement: *A revolving door led into the hotel lobby.* | *The 28-story building is topped by a revolving restaurant that offers ever-changing views of the city.*

rotating /rəʊˈteɪtɪŋ‖ˈrəʊteɪtɪŋ/ [adj only before noun] able to turn with a circular movement – use this especially in technical contexts: *The plastic is cut by a rotating disc.* | *The stones are polished in a rotating drum full of abrasive powder.*

6 to turn your head or your body

- **turn**
- **turn around**
- **turn away**
- **turn your back**
- **turn your head**
- **turn on your heel**
- **swing around**
- **spin around**
- **swivel**

turn /tɜːʳn/ [v I] to **turn** your head or body so that you are looking in a different direction: *Campbell turned and walked out of the room.* | **+ to** *'What do you think we should do?' she said, turning to her husband.* | **+ to do sth** *She heard the door opening and turned to see who was coming in.*

turn around ALSO **turn round** British /ˌtɜːʳn əˈraʊnd, ˌtɜːʳn ˈraʊnd/ [phr v I] to turn your body so that you are looking in the opposite direction: *Ian, turn round and face the front!* | *I turned around quickly to see if anyone was following me.* | *'Does my dress look OK?' 'Turn around and let me see the back.'*

turn away /ˌtɜːʳn əˈweɪ/ [phr v I] to turn so that you are no longer facing someone, especially because you want to avoid them: *Alice turned away with tears in her eyes.* | *The scene was so sickening I had to turn away.* | **+ from** *She frowned and turned away from him without speaking.*

turn your back /ˌtɜːʳn jɔːʳ ˈbæk/ [v phrase] to turn so that you are no longer facing someone, especially because you are angry or disappointed, or because you are deliberately ignoring them: *As soon as I turn my back, the children start to misbehave.* | **+ on** *Don't turn your back on me – I'm talking to you!* | *She turned her back on him and began to walk away.*

turn your head /ˌtɜːʳn jɔːʳ ˈhed/ [v phrase] to **turn your head** in order to look at someone or in order to look away from someone: *She turned her head to avoid making eye contact with the beggar.* | *Whenever Suzie walks into a room all the men immediately turn their heads.*

turn on your heel /ˌtɜːʳn ɒn jɔːʳ ˈhiːl/ [v phrase] to quickly and suddenly turn, especially before walking away: *David angrily turned on his heel and marched towards the door.* | *When her ex-husband entered the room, she turned on her heel and left.*

swing around ALSO **swing round** British /ˌswɪŋ əˈraʊnd, ˌswɪŋ ˈraʊnd/ [phr v I] to turn around suddenly and quickly, especially because you are angry or surprised: *He swung around at the sound of her voice and smiled at her.* | *I felt a hand on my shoulder and swung round quickly to find Chris standing behind me.*

spin around ALSO **spin round** British /ˌspɪn əˈraʊnd, ˌspɪn ˈraʊnd/ [phr v I] to turn around very quickly, especially because you are angry or because something unexpected has suddenly happened: *The sudden crash made her spin round and look back down the passage.* | *Dobbs yelled back and spun around with clenched fists, ready to fight.*

swivel /ˈswɪvəl/ [v I] to turn around quickly as if you are fixed to a central point, or when you are sitting in a chair which can turn round: *Ralph swivelled in his chair and looked directly at Meg.* | **+ around** ALSO **+ round** British *Mr Tench swivelled round in astonishment as the men burst through his office door.*

7 to turn your body when you are lying down

- **turn over**
- **roll over**

turn over /ˌtɜːʳn ˈəʊvəʳ/ [phr v I] to change the position of your body while you are lying down, so that you are facing in a different direction: *The bed squeaks every time I turn over.* | *Turn over and I'll give you a massage.* | *He opened his eyes and turned over on his side, facing her.*

roll over /ˌrəʊl ˈəʊvəʳ/ [phr v I] to turn your body so that it is facing the opposite direction, in a single smooth movement: *The cat purred, rolled over on its back, and stretched.* | *I heard the alarm clock, but I rolled over and went back to sleep.*

8 to change your direction when you are walking or driving

- **turn**
- **change direction**
- **change course**
- **veer**
- **swerve**

turn /tɜːʳn/ [v I/T] to change your direction when you are walking or driving: *He saw a police car up ahead, so he turned and went down a side street.* |

Soon after leaving harbour, the ships turned and headed north. | **turn left/right** *Turn left at the next intersection.* | **+ back** *It's getting late – I think we should turn back before it gets dark.* | **+ off** (=leave a street in order to go down another street) *Turn off Delaney Road just after the church.* | **+ onto/into** (=start going along another street after changing direction) *Turn onto Lowell Street, then go straight for three blocks.* | **turn a corner** *I turned a corner and nearly ran into Caroline.*

change direction /ˌtʃeɪndʒ dəˈrekʃən/ [v phrase] to turn while you are moving so that you start going in a different direction: *The horse abruptly changed direction, nearly throwing the rider off.* | *Changing direction on skis isn't difficult once you've learned the technique.*

change course /ˌtʃeɪndʒ ˈkɔːʳs/ [v phrase] if a vehicle, ship, or aircraft **changes course**, it changes the direction in which it is travelling: *The yacht changed course and approached the island.* | *The plane must change course to avoid flying through the storm.*

veer /vɪəʳ/ [v I] if a vehicle or moving object **veers**, it suddenly and unexpectedly changes direction **+ off/away/across etc** *The car suddenly veered across the road into oncoming traffic.* | *The boat was heading for the rocks but at the last minute veered off in another direction.*

swerve /swɜːʳv/ [v I] if a vehicle or moving object **swerves**, it suddenly changes direction, especially in order to avoid hitting something: *The driver swerved to avoid a child, and crashed into a signpost.* | **+ across/into/towards etc** *Dozens were injured when a passenger bus swerved into the wrong lane and slammed into another bus.*

9 when a road or river changes direction

- bend
- curve
- turn
- wind
- twist
- weave

bend /bend/ [n C] the place where a road or river turns: *The taxi went around the bend at an alarming speed.* | **+ in** *The balcony overlooked a wide bend in the river.* | **round a bend** *As we rounded the bend, I could see the town up ahead.*

curve /kɜːʳv/ [n C] a place where there is a bend in the road: *He lost control of the car on a sharp curve.* | **round a curve** *I rounded the curve looking for a place to pull over.* —**curve** [v I] *The road curves to the left as you go up the hill.*

turn ALSO **turning** British /tɜːʳn, ˈtɜːʳnɪŋ/ [n C] a place where you can **turn** and go into another road: *Take the first turning after the traffic lights.* | *We were supposed to take Highway 12, but I think we missed the turn.*

wind /waɪnd/ [v I] if a road, path, or river **winds**, it frequently turns and changes direction, in smooth curves **+ between/through/up etc** *A narrow road wound up the hillside towards the little house.* | *The path wound through the orchard and between small beds of flowers.* | **wind its way** *The staircase appears almost to be floating on air, as it winds its way up three stories.* —**winding** [adj only before noun] *She hated driving on the winding mountain roads at night.*

twist /twɪst/ [v I] to frequently turn and change direction, especially in small but sharp turns **+ up/through/towards etc** *A dry stream bed twisted through thick tree roots.* | **twist its way** *We approached Assisi via the dusty road that twists its way up Monte Subasio.* —**twisting** [adj only before noun] *Wild flowers grew on either side of the twisting path.*

weave /wiːv/ [v I/T] to turn and change direction, especially around things, in smooth curves **+ through/up/across etc** *The river weaved across the plain, towards the sea.* | **weave its way** *The old highway weaved its way through Tucson.*

10 when a vehicle, ship etc turns over in an accident

- turn over
- roll over
- capsize
- overturn

turn over /ˌtɜːʳn ˈəʊvəʳ/ [phr v I] if a vehicle **turns over**, it turns upside down, especially as a result of an accident: *The car smashed into the post, turned over, and burst into flames.* | *The train was travelling so fast that when it came off the rails it turned over onto its roof.*

roll over /ˌrəʊl ˈəʊvəʳ/ [phr v I] if a vehicle or ship **rolls over**, it turns upside down because it is not correctly balanced: *The truck jack-knifed and then rolled over.* | *Ships have stabilizers to prevent them from rolling over in rough seas.*

capsize /kæpˈsaɪz‖ˈkæpsaɪz/ [v I/T] if a boat **capsizes**, or someone or something **capsizes** it, it turns over in the water: *The ship capsized in rough waters with the loss of 208 lives.* | *People were fighting for places in the lifeboat, and there was a real danger of it capsizing.* | *A huge wave struck the side of our boat, almost capsizing it.*

overturn /ˌəʊvəʳˈtɜːʳn/ [v I/T] if a vehicle or boat **overturns**, or someone or something **overturns** it, it turns over: *The truck had overturned, but the driver was not injured.* | *The whole crew was drowned when their boat overturned in a storm.* | *During the riots several cars were overturned and set on fire.*

11 to turn something upside down

- turn over
- turn
- flip
- invert

turn over /ˌtɜːʳn ˈəʊvəʳ/ [phr v T] **turn sth over** *Do not turn your exam papers over until I tell you to.* | *She turned the envelope over and began making notes on the back.* | **turn over sth** *The children were turning over the rocks to see what was underneath.*

turn /tɜːʳn/ [v T] to **turn** something so that the other side of it is facing upwards or outwards: *Continue to turn the fritter until both sides are golden brown.* | *I'll read the story and you turn the pages. OK, honey?* | **turn sth upside down** *Take out the spark plugs and turn the cylinder block upside down.*

flip /flɪp/ [v T] to turn something over with a quick, sharp movement: *Come help me flip this mattress.* | **flip sth over** *She flipped the pancakes over with one smooth movement.* | **flip over sth** *I flipped over the card to see what was written on the other side.*

invert /ɪnˈvɜːʳt/ [v T] formal to turn something upside down: *A camera inverts the image it receives.* | *Invert the cake and pan on a wire rack and remove the pan.*

two

1 two

▸ two ▸ a couple

two /tu:/ [quantifier] 2: *We've got two dogs and three cats.* | *There used to be five churches in the town. Now there are only two.* | *It takes two hours to get there.* | **+ of** *Two of the boys in the hockey team were sick.*

a couple /ə 'kʌpəl / [quantifier] **informal** two: *I haven't got any stamps – could you lend me a couple?* | **+ of** *I've got a couple of tickets for the game on Saturday.* | *She lived in Japan for a couple of years.*

2 two people

▸ couple ▸ duo
▸ pair

couple /'kʌpəl/ [n C] two people who are together, especially because they are married or have a sexual relationship: *the couple who live next door to me* | *A young couple were walking hand in hand along the beach.* | **a married couple** (=a couple who are married) *The house was bought by a young married couple.*

pair /peəʳ/ [n C] two people who are doing something together, or who are similar or connected in some way **+ of** *They felt like a pair of burglars, enjoying themselves in someone else's house while the owner was away.* | **in pairs** (=working in groups of two) *Do the next exercise in pairs.* | **a strange/funny/friendly etc pair** *Bill and his brother were a rather odd-looking pair.*

duo /'dju:əʊ‖'du:-/ [n C] two people who work or perform together: *a brilliant young comedy duo* | *the successful management duo of Doug Livermore and Ray Clemence*

3 two things of the same type that are used together

▸ pair ▸ twin

pair /peəʳ/ [n C] two things of the same type that are used together **a pair of shoes/socks/gloves/earrings etc** *I need a new pair of shoes.*

twin /twɪn/ [adj only before noun] use this to talk about two things that are the same as each other and exist together or are used together: *the new twin bridges over the river Clyde* | *a PC with twin disk drives* | **twin beds** *I asked for a room with twin beds.*

4 each one of two people or things

▸ both ▸ neither
▸ each ▸ each other/one another
▸ either

both /bəʊθ/ [predeterminer/quantifier] use this to talk about two people or things together: *We both really enjoyed the evening.* | *I can't decide which dress to buy, I like them both.* | *Both drivers were injured, but not seriously.* | **+ of** *Both of us felt ill the next day.* | *Both of the windows had been broken.* | **both the/these/my etc** *Both her attackers were wearing masks and gloves.* | *Both her parents are doctors.*

each /i:tʃ/ [determiner/pron] use this to talk about two or more people or things when you think of them as separate: *My wife and I each have our own bank account.* | **+ of** *In the cup final, each player gets a medal, even the substitutes.*

either /'aɪðəʳ‖'i:-/ [determiner/pron] use this to talk about one of two people, places, or things, especially when it does not matter which one: *'Would you like tea or coffee?' 'Either – I don't mind.'* | *You can enjoy the view from either window.* | **+ of** *If you see either of these men, contact the police immediately.* | *She says she has never seen either of them before.* | **either sb/sth or sb/sth** *I usually drink either coke or beer.*

neither /'naɪðəʳ‖'ni:-/ [determiner/pron] not one of two people, places, or things, and not the other: *'Do you want milk or lemon in your tea?' 'Neither thanks.'* | *The game wasn't very exciting. Neither team played well.* | **+ of** *Luckily, neither of the passengers was hurt in the crash.* | **neither sb/sth nor sb/sth** *Neither Mary nor the doctor was willing to use the word 'cancer'.*

each other/one another /i:tʃ 'ʌðəʳ, ˌwʌn ə'nʌðəʳ/ [pron] use this to say that each of two people does the same thing to the other, or has the same feeling about the other: *The twins looked at one another and giggled.* | *We don't see each other so often now.* | **each other's/one another's** *They used to borrow each other's clothes.*

5 someone whose brother or sister was born at the same time

▸ twin

twin /twɪn/ [n C] one of two children who were born on the same day to the same mother: *I never realized that you and Sammy were twins.* | *Joey's my twin.* | **twin brother/sister** *Sally and her twin sister still spend a lot of time together now that they are adults.* | **identical twins** (=twins who look exactly the same) *There have been a lot of interesting studies done on identical twins separated at birth.* | **fraternal twins** (=twins who do not look the same) *Noelle and Craig are fraternal twins.*

6 intended for two people

▸ for two ▸ two-man
▸ double

for two /fəʳ 'tu:/ [adv] use this about something that is intended for only two people: *We'd like a table for two please.* | *a romantic weekend in Paris for two*

double /'dʌbəl/ [adj only before noun] **double room/bed/mattress** a room, bed etc that is intended for two people: *The room contained a double bed, a wardrobe, and a small chest of drawers.* | *Double rooms cost $80, single rooms are $50.*

two-man /'tu: mæn/ [adj only before noun] **two-man tent/canoe** a tent etc that is designed for two people: *We all squeezed into Ralph's small two-man tent.* | *They paddled down the river in a two-man canoe.*

7 twice the normal size

▸ double

double /'dʌbəl/ [adj only before noun] twice the amount, number etc: *The band has just released a new double album.* | *Last year she suffered the double blow of losing her father and discovering that she had cancer.* | **double whiskey/brandy etc** *A double brandy,* *please.* | **a double portion of sth** *I ordered fish and a double portion of chips.* —**double** [n C] *Three whiskeys, please – two singles and one double.*

8 when something happens two times

- twice
- a couple of times

twice /twaɪs/ [adv] *The weather was great – it only rained twice in three weeks.* | *She's been married twice before.* | **twice a day/month/year etc** (=when something happens regularly two times every day, month etc) *I play golf twice a week.* | *Staff meetings are held twice a month.* | **twice over** British *You should read the exam question twice over before answering it.* | *The company's accounts were checked twice over, the second time by an independent auditor.*

a couple of times /ə 'kʌpəl əv taɪmz/ [adv] informal two or three times: *I've been out with Harry a couple of times, but I wouldn't call him my boyfriend.*

9 consisting of two things of the same type

- double
- dual
- twofold

double /'dʌbəl/ [adj only before noun] *I pushed the double doors open and walked into the office.* | *The report and photographs fitted nicely onto a double page.* | *You cannot park on double yellow lines.*

dual /'djuːəl‖'duːəl/ [adj only before noun] having two types of one particular thing: *It's much safer if you learn to drive in a car which has dual controls.* | *He found it difficult to cope with the dual pressures of work and home life.* | **dual role/function/purpose/aim** *Don Jose continued in his dual role of father and teacher to his son.* | *The magistrate's court has a dual function: to try minor cases and consider whether in more serious cases there is enough evidence for a trial to take place.* | **dual nationality/citizenship** (=when someone has the legal right to live in two different countries) *He has dual nationality because his father was born in Pakistan and his mother is British.*

twofold /'tuːfəʊld/ [adj] formal if the reasons, aims, or effects etc, of something are **twofold**, there are two reasons, aims, or effects: *My reasons for leaving are twofold.* | *This new legislation will have a twofold effect on businesses.*

10 when a number or amount is twice as big as another

- twice
- double
- twofold

twice /twaɪs/ [predeterminer/adv] **twice as big/fast/much/many etc** bigger, faster etc by 100%: *This sweater would have cost twice as much if I'd bought it in England.* | **twice the size/my salary/his age etc** *He married a woman who was twice his age.* | *It's about twice the length of a football field.* | *Full cream milk contains about twice the fat of skimmed milk.*

double /'dʌbəl/ [predeterminer] twice as much as an amount, number etc **double the amount/number/weight/size/cost etc** *Over 30% of marriages end in divorce, which is double the number 20 years ago.* | *The house is now worth double the amount we paid for it.*

twofold /'tuːfəʊld/ [adj only before noun] two times as much or as many of something **a twofold increase** *The last ten years have seen a twofold increase in the numbers of deaths on the road.*

type

RELATED WORDS

- to write something with a typewriter *see* **write**

1 a type of person or thing

- type/kind/sort
- style
- category
- class
- variety
- genre
- form
- nature
- of that/his/their etc ilk
- like this/like that

type/kind/sort /taɪp, kaɪnd, sɔːʳt/ [n C] a group of things or people that are similar to each other in some way, or a thing or person that belongs to such a group. **Kind** and **sort** are more common than **type** in spoken English. Use **type** when you are talking about technical subjects or when you are describing something in an exact way: *I'll get you some ice-cream. What kind would you like?* | **+ of** *The floor was made of three different types of wood.* | *What sort of fish is this?* | *'What type of music do you like?' 'Mainly dance music and some indie.'* | *She's the kind of person you can always rely on.* | *There are two sorts of politician – the ones who really want to help people, and the ones who just want power.* | **of this/that type etc** *Accidents of this type are extremely common.* | *It's a club for writers and actors and people of that sort.* | **of various/many/different types etc** *They export farming machinery and tools of various kinds.*

style /staɪl/ [n C] a particular type of building, art, literature, music etc: *The new library is a blend of various architectural styles.* | **+ of** *a completely new style of painting* —**style** [adj/adv] **western-style/Japanese style etc** *The room was simply furnished, Japanese-style.*

category /'kætɪ̥gəri‖-gɔːri/ [n C] a group that people or things of the same type are divided into for a particular purpose – use this when there are several groups and there is a clear system for deciding which group something belongs to: *Emma Thompson won an Oscar in the Best Actress category.* | *The novels are divided up into three categories: historical, romantic, and crime.* | **+ of** *Insurance companies identify six main categories of driver.*

class /klɑːs‖klæs/ [n C] a number of people or things that are considered as being of the same group because they have the same physical features, qualities etc **+ of** *French is one of a class of languages known as the Romance languages.* | *Doctors are reluctant to prescribe a new class of drugs, especially ones which need to be taken for long periods of time.*

variety /və'raɪəti/ [n C] a type of thing that is different from another similar type **+ of** *The French make many varieties of cheese, from both cows' and goats' milk.* | *At that time, all newsreaders spoke a variety of English spoken in southern England, known as Received Pronunciation.*

genre /'ʒɒnrə‖'ʒɑːnrə/ [n C] formal a type of literature, film, or work of art: *Science fiction as a genre is relatively new.* | *Italian filmmakers made their own versions of the classic Hollywood genres – the western, the gangster film, the musical.*

form /fɔːʳm/ [n C] a **form** of something is one type of it of all the ones that are possible **+ of** *Melanoma is a form of skin cancer.* | *Britain has a constitutional form of government.* | *Sugar in chocolate and other forms of confectionery is one of the major causes of tooth decay.*

nature /ˈneɪtʃəʳ/ [n singular] a particular type of thing **of a political/historical/technical/scientific/ sexual nature** *The support being given is primarily of a practical nature.* | *books of an erotic nature* | **of a different/similar nature** *On the plains the farmers have to deal with frequent floods, but up in the hills their problems are of a different nature.* | **of that nature** *Children at this age commonly refer to being eaten up by tigers and lions and things of that nature.* | **be in the nature of sth** (=to be like something) *The cruise was to be in the nature of a 'rest cure'.*

of that/his/their etc ilk /əv ˌðæt ˈɪlk/ [adj phrase] of that type, his type etc – use this especially about types that you do not like or respect: *Environmentalists, feminists, and others of that ilk regularly try to drive shows like this off the air.* | *Desserts ($5) were of the tiramisu, crème brûlée, chocolate torte ilk.*

like this/like that /laɪk ˈðɪs, laɪk ˈðæt/ [adj phrase] **especially spoken** of the type that you have just been talking about: *The children need new pens and pencils and things like that.* | *People like that really annoy me.* | *I'm not sure what to do. I've never been in a situation like this before.*

2 a type of plant or animal

- species
- breed
- variety
- strain

species /ˈspiːʃiːz/ [n C] a group of animals or plants that are all similar and can breed together to produce young animals or plants of the same type **+ of** *There are over forty species of bird living on the island.* | *Scientists have discovered a new species of Eucalyptus tree.* | **endangered species** (=one that might not exist for much longer) *The giant panda is an endangered species. There are fewer than a thousand living in the wild.*

breed /briːd/ [n C] a type of animal, especially one that has been developed by man, such as a dog, cat, or a farm animal: *Most dairy herds today are of Friesian or Holstein breeds.* | **+ of** *What breed of dog is that? I've never seen one like it before.* | *It's a very unusual breed of goat, dating back to the time of Cleopatra.*

variety /vəˈraɪəti/ [n C] a type of plant or animal that is different from another similar type: *South American growers use the best US seed varieties.* | **+ of** *This is a new variety of apple; we're selling it for the first time.* | *It may be possible to create varieties of fish that have resistance to common diseases.*

strain /streɪn/ [n C] a type of plant, animal, bacteria etc that has one particular feature that makes it different from others of the same type – use this in scientific or technical contexts **+ of** *A pure-bred strain of barley is required in the production of this whisky.* | *A particularly hardy strain of the virus can make you ill for over a week.*

3 a type of product

- brand
- make
- model

brand /brænd/ [n C] a type of product made by a particular company – use this about products that you use every day such as food or drink or cleaning materials: *They sell all the usual kinds of coffee, but also some less well-known brands.* | **+ of** *Coke and Pepsi are the most popular brands of cola.* | *my favourite brand of toothpaste*

make /meɪk/ [n C] a type of product made by a particular company – use this about things such as machines, equipment, and cars, not about food or drink: *What make is your washing machine?* | **+ of** *'What make of car was she driving?' 'A Mercedes.'*

model /ˈmɒdl‖ˈmɑːdl/ [n C] one particular type of car or machine from among the various types that a company produces: *'What make is the car?' 'It's a Ford.' 'And what model?' 'An Escort 1.8L.'* | *We produce a range of different computers, but this is our most popular model.*

4 to say that someone or something belongs to a particular type

- categorize
- classify
- stereotype
- pigeonhole
- under

categorize ALSO **categorise** British /ˈkætɪ̯gəraɪz/ [v T] to decide that someone or something belongs to a particular group of people or things that have similar qualities **categorize sb/sth as sth** *Dali was categorized as a surrealist painter.* | *Forecasts suggest that by the year 2010, only about 30 percent of U.S. households will be categorized as middle class.*

classify /ˈklæsɪ̯faɪ/ [v T] to put things or people into particular groups, especially according to an official or scientific system **classify sb/sth as sth** *Carpentry and furniture making are usually classified as skilled trades.* | **classify sb/sth by/according to sth** *Wines can be classified according to their sugar content – that is dry, medium or sweet.* | *Eggs are classified by weight as Extra Large, Large, Medium, Small, and Peewee.*

stereotype /ˈsteriətaɪp/ [v T] to decide unfairly, that certain people have particular qualities, abilities, or needs, for example because they are of a particular sex, race, or social class: *Teachers often stereotype kids who speak with strong regional accents.* | **stereotype sb as sth** *There is a tendency to stereotype childless women as being hard and career-orientated.*

pigeonhole /ˈpɪdʒɪ̯nhəʊl/ [v T] to say that someone or something can be described as a particular type or group, in a way that is too simple and therefore unfair: *You shouldn't pigeonhole people according to your first impressions of them.* | *When your band becomes successful, people immediately try to pigeonhole you, but we're into all kinds of music – dance, rock, jazz, blues.*

under /ˈʌndəʳ/ [prep] if you include something **under** a particular category or heading, you decide that it belongs to that particular group of things **classify/categorize/file/list sth under sth** *In our library, novels are classified under Crime, Romance, and General.* | *The Association of British Travel Agents is listed under 'Trade Associations and Professional Bodies' in the Yellow Pages.*

typical

when something or someone is a good example of the type that they belong to

RELATED WORDS

▸ *see also* **usually, normal/ordinary, unusual**

1 a typical person or thing

- ▸ typical
- ▸ representative
- ▸ archetypal
- ▸ classic
- ▸ textbook case/example
- ▸ stereotype

typical /ˈtɪpɪkəl/ [adj] *With his shorts and camera around his neck, he looked like a typical tourist.* | *'Is there a typical New York breakfast?' 'Bagels and coffee.'* | *On a typical day, the president receives more than 4,500 letters.* | *a typical American diner, with twangy-voiced waitresses and vinyl booths* | **+ of** *This painting is typical of Manet's portraits of Morisot – a beautiful woman, gazing sadly out at the viewer.* —**typically** [adv] *Everyone admired his typically Greek fearlessness when dealing with any official.*

representative /ˌreprɪˈzentətɪv/ [adj] formal someone or something that is **representative** of the group that they belong to is typical of it, and shows what the others in the group are like **+ of** *These paintings are representative of the kind of work being done by young artists nowadays.* | *Would you say that his views were representative of the majority of French voters?* | **representative sample** *For our survey we asked a representative sample of voters to give us their opinions.*

archetypal /ˈɑːʳkɪtaɪpəl/ [adj usually before noun] the **archetypal** person or thing is the most typical example of that kind of person or thing, and has all their most important qualities: *Indiana Jones is the archetypal adventure hero.* | *the archetypal pushy Hollywood mother* —**archetype** [n C] *Merlin is the archetype of the Wise Old Man.*

classic /ˈklæsɪk/ [adj usually before noun] a **classic** example of something is a very typical and very good example of it **+ of** *The misunderstanding was nobody's fault and was a classic example of bad communication.* | *The invention of the X-ray was a classic case of discovering something by accident.* | *She made the classic mistake of trying to drive away without releasing the hand brake.*

textbook case/example /ˈtekstbʊk ˌkeɪs, ɪgˌzɑːmpəl‖-ɪgˌzæm-/ [n C] a situation in which things happen in a very typical and expected way **+ of** *The Apple Computer company was a textbook case for business schools about how two guys working out of a garage could change the world.* | *This is a textbook example of how Hollywood undermines its best ideas, by insisting on happy endings, even when they are completely implausible.*

stereotype /ˈsteriətaɪp/ [n C] a fixed idea which most people have in their minds about what people of a particular type or from a particular country are like, but which is not actually true: *The film is full of stereotypes: a stupid blonde, a fat American tourist, and a gay man with huge muscles.* | **+ of** *Charles quite plainly did not fit the stereotype of a successful, high powered businessman.* | **racial/sexual stereotype** *They rejected the sexual stereotype of blue for a boy and pink for a girl, and dressed their baby in other colors instead.* | *the racial stereotype of Asian girls as quiet and hard-working* —**stereotypical** /ˌsteriəˈtɪpɪkəl◂/ [adj] *Some people find his novels offensive because of the stereotypical black people he portrays.*

2 typical behaviour or qualities

- ▸ typical
- ▸ characteristic
- ▸ just what you'd expect
- ▸ be just like
- ▸ that's sb all over
- ▸ true to form
- ▸ would
- ▸ the inevitable
- ▸ be in character

typical /ˈtɪpɪkəl/ [adj] behaviour or actions that are **typical** of a person are just what you usually expect them to do, especially when this is something bad or annoying: *'Dad forgot to mail the letter.' 'That's just typical!'* | *Mrs Quilley greeted the guests with typical charm and confidence.* | *This is typical adolescent behaviour – part of the process of becoming independent from your parents.* | **it is typical of sb to do sth** *It's typical of Ramon to waste time when he knows we're already late.* —**typically** [adv] *Aunt Lilly's gifts were typically generous, and reflected her impeccable taste.*

characteristic /ˌkærᵻktəˈrɪstɪk◂/ [adj] very typical of a particular type of thing, or of someone's character or usual behaviour: *Each species of bird has its own characteristic song.* | *Larry, with characteristic generosity, invited everyone back to his house.* | **+ of** *This pattern is characteristic of the local architecture.* —**characteristically** [adv] *Mrs Bhalla started to apologise in her characteristically nervous manner.*

just what you'd expect /ˌdʒʌst wɒt juːd ɪkˈspekt/ [adj phrase] if you say that something is **just what you'd expect**, you mean that it is exactly what your idea of someone makes you expect them to do: *Jenny's house is very clean and neat, just what you'd expect.* | *He was annoyed, but he soon got over it – just what you'd expect, in fact.*

be just like /biː ˌdʒʌst ˈlaɪk/ [v phrase] if you say that someone's action or behaviour is **just like** them, you mean that it is typical of them in a way that annoys you: *You have left everything to the last minute. That's just like you.* | **it is just like sb to do sth** *It's just like Uncle Roy to invite us all to lunch and then forget to tell Aunt Sarah.* | *It would be just like my son to get the measles twice.*

that's sb all over /ðæts (sb) ɔːl ˈəʊvəʳ/ used for saying that you are not surprised that someone has done something or behaved in a particular way, because it's the kind of thing they often do: *He was late, of course, but that's Tim all over.* | *'That's Dora all over,' interrupted Rose with a sniff. 'Once she gets an idea into her head, nothing will stop her.'*

true to form /ˌtruː tə ˈfɔːʳm/ [adv] if you say that someone does something **true to form** you mean it is very typical of them, especially when it is something annoying: *True to form, Oliver turned up late and drunk.* | *They promised to pay by Friday and yes, true to form, the money didn't arrive till Wednesday.*

would /wʊd/ [modal verb] you say someone **would** do something when they do something that is typical of them and you want to criticize them for it: *'Janice is going to be late for the meeting.' 'She would be!'* | *'And then Harry got drunk.' 'He would do, wouldn't he!'*

the inevitable /ði ɪˈnevᵻtəbəl/ [adj phrase only before noun] usual and expected for a particular person or type of person or a situation – you can often use this in humorous contexts: *It was a typical student's room with the inevitable Van Gogh print on the wall.* | *Dinner started with the inevitable chicken* *soup.* | *In the subway I got cornered by the inevitable drunkard wanting to give me some advice.*

be in character /biː ɪn ˈkærəktəʳ/ [v phrase] an action or remark that **is in character** is typical of someone's character: *Julie said that? That doesn't seem to be in character at all.* | *His reaction was quite in character. The man had no respect for education, and it was no surprise when he took his son out of school.*

3 to be a typical example of someone or something

- be a good/excellent/perfect etc example
- characterize
- typify
- epitomize
- be the epitome of
- personify

be a good/excellent/perfect etc example /biː ə ˌgʊd ɪgˈzɑːmpəl‖-ˈzæm-/ [v phrase] something that **is a good**, **excellent**, or **perfect example** of a group or type of thing, has all the usual and typical qualities of that group or type: *There are many beautiful Norman churches in this part of England. Iffley church is a good example.* | *If you want to know how not to make a video, this is a perfect example!* | *France produces some of the world's best dessert wines, and this is an excellent example.* | **+ of** *The fox is a good example of a wild animal that has adapted to living in towns.*

characterize ALSO **characterise** British /ˈkærəktəraɪz/ [v T not in progressive] to be typical of a person, place, or thing: *We approached the big empty square that characterizes the centre of Chinese cities.* | *Bright, vibrant colors characterize his paintings.* | *Robinson's photographs are characterized by the intense contrasts of dark and light areas, and the consequent loss of detail.*

typify /ˈtɪpəfaɪ/ [v T not in progressive] to be a typical example of a type of person, thing, attitude, or situation: *This letter typifies his loyalty and consideration.* | *Burke's arrogance seems to typify this government's approach.* | *Mrs Maugham's attitude towards the television typified her whole moral outlook.*

epitomize ALSO **epitomise** British /ɪˈpɪtəmaɪz/ [v T not in progressive] to be the most typical example of a type of person, thing, attitude or situation: *His poems epitomize the feelings of the generation of soldiers that fought in World War I.* | *The auto assembly line epitomizes the conditions that contribute to employee dissatisfaction.*

be the epitome of /biː ði ɪˈpɪtəmi ɒv/ [v phrase] to be the best possible example of a particular type of person or thing or of a particular quality: *Christine's clothes are the epitome of good taste.* | *With her neat hair and her flat, sensible shoes, she was the epitome of the traditional librarian.*

personify /pəʳˈsɒnəfaɪ‖-ˈsɑː-/ [v T not in progressive] if someone **personifies** a particular quality, they are the perfect example of someone who has that quality: *The little boy seemed to personify the poverty and famine of his country.* | *To the school children, kindness and beauty were personified by their teacher Miss Appleby.*

4 not typical

- atypical
- uncharacteristic
- not be like/be unlike
- be out of character
- untypical

atypical /eɪˈtɪpɪkəl/ [adj] belonging to a type or group, but not having the usual qualities of that type or group: *Such letters of complaint are atypical; the foundation usually receives nothing but praise and admiration for our work.* | **+ of** *This bird is atypical of most species here in that it does not build a nest.*

uncharacteristic /ˌʌnkærəktəˈrɪstɪk/ [adj] not typical of a situation or of someone's character, and therefore surprising: *It was summer and despite the uncharacteristic chill in the air, the tourists were swarming the beaches.* | *With uncharacteristic modesty, Will explained his contribution to the development of the film medium.* —**uncharacteristically** [adv] *In the morning Narendra was uncharacteristically quiet, and I asked her what was wrong.*

not be like/be unlike /nɒt biː ˈlaɪk, biː ʌnˈlaɪk/ [v phrase] if you say it **is not like** someone or **is unlike** them to do something, you mean it is not typical of them to behave in that way, and it is strange or surprising: *Cheer up Maria. It isn't like you to be as depressed as this.* | *It's unlike him to drink so much – I hope he is all right.* | *I don't understand why Mr Beanie is being so nice today – it's just not like him.*

be out of character /biː ˌaʊt əv ˈkærəktəʳ/ [v phrase] an action which is **out of character** is not typical of someone's character and usual behaviour: *I can't believe Andrew wrote this letter – it seems so out of character.* | *'Jane never said a word all morning.' 'That sounds very out of character to me.'*

untypical /ʌnˈtɪpɪkəl / [adj] not typical of the usual behaviour of a person or group: *The train's 20-minute delay, my Japanese friend informed me, was most untypical.* | *For some reason, and with untypical boldness, she took a step forward and walked into the room.* | **+ of** *The solemn tone of this story is untypical of her usual style.*

Uu

ugly

RELATED WORDS

opposite: **beautiful**

▸ *see also* **look (9-10)**

1 person

- ugly
- hideous
- repulsive
- grotesque
- unsightly
- he's/she's no oil-painting

ugly /ˈʌgli/ [adj] extremely unattractive, with a face that is not at all nice to look at: *We hated our uncle. He was fat and ugly, with tiny eyes and a long, pointed nose.* | *An ugly little man came over and offered to buy me a drink.*

hideous /ˈhɪdiəs/ [adj] extremely ugly, especially because you were born with something wrong with you: *In fairy stories the Prince is always very handsome, and the witch hideous.* | *a man with a hideous twisted lip*

repulsive /rɪˈpʌlsɪv/ [adj] very ugly and extremely

unpleasant to look at, especially so that people do not like to look at you: *Delia was frightened of the operation, because afterwards she knew she would look repulsive.* | **+ to** *The patient's disease was so terrible that his own skin was repulsive to him.*

grotesque /grəʊˈtesk/ [adj] extremely ugly in a strange or unnatural way: *The boy was twisting one side of his face in grotesque imitation of his grandfather.* | *Suddenly the grotesque figure of the hunchback Quasimodo loomed out of the darkness.* —**grotesquely** [adv] *Jacob lay on the bed with his mouth open. His face was purple and grotesquely swollen.*

unsightly /ʌnˈsaɪtli/ [adj usually before noun] an **unsightly** spot, mark, hair on your face etc is very unattractive **unsightly scar/fat/mark/spot/hair etc** *The accident left Simon with unsightly scars.* | *Electrolysis gets rid of unsightly facial hair.*

he's/she's no oil-painting British **/she's no Miss America** American /hiːz, ʃiːz nəʊ ˈɔɪl peɪntɪŋ, ʃiːz nəʊ mɪs əˈmerɪkə/ informal use this as a humorous way of saying that someone is ugly: *'What's Anna's new boyfriend like?' 'Well, he's nice, but he's no oil painting.'*

2 not good-looking

- not very good-looking
- unattractive/not attractive
- plain
- homely
- not much to look at

not very good-looking /nɒt veri ˌgʊd ˈlʊkɪŋ/ [adj phrase] not nice to look at – use this as a less direct way of saying someone is unattractive: *He's a nice guy, but not very good-looking.*

unattractive/not attractive /ˌʌnəˈtræktɪv◂, nɒt əˈtræktɪv/ [adj] not nice to look at and not sexually attractive in a physical way: *Like many teenage girls, she was worried that she was unattractive.* | *He wasn't a particularly attractive man, but there was something about him that women liked.* | **find sb unattractive** (=think that someone is unattractive) *She was crazy about Carl, and couldn't understand why we found him unattractive.*

plain /pleɪn/ [adj] someone who is **plain**, especially a woman, is not ugly but is not at all good-looking: *Catherine, who had been rather plain as a child, was now an attractive young woman.* | *Miles was the plain one in an otherwise good-looking family.*

homely /ˈhəʊmli/ [adj] American someone who is **homely** is not at all good-looking: *The waitress was a homely girl from Kansas.* | *Brad was a serious boy, very ordinary-looking but not downright homely.*

not much to look at /nɒt ˌmʌtʃ tə ˈlʊk æt/ [adj phrase] if you say that someone is **not much to look at**, you mean that they are not good-looking, especially when other things about them are attractive: *Edward's not much to look at, but he has a great personality.*

3 object/building etc

- ugly
- unsightly
- unattractive
- hideous
- revolting
- monstrosity
- an eyesore
- blot on the landscape

ugly /ˈʌgli/ [adj] very unpleasant to look at: *Local residents think that the new shopping centre is one of the ugliest buildings in the city.* | *The room was bare except for a few pieces of ugly furniture.*

unsightly /ʌnˈsaɪtli/ [adj] something that is **unsightly** is unpleasant to look at, and spoils the appearance of the things around it: *Bushes and plants make the perfect screen for unsightly objects such as dustbins.* | *Tight bras and knickers can cause unsightly bulges under close-fitting clothes.*

unattractive /ˌʌnəˈtræktɪv◂/ [adj] not at all pleasant to look at: *The town is surrounded by large, unattractive housing estates that nobody wants to live in.* | *Wearing an unattractive blouse and old-fashioned skirt, Lisa looked older than she was.*

hideous /ˈhɪdiəs/ [adj] extremely ugly: *One of our wedding presents was a hideous clock.* | *Emma was wearing an absolutely hideous purple and orange dress.*

revolting /rɪˈvəʊltɪŋ/ [adj] something that is **revolting** is so ugly that you do not like to look at it: *Remember that three piece suite Mrs Killeen had? It was grey and mustard. It was absolutely revolting!* | *Who's that TV presenter who always wears those revolting sweaters?*

monstrosity /mɒnˈstrɒsəti‖mɑːnˈstrɑː-/ [n C] a very large ugly building or object: *I rented a Spanish-style monstrosity in Beverly Hills while my apartment was redecorated.* | *This building is another monstrosity celebrated as a brilliant piece of architecture.*

an eyesore /ən ˈaɪsɔːʳ/ [n singular] a large and very ugly building that you cannot avoid seeing: *They built a huge office block right next to the old cathedral – what an eyesore!* | *Intended to be the world's largest casino, it now stands as an eyesore near the big tourist and convention hotels of New Orleans.*

blot on the landscape /ˌblɒt ɒn ðə ˈlændskeɪp‖ˌblɑːt-/ [n phrase] British something that spoils the view, especially an ugly building: *The container site at North Farm is a real blot on the landscape.*

uncertain

RELATED WORDS

opposite: —— **certainly/definitely**

▸ *see also* **sure/not sure, know/not know, doubt**

1 something that you cannot be certain about

- uncertain/not certain
- unclear/not clear
- be up in the air
- there is uncertainty about/over sth

uncertain/not certain /ʌnˈsɜːʳtn, nɒt ˈsɜːʳtn/ [adj] something that is **uncertain**, has not been definitely shown or decided: *The cause of the accident is uncertain.* | *Exactly how and when these plant species came to the Great Plains is not certain.* | **it is uncertain whether/if** *It is still uncertain whether the conference will actually take place.* | **it is uncertain how/why/when/that** *It's uncertain when the trial will begin.* | *It is not at all certain that Christopher Columbus was the first European to discover America.*

unclear/not clear /ʌnˈklɪəʳ, nɒt ˈklɪəʳ/ [adj] a situation that is **unclear**, is one that people do not know enough or understand enough to be sure about it: *The causes of the dispute are not entirely clear.* | *At* *this hour, the fate of the passengers and crew is still unclear.* | **it is unclear how/why/whether etc** *It isn't clear how the fire started.* | *It's not yet clear whether the disease is caused by a virus.* | *It was unclear when the two sides would meet again to discuss the budget.* | **it is not clear that** *It's not clear that the problems with the new computer system have been worked out.*

be up in the air /biː ˌʌp ɪn ði ˈeəʳ/ [v phrase] informal use this about something that is uncertain because a decision has not yet been made: *I might be going on a training course next week, but it's still up in the air.* | *They still haven't said if I've got the job – it's all up in the air at the moment.*

there is uncertainty about/over sth /ðeər ɪz ʌnˈsɜːʳtnti əbaʊt, əʊvəʳ (sth)/ use this to say that people do not feel certain about what has happened or will happen, and are worried about it – used especially in newspapers and public speeches: *The Principal said there was uncertainty about the candidate's qualifications.* | *There is some uncertainty over where the refugees are going to be housed.*

2 when a situation is uncertain, and something bad may happen

- uncertain
- be/look/remain etc doubtful
- be in doubt
- it's touch and go
- be/hang in the balance
- iffy

uncertain /ʌnˈsɜːʳtn/ [adj] *The situation on the island is still very uncertain and the army is on full alert.* | *The long-term benefits of the treatment are extremely uncertain.* | *The economic outlook is so uncertain that I would think carefully before investing any money.* | **highly uncertain** (=very uncertain) *The company faces a highly uncertain future.*

be/look/remain etc doubtful /biː ˈdaʊtfəl/ [v phrase] to be uncertain and likely to be bad: *The result of the President's re-election campaign remains doubtful.* | *With more and more cuts in government spending, the program's future now seems doubtful.* | **it is doubtful if/whether** *It is doubtful if she will survive the operation.* | *It is extremely doubtful whether the aid is actually reaching the people who need it most.* | **it is doubtful that** *It is doubtful that the governor's proposed tax increase will be popular with voters.*

be in doubt /biː ɪn ˈdaʊt/ [v phrase] if someone or something's future or success **is in doubt**, it seems very uncertain and they may not be able to continue or to succeed: *After yet another injury, his football career is in doubt.* | *The building's future remained in doubt until the government agreed to restore it.*

it's touch and go /ɪts ˌtʌtʃ ən ˈgəʊ/ spoken you say **it's touch and go** when a situation seems extremely uncertain and you are worried that something may not happen in the way you want: *It was touch and go for a few hours, but we were able to get everything out of the basement before it flooded.* | *An urgent operation was needed to save his life, and doctors said it was touch and go until the end of the procedure.* | **+ whether** *Traffic was really heavy, and for a while it was touch and go whether they'd get to the wedding on time.*

be/hang in the balance /biː, ˌhæŋ ɪn ðə ˈbæləns/ [v phrase] if something **is in the balance** or **hangs in the balance**, there is a risk that something bad will happen so that it will not continue: *The survival of the African elephant hangs in the balance.* | *His career as a politician hung in the balance.* | *I can't say what the outcome of the talks will be – they're very much in the balance at the moment.*

iffy /ˈɪfi/ [adj not usually before noun] spoken informal use this to describe a plan or situation that seems uncertain and may not succeed or happen as you want: *'What's happening about your new job?' 'The whole thing's rather iffy at the moment.'* | *I was hoping to go to the beach today but it's looking iffy because of the weather.*

3 when two different results are possible

- sth could go either way
- borderline
- there's a fifty-fifty chance
- it's a toss-up

sth could go either way / (sth) kʊd gəʊ ˌaɪðəʳ ˈweɪ‖-ˌiː-/ [v phrase] informal if you say that something such as a game or a decision **could go either way**, you mean that either of two results is equally possible: *Legal experts following the case believe the trial could go either way.* | *Spurs are a goal up but there are ten minutes to go and the match could still go either way.*

borderline /ˈbɔːʳdəʳlaɪn/ [adj] a **borderline** case is a situation in which the decision is not certain, for example about whether someone should pass an exam, get a job etc **borderline case/decision etc** *In borderline cases we look at a student's class work to decide the final exam result.* | *It was a borderline decision whether to send him to prison or not.*

there's a fifty-fifty chance /ðeəʳz ə ˌfɪfti fɪfti ˈtʃɑːns‖-ˈtʃæns/ spoken informal if you say **there is a fifty-fifty chance** of something happening, you mean there is an equal chance of it happening or not happening: *The weather forecast said there was a fifty-fifty chance of rain.* | **be fifty-fifty** (=there is a fifty-fifty chance) *It'll be a tough game – I'd say our chances of winning are fifty-fifty.*

it's a toss-up /ɪts ə ˈtɒs ʌp‖-ˈtɔːs-/ spoken say this when you do not know which of two possibilities someone will choose, and you think each is equally likely: *'Have you decided where to go on holiday?' 'Well, it'll be either Portugal or Turkey – it's a toss-up.'* | **+ between** *I don't know who'll get the job. I guess it's a toss-up between Carl and Steve.*

4 when there are several different opinions about something

- debatable
- questionable
- open to question/debate
- moot point

debatable /dɪˈbeɪtəbəl/ [adj] **it is debatable whether** *It is debatable whether these alternative medical treatments actually work.* | **a debatable point** *Whether or not the government was right to arrest the protesters is an extremely debatable point.*

questionable /ˈkwestʃənəbəl/ [adj] something that is **questionable** seems doubtful and is likely to be wrong or untrue: *The conclusions of the survey are questionable because the research was based on a very small sample of people.* | **it is questionable whether** *It is questionable whether the advertisements will increase sales.*

open to question/debate /ˌəʊpən tə ˈkwestʃən, dɪˈbeɪt/ [adj phrase] something that is **open to question** or **open to debate** seems doubtful and needs to be checked or discussed: *Many people feel that the safety of the drug is now open to question.* | *Just why the guerrillas decided to shoot down the* *unarmed plane remains open to debate.* | **it is open to question/debate whether** *It is open to debate whether the new government is any better than the old one.*

moot point /ˌmuːt ˈpɔɪnt/ [n singular] something that different people have different opinions about: *I'm not sure that bringing in computers has made our job easier. It's a moot point.* | *Whether or not increasing taxes will result in a fairer society remains a moot point.*

unconscious

unable to see, hear, feel etc, because you are injured, ill, drunk etc

RELATED WORDS

opposite: **conscious**

▸ *see also* **drunk, sleep, accident, hit, wake up/get up**

1 unconscious

- ▸ **unconscious**
- ▸ **be in a coma**
- ▸ **be out cold**
- ▸ **dazed**

unconscious /ʌnˈkɒnʃəs‖-ˈkɑːn-/ [adj] not able to see, hear, feel etc, usually for a short time, for example because you have taken a drug or been hit on the head: *There was a woman lying unconscious on the floor.* | *The unconscious man was carefully lifted onto a stretcher.* —**unconsciousness** [n U] *A heavy concentration of the drug may produce dizziness or even unconsciousness.* | *She managed to crawl into a shed, and then lapsed into unconsciousness.*

be in a coma /biː ɪn ə ˈkəʊmə/ [v phrase] to be unconscious for a long time, because of a serious accident or illness: *Marina has been in a coma for the past four months.* | **lie in a coma** *Jo Columbo lay in a coma, paralyzed by bullet wounds.*

be out cold /biː ˌaʊt ˈkəʊld/ [v phrase] especially spoken to be unconscious: *The other boxer was out cold.*

dazed /deɪzd/ [adj] almost unconscious for a short time, and often unable to move, because you have had a shock, been hit on the head etc: *When the realization hit her, she just sat there looking dazed.* | *I stumbled from the room dazed and confused, completely disoriented by what had just happened.*

2 to become unconscious

- ▸ **lose consciousness**
- ▸ **faint**
- ▸ **pass out**
- ▸ **black out/have a blackout**
- ▸ **slip/sink/lapse/fall into unconsciousness**
- ▸ **slip/sink/lapse/fall into a coma**
- ▸ **collapse**

lose consciousness /ˌluːz ˈkɒnʃəsnɨs‖-ˈkɑːn-/ [v phrase] to become unconscious, for example because you are seriously ill or because a doctor has given you a drug before an operation: *I remember looking down and seeing blood, and then I lost consciousness.* | *After Atkins collapsed and lost consciousness at work, she was sent to the hospital for a scan.*

faint /feɪnt/ [v I] to become unconscious so that you fall to the ground for a short time, for example because you are very hot or hungry: *One of the soldiers guarding the palace fainted in the heat.* | *I need to go outside. I feel as if I'm going to faint.* | *I must have fainted, and when I came to I didn't know where I was.*

pass out /ˌpɑːs ˈaʊt‖ˌpæs-/ [phr v I] to become unconscious, usually for a short time, for example because you have had too much to drink, or because you cannot breathe properly: *When I first smoked a cigarette, I almost passed out.* | *I think the poor guy passed out. It looks like he's had a lot to drink.*

black out/have a blackout /ˌblæk ˈaʊt, hæv ə ˈblækaʊt/ [phr v I/v phrase] to become unconscious for a short time, usually without warning and for no clear reason: *Her father's been having blackouts, and the doctor has ordered a brain scan.* | *A man grabbed her and put a piece of cloth to her face. That's the last thing she remembers before blacking out.*

slip/sink/lapse/fall into unconsciousness /ˌslɪp, ˌsɪŋk, ˌlæps, ˌfɔːl ɪntʊ ʌnˈkɒnʃəsnɨs‖-ˈkɑːn-/ [v phrase] to gradually become unconscious, especially because you are seriously ill or near to death – used especially in descriptions of events and in stories: *The patient slipped into unconsciousness at around 7 am.* | *She managed to say a few words before falling into unconsciousness again.*

slip/sink/lapse/fall into a coma /ˌslɪp, ˌsɪŋk, ˌlæps, ˌfɔːl ɪntʊ ə ˈkəʊmə/ [v phrase] to gradually become unconscious, and remain unconscious for a long time, because you are seriously ill or near to death: *The patient slipped into a coma, and died two days later.* | *After the accident she fell into a coma, and was on a life support machine for 6 months before regaining consciousness.*

collapse /kəˈlæps/ [v I] to fall and become unconscious, especially because you are very ill: *Come quickly, one of the passengers has collapsed.* | *After half a dozen glasses of whisky he collapsed and could not be revived.*

3 to make someone unconscious by giving them a drug

- ▸ **anaesthetize**
- ▸ **put sb to sleep**
- ▸ **knock sb out**

anaesthetize ALSO **anesthetize** American /əˈniːs-θətaɪz‖əˈnes-/ [v T usually in passive] to make someone unconscious so that they will feel no pain during an operation by giving them a drug: *Once the patient was fully anesthetized, the surgeon made a small incision in his chest.*

put sb to sleep /ˌpʊt (sb) tə ˈsliːp/ [v phrase] informal to make someone unconscious by giving them a drug: *The doctor told me she was going to put me to sleep.*

knock sb out /ˌnɒk (sb) ˈaʊt‖ˌnɑːk- / [phr v T] if a drug **knocks** you **out**, it makes you unconscious: *I needed something to knock me out – it was the only way to escape from the pain.*

4 to make someone unconscious by hitting them

- ▸ **knock sb out/knock sb unconscious**
- ▸ **beat sb unconscious/beat sb senseless**
- ▸ **stun**

knock sb out/knock sb unconscious /ˌnɒk (sb) ˈaʊt, ˌnɒk (sb) ʌnˈkɒnʃəs‖ˌnɑːk-, -ˈkɑːn-/ [phr v T/v phrase] *There was a fight, and Mark was knocked unconscious.* | **knock sb out** *I hit him on the jaw and knocked him out.* | **knock out sb** *Louis knocked out his opponent in the first round.* | **knock sb out cold** *The impact was so sudden and so fierce, it knocked me out cold.*

beat sb unconscious/beat sb senseless /ˌbiːt (sb) ʌnˈkɒnʃəs‖-ˈkɑːn-, ˌbiːt (sb) ˈsensləs/ [v phrase] to hit someone repeatedly until they become unconscious: *Murphy was attacked by two men and beaten unconscious.* | *She was beaten senseless and left for dead.*

stun /stʌn/ [v T] to make someone unconscious for a short time so that they do not know where they are, what is happening etc: *They had only intended to stun the guard, to give them time to escape.* | *Gamekeepers use special darts to stun the rhinos.*

under/below

RELATED WORDS

opposite: **above**

▸ see also **down**

1 under something that is directly above

▸ **under**
▸ **underneath**
▸ **beneath**

under /ˈʌndəʳ/ [prep] something that is **under** something else has that thing directly above it: *The pen fell under the desk.* | *If there's no one at home, just shove the letter under the door.* | *A small dog scampered into the room and dived under the table.* | *We stood close together under his umbrella, trying to keep dry.*

underneath /ˌʌndəʳˈniːθ/ [prep/adv] directly under another object and close to it: *We found your keys in the sofa underneath a cushion.* | *The cats like to sleep underneath the wood stove when it's cold.* | *Sheets of newspaper had been laid underneath the carpet.* | *A pipe was leaking, so we put a bucket underneath to catch the drips.*

beneath /bɪˈniːθ/ [prep] directly under something – used especially in formal writing or in literature: *The ship passed beneath the Golden Gate Bridge into San Francisco Bay.* | *As he walked across the hall, the boards creaked beneath his feet.*

2 in a lower position or at a lower level than something

▸ **below**
▸ **beneath**

below /bɪˈləʊ/ [prep/adv] at a lower level: *John lives on the top floor and Julie lives on the floor below.* | *They looked down from the mountain to the valley far below.* | *The dog's leg was broken just below the hip.* | *Her hair hangs down below her shoulders.* | *Our pilot spotted two MiG29s flying below us.*

beneath /bɪˈniːθ/ [prep/adv] at a lower level than something and often a little in front or to one side of it – used especially in formal writing or in literature: *Beneath the east window of the church stands the great altar.* | *The army was encamped beneath the castle walls.* | *They stood on the cliff and gazed down at the raging sea beneath.*

3 under the ground or under water

▸ **under**
▸ **beneath**
▸ **underground/below ground**
▸ **subterranean**
▸ **underwater/under water**
▸ **submerged**

under /ˈʌndəʳ/ [prep] *It is one of the largest mountain ranges under the Pacific Ocean.* | *Several of the stolen items were found buried under Mackie's house.* | *When the project is finished, most of Boston's major roads will run under the city.*

beneath /bɪˈniːθ/ [prep] under – used in formal writing or in literature: *Far beneath the waters of the North Atlantic lies the wreck of the great liner, the Titanic.* | *Petroleum occurs in natural deposits beneath the surface of the earth.*

underground/below ground /ˌʌndəʳˈgraʊnd◂, bɪˌləʊ ˈgraʊnd/ [adv] under the ground: *The men work underground for 12 hours a day.* | *The explosives will be stored below ground in concrete bunkers.* | **10 metres underground/two miles underground etc** *The nuclear waste is buried a half-mile underground.* —**underground** [adj only before noun] *an underground parking garage*

subterranean /ˌsʌbtəˈreɪniən◂/ [adj only before noun] below the ground: *A subterranean stream is believed to flow underneath the town.* | *a subterranean explosion* | *Electronic sensors have located a huge subterranean cavern in the Sierre Madre mountain range.*

underwater/under water /ˌʌndəʳˈwɔːtəʳ◂/ [adv] under the water: *I don't like opening my eyes underwater.* | *a camera specially designed for use under water* | *On land the seal is a clumsy creature, but underwater it moves with grace and agility.* —**underwater** [adj only before noun] *The research is done in underwater laboratories, so that scientists can study the creatures in their natural habitat.*

submerged /səbˈmɜːʳdʒd/ [adj] just under the surface of the water: *The boat hit a submerged rock.* | *Sometimes at low tide you can just see the submerged wreck of a large ship.* | **partially/partly submerged** *The flight recorder was found smashed and partially submerged in a creek nearby.*

4 under something such as clothes, skin, or paint

▸ **under/underneath**
▸ **beneath**

under/underneath /ˈʌndəʳ, ˌʌndəʳˈniːθ/ [prep] *I was wearing a thick sweater under my coat, but I was still cold.* | *Scabies is a disease caused by a tiny insect that lays its eggs just underneath the skin.* —**underneath** [adv] *Padding prevents the rug's color from seeping through onto the floor underneath.*

beneath /bɪˈniːθ/ [prep] under a layer of something – used in formal writing or in literature: *The boy lay trembling beneath the bedclothes.* | *The inscription was hidden beneath a layer of dirt and grime.*

understand/ not understand

RELATED WORDS

▸ see also **realize, learn, know/not know, clear/not clear**

1 to understand a situation, idea, or what someone is telling you

- understand
- know what sb means
- see
- get
- comprehend
- grasp
- make sense of
- get the message
- get the picture
- get your head round

understand /ˌʌndəʳˈstænd/ [v I/T not in progressive] *She spoke slowly and clearly so that everyone could understand.* | *I didn't understand the teacher's instructions.* | *When he's old enough to understand, we'll tell him he's adopted.* | **+ what/why/how etc** *Ben asked a few questions to make sure he understood what to do.* | *You don't need to understand how a computer works to use it.* | **+ that** *The witness said he understood that he was swearing to give true and correct information.* | **easy/difficult to understand** *Computer manuals should be written in a way that is easy to understand.* | **understand perfectly** (=understand completely) *Don't worry. I understand perfectly.* | **fully understand** (=understand completely) *Doctors still do not fully understand the process by which the disease is transmitted.*

know what sb means /ˌnəʊ wɒt (sb) ˈmiːnz/ [v phrase not in progressive] to understand what someone is telling you, especially if they have not expressed it very clearly: *I don't think your audience is going to know what you mean by this.* | **you know what I mean?** (=say this to check that someone understands you) *He seems really sad, you know what I mean?* | **I know what you mean** (=say this to show that you understand) *'It's a thing you hold pieces of wood in when you're doing woodwork.' 'Oh, I know what you mean – a vice.'*

see /siː/ [v I/T] especially spoken to understand the truth about a situation, or understand the reasons for something **see what sb means** *Try it for yourself, and you'll see what I mean.* | **+ why/how/what etc** *I can see why people don't like him.* | **I see** (=say this when you understand what someone has told you) *'It goes in the red box, here.' 'Oh, I see.'* | **you see** (=say this when you are explaining something) *Well, you see, he's not really ready to read a book this difficult.* | **+ (that)** *Well, I can see that the logic is somehow wrong, but I don't know why exactly.* | **see any reason** *Can you see any reason why it shouldn't work?* | **see the point** (=understand why something is important) *At fourteen, he couldn't see the point of staying in school.* | **see sb's point** (=understand the main idea or importance of what someone is saying) *I didn't like his attitude, but I could see his point.* | **see the joke** British (=understand why something is funny) *He's just one of those people who never seem to see the joke.*

get /get/ [v T not in progressive or passive] spoken to understand what someone says, what is happening, or why or how something happens **get it** *'Do you understand?' 'Yeah, we've got it,' one of the drivers replied.* | *Barbara Howell and her husband, Kenneth (Barbie and Ken, get it?) run a bed-and-breakfast inn.* | **I don't get it** *Why did you turn down such a fantastic job? I don't get it.* | **get a/the joke** (=understand why something is funny) *John told me one of his stupid jokes, and it took me about five minutes to get it.* | **get the point** (=understand the main idea or importance of something) *I don't think you get the point. Legally, you must give us this information.* | **get the idea** *The students should get the idea that this is a complex issue, with no easy answers.* | **get what/why/how etc** *I just couldn't get what he meant.*

comprehend /ˌkɒmprɪˈhend‖ˌkɑːm-/ [v T] formal to understand something that is complicated or difficult to understand: *Take the time to read, comprehend, and evaluate the report.* | *God cannot truly be seen or comprehended by the human mind.* | **fully comprehend** (=understand something completely) *The significance of the disappearance of the buffalo and the passenger pigeon was not fully comprehended until much later.*

grasp /grɑːsp‖græsp/ [v T not in progressive] to fully understand a fact or an idea, especially one that it is important or difficult to understand: *Obviously, she had barely grasped the subject.* | *Science lessons should be taught in a way that makes the material easier to grasp.* | **hard to grasp** *Fame has come suddenly, and Peyton is finding it hard to grasp.* | **+ that** *The army had failed to grasp that their mission was to protect the navy's ships, not vice versa.* —**grasp** [n U] **beyond sb's grasp** (=too difficult to understand) *Some of the historical nuances are beyond the grasp of most children.* | **have a grasp of sth** *Cordell had an impressive grasp of military issues.*

make sense of /ˌmeɪk ˈsens ɒv/ [v phrase] to understand something that is not clear or easy to understand, especially by spending time thinking about it: *Police are trying to make sense of a bizarre note left by the murderer.* | *There is so much information that it is difficult to make sense of it all.*

get the message /ˌget ðə ˈmesɪdʒ/ [v phrase] informal to understand what someone is telling you or what they want you to do, especially after they have told you several times: *Even the Democrats got the message: voters are concerned about taxes.* | **+ that** *He doesn't seem to get the message that he's not welcome here.*

get the picture /ˌget ðə ˈpɪktʃəʳ/ [v phrase] spoken to understand a situation or arrangement, especially one that someone is explaining to you: *I get the picture. You want me to say you were at my house last night.* | *We don't want any trouble tonight. Do you get the picture?*

get your head round /get jɔːʳ ˈhed raʊnd/ [v phrase] British informal to understand something that is difficult or complicated: *I just couldn't get my head round geometry at school.*

2 to understand how someone feels

- understand
- see
- appreciate
- know how sb feels
- put yourself in sb's place
- understandable

▸ see also **sympathize**

understand /ˌʌndəʳˈstænd/ [v I/T] to **understand** how someone feels, and feel sympathy for them, especially when they are upset or have problems: *I'm sure your teacher will understand.* | **+ how/what/why etc** *I understand how you feel, but I still think you should apologize to her.*

see /siː/ [v I/T] especially spoken to understand how someone feels and why they feel that way, especially because the reasons are very clear **+ why/how/what** *You can see why Clare was so annoyed, can't you?* | **+ that** *I can see that you'd find that upsetting.*

appreciate /əˈpriːʃieɪt/ [v T] formal to understand clearly how someone feels or what problems they have: *Congress did not appreciate the amount of anger that people felt about this issue.* | *Parents have to find ways to show their children that they appreciate their feelings and reactions.* | **+ (that)** *I appreciate that it's not easy for you, but you must try to get here on time.*

know how sb feels /ˌnəʊ haʊ (sb) ˈfiːlz/ to understand how someone feels, because you have had the same feelings or experiences yourself: *I know how you feel. I couldn't watch either – it was too upsetting.* | **know how it feels (to do sth)** *Believe me, I know how it feels to lose.*

put yourself in sb's place /ˌpʊt jɔːʳself ɪn (sb's) ˈpleɪs/ [v phrase] say this when you want someone to imagine they are in the same situation as another person, so that they can understand how the other person feels: *Well, put yourself in her place. Would you like it if someone did that to you?*

understandable /ˌʌndəʳˈstændəbəl/ [adj] feelings or attitudes that are **understandable**, especially feelings of anger, annoyance, or fear, do not surprise you because you can see that there are good reasons for them: *That teachers are annoyed about having so much extra paperwork is understandable.* | *There is understandable anger among the victims' families.* | **it is understandable that** *It's understandable that she doesn't want to see Bill again.* —**understandably** [adv] *Understandably, she just wants to leave as soon as possible.* | *They were, quite understandably, annoyed by the delay.*

3 to understand each part of a story, explanation etc

- follow
- be with
- keep up

follow /ˈfɒləʊ‖ˈfɑː-/ [v T] to understand a story, explanation, or talk that continues for a long time: *I had difficulty following the story – there are so many different characters.* | **difficult/hard/easy to follow** *The lecture was very hard to follow.*

be with /biː ˈwɪð/ [v phrase] informal to have understood everything so far in an explanation that someone is giving: *I'm sorry but I'm not with you. Could you explain that part again?* | *Then you press this button. Are you with me so far?*

keep up /ˌkiːp ˈʌp/ [phr v I] to manage to understand each part of something, especially a very long or complicated explanation or story: *She covers so much in these lectures – I don't know how you manage to keep up.* | **+ with** *It's a complicated film, and some people may find it hard to keep up with the plot.*

4 to understand new facts after studying them

- digest
- take in
- absorb
- assimilate
- sink in

digest /daɪˈdʒest/ [v T] to understand new information, especially when there is a large amount of it or when it is difficult to understand, by thinking about it carefully for a fairly long time: *The pub went silent as the villagers digested the news.* | *By the end of the day, I had a lot of new information to digest.*

take in /ˌteɪk ˈɪn/ [phr v T] to understand and remember new facts or information **take sth in** *I'm not going to my next class. I'm too tired to take anything in.* | **+ what/why/how etc** *I don't think she really took in what I was telling her.* | **take in sth** *She listened attentively, taking in every word he said and asking questions.*

absorb /əbˈsɔːʳb, əbˈzɔːʳb/ [v T] to understand a large amount of new information: *Most people need to read something more than once to absorb all the ideas.* | *He appeared to understand, but whether he absorbed every detail I cannot say.* | *A new baby has an enormous capacity for absorbing new information.*

assimilate /əˈsɪmɪ̈leɪt/ [v T] to understand and use new information or ideas quickly and easily: *The person we are looking for must be flexible, creative, and able to assimilate new ideas.* | *When a child is learning something new, they try to assimilate it in terms of what they already know.*

sink in /ˌsɪŋk ˈɪn/ [phr v I] if a fact, information etc **sinks in**, you gradually understand it: *He paused to let this news sink in.* | *I've been revising all day but I don't think much of it has sunk in.*

5 to understand the meaning of something in a particular way

- make of
- read
- take sth to mean
- see sth as
- interpret
- understand by
- understand sth/sb to mean
- construe sth as

make of /ˈmeɪk ɒv/ [phr v T not in progressive; usually in questions or negative sentences] to believe that something strange, difficult, or unusual has a particular meaning: *Have you read Dawson's letter? What do you make of it?* | *Tom could see that McCarron didn't know what to make of the information.*

read /riːd/ [v T] to think that a remark, an action, an event etc shows that someone has a particular opinion or feeling even though they do not say this directly: *Good managers are usually able to read a situation quickly and take the right action.* | **read sth as sth** *Men shouldn't be surprised if women read this behaviour as threatening.*

take sth to mean /ˌteɪk (sth) tə ˈmiːn/ [v phrase] to choose to understand a particular meaning in someone's words or actions without being sure that this is the correct meaning: *There was a pause, which he took to mean she was angry.* | *Television producers should not take low ratings to mean failure.*

see sth as /ˈsiː (sth) æz/ [phr v T] to understand a remark, a piece of writing, an event etc as having a particular meaning, especially because of your own feelings, opinions, or situation: *I see this poem as an attack on social injustice.* | *Young children often see the birth of a new brother or sister as a great threat.*

interpret /ɪnˈtɜːʳprɪ̈t/ [v T] to choose to understand a piece of information or group of facts in one of several possible ways: *Fairy tales can be interpreted in several different ways.* | **interpret sth as sth** *The statement was interpreted as a threat against the United States.* —**interpretation** /ɪnˌtɜːʳprɪ̈ˈteɪʃən/ [n C] **+ of** *The interpretation of laboratory data is often difficult.*

understand by /ˌʌndəʳˈstænd baɪ/ [v phrase] to find a particular meaning in an expression or in the name of something, even though other people may understand it differently: *What do you understand by the term 'alternative medicine'? | He spoke of profits, by which I understood profits for his company, not for us.*

understand sth/sb to mean /ʌndəʳˌstænd (sth/sb) tə 'miːn/ [v phrase] to think that someone's remarks, a word, a piece of writing etc means something or has a particular message, even though this is not stated directly: *'It's very good. You'll like it,' their mother said, and gave them a look that they understood to mean they must eat it whether they liked it or not.*

construe sth as /kən'struː (sth) æz/ [v phrase] formal to understand a remark or action in a particular way, when there are other possible ways of understanding it: *Such activities by the Americans could be construed as an act of war. | Films that could be construed as offensive are shown after nine o'clock.*

6 to begin to understand something

- begin to understand
- catch on
- get it
- figure/work out
- twig
- cotton on
- click
- fall into place

begin to understand /bɪˌgɪn tʊ ʌndəʳ'stænd/ [v phrase] to slowly **begin to understand** a situation or someone's feelings, because you get more information or because you experience something for yourself: *I think it will be a long time before we even begin to understand how damaging the effect has been. | Patients are given written information and videos so that they can begin to understand more about their condition.* | **+ that** *I was beginning to understand that being alone could be terribly depressing.* | **+ why/how/what etc** *As we walked up the narrow staircases, we began to understand why the Dutch haul their furniture up the outside of the buildings and through the windows.*

catch on /ˌkætʃ 'ɒn / [phr v I] informal to begin to understand something that is not easy to understand: *Thomas isn't catching on as quickly as some of the other children.* | **+ to** *It took Jennifer a long time to catch on to the fact that Mary was taking advantage of her.* | **catch on fast/quickly** *She catches on fast and will soon be promoted.*

get it /'get ɪt/ [v phrase] spoken to finally understand something, especially after it has been explained to you several times: *Okay, I get it. You only get paid if you sell at least ten copies. | 'So the plant takes in carbon dioxide and gives out oxygen.' 'That's it. You've got it.'*

figure/work out /ˌfɪgəʳ, ˌwɜːʳk 'aʊt‖ˌfɪgjər-/ [phr v T] to think about something until you understand it, especially something complicated: *Horgan thought he had it all figured out, but he hadn't.* | **figure/work sth out** *In case you haven't figured it out yet, we've been tricked.* | **+ how/why/what etc** *Detectives are still trying to work out what happened.*

twig /twɪg/ [v I/T] British informal to begin to understand a situation by what you see and hear around you, and not by being told directly: *Oh, I get it, I've twigged at last. How much do you want?* | **+ that** *At last I twigged that I was pregnant* | **+ why/where/what etc** *It took him about two minutes to twig what I was going on about!*

cotton on /ˌkɒtn 'ɒn‖ˌkɑːtn- / [phr v I] informal to begin to understand a situation by what you see and hear around you, and not by being told directly **+ to** *It took him a while to cotton on to what was happening. | Large stores have at last cottoned on to the fact that mothers with pushchairs can't cope with stairs.*

click /klɪk/ [v I] if something **clicks**, especially something you are learning, you suddenly begin to understand it: *Just keep working at it, and suddenly it will all click.*

fall into place /ˌfɔːl ɪntə 'pleɪs/ [v phrase] if several facts **fall into place**, you begin to understand how they are connected and why each one is important, so that you understand a whole situation or subject: *Once the police received this new evidence, things began falling into place.*

7 when you understand something

- comprehension
- understanding
- insight

comprehension /ˌkɒmprɪ'henʃən‖ˌkɑːm-/ [n U] when you understand something, especially a piece of spoken or written language, or the ability to do this: *The teacher gave us a comprehension test. | We tried to explain the causes of the war at a child's level of comprehension.* | **reading comprehension** (=ability to understand what you read) *You need to practise your reading comprehension more.* | **beyond sb's comprehension** (=too difficult to understand) *He was caught up in frightening events far beyond his comprehension.*

understanding /ˌʌndəʳ'stændɪŋ/ [n U] when you understand a situation, subject, idea etc, or someone's ability to do this: *A much greater level of understanding is required to carry out more complex experiments.* | **+ of** *He seems to have very little understanding of economics. | The research may lead to a better understanding of how the disease develops.*

insight /'ɪnsaɪt/ [n C/U] the ability to understand or realize something new about a subject or to more clearly understand the nature of a problem, situation, or subject etc: *Crick soon established himself as a scientist of great insight and creativity.* | **+ into** *We help troubled teenagers gain some insight into their own problems.*

8 easy to understand

- easy to understand/follow
- clear
- comprehensible
- intelligible
- accessible
- coherent

easy to understand/follow /ˌiːzi tʊ ʌndəʳ-'stænd, 'fɒləʊ ‖-'fɑː-/ [adj phrase] *The instructions are easy to follow. | On cards are five easy to follow recipes for you to cut out and keep. | We try to write it in language that is easy to understand.*

clear /klɪəʳ/ [adj] instructions, explanations etc that are **clear** are explained in easy language or stages and are therefore easy to understand: *Most of the 'help' messages you get on computers aren't at all clear to ordinary home users. | Thanks for your directions to the apartment – they were really clear and we had no problems finding it. | Perhaps I didn't make myself clear – there won't be a penny of extra money for this project.*

comprehensible /ˌkɒmprɪ'hensəbəl‖ˌkɑːm-/ [adj] something that is **comprehensible** is easy to understand because it does not contain any complicated information and is expressed in very clear language: *Visual aids can make lessons much more interesting and comprehensible. | Each entry in the guide is brief and immediately comprehensible.* |

+ to *The music was experimental, and not comprehensible to the average concert-goer.*

intelligible /ɪnˈteləd͡ʒəbəl/ [adj] something that is **intelligible**, such as a subject you study or a piece of writing or speech, is fairly easy to understand: *Her English was strongly accented but quite intelligible.* | **+ to** *It is sometimes difficult to discuss medical issues in a way that is intelligible to ordinary people.*

accessible /əkˈsesəbəl/ [adj] books, films, information etc that are **accessible** are written or made in a way that is easy to understand even though they may concern subjects that are complicated: *Philip Glass has produced something very rare – an accessible modern opera.* | *I don't find James Joyce's writing very accessible.* | **+ to** *He was specifically asked to write a play that would be accessible to the local community.*

coherent /kəʊˈhɪərənt/ [adj] a piece of writing or speech that is **coherent** is easy to understand because it is clear and well-planned, so that all the parts fit well together: *I was so confused that I could not give a coherent answer.* | *Rescuers found Campbell, who was conscious and coherent.* | *History could be defined as a coherent account of an event.*

9 to not understand something correctly

- misunderstand
- misunderstanding
- misinterpret
- misread
- miss the point
- take sth the wrong way
- get the wrong end of the stick
- be at cross-purposes
- don't get me wrong
- lose the plot

misunderstand /ˌmɪsʌndəʳˈstænd/ [v I/T] to think that someone means one thing when in fact they mean something else: *I think she misunderstood you.* | *I'm sorry, I must have misunderstood.* | *According to Bennett, you misunderstood the reason you were dropped from the list.*

misunderstanding /ˌmɪsʌndəʳˈstændɪŋ/ [n C/U] a problem caused when someone does not understand something correctly: *There seems to have been a misunderstanding. I didn't order steak.* | *Cultural differences between people from different countries can sometimes lead to misunderstandings.*

misinterpret /ˌmɪsɪnˈtɜːʳprət/ [v T] to not understand the true meaning of someone's actions or words, so that you believe something that is not in fact true: *Your friendliness could easily be misinterpreted.* | *A lot of people misinterpreted what I was saying, and have called me a racist.*

misread /ˌmɪsˈriːd/ [v T] to wrongly believe that someone's actions show that they have a particular opinion or feeling: *Unfortunately, we misread the situation and lost a lot of sales.* | *The intelligence community was criticized for misreading Iraq's intentions.*

miss the point /ˌmɪs ðə ˈpɔɪnt/ [v phrase] if you **miss the point**, you think you understand what someone says or what is important about a situation, but in fact you are wrong: *I soon realised that he had completely missed the point.* | *He's so caught up in the rules that he's missing the point of the game, which is just to have fun.*

take sth the wrong way /ˌteɪk (sth) ðə ˌrɒŋ ˈweɪ‖ -ˌrɔːŋ-/ [v phrase] to be offended or upset by a remark that was not intended to offend or upset you, because you understood it wrongly: *Don't tell Simon that – he might take it the wrong way.* | *No, that's not what I meant. You take everything the wrong way.* | **don't take this the wrong way** (=say this when you want to give advice or ask something that you think might offend someone) *Don't take this the wrong way, but could I stay at your place tonight?*

get the wrong end of the stick /get ðə ˌrɒŋ end əv ðə ˈstɪk‖-ˌrɔːŋ-/ [v phrase] British an informal expression meaning to make a mistake about one part of something that you are told, so that you understand the rest of it in completely the wrong way: *Maybe I got the wrong end of the stick. I thought she was leaving him, not the other way round.*

be at cross-purposes /biː ət ˌkrɒs ˈpɜːʳpəsəz ‖-ˌkrɔːs-/ [v phrase] if two people **are at cross-purposes**, each of them thinks that they understand what the other is talking about, when in fact they are talking about two different things: *I think we're at cross purposes – I'm talking about John, not Nigel.*

don't get me wrong /ˌdəʊnt get miː ˈrɒŋ‖-ˈrɔːŋ/ spoken say this when you do not want someone to understand something wrongly or be upset by what you say: *I like Jenny, don't get me wrong, but I do think she acts a little childishly at times.* | *Don't get me wrong, I love my family, I just don't want to be with them all the time.*

lose the plot /ˌluːz ðə ˈplɒt‖-ˈplɑːt/ [v phrase] British spoken to suddenly be unable to understand what is happening in a situation, especially when people expect you to understand and deal with it: *In the past few days the President seems to have completely lost the plot.*

10 to not understand

- not understand
- can't make head or/nor tail of
- be over sb's head
- be out of your depth
- be none the wiser
- don't/can't see
- be a mystery to me/be beyond me/beats me
- I can't think/can't imagine

not understand /nɒt ʌndəʳˈstænd/ [v phrase] *They didn't understand a single word she said.* | *Tell me if you don't understand.* | *She thought about getting a divorce, but she knew her children would never understand.* | *He made a few references to the CIA and national security, which Wilson did not understand.* | **+ why/how/what/where** *I really can't understand why so many people like her music.*

can't make head or/nor tail of ALSO **can't makes heads or tails (out) of** American /ˌkɑːnt meɪk ˌhed ɔːʳ, nɔːʳ ˈteɪl ɒv, ˌkɑːnt meɪk ˌhedz ɔːʳ ˈteɪlz (aʊt) ɒv‖ˌkænt-/ [v phrase] informal to be unable to understand something at all because it is very complicated or confusing: *I just can't make head or tail of this train timetable.* | *I couldn't make head or tail of this book, and had real trouble finishing it.* | *Consumers can't always make heads or tails out of the way nutrition is labeled on a food package.*

be over sb's head /biː ˌəʊvəʳ (sb's) ˈhed/ [v phrase] to be much too complicated or technical for someone to understand: *It was obvious from her expression that what I was saying was over her head.* | **be way/completely over sb's head** *I went to the lecture, but it was way over my head.*

be out of your depth /biː ˌaʊt əv jɔːʳ ˈdepθ/ [v phrase] to be involved in a situation or activity which is too difficult for you to understand: *She was out of her depth in the advanced class, so they moved her to the intermediate class.* | **be way/completely out of**

your depth *I tried to read the report, but I was way out of my depth.*

be none the wiser /biː ˌnʌn ðə ˈwaɪzəʳ/ [v phrase] to still not understand something after someone has tried to explain it to you: *I've read the manual but I'm still none the wiser.* | **leave sb none the wiser** *His explanations of how it worked left me none the wiser.*

don't/can't see /ˌdəʊnt, ˌkɑːnt ˈsiː‖ˌkænt-/ [v phrase] spoken to not understand the reason for something **+ why/how/what/where** *I didn't see how they could sell it so cheaply.* | *I can't see why you think it's any of your business.*

be a mystery to me/be beyond me/beats me /biː ə ˌmɪstəri tə ˈmiː, biː bɪˌjɒnd ˈmiː‖-ˌjɑːnd-, ˌbiːts ˈmiː/ [v phrase] spoken say this when you cannot understand why something happens or how someone does something, and you find it very surprising **+ how/what/why etc** *It's a mystery to me how he can get so much work done in such a short time.* | *Why anyone would willingly do that job is beyond me.* | **it beats me/it's beyond me etc.** *'Why does she stay with her husband then?' 'It beats me.'*

I can't think/can't imagine /aɪ ˌkɑːnt ˈθɪŋk, ˌkɑːnt ɪˈmædʒɪn‖ -ˌkænt-/ you say **I can't think** or **I can't imagine** how or why someone does something when you cannot think of any reasonable explanation why someone should do it, and are very surprised that they do **+ why/how etc** *He wants to join the army – I can't think why.* | *How such a stupid man ever got to be a politician, I just can't imagine.*

11 difficult or impossible to understand

- puzzling
- baffling
- incomprehensible
- unintelligible
- incoherent
- obscure

puzzling /ˈpʌzlɪŋ/ [adj] a **puzzling** situation makes you feel confused, because you have tried to understand it or explain it, but you cannot: *The police are investigating the puzzling death of a man found on the freeway.* | *Alzheimer's disease is one of medicine's most puzzling and feared illnesses.* | *The fact that many people still do not understand this basic concept is both puzzling and troubling.*

baffling /ˈbæflɪŋ/ [adj] extremely difficult or impossible to understand, and therefore making you feel extremely confused: *To an ordinary person, the legal arguments were baffling.* | *New evidence has provided a clue to one of the most baffling crimes the police have had to deal with.*

incomprehensible /ɪnˌkɒmprɪˈhensɪbəl‖-ˌkɑːm-/ [adj] impossible to understand: *His English was incomprehensible.* | **it is incomprehensible that** *It is incomprehensible that a tragedy like this could be joked about.* | **+ to** *The leaflet was written in jargon that would have been totally incomprehensible to anyone outside the profession.*

unintelligible /ˌʌnɪnˈtelɪdʒɪbəl◂/ [adj] speech or writing that is **unintelligible** is impossible to understand because it is not clear, simple, or well planned: *Joe muttered something unintelligible, clasping his head in his hands.* | *Radio transmissions were often cut off or unintelligible.*

incoherent /ˌɪnkəʊˈhɪərənt◂/ [adj] **incoherent** speech is very difficult to understand, especially because the person who is speaking is drunk, ill, or very angry: *Harris gave rambling, incoherent answers to questions about the case.* | *She was clearly very ill, and at times her speech was incoherent.* —**incoherently** [adv] *Rochester was banging his fists on the wall, raging incoherently.*

obscure /əbˈskjʊəʳ/ [adj] a statement, joke, or idea that is **obscure** is very difficult to understand because the meaning is not clear unless it is carefully explained to you: *Best's art is eccentric and obscure.* | *Publishers would not print his earlier poetry because they felt it was too obscure.*

unfair

RELATED WORDS

opposite: ——— **fair**

▸ *see also* **cruel, unkind, equal/not equal**

1 not treating people in a way that is reasonable or equal

- unfair/not fair
- unreasonable
- undeserved
- biased
- unjust
- favour

unfair/not fair /ˌʌnˈfeəʳ◂, nɒt ˈfeəʳ/ [adj] not treating everyone equally, or not treating people in a way that most people think is right: *The present welfare system is grossly unfair.* | *unfair laws* | *Do you think I'm being unfair?* | *I don't want to be unfair, but you have to admit she behaved stupidly.* | **it's/that's not fair** spoken *Why do I always have to do the laundry? It's not fair!* | *That's not fair – it puts me at a disadvantage!* | **it is unfair that/it is not fair that** *It seems very unfair that she got all the blame.* | **it is unfair/not fair to do sth** *It's not fair to have a dog if you're out at work all day.* | *I told him it wasn't fair to treat her any differently.* | **+ to/on** *This sort of arrangement is not fair on the players, and not fair on the fans.* | *The tax laws are very unfair to the self-employed* | **not fair/unfair of sb (to do sth)** *It's unfair of you to judge all young people in the same way.*

unreasonable /ʌnˈriːzənəbəl/ [adj] not fair or not sensible: *It is possible for telephone companies to make profit without charging unreasonable rates.* | *Some news media have described the government's actions as excessive and unreasonable.* | *She divorced her husband on the grounds of unreasonable behaviour.* | *It didn't seem like an unreasonable request.* | **it is unreasonable (for sb) to do sth** *It's unreasonable to expect people to pay for something they haven't even seen yet.* | *It is not unreasonable for parents to want schools to reinforce the values children are taught at home.*

undeserved /ˌʌndɪˈzɜːʳvd◂/ [adj] a punishment or criticism that is **undeserved** is unfair because you do not deserve it: *He's come in for a lot of criticism, most of it completely undeserved.* | *Unfortunately, Lamarck has developed an undeserved reputation as a loser.* | *an undeserved and unwarranted attack*

biased /ˈbaɪəst/ [adj not usually before noun] unfairly against, or unfairly in favour of a particular group: *The system is so biased that many citizens simply do not register to vote.* | **biased towards/biased in favour of** *Export policy has been biased towards overseas customers.* | *Much of the information the clinics gave people was incomplete and biased in favour of educated middle-class clients.* | **+ against** *University acceptance policies seem to be biased against minorities.*

unjust /ˌʌnˈdʒʌst◂/ [adj] not fair or right according to the principles or ideas of a particular society: *They didn't mind breaking the law because they* *believed the law was unjust.* | *an unjust and pointless war* | *The legal aid charity has helped overturn some notoriously unjust verdicts.* —**unjustly** [adv] *Amnesty International launched a new campaign on behalf of people who have been unjustly imprisoned.*

favour British /**favor** American /ˈfeɪvəʳ/ [v T not usually in progressive] to treat one person in a group better than others, when you should treat all of them the same: *Many teachers favour boys, often without even realizing it.* | **favour sb over sb** *The Federal Republic denied that its policies favored any race over another.*

2 unfair treatment because of someone's race, sex, age etc

- **discrimination**
- **discriminate against**
- **prejudice**
- **inequality**
- **discriminatory**
- **double standards**

▸ *see also* **prejudiced**

discrimination /dɪˌskrɪmᵻˈneɪʃən/ [n U] **+ against** *The Department was notorious for its blatant discrimination against non-U.S. citizen employees.* | *The policy forbids any form of discrimination against gay and lesbian students.* | **racial discrimination** (=discrimination because of someone's race) *a plan to tackle racial discrimination in the police force* | **sexual/sex/gender discrimination** (=discrimination because of someone's sex) *a sex discrimination case* | **age discrimination** (=discrimination because of someone's age, especially if they are quite old) *He believed his boss had violated the age discrimination law.* | **reverse discrimination** (=the practice of treating unfairly a group of people who usually have advantages, in order to be fair to people who do not have those advantages) *White-male fears of reverse discrimination have been widely exaggerated.*

discriminate against /dɪˈskrɪmᵻneɪt əgenst/ [phr v T] to treat someone unfairly because of their race, sex, age etc – use this especially about companies, the police, judges etc: *Shaun says he has definitely been discriminated against because he's black.* | *Why do so many companies think it's OK to discriminate against older people?*

prejudice /ˈpredʒᵊdᵻs/ [n C/U] when people do not like or trust someone who is different, for example because they belong to a different race, country, religion etc: *For years he has fought against prejudice and racial hatred.* | **+ against** *a rising prejudice against gays* | **racial prejudice** (=prejudice because of someone's race) *The number of hate crimes spurred by racial prejudice is increasing in our state.*

inequality /ˌɪnɪˈkwɒlᵻti||-ˈkwɑː-/ [n C/U] when people do not have the same rights or opportunities in their education, their jobs etc, because of their sex, race, or social class **+ in** *The report looks at inequality in education.* | **+ between** *The study shows that large inequalities still exist between men and women.* | **+ of/in** *Most of the complaints centered on the inequality of the justice system.* | **social/sexual/ racial etc inequality** *Social inequality is likely to increase in the 21st century.* | *signs of economic inequality*

discriminatory /dɪˈskrɪmɪnətəri||-tɔːri/ [adj] **discriminatory** laws, systems etc treat one particular group in society, such as women or black people, unfairly: *Congress is to launch an inquiry into discriminatory acts by immigration officials.* | *The government enacted laws to protect women from discriminatory employment practices.* | *Was there evidence of discriminatory treatment?*

double standards /ˌdʌbəl ˈstændəʳdz/ [n plural] an attitude or belief, usually about the way you should behave, that is unfairly thought to be correct for one group in society but not for another: *Their action is designed to call attention to the double standards operating in the Mexican judicial system.* | *What disturbs me most is the racial double standard that exists in foreign policy: Predominantly white countries are given aid and attention while predominantly non-white countries are ignored.*

3 when a report, description etc is unfair

- **unfair**
- **biased**
- **one-sided**
- **slanted**

unfair /ˌʌnˈfeəʳ◂/ [adj] *The press has been accused of unfair coverage of the recent elections.* | *There is nothing unfair about a story that is written from both points of view.*

biased /ˈbaɪəst/ [adj not usually before noun] a **biased** report, account etc is unfair and not correct because it supports one particular group, usually because the writer or newspaper has a connection with that group: *There have been complaints about biased reporting in the tabloid press.* | **biased towards/biased in favour of** *Most newspapers are biased towards one political party or the other.* | **+ against** *Roughly four-fifths of Sun readers believed the paper was biased against the Labour party.*

one-sided /ˌwʌn ˈsaɪdᵻd◂/ [adj] a **one-sided** account, description etc is unfair because it only gives one opinion and not the opposite one, or only tells one part of the story when there are other equally important parts: *Newspapers often give a very one-sided account of political events.* | *Corcoran called the accusations unjust and one-sided.*

slanted /ˈslɑːntᵻd||ˈslæn-/ [adj] presenting facts or information in a way that favours one opinion or side of an argument: *White will make a tough stand against slanted reporting.* | **+ in favour of** *Her arguments are clearly slanted in favour of capital punishment, in spite of her religious convictions.*

4 when one person or group is treated much better than others

- **favouritism**
- **preferential treatment**
- **nepotism**

favouritism British /**favoritism** American /ˈfeɪvərᵻtɪzəm/ [n U] when a teacher, parent, manager etc treats one person in a much better way than the others because they like that person, not because that person deserves it: *Within government, favoritism and nepotism are rampant.* | *If I give Paul the job, I'll be accused of favoritism.* | **+ towards** British /**toward** American *The Labor Secretary said there had been no favoritism toward management in the dispute.*

preferential treatment /ˌprefərenʃəl ˈtriːtmənt/ [n U] if a particular person or group gets **preferential treatment**, they are treated better than other people and therefore have an advantage over them: *She has insisted that she receive no preferential treatment for being an American citizen.* | **give sb preferential treatment** *I get the impression it's busty women who are given preferential treatment around here.* | **receive/get preferential treatment** *Neither I nor my company received any preferential treatment from the White House.*

nepotism /ˈnepətɪzəm/ [n U] when someone in authority gives jobs or special treatment to members of their family – use this to show disapproval: *He resigned, amid rumours of nepotism.* | *Nepotism is an old story in Hollywood circles.*

5 a situation or decision which is very unfair

- injustice
- travesty
- miscarriage of justice

injustice /ɪnˈdʒʌstɪ̈s/ [n C/U] when people are treated with great unfairness, especially in connection with their legal rights: *She will be remembered for her ceaseless campaigning against injustice.* | *These injustices are intolerable, especially when the victims are children.* | **economic/social/racial injustice** *The group, called the Wilmington 10, were active in protests against racial injustices in the schools in the early 1970s.*

travesty /ˈtrævɪ̈sti/ [n C] a situation that is extremely unfair and morally wrong because it has completely the opposite result to the one it is supposed to have: *The Salem witch trials have proved to be a legal travesty.* | **a travesty of justice** *Not allowing her to speak in her own defence was a travesty of justice.*

miscarriage of justice /mɪsˌkærɪdʒ əv ˈdʒʌstɪ̈s/ [n phrase] a situation in which someone is wrongly punished for a crime that they were not responsible for: *Whenever a miscarriage of justice is discovered, people lose respect for the law.* | *The safeguards are intended to prevent a miscarriage of justice.* | **a gross miscarriage of justice** (=a very serious miscarriage) *The execution was a gross miscarriage of justice against an innocent man.*

unfortunately

RELATED WORDS

- to feel sorry for someone who is unhappy *see* **sympathize**
- to wish you had not done something *see* **regret**
- *see also* **sorry, unlucky**

1 when you wish that something had not happened or was not true

- unfortunately
- sadly
- it's a pity/shame
- it's sad
- too bad
- it's unfortunate
- more's the pity
- regrettably

unfortunately /ʌnˈfɔːʳtʃənɪ̈tli/ [adv] use this to show that you wish something had not happened, or you wish something was not true: *There's nothing I can do about it, unfortunately.* | *Unfortunately, Dr Cole cannot spend as long with each patient as she would like.* | *We took some fantastic photos, but unfortunately the film got damaged.*

sadly /ˈsædli/ [adv] unfortunately – use this to talk about events or situations that are very sad: *Sadly, this fine old theatre was destroyed by fire in 1993.* | *Alice was rushed to hospital, but sadly she died two hours later.*

it's a pity/shame /ɪts ə ˈpɪti, ˈʃeɪm/ spoken say this to show that you feel disappointed or sad about something that has happened: *It's a pity about the weather – it was so nice yesterday.* | **+ (that)** *It's a shame you can't come with us.* | **what a pity/shame!** (=say this to show that you feel sad or sympathetic about something) *'Janet didn't get that job.' 'Oh, what a pity!'* | **a real/terrible shame** *They've cut down all those beautiful trees. It's a terrible shame.*

it's sad /ɪts ˈsæd/ spoken use this to show that you feel upset about something sad that has happened, and you wish the situation was different **+ (that)** *It's so sad that your father can't be here to see this.* | **+ when** *It's sad when a marriage breaks up, especially after all those years.* | **it's very/terribly sad** *The town centre is dying, and most of the shops have closed down. It's terribly sad.*

too bad /ˌtuː ˈbæd/ especially American use this to say you are disappointed or sad that someone could not do something, or something could not happen: *'Senator Volk's out of town.' 'Too bad! I wanted to meet him and talk about the campaign.'* | **+ (that)** *Too bad Dickie isn't here to enjoy the fun.* | *It's too bad you have to leave, just when we need you most.*

it's unfortunate /ɪts ʌnˈfɔːʳtʃənɪ̈t/ spoken say this when something causes disappointment, suffering or is inconvenient etc: *The wedding was lovely. It was just unfortunate about the rain.* | **+ (that)** *It's unfortunate that you have to travel so far to work.*

more's the pity /ˌmɔːʳz ðə ˈpɪti/ British spoken say this when you wish that the fact that you have just mentioned was not true: *Now I'm too old to fall in love, more's the pity.* | *I'm afraid this car doesn't belong to me, more's the pity.*

regrettably /rɪˈgretəbli/ [adv] formal use this when you consider the existing situation to be unsatisfactory: *Regrettably Jousse's work has not been translated into English.* | *The poor and disadvantaged will, regrettably, be the ones to suffer as a result of the new law.*

2 something that you wish had not happened or was not true

- unfortunate
- regrettable

unfortunate /ʌnˈfɔːʳtʃənɪ̈t/ [adj] *Parents are so busy with their careers that they don't have time to have fun with their children, and that's unfortunate.* | **unfortunate circumstances/event/situation etc** *'It was an unfortunate set of circumstances that no one could have predicted,' a spokesperson said today.*

regrettable /rɪˈgretəbəl/ [adj] formal something that is **regrettable** makes you feel sorry because it has unpleasant results: *'This is an unfortunate and extremely regrettable incident,' the minister told a newspaper.* | *It was decided by the authorities that the building of the dam across the valley was a 'regrettable necessity'.*

unfriendly

RELATED WORDS

opposite: **friendly**

- to reject someone who is trying to be friendly *see* **reject (5)**
- *see also* **unkind, rude, horrible**

1 not friendly

- unfriendly/not friendly
- cold
- inhospitable
- hostile
- antagonistic
- give sb the cold shoulder
- cliquey/cliquish

unfriendly/not friendly /ʌnˈfrendli, nɒt ˈfrendli/ [adj] *It's very difficult to work with Lindsay – she's so unfriendly.* | *I'm sorry if I sounded unfriendly on the phone – I was just tired.* | *The service at the hotel was bad and the staff weren't very friendly.* | **+ to/towards** *The other girls weren't openly unfriendly towards her, but they never invited her along with them.* —**unfriendliness** [n U] *The fact that he didn't invite you had more to do with insecurity than unfriendliness.*

cold /kəʊld/ [adj] behaving towards other people as if you do not like them or care about them: *His manner all evening was cold and unfriendly.* | *Next time she saw Harry he wasn't rude to her, just very cold.* | **+ to** *She was oddly cold to him, and I wondered what had happened.* —**coldly** [adv] *He looked at me coldly, but said nothing.*

inhospitable /ˌɪnhɒˈspɪtəbəl‖ˌɪnhɑː-/ [adj] unfriendly to people who are visiting your home or country by not doing anything to make them feel welcome: *Generally, the people I met in the city were rude and inhospitable.* | *So many tourists had visited the monastery that the monks had grown somewhat inhospitable.*

hostile /ˈhɒstaɪl‖ˈhɑːstl, ˈhɑːstaɪl/ [adj] very unfriendly, and ready to argue with someone, criticize them, or fight with them: *There was a crowd of hostile demonstrators waiting outside her door.* | **+ to/towards** *He was hostile towards me when I arrived, and the situation did not improve over the next few days.* | **openly hostile** *Several of the neighbors had become openly hostile to one another.* —**hostility** /hɒˈstɪlə̣ti‖hɑː-/ [n U] *I thought I detected a little hostility in his voice.* | **open hostility** (=not hiding hostile feelings) *Her cool politeness had given way to open hostility.*

antagonistic /ænˌtægəˈnɪstɪk◂/ [adj] unfriendly and trying to cause arguments with someone: *I can't understand why he's being so antagonistic.* | **+ towards/to** *Why are Kate and John so antagonistic towards each other?* —**antagonism** /ænˈtægənɪzəm/ [n U] **+ between** *The antagonism between her two grown sons was almost too much for Celia to bear.* | **+ towards/to** *The judge's antagonism towards the defendant was clear to everyone.*

give sb the cold shoulder /ˌgɪv (sb) ðə ˌkəʊld ˈʃəʊldəʳ/ [v phrase] informal to ignore someone and be unfriendly to them, especially because they have upset or offended you: *After I got the promotion, a few of my co-workers started giving me the cold shoulder.*

cliquey/cliquish /ˈkliːki, ˈkliːkɪʃ/ [adj] a group of people who are **cliquey** or **cliquish** are friendly to the other people within that group but not to the people outside it: *Everyone at the school was so cliquey, it was hard for me to make new friends.* | *It was a cliquish group, with the older members staying aloof from the younger ones.*

2 when someone prefers not to be with other people

- distant
- aloof
- stand-offish/standoffish
- antisocial
- unapproachable

distant /ˈdɪstənt/ [adj] unfriendly and showing no emotion, as if other people's lives are of no interest to you: *The neighbors seem very distant, although I try to be friendly.* | *As she was growing up, her father was always distant and took little interest in her achievements.*

aloof /əˈluːf/ [adj] unfriendly and not wanting to talk to other people or spend time with them, especially because you think you are better than them: *Barbara remained aloof behind the barrier of her menu.* | *The organization is controlled by aloof intellectuals who do not take an interest in the ordinary members.* —**aloofness** [n U] *Sam had a certain aloofness that made people afraid to approach him.*

stand-offish/standoffish /ˌstænd ˈɒfɪʃ‖-ˈɔːf-/ [adj not usually before noun] behaving in an unfriendly and rather formal way, as if you do not want to get too involved with other people: *She can be quite stand-offish sometimes.* | *He was well-liked by the senior members of the firm, even though his colleagues found him standoffish and arrogant.*

antisocial /ˌæntɪˈsəʊʃəl◂/ [adj] someone who is **antisocial** does not enjoy being with other people and tries to avoid meeting them or talking to them: *Not everyone who likes playing computer games is an antisocial loner.* | *Because she was so shy, people often thought she was antisocial.*

unapproachable /ˌʌnəˈprəʊtʃəbəl◂/ [adj] someone who is **unapproachable** seems unfriendly so that you are nervous about talking to them: *He kept his arms crossed in front of him and seemed somewhat unapproachable.* | *A lot of the guys thought she was attractive, but she seemed so unapproachable that no one dared to talk to her.*

3 when relationships are unfriendly

- unfriendly/not friendly
- cool
- strained
- frosty
- turn sour

unfriendly/not friendly /ʌnˈfrendli, nɒt ˈfrendli/ [adj] *She used to get on well with her neighbours but now things aren't very friendly.* | *Unfriendly relations between the two countries nearly led to war.* | **on unfriendly terms/not on friendly terms** (=with an unfriendly relationship) *They've been on unfriendly terms ever since their argument.*

cool /kuːl/ [adj] less friendly than usual, so that people do not smile at each other, talk to each other in a friendly way etc: *The cool relationship between the two men affected the entire team.* | *When Bill finally arrived, nearly an hour late, he got a rather cool reception.*

strained /streɪnd/ [adj] a situation or relationship that is **strained** is not friendly or relaxed, because people feel worried or do not trust each other: *The meeting took place in a strained atmosphere.* | *Our relationship became very strained because I had refused to lend him money.*

frosty /ˈfrɒsti‖ˈfrɔːsti/ [adj] very unfriendly, especially following an argument or because someone feels offended: *After their quarrel, things between Maria and her father were rather frosty.*

turn sour /ˌtɜːʳn ˈsaʊəʳ/ [v phrase] if a relationship **turns sour**, the people involved in it start to dislike each other and to behave in an unfriendly way towards each other: *After five years their marriage turned sour and ended in divorce.* | *When the company began to lose money, things turned sour between the directors.*

4 when a particular place or situation seems unfriendly

- unfriendly/not friendly
- unwelcoming
- inhospitable
- impersonal
- forbidding

unfriendly/not friendly /ʌnˈfrendli, nɒt ˈfrendli/ [adj] *I don't like going to that bar – it's not very friendly.* | **+ to/towards** *The city has a reputation for being unfriendly to minorities.*

unwelcoming /ʌnˈwelkəmɪŋ/ [adj] making you feel that you are not wanted: *The entrance to the factory is cold, bare, and unwelcoming.* | **+ to/towards** *The new fence is just one example of the city's attempt to make public spaces unwelcoming to the homeless.*

inhospitable /ˌɪnhɒˈspɪtəbəl‖ˌɪnhɑː-/ [adj] unfriendly and difficult to feel relaxed in: *The tribe has lived for generations in the inhospitable mountain regions of the country.* | **+ to/towards** *The brokerage firm has always been extremely inhospitable to women.*

impersonal /ɪmˈpɜːʳsənəl/ [adj] a place or situation that is **impersonal** lacks the normal friendly relations between people who work or do business together, as if such feelings were considered unimportant: *They just handed over the keys and walked out – it was all so impersonal.* | *I had no desire to work for a large, impersonal organization.*

forbidding /fəʳˈbɪdɪŋ/ [adj] a **forbidding** place seems unfriendly, uncomfortable, and a little frightening, so that you do not want to go there: *The school was a large, rather forbidding building.* | *The wood-panelled den looked dark and forbidding.*

unimportant

RELATED WORDS

opposite: **important**

▸ *see also* **small**

1 not important

- not important/unimportant
- minor
- insignificant/not significant
- petty
- trivial
- small
- be of no importance

not important/unimportant /nɒt ɪmˈpɔːʳtənt, ˌʌnɪmˈpɔːʳtənt◂/ [adj] formal not likely to cause problems or to have an important effect on something: *'I forgot to add the olive oil.' 'Don't worry – it's not important.'* | *I don't want to waste time arguing over unimportant details.* | *It is not important that you understand everything at this stage.* | *Critics have dismissed his work as unimportant.*

minor /ˈmaɪnəʳ/ [adj] a **minor** problem, accident, disagreement etc is small and does not have a serious effect or result: *Two car windows were broken and minor damage was done to some shops.* | *She suffered some minor injuries in the accident.* | *We've had a few minor problems with the new computer system.*

insignificant/not significant /ˌɪnsɪgˈnɪfɪkənt, nɒt sɪgˈnɪfɪkənt/ [adj] not important enough to worry about, especially because there are other problems that are much more serious: *The level of radiation was considered 'insignificant' and not a danger to health.* | *There is a slight difference in the way men and women are affected by the drug, but this is not really significant.* | *After a week of negotiations, the differences between the two sides are now relatively insignificant.* | *EU financiers say that recent problems on the US stock markets were not significant for Europe.*

petty /ˈpeti/ [adj] something such as a problem, argument, or worry that is **petty** is so unimportant that it seems silly or selfish for someone to talk or worry about: *We started having arguments over petty little things.* | *The meeting spent too much time on petty issues, and didn't address the real problem.*

trivial /ˈtrɪviəl/ [adj] unimportant and not serious, and not worth worrying about or spending time or effort on: *No, I don't think your question is trivial at all.* | *Why waste time watching trivial TV programs?* | *The issue of where the peace talks will be held may seem trivial, but to the participants it is very important.*

small /smɔːl/ [adj only before noun] not important and not likely to take long to deal with or correct: *Your essay's very good – there are just one or two small points I'd like to discuss.* | *There were a couple of small things I wanted to talk to you about.* | *We had a few small problems when we were putting the design together, but it works fine now.*

be of no importance /biː əv ˌnəʊ ɪmˈpɔːʳtəns/ [v phrase] formal to not be important, and be unlikely to affect anything in a serious way: *If you're capable of doing the job, your age is of no importance.* | *These are small details and probably of no importance.*

2 what you say when something is not important

- it doesn't matter
- it makes no difference/it doesn't make any difference
- it's no big deal / it's not a big deal
- it's nothing

it doesn't matter /ɪt ˌdʌzənt ˈmætəʳ/ spoken say this to tell someone that something is not important and will not cause any serious problems: *'We've missed the train.' 'It doesn't matter – there's another one in 10 minutes.'* | **+ if/whether/what etc** *It doesn't matter if you're a few minutes late. We'll wait for you.* | *It doesn't matter what other people think. You should do what you think is best.*

it makes no difference/it doesn't make any difference /ɪt ˌmeɪks nəʊ ˈdɪfərəns, ɪt ˌdʌzənt meɪk eni ˈdɪfərəns/ say this when you think something is not important enough to affect what happens or change what someone decides: *'Do you want cash or a cheque?' 'It doesn't make any difference.'* | *Even if she had known he was lying it would have made no difference.* | *It doesn't make any difference whether you use fresh berries or frozen ones.* | **it makes no difference/it doesn't make any difference to sb** *It makes no difference to me if you want to go.* | **it makes no difference/it doesn't make any difference to sth** *You can have a single room or a double – it makes no difference to the price.*

it's no big deal / it's not a big deal /ɪts ˌnəʊ bɪg ˈdiːl, ɪts ˌnɒt ə bɪg ˈdiːl/ spoken say this when you do not think something is important or worrying, even though other people may think it is: *My leg's a little sore, but it's no big deal.* | *Just copy your work onto a disk – it's no big deal.* | *She assumed he'd be furious, but the whole incident just wasn't a big deal to him.*

it's nothing /ɪts ˈnʌθɪŋ/ spoken say this when you think something is not important and you do not want other people to worry about it: *'Are you okay?' 'Yeah, it's nothing.'* | *'Why do you want to speak to Danny? Is he in trouble again?' 'No, it's nothing, really. We just want to ask a couple of questions.'*

3 less important than something else

- secondary
- subsidiary
- incidental
- marginal
- peripheral
- be of secondary/minor/less etc importance
- side issue
- pale into insignificance

secondary /'sekəndəri‖-deri/ [adj] less important than the main subject, problem etc: *The government sees unemployment as a secondary issue.* | *The study found that women were often reduced to secondary roles in the workplace.* | **+ to** *Tourism is secondary to oil revenues as a source of income.*

subsidiary /səb'sɪdiəri‖-dieri/ [adj] formal a **subsidiary** idea, question, subject etc is less important than the main one but it is connected with it: *If you take the English literature course, you can do linguistics as a subsidiary subject.* | **+ to** *The formulation of a lasting peace settlement was the main objective, and everything else was seen as subsidiary to it.*

incidental /ˌɪnsə̇'dentl◂/ [adj] happening or existing in connection with or as a result of something else that is more important: *The Red Cross will provide money for food, housing, and incidental expenses.* | **+ to** *The puzzles are fun, but are incidental to the plot of the book.* | **purely incidental** *The concert is just for fun, really. Any profit we make from it will be purely incidental.*

marginal /'mɑːʳdʒə̇nəl/ [adj] too small and unimportant to have any useful or noticeable effect: *The difference between the two cars is marginal.* | *a marginal increase in sales*

peripheral /pə'rɪfərəl/ [adj] relating to the main activity, question, or subject, but much less important than it: *It is a society in which women's rights and concerns are still treated as peripheral.* | *Too much money is being spent on peripheral programs when our kids can't read or do basic math.* | **+ to** *The romance was peripheral to the movie's main plot.*

be of secondary/minor/less etc importance /biː əv ˌsekəndəri ɪm'pɔːʳtəns‖-deri-/ [v phrase] to be not very important compared to other things: *It's the perfect job for him – the salary is of secondary importance.* | *Police are increasingly regarding cannabis use as being of minor importance compared with other forms of crime.* | *We must stop treating mental illness as being of less importance than physical disabilities.*

side issue /'saɪd ˌɪʃuː/ [n C] a subject or question that results from or is connected with the main one being considered, but is much less important: *The meeting seemed to focus on side issues, without ever really addressing the main point.* | *One of the side issues that arose was what to do with the old equipment when the new things arrived.*

pale into insignificance /ˌpeɪl ɪntʊ ɪnsɪg'nɪfɪkəns/ [v phrase] if someone's problems or achievements **pale into insignificance** when they are compared to something else, they are clearly much less important: *Our difficulties pale into insignificance when compared to the problems of the homeless.*

4 someone who is not important

- not important
- insignificant
- the little guy
- lightweight
- a nobody
- nonentity
- small fry

not important /nɒt ɪm'pɔːʳtənt/ [adj] *He's not really an important figure in the organization.* | *Don't worry about the critics. They're not important – they just think they are.*

insignificant /ˌɪnsɪg'nɪfɪkənt/ [adj] not important enough or powerful enough to worry about or treat seriously: *The anti-war group was an insignificant minority within the party.* | *The spies' payroll included insignificant clerks and highly placed officials.*

the little guy /ðə 'lɪtl gaɪ/ [n singular] especially American, informal a person or organization that is not important because they do not have any power or influence: *He got rich trading illegally on the stock market, using the little guy's money.* | *When the big retailers open a store, the little guys lose business.*

lightweight /'laɪt-weɪt/ [n C] someone who is well-known, for example in politics or literature, but is not really respected or considered to be important: *His books are tremendously popular, but most of the critics regard him as a lightweight.* | **political/intellectual/literary etc lightweight** *It would be dangerous to dismiss her as a political lightweight.*

a nobody /ə 'nəʊbədi‖-bɑːdi/ [n C usually singular] informal someone who is considered to be unimportant because they are not famous, powerful, or rich: *He went from being a nobody to being paid $2 million a year.* | *I felt like a complete nobody when I lost my job.*

nonentity /nɒ'nentə̇ti‖nɑː-/ [n C] someone who is not at all important, powerful, or interesting, and has no special qualities or skills: *Next to him, the other dancers seemed like nonentities.* | *He packed his government with nonentities, who would never challenge his leadership.*

small fry /'smɔːl fraɪ/ [n plural] informal a person or group who has very little power or importance compared to other people or organizations: *Environmental groups are small fry against the power of the big multinationals.* | *Only the small fry on the drugs scene got caught by the police.*

5 something that is not important

- trivia

trivia /'trɪviə/ [n U] information or facts that are not important and have no real use or value: *The magazine was full of trivia and gossip.* | *I find that I can remember trivia such as old sports results, but I can't remember the things that I really need to remember.*

6 to make something seem less important than it really is

- trivialize
- play down/downplay
- belittle
- understate
- underestimate

trivialize ALSO **trivialise** British /'trɪviəlaɪz/ [v T] to write or talk about something in a way that makes it seem less serious or important than it really is: *The newspaper's headlines trivialized the war, making it* *seem like a game.* | *Judges feared that showing the trial on television would trivialize the legal process.*

play down/downplay /ˌpleɪ 'daʊn, daʊn'pleɪ/ [phr v T/v T] to pretend that a problem, illness etc is less important or serious than it really is: *He accused drug companies of downplaying the risks of the new drug.* | *She downplayed any suggestion that there had been a leak in the chemical factory.* | **play down sth** *The government is trying to play down the seriousness of the unemployment figures.* | **play sth down** *The plan will cause a lot of changes, but officials are trying to play it down.*

belittle /bɪ'lɪtl/ [v T] to say or do something that makes someone's efforts or achievements seem unimportant or useless: *Good teachers never belittle their students.* | *Does your boss constantly belittle your contribution to the department?*

understate /ˌʌndəʳ'steɪt/ [v T] to describe the size, value, or importance of something in a way that makes it seem less than it really is: *I think you are understating the importance to young people of a stable home life.* | *In the report, the incidence of violent crime is consistently understated.*

underestimate /ˌʌndər'estɪ̌meɪt/ [v T] to wrongly think that something is less important than it really is: *People often underestimate the importance of human relationships in successful companies.* | *Never underestimate the value of really good training.*

unite

RELATED WORDS

▸ *see also* **with/together, join**

1 to join together with other people, organizations, or countries

- ▸ unite
- ▸ team up
- ▸ get together
- ▸ combine
- ▸ join forces
- ▸ come together
- ▸ amalgamate
- ▸ merge

unite /juː'naɪt/ [v I] especially written if people, organizations, or countries **unite**, they start working together or join together as a single unit, for example because they have the same aims as each other **+ to do sth** *In 1960, British and Italian Somaliland united to form Somalia.* | *Various political and religions groups united to oppose the dictatorship.* | **+ against** *Police chiefs called on the local people to unite against the drug dealers.* | **+ behind** *a speech in which he asked America to unite behind the new President*

team up /ˌtiːm 'ʌp/ [phr v I] if two or more people **team up**, they agree to work together, especially in business, music, or theatre **+ with** *I teamed up with a local journalist, and we worked on the story together.* | **+ to do sth** *It all started when Paul McCartney and John Lennon teamed up to form a band.*

get together /get tə'geðəʳ/ [phr v I] if people or organizations **get together**, they join together in order to do something, especially in an informal way: *Designers from both countries got together and held a joint exhibition.* | **+ to do sth** *The whole family needs to get together to decide what to do about the trip.*

combine /kəm'baɪn/ [v I] to join together and work very closely together so that you succeed in achieving the result you want **+ to do sth** *The opposition parties combined to drive the Prime Minister out of office.* | **+ with** *Members of the radical Right combined with communists in holding an illegal meeting.*

join forces /ˌdʒɔɪn 'fɔːʳsɪ̌z/ [v phrase] if people or organizations **join forces**, they join together in order to work together or to fight against an enemy **+ to do sth** *The two manufacturers, who were once bitter rivals, have now joined forces to develop a new sports car.* | **+ with** *The socialists hope to join forces with the communists to fight the next election.*

come together /ˌkʌm tə'geðəʳ/ [phr v I] if people or organizations **come together**, especially ones who usually disagree or compete with each other, they join together in order to do something: *Women from the different organizations have been able to come together and agree on certain basic principles about what they, as women, are fighting for.* | **+ to do sth** *The Conference called on everyone to come together to resist the government's planned educational reforms.*

amalgamate /ə'mælgəmeɪt/ [v I] if two or more organizations **amalgamate**, for example colleges, unions, or hospitals, they join together to form a single organization: *The two schools amalgamated in 1974.* | **+ with** *The women's association has amalgamated with the men's.* | **+ into** *A and B squadrons amalgamated into a single squadron.* —**amalgamation** /əˌmælgə'meɪʃən/ [n U] *the amalgamation of several small farms into one large agricultural unit*

merge /mɜːʳdʒ/ [v I] if two companies or organizations **merge**, they join together to form a single company or organization: *The two banks have announced plans to merge next year.* | **+ with** *In 1969, Cadbury merged with Schweppes, changing the whole character of the company.*

2 when people unite

- ▸ pull together
- ▸ stand together
- ▸ stick together
- ▸ close ranks
- ▸ be united

pull together /ˌpʊl tə'geðəʳ/ [phr v I] if the people in a group **pull together**, they all work together to deal with a difficult situation: *In Japan in the 50s and 60s, the government, bankers and workers all pulled together and brought about what we now call 'the economic miracle'.* | **+ to do sth** *Parents, teachers, and students should all pull together to tackle the school's drugs problem.*

stand together /ˌstænd tə'geðəʳ/ [phr v I] if a group of people **stand together**, they unite and deal with a difficult or dangerous situation as a group: *We must all stand together on this one. I don't want anybody quitting or saying they don't want to get involved.* | *Somehow they stood together and kept the business going in spite of all that was going on.*

stick together /ˌstɪk tə'geðəʳ/ [phr v I] informal if two or more people **stick together**, they continue to support each other even when there are problems or difficulties: *It is important for families to stick together.* | *We should be able to get out of this mess, provided we stick together.*

close ranks /ˌkləʊz 'ræŋks/ [v phrase] if people who belong to a group or organization **close ranks**, they join together to protect each other, especially when the group or its members are being criticized or attacked: *When she applied for promotion, the male managers all closed ranks and made sure she didn't get it.* | *President Nixon's staff were instructed to close ranks in response to the Watergate arrests.*

be united /biː juːˈnaɪtɪ̣d/ [v phrase] if a group of people are united, they support each other or are working together in a difficult situation: *Organisers want the conference to show that the party is united as never before.* | **+ in** *The Council is united in its resolve to maintain and develop standards of professional management.*

3 when people are united

- unity
- solidarity
- spirit

unity /ˈjuːnɪ̣ti/ [n U] *In his speech the Prime Minister stressed the need for party unity.* | *The lack of unity within the women's movement has resulted in a severe lack of power.*

solidarity /ˌsɒlɪ̣ˈdærɪ̣ti‖ˌsɑː-/ [n U] loyalty and support for a person or group whose political views you strongly agree with, especially someone who is fighting against or being badly treated by people who are in authority **+ with** *Workers all over the country went on strike to show their solidarity with the miners.* | **+ between** *There was a feeling of solidarity between all the staff and a common suspicion as to why management had called the meeting.*

spirit /ˈspɪrɪ̣t/ [n U] **team/community/public spirit** a strong feeling of belonging to a particular group and of wanting to help them: *The crew enjoy working together and have developed an excellent team spirit.* | *I am sure that, given the great community spirit here, the fund-raisers will not give up.*

4 to make people, organizations, or countries unite

- unite
- bring together
- rally
- amalgamate
- merge

unite /juːˈnaɪt/ [v T] *President Clinton's rousing speech united the Democrats.* | *What united the two groups was their hatred of fascism in all its forms.* | *She and Picasso had always been friends, but now they shared a secret that united them even more.*

bring together /ˌbrɪŋ təˈgeðəʳ/ [phr v T] if an event or a situation **brings** people **together**, it makes them have a closer, more friendly relationship with each other **bring sb together** *What was it that first brought you two together? Your love of music?* | *In South Africa, cricket has been the one sport that has brought people together.*

rally /ˈræli/ [v T] to persuade or encourage people to unite in order to fight for or against something **rally support/opposition** *The main effect of the new tax was to rally opposition to the government.* | *Recent news reports on the situation in the capital have helped rally support for the war.* | **rally sb** *Churchill's stirring speeches helped rally his countrymen to fight against the enemy.*

amalgamate /əˈmælgəmeɪt/ [v T] to make two or more organizations join together, for example colleges, unions, or hospitals, in order to make a single one: *Worries have been expressed about the current trend of amalgamating sales teams.* | **amalgamate sth into sth** *The 55 army battalions would be amalgamated into 23 units.*

merge /mɜːʳdʒ/ [v T] to make two companies or organizations join together to form a single one: *There are plans to merge the two most successful TV channels.* | **merge sth with sth** *He wanted to merge his company with a South African mining firm.*

unkind

RELATED WORDS

opposite: **kind**

▸ *see also* **cruel, bad, rude**

1 treating someone unkindly

- unkind
- mean
- nasty
- cruel
- spiteful
- be hard on
- give sb a hard time
- take sth out on

unkind /ˌʌnˈkaɪnd◂/ [adj] someone who is **unkind** treats people in a way that makes them unhappy or upset: *Children can be very unkind.* | **+ to** *I felt very sorry for being unkind to her.* | **it is unkind (of sb) to do sth** *It would be unkind to keep him in suspense for too long.* —**unkindly** [adv] *He loves you, Fiona, even though you treat him so unkindly.* | *She laughed unkindly at his misfortune.* —**unkindness** [n U] *I couldn't forgive their unkindness towards me.*

mean /miːn/ [adj] someone who is **mean** deliberately speaks to someone unkindly or does things to annoy them or make them angry: *She hated him for being so mean. Why was he stopping her from seeing her friends?* | *I never thought he was capable of doing such a mean thing to his brother.* | **+ to** *He was mean to those who worked for him and generous to those who he hardly knew.* | **it is mean (of sb) to do sth** *It was mean of you to disturb her when she was having a rest.*

nasty /ˈnɑːsti‖ˈnæsti/ [adj] someone who is **nasty** is deliberately unkind, and seems to enjoy making people unhappy: *When I was a child I did some nasty things to my little brother.* | *I don't mean to be nasty, but I don't think we should work together any more.* | **+ to** *Paul, you mustn't be nasty to the children. You'll make them cry.* —**nastiness** [n U] *She tried to make me look silly. She did it out of sheer nastiness.*

cruel /ˈkruːəl/ [adj] someone who is **cruel** is very unkind, and does not seem to care about other people's feelings: *He didn't seem the sort of man to be cruel on purpose.* | **+ to** *She married a man who was very cruel to her.* | **it is cruel (of sb) to do sth** *It was cruel of you to frighten the poor boy like that.* —**cruelly** [adv] *The other girls teased her cruelly because she was different.* —**cruelty** [n U] *As a result of the scandal, his family was exposed to the cruelty of the press.*

spiteful /ˈspaɪtfəl/ [adj] deliberately unkind to someone because you are jealous of them or angry with them: *Failure had made him bitter and spiteful.* | *That was a wicked and spiteful thing to do.* —**spitefully** [adv] *'I never liked her anyway,' Rob said spitefully.*

be hard on /biː ˈhɑːʳd ɒn/ [v phrase] to be unkind to someone by criticizing them or treating them more severely than is fair: *He's only just started work here – you mustn't be too hard on him.* | *I thought you were a little hard on Denise, not letting her go to the party.*

give sb a hard time /ˌgɪv (sb) ə ˌhɑːʳd ˈtaɪm/ [v phrase] **informal** to be unkind to someone by criticizing them in a way that is not fair: *She left the company because her boss was giving her a really hard time.* | *Stop giving me such a hard time. I'm doing my best.*

take sth out on /ˌteɪk (sth) ˈaʊt ɒn/ [phr v T] to be unkind to someone because you are angry or upset about something else, even though it is not their fault: *I know you've had a bad day at the office, but don't take it out on me.* | *I'm sorry I was rotten to you, but there was no one else to take it out on.*

2 unkind comments or remarks

- unkind
- behind sb's back
- caustic
- cutting
- bitchy
- snide
- vicious

unkind /ˌʌnˈkaɪnd◂/ [adj] something you say to someone that is **unkind**, makes them feel unhappy or upset: *He said some very unkind things about my clothes.* | *She was used to the unkind remarks made by other students.* | **+ about** *Why are you always so unkind about Christina?* | **never say an unkind word about sb** *I never heard her say an unkind word about anyone.*

behind sb's back /bɪˌhaɪnd (sb's) ˈbæk/ [adv] if you talk about someone **behind their back**, you say rude or unkind things about them when they are not present: *I'm sure the other girls are talking about me behind my back.* | *His name is Mr McLeod, but his students call him 'Big Nose' behind his back.*

caustic /ˈkɔːstɪk/ [adj usually before noun] criticizing someone or something in an unkind but clever way: *Hayward made some pretty caustic comments about your poetry.* | **caustic wit/humour** *Some of his students were alienated by his caustic wit.*

cutting /ˈkʌtɪŋ/ [adj] a remark that is **cutting** is very unkind and is intended to hurt someone's feelings, especially by making them feel stupid or unimportant: *Emily always managed to say something cutting whenever we met at a party.* | *At the meeting Mark made some cutting remarks about Sally, who wasn't there to defend herself.*

bitchy /ˈbɪtʃi/ [adj] someone who is **bitchy** or who makes **bitchy** remarks says unkind things about another person, especially about the way they look or behave – used especially by women when talking about other women: *She was always making bitchy comments about people's clothes and make-up.* | **+ about/towards** *The other girls in my class were often bitchy towards me because I studied so hard.*

snide /snaɪd/ [adj usually before noun] a **snide** remark criticizes someone in an unkind way, but is not very direct: *As she uttered these words she realized they sounded snide and insinuating.* | **snide comments/remarks** *The teacher kept making snide comments about my pronunciation, which really embarrassed me.*

vicious /ˈvɪʃəs/ [adj] cruel and deliberately intended to hurt someone's feelings or to make their character seem very bad: *The Senator launched a vicious attack on the former President.* | *Someone is conducting a vicious campaign of false rumours against the Royal Family.* —**viciously** [adv] *Margaret viciously blamed her husband for all that had happened.*

3 unkind, but not deliberately unkind

- thoughtless/inconsiderate
- insensitive
- tactless

thoughtless/inconsiderate /ˈθɔːtləs, ˌɪnkənˈsɪdərɪ̈t◂/ [adj] someone who is **thoughtless** or **inconsiderate** only thinks about their own situation, their own enjoyment etc, and does not think about the effects that their actions will have on other people: *A few thoughtless people have spoiled the holiday for everyone else.* | *I have an inconsiderate neighbour who plays loud music late at night.* | **it is thoughtless/inconsiderate of sb to do sth** *It was thoughtless of him to mention her divorce when she's so upset.* | *I'm sorry, it was inconsiderate of me to phone so early.*

insensitive /ɪnˈsensɪ̈tɪv/ [adj] someone who is **insensitive** does not notice when other people are upset or when something that they do might upset other people: *How could you be so insensitive?* | **insensitive to sb's feelings/needs etc** *Doctors sometimes seem insensitive to their patients' feelings.* —**insensitivity** /ɪnˌsensɪ̈ˈtɪvɪ̈ti/ [n U] *the insensitivity of some police officers in the way they treat rape victims*

tactless /ˈtæktləs/ [adj] someone who is **tactless** says or does things that offend other people or hurt their feelings, without intending to and without realizing that they have done it: *He made all sorts of tactless remarks about her appearance.* | **it is tactless (of sb) to do sth** *It was a bit tactless of you to start talking about her ex-boyfriend.*

4 having no sympathy for other people's problems

- unsympathetic
- hard-hearted

unsympathetic /ˌʌnsɪmpəˈθetɪk/ [adj] someone who is **unsympathetic** does not show you any sympathy when you need help or when you tell them about your troubles: *I explained our problems to the bank manager, but he remained unsympathetic.* | *I'm sorry, I don't mean to be unsympathetic, but I don't see how I can help.* | *Our appeal for government help met with an unsympathetic response.*

hard-hearted /ˌhɑːʳd ˈhɑːʳtɪ̈d◂/ [adj] someone who is **hard-hearted** does not feel any sympathy and does not care at all when people are in trouble or pain and ask for help: *a hard-hearted and unprincipled man* | *I've tried to help in the past, but I think now I have to be hard-hearted and make them help themselves.*

unlucky

RELATED WORDS

opposite: lucky

- *see also* **unfortunately**

1 when someone is unlucky in a particular situation or at a particular time

- unlucky
- unfortunate
- have the misfortune to do sth/have the misfortune of doing sth
- have bad luck
- be out of luck
- a run of bad luck
- it's one of those days/it's not my day
- be in the wrong place at the wrong time

unlucky /ʌnˈlʌki/ [adj not before noun] *'Were you disappointed with the team's performance?' 'No, not really, I think we were just unlucky.'* | **be unlucky (enough) to do sth** *The victims were simply unlucky enough to have been in the restaurant when the gunmen started shooting.* | **+ with** *We were unlucky with the weather. It rained almost every day we were on the island.*

unfortunate /ʌnˈfɔːʳtʃənɪ̈t/ [adj] having bad luck that you do not deserve, especially when this has a serious effect on your life, health etc: *Some of the unfortunate victims were trapped inside the building for over 12 hours.* | **be unfortunate (enough) to do sth** *He was unfortunate enough to lose his job just after his wife had a baby.*

have the misfortune to do sth/have the misfortune of doing sth /hæv ðə mɪsˌfɔːʳtʃən tə 'du: (sth), hæv ðə mɪs,fɔːʳtʃən əv 'duːɪŋ (sth)/ [v phrase not in progressive] formal to be unlucky on a particular occasion, especially when this results in something very unpleasant happening to you: *Bowman had the misfortune of being sent to the area where there was heavy fighting.* | *Women who have the misfortune to be involved with violent men often think it's their own fault.*

have bad luck /hæv ,bæd 'lʌk/ [v phrase] to be unlucky, especially in a way that affects one particular part of your life: *Why do we always have such bad luck when it comes to hiring suitable workers?* | **+ with** *Our kids have had very bad luck with their teachers recently.* | **have the bad luck to do sth** *He had the bad luck to upset the boss's wife at the party.*

be out of luck /biː ,aʊt əv 'lʌk/ [v phrase] to be prevented by bad luck from doing something that you want to do, for example going somewhere, buying something, or seeing someone: *I'm afraid you're out of luck. The director has already left for the day.* | *It looks like we're out of luck – all the hotels are full.*

a run of bad luck /ə ,rʌn əv ,bæd 'lʌk/ [n phrase] a period of time during which a lot of bad things happen to you one after the other: *Mimi's had a terrible run of bad luck this year, what with the car accident and her boyfriend leaving her.* | *Despite the Giant's current run of bad luck, fans are still showing up for the games.*

it's one of those days/it's not my day /ɪts ,wʌn əv ðəʊz 'deɪz, ɪts ,nɒt maɪ 'deɪ/ spoken say this when a lot of bad things have happened to you that day: *I just want to go home, take a bath, and go to bed – it's been one of those days.* | *First I missed the bus, then I spilled coffee on myself, and now my computer is frozen – it's just not my day.*

be in the wrong place at the wrong time /biː ɪn ðə ,rɒŋ ,pleɪs ət ðə ,rɒŋ 'taɪm‖-,rɔːŋ-/ [v phrase] to have something bad happen to you by chance: *The driver was drunk and hit her as she was crossing the road. She was just in the wrong place at the wrong time.*

2 when someone is always unlucky

- unlucky
- with my luck
- just my luck
- be jinxed/be a jinx

unlucky /ʌn'lʌki/ [adj] an **unlucky** person often has bad things happen to them or things often go wrong by chance for them, not because of bad planning, stupidity, or carelessness: *I don't believe anyone is born lucky or unlucky – life is what you make it.* | *Val's one of the unluckiest people I know – on Monday her car was stolen and the day after she fell and broke her arm.* | **+ with** *He seems to be very unlucky with cars – every time he buys one it always has something wrong with it.* | **unlucky in love** *I've never had a girlfriend more than a couple of months – I guess I'm just unlucky in love.*

with my luck /wɪð 'maɪ lʌk/ [adv] spoken say **with my luck** when you think something bad is going to happen to you, and you are not surprised because you think you are an unlucky person: *With my luck all the tickets will be sold by the time we get there.* | *I thought about buying a gun, but then I thought, with my luck, I'd probably end up shooting myself by accident.*

just my luck /,dʒʌst maɪ 'lʌk/ [adv] spoken say **just my luck** when something bad has happened to you and you are not surprised because you think you are an unlucky person: *Married, is he? Just my luck.* | *Just my luck! The one vacation I take all year, and I have to get sick.*

be jinxed/be a jinx /biː 'dʒɪŋkst, biː ə 'dʒɪŋks/ [v phrase] to be very unlucky, so that everything you do or get involved in seems to go wrong, often in a way that affects other people too: *This is the fifth company she's worked for that's gone bankrupt – she's jinxed.* | *The way the team kept losing, I was beginning to think I was some kind of a jinx.*

3 an unlucky situation or event

- unlucky
- unfortunate
- unfortunately
- as bad luck would have it
- be bad luck
- there is a jinx on sth/sth is jinxed

unlucky /ʌn'lʌki/ [adj] an **unlucky** event happens simply because of bad luck, not because of bad planning, carelessness, stupidity etc: *The car in front braked suddenly and I went straight into it – it was just unlucky.* | **it is unlucky (for sb) that** *It was unlucky for Steve that the teacher walked in just at that moment.* —**unluckily** [adv] *Unluckily for us, Melissa had overheard everything we said.*

unfortunate /ʌn'fɔːʳtʃənɪ̩t/ [adj] unlucky – use this especially about something that causes a lot of harm or problems. **Unfortunate** is more formal than **unlucky**: *Quarterback Brady Anderson was injured in an unfortunate collision with one of his team-mates.* | *The mix-up was the result of a set of unfortunate circumstances.* | **it is unfortunate (for sb) that** *It was very unfortunate that someone ended up getting hurt.*

unfortunately /ʌn'fɔːʳtʃənɪ̩tli/ [adv] because of bad luck – use this when something annoying, unpleasant, or dangerous happens as a result of bad luck: *I would have been here an hour ago, but unfortunately I missed the train.* | **unfortunately for sb** *They finally cut down those old trees on our street, but unfortunately for us one of them fell on our car.*

as bad luck would have it /əz ,bæd lʌk wʊd 'hæv ɪt/ [v phrase] use **as bad** or **ill luck would have it** when you are describing something unlucky that happened to you as part of a series of events, and that caused you disappointment, inconvenience etc [adv] *We saw some really amazing things, but as ill luck would have it, I'd forgotten my camera.* | *As bad luck would have it, there was a thick fog the next day and our flight was delayed.*

be bad luck /biː ,bæd 'lʌk/ [v phrase] to happen as a result of bad luck, especially when something bad happens to you that is not your fault: *His medical condition isn't his fault – it's just bad luck.* | **it is bad luck (for sb) that** *It's bad luck for her that they decided to shut down the company right after she started working there.*

there is a jinx on sth/sth is jinxed /ðeər ɪz ə 'dʒɪŋks ɒn (sth), (sth) ɪz 'dʒɪŋkst/ if you say that **there is a jinx on** a plan, occasion etc or that it **is jinxed**, a lot of things go wrong with it without any reason and you think it is because of bad luck: *Three people have quit, we've had computer problems, and now the heating has broken down. There must be a jinx on this office.* | *It's pouring with rain and the flowers haven't arrived – Lynne's convinced the whole wedding is jinxed.*

4 something that is believed to give you bad luck

- unlucky
- be/bring bad luck

unlucky /ʌn'lʌki/ [adj] *I never kill spiders – it's unlucky.* | *Why do you want to get married on the 13th? Thirteen is such an unlucky number.* | **be unlucky to do sth** *Some people think it's unlucky to walk under ladders.*

be/bring bad luck /biː, ˌbrɪŋ bæd 'lʌk/ [v phrase] something that **is bad luck** or **brings bad luck** is believed to make bad things happen: *It's supposed to be bad luck to open an umbrella in the house.* | *For centuries, crows have been thought to bring bad luck.*

5 bad luck

- bad luck
- misfortune

bad luck /ˌbæd 'lʌk/ [n U] the way that bad things happen to someone by chance, not because of bad planning, carelessness, stupidity etc: *She seems to have nothing but bad luck when it comes to men.* | *Talk about bad luck! Last night Ray's car was broken into for the second time this month.*

misfortune /mɪs'fɔːʳtʃən/ [n C/U] formal bad luck, especially when this results in someone having great difficulties in their life, for example being very poor, having a serious accident etc: *It was impossible not to feel sympathy for the family's misfortune.* | *Her misfortunes worsened this year, when her company eliminated her position and she lost her job.*

unsuitable

RELATED WORDS

opposite: **suitable**

see also **wrong**

1 not suitable for a particular purpose, person, or situation

- unsuitable/not suitable
- inappropriate/not appropriate
- unsuited to sth/not suited to sth
- wrong
- hardly the time/place/person
- unfit/not fit

unsuitable/not suitable /ʌn'suːtəbəl, nɒt 'suːtəbəl/ [adj] *We never planted roses here because the climate isn't suitable.* | *The strict laws forbid women to read 'unsuitable material.'* | **+ for** *The road is not suitable for heavy vehicles.* | *The movie contains violence and is unsuitable for children.*

inappropriate/not appropriate /ˌɪnə'prəʊpriɪ̈t, nɒt ə'prəʊpriɪ̈t/ [adj] formal not suitable for a situation or purpose – use this especially about something that has been done or chosen without enough care or thought: *This is not an appropriate use of taxpayers' money.* | *I thought his remarks were inappropriate on such a serious occasion.* | **+ for** *The court found that the sex-education brochures were inappropriate for eighth-grade students.* | **it is inappropriate/not appropriate (for sb) to do sth** *It's completely inappropriate for the President to get so involved in a local issue like this.*

unsuited to sth/not suited to sth /ʌn'suːtɪ̈d tə (sth), nɒt 'suːtɪ̈d tə (sth)/ [adj phrase] not having the qualities or characteristics that are needed for a particular purpose or situation: *The tomatoes didn't grow because they're unsuited to the soil here.* | *Her outfit was completely unsuited to the tropical climate.*

wrong /rɒŋ‖rɔːŋ/ [adj] not the right one for a particular job or purpose: *You're using the wrong spoon – this is the soup spoon.* | *I think you picked the wrong time to call her.* | **+ for** *His brand of nationalism is wrong for our party and wrong for the country.*

hardly the time/place/person [adv] /ˌhɑːʳdli ðə 'taɪm, 'pleɪs, 'pɜːʳsən/ use this when it is completely the wrong time or place in which to do something, or the person doing it is a completely unsuitable person: *This is hardly the place to talk about your sexual problems.* | *I know it's hardly the moment to tell you, but I've quit my job.* | *This little man was hardly the kind of person you'd expect to be in charge of an international gun-smuggling scheme.*

unfit/not fit /ʌn'fɪt, nɒt 'fɪt/ [adj not usually before noun] not good enough for a particular purpose, especially when someone has officially decided this **+ for** *The land is so polluted it is not fit for crops.* | **unfit for human consumption/habitation** (=not fit for humans to eat or live in) *The meat was declared unfit for human consumption.* | **+ to do sth** *Her uncle was mentally unstable and unfit to raise a child.*

2 when someone is not suitable for a particular job or situation

- unsuitable/not suitable
- not be cut out for
- wrong
- ill-suited to sth/not suited to sth
- be/seem/feel/look out of place
- misfit

unsuitable/not suitable /ʌn'suːtəbəl, nɒt 'suːtəbəl/ [adj not usually before noun] *They told me that the reason I was considered unsuitable was that I was over-qualified.* | *We've already rejected several unsuitable candidates.* | **+ for** *The first person we interviewed was clearly not suitable for the job.*

not be cut out for /nɒt biː kʌt 'aʊt fɔːʳ/ [v phrase] informal if you are **not cut out for** a type of work or way of life, you do not have the right qualities to enjoy it or to be successful in it: *Obviously, Paul was not cut out for army life.* | *She'd been married only a year and a half when her husband decided he was not cut out for marriage.*

wrong /rɒŋ‖rɔːŋ/ [adj] completely unsuitable for a particular job: *This is a very important job, so we don't want to choose the wrong person.* | **+ for** *Dave's wrong for this job. He doesn't have enough patience.*

ill-suited to sth/not suited to sth /ˌɪl 'suːtɪ̈d tə (sth), ˌnɒt 'suːtɪ̈d tə (sth)/ [adj phrase] formal unsuitable for a particular job or activity, because you do not have the right qualities for it: *With so little experience, Paula is not really suited to the role of personnel director.* | *The Lieutenant was by nature a man ill-suited to the discomforts of army life.*

be/seem/feel/look out of place /biː, siːm, fiːl, lʊk ˌaʊt əv 'pleɪs/ [v phrase] to be, feel, or look very different from the other people you are with, and therefore seem to not belong with them: *In her old jeans and college sweater, Sarah looked a little out of place in the foyer of the Grand Hotel.* | *Leary later went to Beverly Hills High School, but he felt out of place among the rich kids.*

misfit /'mɪsˌfɪt/ [n C] someone who does not seem to belong in a group or in society because they have different attitudes, a different appearance, different habits etc: *I didn't have a very happy time at school – I suppose I was something of a misfit.* | **social/societal misfit** *He's always blamed his parents for turning him into a social misfit.*

3 when something is not suitable for a place or situation

- be/seem/look out of place
- be out of keeping/not be in keeping
- incongruous

be/seem/look out of place /biː, siːm, lʊk ˌaʊt əv ˈpleɪs/ [v phrase] if something is **out of place**, it seems or looks very different from the other things around it, and therefore seems unsuitable for that particular place or situation: *Extremely informal language is out of place in an academic essay.* | *The Christmas decorations looked somehow out of place in Waikiki.*

be out of keeping/not be in keeping /biː ˌaʊt əv ˈkiːpɪŋ, ˌnɒt biː ɪn ˈkiːpɪŋ/ [v phrase] to not seem right or suitable when seen together with something else that is very different in style or character: *Serious poetry published in newspapers always seems slightly out of keeping.* | **+ with** *Those new windows are not really in keeping with the style of the house.* | *The cheerful cover of the diary was out of keeping with the thoughts I was recording inside.*

incongruous /ɪnˈkɒŋgruəs‖ɪnˈkɑːŋ-/ [adj] something that is **incongruous** seems strange and unsuitable, often in a humorous way, because it is so unexpected in a particular situation, so different from its surroundings etc: *It seemed incongruous having a dance-band at the funeral.* | *He was dressed in a three-piece suit with an incongruous tie shaped like a fish.*

4 when two people are not suitable for each other

- incompatible
- be wrong for/not be right for
- not be sb's type
- not be suited
- ill-matched

▸ *see also* **like**

incompatible /ˌɪnkəmˈpætɪ̈bəl/ [adj] two people who are **incompatible** are unable to form a long relationship with each other because they have very different characters, attitudes, interests etc: *After a week together on vacation it was clear that they were totally incompatible.* | *My parents always seemed incompatible to me, but they stayed together for over 40 years.*

be wrong for/not be right for /biː ˈrɒŋ fɔːʳ‖-ˈrɔːŋ-, nɒt biː ˈraɪt fɔːʳ/ [v phrase] to not be the right type of person to form a relationship with someone else, especially a long or serious relationship: *Everyone told him that she was wrong for him, but he wouldn't listen.* | *I'll introduce you if you want, but I don't think he's really right for you.*

not be sb's type /nɒt biː (sb's) ˈtaɪp/ [v phrase] informal to not be a suitable person to form a relationship or friendship with someone else because you have different attitudes, interests etc or because you are not attracted to someone with particular characteristics: *All he ever talks about is football – he's not really my type.* | *Denise was really nice, but physically she wasn't my type.*

not be suited /nɒt biː ˈsuːtɪ̈d/ [v phrase] if two people **are not suited**, they are not suitable for each other because they have very different attitudes and characters: *I've never thought of going out with her – we're not really suited.* | **+ to/for** *If two people aren't naturally suited to each other, there's no point in pursuing a relationship.*

ill-matched /ˌɪl ˈmætʃt◂/ [adj] formal two people who are having a relationship who are **ill-matched**, have very different characters, interests etc and their relationship is likely to be very difficult or unsuccessful: *They were both strong, vital people, but they made an ill-matched couple.* | *Whenever you see them, they're always arguing – they seem very ill-matched.*

untidy

RELATED WORDS

opposite: **tidy**

▸ *see also* **dirty**

1 place/room

- messy
- be a mess
- cluttered
- dump
- pigsty
- tip

messy ALSO **untidy** British /ˈmesi, ʌnˈtaɪdi/ [adj] if a place is **messy** or **untidy**, things have been left carelessly in different parts of it instead of being neatly arranged: *She felt uncomfortable in such a messy house.* | *He only cleans up his room when it gets really messy.* | *My desk isn't always this messy – I've been working on a major project.* | *Jan found the professor in a small, untidy office.* | *These drawers are so untidy – I can never find what I'm looking for.*

be a mess ALSO **be in a mess** British /biː ə ˈmes, biː ɪn ə ˈmes/ [v phrase] informal if a place **is a mess** or **is in a mess**, it is very untidy and dirty: *Please sit down. Sorry everything's such a mess.* | *My basement is a complete mess and has been for years.* | *The whole house is in a mess, but I didn't have time to clean it up.*

cluttered /ˈklʌtəʳd/ [adj] untidy because there are too many things in a small space: *He works in a cluttered studio that looks like a mechanic's garage.* | *The trailer was cluttered and cramped, with barely enough room to turn around.* | **+ with** *The room was tiny, its walls cluttered with paintings and old photographs.*

dump /dʌmp/ [n singular] informal a place that is untidy and dirty: *The Ewells' place is a real dump.* | *Why don't you do something about your room – it's a dump.*

pigsty ALSO **pit** American /ˈpɪgstaɪ, pɪt/ [n singular] informal an untidy and very dirty place: *This place is a pigsty! Clean it up.* | *I don't know how you can stand living in a pigsty like this.* | *My room's a total pit, but I'm too lazy to clean it.*

tip /tɪp/ [n singular] British informal a very untidy place: *Your room's an absolute tip!* | *It was a very nice house until they moved in and turned it into a tip.*

2 person/clothes/hair

- untidy
- be a mess
- scruffy
- slovenly
- slob
- unkempt
- dishevelled
- bedraggled
- rumpled

untidy British **/messy** American /ʌnˈtaɪdi, ˈmesi/ [adj] someone who is **untidy** does not keep their clothes, hair etc neatly arranged: *The little children were dirty and untidy, but very happy.* | *Her hair was messy and her lipstick was smudged.* | *He was comically tall and thin with a long growth of untidy beard.*

be a mess ALSO **look a mess** British /biː ə 'mes, ˌlʊk ə 'mes/ [v phrase] informal to look very untidy: *I can't go out looking like this – I'm a mess.* | *When the police called, I had just got up, and my hair looked a mess.*

scruffy /'skrʌfi/ [adj] British someone who is **scruffy** is wearing old, untidy clothes: *My parents think I look scruffy in these jeans, but I like them.* | **scruffy clothes/jeans/sweater etc** *She's wearing that scruffy old sweater again.*

slovenly /'slʌvənli/ [adj] extremely untidy and careless, and often dirty: *Their landlady was fat and slovenly.* | *The aide was hired to keep the governor's slovenly brother out of the public eye.*

slob /slɒb‖slɑːb/ [n C] informal someone who is extremely untidy but does not seem to care that they are: *Jo's such a slob – how can you live like that?* | *If you keep dressing like a slob, no one's ever going to ask you for a date.*

unkempt /ˌʌn'kempt◂/ [adj] especially written someone whose clothes or hair are **unkempt**, has made no effort to try to look clean or tidy: *Hoskins beard was tangled and unkempt.* | *She used to dress so neatly, but now her hair and clothes had become unkempt and dirty.*

dishevelled British **/disheveled** American /dɪ'ʃevəld/ [adj] someone who is **dishevelled** has untidy hair and clothes, often because they have been in a hurry, or have been travelling or working hard: *He looked dusty, disheveled, and very tired.* | *The actress was found disheveled and confused in a Los Angeles back yard.* | *She was conscious of her rather dishevelled appearance.*

bedraggled /bɪ'drægəld/ [adj] someone who is **bedraggled** looks untidy, especially because they are wet or muddy: *A rather bedraggled crowd waited outside in the pouring rain.* | *The children walked along the path, looking miserable and bedraggled after the storm.*

rumpled /'rʌmpəld/ [adj] if clothes are **rumpled**, they have lots of creases in them and they look untidy. (Creases are lines where something has been folded.): *Forman was wearing a rumpled sweatsuit and a three-day beard.* | *Her dress was as rumpled as if she'd slept in it.*

3 to make a place messy

- make a mess
- mess up
- clutter/clutter up

make a mess /ˌmeɪk ə 'mes/ [v phrase] to make a place untidy or dirty: *Eric, you're making a mess – I hope you're planning to clean it up.* | *You can bake some cookies if you promise not to make a mess in the kitchen.*

mess up /ˌmes 'ʌp/ [phr v T] informal to make a place untidy or dirty **mess sth up** *Don't mess up the living room – we have company coming tonight.* | **mess up sth** *Who's messed up my nice clean kitchen?*

clutter/clutter up /'klʌtəʳ, ˌklʌtər 'ʌp/ [v T] if a lot of things **clutter** a room, desk etc, they make it untidy, especially because there is not enough space for them: *Toys cluttered the nursery floor.* | **clutter up sth/clutter sth up** *I don't want your old newspapers and magazines cluttering up the house.* | **be cluttered (up) with** *All the available space around her computer is cluttered with papers.* | *His house was cluttered up with the things he had collected.*

4 when things are spread around in a messy way

- mess
- chaos
- clutter
- disaster/disaster area

mess /mes/ [n singular] when things are spread around everywhere in a dirty, untidy way: *We spent the morning tidying up the mess after the party.* | *There were cups and ashtrays everywhere – what a mess!* | *We love having our grandchildren visit, but they always leave such a mess for us to clean up.*

chaos /'keɪ-ɒs‖-ɑːs/ [n U] when everything is very untidy, nothing is organized, and there is no order or system: *We've just moved into the new office and I've no idea where anything is – it's chaos!* | **in chaos** (=in a state of chaos) *I arrived home unexpectedly and found the house in chaos.*

clutter /'klʌtəʳ/ [n U] when a lot of things have been left together in one place, especially unnecessary things that prevent you from moving around easily: *It seemed impossible for her to keep the house free of clutter.* | **+ of** *On the dresser a clutter of compacts, rouges, and lipsticks lie half open.*

disaster/disaster area /dɪ'zɑːstəʳ, dɪ'zɑːstər ˌeəriə‖dɪ'zæs-/ [n C] informal a place that is very messy or dirty: *I'd invite you in, but my place is a disaster.* | *The kids room is always a disaster area.*

until

continuing to a particular time or event and then stopping

RELATED WORDS

- until the present day *see* **now (3)**

- until
- up until/up to
- from ... until/from ... to
- through
- Monday-Friday/6:00-8:00 etc

until ALSO **till** /ən'tɪl, tɪl/ [prep/conjunction] especially spoken if something happens **until** or **till** a time or event, it continues and then stops at that time or event. **Till** is only used in informal speech and writing: *My father worked as a teacher until 1989.* | *I'll be at home until 5:30, if you want to phone me.* | *Vicky polished the car until it shone.* | *David continued living at home until he was 26.* | *The library's only open till five on Saturdays.* | *Just wait till I've finished my coffee. Then we can go.*

up until/up to /'ʌp əntɪl, 'ʌp tuː/ [prep] if something happens **up until** or **up to** a particular time, date etc, it happens continuously before that time but no longer happens after that time: *Up until the nineteenth century wood was commonly used for buildings.* | *She continued to write poetry, up to the day she died.* | *Things had been going very well up until then.* | **right up until/to a time** (=just before) *Right up until the last minute she had hoped that Peter would change his mind.*

from ... until/from ... to /frəm...ən'tɪl, frəm ... tə/ [prep] use this to say that something starts happening at one time and continues until another time: *We worked from seven in the morning until late at night.* | *Max edited the paper from 1950 until he retired in 1989.* | **from May to September/from 9am to 5pm etc** *The hotel is only open during the main tourist season,* *from March to October.* | *Eisenhower was President from 1952 to 1956.*

through /θruː/ [prep] **May through September/Monday through Friday etc** American starting in May and continuing until the end of September, starting on Monday and continuing until the end of Friday, etc: *The store is open Monday through Saturday.* | *Prices are generally lowest from January through March and highest June through August.*

Monday-Friday/6:00-8:00 etc /ˌmʌndi tə ˈfraɪdi, ˌsɪks tʊ ˈeɪt / written starting on Monday and continuing until the end of Friday, starting at 6 o'clock and continuing until 8 o'clock – used on signs and notices: *Visit the exhibition of modern art, open every day, 9:30-6:00.* | *A special fishing licence is required for the season (May-September).*

untrue

RELATED WORDS

opposite: —————— **true**

- when you think something is unlikely to be true *see* **doubt**
- *see also* **false, dishonest, believe, lie, trick/deceive, trust/not trust, rumour/rumor**

1 when what someone says is not true

- not true
- untrue
- false
- not be the case
- there is no truth in/to sth
- misleading
- not ring true
- trumped-up

not true /nɒt ˈtruː/ [adj phrase not before noun] **it's/that's not true** *'No one ever helps me.' 'That's not true.'* | *You're believing what Mike's saying and it's just not true, he doesn't have a clue what's happening.* | **it is not true that** *It is not true that all women want to go out to work.*

untrue /ʌnˈtruː/ [adj not before noun] not true. **Untrue** is more formal than **not true**: *The report has proven this information to be untrue.* | **it is untrue that** *It is untrue that the college broke the terms of the contract.* | **completely/totally/absolutely/simply untrue** *The interviewer made it sound like I thought it was okay to hit a woman, which is totally untrue.*

false /fɔːls/ [adj] not true or not correct: *He gave a false name and address to the police.* | *The article gives a totally false impression of life in Russia today.* | *Decide whether these statements are true or false.* | *Her claims of being able to recall past lives were later proved false.*

not be the case /nɒt biː ðə ˈkeɪs/ [v phrase] if what someone says or believes is happening **is not the case**, it is not happening and what they say or believe is not true: *Recent reports suggest that violent crime is increasing, but this is simply not the case.* | *People think if kids are aware of a particular brand or ad campaign, they'll buy the product, but that's not the case.*

there is no truth in/to sth /ðeər ɪz ˌnəʊ ˈtruːθ ɪn, tə (sth)/ if **there is no truth in** or **to** something that has been said or written, it is completely untrue: *There is no truth in the rumour that Collins and his wife are about to divorce.* | *Robinson says there is no truth to the reports that he is ready to resign.*

misleading /mɪsˈliːdɪŋ/ [adj] **misleading** information or statements make people believe something that is not true, especially by not giving them all the facts: *The holiday brochure is deliberately misleading, because the hotels it shows are not the ones you actually stay in.* | *These statistics give a misleading impression of what is happening to the economy.*

not ring true /nɒt rɪŋ ˈtruː/ [v phrase not in progressive] if an explanation, story etc does **not ring true**, it does not seem to be true even though you are not quite sure why you think it is untrue: *There was something odd about her story, something that didn't ring true.* | *One of the jurors said that Hill's explanation just didn't ring true.*

trumped-up /ˌtrʌmpt ˈʌp◂/ [adj usually before noun] **trumped-up charge/accusation/case etc** something someone says, a legal case etc that is false and has been invented, especially in order to harm someone else for political purposes: *He had been arrested by the secret police on trumped-up charges of spying.* | *Zola believed that the case against Dreyfus was trumped-up and utterly false.*

2 to think of a reason or explanation that is untrue

- make up
- invent

make up /ˌmeɪk ˈʌp/ [phr v T] to think of a reason, explanation, excuse etc that is untrue **make up sth** *I gave her my name, then made up a telephone number with a Los Angeles area code.* | **make sth up** *'You're saying you think Bobby just made it up?' 'I think he believes it, but I'm not sure it's true.'*

invent /ɪnˈvent/ [v T] to think of a reason, explanation, or excuse that is sometimes very complicated but completely untrue: *I began to invent reasons for staying away from work.* | *It was proven that one witness's story had been invented.*

3 an untrue story or explanation

- story/tale
- fiction
- fabrication

- *see also* **lie**

story/tale /ˈstɔːri, teɪl/ [n C] an untrue story or explanation that you use as an excuse or to impress someone **give sb some story** *She gave me some story about Mark being an old friend.* | **tall tale/story** *It's the sort of tall tale about how good they are with women that guys tell in bars.* | **cock-and-bull story** especially British *He gave me a cock-and-bull story about the glass being smashed in the storm, but it looked to me like the two of them had had a fight.*

fiction /ˈfɪkʃən/ [n U] an untrue story or piece of information that someone has deliberately invented: *It can sometimes be difficult to tell fact from fiction.* | **pure fiction** (=completely untrue and invented) *The president denied that he was ill, labelling the report 'pure fiction.'*

fabrication /ˌfæbrɪˈkeɪʃən/ [n C] an untrue story or piece of information that someone has deliberately invented in order to deceive people: *Everything that was written about me in that article was a fabrication.* | **total/pure/complete fabrication** *The defense said that the victim's story was a total fabrication designed to get revenge.*

4 what you say when you think something is untrue

- nonsense/rubbish
- a load of

nonsense/rubbish British spoken ALSO **bull** American spoken /ˈnɒnsəns‖ˈnɑːnsens, ˈrʌbɪʃ, bʊl/ [n U] use this when you think something is totally untrue and stupid: *I don't know where he got that idea, it's total bull.* | *You don't believe that rubbish, do you?* | *That's nonsense. Don't be silly.*

a load of spoken ALSO **a pile of** American spoken /ə ˈləʊd ɒv, ə ˈpaɪl ɒv/ [n phrase] use this when you think everything that someone has said or written about something is stupid and completely untrue **a load of nonsense/rubbish** British *I told Julia what he'd said, and she said that it was a load of nonsense.* | *That article is a load of rubbish, if you ask me.*

unusual

RELATED WORDS

opposite: ——— **normal/ordinary, common**

▸ *see also* **rare/rarely, usually, strange, different**

1 not what usually happens

- unusual
- extraordinary
- exceptional
- uncommon/not common
- you don't usually/often
- out of the ordinary
- special
- freak
- offbeat/off-beat

unusual /ʌnˈjuːʒuəl, -ʒəl/ [adj] *We had snow in April, which is very unusual.* | *She had an unusual last name – Peachtree or Plumtree or something like that.* | *I first met Maria in unusual circumstances – we were both stuck in a Brazilian airport.* | **it is unusual to do sth** *It is unusual to find lakes of this size in Britain.* | **it is unusual for sb to do sth** *We were beginning to worry. It was unusual for David to be so late.* —**unusually** [adv] *The house was unusually quiet.* | *Unusually for a city hotel, it is set in a lush tropical garden.*

extraordinary /ɪkˈstrɔːʳdənəri‖-dn-eri, ˌekstrəˈɔːr-/ [adj] something that is **extraordinary** is very unusual because it would normally be very unlikely to happen or exist: *The man's story was so extraordinary that I didn't know whether to believe him or not.* | *He said it was an extraordinary decision and would send many industries spinning into recession.* | **an extraordinary thing to do/say/happen** *She left her husband, and in 1912 that was an extraordinary thing to do.* | **quite/most extraordinary** British (=very extraordinary) *The whole incident had been quite extraordinary.* —**extraordinarily** [adv] *The level of the sea rose till it was extraordinarily high.*

exceptional /ɪkˈsepʃənəl/ [adj] an **exceptional** situation is very unusual and happens very rarely: *A few of the top executives are women, but this is still exceptional.* | **in exceptional circumstances/cases** *Exit visas are only given in exceptional circumstances.* —**exceptionally** [adv] *This has been an exceptionally busy week.*

uncommon/not common /ʌnˈkɒmən‖-ˈkɑː-, nɒt ˈkɒmən‖ˈkɑː-/ [adj] something that is **uncommon** or **not common** is unusual because it does not happen very often: *The disease mostly affects older people, and is not common among people under 50.* | **it is uncommon/not common (for sb) to do sth** *It is uncommon for small babies to sleep more than four hours without waking.*

you don't usually/often /juː ˌdəʊnt ˈjuːʒuəli, ˈɒfən‖-ˈɔːf-/ spoken say **you don't usually** see, find, hear etc something when it is very unusual to see it, find it etc: *You don't usually see rabbits of this size.* | *You don't often get people ringing up in the middle of the night to say they've found a body in the bath.*

out of the ordinary /ˌaʊt əv ði ˈɔːʳdənri‖-dn-eri/ [adj phrase] unusual and surprising or special: *Something out of the ordinary happened to us that night.* | *The goalkeeper did not have to do anything out of the ordinary to keep his side in the game.*

special /ˈspeʃəl/ [adj usually before noun] a **special** occasion, situation, method etc is one that is different from what normally happens, and usually better: *There were special security arrangements for the President's visit.* | *The prince said he didn't want any special treatment in his new school.* | **special event/occasion** *I would only buy expensive shoes for a special event such as a wedding.* | *a book of recipes for every day and special occasions too* | **in special circumstances** *Prisoners are only allowed to visit their families in special circumstances.*

freak /friːk/ [adj only before noun] **freak accident/storm/conditions etc** an accident, storm etc that is very unusual and unexpected: *He broke his leg in a freak training accident.* | *A freak wave wrecked most of the seafront.* | *Two planes were lifted up and thrown across the tarmac by a freak gust of wind.*

offbeat/off-beat /ˌɒfˈbiːt◂‖ˌɔːf-/ [adj usually before noun] off-beat films, designs, ideas etc are unusual and often seem interesting or humorous because they are so different from the usual ones: *We had some really offbeat ideas for T-shirt designs.* | *Movies featuring original or offbeat material are rarely big box-office successes.*

2 unusually good or impressive

- unusual
- special
- extraordinary
- exceptional
- remarkable
- rare
- quite a/some
- unique

unusual /ʌnˈjuːʒuəl, -ʒəl/ [adj usually before noun] **unusual** beauty, talent etc is much better or more impressive than usual: *Alan's work shows unusual talent and originality.* | *He had an unusual ability to rise above the prejudices of his generation.* —**unusually** [adv] *Mr Elstone is an unusually gifted teacher.*

special /ˈspeʃəl/ [adj] unusually good, impressive, or important: *Joe has a special gift for mathematics.* | *The bond between Sonya and her mother was very special.*

extraordinary /ɪkˈstrɔːʳdənəri‖-dn-eri, ˌekstrəˈɔːr-/ [adj] very much better, more beautiful, or more impressive than what is usual: *He really was a most extraordinary man.* | *The view from up here is extraordinary.* | *Everything about the woman – her hair, eyes, and jewellery – gleamed with extraordinary brilliance.* —**extraordinarily** [adv] *Victoria is an extraordinarily attractive girl.*

exceptional /ɪkˈsepʃənəl/ [adj] an **exceptional** person or thing is so good that they are unusual compared to most other things or people of a similar type: *When it comes to natural footballing ability, Gascoigne is exceptional.* | *Graham Greene had* *exceptional talents as a story-teller.* | *It's one of the best examples of old English furniture I've seen – it truly is exceptional.*

remarkable /rɪˈmɑːʳkəbəl/ [adj] someone or something that is **remarkable** is unusually good or skilled, so that you notice them and admire them: *The record features some remarkable guitar and piano solos.* | *Henry Tippett showed remarkable flair as a hotelier.* | *a remarkable statesman and diplomat* —**remarkably** [adv] *The service in the restaurant is remarkably quick and efficient.*

rare /reəʳ/ [adj only before noun] very special and unusual: *He had that rare gift of being able to impart enthusiasm to others.* | *She bore her illness with rare courage.* | *Huston is a film-maker who has achieved a rare kind of beauty in his work.*

quite a/some /ˈkwaɪt ə, sʌm/ [determiner] informal use this to describe someone or something that is unusually good, impressive, or enjoyable: *This is quite a house.* | *Jane told me I was almost intelligent, which from her is quite a compliment.* | *That was some party last night!* | *'She's some lady,' he said, with admiration.*

unique /juːˈniːk/ [adj] happening or existing extremely rarely – use this especially about the qualities someone or something has or about a chance to do something: *She has a unique ability to communicate with animals of all kinds.* | *This vacation offers a unique opportunity to visit some of the most remote mountain areas of the region.*

3 so unusual that nothing like it has ever happened before

- unprecedented
- unheard of

unprecedented /ʌnˈpresɪdentɪd/ [adj] an **unprecedented** event or situation, especially a good one, has never happened before: *There has been an unprecedented demand for tickets.* | *An unprecedented boom in tourism brought prosperity to the town.* | *In the 1920's the number of Scots who made the journey across the Atlantic was unprecedented.*

unheard of /ʌnˈhɜːʳd ɒv/ [adj] informal a situation or event that is **unheard of** is surprising or shocking because it has never happened before and is difficult to imagine: *Travel for pleasure was almost unheard of in the nineteenth century.* | **an unheard-of luxury/achievement/outburst etc** *When my father was a child, a television was an unheard-of luxury.* | *The band had received six Grammy Awards – an unheard-of achievement in such a short time.*

4 when someone's behaviour is unusual

- unconventional
- it's not like sb

unconventional /ˌʌnkənˈvenʃənəl◂/ [adj] someone who is **unconventional** lives, behaves, or does things in ways that are very different from the way that most ordinary people live or behave: *She comes from an unconventional family.* | *They were both unconventional to the point of eccentricity.* | *unconventional political views*

it's not like sb /ɪts nɒt ˈlaɪk (sb)/ spoken say this when you mean that someone is behaving in a way that they do not usually behave, so you think they may be ill or have some kind of problem: *Don't you want any more to eat? That's not like you.* | **it's not like sb to do sth** *It's not like Sally to get so upset – I think she's been working too hard.*

up

RELATED WORDS

opposite: **down**
- when numbers, prices etc go up *see* **increase**
- *see also* **position/rank, successful, climb, vertical, high**

1 moving up to a higher place

- up
- upwards
- uphill
- upstairs
- higher and higher

up /ʌp/ [prep/adv] *The car went slowly up the hill.* | *Lee gets out of breath just going up the stairs.* | *There's a great view from the top – you should go up and have a look.* | **+ to/into/onto/over/at etc** *The fire sent clouds of smoke up into the sky.* | *Don't let the cat jump up onto the table.* | *We made our way up to the top of the mountain.* | **straight up** *Serena was so scared she jumped straight up in the air.* | **up and down** *Pain was running up and down both his legs.*

upwards ALSO **upward** American /ˈʌpwəʳd(z)/ [adv] towards a higher position, especially towards the sky: *Alan grabbed hold of the ledge and began to climb upward.* | *A few snowflakes fell toward the ground, then blew upward with the next gust of wind.* | *The lighter material floats upwards, carrying heat to the surface of the liquid.* —**upward** [adj only before noun] *She massaged my back with a light upward movement.*

uphill /ˌʌpˈhɪl◂/ [adv] towards a higher position by means of a road or path that goes up a hill: *I don't like cycling uphill.* | *The children were running uphill towards the house.* | *Our guide led us uphill along a steep trail.*

upstairs /ˌʌpˈsteəʳz◂/ [adv] towards a higher floor in a building by means of stairs: *Lucy came rushing upstairs after her sister.* | *Don't go upstairs – Mom's still getting dressed.* | *Flora watched Mrs Brown staggering upstairs with a heavy tray.*

higher and higher /ˌhaɪər ənd ˈhaɪəʳ/ [adv] if something moves **higher and higher**, it continues to move towards a higher position in the sky: *The moon rose higher and higher.* | *The kite went higher and higher into the sky.* | *I watched as the birds flew higher and higher, grew smaller, and then disappeared.*

2 looking, facing, or pointing upwards

- upwards
- up
- face-up

upwards ALSO **upward** American /ˈʌpwəʳd(z)/ [adv] *He held the palms of his hands upward as if he were asking forgiveness.* | *A copy of the book lay on the table, its cover facing upwards.* | *All eyes were turned upward toward the man standing on the ledge.* —**upward** [adj] *Hector gave her an upward glance and then continued reading the paper.*

up /ʌp/ [adv] use this to say where someone or something is looking, facing, or pointing: *Caroline looked up and laughed.* | **+ at/into/from etc** *The boy turned and stared up at her.* | *The receptionist hardly looked up from her book when I came in the office.* | *We stood there for a moment, gazing up into the snow-covered* *branches of the tree.* | **straight up** *He was pointing his rifle straight up in the air.*

face-up /ˌfeɪs ˈʌp/ [adv] if someone or something is lying **face-up**, they are lying with their face pointing upwards: *Police found the body lying face-up in the hall.* | *He put all his cards face-up on the table.*

3 to move upwards through the air

- go up
- rise
- ascend
- climb
- gain height
- shoot up
- soar

go up /ˌgəʊ ˈʌp/ [v phrase] *Mervyn had never invited her to go up in his little plane.* | *If you want to make the kite go up, pull the string hard, then release it slowly.*

rise /raɪz/ [v I] to move straight up into the air: *Hot air rises.* | **+ in/into** *A stream of water rose into the air, arched smoothly, and fell back into the pool.* | **+ up** *Clouds of smoke rose up into the air.*

ascend /əˈsend/ [v I] formal to move up through the air: *A huge flock of red-wing blackbirds ascended from their nests along the side of the road.* | *He leaned out of an upstairs window and felt a current of warm air ascending from the street.*

climb /klaɪm/ [v I] if a bird or a plane **climbs**, it gradually goes higher up into the sky: *As the plane began to climb, Karen started to feel ill.* | *The geese climbed high above us and set off on their long journey south.*

gain height /ˌgeɪn ˈhaɪt/ [v phrase] if an aircraft **gains height**, it gradually moves higher up into the sky: *Investigators are uncertain why the plane failed to gain height after takeoff.* | *Gliders use thermal up-currents to gain height.*

shoot up /ˌʃuːt ˈʌp/ [phr v I] to suddenly go up into the air very quickly: *Flames shot up into the air and clouds of smoke poured out of the windows.* | *I saw a spray of white water shoot up into the sky and knew that there were whales nearby.*

soar /sɔːʳ/ [v I] to go quickly upwards to a great height in the air **+ upwards/up/above/into etc** *The ball soared high into the air.* | *The snow goose flew down low over the field and then soared back up gracefully.*

4 when something moves upwards into the air

- leave the ground
- take off
- lift off
- blast off
- launch

leave the ground /ˌliːv ðə ˈgraʊnd/ [v phrase] *Gunmen started firing at the helicopter as it left the ground.* | *The plane had barely left the ground when it began to experience engine trouble.*

take off /ˌteɪk ˈɒf / [phr v I] if a plane or a bird **takes off**, it leaves the ground and start flying: *Some ducks took off and flew along the river.* | *We had to wait on the runway for a half an hour before we finally took off.* | **+ from** *The president's plane took off from Andrews Air Force Base at 9:45 am.* —**takeoff/take-off** /ˈteɪkɒf‖-ɔːf/ [n C/U] *The takeoff and landing were a little rough, but the rest of the flight was very smooth.*

lift off /ˌlɪft ˈɒf / [phr v I] if a space ship **lifts off**, it leaves the ground and starts its journey into space: *There was a burst of flame as the rocket lifted off into the sky.* | *Thousands of people had gathered at Cape Canaveral to watch the rocket lift off.* —**lift-off** /ˈlɪft ɒf/ [n C/U] *This is Houston. We have lift-off* (=the rocket is now lifting off).

blast off /ˌblɑːst ˈɒf‖ˌblæst- / [phr v I] if a space ship **blasts off**, it leaves the ground with an explosion of fire and starts its journey into space: *The space shuttle is set to blast off on a nine-day mission tomorrow at 4:18 a.m.* —**blast-off** /ˈblɑːst ɒf‖ˈblæst-/ [n C/U] *Minutes after blast-off the rocket exploded.*

launch /lɔːntʃ/ [v T] to send a rocket up into the air or into space **launch a rocket/missile/satellite etc** *China is planning to launch a space rocket later this month.* | *On the first day of the war over 400 missiles were launched.* —**launch** [n C/U] *During the launch, two rockets boost the shuttle before separating and falling back into the sea.*

5 to move up a slope or upstairs

- go up
- climb/climb up
- ascend

go up /ˌgəʊ ˈʌp/ [v T not in passive] *You have to go up two flights of stairs, and then it's the second door on your right.* | *Hundreds of people lined the street, cheering the runners as they went up the hill.*

climb/climb up /klaɪm, ˌklaɪm ˈʌp/ [v T] to go up a steep slope, especially with a lot of effort: *The old man slowly climbed up the stairs to his room.* | *We had to climb a pretty big hill to get to the temple.* —**climb** [n singular] *The tour begins with a steep climb up one of the city's many hills.*

ascend /əˈsend/ [v T] formal to go up a slope, a ladder, or stairs: *He was turning to ascend the ladder to the engine room when the ship's fire alarm sounded.* | *Bianca walked regally across the hall and ascended the marble staircase.*

6 when a road or path goes upwards

- go up
- climb

go up /ˌgəʊ ˈʌp/ [v phrase] *The road goes up from the beach into the forest.* | *I could see a tiny track going up ahead of us.*

climb /klaɪm/ [v I] to go up steeply: *The road climbs steadily, reaching 6,000 feet after 18 miles.* | *The path climbs high into the hills above the village of Glenridding.*

7 when the level of water goes up

- rise

rise /raɪz/ [v I] if the level of water **rises**, it goes up, especially in a way that causes danger, problems etc: *The level of the water in the lake was rising fast.* | *In 1956 the river rose to a height of more than 6 metres.* | *The waves rose higher and higher till the rocks behind them were hidden.* | *Floodwaters continue to rise as the rain continues to fall.*

8 when the sun or moon comes up into the sky

- rise
- come up

rise /raɪz/ [v I] if the sun or the moon **rises**, it goes above the level of the horizon or it goes further up into the sky: *A full moon rose over the valley.* | *What time does the sun rise tomorrow morning?* | *The* *moon rises nearly an hour later each night. | By midday the sun had risen high in the sky and was burning down on us.*

come up /ˌkʌm ˈʌp/ [phr v I] if the sun or the moon **comes up**, it moves above the level of the horizon: *The moon came up slowly over the pine trees. | The sun was coming up and you could just see the tops of the mountains.*

9 to move a part of your body upwards

- raise
- lift/lift up
- put up

raise /reɪz/ [v T] *She raised her head and looked at him. | If you want to ask a question, please raise your hand first. | 'Oh really?' Zack said, raising an eyebrow.*

lift/lift up /lɪft, ˌlɪft ˈʌp/ [v T] to raise part of your body such as your arm or your leg, especially carefully or with effort: *Her shoulder muscles had become so weak that she could not lift her arms.* | **lift up sth** *It took him a great deal of effort just to lift up his arm a few inches.* | **lift sth up** *OK, now lift your right leg up as far as it will go.*

put up /ˌpʊt ˈʌp/ [phr v T] to raise your hand or arm **put up sth** *I gasped and put up a hand to cover my mouth. | He swore at us and put up his fists as if he was going to punch one of us.* | **put sth up** *Rachel put both her hands up to shield her eyes from the sun.*

10 to move up in a list

- move up
- rise
- climb
- shoot up

move up /ˌmuːv ˈʌp/ [v I/T] *With this win Williams moves up to third place in the world rankings.* | **move up sth** *FC Roma are slowly moving up the league table.*

rise /raɪz/ [v I] to gradually move up in a list or group of people, teams, records etc: *Hobson's novel has risen steadily up the bestseller list since it's release last August.* | **+ to** *Borland rose to the top of the computer software industry by a mixture of innovation and good marketing.*

climb /klaɪm/ [v I/T] to move up in a list of teams, records etc, especially a long way up the list **+ to** *Jennifer Lopez's new single has climbed to number two in the US charts.* | **climb the table/charts etc** *Towards the end of the season Benfica suddenly climbed the league table and finished third.*

shoot up /ˌʃuːt ˈʌp/ [v I/T] to move up very quickly in a list of people, teams, records etc **+ in** *Since the debate Robertson has shot up in the polls.* | **shoot up sth** *The new detective series quickly shot up the TV ratings.*

upset

RELATED WORDS

see also **sad, offend, criticize, insult, cry**

1 feeling upset

- upset
- hurt
- distressed
- distraught
- be in a state

upset /ʌpˈset/ [adj not before noun] unhappy because something very unpleasant or disappointing has happened, so that you feel shocked or you want to cry: *Miss Hurley is too upset to speak to anyone at the moment. | The children were very upset when we told them that we wouldn't be going to Disneyland.* | **+ about** *She's still upset about her uncle's death.* | **+ (that)** *The organizers were upset that so few people visited the exhibition.*

hurt /hɜːʳt/ [adj not before noun] upset and shocked because someone has been unkind to you, especially someone that you trusted and thought was a friend: *Bill felt very hurt when he realized she had lied to him.* | **+ (that)** *Gretta was really hurt that none of her friends came to visit her in the hospital.* | **deeply hurt** (=extremely hurt) *Jackson was said to be 'deeply hurt' by the newspaper reports about him.*
—**hurt** [n U] *Sylvie could still remember the hurt of being treated like an outsider.*

distressed /dɪˈstrest/ [adj] extremely upset and shocked about something very unpleasant that has happened, so that you cry or become confused: *Herman becomes distressed when anyone asks him about the accident. | The airport was full of distressed relatives waiting for news of the crash.* | **+ by/about/at** *Everyone in the office was distressed by Maggie's unexpected death. | Nelson's supporters were distressed about his use of racial slurs.* | **+ that** *I was crying all the time, and my mother was distressed that she could do nothing to comfort me.* | **+ to hear/learn/see/find etc** *We were all distressed to hear that Stuart had been attacked the night before.* | **deeply distressed** (=extremely distressed) *She was deeply distressed to see the animal in so much pain.*
—**distress** [n U] *Mr and Mrs Roberts spoke with obvious distress about their missing daughter.*

distraught /dɪˈstrɔːt/ [adj] extremely upset, usually because you are very worried about something, so that you cry a lot or seem confused: *He could see that I was distraught, but he still kept asking me questions. | The distraught parents of the missing baby have made a public appeal for her return.* | **+ at/over/about** *We were all distraught about the accident, but Mama was the most upset. | Benson was so distraught over the breakup of his marriage that he committed suicide.* | **+ that** *Casey was totally distraught that they were throwing him out of school.*

be in a state /biː ɪn ə ˈsteɪt/ [v phrase] British informal to be so upset that you cannot stop crying or control your emotions: *Stephan called me in a state, saying he was thinking of killing himself. | The children were in such a state that the police couldn't question them.* | **be in an awful/terrible/shocking etc state** *He's been in a terrible state since Julie left him.*

2 to make someone feel upset

- upset
- hurt
- hurt sb's feelings
- distress

upset /ʌpˈset/ [v T] *I'm sorry if I upset you – I didn't mean to. | 'Why's he crying?' 'I don't know – something must have upset him.' | Try not to upset your father. He's had a hard day.* | **it upsets sb to see/hear/think etc** *It still upsets me to think about my parents' divorce.* | **what upsets sb is** *What upsets me most is the way she lied to me.*

hurt /hɜːʳt/ [v T] to make someone feel upset by being unkind to them or not thinking enough about their feelings, especially someone who trusts you and thinks you are their friend: *I would never do anything to hurt her. | The fact that his parents take little* *interest in his life hurts him more than he admits.* | **it hurts sb to see/hear/learn etc** *It hurts me to think that you still don't trust me.*

hurt sb's feelings /ˌhɜːʳt (sb's) ˈfiːlɪŋz/ [v phrase] to make someone feel upset or offended by something that you say or do, often unintentionally: *I'm sorry if I hurt your feelings, but I was just being honest.* | *Don't tell your sister what William said – you'll only hurt her feelings.* | *I didn't tell him I don't like his haircut – I don't want to hurt his feelings.*

distress /dɪˈstres/ [v T] formal to make someone feel extremely upset or worried: *The number of young men who called asking for Marie distressed her mother.* | **it distresses sb to see/hear etc** *It distressed him to see Susie cry.*

3 to become upset

- get upset
- get worked up
- take sth to heart
- get het up

get upset /ˌget ʌpˈset/ [v phrase] *I get upset when I see people being cruel to animals.* | *At the slightest mention of her ex-husband's name she gets upset.* | **+ about** *It was an awful thing for him to say, but there's no point in getting upset about it.*

get worked up /get ˌwɜːʳkt ˈʌp/ [v phrase] informal to become very upset or angry, so that you think things are worse than they really are: *I'll tell you what he said, but promise you won't get worked up.* | **+ about/over** *It's not worth getting worked up about. Anyone can make a mistake.* | **get (yourself) all worked up** *If there's nothing you can do, why get yourself all worked up, honey?*

take sth to heart /ˌteɪk (sth) tə ˈhɑːʳt/ [v phrase] to be more upset by what someone says than they intended you to be: *Don't take anything he said to heart – he was drunk.* | *Brian is a very sensitive kind of person and he takes criticism very much to heart.*

get het up /get ˌhet ˈʌp/ [v phrase] especially British, informal to become very upset about something in a way that other people think is unnecessary: *There's no need to get so het up – it's only a driving test!*

4 making you feel upset

- upsetting
- distressing
- painful
- harrowing
- traumatic

upsetting /ʌpˈsetɪŋ/ [adj] *She can't talk about her son's death – she finds it too upsetting.* | *Many adults manage to forget their more upsetting childhood experiences.* | **it is upsetting to do sth** *It was upsetting to have to say goodbye so soon.*

distressing /dɪˈstresɪŋ/ [adj] making you feel extremely upset or worried: *U.N. officials have called the recent arrest of political opponents 'distressing.'* | *Being in a strange city with no money was an extremely distressing situation.*

painful /ˈpeɪnfəl/ [adj] a **painful** experience or memory makes you feel extremely upset and sad: *It's five years since we separated, but I still find the memories quite painful.* | *For those involved, the scandal has been a very painful experience.* | **+ to** *Colin's death is painful to me and everyone who knew him.* | **it is painful to see/hear etc** *It was so painful to see how frail she had become in just a few months.*

harrowing /ˈhærəʊɪŋ/ [adj] an experience or event that is **harrowing** makes you feel extremely upset because it is very frightening or shocking: *The film contained harrowing scenes of starving children.* | *After a harrowing bus ride through the mountains, we arrived at the port of Heraklion.*

traumatic /trɔːˈmætɪk/ [adj] an experience or event that is **traumatic** makes you feel so upset that it affects the way you think or behave for a very long time: *Len's slow and painful death was traumatic for the entire family.* | *Learning to swim was the most traumatic experience of my childhood.*

5 getting upset easily

- sensitive
- oversensitive/overly sensitive

sensitive /ˈsensɪ̈tɪv/ [adj] *My brother pretends he's tough, but he's actually pretty sensitive.* | **+ about** *I didn't realize that Lee was so sensitive about her family.* | **sensitive to criticism** *If you are a public figure you can't afford to be too sensitive to criticism.*

oversensitive/overly sensitive /ˌəʊvəˈsensɪ̈tɪv◂, ˌəʊvəʳli ˈsensɪ̈tɪv/ [adj] use this about someone who you think gets upset too easily: *When I complain about the mean things he says, he just tells me I'm being oversensitive.* | *Overly sensitive children have trouble making friends with other children.*

use

RELATED WORDS

- get used to something *see* **used to/accustomed to**

WHAT'S HERE

- **to use sth for a purpose** see **1 to 15**
- **to use/consume** see **16 to 19**
- **to use a person to your own advantage** see **20 to 21**

to use sth for a purpose

RELATED WORDS

- use something that belongs to some else *see* **borrow**
- not being used *see* **available/not available**
- *see also* **way (1-6), purpose**

1 to use something for a purpose

- use
- with
- make use of

use /juːz/ [v T] *Do you mind if I use your phone?* | *Are we allowed to use a dictionary in the test?* | *They rebuilt the church using local stone.* | **use sth to do sth** *Use a calculator to check your answers.* | **use sth for doing sth** *We use the shed for storing our firewood.* | **use sth as sth** *We decided to use the second bedroom as a junk room.*

with /wɪð, wɪθ/ [prep] if you do something **with** a tool, piece of equipment etc you use a tool, piece of equipment etc to do it: *Beat the egg with a fork.* | *Do you have anything I can open the bottle with?*

make use of /ˌmeɪk ˈjuːs ɒv/ [v phrase] to use something you have available for a particular purpose:

To build the shelter, they had to make use of whatever bits of wood or plastic they could find. | **+ to do sth** *The Romans made use of volcanic ash to produce concrete.* | **+ as** *Who were the first to make use of pigeons as messengers?*

2 to use particular methods, knowledge, skills etc

- use
- make use of
- put sth to use
- apply
- exercise
- utilize
- draw on
- exploit

use /juːz/ [v T] *Researchers often use questionnaires in their work.* | *I can't tell you what to do – you must use your own discretion.* | **use sth to do sth** *The nurse must use her communication skills to make the patient feel at ease.* | *These new techniques are already being used to produce special effects in films.* —**use** /juːs/ [n U] *There have been complaints about the use of excessive force by the police.*

make use of /ˌmeɪk ˈjuːs ɒv/ [v phrase] to use a method, skill, or piece of information that is available to you: *People asked her why she didn't make use of her musical talent and give singing lessons.* | *We might as well make good use of his expertise while he's here.*

put sth to use /ˌpʊt (sth) tə ˈjuːs/ [v phrase] to start to use something, especially knowledge or a skill that has not been used before: *Your knowledge of computers can finally be put to use when the office buys a new system next month.* | *When governments acquire personal information about people they always try to put it to political use.* | **put sth to good use** *I finally feel that I can put all my education to good use in this job.*

apply /əˈplaɪ/ [v T] to use something such as a method, idea, or system in a particular situation, activity, or process **apply sth to sth** *New technology is being applied to almost every industrial process.* | *You can't apply policies designed for a big country like the United States to a small country like Cuba.* | **apply sth to do sth** *There are several tests you can apply to find out how old a tree is.*

exercise /ˈeksəʳsaɪz/ [v T] to use your authority, influence etc effectively in order to achieve something: *Parents sometimes need to exercise their authority and say 'no' to their children.* | *The Congress must decide whether to exercise its veto or not.* | *Many people are exercising their right to leave the state pension plan.*

utilize ALSO **utilise** British /ˈjuːtɪ̬laɪz/ [v T] formal to use something that is available to you: *Employers must utilize their workers more effectively if the region is to become an economic success.*

draw on /ˈdrɔː ɒn/ [phr v T] to use information, knowledge, or experience that you have learned in the past, in order to do something more effectively: *As a teacher, she drew on her knowledge of her own children.* | *Journalists draw on both published and unofficial information from many different sources.* | *It was a challenge, but luckily we had the experience to draw on.*

exploit /ɪkˈsplɔɪt/ [v T] to use something as fully and effectively as possible in order to gain as much as possible from it: *Britain consistently fails to exploit the scientific discoveries made in its universities.* | *The country's natural resources have not yet been fully exploited.*

3 to use a service that is available

- use
- make use of

use /juːz/ [v T] *How often do you use the library?* | *Now that we have a car we very rarely use the buses.* | *The hotel used to offer a baby-sitting service, but no one ever used it.* —**use** /juːs/ [n U] *There has been a decline in the use of the subway system over recent years.*

make use of /ˌmeɪk ˈjuːs ɒv/ [v phrase] to use something that is available, especially in order to enjoy it or to get something that you want from it: *Not enough people are making use of the company's fitness centre.* | **make good use of sth** *Students are encouraged to make good use of all the computing facilities.*

4 someone who uses something

- user

user /ˈjuːzəʳ/ [n C] *Software should be designed to be as accessible as possible to users.* | **road/phone/library etc user** *Drunken drivers are a menace to themselves and other road users.* | *A new information service will soon be available to library users.* | **end user** (=the person who uses a product) *Computers are sold direct to end users as well as through dealers.*

5 to use a situation in order to gain an advantage

- use
- exploit
- make use of
- take advantage of
- play on
- capitalize on

use /juːz/ [v T] **use sth to do sth** *She used her position as manager to get jobs for her friends.* | *The prisoners used the confusion caused by the fire to conceal their escape.* | **use sth for sth** *Charles was able to use his family connection for his own personal advancement.* | **use sth as sth** *Right-wing activists used people's fear of unemployment as a way of stirring up extremism.*

exploit /ɪkˈsplɔɪt/ [v T] to use a situation in order to gain as much advantage for yourself as possible, especially in a way that people disapprove of: *Opposition leaders were quick to exploit government embarrassment over the incident.* | **exploit sth to do sth** *The country could exploit its position as a major oil producer to push up world oil prices.*

make use of /ˌmeɪk ˈjuːs ɒv/ [v phrase] to use a situation in order to gain an advantage for yourself, especially when that situation has already existed for some time: *I made use of my old contacts to get a job when I come back from Australia.* | *The Republicans were making use of their large majority in congress to block legislation on taxes.*

take advantage of /ˌteɪk ədˈvɑːntɪdʒ ɒv‖-ˈvæn-/ [v phrase] to use an opportunity in order to do what you want or need to do: *Shoppers flocked to take advantage of a supermarket price war which cut the price of many goods.* | **+ to do sth** *Many small investors are taking advantage of these attractive share offers to make a quick profit.*

play on /ˈpleɪ ɒn/ [phr v T] **play on sb's fears/greed/sympathy/prejudices etc** to use someone's fears, sympathy etc in order to gain an advantage for yourself: *A common sales tactic is to play on people's greed in order to make them buy more than they* *need.* | *Disguised as an electrician, he played on people's trust to trick them out of money.*

capitalize on /ˈkæpɪtl-aɪz ɒn/ [phr v T not in passive] to use a situation in order to gain an advantage and make yourself more successful or more effective: *Teachers can capitalize on young children's natural curiosity.* | **fail to capitalize on sth** *The generals failed to capitalize on the weaknesses and divisions in the enemy camp.* | **+ to do sth** *Will the President capitalize on his immense popularity to exert strong leadership?*

6 used for a particular purpose

- be used
- be for
- serve as
- double as

be used /biː ˈjuːzd / [v phrase] **+ as** *Three extra rooms were used as classrooms when necessary.* | *An old Chianti bottle can be used as an attractive base for a table-lamp.* | **+ for** *The tanks are used for storing chemicals.* | **+ to do sth** *Hypnosis is sometimes used to help people give up smoking.*

be for /biː ˈfɔːʳ/ [v phrase] to be intended to be used for a particular purpose: *'What are these buttons for?' 'They're for controlling the heating system.'* | *The phones are for internal communication only.*

serve as /ˈsɜːʳv æz/ [v phrase not usually in progressive] to be used for a particular purpose, especially a different purpose from its original one: *The old hospital in London Road now serves as a hostel for the homeless.* | *They had no bathroom, so a hole in the ground served as a toilet.*

double as /ˈdʌbəl æz/ [phr v T not usually in progressive] if something **doubles as** something else, it is used for that purpose as well as for its original purpose: *The village post-office doubles as a store.* | *Lingerie that doubles as clothing was very fashionable at the time.*

7 what something can be used for

- use
- application
- function

use /juːs/ [n C] a way in which something can be used: *Robots have many different uses in modern industry.* | *The land has been developed for tourism and other recreational uses.* | **+ of** *the use of animals in scientific experiments*

application /ˌæplɪˈkeɪʃən/ [n C] a practical use of something, especially in science or industry **+ of** *The possible applications of this invention are limitless.* | **practical application** *scientific research and its practical applications*

function /ˈfʌŋkʃən/ [n C] the purpose for which something is intended or the way people use it: *What is the function of literature in our society?* | **+ of** *The main function of the bars is to protect the driver's legs.*

8 being used now

- be in use
- be occupied
- be taken
- be engaged

be in use /biː ɪn ˈjuːs/ [v phrase] if a room or machine **is in use**, it is being used by someone at the present time: *The meeting room is in use at the moment, so we'll have to go somewhere else.* | *All the photocopiers are in use. Could you come back later?*

be occupied /biː ˈɒkjəpaɪd‖-ˈɑːk-/ [v phrase] if seats, rooms, beds etc **are occupied**, they are being used and are therefore not available for anyone else to use: *All the chairs in the hall were occupied and at least 100 people had to stand.* | *We're having to turn patients away because all the beds are occupied.*

be taken /biː ˈteɪkən/ [v phrase] if a seat in a train, theatre, restaurant etc **is taken**, it is not available because someone else is already sitting there or will be soon: *I'm sorry. This seat's taken.* | *There was nowhere to sit down in the hall. All the seats were taken.*

be engaged /biː ɪnˈgeɪdʒd/ [v phrase] British if a telephone line or a public toilet **is engaged**, someone else is using it: *Every time I try to call her, the line's engaged.* | *When the toilet is engaged, a red light shows above the door.*

9 something that can be used

- available
- free
- usable
- valid
- current

available /əˈveɪləbəl/ [adj] something that is **available** can be used, for example because no one else is using it or it is not being used for anything else: *This program will take up a lot of your available disk space.* | **every available** *Houses were being built on every available plot of land.* | **whatever is available** *Use whatever seasonal vegetables are available.*

free /friː/ [adj] use this about a chair, room, table etc that you can use because no-one else is using it: *The office next door is free if you need somewhere to work.* | *There's just one free table, over there in the corner.*

usable /ˈjuːzəbəl/ [adj] something that is **usable** can be used, because it works well or because it has been made ready for use: *I know the bicycle's old, but it's still usable.* | *The refinery turns crude oil into usable products such as gas and tar.* | *The program has some nice features that make it more usable than most.*

valid /ˈvælɪ̇d/ [adj] if a ticket, passport etc is **valid**, you can legally use it and it will be officially accepted.: *Do you have a valid driver's license?* | **+ for** *Your ticket is valid for travel at any time of the day.* | **valid for 10 years/two months/one week etc** *My passport is valid for 10 years.*

current /ˈkʌrənt‖ˈkɜːr-/ [adj usually before noun] a **current** official document has not yet reached the date after which it can no longer be used: *Acceptable forms of ID include a current passport or a birth certificate.*

10 something that can be used in various ways

- versatile
- multi-purpose
- all-purpose

versatile /ˈvɜːʳsətaɪl‖-tl/ [adj] something that is **versatile** can be used in many different ways: *Few foods are as versatile as cheese.* | *Because lavender oil is versatile and cheap, it is the most used in aromatherapy.* | *a versatile work table*

multi-purpose /ˌmʌlti ˈpɜːʳpəs◂/ [adj only before noun] a **multi-purpose** tool, machine, piece of equipment etc has been specially designed to have many different uses: *The emergency box contains a multi-purpose knife with screwdriver, scissors and a can-opener.* | *The new multi-purpose bank card gives access to your checking accounts and can also be used as a credit card.*

all-purpose /ˈɔːl ˌpɜːʳpəs/ [adj only before noun] an **all-purpose** product has been specially made for all the uses which that type of product has: *You can buy an all-purpose greetings card, with blank space, for you to write in your own message.* | *an all-purpose cleaning fluid*

11 to use something again

▸ reuse ▸ recycle

reuse /ˌriːˈjuːz/ [v T] to use something more than once: *The supermarket encourages shoppers to reuse plastic bags.* | *The bottles are designed to be reused up to 20 times.*

recycle /ˌriːˈsaɪkəl/ [v T] to put bottles, newspapers, cans etc through a process so that they can be used for making new glass products, paper etc: *New techniques for recycling plastics are being introduced.* —**recyclable** [adj] *Most cans are recyclable.* —**recycled** [adj] *All our envelopes are made from recycled paper.* —**recycling** [adj only before noun] *a recycling bin*

12 to use something wrongly

▸ misuse ▸ abuse

misuse /ˌmɪsˈjuːz/ [v T] to use something wrongly, for a purpose that was not intended: *Measures must be taken to prevent confidential data from being misused.* | *He is accused of misusing public funds.* —**misuse** /ˌmɪsˈjuːs/ [n C/U] *Opponents of genetic engineering see it as a misuse of scientific knowledge.*

abuse /əˈbjuːz/ [v T] to use something for a bad purpose, especially to use a position of power or trust in order to get a personal advantage: *Local politicians abused their privileges to make themselves rich.* | *people who abuse the welfare system* —**abuse** /əˈbjuːs/ [n U] *This is an obscene abuse of political power.*

13 words, remarks, ideas etc that have been used too much

▸ over-used ▸ be wearing thin
▸ stale ▸ clichéd
▸ trite ▸ hackneyed

over-used /ˌəʊvəʳ ˈjuːzd◂/ [adj] used too much and therefore no longer interesting or effective: *'Creative' is an over-used word nowadays and is difficult to define.* | *His lecture turned out to be full of unoriginal material and over-used examples.*

stale /steɪl/ [adj] no longer interesting or exciting because of having been used too much: *Nicholson's routine was full of stale old jokes that we'd all heard before.* | *stale advertising images*

trite /traɪt/ [adj] a **trite** remark, idea etc has been used so often, that is seems boring or not sincere: *I know it might sound like a trite remark, but mothers usually know best.*

be wearing thin /biː ˌweərɪŋ ˈθɪn/ [v phrase] if an excuse, an argument, someone's behaviour etc **is wearing thin**, it has been used so often that it no longer has any effect and is annoying: *Her rebellious teenager act is wearing thin. After all, she's nearly twenty-five.* | **be wearing a bit/a little thin** *That joke is wearing a bit thin now, Stuart.*

clichéd /ˈkliːʃeɪd‖kliːˈʃeɪd/ [adj] speech, writing or an idea that is **clichéd** is boring and without real meaning, because it is not original at all: *the clichéd openings of jokes like, 'Have you heard the one about … ?'* | *We work well together and we are really good friends. I know it sounds clichéd but it's the truth.*

hackneyed /ˈhæknid/ [adj] a **hackneyed** phrase, statement etc is boring and does not have much meaning because it has been used so often before: *Politicians tend to repeat the same hackneyed expressions over and over again.* | *All those slogans we used to chant sound so hackneyed now.*

14 no longer being used

▸ disused ▸ gather dust
▸ unused ▸ fall into disuse
▸ idle

disused /ˌdɪsˈjuːzd◂/ [adj only before noun] especially British a **disused** factory, mine, railway etc is old and not used any more: *The drugs were found in a disused warehouse.* | *They have been given a grant to convert the disused church into luxury flats.*

unused /ˌʌnˈjuːzd◂/ [adj] something that is **unused** has not yet been used or has not been used for a long time: *His old car sat in the garage, unused.* | *Batteries which are unused for long periods may have to be recharged.* | *Unused muscles can feel very sore when you start exercising.*

idle /ˈaɪdl/ [adj not before noun] if machines or factories are **idle**, they are not being used: | **stand/sit/lie idle** *Most of the factory stood idle during the strike.* | *The new machines may sit idle for months until they have been paid for.* | *Why is millions of pounds worth of state-of-the-art equipment lying idle?*

gather dust /ˌgæðəʳ ˈdʌst/ [v phrase] if something such as a machine or a plan **gathers dust**, it is not being used, especially when it could be useful: *Some of the new equipment is just gathering dust because the staff have not been trained to use it.* | *The plans lie gathering dust in some government office.*

fall into disuse /ˌfɔːl ɪntə dɪsˈjuːs/ [v phrase] if something **falls into disuse**, people gradually stop using it because they no longer need or want it: *The canal system fell into disuse around the end of the nineteenth century.* | *When the old woman died, the house fell into disuse.*

15 documents, tickets etc that can no longer be used

▸ invalid ▸ null and void
▸ out of date

invalid /ɪnˈvælɨd/ [adj] a ticket, passport etc that is **invalid** cannot legally be used and it will not be officially accepted: *I'm afraid your ticket is invalid on this route.* | *This passport is invalid. Look at the expiry date.*

out of date /ˌaʊt əv ˈdeɪt/ [adj/adv] a ticket, passport etc that is **out of date** cannot be used because the time during which it could be used has passed: *Are you aware that your passport is out of date?* | **days/months/years out of date** *He tried to get on the train using a pass that was months out of date.*

null and void /ˌnʌl ən ˈvɔɪd/ [adj phrase] a document such as a contract that is **null and void** has no legal force and cannot be used for any purpose – used in legal contexts: *If the contract has not been signed by witnesses, it is considered null and void.*

to use/consume

RELATED WORDS

- use all of something *see* **finish**
- *see also* **waste**

16 to use an amount of something

- use
- use up
- consume
- get/go through
- burn up
- eat up
- take up
- expend

use /juːz/ [v T] to **use** an amount of something such as fuel, water, or food: *Who's used all the hot water?* | *We use about six pints of milk a week.* | *Planning is essential to make sure that resources are used effectively.* | *The average Westerner uses over 260 lbs of paper every year.*

use up /ˌjuːz ˈʌp/ [phr v T] to use all of something, so that there is none left **use up sth** *We should use up everything in the fridge before we go on vacation.* | *The country's oil reserves will soon be used up.* | **use sth up** *That is to say, once we have used our fossil fuels up, there won't be any more.*

consume /kənˈsjuːm‖-ˈsuːm/ [v T] formal to use fuel, energy, water, and other natural products – use this especially to talk about the amount of fuel, energy etc used by people in general: *The US imports 45% of the oil that it consumes.* | *Industrialized countries consume natural resources in huge quantities.*

get/go through /ˈget, ˈgəʊ θruː/ [phr v T] to use a large amount of something in a short period: *Sometimes I go through a whole pack of cigarettes in a single afternoon.* | *We went through our food supplies at an alarming rate.*

burn up /ˌbɜːʳn ˈʌp/ [phr v T] to use a lot of something, especially energy or fuel: *In the typical Western diet, all the energy in protein is burned up daily.* | **burn up calories** (=to use energy, for example by exercising) *Women tend to burn up calories less efficiently than men.*

eat up /ˌiːt ˈʌp/ [phr v T] if something **eats up** money, gas, electricity etc, it uses it very quickly and in large amounts: *My rent eats up most of my money.* | *Non-energy saving light bulbs just eat up electricity.* | *The V8 is a very powerful engine, but it really eats up gas.*

take up /ˌteɪk ˈʌp/ [phr v T] to use space or time, especially a lot of it: *Filing cabinets are very useful but they take up a lot of space.* | *I'll go now – I don't want to take up too much of your time.*

expend /ɪkˈspend/ [v T] formal **expend energy/time/effort etc** to use energy, time etc when you are doing something, usually too much of it: *The final result hardly justifies the amount of time and energy that has been expended.* | **expend sth on/upon sth** *We expend a lot of effort every day upon quite pointless activities.*

17 the amount of something that is used

- consumption

consumption /kənˈsʌmpʃən/ [n U] the amount of fuel, energy etc that people use **water/fuel/energy etc consumption** *The government is urging people to reduce their water consumption.* | *Most people are aware of the need to reduce energy consumption.* | **+ of** *declining consumption of coal, oil and gas*

18 someone that regularly uses amounts of something

- user
- consumer

user /ˈjuːzəʳ/ [n C] *Part of the increase in price will be passed on to private users.* | *one of the heaviest users of fossil fuels in the world* | **drug user** *There is a growing concern about the spread of AIDS among drug users.*

consumer /kənˈsjuːməʳ‖-ˈsuː-/ [n C] someone who buys and uses products and services: *Only 25% of the price a consumer pays for vegetables goes to the farmer.* | **consumer demand/behaviour/preferences etc** *Supermarkets are responding to increased consumer demand for organic products.* | *Improved consumer choice is one of the benefits of a free market.* | **the consumer** (=consumers generally) *Any increase in the cost of transporting goods will be passed on to the consumer.*

19 amounts of something that have not been used

- unused
- untouched
- untapped

unused /ˌʌnˈjuːzd◂/ [adj usually before noun] something that is **unused**, has not been used, especially because it has not been needed: *Any unused wool can be returned to the shop.* | *Unused ammunition was dumped by US planes over Laos.* | *the safe disposal of unused stocks of pharmaceutical products*

untouched /ˌʌnˈtʌtʃt◂/ [adj] not used at all – use this when it is unusual or surprising that something has not been used: *The guests had disappeared and the food was untouched.* | **leave sth untouched** *We managed to leave our savings untouched when we bought the new car.*

untapped /ˌʌnˈtæpt◂/ [adj] **untapped** supplies of something, especially a natural product, have not been used: *Untapped reserves of oil and minerals are thought to lie beneath the desert.* | *The firm recognized that the potential of their databases went largely untapped.* | **untapped resources** *The plants of the Australian outback represent a vast untapped resource.*

to use a person for your own advantage

RELATED WORDS

- *see also* **force sb to do sth, trick/deceive**

20 to use someone for your own advantage

- use
- take advantage of
- exploit
- manipulate
- can wrap/wind sb around your little finger

use /juːz/ [v T] *Can't you see they're just using you?* | *She lets herself be used and then dropped by almost every man she meets.* | **use sb to do sth** *The drug smugglers used innocent travellers to carry the drugs through customs.* | **use sb for your own ends** (=for your own advantage) *In his political life, he was not above using his family for his own ends.*

take advantage of /ˌteɪk ədˈvɑːntɪdʒ ɒv‖-ˈvæn-/ [v phrase] to use someone for your own advantage, especially someone who is very generous or is easily persuaded or deceived: *Don't let them take advantage of you. Stand up for yourself.* | *Older brothers and sisters often take advantage of the younger children in a family.* | **take advantage of sb's good nature** *She's always willing to babysit, but I don't want to take advantage of her good nature.*

exploit /ɪkˈsplɔɪt/ [v T] to use someone in order to get what you want, especially to make money from their work: *Many employers are only too ready to exploit and underpay female part-time workers.* | *Peasants in remote areas of the country were being shamelessly exploited by wealthy land owners.* —**exploitation** /ˌeksplɔɪˈteɪʃən/ [n U] *protests against the exploitation of children in the clothing industry*

manipulate /məˈnɪpjəleɪt/ [v T] to make someone do exactly what you want them to do by influencing them in a clever and dishonest way: *He's so crazy about her he doesn't realize he's being manipulated.* | **manipulate sb into (doing) sth** *He managed to manipulate her into lending his company £500,000.* | *He's such a nice man, I could imagine him getting manipulated into a situation like that.* —**manipulation** /məˌnɪpjəˈleɪʃən/ [n U] *the manipulation of public opinion by the media* —**manipulative** /məˈnɪpjələtɪv‖-leɪtɪv/ [adj] good at manipulating people: *Small children can be quite manipulative.*

can wrap/wind sb around your little finger /kən ˌræp, ˌwaɪnd (sb) əraʊnd jɔːʳ ˌlɪtl ˈfɪŋgəʳ/ [v phrase] informal to be able to persuade someone to do anything you want, especially someone who likes or loves you: *Young girls quickly learn how to wind Daddy around their little finger.* | **have sb wound/wrapped around your little finger** *It was obvious she had her mother wrapped around her little finger.*

21 someone who is used by someone else

- pawn
- puppet
- tool
- stooge
- instrument

pawn /pɔːn/ [n C] someone who is used by a more powerful person or group as part of their plans for getting power, especially when the person being used does not realize this: *The soldiers were nothing more than pawns, regarded as dispensable by their officers.* | **use sb as a pawn** *The ambassador was being used as a pawn in the struggle between the two superpowers.*

puppet /ˈpʌpət/ [n C] a ruler or government that seems to be independent but is really controlled by the government of another more powerful country **a puppet ruler/regime/government** *In 1290, Edward I set up a puppet government in the Scottish lowlands.* | **+ of** *During the 70s many Eastern European leaders were merely puppets of the Kremlin.*

tool /tuːl/ [n C] someone who is controlled and used unfairly by another person or group, especially to do something bad **+ of** *The king was merely a tool of the military regime.*

stooge /stuːdʒ/ [n C] someone who always does what another person or group wants: *Community leaders in the area are widely regarded as police stooges.* | **+ of** *He accused her of being a stooge of the Tory Party.*

instrument /ˈɪnstrəmənt/ [n C] someone who is used and controlled by someone or something more powerful **+ of** *Even small children were used as instruments of the regime, encouraged to spy on and report their parents.* | *The Committee on Ethics in Public Life was regarded by many as being a mere instrument of the government.*

used to/ accustomed to

when something seems normal to you because you have often done it or experienced it before

RELATED WORDS

- used to do sth in the past *see* **past (3)**

1 to be used to something

- be used to
- be accustomed to
- be/feel at home with

be used to /biː ˈjuːst tuː/ [v phrase] if you are **used to** something, you have often done it or experienced it before, so it does not seem strange, new, or difficult to you: *At first Omar hated the rain in England, but he's used to it now.* | *The car breaks down so often, I suppose I should be used to it by now.* | **be used to doing sth** *She grew up on a farm, so she's used to getting up early.* | *My grandfather was used to having everything done for him.*

be accustomed to /biː əˈkʌstəmd tuː/ [v phrase] formal to be used to something, especially because it is a normal part of your life: *Americans are much more accustomed to computer technology these days.* | **be accustomed to doing sth** *They were already accustomed to waiting, so no one complained.* | *A few of the men in the office weren't accustomed to taking orders from women.*

be/feel at home with /biː, ˌfiːl ət ˈhəʊm wɪð/ [v phrase] to be so used to something that you feel comfortable and happy with it, especially because you have learned how to do it well: *Jim has lived in Tokyo for 20 years, so he is perfectly at home with Japanese customs.* | *Practise using the computer until you feel at home with the mouse and keyboard.*

2 something that you are used to

- familiar

familiar /fəˈmɪliəʳ/ [adj] a **familiar** place, idea, situation etc is one that you are used to and that you know well: *It was good to be back in familiar surroundings.* | *We heard the familiar sound of coyotes in the distance.* | **+ to** *This kind of problem will be familiar to many married couples.* | **old familiar** *That morning she heard an old familiar voice on the kitchen radio.* | **that familiar sth** *Robbie got that familiar goofy expression on his face as I told him the story.*

3 to gradually become used to something

- get used to
- become/grow accustomed to
- adjust to
- adapt to
- acclimatize/become acclimatized

get used to /ˌget ˈjuːst tuː/ [v phrase] *Once you get used to a routine, it's hard to change.* | *Paul had* *finally gotten used to Heidi's mood swings.* | **get used to (doing) sth** *Mary never really got used to living on her own after her husband died.* | *It took me a while to get used to the casual atmosphere in the office.*

become/grow accustomed to /bɪˌkʌm, ˌgrəʊ əˈkʌstəmd tuː/ [v phrase] formal written to get used to something: *After a while Edward's eyes grew accustomed to the dark.* | *Living so near the airport, they've grown accustomed to the sound of planes overhead.* | **become/grow accustomed to doing sth** *She had become accustomed to cooking for everyone in the house.* | *Larry remained completely relaxed – he was accustomed to dealing with difficult customers.*

adjust to /əˈdʒʌst tuː/ [v phrase] to get gradually used to a new situation, by changing your attitudes or the way you do things: *It took us a while to adjust to the tropical climate.* | *Some of the staff found it hard to adjust to all the changes in technology and working methods.* | **adjust to doing sth** *Kids need help to adjust to having a new baby in the house.*

adapt to /əˈdæpt tuː/ [v phrase] to gradually change your behaviour and attitudes, so that you get used to a new situation and can deal with it effectively: *Slowly the country is adapting to the new market economy.* | **adapt to doing sth** *She adapted remarkably well to eating a limited diet, and she's lost a great deal of weight.* | *After living in a house with a garden, it's hard to adapt to living in a flat.*

acclimatize/become acclimatized ALSO **acclimatise/become acclimatised** British ALSO **acclimate/become acclimated** American /əˈklaɪmətaɪz, bɪˌkʌm əˈklaɪmətaɪzd, əˈklaɪmət‖ˈækləmeɪt, bɪˌkʌm əˈklaɪmətɪ̬d‖-ˈækləmeɪ-/ [v I/v phrase] to get used to a new place or a different type of weather: *When first arriving in the Himalayas, mountaineers must give themselves time to acclimatize.* | **+ to** *As the immigrants became acclimatized to life in America, they abandoned some of their old traditions.* | *I flew to Hong Kong a day early to give myself a chance to acclimatise to the time difference.* | **get acclimatized/acclimatised/acclimated** *The team wants to have a few practices to get acclimated to the ball park.* | **acclimatize/acclimatise/acclimate yourself** *After a while, if you acclimatise yourself to the heat, you can get by with two canteens of water a day.*

4 to get used to a new job or way of life

- settle in
- find your feet
- find your way around

settle in /ˌsetl ˈɪn/ [phr v I] to gradually get used to a new place or a new way of life, so that you feel relaxed and confident: *Paul never really settled in at his last school.* | *We normally give new employees a little while to settle in before we overload them with responsibilities.* | **settle into sth** *It didn't take Charlie long to settle into his new job.* | *Within a month she had settled into a moderate exercise regimen.*

find your feet /ˌfaɪnd jɔːʳ ˈfiːt/ [v phrase] to get used to a new type of work or a new way of life, especially one that is difficult at first and takes time to learn: *I asked Susie if I could stay with her till I found my feet.* | *This organization's role is to help refugees find their feet when they arrive in the host country.*

find your way around /ˌfaɪnd jɔːʳ weɪ əˈraʊnd/ [v phrase] to get used to a new place where you have come to live or work, especially so that you know where everything is: *Whenever I move into a new neighborhood I like to spend a couple of weeks just finding my way around.* | **find your way around sth** *The university campus is quite large and it takes new students a while to find their way around it.*

5 to be used to something difficult or unpleasant

- be used to
- be hardened to
- be no stranger to
- be inured to

be used to /biː ˈjuːst tuː/ [v phrase] *Living so far north, they're used to the very cold winters.* | **be used to doing sth** *It's a small company, so everyone is used to working late and on weekends.*

be hardened to /biː ˈhɑːʳdnd tuː/ [v phrase] to have become used to something unpleasant or shocking because you have seen or experienced it many times before: *The relief workers are hardened to the sight of people dying from starvation.* | **be hardened to doing sth** *Violence is stressful even to those who are hardened to seeing it every day.* —**hardened** [adj only before noun] *Many of the soldiers are hardened veterans of the war in Afghanistan.*

be no stranger to /biː nəʊ ˈstreɪndʒəʳ tuː/ [v phrase] to be used to sad or unpleasant situations because you have experienced them many times before: *Amanda is no stranger to sorrow – both of her parents died this past year.* | *As a writer he is no stranger to controversy.*

be inured to /biː ɪˈnjʊəʳd tuː/ [v phrase] to be used to something difficult or unpleasant so that you are able to bear it, because it has happened so much or for so long – used in formal or literary contexts: *Diego looked like a man who was inured to disappointment.* | *After years in politics, Gramm seems to be inured to criticism.*

6 not used to something

- not be used to
- not be accustomed to
- unaccustomed/unused to

not be used to /nɒt biː ˈjuːst tuː/ [v phrase] *I'm not used to cold weather.* | *She's still not used to the new phone system.* | **not be used to doing sth** *We're not used to losing, so the defeat came as a surprise.* | *Like most jazz musicians, Dan wasn't used to getting up so early in the morning.*

not be accustomed to /nɒt biː əˈkʌstəmd tuː/ [v phrase] formal to not be used to something, especially because it is not a normal part of your life: *Sorry, but I need to sit down and rest – I'm not accustomed to the heat.* | *Helen wasn't accustomed to such a big breakfast.* | **not be accustomed to doing sth** *Mr Tench was not accustomed to being treated with disrespect.*

unaccustomed/unused to /ˌʌnəˈkʌstəmd, ʌnˈjuːst tuː/ [v phrase] to be not used to something new or different, especially so that you find it unpleasant or hard to accept: *Coming from the country, I was entirely unused to city traffic.* | *My mother was unaccustomed to the hard physical work that was expected of her.* | **be unaccustomed/unused to doing sth** *He was a successful man, unused to sitting still.*

7 something that you are not used to

- unfamiliar
- strange

unfamiliar /ˌʌnfəˈmɪliəʳ◂/ [adj] an **unfamiliar** place, idea, situation etc is one that you are not used to or do not know much about: *Driving on the left-*

hand side of the road was unfamiliar and a little frightening. | *She needs your support even more now that she's in an unfamiliar environment.* | *The army uses satellites to help soldiers navigate unfamiliar terrain.* | **+ to** *Some of these expressions may be unfamiliar to your students.*

strange /streɪndʒ/ [adj only before noun] a **strange** country, food, custom etc is one that you are not used to because you have never been there before, experienced it before etc, and this may make you feel anxious: *The strange food made her ill.* | *He was a little nervous about moving to a strange country where he didn't know anyone.*

useful

RELATED WORDS

opposite: —————— **useless**

▸ *see also* **convenient**

1 useful

- ▸ **useful**
- ▸ **be of use**
- ▸ **handy**
- ▸ **practical**
- ▸ **be good for (doing) sth**
- ▸ **helpful**
- ▸ **valuable**
- ▸ **be worth it**

useful /ˈjuːsfəl/ [adj] something that is **useful** makes it easier for you to do something: *See page 35 for a list of useful addresses.* | *The bank gave us a lot of useful advice about starting our own business.* | **+ for (doing) sth** *Scotch tape is very useful for making quick repairs.* | **+ to** *information that may be useful to the enemy* | **+ in (doing) sth** *This equipment will prove useful in testing premature babies who we suspect might have hearing problems.*

be of use /biː əv ˈjuːs/ [v phrase] formal to be useful: *If there are items in the newspaper files which could be of use, please take a copy of them.* | **+ to** *This book will be of use to all teachers.* | **be some/any use** *Would these computer cleaners be any use to you?* | **be of some use** (=be fairly useful) *The information is slightly out-of-date, but it could still be of some use.*

handy /ˈhændi/ [adj] informal useful and easy to use: *This handy booklet tells you everything you need to know about getting connected to the Internet.* | *a handy chart for converting pounds into kilos* | **+ for (doing) sth** *There's a special brush you can attach to the vacuum cleaner, which is handy for cleaning the stairs.*

practical /ˈpræktɪkəl/ [adj] designed to be useful rather than attractive – use this especially about clothes and things you use in your house: *The company specializes in making practical footwear for the leisure sports market.* | *a type of floor covering that is simple, practical, and cheap*

be good for (doing) sth /biː ˌgʊd fəʳ (ˈduːɪŋ) (sth)/ [v phrase] especially spoken to be suitable and useful for a particular job or purpose: *The table does take up a lot of space, but it's good for parties.* | *The big jars are good for storing pasta.*

helpful /ˈhelpfəl/ [adj] something that is **helpful** is useful because it helps you to do something: *I found these cassettes very helpful when I was learning Spanish.* | *The Student Cook Book provides basic helpful advice without sounding patronising.* | **+ in doing sth** *The drug Prozac can be helpful in treating anxiety.* | **it is helpful to do sth** *I think it would be helpful to summarize what we agreed at the last meeting.*

valuable /ˈvæljuəbəl, -jᵿbəl‖ˈvæljᵿbəl/ [adj] help, advice, knowledge etc that is **valuable** is very useful in helping you do something: *Joyce gave us a lot of valuable advice when we first started the company.* | **+ to** *Your knowledge and experience would be very valuable to us.* | **it is valuable for sb to do sth** *While it is valuable for children to have individual responsibilities, it is also good to share jobs with them.* | **valuable contribution** *Nuclear power makes a valuable contribution to the environment by curbing carbon dioxide emissions.*

be worth it /biː ˈwɜːʳθ ɪt/ [v phrase] use this to say that something you do has a useful result: *I didn't bother looking at the instructions – I didn't think it was worth it.* | **be worth doing/trying etc** (=used especially to suggest doing something) *It may be worth putting an advertisement in the local paper.*

2 extremely useful

- ▸ **invaluable**
- ▸ **indispensable**
- ▸ **can't do/manage without**

invaluable /ɪnˈvæljuəbəl, -jᵿbəl‖ɪnˈvæljᵿbəl/ [adj] *This book has been invaluable as a source of teaching materials.* | *Contact with Western medical techniques proved invaluable, and the student doctors have benefited greatly.* | **+ to** *Margaret's sensible suggestions have been invaluable to us.* | **+ for/in doing sth** *Improved sewage and water services were invaluable in preventing disease.*

indispensable /ˌɪndɪˈspensəbəl/ [adj] someone or something that is **indispensable** is so useful and important that you cannot do something without them: *For mountain-climbing a really good sleeping-bag is indispensable.* | *She soon became an indispensable member of staff.* | **+ to** *A knowledge of classical music is indispensable to anyone who wants to apply for this job.*

can't do/manage without /ˌkɑːnt duː, ˌmænɪdʒ wɪðˈaʊt‖ˌkænt-/ [v phrase] spoken use this about someone or something that is so useful that it would be very difficult to do something without them: *Of course we all have concerns about the environment but you can't do without a car out here in the countryside with no public transport.* | *Top TV chef Billy Williams says he couldn't manage without his food processor: 'It cuts down preparation time by about half and saves you all those fiddly tasks.'*

3 useful only in particular situations

- ▸ **come in handy**
- ▸ **have its uses**

come in handy informal ALSO **come in useful** British informal /ˌkʌm ɪn ˈhændi, ˌkʌm ɪn ˈjuːsfəl/ [v phrase] something that **comes in handy** is not always necessary, but is good to have because it can be very useful in particular situations: *My knowledge of Spanish came in handy when the car broke down near Madrid.* | *Sometimes there are problems that are too big for you to sort out on your own. That's when professional advice comes in useful.* | **+ for (doing) sth** *A hacksaw always comes in handy for cutting plastic pipes.* | **+ as** *I suppose you thought I might come in useful as a translator.*

have its uses /ˌhæv ɪts ˈjuːsᵻz/ [v phrase not in progressive] informal use this to say that something is more useful than it seems: *This typewriter may be old, but it has its uses.* | *A knowledge of Latin can have its uses – for instance, it can help you if you are learning Italian.*

4 the quality of being useful

- usefulness
- utility

usefulness /ˈjuːsfəlnəs/ [n U] *Statistics have some usefulness in the study of public health issues.* | **outlive its usefulness** (=not be useful any more) *We are beginning to think that this factory has outlived its usefulness as our main supplier.*

utility /juːˈtɪləti/ [n U] formal how useful and effective something is: *Demonstrations allow customers to get an immediate idea of a product's utility.* | *I have severe doubts about the utility of examinations on subjects which have been learned parrot-fashion.*

useless

RELATED WORDS

opposite: **useful**

▸ see also **purpose**

1 when something is not useful

- useless
- be no good
- be (of) no use
- be (of) no help
- have got no use for

useless /ˈjuːsləs/ [adj] not at all useful: *The lifejackets turned out to be useless, because they didn't inflate properly.* | *a useless piece of information* | *She gave me a video, but of course it's useless without a player.* | **completely/totally/utterly/absolutely useless** *Presumably, my files will be completely useless to whoever stole them.* | *It's time you traded the car in, before it becomes utterly useless.* | **useless for (doing) sth** *That's a nice watch, but it's useless for going underwater.* | *Jay's car was 20 years old, and useless for anything but a short journey to the local shops.* —**uselessly** [adv] *His injured arm hung uselessly by his side.*

be (of) no use /biː (əv) ˌnəʊ ˈjuːs/ [v phrase] to be useless: *This map's no use – it doesn't show the minor roads.* | *I'm freezing, and these heaters are no use either.* | **+ to** *All this information is of no use to me now. It's too late.* | **be of no use for doing sth** *It's a great rifle – but no use for shooting anything bigger than a rabbit.*

have got no use for /həv gɒt nəʊ ˈjuːs fɔːʳ‖-gɑːt-/ [v phrase] British if you **have no use for** something, you do not want it or need it because you cannot use it for anything: *You may as well stop giving me these magazines – I've got no use for them, and they just go straight in the bin.*

be no good /biː ˌnəʊ ˈgʊd/ [v phrase] informal to be useless: *These matches must have got wet – they're no good at all.* | *Yeah, Clancy's Bar is a lively place, but it's no good if you just want a quiet drink with a friend.* | **be no good for (doing) sth** *These glasses are no good for champagne.* | *We found out that the vehicle was not much good for transporting heavy loads.* | **+ to** *You're no good to me if you can't drive a car.* | *Do you want these bike parts? They're no good to me.*

be (of) no help /biː (əv) ˌnəʊ ˈhelp/ [v phrase] to not be helpful in a particular situation: *Johnny had drawn me a map, but that was no help.* | *Seat belts are of no help at all in 30% of car accidents.* | *I looked at the departures screen, but that was no help because it was out of order.* | **+ to** *It was the nicest thing she could think of to say, but it was really no help to me.* | *The follow-up seminar on women's issues was of no help to me, so I left early.* | **be (of) no help in doing sth** *In-store videos were of no help in identifying the criminals.*

2 objects that are useless and not needed

- junk
- garbage

junk /dʒʌŋk/ [n U] objects that have little value because they are old, useless, broken, or unwanted: *a market stall selling junk and old clothes* | *a pile of old junk* | *Her cupboards were full of junk which she had accumulated over the years.*

garbage /ˈgɑːʳbɪdʒ/ [n U] especially American, informal things that are useless because they are badly made, old, or broken: *Don't buy from that store – most of the stuff there is garbage.* | *You can throw out all the stuff in that cupboard, it's garbage.* | *The attic was full of all kinds of garbage, including an old stereo and boxes of broken toys.*

3 actions or activities that are useless

- pointless
- useless
- futile

pointless /ˈpɔɪntləs/ [adj] if someone does something that is **pointless**, it does not seem to have any useful purpose and will not help anyone: *The argument was completely pointless.* | *pointless drug testing on animals* | **a pointless exercise** (=something that you have to do that does not seem to have any purpose) *We had to change the sheets daily, which always seemed to me to be a pointless exercise.* | **it is pointless doing sth** British *It's pointless trying to speak to the manager – she's always too busy.* | *Look, it's pointless us both waiting here – I'll go and find a phone.* | **it is pointless to do sth** *The company says it is pointless to compete in the air package holiday market.* | *Simon was probably dead, and it was pointless to think he was coming back.* —**pointlessly** [adv] *'When ... ? How ... ?' I stammered pointlessly. I already knew the answers.* —**pointlessness** [n U] *Trevor began explaining the pointlessness of a classical education.*

futile /ˈfjuːtaɪl‖-tl/ [adj] a **futile** effort or attempt to do something is completely pointless because there is no chance of its being effective or successful: *Kevin made one last futile attempt to persuade Sandra to go with him, then left.* | *Demonstrators condemned the summit as a futile and fruitless exercise.* | **prove futile** (=when an attempt ends without being successful) *All efforts to save the child proved futile.* | *Until attitudes at work are changed, attempts to improve performance are likely to prove futile.* | **it is futile to do sth** *The goal is not to punish the rebels, but to convince them that it is futile to resist.* —**futility** /fjuːˈtɪləti/ [n U] *Wilfrid Owen's poems stress the absolute futility of war.* | **an exercise in futility** (=something that would be pointless to try doing) *Signing a trade agreement would be an exercise in futility.*

useless /ˈjuːsləs/ [adj] if an activity is **useless**, it does not achieve anything or does not help anyone: *Numerous studies show that dieting is useless and may even cause weight gain.* | *I had to remind myself that worrying is a useless activity.* | **it is useless to do sth** *It was useless now to ask for help from my mother.* | *He knew it was useless to pretend to be innocent.* | **it is useless doing something** British *It's useless* *trying to talk to you when you've had a drink.* | *I think it would be useless writing to the company – they haven't even returned my calls.*

4 ways of telling someone that it is useless to do something

- there's no point/what's the point
- be a waste of time/be wasting your time
- it's not worth it
- it won't do you any good/it won't get you anywhere
- it's/there's no use

there's no point/what's the point /ðeəʳz ˌnəʊ ˈpɔɪnt, ˌwɒts ðə ˈpɔɪnt/ especially spoken say this when you think that it is useless to do something because it will not achieve any useful purpose: *'Why don't you try and sort out your argument with Mike?' 'There's no point – he never listens.'* | *Don't try working out what your exam results will be – there's no point.* | **there's no point (in) doing sth** *There's no point kidding yourself, Karen – he just isn't interested in you anymore.* | *It's frustrating, but there's no point in getting angry.* | **what's the point of doing sth?** spoken *You've already decided, so what's the point of discussing it?* | **see no point/not see the point** *I didn't see the point of waiting around, so I left.* | *I figured I'd be in town a while, and I saw no point in making enemies when I didn't have to.*

be a waste of time/be wasting your time /biː ə ˌweɪst əv ˈtaɪm, biː ˌweɪstɪŋ jɔːʳ ˈtaɪm/ [v phrase] spoken use this when you think that someone should not spend their time doing something because it will definitely not achieve anything **be a waste of time doing sth/wasting your time doing sth** *You're wasting your time trying to start that car. The battery's completely flat.* | *I told you it would be a waste of time applying for a visa.* | *Why waste your time trying to convince him? He won't change his mind.*

it's not worth it /ɪts ˌnɒt ˈwɜːʳθ ɪt/ spoken say this when you think that something someone wants to do is not important enough to spend any time or money on: *Don't get angry. It's not worth it.* | *'You should have your car serviced.' 'It isn't worth it. I hardly ever drive now.'*

it won't do you any good/it won't get you anywhere /ɪt ˌwəʊnt duː juː ˌeni ˈgʊd, ɪt ˌwəʊnt get juː ˈeniweəʳ/ spoken say this when you think that someone will not be able to change a situation or persuade someone by doing something: *Worrying about the test won't do you any good.* | *I don't think this is getting us anywhere. Can we change the subject?* | *Flattery won't get you anywhere – I'm not doing it.* | *All this speculation isn't doing anyone any good.*

it's/there's no use spoken ALSO **it's/there's no good** British spoken /ɪts, ðeəʳz ˌnəʊ ˈjuːs, ɪts, ðeəʳz ˌnəʊ ˈgʊd/ say this when something you are doing is not working so it is pointless to continue **no use (in) doing sth** *It's no use talking to me about interest rates and mortgages – I find it all too confusing.* | *It's no use lying about it because I saw you do it!* | *There's no use in getting upset about it now.* | **be no good doing sth** British *It's no good sitting here feeling sorry for yourself.* | *There's no good punishing him hours later, because he won't remember what he's done wrong.*

5 when it is useless to try to persuade someone

- it's like talking to a brick wall
- be wasting your breath
- till you're blue in the face

it's like talking to a brick wall ALSO **might as well talk to a brick wall** British /ɪts laɪk ˌtɔːkɪŋ tʊ ə ˌbrɪk ˈwɔːl, maɪt əz wel ˌtɔːk tʊ ə ˌbrɪk ˈwɔːl/ spoken use this to say that it is useless to try to persuade someone or argue with them, because they will not listen to what you are saying: *I wouldn't bother arguing with Francis – it's like talking to a brick wall.* | *I told you I don't want to go out again tonight – honestly, I might just as well talk to a brick wall!*

be wasting your breath /biː ˌweɪstɪŋ jɔːʳ ˈbreθ/ [v phrase] spoken use this to tell someone that there is no point in trying to argue with someone or persuade them about something because they will not change their opinion: *It's no good trying to make Kit change her mind – you'd just be wasting your breath.* | *He's wasting his breath. There's no way they're going to lend him the money.*

till you're blue in the face /tɪl jɔːʳ ˌbluː ɪn ðə ˈfeɪs/ [adv] spoken if you talk, argue etc with someone **till you're blue in the face**, you talk or argue with them for a very long time when it is pointless to do this because they will not listen or understand: *You can argue till you're blue in the face, but it won't do you any good.* | *Politicians can claim until they are blue in the face that students have never had it so good, but the fact is, they cannot justify those claims.*

usually

RELATED WORDS

opposite: **unusual**

- a situation or behaviour that is not unusual *see* **normal/ordinary**
- *see also* **often, always, typical, habit, in general**

1 ways of saying that something usually happens

- usually/generally
- normally
- as a (general) rule
- nine times out of ten
- routinely
- typically

usually/generally /ˈjuːʒuəli, ˈdʒenərəli/ [adv] *I don't know where Jack is – he's usually home by this time.* | *Wolves usually hunt in packs.* | *What's come over Jim? He isn't usually this grumpy.* | *The sea here is generally calm.* | *Generally, these small stores do not keep fresh meat or vegetables.* | *We're generally finished by about 4:30.*

normally /ˈnɔːʳməli/ [adv] on most occasions, unless something unusual happens: *The museum isn't normally as crowded as this.* | *His normally cheerful face looked sad for a moment.*

as a (general) rule /əz ə (ˌdʒenərəl) ˈruːl/ [adv] use this to say what usually happens: *As a general rule, the police may only enter your house if you invite them in.* | *We do not, as a rule, provide funds for this type of project.*

nine times out of ten /ˌnaɪn taɪmz aʊt əv ˈten/ [adv] almost always: *Nine times out of ten I just skip breakfast and have a coffee.* | *Nine times out of ten, jobs that become vacant are filled from inside the organization.*

routinely /ruːˈtiːnli/ [adv] if something is **routinely** done, tested, checked etc, it is usually done as part of the normal process of working, doing a job etc: *The cars are routinely tested for safety and reliability before leaving the factory.* | *We routinely test patients for high blood pressure and diabetes.* | *It later emerged that prisoners at the camp were routinely tortured, and many executed.*

typically /ˈtɪpɪkli/ [adv] in the way that a particular type of thing usually happens, for example what type of person is usually involved, what group something usually affects etc: *Victims of mugging are typically young men in their early 20s.* | *This disease typically affects young cattle.* | *Typically, gasoline taxes are used to fund road-building programs.*

2 in the same way as things usually happen

- as usual
- as ever/as always
- as per usual

as usual /əz ˈjuːʒuəl/ [adv] in the same way as things usually happen: *Sam was in a bad mood as usual.* | *There will be discounts available for students as usual.* | *As usual, there was far too much food.*

as ever/as always British **/like always** American informal /əz ˈevəʳ, əz ˈɔːlweɪz, laɪk ˈɔːlweɪz/ [adv] spoken use this to say that something is not surprising because it is what almost always happens: *Jim was the first to arrive, as always.* | *As ever, her work has been excellent this term.* | *When he arrived he stank of whiskey and tobacco, like always.*

as per usual /ˌæz pəʳ ˈjuːʒuəl/ [adv] British spoken say this when you are annoyed because something bad that usually happens has just happened again: *I'm in trouble at work, as per usual.* | *She was three hours late as per usual.* | *He said he'd phone, but he won't. As per usual!*

3 usual

- usual
- normal
- be the norm
- customary
- routine
- same old
- stock

usual /ˈjuːʒuəl, ˈjuːʒəl/ [adj] use this about something that usually happens or something that someone usually does or uses: *She was sitting in her usual chair by the fire.* | *All the usual people were there.* | **colder/better/slower etc than usual** *It seemed colder than usual in the house.* | *We've sold more than the usual amount of coal this year.* | **it is usual for sb to do sth** *Is it usual for him to be so late?*

normal /ˈnɔːʳməl/ [adj] someone's **normal** behaviour or habit is what they usually do in a particular situation: *She went to bed at her normal time of eleven o'clock.* | *It used to be normal practice to live at home with your parents until you got married.* | **+ for** *Don't worry if Mike seemed rude – that's normal for him.* | **be normal for sb to do sth** *It's normal for young children to misbehave sometimes.*

be the norm /biː ðə ˈnɔːʳm/ [v phrase] to be the thing that most people do or think: *Going to church on Sunday used to be the norm in most households.* | *In the building industry, short-term employment contracts are the norm.* | *Smoking is no longer the norm but the exception.*

customary /ˈkʌstəməri‖-meri/ [adj] usually done on a particular occasion or at a particular time of year: *We were presented with the customary bottle of champagne.* | **it is customary to do sth** *It's customary to kiss the bride at a wedding.* | **as is customary** *As is customary, you will be paid a fixed fee for the job.*

routine /ˌruːˈtiːn◂/ [adj] something that is **routine** is done as part of the normal process of working, doing a job etc: *A major electrical fault was found during a routine safety inspection.* | *The hospital carried out some routine tests.* | *Do you mind if I ask you a few questions? It's just routine.*

same old /ˈseɪm əʊld/ [adj phrase only before noun] informal use this about something that you have seen or heard many times before: *They always come up with the same old excuses for why they can't deliver on time.* | *They still sing the same old songs, but the audiences love it!* | **the same old story** (=use this when it is annoying that the same thing always happens) *It's always the same old story. They're two or three goals up, and then they relax and end up losing.*

stock /stɒk‖stɑːk/ [adj only before noun] **stock** phrases, questions, answers, excuses etc are the ones that people usually use – use this about phrases, questions etc that have been used so often that they are no longer effective: *Her speech contained all the stock phrases about increasing productivity and reducing costs.* | *The same questions seem to be asked every time, and he gives his stock answers.*

4 what people usually do

- habit
- routine
- standard practice

habit /ˈhæbɪ̈t/ [n C] something that you do regularly without thinking about it, because you have done it so many times before: *My father had some rather strange habits, like reading the newspaper in the bath.* | **be in the habit of doing sth** *She was in the habit of taking a walk in the early evening.* | **not be in the habit of doing sth** *I'm not in the habit of going to bars during the day.* | **get into the habit of doing sth** *He had got into the habit of phoning home during the day.*

routine /ruːˈtiːn/ [n C] a series of things that someone usually does in the same order, especially when it is the same every day: *His routine consisted of work, dinner, then TV and bed.* | *Most babies soon develop a daily routine of eating and sleeping.* | *She does not like having her work routine interrupted.*

standard practice /ˌstændəʳd ˈpræktɪ̈s/ [n U] the way that something is usually done in a particular situation or within a particular organization: *Checking police records of new staff is standard practice these days.* | **it is standard practice (for sb) to do sth** *In the 1930s, it was standard practice for workers to have seven days' holiday a year.* | *It's standard practice for the architects and builders to haggle over costs.*

Vv

value

the amount of money that something is worth

RELATED WORDS

▸ *see also* **cost, expensive, cheap**

1 what the value of something is

▸ value
▸ be worth
▸ be valued at

value /ˈvæljuː/ [n C/U] the amount of money that something expensive, rare, or old would cost if it was sold – use this to talk about things like houses, cars, jewellery, paintings, or furniture **+ of** *The value of the sculpture was estimated at $500,000.* | **increase/fall in value** *Some fine wines increase in value as they get older.*

be worth /biː ˈwɜːʳθ/ [v phrase] if something **is worth** £1, £10, $100 etc, that is how much money it would cost if it was sold: *How much is your ring worth?* | **be worth $500/£10 etc** *I guess their house must be worth about £500,000.* | *That old piano can't be worth more than $200.*

be valued at /biː ˈvæljuːd æt/ [v phrase] to have a particular value, especially a very high value which has been calculated: *As a wedding present he gave her some pearls valued at $350,000.* | *They have a classic car which has been valued at a higher price than they paid for it.* | *At current market prices their holding in the company is valued at over $25 million.*

2 worth a lot of money

▸ valuable
▸ of great value
▸ be worth a lot
▸ be worth a fortune
▸ precious
▸ priceless

valuable /ˈvæljuəbəl, -jᵍbəl‖ˈvæljᵍbəl/ [adj] worth a lot of money and expensive to buy or replace: *Don't lose this ring – it's very valuable.* | *Besides her studio apartment, she also owns a valuable estate in Italy.* | *Rogers had purchased a valuable Hebrew manuscript from a dealer in Jerusalem.*

of great value /əv ˌgreɪt ˈvæljuː/ [adj phrase] something that is **of great value** is worth a lot of money, especially a personal possession such as a work of art or a piece of jewellery: *He has a few medals of great value.* | *The burglars stole the television and video, but nothing of great value.*

be worth a lot /biː ˌwɜːʳθ ə ˈlɒt‖-ˈlɑːt/ [v phrase] informal if something **is worth a lot,** you can get a lot of money if you sell it: *You should look after those old dolls – one day they could be worth a lot.*

be worth a fortune /biː ˌwɜːʳθ ə ˈfɔːʳtʃən/ [v phrase] if something **is worth a fortune** it is worth a very large amount of money: *He was very poor when he died, but now his paintings are worth a fortune.*

precious /ˈpreʃəs/ [adj only before noun] **precious metal/stone** a valuable metal such as gold or a jewel such as a diamond: *The robe was encrusted with precious metals and stones.*

priceless /ˈpraɪsləs/ [adj] worth so much money that it is impossible to calculate the price – use this about objects that are old and rare such as paintings, furniture, or jewellery: *The house was full of priceless antiques.* | *a priceless oil painting*

3 valuable objects or possessions

▸ valuables
▸ treasures

valuables /ˈvæljuəbəlz, -jᵍbəlz‖-jᵍbəlz/ [n plural] valuable personal possessions such as jewellery, cameras, and important documents: *The hotel management advises guests to deposit their valuables in the hotel safe.* | *Thieves will take any bags, wallets, and other valuables they can find.*

treasures /ˈtreʒəʳz/ [n C] very valuable works of art, especially ones that are very old: *The exhibition shows treasures from ancient China.* | **art treasures** *Some of Spain's most valuable art treasures are housed in El Prado.*

4 to decide what the value of something is

▸ value

value British **/appraise** American /ˈvæljuː, əˈpreɪz/ [v T] to decide what the **value** of something is, especially when it is your job to do this: *He works for an antique firm, valuing furniture.* | *The apartment was appraised, and Stephen gave Julie a check for half the amount.* | **value/appraise sth at $100/$500 etc** *The builder valued the work already done at $400.* | **have sth valued/appraised** (=get a professional person to value it for you) *Those silver bowls could be worth a lot of money – you ought to have them appraised.* —**valuation** /ˌvæljuˈeɪʃən/ British **/appraisal** American [n U] *I took the ring to a shop for valuation.* —**valuer** British **/appraiser** American [n C] *The valuer* (=person whose job is to value things) *said the plate was worth £500.*

5 to become more valuable

▸ increase/rise/go up in value
▸ appreciate
▸ double/triple in value

increase/rise/go up in value /ɪnˌkriːs, ˌraɪz, gəʊ ˌʌp ɪn ˈvæljuː/ [v phrase] *They bought a Ferrari knowing that it would increase in value.* | *Through clever marketing, the shares have gone up in value quite quickly.* | *The pound has risen in value against the yen over the weekend.*

appreciate /əˈpriːʃieɪt/ [v I] to become gradually more valuable over a period of time: *This property has appreciated rapidly during the last ten years.* | *Most investments are still expected to appreciate at a steady rate.*

double/triple in value /ˌdʌbəl, ˌtrɪpəl ɪn ˈvæljuː/ [v phrase] to become two or three times more valuable: *Fortunately, when I sold my apartment it had almost doubled in value since I bought it.* | *Production of iron and steel more than tripled in value during the 1950s.*

6 to become less valuable

▸ fall/decrease/go down in value
▸ depreciate

fall/decrease/go down in value /ˌfɔːl, dɪˌkriːs, gəʊ ˌdaʊn ɪn ˈvæljuː/ [v phrase] *Gold and silver have* *gone down in value.* | *Most European currencies fell in value yesterday.*

depreciate /dɪˈpriːʃieɪt/ [v I] to become gradually less valuable over a period of time: *A new car depreciates more quickly than a second-hand one.* | *US investors anticipate that the Deutschmark will, in the long term, depreciate relative to the dollar.* —**depreciation** /dɪˌpriːʃiˈeɪʃən/ [n U] *The price of the equipment must reflect depreciation.*

7 without any value

- worthless
- not be worth anything

worthless /ˈwɜːʳθləs/ [adj] *When he died, all my uncle left me was a worthless plot of land.* | *The jewellery turned out to be completely worthless.* | *I'm afraid this banknote is a forgery; it's just a worthless piece of paper.*

not be worth anything /nɒt biː ˈwɜːʳθ ˌeniθɪŋ/ [v phrase] to have no value: *I don't think my stereo is worth anything now, but it was quite expensive when I bought it.*

various/of different kinds

RELATED WORDS

- *see also* **different, lot**

1 words for describing things or people that are of different kinds

- different
- various
- a variety of sth
- differing
- varying
- an assortment of sth
- assorted
- a mix of sth
- a mixture of sth

different /ˈdɪfərənt/ [adj only before noun] use this about several people or things of the same general type, when you are comparing them with each other and noticing the differences between them: *His hair was dyed in at least three different colors.* | *I always check the prices of different brands before I make a major purchase.* | *The drug affects different people in different ways.* | *The word can have completely different meanings depending on the context.*

various /ˈveəriəs/ [adj only before noun] use this when you want to emphasize that there are several different people or things: *The study evaluates various methods of weight loss.* | *The committee has asked various people for their opinions.* | *I had to sign various documents before they would let me into the country.*

a variety of sth /ə vəˈraɪəti əv (sth)/ [n phrase] especially written a lot of things that are different from each other, but of the same general type: *Children do badly at school for a variety of reasons.* | *The reef fishes display an almost endless variety of colors and patterns.* | **a wide variety of sth** (=a large variety) *The college offers a wide variety of language courses.*

differing /ˈdɪfərɪŋ/ [adj only before noun] different from each other, especially very different in degree, amount, character etc: *We aim to satisfy the differing needs of our customers.* | *Survivors sustained injuries with differing degrees of severity.* | **widely differing** *There are widely differing views among community leaders on how best to deal with the homeless issue.*

varying /ˈveəriɪŋ/ [adj only before noun] different from each other in degree, amount, condition etc: *The program teaches children of varying ages.* | *It is now possible to grow satisfactory crops under varying climatic conditions.* | **varying degrees/levels/amounts etc of sth** *She has tried numerous diets with varying degrees of success.* | *Test-takers must complete ten tasks with varying levels of complexity.*

an assortment of sth /ən əˈsɔːʳtmənt əv (sth)/ [n phrase] several things that are of the same general kind but are not all exactly alike: *Police confiscated an assortment of weapons from the gang.* | *Every good cook needs an assortment of knives for different jobs in the kitchen.* | *The basket contained an assortment of sandwiches, cheese, and fruit.*

assorted /əˈsɔːʳtɪ̈d/ [adj only before noun] various things of the same general kind, all together in the same place – often used about products: *In the centre of the table was a plate of assorted biscuits.* | *a box of assorted bandages* | *The website contains links to assorted investment sites.*

a mix of sth /ə ˈmɪks əv (sth)/ [n phrase] an interesting or useful variety of different people or things: *The ideal lesson contains a good mix of activities and subjects.* | *A mix of young people and old people attended the meeting.* | *The band's music is an exciting mix of jazz, swing, and rock 'n' roll.*

a mixture of sth /ə ˈmɪkstʃər əv (sth)/ [n phrase] a variety of people or things, especially when they have been deliberately chosen to be together: *The film is largely a mixture of music, dance, and comedy.* | *Indonesian civilization is an extreme mixture of races, religions, and cultures.* | *Yiddish is a dialect of German with a mixture of Polish and Hebrew added.*

2 words for describing things or people of many different kinds

- all sorts/kinds of sth
- diverse
- all manner of sth
- from/in all walks of life

all sorts/kinds of sth /ɔːl ˈsɔːʳts, ˈkaɪndz əv (sth)/ [n phrase] especially spoken a lot of people or things that are different from each other, but of the same general type: *I meet all sorts of people in my job.* | *The bureau provides advice on all kinds of housing problems.* | *My landlady has all kinds of junky stuff in the basement.* | *Pregnancy causes all sorts of hormonal changes in your body.*

diverse /daɪˈvɜːʳs‖ dɪ̈-, daɪ-/ [adj] very different from each other, though belonging to the same group or being connected in some way: *Indian cinema shows several diverse influences.* | *It is difficult to design a program that will meet the diverse needs of all our users.* | *The category of 'mammals' contains creatures as diverse as whales, elephants, and human beings.* —**diversity** [n U] *The diversity of languages among our schoolkids should be seen as a benefit, and not as a disadvantage.*

all manner of sth /ɔːl ˈmænər əv (sth)/ [n phrase] many very different or surprisingly different kinds of things: *All manner of foodstuffs lay scattered on the kitchen table.* | *Health food stores promote all manner of herbs to prevent colds.*

from/in all walks of life /frəm, ɪn ˌɔːl wɔːks əv ˈlaɪf/ [adj phrase] from or in every kind of job and every social class: *Members of the organization* *come from all walks of life.* | *The Internet has affected the everyday existence of children and adults in all walks of life.* | *Golf used to be a game for the rich, but now it attracts people from all walks of life.*

3 including many different people, things, activities etc

- varied
- variety
- diverse
- wide-ranging
- mixed
- multicultural/multiracial

varied /ˈveərid/ [adj] consisting of or including many different people, things, activities etc: *He had a varied and outstanding career.* | *Grain products, vegetables, and fruit are important parts of a varied diet.* | *Sandra's circle of friends was varied, and often a little strange.*

variety /vəˈraɪəti/ [n U] the differences within a group, set of actions etc that make it interesting: *She's always complaining that her job doesn't have enough variety.* | *The music on her latest CD shows a great deal of variety.* | **+ of** *The doctor encouraged him to increase the variety of food that he eats.*

diverse /daɪˈvɜːˈs‖də-, daɪ-/ [adj] a **diverse** group of people or things contains a lot of very different types of people or things: *The project studied a diverse group of 20,000 teenagers from nine high schools.* | *We believe the committee should reflect the diverse make-up of our community.* | *The region's economy is more diverse now than it was 10 years ago.*

wide-ranging /ˌwaɪd ˈreɪndʒɪŋ◂/ [adj] including many different subjects, ideas, or things: *Climate change is likely to have a wide-ranging impact on human health.* | *Our discussions were wide-ranging and substantive.* | *A wide-ranging survey found growing dissatisfaction among workers.*

mixed /mɪkst/ [adj usually before noun] including two or more different things of the same type, or people of different types, **mixed** together: *The show draws a mixed audience of children and adults.* | *After beating the cake mixture, add a handful of mixed nuts.* | *This is a very mixed neighborhood, both racially and socially.*

multicultural/multiracial /ˌmʌltiˈkʌltʃərəl◂, ˌmʌlti ˈreɪʃəl◂/ [adj usually before noun] including or concerning people of different races or religions, especially those who live together in the same society, go to the same schools etc: *Most of today's teachers are committed to multicultural education.* | *He grew up in a multiracial area in London's East End.* | *Government policies should reflect the multiracial nature of our society.*

4 seeming to be together for no particular reason

- miscellaneous
- motley
- mixed bag
- this, that, and the other

miscellaneous /ˌmɪsəˈleɪniəs◂/ [adj only before noun] *You'll need enough money for food, transport, and other miscellaneous costs.* | *Their junk shop was full of chairs, trunks, ornaments, and other miscellaneous objects.* | *The seminar was attended by a miscellaneous collection of students, businessmen, and housewives.*

motley /ˈmɒtli‖ˈmɑːtli/ [adj only before noun] **motley crew/bunch/assortment etc** a group of people of very different kinds, especially people that you disapprove of: *The people who travelled with us to Mexico were a motley crew.* | *A motley bunch of students, ex-convicts and unemployed artists worked together to repair the building.*

mixed bag /ˌmɪkst ˈbæg/ [n singular] informal a group of people or things of very different kinds which do not seem to have much connection with each other: *Downtown is a mixed bag of upscale retailers and discount stores.* | *Today, healthcare depends on a mixed bag of medical professionals, charity workers, and patients' families.*

this, that, and the other ALSO **this, that, and the other thing** American /ˌðɪs, ˌðæt, ən ði ˈʌðəʳ, ˌðɪs, ˌðæt, ən ði ˈʌðəʳ θɪŋ/ [n phrase] spoken say this about a variety of things that someone says or does: *We spent the evening chatting about this, that, and the other.* | *The casting agents always want me to prove that I can do this, that, and the other thing.*

5 a set of different things of the same general type

- a range of sth
- spectrum
- selection
- gamut

a range of sth /ə ˈreɪndʒ əv (sth)/ [n phrase] a set of many different things of the same general type that are available in the same place for the same use: *She has an interesting range of hobbies, from stamp-collecting to astronomy.* | **a wide/broad range of sth** *Atkins is extremely well educated and able to talk on a broad range of topics.* | *It was difficult to choose from such a wide range of dishes on the menu.*

spectrum /ˈspektrəm/ [n C usually singular] a complete range of different types of things or people, especially when those at one end of the range are the opposite of those at the other end **+ of** *The spectrum of protest activity goes from peaceful to extremely violent.* | **broad/wide/whole/entire spectrum** *Their songs appeal to a broad spectrum of music lovers.* | *You can find therapists along the whole spectrum, from caring and honest to cool and manipulative.* | **at one end/the other end of the spectrum** *At one end of the spectrum were the Communists, and at the other, the Nationalists.* | **political spectrum** (=range of political opinions) *The announcement has upset people all across the political spectrum.*

selection /sə̇ˈlekʃən/ [n C] a number of different things of the same kind that are available for you to choose or use: *Customers are invited to view the selection at any time.* | **+ of** *The library also has a selection of foreign language videos on the third floor.* | **wide/broad selection** *The shop offers a wide selection of glasses frames to choose from.*

gamut /ˈgæmət/ [n singular] a complete range of every possible emotion, problem, experience etc **+ of** *'Fear' is a word that covers a gamut of different feelings.* | **a/the whole gamut** *Alternative therapies have been successful with a whole gamut of health problems.* | *New mothers can experience the whole gamut of emotions, from intense joy to deep depression.* | **run the gamut** *Lodgings run the gamut from rustic cabins to plush hotels.*

6 to start to get involved in new activities

- branch out
- diversify

branch out /ˌbrɑːntʃ ˈaʊt‖ˌbræntʃ-/ [phr v I] *When you don't allow employees to branch out, they become bored.* | *The clothing designer has branched out and* *now has his name on a line of perfume.* | **+ into** *Many businesses are unwilling to branch out into new and unfamiliar areas.*

diversify /daɪ'vɜːʳsᵻfaɪ‖dᵻ-, daɪ-/ [v I] if a business or organization **diversifies**, it begins to make new products or get involved in new areas of business in addition to what it was doing before: *The company is diversifying to find new sources of income.* | **+ into** *We started out making cash registers, but have diversified into computer systems of all sorts.*

7 to make something different and more varied

- vary
- add variety to

vary /'veəri/ [v T] *To obtain the nutrients you need, vary the foods you eat.* | *Good writers vary the length and structure of their sentences.*

add variety to /ˌæd və'raɪəti tuː/ [v phrase] to make something more varied, especially in order to make it more interesting: *Tutoring younger students can add variety to older students' days, and make them feel important.* | *Bartlett argued that billboards add color and variety to our city streets.*

vertical

a vertical line or surface goes straight up or down

RELATED WORDS

opposite: **flat**

▸ *see also* **up**

1 standing, pointing, or moving straight up or down

- vertical
- upright
- straight up
- perpendicular
- erect
- sheer

vertical /'vɜːʳtɪkəl/ [adj] *The wallpaper has vertical pink and white stripes.* | *In some places the cliff was almost vertical, and much too dangerous to climb.* | *The vertical line on the graph represents the time taken, and the horizontal line represents the distance travelled.* | *a fairground ride that ends with a vertical drop of a hundred feet* — **vertically** [adv] *a sheet of paper divided vertically into two*

upright /'ʌp-raɪt/ [adv] in a vertical position **sit/stand upright** *The ceiling was so low that he couldn't stand upright.* | **hold/keep sth upright** *Keep the bottle upright, in case it leaks.* | *She sat quietly, her violin held upright in her lap.*

straight up /ˌstreɪt 'ʌp/ [adv] in a vertical direction, into or towards the sky **point/rise/travel etc straight up** *The rocket shot straight up and exploded overhead.* | *The towers of the hospital rose straight up from the edge of the highway.* | *A thin crack running straight up the wall had appeared.* | *At this point, the base of the golf club should point straight up into the air.*

perpendicular /ˌpɜːʳpən'dɪkjᵊləʳ◂/ [adj] perfectly vertical in relation to the ground, or in relation to another line – used especially in technical contexts: *Behind them, there was a perpendicular wall of rock.* | *Ensure that the plumbline is perpendicular before you start to draw the line.* | **+ to** (=at an angle of 90 degrees to another line or surface) *In a graph, the x-axis is perpendicular to the y-axis.*

erect /ɪ'rekt/ [adj] in a very straight, stiff, vertical position: *The headstones were all erect and orderly.* | *The rabbit looked all around, with its ears erect.* | **sit/stand/walk etc erect** *The magistrate sat there, stern and erect, as the charge was read out.* | *She holds her head erect, with her blonde curls falling down her back.*

sheer /ʃɪəʳ/ [adj only before noun] a **sheer** surface or slope is very steep, almost vertical **sheer cliff/drop/slope etc** *The coastguard patrols paths at the top of high and sheer cliffs.* | *I stood at the edge of the old chalk quarry, with a sheer drop of ten or twenty metres below me.*

2 to put something into a vertical position

- stand up
- stand sth on end

stand up /ˌstænd 'ʌp/ [phr v T] to put something into a vertical position, especially when this is its usual position **stand sth up** *Tom stood the statue up and looked at it.* | *Stand the wine bottle up for a few hours in a warm place before drinking.* | **stand up sth** *The bartender had to go round standing up all the stools that had been knocked down in the fight.*

stand sth on end /ˌstænd (sth) ɒn 'end/ [v phrase] to put something in a vertical position, when this is not its usual position: *We had to stand the table on end to get it through the door.*

very

RELATED WORDS

▸ *see also* **completely, too/too much, fairly/quite**

1 very

- very
- really
- highly
- deeply
- real
- so
- one
- decidedly
- quite

very /'veri/ [adv] *Juan is a very good dancer.* | *Your house is very different from the way I'd imagined it.* | *'Was it a good movie?' 'Yes, very.'* | *This meeting is very important, so be on time.* | *During our time working together I got to know her very well.* | *Everything was happening very quickly, and I don't remember it all.* | *The ambassador made a brief statement, saying that the talks had been very productive.*

really /'rɪəli/ [adv] especially spoken use this especially to talk about your feelings or what you think about something: *It's really cold out there.* | *I'm always really hungry by noon.* | *That's a really pretty dress – where did you get it?* | *Considering this was your first time, I think you did really well.*

highly /'haɪli/ [adv] formal very – use this only with particular adjectives **highly dangerous/toxic/flammable** *Danger: highly flammable materials!* | **highly skilled/educated/ trained/intelligent** *Our engineers are highly skilled and very difficult to replace when they leave.* | **highly likely/unlikely/probable/doubtful/suspicious** *I think it's highly unlikely that Bob had anything to do with the theft.* | **highly successful/productive** *She arrived in Australia as a refugee, but went on to become a highly successful lawyer.*

deeply /ˈdiːpli/ [adv] use this to describe very strong or very sincere feelings: *We are all deeply saddened by Bill's sudden death.* | *The ceremony was short but deeply moving.* | *Senator McCain is deeply committed to campaign finance reform.* | *I want you to know how deeply grateful I am for everything you've done for me.* | *Local residents are deeply concerned about the threat to health posed by the power station.*

real /rɪəl/ [adv] American spoken very: *I think it was real sweet that she called me herself.* | *The sidewalk was real wet and slippery.* | *He got up real close to the bear and took a picture.*

so /səʊ/ [adv] use this to emphasize how you feel about something: *It all happened so fast.* | *You've been so kind. I hope I can repay you some day.* | *The dresses were lovely, and the colours were so pretty.* | *That puppy is so cute!*

one /wʌn/ [determiner] especially American, spoken use this to emphasize a description of someone or something: *She's one crazy lady!* | *That's one fancy car you've got there.*

decidedly /dɪˈsaɪdədli/ [adj] definitely or in a way that is easily noticed: *The weather had turned decidedly chilly.* | *The play has received decidedly negative reviews.*

quite /kwaɪt/ [adv] especially British use this with words that mean 'excellent': *Thank you, Gloria. That meal was quite delicious!* | *The concert was quite wonderful. I'm sorry you couldn't make it.*

2 extremely

- extremely
- absolutely
- awfully/terribly/terrifically
- very, very
- incredibly/unbelievably
- ridiculously
- enormously/hugely
- dreadfully
- remarkably/exceptionally

extremely /ɪkˈstriːmli/ [adv] especially written use this when you want to use a stronger word than 'very': *The conference was extremely badly organized.* | *The fungus is extremely difficult to get rid of.* | *Regular visits to the doctor are extremely important for pregnant mothers.*

absolutely /ˈæbsəluːtli, ˌæbsəˈluːtli/ [adv] as much as it is possible to imagine – use this to emphasize adjectives that already have a strong meaning **absolutely marvellous/wonderful/delicious etc** *We had an absolutely marvellous day.* | *The costumes were absolutely stunning.* | **absolutely filthy/disgusting/awful etc** *When they came in from the yard, they were absolutely filthy.* | **absolutely terrified/exhausted/delighted/furious etc** *She stood in the middle of the stage looking absolutely terrified.* | **absolutely necessary/essential** *Don't call me unless it's absolutely necessary.*

awfully/terribly/terrifically /ˈɔːfəli, ˈterəbli, təˈrɪfɪkli/ [adv] spoken extremely: *Our Internet connection is awfully slow today.* | *He's been terribly ill for the last two weeks.* | *The plot is terrifically complicated and difficult to follow.* | *That box looks awfully heavy – are you sure you don't need any help?*

very, very /ˈveri veri/ [adv] spoken say this when you want to emphasize 'very': *I'm very, very angry with her.* | *This is a very, very important decision – please give it your full attention.* | *We've been working on this deal for a very, very long time.*

incredibly/unbelievably /ɪnˈkredəbli, ˌʌnbəˈliːvəbli/ [adv] use this when something is so good, so bad, so fast etc that you are surprised by it or you find it hard to believe: *Everyone in the company works incredibly hard.* | *Their house is incredibly cold – I don't think they heat it at all.* | *What they did was unbelievably stupid.* | *The apartment is unbelievably cheap – there must be something wrong with it.*

ridiculously /rɪˈdɪkjələsli/ [adv] use this to emphasize how unreasonable or stupid something is: *The questions seemed ridiculously easy.* | *The amount they offered for the car was ridiculously low.*

enormously/hugely /ɪˈnɔːʳməsli, ˈhjuːdʒli/ [adv] use this especially to emphasize how popular, successful, or powerful someone or something is: *Barry's novels have been hugely successful.* | *'The Wizard of Oz' remains enormously popular with children.* | *Davis plays an enormously influential role in city politics.*

dreadfully /ˈdredfəli/ [adv] British use this to emphasize how bad something is, or how sad or unhappy someone is: *You must be dreadfully disappointed!* | *Dreadfully overcrowded trains and frequent cancellations made commuting an ordeal.*

remarkably/exceptionally /rɪˈmɑːʳkəbli, ɪkˈsepʃənəli/ [adv] use this to emphasize how unusual, impressive, or surprising something is: *Mills' predictions turned out to be remarkably accurate.* | *The old documents are remarkably well preserved.* | *Nadine's daughter has an exceptionally fine singing voice.* | *The heavy soil of the delta produces exceptionally high yields of rice and millet.*

violent

RELATED WORDS

▸ *see also* **cruel, dangerous, fight, attack, kill, threaten, hit, crime**

1 people and their behaviour

- violent
- brutal
- aggressive
- vicious
- savage
- ferocious
- rough

violent /ˈvaɪələnt/ [adj] someone who is **violent** attacks people physically, especially because this is part of their character. A **violent** action involves physical attacks on people: *My father was a violent man who couldn't control his temper.* | *There was a violent protest outside the court, and a police officer was injured.* | **violent crime** *Everyone is worried about the increase in violent crime.* | **turn violent** (=suddenly start to behave violently) *Travellers to the country have been urged to avoid large crowds, which have occasionally turned violent in the past.* —**violently** [adv] *He was violently attacked by a gang of youths.*

brutal /ˈbruːtl/ [adj] very cruel and violent, and without any pity: *The police are searching for the brutal attacker of a 98-year-old woman.* | *Some of the prison guards were brutal and corrupt.* | *a brutal dictator* | **brutal murder/attack/killing etc** *Carter was jailed for the brutal murder of a young mother of three.* —**brutally** [adv] *The boy's body was found on wasteland, brutally stabbed to death.*

aggressive /əˈgresɪv/ [adj] someone who is **aggressive** behaves in an angry way, and seems to want to fight or argue, often when this is a part of their character: *Some of the crowd were very aggressive, shouting and banging on windows.* | *Kids who* *play violent video games show much more aggressive behaviour than those who don't.* —**aggressively** [adv] *The driver of the truck leant out of the window and yelled at me aggressively.*

vicious /ˈvɪʃəs/ [adj] someone who is **vicious** is violent and dangerous and seems to enjoy hurting people for no reason: *We found ourselves surrounded by a gang of vicious young thugs, armed with belts, sticks and stones.* | *'It was a particularly vicious crime,' a police spokesman said.* | **vicious attack/assault** *Apparently the girl was the victim of a vicious sex attack.* —**visciously** [adv] *The baby had been viciously battered to death.*

savage /ˈsævɪdʒ/ [adj] hurting people in a particularly cruel way: *Police are hunting the savage killer of five men in South London.* | *There was savage fighting in and around the eastern border towns.* | *Fussell described the war as 'appallingly cruel and savage.'* —**savagely** [adv] *It is alleged that Davies savagely attacked Mrs Cousins with a knife.*

ferocious /fəˈrəʊʃəs/ [adj] a **ferocious** attack or fight is extremely violent: *It was one of the most ferocious attacks on prison officers I have ever seen.* | *Defence lawyers claimed that the shooting was a spontaneous reaction, ferocious, but not part of a plan.* —**ferociously** [adv] *The boy fought ferociously.*

rough /rʌf/ [adj] using force or violence but not causing serious injury: *Some of the boys were being a bit rough with the younger kids.* | **rough treatment/handling** *The hostages received some rough treatment during their long period of captivity.* | *The police have been criticized for their rough handling of the demonstrators.* —**roughly** [adv] *A man on the subway grabbed her roughly, asking for money.*

2 a violent person

- thug
- brute
- hooligan
- psychopath

▸ *see also* **bad, crazy**

thug /θʌg/ [n C] a man, especially a criminal, who has rough manners and uses violent methods: *A policeman is fighting for his life after young thugs threw a brick through his patrol car windscreen.* | *A gang of thugs was waiting for him round the back. He didn't have a chance.*

brute /bruːt/ [n C] if you call a man a **brute**, you mean he is cruel and violent and does not care if he hurts people: *She spun round and screamed, 'Leave him alone, you brute!'* | **a brute of a man** *Milly had a husband – a great brute of a man who knocked her about.*

hooligan ALSO **hoodlum** American /ˈhuːlɪgən, ˈhuːdləm/ [n C] a violent young man, often a member of a group, who enjoys causing damage and hurting people, especially in public places: *According to the report, the riots had been started by a group of young hoodlums.* | *Football hooligans caused over £30,000 of damage in bars and restaurants near the stadium.* | *His father was attacked by a gang of hooligans in a back street.*

psychopath /ˈsaɪkəpæθ/ [n C] a mentally ill person who behaves violently and kills people, and is unable to feel sorry: *Police described the killer as a psychopath.* | *The main character in the movie is Dr Hannibal Lector, who displays all the characteristics of a psychopath.*

3 animals

- fierce
- vicious
- savage
- ferocious

fierce /fɪəʳs/ [adj] a **fierce** animal looks very frightening and is ready to attack people: *The dog was standing at the gate, looking fierce and growling.* | *Swans are always fierce in defence of their young.* —**fiercely** [adv] *The female spider often reacts fiercely to the male's advances.*

vicious /ˈvɪʃəs/ [adj] a **vicious** animal is likely to attack and cause injury, often suddenly and for no reason: *Keep away from that horse – he can be vicious.* | *Rottweilers are vicious dogs, far too dangerous to have as pets.* —**viciously** [adv] *I put out my hand to stroke the cat but it spat at me viciously.*

savage /ˈsævɪdʒ/ [adj] violent in a completely uncontrolled way, and always ready to attack: *They caught the monkey, but it was so savage that no one could get near enough to feed it.* | *At night, packs of savage dogs roamed the streets.* —**savagely** [adv] *The dog snarled savagely as soon as we came near.*

ferocious /fəˈrəʊʃəs/ [adj] violent and frighteningly powerful, and so able to cause great harm: *The tiger is a ferocious beast which has already killed ten villagers.* | *These bears look ferocious, but attacks by them are extremely rare.* —**ferociously** [adv] *The eagle tears at its prey ferociously with its beak.*

4 stories, films etc

- violent
- gory

violent /ˈvaɪələnt/ [adj] **violent** films, stories, or television programmes contain a lot of fighting and killing: *I think Tarantino's films are too violent.* | *Do violent programmes and video games really cause people to become more aggressive?*

gory /ˈgɔːri/ [adj] **gory** films, descriptions etc clearly show or describe violent injuries, blood, death etc: *The book's descriptions of the killings were unbelievably gory.* | *a gory horror movie*

5 violent behaviour

- violence
- aggression
- brutality
- savagery
- ferocity
- force

violence /ˈvaɪələns/ [n U] fighting, killing, and other violent behaviour: *In some parts of the city, teachers have to deal with violence in the classroom.* | *complaints about sex and violence on TV* | **+ against** *The statistics show that male violence against women is widespread.*

aggression /əˈgreʃən/ [n U] angry feelings or behaviour that often results in fighting: *In a prison, drugs sometimes have to be used to control aggression.* | **+ in** *Some people think that aggression in children may be caused by the food they eat.* | **+ towards/toward** *Low-ranking male chimpanzees eat with the dominant females, who show no aggression towards them.*

brutality /bruːˈtælɪti/ [n U] deliberately cruel and violent behaviour that shows no pity for the person who is injured or killed: *Civil rights activists were appalled by the brutality of the police.* | **mindless brutality** (=used to emphasize that there is no good reason for a violent action) *The killings were an act of mindless brutality.*

savagery /ˈsævɪdʒəri/ [n U] extreme and uncontrolled violence in which people are attacked and killed: *Thompson condemned the murder as 'an appalling attack of savagery'.* | *The book tells of the boys' rapid descent into savagery, and the use of torture and terror.*

ferocity /fəˈrɒsɪ̇ti‖fəˈrɑː-/ [n U] extreme violence in fighting or in attacking someone: *Further attacks escalated rapidly in extent and ferocity.* | **the ferocity of sth** *The knife had snapped in two from the ferocity of the attack.* | *The ferocity of the piranha fish has made it famous.*

force /fɔːʳs/ [n U] violent action, used in order to make someone do something: *We want to end the demonstration without force.* | **use force** *The police do not use force when arresting people unless it's absolutely necessary.* | **by force** (=using force) *Her husband tried to get the children back by force.*

6 a violent situation

- riot
- unrest
- disturbance

riot /ˈraɪət/ [n C] a situation in which a large crowd of people is behaving in a violent and uncontrolled way, especially when they are protesting about something: *More than 150 officers battled to end the riots outside the embassy.* | **race riots** (=between people of different races) *In 1943 there were violent race riots in Detroit in which 25 black people died.* | **prison/student etc riots** *the student riots in Paris in the 1960s* | **riots erupt/break out** (=start suddenly and violently) *Riots erupted in the capital after police banned two anti-government demonstrations.* | **put down a riot** (=stop a riot) *The army was called in to put down the riots.* | **riot police** (=police whose job is to stop riots) *Riot police used tear gas against the protestors.*

unrest /ʌnˈrest/ [n U] a social or political situation in which people protest and often behave violently: *In the unrest since January, 103 people have died.* | **civil/industrial/political/social etc unrest** *The Foreign Office is advising people not to travel to the area, because of civil unrest.* | *a wave of nation-wide strikes and industrial unrest* | **a state of unrest** *For several weeks students at the university have been in a state of unrest.*

disturbance /dɪˈstɜːʳbəns/ [n C usually plural] a situation in which people fight or behave violently in public: *The government is introducing special new measures to deal with prison riots and disturbances.* | **civil disturbances** *Israel was reported to be offering guidance to the army on controlling civil disturbances.* | **minor/major disturbances** *There were minor disturbances in Amman during the recent by-elections.*

7 deliberately avoiding violence

- peaceful
- non-violent

peaceful /ˈpiːsfəl/ [adj] *The revolution turned out to be less peaceful than we had hoped.* | *On May 13th, there was a peaceful demonstration of students calling for the resignation of the military regime.* —**peacefully** [adv] *The protest march began peacefully, but soon descended into violence.*

non-violent /nɒn ˈvaɪələnt/ [adj] **non-violent** methods, protests, organizations etc deliberately avoid using violence: *Our organization has always been non-violent and non-partisan.* | *In 1942, the Congress Party demanded immediate independence, and threatened massive though non-violent resistance.* —**non-violence** [n U] *It was in South Africa that Gandhi first used methods of non-violence, by staging sit-ins for the 'coloured' population.*

visit

to go and spend time in a place or with a person

RELATED WORDS

▸ *see also* **travel, holiday/vacation, stay (4-8)**

1 to visit a person

- visit
- go to see/go and see
- go over/go around/go round
- come over/come around/come round
- pay a visit
- look up
- descend on/upon

visit /ˈvɪzɪ̇t/ [v I/T] to go and spend time with someone, especially in their home: *I visit my grandparents at least once a month.* | *Paul visited her every day when she was in hospital.* | *We won't be that far away – you'll be able to come and visit.*

go to see/go and see /ˌɡəʊ tə ˈsiː, ˌɡəʊ ən ˈsiː/ [v phrase] spoken to visit someone: *I'm going to see my brother and his family tomorrow.* | *Better go and see your father tonight.* | *Why don't you go and see your mother?* | **go see** American spoken *You really should go see Mattie some time.*

go over/go around/go round /ˌɡəʊ ˈəʊvəʳ, ɡəʊ əˈraʊnd, ˌɡəʊ ˈraʊnd/ [phr v I] to visit someone at their house, especially if they live close to you: *I saw your Mum today, and I promised that we'd go round later.* | **+ to** *Let's get a bottle of wine and go over to Simon's place.*

come over/come around/come round /ˌkʌm ˈəʊvəʳ, ˌkʌm əˈraʊnd, ˌkʌm ˈraʊnd/ [phr v I] if someone **comes over** or **comes round**, they visit you at your house, especially if they live close to you: *I'll come over at about 7 o'clock,* | *Why don't you come round later and we'll discuss it over dinner?*

pay a visit /ˌpeɪ ə ˈvɪzɪ̇t/ [v phrase] to visit someone, especially for a particular reason **pay a visit to sb** *Your hand looks very swollen, I think you should pay a visit to the doctor.* | **pay sb a visit** *Isn't it time you paid your mother a visit?*

look up /ˌlʊk ˈʌp/ [phr v T] to visit someone that you have not seen for a long time, while you are spending some time in the area where they live **look sb up** *I'll give you my address so you can look me up whenever you're in London.* | **look up sb** *I looked up a few old friends while I was in Birmingham.*

descend on/upon /dɪˈsend ɒn, əˌpɒn / [phr v T] if a lot of people, especially members of your family, **descend on** you, all of them suddenly visit you at the same time: *Sorry for just descending on you like this, Pam – we had nowhere else to stay.* | *The following week all my family descended upon me.*

2 to visit someone for a short time

- call on/call in on
- drop in/drop by
- pop in
- call round/call in

call on/call in on /ˈkɔːl ɒn, ˌkɔːl ˈɪn ɒn/ [phr v T] especially British to visit someone for a short time: *Why don't you call on Matt on your way back from work and see how he is?* | *One of our salesmen would be delighted to call in on you in your own home.*

drop in/drop by /ˌdrɒp ˈɪn, ˌdrɒp ˈbaɪ‖ˌdrɑːp-/ [phr v I] especially spoken to visit someone for a short time, especially when they are not expecting you: *Lizzie said she'd drop in later to let us know what the arrangements are for tonight.* | *Kate dropped by this morning.* | **drop in to see sb** *I'll drop in to see you later.*

pop in /ˌpɒp ˈɪn‖ˌpɑːp-/ [phr v I] British informal to visit someone for a very short time: *I might be able to pop in for about half an hour.* | *Just pop by when you've got a minute and I'll show you our holiday photographs.* | **pop in to see sb** *I popped in to see Keith on my way home.*

call round/call in /ˌkɔːl ˈraʊnd, ˌkɔːl ˈɪn / [phr v I] British to visit someone who lives near you for a short time: *Fred calls round sometimes on his way to the sports centre.* | *I'll call in tomorrow then, Mum.*

3 to visit a place as a tourist

- visit
- pay a visit
- go to see/go and see
- see the sights
- sightseeing
- do

visit /ˈvɪzət/ [v T] *Every year thousands of tourists visit Turkey.* | *We spent the day visiting temples and other historic buildings.*

pay a visit /ˌpeɪ ə ˈvɪzət/ [v phrase] to visit a place, especially because you are near it: *We were near Edinburgh, so we decided to pay a visit.* | **+ to** *We paid a quick visit to New York before flying home.*

go to see/go and see ALSO **go see** American spoken /ˌgəʊ tə ˈsiː, ˌgəʊ ən ˈsiː, ˌgəʊ ˈsiː/ [v phrase] to visit a well-known place or building while you are in a city or country: *If you're in Paris, you must go to see the Pompidou Centre.* | *Let's go and see the cathedral.* | *Why don't we go see the Statue of Liberty?*

see the sights /ˌsiː ðə ˈsaɪts/ [v phrase] to visit a city or country and look at the famous and interesting places there: *I wanted to look round Moscow and see the sights.* | **+ of** *We're going on a bus tour today, to see the sights of Copenhagen.*

sightseeing /ˈsaɪtˌsiːɪŋ/ [n U] the activity of visiting and travelling around a place to look at the famous and interesting places there: *After an afternoon's sightseeing we were all exhausted.* | *We spent the days sightseeing and the evenings sitting in cosy bars drinking the local wine.* | **go sightseeing** *Why don't we go sightseeing tomorrow?*

do /duː/ [v T not in passive] spoken to visit a particular famous place while you are on holiday: *I think we ought to do St Paul's while we're in London.* | *We did the Eiffel Tower yesterday.*

4 to visit a place as part of your official duties

- visit

visit /ˈvɪzət/ [v I/T not in passive] *The Ambassador last visited Hong Kong in 1982.* | *This afternoon the Queen will visit Great Ormond Street Children's Hospital.* | *A police officer will be visiting next week to give the children a talk on crime prevention.* —**visiting** [adj only before noun] *We all had to attend a reception for some visiting dignitaries.*

5 to visit a person or place on the way to somewhere else

- stop by
- look in on
- call in
- stop off
- stop over

stop by ALSO **stop in** American /ˌstɒp ˈbaɪ, ˌstɒp ˈɪn‖ˌstɑːp-/ [phr v I] to visit a person for a short time while you are on your way to somewhere else: *I just stopped in to say goodbye before I go on vacation.* | *Stop by for a drink on your way home from work.*

look in on /ˌlʊk ˈɪn ɒn / [phr v T] to make a short visit to someone, while you are on your way somewhere, especially if they are ill or need help: *I promised to look in on Dad and see if he's feeling better.* | *Tom will look in on you later to see if you need anything.*

call in British **/come by** American /ˌkɔːl ˈɪn, ˌkʌm ˈbaɪ/ [phr v I] to visit a person or place for a short time while you are on your way to somewhere else: *Why don't you call in on your way up north?* | *Come by on Saturday and we'll have a drink together.* | **call in on sb** *I called in on Sally yesterday.*

stop off /ˌstɒp ˈɒf‖ˌstɑːp-/ [phr v I] to make a short visit to a place during a journey: *We'll stop off and see you on our way back.* | **+ in/at** *He stopped off in Paris for a couple of days.*

stop over /ˌstɒp ˈəʊvəʳ‖ˌstɑːp-/ [phr v I] to visit somewhere for a short time during a long journey, especially a plane flight **+ in** *The flight to Australia takes 28 hours but we stop over in Singapore for a night.* —**stopover** /ˈstɒpəʊvəʳ‖ˈstɑːp-/ [n C] *The journey includes a two-day stopover in Miami before flying on to Mexico.*

6 someone who visits someone else

- visitor
- guest
- caller
- have company/visitors/guests

visitor /ˈvɪzətəʳ/ [n C] *We have nowhere for visitors to sleep at the moment as the spare room is being decorated.* | *Colette offered her visitor a glass of wine.* | *I've been asked to show some important visitors round the department.*

guest /gest/ [n C] someone who you have invited to visit you at your home: *You're not supposed to do the dishes – you're a guest.* | *Among the guests was the television presenter Jo Everton.* | *She felt she had to stay in and entertain her guests.* | **have a guest** *We had a couple of guests for the weekend.*

caller /ˈkɔːləʳ/ [n C] especially British someone who you do not know who visits you at home for a short time: *I don't seem to have many callers these days.* | *When answering the door, always check the identity of callers.*

have company/visitors/guests /hæv ˈkʌmpəni, ˈvɪzətəʳz, ˈgests/ [v phrase] if you **have company**, **visitors** etc someone is visiting you in your home: *I didn't realise you had company, I'll call back tomorrow.* | *There's a surprise waiting for you at home – we have unexpected guests.*

7 an occasion when someone visits a place or person

- visit
- flying visit

visit /ˈvɪzət/ [n C] *We're all looking forward to your visit.* | **+ from** *The girls were quite excited because* *they were expecting a visit from their parents.* | **+ to** *The Senator's visit to the Military Academy at Andover was a great success.* | **make/pay a visit to** (=visit a person or place) *The president will make a brief visit to Britain before returning home.* | *The Queen will pay a state visit to China later this year.*

flying visit /ˌflaɪ-ɪŋ ˈvɪzət/ [n C] a very short visit, made especially when you are on your way to another place and you do not have much time: *I'm afraid this is only a flying visit – we have to get to the station by three.* | **make a flying visit to** *We're making a flying visit to Monte Carlo on our way back.*

voice

RELATED WORDS

▸ *see also* **sound, speak, talk, shout, scream, high (7), low (2)**

1 the sounds someone makes when they speak

▸ **voice** ▸ **tone**

voice /vɔɪs/ [n C] *She has a very high, squeaky voice.* | *I could hear Dan's angry voice shouting 'stupid idiot'.* | *There was a note of irritation in her voice.* | *She was startled to hear voices coming from upstairs.* | **in a loud/high/deep etc voice** *'Sorry I'm late', she said, in a low voice.*

tone /təʊn/ [n C/U] the way someone speaks, especially when this shows the way they feel: *He kept his tone formal.* | **+ of** *I often detect a tone of regret in her voice.* | **in an friendly/angry/embarrassed etc tone** *'This is Julia', Jo said, in a friendly tone.* | *She was speaking in a rather irritated tone.* | **in hushed tones** (=quietly) *Mary ushered her into the church, speaking in hushed tones.* | **tone of voice** *She was almost hypnotised by his mellow tone of voice.*

2 a rough voice

▸ **rough** ▸ **gruff**
▸ **throaty** ▸ **hoarse**
▸ **husky**

rough /rʌf/ [adj] not sounding soft or gentle, especially because the person speaking is angry or rude: *'What are you doing in here?' shouted the farmer in a rough voice.* | **+ with** *Fran was shaking her urgently, his voice rough with concern.* —**roughly** [adv] *'Well, what are you waiting for? Get a move on!' said the guard roughly.*

throaty /ˈθrəʊti/ [adj] deep and rough, as if the sounds are produced deep down in your throat: *Julie had a throaty voice that made her sound older than she was.* | *She always spoke with a throaty German accent.*

husky /ˈhʌski/ [adj] slightly rough, as though you have a sore throat, but also attractive and deep: *Stephen put his arms around her and his voice became a soft, husky whisper.* | *Caron Wheeler's rich, husky vocal is perfect for the song's mellow soulfulness.* —**huskily** [adv] *Mel cleared his throat and chuckled huskily.*

gruff /grʌf/ [adj] deep and rough, especially when the speaker is feeling annoyed or being rude and does not want to talk much: *'If this happens again,' said Dad, in a gruff voice, 'I shall be extremely angry!'* | *He was an irritable old man, who seldom spoke except to say a gruff hello.* —**gruffly** [adv] *The doorman asked me gruffly for my identity card.*

hoarse /hɔːʳs/ [adj] rough and not very clear, especially because your throat is sore as a result of illness or too much shouting, singing etc: *You sound very hoarse. Do you have a cold?* | *His voice dropped to a hoarse whisper.* | **shout yourself hoarse** British (=shout so much that you become hoarse) *He had shouted himself hoarse in his frenzied efforts to attract attention.* —**hoarsely** [adv] *'Sorry, I'm losing my voice,' Sam whispered hoarsely.* —**hoarseness** [n U] *The hoarseness in Brenda's voice made it very difficult to hear her over the phone.*

3 a high voice

▸ **high** ▸ **shrill**
▸ **high-pitched** ▸ **squeaky**
▸ **piercing**

high /haɪ/ [adj] *I recognized Juliet's high, excited voice on the phone immediately.*

high-pitched /ˌhaɪ ˈpɪtʃt◂/ [adj] high and often unpleasant or annoying to listen to: *Her voice was clear but rather high-pitched.* | *The commentary was punctuated by high-pitched giggles.*

piercing /ˈpɪəʳsɪŋ/ [adj] very high and loud, and unpleasant or painful to listen to: *Her voice was nasal and piercing.* | *He raised his hands and let out a piercing shriek.* | *There came a piercing cry from the back of the cinema.*

shrill /ʃrɪl/ [adj] very high and loud and unpleasant to listen to: *As Sophie became angry her voice got shriller.* | *Sylvie burst out in a shrill laugh before leaving the room.*

squeaky /ˈskwiːki/ [adj] a **squeaky** voice keeps changing between being too high and being normal, especially because there is something wrong with your throat: *He's had a throat infection for over a week and his voice has gone squeaky.* | *a band with a squeaky vocal style*

4 a low voice

▸ **low** ▸ **rich**
▸ **deep** ▸ **resonant**

low /ləʊ/ [adj] *Martin's voice was low, with a note of sadness in it.* | *Gripping his stomach, he let out a low moan.*

deep /diːp/ [adj] if a man's voice is **deep**, it is very low, especially in an attractive way. If a woman's voice is **deep**, it is very low, like a man's voice: *He has a deep, reassuring voice,* | *I tried to make my voice sound deeper when I answered the phone.*

rich /rɪtʃ/ [adj] a **rich** voice is low, strong, and pleasant to listen to: *The lead actor's rich voice claimed the attention of the audience.* | *He sang in a deep, rich baritone.*

resonant /ˈrezənənt/ [adj] a **resonant** voice is deep, loud, and clear: *Billy's voice had a deep, resonant tone that was a pleasure to hear.* | *'Listen,' Toranaga interrupted in his resonant, commanding voice.*

vote

RELATED WORDS

▸ *see also* **government, politics, represent, choose, power (5)**

1 to vote

- vote
- have/take a vote
- cast a vote
- put sth to the/a vote
- veto
- ballot
- go to the polls
- the ballot box

vote /vəʊt/ [v I/T] to formally choose someone such as a political representative or show your support or disapproval of something, for example by putting a mark on a piece of paper in an election: *In tomorrow's election, many young people will be voting for the first time.* | *Hundreds of people lost their lives in the past fighting for the right to vote.* | **+ for** (=vote to support them) *I haven't decided who I'm going to vote for.* | *70% of the population voted for independence.* | **+ against** *Only two people voted against the expansion of the business.* | **vote in favour of sth** *The vast majority of people voted in favour of closer links with Europe.* | **+ on** *Teachers will be voting on a proposal to accept the 5% pay offer.* | **vote Republican/Labour etc** (=vote for a political party) *I've voted Democrat all my life.*

have/take a vote /ˌhæv, ˌteɪk ə ˈvəʊt/ [v phrase] if a group of people **have** or **take a vote**, they each make it known which idea they agree with, as a formal way of deciding what to do: *We couldn't agree on a way forward, so we decided to have a vote.* | **+ on** *I think we should take a vote on whether or not to accept their offer.*

cast a vote ALSO **cast a ballot** American /ˌkɑːst ə ˈvəʊt, ˌkɑːst ə ˈbælət‖ˌkæst-/ [v phrase] to vote in a political election: *By the end of the day, less than 40% of the population had cast their votes.* | *Over three quarters of the votes cast were for the Liberal candidate.* | *Not until all the ballots have been cast can they be counted.*

put sth to the/a vote /ˌpʊt (sth) tə ðə, ə ˈvəʊt/ [v phrase] to ask a group of people to vote on something that has been discussed in order to come to an official decision about it: *Let's put it to the vote. All those in favour raise your hands.* | *When the matter was put to a vote, the staff voted overwhelmingly not to go on strike.*

veto /ˈviːtəʊ/ [v T] if someone **vetoes** a decision that other people have agreed on, they use their official power to refuse to allow it: *The president has the right to veto any piece of legislation.* | *The deal was agreed by the board but vetoed by the chairman.*

ballot /ˈbælət/ [v T] to decide something by asking the members of an organization to formally vote on it: *The union will now ballot its members on whether to go ahead with strike action.*

go to the polls /ˌgəʊ tə ðə ˈpəʊlz/ [v phrase] if the people of a country or area **go to the polls**, they vote in a political election – used especially in newspapers and on television or radio: *The people of Houston will go to the polls next week to elect a new mayor.* | *With only two days left before France goes to the polls, all parties are campaigning hard.*

the ballot box /ðə ˈbælət bɒks‖-bɑːks/ [n phrase] the system of choosing a government by voting – used especially in newspapers and on television or radio: *They are determined to win power through the ballot box, not by violence.* | *The voters have expressed their views at the ballot box.*

2 to choose a government, leader, or representative by voting

- elect
- vote in/into
- re-elect
- return
- nominate

elect /ɪˈlekt/ [v T] to choose a government, leader, or representative by voting: *I think we should start by electing a new chairman.* | **elect sb leader/chairman/president etc** *Ken Livingstone was elected mayor of London in May 2000.*

vote in/into /ˌvəʊt ˈɪn, ˈɪntuː/ [phr v T] give someone a position of political power by voting for them **vote sb/sth in** *They always seem to vote in these corrupt, incompetent governments.* | **vote sb into power/office** *The conservatives have promised to cut taxes if they are voted into office.*

re-elect /ˌriːɪ̵ˈlekt/ [v T] to elect someone to a position that they have had since the previous election: *The chairman and treasurer have both been re-elected for another year.* | **re-elect sb as sth** *Simon Mungford has been re-elected as party leader.*

return /rɪˈtɜːʳn/ [v T] British to elect a politician as a member of parliament – used especially in news reports: *Only 96 Conservative MPs were returned at the last election.*

nominate /ˈnɒmɪ̵neɪt‖ˈnɑː-/ [v T] to formally suggest that someone should become one of the people who will be voted for in an election: *Whoever is nominated today will go forward to the leadership elections.* | **nominate sb for sth** *By now it was clear that Bush was going to be nominated for President.* | **nominate sb as sth** *I was nominated as chairman.* —**nomination** /ˌnɒmɪ̵ˈneɪʃən‖ˌnɑː-/ [n C] the name of a person who has been nominated: *All nominations must be in by three o'clock on March 21st.*

3 an occasion when people vote

- election
- electoral
- referendum
- ballot
- polls
- polling
- show of hands

election /ɪˈlekʃən/ [n C] when people vote to choose a government or leader: *It will be interesting to see what happens at the next election.* | **hold an election** *South Africa held its first multi-racial elections in 1994.* | **call an election** (=to say officially that there will be an election) *The government may decide to call an election early.* | **presidential/gubernatorial election** (=an election to choose a president or governor) *America is preparing for the presidential elections, which will take place in two weeks' time.* | **general election** British (=an election to choose a government) *Taxation will be one of the major issues at the next general election.*

electoral /ɪˈlektərəl/ [adj only before noun] relating to an election: *Support for electoral reform is growing.* | *This was the first of her many electoral successes.* | *Electoral systems vary from country to country.*

referendum /ˌrefəˈrendəm/ [n C] when everyone in a country votes on a particular important political subject: *How will you be voting in the referendum?* | **hold a referendum** *The government has promised to hold a referendum and let the people choose.* | **+ on** *The Irish people voted 'no' in a referendum on divorce in 1986.*

ballot /ˈbælət/ [n C] when the members of an organization vote on something by marking what they want on a piece of paper, especially in order to make sure that it is secret: *The result of the ballot showed that nurses were not in favour of a strike.* | **+ of** *He was elected by a ballot of all the teaching staff in the college.* | **hold a ballot** *It was decided to hold a ballot of all party members.* | **secret ballot** (=when no-one knows what you voted for) *Voting will be by secret ballot.*

polls /pəʊlz/ [n plural] a political election – used especially in news reports: *The party is still trying to recover from the losses it suffered at last year's polls.* | **at the polls** *Richards won a huge victory at the polls.* | **the polls** *Voters have been flocking to the polls to elect a new president.*

polling /ˈpəʊlɪŋ/ [n U] the process of voting in a political election: *Polling has been going on since 9 am.* | *The announcement of her resignation came just two days before polling was to begin.* | **polling day** British (=the day when an election is held) *Polling day is 30 May.* | **polling booth/station** (=a place where people vote) *Security was tight at the polling stations.*

show of hands /ˌʃəʊ əv ˈhændz/ [n phrase] when the people in a group are asked to vote informally by raising their hands: *A show of hands suggested that Martins had little support.* | *She was elected by a show of hands.*

4 someone who votes

- voter
- electorate

voter /ˈvəʊtəʳ/ [n C] someone who votes in a political election: *Italian voters have shown that they are ready for a change of government.* | **Republican/Labour etc voters** *There is disappointment among Labour voters that the party has not done more to help traditional industries.*

electorate /ɪˈlektərɪ̇t/ [n singular] all the people who can vote in a country or area: *Research has shown that thirty percent of the electorate have still not decided how they will vote.* | *He has been accused of misleading the electorate.*

5 the right to vote

- the vote
- have a vote
- suffrage
- franchise
- enfranchise
- disenfranchise

the vote /ðə ˈvəʊt/ [n singular] the right to vote in an election: *People are campaigning for civil rights and especially for the vote.* | **have the vote** *The majority of immigrant workers do not have the vote.* | **get the vote** *In 1928 in Britain, women got the vote at 21 on equal terms with men.*

have a vote /ˌhæv ə ˈvəʊt/ [v phrase not in progressive] if you **have a vote**, you have the right to vote: *In Britain, everyone over 18 has a vote.* | *The secretary is allowed to attend meetings, but does not have a vote.*

suffrage /ˈsʌfrɪdʒ/ [n U] formal the right to vote in elections – use this especially to talk about people's fight to be allowed to vote: *There was a fierce struggle for women's suffrage in Britain early this century.* | *Suffrage reforms took place in the 18th, 19th and 20th centuries.* | **universal suffrage** (=the right of every adult in a country to vote) *Even now, not every country in Europe has universal suffrage.*

franchise /ˈfræntʃaɪz/ [n singular] formal the right to vote in political elections: *The franchise was later extended to any person over 18 years old.*

enfranchise /ɪnˈfræntʃaɪz/ [v T] formal to give a person or a group of people the right to vote in political elections: *This legislation enfranchised many thousands of people.* | *The group works in developing countries to increase literacy and enfranchise women.*

disenfranchise /ˌdɪsɪnˈfræntʃaɪz/ [v T] formal to take away someone's right to vote in an election: *If you don't get your name on the electoral register you may be disenfranchised.*

6 ways of saying how many votes are made or received

- the vote
- receive/get
- poll

the vote /ðə ˈvəʊt/ [n singular] the total number of votes made in a political election: *63% of the vote went to the National Party.* | **sb's share of the vote** *Once again, the Democrats increased their share of the vote.*

receive/get /rɪˈsiːv, get/ [v T] if a candidate **receives** or **gets** a particular number of votes, that is the number of people who have voted for him or her. **Receive** is more formal than **get**: *Standord received 50% of the male vote.* | *The Green Party candidate got only one more vote than the Socialists.*

poll /pəʊl/ [v T] British to receive a particular number of votes in an election: *He polled 23,579 votes.* | *The Labour candidate polled 52% of the votes.*

7 to try to get elected

- run
- fight
- candidate

run ALSO **stand** British /rʌn, stænd/ [v I] *Ellis has not yet announced whether or not he will run.* | *I hope Ian will decide to stand because he'd make an excellent president.* | **+ for** *Only eight percent of those standing for the National Party were women.* | **+ against** *We've got an excellent candidate to run against Harwood in the election.* | **stand for Parliament** British *He first stood for Parliament in 1974 but failed to get in.* | **stand for election** British *If you want to change the way the committee does things, you should stand for election yourself.* | **run for President/mayor/office etc** *There are rumors going around that I'm running for President, but they're not true.*

fight /faɪt/ [v T] especially British to try very hard to get elected, especially when this is difficult **fight an election** *The Prime Minister has decided to stay on to fight another election.* | **fight sb for sth** *Neil Phillips will now fight Adams for leadership of the party.*

candidate /ˈkændɪ̇dɪ̇t‖-deɪt, -dɪ̇t/ [n C] someone who tries to get elected: *I think Reid is definitely the best candidate.* | **+ for** *She stood as the candidate for Hackney East.* | **Conservative/Nationalist/Communist etc candidate** *My name is Andrew Fraser. I'm your Labour candidate.* | *the Democratic candidate*

8 political activities before an election

- campaign
- electioneering
- canvass

campaign /kæm'peɪn/ [n C] the activities and advertising used over a period of time to persuade people to vote for a particular party or person: *Richards and his team have already started planning his campaign for election as party leader.* | *Throughout the campaign, Baldwin looked the most likely to win.* | **election campaign** *The government does not want this kind of bad publicity in the middle of an election campaign.* —**campaign** [v I] *The Prime Minister will be campaigning in Scotland next week.*

electioneering /ɪˌlekʃə'nɪərɪŋ/ [n U] activities such as visiting places and talking to people to try to persuade them to vote for a particular person or party – use this especially when you think politicians are not being sincere when they do this: *Modern electioneering is sophisticated and highly organised.* | *Critics have dismissed his visit to a shelter for the homeless as an obvious piece of electioneering.*

canvass /'kænvəs/ [v I/T] to go around an area or to people's houses in order to find out if they intend to vote for you or your party and, if not, to try to persuade them that they should: *She was canvassing in the Greenside area of town yesterday.* | *I spent the whole afternoon canvassing voters.* | **+ for** *I canvass for the Democrats at election times.*

Ww

wait

RELATED WORDS

- to believe that something will happen *see* **expect**
- *see also* **delay, later**

1 to wait

- wait
- hold on/hang on
- hang around
- stand by
- wait your turn
- sit out
- await
- long-awaited

wait /weɪt/ [v I] to spend time not doing very much, while you are expecting something to happen or expecting someone to arrive: *Wait here until I get back.* | *Hurry up, everyone's waiting.* | **wait for sb** *I'll stay here and wait for Suzie.* | **wait for sth** *We spent almost an hour just waiting for the bus.* | **wait (for) a minute/two hours/a long time etc** *Where have you been? I've been waiting since 7:00.* | *You'll have to wait a few minutes – I'm not ready yet.* | **wait to do sth** *Are you waiting to use the phone?* | **wait for sb/sth to do sth** *She waited for him to reply.* | *He waited for the applause to die down before he continued speaking.* | **keep sb waiting** (=make someone wait, for example by arriving late) *I'm so sorry I kept you waiting.* | **wait and see** (=wait to find out what will happen) *I've done as much as I can – now all I can do is wait and see what happens.* | **wait-and-see attitude/position/approach etc** *The airline industry has adopted a wait-and-see attitude to the report's proposals.*

hold on/hang on /ˌhəʊld 'ɒn, ˌhæŋ 'ɒn/ [phr v I] spoken to wait, especially in a difficult situation, hoping that something good will happen: *Captain Damas decided it was best to hold on and wait for the other ship to arrive.* | *We knew that if we hung on long enough, things were bound to change.*

hang around ALSO **hang about** British informal /ˌhæŋ ə'raʊnd ˌhæŋ ə'baʊt/ [phr v I] informal to wait in one place without doing anything, so that you are wasting time: *Sally hung around for over an hour but no-one came.* | *I wish we could get on with the job. I hate all this hanging about.* | **+ for** British *We spent half an hour hanging about for Kerry.* | **hang around for hours/ages etc** *We were hanging around for hours before they opened the gates.* | **keep sb hanging around** *We can't keep our troops hanging around forever, doing nothing.*

stand by /ˌstænd 'baɪ/ [phr v I] to wait and be ready to do something if needed: *The family stood by, knowing that she might wake up any minute.* | **+ for** *The crew was ordered to stand by for take-off.* | **+ to do sth** *The Foreign Minister had a helicopter standing by to whisk him to the northern city of Afula.*

wait your turn /ˌweɪt jɔːʳ 'tɜːʳn/ [v phrase] to wait before doing something that other people are also waiting to do, because some of them have the right to do it before you: *Everyone has to wait their turn.* | **+ to do sth** *A long line of people waited their turn to shake his hand.*

sit out /ˌsɪt 'aʊt/ [phr v T] to wait until something has finished, especially something unpleasant or boring **sit it out** *If the plane's late, there's nothing we can do except sit it out.* | **sit sth out** *Tony forced himself to sit the play out.* | **sit out sth** *Like many people in the community, we sat out the storm at home, hoping no disasters would occur.*

await /ə'weɪt/ [v T] formal to wait for something: *The committee is awaiting a decision from head office before it takes any action.* | *Two men have been charged with murder and are now in prison awaiting trial.*

long-awaited /ˌlɒŋ ə'weɪtɪ̈d◂‖ˌlɔːŋ-/ [adj only before noun] used to describe things that you have waited for for a long time: *The next morning we received the long-awaited order to attack.* | *It is hoped that these measures will trigger the long-awaited upturn in the economy.*

2 what you say to tell someone to wait

- wait
- just a minute/second
- hold on
- wait and see
- see how things go
- wait up
- I'll be right with you/be right there
- bear with me
- hold your horses
- all in good time

wait /weɪt/ *Wait, I have a better idea.* | *Wait! We haven't talked to Vicky yet.* | **wait a minute/moment/second etc** *Wait a minute. I forgot to turn off the lights.* | *Wait a second, don't rush off!*

just a minute/second /ˌdʒʌst ə 'mɪnɪ̈t, 'sekənd/ say this when you want someone to wait a short time: *Just a minute, I'm almost ready.* | *Just a second, let me just check I've got my keys with me.*

hold on ALSO **hang on** especially British /ˌhəʊld 'ɒn, ˌhæŋ 'ɒn/ use this to tell someone to wait for a short time: *Hold on – I haven't finished yet.* | **hold on a minute/moment/second etc** *Hang on a minute while I find her phone number.*

wait and see /ˌweɪt ən 'siː/ use this to tell someone to be patient because they will find out about something later: *'So what's this surprise you've got* *for me then?' 'Wait and see.' | I'm not going to tell you who else I've invited – you'll just have to wait and see.*

see how things go /ˌsiː haʊ θɪŋz ˈgəʊ/ [v phrase] say this when you are advising someone to wait before deciding something, in order to see how the situation develops: *Let's load up the program and see how things go. | See how things go for another week, and if you're no better we'll change the treatment.*

wait up /ˌweɪt ˈʌp/ American use this to tell someone to stop, because you want to talk to them or go with them: *Wait up, you guys! I can't walk that fast.*

I'll be right with you/be right there /aɪl biː ˌraɪt ˈwɪð juː, biː ˌraɪt ˈðeəʳ/ say this when you want someone to know that you will be able to see them or talk to them very soon: *I'm sorry for the delay, sir – I'll be right with you. | Hang your coat up and make yourself at home – I'll be right there.*

bear with me /ˈbeəʳ wɪð miː/ formal use this to ask someone to wait patiently while you explain something or while you finish what you are doing: *If you'll just bear with me, I'll explain. | Bear with me for just a couple of minutes while I find my notes.*

hold your horses /ˌhəʊld jɔːʳ ˈhɔːʳsɪ̮z/ say this to someone who is hurrying too much, when you want them to slow down: *Hold your horses – I haven't even said I'll do the job yet!*

all in good time /ˌɔːl ɪn gʊd ˈtaɪm/ spoken say this to someone who wants you to hurry, to tell them that you are not going to: *'When are we going to open the presents?' 'All in good time.'*

3 a period of time when you have to wait

- wait

wait /weɪt/ [n singular] *I'm sorry you have had such a long wait. | Relatives now face an anxious wait while the emergency services search the wreckage for survivors.* | **a ten-minute/two-hour etc wait** *After a four-hour wait at the airport, we finally got on a flight to New York. | A lot of patients face a two-year wait for treatment.*

4 to make someone wait

- keep sb waiting
- make sb wait
- keep sb in suspense
- keep sb hanging on

keep sb waiting /ˌkiːp (sb) ˈweɪtɪŋ/ [v phrase] to make someone wait, especially by arriving late: *I'm sorry to keep you waiting. | She was annoyed because she had been kept waiting.* | **+ for** *Lott kept us waiting for 40 minutes while he attended another meeting.*

make sb wait /ˌmeɪk (sb) ˈweɪt/ [v phrase] to deliberately make someone wait: *Shaw made us wait a few days before giving us an answer. | They made me wait for half an hour before allowing me to see my father.*

keep sb in suspense /ˌkiːp (sb) ɪn səˈspens/ [v phrase] to make someone wait anxiously or excitedly before you tell them something that they are eager to know: *Come on – don't keep us in suspense – who won? | The audience is kept in suspense to the very end of the play.*

keep sb hanging on /ˌkiːp (sb) ˌhæŋɪŋ ˈɒn/ [v phrase] to make someone wait a long time for something that you are not actually going to give them: *They kept me hanging on for three weeks before they finally told me they weren't going to give me the job.*

5 when you stand in a line of people waiting

- queue (up)
- stand/wait in line
- line up
- queue
- be in the queue
- jump the queue
- push in/cut in

queue (up) /ˌkjuː (ˈʌp)/ [v I] British to stand in a line of people who are all waiting for the same thing: *Students were queuing up at the bus-stop.* | **+ to do sth** *It's worth queuing up to get the best tickets.* | **+ for** *I hope we don't have to queue for tickets.*

stand/wait in line /ˌstænd, ˌweɪt ɪn ˈlaɪn/ [v phrase] American to stand in a line of people who are all waiting for the same thing: *Go and wait in line like everyone else.* | **+ for** *There were about 50 people standing in line for tickets outside the club.* | **+ to do sth** *People stood in line to touch him, believing his body had healing powers.*

line up /ˌlaɪn ˈʌp/ [phr v I] if people **line up**, they go and stand in a line and wait to do something or be given something: *The guard ordered us to line up by the wall.* | **+ to do sth** *Christopher and the other children lined up to receive their awards.*

queue British **/line** American /kjuː, laɪn/ [n C] a group of people, standing one behind the other, who are all waiting for the same thing: *The queue went right round the block.* | **+ for** *There was a long queue for the toilets.* | **the front/back of the queue/line** *After waiting for an hour, we finally got to the front of the line.* | **join a queue/get in line** *I joined the queue for a taxi. | Two people tried to get in line ahead of us.*

be in the queue British **/be in (the) line** American /biː ɪn ðə ˈkjuː, biː ɪn (ðə) ˈlaɪn/ [v phrase] to be waiting in a line with people who are all waiting for the same thing: *While I was in the queue at the bank I met an old school friend. | Kerry started talking to the people who were in line ahead of us.* | **+ for** *Several people in the line for the rollercoaster gave up and left.*

jump the queue /ˌdʒʌmp ðə ˈkjuː/ [v phrase] British to get something before other people who have been waiting for it longer than you: *My official uniform meant that we could jump the queue. | While ordinary citizens had to wait months to get hospital treatment, government officials were able to jump the queue.*

push in/cut in /ˌpʊʃ ˈɪn, ˌkʌt ˈɪn/ [phr v I] informal to join a line in front of other people who are already waiting, so that you get something before them: *I hate people who push in in front of me! | Hey, that guy just cut in line!*

6 when someone is waiting for something to happen

- patient
- impatient
- look forward to
- can't wait
- hold your breath
- expectant

patient /ˈpeɪʃənt/ [adj] able to wait calmly without becoming annoyed or bored: *I'm sure she'll write soon. Just try to be patient. | Halle was patient, waiting for the boy to finish his explanation.* —**patiently** [adj] *The audience waited patiently for the show to begin.* —**patience** [n U] when you can wait calmly without becoming annoyed or bored: *It's easy to grow your own plants – all you need is a little time and patience.*

impatient /ɪmˈpeɪʃənt/ [adj] becoming annoyed because you have been waiting for a long time:

Don't be so impatient. I'm working as fast as I can. | *By this time there was a queue of impatient customers waiting to be served.* | **+ for** *The new minister was almost immediately the object of attack by politicians and press impatient for results.* | **get/become/grow impatient (with)** *I could see that Max was getting impatient with me.* —**impatiently** [adj] *The customs officer waved them on impatiently.* —**impatience** [n U] annoyance caused by waiting for a long time: *People were beginning to show signs of impatience.*

look forward to /ˌlʊk ˈfɔːʳwəʳd tuː/ [phr v T] to wait happily or excitedly for something that is going to happen: *I'm really looking forward to this trip to Japan.* | *We used to look forward to the weekends because that was when we could spend some time together.* | **+ to doing sth** *I look forward to meeting you next month.*

can't wait /ˌkɑːnt ˈweɪt‖ˌkænt-/ [v phrase] if you say you **can't wait**, you mean you feel excited and impatient because something good is going to happen and you want it to happen as soon as possible: *We're flying to Austria on Friday. I can't wait!* | **+ for** *I can't wait for Christmas!* | *School is so boring. I can't wait for the holidays to come.* | **+ to do sth** *I can't wait to see their new house.* | *She couldn't wait to quit her job and get married.*

hold your breath /ˌhəʊld jɔːʳ ˈbreθ/ [v phrase] to wait anxiously to see what is going to happen, especially when there is a possibility that something bad may happen: *Rachel held her breath as she waited for his answer.* | *The art world will be holding its breath to see how much these paintings sell for at auction.*

expectant /ɪkˈspektənt/ [adj usually before noun] waiting hopefully and excitedly for something to happen: *Bright expectant faces were turned upward toward the stage.* | *Expectant crowds waited outside the theatre.* | *The darkened assembly room became suddenly hushed and expectant as the picture appeared on the screen.* —**expectantly** [adv] *Patrick looked at me expectantly.*

wake up/get up

RELATED WORDS

▸ *see also* **sleep, tired/tiring, early (3)**

1 to stop sleeping

▸ wake/wake up
▸ awake
▸ come around
▸ stir

wake/wake up /weɪk, ˌweɪk ˈʌp/ [v I] to stop sleeping. **Wake** is more formal than **wake up** and is usually used in writing.: *She woke early the next morning, and slipped out of the house unseen.* | *Babies often wake because they are hungry.* | *The dog suddenly woke up and started barking.* | **wake up at 5 a.m./12 noon etc** *I woke up at five o'clock and couldn't get back to sleep again.*

awake /əˈweɪk/ [adj not before noun] not asleep **be awake** *'Are you awake, Lucy?' she whispered.* | *I'm usually awake before anyone else.* | **be wide awake** (=be completely awake) *It was nearly three in the morning, but Jill was still wide awake.* | **be half awake/barely awake** (=be not quite awake) *He listened, only half awake, as the teacher's voice droned on.* | *Barely awake, we stumbled out of the tent to find ourselves in a foot of water.* | **keep sb awake** *I've stopped drinking coffee in the evenings, as it tends to keep me awake at night.* | **stay awake** *Some members of the audience were clearly having difficulty staying awake.* | **lie awake** (=be unable to sleep at night) *Ben lay awake, worrying about next day's exam.* | *I've lain awake at nights, turning the problem over and over in my mind.*

come around ALSO **come round** British /kʌm əˈraʊnd, kʌm ˈraʊnd/ [phr v I] to gradually become conscious again after being given a drug or being hit on the head: *She was coming round after her operation, but she still felt dizzy and very sleepy.* | *Henry's eyelids flickered. 'He's coming around!' Marie cried.*

stir /stɜːʳ/ [v I] to move slightly and wake for a short time, then go back to sleep again: *As I entered the room, she stirred slightly, then went back to sleep.* | *Roger momentarily stirred, turned in the bed and murmured something inaudible.*

2 to make someone stop sleeping

▸ wake/wake up
▸ disturb
▸ rouse
▸ get sb up/get sb out of bed

wake/wake up /weɪk, ˌweɪk ˈʌp/ [v T/phr v T] *Be quiet or you'll wake my parents.* | *We were woken by a loud banging on the door.* | *He shook her arm to try and wake her.* | **wake sb up** *The alarm clock woke me up at 8 o'clock.* | *Why didn't you wake me up this morning? I was late for work.* | **wake up sb** *They were making enough noise to wake up the whole street!* | **wake up!** spoken (=what you say to someone when you want to stop them sleeping) *Come on honey, wake up! You'll be late!*

disturb /dɪˈstɜːʳb/ [v T] to accidentally wake someone who is sleeping, by making a noise or movement: *I got undressed in the bathroom to avoid disturbing her.* | *I hope my snoring won't disturb you too much.* —**disturbed** [adj] *a disturbed night's sleep*

rouse /raʊz/ [v T] formal to wake someone with difficulty because they are sleeping very deeply: *He found Paula fast asleep in bed, and nothing would rouse her.* | **rouse sb from their sleep/slumbers** *I was roused from my sleep by the sound of a door banging shut.*

get sb up/get sb out of bed /ˌget (sb) ˈʌp, ˌget (sb) aʊt əv ˈbed/ [phr v T/v phrase] to wake someone up and make them get out of their bed: *Go and get your brother up. It's time for him to go to work.* | *Did you get me up just to tell me that?* | *I'm sorry for calling so early – I hope I didn't get you out of bed.*

3 to get out of bed

▸ get up
▸ get out of bed
▸ be up
▸ surface

get up /ˌget ˈʌp/ [phr v I] to get out of bed, especially in the morning in order to get ready for the day: *What time do you need to get up tomorrow?* | *Why is it always me who gets up first?* | **get up at 7.00 a.m./dawn etc** *Frank gets up at half past five every morning.* | **get up early/late** *I think we should get up early and leave before breakfast.* | *She goes to bed late and gets up late.*

get out of bed /get ˌaʊt əv ˈbed/ [v phrase] *I couldn't face getting out of bed this morning.* | *Isn't it about time you got out of bed?*

be up /biː ˈʌp/ [v phrase] to be out of bed and doing things: *Is Harry up yet?* | *I was up at six this morning.* | *Jake had been up since dawn.* | **be up early** *You're up early!*

surface /ˈsɜːʳfɨ̞s/ [v I] spoken informal to get up, especially late and after being in bed for a long time: *'Have you seen Cathy?' 'No, she hasn't surfaced yet.'*

4 to stay in bed until late in the morning

- get up late
- have a lie in/sleep late
- stay in bed
- oversleep
- sleep in

get up late /ˌget ʌp ˈleɪt/ [v phrase] to get out of bed later than usual in the morning: *We usually get up late on Sundays.* | *Jackson's not here. He must have gotten up late again.* | *I got up late, and then Brian was in the bathroom, so I just rushed straight here.*

have a lie in/sleep late /hæv ə ˈlaɪ ɪn, ˌsliːp ˈleɪt/ [v phrase] to stay in bed longer than usual in the morning, especially because you do not need to get up: *It's Saturday tomorrow, so I can have a lovely long lie in.* | *We slept late, and when we woke the sun was blazing in through the windows.*

stay in bed /ˌsteɪ ɪn ˈbed/ [v phrase] to not get out of bed, even though you are not asleep: *If you're not well, you'd better stay in bed.* | *We stayed in bed all morning, reading the papers and drinking coffee.*

oversleep /ˌəʊvəʳˈsliːp/ [v I] to accidentally sleep longer than you intended, so that you are late for something: *Sorry I'm late – I overslept.* | *They were afraid of oversleeping and missing the plane.* | *He had overslept on the day he was supposed to take the entrance exam.*

sleep in /ˌsliːp ˈɪn/ [phr v I] to deliberately get up later than usual because you do not have to get up at a fixed time: *I think I'll go to bed late tonight and sleep in tomorrow.* | *She doesn't even like sleeping in, even on Sundays.*

5 someone who is easily woken by noise

- light sleeper

light sleeper /ˌlaɪt ˈsliːpəʳ/ [n C] *Mr and Mrs Carlton are both light sleepers, so be very quiet when you come in at night.* | *If you are a light sleeper, ask for a room that doesn't face the street.*

6 someone who usually gets up early in the morning

- early riser

early riser /ˌɜːʳli ˈraɪzəʳ/ [n C] *He'd been an early riser ever since he was a child.* | *A few early risers were already sipping their cappuccinos in the bars facing the square.*

walk

RELATED WORDS

▸ *see also* **go, travel, run, fall, road/path**

1 to walk

- walk
- on foot

walk /wɔːk/ [v I] *Anna missed the bus, so she decided to walk.* | *How old was Daisy when she first started walking?* | **+ into/out of/along/back etc** *Jed walked out of the station and got into a taxi.* | *I was walking along Main Street when I met Pierre.* | **walk home** *She hates walking home alone at night.* | **walk two miles/100 metres etc** *We must have walked about five miles today.*

on foot /ɒn ˈfʊt/ [adv] if you go somewhere **on foot**, you walk instead of going by car, bus, train etc: *It's not far. It'll take you about ten minutes on foot.* | **go on foot** *The bus left us at the bottom of the hill, and we went the rest of the way on foot.*

2 to walk quickly

- stride
- march
- pace

stride /straɪd/ [v I] to walk quickly, taking big steps, in an angry, determined or confident way **+ into/out of/towards etc** *Brian strode out of the room without speaking.* | *The Principal came striding towards me, and shook my hand.*

march /mɑːʳtʃ/ [v I] to walk quickly and with firm steps, especially because you feel angry or determined **+ into/off/towards etc** *Sheila marched straight into the office and demanded an apology.* | *'I'll never forgive you for this,' Marge said, and she marched off without a backward glance.*

pace /peɪs/ [v I/T] to walk backwards and forwards within a small area, especially because you are nervous, bored, or angry **pace back and forth/up and down** *'We're going to be late,' Jordan said irritably, pacing up and down the room.* | *Sarah paced back and forth along the corridor, waiting for the doctor to come back.* | *A lion paced up and down the cage, growling.* | **pace the room/floor etc** *Meryl was also awake, pacing the floor in her dressing-gown.*

3 to walk slowly in a relaxed way

- stroll
- amble
- saunter

stroll /strəʊl/ [v I] to walk in a slow and relaxed way, especially for pleasure **+ along/through/around etc** *They strolled along the riverbank, enjoying the evening sun.* | *We drove to Penrhyn Castle, and strolled around the beautiful gardens there.*

amble /ˈæmbəl/ [v I] to walk in a slow and relaxed way, especially when you are going a short distance, or not going anywhere in particular **+ across/along/towards etc** *An old man appeared from behind the house and ambled across the yard.* | *One of the horses, a white one, slowly ambled towards me.* | *Cecil was ambling along as usual without a care in the world.*

saunter /ˈsɔːntəʳ/ [v I] to walk in a slow and lazy way, often when you should be hurrying to do something **+ down/into/across etc** *'Shouldn't you be in class?' Mr Harris asked the girls who were sauntering down the corridor.* | *I sauntered into the garden, where some friends were chatting near the barbecue.* | *As usual, Ron sauntered into the office twenty minutes late.*

4 to walk slowly because you are tired

- trudge/plod
- traipse

trudge/plod /trʌdʒ, plɒd‖plɑːd/ [v I] to walk slowly and with heavy steps, especially because you are tired, it is difficult to walk, or you do not want to go somewhere **+ through/back/along etc** *She trudged back up the hill, loaded down with heavy bags of groceries.* | *We trudged to school through the snow, wishing we could be playing in it.* | *The donkey was plodding slowly along under its heavy load.*

traipse /treɪps/ [v I] to walk a long way, especially when you are looking for something or visiting different places, so that you become tired **+ around/about/in and out etc** *We traipsed around every store in town, trying to find the right color paint.* | *Traipsing round museums all day is not my idea of fun.*

5 to walk slowly because you are in pain or weak

- hobble
- limp
- shuffle
- shamble

hobble /'hɒbəl‖'hɑː-/ [v I] to walk with difficulty in a slow and unsteady way because it is painful for you to walk: *My knee was stiff and painful, and I could only hobble.* | **+ across/along/towards etc** *Aunt Sophy hobbled slowly across the room on her crutches.*

limp /lɪmp/ [v I] to walk with difficulty because you have hurt one of your legs: *I noticed that one of the horses was limping, and called for the vet.* | **+ along/over/towards etc** *She limped painfully over to a chair and sat down.* —**a limp** [n singular] a limping movement: *Josie walked with a slight limp.*

shuffle /'ʃʌfəl/ [v I] to walk slowly and noisily, without lifting your feet off the ground properly **+ along/towards/down etc** *Supporting herself on Ali's arm, the old woman shuffled towards the door.* | *I heard Bob shuffling around the kitchen in his slippers.*

shamble /'ʃæmbəl/ [v I] to walk slowly and rather awkwardly, bending forwards in a tired or lazy way **+ along/past/out etc** *Looking tired and fat, Parker shambled onto the stage and started playing.* | *An old tramp shambled along, looking for money or cigarette ends on the floor.*

6 to walk in an unsteady way

- stagger
- stumble
- lurch

stagger /'stægəʳ/ [v I] to walk very unsteadily, with your body moving from side to side and almost falling, especially because you are injured, very tired, or drunk **+ in/out/home etc** *Something hit me on the head, and I staggered across the room.* | *My father was staggering under the weight of a huge parcel.*

stumble /'stʌmbəl/ [v I] to walk unsteadily, often hitting things with your feet and almost falling, especially because it is dark, the ground is uneven, or because you are tired or drunk **+ in/out/across etc** *The room was dark, and Stan nearly fell over a chair as he stumbled to the phone.* | *I finished the whiskey, then stumbled upstairs and into bed.*

lurch /lɜːʳtʃ/ [v I] to walk very unsteadily, moving forward or from side to side with sudden, irregular movements **+ backwards/towards/forwards etc** *Paul lurched sideways as the boat rolled suddenly.* | *Harriet lurched towards the bathroom, clutching her stomach in pain.*

7 to walk with heavy, noisy steps

- stomp
- clump

stomp /stɒmp‖stɑːmp, stɔːmp/ [v I] to walk with heavy steps, making a lot of noise to show that you are angry **+ out/away/off etc** *My sister stomped out of the house, slamming the door behind her.* | *Kevin looked furious as he stomped into his office. 'What the hell is going on here?' he yelled.*

clump /klʌmp/ [v I] to walk with slow, heavy, noisy steps, for example because you are wearing heavy shoes **+ up/about/across etc** *The three of us clumped up the steps in our heavy ski boots.* | *The walls are so thin we can hear the man next door clumping about all day.*

8 to walk quietly

- tiptoe
- creep
- sneak
- pad

tiptoe /'tɪptəʊ/ [v I] to walk on your toes because you do not want to make any noise **+ into/out of/past etc** *He tiptoed out of the room, trying not to wake the baby.* | *I tiptoed along the passage to Claire's door and peeped in.*

creep /kriːp/ [v I] to walk quietly and carefully because you do not want anyone to notice you **+ in/through/across etc** *Ron unlocked the back door and crept out into the yard.* | *No-one noticed that the little boy had crept into the room and was sitting there, listening.* | **creep/sneak up behind sb** (=walk quietly up behind someone in order to surprise them) *She crept up behind him and put her hands over his eyes.*

sneak /sniːk/ [v I] to walk quietly so that no-one notices you, especially because you are doing something wrong and do not want to be caught **+ in/up/around etc** *The thieves sneaked in while the guard had his back turned.* | *Molly snuck around the house.* | **sneak off** (=sneak away from a place) *We tried to sneak off from work early.*

pad /pæd/ [v I] to walk quietly and steadily, without shoes or with soft shoes, or on a soft surface **+ along/down/in etc** *Michelle got out of bed, and padded across to the window.* | *The cat came padding softly across the kitchen floor, and jumped onto my lap.*

9 to walk proudly

- swagger
- strut
- parade

swagger /'swægəʳ/ [v I] to walk proudly, swinging your shoulders, in a way that shows too much self-confidence **+ into/down/across etc** *Ali swaggered arrogantly into the boxing ring, as if he had already won the fight.* | *Sally's boyfriend came swaggering down the steps with his hands in his pockets.* —**swagger** [n singular] *Bernard left the room with a swagger, clearly pleased with himself.*

strut /strʌt/ [v I] to walk proudly with your head high, shoulders back, and chest pushed forwards in a way that shows you think you are important or impressive **+ in/through/around etc** *He strutted across the stage like Mick Jagger.* | *The hotel was full of rich people strutting around in fur coats and Rolex watches.*

parade /pə'reɪd/ [v I] to walk proudly around a place, in a way that shows you want people to notice and admire you **+ around/through/up etc** *On Sunday mornings, fashionable young couples parade up and down the Boulevard St Michel.*

10 to walk without going in one particular direction

- walk around
- wander
- roam
- prowl

walk around ALSO **walk round** British /ˌwɔːk əˈraʊnd, ˌwɔːk ˈraʊnd/ [phr v I/T] *I keep seeing these two strange men walking around. I'm sure they're up to something.* | *We walked round the market for a while, and then we went to the beach.*

wander /ˈwɒndəʳ‖ˈwɑːn-/ [v I/T] to walk around with no particular aim and in no particular direction, especially in a place you do not know or when you are lost **+ about/around/through etc** *For an hour and a half we wandered around the old city, totally lost.* | *We wandered along the river bank, looking for a place to cross.* | **wander the streets/hills/town etc** *After dinner Carol left the hotel to wander the crowded streets.*

roam /rəʊm/ [v I/T] to walk around freely and with no particular aim **+ about/around/over etc** *Tourists love roaming about the old town.* | *Great herds of wild deer roam freely over the hills.* | **roam the streets/desert/hills etc** *Residents of the Red Hall estate claim to be living in fear of gangs who roam the streets after dark.*

prowl /praʊl/ [v I/T] to quietly walk around an area or building, trying not to be seen or heard, especially in order to steal something or attack someone **+ around/round** *Several wolves prowled round the camp, but were kept at bay by the fire.* | *The babysitter said she could hear someone prowling around in the garden.* | **prowl the streets/neighbourhood/city etc** *Police have warned the public that the killer may still be prowling the streets.*

11 to walk for pleasure or exercise

- walk
- go for a walk/take a walk
- go for a stroll
- hike
- trek
- stretch your legs
- walk the dog

walk /wɔːk/ [v I] *Walking instead of driving is an excellent way of losing weight.* | **+ in/across/along etc** *Sheena's up at six every morning to walk along the beach.* | *I like to go walking in the woods, just to breathe the air.* —**walker** [n C] *The park was full of Sunday afternoon walkers.*

go for a walk/take a walk /ˌgəʊ fər ə ˈwɔːk, ˌteɪk ə ˈwɔːk/ [v phrase] to walk somewhere for pleasure or for exercise. **Go for a walk** is more common in spoken English than **take a walk**: *It's a lovely evening. Let's go for a walk.* | **+ along/through/across etc** *He said he was going for a walk around the block to clear his head.* | *We arrived in St Louis at noon, and took a walk down by the Mississippi River.*

go for a stroll /ˌgəʊ fər ə ˈstrəʊl/ [v phrase] to walk in a slow and relaxed way, especially for pleasure **+ along/through/across etc** *Dave strolled along the riverbank, enjoying the evening sun.* | *They decided to go for a stroll along the beach.*

hike /haɪk/ [v I] to take a long walk in the countryside: *Patricia likes doing active things like canoeing, hiking, and horse-riding.* | *We're going to hike to the top of that hill over there.* | **go hiking** *We're going hiking in Scotland this summer.*

trek /trek/ [v I] especially British to walk a very long way, especially in the mountains, for enjoyment: *We trekked up Mount Calahi for five days.* | *The scouts will have to trek 40km back to the base camp.* | **go trekking** *Maria's going trekking in the Himalayas this year.*

stretch your legs /ˌstretʃ jɔːʳ ˈlegz/ [v phrase] to walk around for a little exercise after a long time sitting down: *After so long on the train, we couldn't wait to get out and stretch our legs.* | *Do you feel like stopping here and stretching your legs?*

walk the dog /ˌwɔːk ðə ˈdɒg‖-ˈdɔːg/ [v phrase] to take your dog for a walk: *I get quite a lot of exercise myself by walking the dog.* | *Geoff wants a Walkman for when he walks the dogs.*

12 to walk through water

- wade
- paddle

wade /weɪd/ [v I] to walk through deep water **+ across/towards/through etc** *They waded across the river.*

paddle British **/wade** American /ˈpædl, weɪd/ [v I] to walk in water that is not very deep, for enjoyment: *One of my earliest memories is paddling in the sea with my parents.* | *Ryan took off his shoes and socks to wade in the stream.*

13 to walk with regular steps with other people

- march
- in step

march /mɑːʳtʃ/ [v I] if soldiers **march**, they all walk together with regular steps **into/through/past etc** *Thousands of US soldiers marched through the streets of Paris.*

in step /ɪn ˈstep/ [adv] if a group of people walk **in step**,they walk at the same speed and move their feet forward at exactly the same time: *The regiment had finally learned to march in step.* | **+ with** *Steve wasn't walking in step with the rest of the class.*

14 to walk slowly and carefully

- pick your way
- edge

pick your way /ˌpɪk jɔːʳ ˈweɪ/ [v phrase] to walk carefully and slowly because the ground is not level or because you have to step over things, lifting your feet higher off the ground than usual **+ over/through/across etc** *The boy began to pick his way over the rocks towards the ocean.* | *I picked my way across the crowded field, towards the main stage.*

edge /edʒ/ [v I] to walk slowly and carefully, especially sideways, along or through a small space, because you do not have enough room to walk normally: *Mervyn edged sideways through the front door, which seemed to be stuck.* | **edge your way** *Edging my way through the crowd, I eventually managed to get to the bar.*

15 a trip that you make by walking

- walk
- hike
- trek

walk /wɔːk/ [n C] a journey that you make by walking, either for pleasure or exercise, or in order to go somewhere: *It was a pleasant walk, under cool, shady trees.* | *Emily enjoyed her walks in the park with her father.* | **go for a walk** (=walk for pleasure or exercise) *I love going for walks in the countryside.*

hike /haɪk/ [n C] a long walk in the countryside: *They set off on a 10 mile hike across the island.* | *The hike back was through the first real jungle I had ever been in.* | **go on a hike** *We went on lots of great hikes.*

trek /trek/ [n C] a long and difficult walk in the country, mountains, desert etc: *You'll need a guide for your treks in the mountains.* | *I took my backpack and joined some Egyptian friends for a trek in the Sahara.* | *The trek to the campsite was along bush tracks and down cliffs.*

16 a single movement when you are walking

- step
- footstep
- pace
- stride

step /step/ [n C] the single movement that you make when you put one foot in front of the other when you are walking: *I was so breathless, I could only manage a few steps.* | **take a step** *Zoe took a step forward to let the man pass.* | **with short/heavy/light etc steps** *She walked briskly, with quick, short steps.*

footstep /ˈfʊtstep/ [n C usually plural] the sound of someone's foot being placed on the ground when they are walking or running: *Suddenly Rachel heard footsteps behind her in the dark street.* | *I could always recognise my mother's footsteps as she scurried up the stairs.*

pace /peɪs/ [n C] the distance you go when you take a single step: *He took a couple of paces forward, then stopped.* | *Eddie walked a few paces behind his mother, his head hung low.* | *I'd gone about ten paces, when I heard a strange sound behind me.*

stride /straɪd/ [n C] a long step you take when you are walking quickly: *In four angry strides, Stuart was through the front gate.* | *Doctor Jameson hurried past us, taking long strides.*

17 the way someone walks

- walk
- gait

walk /wɔːk/ [n singular] *The woman's stiff, agitated walk showed how nervous she was.* | *Janet had the slow, leaning walk of an expectant mother.*

gait /geɪt/ [n singular] written the way someone walks, especially when it is a little strange or unusual: *Melanie walked with the slightly awkward gait of a very tall person.* | *The old man approached the counter with a stooped, shuffling gait.*

18 someone who is walking

- pedestrian
- walker/hiker

pedestrian /pɨˈdestriən/ [n C] someone who is walking in a town, rather than travelling in a car, bus etc: *Banning traffic from the shopping areas has made life much more pleasant for pedestrians.* | *The man lost control of his car, killing a pedestrian.*

walker/hiker /ˈwɔːkəʳ, ˈhaɪkəʳ/ [n C] someone who walks long distances in the countryside for pleasure: *There's a rough track through the woods for riders and walkers.* | *They ran a hostel for hikers in the White Mountains.*

want/not want

RELATED WORDS

▸ *see also* **prefer, willing, need/necessary, like/not like**

1 to want something or want to do something

- want
- would like
- feel like
- wouldn't mind
- wish
- I wouldn't say no
- be interested in
- fancy
- take your fancy

want /wɒnt‖wɑːnt, wɔːnt/ [v I/T not in progressive or passive] *My parents moved out of London because they wanted a bigger house.* | *Do you want milk in your coffee?* | **+ to do sth** *What do you want to do at the weekend?* | *Stacey wants to be a doctor.* | **want sb to do sth** *She wants Tom to come to her party.* | **what sb wants is** *What we want is a car that's cheap and reliable.* | **if you want (to)** *You can go back to bed for a while if you want.*

would like /wʊd ˈlaɪk/ [v T] especially spoken use this as a polite way of asking for something, offering something, or saying what you want to do: *We'd like some information about flights to Chicago, please.* | *Would you like some more coffee?* | **+ to do sth** *I'd like to reserve a room for Saturday.* | *Would you like to borrow this book?* | **would like sb to do sth** *We would like you to attend an interview at 3:30 on Friday.*

feel like /ˈfiːl laɪk/ [v phrase not in progressive or passive] especially spoken to want to have something or do something, because you think you would enjoy it: *I feel like a long, hot soak in the bath.* | *It's a lovely day – do you feel like a walk?* | **feel like doing sth** *I feel like watching a movie tonight.*

wouldn't mind /ˌwʊdnt ˈmaɪnd/ [v phrase] spoken to want to do or have something, but not very strongly: *I wouldn't mind another cup of coffee. How about you?* | **I wouldn't mind doing sth** *It was a really good play. I wouldn't mind seeing it again.*

wish /wɪʃ/ [v I/T not in progressive or passive] formal to want to do something **+ to do sth** *I wish to purchase a second house in the UK for investment purposes.* | *Anyone wishing to order the book should send a cheque to the publishers.* | **if you wish** *Everyone has the right to smoke if they wish, but not the right to ruin the health of those around them.*

I wouldn't say no /aɪ ˌwʊdnt seɪ ˈnəʊ/ say this when you would like to do or have something: *'How about a girls' night out on the town?' 'I wouldn't say no!'* | **+ to** *I wouldn't say no to a glass of whisky!*

be interested in /biː ˈɪntrɨstɨd ɪn/ [v phrase] to think that you may want to do something, buy something, or get involved in something: *Melanie wants to be a lawyer, and Sam's interested in a career in teaching.* | **be interested in doing sth** *We're interested in buying an apartment downtown.* | *Would you be interested in going to the theatre with me on Friday? I have two tickets for 'The King and I'.*

fancy /ˈfænsi/ [v T not in progressive or passive] British informal to want to have or do something: *Do you fancy a drink?* | *I think he's always fancied a car like Lizzie's.* | **fancy doing sth** *I really fancy going for a swim.*

take your fancy /ˌteɪk jɔːʳ ˈfænsi/ [v phrase not in progressive] informal if something **takes your fancy**, you want to do or have it as soon as you see it or think of it: *We could go to the movies or go out for a meal – whatever takes your fancy.* | *She wandered around the market stalls, stopping occasionally to look at something that took her fancy.*

2 to want something very much

- wish
- would love
- would do anything/would give anything/ would give your right arm
- be eager to do sth
- be anxious to do sth
- be dying
- be desperate
- can't wait
- be itching to do sth
- need
- crave

wish /wɪʃ/ [v T not in progressive or passive] to want something to happen, when it is unlikely or impossible that it will happen, or when you cannot control what will happen **+ (that)** *I wish I had a car like that.* | *Beth wished she could stay there forever.* | **wish sb/sth would do sth** *I wish they would turn that music down.*

would love /wʊd 'lʌv/ [v phrase] especially spoken to want something very much, and feel that you would be happy if you had it: *I would love a cup of coffee.* | **would love to do sth** *She would love to have children, but she hasn't met the right man.* | *'Would you like to go on a Caribbean cruise?' 'I'd love to!'* | **would love sb to do sth** *My mother would love me to come and live in New York with her.*

would do anything/would give anything/would give your right arm /wʊd duː 'eniθɪŋ, wʊd ˌɡɪv 'eniθɪŋ, wʊd ˌɡɪv jɔːʳ ˌraɪt 'ɑːʳm/ [v phrase] if you say that you **would do anything**, **would give anything** or **would give your right arm**, you mean you very much want to have something or do something, especially something that is impossible to get or do **+ for** *I would do anything for a drink right now!* | *I would give anything for a look at that file.* | **+ to do sth** *When she first started writing, she would have done anything to get an article printed.* | *I'd give my right arm to be 21 again.*

be eager to do sth ALSO **be keen to do sth** British /biː ˌiːɡəʳ tə 'duː (sth), biː ˌkiːn tə 'duː (sth)/ [v phrase] to want to do something very much, especially because you think it will be interesting or enjoyable or it will help other people: *He's really keen to meet you.* | *I was eager to get my hands on these rare recordings.* | *Donna is very eager to prove her worth to the group.* | **be keen for sb to do sth** *My parents were keen for me to be independent, and let me have a lot of freedom.*

be anxious to do sth /biː ˌæŋkʃəs tə 'duː (sth)/ [v phrase] to want very much to do or achieve something, so that you make a great effort: *Miles was anxious to gain his boss's approval, and was always the last to leave the office in the evening.* | *A newly-arrived executive is usually anxious to make his mark in a new firm.* | **be anxious for sb/sth to do sth** *After the war, the government was anxious for the tourist industry to be revived.*

be dying /biː 'daɪ-ɪŋ/ [v phrase] to want something very much, and feel that you must have it or do it immediately **+ to do sth** *I'm dying to meet Lisa's new boyfriend.* | **+ for** *I'm dying for a drink – let's go to a bar.*

be desperate /biː 'despərɨt/ [v phrase] especially British to want or need something so much that you will be very unhappy or disappointed if you do not get it: *I could see that they were desperate and needed help.* | **+ to do sth** *After having four boys, the couple were desperate to have a little girl.* | *We were desperate to view the inside of the house once we saw the garden.* | **+ for** *Newspapers are always desperate for stories.*

can't wait /ˌkɑːnt 'weɪt‖ˌkænt-/ [v phrase] spoken say this when you want something to happen as soon as possible, because you know you will enjoy it and you are very excited about it: *'You're going on holiday soon, aren't you?' 'Yes, I can't wait.'* | **I can't wait to do sth** *I can't wait to see Bill again – it's been a long time.* | **+ for** *I can't wait for Christmas.*

be itching to do sth /biː ˌɪtʃɪŋ tə 'duː (sth)/ [v phrase] to be impatient to do something that you are excited about, especially something you have not done before: *She's just itching to tell you about her new boyfriend.* | *Despite her success, however, it just wasn't much fun anymore. Liz was itching to try something different.*

need /niːd/ [v T not in progressive or passive] a word used especially in spoken English meaning to want something very much, especially something to eat, drink etc: *I need a drink – coming to the bar?* | *Dave's been working really hard – he needs a holiday.*

crave /kreɪv/ [v T] to want as much of something as you can get, especially food, attention, or a drug: *I've always craved love and acceptance.* | *The review gave Picasso a taste of the recognition he craved.*

3 to want something very much and be determined to get it

- set your sights on
- set your heart on

▸ *see also* **determined**

set your sights on /ˌset jɔːʳ 'saɪts ɒn/ [v phrase] to decide that you want something that will be hard for you to get, and to make a very determined effort to achieve it: *Now she's set her sights on the manager's job, nothing will stop her.* | *Quite consciously, I set my sights on the best-looking boy in the whole school.*

set your heart on /ˌset jɔːʳ 'hɑːʳt ɒn/ [v phrase] to want something so much that you will be very disappointed if you cannot have it or get it: *We've set our hearts on this little house in the country.* | **set your heart on doing sth** *I had set my heart on becoming a pilot.*

4 to want something that you are very unlikely to get

- dream of
- long
- yearn
- hanker after/for sth

dream of /'driːm ɒv/ [v T] to want something that you have wanted for a long time, but which you are unlikely to get: *It was the kind of house I'd always dreamed of having.* | *To think that what I've dreamt of all my life is coming true!* | **dream of doing sth** *She dreamt of becoming a famous novelist.* | *Every jazz-lover at some time of his life has dreamed of assembling a band of his own favourite musicians.*

long /lɒŋ‖lɔːŋ/ [v I] to very much want to have something or do something, especially when this used to happen or exist in the past, or when it may do in the future – used especially in stories or literature **+ for** *He longed for the good old days when teachers were shown respect.* | *He was longing for everyone to leave, so that he could think in peace about what had happened that day.* | **+ to do sth** *More than anything, I long to have someone who loves me for myself.* —**longed-for** /'lɒŋd fɔːʳ‖'lɔːŋd-/ [adj only before noun]

The day of the longed-for visit (=that people had been longing for) *eventually arrived.*

yearn /jɜːʳn/ [v I] to want something so much that you do not feel happy or complete without it **+ for** *The people yearned for peace, and the chance to rebuild their shattered lives.* | *Hannah yearned for a child, and felt desperately sad whenever she saw other women with their babies.* | **+ to do sth** *I have always yearned to travel.*

hanker after/for sth /ˈhæŋkər ɑːftəʳ, fəʳ (sth) ‖-æf-/ [phr v T] to want something that you are unlikely to get very much, especially secretly, and over a long period of time: *Paula had always hankered after a traditional white wedding.* | *I had a good job and a nice apartment, but I still hankered for the country life.*

5 to have an aim in life that you want to achieve

- want
- aspire to
- would-be
- aspiring

▸ *see also* **ambitious**

want /wɒnt‖wɑːnt, wɔːnt/ [v T not in progressive or passive] **to be sth** *What do you want to be when you grow up, Clare?* | *You don't really want to be a hairdresser, do you?* | **to do sth** *I never want to work in a factory, having seen the effect it had on my father.* | *I want to see life, to travel the world, and write about what I see.*

aspire to /əˈspaɪəʳ tuː/ [v phrase] formal to want a better job, way of life, position etc than the one you have now: *She was a struggling writer aspiring to fame.* | *He aspired to artistic perfection in all his paintings.* | **aspire to do sth** *He aspired to become President.*

would-be ALSO **wannabe** informal /ˈwʊd biː, ˈwɒnəbiː‖ˈwɑː-/ [adj only before noun] **would-be actor/writer etc** someone who hopes to be an actor, writer etc: *The Drama Centre is a great help for all would-be actors and actresses.* | *Moon beat all the other wannabe quarterbacks, and was signed by the Seattle Seahawks.*

aspiring /əˈspaɪərɪŋ/ [adj only before noun] **aspiring teacher/model/poet etc** someone who wants to be a teacher, model, poet etc and is just starting work or training: *a part-time course for aspiring chefs* | *Like a lot of aspiring New York artists, Lara worked in bars and restaurants in the evenings.*

6 a feeling that you want to do or have something

- desire
- wish
- longing/yearning
- craving
- lust
- appetite
- temptation
- compulsion

desire /dɪˈzaɪəʳ/ [n C] especially written a strong feeling of wanting to have something or wanting to do something, especially something important, which makes you try very hard to have it or do it **+ to do sth** *Young children have a keen desire to learn and succeed.* | **+ for** *After so many years of war, there was a great desire for peace.* | **a strong/keen/burning desire** *Young Peryoux left home for Paris, armed with a guitar, and a burning desire to succeed.*

wish /wɪʃ/ [n C] formal something that you want to happen, especially when this is very important to you: *His last wish was that his body should be buried in his home town.* | **sb's dearest/greatest wish** (=the thing they want most of all) *She always wanted to see her grandchildren again – it was her dearest wish.*

longing/yearning /ˈlɒŋɪŋ‖ˈlɔːŋ-, ˈjɜːʳnɪŋ/ [n C/U] a very strong and long-lasting desire for something that you are unlikely to get – used especially in stories and literature **+ for** *She felt a great longing for the sights, sounds and smells of home.* | *The story gives a sensitive account of Paul's innocent yearning for love and affection.* | **+ to do sth** *At 18 I had a strong yearning to leave my small town, and see the world.*

craving /ˈkreɪvɪŋ/ [n C] a very strong and uncontrollable desire to have something that you think about all the time, especially food, attention, or a drug: *After a week without smoking, the craving began to disappear.* | **+ for** *The symptoms include a craving for sweet foods.*

lust /lʌst/ [n C/U] a very strong desire to have something, such as money or power, that can make you do evil things to get what you want **+ for** *Throughout his career he was motivated by a lust for power.* | *Her lust for money is insatiable.*

appetite /ˈæpɪtaɪt/ [n C] a strong desire to have something regularly or do something regularly **+ for** *He has a tremendous appetite for hard work.* | **insatiable appetite** (=extremely strong appetite) *The public has an insatiable appetite for scandal and political controversy.* | **whet sb's appetite** (=make it stronger) *The dangers of the climb up Mt. Washington only whetted our appetite for more adventure.*

temptation /tempˈteɪʃən/ [n C] a strong desire to do something, even though you know it is wrong, dangerous, unnecessary etc **+ to do sth** *There is always a temptation to blame others for your own problems.* | **resist the temptation** (=not do something, even though you want to) *Resist the temptation to get involved. After all, it's not your problem.* | **give in to temptation** (=to do something, after trying not to) *In the end, he gave in to temptation, and lit his first cigarette in five days.*

compulsion /kəmˈpʌlʃən/ [n C] an extremely strong desire, usually an unreasonable one, that is difficult or impossible to control: *The patient had a compulsion that caused him to wash his hands 20 or 30 times a day.* | **+ to do sth** *He felt a sudden compulsion to laugh out loud.*

7 a sudden feeling of wanting something

- urge
- whim
- impulse

urge /ɜːʳdʒ/ [n C] a sudden strong feeling that you want to do something, especially a feeling that is difficult to control **+ to do sth** *She was seized with the urge to drag Alice from her chair and shake her.* | **feel/have an urge** *I felt a sudden urge to tell him all my problems.* | **fight an urge** (=try not to do something) *He was fighting the urge to drink as he waited for her to come down.* | **resist an urge** (=not do something, even though you want to) *Sheena resisted the urge to get in her car and go home.*

whim /wɪm/ [n C] a sudden feeling that you would like to do something, especially when this is not sensible or when there is no reason at all to do it: *I don't know why I bought it. I suppose it was just a whim.* | **do sth on a whim** (=do something because you feel a whim) *I went to visit her on a whim.*

impulse /ˈɪmpʌls/ [n C] a sudden strong desire to do something before thinking about whether it is the right or sensible thing to do: *My first impulse was to go straight to Henry and tell him my news, but on* *reflection I thought better of it.* | *He has to learn to control his violent impulses.* | **on (an) impulse** (=because you feel an impulse) *It was an outfit that I had bought on impulse, and never worn.*

8 something that you want to achieve in your life

- dream
- ambition
- goal
- target
- aspirations

▸ *see also* **purpose (1)**

dream /driːm/ [n C] something very special that you want to do and that you think about a lot, especially something that is not very likely to happen **sb's dream is to do sth** *Her dream was to go to Hollywood and become a movie star.* | **dream of doing sth** *After the accident, Clarke had to give up his dream of becoming a racing driver.* | **sb's dream comes true** (=they finally do what they want) *Last year her dream came true and she was offered a chance to study in America.*

ambition /æmˈbɪʃən/ [n C] something which you want to achieve in the future, especially in your work, and which you will try hard to achieve **sb's ambition is to do sth** *Her ambition was to go to law school and become an attorney.* | **achieve/fulfil your ambition** (=finally do what you wanted to do) *Earlier this year, he achieved his ambition of competing in the Olympic games.*

goal /gəʊl/ [n C] something important that a person, company, or government hopes to achieve in the future, even though it may take a long time **achieve/reach a goal** *By 1975, they had achieved their goal of providing free education for every child.* | **sb's goal is to do sth** *Our goal is to become the biggest-selling brand of coffee in the country.* | **short-term goal/long-term goal** (=one that you hope to achieve soon/a long time in the future) *I took a job as a teacher with the long-term goal of becoming a principal of a school.*

target /ˈtɑːʳgɪ̇t/ [n C] a particular amount or total that you want to achieve, for example an amount of products you must sell or produce: *We produced 16,000 cars this year, but our target was 17,500.* | **achieve/reach/meet a target** *The Government is struggling to reach its target of $23 billion in spending cuts.* | **set (sb) a target** (=say what the target is) *I set myself a target of learning 20 new words each week.*

aspirations /ˌæspɪ̇ˈreɪʃənz/ [n plural] a word meaning the important things that people want from their lives, used especially when you are talking about all of society or large groups within it: *A government should reflect the hopes, values and aspirations of society.* | *the aspirations of the people of Eastern Europe* | **+ for** *What are our aspirations for the future?* | *The parents have very high aspirations for their children.* | **career/democratic/economic/political etc aspirations** *a handsome and rich young senator with presidential aspirations* | **high aspirations** *The immigrants who came to settle in America were determined people with high aspirations.*

9 to not want to do or have something

- not want
- not feel like doing sth
- I'd rather not
- be unwilling to do sth
- you are welcome to sth/you can keep sth
- have no desire to do sth
- I'd rather die

not want /nɒt ˈwɒnt‖-ˈwɑːnt/ [v phrase] **+ to do sth** *She doesn't want to see me anymore.* | *We asked him to come with us, but he said he didn't want to.* | **not want sb to do sth** *'Why didn't he tell me he was sick?' 'He didn't want you to worry.'*

not feel like doing sth /nɒt ˌfiːl laɪk ˈduːɪŋ (sth)/ [v phrase] especially spoken to not want to do something, especially because you think you would not enjoy it or because you feel too lazy: *I don't feel like writing that essay today.* | *Some days she just doesn't feel like going to work.*

I'd rather not /aɪd ˌrɑːðəʳ ˈnɒt‖-ˌræ-/ spoken say this when you do not want to do something, especially because you think it may cause problems for you: *I could lend him the money, but to be honest, I'd rather not.* | **I'd rather not do sth** *I'd rather not talk about it right now.*

be unwilling to do sth /biː ʌnˌwɪlɪŋ tə ˈduː (sth)/ [v phrase] formal to not want to do something, even though you should do it or someone wants you to do it: *She is unwilling to admit that she was wrong.* | *Most people here are unwilling to give up their cars and use buses and trains instead.*

you are welcome to sth/you can keep sth /juː ɑːʳ ˈwelkəm tə (sth), juː kən ˈkiːp (sth)/ informal you say that someone **is welcome to** something when you do not like it and you are happy for them to have it instead of you: *She's welcome to her smart friends and glittering parties – I'll take the quiet life anytime.* | *He can keep his money – he's not going to bribe me!*

have no desire to do sth /hæv ˌnəʊ dɪˌzaɪəʳ tə ˈduː (sth)/ [v phrase] formal to not want to do something, especially something that you are being asked or forced to do: *Sarah had been to Harlow before, and had no desire to go there again.* | *Richards tried to enlist my support, but I had no desire to get involved.*

I'd rather die /aɪd ˌrɑːðəʳ ˈdaɪ‖-ˌræ-/ spoken use this to say strongly that you really do not want to do something that someone has suggested or mentioned: *Apologize to that creep! I'd rather die!*

10 something that you do not want

- undesirable
- unwanted
- unwelcome

undesirable /ˌʌndɪˈzaɪərəbəl◂/ [adj] something that is **undesirable** is not wanted because it could affect a person or situation in a bad way: *The drug is effective, but has undesirable side effects, and long-term use can result in liver damage.* | **undesirable consequences/effects** *The incident could have undesirable consequences for the government.* | *Environmentalists claim that the development will have undesirable effects on animal habitats in the area.*

unwanted /ʌnˈwɒntɪ̇d‖-ˈwɔːnt-, -ˈwɑːnt-/ [adj] use this about something that you are given or that happens to you that you do not want and did not ask for: *There are several ways that you can remove unwanted hair, including waxing or electrolysis at a salon.* | *Jones claimed that the President made unwanted sexual advances towards her, in a Little Rock hotel room.* | **unwanted pregnancy** *The pill was once expected to limit the number of unwanted pregnancies, but instead the number has soared.*

unwelcome /ʌnˈwelkəm/ [adj] likely to upset or cause problems for someone and therefore not wanted: *Philippides returned with the unwelcome news that the army would not be ready to march for several days.* | **unwelcome publicity/attention** *Environmentalists had been drawing unwelcome atten-*

tion to the discharge of radioactive waste from nuclear power-stations. | **unwelcome intruder/intrusion** *Many people saw the immigrants as unwelcome intruders in their town.* | **unwelcome visitors/guests/callers** *Time is precious enough, without having to cope with unwanted visitors.*

war

RELATED WORDS

opposite: —— **peace**

▸ *see also* **fight, army, kill, attack, defend, rebellion/revolution, enemy, weapon, explode**

1 fighting between countries or armies

- ▸ **war**
- ▸ **conflict**
- ▸ **rebellion**
- ▸ **fighting**
- ▸ **warfare**
- ▸ **hostilities**
- ▸ **battle**
- ▸ **skirmish**

war /wɔːʳ/ [n C/U] a long period of fighting, when the armies, ships, and planes of two or more countries fight against each other: *the Vietnam War* | *When the war ended in 1945, Europe was in chaos.* | **win/lose a war** *Who won the Franco-Prussian War?* | **civil war** (=war between groups of people from the same country) *More Americans died in the Civil War than in World War II.* | **+ against/with** *Iran's seven-year war with Iraq* | **war breaks out** (=war begins) *In 1874, war broke out in Europe again.* | **the outbreak of war** (=the time when a war begins) *In the months leading up to the outbreak of war, both countries were involved in a massive arms build-up.* | **war hero** *a war hero and former fighter pilot* | **war veteran** (=a former soldier who fought in a war) *War veterans claim that they were exposed to chemical weapons while fighting in the Gulf.*

conflict /ˈkɒnflɪkt‖ˈkɑːn-/ [n C/U] a situation in which two countries or groups are fighting against each other – used especially in news reports: *the conflict in the Middle East* | *Can this peace settlement bring an end to years of conflict?* | *The conflict began early in December 1994.*

rebellion /rɪˈbeljən/ [n C] an organized attempt to change or destroy the government by fighting against it: *The rebellion spread quickly through the Western Provinces.* | **+ against** *an armed rebellion against the government* | **crush/put down a rebellion** (=use force to stop it) *The army was brought in to crush the rebellion.*

fighting /ˈfaɪtɪŋ/ [n U] when soldiers fight against each other during a war or battle: *The UN had failed to stop the fighting in Rwanda.* | **heavy/fierce fighting** (=a lot of fighting when many people are hurt) *The streets of the capital are now quiet again, after three weeks of heavy fighting.* | **renewed fighting** (=fighting that starts again after it had stopped) *Some 15,000 people have fled the city, following renewed fighting.*

warfare /ˈwɔːʳfeəʳ/ [n U] the activity of fighting in a war – use this especially to talk about the methods of fighting that are used in war: *the history of modern warfare* | **nuclear/chemical warfare** (=fighting with nuclear bombs or poison gas) *a secret underground chemical warfare plant* | *Many people believe that what happened in 1940 was a British chemical warfare experiment that went wrong.* | **guerrilla warfare** (=when small unofficial military groups fight against the government) *The rebels aimed to overthrow the government through protracted guerrilla warfare.*

hostilities /hɒˈstɪlətiz‖hɑː-/ [n plural] written when two armies or opposing groups are fighting: *Land mines maim and kill innocent people, long after hostilities have ceased.* | *Mexican forces were ordered to avoid all hostilities with the American troops.* | **end hostilities** *The two sides reach an agreement to end hostilities.* | **the start/outbreak of hostilities** *The Japanese navy scored a success only two days after the start of hostilities, by sinking two British battleships.*

battle /ˈbætl/ [n C] a fight in one area between two armies, or two groups of ships or planes: *a naval battle in the North Sea* | **+ of** *the Battle of the Somme* | **win/lose a battle** *The French lost the Battle of Agincourt in 1415.* | **die/be wounded/be killed in battle** *King Olaf died in battle, in 1030.* | **lead/send sb into battle** *Lyndon Johnson first sent U.S. combat troops into battle in March 1965.*

skirmish /ˈskɜːʳmɪʃ/ [n C] a short, unplanned, and usually not very important fight between two small groups of soldiers: *Last night skirmishes were reported along the border.* | *Government soldiers ran into a group of rebels, and a skirmish followed.*

2 to fight in a war or be in a war

- ▸ **fight**
- ▸ **clash**
- ▸ **be at war**
- ▸ **wage war**
- ▸ **make war**
- ▸ **warring**

fight /faɪt/ [v I/T] to take part in a war or battle: *His grandfather fought on the Republican side in the Spanish Civil War.* | *The Boers were fighting the British at this time.* | **+ for** *Most of these young soldiers don't even know what they're fighting for.* | **+ in** *My grandfather fought in World War II.* | **fight a war/battle** *They were fighting a war of independence against a powerful enemy.*

clash /klæʃ/ [v I] if two armies or groups **clash**, they suddenly start fighting each other, especially for a short time – used especially in news reports: *Iranian and Iraqi troops clashed on the border.* | **+ with** *US planes clashed with enemy fighter aircraft again today.* — **clash** [n C] *border clashes between India and Pakistan*

be at war /biː ət ˈwɔːʳ/ [v phrase] if two countries **are at war** with each other, they are fighting a war against each other: *Europe had been at war for nearly two years.* | *He could not remember a time when his country had not been at war.* | **+ with** *In 1792 England was at war with America.*

wage war /ˌweɪdʒ ˈwɔːʳ/ [v phrase] to start and continue a war, especially for a long period: *In his speech he promised full support to wars of independence waged by colonial peoples.* | **+ on/against** *Many Americans now question whether the US should have waged war on Vietnam.*

make war /ˌmeɪk ˈwɔːr/ [v phrase] to fight a war, especially by suddenly attacking a country that does not threaten your country: *He believes that men make war because they are by nature aggressive.* | **+ on** *Throughout the nineteenth century the colonial powers made war on poorer countries in order to gain territory.*

warring /ˈwɔːrɪŋ/ [adj only before noun] **warring factions/nations/tribes/groups etc** nations etc that are fighting against each other: *Fighting between the various warring factions was destroying the country.* | *All attempts to reconcile the two warring groups have failed.*

3 to start a war

- declare war
- go to war

declare war /dɪˌkleəʳ ˈwɔːʳ/ [v phrase] if a country **declares war** on another country, it makes an official public statement that it is going to fight a war against that country: *He was visiting his parents in Torino when war was declared.* | *Within hours of the incident, both countries had declared war.* | **+ on** *In April the Americans declared war on Germany and entered the war.*

go to war /ˌgəʊ tə ˈwɔːʳ/ [v phrase] if someone **goes to war** they leave home to fight in a war. If a country or group **goes to war** it begins to fight another country, group etc: *The women stayed at home and farmed the land, while the men went to war.* | *The two countries went to war over a small, but important, area of land.*

4 during a war

- wartime
- wartime
- in the war
- in action

wartime /ˈwɔːʳtaɪm/ [adj only before noun] during or relating to the time when there is a war: *He died on a wartime bombing mission.* | *My grandmother's wartime experiences were still fresh in her memory.* | *She grew up in Africa, far away from the hardships of wartime Europe.* | *wartime President, Franklin D. Roosevelt*

wartime /ˈwɔːʳtaɪm/ [n U] the time when there is a war: *I longed for a bar of chocolate, but this was wartime, and such luxuries were not available.* | **in wartime** *the importance of secrecy in wartime*

in the war /ɪn ðə ˈwɔːʳ/ [adv] during the particular war that you are talking about: *What did your father do in the war?* | *Three of his brothers were killed in the First World War.*

in action /ɪn ˈækʃən/ [adv] **be killed/wounded in action** to be killed or injured while fighting in a battle during a war – used especially in official military statements: *a memorial to the thousands of soldiers killed in action*

5 the place where a war is fought

- battlefield
- the front line/the front
- war zone
- the field (of battle)
- theatre
- war-torn

battlefield /ˈbætlfiːld/ [n C] the place where two armies fight a battle: *Thousands died on the battlefields of northern France.*

the front line/the front /ðə ˌfrʌnt ˈlaɪn, ðə ˈfrʌnt/ [n phrase] the place where an army is closest to the enemy and where the fighting takes place: *We were now just a few kilometres behind the front line.* | **the Western/Eastern/Russian etc front** *Her grandfather had four years on the Western Front.*

war zone /ˈwɔːʳ zəʊn/ [n C] an area which is very dangerous because a war is being fought there: *the latest news from the war zone* | *Aid workers returning from the war zone reported seeing groups of rebels waving white flags.*

the field (of battle) /ðə ˌfiːld (əv ˈbætl)/ [n singular] the time or the place where there is fighting – use this especially to talk about fighting in general **on the field of battle** *It is better to negotiate than to settle political disputes on the field of battle.* | **in the field** *The new weapon has not yet been tried out in the field.* | *He was awarded a medal for distinguished service in the field.*

theatre British **/theater** American /ˈθɪətəʳ/ [n singular] a large area in which a war is being fought, especially when the war is taking place in several different areas or countries **Pacific/European/Middle East etc theatre** *It was in the Pacific theater of the war that the US won its first major victories.* | *Many of NATO's nuclear weapons in the European theatre are obsolete.*

war-torn /ˈwɔːʳ tɔːʳn/ [adj only before noun] relating to an area where a lot of damage has been caused by war and fighting: *In 1941, Margaret E. Ray escaped war-torn France and landed in New York.* | *The plan offered long-term aid to war-torn Europe.*

6 the people you are fighting against in a war

- enemy

enemy /ˈenəmi/ [n C] someone that you are fighting against in a war: *Even though these soldiers were our enemies, I felt desperately sorry for them.* | **the enemy** (=the army or country that your army or country is fighting against in a war) *They accused him of giving secret information to the enemy.*

7 someone who is keen to start a war

- warmonger
- militarist
- hawk

warmonger /ˈwɔːʳˌmʌŋgəʳ‖-ˌmɑːŋ-, -ˌmʌŋ-/ [n C] someone, especially a politician or a military leader, who is too keen to start wars or to settle arguments by starting a war: *Some saw him as a great statesman, but others saw him as a ruthless warmonger.*

militarist /ˈmɪlɪtərɪ̇st/ [n C] someone, especially a politician or a military leader, who is too keen to increase the size and power of their country's armed forces so that it can attack other countries: *The militarists wanted Japan to invade China.*

hawk /hɔːk/ [n C] a person, especially a politician, who supports the use of military force and strong action in order to settle arguments with other countries: *The hawks in the government would never permit any talks with the enemy.* | *We don't yet know whether the new President is a hawk or a dove* (=someone who prefers peaceful methods). —**hawkish** [adj] supporting the use of military force, even when other people think this is unnecessary: *the hawkish element in the opposition party*

warn

RELATED WORDS

▸ *see also* **advise, threaten, dangerous**

1 to warn someone about something

- warn
- give sb a warning
- warn off
- caution
- tip off
- alert
- sound/raise the alarm
- forewarn
- I told you!/I told you so!

warn /wɔːʳn/ [v I/T] to tell someone about something unpleasant or dangerous that might happen, so that they can avoid it or prevent it: *We tried to warn her, but she refused to listen.* | *The consequences could be serious – I just wanted to warn you.* | **+ (that)** *The local people were warned that the volcano might erupt at any time.* | *We were warned there were going to be delays on the motorway, so we came back by a different route.* | **warn sb about sth** especially spoken *I was going for a swim, until the people in the hotel warned me about the jellyfish.* | **warn (sb) of sth** especially written *Weather forecasters warned of possible flooding in coastal regions.* | **warn sb (not) to do sth** *Police are warning drivers not to go out on the roads unless their journey is really necessary.* | **warn sb against doing sth** *Tourists are warned against going to remoter regions.*

give sb a warning /ˌgɪv (sb) ə ˈwɔːʳnɪŋ/ [v phrase] to tell someone that if they continue to behave in an unsatisfactory way, they will be punished: *So you've given her a warning about her conduct in future?* | **+ that** *The US gave a warning that, if the hostages were not released, they would be forced to take military action.* | **give sb a final warning** *One day Monica's boss gave her a final warning. If she messed up again, she was fired.*

warn off /ˌwɔːʳn ˈɒf/ [phr v T] to try to prevent someone from doing something by warning them about the trouble or problems it could cause for them **warn sb off** *The army had put signs up around the area where the mines were, to warn people off.* | **warn sb off doing sth** *Even though we'd been warned off going into the mountains, we couldn't resist it.* | **warn off sb** *The female rattlesnake warns off intruders by making a loud noise.*

caution /ˈkɔːʃən/ [v T] formal to warn someone not to do something because it is likely to be dangerous or have a bad result: *'Be careful now,' Sarah cautioned. 'Don't do anything stupid.'* | **caution sb against doing sth** *The policeman cautioned the children against talking to strangers.* | **caution against (doing) sth** *Marshall cautioned against pouring millions of pounds into taking legal action when there was no guarantee of victory.*

tip off /ˌtɪp ˈɒf/ [phr v T] to warn someone about something that is going to happen, especially to warn the police about a crime, so that they can try to prevent it **be tipped off about** *The police had been tipped off about the gang's arrival.* | **be tipped off that** *Customs officers had been tipped off that the drugs were hidden in a child's rucksack.* | **tip sb off** *Someone must have tipped the press off about the princess's visit.* | **tip off sb** *A farmer noticed our foreign accents and tipped off the Security Police.*

alert /əˈlɜːʳt/ [v T] to officially or publicly warn people of possible danger so that they can be ready to deal with it: *When he realized that one engine was not working, the pilot alerted air traffic control.* | **alert sb to sth** *a poster campaign to alert people to the disease* | **alert sb that** *Drivers are being alerted that an escaped prisoner has been seen hitch-hiking on the road to Frankfurt.*

sound/raise the alarm /ˌsaʊnd, ˌreɪz ði əˈlɑːʳm/ [v phrase] to warn everyone about something bad or dangerous that is already happening so that they can take action to stop it or avoid it: *Leighton was told to stand at the door, and to raise the alarm if a guard came.* | **+ about** *The Red Cross has sounded the alarm about the danger of further famine in the region.* | *The problem is that if you sound the alarm about fraud in your company, you might end up out of a job.*

forewarn /fɔːʳˈwɔːʳn/ [v T] formal to warn someone about something bad that is going to happen soon, so that they have enough time to prepare for it: *Barry Hearn forewarned me that the meeting was going to be tough.* | **be forewarned of sth** *A police team, forewarned of the raid, had taken up positions inside the bank.*

I told you!/I told you so! /aɪ ˈtəʊld juː, aɪ ˈtəʊld juː ˌsəʊ/ spoken say this when you had warned someone about a possible danger that has now happened, especially if they ignored your warning: *I told you he had a violent temper! Why did you argue with him?* | *I told you so! It was obvious she was going to disappear as soon as she got the money.* | *I hate to say 'I told you so', but maybe you should listen to me next time.*

2 what you say when you want to warn someone

- look out/watch out
- mind
- watch it/watch out
- be careful
- beware
- you'd better
- sth ends in tears

look out/watch out /ˌlʊk ˈaʊt, ˌwɒtʃ ˈaʊt‖ˌwɑːtʃ-/ spoken say this to urgently warn someone that they will have an accident if they do not immediately try to avoid it: *'Look out!' yelled Willie. 'He's got a gun!'* | *Look out! There's a train coming!* | *Watch out! You nearly hit that car.*

mind /maɪnd/ British spoken use this to warn someone not to touch something or do something that would be dangerous or cause trouble: *Mind the table Charlotte, there are drinks on it.* | **mind/mind out** *Mind! The plate's hot.* | *Mind out! There's a motorcycle!* | **mind you don't do sth** *The cat's down there – mind you don't tread on him.* | **mind how you go** (=used to warn someone to walk carefully to avoid slipping or falling) *Mind how you go. The path's a bit slippery.*

watch it/watch out /ˈwɒtʃ ɪt, ˌwɒtʃ ˈaʊt‖ˈwɑːtʃ-/ use this to warn someone that what they are doing could be dangerous: *'Watch out!' yelled the driver, as the truck veered towards his car.* | *Watch it! You nearly knocked my head off with that ladder.*

be careful /biː ˈkeəʳfəl/ spoken use this to warn someone that what they are doing could be dangerous: *I handed Phil the heavy revolver. 'Be careful, it's loaded.'* | *Be careful, it's very hot.* | **+ with** *Hey! Be careful with that cigarette!* | **be careful/take care not to do sth** *Be careful not to do anything that might make him angry.*

beware /bɪˈweəʳ/ [v I only in imperative and infinitive] especially written used to warn people about something dangerous – usually seen on signs and official statements: *Beware. Deep water.* | **+ of** *Beware of the dog.* | *Beware of falling rocks.* | *The police warn tourists to beware of pickpockets, especially in crowded places.* | **beware of doing sth** *Beware of accidentally starting the engine while you are cleaning the blades.*

you'd better /juːd ˈbetəʳ/ spoken informal use this to warn or advise someone that they should do something in order to avoid trouble: *'I suppose I ought to apologize.' 'Yes, you'd better, or she might make things difficult for you.'* | **you'd better do sth** *You'd better tell the police in case they think it was your fault.* | *The train leaves in twenty minutes, so you'd better hurry up!*

sth ends in tears /(sth) ˌendz ɪn ˈtɪəʳz/ British spoken say this to warn someone that something they are determined to do is not sensible and will probably end badly: *Never have an affair with a work colleague – they usually end in tears.* | **it'll (all) end in tears** *My common sense told me: 'Stay away! It'll end in tears!'*

3 making you realize that something bad could happen

- warn
- be a warning
- set (the) alarm bells ringing
- ominous
- warning
- cautionary

warn /wɔːʳn/ [v I/T] **warn sb (that)** *Something warned Lucy that she must stop him.* | *The bleached bones of cattle warn the traveler how hot it can be in Death Valley.* | **+ of** *Dark clouds warned of the approaching storm.*

be a warning /biː ə ˈwɔːʳnɪŋ/ [v phrase] if an event or fact **is a warning**, it shows that something bad could happen or is going to happen: *The story of the Titanic is a warning to anyone who trusts too much in their technology.* | *The only warning was a low rumbling sound.* | **+ of** *Pain in the shoulder and arm can be a warning of a heart attack.*

set (the) alarm bells ringing /ˌset (ði) əˈlɑːʳm belz ˌrɪŋɪŋ/ [v phrase] if something **sets (the) alarm bells ringing** it makes you realize that something seriously wrong or very dangerous is happening: *There were no lights on when I got home. That immediately set alarm bells ringing.* | *A brief study of the company's accounts set the alarm bells ringing – there was no trace of the $56 million loan.*

ominous /ˈɒmɪ̈nəs‖ˈɑː-/ [adj] making you think that something bad has happened or is likely to happen soon: *Another wave crashed onto the deck and the mast made an ominous creaking sound.* | *Katy answered the phone. There was an ominous silence.* | **sth sounds ominous** *My manager asked for an appointment at nine o'clock on a Monday morning: it sounded ominous.* —**ominously** [adv] *When the army moved into the city, the streets were ominously silent.*

warning /ˈwɔːʳnɪŋ/ [adj only before noun] intended to or likely to warn you that something bad will happen if you continue to do something or do not do something: *Aunt Lou shot a warning glance at father just as he was about to speak.* | *He grabbed her pistol and fired a warning shot. The intruder ran back out into the hall.* | *From the trees there came a warning screech and the whole flock took to the air.*

cautionary /ˈkɔːʃənəri‖-neri/ [adj only before noun] **cautionary tale/note** something that provides a warning of something bad that could happen or a warning against particular actions or behaviour: *The rise and fall of this company is a cautionary tale for anyone investing in the property market.* | *The director ended her speech on a cautionary note, when she said that next year would be even harder than this year.*

4 a spoken or written statement that warns people

- warning
- tip-off
- caution

warning /ˈwɔːʳnɪŋ/ [n C] something that you say or do to warn people about danger or to warn them not to do something: *All cigarette packets carry a government health warning.* | **give a warning** *The weather report gave a warning of more snow and icy roads.* | **+ to** *Two of the prisoners were publicly beaten, as a warning to the others.* | **without (any) warning** (=without giving a warning) *Soldiers began firing into the crowd without any warning.*

tip-off /ˈtɪp ɒf/ [n C] a warning that something bad is going to happen, especially a warning about a crime that is given to the police in time for them to stop it happening: *Police were called to the hotel after a tip-off.* | **acting on a tip-off** (=doing something because of a tip-off) *Acting on a tip-off, customs officers seized 50 kilos of cocaine from a house in Leicester.*

caution /ˈkɔːʃən/ [n C] formal a warning to someone about a possible danger, especially a warning added to the end of a statement or piece of information: *This caution cannot be overstated: if the belts are incorrectly adjusted they are useless.* | *Caution: do not install electrical equipment near or around water sources.*

wash

RELATED WORDS

- to remove dirt, marks etc from something *see* **remove (3)**
- *see also* **clean, dirty, mark, shine/shiny**

1 to wash your hands/face/body etc

- wash
- have a wash
- freshen up
- get cleaned up
- spruce yourself up/get spruced up
- brush your teeth
- wipe
- cleanse
- shampoo

wash /wɒʃ‖wɔːʃ, wɑːʃ/ [v I/T] to clean yourself with soap and water: *Harry went upstairs to wash.* | **wash your hands/face/hair etc** *She was washing her hair when the phone rang.* | *Have you boys washed your hands yet?* —**wash** [n singular] *He looks as if he could do with a good wash.*

have a wash [v phrase] British **/wash up** [phr v I] American /hæv ə ˈwɒʃ, ˌwɒʃ ˈʌp ‖ -ˈwɔːʃ/ to wash your hands and face: *You'll feel better once you've had a wash and something to eat.* | *You kids go wash up now – dinner's nearly ready.*

freshen up /ˌfreʃən ˈʌp/ [phr v I] especially spoken to wash your face and hands so that you feel more comfortable, for example when you have been working hard or travelling: *The bathroom's on the right if you'd like to freshen up.* | *She hoped there would be time to freshen up before the interview.*

get cleaned up /get ˌkliːnd ˈʌp/ [v phrase] to wash yourself after you have got dirty doing something: *I'll make the dinner – just give me chance to get cleaned up first.* | *He's upstairs in the bathroom getting cleaned up.*

spruce yourself up/get spruced up /ˌspruːs jɔːʳself ˈʌp, get ˌspruːst ˈʌp/ [v phrase] to get washed and make yourself look tidy or change your clothes: *She went into the washroom at the airport to get spruced up before meeting the others.*

brush your teeth ALSO **clean your teeth** British /ˌbrʌʃ jɔːʳ ˈtiːθ, ˌkliːn jɔːʳ ˈtiːθ/ [v phrase] to clean your teeth with a small brush: *Have you brushed your teeth this morning?* | *I cleaned my teeth, flattened down my hair, and rushed out of the door.*

wipe /waɪp/ [v T] to clean your hands or face by gently rubbing them with a cloth or with your hand: *Wipe your face. There's chocolate all around your mouth.* | *Wiping his oily hands on a piece of cloth, he* *reached into his pocket and handed me the bill.* —**wipe** [n singular] *Give your nose a wipe* (=wipe it).

cleanse /klenz/ [v T] to clean your skin, especially using a special liquid cream: *This lotion cleanses your skin deep down, while preserving its natural pH balance.*

shampoo /ʃæm'puː/ [v T] to wash your hair with shampoo (=a special liquid soap for washing hair): *It's a new conditioner. Simply shampoo your hair, towel dry, and spray it in.*

2 to wash in a bath or shower

- have a shower
- have a bath
- be in the bath
- shower
- bath

have a shower British **/take a shower** /ˌhæv ə 'ʃaʊəʳ, ˌteɪk ə 'ʃaʊəʳ/ [v phrase] to wash your whole body while standing under a shower: *I'll just have a quick shower and get changed.* | *She decided to take a shower before dinner.*

have a bath British **/take a bath** American /ˌhæv ə 'bɑːθ, ˌteɪk ə 'bɑːθ‖-'bæθ/ [v phrase] to wash your whole body while sitting in a bath full of water: *Is there enough hot water for me to have a bath?* | *I just had time to take a bath and change before we had to go out again.*

be in the bath British **/be in the bathtub** American /biː ɪn ðə 'bɑːθ, ɪn ðə 'bɑːθtʌb‖-'bæθ-/ [v phrase] to be sitting in a bath washing your whole body: *'Where's Barry?' 'He's in the bath.'* | *My wife was still in the bathtub when I got back from work.*

shower /'ʃaʊəʳ/ [v I] to have a shower: *I got up early as usual, and showered and shaved.* | *It's so hot there, you have to shower three or four times a day.*

bath British **/bathe** American /bɑːθ‖bæθ, beɪð/ [v T] to wash someone, especially a baby or a child, in a bath: *Make sure you bathe the kids and put them to bed before eight.* | *Louise loved being bathed when she was a baby.*

3 to wash a car/floor/wall etc

- wash
- clean
- mop
- scrub
- wash down
- wash out

wash /wɒʃ‖wɔːʃ, wɑːʃ/ [v T] to clean something using a lot of water, and usually soap: *I really must wash the car this weekend.* | *When we moved in, we spent a whole day washing all the floors and paintwork.* | **+ in** *The spinach leaves should be washed in cold water.*

clean /kliːn/ [v T] to **clean** something using soap and water, and usually by rubbing with a cloth or brush: *Where's that stuff you use for cleaning the bathtub?* | *I usually clean the windows about once a month.*

mop /mɒp‖mɑːp/ [v T] to wash a floor using a special tool with a long handle that is dipped in a bucket of water: *Dan has to mop the floor of the café every night.*

scrub /skrʌb/ [v I/T] to make something very clean, using a stiff brush and water, or soap and water: *Martin washed the mud off his hands and scrubbed his nails.* | *Lou was on her knees, scrubbing the kitchen floor.* | *Scrub the potatoes, then put them in a pan of boiling water.*

wash down /ˌwɒʃ 'daʊn‖ˌwɔːʃ-/ [phr v T] to wash something large with a lot of water **wash down sth** *Wash down the walls and leave them to dry before putting up new wallpaper.* | **wash sth down** *Carol washed the van down and checked the oil and tyres.*

wash out /ˌwɒʃ 'aʊt‖ˌwɔːʃ-/ [phr v T] to wash the inside of a cup, glass, pan, or container **wash out sth** *I'll just go and wash out these glasses.* | **wash sth out** *When the bottle is empty, wash it out thoroughly before refilling.*

4 to wash clothes

- wash
- dry-clean
- do the washing
- hand wash/handwash
- be in the wash
- laundry
- washable

wash /wɒʃ‖wɔːʃ, wɑːʃ/ [v I/T] to **wash** clothes, especially in a washing machine: *Could you wash this shirt for me?* | *I seem to spend all my time washing and ironing these days.* | *You ought to wash that sweater by hand.*

dry-clean /ˌdraɪ 'kliːn/ [v T] to clean clothes by using special chemicals instead of soap and water: *Don't put that dress in the washing machine – the label says it should be dry-cleaned.* —**dry-cleaner's** [n C] a shop where you can get your clothes dry-cleaned: *Could you collect my suit from the dry-cleaner's?*

do the washing British **/do the laundry** American /ˌduː ðə 'wɒʃɪŋ‖-'wɔːʃ-, ˌduː ðə 'lɔːndri/ [v phrase] to wash clothes that need to be washed: *Did you do the laundry this morning?* | *I had to go to the laundromat to do the washing.*

hand wash/handwash /'hænd wɒʃ‖-wɔːʃ, -wɑːʃ/ [v T] to wash clothes by hand, not in a washing machine: *I usually hand wash the socks and underwear, and put the rest in the machine.* | *Delicate garments and woollens should be handwashed.*

be in the wash /biː ɪn ðə 'wɒʃ‖-'wɔːʃ/ [v phrase] clothes that **are in the wash** are being washed or are waiting to be washed: *'Where's my yellow blouse?' 'It's in the wash'.* | *You'll have to wear these – your other pants are in the wash.*

laundry ALSO **washing** British /'lɔːndri, 'wɒʃɪŋ‖'wɔːʃ-/ [n U] clothes that need to be washed, are being washed, or have just been washed: *a basket of laundry* | *There was dirty washing all over the floor.*

washable /'wɒʃəbəl‖'wɔːʃ-, 'wɑːʃ-/ [adj] able to be washed in water without being spoiled: *Let's have a look at the label on those trousers. Are they washable?* | *I always buy cotton clothes that are easily washable.*

5 to wash cups/plates/knives etc

- wash the dishes/do the dishes
- do the washing up/wash up

wash the dishes/do the dishes /ˌwɒʃ ðə 'dɪʃɪ̆z‖ˌwɔːʃ-, ˌduː ðə 'dɪʃɪ̆z/ [v phrase] to wash all the cups, plates, knives etc that you have used during a meal: *My mom always makes me wash the dishes.* | *Can I help you do the dishes?*

do the washing up/wash up /duː ðə ˌwɒʃɪŋ 'ʌp, ˌwɒʃ 'ʌp‖-ˌwɔːʃ-/ [v phrase/phr v I/T] British to wash all the cups, plates, knives etc that you have used during a meal: *If you do the cooking tonight, I'll do the washing up.* | *Who's going to wash up?* —**washing-up** [n C] the dirty plates, dishes, knives etc that have to be washed: *The sink was full of washing-up.*

6 to wash something using water but without soap

- rinse
- soak/leave sth to soak

rinse /rɪns/ [v T] to wash something with water in order to remove soap or dirt: *I'll just rinse the lettuce under the tap.* | *Rosie rinsed her mouth to get rid of the taste.* | **rinse out sth** (=quickly clean a container, just using water) *He rinsed out a glass and poured himself a whiskey.* —**rinse** [n singular] **give sth a rinse** *Pass me your cup, and I'll give it a quick rinse.*

soak/leave sth to soak /səʊk, ˌliːv (sth) tə ˈsəʊk/ [v T/v phrase] to leave something in water for a long time in order to clean it or make it easier to wash later: *You'll have to soak that shirt to get the blood off it.* | **leave sth to soak** *Just leave that pan to soak overnight.*

waste

to use something in a way that is not useful, or to use too much of something

RELATED WORDS

opposite: —— **save**

- to spend a lot of money carelessly *see* **spend money/time (3)**
- to waste time *see* **spend time/money (12)**
- *see also* **rubbish/garbage, get rid of, efficient**

1 to waste something

- waste
- wasted
- go to waste
- squander
- fritter away
- dissipate
- money down the drain

waste /weɪst/ [v T] to use time, money, food etc in a way that is not useful or sensible, or use more of something than is necessary: *I wasted 40 minutes waiting for a bus this morning.* | *Don't leave the light on – you're wasting electricity.* | *The school kitchen wastes an awful lot of food.* | **waste money/time on sth** *Bill wastes all his money on beer and cigarettes.* | *Let's not waste any more time on this.*

wasted /ˈweɪstɪ̇d/ [adj] something that is **wasted** is not used in a sensible way, or does not produce a useful result: *I felt as if my education had been wasted when I couldn't get a job.* | **a wasted trip/journey** *I'm sorry, you've had a wasted trip. Mr Newton isn't here at the moment.* | **wasted life/years** *She thought back over the past four years – four wasted years married to a man who almost destroyed her.* | **a wasted opportunity** *The government could have dealt with the problem there and then. It was a wasted opportunity.*

go to waste /ˌgəʊ tə ˈweɪst/ [v phrase] if something **goes to waste** or if you let something **go to waste**, it is wasted because it is not used: *Local produce often goes to waste because people prefer to buy imported food.* | *If no one else wants this, I'll eat it – I hate to see good food go to waste.* | *We can't let all our hard work go to waste.*

squander /ˈskwɒndəʳ‖ˈskwɑːn-/ [v T] to waste something valuable by using it in a stupid way that brings no useful results: *His family felt he had squandered his musical talent.* | **squander a chance/opportunity** *England squandered a golden opportunity to score, seconds before the final whistle.* | **squander away sth** *Howard was a terrible gambler, and had squandered away the family fortune.*

fritter away /ˌfrɪtər əˈweɪ/ [phr v T] to waste something such as time or money in a silly way by using small amounts of it on things you do not need **fritter away sth** *So many students seem to fritter away their time at college.* | **fritter sth away** *Michelle had frittered her inheritance away on extravagant parties and fancy clothes.*

dissipate /ˈdɪsɪ̇peɪt/ [v T] formal to gradually waste something such as money or energy by trying to do a lot of different and often unnecessary things: *She had dissipated her fortune by the time she was twenty-five.*

money down the drain /ˌmʌni daʊn ðə ˈdreɪn/ [n phrase] money that is wasted **be money down the drain** *Buying nice clothes for you was just money down the drain. All you ever wear are jeans and T-shirts.* | **throw money down the drain** *The government is throwing tax payers' money down the drain.*

2 something that wastes time, money etc

- be a waste of sth
- wasteful
- inefficient

be a waste of sth /biː ə ˈweɪst əv (sth)/ [v phrase] if something **is a waste of** time, money, energy etc, it annoys you because it uses time, money etc in a way that has no useful results: *a pointless war that was a terrible waste of human life* | *That class was a complete waste of time – I didn't learn anything.* | *My parents think going to football games is a waste of money.*

wasteful /ˈweɪstfəl/ [adj] an activity or method that is **wasteful** uses too much money, food, energy etc, without any useful results: *Many people see the new £60 million building as wasteful and extravagant.* | *wasteful packaging*

inefficient /ˌɪnɪ̇ˈfɪʃənt◂/ [adj] an organization or system that is **inefficient** does not work well, so it uses more time, money, or energy than it needs to: *an inefficient heating system* | *Local government in the area is seen as being corrupt and inefficient.* | *The factory is inefficient, and its working practices and machinery dated.*

watch

to look at and pay attention to something that is happening

RELATED WORDS

- to look at people, scenery, pictures etc that are not moving *see* **look**
- to notice something with your eyes *see* **see**
- *see also* **attention**

1 to watch someone or something

- watch
- see
- observe
- look on

watch /wɒtʃ‖wɑːtʃ, wɔːtʃ/ [v I/T] to look for some time at something that is happening or moving, and pay attention to what you see: *She watched the man with interest as he made his way through the crowd.* | *Do you want to join in or just sit and* *watch?* | **+ as** *I watched as the small boat disappeared over the horizon.* | **watch sb do/doing sth** *They watched the runners go past.* | *We watched the children playing on the beach.* | **watch television/a video/the tennis etc** *Did you watch that programme about real life murders last night?* | *The Presidential debate was watched by over 10 million people.*

see /siː/ [v T not in progressive] to look at something or someone: *Did you see the news last night?* | *We went to see the new 'Star Wars' film last weekend.* | **see sb do/doing sth** *He saw a man get out of the car and walk to the side of the road.* | *The driver saw two men attacking a middle-aged woman.*

observe /əbˈzɜːʳv/ [v T] to watch someone or something carefully in order to learn more about them: *I love to observe people at work.* | **+ how/what** *Visitors are encouraged to look around and observe how things work.* —**observation** /ˌɒbzəʳˈveɪʃən‖ˌɑːb-/ [n U] *We have reached these conclusions after months of careful observation and experiment.*

look on /ˌlʊk ˈɒn / [phr v I] to watch something happening, without taking part or trying to stop it: *Sarah set off after the man, while her friends looked on in amazement.* | *The women looked on, nodding and smiling.* | *Mr Parsons began to cough again, while his wife looked on helplessly.*

2 to watch someone or something continuously

- not take your eyes off
- stand over

not take your eyes off /nɒt teɪk jɔːr ˈaɪz ɒf / [v phrase] to watch someone or something continuously because they are very interesting, exciting or attractive: *The woman had hardly taken her eyes off him all evening.* | *The dog scuttled across to the other side of the room, without taking his eyes off me.* | **can't/couldn't take your eyes off** *Charlie couldn't take his eyes off Rose.*

stand over /ˈstænd əʊvəʳ/ [phr v T] to stand next to someone and watch what they are doing, especially because you want to make sure that they do it right: *Do I have to stand over you to make sure you do your homework?* | *Liz dragged her out of bed and stood over her while she got dressed.*

3 to watch to make sure that nothing bad happens to someone or something

- watch
- keep an eye on
- can't take your eyes off
- observation

watch /wɒtʃ‖wɑːtʃ, wɔːtʃ/ [v T] *Stay here and watch our bags while I go and buy some food.* | *Don't let children play near water without an adult to watch them.*

keep an eye on /ˌkiːp ən ˈaɪ ɒn/ [v phrase] especially spoken to watch someone or something by occasionally going to look at them over a long period of time: *Keep an eye on the baby, in case he gets too near the fire.* | *Ask a neighbour to keep an eye on the house for you while you're away.* | *You'd better come into hospital where we can keep an eye on you.*

can't take your eyes off /ˌkɑːnt teɪk jɔːr ˈaɪz ɒf ‖ˌkænt-/ [v phrase] to have to watch someone very carefully all the time because you think something bad might happen to them: *You have to be so careful with small children – you can't take your eyes off them for a minute.*

observation /ˌɒbzəʳˈveɪʃən‖ˌɑːb-/ [n U] when doctors watch a patient carefully because they think they might suddenly become more ill **keep sb in (the hospital) for observation** *They kept him in overnight just for observation.* | **under observation** *She spent two nights in hospital under observation, before being allowed home.*

4 to pay attention to the way a situation develops

- watch
- monitor
- keep an eye on

watch /wɒtʃ‖wɑːtʃ, wɔːtʃ/ [v T] *Both candidates are watching the opinion polls carefully.* | **watch sb do sth** *We have watched hundreds of small firms collapse over the last few years.* | **+ how/when/what etc** *Many swimmers are videoed during training so they can watch how their performance improves.*

keep an eye on /ˌkiːp ən ˈaɪ ɒn/ [v phrase] to watch a situation carefully over a period of time, especially so that you are prepared for anything bad that might happen: *If I were you, I'd keep an eye on house prices for a while before you decide to sell.* | **keep a close/careful eye on sth** *Government experts will be keeping a close eye on the new currency to see whether it proves successful.*

monitor /ˈmɒnətəʳ‖ˈmɑː-/ [v T] to carefully watch a situation over a period of time, to see how it changes or develops: *Doctors monitored her progress during the night.* | *We will of course monitor the campaign to assess its effectiveness.*

5 to secretly watch a person or place

- watch
- surveillance
- spy on sb
- observation
- keep a watch on

watch /wɒtʃ‖wɑːtʃ, wɔːtʃ/ [v T] *The thieves had obviously been watching his house and knew when he was likely to be out.* | *He had the feeling that he was being watched.* | **watch sb's movements** (=watch someone as they go to different places) *Detectives have been watching Mr Heskey's movements for some time.*

spy on sb /ˈspaɪ ɒn (sb)/ [phr v T] to watch someone secretly, in order to find out information about them: *Mathers admitted he had followed Ms Evans and spied on her.*

keep a watch on /ˌkiːp ə ˈwɒtʃ ɒn‖-ˈwɑːtʃ-/ [v phrase] if the police **keep a watch on** a person or place, a group of them are organized to watch that person or place continuously: *Our orders were to keep a 24-hour watch on the cottage where the men were staying.*

surveillance /sɜːʳˈveɪləns/ [n U] when people, especially the police or government officials secretly watch a place or person, especially for a long period, often using special equipment such as hidden cameras: *Television surveillance in public areas should help to make housing developments safer.* | **surveillance camera** *Banks are installing surveillance cameras to prevent robberies.* | **under surveillance** (=being secretly watched) *The men had been under surveillance by customs officers for some time before their arrest.* | **keep sb/sth under surveillance** (=secretly watch someone or something) *The terrorists had been kept under constant surveillance by our officers.*

observation /ˌɒbzəʳˈveɪʃən‖ˌɑːb-/ [n U] when people watch a place or person carefully for a period of time **under observation** (=being watched) *A patrol car spotted us and the officers inside made it clear that we were under observation.* | **keep sb/sth under observation** (=watch someone or something) *We want that place kept under constant observation.*

6 someone who is watching an event or performance

- spectator
- viewer
- audience
- onlooker
- observer

spectator /spekˈteɪtəʳ‖ˈspekteɪtər/ [n C] someone who is watching an event or game: *The game was watched by over 50,000 spectators.* | *There are no facilities for spectators at the pool.* | *Someone was juggling in the street, and a small group of spectators had gathered to watch.*

viewer /ˈvjuːəʳ/ [n C] someone who watches a television programme – used especially in newspapers and news reports: *The concert was seen by 500 million viewers around the world.* | *Millions of television viewers tuned in to the president's speech.*

audience /ˈɔːdiəns‖ˈɔː-, ˈɑː-/ [n C with singular or plural verb in British English] a group of people who have come to a place to watch a play, concert, film etc: *Actors, wearing masks, came down among the audience.* | *I'm not sure that this film will appeal to British audiences.* | *The show has delighted television audiences in the United States and Britain.* | **in the audience** *There seemed to be quite a lot of young people in the audience.*

onlooker /ˈɒnˌlʊkəʳ‖ˈɑːn-, ˈɔːn-/ [n C] someone who is watching an event, especially when they did not come specially to watch it but just happened to see it: *The child glanced fearfully around the small circle of onlookers.* | *The last few runners appeared, to an accompanying cheer from the crowd of onlookers.*

observer /əbˈsɜːʳvəʳ/ [n C] someone who watches an event, activity, or situation, especially someone who has been officially sent there in order to report back about it to an organization or country: *She's been sent as an observer to the UN aid conference.* | *Most political observers believe that the president will now have to resign.* | *Military observers have been allowed into the area to monitor the ceasefire.*

7 always watching to see what happens

- alert
- be on the alert
- keep your eyes open/peeled
- look/watch out for
- watchful
- vigilant

alert /əˈlɜːʳt/ [adj] someone who is **alert** is always watching, and notices if anything strange or unusual happens: *Passengers should try to stay alert at all times, and report any suspicious packages to the police immediately.* | *She owes her life to an alert farmer, who spotted her car in a ditch and called the emergency services.*

be on the alert /biː ɒn ðə əˈlɜːʳt/ [v phrase] to watch carefully because you think that something bad might happen: *We ask you all to be on the alert and to report anything suspicious immediately.* | **+ for** *Staff have been warned to be on the alert for bombs.*

keep your eyes open/peeled /ˌkiːp jɔːr ˈaɪz ˌəʊpən, ˌpiːld/ [v phrase] spoken say this to tell someone to keep watching carefully so that they will see something that they are hoping or expecting to see: *We might see a dolphin if we're lucky, so keep your eyes open.* | **+ for** *I always keep my eyes open for discounts and special offers.* | *Keep your eyes peeled for Robert – he should be here any minute.*

look/watch out for /ˌlʊk, ˌwɒtʃ ˈaʊt fəʳ‖ˌwɑːtʃ-/ [phr v T] to keep watching so that you will notice someone or something: *Look out for the old college buildings on your left.* | *We had to watch out for potholes in the road.*

watchful /ˈwɒtʃfəl‖ˈwɑːtʃ-, ˈwɔːtʃ-/ [adj] always watching to see what happens, either to make sure that nothing bad happens, or simply because you are interested: *The fans left the ground quietly, under the watchful gaze of security cameras.* | *Alan became more watchful and uneasy as the evening went on.* | **keep a watchful eye on** (=keep watching someone to make sure they do not get into trouble, hurt themselves etc) *Bill was in the kitchen, keeping a watchful eye on the children as he prepared lunch.*

vigilant /ˈvɪdʒələnt/ [adj] someone who is **vigilant** is always watching to see what happens, especially to see if anyone is doing anything wrong or illegal: *To combat thieves, it is important for staff to be vigilant at all times.* —**vigilance** [n U] *Constant public vigilance is required to combat this kind of terrorism.*

water

RELATED WORDS

- float *see* **on/on top of**
- *see also* **liquid, wet, pour**

1 water

- water
- moisture

water /ˈwɔːtəʳ‖ˈwɔː-, ˈwɑː-/ [n U] *Could I have a glass of water, please?* | *Humans can't survive for more than a few days without water.* | *This reservoir supplies water to half of Los Angeles.* | **shallow/deep water** *Stonefish lie on the ocean bed, often in shallow water.* | **rain/sea water** *Some of the bacteria are found in rivers, lakes, mud, and even rain water.* | *Never drink sea water.* | **running water** (=water that is flowing or that comes out of taps) *As we got deeper into the forest we could hear the sound of running water.* | *All the rooms in the hotel have hot and cold running water.* | **water shortage** (=when there is not much water available) *By the end of the hot summer of '76, there was a serious water shortage.* | **water level** (=the level of water in rivers, the sea etc, which rises and falls) *The water level of the River Thames has risen 14" in the past few days.* | **water content** (=how much water there is in something) *Condensed milk is produced by removing about 50% of the water content of whole milk.*

moisture /ˈmɔɪstʃəʳ/ [n U] the amount of wetness in something, especially in the earth or in the air, caused by the presence of water: *In the summer, temperatures rose to 90 or 100 degrees, and the air was constantly heavy with moisture.* | *Moisture is essential for keeping your skin fresh and youthful.* | **moisture content** (=how much moisture there is in something) *Nearby ditches and walls affect the moisture content of the soil.*

2 when a lot of water covers a place that is usually dry

- flood
- flooding
- deluge
- flood

flood /flʌd/ [n C] very large amounts of water covering an area of land or filling a building, caused by heavy rains and usually causing serious damage: *Last winter, the town suffered the worst floods for fifty years.* | *There has been an extensive programme of restorations in Venice since the 1966 flood.* | **flood damage** *Yosemite National Park is restricting access to the Park in order to cope with the flood damage.* | **flood water/waters** *Helicopters continued to search for others who had climbed trees to escape from the flood waters.* | **flood plain** (=the area of land near a river that floods) *the wide flood plains of the River Nile*

flooding /'flʌdɪŋ/ [n U] a situation in which an area of land or part of a building is covered with water, for example as a result of heavy rain or burst water pipes: *Parts of the harbour wall collapsed, causing serious flooding in the town.* | *The government is to receive £200,000 in emergency European Community aid, to help victims of the flooding.*

deluge /'delju:dʒ/ [n C usually singular] written a situation in which an area of land is covered with very large amounts of water as a result of heavy rain: *Many homes in Jakarta were flooded in the Indonesian capital's worst deluge for years.*

flood /flʌd/ [v I/T] if a river **floods**, or heavy rain, snow etc **floods** an area of land, it causes the land to become covered with very large amounts of water: *Three major rivers have already flooded, and two more are on red alert.* | *After two days of continuous rain, the village was flooded.* | *Melting snow floods the valleys each spring.* —**flooded** [adj] *Emergency officials will tour flooded areas to assess the extent of the damage.*

3 a continuous movement of water

- current
- torrent

current /'kʌrənt‖'kɜ:r-/ [n C] a continuous movement of water in a particular direction in the sea or in a river: *The currents in these parts could carry a boat miles out to sea.* | **a strong current** *It's dangerous to swim in the sea here because the current is so strong.* | **river/ocean/sea currents** *The tiny young drift on the ocean currents, until a few are lucky enough to land in a suitable place and begin a new life.*

torrent /'tɒrənt‖'tɔ:-, 'tɑ:-/ [n C] a large amount of water that moves quickly and strongly in a particular direction: *The river occasionally becomes a torrent after a downpour, and may even cause flooding.* | **torrent of water** *A torrent of water flowed down the street.* | **raging torrent** (=very violent torrent) *After five days of heavy rain the Telle River was a raging torrent.* | **in torrents** *There was no shelter anywhere and the rain was coming down in torrents.* —**torrential** /tə'renʃəl/ [adj] **torrential rain** *Torrential rain and gale-force storms left many coastal roads impassable.*

4 to supply farmland, plants etc with water

- water
- irrigate

water /'wɔ:təʳ‖'wɔ:-, 'wɑ:-/ [v T] to pour **water** on plants, crops, or grass in order to make them grow: *Would you mind watering my plants while I'm away?* | *During the drought, residents were barred from watering their gardens, or washing their cars.* | *Many farmers use low-flying aircraft to water their crops.*

irrigate /'ɪrɪ̈geɪt/ [v T] to provide a regular supply of water to large areas of land, in order to grow crops there, for example by using a system of pipes or long holes in the ground: *The stored water is then used to irrigate nearby agricultural land.* | *A system of channels carries water down from the mountains to irrigate the soil.* —**irrigation** /ˌɪrɪ̈'geɪʃən/ [n U] *methods of irrigation*

5 to add water to another liquid

- dilute
- water down

dilute /ˌdaɪ'lu:t/ [v T] to add a liquid, especially water, to another liquid in order to make it weaker or thinner: *Pour a little of the antiseptic into a bowl and dilute it before bathing the cut.* | **+ with** *To make citron pressé, dilute fresh lemon juice with water and add sugar.* | *Continue diluting the tomato sauce with red wine, according to taste.* —**diluted** [adj] *Try giving the baby diluted fruit juice* (=fruit juice diluted with water) | *once or twice a day.*

water down /ˌwɔ:təʳ 'daʊn/ [phr v T] to add water to another liquid, in order to make it weaker or to increase the amount – use this especially to show disapproval: *I'm sure they water down the tomato ketchup at school.* | **water sth down** *You'll find the paint drips everywhere if you water it down too much.* | *It's a very good whisky. Much too good to water down.* —**watered-down** [adj] *They served us some disgusting watered-down wine.*

6 living in water

- aquatic
- amphibious

aquatic /ə'kwætɪk, ə'kwɒ-‖ə'kwæ-, ə'kwɑ:-/ [adj] formal an **aquatic** animal or plant lives or grows in water: *These fish are particularly fond of vegetable foods, and will usually eat tender aquatic plants.* | *The hippopotamus is semi-aquatic* (=lives partly in water and partly on the land). | *Unfortunately, fertilizers from surrounding farmland have reduced the aquatic life.*

amphibious /æm'fɪbiəs/ [adj] animals that are **amphibious** are able to live both in water and on land: *Most species of frogs are amphibious.* | *Dinosaurs were probably the first ancestors of amphibious reptiles and fish.*

7 something that does not let water pass through it

- waterproof
- watertight

waterproof /'wɔ:təʳpru:f‖'wɔ:-, 'wɑ:-/ [adj] something such as a container or material that is **waterproof** does not let water pass through it: *A warm, waterproof jacket is the first thing you need for mountain walking.* | *The Gore-tex fabric manages to be completely waterproof, and yet allows body moisture to escape.* | *a waterproof watch*

watertight /'wɔ:təʳtaɪt‖'wɔ:-, 'wɑ:-/ [adj] something such as a box or roof that is **watertight** does not let water pass through it so that what is inside does not get wet: *The cameras had been stored in watertight containers.* | *Most wooden ships were watertight in harbour, but they all leaked when they got out to sea.*

way

WHAT'S HERE

- **a way of doing sth** see **1 to 6**
- **the way sb behaves** see **7 to 8**
- **the way you go from one place to another** see **9 to 10**

a way of doing sth

RELATED WORDS

▸ *see also* **system, plan**

1 a way or method of doing something

- ▸ **way**
- ▸ **method**
- ▸ **approach**
- ▸ **technique**
- ▸ **strategy**
- ▸ **system**
- ▸ **tactics**

way /weɪ/ [n C] *Websites can be designed in many different ways.* | **+ to do sth** *Visiting a country is a great way to learn its language.* | *There's more than one way to build a house – all builders work differently.* | *I tried every way I could to make the child go to bed, but she refused.* | **+ of doing sth** *Is there any way of controlling the heating in here?* | **the way (that) sb does sth** *I'll show you the way we calculate the figures.* | **the best/only way** *What's the best way to remove wine stains?* | *The only way to lose weight is to eat less.* | **the right/wrong way** *The government does not believe that this approach is the right way to deal with the problem.* | **the way to go about sth** *I think you're going about this in completely the wrong way.*

method /ˈmeθəd/ [n C] a way of doing something, especially one that is well known and often used: *Printing methods have changed completely in the last twenty years.* | *In this school, staff are given complete freedom in their choice of language teaching methods.* | *Make a list of the different methods you could use in conducting a survey.* | **+ of** *You can choose whichever method of payment you prefer.* | **method of/for doing sth** *Medical science has not yet found a satisfactory method of treating cholera.* | *an environmentally-friendly method for treating household waste*

approach /əˈprəʊtʃ/ [n C] a way of dealing with a particular problem or situation, especially a way that has been carefully thought about or planned: *The main advantage of this approach is its simplicity.* | **+ to** *Today's approach to raising children is very different from 40 years ago.* | *Space scientists had to adopt a whole new approach to design and construction.*

technique /tekˈniːk/ [n C] a particular way of doing something, for which you need a skill that has to be learned and practised: *More and more heart patients are surviving thanks to improved surgical techniques.* | *helpful tips on how to improve your exam technique* | **+ for doing sth** *Chapter 6 describes useful techniques for creating on-screen filing systems that really work.*

strategy /ˈstrætɪ̈dʒi/ [n C] a set of carefully planned methods for achieving something that is difficult and may take a long time: *We will continue to update our sales strategy.* | **+ for (doing) sth** *The government has no long-term strategy for reducing crime.* | **+ to do sth** *a strategy to reduce the level of teenage smoking*

system /ˈsɪstɪ̈m/ [n C] a planned and effective way of doing something that you use every time you do it: *I do the cooking and Andrew does the shopping; it's an excellent system.* | **+ of doing sth** *I work a lot more quickly now I've developed an efficient system of working.* | **+ for doing sth** *Ryan thinks he's discovered a system for winning at roulette.*

tactics /ˈtæktɪks/ [n plural] methods that you use in order to achieve what you want, especially in a game or competition: *Salesmen use all sorts of clever tactics to persuade people to buy from them.* | *The team was busy discussing tactics for the game.* | *He played with the confidence of a winning captain, instinctively changing tactics when necessary.*

2 the correct way of doing something

- ▸ **how to do sth**
- ▸ **procedure**

how to do sth /ˌhaʊ tə ˈduː (sth)/ *For details on how to install the program, see the instructions on the right.* | **show/teach/tell etc sb how to do sth** *Could you show me how to work the photocopier?* | *My father taught me how to make and mend fishing nets* | **know how to do sth** *I don't know how to load this thing.* | **learn/find out/work out etc how to do sth** *Find out how to decorate your own Easter eggs on pages 30-31.*

procedure /prəˈsiːdʒəʳ/ [n C] the correct or official way of doing something, especially something that has several stages: *I want to get a new passport but I don't know the procedure.* | **+ for doing sth** *What is the procedure for opening a bank account?* | **follow/observe a procedure** *It is very important to follow the safety procedures laid down in the handbook.* | *Always observe the correct procedure for the use of ski-lifts.* | **correct/proper/standard procedure** *Stewards spent hours rehearsing the proper procedure for marshalling the huge crowds expected in the stadium.* | *Sorry about the body search. It's just standard procedure.*

3 the method you use to achieve something

- ▸ **means**
- ▸ **tool**
- ▸ **tactic**
- ▸ **medium**
- ▸ **vehicle**
- ▸ **avenue**

means /miːnz/ [n C] a method, system, machine etc that you use to do something or achieve something: *We aim to use peaceful means to bring about change.* | **+ of doing sth** *Education and training are the most effective means of improving the nation's economy.* | **by means of sth** (=using a particular method or system) *He came to power by means of a military coup in 1960.* | **by peaceful/political/unlawful etc means** *The judge ruled that Smith had been elected by unlawful means.* | **means of communication/transport/transportation** *E-mail has become an increasingly important means of business communication.* | **means to an end** (=something that you do only as a way of achieving something else) *You should not regard the course simply as a means to an end.*

tool /tuːl/ [n C] a particular method or system that you use to get a result, especially in business or politics: *Pictures of fleeing refugees were used as an effective propaganda tool against the Communists.* | **+ of** *Interest rates are one of the Finance Minister's main tools of economic policy.* | **+ for (doing) sth** *Dance and aerobics classes are a useful tool for encouraging girls back to school P.E. lessons.*

tactic /ˈtæktɪk/ [n C] a carefully planned way of trying to get what you want: *He's threatening to sue us? That's a tactic he's used before.* | *Giving out criticism rather than praise is a tactic that rarely works in the workplace.* | **delaying tactic** (=something you do to gain more time for yourself) *The question was just a delaying tactic to stop her leaving the room.*

medium /ˈmiːdiəm/ [n C] PLURAL **media** /-diə/ **formal** a physical or electronic method used for giving people information, for example the telephone, television, newspapers etc: *The wide variety of electronic media available on the Internet.* | **+ for (doing) sth** *DVDs have quickly become an extremely popular medium for film viewing.*

vehicle /ˈviːɪkəl/ [n singular] **written** something you use as a way of expressing your ideas, communicating something to people, or achieving what you want **+ for (doing) sth** *the use of TV soap operas as a vehicle for spreading public information* | *The secret ballot was an important vehicle for freer elections.*

avenue /ˈævɪ̇njuː‖-nuː/ [n C] a way of achieving something – use this especially when there are several different ways and you are trying to find the best one or the only one that is really possible: *We explored every possible avenue, but still couldn't come up with a solution.*

4 a way of achieving success, happiness etc

- route/path
- the key
- secret

route/path /ruːt, pɑːθ‖pæθ/ [n C usually singular] *Her political career followed the usual route of local and then national government.* | **+ to** *There's more than one route to a successful marriage.* | *the path to happiness and enlightenment*

the key /ðə ˈkiː/ [n singular] the most important means of making progress or achieving success: *In all types of advice work, listening is the key.* | **+ to** *What's the key to getting a good night's sleep?* | *We feel that our policy of low-price products in plain packaging is the key to our success.*

secret /ˈsiːkrɪ̇t/ [n singular] a way of becoming happy, healthy, successful etc that not everyone knows about or knows how to do: *I don't know what her secret is but she always gets top marks in exams.* | *Hollywood stars reveal their beauty secrets in next month's edition.* | **the secret of sb's/sth's success** *Mr. Ritchie, you're a millionaire at the age of twenty. What's the secret of your success?*

5 a clever or dishonest way of getting what you want

- ploy
- device
- ways and means

ploy /plɔɪ/ [n C] a clever way of gaining an advantage, for example by making people feel concerned about you or making them feel grateful towards you: *The religious element of their election campaign was a cynical ploy.* | **+ to do sth** *He's not really ill, it's just a ploy to make us feel sorry for him.*

device /dɪˈvaɪs/ [n C] something that is intended to achieve a particular aim, especially an aim that is slightly dishonest or unacceptable **+ to do sth** *He used every device possible to prevent inspectors from entering the premises.* | *Commissions and inquiries are little more than a device to allow politicians to put off taking decisions.*

ways and means /ˌweɪz ən ˈmiːnz/ [n phrase] clever ways of getting an advantage, especially by doing something that is unusual or secret **+ of doing sth** *Dealers have ways and means of making people smuggle drugs for them.*

6 the way in which something is done

- how
- like this
- somehow
- by
- by means of

how /haʊ/ [adv] use this to say or ask the way that someone does something: *How do you get your CD player to work?* | *We don't know how she managed to escape.* | **+ to do sth** *My dad's teaching me how to use email.* | *She told me how to get to the Johnsons' house.*

like this /laɪk ˈðɪs/ [adv] **spoken** in this way – say this when you are showing someone the way to do something: *You have to fold the corners back like this.* | **something like this** *The program works something like this.*

somehow /ˈsʌmhaʊ/ [adv] if you do something **somehow**, you do it by using any method that is available: *There's a bus strike, but I'm sure Ian will get here somehow.* | *The newspaper had somehow got hold of some secret government papers.* | **somehow or other** *I'll find out her address somehow or other.*

by /baɪ/ [prep] using a particular method **by doing sth** *They got the information by bribing officials.* | *She earns a living by selling insurance.*

by means of /baɪ ˈmiːnz ɒv/ [prep] using a particular method, tool, object etc: *FBI officers recorded the conversation by means of a tiny bug hidden in the phone.* | *She paid for the goods by means of a stolen credit card.*

the way sb behaves

RELATED WORDS

- *see also* **behave, character**

7 the way someone behaves or does something

- way
- manner
- how sb does sth
- style

way /weɪ/ [n C] *Losing a job affects different people in different ways.* | **the way (that) sb does sth** *I just love the way she laughs.* | *I could tell by the way he looked at me that he was annoyed.* | **sb's way of doing sth** *The younger girls admired Louise, and tried to copy her way of dressing and talking.* | **in the same/a different way** *We try to treat all the children in the same way.*

manner /ˈmænəʳ/ [n singular] the way that someone behaves towards someone else and talks to them: *The doctor had a relaxed and friendly manner.* | **not like sb's manner** *a young man with a slightly shy, awkward manner*

how sb does sth /ˌhaʊ (sb) ˈdʌz (sth)/ [adv] use

this to talk about the way someone behaves or does something: *Have you noticed how she reacts when you mention her husband?* | *Just watch how he tricks the other player into going in the wrong direction.*

style /staɪl/ [n C] the particular way that someone does something or deals with other people, especially if this way has been chosen from several possible ways: *Cameron found my style aggressive, although I thought I was just being direct and honest.* | **+ of** *Her friendly style of management works well with small groups of people.* | *an authoritarian style of leadership*

8 done in a particular way

- in a ... way/manner
- in a ... fashion
- with
- like
- -style
- along ... lines
- as if/as though
- with an air of

in a ... way/manner /ɪn ə ... 'weɪ, 'mænəʳ/ [adv] *She was looking at me in a very strange way.* | *The wedding ceremony was conducted in quite a formal manner.*

in a ... fashion /ɪn ə ... 'fæʃən/ [adv] formal if you do something **in a** particular **fashion**, you do it in a particular way: *There's no reason why we can't behave in a civilized fashion even though we're getting divorced.*

with /wɪð, wɪθ/ [prep] **with enthusiasm/care/envy/delight etc** enthusiastically, carefully etc: *A sign warned motorists to drive with care.* | *He has borne his illness with great courage.* | *They set about tackling the problem with a great deal of enthusiasm.* | *'My daughter's been selected for the Olympic team,' she said, with understandable pride.*

like /laɪk/ [prep] in a particular way **+ this/that** *You mustn't talk to people like that – it's very rude.* | *They were all waving their arms around, like this.* | **like sb** (=in the same way as someone) *He stood bolt upright, like a soldier.* | *He moves and talks just like his father.*

-style /staɪl/ done or made in a way that is typical of a place, group of people etc – use this after another noun or adjective: *Although he was educated in India, he went to an English-style boarding school.* | *They live in a beautiful little country-style house on the edge of town.* | *He wore his gun at the hip, cowboy-style.*

along ... lines /əˌlɒŋ ... 'laɪnz‖əˌlɔːŋ-/ [adv] if something is done **along** particular **lines**, it is done in a way that is similar to the way you have mentioned **along socialist/military/institutional etc lines** *The school was run along almost military lines.* | **along the same/similar lines** *We must have been thinking along the same lines, because we both said together, 'Let's get out of here!'*

as if/as though /əz 'ɪf, əz 'ðəʊ/ [conjunction] in a way that seems to show that something has happened, something is true etc, even though this might not always be what has happened, what is true etc: *Dreen looked as if he'd seen a ghost.* | *She moved her legs slowly, as though in pain.*

with an air of /wɪð ən 'eər ɒv/ [prep] formal in a particular way – used in literature: *The affair had been conducted with an air of mystery which he disliked.* | *Lila came out into the yard with an air of happy confidence.*

the way you go from one place to another

RELATED WORDS

see also **direction, go, travel**

9 the way to go from one place to another

- way
- how to get
- route
- short cut
- directions

way /weɪ/ [n singular] the road, path etc that you must follow in order to get to a place: *The road was blocked, so we came back a different way.* | **be the way** *Are you sure this is the way?* | **+ to/into/home etc** *Is this the way to Grand Central Station?* | *I think this is the quickest way into town.* | *Do you think you can find the way home by yourself?* | **the right/wrong way** *I don't recognize this part of town – we must have come the wrong way.* | **know the way** (=know how to get somewhere) *Will you come with me? I don't know the way.*

how to get /ˌhaʊ tə 'get/ if you ask or tell someone **how to get** somewhere, you ask or tell them the way to a place **+ to** *Can you tell me how to get to the Piazza Venezia?* | **how to get there/back/home** *Come with me. I know how to get there.*

route /ruːt‖ruːt, raʊt/ [n C] the way from one place to another, especially a way that is used regularly and can be shown on a map: *If you don't enjoy driving on the main highways, try some of the rural routes.* | *It looked as though the most direct route was through the forest.* | *I try to vary my route to and from work a little.* | **take a route** (=follow a route) *There are two routes we can take – this one along the coast or this one through the mountains.*

short cut /ˌʃɔːt 'kʌt‖'ʃɔːrt kʌt/ [n C] a way of getting somewhere that is shorter than the usual way: *Taxi-drivers know all the short cuts.* | **take a short cut** (=use a short cut) *Let's take a short cut across the field.*

directions /d$_{\frac{1}{2}}$'rekʃənz, daɪ-/ [n plural] instructions on how to get to a place: *I checked the directions and turned left as I was told to.* | **+ to** *The letter contained a wedding invitation and directions to the church.* | **follow directions** *If you follow these directions you'll have no problem finding the house.*

10 to find out how to get to a place by using maps

- find your way
- navigate

find your way /ˌfaɪnd jɔːʳ 'weɪ/ [v phrase] to manage to get to a place, either by remembering the way from previous journeys, or by going the way you think is right: *Unable to find our way, we stopped at a local hotel to ask directions.* | **find your way to/home/out/back etc** *Somehow, I managed to find my way out of the forest.* | **find your own way** (=without anyone else's help) *If I take you there, do you think you'll be able to find your own way back?*

navigate /'næv$_{\frac{1}{2}}$geɪt/ [v I] to find the way to a place using maps or by carefully remembering the position of various objects or places: *I don't mind driving but I'd like you to navigate.* | **+ by** *Some birds fly at night and navigate by the stars.* —**navigation** /ˌnæv$_{\frac{1}{2}}$'geɪʃən/ [n U] *The fog and heavy rain made navigation difficult.*

weak

RELATED WORDS

opposite: **strong**

- not brave *see* **brave/not brave**
- not good at making decisions quickly and firmly *see* **decide**
- weak taste *see* **taste (8)**
- *see also* **break**

1 physically weak

- weak
- frail
- feeble
- fragile
- shaky
- puny
- weedy
- weakling
- weed

weak /wiːk/ [adj] someone who is **weak** is not strong enough to lift heavy things or do a lot of physical work, especially because they are ill: *When you have flu, you feel tired and weak for a long time.* | *The child was too weak to undergo a transplant operation.* | *I can't go running – I've got a weak heart.* | **+ from/with** *The soldiers were weak from hunger and exhaustion.* | *She felt weak with emotion at the sight of him.* —**weakness** [n U] *In spite of his physical weakness Harry kept himself as busy and active as possible.*

frail /freɪl/ [adj] someone who is **frail** is thin and weak, especially because they are old: *a frail 85-year-old lady* | *She sat up a little straighter, raising her frail body in the bed.* —**frailty** [n U] *We hadn't seen her for many years and were shocked by her frailty.*

feeble /ˈfiːbəl/ [adj] not physically strong because of being very young, old, ill etc,: *My grandmother's very feeble now and needs someone at home full-time to look after her.* | *He did not remember his sister at all, except as a tiny, feeble baby.* —**feebly** [adv] *I watched him as he tried, very slowly and feebly, to get out of bed.*

fragile /ˈfrædʒaɪl‖-dʒəl/ [adj] someone who is **fragile** is so weak and delicate that they look as if they could easily be hurt: *The baby felt so fragile in his arms.* | *Two ambulance attendants picked up his fragile body and put him carefully onto a stretcher.*

shaky /ˈʃeɪki/ [adj] feeling weak in your legs and only able to walk slowly and unsteadily: *Even after the long months of therapy Owen was still very shaky.* | **be shaky on your feet** *Her grandfather was a little shaky on his feet after the fall.* | **shaky steps** *The baby's taken her first few shaky steps.* —**shakily** [adv] *As I entered the room, he reached for his stick and got shakily to his feet.*

puny /ˈpjuːni/ [adj] especially written a man or boy who is **puny** is small, thin, and looks very weak: *Pete was a puny little boy with short hair and glasses.* | *His wife was such a big strong woman, she made him look puny.*

weedy /ˈwiːdi/ [adj] British informal a man or boy who is **weedy** is thin and looks weak: *Mouse got his nickname because he was small and weedy.*

weakling /ˈwiːklɪŋ/ [n C] someone, especially a boy or young man, who is weak and is not willing to fight or defend himself: *Most of the kids were weaklings and were frightened of getting in a fight.*

weed /wiːd/ [n C] British informal someone, especially a boy or young man, who is thin and weak – sometimes used humorously: *Everyone called me a weed when I was at school because I was so bad at sports.*

2 not powerful

- weak

weak /wiːk/ [adj] a **weak** leader, manager, or government does not have clear ideas about what should be done, and is too easily influenced by other people. A **weak** country does not have the power to defend itself: *He came across as a weak and indecisive leader.* | *Weak management led to failure of the business.* | *In 1949-50 China was a weak, vulnerable country, devastated by war.* —**weakness** [n U] *The President has often been accused of weakness.*

3 easy to attack or harm

- vulnerable
- defenceless

vulnerable /ˈvʌlnərəbəl/ [adj] someone who is **vulnerable** can easily be harmed or attacked: *a small vulnerable child in need of protection* | *Wild animals are at their most vulnerable when they are asleep.* | **+ to** *The virus leaves sufferers vulnerable to a range of infections.*

defenceless British **/defenseless** American /dɪˈfensləs/ [adj] not strong enough or not able to protect yourself against an attack: *No one is doing anything to help these poor defenceless children.* | *While the mother bird searches for food she has to leave her chicks alone and defenseless in the nest.* | **+ against** *He closed the door behind him, leaving her cruelly defenceless against his bitter attack.*

4 to make someone or something weak

- weaken
- sap sb's strength/energy
- debilitating

weaken /ˈwiːkən/ [v T] *Her long illness has weakened her so much that she has difficulty walking.* | *The city's defences had been weakened by enemy shelling.*

sap sb's strength/energy /ˌsæp (sb's) ˈstreŋθ, ˈenəʳdʒi/ [v phrase] if something such as too much work or worry **saps your strength** or **energy**, it gradually takes away your energy and makes you weaker: *They were travelling very slowly, and the heavy load they were carrying sapped their strength.* | *The constant tension was sapping my energy.*

debilitating /dɪˈbɪlɪteɪtɪŋ/ [adj] written a **debilitating** disease or condition makes you physically or mentally weak: *He was still suffering the debilitating effects of flu.* | *The conditions under which doctors work are increasingly unhealthy and debilitating.*

5 to become weak

- weaken
- crumble

weaken /ˈwiːkən/ [v I] if someone's power, strength, or determination **weakens**, it becomes weaker: *By 1945, the country's power was weakening considerably.* | *The soldiers' morale was beginning to weaken.*

crumble /ˈkrʌmbəl/ [v I] if your determination, courage etc **crumbles**, it becomes weak or fails: *Briggs' resolve crumbled and he reached for the whisky bottle.*

6 when a plant becomes weak

▸ wilt ▸ droop

wilt /wɪlt/ [v I] if a plant or flower **wilts**, it becomes weak and loses its colour, freshness etc, especially because of heat or lack of water: *Marigolds are a strong breed, less likely to wilt than other plants.* | *The plant in the corner was wilting, its brilliant yellow petals scattered on the floor.*

droop /druːp/ [v I] if a plant or flower **droops**, it starts to hang down, especially because it is not getting enough water, and begins to die: *These flowers are beginning to droop. You'd better water them.* | *He watered the vines so little that the leaves drooped and the tendrils withered.*

weapon

RELATED WORDS

▸ *see also* **army, shoot, kill, destroy, hurt/injure, explode, attack, defend**

1 a weapon

▸ weapon ▸ weaponry
▸ arms ▸ arsenal
▸ ammunition

weapon /ˈwepən/ [n C] something that you use to fight with, such as a gun, bomb, or knife: *The men were finally persuaded to come out and hand over their weapons to the police.* | **carry a weapon** *The three men had blackened faces and were carrying weapons.* | **murder weapon** (=a weapon used to kill someone) *Police have not yet found the murder weapon.* | **an offensive weapon** (=one that can be used to attack someone) *He was arrested by police and charged with carrying an offensive weapon.* | **nuclear/chemical/conventional weapons** (=atom bombs, poisonous gases, or ordinary weapons) *a treaty to reduce the number of nuclear weapons*

arms /ɑːʳmz/ [n plural] weapons such as guns and bombs that are used for fighting against large numbers of people: *European governments have been supplying arms to the rebels.* | **carry arms** *Only certain members of the police force are allowed to carry arms.* | **lay down your arms** (=stop using arms) *The government has called on the terrorists to lay down their arms.* | **arms control** (=agreements between countries to limit the number of weapons they have) *The two countries have just signed a new agreement on arms control.*

ammunition /ˌæmjəˈnɪʃən/ [n U] bullets and other things that are fired from large or small guns: *The soldiers kept on firing until they had no more ammunition.* | *The terrorist group is believed to have significant quantities of guns, ammunition, and explosives.* | **round of ammunition** (=a single bullet) *We now knew that we were trapped, with only a few rounds of ammunition left.*

weaponry /ˈwepənri/ [n U] weapons used for fighting wars – use this especially when talking about how effective, modern etc they are: *It is a highly-trained army, with very sophisticated modern weaponry.* | **nuclear/conventional weaponry** *Many of the world's poorer countries are now beginning to invest in nuclear weaponry.*

arsenal /ˈɑːʳsənəl/ [n C] all of the weapons and military equipment that a country or fighting force has: *Their arsenal includes both SAM 7 missiles and anti-tank weapons.* | **+ of** *Police have discovered an arsenal of guns and ammunition in a London house.*

2 having weapons

▸ armed

armed /ɑːʳmd/ [adj] someone who is **armed** is carrying a gun or other weapon: *The two men may be armed, and should not be approached by members of the public.* | *Over £60,000 worth of jewellery has been stolen by an armed gang in north London.* | **+ with** *The men were masked and armed with machine guns.* | **heavily armed** (=with lots of weapons) *a group of heavily armed soldiers*

3 having no weapons

▸ unarmed ▸ defenceless

unarmed /ˌʌnˈɑːʳmd◂/ [adj] someone who is **unarmed** is not carrying a gun or other weapon: *It was later discovered that the hijacker was unarmed.* | **unarmed civilians** *The army allegedly shot dead over 300 unarmed civilians.*

defenceless British **/defenseless** American /dɪˈfensləs/ [adj] a person, place, ship etc that is **defenceless** has no weapons and cannot defend itself against an attack: *In the first weeks of the war, dozens of defenceless ships were sunk by submarines.* | *The stick splintered under the blow and Alex was left defenseless.*

4 to get weapons or provide someone with weapons

▸ arm ▸ rearm

arm /ɑːʳm/ [v T] to provide someone with weapons: *The rebels were trained, armed, and financed by foreign governments.* | *The majority of people still do not believe we should arm our police force.* | **arm yourself with sth** *We armed ourselves with whatever we could find – sticks, knives, bricks.*

rearm /riːˈɑːʳm/ [v I] if a country **rearms**, it gets new or better supplies of weapons in order to prepare for fighting a war, especially after a period of peace: *They remain opposed to any suggestion that the country should be allowed to rearm.*

weather

RELATED WORDS

▸ *see also* **hot, cold, wet, dry, environment**

1 weather

▸ weather ▸ climate
▸ it ▸ conditions

weather /ˈweðəʳ/ [n U] use this to talk about whether it is hot or cold outside or whether it is raining, snowing, windy etc: *Weather patterns have been changing as a result of global warming.* | **the weather** *What was the weather like on your vacation?* | *We want to have a picnic on Saturday, but it depends on the weather.* | **hot/warm/wet etc weather** *a period of warm sunny weather* | *I don't like going to work on my bike in wet weather.* |

weather permitting (=if the weather is suitable) *We'll play softball in the park tomorrow, weather permitting.*

it /ɪt/ [pron] spoken use this to talk about what the weather is like: *What's it like in Spain at this time of year? Is it really hot?* | **it's cold/sunny/cloudy etc** *The weather forecast says it's going to be cloudy tomorrow.* | *It was cool and sunny when we left this morning.*

climate /ˈklaɪmɪ̈t/ [n C] the usual weather conditions in a particular country or area: *Queensland has a warm tropical climate.* | *These flowers will not grow in a cold climate.* | **+ of** *The climate of southern Florida attracts thousands of tourists each winter.* | **climate change** (=changes in average temperature, weather conditions etc) *The recent floods are said to be caused by climate change in the northern hemisphere.*

conditions /kənˈdɪʃənz/ [n plural] the weather at a particular time, especially when considering how this will affect an event or activity that has been planned, such as a journey or a race: *Conditions are perfect for today's boat race.* | *If the conditions are really bad we'll have to postpone the trip and stay at home.* | **weather conditions** *We can expect a return to normal weather conditions this weekend.* | **freezing/icy/stormy etc conditions** *Freezing conditions are making the roads extremely hazardous and drivers are warned to take extra care.*

2 connected with the weather

- climatic
- meteorological
- atmospheric

climatic /klaɪˈmætɪk/ [adj only before noun] especially written connected with the weather in a large area over a long period of time: *toxic gases that threaten the earth's climatic balance* | *The types of rice grown in a country depend on climatic conditions.* | *Climatic changes are caused by the increasing levels of carbon dioxide in the atmosphere.*

meteorological /ˌmiːtiərəˈlɒdʒɪkəl‖-ˈlɑː-/ [adj only before noun] connected with the scientific study of the weather: *Meteorological reports are fed into a computer, which helps scientists make accurate predictions about the weather.* | *His meteorological observations resulted in a theory of how tropical storms arise in the Gulf of Mexico.*

atmospheric /ˌætməsˈferɪk◂/ [adj only before noun] connected with the air that surrounds the earth and how it affects the weather: *Snow crystals form when atmospheric conditions turn water vapour into ice.* | *The cylinder swelled and contracted with the changing atmospheric pressure.*

3 information about the weather

- weather forecast
- weather report
- the weather
- the outlook

weather forecast /ˈweðəʳ ˌfɔːʳkɑːst‖-kæst/ [n C] a description of what the weather will probably be like in the near future, for example on the radio, television, or in newspapers: *The weather forecast predicted blizzards for Scotland.* | *'Do you think it's going to rain?' 'Well it said so on the weather forecast'.*

weather report /ˈweðəʳ rɪˌpɔːʳt/ [n C] a description of the weather conditions now and in the near future, especially one on the radio or television: *There are weather reports every hour to keep you up to date with driving conditions in your area.* | *And now over to the London Weather Centre for the latest weather report.*

the weather /ðə ˈweðəʳ/ [n singular] informal a short radio, television, or newspaper report saying what **the weather** is likely to be in the near future: *The news from your area will follow the weather in five minutes time.*

the outlook /ði ˈaʊtlʊk/ [n singular] what the weather will probably be like for the next few days, especially according to information provided by the radio, television, or newspapers: *I'm afraid the outlook isn't very good – they say it's going to rain tomorrow.* | **the outlook for tomorrow/the weekend etc** *The outlook for the weekend is for continued sunny weather.*

4 good weather

- good weather
- beautiful/gorgeous/glorious
- nice
- fine
- dry
- sunny
- sunshine
- in the sun

good weather /gʊd ˈweðəʳ/ [n U] weather that is sunny and warm **get/have good weather** *We go to Greece every Easter, and we usually get good weather.* | *We had good weather apart from one day of heavy rain.* | **a spell/run of good weather** *You must be ready to take advantage of any spell of good weather.* | **in good weather** *Sometimes, in good weather, he walked to work across the fields.*

beautiful/gorgeous/glorious /ˈbjuːtɪ̈fəl, ˈgɔːʳdʒəs, ˈglɔːriəs/ [adj] especially spoken very sunny and warm: *It was a glorious day with blue skies.* | *We had three weeks of absolutely gorgeous weather.* | **it is beautiful/gorgeous/glorious** *What's happened to the weather? It was beautiful last week.*

nice spoken ALSO **lovely** especially British, spoken /naɪs, ˈlʌvli/ [adj] pleasantly warm and sunny: *Morning, Bill. Nice weather, isn't it?* | **it's a nice day/it's a lovely morning etc** *It's a lovely day – why don't we go for a walk?*

fine /faɪn/ [adj] especially British if the weather is **fine**, it is not raining and the sky is clear: *Next week will be fine but a little cooler.* | *a fine spring evening* | *It can take several days of fine weather for the grass to dry out.*

dry /draɪ/ [adj] if the weather is **dry**, it does not rain: *The dry weather will continue for several days* | *Southern areas should stay dry until the early evening.* | **the dry season** (=the time of year when there is little or no rain) *During the dry season, many of the swamps turn to hard-baked mud.*

sunny /ˈsʌni/ [adj] if the weather is **sunny**, the sun is shining: *a lovely sunny afternoon* | *It's going to be sunny all day.* | **sunny spells/intervals** especially British (=short periods of sunny weather) *The weather will remain dry with sunny spells.*

sunshine /ˈsʌnʃaɪn/ [n U] warm bright light from the sun: *We sat on the patio enjoying the autumn sunshine.* | *Northern regions will start dry with some sunshine.*

in the sun /ɪn ðə ˈsʌn/ [adv] where the sun is shining down: *I get a rash every time I go in the sun.* | *Put the plant on a window sill in the sun.* | **lie/laze/bask etc in the sun** *We spent all day lazing around in the sun.*

5 bad weather

- bad weather
- awful/terrible/horrible

bad weather /bæd ˈweðəʳ/ [n U] when it is raining, snowing, or very cold: *The game was cancelled because of bad weather.* | **a spell/run of bad weather** *Once this spell of bad weather is over, we can start work on the garden.* | **in bad weather** *At least 20 people died when the aircraft crashed in bad weather.*

awful/terrible/horrible /ˈɔːfəl, ˈterɨbəl, ˈhɒrɨbəl‖ˈhɔː-/ [adj] especially spoken very unpleasant, cold, wet etc: *Awful weather, isn't it?* | *'What's it like outside?' 'Terrible.'* | **it is awful/terrible/horrible** *It's been absolutely horrible all day.*

6 weather that changes a lot

- unsettled
- changeable

unsettled /ʌnˈsetld/ [adj] if the weather is **unsettled**, it keeps changing and it often rains: *More unsettled weather is forecast for the weekend.* | **continue unsettled** British (=used in weather forecasts) *Tomorrow will continue unsettled, with showers in most areas.*

changeable /ˈtʃeɪndʒəbəl/ [adj] especially British likely to change suddenly: *The British weather is very changeable.* | *The changeable weather that November brings can lead to foggy conditions.*

7 hot weather

- hot
- boiling/scorching
- warm
- mild
- humid

▸ *see also* **sweat**

hot /hɒt‖hɑːt/ [adj] *We had three weeks of very hot weather.* | *It was the hottest summer this century.* | **it is hot** *Isn't it hot today?*

boiling/scorching /ˈbɔɪlɪŋ, ˈskɔːʳtʃɪŋ/ [adj] especially spoken extremely hot **it is boiling/scorching** *It's boiling out here! Let's go inside and get a cool drink.* | **boiling hot/scorching hot** *It was a boiling hot day, and the kids were out playing in the pool.*

warm /wɔːʳm/ [adj] pleasantly hot, but not too hot: *I'm looking forward to some warmer weather.* | **nice and warm** *It was nice and warm in the sunshine.*

mild /maɪld/ [adj] **mild** winter weather is pleasant because it is not as cold as it usually is: *It seems quite mild for February.* | *Some plants will survive outside during a mild winter.*

humid /ˈhjuːmɨd/ [adj] if the weather is **humid**, the air is hot and wet in a way that makes you feel uncomfortable: *Tokyo is very humid in summer.* | *It was a hot, humid day, and the only sound was the buzzing of insects.*

8 cold weather

- cold
- cool
- chilly
- freezing

cold /kəʊld/ [adj] *I'd hate to live somewhere where it's always cold.* | *The car is difficult to start, especially on cold winter mornings.* | *It's so cold. I wish I was back home in Morocco.* —**the cold** [n singular] cold weather outside: *Come in out of the cold.*

cool /kuːl/ [adj] pleasantly cold, especially compared to the heat of the sun: *It gets much cooler in the evenings.* | *We stopped at a cool, grassy area, under the shade of the trees.* —**the cool of** [n phrase] *He liked to take a stroll in the cool of the evening.*

chilly /ˈtʃɪli/ [adj] a little cold, in a way that makes you feel uncomfortable: *It was getting chilly outside, so we went back into the house.* | *Despite the chilly autumn afternoon, she was wearing a thin cotton dress.*

freezing /ˈfriːzɪŋ/ [adj] especially spoken extremely cold: *Supporters queued for tickets all night in freezing conditions.* | **it is freezing** *Can't we go inside? It's freezing out here.* | **freezing cold** *a freezing cold day in January*

9 rain

- rain
- rain
- it's raining
- it's pouring
- it's drizzling
- it's sprinkling
- wet/rainy
- shower
- the wet
- the rainy season/the Monsoon

▸ *see also* **wet**

rain /reɪn/ [n U] water that falls from the sky in small drops **the rain** *The rain was beating against the window.* | **in the rain** *I like walking in the rain* | **heavy/torrential rain** (=a lot of rain) *The roads are flooded after a period of exceptionally heavy rain.* | *The coast has been battered by torrential rain all week.* | **light rain** (=a little rain) *Some light rain is likely in the Boston area.* | **rain falls** (=comes down from the sky) *Four inches of rain have fallen in four days.* | **acid rain** (=rain that contains harmful chemicals from industry) *When acid rain falls, it affects the pH balance of the soil.*

rain /reɪn/ [v I] if it **rains**, water falls from the sky in the form of small drops **it rains** *It rained all night, and half the day after.* | *Take an umbrella in case it rains.*

it's raining /ɪts ˈreɪnɪŋ/ spoken use this to say that rain is falling now: *Look, it's raining again.* | *Is it still raining?* | **it's raining hard/heavily** (=raining a lot) *It had been raining heavily and the ground was very soft.*

it's pouring /ɪts ˈpɔːrɪŋ/ spoken use this to say that it is raining very hard: *As soon as I got outside it started pouring.* | **it's pouring with rain** British *It was pouring with rain and she had forgotten her umbrella.*

it's drizzling /ɪts ˈdrɪzlɪŋ/ spoken use this to say that it is raining a little, with very small drops of rain: *I think I'll walk to work – it's only drizzling.*

it's sprinkling /ɪts ˈsprɪŋklɪŋ/ American spoken use this to say that it is raining a little, usually when it will not last long: *'Is it raining out?' 'It's just sprinkling.'* —**sprinkle** [n C] a short light rain: *There were a few sprinkles this afternoon, but the sun was shining through it all.*

wet/rainy /wet, ˈreɪni/ [adj] if the weather is **wet** or **rainy**, it rains a lot: *It's been wet all week.* | *You should bring a waterproof jacket and strong boots in case of wet weather.* | *a rainy weekend in November*

shower /ˈʃaʊəʳ/ [n C] a short period of rain, especially light rain: *It was just a shower, so we didn't get too wet* | **heavy showers** (=when a lot of rain falls for short periods) *Heavy showers are forecast for the weekend.* | **light showers** (=when a small amount of rain falls during short periods) *The weather will be cloudy with light showers in places.*

the wet /ðə 'wet/ [n phrase] spoken wet weather outdoors: *Come on in out of the wet.*

the rainy season/the Monsoon /ðə 'reɪni ˌsiːzən, ðə mɒn'suːn‖-mɑːn-/ [n singular] a time of the year when it rains a lot in hot countries: *The seeds must be planted in time for the rainy season.* | *At this time of year, before the Monsoon, the river is at its lowest.* | **monsoon rains** *During the monsoon rains, torrents of water spill down the mountains.*

10 snow and ice

- snow
- snow
- it's snowing
- hail/hail stones
- sleet
- frost
- icy

snow /snəʊ/ [n U] soft white pieces of frozen water that fall from the sky in cold weather: *The tops of the mountains were still covered in snow.* | *Tony and I trudged home through the deep snow.* | *When climbing in snow and ice, it is essential to use the correct gear.* | **snow falls** *Some snow is expected to fall in the Rockies tonight.* | **snow storm** *She disappeared without trace in a heavy snow storm.* | **virgin snow** (=snow on the ground that looks clean and white because no-one has stepped on it, driven on it etc) *There was a single line of footprints in the virgin snow.*

snow /snəʊ/ [v I] if **it snows**, soft white pieces of frozen water fall from the sky when the weather is cold **it snows** *It snowed continually for three weeks.*

it's snowing /ɪts 'snəʊɪŋ/ spoken use this to say that it is snowing now: *It was snowing when he left the house.*

hail/hail stones /heɪl, 'heɪl stəʊnz/ [n U] frozen raindrops that fall as small balls of ice: *There were frequent showers of rain and hail.* | *Even in England, half-inch diameter hail stones are not unusual.*

sleet /sliːt/ [n U] a mixture of snow and rain: *We couldn't see anything because of the sleet and snow.*

frost /frɒst‖frɔːst/ [n U] ice that looks white and powdery and covers things when the temperature is very cold: *The grass and trees were white with frost.* | *Frost covered all the windows.*

icy /'aɪsi/ [adj] covered in ice and very slippery: *Be careful – the roads are icy this morning.* | *Despite the icy ground, he was urging his horse on faster and faster.*

11 cloudy

- cloudy
- dull
- grey
- overcast
- cloud
- fog
- mist

cloudy /'klaʊdi/ [adj] if the weather is **cloudy**, there are a lot of clouds in the sky: *You can still get sunburnt on a cloudy day.*

dull /dʌl/ [adj] if the weather is **dull**, it is cloudy and there is no sunshine: *It will be dry but dull this morning, with the possibility of showers later in the day.*

grey ALSO **gray** American /greɪ/ [adj] especially written cloudy and not at all bright: *It was a grey winter morning.*

overcast /ˌəʊvəʳ'kɑːst◂‖-'kæst◂/ [adj] if the sky is **overcast**, it is very cloudy and dark, and there will probably be rain: *The sky was overcast, and a light rain began to fall.*

cloud /klaʊd/ [n C/U] a white or grey mass in the sky that rain falls from: *There wasn't a single cloud in the sky.* | **thick/dense cloud** *Dense cloud prevented the rescue helicopter from taking off.*

fog /fɒg‖fɑːg, fɔːg/ [n U] thick cloudy air near the ground that is very difficult to see through **the fog** *I could just make out a dim figure coming towards me in the fog.* | **patch of fog** *Watch out for patches of fog in low-lying areas.* | **thick/dense fog** *Dense fog is making driving conditions difficult on many roads.* | **the fog lifts/clears** (=it goes away) *The fog has almost cleared – our plane will be able to take off soon* — **foggy** [adj] *a foggy November evening*

mist /mɪst/ [n singular/U] wet light cloud near the ground, which is difficult to see through clearly: *A light mist lay in the valley.* | *The mist along the river banks had gone by mid-morning.* | **shrouded/veiled in mist** (=be covered in mist) *From Primrose Hill, London looked like a ruined city shrouded in mist.* — **misty** [adj] *It may be misty in the east in the morning.*

12 windy

- windy
- wind
- breeze
- gale

windy /'wɪndi/ [adj] if the weather is **windy**, there is a lot of wind: *It was a bright windy day in October.* | *The windy conditions made it difficult to put the tent up.*

wind /wɪnd/ [n C/U] a moving current of air near the ground: *We walked home through the wind and the rain.* | **the wind blows** *A bitter wind was blowing from the East* | **in the wind** *The flags fluttered gently in the wind.* | **strong/high wind** *Strong winds caused damage to many buildings.* | **gust of wind** (=when the wind suddenly blows strongly) *A sudden gust of wind blew the paper out of his hand.*

breeze /briːz/ [n C] a gentle pleasant wind: *A cool breeze blew in off the sea.* | **slight/gentle breeze** *A gentle breeze ruffled her hair.* | **in the breeze** *Her black hair was blowing in the breeze as she waved goodbye to me.*

gale /geɪl/ [n C] a very strong wind: *The fence was blown down in the gale last night.* | **a howling gale** (=a very strong gale) *A howling gale and torrential rain lashed the windows.*

13 storm

- storm
- thunderstorm
- thunder
- lightning
- blizzard
- hurricane/typhoon
- tornado

storm /stɔːʳm/ [n C] a period of very bad weather, when there is a lot of rain, wind, and sometimes thunder and lightning: *The Spanish ships were wrecked in the storm.* | **a severe storm** *There had not been such severe storms in southern England for hundreds of years.* | **storm cloud** *The storm clouds were gathering over the sea.* —**stormy** [adj] *stormy weather* | *The sky was starting to look stormy.*

thunderstorm /'θʌndəʳstɔːʳm/ [n C] a storm where there is a lot of thunder and lightning: *There was a spectacular thunderstorm that night.*

thunder /'θʌndəʳ/ [n U] the loud crashing noise that you hear in a storm **thunder rumbles/crashes** *They could hear thunder rumbling in the distance.* | **clap of thunder/thunder clap** (=one sudden noise of thunder) *There was a thunder clap followed instantly by lightning.* | **thunder and lightning** *The* *thunder and lightning seemed to have moved away, but the rain continued to pour.*

lightning /ˈlaɪtnɪŋ/ [n U] a bright flash of light in the sky during a storm **flash of lightning** *A flash of lightning lit up the whole sky.* | **thunder and lightning** *There was a great summer storm, with thunder and lightning and heavy rain.*

blizzard /ˈblɪzəʳd/ [n C] a storm with a lot of snow and strong winds: *Eliot had to drive home in the blizzard.*

hurricane/typhoon /ˈhʌrɪ̥kən‖ˈhɜːrɪ̥keɪn, ˌtaɪˈfuːn◂/ [n C] a severe storm with very strong winds that causes a lot of damage. **Hurricanes** happen in the western Atlantic Ocean. **Typhoons** happen in the western Pacific Ocean.: *The hurricane devastated Florida and killed at least 40 people.* | *The typhoon brought 30 foot waves crashing down on to the sea walls.*

tornado /tɔːʳˈneɪdəʊ/ [n C] a small but very powerful twisting mass of air that causes a lot of damage. **Tornadoes** are most common in the central area of the US: *A tornado destroyed twelve homes in Ashport, Tennessee yesterday.*

14 happening or used in any kind of weather

- rain or shine
- in all weathers
- all-weather

rain or shine /ˌreɪn ɔːʳ ˈʃaɪn/ [adv] if something happens **rain or shine**, it always happens or it will definitely happen whether the weather is good or bad: *My husband plays golf every weekend, rain or shine.* | **come rain or shine** *Organizers say the concert in Central Park will go ahead come rain or shine.*

in all weathers /ɪn ˌɔːl ˈweðəʳz/ [adv] British if someone does something **in all weathers**, they do it in all kinds of weather, even when the weather is very unpleasant: *There are homeless people sleeping on the streets of London in all weathers.* | *She loves gardening – she's out in her garden in all weathers.*

all-weather /ˈɔːl weðəʳ/ [adj only before noun] use this about a sports ground or sports equipment which can be used in any weather conditions: *The team now have their own all-weather stadium, and matches are rarely cancelled.* | *an all-weather jacket*

weigh

RELATED WORDS

▸ *see also* **heavy, light/not heavy, measure**

1 ways of saying how heavy something or someone is

- weigh
- weight
- be 5 kilos/10 pounds etc
- how heavy
- weigh in at

weigh /weɪ/ [v not in progressive] *How much do you weigh, Diane?* | *At all ages, men weigh more than women.* | **weigh 20 lbs/2 tonnes/3.5 kilos etc** *I weigh eight stone now, exactly.* | *I've never seen anything like it – some of those cabbages must have weighed 8 pounds at least.* | **weigh a ton** informal (=be very heavy) *It'll take two of us to get it out of the car, it weighs a ton!*

weight /weɪt/ [n U] the amount that someone or something weighs: *Your weight is about right for someone of your height.* | *Top quality hams range in weight from eight to eighteen pounds.* | **+ of** *The cost of postage depends on the weight of the package* | **12 tonnes/3 kilos/2 pounds etc in weight** *The average sperm whale is 72 feet long and about 90 tons in weight.* | **gain/put on weight** (=become heavier than you were before) *It's true, people who stop smoking do tend to gain weight.* | *I think he looks better now that he's put on some weight.* | **lose weight** (=become less heavy than you were before) *I've been trying to lose weight for over a year now.* | **weight loss** (=when someone begins to weigh less than they did before) *Sudden or unexplained weight loss may be an early indication of health problems.* | **birth weight** (=what a baby weighs when it is born – used in technical contexts) *Twins and triplets are expected to have lower birth weights than single infants.*

be 5 kilos/10 pounds etc /biː ˌfaɪv ˈkiːləʊz/ [v phrase] to weigh 5 kilos, 10 pounds etc: *Sandra's baby was only 4lb 7oz when it was born.* | *If the parcel is over 2 kilos, you have to pay 50p more.*

how heavy /ˌhaʊ ˈhevi/ [adj phrase] use this to ask or say how much something weighs, especially something that is very heavy: *How heavy is the average small car?* | *I didn't realise how heavy each brick was until I tried to pick one up.* | *You'd be surprised how heavy these sacks are.*

weigh in at /ˌweɪ ˈɪn æt/ [v] if a sports person **weighs in at** a particular weight, that is what they weigh just before a sports event **weigh in at 250 pounds/80 kilos etc** *The champion weighed in at 225 pounds before his last fight.*

2 to measure how much something or someone weighs

- weigh

weigh /weɪ/ [v T] to measure the weight of a person or thing: *You have to weigh the sugar exactly when you make wine.* | *a special machine that weighs each truck and its cargo* | **weigh yourself/himself etc** *Have you weighed yourself lately?*

well-dressed

RELATED WORDS

▸ *see also* **fashionable, style/elegance, clothes**

1 wearing good clothes and looking tidy

- well-dressed
- smart
- neat
- presentable
- well-groomed
- sharp
- dapper
- well turned out
- snazzy

well-dressed /ˌwel ˈdrest◂/ [adj] wearing good or expensive clothes: *The photograph showed a well-dressed man in his early 50s.* | *The young woman with the children looked too well-dressed to be a nanny.* | *He walked into the party with a beautiful well-dressed blonde on his arm.*

smart /smɑːʳt/ [adj] British if you look **smart** or your clothes are **smart**, you are dressed in an attractive way and you look very tidy: *The editor was slim, smart and dark-haired.* | *You look really smart today, Chris. Have you got a job interview?* | *The waitresses were the smartest ones I'd ever seen.* | *That's a smart suit, Sam.* —**smartly** [adv] *The children stood in neat rows, smartly dressed in school uniform.*

neat /niːt/ [adj] If you look **neat** or if you have **neat** clothes, the clothes you are wearing are clean, ironed, and fit you properly: *She had been waiting there all night, but she still looked neat.* | *A man in a neat gray suit sat on the other side of the bar.* | **neat and clean** *They didn't have much money, but the children were always neat and clean.* —**neatly** [adv] *He was polite and neatly dressed.*

presentable /prɪˈzentəbəl/ [adj] well-dressed enough for meeting people, socially or in your job: *We don't have to wear suits for work, but we do have to look presentable.* | *Arnold was a very presentable young fellow.*

well-groomed /ˌwel ˈgruːmd◂/ [adj] someone who is **well-groomed** has clean, neat hair, wears good clothes, and looks as if they have spent a lot of time and money on their appearance: *She's marrying a well-groomed successful businessman named Paul.* | *Ambassadors' wives are expected to look fashionable and well-groomed.*

sharp /ʃɑːʳp/ [adj] dressed in a way that shows you have good judgement about what clothes look good on you and what other people will admire: *Hey, you look sharp. Where'd you get the suit?* | **sharp dresser** *Paula's a very sharp dresser, so I always have her go shopping with me.*

dapper /ˈdæpəʳ/ [adj] a man, especially a small man, who is **dapper** wears neat, tidy clothes and is generally very smart in appearance: *The Captain was a dapper little man with a neat moustache and shiny shoes.* | *Graham walked into the restaurant, looking dapper in a grey business suit.*

well turned out /ˌwel tɜːʳnd ˈaʊt◂/ [adj phrase] someone who is **well turned out** has taken care that their clothes and general appearance are clean and neat, for example for a special occasion: *Nico looked trim and well turned out in a new dark suit.* | *The principal expected everyone to be well turned out on graduation day.*

snazzy /ˈsnæzi/ [adj] informal clothes that are **snazzy** are bright, colourful, and attractive: *I love those snazzy little silk dresses.* | *There were racks and racks of snazzy swimming trunks.* | *Dale spun around the dance floor in a snazzy blue suit.*

2 to make yourself look well-dressed and tidy

- smarten yourself up
- spruce (yourself) up/get spruced up
- make yourself presentable

smarten yourself up /ˌsmɑːʳtn jɔːʳself ˈʌp/ [v phrase] British if you **smarten yourself up**, you make yourself look smart by changing your clothes, arranging your hair etc: *She's smartening herself up in the ladies' room.* | *Jeremy, go smarten yourself up before dinner.* | **smarten up** *Smarten up! It's time for inspection.*

spruce (yourself) up/get spruced up /ˌspruːs (jɔːʳself) ˈʌp, get ˌspruːst ˈʌp/ [v phrase] to wash, tidy your hair, put on good clothes etc before doing something or going somewhere: *On Saturdays we got spruced up and headed off into town.* | *He spent a few minutes sprucing up in front of the mirror and he was ready to go.* | *I think I'll go and spruce myself up before dinner.*

make yourself presentable /ˌmeɪk jɔːʳself prɪˈzentəbəl/ [v phrase] to wash, put on nice enough clothes, and tidy your hair so that you can meet people: *Give me a few more minutes to make myself presentable and I'll be with you.*

wet

RELATED WORDS

opposite: —— **dry**

▸ *see also* **water, liquid, weather**

1 wet

- wet
- soaked
- soaking/sopping/dripping wet
- be soaking
- drenched
- soggy
- sodden
- saturated
- waterlogged
- awash

wet /wet/ [adj] if something is **wet**, it has a lot of liquid on it or in it; if someone is **wet**, their clothes, skin, and hair are wet: *I can't come out yet – my hair's still wet.* | *You'd better change out of those wet clothes.* | *Let's not sit here – the grass is wet.* | *Freshly wet roads are dangerous because oil and dust mix with the water to make them slippery.* | **get wet** *Hurry up with the umbrella – I'm getting wet!* | **all wet** informal *When he got out of the boat, the sleeves of his sweater were all wet.* | **wet paint/ink** (=that has not yet dried) *All the benches had been painted and had 'wet paint' signs on them.*

soaked /səʊkt/ [adj not before noun] very wet all the way through: *Your clothes are soaked. Leave them in front of the fire to dry.* | *Don't leave the cushions in the garden. They'll get soaked if it rains.* | **+ with** *Panting and soaked with sweat, Ron came running into the house.* | **soaked to the skin** *When the men came in from the storm, they were soaked to the skin.* | **soaked through** (=extremely wet) *After a morning walk through the meadow, my shoes were completely soaked through.*

soaking/sopping/dripping wet ALSO **wringing wet** British /ˌsəʊkɪŋ, ˌsɒpɪŋ, ˌdrɪpɪŋ ˈwet‖-ˌsɑːp-, ˌrɪŋɪŋ ˈwet/ [adj not usually before noun] someone or something that is **soaking wet** etc is so wet that drops of water fall from them: *We were soaking wet by the time we got out of the rain.* | *There's no way I can wear this shirt tonight – it's still sopping wet.* | *Can I call you back in five minutes? I just got out of the shower and I'm dripping wet.*

be soaking /biː ˈsəʊkɪŋ/ [v phrase] someone who is **soaking** is very wet, so that drops of water fall from their clothes or hair: *You're soaking. Take those wet clothes off before you catch a cold.* | *Someone had pushed Sally into the swimming pool, and she was soaking.*

drenched /drentʃt/ [adj not before noun] if a person or area is **drenched**, it is completely wet, because a lot of rain or water has poured onto them: *Everyone got completely drenched when a huge wave hit the boat.* | *The two and a half hour walk in the wind and rain left us drenched.*

soggy /ˈsɒgi‖ˈsɑːgi/ [adj] something that is **soggy** is softer than usual and looks or feels unpleasant, because it has become wet: *Breakfast was terrible – the eggs were burnt and the toast was soggy.* | *A soggy pile of old leaves lay in the corner of the yard.*

sodden /ˈsɒdn‖ˈsɑːdn/ [adj] especially British something that is **sodden** is very wet and heavy, and is usually spoiled because there is so much water in it: *His shoes were sodden and covered with mud.* | *Mary tried to read the writing in her sodden address book, but it was impossible.*

saturated /ˈsætʃəreɪtəd/ [adj not before noun] something that is **saturated** is so wet that it cannot hold any more water or liquid: *When the summer rains begin, the soil quickly becomes saturated.* | **+ with** *The bandage around his knee was already saturated with blood.*

waterlogged /ˈwɔːtərlɒgd‖-lɔːgd, -lɑːgd/ [adj] ground that is **waterlogged** has water on its surface, because it is so wet it cannot hold any more water: *The game was cancelled because the field was waterlogged.* | *You can plant the seeds anytime, as long as the soil is not frozen or waterlogged.*

awash /əˈwɒʃ‖əˈwɔːʃ, əˈwɑːʃ/ [adj not before noun] written if a floor or area is **awash**, it is covered with a lot of water: *The ship leaned further to starboard and soon the decks were awash.* | **+ with/in** *The toilet leaks, leaving the bathroom floor awash in slimy water.*

2 slightly wet

- damp
- moist
- clammy

damp /dæmp/ [adj] slightly wet, especially in an unpleasant way: *Don't put that shirt on. It's still damp.* | *Clean the counter with a damp cloth.* | *Be careful you don't slip – the grass is damp.* | *There was a damp spot on the ceiling.*

moist /mɔɪst/ [adj] something that is **moist** is slightly wet, and this is the way it should be: *The mixture should be slightly moist, but not sticky.* | *Water the plants regularly to keep the soil moist.* | *The sandwiches are made with moist slices of chicken breast, topped with various ingredients.*

clammy /ˈklæmi/ [adj] something that is **clammy**, especially someone's skin, is slightly wet and feels unpleasantly cold and sticky: *As soon as the interview began, I felt my hands go clammy.* | *We were left waiting in our clammy clothes for over an hour.* | **+ with** *His whole body was clammy with sweat as a result of the malaria.*

3 when the air feels wet

- humid
- damp
- muggy
- sticky
- dank

humid /ˈhjuːməd/ [adj] **humid** air or weather is hot and wet in a way that makes you feel uncomfortable: *Summers in Tokyo are hot and humid.* | *Her clothes were sticking to her, but the humid air didn't seem to bother Ralph.* | *The entire island is covered by thick humid jungle.* —**humidity** /hjuːˈmɪdəti/ [n U] *The humidity makes it feel even hotter here.*

damp /dæmp/ [adj] **damp** air or weather is slightly wet in an unpleasant way, and makes you feel cold: *It's cold and damp outside – make sure you wear a warm coat.* | *At first I hated the damp weather in Britain.* —**damp/dampness** [n U] *The constant cold and damp made Tony feel even worse.*

muggy /ˈmʌgi/ [adj] **muggy** weather is very warm and wet, and there is no wind, so that you feel very uncomfortable: *When it's hot and muggy, no one feels like working.* | *It was a warm muggy afternoon, and it looked like it would rain.*

sticky /ˈstɪki/ [adj] very hot and wet, making you feel uncomfortable and dirty: *We left Rome on a hot sticky day in August.* | *Something about the sticky humid weather made people feel a little angry.*

dank /dæŋk/ [adj] air that is **dank**, especially the air in an enclosed room or space, is unpleasantly wet and cold and smells bad: *The air in the room was heavy and dank, and I couldn't sleep.* | *I'm not surprised he's miserable, living in that dank old house.* | *The bag had been sitting in a dank tent for three days and smelled like an old laundry hamper.*

4 to make someone or something wet

- get sth wet
- wet
- soak
- splash
- drench
- flood
- swamp
- saturate

get sth wet /ˌget (sth) ˈwet/ [v phrase] especially spoken to make something wet, especially by not taking enough care to keep it dry: *Don't splash me – I don't want to get my hair wet.* | *How did you manage to get the bathroom floor so wet?* | *She can't wash the dishes without getting the front of her clothes all wet.*

wet /wet/ [v T] to deliberately put water or other liquid onto something: *The other hairdresser usually wets my hair before she cuts it.* | *She wet her index finger and cleaned the spot off the mirror.* | *Wetting the toothbrush before you put the toothpaste on makes the bristles softer.*

soak /səʊk/ [v T] if you **soak** something, you leave it in water for a long time in order to make it clean, soft etc. If water or another liquid **soaks** something, it makes it very wet: *Soak the beans overnight before cooking.* | *The rain had come in through the bottom of our tent and completely soaked our clothes.* | **soak sth in sth** *Soak a piece of cotton in water and use it to clean the wound.*

splash /splæʃ/ [v T] to make someone or something wet by making a lot of small drops of water fall onto them, either deliberately or accidentally: *The kids were playing around in the pool, splashing each other.* | **+ on/over** *He knocked over her cup and splashed coffee all over her new dress.* | **splash sb/sth with sth** *A motorcycle sped past, splashing all the spectators with mud.*

drench /drentʃ/ [v T] to make someone or something extremely wet with a large amount of water: *He turned the hose on us and drenched us all.* | *Blood was pouring from the cut, drenching his shirt.*

flood /flʌd/ [v T] to cover an area of land with a large amount of water: *Farmers flood the fields in order to grow rice.* | *In the rainy season the river can rise rapidly to flood the valley in a few hours.* —**flooded** [adj] *We waded up the flooded garden path to the house.*

swamp /swɒmp‖swɑːmp, swɔːmp/ [v T] to suddenly cover something completely with a large amount of water, especially in a way that causes damage: *Water the young plants well, but don't swamp them.* | *The dam burst, swamping the valley and hundreds of homes.* | *About 3000 years ago a tidal wave swamped the coastal lowlands of Greece, causing massive destruction.*

saturate /ˈsætʃəreɪt/ [v T] to completely cover or fill something with liquid, so that it is wet all the way through: *Heavy rains had saturated the ground, turning the streets into rivers.* | *Saturate the label with vinegar and let it sit before you try to scrape it off the bottle.*

5 to make something slightly wet

▸ dampen ▸ moisten

dampen /'dæmpən/ [v T] to make something slightly wet by putting a little water on it: *Dampen the soil a little before you put the seeds in.* | *She dampened a cloth and held it to his forehead.* | *If you dampen your piece of paper before you start painting it will be easier to paint evenly.*

moisten /'mɔɪsən/ [v T] to make something slightly wet by putting a small amount of water or another liquid on it, especially to stop it from getting too dry: *Add just enough water to moisten the cake mixture without making it too watery.* | *Tom paused and moistened his lips.* | *When the clay becomes dry, moisten it lightly before you continue to shape it.*

when

RELATED WORDS

▸ *see also* **time, during**

1 at or immediately after the time when something happens

▸ when

when /wen/ [conjunction] *When I give the signal, turn on the engine.* | *When I told her what had happened she was really shocked.* | *We'd only just finished cleaning the house when our guests arrived.* | *You can change when you get back.* | *I quit school when I was 15.* | *When completed, the road will link four major cities.*

2 when one thing always happens when another thing happens

▸ when ▸ every time
▸ whenever

when /wen/ [conjunction] *Her nose crinkles up when she laughs.* | *When the demand for a product is high, its price tends to rise.* | *I can't understand you when you mumble.* | *You know what she's like when she's on the phone.*

whenever /wen'evəʳ/ [conjunction] use this when you want to emphasize that something always happens when another thing happens: *Whenever we come here, we see somebody we know.* | *You should come and talk to me whenever you have a problem.* | **whenever you can** *I try to rest whenever I can.* | *He still visited her whenever he could.* | **whenever possible** *She still visits her old schoolfriends whenever possible.*

every time /ˌevri 'taɪm/ [conjunction] use this when you want to emphasize that something always happens when another thing happens: *Every time she sees me she says looks away.* | *Every time it rains we get a flood in the bedroom.* | *Don't ask me for money every time you want to buy a drink.*

3 when one thing happens during the time that something else is happening

▸ when ▸ while

when /wen/ [conjunction] *I hurt my shoulder when I was playing football.* | *All this happened when we were living abroad.* | *When she was at college she wrote for a student newspaper.* | *Why were you downstairs when everyone else was in bed?*

while ALSO **whilst** British formal /waɪl, waɪlst/ [conjunction] during the time that something is happening – use this to emphasize that something is continuing: *My car was stolen while I was on holiday.* | *While she was out of the room, he took a quick look at the papers on her desk.* | *While Sandy was filling out the forms, I called Jimmy from the airport.* | *Patients often comment upon lack of sleep whilst in hospital.* | *They keep the animals under sedation whilst they're being transported.* | **while/whilst doing sth** *They were killed while attempting to reach the summit.*

4 ways of asking or mentioning when something happened or will happen

▸ when ▸ at what point
▸ what time

when /wen/ [adv/conjunction] *When are you leaving for Norway?* | *When did you last have something to eat?* | *Do you know when the concert will be held?* | *I can't remember when I bought this.*

what time /ˌwɒt 'taɪm/ [adv/conjunction] exactly when: *What time is dinner?* | *What time did you get in last night?* | *What time do you usually get home from work?* | *I don't know what time she's coming home.*

at what point /ət ˌwɒt 'pɔɪnt/ [adv/conjunction] at what particular time during a process, situation, or activity: *At what point did you try to stop the fight?* | *At what point did you realize that your book would never be published?* | *I'm not sure at what point he began to suspect the truth.*

wide

RELATED WORDS

opposite: —— **narrow**

▸ when people or things are spread over a wide area *see* **spread (4-5)**

▸ *see also* **fat, thick, long, thin**

1 a long distance from one side to another

▸ wide ▸ broad

wide /waɪd/ [adj] if a road, river, space, object etc is **wide**, there is a large distance between one side of it and the other: *The girl led me down a wide corridor into a large office.* | *The doorway wasn't quite wide enough to get the piano through.* | *a wide leather belt*

broad /brɔːd/ [adj] written wide – use this especially to describe roads, paths, or parts of someone's body: *We drove down the broad tree-lined avenue.* | *He was six feet tall with broad shoulders and strong arms.*

2 how wide something is

▸ how wide ▸ 2 miles across/20 metres across etc
▸ 2 miles wide/20 metres wide etc ▸ width

how wide /haʊ 'waɪd/ [adj phrase] use this to ask or talk about **how wide** something is: *How wide is the main hall?* | *I'm not sure how wide the window is.*

2 miles wide/20 metres wide etc /ˌtuː maɪlz ˈwaɪd/ [adj phrase] use this to say exactly how wide something is: *The river is over a mile wide here.* | *Cut a strip of paper 3cm wide.*

2 miles across/20 metres across etc /ˌtuː maɪlz əˈkrɒs‖-əˈkrɔːs/ [adj phrase] use this to say exactly how wide something is: *a narrow opening only a few metres across*

width /wɪdθ/ [n C/U] how wide something is: *Carpets are available in several different widths.* | **+ of** *The huge vehicle took up the whole width of the road.* | *Can you just measure the width of the door?*

3 to become wider

- become/get wider
- widen

become/get wider /bɪˌkʌm, ˌget ˈwaɪdəʳ/ [v phrase] *The river starts to get wider at Lyon.* | *The gap between the boat and the pier was getting wider and wider.* | *The path gradually became wider as we came down off the mountain.*

widen /ˈwaɪdn/ [v I] to become wider – use this especially in written descriptions of places: *The road widened again when we came out of the tunnel.* | *From Horton, the valley widens, becoming broader and more expansive.*

4 to make something wider

- make sth wider
- widen

make sth wider /ˌmeɪk (sth) ˈwaɪdəʳ/ [v phrase] *I think we'll have to make the door a bit wider so that wheelchairs can get through.* | *Why don't you make the table wider?*

widen /ˈwaɪdn/ [v T] to make something such as a road wider, especially in a deliberately planned way: *A lot of local residents are against council plans to widen the road.* | *Later the tunnel was widened to accommodate larger vehicles.*

willing

RELATED WORDS

opposite: **force sb to do sth**

- *see also* **want/not want, can/can't**

1 to be willing to do something

- be willing to do sth
- be ready to do sth
- not mind doing sth
- be glad/happy/pleased to do sth
- agree to do sth
- be prepared to do sth
- willing
- be game

be willing to do sth /biː ˌwɪlɪŋ tə ˈduː (sth)/ [v phrase] if you **are willing to** do something that is necessary or that you have been asked to do, you will do it fairly happily: *He's willing to tell the police everything he knows.* | *To do well as a journalist, you have to be willing to change jobs very frequently.* | *Investors are willing to pay more for stocks when interest rates are low.*

be ready to do sth /biː ˌredi tə ˈduː (sth)/ [v phrase] to be willing to do something at any time, whenever it needs to be done: *I'm always ready to help if you need me.* | *We are ready to consider any serious proposals.* | *If you really want to sell, price your house sensibly and be ready to make a deal.*

not mind doing sth /nɒt ˌmaɪnd ˈduːɪŋ (sth)/ [v phrase not in progressive] spoken to be willing to do something that someone wants you to do, even though you might prefer not to: *I don't mind driving if you're tired.* | *If you don't mind waiting a few minutes, we can check our records for you.*

be glad/happy/pleased to do sth /biː ˌglæd, ˌhæpi, ˌpliːzd tə ˈduː (sth)/ [v phrase] to be very willing to do something that will help someone else: *Our sales staff are always pleased to help.* | *'Could you do me a favor?' 'Sure, I'd be glad to.'* | *John says he'd be happy to give you a hand with the gardening.* | **be only too glad/happy/pleased to do sth** (=be very willing) *I'd be only too pleased to look after the kids for you.*

agree to do sth /əˌgriː tə ˈduː (sth)/ [v phrase] to say that you are willing to do something that someone has asked you to do, especially when this will take some effort or be inconvenient: *I've agreed to help Sarah move house this weekend.* | *One of the jurors agreed to talk about the experience, but did not want to be named.* | **kindly agree to do sth** formal *Officer Browning has kindly agreed to come into school and give us a talk on crime prevention.*

be prepared to do sth /biː prɪˌpeəʳd tə ˈduː (sth)/ [v phrase] to be willing to do something, especially something difficult or unpleasant: *He was prepared to use force if necessary.* | *You'll never learn to speak another language unless you're prepared to make an effort.* | *Griffiths was prepared to spend up to $500,000 to renovate the old theater.*

willing /ˈwɪlɪŋ/ [adj] eager, hard-working, and **willing** to do anything you are asked to do: *He's not a very bright boy, but he's young, strong, and willing.* | *She's an enthusiastic, willing learner.*

be game /biː ˈgeɪm/ [v phrase] informal to be willing to try something dangerous, new, difficult, or risky: *'Want to go climbing with us?' 'Yeah, I'm game.'* | **+ to do sth** American *She's one of those people who's game to try anything.* | **+ for** British *Tim's always game for a laugh.* (=willing to do things that might be fun)

2 when you do something willingly

- willingly
- voluntarily
- willing
- of your own free will
- voluntary
- readily
- freely
- gladly

willingly /ˈwɪlɪŋli/ [adv] *I'd willingly pay higher taxes if the money was spent on health and education.* | *Hundreds of teenagers volunteer willingly to help in service organizations.* | *She willingly cut her beautiful long hair in order to play Joan of Arc in Shaw's play.*

voluntarily /ˈvɒləntərəli, ˌvɒlənˈterəli‖ˌvɑːlənˈterəli/ [adv] if you do something **voluntarily**, especially something difficult, unpleasant, or inconvenient, you do it willingly and not because you are forced to: *She wasn't fired or asked to resign; she left voluntarily.* | *The company has voluntarily recalled the product to check for defects.*

willing /ˈwɪlɪŋ/ [adj only before noun] **willing accomplice/partner/participant etc** someone who takes part in an activity with someone else without being forced to, especially a dishonest or criminal activity: *The police believe Davison was a willing participant in the murder.* | *Get a bike, find a willing friend, and explore the bike trails.*

of your own free will /əv jɔːr ˌəʊn friː ˈwɪl/ [adv]

if you do something **of your own free will**, you do it because you choose to and want to, and not because you are forced to: *Nobody forced her to go – she left of her own free will.* | *How many of our teenage children actually help around the house of their own free will?*

voluntary /ˈvɒləntəri‖ˈvɑːlənteri/ [adj] actions that are **voluntary** are done willingly, not because you are forced to do them or have a legal duty to do them: *Most charities rely on voluntary contributions from the public.* | *Playing sport on Saturday at school was entirely voluntary.* | *The district is calling for a voluntary ban on using wood-burning stoves, in order to improve air quality.*

readily /ˈredəli/ [adv] written if you do something **readily**, you do it very willingly and without needing to think about whether you should do it or not: *He readily agreed to all our suggestions.* | *Beth was very tired and readily accepted a seat when it was offered.* | *Parsons readily took responsibility for the show's failure.*

freely /ˈfriːli/ [adv] if you **freely** do or say something, you do or say it willingly, even though it is something that other people might be embarrassed to do or say: *Mrs. Atwood's note said that she freely chose to end her life.* | **freely admit/acknowledge** *I freely admit I made many mistakes.* | *Ms. Tate freely acknowledges that she hasn't paid the fines, but argues she should not have to.*

gladly /ˈglædli/ [adv] if you do something **gladly**, you are very willing and pleased to do it: *If only I had more money in the bank, I would gladly retire.* | *When businesses heard about the reason for the fund-raiser, they gladly gave us donations.*

3 to not be willing to do something

- unwilling/not willing
- reluctant
- drag your feet
- be loath to do sth

unwilling/not willing /ʌnˈwɪlɪŋ, ˌnɒt ˈwɪlɪŋ/ [adj] not willing to do something, even though you should do it or someone else wants you to do it: *According to his lawyer, Stuart was an unwilling participant in the shooting.* | **+ to do sth** *She's unwilling to admit that she was wrong.* | *Most people are unwilling to give up their cars and use public transportation.* | *Put away any toys the child is not willing to share, to avoid any problems.* —**unwillingness** [n U] **+ to do sth** *No agreement was reached because of the unwillingness of either side to compromise.*

reluctant /rɪˈlʌktənt/ [adj] someone who is **reluctant** is not willing to do something, although they may be persuaded after refusing for a while: *Stores have cut prices to attract reluctant shoppers.* | *Becoming a donor is a simple process, but many people remain reluctant.* | **+ to do sth** *He seemed somewhat reluctant to explain, but finally did so.* | *Some of the older staff were reluctant to use the new equipment.* —**reluctance** [n U] **+ to do sth** *The U.S. has been criticized for its reluctance to deal with the problem of global warming.*

drag your feet /ˌdræg jɔːʳ ˈfiːt/ [v phrase] to take too much time to do something because you are unwilling to do it: *The White House has accused Congress of dragging its feet.* | **+ over/on** *They urged Parliament not to drag its feet on the bill.* | **drag your feet in doing sth** *Demonstrators say the administration is dragging its feet in establishing a housing program.*

be loath to do sth /biː ˌləʊθ tə ˈduː (sth)/ [v phrase] to be very unwilling to do something, especially something which affects you personally and which you may find upsetting or unpleasant to do: *His mother was still asleep and he was loath to wake her.* | *Congressmen are loath to limit the amount of time they can be in office.*

4 doing something unwillingly

- unwillingly
- reluctantly
- against your will
- grudgingly

unwillingly /ʌnˈwɪlɪŋli/ [adv] if you do something **unwillingly**, you do it slowly or without any eagerness, in a way that shows you are unwilling: *Johnson unwillingly admitted he'd been drinking that evening.* | *He pointed at a chair, and Alfred sat down unwillingly.*

reluctantly /rɪˈlʌktəntli/ [adv] if you do something **reluctantly**, you do it even though you are not very willing to do it: *Reluctantly, he gave the officer his name and address.* | *He reluctantly consented to his daughter's marriage.* | *Mrs. Bernson reluctantly agreed to help prepare for the conference.*

against your will /əˌgenst jɔːʳ ˈwɪl/ [adv] if you do something **against your will**, you do not want to do it but you are forced to: *The refugees were sent back against their will.* | *No one should be forced to marry against their will.*

grudgingly /ˈgrʌdʒɪŋli/ [adv] if you do something or say something **grudgingly**, especially something that gives help or praise or pleasure to someone else, you do it very unwillingly: *The city council has grudgingly given $100,000 towards the new after-school care program.* | *Steve grudgingly admitted that Matthew had played a better game.* —**grudging** [adj] *Charles listened to the speech with grudging admiration.*

win

RELATED WORDS

opposite: **lose**

- to beat someone in a game or competition *see* **beat/defeat**
- *see also* **sport/game, compete/with, war, fight, competition, against/oppose, gambling, succeed/successful**

1 to win a race, competition etc

- win
- finish first/be first/come in first
- first place
- get in

win /wɪn/ [v I/T] to **win** a race, competition, election etc, for example by getting more points, votes etc than everyone else or by being the first to finish: *No-one really expected the Socialist Party to win.* | **win a race/game/election etc** *Chang won the first set but lost the next two.* | *The competition was won by a Nigerian student.* | **win a prize/medal/cup etc** *His book won the Pulitzer Prize for literature.* | *What would you do if you won $1 million?* | **win by 6 votes/2 goals etc** (=win by getting 6 votes etc more than the other person or team) *He went ahead of Nolan, winning by 15 seconds.* | **win 4-2/20-12 etc** (=use this to show the final result of a game) *Do you remember our first game of the season? We won 3-1.* | **win at cards/chess/tennis etc** *She always wins at Scrabble.*

finish first/be first/come in first ALSO **come first** British /ˌfɪnɪʃ 'fɜːʳst, biː 'fɜːʳst, ˌkʌm ɪn 'fɜːʳst, ˌkʌm 'fɜːʳst/ [v phrase not in progressive] to win a race or competition in which more than two people or teams are competing: *Who do you think will finish first?* | *The British team was first, followed closely by the Americans.* | *André Etienne came in first, having completed the course in record time.* | **+ in** *An Australian runner came first in the marathon.* | *Sue finished first in two races – the 50m backstroke and the 100m front crawl.*

first place /ˌfɜːʳst 'pleɪs/ [n singular] the position of the person or team that wins a race or competition **in first place** *Johnson finished in first place, narrowly ahead of Green.* | **win first place in** *My greatest achievement was winning first place in the Young Artist competition.*

get in /ˌget 'ɪn/ [phr v I not in progressive] British if a political party **gets in**, they win an election, and have the right to form a government: *Do you think Labour will get in again at the next election?*

2 to win an argument, fight, war, etc

- win
- come out on top
- prevail
- carry the day
- win the day

win /wɪn/ [v I/T] to argue, fight etc more successfully than someone else: *The court case has been dragging on for months, and it's increasingly unlikely that she'll win.* | *I could never win an argument with my father.* | *Who won the first Civil War?* | **win a victory** *This was the first of many victories won by women's rights campaigners.*

come out on top /ˌkʌm aʊt ɒn 'tɒp‖-'tɑːp/ [v phrase not in progressive] informal to win something, especially something that other people are judging or deciding: *In a survey of customer preference, one model came consistently out on top.* | *In all action movies, the hero always comes out on top.*

prevail /prɪ'veɪl/ [v I] formal if an idea or way of doing something **prevails**, it is finally accepted as being better or more important than something else, especially after a lot of arguing: *Fortunately, in this case, common sense has prevailed.* | **+ over** *She seems to think that animal rights should prevail over everything else.*

carry the day /ˌkæri ðə 'deɪ/ [v phrase not in progressive] British to win by persuading people to accept a plan, proposal, or idea, especially after a lot of talking and arguing: *Anti-gun campaigners feel they have enough support to carry the day in tomorrow's vote.* | *His appeal to reason and common sense was what finally carried the day.*

win the day /ˌwɪn ðə 'deɪ/ [v phrase not in progressive] British to finally win an argument or political struggle, especially when this has been difficult – used especially in news reports: *On this occasion the strikers won the day and were given a pay increase of 20%.*

3 to be winning a game, race etc that has not yet finished

- be winning
- lead/be in the lead
- be ahead

be winning /biː 'wɪnɪŋ/ [v phrase] to have more points or votes than your opponents in a game or election, or to be at the front in a race when the game, race etc has not yet finished: *Senna was winning when the race was brought to a halt because of a crash.* | **be winning sth** *It looked as though Bush was winning the election battle.*

lead/be in the lead /liːd, biː ɪn ðə 'liːd/ [v I/T/v phrase] to be winning a game, race, election etc: *The High School team were leading with 60 points.* | *The Dolphins are still in the lead with only 2 minutes left to play.* | **lead by 10 points/three meters etc** *Agassi was leading by two sets when rain stopped play.*

be ahead /biː ə'hed/ [v phrase] to be doing better than someone else in a game, competition, race, or election: *She was still ahead in the polls just a week before the election.* | **+ of** *Waylan was ahead of Miller by three shots.* | **put sb ahead** *Shortly afterwards Smith put the Dodgers ahead with a stunning home run.* | **be 12 points/5 games etc ahead** *Damon Hill is now 14 points ahead of his nearest rival.* | **by way ahead** *By the final lap, Molly was way ahead of all the other girls.* | **be ahead by 12 points/5 games etc** *Houston was ahead by 3 points at half-time.*

4 to win easily

- win easily
- win hands down
- be no contest
- run away with
- be a shoo-in
- sweep to victory
- romp home

win easily /ˌwɪn 'iːzəli/ [v phrase] *Everyone expected the Democrats to win easily.* | **win sth easily** *She won the race easily with seconds to spare.*

win hands down /wɪn ˌhændz 'daʊn/ [v phrase] to win very easily without having any problems: *The Socialists will win hands down if the election is free and fair.* | *The newer model wins hands down when it comes to speed and capacity.*

be no contest /biː ˌnəʊ 'kɒntest‖-'kɑːn-/ [v phrase] if a game, competition etc **is no contest**, one person or team wins so easily that it is impossible for their opponent to win: *In the end it was no contest. New Labour won more votes than even they thought possible.*

run away with /ˌrʌn ə'weɪ wɪð/ [phr v T] to win a game or competition very easily, especially because you are much better than your opponents: *United have established a clear lead, and are threatening to run away with the championship.*

be a shoo-in /biː ə 'ʃuː ɪn/ [v phrase] American to be very likely to easily win an election, competition etc, by having many more points, votes etc than you opponents: *He looked like a shoo-in to win South Carolina's Republican presidential primary.*

sweep to victory /ˌswiːp tə 'vɪktəri/ [v phrase] to win very easily, in a way that impresses people – used especially in news reports: *Olson scored twice as the Rams swept to victory.* | *Nixon swept to victory by 47 million votes to 29 million.*

romp home /ˌrɒmp 'həʊm‖ˌrɑːmp-/ [v phrase] British informal to win a race or game easily: *No goals were scored in the first half but Spurs romped home in the second, scoring four.*

5 to win when you almost lost

- win by a narrow margin
- scrape home
- be close

win by a narrow margin /ˌwɪn baɪ ə ˌnærəʊ 'mɑːʳdʒən/ [v phrase] if someone wins something or is elected **by a narrow margin**, they win by getting only a few more points, votes etc than their opponent: *We won the debate by a narrow margin.* | *Win-*

ning by a narrow margin, the Lakers now go on to play in the championships.

scrape home /ˌskreɪp ˈhəʊm/ [v phrase] British to win by a very small number of votes or points, or by a very small distance in a race: *The Green Party scraped home in the local elections.* | *The referees decided that Foreman had just scraped home.*

be close ALSO **be a close-run thing** British /biː ˈkləʊs, biː ə ˌkləʊs rʌn ˈθɪŋ/ [v phrase] if a race, competition, election etc **is close** or **is a close-run thing**, any person or party could win because they all have nearly the same number of points, votes etc, or are close to each other in the race: *The election was very close – a handful of votes decided it.* | *The champions have kept their title, but it was a close-run thing.*

6 when someone wins

- victory
- win
- triumph
- success
- conquest
- walkover
- landslide

victory /ˈvɪktəri/ [n C/U] when a country, player, team etc wins a battle, game, race etc: *The crowds were celebrating Italy's victory.* | *We're very confident of victory.* | *victory celebrations* | **+ over/against** *Their 2-1 victory over the Australians was completely unexpected.* | **win a victory** *He had won a comfortable victory in the general election.*

win /wɪn/ [n C] when a team or player wins in a sport or competition – used especially in news reports: *It was an important win for Manchester United.* | *A couple from London are celebrating a big lottery win.* | **+ over/against** *a 2-0 win over their oldest rivals*

triumph /ˈtraɪəmf/ [n C/U] written an important victory after a long, difficult struggle, especially in war or politics: *Despite many local triumphs, their party stands little chance of winning a national election.* | *Arsenal's recent League Cup triumph.*

success /səkˈses/ [n C/U] a victory, especially in a series of games, fights etc: *With such a strong team, France are heading for certain success.* | *their fourth success in a row*

conquest /ˈkɒŋkwest‖ˈkɑːŋ-/ [n C/U] a victory in which one country wins a war against another country and takes control of it: *The palace was built in Cordoba, Spain, following the Arab conquest.* | *The Roman legions left, opening the way for the conquest of the British Isles by the Germanic tribes.*

walkover /ˈwɔːkˌəʊvəʳ/ [n singular] informal a situation in which someone wins very easily, especially in a sport, because they are much better than the people they are playing against: *If they were expecting this game to be a walkover, they were very wrong.*

landslide /ˈlændslaɪd/ [n singular] when one party or candidate gets far more votes than their opponents in an election: *The newspapers were predicting a landslide for Thatcher.* | **by a landslide** *He was re-elected in 1984 by a landslide.* | **landslide victory** *Few people had expected Labour's landslide victory in 1945.*

7 the person or team that wins

- winner
- champion
- winning
- victor
- victorious

winner /ˈwɪnəʳ/ [n C] *The winner will receive a prize of $500.* | *The crowd roared as the winner crossed the finishing line.* | **+ of** *On Thursday the judges will be announcing the winner of this year's Booker Prize.*

champion /ˈtʃæmpiən/ [n C] a person who has won a competition, especially in sport: *Mohammed Ali, the former world heavyweight boxing champion, will appear on the 'Tonight' show next week.* | **defending champion** (=the person who won last time and is trying to win again) *As defending champion, he is expected to reach the final.* | **reigning champion** (=the present champion who won the competition last time) *Bjorn Borg was the reigning Wimbledon champion for five years.*

winning /ˈwɪnɪŋ/ [adj only before noun] **winning team/player/horse etc** (=the team, player etc that wins) *The winning team will go through to the grand final in London.* | *A group of reporters followed the winning jockey and horse into the winner's enclosure.*

victor /ˈvɪktəʳ/ [n C] written the winner in a war, election, or important sporting event: *After the war, the victors returned in triumph.* | *The victors are waving to the crowd as they do their lap of honour.*

victorious /vɪkˈtɔːriəs/ [adj] having won an important fight, competition, election, etc: *He shook hands with his victorious opponent.* | *Three young men from the victorious team came forward to collect their trophy.*

8 to be the person or team that is expected to win

- be (the) favourite
- frontrunner
- be in the running

be (the) favourite British **/be the favorite** American /biː (ðə) ˈfeɪvərɪ̆t/ [v phrase] to be the person or team that everyone expects to win **+ for** *The Danish runner was the favorite for the 100m sprint.* | **be (the) favourite to win** *Thatcher was favourite to win the 1983 election.* | **be (the) clear favourite** *The Luxembourg entry is clear favourite to win the Eurovision Song Contest.*

frontrunner /ˌfrʌntˈrʌnəʳ/ [n C] the person or team that is most likely to win a race, election, or competition: *He will certainly be a frontrunner in the Democratic primaries.* | *The Greens have never really been among the frontrunners in British politics.*

be in the running /biː ɪn ðə ˈrʌnɪŋ/ [v phrase] to be one of the people who has a good chance of winning: *Spain still has several athletes in the running.* | **+ for** *Anthony Hopkins was in the running for an Oscar.*

9 something that you get when you win

- prize
- cup
- medal
- trophy
- jackpot
- winnings

prize /praɪz/ [n C] something that is given to the person who wins a competition, game, or race: *The prize is a 3-week holiday in the Bahamas.* | **first/second/third etc prize** *Second prize is a book token.* | **win/get a prize** *She won the Booker Prize for her novel 'The Blind Assassin'.* | **prize winner** *A list of prize winners will appear in net week's issue.*

cup /kʌp/ [n C] a special silver or gold container, shaped like a large **cup** with two handles, that is given to the winner of a sports competition: *The*

Queen presented the cup to the captain of the winning team.

medal /'medl/ [n C] a round flat piece of metal that is given to someone who has won a race, game, or competition: *The winning team went up to collect their medals* | **gold/silver/bronze medal** (=a medal for coming first/second/third) *The gold medal was won by Anna Svensen.*

trophy /'trəʊfi/ [n C] an object or special cup that is given to the winner of a race, game, or competition, especially in sports: *The winner went to receive her trophy.* | *They became the first British team to win a major European trophy.*

jackpot /'dʒækpɒt‖-pɑːt/ [n singular] the largest amount of money that can be won in a game of chance: *The jackpot is worth $1 million this week.* | **hit the jackpot** (=win it) *Unemployed roadsweeper Mickey Reid hit the jackpot when his £4 Lotto ticket won him £1.8m.*

winnings /'wɪnɪŋz/ [n plural] money that you win by playing games for money: *She collected her winnings and put them into her bag.* | *Scooping up his winnings, he went off to invest them at the blackjack table.*

with/together

RELATED WORDS

opposite: **alone**

- to join together with other people, countries etc in order to achieve something *see* **unite**
- to join two or more things together *see* **join**
- at the same time *see* **time (19-21)**

1 in the same place with another person

- with
- together
- join
- be accompanied by
- company
- in sb's company
- in sb's presence
- live side by side

with /wɪð, wɪθ/ [prep] *Don't leave me alone with her.* | *'Where's Jill?' 'I don't know, I thought she was with you.'* | *I try to make sure I have a couple of hours to spend with David every evening.* | *We live with my parents-in-law.* | *At the moment, she's in a meeting with the President.* | **arrive/leave/go out etc with sb** *Lindsay arrived with her husband but left by herself.* | *I saw Rick go out of the building with Susan.*

together /tə'geðəʳ/ [adv] *Nicola and I were at school together.* | *Each year the whole family spends Christmas together.* | *For years, these people who are now at war lived together very peacefully.* | *We'd better stay together, or we might get lost.*

join /dʒɔɪn/ [v T] to go to the place where someone else is, in order to be with them or do something with them: *We're sitting over there. Why don't you join us?* | *Her parents are going to Paris next week and she will join them later.*

be accompanied by /biː ə'kʌmpənid baɪ/ [v phrase] to be with someone, especially when this person's presence gives you support or protection: *Children under fourteen must be accompanied by an adult.* | *Wherever she goes she has to be accompanied by a bodyguard.* | *The Prince, accompanied by the Princess, spoke to many of the disaster victims in the hospital.*

company /'kʌmpəni/ [n U] the presence of another person or other people, that gives you someone to talk to and stops you feeling lonely: *I was grateful for Jean's company on the long journey up to Edinburgh.* | **have (some) company** *'Do you mind if I join you?' 'No of course not, it's nice to have some company.'* | **do sth for the company** *I go to French evening classes, for the company as much as for the French.* | **miss sb's company** *Now that she's gone, I really miss her company.*

in sb's company /ɪn (sb's) 'kʌmpəni/ [adv] when you are with a particular person: *I always feel very relaxed in Nick's company.* | **in the company of sb** *Many people are uneasy in the company of strangers.*

in sb's presence /ɪn (sb's) 'prezəns/ [adv] if you are **in someone's presence**, especially someone important or famous, you are with them or in the same place as them: *What was it like to be actually in the Queen's presence?* | **in the presence of sb** *I could think of very little to say in the presence of so many important people.*

live side by side /lɪv ˌsaɪd baɪ 'saɪd/ [v phrase] if people **live side by side**, they live together peacefully even though there are big differences between them: *It was a great experience – people from so many very different backgrounds living side by side.* | *The Muslim residents say they are ready and willing to live side by side with their neighbors again.*

2 doing something with another person/group etc

- with
- together
- side by side
- collectively
- jointly
- in conjunction with
- in partnership with
- in collaboration with
- shoulder to shoulder with sb

with /wɪð, wɪθ/ [prep] *My family and I went camping in the mountains with some old friends of ours.* | *I'd like you to work with the person sitting beside you and see if we can come up with some new ideas,*

together /tə'geðəʳ/ [adv] *There's no point in taking two cars – let's go together.* | *The police and army worked together to track down the terrorists.*

side by side /ˌsaɪd baɪ 'saɪd/ [adv] if two groups work or fight **side by side**, they work closely together to achieve something, even though there may be big differences between them: *It was a strange situation with Washington, Pretoria and Peking fighting side by side.* | **+ with** *Soldiers worked side by side with civilians to rebuild the city.*

collectively /kə'lektɪvli/ [adv] if people do something **collectively**, they do it by working together as equal members of an organized group: *The team collectively must decide what resources they need and how they are to be used.* | *Individually, people have little power, but collectively they can be more influential.*

jointly /'dʒɔɪntli/ [adv] **jointly managed/owned/published/funded etc by sb** managed, owned etc by two or more people or organizations working together equally: *The business is jointly owned and run by six TV companies.* | *It was a major research project, jointly funded by the university and the Health Department.*

in conjunction with /ɪn kən'dʒʌŋkʃən wɪð/ [prep] if something is done by one organization or group of people in **conjunction with** another organization or group, it is done by both of them working together: *The exhibition is sponsored by the Arts Council in conjunction with British Airways.* | *Sten-*

mann is working in conjunction with leading scientists and has invested $5 million in the scheme.

in partnership with /ɪn 'pɑːʳtnəʳʃɪp wɪð/ [prep] if people, organizations, or countries work **in partnership with** each other, they work together to do something important or useful: *The city council is working in partnership with local businesses to build new sports facilities in the area.*

in collaboration with /ɪn kəˌlæbə'reɪʃən wɪð/ [prep] if you work on a plan or do something **in collaboration with** another person or organization, you work very closely with them in order to achieve it: *I wrote the article in collaboration with a number of my colleagues.* | *This course has been developed in collaboration with major professional bodies involved in the financial services sector.*

shoulder to shoulder with sb /ˌʃəʊldəʳ tə 'ʃəʊldəʳ wɪð (sb)/ [prep] if one group of people stands or fights **shoulder to shoulder with** another group of people, they support them or fight together with them against an enemy: *British soldiers fought shoulder to shoulder with American and French troops.* | *Mitterrand, although a socialist, stood shoulder to shoulder with the NATO allies during the challenges of the early 1980s.*

3 when people do something together in a dishonest way

- be in league with
- in collusion with
- be in cahoots (with)
- hand in glove with sb

be in league with /biː ɪn 'liːg wɪð/ [prep] if someone **is in league with** a group of people, they are secretly planning and working with them in order to do something dishonest or illegal: *Anyone suspected of being in league with the rebels was arrested.* | *There was a suggestion that the authorities were in league with the drug dealers.*

in collusion with /ɪn kə'luːʒən wɪð/ [prep] if one group of people is **in collusion with** another group, they are all working secretly together to do something dishonest: *Some of the police force were working in collusion with the Mafia.* | *Journalists suspected that the army was acting in collusion with the terrorists.*

be in cahoots (with) /biː ɪn kə'huːts (wɪð)/ [prep] working secretly and closely with another person or group in order to do something dishonest or cheat someone: *Assassins, in cahoots with the army, were sent to kill two top members of the parliament.* | *By the middle of the book we've learned that the church and the local politicians are in cahoots to try to slow Sonja's research.*

hand in glove with sb /ˌhænd ɪn 'glʌv wɪð (sb)/ [prep] British if one organization is **hand in glove with** another organization, they work together very closely in order to do something dishonest, or dishonestly get power: *The politicians are hand in glove with the military, everyone knows that.*

4 to work together

- work together
- cooperate
- collaborate

work together /ˌwɜːʳk tə'geðəʳ/ [v phrase] *We can only succeed if we all work together as a team.* | **+ to do sth** *Both sides are going to have to work together to find other ways of settling their differences.*

cooperate ALSO **co-operate** British /kəʊ'ɒpəreɪt‖-'ɑːp-/ [v I] if two people or groups **cooperate** with each other, they work together and help each other in order to achieve something that will be good for both of them **+ with** *The president said that Mexico would continue to cooperate with the US in the fight against drugs.* | **+ to do sth** *Aid agencies and UN forces are cooperating to get food supplies to the people who need them.* | **cooperate closely** (=help each other as much as possible) *Finance ministers and central bankers agreed to cooperate closely to sustain the strength of the pound.* | **+ in/on** *Traditionally management has called upon workers to cooperate in increasing productivity.* —**cooperation/co-operation** /kəʊˌɒpə'reɪʃən‖-ˌɑːp-/ [n U] *In the future there will be greater military cooperation among all the nations of Europe.*

collaborate /kə'læbəreɪt/ [v I] to work together, especially on a specific piece of scientific, artistic, or industrial work **+ to do sth** *Researchers in Stanford and Princeton collaborated to manufacture a completely new waterproof textile.* | **+ with** *Hewlett Packard collaborated with Nokia to produce the palmtop-telephone.* | **+ on/in** *Fellini collaborated with Rossellini on the script of the film.* | *Educators and employers need to collaborate in preparing the next generation for employment and adulthood.* —**collaboration** /kəˌlæbə'reɪʃən/ [n U] *We couldn't have done it without their collaboration* (=if they had not collaborated with us).

5 someone who does something with someone else

- partner
- fellow
- companion
- sidekick
- accomplice

partner /'pɑːʳtnəʳ/ [n C] someone who takes part in a sport or game, or a business or social activity with you: *Have you got a partner for the dance on Saturday?* | *The firm was so successful that she took on a partner.* | *We called a meeting with Russco, our partners in the construction project.* | **a business/trading partner** *Manson and I were business partners, but not friends.* | **a marriage/sexual partner** *People who have many sexual partners are more at risk from AIDS.* | **be partners** *Let's have a game of cards – you and Frank can be partners.*

fellow /'feləʊ/ [adj only before noun] **fellow passenger/worker/student etc** someone who is travelling, working, studying etc with you: *The accident happened when Roland was walking home with fellow student Karl Xavier.* | *Toni's views on the Kyoto Treaty were echoed by her fellow workers.*

companion /kəm'pænjən/ [n C] someone that you spend a lot of time with, especially someone that provides friendship or conversation while you are doing something, for example travelling: *Mum and Dad didn't seem to approve much of my new companions.* | *He left the major part of his £60 million fortune to his close friend and companion, Jerry Edwards.* | **a drinking/travelling etc companion** *Ed is a great travelling companion – funny and sensible at the same time.*

sidekick /'saɪdˌkɪk/ [n C] informal someone who spends a lot of time with another person, and is usually less important or powerful than them: *Tom and his sidekick Larry sauntered into the bar, plainly looking for a fight.* | *Sherlock Holmes and his sidekick Dr Watson*

accomplice /ə'kʌmplɪ̈s‖ə'kɑːm-, ə'kʌm-/ [n C] someone who helps another person to commit a crime: *After the robbery, the men escaped in a stolen* *car driven by an accomplice.* | **+ in** *Two other boys were accused of being accomplices in the attack.*

6 done by people working together

▸ **joint** ▸ **collective**
▸ **combined** ▸ **collaborative**

joint /dʒɔɪnt/ [adj only before noun] a **joint** decision, statement, effort, report etc is made by people or groups working together, not by just one of them: *We both wanted to move to Canada – it was a joint decision.* | *a joint declaration by Israeli and Palestinian leaders* | **a joint effort** *'Did you cook the dinner, Jane?' 'No, it was a joint effort.'*

combined /kəm'baɪnd/ [adj only before noun] **combined** actions are done by people or groups who try to do something together which they could not do alone: *The combined efforts of four police officers and two paramedics were needed to lift the driver from the wreckage.* | *It was a combined operation involving troops from the US and Europe.*

collective /kə'lektɪv/ [adj only before noun] a **collective** decision, action, or agreement is made by everyone in a group or organization, not by just one or two of its members: *A jury's verdict is the result of a collective agreement.* | *Kerry called the labor laws 'a legitimate collective effort to protect our children' and said he supported them.* | **collective responsibility (for sth)** (=when everyone in a group shares responsibility for its decisions and actions) *The bureau was without a manager for some time, so the staff took collective responsibility for all the tasks.*

collaborative /kə'læbərətɪv‖-reɪ-/ [adj only before noun] use this about an activity that involves people working together, especially in order to achieve something that will bring an advantage to both of them **a collaborative effort** *A manager's main task is to coordinate the collaborative efforts of a number of people.* | **collaborative project/research/venture etc** *The new system was the product of a collaborative project between Apple and IBM.* | *a collaborative youth training program involving several businesses*

7 people or groups who work together

▸ **partnership** ▸ **alliance**

partnership /'pɑːʳtnəʳʃɪp/ [n C] a relationship between people or groups working closely together: *The song-writing partnership has been very productive.* | **+ between** *Crime prevention is most effective when it is a partnership between the police and the public.* | **form a partnership** *Elliot and Elver decided to form a partnership and launch their own business.*

alliance /ə'laɪəns/ [n C] an arrangement involving two or more different groups or countries to work together to oppose an enemy, to do business, or to work together for something that they both believe in: *NATO is a formal military alliance with America at its head.* | **enter into an alliance/form an alliance** *The two countries entered into a defensive alliance.* | *Apple and online service provider America Online formed an alliance.*

8 to be together again after being separated

▸ **be back together** ▸ **be reunited**

be back together /biː ˌbæk tə'geðəʳ/ [v phrase] to be together again after being separated, used especially about couples who have started a romantic relationship again: *Did you know that Denise and Jonathon are back together?* | *It's so nice to have all the family back together again.* | **+ with** *I'm back together with Johnny now and things are going pretty well.* | **get back together** *Jack wants to get back together, but I've really had enough.*

be reunited /biː ˌriːjuː'naɪtɪ̇d/ [v phrase] to be brought together again with someone that you lost or were unable to see for a long time, especially when someone helps you to be with them again: *After 50 years apart, the twin sisters were eventually reunited.* | **+ with** *In the early hours of this morning, the hostages were reunited with their families at Point Reach airbase.*

9 with another thing or other things

▸ **with** ▸ **come with**
▸ **together** ▸ **accompanying**
▸ **along with**

with /wɪð, wɪθ/ [prep] *I've put our passports in your handbag with the travellers cheques.* | *I hope you haven't thrown that letter out with the garbage!* | *a traditional Christmas dinner of roast turkey with all the trimmings*

together /tə'geðəʳ/ [prep] **together** in the same place, or added **together**, not separately: *Mix the butter and the sugar together.* | *That skirt and jacket look really good together.* | *Together these two paintings are worth more than $10,000.*

along with /ə'lɒŋ wɪð‖ə'lɔːŋ-/ [prep] in the same place as another thing or other things: *I keep my insurance policy in the top drawer, along with my other important documents.* | *Put it over there along with the other presents.*

come with /'kʌm wɪð/ [phr v T not in progressive or passive] if something that you buy **comes with** something else, it is sold with an additional object that is included in the price: *Every new camera comes with a leather case and free film.* | *All the main courses come with salad and chips.* | *We have 5000 log cabins to rent. All come with their own private sauna.*

accompanying /ə'kʌmpəni-ɪŋ/ [adj only before noun] an **accompanying** book, document etc, is one that you get together with something that you buy, and which gives you more information about it **accompanying booklet/volume/letter etc** *The video recorder has an accompanying booklet which contains full instructions.* | *Each coursebook has an accompanying workbook for grammar practice.*

10 when something is used together with something else

▸ **together** ▸ **in conjunction with**
▸ **together with** ▸ **alongside**
▸ **combined with** ▸ **compatible**
▸ **in combination**

together /tə'geðəʳ/ [adv] *The shampoo and conditioner should be used together for the best possible result.* | *When you're slowing down, use the gears and the brakes together.*

together with ALSO **along with** American /tə'geðəʳ wɪð, ə'lɒŋ wɪð‖ə'lɔːŋ-/ [prep] *A sensible diet along with regular exercise is the best way to lose weight.* | *I love Italian food, together with a good bottle of red wine.*

combined with /kəm'baɪnd wɪð/ [adj phrase] if a treatment, method, drug etc is **combined with** another, it is used with it because this will have the most effect: *Small children need firmness combined with loving care.* | *The standard treatment is surgery, often combined with radiation.*

in combination /ɪn ˌkɒmbəˈneɪʃən‖-ˌkɑːm-/ [adv] if two or more things or methods are used **in combination**, they are used together at the same time, in order to achieve a particular effect: *The drug company recommended using Losec in combination with antibiotics for the treatment of ulcers.* | **+ with** *The flavor of paprika, in combination with sour cream, is used in many Eastern European cuisines.*

in conjunction with /ɪn kən'dʒʌŋkʃən wɪð/ [prep] if one thing is used **in conjunction with** another, it is used with it, in order to help you do something more easily: *Learners will benefit from using the book in conjunction with the video.* | *The file viewing functions can be used in conjunction with file manager.*

alongside /əˌlɒŋ'saɪd‖əˌlɔːŋ-/ [prep] different types of things, methods, ideas etc that are used or exist **alongside** each other, are being used together or exist together at the same time: *The new advertisement will be broadcast alongside AMV's two existing commercials during prime time viewing.* | *Only the island of Bali preserved, alongside its own traditions, the Brahman heritage of those ancient times.*

compatible /kəm'pætəbəl/ [adj] different machines, methods, ideas etc that are **compatible** can exist together or be used together without producing problems: *Certain kinds of drug are not compatible and should never be taken together.* | *The two businesses have compatible aims, and a merger would be to everyone's advantage.* | **+ with** *Unfortunately he bought a printer that was not compatible with his computer.*

11 several different things or people considered together

- together
- collectively

together /tə'geðəʳ/ [adv] *The Executive, Legislative, and Judiciary branches together make up the US government.* | **taken together** (=considered as a group) *Taken together, these measures should ensure a rapid return to financial stability.*

collectively /kə'lektɪvli/ [adv] *Collectively, these studies showed a clear link between smoking and cancer.* | **collectively called/collectively known as/collectively referred to as etc** *Belgium, Luxembourg, and the Netherlands are collectively known as the 'Benelux' countries.* | *These substances are referred to collectively as ketone bodies.*

woman

RELATED WORDS

- *see also* **mother, girlfriend/boyfriend, sex, man, character**

1 a woman

- woman
- lady
- girl

woman /'wʊmən/ [n C] a female adult: *Rebecca Stephens was the first British woman to climb Mount Everest.* | *Who's that woman you were talking to just now?* | *In some African countries, the women do most of the agricultural work.*

lady /'leɪdi/ [n C] a polite word for a woman, especially a woman who is there when you are speaking about her: *There's a lady here who wants to speak to you about her account.* | **old lady** *Ella is the elderly lady who lives next door.* | **ladies and gentlemen** (=use this when you are talking to an audience, making a speech etc) *Ladies and gentlemen, I am delighted to welcome you here tonight.*

girl /gɜːʳl/ [n C] a young woman: *He's going out with that girl who works in the library.* | *On Saturday night, the streets are full of teenage girls and boys, out for a good time.* | **young girl** *In Britain, some young girls are choosing parenthood as an alternative to employment.*

2 a woman who does a particular job or activity

- woman
- female
- lady

woman /'wʊmən/ [n C] **woman writer/teacher/priest/driver etc** *Mrs Thatcher was Britain's first woman prime minister.* | *an exciting new collection of short stories by women writers* | *Not long ago, the Church of England voted to ordain women priests.* | *Women drivers tend to be much more careful than men.* | **policewoman/businesswoman/publicity woman etc** *A young policewoman was standing at the door.* | *I was impressed by some of the high-flying businesswomen at the conference.*

female /'fiːmeɪl/ [adj usually before noun] formal a **female** worker, teacher, singer etc is a woman or girl – use this to contrast women with men who are doing the same thing: *Emma is the only female lawyer that the firm has ever employed.* | *Female students tend to get better grades than male students.* | *In Tokyo, the number of female taxi drivers is up 75% since 1972.*

lady /'leɪdi/ [adj only before noun] a polite word, which some women may find offensive, for a woman who does an important or professional job **lady doctor/councillor etc** *I'd rather see a lady doctor, if that's possible.* | *The town has had a lady mayor for a couple of years now.*

3 what you call a woman when you speak to her or write to her

- Mrs
- Miss
- Ms
- madam
- ma'am

Mrs British **/Mrs.** American /'mɪsəz/ use this before the family name of a woman who is married: *Mrs Thomas, the doctor is ready to see you now.* | *'Dear Mrs. Gilman,' the letter said ...* | *It's Mrs Hawksworth's 70th birthday this weekend.*

Miss /mɪs/ use this before the family name of a woman who has never been married: *The children were told that they should call their new teacher Miss Watts.* | *My secretary, Miss Evans, will meet you in reception.*

Ms British **/Ms.** American /mɪz, məz/ use this before a woman's family name if you do not know whether she is married, or if it is not important whether she is married: *Would you prefer to be called Mrs or Ms Cawley?* | *Does anyone know a Ms. Jacobs? There's a letter for her here.*

madam /ˈmædəm/ formal use this when writing a formal letter to a woman. In British English this is also used when talking to a customer in a shop, hotel, restaurant etc: *Can I help you, madam?* | *Dear Madam, I am writing in response to your advertisement.* | **Madam Chairman** (=use this to address a female chairman in a formal discussion) *Madam Chairman, I would like to reply to that point.*

ma'am /mæm, mɑːm, məm‖mæm/ American spoken a polite word used when talking to a woman who you do not know: *Would you like some help, ma'am?*

4 for women or relating to women

- women's
- ladies'
- female
- feminine
- effeminate
- womanly

women's /ˈwɪmɪnz/ [adj only before noun] use this about things that are designed for women or done by women, and not designed for or done by men: *She's the fashion editor for a women's magazine.* | *Why don't they ever show women's football on TV?* | *the latest and most fashionable trends in women's clothes*

ladies' /ˈleɪdiz/ [adj only before noun] formal used, especially in the past, about things that are designed for women or done by women, and not designed for or done by men: *I managed to get a place on the university ladies' golf team.* | *the ladies' tennis tournament* | *Ladies' fashions are on the first floor.* | **the ladies' room/the ladies'** (=the women's toilets in a public place) *Could you tell me where the ladies' room is?*

female /ˈfiːmeɪl/ [adj only before noun] use this about behaviour or personal qualities that are traditionally thought to be typical of women, or about physical characteristics that belong to women: *Many women reject the traditional female roles of wife and mother.* | *Patience and kindness are often seen as female qualities.* | *the female reproductive system*

feminine /ˈfemənən/ [adj] looking attractive in a way that is traditionally thought to be typical of a woman: *Hairstyles this autumn are long, soft and very feminine.* | *Lindsay wears very feminine clothes – pretty dresses with flowers on and things like that.* | *the rounded feminine shape* —**femininity** /ˌfeməˈnɪnəti/ [n U] *ideas of femininity*

effeminate /ɪˈfemənət/ [adj] use this about a man who behaves like a woman or looks like a woman: *He was very young and handsome in a slightly effeminate way.* | *The way he walks is a bit effeminate, and he sounds effeminate too.*

womanly /ˈwʊmənli/ [adj] **womanly** qualities are typical of a grown woman, especially one who is sensible, kind etc: *She had a plump, womanly figure.* | *the conventional womanly virtues of patience and sense* | *He thought that since she'd had children, she'd grown more attractive and womanly.*

5 believing in equal rights for women

- feminism
- feminist

feminism /ˈfemənɪzəm/ [n U] a set of beliefs based on the principle that women are equal to men and should be treated equally: *There were many close links between social reform movements and feminism.* | *the civilising influence of feminism*

feminist /ˈfemənəst/ [n C] someone who believes strongly in the principle that men and women should be treated equally, and that society should be changed so that this can happen: *The feminists marched in thousands when David Laing urged married women to give up their jobs and stay at home.* | **radical feminist** (=someone with extreme feminist views) *In the 1960's I saw myself as a revolutionary and a radical feminist.* —**feminist** [adj] *the early feminist movement*

word/phrase/ sentence

RELATED WORDS

- see also **language, write, read, talk, listen, meaning, translate**

1 a word or group of words

- word
- phrase
- expression
- term
- idiom
- figure of speech
- catchword

word /wɜːʳd/ [n C] *Are there any words in the passage that you don't understand?* | *Look up any words you don't know in a dictionary.* | *Is 'lunchtime' one word or two?* | *The word 'origami' comes from Japanese.* | **word for sth** (=word that means something) *'Casa' is the Italian word for 'house'.* | *What's another word for 'way out'?*

phrase /freɪz/ [n C] a combination of two or more words that has a particular meaning: *There are some useful words and phrases at the end of each chapter in the Student's Book.* | *Are you familiar with the phrase 'the old boy network'?* | **use a phrase** *I was criticized for using the phrase 'gay lifestyles'.* | *His campaign is, to use one of his favourite phrases, 'as dead as Elvis'.* | **in sb's phrase** (=according to a phrase which someone used) *The battle of El Alamein was, in Churchill's phrase, 'the end of the beginning'.* | **coin a phrase** (=invent a phrase) *Who first coined the phrase 'Iron Curtain'?* | **turn of phrase** (=a particular phrase or word that someone uses) *The head of the bank described the salary cuts as 'peanuts', a turn of phrase which angered many bank workers.*

expression /ɪkˈspreʃən/ [n C] a group of words that is used to talk about or say a particular thing: *'It'll be alright in the end' – that was my mother's favourite expression.* | *'Shadow-boxing'? I've never heard that expression before!* | **use an expression** *I don't normally use that expression myself, but I've heard other people use it sometimes.* | *He said he didn't care – well actually he used a rude expression that I can't repeat!*

term /tɜːʳm/ [n C] a word or group of words that are used in a technical or scientific subject and have an exact meaning in that subject: *Mr Hicks used the term 'neighbourhood schools' for what in effect were segregated black schools.* | *It's very difficult to give a definition of a term like 'cyberspace'.* | **medical/legal/scientific etc term (for sth)** *The medical term for losing your hair is 'alopecia'.*

idiom /ˈɪdiəm/ [n C] a group of words that are used together and have a special meaning that you cannot guess from the meanings of each separate word: *'Full of beans' is an idiom which means lively and energetic.* | *In Hollywood, white stars are adopting black idioms, dress styles and manners.* —**idiomatic** /ˌɪdiəˈmætɪk◂/ [adj] *Some idiomatic phrases don't translate literally, so you have to find an equivalent.*

figure of speech /ˌfɪgər əv ˈspiːtʃ‖ˌfɪgjər-/ [n C] a group of words that are used to describe someone or something in an unusual or poetic way: *We describe our genes as 'selfish' or 'ruthless', but of course this is only a figure of speech.* | *When I said we spent the night together, it was just a figure of speech. I didn't sleep with her.*

catchword /ˈkætʃwɜːʳd/ [n C] a word or phrase that people use in a particular situation, because it describes what is important in that situation: *Variety will be the catchword at the new venue, with acts ranging from stand-up comedy to poetry readings.* | *After World War II, the catchword for a newly health-conscious society was 'protein'.*

2 a sentence or part of a sentence

- sentence
- clause
- phrase

sentence /ˈsentəns/ [n C] a group of words that begins with a capital letter, ends with a full stop, and includes a verb: *Write a complete sentence for each answer.* | *Try to write using short, punchy sentences.* | *Describe your best friend in a single sentence.* | *The opening sentence of the book defines the concept of Tai-Chi-Chuan.*

clause /klɔːz/ [n C] a group of words that has a subject and a verb and that is part of a sentence **main clause** (=the clause that describes the main action) *We will go to the theatre tonight [main clause] if we can get tickets [subordinate clause].* | **subordinate clause/dependent clause** (=a clause that is not the main clause) *In the sentence 'Can you tell me what time it is?' 'Can you tell me' is the main clause, and 'what time it is' is a subordinate clause.*

phrase /freɪz/ [n C] a small group of words which together form a single unit in a sentence – used in technical contexts: *The phrase 'a big black dog' is the subject of the sentence.* | **noun/adverb/verb etc phrase** *'A bottle of whisky' is a noun phrase, and 'really rather foolishly' is an adverb phrase.*

3 a phrase or sentence that is well known or often used

- saying
- proverb
- buzzword
- cliché
- platitude
- quotation
- slogan
- catchphrase
- motto

saying /ˈseɪ-ɪŋ/ [n C] a short sentence that contains advice, or says what is usually true in a particular situation. **Sayings** have usually been used for a long time: *'You're only as old as you feel' – that's one of my favourite sayings.* | **old/famous/well-known saying** *The more often you play the flute, the better you'll get. Remember the old saying, practice makes perfect.* | *How many times have we heard the famous saying, 'Physician heal thyself'?* | **as the saying goes** (=according to a saying) *What followed, as the saying goes, shook the world.* | *Like father, like son, as the saying goes – by the time Tim was eight, he was already a budding entrepreneur.*

proverb /ˈprɒvɜːʳb‖ˈprɑː-/ [n C] a well-known saying that gives advice or says something about human life, especially using words that represent a wider meaning: *Do you remember this old proverb: 'When poverty comes in the door, love flies out of the window'?* | **Chinese/Arabic/French etc proverb** *An Irish proverb is relevant here – 'You've got to do your own growing, no matter how tall your grandfather is.'* | **cite/quote a proverb** *In reply, he quoted a Sanskrit proverb: 'Forgiveness is the ornament of the brave'.*

buzzword /ˈbʌzwɜːʳd/ [n C] a word or phrase from one special area of knowledge that people suddenly start using a lot, especially because they think it means something important: *The big Internet buzzword at the moment is 'push technology'.* | *Customer-friendliness was the buzzword in British business circles.* | *'Going snap' on a decision was the latest buzzword in our office.*

cliché /ˈkliːʃeɪ‖kliːˈʃeɪ/ [n C] a phrase that is used so often that it seems boring, annoying, or silly: *It's a cliché, I know, but the game isn't over till the final whistle blows.* | **old/tired cliché** *At the risk of repeating an old cliché, what doesn't kill you makes you stronger.* | **become a cliché** *It's become a cliché to say that presidential candidates are being marketed like bars of soap or boxes of cereal.* —**clichéd** [adj] *Without sounding too clichéd about it, there should be more to life than that.* | *Poor production, dreary guitar chords and clichéd lyrics – this latest album is truly awful.*

platitude /ˈplætɪ̣tjuːd‖-tuːd/ [n C] a phrase that is so clearly true that it has no useful meaning and is therefore annoying, especially because the person using it seems insincere and unsympathetic: *The management tried to satisfy staff with some platitudes about the need to make sacrifices for the benefit of the company.* | **empty platitude** (=one that is meaningless) *The marriage counsellor could only offer us a string of empty platitudes.* | **mouth/spout platitudes** *Mr Gringold droned on, mouthing the usual platitudes about motivation and self-reliance.*

quotation /kwəʊˈteɪʃən/ [n C] a sentence or phrase from a book, play, poem etc that is used to explain or show something: *If you do use quotations in your essay, select them carefully.* | *a dictionary of theatrical quotations* | **+ from** *The book begins with a quotation from The Book of Common Prayer.* | **attribute a quotation to sb** (=say that they are the first person to say it) *The quotation is attributed to Chu Hsi, an ancient Chinese philosopher.*

slogan /ˈsləʊgən/ [n C] a short phrase that is easy to remember, especially one that is used by advertisers, politicians, or entertainers: *Bloomingdale's has as its slogan 'Like no other store in the world'.* | *Young men risked their lives to daub buildings with anti-government slogans.* | **+ of** *'Liberte, egalite, fraternite' was the slogan of the French Revolution.* | **advertising/marketing/campaign slogan** *They've come up with a new advertising slogan for the product.*

catchphrase /ˈkætʃfreɪz/ [n C usually singular] a short, well-known phrase used regularly by an entertainer or other public figure: *The public soon learned to associate the catchphrase 'Ooh, you are awful' with the inimitable Dick Emery.* | *His catchphrases like'What a peach of a shot' and 'That's a dream of a pass' are now part of tennis language.*

motto /ˈmɒtəʊ‖ˈmɑː-/ [n C usually singular] a word or phrase that expresses a person or organization's aims or beliefs: *The school's motto was 'Work hard and play hard'.* | *'All my life,' said Sir Humphrey, 'my motto has been "aim high".'* | **family motto** *The Mortimer family motto is inscribed above the door – 'Humilitas'.*

4 all the words someone knows or uses

- vocabulary
- terminology

vocabulary /vəˈkæbjələri, vəʊ-‖-leri/ [n C usually singular] someone's **vocabulary** is all the words that they know or use: *These stories are written for students with a vocabulary of about 2000 words.* | *Reading is a good way to increase your vocabulary.* | *a vocabulary test* | *How big is the average 4-year-old's vocabulary?*

terminology /ˌtɜːʳməˈnɒlədʒi‖-ˈnɑː-/ [n U] all the technical words or expressions that are used in connection with a particular subject: *One of the hardest things when studying linguistics is learning all the right terminology.* | **legal/medical/scientific etc terminology** *In legal terminology, a widow is the 'relict' of her late husband.* | *Kelly wants to be a nurse, and is taking a medical terminology class at night.*

work

RELATED WORDS

▸ *see also* **job, earn, work for sb, work hard, business, company**

WHAT'S HERE

- **work that sb does** see **1 to 6**
- **to work/do work** see **7 to 9**
- **sth you have to do** see **10 to 12**

work that sb does

1 work that someone does as part of their job

▸ work ▸ duties
▸ business

work /wɜːʳk/ [n U] the things that you have to do in your job, which need time and effort: *What kind of work are you looking for?* | *He liked the work, and he was good at it too.* | **do some/more etc work** *Scott's doing some work for me at the moment, as it happens.* | *I didn't get much work done today.* | *Being in the police isn't all action. Administration is a large part of the work we do.* | **personnel/secretarial/bar etc work** *Have you ever done bar work before?* | *He's doing construction work these days.* | *It's clerical work mainly – pretty boring.* | **voluntary/charity work** (=work that you do not get paid for) *She does two afternoons voluntary work at the playgroup.* | *Are you still involved in charity work?* | **extra/more/additional work** *The last thing I want is extra work.*

business /ˈbɪznəs/ [n U] work that you do in your job, especially work that involves buying and selling, travelling to different places, or discussing things such as contracts with people: *I was in London last month because I had some business there.* | *Gerald left, saying he had some important business to attend to.* | *Some insurance companies offer lower rates for drivers who do not use their cars for business.* | *'Is this trip for business or pleasure?' 'Business, I'm afraid.'* | **do business** *The paper claims to provide proof that some drug lords are doing business from their jail cells.* | **business trip/meeting/traveller etc** *'Where's Michael?' 'He's at a business meeting.'* | *This is strictly a business trip.* | *Our main market is the business traveler looking for cheap overnight accommodation.* | **on business** (=for business, not pleasure) *I have to go to Tokyo next month on business.*

duties /ˈdjuːtiz‖ˈduː-/ [n plural] the various things that you have to do as part of your job – used especially in contracts or other official documents **sb's duties** *In addition to secretarial and general office work, your duties will include providing the directors with refreshments.* | *As soon as she returned home from her honeymoon, she resumed her medical duties at the clinic.* | **go about/perform/fulfil duties** *A teacher can be dismissed for not performing his or her contractual duties.* | *She is a member of staff, and like all of us, she has duties to fulfil.* | *I admired him, especially because of the way he went about his duties efficiently.* | **suspend sb/relieve sb from duties** (=to stop them doing their job for a period of time) *Three instructors have been suspended from duties while sexual harassment charges are investigated.* | *Nine officers were relieved of their duties after McDuffie's death.*

2 work that a student does

▸ homework ▸ coursework
▸ classwork ▸ studies
▸ schoolwork

homework /ˈhəʊmwɜːʳk/ [n U] the work that a student has to do at home as part of their studies: *My brother always used to help me with my homework.* | **do (your) homework** *I'm sorry Gail, but Amber has to stay home and do her homework.* | *Oh, I've got so much homework to do!* | *Did you get your homework done Jason?* | **have homework** *I don't have any homework tonight.* | *Have you got a lot of homework then?* | **for homework** *For homework, I'd like you to finish exercises 2 and 3 on page 24.* | **English/geography etc homework** *Dave, have you done your French homework?*

classwork /ˈklɑːswɜːʳk‖ˈklæs-/ [n U] the work that a student does when they are at school, rather than work they do at home: *Mrs Hoffmann, I'm calling about Mike's classwork. There are some problems.* | *The units are ideal for classwork, but can also be used by students at home.*

schoolwork /ˈskuːlwɜːʳk/ [n U] all the work that a student has to do for their studies: *Johnny's had a lot of problems at home recently and it's starting to affect his schoolwork.* | *The program combines schoolwork with job experience.* | *Tim, a third-grader, had difficulty with his schoolwork, and also found it hard to make friends.*

coursework /ˈkɔːʳswɜːʳk/ [n U] British the work that a student has to do for the course that they are studying, especially when this is compared with work done in examinations: *Half of the marks are for the exam, the rest are for coursework.* | *None of the coursework seemed to have much relevance to being a nurse in a busy hospital.* | *I'm just so behind on the coursework.*

studies /ˈstʌdiz/ [n plural] formal the work that a student does at a school or university **sb's studies** *After the war, he resumed his studies at the University of Turin.* | *Her parents insisted that she give up the vacation job, as they felt it was interfering with her studies.* | **finish/complete your studies** *After completing her studies at the University, she worked as a nurse for six years.*

3 work that you have to do in your home

▸ housework ▸ work

housework /ˈhaʊswɜːʳk/ [n U] work that needs to

be done in your home, for example, cleaning, washing clothes, or keeping rooms tidy: *None of her kids ever help with the housework.* | *I've got to catch up on the housework this weekend.* | **do housework** *Well, I did all my housework this morning, though you wouldn't think it to look at the place now.*

work /wɜːʳk/ [n U] the things that you have to do in your home, for yourself or your family: *The garden needs a bit more work, but it's almost finished.* | *Use the best tools and materials you can afford to give a professional finish to your DIY work.* | **do some/any more/a bit of etc work** *'Where's Dave?' 'He's outside, doing some work on the car, I think.'* | **+ on** *I'm not doing any more work on the house this year, I can't be bothered.*

4 a piece of work done by an artist, musician etc

- work
- piece

work /wɜːʳk/ [n C usually plural] something such as a painting, film, book, or long piece of music produced by an artist, writer etc: *The painting is one of Picasso's earlier works.* | *A major new work by one of Poland's leading film directors will be shown next Saturday.* | **work of art** (=a painting or sculpture, especially a famous, important, or very valuable one) *The highest price paid for a work of art was the £30.2 million for Van Gogh's 'Irises'.* | **complete works of sb** (=all the things that someone has produced) *the complete works of William Shakespeare*

piece /piːs/ [n C] something that has been produced by an artist, musician, or writer, for example a painting or drawing or a short **piece** of music or writing: *The concert began with three short pieces by the Brazilian composer Villa-Lobos.* | *The collection includes pieces in both oils and watercolours, with a range of still life paintings.* | **piece of music/writing/work etc** *Another typical piece of Owen's work is the poem, 'The Sentry'.* | *a truly impressive piece of Greek sculpture*

5 the effort involved in working

- work
- effort
- labour
- commitment

work /wɜːʳk/ [n U] *David tries to avoid work at all times.* | *It seems to be an awful lot of work to keep this place looking tidy.* | **hard work** *Finally, I would like to thank all the staff for their hard work this year.* | *My daughter gained her grades through sheer hard work and determination.* | **put work into sth** *His last few speeches had been awful, and he knew he had to put more work into them.* | *Phil has had the car for two years and has put hours of work into it.* | **a considerable/huge/immense etc amount of work** *A considerable amount of work was necessary to establish even this basic framework.* | *The students have put a huge amount of work into the scheme.* | **good/sterling work** (=used to say that the effort someone has made is good) *Well done Peter – keep up the good work.* | *I hope you'll join me in paying tribute to the sterling work done by the committee this year.*

effort /ˈefəʳt/ [n U] the physical or mental energy that is needed to do something: *It seemed like a lot of effort for a very small gain.* | *His last piece does require some effort from the listener, but it's well worth it.* | **with effort** *He mounted the slope with effort, breathing hard.* | **a waste of effort** *I could have told you it would be a waste of effort.* | **put effort in/into sth** *After all the effort I put in, they had better be satisfied!* | *Vicki has hardly put in any effort, yet she's expecting the same rewards as everyone else.* | **take/require effort** *This exercise isn't difficult – it shouldn't require much effort.* | *The former method takes a bit more effort, but the results are more reliable.* | **be (well) worth the effort** (=use this when the energy you use is worth using, because the result is good) *Children are hard work, of course, but worth the effort.* | *The climb is arduous, but well worth the effort, as the views from the top are spectacular.* | **time and effort** *I've spent a lot of time and effort getting this far. I'm not giving up now.*

labour British **/labor** American /ˈleɪbəʳ/ [n U] hard physical work, such as digging, lifting, or cleaning: *Many women do all the work in the home, and their labour is unpaid.* | *Marx defined the working class as people who sell their labour to employers.* | **manual/physical labour** *You don't look as if you could do physical labor.* | **farm/agricultural labour** *rising opportunities in agricultural labor in the North*

commitment /kəˈmɪtmənt/ [n U] the hard work and loyalty that someone gives to an organization, activity, or piece of work, because they really care about it and believe in it: *Thanks to your energy and commitment, the fundraiser was a great success.* | **+ to** *Your commitment to the project is very much appreciated by management.* | **total/absolute/full commitment** *He is adamant that he wants total commitment and effort in the build-up to the match.* | *Lawrence promised full commitment in his drive to make Santa Barbara College the most successful school in the region.*

6 unpleasant or boring work

- grind
- be a slog
- donkey work
- drudgery
- toil

grind /graɪnd/ [n singular] things that you have to do every day, especially as part of your job, which are boring and make you feel tired **+ of** *Work feels like such a grind lately.* | *The relentless grind of hard labour and ill-health had taken its toll on Booth.* | **the daily grind** *The daily grind of meetings and tutorials went on.* | **hard grind** British *The Prime Minister is pictured taking a break from the hard grind of political life.*

be a slog /biː ə ˈslɒg‖-ˈslɑːg/ [v phrase] British use this to say that work is difficult, boring, and tiring: *The journey across the valley to the farm is going to be a slog.* | **hard/long slog** *It's a hard slog isn't it? I wish we'd got further yesterday.* | *Cutting all the wood before nightfall was a long, hard slog.*

donkey work British **/grunt work** American /ˈdɒŋki wɜːʳk‖ˈdɑːŋki-, ˈgrʌnt wɜːʳk/ [n U] informal work that is boring or takes a lot of time and effort, but that has to be done as part of a job or larger piece of work: *I was doing grunt work for the secretary in the department, twenty hours a week.* | *The real donkey work was actually done by those guys.*

drudgery /ˈdrʌdʒəri/ [n U] work that is hard and unpleasant because it is very boring, takes a long time to do, and often involves a lot of physical effort: *Technological advances have taken much of the drudgery out of the assembly line and car plant.* | *What seemed a promising job turned into months of boredom and drudgery.* | **the drudgery of sth** *The data management system has eliminated much of the drudgery of filing.* | *Calculators were introduced to relieve students of the drudgery of pencil-and-paper number-crunching.*

toil /tɔɪl/ [n U] formal difficult and boring work that takes a long time: *Here began their arduous toil to force a living from the land.* | *man's desire for freedom from physical toil*

to work/do work

7 to do a job that you get paid for

- work
- be
- go into
- practise

work /wɜːʳk/ [v I] *I haven't worked since I had my first child seven years ago.* | *His illness eventually prevented him from working.* | *Four teachers agreed to work without pay until things were settled.* | **+ for** *For nineteen years, my father worked for the General Electric Corporation.* | *The company Jack worked for gave him fully paid leave during his wife's illness.* | **+ in/on/at** *I'd never worked in a lab before I came here.* | *Five mornings a week, she worked on campus.* | *Over the years, I'd gotten used to all the perks of working at a posh downtown Miami law firm.* | **work as a consultant/secretary/builder etc** *He's changed his job and is now working as a consultant for a German firm.* | *Her father was an artist who sometimes worked as a salesman and labourer.* | **work somewhere** *Sorry, Bethany doesn't work here any more.* | *Where do you work?* | **work long hours/Sundays/nights/full-time etc** *He only works three days a week now.* | *There's always someone in – I'm working nights so I'm here in the days.* | *I was working full-time, so I didn't see much of my girlfriend.* | *Are you prepared to work longer hours occasionally, to get the work done?* | **work hard** *My staff work hard, and they trust me. That's important.*

be /biː/ [v] if someone **is** a teacher, farmer, doctor etc, that is their job: *'What do you do?' 'I'm a journalist.'* | *She was a teacher for over twenty years.* | *Before becoming a writer, Schwarz had been a cook, a cab driver and a door-to-door salesman.*

go into /ˈgəʊ ɪntuː/ [v T] **go into teaching/nursing/politics/journalism etc** to start working as a teacher, nurse etc, because you have decided that this is the job you would like to do: *Janet says she'd like to go into teaching after she finishes college.* | *Mills was wealthy even before he went into politics.* | *Snyder went into business for herself as an independent consultant.*

practise British **/practice** American /ˈpræktɪ̈s/ [v I/T] to work in a professional job as a doctor, lawyer, dentist etc: *Although he is a qualified dentist, he ceased to practice several years ago.* | *Kingsley has been practising from the London Hydrotherapy Centre since 1960.* | **practise medicine/law etc** *I graduated from Manchester Law school and practised law with the firm of Arthur & Madden of Birmingham.* | **+ as** *A small proportion of those who complete their training do not practise as doctors.* —**practising** [adj only before noun] *Jenny is a practising psychotherapist.*

8 to do work that is not part of your job

- work
- do

work /wɜːʳk/ [v I] to do an activity that needs effort and takes time: *I've been working all day in the garden.* | *We had to work non-stop to get the boat ready for the race.* | **+ on** *I have to work on the Jeep over the weekend.*

do /duː/ [v T] **do the housework/gardening/cleaning etc** to **do** work that must be done regularly in your home: *I'm always the one who does the cooking and cleaning and stuff around here.* | *It's about time the laundry was done.* | *Hey, the washing-up's been done. That must have been Cynthia.*

9 to be at the place where you work

- be at work
- be on duty
- on business
- be on call

be at work /biː ət ˈwɜːʳk/ [v phrase] to be doing your job at the place where you work, especially at a factory, office etc owned by your employer: *I'm afraid Fran's not here at the moment – he's at work.* | *What time do you have to be at work?* | *I'll tell you, I wish I had these DAT machines at work.*

be on duty /biː ɒn ˈdjuːti‖-ˈduːti/ [v phrase] to be at work in a job where there must always be someone working, for example if you are a nurse or a police officer: *You can't drink while you're on duty.* | **on duty 24 hours/from 6.00 p.m./on Mondays etc** *I'm on duty from 8 a.m. on Monday till 12 midday on Thursday.* | *We're on duty tonight at half past ten.*

on business /ɒn ˈbɪznɪ̈s/ [adv] if someone goes somewhere **on business**, they go somewhere as part of their job, especially to another city or country: *She drives to Tijuana several times a month on business.* | *The family was living in the Palace Hotel in Japan because my father was there on business.* | *Do you travel abroad on business more than three times a year?* | **be away on business** *With her husband frequently away on business, Berenice turns to a close friend for help and support.*

be on call /biː ɒn ˈkɔːl/ [v phrase] if someone such as a doctor, lawyer, or engineer **is on call**, they can be telephoned and will work if they are needed: *Doctor Lalor won't be at the surgery this afternoon, but she's on call until midnight.* | *If the machine breaks down at any time, there's always a technician on call.* | *Construction managers must be on call to deal with emergencies.* | **be on call 24 hours a day/3 days a week etc** *Resident managers live in hotels and are on call 24 hours a day.*

sth you have to do

10 a piece of work that you have to do

- job
- task
- something to do/some work to do
- piece of work
- assignment
- chore
- errand
- duty

job /dʒɒb‖dʒɑːb/ [n C] a specific piece of work that you have to do, often one that you are not paid for: *Repairing the roof – that's going to be the biggest job.* | *Cleaning the car's one of my least favorite jobs.* | **do a job** *Well, I must go now. I've lots of jobs to do around the house.* | **do a good/nice/beautiful etc job** (=do a job well) *I always take my car to York Street garage. They're expensive, but they do a good job.* | *Irene did a nice job on those clothes didn't she?* | **get on with a job** (=continue doing a job) *He didn't complain or criticize, he just got on with the job.* | **odd jobs** (=jobs of different kinds that are not regular) *He does odd jobs for people in his spare time.* | **the job in/at hand** (=the job you have to do at the moment) *Let's just concentrate on the job in* *hand, shall we? | She was upset, and found it difficult to keep her mind on the job at hand.*

task /tɑːsk‖tæsk/ [n C] formal a piece of work that you have to do – use this especially about a difficult or unpleasant job, or about a specific part of your work: *One of the first tasks Eva set herself was learning the local language.* | **impossible/difficult/arduous etc task** *The UN Peacekeeping Force faces an almost impossible task.* | *We knew what had to be done, but it wasn't an easy task.* | **+ of** *Recovery crews continued the grim task of retrieving bodies from the wreckage.* | **face/begin/continue a task** *By 2001, we had begun the task of collecting the materials and information needed for the study.* | *This is one of the most difficult and complex tasks we face.* | **perform a task/carry out a task** *Most of the workers did not have the skills required to perform the most basic tasks.* | *The massacre was never fully investigated because the police were incapable of carrying out the task.* | **thankless task** (=one that no one wants to do because they will get no satisfaction from it) *Who on earth would volunteer for such a thankless task?*

something to do/some work to do /ˌsʌmθɪŋ tə ˈduː, səm ˈwɜːʳk tə duː/ [v phrase] a job that you have to do, either for your work or for yourself, especially things that you have to leave your office or house to do: *I'll pick the laundry up on Saturday – I have some shopping to do anyway.* | *I've got some work to do this evening.*

piece of work /ˌpiːs əv ˈwɜːʳk/ [n phrase] something that you have to do, especially something that involves writing or drawing and a lot of thinking **do/hand in/submit a piece of work** *Do you actually fail the year if you don't hand in a piece of work?* | *I've got a merit for every piece of work I've done.* | **good/excellent etc piece of work** *I think this is a very fine piece of work and it deserves a first class mark.* | *Look at that piece of work and ask yourself the question – 'Is this the best I can do?'*

assignment /əˈsaɪnmənt/ [n C] a piece of work that someone gives you to do, as part of your job or as part of your studies: *Bart's first assignment for the newspaper was to report on the French elections.* | *This is a really tough assignment, and I believe you're the only person who can handle it.* | **finish/complete an assignment** *She stayed late to complete a class assignment.* | **history/homework/school/military etc assignment** *Robin spent many lunch hours poring over her math assignments.* | *I eventually got a teaching assignment at Xibei.* | **one-year/two week etc assignment** *'I figure this will either make or break us,' Cheyne said of the 1-year assignment to get the camp up and running.*

chore /tʃɔːʳ/ [n C] an unpleasant or boring job, especially one that you have to do regularly in your home: *Washing the kitchen floor was a daily chore, and it was the one I hated most.* | *When we opened the store, our ambition was to make shopping less of a chore, more of a pleasure.* | *When I got old enough I started to have chores around the house.* | **do the/your chores** (=do all the cleaning etc that needs doing in a home) *Michael, come on. Do your chores, bud.* | **household chores** (=chores in the home, such as cleaning or cooking) *Husbands should be prepared to do their share of the household chores.*

errand /ˈerənd/ [n C] a small job that you need to do or that someone has asked you to do, such as buying something, posting something, taking somebody to a place etc **do/run an errand (for sb)** *Before you disappear, I want you to do an errand for me.* | *Peter cleaned equipment, ran errands, answered the phone – it was all routine.* | *I used to pick up her dry cleaning and run errands for her.*

duty /ˈdjuːti‖ˈduːti/ [n C usually plural] something that you have a responsibility to do, especially as a regular part of your job: *For the most part, there was not much to do, other than cleanup duty around the prison camp.* | *Part of a park ranger's official duties is to ensure public safety.* | *clerical and secretarial duties* | **have a duty to do sth** formal *Teachers have a duty to ensure that students are not injured whilst they are in their care.* | **perform a duty** *And now I have a very pleasant duty to perform. I am going to present the prizes to the winning competitors.* | **tour of duty** (=a period of time that a soldier or other member of the armed forces spends in a particular place) *He recently completed a tour of duty in Seoul as assistant to the US ambassador there.*

11 an important piece of work

- project
- mission
- undertaking

project /ˈprɒdʒekt‖ˈprɑː-/ [n C] an important piece of work that an organization, group, or person plans carefully in order to achieve a particular aim over a long period of time: *The federal government will help fund this immense project, which includes the building of 150 day-care centers.* | *The government scrapped the project after ruling that the costs were too high.* | *I've been working on the Inner City Development Project for the last five years.* | **educational/construction/research etc project** *a joint US–British research project* | *These are encouraging signs that the ballpark project is moving from blueprint to reality.*

mission /ˈmɪʃən/ [n C] an important job that someone is sent to do in another place, especially for a military or political purpose: *He was immediately sent to Paris. His mission was to negotiate a cease-fire.* | *He volunteered to embark on a dangerous secret mission into occupied France.* | *a rescue mission to salvage a satellite* | **combat/military mission** *I flew on over 280 combat missions in two wars, so I'm used to danger.*

undertaking /ˌʌndəˈteɪkɪŋ‖ˈʌndərteɪ-/ [n C usually singular] a big or important job, which you decide or agree to do, and which you will be responsible for **huge/major/big etc undertaking** *In the late 1980s, the US embarked on a major undertaking: the human genome project.* | *Everybody needs to realise that this is a huge undertaking.* | *Covering an Olympics is an extraordinary undertaking for any television company.*

12 to give someone work to do

- give
- assign
- set
- commission
- saddle sb with

give /gɪv/ [v T] if you **give** someone a job, some work etc, you offer them the job, work etc, or ask them to do it for you **give sb sth** *I asked Joel's teacher if we should give him some Level 4 work.* | *We were given some grammar assignments for homework.* | **give sth to sb** *Angie did a really good interview, but they gave the job to someone with more experience.* | **give sb sth to do/give sth to sb to do** *What can I give Helen to do? She's finished the filing.* | *OK, you open the parcels. That'll give you something to do.* | *'Have you peeled the carrots?' 'No, I gave them to Dad to do.'*

assign /əˈsaɪn/ [v T usually in passive] formal to give a particular job to a particular person **be assigned sth** *You have been assigned the task of keeping the* *records up to date.* | *After her promotion took effect, she was assigned a research job.* | **be assigned to sb** *The job of producing a development program was assigned to the junior minister.* | *He was asked to assign two of his employees to the inventory control department.*

set /set/ [v T] especially British if a teacher or employer **sets** you a piece of work, they give it to you to do, and you must finish it by a particular time or date **set homework/a task/work etc** *Mr Harris always sets a lot of homework.* | *Is that all – or has she set some other task for you as well?* | *Anneka was set the huge task by Christian Aid on behalf of a family who fled from war-torn Mozambique.* | **set sb sth** *She set us some work to do in groups.* | *At the end of the session, they were set a homework task.*

commission /kəˈmɪʃən/ [v T] to appoint someone to do a piece of work for you, for example to write a report or to produce some artistic or scientific work: *The Philadelphia Medical Society commissioned a report on alcoholism.* | **be commissioned for/by/from etc** *His 'Landscapes' Symphony was commissioned for the inaugural concert of the Shepherd School.* | *Seventy-five percent of Americans think that women are more sensual than men, according to a survey commissioned by Revlon.* | *The Left-Hand Piano Concerto was the first of several works commissioned from distinguished composers.* | **commission sb to do sth** *In 1506, Bramante was commissioned by Pope Julius II to rebuild St Peter's church.* | *The gallery is housed in the new wing, which he commissioned Adams to build 18 years ago.*

saddle sb with ALSO **lumber sb with** British informal /ˈsædl (sb) wɪð, ˈlʌmbəʳ (sb) wɪð/ [phr v T] to give someone an unpleasant or difficult job to do **be/get saddled with sth** *Campaign adviser Ken Polaski has been saddled with the job of explaining the recent presidential gaffes.* | *'I'm sorry you've been lumbered with running me back home,' said Ashley stiffly.* | **saddle sth with sth** *The Hong Kong Rugby Union has saddled Simpkin with the post of national coach to the ailing team.*

work for sb

RELATED WORDS

▸ *see also* **job, work, business, company, position/rank, manager, in charge of**

1 to work for a company, person etc

- work for
- be employed
- be on the payroll
- be on the staff
- be with sb
- employer

work for /ˈwɜːʳk fɔːʳ/ [v T not in passive] to do **work for** a person, company, or organization: *How long have you worked for Mr Jackson?* | *My Dad's been working for IBM for over twenty years.* | **work as sth for** *Russell is working as a software developer for Microsoft.*

be employed /biː ɪmˈplɔɪd/ [v phrase] to work for a company or organization, especially when you have an official contract and a permanent job **+ by** *She was the first woman pilot to be employed by a commercial airline.* | **+ in** *The number of people employed in the construction industry has been falling for many years.*

be on the payroll /biː ɒn ðə ˈpeɪrəʊl/ [v phrase] to officially work for a company or organization and to receive regular payments for your work: *Just before the company closed in 1968, there were 300 people on the payroll.* | **+ of** *Ames exposed 34 intelligence agents on the payroll of the US or its allies.*

be on the staff /biː ɒn ðə ˈstɑːf‖-ˈstæf/ [v phrase] to be one of the people who work for a company or organization, especially when you have a permanent job there: *Police questioned everyone on the staff at the hotel.* | **+ of** *Valerie has been on the staff of the French Department at Reading University since 1992.*

be with sb /biː wɪð (sb)/ [v T] informal to work for a company, especially a large well-known one: *I believe he's with Random House now.* | *I used to be with the BBC, but then I got the chance of being a producer for Channel Four.*

employer /ɪmˈplɔɪəʳ/ [n C] the person, company, or organization that you work for: *We will need a reference from your last employer before we can send you a contract.* | *She applied to her employer for a redundancy payment, but she was refused.*

2 to work independently and not for someone else

- self-employed
- have/run your own business
- freelance
- be your own boss

self-employed /ˌself ɪmˈplɔɪd◂/ [adj] someone who is **self-employed** does not have a job with one particular employer, but instead works independently and does work for many different people: *Martin is a self-employed builder.* | *Most fashion models are self-employed, and find work through agencies.* | **the self-employed** (=people who are self-employed) *The government gives generous tax allowances to the self-employed.*

have/run your own business /ˌhæv, ˌrʌn jɔːr əʊn ˈbɪznɪs/ [v phrase] to own and manage a business, especially a small one such as a shop or restaurant: *She runs her own business, making and selling hand-knitted clothes.* | *It's always been Maria's ambition to have her own business.* | **set up your own business** (=begin running your own business) *People wanting to set up their own business should take expert financial advice.*

freelance /ˈfriːlɑːns‖-læns/ [adj] working for several different organizations instead of being employed by only one – use this especially about people such as writers, designers, and photographers **freelance designer/journalist/photographer** *Jamie's trying to earn a living as a freelance photographer.* | **freelance work/writing/photography etc** *Karen stayed at home while the children were small, and made a little money from freelance writing.* —**freelance** [adv] *If you work freelance from home, your hours are completely flexible.* | **go freelance** (=start working freelance after being employed by one organization) *I'd built up a number of contacts in the world of graphic design, so in the end I went freelance.*

be your own boss /biː jɔːr ˌəʊn ˈbɒs‖-ˈbɔːs/ [v phrase] informal to work independently and not be employed by other people, and therefore be able to decide by yourself what you should do: *I'm not good at taking orders from anybody – I prefer being my own boss.* | *Jim sacrificed a television career to set up in business and be his own boss.*

3 someone who works for a company or organization

- worker
- employee
- member of staff/staff member

worker /ˈwɜːʳkəʳ/ [n C] someone who works for an organization but is not a manager: *We need better communication between the management and the workers.* | **manual worker** (=someone who does physical work, for example in a factory, rather than working in an office) *The report shows that male manual workers earn twice as much as female workers.* | **post office/factory/office etc worker** *Tony was a retired post-office worker.* | *Ambulance workers threatened to refuse all calls for twenty-four hours on New Year's Eve.* | **skilled/unskilled worker** (=someone who has or does not have special skills) *Despite the high unemployment rate, there is a shortage of skilled workers in some sectors.* | **white-collar workers** (=people who work in offices, banks etc, rather than in factories or with their hands) *There is increasing social mobility among senior white collar workers, who are able to move quite rapidly between organizations.* | **blue collar workers** (=people who do unskilled or manual work) *The report showed that blue collar workers lost ten days a year due to ill health, compared with five days for white collar workers.*

employee /ɪmˈplɔɪ-iː, ˌemplɔɪˈiː/ [n C] someone who has a job, especially a permanent job, with a particular company or organization: *We are a multinational corporation with 140,000 employees worldwide.* | **+ of** *Employees of American Airlines get generous reductions on the cost of flights.*

member of staff/staff member /ˌmembər əv ˈstɑːf, ˈstɑːf ˌmembəʳ‖-ˈstæf/ [n phrase] someone who is employed by a company, organization, school etc, along with other people: *Training opportunities are available to all members of staff.* | *At certain stages of a project, most staff members are expected to work additional hours when needed.* | *Mr Vickers has been with the firm for forty years, and is their longest-serving member of staff.* | **senior/junior member of staff** *All employees have a formal annual interview with the senior member of staff responsible for their work.*

4 all the people who work in a company, organization, or country

- staff
- workforce
- labour
- personnel
- manpower

staff /stɑːf‖stæf/ [n C/U with singular or plural verb in British English] all the people who work in a company, organization, school etc: *The staff were clearly worried about rumours of job losses.* | **library/office/hospital/security etc staff** *Our library staff will be happy to help if you are unable to find the book you want.* | *Ford is looking for part-time sales staff.* | **join the staff** *In 1998, she joined the President's personal staff in the White House.*

workforce /ˈwɜːʳkfɔːʳs/ [n C usually singular] all the people that work in a country, industry, or large organization: *Women make up 41% of the workforce.* | *Cook began his cost-cutting campaign by getting rid of a third of his workforce.*

labour British **/labor** American /ˈleɪbəʳ/ [n U] all the people that work in an industry or country, especially people whose jobs involve working with their hands, in factories etc rather than managing other people: *Large-scale growth in this type of farming is limited by the climate and the high cost of labour.* | **skilled/unskilled labour** (=people who have or do not have special skills) *Many industries are reporting a shortage of skilled labor.* | **labour force** (=all the people who work or are available to work in a particular country or organization) *The labour force is growing at a rate of 4% a year.* | **cheap labour** (=people whose wages are very low) *Our produce prices cannot compete with those of Spain, with its cheap labour and sunshine.*

personnel /ˌpɜːʳsəˈnel/ [n plural] the people employed by a particular company, organization etc – used in official or business contexts: *In the event of a fire, all personnel must report to the reception area.* | *One of her responsibilities is recruiting highly trained personnel.*

manpower /ˈmænˌpaʊəʳ/ [n U] all the workers that an employer or a country has available to do work: *The police say they don't have sufficient manpower to patrol the area.* | *At the time there was a major shortage of trained manpower in computer science in the US.* | **manpower levels/resources/shortages etc** *The Commission was set up to look at the management of the manpower resources of the National Health Service.*

5 someone that you work with

- colleague
- workmate
- co-worker

colleague /ˈkɒliːg‖ˈkɑː-/ [n C] someone you work with – use this especially about people who do professional jobs in offices, schools, government etc: *I'd like you to meet a colleague of mine, Jean-Michel Blanc from our Paris office.* | *Jenny is a conscientious manager, very popular with her colleagues.*

workmate /ˈwɜːʳkmeɪt/ [n C] someone you work with, especially someone who works closely with you and who you are friendly with: *Having the support of close family, friends and workmates is important to us all.* | *Kevin had come home really upset after a quarrel with a workmate.*

co-worker /ˈkəʊ ˌwɜːʳkəʳ/ [n C] especially American someone you work with, especially someone who works closely with you or does a similar job: *Wantz's job is to teach employees how to handle difficult bosses and co-workers.* | *The manual explains what to do if a co-worker is injured and in need of medical attention.*

6 when there are not enough people working in a company etc

- be understaffed
- be short-staffed

be understaffed /biː ˌʌndəʳˈstɑːft‖-ˈstæft/ [v phrase] a company or organization that **is understaffed** does not have enough people working in it because it cannot or will not employ more people: *It's crazy that unemployment is sky-high while so many companies are still understaffed.* | *The few public health clinics that existed were filthy and understaffed.*

be short-staffed especially British ALSO **be short-handed** especially American /biː ˌʃɔːʳt ˈstɑːft‖-ˈstæft, biː ˌʃɔːʳt ˈhændɪ̣d/ [v phrase] to not have the number of people you need to do a job properly or on time, especially because some of the people who usually work are ill, on holiday etc: *Schools in inner city areas are often short-staffed because the work is particularly* *stressful.* | *After three hours, Mrs Morrison was told that her operation had been cancelled because the hospital was short-staffed.* | *Let me know if you're short-handed – I'll get a couple of the boys to help out.*

work hard

RELATED WORDS

▸ *see also* **work, work for sb, job, earn, business, company**

1 to work hard

- work hard
- put a lot of effort into sth
- work at
- be hard at work
- push yourself
- beaver away
- labour

work hard /ˌwɜːʳk ˈhɑːʳd/ [v phrase] to **work hard** when you are doing your job, your schoolwork, or anything that takes time and effort: *Bruno had been working hard in the kitchen all morning.* | *I wouldn't mind working so hard if they paid us more.*

put a lot of effort into sth /ˌpʊt ə lɒt əv ˈefəʳt ɪntə (sth) ‖-lɑːt-/ [v phrase] to work hard because you think something is important and you want to do it well: *Stella had obviously put a lot of effort into her assignment, and got a good grade.* | *The company puts a great deal of effort into training its staff.*

work at /ˈwɜːʳk æt/ [v T not in passive] to try hard to improve something or to improve the way you do something: *The only way to be successful in athletics is to really work at it.* | *You should be able to take your music exam in the summer, if you work at it between now and then.*

be hard at work /be hard at it British /biː ˌhɑːʳd ət ˈwɜːʳk, biː ˌhɑːʳd ˈæt ɪt/ [v phrase] informal to be working very hard and continuously: *Mike's been hard at it all afternoon and he still hasn't finished mending the car.* | **be hard at work on sth** *Since January, Leane's been hard at work on a self-help book on how to launch a business.* | **be hard at work doing sth** *They've been hard at work getting the house decorated.*

push yourself /ˈpʊʃ jɔːʳself/ [v phrase] to force yourself to work or train very hard at something: *If you really push yourself, you should get all the work done on time.* | **push yourself hard** *Warm up your body before you start exercising, and avoid pushing yourself too hard or too fast.*

beaver away British **/plug away** American /ˌbiːvər əˈweɪ, ˌplʌg əˈweɪ/ [phr v I] informal to work very hard for a long time in a determined way: *American investment bankers are still plugging away, looking for business in developing countries like Thailand, Indonesia, or Malaysia.* | **+ on/at** *Haven't you finished? You've been beavering away on that report all morning.*

labour British **/labor** American /ˈleɪbəʳ/ [v I] formal to work hard, especially doing hard physical work, or doing something difficult or boring: *Sheffield is a city where steel-workers once laboured in their thousands.* | **+ over** *Shipman was seated in his office, labouring over his paperwork, when I came in.* | **+ to do sth** *The goal was just what the team needed, at the end of a game in which they had laboured hard to overcome Chelsea.*

2 to work extremely hard

- slave away
- work your fingers to the bone
- work your butt/ass off
- toil

slave away /ˌsleɪv əˈweɪ/ [phr v I usually in progressive] informal to work very hard at something you do not enjoy and do not want to do: *I've been slaving away all week and I've had enough of it!* | **+ at** *Ed had been slaving away at his essay for hours, but it still wasn't finished.* | **+ to do sth** *The poor man spent ten years of his life slaving away to pay back the money they had borrowed.*

work your fingers to the bone /wɜːʳk jɔːʳ ˌfɪŋgəʳz tə ðə ˈbəʊn/ [v phrase] informal to work extremely hard for a long time – use this when you are complaining about how hard you have to work: *In those days we got up at 5 in the morning, and worked our fingers to the bone.* | *His mother had had a hard life – had worked her fingers to the bone bringing up six children.*

work your butt/ass off /ˌwɜːʳk jɔːʳ ˈbʌt, ˈæs ɒf/ [v phrase] American spoken to work very hard, especially for a period of time on one particular thing – use these only in situations where you know people well as they are considered impolite by many people: *It hasn't been easy. The truth is I've worked my ass off for everything I've achieved.* | **+ to do sth** *Lea worked her butt off to graduate with honors and big scholarships.*

toil /tɔɪl/ [v I] formal to work hard for a long time, especially doing work that is boring or difficult: *Men. women and children spent long hours toiling in the fields, whatever the weather conditions.* | **+ to do sth** *Roger and his wife toiled round the clock for seven years to make a success of their business.*

3 to work too hard

- overworked
- overdo it
- drive/push yourself too hard
- work/drive yourself into the ground

overworked /ˌəʊvəʳˈwɜːʳkt/ [adj] someone who is **overworked** has too much work to do: *Teachers often complain that they are overworked and underpaid.* | *I'd been six months without any holiday, and I was tired and overworked.* —**overwork** [n U] *She had a heart condition caused by heavy smoking and overwork.* (=being overworked)

overdo it /ˌəʊvəʳˈduː ɪt/ [v phrase] informal to work so hard that you become ill: *The doctor told me to relax and not overdo it.* | *The President's advisers are worried that he might have been overdoing it lately.*

drive/push yourself too hard /ˌdraɪv, ˌpʊʃ jɔːʳself tuː ˈhɑːʳd/ [v phrase] to force yourself to work too hard, especially because you want very much to be successful: *You should slow down. You're pushing yourself too hard.* | *It's no wonder that she had a nervous breakdown – she's been driving herself too hard for months.*

work/drive yourself into the ground /ˌwɜːʳk, ˌdraɪv jɔːʳself ɪntə ðə ˈgraʊnd/ [v phrase] informal to force yourself to work very hard, so that you become extremely tired or ill: *It's good to work hard. But don't drive yourself into the ground.* | *By the time the great day arrived, I'd worked myself into the ground making sure everything would be just right.*

4 someone who works hard

- hardworking
- workaholic
- industrious
- dedicated
- committed
- studious
- swot

hardworking /ˌhɑːʳdˈwɜːʳkɪŋ◂/ [adj] *Colleagues described him as a quiet, hardworking young man.* | *She's not our best employee, but at least she's hardworking.* | *Unfortunately, the school has just lost two of its best and most hardworking teachers.*

workaholic /ˌwɜːʳkəˈhɒlɪk‖-ˈhɔː-/ [n C] someone who wants to work all the time and who cannot relax when they are not working: *Steve's doing a sixty-hour week at the moment – I never realized he could be such a workaholic.* | *Selling is a career that seems to attract workaholics.*

industrious /ɪnˈdʌstriəs/ [adj] someone who is **industrious** works hard and effectively: *Most of the students I knew at college were serious and industrious.* | *The Omanis are industrious people, striving to make their country prosperous.*

dedicated /ˈdedɪkeɪtɪd/ [adj] someone who is **dedicated** works very hard at something because they care about it a lot, even though the job is difficult or does not earn them much money: *Janie's a wonderful nurse – completely dedicated.* | *The lifeboat service is run by a team of dedicated volunteers.* | **+ to** *The group is dedicated to the conservation of the environment.* | **+ to doing sth** *Worknet has a staff of 28 people, dedicated to assisting the community in their search for employment or training.* | **dedicated sportsman/gardener etc** (=someone who is dedicated to their sport, gardening etc) *As a dedicated sportsman, Steven trained every day of the week.*

committed /kəˈmɪtɪd/ [adj] if a person, organization, or country is **committed** to a particular job or idea, they really believe in it and want it to succeed, and are willing to work very hard to achieve this **+ to** *Edinburgh sees itself as a university of the new millennium, committed to research and teaching.* | **+ to doing sth** *Tanzania is a country committed to building socialism in the long term.* | **highly committed** *The company looks for highly committed people, who are willing to study for further professional qualifications in their own time.*

studious /ˈstjuːdiəs‖ˈstuː-/ [adj] someone who is **studious** likes to spend their time reading and studying in order to be more successful at school, college etc: *Francis didn't bother with clothes or make-up. She was an extremely serious and studious young girl.* | *Angus's round glasses made him look studious.*

swot British **/grind** American /swɒt‖swɑːt, graɪnd/ [n C] informal someone who spends too much time studying: *Everyone else in the class hated him because they thought he was a real swot.*

5 someone who does the hardest or most boring work

- drudge
- dogsbody

drudge /drʌdʒ/ [n C] someone who works hard at something that is difficult and boring, especially for people who do not realize or care that the work is difficult and boring: *The work I was given was the same, day after day; I felt like a drudge.* | **a household drudge** (=someone who stays at home doing nothing except boring tasks around the house) *One of the women said that since having four children, she felt she'd been reduced to a household drudge.*

dogsbody British **/peon** American /ˈdɒgzˌbɒdi‖ˈdɔːgzˌbɑːdi, ˈpiːən‖ˈpiːɑːn/ [n C] informal a person who does the boring or unimportant jobs that no one else wants to do: *You have to be prepared to be a peon when you start – sweeping floors, delivering, that kind of thing.* | **a general dogsbody** *I got myself a job as a typist and general dogsbody on a small magazine.*

6 to make people work hard

- work sb hard
- slave driver

work sb hard /ˌwɜːʳk (sb) ˈhɑːʳd/ [v phrase] to make someone work hard, especially unreasonably hard: *Sometimes I think that they work us too hard in this office.* | *The bank's managers admit that they work their employees hard, but on the other hand they pay good wages.*

slave driver /ˈsleɪv ˌdraɪvəʳ/ [n C] informal someone who makes people work too hard: *She's a real slave driver. One of her secretaries had a nervous breakdown last year.*

7 what you say to tell someone to work harder

- put some effort into it
- pull/get your finger out

put some effort into it ALSO **put your back into it** British **/put some muscle into it** American /ˌpʊt səm ˈefəʳt ɪntʊ ɪt, ˌpʊt jɔːʳ ˈbæk ɪntʊ ɪt, ˌpʊt səm ˈmʌsəl ɪntʊ ɪt/ [v phrase] use this to tell someone to work harder at what they are doing: *You'll have to put your back into it – I want to see all these boxes moved by tonight.* | *Come on you guys, let's see you put some muscle into it!*

pull/get your finger out /ˌpʊl, ˌget jɔːʳ ˈfɪŋgər aʊt/ [v phrase] British informal say this to tell someone to do something faster or work harder: *You could easily finish your essay if you just sit down and pull your finger out!*

8 to not work hard enough

- not pull your weight
- skive
- goof off
- not do a stroke of work
- slack
- malinger

not pull your weight /nɒt ˌpʊl jɔːʳ ˈweɪt/ [v phrase] to not do as much work as other people, when you are working in a group or team: *If you think that Alan isn't pulling his weight, you must tell him either to improve or leave.* | *Of all the people sharing the house with us, only Lizzie didn't pull her weight.*

skive /skaɪv/ [v I] British informal to not do the work that you should be doing, or to be away from your place of work without a good reason: *She says she's been ill for the past week, but I think she's just skiving.* | **skive off** (=not be at your place of work) *Harry's going to get into trouble if he keeps skiving off on Friday afternoons.* —**skiver** [n C] *Everyone knew that Ned was the biggest skiver in the class.*

goof off /ˌguːf ˈɒf/ [phr v I] American informal to not work when you are supposed to be working: *Hey you two! Quit goofing off and do some work!* | **goof off on the job** *Anyone who does consistently good work doesn't need to worry about occasionally goofing off on the job.*

not do a stroke of work /nɒt duː ə ˌstrəʊk əv ˈwɜːʳk/ [v phrase] British informal to do no work at all: *The* *telephone's been ringing and I haven't managed to do a stroke of work yet today.* | *Duncan found a wealthy woman, married her, and he's never done a stroke of work since!*

slack /slæk/ [v I usually in progressive] British informal to deliberately do less work than you should: *She called me into her office and accused me of slacking and taking too many holidays!* | **no slacking** (=use this to tell someone to work as hard as possible) *'You start tomorrow at nine,' he told them, 'and no slacking, or there'll be trouble.'*

malinger /məˈlɪŋgəʳ/ [v I usually in progressive] formal to avoid going to work by pretending to be ill: *I'm sure he's not malingering. He looked awful when I saw him last night.* | *The report claimed that women may be more likely to malinger than men.* —**malingering** [n U] *There've been so many cases of malingering that now you need a doctor's note if you're absent.*

working

when a machine/system etc works properly

RELATED WORDS

opposite: **broken/not broken**
- to have a job *see* **job (4)**
- *see also* **repair**

- work
- be in working order
- go
- be up and running
- operational
- on-stream

work /wɜːʳk/ [v I] if a machine or piece of equipment **works** or **is working**, it can be used without any problems because there is nothing wrong with it: *Does the old tape recorder still work?* | *We had to go to the laundromat because the washing-machine wasn't working.* | **work fine/be working fine** *We tested the cable and it seems to be working fine.* | **work well/be working well** *The new computers seem to work perfectly well, despite everyone's worries.*

be in working order /biː ɪn ˌwɜːʳkɪŋ ˈɔːʳdəʳ/ [v phrase] if something **is in working order**, it is working well and safely, especially because it has been well-cared for: *The mill was built in the 16th century and is still in working order.* | **be in good/perfect/top working order** *The guns were all clean and in good working order.* | *As far as he could tell the engine was in perfect working order.*

go British spoken **/run** American spoken /gəʊ, rʌn/ [v I] to be working properly – use this especially about a car, clock, or watch: *I dropped my watch, but it's still going.* | *I don't mind what kind of car we rent as long as it runs.*

be up and running /biː ˌʌp ən ˈrʌnɪŋ/ [v phrase] to be working well and without any problems – use this about computers or systems: *As soon as the new computer system is up and running, we can transfer our records onto it.* | *The new hiring process should be up and running by the end of the year.*

operational /ˌɒpəˈreɪʃənəl◂‖ˌɑː-/ [adj] a place, system, or large piece of machinery that is **operational** is working and ready to be used at any time: *At least eight countries are known to have operational nuclear weapons.* | **fully operational** *The terminal is fully operational and airlines will begin using it next week.*

on-stream especially British ALSO **on-line** American /ˌɒn ˈstriːm◂, ˌɒn ˈlaɪn◂/ [adj not before noun] a new system or large piece of machinery that is **on-stream** or **online**, is ready to be used – used especially in business: *All the oil refineries in the region are now back on-stream.* | **come on-stream/on-line** *Another nuclear reactor is scheduled to come on-line in January.* | **bring sth on-stream/on-line** *With so much money in grants, we need to start thinking now about the projects we want to bring on-stream.*

world

RELATED WORDS

- an area of the world *see* **area**
- *see also* **country, everywhere**

1 the world

- the world
- earth/Earth
- the planet
- the globe

the world /ðə ˈwɜːʳld/ [n singular] the planet we live on, and all the places on it: *In some parts of the world, clean drinking water is very scarce.* | **all over the world** *You can buy Coca-Cola all over the world.* | **around the world** (=in every part of the world) *Scientists around the world have been conducting similar experiments.* | *The ceremony was seen on television around the world.* | **the whole world** (=everyone and everything in the world) *For South Africa, and indeed for the whole world, 1990 was a year of great change.* | *The two countries are trying to work out a peace deal with the whole world watching.* | **the best, fastest etc in the world/the world's best, fastest etc** *It's the world's tallest building.* | *At age 116, she was believed to be one of the oldest people in the world.*

earth/Earth /ɜːʳθ/ [n singular/U] use this especially when you are comparing our world with the moon, stars, and other places in space: *Light from the stars can take millions of years to reach Earth.* | **the earth/the Earth** *The earth revolves around the sun.* | *Water is one of the Earth's most important resources.* | **the largest/oldest/poorest sth on earth** *Vietnam is among the poorest nations on Earth.* | *The blue whale is the largest animal on Earth.* | **to earth** *The space shuttle returned safely to earth on December 9th.*

the planet /ðə ˈplænɪ̣t/ [n singular] use this especially when you are talking about problems that affect the environment: *The massive volcanic eruption could affect the climate of the whole planet.* | *Energy conservation is vital for the future of the planet.* | *Ozone shields the planet from the effects of the sun's ultraviolet radiation.*

the globe /ðə ˈgləʊb/ [n singular] use this especially when you want to emphasize the great distances or areas involved in something that happens or exists in the world: *Water covers over half of the globe.* | *Using satellites, television pictures can be seen on the other side of the globe almost instantly.* | **all over the globe** (=everywhere in the world) *This garden has exotic plants from all over the globe.*

2 things that affect or happen everywhere in the world

- world
- global
- worldwide
- globalization

world /wɜːʳld/ [adj only before noun] use this to talk about something that exists everywhere in the world, affects the whole **world**, or is the best or most important in the world: *The top 50 multi-*

national companies control about 80% of world trade. | *At that time Britain was a major world power.* | *Islam is one of the great world religions.* | **world champion/record/expert** (=the best in the world) *The ice skating show features twelve Olympic and world champions.* | *Jones is a world expert in genetics.*

global /ˈgləʊbəl/ [adj only before noun] affecting the whole world – use this especially to talk about political or economic situations: *Campaigners have called for a global ban on landmines.* | *Multinational companies create, in effect, a global economy.* | **global warming** (=a global increase in temperature) *Scientists at an international conference have been discussing global warming and its possible effects.*

worldwide /ˌwɜːʳldˈwaɪd◂/ [adj only before noun] existing or happening in every country of the world: *There is a worldwide shortage of oil.* | *The concert attracted a worldwide television audience of over a billion people.* —**worldwide** [adv] *Sea levels are expected to rise worldwide by 2100.*

globalization ALSO **globalisation** British /ˌgləʊbəlaɪˈzeɪʃən‖-lə-/ [n U] when companies from one country operate in and affect countries all over the world, for example by selling their goods there, having factories there, employing people there etc: *Some see the spread of English as an international language as just another consequence of globalization.* | *Globalization often means that poorer countries become too dependent on foreign investment, with the result that their own development suffers.* | *There were widespread anti-globalization demonstrations at the World Environmental summit yesterday, leading to the arrest of dozens of protestors.*

worried/ worrying

RELATED WORDS

- *see also* **nervous, frightened/frightening, problem, relax/relaxed**

1 feeling worried

- worried
- anxious
- nervous
- concerned
- apprehensive
- uneasy
- dismayed
- not like the look/sound of

worried /ˈwʌrid‖ˈwɜːrid/ [adj] not feeling happy or relaxed, because you keep thinking about a problem or about something bad that might happen: *Dave could see how worried she was, and he tried to reassure her.* | **look worried** *You look worried – what's the matter?* | **+ about** *Marion was worried about losing her job.* | *We're very worried about Grandma.* | *I'm not really worried about how much it will cost.* | **+ (that)** *She rushed to the station, worried that she might miss her train.* | *I was worried if I washed it, it might shrink.* | **get worried** *I'm getting worried because my account still hasn't registered a check I deposited a while ago.* | **a worried look/frown/glance etc** *She had such a worried look on her face!* | *Helen looked at me with a worried expression.*

anxious /ˈæŋkʃəs/ [adj] especially written very worried because you think that something bad has happened or may happen, and you feel that you have no control over the situation: *Anxious relatives waited at the airport for news of the plane crash.* | **feel/sound anxious** *She knew it was a simple operation, but she still felt anxious.* | **+ about** *Helen is always anxious about travelling alone.* | *When you become anxious about sleeplessness, you actually make the problem worse.* | **an anxious face/voice/expression etc** *'Please come with me,' she said in an anxious voice.* | *Mae cast an anxious look in his direction.* —**anxiously** [adv] *'Is he going to be all right?' she asked anxiously.*

nervous /ˈnɜːʳvəs/ [adj] worried and slightly frightened about something that is going to happen or something new or difficult that you have to do: *I'm always nervous before exams.* | **get nervous** *Mum gets nervous if we don't call to say we're late.* | **look/feel/sound nervous** *Bill looked nervous, and I could see that his hands were shaking.* | *Harry began to feel nervous again as the plane made its descent.* | **make sb (feel) nervous** *The sounds outside were making me feel nervous.* | *Stop tapping your feet! You're making me nervous.* | **+ about** *Kelly was so nervous about her interview that she couldn't sleep.* —**nervously** [adv] *Nervously, she twisted her handkerchief in her fingers.* | *Carrie peeped out nervously.*

concerned /kənˈsɜːʳnd/ [adj] worried about someone else's problems, health, safety etc: *A TV programme about cruelty to children brought hundreds of letters from concerned viewers.* | **+ about** *I'm very concerned about Veronica. She looks so pale, and she has no appetite.* | *World governments are becoming increasingly concerned about rising global temperature levels.* | **+ for** *Rescuers are concerned for the safety of two men trapped in the mine.*

apprehensive /ˌæprɪˈhensɪv◂/ [adj] formal worried and a little frightened about something that you are going to do or about the future, because you are not sure what it will be like: *Dr Gottlieb reassures apprehensive patients that the operation is a simple procedure.* | **+ about** *I must admit that before my baby was born I was very apprehensive about motherhood.* | *No one need be apprehensive about their personal safety; everything is under control.* —**apprehensively** [adv] *She looked at her father apprehensively, frightened of what his reaction would be.*

uneasy /ʌnˈiːzi/ [adj] worried and not happy with a situation, because you feel there may be something wrong and you are not sure what is going to happen **make sb uneasy** *When I answered the telephone, no one was there, which made me uneasy.* | **feel uneasy** *After a while she started to feel uneasy, and then scared.* | **+ about** *Roger was a bit uneasy about the plan, but he agreed.* | *75 percent of consumers said they were uneasy about using their credit cards over the Internet.* | **distinctly uneasy** (=very uneasy) *I was distinctly uneasy in his company, but I couldn't explain why.* | **have the/an uneasy feeling** *She had the uneasy feeling that he wasn't going to come back.* —**uneasily** [adv] *Deborah shifted uneasily in her seat.*

dismayed /dɪsˈmeɪd/ [adj not usually before noun] very worried, disappointed, and upset by something that has happened: *Hardeep's lawyer said his client was 'shocked and dismayed' after hearing the court's decision.* | **+ at/by** *American historians are dismayed at the condition of the texts stored in the library.* | **dismayed to see/hear etc** *We were dismayed to discover that our daughter Louise had started experimenting with heroin.* | **+ that** *Danby was dismayed that Watt had opposed him in the vote.* | *Many of the nurses are dismayed that the management intends to make further service reductions.*

not like the look/sound of /nɒt ˌlaɪk ðə 'lʊk, 'saʊnd ɒv/ [v phrase not in progressive] informal if you **do not like the look** or **sound of** something, it makes you feel worried and unhappy because it seems threatening or dangerous: *I don't like the look of that rash on your chest.* | *The captain's face darkened as he listened. 'I don't like the sound of this,' he said.* | *Don't let anyone into your home that you don't like the look of.*

2 to make someone feel worried

- worry
- trouble
- concern
- bother
- cause concern/be a cause for concern
- prey on your mind

worry /'wʌri‖'wɜːri/ [v T] *The changes in the Earth's climate began to worry some scientists.* | *'Why didn't you tell me?' 'I didn't want to worry you.'* | **it worries sb that** *Doesn't it worry you that Stephen spends so much time away from home?* | **what worries sb is** *What worries me is the difference in age between Rosie and her boyfriend.* | *One thing that worried me was that information had been leaked to the press.*

trouble /'trʌbəl/ [v T] if a problem **troubles** you, it makes you feel worried because you do not know what to do about it: *You must talk to your daughter and find out what's troubling her.* | *The incident troubled me – it wasn't like Sarah to be so secretive.* | **be troubled by sth** *She is troubled by the fact that her son already shows signs of inheriting his father's mental problems.* —**troubled** [adj] *Kemp looked troubled. 'I'm not sure what's wrong,' he said.* | *He caught her troubled expression, and put an arm around her shoulders.*

concern /kən'sɜːʳn/ [v T not in passive] if someone else's problems, health, safety etc **concern** you, you worry about them because you think they are important, even when they may not affect you personally: *Kate's behaviour at school is starting to concern her parents.* | **it concerns sb that** *It concerns me that some tutors are meeting with students outside college hours.* | **what concerns sb is** *What concerns me most is that despite pay increases, production has not improved.*

bother /'bɒðəʳ‖'bɑː-/ [v T] if something **bothers** you, it slightly worries you – use this especially about problems that do not seem serious: *The only thing that bothers me is how I'm going to get from the station to the farm.* | *You shouldn't let little things like that bother you.* | **what bothers sb is** *What bothers me is that you didn't feel you could talk to me or your father about it.*

cause concern/be a cause for concern ALSO **give sb cause for concern** /ˌkɔːz kən'sɜːʳn, biː ˌkɔːz fəʳ kən'sɜːʳn, gɪv (sb) ˌkɔːz fəʳ kən'sɜːʳn/ [v phrase] if something that is happening **causes concern** or **is a cause for concern**, it makes someone, especially someone in an official position, feel worried, because it is unsatisfactory or possibly dangerous – used especially in official situations: *We have to inform you that your son's behaviour has been causing concern for some time now.* | *Two dozen cases of water poisoning in the space of a week certainly is a cause for concern, and we shall be taking action.* | *The Secretary General said that the recent developments are giving him cause for concern.* | **cause sb concern** *Your husband has almost recovered – the only thing that's still causing us concern is his high blood pressure.* | **cause concern among** *The decision has caused concern among human rights groups.*

prey on your mind /ˌpreɪ ɒn jɔːʳ 'maɪnd/ [v phrase] if a problem or something bad that has happened **preys on your mind**, it worries you continuously even though you do not want to think about it: *It was starting to prey on my mind so much that I went to the hospital.* | *The old woman's warning preyed on Mary's mind as she continued her journey.*

3 to feel worried about something

- worry
- fret
- brood
- be worried sick
- frantic
- be at your wits' end
- have qualms

worry /'wʌri‖'wɜːri/ [v I] *My husband worries when I'm late home from work.* | *Don't worry, there's plenty of time.* | *Mom, stop worrying. I'll be fine.* | **+ (that)** *He began to worry he might lose his job.* | *I was worried that Shannon was too small, but the doctor says she's fine.* | **+ about** *I was really worried about it at the time.* | *I don't know what you're worrying about.*

fret /fret/ [v I] to worry a lot about something, especially something that is not very serious: *She worries and frets all the time – I think it's because she's got no one to talk to about her problems.* | **+ about/over** *I'd sit in meetings, fretting about what was happening at home.* | *There's no point in fretting over it now.* | **+ that** *Opponents fret that the system might not provide enough help in times of rural economic crisis.*

brood /bruːd/ [v I] to keep thinking about and worrying about a problem for a long time after it has happened: *There's no point in brooding – forget about her.* | *Dad alternately brooded and raged, and Mum wasn't much better.* | **+ about/over/on** *Don't sit at home brooding about how badly you've been treated.* | *Achilles sits in his tent, brooding over the wrongs done to him.*

be worried sick /biː ˌwʌrid 'sɪk‖-ˌwɜːr-/ [v phrase] to be very worried and upset about something: *Where were you last night? I was worried sick.* | **+ about** *She's worried sick about the possibility of losing her job.* | *I'm worried sick about Sandy. I haven't heard from her for days.* | **worry yourself sick** *Jenny had worried herself sick trying to think of a way to pay back the money.*

frantic /'fræntɪk/ [adj] extremely worried and frightened about a situation and unable to think or behave calmly: *Inspector Grimes was used to dealing with frantic parents.* | **get/grow/become frantic** *The knocking on the door and shouts became frantic.* | *There is still no news of the missing child and her parents are getting frantic.* | *The dog's barking grew frantic as I approached.* | **frantic with worry/fear** *Her eyes were frantic with fear, and she couldn't keep still.* —**frantically** [adv] *She hung on frantically, terrified by the steep drop below.*

be at your wits' end /biː ət jɔːʳ ˌwɪts 'end/ [v phrase] to be very worried about a problem, especially something that has been happening for a long time that you feel you cannot deal with any longer: *I don't know what I can do to keep our marriage together – I'm at my wits' end!* | *It was two days before the baby was due, and Robert was at his wits' end.*

have qualms /hæv 'kwɑːmz/ [v phrase] to be worried that something you are going to do might be morally wrong: *Few so-called animal lovers have qualms when they purchase meat from supermarkets.* | *Despite my qualms, I accepted the job.* | **+ about** *Shareholders seem to have few qualms about companies sponsoring overseas abortion programs.*

4 to feel worried all the time

- have a lot on your mind
- be under stress/be under (a) strain
- stressed out
- preoccupied
- paranoid

have a lot on your mind /hæv ə ˌlɒt ɒn jɔːʳ ˈmaɪnd‖ -ˌlɑːt-/ [v phrase] to have a lot of problems to worry about, especially when this means that you do not concentrate on other things: *Since the divorce, Linda's had a lot on her mind.* | *I'm sorry I wasn't paying attention, I have a lot on my mind at the moment.*

be under stress/be under (a) strain /biː ˌʌndəʳ ˈstres, biː ˌʌndər (ə) ˈstreɪn/ [v phrase] to have a lot of work to do or have a lot of problems to deal with, so that you feel worried and tired or get upset easily: *Although I was under a strain, and drinking a lot at the time, I remember very clearly what happened.* | *This investigation has placed her under additional stress.* | **be under a lot of stress/strain** *Mr Payne, have you been under a lot of stress recently?*

stressed out /ˌstrest ˈaʊt◂/ [adj] informal so worried and tired from problems you have to deal with continuously that you cannot relax: *By the end of the tour, the band was totally stressed out.* | *One of my adult students was a stressed-out working mother.* | **feel stressed out** *I'm trying to have a few early nights because I'm feeling stressed out at the moment.*

preoccupied /priːˈɒkjᵍpaɪd‖-ˈɑːk-/ [adj] worrying so much about a particular problem that you cannot think about anything else: *I admit I'm preoccupied and snappy at the moment – I'm sorry.* | *Alison had entered the room, but he was too preoccupied to notice.* | **look/seem preoccupied** *She seemed preoccupied and kept glancing toward the window.* | **preoccupied look/expression etc** *Prajapat glanced up with a preoccupied smile, then went back to the map.* | **+ with** *He was far too preoccupied with his own marital difficulties to give any thought to his friend's problems.*

paranoid /ˈpærənɔɪd/ [adj] someone who is **paranoid** is worried all the time that people do not like them, that bad things are going to happen to them etc, when this is not true: *I was so paranoid at one point, that I was refusing to answer the door.* | **feel paranoid** *The mysterious phone calls were beginning to make him feel paranoid.* | **+ about** *By 1982, he was so paranoid about his health that he wore plastic gloves at all times.* —**paranoia** /ˌpærəˈnɔɪə/ [n U] the feeling or medical condition of being paranoid: *Just forget it – it's pure paranoia.* | *the paranoia of the Nixon years* | **sb's paranoia** *His words only added to her fear and paranoia.*

5 making you feel worried

- worrying
- stressful
- anxious
- alarming
- tense
- niggling
- alarmist

worrying ALSO **worrisome** American /ˈwʌri-ɪŋ‖ ˈwɜːri-, ˈwʌrisəm‖ˈwɜːri-/ [adj] *The possibility that I might lose my job is very worrying.* | *It must have been a worrying time for you.* | **it's worrying that/when etc** *It's always a little worrisome when a company is praised for making a smaller loss than expected.* | *a worrying upsurge in violence*

stressful /ˈstresfəl/ [adj] a **stressful** job or situation makes you feel worried and tired all the time, for example because you have too many problems or too much work to do: *Looking after small children can be very stressful.* | *What's the most stressful aspect of your job?* | *It was a stressful time for the whole family.*

anxious /ˈæŋkʃəs/ [adj only before noun] **anxious time/wait/hours etc** a time during which you feel worried and nervous, because the situation is dangerous and you do not know what is going to happen: *For one anxious moment, I thought the rope was going to break.* | *After an anxious wait, Audrey was told her father had died.* | *In the anxious days that followed, Henry tried to keep his mind off his results.*

alarming /əˈlɑːʳmɪŋ/ [adj] changing or increasing in a way that is worrying and frightening: *Even more alarming is the increase in child porn sites on the Internet.* | *an alarming rise in crime* | **it's alarming that/when etc** *It's alarming to think how many people are at risk.* | **alarming rate/number** *The epidemic is spreading at an alarming rate.* | *There are no easy answers to the alarming number of mass killings taking place in our cities.* | **in alarming numbers** *The young girls she treats in alarming numbers are the victims of broken homes and parental neglect.* | **at an alarming rate** *Agricultural open space is disappearing at an alarming rate.* | **with alarming frequency/regularity** *Baggage seems to go missing with alarming frequency on these flights.* —**alarmingly** [adv] *Infant mortality among the population is alarmingly high.*

tense /tens/ [adj] a situation or time that is **tense** makes you feel worried and nervous that something bad might happen at any time: *The atmosphere in the waiting room was extremely tense.* | *In the program, the hostages re-live the tense days they spent under guard in East Africa.* | *In the tense silence that followed, the boys fidgeted uneasily.* | **tense face/expression etc** *Her tone was anxious now, her face tense.*

niggling /ˈnɪgəlɪŋ/ [adj only before noun] **niggling feeling/worry/doubt etc** something that continues to worry you, even though you do not really want to think about it: *The suspect seemed to have proved his innocence, but a niggling doubt remained in my mind.* | *I couldn't shake off a niggling worry. Had I forgotten to lock the office door?*

alarmist /əˈlɑːʳmᵻst/ [adj] making people worried about dangers that do not really exist: *I do not wish to be alarmist, but the situation in the region is worse than it has been in many months.* | *The ambassador dismissed these views as excessively alarmist.* | *alarmist propaganda*

6 something that makes you feel worried

- worry
- concern
- stresses and strains
- hang-up
- cares

worry /ˈwʌri‖ˈwɜːri/ [n C] *It's important that children can discuss their worries with their parents.* | *His remarks reflect a widespread worry that Canada may be going the same way as the US.* | **+ about/over** *Worries about the tire company's performance sent its shares tumbling.* | *The launch was delayed because of worries over protestors.* | **greatest/biggest/main etc worry** *Roosevelt's chief worry at the time was that an attack on Britain would put the US at a strategic disadvantage.*

concern /kənˈsɜːʳn/ [n C] a situation that makes you feel worried, especially a problem that affects a lot of people, but that may not affect you personally: *The hospital's main concern is that doctors are overworked.* | *The survey suggests that rising crime is the top of the average American's concerns.* | **+ about/over** *My only concern about the match is that Price will be fit enough to take part.* | *The committee brushed aside concerns about racism and prejudice in local government.* | **raise concerns** (=cause concerns) *The incident has raised concerns that the government may retaliate.*

stresses and strains /ˌstresɪ̈z ən ˈstreɪnz/ [n phrase] all the things in a job or situation that make you feel worried and tired, especially when your work or life is very difficult: *Despite many stresses and strains, the team has held together, and I'm proud of that.* | **+ of** *the stresses and strains of modern living* | *Do some gentle exercises to relieve the stresses and strains of your day.*

hang-up /ˈhæŋ ʌp/ [n C] informal if you have a **hang-up** about something, for example your appearance, or your relationships with other people, you feel worried and embarrassed about it, and this makes you feel less confident: *I want the children to understand sex and grow up without any hang-ups.* | **have a hang-up about** *Sarah has a hang-up about her nose – she thinks it's too big.* | *They're just ordinary people with all the usual hang-ups about love.*

cares /keəʳz/ [n plural] written problems or responsibilities in your life that make you worry: *She was not really ready for the cares and responsibilities of running a family.* | *'Forget all your cares and worries', as the song goes.*

7 the feeling of being worried

- worry
- stress
- concern
- anxiety
- strain
- angst

worry /ˈwʌri‖ˈwɜːri/ [n U] *The meningitis outbreak is a major cause of worry at the moment.* | *The rage and disappointment had disappeared, but the worry in Jim's face was starting to show.* | **+ over/about** *This constant worry about your debts isn't doing you any good at all.* | **be sick with worry** *The poor mother was sick with worry over her missing daughter.*

stress /stres/ [n C/U] the feeling of being worried all the time, for example about work or personal problems, which can make you ill or very tired: *Her financial problems were causing her a lot of stress.* | *methods for reducing stress* | *Air travelers can enjoy stress-free trips if they follow a few guidelines.* | **+ of** *The city's many parks offer a comforting relief from the stress of modern life.* | **mental/emotional/psychological stress** *Geoff is having trouble dealing with the emotional stress of his recent divorce.* | **stress-related illnesses/disorders/conditions etc** (=illnesses, conditions etc caused by stress) *His wife has also suffered stress-related health problems.* | **be under stress** (=be feeling stress) *She had been under a lot of stress just before the baby was born.* | *Workers are under such stress right now, and they have less time to spend relaxing with their families.*

concern /kənˈsɜːʳn/ [n U] a worried feeling – use this especially when many people are worried about a problem that affects everyone: *The shortage of water is beginning to cause widespread concern.* | **+ about/over** *There is also some concern about the safety of the structure.* | **express/voice concern** *I did voice my concern about the financial management, but was told to stay quiet.* | **deep/grave concern** *This is a matter of grave concern to the hospital management.*

anxiety /æŋˈzaɪəti/ [n U] the feeling of being worried because you think that something bad has happened or will happen, and you feel that you have no control over the situation: *I knew I had to give a speech, but the thought filled me with anxiety.* | *feelings of guilt and anxiety* | *The increase in the tax on heating fuel is causing a lot of anxiety among elderly people.* | **+ about** *Her anxiety about the pain of childbirth is understandable.*

strain /streɪn/ [n C/U] a feeling of being worried that is caused by having to continuously deal with a difficult problem or having to work very hard for a long period of time: *The strain of managing such a huge company became too much for Anita.* | *He could see the strain in her face as she told him what she was going through.* | **be a strain on** *The legal fight has been an enormous strain on my wife.* | **put (a) strain on sth** *The company wanted 110% commitment, and that put a strain on our marriage.* | **be under strain** *She had a busy week, and she's under a lot of strain at the moment.*

angst /æŋst/ [n U] a strong feeling of worry and anxiety, especially about things that you cannot change: *Wallowing in angst about the unfairness of it all will just make the problem worse.* | *a period of national angst* | *a touching story of teenage angst*

8 someone who worries a lot

- worrier
- worrywart
- neurotic

worrier /ˈwʌriəʳ‖ˈwɜː-/ [n C] the type of person who worries a lot, even when they do not need to: *He admitted to the doctor that he was a worrier and found it hard to relax.* | *My grandmother was always a worrier, and I take after her.*

worrywart /ˈwʌriwɔːʳt‖ˈwɜː-/ [n C] American informal someone who worries too much: *Don't be such a worrywart!* | *The cast also included Norman Fell as the worrywart producer.*

neurotic /njʊˈrɒtɪk‖nʊˈrɑː-/ [adj] always very worried and nervous about unimportant things or about dangers that do not really exist: *He was a shy, neurotic man who found it difficult to make friends.* | *In many respects, Mozart had a typically neurotic personality.* —**neurotic** [n C] *She is a complete neurotic – I don't think I've ever seen her sit down and relax.*

9 not worried

- not worried/concerned
- relieved
- be a weight off sb's mind
- relief
- not lose sleep over
- have no qualms
- carefree
- without a care in the world/not have a care in the world
- laugh off

not worried/concerned ALSO **unconcerned** formal /nɒt ˈwʌrid, kənˈsɜːʳnd‖-ˈwɜːrid, ˌʌnkənˈsɜːʳnd/ [adj] *Sam had stayed out late before, so we weren't particularly worried when he didn't return.* | *Brian didn't seem at all concerned when the car broke down.* | **+ about** *He insists that he is not worried about the poor showing his party made in the recent local elections.* | *For once, Karen seemed unconcerned about the possibility of being late for class.* | **not in the least bit worried etc** (=not at all worried) *Even after losing her job, she doesn't seem in the least bit worried.*

relieved /rɪˈliːvd/ [adj not before noun] feeling relaxed again because you do not need to worry about something that you worried about before: *'Oh,' she said, relieved. 'I'm so glad you're back.'* | **seem/feel/look/appear relieved** *The hostages simply look relieved to be going home.* | **+ that** *I was relieved that John was there to help me explain.* | *The government will be relieved that a crisis has been averted.* | **+ at** *Sahlin appeared relieved at my news.* | **relieved to know/hear/find/learn etc sth** *I'm so relieved to see you!* | *Polly was relieved to learn that her mother's illness was not a serious one.* | *Andrew was relieved to discover that he was not himself under suspicion.*

be a weight off sb's mind /biː ə ˌweɪt ɒf (sb's) ˈmaɪnd/ [v phrase] spoken if something **is a weight off your mind** you do not have to worry any more because something has happened to make you feel happier about it **be a great/big/enormous weight off sb's mind** *No doubt the news will be a huge weight off his mind.* | **take a weight off sb's mind** *Now that Peter has passed all his exams, it's taken a great weight off my mind.*

relief /rɪˈliːf/ [n singular/U] the pleasant feeling you have when you no longer have to worry about something: *A white envelope lay on the mat. Holmes felt considerable relief.* | **a feeling/sense of relief** *Edwards commented that the convictions give him a feeling of relief that he hopes the victim shares.* | **with relief** *To her own surprise, she began sobbing with relief.* | **to sb's relief** (=making them feel relieved) *To Greg's relief, nobody asked to check his ticket.* | *The rains came this weekend, much to the relief of tomato growers in Florida.* | **breathe/heave a sigh of relief** (=show by your behaviour that you are no longer worried about something) *You could hear the students breathing a collective sigh of relief when the final bell rang.* | **it is a relief to know/hear/see/find etc** *It was such a relief to see Liz looking healthy again.* | *Mary says it's a relief to have someone to talk to at last.* | **come as a relief** *The decision, announced on Thursday, came as a huge relief to the factory's 300 workers.*

not lose sleep over /nɒt ˌluːz ˈsliːp əʊvəʳ/ [v phrase] to not be worried by a problem because you do not think it is important enough: *I tried my best, and I certainly won't be losing any sleep over the result.* | *It's not that serious. I wouldn't lose sleep over it if I were you.*

have no qualms /hæv ˌnəʊ ˈkwɑːmz/ [v phrase] if you **have no qualms** about something, you are not worried about it, especially because you are sure it is the right thing to do **+ about** *One protestor said he would have no qualms about bombing the clinic.* | *He was a man who had no qualms about preaching one thing and practising another in his private life.*

carefree /ˈkeəʳfriː/ [adj] cheerful and not worried about anything, because you do not have any real problems or responsibilities in your life: *I felt carefree for the first time in my life.* | *They both laughed, feeling like two carefree schoolgirls.*

without a care in the world/not have a care in the world /wɪðaʊt ə ˌkeər ɪn ðə ˈwɜːʳld, nɒt hæv ə ˌkeər ɪn ðə wɜːʳld/ [adv] if someone is **without a care in the world**, they are not worried about anything at all and are happy: *I was just sixteen, young, confident and without a care in the world.* | *He puffed away on his pipe as if he didn't have a care in the world.*

laugh off /ˌlɑːf ˈɒf‖ˌlæf-/ [phr v T] to laugh and refuse to worry or be serious about a problem, when someone is trying to talk to you about it **laugh off sth** *Venables laughed off suggestions that he will be asked to retire.* | *She took praise with delight, and laughed off any criticisms with good humour.* | **laugh it off** *She was genuinely angry, but Luke just tried to laugh it off.*

10 to make someone feel less worried

- reassure
- set/put sb's mind at rest
- put sb out of their misery

reassure /ˌriːəˈʃʊəʳ/ [v T] to make someone feel less worried, especially by saying something to comfort them: *I tried to reassure her by saying that the police would arrive soon.* | *'No one can ever take your spirit away from you,' my mother reassured me.* | **+ that** *The company has reassured its workers that there will be no job losses this year.* | *She returned to her motel, reassured by the nurses that her husband would be quite all right.* —**reassuring** [adj] *He stroked her hand and murmured reassuring words.* | *There was something very reassuring about Jacob's voice.* | **find sth reassuring** *I saw a sign reading 'Welcome Visitors', which I found reassuring.*

set/put sb's mind at rest ALSO **set/put sb's mind at ease** /ˌset, ˌpʊt (sb's) ˈmaɪnd ət ˌrest, set, ˌpʊt (sb's) ˈmaɪnd ət ˌiːz/ [v phrase] to make someone feel less worried, especially by giving them information that shows they do not need to worry: *The doctor set my mind at rest by explaining exactly what effect the drug would have on me.* | *Just to put your mind at ease, we will get a second opinion from a cardiac specialist.*

put sb out of their misery /ˌpʊt (sb) aʊt əv ðeəʳ ˈmɪzəri/ [v phrase] informal to tell someone something that they have been waiting anxiously to find out: *Come on Robyn, put me out of my misery. Who won?* | *Eventually, we put him out of his misery and told him he'd passed.*

11 what you say to tell someone not to worry

- don't worry
- it's/everything's all right
- nothing to worry about

don't worry /ˌdəʊnt ˈwʌri‖-ˈwɜːri/ *'Don't worry, there's plenty of food for anyone who wants to come.'* | **+ about** *'Don't worry about me – I'll be fine,' said Billie.* | *Don't worry about it. You can pay me back tomorrow.*

it's/everything's all right ALSO **it's/everything's ok** /ɪts, ˌevriθɪŋz ɔːl ˈraɪt, ɪts, ˌevriθɪŋz əʊˈkeɪ/ use this to try to make someone feel better when they are worrying: *It's all right, honey, don't cry.* | *It'll all be over soon, and everything's going to be ok.*

nothing to worry about /ˌnʌθɪŋ tə ˈwʌri əbaʊt‖-ˈwɜːri-/ use this to tell someone that there is no reason to worry **there's/it's nothing to worry about** *It's just a simple check-up. There's nothing to worry about.* | **sb has nothing to worry about** *You're a bright girl, and you've got nothing to worry about, as long as you finish all your assignments.*

worse

RELATED WORDS

opposite: ———————— **better**

▸ *see also* **bad, improve**

1 worse

- ▸ worse
- ▸ not as good
- ▸ inferior
- ▸ not be in the same league/can't compare with
- ▸ not be a patch on

worse /wɜːʳs/ [adj] more unpleasant, annoying, bad etc, or of a lower standard or quality than someone or something else that is also bad: *I really don't think the situation could be any worse.* | **+ than** *Conditions in the prison were worse than anything I had seen before.* | *Stop it Gary, you're worse than the kids!* | **even/far worse** (=worse than something that is very bad) *Duncan's handwriting is even worse than his sister's.* | *a terrible script and even worse acting* | **a lot worse/much worse** *The traffic is a lot worse after five o'clock.* | *The next morning, the weather was much worse, and the team stayed at base camp.* | **make sth worse** *I tried to fix the computer myself, but that just made it worse.*

not as good /ˌnɒt əz ˈgʊd/ [adj phrase] of a lower standard, quality, or level than something else that is good: *I like this town better than Harrisburg, but the schools aren't as good.* | **+ as** *This book is not as good as her last one.* | *The fishing out there isn't as good as it used to be.* | **not nearly as good as/nowhere near as good as** (=use to emphasize that the difference in quality is quite big) *Their latest album isn't nearly as good as their last one.* | *Cheap, plastic-wrapped cheese is nowhere near as good as the real thing.*

inferior /ɪnˈfɪəriəʳ/ [adj] formal of a lower quality than something else, or less good at doing something than someone else: *Consumers are tired of paying a high price for what is an increasingly inferior service.* | *California oil is a heavier and inferior grade of oil, compared with other crude oils.* | **+ to** *Old Mr Carter was convinced that women doctors were inferior to men.* | **inferior in quality/status/worth etc** *White bread is generally inferior in nutritional value.* | **of inferior quality/materials/status etc** *Their furniture is certainly cheaper, but it's of inferior quality.*

not be in the same league/can't compare with /nɒt biː ɪn ðə ˌseɪm ˈliːg, ˌkɑːnt kəmˈpeəʳ wɪð‖ˌkænt-/ [v phrase] especially spoken use this to emphasize that someone or something is not nearly as good as someone or something else: *How can you compare him to Ivan Lendl? He's not in the same league at all.* | *Vinyl is strong and looks good but it doesn't compare with real leather.* | **not be in the same league as** *It's quite a good movie but not in the same league as 'High Noon' or 'The Magnificent Seven'*

not be a patch on /nɒt biː ə ˈpætʃ ɒn/ [v phrase] British informal use this to emphasize that something is not nearly as good as something else, especially something that came before it: *Shop-bought pasta sauces aren't a patch on home-made.* | *This year's charity marathon wasn't a patch on last year's.*

2 to become worse

- ▸ get worse
- ▸ deteriorate
- ▸ go down/decline
- ▸ worsen
- ▸ go from bad to worse
- ▸ go downhill
- ▸ suffer
- ▸ slip
- ▸ deepen
- ▸ degenerate

get worse /ˌget ˈwɜːʳs/ [v phrase] *The food here gets worse every day.* | *My eyesight must be getting worse.* | *I don't think things can get much worse!* | **get worse and worse** *The tension in the flat got worse and worse, and Kate thought about moving out.* | *Paul's behaviour seems to get worse and worse.*

deteriorate /dɪˈtɪəriəreɪt/ [v I] formal to gradually become worse: *If the dispute drags on, conditions in the city could deteriorate.* | *The US trade position has deteriorated over the past few years.* | **deteriorate rapidly** *Air quality is rapidly deteriorating in our cities.* | **deteriorate to the level/point/stage where...** (=to deteriorate so much that a particular problem is caused) *School buildings have deteriorated to the point where they pose a health threat to both students and teachers.* —**deterioration** /dɪˌtɪəriəˈreɪʃən/ [n U] *the further deterioration of relations between the two countries* —**deteriorating** [adj] *our deteriorating road network* | *deteriorating standards of living*

go down/decline /ˌgəʊ ˈdaʊn, dɪˈklaɪn/ [v I] to become gradually worse – use this especially about the quality or standard of something: *He's been very unhappy and depressed recently, and his work has definitely gone down.* | *The quality of life for pensioners in this country has certainly declined recently.* | **go right down** British *The standard of service has gone right down since the company was privatized.* —**declining** [adj] *Educationalists are worried about what they see as declining standards of literacy.*

worsen /ˈwɜːʳsən/ [v I/T] if a bad situation **worsens**, or something **worsens** it, it becomes worse: *The weather worsened during the night.* | *The government's bungling attempts to help have only worsened the refugees' plight.* | *The situation was worsened by Roy's tendency to drink heavily in times of stress.* —**worsening** [adj] *The worsening economic conditions here have destroyed many small businesses.* | *worsening air pollution*

go from bad to worse /ˌgəʊ frəm ˌbæd tə ˈwɜːʳs/ [v phrase] if a situation **goes from bad to worse**, it is already bad and then becomes even worse: *The rail service has gone from bad to worse since it was privatised.* | *Things went from bad to worse, and soon the pair were barely talking to each other.*

go downhill /ˌgəʊ daʊnˈhɪl/ [v phrase] to start getting worse, especially after a particular time or event: *Moving in together was a mistake, and things rapidly went downhill.* | *When things started to go downhill, Kyle began looking for another job.* | *I said I didn't like baseball, and the interview went downhill from then on.*

suffer /ˈsʌfəʳ/ [v I] if the quality of something **suffers**, it becomes worse as it begins to be affected by something: *His school work suffered because he was continually worried about his mother.* | *The ferry line denied that safety would suffer if costs were cut.* | *Her husband, a lawyer, suffered professionally for having to leave the office early every night.*

slip /slɪp/ [v I] if standards **slip**, they get worse, because people are not trying hard enough to keep the standards high: *Standards have slipped in the past few months, and we have to try and improve our* *performance.* | **let things slip** *He used to make sure his apartment was in immaculate condition, but he's let things slip recently.*

deepen /ˈdiːpən/ [v I] if a bad situation **deepens**, it gets worse – use this especially about serious political or military problems: *As the crisis deepened, it became clear that the government was losing control.* | *The company's legal and financial problems are deepening.* —**deepening** [adj] *There was an atmosphere of deepening discontent in the country.* | *deepening political and economic troubles*

degenerate /dɪˈdʒenəreɪt/ [v I] formal if a situation **degenerates**, it becomes much worse: *There's no denying that our relationship has degenerated over the years.* | **+ into** *Attempts by the UK government to prop up the pound on the exchange markets degenerated into chaos.* | *What should have been a civilised debate degenerated into an unseemly row between the two sides.* | *Don't allow your comments to degenerate into a personal attack on the employee.*

3 to make a bad or difficult situation worse

- make things worse/make it worse
- to make matters/things worse
- aggravate
- exacerbate
- compound
- to add insult to injury

make things worse/make it worse /ˌmeɪk θɪŋz ˈwɜːʳs, ˌmeɪk ɪt ˈwɜːʳs/ [v phrase] to make a bad or difficult situation even worse, especially when you were trying to improve it: *Don't interfere. You'll only make things worse.* | *Trying not to laugh aloud made it worse, and for a moment or two, they were both helpless with suppressed laughter.* | *Why not try running the anti-virus software? It can't make things any worse, can it?*

to make matters/things worse /tə ˌmeɪk mætəʳz, θɪŋz ˈwɜːʳs/ [adv] use this to talk above something that makes a bad situation even worse: *To make matters worse, the director's gone on holiday without leaving anyone in charge.* | *To make things worse, Jimmy suddenly announced he'd left his passport at home.*

aggravate /ˈægrəveɪt/ [v T] to make a bad or difficult situation even worse: *Air pollution may aggravate a child's asthma.* | *Is the pain aggravated by coughing or laughing?* | *Any talk of price rises now will only aggravate an already serious situation.*

exacerbate /ɪgˈzæsəʳbeɪt/ [v T] formal to make a bad or difficult situation even worse: *The family's problems were exacerbated when Walter lost his job.* | *Ironically, the government's reassurances may have exacerbated fear about the disease.*

compound /kəmˈpaʊnd/ [v T usually in passive] if something **compounds** a problem, mistake, or difficulty, it adds to the existing problem so that the general situation gets even worse than before: *Strong nationalist sentiment is compounding the deep political problems faced by the President.* | **be compounded by** *John and Val's domestic problems were compounded by stress at work.* | *The effects of the East Coast snows this year were compounded by severe storms in the spring.*

to add insult to injury /tʊ æd ˌɪnsʌlt tʊ ˈɪndʒəri/ [adv] use that to say that something makes a bad situation worse for someone, by unfairly giving them another problem that relates to or is a result of the original one: *The bank not only refused to refund the money but, to add insult to injury, charged me for the letter telling me so!*

4 worst

- worst
- hit/reach rock bottom
- sth takes the cake

worst /wɜːʳst/ [adj only before noun] worse than anything else or worse than at any time before: *In my opinion, that's the worst movie of all time.* | *The doctor said it was one of the worst cases of food poisoning he'd ever seen.* | *UN workers were withdrawn from the western areas, where the worst bloodshed has occurred.* | **by far the worst** (=much worse than any other) *It's by far the worst neighborhood in the whole city.* | *First thing in the morning is by far the worst time to ask Dad a favour.*

hit/reach rock bottom /ˌhɪt, ˌriːtʃ rɒk ˈbɒtəm‖-rɑːk ˈbɑːtəm/ [v phrase] if a situation **hits** or **reaches rock bottom**, it is worse than it has ever been before, and cannot get any worse than that: *After we lost the contract, morale in the office reached rock bottom.* | *Confidence in the city's police force has hit rock bottom.*

sth takes the cake ALSO **sth takes the biscuit** British / (sth) ˌteɪks ðə ˈkeɪk, (sth) ˌteɪks ðə ˈbɪskɪ̣t/ [v phrase] spoken informal use this to say that something is the worst of its kind – used especially in a humorous way: *I've known some idiots in my time, but you really take the cake.* | *This last little escapade really takes the biscuit, Tom.*

5 when someone who is ill becomes worse

- get worse
- deteriorate
- relapse

get worse /ˌget ˈwɜːʳs/ [v phrase] if someone who is ill **gets worse** or their condition **gets worse**, they become more seriously ill: *I'm afraid your father is getting worse, and we'll have to keep him in hospital.* | *The chest pains got worse, and the family doctor was called.*

deteriorate /dɪˈtɪəriəreɪt/ [v I] formal if someone's medical condition **deteriorates**, it gets worse: *Nina's hearing had deteriorated considerably since I last saw her.* | *His condition deteriorated rapidly during the night.*

relapse /rɪˈlæps/ [v I not in progressive] if someone who has a serious illness **relapses**, they get worse when they had previously been getting better: *On vacation at home, he relapsed and had to return to hospital for further tests.* | *Most drug abusers relapse within a year.* —**relapse** [n C usually singular] **have/suffer a relapse** *Grandad had an unexpected relapse and died within a week.* | *These herbal remedies become less effective if the patient suffers a relapse.*

write

RELATED WORDS

- when a piece of writing is short *see* **short (2)**
- *see also* **read, message, letter, word/phrase/sentence, draw, summarize**

1 to write with a pen, pencil, etc

- write
- put
- take notes
- make a note of something/note down something
- take down/get down
- put sth in writing
- print
- writing/handwriting
- scrawl

write /raɪt/ [v I/T] to **write** words or numbers: *By third grade they can all read and write pretty well.* | *At the bottom he wrote: 'with sincere love from your oldest friend'.* | *Over 15 percent of adults have never learned to write.* | *Helga wrote her comments neatly in pencil.* | **+ on/in/at etc** *She quickly wrote the license plate number on her hand.* | *Hang on, let me just get something to write on.* | *Write your name at the top of the page.* | **write down sth** *I wrote down all the things we have to do today.* | **write sth down** *Do you want me to write that down for you?*

put /pʊt/ [v T] **especially spoken** to write something: *I wrote to Marian, but I didn't put anything about Bill being arrested.* | **put sth in/on/at etc** *Put your name at the top of each answer sheet.* | *Just put 'with love from Jason' on the card.*

take notes /teɪk 'nəʊts/ [v phrase] to write down short pieces of information about something, especially in order to remind yourself about what someone said or what was happening: *Did you take any notes at the lecture?* | *I read the first three chapters and took some notes.*

make a note of sth/note down sth /ˌmeɪk ə 'nəʊt əv (sth), ˌnəʊt 'daʊn (sth)/ [v phrase] to write down information as soon as you get it, so that you will be able to use it later: *OK, let me make a note of that before I forget it.* | *Did you make a note of the train times?* | **note down sth** *Taking out a pen, she noted down the phone number.* | **note sth down** *Colin noted everything down in a little black book.*

take down/get down /ˌteɪk 'daʊn, ˌget 'daʊn/ [phr v T] to write down what someone says, at the same time as they are saying it **take down sth/get down sth** *A group of reporters was following the Senator, trying to get down every word he said.* | *Could I just take down your name and address?* | **take sth down/get sth down** *Do you want me to take all this down?* | *Before he left, Mark got most of what she'd said down on paper.*

put sth in writing /ˌpʊt (sth) ɪn 'raɪtɪŋ/ [v phrase] to give someone a written agreement, promise, offer etc in order to show them that you are serious about it: *Following an informal discussion, Chris decided to put her proposals in writing.* | *A deal was made, but apparently nothing was ever put in writing.*

print /prɪnt/ [v I/T] to write something using separate letters, in order to make your writing clearer: *Please print your name in block capitals.*

writing/handwriting /'raɪtɪŋ, 'hændraɪtɪŋ/ [n U] the way someone writes with a pen, pencil etc: *I can barely read your writing.* | *The children spent hours practising their handwriting.*

scrawl /skrɔːl/ [n U] careless and untidy writing that is difficult to read: *What does it say? I can't read your scrawl!*

2 to write something quickly or carelessly

- jot down
- scribble
- scrawl
- dash off

jot down /ˌdʒɒt 'daʊn‖ˌdʒɑːt-/ [phr v T] to quickly write down ideas, notes, or facts **jot down sth** *Let me jot down the name of that restaurant.* | **jot sth down** *If anyone has any suggestions, jot them down on a piece of paper and give them to me.*

scribble /'skrɪbəl/ [v I/T] to write something quickly and untidily: *Andrew scribbled a quick note and handed it to the chairman.* | **scribble sth down** *Sorry, I scribbled her phone number down, and now I can't read my own writing!* | **scribble down sth** *We'll all scribble down some suggestions, and then compare them.* — **scribbled** [adj] *scribbled notes*

scrawl /skrɔːl/ [v T] to write something carelessly and untidily: *Someone had scrawled a strange symbol on the wall above the bed.* | *Three students were excluded for scrawling graffiti on a school wall.*

dash off /ˌdæʃ 'ɒf / [phr v T] to write a letter, note, story etc quickly and without thinking carefully about it **dash off sth** *He was furious when he saw the article, and dashed off a letter to the editor immediately.* | **dash sth off** *The publishers wanted a summary that afternoon, so I dashed it off in an hour or so.*

3 to write something on a computer, typewriter etc

- write
- type
- key in
- enter
- print
- print/print out

▸ *see also* **computers/internet/email**

write /raɪt/ [v I/T] to **write** something using a computer: *Most of our students write their essays on screen.* | *While I was writing, the computer went down and I lost all my work.*

type /taɪp/ [v I/T] to write with a computer or a typewriter: *I'm afraid I don't type very fast.* | *Could you type those letters for me?* | **type sth out/up** (=to type something that has been written on paper) *We'll have someone type it out and put it in alphabetical order.* | *I asked Michelle to type up my assignment so I could mail it in today.* | **type in sth** (=type something in a blank space, for example on a form) *Bring up the customer database, and type in the amount on the invoice.* — **typing** [n U] writing with a typewriter or computer: *Marion says she'll do some typing for us.* | *We need a secretary with good typing speeds.* (=who can type fast)

key in /ˌkiː 'ɪn/ [phr v T] **especially British** to write something on a computer, especially something that you are copying **key in sth** *I keyed in my password, but the file still won't open.* | **key sth in** *Find out the name of the file, key it in, and it will appear on the screen*

enter /'entəʳ/ [v T] to make words or numbers appear on a computer screen by pressing the keys: *Enter the filename and click 'OK'.* | *She entered Jim's postcode, and watched as a street map appeared on the screen.* | **enter sth in/into** *The patients' medical records are entered into a database.*

print /prɪnt/ [v T usually in passive] to produce copies of a book, letter, newspaper etc using a printing machine: *Most of our books are printed abroad.* | *This book was printed on recycled paper.* | *Where did you get your wedding invitations printed?*

print/print out /prɪnt, ˌprɪnt 'aʊt/ [v I/T] to produce a copy of something you have written on a computer using a special machine connected to it: *My printer prints out at 8 pages per minute.* | *She printed three copies of the letter.*

4 to write a letter or message

- write
- write off
- e-mail
- drop sb a line
- get in touch with sb
- contact
- keep/stay in touch
- correspond

write /raɪt/ [v I/T] to **write** someone a letter: *Sorry, I haven't had time to write.* | *Keith hasn't written for a while.* | **write a letter/postcard etc to sb** *I try to write a cheerful letter to her at least once a week.* | *We wrote about 20 postcards while we were in Greece.* | *I wasn't happy, so I wrote a nasty letter asking for my money back.* | **+ to** *He wrote to his father, asking for more money.* | **write sb** American (=write a letter to someone) *I just wrote him saying how much I missed him being around.* | **write back** (=write a letter to someone after they have written one to you) *Why didn't you write back?* | **write in** (=to write and send a letter to an organization) *A lot of listeners wrote in and complained about the programme.* —**writer** [n C] the person who writes a letter or message: *The writer forgot to put her address.* | *Sarah's a good letter writer, she's very funny.*

write off /ˌraɪt ˈɒf/ [phr v I] to write a letter and send it in order to buy something, take part in a competition, have something sent to you etc **write off for sth** *Write off today for your free Batman poster!* | **write off to sb** *I wrote off to Friends of the Earth and they sent me some leaflets.*

e-mail ALSO **email** /ˈiː meɪl/ [v T] to send someone a message using the Internet: *Please e-mail your CV to the address below.* | **e-mail sb** *So, if you e-mail someone in California, you only pay local phone rates.* | **e-mail sb with sth** *She e-mailed me with her new address, but I deleted it by mistake.* —**e-mail** [n C/U] *Nikki and I keep in touch by e-mail.* | *Did you get my last e-mail?* | **send sb an email** *I sent him an e-mail asking for a copy of his article.* | **check your e-mail** (=connect to the Internet to find out whether you have any e-mails) *I didn't even check my e-mail this morning, so I'll check it now.*

drop sb a line /ˌdrɒp (sb) ə ˈlaɪn‖ˌdrɑːp- / [v phrase] spoken informal to send someone a letter: *Why don't you give me a call or drop me a line sometime?* | *What do you think? Drop me a line at the Washington Post Weekend section and share your thoughts.*

get in touch with sb /ˌget ɪn ˈtʌtʃ wɪð (sb)/ [v phrase] to write to someone, or phone them, especially someone you have not seen or written to for a long time: *I'd love to get in touch with Monique again. Do you have her new address?* | *We help adopted children who want to get in touch with their natural parents.*

contact /ˈkɒntækt‖ˈkɑːn-/ [v T] to write to someone that you do not know, or phone them, especially in order to ask for help or information: *Elsa contacted several companies to ask if they could offer her part-time work.* | *If the problem continues, try contacting a software expert.*

keep/stay in touch /ˌkiːp, ˌsteɪ ɪn ˈtʌtʃ/ [v phrase] to continue to write to someone or phone them, when you no longer work with them or live near them: *I met Pia in Sweden and we've stayed in touch ever since.* | **+ with** *Do you keep in touch with any of your friends from school?*

correspond /ˌkɒrɪ̈ˈspɒnd‖ˌkɔːrɪ̈ˈspɑːnd, ˌkɑː-/ [v I] formal to write letters to someone and receive letters from them, especially regularly: *They started to correspond two years ago.* | **+ with** *I'm a 21-year old Kenyan student who wishes to correspond with students from Britain or the US.*

5 to write a story, book, newspaper article etc

- write
- compile
- compose

write /raɪt/ [v I/T] to **write** a book, story, newspaper article etc: *I can't come out tonight. I have an essay to write.* | *Who wrote 'Madame Bovary'?* | *Anna enjoys writing, and she's quite good at it.* | **+ about/on** *She writes very amusingly about her childhood in Moscow.* | *He wrote several scholarly articles on ancient Chinese texts.* | **well/badly written** *It's a fascinating article, and very well written.*

compile /kəmˈpaɪl/ [v T] to make a list, or a document, book etc that contains lists of information, for example a dictionary: *They are compiling a dictionary of new words.* | *The book was compiled by a panel of experts, working in conjunction with the publisher.*

compose /kəmˈpəʊz/ [v T] formal to write a poem, letter, or song, thinking very carefully about what to say and how to say it: *These love poems are believed to have been composed by a poet at the court of King Henry II.* | *Tom tried to compose a letter, but he couldn't concentrate.*

6 someone who writes books, articles, stories etc

- writer
- author
- journalist

writer /ˈraɪtəʳ/ [n C] someone whose job is to write books, stories etc: *When I was young, I wanted to be a writer.* | *I enjoy reading American writers.* | *a political writer for the New York Times* | *He's a good speech writer* (=someone who writes speeches for other people), *and much in demand among politicians.* | **+ of** *a writer of romantic novels*

author /ˈɔːθəʳ/ [n C] someone who writes books, or who wrote a particular book: *Dickens is one of my favourite authors.* | *The author recalls scenes from her childhood.* | **+ of** *The author of 'Surfing on the Internet', JC Hertz, will be on tonight's show.* | **co-author** (=someone who writes a book with someone else) *Phil Duncan, co-author of 'Politics in America'*

journalist ALSO **reporter** American /ˈdʒɜːʳnəl-ɪ̈st, rɪˈpɔːʳtəʳ/ [n C] someone whose job is to write articles for newspapers or magazines: *She works as a journalist on the Sunday Times.* | **financial/sports etc journalist** *After he retired from football, he became a sports reporter for the Gazette.* | *Lee is one of the highest-paid financial journalists in the country.*

7 to write the letters of a word

- spell
- spelling

spell /spel/ [v I/T] to write a word using the correct letters in the correct order: *In American English, 'organize' is always spelled with a 'z'.* | *How do you spell your surname?* | *I've never been able to spell very well in English.* | **spell sth out** (=to say each letter of a word in the right order) *And your last name is Aitchson? Could you spell that out for me please?*

spelling /ˈspelɪŋ/ [n C/U] the way a word is spelled, or someone's ability to spell words correctly: *British and American spellings* | *Your spelling is atrocious!* | *This essay is full of spelling mistakes.*

8 to write your name

- sign
- initial
- countersign
- signature
- autograph

▸ *see also* **name**

sign /saɪn/ [v I/T] to write your name at the end of a letter, document etc, in order to prove who you are or show that you wrote it: *Sign here please.* | *Did the doctor ask you to sign a consent form Mrs Harris?* | *You forgot to sign the credit card slip.* | **sign your name** *Where do you want me to sign my name?* | **sign for sth** (=to show that you have received it) *Could you sign for this package, please?*

initial /ɪˈnɪʃəl/ [v T] to write the first letter of each of your names on something such as a document to show that you agree to it, have read it etc: *The memo had been initialled by the President.* | *If you alter something you have written on a cheque, you must initial the change.*

countersign /ˈkaʊntəʳsaɪn/ [v T] to write your signature on an official document, especially one that has already been signed by someone else, in order to approve it: *You have to get your visa countersigned by someone at the embassy.*

signature /ˈsɪgnətʃəʳ/ [n C] your name written by you, for example on a document or at the end of a letter, in order to prove who you are or show that you wrote it: *Who's it from? I can't read the signature.* | *Put your signature here, then print your name underneath.* | *You have to get the signature of the child's parent or guardian.* | **+ on** *I just need your signature again on this last sheet here.*

autograph /ˈɔːtəgrɑːf‖-græf/ [n C] the name of a famous person, written by them on a photograph, in a book etc for someone to keep: *She has the autograph of every player in the team.* | **sign autographs** (=to sign your name for people when they ask) *He refused to sign autographs at a charity event last year.* —**autographed** [adj] *I have an autographed picture of John Lennon that's worth quite a lot.*

9 to write information on an official document

- fill in sth/fill out sth
- write out/write
- make out

fill in sth/fill out sth /ˌfɪl ˈɪn (sth), ˌfɪl ˈaʊt (sth)/ [phr v T] to write information or answer questions on an official document, for example giving your name, address, and age: *Passengers must fill in a boarding card before boarding the plane.* | *I must have filled out the order form incorrectly.* | **fill sth in/fill sth out** *You just fill it out, then send it in to the passport office.*

write out/write /ˌraɪt ˈaʊt, raɪt/ [phr v T] to write information, such as your name, the date etc on something such as a cheque or a form **write (out) sth** *I'll write out a cheque for $500 to cover expenses.* | **write sb (out) sth** *Why don't you get the doctor to write you a prescription for some painkillers?* | **write sth out** *Write the information out here on this form, and I'll order the books for you.*

make out /ˌmeɪk ˈaʊt/ [phr v T] to write the necessary details on an official document such as a cheque or ticket, including the name of the person or organization it should go to **make out sth** *He made out a cheque for $100.* | **make sth out (for sb)** *Would you like me to make out a receipt for you?* | *He's just making the booking form out.* | **make out a cheque to sb** (=write on a cheque the name of the person you are paying it to) *Who should I make the cheque out to?* | *If you want to pay by check, make it out to GK Fisher.*

10 to write something that you intend to improve or finish later

- draft
- rough

draft /drɑːft‖dræft/ [v T] to write a letter, speech, official document etc with the intention of changing and improving it before you use it: *She's busy drafting her speech for next week's conference.* | *The prisoners sat down together to draft a letter to the governor.* —**draft** [n C] a first copy of a letter, book, agreement etc which will be improved before it is finally used: *By the end of the year, Jim had produced a first draft of his new novel.*

rough /rʌf/ [adj usually before noun] a **rough** copy of a document is the first one you write which has all the main ideas but does not have all the details and is not finished **rough copy/draft** *This is only a rough copy. I'm going to write it out again.* | *It's just a rough draft, but I'd like you to read it and tell me what you think.* —**in rough** [adv] written in this way: *Write your experiment in rough then read it through carefully before finalizing it.*

11 to write something again

- write out
- rewrite
- write up

write out /ˌraɪt ˈaʊt/ [phr v T] to write something again in a better or more complete way **write sth out** *First I think up the basic plot, then I write the story out in more detail.* | *Find out what is wrong with the example sentences, then write them out correctly.* | **write out sth** *I've written out what everyone owes for the phone bill – it's over there.*

rewrite /ˌriːˈraɪt/ [v T] to write something again using different words, or a different style, in order to make it better or more acceptable: *Perhaps you ought to rewrite the first paragraph to make it a little clearer.* | *The script was rewritten to give it a happier ending.*

write up /ˌraɪt ˈʌp/ [phr v T] to write out notes in complete form, making them into full sentences so that they can be read easily later **write up sth** *I must write up my history notes tonight.* | *I think I'm probably ready to start writing up the first part of the study.* | **write sth up** *We're trying to get all the results organized, so we can write them up.*

12 to write a song/music

- write
- compose
- composer
- songwriter

write /raɪt/ [v T] to **write** music or songs: *Lennon and McCartney wrote over 100 songs.* | *Who wrote the film soundtrack for 'The Bodyguard'?*

compose /kəmˈpəʊz/ [v T] to write a piece of music, especially serious music: *Mozart composed his first symphony when he was still a child.* | *The music was composed and performed by Keith Jarrett.*

composer /kəmˈpəʊzəʳ/ [n C] someone who writes music, especially serious music: *My favourite composer is Beethoven.* | *the composer Philip Glass*

songwriter /'sɒŋˌraɪtəʳ‖'sɔːŋ-/ [n C] someone who writes songs, especially modern, popular songs: *songwriter Bernie Taupin* | **singer-songwriter** (=someone who writes and performs their own songs) *Kaylie is a very talented singer-songwriter.*

13 something that has been written or printed

- writing
- words
- text
- manuscript
- inscription
- graffiti
- document

writing /'raɪtɪŋ/ [n U] *There's some writing on the back of this photo, but I can't make out what it says.* | **in writing** *All bids must be submitted in writing to the above address.* | **piece of writing** *Below each picture was a short piece of writing in Arabic script.*

words /wɜːʳdz/ [n plural] writing, especially a small amount of writing **the words** *The words were very faint but I could make out the name 'Alex'.* | *She scrawled the words 'I love you' on my desk.*

text /tekst/ [n U] the written part of a book, newspaper etc, not including notes, pictures etc: *The front page had no text, just a photograph of the Princess and a huge headline.* | *You can cut and paste whole blocks of text very easily on screen.*

manuscript /'mænjəskrɪpt/ [n C] a copy of a book which is written by hand or typed, often before it is printed: *The finished manuscript was sent to the publisher on 3 January.* | *We were shown some of the ancient manuscripts and rare books that are kept in the British Library.*

inscription /ɪn'skrɪpʃən/ [n C] a piece of writing written on, or cut into, the surface of a stone, coin etc: *We read the inscriptions on the graves, and wondered what each of those lives had been like.* | *It was an engraved silver plate bearing the inscription 'Made for His Majesty George III June 1737'.*

graffiti /græ'fiːti, grə-/ [n U] rude, humorous, or political writing on the walls of buildings, trains etc: *The corridors are very dirty, and the walls are covered with graffiti.*

document /'dɒkjəmənt‖'dɑːk-/ [n C] a piece of writing. A paper document is usually an official or legal one. A document that you produce on a computer is something you type into a particular file: *Several secret documents went missing from the government's Information department.* | *Your birth certificate is an important document, which should be kept safe at all times.* | *Open a new document* (=on a computer) *and name it 'resume'.* | *You can attach any documents to an email and send them to friends or colleagues.*

14 written not spoken

- written
- in writing
- on paper
- handwritten

written /'rɪtn/ [adj] *Some expressions are more common in spoken English than in written English.* | *She was illiterate, and could not understand the written details on the insurance form.* | *Don't sign any written agreement until you have read every word of the contract.*

in writing /ɪn 'raɪtɪŋ/ [adv] if you get or give information **in writing**, it is written down, not spoken, so you can prove later what was actually said: *Please confirm in writing the date you intend to leave.* | *I don't have anything in writing, but they said they expected me to start work Monday.* | **put sth in writing** *You should have asked them to put what they agreed in writing.*

on paper /ɒn 'peɪpəʳ/ [adv] if you put ideas or suggestions **on paper**, you write them down so that you can remember them or organize them more clearly: *If you have any suggestions for improving the course, put them on paper and we'll discuss them.* | *Felton had made the same allegations on paper, and had sent a copy to the FBI.*

handwritten /ˌhænd'rɪtn◂/ [adj] written by hand: *Please attach a covering letter (typed, not handwritten).* | *The scene of the accident was surrounded by flowers, many with handwritten cards expressing sympathy.*

wrong

WHAT'S HERE

- not correct — see **1 to 4**
- not reasonable or necessary — see **5**

not correct

RELATED WORDS

opposite: — **correct**

- not suitable *see* **suitable/not suitable**
- *see also* **mistake, stupid**

1 information/numbers/calculations etc

- wrong
- incorrect
- misleading
- inaccurate
- bad
- be out
- be way off the mark

wrong /rɒŋ‖rɔːŋ/ [adj] not correct: *For every answer that is wrong, you lose five points.* | *I think that clock must be wrong* (=showing the wrong time). | **get sth wrong** *You must have got my email address wrong.* | **wrong (telephone) number/address/name etc** *I tried to phone him, but it was the wrong number.* | *This must be the wrong address – no one of that name lives here* — **wrong/wrongly** [adv] *You've spelled my name wrong – there should be an 'e' at the end.* | *I think you've added it up wrongly.*

incorrect /ˌɪnkə'rekt◂/ [adj] facts, figures, answers etc that are **incorrect** are wrong because they are not the same as the correct ones: *The information about current prices was incorrect.* | *incorrect spelling* | *They discovered later that the doctor had made an incorrect diagnosis.* | **it is incorrect to do/say sth** *It's simply incorrect to say that tobacco advertising does not influence young people.* —**incorrectly** [adv] *If a player answers incorrectly, the question is given to the other team.*

misleading /mɪs'liːdɪŋ/ [adj] a statement or piece of information that is **misleading** makes people believe something that is not true, especially because it does not give all the facts: *The article was deliberately misleading, and the newspaper has apologized.* | *misleading statistics* | *The Advertising Review Board says the adverts are deliberately misleading.* | **give a misleading impression/statement etc** *Agents often gave a false or misleading description of the houses they were selling.*

inaccurate /ɪn'ækjərɪt/ [adj] information, numbers etc that are **inaccurate** are not exactly right or contain some mistakes: *The old maps were usually inaccurate or incomplete.* | *TV ratings figures are often inaccurate.* | *He admitted he had given the committee 'inaccurate, incomplete and unreliable information'.* | **totally/wildly inaccurate** (=very inaccurate) *Figures quoted in the article are wildly inaccurate.*

bad /bæd/ [adj] **bad grammar/English/Italian etc** not spoken or written correctly: *You will lose marks for bad grammar in the exam.* | *Robert ordered two beers in very bad Spanish.* | *Masanori is the worst student in the class – his spelling's bad and his grammar's terrible.*

be out British **/be off** American /biː 'aʊt, biː 'ɒf/ [phr v I] if a measurement, result, figure etc **is out**, it is wrong because the numbers have not been calculated correctly: *These sales figures must be out. We certainly haven't made that much money this year.* | **be out by $10/50 centimetres etc** *My last bank statement was off by $60.*

be way off the mark /biː 'weɪ ɒf ðə ˌmɑːʳk/ [v phrase] if someone's guess, opinion etc **is way off the mark**, their idea about a situation is completely wrong: *No, you're way off the mark – he was born in 1736.*

2 beliefs/ideas/actions etc

- wrong
- mistaken
- false
- erroneous
- misplaced
- misguided
- wrongheaded

wrong /rɒŋ‖rɔːŋ/ [adj] *People used to believe that the world was flat, but we now know this is wrong.* | *Alice felt she had made the wrong decision.* | **get the wrong impression** *I wouldn't like you to get the wrong impression – I do enjoy the course, but I just find it very hard work.*

mistaken /m$_{\text{ə}}^{\text{I}}$'steɪkən/ [adj only before noun] **mistaken idea/belief/impression etc** an idea, belief etc that people believe is right but is in fact wrong – use this as a polite way of saying someone is wrong: *Many people have the mistaken idea that AIDS cannot spread through heterosexual sex.* | **under the mistaken belief/impression etc** *Pauline was under the mistaken impression that I didn't like her.*

false /fɔːls/ [adj] based on wrong ideas or incorrect information: *He gave false and misleading statements to the court.* | *My mother avoided visiting Bali on the quite false assumption that the place is full of tourists.* | **give a false impression/belief** *The title gives a false impression of what the book is actually about.*

erroneous /ɪ'rəʊniəs/ [adj] formal based on incorrect or incomplete information: *There were erroneous reports that the company had issued false statements.* | **erroneous assumption/view/belief etc** *Ricci's book tries to correct this erroneous view of ancient China.* —**erroneously** [adv] *It is sometimes erroneously believed that cutting interest rates will cure all our economic problems.*

misplaced /ˌmɪs'pleɪst◂/ [adj] **misplaced trust/loyalty/admiration/concern etc** trust, loyalty etc that is wrong because there is no good reason for feeling it: *Richards said, with misplaced confidence, that the ship was 'unsinkable'.* | *I suppose her chief fault was misplaced trust, rather than any real crime.* | **(do sth out of) a sense of misplaced loyalty/admiration etc** *Despite her doubts, she supported the new legislation out of a misplaced sense of loyalty to the leadership.*

misguided /mɪs'gaɪd$_{\text{ə}}^{\text{I}}$d/ [adj] done with good intentions but based on information or an idea that is wrong: *These decision now seem misguided, if not downright wrong.* | **misguided efforts/attempt/action etc** *It was another of his misguided attempts to save money.* | **(do sth in the) misguided belief/hope** *The taxes were introduced in the misguided belief that they would reduce foreign competition.*

wrongheaded /ˌrɒŋ'hed$_{\text{ə}}^{\text{I}}$d◂‖ˌrɔːŋ-/ [adj] wrong and a little stupid, because of being based on a lack of understanding: *The young man's speech was full of wrongheaded ideas about 'the evils of capitalism'.* | *wrongheaded economic policies*

3 to believe something that is wrong

- be wrong
- be mistaken
- be misinformed
- be on the wrong track/tack
- kid/delude yourself

be wrong /biː 'rɒŋ‖-'rɔːŋ/ [v phrase] if you **are wrong**, you think or say something that is not correct: *I thought a holiday in Greece would be cheap, but I was wrong.* | *Maybe I'm wrong, but I could have sworn the class was at 9.30 a.m.* | *Why won't he admit he was wrong?* | **+ about** *You were wrong about that train – it left at 10.30.* | **be wrong in thinking/believing etc sth** *You'd be wrong in thinking we don't encourage disabled students to come to the college.*

be mistaken /biː m$_{\text{ə}}^{\text{I}}$'steɪkən/ [v phrase] formal to have an incorrect opinion or belief about something – use this as a polite way of saying someone is wrong: *I thought it was an accident, but I was mistaken.* | **+ about** *Anna realised she had been mistaken about Dennis.* | **you must be mistaken** *I think you must be mistaken. He could not have obtained a key to your room.*

be misinformed /biː ˌmɪsɪn'fɔːʳmd/ [v phrase] to be wrong because you have been given information that is incorrect or untrue: *I think you must have been misinformed – we don't teach any courses in business studies here.* | **+ about** *The documents clearly show that the public was misled and misinformed about the crisis.*

be on the wrong track/tack /biː ɒn ðə ˌrɒŋ 'træk, 'tæk‖-ˌrɔːŋ-/ [v phrase] to have the wrong idea about a situation, so that you are unlikely to get the result you want or the right answer to a problem: *I feel that this advertising campaign is on completely the wrong tack.* | **get sb off on the wrong tack/track** *He admitted that he had gotten us off on the wrong tack, and that we'd need to start again.*

kid/delude yourself /'kɪd, dɪ'luːd jɔːʳself/ [v phrase] to wrongly and stupidly let yourself believe something that you want to believe, but which is not true: *He's kidding himself if he thinks he's going to be a great film director.* | *Don't delude yourself. They have no intention of offering you a job.*

4 in the wrong position

- wrong
- the wrong way around
- back to front
- inside out
- upside down

wrong /rɒŋ‖rɔːŋ/ [adj only before noun] *Someone had moved the road sign so it was pointing in the wrong direction.* | *You're heading in the wrong direction for the city centre.* | *The files had been put back in the wrong order.*

the wrong way around ALSO **the wrong way round** British /ðə ˌrɒŋ weɪ əˈraʊnd, ðə ˌrɒŋ weɪ ˈraʊnd‖-ˌrɔːŋ-/ [adv] if something is **the wrong way around**, it is pointing in the opposite direction to the one it should be pointing in: *Tom often writes 'b' and 'd' the wrong way round.* | *That hat looks a bit strange – have you got it on the wrong way around?* | *The torch won't work if you put the batteries in the wrong way round.*

back to front British ALSO **backwards** British **/backward** American /ˌbæk tə ˈfrʌnt, ˈbækwəʳd(z)/ [adv] if something, especially a piece of clothing, is **back to front**, the back of it is where the front should be: *You've got your sweater on back to front.* | *Dan appeared in jeans, wearing his cap backward as usual.*

inside out /ˌɪnsaɪd ˈaʊt/ [adv] if something, especially a piece of clothing, is **inside out**, the inside of it is on the outside and the outside of it is on the inside: *I put my socks on inside out by mistake.* | *The wind was so strong, it blew her umbrella inside out.* | **turn sth inside out** *I turned the jeans inside out to repair the hem.*

upside down /ˌʌpsaɪd ˈdaʊn/ [adv] if something is **upside down**, the top of it is at the bottom and the bottom of it is at the top: *You're holding the picture upside down.* | *The monkey was hanging upside down from a tree.* | **turn sth upside down** *Turn the cups upside down and leave them to dry.*

not reasonable or necessary

RELATED WORDS

opposite: —— **right**

- morally wrong *see* **bad (13)**
- *see also* **fair/unfair**

5 not reasonable or necessary

- **wrong**
- **unjustified**
- **unjustifiable**
- **unreasonable**
- **unwarranted**
- **gratuitous**
- **unprovoked**
- **without good reason**

wrong /rɒŋ‖rɔːŋ/ [adj] *I don't deny that what I did was wrong, but I had no choice at the time.* | *Do you think violence is always wrong, even in self-defence?* | **+ with** *There's nothing wrong with making money, is there?* | **be wrong (of sb) to do sth** *It is wrong to treat people this way – they should be given a chance to defend themselves.* | *It was wrong of Sophie to take the money without asking.* —**wrongly** [adv] *Rightly or wrongly, employees see 'performance pay raises' as unfair.* | *The police chief admitted that some prisoners had been wrongly punished.*

unjustified /ʌnˈdʒʌstɪ̇faɪd/ [adj] something such as criticism or bad treatment of someone that is **unjustified** is unfair and cannot be shown to have a good reason: *Many disabled people suffer from unjustified discrimination when they apply for jobs.* | *Brian has the reputation, unjustified in my opinion, of being a bit of a bore.* | **totally/completely unjustified** *I think your criticisms of Mr Ward are completely unjustified.*

unjustifiable /ʌnˈdʒʌstɪ̇faɪəbəl/ [adj] not fair, reasonable, or true: *It is morally unjustifiable to punish a whole class for the actions of one or two of its members.* | *unjustifiable accusations*

unreasonable /ʌnˈriːzənəbəl/ [adj] **unreasonable** demands, requests, orders etc are unfair and not based on any good reason: *I think your attitude is most unreasonable.* | *I don't think the amount of homework they get is unreasonable.* | *Even the most caring parents will sometimes make unreasonable demands on their children.* | **it is unreasonable to do sth** *Don't you think it's a little unreasonable to charge someone $75 just for parking their car?* —**unreasonably** [adv] *Some investors had unreasonably high expectations of the new dotcom companies.*

unwarranted /ʌnˈwɒrəntɪ̇d‖-ˈwɔː-, -ˈwɑː-/ [adj] an **unwarranted** action or criticism is not deserved and is not based on any good reason: *Many sportsmen and women consider random drug-testing to be an unwarranted invasion of their privacy.* | *His attorney called the punishment 'excessively severe' and 'unwarranted'.* | **unwarranted assumptions/beliefs/conclusions** *He warned members of the public not to jump to any unwarranted conclusions about the tragedy.*

gratuitous /grəˈtjuːɪ̇təs‖-ˈtuː-/ [adj] done for no good reason and causing unnecessary harm or offence: *He has criticised the film industry for its use of gratuitous sex and violence.* | *There's no point in exchanging gratuitous insults with them.* —**gratuitously** [adv] *A lot of the jokes were just gratuitously offensive.*

unprovoked /ˌʌnprəˈvəʊkt◂/ [adj] an **unprovoked** attack or criticism is directed at someone who did nothing to deserve it: *A man died in an apparently unprovoked attack in central Oxford last night.* | *Troops have been accused of unprovoked aggression against innocent civilians.*

without good reason /wɪðaʊt ˌgʊd ˈriːzən/ [adv] if someone does something **without good reason**, they do not have a good reason for doing it, and this may lead to trouble or punishment: *Anyone who is late without good reason will be punished.* | *An employer is unlikely to dismiss an employee without good reason.*

Yy

yes

RELATED WORDS

opposite: —— **no**

- *see also* **agree, accept**

1 when someone asks you a question

- **yes**
- **yeah**
- **sure**
- **definitely**
- **of course**
- **I'm afraid so**
- **answer/reply in the affirmative**

yes /jes/ spoken *'Have you lived here long?' 'Yes, about 10 years.'* | *'Did you watch 'Trial and Retribution' last night?' 'Yes, wasn't it good?'* | *If you're asking me whether I think we should do it, the answer is yes.* | **yes, please** (=say this to politely accept something that someone offers you) *'Would you like some wine?' 'Yes, please.'*

yeah /jeə/ spoken informal *'Are you ready, Chrissie?' 'Yeah, yeah, I'm just coming.'* | *'Was it £2000 that your car cost?' 'Yeah, that's right.'* | *'Do you think you may have to retire from athletics soon?' 'Well, yeah, I suppose so.'*

sure /ʃʊəʳ/ spoken informal especially American *'Do you have the time, please?' 'Sure, it's three o'clock.'* | *'We're going to the beach this afternoon – want to come?' 'Sure, that 'd be great.'*

definitely /ˈdef₃n₃tli/ spoken say this when you want to agree strongly with something, or to make it clear that you are **definitely** going to do something: *'I think Mark would make a good team captain, don't you?' 'Definitely!'* | *'Are you going to Sonya's party?' 'Definitely! It should be really fun.'*

of course /əv ˈkɔːʳs/ spoken say this when you are surprised or annoyed that someone has asked you something, or to make your answer strong: *'Do you know when my birthday is?' 'Of course, it's next Wednesday.'* | **of course I am/she is/you can etc** *'Are you feeling nervous?' 'Of course I am, it's a very important speech.'*

I'm afraid so /aɪm əˌfreɪd ˈsəʊ/ spoken say this when you think the person asking the question is hoping for a different answer: *'You're not going out, are you?' 'I'm afraid so. But I won't be long.'* | *'School doesn't start again next week, does it?' 'Yes, I'm afraid so, Charlie.'*

answer/reply in the affirmative /ˌɑːnsəʳ, rɪˌplaɪ ɪn ði əˈfɜːʳmətɪv‖ˌæn-/ [v phrase] formal written to say yes – use this when someone says yes in a formal or public situation, for example in a law court: *When asked if he recognized the defendant, the witness replied in the affirmative.* | *Are men more mechanical than women? 67% of all men responding to our poll answered in the affirmative.*

2 when someone asks you for permission to do something

- yes
- ok/okay
- sure
- of course
- certainly
- go ahead
- by all means
- no problem

yes /jes/ spoken *'Is it all right if I use this computer?' 'Yes, that's fine.'* | *'Do you have a pen I can borrow?' 'Yes, what color do you want?'* | *I asked her if I could come too, and she said yes.*

ok/okay /əʊˈkeɪ/ spoken say this when you agree to give permission but you are not completely happy about it: *'Mum, can I borrow your car for an hour?' 'OK, but don't be any longer than that.'* | *Ed asked if he could stay over at Matt's house so I said okay.*

sure /ʃʊəʳ/ spoken informal especially American *'Can I call you this evening?' 'Sure. I'll be home about seven thirty.'* | *'Do you have a photo of the baby I can see?' 'Sure,' said Maddy, pulling out her wallet.*

of course /əv ˈkɔːʳs/ spoken use this to say clearly and definitely that you are very willing to give your permission for something: *'Do you think I could borrow some money?' 'Of course. How much do you need?'* | **of course you can/we will etc** *'Will we be able to go to Disney World?' 'Of course we will, that's why we're here.'*

certainly /ˈsɜːʳtnli/ spoken say this especially when you are being polite to someone in a formal situation: *'Can I change the date of my return flight to London?' 'Certainly, which date would you prefer?'* | *'I'd like to use the hotel sauna, please.' 'Certainly, Madam. It's down the corridor on the left.'*

go ahead /ˌgəʊ əˈhed/ spoken say this when someone asks your permission to use something that belongs to you, or asks to do something that affects you in some way: *'Is it OK if I smoke?' 'Sure, go ahead.'* | *'Do you mind if I use your phone?' 'Not at all – go ahead.'*

by all means /baɪ ˌɔːl ˈmiːnz/ spoken formal say this to show that you are very willing to give permission: *'Do you think I could stay at your house for a few days?' 'By all means, but you may have to sleep on the floor.'*

no problem /ˌnəʊ ˈprɒbləm‖-ˈprɑːb-/ spoken say this to show that you are very willing to give permission, and it is not at all inconvenient for you: *'Would it be all right if I leave work a bit early tomorrow? I've got a dentist's appointment.' 'No problem – thanks for letting me know.'*

3 when someone asks or tells you to do something

- yes
- ok/okay
- all right/alright
- right
- sure
- no problem

yes /jes/ spoken *'Will you type this letter for me, please.' 'Yes, but I'll have to finish this first.'* | *'Clean the pans and scrub the floor, I want this place spotless.' 'Yes, sir,' he replied.*

ok/okay /əʊˈkeɪ/ spoken say this when you agree to do something but you are not completely happy about it: *'Could you pick me up at about 12 o'clock?' 'Okay, if you're sure it won't be any later than that.'* | *'Go and wake Ted up, will you?' 'OK, but he isn't going to be too pleased.'*

all right/alright /ˌɔːl ˈraɪt/ spoken say this especially when you do not really want to do what someone is asking or telling you to do: *'Dad, can you help me with this maths homework?' 'Alright, but shouldn't you really do it by yourself?'* | **all right then** *'I'd really like to see you some time this week.' 'Oh, all right then, how about a quick drink after work?'*

right /raɪt/ spoken especially British say this especially when you want to show that you have understood what someone wants you to do and you are going to do it: *'We seem to have run out of eggs, too.' 'Right, how many do you want?'* | *'I'll need ten copies of this letter.' 'Right, I'll do it straight away.'*

sure /ʃʊəʳ/ spoken informal especially American say this when you are happy to do something which someone asks or tells you to do: *'Will you be able to help with Jimmy's birthday party?' 'Sure, I love kids.'* | *'Just go out to the garage, will you, and get my tools.' 'Sure, I'll be right back.'*

no problem /nəʊ ˈprɒbləm‖-ˈprɑː-/ spoken say this when you are very happy to do something that someone has asked you to do: *'Can you have the car ready for me by 5 o'clock?' 'No problem, sir.'* | *'Could you get me down that box on the top shelf?' 'Sure, no problem at all.'*

young

RELATED WORDS

opposite: —— **old**

▸ *see also* **age, child, baby**

1 young

- young
- little
- small

young /jʌŋ/ [adj] *You're too young to smoke.* | *a single mother with two young children* | *When I was younger, I used to play a lot of baseball.* | *Her youngest son works for a television company.* | *At 35, he is the youngest person to hold this office.*

little /ˈlɪtl/ [adj] **especially spoken** very young – use this to talk about a young child: *When I was little we used to go camping a lot.* | *There were three bridesmaids at the wedding, and even the little one behaved beautifully.* | **little boy/girl** (=a young child, or a young son or daughter) *They've been married for ten years and have two little girls.* | *Who's that little boy in the blue sweater?*

small /smɔːl/ [adj] young, usually less than about ten years old: *We loved going to the zoo when we were small.* | *The kids were too small to really understand.* | **small children** *She soon discovered that looking after small children was very tiring.*

2 younger than someone else

- younger
- junior

younger /ˈjʌŋgəʳ/ [adj] *At school, the younger children go home an hour before the rest.* | *He is the most influential of the younger French photographers.*

junior /ˈdʒuːniəʳ/ [n singular] **ten years/18 months etc sb's junior** formal ten years, etc younger than someone else: *Sarah is six years my junior.* | *He was replaced by a young graduate, 10 years his junior.*

3 a brother or sister who is younger than you

- younger sister/brother
- little sister/brother
- kid sister/brother

younger sister/brother /ˌjʌŋgəʳ ˈsɪstəʳ, ˈbrʌðəʳ/ [n C] *Tony's the oldest – he has two younger sisters.* | *The king was killed by his younger brother.*

little sister/brother /ˌlɪtl ˈsɪstəʳ, ˈbrʌðəʳ/ [n C] a younger sister or brother, especially one who is still a child: *Mike's little brother is doing much better at school than he is.* | *She went to the ballet class with her little sister every week.*

kid sister/brother /ˌkɪd ˈsɪstəʳ, ˈbrʌðəʳ/ [n C] informal a younger sister or brother, who is usually still a child: *He has a kid sister in the fourth grade at school.* | *I suddenly realized Bobby was more than just an annoying kid brother who always wanted to use my stuff.*

4 a young person

- teenager
- youth
- in your teens
- adolescent
- minor

▸ *see also* **child**

teenager /ˈtiːneɪdʒəʳ/ [n C] someone who is between 13 and 19 years old: *River Phoenix became a famous actor while still a teenager.* | *The survey shows that four out of five teenagers have experimented with illegal drugs.* —**teenage** [adj only before noun] *Jenny has three teenage children.*

youth /juːθ/ [n C usually plural] a young man between about 15 and 25 years old – use this especially about groups of young men who behave badly or do something illegal: *One of the youths pushed her against the wall and took her bag.* | *The police had questioned three youths, but then later released them without charge.* | *a gang of youths on motorbikes*

in your teens /ɪn jɔːʳ ˈtiːnz/ [adv] someone who is **in their teens** is between 13 and 19 years old: *She had run away from home several times in her teens.* | **in your early/mid/late teens** *Most of the girls at the concert were in their early teens.*

adolescent /ˌædəˈlesənt◂/ [n C] someone who is at the age when they change from being a child into a young adult – use this especially when talking about problems that young people have at this age: *John changed from a friendly and cheerful young boy into a confused adolescent.* | *An estimated 62 million Americans smoke, including 4.1 million adolescents aged 12-17.* —**adolescent** [adj] *Parents tend to worry more about adolescent daughters than adolescent sons.*

minor /ˈmaɪnəʳ/ [n C] a person under the age when they legally become an adult – used in legal contexts: *Stores are forbidden to sell alcohol and cigarettes to minors.*

5 young people in general

- the young
- the youth

the young /ðə ˈjʌŋ/ [n plural] *The show is extremely popular, especially with the young.* | *Living together without getting married is increasingly common among the young.*

the youth /ðə ˈjuːθ/ [n plural] the young people of a particular time or place **+ of** *The youth of today have much more money than we had 50 years ago.* | *The youth of industrialized nations need to be made aware of global problems.*

6 the time when you were young

- childhood
- youth
- adolescence

childhood /ˈtʃaɪldhʊd/ [n C/U] the time when you are a child: *Nina had happy memories of her childhood on the farm.* | **early childhood** (=when you are a young child) *His early childhood was spent with his father in Chicago.* —**childhood** [adj only before noun] *My own childhood hero was Stirling Moss, the racing car driver.* | **childhood illness/memory/friend/experience** *The smell of the sea brought back childhood memories of long summer holidays spent on the beach.*

youth /juːθ/ [n U] the time when you are young, especially the time between 15 and 25 when you are no longer a child: *She revisited all the places where she had spent her youth.* | **in sb's youth** (=when they were young) *Caroline had been a ballet dancer in her youth.*

adolescence /ˌædəˈlesəns/ [n U] the time when a young person is changing from being a child into a young adult – use this especially when talking about the problems that young people have at this age: *During adolescence, boys are sometimes very shy and lacking in self-confidence.*

7 affecting or involving young people

- youth
- juvenile
- teenage

youth /juːθ/ [adj only before noun] **youth club/group/organization etc** a club, group etc for young people: *I met her at the local youth club.* | *a concert by the National Youth Orchestra*

teenage /ˈtiːneɪdʒ/ [adj only before noun] use this about things produced for teenagers, or things that teenagers do: *the teenage music scene* | **teenage fashions/magazines/pregnancy/drug-taking etc** *There has been a significant increase in teenage pregnancies recently.*

juvenile /ˈdʒuːvənaɪl‖-nəl, -naɪl/ [adj only before noun] use this about crimes by young people **juvenile crime/offender** (=crime by young people/a young person who is a criminal) *Juvenile crime is an increasing problem in big cities.* | *Many juvenile offenders were being put in adult prisons.* | **juvenile delinquency** (=illegal or bad behaviour by young people) *The public housing units have frequently become slums and hotbeds of crime, especially juvenile delinquency.* | **juvenile court** (=a court that deals with crimes by young people) *O'Brien, 15, will face murder charges in a juvenile court.* —**juvenile** [n C] a young person who has done something illegal: *the treatment of juveniles in the criminal justice system*

8 looking or behaving like a young person

- youthful
- look young for your age
- mutton dressed as lamb

youthful /ˈjuːθfəl/ [adj] looking or behaving like a young person, even though you are no longer young: *At 61, she seems remarkably youthful.* | *Although middle-aged, he had a youthful appearance.* | *She still manages to bring a youthful enthusiasm and energy to her work.*

look young for your age /lʊk ˌjʌŋ fəʳ jɔːr ˈeɪdʒ/ [v phrase] to look younger than you really are: *Veronique looks very young for her age, and people often think that her daughter is her sister.*

mutton dressed as lamb /ˌmʌtn drest əz ˈlæm/ [n phrase] British someone who dresses in clothes that are only suitable for a much younger person in order to seem younger – use this to say that you think this makes them look silly or embarrassing: *Some people might think that she was 'mutton dressed as lamb', but tonight Moira really didn't care.*

Longman Language Activator®

▸ Index

▸ Index

a

e

h

i

j

k

l

m

n

neck ▸ KISS 2
be a pain in the neck ▸ ANGRY 9; DIFFICULT 1, 7
be breathing down sb's neck ▸ FORCE SB TO DO STH 1
be neck and neck ▸ EQUAL/NOT EQUAL 4
be up to your ears/neck in ▸ BUSY/NOT BUSY 1
be up to your neck/ears in debt ▸ OWE 2
risk your neck ▸ DANGEROUS 4
stick your neck out ▸ RISK 3
need ▸ NEED/NECESSARY 1, 5, 6; WANT/NOT WANT 2
be in need of ▸ NEED/NECESSARY 1
don't need ▸ NEED/NECESSARY 8
fill a need ▸ NEED/NECESSARY 7
have no need of ▸ NEED/NECESSARY 8
meet/satisfy a need ▸ NEED/NECESSARY 7
needy/in need ▸ POOR 1
not need to do sth/needn't do sth ▸ MUST/DON'T HAVE TO 5
there is a need for ▸ NEED/NECESSARY 1
there is no need to do sth ▸ MUST/DON'T HAVE TO 5
need to do sth ▸ MUST/DON'T HAVE TO 1
needless ▸ NEED/NECESSARY 9
needn't
not need to do sth/needn't do sth ▸ MUST/DON'T HAVE TO 5
needs
meet sb's needs ▸ ENOUGH/NOT ENOUGH 1
special needs ▸ DISABLED 1
needy
poor people/the poor/the needy ▸ POOR 4
needy/in need ▸ POOR 1
negate
cancel out/negate ▸ EFFECTIVE/NOT EFFECTIVE 5
negative ▸ CRITICIZE 6; HARM 3; NONE/NOTHING 3; PROVE 2
answer/reply in the negative ▸ NO 2
have a negative impact on ▸ EFFECT/AFFECT 2
neglect ▸ LOOK AFTER 6
neglect to do sth ▸ DO/NOT DO 13
negligence ▸ CARELESS 2
negligible ▸ LITTLE 4, 7
negotiable ▸ DISCUSS 4
negotiate ▸ DISCUSS 2
negotiation
be open to discussion/negotiation ▸ DISCUSS 4
negotiations ▸ DISCUSS 5
neighbourhood ▸ AREA 2
neighbouring ▸ NEAR 1
neither ▸ BOTH 1; NOT 1, 3; TWO 4
neither ... nor ▸ NOT 3
neither here nor there ▸ CONNECTED WITH/RELATED 7
neither one thing nor the other ▸ NOT 3
nepotism ▸ UNFAIR 4
nerve ▸ BRAVE/NOT BRAVE 4
have the nerve ▸ RUDE 5
have the nerve to do sth ▸ BRAVE/NOT BRAVE 5
lose your nerve ▸ BRAVE/NOT BRAVE 7
not have the nerve ▸ BRAVE/NOT BRAVE 7
nerve-wracking ▸ NERVOUS 5
nerves ▸ NERVOUS 4
be a bundle of nerves ▸ NERVOUS 2
get on sb's nerves ▸ ANGRY 7
steady your nerves ▸ CALM 3
nervous ▸ FRIGHTENED/FRIGHTENING 7; NERVOUS 1, 3; WORRIED/WORRYING 1
a nervous/jealous etc disposition ▸ CHARACTER 1
be a nervous wreck ▸ NERVOUS 2
have a (nervous) breakdown ▸ MENTALLY ILL 3
make sb nervous ▸ NERVOUS 6
nest egg ▸ SAVE 3
Net
(the) Internet/(the) Net ▸ COMPUTERS/INTERNET/EMAIL 8
surf the Internet/Net/Web ▸ COMPUTERS/INTERNET/EMAIL 9
net ▸ EARN 2
net result/effect ▸ RESULT 2
netiquette ▸ RULE/REGULATION 2
network ▸ COMPUTERS/INTERNET/EMAIL 1; MEET 2; SYSTEM 1; TELEVISION/RADIO 6
neurotic ▸ WORRIED/WORRYING 8
neutral ▸ FAIR 3
neutralize ▸ EFFECTIVE/NOT EFFECTIVE 5
never ▸ NEVER 1
better late than never ▸ LATE 2
have never been known to do sth ▸ NEVER 1
I will never forget ▸ REMEMBER 4
there's never a dull moment ▸ INTERESTING 3
you never know ▸ MAYBE 1; POSSIBLE 2
never been done/attempted/tried before ▸ FIRST 5
never ever/never, never ▸ NEVER 1
never fails/can't fail/works every time ▸ EFFECTIVE/NOT EFFECTIVE 3
never for a moment/not for a moment ▸ NEVER 1
never forgive ▸ FORGIVE/NOT FORGIVE 4
never mind ▸ FORGIVE/NOT FORGIVE 2; NO MATTER WHAT/HOW MUCH ETC 1
never-ending ▸ ALWAYS 6
endless/unending/never-ending ▸ CONTINUE 7
never/not in a million years ▸ NEVER 1
nevertheless
however/nevertheless/nonetheless ▸ BUT 1
new ▸ DIFFERENT 5; NEW 1, 2, 4, 5, 6, 7, 8, 9
as good as new ▸ CONDITION 2
be new to sth ▸ EXPERIENCED/NOT EXPERIENCED 3
brand new ▸ NEW 2
break new ground ▸ FIRST 5
new arrival ▸ NEW 7
new blood ▸ NEW 7
new leaf
turn over a new leaf ▸ BEHAVE 4
new man ▸ MAN 1
new start
start afresh/make a fresh start/make a new start ▸ START 7
newbie ▸ NEW 7
newborn ▸ BABY 1, 2
newcomer ▸ NEW 7
newfound ▸ NEW 8
newly ▸ RECENTLY 1
newly discovered ▸ NEW 6
newlyweds ▸ MARRY 10
news ▸ NEWS 1, 2
be in the news ▸ NEWS 5
break the news (to sb)/break it to sb ▸ TELL 1
make the news/make news ▸ NEWS 5
the news ▸ NEWS 2
update/news update ▸ NEWS 2
news bulletin ▸ NEWS 2
newsagent
newsagent's/newsagent ▸ SHOP/STORE 2
newsagent's/newsagent ▸ SHOP/STORE 2
newsflash ▸ NEWS 2
newspaper/paper ▸ NEWSPAPERS 1
newsreader ▸ NEWS 6; TELEVISION/RADIO 8
newsstand
newstand/newsstand ▸ SHOP/STORE 2
newstand/newsstand ▸ SHOP/STORE 2
next ▸ AFTER 1, 4, 8; THEN 1
be/come next ▸ AFTER 9
the next ▸ AFTER 6; NEAR 4; NEXT TO 2
next door ▸ NEXT TO 1
next in line ▸ AFTER 6
next of kin ▸ FAMILY 3
next to ▸ NEXT TO 1
be next to ▸ NEXT TO 3
next to last/second to last ▸ LAST 3
next to nothing ▸ LITTLE 4, 7
nibble ▸ EAT 7
nice ▸ FRIENDLY 1; GOOD 1, 6; KIND 1; NICE 1, 2; WEATHER 4
have a nice day/good weekend/great time etc ▸ GOODBYE 1
not very nice ▸ HORRIBLE 1, 2, 3
pleased/good/nice to meet you ▸ HELLO 2
nice to meet you/nice meeting you ▸ GOODBYE 1
nice-looking ▸ BEAUTIFUL 1, 2
nick ▸ CUT 3
in good nick ▸ CONDITION 2
in the nick of time ▸ ON TIME 3
nick/pinch ▸ STEAL 1
nickname ▸ CALL/DESCRIBE AS 3; NAME 2
niggling ▸ WORRIED/WORRYING 5
night
all day/night/summer etc long ▸ ALWAYS 3
all day/night/year/week ▸ TIME 10
by day/by night ▸ DURING 1
day and night/night and day ▸ CONTINUE 6
goodnight/night ▸ GOODBYE 2
last thing at night ▸ LATE 7
restless night ▸ SLEEP 6
sleepless night ▸ SLEEP 6
stag night ▸ MARRY 7

O

p

S

t

W

x

y

Z